W9-CAB-953

ENCYCLOPEDIA OF
ASSOCIATIONS®

AN ASSOCIATIONS UNLIMITED REFERENCE

ISSN 0071-0202

ENCYCLOPEDIA OF
ASSOCIATIONS®

AN ASSOCIATIONS UNLIMITED REFERENCE

A Guide to More Than 24,000 National and International Organizations, Including: Trade, Business, and Commercial; Environmental and Agricultural; Legal, Governmental, Public Administration, and Military; Engineering, Technological, and Natural and Social Sciences; Educational; Cultural; Social Welfare; Health and Medical; Public Affairs; Fraternal, Nationality, and Ethnic; Religious; Veterans', Hereditary, and Patriotic; Hobby and Avocational; Athletic and Sports; Labor Unions, Associations, and Federations; Chambers of Commerce and Trade and Tourism; Greek Letter and Related Organizations; and Fan Clubs.

45th
EDITION

VOLUME 1
NATIONAL ORGANIZATIONS OF THE U.S.

PART 2 (SECTIONS 7-18)
Entries 10980-24421

Kristy A. Swartout, Project Editor

THOMSON

GALE

Detroit • New York • San Francisco • New Haven, Conn. • Waterville, Maine • London

Encyclopedia of Associations, 45th Edition

Project Editor
Kristy A. Swartout

Editorial
Tara Atterberry, Verne Thompson

Editorial Support Services
Natasha Mikheyeva

Composition and Electronic Prepress
Gary Oudersluys

Manufacturing
Rita Wimberley

Product Management
David Forman

ISBN-13:
978-0-7876-9686-3 (Volume 1, 3-part set)
978-0-7876-9687-0 (Volume 1, Part 1)
978-0-7876-9688-7 (Volume 1, Part 2)
978-0-7876-9689-4 (Volume 1, Part 3)
978-0-7876-9690-0 (Volume 2)

ISBN-10:
0-7876-9686-2 (Volume 1, 3-part set)
0-7876-9687-0 (Volume 1, Part 1)
0-7876-9688-9 (Volume 1, Part 2)
0-7876-9689-7 (Volume 1, Part 3)
0-7876-9690-0 (Volume 2)

ISSN 0071-0202

Printed in the United States of America
10 9 8 7 6 5 4 3 2 1

Contents

The *Encyclopedia of Associations (EA),* Volume 1, is the only comprehensive source of detailed information concerning more than 24,000 nonprofit American membership organizations of national scope. For over fifty years and through 44 earlier editions, *EA's* listing of associations and professional societies is unsurpassed as a 'switchboard' connecting persons needing information to highly qualified sources.

Frequently, a phone call, fax, or email to one of the thousands of organizations formed around a specific interest or objective produces more information faster than research in books, periodicals, and other printed materials.

Organizations often operate with small, volunteer staffs. *Many such groups have requested that all written inquiries be accompanied by stamped, self-addressed envelopes.* Replies can then be expedited and costs to the organization kept to a minimum.

Preparation of This Edition

The editorial objective for each edition of *EA* is complete verification or updating of existing entries and the identification and description of new or previously unlisted organizations. This intensive effort includes direct contact by correspondence and telephone with non-responding groups.

Scope of the Encyclopedia

The organizations described in *EA* fall into the following seven general categories:

National, nonprofit membership associations, which represent the largest number of organizations listed;

International associations, which are generally North American in scope and membership or binational, representing a direct link between the United States and another country or region; also includes American or North American sections, chapters, or divisions of associations headquartered outside of the United States;

Local and regional associations, only if their subjects or objectives are national in interest;

Nonmembership organizations, if they disseminate information to the public as well as to the researcher;

For-profit associations, if their names suggest that they are nonprofit organizations;

Defunct associations, which appear only in the index with the appropriate 'defunct' annotation;

Untraceable associations, which are listed without address with the annotation 'address unknown since [edition year]' in place of contact information. (After requests for updated information have remained unanswered for two editions, these associations are listed in the index only, with the annotation 'address unknown.')

Available in Electronic Formats

Licensing. National Organizations of the U.S. is available for licensing. The complete database is provided in a fielded format and is deliverable on such media as disk or CD-ROM. For more information, contact Gale's Business Development Group at 1-800-877-GALE, or visit us on our web site at www.gale.com/bizdev.

Online. The complete *Encyclopedia of Associations (EA)* series (including associations listed in the international and regional, state and local editions) is available online as File 114 through The Dialog Corporation's DIALOG service and as File ENASSC through LexisNexis. For more information, contact The Dialog Corporation, 11000 Regency Parkway, Ste. 10, Cary, NC 27511, phone: (919) 462-8600; toll-free: 800-3-DIALOG; or LexisNexis, PO Box 933, Dayton, OH 45401-0933, phone (937) 865-6800, toll-free: 800-227-4908.

Associations Unlimited. Associations Unlimited is a modular approach to the *Encyclopedia of Associations* database, allowing customers to select the pieces of the series that they want to purchase.

The four modules include each of the *EA* series (national, international, and regional) as well as one module featuring U.S. government data on more than 450,000 nonprofit organizations.

Associations Unlimited is available on a subscription basis through InfoTrac, Gale's online information resource that features an easy-to-use end-user interface, powerful search capabilities, and ease of access through the World-Wide Web. For more information, call 800-877-GALE.

The complete *EA* database is also available through InfoTrac as part of *Gale's Ready Reference Shelf.*

Acknowledgments

The editors are grateful to the large number of organization officials in the United States and abroad who generously responded to our requests for updated information, provided additional data by telephone, fax, email or website and helped in the shaping of this edition with their comments and suggestions throughout the year. Special thanks go to Jeannine M. James for her research contributions. Appreciation is also extended to the American Society of Association Executives for its ongoing support.

Comments and Suggestions Welcome

Matters pertaining to specific listings in *EA,* as well as suggestions for new listings, should be directed to Kristy Swartout, Editor, *Encyclopedia of Associations.*

Please write or call:
Encyclopedia of Associations
The Gale Group
27500 Drake Rd.
Farmington Hills, MI 48331-3535

Phone: (248) 699-4253
Toll-free: 800-347-GALE
Fax: (248) 699-8075
Email: Kristy.Swartout@Thomson.com

Descriptive Listings

Entries in *EA* are arranged into 18 subject sections, as outlined on the Contents page. Within each section, organizations are arranged in alphabetical order, with numeric listings appearing first, according to the assigned principal subject keyword that appears as a subhead above the organization names. An alphabetical list of keywords used throughout *EA* follows the 'Abbreviations and Symbols' list. Within each keyword, entries are listed alphabetically by organization name.

Access to entries is facilitated by the alphabetical *Name and Keyword Index* found in Part 3 of this edition. An explanation of this index follows the discussion of the sample entry.

Sample Entry

The number preceding each portion of the sample entry designates an item of information that might be included in an entry. Each numbered item in the sample entry is explained in the paragraph of the same number following the diagram.

❚1❚ Storytelling

❚2❚ 3348 ■ **❚3❚** Association of Eclectic Storytellers **❚4❚** (AES)
❚5❚ 123 Amanda Ave.
PO Box 1992
Eldridge, NY 13201
❚6❚ Ph: (315)555-9500
❚7❚ Free: (800)555-2000
Fax: (315)555-9505
Telex: 123456
❚8❚ E-mail: harmersway@aes.org
❚9❚ Website: http://www.aes.org
❚10❚ Contact: Grant Smith, Pres.
❚11❚ Founded: 1950. **❚12❚ Members:** 150,000. **❚13❚ Membership Dues:** individual, $50 (annual). **❚14❚ Staff:** 15. **❚15❚ Budget:** $1,000,000. **❚16❚ Regional Groups:** 10. **Local Groups:** 20. **❚17❚ Languages:** English, Dutch. **❚18❚ Multinational. ❚19❚ Description:** Professional society of storytellers, focusing on storytellers that enjoy eclectic themes and others with an interest in this field. Promotes the study and tradition of storytelling. Conducts special programs for various types of audiences. Sponsors special seminars and courses on traditional forms of storytelling. **❚20❚ Libraries: Type:** lending. **Holdings:** 15,000; archival material, artwork, books, periodicals. **Subjects:** folktales, traditional stories, fairytales. **❚21❚ Awards:** Yaeko Abe Excellence Endowment. **Frequency:** annual. **Type:** monetary. • Michelle Eads's Founder Prize. **Frequency:** quarterly. **Type:** recognition. **❚22❚ Computer Services:** database on literature • publishing capabilities. **❚23❚ Telecommunication Services:** electronic bulletin board, (201)836-7569 • teleconference • teletype. **❚24❚ Committees:** Career Counseling; Cultural Studies; History of Stories. **Divisions:** Education; Literature. **❚25❚ Affiliated With:** Storytelling Institute. **❚26❚ Also Known As:** Story Time Society. **❚27❚ Formerly:** (1975) Storytelling Society of America. **❚28❚ Publications:** *AES News,* monthly. Newsletter. Contains happenings in the storytelling world, book reviews, and listing of seminars and courses offered. **❚29❚ Price:** $25. **❚30❚ ISSN:** 1234-5678. **❚31❚ Circulation:** 5000. **❚32❚ Advertising:** accepted. **❚33❚ Alternate Formats:** online. **❚34❚ Also Cited As:** *American Society of Eclectic Storytellers.* **❚35❚ Conventions/Meetings:** annual (with exhibits) - 2007 Sept. 14-16, Ypsilanti, MI; 2008 Nov. 1-9, Boulder, CO.

Description of Numbered Elements

❚1❚ Keyword. In each of the sections, keywords are given as subheadings and listed alphabetically. Organizations are listed in alphabetical order under their principal keyword subheading. Since the listings are arranged by keyword, the user will find organizations having similar interests grouped together within each keyword subheading.

❚2❚ Entry Number. Entries are numbered sequentially and the entry number (rather than the page number) is used in the Name and Keyword Index to refer to the organization. To facilitate location of the entries in the text, the first entry number on each left-hand page and the last entry number on each right-hand page are provided at the top outer corners of the pages.

❚3❚ Organization Name. The formal name is given; 'The' and 'Inc.' are omitted in most listings, unless they are an integral part of the acronym used by the association.

❚4❚ Acronym. Indicates the short form or abbreviation of the organization's name, usually composed of the initial letter or syllable of each word in it.

❚5❚ Address. The address is generally that of the permanent national headquarters, or of the chief official for groups that have no permanent office.

❚6❚ Telephone Numbers. These are listed when furnished by the organization.

❙7❙ Toll-free, Fax, and Telex. These are listed when furnished by the organization.

❙8❙ E-mail. This is listed when furnished by the organization.

❙9❙ Website. The primary web address for the organization or contact person listed.

❙10❙ Chief Official and Title. The name of a full-time executive, an elected officer, or other contact person designated by the association is provided.

❙11❙ Founding Date. Indicates the year in which the organization was formed. If the group has changed its name, the founding date is for the earliest name by which it was known. If, however, the group was formed by a merger or supersedes another group, the founding date refers to the year in which this action took place.

❙12❙ Members. The figure represents individuals, firms, institutions, other associations, or a combination of these categories. Since membership constantly fluctuates, the figure listed should be considered an approximation. If an organization describes itself as nonmembership, such notation is made in the entry preceding the descriptive text.

❙13❙ Membership Dues. Fees required of members as reported by the organization. Dues often vary according to membership category.

❙14❙ Staff. Many associations operate with a small paid or volunteer staff. The fact that an organization has no paid staff does not mean it has a limited program. Many groups carry on extensive activities through volunteer workers and committees.

❙15❙ Budget. The approximate annual budget for all activities is listed as reported by the organization.

❙16❙ Regional, State, and Local Groups. Indicates the number of regional, state, and local associations, chapters, clubs, councils, and posts affiliated with the national organization.

❙17❙ Languages. The official and/or working languages of the organization are listed, if other than English.

❙18❙ Geographic Scope. The boldface word **Multinational** indicates a multinational scope of the organization; otherwise, the geographic scope is assumed to be National.

❙19❙ Description. The description briefly outlines the membership, purpose, and activities of the association. Where no description is given, the title of the group usually is self-explanatory; in some cases, no summary of activities could be obtained.

❙20❙ Libraries. Provides information for organizations that maintain a library. Includes type of collection, holdings, and subject matter of collection, if available.

❙21❙ Awards. Provides information for organizations that offer awards. Includes name, frequency, type, and recipient of award.

❙22❙ Computer Services. Lists computer-based services offered by the organization, including online services and databases, bibliographic or other search services, automated mailing list services, and electronic publishing capabilities.

❙23❙ Telecommunication Services. Notes special communications services sponsored by the organization. Services included are hotlines, electronic mail/bulletin boards, and telephone referrals.

❙24❙ Subgroups. Lists those subgroups, including committees, sections, divisions, councils, departments, etc., that give an indication of the activities of the group, as distinguished from such administrative committees such as membership, finance, and convention. This information often supplements the description (see paragraph 19) by providing details about the organization's programs and fields of interest. Geographic divisions are omitted.

❙25❙ Affiliated With. Lists organizations sponsored by or directly related to the listed group. Organizations listed under this rubric can be found in *EA* or in *International Organizations.*

❙26❙ Also Known As. If the group is also known by another name, legally doing business under another name, or otherwise operates under a name different than its official title, that name is provided here.

❙27❙ Supersessions, Mergers, and Former Names. If the group superseded another organization or was formed by a merger, the original organizations are listed. Former names and the date of change to a new name, if available, are also listed.

❙28❙ Publications. The official publications are listed in alphabetical order with frequencies. When available, a brief description of the publication is provided. Additional publications, such as newspaper columns, are listed following the words 'Also publishes.' When provided, languages in which the publications are available are noted. If the group has indicated that no publications are issued, this is noted in the entry's main body.

❙29❙ Price. The figures are as provided by the organization.

❙30❙ ISSN. The International Standard Serial Number is a unique code for the purpose of identifying a specific serial publication. It is listed when provided by the organization; not all publications have been assigned an ISSN.

❙31❙ Circulation. This figure is as reported by the organization.

❙32❙ Advertising. Indicates whether or not the association accepts advertising in the publication.

❙33❙ Alternate Formats. Notes online, CD-ROM, diskette, and microform (includes microfiche and microfilm) availability.

❙34❙ Also Cited As. Lists any alternate or former names of the publication.

❙35❙ Conventions/Meetings. The frequency of national or international sessions and the dates and locations (city, state, and country), of the association's conventions, meetings, or conferences are given, if available at the time of publication. Also noted is the inclusion of commercial exhibits. If the group has indicated that no conventions or meetings are held, this is noted in the entry's main body.

Name and Keyword Index

A comprehensive alphabetical Name and Keyword index is provided in Part 3 of this edition of the Encyclopedia. Note that *each reference refers to the entry number, rather than the page on which the entry is listed.* Alphabetization rules ignore articles, prepositions, and conjunctions. A collection of references in this index would appear this way:

❙1❙ Amer. Soc. of Earth Sciences [6359], 123 Salina St., Syracuse, NY 13201 (315)222-950
❙2❙ Earth Sciences, Amer. Soc. of [6359]
❙3❙ Earth Sciences Soc., USA [★6359]
❙4❙ Geology
　　Amer. Soc. of Earth Sciences [6359]
❙5❙ *Highways* Asphalt Recycling and Reclaiming Assn [3728]
❙6❙ Natl. Soc. of Constitutional Training —Address unknown since 1988
❙7❙ Soc. for the Advancement of Space Travel—Defunct
❙8❙ Turkish Air Assn. [IO]

Description of Numbered Index References

❙1❙ Each association's primary reference includes the mailing address and telephone number of the group.

❙2❙ Associations are alphabetized by important words in the name. These references aid in locating organizations whose correct name is unknown to the user.

❙3❙ Any reference with a ★ preceding the entry number indicates that the organization is not listed separately, but is mentioned within the description of another entry. These references would include the organization's former or alternate name as well as names of important committees, projects, or programs.

❙4❙ Associations appear alphabetically by primary and added keywords (see keyword list in this volume). These references allow the user to access all organizations within a particular field of interest.

❙5❙ Keywords that are italicized are added keywords and do not appear as subject headings within a section.

❙6❙ Organizations that are untraceable are noted as 'address unknown.'

❙7❙ Defunct associations are listed as such.

❙8❙ This index includes references to associations listed in the *Encyclopedia of Associations: International Organizations.*

Geographic Index

Entries in *EA*'s Geographic Index are listed according to the state in which the organization's headquarters are located. They are then sub-arranged by city and listed alphabetically according to the names of the organizations within each city.

A sample entry is shown below.

❙1❙ Amer. Soc. of Earth Sciences ❙2❙ [3348]
❙3❙ 123 Salina St.
　　PO Box 1992
　　Allen Park, NY 13201
❙4❙ Ph: (315)555-9500
❙5❙ Patsy Rachel, Pres.

Description of Numbered Elements

❙1❙ **Organization Name.** The formal name is given; 'The' and 'Inc.' are omitted in most listings, unless they are an integral part of the acronym used by the association.

❙2❙ **Entry Number.** Refers to the sequential entry number (rather than the page number) assigned to the organization's main entry in Volume 1, where other details concerning membership, objectives and activities, and publications can be found.

❙3❙ **Address.** The address is generally that of the permanent national headquarters, or of the chief official for groups that have no permanent offices. The city appears in **boldface.**

❙4❙ **Telephone Number.** A telephone number is listed when furnished by the organization.

❙5❙ **Chief Official and Title.** Lists the name of a full-time executive, an elected officer, or other contact person designated by the association.

Executive Index

Entries in *EA*'s Executive Index are listed alphabetically according to the surname of the chief executive of the organization. When an individual is listed as the chief executive of more than one organization, entries are arranged by organization name.

A sample entry is shown below.

❙1❙ Rachel, Patsy, Pres.
❙2❙ Amer. Soc. of Earth Sciences ❙3❙ [3348]
❙4❙ 123 Salina St.
　　PO Box 1992
　　Allen Park, NY 13201
❙5❙ Ph: (315)555-9500

Description of Numbered Elements

❙1❙ **Chief Official and Title.** Lists the name of a full-time executive, an elected officer, or other contact person designated by the association.

❙2❙ **Organization Name.** The formal name is given; 'The' and 'Inc.' are omitted in most listings, unless they are an integral part of the acronym used by the association.

❙3❙ **Entry Number.** Refers to the sequential entry number (rather than the page number) assigned to the organization's main entry in Volume 1, where other details concerning membership, objectives and activities, and publications can be found.

❙4❙ **Address.** The address is generally that of the permanent national headquarters, or of the chief official for groups that have no permanent offices. The city appears in boldface.

❙5❙ **Telephone Number.** A telephone number is listed when furnished by the organization.

Geographic Abbreviations

United States and U.S. Territories

AK Alaska
AL Alabama
AR Arkansas
AZ Arizona
CA California
CO Colorado
CT Connecticut
DC District of Columbia
DE Delaware
FL Florida
GA Georgia
GU Guam
HI Hawaii
IA Iowa
ID Idaho
IL Illinois
IN Indiana
KS Kansas
KY Kentucky
LA Louisiana
MA Massachusetts
MD Maryland
ME Maine
MI Michigan
MN Minnesota
MO Missouri
MS Mississippi
MT Montana
NC North Carolina
ND North Dakota
NE Nebraska
NH New Hampshire
NJ New Jersey
NM New Mexico
NV Nevada
NY New York
OH Ohio
OK Oklahoma
OR Oregon

PA Pennsylvania
PR Puerto Rico
RI Rhode Island
SC South Carolina
SD South Dakota
TN Tennessee
TX Texas
UT Utah
VA Virginia
VI Virgin Islands
VT Vermont
WA Washington
WI Wisconsin
WV West Virginia
WY Wyoming

Table of Abbreviations Used in Addresses and the Index

Acad   Academy
AFB   Air Force Base
Amer   American
APO   Army Post Office
Apt   Apartment
Assn   Association
Ave   Avenue
Bd   Board
Bldg   Building
Blvd   Boulevard
Br   Branch
Bur   Bureau
c/o   Care of
Co   Company
Coll   College
Comm   Committee
Commn   Commission
Conf   Conference
Confed Confederation
Cong   Congress
Corp   Corporation
Coun   Council
Ct   Court

Dept   Department
Div   Division
Dr   Drive
E   East
Expy   Expressway
Fed   Federation
Fl   Floor
Found   Foundation
FPO   Fleet Post Office
Ft   Fort
Fwy   Freeway
Govt   Government
GPO   General Post Office
Hwy   Highway
Inc   Incorporated
Inst   Institute
Intl   International
Ln   Lane
Ltd   Limited
Mfrs   Manufacturers
Mgt   Management
Mt   Mount
N   North
Natl   National
NE   Northeast
No   Number
NW   Northwest
Pkwy   Parkway
Pl   Place
PO   Post Office
Prof   Professor
Rd   Road
RD   Rural Delivery
RFD   Rural Free Delivery
Rm   Room
RR   Rural Route
Rte   Route
S   South
SE   Southeast
Sect   Section
Soc   Society

Sq	Square	Subcommn	Subcommission	UN	United Nations
St	Saint, Street	SW	Southwest	Univ	University
Sta	Station	Terr	Terrace, Territory	U.S.	United States
Ste	Sainte, Suite	Tpke	Turnpike	U.S.A.	United States of America
Subcomm	Subcommittee	T.V.	Television	W	West

Currency Abbreviations and Definitions

Arranged by Currency Abbreviation

Abbr.	Currency Unit	Country
$	U.S. dollar	American Samoa, British Virgin Islands, Guam, Marshall Islands, Federated States of Micronesia, U.S.
$A	Australian dollar	Australia, Kiribati, Nauru, Norfolk Island, Tuvalu
$B	Belizean dollar	Belize
$b	boliviano	Bolivia
$F	Fijian dollar	Fiji
œ	pound sterling	England, Northern Ireland, Scotland, Wales
œC	Cyprus pound	Cyprus
œE	Egyptian pound	Egypt
œG	Gibraltar pound	Gibraltar
œS	Sudanese pound	Sudan
Syr	Syrian pound	Syria
A	Argentinian austral	Argentina
Af	afghani	Afghanistan
AF	Aruban florin	Aruba
AS	Austrian Schilling	Austria
B	balboa	Panama
B$	Bahamian dollar	Bahamas
BD	Bahraini dinar	Bahrain
BD$	Barbados dollar	Barbados
BFr	Belgian franc	Belgium
Bht	baht	Thailand
Bm$	Bermuda dollar	Bermuda
Br$	Brunei dollar	Brunei Darussalam
Bs	bolivar	Venezuela
C	colon	Costa Rica, El Salvador
Cd	cedi	Ghana
C$	Canadian dollar	Canada
C$	new cordoba	Nicaragua
CFP	Colonial Francs Pacifique	New Caledonia
ChP	Chilean peso	Chile
CI$	Cayman Island dollar	Cayman Islands
CoP	Colombian peso	Colombia
Cr$	cruzado	Brazil
CRs	Ceylon rupee	Sri Lanka
CuP	Cuban peso	Cuba
D	dalasi	Gambia
DA	dinar	Algeria
Db	dobra	Sao Tome and Principe
DFr	Djibouti franc	Djibouti
Dg	dong	Vietnam
Dh	dirham	Morocco
Din	dinar	Bosnia-Hercegovina, Croatia, Macedonia, Slovenia, Yugoslavia
DKr	Danish krone	Denmark, Faroe Islands, Greenland
DM	Deutsche Mark	Germany
DP	Dominican peso	Dominican Republic
Dr	drachma	Greece
Ec	escudo	Cape Verde
EC$	East Caribbean dollar	Antigua-Barbuda, Dominica, Grenada, Montserrat, St.Christopher-Nevis, St. Lucia, St. Vincent and the Grenadines
ECU	European currency unit	European Economic Community
E$	Ethiopian birr	Ethiopia
Eg	emalangeni	Swaziland
Esc	escudo	Portugal
EUR	Euro	Austria, Belgium, Finland, France, Germany, Greece, Ireland, Italy, Luxembourg, Netherlands, Portugal, Spain
f	florin	Netherlands
FM	Finnish mark	Finland
Fr	franc	Andorra, France, French Guiana, Guadeloupe, Martinique, Monaco, Reunion Island, St. Pierre and Miquelon
FrB	Burundi franc	Burundi
Fr CFA	Communaute Financiere Africaine franc	Benin, Burkina Faso, Cameroon, Central African Republic, Chad, Comoros, Congo, Cote d'Ivoire, Equatorial Guinea, Gabon, Mali, Niger, Senegal, Togo
Ft	forint	Hungary
G	gourde	Haiti
GBP	Guinea-Bissau peso	Guinea-Bissau
G$	Guyana dollar	Guyana
GFr	Guinea franc	Guinea
Gs	guarani	Paraguay
HK$	Hong Kong dollar	Hong Kong
ID	Iraqi dinar	Iraq
IKr	Icelandic krona	Iceland
IRœ	Irish pound	Republic of Ireland
IS	Israel shekel	Israel
It	inti	Peru
J$	Jamaican dollar	Jamaica
JD	Jordanian dinar	Jordan
K	kina	Papua New Guinea
K	new kip	Laos
Kcs	koruna	Czech Republic, Slovakia
KD	Kuwaiti dinar	Kuwait
KSh	Kenyan shilling	Kenya
Ky	kyat	Myanmar (Burma)
Kz	kwanza	Angola
L	leu	Romania
L$	Liberian dollar	Liberia
LD	Libyan dinar	Libya
Le	leone	Sierra Leone
LFr	Luxembourg franc	Luxembourg
Lk	lek	Albania
Lp	lempira	Honduras
L£	Lebanese pound	Lebanon
Lr	lira	Italy, San Marino
Lv	leva	Bulgaria
M$	Malaysian dollar	Malaysia
MFr	Malagasy franc	Madagascar
MKw	Malawi kwacha	Malawi
Ml	maloti	Lesotho
ML	Maltese lira	Malta

MP	Mexican peso	Mexico
MRs	Mauritius rupee	Mauritius
MRu	Maldivian rufiya	Maldives
Mt	metical	Mozambique
N	naira	Nigeria
NAf	Antillean florin	Netherlands Antilles
Ng	ngultrum	Bhutan
NKr	Norwegian krone	Norway
NP	nuevo peso	Uruguay
NRs	Nepalese rupee	Nepal
NTs	New Taiwanese dollar	Taiwan
NZ$	New Zealand dollar	Cook Islands, New Zealand, Niue
Og	ouguiya	Mauritania
P	pula	Botswana
PP	Philippine peso	Philippines
PRs	Pakistan rupee	Pakistan
Ptas	peseta	Spain
Ptcs	pataca	Macao
Q	quetzal	Guatemala
QRl	riyal	Qatar
R	rand	South Africa, Namibia
Rb	ruble	Armenia, Azerbaijan, Belarus, Estonia, Georgia, Kazakhstan, Kirgizstan, Latvia, Lithuania, Moldova, Russia, Tajikstan, Turkmenistan, Ukraine, Uzbekistan
RFr	Rwandan franc	Rwanda
riel	riel	Cambodia
Rl	Iranian rial	Iran
Rlo	rial Omani	Oman
Rp	rupiah	Indonesia
Rs	rupee	India
S	sucre	Ecuador
S$	Singapore dollar	Singapore
Sf	Suriname florin	Suriname
SFr	Swiss franc	Switzerland, Liechtenstein
SI$	Solomon Island dollar	Soloman Islands
SKr	Swedish krona	Sweden
SRl	Saudi riyal	Saudi Arabia
SRs	Seychelles rupee	Seychelles
SSh	Somali shilling	Somalia
T$	pa'anga	Tonga
TD	Tunisian dinar	Tunisia
Tg	tugrik	Mongolia
Tk	taka	Bangladesh
TL	Turkish lira	Turkey
TSh	Tanzanian shilling	Tanzania
TT$	Trinidad and Tobagoan dollar	Trinidad and Tobago
USh	Ugandan shilling	Uganda
V	vatu	Vanuatu
W	won	Democratic People's Republic of Korea, Republic of Korea
Y	yen	Japan
YRl	Yemen rial	Yemen
Yu	yuan	People's Republic of China
Z	Zaire	Zaire
Z$	Zimbabwe dollar	Zimbabwe
ZKw	Zambian kwacha	Zambia
Zl	zloty	Poland

Following is a list of keywords used in EA. The section(s) in which each keyword appears are listed after each keyword. Within each keyword, entries are arranged alphabetically by organization name.

Abortion. 7, 8, 9
Academic Freedom 5
Academic Placement 5
Accounting 1, 3, 8, 9, 17
Accreditation 5, 7, 8, 9
Acid Maltase Deficiency 8
Acoustics 4
Acquisitions. 1
Acrobatics. 14
Actors. 1, 18
Acupuncture 8
Adhesives 1
Adirondacks 6
Administration 5
Administrative Services 1, 3, 15
Admissions 5
Adoption 7
Adult Education 5, 17
Adventist 7, 11
Advertising 1, 5, 13, 17
Advertising Auditors. 1
Aerobics. 14
Aerospace. 1, 4, 5, 6, 12, 13, 14
Aerospace Medicine 8
Afghan. 16
Afghanistan 6, 7, 9
Africa 1, 7, 9
African. 5, 6, 10
African-American . . .1, 3, 4, 5, 6, 7, 9, 10
Agents 1
Aging. 7, 8
Agribusiness 2
Agricultural Development. 2
Agricultural Education 2, 5, 17
Agricultural Engineering. 17
Agricultural Equipment. 1, 2
Agricultural Law 3
Agricultural Science 2
Agriculture 1, 2, 3, 4, 9, 15, 17
Agroforestry 2
AIDS 7, 8, 9
Aikido. 5, 14
Air Force 3, 12
Aircraft. 1, 6, 15
Albanian 9, 10

Alcohol 8
Alcohol Abuse 7
Alcoholic Beverages 1, 3, 9, 13
Alleghenies. 6
Allergy. 8
Alpine 16
Alternative Education 5
Alternative Lifestyles 8
Alternative Medicine 8, 11
Alternative Technology 4
Alumni. 10, 17
Alzheimer's Disease 8
Amateur Radio 13
Ambulatory Care. 8
Amegroid 6
American 6, 9
American Indian 9, 10, 11
American Legion 12
American Revolution 6, 7, 12
American South 6
American West. 6
Americans Overseas 10
Americas 9
Amish 11
Amusement Parks 1, 13
Amyotrophic Lateral Sclerosis 8
Anarchism 9
Anatomy 5, 8
Andean 6
Anesthesiology. 8
Anglican 5, 11
Anglican Catholic. 11
Anguilla 16
Animal Breeding 2, 13
Animal Research 4, 8
Animal Rights 7
Animal Science 1, 2, 4, 17
Animal Welfare. 2, 7, 8, 9, 11
Animals 2, 7, 8, 13, 18
Animation. 6
Anthropology 4, 5, 17
Anthroposophical. 11
Anti-Communism 9
Anti-Poverty 7
Anti-Racism 7

Antiques 1, 13
Antiquities 6
Aphasia 8
Apheresis 8
Apiculture. 2
Appalachian 6, 10
Apparel 1
Appliances. 1, 13, 15
Appraisers 1
Appropriate Technology. 9
Aquaculture. 2
Aquatics. 5
Arab. 5, 9, 10, 16
Arabic 5, 6, 10
Arbitration and Mediation 3, 7
Archaeology 4
Archery 14
Architecture. 1, 3, 4, 5, 17
Archives 1, 6
Argentina 16
Armed Forces 3, 7, 10, 12
Armenian 5, 6, 10, 11
Arms. 13
Armwrestling 14
Army 3, 12
Art 1, 6, 8, 13, 15
Art History. 5, 6
Art Therapy. 8
Artifacts. 6, 13
Artificial Intelligence 4
Artificial Organs 8
Artists. 1, 6, 9, 13
Arts 1, 2, 5, 6, 7, 8, 13, 17
Arts and Crafts. 1, 7, 13
Arts and Sciences 6, 17
Arumanian 10
Asatru 11
Asbestos 1
Ascended Masters 11
Asia 9
Asian 3, 5, 6, 10
Asian Studies 5
Asian-American. 6, 10, 15
Asian-Indian 16
Assault 7

Shuffleboard 14	Sports Law 3	Technology Education 1, 4, 5, 7
Sicilian. 10	Sports Medicine 8	Telecommunications 1, 3, 4, 8
Sickle Cell Anemia 8	Sports Officials 14	Telegraphy 13
Sikh. 8, 11	Squash 14	Telemetry 4
Sinatra, Frank 18	Sri Lanka 16	Telephone Service. 1
Singles 7	Sri Lankan 10	Telephones 13
Skating 14	Standards 3, 4, 5, 9	Television 9, 18
Skiing. 6, 14	Star Trek 18	Temperance 7
Slavic 5, 6, 10	Star Wars 18	Tennis 14
Sleep. 8, 9	State Government. 3	Terrorism 9
Slovak 6, 10	States Rights. 9	Testing 4, 5
Slovenian 6, 10	Stationery. 1	Textbooks. 5
Small Business 1	Statistics 4	Textiles 1, 4, 13, 15
Smoking 8	Steam Engines 13	Thanatology 7
Snow Sports 14	Stoker, Bram 18	Theatre. 1, 5, 6, 17
Snowshoe Racing 14	Stone 1, 13	Theology 5, 11
Soap Box Derby 14	Storytelling 6	Theosophical 11
Soccer. 14	Strategic Defense Initiative. 9	Therapy 7, 8
Social Action 9	Stress 8	Thermal Analysis 4, 8
Social Change 1, 7, 9	Stress Analysis. 4	Thoracic Medicine. 8
Social Clubs 10	Stress Management. 8	Thyroid 8
Social Fraternities 17	Stroke 8	Tibet. 9
Social Issues 7, 9	Student Services 5, 7	Tibetan 6
Social Justice. 3, 5, 7, 9	Students 5	Time. 6
Social Responsibility 9	Stuttering 8	Time Equipment 1
Social Sciences 4, 7, 17	Substance Abuse 3, 5, 7, 8, 9	Timepieces. 5, 13
Social Security 3, 9	Subterranean Construction. 4	Tires 1, 4
Social Service 7, 11	Subud 11	Tissue. 8
Social Sororities 17	Sudden Infant Death Syndrome 8	Tithing 9, 11
Social Studies 5	Sugar. 1, 2	Tobacco 1, 2, 8, 9
Social Welfare 3, 5, 7, 9, 11	Suicide 7	Touch-Healing 8
Social Work. 5, 7	Summer School 5	Tourism. 1, 16
Socialism 3, 9	Support Groups. 7, 8	Toxic Exposure 7, 8, 9
Sociology 4, 9, 17	Surfing. 14	Toxicology 4, 8
Softball 14	Surgery 8	Toys 1, 13, 15
Soil. 2, 4	Surplus 1	Track and Field. 14
Soil Conservation 2	Surrogate Parenthood 7	Tractor Pulling 14
Solar Energy 4, 9	Surveying 1, 4	Tractors 13
Somalia 10	Survival 5	Trade 1
Sonography 8	Swedish 6, 10	Traffic 3, 9
Sororities 17	Swimming 14	Trails 6, 14
South Africa 9, 16	Swine 2, 13	Trainers. 1, 14
Southern Africa. 16	Swiss 6, 10	Transgender 7
Southern Asians 9	Switzerland 16	Translation 1, 4, 6
Space 1, 4, 5, 9	Systems Integrators 1	Transplantation. 8
Spain 16	T'ai Chi. 8, 14	Transportation . . . 1, 3, 4, 7, 9, 13, 15, 17
Spanish. 6, 9, 10, 17	Table Tennis 14	Trapping 2
Spanish American War 12	Tableware. 1	Trauma 8
Spanish Civil War 12	Taiwan 5, 9	Travel 1, 2, 3, 5, 7, 12, 13, 16
Special Days 9, 13	Taiwanese. 10	Travel Services 1
Special Education 5	Tallness 7	Trees 1
Special Forces 12	Tangible Assets 1	Trees and Shrubs 2
Spectroscopy. 4	Tarot 13	Trial Advocacy 3, 5
Speech 5, 9, 17	Tattooing 1, 6, 11	Tropical Medicine 8
Speech and Hearing. 7, 8	Tax Reform 9	Tropical Studies 4
Speleology 4	Taxation. 1, 3, 9	Trucking 7, 11
Spina Bifida 8	Taxidermy. 1	Trucks. 13, 14
Spinal Injury 8	Tea 2	Tug of War 14
Spiritual Life 6, 11	Teacher Education. 5	Turkey 9, 16
Spiritual Understanding. 5, 11	Teachers 5	Turkish 5, 6, 10
Sporting Goods 1	Technical Consulting 1, 4	Tutoring 5
Sports. 1, 13, 14, 15, 18	Technical Education 5	Twins 8
Sports Facilities 1, 14	Technology 1, 4, 5, 7, 8, 17	Ukrainian 6, 9, 10

Abortion

10980 ■ Abortion Access Project (AAP)
552 Massachusetts Ave., Ste.215
Cambridge, MA 02139
Ph: (617)661-1161
Fax: (617)492-1915
E-mail: info@abortionaccess.org
URL: http://www.abortionaccess.org
Contact: Susan Yanow, Dir. of Training Initiatives
Founded: 1992. **Description:** Works to ensure access to abortion for all women by increasing abortion services, training new abortion providers, and raising awareness. **Projects:** Hospital. **Publications:** Newsletter, quarterly ● Report.

10981 ■ Life and Liberty for Women
PO Box 271778
Fort Collins, CO 80527-1778
Ph: (970)416-6872
E-mail: info@lifeandlibertyforwomen.org
URL: http://www.lifeandlibertyforwomen.org
Contact: Peggy Loonan, Pres./Exec. Dir.
Description: Women. Advocates for safe abortion. Provides newsletters, research and information covering abortion issues. **Publications:** Newsletter.

10982 ■ Pro-Choice Public Education Project (PEP)
PO Box 3952
New York, NY 10163
Free: (888)253-CHOICE
Fax: (212)977-4578
E-mail: pep@protectchoice.org
URL: http://www.protectchoice.org
Contact: Aimee R. Thorne-Thomsen, Exec. Dir.
Description: Seeks to educate young women about reproductive freedom and choice. **Computer Services:** Mailing lists.

Accreditation

10983 ■ Association for the Accreditation of Human Research Protection Programs (AAHRPP)
915 15th St. NW, Ste.400
Washington, DC 20005
Ph: (202)783-1112
Fax: (202)783-1113
E-mail: accredit@aahrpp.org
URL: http://www.aahrpp.org
Contact: Marjorie Speers PhD, Exec. Dir.
Founded: 2001. **Description:** Offers accreditation to organizations that conduct or review research with humans. Strives to protect the rights and welfare of research participants. Promotes scientifically meritorious and ethically sound research by fostering and advancing the ethical and professional conduct of persons and organizations engaged in research with human participants. Seeks to ensure that organizations comply with federal regulations when conduct-

ing their research. **Telecommunication Services:** electronic mail, mspeers@aahrpp.org. **Publications:** *AAHRPP Advance*, quarterly. Newsletter. Alternate Formats: online.

Adoption

10984 ■ AASK - Adopt a Special Kid
8201 Edgewater Dr., Ste.103
Oakland, CA 94621
Ph: (510)553-1748
Free: (888)680-7349
Fax: (510)553-1747
E-mail: info@aask.org
URL: http://www.adoptaspecialkid.org
Contact: Vali Ebert, Exec. Dir.
Founded: 1973. **Staff:** 10. **Budget:** $1,000,000. **Description:** Promotes adoption for children who have special needs; develops adoptions services and programs; advocates systemic and legislative remedies to improve special needs adoptions and develops and implements special events. **Formerly:** (2003) Adopt a Special Kid. **Conventions/Meetings:** monthly Bring A Child Into Your Life - workshop.

10985 ■ Adopt America Network (AAN)
1025 N Reynolds Rd.
Toledo, OH 43615
Ph: (419)534-3350
Free: (800)246-1731
Fax: (419)534-2995
E-mail: adoption@adoptamericanetwork.com
URL: http://www.adoptamericanetwork.com
Contact: Jani Miller, Chm.
Founded: 1983. **Description:** Strives to find good families for the children who wait in foster care. Increases public awareness of adoption concerns. Provides family adoption preparation and training, home studies and post-adoption services. **Publications:** *Visions*, semiannual. Newsletter. Alternate Formats: online.

10986 ■ Adoptee-Birthparent Support Network (ABSN)
6439 Woodridge Rd.
Alexandria, VA 22312-1336
Ph: (301)442-9106 (804)692-1285
E-mail: absnmail@verizon.net
URL: http://www.metroreunionregistry.org/ABSN.html
Contact: Suzanne Ashford, Contact
Founded: 1986. **Members:** 200. **Membership Dues:** full, $20 (annual). **Budget:** $5,000. **Description:** Adoptees, adoptive parents, birthparents (biological parents), and siblings; social workers, and adoption professionals. Seeks to provide support, information, and education to members and help them come to terms with the effects of adoption. Provides search assistance to adoptees and birthparents who wish to locate their biological relatives. Administers public outreach and education programs; conducts legislative efforts. **Libraries: Type:** reference. **Holdings:** 100; audio recordings, books, video recordings. **Com-

puter Services:** database, national search and reunion registry. **Committees:** Adoptee Searches; Birthparent Searches; Hospitality; Legislative; Public Education; Publicity. **Publications:** *The Network News*, quarterly. Newsletter. **Price:** included in membership dues. **Conventions/Meetings:** monthly meeting - always second Sunday, alternately in Kensington, MD and Springfield, VA ● monthly workshop.

10987 ■ Adoption Identity Movement (AIM)
PO Box 9783
Grand Rapids, MI 49509
Ph: (616)531-1380
Fax: (616)532-5589
Contact: Peg Richer, Dir.
Founded: 1977. **Membership Dues:** lifetime donation, $30. **State Groups:** 8. **Description:** Birthparents, adoptive parents, and adoptees; others affected by or interested in adoption. Promotes the opening of sealed adoption records for adoptees and birth parents searching for their biological families. Conducts lobbying activities. Provides support services and referrals for those engaged in searches for biological family members. Maintains search registry and speakers' bureau; conducts educational programs. Confidential intermediary for the courts of Michigan. **Libraries: Type:** reference. **Holdings:** 85; archival material, books, clippings, periodicals. **Subjects:** adoption. **Computer Services:** database, soc. sec.deathindex, phone index, national name sweep ● online services. **Telecommunication Services:** phone referral service. **Conventions/Meetings:** semimonthly meeting - always first and third Wednesday of the month; **Avg. Attendance:** 20.

10988 ■ Adoption Information Services (AIS)
558 Dovie Pl.
Lawrenceville, GA 30045
Ph: (770)339-7236
Fax: (770)277-6912
E-mail: aismarcia@comcast.net
URL: http://www.adoptioninfosvcs.com
Contact: Marcia S. Barker, Exec. Dir./Founder
Founded: 1983. **Members:** 25. **Budget:** $150,000. **Regional Groups:** 1. **State Groups:** 1. **Description:** Adoptive parents, adoptees, birth parents. Dedicated to providing information regarding adoption, long term foster care opportunities and search information. Sponsors adoption information events. **Computer Services:** Mailing lists, of members. **Affiliated With:** Resolve, The National Infertility Association. **Publications:** *Exchange List*. Contains agencies, attorneys, social workers, and community groups involved in adoption. **Conventions/Meetings:** annual Adoption Fair - meeting.

10989 ■ Adoptions Together
10230 New Hampshire Ave., Ste.200
Silver Spring, MD 20903
Ph: (301)439-2900
Fax: (301)439-9334

E-mail: info@adoptionstogether.org
URL: http://www.adoptionstogether.org
Contact: Janice Goldwater, Founder/Exec. Dir.
Founded: 1990. **Multinational. Description:** Provides child placement services. Offers prenatal support and counseling for pregnant women. Provides birth parents with education, guidance and support in making the best decision for their child. **Computer Services:** database, waiting families ● database, waiting kids ● information services, adoption resources. **Programs:** AdoptionWorks; Domestic Adoption; International Adoption. **Projects:** If Not Us. **Publications:** *Conversation,* quarterly. Newsletter. Alternate Formats: online.

10990 ■ ALMA Society - Adoptees' Liberty Movement Association (ALMA)
PO Box 85
Denville, NJ 07834
E-mail: manderson@almasociety.org
URL: http://almasociety.org
Contact: Marie Anderson, Coor.
Founded: 1971. **Membership Dues:** life, $50. **Description:** Adults (persons over 18) who were adopted or foster children, birth parents who have given children up for adoption, adoptive parents, and individuals separated by adoption. Seeks to increase public awareness of what the group feels is the injustice of laws that seal birth and adoption records from adoptees. Provides mutual assistance to members searching for their birth parents or children. **Computer Services:** database, vital statistics of adoptees, natural parents, and other persons separated by adoption. **Committees:** Search.

10991 ■ American Adoption Congress (AAC)
PO Box 42730
Washington, DC 20015
Ph: (202)483-3399
E-mail: ameradoptioncong@aol.com
URL: http://www.americanadoptioncongress.org
Contact: Paul Schibbelhute, Pres.
Founded: 1978. **Members:** 1,000. **Membership Dues:** individual, $50 (annual) ● student, $40 (annual) ● senior, $45 (annual) ● household, $60 (annual) ● search/support group, $70 (annual) ● friend of AAC, $110 (annual) ● organization, adoption agency, $160 (annual). **Regional Groups:** 7. **State Groups:** 50. **Local Groups:** 800. **Description:** Adopted persons, birthparents, and adoptive parents; members of related organizations devoted to leadership in adoption reform. Purposes are to: further information on adoptions and related social-psychological issues in the U.S. by study, research, teaching, and conferences; collect, publish, and disseminate information; act as a national clearinghouse and public information center. Develops alternative model plans for adoption; conducts regional educational conferences; provides research referrals to adoption-related services. **Awards:** Emma May Vilardi Award. **Frequency:** annual. **Type:** recognition. **Recipient:** for lifelong contribution to adoption advocacy. **Computer Services:** Mailing lists. **Committees:** Communications; Education; Finance; Legislation; Membership; Organization Development; Professional Relations; Publications. **Publications:** *Decree,* quarterly. Contains adoption-related articles, reports, stories, legislation and education. ● *Legislative Report.* Includes updates in publications "Decree" and "GoodCause". **Conventions/Meetings:** annual conference (exhibits) - always April.

10992 ■ American World War II Orphans Network (AWON)
5745 Lee Rd.
Indianapolis, IN 46216
Ph: (540)310-0750
E-mail: awon@aol.com
URL: http://www.awon.org
Contact: Judith Hoffman, Pres.
Founded: 1991. **Members:** 600. **Membership Dues:** individual, $30 (annual). **Budget:** $35,000. **State Groups:** 52. **Description:** Sons and daughters of American military personnel listed as killed or missing during World War II. Works to keep the memory of their parents alive, and to locate all individuals

orphaned during World War II. Supports pilgrimages to cemeteries and battlesites; maintains index of Americans killed in action during World War II whose names are listed on memorials nationwide; assists members in locating their parents' war buddies and family members. Operates speakers' bureau; compiles statistics; organizes educational conferences. **Libraries: Type:** not open to the public. **Holdings:** 200. **Subjects:** American casualties in World War II, war orphans, World War II history. **Awards: Frequency:** biennial. **Type:** recognition. **Recipient:** to members for service. **Computer Services:** database, World War II casualties and their family members, war orphans ● mailing lists, gatherings locally and nationally ● online services, website. **Telecommunication Services:** electronic bulletin board, members and nonmembers may post messages about the orphan experience or asking for assistance in research. **Publications:** *The Star,* quarterly. Newsletters. Documents orphans' search for information about their fathers; local get togethers; national conferences; and information about the organization. **Circulation:** 2,000. **Conventions/Meetings:** biennial conference, educational meeting with speakers and sharing circles for members to share stories about experiences and research (exhibits).

10993 ■ Association of Administrators of the Interstate Compact on Adoption and Medical Assistance (AAICAMA)
810 1st St. NE, Ste.500
Washington, DC 20002
Ph: (202)682-0100
Fax: (202)289-6555
E-mail: rbockweg@aphsa.org
URL: http://aaicama.aphsa.org
Contact: Elizabeth Oppenheim JD, Prog.Dir.
Founded: 1986. **State Groups:** 42. **Description:** Promotes special needs adoption. **Affiliated With:** American Public Health Association. **Publications:** *Bridges,* 3/year. Newsletter. Provides timely information to adoption professionals dealing with special needs adoption. **Price:** $25.00/year. Alternate Formats: online ● *Compilation of PIQs, PAs, and Ims.* **Price:** $45.00 ● *Issue briefs.* Papers. Provide analyses and advice on implementing policy affecting the Title IV-E Adoption Assistance Program and service delivery. **Price:** $125.00 complete set that includes index ● Reports. Cover research and conduct surveys of member states. **Conventions/Meetings:** annual conference ● regional meeting.

10994 ■ Bastard Nation: The Adoptee Rights Organization (BN)
PO Box 1469
Edmond, OK 73083-1469
Ph: (415)704-3166
Fax: (415)704-3166
E-mail: bn@bastards.org
URL: http://www.bastards.org
Contact: Marley Greiner, Exec. Chair
Founded: 1996. **Membership Dues:** bastard/friend of bastard/organization, $35 (annual) ● group/family, $75 (annual) ● sponsor, $100 (annual) ● patron, $250 (annual) ● benefactor, $500 (annual) ● senior/student/hardship, $15 (annual). **Description:** Works to establish respect, dignity and equal rights for adoptees, including the restoration of the right of access to adult adoptees, of government documents pertaining to the adoptee's historical, genetic, and legal identity, including the original birth certificate and adoption decree. **Publications:** *Baby Dump News: A Weekly E-Chronicle of Newborn Abandonment, Noenaticide, Safe Haven Legislation and Related Issues.* **Price:** free ● *The Bastard Byline,* every 4-6 weeks. Newsletter. **Price:** free. Alternate Formats: online ● *The Bastard Quarterly (BQ).* Newsletters. **Price:** free for members. **Advertising:** accepted. Alternate Formats: online.

10995 ■ Children with AIDS Project of America (CWA)
PO Box 23778
Tempe, AZ 85285-3778
Ph: (480)774-9718
Fax: (480)921-0449

E-mail: jimjenkins@aidskids.org
URL: http://www.aidskids.org
Contact: Jim Jenkins, Co-Founder
Description: Works to recruit families to adopt HIV children, AIDS orphans and drug addicted infants, refer them to private homes and public adoption agencies. **Computer Services:** database, families caring for children ● database, national resources pertaining to adoption, foster care, respite, children with AIDS, drug abandoned babies.

10996 ■ Children Awaiting Parents (CAP)
595 Blossom Rd., Ste.306
Rochester, NY 14610
Ph: (585)232-5110
Free: (888)835-8802
Fax: (585)232-2634
E-mail: info@capbook.org
URL: http://www.capbook.org
Contact: Ms. Maryjane K. Link, Exec. Dir.
Founded: 1969. **Staff:** 5. **Description:** Commits to find families for America's longest waiting children in the foster care system. **Additional Websites:** http://www.childrenawaitingparents.org. **Publications:** *The CAP Book,* with biweekly updates. Provides national listing of waiting children's photos and biographies. **Price:** $65.00/year. Alternate Formats: CD-ROM. **Conventions/Meetings:** annual Adoption Awareness Walk - meeting.

10997 ■ Concerned Persons for Adoption (CPFA)
c/o Jean Giouvanos, Membership Dir.
11 Crestwood Rd.
Rockaway, NJ 07866
URL: http://www.cpfanj.org
Contact: Kathleen Walz, Pres.
Founded: 1972. **Members:** 350. **Membership Dues:** regular, $25 (annual). **Staff:** 20. **State Groups:** 1. **Description:** Volunteer support group dedicated to the belief that every child deserves a family; is not an adoption agency. Objective is to offer support and information to the adoption community. Recruits prospective parents; assists individuals interested in adopting; provides educational and social assistance to adoptive parents. Offers Adoption Awareness Program in high schools; maintains research group; provides calendar of cultural events reflecting biological heritage of children; sponsors social events. Monitors related legislative activities and encourages involvement in the legislative process; collects and distributes items and supplies such as clothing, medicine, food, and medical equipment for children in orphanages. **Libraries: Type:** not open to the public. **Holdings:** 30; audio recordings, books. **Subjects:** adoption. **Committees:** Charity; Domestic; International; Legislative; Newsletter; Older Child Advocate; Publicity; Social. **Publications:** *Adoption Today Newsletter,* monthly. **Price:** included in membership dues. **Circulation:** 350. **Advertising:** accepted ● Also publishes agency fact sheets and brochures. **Conventions/Meetings:** annual Let's Talk Adoption - conference, adoption agencies and child welfare organizations (exhibits).

10998 ■ Concerned United Birthparents (CUB)
PO Box 503475
San Diego, CA 92150-3475
Free: (800)822-2777
Fax: (858)712-3317
E-mail: info@cubirthparents.org
URL: http://www.cubirthparents.org
Contact: Margy McMorrow, Pres.
Founded: 1976. **Members:** 500. **Membership Dues:** regular, $40 (annual). **Staff:** 1. **Regional Groups:** 6. **State Groups:** 12. **Local Groups:** 3. **Description:** Birthparents and others who support adoption reform. Works to open birth records for adoptees and their birthparents; develop alternatives to the current adoption system; assist members in coping with ongoing suffering and problems of adoption separation. Provides "informed choice" for all women considering releasing a child for adoption. Supports vulnerable families in an effort to prevent unnecessary separation of families by adoption. Provides speakers to

interested groups; sponsors legislative action; generates publicity; engages in research; provides advocacy service for its membership with agencies and referrals to search groups. Compiles statistics. statistics. **Publications:** *Concerned United Birthparents—Communicator*, monthly. Newsletter. Covers adoption issues for people affected by adoption separation; includes histories and information on finding adoption-separated relatives. **Price:** included in membership dues ● *What you should know if you're considering adoption for your baby*. Booklet. **Price:** $2.00. Alternate Formats: online ● Books ● Papers. **Conventions/Meetings:** monthly meeting ● annual retreat.

10999 ■ Families Adopting Children Everywhere (FACE)
PO Box 28058
Baltimore, MD 21239
Ph: (410)488-2656
E-mail: info@faceadoptioninfo.org
Contact: M.R. Evans, Pres.
Founded: 1975. **State Groups:** 10. **Description:** Offers comprehensive course that covers practical topics on adoption, such as picking an adoption agency, current information on trends in domestic and inter-country adoptions, various choices in adoption, the terminology, the emotions, the monetary costs, etc. **Publications:** *The FACE Adoption Resource Manual*, annual. **Advertising:** accepted. **Conventions/Meetings:** quarterly Family Building through Adoption Courses - seminar.

11000 ■ Families with Children from China (FCC)
c/o Susan Caughman
255 W 90th St., 11C
New York, NY 10024
E-mail: caugh@aol.com
URL: http://www.fwcc.org
Contact: Susan Caughman, Contact
Description: Provides support to families who have adopted children from China. **Publications:** Newsletter ● Membership Directory. **Conventions/Meetings:** dinner ● picnic.

11001 ■ Families for Private Adoption (FPA)
PO Box 6375
Washington, DC 20015-0375
Ph: (202)722-0338
E-mail: info@ffpa.org
URL: http://www.ffpa.org
Contact: Debby Ballweg, Pres.
Founded: 1984. **Members:** 400. **Membership Dues:** regular, $45 (annual) ● sponsoring, $75 (annual) ● sponsoring professional, $100 (annual). **Description:** Individuals who are interested in or have already adopted children through private adoption; attorneys, physicians, and social workers. Assists people who are considering private adoption, which is adoption without the use of an adoption agency. Provides information on adoption procedures and legal concerns; offers referrals to doctors, lawyers, and social workers. Organizes workshops and professional and peer support groups. **Convention/Meeting:** none. **Telecommunication Services:** electronic mail, gertdog4@earthlink.net. **Publications:** *FPA Bulletin*, quarterly. **Price:** included in membership dues ● *Successful Private Adoption*. Handbook ● Newsletter.

11002 ■ Friends in Adoption (FIA)
44 South St.
PO Box 1228
Middletown Springs, VT 05757-1228
Ph: (802)235-2373
E-mail: fia@friendsinadoption.org
URL: http://www.friendsinadoption.com
Contact: Dawn Smith-Pliner, Founder/Dir.
Founded: 1982. **Members:** 40. **Membership Dues:** family, $20 (annual). **Regional Groups:** 1. **Description:** Families who have adopted children and families interested in adopting. Works to provide emotional support and encouragement to people involved in the adoption process. Provides a forum for discussing adoption issues and an opportunity to meet other families who've been touched by adop-

tion; conducts social events such as Waiting Parents Tea, family outings and adult gatherings; conducts educational programs. **Libraries: Type:** lending. **Holdings:** 50; books, periodicals. **Subjects:** adoption and parenting. **Subcommittees:** Wish (Waiting Is So Hard). **Publications:** Newsletter, semiannual ● Brochure. **Conventions/Meetings:** board meeting - 3/year ● monthly support group meeting, with speakers.

11003 ■ Independent Search Consultants (ISC)
PO Box 10192
Costa Mesa, CA 92627
E-mail: referrals@iscsearch.com
URL: http://www.iscsearch.com
Contact: Patricia Sanders, Pres./Exec. Dir.
Founded: 1980. **Multinational. Description:** Individuals assisting in searches for birth-families separated by adoption. Seeks to: provide a means of certification for active search consultants; promote ethical standards of conduct and quality assistance; encourage public understanding of the rights of the adoptee, the adoptive parent, and the birthparent; serve as a professional association for search consultants. Offers search consultant certification on national, state, and specialized levels. Individuals qualify for certification by taking an exam, documenting 500 hours of search assistance or volunteer service, and securing personal recommendations. Sponsors panels, seminars, and workshops on adoption search. Offers speakers on all aspects of adoption education and referrals to search agencies, support groups, and certified consultants. **Libraries: Type:** reference. **Holdings:** 100. **Subjects:** adoption, heredity, state laws. **Committees:** Educational. **Departments:** Publications. **Divisions:** Board of Certification. **Publications:** *Consultant Newsletter*, monthly ● *Consultants Directory*, annual ● *State Search Books*.

11004 ■ Institute for Adoption Information
PO Box 4405
Bennington, VT 05201
Ph: (802)442-2845
E-mail: info@adoptioninformationinstitute.org
URL: http://www.adoptioninformationinstitute.org
Contact: Kathryn Creedy, Exec. Dir.
Founded: 1995. **Staff:** 1. **Nonmembership. Description:** Represents adoptees, birth parents, adoptive parents, and adoption professionals. Promotes adoption. Provides positive support to members of adoption triad, and enhances the understanding of adoption. **Awards:** David P. Schwartz Foundation Grant. **Type:** monetary. **Formerly:** (2003) Celebrate Adoption. **Publications:** *A Guide to Adoption for Health Care and Counseling Professionals*. Book. **Price:** $8.00 ● *A Journalist's Guide to Adoption*. Book. **Price:** free. Alternate Formats: online ● *An Educator's Guide to Adoption*. Book. Serves as a guide to understand how classroom assignments impact children from non-traditional families and what teachers can do to help. **Price:** $8.00 ● *Why Should You Understand Adoption - How Social Bias Against Adoption Impacts Society*. Brochure.

11005 ■ International Soundex Reunion Registry (ISRR)
PO Box 2312
Carson City, NV 89702
Ph: (775)882-7755
E-mail: webmaster@isrr.net
URL: http://www.isrr.net
Founded: 1975. **Description:** Serves as a central reunion registry for adults (18 years or older) who were adopted, orphaned, or separated from their parents by war or divorce, or were foundlings, foster children, or wards of the state, and their blood relatives. Provides a free mutual consent registry system for matching persons who desire contact with their next of kin-by-birth. Conducts surveys; compiles statistics. **Libraries: Type:** open to the public. **Committees:** Genetic Guidance Evaluation. **Publications:** *Financial Report*, annual ● *Statistical Report*, annual. **Conventions/Meetings:** annual board meeting.

11006 ■ Jewish Children's Adoption Network (JCAN)
PO Box 147016
Denver, CO 80214-7016
Ph: (303)573-8113
Fax: (303)893-1447
E-mail: jcan@qwest.net
URL: http://www.users.qwest.net/~jcan
Contact: Vicki Krausz, Exec. Dir.
Founded: 1990. **Staff:** 2. **Budget:** $50,000. **Languages:** English, Hebrew, Yiddish. **Description:** Dedicated in finding appropriate homes for Jewish children, many of who have special needs. **Convention/Meeting:** none. **Libraries: Type:** reference; open to the public; by appointment only. **Holdings:** 500; articles, audiovisuals, books, monographs, periodicals. **Subjects:** adoption, infertility, special needs. **Publications:** Newsletter, quarterly. Contains information on adoption and children with special needs. **Price:** free. **Circulation:** 2,800. **Advertising:** accepted.

11007 ■ Joint Council on International Children's Services (JCICS)
117 S St. Asaph St.
Alexandria, VA 22314
Ph: (703)535-8045
Fax: (703)535-8049
E-mail: jcics@jcics.org
URL: http://www.jcics.org
Contact: Rick Gibson, Pres.
Membership Dues: agency (with 25-250 number of clients), $478-$3,187 (annual) ● non-profit parent group/child advocacy organization (99-250 or more members), $105-$210 (annual) ● non-profit medical clinic, $210 (annual). **Multinational. Description:** Advocates on behalf of children in need of permanent families by promoting ethical practices in inter-country adoptions. **Publications:** *The Adoptive Parent Preparation Manual*. **Price:** $30.00 suggested donation. Alternate Formats: online ● *The Bulletin*, quarterly. Newsletter ● *White Paper on International Child Welfare*. Alternate Formats: online ● Membership Directory. Alternate Formats: online. **Conventions/Meetings:** annual conference.

11008 ■ Kidsave International
11835 W Olympic Blvd., Ste.295
Los Angeles, CA 90064
Ph: (310)479-5437
Free: (888)KID-SAVE
Fax: (310)479-5434
E-mail: info@kidsave.org
URL: http://www.kidsave.org
Contact: Randi Thompson, Exec. Dir./CEO/Co-Founder
Multinational. Description: Increases the number of older children living in permanent, adoptive families. Builds awareness of the plight of children worldwide living in orphanages and foster care. Tests and promotes successful models for change that are focused on moving children out of institutions and into permanent families. **Publications:** Annual Report. Alternate Formats: online.

11009 ■ Latin America Parents Association (LAPA)
PO Box 339-340
Brooklyn, NY 11234
Ph: (718)236-8689
E-mail: info@lapa.com
URL: http://www.lapa.com
Contact: Andrea Quatrale, Pres.
Founded: 1975. **Members:** 300. **Membership Dues:** regular, $50 (annual). **Regional Groups:** 5. **Description:** Adoptive parents and supporters. Seeks to: aid persons seeking to adopt children from Latin America and assist families after they have adopted; distribute information regarding adoption and offer moral support before, during and after the adoption process. Keeps records on procedures, expenses, and new sources for adoption throughout Latin America; offers a forum providing educational and social information for the adoptive family. Provides financial support to Latin American orphanages. Offers workshops and seminars on adoption procedures, parenting issues.

Hosts a teens-only event, picnic, weekend getaway, and Latin Culture Night. **Committees:** International Adoptions; International Relief. **Publications:** *Que Tal*, periodic. Newsletter. Alternate Formats: online.

11010 ■ Liberal Education for Adoptive Families (LEAF)

1295 Omaha Ave. N
Stillwater, MN 55082
Ph: (651)436-2215
Contact: Cheryl Hall-Rock, Dir.
Founded: 1975. **Description:** A post-adoption service organization providing legislative and agency policy reform, client counseling (including search assistance and referrals), training and technical assistance for public and private agencies, public education seminars, and media presentations. Cosponsors Minnesota Reunion Registry, which is fed into the system of the International Soundex Reunion Registry, which contains input from adoptees and birthparents throughout the U.S., Mexico, Canada, and abroad.

11011 ■ National Adoption Center (NAC)

1500 Walnut St., Ste.701
Philadelphia, PA 19102
Ph: (215)735-9988
Free: (800)TO-ADOPT
Fax: (215)735-9410
E-mail: kmullner@nacenter.adopt.org
URL: http://www.adopt.org
Contact: Ken Mullner, Exec. Dir.
Founded: 1972. **Staff:** 26. **Description:** Expands adoption opportunities for children throughout the United States, particularly the adoption of children with special needs and children from minority cultures, through public awareness and information and referral with families nationwide. Pictures and descriptions of waiting children are highlighted on Website. **Libraries: Type:** reference. **Holdings:** articles, books. **Subjects:** adoption. **Additional Websites:** http://www.adoptionclubhouse.org. **Publications:** *Adoption Update*, semiannual. Newsletter. Provides information on adoption legislation, children waiting for adoption, and children with special needs. **Price:** free. **Circulation:** 12,500 ● *NACzine*, monthly. Magazine. Alternate Formats: online ● *Photolisting*, quarterly ● Bibliography ● Brochures ● Films ● Pamphlets ● Videos. On adoption and foster care.

11012 ■ National Council for Adoption (NCFA)

225 N Washington St.
Alexandria, VA 22314
Ph: (703)299-6633
Fax: (703)299-6004
E-mail: ncfa@adoptioncouncil.org
URL: http://www.adoptioncouncil.org
Contact: Thomas Atwood, Pres./CEO
Founded: 1980. **Members:** 1,200. **Staff:** 14. **Budget:** $7,000,000. **Languages:** English, Spanish. **Description:** Represents voluntary agencies, adoptive parents, adoptees, and birthparents. Works to protect the institution of adoption and ensure the confidentiality of all involved in the adoption process. Promotes appropriate adoption practice with legislators, policymakers, human service agencies and staff, and the public. Strives for the regulation of all adoptions to ensure the protection of birthparents, children, and adoptive parents. Serves as an information clearinghouse; provides technical assistance. Conducts research programs; monitors state and national legislation affecting adoption and maternity services. Maintains hall of fame. Compiles statistics. Operates speakers' bureau; compiles statistics. **Libraries: Type:** reference. **Holdings:** 8,000. **Subjects:** adoption, maternity services, infertility, child welfare, youth development. **Awards:** Adoption Hall of Fame. **Type:** recognition ● Friend of Adoption. **Frequency:** annual. **Type:** recognition. **Programs:** Infant Adoption Awareness Training. **Formerly:** (1992) National Committee for Adoption. **Publications:** *Adoption Factbook III*. Includes data on international adoption trends and analyses of important policy questions. **Price:** $39.95. **Circulation:** 6,000. Alternate Formats: online ● *National Adoption Reports*, quarterly.

Newsletter. Provides information for those who have already adopted a child or are considering adopting, legal information or pregnancy counseling services. **Circulation:** 5,200. Alternate Formats: online ● *NCFA Directory of Member Agencies*, periodic. Lists member agencies by state. **Price:** free. **Conventions/Meetings:** annual conference (exhibits) - always spring, usually Washington, DC.

11013 ■ National Council for Single Adoptive Parents (NCSAP)

PO Box 567
Mount Hermon, CA 95041-0567
Free: (888)490-4600
E-mail: info@ncsap.com
Contact: Hope Marindin, Exec.Dir.
Founded: 1973. **Staff:** 1. **Description:** Single persons who have adopted or wish to adopt children. Provides subscribers with information and assistance; informs public and private agencies of legislation and research applying to single-person adoption; supports the adoption "of adoptable children to loving families, regardless of any difference in race, creed, color, religion or national origin, or of any handicap the children may have." **Convention/Meeting:** none. **Awards: Frequency:** biennial. **Type:** recognition ● **Frequency:** biennial. **Type:** recognition. **Formerly:** (1975) Single Parents Committee; (1995) Committee for Single Adoptive Parents. **Publications:** *Handbook for Single Adoptive Parents*, biennial. A how to book. **Price:** $25.00. ISSN: 9634-0452.

11014 ■ North American Council on Adoptable Children (NACAC)

970 Raymond Ave., Ste.106
St. Paul, MN 55114
Ph: (651)644-3036
Fax: (651)644-9848
E-mail: info@nacac.org
URL: http://www.nacac.org
Contact: Joe Kroll, Exec. Dir.
Founded: 1974. **Members:** 2,500. **Membership Dues:** individual, parent group, $45 (annual) ● organization, enhanced parent group, $200 (annual) ● national/corporate, $1,000 (annual). **Staff:** 33. **Budget:** $1,800,000. **State Groups:** 50. **Local Groups:** 400. **National Groups:** 139. **Description:** Members of citizen adoption groups (composed primarily of adoptive parents of "special needs" children) and other individuals from judicial, child welfare, and legislative areas. Advocates the right of every child to a permanent, loving home. Provides direct assistance to local and state adoption advocacy efforts; acts as a clearinghouse for adoption information; liaises with other adoption organizations. Sponsors an annual national training conference. Also sponsors Adoption Awareness Month. Conducts extensive education and outreach through the media and pre- and post-adoptive support programs. Provides resources for local advocacy programs. **Awards: Type:** recognition. **Computer Services:** database, adoption-related support groups. **Telecommunication Services:** information service, provides information and referrals on adoption and adoption services via phone, email, fax or letter. **Publications:** *Achieving Permanence for Every Child: The Effective Use of Adoption Subsidies*. Book. Presents comparison of the differences between foster care and adoption subsidy rates. Alternate Formats: online ● *Adoptalk*, quarterly. Newsletter. Provides legal and activity updates related to adoption and foster care. **Price:** free for members. ISSN: 0273-6497. **Circulation:** 4,000 ● *Adoption Assistance in America: A Programmatic Analysis Fifteen Years after Federal Implementation*. Report. Identifies eligibility rules, practices and policies affecting program effectiveness. ● *Forever Families*. Report. Alternate Formats: online ● *Parenting Resource Manual*. Features articles about the realities faced by multiracial families. ● *While You Wait*. Bulletin. Contains information and advice for parents in preparing for adoption. Alternate Formats: online ● Also publishes adoption-related materials. **Conventions/Meetings:** annual conference, provides training on adoption-related issues (exhibits).

11015 ■ Operation Identity (OI)

7045 Maynardville Pike
Knoxville, TN 37918
Ph: (865)922-9099
Fax: (865)922-9098
E-mail: todd@operationidentity.com
URL: http://www.operationidentity.com
Contact: Sally File, Coor.
Founded: 1979. **Members:** 100. **Regional Groups:** 20. **State Groups:** 1. **Local Groups:** 1. **Description:** Individuals 18 years of age or older in search of their biological parents (from whom they were separated as a result of adoption or divorce); family members, friends, and interested persons. Educates and informs the public on facts relating to adoption; aids searching adults by supplying information on searching procedures and methods and by advising on the use of available research sources; offers emotional support to adult adoptee, adoptive parents, and birthparents. Provides information on legislation and court actions concerning adoption records. Maintains small collection of adoption and search-related books; operates speakers' bureau. **Publications:** Newsletter, quarterly. **Conventions/Meetings:** annual conference ● monthly meeting - always fourth Thursday.

11016 ■ Organized Adoption Search Information Services (OASIS)

PO Box 53-0761
Miami Shores, FL 33153
Ph: (305)947-8788
E-mail: rayrivers@netzero.com
Contact: Rachel S. Rivers, Dir.
Founded: 1980. **Membership Dues:** life, $70. **For-Profit. Description:** Offers individual assistance to adult adoptees, birth and/or adoptive parents and others who are searching for or wish to be reunited with members of birth families. Maintains confidential search files for each searching member and a cross-match birth index registry. **Affiliated With:** American Adoption Congress; International Soundex Reunion Registry.

11017 ■ ORIGINS

c/o Mary Anne Cohen, Co-Founder
PO Box 556
Whippany, NJ 07981
Ph: (973)428-9683
E-mail: maireaine@hexatron.com
Contact: Mary Anne Cohen, Co-Founder
Founded: 1980. **Members:** 200. **Description:** Women whose children have been surrendered for adoption. Works to: recognize the emotional needs of these mothers and help them deal with the continuing guilt, anguish, and concern for their lost children; unite women in similar situations; provide moral support and help in searching for their children, for the purpose of learning whether the children are alive, well, and in loving homes. Sponsors search clinics which include advice on methodology and contacts. Provides search assistance to fathers, siblings, grandparents, and other relatives. Maintains collection of books and clippings on adoption, search, and contact. Keeps mailing list and membership records. Operates speakers' bureau. Provides referrals. **Affiliated With:** American Adoption Congress. **Publications:** Newsletter, quarterly. **Price:** $20.00/year. **Circulation:** 180.

11018 ■ Orphan Voyage (OV)

c/o Gay Swearington
13906 Pepperrell Dr.
Tampa, FL 33624
Ph: (813)961-1393
Fax: (904)396-8523
E-mail: asyman@aug.com
URL: http://www.geocities.com/orphanvoyage1953
Contact: Alice Syman, Contact
Founded: 1953. **Members:** 500. **Description:** Adult adopted people, adoptive parents, and professionals engaged in adoption practice or related to people in adoption; natural parents of children who were adopted. Assists in building relationships between adult adopted people and their birth families; informs adoptive parents and professionals of the needs of

adopted children; offers guidance and hope to birth parents whose children were adopted. Maintains liaison with groups and individuals working along similar lines through correspondence and distribution of materials. Develops museum. **Libraries: Type:** reference. **Holdings:** 900. **Subjects:** materials to assist in understanding differentiation of orphans. **Formerly:** (1962) Life History Study Center. **Publications:** *A Proper Response*, quarterly. Newsletter. **Price:** $10.00/year. **Circulation:** 200 ● *The Adopted Break Silence*. Book. **Price:** $8.00 ● *Friendly Debate Across the Waters*. Contains correspondence between Mr. S. Lipson and Jean Paton. **Price:** $3.50 ● *Pioneer for Adoption Reform*. Interview of Jean Paton. **Price:** $3.00 ● *They Serve Fugitively*. Poem. **Price:** $5.00 ● Report. Contains reports of interviews with adopted people living in various parts of lower Michigan. **Price:** $9.00 ● Books ● Pamphlets. **Conventions/Meetings:** periodic regional meeting.

11019 ■ Stars of David International (SDI)
3175 Commercial Ave., Ste.100
Northbrook, IL 60062-1915
Ph: (847)509-9929
Free: (800)STAR-349
Fax: (847)509-9545
E-mail: info@starsofdavid.org
URL: http://www.starsofdavid.org
Contact: Elyse Flack, Dir.
Founded: 1984. **Membership Dues:** individual or family, $50 (annual) ● professional or agency, $125 (annual). **Multinational. Description:** Works as a Jewish adoption information and support network. Provides a network of support, adoption information and education to prospective parents, adoptive families, adult adoptees, birth families, and the Jewish community. **Libraries: Type:** reference. **Subjects:** adoption. **Formerly:** (1989) Stars of David. **Publications:** *Star Tracks*, quarterly. Newsletter.

11020 ■ WAIF
Address Unknown since 2006
Founded: 1955. **Members:** 3,000. **Staff:** 4. **Budget:** $250,000. **Description:** Founded by actress Jane Russell and dedicated to the principle of "a permanent and loving family for every child." Operates national and local adoption recruitment, public information, and advocacy programs. Sponsors Project Adopt, which finds families for older and handicapped children. Provides information on adoption procedures; trains social workers and volunteers in fundraising, public relations, publicity, and education concerning adoption. Refers individuals and families to licensed local adoption agencies. **Awards:** National Humanitarian Award. **Frequency:** periodic. **Type:** recognition. **Recipient:** for outstanding contributions to adoption and/or waif ● Outstanding Service Award. **Type:** recognition. **Recipient:** for outstanding service to the field of adoption. **Publications:** *Update*, periodic. Newsletter. Reports on WAIF's efforts to promote adoption of children; includes information on legislation and fundraising and case histories. **Price:** free. **Conventions/Meetings:** periodic conference.

11021 ■ World Partners Adoption (WPAdopt)
c/o Cindy Harding, Exec. Dir.
2205 Summit Oaks Ct.
Lawrenceville, GA 30043
Ph: (770)962-7860
Free: (800)350-7338
Fax: (770)513-7767
E-mail: wpadopt@aol.com
URL: http://www.worldpartnersadoption.org
Contact: Cindy Harding, Exec. Dir.
Founded: 1999. **Multinational. Description:** International child placement agency specializing in international adoptions from the Republic of Kazakhstan, China, Ukraine, and Russia. Children waiting for immediate adoption are age 6 months to 10 years old. Provides families with comprehensive and compassionate assistance during the entire adoption process.

Adventist

11022 ■ Adventist World Aviation (AWA)
PO Box 251
Berrien Springs, MI 49103-0251

Ph: (269)473-0135
Fax: (269)471-4049
E-mail: info@flyawa.org
URL: http://www.flyawa.org
Contact: Donald B. Starlin, Pres.
Founded: 1995. **Staff:** 6. **Budget:** $340,000. **Nonmembership. Multinational. Description:** Serves as missionary-sending agency that provides aviation, communications, and logistical support to organizations that provides for people in need. **Affiliated With:** Adventist-Laymen's Services and Industries. **Publications:** *Flight Log Newsletter*, quarterly. Contains project news. **Price:** free. **Circulation:** 2,400. Alternate Formats: online. **Conventions/Meetings:** annual convention (exhibits).

Afghanistan

11023 ■ America's Fund for Afghan Children
c/o The White House
1600 Pennsylvania Ave. NW
Washington, DC 20500
Ph: (202)456-1111 (202)456-1414
Fax: (202)456-2461
E-mail: comments@whitehouse.gov
URL: http://www.whitehouse.gov/afac
Description: Fund created by President George W. Bush, asking American children to help Afghan children by contributing one dollar individually or collectively.

Africa

11024 ■ Malawi Project
3314 Van Tassel Dr.
Indianapolis, IN 46240
E-mail: info@malawiproject.org
URL: http://www.malawiproject.org
Contact: Richard Stephens, Exec. Dir./Chm.
Founded: 1993. **Multinational. Description:** Provides medical supplies, health care and other humanitarian aid to the African nation of Malawi. Improves the agriculture and education of Malawi individuals. Offers food aid and health care programs. **Publications:** Newsletter. Alternate Formats: online.

11025 ■ Touching Hearts
PO Box 761
Novi, MI 48376
E-mail: mdixon@touchinghearts.net
URL: http://www.touchinghearts.net
Contact: Michele Dixon, Pres./Co-Founder
Founded: 2001. **Multinational. Description:** Focuses on the needs of Malawi, Africa. Aims to raise awareness of the needs of people in Africa and to empower people to respond to those needs. Offers resources and education necessary for the self-reliance of communities. **Telecommunication Services:** electronic mail, hallen@touchinghearts.net. **Publications:** Brochure.

African-American

11026 ■ African American Life Alliance (AALA)
1 Staton Dr.
Upper Marlboro, MD 20774-1717
Ph: (301)249-2738 (301)249-0074
Fax: (301)249-0070
E-mail: contact@lifedrum.org
URL: http://www.lifedrum.org
Contact: Paulette Roseboro, Exec. Dir.
Founded: 1991. **Description:** Works to educate black community about how sexual promiscuity and illicit moral activities have invaded the communities and are eroding the families, organizations, schools and churches. **Publications:** *Life Drum Newsletter*, 1-2/year. Provides information regarding the social and health problems abortion and contraceptive drugs and devices has caused in the African American community.

Aging

11027 ■ 60 Plus Association
1600 Wilson Blvd., Ste.960
Arlington, VA 22209
Free: (888)560-7587
Fax: (703)807-2073
E-mail: info@60plus.org
URL: http://www.60plus.org
Contact: James L. Martin, Pres.
Founded: 1992. **Members:** 500,000. **Staff:** 7. **Budget:** $650,000. **Description:** Individuals aged 60 years or older. Promotes adoption of a "less government, less taxes approach to seniors' issues". Conducts lobbying and advocacy activities. **Awards:** Ben Franklin Awards. **Type:** recognition. **Recipient:** to members of Congress who have sponsored legislation to repeal the "death" tax ● Guardian of Seniors' Rights. **Frequency:** annual. **Type:** recognition. **Recipient:** for lawmakers or parties judged to be "pro-senior". **Publications:** *Scorecard*, periodic. Report ● *Senior Voice*, periodic. Newsletter.

11028 ■ Aging in America (AIA)
1000 Pelham Pkwy. S
Bronx, NY 10461
Ph: (718)409-8200
E-mail: pointofentry@aiamsh.org
URL: http://www.aginginamerica.org
Contact: Charlotte Ostman, Contact
Founded: 1979. **Budget:** $3,700,000. **Description:** Research and service organization for professionals in gerontology. Objectives are: to produce, implement, and share effective and affordable programs and services that improve the quality of life for the elderly community; to better prepare professionals and students interested in, or currently involved with, aging and the aged. Conducts research projects, educational and training seminars, and in-service curricula for long-term and acute care facilities. Operates: Education and Training Program to educate professionals and para-professionals; Projects With Industry Program to help both able-bodied and disabled elderly individuals enter into the work force. Conducts local programs in New York City including: In-Home Services, which provides Meals-on-Wheels, transportation, and housekeeping; Alzheimer's Day Care; Respite and Long-Term Residence; Self-Governing Senior Centers. Provides social services, including case management, information, referral, and advocacy; Research. Maintains speakers' bureau; compiles statistics. **Awards: Type:** recognition. **Formerly:** (1952) Morningside House. **Publications:** *Sharing Newsletter*, quarterly ● Brochure. Outlines various programs.

11029 ■ Alliance for Aging Research (AAR)
2021 K St. NW, Ste.305
Washington, DC 20006-1003
Ph: (202)293-2856
Free: (800)497-0360
Fax: (202)785-8574
E-mail: info@agingresearch.org
URL: http://www.agingresearch.org
Contact: Daniel Perry, Exec. Dir.
Founded: 1986. **Staff:** 11. **Budget:** $2,300,000. **Description:** Represents gerontologists and other medical professionals, executives, and members of Congress. Works to increase private and public research into aging. Supports policies concerning: productive aging; independence for older Americans; successful aging; human genome initiative. **Publications:** *Aging Research on the Threshold of Discovery* ● *Alliance Reports* ● *Americans' View on Aging* ● *Health Care Options under MEDICARE: The Choice is Yours*. Report ● *How to Help Your Patients with Age-Related Macular Degeneration*. Booklet. **Price:** free. Alternate Formats: online ● *Independence for Older Americans: Task Force for Aging Research Funding* ● *Investing in Older Women's Health* ● *Issue Reports*, periodic ● *It's Time for a Heart to Heart*. Brochure. Contains an educational kit for CHF. **Price:** free. Alternate Formats: online ● *Living Longer & Loving It!*, quarterly. Newsletter. Alternate Formats: online ● *Meeting the Medical Needs of the Senior*

Boom: The National Shortage of Geriatricians ● *Putting Aging on Hold—Delaying the Diseases of Old Age.* Report. **Price:** $8.00. Alternate Formats: online ● *Report on Public Opinion* ● *The Research Gap* ● *Seven Deadly Myths: Uncovering the Facts About the High Cost of the Last Year of Life.* Report. **Price:** $8.00. Alternate Formats: online ● *Will You Still Treat Me When I'm 65?.* Report. **Price:** $8.00. Alternate Formats: online. **Conventions/Meetings:** periodic conference.

11030 ■ American Association of Homes and Services for the Aging (AAHSA)
2519 Connecticut Ave. NW
Washington, DC 20008-1520
Ph: (202)783-2242
Fax: (202)783-2255
E-mail: info@aahsa.org
URL: http://capwiz.com/aahsa/home
Contact: William L. Minnix Jr., Pres./CEO
Founded: 1961. **Members:** 5,600. **Membership Dues:** national/state/local organization, $575 (annual) ● alliance, $900 (annual) ● law firm, $1,050 (annual) ● attorney, $350-$675 (annual) ● individual, $90 (annual) ● business firm (based on number of employees), $575-$1,050 (annual) ● bronze, $10,000 (annual) ● silver, $25,000 (annual) ● gold, $50,000 (annual) ● platinum, $100,000 (annual). **Staff:** 95. **Budget:** $17,000,000. **Regional Groups:** 3. **State Groups:** 40. **Multinational. Description:** Works to advance the vision of healthy, affordable, ethical aging services for America. Represents 5,600 mission-driven, not-for-profit nursing homes, continuing care retirement communities, assisted living and senior housing facilities, and community service organizations throughout the U.S. **Awards: Frequency:** annual. **Type:** recognition. **Departments:** Accreditation; Advocacy; Education and Conferences; International; Marketing and Member Communications; Member Services; Public Affairs; Research; Technology and Business Development. **Formerly:** American Association of Homes for the Aging. **Publications:** *American Association of Homes and Services for the Aging Publications Catalog.* Alternate Formats: online ● *Best Practices*, bimonthly. Magazine ● *Directory of Members*, annual. Membership Directory ● *Weekly Perspectives.* Newsletter. Provides legislative and regulatory highlights. **Price:** included in membership dues. **Conventions/Meetings:** conference and meeting - every fall and spring ● semiannual Future of Aging Services - conference - 2008 Mar. 31-Apr. 2, Washington, DC ● annual meeting (exhibits) - 2007 Oct. 22-25, Orlando, FL; 2008 Oct. 13-16, Philadelphia, PA; 2009 Nov. 9-12, Chicago, IL; 2010 Oct. 31-Nov. 3, Los Angeles, CA.

11031 ■ American Association for International Aging (AAIA)
Address Unknown since 2007
Founded: 1983. **Description:** Advocates for the aged; organizations, corporations, foundations, and individuals concerned about the interests and needs of the aged worldwide, particularly in the Third World. Seeks to improve the socioeconomic conditions of older, low-income persons in developing countries through selfhelp, mutual support, and economic development activities. Sponsors international developmental education programs for retired Americans. Provides small grants assistance to economic-development projects for Third World aging; sponsors an information exchange program. **Convention/Meeting:** none. **Supersedes:** Help the Aged. **Publications:** *Aging and the Global Agenda for Women: Conversations in Nairobi* ● *American Association for International Aging Reports*, quarterly. Newsletter. Highlights activities benefiting aging persons worldwide. ● *International Directory of Organizations in Aging* ● *Retired Americans Look at International Development.*

11032 ■ American Society on Aging (ASA)
833 Market St., Ste.511
San Francisco, CA 94103-1824
Ph: (415)974-9600
Free: (800)537-9728
Fax: (415)974-0300

E-mail: info@asaging.org
URL: http://www.asaging.org
Contact: Robert Stein, Pres./CEO
Founded: 1954. **Members:** 10,000. **Membership Dues:** individual, $155 (annual) ● reduced rate, $80 (annual) ● full-time student, $60 (annual) ● organizational, $385 (annual) ● organizational affiliate, $95 (annual). **Staff:** 35. **Budget:** $3,000,000. **Description:** Health care and social service professionals, educators, researchers, administrators, businesspersons, students, and senior citizens. Works to enhance the well-being of older individuals and to foster unity among those working with and for the elderly. Offers 25 continuing education programs for professionals in aging-related fields. **Awards:** Business of the Year Award. **Frequency:** annual. **Type:** recognition ● Media Award. **Frequency:** annual. **Type:** recognition ● New Products and Designs for New Makers Market. **Frequency:** annual. **Type:** recognition. **Recipient:** for best new market product. **Computer Services:** Mailing lists, of members, journal subscribers, and conference attendees. **Committees:** Education and Training; Minority Concerns; Public Policy; Research. **Subgroups:** Business Forum on Aging; Forum on Religion and Aging; Healthcare and Aging Network; International Society for Retirement Planning; Lesbian and Gay Aging Issues Network; Lifetime Education and Renewal Network; Mental Health and Aging Network; Multicultural Aging Network; Network on Environments, Services & Technologies for Maximizing Independence. **Formerly:** (1985) Western Gerontological Society. **Publications:** *Aging Today*, bimonthly. Newspaper. Features critical events and issues in the field of aging, including legislative news, new products and designs, and research. **Price:** included in membership dues; $14.95 /year for nonmembers. **Circulation:** 12,000. **Advertising:** accepted ● *ASA Connection.* Newsletter. Features timely announcements, news briefs, articles, policy and member news. Alternate Formats: online ● *Generations*, quarterly. Journal. Provides practical, current information in the field of aging, with emphasis on medical and social practice, research, and policy. **Price:** included in membership dues; $38.00 /year for nonmembers; $50.00 for institutions. ISSN: 0738-7806. **Circulation:** 15,000. **Advertising:** accepted. **Conventions/Meetings:** annual Invest in Aging: Strengthening Families, Communities and Ourselves - conference (exhibits).

11033 ■ Association of Brethren Caregivers (ABC)
1451 Dundee Ave.
Elgin, IL 60120-1949
Ph: (847)742-5100
Free: (800)323-8039
Fax: (847)742-6103
E-mail: abc@brethren.org
URL: http://www.brethren.org/abc
Contact: Kathryn G. Reid, Exec. Dir.
Founded: 1968. **Members:** 24. **Membership Dues:** retirement community, $500 (annual). **Staff:** 5. **Budget:** $650,000. **Description:** Develops resources, leadership, and programs within the caring ministries of the Church of the Brethren and the wider community. **Formerly:** (1989) Church of the Brethren Homes and Hospitals Association; (1990) Board of Brethren Homes and Older Adult Ministries; (1993) Brethren Homes and Older Adult Ministries. **Publications:** *Caregiving*, quarterly. Newsletter. Contains information for the Church of the Brethren on caregiving issues. **Price:** $10.00/year. **Conventions/Meetings:** biennial Caring Ministries Assembly - conference (exhibits) - always late summer ● annual Fellowship of Brethren Homes Forum - retreat, with networking opportunities - early summer.

11034 ■ Association of Jewish Aging Services (AJAS)
316 Pennsylvania Ave. SE, Ste.402
Washington, DC 20003
Ph: (202)543-7500
Fax: (202)543-4090
E-mail: harvey@ajas.org
URL: http://www.ajas.org
Contact: Harvey Tillipman MBA, Pres./CEO
Founded: 1960. **Members:** 125. **Staff:** 3. **Budget:** $500,000. **Multinational. Description:** Non-profit

charitable Jewish homes and nursing homes; retirement and housing units; independent and assisted living, geriatric hospitals, and special facilities for Jewish aged and chronically ill. Conducts institutes and conferences; undertakes legislative activities; compiles statistics. Conducts studies and maintains demographic and other information on Jewish aging. Publishes journals and periodicals on aging. **Awards:** AJAS Jewish Programming Award. **Type:** recognition. **Recipient:** for Jewish programs developed and implemented by AJAS organizations ● AJAS Trustee of the Year Award. **Frequency:** annual. **Type:** recognition. **Recipient:** to an outstanding trustee ● Award of Honor. **Frequency:** annual. **Type:** recognition. **Recipient:** for contributions to the field ● Professional Award. **Type:** recognition. **Recipient:** to an outstanding AJAS professional ● Young Leadership Award. **Frequency:** annual. **Type:** recognition. **Committees:** Legislative. **Affiliated With:** American Association of Homes and Services for the Aging; Jewish Communal Service Association of North America. **Formerly:** (1982) National Association of Jewish Homes for the Aged; (1998) North American Association of Jewish Homes and Housing for the Aging. **Publications:** *E-Update*, monthly. Newsletter. **Advertising:** accepted. Alternate Formats: online ● *Journal on Jewish Aging*, semiannual. **Advertising:** accepted ● *Scribe*, quarterly. Newsletter. Provides immediate and ongoing information about members and activities. **Advertising:** accepted. Alternate Formats: online ● Membership Directory, annual. **Conventions/Meetings:** annual convention (exhibits).

11035 ■ Beverly Foundation (BF)
566 El Dorado St., No. 100
Pasadena, CA 91101-2505
Ph: (626)792-2292
Fax: (626)792-6117
E-mail: info@beverlyfoundation.org
URL: http://www.beverlyfoundation.org
Contact: Don Pearson, Chm.
Founded: 1979. **Staff:** 4. **Budget:** $400,000. **Description:** Aims to enhance the quality of life and care until the last moment of life, thus bettering the well being of older adults, their caregivers, and their families. Engages in research, education and demonstration. Addresses special concerns through programs such as: mobility and transportation within the community; service delivery and care support within institutional and home settings; life enrichment of the body, mind, and spirit for those who live independently and in institutions. Provides technical and informational assistance to professionals, caregivers, and families. Influences other organizations and groups through communication, collaboration, and limited financial support to program partners. Funds activities through efficient use of its own resources and the contributions of others. **Awards:** STAR Award for Excellence. **Frequency:** annual. **Type:** monetary. **Recipient:** to senior transportation provider. **Computer Services:** database, national listing of supplemental transportation programs for seniors.

11036 ■ Center for Advocacy for the Rights and Interests of the Elderly (CARIE)
100 N 17th St., Ste.600
Philadelphia, PA 19103
Ph: (215)545-5728
Free: (800)356-3606
Fax: (215)545-5372
E-mail: menio@carie.org
URL: http://www.carie.org
Contact: Diane Menio, Exec. Dir.
Founded: 1977. **Staff:** 21. **Languages:** English, Spanish. **Description:** Works to improve the quality of life for vulnerable older people. Maintains speaker's bureau. **Computer Services:** Online services, consultation and advocacy service for adults. **Programs:** Abuse Prevention Training; Health Care Fraud Education; Line; Ombudsman. **Publications:** Brochures ● Newsletter, periodic ● Booklets.

11037 ■ The Center for Social Gerontology (TCSG)
2307 Shelby Ave.
Ann Arbor, MI 48103
Ph: (734)665-1126

Fax: (734)665-2071
E-mail: tcsg@tcsg.org
URL: http://www.tcsg.org
Contact: Penelope A. Hommel, Co-Dir.
Founded: 1972. **Staff:** 7. **Budget:** $450,000. **Description:** Purpose is to advance the well-being of older people in the U.S. through research, education, technical assistance, and training. Focuses primarily on legal rights, guardianship and alternative protective services, delivery of legal services, and issues of tobacco and older persons. Provides consulting services. Develops and researches standards for the provision of guardianship services for older people; works to improve the court processes for determining the need for guardianship through development and evaluation of a new model. Conducts periodic training on Legal rights and Legal resources, for legal advocates, nonlawyers who work with the elderly, and older consumers. **Libraries: Type:** reference. **Subjects:** legal and policy issues. **Projects:** Smoke-Free Environments Law. **Formerly:** (1985) International Center for Social Gerontology. **Publications:** *Adult Guardianship Mediation.* Manual. **Price:** $75.00 ● *Adult Guardianship Mediation: An Introduction.* Video. **Price:** $50.00 ● *Best-Practice Notes on Delivery of Legal Services to Older Persons,* quarterly. Bulletin ● *Comprehensive Guide to Delivery of Legal Assistance to Older Persons.* Manual. **Price:** $40.00 ● *Guidelines for Planning and Evaluating Legal Assistance Programs Funded Under the Older Americans Act.* **Price:** $15.00 ● *Legal Services Developers' Resource Manual.* **Price:** $20.00 ● Audiotapes ● Reports ● Adult Guardianship Mediation Manual, Guardianship & Alternatives: A Guide to Personal, Health Care & Financial Management Options, and National Study of Guardianship Systems: Findings & recommendations.

11038 ■ Center for the Study of Aging of Albany (CSA)
706 Madison Ave.
Albany, NY 12208
Ph: (518)465-4927
Fax: (518)462-1339
E-mail: iapaas@aol.com
URL: http://www.centerforthestudyofaging-albany.org
Contact: Sara Harris, Founder/Dir.
Founded: 1957. **Staff:** 3. **Budget:** $150,000. **Description:** Participants include behavioral scientists, educators, gerontologists, physicians, and other health professionals. Promotes education, research, and training; provides leadership in the field of health and fitness for older people. Includes: programs for volunteers and professionals in aging, gerontology, geriatrics, wellness, physical fitness, and mental health; consultant services include adult day care, nutrition, physical and mental fitness, nursing home, housing, and retirement; speakers' bureau. Develops national and international conferences on health, fitness, and prevention. Provides expert assistance in research, institutional and community program development, planning, and organization; offers consultation addressing the development of library resource centers and collections of books on aging. Conducts seminars and offers information and referral services. **Libraries: Type:** reference. **Holdings:** 5,000; books, periodicals. **Subjects:** aging, medicine, mental health, physical activity, sports, psychology, social work, topics of interest to women, housing, nutrition, long-term care, prevention. **Awards:** Raymond Harris Memorial Award. **Frequency:** periodic. **Type:** recognition. **Recipient:** for outstanding contribution to improving quality of life for older men and women. **Also Known As:** International Association of Physical Activity. **Publications:** *Classics in Aging.* Book ● *Environment and Aging.* Book ● *Life Long Health and Fitness: Volume I - Prevention and Human Aging,* annual. Bibliographies. Covers health and fitness. **Price:** $19.95 each ● *Physical Activity, Aging and Sports (Volume I: Prevention and Human Aging).* Manual. **Price:** $39.95 each ● *Physical Activity, Aging and Sports (Volume II: Practice, Program, and Policy).* Manual. **Price:** $39.95 each ● *Physical Activity Aging and Sports (Volume III: Toward Healthy Aging Part I).* Manual. **Price:** $39.95 each ● *Physical Activity Aging and Sports (Volume III: Toward Healthy*

Aging Part II). Manual. **Price:** $39.95 each ● *Safe Therapeutic Exercise for the Frail Elderly.* Manual. **Price:** $19.95 each ● *Senior Citizen School Volunteer Program: A Manual for Program Implementation* ● *Who? Me!? Exercise: Safe Exercise for People Over Fifty.* Manual. Contains sensible advice, reasonable guidelines and alternatives for those with physical problems. **Price:** $5.00 each ● Books. **Conventions/Meetings:** periodic International Conference on Physical Activity, Aging and Sports (exhibits) - every three or four years ● Preventicare: The Key to Health for Life - conference (exhibits).

11039 ■ Children of Aging Parents (CAPS)
PO Box 167
Richboro, PA 18954
Ph: (215)355-6611
Free: (800)227-7294
Fax: (215)355-6824
E-mail: admin@caps4caregivers.org
URL: http://www.caps4caregivers.org
Contact: Karen Rosenberg, Contact
Founded: 1977. **Members:** 900. **Membership Dues:** individual, $25 (annual) ● business, $100 (annual) ● benefactor, $500 (annual) ● sustaining friend, $1,000 (annual). **Staff:** 1. **Budget:** $100,000. **Description:** Gives information and referral service for caregivers of the elderly. Provides information and emotional support on day-to-day caregiver issues. Organizes and promotes caregiver support groups and responds to requests for assistance nationally. **Libraries: Type:** reference. **Holdings:** 400; books, monographs. **Subjects:** caregiving issues, grief, caring for aging parents, stress, aging. **Awards:** Annual Co-Founders Caregiver Award. **Frequency:** annual. **Type:** recognition. **Recipient:** for dedicated care of elderly parent. **Publications:** *The Capsule,* quarterly. Newsletter. Reports on concerns of elderly persons and their families. Includes publications listing, book reviews, and research news. **Price:** included in membership dues. ISSN: 1076-4623. **Circulation:** 2,000. **Advertising:** accepted ● Publishes fact sheets on caregiving issues. **Conventions/Meetings:** annual Conference on Caregiving for Caregivers, for caregivers and professionals involved with elder care (exhibits).

11040 ■ Consumer Consortium on Assisted Living (CCAL)
2342 Oak St.
Falls Church, VA 22046
Ph: (703)533-8121
E-mail: ccal@starpower.net
URL: http://www.ccal.org
Contact: Kathleen Cameron MPH, Chair
Founded: 1995. **Description:** Focuses on the needs, rights and protection of assisted living consumers, their caregivers and loved ones. Educates consumers, trains professionals and advocates for assisted living issues. Works collaboratively with a broad spectrum of people and organizations to support quality assisted living. Provides options for individuals with low incomes. **Computer Services:** Information services, consumers and caregivers facts and issues ● mailing lists, of members (E-updates). **Publications:** *Assisted Living: What You Should Know as a Consumer.* Paper. Alternate Formats: online ● *Future of Quality Care in Assisted Living.* Paper. Alternate Formats: online ● *Not Going to Take It Anymore.* Paper. Alternate Formats: online ● *Why Bother Working Together.* Paper. Alternate Formats: online.

11041 ■ Ebenezer Society (ES)
2722 Park Ave. S
Minneapolis, MN 55407
Ph: (612)874-3460
Fax: (612)874-3465
URL: http://www.fairviewebenezer.org
Contact: Mark Thomas, Pres./CEO
Founded: 1917. **Members:** 45. **Description:** Lutheran congregations and their delegates. Works to provide quality services and facilities for older people with varying needs; to make their lives more healthful, meaningful, and secure. Services are not limited to Lutheran clients. Offers nursing home care for low-income elderly; provides home services, including

medical treatment, to help persons remain in their own homes as long as possible. Sponsors Ebenezer Center for Aging and Human Development which provides consultative services, conducts educational events and applied research, and issues publications. Maintains Ebenezer Foundation as the support arm of the society. Compiles research statistics; offers placement service. Ebenezer means "stone of help". **Libraries: Type:** reference. **Holdings:** archival material. **Affiliated With:** Advocate Health Care; American Association of Homes and Services for the Aging; Minnesota Health and Housing Alliance. **Conventions/Meetings:** annual meeting ● periodic seminar, for administrators and managers.

11042 ■ Elder Craftsmen (EC)
307 7th Ave., Ste.1401
New York, NY 10001
Ph: (212)319-8128
Fax: (212)319-8141
E-mail: info@eldercraftsmen.org
URL: http://www.eldercraftsmen.org
Contact: Patricia Manzione, Exec. Dir./Sec.
Founded: 1955. **Staff:** 5. **Budget:** $205,000. **Description:** Helps men and women 55 and older be creative, productive, and independent. Seeks broader recognition by the general public of the skills and capabilities of older people. Sponsors craft training workshops for representatives of Senior Centers. Sponsors community service projects with older adults making items for people in need. **Affiliated With:** New York State Coalition for the Aging. **Publications:** *Elder Craftnotes,* semiannual. Newsletter ● *What's This Got to do With Quilting: Nine Stories of Southern Women Quilters.* Booklet.

11043 ■ Families U.S.A. Foundation
1201 New York Ave. NW, Ste.1100
Washington, DC 20005-6100
Ph: (202)628-3030
Fax: (202)347-2417
E-mail: info@familiesusa.org
URL: http://www.familiesusa.org
Contact: Ron Pollack, Exec. Dir.
Founded: 1981. **Budget:** $2,500,000. **Description:** Issues reports and other materials on health care and long-term care for use by consumer organizations, policymakers, the media, and state-based coalitions working on health care and long term care reform. **Formerly:** (1989) Villers Foundation. **Publications:** *Crossing to Mexico: Priced Out of American Health Care.* Survey. Surveys Mexican doctors and American consumers about the reasons Americans go to Mexico for routine medical care. **Price:** $5.00 ● *The Crunch: The Health Insurance Crisis Comes to America's Charities.* Survey. Covers the problems of the small business market for health insurance by examining the experiences of 500 nonprofit groups surveyed. **Price:** $5.00 ● *Half of Us: Families Priced Out of Health Protection.* Report. Provides an analysis of government survey data. **Price:** $10.00 ● *The Health Cost Squeeze on Older Americans.* Report. Provides an analysis of elderly out-of-pocket health care costs; compares current costs to those prior to the enactment of Medicare. **Price:** $5.00 ● *The Heavy Burden of Home Care.* Report. Provides an analysis of home care expenditures and the high out-of-pocket costs consumers pay to provide home care. **Price:** $5.00 ● *Making Them Wait For Social Security Disability Benefits.* Report. Provides an analysis of the waiting times and backlogs for people applying for Social Security and SSI Disability benefits. **Price:** $5.00 ● *The Medicare Buy-in: A Promise Unfulfilled.* Report. Describes the Medicare buy-in benefits, the Qualified Medicare Beneficiary and Specified Low-income Medicare Beneficiary. **Price:** $5.00 ● *No Sale: The Failure of Barebones Insurance.* Book. Examines state barebones policies and their ability to provide affordable coverage and to expand insurance to the uninsured population. **Price:** $15.00 ● *Nursing Home Insurance: Who Can Afford It?.* Book. Provides an analysis of the affordability of providing nursing home insurance policies for today's elderly population. **Price:** $5.00 ● *Prescription Costs: America's Other Drug Crisis.* Book. Provides an analysis (for years 1985-1991) of the prices of America's 20 top

selling drugs and the pharmaceutical companies' profits. **Price:** $5.00 ● *They Make That Much.* Survey. Contains salaries of medical specialists, CEOs of drug and insurance companies and large hospitals. **Price:** $5.00 ● Manuals ● Videos. **Conventions/Meetings:** annual Health Advocacy - conference, in conjunction with a wide range of national organizations in Washington, DC - every January.

11044 ■ Gray Panthers (GP)
1612 K St. NW, Ste.300
Washington, DC 20006
Ph: (202)737-6637
Free: (800)280-5362
Fax: (202)737-1160
E-mail: info@graypanthers.org
URL: http://www.graypanthers.org
Contact: Tim Fuller, Exec. Dir.
Founded: 1970. **Members:** 40,000. **Membership Dues:** regular, $20 (annual). **Staff:** 4. **Budget:** $250,000. **Local Groups:** 60. **Description:** Consciousness-raising activist group of older adults and young people. Aims to combat ageism - the discrimination against persons on the basis of chronological age. Believes that both the old and the young have much to contribute to make society more just and humane. Advises, acts as a catalyst for, and organizes local groups of young, middle-aged, and older persons to work on issues of their choosing. Conducts work on eight national interests: national health care, affordable housing, environmental preservation, peace, ending discrimination, education, economic and tax justice, and social justice. **Libraries: Type:** open to the public. **Holdings:** books, periodicals, video recordings. **Subjects:** ageism, healthcare, social security, discrimination. **Awards:** Mahler Grant. **Frequency:** semiannual. **Type:** grant. **Computer Services:** Mailing lists ● online services. **Also Known As:** Gray Panthers Project Fund. **Publications:** *Gray Panther Network*, bimonthly. Newsletter. Contains articles on ageism, health care, housing, disarmament, and other intergenerational issues. **Price:** included in membership dues; $20.00 /year for nonmembers; $35.00/year for organizations. **Advertising:** accepted ● *Network Newsletter*, bimonthly. Covers national Gray Panther issues like housing, health care, and environmental protection. **Circulation:** 40,000. **Advertising:** accepted. **Conventions/Meetings:** semiannual board meeting, on age-related issues, social and justice issues, environment, place, labor ● biennial convention (exhibits).

11045 ■ Health Promotion Institute (HPI)
c/o National Council on Aging
1901 L St. NW, 4th Fl.
Washington, DC 20036
Ph: (202)479-1200
Free: (800)373-4906
Fax: (202)479-0735
E-mail: info@ncoa.org
URL: http://www.ncoa.org/content.cfm?sectionID=37
Contact: James Firman, Pres./CEO
Founded: 1986. **Members:** 700. **Description:** A program of the National Council on Aging. Seeks to aid professionals who are interested in developing and implementing health promotion programs for senior citizens and serving older consumers. Promotes optimal quality of life for older adults, including physical, emotional, and mental health as well as social and spiritual well-being. Advocates for and empowers older adults to achieve health and well-being through a multidisciplinary approach. Provides information and materials on health promotion programs. **Affiliated With:** National Council on Aging. **Formerly:** (1991) National Center for Health Promotion and Aging. **Conventions/Meetings:** annual conference, held in conjunction with NCOA (exhibits).

11046 ■ International Association of Homes and Services for the Ageing (IAHSA)
2519 Connecticut Ave. NW
Washington, DC 20008
Ph: (202)508-9468
Fax: (202)220-0041

E-mail: iahsa@aahsa.org
URL: http://iahsa.net
Contact: Virginia D. Nuessle, Exec. Dir.
Founded: 1994. **Membership Dues:** corporate, government, NGO, business, $550 (annual) ● single site/facility, $150 (annual) ● individual, $100 (annual). **Multinational. Description:** Aims to enhance the quality of care for the elderly. Connects and supports care and service providers worldwide. Fosters an international forum for exchange of research, services, products and training that benefit aged care service providers. Maintains a compilation of a general overview of the aging service systems in various countries. **Publications:** *Alliance*, monthly. Newsletter. Contains news about trends and issues on the global aging agenda, insight into best practices and profiles of aging services worldwide. Alternate Formats: online. **Conventions/Meetings:** biennial international conference (exhibits).

11047 ■ Jewish Association for Services for the Aged (JASA)
132 W 31st St., 15th Fl.
New York, NY 10001
Ph: (212)273-5272 (212)273-5290
Fax: (212)695-3083
E-mail: help@jasa.org
URL: http://www.jasa.org
Contact: Aileen Gitelson, CEO
Founded: 1968. **Staff:** 2,200. **Budget:** $70,000,000. **Local Groups:** 61. **Description:** Provides services necessary to enable the older adult to remain in the community. Maintains 18 community service offices and 24 local senior citizens centers in New York City and Nassau and Suffolk Counties, NY. Services include: case management; information and referral to appropriate health, welfare, educational, social, recreational, and vacation services, and on government benefits and entitlements; personal counseling; financial assistance; health and medical service counsel; counsel on housing and long-term care; homemaker service; group educational and recreational activities through senior citizens centers; information and guidance for social action on legislative issues affecting the elderly; hot lunch programs; referral to summer camps; legal services; protective services; reaching out to the isolated; programs for independent senior clubs; volunteer service opportunities. Conducts programs for elderly Soviet Jewish immigrants. Operates home attendant agencies in Brooklyn and Queens, NY. Trains students from the New York University School of Social Work, Hunter College School of Social Work, Yeshiva University School of Social Work, and Adelphi University School of Social Work. **Affiliated With:** United Jewish Appeal - Federation of Jewish Philanthropies of New York. **Publications:** *JPAC Action Memo/Senior Citizens Advocate*, 10/year. Report. Addresses the issues of interest to senior citizens, especially those with low income. **Price:** free. ISSN: 0882-9403. **Circulation:** 3,000. **Conventions/Meetings:** semiannual workshop.

11048 ■ John A. Hartford Foundation (JAHF)
55 E 59th St., 16th Fl.
New York, NY 10022-1178
Ph: (212)832-7788
Fax: (212)593-4913
E-mail: mail@jhartfound.org
URL: http://www.jhartfound.org
Contact: Corinne H. Rieder, Exec. Dir./Treas.
Founded: 1929. **Members:** 9. **Staff:** 16. **Budget:** $29,000,000. **Description:** Works to promote health care, training, research, and service related to older adults. **Awards: Type:** grant. **Telecommunication Services:** electronic mail, corinne.rieder@jhartfound.org. **Publications:** *The Hartford Foundation Report*, quarterly. Newsletter. Alternate Formats: online.

11049 ■ Latino Gerontological Center (Centro Gerontologico Latino)
75 Maiden Ln., Ste.208
New York, NY 10038
Ph: (212)402-5474

E-mail: info@gerolatino.org
URL: http://www.gerolatino.org
Contact: Mario E. Tapia, Pres./CEO
Founded: 1991. **Members:** 300. **Membership Dues:** individual, $25 (annual) ● organization, $100 (annual) ● senior/student, $5 (annual). **Staff:** 3. **Budget:** $150,000. **Languages:** English, Spanish. **Multinational. Description:** Works to improve the quality of life of Hispanic seniors. Provides Thanksgiving meals to needy families; operates cable television show in Manhattan, NY. Writes question and answer column in New York paper "El Diario" to provide information to Hispanic seniors. **Awards:** Golden Age Award. **Frequency:** annual. **Type:** recognition. **Recipient:** for an individual who has made significant contributions to Latino-Hispanic communities throughout the world. **Conventions/Meetings:** periodic Interamerican Conference on Gerontology (exhibits) ● periodic Northeastern Conference on the Hispanic Elderly (exhibits).

11050 ■ Leadership Council of Aging Organizations (LCAO)
c/o Scott Frey
10 G. St. NE, Ste.600
Washington, DC 20002
Ph: (202)216-8380
Fax: (202)216-0445
E-mail: freys@ncpssm.org
URL: http://www.lcao.org
Contact: Scott Frey, Contact
Founded: 1978. **Members:** 37. **Membership Dues:** individual, $100 (annual). **Description:** Professional groups serving older persons. Objective is to further the public's understanding of the potential and needs of older persons. Responds to public or private initiatives concerning the aging. Acts as coordinating body in reviewing and acting on public policy issues. Compiles statistics on aging. **Publications:** Monographs ● Papers.

11051 ■ Lifespan Resources (LR)
PO Box 995
New Albany, IN 47151-0995
Ph: (812)948-8330
Free: (888)948-8330
Fax: (812)752-4264
E-mail: information@lsr14.org
URL: http://www.lsr14.org
Founded: 1979. **Staff:** 1. **Budget:** $100,000. **Nonmembership. Description:** Designs, implements, and develops innovations for programs involving interaction between youth and senior citizens, emphasizing mentoring. Develops policy initiatives to assist states in determining their intergenerational program needs; is concerned with multicultural issues and economic development for youth and senior citizens. Conducts surveys; operates speakers' bureau. **Libraries: Type:** reference. **Holdings:** archival material, artwork, audiovisuals, books, clippings, periodicals. **Subjects:** intergenerational programs, working with at-risk populations, strengthening families. **Awards:** National Lifespan Reward to Most Creative Use of Generations in Schools. **Frequency:** periodic. **Type:** recognition. **Affiliated With:** Generations United. **Formerly:** (1990) New Age. **Publications:** *Guide for Mentoring At-Risk Youths*, daily. Manuals ● *Guide to Intergenerational Programs*. Booklets ● *What We Have*. Film ● Reports. **Conventions/Meetings:** periodic meeting (exhibits).

11052 ■ Little Brothers - Friends of the Elderly (LBFE)
28 E Jackson Blvd., Ste.405
Chicago, IL 60604-2357
Ph: (312)786-1032
Fax: (312)786-1067
E-mail: national@littlebrothers.org
URL: http://www.littlebrothers.org
Contact: Ms. Liz Drew, Natl. Exec. Dir.
Founded: 1959. **Members:** 6,200. **Staff:** 105. **Budget:** $100. **State Groups:** 9. **Languages:** English, Spanish. **Description:** Seeks to combat the isolation and loneliness often experienced by elderly people by providing friendship and special assistance. Sponsors visitation programs, holiday and birthday parties,

and summer vacations. Provides transportation for shopping and doctor's visits, food packages, and other "special touches." Also offers information, referrals, and contacts with other public or private agencies. **Also Known As:** Little Brothers of the Poor. **Publications:** *Little Brothers Bulletin*, 3/year. Newsletter. For donors and volunteers. **Circulation:** 19,000 ● *Volunteer Newsletter* ● Annual Report, annual ● Brochure. **Conventions/Meetings:** biennial general assembly.

11053 ■ Mature Market Resource Center (MMRC)
c/o Janet Jesse
1850 W Winchester Rd., Ste.213
Libertyville, IL 60048
Ph: (847)816-8660
Free: (800)828-8225
Fax: (847)816-8662
E-mail: seniorprograms@aol.com
URL: http://www.seniorprograms.com
Contact: Pat Ford, Associate Dir.
Founded: 1993. **Membership Dues:** individual, $149 (annual) ● corporate, $295 (annual). **Staff:** 4. **For-Profit. Description:** Acts as a clearinghouse of resources for the mature market. Provides research and information on new trends and discoveries in senior health and fitness. Produces resource books. National Senior Health and Fitness Day and various Mature Fitness Awards USA. **Convention/Meeting:** none. **Libraries: Type:** reference; not open to the public; by appointment only. **Holdings:** archival material, articles, audiovisuals, books, clippings, periodicals. **Subjects:** older adults. **Awards:** National Mature Media Awards. **Frequency:** annual. **Type:** recognition. **Computer Services:** database, 20,000 senior program directors in 30 categories ● mailing lists ● online services. **Telecommunication Services:** electronic mail, info@seniorprograms.com. **Publications:** *Mature Market Calendar of Events*, annual. Directory ● *Mature Markets*, annual. Directory ● *Mature Markets Online*, annual. Directory ● *Resources for Senior Programs Catalog*, annual. **Circulation:** 20,000 ● *What's New in senior Health and Fitness Action Cards*, annual. **Circulation:** 20,000. **Advertising:** accepted.

11054 ■ National Academy for Teaching and Learning About Aging (NATLA)
PO Box 310919
Denton, TX 76203-0919
Ph: (940)565-3450 (940)565-4764
Fax: (940)565-3141
E-mail: louis@scs.unt.edu
URL: http://www.cps.unt.edu/natla
Contact: Don Louis PhD, Interim Dir.
Founded: 1983. **Members:** 250. **Staff:** 4. **Budget:** $100,000. **Description:** Professionals in gerontology, education, health care, and other fields interested in developing aging education and intergenerational programming. Seeks to dispel myths about aging and old age; encourages communication among generations and works to create a social environment where people of all ages can live together. Serves as a clearinghouse of information on issues of aging and intergenerational programs; provides consultation and presentation services to individuals or groups that wish to develop aging education programs. Maintains resources for aging education and intergenerational programming. **Libraries: Type:** reference. **Holdings:** 500. **Formerly:** Center for Understanding Aging; (1996) Center for Understanding Aging. **Supersedes:** Teaching and Learning About Aging Project. **Publications:** *AgeShare* ● *Schools in an Aging Society*. Features six interrelated curriculum guides which provide education, for, with, and about older adults. **Price:** $55.00 ● Teaching about Aging: Enriching Lives across the Lifespan (published by the National Retired Teachers Association; free & available from NRTA/AARP). **Conventions/Meetings:** annual Gerontology for Educators - meeting (exhibits) - summer.

11055 ■ National Adult Day Services Association
2519 Connecticut Ave. NW
Washington, DC 20008

Ph: (202)508-1205
Free: (800)558-5301
Fax: (202)783-2255
E-mail: info@nadsa.org
URL: http://www.nadsa.org
Contact: Merle D. Griff PhD, Chair
Founded: 1979. **Members:** 500. **Membership Dues:** individual, $150 (annual) ● individual consultant, $250 (annual) ● corporate, $1,000 (annual) ● regular-level 1, $300 (annual) ● regular-level 2, $500 (annual) ● regular-level 3, $800 (annual) ● regular-level 4, $1,400 (annual) ● regular-level 5, $3,000 (annual) ● regular-level 6, $5,000 (annual). **Staff:** 1. **Budget:** $600,000. **Description:** Adult daycare practitioners; health and social service planners; individuals involved in planning and providing services for older persons. (Daycare centers offer services in a group setting ranging from active rehabilitation to social and health care.) Promotes and enhances adult daycare programs; provides services and activities for disabled older persons on a long-term basis; provides training and technical assistance and consultation services for daycare personnel; organizes funding; develops standards and guidelines for adult daycare programs; encourages adult daycare centers to participate in local area health planning activities to heighten the effectiveness of adult daycare. Plans and conducts training events for annual meeting and related conferences; maintains annotated bibliography; lobbies for approved public policy positions; surveys state adult daycare regulations and legislation. **Awards:** Ruth Von Behren Award. **Frequency:** annual. **Type:** recognition. **Recipient:** to a daycare provider or leader in daycare programs. **Committees:** Education & Training; Finance; Membership; Nominating; Public Policy. **Publications:** *Adult Day Services: Secrets, Systems, and Strategies for Excellence: Leaders Guide*. Book. Contains guidance on goals, the main message and key points, the teasing out of management skills, handouts, and thought-provoking questions. **Price:** $29.00 for members; $55.00 for nonmembers ● *NADSA Voice*, quarterly. Newsletter. Reports on adult day care and other aging issues with a focus on public policy. **Price:** free, for members only. **Circulation:** 2,000. **Advertising:** accepted. **Conventions/Meetings:** annual conference (exhibits) ● Educational Conference ● Legislative Conference.

11056 ■ National Alliance of Senior Citizens (NASC)
Address Unknown since 2007
Founded: 1974. **Members:** 117,000. **Staff:** 4. **Budget:** $1,000,000. **Description:** Persons advocating the advancement of senior Americans through sound fiscal policy and through belief in the American system of individuality and personal freedom. Purpose is to inform the membership and the American public of the needs of senior citizens and of the programs and policies being carried out by the government and other specified groups. Represents the views of senior Americans before Congress and state legislatures. Maintains Golden Age Hall of Fame honoring individuals for outstanding service to the senior community. Conducts educational program; compiles statistics. Project "Life with Dignity: Compassionate Care for the Dying" helps to improve quality of life for people with terminal illness. Advocates living will and patients rights. **Libraries: Type:** reference. **Awards: Type:** recognition. **Computer Services:** Mailing lists. **Subgroups:** Adult Education; Budgeting; Consumerism; Crime; Economics; Election Laws; Employment Security; Environmental Protection; Family Life; Farm and Rural Life; Gerontology; Health Care; Housing; Nursing Homes; Nutrition; Organized Labor; Pension and Retirement Benefits; Planning and Zoning; Political Action; Productivity; Psychologist on Aging; Retirement Centers; Rural Transportation; Social Security; Sociologist on Aging; Taxation; Urban Transportation; Veterans Affairs; Volunteerism; Welfare. **Publications:** *Senior Guardian*, bimonthly. **Advertising:** accepted. **Conventions/Meetings:** periodic meeting.

11057 ■ National Asian Pacific Center on Aging (NAPCA)
1511 3rd Ave., Ste.914
Seattle, WA 98101

Ph: (206)624-1221
Free: (800)336-2722
Fax: (206)624-1023
E-mail: website@napca.org
URL: http://www.napca.org
Contact: David L. Kim, Chm.
Founded: 1979. **Membership Dues:** senior, $10 (annual) ● individual/professional, $20 (annual) ● nonprofit agency, $100 (annual) ● corporate, $500 (annual). **Staff:** 15. **Regional Groups:** 4. **Description:** Aims to ensure and improve the delivery of health and social services to elderly Pacific/Asians; increase the capabilities of community-based services by expanding their information and technical base; include Pacific/Asians in planning and organizational activities, thus maintaining a strong link between the center and the community. Provides technical assistance to the generic service delivery system on program development and organizational capacity building and training. Compiles statistics. **Convention/Meeting:** none. **Libraries: Type:** reference. **Holdings:** 500. **Programs:** Senior Community Service Employment; Senior Environmental Employment. **Projects:** Advocacy and Demonstration. **Formerly:** (1993) National Pacific/Asian Resource Center on Aging. **Publications:** *Asian Pacific Affairs*, quarterly. Newsletter. **Circulation:** 10,000. **Advertising:** accepted. Alternate Formats: online ● *Demographic and Socio-Economic Characteristics of Elderly Asian and Pacific Island Americans* ● *Directory of Pacific/Asian Media Sources* ● *Pacific/Asian Elderly Bibliography*. Directory ● *Registry of Services for Pacific/Asian Elderly*, biennial. Directory.

11058 ■ National Association of Area Agencies on Aging (N4A)
1730 Rhode Island Ave. NW, Ste.1200
Washington, DC 20036
Ph: (202)872-0888
Free: (800)677-1116
Fax: (202)872-0057
E-mail: smarkwood@n4a.org
URL: http://www.n4a.org
Contact: Sandy Markwood, CEO
Founded: 1975. **Members:** 665. **Staff:** 9. **Budget:** $2,000,000. **Description:** Members are Area Agencies on Aging, established under the provisions of the Older Americans Act of 1965; also offers corporate and cooperating memberships. Promotes the achievement of a reasonable and realistic national policy on aging; assists the process of partnership and regular communication within a national network on aging. Acts as advocate for the needs of older persons at the national level. Maintains communication among members to enable an effective response to federal legislation and regulations. Disseminates information to the federal government, the private sector, and the public. Provides general administrative, training, and technical assistance to area agencies. **Libraries: Type:** reference. **Awards: Type:** recognition. **Computer Services:** Mailing lists. **Committees:** Public Policy; Training. **Programs:** Making the Link; Older Driver Safety; Volunteer Promotion Project. **Publications:** *In Step with N4A*, monthly. Newsletter. **Advertising:** accepted. Alternate Formats: online ● *National Directory for Eldercare Information and Referral*, biennial. Manuals. Contains listings of all area agencies throughout the US. **Price:** $49.95 ● Annual Report, annual. Alternate Formats: online. **Conventions/Meetings:** annual conference (exhibits) - always summer.

11059 ■ National Association of County Aging Programs (NACAP)
c/o Marilina Sanz, Legislative Dir.
25 Massachusetts Ave. NW
Washington, DC 20001-1430
Ph: (202)942-4260
Fax: (202)942-4281
E-mail: msanz@naco.org
URL: http://www.naco.org
Contact: Marilina Sanz, Legislative Dir.
Founded: 1978. **Description:** Assists counties in their plans for providing services to the aging of the community. **Telecommunication Services:** elec-

tronic mail, koskandy@email.com. **Affiliated With:** National Association of Counties.

11060 ■ National Association for Human Development (NAHD)
PO Box 100
Washington, DC 20036
Ph: (202)328-2191
Fax: (202)265-6682
Contact: Anne Radd, Exec.VP
Founded: 1974. **Budget:** $700,000. **Description:** Seeks to help people establish and maintain physical and emotional health and vigor. Operates model demonstration projects and evaluation, research and training programs; conducts multimedia community awareness activities; sponsors "Active People Over 60" campaign. Provides specialized education in motivational communications; develops and implements employment training programs. Develops drug prevention educational programs, activities, and materials for minority populations; advocates on behalf of troubled children and youth. Offers resource development and technical assistance to other organizations. **Publications:** *Digest*, quarterly ● Booklets ● Manuals ● Also publishes evaluation sheets and audiovisual and media-oriented materials. **Conventions/Meetings:** seminar, on health and career education and professional training ● workshop, local.

11061 ■ National Association of Senior Companion Project Directors (NASCPD)
c/o Camellia Pisegna, Pres.
Region IV Area Agency on Aging
2900 Lakeview Ave.
St. Joseph, MI 49085
Ph: (269)983-7058
Fax: (269)983-2483
E-mail: camelliapisegna@areaagencyonaging.org
URL: http://www.nascpd.com
Contact: Camellia Pisegna, Pres.
Founded: 1978. **Members:** 187. **Membership Dues:** professional, $100 (annual) ● supporting, $50 (annual). **Staff:** 1. **Budget:** $20,000. **Regional Groups:** 5. **Description:** Project directors from the Corp. for National Service's Senior Companion Program. Works to address the needs of SCP. Provides opportunities for expression and education for and by SCP project directors. Fosters communication between project directors, organizations, and agencies serving the SCP and the Corp. for National Service offices. Encourages the support and exchange of services among programs benefiting the aging. Seeks to prevent duplication and maximize the quality and level of services. Expands and promotes opportunities for senior companions worldwide. Assists in preserving government funding for SCP projects; works for increased stipends for volunteers. Works with Washington representatives on behalf of legislative changes affecting Corp. for National Service's and the SCP. Offers professional training and development. Conducts surveys. Operates speakers' bureau; compiles statistics. **Awards: Type:** recognition. **Affiliated With:** American Society on Aging; Generations United; National Council on the Aging. **Publications:** *NASCPD Newsletter*, periodic. **Conventions/Meetings:** semiannual conference and board meeting.

11062 ■ National Association of State Units on Aging (NASUA)
1201 15th St. NW, Ste.350
Washington, DC 20005
Ph: (202)898-2578
Free: (800)677-1116
Fax: (202)898-2583
E-mail: info@nasua.org
URL: http://www.nasua.org
Contact: Diane Justice, Exec. Dir.
Founded: 1964. **Members:** 57. **Staff:** 16. **Budget:** $1,200,000. **Description:** Public interest organization that provides information, technical assistance, and professional development support to State Units on Aging. (A state unit is an agency of state government designated by the governor and state legislature to administer the Older Americans Act and to serve as a

focal point for all matters relating to older people.) Serves as organized channel for officially designated state leadership in aging to exchange information and mutual experiences, and to join together for appropriate action on behalf of the elderly. Services include: information on federal policy and program developments in aging; training and technical assistance on a wide range of program and management issues; liaison with organizations representing the public and private sectors. **Libraries: Type:** not open to the public. **Awards:** Louise B. Gerrard Award. **Frequency:** annual. **Type:** recognition. **Recipient:** for contributions to rural older Americans. **Telecommunication Services:** electronic mail, djustice@nasua.org. **Committees:** Elder Rights; Health and Long Term Care; Workforce Development. **Divisions:** Communications and Development; Community-Based Long Term Care; Management Forum on Aging. **Programs:** Adult Protective Service/Elder Abuse; Legal Services; Long Term Care Ombudsman; State Health Insurance. **Publications:** *Directory of State Units on Aging*, periodic ● Books ● Manuals ● Reports ● Also publishes materials on aging policy and programs, policy briefs, legislative updates, and technical assistance documents. **Conventions/Meetings:** semiannual meeting - usually June in Washington, DC.

11063 ■ National Caucus and Center on Black Aged (NCBA)
1220 L St. NW, Ste.800
Washington, DC 20005
Ph: (202)637-8400
Fax: (202)347-0895
E-mail: info@ncba-aged.org
URL: http://www.ncba-aged.org
Contact: Karyne Jones, Pres./CEO
Founded: 1970. **Members:** 3,000. **Staff:** 64. **Budget:** $24,000,000. **Local Groups:** 45. **Description:** Seeks to improve living conditions for low-income elderly Americans, particularly blacks. Advocates changes in federal and state laws in improving the economic, health, and social status of low-income senior citizens. Promotes community awareness of problems and issues effecting low-income aging population. Operates an employment program involving 2000 older persons in 14 states. Sponsors, owns, and manages rental housing for the elderly. Conducts training and intern programs in nursing home administration, long-term care, housing management, and commercial property maintenance. **Awards: Type:** recognition ● **Type:** scholarship. **Divisions:** Economic Development and Research; Employment; Health; Housing; Training. **Programs:** Health and Wellness; Senior Community Service Employment; Senior Environment Employment. **Formed by Merger of:** National Center on Black Aged; National Caucus on the Black Aged. **Publications:** *Golden Page*, quarterly. Newsletter. Reports developments concerning elderly blacks. Includes association news and legislative update. **Price:** included in membership dues ● *The Healing Zone Health Update*, quarterly. Newsletter. Provides information about the problem of overweight and obesity, useful ways of managing weight and ideas for healthy activities. ● *Senior Environmental Employment Program*, quarterly. Newsletter. Provides SEE program enrollees' information about the SEE program, activities, health and wellness, and other useful resources. ● Bulletin. **Conventions/Meetings:** annual conference.

11064 ■ National Coalition on Rural Aging (NCRA)
c/o National Council on Aging
1901 L St. NW, 4th Fl.
Washington, DC 20036
Ph: (202)479-1200 (202)479-6674
Fax: (202)479-0735
E-mail: info@ncoa.org
URL: http://www.ncoa.org
Contact: Ronald W. Schoeffler EdD, Chm.
Founded: 1978. **Members:** 500. **Description:** Planners and providers of services for the aging, academicians and students, and others interested in issues related to older persons living in rural areas. Purposes are to develop social and public policies related to

the needs and interests of rural older adults; to improve and increase services to rural older adults by working with national organizations and government agencies at all levels; to provide guidance to supportive organizations and communities; to encourage action on legislative, public policy, and service delivery issues. Disseminates information and promotes research and demonstration projects on the aging in rural America. Conducts training for individuals working with rural older adults, emphasizing the cultural mores of rural America and the methods of service provision which have proven adaptable to rural areas. Provides technical assistance and consultation significant to rural program planning and implementation. **Formerly:** (1999) National Center on Rural Aging. **Conventions/Meetings:** annual conference, held in conjunction with National Council on the Aging ● seminar ● workshop.

11065 ■ National Committee for the Prevention of Elder Abuse (NCPEA)
1612 K St. NW
Washington, DC 20006
Ph: (202)682-4140
Fax: (202)223-2099
E-mail: ncpea@verizon.net
URL: http://www.preventelderabuse.org
Contact: Randolph W. Thomas, Pres.
Founded: 1988. **Members:** 450. **Membership Dues:** individual, $60 (annual) ● institutional, $200 (annual) ● student, retired person, $45 (annual) ● associate, $35 (annual). **State Groups:** 3. **Local Groups:** 10. **Description:** Aims to promote a greater understanding of the problem and the development of services to protect older persons and disabled adults in order to reduce the likelihood of their abuse and neglect. Performs research, advocacy, public awareness, and training services. **Publications:** *Elder Abuse And Neglect In The Family: A Videotape Series*. Videos. Contains training series. **Price:** $75.00 individual tape; $180.00 series ● *Journal of Elder Abuse and Neglect*, quarterly. **Price:** included in membership dues. **Circulation:** 800 ● *Nexus*, bimonthly. Newsletter. Provides updates on the affiliates' activities. **Price:** included in membership dues ● Membership Directory. **Conventions/Meetings:** semiannual board meeting ● annual meeting, for membership.

11066 ■ National Council on the Aging (NCOA)
1901 L St. NW, 4th Fl.
Washington, DC 20036
Ph: (202)479-1200
Free: (800)373-4906
Fax: (202)479-0735
E-mail: info@ncoa.org
URL: http://www.ncoa.org
Contact: Dr. James P. Firman EdD, Pres./CEO
Founded: 1950. **Members:** 3,800. **Membership Dues:** organization, $195 (annual) ● individual, $95 (annual) ● student/retired, $47 (annual) ● life, $1,500. **Staff:** 70. **Description:** Serves as a national voice and powerful advocate on behalf of older Americans. Has developed programs such as Benefits CheckUp, Foster Grandparents and Family Friends. Works with thousands of its community organization members nationwide to provide needed services to the elderly. Members include senior centers, area agencies on aging, employment services, congregate meal sites, faith congregations, health centers and senior housing. Accredits senior centers nationally; provides consumer information for older Americans on health care and related programs and insurance; directs an intergenerational volunteer program that matches mature men and women with children and families at risk; Best Practices encompasses a series of research projects that have provided best practices for senior centers and other community based organizations in health care and other areas; administers two federal programs (Senior Community Service Employment Service and Senior Environmental Program), and the Maturity Works partnership that provide employment and training opportunities for mature adults through offices nationwide. **Awards:** Geneva Mathiasen Award. **Frequency:** annual. **Type:** recognition. **Recipient:** for

major contributions to the NCOA and its programs ● Ollie A. Randall Award. **Frequency:** annual. **Type:** recognition. **Recipient:** for outstanding contributions on behalf of older people. **Telecommunication Services:** TDD, (202)479-6674. **Programs:** Access to Benefits Coalition; Benefits CheckUp; Center for Healthy Aging; Consumer Direction; Family Friends; RespectAbility; Senior Center National Accreditation; Use Your Home to Stay at Home. **Affiliated With:** Health Promotion Institute; National Coalition on Rural Aging; National Institute on Community-Based Long-Term Care; National Institute of Senior Centers; National Institute of Senior Housing; National Interfaith Coalition on Aging. **Formerly:** (1960) National Committee on Aging of National Social Welfare Assembly. **Publications:** *Abstracts in Social Gerontology: Current Literature on Aging*, quarterly. Journal. Features books, reports, and articles on a variety of aging issues. Includes author and subject index. **Price:** free for members. ISSN: 1047-4862. **Circulation:** 8,000 ● *Innovations in Aging*, quarterly. Magazine. Covers issues and developments in the field of aging. **Price:** available to members only and by subscription. ISSN: 0096-2740. **Circulation:** 4,000. **Advertising:** accepted ● *Senior Focus*, monthly. Newsletter. Contains information on health, wellness, lifestyle, and financial issues for seniors and people who work with them. **Price:** included in membership dues. Alternate Formats: online ● Books ● Brochures ● Pamphlets. **Conventions/Meetings:** annual Vital Aging Conference, joint with American Society on Aging (exhibits).

11067 ■ National Hispanic Council on Aging (NHCOA)

734 15th St. NW, Ste.1050
Washington, DC 20005
Ph: (202)347-9733
Fax: (202)347-9735
E-mail: nhcoa@nhcoa.org
URL: http://www.nhcoa.org
Contact: Ms. Yanira L. Cruz MPH, Pres./CEO
Founded: 1979. **Members:** 70,000. **Membership Dues:** student, $50 ● standard, $100 ● senior, $25 ● organization, $300. **Staff:** 16. **Budget:** $2,500,000. **Regional Groups:** 4. **State Groups:** 38. **Local Groups:** 20. **National Groups:** 25. **Languages:** English, Spanish. **Description:** Individuals and groups who work in administrative, planning, direct services, research, or educational areas that have a concern for the Hispanic elderly. Fosters the well-being of the Hispanic elderly through research, policy analysis, demonstration projects, development of educational resources, and training. Compiles research data and provides a network for organizations and community groups interested in the Hispanic elderly. Maintains speakers' bureau. **Libraries:** Type: reference. **Holdings:** 3. **Subjects:** retired elderly, health, income, demographic info. **Computer Services:** database, membership list ● mailing lists. **Publications:** *The Hispanic Elderly: A Cultural Signature, Latino Elderly: Issues and Solutions for 20th Century Triple Jeopardy: Aged, Hispanic Women*, quarterly. Book. **Price:** $18.45 portage per book. **Circulation:** 10,000. **Advertising:** accepted. Alternate Formats: online ● *Hispanic Elderly: Issues and Solutions for the 21st Century*. Book ● *Noticias on Hispanic Elderly Issues* (in English and Spanish), quarterly. Newsletter. Publicizes the activities of NH-COA. Includes calendar of events, legislative news, and notices of publications available. **Price:** $25.00/year. **Circulation:** 3,000. **Advertising:** accepted ● *Triple Jeopardy: Hispanic Older Women*. Book. **Conventions/Meetings:** semiannual conference (exhibits).

11068 ■ National Indian Council on Aging (NICOA)

10501 Montgomery Blvd. NE, Ste.210
Albuquerque, NM 87111-3846
Ph: (505)292-2001
Fax: (505)292-1922
E-mail: traci@nicoa.org
URL: http://www.nicoa.org
Contact: Traci L. McClellan, Exec. Dir.
Founded: 1976. **Members:** 1,037. **Membership Dues:** voting, $50 (annual) ● associate, $100 (an-

nual) ● organization, $200 (annual). **Staff:** 26. **Description:** American Indian/Alaska Native populations. Seeks to bring about improved comprehensive services to the American Indian and Alaska Native elderly. Aims to interact with service provider agencies and advocacy organizations in the aging network, to disseminate information to Indian communities and to provide technical assistance and training opportunities to organizations. Conducts research and acts as a clearinghouse for current issues affecting the American Indian and Alaska Native elderly. **Divisions:** Department of Labor/Senior Community Service Employment Program; Program Development; Training and Technical Assistance. **Publications:** *Elder Visions*, quarterly. Newsletter. **Price:** $5.00 for nonmembers ● *Mapping Indian Elders*. Reports. **Price:** $25.00 ● Monographs ● Proceedings. **Conventions/Meetings:** semiannual National Conference on Indian Aging (exhibits) - usually late summer.

11069 ■ National Institute on Community-Based Long-Term Care (NICLC)

c/o National Council on Aging
1901 L St. NW, 4th Fl.
Washington, DC 20036
Ph: (202)479-1200
Fax: (202)479-0735
E-mail: info@ncoa.org
URL: http://www.ncoa.org/content.cfm?sectionID=42
Contact: Paul H. Bennett, Chm.
Founded: 1984. **Members:** 3,200. **Staff:** 44. **Budget:** $44,000,000. **Description:** Serves as a unit of the National Council on Aging (see separate entry). Seeks to promote a comprehensive long-term care system that will integrate home-and community-based services, enabling older adults to live in their own homes as long as it is medically, socially, and economically feasible. Serves as information clearinghouse for long-term care professionals. Advocates public policies that support home and community-based services. Maintains speakers' bureau; offers educational sessions; compiles statistics. **Telecommunication Services:** TDD, (202)479-6674. **Committees:** Communications; Education; Membership; Public Policy. **Publications:** *Care Management Standards*. Book ● *NCOA Networks*, bimonthly. Newsletter ● *Perspective on Aging*, periodic. Journal. Provides information on aging issues. **Conventions/Meetings:** annual conference.

11070 ■ National Institute of Senior Centers (NISC)

c/o National Council on the Aging
1901 L St. NW, 4th Fl.
Washington, DC 20036
Ph: (202)479-1200
Free: (800)424-9046
Fax: (202)479-0735
E-mail: info@ncoa.org
URL: http://www.ncoa.org/content.cfm?sectionID=44
Contact: Constance Todd, Dir.
Founded: 1970. **Members:** 3,000. **Description:** Individuals or organizations who are affiliated with senior centers at the local, state, or national level. (Senior centers are places where senior citizens can go for services, recreation, and information on topics such as nutrition, employment, and housing.) Assists senior centers, organizations, and communities in developing new centers and upgrading existing operations. Promotes professionalism within the senior center field and develops standards for senior centers nationwide. Maintains advocacy and public policy positions for senior centers; provides management training for persons working with senior centers. **Publications:** *NCOA Week*, weekly. Newspaper. Electronic newsletter, reports on senior citizen centers, including legislative updates, program and funding information, and current issues. **Price:** free, for members only. **Circulation:** 8,000. **Advertising:** accepted. Alternate Formats: online ● *Senior Center Operation: A Guide to Organization and Management* ● *Senior Center Standards*. **Conventions/Meetings:** seminar ● workshop.

11071 ■ National Interfaith Coalition on Aging (NICA)

c/o National Council on the Aging
1901 L St. NW, 4th Fl.
Washington, DC 20036
Ph: (202)479-6655
Free: (800)424-9046
Fax: (202)479-0735
E-mail: info@ncoa.org
URL: http://www.ncoa.org/content.cfm?sectionID=41
Contact: Rita K. Chow EdD, Dir.
Founded: 1972. **Members:** 300. **Staff:** 1. **National Groups:** 13. **Description:** Shares administrative capabilities and resources with National Council on the Aging. Religious and secular organizations and individuals concerned with the U.S. religious community's response to the problems of aging, and about the spiritual well-being of the elderly. Promotes communication and cooperative effort among religious organizations and individuals concerned about older people; assists churches and synagogues that attempt to respond to the needs of the elderly; identifies and supports programs and services for the elderly that are best implemented by religious organizations; facilitates continued participation in community affairs by the elderly. Serves as a resource and gerontological training agency for clergy and religious workers. **Awards:** Spirituality and Aging. **Frequency:** annual. **Type:** recognition. **Telecommunication Services:** electronic mail, rita.chow@ncoa.org. **Councils:** Delegate; NICA Delegate. **Affiliated With:** National Council on the Aging. **Publications:** *Journal of Religion, Spirituality and Aging*, quarterly. Contains articles about developments in religious gerontology and religious concerns of aging. Includes book reviews and research reports. **Price:** $40.00/year. Also Cited As: *Journal of Religious Gerontology*. **Conventions/Meetings:** annual Joint Conference of the National Council on Aging and The American Society on Aging - meeting, held concurrently with NCOA conference with Wingspread Conference and Religion and Spirituality Special Programs (exhibits).

11072 ■ National Meals on Wheels Foundation

Address Unknown since 2007
URL: http://www.nationalmealsonwheels.org/
Founded: 1977. **Members:** 1,000. **Membership Dues:** regular, $100 (annual) ● associate and corporate, $200 (annual). **Staff:** 3. **Description:** Grants-making organization. **Awards:** Golden Apple Award. **Type:** recognition. **Computer Services:** database, nutrition projects ● mailing lists. **Committees:** Government Relations; Legislative. **Task Forces:** Peer and Association; Private Industry. **Formerly:** (1978) National Association of Title Seven Directors. **Publications:** *Collection of Innovative Models* ● *Monthly Membership Updates* ● *NANASP News*, quarterly. Newsletter. Contains legislative and membership updates, and new product information. **Price:** included in membership dues. **Advertising:** accepted ● *National Standards for Congregate Meals* ● *National Standards for Home-Delivered Meals* ● *Preparing Nutrition Programs for the Nineties* ● *Special Bulletins*, monthly ● *Special Report to Members*, quarterly. Newsletter. **Price:** included in membership dues. **Circulation:** 1,000. **Advertising:** accepted ● *Annual Report*, annual. **Conventions/Meetings:** seminar ● annual Training Conference (exhibits) ● workshop.

11073 ■ National Senior Citizens Law Center (NSCLC)

1101 14th St. NW, Ste.400
Washington, DC 20005
Ph: (202)289-6976
Fax: (202)289-7224
E-mail: nsclc@nsclc.org
URL: http://www.nsclc.org
Contact: Michael Kelly, Exec. Dir.
Founded: 1972. **Staff:** 10. **Budget:** $900,000. **Description:** Legal services support center specializing in the legal problems of the elderly poor. Acts as advocate on behalf of elderly, poor clients in litigation and administrative affairs. Sponsors conferences and

workshops on areas of the law affecting the elderly. **Libraries: Type:** reference. **Publications:** *Nursing Home Law Letter*, quarterly. Articles. Includes articles exploring legal issues relating to nursing facilities and/or residential care facilities. **Price:** $175.00/year ● *Washington Weekly*. Newsletter. Provides the latest case information, administration and congressional developments of importance to the elderly. **Price:** $295.00/year for multiple offices; $195.00/year for single office ● Also publishes handbooks, guides, and testimonies. **Conventions/Meetings:** annual Joint Conference on Law and Aging (exhibits).

11074 ■ Old Lesbians Organizing for Change (OLOC)
PO Box 5853
Athens, OH 45701
Ph: (704)448-6424
E-mail: info@oloc.org
URL: http://www.oloc.org
Founded: 1989. **Members:** 1,000. **Membership Dues:** individual, $25 (annual). **Staff:** 1. **Description:** Lesbians 60 years or older. Serves as a network to reduce ageism. Exchanges information on diversity of races, ethnicities, class backgrounds, and histories of members. Develops and disseminates educational materials on ageism and how to combat discrimination. **Also Known As:** Old Lesbians Organizing. **Publications:** *Facilitator's Handbook: Confronting Ageism, Consciousness Raising for Lesbians 60 and Over.* **Price:** $25.00. **Circulation:** 700. **Conventions/Meetings:** biennial meeting.

11075 ■ Retirement Research Foundation (RRF)
8765 W Higgins Rd., Ste.430
Chicago, IL 60631-4170
Ph: (773)714-8080
Fax: (773)714-8089
E-mail: info@rrf.org
URL: http://www.rrf.org
Contact: Edward J. Kelly, Chm.
Founded: 1978. **Description:** Works to promote aging and retirement issues. Supports efforts that improve care for the aging, and enable older adults to live at home or in residential settings that facilitate independent living. **Awards: Type:** grant.

11076 ■ The Seniors Coalition (TSC)
4401 Fair Lakes Ct., Ste.210
Fairfax, VA 22033-3848
Ph: (703)631-4211
Free: (800)325-9891
Fax: (703)631-4283
E-mail: tsc@senior.org
URL: http://www.senior.org
Contact: Mary M. Martin, Chair
Founded: 1989. **Membership Dues:** individual, $10 (annual) ● couple, $13 (annual). **Description:** Represents the interests and concerns of America's senior citizens at state and federal levels. **Awards:** Senior Activist Award. **Type:** recognition. **Recipient:** to a member of Congress for his or her commitment to issues important to older Americans. **Programs:** Senior Congress. **Publications:** *The Senior Advocate*, quarterly. Magazine. **Conventions/Meetings:** periodic seminar, with congressional legislative staff and senior citizens.

11077 ■ Significant Living
1559 E Howard St.
Pasadena, CA 91104
Ph: (626)398-2394
Free: (800)443-0227
Fax: (626)398-2386
E-mail: email@significantliving.org
URL: http://significantliving.org
Contact: Marc Whitmore, Pres.
Founded: 1993. **Members:** 40,000. **Membership Dues:** silver, $19 (annual) ● gold, $39 (annual). **Staff:** 10. **Budget:** $650,000. **Description:** Seeks to improve, encourage and create a better quality of life to those ages 50 and older; offers discount travel and volunteer opportunities. **Computer Services:** Online services. **Additional Websites:** http://gocasa.org. **Also Known As:** (2006) Christian Association of

Senior Adult Ministries. **Formerly:** (2005) Christian Association of Primetimers. **Publications:** *Significant Living Today*, bimonthly. Newsletter. Provides updates on new benefits, travel opportunities, and CAP activities. **Advertising:** accepted. **Conventions/Meetings:** biennial Senior Summit - conference, for church leaders, para-churches, denominations, educational institutions, extended care facilities, and those who minister to persons over 50.

11078 ■ Support Our Aging Religious (SOAR!)
900 Varnum St. NE
Washington, DC 20017
Ph: (202)529-7627
Fax: (202)529-7633
E-mail: info@soar-usa.org
URL: http://www.soar-usa.org
Contact: Bernard J. Casey, Chm.
Founded: 1986. **Description:** Represents individuals committed to assuring a financially stable and secure future for elderly and frail members of Catholic religious congregations in the United States. Raises and provides funds for congregations to meet the immediate needs of their retired members. Educates the public about the serious retirement needs of religious elderly. **Awards:** Retirement Needs Grant. **Frequency:** annual. **Type:** grant. **Recipient:** to religious orders with retired, aged, and infirm members. **Programs:** Education; Fundraising; Networking.

11079 ■ United Seniors Association (USA)
PO Box 2038
Purcellville, VA 20132
Ph: (703)359-6500
E-mail: info@usanext.org
URL: http://www.unitedseniors.org
Contact: Charles W. Jarvis, Chm./Chief Exec.
Founded: 1991. **Members:** 550,000. **Membership Dues:** individual/household, $12 (annual). **Staff:** 14. **Budget:** $12,000,000. **Description:** Seeks to educate and mobilize senior citizens about Social Security, Medicare, taxes, and other related issues. **Telecommunication Services:** electronic mail, ltrost@unitedseniors.org. **Publications:** *The Senior American*, quarterly. Newsletter. **Price:** included in membership dues. **Circulation:** 400,000. **Advertising:** accepted.

AIDS

11080 ■ AIDS Action
1730 M St. NW, Ste.611
Washington, DC 20036
Ph: (202)530-8030
Fax: (202)530-8031
E-mail: aidsaction@aidsaction.org
URL: http://www.aidsaction.org
Contact: Rebecca Haag, Exec. Dir.
Founded: 1984. **Members:** 3,200. **Staff:** 20. **Description:** Represents national AIDS service organizations; dedicated to responsible federal policy for improved HIV/AIDS care and services, vigorous medical research and effective prevention. Operates the Pedro Zamora Center National AIDS Youth Advocacy Program.

11081 ■ AIDS Treatment Activists Coalition (ATAC)
PO Box 1514
Old Chelsea Sta.
New York, NY 10113
Ph: (212)367-1237
Fax: (212)367-1235
E-mail: askatac@atac-usa.org
URL: http://www.atac-usa.org
Contact: Kristen Lepore, Coor.
Description: Encourages greater and more effective involvement of people with HIV/AIDS in the decisions that affect their lives by identifying, mentoring and empowering treatment activists in all communities affected by the epidemic. Develops within all communities affected by HIV/AIDS and related co-infections

the leadership to provide the knowledge and skills needed to advocate for improved research, treatment and access to care. Enables treatment activists to speak with a united voice to provide meaningful input into issues concerning HIV disease and related complications and coinfections. **Telecommunication Services:** electronic mail, kristen@atac-usa.org ● electronic mail, steeringcommittee@atac-usa.org.

11082 ■ Artists Against AIDS Worldwide (AAAW)
1225 Connecticut Ave. NW, Ste.401
Washington, DC 20036
Fax: (202)296-0261
E-mail: info@aaaw.org
Founded: 2001. **Multinational. Description:** Raises awareness and funds needed to bring direct care to those affected by AIDS worldwide, especially in Africa.

11083 ■ Broadway Cares/Equity Fights AIDS (BC/EFA)
165 W 46th St., Ste.1300
New York, NY 10036
Ph: (212)840-0770
Fax: (212)840-0551
E-mail: info@bcefa.org
URL: http://www.broadwaycares.org
Contact: Tom Viola, Exec. Dir.
Founded: 1992. **Description:** American theatre community working as an AIDS fundraising and grant making organization. **Awards: Type:** grant. **Programs:** Classical Action; Dancers Responding to AIDS; International Grants; National Grants; School Outreach. **Publications:** Annual Report, annual. **Alternate Formats:** online. **Conventions/Meetings:** Broadway Bares - show ● annual Easter Bonnet Competition ● annual Gypsy of the Year Competition.

11084 ■ Cable Positive
1775 Broadway, Ste.433
New York, NY 10019
Ph: (212)459-1605 (212)459-1506
Fax: (212)459-1631
E-mail: info@cablepositive.org
URL: http://www.cablepositive.org
Contact: Steve Villano, Pres./CEO
Founded: 1992. **Description:** Mobilizes the talents, resources, access and influence of the cable and telecommunications industry to raise HIV/AIDS awareness. Supports HIV/AIDS education, prevention and care. Strives to create a more compassionate climate for people whose lives have been affected by HIV or AIDS. **Awards:** Brad Wojcoski Memorial Award. **Frequency:** annual. **Type:** recognition. **Recipient:** for local support to Cable Positive's local programs ● Joel A. Berger Memorial Award. **Frequency:** annual. **Type:** recognition. **Recipient:** for exceptional support to national AIDS awareness ● Pop Awards. **Frequency:** annual. **Type:** recognition. **Recipient:** for HIV/AIDS related program originally produced and aired in the United States. **Computer Services:** Information services, HIV/AIDS resources ● mailing lists. **Telecommunication Services:** electronic mail, steve@cablepositive.org. **Programs:** Cable Positive Tony Cox Community Fund; Employee Assistance. **Publications:** *Positive Outlook*. Newsletter ● Newsletter, monthly. **Alternate Formats:** online.

11085 ■ Design Industries Foundation Fighting AIDS (DIFFA)
200 Lexington Ave., Ste.1016
New York, NY 10016
Ph: (212)727-3100
Fax: (212)727-2574
E-mail: info@diffa.org
URL: http://diffa.org
Contact: David Sheppard, Exec. Dir.
Founded: 1984. **Staff:** 14. **Budget:** $2,500,000. **Local Groups:** 15. **Description:** Serves as a foundation bestowing grants to AIDS organizations and programs providing direct patient care and services; preventive, post-diagnostic, and community education; housing, meals, emergency assistance, and legal advocacy; treatment and community-based

research. **Awards: Frequency:** annual. **Type:** grant. **Recipient:** to organizations engaged in HIV and AIDS activities. **Computer Services:** Mailing lists, of members. **Telecommunication Services:** electronic mail, dsheppard@diffa.org. **Formerly:** Design Industries Foundation for AIDS. **Publications:** *Good Magazine*, quarterly. Contains information on managing care and commerce. **Price:** $35.00. **Circulation:** 25,000. **Advertising:** accepted. Alternate Formats: online. **Conventions/Meetings:** annual meeting ● annual regional meeting.

11086 ■ Global Business Coalition on HIV/AIDS (GBC)
1230 Avenue of the Americas, 4th Fl.
New York, NY 10020
Ph: (212)698-2113
Fax: (212)698-7056
E-mail: info@businessfightsaids.org
URL: http://www.businessfightsaids.org
Contact: Richard Holbrooke, Pres./CEO

Members: 200. **Membership Dues:** company, $25,000 (annual). **Languages:** Chinese, English, French, Russian. **Multinational. Description:** Combats the AIDS epidemic through the business sector's skills and expertise. Raises the number and diversity of companies committed to fighting the global HIV/AIDS pandemic. Increases business action against HIV/AIDS and improves the quality and reach of company anti-AIDS workplace and community programs. Enhances and facilitates the use of companies' core competencies and products in the fight against HIV/AIDS. Uses business power to advocate for HIV/AIDS issues. **Awards:** Awards for Business Excellence. **Frequency:** annual. **Type:** recognition. **Recipient:** to member companies for business excellence. **Publications:** *Addressing Stigma as a Key Barrier to HIV Prevention.* Report. Alternate Formats: online ● *Business & AIDS Magazine*, quarterly. **Price:** included in membership dues. Alternate Formats: online ● *GBC Newsletter.* **Price:** included in membership dues. Alternate Formats: online ● *Outstanding Business Action on HIV/AIDS.* Booklet. Alternate Formats: online ● Brochure. Alternate Formats: online.

11087 ■ Grassroot Soccer (GRS)
2456 Christian St., Ste.102
White River Junction, VT 05001
URL: http://www.grassrootsoccer.org
Contact: Thomas Clark MD, Exec. Dir./Founder

Founded: 2002. **Multinational. Description:** Seeks to reduce the spread of HIV and AIDS by training well-known soccer players to educate at-risk youth about the dangers of HIV infection and ways to protect themselves.

11088 ■ Health Global Access Project (HGAP)
973 St. Johns Pl., No. 2
Brooklyn, NY 11213
Ph: (646)645-5225
Fax: (917)591-3353
E-mail: info@healthgap.org
URL: http://www.healthgap.org
Contact: Brook Baker, Contact

Founded: 1999. **Description:** Aims to eliminate barriers to global access to affordable life-sustaining medicines for people living with HIV/AIDS. Campaigns for access to drugs and resources necessary to sustain people with HIV/AIDS across the globe. Works with affiliate organizations in formulating policies that promote access. Confronts governmental policy makers, the pharmaceutical industry, and international agencies when their policies or practices block access to drugs and resources. **Computer Services:** Information services, downloadable resources; press center ● online services, search. **Committees:** National Steering. **Funds:** Funding for AIDS. **Programs:** Action Alerts; Free Trade of the Americas; Patents and Medicine; Presidential Campaign. **Publications:** Papers. Alternate Formats: online ● Reports. Alternate Formats: online.

11089 ■ National Episcopal AIDS Coalition (NEAC)
520 Clinton Ave.
Brooklyn, NY 11238-2211
Ph: (718)857-9445
Free: (800)588-6628
Fax: (718)638-3039
E-mail: neac@neac.org
URL: http://www.neac.org
Contact: Rev. Richard F. Brewer MHA, Admin. Sec.

Founded: 1988. **Members:** 1,400. **Membership Dues:** individual, $35 (annual) ● household, $50 (annual) ● organization, $100 (annual). **Staff:** 1. **Budget:** $100,000. **Description:** Works to educate all Episcopalians about HIV/AIDS issues. Advocates for the physical, emotional and spiritual health of and the pastoral care for HIV/AIDS infected people. Develops support networks and communities. **Publications:** *NEACtion*, quarterly. Newsletter. **Circulation:** 600. Alternate Formats: online.

11090 ■ River Fund
11155 Roseland Rd., No. 16
Sebastian, FL 32958
Ph: (772)589-5076
Fax: (253)390-3985
E-mail: theriverfund@aol.com
URL: http://www.riverfund.org
Contact: Jaya Canterbury-Counts MEd, Exec. Dir.

Founded: 1990. **Description:** Provides physical, emotional, spiritual, educational support to those living with or affected by HIV/AIDS and other life challenging illnesses.

Alcohol Abuse

11091 ■ Leadership to Keep Children Alcohol Free
c/o The CDM Group, Inc.
7500 Old Georgetown Rd., Ste.900
Bethesda, MD 20814
Ph: (301)654-6740
Fax: (301)656-4012
E-mail: leadership@alcoholfreechildren.org
URL: http://www.alcoholfreechildren.org

Founded: 1999. **Description:** Represents governors' spouses, federal agencies, and public and private organizations committed to preventing the use of alcohol by children ages 9-15. **Publications:** *Alcohol Alerts*, quarterly. Newsletter. **Price:** free. Alternate Formats: online ● *Leadership Weekly Update.* Newsletter. **Price:** free. Alternate Formats: online ● Brochures.

American Revolution

11092 ■ Junior American Citizens (JAC)
1776 D St. NW
Washington, DC 20006-5303
Ph: (202)628-1776 (202)628-4780
URL: http://www.dar.org/natsociety/content.
    cfm?id=266&fo=y&hd=n
Contact: Presley Meritt Wagoner, Pres. Gen.

Founded: 1901. **State Groups:** 50. **Description:** Pre-school through high school age students. Promotes education and patriotism. Conducts conservation activities including recycling, planting trees, and adopting animals. Conducts patriotic activities including how to treat the American flag, learning U.S. history, and visiting museums, courts, and government offices. Offers safety programs; conducts charitable and educational programs. Sponsors a contest in art, community service, and creative expression for students in grades 1-12. **Libraries: Type:** open to the public. **Affiliated With:** National Society, Daughters of the American Revolution. **Formerly:** Children, Sons and Daughters of the United States of America.

Animal Rights

11093 ■ Mercy For Animals (MFA)
PO Box 363
Columbus, OH 43216
Free: (866)MFA-OHIO

E-mail: info@mercyforanimals.org
URL: http://www.mercyforanimals.org
Contact: Nathan Runkle, Exec. Dir.

Founded: 1999. **Members:** 6,000. **Description:** Represents the interests of individuals dedicated to establishing and defending the rights of all animals. Works to end animal abuse and create a culture where all animals are treated with respect and compassion. Provides public education, advertisement campaigns, research, investigations and rescues. **Publications:** *Outrage*, biennial. Magazine. Contains information on recent campaigns, investigations and more. ● Newsletter. Alternate Formats: online.

11094 ■ Student Animal Rights Alliance (SARA)
275 Seventh Ave., 23rd Fl.
New York, NY 10001
Ph: (212)696-7911
E-mail: info@defendanimals.org
URL: http://www.defendanimals.org
Contact: Patrick Kwan, Founder/Exec. Dir.

Founded: 2001. **Description:** Represents the interests of individuals dedicated to youth mobilization, education and leadership development to build a youth movement for animal protection. Helps build a culture of respect for animal rights with the leadership of youth. Supports and connects young animal advocates.

Animal Welfare

11095 ■ Activists for Protective Animal Legislation (A-PAL)
PO Box 11743
Costa Mesa, CA 92627
Ph: (714)540-0583
Fax: (714)540-0365
Contact: Judy B. Stricker, Chair

Founded: 1980. **Members:** 500. **Description:** Animal welfare groups and individuals united to inform the general public on legislation pertaining to animal welfare. Monitors all legislation dealing with animal welfare; advises and assists lawmakers who support humane animal legislation. **Publications:** *Political Watchdog*, quarterly. Newsletter ● Also publishes special bulletins. **Conventions/Meetings:** quarterly meeting.

11096 ■ Actors and Others for Animals (A&O)
11523 Burbank Blvd.
North Hollywood, CA 91601-2309
Ph: (818)755-6045 (818)755-6323
Fax: (818)755-6048
E-mail: webmistress@wom-designs.com
URL: http://actorsandothers.com
Contact: Earl Holliman, Pres.

Founded: 1971. **Members:** 10,000. **Membership Dues:** regular, $15 ● senior, $10. **Staff:** 7. **Description:** Serves as an animal welfare organization that provides care and protection of animals; works to eliminate the problem of pet overpopulation through sterilization; educates the public toward these goals through human education and resource services; assists pet therapy program. **Publications:** *Actors and Others Newsletter*, semiannual. Alternate Formats: online. **Conventions/Meetings:** biennial Celebration of Caring - meeting and luncheon, with celebrity fashion show ● annual luncheon.

11097 ■ Adopt a Husky, Inc. (AAHI)
PO Box 275
Salem, WI 53168-0275
Ph: (262)909-2244
Fax: (262)878-1890
E-mail: adoptahusky@adoptahusky.com
URL: http://www.adoptahusky.com
Contact: Lois Leonard, Sec.-Treas.

Founded: 1998. **State Groups:** 4. **Description:** Strives to place stray, abandoned, abused, or otherwise homeless purebred Siberian Huskies in permanent, loving adoptive homes. **Conventions/Meetings:** Husky Hike - meeting.

11098 ■ Akita Rescue Society of America (ARSA)
237 Venus St.
Thousand Oaks, CA 91360-2958
URL: http://www.akitarescue.com
Contact: Barbara Bouyet, Contact
Founded: 1976. **Staff:** 6. **State Groups:** 8. **Description:** Interested individuals. Rescues dogs of the Akita breed from shelters. Disseminates information about Akitas, including health and behavior. Provides lost and found services.

11099 ■ Alaskan Malamute Assistance League (AMPL)
PO Box 691
Mount Vernon, OH 43050
Ph: (419)512-2423
E-mail: contact@malamuterescue.org
URL: http://www.malamuterescue.org
Contact: Catherine White, Pres.
Founded: 1986. **Members:** 300. **Membership Dues:** individual, $20 (annual) ● family, $5 (annual) ● benefactor, $100 (annual). **Staff:** 6. **State Groups:** 32. **Description:** Owners of Alaskan malamute dogs; malamute rescue groups; interested individuals. Functions as a support network; provides clerical assistance to malamute rescue groups. Maintains files on lost, found, and homeless malamutes and people interested in adopting a dog; compiles statistics. Monitors legislation affecting breed. Conducts fundraising activities. **Formerly:** (2002) Alaskan Malamute Protection League. **Publications:** Newsletter, semimonthly. **Circulation:** 300. **Advertising:** accepted ● Books. **Conventions/Meetings:** annual meeting (exhibits).

11100 ■ Alley Cat Allies (ACA)
7920 Norfolk Ave., Ste.600
Bethesda, MD 20814-2525
Ph: (240)482-1980
Fax: (240)482-1990
E-mail: alleycat@alleycat.org
URL: http://www.alleycat.org
Contact: Donna Wilcox, Exec. Dir.
Founded: 1990. **Members:** 75,000. **Membership Dues:** individual, $25 (annual) ● sponsorship, $25. **Staff:** 10. **Budget:** $1,500,000. **Description:** Network of individuals with an interest in controlling domestic and feral cat populations in the U.S. Promotes humane feral cat population control through trapping and sterilization programs. Acts as a clearinghouse of information for individuals seeking feline population control methods. Conducts educational programs; maintains a speakers' bureau. **Libraries: Type:** open to the public. **Subjects:** feral cats, cat population control, feline health. **Computer Services:** database, Feral Friends Network ● mailing lists, Feral Power. **Departments:** Administrative; Development; Programs/Publications. **Funds:** Compassion; Human Education. **Programs:** The Cat-alyst Society; DC CAT; Wild About Cats. **Publications:** Alley Cat Action, quarterly. Newsletter. **Price:** $10.00. **Circulation:** 75,000. Alternate Formats: online ● Feral Cat Activist, semiannual. Newsletter. Alternate Formats: online ● How to Build a Feral Cat Shelter. Pamphlet ● How to Implement Humane Methods of Control. Pamphlet ● How to Tame Feral Kittens. Pamphlet ● Notes for Veterinarians Treating Ferals. Pamphlet ● Rabies and Feral Cats. Pamphlet ● Relocation of Feral Cats. Pamphlet ● Annual Report, annual. Alternate Formats: online ● Articles. Alternate Formats: online. **Conventions/Meetings:** periodic Focus on Ferals - workshop.

11101 ■ Alliance for Animals (AFA)
232 Silver St.
South Boston, MA 02127-2206
Ph: (617)268-7800
E-mail: shelter@afa.arlington.ma.us
URL: http://www.afaboston.org
Contact: Donna Bishop, Pres.
Founded: 1988. **Members:** 3,500. **Membership Dues:** student/senior, $25 (annual) ● animal lover,

$25 (annual) ● sponsor, $50 (annual) ● patron, $100 (annual) ● life, $1,000. **Staff:** 11. **Budget:** $400,000. **Description:** Individuals concerned with animal rights. Dedicated to creating an awareness of animal suffering and reducing the use of animals in research, entertainment, agriculture, and fashion industries. Provides low-cost spay/neuter assistance services; operates a shelter and adoption services for abandoned animals. Offers educational programs. Operates low-cost veterinary clinic. **Convention/Meeting:** none. **Publications:** Ally, quarterly. Newsletter. **Circulation:** 5,000. **Advertising:** accepted ● Brochures. Covers animal rights. ● Also prints ads, bumper stickers, buttons, and public service announcements.

11102 ■ American Anti-Vivisection Society (AAVS)
801 Old York Rd., Ste.204
Jenkintown, PA 19046
Ph: (215)887-0816
Fax: (215)887-2088
E-mail: aavs@aavs.org
URL: http://www.aavs.org
Contact: Sue Leary, Pres.
Founded: 1883. **Members:** 11,000. **Membership Dues:** supporting, $150 (annual) ● individual, $25 (annual) ● sustaining, $75 (annual) ● advocate, $45 (annual) ● student, senior, $15 (annual) ● sponsor, $250 (annual). **Staff:** 10. **Budget:** $1,000,000. **Description:** Dedicated to ending experiments on animals in education, research and testing. Gives grant to scientists working on alternatives to animal experiments. Dissection alternatives available, free on loan to students and teachers. **Libraries: Type:** reference. **Holdings:** 400. **Subjects:** vivisection, alternatives, science, biology. **Awards:** Alternatives Research & Development Foundation. **Frequency:** annual. **Type:** grant. **Recipient:** for research performed that does not use animals or animal by-products. **Subgroups:** Animalearn. **Publications:** Activate for Animals, bimonthly. Newsletter. Features latest news on animal protection including phone numbers of companies and government agencies to contact animal cruelty. **Price:** included in membership dues ● The AV, quarterly. Magazine. **Price:** included in membership dues. Alternate Formats: online ● Frog Fact Kit, quarterly. Teacher resource kit. **Price:** included in membership dues ● Guide to Compassionate Shopping ● Guide to Cruelty-Free Health Charities ● Health and Humane Research. Book ● Problems with Product Testing ● Rat Pack Resource Kit ● So! You Love Animals. Book ● Vegetarian Fact Book ● Vivisection and Dissection and the Classroom: A Guide to Conscientious Objection. Pamphlets ● The Witness. Videos ● Xenotransplantation ● Catalog. Alternate Formats: online.

11103 ■ American Boxer Rescue Association (ABRA)
c/o Beth Moody, Membership Chair
PO Box 134
Mount Morris, MI 48458
Ph: (207)998-4594
E-mail: boxersrrescued@aol.com
URL: http://www.americanboxerrescue.org
Contact: Gail Lombard, Pres.
Membership Dues: general, $25 (annual). **Description:** Educates the public and breeders on responsible dog ownership. Provides information and support to breed clubs and breeders to ensure the humane and effective rescue of Boxer dogs. **Computer Services:** Mailing lists. **Telecommunication Services:** electronic mail, lilibet@peoplepc.com. **Committees:** Auction; Ethics and Standards; Rescue Telephone Hotline Coordinator; Ways and Means. **Publications:** Newsletter.

11104 ■ American Dog Owner's Association (ADOA)
PO Box 186
Castleton, NY 12033
Ph: (518)732-7600
Free: (800)226-6233
Fax: (518)732-7611

E-mail: adoa@adoa.org
URL: http://www.adoa.org
Contact: Dr. Leon S. Sohn, Pres.
Founded: 1970. **Members:** 3,700. **Membership Dues:** individual, $15 (annual) ● couple, $25 (annual) ● business, $100 (annual). **Staff:** 2. **Description:** Volunteer organization of dog owners. Seeks to educate the public on the responsibilities of pet ownership. Advocates stringent laws applying to vicious dogs and their owners. Maintains speaker's bureau. **Awards:** Duncan G. Wright Award. **Frequency:** periodic. **Type:** recognition ● Kathryn M. Birk Memorial Award. **Frequency:** annual. **Type:** recognition. **Computer Services:** Mailing lists. **Telecommunication Services:** electronic mail, adoamail@yahoo.com. **Publications:** Educational Brochures ● Newsletter, quarterly. **Price:** available to members only. **Conventions/Meetings:** annual meeting - usually September.

11105 ■ American Pet Society (APS)
c/o World Wide Pet Industry Association
135 W Lemon Ave.
Monrovia, CA 91016
Ph: (626)447-2222
Free: (800)999-7295
Fax: (626)447-8350
E-mail: info@wwpia.org
URL: http://www.wwpia.org
Contact: Doug Poindexter CAE, Exec. VP
Founded: 1951. **Membership Dues:** regular, $550 (annual). **Staff:** 6. **Budget:** $750,000. **Description:** Promotes responsible pet ownership. Sponsors charitable and educational programs; offers children's services. **Awards: Type:** recognition. **Conventions/Meetings:** annual America's Family Pet Expo - show, for consumer pet owners (exhibits).

11106 ■ American Society for the Prevention of Cruelty to Animals (ASPCA)
424 E 92nd St.
New York, NY 10128-6804
Ph: (212)876-7700
Fax: (212)876-9571
E-mail: humanel@aspca.org
URL: http://www.aspca.org
Contact: Ed Sayres, Pres.
Founded: 1866. **Members:** 672,000. **Membership Dues:** regular, $25-$100 (annual) ● Founder's Society, $500 (annual). **Staff:** 264. **Budget:** $37,000,000. **Description:** Seeks to: provide effective means for the prevention of cruelty to animals; enforce all laws for the protection of animals; promote appreciation for and humane treatment of animals; maintain shelter for unwanted animals; operate a veterinary hospital and a major low-cost spay/neuter clinic. Conducts educational programs and disseminates animal-related information for children and adults. Maintains 1 shelter in New York City. Promotes campaigns for legislation to improve animal welfare. Offers national and international legislative, consulting, and educational programs. **Libraries: Type:** not open to the public. **Holdings:** 200; articles, books, periodicals. **Subjects:** animal-related issues. **Awards:** ASPCA Cares Award. **Frequency:** annual. **Type:** recognition. **Recipient:** to a member of the community who works to better the lives of New York City's animals ● Board of Directors Award. **Frequency:** annual. **Type:** recognition ● Chairman's Emergency Relief Award. **Frequency:** annual. **Type:** recognition. **Recipient:** to government employees in recognition of their outstanding efforts in facilitating disaster relief work ● Duncan Gibbons Award for Heroism. **Type:** recognition ● Founder's Award. **Frequency:** annual. **Type:** recognition ● Henry Bergh Medal of Honor. **Frequency:** annual. **Type:** medal. **Recipient:** for individuals who dedicate their lives to making the world a kinder, more humane place for animals ● President's Award for Outstanding Veterinarians. **Type:** recognition ● Trooper Award for Animal Heroism. **Frequency:** annual. **Type:** recognition. **Recipient:** to Nuggets. **Additional Websites:** http://www.animaland.org. **Departments:** Animal Cruelty/Humane Law Enforcement; Animal Placement; Animal Poison Control Center; Corporate Partnerships; Development; Government Affairs and

Public Policy; Humane Education; Legal; Member and Donor Services; National Outreach; Public Information; Special Events; Veterinary Hospital and Clinic. **Publications:** *Animal Watch*, quarterly. Magazine. Covers animal welfare issues. Includes articles on animal farming, genetic engineering of animals for food, and animal experimentation. **Price:** included in membership dues. **Circulation:** 345,000. **Advertising:** accepted ● *ASPCA Action*, quarterly. Newsletter. **Price:** included in membership dues ● *ASPCA News Alert*, weekly. Newsletter. **Price:** included in membership dues. Alternate Formats: online ● Also publishes information and educational brochures; produces videotapes on animal issues. **Conventions/Meetings:** annual Dogwalk - rally - October in New York City ● annual Humane Awards Luncheon, includes awards presentation and fundraising event.

11107 ■ Animal Legal Defense Fund (ALDF)
170 E Cotati Ave.
Cotati, CA 94931
Ph: (707)795-2533
Fax: (707)795-7280
E-mail: info@aldf.org
URL: http://www.aldf.org
Contact: Stephen Wells, Exec. Dir.
Founded: 1979. **Members:** 120,800. **Membership Dues:** attorney, $25 (annual) ● paralegal, $10 (annual) ● law student, $10 (annual) ● supporting, $15 (annual). **Staff:** 18. **Description:** Attorneys and law students who protect the lives and interests of animals through the legal system. Represents people and organizations working for animal rights and welfare. **Formerly:** (1984) Attorneys for Animal Rights. **Publications:** *ALDF Update for Law Professionals*, quarterly. Newsletter. **Price:** included in Law Professional membership dues. **Circulation:** 1,000 ● *Animal Legal Defense Fund—Newsletter-The Animals Advocate*, quarterly. **Price:** included in membership dues; $15.00 /year for nonmembers. **Circulation:** 65,000.

11108 ■ Animal Liberation Action Group
Univ. of Wisconsin Oshkosh
Campus Connection, Reeve Memorial Union
748 Algoma Blvd.
Oshkosh, WI 54901-3512
Ph: (920)424-0265 (920)235-4887
Fax: (920)424-7317
E-mail: animallib@uwosh.edu
URL: http://www.uwosh.edu/organizations/alag
Contact: Kara Naramore, Pres.
Description: Works to advance the knowledge of animal exploitation; seeks to end prejudice and unjustifiable discrimination against animals. **Computer Services:** Mailing lists. **Publications:** *Humans and Animals: Bridging the Gap*. Video. **Conventions/Meetings:** meeting.

11109 ■ Animal Medical Center (AMC)
510 E 62nd St.
New York, NY 10021-8314
Ph: (212)838-8100 (212)838-7053
E-mail: webmaster@amcny.org
URL: http://www.amcny.org
Contact: Gleniss Schonholz, Interim CEO
Founded: 1910. **Staff:** 350. **Budget:** $18,000,000. **Description:** Provides quality medical and surgical care for small pets; conducts educational programs for veterinarians, students, and technicians; conducts clinical investigations in veterinary and comparative medicine. Sponsors charitable outreach programs including bereavement counseling, pet therapy, and subsidized care for indigent elderly pet owners and guide dog owners. **Convention/Meeting:** none. **Libraries: Type:** by appointment only. **Holdings:** 2,500; books, periodicals. **Subjects:** veterinary medicine, human medicine. **Awards:** Employee of the Year. **Frequency:** annual. **Type:** recognition ● Intern of the Year. **Frequency:** annual. **Type:** recognition ● Teacher of the Year. **Frequency:** annual. **Type:** recognition ● Veterinarian of the Year. **Frequency:** annual. **Type:** recognition. **Departments:** Medicine; Pathology; Surgery. **Programs:** Companion Animal Clinical; Graduate Veterinary Clinical; Internship;

Residency; Senior Veterinary Clinical. **Formerly:** (1959) New York Women's League for Animals. **Publications:** *The AlumniScope*, semiannual ● *Animal Medical Center Annual Report*, annual ● *Animal Medical Center News*, quarterly. Newsletter. Alternate Formats: online.

11110 ■ Animal Place
PO Box 5910
Vacaville, CA 95696-5910
Ph: (707)449-4814
Fax: (707)449-8775
E-mail: info@animalplace.org
URL: http://animalplace.org
Contact: Kim Sturla, Co-Founder/Exec. Dir.
Founded: 1989. **Description:** Provides sanctuary for abused and discarded farmed animals. Develops educational materials to provide the public, mainly young people, with information on "why they should view farmed animals as more than just food". Runs open-house events, "adoption" of residents online or via mail, and Veggie Cook-Off. **Programs:** Foster Parent. **Publications:** *Animal Place: Where Magical Things Happen*. Book. **Price:** $6.00 ● *The Internet*. Book. Features a comic illustration of issues relating to young children and teenagers. **Price:** free ● *Justice for All*. Book. Features a comic illustration of issues relating to young children and teenagers. **Price:** $1.00/additional copy; free (first copy) ● *Sausage Patty*. Book. **Price:** $4.00 ● Books. Includes vegetarian cookbooks.

11111 ■ Animal Protection Institute of America (API)
PO Box 22505
Sacramento, CA 95822
Ph: (916)447-3085
Fax: (916)447-3070
E-mail: info@api4animals.org
URL: http://www.api4animals.org
Contact: Gary Pike, Chm.
Founded: 1968. **Members:** 75,000. **Membership Dues:** individual in U.S., $15 (annual) ● family, $25 (annual) ● protector, $100 (annual) ● advocate, $500 (annual) ● circle of compassion, $1,500 (annual). **Staff:** 20. **Budget:** $2,300,000. **Description:** Dedicated to ending animal abuse and exploitation. Operates a primate sanctuary in Dilley, TX, for more than 400 rescued primates. **Libraries: Type:** reference. **Holdings:** archival material, papers. **Subjects:** animal protection. **Awards: Type:** recognition. **Recipient:** for individuals furthering the efforts of animal protection. **Publications:** *Animal Issues*, quarterly. Magazine. Features articles. **Price:** $15.00/year. **Circulation:** 28,000 ● *Animal Protection*. Brochures. **Price:** free. Alternate Formats: online ● Newsletter, 5/year. Contains timely issues requiring API and/or member action. **Price:** free for members. Alternate Formats: online.

11112 ■ Animal Rights Coalition (ARC)
PO Box 8750
Minneapolis, MN 55408
Ph: (612)822-6161
E-mail: animalrightscoalition@msn.com
URL: http://www.animalrightscoalition.com
Founded: 1980. **Membership Dues:** individual, $35 (annual). **Description:** Seeks to end the suffering, abuse, and exploitation of non-human animals through information, education, and advocacy. **Libraries: Type:** reference. **Publications:** *Animal Rights Coalition News*, semiannual. Newsletter. **Price:** included in membership dues. **Advertising:** accepted ● *Children and Dogs* ● *Dissection: Biology or Cruelty?* ● *Factory Farming: Mechanized Madness* ● *Kids: Lets Talk About Animal Rights* ● *Pet Shops: Love for Sale* ● *The Real Price of Fashion*. **Conventions/Meetings:** monthly meeting - every 2nd Saturday.

11113 ■ Animal Rights International (ARI)
PO Box 1292
Middlebury, CT 06762
Ph: (203)598-0554

E-mail: info@ari-online.org
URL: http://www.ari-online.org
Contact: Sarah Whitman, Admin. Off.
Founded: 1985. **Staff:** 2. **Description:** Represents individuals and organizations united to: reduce or eliminate the use of animals in testing, research, and education, without compromising human safety. Promotes nonviolent food. Encourages companies that conduct tests on animals to sponsor research into devising substitute tests of equal or greater accuracy that do not require the use of animals, or that use fewer animals and minimize their pain and suffering; encourages agribusinesses to employ economically viable techniques that take into account the well-being of food animals. Develops fact sheets and position papers on topics related to alternative methods of testing. Promotes vegetarianism. **Libraries: Type:** reference. **Holdings:** archival material. **Subjects:** farm and laboratory animal welfare. **Committees:** Science Advisory. **Affiliated With:** Coalition for Non-Violent Food. **Publications:** *Coordinator's Report*, periodic. **Conventions/Meetings:** periodic meeting.

11114 ■ Animal Rights Mobilization (ARM)
PO Box 805859
Chicago, IL 60680
Ph: (773)282-8918
E-mail: spayneuterchicago@earthlink.net
URL: http://animalrightsmobilization.org
Contact: Kay Sievers, Pres./Dir.
Founded: 1981. **Description:** Animal rights advocates dedicated to the elimination of animal exploitation and abuse. Works to: develop a comprehensive educational program; expose specific cases of animal abuse and seek redress through persuasive and legal means; protest, nonviolently, against abuse of animals; foster cooperation within the rights movement; promote awareness of the natural relationship between human and animal liberation. Prompts national and international involvement on local animal rights issues. Conducts campaigns such as Campaign for a Fur Free America and a campaign to end the use of animals in laboratory experiments and product testing. Promotes spaying/neutering and the strengthening of regulations for protection of laboratory animals. Offers presentations and educational programs on animal rights issues; maintains speakers' bureau. **Libraries: Type:** reference; lending; open to the public. **Holdings:** archival material, audiovisuals, books, business records, clippings, periodicals. **Subjects:** animal research, factory farming, hunting, trapping, fur industry, marine mammals, environmental. **Formerly:** (1990) Trans-Species Unlimited. **Publications:** Pamphlets ● Also publishes educational materials.

11115 ■ Animal Rights Network/Institute for Animals and Society (ARN/IAS)
3500 Boston St., Ste.325
Baltimore, MD 21224
Ph: (410)675-4566
Fax: (410)675-0066
E-mail: kim.stallwood@animalsandsociety.org
URL: http://www.animalsandsociety.org
Contact: Kim W. Stallwood, Exec. Dir.
Founded: 1979. **Staff:** 3. **Budget:** $200,000. **Description:** Advances animal advocacy issues in public policy development by conducting scholarly research and analysis, providing education and training, and fostering cooperation with other social movements and interests. **Formerly:** (2004) Animal Rights Network/Animals' Agenda.

11116 ■ The Animal Society (TAS)
723 S Casino Center Blvd., 2nd Fl.
Las Vegas, NV 89101
Ph: (702)477-9677
Free: (877)227-7487
E-mail: support@animalsociety.org
URL: http://www.animalsociety.org
Contact: Ari Burton, Pres.
Founded: 2000. **Staff:** 4. **Nonmembership. Multinational. Description:** Works to prevent the suffering, neglect, abuse, and cruelty to animals worldwide. Promotes responsible pet ownership, and kindness

toward all living things. Raises money for shelters and animal rights support groups. **Also Known As:** USASPCA - United States Animal Society for the Prevention of Cruelty to Animals.

11117 ■ Animal Transportation Association (AATA)
111 East Loop N
Houston, TX 77029
Ph: (713)532-2177
Fax: (713)532-2166
E-mail: info@aata-animaltransport.org
URL: http://www.aata-animaltransport.org
Contact: Lisa Schoppa, Pres.

Founded: 1976. **Members:** 300. **Staff:** 2. **Budget:** $100,000. **Description:** Transportation manufacturers, carriers, and shippers; animal shippers and forwarders; humane and animal welfare groups, zoos, and animal breeders. Seeks to improve conditions for safe and humane transportation of animals by all modes of transit. **Committees:** European Council; Exotics and Wildlife; Horses; Livestock; Research and Technology; Rowsell Foundation; Small Animals. **Formerly:** (1990) Animal Air Transportation. **Publications:** *AATA Resource List* ● *Conference Proceedings*, annual. **Price:** $15.00. **Advertising:** accepted. Alternate Formats: online ● Newsletter, quarterly. **Price:** available to members only. **Circulation:** 500. **Advertising:** accepted. Alternate Formats: online ● Manuals. Alternate Formats: online ● Also provides reprint service. **Conventions/Meetings:** annual conference (exhibits).

11118 ■ Animal Welfare Institute (AWI)
PO Box 3650
Washington, DC 20027
Ph: (703)836-4300
Fax: (703)836-0400
E-mail: awi@awionline.org
URL: http://www.awionline.org
Contact: Cathy Liss, Pres.

Founded: 1951. **Members:** 5,800. **Membership Dues:** regular, $25 (annual) ● student or senior citizen, $5 (annual) ● supporting, $50 (annual) ● friend, $100 (annual) ● patron, $500 (annual) ● benefactor, $1,000 (annual). **Staff:** 11. **Description:** Works to reduce the sum total of pain and fear inflicted on animals by humans. Specifically aims to abolish factory farms and achieving humane slaughter for all animals raised for meat; improve the housing and handling of animals used for experimentation and pushing for the development of animal research alternatives; end the use of steel-jaw leghold traps and reform other cruel methods of controlling wildlife populations; preserve species threatened with extinction and protect wildlife in international trade; enforce strict regulation of transport conditions for all animals; encourage animal-friendly science teaching; and prevent painful experiments on animals by students. **Libraries: Type:** not open to the public. **Holdings:** 400. **Subjects:** endangered species, primates, predators, dogs, cats, philosophy and history of animal protection, whales and dolphins. **Awards:** Albert Schweitzer Medal. **Type:** medal. **Recipient:** for outstanding contributions to animal welfare. **Publications:** *Alternative Traps*. Book. **Price:** $3.00 ● *The Animal Dealers: Evidence of Abuse of Animals in the Commercial Trade 1952-1997*. Book ● *Animal Welfare Institute—Annual Report* ● *Animals and Their Legal Rights*. Book ● *AWI Quarterly*. Newsletter. Reports on the treatment of animals in laboratories, commercial trade, and traplines. Includes book reviews. **Price:** included in membership dues; $25.00 /year for nonmembers; free for libraries. Alternate Formats: online ● *Beyond the Laboratory Door*. Book. Includes two new sections: "Unjustifiable by Any Standard" and "Photographs of Experimental Animals". **Price:** $1.00 ● *The Bird Business*. Book ● *Endangered Species Handbook (in press)*. For teachers. ● *Factory Farming: The Experiment that Failed*. Book ● *Facts About Fur*. Book. **Price:** $3.00 ● *First Aid and Care of Small Animals*. Book. For primary school teachers. ● *Physical and Mental Suffering of Experimental Animals*. Book ● *Whales vs. Whalers*. Book.

11119 ■ Animals Voice
1354 E Ave., No. R-252
Chico, CA 95926
Ph: (530)343-2498
Free: (800)82-VOICE
Fax: (530)343-2498
E-mail: info@animalsvoice.com
URL: http://www.animalsvoice.com
Contact: Laura Moretti, Pres./Co-Founder

Founded: 2000. **Multinational. Description:** Represents animal rights activists. Promotes activism on behalf of animals worldwide. **Telecommunication Services:** electronic mail, veda@animalsvoice.com. **Publications:** *Animals Voice Magazine*, quarterly. **Price:** $5.00/copy; $20.00/year. **Advertising:** accepted. Alternate Formats: online.

11120 ■ Anti-Cruelty Society (ACS)
157 W Grand Ave.
Chicago, IL 60610
Ph: (312)644-8338
Fax: (312)644-3878
E-mail: info@anticruelty.org
URL: http://www.anticruelty.org
Contact: David Dinger, VP

Founded: 1899. **Staff:** 70. **Budget:** $3,400,000. **Description:** Strives to eliminate cruelty to animals, to educate children on responsibilities of pet ownership, and to provide refuge for abandoned or abused animals. Investigates reports of cruelty and abuse of animals; spays and neuters animals; places animals in permanent homes. Operates low-income clinic. Conducts humane education programs and workshops. Disseminates information to the public. **Convention/Meeting:** none. **Libraries: Type:** reference. **Holdings:** audio recordings, books, clippings, periodicals, video recordings. **Subjects:** animal behavior, wildlife. **Programs:** Humane Education. **Also Known As:** SPCA of Illinois. **Publications:** *Animal Crackers*, quarterly. Newsletter. **Price:** free for donors. **Circulation:** 85,000.

11121 ■ Arabian F.O.A.L. Association
PO Box 198
Parksville, NY 12768-0198
Ph: (505)531-2977
Fax: (505)531-2978
E-mail: elizabethanarab@hotmail.com
URL: http://www.foalinfo.org
Contact: Frederick A. Metcalf, Pres.

Description: Works to fight off "Arabian lethals". Reduces the incidence of lethals by disclosing known information to prospective users or buyers of breedable animals on request. Supports genetic research. Funds educational programs. **Computer Services:** database, Gold Patron Farm directory ● information services, Arabian lethals resources.

11122 ■ Associated Humane Societies (AHS)
124 Evergreen Ave.
Newark, NJ 07114-2133
Ph: (973)824-7080
Fax: (973)824-2720
E-mail: contactus@ahcares.org
URL: http://www.associatedhumanesocieties.org
Contact: Roseann Trezza, Exec. Dir.

Founded: 1906. **Members:** 75,000. **Membership Dues:** regular, $10 (annual). **Staff:** 94. **Budget:** $4,500,000. **Regional Groups:** 4. **Languages:** English, Spanish. **Description:** Represents humane societies that seek to assist wild and domestic animals. Works toward legislation supporting animal welfare. Maintains shelters for injured and abandoned animals; operates Popcorn Park Zoo; conducts educational presentations in schools and operates two animal hospitals in Newark and Forked River. **Committees:** Fundraising. **Departments:** Animal Control; Medical. **Programs:** Foster Pet. **Projects:** Popcorn Park-Wildlife Club; Share-A-Pet; Zoological Society. **Affiliated With:** American Humane Association. **Formerly:** (1976) Associated Humane Societies of New Jersey. **Publications:** *Being Homeless is Nothing to Sneeze At*. Magazine. **Circulation:** 89,000. **Advertising:** accepted ● *Coloring Book* ● *How to Raise a Baby Squirrel* ● *Humane News*, bimonthly. Newsletter. **Price:** included in membership

dues; $10.00 /year for nonmembers. **Circulation:** 89,000. **Advertising:** accepted ● *Lil Herbie*. Book ● Directory, annual. **Conventions/Meetings:** annual board meeting.

11123 ■ The Association of Sanctuaries (TAOS)
PO Box 925
Stillwater, MN 55082
Ph: (763)772-3087
Fax: (651)275-0457
E-mail: info@taosanctuaries.org
URL: http://www.taosanctuaries.org
Contact: Eileen McCarthy, Pres./Office Admin.

Founded: 1992. **Description:** Animal sanctuary accrediting organization. Provides sanctuaries as a refuge for abused, neglected, homeless, impounded, abandoned, or displaced animals for their lifetime. **Publications:** *TAOS Horizons*. Newsletter. **Price:** included in membership dues. **Conventions/Meetings:** annual conference.

11124 ■ Association of Veterinarians for Animal Rights (AVAR)
PO Box 208
Davis, CA 95617-0208
Ph: (530)759-8106
Fax: (530)759-8116
E-mail: info@avar.org
URL: http://avar.org
Contact: Teri A. Barnato MA, Natl. Dir.

Founded: 1981. **Members:** 2,500. **Membership Dues:** veterinarian, $30 (annual) ● veterinary medical student, $10 (annual) ● veterinary medical technician, financial supporter, $20 (annual). **Staff:** 2. **Budget:** $200,000. **Description:** Works to educate the public and the veterinary profession about society's use of animals. Actively seeks rights for animals. Sponsors educational programs. **Libraries: Type:** reference. **Holdings:** audiovisuals, books. **Publications:** *Alternatives*. Newsletter. Alternate Formats: online ● *Comparison of Alternatives Offered by Veterinary Medical Schools*. Report. Alternate Formats: online ● *Directions*, quarterly. Newsletter. Alternate Formats: online ● *Early Age Sterilization*. Video ● *Guide to Congenital and Heritable Disorders in Dogs*. Booklet ● *Position Statements*. Pamphlet. Alternate Formats: online. **Conventions/Meetings:** board meeting.

11125 ■ Beardies and Others Needing Emissaries (BONE)
6357 Chestnut Pkwy.
Flowery Branch, GA 30542
E-mail: twcasavage@mindspring.com
URL: http://beardie.net/bone
Contact: Carolyn Savage, Treas.

Description: Committed to assisting in rescues of beardies and beardie mixed collies.

11126 ■ Best Friends Animal Society
5001 Angel Canyon Rd.
Kanab, UT 84741-5000
Ph: (435)644-2001
E-mail: info@bestfriends.org
URL: http://www.bestfriends.com
Contact: Michael Mountain, Pres.

Members: 250,000. **Description:** Works as no-kill animal sanctuary for abused and abandoned cats, dogs, and other animals. Sets up adoptions. **Programs:** No More Homeless Pets Campaign. **Formerly:** (2004) Best Friends Animal Sanctuary. **Publications:** *Best Friends*. Magazine. **Circulation:** 200,000. Alternate Formats: online ● Newsletter, weekly. Features articles from the sanctuary. ● Reports. **Conventions/Meetings:** semiannual No More Homeless Pets Conference ● seminar ● tour - available daily, booked in advance ● workshop.

11127 ■ Bide-A-Wee Home Association
410 E 38th St.
New York, NY 10016
Ph: (212)532-6395
Fax: (212)532-4210

E-mail: info@bideawee.org
URL: http://www.bideawee.org
Contact: William A. Dueker Jr., Chm.
Founded: 1903. **Staff:** 125. **Budget:** $9,000,000.
Description: Humane society for the adoption and care of dogs, cats, puppies, and kittens. Shelters unwanted pets. Provides pet adoption services, veterinary clinic services, and burial/cremation services at pet memorial parks. Offers free pet bereavement counseling. Conducts community outreach programs by visiting schools and community centers. Provides pet-assisted therapy programs to hospitals, nursing homes, and other health-related facilities. Offers volunteer opportunities and special discounted adoption program for the elderly. **Publications:** *Bide-A-Wee Brochure* ● *Bide-A-Wee News*, quarterly. Newsletter. **Price:** free. **Circulation:** 70,000. Alternate Formats: online ● *Pet Memorial Parks Brochure*.

11128 ■ Canine Defense Fund (CDF)
c/o American Dog Owners Association
PO Box 186
Castleton, NY 12033
Ph: (518)477-8469 (518)732-7600
Free: (800)226-6233
Fax: (518)477-4034
E-mail: adoa@adoa.org
URL: http://www.adoa.org
Contact: Dr. Leon S. Sohn, Pres.
Founded: 1984. **Membership Dues:** individual, $15 (annual) ● husband and wife, couple, $25 (annual). **Description:** Established by the American Dog Owners Association, American Kennel Club, and the United Kennel Club. Opposes breed-specific ordinances restricting pet ownership in certain U.S. communities. Advocates laws that would apply to all dogs and hold an owner responsible for personal injury or damage caused by his or her dog. By-laws revised to allow dialogue with all levels of legislative bodies when legislation is proposed that is detrimental to the dog/pet owning public. **Computer Services:** Mailing lists, of members. **Affiliated With:** American Dog Owner's Association; American Kennel Club; United Kennel Club. **Publications:** Newsletter. **Price:** included in membership dues. **Conventions/Meetings:** annual board meeting.

11129 ■ Carver-Scott Humane Society (CSHS)
PO Box 215
Chaska, MN 55318
Ph: (952)368-3553
E-mail: info@carverscotths.org
URL: http://www.carverscotths.org
Contact: Jim Colbert, Pres.
Founded: 1989. **Members:** 250. **Membership Dues:** active, $25 (annual) ● senior active, $10 (annual) ● associate, $15 (annual). **Budget:** $35,000. **Local Groups:** 1. **Description:** Works to prevent cruelty to animals; promotes humane education and enforcement of animal protection laws. Maintains foster home network; seeks to return or find homes for lost animals; conducts fund-raisers. **Awards:** Type: recognition. **Publications:** *Furry Footnotes*, quarterly. Newsletter. Features educational animal care and issues, information about humane society itself and other events. **Price:** included in membership dues. **Circulation:** 2,000. **Advertising:** accepted. Alternate Formats: online. **Conventions/Meetings:** monthly board meeting.

11130 ■ Citizens to End Animal Suffering and Exploitation (CEASE)
PO Box 440456
Somerville, MA 02144
Ph: (617)628-9030
E-mail: info@ceaseboston.org
URL: http://www.ceaseboston.org
Founded: 1979. **Members:** 20,000. **Membership Dues:** individual, $20 (annual) ● family, $30 (annual) ● student, $15 (annual) ● senior citizen, $10 (annual) ● life, $300. **Staff:** 2. **Budget:** $75,000. **Description:** Individuals interested in animal rights. Seeks to raise public awareness of animal issues through outreach, legislation, protest, and education.

Campaigns against hunting, trapping, fur, animals in entertainment, and animal research. **Publications:** *Cease Newsline*, quarterly. Newsletter. Includes legislative updates. **Price:** $20.00/year. **Conventions/Meetings:** annual meeting.

11131 ■ Civitas
2210 W North Ave.
Chicago, IL 60647
Ph: (312)226-6700
Fax: (312)226-6733
E-mail: contactus@civitas.org
URL: http://www.civitas.org
Contact: Ashley Dinneen Rolls MA, Exec. Dir.
Founded: 1993. **Description:** Works to educate front-line professionals working on behalf of abused and neglected children. Gathers cutting-edge research on early childhood development and transform this content into bilingual educational tools. **Councils:** Advisory. **Publications:** *Begin with Love*. Video. **Price:** $16.95 ● *Connecting Through Child Care*. Video. **Price:** $70.00 ● *Understanding Children*. Book. Contains topics and latest research on child development. **Price:** $25.00 ● *Vivisection: A Crime Against Humanity*.

11132 ■ Coalition for Non-Violent Food (CONF)
c/o Animal Rights International
PO Box 1292
Middlebury, CT 06762
Ph: (203)598-0554
E-mail: info@ari-online.org
URL: http://www.ari-online.org
Contact: Sarah Whitman, Admin. Off.
Founded: 1986. **Description:** Organizations and individuals who promote reduction in the pain and suffering of farm animals by advocating eating only nonviolent foods. (Nonviolent foods are those not derived from animals killed for their meat.) Fosters a reduction in the number of animals used for food; encourages alternatives to animal food products. Advocates refining current agribusiness methods in order to reduce the pain and distress suffered by factory farm animals. Promotes vegetarianism. A program of Animal Rights International. **Libraries:** Type: reference. **Holdings:** archival material. **Committees:** Science Advisory. **Affiliated With:** Animal Rights International. **Publications:** *Coordinator's Report*, periodic ● *Factories of Despair*. Brochure ● Also publishes fact sheets and position papers. **Conventions/Meetings:** periodic meeting.

11133 ■ Coalition to Protect Animals in Entertainment (CPAE)
Address Unknown since 2007
Founded: 1987. **Description:** Networks with organizations interested in protecting animals in the entertainment industry. A task force of United Activists for Animal Rights. Provides follow-up investigation and action on reported animal abuse cases. Fosters elimination of the profiting aspect of animal cruelty in movies, T.V., commercials, circuses, zoos, rodeos, and all areas of entertainment. CPAE was originally formed to investigate alleged abuses uncovered in the 1987 movie Project X. Maintains that the American Humane Association, which was present on the Project X set, is neglecting its responsibilities. Believes that animals used for "entertainment" purposes are not adequately protected. **Publications:** *Alerts*, periodic.

11134 ■ Coalition to Protect Animals in Parks and Refuges (CPAPR)
PO Box 26
Swain, NY 14884-0026
E-mail: civitas@linkny.com
URL: http://web.linkny.com/~civitas/index.html
Founded: 1983. **Members:** 1,500. **Membership Dues:** $5 (annual). **Staff:** 1. **Budget:** $800. **Description:** Promotes habitat preservation and wildlife protection in general. **Libraries:** Type: reference. **Holdings:** 67. **Also Known As:** (2000) CIVITAS: Citizens for Planetary Health. **Publications:** *C-Paper*, quarterly. Newsletter. Provides wildlife and environment news. **Price:** included in membership dues.

Circulation: 2,000. Alternate Formats: online. **Conventions/Meetings:** periodic seminar ● periodic workshop.

11135 ■ Committee to Abolish Sport Hunting (CASH)
PO Box 562
New Paltz, NY 12561
Ph: (845)256-1400
Fax: (845)818-3622
E-mail: cash@cashwildwatch.org
URL: http://www.all-creatures.org/cash
Contact: Anne Muller, Pres.
Founded: 1976. **Members:** 11,500. **Membership Dues:** basic, $35 (annual) ● basic plus, $50 (annual). **Staff:** 1. **Budget:** $20,000. **Description:** Works to abolish all forms of recreational hunting through social, political, and legal pressure. Maintains that sport hunters are not conservationists or champions of the environment, rather a danger to wildlife and ecosystems. Seeks to change current government wildlife management programs, as CASH maintains that government policies are designed primarily to provide recreational opportunities for hunters at taxpayer expense. Issues committee reports and action alerts; interviews and debates on radio and television. Involved with demonstrations, affiliated with wildlife rehabilitation programs; maintains speakers' bureau. **Libraries:** Type: open to the public. **Holdings:** archival material, audio recordings, books, video recordings. **Additional Websites:** http://www.wildwatch.org, http://www.canadageese.org. **Publications:** *CASH Courier*, quarterly. Newsletter. **Price:** included in membership dues. Alternate Formats: online ● Also publishes videos and pamphlets.

11136 ■ Compassion for Animals Campaign
PO Box 322
Feasterville, PA 19053
Ph: (215)721-6661
Fax: (415)962-0659
E-mail: marialiberati@liberaticorporation.com
Contact: Maria Liberati, Spokesperson
Founded: 1987. **Members:** 10,000. **Membership Dues:** $25 (annual). **Staff:** 6. **Budget:** $250,000. **Regional Groups:** 62. **State Groups:** 3. **Local Groups:** 2. **Languages:** English, French, Italian. **Description:** Promotes public awareness of animal testing performed in the cosmetic and pharmaceutical industries. Encourages support for those companies that do not employ animal testing. Provides strategies to encourage companies to abandon animal testing; offers consulting services for manufacturers seeking alternative testing methods. Conducts charitable activities. Maintains speakers' bureau; conducts research and educational programs. **Libraries:** Type: reference. **Awards:** Type: recognition. **Computer Services:** database ● mailing lists. **Committees:** Political Action. **Affiliated With:** People for the Ethical Treatment of Animals. **Publications:** *Be Beautiful, Not Cruel* ● *Compassion Campaign*, quarterly. Newsletter. **Circulation:** 15,000. **Advertising:** accepted ● *Compassionate Beauty* ● *Directory of Cruelty Free Beauty and Personal Care Companies*, semiannual. **Price:** included in membership dues; $5.00 for nonmembers. **Circulation:** 20,000. **Advertising:** accepted ● *Eat Yourself Beautiful*.

11137 ■ Compassion Over Killing (COK)
PO Box 9773
Washington, DC 20016
Ph: (301)891-2458
E-mail: info@cok.net
URL: http://www.cok.net
Contact: Erica Meier, Dir.
Description: Works to end animal abuse. Focuses on cruelty to animals in agriculture. Promotes vegetarian eating as a way to build a kinder world for both human and nonhuman. **Publications:** *The Abolitionist*. Magazine. Alternate Formats: online ● *Compassionate Action*. Newsletter. Alternate Formats: online.

11138 ■ Concern for Helping Animals in Israel (CHAI)
PO Box 3341
Alexandria, VA 22302

Ph: (703)370-0333
Free: (866)308-0333
Fax: (703)370-1314
E-mail: chai.usa@verizon.net
URL: http://www.chai-online.org
Contact: Nina Natelson, Dir.
Founded: 1984. **Members:** 5,000. **Membership Dues:** individual, $18 (annual) ● family, $25 (annual) ● supporter, $50 (annual) ● sponsor, $100 (annual) ● patron, $500 (annual) ● benefactor, $1,000 (annual). **Staff:** 4. **Budget:** $175,000. **Multinational.** **Description:** Individuals and organizations interested in improving the condition and treatment of animals in Israel. Seeks to aid the Israeli animal welfare community in the construction of animal shelters and the expansion and modernization of the few, existing shelters. Provides veterinary medical equipment, supplies, and medications. Promotes animal protection legislation. Works to eliminate cruelty to animals; makes humane education materials available to schoolchildren, teachers, and summer camps in the U.S. and Israel. Is constructing a Humane Education Center in Israel. Sponsors traveling photo exhibit and a program to bring Jewish and Arab children together to learn about animals and participate in projects to help them. Sponsors conferences on relevant issues such as the child/animal abuse link and alternatives to animals in laboratories. Aims to construct a horse and donkey sanctuary; provides a mobile spay/neuter clinic offering low cost services; travels to schools throughout Israel to teach humane education to teachers and children. **Computer Services:** Mailing lists, of members. **Publications:** *CHAI Lights*, quarterly. Newsletter. Describes CHAI's efforts to promote positive treatment of animals in Israel. Includes book reviews and profiles of the animal welfare community. **Price:** included in membership dues. **Circulation:** 5,000. Alternate Formats: online ● *Future Medical Research without the Use of Animals: Facing the Challenge.* Proceedings ● *Preventing Violence in Society through Education.* Proceedings ● Also publishes humane education materials based on Biblical and Judaic teachings. **Conventions/Meetings:** periodic Alternatives to Laboratory Animals - meeting.

11139 ■ Culture and Animals Foundation (CAF)

3509 Eden Croft Dr.
Raleigh, NC 27612
Ph: (919)782-3739
Fax: (919)782-6464
E-mail: nancy@cultureandanimals.org
URL: http://www.cultureandanimals.org
Contact: Tom Regan, Pres.
Founded: 1985. **Members:** 14,000. **Membership Dues:** individual, $25 (annual) ● family, $40 (annual). **Staff:** 4. **Budget:** $40,000. **Description:** Promotes the understanding and appreciation of animals through dance, music, painting, poetry, theater, and sculpture. **Awards:** Type: grant. **Recipient:** for individuals whose art or literature expresses a positive concern for animals. **Publications:** *The Philosophy of Animal Rights.* Booklet. **Price:** $3.00 ● *Vegetarianism and Friendship.* Booklet. **Price:** $3.00. **Conventions/Meetings:** annual International Compassionate Living Festival (exhibits) - 1st weekend of October, Raleigh, NC.

11140 ■ Dachshund Rescue of North America (DRNA)

7821 Sabre Ct.
Manassas, VA 20109
E-mail: jane.lantz@verizon.net
URL: http://www.drna.org
Contact: Jane Lantz, Contact
Description: Committed to the rescue, rehabilitation and re-homing of dachshunds and mostly-dachshunds mixes. **Conventions/Meetings:** annual Mid-Atlantic Dachshund Phest - festival - 2007 Oct. 6, Manassas, VA.

11141 ■ Doing Things for Animals

59 S Bayles Ave.
Port Washington, NY 11050-3728
Ph: (516)883-7767

Fax: (516)944-5035
E-mail: dtfafetsvr@aol.com
URL: http://www.dtfa.org
Contact: Lynda Foro, Pres.
Founded: 1994. **Staff:** 1. **Budget:** $30,000. **Description:** Animal welfare group working for education and charity through communication, research, and service. Works in conjunction with other groups to promote alternatives to killing healthy homeless animals. **Libraries:** Type: reference. **Subjects:** no-kill groups in the United States. **Awards:** Voice for the Animals. **Frequency:** annual. **Type:** recognition. **Recipient:** for significant contributions to save animals' lives. **Computer Services:** database, no-kill humane organizations in the United States ● mailing lists. **Affiliated With:** Pet Savers Foundation. **Publications:** *No-Kill Directory*, annual. Contains listing of humane organizations that limit euthanasia. Is indexed by state, species and alphabetically. **Price:** $30.00/issue. **Advertising:** accepted ● *No-Kill News*, quarterly. Newsletter. **Conventions/Meetings:** annual No Kill Conference, an international educational event to explore the options for saving the lives of homeless animals (exhibits) - usually September.

11142 ■ Doris Day Animal League (DDAL)

2100 L St. NW
Washington, DC 20037
Ph: (202)452-1100
E-mail: info@ddal.org
URL: http://www.ddal.org
Contact: Holly Hazard, Exec. Dir.
Founded: 1987. **Membership Dues:** regular, $10 (annual). **Staff:** 12. **Description:** Serves as lobbying organization on Capitol Hill. Seeks to increase protection of animals and public awareness of animal suffering. Gathers and disseminates information on animal testing to legislators and the general public. Works to improve federal and state legislation and regulations, including the reduction of pet overpopulation and toxicity testing. **Publications:** *Animal Guardian*, quarterly. Magazine. Contains current issues about the society. **Price:** included in membership dues. Alternate Formats: online ● *Legislative Tracks*, quarterly. Newsletter. **Price:** free. Alternate Formats: online ● *U.S. Congressional Handbook.* Includes contact information for select federal agencies and a glossary of terms in the legislative process. **Price:** $15.00 plus shipping and handling ● Annual Report, annual ● Brochures.

11143 ■ Echo Dogs White Shepherd Rescue (EDWSR)

PO Box 240028
Ballwin, MO 63024
E-mail: info@echodogs.org
URL: http://www.echodogs.org
Contact: Susan Fishbein, Pres.
Founded: 1999. **Description:** Rescues neglected and abused dogs. Promotes responsible pet care. Educates the public about the breed. Provides training support and advice to adopters after dogs have been placed in their homes. Teaches dogs house manners and basic obedience skills while in foster care. **Telecommunication Services:** electronic mail, whitesheplover2@aol.com.

11144 ■ Elephant Sanctuary in Tennessee

PO Box 393
Hohenwald, TN 38462
Ph: (931)796-6500
Fax: (931)796-1360
E-mail: sharon@elephants.com
URL: http://www.elephants.com
Contact: Ann M. Bilanzich, Contact
Founded: 1995. **Members:** 62,000. **Membership Dues:** family, $50 (annual) ● individual, $30 (annual) ● elder, student, $10 (annual). **Staff:** 25. **Budget:** $5,300,000. **Description:** Provides haven for old, sick or needy elephants in a setting of green pastures, old-growth forests, spring-fed ponds and a heated barn for cold winter nights. Provides education about the crisis facing social, sensitive, passionately intense, playful, complex, exceedingly intelligent and endangered creatures. **Libraries:** Type: not open to

the public. **Holdings:** archival material. **Publications:** *Trunklines.* Newsletter. Alternate Formats: online.

11145 ■ English Springer Rescue America (ESRA)

2721 Walker Lee Dr.
Los Alamitos, CA 90720-4935
Free: (800)921-1047
E-mail: info@springerrescue.org
URL: http://www.springerrescue.org
Contact: Caryn Pola, Pres.
Founded: 1998. **Members:** 400. **Description:** Provides assistance for English Springer Spaniels who are unwanted, abused, and abandoned; offers adoption referral service to assist shelters and animal control facilities in the re-homing of impounded Springers. Referral assistance is available to owners who can no longer care for their Springer.

11146 ■ Equine Advocates

c/o Susan Wagner, Pres./Founder
PO Box 354
Chatham, NY 12037-0354
Ph: (518)245-1599
URL: http://www.equineadvocates.com
Contact: Susan Wagner, Pres./Founder
Founded: 1996. **Description:** Aims to rescue, protect, and prevent the abuse of horses through education, investigation rescue operations, and the dissemination of information to the public. **Publications:** *Horse Slaughter: An American Disgrace.* Pamphlet. Contains facts and figures to help understand the current situation.

11147 ■ Equine Rescue League (ERL)

PO Box 4366
Leesburg, VA 20177
Ph: (703)771-1240
E-mail: bubbasays2@aol.com
URL: http://www.equinerescueleague.org
Contact: Patricia Rogers, Founder
Founded: 1990. **Members:** 2,500. **Membership Dues:** regular, $20 (annual) ● junior, $10 (annual) ● family, $40 (annual) ● professional, $100 (annual) ● life, $500. **Staff:** 3. **Budget:** $100,000. **Description:** Seeks to increase public awareness about horse neglect and abuse. Works for adoption of horses by qualified people. Provides transportation and holding facilities for animals seized by humane officials. Works to find "caring homes" for horses. Conducts educational programs on horse health care. **Libraries:** Type: reference. **Holdings:** articles. **Programs:** Adoption; Foster; Volunteer. **Publications:** *The Equine Rescuer*, quarterly. Newsletter. **Circulation:** 3,000 ● Articles. Alternate Formats: online. **Conventions/Meetings:** monthly board meeting ● annual meeting.

11148 ■ Exotic Bird Rescue (EBR)

317 H. Goodpasture Island Rd.
Eugene, OR 97401
Ph: (541)461-4333
E-mail: ebr@rescuebird.com
URL: http://www.rescuebird.com
Contact: Ms. Andrea Larsen, Chair
Founded: 1994. **Membership Dues:** regular, $20 (annual). **Description:** Works to provide education and support for bird owners; ensures exotic birds receive proper care. **Libraries:** Type: by appointment only; lending; not open to the public. **Holdings:** 30. **Subjects:** parrots.

11149 ■ FARM (Farm Animal Reform Movement)

10101 Ashburton Ln.
Bethesda, MD 20817
Ph: (301)530-1737
Free: (888)ASK-FARM
Fax: (301)530-5747
E-mail: dawn@farmusa.org
URL: http://www.farmusa.org
Contact: Dawn Moncrief, Exec. Dir.
Founded: 1981. **Members:** 18,000. **Membership Dues:** regular, $15 (annual) ● supporter, $35 (annual) ● friend, $100 (annual) ● sponsor, $250 (annual) ● idealist, $500 (annual) ● benefactor, $1,000

(annual) ● partner, $5,000 (annual) ● founder, $10,000 (annual). **Staff:** 10. **Budget:** $300,000. **Description:** Promotes a plant-based diet and exposes abuse of farm animals and other adverse impacts of animal agriculture. Holds demonstrations and print, radio, and television interviews. Promotes observance of the Great American Meatout on March 20, World Farm Animals Day on October 2, and choice of plant-based diet in schools. **Libraries: Type:** reference. **Holdings:** 300; books, video recordings. **Subjects:** farm animal abuse and other destructive impacts of animal agriculture, diet and health, environmental impacts. **Awards:** Bill Rosenberg Award. **Frequency:** annual. **Type:** recognition. **Recipient:** for youth activists who have made significant contributions to end farm animal abuse ● Sabina Fund. **Type:** grant. **Recipient:** for grassroots organizations. **Additional Websites:** http://www.meatout.org, http://www.animalrights2003.org. **Absorbed:** Vegetarian Information Service. **Formerly:** (1982) Farm Animal Task Force. **Publications:** *The FARM Report*, quarterly ● *Meatout Mondays*, weekly. Newsletter. Alternate Formats: online ● Annual Report ● Also publishes news releases and fact sheets. **Conventions/Meetings:** annual convention, with speakers (exhibits).

11150 ■ Farm Sanctuary
PO Box 150
Watkins Glen, NY 14891
Ph: (607)583-2225
Fax: (607)583-2041
E-mail: info@farmsanctuary.org
URL: http://www.farmsanctuary.org
Contact: Mr. Gene Baur, Pres.
Founded: 1986. **Members:** 150,000. **Membership Dues:** regular, $20 (annual). **Staff:** 50. **Budget:** $3,000,000. **Description:** Representatives working to end factory farm animal abuses. Works to: eliminate what the organization terms abusive animal agricultural practices; educate the public on factory farming; promote alternatives to factory farm products. Sponsors Farm Animal Alert to monitor and inform people of legislative efforts to end factory farming. Organizes Veal Boycott and Veal Calf Refuge campaign to protest the abuse of veal calves. Sponsors Adopt-A-Turkey campaigns to draw media attention to the problems of factory farming. Operates referral, placement, and shelter services for abused and abandoned farm animals; maintains educational center and speakers' bureau; conducts outreach and educational activities and training sessions on farm animal issues. **Libraries: Type:** reference. **Subjects:** animal welfare, animal agriculture, vegetarianism. **Programs:** Adopt-A-Farm Animal; Cruelty Investigation and Action; Education and Outreach; Farm Animal Alert; Sanctuary for Farm Animals. **Publications:** *Farm Sanctuary News*, quarterly. Newsletter. Contains legislative and shelter updates. **Price:** included in membership dues. **Circulation:** 60,000. Alternate Formats: online ● *Guide to Veg Living*. Booklet. **Price:** free. Alternate Formats: online ● *Life Behind Bars*. Booklet. **Price:** free. Alternate Formats: online ● Annual Report, annual. Includes information on programs and fiscal revenue and expenditures. ● Videos ● Also publishes fact sheets.

11151 ■ Feminists for Animal Rights (FAR)
PO Box 41355
Tucson, AZ 85717-1355
Ph: (520)825-6852
E-mail: far@farinc.org
URL: http://www.farinc.org
Contact: Michelle Taylor, Dir.
Founded: 1982. **Members:** 600. **Membership Dues:** angel, $1,000 (annual) ● regular, $25 (annual) ● matron, $100 (annual) ● friend, $26-$100 (annual). **Staff:** 1. **Regional Groups:** 8. **Description:** Feminist vegetarians dedicated to ending all forms of violence against women and animals. Believes that violence against animals is directly related to violence against women and stems from the hierarchical system which works for the powerful against the powerless. Advocates a plant-based diet as an actualization of the feminist belief that "the personal is political." Provides educational materials. Offers a rescue program for companion animals of battered women. **Publica-**

tions: *The Ecofeminist Journal*. Contains information on feminist, animal advocacy, and environmental issues and the connections between them. ● *Feminists for Animal Rights Newsletter*, semiannual. **Price:** free for members; $3.50 for nonmembers. **Advertising:** accepted ● Bibliography. **Price:** $7.50 ● Brochure. **Price:** free (provide stamped self-addressed envelope).

11152 ■ Friends of Animals (FoA)
777 Post Rd., Ste.205
Darien, CT 06820
Ph: (203)656-1522
Fax: (203)656-0267
E-mail: info@friendsofanimals.org
URL: http://www.friendsofanimals.org
Contact: Priscilla Feral, Pres.
Founded: 1957. **Members:** 200,000. **Membership Dues:** regular, outside U.S., $35 (annual) ● regular, in U.S., $25 (annual). **Staff:** 24. **Description:** Works to reduce and eliminate animal suffering and abuse, and creates respect for all animals by advocating animal rights and veganism. Offers low-cost spay/neuter program. Active in: wildlife and habitat protection; banning hunting and trapping; anti-fur and ivory campaigns. **Publications:** *Action Line*, quarterly. Magazine. Reports/updates on efforts to protect animals. **Price:** included in membership dues. **Circulation:** 160,000 ● Also publishes bulletins.

11153 ■ Fund for Animals
200 W 57th St.
New York, NY 10019
Ph: (212)246-2096
Free: (888)405-FUND
Fax: (212)246-2633
E-mail: info@fundforanimals.org
URL: http://www.fundforanimals.org
Contact: Tracey McIntire, Contact
Founded: 1967. **Members:** 200,000. **Membership Dues:** individual, $10 (annual) ● supporting, $50 (annual) ● sustaining, $100 (annual) ● sponsor, $500 (annual) ● patron, $1,000 (annual). **Staff:** 65. **Budget:** $7,000,000. **Description:** Works to protect wildlife and fight cruelty to animals, both domestic and wild, by means of legal action, direct activism, public education, and lobbying. Publicizes and influences public opinion on environmental and animal issues through books, press releases, articles, meetings, and special events. Exposes over network television, the cruelty of bullfighting, the clubbing of baby seals, the use of the leghold trap, and the sport hunting. Initiates national debates on issues such as fox hunting, greyhound racing, and dog fighting. Places over 400 animal species on the endangered species list. Owns and operates Black Beauty Ranch for homeless and abused hooved animals in Texas and the Animal Trust Wildlife Sanctuary, a wildlife rehabilitation facility in Ramona, CA. **Publications:** Annual Report, annual. Alternate Formats: online.

11154 ■ Fur Commission U.S.A. (FCUSA)
826 Orange Ave.
PMB 506
Coronado, CA 92118-2619
Ph: (619)575-0139
Fax: (619)575-5578
E-mail: info@furcommission.com
URL: http://www.furcommission.com
Contact: Teresa Platt, Exec. Dir.
Founded: 1994. **Members:** 650. **Staff:** 3. **Description:** Represents 420 mink-farming families on 330 farms in 28 states. Works to ensure the best standards of animal husbandry through a certification program, and to educate the public about responsible fur farming and the merits of fur. Promotes humane care practices for fur farm animals. Establishes care guidelines and conducts veterinarian inspections; involved in public education. Compiles statistics and conducts research. **Libraries: Type:** not open to the public. **Awards:** Merit Award. **Type:** recognition. **Recipient:** for excellent animal husbandry skills ● **Type:** recognition. **Committees:** Animal Welfare; Government Affairs; Research. **Affiliated With:** American Farm Bureau Federation; American Sheep Industry Association; American Veterinary Medical Associa-

tion; Americans for Medical Progress Educational Foundation; Animal Agriculture Alliance; Association of Fish and Wildlife Agencies; Center for the Defense of Free Enterprise; Convention on International Trade in Endangered Species of Wild Fauna and Flora; Countryside Alliance; Empress Chinchilla Breeders Cooperative; Fur Information Council of America; Fur Institute of Canada; International Fur Trade Federation; Leather Apparel Association; Museum of the Fur Trade; National Anxiety Center; National Association for Biomedical Research; National Trappers Association; North American Trap Collector Association; Ohio State Trappers Association; Pet Industry Joint Advisory Council. **Publications:** *Fur Animal Research*, quarterly. Newsletter ● *Fur Farm Letter*, quarterly. Newsletter. Alternate Formats: online. **Conventions/Meetings:** annual board meeting.

11155 ■ Great Ape Project (GAP)
806A NW 51st St.
Seattle, WA 98107
Ph: (206)579-5975
E-mail: info@greatapeproject.org
URL: http://www.greatapeproject.org
Contact: Peter Singer, Pres./Co-Founder
Founded: 1993. **Multinational. Description:** Provides non-human great apes with the right to life, the freedom of liberty and protection from torture. Works for the global removal of non-human great apes from the category of mere property, and for their immediate protection. Seeks to implement basic legal principles designed to provide non-human great apes the fundamental moral and legal protections. **Publications:** Books.

11156 ■ Greyhound Adoption Center (GAC)
PO Box 2433
La Mesa, CA 91943-2433
Free: (877)478-8364
E-mail: greyhound@greyhoundog.org
URL: http://www.greyhoundog.org
Contact: Kathy Johnson, Pres.
Founded: 1987. **Members:** 619. **Membership Dues:** advocate, $30 (annual) ● supporting, $50 (annual) ● sustaining, $75-$150 (annual) ● benefactor, $200-$500 (annual) ● angel, $1,000 (annual). **Staff:** 5. **Budget:** $340,000. **State Groups:** 3. **Local Groups:** 1. **Description:** Volunteers. Works to provide quality homes for Greyhounds that fails to qualify or no longer qualify at racetracks throughout the U.S. Disseminates information on the Greyhound breed to public. Rescues abandoned Greyhounds from animal shelters. Works toward ending Greyhound abuse. **Computer Services:** Online services, catalog of Greyhound-related information. **Formerly:** (2001) Greyhound Pets of America. **Publications:** *Offtrack Greyhound*, quarterly. Newsletter. Includes articles of general interest of Greyhounds and efforts of the center. **Price:** free. **Circulation:** 8,000. Alternate Formats: online ● Booklet. **Conventions/Meetings:** annual meeting and workshop - usually in September.

11157 ■ Greyhound Friends
167 Saddle Hill Rd.
Hopkinton, MA 01748
Ph: (508)435-5969
Fax: (508)435-0547
E-mail: ghfriend@greyhound.org
URL: http://www.greyhound.org
Contact: Louise Coleman, Exec. Dir.
Founded: 1983. **Membership Dues:** basic, $25 (annual). **Staff:** 3. **Budget:** $400,000. **Regional Groups:** 5. **Description:** Organizations who contribute to animal welfare; individuals who have adopted greyhounds or who are interested in the fate of retired greyhound racing dogs. Works to save racetrack greyhounds and placing them in responsible homes. Maintains a kennel for 20 greyhounds; arranges adoptions; presents open houses. Offers educational and charitable programs; maintains Speaker's Bureau. **Libraries: Type:** reference; open to the public. **Subjects:** greyhound history. **Awards:** Mickey Award. **Type:** recognition. **Recipient:** for people who have done an outstanding job of helping greyhounds. **Computer Services:** Mailing lists, of members. **Publications:** *The Home Stretch*, quarterly. Newsletter.

Price: included in membership dues. **Conventions/ Meetings:** semiannual board meeting.

11158 ■ Habitat for Horses (HfH)
PO Box 213
Hitchcock, TX 77563
Ph: (409)935-0277
Free: (866)HFH-LSER
Fax: (409)935-0424
E-mail: admin@habitatforhorses.org
URL: http://www.habitatforhorses.org
Contact: Mr. Jerry Finch, Admin.
Membership Dues: general, $25 (annual) ● organizational, $75 (annual) ● sponsoring, $10 (monthly) ● life, $1,500. **Description:** Promotes and secures the safety and well being of horses, both mentally and physically. **Publications:** Newsletter. **Price:** included in membership dues.

11159 ■ Harmony House for Cats (APA)
PO Box 18098
Chicago, IL 60618-0098
Ph: (773)463-6667
E-mail: hhforcats@yahoo.com
URL: http://hhforcats.org
Contact: Annette Grennell, Dir.
Founded: 1970. **Membership Dues:** supporting, $50 (annual) ● family, $75 (annual) ● sustaining, $100 (annual) ● life, $500 ● youth, senior citizen, $25 (annual). **Staff:** 6. **Budget:** $200,000. **Description:** Aims to protect, heal, and rehome cats and kittens in need. Maintains homelike, no-kill shelter and adoption center. Offers volunteer program, pet counseling and humane education. **Formerly:** (1995) Animal Protective Association. **Publications:** Newsletter, quarterly. **Price:** free. **Circulation:** 5,000.

11160 ■ Hearts United for Animals (HUA)
Box 286
Auburn, NE 68305
Ph: (402)274-3679
Fax: (402)274-3689
E-mail: hua@hua.org
URL: http://www.hua.org
Description: Serves as a national no-kill animal shelter and sanctuary for animals. Works for the relief of suffering of animals. Rescues animals from all over the country and specializes in long distance adoptions of animals. **Programs:** Community Outreach; Jet Set Dogs; Puppy Rescue; Spay/Neuter. **Publications:** Newsletter, 3/year.

11161 ■ Helping Hands Rescue
PO Box 1975
Lewiston, ID 83501
Ph: (208)746-2777 (208)743-6855
E-mail: info@lctoday.net
URL: http://www.lctoday.net/nonprofit/helpinghand-srescue.htm
Multinational. Description: Works to re-home companion animals that are homeless. Provides a hotline to coordinate animal adoptions. Networks with other shelters to rescue animals in the U.S. and Canada and transport them to new homes or rescue organizations for their breed.

11162 ■ Hooved Animal Humane Society (HAHS)
10804 McConnell Rd.
Woodstock, IL 60098
Ph: (815)337-5563
Fax: (815)337-5569
E-mail: info@hahs.org
URL: http://www.hahs.org
Contact: Barbara Geittmann, Exec. Dir.
Founded: 1971. **Members:** 5,000. **Membership Dues:** junior (18 and under) and senior (65 and better), $15 (annual) ● adult, $35 (annual) ● club, $100 (annual) ● family, $50 (annual) ● sustaining, $500 (annual) ● life, $1,000 ● patron, $5,000 (annual) ● benefactor, $10,000 (annual). **Staff:** 5. **Description:** Aims to promote the humane treatment of hooved animals through education, legislation, investigation and if necessary intervention; abused and or neglected animals receive proper veterinary care, feed, and are rehabilitated on the association's farm and

adopted out to prequalified permanent homes. **Boards:** Advisory. **Programs:** Adopt a Hoof; Internship; Volunteer. **Publications:** Basics of Horse Care. Booklet. Alternate Formats: online ● Hoofprints, quarterly. Newsletter. Contains articles on horse health, and humane issues. **Price:** included in membership dues. **Circulation:** 6,500 ● The Misuse of Drugs in Horseracing. Book. **Conventions/Meetings:** annual picnic, with games, pony and wagon rides, vendors and tours.

11163 ■ Horseaid Equine Relief Programme (HERP)
c/o International Generic Horse Association
PO Box 6778, Eastview Sta.
San Pedro, CA 90734-6778
E-mail: volunteer@equinerescue.net
URL: http://www.igha.org
Contact: Enzo Giobbe, CEO/Founder
Founded: 1984. **Description:** Individuals and organizations with an interest in horses. Promotes responsible horse ownership and humane treatment of horses. Rescues abused horses; maintains horse adoption and placement program. **Publications:** HorseAid Update, periodic. Newsletter. Alternate Formats: online ● IHG/HA Informational Brochure, periodic.

11164 ■ House Rabbit Network (HRN)
PO Box 2602
Woburn, MA 01888-1102
Ph: (781)431-1211
E-mail: info@rabbitnetwork.org
URL: http://www.rabbitnetwork.org
Contact: Suzanne Trayhan, Contact
Founded: 2000. **Membership Dues:** Netherland Dwarf, $15 (annual) ● Mini lop, $25 (annual) ● New Zealand, $50 (annual) ● Flemish giant, $100 (annual). **Description:** Committed to the rescue of homeless rabbits, including foster care for discarded domestic rabbits and finding them permanent indoor homes; assisting humane societies and shelters with rabbits; providing spay/neuter surgery and veterinary care; rehabilitating and socializing mistreated or neglected animals; permanently caring for animals who cannot be placed in adoptive homes due to serious health or behavioral problems; and educating the public on responsible pet ownership and humane practices. **Publications:** Rabbit Tracks, 3/year. Newsletter.

11165 ■ House Rabbit Society
148 Broadway
Richmond, CA 94804
Ph: (510)970-7575
Fax: (510)970-9820
E-mail: membership@rabbit.org
URL: http://www.rabbit.org
Contact: Margo DeMello, Financial Dir.
Founded: 1988. **Members:** 7,000. **Membership Dues:** regular, $18 (annual). **Staff:** 3. **Budget:** $150,000. **State Groups:** 18. **Local Groups:** 9. **Description:** Volunteers who live with or care about rabbits. Aims to share information and support. Works to educate the public on popular misconceptions about rabbits as pets. Rescues rabbits from shelters and seeks homes for them. **Convention/Meeting:** none. **Publications:** House Rabbit Journal, quarterly. Contains information on rabbit diet, behavior, and environment. Features articles made by veterinarians. **Price:** included in membership dues. **Circulation:** 6,000.

11166 ■ Humane Farming Association (HFA)
PO Box 3577
San Rafael, CA 94912
Ph: (415)771-2253
Fax: (415)485-0106
E-mail: hfa@hfa.org
URL: http://www.hfa.org
Contact: Bradley S. Miller, Natl. Dir.
Founded: 1985. **Members:** 135,000. **Staff:** 8. **Local Groups:** 1. **Description:** Protects farm animals from cruelty and abuse, the public from the dangerous use of antibiotics, hormones, and other chemicals used in factory farming, and the environment from the

devastating impacts of industrialized animal factories. Designs campaigns to expose to the American public the horrors of factory farming and to see to it that farm animal abuse is outlawed.

11167 ■ Humane Society of the United States (HSUS)
2100 L St. NW
Washington, DC 20037
Ph: (202)452-1100 (301)258-8276
Fax: (301)258-3078
E-mail: membership@hsus.org
URL: http://www.hsus.org
Contact: Wayne Pacelle, Pres./CEO
Founded: 1954. **Members:** 1,750,000. **Membership Dues:** individual, $25 (annual) ● family, $35 (annual) ● supporting, $50 (annual) ● sustaining, $100 (annual) ● sponsor, $500 (annual) ● patron, $1,000 (annual). **Regional Groups:** 10. **Description:** Promotes public education to foster respect, understanding, and compassion for all creatures. Programs include: reducing the overbreeding of cats and dogs and promoting responsible pet ownership; eliminating cruelty in hunting and trapping; exposing and eliminating painful uses of animals in research and testing; eliminating the abuse of animals in movies, television productions, circuses, and competitive events such as dogfights, racing, pulling contests, and shows; correcting inhumane conditions for animals in zoos, menageries, pet shops, puppy mills, and kennels; stopping cruelty in the raising, handling, and transporting of animals used for food; addressing critical environmental issues in terms of their impact on animals and humans; protecting endangered wildlife and marine mammals; making national wildlife refuges and parks into true sanctuaries for wildlife; halting the cruelty and destruction of the international trade in wildlife, especially exotic birds and elephant ivory; campaigns to create public awareness and rejection of harvested or farm-raised fur-bearing animals. Campaigns for or against legislation affecting animal protection and monitors enforcement of existing animal protection statutes; works with animal control agencies and local humane societies to establish effective and humane programs. Assists local humane societies in improving their administrative, organizational, and sheltering techniques. Sponsors HSUS Animal Control Academy and the National Association for Humane and Environmental Education. **Affiliated With:** National Association for Humane and Environmental Education; World Society for the Protection of Animals - England. **Publications:** Animal Activist Alert, quarterly. Newsletter. Covers animal legislation. **Price:** included in membership dues ● HSUS Close-Up Reports, quarterly. Covers critical problems affecting animals. ● HSUS News, quarterly. Magazine. Covers society activities. **Price:** included in membership dues ● Kind News, 9/year. **Price:** $18.00/year ● Kind Teacher, annual. Contains educational program information and activities for teachers and students. **Price:** $18.00/year ● Shelter Sense, 10/year. Newsletter. Designed for individuals employed in or concerned with community animal control. **Price:** $8.00/year. ISSN: 0734-3078. **Circulation:** 3,000 ● Pamphlets. **Conventions/ Meetings:** annual conference.

11168 ■ In Defense of Animals (IDA)
3010 Kerner Blvd.
San Rafael, CA 94901
Ph: (415)388-9641
Fax: (415)388-0388
E-mail: ida@idausa.org
URL: http://www.idausa.org
Contact: Dr. Elliot M. Katz DVM, Pres.
Founded: 1983. **Members:** 75,000. **Staff:** 32. **Budget:** $2,500,000. **Regional Groups:** 7. **Local Groups:** 3. **Description:** Individuals interested in taking direct action to protect animals from cruel treatment. Attempts to come to the aid of animals experiencing "cruel treatment in the name of science". Promotes and disseminates information about animal advocacy. Conducts demonstrations and protests at experimental laboratories. Plans to establish speakers' bureau. Provides children's services and educational programs. **Libraries: Type:** reference. **Sub-**

jects: animal advocacy, wildlife protection. **Computer Services:** database, activist ● database, pet theft. **Telecommunication Services:** hotline, pet theft hotline, (800)STOLEN-PET. **Formerly:** (1985) Californians for Responsible Research. **Publications:** *A Behind the Scenes Look at Primate Experimentation.* Brochure ● *Can A Student Help Animals and the Environment?.* Brochure ● *EPA Animal Tests: Inhumane and Ineffective.* Brochure ● *The Heart of Technology: A Look at Modern Scientific Research Methods that Do Not Harm or Kill Animals.* Brochure ● *The Pet Theft Conspiracy.* Brochure ● *Twelve Things You Can Do In Defense of Animals.* Brochure ● Newsletter, quarterly. **Conventions/Meetings:** quarterly board meeting ● competition.

11169 ■ International Defenders of Animals (IDA)

PO Box 5634
Weybosset Hill Sta.
Providence, RI 02903-0634
Ph: (401)738-3710
E-mail: dennis@defendersofanimals.org
URL: http://www.defendersofanimals.org
Contact: Dennis Tabella, Dir./Founder
Founded: 1978. **Membership Dues:** regular, $25 (annual) ● senior/student, $20 (annual). **Languages:** English, Spanish. **Description:** Individuals interested in animal welfare and in the abolition of vivisection. Activities include: humane education; birth control of domestic pets; pet adoption service; care for sick, injured, or homeless animals; investigation of cases of cruelty to animals. Promotes general interest in birds, animals, and all creatures. **Awards: Frequency:** periodic. **Type:** recognition. **Publications:** *Jelly Side Down,* monthly. Newsletter. **Price:** included in membership dues ● *Orphans of the Storm.* Book. Features Virginia Gillas' life of rescuing, sheltering, caring for and adopting of companion animals. ● Articles (in English and Spanish). **Price:** free ● Brochures. Covers various subjects including chained dogs, downed cows, bullfights, rodeos, circus, and zoos. **Conventions/Meetings:** annual meeting.

11170 ■ International Foundation for Ethical Research (IFER)

53 W Jackson Blvd., Ste.1552
Chicago, IL 60604
Ph: (312)427-6025
Fax: (312)427-6524
E-mail: ifer@navs.org
URL: http://www.ifer.org
Contact: Mr. Peter O'Donovan, Exec. Dir.
Founded: 1985. **Staff:** 2. **Description:** Promotes the discovery, development, and implementation of scientifically valid alternatives to the use of live animals in research, testing, and technology. Maintains speakers' bureau and charitable program. **Awards:** Graduate Fellowships in Alternatives in Scientific Research. **Frequency:** annual. **Type:** fellowship. **Recipient:** to students who are enrolled in Master's and PhD programs in sciences, humanities, psychology, and journalism ● **Type:** grant. **Boards:** Scientific Advisory. **Publications:** *The IFER Newsletter,* quarterly. Alternate Formats: online ● *International Forum Addresses Alternatives in Animal Research.* Report. Alternate Formats: online ● Proceedings, annual. **Conventions/Meetings:** annual conference and symposium ● seminar ● workshop.

11171 ■ International Fund for Animal Welfare (IFAW)

411 Main St.
PO Box 193
Yarmouth Port, MA 02675-0193
Ph: (508)744-2000
Free: (800)932-4329
Fax: (508)744-2009
E-mail: info@ifaw.org
URL: http://www.ifaw.org
Contact: Frederick O'Regan, Pres.
Founded: 1969. **Members:** 1,500,000. **Staff:** 200. **Budget:** $54,000,000. **Multinational. Description:** Works to improve the welfare of wild and domestic animals throughout the world by reducing commercial exploitation of animals, protecting wildlife habitats

and assisting animals in distress. Seeks to motivate the public to prevent cruelty to animals and to promote animal welfare and conservation policies that advance the well being of both animals and people. **Libraries: Type:** not open to the public. **Holdings:** 10,000; photographs, video recordings. **Publications:** *IFAW News.* Newsletter. Alternate Formats: online ● Annual Report, annual. Alternate Formats: online.

11172 ■ International Hedgehog Association (IHA)

PO Box 1060
Divide, CO 80814
Ph: (719)687-8087
Free: (800)735-3160
Fax: (719)687-8082
E-mail: info@hedgehogclub.com
URL: http://www.hedgehogclub.com
Contact: Zug G. Standing Bear, Treas./Research Coor.
Founded: 1999. **Members:** 150. **Membership Dues:** individual, $20 (annual) ● family, $30 (annual) ● junior, $12 (annual) ● breeder, $40 (annual) ● veterinarian/veterinary clinic, $15 (annual) ● life (individual), $250 ● life (family), $350 ● life (breeder), $450. **Staff:** 2. **Budget:** $10,000. **Multinational. Description:** Strives to educate the public in the care and betterment of hedgehogs and to facilitate the rescue, welfare, promotion and care of hedgehogs. **Libraries: Type:** not open to the public. **Holdings:** 40. **Subjects:** hedgehogs; includes technical works, general information, pet care, folklore, children's stories in English, German and Dutch. **Awards:** Rescue Fund. **Type:** monetary. **Computer Services:** database ● mailing lists, of members. **Formerly:** (1999) International Hedgehog Fanciers Society; (2002) International Hedgehog Club. **Publications:** Newsletter.

11173 ■ International Primate Protection League (IPPL)

PO Box 766
Summerville, SC 29484-0766
Ph: (843)871-2280
Fax: (843)871-7988
E-mail: info@ippl.org
URL: http://www.ippl.org
Contact: Dr. Shirley McGreal, Chair
Founded: 1973. **Members:** 15,000. **Membership Dues:** patron, $100 (annual) ● student/hardship, $10 (annual) ● regular, $20 (annual). **Staff:** 11. **Budget:** $800,000. **Multinational. Description:** Zoologists, primate field workers, anthropologists, and other interested individuals; humane societies and animal welfare organizations. Fosters the conservation and protection of nonhuman primates worldwide. Works to protect the native habitat of primates; to monitor and reduce international trade and smuggling; to improve conditions of zoo and laboratory primates in nonhabitat countries. Compiles trade statistics. **Awards: Frequency:** 3/year. **Type:** grant. **Recipient:** to overseas projects. **Programs:** Wildlife Protection and Conservation. **Publications:** *International Primate Protection League News,* 3/year. Magazine. Covers developments in the field of primate protection and conservation. Includes updates on IPPL's activities and news on endangered primates. **Price:** included in membership dues; $20.00 for nonmembers. ISSN: 1040-3027. **Circulation:** 16,000. **Conventions/Meetings:** biennial conference, for members only - even-numbered years, always held at IPPL Headquarters in Summerville.

11174 ■ International Society for Animal Rights (ISAR)

965 Griffin Pond Rd.
Clarks Summit, PA 18411-9214
Ph: (570)586-2200
Free: (800)543-ISAR
Fax: (570)586-9580
E-mail: info@isaronline.org
URL: http://www.isaronline.org
Contact: Susan Altieri, Pres.
Founded: 1959. **Members:** 50,000. **Membership Dues:** regular (minimum), $15 (annual). **Staff:** 8.

Description: Promotes animal rights through educational programs and legislation. Seeks to prevent exploitation and abuse in animals. Provides and distributes literature on subjects of animal abuse and exploitation; circulates a documentary film collection to schools and colleges throughout the U.S; sponsors seminars and organizes demonstrations. Serves as an information resource for the media, writers, and other humane organizations; drafts legislation and works actively to advance the animal rights cause. **Formerly:** (1972) National Catholic Society for Animal Welfare; (1983) Society for Animal Rights. **Publications:** *International Society for Animal Rights—Report,* quarterly. Newsletter. Reports on legal cases and other programs undertaken by ISAR on legislative issues affecting animals; includes global news on animal rights. **Price:** included in membership dues. **Circulation:** 80,000 ● Pamphlets. Covers topics related to animal rights and books.

11175 ■ International Veterinary Assistance (IVA)

c/o Dr. Angela L. Witt, DVM, Sec.
1972 Woodcrest Cir.
Mosinee, WI 54455
E-mail: info@dvmassist.org
URL: http://www.dvmassist.org
Contact: Dr. Angela L. Witt DVM, Sec.
Multinational. Description: Promotes the humane management of stray and feral companion animals abroad. Mobilizes local and international veterinary resources. Collaborates with animal protection societies, the tourism sector, businesses and organizations with strong commitments to animal welfare and individual animal lovers to create and support change. **Publications:** *IVA News,* semiannual. Newsletter. Alternate Formats: online.

11176 ■ Jehovah's Witnesses for Animal Rights (JWAR)

1090 Sunnyvale Saratoga Rd., No. 19
Sunnyvale, CA 94087-2513
Ph: (408)737-0935
Contact: Jonathan Ross, Pres.
Founded: 1980. **Local Groups:** 1. **Languages:** English, German, Spanish. **Description:** Jehovah's witnesses. Seeks to increase awareness of animal rights. Disseminates materials on animal rights and conducts research and educational programs. **Convention/Meeting:** none. **Libraries: Type:** lending; reference; open to the public. **Holdings:** 100; archival material, books, clippings, periodicals. **Subjects:** Jehovah's Witnesses, animal liberation, animal welfare. **Publications:** *The Arian,* quarterly. Newsletter. **Price:** free. **Circulation:** 350. **Advertising:** accepted.

11177 ■ Jews for Animal Rights (JAR)

255 Humphrey St.
Marblehead, MA 01945
Ph: (781)631-7601
Free: (877)268-9963
E-mail: micah@micahbooks.com
URL: http://www.micahbooks.com/JAR.html
Contact: Roberta Kalechofsky, Contact
Founded: 1985. **Membership Dues:** student/senior citizen, $9 (annual) ● regular, $18 (annual). **Staff:** 2. **Description:** Jews promoting animal rights and the alleviation of animal suffering. Believes that "the earth and all life is sacred because God created it." Encourages vegetarianism and preventive medicine and alternatives to animal research. Provides materials on celebrating bar/bat mitzvahs, confirmations, and other holidays. Sponsors community action organizations, discussion groups, and educational programs. Maintains speakers' bureau. Operates Micah as publishing arm. **Libraries: Type:** open to the public. **Holdings:** 15. **Subjects:** Jewish vegetarianism, animal rights, cookbook. **Computer Services:** Mailing lists. **Publications:** *A Boy, A Chicken, and The Lion of Juelah - How Ari Became a Vegetarian.* Book. **Price:** $8.00 ● *Autobiography of a Revolutionary: Essays on Animal and Human Rights.* Book. **Price:** $12.00 ● *The Dark Face of Science.* Book. **Price:** $12.00 ● *In Pity and in Anger.* Book. **Price:** $10.00 ● *JAR Newsletter,* semiannual. **Price:** free for members

● *The Jewish Vegetarian Year Cookbook*. Contains advice about where to find vegetarian pareve products, how to make tofu delicious, useful addresses and bibliography. **Price:** $18.95/copy ● *Judaism and Animal Rights: Classical and Contemporary Responses*. Book. Features an anthology of 41 articles from classical and contemporary sources by rabbis, veterinarians and conservationists. **Price:** $17.95/copy ● *My Time*. Book. **Price:** $4.95 ● *Rabbis and Vegetarianism: An Evolving Tradition*. Book. Testifies to a revolution taking place in the traditional Jewish diet. Includes brief biographies. **Price:** $10.00/copy ● *The 6th Day of Creation - A Prose Poem About Vivisection*. Book. Delineates a pattern of thought from Descartes to the modern Weltanschauung, which has created the moral subterranean world of animal experimentation. **Price:** $10.00/copy ● *Vegetarian Judaism: A Guide for Everyone*. Book. Includes practical information about organizations and activism. **Price:** $15.95/copy ● Videos.

11178 ■ Johns Hopkins Center for Alternatives to Animal Testing (CAAT)

111 Market Pl., Ste.840
Baltimore, MD 21202-6709
Ph: (410)223-1692
Fax: (410)223-1603
E-mail: caat@jhsph.edu
URL: http://caat.jhsph.edu
Contact: Alan M. Goldberg PhD, Dir.
Founded: 1981. **Description:** Serves as a resource to academic, industrial and government scientists, the media and the general public on issues related to the development of reduction alternatives, refinement alternatives and replacement alternatives in research and testing. Supports the creation, development, validation, acceptance, and use of alternatives to animal testing. **Awards:** Research grants. **Frequency:** annual. **Type:** grant. **Recipient:** for international research. **Boards:** Advisory. **Programs:** Grant; Information; Refinement; Workshops. **Publications:** *Alternative Methods in Toxicology*. Books. Presents a series of books on toxicology. ● *Animals and Alternatives in Testing: History, Science, and Ethics*. Book ● Reports. **Conventions/Meetings:** annual symposium.

11179 ■ Last Chance for Animals (LCA)

8033 Sunset Blvd., No. 835
Los Angeles, CA 90046
Ph: (310)271-6096
Free: (888)882-6462
Fax: (310)271-1890
E-mail: development@lcanimal.org
URL: http://www.lcanimal.org
Contact: Chris DeRose, Pres./Founder
Founded: 1984. **Members:** 60,000. **Membership Dues:** student, $15 ● senior, $20 ● regular, $25 ● friend, $50 ● advocate, $100 ● guardian, $250 ● partner, $500 ● President's Circle, $1,000. **Staff:** 8. **Budget:** $1,000,000. **Description:** Individuals with an interest in animal welfare. Seeks to abolish the use of animals for food, entertainment, clothing, or "scientific curiosity." Conducts nonviolent protests of what the group believes are inappropriate uses of animals. Serves as a clearinghouse on animal rights and abuse. **Computer Services:** Mailing lists, of members. **Publications:** *Fighting Chance*, quarterly. Newsletter.

11180 ■ Last Chance Corral (LCC)

5350 Pomeroy Rd.
Athens, OH 45701
Ph: (740)594-4336
E-mail: lccorral@frognet.net
URL: http://www.lastchancecorral.org
Contact: Victoria Goss, Pres.
Founded: 1986. **Description:** Offers all horses "hope, shelter and opportunity" regardless of their situation or problems. Alleviates the suffering and "senseless slaughter" of domestic equines. Provides an environment for rehabilitation and carefully adoptive homes that are appropriate for each horse's individual needs and abilities. **Affiliated With:** American Horse Protection Association. **Publications:**

Newsletters. Contains updates on programs and individual animal accounts.

11181 ■ Latham Foundation (LF)

Latham Plaza Bldg.
1826 Clement Ave.
Alameda, CA 94501
Ph: (510)521-0920
Fax: (510)521-9861
E-mail: info@latham.org
URL: http://www.Latham.org
Contact: Mr. Hugh H Tebault III, Pres.
Founded: 1918. **Members:** 70. **Membership Dues:** regular, $30 (annual). **Staff:** 4. **Budget:** $300,000. **Languages:** English, German, Hungarian. **Multinational. Description:** Promotes the ideas of: interdependence of all living things; justice, kindness, and compassion for all life. Acts as a clearinghouse for the exchange of ideas and resources on the mutual relationship between animals and humans. Has produced and distributed documentaries on topics including: wildlife; the environment; basic pet care responsibility; and animal therapy programs. Other topics include: AIDS, child/animal abuse and the disabled. **Publications:** *The Latham Letter*, quarterly. Magazine. **Price:** $15.00 in U.S.; $20.00 in Canada and Mexico. **Conventions/Meetings:** semiannual meeting - always December and June ● seminar.

11182 ■ Llama Rescue Net (LRN)

c/o Jim Krowka, Pres.
PO Box 215
Bow, WA 98232-0215
Ph: (541)937-2507
E-mail: lrnoffice@llamarescue.org
URL: http://www.llamarescue.org
Contact: Jim Krowka, Pres.
Founded: 1999. **Nonmembership. Description:** Aims to respond to situations in which the well-being of one or more llamas is compromised, offers information and support to llama owners and caretakers or rehabilitates and finds adoption placement for the llama.

11183 ■ Morris Animal Foundation (MAF)

45 Inverness Dr. E
Englewood, CO 80112
Ph: (303)790-2345
Free: (800)243-2345
Fax: (303)790-4066
E-mail: mailbox@morrisanimalfoundation.org
URL: http://www.morrisanimalfoundation.org
Contact: Patricia N. Olson DVM, Pres./CEO
Founded: 1948. **Members:** 15,000. **Staff:** 22. **Budget:** $5,000,000. **Multinational. Description:** Seeks to improve the health and well-being of companion animals and wildlife by funding humane health studies and disseminating information about these studies. **Awards:** Ballard Student Program. **Frequency:** biennial. **Type:** monetary. **Recipient:** for 2nd or 3rd year veterinary students. **Divisions:** Canine; Equine; Feline; Llama/Alpaca; Veterinary; Wildlife/Special Species. **Publications:** *AnimalNews*, 3/year. Newsletter. Contains information about the organization-sponsored animal health studies; disseminates information about animal health advancements. **Price:** free. **Circulation:** 150,000. **Conventions/Meetings:** annual meeting, reviews grant proposals, conducts Foundation business and holds a special event for donors and supporters - every June ● annual Trustee Meeting - always first weekend of December.

11184 ■ MSPCA-Angell

350 S Huntington Ave.
Boston, MA 02130
Ph: (617)522-7400
Fax: (617)522-4885
E-mail: questions@mspca.org
URL: http://www.mspca.org
Contact: Carter Luke, CEO
Founded: 1889. **Staff:** 1. **Budget:** $150,000. **Description:** Works to promote humane attitudes and behavior towards animals and people. **Libraries: Type:** reference. **Holdings:** archival material, audio recordings, books, clippings, periodicals, video

recordings. **Subjects:** humane education, animals and environment, children's literature. **Also Known As:** (2005) American Humane Education Society. **Publications:** *Companion*, semiannual. Newsletter. Features pet-care tips and stories about people who love and care for companion animals. **Price:** $10.00. Alternate Formats: online.

11185 ■ National Animal Control Association (NACA)

PO Box 480851
Kansas City, MO 64148-0851
Ph: (913)768-1319
Fax: (913)768-1378
E-mail: naca@interserv.com
URL: http://www.nacanet.org
Contact: Mark Byers, Pres.
Founded: 1978. **Members:** 4,200. **Membership Dues:** regular in U.S., $35 (annual) ● regular outside U.S., $50 (annual) ● agency in U.S., $125 (annual) ● agency outside U.S., $150 (annual). **Staff:** 4. **Budget:** $300,000. **Description:** Animal control agencies, humane societies, public health and safety agencies, corporations, and individuals. Works to educate and train personnel in the animal care and control professions. Seeks to teach the public responsible pet ownership; operates the NACA Network to provide animal control information; evaluates animal control programs. Provides training guides for animal control officers; makes available audiovisual materials. Conducts research. Operates placement service and speakers' bureau. **Libraries: Type:** not open to the public. **Holdings:** 1,000; articles, books, periodicals, video recordings. **Subjects:** animal control, animal welfare. **Awards:** Animal Control Employee of the Year Award. **Frequency:** annual. **Type:** recognition. **Recipient:** for a single outstanding achievement in animal control ● Bill Lehman Memorial Award. **Frequency:** annual. **Type:** recognition. **Recipient:** for exceptional awareness in animal control matters ● Diane Lane Memorial Award. **Frequency:** annual. **Type:** recognition. **Recipient:** for outstanding volunteer service in animal welfare related fields ● Outstanding Animal Control Agency. **Frequency:** annual. **Type:** recognition. **Recipient:** for a member agency with effective training programs for personnel, outstanding public education programs, active community involvement, and a 20-minute average officer response time to calls for assistance ● Outstanding State Association Award. **Frequency:** annual. **Type:** recognition. **Recipient:** for noticeable improvement in the quality of animal control within their state ● R.D. Bob Ward DVM Memorial Posthumous Award. **Frequency:** annual. **Type:** recognition. **Recipient:** for animal control officers killed in the line of duty (posthumous). **Computer Services:** Mailing lists. **Publications:** *NACA News*, bimonthly. Magazine. **Price:** $25.00 in U.S.; $35.00 outside U.S. **Circulation:** 4,600. **Advertising:** accepted ● *National Animal Control Association Training Guide*. **Price:** $35.00 for members; $50.00 for nonmembers. **Conventions/Meetings:** annual Training Conference (exhibits).

11186 ■ National Animal Interest Alliance (NAIA)

PO Box 66579
Portland, OR 97266
Ph: (503)761-1139
Fax: (503)761-1289
E-mail: president@naiaonline.org
URL: http://www.naiaonline.org
Contact: Dr. Larry S. Katz, Pres.
Founded: 1991. **Members:** 11,000. **Membership Dues:** companion, $35 (annual) ● champion, $100 (annual) ● steward, $250 (annual) ● patron, $500 (annual) ● guardian, $150 (annual) ● angel, $1,000 (annual). **Staff:** 5. **Budget:** $55,000. **Regional Groups:** 50. **State Groups:** 50. **Description:** Business, agriculture, scientific and recreational interests. Strives to protect and promote humane practices and relationships between people and animals. Distributes information packets to the media, sponsors conferences such as the purebred rescue symposium, and writes articles for national journals and magazines. **Libraries: Type:** reference. **Holdings:** archival mate-

rial, articles, periodicals. **Subjects:** animal welfare, biomedical research, agriculture, environment, human-animal bond, animal rights, animal husbandry, reasonable laws. **Publications:** *NAIA E-News.* Bulletin. Alternate Formats: online ● *NAIA News,* quarterly. Newspaper. **Price:** included in membership dues. **Circulation:** 11,000. Alternate Formats: online ● Brochures. Alternate Formats: online. **Conventions/Meetings:** Dog Training - conference.

11187 ■ National Anti-Vivisection Society (NAVS)
53 W Jackson Blvd., Ste.1552
Chicago, IL 60604
Ph: (312)427-6065
Free: (800)888-NAVS
Fax: (312)427-6524
E-mail: feedback@navs.org
URL: http://www.navs.org
Contact: Mary Margaret Cunniff, Exec. Dir.
Founded: 1929. **Members:** 75,000. **Membership Dues:** individual, $40 (annual) ● student, senior, $15 (annual) ● life partner, $1,000 ● life sponsor, $100 ● life benefactor, $500. **Staff:** 9. **Budget:** $2,000,000. **Description:** Conducts educational programs and distributes information to acquaint the public with the problems associated with vivisection of animals. Concerned with animal use in research, product testing, and education. Compiles statistics on laboratory experiments using animals and the purposes and costs of such experiments. Underwrites alternatives to animal use; operates speakers' bureau. **Libraries: Type:** reference. **Holdings:** 300. **Subjects:** live animal usage in laboratory experimentation from scientific, religious, historical, legal, and philosophical perspectives. **Awards: Type:** recognition. **Affiliated With:** International Foundation for Ethical Research. **Publications:** *National Anti-Vivisection Society—Animal Action Report,* every 8-10 weeks. Newsletter. Includes book reviews. **Price:** free for members. **Circulation:** 50,000 ● *NAVS Animal Action Report* ● *Objecting to Dissection - High School and College* ● *Personal Care for People Who Care,* annual. Booklets. Contains guide to cruelty-free products. **Price:** $13.50 plus shipping and handling; included in membership dues. **Advertising:** accepted ● *Saying No to Dissection - Elementary.* **Conventions/Meetings:** annual meeting (exhibits) - always Chicago, IL.

11188 ■ National Association for Humane and Environmental Education (NAHEE)
67 Norwich Essex Tpke.
East Haddam, CT 06423-1736
Ph: (860)434-8666
E-mail: nahee@nahee.org
URL: http://www.nahee.org
Contact: Bill DeRosa, Exec. Dir.
Founded: 1973. **Staff:** 13. **Description:** Seeks to instill good character in children, with a strong emphasis on the humane treatment of animals and respect for natural habitats, by providing publications and programs to teachers, students, and animal sheltering professionals. **Libraries: Type:** reference. **Awards:** Humane Teen of the Year Award. **Frequency:** annual. **Type:** recognition. **Recipient:** to a teenager with significant contribution to animal protection ● Kind Children's Book Award. **Frequency:** annual. **Type:** recognition. **Recipient:** for outstanding work of fiction or nonfiction about animals or the environment written for children at the elementary level ● Kind Club Achievement Award. **Frequency:** annual. **Type:** recognition. **Recipient:** for an elementary level class that has demonstrated exceptional commitment to the principle of kindness to people, animals or the earth ● National KIND Teacher Award. **Frequency:** annual. **Type:** recognition. **Recipient:** for a K-6 teacher who consistently includes lessons about kindness to people, animals and the earth in his/her curriculum. **Telecommunication Services:** electronic mail, obrien@nahee.org. **Affiliated With:** Humane Society of the United States. **Absorbed:** Norma Terris Humane Education Center. **Formerly:** (1989) National Association for the Advancement of Humane Education. **Publications:** *KIND News,* 9/year. Newspaper. Contains facts about animals, tricky brainteasers, KIND Club projects, and inspira-

tional celebrity profiles. **Price:** $30.00. **Circulation:** 1,203,200. Alternate Formats: online ● *KIND Teacher,* annual. Magazine. Contains a wealth of humane education resources for teachers. **Price:** free with yearly subscription to KIND News. **Circulation:** 37,600. Alternate Formats: online.

11189 ■ National Cat Protection Society (NCPS)
6904 West Coast Hwy.
Newport Beach, CA 92663-1306
Ph: (949)650-1232
Fax: (949)650-7367
E-mail: natcatnewport@gmail.com
URL: http://www.natcat.org
Contact: Denise Johnston, Pres.
Founded: 1968. **Membership Dues:** regular, $10 (annual) ● supporting, $250 (annual) ● life, $1,000. **Description:** Seeks to control cat breeding through spaying and neutering; to provide a shelter for homeless cats; and to educate the public regarding humane treatment of animals. Campaigns to protect cats. Disseminates information about the need for cat protection. **Publications:** *Feline Defenders.* Booklet ● *Shelter News.* Newsletter. **Conventions/Meetings:** annual National Cat Open House - meeting.

11190 ■ National Congress of Animal Trainers and Breeders (NCATB)
23675 W Chardon Rd.
Grayslake, IL 60030
Ph: (847)546-0717
Fax: (847)546-3454
Contact: John F. Cuneo Jr., Pres.
Founded: 1975. **Members:** 300. **Staff:** 1. **Description:** Animal trainers and breeders of rare animals; circuses and breeding compounds are institutional members; others concerned with endangered species are associate members. Seeks to prevent the extinction of rare animals by opposing endangered species laws and government regulations that prohibit the sale or trade of such animals and thus prevent breeding. Monitors government activities regarding animal legislation; testifies at government hearings on pending legislation. Maintains lists of "animal people" throughout the world. Compiles statistics. **Publications:** none. **Libraries: Type:** reference. **Subjects:** federal and state regulations.

11191 ■ National Dog Registry (NDR)
PO Box 116
Woodstock, NY 12498-0116
Free: (800)NDR-DOGS
E-mail: info@nationaldogregistry.com
URL: http://www.nationaldogregistry.com
Contact: Bette A. Rapoport, Pres.
Founded: 1966. **Members:** 6,500,000. **Membership Dues:** life, $38. **Staff:** 8. **For-Profit. Description:** Seeks to reduce the traffic in stolen pets and expedite the identification of lost, strayed, injured, or dead animals. Since a pet loses its identity as soon as it loses its tag, the registry encourages owners to have an identification number tattooed on the right hind leg of their pet as permanent identification or microchipped and, for a small fee, to register this number. Officials in laboratories, law enforcement agencies, humane societies, and others who encounter stray animals cooperate with the registry by calling in the tattooed or microchipped information on pets that come into their custody. The registry can then notify owners who have placed information on file. Educates girl/boy scouts, schools, and 4-H clubs on responsible pet care. Maintains speakers' bureau. Provides missing pet counseling services. Sponsors Pekinese and Schipperke rescue for the Northeast. **Awards: Type:** recognition. **Publications:** *Agent Update.* Newsletter. Features information for tattooers and veterinarians. **Circulation:** 6,000. Alternate Formats: online ● *National Dog Registry Product Catalog.*

11192 ■ National Endowment for the Animals (NEA)
PO Box 1161
Boulder, CO 80306
Ph: (720)252-8449

E-mail: info@neaforever.org
URL: http://www.neaforever.org
Contact: Matt Bear, Founder
Founded: 2003. **Description:** Works to end violence toward animals by offering grants to support grassroots groups that focus on animals, animal advocacy and protecting wilderness areas. Expands the circle of compassion through projects, programs and educational campaigns. Encourages humane, nonviolent and sustainable investing through research.

11193 ■ National Greyhound Adoption Program (NGAP)
10901 Dutton Rd.
Philadelphia, PA 19154
Ph: (215)331-7918
Free: (800)348-2517
Fax: (215)331-1947
E-mail: ngap@ix.netcom.com
URL: http://www.ngap.org
Contact: David G. Wolf, Dir.
Founded: 1990. **Members:** 4,000. **Membership Dues:** benefactor, $100 (annual) ● donor, $75 (annual) ● sponsor, $50 (annual) ● subscriber, $25 (annual) ● life and benefactor, $1,000. **Staff:** 12. **Budget:** $600,000. **Regional Groups:** 3. **Description:** Seeks to find homes for retired greyhounds (a type of dog that is often used for racing). Promotes retired greyhounds as loving, beautiful pets. **Libraries: Type:** open to the public. **Holdings:** articles, clippings. **Subjects:** greyhounds and greyhound rescue. **Computer Services:** Mailing lists, of members. **Publications:** *Greyhound Update,* 3/year. Newsletter. **Price:** available to members only. **Circulation:** 2,500. **Advertising:** accepted. **Conventions/Meetings:** annual picnic.

11194 ■ National Horse Protection Coalition (NHPC)
PO Box 1252
Alexandria, VA 22313
Ph: (703)836-4300
Fax: (703)997-1134
E-mail: info@horse-protection.org
Contact: John Hettinger, Chm./Dir.
Description: Works to end horse slaughter in the United States. Advocates for the protection of American horses from abuse and neglect. Aims to educate the public on issues pertaining to the transport and slaughter of horses for human consumption within the United States and deliver a message to policymakers that the practice should be prohibited.

11195 ■ National Humane Education Society (NHES)
PO Box 340
Charles Town, WV 25414-0340
Ph: (304)725-0506
Fax: (304)725-1523
E-mail: nhesinformation@nhes.org
URL: http://www.nhes.org
Contact: Michael Mahrer, Dir. of Development and Marketing
Founded: 1948. **Members:** 350,000. **Staff:** 40. **Regional Groups:** 2. **Description:** Works for animal welfare. Conducts humane education program and rescue and relief services. Educates the public about all aspects of humane issues. **Libraries: Type:** open to the public. **Holdings:** 45; video recordings. **Subjects:** humane topics. **Publications:** *NHES Journal,* quarterly. Newsletter. Features information on humane education. **Price:** free. Alternate Formats: online. **Conventions/Meetings:** quarterly board meeting.

11196 ■ National Pet Alliance (NPA)
PO Box 53385
San Jose, CA 95153
Ph: (408)363-0700
E-mail: karenj115@aol.com
URL: http://www.fanciers.com/npa/
Contact: Karen Johnson, Contact
Description: Promotes the well-being and responsible ownership of domesticated cats and dogs. Sets a standard of excellence among dog and cat fanciers

with regard to the care and housing of animals. Focuses on animal welfare issues, such as improving the standard of animal care, controlling the surplus of dogs and cats at the shelters, and defending the rights of responsible pet owners. Conducts comprehensive studies and provides mentoring programs on animal breeding and exhibition.

11197 ■ Patriotic Pets
PO Box 95706
Atlanta, GA 30347
Ph: (404)879-1053
Fax: (770)798-9120
E-mail: patrioticpets@hotmail.com
URL: http://www.patrioticpets.org
Description: Helps service personnel find and reserve temporary homes for their pets during military deployment. Provides detailed profiles to the military owners, allowing them to locate an environment that closely resembles their pet's current situation. Registers military pet owners, recruits guardian homes and matches the military pet to the best temporary home.

11198 ■ PAWS for a Cause
2708 Freeman Mill Rd.
Suffolk, VA 23438
Ph: (757)986-2287
E-mail: pawonit@aol.com
URL: http://paws4acause.bizland.com
Contact: Brenda Beck, Pres.
Founded: 1998. **Members:** 20. **Staff:** 3. **Budget:** $184,674. **Description:** Committed to saving helpless, homeless, neglected and abused animals, offering shelter, food and medical care, and an adoptive home.

11199 ■ People for the Ethical Treatment of Animals (PETA)
501 Front St.
Norfolk, VA 23510
Ph: (757)622-7382
Fax: (757)622-0457
E-mail: info@peta.org
URL: http://www.peta.org
Contact: Ingrid E. Newkirk, Pres.
Founded: 1980. **Members:** 1,000,000. **Membership Dues:** regular, $16 (annual). **Staff:** 156. **Budget:** $27,500,000. **Multinational. Description:** Educational and activist group that opposes all forms of animal exploitation. Seeks to educate the public against speciesism and human chauvinist attitudes toward animals through documentary films, slides, and pictures of current conditions in slaughterhouses and animal experimentation laboratories. Conducts rallies and demonstrations to focus attention on the four major institutionalized cruelty issues: the exploitation and abuse of animals in experimentation, use of animals for clothing, abuse of animals in the entertainment industry, and slaughtering for human consumption. Offers children's services; conducts research and charitable programs; compiles statistics; maintains speakers' bureau. Provides low-cost spaying and neutering for local dogs and cats, free doghouses to locals with backyard dogs; provides hands-on rescue of local animals; provides services for students; maintains a print and an audio-visual library, and will provide information or other literature to the public. **Libraries: Type:** reference. **Holdings:** 4,100. **Subjects:** animal abuse, vegetarianism, holistic health care for animals, alternatives to animal abuse. **Awards:** Humanitarian Award. **Frequency:** semiannual. **Type:** recognition. **Recipient:** for proven dedication on the part of public figures to easing animal suffering ● Litterbox and Glitterbox Awards. **Frequency:** annual. **Type:** recognition. **Recipient:** for companies that depict animals either in a disrespectful manner (Litterbox) or in a positive and compassionate way (Glitterbox) ● The Proggy Awards. **Frequency:** annual. **Type:** recognition. **Recipient:** for innovative animal-friendly events, products, and companies. **Additional Websites:** http://www.petakids.com, http://www.animalactivist.com. **Departments:** Communications; Education; Outreach; Research and Investigations. **Publications:** *The Compassionate Cook: A Vegetarian Cookbook.*

Contains recipes for vegetarians. ● *Cooking With PETA.* Book ● *50 Awesome Ways Kids Can Help Animals.* Book ● *Guide to Animal Liberation.* Includes an overview of animal rights issues. ● *Making Kind Choices.* Book ● *People for the Ethical Treatment of Animals—Action Alerts*, periodic. Alternate Formats: online ● *PETA's Animal Times*, quarterly. Magazine. Focuses on efforts to end animal exploitation, reports on animal research laboratories; animals in entertainment, food and clothing industries. **Price:** $16.00/year. **Circulation:** 350,000. Alternate Formats: online ● *Save the Animals! 101 Easy Things You Can Do.* Book ● *Shopping Guide for Caring Consumers*, annual. Book. Lists companies that do and do not test products on animals. **Price:** $8.95. **Circulation:** 8,500. **Advertising:** accepted ● *250 Things You Can Do To Make Your Cat Adore You* ● *You Can Save The Animals!.* Book ● Pamphlets ● Videos. **Conventions/Meetings:** periodic Speaking Up For Animals Conference - seminar.

11200 ■ People Protecting Animals and Their Habitats (PATH)
PO Box 850861
New Orleans, LA 70185
Ph: (617)354-2826
E-mail: animalpath@aol.com
URL: http://www.ppath.org
Contact: Kelly Overton MPH, Exec. Dir.
Multinational. Description: Advocates for the humane treatment of all animals. Promotes the conservation and protection of areas that are vital to the survival of endangered or threatened species. Develops and operates programs that combine animal welfare, education and community development. Provides communities with educational and vocational opportunities that provide realistic and sustainable solutions that both improve the quality of animals' lives and stop habitat destruction.

11201 ■ Performing Animal Welfare Society (PAWS)
PO Box 849
Galt, CA 95632
Ph: (209)745-2606
Fax: (209)745-1809
E-mail: info@pawsweb.org
URL: http://www.pawsweb.org
Contact: Pat Derby, Founder
Founded: 1984. **Members:** 45,000. **Membership Dues:** regular, $25 (annual) ● student, senior, $15 (annual). **Staff:** 11. **Budget:** $3,600,000. **Description:** Works to assist performing animals that are victims of abuse. Rescues animals through intervention, legislation, and purchase; maintains 30-acre sanctuary for rescued animals that cannot be placed in humane facilities. Conducts public education campaigns; lobbies on behalf of exotic and performing animals. Investigates reports of animal abuse. **Libraries: Type:** not open to the public. **Holdings:** 500; articles, books, video recordings. **Subjects:** circus, captive wildlife. **Awards:** Amanda Blake Award. **Frequency:** annual. **Type:** recognition. **Recipient:** for outstanding achievement in captive wildlife. **Publications:** *Sanctuary*, quarterly. Newsletter. Reports cases of animal abuse and provides updates on legislative and judicial proceedings. **Price:** included in membership dues. **Circulation:** 20,000. **Conventions/Meetings:** annual Captive Wildlife Conference - always September in Sacramento, CA ● annual Gala and Celebrity Auction - meeting.

11202 ■ Pet Care Trust (PCT)
c/o Debbie Mazur, Admin.
406 S 1st Ave.
Arcadia, CA 91006-3829
Ph: (626)566-2293
Fax: (626)447-8350
E-mail: petcaretrust@aol.com
URL: http://www.petcaretrust.org
Contact: Lew Sutton, Pres.
Founded: 1990. **Members:** 200. **Staff:** 1. **Budget:** $195,000. **Description:** Promotes public understanding regarding the value of and the right to enjoy companion animals; enhances society's knowledge about companion animals through research and

education; promotes professionalism among members of the companion animal community. Compiles statistics. Provides animals in the classroom teacher education workshops. **Awards: Frequency:** annual. **Type:** grant. **Recipient:** for research on specific programs on animal health and welfare ● Sue J. Busch Companion Award. **Frequency:** annual. **Type:** recognition. **Recipient:** for research, education, and achievement. **Conventions/Meetings:** board meeting - 3/year.

11203 ■ Pet Pride (PP)
PO Box 1055
Pacific Palisades, CA 90272
Ph: (310)836-5427
E-mail: ruth@petpride.org
URL: http://www.petpride.org
Contact: Ruth C. Argust, Pres.
Founded: 1965. **Members:** 45,000. **Description:** Serves as a national humane society for cats. Conducts nonprofit shelter and clinic; offers public education programs on proper cat care. Maintains placement service, hall of fame, and speakers' bureau. **Awards: Type:** recognition. **Computer Services:** Mailing lists. **Absorbed:** (1984) Cat Fund. **Publications:** *Pet Pride Purr-/Ress*, quarterly. Newsletter ● Booklets. Contains information on cat care and feeding. **Conventions/Meetings:** annual meeting - always in California.

11204 ■ Pet Savers Foundation
59 S Bayles Ave.
Port Washington, NY 11050-3728
Ph: (516)944-5025
E-mail: info@petsavers.org
URL: http://www.petsavers.org
Contact: Tammy Kirkpatrick, Assoc. Dir.
Founded: 1992. **Staff:** 4. **Description:** Works to save and enhance the lives of dogs and cats through shelter assistance and population control programs. **Computer Services:** Mailing lists, of members. **Programs:** Buyers' Co-op; Pet Med Care; Seniors for Seniors; Shelter on Wheels; SPAY/USA. **Publications:** *Paws To Think*, quarterly. Magazine. **Circulation:** 32,000. Alternate Formats: online ● *SPAY/USA Network News*, quarterly. Newsletter.

11205 ■ Pot Belly Pig Rescue
19025 Parthenia St., Dept. IN
Northridge, CA 91324
Ph: (818)701-1534
Fax: (818)993-0194
E-mail: pigresq@hotmail.com
URL: http://www.jojoba-ksa.com/pig.htm
Contact: Kathie Ward, Contact
Description: Committed to the rescue of abandoned or unwanted pot belly pigs; provides adoption program and disseminates information regarding the care of the animals. Provides worldwide matching program of individuals wanting to rescue a pot belly pig and individuals that can no longer keep their pet. Operates a shot clinic that administers annual booster shots, de-worming, tusk cutting, and nail cutting.

11206 ■ Prevent a Litter Coalition (PaLC)
2579 John Milton Dr., Ste.105 - PMB 143
Herndon, VA 20171
Ph: (703)818-8009
Fax: (801)516-8601
E-mail: contact@palc.org
URL: http://www.palc.org
Contact: Sara Khurody-Downs, Pres./CEO
Founded: 1992. **Staff:** 5. **Budget:** $100,000. **Regional Groups:** 1. **State Groups:** 1. **Local Groups:** 1. **Description:** Works toward community, preventative, and sustainable solutions to pet population, care and control issues. **Computer Services:** Mailing lists. **Additional Websites:** http://www.americanpartnershipforpets.org. **Committees:** Humane Education; Pet Care; Pet Population; Spay/Neuter. **Publications:** *American Partnership for Pets Newsletter*. Alternate Formats: online ● *Friends of PaLC*, periodic. Newsletter. Alternate Formats: online. **Conventions/Meetings:** semiannual workshop - always spring and fall.

11207 ■ Primarily Primates, Inc. (PPI)
c/o Wallace W. Swett, Pres.
PO Box 207
San Antonio, TX 78291-0207
Ph: (830)755-4616 (702)804-8562
Fax: (830)981-4611
E-mail: primarilyprimates@friendsofanimals.org
URL: http://primarilyprimates.org
Contact: Stephen Rene Tello, Contact
Founded: 1978. **Members:** 18,000. **Staff:** 12. **Budget:** $1,000,000. **Description:** Provides sanctuary, rehabilitation, lifetime care, and shelter to abused or unwanted, non-native species of primates, birds, mammals, and reptiles. Serves as a clearinghouse for the exchange of information on animal care, endangered species husbandry, animal welfare issues, and cruelty cases. Works with the International Union for the Conservation of Nature and Natural Resources to return sheltered animals to their native habitats. **Libraries: Type:** reference. **Holdings:** photographs. **Awards:** Gift O Life Award. **Frequency:** annual. **Type:** recognition. **Computer Services:** Mailing lists. **Publications:** *Primarily Primates Newsletter,* periodic. **Circulation:** 18,000. **Advertising:** accepted.

11208 ■ Primate Rescue Center
5087 Danville Rd.
Nicholasville, KY 40356
Ph: (859)858-4866
Fax: (859)858-0044
E-mail: kyprimatejen@earthlink.net
URL: http://www.primaterescue.org
Contact: April D. Truitt, Pres.
Founded: 1987. **Description:** Provides sanctuary or referral to rescued primates; works to end illegal trade in primates; assists zoo personnel. **Publications:** *Reaching Out.* Newsletter. Alternate Formats: online.

11209 ■ Project BREED (Breed Rescue Efforts and Education)
Address Unknown since 2006
Founded: 1991. **Members:** 12,000. **Staff:** 2. **Description:** Breed-specific and species-specific animal rescue volunteers. A national network for animal rescue, rehabilitation, adoption, and humane education on animal protection efforts. Pursues innovative solutions to major animal protection problems. Provides educational programs on animal sterilization; disaster relief for animals; temporary shelter for adoptable pets; financial assistance for veterinary costs; and grants to other groups and individuals pursuing solutions to animal protection problems. **Convention/Meeting:** none. **Telecommunication Services:** phone referral service, hotline service to directory users. **Formerly:** (1987) Network for Ani-Males and Females, Project BREED. **Publications:** *Project BREED Directory Series.* The Green Book contains contacts and rescues for over 300 breeds of dogs and other species of pets, farm animals and wildlife. **Price:** $35.00 plus 4 shipping and handling. **Circulation:** 10,000. **Advertising:** not accepted.

11210 ■ Safe Harbour Animal Refuge
PO Box 275
London, TX 76854-0275
E-mail: info@safeharbour.org
URL: http://www.safeharbour.org
Founded: 1999. **Description:** Works to protect pigs that have been raised as pets or saved from abandonment. **Formerly:** (2006) Safe Harbour Pig Refuge.

11211 ■ Scientists Center for Animal Welfare (SCAW)
7833 Walker Dr., Ste.410
Greenbelt, MD 20770
Ph: (301)345-3500
Fax: (301)345-3503
E-mail: info@scaw.com
URL: http://www.scaw.com
Contact: Ms. Lee Krulisch, Exec. Dir.
Founded: 1978. **Members:** 2,000. **Membership Dues:** regular, $60 (annual) ● student, $30 (annual) ● foreign, $85 (annual) ● patron, $1,000 (annual) ● sustaining, $500 (annual) ● institutional (level A), $5,000 (annual) ● institutional (level B), $2,000 (an-

nual) ● institutional(level C), $1,000 (annual) ● institutional (level D), $500 (annual). **Staff:** 5. **Budget:** $350,000. **Description:** Scientists and others concerned with research animal welfare. Supports responsible and humane research on animals. Provides a forum for the discussion of public accountability, public policy, and the scientist's responsibilities regarding standards of animal care and use; promotes ethical discourse on biomedical, agricultural, and wildlife research procedures. Develops educational resource material on Institutional Animal Care Use Committees, animal pain, and national guidelines on humane research using animals. Conducts workshops, training for investigators, and surveys; maintains speakers' bureau. **Libraries: Type:** reference. **Holdings:** audiovisuals, books, clippings, periodicals. **Subjects:** biomedical and other research animals. **Awards:** Harry C. Rowsell Award. **Frequency:** annual. **Type:** recognition. **Recipient:** for fostering good science and the humane treatment of animals. **Publications:** *Canine Research Environment.* **Price:** $30.00 ● *The Care and Use of Amphibians, Reptiles and Fish in Research.* **Price:** $55.00 ● *Field Research Guidelines: Mammalogy; Wild Birds; Live Amphibians and Reptiles; Fishes.* **Price:** $10.00 ● *Guidelines for the Well-Being of Rodents in Research.* **Price:** $30.00 ● *Research Animal Anesthesia, Analgesia, and Surgery.* **Price:** $25.00 ● *Rodents and Rabbits: Current Research Issues.* **Price:** $25.00 ● *Scientists Center of Animal Welfare—Newsletter,* quarterly. Covers legislation, regulations, and national policies regarding animal experimentation, as well as the social and bioethical issues. **Price:** included in membership dues; $40.00/year in U.S.; $50.00/year outside U.S. ISSN: 0742-5260. **Circulation:** 3,500 ● *Summary of New Animal Welfare Regulations.* **Price:** $4.50 ● *The Well-Being of Agricultural Animals in Biomedical and Agricultural Research.* **Price:** $45.00 ● *The Well-Being of Animals in Zoo and Aquarium Sponsored Research.* **Price:** $50.00 ● *Well-Being of Non-Human Primates in Research.* **Price:** $30.00 ● Newsletter ● Articles. **Conventions/Meetings:** periodic conference.

11212 ■ Simian Society of America (SSA)
c/o Mel Orr, Sec.
6 Stephens St.
Dillsburg, PA 17019
Ph: (717)432-9205
E-mail: mnkylady@gte.net
URL: http://www.simiansociety.org
Contact: Mel Orr, Sec.
Founded: 1957. **Members:** 500. **Membership Dues:** individual, family, $30 (annual) ● senior, $24 (annual) ● life, $750. **Regional Groups:** 4. **Local Groups:** 17. **Description:** Membership includes private caretakers committed to providing permanent, healthy environments for captive primates; veterinarians, professional primatologists, humane workers, and anyone fascinated with monkeys. Promotes better husbandry and living conditions for monkeys in captivity. Exchanges information on the biological and psychological needs of monkeys in captivity and on humane and conservation activities. Distributes material on basic monkey care; provides adoption and relocation service for unwanted simians; contributes to monkey sanctuaries throughout the U.S. **Libraries: Type:** reference. **Holdings:** books, films, video recordings. **Awards: Type:** recognition. **Telecommunication Services:** electronic mail, simiansociety@yahoo.com. **Divisions:** Animal Legislation; Primate Care; Professional Relations; Research; Sanctuary; Tapes and Films; VHS Video Library. **Publications:** *The Primate Care Journal,* quarterly ● *The Simian,* monthly. Newsletter. Provides information on the biological and psychological needs of monkeys and on humane and conservation activities. **Price:** included in membership dues. **Advertising:** accepted. **Conventions/Meetings:** biennial convention - even numbered years.

11213 ■ Society Against Vivisection (SAV)
Address Unknown since 2007
Description: Grass roots organization seeking to abolish vivisection. Subsidizes pet spaying and neutering. Provides animal rescue services. Dis-

seminates free literature. **Telecommunication Services:** hotline, educational. **Affiliated With:** Activists for Protective Animal Legislation. **Publications:** Newsletter, periodic.

11214 ■ Society for Animal Protective Legislation (SAPL)
PO Box 3719
Washington, DC 20027
Ph: (703)836-4300
Fax: (703)836-0400
E-mail: sapl@saplonline.org
URL: http://www.saplonline.org
Contact: Chris Heyde, Contact
Founded: 1955. **Budget:** $150,000. **Description:** A division of the Animal Welfare Institute. Aims to protect animals through legislation. Prepares information for use by members of Congress and their staffs. Disseminates information, through correspondence, to persons interested in progress of proposed state and federal legislation for the protection of animals. **Convention/Meeting:** none. **Publications:** none. **Affiliated With:** Animal Welfare Institute.

11215 ■ Society and Animals Forum
PO Box 1297
Washington Grove, MD 20880-1297
Ph: (301)963-4751
Fax: (301)963-4751
E-mail: kshapiro@societyandanimalsforum.org
URL: http://www.psyeta.org
Contact: Kenneth Shapiro PhD, Exec. Dir./Co-Founder
Founded: 1981. **Members:** 5,500. **Membership Dues:** student, senior, $25 (annual) ● full, $35 (annual) ● supporting organization, $500 (annual). **Staff:** 6. **Budget:** $120,000. **Description:** Works to reduce the suffering and exploitation of nonhuman animals through education and psychology. **Libraries: Type:** reference. **Holdings:** 900; articles, books, periodicals. **Subjects:** animal welfare, animal rights. **Programs:** AniCare Model of Treatment for Animal Abuse. **Projects:** Beyond Violence. **Also Known As:** (1999) Animal Care Committee. **Formerly:** (2004) Psychologists for the Ethical Treatment of Animals. **Publications:** *Animal Models of Human Psychology.* Book. ISSN: 8893-7189 ● *Forum FOCUS,* 3/year. Newsletter. **Price:** included in membership dues. Alternate Formats: online ● *Journal of Applied Animal Welfare Science,* quarterly. **Price:** $22.50 for members; $255.00 /year for individuals, /year for libraries; $45.00 for nonmembers. ISSN: 1088-8705. **Advertising:** accepted ● *Society and Animals: Journal of Human-Animal Studies,* quarterly. **Price:** $44.00 for members; $123.00 /year for individuals; $61.00 for nonmembers. **Conventions/Meetings:** annual meeting.

11216 ■ Stolen Horse International (SHI)
PO Box 1341
Shelby, NC 28151
Ph: (704)484-2165
E-mail: stolenhorse@netposse.com
URL: http://www.netposse.com
Contact: Debi Metcalfe, Pres.
Multinational. Description: Provides comprehensive theft awareness program to the horse industry. Offers educational opportunities for horse enthusiasts. Establishes a global resource to aid in the search for missing and stolen horses. Provides educational opportunities to improve public awareness of horse theft and identification methods through seminars, presentations and exhibits. Provides resources and information to the law enforcement community. **Computer Services:** Information services, horse identification, theft prevention, missing and stolen horse resources. **Publications:** *Horse Theft, Been There Done That.* Book. Contains prevention and recovery tips, identification methods and helpful forms. **Price:** $15.50.

11217 ■ Tattoo-a-Pet (PSU)
6571 SW 20th Ct.
Fort Lauderdale, FL 33317
Ph: (954)581-5834
Free: (800)828-8667
Fax: (954)581-0056

E-mail: info@tattoo-a-pet.com
URL: http://www.tattoo-a-pet.com
Contact: Julie S. Moscove, Exec. Dir.
Founded: 1972. **For-Profit. Description:** Provides permanent identification of animals by tattoo registration under the trademark Tattoo-A-Pet; promotes its use by veterinarians, pet shops, and groomers as a service to pet owners for protection of their pet against loss, theft, and laboratory use. Registration includes tattoo number (inscribed painlessly on the pet), warning decals for home and car as a deterrent to dognappers, collar tag, and permanent computer record of tattoo number. Educates the public to the need for registering animals by tattoo; conducts professional training sessions. Provides services to seeing-eye and working dogs, humane societies, and adoption agencies on a nonprofit basis as a way to prevent the abandonment of adopted animals. Maintains charitable program and fundraising system; compiles statistics. **Awards: Type:** recognition. **Computer Services:** database, registered pet owners and pets nationwide. **Telecommunication Services:** additional toll-free number, (800)828-8007. **Formerly:** (1976) Ident-A-Pet. **Publications:** *Directory of Tattoo-A-Pet Agents*, periodic ● *Directory of U.S. Tatoo Registration Services*, annual ● *Tatoo-A-Pet News*, quarterly. Newsletter ● *This Tatoo Means I Love You.* Video ● *Welcome to Tattoo-A-Pet.* Video ● Bulletin, periodic. **Conventions/Meetings:** seminar and competition.

11218 ■ Tree House Animal Foundation (THAF)
1212 W Carmen Ave.
Chicago, IL 60640-2999
Ph: (773)784-5488
Fax: (773)784-2332
E-mail: general@treehouseanimals.org
URL: http://www.treehouseanimals.org
Contact: David De Funiak, Exec. Dir.
Founded: 1971. **Members:** 10,000. **Staff:** 30. **Budget:** $1,000,000. **Description:** Seeks to develop and implement model programs in animal welfare, public education, and the human/animal bond. Works to reduce and prevent animal overpopulation. Operates cage less "no-kill" shelter, veterinary medical facility, and adoption center. Offers inter agency counseling, animal rescue services and a pet food pantry for owners who can't afford to feed their pets. Conducts cruelty investigations. **Programs:** Pet-Facilitated Therapy; Tree House Education Outreach. **Publications:** *Tree House News*, semiannual. Newsletter. Alternate Formats: online ● Brochures. Covers a variety of areas regarding animal interest or concern. **Price:** free. **Conventions/Meetings:** monthly board meeting.

11219 ■ The True Nature Network (TTNN)
PO Box 20672
Colombus Circle Sta.
New York, NY 10023-1487
Ph: (212)581-1120
E-mail: abull@ix.netcom.com
Contact: Allan Bullington, Exec. Dir.
Founded: 1985. **Membership Dues:** $18 (annual). **Staff:** 2. **Description:** Works to increase public awareness of animal, ecology, and human health through the production and distribution of documentaries and television programs. Coordinates "action campaigns" on ecology and animal issues. Conducts educational programs. **Libraries: Type:** reference. **Holdings:** archival material, audiovisuals. **Subjects:** animal protection, ecology. **Formerly:** (1993) Animal Rights Information Service. **Publications:** *The True Nature Newsletter*, quarterly ● Also makes available video tapes.

11220 ■ Tufts Center for Animals and Public Policy
Tufts Univ.
200 Westboro Rd.
North Grafton, MA 01536
Ph: (508)839-7991
Fax: (508)839-3337

E-mail: patricia.bonner@tufts.edu
URL: http://www.tufts.edu/vet/cfa
Contact: Patricia Bonner, Asst. Dir.
Founded: 1983. **Description:** Supports, coordinates, and provides funds to programs dealing with ethical, legal, scientific, and social issues concerning domestic and farm animals and wildlife. Focuses on the interactions of animals and society. Conducts research regarding the status of animals in society. Current projects include veterinary ethics and jurisprudence; companion animal demographics and control; hunting and trapping in urban society; animal research ethics; and biotechnology. Disseminates information. **Libraries: Type:** reference. **Holdings:** archival material, books, clippings, monographs, periodicals. **Subjects:** animals in society, animal issues. **Publications:** *Alternatives Report*, bimonthly. Newsletter. **Price:** $48.00/year; $65.00/year outside U.S. ● *Animal Policy Report*, quarterly. Newsletter. **Price:** $20.00/year ● *Anthrozoos*, periodic. **Conventions/Meetings:** annual meeting ● periodic seminar and workshop.

11221 ■ Unexpected Wildlife Refuge (UWR)
c/o The New Beaver Defenders
PO Box 765
Newfield, NJ 08344-0765
Ph: (856)697-3541
Fax: (856)697-5182
E-mail: qdi@snip.net
URL: http://users.snip.net/~qdi
Contact: Sarah Summerville, Dir.
Founded: 1968. **Members:** 100. **Description:** Individuals interested in animal welfare. Promotes: education, especially of children, concerning the humane treatment of animals; protection of animals in the refuge; study of wildlife in the field; writing of observations for publication. Operates a 600-acre wildlife refuge, plants trees and crops for the animals, and guides small groups of visitors (by appointment only). **Convention/Meeting:** none. **Libraries: Type:** reference. **Holdings:** 300.

11222 ■ United Action for Animals (UAA)
PO Box 635
New York, NY 10021
Ph: (212)249-9178
E-mail: info@ua4a.org
URL: http://www.ua4a.org
Contact: Gary Kaskel, Pres.
Founded: 1967. **Description:** Promotes ethical standards of conduct and practices in the field of animal welfare and to educate the public on the proper care of animals. Supports the spaying and neutering of companion animals to reduce overpopulation of cats and dogs; subsidizes the costs of initial routine veterinary care, including spaying/neutering of dogs and cats for people who rescue stray and abandoned animals, and assists in finding permanent adoptive homes for these animals. Advocates to improve state and municipal government animal management policies and laws. Seeks to educate the public on matters of animal experimentation and testing, and promotes the advancement of scientific research using modern methods in place of live animals. **Awards:** UFT Humane Education Committee (NYC) Science Fair 1st Prize. **Frequency:** annual. **Type:** monetary. **Recipient:** to the best humane science fair project. **Publications:** Newsletter.

11223 ■ United Activists for Animal Rights (UAAR)
PO Box 2448
Riverside, CA 92516
Ph: (951)776-4040
Fax: (909)776-3617
Contact: Nancy Burnet, Pres.
Founded: 1987. **Description:** Individuals interested in animal rights. Opposes animal cruelty and exploitation. Seeks to abolish the fur industry, vivisection, and factory farming, and end pet overpopulation. Works for the passage of animal rights legislation. **Convention/Meeting:** none. **Divisions:** Coalition to Protect Animals in Entertainment (see separate entry). **Formerly:** Animal Protection Society of America.

11224 ■ United Animal Nations (UAN)
PO Box 188890
Sacramento, CA 95818
Ph: (916)429-2457
Fax: (916)429-2456
E-mail: info@uan.org
URL: http://www.uan.org
Contact: Ms. Nicole Forsyth, Pres./CEO
Founded: 1987. **Members:** 20,000. **Membership Dues:** regular, $25 (annual). **Staff:** 12. **Budget:** $1,500,000. **Description:** Provides emergency animal sheltering and disaster relief services; issues grants to help animal rescuers and caregivers meet the cost of lifesaving veterinary care; educates women about hormone therapy drugs that are made from pregnant mares' urine and helps rescue horses used in this process who are at risk for slaughter; improves animal welfare by advancing legal reform and educating the public on important issues. **Libraries: Type:** by appointment only. **Holdings:** 50. **Subjects:** animals. **Awards:** Animals Choice Award. **Frequency:** annual. **Type:** recognition. **Recipient:** for individuals who have made extraordinary efforts to help animals in need ● Heart and Soul Award. **Frequency:** annual. **Type:** recognition. **Recipient:** for a volunteer who shows outstanding commitment to UAN and a strong personal devotion to animals. **Formerly:** (2000) United Animal Nations U.S.A. **Publications:** *The Journal*, quarterly. Magazine. **Price:** included in membership dues. **Circulation:** 20,000.

11225 ■ United Humanitarians (UH)
PO Box 14587
Philadelphia, PA 19115
Ph: (215)750-0171
E-mail: unitedhum@aol.com
Contact: Adele P. Hudson, Exec.VP
Founded: 1961. **Members:** 10,500. **Staff:** 3. **Budget:** $75,000. **Regional Groups:** 15. **Description:** Persons concerned with the welfare of animals. Establishes humane animal control through mass spaying and neutering of pets and the replacement of the present licensing system with a permit system placing complete responsibility on owners, who would be cited for violations rather than impounding and killing pets found at large. Maintains charitable program and speakers' bureau. **Libraries: Type:** reference. **Awards: Type:** recognition. **Computer Services:** Mailing lists. **Formerly:** (1969) National Humanitarian League. **Publications:** *National Humanitarian*, bimonthly. Magazine ● Also publishes leaflets. **Conventions/Meetings:** annual meeting.

11226 ■ United Poultry Concerns (UPC)
PO Box 150
Machipongo, VA 23405-0150
Ph: (757)678-7875
Fax: (757)678-5070
E-mail: info@upc-online.org
URL: http://www.upc-online.org
Contact: Karen Davis, Pres.
Founded: 1990. **Members:** 7,000. **Membership Dues:** individual, $35 (annual) ● student, $10 (annual). **Staff:** 1. **Budget:** $60,000. **Description:** Individuals concerned about the treatment of fowl by agricultural enterprises, scientific and educational institutions, and the entertainment industry. Works for improved legislation governing the care and handling of poultry raised for egg-laying or slaughter. Promotes nonexplosive treatment of domestic fowl; encourages reduction/elimination in the demand for poultry products by suggesting alternatives. Operates refuge for birds rescued from mistreatment or slaughter. Participates in and speaks at conventions and meetings presented by the animal advocacy movement; animal agribusiness/welfare issues; and state Farm Bureaus. Welcomes speaking engagements on animal welfare, animal welfare/rights philosophy, healthy eating, domesticated fowl, and the poultry industry including the use of poultry in agricultural and biomedical research. Provides research findings on poultry. Conducts educational programs. **Libraries: Type:** reference. **Holdings:** artwork, audiovisuals, books, business records, clippings, periodicals. **Subjects:** animal agriculture, poultry industry, domesticated fowl. **Computer Services:** Mailing lists.

Telecommunication Services: electronic mail, karen@upc-online.org. **Publications:** *A Home for Henny.* Book. **Price:** $4.95 ● *Animals and Women: Feminist Theoretical Explorations.* Book. **Price:** $16.95 ● *Beyond The Law: Agribusiness and the Systematic Abuse of Animals Raised for Food or Food Production.* Book. Pertains to animal farming practices and the status of farmed animals in the United States. **Price:** $4.50 ● *Chicken Flying Contest.* Brochure ● *Chickens.* Brochure ● *Cry Fowl.* Bulletin ● *Debeaking.* Bulletin ● *Hidden Suffering.* Video. **Price:** $17.95 ● *Instead of Chicken, Instead of Turkey: A Poultryless Poultry Potpourri.* Includes artwork, poems and illuminating passages showing chickens and turkeys in an appreciative light. **Price:** $14.95 ● *Intensive Poultry Production: Fowling the Environment.* Bulletin ● *Live Poultry Markets.* Brochure ● *Minny's Dream.* Book. **Price:** $10.00 ● *More Than A Meal.* Book. **Price:** $23.50 ● *Nature's Chicken, The Story of Today's Chicken Farms.* Book. **Price:** $5.95 ● *Ostriches & Emus.* Brochure ● *Poultry Slaughter: The Need for Legislation.* Bulletin ● *PoultryPress,* quarterly. Newsletter. **Price:** $25.00/year. Alternate Formats: online ● *Prisoned Chickens, Poisoned Eggs: An Inside Look at the Modern Poultry Industry.* Book. Alternate Formats: online ● *Raw Footage, Raw Pain.* Video. Shows piles of dead chickens, chickens with open sores, chickens dying in a closed wing. **Price:** $10.00 ● *Replacing School Hatching Projects.* Book ● Also publishes Philosophic Vegetarianism: Acting Affirmatively for Peace. **Conventions/Meetings:** annual Spring Mourning Vigil for Chickens - meeting (exhibits) - April or May; every spring ● annual World Farm Animals Day for Chickens - meeting - always 2nd of October.

11227 ■ U.S.A. Defenders of Greyhounds (USADOG)
PO Box 1256
Carmel, IN 46082
Ph: (317)244-0113 (317)867-1704
E-mail: usadogpresident@aol.com
URL: http://www.usadog.org
Contact: Sally Allen, Pres.
Founded: 1988. **Membership Dues:** affiliate, $15 (triennial). **Description:** Seeks to find homes for retired greyhounds (a type of dog that is often used for racing) as well as greyhounds that have not had successful racing careers. Promotes retired greyhounds as loving, beautiful pets. (Greyhound racing is legal in 18 states; greyhounds that are too old or too slow are put to death.) Sponsors educational programs; maintains speakers' bureau. **Also Known As:** REGAP. **Formerly:** Retired Greyhounds As Pets. **Publications:** Brochures ● Newsletter, 3-4/year. **Price:** $20.00 lifetime subscription ● Also publishes adoption booklet and annual color calendar. **Conventions/Meetings:** annual Greyhounds: Glamour and Glitz Fashion Show - 4th Saturday of October ● annual Hike for the Hounds - meeting, public is invited - first Sunday of May ● annual reunion, for rescued racing greyhounds, their families, and friends - always 2nd Saturday of September.

11228 ■ Vivisection Investigation League (VIL)
PO Box 259
Falls Village, CT 06031
Ph: (860)824-0831
Fax: (860)824-5460
Contact: Jeanne Toomey, Pres.
Founded: 1910. **Staff:** 8. **Budget:** $650,000. **Description:** Protests laboratory experiments on live animals (usually performed without anesthesia). Currently opposes the LD 50 test, required by government agencies, in which lab animals are force-fed household products. Offers "Last Post" haven for cats whose owners have died, or have gone into nursing homes. Provides assistance to limited-income pet owners. Conducts protests and demonstrations. Also objects to experiments on any human being without that individual's informed consent. **Absorbed:** (1972) Anti-Vivisection Society of New York. **Publications:** *Last Post Report,* 2/year. Newsletter. Reports on activities at the Last Post animal sanctuary. **Price:** free. **Circulation:** 4,000 ● Also publishes pamphlets

describing LAST POST. **Conventions/Meetings:** periodic board meeting.

11229 ■ Voice for Animals (VOICE)
PO Box 120095
San Antonio, TX 78212
Ph: (210)737-3138
E-mail: voice@infohiwy.net
URL: http://www.voiceforanimals.org
Contact: Rachel Zepeda Fox, Pres.
Founded: 1987. **Members:** 950. **Membership Dues:** ordinary, $15 (annual). **Budget:** $2,500. **Description:** Individuals with an interest in animal rights. Seeks to raise public awareness of animal rights issues. Works to abolish "the systematic abuse of nonhuman animals." Conducts educational programs. **Libraries: Type:** lending; not open to the public; reference. **Holdings:** audio recordings, books, periodicals, video recordings. **Subjects:** animal rights, vegetarianism. **Publications:** Books ● Videos.

11230 ■ Wild Animal Orphanage (WAO)
PO Box 690422
San Antonio, TX 78269
Ph: (210)688-9038
Fax: (210)688-9514
E-mail: wao@wildanimalorphanage.org
URL: http://www.wildanimalorphanage.org
Contact: Carol Asvestas, Pres./CEO
Founded: 1983. **Members:** 50,000. **Membership Dues:** supporting, $25 (annual). **Staff:** 12. **Budget:** $656,000. **Description:** Individuals and organizations with an interest in the welfare of animals. Maintains sanctuary for unwanted wild and exotic animals, as well as domestic cats. Educates against the ownership of wild and exotic animals as pets. **Publications:** *Wild Means Wild,* bimonthly. Newsletter. Contains stories about animal rescues and education against wild animals as pets. **Circulation:** 12,000. **Advertising:** accepted ● Annual Report, annual. Alternate Formats: online.

11231 ■ Wild Horse Sanctuary
PO Box 30
Shingletown, CA 96088-0030
Ph: (530)335-2241
E-mail: info@wildhorsesanctuary.org
URL: http://www.wildhorsesanctuary.org
Contact: Dianne Nelson, Co-Founder
Founded: 1979. **Members:** 1,200. **Membership Dues:** regular, $50 ● sponsor (feeds one unsponsored horse for one month), $38 ● sponsor (care for an unsponsored horse for 3 months), $114 ● sponsor (sponsors one horse for a year), $456. **Staff:** 2. **Budget:** $200,000. **Description:** Aims to rescue unwanted wild horses and burros and creates a safe home for them. **Publications:** Newsletter. Alternate Formats: online.

11232 ■ Wild Horse Spirit (WHS)
25 Lewers Creek Rd.
Carson City, NV 89704
Ph: (775)883-5488
E-mail: betty@wildhorsespirit.org
URL: http://www.wildhorsespirit.org
Contact: Bobbi Royle, Co-Founder
Founded: 1993. **Description:** Promotes humane treatment, rescue and rehabilitation of injured, sick or jeopardized wild horses; functions as an accredited sanctuary.

11233 ■ Women's Humane Society Animal Shelter
PO Box 1470
Bensalem, PA 19020
Ph: (215)750-3100
Fax: (215)750-5253
URL: http://www.petfinder.org/shelters/PA102.html
Contact: John Foster, Exec. Dir.
Founded: 1869. **Description:** Committed to caring for sick, injured, abused, and abandoned animals; provides veterinary hospital and ambulance service, low-cost medical care for area pets, and serves the needs of shelter animals. Works to prevent animal cruelty through legislation, law enforcement, and education.

11234 ■ World Society for the Protection of Animals (WSPA)
34 Deloss St.
Framingham, MA 01702
Ph: (508)879-8350
Free: (800)883-WSPA
Fax: (508)620-0786
E-mail: wspa@wspausa.org
URL: http://www.wspa-usa.org
Contact: Jennifer Brown, Supporter Liaison
Founded: 1981. **Members:** 20,000. **Multinational.** **Description:** Aims to promote the protection of animals, prevent cruelty to animals, and relieve animal suffering in every part of the world. Supports humane education programmes to encourage respect for animals and responsible stewardship, and laws and enforcement structures to provide legal protection for animals. **Additional Websites:** http://www.wspa-international.org. **Publications:** *Animals International,* semiannual. Newsletter. **Price:** free for members. **Circulation:** 22,000. Alternate Formats: online ● Annual Report, annual. Alternate Formats: online.

Animals

11235 ■ 2nd Chance 4 Pets
1484 Pollard Rd., No. 444
Los Gatos, CA 95032
Ph: (408)871-1133
Fax: (408)866-6659
E-mail: info@2ndchance4pets.org
URL: http://www.2ndchance4pets.org
Contact: Amy Shever, Founder
Description: Aims to educate and inform the public about available solutions to pet owners and to put an end to unplanned, unwanted euthanasia of their pets. Protects animal companions. Prevents pets from becoming orphaned due to owner's death or disability. Provides assistance to pet owners in making lifetime care decisions for their pets. **Boards:** Advisory. **Publications:** *Companion,* quarterly. Newsletter. Alternate Formats: online.

11236 ■ Animals First
153 E 18th St., Ste.22
New York, NY 10003
Ph: (212)505-1073
Contact: John Zeigler, Exec.Dir.
Founded: 1972. **Staff:** 2. **Description:** Seeks to demonstrate to nations that their interests are best served by putting the rights of animals first. Believes that if the needs of animals are addressed as the first priority, a saner and more humane civilization would then be closer to eradicating overpopulation and environmental destruction. **Formerly:** (2000) Speak Out!.

11237 ■ International Sugar Glider Association (ISGA)
824 130th Ave. NE
Bellevue, WA 98005-2612
E-mail: officers@isga.org
URL: http://www.isga.org
Contact: Nancy Shofner, Pres.
Membership Dues: youth, $15 (annual) ● regular, $25 (annual) ● breeder, $35 (annual). **Description:** Informs and educates the public about owing Sugar Gliders as pets; finds homes for lost, abandoned, confiscated and relinquished Sugar Gliders. **Publications:** *ISGA Newsletter.*

11238 ■ Viva! USA
1123 Broadway, Ste.912
New York, NY 10010
Ph: (212)989-8482
Fax: (212)627-6037
E-mail: info@vivausa.org
URL: http://www.vivausa.org
Contact: Lauren Ornelas, Campaign Dir.
Multinational. Description: Campaigns on behalf of animals killed for food. Works to expose the sufferings of animals in factory farms. **Also Known As:**

(2005) Vegetarians International Voice for Animals. **Publications:** *VIVA! Life.* Magazine.

Anti-Poverty

11239 ■ NetAid
75 Broad St., Ste.2410
New York, NY 10004
Ph: (212)537-0500
Fax: (212)537-0501
E-mail: hthompson@netaid.org
URL: http://www.netaid.org
Contact: Kimberly A. Hamilton, Pres.
Founded: 1999. **Staff:** 18. **Budget:** $4,000,000. **Description:** Educates, inspires and empowers young people to fight global poverty. Provides innovative programs to educate young people about global poverty and international development. **Awards:** Global Action Awards. **Frequency:** annual. **Type:** recognition. **Recipient:** for high school students who have taken outstanding actions to fight poverty. **Publications:** *Connections,* monthly. Newsletter. Alternate Formats: online.

Anti-Racism

11240 ■ A World of Difference Institute
Dept. DJ
823 United Nations Plz.
New York, NY 10017
Ph: (212)885-7811
E-mail: webmaster@adl.org
URL: http://www.adl.org/education/edu_awod/
   default_awod.asp
Contact: Erin Lee, Asst. Dir.
Founded: 1985. **Multinational. Description:** Commits to fight bigotry worldwide. **Divisions:** A Campus of Difference; A Classroom of Difference; A Community of Difference; A Workplace of Difference.

Arbitration and Mediation

11241 ■ CPR International Institute for Conflict Prevention and Resolution (CPR)
575 Lexington Ave., 21st Fl.
New York, NY 10022
Ph: (212)949-6490
Fax: (212)949-8859
E-mail: info@cpradr.org
URL: http://www.cpradr.org
Contact: Kathleen Bryan, Acting Pres./CEO
Founded: 1979. **Members:** 550. **Membership Dues:** sustaining, $6,000 (annual) ● contributing, $3,000 (annual). **Staff:** 20. **Multinational. Description:** General counsel from major corporations, senior partners of leading law firms, and prominent legal scholars and public institutions. Develops new Alternate Dispute Resolution (ADR) procedures, educates and trains law departments, law firms, and the courts in ADR; resolves significant public and business disputes through CPR Panels of Distinguished Neutrals. **Libraries: Type:** reference. **Awards:** CPR Awards for ADR Excellence. **Frequency:** annual. **Type:** recognition. **Recipient:** for outstanding achievement in ADR practice and scholarship. **Computer Services:** database, 6800 documents, including ADR practices, litigation management, and preventive practices. **Committees:** Industry; Practice Area. **Formerly:** (1994) Center for Public Resources; (2005) CPR Institute for Dispute Resolution. **Publications:** *Alternatives,* monthly. Newsletter. Covers all business and public institution usage of ADR; includes model ADR agreements and selected conference proceedings. **Price:** $195.00/year. ISSN: 0736-3613. **Circulation:** 2,000. Alternate Formats: online ● *Court ADR: Elements of Program Design.* Book. **Price:** $40.00 ● *Health Industry Dispute Resolution* ● *Judge's Deskbook on Court ADR.* **Price:** $40.00 ● *Manager's Guide to Resolving Legal Disputes* ● *Mediation in Action: Resolving a Complex Business Dispute.* Video ● *Model ADR Practices and Procedures Series.*

Includes twenty-two volumes on substantive and procedural ADR topics. ● *Out of Court: The Minitrial.* Video. **Price:** $100.00 ● *What's the Alternative?.* Video. **Conventions/Meetings:** semiannual meeting.

Armed Forces

11242 ■ AdoptaPlatoon (AAP)
c/o Nanny Fran
PO Box 1457
Seabrook, NH 03874
E-mail: fran@adoptaplatoon.org
URL: http://adoptaplatoon.org
Contact: Nanny Fran, Contact
Founded: 1998. **Description:** Ensures that deployed United States Service members in all branches of the military are not forgotten by providing mail support. Promotes patriotism in schools and communities. Provides a better deployment quality of life. Assists military families. **Computer Services:** Online services, forum. **Telecommunication Services:** electronic mail, info@adoptaplatoon.org. **Projects:** Operation Crayon; Operation Holiday. **Publications:** Newsletter.

11243 ■ Any Soldier
PO Box 29
Hoagland, IN 46745-0029
E-mail: marty@anysoldier.com
URL: http://www.anysoldier.com
Contact: Marty Horn, Pres.
Founded: 2003. **Description:** Encourages individuals to send mail, care packages, food items, health and hygiene items, tactical items and other items to support military needs.

11244 ■ Books for Soldiers (BFS)
353 Jonestown Rd., No. 123
Winston-Salem, NC 27104
URL: http://booksforsoldiers.com
Contact: Storm Williams, Founder
Description: Encourages individuals to send books to men and women in uniform. Facilitates the collection and distribution of donated books to soldiers. **Computer Services:** Mailing lists ● online services, discussion board.

11245 ■ Operation AC (OPAC)
560 Peoples Plz., No. 121
Newark, DE 19702
Ph: (302)836-1008
E-mail: frankiemayo@comcast.net
URL: http://www.operationac.com
Contact: Frankie Mayo, Contact
Founded: 2003. **Description:** Supports the military by sending 110v single phase air conditioners to Iraq. Encourages individuals to donate care packages, food items, health and hygiene items, tactical items and other means to support military needs. **Telecommunication Services:** electronic mail, kim@operationac.com. **Projects:** Afghan Orphanage; Boots from Bikers; Save Ali's Life; School Supplies.

11246 ■ Operation Gratitude (OPG)
c/o Carolyn Blashek, Founder
16444 Refugio Rd.
Encino, CA 91436
Ph: (818)789-0123
E-mail: cblashek@aol.com
URL: http://www.opgratitude.com
Contact: Carolyn Blashek, Founder
Founded: 2003. **Multinational. Description:** Represents the interests of individuals dedicated to support the U.S. military and troops working overseas. Provides civilians anywhere in America a way to express their respect and appreciation to the men and women of the U.S. military through collection drives, letter writing campaigns and donations of requested items or funds for shipping expenses. Seeks to lift U.S. troops' morale by sending care packages and letters of support to service members serving overseas. **Telecommunication Services:** electronic mail, cwalters@opgratitude.com. **Publications:** Newsletter. Alternate Formats: online.

11247 ■ Operation Homelink
25 E Washington, Ste.1735
Chicago, IL 60602
Ph: (312)863-6336
Fax: (312)863-6206
E-mail: contact@operationhomelink.org
URL: http://www.operationhomelink.org
Contact: Dan Shannon, Founder/Pres.
Description: Provides free refurbished computers to either parents or spouses of deployed service men and women in the ranks of E-1 through E-5. Enables e-mail communications between families and their loved ones deployed outside the United States.

11248 ■ Operation Sandbox
PO Box 163
Sarahsville, OH 43779
Ph: (740)732-0130
E-mail: opsandbox@wmconnect.com
Contact: Vicki Thompson, Contact
Founded: 2003. **Description:** Promotes the welfare of soldiers deployed overseas. Supports the needs of military men and women by sending cards, postcards and packages. **Projects:** Post Card and Letter Drive.

11249 ■ Operation ShoeBox
PO Box 1465
Belleview, FL 34421
Ph: (352)553-9362
E-mail: info@operationshoebox.com
URL: http://www.operationshoebox.com
Contact: Mary Harper, Contact
Founded: 2003. **Description:** Encourages citizens to send letters and packages to support the needs of military men and women deployed overseas. **Computer Services:** Mailing lists, of members.

11250 ■ Operation Soldier Support (OSS)
239 Hoover Hwy.
Lowden, IA 52255
E-mail: geneinia@hotmail.com
URL: http://www.operationsoldiersupport.org
Contact: Gene Bowman, Contact
Founded: 1999. **Description:** Helps people make connections with the military men and women stationed away from home. Facilitates the initial contact between military men and women and individuals wishing to provide support. **Computer Services:** Online services, chat ● online services, forum.

11251 ■ Operation: Take a Soldier to the Movies
c/o Hintzke and Associates, Inc.
14775 W Natl. Ave.
New Berlin, WI 53151-4434
Ph: (262)754-4300
E-mail: soldiertomovies@hintzke.com
URL: http://www.soldiertomovies.org
Contact: Bernie Hintzke, Contact
Description: Supports troops in Iraq, Afghanistan and other war zones by "taking a soldier to the movies". Encourages individuals to forward movie-related items to soldiers.

11252 ■ Operation We Do Care
PO Box 604
Holloman AFB, NM 88330
Free: (866)447-3665
E-mail: sue@operationwedocare.org
Contact: Sugin F. Musgrave, CEO
Description: Helps American military members by sending phone cards, care packages and other items to support military needs.

11253 ■ Salute Our Services (SOS)
2100 Reston Pkwy., Ste.300
Reston, VA 20191
Ph: (703)234-1773
Free: (866)863-6867
Fax: (703)234-1701
E-mail: sos@saluteourservices.org
URL: http://www.saluteourservices.org
Contact: Patricia Johnson, CEO
Founded: 2001. **Description:** Augments the existing family programs of the United States military. Encour-

ages and facilitates the use of the Internet as a tool to enhance communication between deployed soldiers and their families. **Programs:** 50 State Salute; Kid Serves 2; SOS Mentor.

11254 ■ A Soldier's Wish List (ASWL)
c/o Mrs. Julieann Najar, Founder
11143 Larimore Rd.
St. Louis, MO 63138
Ph: (314)868-2264
E-mail: soldiersmother2@charter.net
URL: http://www.asoldierswishlist.org
Contact: Mrs. Julieann Najar, Founder
Description: Strives to fulfill the wishes of soldiers serving in Iraq, Afghanistan, Kuwait, Kosovo and Qatar. Provides troops with care packages from their families. Facilitates cooperation and communication among members. **Telecommunication Services:** electronic mail, aswl5000@aol.com.

11255 ■ Support Our Soldiers America (SOS)
55 Bergen St.
Brooklyn, NY 11201
Ph: (718)237-1097
Fax: (718)624-4231
E-mail: barrowlady@aol.com
URL: http://www.sosamericainc.org
Contact: Kathryn Falk, Founder/Pres.
Description: Supports troops overseas by sending books, letters, care packages, and e-mails. **Computer Services:** Mailing lists, of members. **Publications:** Newsletter. Alternate Formats: online.

11256 ■ Tragedy Assistance Program for Survivors (TAPS)
1621 Connecticut Ave. NW, Ste.300
Washington, DC 20009
Ph: (202)588-8277
Free: (800)959-8277
E-mail: info@taps.org
URL: http://www.taps.org
Contact: Bonnie Carroll, Founder/Chair
Founded: 1992. **Description:** Offers peer support and assists the families affected by the death of a loved one serving in the Armed Forces. Educates survivors about the grief process and the traumatic effects of death of one serving in the Armed Forces. **Computer Services:** Information services, facts on trauma ● information services, military benefits resources ● online services, chat. **Telecommunication Services:** electronic mail, help@taps.org. **Programs:** Children's Outreach; Peer Support; Youth. **Publications:** *Military Survivor*, quarterly. Journal. Contains vital issues facing military survivors. ● Brochure. Alternate Formats: online.

Arts

11257 ■ Howard Gilman Foundation
111 W 50th St.
New York, NY 10020
Ph: (212)307-1073
Fax: (212)262-4108
Multinational. Description: Works to preserve the legacy of Howard Gilman by supporting philanthropic programs in his primary areas of interest: performing arts, wildlife conservation and cardiovascular diseases. **Awards: Type:** grant.

11258 ■ Weave a Real Peace (WARP)
PMB 249
3102 N Classen Blvd.
Oklahoma City, OK 73118-3899
E-mail: info@weavearealpeace.org
URL: http://www.weavearealpeace.org
Contact: Cheryl Musch, Admin. Coor.
Founded: 1992. **Members:** 250. **Membership Dues:** regular, in U.S. and Canada, $20 (annual) ● simple living, $10 (annual) ● group, supporting, $30 (annual) ● patron, donor, $100 (annual) ● regular, outside U.S. and Canada, $25 (annual). **Staff:** 1. **Budget:** $15,000. **National Groups:** 11. **Multinational. Description:** Facilitates self-empowerment and betterment of women and communities in need through

textile arts; provides cross-cultural education and support within the textile community; promotes appreciation of textiles that reflect a community's culture or tradition; seeks to enrich the lives of those in the global textile community through cross-cultural exchange. **Publications:** Newsletter, quarterly. Contains information, requests for assistance, technical advice, materials and design expertise, and news of projects. **Price:** included in membership dues. **Advertising:** accepted. Alternate Formats: online ● Membership Directory, annual. **Conventions/Meetings:** annual meeting - usually spring.

Arts and Crafts

11259 ■ ABC Quilts Projects
569 First New Hampshire Tpke., Ste.3
Northwood, NH 03261
Ph: (603)942-9211
Free: (800)536-5694
Fax: (603)942-9210
E-mail: info@abcquilts.org
URL: http://www.abcquilts.org
Contact: Pamela Weeks Worthen, Exec.Dir.
Founded: 1988. **Staff:** 2. **Budget:** $100,000. **Description:** Committed to sending love and comfort to at-risk children, particularly young children infected with HIV/AIDS, alcohol/drug-affected, or abandoned, in the form of handmade baby quilts as a tool for promoting awareness, informed choices and community service.

Assault

11260 ■ STAMP - Survivors Take Action Against Abuse by Military Personnel
500 Greene Tree Pl.
Fairborn, OH 45324
Ph: (937)879-9304
E-mail: dmack500@aol.com
URL: http://www.militarywoman.org/stamp.htm
Contact: Dorothy Mackey, Contact
Description: Offers support to individuals who have survived abuse or mistreatment by a member of the military.

Assyrian

11261 ■ Assyrian Aid Society of America (AAS-A)
350 Berkeley Park Blvd.
Berkeley, CA 94707
Ph: (510)527-9997
Fax: (510)527-6633
E-mail: aas@assyrianaid.org
URL: http://www.assyrianaid.org
Contact: Narsai M. David, Pres.
Founded: 1991. **Multinational. Description:** Works to help Assyrians in need. Promotes Assyrian culture and heritage. Builds a structure capable of responding to unexpected crises that require immediate mobilization. Focuses on the needs and humanitarian concerns of Assyrian people. Funds building programs, education programs, medical projects, irrigation and electrification projects. **Telecommunication Services:** electronic mail, online@assyrianaid. org. **Publications:** *The Tree of Life*, quarterly. Newsletter. Alternate Formats: online.

Bereavement

11262 ■ Alive Alone
c/o Kay Bevington, Founder
1112 Champaign Dr.
Van Wert, OH 45891
E-mail: alivalon@bright.net
URL: http://www.alivealone.org
Contact: Sandy Fox, Chair
Founded: 1988. **Description:** Provides counseling to bereaved parents, whose only child or all children

are deceased. Provides self-help network and publications to promote communication and healing, to assist in resolving their grief, and a means to reinvest their lives for a positive future. **Computer Services:** Online services, message board, guestbook. **Telecommunication Services:** electronic mail, sbrews3165@aol.com. **Publications:** Newsletter, bimonthly. **Price:** $20.00 /year for members. Alternate Formats: online.

11263 ■ Bereaved Parents of the USA (BP/USA)
c/o John Goodrich
PO Box 95
Park Forest, IL 60466-0095
Ph: (708)748-7866
Fax: (708)748-9184
E-mail: jbgoodrich@sbcglobal.net
URL: http://www.bereavedparentsusa.org
Contact: Beverley Hurley, Pres.
Founded: 1995. **Description:** Offers support, understanding, encouragement and hope to bereaved parents, siblings and grandparents after the death of their children, brother, sister or grandchildren, regardless of race, creed or financial status. Educates families about the grief process pertaining to the death of a child at any age and from any cause. **Publications:** *A Journey Together*, quarterly. Newsletter. Contains articles of interest on grief. **Conventions/Meetings:** annual National Gathering - meeting.

Bicycle

11264 ■ Bike and Build
190 N 10th St., Ste.308
Brooklyn, NY 11211
Ph: (718)599-5925
Fax: (661)752-9806
E-mail: info@bikeandbuild.org
URL: http://www.bikeandbuild.org
Contact: Amelia Hanley, Exec. Dir.
Founded: 2002. **Description:** Collaborates with young adults to produce cross-country fundraising cycling trips. Supports fundraising efforts for low-cost housing projects. Educates the public about issues on affordable housing. **Awards:** Bike and Build Grant. **Frequency:** annual. **Type:** grant. **Recipient:** for affordable housing projects chiefly planned and executed by students and young adults, ages 18 to 25. **Publications:** *Rider Handbook*. Includes advice from fellow riders, fundraising tips, and other valuable information. Alternate Formats: online ● Journals. Contains updates on fundraising and cycling activities around the country. Alternate Formats: online.

Bird

11265 ■ Dove Sportsman's Society
PO Box 610
Edgefield, SC 29824
Ph: (803)637-5731 (803)637-5732
Fax: (803)637-0037
E-mail: tsidwell@qu.org
URL: http://www.dovesociety.org
Contact: Tina Sidwell, Contact
Founded: 1999. **Members:** 5,500. **Membership Dues:** regular, $30 (annual) ● mentor, $50 (annual) ● sponsor, $225 (annual) ● youth, $10 (annual). **Staff:** 10. **Description:** Works to conserve and manage Mourning Dove and other native doves and pigeons of North, Central, and South America and to promote the sport of dove hunting. **Libraries: Type:** not open to the public. **Holdings:** articles, artwork, photographs. **Computer Services:** Mailing lists, of members. **Affiliated With:** Quail Unlimited. **Formerly:** (2003) Doves Unlimited. **Publications:** *The Dove Hunter*, bimonthly. Magazine. **Advertising:** accepted.

11266 ■ Parrots and People (P&P)
3930 Glade Rd., No. 108-130
Colleyville, TX 76034
Ph: (817)498-9636
Fax: (817)498-8764
E-mail: info@parrotsandpeople.org
URL: http://www.parrotsandpeople.org
Contact: Kathy Jones Ferguson, Pres.
Membership Dues: Parrotlet (basic single), $35 (annual) ● Quaker (family), $55 (annual) ● Conure, $100 (annual) ● Amazon, $250 (annual) ● Cockatoo, $500 (annual) ● Macaw, life, $2,000 ● commercial, $200 (annual). **Description:** Works to provide individual lifetime solutions for long term care, rehabilitation and rescue of companion birds through programs in collaboration with institutions for people with special needs; aims to develop natural sanctuary where companion birds can retire to live healthy, safe, and with enriched lives. **Publications:** Newsletter.

Burro

11267 ■ Wild Burro Rescue and Preservation Project
PO Box 10
Olancha, CA 93549-0010
Ph: (760)384-8523
Fax: (240)255-8498
E-mail: wildburrorescue@mail.com
URL: http://www.wildburrorescue.org
Contact: Karen Gilligan, Contact
Membership Dues: regular, $25 (annual). **Description:** Works to rescue and preserve those aged, infirmed, psychologically traumatized, physically impaired, as well as pregnant, wild burros from Death Valley region. **Additional Websites:** http://www.help-savethewildburros.org.

Cancer

11268 ■ KIDSCOPE
2045 Peachtree Rd., Ste.150
Atlanta, GA 30309
Ph: (404)892-1437
URL: http://www.kidscope.org
Contact: H. Elizabeth King PhD, Contact
Founded: 1994. **Languages:** English, Spanish. **Description:** Helps children and families understand the effects of cancer or chemotherapy. Develops innovative programs and materials that communicate a message of hope to diverse families coping with cancer.

11269 ■ Reel Recovery
160 Brookside Rd.
Needham, MA 02492
Ph: (781)449-9029
Free: (800)699-4490
Fax: (781)449-9031
E-mail: info@reelrecovery.org
URL: http://www.reelrecovery.org
Contact: Jim Cloud, Pres.
Founded: 2003. **Description:** Helps men in the cancer recovery process by introducing them to the healing powers of the sport of fly-fishing. Provides men a safe and supportive environment to explore their personal experiences with cancer with others who share their stories. Provides expert fly-fishing instruction that enables the participants to learn a new skill, form a healing connection with nature and participate in a sport they can continue throughout their recovery. **Programs:** Reel Recovery Retreat. **Publications:** Articles. Alternate Formats: online ● Brochure.

Career Counseling

11270 ■ International Mentoring Network Organization (IMNO)
766 E 560 N, No. 206
Provo, UT 84606
Ph: (801)361-9942

E-mail: contact@imno.org
URL: http://www.imno.org
Contact: Patrick Tedjamulia, Exec. Dir.
Founded: 2003. **Multinational. Description:** Aims to solve the worldwide need for professional mentoring. Serves as an open source mentoring movement. Gives help and direction to the career development of aspiring professionals. **Telecommunication Services:** electronic mail, ptedjamulia@imno.org. **Publications:** Newsletter, monthly. **Price:** free for members. Alternate Formats: online.

Child Abuse

11271 ■ ASARian
PO Box 605
Durham, NC 27702-0605
E-mail: fuzzy@piglet.asarian.org
URL: http://asarian-host.net/msie.html
Founded: 1991. **Description:** Aims to provide safe Internet services to survivors of any type of childhood abuse. **Computer Services:** Online services, chat programs.

11272 ■ The Linkup - Survivors of Clergy Abuse
PO Box 429
Pewee Valley, KY 40056-0429
Ph: (502)241-5544
Fax: (502)241-0031
E-mail: director@healingall.org
URL: http://www.thelinkup.org
Members: 3,000. **Description:** Commits to prevent clergy abuse and to empower and assist victims to overcome traumatic effects of this abuse. **Computer Services:** Mailing lists, of members ● online services, petition. **Publications:** *Missing Link*, quarterly. Newsletter. **Price:** $35.00 suggested donation. Alternate Formats: online.

11273 ■ RUGMARK Foundation
2001 S St. NW, Ste.430
Washington, DC 20009
Ph: (202)234-9050
Free: (866)784-6275
Fax: (202)347-4885
E-mail: info@rugmark.org
URL: http://www.rugmark.org
Contact: Nina Smith, Exec. Dir.
Founded: 1994. **Staff:** 4. **Multinational. Description:** Works to end child labor and offer educational opportunities to children in India, Nepal, and Pakistan. Assures that no illegal child labor was used to manufacture a rug or carpet. **Telecommunication Services:** electronic mail, nina@rugmark.org.

Child Care

11274 ■ Afterschool Alliance
1616 H St. NW, Ste.820
Washington, DC 20006
Ph: (202)347-2030
Fax: (202)347-2092
E-mail: info@afterschoolalliance.org
URL: http://www.afterschoolalliance.org
Contact: Jodi Grant, Exec. Dir.
Founded: 1999. **Local Groups:** 5. **Description:** Raises awareness of the importance of afterschool programs. Advocates for quality and affordable programs for all children. Engages public will to increase investments in quality afterschool program initiatives. Serves as a source of information on afterschool programs and resources. **Programs:** Help Working Families; Improve Academic Achievement; Keeps Kids Safe.

11275 ■ Child Care Law Center (CCLC)
221 Pine St., 3rd Fl.
San Francisco, CA 94104
Ph: (415)394-7144
Fax: (415)394-7140

E-mail: info@childcarelaw.org
URL: http://www.childcarelaw.org
Contact: Nancy Strohl, Exec. Dir.
Founded: 1978. **Staff:** 10. **Languages:** English, Spanish. **Description:** Provides legal advice, technical assistance, and training programs to attorneys, parents, childcare providers and others working to improve childcare for low-income families. Develops legislative and regulatory policies; monitors legislative issues. Operates an information and referral line. **Libraries: Type:** reference. **Subjects:** legal issues. **Publications:** *A Child Care Advocacy Guide to Land Use Principles* ● *About Child Care in California: Liability Insurance for Family Child Care Providers* ● *ADA Title III Flowchart: When Are You Required to Admit a Child with a Disability?* ● *Administration of Inhaled Medications in Child Care* ● *Caring for Children with Special Needs: The Americans with Disabilities Act (ADA) and Child Care* ● *Child Care and the ADA: Highlights for Parents of Children with Disabilities* ● *Child Care and the ADA: Highlights for Parents of Typically Developing Children* ● *Child Care Contracts: Information for Parents* ● *Child Care Licensing* ● *Child Care Subsidies in California* (in English and Spanish) ● *Legal Issues for Family Child Care Providers: Caring for Mildly Ill and Injured Children* ● *Legal Issues for Family Child Care Providers: Contracts* ● *Legal Issues for Family Child Care Providers in California: Employing an Assistant* ● *Legal Issues for Family Child Care Providers in California: Liability & Insurance* ● *Legal Issues for Family Child Care Providers in California: Reporting Child Abuse* ● *Questions and Answers About CalWORKs Child Care: Appeals & Hearings* (in English and Spanish) ● *Questions and Answers About CalWORKs Child Care: Diversion* ● *Questions and Answers About CalWORKs Child Care: Family Fees* ● *Questions and Answers About CalWORKs Child Care: Introduction* ● *Questions and Answers about the Americans with Disabilities Act: A Quick Reference (Information for Child Care Providers)* ● Offers various additional publications.

11276 ■ Council for Professional Recognition
2460 16th St. NW
Washington, DC 20009
Ph: (202)265-9090
Free: (800)424-4310
E-mail: feedback@cdacouncil.org
URL: http://www.cdacouncil.org
Contact: Josue Cruz PhD, Pres.
Founded: 1985. **Staff:** 50. **Languages:** English, Spanish. **Nonmembership. Description:** Promotes availability of quality child care through the Child Development Associate National Credentialing Program. Credentials are awarded to family child care, center-based infant/toddler and preschool caregivers, and home visitors. Offers annual training program, the CDA Professional Preparation Program. **Computer Services:** database ● mailing lists. **Programs:** The CDA Credentialing; Head Start Fellowships; Regio Children USA; U.S Military School Age Credentials. **Also Known As:** CDA National Credentialing Program. **Formerly:** (1987) Child Development Associate National Credentialing Program; (1999) Council for Early Childhood Professional Recognition. **Supersedes:** Child Development Associate Consortium. **Publications:** *Council News and Views*, 3/year. Newsletter. **Circulation:** 9,000. Alternate Formats: online ● *Essentials* ● *Improving Child Care Through the Child Development Associate Program.* Book ● *Rechild.* Newsletter ● Brochure. Contains information about the assessment processes for the center-based, family child care and home visitor personnel. Alternate Formats: online.

11277 ■ International Nanny Association (INA)
2020 Southwest Fwy., Ste.208
Houston, TX 77098
Ph: (713)526-2670
Free: (888)878-1477
Fax: (713)526-2667
E-mail: ina@nanny.org
URL: http://www.nanny.org
Contact: Patricia Cascio, Pres.
Founded: 1985. **Members:** 450. **Membership Dues:** individual (nanny, nanny employer), $85 (annual) ●

standard, $195 (annual) ● supporting, $275 (annual). **Staff:** 1. **Description:** An educational association for nannies and those who educate, place, employ, and support professional in-home child care. Membership is open to those who are directly involved with the in-home child care profession, including nannies, nanny employers, nanny placement agency owners (and staff), nanny educators, and providers of special services related to the nanny profession. **Awards:** Nanny of the Year. **Frequency:** annual. **Type:** recognition. **Recipient:** for the personal achievements of a working nanny. **Computer Services:** Mailing lists. **Additional Websites:** http://www.internationalnannyassociation.com. **Publications:** A Nanny for Your Family. Brochure ● Beyond Peanut Butter and Jelly. Book. **Price:** $14.95 free shipping ● Directory of Nanny Training Programs, Placement Agencies and Special Services, annual. **Price:** $15.95 /year for members; $29.95 /year for nonmembers. **Circulation:** 1,000. **Advertising:** accepted ● Family and Nanny Agreement. **Price:** $25.00 for members; $50.00 for nonmembers ● INAVision, quarterly. Newsletter. Includes association news and information related to in-home childcare industry. **Price:** included in membership dues. **Circulation:** 1,000. **Advertising:** accepted ● Recommended Competencies for the Education of Nurses ● Recommended Practices for Nannies ● Recommended Practices for Nanny Placement Agencies ● So You Want to Be a Nanny. Brochure. **Conventions/Meetings:** annual conference, for issues related to childcare (exhibits) - in summer.

11278 ■ National AfterSchool Association (NAA)
529 Main St., Ste.214
Charlestown, MA 02129
Ph: (617)778-6020
Free: (800)617-8242
Fax: (617)778-6025
E-mail: phowe@naaweb.org
URL: http://www.naaweb.org
Contact: Peter Howe, COO
Founded: 1981. **Members:** 8,000. **Membership Dues:** individual, $45 (annual). **Staff:** 12. **Regional Groups:** 5. **Local Groups:** 35. **Description:** Professional providers of day care services for school age children outside of school hours. Seeks to advance the profession of school-age child care. Provides support and services to members including coalition building, networking, and group rates for video licensing. **Task Forces:** Accreditation; Database; Financial Sustainability. **Formerly:** (2004) National School-Age Care Alliance. **Publications:** Caring, Stimulating, Responsive. Brochure ● NSACA News, quarterly. Newsletter. **Conventions/Meetings:** annual conference (exhibits).

11279 ■ National Association of Child Care Professionals (NACCP)
PO Box 90723
Austin, TX 78709
Ph: (512)301-5557
Free: (800)537-1118
E-mail: admin@naccp.org
URL: http://www.naccp.org
Contact: Sherry Workman, Exec. Dir./CEO
Founded: 1984. **Members:** 1,200. **Membership Dues:** child care supervisor/manager, $120 (annual) ● associate, $105 (annual) ● vendor, $349 (annual) ● career in caring, $10 (annual). **Staff:** 5. **Budget:** $500,000. **State Groups:** 6. **Description:** Child care supervisors and individuals involved in decision-making at a child care facility. Offers networking opportunities and support services to child care professionals. Dedicated to the professional development of child care directors. Conducts educational programs. **Awards:** National Child Care Director of the Year Award. **Frequency:** annual. **Type:** monetary. **Recipient:** for exceptional contributions to the child care industry. **Computer Services:** Mailing lists, of members. **Publications:** Caring for Your Children, quarterly. Newsletter. Contains information for parents. **Price:** included in membership dues; $39.00 for nonmembers. **Circulation:** 2,000. **Advertising:** accepted ● Immunizing Children Against Disease: A

Guide For Child Care Providers. Booklet. Alternate Formats: online ● Professional Connections, quarterly. Newsletter. Contains management information for directors. **Circulation:** 2,000. **Advertising:** accepted. Alternate Formats: online ● Team Work, quarterly. Newsletter. Directed toward staff members. **Circulation:** 2,000. **Advertising:** accepted ● Directory. Contains contact information for other child care professionals. ● Management Tools of the Trade-Personnel resource management forms specific to child care industry. **Conventions/Meetings:** annual How Successful Directors Manage National Conference (exhibits) ● annual How Successful Directors Manage State Conference (exhibits) ● Training Seminars (exhibits) - 5/year.

11280 ■ National Association of Child Care Resource and Referral Agencies (NACCRRA)
3101 Wilson Blvd., Ste.350
Arlington, VA 22201
Ph: (703)341-4100
Fax: (703)341-4101
E-mail: azephir@naccrra.org
URL: http://www.naccrra.org
Contact: Marsha Thompson, Pres.
Founded: 1987. **Members:** 750. **Membership Dues:** individual, $75 (annual) ● student, child care provider, $25 (annual) ● individual champion, $150 (annual) ● government, nonprofit, $375 (annual) ● government champion, nonprofit champion, $500 (annual) ● corporate, $750 (annual) ● corporate champion, $1,000 (annual). **Staff:** 25. **Budget:** $12,000,000. **Regional Groups:** 8. **State Groups:** 32. **Local Groups:** 600. **Description:** Serves as network of community-based child care resource and referral programs that promote a diverse, high quality child care system with parental choice that is accessible to all families. Provides national leadership to build such system; promotes growth and development of quality resource and referral services. **Telecommunication Services:** electronic mail, membershipservices@naccrra.org. **Conventions/Meetings:** annual conference (exhibits) ● annual symposium.

11281 ■ National Association for Sick Child Daycare (NASCD)
1716 5th Ave. N
Birmingham, AL 35203
Ph: (205)324-8447
Fax: (205)324-8050
E-mail: jackiestewart@nascd.com
URL: http://www.nascd.org
Contact: Dr. Jacqueline W. Stewart, Pres.
Founded: 1988. **Members:** 75. **Membership Dues:** bronze, individual, $65 (annual) ● silver, facility, $125 (annual) ● gold, founder, $500 (annual). **Description:** Works to promote the establishment of sick child daycare programs nationwide. Conducts educational programs; compiles statistics. **Computer Services:** Mailing lists, of members. **Publications:** Survey of Sick Child Care Facilities, quarterly. Newsletter. **Price:** $50.00 facility; $260.00 directory; $75.00 conference synopsis. **Advertising:** accepted ● Brochure ● Newsletters, annual. Alternate Formats: online. **Conventions/Meetings:** annual conference.

11282 ■ National Child Care Association (NCCA)
2025 M St. NW, Ste.800
Washington, DC 20036-3309
Ph: (202)367-1133
Free: (800)543-7161
Fax: (202)367-2133
E-mail: info@nccanet.org
URL: http://www.nccanet.org
Contact: Dawn Hatzer, Exec. Dir.
Founded: 1987. **Members:** 7,000. **Membership Dues:** individual, $88 (annual) ● student, $33 (annual) ● associate, $350 (annual) ● supporter sponsor, $2,000 (annual) ● benefactor sponsor, $3,500 (annual) ● patron sponsor, $6,000 (annual). **Staff:** 7. **Budget:** $800,000. **State Groups:** 25. **Description:** Works to promote and safeguard the interest of quality child care in the United States. Focuses on licensed, private providers of child care and preschool services. Conducts lobbying activities and educational

and research programs; offers casualty insurance programs; provides networking opportunities. **Awards:** National Early Childhood Program Accreditation. **Type:** grant ● **Type:** scholarship. **Computer Services:** Mailing lists, of members. **Committees:** Administration and Bylaws; Conference; Government Relations; Professional Development; Public Relations; Ways and Means. **Publications:** National Focus, quarterly. Newsletter. Includes latest information from Washington. **Circulation:** 8,000. Alternate Formats: online ● Professional Development Video Series. Videos ● Right Path to Quality Child Care Brochures. **Price:** $25.00/100 copies ● Books. **Price:** $20.00 plus shipping and handling ● Annual Report, annual. **Conventions/Meetings:** quarterly board meeting ● annual conference (exhibits) - always March ● annual conference - always September, Washington, DC.

11283 ■ National Child Care and Family Development (NCDCA)
1501 Benning Rd. NE
Washington, DC 20002-4599
Ph: (202)397-3800
Fax: (202)399-2666
E-mail: hardmont@aol.com
Contact: Travis Hardmon, Exec. Dir.
Description: Seeks to provide quality child care services for the Washington, DC area. **Formerly:** National Child Day Care Association.

11284 ■ National Coalition for Campus Children's Centers (NCCCC)
4 Schindler Educ. Ctr.
Univ. of Northern Iowa
Cedar Falls, IA 50614
Ph: (319)273-3113
Free: (800)813-8207
Fax: (319)273-3109
E-mail: ncccc@uni.edu
URL: http://www.campuschildren.org
Contact: Terri Kosik, Pres.
Founded: 1980. **Members:** 680. **Membership Dues:** individual/faculty, $100 (annual) ● single center, $125 (annual) ● associate, $35 (annual). **Staff:** 2. **Regional Groups:** 4. **State Groups:** 22. **Description:** Promotes child care centers on college campuses and provides information on organizing and operating these centers. Believes that campus child care programs should be an integral part of higher education systems and should provide safe and healthy environments for children, developmentally sound educational programs, and services to both parents and campus programs. **Committees:** Clearinghouse; Conference; Executive Conference; Journal; Nominations; Policies and Procedures; Public Policy; Public Relations. **Formerly:** (1997) National Coalition for Campus Child Care; (1998) National Coalition for Children's Centers. **Publications:** Bibliographies ● Books ● Brochure ● Journal, 3/year ● Newsletter, 3/year. **Price:** included in membership dues ● Annual Report, annual. **Price:** included in membership dues. Alternate Formats: online ● Membership Directory. **Price:** included in membership dues. **Conventions/Meetings:** annual conference (exhibits) - always spring.

11285 ■ National Resource Center for Health and Safety in Child Care and Early Education (NRCHSCCEE)
c/o UCHSC at Fitzsimons
Campus Mail Stop F541
PO Box 6508
Aurora, CO 80045-0508
Ph: (303)724-0665
Free: (800)598-KIDS
Fax: (303)724-0960
E-mail: natl.child.res.ctr@uchsc.edu
URL: http://nrc.uchsc.edu
Contact: Marilyn J. Krajicek RN, Dir.
Founded: 1992. **Nonmembership. Description:** Seeks to enhance the quality of childcare by supporting state and local health departments, childcare regulatory agencies, childcare providers, and parents in their effort to promote health and safety in childcare. Provides information services and training and

technical assistance. **Libraries: Type:** reference. **Holdings:** 300. **Subjects:** early childhood health, child care, child safety, child care licensing. **Formerly:** (2007) National Resource Center for Health and Safety in Child Care. **Publications:** Brochure.

11286 ■ Safe Sitter
8604 Allisonville Rd., Ste.248
Indianapolis, IN 46250-1597
Ph: (317)596-5001
Fax: (317)596-5008
E-mail: safesitter@safesitter.org
URL: http://www.safesitter.org
Contact: Dr. Patricia A. Keener, Founder

Founded: 1980. **Description:** Improves the welfare of young children by increasing the availability of young adolescents instructed in safe and nurturing child care techniques. Enhances the lives of young adolescents by providing the opportunity to acquire competencies in rescue skills, basic first aid and safe child care techniques. **Computer Services:** Information services, babysitting activities ● information services, babysitting tips.

Child Custody

11287 ■ National Association of Non-Custodial Moms (NANCM)
614 E Hwy. 50
PMB 246
Clermont, FL 34711
Ph: (352)241-0046
E-mail: bmorris@nancm.com
URL: http://www.nancm.com
Contact: Beverly Morris, Founder/Pres./Treas.

Description: Provides emotional support to all non-custodial parents. Focuses on helping non-custodial moms through the provision of educational and supportive resources. Encourages and educates those involved in custody issues to effectively co-parent their children and reduce post-divorce stress in regard to custody issues.

Child Development

11288 ■ Comprehensive Day Care Programs (CDCP)
Address Unknown since 2007

Founded: 1965. **Members:** 61. **Staff:** 934. **Description:** Day care centers serving 3900 children of low-income families. Aims to help each child fulfill his or her own potential in intellectual, social, emotional, and physical development. Provides opportunities in self-development to parents; seeks to emphasize the parental role and responsibility in the development of the child. Services provided comprise six components: Curriculum; Food Services; Health Services; Parent Involvement; Social Services; Volunteer Services. Is funded by the School District of Philadelphia and the Pennsylvania Department of Public Welfare, under Title XX of the Federal Social Security Act. **Formerly:** (1969) Get Set Pre-Kindergarten Program; (1987) Get Set Day Care Program.

11289 ■ Every Person Influences Children (EPIC)
1000 Main St.
Buffalo, NY 14202
Ph: (716)332-4100
Fax: (716)332-4101
E-mail: nationalinfo@epicforchildren.org
URL: http://www.epicforchildren.org
Contact: Robert T. Russell Jr., Vice Chm.

Founded: 1980. **Description:** Aims to help parents, teachers and community members to raise children to become responsible adults. Provides programs and resources for parents, teachers and school administrators that help adults raise responsible and academically successful children. Offers leadership training in several areas. **Publications:** EPIC Connections. Newsletter. Alternate Formats: online.

11290 ■ Foundation for Child Development (FCD)
145 E 32nd St., 14th Fl.
New York, NY 10016-6055
Ph: (212)213-8337
Fax: (212)213-5897
E-mail: info@fcd-us.org
URL: http://www.fcd-us.org
Contact: Ruby Takanishi, Pres./CEO

Founded: 1900. **Staff:** 7. **Description:** Supports the restructuring of pre-kindergarten, kindergarten, and grades 1 to 3 into a well-aligned first level of public education for children (ages 3-8) in the U.S. through its Mapping the PK-3 Continuum (MAP) Initiative. Promotes New American Children that aims to stimulate basic and applied research on immigrant children (birth through age 10), particularly those living in low-income families. **Awards: Type:** grant. **Programs:** Mapping the PK-3 Continuum; New American Children; Young Scholars. **Formerly:** Association for the Aid of Crippled Children. **Publications:** *Achieving Quality Early Childhood Education For All Insights From the Policy Innovation Diffusion Research.* Papers. Contains working papers from foundation research. Alternate Formats: online ● *Business Leaders As Effective Advocates for Children.* Paper ● *Career Development and Universal Prekindergarten: What Now? What Next?.* Paper ● *Child Care Employment: Implications for Women's Self-Sufficiency and for Child Development.* Paper ● *Economics of Caring Labor: Improving Compensation in the Early Childhood Workforce.* Paper ● *Education for All Young Children: The Role of States and the Federal Government in Promoting Prekindergarten and Kindergarten.* Paper ● *Kindergarten: The Overlooked School Year.* Paper ● *Labor's Role In Addressing the Child Care Crisis.* Paper ● *Let the War on Poverty Line Commence.* Paper ● *Money, Accreditation, and Child Care Center Quality.* Papers. Contains working papers from foundation research. ● *Reducing Poverty Among American Children Through a "Help for Working Parents" Program.* Paper ● *Regulation: An Imperative for Ensuring Quality Child Care.* Paper ● *Subsidizing Child Care by Mothers at Home.* Paper ● *Universal Prekindergarten in Georgia: A Case Study of Georgia's Lottery-Funded Pre-K Program.* Paper ● *The Well-Being of Children in Working Poor Families: Report of a Meeting.* Paper ● *Why Are Early Education and Care Wages So Low? A Critical Guide to Common Explanations.* Paper ● *Working For Worthy Wages: The Child Care Compensation Movement, 1970-2001.* Paper ● *The Working Poor In America: A Bibliographical Resource.* Paper ● Reports, annual.

11291 ■ National Black Child Development Institute (NBCDI)
1101 15th St. NW, Ste.900
Washington, DC 20005
Ph: (202)833-2220
Fax: (202)833-8222
E-mail: moreinfo@nbcdi.org
URL: http://www.nbcdi.org
Contact: Evelyn K. Moore, Pres.

Founded: 1970. **Members:** 3,250. **Membership Dues:** student, $10 (annual) ● regular, $25 (annual) ● agency/sponsoring, $50 (annual) ● sustaining/sponsoring organization, $100 (annual) ● small business/patron, $500 (annual) ● corporation, $1,000 (annual) ● friend, $250 (annual). **Regional Groups:** 42. **Description:** Aims to improving the quality of life for African American children and youth. Conducts direct services and advocacy campaigns aimed at both national and local public policies focusing on issues of health, child welfare, education, and child care. Organizes and trains network of members in a volunteer grassroots affiliate system to voice concerns regarding policies that affect black children and their families. Stimulates communication between black community groups, through conferences and seminars, to discuss and make recommendations that will be advantageous to the development of black children. Analyzes selected policy decisions and legislative and administrative regulations to determine their impact on black children and youth. Informs national policymakers of issues critical to black

children. **Programs:** African American Parents' Project; Center on the Social and Emotional Foundations for Early Learning; Cross Cultural Partnership; Entering the College Zone; Love to Read; Parent Empowerment Project; SPARK-DC. **Publications:** *Black Child Advocate,* quarterly. Newsletter. Provides public policy and legislative updates and information on local service programs. **Price:** included in membership dues; $12.50 for nonmembers ● *Calendar of Black Children,* annual. **Price:** included in membership dues; $12.00 for nonmembers ● *Child Health Talk,* quarterly. Includes topics on nutrition, exercise, childhood stress, dental checkups, behavioral disturbances, and speech and vision problems. **Price:** included in membership dues; $10.00 for nonmembers. **Conventions/Meetings:** annual conference (exhibits).

11292 ■ National Institute on Out-of-School Time (NIOST)
106 Central St.
Wellesley Centers for Women, Waban House
Wellesley, MA 02481
Ph: (781)283-2547
Fax: (781)283-3657
E-mail: niost@wellesley.edu
URL: http://www.niost.org
Contact: Ellen Gannett, Dir.

Description: Provides training and development for out-of-school time programs for children and youth. Conducts research and evaluation on afterschool programs. **Programs:** Consulting. **Projects:** Achieve Boston; After School and Out-of-School Time Program Evaluation; Boston 4Quality Initiative; Cityworks: Building Strong Citywide After School Initiatives; Cross Cities Network for Leaders of Citywide Afterschool Initiatives; Design It!; Explore It!; Jacksonville Children's Commission's After School Program Evaluation Initiatives; Massachusetts Afterschool Research Study; Metlife Discovering Community Initiative; The MOST Initiative; New York City Urban Debate League: Investigating Youth's Experiences in a "Democracy in Action" Afterschool Program; San Jose 4Quality Initiative; Staff Training in Balanced Curriculum; Strategic Planning: Building a Skilled and Stable Out-of-School Time Workforce. **Publications:** *I Wish the Kids Didn't Watch So Much TV: Out-of-School Time in Three Low Income Communities.* Report. Describes the findings of a study of children's out-of-school time. **Price:** $12.00 ● *Links to Learning: Supporting Literacy in Out-of-School Time.* Video. Contains multiple ways that afterschool practitioners can promote and incorporate literacy into their program. **Price:** $25.00 ● *National Study of Before and After School Programs, Executive Summary* ● *School-Age Children With Special Needs: What Do They Do When School Is Out?.* Book. Describes approaches to funding, staffing, administration and training for programs. **Price:** $15.95 ● *Spotlight on MOST,* biennial. Newsletter.

11293 ■ Playing for Keeps
116 W Illinois St., Ste.5E
Chicago, IL 60610
Ph: (312)222-0982
Free: (877)755-5347
Fax: (312)222-0986
E-mail: playingforkeeps@playingforkeeps.org
URL: http://www.playingforkeeps.org
Contact: Susan J. Oliver, Exec. Dir.

Founded: 1998. **Description:** Promotes the importance of constructive play for children aged birth through middle childhood. Fosters constructive play through public education, collaboration and action. Brings together coalition of parents, toy industry leaders, scholars, educators, cultural leaders, health care and human services providers and other professionals dedicated to the optimal development of children. Promotes the need of all children to learn, develop skills and have fun through creative, imaginative and non-violent play. **Telecommunication Services:** electronic mail, soliver@playingforkeeps.org ● electronic mail, info@playingforkeeps.org. **Publications:** Annual Report, annual. Alternate Formats: online.

11294 ■ Prospect Hill Foundation
99 Park Ave., Ste.2220
New York, NY 10016-1601
Ph: (212)370-1165
E-mail: lcallanan@prospect-hill.org
URL: http://fdncenter.org/grantmaker/prospecthill/intro.html
Contact: Laura Callanan, Exec. Dir.
Founded: 1960. **Description:** Strives to support organizations that deal with children and social issues. **Awards: Type:** grant.

11295 ■ Society for Research in Child Development (SRCD)
c/o University of Michigan
3131 S State St., Ste.302
Ann Arbor, MI 48108-1623
Ph: (734)998-6578
Fax: (734)998-6569
E-mail: info@srcd.org
URL: http://www.srcd.org
Contact: Dr. John W. Hagen, Exec. Off.
Founded: 1933. **Members:** 5,500. **Membership Dues:** regular, $150 (annual) ● spouse, $65 (annual) ● graduate student, undergraduate affiliate plus, $75 (annual) ● postdoc, $95 (annual) ● undergraduate affiliate basic, $35 (annual). **Staff:** 15. **Description:** Professional interdisciplinary society composed of anthropologists, educators, nutritionists, pediatricians, physiologists, psychiatrists, psychologists, sociologists, and statisticians. Works to further research in the area of child development. **Telecommunication Services:** electronic mail, jwhagen@umich.edu. **Committees:** Ethnic and Racial; Ethnical Conduct; History; International Affairs; Policy and Communications; Programs; Publications. **Publications:** *Child Development*, bimonthly. Journal. Contains original contributions on topics in child development. **Price:** $325.00/year. ISSN: 0009-3920. **Circulation:** 8,500. **Advertising:** accepted. Alternate Formats: microform. Also Cited As: *CD* ● *Developments*, quarterly. Newsletter. **Advertising:** accepted ● *Monographs of the Society for Research in Child Development*, quarterly. Provides detailed research studies and findings in child development. ISSN: 0037-976X. Alternate Formats: microform ● *Social Policy Report*, quarterly. Serves as a forum for scholarly reviews of developmental research. **Price:** $5.00/issue; $20.00/year. Alternate Formats: online. Also Cited As: *SPR* ● Membership Directory. Alternate Formats: online. **Conventions/Meetings:** biennial meeting (exhibits) - odd numbered years. 2009 Apr. 2-4, Denver, CO.

11296 ■ Supporting Our Sons (SOS)
555 Bryant St., No. 527
Palo Alto, CA 94301
Free: (866)687-7667
E-mail: members@supportingoursons.org
URL: http://www.supportingoursons.org
Contact: Lisen Stromberg, Pres./Chm.
Description: Promotes a better understanding of boyhood. Empowers parents, educators and professionals to support the development of young sons. Addresses the issues affecting boys to support their healthy development and help them become fully integrated adults. **Publications:** Newsletter, monthly.

11297 ■ U.S.A. Toy Library Association (USA-TLA)
1326 Wilmette Ave.
Wilmette, IL 60091
Ph: (847)920-9030
Fax: (847)920-9032
E-mail: usatla@aol.com
URL: http://usatla.deltacollege.org
Contact: Judith Q. Iacuzzi, Exec. Dir.
Founded: 1984. **Members:** 250. **Membership Dues:** individual outside U.S. and Canada, $60 (annual) ● comprehensive outside U.S. and Canada, $175 (annual) ● student, $15 (annual) ● patron, $5,000 (annual) ● sustainer, $1,000-$4,999 (annual) ● contributor, $166-$999 (annual). **Staff:** 1. **Budget:** $20,000. **Regional Groups:** 1. **State Groups:** 1. **Description:** Child care professionals, parents, and others interested in the role of toys and play in child development. Promotes the importance of play and the

development of toy libraries in public and school libraries, hospitals, day care centers, and mobile collections. Seeks to broaden understanding of how toys can educate, increase parent-child interaction, and aid in development and therapy of disabled children. **Awards:** Outstanding Player of the Year. **Frequency:** annual. **Type:** recognition. **Recipient:** for contributions to children and toy library development/expansion. **Committees:** International Representative. **Publications:** *Child's Play*, quarterly. Newsletter. Provides information on toys, preschool child development, events in toy libraries, recommended reading, toy science, and play. **Price:** included in membership dues. **Circulation:** 700. **Advertising:** accepted ● *Directory of Toy Libraries in the United States*, semiannual ● *Play is a Child's Work*. Video. **Price:** $10.00 for members; $20.00 for nonmembers ● *Toy Librarian Operators Manual*, periodic. **Price:** $12.00 for members; $24.00 for nonmembers. **Conventions/Meetings:** periodic National Toy Forum - conference (exhibits) ● regional meeting ● workshop, on play and toy library operations.

11298 ■ William T. Grant Foundation
570 Lexington Ave., 18th Fl.
New York, NY 10022-6837
Ph: (212)752-0071
Fax: (212)752-1398
E-mail: info@wtgrantfdn.org
URL: http://www.wtgrantfoundation.org
Contact: Robert Granger EdD, Pres.
Founded: 1936. **Multinational. Description:** Helps create a society that values young people and enables them to reach their full potential. Invests in research and in activities designed to improve the quality of research and the use of empirical evidence. Supports research on how contexts and settings such as families, schools, and programs affect youth, how these contexts can be improved, and how influential policymakers and practitioners use scientific evidence. **Awards: Type:** grant. **Programs:** Public's View of Youth; Systems Affecting Youth; Youth Development.

11299 ■ World Organization for Human Potential (WOHP)
8801 Stenton Ave.
Wyndmoor, PA 19038
Ph: (215)233-2050
Fax: (215)233-9312
E-mail: institutes@iahp.org
URL: http://www.iahp.org
Contact: Glenn Domann, Founder
Founded: 1968. **Languages:** English, French, German, Italian, Japanese, Spanish. **Description:** Physicians, human developmentalists, anthropologists, and educators engaged in the evaluation and treatment of brain-injured children and in the development of so-called normal children. Objectives are: to identify and promote social, cultural, and political customs and practices that foster and accelerate the progress of children of the world toward achievement of their potential; to abet such customs and practices and encourage their use; to identify and prevent or correct customs and practices that slow or retard the progress of children toward achievement of their potential. Promotes international exchange of information and prominent scholars in the human sciences; encourages recognition of excellence in the achievement of human potential. **Awards:** Spectrum Award. **Frequency:** annual. **Type:** recognition. **Recipient:** for unique contributions to human potential. **Conventions/Meetings:** annual conference - always May, Philadelphia, PA.

Child Health

11300 ■ Child Family Health International (CFHI)
995 Market St., Ste.1104
San Francisco, CA 94103
Ph: (415)957-9000
Free: (866)345-4674
Fax: (415)840-0486

E-mail: info@cfhi.org
URL: http://www.cfhi.org
Contact: Ajoy Mallik MBA, Chair
Founded: 1992. **Staff:** 6. **Budget:** $2,700,000. **Multinational. Description:** Builds and strengthens sustainable healthcare services in underserved communities worldwide. Builds health infrastructure at the community level. Increases access to and efficient use of medical supplies. Promotes cultural competency and awareness of international health issues. **Computer Services:** Mailing lists. **Programs:** Andean Health In Quito, Ecuador; Community Medicine In Ecuador; Cultural Crossroads In Health, Oaxaca, Mexico; Healthcare Challenges In South Africa; Infectious Disease In Mumbai, India; Pediatric Health In La Paz, Bolivia; Recover; Rural Himalayan Rotation, India. **Affiliated With:** Independent Charities of America; International Volunteer Programs Association.

11301 ■ Children's Cross Connection International (CCCI)
c/o Pamela M. Rundle, CEO
220 Avon Dr.
Fayetteville, GA 30215
Ph: (770)716-1926
E-mail: pam@cccinternational.org
URL: http://www.cccinternational.org
Contact: Pamela M. Rundle, CEO
Founded: 1985. **Multinational. Description:** Provides services to underprivileged children worldwide. Expands the availability of medical care to children in different countries. Provides surgical intervention and education for local medical professionals.

Child Welfare

11302 ■ Action for Child Protection (ACP)
2101 Sardis Rd. N, Ste.204
Charlotte, NC 28227
Ph: (704)845-2121
Fax: (704)845-8577
E-mail: kay.thomas@actionchildprotection.org
URL: http://www.actionchildprotection.org
Contact: Kay Thomas, Contact
Founded: 1984. **Staff:** 8. **Budget:** $650,000. **Description:** Offers innovative and assertive strengthening and improvement of the child welfare system. Encourages public and private partnerships through a multi-disciplinary approach. Provides programs and initiatives directed by staff that is strengthened by a national network of multi-disciplinary expert professionals. Works to create opportunities that increase the competence of professionals in child welfare services and to provide tools and processes that enhance the effectiveness of agencies and organizations that are involved in child protection, foster care, adoption, and youth services. **Convention/Meeting:** none. **Publications:** *Assessing Safety Influences*. Video. Presents five interviewing vignettes focusing on the identification and examination of threats to child safety. **Price:** $50.00 ● *The Collins Family*. Video. Consists of a series of interviews with prospective foster parents to assess their appropriateness in providing foster care. **Price:** $75.00 ● *The Dutton - McAdams Family*. Video. Contains a discussion on forming a family partnership to protect the child. **Price:** $75.00 ● *The Leman Family*. Video. Shows interviews with a troubled, depressed 15 year old boy and his depressed, verbally inaccessible, neglectful mother. **Price:** $25.00 ● *The Smith Family*. Video. Provides a demonstration of a family-based approach during initial contact of a substance abuse case situation involving lack of supervision. **Price:** $75.00.

11303 ■ Africamix
Address Unknown since 2006
Multinational. Description: Traveling arts and music festival dedicated to promoting public awareness and funding for the prevention of child abuse and neglect in black communities; provides residential services and therapeutic foster care for abandoned, abused and neglected children. **Telecommunication Services:** electronic mail, beatriceg@africamix.com.

Conventions/Meetings: festival and tour, provides a forum for guest speakers to promote awareness of the ongoing impact of child abuse, will travel around the world covering at least 20 countries - two-days.

11304 ■ Alliance for Transforming the Lives of Children (aTLC)

901 Preston Ave., Ste.400
Charlottesville, VA 22903
Ph: (206)666-4301
Free: (888)574-7580
Fax: (206)666-4301
E-mail: info@atlc.org
URL: http://www.atlc.org
Contact: Meryn Callander, Pres.
Description: Promotes innovative and progressive educational programs, services, products, and public policies that are committed to transforming the lives of children. Encourages a culture of compassionate individuals, families, and communities who have fun with, learn from, and responsively and lovingly interact with children. **Publications:** *aTLC eNews.* Newsletter. Contains information about the organization's activities. Alternate Formats: online ● *Proclamation and Blueprint.* Brochure. **Price:** $2.00 printed copy. Alternate Formats: online.

11305 ■ American Bar Association Center on Children and the Law

740 15th St. NW
Washington, DC 20005-1019
Ph: (202)662-1720
Free: (800)285-2221
Fax: (202)662-1755
E-mail: ctrchildlaw@abanet.org
URL: http://www.abanet.org/child
Contact: Howard Davidson, Dir.
Founded: 1978. **Members:** 400,000. **Staff:** 18. **Description:** Information clearinghouse that provides attorneys with technical assistance, legal advice, and training in the area of children's legal rights. Disseminates information on foster care, termination of parental rights, child abuse reporting, and other children's legal issues. Seeks to influence legislation affecting children's rights; trains state child welfare agency personnel. Conducts legal research on the evolution of children's rights in the U.S. Operated by the Young Lawyer's Division of the American Bar Association. **Libraries: Type:** reference. **Holdings:** books, monographs, periodicals. **Subjects:** children's law. **Awards:** Child Advocate Appreciation. **Frequency:** annual. **Type:** recognition. **Recipient:** for legal advocacy on behalf of children. **Formerly:** (1989) National Legal Resource Center for Child Advocacy and Protection. **Publications:** *ABA Child Law Practice,* monthly. Newsletter. Provides practical advice for child welfare attorneys. **Price:** $199.00 /year for institutions; $169.00 /year for individuals. ISSN: 0887-896X. **Circulation:** 1,000 ● *Children's Legal Rights Journal,* quarterly ● Catalog. **Price:** free. Alternate Formats: online. **Conventions/Meetings:** Children's Legal Rights Conference - every 18 months.

11306 ■ American Humane Association Children's Services (AHA)

63 Inverness Dr. E
Englewood, CO 80112-5117
Ph: (303)792-9900
Free: (800)227-4645
Fax: (303)792-5333
E-mail: children@americanhumane.org
URL: http://www.americanhumane.org/site/
PageServer?pagename=pc_about
Contact: Marie Belew Wheatley, Pres./CEO
Founded: 1877. **Members:** 1,500. **Membership Dues:** individual, $59 (annual) ● agency, $119 (annual). **Staff:** 30. **Budget:** $2,000,000. **Description:** Children's division of the American Humane Association (see separate entry). Individuals and agencies who seek to protect children from neglect and abuse. Works to insure effective and responsive community child protective services. Provides comprehensive in-service training for professionals, including social workers, physicians, teachers, and law enforcement personnel. Offers evaluation and technical assistance

to community and state child protective programs. Conducts ongoing research into the nature and course of child maltreatment. Advocates national and state legislation and policy to protect children. **Libraries: Type:** reference. **Holdings:** 3,000; articles, books, periodicals. **Subjects:** child abuse, child welfare, family violence, public policy. **Awards:** Vincent DeFrancis Award. **Frequency:** annual. **Type:** recognition. **Computer Services:** database ● electronic publishing, catalog of library services. **Affiliated With:** American Humane Association Children's Services. **Formerly:** American Association for Protecting Children; (2000) American Humane Association Children's Division. **Publications:** *Helping in Child Protective Services: A Competency-based Casework Handbook* ● *Innovations for Children's Services in the 21st Century.* Book ● *Partnering with Families to Reform Services: Managed Care in Child Welfare.* Book ● *Protecting Children,* quarterly. Journal. Reports on research and programs concerned with child abuse, protection, and related social work. Includes book reviews and federal legislative news. **Price:** included in membership dues; $40.00 /year for libraries. ISSN: 0893-4231 ● *Understanding the Medical Diagnosis of Child Maltreatment.* Book ● *Visual Assessment of Physical Child Abuse.* Book ● Also distributes children's drawing, stickers and bookmarks. **Conventions/Meetings:** bimonthly roundtable.

11307 ■ American Professional Society on the Abuse of Children (APSAC)

PO Box 30669
Charleston, SC 29417
Ph: (843)764-2905
Free: (877)402-7722
Fax: (803)753-9823
E-mail: apsac@comcast.net
URL: http://www.APSAC.org
Contact: Daphne Wright, Operations Mgr.
Founded: 1987. **Members:** 2,200. **Membership Dues:** student in U.S., $65 (annual) ● individual in U.S. (income under $30,000), $75 (annual) ● individual in U.S. (income between $30,000 and $50,000), $100 (annual) ● individual in U.S. (income over $50,000), $125 (annual). **Staff:** 5. **Budget:** $1,000,000. **State Groups:** 35. **Description:** Psychologists, social workers, physicians, attorneys, nurses, law enforcement personnel, child protective services and mental health workers, administrators, researchers, and allied disciplines in the field of child abuse and neglect. Seeks to ensure that everyone affected by child maltreatment receives the best possible professional response, by promoting effective interdisciplinary approaches to the identification, intervention, treatment, and prevention of child abuse and neglect. Aims to advance professional education by offering interdisciplinary national training programs; works to improve coordination among professionals and to develop national interdisciplinary professional guidelines; encourages research in all fields of child maltreatment; disseminates research to professionals; provides guidance, support, and encouragement for professionals; and educates legislators, the public, and the media about the complex issues of child maltreatment. **Libraries: Type:** reference. **Subjects:** child maltreatment. **Awards:** Outstanding Doctoral Dissertation Award. **Frequency:** annual. **Type:** recognition. **Recipient:** for a doctoral dissertation completed within the past calendar year that made the most outstanding contribution to research on child abuse ● Outstanding Media Coverage Award. **Frequency:** annual. **Type:** recognition. **Recipient:** for outstanding coverage of issues relating to child abuse and neglect ● Outstanding Professional Award. **Frequency:** annual. **Type:** recognition. **Recipient:** for outstanding contributions to the field of child maltreatment and the advancement of APSAC's goals ● Outstanding Research Study Award. **Frequency:** annual. **Type:** recognition. **Recipient:** for authors of a research article or book published that is judged to be the most significant contribution to the study of child abuse during the past year ● Outstanding Service Award. **Frequency:** annual. **Type:** recognition. **Recipient:** for outstanding contributions to APSAC through leadership and service to the society ●

President's Honor Roll Award. **Frequency:** annual. **Type:** recognition. **Recipient:** for members who display exceptional commitment to the field of child maltreatment and the advancement of APSAC's goals ● Research Career Achievement Award. **Frequency:** annual. **Type:** recognition. **Recipient:** for repeated, significant, and outstanding contributions to research on child maltreatment. **Task Forces:** Family Reunification; Investigative Interviewing of Children; Medical Evaluation of Suspected Child Abuse; Prevention of Child Fatalities; Psychological Maltreatment; Psychosocial Evaluation of Suspected Sexual Abuse in Young Children; Psychosocial Evaluation of Trauma History and Memory; Treatment of Sexually Abused Children; Use of Anatomically Detailed Dolls. **Publications:** *APSAC Advisor,* quarterly. Newsletter. Contains articles, reports, book reviews, legislative updates, and conference listings of interest to professionals in the field of child abuse. **Price:** included in membership dues. **Circulation:** 4,000. **Advertising:** accepted ● *APSAC Handbook on Child Maltreatment* ● *APSAC Study Guides on Child Maltreatment* ● *Child Maltreatment,* quarterly. Journal. Contains peer-reviewed research and interdisciplinary articles on child maltreatment. **Circulation:** 45,000. **Advertising:** accepted. **Conventions/Meetings:** annual conference, intensive training seminars and field-generated skills training and research presented by interdisciplinary experts in the field of child abuse and neglect (exhibits).

11308 ■ America's Children Hunger Network (ACHN)

c/o Ruby J. Aime, Pres.
25263 N 67th Dr.
Peoria, AZ 85383
Ph: (623)376-0727
Fax: (623)376-0732
E-mail: rjaime0344@aol.com
URL: http://www.americaschildrenshunger.org
Contact: Ruby J. Aime, Pres.
Multinational. Description: Works to improve the quality of life of needy children and their families. Focuses on the survival of children worldwide. Implements programs that provide food, clothing and spiritual education to children and their families.

11309 ■ Association of Administrators of the Interstate Compact on the Placement of Children (AAICPC)

c/o American Public Human Services Association
810 1st St. NE, Ste.500
Washington, DC 20002
Ph: (202)682-0100
Fax: (202)289-6555
E-mail: icpcinbox@aphsa.org
URL: http://icpc.aphsa.org
Contact: Larry Yarberough, Pres.
Founded: 1974. **Members:** 52. **Staff:** 5. **Description:** State public social service agency personnel who have been appointed compact administrators and who are responsible for the operation of the Interstate Compact on the Placement of Children. (ICPC is a uniform law that has been enacted in 50 states, the District of Columbia, and the Virgin Islands. Governs the placement of children across state lines for foster care and pre-adoptive placement by legally establishing the extension of responsibility and jurisdiction of the sending party, and the concomitant responsibility of the receiving state.) Enhances arrangements for the delivery of protective and supportive services in situations having interjurisdictional considerations. Provides forum for cooperation, consultation, and exchange of information among the states in relation to the placement of children from one state to another. Compiles statistics. **Affiliated With:** American Public Human Services Association. **Publications:** *Compact Administrators' Manual.* Contains the language of ICPC, the regulations that are promulgated under the ICPC, opinions and extensive information about ICPC contact personnel. **Price:** $125.00 plus shipping and handling ● *Guidebook to the ICPC.* Offers a user friendly, comprehensive discussion of the history, purposes and administration of the Compact. Alternate Formats: online ● *Understanding Criminal Records Checks.* Report.

Alternate Formats: online. **Conventions/Meetings:** annual meeting.

11310 ■ Association of Sites Advocating Child Protection (ASACP)
5042 Wilshire Blvd., No. 540
Los Angeles, CA 90036-4305
Ph: (323)908-7864
Fax: (323)734-1577
E-mail: comments@asacp.org
URL: http://www.asacp.org
Contact: Joan Irvine, Exec. Dir.
Founded: 1996. **Membership Dues:** executive, $2,400 (annual) ● crusader, $1,200 (annual) ● guardian, $300 (annual) ● supporter, $50 (annual). **Description:** Helps the adult site industry make a difference in the battle against child pornography. Recognizes sexual child abuse as a heinous crime committed against children. Provides an online hotline for webmasters and surfers to report suspected child pornography. Reviews and reports validated child pornography sites to the appropriate government agencies and related associations. **Telecommunication Services:** electronic mail, info@asacp.org ● electronic mail, membership@asacp.org. **Publications:** Newsletter. **Price:** included in membership dues.

11311 ■ Bethany Christian Services International (BCSI)
901 Eastern Ave. NE
PO Box 294
Grand Rapids, MI 49501-0294
Ph: (616)224-7610 (616)224-7617
Free: (800)BETHANY
E-mail: info@bethany.org
URL: http://www.bethany.org
Contact: Bill Blacquiere, Pres.
Founded: 1944. **Description:** Christian social service organizations operating child welfare programs worldwide. Seeks to improve the quality of life and the availability of educational and economic opportunity for children. Provides support and services to programs pursuing similar goals; conducts religious, educational, public health, and family service programs. **Computer Services:** Online services.

11312 ■ Black Community Crusade for Children (BCCC)
25 E St. NW
Washington, DC 20001
Ph: (202)628-8787
Fax: (202)662-3580
E-mail: cdfinfo@childrensdefense.org
URL: http://www.childrensdefense.org/bccc
Contact: Mrs. Marian Wright Edelman, Founder/Pres.
Description: African-American clergy, educators, policy makers, and community leaders. Seeks to ensure that "no child is left behind, and that every child has a Healthy Start, a Head Start, a Fair Start, a Safe Start, and a Moral Start in life, with the support of caring parents and nurturing communities." Works to mobilize the Black community on behalf of children. Conducts programs in areas including: community building; spiritual, character, and leadership development; intergenerational mentoring; interracial and interethnic communication; interdisciplinary networking; training. Organizes Freedom Schools, which provide meals and education and cultural enrichment programs in local communities. Operates Student Leadership Network for Children (SLNC); maintains farm once owned by African-American author Alex Haley.

11313 ■ Care for Children International (CCI)
c/o Neuropsychological and Family Therapy Associates
400 S Washington St.
Alexandria, VA 22314
Ph: (703)548-0721
E-mail: careforchildren@aol.com
URL: http://www.careforchildreninternational.com
Contact: Dr. Ronald Steven Federici, Pres./CEO
Founded: 1999. **Members:** 40. **Staff:** 2. **Languages:** English, Romanian. **Multinational. Description:** Medical team, specialized experts and volunteers. Provides medical and psychiatric care to children residing in institutions in Eastern Europe and Southeast Asia. **Publications:** Help for the Hopeless Child: A Guide for Families. Book. Contains information on understanding, recognizing symptoms, and treating the effects of institutionalization in adoptive children.

11314 ■ Catholic Guardian Society (CGS)
1011 1st Ave.
New York, NY 10022
Ph: (212)371-1000
Fax: (212)758-5892
E-mail: jfrein@cgshb.org
Contact: John J. Frein, Exec. Dir.
Founded: 1908. **Staff:** 680. **Budget:** $37,000,000. **Description:** Cares for dependent, neglected, abused, and delinquent children. Operates group homes, foster homes, agency-operated boarding homes, and adoption services. Operates intermediate care facilities for profoundly retarded or developmentally disabled children and adults. Provides medical, mental health, and respite care. Offers a foster home program for HIV infected children.

11315 ■ Child Abuse Listening and Mediation (CALM)
1236 Chapala St.
PO Box 90754
Santa Barbara, CA 93101
Ph: (805)965-2376
Fax: (805)963-6707
E-mail: info@calm4kids.org
URL: http://www.calm4kids.org
Contact: Anna M. Kokotovic PhD, Exec. Dir.
Founded: 1970. **Staff:** 45. **Budget:** $1,000,000. **Languages:** English, Spanish. **Description:** Social service program to prevent and treat child sexual abuse, physical abuse, and emotional abuse, and offer early intervention for stressed families. Aims to reach parents "who feel that they cannot cope with their problems and frustrations and who may be in danger of taking out their feelings against their children." Offers parent education and individual or joint counseling to parents who may be in danger of abusing. Maintains speakers' bureau and resource library. Conducts program of public information and education and an in-school education program for students, parents, and teachers on prevention and recognition of child maltreatment. Other services include: individual, marital, and family counseling for high risk families and families involved in physical, emotional, or sexual abuse and neglect, and supports treatment groups for adults who were molested as children. Offers counseling groups for adult offenders legally ordered to seek counseling. Offers in-home family therapy for families referred by county mental health departments; in-house support for families at risk of abuse or neglect; and individual, family, and group counseling for children exposed to domestic violence. All services are offered in English and Spanish. **Committees:** Clinical; Liaison; Outreach; Policy; Public Relations. **Programs:** Family Violence Counseling; Parenting; Therapeutic Foster Care. **Absorbed:** Protecting and Caring Together. **Formerly:** Children's Protective Society. **Publications:** CALMWORD, quarterly. Newsletter ● Chronicle, monthly. Newsletter ● Bibliography. Covers battered child syndrome, child sexual abuse, and a report of CALM's work. ● Annual Report, annual. Alternate Formats: online. **Conventions/Meetings:** annual meeting.

11316 ■ Child Find of America
PO Box 277
New Paltz, NY 12561-0277
Ph: (845)691-4666
Free: (800)I-AM-LOST
Fax: (845)691-7766
E-mail: information@childfindamerica.org
URL: http://www.childfindofamerica.org
Contact: Donna Linder, Exec. Dir.
Founded: 1980. **Staff:** 7. **Budget:** $250,000. **Description:** Purpose is to bring missing children home. Prevents child abduction and locates missing children through investigation, photo distribution, mediation, and public information. Operates location, mediation, and public information programs. **Convention/Meeting:** none. **Telecommunication Services:** additional toll-free number, for mediation, (800)A-WAY-OUT. **Programs:** CAPSS; Location; Mediation; Public Information. **Formerly:** (1986) Child Find. **Publications:** Annual Fiscal Report, annual. Contains fundraising information, and news of missing children. **Price:** free ● Annual Report, annual. Alternate Formats: online.

11317 ■ Child Labor Coalition (CLC)
c/o National Consumers League
1701 K St. NW, Ste.1200
Washington, DC 20006
Ph: (202)835-3323
Fax: (202)835-0747
E-mail: childlabor@nclnet.org
URL: http://www.stopchildlabor.org
Contact: Darlene Adkins, Coor.
Founded: 1989. **Members:** 77. **Staff:** 1. **Budget:** $90,000. **State Groups:** 8. **National Groups:** 69. **Multinational. Description:** Promotes health, safety, education and well being for working minors; seeks to end child labor exploitation. **Publications:** Child Labor Monitor, weekly. Newsletter. **Price:** free. Alternate Formats: online.

11318 ■ Child Quest International (CQI)
1060 N 4th St., Ste.200
San Jose, CA 95112
Ph: (408)287-4673
Free: (888)818-HOPE
Fax: (408)287-4676
E-mail: info@childquest.org
URL: http://www.childquest.org
Founded: 1990. **Staff:** 17. **Budget:** $300,000. **Languages:** English, Spanish. **Multinational. Description:** Works for the protection and recovery of missing, abused, and exploited children, and at-risk adults internationally. Offers technical support and referrals for abused and exploited children nationwide. Provides investigative and photo dissemination worldwide for rescue of runaways, children abducted by non-custodial parents and stranger kidnappings. Provides support and referral services (all services are at no charge and available 24-hours a day.) Conducts educational programs to schools, clubs, and communities. Maintains Speaker's Bureau. **Libraries:** Type: reference; open to the public. **Subjects:** kidnapping prevention, child abuse. **Awards:** Search and Safety Van. **Type:** monetary. **Computer Services:** database, of sex offenders ● information services, child safety tips ● mailing lists. **Programs:** Our Kids are Safe Kids; Vendors Important Contribution Towards Our Recovered Youth. **Publications:** Child Quest International Newsletter, semiannual ● For the Love of a Child, quarterly. Brochure ● Annual Report, annual ● Produces and distributes missing children posters.

11319 ■ Child Relief and You America (CRY America)
PO Box 850948
Braintree, MA 02185-0948
Ph: (339)235-0792 (617)959-1273
E-mail: support@cryamerica.org
URL: http://www.america.cry.org
Contact: Shefali Sunderlal, Pres.
Multinational. Description: Works to restore the basic rights of underprivileged children. Acts as a link between people who want to help the underprivileged child and the child in need. Supports organizations and initiatives that enhance the capacity and quality of grassroots initiatives.

11320 ■ Child Welfare Information Gateway
c/o Children's Bureau/ACYF
1250 Maryland Ave. SW, 8th Fl.
Washington, DC 20024
Ph: (703)385-7565
Free: (800)394-3366
Fax: (703)385-3206

E-mail: info@childwelfare.gov
URL: http://www.childwelfare.gov
Contact: Mary Sullivan, Project Dir.
Founded: 1975. **Staff:** 30. **Languages:** English, Spanish. **Description:** Works to connect professionals and concerned citizens to timely and well-balanced information on programs, research, legislation, and statistics regarding the safety, permanency, and well-being of children and families. **Libraries: Type:** reference. **Holdings:** 39,000. **Subjects:** child abuse and neglect, child welfare, adoption, foster care. **Computer Services:** database, bibliography of professional literature concerning all aspects of child maltreatment and child welfare, including adoption. **Formed by Merger of:** (2005) National Clearinghouse on Child Abuse and Neglect Information and National Adoption Information Clearinghouse. **Formerly:** (1994) Clearinghouse on Child Abuse and Neglect Information. **Publications:** Brochures ● Catalogs ● Manuals ● Pamphlets ● Reports ● Bulletins.

11321 ■ Child Welfare Institute (CWI)

111 E Wacker Dr., Ste.325
Chicago, IL 60601
Ph: (312)949-5640
Fax: (312)922-6736
E-mail: bskidmore@gocwi.org
URL: http://www.gocwi.org
Contact: Elizabeth A. Skidmore, Exec. VP
Founded: 1984. **Staff:** 12. **Budget:** $3,000,000. **Description:** Individuals interested in child welfare issues. Supports programs promoting foster parenting, adoption, reunification of foster children with their birthparents, child abuse and neglect, and other issues. Disseminates information to the public; provides organizational development and training consultation services. Houses the National Resource Center on Child Maltreatment. **Libraries: Type:** reference. **Holdings:** 400. **Computer Services:** database. **Publications:** CWI Commentary, bimonthly. Newsletter. **Circulation:** 500. Alternate Formats: online ● CWI Profiles, bimonthly. Newsletter. **Circulation:** 500 ● Ideas in Action, monthly. Newsletter. **Price:** free. **Circulation:** 500. Alternate Formats: online ● Making a Difference That Matters. Newsletter. Features brief practice articles. Alternate Formats: online. **Conventions/Meetings:** annual Recruitment and Retention - conference and seminar.

11322 ■ Child Welfare League of America (CWLA)

2345 Crystal Dr., Ste.250
Arlington, VA 22202
Ph: (703)412-2400
Fax: (703)412-2401
E-mail: register@cwla.org
URL: http://www.cwla.org
Contact: Shay Bilchik, Pres./CEO
Founded: 1920. **Members:** 1,100. **Staff:** 130. **Budget:** $17,500,000. **Regional Groups:** 6. **Description:** Works to improve care and services for abused, dependent, or neglected children, youth, and their families. Provides training and consultation; conducts research; maintains information service and develops standards for child welfare practice. **Libraries: Type:** reference. **Holdings:** 8,000. **Subjects:** child welfare. **Awards:** Anna Quindlen Award for Journalism. **Frequency:** annual. **Type:** recognition. **Recipient:** for individuals in the field of journalism ● **Frequency:** annual. **Type:** recognition. **Recipient:** for management, board, and direct service ● **Type:** scholarship. **Computer Services:** Mailing lists, subscribers, book buyers, conference attendees, legislative activities, membership information. **Divisions:** Behavioral Health; Juvenile Justice. **Programs:** Adoption; Behavioral Support and Intervention; Child Protection; CWLA Internship; Domestic Violence; Family Preservation and Permanency Planning. **Absorbed:** (1976) Florence Crittenton Association of American. **Publications:** Child Welfare, bimonthly. Journal. Provides articles for policy makers, researchers, and professionals who work with children. **Price:** $84.00/year for students; $110.00 /year for individuals; $150.00 /year for institutions. ISSN: 0009-4021. **Advertising:** accepted. Alternate Formats: microform.

Also Cited As: CWLA Journal ● Children's Monitor. Newsletter. Alternate Formats: online ● Children's Voice, bimonthly. Magazine. Reports on program and policy developments in child welfare services. Covers congressional, federal, and state news, and contains articles. **Price:** included in membership dues; $25.00 /year for nonmembers; $40.00 /year for nonmembers outside U.S. **Advertising:** accepted ● Flagging Child Abuse. Newsletter. **Price:** free. Alternate Formats: online ● The Link, quarterly. Newsletter. Alternate Formats: online ● Residential Group Care Quarterly. Newsletter. Alternate Formats: online ● WeR4Kdz. Bulletin. Alternate Formats: online ● Books ● Monographs. **Conventions/Meetings:** annual conference (exhibits) - always February, Washington, DC ● biennial conference - always even-numbered years.

11323 ■ Childcare Worldwide

715 W Orchard Dr., Ste.7
Bellingham, WA 98225-1767
Ph: (360)647-2283
Free: (800)553-2328
Fax: (360)647-2392
E-mail: info@childcareworldwide.org
URL: http://www.childcareworldwide.org
Contact: Dr. G. Max Lange, Pres./Founder
Founded: 1981. **Staff:** 18. **Nonmembership. Multinational. Description:** Focuses on meeting the needs of the poor, with emphasis on children, through a social, medical and spiritual ministry based on the Gospel of Jesus Christ. Programs help feed hungry children and their families, and help children receive an education that leads to employment. **Telecommunication Services:** electronic mail, gmlange@childcareworldwide.org. **Formerly:** (2006) Childcare International. **Publications:** Newsletter. Alternate Formats: online ● Annual Report, annual. Alternate Formats: online.

11324 ■ Children of the Americas (COA)

c/o W.O. Mills, III, Pres.
PO Box 140165
Dallas, TX 75214-0165
Ph: (214)823-7000
Free: (800)827-3923
Fax: (214)823-7991
E-mail: wom@womills.com
Contact: W.O. Mills III, Pres.
Founded: 1979. **Members:** 600. **Staff:** 2. **Languages:** English, Spanish. **Description:** Individuals and organizations committed to aiding orphaned or abandoned children ages 6 through 16 who live on the streets. Provides first aid and emergency medical care, counseling, and social services. Conducts student/faculty research programs; sponsors student and volunteer street healthcare workers. Efforts are currently concentrated in Santo Domingo, Dominican Republic, and Bogota, Colombia. Maintains speakers' bureau; offers photo service. **Awards: Frequency:** annual. **Type:** recognition. **Committees:** Development; Supplies; Volunteers. **Publications:** A Global Perspective on Gamins. Newsletter ● COA Update, quarterly. Newsletter ● Health Care in the Street. **Conventions/Meetings:** periodic symposium.

11325 ■ Children Now

1212 Broadway, 5th Fl.
Oakland, CA 94612
Ph: (510)763-2444
Fax: (510)763-1974
E-mail: info@childrennow.org
URL: http://www.childrennow.org
Contact: Ted Lempert, Pres.
Founded: 1988. **Staff:** 25. **Budget:** $2,500,000. **Nonmembership. Description:** Research and action organization dedicated to assuring that children grow up in economically secure families, where parents can go to work confident that their children are supported by quality health coverage, a positive media environment, a good early education, and safe, enriching activities after school. Strategies are designed to improve children's lives while at the same time help America build a sustained commitment to putting children first. **Publications:** California County Data Book, biennial. Contains county-level statistics about California children. **Price:** $15.00. Alternate

Formats: online ● California Report Card 2004, annual. Provides a comprehensive snapshot of the status of children in California. Alternate Formats: online ● Fall Colors: Prime Time Diversity Report. Contains analysis of diversity on television. Alternate Formats: online. **Conventions/Meetings:** Media Conference, press briefing on various issues by invitation only.

11326 ■ Children of Russia

4117 Kahala Ave.
Honolulu, HI 96816
Ph: (808)737-5248
Fax: (808)737-7806
E-mail: nowen@lava.net
URL: http://www.leahi.net/russia
Contact: Natasha Owen, Pres./Founder
Founded: 2000. **Multinational. Description:** Advocates for the children of Russia. Works to collects art supplies for classes at a children's oncology center; provides a program of social rehabilitation for children suffering from tuberculosis.

11327 ■ Children's HopeChest

PO Box 8627
Pueblo, CO 81008
Ph: (719)487-7800
Free: (800)648-9575
Fax: (719)487-7799
E-mail: chc@hopechest.org
URL: http://www.hopechest.org
Contact: George Steiner, CEO/Founder
Founded: 1994. **Staff:** 80. **Multinational. Description:** Aids orphans in their journey toward independent living. Provides practical help to orphans while they are in the orphanage and after they have left. Offers programs that take orphans out of the social isolation of the orphanage and place them into a community.

11328 ■ Children's Network International (CNI)

PO Box 911607
Los Angeles, CA 90091
Ph: (323)980-9870
Free: (877)264-2243
Fax: (323)980-9878
E-mail: info@childrensnetworkinternational.org
URL: http://www.childrensnetworkinternational.org
Contact: Roger Presgrove, Founder/Pres./CEO
Multinational. Description: Works to help alleviate the suffering of children and their families throughout the United States and around the world. Provides increased self sufficiency by providing food, clothing, personal care items and medical supplies regardless of political affiliation, religious belief or ethnic identity. Serves a wide variety of people in diverse cultural and economic settings, who suffer emotional, spiritual and physical needs.

11329 ■ The Children's Partnership (TCP)

2000 P St. NW, Ste.330
Washington, DC 20036
Ph: (202)429-0033
Fax: (202)429-0974
E-mail: frontdoordc@childrenspartnership.org
URL: http://www.childrenspartnership.org
Contact: Laurie Lipper, Founder/Co-Pres.
Description: Ensures disadvantaged children have resources necessary to succeed, and involves Americans in children's issues. **Publications:** Reports, monthly. Deals with children-related issues. Alternate Formats: online.

11330 ■ Children's Relief Network (CRN)

PO Box 668
Deerfield Beach, FL 33443
Ph: (561)620-2970
Free: (800)326-6500
Fax: (561)393-3151
E-mail: coh@romanianchildren.org
URL: http://www.romanianchildren.org
Contact: Angie Thomson, Founder
Founded: 1995. **Multinational. Description:** Aims to bring hope to the hurting, impoverished children and the youth of Romania. Improves the quality of

life of underprivileged children in Romania by providing them with physical, medical and educational resources. **Publications:** Newsletter, monthly. Alternate Formats: online.

11331 ■ Children's Rights of America (CRA)
Address Unknown since 2007
Founded: 1982. **Budget:** $200,000. **Description:** Provides services to families of missing and exploited children. Aids in locating and returning missing children to their homes. Offers consultations to lawyers on interstate statutes pertinent to parent abduction cases. Offers "system failure" assistance in child abuse cases. **Telecommunication Services:** hotline, for youths in crisis. **Formerly:** (1983) Children's Rights of Florida. **Publications:** Brochures. **Conventions/Meetings:** seminar, for law enforcement personnel, mental health professionals, parents, and family groups.

11332 ■ Children's Rights Division - Human Rights Watch
c/o Human Rights Watch
350 5th Ave., 34th Fl.
New York, NY 10118
Ph: (212)290-4700
Fax: (212)736-1300
E-mail: hrwnyc@hrw.org
Contact: Kenneth Roth, Exec. Dir.
Founded: 1994. **Multinational. Description:** Promotes protection of international human rights, including the rights of children. Focuses on issues related to children as participants in armed conflict, including a definition of war crimes (international and non-international armed conflict), and penalties. **Formerly:** (2003) Caucus on Children's Rights.

11333 ■ Children's Safety Network (CSN)
c/o Education Development Center, Inc.
55 Chapel St.
Newton, MA 02458-1060
Ph: (617)618-2230
E-mail: csn@edc.org
URL: http://www.childrenssafetynetwork.org
Contact: Lloyd Potter PhD, Dir.
Description: Consists of four resource centers funded by the Maternal and Child Health Bureau of the U.S. Department of Health and Human Services. Promotes public awareness of childhood injury and violence issues. Works with maternal and child health, public health and other injury prevention practitioners to provide technical assistance and information; facilitates the implementation and evaluation of injury prevention programs; and conducts analytical and policy activities that improve injury and violence prevention. **Publications:** Reports, monthly. Talks about injury and violence prevention. Alternate Formats: online ● Bulletin, monthly. Focuses on specific injury prevention topic. Alternate Formats: online.

11334 ■ Children's Watch International
2918 Yarling Ct.
Falls Church, VA 22042
E-mail: vvonstruen@hotmail.com
URL: http://www.webspawner.com/users/childrens-watch
Contact: Vanessa von Struensee, Contact
Founded: 1994. **Description:** Seeks to improve the quality of children's status and to shelter and care for children's human rights. "Represents and publicizes the needs and human rights of children who are victims of violence, in both domestic situations, such as child prostitution or child labor in hazardous industry, and in armed conflicts in national, international, civil, and ethnic conflicts. Develops and evaluates information on the human rights violations of children throughout the world." Organizes celebrations for children. Monitors nation's compliance with the UN convention on the Rights of the Child. **Libraries: Type:** reference. **Holdings:** 500. **Subjects:** children's human rights, street children, indigenous children, child abuse and neglect, pediatric AIDS, child labor, exploitation, education. **Awards:** Child Advocate of the Year. **Frequency:** annual. **Type:** recognition. **Recipient:** for outstanding children's

advocate worldwide. **Computer Services:** database, links to human rights information. **Publications:** *Children's Watch Annual Report*, annual. **Price:** $20.00.

11335 ■ Commission on Missing and Exploited Children (COMEC)
616 Adams Ave.
Memphis, TN 38105
Ph: (901)405-8441
Fax: (901)405-8542
E-mail: comec@comec.org
URL: http://www.comec.org
Contact: Capt. Len Edwards, Exec. Dir.
Founded: 1984. **Members:** 20. **Staff:** 4. **Budget:** $150,000. **Description:** Referral agency for missing or exploited teens. Offers educational programs, speakers' bureau, children's services, and drug tests. **Libraries: Type:** lending; reference; by appointment only. **Holdings:** books. **Subjects:** violence, drugs, truancy, behavior. **Awards:** Law Enforcement Explorer Scholarship. **Frequency:** annual. **Type:** scholarship. **Computer Services:** Mailing lists, of members. **Telecommunication Services:** hotline, Teen Drug, (901)527-DRUG. **Affiliated With:** National Center for Missing and Exploited Children. **Publications:** Brochures. Alternate Formats: online ● Newsletter, bimonthly. **Conventions/Meetings:** monthly board meeting (exhibits).

11336 ■ Committee for Children (CFC)
568 1st Ave. S, Ste.600
Seattle, WA 98104-2804
Ph: (206)343-1223
Free: (800)634-4449
Fax: (206)438-6765
E-mail: info@cfchildren.org
URL: http://www.cfchildren.org
Contact: Debra Boyer PhD, Pres.
Founded: 1981. **Members:** 17. **Staff:** 95. **Budget:** $8,000,000. **Languages:** English, French, Norwegian, Spanish, Tagalog. **Description:** Promotes the safety, well-being, and social development of children by creating quality educational programs for educators, families, and communities. **Supersedes:** Children's Rights, Inc. **Publications:** *A Family Guide to Second Step*. Report ● *Catalog of Committee for Children-Prevention Education Resources*, semiannual. **Price:** free. **Circulation:** 180,000 ● *Prevention Update*, 3/year. Newsletter. Provides articles for professionals and teachers in the field of prevention education. **Price:** free. **Circulation:** 19,000 ● *Second Step: A Violence Prevention Curriculum*. Video. For pre-K through 9th grade. ● Annual Report, annual. Alternate Formats: online. **Conventions/Meetings:** annual conference - always summer.

11337 ■ Community of Caring
c/o University of Utah
1901 E South Campus Dr., No. 1120
Salt Lake City, UT 84112
Ph: (801)587-8990
Fax: (801)581-3113
E-mail: contact@communityofcaring.org
URL: http://www.communityofcaring.org
Contact: Eunice Kennedy Shriver, Founder/Honorary Chair
Founded: 1982. **Description:** Encourages caring, responsibility, respect, trust and family in America's schools through total community involvement. Addresses destructive attitudes resulting in early sexual involvement, teen pregnancy, substance abuse, and quitting school. Provides teacher training, values discussions, student forums, parent involvement, and service learning. **Awards:** Community of Caring Annual Awards. **Frequency:** annual. **Type:** recognition. **Recipient:** for outstanding groups, organizations, and individuals. **Committees:** Coordinating. **Publications:** Newsletter. Alternate Formats: online ● Brochure. Alternate Formats: online.

11338 ■ Coptic Orphans Support Association (CO)
PO Box 2881
Merrifield, VA 22116
Ph: (703)641-8910
Free: (800)499-2989

Fax: (703)641-8787
E-mail: info@copticorphans.org
URL: http://www.copticorphans.org
Contact: Mrs. Nermien Riad, Founder/Exec. Dir.
Founded: 1989. **Members:** 7. **Staff:** 3. **Languages:** Arabic, English. **Description:** Individuals and organizations with an interest in the welfare of orphans and other children in Egypt. Seeks to end poverty and strengthen the family; promotes population control through education. Conducts educational courses; makes available nutrition and health programs. **Programs:** Emergency Housing; Grant Making; Not Alone; Valuable Girl Project. **Also Known As:** Coptic Orphans.

11339 ■ Darkness to Light
7 Radcliffe St., Ste.200
Charleston, SC 29403
Ph: (843)965-5444
Free: (866)367-5444
Fax: (843)965-5449
E-mail: lturner@d2l.org
URL: http://www.darkness2light.org
Contact: Anne Lee, Pres./CEO
Founded: 1997. **Description:** Educates adults in preventing, recognizing and reacting responsibly to child sexual abuse. Provides training programs to help recognize and prevent abuse. **Computer Services:** Information services, child sexual abuse resources. **Committees:** National Advisory. **Programs:** 7 Steps to Protecting Our Children; Stewards of Children. **Publications:** *7 Steps to Protecting Our Children* (in English and Spanish). Booklet. Presents steps on how to protect children from sexual abuse. **Price:** $9.00/package ● Newsletter. Provides information on how to protect children. Alternate Formats: online.

11340 ■ Find the Children
2656 29th St., Ste.203
Santa Monica, CA 90405
Ph: (310)998-8444
Free: (888)477-6721
Fax: (310)998-8282
E-mail: findthechild@earthlink.net
URL: http://www.findthechildren.com
Contact: Karen Strickland, Exec. Dir.
Founded: 1983. **Staff:** 6. **Budget:** $300,000. **Languages:** English, Spanish. **Description:** Assists families and law enforcement officials in locating missing children through investigation and media exposure; serves as a liaison between parents and law enforcement officials; educates parents and children on child safety; assists other child locating agencies; informs media and public of current information concerning missing children; supports legislation that enhances children's safety; and offers referrals for attorneys, private investigators, counseling services, and other child advocacy groups and programs on prevention of child abuse and neglect. **Computer Services:** database, registered missing children. **Programs:** Parenting Sessions; Stranger Safety. **Publications:** Directory, annual. Lists missing children including pictures. **Price:** free.

11341 ■ Foster Care Alumni of America (FCAA)
118 S Royal St., 2nd Fl.
Alexandria, VA 22314
Ph: (703)299-6767
Free: (888)258-6640
E-mail: admin@fostercarealumni.org
URL: http://www.fostercarealumni.org
Contact: Jerry L. Hobbs, CEO/Exec. Dir.
Founded: 2004. **Description:** Works to harness the knowledge and strength of the 12 million alumni of foster care in the U.S. in order to improve the lives of youth currently in foster care. Seeks to enhance research, planning and implementation of approaches in today's foster care system. **Computer Services:** Information services, foster care resources.

11342 ■ Foster Family-Based Treatment Association (FFTA)
294 Union St.
Hackensack, NJ 07601
Ph: (201)343-2246
Free: (800)414-3382
Fax: (201)489-4593
E-mail: ffta@ffta.org
URL: http://www.ffta.org
Contact: Ms. Melissa Cole, Admin.
Founded: 1988. **Members:** 400. **Membership Dues:** TFC agency (based on the amount of budget), $450-$2,000 (annual). **Staff:** 2. **Budget:** $500,000. **State Groups:** 14. **Description:** Represents private and public treatment/therapeutic foster care agencies. Seeks to enhance the lives of children in families through strengthening family-based organizations. Advocates for the development, evaluation, recognition, and expansion of Treatment Foster Care. Provides information, resources, program standards, education, technical assistance, and networking opportunities to treatment foster care agencies and their staff. **Computer Services:** database, membership. **Committees:** Conference; Editorial; Fund Development; Leadership Development; Marketing; Public Policy; Standards and Practices. **Councils:** Chapter Chairs. **Publications:** *FOCUS,* quarterly. Newsletter. Keeps members informed of best practices, developments, and trends in Treatment Foster Care. **Price:** $60.00 for members. **Circulation:** 1,000. **Advertising:** accepted ● *Program Standards for Treatment Foster Care.* Book. Defines the model and set parameters to guide agencies in the private sector that provide Treatment Foster Care. **Price:** $20.00 for nonmembers; $10.00 for members. **Circulation:** 4,000. Alternate Formats: online.

11343 ■ Friends of the Children
44 NE Morris, Ste.2000
Portland, OR 97212-3015
Ph: (503)281-6633
Free: (877)493-2707
Fax: (503)281-6819
E-mail: national@friendsofthechildren.org
URL: http://www.friendsofthechildren.com
Contact: Duncan Campbell, Chm/Founder
Founded: 1993. **Description:** Offers mentoring to transform the lives of at-risk children. **Projects:** Longitudinal Study.

11344 ■ Friends of Rwanda Association (FORA)
c/o Mathilde Mukantabana, Pres.
PO Box 1311
Elk Grove, CA 95759-1311
Ph: (916)683-3356
E-mail: mathilde@friends-of-rwanda.org
URL: http://www.friends-of-rwanda.org
Contact: Mathilde Mukantabana, Pres.
Founded: 1995. **Staff:** 4. **Regional Groups:** 1. **State Groups:** 1. **Local Groups:** 1. **Languages:** English, French, Kinyarwanda. **Description:** Strives to help children of Rwanda orphaned by 1994 genocide. Contributes to local organizations helping those children, especially in education. Conducts fundraising events that include cultural displays, talking engagements and appeals to merchants. **Awards:** FORA Honorary Plaque. **Frequency:** annual. **Type:** recognition. **Conventions/Meetings:** annual meeting, fundraising event with cultural performances and Rwandan food.

11345 ■ Giving Children Hope (GCH)
8332 Commonwealth Ave.
Buena Park, CA 90621
Ph: (714)523-4454
Fax: (714)523-4474
E-mail: global@godaid.com
URL: http://www.gchope.org
Contact: John A. Ditty Jr., CEO
Multinational. Description: Works to improve the quality of life for children and refugees. Upgrades hospitals, clinics, medical institutions and orphanages. Focuses on serving children and the poor

through holistic relief and development. **Publications:** Newsletter. Alternate Formats: online ● Annual Report.

11346 ■ God's Child Project
PO Box 1573
Bismarck, ND 58504
Ph: (701)255-7956
Fax: (701)222-0874
E-mail: godschld@btinet.net
URL: http://www.GodsChild.org
Contact: Patrick J. Atkinson, Exec. Dir.
Founded: 1991. **Staff:** 4. **Budget:** $500,000. **Languages:** English, Spanish. **Description:** Works to assist poor children in Guatemala in their educational, social, physical, and spiritual growth. Provides medical care, schooling, and foster homes for 725 children. Maintains speakers' bureau. **Publications:** Brochure. **Conventions/Meetings:** annual board meeting.

11347 ■ Heart of Romania's Children Foundation
103 S Aurora Dr.
Apopka, FL 32712
Ph: (407)814-9095
E-mail: zamfiram@aol.com
Contact: Zamfira Pauna, Contact
Founded: 2002. **Description:** Aims to help abandoned and orphaned children and to provide assistance to disabled children and adults of Romania. **Projects:** Homeless Children.

11348 ■ Herbalife Family Foundation (HFF)
c/o Joan Kardashian, Exec. Dir.
1800 Century Park E
Los Angeles, CA 90067-1501
Ph: (310)410-9600
Fax: (310)557-3925
E-mail: familyfoundation@herbalife.com
URL: http://www.herbalifefamily.org
Contact: Joan Kardashian, Exec. Dir.
Founded: 1994. **Staff:** 1. **Nonmembership. Multinational. Description:** Works to support charities across the globe that deals with children and family issues. **Affiliated With:** Association of Small Foundations; Council on Foundations.

11349 ■ Hug-A-Tree and Survive (HAT)
c/o Don Abney
ABCANTRA Canine Training
PO Box 248
Abita Springs, LA 70420
Ph: (985)892-6773
URL: http://hugatree.abcantra.com
Contact: Ab Taylor, Pres.
Founded: 1981. **Budget:** $10,000. **Description:** Aims to teach children what to do if they become lost. The name of the program is derived from its primary message: If you're lost, stay put—hug a tree—until help arrives. Produces slide program that is presented by search-and-rescue or sheriff's reserve personnel, who are trained by HAT. Presenters familiarize children with the type of people who will be searching for them if they should be lost, as well as what to do to aid searchers and protect themselves until rescued.

11350 ■ Innocence in Danger - USA (IID)
22 River Terr., PH-G
New York, NY 10282
Free: (866)552-7840
Fax: (646)349-1623
E-mail: info@innocenceindanger.com
URL: http://www.innocenceindanger.com
Contact: Rory J. Cutaia, Dir.
Founded: 1999. **Multinational. Description:** Seeks to bring public attention to the plight of children who have been victims of trafficking and sexual abuse. Raises public awareness of the origins, nature and effects of child abuse. Serves as an advocate to prevent the physical, sexual and emotional abuse of children. Offers education, advocacy and rehabilitation programs to affected children and their families.

11351 ■ Institute for Children and Poverty (ICP)
32A Cooper Sq.
New York, NY 10003
Ph: (212)674-2137
Fax: (212)674-2138
E-mail: info@icpny.org
URL: http://www.homesforthehomeless.com
Contact: Dr. Ralph Nunez, Pres./CEO
Founded: 1990. **Description:** Investigates causes of family homelessness, demographics of family homelessness, and the programs most effective in assisting homeless families to make the transition from poverty to stability and self-sufficiency. **Computer Services:** Mailing lists. **Programs:** Adult Education and Literacy; Children's Education and Recreation; Employment Training and Job Placement; Family Inn Model; Family Support and Assistance. **Publications:** *Children's Book Series.* Books. **Advertising:** accepted ● *Homeless in America: A Children's Story-Part One.* Book. Contains national data sources on homelessness in the country. **Price:** $10.00 ● *Journal of Children and Poverty,* semiannual. Presents research and policy initiatives in the areas of education, social services, public policy, and welfare reform. ● Reports.

11352 ■ International Aid Serving Kids (IASK)
c/o Illens Dort, Pres.
1135 N 650 E
Orem, UT 84097
E-mail: orphans12@comcast.net
URL: http://www.iask4kids.org
Contact: Illens Dort, Pres.
Founded: 2002. **Membership Dues:** regular, $10-$100 (annual). **Multinational. Description:** Aims to improve the living conditions of orphans and abandoned children around the world. Works to find adoptive families and foster homes for these children and to reduce the cause for abandonment through providing education and job training. Organizes humanitarian missions that provide orphanages and poverty-stricken communities with medical care and health education. **Telecommunication Services:** electronic mail, idort@iask4kids.org. **Publications:** Magazine. Alternate Formats: online ● Newsletter. Alternate Formats: online ● Journal. Features events related to the organization, membership records, and a list of past and current donors.

11353 ■ International Child Resource Institute (ICRI)
1581 Leroy Ave.
Berkeley, CA 94708
Ph: (510)644-1000
Fax: (510)525-4106
E-mail: info@icrichild.org
URL: http://www.icrichild.org
Contact: Chou Siv Nuon, Admin. Coor.
Founded: 1981. **Staff:** 30. **Budget:** $3,000,000. **Regional Groups:** 4. **Languages:** English, Portuguese, Spanish, Swedish. **Description:** Individuals interested in issues regarding day care for children, including maternal and child health, child abuse prevention, neglect, and other children's issues. Organizations and companies that furnish or are engaged in child care. Implements model projects to gather information on techniques and practices involved in innovative forms of child care and child health. Provides technical assistance to individuals, corporations, and government agencies that wish to establish and maintain child care centers and other children's programs. Serves as a clearinghouse for information on children's issues. Maintains offices in Kenya, Ghana, Zimbabwe, Norway and Nepal. Conducts speakers' bureau. **Libraries: Type:** reference. **Holdings:** books, clippings, periodicals. **Subjects:** child care, child advocacy, child abuse, education, youth, families, drug abuse, child health, peace education. **Publications:** *News from ICRI.* Newsletter. Alternate Formats: online.

11354 ■ International Committee for the Children of Chechnya (ICCC)
PO Box 381305
Cambridge, MA 02238

E-mail: info@chechenchildren.org
URL: http://www.chechenchildren.org
Contact: Dr. Khassan Baiev, Chm.
Founded: 1996. **Multinational. Description:** Seeks to improve the quality of life of children affected by war in the North Caucasus. Provides immediate and sustainable aid to children affected by war. Supports the work of peacemakers in Chechnya. Works on behalf of the children in Chechnya, to support the efforts of their parents, teachers, and relief workers. **Publications:** Newsletter. Alternate Formats: online.

11355 ■ International Organization for Adolescents (IOFA)
PO Box 25792
Brooklyn, NY 11202-2218
Ph: (718)222-5802
Fax: (718)222-5803
E-mail: iofa@iofa.org
URL: http://www.iofa.org
Contact: Alison Boak MPH, Pres./Co-Founder
Founded: 1999. **Multinational. Description:** Seeks to advance the health and well-being of adolescents throughout the world. Provides technical assistance to communities in 20 countries to develop and implement sustainable programs and services for young people. Seeks to foster the physical, mental, emotional and psychological development of adolescents. Seeks to tackle emerging problems facing young people through partnerships, coalition-building, and the innovative approach of social connectivity. **Programs:** Girls Leadership Development; Girls Talk!; Youth Trafficking Prevention. **Projects:** Dominican Girls. **Publications:** *Smooth Flight: A Guide to Preventing Youth Trafficking.* Book.

11356 ■ International Society for Prevention of Child Abuse and Neglect (ISPCAN)
c/o Secretariat Office
245 W Roosevelt Rd., Bldg. 6, Ste.39
West Chicago, IL 60185
Ph: (630)876-6913
Fax: (630)876-6917
E-mail: ispcan@ispcan.org
URL: http://www.ispcan.org
Contact: Ms. Kimberly Svevo MA, Exec. Dir.
Founded: 1977. **Membership Dues:** individual, $130 (annual). **Multinational. Description:** Supports individuals and organizations working to protect children from abuse and neglect worldwide. **Telecommunication Services:** electronic mail, exec@ispcan.org. **Publications:** Papers. Covers sexual abuse and exploitation. **Conventions/Meetings:** biennial congress (exhibits).

11357 ■ Jacob Wetterling Foundation (JWF)
2314 Univ. Ave. W, Ste.14
St. Paul, MN 55114-1863
Ph: (651)714-4673
Free: (800)325-HOPE
Fax: (651)714-9098
E-mail: info@jwf.org
URL: http://www.jwf.org
Contact: Nancy Sabin, Exec. Dir.
Founded: 1990. **Staff:** 4. **Budget:** $400,000. **Nonmembership. Description:** Works with communities to protect kids and teens from exploitation. Concentrates on the development of innovative, community-based prevention education initiatives. Works with partner agencies to impact the development and passage of legislation in Minnesota and nationally on behalf of the safety and protection of children. Recognizes the growing need to raise awareness of and provide specific tools to address the complex problem of child sexual exploitation and abduction. Offers a number of educational tools and services to both the general public and victim families through its program. Provides resources to victim families and their communities. Maintains community outreach through presentations about online and personal safety for companies, civic and non-profit groups, professional and faith-based organizations, community events, schools and parent groups. **Libraries: Type:** lending; open to the public; reference. **Holdings:** 450; articles, books, clippings. **Subjects:** personal safety of children, online safety, missing

children, sexual exploitation. **Publications:** Newsletter, semiannual. Alternate Formats: online ● Brochures.

11358 ■ Justice for Children International (JFCI)
PO Box 8266
New Haven, CT 06530
Ph: (203)772-4420
Fax: (203)789-1135
E-mail: info@jfci.org
URL: http://www.jfci.org
Contact: Robert Morris, Pres./Co-Founder
Founded: 2004. **Multinational. Description:** Works toward the abolition of child sex trafficking and exploitation through advocacy, prevention and aftercare work. Raises awareness and resources to combat child sex trafficking. Provides "a voice for the victims of modern-day slavery". **Computer Services:** Mailing lists. **Publications:** Newsletter. Alternate Formats: online.

11359 ■ Kempe Children's Center
c/o Donald C. Bross, PhD, Dir. of Education and
 Legal Counsel
1825 Marion St.
Denver, CO 80218
Ph: (303)864-5300
E-mail: info@kempe.org
URL: http://kempecenter.org
Contact: Donald C. Bross PhD, Dir. of Education and Legal Counsel
Founded: 1972. **Staff:** 100. **Budget:** $2,000,000. **Description:** Performs children's services; provides evaluation, treatment, research and education related to child maltreatment. **Libraries: Type:** reference; by appointment only. **Subjects:** child mistreatment. **Computer Services:** Mailing lists, public education. **Programs:** Kempe Child Protection Team; Kempe Community Caring; Kempe Fostering Healthy Futures; Kempe Infants in Foster and Kinship Care Initiative; Kempe Perpetration Prevention; Kempe Primary Care Clinic; Kempe START Team; Kempe Therapeutic Preschool. **Formerly:** (1999) Kempe National Center for the Prevention and Treatment of Child Abuse and Neglect. **Publications:** Newsletter. Alternate Formats: online. **Conventions/Meetings:** biennial conference and congress.

11360 ■ Kids 4 Afghan Kids (K4AK)
c/o Khris Nedam, Exec. Dir.
Amerman Elementary School
847 North Center
Northville, MI 48167
Ph: (248)344-8405 (734)762-0569
Fax: (734)762-9651
E-mail: nedamkh@northville.k12.mi.us
URL: http://www.kids4afghankids.com
Contact: Khris Nedam, Exec. Dir.
Founded: 1998. **Multinational. Description:** Provides humanitarian assistance to the Afghan people to create an opportunity for cooperative efforts between the United States and Afghanistan. Develops and enhances educational and cultural understanding and exchange opportunities. Aims to re-establish equal educational facilities for boys and girls. **Telecommunication Services:** electronic mail, kids4afghankids@yahoo.com. **Projects:** Kids 4 Afghan Kids School.

11361 ■ KIDS COUNT
c/o The Annie E. Casey Foundation
701 St. Paul St.
Baltimore, MD 21202
Ph: (410)547-6600
Fax: (410)547-3610
E-mail: webmail@aecf.org
URL: http://www.aecf.org/kidscount
Contact: Douglas Nelson, Pres.
Description: Collects data and reports on the well being of children.

11362 ■ Kids In Danger (KID)
116 W Illinois, Ste.5E
Chicago, IL 60610-4532
Ph: (312)595-0649

Fax: (312)595-0939
E-mail: email@kidsindanger.org
URL: http://www.kidsindanger.org
Contact: Nancy Cowles, Exec. Dir.
Founded: 1998. **Description:** Educates parents, caregivers and the public about dangerous children's products. Advocates for a legislative and regulatory strategy for children's product safety. Promotes the development of safer children's products. **Awards:** KID Best Friend Award. **Frequency:** annual. **Type:** recognition. **Recipient:** for outstanding commitment to children's product safety. **Computer Services:** Information services, child safety resources ● information services, product hazards. **Telecommunication Services:** electronic mail, nancy@kidsindanger.org. **Programs:** Health Care Providers Outreach; Teach Early Safety Testing; Test It Now. **Publications:** *Action,* semiannual. Newsletter. Alternate Formats: online ● *Are Your Kids Safe?.* Brochure. Alternate Formats: online ● Annual Report, annual. Alternate Formats: online.

11363 ■ Kids With A Cause
400 Corporate Pointe, Ste.300
Culver City, CA 90230
Ph: (310)590-4505
Fax: (310)590-4506
E-mail: info@kidswithacause.org
URL: http://www.kidswithacause.org
Contact: Linda Finnegan, Founder/Exec. Dir.
Founded: 1999. **Membership Dues:** regular, $20 (annual). **Description:** Provides support to children worldwide suffering from such needs as poverty, hunger, sickness, lack of education, abandonment, neglect. **Programs:** Arts, Entertainment and Enrichment; Educational; Environmental; Health and Well-Being.

11364 ■ Kids Without Borders (KWB)
PO Box 24
Bellevue, WA 98009-0024
Ph: (206)484-4830
Fax: (206)374-2944
E-mail: info@kidswithnoborders.org
URL: http://www.kidswithnoborders.org
Contact: Son Michael Pham, Founder
Founded: 2001. **Multinational. Description:** Works to involve and inspire youth helping other youth around the world. Aims to connect children of all ethnic, social and economic backgrounds, ages and religions. Provides support to children worldwide suffering from poverty, hunger, sickness, lack of education and neglect. **Publications:** Newsletter. Alternate Formats: online.

11365 ■ KidsPeace
c/o Kids Peace Hospital
5300 Kids Peace Dr.
Orefield, PA 18069
Free: (800)8KI-D123
E-mail: admissions@kidspeace.org
URL: http://www.kidspeace.org
Contact: David Lyons, VP of Charitable Giving
Founded: 1882. **Description:** Works to give children confidence and protection to overcome crises. **Telecommunication Services:** phone referral service, National Referral Network/National Affiliates Network, (800)543-7283 ● 24-hour hotline, (800)334-4KID. **Divisions:** Continuing Education; Lee Salk Center. **Publications:** *For the Kids,* quarterly. Magazine. Alternate Formats: online ● *Healing,* semiannual. Magazine. Alternate Formats: online ● Brochures. Alternate Formats: online.

11366 ■ Kindness in Suffering (KIS)
114 Long Acre Ct.
Frederick, MD 21702
Ph: (301)668-6127
Fax: (301)668-6127
E-mail: email@kisinternational.org
URL: http://www.kisinternational.org
Multinational. Description: Aims to "reconnect street youths who are socially isolated from the mainstream of life and help build the confidence and life skills they need to lead a full life and achieve their highest potential.".

11367 ■ Light of Cambodian Children (LCC)
181 Market St.
Lowell, MA 01852
E-mail: lccweb@lccweb.org
URL: http://www.lccweb.org
Founded: 1998. **Description:** Youths in Northeastern U.S. concerned for the well being of Cambodian children as well as Khmer children in America. Hosts sports tournaments, fundraising banquet.

11368 ■ Love Humanity - USA
17702 Irvine Blvd., Ste.202
Tustin, CA 92780
Ph: (714)749-3613
Fax: (714)749-3613
E-mail: info@lovehumanity.org
URL: http://www.lovehumanity.org
Contact: Louise Williams, Pres.
Multinational. Description: Empowers children to grow into self-sufficient adults. Provides community awareness of new and alternative ways to raise and treat children. Develops and manages individual family homes where orphaned, neglected and abused children are raised like normal children in a safe and loving family environment. **Telecommunication Services:** electronic mail, volunteerusa@lovehumanity.org. **Programs:** Pilot Family Home; Responsible Childcare Training.

11369 ■ Love Our Children USA
220 E 57th St., 9th Fl., Ste.G
New York, NY 10022
Ph: (212)629-2099
Free: (888)347-KIDS
E-mail: info@loveourchildrenusa.org
URL: http://www.loveourchildrenusa.org
Contact: Ross Ellis, Founder/CEO
Founded: 1999. **Description:** Commits to break the cycle of violence against children. Works to eliminate behaviors that keep children from reaching their potential. Redefines parenting by promoting positive changes in parenting and family attitudes, along with behaviors and prevention strategies through public education. Empowers and supports children, teens, parents and families through information, resources, advocacy, and online youth mentoring. Aims to protect children and strengthen families. **Awards:** **Frequency:** annual. **Type:** scholarship. **Recipient:** for abandoned youth. **Publications:** Newsletter, quarterly.

11370 ■ Mail for Me Club
PO Box 225
Mentone, CA 92359
Ph: (909)794-9676
Fax: (909)794-7956
E-mail: susan@mailformeclub.org
URL: http://www.mailformeclub.org
Contact: Erik Zador, Pres.
Founded: 2000. **Multinational. Description:** Comprised of individuals dedicated to the needs of children with disabilities or terminal illnesses. Provides a monthly package containing various items and special gifts for sick and disabled children. Provides opportunities for sick and disabled children to keep in touch with healthy children through letters and e-mail. **Programs:** Pen Pal. **Publications:** Bulletin, monthly.

11371 ■ Meds and Food for Kids (MFK)
c/o Patricia B. Wolff, MD, Founder/Exec. Dir.
4488 Forest Park Ave., Ste.230
St. Louis, MO 63108
Ph: (314)726-0168
Fax: (314)534-2803
E-mail: pwolff@medsandfoodforkids.org
URL: http://www.medsandfoodforkids.org
Contact: Patricia B. Wolff MD, Founder/Exec. Dir.
Founded: 2004. **Multinational. Description:** Aims to save the lives of children dying of malnutrition in Haiti and other developing countries. Provides children with food, medical services, and education. Works to combat childhood malnutrition and related diseases in Haiti. **Publications:** MFK E-News. Newsletter. Alternate Formats: online.

11372 ■ Miracles of Hope Network
c/o Constance Kosuda
PO Box 621303
Las Vegas, NV 89162
E-mail: admin@miracles-of-hope.com
URL: http://www.miracles-of-hope.com
Contact: Denise Marhoefer, Founder
Multinational. Description: Represents individuals and organizations worldwide interested in child welfare issues. Works to improve care and services for abused and neglected children. Facilitates communication and cooperation among members and other organizations with similar goals and activities. **Telecommunication Services:** electronic mail, defensefoundation@gmail.com.

11373 ■ Mothers Without Borders
125 E Main St., Ste.402
American Fork, UT 84003
Ph: (801)796-5535
E-mail: mail@motherswithoutborders.org
URL: http://www.motherswithoutborders.org
Contact: Kathy Headlee, Founder
Founded: 1996. **Membership Dues:** student, $36 (annual) ● individual, $60 (annual) ● family, $120 (annual) ● sustaining, $600 (annual) ● children's hope, $1,200 (annual) ● orphan's angel, $3,000 (annual). **Local Groups:** 1. **Multinational. Description:** Addresses the needs of orphaned and abandoned children. Supports efforts to provide safe shelter, food, clean water, education and access to caring adults. **Computer Services:** Online services, media resources. **Publications:** Newsletter, quarterly. Contains updates and news on current activities of the group. Alternate Formats: online.

11374 ■ Multicultural Education, Training, and Advocacy
240A Elm St., Ste.22
Somerville, MA 02144
Ph: (617)628-2226
Fax: (617)628-0322
E-mail: rlr@shore.net
Contact: Roger Rice, Exec. Dir.
Founded: 1983. **Members:** 15. **Description:** Attorneys, parents, organizers, and trainers. Serves as an educational defense body for minority children and children from low-income families. Conducts research and educational programs. **Libraries: Type:** reference. **Publications:** A Handbook for Immigrant Parents to Protect the Rights of Your Children, monthly ● Educational Equity. Newsletter.

11375 ■ National Association of Former Foster Care Children of America (NAFFCCA)
5505 5th St. NW
Washington, DC 20011
Ph: (202)291-1603
E-mail: info@naffcca.org
URL: http://www.naffcca.org
Contact: Louis H. Henderson, Founder/Pres./CEO
Founded: 1994. **Description:** Advocates for the needs of children in foster care. Provides children and youth from foster care with the life skills necessary to become fully independent, healthy and productive members of society. Assists teens in transitioning from being in foster care to being an independent adult. **Computer Services:** Information services, foster care resources ● online services, discussion forum. **Programs:** Adult Education; Independent Living.

11376 ■ National Association for Native American Children of Alcoholics (NANACOA)
c/o White Bison, Inc.
6145 Lehman Dr., Ste.200
Colorado Springs, CO 80918
Ph: (719)548-1000
Fax: (719)548-9407
E-mail: info@whitebison.org
URL: http://www.whitebison.org/nanacoa
Contact: Rod Jeffries, Pres.
Founded: 1988. **Members:** 7,000. **Membership Dues:** individual, $15 (annual) ● organizational, $150 (annual). **Staff:** 5. **Budget:** $100,000. **Description:** Native and non-native individuals and organizations.

Promotes awareness of the needs of Native American children of alcoholics. Develops educational and support programs for Native American communities; conducts programs to educate local and national policymakers and thereby influence social change and encourage healthy community development. **Awards:** Generation of Giving. **Frequency:** annual. **Type:** recognition ● Generation of Hope. **Frequency:** annual. **Type:** recognition ● Generation of Strength and Wisdom. **Frequency:** annual. **Type:** recognition. **Publications:** From Nightmare to Vision: A Training Manual for Native American Adult Children of Alcoholics. Video ● The Healing Journey: Hope for Children of Alcoholics. A 30-minute inspirational video about Native American children of alcoholics. **Price:** $50.00 for members; $75.00 for nonmembers ● Healing Our Hearts. Newsletter ● Respect Handbook: A Guide for Helping Native American Children of Alcoholics. **Conventions/Meetings:** annual The Healing Journey - conference, focuses on health and wellness for individuals affected by intergenerational alcoholism (exhibits) - usually in the fall.

11377 ■ National Association to Protect Children
46 Haywood St., Ste.315
Asheville, NC 28801
Ph: (828)350-9350
E-mail: info@protect.org
URL: http://www.protect.org
Contact: Ruby Andrew, Contact
Founded: 1989. **Membership Dues:** general, $35 (annual). **Description:** Protects children from abuse, exploitation and neglect. Provides counseling, medical care and legal representation to child victims. Strengthens the child welfare system. **Conventions/Meetings:** annual international conference.

11378 ■ National Association of Public Child Welfare Administrators (NAPCWA)
810 1st St. NE, Ste.500
Washington, DC 20002
Ph: (202)682-0100
Fax: (202)289-6555
E-mail: napcwa@aphsa.org
URL: http://www.napcwa.org/Home/home_news.asp
Contact: Anita Light, Dir.
Founded: 1983. **Members:** 500. **Membership Dues:** regular, associate, $99 (annual). **Staff:** 4. **Description:** State and local child welfare administrators who belong to the American Public Human Services Association. Seeks to enhance the administration of services promoting the well-being of children; supports the development of public policies to prevent or alleviate family disruptions such as child abuse and juvenile delinquency. Compiles statistics. **Awards:** Award for Excellence in Public Child Welfare Administration. **Frequency:** annual. **Type:** recognition. **Recipient:** for state and local public child welfare administrators ● Award for Leadership in Public Child Welfare. **Frequency:** annual. **Type:** recognition. **Recipient:** for leaders supporting the work of public child welfare agencies. **Publications:** Commitment to Change. Report ● Guidelines for Model Protective Services for Abused and Neglected Children and Their Families. Handbook ● Guidelines for Public Child Welfare Agencies Serving Children and Families Experiencing Domestic Violence. Handbook ● Papers, periodic. **Conventions/Meetings:** conference and workshop - 3/year.

11379 ■ National Center for Missing and Exploited Children (NCMEC)
699 Prince St.
Alexandria, VA 22314-3175
Ph: (703)274-3900
Free: (800)843-5678
Fax: (703)274-2200
URL: http://www.missingkids.com
Contact: Mr. John P. Kelly Jr., Chm.
Founded: 1984. **Staff:** 80. **Budget:** $7,000,000. **Description:** Aims to aid parents and law enforcement agencies in preventing child exploitation and in locating missing children. Serves as a national clearinghouse of information on effective state and federal legislation directed at the protection of children.

Provides technical assistance to individuals, parents, groups, agencies, and state and local governments involved in locating and returning children and in cases of child exploitation. **Awards:** National Law Enforcement Awards. **Frequency:** annual. **Type:** recognition. **Telecommunication Services:** hotline, (800)826-5653, for the hearing impaired. **Divisions:** Administrative Services; Development and Education; Technical Assistance. **Conventions/Meetings:** annual board meeting ● quarterly executive committee meeting.

11380 ■ National Center for Prosecution of Child Abuse (NCPCA)
99 Canal Center Plz., Ste.510
Alexandria, VA 22314
Ph: (703)549-4253
Fax: (703)836-3195
E-mail: ncpca@ndaa.org
URL: http://www.ndaa.org/apri/programs/ncpca/ncpca_home.html
Contact: Ms. Dawn Wilsey, Child Abuse Programs Deputy Dir.

Founded: 1985. **Staff:** 14. **Budget:** $1,500,000. **Description:** Provides technical assistance and training to prosecutors and child abuse professionals. Conducts workshops and symposia and publishes guides. **Boards:** Advisory. **Publications:** *Investigation and Prosecution of Child Abuse.* Manual. **Price:** $64.95 ● *Update*, monthly. Newsletter. **Price:** free to child abuse professionals. Alternate Formats: online ● Contact for publications list. **Conventions/Meetings:** periodic meeting.

11381 ■ National Child Care Development Association (NCCDA)
51 Main St.
Enterprise, FL 32725
Free: (800)777-0219
Fax: (325)692-6813
E-mail: dwmiller1@sbcglobal.net
Contact: David Miller, Chm.

Founded: 1989. **Membership Dues:** regular/affiliate, $10 (annual). **Budget:** $20,000. **Description:** Child care agency with primary responsibility for fund raising, development, public relations, marketing, and/or administration. Provides a network of mutual support and encouragement, as well as a forum where topics of mutual interest and concern can be addressed. Workshops to improve the professional skills and knowledge of its members.

11382 ■ National Children's Alliance (NCA)
516 C St. NE
Washington, DC 20002
Ph: (202)548-0090
Free: (800)239-9950
Fax: (202)548-0099
E-mail: info@nca-online.org
URL: http://www.nca-online.org
Contact: Nancy Chandler, Exec. Dir.

Founded: 1987. **Membership Dues:** full initiation fee, $1,000 ● full, $150 (annual) ● associate initiation fee, $100 ● associate, $75 (annual) ● agency support, $50 (annual) ● individual support, $25 (annual). **Description:** Promotes and supports communities in providing a coordinated investigation and comprehensive response to child victims of abuse. Provides training, technical assistance, and grants to communities seeking to develop or sustain Multidisciplinary Teams and Children's Advocacy Centers. **Committees:** Congressional Spouses' Steering; Congressional Steering; Public Policy. **Publications:** *National Children's Alliance News*, quarterly. Newsletter ● Annual Report, annual ● Manuals ● Videos.

11383 ■ National Coalition for Child Protection Reform (NCCPR)
53 Skyhill Rd., Ste.202
Alexandria, VA 22314-4997
Ph: (703)212-2006
E-mail: info@nccpr.org
URL: http://www.nccpr.org
Contact: Richard Wexler, Exec. Dir.

Founded: 1991. **Description:** Advocates on making the child welfare system to better serve America's most vulnerable children; strives to change policies concerning child abuse, foster care and family preservation. **Telecommunication Services:** electronic mail, rwexler@nccpr.org. **Publications:** Papers. Alternate Formats: online ● Reports. Alternate Formats: online.

11384 ■ National Collaboration for Youth (NCY)
1319 F St. NW, Ste.402
Washington, DC 20004
Ph: (202)347-2080
Fax: (202)393-4517
E-mail: pam@nassembly.org
URL: http://www.nassembly.org
Contact: Irv Katz, Pres./CEO

Members: 49. **Description:** Provides united voice for all youth, advocating for improved conditions and opportunities for positive development. **Computer Services:** Information services, members only. **Telecommunication Services:** electronic mail, irv@nassembly.org. **Projects:** National Youth Development Information Center; National Youth Development Learning Network. **Publications:** *Capturing Promising Practices in Recruitment and Retention of Frontline Youth Workers.* Report ● *Making a Difference in the Lives of Youth.* Report ● *Management Report*, annual ● *Professional Development Series*, quarterly. Newsletter ● *Wingspread Conference Proceedings.* Report ● *Youth Worker News*, quarterly. Newsletter. **Conventions/Meetings:** annual conference.

11385 ■ National Court Appointed Special Advocate Association (NCASAA)
100 W Harrison St., Ste.500
North Tower
Seattle, WA 98119
Ph: (206)270-0072
Free: (800)628-3233
Fax: (206)270-0078
E-mail: inquiry@nationalcasa.org
URL: http://www.nationalcasa.org
Contact: Michael S. Piraino, CEO

Founded: 1982. **Membership Dues:** program, $90 (annual) ● individual, $35 (annual). **Staff:** 18. **Budget:** $1,000,000. **State Groups:** 39. **Local Groups:** 610. **Description:** Supports and maintains a network of programs designed to provide Court Appointed Special Advocates (CASAs) for abused and neglected children involved in juvenile dependency hearings. (A CASA is a specially trained citizen volunteer who advocates on behalf of the child.) Provides technical assistance to communities interested in starting programs. Conducts national training conference; maintains speakers' bureau. **Libraries: Type:** not open to the public. **Awards:** G.F. Bettineski Child Advocate of the Year. **Frequency:** annual. **Type:** recognition. **Recipient:** for CASA volunteers ● Judge of the Year. **Frequency:** annual. **Type:** recognition. **Recipient:** for juvenile court and family court judge ● Kappa Alpha Theta Program Director of the Year. **Frequency:** annual. **Type:** recognition. **Recipient:** for CASA program director. **Additional Websites:** http://www.casanet.org. **Also Known As:** National CASA Association. **Formerly:** Court Appointed Special Advocates Association. **Publications:** *Achieving Diversity* ● *The Connection*, quarterly. Newsletter. Includes updates on developments affecting CASA's work. **Price:** $25.00 /year for nonmembers; included in membership dues. Alternate Formats: online ● *Feedback*, quarterly ● *Guide to Program Development* ● *Guide to Resource Development* ● *NCASAA Communications Manual* ● *Program Survey*, annual ● *Speak Up*, annual ● Annual Report, annual ● *Directory*, semiannual. **Conventions/Meetings:** annual conference and workshop (exhibits).

11386 ■ National Exchange Club Foundation (NECF)
3050 Central Ave.
Toledo, OH 43606
Ph: (419)535-3232
Free: (800)924-2643
Fax: (419)535-1989

E-mail: info@nationalexchangeclub.org
URL: http://www.preventchildabuse.com
Contact: George Mezinko, Exec. Dir.

Founded: 1979. **Staff:** 5. **Budget:** $800,000. **Local Groups:** 85. **Description:** A project of the National Exchange Club (see separate entry). Seeks to combat child abuse by implementing local programs that utilize a parent aide concept for the treatment of abusive parents. The use of parent aides encompasses working directly with abusive parents and children in order to rehabilitate parents and train them in positive, nonviolent coping and child rearing techniques. Sponsors educational activities designed to foster public understanding of the problem and potential solutions to child abuse in the U.S. **Libraries: Type:** reference. **Holdings:** audiovisuals, books, periodicals. **Subjects:** child abuse prevention, parent aides, non-profit board management. **Programs:** National Parent Aide Network. **Formerly:** (2002) National Exchange Club Foundation for the Prevention of Child Abuse. **Publications:** *Training Manual for Parent Aides* ● Brochures. **Conventions/Meetings:** annual symposium.

11387 ■ National Organization Caring for Kids (NOCK)
PO Box 1822
Tacoma, WA 98401
Ph: (253)851-6625
E-mail: info@nockonline.org
URL: http://www.nockonline.org
Contact: Susan Brinkman, CEO

Founded: 2003. **Description:** Improves the quality of life of children disabled by chronic illness. Focuses on programs associated with assistive technology. **Programs:** Expressions; Wheelchairs for Kids. **Formerly:** (2006) National Organization for Chronically Ill Kids. **Publications:** *NOCKS News.* Newsletter ● Annual Report, annual.

11388 ■ National Resource Center for Youth Services (NRCYS)
4502 E 41st St., Bldg. 4W
Tulsa, OK 74135-2512
Ph: (918)660-3700
Fax: (918)660-3737
E-mail: pcorreia@ou.edu
URL: http://www.nrcys.ou.edu
Contact: Peter Correia III, Dir.

Founded: 1973. **Staff:** 47. **Budget:** $3,200,000. **Description:** Works to improve the quality of life for at-risk youth and their families by improving the effectiveness of human services. Seeks to prepare adolescents for the challenges of life. Provides training, management services, information and referral, conference planning and teen conferences. Conducts educational and research programs. Maintains Speaker's Bureau. **Libraries: Type:** reference; by appointment only. **Holdings:** 4,000; articles, audiovisuals, books, clippings, monographs, periodicals. **Subjects:** at-risk youth, child welfare, youth development, youth services. **Computer Services:** Mailing lists, of members. **Publications:** *Daily Living.* Newsletter ● *Reflections on Youth*, 3/year. Newsletter ● Books. **Circulation:** 33,000 ● Manuals ● Catalog. Alternate Formats: online. **Conventions/Meetings:** annual Working with America's Youth - conference (exhibits).

11389 ■ Nationwide Patrol
Address Unknown since 2007

Founded: 1985. **Members:** 50. **Membership Dues:** $100 (annual). **Regional Groups:** 1. **State Groups:** 1. **Local Groups:** 1. **National Groups:** 1. **Multinational. Description:** Volunteers united to help find missing children. Offers assistance to parents who have a missing child; produces flyers for circulation, organizes search parties, and conducts public awareness campaigns. Provides for fingerprinting of children. Conducts research and charitable programs. Provides crime watch patrols throughout the country. **Awards: Type:** recognition. **Publications:** *Nationwide Patrol Directory*, periodic. **Conventions/Meetings:** monthly meeting.

11390 ■ North American Reggio Emilia Alliance (NAREA)

c/o Cheryl Rapaport, Admin. Coor.
Inspired Practices in Early Educ., Inc.
2040 Wilson Ridge Ct.
Roswell, GA 30075
Ph: (770)552-0179
Fax: (770)552-0179
E-mail: contact@regioalliance.org
URL: http://www.reggioalliance.org
Contact: Cheryl Rapaport, Admin. Coor.

Founded: 2000. **Membership Dues:** student, Canada/Mexico resident, $50 (annual) ● U.S. resident (non-student), $75 (annual) ● patron (silver), $200 (annual) ● patron (gold), $500 (annual). **Multinational. Description:** Seeks to elevate both the quality of life and the quality of schools and centers for young children. Serves as a conduit for dialogue and exchange with Reggio Children and other international organizations that promote the rights of young children. Strengthens professional relationships among members by facilitating collaboration and exchange. Strengthens access to professional development initiatives and resources through communication tools. **Telecommunication Services:** electronic mail, narea@mindspring.com. **Publications:** *Innovations in Early Education: The International Reggio Exchange*, quarterly. Newsletter. **Price:** included in membership dues.

11391 ■ One Child At A Time

c/o AIAA/Corporate Office
2151 Livernois, Ste.200
Troy, MI 48083
Ph: (248)362-1207
Fax: (248)362-8222
E-mail: onechilds@aol.com
URL: http://www.onechildatatime.org
Contact: Nancy Fox, Exec. Dir.

Founded: 1975. **Members:** 3,500. **Staff:** 14. **Budget:** $300,000. **Description:** Adopting families and relatives; parent groups; concerned citizens. Promotes international understanding through service to children and those in need; facilitates the international adoption procedure when it is in the best interests of the child; helps parents keep and provide for the child. Provides medical supplies, medical escorting services, overseas family assistance, overseas vocational training assistance, and adoption placement. The group was instrumental in the passage of the Amerasian Bill, passed Oct. 22, 1982. Works with children worldwide, but most frequently in Africa, Korea, India, Vietnam, Russia, Ukraine, Thailand, Romania, and Central and South America. Seeks sponsors for Amerasians aged 18 and over. Maintains Amerasians for International Aid and Adoption, which serves in the adoption placement of children overseas and assists in the collection and distribution of funds. Serves as an information clearinghouse; keeps Americans informed of the plight of Amerasians and compiles statistics. **Committees:** Adoption; Aid; Amerasians; Medical; Sponsorship. **Programs:** Domestic; Overseas; Sponsorship Family. **Formerly:** (1993) Americans for International Aid. **Publications:** Newsletter, quarterly. **Advertising:** accepted. **Conventions/Meetings:** monthly meeting.

11392 ■ Only a Child

PO Box 990885
Boston, MA 02199
Ph: (617)848-8940
Free: (888)593-0083
E-mail: info@onlyachild.org
URL: http://www.onlyachild.org
Contact: George Leger, Founder

Founded: 1994. **Multinational. Description:** Provides help for young men in Guatemala. Maintains a shelter and a carpentry shop for youth. Offers a variety of educational opportunities to give the kids every possible chance to one day lead productive lives. **Publications:** Newsletter. Alternate Formats: online.

11393 ■ Orphan Resources International (ORI)

550 W Trout Run Rd.
Ephrata, PA 17522
Ph: (717)733-7444
Fax: (717)733-8531
E-mail: orphanhelp@aol.com
URL: http://www.orphanresources.org
Contact: Rod Martin, Contact

Multinational. Description: Seeks to restore the lives of orphans. Provides aid to orphanages in Guatemala. Supplies physical necessities and provides volunteers to help with the care of the orphans. **Publications:** Newsletter, quarterly. Alternate Formats: online.

11394 ■ Parents Anonymous (PA)

675 W Foothill Blvd., Ste.220
Claremont, CA 91711-3475
Ph: (909)621-6184
Fax: (909)625-6304
E-mail: parentsanonymous@parentsanonymous.org
URL: http://www.parentsanonymous.org
Contact: Meryl Levine, VP for Development

Founded: 1970. **Budget:** $400,000. **Regional Groups:** 4. **State Groups:** 31. **Local Groups:** 1,200. **Description:** Works for the prevention and treatment of child abuse. Believes that "parenting falls on a continuum and that parents should not be labeled as "good," "bad," "abusive," or "non-abusive," but rather that all parents will experience problems at some time in their parenting careers, and all parents are deserving of help." The treatment model blends traditional support groups with self-help. Support groups encourage peer leadership, and include a volunteer professional sponsor who attends all meetings. Maintains speakers' bureau; operates educational programs. **Awards: Type:** recognition. **Councils:** National Child Abuse Prevention Advisory. **Programs:** Parents Anonymous Children's Program; Parents Anonymous Group; Parents Anonymous Parent Leadership; Shared Leadership in Action. **Formerly:** (1971) Mothers Anonymous. **Publications:** *First Steps. for Baby and Parent.* Booklet. Offers vital information on safety and parenting strategies for mothers, fathers and anyone in a caretaking role. **Price:** $4.00 ● *Innovations*, quarterly. Newsletter. Reports the organization's activities and is widely distributed to the PA national, state, and local organizations and other important constituents. **Price:** free. **Circulation:** 5,000. Alternate Formats: online ● *Parent Leadership Express.* Newsletter. Provides information on best practices, innovative ideas and successful Parent Leadership strategies in the child abuse prevention field. **Price:** free. Alternate Formats: online ● *The Parent Networker.* Newsletter. Includes valuable articles, parents' stories and issues of importance to families. **Price:** free. **Circulation:** 12,000. Alternate Formats: online ● *Program Bulletin - The Model for Effective Parent Education.* Reviews the benefits of the Parent Anonymous model as an effective parent education strategy and resource for families under stress. **Price:** free. Alternate Formats: online ● *Shared Leadership in Action.* Newsletter. Provides information and strategies for implementing Child Welfare System reform through meaningful Parent Leadership and Shared Leadership. **Price:** free. Alternate Formats: online ● *Strengthening Families in Partnership with Communities.* Brochure. Provides an overview of Parents Anonymous and its programs. **Price:** free. Alternate Formats: online.

11395 ■ Pearl S. Buck International (PSBI)

520 Dublin Rd.
Perkasie, PA 18944
Ph: (215)249-0100
Free: (800)220-BUCK
Fax: (215)249-9657
E-mail: psbi@pearlsbuck.org
URL: http://www.psbi.org
Contact: Janet L. Mintzer, Pres./CEO

Founded: 1964. **Members:** 16,000. **Staff:** 25. **Budget:** $4,000,000. **Description:** Provides three distinct functions that operate with one common mission of promoting the legacy and dreams of Pearl S. Buck, her commitment to improving the quality of life and expanding opportunities for children, promoting and understanding the values and attributes of other cultures, the injustice of prejudice, and the need for humanitarianism throughout the world. Welcome House provides children the opportunity to grow in a loving permanent family by providing adoption and support services. International programs provide humanitarian assistance to children and families in Korea, Philippines, Thailand and Vietnam. Pearl S. Buck House and Historic Site preserves a National Historic Landmark and promotes the legacy of Pearl S. Buck through house tours, education programs, and events. **Programs:** Adoption; Education. **Formerly:** (1998) Pearl S. Buck Foundation. **Publications:** *Connections.* Newsletter ● *Outreach*, annual. Magazine. Contains educational information. Includes annual report. **Circulation:** 50,000 ● Pamphlets. **Conventions/Meetings:** quarterly board meeting.

11396 ■ Prevent Child Abuse (PCA)

500 N Michigan Ave., Ste.200
Chicago, IL 60611
Ph: (312)663-3520
Fax: (312)939-8962
E-mail: mailbox@preventchildabuse.org
URL: http://www.preventchildabuse.org
Contact: Anne Reiniger, Chair

Founded: 1972. **Staff:** 35. **Budget:** $3,000,000. **State Groups:** 54. **Description:** Seeks to stimulate greater public awareness of the incidence, origins, nature, and effects of child abuse. Serves as a national advocate to prevent the neglect and physical, sexual, and emotional abuse of children. Facilitates communication about program activities, public policy, and research related to the prevention of child abuse. Fosters greater cooperation between existing and developing resources in the area of prevention. Operates the National Center on Child Abuse Prevention Research; conducts annual national media campaigns and child abuse prevention programs. Provides training and technical assistance. **Programs:** Advocacy; Chapter Network; Healthy Families; National Center on Child Abuse Prevention Research; Prevention Education; Resource Development. **Formerly:** (1974) Family Life Achievement Center; (2003) Prevent Child Abuse. **Publications:** *Monthly Memorandum* ● Booklets ● Catalog ● Monographs ● Pamphlets. **Conventions/Meetings:** annual Leadership Conference.

11397 ■ Project Cuddle (PC)

2973 Harbor Blvd., No. 326
Costa Mesa, CA 92626
Ph: (714)432-9681
Free: (888)628-3353
Fax: (714)433-6815
E-mail: info@projectcuddle.org
URL: http://www.projectcuddle.org
Contact: Debbe Magnusen, Founder

Founded: 1985. **Members:** 2,000. **Staff:** 2. **Description:** Aims to help any pregnant girl or woman regardless of race, creed, religious affiliation, financial status or HIV status. Saves babies from being abandoned. **Awards:** Angel Day. **Frequency:** weekly. **Type:** recognition. **Recipient:** for individuals who have donated $50 or more. **Publications:** *Don't Abandon Your Baby.* Book. Features true stories about girls who have been given help, and babies that have been saved. **Price:** $15.00. **Advertising:** accepted ● *It's Never Dull!.* Book ● Brochures. **Conventions/Meetings:** monthly Auxiliary Meetings, for volunteers who really want to get involved and help make decisions about events and ideas for the charity ● annual Dinner by the Bay - banquet, fun for the whole family, with live music, dinner and dance.

11398 ■ Reach the Children

PO Box 1208
Fairport, NY 14450
Ph: (585)223-3344
Free: (800)275-3003
Fax: (585)223-5477
E-mail: info@reachthechildren.org
URL: http://www.reachthechildren.org
Contact: Kevin Clawson, Pres./CEO

Multinational. Description: Strives to empower the people of Africa. Provides underprivileged children with opportunities to become self-reliant by strengthening families and communities. Focuses on AIDS prevention, education, health, micro-enterprise, orphan care and agriculture. **Publications:** Annual Report, annual. Alternate Formats: online ● Newsletter, quarterly.

11399 ■ Russian Children's Welfare Society (RCWS)
200 Park Ave. S, Ste.1617
New York, NY 10003
Ph: (212)473-6263
Free: (888)732-RCWS
Fax: (212)473-6301
E-mail: main@rcws.org
URL: http://www.rcws.org
Contact: Vladimir P. Fekula, Pres./CEO
Founded: 1926. **Staff:** 2. **Regional Groups:** 3. **State Groups:** 1. **Local Groups:** 1. **Languages:** English, Russian. **Multinational. Description:** Dedicated to helping needy Russian children all over the world. Provides financial aid to organizations serving Russian children and to families living below poverty level. **Publications:** *RCWS NEWS*, annual. Newsletter. Alternate Formats: online. **Conventions/Meetings:** annual meeting.

11400 ■ Safe Kids Worldwide
1301 Pennsylvania Ave. NW, Ste.1000
Washington, DC 20004-1707
Ph: (202)662-0600
Fax: (202)393-2072
E-mail: info@safekids.org
URL: http://www.safekids.org
Contact: Martin R. Eichelberger MD, Chm.
Founded: 1987. **Staff:** 41. **Budget:** $6,200,000. **State Groups:** 34. **Local Groups:** 129. **Languages:** English, Spanish. **Description:** Grass roots coalitions of medical and safety organizations, government leaders, teachers, parents, and interested others working to create safer homes and communities for children. Seeks to raise public awareness of injury prevention through the media. Initiates public policy changes; develops educational programs. Encourages community-based solutions to potential safety hazards, advocates for stronger child-passenger laws. **Libraries: Type:** reference. **Awards:** Coalition Grants. **Type:** grant. **Recipient:** for a coalition in good standing. **Formerly:** (2005) National Safe Kids Campaign. **Conventions/Meetings:** annual Leadership Conference, provides training for coalition leaders (exhibits) - always November.

11401 ■ Special Needs Advocate for Parents (SNAP)
11835 W Olympic Blvd., No. 465
Los Angeles, CA 90064
Ph: (310)479-3755
Free: (888)310-9889
Fax: (310)479-3089
E-mail: info@snapinfo.org
URL: http://www.snapinfo.org
Contact: Susan Bumstead Chanley, Pres.
Founded: 1993. **Description:** Improves the quality of life of children of all ages who have special needs, their parents, or caregivers by serving as a resource that empowers them through information, education, advocacy and referrals. **Programs:** Medical Insurance Empowerment; Teen Volunteer. **Publications:** *SNAP Report*. Newsletter.

11402 ■ Stop it Now!
351 Pleasant St., Ste.B319
Northampton, MA 01060
Ph: (413)585-3500
Free: (888)773-8368
Fax: (413)587-3505
E-mail: info@stopitnow.org
URL: http://www.stopitnow.com
Contact: Ms. Maxine J. Stein, Pres.
Founded: 1992. **Staff:** 9. **State Groups:** 5. **Multinational. Description:** Works to end the sexual abuse of children by educating adults about the ways to stop sexual abuse and increasing public awareness of the trauma of child sexual abuse. Serves as an international network of community-based programs

that provides support, information and resources that adults, families and communities need to prevent sexual abuse before a child is harmed. Seeks to empower individuals and families to keep children safe and create healthier communities. Includes reaching out to adults who are concerned about their own or others' sexualized behavior toward children calling on them to stop and seek help. Manages a confidential, national toll-free helpline for support, resources and referrals. **Publications:** *Parenttalk*, semiannual. Newsletter. Contains information resources by parents and for parents of children with sexual behavioral problems. Alternate Formats: online ● *Stop It Now! News*, quarterly. Newsletter. Contains organizational news and educational articles. Alternate Formats: online.

11403 ■ Supervised Visitation Network (SVN)
2804 Paran Pointe Dr.
Cookeville, TN 38506
Ph: (931)537-3414
Fax: (931)537-6348
E-mail: nancy@svnetwork.net
URL: http://www.svnetwork.net
Contact: Nancy Fallows MS, Exec. Dir.
Founded: 1991. **Members:** 700. **Membership Dues:** individual, $70 (annual) ● agency, $110 (annual) ● affiliate, $30 (annual). **Staff:** 2. **Budget:** $50,000. **State Groups:** 10. **Languages:** English, French, Spanish. **Multinational. Description:** Network of agencies and individuals interested in assuring that children can have safe, conflict-free access to parents with whom they do not reside. **Libraries: Type:** reference. **Subjects:** training and program materials. **Publications:** *Child Sexual Abuse Referrals: A Curriculum for Supervised Visitation Providers*. Manual. **Price:** $66.00 each, purchase of 1-2 copies; $63.00 each, purchase of 3-9 copies; $61.50 each, purchase of more than 10 copies ● *Handbook for Parents*. Booklet. **Price:** $1.45 each, purchase of 1-9 copies; $1.25 each, purchase of 10-49 copies; $1.10 each, purchase of 50-99 copies ● *NYSPCC Professional's Handbook on Providing Supervised Visitation*. **Price:** included in membership dues; $18.00 each, purchase of 1-2 copies, for nonmembers; $16.50 each, purchase of 3-9 copies, for nonmembers; $15.50 each, purchase of more than 10 copies, for nonmembers ● *Sitting In*, quarterly. Newsletter. **Price:** included in membership dues ● *SVN Standards and Guidelines: For Supervised Visitation Practice*. Directory. Contains listing of child access providers. Alternate Formats: online ● Brochure. **Conventions/Meetings:** annual conference, with training and exchange services (exhibits) ● annual meeting and workshop - every spring.

11404 ■ Support A Child International
1130 S Wabash, Ste.304
Chicago, IL 60605
Ph: (312)922-8421
Fax: (312)992-8427
E-mail: sacint@aol.com
URL: http://www.supportachildinternational.com
Founded: 1989. **Multinational. Description:** "Creates a sustainable future for the world's children." Develops and supports international projects that provide education and training to young people, improve the health of children and adolescents, and create entrepreneurial opportunities for mothers. Stimulates the economic revitalization of impoverished communities. **Programs:** Micro-Credit; Nutrition; Urban Kidz. **Projects:** Ghana Soybean Farming.

11405 ■ Survivors And Victims Empowered (SAVE)
1725 Oregon Pike, Ste.106
Lancaster, PA 17601
Ph: (717)569-0550
Fax: (717)569-3039
URL: http://www.childprotectionprogram.org
Description: Helps prevent physical, emotional and sexual abuse of children. Provides support to the survivors of childhood traumas. Works with other organizations to stop the abuse of children and remedy the damaged caused by this abuse. **Com-**

puter Services: Information services, sex offender registries. **Publications:** *The Child Protection eNewsletter*. Alternate Formats: online.

11406 ■ U.S. Fund for UNICEF
333 E 38th St.
New York, NY 10016
Ph: (212)686-5522
Free: (800)553-1200
Fax: (212)779-1670
E-mail: information@unicefusa.org
URL: http://www.unicefusa.org
Contact: Caryl M. Stern, Chief Operating Off.
Founded: 1946. **Staff:** 6,755. **Budget:** $804,000,000. **National Groups:** 37. **Languages:** English, French, Spanish. **Description:** Semi-autonomous U.N. agency working for sustainable human development to ensure the survival, protection, and development of children. Cooperates with governments in the developing world to develop and implement low-cost community-based programs in social service, health, nutrition, education, water and sanitation, environment, and women in development. Works for universal ratification and implementation of the Convention on the Rights of the Child and achievement of the objectives and the goals of the 1990 World Summit for Children. Provides universal immunization against six childhood diseases-diphtheria, measles, poliomyelitis, whooping cough, tetanus, and tuberculosis. Promotes the use of oral rehydration therapy to treat diarrheal dehydration, which is one of the leading causes of death in children in developing countries. Works to eliminate poliomyelitis in selected countries and regions, neonatal tetanus, Vitamin A deficiency, iodine deficiency disorders, and guinea worn diseases. In cooperation with the World Health Organization, has launched a "baby-friendly hospital initiative" to advance breastfeeding. Provides training for health workers and traditional birth attendants; furnishes technical supplies and equipment for health centers. Advocates with and helps governments in strengthening basic education for all, particularly in increasing schooling opportunities for girls. Supports efforts to improve the status of women by enhancing educational and vocational opportunities and supporting small-scale income generating projects and credit schemes to increase the earning power of women. Assists Urban Basic Services programs to address the health and sanitation needs of the urban poor and supports local safe water supply projects. Seeks to help children in especially difficult circumstances, including children in armed conflicts. Provides relief and rehabilitation assistance in response to the needs of children and women affected by emergencies. Works with 37 national committees, mostly in industrialized countries, providing fund-raising and advocacy support. More than 190 Non-Governmental Organizations (NGOs) maintain consultative relationships with the organization. **Libraries: Type:** reference; not open to the public. **Holdings:** 10,000; archival material, audiovisuals, photographs. **Subjects:** children, women, social development. **Awards:** Maurice Pate Award. **Type:** recognition. **Recipient:** for extraordinary and exemplary leadership in and contribution to the advancement of the survival, protection, and development of children. **Absorbed:** Citizens Committee for UNICEF. **Foreign language name:** Fonds des Nations Unies pour l'Enfance. **Formerly:** United Nations International Children's Emergency Fund; (2004) United Nations Children's Fund - USA. **Publications:** *Every Child*, quarterly. Magazine. Contains current issues. ● *Facts and Figures* (in English, French, and Spanish), annual. Brochure. Lists facts and statistical data on children and women. **Price:** free ● *Fifty Years of Service (2002)*, periodic. Catalog. Describes UNICEF's mission, work and accomplishments. **Price:** $10.00/copy. Alternate Formats: CD-ROM ● *First Call for Children* (in English, French, and Spanish), quarterly. Newsletter ● *The Progress of Nations* (in English, French, and Spanish), annual. Report ● *State of the World's Children* (in Arabic, English, French, and Spanish), annual. Book. Offered in 20 other national languages. ● *UNICEF Annual Report* (in English, French, and Spanish), annual. Summarizes UNICEF policies and

programs. ● *UNICEF at a Glance* (in English, French, and Spanish). Newsletter. **Conventions/Meetings:** annual board meeting.

11407 ■ Vanished Children's Alliance (VCA)
991 W Hedding St., Ste.101
San Jose, CA 95126
Ph: (408)296-1113
Free: (800)VANISHED
Fax: (408)296-1117
E-mail: info@vca.org
URL: http://www.vca.org
Contact: Georgia K. Hilgeman-Hammond, Exec. Dir./ Founder
Founded: 1980. **Staff:** 13. **Languages:** English, Spanish. **Description:** Aims to find children who have disappeared, and reuniting them with their parents. Strives to prevent disappearances of children through community education and outreach. Maintains speakers' bureau; compiles statistics; all services are provided free of charge. **Computer Services:** Mailing lists, of members. **Telecommunication Services:** electronic mail, ghilgeman@vca.org. **Departments:** Casework; Outreach. **Programs:** DMV Poster; Northern California Child Identification; School Call Back; Vending Sticker. **Projects:** Public Awareness Recovers Kids. **Publications:** *The Road Home*, semiannual. Newsletter. **Price:** free. Alternate Formats: online ● *Vanished Children's Directory*. Shows pictures of missing children from across the country and presentation information. ● Annual Report, annual. Alternate Formats: online ● Reports. Alternate Formats: online ● Also produces posters and prevention and safety manuals; all materials provided free of charge. **Conventions/Meetings:** monthly Parents Support Group - meeting.

11408 ■ Variety International - The Children's Charity
350 5th Ave., Ste.1233
New York, NY 10118
Ph: (212)695-3818
Fax: (212)695-3857
E-mail: info@varietychildrenscharity.org
URL: http://www.varietychildrenscharity.org
Contact: Michael Forman, Pres.
Founded: 1927. **Members:** 15,000. **Staff:** 2. **Budget:** $400,000. **Regional Groups:** 4. **Multinational. Description:** Serves as an international children's charity with roots in entertainment and leisure-related industries. Sponsors programs to raise funds for children in need such as those in hospitals, special treatment centers, camps, and day nurseries. Focuses on children with special needs; children with serious medical concerns; and children who live in poverty. **Formerly:** (2004) Variety Clubs International. **Publications:** *Convention Journal*, annual ● *The Heart of Variety*, semiannual. Newsletter. An internal publication. **Circulation:** 8,600. **Advertising:** accepted. **Conventions/Meetings:** annual meeting, for reps from Variety worldwide to meet, exchange ideas, and hold business meetings.

11409 ■ Village of Childhelp West
PO Box 247
Beaumont, CA 92223
Ph: (909)845-3155
Fax: (909)845-8412
E-mail: child@discover.net
URL: http://www.childhelpusa.org/regional/california
Contact: Yvonne Fedderson, Pres.
Founded: 1978. **Budget:** $6,800,000. **Languages:** English, Spanish. **Description:** A project of Childhelp U.S.A. (see separate entry). Residential program designed exclusively for abused children and their families. Maintains professional staff including childcare workers, social workers, therapists, teachers, nurses, family and child development specialists, and a consultant staff of physicians, psychiatrists, dentists, and psychologists. Provides care and treatment of the abused child in an environment offering pleasant physical surroundings and caring, nurturing attitudes from adults. Offers professional "crisis care" to victims of child abuse and follows through with long-term treatment for both the child and the parents. Treatment includes counseling, play therapy, exercise, arts

and crafts therapy, and speech, occupational, dance, and music therapy. Parents are taught to cope with their problems, thus preventing further child abuse when the family is reunited. **Convention/Meeting:** none. **Libraries: Type:** not open to the public. **Holdings:** 2,500; books, periodicals. **Subjects:** children's literature. **Programs:** Foster Family Agency; Head Start. **Affiliated With:** Childhelp USA. **Formerly:** (1982) Children's Village U.S.A.; (2000) Village of Childhelp.

11410 ■ Voices for America's Children
1000 Vermont Ave. NW, Ste.700
Washington, DC 20005
Ph: (202)289-0777
Fax: (202)289-0776
E-mail: voices@voices.org
URL: http://www.voicesforamericaschildren.org
Contact: William Bentley, Pres./CEO
Founded: 1984. **Members:** 64. **Staff:** 13. **Budget:** $1,500,000. **State Groups:** 37. **Local Groups:** 7. **Description:** Independent, state and local child advocacy organizations are full members; child advocacy groups who do not meet full membership criteria can be associate members. Serves as a forum for the exchange of ideas and information among members, whose activities impact on state and local public policy issues including basic income, family support service, child welfare, juvenile justice, education, health and nutrition, and child care. Seeks to stimulate the development and increase the effectiveness of state-based child advocacy organizations through multi-state projects. Goals include: increasing the ability of child advocacy organizations to influence public policy; maximizing the effectiveness of existing child advocacy resources and techniques; improving the fundraising methods and overall financial status of members; assisting in the development of new and emerging child advocacy organizations; enhancing public awareness of child advocates as responsible spokespersons for vulnerable children. Provides technical assistance to organizations involved in child advocacy; facilitates the exchange of assistance among members; develops methods of increasing the availability and use of information on children's issues. Maintains skills bank. **Libraries: Type:** reference. **Holdings:** 100; archival material, books, clippings, periodicals. **Subjects:** models of child advocacy materials from around the country. **Awards:** Florette Angel Award. **Frequency:** annual. **Type:** recognition. **Also Known As:** National Association of State-Based Child Advocacy Organizations. **Formerly:** (1993) Association of Child Advocates; (2004) National Association of Child Advocates. **Publications:** Annual Report, annual. Alternate Formats: online. **Conventions/ Meetings:** annual meeting - always June.

11411 ■ War Child USA
PO Box 212
Peterborough, NH 03458
Ph: (603)924-4318
Fax: (603)924-9023
E-mail: info@warchildusa.org
URL: http://www.warchildusa.org
Contact: Ms. Betsy Small-Campbell, Programs Dir.
Founded: 2001. **Staff:** 1. **Nonmembership. Multinational. Description:** Provides immediate, effective and sustainable aid to children around the world affected by war, including rehabilitation programs and counseling, schools and orphanages. **Boards:** Advisory. **Projects:** Bakery; Centre Notre Dame de Sacre Coeur; Displace Camps; Farm; Kindergarten; Orphanage Distribution; School. **Working Groups:** Fund Raising Partners. **Publications:** Newsletter, quarterly. E-newsletter and mail newsletter updating activities in US and abroad. Alternate Formats: online.

11412 ■ Watchlist on Children and Armed Conflict
c/o Women's Commission for Refugee Women and Children
122 E 42nd St., 12th Fl.
New York, NY 10168-1289
Ph: (212)551-3111

Fax: (212)551-3180
E-mail: watchlist@womenscommission.org
URL: http://www.watchlist.org
Contact: Julia Freedson, Dir.
Multinational. Description: Strives to end violations against children in armed conflicts. Works to ensure that the security and rights of children in armed conflicts around the world are protected. Compiles information on violations against children in conflicts in order to inform and influence the UN Security Council, UN and other international agencies, national governments and the public. **Telecommunication Services:** electronic mail, juliaf@womenscommission.org. **Publications:** Reports. Informs and influences the UN Security Council, UN and other international agencies, national governments, and the public. Alternate Formats: online.

11413 ■ World Association for Children and Parents (WACAP)
PO Box 88948
Seattle, WA 98138
Ph: (206)575-4550
Free: (800)732-1887
Fax: (206)575-4148
E-mail: wacap@wacap.org
URL: http://www.wacap.org
Contact: L. Michael Feltman, CEO
Founded: 1976. **Staff:** 40. **Languages:** Chinese, English, Japanese, Norwegian, Russian, Spanish. **Multinational. Description:** Individuals and organizations with an interest in homeless children. Promotes adoption of children unable to remain with their biological parents, and child sponsorship for children who are eligible for adoption but are unable to find homes. Assists families looking to adopt children and agencies seeking to place children with adoptive parents; operates child sponsorship program through which children eligible for adoption who have not yet been placed receive educational, health, and social services; provides technical assistance, financial aid, and equipment to child welfare programs operating in economically disadvantaged areas worldwide. **Programs:** Financial Assistance for Adoptions. **Projects:** Child Assistance and Sponsorship. **Subgroups:** Families Adopting Older Children; Solo Parenting Successfully. **Publications:** *Learning about Adoption (When Fertility is Your Goal)*. Brochure. Contains information about the adoption process, focusing on the struggles infertile couples face. **Price:** free ● *Selecting an Agency for International Adoption*. Pamphlet. Examines the importance of selecting the right agency. ● *WACAP Today*, quarterly. Magazine. **Price:** $25.00/year. Alternate Formats: online ● *WACAP: Where the Children Come First*. Brochure. Contains information about the programs of WACAP. **Price:** free. **Conventions/Meetings:** periodic Adoption Information Meeting - held weekly in Seattle, WA area.

11414 ■ World Orphans
1880 Off. Club Pointe, Ste.2100
Colorado Springs, CO 80920
Ph: (719)487-1700
Free: (888)677-4267
Fax: (719)487-1800
E-mail: info@worldorphans.org
URL: http://www.worldorphans.org
Contact: Paul Myhill, Pres./CEO
Founded: 1993. **Languages:** English, German, Spanish. **Multinational. Description:** Rescues orphaned and abandoned children in developing countries. Funds the construction of orphan homes required for local Christian churches. **Publications:** Newsletter.

11415 ■ Youth Advocate Program International (YAP International)
4545 42nd St. NW, Ste.209
Washington, DC 20016
Ph: (202)244-1986
Fax: (202)244-6396

E-mail: yapi@yapi.org
URL: http://www.yapi.org
Contact: Dr. Mary King, Co-Chair
Founded: 1994. **Multinational. Description:** Promotes and protects the rights and well-being of the world's youth. Fosters the creation, implementation and enforcement of international legal norms and protections for youth. Works to prevent and eliminate the worst forms of child labor, the use of children in armed conflict, and commercial sexual exploitation of children. Protects and ensures rights and services for children affected by war, exploitation, homelessness, discrimination, and internally-displaced children. Serves as an education and information resource for individuals, organizations and agencies throughout the world. **Publications:** Newsletter. **Price:** included in membership dues. Alternate Formats: online ● Annual Report, annual. Alternate Formats: online ● Booklets. **Price:** $6.00 per copy, plus shipping and handling. Alternate Formats: online ● Reports. Alternate Formats: online ● Papers. Alternate Formats: online.

Childbirth

11416 ■ Peaceful Beginnings (PB)
c/o Kari Niedermaier
18119 S Prairie Ave., No. 116
Torrance, CA 90504
Ph: (310)793-1050
E-mail: kari@peacefulbeginnings.net
URL: http://www.peacefulbeginnings.net
Contact: Kari Niedermaier, Contact
Founded: 1985. **Description:** Promotes various aspects of childbirth education including: positive birth options, breastfeeding, coping during the first trimester of pregnancy, perinatal loss, and postpartum adjustment. **Publications:** Booklets ● Also publishes information sheets and makes slides available.

Children

11417 ■ A. L. Mailman Family Foundation
707 Westchester Ave.
White Plains, NY 10604
Ph: (914)683-8089
Fax: (914)686-5519
E-mail: info@mailman.org
URL: http://www.mailman.org
Contact: Ms. Luba H. Lynch, Exec. Dir.
Founded: 1980. **Description:** Strives to enhance the abilities of families and communities to nurture their children by contributing to the building of child care systems, by promoting culturally diverse practices, and by advancing programs and practices that promote social justice. **Awards:** Grant. **Type:** recognition. **Programs:** Early Care and Education; Family Support; Moral Education and Social Responsibility.

11418 ■ African Cradle
1124 13th St.
Modesto, CA 95354
Ph: (209)525-9377
Fax: (209)525-9373
E-mail: info@africancradle.org
URL: http://www.africancradle.org
Contact: Amber Stime MSW, Exec. Dir./Founder
Founded: 1992. **Description:** Works with the Ethiopian government to find homes for children in need of adoption. Provides necessary care to infants and children in Ethiopia.

11419 ■ Angelcare (CAI)
PO Box 600370
San Diego, CA 92160-0370
Ph: (619)795-6234
Free: (888)264-5227
Fax: (619)795-6238
E-mail: info@angelcare.org
URL: http://www.angelcare.org
Contact: Dr. T.J. Grosser, Pres./CEO
Founded: 1977. **Staff:** 6. **Budget:** $5,400,000. **Description:** A "nondenominational charitable organiza-

tion that operates preschools and elementary schools, outreach to homeless street children with educational, medical care, nutrition assistance, community development, parenting training, and emergency relief to the poor and needy in Africa, Southeast Asia, Latin America, and Eastern Europe. Three national projects in the U.S.: 1. Angels on a Mission provides an opportunity for Americans of all ages to live and work among the poor in Third World Countries. Participants are responsible for their expenses. 2. Participates in the USA Today/USA Weekend's annual Make A Difference Day program, offering lesson plans and project suggestions with an "act locally, think globally" plan. 3. The Home Front Campaign gives Americans an opportunity to demonstrate their concern and patriotism by thanking, encouraging, and assisting low ranking military families who have a spouse deployed in the War on Terrorism. Funded through contributions and the operation of a child sponsorship program for children in its schools.". **Projects:** Home Front Campaign. **Study Groups:** The Pelican Patrol. **Also Known As:** Bridges of Hope; Children's Angelcare Aid International; (2005) Home Front Campaign. **Formerly:** (1998) Children's Aid International. **Publications:** *Angelcare Spirit*, quarterly. Newsletter. Includes member news and information on programs. **Price:** free. **Circulation:** 40,000. Also Cited As: *Angelcare Briefs*.

11420 ■ Association for Children for Enforcement of Support (ACES)
3474 Raymont Blvd., 2nd Fl.
University Heights, OH 44118
Free: (800)739-2237
Fax: (800)739-2237
E-mail: aces@childsupport-aces.org
URL: http://www.childsupport-aces.org
Contact: Ms. Debbie Kline, Exec. Dir.
Founded: 1984. **Members:** 50,000. **Staff:** 8. **Budget:** $655,000. **State Groups:** 5. **Local Groups:** 400. **Languages:** English, Spanish. **Description:** Custodial parents seeking legal enforcement of child support. Provides educational information about the legal rights involved in child support enforcement. Advocates improved child support enforcement services from the government. Seeks to increase public awareness of how a lack of child support affects children. Sponsors research and educational programs. Maintains speakers' bureau. **Also Known As:** Association for Children for Enforcement of Support. **Publications:** *Child Support - A Complete Reference Guide*. Book. **Price:** $49.95 plus shipping and handling ($4.50) ● *How to Collect Child Support*. Handbook. **Price:** $9.45 includes shipping ● *Status of Child Support in U.S.* ● Booklets (in English and Spanish). Contains paternity and medical support information. **Price:** free ● Newsletter, semiannual. **Conventions/Meetings:** annual conference and workshop ● monthly meeting.

11421 ■ Believe In Tomorrow National Children's Foundation
6601 Frederick Rd.
Baltimore, MD 21228
Ph: (410)744-1032
Free: (800)933-5470
Fax: (410)744-1984
E-mail: info@believeintomorrow.org
URL: http://www.believeintomorrow.org
Contact: Brian R. Morrison, Founder/CEO
Founded: 1982. **Staff:** 15. **Description:** Provides supportive services to thousands of children with life-threatening illnesses and their families each year. Four unique programs, including Children's Housing, Hands On Adventures, Pain Management and Distraction Technology, and the Dreamsurfer Network, provides ongoing support from the child's diagnosis to the end of the treatment process and ease the stress that families endure. Aims to inspire critically ill children and their families to focus on the promise of the future. Enables families to renew their spirit physically and mentally by providing unique, supportive programs and services. **Computer Services:** Online services, Dreamsurfer Network; a password protected website for critically ill children to share experiences, play games and learn about an illness ● online

services, links adolescent oncology support groups throughout U.S.A. **Programs:** Children's Housing; Hands On Adventure; Print Management and Distraction Technology. **Formerly:** (2002) Grant-A-Wish Foundation. **Publications:** *Dreamcatcher*, quarterly. Newsletter. **Conventions/Meetings:** quarterly board meeting.

11422 ■ Better Boys Foundation (BBF)
1512 S Pulaski Rd.
Chicago, IL 60623
Ph: (773)277-9582
E-mail: lkellman@bbfchicago.org
URL: http://www.bbfchicago.org
Contact: Leon Kellman, Pres.
Founded: 1961. **Staff:** 60. **Budget:** $2,000,000. **Description:** Local organization formed to help youngsters become better students and citizens by providing academic support, cultural enrichment, counseling, and recreational activities. Maintains Nana's House, a 15-bed, temporary living facility for homeless youth. The National Football League Players Association (see separate entry) has designated the foundation as its official charity. **Publications:** Newsletter, quarterly. Includes association news and special events. **Conventions/Meetings:** monthly board meeting.

11423 ■ Big Brothers Big Sisters of America (BBBSA)
230 N 13th St.
Philadelphia, PA 19107
Ph: (215)567-7000
Fax: (215)567-0394
E-mail: lmbmlc@bbbsa.org
URL: http://www.bbbsa.org
Contact: Judy Vredenburgh, Pres./CEO
Founded: 1904. **Staff:** 55. **Budget:** $4,800,000. **Regional Groups:** 11. **State Groups:** 4. **Local Groups:** 510. **Description:** Federation of professionally staffed local agencies administered by volunteer boards of directors. Operates One-To-One program which matches a child from a single parent home with an adult volunteer who serves as a mentor and role model. The match is made with assistance of a professionally trained caseworker who also supervises and supports the One-To-One relationship. Serves local agencies by ensuring compliance with standards and procedures established by the national board of directors. Provides training, evaluation, and technical assistance and consulting in areas of fundraising, recruiting, administration, public relations, publications, information services, and legal services. Compiles statistics; maintains placement service. **Awards: Frequency:** periodic. **Type:** recognition. **Recipient:** for exemplary best practices. **Computer Services:** Online services, pin pals. **Programs:** Little Moments Big Magic Leadership Circle. **Formed by Merger of:** Big Brothers of America; Big Sisters, International. **Publications:** *Agency Directory*, annual ● *Big Brothers Big Sisters of America Annual Report*, annual. Alternate Formats: online ● *Big Brothers Big Sisters of America—Correspondent*, 3/year. Promotes better communication between BBBSA and the public, and serves as a medium for the exchange of information and ideas involving affiliates. **Price:** free. **Circulation:** 13,000. **Advertising:** accepted ● *Experience the Magic*. Video. Alternate Formats: online ● *Little Moments, Big Magic: Inspirational Stories of Big Brothers and Big Sisters and the Magic They Create*. Book. **Price:** $19.95 ● *Pass It On*, periodic. Newsletter. **Conventions/Meetings:** annual conference (exhibits) - always 3rd week in June ● triennial Leadership Summit - conference (exhibits) - always June.

11424 ■ Brass Ring Society (BRS)
500 Macaw Ln., No. 5
Fern Park, FL 32730
Ph: (407)339-6188
Free: (800)666-WISH
Fax: (407)339-6369
E-mail: brassing@brassing.org
URL: http://www.cystic-l.org/handbook/html/the_brass_ring_society__inc.htm
Contact: Ray Esposito, Pres.
Founded: 1983. **Staff:** 1. **Budget:** $250,000. **Local Groups:** 20. **Description:** Represents individuals

who contribute their time, efforts, ideas, compassion, and monetary support toward programs for children including fulfilling the dreams of children with life-threatening illness. **Publications:** *The Carousel.* Newsletter. Describes "dream fulfillment" and other society programs for terminally ill children. Includes chapter, donor and staff and new member news. **Price:** included in membership dues.

11425 ■ Child-Friendly Initiative (CFI)
406 Cortland Ave.
San Francisco, CA 94110
Free: (877)448-0500
URL: http://www.childfriendly.org
Contact: Michele Mason, Founder
Founded: 1999. **Membership Dues:** individual, $25 (annual) ● business, $50 (annual). **Description:** Seeks to improve the lives of children. Creates a forum for public dialogue on the role of children in society. Educates the public about children's unique developmental needs. Promotes child-friendly policies and practices. **Computer Services:** database, child-friendly businesses ● mailing lists, of members. **Programs:** Child-Friendly Seal of Approval. **Publications:** Newsletter, monthly.

11426 ■ Child Trends (CT)
4301 Connecticut Ave. NW, Ste.350
Washington, DC 20008
Ph: (202)572-6000
Fax: (202)362-8420
E-mail: cemig@childtrends.org
URL: http://www.childtrends.org
Contact: Carol Emig, Pres.
Founded: 1979. **Staff:** 40. **Budget:** $5,000,000. **Nonmembership. Description:** Works to improve the lives of children by conducting research. Provides science-based information to improve decisions, programs, and policies that affect children. **Libraries: Type:** reference. **Subjects:** children, families. **Additional Websites:** http://www.childtrendsdatabank. org. **Publications:** *Facts at a Glance*, annual. Newsletter. Provides information on teen childbearing and related issues. **Price:** $5.00. **Circulation:** 10,000. Alternate Formats: online ● *Research Briefs*, bimonthly. Report ● Annual Report, annual. Alternate Formats: online. **Conventions/Meetings:** periodic conference.

11427 ■ Childhelp USA
15757 N 78th St.
Scottsdale, AZ 85260
Ph: (480)922-8212
Fax: (480)922-7061
URL: http://www.childhelpusa.org
Contact: Sara O'Meara, Chair/CEO
Founded: 1959. **Members:** 1,800. **Staff:** 500. **Budget:** $26,300,000. **Regional Groups:** 3. **Local Groups:** 19. **Description:** Serves more than 152,000 children and adults annually whose lives have been traumatized by child abuse. Programs include the Childhelp USA National Child Abuse Hotline, residential treatment facilities, child advocacy centers, group homes, foster family recruitment, training and certification, and child abuse prevention, education and training programs. **Awards: Type:** recognition. **Telecommunication Services:** hotline, Childhelp USA National Child Abuse Hotline, (800)4-A-CHILD, provides services in 140 languages, using translators. **Affiliated With:** Advertising Council. **Formerly:** Children's Village U.S.A.; International Orphans, Inc. **Publications:** *Childhelp USA Newsletter*, periodic ● Annual Report, annual.

11428 ■ Childreach, United States Member of Plan International
155 Plan Way
Warwick, RI 02886
Ph: (401)738-5600
Free: (800)556-7918
Fax: (401)738-5608
E-mail: donorrelations@childreach.org
URL: http://www.childreach.org
Contact: Samuel A. Worthington, Pres./Natl. Exec. Dir.
Founded: 1937. **Staff:** 86. **Budget:** $33,759,000. **Languages:** English, Spanish. **Description:** U.S.

member of Plan International. U.S. sponsors assisting 100,000 needy children in 43 countries of Africa, Asia, Central America, the Caribbean, and South America. Programs combine personal communication with grass roots projects in health, education, family livelihood, and community development to help children and their families lift themselves up out of poverty. Maintains international development education curriculum for fourth and sixth graders and international children's art exhibit. Operates charitable program. Maintains speakers' bureau and library. **Awards: Type:** recognition. **Divisions:** Advertising; Information Systems/Operations; Program Development; Program Development/International Relations; SponsorReach; Sponsorship. **Programs:** Child Centered; Worldwide. **Affiliated With:** Plan Japan. **Formerly:** Child Reach; (1990) Foster Parents Plan - U.S.A.; (1992) PLAN International - U.S.A. **Publications:** *Childreach Magazine*, 3/year. Newsletter. Covers field program activities. **Price:** free. **Circulation:** 80,000 ● Also publishes educational brochures and pamphlets.

11429 ■ Children Before Dogs (CBD)
565 W End Ave.
New York, NY 10024
Ph: (212)873-5507
Contact: Fran Lee, Contact
Founded: 1971. **Description:** Division of Fran Lee Foundation (see separate entry) that deals with consumer problems. Membership includes individuals and groups around the world. Advocates educating the irresponsible pet owner who has lost understanding both of the nature of his pet and of what ownership involves. Tries to bring priorities into a pet-oriented society by stressing that many children are undernourished, while pet food companies thrive. Seeks to educate the public on the danger of disease that can be transmitted from animals to humans, especially between dogs and children; opposes participation of children in Earth Day clean-ups. Maintains speakers' bureau; conducts medical-consumer research programs; acts as resident consumer advocate for many television stations. Advocates the enforcement of pet control laws; is responsible for the prohibition of pets in food stores and restaurants and the declaration of Visceral Larva Migrans as a reportable disease in New York City. Is currently working to compel city officials to enforce litter and dog waste laws ensuring a safe and healthy environment. **Libraries: Type:** reference. **Holdings:** 2,000; archival material.

11430 ■ Children, Inc. (CI)
4205 Dover Rd.
Richmond, VA 23221
Ph: (804)359-4562
Free: (800)538-5381
Fax: (804)353-7541
E-mail: sponsorship@children-inc.org
URL: http://www.childrenincorporated.com
Contact: Marian Cummins, Pres./CEO
Founded: 1964. **Staff:** 34. **Budget:** $5,565,000. **Languages:** English, Spanish. **Multinational. Description:** Aims to assist children of all races and creeds, administering to their physical, mental, and spiritual needs. Works in 24 countries, assisting 16,000 children in more than 300 projects. Provides food, clothing, school supplies, medical needs, and other personal necessities. Assists with the repair of buildings and equipment; furnishes new desks, physical training equipment, and supplementary funds for teacher salaries. Conducts fundraising activities; has received citations from former President Richard Nixon, the Eastern Navajo Tribal Council, the Mayors of Seoul and Pusan, Republic of Korea, the Governor of Kanagawa Prefecture, Japan, and others. **Convention/Meeting:** none. **Publications:** *C.I. News*, quarterly. Newsletter. Contains pictures and descriptions of world-wide affiliated orphanages, schools, and welfare centers; available to sponsors and interested others.

11431 ■ Children's Creative Response to Conflict Program (CCRC)
521 N Broadway
Box 271
Nyack, NY 10960

Ph: (845)353-1796
Fax: (845)358-4924
E-mail: ccrcnyack@aol.com
URL: http://www.planet-rockland.org/conflict
Contact: Priscilla Prutzman, Exec. Dir.
Founded: 1972. **Staff:** 10. **Budget:** $500,000. **Regional Groups:** 35. **Languages:** Arabic, English, French, German, Russian, Serbian, Spanish. **Description:** Seeks to help children learn to live peacefully with others and to acquire the attitudes and skills necessary for resolving conflict. Frequently works directly with children and seeks to share skills with those who work with children. Conducts in-service courses and graduate courses for teachers and others who work with children. **Libraries: Type:** reference. **Holdings:** 2,000. **Subjects:** conflict resolution, BIAS awareness. **Awards:** Certificates of Completion and Appreciation. **Type:** recognition. **Affiliated With:** Fellowship of Reconciliation - USA. **Also Known As:** (2000) Creative Response to Conflict. **Publications:** *A Year of SCRC: 35 Experiential Workshops for the Classroom.* Article. Written by students; creative response to conflict. ● *Friendly Classroom for a Small Planet.* Handbook. **Price:** $17.00 ● *Sharing Space*, 3/year. Newsletter. **Price:** $15.00/year ● *Starting Out Right—Nurturing Young Children As Peacemakers.* Article. Features discussions on nonviolent parenting. **Price:** $9.95 ● Brochures. **Price:** first ten free; $5.00 ● Also publishes a songbook and makes available article reprints and videos. **Conventions/Meetings:** workshop.

11432 ■ Children's Defense Fund (CDF)
25 E St. NW
Washington, DC 20001
Ph: (202)628-8787
Free: (800)233-1200
Fax: (202)662-3510
E-mail: cdfinfo@childrensdefense.org
URL: http://www.childrensdefense.org
Contact: Marian Wright Edelman, Founder/Pres.
Founded: 1973. **Staff:** 150. **Budget:** $13,000,000. **State Groups:** 3. **Local Groups:** 4. **Description:** Provides systematic, long-range advocacy on behalf of the nation's children and teenagers. Engages in research, public education, monitoring of federal agencies, litigation, legislative drafting and testimony, assistance to state and local groups, and community organizing in areas of child welfare, child health, adolescent pregnancy prevention, child care and development, family income, family services, prevention of violence against and by children and child mental health. Works with individuals and groups to change policies and practices resulting in neglect or maltreatment of millions of children. Advocates: access to existing programs and services; creation of new programs and services where necessary; consistent emphasis on prevention; enforcement of civil rights laws; program accountability; strong parent and community role in decision-making; adequate funding for essential programs for children. Compiles statistics. **Libraries: Type:** not open to the public. **Awards:** Beat the Odds Award. **Frequency:** annual. **Type:** scholarship. **Recipient:** for youths (high school age) who have achieved success despite facing such obstacles as poverty, or family problems. **Departments:** Communications; Development; Finance and Administration; Government and Community Affairs; Programs and Policies; Special Projects. **Divisions:** Adolescent Pregnancy Prevention; Child Care; Child Welfare; Education; Family Support; Health; Research; Youth Employment. **Formerly:** (1978) Children's Defense Fund of the Washington Research Project. **Publications:** *CDF Reports*, monthly. Newsletters. Provides articles on issues relating to children and adolescents. Topics include childcare, health, education, and teen pregnancy prevention. **Price:** $29.95/year. ISSN: 0276-6531. **Circulation:** 5,700 ● *The Health of America's Children: Maternal and Child Health Data Book* ● *The State of America's Children*, annual. Examines the status of America's children, youths, and families. Emphasizes ways to improve childcare welfare, and more. ● Books ● Handbooks ● Also publishes posters on issues affecting children. **Conventions/Meetings:** annual Leave No Child Behind - conference (exhibits).

11433 ■ Children's Television Resource and Education Center (C-TREC)
Address Unknown since 2007
Description: Dedicated to helping children develop socially and succeed educationally. Develops curricula, teacher training and technical support projects, media programming and software and presentations, workshops and education products for the family. **Conventions/Meetings:** workshop.

11434 ■ Children's Wish Foundation International (CWFI)
8615 Roswell Rd.
Atlanta, GA 30350-7526
Ph: (770)393-9474
Free: (800)323-WISH
Fax: (770)393-0683
E-mail: contact@childrenwish.org
URL: http://www.childrenswish.org
Contact: Linda Dozoretz, Exec. Dir./Founder
Founded: 1985. **Staff:** 15. **Budget:** $25,000,000. **Multinational. Description:** Seeks to fulfill the wishes of terminally ill children under 18 years old. Maintains speakers' bureau. Provides children's services throughout the world. **Computer Services:** database ● mailing lists. **Programs:** Camp; Hospital Entertainers; Special Outings. **Formerly:** Children's Wish Foundation. **Publications:** *Wishing Well*, quarterly. Newsletter ● Brochures, quarterly. **Price:** free. **Circulation:** 4,000,000. **Conventions/Meetings:** quarterly board meeting.

11435 ■ Christian Children's Fund (CCF)
2821 Emerywood Pkwy.
Box 26484
Richmond, VA 23294
Ph: (804)756-2700
Free: (800)776-6767
Fax: (804)756-2718
E-mail: questions@ccfusa.org
URL: http://www.christianchildrensfund.org
Contact: Dr. John F. Schultz, Pres.
Founded: 1938. **Staff:** 610. **Budget:** $137,000,000. **Multinational. Description:** International, nonsectarian child development organization providing food, clothing, medical care and educational opportunities to children of all races and creeds. Works through the donations of sponsors who maintain personal contact with the child they help support. Provides assistance to needy children and their families in 32 countries including the U.S.A. Member of American Council for Voluntary International Action, and the NGO Committee on UNICEF. **Libraries: Type:** reference. **Holdings:** 2,500. **Subjects:** child care and development; the social, political and economic situations of children. **Programs:** International. **Subgroups:** Finance and Operations; International Fund Raising; Marketing and Sponsor Services. **Supersedes:** China's Children Fund. **Publications:** *Children's Circle News*, quarterly. Newsletter. Contains planned giving news and information. **Price:** free. **Circulation:** 70,000 ● *ChildWire*, monthly. Newsletter. Features updates on the activities of the association. **Price:** free for members. Alternate Formats: online ● *Childworld*, quarterly. Magazine. Includes articles on third world problems of children, families, and communities. **Price:** free. **Circulation:** 300,000 ● Annual Report, annual. **Circulation:** 320,000. Alternate Formats: online. **Conventions/Meetings:** quarterly board meeting ● biennial international conference.

11436 ■ Committee for Mother and Child Rights (CMCR)
6536 Colgate Ave.
Los Angeles, CA 90048-4411
Ph: (323)634-0543
Contact: Elizabeth Owen, Natl.Coor.
Founded: 1980. **Members:** 6,000. **Description:** Serves mothers who have child custody problems related to divorce. Purposes are to help mothers and children who are going through the trauma of contested custody or who have been through it, or have custody but fear losing it, and to educate the public about some of the injustices that are occurring to mothers and children. Aims are to improve the status

of mothers because "when mothers cease to be powerless, children will thrive".

11437 ■ The Dawkins Project
1531 Palmer Dr.
Fayetteville, NC 28303
Ph: (910)488-3953
E-mail: paulandrewdawkins@yahoo.com
Contact: Paul Andrew Dawkins, Founder & Exec.Dir.
Founded: 1990. **Staff:** 2. **Budget:** $25,000. **Non-membership. Description:** Promotes the safety, health, and well-being of children. Provides information on safety issues, such as seat belt and car seat usage, through the Facts for Kids to Grow On series of public service announcements. Conducts educational programs; operates speakers' bureau; compiles statistics. **Libraries: Type:** reference. **Holdings:** archival material. **Awards:** Dawkins Medical Scholars Program. **Frequency:** annual. **Type:** scholarship ● Dawkins Outstanding Educators. **Frequency:** annual. **Type:** scholarship ● Dawkins Teaching Scholars Program. **Frequency:** annual. **Type:** scholarship. **Formerly:** (2000) Paul Andrew Dawkins Children's Project. **Publications:** *A Day in the Life*. Books. Series of 12 books featuring essays written by writers of all ages. ● *Celebrations*. Books. Series of approximately 39 books, featuring letters and photos celebrating loved ones. ● *The Dawkins Report*. Alternate Formats: online ● *Offsprings*, monthly. Newsletter. For children and parents; includes profiles of outstanding individuals and reports on current issues affecting children. **Price:** free. **Advertising:** accepted. **Conventions/Meetings:** annual conference (exhibits) - always January 15-16, Fayetteville, NC.

11438 ■ Dream Factory (DF)
200 W Broadway, Ste.504
Louisville, KY 40202
Ph: (502)561-3001
Free: (800)456-7556
Fax: (502)561-3004
E-mail: info@dreamfactoryinc.com
URL: http://www.dreamfactoryinc.com
Contact: Anne Polivka Bunger, Natl. Dir./CEO
Founded: 1980. **Members:** 3,000. **Staff:** 6. **Budget:** $2,000,000. **State Groups:** 13. **Local Groups:** 19. **Description:** Volunteers devoted to granting the dreams of chronically or critically ill children. Seeks to bring smiles to the faces of seriously ill children. Promotes a better family atmosphere during a prolonged illness. Involves the community in granting wishes to children. Raises funds necessary to provide dreams; has honored requests for meetings with celebrities, trips to Disney World, shopping sprees, pets, everything except for motorized vehicles, medical equipment or weapons. **Additional Websites:** http://www.dreamfactoryinc.org, http://www.dreamfactoryinc.net. **Conventions/Meetings:** annual conference.

11439 ■ Famous Fone Friends (FFF)
Address Unknown since 2007
Founded: 1986. **Members:** 100. **Membership Dues:** individual, $20 (annual) ● gold, $100 (annual). **Budget:** $3,000. **Regional Groups:** 1. **Description:** Seeks to raise the spirits of sick, hospitalized, and homebound children. A sick child's doctor or nurse contacts FFF, which in turn arranges for a well-known actor, athlete, or other celebrity to call the child for a friendly chat. Conducts annual Holiday Calling Day. (Because all participants in the FFF are volunteers, requests for specific stars are not recommended.). **Publications:** *Famous Friend News*, biennial. Includes news updates and membership and entertainer listings. ● *FFF Memo*, 3/year. **Conventions/Meetings:** semiannual meeting.

11440 ■ Foster Grandparent Program (FGP)
c/o Florida Senior Programs, Inc.
7400 Laurel Hill Oaks Cir.
Orlando, FL 32818
Ph: (407)298-4180
Fax: (407)298-2725

E-mail: fgpcf@fostergrandparentprogram.org
URL: http://www.fostergrandparentprogram.org/
    foster_grandpx.html
Contact: Ann Smith, Dir.
Founded: 1965. **Members:** 28,000. **Budget:** $98,500,000. **Local Groups:** 333. **Languages:** English, Spanish. **Description:** A program administered by the Corporation for National Service, part of the federal government. Volunteers are low-income persons (age 60 and over) who provide person-to-person assistance to children with special or exceptional needs. Provides services to abused and neglected children, children with learning disabilities, children with AIDS, teen parents, and juvenile delinquents. Volunteers work in schools and hospitals for retarded, disturbed, and handicapped children, day care centers, correctional institutions, city hospital wards, and other settings. Responsibilities include assisting in physical or speech therapy, teaching parenting skills, feeding and dressing the children, and providing emotional support. **Awards:** FGP. **Type:** grant. **Publications:** *Grand Times*, quarterly. Newsletter. Includes current issues and activities. ● Brochure, periodic. Gives overview of the program. **Price:** free. **Conventions/Meetings:** periodic meeting, training and technical assistance (exhibits).

11441 ■ Friends of Karen (FK)
PO Box 190
Purdys, NY 10578-0190
Ph: (914)277-4547
Fax: (914)277-4967
E-mail: info@friendsofkaren.org
URL: http://www.FriendsofKaren.org
Contact: Stacy Kellner Rosenberg, Exec. Dir.
Founded: 1978. **Staff:** 17. **Budget:** $1,700,000. **Languages:** Cantonese, Chinese, English, Mandarin Dialects, Spanish. **Description:** Provides advocacy and financial and emotional support to children with life-threatening illnesses and to their families. Identifies and coordinates resources and provides direct assistance when needed. Assists over 5000 families in the New York metropolitan area. Encourages the development of similar programs nationally and advises. (Karen MacInnes was the first child to be helped by the late Sheila Petersen, founder of the organization.) Handles a national outreach program for referrals coming outside the organization's primary service area and guidance to similar efforts using Friends of Karen as a model. **Libraries: Type:** reference. **Publications:** Newsletter, semiannual. **Price:** free. **Circulation:** 22,000.

11442 ■ Futures for Children (FFC)
9600 Tennyson St. NE
Albuquerque, NM 87122-2282
Ph: (505)821-2828
Free: (800)545-6843
Fax: (505)821-4141
E-mail: info@futuresforchildren.org
URL: http://www.futuresforchildren.org
Contact: James L. West, Pres./CEO
Founded: 1961. **Membership Dues:** mentorship, $420 (annual). **Staff:** 22. **Budget:** $2,000,000. **Languages:** English, Spanish. **Description:** Ensures the right of Native American children to an education. Through its Circles of Support, encourages student success and leadership. Nationally, 3 out of 10 Native students drop out before graduating high school, however, 95% of Futures students are promoted or graduate from high school and 30-40% enroll in post-secondary education. Seeks support through adult-to-child mentoring, gifts, grants, memorials and bequests to expend its educational services. **Computer Services:** database ● mailing lists. **Publications:** *Guidebook for Community Counselors*. Newsletter ● *Storyteller*, quarterly. Newsletter. Programmatic activities. **Price:** free. **Circulation:** 6,000 ● Annual Report, annual. **Conventions/Meetings:** quarterly workshop.

11443 ■ Give Kids the World Village (GKTW)
210 S Bass Rd.
Kissimmee, FL 34746-6034
Ph: (407)396-1114
Free: (800)995-KIDS

Fax: (407)396-1207
E-mail: dream@gktw.org
URL: http://www.gktw.org
Contact: Pamela Landwirth, Pres.
Founded: 1986. **Staff:** 120. **Budget:** $6,000,000.
Nonmembership. Description: Aims to create magical memories and fulfill wishes for children with life-threatening illnesses and their families. Provides accommodations at its whimsical resort, donated attractions tickets, meals and more for a week-long vacation; has welcomed nearly 75,000 families from all 50 states and 53 countries. **Programs:** Kids Club. **Affiliated With:** Dream Factory; Make-A-Wish Foundation of America. **Formerly:** (1998) Give Kids the World; (2001) Give Kids the World Foundation; (2005) Give Kids the World Trust. **Publications:** *Angel Advisor*, quarterly. Newsletter ● *Clayton's Corner*. Newsletter ● *Miracles and Memories*. Newsletter ● Brochure.

11444 ■ Healing the Children (HTC)

PO Box 9065
Spokane, WA 99209-9065
Ph: (509)327-4281
Free: (800)992-0324
Fax: (509)327-4284
E-mail: administrator@healingthechildren.org
URL: http://www.healingthechildren.org
Contact: Carol Borneman, Natl. Exec. Sec.
Founded: 1979. **Staff:** 1. **Regional Groups:** 14. **Description:** Referral agency seeking to enable underprivileged children worldwide to receive medical care in the U.S. that is unavailable in their native countries. Acts as liaison for patients in making agreements with hospitals and arrangements with foreign governments in obtaining necessary visas; raises funds to provide air fare. Recruits foster families to care for the children in the community where they receive medical care. Compiles statistics. **Committees:** Finance; Public Relations. **Formerly:** (1989) Heal the Children. **Publications:** Brochure ● Newsletter, bimonthly. **Conventions/Meetings:** annual conference.

11445 ■ Holt International Children's Services (HICS)

1195 City View
PO Box 2880
Eugene, OR 97402
Ph: (541)687-2202
Fax: (541)683-6175
E-mail: info@holtinternational.org
URL: http://www.holtintl.org
Contact: Gary Garner, Pres./CEO
Founded: 1956. **Staff:** 100. **Budget:** $11,000,000. **Description:** Aims to deinstitutionalize children in developing countries by rehabilitating biological families, encouraging adoption within the developing country, and arranging inter-country adoption when in the best interest of the child. Offers assistance to children in Korea, India, Philippines, Thailand, Vietnam, Hong Kong, China, Romania, and Latin America, as well as the U.S. Provides funds for food, clothing, housing, and medical care until an adoptive home can be found. Offers nutrition education, foster homes, well-baby clinics, physical, occupational, and speech therapy, and special care and education for the retarded. All services are supported through donations, sponsorships, and adoption fees. **Formerly:** (1978) Holt Adoption Program and Holt Children's Services. **Publications:** *Holt International Children's Services Annual Report*, annual ● *Holt International Ma___ine*, 6/year. Includes list of children read___ ___tion, letter, and photos; for Holt sup___ ___ilies who have adopted child___ ___ries. **Price:** $20.00/year.
___ ___: 20,000.

Giving

E-mail: info@huginternationally.org
URL: http://www.huginternationally.org
Contact: Judy Broom, Pres./Founder/Exec. Dir.
Founded: 1990. **Multinational. Description:** Works to touch the lives of children in need. Supports hospitals and orphanages in areas where economic deprivation, war or natural disasters have resulted in poor living conditions. Provides physical and emotional nurturing, medical and educational training, and humanitarian aid. **Publications:** Newsletter. Alternate Formats: online ● Brochure. Alternate Formats: online.

11447 ■ Institutes for the Achievement of Human Potential (IAHP)

8801 Stenton Ave.
Wyndmoor, PA 19038
Ph: (215)233-2050
Fax: (215)233-9312
E-mail: institutes@iahp.org
URL: http://www.iahp.org
Contact: Janet Doman, Dir.
Founded: 1955. **Staff:** 100. **Languages:** English, French, German, Italian, Japanese, Spanish. **Description:** Promotes the achievement of full potential for all individuals. Maintains Children's Institute which conducts parent orientation and evaluation of brain-injured children with severe disabilities as well as apparently well children who are not realizing full potential. Conducts courses for parents interested in fostering the intellectual development and potential of their children. Sponsors the Institute for Clinical Investigation which promotes improved methods of helping brain-injured children reach a level of performance in accordance with their potential. Operates On-Campus International School and Off-Campus International School. **Libraries: Type:** reference. **Awards:** Leonardo da Vinci Award. **Frequency:** annual. **Type:** recognition. **Recipient:** for recognition of significant action in connection with children ● World Organization for Human Potential Award: The Spectrum Award. **Type:** recognition. **Recipient:** for recognition of achievement in the field. **Telecommunication Services:** additional toll-free number, (800)344-6685, mailbox 2502. **Subgroups:** Temple Fay Institute For Academics. **Affiliated With:** World Organization for Human Potential. **Publications:** *How to Multiply Your Baby's Intelligence* ● *The In Report* (in English, Italian, Japanese, and Spanish), quarterly ● *Kids Who Start Ahead, Stay Ahead* ● *What to Do About Your Brain-Injured Child*. Books. **Conventions/Meetings:** annual meeting - always first week in May, Philadelphia, PA.

11448 ■ International Child Care U.S.A. (ICCUSA)

3620 N High St., Ste.110
Columbus, OH 43214-0485
Ph: (614)447-9952
Free: (800)722-4453
Fax: (614)447-1123
E-mail: iccusa@intlchildcare.org
URL: http://www.intlchildcare.org/index.php
Contact: Mr. Keith Mumma, Natl. Dir.
Founded: 1965. **Budget:** $499,000. **Description:** Seeks to: create a better life for children in Haiti through nutritional care, education, and medical aid; help people of developing countries become self-sufficient and assume responsibility for their own programs. Maintains Grace Children's Hospital in Port-au-Prince, Haiti, which has an inpatient pediatric ward, outpatient adult and pediatric clinics, and community outreach programs. Conducts community-based health programs to provide treatment for contagious illnesses such as TB and HIV and education about basic health practices such as sanitation and hygiene. Sponsors program whereby TB drugs are dispensed at cost to Haitian clinics and hospitals. Trains local leaders in the Dominican Republic in community-based health and rehabilitation promotion programs. Provides children's mission education curriculum to churches and schools in the USA and abroad at no cost. Organizes Mission Education Encounter Teams that travel from North America to Haiti and/or the Dominican Republic for cultural exchange and service learning. **Affiliated With:** International Child Care - Canada. **Formerly:** (1978) Child Care Foundation. **Publications:** *Grace*, quarterly. Newsletter. Alternate Formats: online ● Brochure. **Conventions/Meetings:** periodic board meeting, in conjunction with International Child Care - Canada.

11449 ■ Jack and Jill of America (JJA)

1930 17th St. NW
Washington, DC 20009
Ph: (202)667-7010
Fax: (202)667-6133
E-mail: jackandjill.inc@verizon.net
URL: http://www.jack-and-jill.org
Contact: Alice Leigh Peoples, Natl. Pres.
Founded: 1938. **Members:** 37,000. **Membership Dues:** individual, $55 (annual) ● national, $250 (10/year) ● life-national (member for 15 years), $200 ● life-regional (member for 15 years), $150 ● regional, $200 (10/year) ● life-national (member for 10 years), $250. **Budget:** $400,000. **Regional Groups:** 7. **Local Groups:** 220. **Description:** Parents interested in "PEP" (parenting, education, and political involvement). Objectives are to create a medium of contact among children to stimulate growth and development and to provide them with a constructive cultural, civic, recreational, and social program. Helps parents learn more about their children. Encourages awareness of community needs. Seeks to ensure equal opportunities and advantages for all children. Sponsors Jack and Jill of America Foundation (see separate entry). **Affiliated With:** Jack and Jill of America Foundation. **Publications:** *Intercom*. Newsletter ● *Scope*, annual. Newspaper ● *Up the Hill*, annual. Journal. **Conventions/Meetings:** biennial convention (exhibits) - always even-numbered years ● annual Teen Conference - meeting (exhibits).

11450 ■ Jack and Jill of America Foundation (JJAF)

1930 17th St. NW
Washington, DC 20009
Ph: (202)232-5290
Fax: (202)232-1747
E-mail: administration@jackandjillfoundation.org
URL: http://www.jackandjillfoundation.org
Contact: Grace E. Speights, Pres.
Founded: 1968. **Members:** 26. **Staff:** 2. **Budget:** $200,000. **Description:** Officers of Jack and Jill of America, community leaders, parents, youth representatives, and others. Seeks to improve educational, cultural, and civic opportunities for minority youth. Monitors legislative changes affecting the development of youth. Supports college-level achievement motivation projects, preschool programs, and college preparatory programs for high school students. **Libraries: Type:** reference. **Subjects:** foundation projects. **Awards: Type:** grant. **Recipient:** for exemplary educational community projects throughout the country ● National College Scholarship Award. **Frequency:** annual. **Type:** scholarship. **Recipient:** for African American high school seniors ● **Type:** recognition. **Affiliated With:** Jack and Jill of America. **Publications:** *Intercom*, annual. Newsletter ● Annual Report, annual. **Conventions/Meetings:** annual board meeting.

11451 ■ Kids Fund (KF)

416 Benninghaus Rd.
Baltimore, MD 21212
Ph: (410)532-9330
Free: (877)532-9330
E-mail: info@kidsfundinc.org
URL: http://www.kidsfundinc.org
Contact: George Cooper, Contact
Founded: 1980. **Staff:** 1. **Description:** Seeks to provide young people with tools and resources needed to develop self-respect, to prevent problems growing out of feelings of isolation and despair, and to make wise decisions about critical issues. Provides funds to community organizations for the development of innovative programs in parent-child communication. **Convention/Meeting:** none.

11452 ■ Kids at Hope
2501 W Dunlap Ave.
Phoenix, AZ 85021
Ph: (602)674-0026
Free: (866)275-HOPE
Fax: (602)674-0034
E-mail: kim@kidsathope.org
URL: http://www.kidsathope.org
Contact: Rick Miller, Founder/Chief Treasure Hunter
Founded: 2000. **Description:** Promotes belief system that "all children are capable of success - no exceptions" through trainings, program enhancements, research and technical assistance. **Publications:** *From Youth at Risk to Kids at Hope.* Book ● *Kids at Hope: Every Child Can Succeed, No Exceptions.* Book.

11453 ■ Kids Konnected
27071 Cabot Rd., Ste.102
Laguna Hills, CA 92653
Ph: (949)582-5443
Free: (800)899-2866
E-mail: info@kidskonnected.org
URL: http://www.kidskonnected.org
Contact: Dave Peters, Exec. Dir.
Founded: 1993. **Description:** Provides friendship, understanding, education and support for children who have a parent with cancer or have lost a parent to cancer. Offers summer camps, outreach programs and workshops that teach new skills, confidence and teamwork. Provides programs that are designed to teach kids the grief process and to help them work through and live with their loss. **Publications:** *Gillette Gazette,* quarterly. Newsletter. Features highlights from recent events, information on upcoming activities and informative articles. Alternate Formats: online.

11454 ■ Make-A-Wish Foundation of America (MAWFA)
3550 N Central Ave., Ste.300
Phoenix, AZ 85012-2127
Ph: (602)279-9474
Free: (800)722-9474
Fax: (602)279-0855
E-mail: mawfa@wish.org
URL: http://www.worldwish.org
Contact: David A. Williams, Pres./CEO
Founded: 1980. **Members:** 25,000. **Staff:** 68. **Budget:** $138,000,000. **Regional Groups:** 76. **Multinational. Description:** Grants wishes to children with terminal or life-threatening illnesses, thereby providing these children and their families with special memories and a welcome respite from the daily stress of their situation. Considers the wish of any child with a terminal or life-threatening illness up to the age of 18. Many of the wishes are for trips to Disney World or Disneyland; however, the foundation has also accomplished the following: made one child a fireman, and another a lawyer with a degree; provided an AirEvac plane for a boy who wanted to die at home; sent a teenager to the Super Bowl; brought a girl from the Midwest to Phoenix, AZ in the winter because she missed the sunshine; sent birthday greetings to a boy who wanted nothing more. All expenses are covered by the foundation. **Additional Websites:** http://www.wish.org. **Affiliated With:** Make-A-Wish Foundation of America. **Publications:** Newsletter, quarterly. **Conventions/Meetings:** annual conference - always third week of October ● annual conference - always spring.

11455 ■ Make a Child Smile (MACS)
11110 W Oakland Park Blvd., No. 292
Sunrise, FL 33351
URL: http://www.makeachildsmile.org
Contact: Alexandra Davila, Pres./Dir.
Founded: 1998. **Description:** Provides emotional and financial support to families whose children suffer from chronic or life-threatening illnesses. **Computer Services:** Mailing lists. **Publications:** Newsletter. Alternate Formats: online.

11456 ■ Marine Toys for Tots Foundation
PO Box 1947
Quantico, VA 22134
Ph: (703)640-9433
Fax: (703)640-0917
E-mail: mtftf@toysfortots.org
URL: http://www.toysfortots.org
Contact: Lt. Gen. Matthew T. Cooper, Pres./CEO
Founded: 1991. **Staff:** 8. **Local Groups:** 400. **Description:** Fundraiser and support organization for the U.S. Marine Corps Reserves. Provides supplementary toys, promotion and support materials, as well as financial, administrative, advisory and logistic support. **Affiliated With:** Marine Toys for Tots Foundation. **Also Known As:** (2000) Toys for Tots Foundation. **Formerly:** (2004) Marine Corps Toys for Tots Foundation. **Publications:** *Toys For Tots Newsletter,* semiannual. Provides information about campaigns, corporate sponsors, and future events. ● *Annual Report,* annual. Provides information focusing on previous year's campaign, and information on governance and activities. Alternate Formats: online. **Conventions/Meetings:** board meeting - spring, summer, fall - in Washington, DC ● annual Campaign Kick-Off Luncheon - November in Washington, DC. 2007 Nov. 15, Alexandria, VA ● annual Toys for Tots Coordinator - conference - 2007 Sept. 14-17, Alexandria, VA ● annual Toys for Tots Reception - meeting, recognizes sponsors, donors, supporters and business partners.

11457 ■ Mothers of Murdered Youth (MOMY)
PO Box 17516
Colorado Springs, CO 80935
Ph: (719)231-8234
URL: http://www.momy.org
Contact: Jennifer J. Romero, Dir.
Description: Volunteers, mothers and family affected by murder. Provide support, attend funerals and court proceedings. Promote public awareness. Host vigils, rallies and memorial events.

11458 ■ National Association of Counsel for Children (NACC)
1825 Marion St., Ste.242
Denver, CO 80218
Ph: (303)864-5320
Free: (888)828-NACC
Fax: (303)864-5351
E-mail: advocate@naccchildlaw.org
URL: http://www.naccchildlaw.org
Contact: Mr. Marvin R. Ventrell JD, Pres./CEO
Founded: 1977. **Members:** 2,000. **Membership Dues:** individual, group, $90 (annual). **Staff:** 4. **State Groups:** 18. **Description:** Lawyers, judges, doctors, mental health professionals, social workers, court-appointed advocates, volunteers, and other persons interested in improving legal representation of children. Promotes education, support, and training for attorneys, guardians, and others who act as advocates for children. Seeks to enhance the efficiency and knowledge of children's attorneys by providing a forum for the exchange of information regarding cases; works to develop and improve children's law. Maintains brief bank of cases and briefs and speakers' bureau. **Libraries: Type:** reference. **Holdings:** audio recordings, audiovisuals, books, papers, periodicals, reports. **Awards:** Legal Advocacy Award. **Frequency:** annual. **Type:** recognition. **Computer Services:** database, public online access to membership directory/referral network. **Telecommunication Services:** electronic bulletin board, listserv available to members. **Publications:** *The Guardian,* quarterly. Newsletter. Promotes effective legal representation for children; includes articles on current court cases and decisions, and legal briefs. **Price:** included in membership dues. **Circulation:** 2,000. **Advertising:** accepted. Alternate Formats: online ● Books ● Brochures. **Conventions/Meetings:** annual National Children's Law Conference (exhibits) ● seminar, on issues of children's law.

11459 ■ National Center for Children in Poverty (NCCP)
215 W 125th St., 3rd Fl.
New York, NY 10027
Ph: (646)284-9600
Fax: (646)284-9623
E-mail: info@nccp.org
URL: http://www.nccp.org
Contact: Dr. Jane Kinitzer, Exec. Dir.
Founded: 1989. **Staff:** 35. **Nonmembership. Description:** Seeks to identify and promote strategies that prevent child poverty in the U.S. and that improve the lives of low-income children and families. Offers original research on family economic security, early care and learning, family stability, and child development, synthesis of academic and policy research in these areas, and tools to make this research easy to understand and use. **Publications:** *Children in Low-Income Immigrant Families Series,* periodic. Reports ● *Fact sheets,* quarterly. **Price:** free ● *Low-Income Families in the States: Results from the Family Resource Simulator,* periodic. Reports ● *Project THRIVE Issue Briefs,* periodic. Reports ● *Promoting the Emotional Well-Being of Children and Families Series,* periodic. Reports. Alternate Formats: online ● *Research-to-Policy Connections,* periodic. Reports ● *Statistical Research Reports,* annual. Alternate Formats: online.

11460 ■ National Tribal Child Support Association (NTCSA)
PO Box 154
Ada, OK 74820
Ph: (580)436-7016
E-mail: tlittledave@cherokee.org
URL: http://www.supporttribalchildren.org
Contact: Tracy Gourd Littledave, Pres.
Membership Dues: individual, $25-$35 (annual) ● tribe, $150 (annual) ● associate, $300 (annual). **Description:** Improves the quality of life for Indian children through communication, training and public awareness. **Programs:** Domestic Violence; Head Start; Indian Child Welfare; Tribal and CFR Courts.

11461 ■ Organization for the Lifelong Establishment of Paternity (OLEP)
Address Unknown since 2007
Founded: 1984. **Members:** 3. **Description:** Individuals encouraging the enactment into state law of Section 606 in the latest model code of the Uniform Parentage Act (2000)DNA Paternity Establishment, which permits a non-marital adult to establish paternity at any age, eleven states (as of 2001) have this provision. Conducting research on non-marital father and child relationships in order to determine other appropriate modifications in social attitudes and legal policies. relationships in order to determine other appropriate modifications in social attitudes and legal policies. **Publications:** *Illegitimate Conception: A New Look at This Father-Child Relationship.* **Advertising:** not accepted.

11462 ■ Orphan Foundation of America (OFA)
21351 Gentry Dr., Unit 130
Sterling, VA 20166
Ph: (571)203-0270
Fax: (571)203-0273
E-mail: help@orphan.org
URL: http://www.orphan.org
Contact: Eileen McCaffrey, Exec. Dir.
Founded: 1981. **Members:** 4,000. **Staff:** 4. **Budget:** $1,500,000. **Regional Groups:** 1. **State Groups:** 15. **Local Groups:** 15. **Description:** Orphaned and abandoned youth; volunteers and contributors. Assists orphaned, abandoned, and foster-care youth by providing guidance, support, friendship, and emergency help that is seldom available to children raised outside of the traditional family setting. Advocates orphaned and abandoned youth rights nationwide; administers project that develops public policy initiatives. Offers independent living support services and volunteer referral services. Sponsors Project Bridge Program, a community-based volunteer support network that assists youth in their transition from the child welfare system to independent young adulthood. Adult volunteers guide and assist orphans in planning, independent living and life skills development, job search, maintaining and recreation. Provides research

speakers' bureau, resource center, and orphan hall of fame. **Convention/Meeting:** none. **Libraries: Type:** reference. **Holdings:** archival material. **Subjects:** independent living skills. **Awards:** Casey Family Scholars Scholarship. **Type:** scholarship. **Recipient:** for young people who have spent at least 12 months in foster care and were not subsequently adopted ● Hildegard Lash Merit Scholarship. **Type:** scholarship. **Recipient:** for outstanding scholarship and community service by a college student ● Oliver Award. **Frequency:** annual. **Type:** recognition. **Programs:** Holiday; National Orphan Foundation Scholarship; Orphan Sponsor. **Formerly:** (1988) Orphan Foundation. **Publications:** Newsletter, quarterly.

11463 ■ People for Children
PO Box 13534
San Juan, PR 00908-3534
Fax: (787)754-5444
URL: http://www.rickymartinfoundation.org/english/programs/people_for_children.aspx
Contact: Angel Saltos, Pres.

Founded: 2004. **Description:** Works for educating and supporting the international framework for the elimination of trafficking of persons, especially children; promotes community-based programs that monitor and combat problems relating to exploitation of children, as well as in the areas of debt labor, forced labor, modern day slavery, and prostitution of children.

11464 ■ Project Children (PC)
PO Box 933
Greenwood Lake, NY 10925
Ph: (845)477-3472
Fax: (845)477-2334
E-mail: projectchildren@optonline.com
URL: http://www.projectchildren.com
Contact: Denis Mulcahy, Founder/Chm.

Founded: 1975. **Members:** 70. **Description:** Sponsored by Gaelic Cultural Society. Provides for children from Northern Ireland who are Roman Catholic, Protestant, or relatives of political prisoners to spend 6 weeks during the summer as the houseguests of American families. Sponsors local soccer program. **Awards:** Celt of the Year Award. **Frequency:** annual. **Type:** recognition. **Publications:** Brochure. **Conventions/Meetings:** monthly meeting.

11465 ■ RAINBOWS
2100 Golf Rd., No. 370
Rolling Meadows, IL 60008-4231
Ph: (847)952-1770
Free: (800)266-3206
Fax: (847)952-1774
E-mail: info@rainbows.org
URL: http://www.rainbows.org
Contact: Suzy Yehl Marta, Founder/Pres.

Founded: 1983. **Staff:** 10. **Budget:** $800,000. **State Groups:** 800. **Local Groups:** 800. **National Groups:** 7,200. **Description:** Offers peer support for children, adolescents and adults who are grieving a loss due to death, divorce or any other painful transition. Offers training and curricula for establishing grief peer support groups in schools, churches, and social service agencies; assists teachers, school administrators, and parents to help children through their period of grief. Conducts local training and implementation of programs through authorized registered directors. Operates in 49 state ncluding DC, Puerto Rico, Guam and 17 fo untries. **Divisions:** Adult; Elementary; e; Single Parent. **Formerly:** (1 ll God's Children. **Pub-licati al. Newsletter. Alter- Symphony. Booklet. gs:** annual work- ctors.

ren (RFC)

E-mail: rfc@rfc.org
URL: http://www.rfc.org
Contact: Amber Black, Public Relations Coor.

Founded: 1990. **Members:** 8,500. **Staff:** 3. **Budget:** $200,000. **Description:** Provides assistance for the educational and emotional needs of the children of targeted progressive activists. **Publications:** *AN EXECUTION IN THE FAMILY: One Sons Journey.* Book. **Price:** $20.00 signed hardcover copy (plus $10 if outside U.S.); $10.00 signed paperback copy (plus $10 if outside U.S.) ● *Carry It Forward and Pass It On,* semiannual. Newsletter. Alternate Formats: online.

11467 ■ Save the Children (SCF)
54 Wilton Rd.
Westport, CT 06880
Ph: (203)221-4030
Free: (800)728-3843
E-mail: twebster@savethechildren.org
URL: http://www.savethechildren.org
Contact: Zoe Baird, Pres.

Founded: 1932. **Staff:** 2,474. **Budget:** $105,071,000. **Languages:** Arabic, English, French, Spanish. **Description:** Voluntary, nonsectarian agency that assists children, families, and communities in the U.S. and abroad to achieve social and economic stability through community development and family self-help projects such as health, education and economic opportunities; offers aid to victims of disaster. Programs are designed to "contribute to the growth, dignity, independence and self-reliance of the individual". Conducts programs in Afghanistan, Angola, Armenia, Azerbaijan, Bangladesh, Bhutan, Bolivia, Burkina Faso, Cambodia, Cameroon, Colombia, Costa Rica, Croatia/Bosnian Refugees, Dominican Republic, Egypt, El Salvador, Ethiopia, Gambia, Gaza/West Bank, Georgia, Greece, Haiti, Honduras, Indonesia, Jordan, Korea, Laos, Lebanon, Malawi, Mali, Mexico, Mozambique, Nepal, Nicaragua, Pakistan, Philippines, Somalia, Sudan, Thailand, Tunisia, Vietnam, and Zimbabwe. U.S. programs focus on the southern mountains of Appalachia, inner cities, American Indian reservations, and the rural South. Maintains offices in New York City and Washington, DC. **Departments:** Development; Finance; Management. **Programs:** Literacy. **Affiliated With:** American Association for the Advancement of Science; American Library Association; American Public Health Association; Direct Marketing Association; Foundation Center; Global Health Council; Independent Sector; National Congress for Community Economic Development; National Neighborhood Coalition; Rural Coalition; Society for International Development - Italy; United Nations Association of the United States of America. **Absorbed:** (2000) Community Development Foundation. **Publications:** *Community Reports,* semiannual. Contains information on program areas worldwide. ● *Impact Magazine,* semiannual ● *Save the Children Reports,* periodic ● Annual Report, annual ● Also publishes papers on special issues.

11468 ■ Southern Early Childhood Association (SECA)
PO Box 55930
Little Rock, AR 72215-5930
Ph: (501)221-1648
Free: (800)305-7322
Fax: (501)227-5297
E-mail: gbean@southernearlychildhood.org
URL: http://www.SouthernEarlyChildhood.org
Contact: Glenda Bean, Exec. Dir.

Founded: 1948. **Members:** 17,500. **Staff:** 3. **Budget:** $540,000. **State Groups:** 13. **Description:** Early childhood educators, day care providers, program administrators, researchers, teacher trainers, and parents from the U.S. and abroad who share a common concern for the well-being of young children. Provides a unified voice on vital local, state, and federal issues affecting young children. Exchanges information and ideas through conferences and workshops. Explores contemporary issues in child development and early education through publications. **Awards:** Division for Development Grants. **Frequency:** annual. **Type:** grant. **Recipient:** to support exemplary early childhood project in the South ●

Friend of Children. **Frequency:** annual. **Type:** recognition. **Recipient:** for a strong advocate for children and families ● Helen B. Harley Scholarship. **Frequency:** annual. **Type:** scholarship. **Recipient:** to assist affiliate member to attend annual SECA conference ● Marian B. Hamilton Award. **Frequency:** annual. **Type:** grant. **Recipient:** to a local SECA affiliate of a designated state to support an affiliate project ● President's Award. **Frequency:** annual. **Type:** recognition. **Recipient:** for an outstanding state child advocate selected by designated states. **Computer Services:** Mailing lists. **Formerly:** (1993) Southern Association on Children Under Six. **Publications:** *Dimensions of Early Childhood,* 3/year. Journal. Features a professional informative journal on early childhood development. **Price:** $3.50/copy for non-members; $2.50/copy for members; $25.00/year in U.S.; $35.00/year outside U.S. ISSN: 1068-6177. **Circulation:** 21,000. **Advertising:** accepted ● Books ● Pamphlets ● Also publishes position papers. **Conventions/Meetings:** annual conference, includes products on education (exhibits) - March or April.

11469 ■ A Special Wish Foundation (ASWF)
1250 Memory Ln.
Columbus, OH 43209
Ph: (614)258-3186
Free: (800)486-WISH
Fax: (614)258-3518
E-mail: info@spwish.org
URL: http://www.spwish.org

Founded: 1982. **Members:** 250. **Staff:** 4. **Budget:** $550,000. **Regional Groups:** 17. **Description:** Physicians, nurses, social workers, psychologists, attorneys, and businesspeople. Works to grant wishes of children and adolescents under 20 years of age who are afflicted with a life-threatening disorder; recent wishes granted by the foundation include sending patients to Disney World and other trips and arranging for patients to meet celebrities. Offers in-service programs for hospital staffs. Operates speakers' bureau. **Publications:** Brochures ● Newsletter, quarterly. **Conventions/Meetings:** annual conference.

11470 ■ Starlight Children's Foundation
1850 Sawtelle Blvd., Ste.450
Los Angeles, CA 90025
Ph: (310)479-1212
Free: (800)315-2580
Fax: (310)479-1235
E-mail: info@starlight.org
URL: http://www.starlight.org

Founded: 1983. **Members:** 5,000. **Staff:** 50. **Budget:** $9,000,000. **State Groups:** 10. **Description:** Aims to improve the quality of life for seriously ill children and their families; provides in-hospital and outpatient programs and services. **Awards:** Heart of Gold Award. **Frequency:** annual. **Type:** recognition. **Formerly:** (1998) Starlight Foundation.

11471 ■ Students Helping Street Kids International (SHSKI)
PO Box 24117
Baltimore, MD 21227
Ph: (410)525-1051
Free: (877)543-7697
Fax: (410)525-1051
E-mail: sevans@helpthekids.org
URL: http://www.helpthekids.org
Contact: Stacey Evans Esq., Pres./Sec.

Founded: 1997. **Multinational. Description:** Helps save kids from tragedies of drugs, poverty, abuse and indifference. Provides funding for educational scholarships for needy children in developing countries. Offers service learning opportunity to students involved in fundraising.

11472 ■ Sunshine Foundation (SF)
1041 Mill Creek Dr.
Feasterville, PA 19053
Ph: (215)396-4770
Fax: (215)396-4774

E-mail: philly@sunshinefoundation.org
URL: http://www.sunshinefoundation.org
Contact: Bill Sample, Pres.
Founded: 1976. **Description:** Works to fulfill the wishes of chronically or terminally ill children, many of whom suffer from kidney disease, leukemia, or cancer. Raises funds to send children and their families on vacations together (on advice of the children's doctors); arranges other events (attendance at wrestling matches or plays, meetings with celebrities) to make sick or dying children happy. Since its inception, the foundation has granted more than 19,800 requests. **Libraries: Type:** reference; open to the public. **Computer Services:** Online services, referrals.

11473 ■ Warm Blankets Orphan Care International
5105 Tollview Dr., Ste.155
Rolling Meadows, IL 60008
Ph: (847)577-1070
Free: (877)33-BLANKET
Fax: (847)577-1080
E-mail: information@warmblankets.org
URL: http://www.warmblankets.org
Contact: Craig Muller, Pres./Dir.
Founded: 1999. **Multinational. Description:** Seeks to restore the lives of orphans in partnership with churches, corporations, organizations, and individuals.

11474 ■ A Wish With Wings
917 W Sanford St.
Arlington, TX 76012
Ph: (817)469-9474
Fax: (817)275-6005
E-mail: wish@awishwithwings.org
URL: http://www.awishwithwings.org
Contact: Kim Christian, Exec. Dir.
Founded: 1982. **Staff:** 1. **Budget:** $151,000. **Description:** Fulfills the wish of children (ages 3-18) with life-threatening diseases. Raises funds and makes arrangements with community groups to donate services or funding to make wishes of catastrophically ill children for toys, trips, or introductions to celebrities financially possible. Maintains speakers' bureau. **Committees:** Fund Raising; Public Relations; Screening; Speakers. **Programs:** Charity Motors Car Donation. **Publications:** *Cookin' Up Wishes.* Book. **Price:** $10.00 ● *The Wish Express* (in English and Spanish), quarterly. Newsletter. Features stories about recent wishes granted, donations received and upcoming events. Alternate Formats: online. **Conventions/Meetings:** annual meeting - always January, Arlington, TX.

Circumcision

11475 ■ Doctors Opposing Circumcision (DOC)
2442 NW Market St., Ste.42
Seattle, WA 98107-4137
Ph: (360)385-1882
Fax: (225)381-8200
E-mail: geocdenn@gmail.com
URL: http://www.doctorsopposingcircumcision.org
Contact: Dr. George C. Denniston MD, Pres./CEO
Founded: 1995. **Membership Dues:** doctor, $40 (annual) ● non-doctor, $30 (annual) ● medical student, $10 (annual) ● health care provider, $25 (annual) ● sustaining, $100 (annual) ● patron, $200 (annual). **Staff:** 4. **Description:** Physicians opposed to routine neonatal circumcision. Encourages physicians to have "no role in the painful, unnecessary procedure inflicted on the newborn". Conducts educational programs for doctors and prospective parents. Lawsuits have, of necessity, become part of our modus operandi. **Publications:** *Doctors Re-examine Circumcision.* Book. Contains information for prospective parents. **Price:** $12.00 plus $3 shipping and handling ● *Male and Female Circumcision.* Book. Contains proceedings of the Oxford Conference. ● *Sexual Mutilations.* Book ● *Understanding Circumcision.* Book.

11476 ■ International Coalition for Genital Integrity (ICGI)
1970 North River Rd.
West Lafayette, IN 47906
Ph: (765)497-0150
E-mail: info@icgi.org
URL: http://www.icgi.org
Contact: Dan Bollinger, Exec. Dir.
Multinational. Description: Provides a unified voice to the various, specifically missioned genital integrity groups throughout the world. Seeks affiliation with other ideologically-compatible organizations in protecting non-consenting persons from forced genital mutilations. Creates and disseminates educational information and teaching and learning opportunities for raising consciousness about the forced genital mutilations of minors or others through collective press releases. **Computer Services:** database, file directory ● information services, newsfeed ● online services, downloadable documents; forum.

11477 ■ National Organization of Circumcision Information Resource Centers (NOCIRC)
PO Box 2512
San Anselmo, CA 94979-2512
Ph: (415)488-9883
Fax: (415)488-9660
E-mail: nocirc@cris.com
URL: http://www.nocirc.org
Contact: Marilyn Fayre Milos RN, Exec. Dir.
Founded: 1985. **Staff:** 1. **Budget:** $100,000. **Regional Groups:** 113. **State Groups:** 36. **National Groups:** 15. **Languages:** English, Spanish. **Nonmembership. Multinational. Description:** Serves as an umbrella organization for circumcision information centers internationally; seeks to educate professionals and the public about routine infant male circumcision and the practice of female genital mutilation; defends the body integrity rights of infants and children. Maintains mailing list of 10,000 hospitals, Planned Parenthood clinics, expectant parents, and individual professionals in fields related to health care, law and ethics. Conducts continuing education courses for registered nurses. Operates speakers' bureau. Sponsors the International Symposia on Genital Integrity. **Libraries: Type:** reference. **Subjects:** male circumcision, foreskin restoration, care of intact penis, female genital mutilation. **Awards:** Human Rights Award of International Symposia on Circumcision. **Frequency:** biennial. **Type:** recognition. **Projects:** Attorneys for the Rights of the Child; Nurses for the Rights of the Child. **Affiliated With:** Doctors Opposing Circumcision; National Organization to Halt the Abuse and Routine Mutilation of Males; National Organization of Restoring Men. **Absorbed:** (1987) INTACT Educational Foundation. **Formerly:** Informed Consent. **Publications:** *Answers to Your Questions about Infant Circumcision.* Brochure. **Price:** $25.00/100 copies ● *Answers to Your Questions about NOCIRC.* Pamphlet. Describes NOCIRC, lists NOCIRC centers, and contains the Declaration of the First International Symposium on Circumcision. **Price:** $25.00/100 copies ● *Answers to Your Questions about Premature (Forced) Retraction of Your Son's Foreskin.* Brochure. **Price:** $25.00/100 copies ● *Answers to Your Questions about Your Son's Circumcised Penis.* Brochure. **Price:** $25.00/100 copies ● *Answers to Your Questions about Your Young Son's Intact Penis* (in English and Spanish). Brochure. **Price:** $25.00/100 copies ● *Circumcision: Information, Misinformation, Disinformation.* Proceedings ● *NOCIRC Circumcision Video.* Videos. **Price:** $20.00 ● *Resource Guide.* Brochure. **Price:** free ● Annual Report, annual. Contains the latest medical and legal information on the issue of routine male infant circumcision and female genital mutilation internationally. **Price:** $10.00/year. ISSN: 1070-3721. **Circulation:** 10,000. **Conventions/Meetings:** biennial Genital Integrity: A New Awareness - symposium ● biennial International Symposium on Genital Integrity, forum on genital mutilation of children and rights of children (exhibits).

11478 ■ National Organization to Halt the Abuse and Routine Mutilation of Males (NOHARMM)
PO Box 460795
San Francisco, CA 94146

Ph: (415)826-9351
Fax: (305)768-5967
E-mail: ideas@noharmm.org
URL: http://www.noharmm.org
Contact: Tim Hammond, Founder
Founded: 1992. **Local Groups:** 24. **Description:** Men opposed to routine circumcision. Seeks to educate men about their bodies; organize and empower men to voice their concerns and involve them in efforts to end circumcision. Gathers written documentation of the immediate and long-term effects of infant circumcision; petitions major medical associations; consults with health insurers; seeks to file a class action suit declaring the right of the child to be protected from circumcision. **Publications:** *Action Alert*, periodic. Bulletin. **Price:** free.

11479 ■ National Organization of Restoring Men (NORM)
c/o Mr. R. Wayne Griffiths, Exec. Dir.
3205 Northwood Dr., Ste.209
Concord, CA 94520-4506
Ph: (925)827-4077
Fax: (925)827-4119
E-mail: waynerobb@aol.com
URL: http://www.norm.org
Contact: Mr. R. Wayne Griffiths, Exec. Dir.
Founded: 1989. **Members:** 50,000. **Local Groups:** 31. **National Groups:** 4. **Description:** Represents men who have concerns about being circumcised, are considering foreskin restoration, or are in the process of restoring their foreskins. Provides an arena in which circumcised men can share their concerns without fear of being ridiculed for a desire to be intact and whole again; a safe place is provided to discuss goals and learn about methods and techniques of restoration and to discover those methods that will work best for each individual. Promotes the idea that men should have a choice whether or not to be circumcised. Maintains speakers' bureau and compiles statistics from online survey. Conducts educational programs. **Libraries: Type:** reference. **Holdings:** audiovisuals, books, clippings, periodicals. **Subjects:** circumcision, foreskin restoration. **Affiliated With:** National Organization of Circumcision Information Resource Centers; National Organization to Halt the Abuse and Routine Mutilation of Males. **Formerly:** RECAP (Recover a Penis). **Conventions/Meetings:** monthly support group meeting, restoration devices (exhibits) - usually first Sunday, in Berkeley, CA and other cities in U.S., Canada, and United Kingdom.

11480 ■ Non-Circumcision Educational Foundation (NCEF)
PO Box 251
Oxford, PA 19363
Ph: (717)529-2561
E-mail: jpncef@aol.com
Contact: James E. Peron, Exec.Dir.
Founded: 1973. **Members:** 11,000. **Budget:** $35,000. **Description:** Parents, childbirth educators, nurse-midwives, nurses, doctors, and other interested individuals. Seeks to: stop routine infant circumcision; provide medical information regarding such surgery. Opposes what it calls the unnecessary surgery of baby boys, use of silver nitrate in eyes, and other medical treatments which violate the physical and emotional well-being of the newborn. Conducts research; offers services to parents, educators, and medical staff. Maintains extensive library on infant circumcision, childbirth, and infant and newborn care. Offers speakers' bureau; compiles statistics. Operates educational programs including seminars, lecture series, film and videotape educational services, workshops, and distribution of educational literature. **Computer Services:** Mailing lists. **Affiliated With:** National Organization of Circumcision Information Resource Centers. **Publications:** *Educational Bulletin*, periodic ● Newsletter, semiannual. **Conventions/Meetings:** annual International Symposium on Circumcision (exhibits).

11481 ■ Non-Circumcision Information Center (NCIC)
82 Lexington St.
Weston, MA 02493-2146

Ph: (617)489-4530
E-mail: cheapshott@aol.com
Contact: Roger Saquet, Dir.
Founded: 1973. **Description:** Provides current, accurate, and complete information to the American public regarding the safety and necessity of circumcision; distributes information that discourages routine circumcision; assists in increasing the number of uncircumcised males from 40&percent; to 95&percent;.

11482 ■ Nurses for the Rights of the Child (NRC)
369 Montezuma, No. 354
Santa Fe, NM 87501
Ph: (505)989-7377
E-mail: nrc@cnsp.com
URL: http://nurses.cirp.org
Contact: Mary Conant RN, Pres./Co-Founder
Founded: 1995. **Membership Dues:** individual, $20 (annual). **Staff:** 100. **Description:** Nurses. Seek to protect "the rights of infants and children to bodily integrity". Opposes circumcision "whether in the name of medicine, religion or social custom, is a human rights violation". Provides expectant parents with educational materials regarding circumcision and its effects.

Civil Rights and Liberties

11483 ■ Human and Civil Rights Organizations of America (HCROA)
10 Chestnut St.
Salem, MA 01970-3131
Ph: (978)744-2608
Fax: (978)594-5071
E-mail: info@hcr.org
URL: http://www.hcr.org
Contact: Marshall Strauss, Pres.
Founded: 1994. **Description:** Represents national and international organizations dedicated to stopping racial discrimination, religious bigotry, and promoting equality for all. Screens and certifies human rights charities for programmatic impact and fiscal accountability. Allows affiliated member charities to participate in the combined federal campaign and other workplace fundraising drives. **Publications:** Annual Report, annual. Alternate Formats: online.

Coaching

11484 ■ International Association of Integrative Coaches (IAIC)
c/o Deborah Dowe, Treas.
PO Box 2635
Kennebunkport, ME 04046
E-mail: info@theiaic.com
URL: http://www.theiaic.com
Contact: Deborah Dowe, Treas.
Founded: 2004. **Membership Dues:** association, $250 (annual). **Multinational. Description:** Aims to further and inspire the interests of integrative coaching worldwide. Raises public awareness and understanding of the need for coaching. Serves the public by providing listings of Certified Integrative Coaches and helping potential clients connect with a coach that is best trained to suit their needs. Provides ongoing professional development and accreditation. **Telecommunication Services:** electronic mail, admin@theiaic.com ● electronic mail, deborah@theiaic.com. **Publications:** Newsletter. **Price:** included in membership dues.

Community

11485 ■ Catholic Homesteading Movement (CHM)
Address Unknown since 2007
Founded: 1961. **Members:** 100. **Membership Dues:** $25 (annual). **Staff:** 7. **Budget:** $10,000. **Description:** Purpose is to teach Catholics and non-Catholics

necessary skills for supplying life's basic needs directly from the land using hand tools and horse power, in harmony with the Christian principles of stewardship of the earth, human dignity, and reliance on God. Operates school in the form of a 100-acre working homestead. Intensive courses are presented in the form of demonstrations, discussions, lectures, skits, and workbees with an emphasis on experiential education. Offers week-long instruction in basic homesteading, advanced homesteading, midwifery, Christian customs, herbalism, homebirth, and log cabin construction. Conducts workshops in areas including fruit and nut growing, horse working, and survival and organic gardening. **Libraries: Type:** reference. **Holdings:** 2,000. **Subjects:** homesteading. **Awards:** Basic Homesteading Week Scholarship. **Type:** scholarship. **Recipient:** for inner city and home educated youth. **Publications:** The Homesteader, bimonthly. Newsletter. Provides practical information about Christian homesteading, emphasizing living self-sufficiently from the land. **Price:** 20 first-class stamps. **Circulation:** 1,000. **Advertising:** not accepted. **Conventions/Meetings:** annual Basic Homesteading Week - workshop and lecture, with Organic Gardening Course, Herbalism and Fruit & Nut Workshop, and Log Course - always Oxford, NY.

11486 ■ Center for Self-Sufficiency (CSS)
PO Box 416
Denver, CO 80201-0416
Ph: (303)575-5676
E-mail: mail@gumbomedia.com
Contact: A. C. Doyle, Founder
Founded: 1982. **Membership Dues:** student, $5 (annual) ● family, $10 (annual) ● corporation, $5,000 (annual) ● gold, $1,000 (annual) ● angel, $100 (annual) ● supporting, $50 (annual) ● silver, $500 (annual) ● diamond, $2,000 (annual). **Staff:** 1. **Budget:** $60,000. **Description:** Works to promote and publish information on self-sufficiency, food, housing, clothing and home businesses. Conducts research on self-sufficiency methods and recycling topics; also provides children's stories to explain self-sufficiency. **Libraries: Type:** not open to the public. **Holdings:** articles, reports. **Subjects:** self sufficiency. **Awards:** Be Somebody Be Yourself Award. **Frequency:** annual. **Type:** recognition ● Center for Self Sufficiency Survivor Award. **Frequency:** annual. **Type:** trophy. **Telecommunication Services:** electronic mail, mail@centerforselfsufficiency.org. **Publications:** Center for Self-Sufficiency Update, annual. Newsletter. Explores possibilities for becoming self-sufficient. **Price:** $3.00. ISSN: 0736-3044. Alternate Formats: online ● One Kettle Cookbook ● Recipe Ingredient Replacement as Method of Food Self-Sufficiency ● Self Sufficiency Recipe Pages. **Conventions/Meetings:** Online Workshop, recycling business.

11487 ■ Community-Campus Partnerships For Health (CCPH)
PO Box 354809
Seattle, WA 98195-4809
Ph: (206)543-8178 (206)616-4305
Fax: (206)685-6747
E-mail: ccphuw@u.washington.edu
URL: http://depts.washington.edu/ccph
Contact: Sarena D. Seifer, Exec. Dir.
Founded: 1996. **Members:** 1,000. **Membership Dues:** individual e-membership, $85 ● individual premium, $100 ● student, $30 ● organization, $300. **Description:** Fosters partnership between communities and educational institutions and develops their roles as change agents for improving health professions education, civic responsibility and the overall health of communities. **Awards:** Community Campus Partnerships for Health Award. **Frequency:** annual. **Type:** recognition. **Recipient:** for community-campus partnerships that reflect the organization's principles of good practice. **Telecommunication Services:** electronic mail, sarena@u.washington.edu.

11488 ■ Community Voices
c/o Sherry Adeyemi
210 Guilford Ave., 3rd Fl.
Baltimore, MD 21202
Ph: (410)396-4502

Fax: (410)361-9637
E-mail: sherry.adeyemi@baltimorecity.gov
URL: http://www.communityvoices.org
Contact: Sherry Adeyemi, Contact
Description: Strengthens community support services and helps to ensure the survival of safety-net providers. Promotes sustained increase in access to health services for the vulnerable with a focus on primary care and prevention.

11489 ■ Federation of Egalitarian Communities (FEC)
c/o FEC Sec.
2 Dancing Rabbit Ln.
Rutledge, MO 63563
E-mail: secretary@thefec.org
URL: http://thefec.org
Founded: 1976. **Members:** 225. **Staff:** 9. **Regional Groups:** 9. **Description:** A group of "intentional" communities in North America based on cooperation, equality, and nonviolence. Makes an effort to offer people a communal alternative to a "competitive and consumption-oriented world" and promote the evolution of a more egalitarian society. Members believe that "cooperation holds more potential than competition, taking care of our neighbor is important, and personal achievement and gain can take a back seat to a loving concern for others." Diverse in themselves but similar in ideology, each community: holds its land, labor, and resources in common; assumes responsibility for the needs of its members by distributing products of their labor equally or according to need; practices nonviolence; uses a participatory form of government in which members have either a direct vote or the right to impeach or overrule; does not deny membership through discrimination on grounds of race, creed, age, or sex; assumes responsibility for maintaining the availability of natural resources through ecologically sound production and consumption. **Additional Websites:** http://www.eastwind.org. **Programs:** Communication Skills. **Projects:** Community in the Classroom; Friends of Community; Labor Exchange; Mutual Aid Fund; New Communities Support; PEACH; Systems and Structures. **Publications:** Leaves of Twin Oaks, quarterly. Newsletter. Includes articles, photos, and news tidbits on Twin Oaks. **Price:** $10.00/3 issues. Alternate Formats: online ● Sharing Lives, Changing the World. Brochure ● Soundings, quarterly. Newsletter. Contains news from FEC communities and the assemblies. **Circulation:** 600. Alternate Formats: online ● Windfall, periodic. **Conventions/Meetings:** biennial assembly.

11490 ■ Institute for Local Self-Reliance (ILSR)
927 15th St. NW, 4th Fl.
Washington, DC 20005
Ph: (202)898-1610 (612)379-3815
E-mail: info@ilsr.org
URL: http://www.ilsr.org
Contact: Neil Seldman, Pres.
Founded: 1974. **Staff:** 15. **Budget:** $1,300,000. **Description:** Provides the conceptual framework, strategies, and information to aid the creation of ecologically-sound and economically equitable communities. Works with citizens, activists, policymakers, and entrepreneurs to design systems, policies and enterprises that meet local or regional needs; maximize local human, material, natural, and financial resources; and ensure that the benefits of these systems and resources accrue to all local citizens. **Programs:** Waste to Wealth. **Projects:** The Carbohydrate Economy; The Healthy Building Network; The New Rules. **Publications:** A New Industry Emerges: Making Construction Materials from Cellulosic Waste. Booklet. **Price:** $10.00 ● Alcohol Fuels from Whey: Novel Commercial Uses for a Waste Product. Monograph. **Price:** $10.00 ● Biological Energy: Opportunities and Obstacles. Monograph. **Price:** $10.00 ● Building a Deconstruction Company: A Training Manual for Facilitators and Entrepreneurs. **Price:** $25.00 plus shipping and handling ● The Carbohydrate Economy: Making Chemicals and Industrial Materials from Plant Matter, quarterly. Book. **Price:** $25.00 ● Closer to Home: A Conversation about Lo-

cal Ownership and Community. Proceedings. **Price:** $5.00 ● *Cutting the Waste Stream in Half: Community Record Setters Show How,* Report. **Price:** free. Alternate Formats: online ● *Deconstruction: Salvaging Yesterday's Buildings for Tomorrow's Sustainable Communities.* Book. **Price:** $10.00 ● *Don't Throw Away That Food: Strategies for Record-Setting Waste Reduction.* **Price:** free. Alternate Formats: online ● *The Economic Benefits of Recycling.* Monograph. **Price:** $10.00 ● *Getting the Most From Our Materials: Making New Jersey the State of the Art.* Report. **Price:** $25.00 ● *Green Taxes.* Monograph. Alternate Formats: online ● *Greenhouse Gas Emissions from Ethanol and MTBE: A Comparison.* Monograph. **Price:** $5.00 ● *The Home Town Advantage: How to Defend Your Main Street Against Chain Stores and Why It Matters.* Book. **Price:** $14.00 plus shipping and handling ● *How Much Energy Does It Take to Make a Gallon of Soydiesel?,* quarterly. Monograph. **Price:** $10.00 ● *In Depth Studies of Recycling and Composting Programs: Designs, Costs, Results, Vols. 1-3.* **Price:** $18.00/volume; $45.00 volumes 1-3 ● *New Rules,* quarterly. Journal. **Price:** $5.00. Alternate Formats: online ● *Recycling Economic Development Through Scrap-Based Manufacturing.* Report. **Price:** $20.00 ● *Rural Development, Biorefineries, and the Carbohydrate Economy.* Monograph. **Price:** $5.00 ● *Salvaging the Future: Waste-Based Production.* Monograph. **Price:** $5.00 ● Annual Report, annual. Alternate Formats: online.

Community Action

11491 ■ Association of Community Organizations for Reform Now (ACORN)
2-4 Nevin St., 2nd Fl.
Brooklyn, NY 11217
Ph: (718)246-7900
Free: (877)55A-CORN
Fax: (718)246-7939
E-mail: natexdirect@acorn.org
URL: http://www.acorn.org
Contact: Steve Kest, Exec. Dir.
Founded: 1970. **Members:** 150,000. **Membership Dues:** full, $10 (monthly). **Staff:** 300. **Budget:** $10,000,000. **State Groups:** 28. **Local Groups:** 800. **Description:** Network of community organizations, with over 150,000 low and moderate-income members organized into 800 neighborhood chapters in over 60 cities across the country. Works to build solidly rooted and powerful community organizations that are committed to social and economic justice, has taken action and won victories on thousands of issues of concern to members. Priorities include: better housing for first time homebuyers and tenants; living wages for low-wage workers; more investment in communities, from banks and governments; and better public schools. These goals are achieved through building community organizations that have power to win changes through direct action, negotiation, legislation, and voter participation. **Committees:** ACORN Political Action. **Publications:** *ACORN News.* Newsletters. Contains regular update on the activities of ACORN chapters. Alternate Formats: online ● *United States of ACORN,* bimonthly ● Annual Report, annual. Alternate Formats: online. **Conventions/Meetings:** biennial convention.

11492 ■ Center for Community and Organization Development (CCOD)
DePaul Univ.
2219 N Kenmore Ave.
Chicago, IL 60614-3504
Ph: (773)325-4250 (773)325-7887
Fax: (773)325-4249
E-mail: ccod@depaul.edu
URL: http://condor.depaul.edu/~psych/iowebsite/ccod.html
Contact: Doug Cellar, Dir.
Founded: 1985. **Staff:** 4. **Budget:** $150,000. **Description:** Trainers with backgrounds in social psychology, human services, journalism, planning, and adult education. Objective is to help local citizen groups and agencies become more effective, over-

come internal obstacles, and reach their goals. Organizes sessions tailored to individual groups to aid them in responding effectively to issues that range from human relations to community development to coalition building. Offers consultation services and training materials on organizing, fundraising, the media, and citizen action training. Assists groups or organizations with conference or workshop planning, design, and implementation. **Formed by Merger of:** Citizen Involvement Training Program; Community Education Resource Center. **Publications:** *Citizen Action Manual Series* ● *Partnerships for Community Development.* Manual ● Also publishes information packet. **Conventions/Meetings:** workshop, topics including cultural issues, community development, interorganizational and organizational development, and refugees and immigrant issues.

11493 ■ Midwest Academy (MA)
28 E Jackson St., No. 605
Chicago, IL 60604
Ph: (312)427-2304
Fax: (312)427-2307
E-mail: mwacademy1@aol.com
URL: http://www.midwestacademy.com
Contact: Jackie Kendall, Exec. Dir.
Founded: 1973. **Staff:** 5. **Description:** Educational institution providing assistance to leaders of organizations working for progressive social change. Holds five-day workshops called "Organizing for Social Change" in Chicago, IL and in northeastern, northwestern, and southeastern states. Offers consulting services in planning, strategy, staff and leadership development, teacher training, grassroots fundraising and strategic planning. Conducts on-site training sessions. Maintains speakers' bureau. **Publications:** *Academy Retreat Papers,* annual ● *Organizing for Social Change.* Book. **Price:** $23.95 ● Also publishes books, brochures, and organizing packets. **Conventions/Meetings:** annual conference (exhibits) ● quarterly meeting, training session.

11494 ■ National Association of Neighborhoods (NAN)
1300 Pennsylvania Ave. NW, Ste.700
Washington, DC 20004
Ph: (202)332-7766
Fax: (202)332-2314
E-mail: ricardo@nanworld.org
URL: http://www.nanworld.org
Contact: Ricardo C. Byrd, Exec. Dir.
Founded: 1975. **Members:** 2,000. **Membership Dues:** individual, $10 ● organization, $25 (annual). **Staff:** 5. **Description:** Neighborhood organizations and city-wide coalitions in 120 cities. Promotes better neighborhoods through self-help, welfare reforms, and crime and safety programs. Seeks to help neighborhood leaders secure a political voice and facilitates the exchange of information about programs, issues, structures, and ethics. Has formulated National Neighborhood Platform and Neighborhood Bill of Responsibilities and Rights. Plans to establish a neighborhood leadership training institute. **Awards:** Neighborhood Service Award. **Type:** recognition. **Task Forces:** Citizen Education; Energy; Environmental Issues; Health; Housing and Community Development; Model Legislation; Neighborhood Crime and Fire Prevention; Neighborhood Economic Development; Neighborhood Information; Neighborhood Labor Relations; Participation in Human Rights; Transfer Amendment. **Formerly:** (1977) Alliance for Neighborhood Government. **Publications:** *NAN Bulletin,* quarterly. Includes updates on state and federal legislation affecting neighborhoods. **Price:** included in membership dues; $25.00 /year for nonmembers. **Circulation:** 8,000. **Advertising:** accepted. **Conventions/Meetings:** annual conference (exhibits) ● periodic regional meeting.

11495 ■ National Center for Urban Ethnic Affairs (NCUEA)
PO Box 20, Cardinal Sta.
Washington, DC 20064
Ph: (202)319-6188 (202)232-3600
Fax: (202)319-6289

E-mail: kromkowski@cua.edu
Contact: Dr. John A. Kromkowski, Pres.
Founded: 1970. **Staff:** 4. **Languages:** English, French, German, Greek, Italian, Polish, Spanish, Ukrainian. **Description:** Develops neighborhood programs and policies that are grounded in an appreciation of ethnic cultural diversity. Encourages and enables urban communities, parishes, and congregations to clarify important policy issues. Aids organized networks of neighbors and neighborhood organizations in achieving their goals and objectives. Creates partnerships among neighborhood organizations, government agencies, and the private sector for neighborhood revitalization, self-help development, and cultural programs. Works to improve education, human services, economic opportunities, housing, and culture and heritage for immigrants and in the ethnic and multi-ethnic neighborhoods. Provides technical assistance and advisement training. Develops research proposals; assists neighborhood and ethnic organizations seeking financial support; makes available summer internships in Washington, Dublin, London, and Belgium; sponsors speakers' bureau; compiles statistics on ethnic groups in US. **Libraries:** **Type:** reference. **Holdings:** 8,000. **Awards:** Gloria Aull Award. **Type:** recognition. **Recipient:** for community church leadership. **Publications:** *Building-blocks,* periodic. Newsletter ● *Cultural Heritage and Contemporary Change.* Book ● *Neighborhood Revitalization Series* ● *Neighborhood Strategy Series* ● *Non-Profits with Hard Hats.* Books ● *Race and Ethnic Relations, Annual Editions,* annual ● *Reclaiming the Inner City.* Book ● *Scriptural Faiths and Ethnicity.* Book ● *Urban Ethnic Policy Series* ● *Why 435?.* **Conventions/Meetings:** annual conference and regional meeting ● semiannual workshop.

11496 ■ National Community Action Foundation (NCAF)
810 1st St., Ste.530
Washington, DC 20002
Ph: (202)842-2092
Fax: (202)842-2095
E-mail: info@ncaf.org
URL: http://www.ncaf.org
Contact: David Bradley, Exec. Dir.
Founded: 1981. **Members:** 900. **Staff:** 4. **Regional Groups:** 10. **State Groups:** 70. **Description:** Community action agencies that provide services at the local level, such as Head Start, Meals on Wheels, low-income energy assistance, weatherization services, emergency food and shelter, and job training and placement. Objectives are to assist low-income families in becoming self-sufficient and obtaining employment and decent housing, and to improve communities by developing local solutions to problems and stimulating economic development. Lobbies for federal programs that serve the poor, including employment and training, energy assistance, nutrition, and services to children and senior citizens. Researches energy programs for low-income people; provides information on block grants. Conducts "How Congress Works" programs. **Committees:** Community Action Program Political Action. **Publications:** Newsletter, periodic ● Also publishes research reports. **Conventions/Meetings:** annual conference (exhibits).

11497 ■ National People's Action (NPA)
810 Milwaukee Ave.
Chicago, IL 60622
Ph: (312)243-3038
Fax: (312)243-7044
E-mail: npa@npa-us.org
URL: http://www.npa-us.org
Contact: Alicia Mendoza, Contact
Founded: 1972. **Members:** 302. **Description:** Coalition of neighborhood organizations, unions, senior citizens' groups, and churches concerned with investment in and revitalization of individual neighborhoods. Lobbies for increased involvement on issues concerning: housing; credit and lending policies; community development funds; drugs; utility rates; health care costs. Organizes low- and moderate-income people and was instrumental in passage of legislation, such as the Home Mortgage Disclosure Act and the Com-

munity Reinvestment Act. **Conventions/Meetings:** annual conference, neighborhood groups from across the country.

Community Development

11498 ■ ABLE: Association for Better Living and Education International
7065 Hollywood Blvd.
Los Angeles, CA 90028
Ph: (323)960-3530
Fax: (323)960-3537
E-mail: ableinfo@able.org
URL: http://www.able.org
Contact: Rena Weinberg, Pres.
Founded: 1988. **Membership Dues:** bronze, $50 (annual) ● silver, $100 (annual) ● gold, $250 (annual) ● platinum, $500 (annual) ● life, $2,500. **Multinational. Description:** Enhances the living standard of children and communities. Provides directions and programs to address drug addiction and substance abuse, crime, illiteracy and immorality. **Computer Services:** database, lists of members' information ● mailing lists, of members. **Publications:** Newsletter, weekly. Alternate Formats: online.

11499 ■ Action for Enterprise (AFE)
2009 N 14th St., Ste.301
Arlington, VA 22201
Ph: (703)243-9172
Fax: (703)243-9123
E-mail: info@actionforenterprise.org
URL: http://www.actionforenterprise.org
Contact: Frank Lusby, Exec. Dir./Founder
Founded: 1991. **Staff:** 8. **Budget:** $500,000. **Multinational. Description:** Seeks to design and implement small enterprise development programs, based on a comprehensive analysis of business sectors and the interrelationships of enterprises that function with them. Initiates efforts to develop sustainable business development service providers at the local level. **Formerly:** (1998) Action Consulting Association. **Conventions/Meetings:** periodic workshop.

11500 ■ ActionAid International USA (AAI USA)
1112 16th St. NW, Ste.540
Washington, DC 20036
Ph: (202)835-1240
Fax: (202)835-1244
E-mail: office@actionaidusa.org
URL: http://www.actionaidusa.org
Contact: Mr. Peter O'Driscoll, Exec. Dir.
Founded: 2000. **Description:** Seeks to create change on behalf of the poor and disenfranchised worldwide. Advocates reforms that speak directly to decision-makers on key policies such as poverty reduction, trade, education, agriculture and the expenditure of federal, IMF and World Bank funds. Provides research, monitoring, advocacy and new collaborations to help eliminate hunger. **Publications:** Annual Report, annual ● Reports. Alternate Formats: online.

11501 ■ Africa-America Institute - New York (AAI)
Graybar Bldg.
420 Lexington Ave., Ste.1706
New York, NY 10170-0002
Ph: (212)949-5666
Fax: (212)682-6174
E-mail: aainy@aaionline.org
URL: http://www.aaionline.org
Contact: Mora McLean, Pres./CEO
Founded: 1953. **Staff:** 40. **Description:** National organizations supporting community development efforts in Africa. Promotes appropriate and sustainable development in Africa and understanding between Africans and Americans. Provides support and technical and financial assistance to national community development programs in Africa; sponsors advocacy campaigns to create a constituency for African development in the United States. Conducts educational and leadership training courses for African

development personnel. **Awards:** Atlas Fellowships. **Frequency:** periodic. **Type:** fellowship. **Recipient:** for Africans wishing to participate in undergraduate, graduate, and postgraduate academic programs in the United States. **Boards:** Trustees. **Programs:** African Higher Education and Training; Educational Outreach and Policy. **Publications:** AAIonline, quarterly. Newsletter. Features commentary on AAI program activities, alumni and events. Alternate Formats: online ● Contact Africa. Directory ● Reports. Alternate Formats: online ● Annual Report, annual. **Conventions/Meetings:** periodic seminar.

11502 ■ APPEAL: Asian Pacific Partners for Empowerment and Leadership
300 Frank H. Ogawa Plz., Ste.620
Oakland, CA 94612
Ph: (510)272-9536
Fax: (510)272-0817
E-mail: appeal@aapcho.org
URL: http://www.appealforcommunities.org
Contact: Rod Lew MPH, Exec. Dir.
Founded: 1994. **Members:** 500. **Multinational. Description:** Seeks to prevent the use of tobacco in the Asian, American and Pacific Islander community. Provides network development, capacity building, education, advocacy and leadership development on tobacco control. **Computer Services:** Bibliographic search, research on AAPIs and tobacco ● information services, tobacco resources ● mailing lists. **Programs:** Leadership Development; Technical Assistance and Training; Tobacco Control; Youth Leadership. **Publications:** A Global APPEAL, biennial. Newsletter. Includes articles on tobacco control. Alternate Formats: online.

11503 ■ Architecture for Humanity (AFH)
900 Bridgeway, Ste.2
Sausalito, CA 94965-2100
Ph: (415)332-6273
Fax: (415)332-6283
E-mail: staff@architectureforhumanity.org
URL: http://www.architectureforhumanity.org
Contact: Cameron Sinclair, Exec. Dir./Co-Founder
Founded: 1999. **Multinational. Description:** Aims to promote humanitarian and social design through advocacy and education programs. Promotes architectural and design solutions to global, social and humanitarian crises. Creates opportunities for architects and designers to help communities in need. **Boards:** Advisory. **Projects:** Design Like You Give A Damn; Rethinking City; Tsunami Reconstruction. **Publications:** Newsletter. Alternate Formats: online.

11504 ■ Asia America Initiative (AAI)
1523 16th St. NW
Washington, DC 20036
Ph: (202)232-7020
Fax: (202)232-7023
E-mail: administrator@asiaamerica.org
URL: http://www.asiaamerica.org
Contact: Albert Santoli, Pres./Founder
Staff: 5. **Multinational. Description:** Promotes democratic ideals and strengthens international security in the Asia-Pacific region. Acts as a mediator in conflict-plagued areas of the Asia-Pacific region. Advances national security and the defense of international human rights by enhancing the quality of life, reinforcing opportunities for women, offering alternatives to conflict and denying militant networks the ability to recruit. **Programs:** Adopt A Classroom; Development for Peace in Sulu; Humanitarian Intervention. **Publications:** Asia Security Focus, weekly. Bulletin. Includes development on security, politics, social and economic issues. ● China In Focus, weekly. Bulletin. Features analysis of ongoing events in the People's Republic of China and the region.

11505 ■ Association for the Advancement of Mexican Americans (AAMA)
6001 Gulf Fwy., B1
Houston, TX 77023
Ph: (713)926-4756

Fax: (713)926-8035
URL: http://www.aamainc.us
Contact: Gilbert Moreno, Pres./CEO
Founded: 1970. **Description:** Advances the lives of at-risk and disadvantaged youth and families. Provides innovative programs in the areas of education, health and human services and community development. **Programs:** The Dinosaur; Education/Home; Minorities Action; Proyecto del Corazon.

11506 ■ Benton Foundation
1625 K St. NW, 11th Fl.
Washington, DC 20006
Ph: (202)638-5770
Fax: (202)638-5771
E-mail: benton@benton.org
URL: http://www.benton.org
Contact: Jim Kohlenberger, Contact
Founded: 1981. **Staff:** 20. **Budget:** $6,000,000. **Description:** Works to promote communications as a means for solving social problems. **Libraries: Type:** reference. **Holdings:** reports. **Computer Services:** database, digital divide listing of community technology activities. **Publications:** 101 Things You Can Do For Our Children's Future. Report. Contains information on improving family environments. ● Reports, annual.

11507 ■ Center for Community Action of B'Nai B'rith International
2020 K St. NW, 7th Fl.
Washington, DC 20006
Ph: (202)857-6600 (212)490-3290
Free: (888)388-4224
Fax: (202)857-1099
E-mail: cca@bnaibrith.org
URL: http://www.bnaibrith.org
Contact: Rhonda Love, Exec. Dir.
Founded: 1843. **Members:** 250,000. **Regional Groups:** 18. **Description:** Serves as a department of B'nai B'rith International. Works to resolve social problems such as hunger and poverty through community service; encourages and trains members to become community volunteers. Sponsors food drives, voter registration campaigns, and nursing home visitation services. Provides assistance to veterans, handicapped persons, the elderly, and incarcerated persons. Offers children's services. Provides "hands on" assistance and financial assistance for disasters nationally and internationally. **Task Forces:** Children's Project; Disabled and Hospital; Disaster Relief; Hunger and Homelessness; Older Adult; Overseas Outreach; Planning and Development; Veterans. **Formerly:** Community and Veteran Service; Community Volunteer Services Commission of B'Nai Birth International. **Publications:** International Jewish Monthly, quarterly. Magazine. **Advertising:** accepted ● Also publishes how-to guides on public service programs. **Conventions/Meetings:** biennial international conference ● annual meeting.

11508 ■ Citizens Network for Sustainable Development (CitNet)
c/o ISF
11426 Rockville Pike, Ste.306
Rockville, MD 20852
Ph: (301)770-6375
Fax: (301)770-6377
E-mail: info@isforum.org
URL: http://www.citnet.org
Founded: 1990. **Description:** Brings together US based organizations, communities and individuals working on sustainability issues across the US. Strengthens sustainability movements across the US by providing a framework for information sharing and collaboration across areas, sectors and levels of activity. Promotes broad-based, multi-stakeholder participation in decision making on sustainable development. **Publications:** CitNet News. Newsletter. Contains news items, analysis, opinions and stories by members and friends of the Network. Alternate Formats: online.

11509 ■ Clowns Without Borders - USA (CWB)
540 Alabama, No. 215
San Francisco, CA 94110
Ph: (415)626-7737
Fax: (415)626-7737
E-mail: info@clownswithoutborders.org
URL: http://www.clownswithoutborders.org
Contact: Moshe Cohen, Founder
Founded: 1995. **Multinational. Description:** Improves life in refugee camps and areas of conflict through volunteer artist performances. Provides workshops to children and their educators. Promotes awareness of people and communities affected by war.

11510 ■ Coffee Kids
1305 Luisa St., Ste.C
Santa Fe, NM 87505
Ph: (505)820-1443
Free: (800)334-9099
Fax: (505)820-7565
E-mail: info@coffeekids.org
URL: http://www.coffeekids.org
Contact: Carolyn Fairman, Exec. Dir.
Founded: 1988. **Membership Dues:** business, $300 (annual) ● individual, $25 (annual). **Staff:** 4. **Budget:** $600,000. **Multinational. Description:** Improves the quality of life of children and families who live in coffeegrowing communities. Provides education, healthcare, training and microenterprise for coffee farmers and their families. **Computer Services:** Information services, coffee and community facts. **Projects:** Community Development; Education; Microcredit. **Publications:** Newsletter.

11511 ■ Community Built Association (CBA)
PO Box 115
Parrott, GA 39877
Fax: (931)389-9649
E-mail: cba@communitybuilt.com
URL: http://www.communitybuilt.com
Contact: Sherri Warner Hunter, Pres.
Founded: 1989. **Membership Dues:** business, $100 (annual) ● professional, $40 (annual) ● associate/ student, $25 (annual). **Description:** Furthers and promotes the theory and practice of involving volunteers in the design, organization and creation of community projects that reshape the physical environment. Provides a network for professionals and offers information, education and training to the general public. Offers workshops on community built projects and processes. **Telecommunication Services:** electronic mail, sherriartstudio@aol.com. **Publications:** Newsletter, semiannual ● Brochure. Alternate Formats: online.

11512 ■ Community Development Venture Capital Alliance (CDVCA)
424 W 33rd St., Ste.320
New York, NY 10001
Ph: (212)594-6747
Fax: (212)594-6717
E-mail: info@cdvca.org
URL: http://www.cdvca.org
Contact: Kerwin Tesdell, Pres.
Founded: 1995. **Members:** 100. **Membership Dues:** individual, organization, $500 (annual). **Staff:** 9. **Description:** Ventures capital funds, community development corporations and others working to create jobs among economically disadvantaged populations; provides entrepreneurial solutions to social and environmental problems; and generates long-term capital appreciation. Collects and disseminates industry data; develops case studies; tracks policy and funding trends; provides information, management and technical assistance. **Computer Services:** Mailing lists, of members. **Publications:** *Standard Documents for Community Development Venture Capital Transactions.* **Price:** $39.95. ISSN: 0761-8095. Alternate Formats: CD-ROM. **Conventions/ Meetings:** annual conference, training, networking.

11513 ■ Community Transportation Association of America (CTAA)
1341 G St. NW, 10th Fl.
Washington, DC 20005
Ph: (202)628-1480
Free: (800)891-0590
Fax: (202)737-9197
E-mail: webdesign@ctaa.org
URL: http://www.ctaa.org
Contact: Dale J. Marsico CCTM, Exec. Dir.
Founded: 1975. **Members:** 500. **Membership Dues:** local partner/individual, $125 ● state and national partner/supplier, $225 ● exhibitor, $500 ● friend, $50 ● operator, $30 ● full-time student, $25. **Staff:** 9. **Budget:** $500,000. **Description:** Assists local governments and community-oriented enterprises in small towns and rural areas in meeting their service and developmental needs. Provides technical assistance to the community transportation industry; conducts educational programs. **Awards: Type:** recognition. **Telecommunication Services:** hotline, (800)527-8279. **Divisions:** Center for Community Transportation. **Absorbed:** (1977) Rural Housing Alliance. **Formerly:** (1989) Rural America, Inc. **Publications:** *Community Transportation*, bimonthly. Magazine. Features new transit financing ideas and service modes. **Advertising:** accepted. Alternate Formats: online ● *Community Transportation Reporter: A Voice for Rural and Specialized Transportation*, monthly. Reports on deregulation of the transportation industry, intercity bus service, and lack of rural transportation services. Includes calendar of events. **Price:** $35.00/ year. ISSN: 0895-4437. **Advertising:** accepted. Also Cited As: *Rural Transportation Reporter* ● *CTAA News*, monthly. Membership Directory. **Circulation:** 500. **Advertising:** accepted ● *CTR Buyers' Guide and Resource Guide*, annual. Includes more than 700 company listings indexed by product/service. **Conventions/Meetings:** annual trade show (exhibits).

11514 ■ Eco-Animal Allies
13055 Riverdale Dr. NW, Ste.500-278
Minneapolis, MN 55448
Ph: (763)783-7112
E-mail: info@ecoanimalallies.org
URL: http://www.ecoanimalallies.org
Membership Dues: standard, $25 (annual) ● student/senior, $15 (annual). **Description:** Aims to transform the community into one that respects animals and the environment. Provides and promotes comprehensive humane education. Builds coalitions with other social justice, environmental and animal protection organizations. Investigates and provides aid to sick, neglected and injured animals. Promotes a vegan lifestyle, organic foods, biking and other humane, sustainable practices. **Publications:** *Persevere.* Newsletter.

11515 ■ Egyptians Relief Association (ERA)
c/o Nadia Tadros, Pres.
6121 Winnepeg Dr.
Burke, VA 22015
Ph: (703)503-8816
E-mail: info@egyptiansrelief.org
URL: http://www.egyptiansrelief.org
Contact: Nadia Tadros, Pres.
Founded: 1988. **Members:** 278. **Staff:** 3. **Budget:** $60,000. **Description:** Individuals and organizations working to improve the quality of life of people living in poverty in Egypt. Works to alleviate the causes of poverty. Conducts educational and training programs; facilitates establishment of locally controlled enterprises to insure sustainable, community-based economic development. Sponsors charitable activities. **Computer Services:** database ● electronic publishing, publication ● mailing lists. **Publications:** *Egyptian Relief Newsletter*, bimonthly. Alternate Formats: online ● Directory, periodic.

11516 ■ Engineers for a Sustainable World (ESW)
170 Uris Hall
Ithaca, NY 14853
Ph: (607)255-8996
Fax: (607)254-5000

E-mail: info@esustainableworld.org
URL: http://www.esustainableworld.org
Contact: Regina Clewlow, Exec. Dir.
Members: 3,000. **Membership Dues:** full student, $10 (annual) ● full professional, $45 (annual). **Multinational. Description:** Works to reduce poverty and improve global sustainability. Seeks to mobilize engineers to address the unique challenges of developing communities. Aims to build social capital by creating multi-sectoral partnerships and increasing local ownership of community development programs. Strives to promote a positive image of engineering through outreach, service and international goodwill. **Computer Services:** Mailing lists.

11517 ■ FaithWorks International (FWI)
3121 Middletown Rd., Ste.9D
Bronx, NY 10461
Ph: (347)293-5460
Fax: (347)293-5460
E-mail: questions@faithworksinternational.org
URL: http://www.faithworksinternational.org
Contact: Ms. Virginia Montague, Chair
Founded: 2002. **Staff:** 11. **Languages:** English, Spanish. **Multinational. Description:** Works with faith-based and community-based organizations to develop affordable housing, promote the creation of sustainable businesses, and expand the use of technology in poor communities. Designs, develops, and implements funding plans for housing construction projects. **Computer Services:** Online services, bulletin board. **Publications:** *FaithWorks International Houses of Worship.* Directories. **Price:** $30.00 plus shipping and handling; $100.00 for 4 books series.

11518 ■ Frontiers International (FI)
6031 Crittenden St.
Philadelphia, PA 19138
Ph: (414)354-1851
E-mail: frontiers@frontiersinternational.com
URL: http://www.frontiersinternational.com
Contact: Johnny Moutry Jr., Chm.
Founded: 1936. **Members:** 1,200. **Staff:** 2. **Budget:** $60,000. **Local Groups:** 47. **Description:** Members interested in "social justice to all of the people everywhere through service to the community in which they reside". **Committees:** Buddy Projects; Medical Research Foundation; Women's Auxiliary. **Formerly:** (1961) Frontiers of America. **Publications:** *Frontiersman*, quarterly ● Membership Directory, annual. **Conventions/Meetings:** annual conference.

11519 ■ Gonja Association of North America (GANA)
PO Box 403
Lithonia, GA 30058
E-mail: gana-owner@egroups.com
URL: http://www.geocities.com/mumuni/index.htm
Contact: Alhaji Adam Ibrahim, Pres.
Founded: 1994. **Membership Dues:** regular, $10 (monthly) ● family, $30. **Multinational. Description:** Seeks to advance the political, economic and social well-being of all the people of Gonjaland. Works to aid, counsel, assist and protect the interests of Gonjaland residents in the United States and Ghana. Supports and promotes an appreciation of diversity among Gonjas and its' minorities. Provides a forum for the exchange of ideas about Ghana and Gonjaland. **Awards:** GANA Scholarship. **Frequency:** annual. **Type:** scholarship. **Recipient:** for junior/senior high school students originated from Gonjaland. **Telecommunication Services:** electronic mail, gana-subscribe@egroups.com.

11520 ■ Institute for Sustainable Communities (ISC)
535 Stone Cutters Way
Montpelier, VT 05602
Ph: (802)229-2900
Fax: (802)229-2919
E-mail: isc@iscvt.org
URL: http://www.iscvt.org
Contact: George Hamilton, Pres.
Founded: 1991. **Staff:** 28. **Budget:** $9,300,000. **Multinational. Description:** Helps communities globally

to address environmental, economic, and social challenges. Provides local communities with the training, advice, and grants needed to solve problems. **Publications:** *The Key to Sustainable Cities.* Book. **Price:** $15.00 plus $3 for shipping and handling ● Annual Report, annual. Alternate Formats: online.

11521 ■ International Association of Character Cities (IACC)
520 W Main St.
Oklahoma City, OK 73102
Ph: (405)815-0001
Fax: (405)815-0002
URL: http://www.charactercities.org
Contact: Tom Hill, Founder
Founded: 1998. **Multinational. Description:** Equips families to build character and helps communities reinforce character among citizens. Provides resources, training, contacts, and counsel to leaders who are committed to character development. Urges government and community leaders to use their influence in fostering a community-wide culture where good character is rewarded.

11522 ■ International Relief And Development (IRD)
1621 N Kent St., 4th Fl.
Arlington, VA 22209
Ph: (703)248-0161
Fax: (703)248-0194
E-mail: ird@ird-dc.org
URL: http://www.ird-dc.org
Contact: Dr. Arthur B. Keys Jr., Pres./CEO
Founded: 1998. **Staff:** 41. **Multinational. Description:** Seeks to improve the quality of life of underprivileged people in deprived parts of the world by providing humanitarian relief and development assistance programs. **Programs:** Agriculture Production, Processing and Marketing; Civil Society; Economic Development; Food Security; Health; Infrastructure; Livelihood Security; Relief.

11523 ■ National Association of Community Development Extension Professionals (NACDEP)
PO Box 4033
Bismarck, ND 58502-4033
E-mail: rmaurer@uky.edu
URL: http://nacdep.net
Contact: Rick Maurer, Pres.
Founded: 2002. **Membership Dues:** general, $50 (annual). **Description:** Seeks to improve the visibility, coordination, professional status and resource base of community and economic development extension programs and professionals. Develops, sponsors and promotes educational and training programs and activities that advance sound community development practices. **Committees:** Conference Planning; Marketing and Outreach; Recognition; Resolution and Policy. **Publications:** Proceedings. **Conventions/Meetings:** annual conference.

11524 ■ National Coalition for Asian Pacific American Community Development (National CAPACD)
1001 Connecticut Ave. NW, Ste.730
Washington, DC 20036
Ph: (202)223-2442
Fax: (202)223-4144
E-mail: info@nationalcapacd.org
URL: http://www.nationalcapacd.org
Contact: Gordon Chin, Pres.
Founded: 1999. **Membership Dues:** community, $75-$250 (annual) ● student/senior, $25 (annual) ● individual, $35 (annual) ● national intermediary/trade association, $300 (annual) ● bank/corporation/foundation, $500 (annual). **Description:** Addresses the community development and advocacy needs of the diverse and rapidly growing Asian American and Pacific Islander communities nationwide. Serves as the voice for the unique community development needs of AAPI communities. Strengthens the capacity of community-based organizations to create neighborhoods of hope and opportunity. **Programs:** Connecting AAPIs To Advocate and Lead; Internship.

11525 ■ National Community Building Network (NCBN)
1624 Franklin St., Ste.1000
Oakland, CA 94612
Ph: (510)663-6226
Fax: (510)663-6222
E-mail: network@ncbn.org
Contact: Emanuel Freeman, Pres.
Members: 800. **Membership Dues:** career community builder, $150 (annual) ● volunteer community builder, $25 (annual). **Description:** Promotes and advances community building principles, in practice and policy, to achieve social and economic equity for children and families. Acts as a hub for brokering information and connections among community builders. Integrates community development and human strategies. Fosters broad community participation. **Computer Services:** Information services, community building definition. **Committees:** Annual Meeting and Conference; Membership and Constituency Building; Nominations; Program and Policy.

11526 ■ Operation HOPE, Inc. (OHI)
707 Wilshire Blvd., 30th Fl.
Los Angeles, CA 90017
Ph: (213)891-2900
Free: (877)592-4673
Fax: (213)489-7511
E-mail: wendy.profit@operationhope.org
URL: http://www.operationhope.org
Contact: John Bryant, Founder/Chm./CEO
Founded: 1992. **Description:** Seeks to eradicate poverty and to assist in the development and privatization of inner-city and underserved communities.

11527 ■ Sister Island Project (SIP)
c/o Victoria Santos, Co-Dir.
PO Box 1413
Langley, WA 98260
Ph: (360)321-4012
E-mail: sisterisland@mail2world.com
URL: http://www.sisterislandproject.org
Contact: Victoria Santos, Co-Dir.
Founded: 1999. **Languages:** English, Spanish. **Multinational. Description:** Fosters international friendship and cultural, educational, and technical exchange between the people of the United States and the Dominican Republic. Promotes awareness of issues that challenge developing countries. **Computer Services:** Information services, Dominican Republic resources.

11528 ■ Soccer In The Streets
2323 Perimeter Park Dr. NE
Atlanta, GA 30341
Ph: (770)452-0505 (678)993-2113
Fax: (770)452-1946
E-mail: info@soccerstreets.org
URL: http://www.soccerstreets.org
Contact: Jill Robbins, Exec. Dir.
Description: Teaches less advantaged kids to make positive choices in life so as to better themselves, their families and communities through soccer, educational and life-skill programs. Promotes education, positive values and personal responsibility to "at-risk" kids in urban communities. **Computer Services:** Mailing lists, of members. **Programs:** Positive-Choice Soccer; Street-Box; Urban Soccer Girls. **Publications:** Newsletter. Alternate Formats: online.

11529 ■ Southern Mutual Help Association (SMHA)
3602 Old Jeanerette Rd.
New Iberia, LA 70563
Ph: (337)367-3277
Fax: (337)367-3279
E-mail: smha@southernmutualhelp.org
URL: http://www.southernmutualhelp.org
Contact: Lorna Bourg, Pres./Exec. Dir.
Founded: 1969. **Staff:** 15. **Nonmembership. Description:** Dedicated to finding fair and innovative solutions to challenged rural communities in Louisiana through self-help, partnerships, and the just management of resources. Seeks to end poverty, not by servicing it, but by helping people build viable,

healthy, and prosperous communities. **Programs:** Building Rural Communities; Life Quality; Youth Leadership.

11530 ■ SurfAid International
191 Calle Magdalena, Ste.290b
Encinitas, CA 92024
Ph: (760)753-1103
Fax: (760)753-1167
E-mail: usa@surfaidinternational.org
URL: http://www.surfaidinternational.org
Contact: Andrew Griffiths, CEO
Founded: 2000. **Staff:** 5. **National Groups:** 3. **Multinational. Description:** Improves the health and well being of the indigenous people of Mentawai Islands. Alleviates human suffering through community-based health programs. **Committees:** Programme Design. **Projects:** Childhood Health; Malaria Control. **Publications:** Newsletter. Alternate Formats: online ● Annual Report. Alternate Formats: online.

11531 ■ United Neighborhood Centers of America (UNCA)
11700 W Lake Park Dr.
Milwaukee, WI 53224
Ph: (414)359-1040
Fax: (414)359-1074
E-mail: info@unca.org
URL: http://www.unca.org
Contact: Ian B. Bautista, Pres.
Founded: 1911. **Members:** 150. **Staff:** 5. **Budget:** $250,000. **Regional Groups:** 6. **Local Groups:** 200. **Description:** Develops standards; recruits and refers personnel to member agencies; conducts special studies on neighborhood conditions such as health services, economic development, housing and unemployment, and works for effective legislation in these areas; provides training courses and consultation service to members and to organizers of new neighborhood centers. **Committees:** Budget Affairs; Fund Raising; International; Leadership Development and Training; Public Policy; Public Relations. **Formerly:** (1959) National Federation of Settlements; (1979) National Federation of Settlements and Neighborhood Centers. **Publications:** *News and Roundtable,* quarterly ● *Program Exchange,* bi-monthly ● *Public Policy Review,* monthly ● Journal, annual ● Newsletter, quarterly. Alternate Formats: online. **Conventions/Meetings:** annual meeting, also holds periodic regional meeting (exhibits).

11532 ■ Village Earth: CSVBD
PO Box 797
Fort Collins, CO 80522
Ph: (970)491-5754 (970)491-0633
Free: (800)648-8043
Fax: (970)491-2729
E-mail: csvbd@villageearth.org
URL: http://www.villageearth.org
Contact: Dr. Edwin F. Shinn, Exec. Dir.
Founded: 1995. **Staff:** 7. **Budget:** $115,000. **Languages:** English, Spanish. **Multinational. Description:** Aims to achieve sustainable village-based development by connecting communities with global resources through training, consulting, and networking with organizations worldwide. **Libraries: Type:** reference. **Holdings:** 1,050; books. **Subjects:** areas of village-level and do-it-yourself technologies. **Awards:** AT Library Scholarships. **Type:** scholarship. **Recipient:** to organizations working for sustainable development. **Formerly:** (2002) Consortium for Sustainable Village-Based Development. **Publications:** *Village Earth Newsletter,* quarterly. Contains organizational updates. Alternate Formats: online.

11533 ■ The Waterfront Center (TWC)
PO Box 32129
Washington, DC 20007
Ph: (202)337-0356
Fax: (202)986-0448
E-mail: mail@waterfrontcenter.org
URL: http://www.waterfrontcenter.org
Contact: Ann E. Breen, Co-Dir./Co-Founder
Founded: 1981. **Members:** 1,200. **Membership Dues:** regular, in U.S., $60 (annual) ● regular, in

Canada, C$70 (annual) ● in Mexico, 70 MP (annual) ● all other country, $80 (annual). **Staff:** 3. **Budget:** $300,000. **Languages:** English, French, Spanish. **Description:** State and local governments; architectural, engineering, and design firms; developers; educational institutions; persons in the boating industry; interested others. Helps communities develop waterfronts that facilitate economic growth while providing for public access and recreation. Conducts forums that address problems and opportunities in a particular community; provides on-site analyses and consulting; offers slide presentations; conducts research. **Libraries: Type:** not open to the public. **Awards:** Excellence on the Waterfront Award. **Frequency:** annual. **Type:** recognition. **Recipient:** for built project, comprehensive plan, citizen's efforts. **Publications:** *Caution: Working Waterfront: The Impact of Change on Marine Businesses.* Book. **Price:** $22.00 in U.S., plus shipping and handling ● *Fishing Piers: What Cities Can Do.* Book. **Price:** $22.00 in U.S., plus shipping and handling ● *Urban Waterfront Resource List*, periodic. Provides descriptions and ordering information on current books, reports, planning studies, municipal documents, and other information resources. **Price:** $25.00 for members; $30.00 for nonmembers ● *The Waterfront: A Worldwide Urban Success Story*, annual. Book. Lists member firms, projects, and cities. **Price:** $79.95 for nonmembers; $75.00 for members ● *Waterfront World Spotlight*, quarterly. Communique with information of use to communities planning waterfront projects. ISSN: 0733-0677 ● *Waterfronts: Cities Reclaim Their Edge.* Book. **Price:** $39.00 for nonmembers; $35.00 for members. **Conventions/Meetings:** annual conference (exhibits).

Community Organization

11534 ■ Community Leadership Association (CLA)
Fanning Inst.
1240 S Lumpkin St.
Univ. of Georgia
Athens, GA 30602
Ph: (706)542-0301
Fax: (706)542-7007
E-mail: info@communityleadership.org
URL: http://www.communityleadership.org
Contact: Mr. James D. Maloney, Exec. Dir.
Founded: 1979. **Members:** 425. **Membership Dues:** organization (with budget of $40000 to over $125000), $150-$375 (annual) ● associate, $350 (annual) ● individual, $40 (annual) ● gold, $100 (annual) ● life, $500. **Staff:** 3. **Budget:** $600,000. **Multinational. Description:** Local, regional, and state community leadership organizations. Provides for exchange of creative ideas concerning community leadership; promotes existing community leadership programs and their alumni organizations; helps establish new programs worldwide. Offers training, publications, and volunteer experts to community leadership organizations. Sponsors educational programs; compiles statistics. **Libraries: Type:** reference. **Holdings:** 60. **Subjects:** leadership, management, volunteerism. **Awards:** Distinguished Leadership Award. **Frequency:** annual. **Type:** recognition. **Recipient:** for local leaders ● National Community Leadership Award. **Frequency:** annual. **Type:** recognition. **Recipient:** for organization or individual of international scope ● Preceptor Award. **Frequency:** annual. **Type:** recognition. **Recipient:** for program directors. **Formerly:** (1989) National Association of Community Leadership Organizations; (2000) National Association for Community Leadership. **Publications:** *A Colorful Quilt: The Community Leadership Story.* Book ● *Community Program Resource*, monthly. Newsletter. Alternate Formats: online ● *Exploring Leadership.* Book ● *Leadership News*, quarterly ● *Program Development Guide: Taking Leadership in Hand*, periodic. **Price:** $99.00. **Conventions/Meetings:** annual Leadership Conference (exhibits).

11535 ■ Institute for Social Justice (ISJ)
Address Unknown since 2007
Founded: 1972. **Staff:** 10. **Regional Groups:** 4. **Description:** Offers training and technical assistance

to organizations and individuals interested in community organizing. Offers seminars and a two-day workshop for lawyers, paralegals, church social activists, and law students involved with community groups. Also holds a workshop that teaches basic skills and principles of community organization to persons new to organizing. Provides apprenticeship program and consulting services. **Affiliated With:** Association of Community Organizations for Reform Now. **Formerly:** (1979) Arkansas Institute for Social Justice. **Publications:** *The Organizer*, quarterly ● Also publishes community organizing handbooks. **Conventions/Meetings:** annual Leadership Training Conference (exhibits).

11536 ■ Interreligious Foundation for Community Organization (IFCO)
c/o Rev. Lucius Walker, Jr., Exec. Dir./Founder
402 W 145th St.
New York, NY 10031
Ph: (212)926-5757
Fax: (212)926-5842
E-mail: ifco@igc.org
URL: http://www.ifconews.org
Contact: Rev. Lucius Walker Jr., Exec. Dir./Founder
Founded: 1967. **Budget:** $250,000. **Description:** Member agencies work in more than 40 cities in the fields of political organization, housing, education, job training, and legal aid. Foundation carries out research, offers information, and provides financial and technical assistance to community organization efforts. Helps mobilize poor communities to play a greater role in solving their problems. **Convention/Meeting:** none. **Publications:** *IFCO News*, quarterly. Newsletter. Highlights IFCO programs and projects and provides analysis on social justice issues. Also highlights community organizing efforts nationwide. **Price:** $15.00 /year for individuals; $20.00 /year for institutions. **Circulation:** 10,000. **Advertising:** accepted ● Annual Report, annual.

11537 ■ National Community Development Organization
712A 3rd St. SW
Washington, DC 20024-3104
Fax: (202)488-0735
E-mail: webmail@ncdo.org
URL: http://www.ncdo.org
Contact: Donald Anderson, Exec.Dir.
Founded: 1968. **Members:** 240,000. **Staff:** 25. **Budget:** $650,000. **State Groups:** 7. **Local Groups:** 61. **Description:** Black, low-income individuals in Virginia, North Carolina, South Carolina, and Georgia, Mississippi, Illinois, Ohio, Washington, D.C., Chicago, and Cleveland. Seeks to create local organizations, known as Assemblies, through which low-income people can become involved in local decision-making regarding community services and opportunities. Concentrates on organizing Southern blacks in an effort toward raising levels of health, education, and income. **Libraries: Type:** not open to the public. **Awards: Type:** recognition. **Affiliated With:** National Black United Fund. **Formerly:** (1976) Virginia Community Development Organization; (2001) National Association for the Southern Poor. **Conventions/Meetings:** semiannual Council of Assemblies - conference ● monthly meeting.

11538 ■ National Training and Information Center (NTIC)
810 N Milwaukee Ave.
Chicago, IL 60622
Ph: (312)243-3035
Fax: (312)243-7044
E-mail: ntic@ntic-us.org
URL: http://www.ntic-us.org
Contact: Shel Trapp, Co-Founder
Founded: 1972. **Staff:** 17. **Description:** Resource center dedicated to neighborhood revitalization. Offers community leaders and organizers "how to" courses dealing with issues such as housing, neighborhood reinvestment, community drug problems, block club organizing, issue development, and media usage. Provides on-site consultation services and technical assistance to local groups on organizing campaigns and revitalization efforts. Serves as an

information clearinghouse. Researches mortgage and lending practices, utility rate increases, community development funding, insurance redlining and other issues, and uses the information to pressure industry and regulatory bodies as well as to inform legislative bodies and the public. Sponsors training sessions. **Publications:** *Asset Forfeiture: Getting a Piece of the Pie.* **Price:** $5.00 ● *Basics of Organizing: You Can't Build a Machine without Nuts and Bolts.* Book. **Price:** $5.00 ● *Disclosure*, bimonthly. Newsletter. **Price:** $15.00 /year for individuals and nonprofit organizations; $30.00 for others. **Circulation:** 7,000. Alternate Formats: online ● *Dynamics of Organizing.* Book. **Price:** $5.00 ● *Dynamics of Organizing - Building Power by Developing the Human Spirit.* Book. **Price:** $25.00 ● *Online Reports.* Alternate Formats: online ● *Pass the Buck Back! The Community Reinvestment Handbook* ● *Strategies for Developing A Drug Free Zone.* Book. **Price:** $2.00 ● *Taking Our Neighborhoods Back: A Guide to Organize Against Drugs.* Book. **Price:** $10.00 ● *Who, Me A Researcher? Yes, You!.* Book. **Price:** $5.00. **Conventions/Meetings:** annual meeting.

11539 ■ Organize Training Center (OTC)
508 Johnson Ave.
Pacifica, CA 94044
Ph: (650)557-9720
Fax: (650)557-9720
E-mail: sciplcy@aol.com
URL: http://www.bapd.org/gorier-1.html
Contact: Mike Miller, Dir.
Founded: 1973. **Staff:** 2. **Budget:** $150,000. **Description:** Works to: build effective, democratic, and self-funding community organizations; increase public understanding of the theory and practice of community organization; assist leaders and organizers of community groups. Initiates broadly based community-organizing projects. Assists leaders and organizers in creating plans and structures that can be effective in the development of community organizations. Sponsors and helps organize workshops on the history, philosophy, strategy, and tactics of mass-based organizing. Provides consulting services to community, church, and labor organizations. **Formerly:** (1979) Organize, Inc. **Publications:** *Social Policy*, quarterly. Magazine. Includes compilation of articles on organizing, news stories, research reports, and other relevant material. **Price:** $45.00 /year for individuals; $185.00/year for organizations ● Article ● Additional publications available; write for list.

Community Service

11540 ■ AFL-CIO Community Action Field Mobilization Department
815 16th St. NW
Washington, DC 20006
Ph: (202)637-5309 (202)637-5191
Fax: (202)637-5012
E-mail: feedback@aflcio.org
URL: http://www.aflcio.org
Contact: Marilyn Sneiderman, Dir., Field Mobilization Dept.
Founded: 1955. **Staff:** 8. **Description:** Aims to give working families a voice in their communities. Promotes that Union involvement is human service, coalition-building, and advocacy for the public voluntary human service needs of working people. **Awards:** Presidents' Award. **Type:** recognition. **Recipient:** for outstanding contributions to humanity. **Formed by Merger of:** AFL Community Relations Committee; CIO Community Services Committee. **Formerly:** (1985) AFL-CIO Community Services Activities; (1998) AFL-CIO Department of Community Services. **Conventions/Meetings:** annual National Conference on Community Services.

11541 ■ Call For Action (CFA)
5272 River Rd., Ste.300
Bethesda, MD 20816
Ph: (301)657-8260
Free: (800)647-1756

Fax: (301)657-2914
URL: http://www.callforaction.org
Contact: Shirley L. Rooker, Pres.
Founded: 1963. **Staff:** 2. **Budget:** $250,000. **Regional Groups:** 22. **Description:** A public service program that utilizes the energies of 1,200 volunteers from 24 affiliated radio and television broadcasting networks throughout the U.S., and Argentina. Provides citizens who are unable to solve their consumer problems with free, confidential information and referral assistance. Maintains office which provides help to consumers. Provides consumer education through radio and television reports, brochures, and the Ask the Expert program, which makes professionals such as doctors, pharmacists, lawyers, and financial advisers available to answer questions free of charge. **Awards:** Betty Furness Consumer Media Service Award. **Type:** recognition. **Telecommunication Services:** hotline, (301)657-7490. **Publications:** *Identity Theft - Your Good Name Gone Bad* (in English and Spanish). Brochures. **Price:** free. **Conventions/Meetings:** annual conference.

11542 ■ Joint Action in Community Service (JACS)
5225 Wisconsin Ave. NW, Ste.404
Washington, DC 20015
Ph: (202)537-0996
Free: (800)522-7773
Fax: (202)363-0239
E-mail: info@jacsinc.org
Contact: William Harvey Wise, Exec.Dir.
Founded: 1967. **Staff:** 110. **Budget:** $3,500,000. **Description:** Formed by leaders of national Protestant, Catholic, and Jewish associations. Has developed a local-level network of 5000 volunteers who are available on-call to assist male students formerly in the Job Corps program in dealing with the problems they face in the areas of housing, employment, education, transportation, budget planning, legal and medical aid, training opportunities, and citizenship information. Main focus of program is the availability of a committed and trained volunteer who will work on a one-to-one basis with an individual who has needs and help that individual meet them. Is currently working with young people returning to local communities from Job Corps centers. **Awards:** Jerome Schaller Scholarship. **Frequency:** annual. **Type:** monetary. **Recipient:** to outstanding Job Corps students. **Publications:** *The Volunteer,* quarterly. Newsletter. Recognizes volunteers assisting returning male Job Corps students. Includes award news. **Price:** free. Alternate Formats: online ● Annual Report, annual. Alternate Formats: online. **Conventions/Meetings:** semiannual Regional Directors' Conference.

11543 ■ National Association of Lesbian, Gay, Bisexual and Transgender Community Centers (NALGBTCC)
c/o Terry Stone, Exec. Dir.
1325 Massachusetts Ave. NW, Ste.700
Washington, DC 20005
Ph: (202)824-0450
Fax: (202)824-0453
E-mail: terry@lgbtcenters.org
URL: http://www.nalgbtcc.org
Contact: Terry Stone, Exec. Dir.
Founded: 1995. **Members:** 140. **Local Groups:** 5. **Description:** Seeks to encourage the growth of gay and lesbian community centers throughout the United States. **Publications:** *Nation Directory of Lesbian & Gay Community Centers.* Contains contact information on centers and organizing committees. ● *Resource Manual for Lesbian & Gay Centers.*

11544 ■ National Partnership for Community Leadership (NPCL)
PO Box 5719
Washington, DC 20037
Ph: (202)429-2027
Free: (888)775-6725
Fax: (202)429-2028
E-mail: jjohnson@npcl.org
URL: http://www.npcl.org
Contact: Jeffery M. Johnson PhD, Pres./CEO
Founded: 1996. **Description:** Seeks to improve the lives of children, disadvantaged families and communities. Supports, strengthens and empowers families and communities through education, technology, organizational development, research and policy impact. Fosters support networks and builds system capacities that can provide the tools necessary to strengthen families and communities. **Conventions/Meetings:** annual international conference.

Computers

11545 ■ Geeks Without Borders (GWoB)
1121 Bailey Hill Rd., No. 8
Eugene, OR 97402
Ph: (541)359-1658
E-mail: info@gwob.org
URL: http://www.gwob.org
Multinational. Description: Provides computers and related technology, education and support to schools, clinics, non-profit organizations, and to people with limited resources around the world. **Computer Services:** Mailing lists ● online services, discussion forum.

Conservationists

11546 ■ Alliance for America (AFA)
PO Box 1018
Spearfish, SD 57783
Ph: (518)835-6702
E-mail: afa@allianceforamerica.com
URL: http://www.allianceforamerica.org
Contact: Rose Comstock, Pres.
Members: 500. **Membership Dues:** individual, family, $30 (annual) ● student, senior, $15 (annual) ● sustaining, $100 (annual) ● organization, $100 (annual) ● trade association, $250 (annual). **Description:** Conservationists devoted to bringing human concerns into environmental decision-making, including animal rights vs. human rights, private property rights, natural resources issues. **Telecommunication Services:** electronic mail, comstock@inreach.com. **Conventions/Meetings:** conference.

11547 ■ David and Lucile Packard Foundation
300 Second St.
Los Altos, CA 94022
Ph: (650)948-7658
E-mail: inquiries@packard.org
URL: http://www.packard.org
Contact: Carol S. Larson, Pres./CEO
Founded: 1964. **Multinational. Description:** Works to provide grants to non-profit organizations related to conservation, population, science, children, families, communities, arts, and philanthropy. **Awards: Type:** grant. **Publications:** *The Future of Children.* Journal. Contains information that promotes effective policies and programs for children. ● Annual Report, annual.

11548 ■ Environmental Alliance for Senior Involvement (EASI)
5615 26th St. N
Arlington, VA 22207-1407
Ph: (703)241-4927
Fax: (703)538-5504
E-mail: easi@easi.org
URL: http://www.easi.org
Contact: Thomas P. Benjamin, Pres.
Founded: 1991. **Staff:** 12. **Budget:** $1,200,000. **Description:** Works to promote environmental awareness among seniors to help preserve the environment for future generations. **Awards:** EASI Volunteer Service Award. **Frequency:** periodic. **Type:** recognition. **Additional Websites:** http://www.environmentaleducation.org. **Publications:** *EASI Does It,* bimonthly. Newsletter. **Circulation:** 7,000 ● *Sustainable Communities Review,* biennial. Journal.

Circulation: 3,000. **Advertising:** accepted. **Conventions/Meetings:** annual conference (exhibits).

Conservative

11549 ■ Free Congress Foundation (FCF)
717 2nd St. NE
Washington, DC 20002
Ph: (202)546-3000
Fax: (202)543-5605
E-mail: info@freecongress.org
URL: http://www.freecongress.org
Contact: Paul Weyrich, Chm./CEO
Description: Seeks to return to traditional Judeo-Christian, Western culture. Established Judicial Selection Monitoring Project to expose judicial activists, print and media publishers, satellite and cable television shows. **Publications:** *Weyrich Insider.* Newsletter.

Consumers

11550 ■ Consumer Federation of America Foundation (CFAF)
1424 16th St. NW, Ste.604
Washington, DC 20036
Ph: (202)387-6121
Fax: (202)265-7989
E-mail: cfa@essential.org
URL: http://www.consumerfed.org
Contact: Mel Hall Crawford, Contact
Founded: 1972. **Description:** Consumer advocates. Strives to complement the work of the Consumer Federation of America by assisting state and local organizations, providing consumer information through projects, and conducting consumer research. **Affiliated With:** Consumer Federation of America. **Publications:** *CFAnews,* annual. Newsletter ● Brochures.

Corporate Responsibility

11551 ■ As You Sow Foundation (AYS)
311 California St., Ste.510
San Francisco, CA 94104
Ph: (415)391-3212
Fax: (415)391-3245
E-mail: asyousow@asyousow.org
URL: http://www.asyousow.org
Contact: Michael Passoff, Associate Dir.
Founded: 1992. **Description:** Dedicated to promoting corporate social responsibility. **Programs:** Corporate Social Responsibility; Environmental Enforcement Initiative. **Publications:** *Proxy Season Preview.* Newsletter. Alternate Formats: online ● *Unlocking the Power of the Proxy.* Book. Alternate Formats: online.

Counseling

11552 ■ Access Point
PO Box 6359
Los Osos, CA 93412
Ph: (805)534-1101 (805)534-0827
Fax: (805)534-1718
E-mail: info@accesspt.com
URL: http://www.accesspt.com
Contact: Jill Denton LMFT, Contact
Founded: 1981. **Description:** Provides supportive coaching and counseling to individuals, couples, groups, and businesses nationwide by telephone and locally in California. **Publications:** Newsletter, several times per year. **Conventions/Meetings:** periodic workshop.

11553 ■ Alternative Family Project (AFP)
Ctr. for Alternative Families
425 Divisadero St., Ste.203
San Francisco, CA 94117
Ph: (510)628-9065 (415)436-9000
Fax: (415)431-6404

E-mail: info@altfamilyproject.org
Contact: Robert-Jay Green, Exec.Dir.
Founded: 1993. **Membership Dues:** regular (minimum), $40 (annual). **Staff:** 11. **Budget:** $150,000. **Regional Groups:** 1. **Description:** Provides affordable therapy to individuals, couples, and non-traditional families, especially families with gay, lesbian bi-sexual or transgendered members. Conducts educational and research programs, provides advocacy services for government and media, compiles statistics, maintains speakers' bureau. **Awards:** AFP's Family Service Award. **Frequency:** annual. **Type:** recognition. **Recipient:** for outstanding contribution to the field of alternative families. **Publications:** *The Family Tree*, semiannual. Newsletter. **Price:** free. **Circulation:** 2,000. **Advertising:** accepted. **Alternate Formats:** CD-ROM; diskette. **Conventions/Meetings:** annual Ol' Fashioned Alternative Family Fourth of July Picnic - meeting and support group meeting (exhibits) - always July 4 ● biweekly support group meeting.

11554 ■ American Counseling Association (ACA)

5999 Stevenson Ave.
Alexandria, VA 22304
Free: (800)347-6647
Fax: (800)473-2329
E-mail: ryep@counseling.org
URL: http://www.counseling.org
Contact: Richard Yep, Exec. Dir.
Founded: 1952. **Members:** 51,000. **Membership Dues:** student, new professional, retired, $85 (annual) ● regular, professional, $135. **Staff:** 54. **Budget:** $9,000,000. **State Groups:** 53. **Description:** Counseling professionals in elementary and secondary schools, higher education, community agencies and organizations, rehabilitation programs, government, industry, business, private practice, career counseling, and mental health counseling. Conducts professional development institutes and provides liability insurance. Maintains Counseling and Human Development Foundation to fund counseling projects. **Libraries:** Type: reference. **Holdings:** 5,000; books. **Subjects:** counseling. **Awards:** ACA Extended Research Award. **Frequency:** annual. **Type:** recognition ● ACA Legislative Service Award. **Type:** recognition ● ACA Professional Development Award. **Frequency:** annual. **Type:** recognition ● ACA Research Award. **Type:** recognition ● Arthur A. Hitchcock Award (Distinguished Professional Service). **Frequency:** annual. **Type:** recognition ● Carl D. Perkins Award (Government Relations). **Type:** recognition ● Gilbert and Kathleen Wrenn Award for a Humanitarian and Caring Person. **Frequency:** annual. **Type:** recognition ● Kitty Cole Human Rights Award. **Type:** recognition ● Local, State Branch, and Regional Award. **Frequency:** annual. **Type:** recognition ● National Graduate Student Glen E. Hubele Award. **Type:** recognition ● Ralph F. Berdie Memorial Research Award. **Frequency:** annual. **Type:** recognition. **Computer Services:** database ● mailing lists ● online services. **Telecommunication Services:** TDD, (703)-823-6862. **Committees:** Bylaws; Ethics; Financial Affairs; Human Rights; Interprofessional/International Collaboration; Media; Nominations and Elections; Professional Development; Professionalization; Public Awareness and Support; Public Policy and Legislation; Research and Knowledge; Strategic Planning. **Councils:** Journal Editors. **Divisions:** American College Counseling Association; American Mental Health Counselors Association; American Rehabilitation Counseling Association; American School Counselor Association; Association for Adult Development and Aging; Association for Assessment in Counseling; Association for Counselor Education and Supervision; Association for Counselors and Educators in Government; Association for Gay, Lesbian, and Bisexual Issues in Counseling; Association for Multicultural Counseling and Development; Association for Specialists in Group Work; Association for Spiritual, Ethical and Religious Values and Issues in Counseling; Counseling Association for Humanistic Education and Development; Counselors for Social Justice; International Association of Addictions and Offender Counseling (see separate entries);

International Association of Marriage and Family Counselors; National Career Development Association; National Employment Counseling Association. **Formerly:** (1983) American Personnel and Guidance Association; (1992) American Association for Counseling and Development. **Publications:** *Career Development Quarterly*. Journal. Includes career counseling trends and reviews of current career counseling information. **Price:** included in membership dues; $55.00 /year for nonmembers; $100.00 /year for institutions. ISSN: 0889-4019. **Circulation:** 6,400. **Advertising:** accepted ● *Counseling and Values*, 3/year. Journal. Focuses on the role of values and religion in counseling. **Price:** included in membership dues; $41.00 /year for individuals; $50.00 /year for institutions. ISSN: 0160-7960. **Circulation:** 5,700. **Advertising:** accepted ● *Counseling Today*, monthly. Includes ethical and legal issues, new products, book reviews, association events, and continuing education. **Price:** included in membership dues; $66.00 /year for nonmembers. ISSN: 0017-5323. **Circulation:** 55,000. **Advertising:** accepted. **Alternate Formats:** online ● *Counselor Education and Supervision*, quarterly. **Price:** included in membership dues; $60.00 /year for institutions. ISSN: 0011-0035. **Circulation:** 3,600. **Advertising:** accepted ● *Journal of Addictions and Offender Counseling*, semiannual. **Price:** included in membership dues; $22.00 /year for nonmembers. ISSN: 1055-3835. **Circulation:** 3,300. **Advertising:** accepted ● *Journal of College Counseling*, semiannual. **Price:** $32.00/year. ISSN: 1099-0399. **Circulation:** 3,300. **Advertising:** accepted ● *Journal of Counseling and Development*, quarterly. **Price:** included in membership dues; $128.00 /year for nonmembers and institutions. ISSN: 0748-9633. **Circulation:** 53,500. **Advertising:** accepted ● *Journal of Employment Counseling*, quarterly. **Price:** included in membership dues; $38.00/year. ISSN: 0022-0787. **Circulation:** 1,800. **Advertising:** accepted ● *The Journal of Humanistic Counseling, Education and Development*, quarterly. **Price:** included in membership dues; $32.00 /year for nonmembers. ISSN: 0735-6846. **Circulation:** 2,200. **Advertising:** accepted ● *Journal of Multicultural Counseling and Development*, quarterly. **Price:** included in membership dues; $21.00 /year for nonmembers. ISSN: 0883-8534. **Circulation:** 4,400. **Advertising:** accepted ● *Measurement and Evaluation in Counseling and Development*, quarterly. Journal. **Price:** included in membership dues; $50.00 /year for nonmembers. ISSN: 0748-1756. **Circulation:** 3,200. **Advertising:** accepted ● Journal. **Circulation:** 2,900. **Advertising:** accepted ● Also publishes books, journals, videotapes, home studies and a catalog. **Conventions/Meetings:** annual convention and international conference, includes associations also engaged in the helping professions, and publishers of counseling books (exhibits).

11555 ■ American Family Therapy Academy (AFTA)

1608 20th St. NW, 4th Fl.
Washington, DC 20009
Ph: (202)483-8001
Fax: (202)483-8002
E-mail: afta@afta.org
URL: http://www.afta.org
Contact: Barbro Miles, Admin. Dir.
Founded: 1977. **Members:** 714. **Membership Dues:** regular in U.S., $269 (annual) ● regular outside U.S., early career, retired in U.S., $135 (annual) ● retired international, $90 (annual). **Staff:** 2. **Budget:** $280,000. **Description:** Family therapy teachers, researchers, and practitioners working to advance theory and therapy that regards the family as a unit. Promotes research and professional education in family therapy and allied fields. Disseminates information to practitioners, scientists, and the public. Focuses on improving the knowledge of how families function and how to treat them. **Awards:** Distinguished Contribution to Family Research Award. **Frequency:** annual. **Type:** recognition. **Recipient:** for outstanding research in the field of family therapy ● Distinguished Contribution to Family Therapy Theory and Practice Award. **Frequency:** annual. **Type:** recognition. **Recipient:** for outstanding contributions

to Family Therapy Theory and Practice ● Distinguished Contribution to Social Justice. **Frequency:** annual. **Type:** recognition. **Recipient:** for an outstanding work on social justice ● Innovative Contribution to Family Therapy Award. **Frequency:** annual. **Type:** recognition. **Recipient:** for contributions to Family Therapy Theory and Practice. **Committees:** Awards; Economic and Cultural Diversity; Family Policy; Human Rights; Publications; Research. **Formerly:** American Family Therapy Association. **Publications:** Monograph, semiannual. **Price:** $32.00 /year for nonmembers. **Advertising:** accepted. **Alternate Formats:** online ● Membership Directory, biennial ● Audiotapes. **Price:** $20.00 plus shipping and handling. **Conventions/Meetings:** annual meeting.

11556 ■ AMHS

c/o Integrity International
15702 Tasa Pl.
Laurel, MD 20707
Ph: (301)953-7353
E-mail: helpline@tidalwave.net
URL: http://www.soeken.lawsonline.net/index.htm
Contact: Donald R. Soeken PhD, Pres.
Founded: 1978. **Membership Dues:** $35. **Staff:** 1. **Budget:** $10,000. **Description:** Individuals in consulting, business, and the press concerned with ethical problems and practices. Provides a range of services to assist in the development and promotion of ethical practices in government and business. Conducts seminars on promoting ethical issues in business, government, and individual behavior. Maintains 100 volume library on mental health ethics and whistle blowing. **Libraries:** Type: reference. **Holdings:** 50. **Subjects:** whistle blowing, ethics health. **Awards:** Badge of Courage. **Type:** recognition. **Recipient:** for person of conscience. **Computer Services:** listing of all known whistle blowers in the U.S., Canada, and Europe. **Doing business as:** (2001) Integrity International. **Formerly:** (1987) Association of Mental Health Specialties. **Publications:** *The Lance*, annual. Newsletter. **Advertising:** accepted. **Conventions/Meetings:** annual workshop - always summer.

11557 ■ Association for Counselors and Educators in Government (ACEG)

5999 Stevenson Ave.
Alexandria, VA 22304-3300
Free: (800)347-6647
Fax: (800)473-2329
E-mail: dwilliams14@hot.rr.com
URL: http://www.dantes.doded.mil/dantes_web/organizations/aceg/index.htm
Contact: Doris Williams, Pres.
Founded: 1978. **Members:** 554. **Membership Dues:** regular/professional, $25 (annual) ● student/new professional/retired, $20 (annual). **Regional Groups:** 6. **Description:** Professional counselors who work in the U.S. Armed Services. Encourages and provides counseling to individuals in the service and their dependents, veterans, and civilians employed by the military. Promotes and maintains improved communication with the non-military community. Provides representation for counseling and education professionals working in and for the U.S. Department of Defense. Offers programs to enhance individual growth and development. **Affiliated With:** American Counseling Association. **Publications:** *ACEG Report*, 3/year. Newsletter. **Price:** included in membership dues. **Circulation:** 800. **Advertising:** accepted. **Alternate Formats:** online. **Conventions/Meetings:** annual conference, held in conjunction with ACA; includes professional development institute (exhibits) - always spring.

11558 ■ Association for Multicultural Counseling and Development (AMCD)

c/o Dr. Canary Hogan, Membership Chair
1285 Cheyenne Blvd.
Madison, TN 37115
Ph: (615)876-5117
URL: http://www.bgsu.edu/colleges/edhd/programs/AMCD/HomePage.html
Contact: Dr. Canary Hogan, Membership Chair
Founded: 1972. **Members:** 3,508. **Membership Dues:** regular (ACA and AMCD), $165 (annual) ●

student or retired (ACA and AMCD), new professional (ACA), $124 (annual). **Description:** Represents professionals involved in counseling careers in educational settings, social services, and community agencies; interested individuals and students. Seeks to develop programs aimed at improving ethnic and racial empathy and understanding; foster personal growth and improve educational opportunities for all minorities in the U.S.; defend human and civil rights; provide in-service and pre-service training for members and others in the profession. Works to enhance members' ability to serve as behavioral change agents. Offers placement service. **Awards: Type:** recognition. **Affiliated With:** American Counseling Association. **Formerly:** (1986) Association for Non-White Concerns in Personnel and Guidance. **Publications:** *Journal of Multicultural Counseling and Development*, quarterly. **Price:** included in membership dues; $69.00 /year for individuals nonmember; $80.00 /year for institutions nonmember. ISSN: 0883-8534. **Circulation:** 2,600. **Advertising:** accepted. Alternate Formats: microform ● Newsletter, 3/year. **Conventions/Meetings:** annual conference, held in conjunction with ACA (exhibits).

11559 ■ Association for Specialists in Group Work (ASGW)

c/o Maria Riva, Pres.
2450 S Vine St.
Coll. of Educ.
Univ. of Denver
Denver, CO 80210
Ph: (303)871-2484
E-mail: mriva@du.edu
URL: http://www.asgw.org
Contact: Maria Riva, Pres.
Founded: 1973. **Members:** 1,128. **Membership Dues:** professional (ACA and ASGW), $191 (annual) ● professional (ASGW only), $50 (annual) ● student, new professional, retired (ASGW only), $37 (annual) ● student, new professional, retired (ASGW and ACA), $112 (annual). **Description:** A division of the American Counseling Association (see separate entry). Individuals interested in group counseling holding master's or doctoral degrees, and engaged in practice, teaching, or research in group work; persons holding undergraduate degrees who are interested in group work, but not actively engaged in practice, teaching, or research; students. Seeks to assist and further interests of children, youth, and adults by providing effective services through the group medium, preventing problems, providing maximum development, and remediating disabling behaviors. Sponsors programs to advance group work in schools, clinics, universities, private practice, and mental health institutions. Conducts placement service. **Awards: Type:** recognition. **Affiliated With:** American Counseling Association. **Publications:** *The Group Worker*, 3/year. Newsletter. Includes calendar of events. **Price:** included in membership dues. **Circulation:** 3,000 ● *Journal for Specialists in Group Work*, quarterly. **Price:** included in membership dues; $44.00 /year for nonmembers. ISSN: 0193-3922. **Circulation:** 5,740. **Advertising:** accepted. **Conventions/Meetings:** semiannual conference, held in conjunction with ACA (exhibits).

11560 ■ Association of Traumatic Stress Specialists (ATSS)

PO Box 246
Phillips, ME 04966-0246
Ph: (207)639-2433
Free: (800)991-2877
Fax: (207)639-2434
E-mail: admin@atss.info
URL: http://www.atss.info
Contact: Susy Sanders PhD, Pres.
Founded: 1989. **Members:** 1,200. **Membership Dues:** individual, $85 (annual) ● senior (60), student (proof of status), $45 (annual) ● agency/team (5 members), $225 (annual). **Staff:** 1. **Budget:** $45,000. **Regional Groups:** 2. **Multinational. Description:** Works as an international multidisciplinary organization dedicated to excellence in service, response and treatment to victims of traumatic stress. Establishes and recognizes professional standards for individuals

representing diverse professional disciplines engaged in crisis and emergency response, crisis intervention and victim services, and counseling and treatment practices. **Libraries: Type:** reference. **Subjects:** traumatic incidence, post traumatic stress disorder. **Awards:** Outstanding Contributor for the Advancement of Trauma Treatment. **Frequency:** annual. **Type:** recognition. **Computer Services:** Online services, member section, membership certification, links, calendar. **Boards:** Certification. **Committees:** Education and Training; International; Membership. **Affiliated With:** International Critical Incident Stress Foundation. **Formerly:** (1998) International Association of Trauma Counseling. **Publications:** *Trauma Lines*, quarterly. Newsletter. **Conventions/Meetings:** board meeting - 9/year ● biennial conference (exhibits).

11561 ■ Commission on Rehabilitation Counselor Certification (CRCC)

300 N Martingale Rd., Ste.460
Schaumburg, IL 60173
Ph: (847)394-2104 (847)944-1325
Fax: (847)394-2172
E-mail: info@crccertification.com
URL: http://www.crccertification.com
Contact: Susan Gilpin, CEO
Founded: 1973. **Staff:** 25. **Budget:** $850,000. **Nonmembership. Description:** Serves as national certification board for rehabilitation counselors.

11562 ■ Employee Assistance Society of North America (EASNA)

2001 Jefferson Davis Hwy., Ste.1004
Arlington, VA 22202-3617
Ph: (703)416-0060
Fax: (703)416-0014
E-mail: info@easna.org
URL: http://www.easna.org
Contact: Rich Paul MSW, Pres.
Founded: 1984. **Members:** 300. **Membership Dues:** individual, $140 (annual) ● affiliate, $500 (annual) ● organization (based on number of employees), $500-$2,000 (annual) ● student, $95 (annual). **Staff:** 1. **Budget:** $110,000. **Description:** Individuals in the field of employee assistance, including psychiatrists, psychologists, and managers. Facilitates communication among members; provides resource information; serves as a network for employee assistance programs nationwide. Conducts research. **Awards:** Lifetime Achievement Award. **Frequency:** annual. **Type:** recognition. **Recipient:** for long term (usually over the course of at least ten years) significant, consistent global contribution to the field of employee assistance. **Computer Services:** database ● mailing lists. **Committees:** Credentialing; Ethics; Member Services; Program Accreditation; Regional Affairs; Research. **Publications:** *Accreditation Handbook and Employee Assistance Standards.* **Price:** $18.00 ● *EAP Guidelines.* **Circulation:** 300 ● *Employee Assistance Quarterly.* Journal. **Price:** included in membership dues; $45.00 /year for nonmembers ● *Employee Assistance Society of North America—The Source*, quarterly. Newsletter. **Price:** included in membership dues. **Circulation:** 1,200. **Advertising:** accepted ● *Step by Step.* **Circulation:** 300. **Conventions/Meetings:** annual international conference (exhibits).

11563 ■ International Association of Addictions and Offender Counselors (IAAOC)

PO Box 791006
Baltimore, MD 21279-1006
Free: (800)347-6647
Fax: (800)473-2329
E-mail: cwbroo@wharf.ship.edu
URL: http://www.iaaoc.org
Contact: Ford Brooks EdD, Membership Chm.
Founded: 1972. **Membership Dues:** professional, $145 (annual). **Description:** A division of the American Counseling Association. Promotes counseling and rehabilitation programs for people with substance abuse problems and other addictions. **Affiliated With:** American Counseling Association. **Publications:** *IAAOC Newsletter*, quarterly. **Price:** included in membership dues. Alternate Formats: online ●

Journal of Addictions and Offender Counseling, semiannual. **Price:** $30.00/copy. ISSN: 1055-3835. **Advertising:** accepted. Alternate Formats: microform. **Conventions/Meetings:** annual convention (exhibits).

11564 ■ International Association for Marriage and Family Counselors (IAMFC)

c/o Dr. Robert Smith, Exec. Dir.
Texas A&M Univ. - Corpus Christi
Coll. of Educ.
6300 Ocean Dr.
Corpus Christi, TX 78412
Ph: (361)825-2307
Free: (800)347-6647
E-mail: director@iamfc.com
URL: http://www.counseling.org
Contact: Dr. Robert Smith, Exec. Dir.
Founded: 1989. **Members:** 3,897. **Membership Dues:** regular, professional (joint ACA/IAMFC), $211 (annual) ● regular, professional (IAMFC only), $70 (annual) ● student, retired, new professional (joint ACA/IAMFC), $129 (annual) ● student, retired, new professional (IAMFC only), $54 (annual). **Staff:** 2. **Budget:** $250,000. **Description:** A division of the American Counseling Association. Individuals working in the areas of marriage counseling, marital therapy, divorce counseling, mediation, and family counseling and therapy; interested others. Promotes ethical practices in marriage and family counseling/therapy. Encourages research; provides a forum for dialogue on relevant issues; facilitates the exchange of information. Assists couples and families in coping with life challenges; works to ameliorate problems confronting families and married couples. **Additional Websites:** http://www.iamfc.com. **Publications:** *The Family Digest*, 3/year. Newsletter. Keeps members up to date on the current activities of the organization and abreast of news and developments that are affecting the field. ● *The Family Journal: Counseling and Therapy for Couples and Families*, quarterly. Provides pertinent information to counselors and counselor educators in a number of different areas. **Price:** $38.00. **Circulation:** 10,000 ● *IAMFC Newsletter*, quarterly. **Conventions/Meetings:** annual convention, held in conjunction with ACA (exhibits).

11565 ■ A Minor Consideration

14530 Denker Ave.
Gardena, CA 90247
Fax: (310)523-3691
URL: http://www.minorcon.org
Contact: Paul Petersen, Pres.
Founded: 1990. **Members:** 2,000. **Staff:** 3. **Description:** Former kid star support group working to improve conditions for today's professional children. **Conventions/Meetings:** seminar.

11566 ■ National Association of Peer Programs (NAPP)

PO Box 10627
Kansas City, MO 64188-0627
Free: (877)314-7337
Fax: (866)314-7337
E-mail: napp@peerprograms.org
URL: http://www.peerhelping.org
Contact: Lois Charley, Exec. Sec.
Founded: 1984. **Members:** 500. **Membership Dues:** individual, in U.S., $50 (annual) ● individual, in Canada, $55 (annual) ● international, $60 (annual). **Staff:** 1. **Budget:** $100,000. **State Groups:** 37. **Description:** Individuals interested in peer helping and peer counseling. Seeks to create a network of peer-counseling programs. Encourages the establishment of peer-helping programs in schools, universities, and community-based organizations; works to establish a standard of ethics for the field. Provides information, support, and training to peer counselors. Compiles statistics. **Awards:** Barbara Varenhorst Award of Merit. **Type:** recognition ● NPHA Scholar. **Type:** scholarship ● Peer Program of the Year. **Frequency:** annual. **Type:** recognition ● Professional of the Year. **Frequency:** annual. **Type:** recognition ● Youth of the Year. **Frequency:** annual. **Type:** recognition. **Additional Websites:** http://www.peerprograms.org. **Formerly:** (2006) National Peer Helpers As-

sociation. **Publications:** *Perspectives in Peer Programs*, periodic. Journal. **Price:** included in membership dues. ISSN: 0741-2282. **Advertising:** accepted. **Conventions/Meetings:** annual conference (exhibits) - always June.

11567 ■ National Board for Certified Counselors and Affiliates (NBCC)
3 Terrace Way
Greensboro, NC 27403-3660
Ph: (336)547-0607
Fax: (336)547-0017
E-mail: nbcc@nbcc.org
URL: http://www.nbcc.org
Contact: Ms. Mona Olds, Outreach Coor.
Founded: 1982. **Members:** 37,000. **Staff:** 48. **Budget:** $5,000,000. **Description:** Establishes and monitors professional credentialing standards for counselors. Identifies individuals who have obtained voluntary certification as a National Certified Counselor, one who assists persons with aging, vocational development, adolescence, family, and marital concerns, or a National Certified School Counselor, one who specializes in counseling within the school setting, or a Certified Clinical Mental Health Counselor, one who specializes in working in clinical settings, or a Master Addictions Counselor, one who specializes in addictions counseling. Maintains a database of nearly 37,000 certified counselors. **Computer Services:** Online services, directory of counselors (CounselorFind). **Affiliated With:** American Counseling Association. **Absorbed:** (1993) Academy of Clinical Mental Health Counselors. **Formerly:** (2002) National Board for Certified Counselors. **Publications:** *The National Certified Counselor*, 3/year, every spring, fall and winter. Newsletter. Includes updates on counselor licensure and continuing education information. **Price:** free for certified counselors. ISSN: 0886-7089. **Circulation:** 35,000. **Advertising:** accepted. Alternate Formats: online ● *Preparation Guide for the National Clinical Mental Health Counseling Examination* ● *Preparation Guide for the National Counselor Examination for Licensure and Certification*. Manuals.

11568 ■ National MultiCultural Institute (NMCI)
3000 Connecticut Ave. NW, Ste.438
Washington, DC 20008-2556
Ph: (202)483-0700
Fax: (202)483-5233
E-mail: nmci@nmci.org
URL: http://www.nmci.org
Contact: Elizabeth Pathy Salett MSW, Pres.
Founded: 1983. **Staff:** 12. **Description:** Seeks to work with individuals, organizations, and communities in creating a society that is strengthened and empowered by its diversity. Leads efforts to increase communication, understanding, and respect among diverse groups and addresses important issues of multiculturalism facing society today. Provides organizational training and consulting on diversity issues and develops leading edge projects in the field. Cross-cultural conflict resolution, and initiating cross-cultural dialogues. Programs serve professionals in such fields as management, human resource development, education, health and mental health, social services, refugee resettlement, mediation, and law enforcement. **Awards: Frequency:** annual. **Type:** recognition. **Recipient:** for contribution to NMCI. **Computer Services:** Mailing lists, of members. **Formerly:** (1991) International Counseling Center; (1992) Multicultural Institute of the International Counseling Center. **Publications:** *Crossing Cultures in Mental Health*. Book. **Price:** $29.95 ● *Developing Diversity Training for the Workplace: A Guide for Trainers*. Manual. **Price:** $149.95 ● *Multicultural Case Studies: Tools for Training*. Manual. Contains collection of case studies to be used in diversity training for professionals in all fields. **Price:** $49.95 ● *Race, Ethnicity and Self: Identity in Multicultural Perspective*. Book. Contains collection of articles on the impact of race and ethnicity on individual identity development in the Unites States. **Price:** $29.95 ● *Teaching Skills and Cultural Competency: A Guide for Trainers*. Manual. **Price:** $149.95. **Conventions/Meetings:**

semiannual conference, includes two- and four-day training workshops (exhibits) - always May and November.

11569 ■ Pact Training
PO Box 106
New Kingston, NY 12459-0106
Ph: (845)586-3992
Fax: (845)586-4277
E-mail: office@pacttraining.com
URL: http://www.pacttraining.com
Contact: Joyce St. George, Co-Dir.
Founded: 1980. **Staff:** 4. **Budget:** $300,000. **Description:** Provides custom-designed human dynamics training services for corporations, police, health care organizations and human services agencies. Aims to provide experiential training to help people handle and negotiate sensitive and critical situations. Includes training topics: stress management, conflict and crisis management, preventing workplace violence, diversity and cultural competence, domestic violence, working with emotionally disturbed people, leadership training, among others. **Programs:** Criminal Justice; Education, Human Services/Health Care; Management; Managing Diversity; Victimization. **Formerly:** (1987) Performing Arts for Crisis Training.

11570 ■ Shanti
730 Polk St.
San Francisco, CA 94109
Ph: (415)674-4700
Fax: (415)674-0373
E-mail: jberman@shanti.org
URL: http://www.shanti.org
Contact: Kevin Burns, Exec. Dir.
Founded: 1975. **Staff:** 50. **Budget:** $4,500,000. **Regional Groups:** 1. **Languages:** English, Spanish. **Nonmembership. Description:** Volunteer counseling service offering ongoing support to individuals who face a diagnosis of Acquired Immune Deficiency Syndrome (AIDS), breast cancer and their loved ones in the San Francisco, CA, area. Shanti is a Sanskrit word meaning "inner peace". Provides peer counseling, and practical assistance, including van service, to people with AIDS and breast cancer. Conducts psychosocial training programs for health care professionals, clergy, and laypeople. Serves as a model program for similar services nationwide. **Convention/Meeting:** none. **Committees:** People of Color; Third World; Women. **Programs:** Activities; Care Coordination; Latino; Transportation; Volunteer. **Formerly:** Shanti Project. **Publications:** *Our Times*, quarterly. Newsletter.

11571 ■ Wives-Self-Help Foundation (WSHF)
Smylie Times Bldg., Ste.205
8001 Roosevelt Blvd.
Philadelphia, PA 19152
Ph: (215)332-2311
Fax: (215)332-1873
E-mail: wshfi@rcn.com
Contact: Maxine Schnall, Exec. Dir.
Founded: 1974. **Staff:** 12. **Description:** Persons with an interest in improving their marital, family, or personal lives through trained peer counseling via a Philadelphia, PA-based hotline. Offers immediate emotional support and guidance to clients; develops client potential for self-help. Operates professional in-house counseling which provides therapy for individuals, couples, and families in such areas as stress, depression, marital conflicts, physical abuse, anxiety, sexual problems, and drug and alcohol abuse. Offers services to children and adolescents experiencing difficulties in areas such as substance abuse and conflicts with parents and teachers. Provides information and referral services.

Credit

11572 ■ Alliance Credit Counseling
15720 John J. Delaney Dr., Ste.100
Charlotte, NC 28277
Ph: (704)341-1010
Free: (888)995-7856

Fax: (704)540-5495
E-mail: leadership@knowdebt.org
URL: http://www.knowdebt.org
Contact: Kevin P. Porter, Exec. Dir.
Description: Provides help and hope through personalized education, counseling and support programs that seek to reduce and avoid the burdens of financial crisis, debt stress, bankruptcy and consequences. Provides empowerment to the public through charitable education programs of financial literacy, money management, credit management and debt reduction. Offers services of financial counseling, education and debt management. **Telecommunication Services:** electronic mail, service@knowdebt.org ● electronic mail, management@knowdebt.org ● electronic mail, counseling@knowdebt.org.

Crime

11573 ■ Alliance of Guardian Angels
717 5th Ave., Ste.401
New York, NY 10022
Ph: (212)545-7676
Fax: (212)223-8180
E-mail: marysliwa@guardianangels.org
URL: http://www.guardianangels.org
Contact: Mary Sliwa, Exec. Dir.
Founded: 1979. **Members:** 7,000. **Description:** Unarmed volunteers organized to combat crime in New York City; PA; CA; Denver, CO; Florida; Texas; Boston, MA; Portland, OR; Seattle, WA; Phoenix, AZ; Illinois and other major U.S., Canadian, and European cities. Seeks to "provide positive role models for young people". Patrols subways, buses, streets, ferries, and multiple dwellings. Members wear red berets and are selected only upon recommendation of other Angels. They must act in a calm manner and be capable of self-defense if attacked by one or more persons. Angels must undergo three months of physical and legal training. Members make citizens' arrests but their primary impact is one of deterrence; often their presence prevents crimes. Conducts speakers' bureau on crime prevention and self-protection. Maintains museum. **Libraries: Type:** reference. **Holdings:** archival material. **Awards:** Outstanding High School Student. **Frequency:** annual. **Type:** recognition. **Additional Websites:** http://www.cyberangels.org. **Programs:** Cyber Angels; Junior Angels; Senior Angels; Urban Angels. **Also Known As:** Alliance of Guardian Angels. **Formerly:** (1979) Magnificent 13; (2000) Guardian Angels. **Publications:** Brochure. **Conventions/Meetings:** annual conference (exhibits) - always Labor Day weekend.

11574 ■ American Justice Institute (AJI)
349 Main St., Ste.104
Laurel, MD 20707
Ph: (301)725-5858
Fax: (301)725-7986
E-mail: amerjust@erols.com
URL: http://www.americanjusticeinstitute.com
Contact: Rex C. Smith, Pres.
Founded: 1986. **Members:** 7. **Staff:** 2. **Budget:** $50,000. **Description:** Seeks to help institutions and individuals become more willing and able to reduce the occurrence of crime, delinquency, and related social problems. Conducts research and disseminates information. Provides public and private justice agencies with statistics, demonstrations, and assistance in training and evaluation. **Awards:** Richard A. McGee Award. **Frequency:** quarterly. **Type:** recognition. **Conventions/Meetings:** annual meeting.

11575 ■ Crime Stoppers International (CSI)
3100 Main St., Ste.201
Kansas City, MO 64111
Free: (800)850-7574
E-mail: crimestoppersint@aol.com
URL: http://www.c-s-i.org
Contact: Richard W. Carter, Exec. Dir.
Founded: 1979. **Members:** 1,000. **Membership Dues:** student, $50 (annual) ● II (population under 25,000), $100 (annual) ● III (25,000-49,999 popula-

tion), \$150 (annual) ● IV (50,000-99,999 population), \$200 (annual) ● state or provincial, \$200 (annual) ● V (100,000-249,999 population), \$250 (annual) ● VI (250,000-499,999 population), \$300 (annual) ● VII (500,000-749,999 population), \$400 (annual) ● VIII (750,000-999,999 population), \$500 (annual) ● IX (1 million and more population), \$600 (annual). **Staff:** 3. **Budget:** \$300,000. **Regional Groups:** 15. **Languages:** English, French, Spanish. **Description:** Local and independently organized crime stoppers or crime solver programs that offer anonymity and rewards for information leading to the resolution of serious crimes; associate programs are those that report statistics. Objectives are to: increase the number of crime stopper programs; provide training, guidance, and services to improve the effectiveness of existing programs. Offers assistance in the form of instructional materials, publicity, and on-site visits. Conducts workshops and presentations. Sponsors broadcast competition for television re-enactments or special crime stoppers programs. **Awards:** Civilian Crime Stopper of the Year. **Frequency:** annual. **Type:** recognition ● Coordinator of the Year. **Frequency:** annual. **Type:** recognition ● Productivity Award. **Type:** recognition. **Committees:** Data Processing; Statistics. **Departments:** Programs. **Programs:** Associate. **Formerly:** (1984) Crime Stoppers U.S.A. **Publications:** *The Caller*, monthly. Magazine. Includes statistical information and accounts of Crime Stopper successes. ● Directory, annual. **Conventions/Meetings:** annual conference (exhibits).

11576 ■ International Association for the Study of Organized Crime (IASOC)
c/o Kip Schlegel, Exec. Dir.
Dept. of Criminal Justice
Indiana Univ.
302 Sycamore Hall
Bloomington, IN 47405
Ph: (812)855-0889
Fax: (812)855-5922
E-mail: iasoc_office@yahoo.com
URL: http://www.iasoc.net
Contact: Jay Albanese, Exec. Dir.

Founded: 1984. **Members:** 250. **Membership Dues:** regular, in North America, \$55 (annual) ● regular, outside North America, \$75 (annual). **Staff:** 2. **Budget:** \$10,000. **Description:** Researchers, investigators, educators, journalists, and students representing 20 countries interested in the study of organized crime. Provides a network for those involved in the study of organized crime. **Awards:** **Frequency:** annual. **Type:** recognition. **Committees:** Course Development; International Research; Legal and Legislative; Literature Review. **Publications:** *IASOC UPDATES*, monthly. Newsletter. **Price:** included in membership dues. Alternate Formats: online ● *Trends in Organized Crime*, quarterly. Journal. Includes research information. ● Membership Directory, biennial. **Conventions/Meetings:** annual meeting, held in conjunction with American Society of Criminology - every November.

11577 ■ International Society of Crime Prevention Practitioners (ISCPP)
c/o Richard Cannady, Exec. Dir.
PO Box 476
Simpsonville, SC 29681
Ph: (864)884-8466
E-mail: rcannady@iscpp.org
URL: http://www.iscpp.org
Contact: Cheryl Elliott, Pres.

Founded: 1978. **Members:** 1,300. **Membership Dues:** individual, \$35 (annual). **Staff:** 2. **Budget:** \$150,000. **Multinational. Description:** Crime prevention practitioners, private security officers, and interested individuals from 14 countries. Works to facilitate exchange of ideas on crime prevention practices and programs. Sponsors basic crime prevention training. **Awards:** Business of the Year Award. **Frequency:** annual. **Type:** recognition ● Community Based Program Award. **Frequency:** annual. **Type:** recognition ● George B. Sunderland Award. **Frequency:** annual. **Type:** recognition ● Media of the Year Award. **Frequency:** annual. **Type:** recognition.● State/Province Programs or Associa-

tions Award. **Frequency:** annual. **Type:** recognition ● Unit of the Year Award. **Frequency:** annual. **Type:** recognition ● Volunteer of the Year Award. **Frequency:** annual. **Type:** recognition. **Affiliated With:** National Crime Prevention Council. **Publications:** *International Crime Prevention Specialist Curriculum.* Manual. Contains a complete, revised and updated curriculum guide for basic crime prevention ideas and techniques. **Price:** \$110.00 for members, plus shipping and handling; \$160.00 for nonmembers, plus shipping and handling. **Advertising:** accepted. Alternate Formats: online ● *Practitioner*, quarterly. Newsletter. Contains current crime prevention information. **Price:** included in membership dues. **Circulation:** 2,000. **Advertising:** accepted. Alternate Formats: online ● Membership Directory, annual. **Conventions/Meetings:** annual symposium (exhibits) - October/November.

11578 ■ Milton S. Eisenhower Foundation
1875 Connecticut Ave. NW, Ste.410
Washington, DC 20009-5737
Ph: (202)234-8104
Fax: (202)234-8484
E-mail: info@eisenhowerfoundation.org
URL: http://www.eisenhowerfoundation.org
Contact: Allan Curtis PhD, Pres./CEO

Founded: 1981. **Staff:** 8. **Budget:** \$1,500,000. **Description:** Dedicated to youth investment and economic development in the inner city by reducing the school dropout rate, crime, welfare dependency, drug abuse, unemployment, and family instability. Works as a "mediating institution" to finance, technically assist, and evaluate minority nonprofit organizations. Assists more than 30 local programs based on the themes of: organizing neighborhoods; early intervention for at-risk youth; creating extended families; facilitating employment and remedial education. Also integrates community-oriented policing to assist minority nonprofit-led ventures. Operates international exchanges with Eastern Europe, France, Great Britain, Japan, and other countries. Founded as the private sector continuation of the National Violence Commission and the Kenner Riot Commission, established by former President Johnson. **Formerly:** Eisenhower Foundation for the Prevention of Violence. **Publications:** *Patriotism, Democracy, and Common Sense: Restoring America's Promise at Home and Abroad*. Book. **Price:** \$18.45 ● Reports. Alternate Formats: online ● Publishes commission updates and policy papers.

11579 ■ National Association of Crime Commissions (NACC)
c/o Mr. Bobby Stout, Treas.
Wichita Crime Commn.
125 N Market, Ste.115
Wichita, KS 67202
Ph: (316)267-1235
Fax: (316)263-0011
E-mail: bs@wichitacrimecommission.org
URL: http://www.crimecom.org/naccc
Contact: Mr. Bobby Stout, Treas.

Founded: 1952. **Members:** 25. **Description:** Crime commissions not affiliated with local, state, or federal governments. Facilitates exchanges of mutually helpful information between member commissions and informs the public on dangers of organized crime and effective methods of controlling it. Strives to arouse public interest in clean government and to encourage formation of citizens' crime commissions where needed. **Formerly:** (2005) National Association of Citizens Crime Commissions. **Publications:** *How to Organize and Operate a Citizen's Crime Commission*. **Conventions/Meetings:** annual conference.

11580 ■ National Association of Town Watch (NATW)
PO Box 303
Wynnewood, PA 19096
Ph: (610)649-7055
Free: (800)NIT-EOUT
Fax: (610)649-5456

E-mail: info@natw.org
URL: http://www.natw.org
Contact: Matt A. Peskin, Dir.

Founded: 1981. **Members:** 1,600. **Membership Dues:** basic, \$25 (annual) ● contributor, \$50 (annual). **Staff:** 7. **Description:** Local, state, and regional crime watch organizations and individuals working in cooperation with local law enforcement agencies and crime prevention officers. Promotes, assists, and encourages participation in community crime prevention programs. Sponsors the annual "National Night Out" crime prevention event which culminates on the first Tuesday each August. Since being introduced in 1984 National Night Out has grown to involve more than 33 million people in 10,000 communities nationwide. Compiles statistics. Maintains Advisory Council comprising selected law enforcement professionals and citizen leaders from throughout the U.S. people across the United States in which neighborhood residents spend time in front of their homes to highlight crime prevention programs. Compiles statistics. Maintains Advisory Council comprising selected law enforcement professionals and citizen leaders from throughout the U.S. **Awards:** National Night Out National Awards Program. **Frequency:** annual. **Type:** recognition. **Recipient:** for city or metropolitan area with the best National Night Out Program. **Affiliated With:** International Association of Chiefs of Police; National Crime Prevention Council; National Sheriffs' Association. **Publications:** *New Spirit*, quarterly. Newsletter. **Price:** included in membership dues; \$20.00 /year for nonmembers. **Circulation:** 10,000. **Advertising:** accepted.

11581 ■ National Black on Black Love Campaign (BOBL)
9535 S Cottage Grove Ave.
Chicago, IL 60628-1508
Ph: (773)978-0868
Fax: (773)978-7620
E-mail: info@bobl.org
URL: http://www.bobl.org
Contact: Mrs. Frances Wright, Exec. Dir.

Founded: 1983. **State Groups:** 6. **Description:** Individuals and businesses united to promote the motto, "Replace Black on Black crime with Black on Black love" and foster love and respect in all communities where people are, the group believes, inordinately affected by crime. Organizes No Crime Day in various communities and Adopt a Building Program for businesses. Sponsors youth organizations and seminars in schools and communities to educate the public in ways of dealing with crime. Operates charitable program. Maintains speakers' bureau; compiles statistics. **Convention/Meeting:** none. **Affiliated With:** American Health and Beauty Aids Institute.

11582 ■ National Council on Crime and Delinquency (NCCD)
1970 Broadway, Ste.500
Oakland, CA 94612
Ph: (510)208-0500
Fax: (510)208-0511
E-mail: aboldon@mw.nccd-crc.org
URL: http://www.nccd-crc.org
Contact: Anna Boldon, Contact

Founded: 1906. **Staff:** 60. **Budget:** \$6,500,000. **National Groups:** 2. **Nonmembership. Description:** Promotes effective, humane, fair and economically sound solutions to family, community, and justice problems. Conducts research, promotes reform initiatives, and seeks to work with individuals, public and private organizations, and the media to prevent and reduce crime and delinquency. **Libraries:** **Type:** open to the public. **Holdings:** 100. **Subjects:** criminal justice, injustice, public policy, prison. **Awards:** Don M. Gottfredson Scholarship. **Frequency:** annual. **Type:** scholarship ● PASS (Prevention for A Safer Society). **Frequency:** annual. **Type:** recognition. **Recipient:** for furthering public understanding of crime and prevention. **Computer Services:** Online services, SAFEMEASURES, quality assurance reporting service for child welfare administrators. **Councils:** National Advisory. **Divisions:** Development; Public Education; Research; Training. **Absorbed:** American Parole Association. **Formerly:** (1947) National Probation Association; (1960) National Probation and Parole Association. **Publications:** Booklets, quarterly ● Pamphlets ● Also publishes standard acts, forms, training materials, focus research briefs and NCCD policy statements.

11583 ■ National Crime Prevention Council (NCPC)
1000 Connecticut Ave. NW, 13th Fl.
Washington, DC 20036
Ph: (202)466-6272
Fax: (202)296-1356
E-mail: webmaster@ncpc.org
URL: http://www.ncpc.org
Contact: Alfonso E. Lenhardt, Pres.
Founded: 1982. **Staff:** 65. **Budget:** $17,000,000. **State Groups:** 112. **Local Groups:** 3,800. **National Groups:** 116. **Languages:** English, Spanish. **Description:** Seeks to educate the public to enable citizens to prevent crime and build safer, more caring communities. Sponsors public service advertising, featuring McGruff the Crime Dog and the slogan "Take a Bite Out of Crime," in cooperation with the Advertising Council and the U.S. Department of Justice, corporate foundations, and individual funders. Coordinates activities of the Crime Prevention Coalition, an alliance of 4,000 citizens groups, government agencies, law enforcement bodies, and local, state and national crime prevention and social service and youth-serving organizations. Provides training and technical assistance to crime prevention personnel and community and youth groups; operates demonstration programs focusing on youth and community action; publishes a wide range of material from brochures to books; develops crime prevention/child protection curricula, including the McGruff House and Truck programs. Manages national observance of Crime Prevention Month (October). **Libraries: Type:** not open to the public. **Holdings:** 1,000; articles, books. **Subjects:** crime prevention. **Computer Services:** database. **Additional Websites:** http://www.mcgruff.org. **Telecommunication Services:** electronic mail, media@ncpc.org. **Publications:** *Catalyst*, 10/year. Newsletter. Highlights innovations in crime prevention around the country. **Price:** free. **Circulation:** 17,000. Alternate Formats: online ● Also publishes books, monographs, posters, and pamphlets; develops and distributes brochures, resource guides, youth-oriented materials, and articles for publication, and provides audiovisual programs. **Conventions/Meetings:** biennial meeting and conference, for adults involved in crime prevention (exhibits) - October.

11584 ■ National Crime Prevention Institute (NCPI)
c/o Dr. Deborah Wilson, Acting Dir.
Justice Admin.
Univ. of Louisville
Louisville, KY 40292
Ph: (502)852-0371
Fax: (502)852-0065
E-mail: rmgibb01@gwise.louisville.edu
URL: http://www.louisville.edu/a-s/ja/ncpi
Contact: Dr. Deborah Wilson, Acting Dir.
Founded: 1971. **Members:** 15. **Staff:** 2. **Description:** Trains police officers, criminal justice planners, security personnel in the private sector, and community representatives in crime prevention for the establishment of crime prevention programs; provides information and technical assistance to these groups. **Libraries: Type:** reference. **Conventions/Meetings:** seminar, for crime prevention theory, practice and management, crime prevention through environmental design and security for private industry - 26/year.

11585 ■ Security on Campus (SOC)
133 Ivy Ln., Ste.200
King of Prussia, PA 19406-2101
Ph: (610)768-9330
Free: (888)251-7959
Fax: (610)768-0646
E-mail: soc@securityoncampus.org
URL: http://www.securityoncampus.org
Contact: Catherine Bath, Exec. Dir.
Founded: 1987. **Staff:** 3. **Description:** Seeks to prevent violent crime on college campuses, and to

increase public awareness of campus crime. Undertakes legislative efforts to strengthen campus law enforcement statutes; drafts guidelines for avoidance of crime for college students; works to insure that colleges and universities publicize the rates of crime on their campuses. Provides support and personal assistance to campus crime victims. **Awards:** Jeanne Clery Campus Safety Award. **Frequency:** periodic. **Type:** recognition. **Computer Services:** Online services, publication. **Telecommunication Services:** electronic mail, cbath@securityoncampus.org. **Publications:** *Campus Watch*, semiannual. Newsletter. **Price:** free. **Circulation:** 18,000. Alternate Formats: online.

11586 ■ TIPS Program
1101 Wilson Blvd., Ste.1700
Arlington, VA 22209
Free: (800)GET-TIPS
Fax: (703)524-1487
E-mail: info@gettips.com
URL: http://www.gettips.com
Contact: Adam Chafetz, Pres.
Founded: 1976. **Description:** Provides all schools with awareness, training, evaluation, and technical assistance in the classroom. Assists students in meeting their responsibilities to help ensure the safety and welfare of themselves and others by utilizing protective strategies to reduce their vulnerability to crime. Teaches kindergarten through eighth grade students to positively resolve conflict, resist crime, and protect themselves and their property. Develops and distributes curricula and teaching strategies. Provides personnel to train teachers, administrators, and program instructors. (TIPS is the acronym for Teaching Individual Protective Strategies and Teaching Individuals Positive Solutions). **Also Known As:** Teaching Individual Protective Strategies; Teaching Individuals Positive Solutions.

11587 ■ USCCCN National Clearinghouse on Satanic Crime in America
c/o USCCCN International
PO Box 663
South Plainfield, NJ 07080-0663
Ph: (908)226-8115
E-mail: uscccnii@aol.com
URL: http://uscccnii2000.tripod.com/id1.html
Founded: 1988. **Members:** 80,000. **Staff:** 47. **Languages:** English, French, German, Spanish. **Description:** Educates the public on satanic and occult-related crimes and criminal activities being perpetrated against humans and animals. Disseminates information and intelligence to law enforcement, criminal justice, corrections, clergy, educators, citizens and others through publications, audiobooks, videos, computer software, seminars, workshops, conventions, training programs, and radio, television, and internet programming. Sponsors speakers' bureau; operates referral service. Compiles statistics. Maintains hall of fame. **Libraries: Type:** reference. **Holdings:** 25,000; artwork, audiovisuals, books, clippings, periodicals. **Subjects:** satanism, the occult, cults, deviant movements, violence, death, secret societies, crime and criminal awareness, investigation, crime intervention and prevention, satanic and cult bondage, spiritual counseling, spiritual warfare, deliverance, exorcism, ritual and serial murder. **Awards:** NCSCIA Certificate of Appreciation. **Frequency:** periodic. **Type:** recognition ● NCSCIA Certificate of Merit. **Frequency:** periodic. **Type:** recognition ● NCSCIA Medal of Valor. **Frequency:** periodic. **Type:** medal. **Computer Services:** database ● mailing lists ● online services. **Committees:** Political Action. **Publications:** *The American Focus on Rape Series* ● *The American Focus on Satanic Crime* ● *NCSCIA Focus*, periodic. Newsletter. **Circulation:** 10,000. **Advertising:** accepted. Alternate Formats: online; diskette ● *USCCCN Focus*, periodic. Newsletter. **Circulation:** 10,000. **Advertising:** accepted. Alternate Formats: online; diskette. **Conventions/Meetings:** conference, training conferences - 65/year.

11588 ■ WeTip
PO Box 1296
Rancho Cucamonga, CA 91729-1296

Ph: (909)987-5005
Free: (800)78-CRIME
Fax: (909)987-2477
E-mail: wetiphome@cs.com
URL: http://www.wetip.com
Contact: Susan Aguilar, CEO/VP
Founded: 1972. **Members:** 19,000. **Staff:** 60. **Budget:** $1,250,000. **Regional Groups:** 180. **State Groups:** 6. **Local Groups:** 40. **Languages:** English, Spanish. **Description:** Business, industry, service clubs, private citizens, foundations, insurance companies, chambers of commerce, and veterans' and fraternal groups. Serves as a citizens' self-help program designed to eliminate drug trafficking and major crimes. Aids in murder arrests and successful apprehensions of criminals who have committed robbery, burglary, fraud, rape, drug trafficking, auto theft, or assault. Anonymous tips are conveyed to law officers and arrests are made only after verified law enforcement investigations. Rewards of up to 1000 are given upon verified factual reports from law enforcement agencies that WeTIP information was received prior to arrest and that the information was helpful in the arrest and conviction. Conducts Witness Anonymous Program, which includes corporations, insurance companies, and institutions. Program is dedicated to reducing crime and fear of crime in business communities by providing crime information directly to the concerned corporation, as well as the appropriate law enforcement agency. Maintains speakers' bureau; compiles statistics; conducts educational programs. **Libraries: Type:** reference. **Awards: Type:** recognition. **Computer Services:** database. **Telecommunication Services:** 24-hour hotline, (800)87-FRAUD ● 24-hour hotline, (800)47-ARSON ● 24-hour hotline, (800)47-DRUGS. **Publications:** *Personal Student Identification Handbook* ● *War on Arson Yearbook*, annual ● *We Tip Crimeline*, quarterly. Newspaper. **Price:** free for members. **Circulation:** 60,000. **Advertising:** accepted ● *WeTIP's National Crimefighter*, periodic ● *WeTIP's War on Arson*, periodic. **Conventions/Meetings:** annual conference (exhibits).

Criminal Justice

11589 ■ Academy of Criminal Justice Sciences (ACJS)
PO Box 960
Greenbelt, MD 20768-0960
Ph: (301)446-6300
Free: (800)757-ACJS
Fax: (301)446-2819
E-mail: execdir@acjs.org
URL: http://www.acjs.org
Contact: Mittie D. Southerland, Exec. Dir.
Founded: 1963. **Members:** 3,000. **Membership Dues:** student (with journals), $50 (annual) ● student (without journals), $25 (annual) ● regular, $75 (annual) ● institutional, $250 (annual) ● life, $1,125 ● sustaining, $150 (annual). **Staff:** 3. **Budget:** $500,000. **Regional Groups:** 6. **Description:** Individuals including teachers, administrators, researchers, students, and practitioners involved in the professional advancement of the criminal justice system through education. Purposes are: to foster excellence in education and research in the field of criminal justice in institutions of higher education; to encourage understanding and cooperation among those engaged in teaching and research in criminal justice agencies and related fields; to provide a forum for the exchange of information among persons involved with education and research in the criminal justice field; to serve as a clearinghouse for the collection and dissemination of information related to or produced by criminal justice education and/or research programs; to foster the highest ethical and personal standards in criminal justice educational programs as well as in operational agencies and allied fields. **Awards: Type:** recognition. **Recipient:** for outstanding contributions to criminal justice. **Formerly:** (1971) International Association of Police Professors. **Publications:** *ACJS Employment Bulletin*, weekly, updated every Tuesday and Thursday.

Web listing. **Price:** included in membership dues. Alternate Formats: online ● *ACJS Now*, semiannual. Newsletters ● *ACJS Today*, quarterly. Newsletter. Covers membership activities. Includes calendar of events. **Price:** included in membership dues. **Circulation:** 3,000. **Advertising:** accepted. Alternate Formats: online ● *Journal of Criminal Justice Education*, semiannual. **Price:** included in membership dues; $125.00 for subscription. ISSN: 1051-1253. **Circulation:** 4,000. **Advertising:** accepted ● *Justice Quarterly*. Journal. Contains research in criminal justice and related areas. Includes book reviews. **Price:** included in membership dues; $250.00 for subscription. ISSN: 0741-8825. **Circulation:** 4,000. **Advertising:** accepted. Alternate Formats: microform ● Membership Directory, quarterly. **Price:** included in membership dues. Alternate Formats: online. **Conventions/Meetings:** annual meeting (exhibits) - 2008 Mar. 11-15, Cincinnati, OH; 2009 Mar. 10-14, Boston, MA; 2010 Feb. 23-27, San Diego, CA.

11590 ■ Aid to Incarcerated Mothers (AIM)

434 Massachusetts Ave.
Boston, MA 02118
Ph: (617)536-0058
URL: http://www.catalogueforphilanthropy.org/ma/2003/aid_incarcerated_908.htm
Contact: Jean Fox, Exec. Dir.

Founded: 1980. **Staff:** 5. **Description:** Helps incarcerated mothers in the Boston, MA area meet their parental responsibilities by providing them with the necessary information, resources, and support to do so. Furnishes transportation for family visits. Matches each mother with a volunteer in order to provide friendship and advocacy. Helps mothers learn self-help advocacy skills and their legal rights. Offers post-release support and services to mothers making the transition back to the community. Works to make the social services, the prison system, and the public more aware and responsive to incarcerated mothers' needs. Provides information, advice, and technical support to individuals and groups nationwide. Sends speakers to various groups, organizations, and schools in the community and, occasionally, to other states. **Programs:** Community Outreach; Family Support and Advocacy; Volunteer and Transportation. **Publications:** *Staying Together*, 3/year. Newsletter.

11591 ■ Alston Wilkes Veterans Home (AWS)

c/o Palmetto State Base Camp, Inc.
3519 Medical Dr.
Columbia, SC 29203
Ph: (803)748-7489
Fax: (803)799-5358
E-mail: info@awvh.org
URL: http://www.awvh.org
Contact: Fred Lamphere, Dir.

Founded: 1962. **Members:** 6,000. **Membership Dues:** regular, $25 (annual). **Staff:** 110. **Budget:** $2,600,000. **Local Groups:** 22. **Description:** Operates in South Carolina to assist inmates, homeless veterans, individuals and those being families who are at-risk. These services are provided in order to help them become responsible and productive citizens. Services include: employment and housing assistance, information and referral, crisis intervention, pre-release and parole counseling, individual and group counseling, life skills instruction, and innovative, supportive, and therapeutic prevention projects. Seeks to stimulate public support for progressive prison programs at the state level and for programs of crime prevention. (Named for the late Rev. Eli Alston Wilkes, Jr., a Methodist minister who founded the private correctional services agency.). **Awards: Type:** recognition. **Formerly:** (1963) South Carolina Therapeutic Association; (2000) Alston Wilkes Society. **Publications:** *The Alston Wilkes Society Newsletter*, 3/year. Contains articles and announcements on services and related items of interest. **Price:** free for members ● Annual Report, annual. **Conventions/Meetings:** annual conference, includes national speaker, awards and luncheon - always Thursday preceding Thanksgiving.

11592 ■ American Association for Correctional and Forensic Psychology (AACFP)

c/o David Randall, Treas.
PO Box 7642
Wilmington, NC 28403
Ph: (805)489-0665
E-mail: randall.david@mail.dc.state.fl.us
URL: http://www.aa4cfp.org
Contact: John L. Gannon PhD, Pres./Program Chm.

Founded: 1953. **Members:** 750. **Membership Dues:** individual, $60 (annual). **Staff:** 3. **Description:** Practitioners, academicians, and researchers interested in community and institutional programs for juvenile and adult offenders and their victims. **Awards: Type:** recognition. **Recipient:** for special service ● **Type:** recognition. **Recipient:** for best student thesis and dissertation concerning corrections. **Computer Services:** Mailing lists. **Committees:** ADHOL Standards; Ethics. **Affiliated With:** American Correctional Association; National Commission on Correctional Health Care. **Formerly:** (1983) American Association of Correctional Psychologists. **Publications:** *The Correctional Psychologist*, quarterly. Newsletter. **Price:** free. **Circulation:** 550. **Advertising:** accepted ● *Criminal Justice and Behavior*, bimonthly. **Conventions/Meetings:** annual congress, held in conjunction with American Correctional Association Congress (exhibits) - always August.

11593 ■ American Correctional Association (ACA)

4380 Forbes Blvd.
Lanham, MD 20706-4322
Ph: (301)918-1800
Free: (800)222-5646
Fax: (301)918-0557
E-mail: execoffice@aca.org
URL: http://www.aca.org
Contact: James A. Gondles Jr., Exec. Dir.

Founded: 1870. **Members:** 21,061. **Membership Dues:** professional I, $35 (annual) ● organizational (outside U.S. and Canada), $390 (annual) ● professional I (outside U.S. and Canada), $50 (annual) ● professional II, $75 (annual) ● professional II (outside U.S. and Canada), $110 (annual) ● executive gold, $100 (annual) ● executive gold (outside U.S. and Canada), $150 (annual) ● organizational, $300 (annual) ● supporting patron, $350 (annual) ● supporting patron (outside U.S. and Canada), $440 (annual) ● associate, $15 (annual) ● associate (outside U.S. and Canada), $25 (annual). **Staff:** 100. **Description:** Correctional administrators, wardens, superintendents, members of prison and parole boards, probation officers, psychologists, educators, sociologists, and other individuals; institutions and associations involved in the correctional field. Promotes improved correctional standards, including selection of personnel, care, supervision, education, training, employment, treatment, and post-release adjustment of inmates. Studies causes of crime and juvenile delinquency and methods of crime control and prevention through grants and contracts. Compiles statistics. Conducts research programs and training of correctional professionals. Offers accreditation of institutions and certification for correctional executive, manager, supervisor, and officer. **Libraries: Type:** reference. **Holdings:** 6,000. **Subjects:** corrections, criminal justice. **Awards: Type:** recognition. **Computer Services:** database, directory ● mailing lists. **Committees:** Congress Program Planning; Correctional Awards; Credentials; Legislative Affairs; Resolutions and Policy Development Advisory; Standards. **Councils:** Professional Education; Research. **Affiliated With:** American Association for Correctional and Forensic Psychology; American Correctional Food Service Association; American Correctional Health Services Association; American Institute of Architects; American Jail Association; American Probation and Parole Association; Association of Paroling Authorities International; Association on Programs for Female Offenders; Association of State Correctional Administrators; Correctional Education Association; International Association of Correctional Officers; International Association of Correctional Training Personnel; International Community Corrections Association; National Association of Blacks in Criminal Justice; National Association of Probation Executives; National Correctional Industries Association; National Council on Crime and Delinquency; National Juvenile Detention Association; North American Association of Wardens and Superintendents; Prison Fellowship Ministries; Salvation Army; Texas Corrections Association; Volunteers of America. **Formerly:** National Prison Association; (1954) American Prison Association. **Publications:** *Corrections Compendium*, bimonthly. Journal. Contains research findings and trends. **Price:** $60.00/year. **Circulation:** 1,000. **Advertising:** accepted ● *Corrections Today*, 7/year. Magazine. Contains articles about the field of corrections and criminal justice. Contains advertisers and product indexes and book reviews. **Price:** included in membership dues; $35.00/year. ISSN: 0190-2563. **Circulation:** 23,000. **Advertising:** accepted. Alternate Formats: microform; online ● *Juvenile and Adult Correctional Departments, Institutions, Agencies & Probation & Parole Authorities*, annual. Directory. Contains information on U.S. state and federal, Canadian provincial and federal correctional systems. **Price:** $95.00. **Advertising:** accepted ● *National Jail and Adult Detention Directory*, biennial. Features a complete listing of names, addresses and phone numbers. **Price:** $75.00. **Advertising:** accepted ● *National Juvenile Detention Directory*, triennial. **Price:** $55.00 ● *On the Line*, 5/year. Newsletter. Includes calendar of events, classified, and resource information. **Price:** included in membership dues. **Circulation:** 23,000 ● *Probation and Parole Directory*, triennial. **Price:** $70.00. **Advertising:** accepted ● *Standards and Accreditation Newsletter* ● *Standards for Adult Correctional Institutions, 4th Edition*. Handbook. Standards manual. ● *State of Corrections*, annual. Proceedings. Includes speeches and presentations from the Congress of Correction. **Price:** $5.00 ● Videos. More than 40 titles provided. ● Books ● Manuals ● Also publishes books on corrections, psychology, addictions, standards, guidelines and correspondence courses. **Conventions/Meetings:** annual conference and workshop, with social events (exhibits) - always winter ● annual Congress of Correction - congress and workshop (exhibits) - always summer.

11594 ■ American Criminal Justice Association (Lambda Alpha Epsilon) (ACJA-LAE)

PO Box 601047
Sacramento, CA 95860-1047
Ph: (916)484-6553
Fax: (916)488-2227
E-mail: acjalae@aol.com
URL: http://www.acjalae.org
Contact: Karen K. Campbell, Exec. Sec.

Founded: 1937. **Members:** 4,000. **Membership Dues:** initial (sign-up fee), $36 ● regular, $30 (annual). **Staff:** 1. **Budget:** $150,000. **Regional Groups:** 6. **Description:** Persons employed in an area concerned with the administration of criminal justice; retirees from a career in criminal justice; persons enrolled in a program of study in this field at a college or university, and persons approved by the Executive Board of Grand Chapter involved in volunteer work directly related to the administration of criminal justice. Is dedicated to: furthering the professional standards of criminal justice; fostering assistance and understanding of the problems and objectives of agencies devoted to the administration of criminal justice. Conducts competitive activities. **Awards:** National Scholarship. **Frequency:** annual. **Type:** monetary. **Recipient:** to undergraduate or graduate student members enrolled in criminal justice field ● Student Paper Competitions. **Frequency:** annual. **Type:** monetary. **Recipient:** for entries dealing with issues and problems in the field of criminal justice. **Formerly:** (1970) Lambda Alpha Epsilon. **Publications:** *ACJA/LAE Newsletter*, semiannual. **Price:** free, for members only ● *Journal of the American Criminal Justice Association*, annual. **Price:** $22.00/year. **Conventions/Meetings:** annual competition and seminar - March or April ● annual conference, with workshops, written competitions, physical agility and firearms competitions, banquets and job fair ● seminar ● workshop.

11595 ■ American Jail Association (AJA)

1135 Professional Ct.
Hagerstown, MD 21740-5853
Ph: (301)790-3930

Fax: (301)790-2941
E-mail: gwyns@aja.org
URL: http://www.aja.org
Contact: Gwyn Smith-Ingley, Exec. Dir.
Founded: 1981. **Members:** 4,500. **Membership Dues:** student, $15 (annual) ● affiliate, $100 (annual) ● individual in U.S., $48 (annual) ● agency, $300 (annual) ● corporate, $350 (annual) ● individual in Canada, $54 (annual) ● individual outside U.S. and Canada, $66 (annual). **Staff:** 14. **Budget:** $1,500,000. **State Groups:** 6. **National Groups:** 22. **Description:** Sheriffs, jail administrators, and officers. Works to raise the standards of local adult detention facilities; exchange information on jail management techniques; assure professionalization of jail personnel. Conducts specialized training and education. Administers jail manager and jail officer certification programs. **Libraries: Type:** reference. **Awards:** Civilian Employee of the Year. **Frequency:** annual. **Type:** recognition ● Correctional Administrator of the Year. **Frequency:** annual. **Type:** recognition ● Correctional Officer of the Year. **Frequency:** annual. **Type:** recognition ● Correctional Supervisor of the Year. **Frequency:** annual. **Type:** recognition ● Volunteer of the Year. **Frequency:** annual. **Type:** recognition. **Computer Services:** Mailing lists. **Committees:** ACA Delegate Assembly; Affiliate Member; Awards; Bylaws; Conference Planning; Corrections Workplace; Indian Country Jails; Membership; National Jail Manager's Academy; Nominating; Resolutions; Training. **Affiliated With:** American Correctional Association; American Correctional Food Service Association; American Correctional Health Services Association; American Institute of Architects; American Society for Testing and Materials; Correctional Education Association; International Association of Correctional Officers. **Formed by Merger of:** (1981) National Jail Association; (1981) National Jail Managers Association. **Publications:** *American Jails*, bimonthly. Magazine. Includes advertisers' index, book reviews, calendar of events, state jail association news, foreign coverage, and military jail section. **Price:** included in membership dues. **Circulation:** 8,000. **Advertising:** accepted ● *Exploring Jail Operations*. Book. **Price:** $49.95 ● *Jail and Prison Legal Issues: An Administrator's Guide*, annual. Manual. **Price:** $295.00 for members; $345.00 for nonmembers ● *Jail Managers Bulletin*, monthly. **Price:** $4.00 for members; $6.00 for nonmembers ● *Jail Operations Bulletin*. Videos. **Price:** $895.00/volume of 12 videos; $99.95 individual ● *Product Resource Directory*, annual. **Conventions/Meetings:** annual Training Conference and Jail Expo (exhibits) - 2008 May 4-8, Sacramento, CA; 2009 Apr. 26-30, Louisville, KY; 2010 May 23-27, Portland, OR.

11596 ■ Association on Programs for Female Offenders (APFO)
c/o Judy C. Anderson, Treas.
3119 Heyward St.
Columbia, SC 29250-2632
E-mail: joannmort@aol.com
URL: http://www.apfonews.org
Contact: Dr. Joann Morton, Pres.
Founded: 1975. **Members:** 150. **Membership Dues:** regular, $25 (annual) ● supporting, $50 (annual). **Staff:** 4. **Budget:** $2,000. **Description:** Professionals in corrections or related fields and others interested in issues concerning adult and juvenile female offenders. Develops and sponsors workshops on the topic of female offenders; facilitates sharing of information about programs and research on female offenders. Has sponsored conference workshops including Providing Services for Women in Jail: Whose Responsibility?; Mothers in Prison; and Education, Training, Employment: Resources for Women Inmates. Conducts educational and research programs and charitable activities. Maintains speakers' bureau; compiles statistics; acts as a clearinghouse, fielding and responding to questions from legislators, policymakers, media, academia, authors, and colleagues on a national basis. **Formerly:** (1975) Women's Correctional Association. **Publications:** Newsletter, quarterly. **Circulation:** 150. **Advertising:** accepted. Alternate Formats: online. **Conventions/Meetings:** biennial National Workshop on Adult and Juvenile Female Offenders - meeting, held in conjunction with the American Correctional Association.

11597 ■ Association of State Correctional Administrators (ASCA)
213 Court St., Ste.606
Middletown, CT 06457
Ph: (860)704-6410
Fax: (860)704-6420
E-mail: tech@asca.net
URL: http://www.asca.net
Contact: Camille G. Camp, Co-Exec. Dir.
Founded: 1970. **Members:** 58. **Membership Dues:** associate, $25 (annual). **Staff:** 12. **Description:** Administrators of state and federal correctional systems. Promotes the exchange of ideas among directors of correctional systems; encourages the improvement of correctional standards; seeks support for advances in correctional operations; stimulates public interest toward correctional administration; advocates research into correctional management. Furnishes information to members; conducts training sessions. **Awards:** Michael Francke Award. **Frequency:** annual. **Type:** recognition. **Recipient:** to outstanding members. **Formerly:** Correctional Administrators Association of America. **Publications:** *Alternatives for Financing Prison Facilities*. Report. Alternate Formats: online ● *ASCA Newsletter*, monthly ● *Correctional Directors Best Practices Perspective on Reentry*. Monograph. Alternate Formats: online ● *Survey of High-Risk Inmate Behaviors in the Oregon Prison System*. Alternate Formats: online ● Manuals. Alternate Formats: online. **Conventions/Meetings:** semiannual meeting - always second week in January and third week in August ● seminar.

11598 ■ Center for Studies in Criminal Justice (CSCJ)
c/o The University of Chicago Law School
1111 E 60th St.
Chicago, IL 60637
Ph: (773)702-9494
E-mail: tlmeares@midway.uchicago.edu
URL: http://www.law.uchicago.edu/academics/cj.html
Contact: Prof. Tracey L. Meares, Dir.
Founded: 1965. **Staff:** 5. **Description:** Researches the operation of deterrent processes in criminal law, the relationship of weapons to homicide rates and gun-control measures, administration of justice in juvenile and family courts, prisons, and pre-trial settlement conferences. **Convention/Meeting:** none. **Publications:** *Crime and Justice: An Annual Review of Research* ● *Studies in Crime and Justice* ● Book. Criminal justice textbook.

11599 ■ Citizens United for Rehabilitation of Errants (CURE)
c/o National Cure
PO Box 2310
Natl. Capitol Sta.
Washington, DC 20013-2310
Ph: (202)789-2126
Fax: (202)318-9164
E-mail: cure@curenational.org
URL: http://www.curenational.org
Contact: Charles Sullivan, Co-Founder
Founded: 1972. **Members:** 7,000. **Membership Dues:** prisoner, $5 (annual) ● individual, $10 (annual) ● family, $20 (annual) ● sustaining, $50 (annual) ● life, $100 ● institutional, $75 (annual) ● trustee, $500 (annual). **Staff:** 2. **State Groups:** 30. **Description:** Prisoners and former prisoners, their families, and others concerned with prison reform. Aims to reduce crime through reform of the criminal justice system. **Computer Services:** Mailing lists, of members. **Publications:** Newsletter, quarterly. **Conventions/Meetings:** biennial meeting - always Washington, DC.

11600 ■ Committee to End The Marion Lockdown (CEML)
PO Box 578172
Chicago, IL 60657-8172
Ph: (312)235-0070

E-mail: ceml@aol.com
URL: http://www-unix.oit.umass.edu/~kastor/ceml.html
Contact: Nancy Kurshan, Contact
Founded: 1985. **Description:** Individuals interested in prison reform. Seeks to abolish brutality in the first control unit prison in the United States, located in Marion County, Illinois. Aims to prevent and abolish brutality and racism in control unit prisons nationwide. Maintains speakers' bureau. Conducts educational programs. **Libraries: Type:** reference. **Holdings:** video recordings.

11601 ■ Correctional Education Association (CEA)
8182 Lake Brown Rd., Ste.202
Elkridge, MD 21075
Ph: (443)459-3080 (443)459-3081
Free: (800)783-1232
Fax: (443)459-3088
E-mail: ceaoffice@aol.com
URL: http://www.ceanational.org
Contact: Dr. Stephen J. Steurer, Exec. Dir.
Founded: 1945. **Members:** 2,600. **Membership Dues:** individual, $55 (annual) ● institution/library, $95 (annual) ● corporate, $285 (annual) ● life, $1,000 ● subscription, $55 (annual) ● student/volunteer/retiree, $35 (annual) ● clerical/instructional/support staff, $25 (annual). **Staff:** 4. **Budget:** $250,000. **Regional Groups:** 9. **State Groups:** 20. **Description:** Adult and juvenile educational administrators, academic and vocational educators, correctional officers, child care counselors, clinicians, librarians, and other interested individuals at local, county, state, and federal facilities. Seeks to: increase the effectiveness, expertise, and skills of educators and administrators who provide services to students in correctional settings; increase the quality of educational programs and services; offer timely and practical information to staff members; represent a collective interest of correctional education before government, the media, and the public. Encourages an active and supportive network of professionals who are leaders in the field of correctional education. Maintains speakers' bureau. Compiles statistics. **Libraries: Type:** reference. **Holdings:** archival material. **Awards:** Al Maresh Memorial Award. **Frequency:** annual. **Type:** recognition. **Recipient:** to a teacher of an exemplary computer-assisted program in a correctional ● Austin MacCormick Award. **Frequency:** annual. **Type:** recognition. **Recipient:** for best practices in correctional education ● Correctional Education Association Scholarship. **Frequency:** annual. **Type:** scholarship. **Recipient:** for voting members ● Lifetime Achievement Award. **Frequency:** annual. **Type:** recognition. **Recipient:** to someone who made major contributions to the correctional education field ● Membership Award. **Frequency:** annual. **Type:** recognition. **Recipient:** for recruitment of members ● Teacher of the Year. **Frequency:** annual. **Type:** recognition. **Computer Services:** Mailing lists. **Telecommunication Services:** electronic mail, steurerl@aol.com. **Subgroups:** Community Corrections; Counselors; Evaluation and Training; Jail Network; Juvenile Education; Legislative Network; Librarians; Literacy; Post-Secondary Network; Research; Special Education Network; Vocational Education. **Publications:** *CEA News and Notes*, quarterly, January, April, July, October. Newsletter. **Price:** included in membership dues. **Circulation:** 3,500. **Advertising:** accepted. Also Cited As: *CEA Newsletter* ● *Directory of Correctional Educators*, annual ● *Journal of Correctional Education*, quarterly, March, June, September, December ● *Learning Behind Bars: Selected Educational Programs in Prisons, Jails and Juvenile Facilities* ● *Standards for Adult and Juvenile Correctional Educational Programs*. **Conventions/Meetings:** annual international conference (exhibits) - usually July ● annual Leadership Forum - meeting - always March.

11602 ■ Death Row Support Project (DRSP)
PO Box 600
Liberty Mills, IN 46946

Ph: (260)982-7480
URL: http://www.brethren.org/genbd/witness/drsp.
htm
Contact: Rachel Gross, Contact
Founded: 1978. **Staff:** 1. **Budget:** $800. **State Groups:** 1. **Description:** A project of Church of the Brethren that links concerned individuals with prisoners who have been sentenced to death. Believes correspondence is a way of serving Jesus and brightening the lives of prison inmates, as well as a way of educating the public against the death penalty in the United States.

11603 ■ Families Against Mandatory Minimums Foundation (FAMM)
1612 K St. NW, Ste.700
Washington, DC 20006
Ph: (202)822-6700
Fax: (202)822-6704
E-mail: famm@famm.org
URL: http://www.famm.org
Contact: Julie Stewart, Pres./Founder
Founded: 1991. **Members:** 32,000. **Staff:** 5. **Budget:** $350,000. **Regional Groups:** 30. **State Groups:** 2. **Local Groups:** 1. **Description:** Citizens interested in the reform of statutory mandatory minimum sentences. Opposes mandatory sentencing laws passed by Congress in 1986 as well as state mandatory minimum sentences. Offers information and analysis of mandatory minimum sentences to federal and state legislators, the public, and the media. Encourages legislators to replace such mandatory sentencing with greater use of judicial discretion. **Telecommunication Services:** electronic mail, media@famm.org. **Publications:** *FAMMGram*, quarterly. Newsletter. **Price:** free. **Circulation:** 32,000. Alternate Formats: online ● magnetic tape. **Conventions/Meetings:** annual Sentencing Workshop - assembly and workshop.

11604 ■ Family Justice
625 Broadway, 8th Fl.
New York, NY 10012
Ph: (212)475-1500
Fax: (212)475-2322
E-mail: rfriedman@familyjustice.org
URL: http://www.familyjustice.org
Contact: Carol Shapiro, Founder/Pres./Exec. Dir.
Founded: 2001. **Description:** Provides tools, training, and other resources so that family-based approaches are integrated into criminal justice practice. Seeks to improve community justice supervision and outcomes.

11605 ■ Fathers Behind Bars
525 Superior St.
Niles, MI 49120-3338
Ph: (269)684-5715
E-mail: fathersbehindbars2@msn.com
Contact: Arthur L. Hamilton Jr., Pres.
Founded: 1993. **Members:** 125. **Membership Dues:** imprisoned father, $10 (annual) ● father not in prison, $15 (annual). **Staff:** 15. **State Groups:** 3. **Local Groups:** 1. **National Groups:** 6. **Description:** Assists fathers in prison in reestablishing and maintaining relationships with children, spouses, family, and friends. Works to create a prison environment conducive to family visits and to develop a legal aid referral network in prisons throughout the country. **Publications:** none. **Convention/Meeting:** none. **Libraries:** **Type:** open to the public. **Subjects:** parenting, child abuse, parental responsibility.

11606 ■ Fortune Society (FS)
53 W 23rd St., 8th Fl.
New York, NY 10010
Ph: (212)691-7554
Fax: (212)255-4948
E-mail: kkidder@fortunesociety.org
URL: http://www.fortunesociety.org
Contact: Brian Robinson, Contact
Founded: 1967. **Description:** Ex-offenders and others interested in penal reform. Addresses the needs of ex-offenders and high-risk youth. Promotes greater public awareness of the prison system and of the problems confronting inmates before, after, and during incarceration. Works on a personal basis with men and women recently released from prison; helps ex-offenders find jobs. Offers educational services including literacy training and G.E.D. preparation. Sends teams of ex-offenders to talk to school, church, and civic groups and on radio and television to relate first-hand experiences of prison life and to create a greater understanding of the causes of crime in the United States. Conducts Alternatives to Incarceration programs; offers AIDS and general counseling services. Acts as referral agency for half-way houses and drug and alcohol addiction programs. **Telecommunication Services:** electronic mail, brobinson@fortunesociety.org. **Publications:** *Fortune News*, quarterly. Newsletter. **Price:** free to prison inmates and society sponsors. Alternate Formats: online ● Report, biennial. Alternate Formats: online.

11607 ■ Friends Outside (FO)
PO Box 4085
Stockton, CA 95204
Ph: (209)938-0727
Fax: (209)938-0734
URL: http://www.friendsoutside.org
Founded: 1955. **Staff:** 85. **Budget:** $1,800,000. **Local Groups:** 16. **Languages:** English, Spanish. **Description:** Staff and volunteers seeking to stop the perpetuation of poverty and crime. Assists prison inmates in assuming responsibility for their own successful reintegration into society. Conducts educational, recreational, and social programs; sponsors support groups for adult and juvenile offenders and families of inmates; makes available emergency services. Offers work-furlough and reentry programs for parolees; operates victim and juvenile offenders programs, and mediation and conflict resolution workshops. **Publications:** Newsletter, monthly. **Conventions/Meetings:** annual conference - always September.

11608 ■ Good News Jail and Prison Ministry (GNJPM)
PO Box 9760
Richmond, VA 23228-0760
Ph: (804)553-4090
Free: (800)220-2202
E-mail: info@goodnewsjail.org
URL: http://www.goodnewsjail.org
Contact: Harry L. Greene, Pres./CEO
Founded: 1961. **Description:** Provides ministerial counseling and services to prisoners, ex-offenders, and their families. Assigns chaplains to prisons and institutions in the U.S. and abroad. Conducts a Bible correspondence program. **Councils:** President's. **Also Known As:** Good News Jail and Prison Ministry. **Formerly:** (1999) Good News Mission. **Publications:** *Full Pardon*, quarterly. Newsletter. **Price:** free. Alternate Formats: online ● Brochures.

11609 ■ International Association of Correctional Officers (IACO)
Address Unknown since 2007
Founded: 1977. **Members:** 12,000. **Membership Dues:** individual, $35 (annual) ● supporting, $20 (annual) ● student, $10 (annual). **Staff:** 3. **Budget:** $50,000. **State Groups:** 2. **Description:** Correctional facility officers on the national, state, and local levels; sheriffs; other employees in the corrections field or related fields interested in the study and practice of good corrections principles. Promotes the development of innovative services, evaluation, and inter-professional cooperation in order to increase the effectiveness of correctional facilities. Seeks to advance high standards of training and the professionalization of corrections personnel, thereby securing public confidence and support. Compiles statistics. **Libraries:** **Type:** reference. **Holdings:** books, periodicals. **Subjects:** correctional facilities and personnel, recent court rulings, legislation. **Awards:** Corrections Officer of the Year Award. **Frequency:** annual. **Type:** recognition ● Supervisor of the Year. **Frequency:** annual. **Type:** recognition. **Committees:** Professional Practice; Public Information; Research and Development. **Departments:** Inter-Professional; Program Evaluation; Research. **Formerly:** (1979) American Association of Correctional Facility Officers; (1985) American Association of Correctional Officers. **Publications:** *Keepers Voice Magazine*, quarterly ● Pamphlets. **Conventions/Meetings:** annual conference.

11610 ■ International Association of Correctional Training Personnel
PO Box 6604
Jefferson City, MO 65102
Ph: (573)896-4560
Fax: (573)896-4560
E-mail: iactp@earthlink.net
URL: http://www.iactp.org
Contact: Ms. Kathy Mickle-Askin, Pres.
Founded: 1974. **Members:** 350. **Membership Dues:** individual, $50 (annual) ● library, $65 (annual) ● student, $35 (annual). **Staff:** 1. **Regional Groups:** 9. **Multinational. Description:** Local, state, and federal correctional facilities; community correctional centers and probation and parole agencies; juvenile services, private training, and higher education institutions. Purposes are to: promote the continuous improvement of training programs and staff development standards; encourage and provide a source of communication on developments in correctional staff training; promote professionalism in correctional training; represent the interests of correctional trainers. Conducts workshops, seminars, and research projects in correctional training. **Awards:** Innovative Approaches Award. **Frequency:** annual. **Type:** recognition. **Recipient:** for high quality and state of the art advances in correctional training ● President's Award. **Frequency:** annual. **Type:** recognition. **Recipient:** to a member who has done outstanding service to the association that is above and beyond what would normally be expected ● Specialized Topic Award. **Frequency:** annual. **Type:** recognition. **Recipient:** for high quality training in a particular correctional course, program or subject ● Training System Award. **Frequency:** annual. **Type:** recognition. **Recipient:** for high quality training throughout an entire system or training department. **Committees:** Awards; Editorial Review; Membership; Standards; Training Advocacy. **Affiliated With:** American Correctional Association; American Jail Association. **Formerly:** (1992) American Association Correctional Training Personnel. **Publications:** *Journal of Correctional Training*, quarterly. **Advertising:** accepted. **Conventions/Meetings:** annual conference (exhibits).

11611 ■ International Community Corrections Association (ICCA)
1730 Rhode Island Ave. NW, Ste.403
Washington, DC 20006
Ph: (202)828-5605
Fax: (202)828-5609
E-mail: icca@iccaweb.org
URL: http://www.iccaweb.org
Contact: Jane O'Shaughnessy, Pres.
Founded: 1964. **Members:** 1,300. **Membership Dues:** agency, $150 (annual) ● individual, $50 (annual). **Staff:** 3. **Budget:** $450,000. **Regional Groups:** 12. **State Groups:** 15. **Description:** Agencies and individuals from North America and other countries working in community based correctional programs. Purposes are to assist members in functioning more effectively through the exchange of information regarding management and treatment; promote the development of community-based correctional programs; develop and implement a program of public information and education in the field of community based treatment; assist social institutions within communities to accept the responsibility for coping with crime, substance abuse, mental health, delinquency, and related social problems. Sponsors programs in the areas of corrections. Conducts research programs and Margaret Mead Lecture Series. **Awards:** Margaret Mead Award. **Frequency:** annual. **Type:** recognition. **Recipient:** for contributions to field of community corrections. **Computer Services:** Mailing lists. **Affiliated With:** American Correctional Association; American Probation and Parole Association; United Nations. **Formerly:** International Halfway House Association; (1995) International Association of Residential and Community Alternative. **Publications:** Magazines. **Conventions/Meetings:** annual confer-

ence, research conference and community corrections act conference (exhibits).

11612 ■ International Prison Ministry (IPM)
PO Box 2868
Costa Mesa, CA 92628-2868
Free: (800)327-1212
Fax: (714)972-0557
E-mail: info@chaplainray.com
URL: http://www.chaplainray.com
Contact: Robert Hoekstra, Dir.
Founded: 1972. **Multinational. Description:** Represents individuals concerned about the spiritual well-being of prisoners in the U.S. Seeks to rehabilitate criminals through the processes of Christian conversion and discipleship. Conducts prison crusades and seminars. **Publications:** *Prison Evangelism Newsletter*, quarterly. Alternate Formats: online ● Also publishes Bibles, Bible dictionaries, and inspirational books and pamphlets; makes available videotapes and audiotapes.

11613 ■ John Howard Association (JHA)
300 W Adams St., Ste.423
Chicago, IL 60606
Ph: (312)782-1901
Fax: (312)782-1902
E-mail: info@john-howard.org
URL: http://www.john-howard.org
Contact: Malcolm C. Young, Exec. Dir.
Founded: 1901. **Members:** 352. **Staff:** 4. **Budget:** $350,000. **Description:** Works for prison reform and prevention and control of crime and delinquency. Provides professional consultation and survey services in the crime and delinquency field; encourages and develops volunteer programs; monitors criminal justice programs and services. Staffed by professionals in the correctional field reinforced by active citizen leaders. Conducts research projects and publishes findings; sponsors public information program to promote community understanding. Named after John Howard (1726-90), an 18th century English prison reformer. **Libraries: Type:** open to the public. **Subjects:** corrections. **Publications:** *Update*. Newsletter. **Conventions/Meetings:** annual meeting - always May or June.

11614 ■ Justice Fellowship (JF)
44180 Riverside Pkwy.
Lansdowne, VA 20176
Ph: (703)904-7312
Free: (877)478-0100
Fax: (703)904-7307
E-mail: mail@justicefellowship.org
URL: http://www.justicefellowship.org
Contact: Pat Nolan, Pres.
Founded: 1983. **Staff:** 25. **Budget:** $1,750,000. **Description:** Christians who support reform of the criminal justice system based on Christian biblical teachings of reconciliation, restitution, and restoration. Equips concerned citizens to promote reforms that hold offenders responsible for their acts, protect the public, and help restore victims' losses. Citizen task forces seek reforms that would allow for rights for victims in criminal cases, restitution and community service sentences for nonviolent offenders, and healthy, viable work programs in prisons. **Libraries: Type:** reference; not open to the public. **Holdings:** periodicals. **Subjects:** criminal justice, corrections. **Awards:** Volunteer of the Year. **Frequency:** annual. **Type:** recognition. **Telecommunication Services:** additional toll-free number, customer care center, (877)322-5527. **Affiliated With:** Prison Fellowship Ministries. **Publications:** *Justice eReport*. Alternate Formats: online. **Conventions/Meetings:** annual National Forum on Restorative Justice - conference and lecture.

11615 ■ Justice Research and Statistics Association (JRSA)
777 N Capitol St. NE, Ste.801
Washington, DC 20002
Ph: (202)842-9330
Fax: (202)842-9329

E-mail: cjinfo@jrsa.org
URL: http://www.jrsa.org
Contact: Joan C. Weiss, Exec. Dir.
Founded: 1972. **Members:** 250. **Membership Dues:** individual, $75 (annual) ● student, $40 (annual) ● institution, $300 (annual). **Staff:** 20. **Budget:** $1,500,000. **Description:** Heads of state statistical units in criminal justice are voting members; others are associate members. Seeks to further the collection, analysis, dissemination, and use of data concerning crime and criminal justice at the federal and state levels; assist in the identification and transfer of techniques for analyzing criminal justice data. Acts as clearinghouse and forum for discussion among criminal justice professionals; serves as liaison between the federal Bureau of Justice Statistics and the states. Coordinates the State Evaluation Development (SED) Program funded by the Bureau of Justice Assistance. **Libraries: Type:** reference. **Computer Services:** database, of criminal justice activities and research being conducted in the United States ● online services, index of data sources. **Programs:** JRSA Clearinghouse; Training and Technical Assistance. **Formerly:** (1991) Criminal Justice Statistics Association. **Publications:** *Directory of Justice Issues in the States*, annual. Offers insights into statistical research and analysis being conducted by the states; also includes summaries of state activities. Alternate Formats: online ● *The Forum*, quarterly. Newsletter. Focuses on criminal justice research at the state and national level. Features book reviews, calendar of events, and computer news. **Price:** included in membership dues. Alternate Formats: online ● *Justice Research & Policy*, semiannual. Journal. Contains policy-oriented research articles. **Price:** $55.00/year for individuals; $95.00/year for institutions; $45.00/special issue; $35.00/issue. ISSN: 1525-1071. **Circulation:** 350. **Advertising:** accepted. Alternate Formats: online ● Reports. Alternate Formats: online ● Surveys. Alternate Formats: online. **Conventions/Meetings:** annual conference, features panel and workshop sessions on timely criminal justice topics (exhibits).

11616 ■ National Association of Blacks in Criminal Justice (NABCJ)
1801 Fayetteville St.
Durham, NC 27707
Ph: (919)683-1801
Free: (866)846-2225
Fax: (919)683-1903
E-mail: office@nabcj.org
URL: http://www.nabcj.org
Contact: Fay Lassiter, Pres.
Founded: 1974. **Members:** 4,800. **Membership Dues:** active, $50 (annual) ● full-time student, $15 (annual) ● agency, $300 (annual). **Staff:** 1. **Budget:** $250,000. **State Groups:** 59. **Description:** Criminal justice professionals concerned with the impact of criminal justice policies and practices on the minority community. Advocates with local, state, and federal criminal justice agencies for the improvement of minority recruitment practices and for the advancement of minority career mobility within those agencies. Sponsors regional conferences, career development seminars, and annual training institutes; maintains speakers' bureau. Provides financial and in-kind services to community groups. Compiles statistics on minority involvement in the criminal justice field. **Awards: Type:** recognition. **Affiliated With:** American Correctional Association; National Urban League. **Publications:** *The Commitment*, quarterly. Newsletter ● *NABCJ Minority Criminal Justice Personnel Directory*, annual ● *Proceedings of Annual Conference*, annual ● Annual Report ● Newsletter, quarterly. **Conventions/Meetings:** annual conference (exhibits).

11617 ■ National Center on Institutions and Alternatives (NCIA)
7222 Ambassador Rd.
Baltimore, MD 21244
Ph: (410)265-1490
Fax: (410)597-9656

E-mail: hhoelter@ncianet.org
URL: http://www.ncianet.org
Contact: Herbert J. Hoelter, Chm./CEO
Founded: 1977. **Staff:** 500. **Budget:** $10,000,000. **Regional Groups:** 2. **Nonmembership. Description:** Serves as clearinghouse primarily on decarceration and aids in developing and promoting strategies and actions to reduce the number of people involuntarily institutionalized. Goals include: finding alternatives to mental hospitals; developing, promoting, and supervising enduring alternatives to prison programs; eliminating unnecessary lockup in massive, impersonal prisons, and juvenile training schools. Sponsors the Client Specific Planning Program to provide a systematized development of comprehensive, highly structured, alternative-to-prison, sentencing plans for presentation to the courts. Operates the Augustus Institute, a clinical mental health center which provides psycho-social evaluations and psychotherapy for juveniles and adults involved in the criminal justice system, and for their families; emphasis on violent behavior and sex offenders. Conducts mitigative studies in capital cases. Has completed statistics on the pronounced regional differences in the number of incarcerated youth and a national study of jail suicides. Maintains speakers' bureau. Conducts research programs. **Computer Services:** Mailing lists, Advocate Alert, distributes information on criminal justice issues. **Publications:** *Darkness Closes In - National Study of Jail Suicides*. Monograph ● *The Real War on Crime*. Paper. Analyzes crime and punishment in U.S. **Price:** $15.00 ● *Scared Straight: Second Look*. Report ● *Specialized Foster Care for Hard-to-Place Juveniles*. Manual. **Conventions/Meetings:** annual conference.

11618 ■ National Center for Juvenile Justice (NCJJ)
3700 S Water St., Ste.200
Pittsburgh, PA 15203
Ph: (412)227-6950
Fax: (412)227-6955
E-mail: ncjj@ncjj.org
URL: http://www.ncjj.org
Contact: Hunter Hurst III, Dir.
Founded: 1973. **Staff:** 27. **Budget:** $4,500,000. **Description:** Research division of the National Council of Juvenile and Family Court Judges. Encourages progressive administration of juvenile justice and all its components through research and dissemination of pertinent data. Assumes the responsibility for collecting juvenile court statistics nationally since 1975, and has undertaken to improve both the quality and quantity of the statistics. Provides technical assistance to juvenile courts; conducts comparative analyses of juvenile and family codes and program evaluations. Assesses juvenile justice services; designs programs and facilities; provides consulting on automated information and reporting systems. Operates applied technical assistance resource center. **Computer Services:** database, Bibliographic Kindex. **Publications:** *Children, Families and the Courts - Ohio Bulletin*, quarterly. Contains activities jointly administered by the Supreme Court of Ohio and the Ohio Department of Job and Family Services. Alternate Formats: online ● *Juvenile and Family Law Digest*, monthly. Journal. Summaries case law reported in U.S. organized by topic. **Price:** $160.00/year ● *Juvenile Court Statistics*, annual. Annual Report. Presents national estimates and detailed descriptions of delinquency and status offense cases processed by juvenile courts. **Price:** free through juvenile justice clearinghouse ● *Juvenile Offenders and Victims: A National Report*. Pulls together the most requested on juveniles and the juvenile system. **Price:** free through the juvenile justice clearinghouse ● *KINDEX: An Index to Periodical Literature Concerning Children*, annual. Bibliography. Lists legal periodicals dealing with juvenile justice, arranged by author and topic. **Price:** $83.00/issue. ISSN: 0733-8937 ● *NCJJ in Focus*, periodic. Papers. Contains information regarding approaches to responding to juvenile crime. Alternate Formats: online ● Research Reports ● Also publishes statute analyses and studies.

11619 ■ National Correctional Industries Association (NCIA)
1202 N Charles St.
Baltimore, MD 21201

Ph: (410)230-3972
Fax: (410)230-3981
E-mail: info@nationalcia.org
URL: http://www.nationalcia.org
Contact: Gwyn Smith Ingley, Exec. Dir./Corporate Sec.

Founded: 1941. **Members:** 2,000. **Membership Dues:** agency (based on the number of civilian employees), $500-$2,500 ● corporate, $425 (annual) ● corporate plus, $975 (annual) ● practitioner, $45 (annual) ● individual associate, $45 (annual) ● affiliate, $200 (annual) ● student, $25 (annual) ● corporate associate, $45 (annual). **Description:** Professional correctional industry managers, supervisors, superintendents, and others employed in the industry. Seeks to improve the effectiveness of industrial programs as they relate to the correctional process by providing a forum for the development and exchange of ideas and by providing professional reaction and guidance concerning projected ideas and programs related to correctional industry trends. Compiles statistics. **Awards:** Marketing and Sales Person of the Year Award. **Frequency:** annual. **Type:** recognition. **Recipient:** for outstanding contributors to the field ● McLaughlin Award. **Frequency:** annual. **Type:** recognition. **Recipient:** for outstanding contributors to the field ● Regional Staff Award and NCIA Honor Roll. **Frequency:** annual. **Type:** recognition. **Recipient:** for outstanding contributors to the field ● Rodli Award. **Frequency:** annual. **Type:** recognition. **Recipient:** for outstanding contributors to the field. **Computer Services:** Information services, Cyberwarehouse: online listing service for CI products. **Committees:** Political Liaison; Public Relations. **Publications:** *Industries Directory*, annual. Contains profiles for all federal, state and Canadian industries. **Price:** $65.00 for members; $25.00 cd-rom copy. **Advertising:** accepted. Alternate Formats: CD-ROM ● *NCIA News*, quarterly. Newsletter. Includes member news. **Price:** available to members only. **Circulation:** 1,500. **Advertising:** accepted. Alternate Formats: online. Also Cited As: *CIA Newsletter* ● Newsletter. Alternate Formats: online. **Conventions/Meetings:** annual Enterprise National Training Conference (exhibits).

11620 ■ National Criminal Justice Association (NCJA)
720 7th St. NW, 3rd Fl.
Washington, DC 20001
Ph: (202)628-8550
Fax: (202)628-0080
E-mail: info@ncja.org
URL: http://www.ncja.org
Contact: Cabell C. Cropper, Exec. Dir.

Founded: 1971. **Members:** 700. **Membership Dues:** individual, electronic, $85 (annual) ● individual, hardcopy, $110 (annual) ● student, electronic, $25 (annual) ● student, hardcopy, $50 (annual) ● tribal government, $225 (annual) ● corporate, $2,500 (annual) ● corporate-member of IJIS institute, $2,000 (annual) ● national association, $1,000 (annual) ● state/local association, $225 (annual) ● state/local association (not a member of NCJA), $300 (annual). **Staff:** 9. **Budget:** $1,700,000. **Regional Groups:** 4. **State Groups:** 49. **Languages:** English, Spanish. **Description:** State, tribal and local criminal justice planners, police chiefs, judges, prosecutors, defenders, corrections officials, educators, researchers, and elected officials. Promotes innovation in the criminal justice system through the focused coordination of law enforcement, the courts, corrections, and juvenile justice. Seeks to: focus attention on national issues and developments related to the control of crime; determine and effectively express the states' and tribes' collective views on pending legislative and administrative action encompassing criminal and juvenile justice; improve the states' and tribes' administration of their criminal and juvenile justice responsibilities through the development and dissemination of information to and among justice administrators and policy makers. Conducts technical assistance and training programs. **Projects:** Department of Justice Information Technology Initiative; Electronic Grants Management Systems Initiative; Office for Domestic Preparedness Technical As-

sistance; Protecting Seniors from Fraud; Statewide Communities Initiative. **Formerly:** (1980) National Conference of State Criminal Justice Planning Administrators. **Publications:** *Beltway Short Takes*, bimonthly. Newsletter. Provides information about the availability of funding for justice initiatives by federal agencies, private foundations and organizations. **Price:** free, for members only. Alternate Formats: online ● *Justice Bulletin*, monthly. Covers research projects and activities affecting the criminal justice system at federal and state levels and legislative and regulatory actions. **Price:** included in membership dues. **Circulation:** 1,200. Alternate Formats: online ● Newsletter, monthly. Covers legislative and regulatory actions affecting the criminal justice system at federal and state levels. **Price:** included in membership dues. **Circulation:** 1,400. **Conventions/Meetings:** annual National Forum - meeting (exhibits) - summer.

11621 ■ National Juvenile Detention Association (NJDA)
c/o Eastern Kentucky University
301 Perkins Bldg.
521 Lancaster Ave.
Richmond, KY 40475-3102
Ph: (859)622-6259
Fax: (859)622-2333
E-mail: njdaeku@aol.com
URL: http://www.njda.com
Contact: Earl L. Dunlap, Exec. Dir.

Founded: 1971. **Members:** 750. **Membership Dues:** standard, $39 (annual) ● executive, $69 (annual) ● facility, $200 (annual) ● nonprofit, $199 (annual) ● corporate, $395 (annual). **Staff:** 10. **Budget:** $350,000. **Regional Groups:** 10. **State Groups:** 13. **Description:** Juvenile detention home personnel. Coordinates lines of communication among juvenile detention facilities; conducts training institutes; provides education and consultation to detention facilities and units of government. Conducts research. Compiles statistics. **Libraries:** Type: reference. **Holdings:** archival material. **Awards:** Donald R. Hammeregren Distinguished Service Award. **Frequency:** annual. **Type:** recognition. **Recipient:** for the individual making the most outstanding contribution to the field of juvenile detention ● Merit Award. **Type:** recognition. **Recipient:** for the outstanding line staff person in each detention center. **Computer Services:** database. **Telecommunication Services:** electronic mail, njdaed2@aol.com. **Committees:** Critical Issues and Policy; Political Action. **Affiliated With:** American Correctional Association. **Publications:** *Inside Justice*, quarterly. Newsletter. **Price:** $20.00 /year for nonmembers; included in membership dues. **Circulation:** 1,000. **Advertising:** accepted ● *Journal for Juvenile Justice and Detention Services*, semiannual. Includes articles from professionals in the field. **Price:** $45.00 /year for nonmembers; included in membership dues ● *NJDA Publications*, quarterly. Brochure ● Also makes available training videotapes. **Conventions/Meetings:** annual Joint Conference on Juvenile Services - always October ● annual National Juvenile Training Institute - meeting, for juvenile justice and detention service professionals (exhibits) - always June.

11622 ■ National Prison Project of the ACLU (NPP)
915 15th St. NW, 7th Fl.
Washington, DC 20005
Ph: (202)393-4930
Fax: (202)393-4931
URL: http://www.aclu.org/prisons/prisonsmain.cfm
Contact: Elizabeth Alexander, Dir.

Founded: 1972. **Staff:** 12. **Description:** Aims to provide litigation and educational programs aimed at improving prison conditions and developing alternatives to incarceration. Engages in prisoners' rights litigation. **Libraries:** Type: reference. **Affiliated With:** American Civil Liberties Union. **Publications:** *AIDS in Prison*. Bibliography. Catalogues resource materials on AIDS in prison. **Price:** $10.00/copy ● *National Prison Project Journal*, semiannual. Features reports, legal analyses, legislative news, and other information about the corrections and criminal justice fields.

Price: $30.00/year for non-inmates; $2.00/year for inmates. ISSN: 0748-2655. **Circulation:** 3,000. Alternate Formats: microform. Also Cited As: *NPP Journal* ● *Play it Safer*. Booklet. Describes sexually transmitted diseases, the signs of disease, the importance of safer sex, and the need for treatment. ● *The PLRA: A guide for Prisoners*. Booklet ● *Prisoners' Assistance Directory*, periodic. Identifies and describes organizations and agencies providing assistance to past and present prisoners. **Price:** $30.00/copy ● Reports (in English and Spanish).

11623 ■ North American Association of Wardens and Superintendents (NAAWS)
PO Box 11037
Albany, NY 12211-0037
Ph: (518)786-6801
E-mail: elart26@aol.com
URL: http://corrections.com/naaws
Contact: Arthur A. Leonardo, Exec. Dir.

Founded: 1935. **Members:** 1,150. **Membership Dues:** regular, $25 (annual). **Staff:** 2. **Budget:** $50,000. **Regional Groups:** 5. **State Groups:** 4. **Multinational. Description:** Wardens, superintendents, and heads of detention, penal, and correctional institutions (male and female), including federal, state and local officials in the public and private sector. Seeks to: focus national attention on the problems and programs of correctional institutions; promote better management of institutions and the care, custody, and treatment of committed offenders. **Awards:** National Scholarship. **Frequency:** annual. **Type:** scholarship. **Recipient:** for criminal justice students ● Warden of the Year. **Frequency:** annual. **Type:** recognition. **Recipient:** for outstanding wardens. **Formerly:** (1971) Wardens Association of America; (1980) American Association of Wardens and Superintendents. **Publications:** *The Grapevine*, quarterly. Newsletter. **Price:** available to members only. **Circulation:** 750. **Advertising:** accepted ● *View from the Trenches*. Book. Serves as a warden's manual. **Conventions/Meetings:** semiannual meeting, held in conjunction with American Correctional Association - always January and August.

11624 ■ Osborne Association (OA)
36-31 38th St.
Long Island City, NY 11101
Ph: (718)707-2600
Fax: (718)707-3103
E-mail: info@osborneny.org
URL: http://www.osborneny.org
Contact: Elizabeth Gaynes, Exec. Dir.

Founded: 1931. **Staff:** 155. **Languages:** English, Spanish. **Description:** Offers opportunities for individuals who have been in conflict with the law to transform their lives through innovative, effective, and replicable programs that service the community by reducing crimes and the human and economic costs from crime. Offers assistance for reform and rehabilitation through public education, advocacy, and alternatives to incarceration that respect the dignity of people and honor the capacity to change and achieve self-sufficiency, adopt healthy lifestyles, enter the workforce, form and rebuild families, and rejoin communities. **Awards:** Austin MacCormick Award. **Frequency:** annual. **Type:** recognition. **Recipient:** for work in the human services community ● OA Medal. **Frequency:** annual. **Type:** recognition. **Recipient:** for service in criminal justice. **Telecommunication Services:** hotline, collect hotline for New York State prisoners, (718)378-7022 ● hotline, information hotline for New York State families, (800)-344-3314. **Programs:** Court Advocacy Services; Employment and Training Services; Prevention and Treatment Services; Prison, Reentry and Family Services. **Affiliated With:** American Correctional Association. **Formed by Merger of:** (1995) National Society of Penal Information; Welfare League Association of New York. **Publications:** *How Can I Help?*. Booklet. Offers detailed information for individuals working with children whose parents are sent to jail; a three volume series of booklets. **Price:** $10.00/set ● *Osborne Associations Newsletter*, quarterly. **Price:** free. **Circulation:** 8,000 ● *Osborne Today*, periodic. Newsletter. Alternate Formats: online

● *Parenting from Inside/Out: The Voice of Mothers in Prison.* Book. Details the experience of 11 mothers at the Bedford Hills Correctional Facility who participated in Parenting from a Distance Program. **Price:** $12.00. **Conventions/Meetings:** bimonthly board meeting.

11625 ■ Prison-Ashram Project (PAP)

c/o Human Kindness Foundation
PO Box 61619
Durham, NC 27715
Ph: (919)304-2220
Fax: (919)304-3220
URL: http://www.humankindness.org/project.html
Contact: Sita Lozoff, Dir.
Founded: 1973. **Members:** 40,000. **Staff:** 7. **Budget:** $150,000. **Description:** Prisoners and their families, prison staff and volunteers, and interested individuals. Provides encouragement and advice to prisoners and other shut-ins who want to use their time in spiritual training. Believes "if one is tired enough of being a prison inmate, then he or she can live instead as a prison monk or nun, using the cloistered lifestyle, the regular hours, the inaccessibility of friends, distractions, or entertainment, to one's advantage just as in an ashram". Maintains speakers' bureau. Distributes several books on spiritual growth to prison inmates and staff. A project of the Human Kindness Foundation. **Publications:** *Lineage and Other Stories.* Book ● *Prison-Ashram Project of the Human Kindness Foundation—Newsletter,* quarterly. **Price:** free. **Circulation:** 40,000 ● *We're All Doing Time* (in English, French, and Spanish). Book ● Booklets. **Conventions/Meetings:** workshop, held in prisons, universities, churches, synagogues.

11626 ■ Prison Fellowship International (PFI)

PO Box 17434
Washington, DC 20041
Ph: (703)481-0000
Fax: (703)481-0003
E-mail: info@pfi.org
URL: http://www.pfi.org
Contact: Ronald W. Nikkel, Pres./CEO
Founded: 1979. **Staff:** 30. **Budget:** $1,500,000. **Languages:** English, French, Russian, Spanish. **Description:** National Prison Fellowship organizations devoted to holistic Christian ministry in prisons and welfare communities for prisoners, ex-prisoners, victims, and their families. Promotes restorative justice in the criminal justice system and assists in implementing effective alternatives to incarceration. Offers consultation and assistance in developing additional Prison Fellowship movements. **Councils:** International. **Divisions:** Communications; Field Operations; Training; UN Liaison. **Publications:** *Global Link* (in English, French, Russian, and Spanish), monthly. Newsletter. Equips and provides information to national Prison Fellowship organizations. **Price:** included in membership dues. ISSN: 0738-1530. **Circulation:** 2,800 ● *PFI Global Link Journal* (in English, French, Russian, and Spanish), quarterly. Newsletter. Reports on developments in Prison Fellowship ministries around the world. **Circulation:** 6,000 ● Proceedings, biennial. Features transcripts of speeches of council and convocation meetings. **Price:** included in membership dues. **Circulation:** 1,000. **Conventions/Meetings:** quadrennial convention, attended by representatives from all 110 national ministries and others interested in PFI (exhibits).

11627 ■ Prison Fellowship Ministries (PFM)

PO Box 1550
Merrifield, VA 22116-1550
Ph: (703)554-8440
Free: (800)206-9764
E-mail: volunteers@pfm.org
URL: http://www.prisonfellowship.org
Contact: Mark Earley, Pres./CEO
Founded: 1976. **Staff:** 300. **Budget:** $48,000,000. **Description:** Encourages Christians to work in prisons and to assist communities in ministering to prisoners, ex-offenders, victims, and their families. Works towards a fair and effective criminal justice system. Trains volunteers for in-prison ministries. Sponsors in-prison seminars, bible studies, marriage enrichment seminars, community service projects, correspondence and visitation programs, and programs for ex-offenders and prisoners' families; also sponsors the Prison Fellowship Angel Tree Program, an outreach to prisoners' children at Christmas time, and throughout the year through mentoring and summer camping programs. Records "Break Point" radio program, with Charles Colson, that airs on hundreds of Christian radio stations. **Affiliated With:** American Correctional Association; Evangelical Council for Financial Accountability; Justice Fellowship; Prison Fellowship International. **Formerly:** (1984) Prison Fellowship. **Publications:** *Born Again.* Book ● *Convicted: New Hope for Ending America's Crime Crisis.* Book ● *Inside Journal.* Newsletter ● *Jubilee,* monthly. Newsletter. Features schedule of prison seminars. **Price:** free. ISSN: 0893-1607. **Circulation:** 175,000 ● *Justice Report,* quarterly ● *Kingdoms in Conflict.* Book ● *Life Sentence.* Book ● *Loving God.* Book. **Conventions/Meetings:** triennial international conference.

11628 ■ Prison Ministry of Yokefellow's International

PO Box 482
Rising Sun, MD 21911
Ph: (410)658-2661
E-mail: hal.owens@dol.net
Contact: Rev. Hal E. Owens, Contact
Founded: 1986. **Members:** 2,000. **Staff:** 3. **Budget:** $20,000. **Regional Groups:** 8. **State Groups:** 12. **Local Groups:** 300. **Description:** Helps to serve the religious needs of residents in correctional and penal institutions; attempts to bridge the gulf between persons confined and those in the outside community; demonstrates a continuing concern for offenders against society by promoting employment aid; promotes, supports, and cooperates in the establishment and operation of local community-sponsored Halfway House facilities; participates in programs designed to improve correctional methods; bears concern for the decisions made by those who are responsible for the policies and procedures of rehabilitative efforts. Seeks to develop new life for offenders through the development of small groups within prison walls. **Libraries: Type:** reference. **Holdings:** books. **Subjects:** criminal justice. **Formerly:** (1993) Yokefellowship Prison Ministry. **Publications:** *Yokefellow Handbook.* Brochures ● *Yokefellow News,* quarterly. Newsletter. **Price:** free for members. **Circulation:** 1,000 ● Pamphlets. **Conventions/Meetings:** annual conference.

11629 ■ Prisoners' Rights Union (PRU)

PO Box 161321
Sacramento, CA 95816-1321
Ph: (916)422-2240
Fax: (916)442-2240
URL: http://www.dragonspeaks.org/pru/DefaultKA.htm
Founded: 1971. **Description:** Educates prisoners, parolees, their families, friends, advocates and society that prisoners are people and what rights prisoners do have, where to find them and how to enforce them. **Formerly:** (1987) Prisoner's Union. **Publications:** *Inside/Out Press.* Manuals. Provides self-help legal materials. ● *The Resource Guide,* biennial. Directory.

11630 ■ Safer Society Foundation (SSF)

PO Box 340
Brandon, VT 05733-0340
Ph: (802)247-3132
Fax: (802)247-4233
E-mail: ssfi@sover.net
URL: http://www.safersociety.org
Contact: Ms. Tammy Kennedy, Public Education Dir.
Founded: 1974. **Members:** 7. **Staff:** 5. **Budget:** $500,000. **Description:** Provides referrals for specialized assessment and treatment for youthful and adult sexual victims and offenders. Offers educational materials, training, and networking to the general public as well as professionals who work with sexual offenders and victims. Compiles statistics. **Libraries: Type:** open to the public. **Holdings:** 500. **Subjects:** sexual abuse prevention and treatment. **Computer Services:** database, agencies, institutions, and individual providers. **Affiliated With:** Association for the Treatment of Sexual Abusers. **Formerly:** (1987) Prison Research Education Action Project; (1998) Safer Society Program and Press. **Publications:** Publishes self-help workbooks for adult and juvenile sex offenders, books for victims, professional resources and video- and audiocassettes.

11631 ■ SEARCH - The National Consortium for Justice Information and Statistics

7311 Greenhaven Dr., Ste.145
Sacramento, CA 95831
Ph: (916)392-2550
Fax: (916)392-8440
E-mail: ron.hawley@search.org
URL: http://www.search.org
Contact: Ronald P. Hawley, Exec. Dir.
Founded: 1969. **Members:** 60. **Staff:** 40. **Description:** Gubernatorial appointees representing each of the 50 states. Seeks to improve the criminal justice system through the effective application of information and identification technology. Identifies and works to solve information management problems faced by the state and local criminal justice systems; strives to improve communication and cooperation among criminal justice agencies at all levels. **Libraries: Type:** by appointment only; reference. **Holdings:** 1,200; archival material, books, periodicals. **Subjects:** criminal justice, information management, law, public policy, crime statistics, research. **Awards:** Gary R. Cooper Award. **Frequency:** annual. **Type:** recognition. **Recipient:** for a member with an outstanding work in the field of criminal justice information systems, policy or statistics ● O.J. Hawkins Award. **Frequency:** annual. **Type:** recognition. **Recipient:** for individual who contributes to the criminal justice community's ability to develop and use information. **Computer Services:** database, IT acquisition ● information services, index of criminal justice information systems. **Committees:** Law and Policy; Research and Statistics; Systems and Technology. **Programs:** Criminal History Policy; High-tech Crime; Information Sharing. **Publications:** Reports. Alternate Formats: online ● Bulletins. Features a range of timely issues in criminal justice information management, technology, law and policy. Alternate Formats: online. **Conventions/Meetings:** annual Justice and Public Safety Information Sharing: Effective Decision-making for a Safer America - symposium, provides the tools and techniques needed to properly plan and implement justice and public safety information (exhibits).

11632 ■ Sentencing Project

514 10th St. NW, Ste.1000
Washington, DC 20004
Ph: (202)628-0871
Fax: (202)628-1091
E-mail: staff@sentencingproject.org
URL: http://www.sentencingproject.org
Contact: Marc Mauer, Exec. Dir.
Founded: 1986. **Staff:** 8. **Budget:** $900,000. **Description:** Works for a fair and effective criminal justice system by promoting alternatives to incarceration, reforms in sentencing law and practice, and better use of community-based services and institutions. Seeks to recast the public debate on crime and punishment. **Libraries: Type:** not open to the public. **Holdings:** 250. **Subjects:** government statistics. **Publications:** *Race to Incarcerate.* Book. **Price:** $14.95 paperback edition; $22.95 hardback edition ● Reports. Alternate Formats: online. **Conventions/Meetings:** conference ● regional meeting and conference.

11633 ■ Stop Prisoner Rape (SPR)

3325 Wilshire Blvd., Ste.340
Los Angeles, CA 90010
Ph: (213)384-1400
Fax: (213)384-1411
E-mail: info@spr.org
URL: http://www.spr.org
Contact: Ms. Lovisa Stannow, Co-Exec. Dir.
Founded: 1979. **Staff:** 7. **Budget:** $66,000. **Languages:** English, Spanish. **Description:** Seeks to

end sexual violence against men, women, and youth in all forms of detention; promotes education, outreach, and advocacy. **Libraries: Type:** reference. **Holdings:** 40. **Subjects:** prison rape, incarceration, male and female sexual victimization. **Formerly:** (1993) People Organized to Stop Rape of Imprisoned Persons. **Publications:** *SPR Action Update*, quarterly. Newsletter ● Reports.

11634 ■ Vera Institute of Justice
233 Broadway, 12th Fl.
New York, NY 10279
Ph: (212)334-1300
Fax: (212)941-9407
E-mail: contactvera@vera.org
URL: http://www.vera.org
Contact: Michael P. Jacobson, Dir.
Founded: 1961. **Staff:** 90. **Description:** Seeks to make government policies and practices more fair and humane. Encourages just practices in public services and seeks to improve the quality of urban life. **Libraries: Type:** reference; open to the public. **Holdings:** 1,700; articles, books, periodicals. **Subjects:** criminal justice, public policy. **Formerly:** (1966) Vera Foundation. **Publications:** *Federal Sentencing Reporter*, bimonthly. Journal. Includes cases and commentary on sentencing issues under the federal sentencing guidelines. **Price:** $210.00/year. ISSN: 1053-9867. **Circulation:** 2,400. Also Cited As: *Fed. Sent. R* ● *Just 'Cause*, bimonthly. Newsletter.

11635 ■ Volunteers in Prevention, Probation, Prisons (VIP)
Grand Park Ctre.
28 W Adams, Ste.1310
Detroit, MI 48226
Ph: (313)964-1110
Fax: (313)964-1145
E-mail: staff@vipmentoring.com
URL: http://www.vipmentoring.org
Contact: Jim Comer, Chm.
Founded: 1969. **Members:** 170. **Staff:** 10. **Budget:** $800,000. **Description:** Aims to stimulate the development of citizen participation in juvenile and criminal justice rehabilitative programs. Sponsors a training program for professionals and nonprofessionals. Maintains speakers' bureau; conducts charitable program. **Libraries: Type:** reference. **Holdings:** audiovisuals, books. **Awards: Type:** recognition. **Computer Services:** database, justice volunteer programs. **Formerly:** (1975) Volunteers in Probation; (1984) VIP Division. **Publications:** *VIP Examiner*, quarterly. Newsletter ● *VIP Information Packet*. Booklets. Features teaching-training modules. ● *VIP Mentoring*, bimonthly. Newsletter. Alternate Formats: online. **Conventions/Meetings:** annual National Justice Volunteer Forum - meeting (exhibits) - always October.

11636 ■ We Care Program (WC)
5825 Hwy. 21
Atmore, AL 36502
Ph: (251)368-8818
Fax: (251)368-0932
E-mail: info@wecareprogram.org
URL: http://www.wecareprogram.org
Contact: David Landis, Pres.
Founded: 1970. **Staff:** 30. **Budget:** $570,000. **Description:** Sends Christian workers into prisons to teach inmates how to work through problems, handle culture shock upon reentering society, adjust to family life, gain acceptance in the community, and to share the gospel of Jesus Christ. **Publications:** *The Connection*, 8/year. Newsletter. Contains news, testimonies and editorial. **Price:** included in membership dues. **Circulation:** 4,000. Alternate Formats: online ● *Intercessor's Email Prayer Bulletin*, monthly. Alternate Formats: online. **Conventions/Meetings:** annual PA Banquet, with speaker or former inmate testimony - every spring; first Friday of March ● annual Prison Crusade - assembly.

11637 ■ Women's Prison Association (WPA)
110 2nd Ave.
New York, NY 10003
Ph: (212)674-1163

Fax: (212)677-1981
E-mail: ajacobs@wpaonline.org
URL: http://www.wpaonline.org
Contact: Ann L. Jacobs, Exec. Dir.
Founded: 1844. **Staff:** 128. **Budget:** $7,512,507. **Languages:** English, Spanish. **Description:** Service agency that aids women involved in the criminal justice system and their families. Promotes alternatives to incarceration; sponsors transitional programs for women being released from prison; assists homeless ex-offenders seeking to reunite with their children who are in kinship or foster-care. **Publications:** *A Guide to the New York Child Welfare System*. Manual. Provides information on making informed decisions concerning the care of children when a parent is incarcerated. **Price:** $5.00 ● *A Report on the First Ten Years of the Sarah Powell Huntington House*. Documents the success of the first decade of WPA's transitional shelter. Alternate Formats: online.

Criminology

11638 ■ American Society of Criminology (ASC)
1314 Kinnear Rd., Ste.212
Columbus, OH 43212-1156
Ph: (614)292-9207
Fax: (614)292-6767
E-mail: asc41@infinet.com
URL: http://www.asc41.com
Contact: Chris W. Eskridge, Exec. Dir.
Founded: 1941. **Members:** 2,700. **Membership Dues:** active, $80 (annual) ● partner/spouse, $85 (annual) ● three-year, $225 ● student, $40 (annual) ● student partner/spouse, retired, $45 (annual) ● institutional, $300 (annual). **Staff:** 2. **Budget:** $350,000. **Description:** Represents professional and academic criminologists, students of criminology in accredited universities, psychiatrists, psychologists, and sociologists. Develops criminology as a science and academic discipline. Aids in the construction of criminological curricula in accredited universities. Upgrades the practitioner in criminological fields (police, prisons, probation, parole, delinquency workers). Conducts research programs and sponsors three student paper competitions. Provides placement service at annual convention. **Awards:** Bloch Award. **Frequency:** annual. **Type:** recognition. **Recipient:** for outstanding service contribution to American Society of Criminology ● Michael J. Hindelang Award. **Frequency:** annual. **Type:** recognition. **Recipient:** for a book that made the most outstanding contribution for research in criminology ● Ruth Shonle Cavan Young Scholar Award. **Frequency:** annual. **Type:** recognition. **Recipient:** for an outstanding scholar ● Sellin-Glueck Award. **Frequency:** annual. **Type:** recognition. **Recipient:** for those who reside outside the US who gained international recognition for contributions in criminology ● Sutherland Award. **Frequency:** annual. **Type:** recognition. **Recipient:** for outstanding contributions to theory or research in criminology ● Vollmer Award. **Frequency:** annual. **Type:** recognition. **Recipient:** for an outstanding criminologist. **Telecommunication Services:** electronic mail, ceskridge@unl.edu. **Absorbed:** Association of College Police Training Officials. **Formerly:** (1956) Society for the Advancement of Criminology. **Publications:** *American Society of Criminology—Member Directory*, semiannual. Membership Directory. **Price:** included in membership dues. **Advertising:** accepted ● *The Criminologist*, bimonthly. Newsletter. Includes calendar of events; calls for papers; conference reports; employment opportunities; new members; research reports. **Price:** included in membership dues; $25.00/year in U.S.; $30.00/year outside U.S.; $5.00/per issue. ISSN: 0164-0240. **Circulation:** 2,500. **Advertising:** accepted ● *Criminology: An Interdisciplinary Journal*, quarterly. Examines crime and deviant behavior as found in the disciplines of law, criminal justice, and the social and behavioral sciences. **Price:** included in membership dues; $50.00 /year for individuals; $90.00 /year for institutions in U.S.; $96.00 /year for institutions outside U.S. ISSN: 0011-1384. **Circula-**

tion: 3,250. **Advertising:** accepted. Alternate Formats: microform ● *Criminology and Public Policy*, quarterly. Journal. Contains policy discussions of criminology research findings. **Price:** $130.00/year in U.S.; $150.00/year outside U.S. ● *Proceedings of Annual Meeting*. **Conventions/Meetings:** annual conference (exhibits).

11639 ■ London Club (LC)
Address Unknown since 2007
Founded: 1975. **Members:** 100. **Membership Dues:** $20 (annual). **Staff:** 4. **Multinational. Description:** Criminologists, members of the press, investigative freelancers, educators, and interested individuals. Goals are: to accumulate data; to apply theories and draw conclusions concerning unsolved crimes (such as the Jack the Ripper Whitechapel murders and the Jon Benet Ramsey case), controversial trial verdicts (such as the Lizzie Borden murder and the Lindbergh kidnapping cases) and theories involving alleged criminal conspiracies both past and present (such as the Lincoln and Kennedy assassinations). Seeks to become a mass private sector for research into unsolved crime by bringing together experts and interested individuals on many levels of criminal investigation; foster international communications among members and serve as a forum for their investigative data. Conducts research. **Libraries: Type:** not open to the public. **Holdings:** 500. **Committees:** Editorial. **Divisions:** Specialized Research. **Publications:** *London Club Journal*.

Cultural Resources

11640 ■ Cross-Cultural Solutions
2 Clinton Pl.
New Rochelle, NY 10801
Ph: (914)632-0022
Free: (800)380-4777
Fax: (914)632-8494
E-mail: info@crossculturalsolutions.org
URL: http://www.crossculturalsolutions.org
Contact: Steven C. Rosenthal, Exec. Dir.
Founded: 1995. **Description:** Promotes international understanding and peace through volunteer programs in partnership with sustainable community initiatives.

11641 ■ Robert Sterling Clark Foundation
135 E 64th St.
New York, NY 10021
Ph: (212)288-8900
Fax: (212)288-1033
URL: http://www.rsclark.org
Contact: Margaret C. Ayers, Exec. Dir.
Founded: 1952. **Description:** Strives to support arts and culture, projects that improve the performance and accountability of government agencies responsible for the delivery of human services, and family planning. **Publications:** Annual Report, annual.

Deaf

11642 ■ Abused Deaf Women's Advocacy Services (ADWAS)
8623 Roosevelt Way NE
Seattle, WA 98115
Ph: (206)726-0093
Free: (800)787-3224
Fax: (206)726-0017
E-mail: adwas@adwas.org
URL: http://www.adwas.org
Contact: Marilyn J. Smith, Exec. Dir.
Founded: 1986. **Staff:** 18. **Description:** Provides support for deaf, deaf-blind, and hard-of-hearing victims of domestic violence and sexual assault. **Telecommunication Services:** hotline, (206)236-3134. **Programs:** Children's Advocacy; Community Advocacy; Domestic Violence Services; Education/Outreach Services; Medical Advocacy. **Publications:** Newsletter, quarterly. **Conventions/Meetings:** workshop.

11643 ■ Deaf Friends International (DFI)
PO Box 13192
Hamilton, OH 45013
E-mail: dfi@workersforjesus.com
URL: http://www.workersforjesus.com/dfi/front-eng. · htm
Contact: Jeanne Griffin, Dir.
Founded: 1992. **Multinational. Description:** Provides financial help to deaf children and adults around the world. Provides school supplies, medical assistance, scholarships, disaster relief and hearing aids to deaf people. **Computer Services:** Information services, deaf resources. **Publications:** Magazine. Alternate Formats: online.

11644 ■ Deaf Women United (DWU)
PO Box 152795
Austin, TX 78715-2795
E-mail: dwu05board@dwu.org
URL: http://www.dwu.org
Contact: Melissa S. Draganac-Hawk, Pres.
Founded: 1985. **Membership Dues:** regular (under age 62), $25 (annual) ● senior citizen (age 62 plus), student, $15 (annual) ● supporting (hearing women only), $20 (annual) ● special individual (with proof of public assistance), junior (under 18, deaf, hard of hearing, deaf-blind), $10 (annual) ● affiliate/organization (at least 75 percent of deaf women), $50 (annual). **Description:** Promotes opportunity for deaf women in the areas of deaf culture, politics, employment and education, social activities and networking. Provides tools, information and training in organizational management, personal growth and empowerment; assists in setting up a home office that becomes a clearinghouse of resource information; maintains mentoring system. **Awards:** Deaf Women of Achievement. **Type:** recognition. **Recipient:** for deaf or hard of hearing women with significant contribution to the deaf community ● Wall of Honors. **Type:** recognition. **Recipient:** for women with outstanding contributions to the local communities. **Publications:** Newsletter, quarterly. Features health care articles, editorial columns, board reports and upcoming events. **Advertising:** accepted. **Conventions/Meetings:** conference.

11645 ■ National Deaf Education Network and Clearinghouse
c/o Laurent Clerc National Deaf Education Center
800 Florida Ave. NE
Washington, DC 20002
Ph: (202)651-5051 (202)651-5031
Fax: (202)651-5054
E-mail: clearinghouse.infotogo@gallaudet.edu
URL: http://clerccenter.gallaudet.edu
Contact: Anita Glibert, Information Specialist
Description: Information dissemination at the Gallaudet University Laurent Clerc National Deaf Education Center on diverse topics related to deaf and hard of hearing children, ages birth to 21 years old. **Publications:** *Odyssey Magazine.* Reports on Clerc Center projects and contains peer-reviewed articles from contributors. **Price:** free for members; $5.00 for nonmembers ● *World Around You.* Magazine. Provides motivation for independent and assisted reading, creative writing, and drawing for deaf and hard of hearing teens.

Death and Dying

11646 ■ Aiding Mothers and Fathers Experiencing Neonatal Death (AMEND)
c/o Martha Eise
1559 Ville Rosa
Hazelwood, MO 63042
Ph: (314)291-0892
E-mail: martha@amendgroup.com
URL: http://www.amendgroup.com
Contact: Martha Eise, Contact
Founded: 1974. **Description:** Provides free counseling services to parents who have experienced the loss of an infant through miscarriage, stillbirth or neonatal death. Offers support and encouragement

to parents having a normal grief reaction to the loss of their baby. **Publications:** Booklets.

11647 ■ American Institute of Life Threatening Illness and Loss (Division of Foundation of Thanatology) (FT)
c/o Dr. Austin H. Kutscher, Pres.
Columbia-Presbyterian Medical Ctr.
630 W 168th St.
New York, NY 10032
Ph: (718)601-4453
Fax: (718)549-7219
E-mail: fndtn@lifethreat.org
URL: http://www.lifethreat.org
Contact: Dr. Austin H. Kutscher, Pres.
Founded: 1967. **Members:** 400. **Staff:** 4. **Description:** Health, theology, psychology, and social science professionals devoted to scientific and humanistic inquiries into death, loss, grief, and bereavement. Promotes improved psychosocial and medical care for critically ill and dying patients and assistance for their families. Stimulates and coordinates professional, educational, and research programs concerned with mortality and the management of grief. Maintains research programs, speakers' bureau, biographical archives, and library. **Formerly:** (1991) Foundation of Thanatology. **Publications:** *Advances in Thanatology,* quarterly ● *Archives of the Foundation of Thanatology,* quarterly ● *Loss, Grief and Care,* quarterly. Journal ● *National Directory,* periodic ● *Thanatology Abstracts,* annual ● *Thanatology News,* periodic. **Conventions/Meetings:** symposium - 3-4/year.

11648 ■ Association for Death Education and Counseling (ADEC)
60 Revere Dr., Ste.500
Northbrook, IL 60062
Ph: (847)509-0403
Fax: (847)480-9282
E-mail: info@adec.org
URL: http://www.adec.org
Contact: Sherry Schachter PhD, Pres.
Founded: 1976. **Members:** 2,000. **Membership Dues:** individual, $135 (annual) ● institutional, $275 (annual) ● senior, $70 (annual) ● student, $60 (annual). **Staff:** 5. **Regional Groups:** 10. **Description:** Individuals and institutions interested in responsible and effective death education and counseling. Goals are: to upgrade the quality of death education and patient care in hospitals, residential care facilities, churches, schools, community organizations, and government facilities; to upgrade the quality of counseling in the areas of death, dying, and bereavement. Formulates codes of ethics and certifies death educators and counselors. Conducts workshops and conferences to improve the lifestyle of the dying and their survivors. **Awards:** ADEC Service Award. **Frequency:** annual. **Type:** recognition. **Recipient:** for individuals who demonstrate excellence in service to the association ● Clinical Practice Award. **Frequency:** annual. **Type:** recognition. **Recipient:** for individuals who demonstrate excellence in clinical practice ● Death Education Award. **Frequency:** annual. **Type:** recognition. **Recipient:** for individuals with expertise in the field of death education ● Research Recognition Award. **Frequency:** annual. **Type:** recognition. **Recipient:** for a research that contributes significantly to death and loss studies ● Student Paper Awards. **Frequency:** annual. **Type:** recognition. **Computer Services:** Mailing lists, for a fee. **Telecommunication Services:** electronic mail, adec@adec.org. **Committees:** Certification Review Board; Conference Steering; Disaster Resource Team; Human Resources; Professional and Program Development; Professional Standards and Ethics; Special Interest Groups; Test. **Formerly:** (1986) Forum for Death Education and Counseling. **Publications:** *Forum Newsletter,* quarterly. Includes book reviews and calendar of events and professional articles. **Price:** included in membership dues. ISSN: 1091-4846. **Circulation:** 2,000. **Advertising:** accepted. Alternate Formats: online ● *International Conference Program Book,* annual. Includes abstracts. ● *Directory,* monthly. Includes a listing of ADEC members. **Price:** included in membership

dues. **Circulation:** 2,000. Alternate Formats: online. **Conventions/Meetings:** annual conference, books, posters, and videos (exhibits) ● annual International Conference on Grief in Contemporary Society (exhibits).

11649 ■ Choice in Dying
c/o Choices Education Group
1100 Dexter Ave. N
Seattle, WA 98109
Free: (888)246-4237
Fax: (206)273-7777
E-mail: info@choices.org
URL: http://www.choices.org
Contact: John Waechter, Pres.
Description: Represents people interested in the choices related to dying. Aims to help patients and their families participate in decisions about end-of-life medical care. Provides legal documents, counseling line, educational materials and subscriptions for professionals.

11650 ■ Sacred Dying Foundation
PO Box 210328
San Francisco, CA 94121
Ph: (415)585-9455
E-mail: foundation@sacreddying.org
URL: http://www.sacreddying.org
Contact: Megory Anderson, Exec. Dir./Founder
Founded: 1996. **Description:** Seeks to transform the dying experience by reintegrating spiritual and religious practices, and to change the way society experiences death and dying. **Publications:** *Reviews of Sacred Dying: Creating Rituals for Embracing the End of Life.* Article ● *Sacred Dying: Creating Rituals for Embracing the End of Life.* Book. **Conventions/Meetings:** conference ● retreat ● seminar ● Training Sessions and Classes - lecture ● workshop.

Democracy

11651 ■ Artists for a New South Africa (ANSA)
2999 Overland Ave., Ste.102
Los Angeles, CA 90064
Ph: (310)204-1748
Free: (877)423-7422
Fax: (310)204-4277
E-mail: info@ansafrica.org
URL: http://www.ansafrica.org
Contact: Sharon Gelman, Exec. Dir.
Founded: 1989. **Staff:** 5. **Multinational. Description:** Combats the African AIDS pandemic and advances democracy and equality in South Africa. Safeguards civil and voting rights in the United States. **Computer Services:** Information services, HIV/AIDS resources ● mailing lists. **Boards:** Amandla AIDS Fund Advisory. **Projects:** Aid for South Africa People; AIDS Advocacy; Amandla AIDS Fund; Election Protection; It Takes A Village; Voices from the Frontlines.

Dentistry

11652 ■ Consumers for Dental Choice (CDC)
17525 K St. NW, Ste.511
Washington, DC 20006
Ph: (202)822-6307
Fax: (202)822-6309
E-mail: info@toxicteeth.org
URL: http://www.toxicteeth.org
Contact: Sandy Duffy, Pres.
Founded: 1996. **Description:** Protects the health of dental consumers and the environment by abolishing the use of mercury amalgam dental fillings. Educates the public about the health and environmental dangers of mercury fillings. Ensures the integrity of scientific research on amalgam. Brings about environmental awareness of the colossal contribution of mercury from amalgam.

Disabled

11653 ■ Abilities!

201 I.U. Willets Rd.
Albertson, NY 11507
Ph: (516)465-1400 (516)747-5400
Fax: (516)465-1591
E-mail: ecortez@ncds.org
URL: http://www.ncds.org
Contact: Edmund L. Cortez, Pres./CEO
Founded: 1952. **Staff:** 425. **Budget:** $20,000,000.
Description: Serves as a center providing educational, vocational, rehabilitation, and research opportunities for persons with disabilities. Work is conducted through the following: Abilities Health and Rehabilitation Services, a New York state licensed diagnostic and treatment center which offers comprehensive outpatient programs in physical therapy, occupational therapy, speech therapy, and psychological services; Career and Employment Institute, which evaluates, trains, and counsels more than 600 adults with disabilities each year, with the goal of productive competitive employment; Henry Viscardi School, which conducts early childhood, elementary, and secondary programs, as well as adult and continuing education programs; Research and Training Institute, which conducts research on the education, employment, and career development of persons with disabilities, and holds seminars and workshops for rehabilitation services professionals. Maintains library and speakers' bureau; compiles statistics; offers placement service; conducts research and educational programs. **Awards:** Henry Viscardi, Jr. Legacy Award. **Frequency:** annual. **Type:** recognition. **Recipient:** to corporate leaders who have supported the education and employment of people with disabilities ● President's Service Award. **Type:** recognition. **Additional Websites:** http://www.abilitiesinc.org. **Councils:** National Business and Disability. **Programs:** Edwin W. Martin, Jr. Career and Employment Institute; Global Institute; Henry Viscardi School; Mary Jean and Frank P. Smeal Learning Center; Nathaniel H. Kornreich Technology Center; Research and Evaluation Center. **Affiliated With:** National Business and Disability Council. **Formerly:** (1991) Human Resources Center; (2004) National Center for Disability Services. **Conventions/Meetings:** semiannual conference.

11654 ■ Advocating Change Together (ACT)

1821 Univ. Ave. W, Ste.306-S
St. Paul, MN 55104
Ph: (651)641-0297
Free: (800)641-0059
Fax: (651)641-4053
E-mail: act@selfadvocacy.org
URL: http://www.selfadvocacy.org
Contact: Rick Cardenas, Co-Dir.
Description: Represents the interests of people with developmental and other disabilities. Helps people across disabilities to see themselves as part of a larger disability rights movement and make connections to other civil and human rights struggles. Provides information, skill building and leadership opportunities to individuals with disabilities. **Telecommunication Services:** electronic mail, cardenas@selfadvocacy.org.

11655 ■ Alliance for Technology Access (ATA)

1304 Southpoint Blvd., Ste.240
Petaluma, CA 94954
Ph: (707)778-3011
Free: (800)914-3017
Fax: (707)765-2080
E-mail: atainfo@ataccess.org
URL: http://www.ataccess.org
Contact: Mary Lester, Co-Founder/Exec. Dir.
Founded: 1987. **Membership Dues:** individual, $50 (annual) ● organization, $100 (annual). **Description:** Serves as a network of community-based resource centers, developers, vendors and associates dedicated to providing information and support services to children and adults with disabilities. Increases the use of technology by children and adults with dis-

abilities and functional limitations. Encourages and facilitates the empowerment of people with disabilities to participate fully in their communities through public education, information, referral and advocacy. **Awards:** Jacquelyn Brand Leadership in Technology Award. **Frequency:** annual. **Type:** recognition. **Recipient:** for an outstanding individual who advocates for the use of technology ● Tom Morales Leadership in Technology Award. **Frequency:** annual. **Type:** recognition. **Recipient:** for an individual working to increase the use of technology by people with disabilities. **Telecommunication Services:** electronic mail, martinsweeney@ataccess.org ● electronic mail, toddplummer@ataccess.org ● teletype, (707)778-3015. **Publications:** *Computer Resources for People with Disabilities.* Book. Contains updates on technologies that can benefit people with disabilities. **Price:** $24.95 paperback; $31.95 spiral bound.

11656 ■ American Amputee Foundation (AAF)

PO Box 250218
Little Rock, AR 72225
Ph: (501)666-2523
Fax: (501)666-8367
E-mail: info@americanamputee.org
URL: http://www.americanamputee.org
Contact: Catherine J. Walden LSW, Exec. Dir.
Founded: 1975. **Membership Dues:** individual, $25 (annual) ● professional, $150 (annual) ● professional plus link, $250 (annual). **Staff:** 5. **Budget:** $200,000. **Local Groups:** 1. **National Groups:** 8. **Description:** Provides information and referral service to new amputees and their families to aid them in their adjustment to amputation. Sponsors programs and resources on state-of-the-art prosthetics, coalition building, self-help, life care planning services to those with catastrophic injury, and aid in obtaining prosthetics for amputees who qualify. **Libraries:** Type: reference. **Holdings:** audiovisuals, books, periodicals. **Subjects:** amputation, spinal injury, medical, abledata, product information. **Computer Services:** database, life care planning, product research. **Committees:** Direct Aid. **Publications:** *Active Living*, quarterly. Magazine ● *National Resource Directory*, biennial. Features national listings of organizations and agencies of interest to individuals with disabilities. **Price:** $10.00. **Advertising:** accepted ● Books. Provides information on self-help methods. ● Newsletter.

11657 ■ American Association of People with Disabilities (AAPD)

1629 K St. NW, Ste.503
Washington, DC 20006
Ph: (202)457-0046
Free: (800)840-8844
Fax: (202)457-0473
E-mail: aapd@aol.com
URL: http://www.aapd-dc.org
Contact: Helena Berger, COO
Founded: 1995. **Members:** 28,000. **Membership Dues:** individual, $15 (annual). **Staff:** 10. **Budget:** $1,500,000. **Description:** Promotes economic and political empowerment of persons with disabilities; educating businesses and general public about disability issues. **Awards:** Paul G. Heane/AAPD Leadership Awards. **Frequency:** annual. **Type:** monetary. **Recipient:** for leadership achievements that show a positive impact on the community of people with disabilities or within their area of disability interest. **Publications:** *AAPD News*, quarterly. Newsletter. Also available in Braille. **Price:** included in membership dues. **Circulation:** 15,000. **Alternate Formats:** diskette; online ● Annual Report, annual. Alternate Formats: online. **Conventions/Meetings:** annual Leadership Gala - convention, leadership awards ceremony.

11658 ■ American Disability Association (ADA)

2201 Sixth Ave. S
Birmingham, AL 35233
Ph: (205)328-9090

Fax: (205)251-7417
Contact: Bill Freeman, Pres.
Founded: 1991. **Members:** 60,000. **Staff:** 3. **Budget:** $125,000. **Regional Groups:** 20. **State Groups:** 40. **Description:** Serves as a support group for individuals with disabilities. Provides exchange of information on disability issues. Makes available children's services, educational and research programs, and charitable services. **Libraries:** Type: reference. **Subjects:** spinal injury, cerebral palsy, welfare, medicine, cancer, AIDS, civil rights, politics, independent living, law. **Publications:** *Journal of the American Disability Association*, monthly. **Price:** free. **Circulation:** 45,000. **Advertising:** accepted. Alternate Formats: online. **Conventions/Meetings:** annual congress (exhibits).

11659 ■ American Society of Handicapped Physicians (ASHP)

Address Unknown since 2007
Founded: 1981. **Members:** 1,200. **Description:** Handicapped physicians and others concerned with the problems faced by handicapped physicians. Acts as a forum to address the needs of physically disabled physicians. Works against discrimination of the handicapped and serves as a support group and legal and career counselor. Disseminates information about resources for handicapped physicians. Plans to offer rehabilitation services. Maintains speakers' bureau and placement service; compiles statistics; offers specialized education. Founded by the late Spencer B. Lewis, M.D. and Terry Winkler, M.D. **Convention/Meeting:** none. **Awards:** Type: recognition. **Committees:** Ad Hoc for AMA Liaison; Ad Hoc for Insurance; Fund Raising; Legal and Legislative; Public Relations and Newsletter; Resource and Rehabilitation. **Publications:** *American Society of Handicapped Physicians—SYNAPSE*, quarterly. Includes book reviews and research updates. **Price:** free. **Circulation:** 1,000 ● Directory, annual.

11660 ■ Americans With Disabilities Act (ADA)

9841 SW 100 Ave.
Miami, FL 33176
Ph: (305)271-0012 (305)271-0011
Fax: (305)273-1221
E-mail: ergobob@consultant.com
URL: http://www.rehabserv.com
Contact: Robert L. Lessne PhD, Contact
Founded: 1990. **Members:** 100. **Staff:** 2. **Budget:** $25,000. **Description:** Individuals and organizations united to ensure compliance with the Americans With Disabilities Act of 1992. Compiles statistics; sponsors competitions; maintains Speaker's Bureau; and operates a museum with cones for visually impaired individuals. **Libraries:** Type: reference. **Holdings:** audio recordings, books, clippings, monographs, periodicals, video recordings. **Publications:** *ADA Compliance Kit*. Booklet. Alternate Formats: online ● *ADA Compliance Sourcebook*. **Conventions/Meetings:** annual seminar.

11661 ■ Amputees in Motion, International (AIM)

Address Unknown since 2006
Founded: 1973. **Members:** 80. **Membership Dues:** individual, $10 (annual) ● family, $15 (annual) ● lifetime, $200. **Budget:** $3,500. **Languages:** English, Spanish. **Local. Description:** Amputees and their families. Helps amputees of any age reestablish an active and satisfying life through visitation program and civic, social, and recreational participation. Attempts to prove that losing a limb doesn't mean losing the ability to participate in physical activities. Works with physicians, physical therapists, prosthetists, and others as part of the amputee rehabilitation team. Makes available sporting and social activities. Provides speakers who talk before professional and civic organizations regarding amputees. **Libraries:** Type: open to the public. **Subjects:** amputee current news/affairs. **Awards:** Person of the Year. **Frequency:** annual. **Type:** recognition. **Recipient:** committee. **Formerly:** (2000) Amputees in Motion. **Publications:** *Amputees in Motion Newsletter*, 3/year. Includes membership meeting information. **Price:**

free. **Advertising:** accepted. **Conventions/Meetings:** monthly general assembly, for members, their families and friends and health care professionals - most months; **Avg. Attendance:** 15.

11662 ■ Assistance Dogs of America, Inc. (ADAI)
8806 State Rte. 64
Swanton, OH 43558
Ph: (419)825-3622
Fax: (419)825-3710
E-mail: info@adai.org
URL: http://www.adai.org
Contact: Chris Diefenthaler, Exec. Dir.
Founded: 1984. **Members:** 4,500. **Staff:** 5. **Budget:** $250,000. **Description:** Promotes increased independence for people with disabilities. Locates, trains, and places highly skilled service and therapy dogs with disabled adults and children. **Affiliated With:** Assistance Dogs International; Ohio Association of Nonprofit Organizations; Swanton Chamber of Commerce. **Formerly:** (1989) Dogs for the Handicapped, Inc. **Publications:** *Hearts and Harness*, 3/year. Newsletter. Features stories about graduates, volunteers, supporters, staff, special events and community activities. **Conventions/Meetings:** annual meeting.

11663 ■ Assistance Dogs International (ADI)
PO Box 5174
Santa Rosa, CA 95402
Ph: (707)571-0427
E-mail: info@adionline.org
URL: http://www.adionline.org
Contact: Suzi Hall, Coor.
Founded: 1987. **Members:** 79. **Membership Dues:** full, $50 (annual) ● provisional, $250 (annual). **Multinational. Description:** Represents not-for-profit organizations that train and place Assistance Dogs. Aims to improve the areas of training, placement, and utilization of Assistance Dogs, as well as staff and volunteer education. Members meet annually to share ideas, attend seminars and conduct business regarding such things as educating the public about Assistance Dogs, and the legal rights of people with disabilities partnered with Assistance Dogs, setting standards and establishing guidelines and ethics for the training of these dogs, and improving the utilization and bonding of each team. **Publications:** *Legal Rights of Guide Dogs, Hearing Dogs, and Service Dogs.* Book. Contains information regarding access by disabled individuals with their Assistance Dogs. **Price:** $6.00 ● Book. **Price:** $6.00. **Conventions/Meetings:** annual conference.

11664 ■ Association of Rehabilitation Programs in Computer Technology (ARPCT)
Western Michigan Univ.
Educational Stud. Off.
3421 Sangren Hall
Kalamazoo, MI 49008
Ph: (269)387-2053
Fax: (269)387-3696
E-mail: janisk@cprf.org
URL: http://www.arpct.org
Contact: Janis Krohe, Pres.
Founded: 1978. **Members:** 70. **Membership Dues:** individual, $325 (annual) ● associate, $50 (annual). **Description:** Rehabilitation training programs; business and community leaders and rehabilitation trainers are associate members. Dedicated to providing data processing as a career path for handicapped persons. Purposes are to: promote communications among the programs designed to train and place handicapped persons in the data processing field; foster and provide assistance for new projects and programs; establish standards and procedures for programs to ensure the maximum benefit for the disabled persons served. Promotes the involvement of the education and research communities. Offers professional training; compiles statistics; sponsors competitions. **Awards:** Employer Award. **Type:** recognition ● National Leadership Award. **Type:** recognition ● Outstanding Students Award. **Type:** recognition ● Outstanding Trainer Award. **Type:** recognition. **Committees:** Communications; New

Programs. **Formerly:** (1996) Association of Rehabilitation Programs in Data Processing. **Publications:** *Handbook for Implementing New Projects* ● *Viewpoint*, quarterly. Newsletter ● Membership Directory, annual. **Conventions/Meetings:** annual conference - always spring ● annual Leader Conference - always fall.

11665 ■ Canine Assistants
3160 Francis Rd.
Alpharetta, GA 30004
Ph: (770)664-7178
Free: (800)771-7221
Fax: (770)664-7820
E-mail: info@canineassistants.org
URL: http://www.canineassistants.org
Contact: Jennifer Arnold, Exec. Dir./Founder
Founded: 1991. **Description:** Promotes the benefits of service dogs for people with disabilities. Trains and provides service dogs for children and adults with physical disabilities and special needs.

11666 ■ Canine Companions for Independence (CCI)
PO Box 446
Santa Rosa, CA 95402-0446
Ph: (707)577-1700
Free: (800)572-2275
E-mail: info@caninecompanions.org
URL: http://www.caninecompanions.org
Contact: Ted Rogahn, Pres.
Founded: 1975. **Staff:** 130. **Budget:** $9,000,000. **Regional Groups:** 5. **State Groups:** 3. **Description:** Provides to people with disabilities, specially-bred and trained dogs enabling them to lead more personally fulfilling and socially productive lives. Believes that human attendant care is reduced with the aid these dogs provide. Provides four types of Canine Companions: Hearing Dogs trained to alert the hearing-impaired to sounds such as the doorbell, smoke alarm, or a baby's cry; skilled companion dogs used for children and adults with disabilities, people with developmental disabilities, or anywhere the supervision of a third party is required; Service Dogs trained to provide physical assistance, such as retrieving dropped objects, operating elevator buttons and light switches, and pulling wheelchairs and Facility dogs placed with professionals in facilities where interaction with a dog will be beneficial to the mental or physical health of those in their care. Works to expand services to aid more persons with disabilities. Sponsors puppy raising programs where puppies are placed and raised in volunteer homes for 13 months; advanced training takes about 6-8 months to master over 60 required working commands. Conducts ongoing research in canine breeding, training, and nutrition. **Telecommunication Services:** TDD, (707)577-1756. **Publications:** *Canine Companion Courier*, quarterly. Newsletter. **Price:** free. **Circulation:** 45,000. **Alternate Formats:** online ● Annual Report. **Alternate Formats:** online ● Brochures ● Manuals.

11667 ■ Canines for Disabled Kids (CDK)
299 Redemption Rock Trail S
Princeton, MA 01541
Ph: (978)422-5299
Free: (888)KID-DOGS
Fax: (978)422-3255
E-mail: info@caninesforkids.org
URL: http://www.caninesforkids.org
Founded: 1998. **Description:** Enhances the education and independence of children with disabilities across the USA. Sponsors and trains dogs to assist disabled children with everyday tasks. Helps educate the public about assistance dogs. **Telecommunication Services:** TDD, (978)422-9064.

11668 ■ Center on Human Policy (CHP)
Syracuse Univ.
805 S Crouse Ave.
Syracuse, NY 13244-2280
Ph: (315)443-3851
Free: (800)894-0826
Fax: (315)443-4338

E-mail: thechp@syr.edu
URL: http://thechp.syr.edu
Contact: Steven Taylor PhD, Dir.
Founded: 1971. **Staff:** 14. **Description:** Consumers and students; parents of persons with disabilities; human services administrators and staff members; professionals in psychology, special education, rehabilitation, sociology, law, social work, and planning. Promotes the inclusion of persons with severe disabilities into the mainstream of society. Disseminates information to families, human services professionals, and others on laws, regulations, and programs affecting children and adults with disabilities, focusing on those with developmental disabilities. Provides speakers to professional gatherings and parents' groups. Documents outstanding community living and educational programs and assists in creating exemplary services. Evaluates public policies to determine their impact on people with disabilities. Participates in public forums, legislative hearings, national conventions, and other community events involving issues relating to people with disabilities. Operates National Resource Center on Supported Living and Choice for people with developmental disabilities. Offers technical assistance, consultation, and training on service system issues to local, regional, state, and national organizations and agencies. Conducts research related to community inclusion. **Telecommunication Services:** TDD, (315)443-4355.

11669 ■ Center for Workers with Disabilities (CWD)
810 1st St. NE, Ste.500
Washington, DC 20002
Ph: (202)682-0100
Fax: (202)204-0071
E-mail: asuchman@aphsa.org
URL: http://cwd.aphsa.org
Contact: Alexandra Suchman, Policy Analyst
Founded: 2001. **Description:** Aids participating states to implement provisions of "Ticket to Work and Work Incentives Improvement Act of 1999". **Publications:** *Working for Tomorrow*, monthly. Newsletter. Alternate Formats: online ● Report, periodic. **Conventions/Meetings:** annual meeting and conference, a joint conference which will include over 150 states, federal and private sector disability experts - 2007 Nov. 12-14, Washington, DC.

11670 ■ Challenged Conquistadors
c/o Shaun Best, Pres./Founder
1110 Pine Cir.
Smackover, AR 71762
Ph: (870)725-3612
E-mail: shaun_best_2000@yahoo.com
URL: http://www.SpeakersQuest.com/speakers/Best.htm
Contact: Shaun Best, Pres./Founder
Founded: 1993. **Members:** 10,000. **Staff:** 1. **Budget:** $500. **Local Groups:** 1. **Description:** Works to increase self preservation, reduce dependency, and eradicate negative stereotypes, myths, and stigmas about persons with brain injuries. Targets active, positive, challenged role models to show others that success is obtainable. Reinforces individual empowerment and capabilities to reveal the talents inherent in all challenged individuals and reap rewards as opposed to the "stagnation and destruction that many social programs have achieved." Offers educational and research programs. **Libraries: Type:** reference. **Subjects:** traumatic brain injuries.

11671 ■ Christian Council on Persons with Disabilities (CCPD)
4700 Millenia Blvd., Ste.175
Orlando, FL 32839
Ph: (407)210-3917
Fax: (407)210-3901
E-mail: ccpd@ccpd.org
URL: http://www.ccpd.org
Contact: Jim Hukill, Interim Exec.Dir.
Founded: 1989. **Membership Dues:** individual, $50 (annual) ● student, $25 (annual) ● church/non-profit organization, $100 (annual) ● contributor, $250 (annual) ● benefactor, $500 (annual) ● corporate,

$1,000 (annual). **Multinational. Description:** Christian disability advocacy organization promoting the spiritual well-being of people with physical, mental or emotional disabilities. **Awards:** Aaron Award. **Frequency:** annual. **Type:** recognition. **Recipient:** to an individual who "holds up the arms" of those who are in the forefront of disability ministry ● Camp Recognition. **Frequency:** annual. **Type:** recognition. **Recipient:** for Christian Camping programs that seek to serve the needs of adults and/or children with disabilities ● Caring Church. **Frequency:** annual. **Type:** recognition. **Recipient:** for churches that are sensitive to the needs of people with disabilities ● Vision Award. **Frequency:** annual. **Type:** recognition. **Recipient:** to an individual who saw a need in the disability ministry community. **Telecommunication Services:** information service, networking message board. **Affiliated With:** National Association of Evangelicals. **Publications:** *CCPD News*, quarterly. Newsletter. Contains information in the field of Christian disability ministry and developments in the U.S. and worldwide. Available in Braille and large print. **Price:** included in membership dues. Alternate Formats: online. **Conventions/Meetings:** annual conference (exhibits) - April.

11672 ■ Christian Overcomers (CO)
PO Box 2007
Garfield, NJ 07026
Ph: (973)253-2343
Fax: (973)253-2351
E-mail: overcomers2007@optonline.net
URL: http://www.christian-overcomers.org
Contact: Debbie Neilley, Program Dir.

Founded: 1977. **Staff:** 3. **Description:** Individuals with physical disabilities and volunteers. Provides holistic physical and spiritual guidance to help members live with their disabilities. Sponsors camp program that provides Bible study, worship, recreational and social activities, and encourages "commitment to Jesus Christ and each other." Functions as a resource for local groups that wish to conduct activities including athletic events, outings, dinners, and other socially oriented educational programs for physically disabled individuals. Maintains Speaker's Bureau. Provides volunteer training. **Publications:** *Library Catalog*, annual ● *The Overcomer*, quarterly. Newsletter ● Brochure. **Conventions/Meetings:** annual banquet.

11673 ■ Clearinghouse on Disability Information (CDI)
Off. of Special Educ. and Rehabilitative Services
Commun. and Media Support Services
U.S. U.S. Department of of Educ.
500 12th St. SW, Rm. 5133
Washington, DC 20202-2550
Ph: (202)245-7307 (202)205-5637
Free: (800)437-0833
Fax: (202)245-7636
URL: http://www.ed.gov/about/offices/list/osers/codi.html
Contact: Carolyn Corlett, Technical Asst.

Founded: 1973. **Staff:** 4. **Description:** Provides information to people with disabilities, or anyone requesting information, by doing research and providing documents in response to inquiries. Information provided includes areas of federal funding for disability-related programs. Clearinghouse staff is trained to refer requests to other sources of disability related information, if necessary. **Formerly:** (1989) Clearinghouse on the Handicapped. **Publications:** *Pocket Guide to Federal Help for Individuals With Disabilities*. Booklet.

11674 ■ Council of Citizens With Low Vision International (CCLVI)
c/o American Council of the Blind
1155 15th St. NW, Ste.1004
Washington, DC 20005
Ph: (703)642-1909 (703)578-6513
Free: (800)733-2258
Fax: (703)671-9053

E-mail: pbeattie@nib.org
URL: http://www.cclvi.org
Contact: Bernice Kandarian, Pres.

Founded: 1979. **Members:** 2,000. **Membership Dues:** individual, $15 (annual) ● agency, $25 (annual) ● life, $150. **Budget:** $12,000. **State Groups:** 11. **Description:** Partially sighted and low-vision individuals, their families, and professional workers. Provides a vehicle through which partially sighted people may voice their needs, preferences, and interests. Promotes the concept that partially sighted and low-vision individuals are not blind and that they have the right to maximize the use of residual vision through the use of any visual aid, service, or technology. Keeps abreast of all developments benefiting partially sighted persons. Promotes educational, engineering, medical, rehabilitative, scientific, and social research that facilitates the lives of individuals with residual vision. Supports the development of pre-service professional training programs for the establishment and expansion of multidisciplinary low-vision services. Strives to educate the public about the existence, capabilities, and needs of such individuals. Establishes outreach programs to insure access to available services for partially sighted persons. Maintains speakers' bureau. **Awards:** Carl Foley Scholarship. **Frequency:** annual. **Type:** scholarship ● Telesensory Scholarship. **Frequency:** annual. **Type:** scholarship. **Committees:** Scholarship. **Projects:** Insight. **Affiliated With:** American Council of the Blind. **Formerly:** (2004) Council of Citizens With Low Vision. **Publications:** *Vision Access*, quarterly. Journal. Reports on research and resources. Available on audiocassette and in large print. **Price:** included in membership dues. **Circulation:** 2,000. Alternate Formats: online; diskette. **Conventions/Meetings:** annual conference (exhibits) - always July.

11675 ■ Council for Disability Rights (CDR)
30 E Adams, Ste.1130
Chicago, IL 60603
Ph: (312)444-9484
Fax: (312)444-1977
E-mail: webmaven@disabilityrights.org
URL: http://www.disabilityrights.org
Contact: Jo Holzer, Exec. Dir.

Founded: 1981. **Description:** Advances the rights of people with disabilities. Promotes public policy and legislation and public awareness through education. Provides information and referral services. **Awards:** Gargoyle Awards. **Frequency:** annual. **Type:** recognition. **Recipient:** for individual acts of advocacy which inspire other people with disabilities to speak up and be heard. **Computer Services:** Information services. **Telecommunication Services:** TDD, (312)444-1967. **Publications:** *Inclusion: A Special Education Dilemma*. Video. Presents a roundtable discussion on the issue of bringing children with disabilities into general education classrooms. **Price:** $33.50 includes shipping cost ● Annual Report, annual. Alternate Formats: online.

11676 ■ DateAble
15520 Bald Eagle School Rd.
Brandywine, MD 20613
Ph: (301)888-1177 (301)657-3283
Fax: (301)657-4327
E-mail: robert@dateable.org
URL: http://www.dateable.org
Contact: Robert Watson, Exec. Dir.

Founded: 1987. **Members:** 600. **Membership Dues:** individual, $125 (annual). **Staff:** 3. **Budget:** $50,000. **Local Groups:** 1. **Description:** Brings together those with disabilities for love and friendship. Provides individual counseling and support network. **Convention/Meeting:** none. **Awards:** Date Able Image Award. **Frequency:** annual. **Type:** recognition. **Recipient:** for positive contribution to the image of people with disabilities. **Computer Services:** database, members' profiles. **Formerly:** Dateable International; (1994) Handicap Introductions; (1997) DateAble/HI. **Publications:** *DateLine*, annual. Newsletter. **Price:** free. **Circulation:** 1,500 ● *News, Views and the Calendar Too!*, semiannual. Newsletter. Contains

information on upcoming events, essays and articles by members, and a photo gallery of recent events.

11677 ■ Disability Central
4744 Adenmoor Ave.
Lakewood, CA 90713-2302
E-mail: docstein@disabilitycentral.com
Description: People with disabilities. Promote disability awareness. Provide information and resources.

11678 ■ Disability Resources
4 Glatter Ln.
Centereach, NY 11720-1032
Ph: (631)585-0290
Fax: (631)585-0290
E-mail: info@disabilityresources.org
URL: http://www.disabilityresources.org
Contact: Avery Klauber, Exec. Dir.

Founded: 1993. **Staff:** 2. **Budget:** $25,000. **Description:** Works to promote and improve awareness, availability and accessibility of information to help people with disabilities to live independently. Advises libraries, independent living centers, rehabilitation professionals, hospitals, health and social service organizations, and consumers of resources and publications concerning independent living. **Convention/Meeting:** none. **Libraries:** Type: reference. **Holdings:** articles, audiovisuals, books, clippings, periodicals. **Subjects:** nonmedical disabilities. **Computer Services:** database. **Publications:** *An Enabling Collection for People with Disabilities*. Articles. **Price:** $2.00 in U.S.; $3.00 outside U.S. ● *Disability Information at Your Fingertips, 3rd Edition*. Book. **Price:** $10.00 ● *Disability Resources Monthly*. Newsletter. Reports on and reviews resources for independent living. **Price:** $33.00/year in U.S.; $43.00/year outside U.S. ISSN: 1070-7220. Alternate Formats: magnetic tape. Also Cited As: *DRM* ● *Living Well with a Disability: How Libraries Can Help*. Articles. **Price:** $2.00 in U.S.; $3.00 outside U.S. ● *Toy Story - How to Select and Buy Adaptive Toys*. Articles. **Price:** $2.00 in U.S.; $3.00 outside U.S.

11679 ■ Disability Rights Center (DRC)
PO Box 2007
Augusta, ME 04338-2007
Ph: (207)626-2774
Free: (800)452-1948
Fax: (207)621-1419
E-mail: advocate@drcme.org
URL: http://www.drcme.org
Contact: Kim Moody, Exec. Dir.

Founded: 1976. **Staff:** 3. **Description:** Represents public interest research group committed on educating society about the disability rights movement. Aims to inform the public, political activists, consumer activists, advocates, and students on the disability movement. Seeks to involve as many disabled citizens as possible in processes that directly affect their lives, to work closely with other disability-related, consumer-based advocacy groups, and to educate the public in the legitimate demands and needs of the disabled. Compiles statistics. **Publications:** *Advance Health Care Directives*. Manual. **Price:** $4.00. Alternate Formats: online ● *DRC News*. Newsletter. Alternate Formats: online ● *Involuntary Hospitalization Laws*. Manual. **Price:** $2.65. Alternate Formats: online ● *Parent Advocate Handbook*. Alternate Formats: online ● *Your Rights Under the AMHI Consent Decree*. Pamphlet. Alternate Formats: online.

11680 ■ Disability Rights Education and Defense Fund (DREDF)
2212 6th St.
Berkeley, CA 94710
Ph: (510)644-2555
Free: (800)348-4232
Fax: (510)841-8645
E-mail: info@dredf.org
URL: http://www.dredf.org
Contact: Susan Henderson, Managing Dir.

Founded: 1979. **Staff:** 19. **Description:** Believes in the principle that people with disabilities have the right to lead full and integrated lives, with the freedom of choice and dignity. Seeks to educate the public and policymakers in order to further the civil rights and liberties of people with disabilities. Conducts educational activities such as: training state and local government officials, attorneys, and judges on disability rights compliance requirements such as the Americans with Disabilities Act; prepares materials pertaining to the right of children with disabilities to a free and appropriate public education. Houses the Disability Rights Clinical Legal Education Program which educates law students about disability rights laws and represents people with disabilities who have experienced unlawful discrimination. Provides technical assistance. **Convention/Meeting:** none. **Computer Services:** Mailing lists. **Telecommunication Services:** TDD, (510)644-2626. **Publications:** *Disability Rights News*, quarterly ● *DREDF News*, periodic. Newsletter. Alternate Formats: online ● *Explanation of the Contents of the ADA*. Book. **Price:** $118.00 ● Manuals.

11681 ■ Disabled and Alone/Life Services for the Handicapped
61 Broadway, Ste.510
New York, NY 10006
Ph: (212)532-6740
Free: (800)995-0066
Fax: (212)532-3588
E-mail: info@disabledandalone.org
URL: http://www.disabledandalone.org
Contact: Roslyn Brilliant, Exec. Dir.
Founded: 1988. **Members:** 40. **Membership Dues:** family (with a disabled member), $3,000. **Staff:** 5. **Budget:** $500,000. **Regional Groups:** 1. **Description:** Helps families plan for the time when they will not be able to care for their disabled children. Functions as quasi/surrogate parents for disabled people whose families have left assets for their care. Conducts educational programs on lifetime planning for families with a disabled member. Maintains Speaker's Bureau. **Libraries: Type:** reference. **Holdings:** 50; articles, books, clippings. **Subjects:** lifetime care (future care) planning for a person with a disability. **Awards:** Leadership Award. **Frequency:** annual. **Type:** recognition. **Recipient:** for contributions that improve the lives of persons with disabilities. **Formerly:** (2000) Life Services for the Handicapped. **Publications:** *How to be a Friend to the Handicapped*. Book. **Price:** $50.00 for a prepaid shipment of 10 books; $6.95 for 1 book including postage ● *Lifelines*, 3/year. Newsletter. Provides information about "lifetime care" (future care) planning for a person with a disability. **Price:** free. **Circulation:** 5,000 ● Also publishes brochures, prospectus, articles about "lifetime care" (future care) planning for a person with a disability. **Conventions/Meetings:** periodic You Can't Replace a Mother, But. - workshop, families learn how to create a "lifetime care" (future care) plan for a person with a disability.

11682 ■ Disabled Womyn's Educational Project
PO Box 8773
Madison, WI 53708-8773
Ph: (608)256-8883
Fax: (608)256-8883
E-mail: catherine-odette@juno.com
Contact: Catherine Odette, Exec. Off.
Founded: 1988. **Staff:** 6. **Description:** Lesbians with disabilities. Promotes members' interests. Supports legislation sensitive to members' needs. Maintains speakers' bureau. **Convention/Meeting:** none. **Libraries: Type:** reference. **Holdings:** artwork, books, business records, clippings, periodicals. **Computer Services:** Mailing lists. **Committees:** Political Action. **Publications:** *Building Community Through Access* ● *Dykes, Disability, and Stuff*, quarterly. Newsletter. Available in the format of audiocassette, Braille, DOS diskette, large print, modem transfer, audio tape. **Price:** $25.00/year. **Circulation:** 750. **Advertising:** accepted. Alternate Formats: diskette ● *The Time for Access is Now*.

11683 ■ Dream Catchers, USA
c/o Nancy J. Copeland, Exec. Pres.
PO Box 701
Killen, AL 35645
Ph: (256)272-0286 (315)252-5464
Fax: (256)272-0286
E-mail: dreamcatchermail@aol.com
URL: http://www.dreamcatchersusa.org
Contact: Nancy J. Copeland, Exec. Pres.
Founded: 1999. **Members:** 200. **Budget:** $10,000. **Regional Groups:** 5. **State Groups:** 35. **Description:** Works to advance independence, productivity and confidence of those with disabilities and the terminally ill through assisted fishing trips, assisted hunting trips, shooting competitions, demonstrations, and other outdoor adventures. **Libraries: Type:** by appointment only; lending; reference. **Holdings:** 2; articles, audiovisuals, business records, clippings, photographs, video recordings. **Subjects:** fiscal year business reports. **Computer Services:** Information services, application forms, fact sheets, general information and resource list of outdoor links and web sites.

11684 ■ Easter Seals
230 W Monroe St., Ste.1800
Chicago, IL 60606
Ph: (312)726-6200
Free: (800)221-6827
Fax: (312)726-1494
E-mail: info@easterseals.com
URL: http://www.easterseals.com
Contact: James E. Williams Jr., Pres./CEO
Founded: 1919. **Members:** 90. **Staff:** 100. **Budget:** $700,000,000. **State Groups:** 52. **National Groups:** 2. **Languages:** English, Spanish. **Description:** Provides services for children and adults with disabilities or special needs, and supports their families. Provides services such as: medical rehabilitation, early intervention, physical therapy, occupational therapy, speech and hearing therapy, job training and employment, inclusive childcare, adult day services, camping and recreation. **Awards: Type:** recognition. **Telecommunication Services:** TDD, (312)726-4258. **Committees:** Office of Public Affairs; Volunteers. **Councils:** National Advisory; Professional Advisory. **Formerly:** (1998) National Easter Seal Society. **Publications:** *Publications*. Catalog. **Conventions/Meetings:** annual meeting - always November.

11685 ■ Extensions for Independence (EI)
555 Saturn Blvd., No. B-368
San Diego, CA 92154
Ph: (619)423-7709
Free: (866)632-7149
Fax: (619)423-7709
E-mail: info@mouthstick.net
URL: http://www.mouthstick.net
Contact: Arthur Heyer, Pres.
Founded: 1976. **Staff:** 10. **For-Profit. Description:** Develops, manufactures, and markets vocational equipment for the physically handicapped. Promotes improvements in design, materials, production, and quality of products while maintaining affordable prices. Products include the Multi-Tip Telescoping H-A Modular Mouthstick that enables individuals to talk and swallow while drawing, turning pages, loading and unloading computer software, and performing other tasks. **Conventions/Meetings:** annual Exposition - meeting.

11686 ■ Foundation for Science and Disability (FSD)
c/o Dr. E.C. Keller, Jr., Treas./Newsletter Ed.
West Virginia Univ.
Biology Dept.
Morgantown, WV 26506-6057
Ph: (304)293-5201
E-mail: ekeller@wvu.edu
URL: http://www.as.wvu.edu/~scidis/organize/fsd.html
Contact: Dr. E.C. Keller Jr., Treas./Newsletter Ed.
Founded: 1975. **Members:** 206. **Membership Dues:** non-student, $25 (annual) ● student, $5 (annual) ● sustaining, $100 (annual). **Budget:** $2,000. **Description:** Disabled scientists and interested individuals. Offers consultation and advice concerning problems faced by persons with disabilities in scientific fields. **Libraries: Type:** reference. **Holdings:** 28; periodicals. **Subjects:** disability, science. **Awards:** Disabled Graduate Students in Science. **Frequency:** annual.

Type: grant. **Recipient:** for U.S. graduate students with disabilities. **Affiliated With:** American Association for the Advancement of Science. **Formerly:** (1993) Foundation for Science and the Handicapped. **Publications:** *The Abled Disabled in Science*, periodic. Book ● *FSD News*, semiannual. Newsletter. **Price:** available to members only. **Circulation:** 210. Alternate Formats: online. **Conventions/Meetings:** annual convention, held in conjunction with AAAS (exhibits) - usually late February.

11687 ■ Free Wheelchair Mission (FWM)
9341 Irvine Blvd.
Irvine, CA 92618
Ph: (949)273-8470
Free: (800)733-0858
Fax: (949)273-8471
E-mail: involve@freewheelchairmission.org
URL: http://www.freewheelchairmission.org
Contact: Don Schoendorfer PhD, Founder/Pres.
Founded: 2001. **Multinational. Description:** Aims to improve the quality of life for people with physical disabilities. Offers the least expensive wheelchair capable of satisfying the needs of poor people with physical immobility. Provides free wheelchairs to the physically disabled poor in developing countries. **Publications:** *Free Wheeling*, quarterly. Newsletter. Alternate Formats: online ● Annual Report, annual. Alternate Formats: online ● Articles. Alternate Formats: online.

11688 ■ Glenkirk
3504 Commercial Ave.
Northbrook, IL 60062
Ph: (847)272-5111
Fax: (847)272-7350
E-mail: info@glenkirk.org
URL: http://www.glenkirk.org
Contact: Alan G. Spector, Pres./CEO
Founded: 1954. **Description:** Advocacy for, and support and service to empower individuals with developmental disabilities in order for them to participate fully in all areas of life, including day and residential services.

11689 ■ Goodwill Industries International (GII)
15810 Indianola Dr.
Rockville, MD 20855
Ph: (301)530-6500
Free: (800)741-0186
E-mail: contactus@goodwill.org
URL: http://www.goodwill.org
Contact: George W. Kessinger, Pres./CEO
Founded: 1902. **Members:** 207. **Staff:** 84. **Budget:** $14,300,000. **Regional Groups:** 19. **Local Groups:** 173. **Languages:** English, French, Spanish. **Multinational. Description:** Federation of Goodwill Industries organizations across North America and the world concerned primarily with providing employment, training, evaluation, counseling, placement, job training, and other vocational rehabilitation services and opportunities for individual growth for people with disabilities and other special needs. Collects donated goods and sell them in Goodwill retail stores as a means of providing employment and generating income. Conducts seminars and training programs; compiles statistics. **Awards: Frequency:** annual. **Type:** recognition. **Telecommunication Services:** TDD, (301)530-9759. **Committees:** Board Development; Finance and Administrative Services; Public Policy; Research and Resource Development; Strategic Issues/Planning. **Councils:** Conference of Executives; Goodwill Industries Volunteer Services; Membership Standards and Services. **Departments:** Executive (Legal Services & Goodwill Global, Inc.); Marketing and Communications; Membership and Enterprise Development; Membership Support Services; Operations (HR, Finance, Information Technology, Building Services). **Formerly:** (1910) Morgan Memorial and Cooperative Industries and Stores; (1946) National Association of Goodwill Industries; (1994) Goodwill Industries of America. **Publications:** *Corporate Brochure*, annual ● *Internal Membership Directory*, annual ● *Working!*, quarterly. Magazine ● Annual Report. **Circulation:** 7,000 ● Also publishes

promotional materials. **Conventions/Meetings:** annual assembly (exhibits) - always June ● board meeting - 3/year ● annual conference - always February.

11690 ■ Goodwill Industries Volunteer Services (GIVS)

c/o Goodwill Industries International Inc.
15810 Indianola Dr.
Rockville, MD 20855
Free: (800)741-0186
E-mail: contactus@goodwill.org
URL: http://www.goodwill.org
Contact: George W. Kessinger, Pres./CEO

Founded: 1933. **Members:** 3,000. **Local Groups:** 71. **Description:** Persons interested in volunteer work in programs serving people with disabilities or other barriers to employment. Supports the efforts of national and local Goodwill Industries International, Inc., programs through volunteer services. Provides programs that vary according to local needs and includes such activities as direct program services, fundraising, and public relations. **Committees:** Ideas and Exchange. **Formerly:** National Auxiliary of Goodwill Industries; National Women's Auxiliary to the Goodwill Industries. **Publications:** *Giving*, quarterly. Directory ● *Goodwill Volunteer Services Directory*, annual ● *Goodwill Volunteer Services Handbook*, annual ● Annual Report, annual. **Conventions/Meetings:** annual convention, held in conjunction with GII delegate assembly (exhibits).

11691 ■ Indoor Sports Club (ISC)

16 Liberty St.
Larkspur, CA 94939
Ph: (415)924-3549
Fax: (415)927-9556
E-mail: russab@earthlink.net
URL: http://www.localcommunities.org/servlet/lc_
  ProcServ/DBPAGE=page&GID=
  01002011550942360442522615
Contact: Russ Bohlke, Exec. Sec.

Founded: 1930. **Members:** 300. **Membership Dues:** $12 (annual). **Regional Groups:** 6. **Local Groups:** 15. **Description:** Social, benevolent, educational, and rehabilitative organization for persons with physical disabilities. Provides entertainment and amusement for disabled persons and shut-ins; seeks aid for needy disabled persons; provides opportunities for active participation in civic affairs; and promotes a better understanding and acceptance of the seriously disabled by the able-bodied. **Awards:** Certificate of Appreciations. **Type:** recognition. **Recipient:** for service to physically disabled persons. **Committees:** Architectural Design; Legislative Research; Social Welfare. **Publications:** *National Hookup*, bimonthly. Newsletter. **Price:** $6.50/year. **Circulation:** 350. **Conventions/Meetings:** annual National Indoor Sports Convention - always August.

11692 ■ Inspiration Ministries (IM)

PO Box 948
Corner State Rd. 67 and County F
Walworth, WI 53184
Ph: (262)275-6131
Fax: (262)275-3355
E-mail: info@inspirationministries.org
URL: http://www.inspirationministries.org
Contact: Tim Schnake, VP of Resident Services

Founded: 1948. **Members:** 90. **Description:** Seeks to provide fully accessible, permanent residence with attendant care in room and board facility for physically disabled adults. Conducts summer camping program for disabled persons and retreat opportunities for groups. **Councils:** Resident. **Formerly:** (2001) Christian League for the Handicapped. **Publications:** *Seasons*, quarterly. Newsletter. **Price:** free. **Conventions/Meetings:** monthly meeting, chapter meetings in various cities.

11693 ■ International Association of Laryngectomees (IAL)

c/o Gary L. Miner, Sr., Pres.
1203 Wolf Swamp Rd.
Jacksonville, NC 28546
Ph: (910)340-4519

E-mail: ialhq@larynxlink.com
URL: http://www.larynxlink.com
Contact: Gary L. Miner Sr., Pres.

Founded: 1952. **Members:** 250. **Staff:** 1. **Regional Groups:** 200. **Description:** Persons who have had their larynx removed; physicians, surgeons, speech therapists, rehabilitation experts, nurses, and others interested in the rehabilitation of laryngectomees. Encourages exchange of ideas and methods for training and teaching of alaryngeal methods of communication. Fosters recognized standards for the rehabilitation of laryngectomees. Maintains the Voice Rehabilitation Institute for training teachers of alaryngeal voice and the Lost Chord Clubs. Organizes support groups for laryngectomees and their families. **Libraries:** **Type:** reference. **Holdings:** books, periodicals, video recordings. **Committees:** Medical Affairs; Rehabilitation and Public Affairs; Speech Standards. **Affiliated With:** American Cancer Society. **Publications:** *IAL News*, 3/year. Newsletter. **Price:** free. **Circulation:** 5,000. **Advertising:** accepted ● Directory, annual ● Films. Provides information on first aid and post-laryngectomy speech. ● Pamphlets. Provides information on laryngectomees, esophageal voice, and rehabilitation. **Conventions/Meetings:** annual dinner, training for speech language pathologists, and speech instruction and other rehabilitation issues for laryngectomees (exhibits) - usually July or August.

11694 ■ International Child Amputee Network (I-CAN)

PO Box 514
Abilene, TX 79604-0514
Ph: (325)675-6434
E-mail: joycebaughn@sbcglobal.net
URL: http://www.child-amputee.net
Contact: Joyce Baughn, Pres.

Multinational. Description: Serves people who have limb differences, their families and healthcare providers. Provides information, support contacts and education to children with absent or underdeveloped limbs. **Computer Services:** Information services, child amputee resources ● mailing lists.

11695 ■ Job Accommodation Network (JAN)

PO Box 6080
Morgantown, WV 26506-6080
Ph: (304)293-7186
Free: (800)526-7234
Fax: (304)293-5407
E-mail: jan@jan.wvu.edu
URL: http://www.jan.wvu.edu
Contact: D.J. Hendricks EdD, Project Mgr.

Founded: 1984. **Staff:** 31. **Languages:** English, Spanish. **Description:** A service of U.S. Department of Labor's Office of Disability Employment Policy. An international toll-free consulting service that provides information about job accommodation and the employability of people with disabilities. Calls are answered by consultants who understand the limitations associated with disabilities and who have instant access to the most comprehensive and up-to-date information about accommodation methods, devices, and strategies. **Telecommunication Services:** TDD, (877)781-9403. **Publications:** Newsletter, quarterly. Contains information on changes at JAN. Alternate Formats: online.

11696 ■ Joni and Friends

PO Box 3333
Agoura Hills, CA 91376-3333
Ph: (818)707-5664
Free: (800)523-5777
Fax: (818)707-2391
URL: http://www.joniandfriends.org
Contact: Joni Eareckson Tada, Founder/Pres.

Founded: 1979. **State Groups:** 9. **Local Groups:** 7. **Multinational. Description:** Advocates for a biblical response toward disabilities, both visible and invisible. Provides opportunities for disability awareness. Educates the church community in practical ways of serving disabled persons. Assists persons with disabilities in their progress toward independence and fulfillment. **Computer Services:** Information services, resource center ● online services, daily devotional;

online shop. **Telecommunication Services:** teletype, (818)707-7006. **Programs:** Christian Fund for the Disabled; Family Retreats; Wheels for the World.

11697 ■ Just One Break (JOB)

570 Seventh Ave.
New York, NY 10018
Ph: (212)785-7300
Fax: (212)785-4513
E-mail: jobs@justonebreak.com
URL: http://www.justonebreak.com
Contact: Ms. Lana Smart, Program Dir.

Founded: 1947. **Staff:** 8. **Description:** Serves as an employment service for people with disabilities, to help them find jobs and lead to productive lives. Finds competitive employment for people with disabilities by bringing together leading employers and qualified JOB applicants. Concentrates efforts in New York, and is working to include New Jersey and Connecticut, but advises companies nationwide. Offers placement services, employment counseling, skills evaluation, college recruitment, resume writing assistance service referrals, and computer access. Provides JOB's Student Internship Program (SIP), a hands-on work experience for college students with disabilities and works in collaboration with college disability and career service offices. Provides on-site disability awareness training to support initiatives related to interviewing, hiring, and retaining employees with disabilities. **Libraries:** **Type:** open to the public. **Holdings:** 100. **Subjects:** disabilities, Americans with Disabilities Act. **Awards:** Ability First. **Frequency:** annual. **Type:** recognition. **Recipient:** for persons with disabilities who inspire and encourage others on similar journeys and who help enlighten those just learning about people with disabilities; for companies or organizations that have made tremendous progress in hiring and/or retaining disabled ● **Frequency:** annual. **Type:** recognition. **Recipient:** for persons with disabilities who encourage and inspire others on similar journeys, and for hiring champions who are committed to having a diverse workforce as part of a strategy to achieve business objectives. **Telecommunication Services:** TDD, (212)785-4515. **Boards:** Directors. **Committees:** Business Advisory; Information Advisory in Southwestern Connecticut and New Jersey. **Affiliated With:** Abilities!; Rehabilitation International. **Publications:** *Gale Journal*, annual. **Advertising:** accepted ● *Informational Brochure* ● *Just One Breaking News*, periodic. Newsletter. Alternate Formats: online ● Annual Report, annual. **Advertising:** accepted. **Conventions/Meetings:** annual Job Fair - workshop (exhibits).

11698 ■ Knowbility

3925 W Braker Ln., 3rd Fl.
Austin, TX 78759
Ph: (512)305-0310
Free: (800)735-2989
E-mail: knowbility@knowbility.org
URL: http://www.knowbility.org
Contact: Sharron Rush, Co-Founder/Exec. Dir.

Founded: 1999. **Description:** Promotes the development of accessible technology to support the independence of children and adults with disabilities. Seeks to increase public awareness of information technology's potential for creating opportunities for people with disabilities. Provides consulting services to help organizations meet federal government and other institutional mandates for accessibility. **Telecommunication Services:** electronic mail, srush@knowbility.org. **Programs:** Accessibility Internet Rally; Community Training.

11699 ■ Landmine Survivors Network (LSN)

2100 M St. NW, Ste.302
Washington, DC 20037
Ph: (202)464-0007
Fax: (202)464-0011
E-mail: info@landminesurvivors.org
URL: http://www.landminesurvivors.org
Contact: Jerry White, Exec. Dir./Co-Founder

Founded: 1997. **Description:** Survivors of landmines. Aims to empower individuals, families and communities affected by landmines to recover from trauma, reclaim their lives, and fulfill their rights. **Libraries: Type:** reference. **Holdings:** articles, photographs, reports, video recordings. **Publications:** *Survivor Report*, monthly. Newsletter. Alternate Formats: online.

11700 ■ Logan Community Resources

2505 E Jefferson Blvd.
South Bend, IN 46615
Ph: (574)289-4831
Fax: (574)234-2075
E-mail: logan@logancenter.org
URL: http://logancenter.org
Contact: Mr. Patrick Pinnick, Treas.
Description: Individuals, families, volunteers, neighbors, employers, donors. Strives to create opportunities for persons with developmental disabilities. Offers person directed planning.

11701 ■ Mobility International USA (MIUSA)

132 E Broadway, Ste.343
Eugene, OR 97401
Ph: (541)343-1284
Fax: (541)343-6812
E-mail: info@miusa.org
URL: http://www.miusa.org
Contact: Susan Sygall, CEO/Exec. Dir.
Founded: 1981. **Members:** 300. **Staff:** 15. **Languages:** Arabic, English, French, Greek, Hungarian, Japanese, Romanian, Russian, Spanish. **Multinational. Description:** Focuses on empowering people with disabilities through international exchange opportunities. Organizes international exchange programs annually. Provides information on the range of international exchange opportunities available including work, study, research, and volunteering. Provides information to international exchange organizations on accessibility, homestays, recruiting and inclusion in international development programs. **Libraries: Type:** reference. **Subjects:** transportation policy, urban planning, international development. **Formerly:** (1989) Haitian Development Fund. **Publications:** *A World Awaits You: A Journal of Success of People with Disabilities in International Exchange.* **Price:** free ● *A World of Options: A Guide to International Educational Exchange, Community Service, and Travel for Persons with Disabilities.* Book. **Price:** $18.00 ● *All Aboard!* (in English and Japanese). Video. Available with or without audio description and with captions; for People with Disabilities Interested in International Exchange. **Price:** $49.00. Alternate Formats: CD-ROM ● *Building an Inclusive Development Community: A Manual on Including People with Disabilities in International Development Programs.* Book. Offers opinions, techniques and guidelines, resource lists, and examples of best practices from around the world. **Price:** $40.00 plus $5 domestic and $12 international shipping ● *Building Bridges: A Manual on Including People with Disabilities in International Exchange Programs.* **Price:** $20.00 ● *Building Bridges: A Training Video on Including People with Disabilities in International Exchange Programs.* Available with captions and with or without audio description. **Price:** $49.00. Alternate Formats: CD-ROM ● *Loud, Proud and Passionate* (in English, Russian, and Spanish). Video. Available with captions. **Price:** $49.00 ● *Loud, Proud and Passionate Including Women with Disabilities in International Development Programs* (in English, Russian, and Spanish), quarterly. Book. Available with captions. **Price:** $30.00. **Advertising:** accepted ● *Loud, Proud and Prosperous: Microcredit Projects By and For Women with Disabilities in South Africa* (in Aramaic, English, French, and Spanish). Video. Available with captions. **Price:** $49.00 ● *MIUSA's Global Impact,* semiannual. Newsletter. Also available on audiocassette. **Price:** included in membership dues. **Advertising:** accepted ● *Survival Strategies for Going Abroad: A Guide for People with Disabilities.* Book. Contains stories, tips and resources told by twenty experienced travelers with disabilities. **Price:** $16.95.

11702 ■ MOVE International: Mobility Opportunities Via Education - USA

1300 17th St.
City Centre
Bakersfield, CA 93301-4504
Free: (800)397-6683

Fax: (661)636-4045
E-mail: move-international@kern.org
URL: http://www.move-international.org
Contact: David Schreuder, Exec. Dir.
Multinational. Description: Helps children and adults with disabilities acquire increased independence in sitting, standing and walking to experience, learn and gain more mobility, better health and enhanced personal dignity. Improves the quality of life for people with severe disabilities through instruction and adaptive equipment that enhances independent mobility. **Computer Services:** Online services, discussion forum. **Councils:** Professional Development. **Publications:** *MOVE Newsletter.* Alternate Formats: online.

11703 ■ National Accessible Apartment Clearinghouse (NAAC)

4300 Wilson Blvd., Ste.400
Arlington, VA 22203
Ph: (703)518-6141
Free: (800)421-1221
Fax: (703)248-9440
E-mail: clearinghouse@naahq.org
URL: http://www.accessibleapartments.org
Contact: Ms. Shelly Cook, Coor.
Nonmember. Description: Dedicated to providing an effective means to connect individuals with disabilities with apartments designed for an individual's particular needs. **Computer Services:** Online services, accessible apartment search.

11704 ■ National AMBUCS

4285 Regency Ct.
High Point, NC 27265
Free: (800)838-1845
Fax: (336)852-6830
E-mail: joec@ambucs.org
URL: http://www.ambucs.org
Contact: J. Joseph Copeland, Exec. Dir.
Founded: 1927. **Members:** 5,600. **Membership Dues:** friend, $25 (annual). **Staff:** 6. **Regional Groups:** 6. **Local Groups:** 125. **Description:** Dedicated to creating opportunities for independence for people with disabilities. Performs community service; provides physically challenged children with tricycles that can be operated by hand, foot or both: operates the Living Endowment Fund. **Awards:** AMBUC of the Year. **Frequency:** annual. **Type:** recognition. **Recipient:** to the most outstanding member of AMBUC ● Scholarships for Therapists. **Frequency:** annual. **Type:** scholarship. **Recipient:** for students majoring in occupational, physical, therapy, speech pathology, hearing audiology. **Committees:** Attendance and Reception; Big Hat; Fun; Recruitment; Retention. **Programs:** AmTryke; Scholarships for Therapists. **Formerly:** American Business Clubs Spastic Paralysis Fund. **Publications:** Magazine, quarterly. **Circulation:** 7,000. **Advertising:** accepted. **Conventions/Meetings:** annual conference - always July.

11705 ■ National Amputation Foundation (NAF)

40 Church St.
Malverne, NY 11565
Ph: (516)887-3600
Fax: (516)887-3667
E-mail: amps76@aol.com
URL: http://www.nationalamputation.org
Contact: Paul Bernacchio, Pres.
Founded: 1919. **Members:** 2,500. **Membership Dues:** honorary, $25 (annual). **Description:** Veterans with service-connected amputation. Assists all amputees, including non-veterans, in employment, social, and mental rehabilitation. Provides services, including legal counsel, vocational guidance and placement, social activities, liaison with other groups, and psychological aid. Sponsors Amp-to-Amp program arranging for amputees who have returned to a normal life to visit new amputees. **Libraries: Type:** reference. **Subjects:** amputees, amputations. **Awards:** **Type:** recognition. **Programs:** AMP-to-AMP; Medical Equipment Give-A-Way. **Publications:** *The Amp,* bimonthly. Newsletter. **Advertising:** accepted. **Conventions/Meetings:** annual meeting - always February, New York City.

11706 ■ National Association of the Physically Handicapped (NAPH)

1375 Dewitt Dr.
Akron, OH 44313
Ph: (330)724-1994
Free: (800)743-5008
E-mail: trumanjm@aol.com
URL: http://www.naph.net
Contact: Jerry Snyder, Pres.
Founded: 1958. **Members:** 700. **Membership Dues:** at large, $10 (annual) ● chapter, $6 (annual). **Budget:** $25,000. **State Groups:** 1. **Local Groups:** 13. **Description:** Physically handicapped persons; associate members are nonhandicapped. Seeks to advance the social, economic, and physical welfare of the physically handicapped persons. Promotes involvement of the physically handicapped in the planning and administration of all programs in their interest. Sponsors fundraising activities. **Telecommunication Services:** electronic mail, jrs1375@aol.com. **Committees:** Awards; Employment; Housing; Legislation; Membership; Social; Transportation; Ways and Means. **Publications:** *NAPH National Newsletter,* quarterly. **Price:** included in membership dues; $12.00 /year for nonmembers. ISSN: 0741-1405. **Circulation:** 1,000. **Advertising:** accepted ● Brochure. **Conventions/Meetings:** annual convention (exhibits) - usually August.

11707 ■ National Council on Independent Living (NCIL)

1710 Rhode Island Ave. NW, 5th Fl.
Washington, DC 20036
Ph: (202)207-0334 (202)207-0340
Free: (877)525-3400
Fax: (202)207-0341
E-mail: ncil@ncil.org
URL: http://www.ncil.org
Contact: John Lancaster, Exec. Dir.
Founded: 1982. **Members:** 380. **Budget:** $400,000. **Local Groups:** 80. **Description:** Independent living centers, organizations that provide support to independent living centers, and individuals. Encourages the integration of people with disabilities into society; promotes independent lifestyles and decision-making for people with disabilities; works to strengthen independent living centers. Offers technical assistance and encourages cooperation among independent living centers. Seeks to develop leadership skills among people with disabilities; works to increase public awareness of the rights and needs of disabled individuals. Provides information and referral service; sponsors Peer Technical Assistance Network. Maintains speakers' bureau and placement service. **Awards:** **Type:** recognition. **Committees:** Communication Access; Evaluation; Legislative and Advocacy; Minority; Technical Assistance. **Subcommittees:** Civil Rights; Developmental Disabilities; Housing; Long-Term Care; Rehabilitation Act; Social Security; Transportation. **Formerly:** (1985) National Coalition of Independent Living Programs. **Publications:** *NCIL Newsletter,* quarterly ● *President's Bulletin,* monthly. **Conventions/Meetings:** annual meeting ● annual National Conference on Independent Living.

11708 ■ National Cristina Foundation (NCF)

500 W Putnam Ave.
Greenwich, CT 06830
Ph: (203)863-9100
Fax: (203)863-9230
E-mail: info@cristina.org
URL: http://www.cristina.org
Contact: Yvette Marrin PhD, Pres.
Founded: 1985. **Staff:** 10. **Multinational. Description:** Seeks donations of used computer equipment and directs those donations to non-profit organizations, schools, and public agencies that provide training and education to people with disabilities, students at risk, and those that are otherwise disadvantaged. Individuals, small businesses and large corporations (throughout the US and Canada) can donate computers that are pledged through their website using their online donor submission form and then matched appropriately with one of their thousands of partner organizations in need of technology. **Affiliated With:**

Computing Technology Industry Association. **Publications:** *Cristina Connections.* Magazine. Alternate Formats: online.

11709 ■ National Disability Rights Network (NDRN)

900 2nd St. NE, Ste.211
Washington, DC 20002
Ph: (202)408-9514
Fax: (202)408-9520
E-mail: info@ndrn.org
URL: http://www.napas.org
Contact: Curtis L. Decker JD, Exec. Dir.
Founded: 1978. **Members:** 96. **Staff:** 16. **Budget:** $1,500,000. **Regional Groups:** 5. **State Groups:** 96. **Description:** Executive directors and designees of state or territorial Developmental Disability, Mentally Ill Protection and Advocacy Systems, and Client Assistance Programs. Furthers the human, civil, and legal rights of persons with disabilities; advances the interests of protection and advocacy systems; facilitates coordination and mutual support among such systems and enhance their capacity to provide optimal services. Offers professional training; collects data. **Telecommunication Services:** teletype, (202)-408-9521. **Formerly:** (2005) National Association of Protection and Advocacy Systems. **Publications:** *State Protection and Advocacy Agencies,* annual. Directory ● Newsletter, periodic ● Manuals ● Reports. **Conventions/Meetings:** periodic conference (exhibits).

11710 ■ National Dissemination Center for Children with Disabilities (NICHCY)

PO Box 1492
Washington, DC 20013-1492
Ph: (202)884-8200
Free: (800)695-0285
Fax: (202)884-8441
E-mail: nichcy@aed.org
URL: http://www.nichcy.org
Contact: Suzanne Ripley, Dir.
Founded: 1970. **Staff:** 16. **Budget:** $1,000,000. **Languages:** English, Spanish. **Description:** Serves as central source of information on: IDEA, the nation's special education law; No Child Left Behind (as it relates to children with disabilities); and research-based information on effective educational practices; funded by the Office of Special Education Programs, U.S. Department of Education. **Libraries: Type:** open to the public. **Holdings:** 1,500; archival material, articles, books, periodicals. **Subjects:** disability. **Formerly:** National Information Center for the Handicapped; National Special Education Information Center; (1982) Parents Campaign for Handicapped Children and Youth; (1987) National Information Center for Handicapped Children and Youth; (1991) National Information Center for Children and Youth with Handicaps; (2004) National Information Center for Children and Youth with Disabilities. **Publications:** *Disability Fact Sheet,* annual ● *News Digest,* periodic. Newsletter. Addresses current issues affecting individuals concerned with handicapped children and youth with disabilities. **Price:** free. **Circulation:** 30,000 ● *Parent Guide* ● *State Resource Sheet,* annual ● *Transition Summary* ● Booklets ● Papers.

11711 ■ National Institute for Rehabilitation Engineering (NIRE)

PO Box T
Hewitt, NJ 07421
Ph: (973)853-6585
Free: (800)736-2216
E-mail: nire@theoffice.net
URL: http://www.angelfire.com/nj/nire2
Contact: Donald Selwyn, Exec. VP
Founded: 1967. **Membership Dues:** regular, $50 (annual). **Staff:** 400. **Description:** Multidisciplinary research, training, and service organization providing custom-designed and custom-made tools and devices, along with intensive personal task-performance and driver training, to aid the handicapped person in becoming more self-sufficient and independent. Often an organization of "last resort" for permanently, severely, or multihandicapped persons, the NIRE is staffed by electronics engineers, physicists, psycho-

gists, optometrists, and other volunteers who work as a team with the handicapped person. These specialists review the handicapped person's abilities, disabilities, and task-performance goals and are thus able to help advise, plan, and implement programs to increase the person's abilities to perform desired tasks, using a combination of methods involving different practitioners and disciplines. Staff members also adapt, modify, and construct equipment specially suited to the individual client's need. No handicapped person is denied the institute's services due to an inability to pay, and fees for others are based on each person's income and means. Conducts occasional seminars for the handicapped and for professionals serving the handicapped. Provides speakers and seminar participants for other agencies' programs. Compiles statistics. **Departments:** ADA Compliance; Communications; Computer Technology; Consumer Advisory; Counseling; Driver Evaluation and Training; Employment and Job Accommodation; Engineering; Geriatric Rehabilitation; Hearing and Speech; Housing; Medical; Pediatric Rehabilitation; Vision & low-vision. **Publications:** *Rehabilitation Newsletter,* quarterly. Features announcements of upcoming seminars. **Price:** included in membership dues. **Circulation:** 400. **Advertising:** accepted. **Conventions/Meetings:** semiannual meeting.

11712 ■ National Network for the Disabled

PO Box 3574
Gardena, CA 90247-7274
Ph: (310)638-5717
Fax: (310)638-5986
Contact: Linda Walls, Founder/Pres.
Founded: 1980. **Members:** 11,000. **Staff:** 7. **Languages:** English, Spanish. **Description:** Provides support, companionship, and networking opportunities for elderly individuals and parents of disabled children. Conducts research. Sponsors education on such topics as assertiveness, resources, and medical options. Provides transportation and emergency services, including a food program through which meals are delivered to homes. Conducts special events for parents and children, including picnics and field trips; special programs on nutrition and accessible travel with groups. **Libraries: Type:** reference; not open to the public. **Holdings:** video recordings. **Subjects:** music. **Awards: Type:** scholarship. **Formerly:** Parent Networking Program. **Publications:** Brochure, monthly ● Newsletter, monthly. **Conventions/Meetings:** annual Christmas Party (exhibits).

11713 ■ National Odd Shoe Exchange (NOSE)

PO Box 1120
Chandler, AZ 85244-1120
Ph: (480)892-3484
URL: http://www.oddshoe.org
Founded: 1943. **Multinational. Description:** Provides new single shoes to amputees and pairs of different sizes to people with feet of significantly different sizes due to disease, injury, and genetic disorders. **Convention/Meeting:** none. **Awards:** Certificate of Appreciation. **Frequency:** annual. **Type:** recognition. **Recipient:** for people who donate shoes, money, or time. **Computer Services:** database ● mailing lists ● online services.

11714 ■ Networking Project for Young Adults with Disabilities (NPDWG)

50 Broadway, 13th Fl.
New York, NY 10004
Ph: (212)755-4500
Fax: (212)838-1279
E-mail: info@ywcanyc.org
URL: http://www.ywcanyc.org
Contact: Miyilyn Parra, Networking Coor.
Founded: 1984. **Staff:** 3. **Description:** A project of the Young Women's Christian Association (see separate entry) of New York City. Aims to increase the educational, social, and career aspirations of adolescents with disabilities by linking them to successful, disabled role models. Provides support groups; offers advocacy training, pre-employment skills development, and one-to-one mentoring. Organizes visits to the role model's workplace. Oper-

ates in the New York City area and provides technical assistance to facilitate replication at several sites throughout the country. **Telecommunication Services:** electronic mail, mparra@ywcanyc.org. **Publications:** *Replication Manual* ● Books. **Conventions/Meetings:** periodic meeting - usually in New York City.

11715 ■ NISH

8401 Old Courthouse Rd., Ste.200
Vienna, VA 22182
Ph: (571)226-4660
Fax: (703)849-8741
E-mail: info@nish.org
URL: http://www.nish.org
Contact: Robert Sullivan, Exec. Dir.
Founded: 1974. **Members:** 550. **Budget:** $17,000,000. **Regional Groups:** 6. **Description:** Provides employment opportunities for people with severe disabilities under the Javits-Wagner O'Day Act. Promotes their placement into competitive industry. Conducts research and development to identify to the government commodities and services, which are feasible for production and/or performance by work centers. (Work centers are nonprofit agencies that provide rehabilitative, training, and vocational services for persons with severe disabilities). Provides training and technical assistance in the form of industrial engineering, production planning, quality control, inventory management, cost analysis, procurement, and contract administration. Acts as a liaison between work centers and the federal government. **Telecommunication Services:** TDD, (703)-560-6512. **Formerly:** (1991) National Industries for the Severely Handicapped. **Publications:** *NISH News,* monthly. Newsletter. Reports on work centers employing persons with severe disabilities, and legislation and regulations affecting these centers. **Price:** free to participants of the J-W O'Day Program ● Annual Report. **Price:** free. **Circulation:** 4,800 ● Brochure. **Conventions/Meetings:** annual conference (exhibits).

11716 ■ The One Shoe Crew (TOSC)

PO Box 285
Rio Linda, CA 95673
Ph: (916)991-0412
Fax: (916)685-8746
E-mail: sally_tavarez@hotmail.com
Contact: Sally Tavarez, Contact
Founded: 1986. **Members:** 2,500. **Membership Dues:** life, $3. **Staff:** 1. **Description:** Provides services for adults or teens whose feet have stopped growing. Includes individuals with mismatched feet, amputees, and people wearing a brace on one foot, and anyone with a one-sided foot problem who still wear one regular shoe. Possesses thousands of new, unused shoes and over 3,000 pairs of mismatched shoes (same shoe, different size) are available free to clients; shipping must be prepaid; requests donation of $5 per shoe. Indicates the preferred general shoe style by clients. Provides services that are free for US Veterans. **Libraries: Type:** open to the public. **Computer Services:** database, members, sizes, handicaps, shoe information ● mailing lists, client list by shoe size. **Affiliated With:** Amputee Coalition of America.

11717 ■ Opportunity Plus

Address Unknown since 2007
Founded: 1979. **Staff:** 3. **Budget:** $260,000. **Regional Groups:** 5. **Description:** Works with the physically disabled community by providing the opportunity to be independent through mentoring, training, and employment programs, and by educating the community at large through information, referral, and networking. **Awards:** Phoenix Award. **Frequency:** annual. **Type:** recognition. **Recipient:** for physically disabled professional who raises image of people with physical disabilities. **Programs:** Mentorship Plus. **Also Known As:** (2002) Learning How. **Formerly:** (1987) Handicapped Organized Women; (1988) HOW. **Publications:** *Mentor Newsletter,* quarterly. Includes client updates, resources, and legislative updates. **Advertising:** not accepted.

11718 ■ Paws With a Cause (PAWS)
4646 S Div.
Wayland, MI 49348
Ph: (616)877-7297
Free: (800)253-PAWS
Fax: (616)877-0248
E-mail: paws@pawswithacause.org
URL: http://www.pawswithacause.org
Contact: Ms. A.J. Sapp, CEO
Founded: 1979. **Members:** 526. **Membership Dues:** individual, $35 (annual) ● family, $65 (annual) ● corporate, $125 (annual). **Staff:** 56. **Budget:** $4,300,000. **Regional Groups:** 4. **National Groups:** 38. **Description:** Trains Assistance Dogs nationally for people with disabilities and provides lifetime team support which encourages independence. Promotes awareness through education. **Councils:** National Advisory. **Affiliated With:** Assistance Dogs International; United Way of America. **Formerly:** (1988) Ears for the Deaf. **Publications:** *Dogs for Dignity*, quarterly. Newsletter. **Price:** included in membership dues. **Circulation:** 35,000 ● *The Story of Trapper*. Book. A children's story about the life of a service dog who changes the life of a family. **Conventions/Meetings:** annual Swing for Independence - meeting, golf outing for primary fundraiser - first Monday of May, in Grand Rapids, MI.

11719 ■ People-to-People Committee on Disability (PPCOD)
c/o Marc L. Bright, Deputy CEO/Exec.VP
510 E Armour Blvd.
Kansas City, MO 64109-2200
Ph: (816)531-4701
Fax: (816)561-7502
E-mail: marcb@ptpi.org
Contact: Marc L. Bright, Deputy CEO/Exec.VP
Founded: 1956. **Members:** 250. **Staff:** 3. **Budget:** $16,000. **Description:** A program of People to People International. Individuals concerned about the circumstances of disabled people throughout the world. Disseminates information; acts as consultant in promoting exchange activities; coordinates special assistance projects in developing countries. Compiles statistics. **Awards:** Arneson Award. **Frequency:** annual. **Type:** recognition ● HC of Year. **Frequency:** annual. **Type:** recognition ● One-of-a-Kind Award. **Frequency:** annual. **Type:** recognition ● Pope Memorial. **Frequency:** annual. **Type:** recognition ● Preminger Medallion. **Frequency:** annual. **Type:** recognition. **Affiliated With:** People to People International. **Formerly:** (1994) People-to-People Committee for the Handicapped. **Publications:** Newsletter, quarterly ● Also publishes reports and surveys. **Conventions/Meetings:** annual meeting - always April/May.

11720 ■ Post-Polio Health International (PHI)
4207 Lindell Blvd., No. 110
St. Louis, MO 63108-2930
Ph: (314)534-0475
Fax: (314)534-5070
E-mail: info@post-polio.org
URL: http://www.post-polio.org
Contact: Joan L. Headley, Exec. Dir.
Founded: 1960. **Members:** 4,000. **Membership Dues:** subscriber, $25 (annual) ● subscriber plus, $45 (annual) ● contributor, $75 (annual) ● sustainer, $125 (annual). **Staff:** 3. **Budget:** $200,000. **Multinational. Description:** Polio survivors, ventilator users, other individuals with neuromuscular diseases, health care personnel, government agencies, independent living centers, and interested others. Works to inform, encourage, dignify, and sustain people with disabilities. Seeks to create a communications network to provide information on issues related to disabilities. Serves as clearinghouse for information on polio, ventilators, neuromuscular diseases, and independent living. Sponsors seminars. Coordinates International Ventilator Users Network. **Awards:** Research Awards. **Frequency:** periodic. **Type:** monetary. **Recipient:** for research into post-polio or neuromuscular respiratory disorders. **Absorbed:** Care for Life; (2003) International Polio Network. **Formerly:** (1983) Rehabilitation Gazette; (2003) Gazette International Networking Institute. **Publications:** *Handbook on the*

Late Effects of Poliomyelitis for Physicians and Survivors. **Price:** $11.50/copy; $12.50 for nonmembers outside U.S.; $9.00 for contributor and sustainer members only ● *Information About Ventilator-Assisted Living.* Pamphlet ● *The Late Effects of Polio: An Overview* (in English, French, German, and Portuguese). Pamphlet. Alternate Formats: online ● *Polio and Post-Polio Fact Sheet* (in English and Farsi). Pamphlet. Alternate Formats: online ● *Post-Polio Directory*, annual. Lists self-identified clinics, health professionals, and support groups knowledgeable about the late effects of polio. **Price:** $8.00/copy for individuals; $10.00 in Canada and Mexico; $12.00 outside U.S. ● *Post-Polio Health*, quarterly. Contains information about the late effects of polio and topics related to disability. **Price:** included in membership dues ● *Resource Directory for Ventilator-Assisted Living*, annual. **Price:** $8.00/copy ● *Ventilator-Assisted Living*, quarterly. Newsletter. Includes information for those interested in home mechanical ventilation. **Price:** included in membership dues. **Circulation:** 1,800 ● Pamphlet (in English, Farsi, French, German, and Japanese). Alternate Formats: online. **Conventions/Meetings:** periodic International Post-Polio and Independent Living Conference (exhibits).

11721 ■ P.R.I.D.E. Foundation - Promote Real Independence for the Disabled and Elderly (P.R.I.D.E. Fdn.)
391 Long Hill Rd.
Groton, CT 06340-1293
Ph: (860)445-7320
Free: (800)332-9122
Fax: (860)445-1448
E-mail: sewtique@aol.com
URL: http://www.sewtiqueonline.com/pride.htm
Contact: Evelyn S. Kennedy, Pres./Founder
Founded: 1978. **Staff:** 2. **Languages:** English, Italian. **Description:** Provides rehabilitation assistance for the handicapped and elderly in the areas of home management, independent dressing, and personal grooming. Designs and develops special garments that will help the handicapped feel more comfortable and dress independently; designs assistive devices for use in the kitchen, bedroom, and bathroom. Provides discussion leaders for community outreach and assistance to health agencies, social service groups, and volunteer organizations. Conducts workshops and educational forums for rehabilitation centers, educational institutions, and community agencies. Sponsors Project Pride, an in-class training program providing physically and mentally handicapped individuals with entry-level occupational skills in the sewing field. Conducts public exhibitions and demonstrations of clothing and adaptive devices. **Libraries: Type:** reference. **Holdings:** 500. **Subjects:** fashion, rehabilitation utilizing clothing, clothing, home management assistance, employment opportunities in the clothing industry. **Publications:** *Children's Fashions and Special Needs.* Paper ● *Dressing With Pride.* Book. **Price:** $15.00 ● *Fashion and Clothing Accessibility.* Book ● *Resources and Clothing for Special Needs* ● *Scoliosis and Fashion.* Paper. **Price:** $4.50. **Conventions/Meetings:** Dressing with Pride - Fashion and Fit for Special Needs - seminar (exhibits).

11722 ■ Rehabilitation Engineering and Assistive Technology Society of North America (RESNA)
1700 N Moore St., Ste.1540
Arlington, VA 22209-1903
Ph: (703)524-6686 (703)524-6639
Fax: (703)524-6630
E-mail: info@resna.org
URL: http://www.resna.org
Contact: Thomas A. Gorski, Exec. Dir.
Founded: 1980. **Members:** 1,250. **Membership Dues:** student, $50 (annual) ● regular, $150 (annual) ● non-profit, $500 (annual) ● student with journal, $80 (annual) ● sustaining, $200 (annual) ● consumer, $50 (annual) ● consumer with journal, $80 (annual) ● for profit, $800 (annual). **Staff:** 9. **Budget:** $1,200,000. **Description:** Rehabilitation professionals, providers, and consumers. Serves as an interdis-

ciplinary association for the advancement of rehabilitation and assistive technologies. Seeks to improve the quality of life for disabled persons through the application of science and technology; influence policy relating to delivery of technology to disabled persons. Works for the design and development of rehabilitation devices and the modification of housing and transportation systems. **Awards: Frequency:** annual. **Type:** fellowship. **Recipient:** for contributions to the field. **Committees:** Consumer Involvement; Education; Industrial Relations; Society and Government Relations; Special Interest Groups. **Special Interest Groups:** Assistive Robotics and Mechatronics; Augmentative and Alternative Communication; Computer Applications; Dysphasia; Electrical Stimulation; Gerontology; Information Networking; International Appropriate Technology; Job Accommodation; Personal Transportation; Quantitative Functional Assessment; Rural Rehabilitation; Sensory Aids; Service Delivery and Public Policy; Special Education; Tech Act; Technology Transfer; Wheeled Mobility and Seating. **Subgroups:** Occupational Therapists; Orthotists and Prosthetists; Physical Therapists; Rehabilitation Engineers; Speech-Language Pathologists/Audiologists; Suppliers and Manufacturers. **Formerly:** (1988) RESNA: Association for the Advancement of Rehabilitation Technology. **Publications:** *Assistive Technology*, semiannual. Journal. **Price:** $75.00 /year for institutions, in U.S. and Canada; $65.00 /year for individuals, in U.S. and Canada; $90.00 /year for institutions, other countries; $80.00 /year for individuals, other countries. Alternate Formats: online ● *Assistive Technology Sourcebook.* **Price:** $30.00. ● *Augmentative Communication: Finding a Voice.* Video. Contains information on augmentative and alternative communication systems for funding sources and case managers. **Price:** $30.00 ● *Backs: Correction or Accommodation.* Video. Contains information about static and adjustable back supports for funding sources and case managers. **Price:** $30.00 ● *Communication: The Key to Teamwork.* Video. Includes explanations of assistive technology by rehabilitation experts for funding sources and case managers. **Price:** $30.00 ● *Manual Mobility: Finding the Right Wheels.* Video. Contains information about rigid, folding, and lightweight wheelchairs for funding sources and case managers. **Price:** $30.00 ● *RESNA News*, quarterly. Newsletter ● *Understanding the Technology When Selecting Wheelchairs.* **Price:** $10.00 ● Brochures ● Manuals ● Membership Directory, annual ● Monographs ● Proceedings, annual. Alternate Formats: online ● Reports ● Also publishes an education series. **Conventions/Meetings:** annual conference, with instructional courses (exhibits) - always June ● annual Paralyzed Veterans of America Student Design Competition, recognizes students' prototype designs for rehabilitation devices (exhibits).

11723 ■ Research and Training Center on Independent Living (RTC/IL)
Univ. of Kansas
1000 Sunnyside Ave.
Dole Ctr., Ste.4089
Lawrence, KS 66045-7755
Ph: (785)864-4095
Fax: (785)864-5063
E-mail: rtcil@ku.edu
URL: http://www.rtcil.org
Contact: Dr. Glen W. White PhD, Dir.
Founded: 1980. **Members:** 180. **Staff:** 19. **Languages:** English, Spanish. **Description:** U.S. independent living centers helping individuals with severe disabilities lead independent lives. Works to: identify attributes of successful self-help support groups; develop and test instruments to assess social support levels within self-help support groups; implement and evaluate intervention strategies for accurate and positive portrayals of people with disabilities by the media; deter unlawful parking in handicapped-designated parking spaces and enhance public awareness of issues related to disability and independent living; establish accreditation standards to evaluate ILC programs, services, and management. Has developed: Personal Attendant Care Management Training model in seven states to increase the ability of consumers to manage attendants and reduce

management problems and institutionalization; program to assist ILC consumers in identifying personal goals and initiating behavioral changes to attain them. Provides direct training and technical assistance to individuals, ILCs, state agencies, and consumers' groups; university courses, and presentations. Places an emphasis on the needs of under-served populations, including the mentally ill, patients with brain injuries, minorities, the elderly, and persons living in rural areas. **Libraries: Type:** reference. **Holdings:** 220. **Telecommunication Services:** TDD, (785)864-0706. **Committees:** Research; Technical Assistance; Training. **Publications:** *Action Letter Portfolio.* Manual. **Price:** $30.00 ● *Building Consumer Consensus on Independent Living.* Report. **Price:** $1.35 ● *Catalogue of Publications* (in English and Spanish), annual. Lists publications available from the center; includes abstracts. ● *Consumers as Collaborators in Research and Action.* Paper. **Price:** $5.00 ● *Guidelines for Reporting and Writing About People with Disabilities.* Brochure. **Price:** free. Alternate Formats: online ● *How-to Guide: Condensing and Translating.* Manual. **Price:** $5.00 ● *The Self-Help Group Leader's Handbook: Leading Effective Meetings.* **Price:** $5.00 ● Manuals ● Monographs. **Conventions/Meetings:** workshop.

11724 ■ Responsible Hospitality Institute (RHI)
740 Front St., Ste.318
Santa Cruz, CA 95060
Ph: (831)469-3396
Fax: (831)469-3916
E-mail: jim@rhiweb.org
URL: http://www.rhiweb.org
Contact: Jim Peters, Pres.
Founded: 1983. **Members:** 300. **Membership Dues:** regular, $80 (annual). **Staff:** 11. **Budget:** $500,000. **Local Groups:** 1. **Description:** Individuals in the U.S., Canada, New Zealand, and Australia concerned with: accessibility of restaurants and other hospitality businesses to disabled persons; responsible operation of establishments selling alcoholic beverages. **Formerly:** Intermission. **Publications:** *Hospitality Insighter,* monthly. Newsletter. **Price:** $60.00. **Circulation:** 1,000. **Advertising:** accepted ● *Networker* ● Directory. Alternate Formats: online. **Conventions/ Meetings:** annual Symposium on Responsible Hospitality - conference.

11725 ■ Rural Institute
Univ. of Montana Rural Inst.
52 Corbin Hall
Missoula, MT 59812
Ph: (406)243-5467
Free: (800)732-0323
Fax: (406)243-4730
E-mail: rural@ruralinstitute.umt.edu
URL: http://ruralinstitute.umt.edu
Contact: Jo York, Office Mgr.
Founded: 1979. **Description:** Aims to support the independence, productivity, and inclusion into the community of persons with developmental disabilities and their families. **Projects:** Adult Community Services and Supports; Child Care Plus; Child Find; Dynamic Community Connections; Hearing Conservation; Montana Works; Montana's Special Needs Subsidy; Montana's State Improvement Grant; Rural Independent Living Leadership Mentoring Initiative. **Publications:** *Montana's Programs for Individuals with Developmental Disabilities.* Pamphlet. Alternate Formats: online. **Conventions/Meetings:** Montana Conference on Developmental Disabilities.

11726 ■ Siblings for Significant Change (SSC)
Empire State Bldg.
350 5th Ave., Ste.627
New York, NY 10118
Ph: (212)643-2663
Free: (800)841-8251
Fax: (212)643-1244
E-mail: gerriscfu@aol.com
Contact: Gerri Zatlow, Exec. Dir.
Founded: 1982. **Members:** 75. **Staff:** 1. **Description:** Siblings of disabled individuals; parents, educa-

tors, social workers, medical professionals, and researchers interested in siblings of disabled individuals. Provides peer support, legal assistance, and psychological counseling to siblings of the handicapped. Coordinates social activities for families with handicapped members and works on projects and audiovisual programs designed to increase national awareness of the difficulties faced by families of disabled individuals. Maintains speakers' bureau. Division of Special Citizens Futures Unlimited, a New York state organization that offers ongoing programs for autistic and autistic-like adults. **Libraries: Type:** reference. **Publications:** *Directory of Sibling Related Services* ● Journal, semiannual ● Newsletter, periodic. **Conventions/Meetings:** competition, essay, art, and photography contest for sibling members ● monthly meeting ● seminar ● annual symposium.

11727 ■ Society for Disability Studies (SDS)
c/o Joy Hammel, PhD, Exec. Off.
Univ. of Illinois at Chicago, MC626
Dept. of Disability and Human Development
1640 W Roosevelt Rd., No. 236
Chicago, IL 60608-1316
Ph: (312)996-4664
Fax: (312)996-7743
E-mail: hammel@uic.edu
URL: http://www.uic.edu/orgs/sds
Contact: Joy Hammel PhD, Exec. Off.
Founded: 1986. **Members:** 300. **Membership Dues:** special, life, $1,000 ● sponsoring, $200 (annual) ● regular, $95 (annual), low-income, student, $30 (annual). **Budget:** $25,000. **Description:** Social scientists and scholars studying the problems of disabled people in society. Strives to develop theoretical and practical knowledge about disability and promotes equal participation in society for individuals with disabilities. **Awards:** Irving Kenneth Zola Emerging Scholar Award. **Frequency:** annual. **Type:** scholarship. **Recipient:** for research and scholarship in disability studies. **Publications:** *Disability Studies Quarterly.* Journal. **Price:** $95.00 /year for individuals; $200.00 /year for institutions. Alternate Formats: online ● Proceedings, annual. **Price:** $25.00. **Conventions/Meetings:** annual conference (exhibits).

11728 ■ Special Recreation for disABLED International (SRDI)
701 Oaknoll Dr.
Iowa City, IA 52246-5168
Ph: (319)466-3192 (319)351-1720
Fax: (319)351-6772
E-mail: john-nesbitt@uiowa.edu
URL: http://www.globalvisionproject.org
Contact: Prof. John A. Nesbitt EdD, Pres./CEO
Founded: 1978. **Staff:** 1. **Languages:** English, Spanish. **Multinational. Description:** Seeks to serve and advocate special and therapeutic play and recreation for infants, children, youth, adults, and seniors throughout the world. Services include advisory and consultation, awards, employment information, professional education, public education, publishing, research, resource information and referral, technical assistance on programs and management methods, and an international library. Does international service work to: collect and disseminate international information on special recreation services for disabled persons, special recreation programs, and personnel training; conduct, provide, and support international exchange of technical, professional, and general information on special recreation for the disabled; cooperate with both governmental and voluntary organizations on national and international levels. Offers career guidance and placement service. Maintains speakers' bureau; compiles statistics. **Libraries: Type:** reference. **Holdings:** 5,000; archival material, biographical archives. **Awards:** Special Recreation Award. **Frequency:** annual. **Type:** recognition. **Computer Services:** database, SRDI ERIC: 2750 pages of SR documents in 1000 libraries in 25 nations. **Programs:** Public Information; Research and Studies; Service; Special Recreation Day/Week; Training. **Projects:** Stop Fireworks Victimization Campaign. **Affiliated With:** American Recreation Coalition. **Formerly:** (1998) Special Recreation for Disabled. **Publications:**

Camping/Outdoor Recreation, National Institute on Camping for DisABLED. Monograph ● *Community-Based Special Recreation, National Institute on New Models of Community-Based Special Recreation for DisABLED.* Monograph ● *Deaf-Blind, National Institute on Play and Recreation for Deaf-Blind.* Monograph ● *Mental Health, World Seminar on Special Recreation, World Congress of the World Federation for Mental Health, Manila, Philippines.* Monograph. **Conventions/Meetings:** annual board meeting - always November in Iowa City, IA.

11729 ■ Support Dogs, Inc. (SDI)
11645 Lilburn Park Rd.
St. Louis, MO 63146
Ph: (314)997-2325
Fax: (314)997-7202
E-mail: rkjames@supportdogs.org
URL: http://www.supportdogs.org
Contact: Robyn James, Exec. Dir.
Founded: 1981. **Members:** 15,000. **Staff:** 6. **Budget:** $300,000. **Description:** Helps people with special needs achieve greater independence and improve the quality of their lives by providing them with professionally trained dogs. Dogs are prematched and custom trained for each individual and assist their owners with tasks such as: opening mall and house doors; pulling wheelchairs long distances and up ramps; loading wheelchairs into vehicles; retrieving a dropped or distant object; bringing the phone and operating an emergency assistance switch; rising to high counters to assist with business transactions. **Computer Services:** database. **Programs:** Paws for Reading; Puppy Raising; Signal Dog; TOUCH; Youth Service Dog. **Projects:** Service Dogs; Social Dogs; Therapy Dogs. **Affiliated With:** Assistance Dogs International; Delta Society. **Formerly:** Support Dogs for the Handicapped. **Publications:** *Paw Prints,* quarterly. Newsletter. Contains education about service dogs. **Price:** free. **Circulation:** 15,000. Alternate Formats: online. **Conventions/Meetings:** annual Volunteer Appreciation - conference - always May, St. Louis, MO.

11730 ■ TASH
1025 Vermont Ave., 7th Fl.
Washington, DC 20005
Ph: (202)263-5600
Fax: (202)637-0138
E-mail: btrader@tash.org
URL: http://www.tash.org
Contact: Barbara Trader, Exec. Dir.
Founded: 1975. **Members:** 6,300. **Membership Dues:** individual, $113 (annual) ● associate, $65 (annual) ● organizational, $275 (annual) ● life, $1,500 ● life (organization), $2,800. **Staff:** 13. **Regional Groups:** 2. **State Groups:** 35. **Description:** Teachers, therapists, parents, administrators, university faculty, lawyers, and advocates involved in all areas of service to people with severe disabilities. Seeks to ensure an autonomous, dignified lifestyle for all people with severe disabilities; advocates quality education, from birth through adulthood, for disabled individuals. Disseminates updated information on solutions to problems, research findings, trends, and practices relevant to people with severe disabilities. Provides information and referral service. **Awards: Type:** recognition. **Committees:** ACA Communication Issues; Accessibility Issues; Community Living; Criminal Justice Issues; Early Childhood; Employment and Transition; Family Issues; Guardianship Alternatives. **Formerly:** (1984) The Association for the Severely Handicapped; (2000) Association for Persons with Severe Handicaps. **Publications:** *Research & Practice for Persons with Severe Disabilities,* quarterly. Journal. **Price:** included in membership dues. Alternate Formats: online. Also Cited As: *RPPSD* ● *TASH Connections,* 10/year. Magazine. **Price:** included in membership dues. Alternate Formats: online. **Conventions/Meetings:** annual conference (exhibits).

11731 ■ United States International Council on Disabilities (USICD)
c/o Tapan Banerjee Exec. Dir.
1710 Rhode Island Ave. NW, 5th Fl.
Washington, DC 20036

Ph: (202)207-0338
Fax: (202)207-0334
E-mail: usicd@ncil.org
URL: http://www.usicd.org
Contact: John Lancaster, Pres.
Founded: 1988. **Membership Dues:** individual, $30 (annual) ● associate, $300 (annual) ● federal agency, $1,000-$2,000 (annual). **Staff:** 1. **National Groups:** 90. **Multinational. Description:** Promotes human and civil rights of children and adults with disabilities. Increases participation of disabled people in international activities. Educates the community on international issues affecting disabled people. **Computer Services:** Information services, disability resources.

11732 ■ VSA arts
818 Connecticut Ave. NW, Ste.600
Washington, DC 20006
Ph: (202)628-2800
Free: (800)933-8721
Fax: (202)429-0868
E-mail: info@vsarts.org
URL: http://www.vsarts.org
Contact: Soula Antoniou, Pres.
Founded: 1974. **State Groups:** 49. **National Groups:** 66. **Languages:** English, French, Spanish. **Multinational. Description:** Promotes educational and lifelong learning opportunities through the arts for people of all abilities. The Organization's educational programs use alternative curricula and teaching strategies designed to promote optimal learning experiences in a fully inclusive environment, providing youth and adults with an artistic means of self-expression, creating self-confidence and teaching marketable skills while fostering communication and independence. Offers comprehensive programs in literary, performing, and visual arts, in collaboration with local educational agencies, cultural institutions, institutions of higher education, arts agencies, disability associations, and health and rehabilitation organizations in 49 states and DC, and in more than 60 countries worldwide. **Awards:** Playwright Discovery Teacher Award. **Frequency:** annual. **Type:** monetary. **Recipient:** to teachers in middle and high schools who creatively bring disability awareness to their classrooms through the art of playwriting ● Young Soloists Award. **Frequency:** annual. **Type:** monetary. **Recipient:** to any individual musician with disability. **Telecommunication Services:** TDD, (202)737-0645. **Formerly:** (2000) Very Special Arts. **Publications:** *The Creative Spirit*, quarterly. Magazine. Includes latest news, events and accomplishments of the organization and its affiliates across the country and around the world. ● *Disability Awareness Guide*, periodic. Book. Serves as an informational tool for those who want to gain additional knowledge about disability and tips for social etiquette. ● *Express Diversity*. Booklet. Provides arts-based activities. Alternate Formats: CD-ROM; diskette ● *Start with the Arts*. Book. Promotes the development of basic literacy skills and offers engaging arts activities teachers can apply in all curricular areas. **Price:** $59.00/package ● *Tips for Parents*. Articles. Contains suggestions for fun, educational arts activities that parents can enjoy with their children. ● *Year in Retrospect*, annual. Annual Report. Contains educational opportunities through the arts of people with disabilities. ● Also publishes manuals and guides and makes available videotapes. **Conventions/Meetings:** annual conference ● regional meeting and conference.

11733 ■ Wheels for the World
c/o Joni and Friends
PO Box 3333
Agoura Hills, CA 91376-3333
Ph: (818)707-5664
Free: (800)523-5777
Fax: (818)707-2391
E-mail: wftw@joniandfriends.org
URL: http://www.joniandfriends.org/pg_wheelchair.php
Contact: Joni Eareckson Tada, Founder/CEO
Founded: 2003. **Multinational. Description:** Aims to meet the physical and spiritual needs of the disabled around the world by providing wheelchairs

and sharing the Gospel of Jesus Christ. Promotes disability awareness. Educates and trains local churches in disability ministry. **Programs:** International Outreach.

11734 ■ World Ability Federation (WAF)
120 S Riverside Plz., Ste.1050
Chicago, IL 60606
Ph: (312)207-0000
Fax: (312)207-0017
E-mail: info@worldabilityfederation.com
Contact: William A. Smith, Managing Dir./Co-Founder
Founded: 2002. **Multinational. Description:** Seeks to improve the quality of life for people who have a disability. Provides programs to educate the public on issues faced by people who have a disability. Provides research and information to foundations and corporate giving programs about the needs of organizations that serve or advocate for people with disabilities. Produces information to help remove the negative stigmatization often associated with disabilities. **Awards:** Ability Through Education Scholarship Program. **Frequency:** annual. **Type:** scholarship. **Recipient:** for students who study disciplines that directly benefit people who have a disability ● World Ability Awards. **Frequency:** annual. **Type:** trophy. **Recipient:** for individuals and organizations that improve the lives of people who have a disability. **Telecommunication Services:** electronic mail, media@worldabilityfederation.com ● electronic mail, legal@worldabilityfederation.com.

11735 ■ World Institute on Disability (WID)
510 16th St., Ste.100
Oakland, CA 94612
Ph: (510)763-4100
Fax: (510)763-4109
E-mail: wid@wid.org
URL: http://www.wid.org
Contact: Ms. Kathy Martinez, Exec. Dir.
Founded: 1983. **Staff:** 16. **Budget:** $2,430,000. **Nonmembership. Description:** International public policy center that conducts research on disability issues and overcoming obstacles to independent living for all people with disabilities. **Telecommunication Services:** TDD, (510)208-9493. **Divisions:** Access to Assets; California Work Incentives Initiative; Health Access and Long Term Care; International Disability and Development; Proyecto Vision. **Publications:** *An Independent Living Approach to Disability Policy Studies*. Report. **Price:** $17.50 ● *The Cost of Program Models Providing Personal Assistance Services for Independent Living*. Report. **Price:** $10.00 ● *Ethical Issues in Disability and Rehabilitation: A Report on an International Conference*. Monograph. **Price:** $10.00 ● *How to Create Disability Access to Technology: Best Practices in Electronic and Information Companies*. Booklets. **Price:** $12.00 ● *Treating Adults with Physical Disabilities: Access and Communication*. Video. **Price:** $152.00.

11736 ■ World Rehabilitation Fund (WRF)
16 E 40th St., Ste.704
New York, NY 10016
Ph: (212)532-6000
E-mail: wrfnewyork@msn.com
URL: http://www.worldrehabfund.org
Contact: Dr. Nadim Karam, Acting Exec. Dir.
Founded: 1955. **Staff:** 30. **Description:** Works to create and implement comprehensive programs in post-conflict and developing nations in order to assist persons with disabilities, including landmine survivors, to regain economic and social independence through community reintegration and employment. Partners with local organizations to provide technical and professional training to aid in the physical, psychosocial and socio-economic rehabilitation of people with disabilities. **Conventions/Meetings:** semiannual meeting.

11737 ■ Yes I Can! Foundation for Exceptional Children
1110 N Glebe Rd., Ste.300
Arlington, VA 22201-5704
Ph: (703)264-3660
Free: (800)224-6830

Fax: (703)264-9494
E-mail: yesican@cec.sped.org
Contact: Bill Bogdan, Pres.
Founded: 1922. **Members:** 50,000. **Staff:** 80. **State Groups:** 51. **Multinational. Description:** Advocates for quality education for all individuals with physical disabilities, multiple disabilities, and special health care needs served in schools, hospitals, or home settings. Advocates for gifted and talented children and youth. Operates the ERIC Clearinghouse on Disabilities and Gifted Education, and the National Clearinghouse for Professions in Special Education. Develops programs to help teachers, administrators, and related services professionals improve their practice. **Libraries: Type:** reference; open to the public. **Holdings:** articles, books, periodicals. **Subjects:** special education, gifted education. **Awards:** Business Awards. **Frequency:** annual. **Type:** recognition. **Recipient:** for business leaders who are involved with children and youth with exceptionalities in local communities ● D.C. Awards Program. **Frequency:** annual. **Type:** monetary. **Recipient:** for children and youth with disabilities and/or gifts/talents, who attend District of Columbia public schools ● Joan Wald Baaken Award. **Frequency:** annual. **Type:** recognition ● Mini-Grants. **Frequency:** annual. **Type:** monetary. **Recipient:** to teachers in support of innovative projects ● Outstanding Leadership. **Frequency:** annual. **Type:** recognition ● Outstanding Public Service Award. **Frequency:** annual. **Type:** recognition ● Special Education Research. **Frequency:** annual. **Type:** recognition ● Stanley Jackson Scholarships. **Frequency:** annual. **Type:** monetary. **Recipient:** to high school youth graduating with special needs and entering post-secondary education in a university or trade school. **Telecommunication Services:** teletype, (703)620-3660. **Formerly:** (1968) Association of Educators for Homebound and Hospitalized Children; (1979) Division on Physically Handicapped, Homebound and Hospitalized; (1993) Division for Physically Handicapped; (2002) Foundation for Exceptional Children. **Publications:** *DPHD Newsletter*, quarterly. Covers information regarding the education of individuals with physical disabilities and health impairments. **Price:** included in membership dues. **Circulation:** 1,600. **Advertising:** accepted ● *Exceptional Child Education Resources*, quarterly. Journal. Includes abstracts of book, non-print media, and journal literature. Alternate Formats: online ● *Exceptional Children*, quarterly. Journal. Covers special education and research. **Price:** included in membership dues; $58.00 /year for nonmembers ● *Teaching Exceptional Children*, bimonthly. Magazine. Includes classroom-oriented information about instructional methods, materials, and techniques for students of all ages with special needs. **Price:** included in membership dues; $58.00 /year for nonmembers ● Audiotapes ● Books ● Films ● Videos. **Conventions/Meetings:** annual meeting, held in conjunction with the Council for Exceptional Children (exhibits) - always spring.

Disaster Aid

11738 ■ Action Against Hunger (AAH)
247 W 37th St., 10th Fl.
New York, NY 10018
Ph: (212)967-7800
Free: (877)777-1420
Fax: (212)967-5480
E-mail: info@actionagainsthunger.org
URL: http://www.aah-usa.org
Contact: Kiera Downes-Vogel, Human Resources Asst.
Founded: 1979. **Staff:** 42. **Multinational. Description:** Strives to deliver emergency aid and longer-term assistance to those suffering from the consequences of natural disasters or manmade crisis. **Programs:** Food Security; Health; Nutrition; Water/Sanitation. **Publications:** *Assessment & Treatment of Malnutrition in Emergency Situations* (in English and French). Manual. **Price:** $33.95 plus shipping and handling ● *The Geopolitics of Hunger* (in English, French, and Spanish). Book. **Price:** $33.95 paper-

back; $50.00 hardcover ● *Providing Water to Threatened Populations* (in English and French). Book. **Price:** $33.95 paperback ● *RESPONSE*. Newsletter. **Conventions/Meetings:** annual conference, with dinner and live auction.

11739 ■ American Disaster Reserve (ADR)
3355 N Acad. Blvd., No. 232
Colorado Springs, CO 80917-5103
E-mail: wgreen@disasterreserve.us
URL: http://www.disasterreserve.us
Contact: Walter G. Green III, Natl. Commander
Membership Dues: regular, $30 (annual). **Description:** Aims to expand the disaster management capabilities of state and local jurisdictions and voluntary agencies. Provides services to disaster victims and serves as a training ground for disaster responders and voluntary recovery organizations. Advocates cooperation, communication, coordination and collaboration for effective rescue operations. **Awards:** Commendation. **Type:** recognition. **Recipient:** for individual performance of duty contributing to the success of battalions or companies over a sustained period of time ● Distinguished Service. **Type:** recognition. **Recipient:** for leadership or management of operations or programs ● Exceptional Service. **Type:** recognition. **Recipient:** for performance by Commanders, Deputy Commanders, and Chiefs of Staff that contributes to the success of divisions and brigades ● Life Saving. **Type:** recognition. **Recipient:** for action resulting in preservation of life threatened by disaster or emergency ● Meritorius Service. **Type:** recognition. **Recipient:** for individual performance of duty contributing to the success of divisions and brigades ● Presidential Disaster Service. **Type:** recognition. **Recipient:** for completion of one shift of active work in an assignment during a disaster ● Unit Citation. **Type:** recognition. **Recipient:** for units that make outstanding contribution to the success of a supported agency's disaster operations ● Unit Performance. **Frequency:** annual. **Type:** recognition. **Recipient:** for units that meet the annual national recruiting, training, and disaster operations goals in support of ADR's strategic plan. **Computer Services:** Information services, operations portal resources ● mailing lists, of members. **Programs:** Communications; National Training. **Affiliated With:** National Voluntary Organizations Active in Disaster. **Formerly:** (2004) United States Service Command. **Publications:** *The Volunteer*, monthly. Newsletter. Alternate Formats: online ● Reports, monthly. Alternate Formats: online ● Annual Report, annual. Alternate Formats: online.

11740 ■ Center for International Disaster Information (CIDI)
4100 N Fairfax Dr., Ste.302
Arlington, VA 22203-1629
Ph: (703)276-1914
E-mail: cidi@cidi.org
URL: http://www.cidi.org
Contact: Suzanne Brooks, Dir.
Multinational. Description: Provides tools and information regarding preparedness, mitigation, prevention activities and disaster response through training, hotline service and other programs to increase public and private sector awareness about international disaster response. Develops outreach program for individuals, groups, corporations, foreign embassies and other institutions in support of appropriate international disaster assistance. **Computer Services:** Information services, disaster related resources ● mailing lists, of members. **Affiliated With:** National Voluntary Organizations Active in Disaster.

11741 ■ September 11 Widows and Victims' Families Association (9-11-WVFA)
22 Cortlandt St., 20th Fl.
New York, NY 10007
Ph: (212)422-3520
E-mail: info@911wvfa.org
URL: http://www.911families.org
Contact: Jennifer Adams, Exec. Dir.
Founded: 2001. **Description:** Seeks to ensure dignified recovery of loved ones from the 9-11 terrorist at-

tacks; provides accurate information; addresses family hardships; liaisons with Mayor's Office, Fire Commissioner and Unions. **Conventions/Meetings:** meeting.

11742 ■ Tuesday's Children
390 Plandome Rd., Ste.217
Manhasset, NY 11030
Ph: (516)562-9000
Fax: (516)627-4736
E-mail: info@tuesdayschildren.org
URL: http://www.tuesdayschildren.org
Contact: Jonathan S. Barnett, Chm./Interim Pres.
Description: Seeks to address the ongoing needs of children coping with the September 11 tragedy. Provides educational and career guidance for teens. Offers mentoring programs for children and life management skills for adults. **Programs:** Career Paths; First Steps; Mentoring; Next Steps. **Publications:** *The Big Umbrella*, semiannual. Newsletter. Features articles about the organization's programs, events and latest news. Alternate Formats: online.

11743 ■ Windows of Hope Family Relief Fund
c/o Bloomberg LP
731 Lexington Ave.
New York, NY 10022
Ph: (212)617-3710
Fax: (212)617-4367
E-mail: ddwyer@bloomberg.net
URL: http://www.windowsofhope.org
Contact: Darlene Dwyer, Exec. Dir.
Multinational. Description: Provides aid, future scholarships and funds to families of victims of the World Trade Center tragedy in New York City on September 11, 2001, who worked in food, beverage and hospitality professions.

Divorce

11744 ■ American Society of Separated and Divorced Men (ASDM)
575 Keep St.
Elgin, IL 60120
Ph: (847)695-2200 (847)909-4141
Contact: Richard Templeton, Pres.
Founded: 1968. **Membership Dues:** in state, $125 (annual) ● out of state, $75 (annual). **Staff:** 3. **Description:** Separated and divorced men. Works to assist men "in fighting the divorce racket." Dedicated to the elimination of unreasonable alimony, child support, custody, and property settlement awards. Devoted to establishing respect for marriage in the courts, and to upholding the rights of fathers to their children. Educates the public about divorce customs and practices. Conducts interviews in the office or over the phone with divorced and separated men to discuss their situations and offer help if possible. Also provides pro-male attorney referrals. **Formerly:** (1968) America's Society of Divorced Men.

11745 ■ Child Support Resistance (CSR)
1464 Ticonderoga Dr.
Southaven, MS 38671
Fax: (530)453-3799
E-mail: bobevenson@yahoo.com
Contact: Robert M. Evenson, Dir.
Founded: 1992. **Description:** Individuals who oppose child support laws and their enforcement. Seeks to abolish all such laws and the agencies that enforce them. Views child support as a "private matter for all parents," and believes that "divorced parents should not be singled out and discriminated against by the legal system." Acts as clearinghouse for information and advice on resisting child support orders.

11746 ■ Children's Rights Council (CRC)
6200 Editors Park Dr., Ste.103
Hyattsville, MD 20782
Ph: (301)559-3120 (202)547-6227
Free: (800)787-KIDS
Fax: (301)559-3124

E-mail: crcdc@erols.com
URL: http://www.gocrc.com
Contact: John L. Bauserman Jr., Pres.
Founded: 1985. **Members:** 2,500. **Membership Dues:** new, $50 ● sustaining, $60 (annual) ● sponsor, $125 (annual) ● life, $500 ● full, $20 (annual). **Staff:** 11. **Budget:** $350,000. **Regional Groups:** 4. **State Groups:** 38. **Local Groups:** 3. **National Groups:** 3. **Description:** Promotes strengthened families through education and advocacy. Works to achieve divorce and custody reforms, and to minimize hostilities between parents involved in marital disputes. Favors shared parenting, parenting education, mediation, access enforcement, emotional and financial child support, family formation, family preservation, and school-based programs for children at risk. Files amicus curiae briefs in appeal cases of domestic relations matters such as joint custody (shared parenting), and access/visitation/parenting time issues. Conducts research and compiles statistics; monitors legislation; maintains speakers' bureau. **Libraries: Type:** reference. **Holdings:** 250; artwork, audiovisuals, books, clippings, monographs, periodicals. **Subjects:** custody, access/visitation, parenting. **Awards:** Chief Justice Warren E. Burger "Healer" Award. **Frequency:** annual. **Type:** recognition. **Recipient:** to judges, lawyers, and others who promote healing, not just litigation, in the domestic relations area ● Media Award. **Frequency:** annual. **Type:** recognition. **Recipient:** for best in media affecting children of separation and divorce ● Positive Parenting Award. **Frequency:** annual. **Type:** recognition. **Recipient:** to organizations and individuals who promote active parenting by both parents. **Computer Services:** database, custody and divorce reform groups in the U.S., mediators, and mental health professionals. **Committees:** Early Childhood Education; Research. **Affiliated With:** Stepfamily Association of America. **Formerly:** National Council for Children's Rights. **Publications:** *The Best Parent Is Both Parents*. Book. Published in 1993. ● *Catalog of Resources*, periodic. Lists books, reports, and cassettes. ● *Helping Your Child Succeed After Divorce*. Book. **Price:** $9.95 ● *How to Win as a Stepfamily*. Book. Contains specific suggestions for adults to make their stepfamilies work. **Price:** $13.95 ● *I Think Divorce Stinks*. Book. **Price:** $4.95 ● *Kid's Guide to Divorce*. Book ● *Mom's House, Dad's House (Revised)*. Book. Features ways on how parents can make two homes for their children after divorce. **Price:** $20.00 ● *My Mom and Dad are Getting a Divorce*. Book. **Price:** $3.95 ● *Parenting Directory*, annual. Lists 1,200 parenting groups in the U.S. ● *Speak Out for Children*, quarterly. Newsletter. Includes book reviews. **Price:** included in membership dues; $20.00 /year for libraries. ISSN: 1042-3559. **Circulation:** 5,000. **Advertising:** accepted ● Audiotapes, annual. Contains conference proceedings. **Price:** $10.00/tape ● Reports ● Videos ● Also publishes legal briefs, model bills, and books on parenting. **Conventions/Meetings:** annual conference (exhibits) - usually in Washington, DC.

11747 ■ Dads Rights
3140 De La Cruz Blvd., Ste.200
Santa Clara, CA 95054
Ph: (415)853-6877
URL: http://www.dadsrights.org
Contact: Anne P. Mitchell Esq., Founder/Exec.Dir.
Founded: 1991. **Members:** 1,250. **Membership Dues:** general, $95 (annual). **Staff:** 5. **State Groups:** 45. **National Groups:** 3. **Description:** Acts as advocate in issues relating to noncustodial fathers. Offers educational programs, referrals, and support. **Computer Services:** Mailing lists, of members ● online services, discussion lists. **Formerly:** (2005) Fathers Rights and Equality Exchange. **Publications:** *F.R.E.E. Thoughts*, quarterly. Newsletter. **Price:** included in membership dues. **Advertising:** accepted. Alternate Formats: online. **Conventions/Meetings:** annual meeting.

11748 ■ Ex-Partners of Servicemembers for Equality (EX-POSE)
PO Box 11191
Alexandria, VA 22312-0191
Ph: (703)941-5844

Fax: (703)212-6951
E-mail: ex-pose@juno.com
URL: http://www.ex-pose.org
Contact: Ms. Nancy Davis, Office Admin.
Founded: 1980. **Members:** 2,700. **Membership Dues:** individual, $20 (annual) ● attorney, $50 (annual) ● life (individual), $200 ● life (attorney), $500. **Description:** Represents the interests of military spouses and the attorneys who represent them. Provides information resources and materials about the rights and benefits of spouses in the process of separation and divorce from a service member. Seeks legislation that treats marriage as an economic partnership. Has achieved legislation for the direct payment of court-awarded monies from ex-spouses' retirement pay for alimony, child support, property settlement, and the courts' ability to award survivor benefits. **Computer Services:** Information services, membership and general information about military divorce. **Publications:** *Ex-Partners of Servicemembers for Equality—Newsletter*, quarterly. **Price:** free for members. **Circulation:** 3,000 ● *Guide for Military Separation or Divorce.* Booklet. **Conventions/Meetings:** annual meeting - usually third Saturday in June.

11749 ■ Fathers for Equal Rights (FER)
701 Commerce St., Ste.302
Dallas, TX 75202
Ph: (214)953-2233
Fax: (214)749-4622
E-mail: info@fathers4kids.com
URL: http://www.fathers4kids.com/html/FER.htm
Contact: Doug Clark, Exec. Dir.
Founded: 1973. **Members:** 3,000. **Membership Dues:** regular, $160 (annual). **Staff:** 4. **Regional Groups:** 2. **State Groups:** 4. **Local Groups:** 2. **Languages:** English, Spanish. **Description:** Parents and grandparents involved in divorce and child custody disputes. Provides support for men in divorce cases involving custody issues. Strives to prevent children from becoming victims of the legal divorce process. Seeks to educate the public about the ramifications of the absence of a father figure in the family. Works to establish minimum standards of competence for attorneys in child custody cases. Serves as clearinghouse on matters involving child custody litigation; makes recommendations to the legislature and courts. Researches issues such as the single parent family in America and the changing family unit. Offers referral service. Maintains certain "Pro Se" legal forms for sale for persons to file their own Court and legal papers in Court without having to pay or hire or be at the mercy of a lawyer. **Libraries: Type:** open to the public. **Holdings:** 400; audio recordings, video recordings. **Subjects:** divorce, child custody, father's rights. **Computer Services:** database. **Publications:** Newsletter, annual. Includes list of publications. **Conventions/Meetings:** monthly workshop and seminar.

11750 ■ Joint Custody Association (JCA)
c/o James A. Cook, Pres.
10606 Wilkins Ave.
Los Angeles, CA 90024
Ph: (310)475-5352
URL: http://www.ncfc.net/cook.html
Contact: James A. Cook, Pres.
Founded: 1980. **Members:** 5,000. **Description:** Psychologists, psychiatrists, physicians, social workers, marital and family counselors, attorneys, judges, concerned parents, authors of texts on joint custody, and others concerned with joint custody of children and related divorce issues. Disseminates information on joint custody for the children of divorce; surveys court decisions and their consequences. Assists children, parents, attorneys, counselors, and jurists with implementation of joint custody practices. Fosters introduction of legislation in several states regarding joint custody for children involved in divorce. **Libraries: Type:** reference. **Holdings:** archival material. **Subjects:** joint custody. **Publications:** *Joint Custodian*, periodic. Newsletter.

11751 ■ National Action for Former Military Wives (NAFMW)
2090 N Atlantic Ave., Apt. P-2
Cocoa Beach, FL 32931-5010

Ph: (321)783-2101
Fax: (321)783-2101
E-mail: jeanniebythesea@earthlink.net
Contact: Jeanne Buchan, Pres.
Founded: 1979. **Members:** 5,000. **Membership Dues:** $12 (annual). **Description:** Seeks federal legislation that provides for prospective pro-rata sharing of military retirement pay as a "marital property right" based on the length of marriage, concurrent with military spouse's active duty time. Also seeks mandatory assignment of the Survivors Benefit Plan to current and former spouses, members and the restoration of all medical, commissary, and exchange privileges to former spouses who were married for at least ten years during their military spouses active duty service. Works for Legislation that prevents instances of double taxation on benefits shared by ex-spouses. Compiles statistics. **Formerly:** (1983) Action for Former Military Wives. **Publications:** Newsletter, 2-4/year. **Conventions/Meetings:** monthly support group meeting, for former military wives and those in the process of divorce.

11752 ■ North American Conference of Separated and Divorced Catholics (NACSDC)
PO Box 10
Hancock, MI 49930-0010
Ph: (906)482-0494
Fax: (906)482-7470
E-mail: office@nacsdc.org
URL: http://www.nacsdc.org
Contact: Irene Varley, Exec. Dir.
Founded: 1974. **Members:** 2,000. **Membership Dues:** individual, $35 (annual) ● sustaining, $100 (annual) ● professional/group, $60 (annual) ● diocesan I, $150 (annual) ● diocesan II, $225 (annual). **Staff:** 1. **Budget:** $124,000. **Regional Groups:** 15. **Description:** Regional representatives of separated and divorced Catholics. Offers support and comfort to these individuals. Works to assist in the formation of new groups; develops programs for existing groups and disseminates information. Emphasis is on lay ministry, those with similar experiences aiding each other. Organizes workshops, retreats, educational and training programs, and experiential opportunities. Maintains speakers' bureau and offers programs and services for children of divorce. **Awards:** James J. Young Ministry Award. **Frequency:** annual. **Type:** recognition. **Recipient:** for outstanding service to the separated and divorced ministry. **Telecommunication Services:** electronic mail, bob@nacsdc.org. **Publications:** *Jacob's Well Professional*, quarterly. Newsletter. Provides information for divorced Catholics. Includes articles on being a single parent and helping the children of divorced parents. **Price:** included in membership dues. **Circulation:** 4,000 ● Books ● Brochure. Alternate Formats: online ● Also distributes resource packets, tapes, and training programs. **Conventions/Meetings:** annual A Whisper through the Darkness - international conference and workshop, with speakers - always June/July.

11753 ■ United Fathers of America (UFA)
1651 E Fourth St., Ste.122
Santa Ana, CA 92701
Ph: (714)558-7949
E-mail: help@unitedfathers.org
URL: http://www.unitedfathers.org
Contact: Marvin Chapman, Pres.
Founded: 1976. **Members:** 450. **Membership Dues:** regular, $400 (annual). **Staff:** 2. **Budget:** $85,000. **State Groups:** 3. **Description:** Assists individuals experiencing family disruption due to divorce. Seeks to establish equal rights for fathers with regard to child custody in divorce cases and provide the best possible environment for the children of divorce. Provides counseling and support services. Conducts educational programs. Monitors legislation pertaining to custody and divorce and disseminates information about this legislation to the public. Conducts research; offers referral service; operates speakers' bureau.

Dog

11754 ■ American Kuvasz Association (AKA)
c/o Agi Hejja
3831 Broad St. Rd.
Gum Spring, VA 23065-2135

E-mail: ederrakuv@aol.com
URL: http://www.kuvasz.org
Contact: Maria Arechaederra, Pres.
Membership Dues: regular - single, $36 ● regular - joint, $42 ● associate, $30. **Description:** Represents individuals devoted to the promotion and protection of the Kuvasz. Works to identify threats to the well-being of all Kuvasz. Provides assistance to Kuvasz owners. Attempts to place homeless Kuvasz into good homes and provide new owners with a loving companion. **Computer Services:** Information services, Kuvasz resources. **Telecommunication Services:** electronic mail, ahejja@aol.com. **Committees:** Health; Rescue. **Programs:** Mentor. **Publications:** *The Kuvasz Times*. Newsletter.

11755 ■ Dogs Deserve Better (DDB)
PO Box 23
Tipton, PA 16684
Ph: (814)941-7447
Free: (877)636-1408
E-mail: info@dogsdeservebetter.org
URL: http://www.dogsdeservebetter.com
Contact: Tammy Sneath Grimes, Founder
Founded: 2002. **Membership Dues:** student/senior, $15 (annual) ● silver, $25 (annual) ● gold, $50 (annual) ● platinum, $100 (annual) ● diamond, $500 (annual) ● benefactor, $1,000 (annual). **Description:** Represents the interests of individuals dedicated to rescuing and freeing chained dogs and bringing them into the home and family. Promotes the stopping of chained and penned dogs and other forms of abuse to dogs. Creates public awareness of the rights of animals. Seeks to highlight the mistreatment of dogs in the community. **Publications:** Newsletter, quarterly. **Price:** included in membership dues ● Brochure (in English and Spanish). **Price:** $2.50/50 pieces, plus shipping and handling; $3.25/75 pieces, plus shipping and handling; $4.00/100 pieces, plus shipping and handling.

11756 ■ Heart Bandits American Eskimo Dog Rescue
PO Box 4322
Fresno, CA 93744-4322
Ph: (559)787-2459
E-mail: contact@heartbandits.com
URL: http://www.heartbandits.com
Contact: Dan Senke-Rocka, Exec. Dir.
Founded: 1996. **Membership Dues:** general, $25 (annual). **Multinational. Description:** Provides care and shelter to homeless, or about to become homeless, American Eskimo dogs. Seeks to reunite lost dogs with their lawful owners. Provides veterinary care to dogs in need of such care. Secures appropriate adoptive homes for stray dogs. Educates the public about the responsible care of dogs. Provides guidance to existing dog owners.

11757 ■ North American Border Terrier Welfare (NABTW)
c/o Jo Ellen Wolf, U.S. Coor.
132 Buckboard Dr.
Martinez, GA 30907
Ph: (706)863-0951
E-mail: jo-wolf@webtv.net
URL: http://clubs.akc.org/btcoa/rescue.htm
Contact: Jo Ellen Wolf, U.S. Coor.
Description: Provides caring, rescue services and rehabilitation of purebred Border Terriers across the United States. Prevents the future need for rescue or re-homing. Provides education and information to individuals about the health, behavior and training of Border Terriers.

Domestic Violence

11758 ■ AMEND
2727 Bryant St., Ste.350
Denver, CO 80211
Ph: (303)832-6363
Fax: (303)480-9661

E-mail: central@amendinc.org
URL: http://www.amendinc.org
Contact: Linda Loflin Pettit, Exec. Dir.

Founded: 1977. **Staff:** 20. **Budget:** $656,917. **Regional Groups:** 6. **Local Groups:** 6. **Languages:** English, Spanish. **Description:** Provides psychotherapy for abusive men, advocacy for women, violence prevention programs in the schools, and educational programs on violence and its prevention. Sponsors training programs. Operates 6 county offices and 1 satellite office. Maintains speakers' bureau. Offers community education presentations and trainings across the U.S. when asked and when feasible. **Libraries:** Type: reference. **Holdings:** 100; audiovisuals, books. **Subjects:** domestic violence, child abuse, victimology. **Also Known As:** Abusive Men Exploring New Directions. **Formerly:** (1992) AMEND Network. **Publications:** *Time Out*, semiannual. Newsletter. **Price:** free. **Circulation:** 1,100. **Conventions/Meetings:** semiannual conference.

11759 ■ American Women Overseas Domestic Violence Fund (AWOS)

3300 NW 185th, Ste.133
Portland, OR 97229
Ph: (503)846-8748
Free: (866)879-6636
Fax: (503)907-6554
E-mail: a866uswomen@866uswomen.org
URL: http://www.awoscentral.com
Contact: Paula Lucas, Exec.Dir.

Multinational. Description: Provides necessary tools for American women and children living overseas to end domestic violence.

11760 ■ Asian and Pacific Islander Institute on Domestic Violence

450 Sutter St., Ste.600
San Francisco, CA 94108
Ph: (415)954-9988
Fax: (415)954-9999
E-mail: apidvinstitute@apiahf.org
URL: http://www.apiahf.org/apidvinstitute/default.htm
Contact: Firoza Chic Dabby, Dir.

Description: Seeks to eliminate domestic violence in Asian and Pacific Islander communities by increasing awareness about the extent and depth of problem. **Computer Services:** database, trainers, experts, organizers ● mailing lists, of members. **Working Groups:** Intervention; Policy; Prevention; Research. **Conventions/Meetings:** regional meeting.

11761 ■ Batterers Anonymous - Beyond Abuse (BA)

c/o Sojourner Truth House, Inc.
PO Box 080319
Milwaukee, WI 53208
Ph: (414)643-4799
Fax: (414)643-1790
E-mail: sojour@sojournertruthhouse.org
URL: http://www.sojournertruthhouse.org/services.htm
Contact: Kathie Stolpman, Exec. Dir., Sojourner Truth House

Founded: 1980. **Staff:** 1. **Budget:** $25,000. **National Groups:** 20. **Description:** Self-help program designed to rehabilitate men who are abusive toward women. Aims to achieve the complete elimination of physical and emotional abuse and seeks positive alternatives to abusive behavior. Batterers attend weekly informal meeting with other persons who have similar difficulties. Each group is aided by a professional or paraprofessional sponsor and a group leader. A "Buddy System" is encouraged to provide reassurance and support to the batterer. It is believed that through increased awareness of their problem, batterers are better able to cope with abuse issues and develop skills for handling stress. **Convention/Meeting:** none. **Publications:** *National Directory*, annual ● *Self-Help Counseling for Men Who Batter Women*. **Price:** $9.95 ● Also publishes handbook for members.

11762 ■ Break the Cycle

5200 W Century Blvd., Ste.300
Los Angeles, CA 90045
Ph: (310)286-3383
Free: (888)988-TEEN
Fax: (310)286-3386
E-mail: info@breakthecycle.org
URL: http://www.breakthecycle.org
Contact: Jessica Aronoff Esq., Exec. Dir.

Nonmembership. Description: Engages, educates and empowers youth to build lives and communities free from domestic and dating violence.

11763 ■ Corporate Alliance to End Partner Violence (CAEPV)

2416 E Washington St., Ste.E
Bloomington, IL 61704
Ph: (309)664-0667
Fax: (309)664-0747
E-mail: caepv@caepv.org
URL: http://www.caepv.org
Contact: Jane Randel, Pres.

Founded: 1995. **Membership Dues:** general (minimum; based on number of employees), $500 (annual). **Description:** Works to aid in the prevention of partner violence by leveraging the strength and resources of the corporate community. Enhances corporate profitability through reduction of rising expenses related to partner violence.

11764 ■ Emerge: Counseling and Education to Stop Domestic Violence

2464 Massachusetts Ave., Ste.101
Cambridge, MA 02140-1645
Ph: (617)547-9879
Fax: (617)547-0904
E-mail: emergedv@aol.com
URL: http://www.emergedv.com
Contact: David Adams, Co-Dir.

Founded: 1977. **Staff:** 28. **Budget:** $450,000. **Local Groups:** 1. **Languages:** English, Spanish, Vietnamese. **Description:** Counseling agency in the Boston, MA, area dedicated to assisting men in the prevention of domestic violence. National activities include: technical assistance and training programs for human service and law enforcement professionals on counseling techniques; information and telephone referral service. Seeks to serve as model for the establishment of similar groups. Conducts research and training workshops on the abuse of women and for teen perpetrators of dating and/or domestic violence. **Libraries:** Type: reference. **Holdings:** 1; articles, books. **Subjects:** domestic violence, treatment of batterers. **Formerly:** (1993) Emerge: A Men's Counseling Service on Domestic Violence; (1998) Emerge: Counseling and Education to Stop Male Violence. **Publications:** *Emerge - A Group Education Model for Abusers*. Article. **Price:** $4.00 ● *Program Manual* (in English and Spanish). Covers domestic violence. **Price:** $50.00 ● *To Have and To Hold*. Film. Examines the problem of spouse abuse from a male perspective. ● *Treatment Program for Batterers*. Article. Contains an overview of batterer intervention programs in U.S. and Canada. **Price:** $3.50 ● *What You Should Know About Your Abusive Partner*. Pamphlets ● Newsletter, annual. **Conventions/Meetings:** Counseling Men Who Batter: A Four Day Intensive Course - meeting - always fall, winter and spring.

11765 ■ FaithTrust Institute

2400 N 45th St., No. 10
Seattle, WA 98103
Ph: (206)634-1903
Free: (877)860-2255
Fax: (206)634-0115
E-mail: info@faithtrustinstitute.org
URL: http://www.faithtrustinstitute.org
Contact: Rev. Kathryn Jans, Exec. Dir.

Founded: 1977. **Staff:** 8. **Description:** Works to address issues of sexual and domestic violence; seeks to engage religious leaders to help end abuse and prepare human service professionals to recognize and attend to the religious questions and issues that may arise in their work with women and children in crisis, focusing on education and prevention.

Projects: Seminary. **Publications:** *A Sacred Trust*. Video ● *Domestic Violence*. Video ● *Educational Resources*. Video ● *Family Violence & Religion*. Video ● *The Healing Years*. Video ● *Love - All That and More*. Video ● Numerous Educational Books and Brochures ● *Working Together*. Newsletter ● Annual Report, annual. **Conventions/Meetings:** Bi-National Sermon Contest - seminar ● competition ● conference.

11766 ■ Family Violence Prevention Fund (FVPF)

383 Rhode Island St., Ste.304
San Francisco, CA 94103-5133
Ph: (415)252-8900
Free: (800)252-4889
Fax: (415)252-8991
E-mail: info@endabuse.org
URL: http://www.endabuse.org
Contact: Esta Soler, Founder/Pres.

Founded: 1980. **Membership Dues:** limited income/student/senior, $15 (annual) ● individual, $35 (annual) ● organization, $50 (annual) ● sponsor, $100 (annual). **Staff:** 30. **Languages:** English, Spanish. **Description:** Individuals, corporations, health care professionals, child welfare and community organizations committed to ending domestic violence. Focuses on domestic violence education, prevention, and public policy reform. Works on the local, state, and national level to promote prevention and intervention. Distributes information to medical researchers and health care professionals. Provides specialized services and training on domestic violence to judges, health care professionals and service providers, and workplace leaders. **Libraries:** Type: reference. **Subjects:** health resources. **Additional Websites:** http://www.fvpf.org. **Projects:** Battered Immigrant and Refugee Women's Rights; Child Welfare; Economic Independence; Health Care Response; Judicial Education; Public Education; Public Policy; Workplace Education: Community Localization. **Publications:** *Domestic Violence in Immigrant and Refugee Communities: Asserting the Rights of Battered Women*. Manual. Written for domestic violence program staff, immigration and refugee service providers, and social workers. **Price:** $85.00 for private attorneys/firms; $50.00 for nonprofit organizations ● *Domestic Violence: The Crucial Role of the Judge in Criminal Court Cases A National Model for Judicial Education*. Manual. Assists judicial educators and domestic violence workers in developing a judicial education program on domestic violence. **Price:** $50.00/manual; $25.00/disk. Alternate Formats: diskette ● *News from the Homefront*, semiannual. Newsletter. **Price:** included in membership dues ● Newsletter. Alternate Formats: online ● Offers domestic violence prevention posters and camera-ready art.

11767 ■ House of Ruth

5 Thomas Cir. NW
Washington, DC 20005
Ph: (202)667-7001
Fax: (202)667-7047
E-mail: houseofruth@houseofruth.org
URL: http://www.houseofruth.org
Contact: Christel Nichols, Pres.

Founded: 1976. **Staff:** 65. **Description:** Supported by individuals, churches, synagogues, service organizations, businesses, foundations, and local and federal government sources. Guides women and children in crisis to long-term stability and independence. Provides emergency shelter, counseling, food, and case management; job training and experience in the food service industry; transitional housing for women who are working or seeking employment; free food and clothing for men and women living on the streets; comprehensive care for women and the infants of women who are pregnant or post-partum and recovering from substance abuse; emergency and transitional housing, counseling, and legal and medical services for women and their children who are fleeing domestic violence; a 24-hour hotline to link victims of abuse to support services; and developmental day care and family support services for children who are homeless, delayed, abused, or at risk. **Publications:** *House of Ruth Annual Report*, annual. **Price:** free. Alternate Formats: online ● *House of Ruth Newsletter*, semiannual. **Price:** free.

11768 ■ Illusion Theater (IT)
528 Hennepin Ave., Ste.704
Minneapolis, MN 55403
Ph: (612)339-4944
Fax: (612)337-8042
E-mail: info@illusiontheater.org
URL: http://www.illusiontheater.org
Contact: Michael H. Robins, Exec. Producing Dir.

Founded: 1974. **Staff:** 17. **Budget:** $1,200,000. **Regional Groups:** 9. **State Groups:** 9. **Local Groups:** 22. **Description:** Theatrical organization committed to the creation of new works for the American Theater by emerging and established artists who reflect a variety of cultural backgrounds. Collaborates annually with over 150 playwrights, directors, actors, composers, designers, and human service professionals. Nationally renowned Education Program works to raise awareness and promote communication about issues relevant to youth, adults, families, and communities including sexual abuse, HIV/STDs, interpersonal violence, sexual harassment, breast cancer, mental health, tobacco use, eating disorders and diversity. **Divisions:** Development; Education Programming; Marketing and Communications; Outreach; Production. **Affiliated With:** Greater Minneapolis Convention and Visitors Association; Theatre Communications Group. **Also Known As:** Illusion Theater and School. **Publications:** *Building Blocks to Strengthen Families*. Booklet ● *How to Take the First Steps*. Booklet. Discusses child sexual abuse prevention. ● *In Touch*, semiannual. Newsletter. **Price:** free ● *No Easy Answers*. Video. Discusses adolescent sexual abuse prevention. ● *No Easy Answers Curriculum*. Adolescent sexual abuse prevention curriculum. ● *Sponsor Information Packet, Licensing Summary and Procedures* ● *Touch*. Video. Discusses adolescent sexual abuse prevention.

11769 ■ Leadership Council on Child Abuse and Interpersonal Violence
191 Presidential Blvd., Ste.C-132
Bala Cynwyd, PA 19004
Ph: (610)664-5007
Fax: (610)664-5279
E-mail: desk@leadershipcouncil.org
URL: http://www.leadershipcouncil.org
Contact: Dr. Paul J. Fink MD, Pres.

Founded: 1998. **Description:** Comprised of scientists, clinicians, educators, legal scholars, journalists and public policy analysts. Promotes psychological science and provides current materials and information for mental health issues. **Formerly:** (2005) Leadership Council for Mental Health, Justice and the Media.

11770 ■ National Center for Assault Prevention (NCAP)
606 Delsea Dr.
Sewell, NJ 08080
Ph: (856)582-8282
E-mail: jcollins@eirc.org
URL: http://www.ncap.org
Contact: Jeannette Collins, Dir. of Curriculum

Founded: 1978. **Regional Groups:** 200. **Description:** Seeks to prevent interpersonal violence against vulnerable populations through education, prevention training, and research. Provides services to children aged two and one half years through adolescence, children and adults with mental retardation and developmental disabilities, and older citizens. Conducts research on the causes, consequences, and prevention of interpersonal violence. Provides three-day training sessions in the Child Assault Prevention model; sponsors workshops. Compiles statistics; operates speakers' bureau. **Convention/Meeting:** none. **Formed by Merger of:** Assault Prevention Training Project; Child Assault Prevention. **Formerly:** National Assault Prevention Center. **Publications:** *Strategies for Free Children*. Manual.

11771 ■ National Center on Elder Abuse (NCEA)
1201 15th St. NW, Ste.350
Washington, DC 20005-2800
Ph: (202)898-2586
Fax: (202)898-2583
E-mail: ncea@nasua.org
URL: http://www.elderabusecenter.org
Contact: Sara Aravanis, Dir.

Founded: 1998. **Languages:** English, French, German, Italian, Spanish. **Description:** Provides elder abuse research, information, and technical assistance to professionals and the public. **Libraries: Type:** reference. **Subjects:** elder abuse, neglect, exploitation. **Computer Services:** Bibliographic search, clearing house on abuse and neglect of the elderly ● information services, state elder abuse hotline list ● mailing lists, elder abuse listserv. **Telecommunication Services:** information service, clearing house on abuse and neglect of the elderly, (202)831-3525. **Publications:** Newsletter, monthly. Contains current issues, events, and promising practices. Alternate Formats: online.

11772 ■ National Coalition Against Domestic Violence (NCADV)
PO Box 18749
Denver, CO 80218
Ph: (303)839-1852
Fax: (303)831-9251
E-mail: mainoffice@ncadv.org
URL: http://www.ncadv.org
Contact: Rita Smith, Exec. Dir.

Founded: 1978. **Members:** 1,300. **Membership Dues:** individual, $30 (annual) ● student, $20 (annual) ● supporting, $50 (annual) ● sponsoring, $75 (annual) ● government agency, $200 (annual) ● state coalition, $400 (annual). **Staff:** 8. **Budget:** $800,500. **State Groups:** 56. **Local Groups:** 2,000. **Description:** Grass roots coalition of battered women's service organizations and shelters. Supplies technical assistance and makes referrals on issues of domestic violence. Provides training personnel; offers child advocacy training. Maintains speakers' bureau. Compiles statistics. Conducts National Public Policy work. **Libraries: Type:** reference. **Holdings:** archival material, books, business records, films. **Subjects:** domestic violence, intimate partner abuse. **Computer Services:** Mailing lists. **Caucuses:** Child Advocacy; Formerly Battered Women; Jewish Women; Lesbian/Bisexual/Transgendered Women; Queers of Color; Women of Color. **Absorbed:** (1981) National Communications Network for the Elimination of Violence Against Women. **Publications:** *Grassroots Connection*, 3/year. Newsletter. **Price:** included in membership dues. **Advertising:** accepted ● *Guidelines for Mental Health Practitioners in Domestic Violence Cases* ● *Naming the Violence: Speaking Out About Lesbian Battering* ● *National Coalition Against Domestic Violence—Voice*, quarterly. Journal. **Price:** included in membership dues for organizations; $50.00 for individuals. **Advertising:** accepted ● *National Directory of Domestic Violence Programs*, periodic ● *Open Minds, Open Doors*. Manual. Includes topics for working with women with disabilities. ● *Rural Task Force Resource Packet* ● *Teen Dating Violence Resource Manual*. **Conventions/Meetings:** biennial National Domestic Violence - conference (exhibits).

11773 ■ National Coalition for Domestic Abuse Awareness (NCDAA)
Address Unknown since 2006

Description: Reduces crime through accurate information to domestic abuse professionals.

11774 ■ National Council on Child Abuse and Family Violence (NCCAFV)
1025 Connecticut Ave. NW, Ste.1000
Washington, DC 20036
Ph: (202)429-6695
Fax: (202)521-3479

E-mail: info@nccafv.org
URL: http://www.nccafv.org
Contact: Alan Davis, Pres./Sec.

Founded: 1984. **Staff:** 6. **Nonmembership. Description:** Assists community-based non-profit organizations that work to provide safety from violence within the family — whether child abuse, spouse/partner abuse (domestic violence), or elder abuse. Believes in prevention when possible and integrated, coordinated intervention when necessary. Supports community-based prevention and treatment programs that provide assistance to children, women, the elderly, and families who are victims of abuse and violence; concerned with the cyclical and inter-generational nature of family violence and abuse. Seeks to increase public awareness of family violence and promote private sector financial support for prevention and treatment programs. Serves as Secretariat for the International Network on Family Violence (INFV), its World Congress on Family Violence (WCFV), and Child Welfare Fund International (CWFI). Collects and disseminates information regarding child abuse, domestic violence, and elder abuse. **Computer Services:** Electronic publishing. **Telecommunication Services:** hotline, National Domestic Violence hotline, (800)799-7233 ● hotline, National Domestic Violence hotline, (800)787-3244 ● hotline, National Child Abuse hotline, (800)422-4453. **Programs:** American Campaign for Prevention of Abuse and Family Violence; Awareness Campaign; Community Volunteer Councils on Child Abuse and Family Violence; Information Services; Professional Planning; Technical Assistance; Volunteer Recruitment and Training. **Also Known As:** American Campaign for Prevention of Child Abuse and Family Violence.

11775 ■ National Domestic Violence Hotline (NDVH)
PO Box 161810
Austin, TX 78716
Ph: (512)794-1133
Free: (800)799-7233
Fax: (512)794-1199
E-mail: ndvh@ndvh.org
URL: http://www.ndvh.org
Contact: Sheryl Cates, CEO

Founded: 1996. **Languages:** English, Spanish. **Description:** Provides crisis intervention, referrals, information and support in many languages. **Telecommunication Services:** electronic mail, deafhelp@ndvh.org ● TDD, (800)787-3224.

11776 ■ National Latino Alliance for the Elimination of Domestic Violence
PO Box 672
New York, NY 10035
Ph: (646)672-1404
Free: (800)342-9908
Fax: (646)672-0360
E-mail: amedina@dvalianza.org
URL: http://www.dvalianza.org
Contact: Adelita Michelle Medina, Exec. Dir.

Founded: 1997. **Languages:** English, Spanish. **Description:** Addresses the domestic violence needs and concerns of underserved populations. Represents a growing network of Latina and Latino advocates, practitioners, researchers, community activists, and survivors of domestic violence. Aims to promote understanding, initiate and sustain dialogue, and generate solutions that move toward the elimination of domestic violence affecting Latino communities, with an understanding of the sacredness of all relations and communities. **Computer Services:** Mailing lists. **Telecommunication Services:** electronic mail, inquiry@dvalianza.org ● additional toll-free number, (800)216-2404. **Programs:** Community Education and Development; Public Policy; Research; Training and Technical Assistance.

11777 ■ National Network to End Domestic Violence (NNEDV)
660 Pennsylvania Ave. SE, Ste.303
Washington, DC 20003
Ph: (202)543-5566
Fax: (202)543-5626

E-mail: nnedv@nnedv.org
URL: http://www.nnedv.org
Contact: Lynn Rosenthal, Pres.
Founded: 1990. **Members:** 54. **Staff:** 5. **Regional Groups:** 6. **State Groups:** 54. Seeks to strengthen cooperation and coordination of programs offered by members. Provides technical assistance to programs benefiting battered women; conducts educational programs to raise public awareness of domestic violence issues; lobbies for public policies responsive to the needs of victims of domestic violence. **Telecommunication Services:** hotline, National Domestic Violence hotline, (800)799-7233 ● hotline, National Domestic Violence hotline, (800)787-3224.

11778 ■ Stop Abuse for Everyone (SAFE)
PO Box 951
Tualatin, OR 97062
Ph: (319)441-1010
E-mail: safe@safe4all.org
URL: http://www.safe4all.org
Contact: Mr. Philip Cook, Exec. Dir.
Founded: 1996. **Members:** 100. **Membership Dues:** charter, $15 (annual). **Staff:** 2. **State Groups:** 4. **Description:** Seeks to end abuse in families. Provides community resource information, public education to community leaders, health organizations, criminal justice agencies and individuals regarding the effects of family violence; conducts research on domestic violence. Advocates for men and women who are victims and perpetrators of domestic violence, particularly against men, gay men, lesbian women, teens and elderly. **Awards:** Best News Media Coverage of Domestic Violence, Radio, TV, Newspaper, Magazine. **Frequency:** annual. **Type:** recognition. **Recipient:** for best news media coverage of domestic violence on radio, television, in newspapers or magazines. **Computer Services:** Mailing lists, updates on SAFE's activities, research developments and more. **Publications:** Newsletter, monthly. **Price:** included in membership dues. **Advertising:** accepted. Alternate Formats: online.

Down's Syndrome

11779 ■ National Down Syndrome Society (NDSS)
666 Broadway
New York, NY 10012
Ph: (212)460-9330
Free: (800)221-4602
Fax: (212)979-2873
E-mail: info@ndss.org
URL: http://www.ndss.org
Contact: Jonathan Colman, COO
Founded: 1979. **Staff:** 22. **Languages:** English, Spanish. **Description:** Aims to benefit people with Down syndrome and their families through national leadership in education, research and advocacy. **Telecommunication Services:** electronic bulletin board, maintains message boards that parents and professionals can use to ask questions and obtain information ● information service, through 800-line and email, NDSS responds to questions, makes referrals and distributes educational materials to parents, professionals, and others. **Boards:** Affiliate Advisory; Clinical and Science Advisory; Honorary Board of Governors; Self-Advocate Advisory. **Publications:** A Promising Future Together. Video ● Clinical Care Booklets ● Down Syndrome: An Introduction. Brochure. Designed for new parents of Down syndrome children. **Price:** free ● Inclusion, Making Plans, Transition, A Promising Future Together: A Guide for New and Expectant Parents. Booklets. Educational materials regarding Down syndrome. ● UpBeat. Magazine ● Also publishes fact sheets and a variety of written materials in both English and Spanish.

Drug Abuse

11780 ■ DanceSafe
536 45th St.
Oakland, CA 94609

E-mail: dsusa@dancesafe.org
URL: http://www.dancesafe.org
Contact: Marc Brandl, Exec. Dir.
Multinational. Description: Promotes health and safety within the rave and nightclub community. Creates peer-based educational programs to reduce drug abuse and empower young people to make healthy, informed lifestyle choices. Trains volunteers to be health educators and drug abuse prevention counselors. Utilizes the principles and methods of harm reduction and popular education. **Telecommunication Services:** electronic mail, marc@dancesafe.org. **Publications:** DanceSafe E-News, monthly. Newsletter. Includes harm reduction news, information, culture, and policy news. Alternate Formats: online.

11781 ■ Harm Reduction Coalition (HRC)
22 W 27th St., 5th Fl.
New York, NY 10001
Ph: (212)213-6376
Fax: (212)213-6582
E-mail: hrc@harmreduction.org
URL: http://www.harmreduction.org
Membership Dues: individual, $35-$125 ● organizational, $100 ● organizational (international), $175 ● senior, $250 ● core, $500 ● harm reduction partner, $1,000. **Multinational. Description:** Seeks to reduce drug-related harm to individuals and communities. Promotes local, regional and national reduction education and intervention. Promotes alternative models to conventional health and human services and drug treatment. **Computer Services:** database, youth services ● information services, health resources ● information services, syringe exchange resources ● online services, message board. **Programs:** African American Capacity; Harm Reduction Training. **Projects:** Hepatitis C. **Publications:** Harm Reduction Communication. Magazine.

11782 ■ MAD DADS (Men Against Destruction—Defending Against Drugs and Social Disorder)
c/o Eddie Staton
2221 N 24th St.
Omaha, NE 68110
Ph: (402)451-3500
Fax: (402)451-3477
URL: http://www.nal.usda.gov/pavnet/cf/cfmaddad.htm
Contact: Eddie Staton, Contact
Description: Coalition of fathers who aim to prevent violence and help troubled youth through community services and role modeling. **Publications:** Training Manual.

Economic Development

11783 ■ Enterprise Development International
7910 Woodmont Ave., Ste.800
Bethesda, MD 20814
Ph: (240)396-1146
Free: (800)9-ENABLE
Fax: (240)235-3550
E-mail: info@endpoverty.org
URL: http://www.endpoverty.org
Contact: Larry Roadman, Chm.
Founded: 1985. **Staff:** 10. **Budget:** $1,500,000. **Multinational. Description:** Works to enable the poor in the United States and in the developing world to free themselves from poverty. **Publications:** Enterprising Times, quarterly. Newsletter. **Price:** free. Alternate Formats: online ● Annual Report, annual. Alternate Formats: online.

11784 ■ Structured Employment Economic Development Corporation (Seedco)
915 Broadway, 17th Fl.
New York, NY 10010
Ph: (212)473-0255 (212)204-1329
Fax: (212)473-0357

E-mail: info@seedco.org
URL: http://www.seedco.org
Contact: William Grinker, CEO
Founded: 1987. **Description:** Creates opportunities for low-wage workers and their families to develop, operate and learn from model programs that help people join the workforce and achieve economic self-sufficiency. Assists small businesses. Promotes asset building for residents and businesses in economically distressed communities. Provides financial and technical assistance to the networks of neighborhood-based partners. **Computer Services:** Information services, capacity building resources ● information services, lending resources. **Programs:** Affordable Homeownership; Economic Development; Workforce Development. **Publications:** Fieldnotes. Newsletter. Alternate Formats: online ● Reports. Alternate Formats: online.

Economics

11785 ■ Center for Economic and Social Justice (CESJ)
PO Box 40711
Washington, DC 20016
Ph: (703)243-5155
Fax: (703)243-5935
E-mail: thirdway@cesj.org
URL: http://www.cesj.org
Contact: Norman G. Kurland, Pres.
Founded: 1984. **Members:** 500. **Membership Dues:** basic in U.S., $25 (annual) ● basic outside U.S., $30 (annual) ● family (same residence), $40 (annual) ● sustaining, $25 (monthly) ● sustaining, $300 (annual) ● life, $10,000. **Staff:** 4. **Multinational. Description:** Promotes a free enterprise approach to global economic justice through expanded capital ownership. **Publications:** Capital Homesteading for Every Citizen: A Just Free Market Solution for Saving Social Security. Book ● Curing World Poverty: The New Role of Property. Book ● Toward Economic & Social Justice: The Founding Principles of CESJ. Pamphlet. **Conventions/Meetings:** quarterly board meeting ● monthly executive committee meeting ● annual meeting, with anniversary celebration ● periodic seminar and workshop, educational.

11786 ■ John M. Olin Foundation
330 Madison Ave., 22nd Fl.
New York, NY 10017
Ph: (212)661-2670
Fax: (212)661-5917
E-mail: inquiry@jmof.org
Contact: James Piereson, Exec.Dir.
Founded: 1953. **Description:** Works to provide support for projects that are related to economic, political, and cultural institutions. Encourages the study of connections between economic and political freedoms. **Awards: Type:** grant.

Education

11787 ■ Arthur Vining Davis Foundations
c/o Dr. Jonathan T. Howe, Exec. Dir.
225 Water St., Ste.1510
Jacksonville, FL 32202-5185
Ph: (904)359-0670
E-mail: arthurvining@bellsouth.net
URL: http://www.avdfdn.org
Contact: Dr. Jonathan T. Howe, Exec. Dir.
Founded: 1952. **Staff:** 6. **Description:** Board of Trustees. Strives to provide financial assistance to educational, cultural, scientific, and religious institutions with a focus on private higher education, secondary education, graduate theological education, health care, and public television. **Awards: Frequency:** annual. **Type:** grant.

11788 ■ Books for the Barrios (BftB)
2350 Whitman Rd., Ste.D
Concord, CA 94518-2541
Ph: (925)687-7701
Fax: (925)687-8298

E-mail: joinus@booksforthebarrios.com
URL: http://www.booksforthebarrios.com
Contact: Nancy Harrington, Exec. Dir.
Founded: 1981. **Multinational. Description:** Aims to improve the quality of education in the Philippines. Strengthens public elementary school education in the Philippines to allow equal access to quality education for disadvantaged children. Offers programs designed to help students and teachers, both in the U.S. and in the Philippines.

11789 ■ Henry Luce Foundation
51 Madison Ave., 30th Fl.
New York, NY 10010
Ph: (212)489-7700
Fax: (212)581-9541
E-mail: hlf@hluce.org
URL: http://www.hluce.org
Contact: Margaret Boles Fitzgerald, Chair
Founded: 1936. **Description:** Strives to promote higher education, the study of religion and theology, American art, environmental programs, opportunities for women in science and engineering, and public policy issues. **Awards: Type:** grant.

11790 ■ Joseph Drown Foundation
1999 Ave. of the Stars, Ste.2330
Los Angeles, CA 90067
Ph: (310)277-4488
Fax: (310)277-4573
E-mail: staff@jdrown.org
URL: http://www.jdrown.org
Contact: Norman C. Obrow, Chm. of the Board/Pres.
Founded: 1953. **Description:** Strives to assist individuals in becoming successful, self-sustaining, contributing citizens, and focuses on education, medical and scientific research; community, health, and social services; and arts and humanities.

11791 ■ Parents for Public Schools (PPS)
3252 N State St.
Jackson, MS 39216
Ph: (601)713-3229
Free: (800)880-1222
Fax: (601)713-3099
E-mail: ppschapter@parents4publicschools.com
URL: http://www.parents4publicschools.com
Contact: Ken Rolling, Exec. Dir.
Founded: 1989. **Membership Dues:** chapter, $250 (annual). **Description:** Works to strengthen public schools through broad-based enrollment. Promotes and focuses positive attention on public schools. Strives to maximize parent involvement and consolidate community resources by working together to ensure a quality and equitable education for all children. **Telecommunication Services:** electronic mail, kencrolling@aol.com. **Publications:** *Parent Press*, 3/year. Newsletter. **Price:** included in membership dues. Alternate Formats: online.

11792 ■ Room to Read
PO Box 29127
San Francisco, CA 94129
Ph: (415)561-3331
Fax: (415)561-4428
E-mail: info@roomtoread.org
URL: http://www.roomtoread.org
Contact: John Wood, Founder/CEO
Founded: 2000. **Multinational. Description:** Seeks to intervene early in the lives of children and help provide them with education. Partners with communities in building schools. Establishes bilingual libraries. Establishes computer and language laboratories. Provides long-term scholarships to girls. **Publications:** Annual Report, annual. Alternate Formats: online.

11793 ■ Spencer Foundation
625 N Michigan Ave., Ste.1600
Chicago, IL 60611
Ph: (312)337-7000
Fax: (312)337-0282

E-mail: mnatonski@spencer.org
URL: http://www.spencer.org
Contact: Mary Ellen Natonski, Admin. Asst.
Founded: 1962. **Description:** Works to support research, which contributes to the understanding and improvement of education. Hosts conferences. **Awards: Type:** grant. **Publications:** Annual Report, annual. Alternate Formats: online.

11794 ■ Wallace-Reader's Digest Funds
5 Penn Plz., 7th Fl.
New York, NY 10001
Ph: (212)251-9700
Fax: (212)251-6990
E-mail: webmaster@wallacefoundation.org
URL: http://www.wallacefunds.org
Contact: M. Christine DeVita, Pres.
Founded: 1950. **Description:** Works to develop educational leaders, provide informal learning opportunities, and promote new standards of practice to increase participation in the arts. **Awards: Type:** grant.

Educational Funding

11795 ■ Edge-ucate
PO Box 126
Englewood, CO 80151-0126
E-mail: info@edge-ucate.org
URL: http://www.edge-ucate.org
Contact: Justin Kaliszewski, Exec. Dir.
Multinational. Description: Seeks to build and operate schools in some of the most underdeveloped countries in the world. Selects non-traditional sites for project schools.

Educators

11796 ■ Association of Professional Humane Educators (APHE)
c/o The Latham Foundation
Latham Plaza Bldg.
1826 Clement Ave.
Alameda, CA 94501
E-mail: aphe@aphe.org
URL: http://aphe.org
Contact: Sheryl L. Pipe PhD, Pres.
Membership Dues: individual, $25 (annual). **Description:** Provides professional development opportunities and networking for humane educators. Promotes humane attitudes toward people, animals and environment. Upholds the standards of practice on humane education. **Computer Services:** Mailing lists, of members. **Committees:** Education; Fundraising; Marketing; Ways and Means. **Publications:** *Packrat*, quarterly. Newsletter. **Price:** free for members. Alternate Formats: online.

Electronic Publishing

11797 ■ Internet Content Rating Association (ICRA)
666 11th St. NW, Ste.1100
Washington, DC 20001
Ph: (202)331-8651
Fax: (202)331-8652
E-mail: mlkenny@icra.org
URL: http://www.icra.org
Contact: Stephen Balkam, CEO
Membership Dues: associate, $100 (annual). **Languages:** English, French, German, Italian, Spanish. **Multinational. Description:** Organizations with Websites. Strives to protect children from explicit information on the Web and protect free speech rights on the Internet.

Emergency Services

11798 ■ Federal Alliance For Safe Homes (FLASH)
1427 E Piedmont Dr., Ste.2
Tallahassee, FL 32308
Free: (877)221-SAFE

Fax: (850)201-1067
E-mail: flash@flash.org
URL: http://flash.org
Contact: Leslie Chapman-Henderson, Pres./CEO
Founded: 1998. **Description:** Promotes disaster safety and property loss mitigation. Upholds life safety, property protection and economic well-being. Provides information and services on natural and man-made disasters. **Computer Services:** Information services, safe homes and disaster resources ● online services, interactive tools. **Programs:** A Tale of Two Houses; Animated Homeowner How-Tos; Blueprint for Safety; Cards; Firewise; Florida Prepares; On the Air; Turn Around Don't Drown. **Publications:** *Blueprint for Safety*. Newsletter. Alternate Formats: online ● Newsletter, quarterly.

11799 ■ Fire and Emergency Manufacturers and Services Association (FEMSA)
PO Box 147
Lynnfield, MA 01940-0147
Ph: (781)334-2771
Fax: (781)334-2771
E-mail: info@femsa.org
URL: http://www.femsa.org
Contact: Karen H. Burnham, Exec. Asst.
Founded: 1966. **Members:** 150. **Budget:** $100,000. **Description:** Fire and emergency industry manufacturers and service providers. Works to promote the growth of the overall industry by maintaining and expanding its user information guide program, marketing products and services, educating the marketplace and members and fighting for product liability reform. **Publications:** *FEMSA News*, quarterly. Newsletter. **Price:** included in membership dues. **Circulation:** 500. **Advertising:** accepted. Alternate Formats: CD-ROM; diskette; online ● *Personal Responsibility Code*. Paper. **Conventions/Meetings:** annual meeting.

Employee Rights

11800 ■ Verite
44 Belchertown Rd.
Amherst, MA 01002
Ph: (413)253-9227
Fax: (413)256-8960
E-mail: verite@verite.org
URL: http://www.verite.org
Contact: Dan Viederman, Exec. Dir.
Founded: 1995. **Multinational. Description:** Aims to improve the lives of workers and assists the corporations that employ these workers to better balance profitability with social responsibility. Monitors independent factories from different industry sectors to ensure that employees work under safe, fair, and legal labor conditions. Conducts research in all aspects of workplace conditions. Provides social audits, factory remediation, corporate training, labor research, and worker education worldwide. **Publications:** *Monitor*, quarterly. Newsletter. Features articles concerning issues about global labor and manufacturing trends. Alternate Formats: online.

11801 ■ Workplace Fairness
44 Montgomery St., Ste.2080
San Francisco, CA 94104
Ph: (415)362-7373
Fax: (415)677-9445
URL: http://www.workplacefairness.org
Contact: Paula Brantner, Program Dir.
Founded: 2001. **Description:** Promotes public policies that advance employee rights. **Affiliated With:** National Employment Lawyers Association. **Formerly:** National Employee Rights Institute. **Publications:** *Workplace Week*. Newsletter. Covers news and commentary on critical issues affecting employees and their advocates. Alternate Formats: online ● Brochure. Alternate Formats: online.

Employment

11802 ■ AFL-CIO Working for America Institute
815 16th St. NW
Washington, DC 20006

Ph: (202)508-3717
Fax: (202)508-3719
E-mail: info@workingforamerica.org
URL: http://www.workingforamerica.org
Contact: Nancy Mills, Exec. Dir.
Founded: 1968. **Staff:** 25. **Description:** Serves as the employment and training arm of the AFL-CIO (see separate entry). Works to assure full labor participation in employment and training programs funded under the Job Training Partnership Act. Assists in developing JTPA programs for dislocated and economically disadvantaged workers; provides technical services in support of plant-operated programs. Offers job search and placement services for disabled persons and early intervention and return-to-work services for recently disabled union members. Sponsors demonstration program to develop effective ways of improving workers' skills through structured workplace training; also offers workplace literacy study. Works with affected labor groups to help workers displaced by plant closings. Provides education and training to labor members of JTPA planning councils, labor leaders, and employment and training professionals. **Publications:** *Achieving Fiscal Integrity*. Manual ● *Connections*, bimonthly. Newsletter. Includes legislative news. **Price:** free to employment and training community. **Circulation:** 3,500 ● Brochure. **Price:** free. **Conventions/Meetings:** annual conference ● seminar ● workshop.

11803 ■ American Association for Affirmative Action (AAAA)
888 16th St. NW, Ste.800
Washington, DC 20006
Ph: (202)349-9855
Free: (800)252-8952
Fax: (202)355-1399
E-mail: execdir@affirmativeaction.org
URL: http://affirmativeaction.org
Contact: Shirley J. Wilcher JD, Exec. Dir.
Founded: 1974. **Members:** 2,000. **Membership Dues:** individual, $125 (annual) ● organizational (with over 1000 employees), $475 (annual) ● student, $25 (annual) ● retiree, $50 (annual) ● large organization (with 501-1000 employees), $400 (annual) ● small organization, $250 (annual). **Staff:** 3. **Budget:** $160,000. **Regional Groups:** 10. **State Groups:** 32. **Description:** Equal Opportunity/Affirmative Action officers at educational institutions and industrial firms; public administration and representatives from national, state, and local EO/AA related agencies. Purposes are: to foster the implementation of affirmative action and equal opportunity in employment and in education nationwide; to provide formal liaison with federal, state, and local agencies involved with equal opportunity compliance in employment and education. Is developing speakers' bureau and training program. **Awards:** Cesar Chavez Award. **Frequency:** annual. **Type:** recognition. **Recipient:** to an individual who has demonstrated leadership in support of workers' rights ● Corporate Friends Award. **Frequency:** annual. **Type:** recognition. **Recipient:** to one or more companies, agencies or enterprises that have accomplished the goals of affirmative action and serve as models for other organizations ● President's Award. **Frequency:** annual. **Type:** recognition. **Recipient:** to a member who has made major contributions to the growth, development and accomplishments of the national organization ● Rosa Parks Award. **Frequency:** annual. **Type:** recognition. **Recipient:** to individuals who served as role models and leaders for others. **Computer Services:** database ● mailing lists ● online services. **Committees:** Action; Professional Ethics and Standards; Training Program Development. **Publications:** *American Association for Affirmative Action—Membership Directory*, annual. **Price:** $50.00. **Circulation:** 3,000. **Advertising:** accepted ● *American Association for Affirmative Action—Newsletter*, quarterly. Includes employment listings. **Price:** included in membership dues; $50.00 /year for nonmembers. **Circulation:** 1,200. **Advertising:** accepted. **Conventions/Meetings:** annual conference (exhibits).

11804 ■ American Association of Working People (AAWP)
4435 Waterfront Dr., Ste.101
Glen Allen, VA 23060

Ph: (804)527-1905
Fax: (804)747-5316
E-mail: info@aawp.org
URL: http://www.aawp.org
Contact: Bill Williams MD, Pres.
Founded: 1992. **Membership Dues:** life (individual, family), $250. **Staff:** 12. **Description:** Working Americans. Seeks to address the special interests and needs of working Americans and their families. Conducts research, educational, and charitable programs; provides children's services; maintains Speaker's Bureau. **Publications:** *American Destiny*, quarterly. Newsletter. **Price:** free for members.

11805 ■ American Institute for Full Employment (AIFE)
2636 Biehn St.
Klamath Falls, OR 97601
Ph: (541)273-6731
Free: (800)562-7752
Fax: (541)273-6496
E-mail: info@fullemployment.org
URL: http://www.fullemployment.org
Contact: Ted Abram, Exec. Dir.
Founded: 1994. **Staff:** 7. **Multinational. Description:** Supports privatization of social security. Works towards the goal of full employment through research and development of public assistance, employment and retirement policies. Supports community efforts to address societal problems. Serves as a source of information for state and local officials who want to know how their workforce and public assistance programs compare to those in other areas.

11806 ■ Asian Resources (ARI)
5709 Stockton Blvd.
Sacramento, CA 95824
Ph: (916)454-1892
Fax: (916)454-1895
E-mail: info@asianresources.org
URL: http://www.asianresources.org
Contact: Ms. Stephanie Nguyen, Pres.
Founded: 1980. **Staff:** 18. **Budget:** $100,000,000. **Languages:** English, Laotian, Russian, Spanish, Vietnamese. **Description:** Provides information on employment opportunities to individuals who are unemployed with no other means of income and to disadvantaged individuals. Offers educational seminars and skilled labor training sessions to refugees. Provides placement services. **Programs:** California Works for Better Health; Job Club/Job Search; On-the-Job Training; Refugee; Sacramento Works Career Center; Youth Development; Youth Internship. **Publications:** Newsletter, monthly. Lists employment and training opportunities as well as upcoming community events. **Conventions/Meetings:** annual Youth Conference, for youth to prepare them for life after high school, jobs, further education and leadership (exhibits).

11807 ■ Career Planning and Adult Development Network (CPADN)
c/o Administrative Office
PO Box 1484
Pacifica, CA 94044
Ph: (650)359-6911
Fax: (650)359-3089
E-mail: admin@careernetwork.org
URL: http://www.careernetwork.org
Contact: Richard L. Knowdell, Exec. Dir./Founding Ed.
Founded: 1979. **Members:** 900. **Membership Dues:** in U.S., $49 (annual) ● outside U.S., $64 (annual). **Staff:** 2. **Budget:** $60,000. **Description:** Counselors, trainers, consultants, therapists, educators, personnel specialists, and graduate students who work in business, educational, religious, and governmental organizations, and focus on career planning and adult development issues. Seeks to: establish a link between professionals working with adults in a variety of settings; identify and exchange effective adult development methods and techniques; develop a clearer understanding of the directions and objectives of the career planning and the adult development movement. Keeps members informed of developments in career decision-making, career values

clarification, preretirement counseling, dual-career families, job search techniques, and mid-life transitions. Cosponsors professional seminars; maintains biographical archives. **Libraries: Type:** not open to the public. **Holdings:** 1,200. **Subjects:** career planning, assessment, development. **Awards:** Professional Resource Award. **Frequency:** annual. **Type:** recognition. **Recipient:** for leadership and volunteerism. **Computer Services:** Mailing lists. **Publications:** Journal, quarterly. Features bibliography, book reviews, and research reports. **Price:** included in membership dues; $7.50/issue for nonmembers. ISSN: 0736-1920. **Circulation:** 1,500 ● Newsletter, bimonthly. Includes book reviews, calendar of events, and information on employment opportunities, network contacts, and new materials. **Price:** included in membership dues; $4.50/issue for nonmembers; $6.00/issue overseas. ISSN: 0898-1353. **Circulation:** 1,500. **Conventions/Meetings:** annual International Career Development Conference (exhibits) - late October or early November.

11808 ■ Career Transition For Dancers (CTFD)
c/o The Caroline and Theodore Newhouse Centre for Dancers
165 W 46th St., Ste.701
The Actors' Equity Bldg.
New York, NY 10036-2501
Ph: (212)764-0172
Free: (800)581-2833
Fax: (212)764-0343
E-mail: info@careertransition.org
URL: http://www.careertransition.org
Contact: Cynthia Fischer Esq., Pres.
Founded: 1985. **Staff:** 6. **Description:** Provides assistance free of charge to professional dancers including career counseling, vocational self-assessment, career management, financial planning, networking, resume writing, workshops and seminars. **Libraries: Type:** not open to the public. **Holdings:** books. **Subjects:** job opportunities, education, career. **Awards:** Scholarship Fund. **Type:** scholarship. **Recipient:** for professional dancer age 27 or older needing financial assistance for education and retraining. **Affiliated With:** Actors' Fund of America. **Publications:** *Changing Steps*, 3/year. Newsletter ● *Moving On*. Newsletter. Alternate Formats: online.

11809 ■ Center for the Child Care Workforce, A Project of the American Federation of Teachers Educational Foundation (CCW/AFTEF)
555 New Jersey Ave. NW
Washington, DC 20001
Ph: (202)662-8005
Fax: (202)662-8006
E-mail: ccw@aft.org
URL: http://ccw.cleverspin.com
Contact: Marci P. Young, Dir.
Founded: 2002. **Membership Dues:** general, $40 (annual) ● life, $500. **Staff:** 3. **Budget:** $50,000. **Description:** Purposes are: to develop innovative solutions to the child care crisis to improve salaries, working conditions, and status of child care workers; to increase public awareness about the importance of child care work and the training and skill it demands; to develop resources and create an information sharing network for child care workers nationwide. Gathers current information on salaries and benefits; offers consultation services. Sponsors research projects; compiles statistics; operates speakers' bureau. Maintains extensive file of materials on working conditions and research on child care workers. **Boards:** Research Advisory. **Formerly:** (1979) East Bay Workers in Child Care; (1993) Child Care Employee Project; (1998) National Center for the Early Childhood Workforce; (2003) Center for the Child Care Workforce. **Publications:** *The American Teacher*. **Price:** included in membership dues ● *Child Care Employee Rights Guide* ● *Curriculum Guide on Childhood Education*. Report ● *Rights, Raises, Respect: News and Issues for the Child Care Workforce*, monthly. Newsletter. **Price:** included in membership dues. Alternate Formats: online ● *Taking on*

Turnover ● Also publishes more material on recent research findings related to child care staffing issues.

11810 ■ Center for Economic Options (CEO)
910 Quarrier St., Ste.206
Charleston, WV 25301
Ph: (304)345-1298
Fax: (304)342-0641
E-mail: info@economicoptions.org
URL: http://www.centerforeconomicoptions.org
Contact: Pam Curry, Exec. Dir.
Founded: 1979. **Members:** 1,450. **Budget:** $350,000. **State Groups:** 2. **Description:** Seeks to improve the economic position and quality of life for women, especially low-income and minority women. Works to provide access to job training and employment options to women. Supports self-employed women and small business owners by offering training and technical assistance and information. Advocates women's legal right to employment, training, education, and credit. Seeks to inform the public on economic issues related to women; while activities are conducted on local and state levels, group cooperates with national and international organizations on issues relating to employment and economic justice for women. Maintains speakers' bureau and library. Compiles statistics; conducts research. **Formerly:** Women and Employment. **Publications:** *Women and Employment News*, quarterly. Includes association activities and information on economic and employment issues relating to women. **Conventions/Meetings:** annual conference ● quarterly workshop.

11811 ■ Consortium of Doctors (COD)
c/o Dr. Jacqualine Desmona Myers, Dir.
501 Deerfield Dr.
Montgomery, AL 36109
Ph: (334)272-1271
URL: http://www.consortiumofdoctors.com
Contact: Dr. Abigail Jordan, Founder
Founded: 1991. **Members:** 162. **Budget:** $50,000. **Regional Groups:** 1. **State Groups:** 6. **National Groups:** 15. **Description:** Minority women who have earned a doctorate degree from an established, accredited institution. Assists members in finding jobs suitable to their training. Conducts charitable, educational, and inspirational programs. **Awards:** Award of Perseverance. **Type:** recognition ● Humanitarian Award. **Frequency:** annual. **Type:** recognition ● Seminole Award. **Frequency:** annual. **Type:** recognition. **Publications:** *COD Newsletter*, quarterly. **Price:** free. **Circulation:** 1,000. Alternate Formats: online. **Conventions/Meetings:** annual conference and banquet.

11812 ■ Corporate and Foundation Relations
Univ. of Colorado Found.
4740 Walnut St.
PO Box 1140
Boulder, CO 80306-1140
Ph: (303)735-9818
Fax: (303)735-9001
E-mail: info@cufund.org
URL: http://www.cufund.org
Contact: Robert Willis, Asst. VP
Founded: 1934. **Staff:** 2,400. **Budget:** $97,000,000. **Description:** Voluntary, nonsectarian community human service agency. Serves more than 50,000 persons annually in over 117 locations with individual and group career development services, including psychological testing, job placement, and vocational rehabilitation, as well as mental health, residential, developmental, clinical, and youth services. Provides programs in economic development and criminal justice. Maintains business and trade schools; offers outplacement corporate services and a full range of family services, including domestic violence, substance abuse, and family counseling. Emphasizes employment aid for a "generic population", but also has a tradition of employment aid to the disabled, hard-to-place, older, retarded, disadvantaged, new immigrant, drug addicted, and emotionally disturbed workers. Activities concentrated in the greater New York area. Maintains Professional Development Institute, which sponsors seminars for vocational,

career, and human resource counselors. **Absorbed:** (1976) American Rehabilitation Committee; (1990) Altro Rehabilitation Agency Programs; (1993) Jewish Community Services of Long Island. **Formerly:** (2000) Federation Employment and Guidance Service.

11813 ■ Disabled Businesspersons Association (DBA)
San Diego State Univ. Interwork Indus.
3590 Camino del Rio N
San Diego, CA 92108-1716
Ph: (619)594-8805
Fax: (619)594-4208
E-mail: info@disabledbusiness.com
URL: http://www.ChallengedAmerica.org
Contact: Mr. Urban Miyares, Pres.
Founded: 1985. **Members:** 12,000. **Membership Dues:** individual, business/corporate, non-formal, not-required, $25 (annual). **Staff:** 5. **Budget:** $725,000. **Description:** Assists active and enterprising individuals with disabilities maximize their rehabilitation and potential in the workplace and business, and work with vocational rehabilitation, government, education and business. Encourages the participation and enhances the performance of the disabled in the work force. Membership is not a prerequisite for services or assistance. **Additional Websites:** http:// www.disabledbusiness.org. **Programs:** Challenged America; Veterans Business Resource Center; Young Entrepreneurs with Disabilities. **Publications:** *Challenged America Newsletter*, quarterly. Features recreational rehabilitation and adaptive-sailing program for the disabled. Alternate Formats: online ● *dba Advisor*, quarterly. Newsletter. **Circulation:** 12,000. **Advertising:** accepted. Alternate Formats: online.

11814 ■ Employment Policy Foundation (EPF)
1015 15th St. NW; Ste.1200
Washington, DC 20005
Ph: (202)789-8685
Fax: (202)789-8684
E-mail: info@epf.org
Contact: Janemarie Mulvey PhD, Pres.
Founded: 1983. **Staff:** 8. **Budget:** $1,000,000. **Description:** Seeks to provide policymakers and the public with the highest quality economic analysis and commentary on U.S. employment policies affecting the competitive goals of American industry and the people it employs. The Foundation conducts studies of the economic and productivity consequences of employment legislation, executive orders, regulations and court decisions. Provides a sound basis for assessing the utility of existing employment policies and proposals for reform. **Libraries: Type:** not open to the public. **Holdings:** 54; monographs, papers. **Subjects:** employment policies, annual American Workplace report, cost studies and analysis of paid family leave, comparable worth, gainsharing, workforce demographics, contingent workforce. **Affiliated With:** Equal Employment Advisory Council; HR Policy Association. **Formerly:** (1987) National Foundation for the Study of Equal Employment; (1991) National Foundation for the Study of Employment Policy. **Publications:** *A Compliance Guide to the Americans with Disabilities Act*. Monograph. **Price:** $40.00 for members; $100.00 for nonmembers ● *Above the Law: Covering Congress Under Federal Employment Laws*. Monograph. **Price:** $20.00 for members; $25.00 for nonmembers ● *Alternative Dispute Resolution Techniques: Options and Guidelines to Meet Your Company's Needs*. Monograph. **Price:** $20.00 for members; $25.00 for nonmembers ● *Developing Effective Affirmative Action Plans*. Manuals. **Price:** $100.00 for members; $125.00 for nonmembers ● *Disability Etiquette in the Workplace*. Manuals. **Price:** $16.00 for members; $20.00 for nonmembers ● *Effective Handling of EEO Charges: A Guide for Employers*. Manuals. **Price:** $40.00 for members; $50.00 for nonmembers ● *Effects on Union Status on Employee Involvement: Diffusion and Effectiveness*. **Price:** $12.00 for members; $15.00 for nonmembers ● *Equity at Work: A Manager's Guide to Fair Employment Laws and Practices*. Manuals. **Price:** $28.00 for

members; $35.00 for nonmembers ● *Keeping America Competitive: Employment Policy for the Twenty-First Century*. Monograph. **Price:** $25.00 for members; $27.95 for nonmembers ● *Loading the Scales: Is the Balance Between the Right to Strike and the Right to Operate in Need of Reform?*. Monograph. **Price:** $20.00 for members; $25.00 for nonmembers ● *Managing Diversity in an Equal Opportunity Workplace*. **Price:** $20.00 for members; $25.00 for nonmembers ● *Statistics for Nonstatisticians*. Manuals. **Price:** $24.00 for members; $30.00 for nonmembers.

11815 ■ Employment Support Center (ESC)
1556 Wisconsin Ave. NW
Washington, DC 20007
Ph: (202)628-2919
Fax: (202)628-2919
E-mail: jobclubs@hotmail.com
URL: http://www.angelfire.com/biz/jobclubs
Contact: Ms. Ellie Wegener, Founder/Exec. Dir.
Founded: 1984. **Membership Dues:** part-time/ unemployed, $50 (annual) ● full-time/employed, $100 (annual) ● associate, $1,000 (annual) ● gold, $2,000 (annual). **Description:** Trains individuals to facilitate support groups for job-seekers. Operates a job bank for employment assistance; helps people learn to network for job contacts; provides technical assistance to employment support self help groups. Maintains speakers' bureau. Provides job-search skills training. **Libraries: Type:** open to the public. **Holdings:** 150; articles, books, periodicals. **Subjects:** employment, networking, self-esteem, starting your own business. **Computer Services:** database, job bank. **Subgroups:** Capitol Hill Job Support. **Affiliated With:** National Neighborhood Coalition. **Publications:** *ESC Newsline*, monthly. Newsletter. Contains information for jobseekers and entrepreneurs. **Circulation:** 400. **Advertising:** accepted ● *Portfolio of Self-Help Materials to Start a Self-Help Group for Job Seekers* ● *The Self-Help Bridge to Employment*. Manual. **Price:** $25.00. **Conventions/Meetings:** monthly Network Meeting (exhibits) - always in Washington, DC ● periodic seminar.

11816 ■ Equal Employment Advisory Council (EEAC)
1015 15th St. NW, Ste.1200
Washington, DC 20005
Ph: (202)789-8650
Fax: (202)789-2291
E-mail: info@eeac.org
URL: http://www.eeac.org
Contact: Jeffrey A. Norris, Pres.
Founded: 1976. **Members:** 342. **Membership Dues:** regular, $5,000 (annual). **Description:** Promotes and presents the mutual interests of employers and the public regarding affirmative action and equal employment opportunity practices. Provides members with regulatory and legislative developments. **Publications:** *Member Services*. Brochure ● Manuals ● Pamphlets ● Reports, annual. **Conventions/Meetings:** meeting - 3/year.

11817 ■ Experience Works
2200 Clarendon Blvd., Ste.1000
Arlington, VA 22201
Ph: (703)522-7272
Free: (866)EXP-WRKS
Fax: (703)522-0141
E-mail: info@experienceworks.org
URL: http://www.experienceworks.org
Contact: Cynthia A. Metzler, Pres./CEO
Founded: 1965. **Staff:** 526. **Budget:** $110,000,000. **State Groups:** 44. **Multinational. Description:** Provides training and employment services for mature workers. Reaches more than 125,000 mature individuals. **Awards:** America's Oldest Worker. **Frequency:** annual. **Type:** recognition ● Outstanding Employer of Older Workers. **Frequency:** annual. **Type:** recognition ● Outstanding Older Worker. **Frequency:** annual. **Type:** recognition. **Formerly:** (2002) Green Thumb. **Publications:** Annual Report, annual. Alternate Formats: online. **Conventions/Meetings:** quarterly meeting.

11818 ■ Homeworkers Organized for More Employment (HOME)
PO Box 10
Orland, ME 04472
Ph: (207)469-7961
Fax: (207)469-1023
E-mail: info@homecoop.net
URL: http://www.homecoop.net
Contact: Randy Eldridge, Volunteer Coor.
Founded: 1970. **Members:** 1,350. **Membership Dues:** general, $5 (annual). **Staff:** 40. **Budget:** $1,000,000. **Regional Groups:** 1. **Languages:** English, Spanish. **Description:** Individuals who produce home crafts made by Maine people in their homes for income. Aims to provide supplemental income for low-income families through sale of their crafts through retail, catalog, and wholesale departments. Conducts education classes, craft fairs, and craft shows. Offers counseling and crisis intervention services. Sponsors Project Woodstove, a program that provides elderly and low-income families with firewood; also provides low-income persons with shelter, clothing, food, and transportation; has built 38 houses through the Covenant Community Land Trust. Maintains a crafts and stitchery museum. **Libraries: Type:** reference. **Holdings:** 1,000. **Subjects:** psychology, history. **Divisions:** Education; Marketing; Outreach. **Programs:** Adult Basic Education; Alternative High School; College. **Publications:** *This Time*, quarterly. Newspaper. **Price:** $5.00/year ● Catalogs. **Conventions/Meetings:** annual Craft and Farm Fair - festival, old-fashioned country fair with wagon rides, barbecues, entertainment, music, crafts (exhibits) - in October ● annual dinner and meeting, pot luck dinner (exhibits) - usually in April.

11819 ■ International Union of Painters and Allied Trades/Joint Apprenticeship and Training Fund
1750 New York Ave. NW
Washington, DC 20006
Ph: (202)637-0700
Free: (800)554-2479
E-mail: mail@iupat.org
URL: http://www.iupat.org
Contact: James A. Williams, Gen. Pres.
Founded: 1971. **Members:** 140,000. **Staff:** 8. **Budget:** $3,000,000. **Regional Groups:** 50. **Local Groups:** 426. **Description:** Representatives of labor and management. Labor is represented by the International Brotherhood of Painters and Allied Trades management by the Finishing Contractors Association. Seeks to increase apprenticeship and training activities so that prospective apprentices can obtain the training necessary to equip themselves and to assume a high level of skill and responsibility. Develops and supplies materials necessary for training tradespersons and journeypersons with emphasis on changing techniques, materials, and tools of the trade; maintains library. Holds workshops and seminars for instructors and coordinators; sponsors international Apprenticeship Panel contests and sponsors college degree programs. **Committees:** Curriculum; Public Relations. **Formerly:** National Painting, Decorating, and Drywall Apprenticeship and Manpower Training Fund; International Brotherhood of Painters and Allied Trades; (1969) Brotherhood of Painters, Decorators and Paperhangers of America; (1992) National Joint Painting, Decorating, and Drywall Apprenticeship and Training Committee; (2001) International Joint Painting, Decorating and Drywall Apprenticeship and Manpower Training Fund. **Conventions/Meetings:** quarterly meeting.

11820 ■ A Job is a Right Campaign (AJRC)
PO Box 06053
Milwaukee, WI 53206
Ph: (414)374-1034
Fax: (414)374-1034
E-mail: ajrc@execpc.com
URL: http://my.execpc.com/~ajrc
Contact: Phil Wilayto, Coor.
Founded: 1993. **Description:** Strives to fight growing unemployment. Organizes protest marches, rallies, and demonstrations to oppose layoffs and plant closings. **Publications:** Newsletter, periodic. Alternate Formats: online.

11821 ■ Jobs for America's Graduates (JAG)
1729 King St., Ste.100
Alexandria, VA 22314
Ph: (703)684-9479
Fax: (703)684-9489
E-mail: ken.smith@jag.org
URL: http://www.jag.org
Contact: Mr. Kenneth M. Smith, Pres./CEO
Founded: 1980. **Members:** 48,000. **Staff:** 10. **Budget:** $1,200,000. **State Groups:** 28. **Description:** Develops statewide systems dedicated to serving at-risk youth who are most likely to leave school before graduation or who have already left school. Implements the JAG model and the appropriate program applications. Provides job programs for at-risk and disadvantaged students who have limited work experience and do not plan to attend college immediately upon graduation or are at risk of dropping out. **Libraries: Type:** reference. **Holdings:** 1,400; books. **Subjects:** school-to-work, dropout prevention, dropout recovery, learning. **Awards:** National Leadership. **Frequency:** annual. **Type:** recognition. **Recipient:** for significant service to the organization. **Computer Services:** database ● mailing lists, of members. **Programs:** Dropout Prevention; Dropout Recovery; School-to-Career. **Publications:** *Crossroads*, semiannual. Newsletter. Features articles and news items submitted by affiliates. **Price:** free. Alternate Formats: online ● Annual Report, annual. Alternate Formats: online ● Publishes various research studies, news briefs, federal legislation updates, curriculum guides, staff development guides, and handbooks. **Conventions/Meetings:** semiannual National Training Seminar - meeting, leadership/development training (exhibits) - February and July.

11822 ■ Jobs for the Future (JFF)
88 Broad St.
Boston, MA 02110
Ph: (617)728-4446
Fax: (617)728-4857
E-mail: info@jff.org
URL: http://www.jff.org
Contact: Arthur H. White, Interim Chm./Co-Founder
Founded: 1983. **Staff:** 40. **Description:** Seeks to integrate quality education and work opportunities. Offers technical assistance and training to educators, executives, and policy makers. Conducts research and disseminates results on trends in learning among students and employees. **Publications:** *Newswire*, bimonthly. Newsletter. Alternate Formats: online ● Annual Report, annual. **Conventions/Meetings:** annual conference.

11823 ■ Mothers And More
PO Box 31
Elmhurst, IL 60126
Ph: (630)941-3553
Fax: (630)941-3551
E-mail: nationaloffice@mothersandmore.org
URL: http://www.mothersandmore.org
Contact: Joanne Brundage, Exec. Dir.
Founded: 1987. **Members:** 7,500. **Membership Dues:** regular in U.S., $45 (annual) ● regular outside U.S., $55 (annual). **Local Groups:** 175. **Description:** Dedicated to improving the lives of mothers through support, education and advocacy. Addresses mothers' needs as individuals and members of society, and promotes the value of all the work mothers do. Provides nationwide network of local chapters for mothers who are, by choice or circumstance, altering their participation in the paid workplace over the course of their active parenting years. **Formerly:** (2002) Formerly Employed Mothers at the Leading Edge. **Publications:** *The Forum*, bimonthly. Newsletter. Focuses on work and family issues, survival techniques for life at home and at work, book reviews, personal enrichment, author interviews etc. **Price:** included in membership dues ● Brochure.

11824 ■ National Association of Workforce Boards (NAWB)
4350 N Fairfax Dr., Ste.220
Arlington, VA 22203
Ph: (703)778-7900
Fax: (703)778-7901
E-mail: nawb@nawb.org
URL: http://www.nawb.org
Contact: Michael Sotire, Natl. Dir.
Founded: 1979. **Members:** 767. **Staff:** 11. **Budget:** $1,700,000. **Description:** Represents private industry councils' workforce investment boards, and other business-oriented organizations seeking to provide job training opportunities for the unemployed and economically disadvantaged. Aims to facilitate private sector involvement in federal employment and training policy. Provides information on federal employment and training legislation; affords members the opportunity to meet with congressional and executive staff. Offers technical assistance to members. **Computer Services:** database ● mailing lists. **Programs:** Ticket to Work. **Formerly:** (1999) National Association of Private Industry Councils. **Publications:** *NAPIC Reports to.*, monthly. Newsletter. **Price:** included in membership dues. **Circulation:** 2,000 ● *Workforce Brief.* Bulletin. Alternate Formats: online ● Report. **Conventions/Meetings:** annual Forum - conference.

11825 ■ National Association of Workforce Development Professionals (NAWDP)
c/o Mr. C. Paul Mendez, Pres.
810 1st St. NE, Ste.525
Washington, DC 20002-4282
Ph: (202)589-1790
Fax: (202)589-1799
E-mail: nawdp@aol.com
URL: http://www.nawdp.org
Contact: Mr. C. Paul Mendez, Pres.
Founded: 1989. **Members:** 4,500. **Membership Dues:** regular, $50 (annual) ● life, $750. **Staff:** 2. **Budget:** $600,000. **Description:** Represents professionals in the employment and training industries including welfare to work, incumbent worker, older worker, youth, corrections and community colleges. Has front line staff and management that are provided with industry information and professional development services including certification, conferences, workshops and committee participation. **Awards:** Advancing the Profession Award. **Frequency:** annual. **Type:** recognition. **Computer Services:** Mailing lists. **Committees:** Advocacy; Certification; Conference; Professional Development. **Formerly:** (1998) Partnership for Employment and Training Careers. **Publications:** *The Journal of Workforce Development*, semiannual. **Price:** $50.00 for members. ISSN: 1556-1127. **Circulation:** 4,500 ● *NAWDP Advantage*, monthly. Newsletter. **Price:** $45.00/year. ISSN: 1084-0869. **Circulation:** 4,500. **Advertising:** accepted. **Conventions/Meetings:** annual conference (exhibits).

11826 ■ National Business and Disability Council (NBDC)
201 I.U. Willets Rd.
Albertson, NY 11507
Ph: (516)465-1516
Fax: (516)465-3730
E-mail: lbroder@abilitiesonline.org
URL: http://www.nbdc.com
Contact: Edmund L. Cortez, Pres./CEO
Founded: 1977. **Members:** 195. **Staff:** 15. **Budget:** $300,000. **Regional Groups:** 7. **Languages:** English, Spanish. **Description:** Acts as a resource for employers seeking to integrate people with disabilities into the workplace and companies seeking to reach them in the consumer market. **Libraries: Type:** reference. **Holdings:** 1,000; audio recordings, audiovisuals, periodicals. **Subjects:** issues concerning disability in the workplace and marketplace, disability specific. **Awards:** Advertiser of the Year. **Type:** recognition ● Award of Honor. **Frequency:** annual. **Type:** recognition. **Recipient:** to outstanding disabled workers and to corporate and labor representatives for exceptional efforts in affirmative action ● Employee of the Year. **Frequency:** annual. **Type:**

recognition. **Recipient:** to an employee with disability who is engaged in competitive employment ● Employer of the Year. **Frequency:** annual. **Type:** recognition. **Recipient:** to an employer who is recognized by staff and associates as a leader in expanding employment for people with disabilities ● Manager of the Year. **Type:** recognition. **Recipient:** to a management level employee who has been instrumental in enhancing employment opportunities for people with disabilities ● Outstanding Advertising Campaign. **Frequency:** annual. **Type:** recognition. **Recipient:** to advertising agency that has created an effective advertising campaign ● Product of the Year. **Frequency:** annual. **Type:** recognition. **Recipient:** for individual or company that has designed, or is responsible for manufacturing and distributing a product that has enhanced the lives of the people with disabilities ● Valued Customer Award. **Frequency:** annual. **Type:** recognition. **Recipient:** for outstanding company that considers the people with disabilities as valued customers. **Computer Services:** Information services, recruitment services, news services, training services, events. **Affiliated With:** Abilities!. **Publications:** *The Americans with Disabilities Act Training Module* ● *Emergency Evacuation Checklist to Include People with Disabilities.* **Price:** $70.00 ● *Giving Us the Tools: A Human Resources Training Package on Employing Individuals with Disabilities.* Video ● *Interviewing Individuals with Disabilities.* Video ● *NBDC News,* quarterly. Newsletter. Alternate Formats: online ● *Steps to Success: A Blueprint for Employing Individuals with Disabilities.* **Conventions/Meetings:** seminar ● annual Spring Orientation - meeting ● annual Tools for Disability Employment and Marketing - conference - usually April ● workshop.

11827 ■ National Career Development Association (NCDA)
305 N Beech Cir.
Broken Arrow, OK 74012
Ph: (918)663-7060
Free: (866)367-6232
Fax: (918)663-7058
E-mail: dpennington@ncda.org
URL: http://www.ncda.org
Contact: Deneen Pennington, Exec. Dir.
Founded: 1913. **Members:** 4,500. **Membership Dues:** regular, $55 (annual) ● student, professional, $23 (annual) ● retired, $35 (annual). **Staff:** 4. **Budget:** $750. **State Groups:** 37. **Description:** Represents professionals and others interested in career development or counseling in various work environments. Supports counselors, education and training personnel, and allied professionals working in schools, colleges, business/industry, community and government agencies, and in private practice. Provides publications, support for state and local activities, human equity programs, and continuing education and training for these professionals. Provides networking opportunities for career professionals in business, education, and government. **Affiliated With:** American Counseling Association. **Formerly:** (1985) National Vocational Guidance Association. **Publications:** *Career Convergence Web Magazine,* monthly. Includes annual index. **Price:** included in membership dues; $45.00 /year for nonmembers. **Circulation:** 7,653 ● *Career Development Quarterly.* Journal. Includes annual index. **Price:** included in membership dues; $45.00 /year for nonmembers. ISSN: 0889-4019. **Circulation:** 7,653 ● *Career Developments,* quarterly. Newsletter. Alternate Formats: online ● *Counselor's Guide to Career Assessment Instruments.* Book. **Conventions/Meetings:** annual Global Career Development - convention (exhibits).

11828 ■ National Employment Counseling Association (NECA)
c/o American Counseling Association
5999 Stevenson Ave.
Alexandria, VA 22304
Free: (800)347-6647
Fax: (703)461-9260
E-mail: jobfields@aol.com
URL: http://www.employmentcounseling.org/neca.html
Contact: Cheryl West, Pres.
Founded: 1964. **Members:** 1,694. **Membership Dues:** professional, regular, $58 (annual) ● profes-

sional, student, retired, $34 (annual). **Description:** Serves as a division of the American Counseling Association (see separate entry). Represents individuals who are engaged in employment counseling, counselor education, research, administration or supervision in business and industry, colleges and universities, and federal and state governments; students. Offers professional leadership and development services; provides opportunities for professional growth through workshops and special projects. **Awards: Type:** recognition. **Affiliated With:** American Counseling Association. **Publications:** *Journal of Employment Counseling,* quarterly. **Price:** included in membership dues; $38.00 for nonmembers; $50.00 /year for institutions. ISSN: 0022-0787. **Circulation:** 1,200. **Advertising:** accepted. Alternate Formats: microform ● *NECA News,* quarterly. Newsletter. **Conventions/Meetings:** annual Balancing the Needs of Workforce Development - workshop, held in conjunction with ACA (exhibits).

11829 ■ National Employment Law Project (NELP)
80 Maiden Ln., Ste.509
New York, NY 10038
Ph: (212)285-3025
Fax: (212)285-3044
E-mail: nelp@nelp.org
URL: http://www.nelp.org
Contact: Bruce Herman, Exec. Dir.
Founded: 1969. **Staff:** 14. **Description:** Works to develop and implement program assistance to legal services and public interest and pro bono attorneys through litigation and limited policy advocacy in the area of employment problems of the poor. Concentrates on the following areas: unemployment insurance; employment discrimination; abusive discharge; labor relations; employment aspects of federal work programs; Job Training Partnership Act; employment rights of the disabled. Includes project attorneys that are available to conduct specialized employment law seminars. Maintains library. **Publications:** *Abusive Discharge.* Manual ● *Employment Law News,* quarterly ● *NELP Update,* quarterly. Newsletter. Alternate Formats: online ● *Representing the Handicapped Employee.* Manual ● *Rising Stakes of Job Loss.* Report ● *Sex Discrimination and the Sexually Charged Work Environment.* Manual ● Monographs.

11830 ■ National Job Corps Alumni Association (NJCAA)
PO Box 1885
Gresham, OR 97030
Free: (800)424-2866
E-mail: dorseyj@execpc.com
URL: http://www.jcalum.org
Contact: Dorsey Jackson, Pres.
Founded: 1980. **Members:** 27,000. **Membership Dues:** associate individual, $25 (annual) ● associate family, $35 (annual) ● regular, $5 (annual). **Staff:** 13. **Regional Groups:** 10. **Local Groups:** 50. **Description:** Former members of the Job Corps and its supporters. Objectives are to: enhance the public awareness and image of the Job Corps (a nationwide federally-sponsored training program offering education, vocational training, and work experience in urban, rural, or inner city residential centers to disadvantaged youth aged 16 to 24) and its alumni; conduct programs and provide services in response to the needs and interests of the Job Corps; support the educational and career development of Job Corps members; provide a forum for social interaction and group support for Job Corps alumni. Conducts educational programs on communications, job search skills, public relations, and community service; sponsors social programs such as local reunions, dances, theme parties, and dinners; coordinates benefits program which include club membership and automobile discounts; makes available employment information. Maintains hall of fame. **Awards: Type:** recognition. **Affiliated With:** Joint Action in Community Service. **Publications:** *The Proof Sheet.* Newsletter ● Newsletter, quarterly. Includes chapter news and features. **Price:** free. **Circulation:** 17,000.

11831 ■ New Ways to Work (NWW)
103 Morris St., Ste.A
Sebastopol, CA 95472
Ph: (707)824-4000
Fax: (707)824-4410
E-mail: newways@newwaystowork.org
URL: http://www.nww.org
Contact: Steve Trippe, Pres./Exec. Dir.
Founded: 1972. **Members:** 300. **Staff:** 7. **Budget:** $750,000. **Description:** Helps communities build systems that connect schools, community organizations and businesses, and improve the services, educational programs and support the community provides for its youth. Engages and supports local communities in the invention and renewal of connected, comprehensive youth-serving systems. **Libraries: Type:** not open to the public. **Holdings:** 650; artwork, books, periodicals. **Subjects:** reduced and restructured work options, flexible staffing arrangements. **Publications:** Reports ● Also publishes studies and "how to" materials.

11832 ■ NTID's Center on Employment (NCE)
Lyndon Baines Johnson Bldg.
Rochester Inst. of Tech.
52 Lomb Memorial Dr.
Rochester, NY 14623-5604
Ph: (585)475-6219 (585)475-6217
Fax: (585)475-7570
E-mail: ntidcoe@rit.edu
URL: http://www.ntid.rit.edu/nce
Contact: Allen Vaala, Dir.
Founded: 1968. **Staff:** 11. **Description:** Operated by the National Technical Institute for the Deaf. Promotes successful employment of Rochester Institute of Technology's deaf students and graduates. Offers resources and training for employers. **Formerly:** (1993) National Center on Employment of the Deaf. **Conventions/Meetings:** Working Together: Deaf and Hearing People - workshop, available on-site.

11833 ■ Opportunities Industrialization Centers of America (OICA)
1415 N Broad St.
Philadelphia, PA 19122-3323
Ph: (215)236-4500
Free: (800)621-4642
Fax: (215)236-7480
E-mail: info@oicofamerica.org
URL: http://oicofamerica.org
Contact: Thomasenia G. Cotton, Pres./COO
Founded: 1964. **Description:** Network of employment and training programs. Serves disadvantaged and underskilled Americans of all races. Seeks to develop the "whole person" and enables individuals to become self-sufficient, productive workers. Represents its community and strives to meet the needs of the local labor market, while preparing trainees for the world of work. **Awards: Frequency:** annual. **Type:** recognition. **Councils:** National Industrial Advisory; National Technical Advisory. **Publications:** *OIC Forging Ahead.* Newsletter. Alternate Formats: online ● *OIC Key News,* quarterly. Newsletter. **Price:** free. **Circulation:** 5,000 ● *Opportunities Industrialization Centers of America—Annual Report.* Includes an audited financial statement. **Circulation:** 5,000. **Conventions/Meetings:** annual meeting (exhibits).

11834 ■ Professional Association of Resume Writers and Career Coaches (PARW/CC)
1388 Brightwaters Blvd., NE
St. Petersburg, FL 33704-1336
Ph: (727)821-2274
Free: (800)822-7279
Fax: (727)894-1277
E-mail: parwhq@aol.com
URL: http://www.parw.com
Contact: Frank Fox, Exec. Dir.
Founded: 1990. **Members:** 750. **Membership Dues:** active, $150 (annual). **Staff:** 2. **For-Profit. Description:** Represents the interests of professional resume writers, employment interview trainers, and career coaches. Acts as a clearinghouse for information on career topics. Provides educational programs. Offers certification for Certified Professional Resume Writers (CPRW) and for Certified Employment Interview

Professionals (CEIP). **Awards:** Certified Professional Resume Writer. **Type:** recognition. **Recipient:** for passing all the four modules of exam. **Publications:** *The Spotlight,* monthly. Newsletter. **Price:** included in membership dues. **Circulation:** 850. **Advertising:** accepted. **Conventions/Meetings:** annual convention and workshop (exhibits).

11835 ■ PUSH Commercial Division (PITB)
930 E 50th St.
Chicago, IL 60615-2702
Ph: (773)373-3366
Fax: (773)373-3571
E-mail: info@rainbowpush.org
URL: http://www.rainbowpush.org
Contact: Rev. Willie T. Barrow, Board Member
Founded: 1982. **Members:** 300. **Membership Dues:** $250 (annual). **Description:** A bureau of Operation PUSH. Minority-owned franchises and small businesses; minority individuals who are self-employed. Seeks the creation of a black common market in the U.S. Works to facilitate the opening of new markets for black-owned businesses. Provides technical assistance to members, including market research and analysis, financial counseling, and packaging and marketing services. Negotiates with major U.S. corporations to help create business opportunities for blacks. Conducts workshops on job hunting and business management. Maintains archive. **Awards:** Black Diamond Award. **Type:** recognition. **Recipient:** to businesses and individuals who have done the most to improve the economic status of blacks in the US. **Formerly:** PUSH International Trade Bureau. **Publications:** *Membership List,* quarterly. Membership Directory. **Advertising:** accepted ● Newsletter, monthly ● Also publishes brochure. **Conventions/Meetings:** annual convention, held in conjunction with Operation PUSH - always June.

11836 ■ Senior Community Service Employment Program (SCSEP)
c/o Division of Older Worker Programs
U.S. Dept. of Labor, Employment and Training Admin.
200 Constitution Ave. NW, Rm. N-4641
Washington, DC 20210
Ph: (202)693-3758
Free: (866)4US-ADOL
E-mail: gibson.gale@dol.gov
URL: http://www.doleta.gov/seniors
Contact: Gale Gibson, Contact
Founded: 1969. **Description:** Comprises eight employment programs organized under Title V of the Older Americans Act and funded by the federal government. Provides programs that are designed to provide on-the-job training in community service agencies for workers 55 years of age or older who are economically disadvantaged, in order that they might gain the experience needed to find permanent employment. Conducts individual programs that are sponsored by the U.S. Forest Service. **Affiliated With:** AARP; Experience Works; National Caucus and Center on Black Aged; National Council on the Aging; National Urban League.

11837 ■ SER - Jobs for Progress National
5215 N O'Connor Blvd., Ste.2550
Irving, TX 75039
Ph: (972)506-7815
Fax: (972)506-7832
E-mail: info@ser-national.org
URL: http://www.ser-national.org
Contact: Ignacio Salazar, Pres./CEO
Founded: 1964. **Members:** 42. **Staff:** 25. **Budget:** $6,500,000. **Regional Groups:** 4. **Local Groups:** 100. **Languages:** English, Spanish. **Description:** Aims to provide employment training and opportunities for Spanish-speaking and disadvantaged Americans. Seeks to increase business and economic opportunities for minority communities and ensure optimum participation by the Hispanic community in public policy forums. Gives funds to SER performance contracts that are funded by the federal government. (The acronym SER stands for service, employment, and redevelopment.) Organizes its own training and management program and is responsible for recruit-

ment and selection of job trainees, counseling, pre-job orientation and vocational preparation, basic education, employer relations, and follow-up services to trainees after training and job placement. **Awards:** SER Hispanic Scholarship. **Frequency:** annual. **Type:** scholarship. **Recipient:** for SER participants and/or children of SER employees. **Computer Services:** database. **Departments:** Comptroller; Corporate Relations. **Affiliated With:** American GI Forum of United States; League of United Latin American Citizens. **Also Known As:** Operation SER. **Formerly:** (1976) SER; (1993) SER - Jobs for Progress. **Publications:** *SER America,* quarterly. Magazine. **Advertising:** accepted ● *SER—Jobs for Progress—Annual Report.* Contains financial information, statistics, description of programs offered, and training center locations. **Price:** free. **Circulation:** 5,000 ● *SER—Jobs for Progress—Network Directory,* annual. Includes main offices of local SER corporations, affiliates, and satellites. **Price:** free. **Circulation:** 3,300. **Conventions/Meetings:** annual Yesterday, Today, And Tomorrow - conference (exhibits).

11838 ■ Tradeswomen
1433 Webster St.
Oakland, CA 94612
Ph: (510)891-8773
Fax: (510)891-8775
E-mail: beth@tradeswomen.org
URL: http://tradeswomen.org
Contact: Ms. Beth Youhn, Exec. Dir.
Founded: 1979. **Members:** 1,000. **Staff:** 1. **Description:** Women who work in nontraditional, blue-collar occupations including construction, transportation, and industrial work; women who seek to enter these fields or who support the right of others to do so. Serves as a network for women in the trades. Conducts social gatherings and local and regional forums on topics such as: health and safety on the job; racism and sexism in the trades; sexual harassment; working within unions. Maintains speakers' bureau. Compiles statistics. **Libraries:** **Type:** reference. **Holdings:** 17. **Subjects:** tradeswomen. **Awards:** **Frequency:** annual. **Type:** recognition. **Recipient:** to community activists and tradeswomen. **Computer Services:** database ● mailing lists. **Publications:** *Little Tradeswomen Coloring Book.* **Price:** $4.00 ● *Tradeswomen Magazine.* **Price:** $5.00 plus shipping and handling ● Pamphlets ● Videos ● Newsletter, periodic. Alternate Formats: online. **Conventions/Meetings:** periodic regional meeting.

11839 ■ Uglies Unlimited (UU)
1906 Juniper Ln.
Lufkin, TX 75904
Ph: (936)634-1429
Fax: (936)675-5169
E-mail: teamwardbound@yahoo.com
URL: http://www.ugliesunlimited.com
Contact: Danny McCoy, Founder
Founded: 1973. **Members:** 100. **Membership Dues:** research, $25 (annual). **Staff:** 2. **Budget:** $25,000. **Regional Groups:** 85. **Description:** Unattractive individuals who are vexed by discrimination against "uglies." Purposes are to: serve as the guardian of ugly human beings; encourage society and employers to accept people for what they are instead of what they look like; assists members in finding a new self-image. Solicits more exposure for uglies in mass media advertising ("Uglies can sell products too!"). Pickets, boycotts, and files complaints with Equal Employment Opportunity Commission. Conducts public awareness program. Holds Ugly Stick Competition (prizes are awarded by a "select committee of washed-out judges of past beauty pageants"). Compiles statistics. **Awards:** Ugly Stick. **Frequency:** annual. **Type:** recognition. **Recipient:** for promotion of discrimination awareness based on appearance. **Committees:** Ugly Stick Competition. **Conventions/Meetings:** annual meeting - always October. 2007 Oct. 23-27, Portland, OR - **Avg. Attendance:** 50.

11840 ■ Vocational Foundation, Inc. (VFI)
52 Broadway, 6th Fl.
New York, NY 10004
Ph: (212)823-1001

Fax: (718)230-8784
E-mail: erodriguez@vfinyc.org
URL: http://www.vfinyc.org
Contact: Hector Batista, CEO
Founded: 1936. **Members:** 23. **Staff:** 34. **Budget:** $2,800,000. **Description:** Serves as a free voluntary vocational training, guidance, and job placement service for economically and educationally disadvantaged young people (ages 16-21) who are referred by other accredited public and voluntary agencies in New York City. Seeks to aid high school dropouts and young people with correctional and drug abuse histories. Conducts GED prep and testing. **Formerly:** (1954) Vocational Foundation Bureau of the Association for the Prevention of Crime.

11841 ■ W. E. Upjohn Institute for Employment Research
300 S Westnedge Ave.
Kalamazoo, MI 49007-4686
Ph: (269)343-5541 (269)343-4330
Free: (888)227-8569
Fax: (269)343-3308
E-mail: publications@we.upjohninstitute.org
URL: http://www.upjohninstitute.org
Contact: Randall W. Eberts, Exec. Dir.
Founded: 1945. **Staff:** 55. **Budget:** $5,000,000. **Description:** Focuses its resources in research to find out the causes and consequences of unemployment. Conducts research on social insurance and income maintenance programs, earnings and benefits, economic development and local labor markets, family labor issues, work arrangements, education and training issues for the workplace, and other methods of alleviating problems related to unemployment. Administers federal and state funded employment programs and services in a two-county area. Compiles statistics. Maintains job-training program for the disadvantaged in on-the-job training by contract with Kalamazoo County, MI. Operates publishing program. **Libraries:** **Type:** by appointment only. **Holdings:** 12,000; books, periodicals. **Subjects:** labor economics, regional and urban development. **Awards:** Dissertation. **Frequency:** annual. **Type:** monetary ● W.E. Upjohn Institute for Employment Research Dissertation Award. **Frequency:** annual. **Type:** monetary. **Recipient:** for best dissertation on a topic dealing with labor economics. **Computer Services:** Mailing lists. **Programs:** Grant; Research. **Formerly:** (1959) W. E. Upjohn Institute for Community Research. **Publications:** *Business Outlook for West Michigan,* quarterly. Journal. Features indicators of future economic conditions, analyses of current business conditions, and special articles on business topics. **Price:** $50.00/year. ISSN: 0748-4216. Alternate Formats: online. Also Cited As: *Business Outlook* ● *Employment Research,* quarterly. Newsletter. Contains current issues dealing with labor economics. **Price:** free. Alternate Formats: online ● Books, 8/year. Covers topics dealing with labor economics and industrial relations. ● Reports ● Also issues periodic national and local research studies. **Conventions/Meetings:** annual conference, for varying policy issues.

11842 ■ WAVE
525 School St. SW, Ste.500
Washington, DC 20024-2795
Ph: (202)484-0103
Free: (800)274-2005
Fax: (202)484-7595
E-mail: info@waveinc.org
URL: http://www.waveinc.org
Contact: Larry Brown, Pres.
Founded: 1969. **Staff:** 36. **Budget:** $1,000,000. **Local Groups:** 150. **Description:** Helps disadvantaged 16-21 year old high school dropouts and students at risk of dropping out to find unsubsidized jobs and careers. Provides classes for students to prepare for their high school equivalency diplomas and to learn basic living skills, such as how to find an apartment, how to dress for a job interview, and how to balance a checkbook. Holds seminars and competitions that foster motivation and leadership and conducts national employment and training seminars for enrollees, and annual staff training institutes. **Divi-**

sions: Communications; Corporate Development; Field Operations; Program Development. **Formerly:** 70001—The Youth Employment Company; (1991) 70001 Training and Employment Institute. **Supersedes:** Project 70,001. **Publications:** *Annual Corporate Report*, annual ● *The Rising Tide*, quarterly. Includes articles, drawings, poetry, and achievements written by the youth participants of WAVE programs. **Circulation:** 20,000. **Advertising:** accepted ● Newsletter. Alternate Formats: online. **Conventions/Meetings:** annual National Youth Professionals' Institute - meeting.

11843 ■ Wider Opportunities for Women (WOW)
1001 Connecticut Ave. NW, Ste.930
Washington, DC 20036
Ph: (202)464-1596
Fax: (202)464-1660
E-mail: info@wowonline.org
URL: http://www.wowonline.org
Contact: Joan A. Kuriansky Esq., Exec. Dir.
Founded: 1964. **Membership Dues:** regular, $100 (annual). **Staff:** 15. **Budget:** $1,000,000. **Regional Groups:** 500. **Local Groups:** 500. **Description:** Expands employment opportunities for women through information, employment training, technical assistance, and advocacy. Works to overcome barriers to women's employment and economic equity, including occupational segregation, sex stereotyped education and training, discrimination in employment practices and wages. Sponsors Women's Work Force Network, a national network of 500 women's employment programs and advocates. Monitors current policies to increase the priority given to employment needs of women; provides information to congressional staffs to clarify the impact of various legislative proposals on women; issues public policy alerts and informational materials when relevant federal policy is being proposed or undergoing revision; conducts investigative projects to assess how legislative programs are implemented and their impact on women. Offers technical assistance to education institutions, government agencies, and private industry on programs to increase women's participation in non-traditional employment and training. Maintains National Commission on Working Women and Industry Advisory Councils. **Awards:** Women at Work Awards. **Frequency:** annual. **Type:** recognition. **Publications:** *A More Promising Future: Strategies to Improve the Workplace.* Book ● *Growing Up in Prime Time: An Analysis of Adolescent Girls on Television.* Book ● *Women at Work*, quarterly ● Books ● Pamphlets ● Also publishes workbooks and fact sheets. **Conventions/Meetings:** periodic meeting ● periodic regional meeting and workshop.

11844 ■ Wildcat Service Corporation (WSC)
17 Battery Pl.
New York, NY 10004
Ph: (212)209-6000
E-mail: rmandor@wildcatatwork.org
Contact: Mary Ellen Boyd, Pres.
Founded: 1972. **Staff:** 250. **Budget:** $55,000,000. **Languages:** Chinese, English, Spanish. **Description:** Provides transitional employment and training for chronically unemployed persons (former substance abusers, ex-offenders, welfare mothers, out-of-school youth, and illiterate and delinquent youth). Systematically prepares and grooms employees to accept the full responsibility of full-time work within a 12-month time period. Placement rate of terminees is about 70&percent; in a variety of industries. Operates clerical work in basic and advanced office practices; conducts specialized "life skills" educational program. Compiles statistics; maintains placement service. Operates three high schools. **Convention/Meeting:** none. **Publications:** *The Wildcatter.* Newsletter. Alternate Formats: online.

11845 ■ Women Employed (WE)
111 N Wabash, Ste.1300
Chicago, IL 60602
Ph: (312)782-3902
Fax: (312)782-5249

E-mail: info@womenemployed.org
URL: http://www.womenemployed.org
Contact: Anne Ladky, Exec. Dir.
Founded: 1973. **Members:** 1,600. **Staff:** 12. **Description:** Working women and women seeking employment. Helps women improve their jobs and employment opportunities. Conducts advocacy efforts on issues including pay equity, sexual harassment, and nontraditional jobs for women. Offers career development services that include seminars, counseling, networking opportunities and a job-bank. Monitors government enforcement of equal opportunity laws. Conducts public education programs on issues concerning working women. Sponsors Women Employed Institute. **Affiliated With:** Women Employed Institute. **Publications:** *Newsbyte*, monthly. Article. Alternate Formats: online ● *Women Employed News*, quarterly. Newsletter. **Price:** included in membership dues. **Circulation:** 1,800 ● Reports. **Conventions/Meetings:** annual Career Conference - usually March or April in Chicago, IL.

11846 ■ Women Employed Institute (WEI)
111 N Wabash, Ste.1300
Chicago, IL 60602
Ph: (312)782-3902
Fax: (312)782-5249
E-mail: info@womenemployed.org
URL: http://www.womenemployed.org
Contact: Anne Ladky, Exec. Dir.
Founded: 1973. **Members:** 2,500. **Membership Dues:** regular, $50 (annual). **Staff:** 12. **Description:** Serves as a research and education division of Women Employed (see separate entry) devoted to promoting economic equity for women. Analyzes government programs and employer policies; develops recommendations for public and corporate policy to promote equal opportunity. Sponsors advocacy programs to increase women's accessibility to vocational education and training for higher paying and nontraditional jobs. Develops model employment awareness/readiness programs for disadvantaged women. Conducts research projects; compiles statistics on women's economic status. **Affiliated With:** Women Employed. **Publications:** *Bridges to Careers for Low-Skilled Adults: A Program Development Guide.* Handbook ● *Directory of Work/Family Benefits Offered by Chicago-Area Employers* ● *News Byte*, monthly. Article. Alternate Formats: online ● *Workers and Families: A Policy Guide for Employers* ● Also publishes factsheets on sexual harassment prevention affirmative action, welfare-to-work debate, and pregnancy rights on the job.

11847 ■ Work Fairness
39 W 14th St., Rm. 206
New York, NY 10011
Ph: (212)633-6646
Fax: (212)633-2889
E-mail: iacenter@iacenter.org
URL: http://www.iacenter.org
Contact: Von dora Jordan, Co-Coor.
Founded: 1992. **Description:** Works on a grass roots basis to fight homelessness and unemployment. Sponsors educational programs. **Publications:** Newsletter, periodic. **Conventions/Meetings:** meeting.

Engineering

11848 ■ Engineers Without Borders - USA (EWB-USA)
c/o Ann Geesaman, Membership and Admin. Asst.
1880 Indus. Cir., Ste.B3
Longmont, CO 80501
Ph: (303)772-2723
Fax: (303)772-2699
E-mail: cathy.leslie@ewb-usa.org
URL: http://www.ewb-usa.org
Contact: Cathy Leslie, Exec. Dir.
Founded: 2000. **Membership Dues:** professional, $100 (annual) ● student, $15 (annual) ● supporting, $150 (annual) ● life, $1,000. **Multinational. Description:** Partners with disavantaged communities to

improve their quality of life through implementation of environmentally and economically sustainable engineering projects. Helps develop internationally responsible engineering students. Strives to provide the disadvantaged communities with adequate sanitation, safe drinking water and the resources to meet other economic development needs. **Computer Services:** database, technology products catalog. **Committees:** Technical Advisory. **Projects:** Agriculture; Energy; Information and Communication System; Microenterprise; Sanitation and Waste Treatment; Structures and Construction; Water Supply. **Publications:** Newsletter, monthly. Alternate Formats: online.

Entertainers

11849 ■ Actors' Fund of America
729 Seventh Ave., 10th Fl.
New York, NY 10019
Ph: (212)221-7300
Fax: (212)764-0238
E-mail: jbeninca@actorsfund.org
URL: http://www.actorsfund.org
Contact: Joseph P. Benincasa, Exec. Dir.
Founded: 1882. **Members:** 6,000. **Staff:** 130. **Budget:** $21,000,000. **Regional Groups:** 3. **Description:** Helps all professionals - both performers and those behind the scenes - in performing arts and entertainment. Serves those in film, theatre, television, music, opera, and dance with a broad spectrum of programs including comprehensive social services, health services, supportive and affordable housing, emergency financial assistance, employment and training services, and skilled nursing and assisted living care. Administered from offices in New York, Los Angeles, and Chicago, it serves as a safety net, providing programs and services for those who are in need, crisis, or transition. **Awards:** Lee Strasberg Artistic Achievement Award. **Frequency:** annual. **Type:** recognition. **Recipient:** for performers who have upheld a consistent standard of excellence in their work. **Boards:** Trustees. **Committees:** Artist. **Divisions:** External Affairs; Social Service. **Programs:** Actors' Work; Chemical Dependency; HIV/AIDS Initiative; Musicians Assistance; Senior and Disabled; Supportive and Affordable Housing. **Publications:** *Marquee*, 3/year. Newsletter ● Annual Report, annual. Includes membership and memoriam listing, and financial report. **Conventions/Meetings:** annual meeting - always May in New York City.

11850 ■ Bread and Roses (B&R)
233 Tamalpais Dr., Ste.100
Corte Madera, CA 94925-1415
Ph: (415)945-7120
Fax: (415)945-7128
E-mail: info@breadandroses.org
URL: http://www.breadandroses.org
Contact: Cassandra Flipper, Exec. Dir.
Founded: 1974. **Staff:** 9. **Budget:** $800,000. **Description:** Coordinates volunteer entertainers to bring free, live entertainment to people in Bay area institutions such as convalescent homes, children's centers, AIDS facilities, and psychiatric wards; entertainers donate their time and talents to people who "desperately need and appreciate the pleasure and human contact that live performance provides." Acquires benefit from a "sympathetic, noncommercial environment in which to perform.". **Publications:** Newsletter, semiannual. **Price:** $20.00/year. **Circulation:** 3,000 ● Handbook. Provides information on developing similar organizations.

11851 ■ Entertainment Industry Foundation (EIF)
1201 W 5th St., Ste.T-700
Los Angeles, CA 90017
Ph: (213)240-3900
E-mail: admin@eifoundation.org
URL: http://www.eifoundation.org
Contact: Lisa C. Paulsen, Pres./CEO
Founded: 1969. **Members:** 133. **Staff:** 12. **Description:** Conducts annual fundraising campaign within

the motion picture, radio, television, recording, advertising, and allied industries to channel funds to publicly supported health and welfare services throughout the Greater Los Angeles, CA, area; allocations are made to agencies involved with national charitable organizations conducting local fund appeals. Recognizes AIDS, environment, gay violence, hunger and homelessness, literacy, health and medicine, children, senior citizens, and substance abuse, as well as committee members through 20 industry groups representing management, talent guilds, and craft unions and guilds. **Formerly:** (1998) Permanent Charities Committee of the Entertainment Industries.

11852 ■ Motion Picture and Television Fund (MPTF)
22212 Ventura Blvd., Ste.300
Woodland Hills, CA 91364
Ph: (818)876-1900
Free: (800)876-8320
Fax: (818)876-1940
E-mail: webmaster@securemptvfund.org
URL: http://www.mptvfund.org
Contact: David Tillman MD, Pres./CEO
Founded: 1921. **Members:** 55. **Staff:** 680. **Budget:** $30,000,000. **Description:** Serves as welfare agency of the motion picture and television industry, supported by contributions (1-2&percent; of salary) from employees in the industry. Conducts drug and alcohol abuse programs; provides maintenance and medical care. Operates Motion Picture Country House/Hospital, permanent home for the elderly, and five outpatient health centers. **Convention/Meeting:** none. **Programs:** Junior Volunteer; Pastoral Volunteer. **Formerly:** Motion Picture Relief Fund.

11853 ■ Veterans Bedside Network (VBN)
10 Fiske Pl., Rm. 301
Mount Vernon, NY 10550-3205
Ph: (914)699-6069
Fax: (914)667-0405
URL: http://www.veteransbedsidenetwork.org
Contact: Douglas Lutz, Pres.
Founded: 1948. **Members:** 130. **Membership Dues:** individual, $25 (annual). **Staff:** 1. **Budget:** $93,000. **Description:** Professional actors, writers, producers, musicians, engineers, and others in radio and television who serve as weekly volunteers in Veterans Administration hospitals. Objectives are to provide recreation-therapy programs for hospitalized veterans and to help them produce and perform in their own radio and television programs. The taped all-patient shows feature professional network scripts, with music and sound effects provided by VBN. Additionally, more than 100 hospitals across the country participate in the "Script Kit" project. Escorts patients to entertainment and sports events. Serves as media consultant to the Veterans Administration in New York City. New York City. Serves as media consultant to the Veterans Administration in New York City. **Libraries: Type:** reference. **Holdings:** 100; audio recordings, books, video recordings. **Subjects:** radio and television scripts. **Awards:** Helping Hand Award. **Frequency:** annual. **Type:** recognition. **Recipient:** for the person who did the most in preceding year to advance VBN's mission. **Committees:** Finance/Fund Raising; Hospital Relations and Activities; National Affiliates; Public Information; Radio/TV; Special Events. **Also Known As:** Veterans Hospital Radio and Television Guild. **Publications:** *Presidents Newsletter*, semiannual. **Circulation:** 1,250. **Conventions/Meetings:** monthly board meeting and executive committee meeting ● annual executive committee meeting.

Environment

11854 ■ Coalition for Environmentally Safe Communities (CESC)
6642 Fisher Ave.
Falls Church, VA 22046
Ph: (703)534-8334
Fax: (703)534-8332

E-mail: japhoenix@cesckids.org
URL: http://www.cesckids.org
Contact: Janet A. Phoenix MD, Exec. Dir.
Founded: 1998. **Description:** Seeks to implement community-based programs to make homes safe environments. Provides training on lead hazard prevention, lead abatement and control, asthma prevention and the control of other indoor environmental hazards. Works to increase the capacities within community-based organizations to reduce the incidence of lead poisoning in their communities. Helps provide temporary "safe housing" as needed for relocation purposes.

11855 ■ Educational Foundation of America (EFA)
35 Church Ln.
Westport, CT 06880
Ph: (203)226-6498
Fax: (203)227-0424
E-mail: efa@efaw.org
URL: http://www.efaw.org
Contact: Elaine P. Hapgood, Pres.
Founded: 1959. **Multinational. Description:** Strives to promote environmental preservation and conservation, and works to educate the public about overpopulation. **Publications:** Annual Report. Alternate Formats: online.

11856 ■ Pacific Institute for Studies in Development, Environment, and Security
654 13th St., Preservation Park
Oakland, CA 94612
Ph: (510)251-1600
Fax: (510)251-2203
E-mail: info@pacinst.org
URL: http://www.pacinst.org
Contact: Dr. Peter H. Gleick, Pres.
Founded: 1987. **Membership Dues:** basic, $35 (annual). **Description:** Works to protect the natural world, encourage sustainable development, and improve global security. Provides independent research and policy analysis on issues at the intersection of development, environment, and security. Aims to find real-world solutions to problems like water shortages, habitat destruction, global warming, and environmental terrorism. Conducts research, publish reports, recommend solutions, and work with decision makers, advocacy groups, and the public to change policy; known for independent, innovative thinking that cuts across traditional areas of study. Brings opposing groups together to forge effective real-world solutions through interdisciplinary approach. **Libraries: Type:** by appointment only. **Holdings:** 35; books, papers, reports. **Subjects:** freshwater resources, climate change, water and conflict, desalination, water privatization, human right to water, environmental indicators, diesel pollution, globalization, ISO, international standards, Salton Sea, Colorado River, environmental justice, goods movement, agricultural water, California water, World Water, climate change and water. **Computer Services:** Bibliographic search, water and climate ● bibliographic search, water and conflict ● electronic publishing, monthly email newsletter ● online services, integrity of science blog. **Also Known As:** (2006) Pacific Institute. **Publications:** *Pacific Institute Online Update*, monthly. Newsletter. Features updates on research and publications. Alternate Formats: online ● Reports. Alternate Formats: online.

Epidemiology

11857 ■ Community Information and Epidemiological Technologies (CIET)
511 Ave. of the Americas, No. 132
New York, NY 10011
Ph: (212)242-3428
Fax: (212)504-0848
E-mail: cietinter@ciet.org
URL: http://www.ciet.org
Founded: 1994. **National Groups:** 8. **Multinational. Description:** Brings scientific research methods to community levels by involving local people in informa-

tion gathering and analysis. Shares its collective skills and its methods with national, regional, and local partners to help develop local stakeholder information systems and build indigenous capacities for evidenced-based planning and action. **Libraries: Type:** reference. **Holdings:** articles, clippings. **Subjects:** research, sustainable development, economy, corruption. **Computer Services:** Information services, media releases. **Projects:** Aboriginal Health; Appropriate Technology; Breastfeeding; Capacity Building; Child Rights; Corruption; Eco-system Health; Gender. **Publications:** Articles. Alternate Formats: online.

Ethics

11858 ■ American Institute of Medical Ethics
409 Encina Ave.
Davis, CA 95616
Ph: (530)758-0739
Contact: Dr. John Monagle PhD, Pres.
Founded: 1987. **Staff:** 3. **Description:** Works to uphold ethics in medicine. Conducts education and consultation in hospitals. **Libraries: Type:** reference; by appointment only. **Subjects:** bioethics, philosophy, literature, healthcare risk management. **Publications:** Publishes informational materials on risk management and medical ethics. **Conventions/Meetings:** periodic meeting, held in hospitals.

11859 ■ Americans for the Enforcement of Attorney Ethics (AEAE)
PO Box 35189
Chicago, IL 60707-0189
Ph: (773)283-3880
Fax: (708)453-0083
E-mail: aeae@rentamark.com
Contact: Leo Stoller, Exec.Dir.
Founded: 1989. **Members:** 50,000. **Membership Dues:** professional, $95 (annual). **Staff:** 10. **Description:** Believes that all attorneys should adhere to the American Bar Association rules of professional conduct. Files charges of professional misconduct against members of the bar who do not abide by the ABA rules. **Libraries: Type:** reference. **Holdings:** 10,000. **Subjects:** attorney ethics. **Awards:** Attorney Ethics Award. **Frequency:** annual. **Type:** recognition. **Recipient:** for attorneys who have uphold the rules of professional conduct ● Disciplinary Commission Award. **Frequency:** annual. **Type:** recognition. **Recipient:** for vigorously enforcing the rules of professional conduct. **Computer Services:** Mailing lists, of members. **Committees:** Political Action. **Also Known As:** (2000) Attorney Ethics Association. **Publications:** *Ethics Report*, quarterly. Magazine. **Price:** $2.50. **Circulation:** 100,000. **Advertising:** accepted. Alternate Formats: online ● Newsletter. Invites authors to submit articles in MS Word format. **Conventions/Meetings:** annual convention.

11860 ■ Americans for the Enforcement of Judicial Ethics (AEJE)
PO Box 35215
Chicago, IL 60707-0215
Ph: (708)453-0080
Fax: (708)453-0083
E-mail: law@rentamark.com
Contact: Leo Stoller, Exec.Dir.
Founded: 1989. **Members:** 69,532. **Membership Dues:** business, $100 (annual) ● corporate sponsor, $250 (annual) ● individual, $25 (annual). **Staff:** 50. **Description:** Serves as a watchdog group overseeing the strict enforcement of the code of judicial conduct. Brings formal complaints against judges who fail to follow the code of judicial conduct. Offers member education through approved legal books. Provides benefits. **Libraries: Type:** reference. **Holdings:** 1,000. **Subjects:** code of judicial ethics. **Awards:** Code of Judicial Conduct. **Frequency:** annual. **Type:** recognition. **Recipient:** for judges who follow the code of judicial conduct. **Computer Services:** Mailing lists, of members. **Committees:** Political Action. **Publications:** *Judicial Code of Conduct Report*, monthly. Magazine. **Price:** free for

members. **Circulation:** 100,000. **Advertising:** accepted. Alternate Formats: online. **Conventions/Meetings:** annual conference and convention.

11861 ■ Hastings Center (HC)
21 Malcolm Gordon Rd.
Garrison, NY 10524-4125
Ph: (845)424-4040
Fax: (845)424-4545
E-mail: mail@thehastingscenter.org
URL: http://www.thehastingscenter.org
Contact: Thomas H. Murray, Pres.
Founded: 1969. **Members:** 6,000. **Membership Dues:** individual in U.S., $76 (annual) ● individual outside U.S., $94 (annual) ● library/institution in U.S., $115 (annual) ● library/institution outside U.S., $129 (annual) ● senior in U.S. (age 65 or older), $50 (annual) ● senior outside U.S. (age 65 or older), $72 (annual). **Staff:** 28. **Description:** Individuals concerned with medical, professional, and environmental ethics including physicians, nurses, lawyers, administrators, public policymakers, and other academic and health care professionals. Conducts research on issues relevant to ethics. Offers consulting services. Provides in-house and international educational opportunities including student intern, visiting scholar, and international fellowship programs. **Libraries: Type:** open to the public; by appointment only. **Holdings:** 8,000; books, periodicals. **Subjects:** medical ethics, philosophy, environment. **Awards:** Henry Knowles Beecher Award. **Frequency:** triennial. **Type:** recognition. **Recipient:** for contributions to ethics and the life sciences. **Formerly:** (1987) Institute of Society, Ethics, and the Life Sciences. **Publications:** *Hastings Center Report*, bimonthly. Journal. Contains articles, case studies, regular columns and letters - explores a wide range of issues and perspectives in bioethics and environment. **Price:** included in membership dues; $76.00 for nonmembers in U.S.; $115.00 for institutions and libraries in U.S.; $94.00 for nonmembers outside U.S. ISSN: 0093-0334. **Circulation:** 10,000. Alternate Formats: online ● *IRB: Ethics and Human Research*, bimonthly. Journal. Helps clarify fundamental ethical concerns, explore regulatory developments, and share insights and experiences as resources for all. **Price:** $55.00 for individuals in U.S.; $66.00 for individuals outside U.S.; $74.00 for institutions and libraries in U.S.; $89.00 for institutions and libraries outside U.S. ● Books. Devoted to questions of the ethics and regulations of human subject research. ● Monographs ● Reports. Covers topics such as patient safety, palliative care, genetic research and international medicine. **Price:** $10.00 for single copy (varies with number of purchase).

11862 ■ International Network on Feminist Approaches to Bioethics (FAB)
c/o Anne Donchin, Treas.
5 Riverpoint Rd.
Hastings on Hudson, NY 10706
Ph: (914)674-0122
Fax: (914)478-2885
E-mail: adonchin@iupui.edu
URL: http://www.fabnet.org
Contact: Anne Donchin, Treas.
Founded: 1992. **Members:** 380. **Membership Dues:** individual (with annual income level under $20,000), $10 (annual) ● individual (with annual income level of $35,000-$20,000), $15 (annual) ● individual (with annual income level of $50,000-$35,000), $20 (annual) ● individual (with annual income level over $50,000), $25 (annual). **Staff:** 15. **Budget:** $5,000. **Languages:** English, French, German, Hindi, Italian, Japanese, Portuguese, Spanish. **Multinational. Description:** Committed to a non-hierarchical model of organizations and seeks to include all who share the goals and will strive to advance them. Academics, professionals, grassroots activists, concerned persons from all fields are welcome to join FAB. Exchanges information with many organizations. Aims to develop a more inclusive theory of bioethics encompassing the standpoints and experiences of women and other marginalized social groups; to examine presuppositions embedded in the dominant bioethical discourse that privilege those already

empowered; and to create new methodologies and strategies responsive to the disparate conditions of women's lives across the globe. Bioethics is a discipline dealing with the ethical implications of matters related to health care practice, systems, institutions, and decisions. Conducts exchange of information about research initiatives; organizes presentations at national and international bioethics conferences; and develops collaborative research projects. **Computer Services:** Information services, listserv for members. **Formerly:** (2002) Network on Feminist Approaches to Bioethics; (2004) International Feminist Approaches to Bioethics. **Publications:** *The International Network on Feminist Approaches to Bioethics*, semiannual. Newsletter. **Price:** free for members. **Circulation:** 300. Alternate Formats: online. **Conventions/Meetings:** biennial Feminist Approaches to Bioethics - conference, in conjunction with International Association of Bioethics (exhibits).

11863 ■ Society for Business Ethics (SBE)
c/o Joe DesJardins, Exec. Dir.
Dept. of Philosophy
Coll. of St. Benedict, St. John's Univ.
Coll. Ave.
St. Joseph, MN 56374
Ph: (320)363-5915
E-mail: jdesjardins@csbsju.edu
URL: http://www.societyforbusinessethics.org
Contact: Joe DesJardins, Exec. Dir.
Founded: 1980. **Members:** 800. **Membership Dues:** individual, $60 (annual) ● institutional, $165 (annual) ● student, $30 (annual). **Staff:** 5. **Budget:** $70,000. **Multinational. Description:** Philosophy and theology professors, business school professors, and business executives. Facilitates information exchange regarding research and activities in business ethics. **Affiliated With:** Academy of Management; American Philosophical Association. **Publications:** *Business Ethics Quarterly*. Journal. Publishes scholarly articles and book reviews on all aspects of ethics in business. **Price:** included in membership dues. **Circulation:** 1,000. **Advertising:** accepted. Alternate Formats: CD-ROM; online. Also Cited As: *BEQ* ● *Society for Business Ethics Newsletter*, quarterly. **Price:** included in membership dues. Alternate Formats: online. **Conventions/Meetings:** annual conference, held in conjunction with the Academy of Management (exhibits) - always summer ● annual meeting, held in conjunction with APA.

11864 ■ Society of Christian Ethics (SCE)
PO Box 5126
St. Cloud, MN 56302
Ph: (320)253-5407
Fax: (320)252-6984
E-mail: sce@cord.edu
URL: http://www.scethics.org
Contact: Stewart W. Herman, Exec. Dir.
Founded: 1959. **Members:** 1,100. **Membership Dues:** unemployed, student, retired, $30 ● full, $30-$160. **Staff:** 1. **Budget:** $100,000. **Regional Groups:** 1. **Description:** Teachers of Christian or social ethics; persons teaching in fields concerned with the relation of Christian ethics to their subject matter; persons whose full-time professional work in churches, government, social agencies, or elsewhere is related to the concerns of the society. Promotes scholarly work in the field of Christian ethics, in relation to other traditions of ethics, and to social, economic, political, and cultural problems. Encourages and works to improve the teaching of Christian ethics in colleges, universities, and theological schools. Provides a fellowship of discourse and debate for those in the field of Christian ethics and social policy. **Affiliated With:** Council of Societies for the Study of Religion. **Formerly:** American Society of Christian Social Ethics in the United States and Canada; (1980) American Society of Christian Ethics. **Publications:** *Journal of the Society of Christian Ethics*, semiannual. **Price:** included in membership dues; $22.00 /year for libraries. ISSN: 1540-7942. **Circulation:** 1,200. **Advertising:** accepted. Also Cited As: *Selected Papers of the American Society of Christian*

Ethics. **Conventions/Meetings:** annual meeting (exhibits) - always January. 2008 Jan. 3-6, Atlanta, GA.

Euthanasia

11865 ■ Citizens United Resisting Euthanasia (CURE)
303 Truman St.
Berkeley Springs, WV 25411
Ph: (304)258-5433
Fax: (304)258-5433
E-mail: cureltd@verizon.net
URL: http://mysite.verizon.net/cureltd/index.html
Contact: Earl Appleby Jr., Dir.
Founded: 1981. **Nonmembership. Description:** Individuals "bound together in a common cause: uncompromising opposition to euthanasia". Promotes increased awareness of alternatives to voluntary euthanasia. Provides practical help to families besieged by euthanasia practitioners; makes available legal assistance to individuals contemplating voluntary euthanasia; conducts research; lobbies to strengthen statutes criminalizing euthanasia. **Publications:** *Life Matters*. Brochure ● Reports ● Articles. **Conventions/Meetings:** biennial meeting and conference.

11866 ■ Compassion in Dying Federation (CID)
c/o Barbara Coombs Lee, Pres./CEO
6312 SW Capitol Hwy., No. 415
Portland, OR 97239
Ph: (503)221-9556
Fax: (503)228-9160
E-mail: info@compassionandchoices.org
Contact: Barbara Coombs Lee, Pres./CEO
Founded: 1993. **State Groups:** 6. **Description:** Provides information, counseling, and emotional support to terminally ill patients who are deciding how life should come to an end. Includes counseling patients and families about intensive pain management, comfort or hospice care, and safe, effective methods for hastening death. **Formerly:** (1998) Compassion in Dying. **Publications:** *Compassion and Choices*, quarterly. Magazine. **Circulation:** 50,000 ● *In Thought and Action*, monthly. Newsletter. **Circulation:** 25,000. Alternate Formats: online.

11867 ■ End-of-Life Choices
PO Box 101810
Denver, CO 80250-1810
Ph: (303)639-1202
Free: (800)247-7421
Fax: (303)639-1224
E-mail: info@endoflifechoices.org
URL: http://www.compassionandchoices.org
Contact: David Goldberg, Contact
Founded: 1980. **Members:** 34,000. **Membership Dues:** individual, $35 (annual) ● couple, dual, $43 (annual) ● individual (life), $350 ● couple, dual (life), $430 ● benefactor, $100 (annual). **Staff:** 17. **Budget:** $3,100,000. **Regional Groups:** 91. **State Groups:** 10. **Local Groups:** 86. **Description:** Maximizes options for dignified death, including voluntary physician aid in dying for mentally competent, terminally ill adults who request it, within the context of legal safeguards. Serves as the voice of a national grassroots movement, provides materials and information to the public, the media, health care professionals, and legislators through education, research, and legislation. Promotes the importance of living wills, powers of attorney, and advance health care directives. Approves suicide prevention work and does not advocate self-deliverance for any primary reason other than terminal illness under legal and ethical protocols. **Libraries: Type:** reference. **Holdings:** audio recordings, books, clippings, video recordings. **Subjects:** legal, medical, and social aspects of the right-to-die movement. **Formerly:** (1993) Hemlock Society; (2003) Hemlock Society U.S.A. **Publications:** *EOL Choices*, quarterly. Magazine. **Price:** included in membership dues. **Circulation:** 34,000. **Advertising:** accepted ● Books. Covers death and

dying and physician aid in dying. ● Also publishes source materials. **Conventions/Meetings:** biennial National Conference on Right to Die (exhibits).

11868 ■ Euthanasia Research and Guidance Organization (ERGO)
24829 Norris Ln.
Junction City, OR 97448-9559
Ph: (541)998-1873
Fax: (541)998-1873
E-mail: ergo@efn.org
URL: http://www.finalexit.org
Contact: Derek Humphry, Pres.
Founded: 1993. **Members:** 4,755. **Membership Dues:** nonvoting, $10 (annual). **Staff:** 1. **Description:** Individuals supporting voluntary euthanasia. Promotes greater public awareness of euthanasia and related issues. Conducts research and develops guidelines for euthanasia; provides counseling to individuals with terminal conditions; briefs scholars and the media on historical and ethical issues surrounding euthanasia. **Computer Services:** Mailing lists. **Publications:** *Final Exit: The Practicalities of Self-Deliverance and Assisted Suicide for the Dying*, quadrennial. Book. Includes interim addenda. **Price:** $15.00/copy ● *The Good Euthanasia Guide 2005: Where, What and Who In Choices In Dying*. Book. **Price:** $14.00 ● *The Good Euthanasia Guide 2004: Where, What and Who In Choices In Dying*, annual. Book. **Price:** $5.00/copy ● *Right-to-die News*, daily. Newsletter. **Price:** $5.00/copy. Alternate Formats: online ● Newsletter, periodic.

11869 ■ International Task Force on Euthanasia and Assisted Suicide (ITF)
PO Box 760
Steubenville, OH 43952
Ph: (740)282-3810
Free: (800)958-5678
Fax: (740)282-0769
E-mail: rmarker@internationaltaskforce.org
URL: http://www.internationaltaskforce.org
Contact: Rita L. Marker Esq., Exec. Dir.
Founded: 1988. **Description:** Provides information on euthanasia, suicide, assisted suicide, and related issues. Promotes and defends the right of all persons to be treated with respect, dignity, and compassion. Maintains speakers' bureau, and film resources; provides speakers' training, news service, background information services for media, and information on advocacy and disability rights; conducts legislative and curriculum analyses, news service, background information services for media, and information on advocacy and disability rights; conducts legislative and curriculum analyses. **Libraries:** Type: reference. **Subjects:** bioethics, assisted suicide, euthanasia. **Formerly:** (2001) International Anti-Euthanasia Task Force. **Publications:** *Deadly Compassion*. Book. Relates the explosive details of this tragic death and the dark side of the euthanasia movement. **Price:** $6.60/copy (includes postage and handling) ● *False Light*. Video. Addresses points which are most apt to cause people to question the advisability of legalizing assisted death. **Price:** $24.95 each (1-4 copies); $19.95 each (5-9 copies); $10.95 each (100-299 copies); $5.50 each (over 500 copies) ● *ITF Update*, periodic. Newsletter. **Price:** $25.00 donation requested ● Informational packets and other publications on euthanasia-related issues. **Conventions/Meetings:** seminar and workshop.

Families

11870 ■ Ackerman Institute for the Family
149 E 78th St.
New York, NY 10021-0405
Ph: (212)879-4900
Fax: (212)744-0206
E-mail: ackerman@ackerman.org
URL: http://www.ackerman.org
Contact: Dr. Louis Braverman, Pres./CEO
Founded: 1960. **Staff:** 35. **Budget:** $1,200,000. **Description:** Conducts research projects on issues as diverse as urgent family crises, depression, and child-

hood learning disabilities; research also evolves into "new insight about family dynamics and methods of treatment.". **Formerly:** (1971) Family Institute; (1977) Nathan W. Ackerman Family Institute; (1998) Ackerman Institute for Family Therapy. **Publications:** Report ● Newsletter. **Conventions/Meetings:** periodic meeting - always New York City.

11871 ■ Advocates for Fair Family Support
c/o Henry A. Freedman
275 7th Ave., Ste.1205
New York, NY 10001-6708
Ph: (212)633-6967
Fax: (212)633-6371
E-mail: wlc@welfarelaw.org
URL: http://www.welfarelaw.org
Contact: Henry A. Freedman, Exec.Dir.
Description: Works with and on behalf of low-income people to ensure that adequate income support and public funding are provided on the basis of need.

11872 ■ Alliance for Children and Families (ACF)
11700 W Lake Park Dr.
Milwaukee, WI 53224-3099
Ph: (414)359-1040
Free: (800)221-3726
Fax: (414)359-1074
E-mail: info@alliance1.org
URL: http://www.alliance1.org
Contact: Mr. Peter Goldberg, Pres./CEO
Founded: 1911. **Members:** 450. **Membership Dues:** state council/association, $750 (annual). **Staff:** 50. **Budget:** $6,000,000. **Multinational. Description:** Membership organization of local agencies in more than 1,000 communities providing family counseling, family life education and family advocacy services, and other programs to help families with parent-child, marital, mental health, and other problems of family living. Assists member agencies in developing and providing effective family services. Works with the media, government, and corporations to promote strong family life. Compiles statistics; conducts research. Maintains extensive files of unpublished materials from member agencies. Offers career placement services. **Libraries:** Type: reference. **Holdings:** 2,000. **Subjects:** social work, family life, psychology, non-profit agency management, residential care for children. **Awards:** Barksdale-Brown Award. **Frequency:** semiannual. **Type:** recognition. **Recipient:** for excellence in volunteerism ● Robert Rice Award. **Frequency:** semiannual. **Type:** recognition. **Recipient:** for an innovative program. **Computer Services:** database, member agency information on personnel, income, and programs. **Departments:** Member Services; Public Policy; Severson National Information Center. **Formerly:** Family Welfare Association of America; (1983) Family Service Association of America; (1990) National Association of Homes for Children; (1998) Family Association of America; (1998) National Association of Homes and Services for Children. **Publications:** *Alliance E-News*. Newsletter. **Price:** available to members only ● *Alliance for Children and Families—Directory of Member Agencies*, annual. Membership Directory. Lists member agencies by state. **Price:** free to each member headquarters; $350.00 for nonmembers; $40.00 for non-profit organizations. **Circulation:** 800. **Advertising:** accepted ● *Families in Society: The Journal of Contemporary Human Services*, quarterly ● Magazine, 3/year ● Books ● Manuals. **Conventions/Meetings:** annual convention, software, insurance, non-profit publications, office products (exhibits) - always September or October.

11873 ■ American College of Counselors (ACC)
2750 E Sunshine St.
Springfield, MO 65804-2047
Ph: (317)826-3168
Free: (800)205-9165
Fax: (317)826-3168
E-mail: wmsloane@widener.edu
URL: http://www.freewebs.com/counselors
Contact: William Martin Sloane PhD, Chm.
Founded: 1976. **Members:** 250. **Membership Dues:** certification, fellow, diplomate, $120 (annual). **Staff:**

2. **Budget:** $10,000. **Regional Groups:** 4. **State Groups:** 10. **Local Groups:** 3. **Languages:** Dutch, English, French, German, Spanish. **Description:** Represents individuals who are active in counseling in related fields of human services. Fosters values that enrich human growth and development. Works to establish guidelines and standards that will be in common with all specialties. Aims to increase knowledge and awareness of complex behavioral and emotional problems. Promotes objectivity and integrity; high standards of inquiry and communication; responsibility and competence in objectively reporting findings. **Libraries:** Type: open to the public. **Holdings:** 2. **Subjects:** counseling techniques. **Awards:** Annual Symposium Scholarship. **Frequency:** annual. **Type:** scholarship. **Computer Services:** Mailing lists. **Telecommunication Services:** additional toll-free number, (800)423-9737. **Committees:** Certification; Continuing Education; Legislation and Research; Public and Professional Education; Public Relations. **Formerly:** National Academy of Counselors and Family Therapists; (1984) National Alliance for Family Life. **Publications:** *ACC Courier*, 3/year. Journal. **Price:** included in membership dues; $20.00 /year for nonmembers. **Circulation:** 200. **Advertising:** accepted ● *CON-TEXT: Journal of the ACC*, annual. **Price:** included in membership dues; $10.00 for nonmembers. **Conventions/Meetings:** annual meeting - always spring ● annual symposium and conference - usually fall.

11874 ■ American Family Communiversity (AFCO)
PO Box 121187
Chicago, IL 60612
Ph: (312)738-2275 (312)545-6651
Fax: (312)738-2275
E-mail: afcomveristy@netscape.com
Contact: Dr. Les Kohut Ed.D., Pres.
Founded: 1966. **Description:** Multidisciplinary action and education agency engaged on the systems level in upgrading the various policies, practices, procedures, professions, systems and institutions affecting the stability and viability of marriages. **Absorbed:** (1976) Family Law Research Foundation. **Formerly:** (1966) Association for the Advancement of Family Stability; (1972) Family Cause. **Publications:** *Divorce for the Unbroken Marriage*. Book ● *Needless Divorce in America*. Monographs ● *Therapeutic Family Law*. Book ● Also publishes numerous monographs.

11875 ■ American Mothers, Inc. (AMI)
Carlyle Crescent Ctr.
1940 Duke St., Ste.200
Alexandria, VA 22314
Ph: (703)486-5760
Free: (877)242-4624
Fax: (703)486-5761
E-mail: info@americanmothers.org
URL: http://www.americanmothers.org
Contact: Sue Hickenlooper, Pres.
Founded: 1935. **Members:** 4,000. **Membership Dues:** general, national, $20 (annual) ● life, $1,000. **Staff:** 2. **Budget:** $100,000. **State Groups:** 52. **Languages:** English, Spanish. **Description:** Seeks to strengthen the moral and spiritual foundations of the American home and family and to give the observance of Mother's Day "a spiritual quality representative of ideal motherhood." Offers counselor service to young mothers; sponsors young mothers study groups. Sponsors Mother mentoring and Project Pledge, a program encouraging family commitment to integrity, honesty, a good work ethic, and prayer in the home. Maintains Hall of Fame of Mothers at the Waldorf Astoria Hotel NYC and National Mothers Chapel (Colorado Springs, CO). **Awards:** American Mother of the Year. **Frequency:** annual. **Type:** recognition. **Recipient:** for an outstanding mother ● **Type:** recognition. **Recipient:** for literature, music, arts, and crafts. **Committees:** Annual Interfaith Event; Art Competition; Character Education; Education; International; Literacy; Literary and Craft Awards; Marketing; Memorial; Men's Booster; Mother Mentoring; Music Competition; United Nations. **Formerly:** (1981) American Mothers Committee. **Publications:**

The American Mother, quarterly. Magazine. Includes award news, book reviews, calendar of events, legislative news, and obituaries-parenting articles. **Price:** included in membership dues. **Circulation:** 4,000. **Advertising:** accepted ● *American Mothers, Inc.—Yearbook*, annual. Includes convention news, short biographies, and reports on contest and award winners. **Price:** $10.00/year. **Circulation:** 600. **Advertising:** accepted ● *Literary Awards Journal*, annual. Features recipients of the annual Alice Abel Cultural Arts Literary Contest. Contains articles, stories, and poetry. **Price:** $10.00. **Circulation:** 300 ● *Mothers of Achievement in American History, 1776-1976*. Book. **Conventions/Meetings:** annual convention, meetings for training, choosing mother of the year; education workshops (exhibits) - always April in Bismarck, ND.

11876 ■ America's Angel
4460-16 Redwood Hwy.
San Rafael, CA 94903
E-mail: infoangel@americasangel.org
URL: http://www.americasangel.org
Contact: Morgan Rose MS, Exec. Dir.
Description: Promotes national awareness of health parenting as the cornerstone of democracy and the highest act of patriotism. Provides parents the respect, research and resources required to raise happy, healthy, whole children to strengthen America's future. Seeks to enroll one hundred respected celebrities, athletes and experts in a national celebrity media campaign in support of the nation's parents and families.

11877 ■ Association of MultiEthnic Americans (AMEA)
PO Box 29223
Los Angeles, CA 90029-0223
E-mail: info@ameasite.org
URL: http://www.ameasite.org
Contact: Ms. Jungmiwha Bullock ABD, Pres.
Founded: 1988. **Membership Dues:** individual (lower rate for students and seniors), $10-$15 (annual) ● family/student group, $25 (annual) ● affiliate organization, $50-$1,000 (annual) ● affiliate ally organization, $100-$2,000 (annual). **National Groups:** 11. **Description:** Advocates on behalf of the multiracial, multiethnic, and transracial adoption community. Promotes the advancement of diverse families, and welcomes all people. Conducts educational programs. Develops a national center for multiracial/multiethnic information through the Mixed Heritage Center. **Affiliated With:** Interracial-Intercultural Pride. **Conventions/Meetings:** annual meeting - always June.

11878 ■ Better World J. L. Institute
Address Unknown since 2007
Founded: 1982. **Staff:** 1. **Description:** Believes that a better world begins with the family. Promotes "sensitivity to parenthood as a noble profession"; upholds basic spiritual, ethical, and moral values the institute considers vital to the development of youth. Seeks recognition of the first Sunday in June as Family Day. Promotes Junior Good Will Ambassadors for a Better World, a project in which talented students from UN countries pledge their dedication to universal peace and the advancement of human dignity and represent their countries at international seminars. Work of the institute is supported by the Better World J. N. L. Foundation. **Also Known As:** Better World Builders J. L. Institute. **Publications:** *The Better World Builder*, periodic ● Newsletter, bimonthly. **Advertising:** not accepted.

11879 ■ Bonus Families
PO Box 1926
Discovery Bay, CA 94514
Ph: (925)516-2681
Fax: (925)634-3300
E-mail: jann@bonusfamilies.com
URL: http://www.bonusfamilies.com
Contact: Jann Blackstone-Ford MA, Dir./Co-Founder
Founded: 1999. **Membership Dues:** regular, $29 (annual). **Multinational. Description:** Works to improve the quality of life for stepfamilies. Promotes

peaceful coexistence between divorced or separated parents and their new families. Provides information, advice and support services to parents. Offers mediation, conflict management, and education to people attempting to combine families after a divorce or separation. Acts as a support network for stepparents, remarried parents, and their children. **Publications:** *Bonus Families Support*, monthly. Newsletter. **Price:** included in membership dues. Alternate Formats: online.

11880 ■ Center for Work and the Family
c/o Leah Fisher, Co-Dir.
910 Tulare Ave.
Berkeley, CA 94707
Ph: (925)258-5400
Fax: (925)376-3766
E-mail: cwfseminar@aol.com
URL: http://www.centerforworkandfamily.com
Contact: Leah Fisher, Co-Dir.
Founded: 1990. **Description:** Promotes the well being of families through community and workplace responsiveness. Strengthens families throughout communities; the Center's work falls into three broad categories: research, education, and policy analysis. **Libraries: Type:** by appointment only. **Holdings:** articles, audiovisuals, books, clippings, periodicals. **Subjects:** work, communities, families. **Publications:** *Work/Family Prevention: Research and Practice*. Paper. **Price:** $7.50.

11881 ■ Child and Family Policy Center (CFPC)
218 6th Ave., Ste.1021
Des Moines, IA 50309-4013
Ph: (515)280-9027
Fax: (515)244-8997
E-mail: info@cfpciowa.org
URL: http://www.cfpciowa.org
Contact: Charles Bruner, Exec. Dir.
Founded: 1989. **Staff:** 13. **Description:** Works to link research and policy concerning children and families in order to develop more comprehensive, community-based service systems and improve human services for children, youth and families living in poverty. Conducts research programs; compiles statistics. **Publications:** *Financing School Readiness Strategies: An Annotated Bibliography*. **Price:** $10.00/copy. Alternate Formats: online ● *Information Systems to Support Comprehensive Human Service Delivery: Emerging Approaches, Issues and Opportunities*. Report. **Price:** $12.00 ● *Service Integration: An Annotated Bibliography*. **Price:** $4.00.

11882 ■ Christian Family Life (CFL)
PO Box 50180
Nashville, TN 37205-0180
Free: (800)264-3876
E-mail: info@christianfamilylife.com
URL: http://www.christianfamilylife.com
Contact: Don Meredith, Contact
Founded: 1971. **Staff:** 3. **National Groups:** 100. **Languages:** English, Hungarian, Russian. **Description:** Serves as a counseling and consulting ministry for laypersons and businesses. Conducts seminars on marriage, parent-child relationships, and single adults. Maintains a collection of cassettes on marriage for use in seminars, home Bible studies, Sunday school, and marital and premarital counseling. Has developed a 12-week discipleship course on marriage called, "Two Becoming One". **Libraries: Type:** open to the public. **Subjects:** marriage. **Study Groups:** Two Becoming One. **Publications:** *Two Becoming One*. Book. Contains information that is helpful to couples. **Price:** $14.95. **Circulation:** 200,000.

11883 ■ Christian Family Movement (CFM)
PO Box 925
Evansville, IN 47706-0925
Ph: (812)962-5508
Fax: (812)962-5509

E-mail: office@cfm.org
URL: http://www.cfm.org
Contact: Paul Leingang, Exec. Dir.
Founded: 1949. **Members:** 4,000. **Membership Dues:** family, $35 (annual). **Staff:** 3. **Budget:** $60,000. **Regional Groups:** 18. **Local Groups:** 300. **Languages:** English, Spanish. **Multinational. Description:** Promotes Christian way of life in the family through interaction with a network of small faith communities. Maintains archives which are housed at University of Notre Dame. **Libraries: Type:** reference. **Holdings:** 57. **Affiliated With:** National Association of Catholic Family Life Ministers. **Publications:** *Act*, 8/year. Newsletter. Focuses on family issues and social action. **Price:** included in membership dues; $8.00 /year for nonmembers. ISSN: 0001-5083. **Circulation:** 2,000 ● *Annual Programs on Christian Family Development Through Social Action Families: Whole and Holy - 1995* ● *Christian Families: Into the New Millennium - 1996* ● *Families of Faith I - 1998* ● *Families of Faith II - 1999* ● *Living the Jubilee: New Growth From Fallow Fields - 2000* ● *Love Still Happens in Families - 2001* ● *Seasons of the Spirit - 1997*. **Conventions/Meetings:** triennial Fanning the Fire of Faith - conference.

11884 ■ CoMamas Association
PO Box 231804
Encinitas, CA 92023-1804
Ph: (760)942-4572
Fax: (760)918-0680
E-mail: feelgood@comamas.com
URL: http://www.comamas.com
Contact: Lynne Oxhorn-Ringwood, Co-Founder
Description: Works to develop cooperative and respectful relationships for stepwives and their families. Maintains Speakers' Bureau. **Publications:** *CoMamas Workbook*. **Price:** $25.00 plus shipping and handling of $4.99 ● *Stepwives*. Book. **Price:** included in membership dues; $11.00 for nonmembers; $13.00 with theme song on CD-Rom; $34.00 autographed copy with The CoMamas Workbook ● Newsletter. **Price:** free.

11885 ■ Council on Contemporary Families (CCF)
Univ. of Illinois at Chicago
MC 312, 1007 W Harrison St.
Chicago, IL 60607
Ph: (312)996-3074
E-mail: brisman@uic.edu
URL: http://www.contemporaryfamilies.org
Contact: Barbara Risman, Exec. Off.
Founded: 1996. **Membership Dues:** regular, $100 ● student, $50. **Description:** Represents the interests of family researchers, mental health and social work practitioners, and clinicians. Seeks to meet the needs of contemporary families through the dissemination of educational materials, media coverage, conferences, and seminars. Seeks to help the media find experts in various arenas of family research and practice. Provides information about the condition of America's families. **Telecommunication Services:** electronic mail, brisman@uic.edu.

11886 ■ Dads and Daughters (DADS)
2 W 1st St., Ste.101
Duluth, MN 55802
Ph: (218)722-3942
Fax: (218)728-0314
E-mail: info@dadsanddaughters.org
URL: http://www.dadsanddaughters.org
Contact: Nancy Gruver, Exec. Dir.
Founded: 1999. **Members:** 1,000. **Staff:** 5. **Budget:** $1,700,000. **Description:** Aims to inspire fathers to actively and deeply engage in the lives of their daughters and galvanizes fathers and others to transform the pervasive cultural messages that devalue girls and women. **Publications:** *Daughters*, bimonthly. Newsletter. Features educational information for parents of girls. **Price:** $25.00. ISSN: 1521-4273. **Circulation:** 24,000. **Conventions/Meetings:** workshop.

11887 ■ Education and Enrichment Section of the National Council on Family Relations (EES)

3989 Central Ave. NE, Ste.550
Minneapolis, MN 55421
Ph: (763)781-9331
Free: (888)781-9331
Fax: (763)781-9348
E-mail: info@ncfr.org
URL: http://www.ncfr.org
Contact: Donald W. Bower, Chm.

Founded: 1938. **Members:** 652. **Description:** A section of the National Council on Family Relations (see separate entry). Professors, school teachers, enrichment leaders, family agency personnel, and others involved in teaching on the subject of family relations. Seeks to improve the quality of family relations education by specifying necessary competencies for educators; disseminates information on aspects of such teaching; promotes exchange of information among members. **Awards:** Ernest B. Osborne Award. **Type:** recognition. **Recipient:** for excellence in teaching family subjects. **Committees:** Certification Review; Continuing Education for Family Life Educators; Public Policy. **Affiliated With:** National Council on Family Relations. **Formerly:** (1991) Education and Enrichment Section. **Conventions/Meetings:** annual convention (exhibits) - always November.

11888 ■ Families and Work Institute (FWI)

267 5th Ave., 2nd Fl.
New York, NY 10016
Ph: (212)465-2044
Fax: (212)465-8637
E-mail: mlambert@familiesandwork.org
URL: http://www.familiesandwork.org
Contact: Ellen Galinsky, Pres.

Founded: 1989. **Membership Dues:** corporate benefactor, $15,000 ● corporate patron, $14,999 ● corporate sponsor, $5,000-$9,999 ● corporate friend, $3,000-$4,999. **Staff:** 22. **Description:** Conducts research on: business, government, and community efforts to help families balance their work and family responsibilities; pressing policy questions in the public and private sectors; demographic trends. **Publications:** *An Examination of the Impact of Family-Friendly Policies on The Glass Ceiling.* Article ● *Ask the Children: The Breakthrough Study that Reveals How to Succeed at Work and Parenting.* Book. **Price:** $25.00 hardcover; $14.00 paperback ● *The Changing Workforce: Highlights from the National Study.* Report. **Price:** $25.00 ● *Corporate Reference Guide to Work-Family Programs.* Book. **Price:** $35.00 ● *The Family Child Care Training Study.* Book ● *Feeling Overworked: When Work Becomes Too Much.* Book. **Price:** $34.00 ● *State Reference Guide to Work-Family Programs for State Employees.* Book. **Conventions/Meetings:** annual conference, work-family conference for human resources managers in conjunction with the conference board ● seminar.

11889 ■ Family Research Council (FRC)

801 G St. NW
Washington, DC 20001
Ph: (202)393-2100
Fax: (202)393-2134
URL: http://www.frc.org
Contact: Tony Perkins, Pres.

Founded: 1983. **Members:** 450,000. **Staff:** 100. **Budget:** $11,500,000. **Languages:** English, Spanish. **Description:** Provides expertise policy research and analysis for the legislative, executive, and judicial branches of government. Seeks to inform the news media, the academic community, business leaders and the general public about policy decisions and legislative initiatives that benefit and support the family or adversely impact the traditional family unit. **Libraries: Type:** reference; not open to the public. **Holdings:** 1,500; books, periodicals. **Subjects:** family life issues, religion, education, culture, parenting, government, economics. **Awards:** Family Faith and Freedom. **Frequency:** periodic. **Type:** recognition. **Recipient:** for significant contribution and outstanding leadership in promoting family values. **Computer Services:** database, policy paper, email alert system, email subscriptions. **Programs:** Educational; Wither-

spoon Fellowship. **Formerly:** (1983) Family Research Group; (1989) Family Research Council of America. **Publications:** *The ACLU vs. America: Exposing the Agenda to Redefine Moral Values.* Book. **Price:** $15.00 ● *2005 State Model Legislation.* Booklet. Incorporates well thought-out-pro-family policies from around the country. **Price:** $5.00 ● *War and Faith in Sudan.* Book. Offers a deeper understanding of cultural, racial, and religious fault lines that divide the world at the beginning of the twenty-first century. **Price:** $20.00 ● *Washington Watch*, monthly. Newsletter. **Price:** free. **Circulation:** 110,000. Alternate Formats: online. **Conventions/Meetings:** annual Washington Briefing - meeting, private briefings by policy makers and commentators.

11890 ■ Family Support America

307 W 200 S, Ste.2004
Salt Lake City, UT 84101
Free: (877)338-3722
E-mail: admin@familysupportamerica.org
URL: http://www.familysupportamerica.org
Contact: Nancy Cohen, Exec. Admin.

Founded: 1981. **Members:** 2,000. **Membership Dues:** individual, $60 (annual) ● organization, $100 (annual) ● retiree, student, $30 (annual). **Staff:** 60. **Budget:** $5,500,000. **Languages:** Spanish. **Description:** Membership, consulting, and advocacy organization that has been advancing the movement to strengthen and support families since 1981. Seeks to strengthen and empower families and communities so that they can foster the optimal development of children, youth and adult family members. Builds networks, produces resources, advocates for public policy, provides consulting services, and gathers knowledge to help the family support movement grow. **Libraries: Type:** reference. **Holdings:** 6,000; audio-visuals, books, monographs, periodicals. **Subjects:** family support, welfare reform. **Computer Services:** database, family support programs ● online services, Dialog and Lexis. **Projects:** National Mapping. **Special Interest Groups:** African-American; Latino. **Formerly:** (2000) Family Resource Coalition of America. **Publications:** *America's Family Support Magazine*, quarterly. Includes articles on family support programs, policy, and practice. **Price:** $5.00 for members; $10.00 for nonmembers ● *Family Support Center: A Program Manager's Toolkit* ● *Guidelines for Family Support Practice* ● *How Are We Doing? A Program Self-Assessment Toolkit for the Family Support Field* ● *Know Your Community: A Step-By-Step Guide to Needs and Resources Assessment* ● *Learning to be Partners: An Introductory Training Program for Family Support Staff* ● *Making Case for Family Support.* Booklet ● *Making Room at the Table: Fostering Family Involvement in the Planning and Governance of Formal Support Systems* ● *Standards for Prevention Programs: Building Success through Family Support.* Monograph ● Newsletter, quarterly. Alternate Formats: online. **Conventions/Meetings:** periodic conference, topical and regional - odd numbered years ● biennial National Family Support Conference, workshops, seminars, speeches and networking (exhibits) - even numbered years.

11891 ■ Family Supports

c/o Charles B. Hennon, Assoc. Dir.
Center for Human Development, Learning, and Tech.
101D McGuffey Hall
Miami Univ.
Oxford, OH 45056
Ph: (513)529-2323
Fax: (513)529-6468
URL: http://www.units.muohio.edu/chdlt/familysupports
Contact: Charles B. Hennon, Assoc. Dir.

Founded: 1970. **Multinational. Description:** Promotes interdisciplinary research, information dissemination, and training on family issues and topics that can extend knowledge and practice in support of families, especially those at risk for stress and disruption. Helps families and communities build capacity for families to flourish. Encourages a global, multicultural, and multidisciplinary focus. **Formerly:** Family and Child Studies Center.

11892 ■ Feminism and Family Studies Section of the National Council on Family Relations (FFS)

3989 Central Ave. NE, Ste.550
Minneapolis, MN 55421
Ph: (763)781-9331
Free: (888)781-9331
Fax: (763)781-9348
E-mail: info@ncfr.org
URL: http://www.ncfr.org
Contact: Lee Ann De Reus, Chair

Founded: 1985. **Members:** 414. **Description:** Family researchers and practitioners. Aims to integrate feminist perspectives into theory and family counseling. Is establishing a collection of teaching materials with a feminist perspective and a mentoring network. As a section of the National Council on Family Relations, organizes sessions on feminism and family studies and presents distinguished lecturers. **Awards:** Outstanding Contribution to Feminist Scholarship. **Frequency:** annual. **Type:** recognition ● Outstanding Research Proposal from a Feminist Perspective. **Frequency:** annual. **Type:** recognition. **Affiliated With:** National Council on Family Relations. **Formerly:** (1991) National Council of Family Relations Feminism and Family Studies Section. **Publications:** Newsletter, periodic. **Conventions/Meetings:** annual conference (exhibits) - always November. 2007 Nov. 5-10, Pittsburgh, PA; 2008 Nov. 3-2007 Nov. 8, Little Rock, AR; 2009 Nov. 10-14, San Francisco, CA.

11893 ■ Focus on the Family (FOTF)

8605 Explorer Dr.
Colorado Springs, CO 80920
Ph: (719)531-5181
Free: (800)232-6459
Fax: (719)531-3424
E-mail: paul.hetrick@fotf.org
URL: http://www.family.org
Contact: Jim Daly, Pres./CEO

Founded: 1977. **Staff:** 1,300. **Budget:** $128,000,000. **State Groups:** 33. **Languages:** Afrikaans, Arabic, Bulgarian, Chinese, Croatian, Czech, Danish, English, Finnish, French, German, Greek. **Multinational. Description:** Promotes traditional Judeo-Christian values and strong family ties. Gathers and disseminates practical resource information on marriage, parenting, and other subjects related to family life. Produces fourteen different radio programs, aired in 96 countries. Conducts research and educational programs; sponsors charitable activities; makes available children's services; maintains speakers' bureau. Broadcasts and resources are also available in Hebrew, Hungarian, Indonesian, Italian, Japanese, Korean, Lithuanian, Norwegian, Polish, Portuguese, Romanian, Russian, Slovakian, Spanish, Swedish, Thai, Ukrainian and Zulu. **Libraries: Type:** reference. **Additional Websites:** http://www.focusonthefamily.com. **Affiliated With:** Focus on the Family - Canada. **Publications:** *Boundless*, weekly. Magazine. Contains information for college students. Alternate Formats: online ● *Breakaway*, monthly. Magazine. Contains articles for teen boys. **Circulation:** 97,000 ● *Brio*, monthly. Magazine. Contains articles for teen girls. **Circulation:** 190,000 ● *Clubhouse*, monthly. Magazine. Contains articles for children ages 8-12. **Circulation:** 113,000 ● *Clubhouse, Jr.*, monthly. Magazine. Contains articles for children ages 4-8. **Circulation:** 95,000 ● *Focus on the Family Citizen*, monthly. Magazine. Covers social and public policy issues. Evaluates current events, and state and federal legislative activities from a pro-family values perspective. **Circulation:** 64,000 ● *Focus on the Family Physician*, bimonthly. Magazine. Covers current topics in science, medicine, and medical ethics from a traditional family values perspective. **Circulation:** 89,000 ● *LifeWise*, bimonthly. Magazine. Contains information for senior adults. **Circulation:** 43,000 ● *Plugged In*, monthly. Magazine. Covers positive and negative content in films, videos, music, and popular culture. **Circulation:** 52,000 ● Magazine, monthly. Covers family matters and inspirational stories from a traditional family values perspective. **Circulation:** 2,600,000 ● Also produces films and videos. **Conventions/Meetings:** biennial Attorneys

Conference ● periodic Counseling Enrichment Program - seminar ● periodic Crisis Pregnancy Center Directors Conference ● periodic Love Won Out - seminar ● annual Physicians Conference ● annual Pillars - seminar ● periodic Rebuilding the Walls/Focus Over Fifty - conference.

11894 ■ Institute for American Values (IAV)
1841 Broadway, Ste.211
New York, NY 10023
Ph: (212)246-3942
Fax: (212)541-6665
E-mail: info@americanvalues.org
URL: http://www.americanvalues.org
Contact: David Blankenhorn, Pres.
Founded: 1987. **Staff:** 9. **Budget:** $1,500,000. **Nonmembership. Multinational. Description:** Participants include academics, public policy and family service professionals, business and labor leaders, and grassroots constituency leaders. Serves as a research organization focusing on issues affecting the well-being of families and children and issues regarding civil society in the U.S. and abroad. **Libraries: Type:** reference. **Holdings:** articles, books, periodicals, reports. **Subjects:** family issues, civil society. **Publications:** *A Call to Civil Society: Why Democracy Needs Moral Truths.* Report. **Price:** $7.00 ● *Between Two Worlds: The Inner Lives of Children of Divorce.* Book ● *The Consequences of Marriage for African Americans.* Report ● *Fatherless America.* Book. **Price:** $15.00 ● *Hardwired to Connect: The New Scientific Case for Authoritative Communities.* Report. **Price:** $7.00 ● *The Islam/West Debate: Documents from a Global Debate on Terrorism, U.S. Policy and the Middle East.* Book ● *The Marriage Movement: A Statement of Principles.* Report. **Price:** $5.00 ● *The Motherhood Study: Fresh Insights on Mothers' Attitudes and Concerns.* Report ● *Promises to Keep: Decline and Renewal of Marriage in America.* Book. **Price:** $25.00 plus shipping and handling ● *Rebuilding the Nest: A New Commitment to the American Family.* Book ● *Seedbeds of Virtue: Sources of Competence, Character, and Citizenship in American Society.* Book. **Price:** $27.00 plus shipping and handling ● *Why Marriage Matters: Twenty-Six Conclusions from the Social Sciences: Second Edition.* Report. **Conventions/Meetings:** annual Family Policy - symposium.

11895 ■ International Section of the National Council on Family Relations
3989 Central Ave. NE, Ste.550
Minneapolis, MN 55421
Ph: (763)781-9331
Free: (888)781-9331
Fax: (763)781-9348
E-mail: ritblatt@mail.sdsu.edu
URL: http://www.ncfr.org
Contact: Shulamit N. Rittblatt, Chair
Founded: 1964. **Members:** 195. **Description:** A section of the National Council on Family Relations. Governmental and nongovernmental employees, social workers, and individuals interested in generating a better understanding of the variations of family process throughout the world. Seeks to: promote transnational family research; facilitate communication among family scholars; share information on current and proposed research projects; maintain ties with international organizations engaged in family research. Sponsors family education programs, presentations, and seminars. **Awards:** Jan Trost Award. **Frequency:** annual. **Type:** recognition. **Recipient:** for outstanding contributions in comparative family studies. **Affiliated With:** National Council on Family Relations. **Publications:** *International Section Newsletter,* periodic. Includes information on research, family policy, and section news. **Conventions/Meetings:** annual What is the Future of Marriage? - conference (exhibits).

11896 ■ Interracial Family Alliance of Houston (IFA)
Address Unknown since 2007
Founded: 1983. **Members:** 50. **Staff:** 3. **Description:** Families that are interracial through marriage, adoption across racial lines, or biracial birth. Purposes

are to: strengthen and support the interracial family unit; promote acceptance of interracial families by the public; focus on solutions to problems unique to interracial families such as developing self-esteem in biracial children. Conducts social activities involving biracial children; sponsors educational programs. **Convention/Meeting:** none. **Libraries: Type:** reference. **Holdings:** articles, books, video recordings. **Computer Services:** Mailing lists, national network of interracial family organizations. **Formerly:** (2003) Interracial Family Alliance.

11897 ■ Interracial Family Circle (IFC)
4923 E Chalk Point Rd.
West River, MD 20778
E-mail: info@interracialfamilycircle.org
URL: http://www.interracialfamilycircle.org
Contact: Nancy McFall Jean, Pres.
Founded: 1984. **Members:** 300. **Membership Dues:** general, $35 (annual). **Budget:** $5,000. **Local Groups:** 1. **Description:** Interracial couples with and without children, same-race couples who have adopted transracially, single parents of biracial children, biracial/multiracial adults, foster parents, and individuals supporting the concept of interracial families. Seeks to provide a supportive environment and affirm the intercultural family as a viable unit. Coordinates discussion groups to explore the issues of interracial family life. Publicly represents the interests of interracial families. Conducts educational programs; maintains speaker's bureau. **Libraries: Type:** reference. **Holdings:** archival material, articles, books. **Publications:** *Collage,* monthly. Newsletter. **Price:** $12.50 /year for nonmembers; included in membership dues. **Circulation:** 350. **Advertising:** accepted. **Conventions/Meetings:** monthly meeting ● annual seminar ● workshop.

11898 ■ Interracial-Intercultural Pride (iPride)
PO Box 11811
Berkeley, CA 94712-2811
Ph: (510)644-1000
Fax: (501)525-4106
E-mail: info@ipride.org
URL: http://www.ipride.org
Contact: Marcus Ruiz Barrios Evans, Dir.
Founded: 1979. **Members:** 250. **Membership Dues:** regular, $25 (annual) ● student, $15 (annual). **Description:** Members of interracial and intercultural families; concerned individuals. Supports and encourages the well-being and development of children and adults who are of more than one ethnic or cultural heritage. Conducts educational forums and workshops. Maintains library and speakers' bureau; membership is currently concentrated in the San Francisco, CA area. **Telecommunication Services:** electronic mail, iprideca@aol.com. **Committees:** Adoption Support Group; Biracial Adult Group; Children's Group; Discussion/Support; Education; Interracial Couples Issues Discussion Group; Preteen Group; Single Parent Support Group; Social Action; Special Events; Teen Group; Toddler Group. **Conventions/Meetings:** annual conference.

11899 ■ National Alliance for Caregiving (NAC)
4720 Montgomery Ln., 5th Fl.
Bethesda, MD 20814
E-mail: info@caregiving.org
URL: http://www.caregiving.org
Founded: 1996. **Members:** 40. **Description:** Provides support to family caregivers and professionals, and issues facing family caregiving. **Computer Services:** database, reviews and ratings of books, websites, resources for family caregivers. **Publications:** *Caregiving in the U.S.: Findings From the National Caregiver Survey.* Alternate Formats: online ● *Conference proceedings* ● *Tips for Family Caregivers* ● Reports. Alternate Formats: online ● Brochures. Alternate Formats: online. **Conventions/Meetings:** annual conference.

11900 ■ National Council on Family Relations (NCFR)
3989 Central Ave. NE, Ste.550
Minneapolis, MN 55421
Ph: (763)781-9331
Free: (888)781-9331

Fax: (763)781-9348
E-mail: info@ncfr.org
URL: http://www.ncfr.org
Contact: Diane Cushman MPH, Exec. Dir.
Founded: 1938. **Members:** 3,900. **Membership Dues:** regular, $90 (annual). **Staff:** 11. **Budget:** $1,100,000. **Regional Groups:** 3. **State Groups:** 22. **Local Groups:** 4. **Description:** Multidisciplinary group of family life professionals, including clergy, counselors, educators, home economists, lawyers, nurses, therapists, librarians, physicians, psychologists, social workers, sociologists, and researchers. Seeks to provide opportunities for members to plan and act together to advance marriage and family life through consultation, conferences, and the dissemination of information and research. **Awards:** Media Awards. **Frequency:** annual. **Type:** recognition ● NCFR Awards. **Frequency:** annual. **Type:** recognition. **Recipient:** for research, teaching, publication, service to families, and videotapes. **Computer Services:** database ● online services. **Sections:** Education and Enrichment; Ethnic Minorities; Family and Health; Family Policy; Family Science; Family Therapy; Feminism and Family Studies; International; Religion and Family Life; Research and Theory. **Formerly:** (1948) National Conference of Family Relations. **Publications:** *Family Relations,* quarterly. Journal. **Circulation:** 4,200. **Advertising:** accepted. Alternate Formats: online. Also Cited As: *The Family Coordinator* ● *Journal of Marriage and Family,* quarterly. Presents original theory, research, interpretation, and critical discussion of materials related to marriage and the family. **Circulation:** 6,200. Alternate Formats: online ● *NCFR 2000.* Catalog ● Directory, periodic. **Conventions/Meetings:** annual Families, Stress, and Coping - conference - always November ● annual Visions for Family - conference, continuity and change across cohorts and generations (exhibits) - always November. 2007 Nov. 5-10, Pittsburgh, PA; 2008 Nov. 3-8, Little Rock, AR.

11901 ■ Religion and Family Life Section of the National Council on Family Relations (RFL)
c/o National Council on Family Relations
3989 Central Ave. NE, Ste.550
Minneapolis, MN 55421
Ph: (763)781-9331
Free: (888)781-9331
Fax: (763)781-9348
E-mail: info@ncfr.org
URL: http://www.ncfr.org
Contact: Angela R. Wiley, Chair
Founded: 1985. **Members:** 311. **Description:** A section of the National Council on Family Relations. Family counselors, social workers, educators, sociologists, psychologists, and clergy members. Provides a forum for the discussion of issues pertaining to religion and family. **Telecommunication Services:** electronic mail, awiley@uiuc.edu. **Affiliated With:** National Council on Family Relations. **Formerly:** (1991) Religion and Family Life Section. **Publications:** Newsletter, periodic. **Conventions/Meetings:** annual conference (exhibits) - always November. 2007 Nov. 5-10, Pittsburgh, PA; 2008 Nov. 3-8, Little Rock, AR.

11902 ■ Save a Family Plan (SAFP)
PO Box 611832
Port Huron, MI 48061-1832
Ph: (519)672-1115
Fax: (519)672-6379
E-mail: safpinfo@safp.org
URL: http://www.safp.org
Contact: Mrs. Lesley Porter, Exec. Dir.
Founded: 1965. **Members:** 13,000. **Staff:** 9. **Budget:** C$5,000,000. **Multinational. Description:** Builds partnership with poor families in India through family and community development programming such as monthly assistance, housing, job training, health and sanitation, income generation and the environment to enable these families to become self-sufficient. Started 2,000 people's organizations, called "sangams", with democratically elected leadership, through which the programming is accomplished at the grassroots level. These community groups

empower the people to successfully identify their needs and implement, monitor and evaluate the programs to better their lives; these groups also initiate progressive social action in their local communities. **Libraries: Type:** reference. **Holdings:** periodicals. **Subjects:** international development. **Computer Services:** database, of contributors and beneficiaries. **Programs:** Family and Community Development; Family to Family Development. **Projects:** Haiti. **Publications:** *News and Views*, annual. Newsletter. **Circulation:** 15,000. Alternate Formats: online; CD-ROM ● Annual Report, annual. **Circulation:** 15,000. Alternate Formats: online; CD-ROM. **Conventions/Meetings:** quarterly board meeting.

11903 ■ Secretariat for Family, Laity, Women, and Youth
3211 4th St. NE
Washington, DC 20017-1194
Ph: (202)541-3000
Fax: (202)541-3176
E-mail: flwymail@usccb.org
URL: http://www.nccbuscc.org/laity
Contact: H. Richard McCord, Exec. Dir.
Staff: 6. **Nonmembership. Description:** Division of the United States Conference of Catholic Bishops. Works to provide service in the areas of laity, marriage and family, women in church and society, and youth. Develops national policy in areas for the body of bishops. **Affiliated With:** United States Conference of Catholic Bishops. **Formerly:** Secretariat on Laity and Family Life; Youth Ministry, United States Catholic Conference; Family Life Bureau; National Catholic Conference on Family Life; (1982) Family Life Division, United States Catholic Conference; (1987) Family Life Ministry, United States Catholic Conference. **Publications:** *Message to Youth* (in English and Spanish). Brochure. Contains a letter written to teens from the bishops of the Laity Committee and the Youth Subcommittee. ● *When I Call for Help: A Pastoral Response to Domestic Violence Against Women* (in English and Spanish). Pamphlet. Offers practical advice to women who are abused, their abusers, and pastors and pastoral staff.

11904 ■ Stepfamily Association of America (SAA)
650 J St., Ste.205
Lincoln, NE 68508
Free: (800)735-0329
Fax: (402)477-8317
E-mail: saa@saafamilies.org
URL: http://www.saafamilies.org
Contact: Margorie Engel PhD, Pres./CEO
Founded: 1979. **Members:** 800. **Membership Dues:** regular, $40 (annual). **Staff:** 2. **Budget:** $100,000. **National Groups:** 47. **Description:** Families interested in stepfamily relationships. Acts as a support network and national advocate for stepparents, remarried parents, and their children. Works to improve the quality of life for American stepfamilies and affirm the value of step relationships. Helps the community and members of stepfamilies understand and deal with differences in positive ways that bring satisfaction and a sense of personal growth and accomplishment. Provides education and children's services, chapter meetings, stepfamily survival courses, support groups, communication courses, and referral services. Conducts mutual help groups consisting of couples who meet on a regular basis to share experiences and discuss their remarriage and stepfamily situations. Conducts research programs. **Publications:** Handbook. **Price:** free ● Magazine, bimonthly. **Price:** included in membership dues.

11905 ■ Stepfamily Foundation (SF)
333 W End Ave.
New York, NY 10023
Ph: (212)877-3244
Free: (800)SKY-STEP
Fax: (212)362-7030
E-mail: staff@stepfamilyfoundation.org
URL: http://www.stepfamily.org
Contact: Jeannette Lofas, Pres.
Founded: 1975. **Members:** 5,000. **Membership Dues:** initial, $70 ● individual, $20 (annual). **Staff:** 5.

Budget: $80,000. **Regional Groups:** 6. **Languages:** English, French, German, Spanish. **Description:** Remarried persons with children, interested professionals, and divorced persons. Gathers information on the stepfamily and stepfamily relationships. Provides counseling on stepfamily relationships to individuals, couples, and groups. Trains and certifies professionals in October and April seminars. Conducts research and educational programs; operates speakers' bureau; compiles statistics. **Libraries: Type:** reference; not open to the public. **Holdings:** 700. **Subjects:** remarriage, divorce, step relationships, coparenting. **Computer Services:** Mailing lists ● online services. **Committees:** Clinical. **Publications:** *Dynamics of Step*, quarterly. Newsletter. **Price:** included in membership dues; $20.00 /year for nonmembers. **Advertising:** accepted ● *The Family Rules*, quarterly. Newsletter. **Price:** included in membership dues; $20.00 /year for nonmembers. **Advertising:** accepted ● *History of the Stepfamily Foundation*. Book ● *How to StepParent*. Book ● *Living in Step*, quarterly. Book. **Price:** $25.00/year. **Circulation:** 2,000. **Advertising:** accepted ● *New American Family*, quarterly. Video. **Price:** $25.00/year. **Circulation:** 2,000. **Advertising:** accepted ● *The Realities of Step*. Video ● *Step Parenting*. Book ● *Stepfamily Statistics* ● *10 Steps for Step* ● Also publishes digest. **Conventions/Meetings:** semiannual Stepfamily Foundation Certification Seminar for Professional & Coaches - seminar and workshop (exhibits) - 3-days, always April and October, New York City.

11906 ■ Teaching-Family Association (TFA)
PO Box 2007
Midlothian, VA 23113
Ph: (804)632-0155
Fax: (804)639-9212
E-mail: peggymcelgunn@comcast.net
URL: http://www.teaching-family.org
Contact: Ms. Peggy McElgunn JD, Exec. Dir.
Founded: 1977. **Members:** 400. **Membership Dues:** individual, $40 (annual). **Staff:** 4. **Budget:** $178,000. **Regional Groups:** 31. **Description:** Practitioners (individuals trained in providing family services to youths living in group home situations); others include evaluators, trainers, program consultants, and administrators not involved in a live-in group home situation. Ensures that minimum standards of quality are met in all of the programs throughout the U.S. and Canada. Evaluates and certifies teaching family sites. **Awards:** Distinguished Contributor Award. **Frequency:** annual. **Type:** recognition ● Lonnie and Elaine Phillips Award. **Frequency:** annual. **Type:** recognition. **Committees:** Awards and Recognitions Administrator; Certification and Ethics; Long Range Planning; Organization Dissemination; Practitioner; Publications. **Formerly:** (1992) National Teaching-Family Association. **Publications:** *Directory of the Teaching-Family Association*, annual ● *Standards of Ethical Conduct* ● *Teaching-Family Bibliography* ● *Teaching-Family Newsletter*, quarterly. Includes articles on training sites and children's issues. **Circulation:** 1,500 ● Brochures. **Conventions/Meetings:** semiannual conference and meeting.

11907 ■ TV-Turnoff Network
1200 29th St. NW
Lower Level No. 1
Washington, DC 20007
Ph: (202)333-9220
Fax: (202)333-9221
E-mail: email@tvturnoff.org
URL: http://www.tvturnoff.org
Contact: Robert Kesten, Exec. Dir.
Founded: 1994. **Members:** 18,000. **Membership Dues:** organizer, $30 (annual) ● regular, $25 (annual) ● couch potato masher, $100 (annual). **Staff:** 4. **Budget:** $275,000. **Description:** Encourages children and adults to watch less television in order to promote healthier lives and communities. Organizes the National TV-Turnoff Week, featuring screen-free activities to foster social, physical, academic and creative development. Conducts educational and research programs; offers children's services; compiles statistics. **Libraries: Type:** reference; not open to the public. **Holdings:** books, clippings, periodicals.

Subjects: TV industry, advertising, health, environment. **Formerly:** (2003) TV-Free America. **Publications:** *The TV-Free American*, quarterly. Newsletter. **Circulation:** 4,000 ● *TV-Turnoff "Organizers Kit"*. Book.

Family Law

11908 ■ National Association for Family and Child Care (NAFCC)
5202 Pinemont Dr.
Salt Lake City, UT 84123-4607
Ph: (801)269-9338
Free: (800)359-3817
Fax: (801)268-9507
E-mail: nafcc@nafcc.org
URL: http://www.nafcc.org
Contact: Linda Geigle, Exec. Dir.
Founded: 1978. **Members:** 7,500. **Membership Dues:** individual, $25 (annual) ● association, $50 (annual) ● agency, $100 (annual). **Staff:** 15. **Budget:** $285,000. **Languages:** English, Spanish. **Description:** Provides technical assistance to family child care associations through leadership and professional development, addressing issues of diversity, and by promoting quality and professionalism. **Libraries: Type:** reference. **Computer Services:** Mailing lists, of members. **Publications:** *The National Perspective*, quarterly. Newsletter. **Circulation:** 7,500. **Advertising:** accepted. **Conventions/Meetings:** annual conference and board meeting (exhibits) - always July.

11909 ■ National Congress for Fathers and Children (NCFC)
9454 Wilshire Blvd., Ste.907
Beverly Hills, CA 90212
Ph: (310)247-6051 (760)758-0268
Free: (800)SEE-DADS
E-mail: ncfc@sbcglobal.net
URL: http://www.ncfc.net
Contact: Larry Hellmann, Pres.
Founded: 1981. **Membership Dues:** individual, $75 (annual) ● life (family, individual, major donor), $500 ● life (professional), $1,000 ● family, $90 (annual) ● professional, $150 (annual) ● associate, $50 (annual). **Description:** Advocates for equal parental responsibility and protection of the father-child relationship; assists state and local efforts to assist parents to remain actively involved in their children's lives, regardless of marital status; seeks to coordinate local efforts, impact national initiatives, and promotes public awareness; supports the Equal Rights Amendment and urges its application to men as well as women. **Committees:** Annual National Convention; Legislative Advisory; Litigation Action; Marketing and Media Relations; Nominating. **Publications:** *Membership Manual*. Alternate Formats: online ● *NCFC Network*. Newsletter. Alternate Formats: online.

Family Planning

11910 ■ Advocates for Youth
2000 M St. NW, Ste.750
Washington, DC 20036
Ph: (202)419-3420
Fax: (202)419-1448
E-mail: information@advocatesforyouth.org
URL: http://www.advocatesforyouth.org
Contact: Amanda Deaver, Chair
Founded: 1980. **Staff:** 30. **Budget:** $3,500,000. **Languages:** English, French, Spanish. **Nonmembership. Description:** Creates programs and promotes policies that help young people make informed and responsible decisions about their sexual and reproductive health. Provides information, training and advocacy to youth-serving Organization, youth leaders, policymakers, and the media in the U.S. and developing countries. Implements numerous programs and promotes evidence-based policies on effective pregnancy and HIV/STI prevention for youth; sexuality education; gay, lesbian, bisexual and transgender youth issues, in addition to forming online

communities for sexual health activists. The Resource Center online offers journal databases of information on youth sexual health, as well as model programs in developing countries. **Libraries: Type:** reference. **Holdings:** 10,000; audiovisuals, books, clippings, monographs, periodicals. **Subjects:** sexuality education, family planning, adolescent fertility, HIV/AIDS, abortion, adolescent pregnancy, pregnancy prevention, sexual orientation. **Awards:** SHINE Awards (Sexual Health in Entertainment). **Frequency:** annual. **Type:** recognition. **Recipient:** for outstanding media and television portrayals of family planning, sexuality and reproductive health issues. **Formerly:** Center for Population Options. **Publications:** Also publishes fact sheets, resource guides, and life planning education curricula. **Conventions/Meetings:** semiannual meeting - always fall.

11911 ■ Advocates for Youth's Media Project
3940 Laurel Canyon Blvd., No. 237
Studio City, CA 91604
Ph: (323)318-0825
Fax: (323)650-6558
E-mail: healthytv@themediaproject.com
URL: http://www.themediaproject.com
Founded: 1983. **Staff:** 5. **Budget:** $325,000. **Description:** Serves as an advisory and information resource for the entertainment industry to encourage positive and relevant messages about family planning, sexuality, and reproductive health, especially in programming directed toward adolescents. Operates speakers' bureau. **Awards:** The SHINE Awards. **Frequency:** annual. **Type:** recognition. **Recipient:** for media accomplishments. **Computer Services:** Mailing lists, of members. **Affiliated With:** Advocates for Youth. **Formerly:** Center for Population Options' Media Project.

11912 ■ Alan Guttmacher Institute (AGI)
120 Wall St., 21st Fl.
New York, NY 10005
Ph: (212)248-1111
Free: (800)355-0244
Fax: (212)248-1952
E-mail: info@guttmacher.org
URL: http://www.guttmacher.org
Contact: Sharon Camp, Pres./CEO
Founded: 1968. **Staff:** 70. **Budget:** $11,000,000. **Nonmembership. Multinational. Description:** Advances sexual and reproductive health through an interrelated program of social science research, policy analysis and public education. Promotes sound policy and program development, and informs individual decision making. **Awards:** The Darroch Award for Excellence in Sexual and Reproductive Health. **Frequency:** biennial. **Type:** monetary. **Recipient:** for an emerging leader in the field of sexual and reproductive health, where scientific evidence is essential to guiding the policies and programs of the future. **Divisions:** Office of the President; Public Education; Public Policy; Research. **Formerly:** (1975) Center for Family Planning Program Development; (1977) Research and Development Division of Planned Parenthood Federation of America. **Publications:** *Guttmacher Policy Review*, quarterly. Journal. Also Cited As: *The Guttmacher Report on Public Policy* ● *International Family Planning Perspectives*, quarterly. Journal ● *Perspectives on Sexual and Reproductive Health*, quarterly. Journal. Also Cited As: *Family Planning Perspectives*. **Conventions/Meetings:** board meeting - 3/year.

11913 ■ Asociacion Puertorriquena Pro-Bienestar de la Familia (APPBF)
PO Box 192221
San Juan, PR 00919-2221
Ph: (787)765-7373
Fax: (787)766-6920
E-mail: profamilia@profamilia.org.pr
URL: http://www.ippfwhr.org/profiles/association_e.asp?AssociationID=19
Contact: Sra. Carmen Rivera Cespedes, Exec. Dir.
Founded: 1954. **Multinational. Description:** Promotes increased availability of family planning services. Conducts educational programs to raise public awareness of population issues and family

planning services; provides support and assistance to reproductive health and family planning clinics. **Additional Websites:** http://www.profamiliapr.org.

11914 ■ Association of Reproductive Health Professionals (ARHP)
2401 Pennsylvania Ave. NW, Ste.350
Washington, DC 20037-1718
Ph: (202)466-3825
Fax: (202)466-3826
E-mail: arhp@arhp.org
URL: http://www.arhp.org
Contact: Wayne C. Shields, Pres./CEO
Founded: 1963. **Members:** 2,000. **Membership Dues:** physician, $175 (annual) ● advanced practice clinician, researcher, educator, $110 (annual) ● student, resident, retired, $40 (annual) ● joint, $100 (annual). **Staff:** 10. **Budget:** $4,000,000. **Description:** Professionals in reproductive health, including obstetricians, gynecologists, family practitioners, pediatricians, nurse clinicians, researchers, educators, counselors, and administrators. Interested in contraception, sexually transmitted diseases, HIV/AIDS, menopause, urogenital disorders, sexuality, cancer prevention/detection, abortion and infertility. Maintains speakers' bureau; sponsors clinical and public educational programs. **Libraries: Type:** reference. **Holdings:** archival material, audiovisuals, books, clippings, monographs, periodicals. **Subjects:** reproductive health. **Computer Services:** Mailing lists. **Formerly:** (1973) American Association of Parenthood Physicians; (1982) Association of Planned Parenthood Physicians; (1987) Association of Planned Parenthood Professionals. **Publications:** *ARHP Update*, bimonthly. Newsletter. Contains information for and about ARHP members. Alternate Formats: online ● *Clinical Proceedings*, monthly-bimonthly ● *Contraception: An International Journal*, monthly ● *Health and Sexuality*, quarterly. Magazine. **Circulation:** 15,000. Alternate Formats: online ● Journals ● Videos. **Conventions/Meetings:** annual Reproductive Health Conference, held in conjunction with Planned Parenthood (exhibits) ● biennial Women's Health in the Perimenopause - conference.

11915 ■ CHOICE
1233 Locust St., Ste.301
Philadelphia, PA 19107
Ph: (215)985-3355 (215)985-3350
Free: (800)848-3367
Fax: (215)985-2938
E-mail: info@choice-phila.org
URL: http://www.choice-phila.org
Contact: Lynn H. Green PhD, Exec. Dir.
Founded: 1971. **Staff:** 30. **Budget:** $1,000,000. **Description:** Dedicated to increasing awareness of and access to sexual and reproductive health services, especially among underserved minority populations who experience barriers to care. **Libraries: Type:** reference. **Telecommunication Services:** hotline, health information, (215)985-3300 ● hotline, child care telephone counseling and referrals, (215)985-3301 ● hotline, AIDS and HIV-related information, (215)985-2437 ● hotline, State-wide AIDS and HIV-related information, (800)662-6080. **Also Known As:** Concern for Health Options - Information, Care and Education. **Publications:** *Changes: You and Your Body*, periodic. Directory. Features a directory of sexual and reproductive health services for teens. **Circulation:** 15,000 ● *Where to Find*, periodic. Directory. Lists family planning services. **Price:** free. **Circulation:** 8,800. **Conventions/Meetings:** seminar ● workshop.

11916 ■ Clayton Fund
3505-M Cadillac Ave.
Costa Mesa, CA 92626
Ph: (714)751-7433
E-mail: judy@cyclenews.com
URL: http://www.cyclenews.com/about/clayton.html
Contact: Sharon Clayton, Chair
Description: Strives to fund programs related to children, the environment, family planning, education, agriculture, arts and culture.

11917 ■ EngenderHealth
440 9th Ave.
New York, NY 10001
Ph: (212)561-8000
Free: (800)564-2872
Fax: (212)561-8067
E-mail: info@engenderhealth.org
URL: http://www.engenderhealth.org
Contact: Stasia A. Obremsky, Chair
Founded: 1943. **Members:** 8,000. **Membership Dues:** general, $25 (annual). **Staff:** 300. **Budget:** $25,000,000. **Languages:** Arabic, English, Filipino, French, Hindi, Malay, Russian, Spanish, Swahili. **Description:** Works to improve the lives of individuals by making reproductive health services safe, available and sustainable. Provides technical assistance, training and information, with a focus on practical solutions that improve services where resources are scarce. Coordinates with governments, institutions, and health care professionals to make this right a reality. **Formerly:** (1985) Association for Voluntary Sterilization; (1994) Association for Voluntary Surgical Contraception; (2001) AVSC International. **Publications:** *EngenderHealth Update*, quarterly. Newsletter. **Price:** included in membership dues ● Brochures ● Also publishes clinical guides and resources for family planning professionals. **Conventions/Meetings:** annual meeting.

11918 ■ Family Health International (FHI)
PO Box 13950
Research Triangle Park, NC 27709
Ph: (919)544-7040
Fax: (919)544-7261
E-mail: services@fhi.org
URL: http://www.fhi.org
Contact: Albert J. Siemens PhD, CEO
Founded: 1971. **Members:** 300. **Staff:** 300. **Multinational. Description:** Biomedical researchers and technical assistants. Promotes increased availability, safety, effectiveness, acceptability, and ease of using family planning methods. Works to improve the delivery of voluntary fertility and primary health care services, and reduces the spread of sexually transmitted diseases, especially HIV infection. Conducts, analyzes, and disseminates research on contraception and distribution of family planning services. Supports a program of contraceptive safety and health records. Maintains library of 8000 monographs, journals, and reports. Operates computerized services. **Libraries: Type:** not open to the public. **Holdings:** 8,000. **Subjects:** reproductive health, sexually transmitted diseases, family planning. **Divisions:** Behavioral and Social Sciences Research Group; Biostatistics; Clinical Research; Data Management; Field, Information, Training Services; Health Services Research; HIV Prevention and Care; HIV Prevention Trials; Regulatory Affairs/Quality Assurance. **Formerly:** (1982) International Fertility Research Program. **Publications:** *Family Health International—Network*, quarterly. Bulletin. Covers reproductive health and family planning for health care personnel and policymakers in developing countries. **Price:** free. **ISSN:** 0270-3637. **Circulation:** 70,000.

11919 ■ Healthy Teen Network (HTN)
509 2nd St. NE
Washington, DC 20002
Ph: (202)547-8814
Fax: (202)547-8815
E-mail: healthyteens@healthyteennetwork.org
URL: http://www.healthyteennetwork.org
Contact: Pat Paluzzi, Pres./CEO
Founded: 1979. **Members:** 2,000. **Membership Dues:** individual, $100 (annual) ● organization, $250 (annual) ● student, $30 (annual) ● individual, $185 (biennial) ● individual, $180 (triennial) ● organization, $470 (biennial) ● organization, $700 (triennial). **Staff:** 4. **Description:** Professionals, policy makers, community and state leaders, and other concerned individuals and organizations. Promotes comprehensive and coordinated services designed for the prevention and resolution of problems associated with adolescent pregnancy, parenthood and prevention. Supports families in expanding their capability of

nurturing children and setting standards that encourage their healthy development through loving, stable relationships. Programs include: providing advocacy services at local, state, and national levels for adolescent pregnancy issues; sharing information and promoting public awareness; conducting conferences, training institutes and workshops to encourage the establishment of effective programs; coalition building assistance. **Awards: Frequency:** annual. **Type:** recognition. **Recipient:** for an outstanding contribution to the prevention of adolescent pregnancy. **Formerly:** (1993) National Organization of Adolescent Pregnancy and Parenting; (2005) National Organization on Adolescent Pregnancy, Parenting and Prevention. **Publications:** *NOAPPP Network Newsletter*, quarterly. Contains resource and research reviews, state highlights, legislative focus, and successful program models. **Conventions/Meetings:** annual conference (exhibits) ● workshop - 4-6/year.

11920 ■ International Consortium for Emergency Contraception (ICEC)
c/o Meridian Development Foundation
588 Broadway, Ste.503
New York, NY 10012
Ph: (212)941-5300
E-mail: info@cecinfo.org
URL: http://www.cecinfo.org
Contact: Elizabeth Westley, Consortium Coor.
Founded: 1995. **Languages:** English, Spanish. **Multinational. Description:** Expands access to and ensures safe and locally appropriate use of emergency contraception worldwide within the broader context of family planning and reproductive health, with emphasis on developing countries. Serves as an authoritative source of information about emergency contraception, as well as a voice for expanded access emergency contraception. Facilitates information sharing and networking among members and other groups working to broaden knowledge of emergency contraception. **Computer Services:** database, search for articles, materials, and EC pill formulations ● information services, resources for programs, country experiences, emergency contraception. **Committees:** Communications and Advocacy; Products; Science; Steering; Youth. **Programs:** Arab Region; Asia Pacific Network on EC; Eastern Europe and the Balkans/NIS; ECafrique; Latin American Consortium for Emergency Contraception. **Affiliated With:** Advocates for Youth; Family Care International; International Planned Parenthood Federation - United Kingdom; International Planned Parenthood Federation, Western Hemisphere Region; Population Council; Program for Appropriate Technology in Health; World Health Organization. **Publications:** *Emergency Contraceptive Pills: Medical and Service Delivery Guidelines*. Handbook. Alternate Formats: online ● *Resources for Emergency Contraceptive Pill Programming: A Toolkit*. Manual. Alternate Formats: online ● Newsletter, periodic. Includes information on international activities as well as news from related organizations. Alternate Formats: online.

11921 ■ International Planned Parenthood Federation, Western Hemisphere Region (IPPF/WHR)
120 Wall St., 9th Fl.
New York, NY 10005
Ph: (212)248-6400
Fax: (212)248-4221
E-mail: info@ippfwhr.org
URL: http://www.ippfwhr.org
Contact: Alexander C. Sanger, Chm.
Founded: 1954. **Members:** 46. **Staff:** 45. **Budget:** $8,787,361. **Languages:** English, Spanish. **Description:** Provides more than 12 million sexual and reproductive health services and information each year to men, women and youth throughout Latin America and the Caribbean. **Awards:** Rosa Cisneros Award. **Frequency:** annual. **Type:** recognition. **Computer Services:** database ● online services. **Programs:** Emergency Contraception; Gender-Based Violence; Service Delivery; Youth. **Affiliated With:** International Planned Parenthood Federation - United Kingdom. **Publications:** *NewsNewsNews* (in English and Spanish), weekly. Newsletter. Includes transla-

tions of selected articles and briefs on sexual and reproductive health. ● *Reaching Out*, semiannual. Newsletter. Features articles on IPPF/WHR's participation during the Commission on the Status of Women at the UN. ● Magazine (in English and Spanish), annual. Includes in-depth studies of sexual and reproductive health program in Latin America and the Caribbean. Alternate Formats: online ● Annual Report (in English and Spanish) ● Also publishes occasional monographs, studies, and position papers. **Conventions/Meetings:** annual meeting - always September/October.

11922 ■ National Abortion Federation (NAF)
1755 Massachusetts Ave. NW, Ste.600
Washington, DC 20036
Ph: (202)667-5881
Free: (800)772-9100
Fax: (202)667-5890
E-mail: naf@prochoice.org
URL: http://www.prochoice.org
Contact: Vicki Saporta, Pres./CEO
Founded: 1977. **Members:** 400. **Staff:** 30. **Budget:** $6,000,000. **Description:** Abortion service providers (physician offices, clinics, feminist health centers, Planned Parenthood affiliates) and others committed to making safe, legal abortions accessible to all women. Unites abortion service providers into a professional community dedicated to health care; upgrades abortion services by providing continuing medical education, standards, and guidelines; serves as clearinghouse of information on variety and quality of services offered; keeps abreast of educational, legislative, and public policy developments in reproductive health care. Provides referrals. **Libraries: Type:** reference. **Holdings:** 225. **Subjects:** abortion, contraception, sexuality, sociology, health issues. **Awards: Type:** recognition. **Computer Services:** database, violence directed against abortion providers. **Additional Websites:** http://www.earlyoptions.org, http://www.supremecourtwatch.org, http://www.cliniciansforchoice.org. **Absorbed:** (1977) Association for the Study of Abortion. **Formed by Merger of:** National Abortion Council; National Association of Abortion Facilities. **Publications:** *A Clinician's Guide to Medical and Surgical Abortion*. Book ● *Choice*. Newsletter. Contains the most current developments in abortion policy, advances in science, progress in NAF's work, and accomplishments of NAF members. Alternate Formats: online ● *Clinical Training Curriculum in Abortion Practice*. Curriculum for residency training, medical reference. Price: $130.00 ● *Unsure About Your Pregnancy? A Guide to Making the Right Decision for You* ● Bulletins ● Annual Report, annual. Alternate Formats: online ● Also publishes fact sheets, bulletins, and position papers on abortion, and resource materials for abortion providers. **Conventions/Meetings:** annual meeting ● semiannual Risk Management Meeting, continuing medical education conferences (exhibits) - spring and fall.

11923 ■ National Family Planning and Reproductive Health Association (NFPRHA)
1627 K St. NW, 12th Fl.
Washington, DC 20006
Ph: (202)293-3114
Fax: (202)293-1990
E-mail: info@nfprha.org
URL: http://www.nfprha.org
Contact: Mary Jane Gallagher, Pres./CEO
Founded: 1971. **Members:** 1,000. **Membership Dues:** corporate, $5,000 (annual) ● sustaining, $3,000 (annual) ● professional, $250 (annual) ● institutional (with annual family planning budget of 1500000 or more), $1,500 (annual) ● institutional (with annual family planning budget of 500000 to 1500000), $1,000 (annual) ● institutional (with annual family planning budget of less than 500000), $500 (annual) ● advocate, $75 (annual) ● student, $25 (annual). **Staff:** 11. **Budget:** $1,250,000. **Description:** Hospitals, state and city departments of health, health care providers, private nonprofit clinics, and consumers concerned with the maintenance and improvement of family planning and reproductive health services. Serves as a national communications network and advocacy organization. Maintains

contact with Congress and government agencies in order to monitor government policy and regulations. **Awards:** Distinguished Public Service. **Frequency:** annual. **Type:** recognition ● Outstanding Clinic. **Frequency:** annual. **Type:** recognition ● Outstanding Educator. **Frequency:** annual. **Type:** recognition. **Computer Services:** database ● mailing lists. **Committees:** International and Domestic Public Affairs; Leadership & Diversity; Service Delivery. **Programs:** Leadership Development Institute. **Formerly:** (1979) National Family Planning Forum. **Publications:** *NFPRHA Quarterly*. Newsletter. **Circulation:** 1,500 ● *NFPRHA Report*. Reports on public policy affecting family planning and reproductive health. **Price:** included in membership dues; $200.00 for nonmembers. Alternate Formats: online ● Annual Report, annual ● Also publishes professional papers and educational materials. **Conventions/Meetings:** annual meeting and conference, public policy and service delivery workshop with award presentation (exhibits).

11924 ■ Pathfinder International (PI)
9 Galen St., Ste.217
Watertown, MA 02472
Ph: (617)924-7200
Fax: (617)924-3833
E-mail: information@pathfind.org
URL: http://www.pathfind.org
Contact: Henry W. Foster Jr., Chm.
Founded: 1957. **Staff:** 300. **Budget:** $50,000,000. **Nonmembership. Multinational. Description:** Works to find, demonstrate, and promote new and more efficient family planning programs in developing countries. Aims to introduce and expand the availability of effective family planning services; improve the welfare of families in developing countries; assist developing countries in implementing population policies favorable to national development. Conducts activities with a concern for upholding human rights, enhancing the status and role of women, and respecting the views of family planning clients. **Convention/Meeting:** none. **Libraries: Type:** open to the public. **Holdings:** 2,000; articles, books, periodicals. **Subjects:** family planning, women in development, maternal and child health. **Also Known As:** PF. **Publications:** *Pathways*, semiannual. Newsletter. Provides information on programs and updates on services. **Circulation:** 6,000 ● Annual Report, annual.

11925 ■ Planned Parenthood Federation of America (PPFA)
434 W 33rd St.
New York, NY 10001
Ph: (212)541-7800
Free: (800)230-7526
Fax: (212)245-1845
E-mail: pponline@ppfa.org
URL: http://www.plannedparenthood.org
Contact: Cecile Richards, Pres.
Founded: 1916. **Staff:** 11,160. **Budget:** $819,000,000. **Regional Groups:** 117. **Description:** Provides leadership in making effective means of voluntary fertility regulation, including contraception, abortion, sterilization, and infertility services. Stimulates and sponsors relevant biomedical, socioeconomic, and demographic research; develops appropriate information, education, and training programs to increase knowledge about human reproduction and sexuality. Supports and assists efforts to achieve similar goals worldwide. Operates more than 900 centers that provide medically supervised reproductive health services and educational programs. **Libraries: Type:** reference. **Holdings:** 6,500. **Subjects:** contraception, abortion, sterilization, family planning, population, sexuality education. **Awards:** PPFA Maggie Awards. **Frequency:** annual. **Type:** recognition. **Recipient:** for media excellence ● PPFA Margaret Sanger Award. **Frequency:** annual. **Type:** recognition. **Recipient:** for leadership, excellence, and outstanding contributions to the reproductive health and rights movement. **Absorbed:** World Population Emergency Campaign. **Also Known As:** Planned Parenthood; Planned Parenthood/World Population. **Formerly:** (1939) American Birth Control

League. **Publications:** Annual Report, annual. Alternate Formats: online ● Books ● Pamphlets. **Conventions/Meetings:** annual meeting (exhibits) - always fall.

Farming

11926 ■ Center for Farm Health and Safety
Eastern Washington Univ.
314 Patterson Hall
Cheney, WA 99004
Ph: (509)359-7995
Fax: (509)359-6583
E-mail: pelkind@ewu.edu
URL: http://www.ewu.edu/x11667.xml
Contact: Dr. Pamela Elkind, Dir.
Founded: 1989. **Staff:** 7. **Description:** Facilitates the study and promotion of the health and well being of the rural and farm communities in Eastern Washington. Builds coalitions, conducts research and fosters community programs.

Financial Planning

11927 ■ Money Management International (MMI)
9009 W Loop S, 7th Fl.
Houston, TX 77096-1719
Free: (866)889-9347
E-mail: cate.williams@moneymanagement.org
URL: http://www.moneymanagement.org
Contact: Cate Williams, VP of Financial Literacy
Nonmembership. Description: Serves as a full service credit-counseling agency. Provides professional financial guidance, counseling, community-wide educational programs and debt management assistance to consumers. **Publications:** Newsletter ● Annual Report, annual. Alternate Formats: online ● Articles, monthly. Alternate Formats: online.

Food

11928 ■ Community Food Security Coalition (CFSC)
PO Box 209
Venice, CA 90294
Ph: (310)822-5410
Fax: (310)822-1440
E-mail: andy@foodsecurity.org
URL: http://www.foodsecurity.org
Contact: Andy Fisher, Exec. Dir.
Founded: 1994. **Members:** 325. **Membership Dues:** individual, $35 (annual) ● small organization (less than $100000 budget), $50 (annual) ● large organization (more than $100000 budget), $100 (annual) ● life, $500 ● low income individual, student and senior, $1-$35 (annual). **Staff:** 12. **Multinational. Description:** Seeks to build strong, sustainable, local and regional food systems that ensure access to affordable, nutritious and culturally appropriate food to people at all times. Seeks to develop self-reliance among communities in obtaining their food. Creates a system of growing, manufacturing, processing, making available and selling food. **Computer Services:** Mailing lists, COMFOOD listserv. **Committees:** Farm to Cafeteria; Food and Faith; Food Retail; International Links; Outreach and Diversity; Policy; Training and Technical Assistance; Urban Agriculture. **Publications:** Community Food Security News. Newsletter. Includes articles related to community food security. Alternate Formats: online.

Foster Parents

11929 ■ Partners in Foster Care
c/o Cora E. White, Pres.
PO Box 2534
Madison, WI 53701
Ph: (608)274-9111

E-mail: cwhite@fostering.us
URL: http://www.fostering.us
Contact: Cora E. White, Pres.
Founded: 1988. **Membership Dues:** friend, $25-$99 (annual) ● supporter, $100-$249 (annual) ● advocate, $500 (annual). **Description:** Seeks to improve the lives of foster children. Supports foster and adoptive families and the children living in their homes. Provides social, cultural, and educational activities to disadvantaged, medically fragile, abused, and neglected children living in out of home care. **Publications:** Newsletter, quarterly. **Price:** included in membership dues.

Free Enterprise

11930 ■ Global Envision
c/o Mercy Corps
3015 SW, 1st Ave.
Portland, OR 97201
E-mail: contact@globalenvision.org
URL: http://www.globalenvision.org
Contact: William Early, Founder/Contributor
Multinational. Description: Promotes free market system as a starting point for reducing world poverty. Advocates for "a better world, reduction of poverty and improved living standards". **Computer Services:** Online services, forum ● online services, global blogs. **Boards:** Advisory. **Publications:** Newsletter, biweekly.

Fundraising

11931 ■ American Charities for Reasonable Fundraising Regulation (ACFRFR)
9112 Tetterton Ave.
Vienna, VA 22182
Ph: (703)938-1809
Fax: (703)938-2207
E-mail: gpeters@gpeters.net
URL: http://www.charity-reg.org
Contact: Mr. Geoffrey Peters Esq., Pro-bono Gen. Counsel
Membership Dues: fundraising, nonprofit, vendor, other supporter, $1,000 (annual). **Description:** Works to combat excessive regulation of nonprofits and of fundraising by means of litigation on behalf of the nonprofit sector. Alerts other nonprofit associations and fundraising organizations about regulatory matters; has litigated successfully in Federal District Court, U.S. Court of Appeals, and Supreme Court of the United States. **Affiliated With:** Association of Fundraising Professionals; Council for Advancement and Support of Education; Direct Marketing Association; National Catholic Development Conference; National Health Council.

11932 ■ America's Charities (AC)
14150 Newbrook Dr., Ste.110
Chantilly, VA 20151
Ph: (703)222-3861
Free: (800)458-9505
Fax: (703)222-3867
E-mail: ljones@charities.org
URL: http://www.charities.org
Contact: Edwin Washington, Field Operations Dir.
Founded: 1980. **Members:** 81. **Description:** Works to meet community needs through member charity services impacting health, human service, education, human and civil rights, and the environment. "A 20-year tradition of giving and caring". **Telecommunication Services:** electronic mail, ewashington@charities.org. **Formerly:** (1994) National Service Agencies.

11933 ■ Association of Fundraising Professionals (AFP)
4300 Wilson Blvd., Ste.300
Arlington, VA 22203
Ph: (703)684-0410
Free: (800)666-FUND
Fax: (703)684-0540

E-mail: afp@afpnet.org
URL: http://www.afpnet.org
Contact: Mr. Michael Nilsen, Public Affairs Dir.
Founded: 1960. **Members:** 28,000. **Membership Dues:** active/associate, $220 (annual) ● introductory (initial), $100 ● regular, $150 (annual). **Staff:** 50. **Budget:** $8,000,000. **Local Groups:** 185. **Multinational. Description:** Fundraising executives who work for non-profit and philanthropic organizations. Purposes are: to foster the development and growth of professional fundraising executives committed to the philanthropic process; to establish professional ethical standards and to require its members to adhere to those standards; to provide guidance and assistance to philanthropic institutions and agencies with fundraising programs; to offer continuing professional education and career enhancement services for philanthropic fundraising professionals. Maintains speakers' bureau. **Libraries:** Type: reference. **Holdings:** 3,800. **Subjects:** philanthropy. **Formerly:** National Society of Fund Raisers; (2001) National Society of Fund Raising Executives. **Publications:** *Advancing Philanthropy*, bimonthly. Magazine. Reports on capital and annual campaigns, major gifts and donors, and other information about philanthropy and philanthropic fundraising. **Price:** included in membership dues; $50.00/year for extra subscription; $80.00 /year for nonmembers. ISSN: 1056-2443. **Circulation:** 24,000. **Advertising:** accepted. Alternate Formats: CD-ROM; online; diskette ● *AFP eWire*, weekly. Newsletter. Alternate Formats: online ● Membership Directory, annual. Lists members by state and chapter. Includes roster of consultants. **Price:** included in membership dues. **Circulation:** 18,500. **Advertising:** accepted ● Annual Report, annual. Contains information about the foundation. Alternate Formats: online. **Conventions/Meetings:** annual International Conference on Fund Raising (exhibits).

11934 ■ Association of Professional Researchers for Advancement (APRA)
401 N Michigan Ave., Ste.2200
Chicago, IL 60611
Ph: (312)321-5196
Fax: (312)673-6966
E-mail: info@aprahome.org
URL: http://www.aprahome.org
Contact: Julie Sutter, Exec. Dir.
Founded: 1988. **Members:** 1,900. **Membership Dues:** institution, individual, $150 (annual). **Regional Groups:** 27. **Description:** Individuals involved in educational, medical, cultural, and religious organizations; fundraising consultants. Facilitates education and dissemination of information about prospect research; encourages professional development and cooperative relationships among members. Prospect research is aimed at securing gifts, grants, and charitable donations for nonprofit organizations. **Awards:** APRA Foundation Margaret Fuhry Grant. **Frequency:** annual. **Type:** grant. **Recipient:** for a researcher with outstanding leadership, mentorship, volunteerism and dedication to the profession ● APRA Visionary Award. **Frequency:** annual. **Type:** recognition. **Recipient:** for a member who has served as a pioneer or trailblazer in the field ● Distinguished Service Award. **Frequency:** annual. **Type:** recognition. **Recipient:** for an individual who has contributed exceptional service for the advancement of the research profession ● Researcher of the Year. **Frequency:** annual. **Type:** recognition. **Recipient:** for outstanding skills and accomplishments. **Formerly:** (1995) American Prospect Research Association. **Publications:** *APRA Member Directory*, annual. Membership Directory. **Advertising:** accepted ● *Connections*, quarterly. Journal. Contains articles about advancement research, management, and other fundraising issues. **Price:** included in membership dues; $10.00 back issues, for members; $20.00 back issues, for nonmembers. **Advertising:** accepted. Alternate Formats: online ● *Quarterly* ● Bulletin ● Annual Report, annual. Highlights past year's accomplishments and graphical summary of finances of the organization. Alternate Formats: online. **Conventions/Meetings:** annual conference (exhibits) ● annual international conference, with sessions for the

advancement of researchers at every level of professional development - 2008 Aug. 17-23, Denver, CO.

11935 ■ CASE Matching Gifts Clearinghouse
1307 New York Ave. NW, Ste.1000
Washington, DC 20005-4701
Ph: (202)478-5656 (301)604-2068
Free: (800)554-8536
Fax: (301)206-9789
E-mail: memberservicecenter@case.org
URL: http://www.case.org/matchinggifts
Contact: John Lippincott, Pres.
Founded: 1955. **Staff:** 3. **Description:** A division of the Council for Advancement and Support of Education. Assists non-profit organizations that receive corporate matching gifts and corporations that have matching gift programs. (Corporate matching gifts are company donations that are equivalent or in variable proportions to monies contributed by employees for charitable causes.) Collects and disseminates information on the nearly 7100 companies with matching gift programs. Offers assistance to companies seeking to initiate matching gift programs and to non-profit organizations requesting increased donations through existing programs. Compiles statistics; conducts surveys. **Affiliated With:** Council for Advancement and Support of Education. **Formerly:** (1998) National Clearinghouse for Corporate Matching Gift Information. **Publications:** *Double Your Dollars,* annual. Brochure. Leaflets listing companies that match gifts to higher education, secondary/elementary education; arts and community service organizations. ● *Matching Gift Company Online.* Brochure. Alternate Formats: online ● *Matching Gift Details,* annual. Directory. Contains corporate matching gift program guidelines. **Conventions/Meetings:** annual Matching Gift Symposium - conference (exhibits) - usually early spring.

11936 ■ Community Health Charities
200 N Glebe Rd., Ste.801
Arlington, VA 22203
Ph: (703)528-1007
Free: (800)654-0845
Fax: (703)528-1365
E-mail: info@healthcharities.org
URL: http://www.healthcharities.org
Contact: Thomas Bognanno, Pres./CEO
Founded: 1956. **Members:** 65. **Membership Dues:** health organization, $1,000 (annual). **Staff:** 10. **Budget:** $5,000,000. **State Groups:** 50. **Local Groups:** 50. **National Groups:** 50. **Description:** Represents national health agencies. Generates funds through workplace charitable solicitation and distributes them to member agencies. **Computer Services:** database, informational. **Subcommittees:** Budget; Domestic Activities; Eligibility. **Formerly:** (1975) National Committee of the Federal Service Campaign for National Health Agencies; (1985) National Health Agencies Committee for the Combined Federal Campaign; (1999) National Voluntary Health Agencies. **Publications:** *NVHA National Newsletter,* quarterly. **Conventions/Meetings:** semiannual meeting.

11937 ■ Intimate Apparel Square Club (IASC)
326 Field Rd.
Clinton Corners, NY 12514
Ph: (845)758-5752
Fax: (845)758-2546
E-mail: amasry@yahoo.com
URL: http://thehugaward.org
Contact: Adam Masry, Sec.
Founded: 1955. **Members:** 85. **Membership Dues:** regular, $50 (annual). **Description:** Members of the women's and children's intimate apparel industry. Works with other charity groups in the greater New York City area. Strives to "help those who cannot help themselves". Provides support to needy medical school students and makes contributions to children's organizations and rehabilitation clinics, primarily Rusk Institute. **Awards:** Al Jaffin Award. **Frequency:** annual. **Type:** recognition. **Recipient:** to members. **Committees:** Al Jaffin Award; Charity; Dinner Dance; Entertainment; Events; Fund Raising; Good and Welfare; Public Relations. **Publications:** Journal, annual ● Newsletter. Alternate Formats: online.

11938 ■ National Network of Grantmakers (NNG)
2801 21st Ave. S, Ste.132
Minneapolis, MN 55407-1227
Ph: (612)724-0702
Fax: (612)724-0705
E-mail: nng@nng.org
URL: http://www.nng.org
Contact: Ellery July, Contact
Founded: 1980. **Members:** 400. **Membership Dues:** individual, $200 (annual) ● supporting institution, $1,000 (annual). **Staff:** 5. **Budget:** $600,000. **Languages:** English, Spanish. **Description:** Individuals who are staff/trustees of corporate and independent foundations and religious giving programs; philanthropists; staff of nonprofit organizations servicing grantmakers; government officials involved in grantmaking programs. Aims to establish a communications link for sharing information and ideas on grantmaking; provide a network of support for individuals working on similar concerns in grantmaking environments; discuss issues and grantmaking approaches as well as receive feedback from other members; act as a voice for social and economic justice issues within the philanthropic community and in other sectors, including government, business, labor, and education. Sponsors workshops for grantmakers. **Computer Services:** Mailing lists. **Caucuses:** People of Color; Queer; Women's; Youth. **Committees:** Communications; Philanthropic Reform. **Working Groups:** Family Philanthropy; Grantmakers without Borders. **Publications:** *Exemplary Grantmaking Practices* ● *Grantmakers Directory 2000-2001,* annual. Membership Directory. Indexed alphabetically, geographically, and by grantmaking interest. **Price:** $50.00 ● *The Network Newsletter,* quarterly. Alternate Formats: online ● *Welcome to Philanthropy.* Brochure. **Conventions/Meetings:** annual conference ● periodic regional meeting.

11939 ■ TelecomPioneers
930 15th St., 12th Fl.
Denver, CO 80202
Ph: (303)571-1200
Free: (800)872-5995
Fax: (303)572-0520
E-mail: info@telecompioneers.org
URL: http://www.telecompioneers.org
Contact: Marty Lee, Pres.
Founded: 1911. **Members:** 800,000. **Membership Dues:** regular, $15 (annual). **Staff:** 13. **Budget:** $3,000,000. **Regional Groups:** 7. **Local Groups:** 150. **Description:** Active and retired telecommunications employees. Programs embrace a wide range of fellowship and service activities, including such community projects as services to the blind (talking book recording), volunteer hospital services, literacy aid, educational programs, work with troubled teens and the aged, and Habitat for Humanity. **Libraries: Type:** not open to the public. **Awards:** People Who Care Award. **Frequency:** annual. **Type:** recognition. **Telecommunication Services:** electronic mail, mlee@telecompioneers.org. **Formerly:** (2003) Telephone Pioneers of America. **Publications:** *The Pioneer,* semiannual. Newsletter. **Price:** included in membership dues. **Circulation:** 875,000 ● Manuals. Alternate Formats: online. **Conventions/Meetings:** annual convention and general assembly ● quarterly meeting.

11940 ■ United Black Fund (UBF)
PO Box 7051
Washington, DC 20032
Ph: (202)783-9300
URL: http://www.ubfinc.org
Contact: Wilhelmina J. Rolark Esq., Pres./CEO
Founded: 1969. **Description:** Provides human care services to low-income or disabled blacks and other minorities. Assists disadvantaged blacks and other minorities in becoming self-sufficient by providing funds to member agencies for the establishment of health and welfare programs. Sponsors fundraising activities to support day care service, education, senior citizens, and drug and alcohol rehabilitation programs; monitors the establishment and development of such programs. **Formerly:** (2002) United

Black Fund of America. **Publications:** *United Black Fund Agency Directory,* annual. **Conventions/Meetings:** annual meeting - always in Washington, DC.

11941 ■ United Way of America (UWA)
701 N Fairfax St.
Alexandria, VA 22314
Ph: (703)836-7100
Fax: (703)683-7840
URL: http://national.unitedway.org
Contact: Brian A. Gallagher, Pres./CEO
Founded: 1918. **Members:** 1,400. **Staff:** 200. **Budget:** $40,000,000. **Regional Groups:** 5. **State Groups:** 23. **Local Groups:** 2,100. **Description:** Local United Way organizations in the U.S. Provides national, regional, and local program support and consulting to United Ways in the areas of fundraising, budgeting, management, fund distribution, planning, and communications. Assists in fundraising by cultivating increased corporate giving by selected companies through the National Corporate Leadership Program. Administers staff and volunteer development training through the National Academy for Voluntarism. Acts as liaison between United Ways, the federal government, national labor unions, and national nonprofit agencies. Provides national media support and produces films, audiovisual materials, publications, and similar aids for members. Compiles statistics. **Awards:** Alexis de Tocqueville Society Award. **Type:** recognition. **Recipient:** for outstanding volunteer leaders/supporters ● Diversity Awards. **Type:** recognition ● Spirit of America Award. **Type:** recognition. **Formerly:** (1956) Community Chests and Councils of America; (1970) United Community Funds and Councils of America. **Publications:** *Executive Newsletter,* biweekly ● *International Directory,* annual ● Annual Report. **Conventions/Meetings:** annual Community Leaders Conference, for corporate supporters and partners (exhibits).

11942 ■ United Way International (UWI)
701 N Fairfax St.
Alexandria, VA 22314-2045
Ph: (703)519-0092
Fax: (703)519-0097
E-mail: uwi@unitedway.org
URL: http://www.uwint.org/gppweb/index.aspx
Contact: Teresa Halls Bartels, Chair
Founded: 1974. **Members:** 43. **Staff:** 15. **Budget:** $2,600,000. **Languages:** English, French, Hindi, Japanese, Korean, Russian. **Description:** Assists multi-national corporations with their Global Philanthropy Programs. Provides technical assistance to members. Offers information exchange, training for volunteers, professionals, and charitable programs. Helps with start-up of United Way type organizations in counties without one. **Conventions/Meetings:** biennial World Assembly.

11943 ■ Women, Children and Family Service Charities of America (WCFSCA)
21 Tamal Vista Blvd., Ste.209
Corte Madera, CA 94925
Free: (800)626-6481
Fax: (415)924-1379
E-mail: info@womenandchildren.org
URL: http://www.womenandchildren.org
Contact: Zanna Curry, Pres.
Members: 45. **Description:** National charitable organizations in the United States. Seeks to represent charities that meet the highest standards of public accountability and program effectiveness to prospective givers in fund drives conducted at work. Provides support and assistance to charitable organizations wishing to conduct workplace fundraising campaigns. Screens, certifies, and presents charities for giver consideration. **Publications:** Annual Report, annual. Alternate Formats: online.

Gambling

11944 ■ Association of Problem Gambling Service Administrators (APGSA)
c/o Arizona Office of Problem Gambling
202 E Earll Dr., Ste.200
Phoenix, AZ 85012

Ph: (602)266-8299
E-mail: tchristensen@problemgambling.az.gov
URL: http://www.apgsa.org
Contact: Tim Christensen, Pres.
Founded: 2000. **Membership Dues:** general, $500-$1,500 (annual). **Description:** Supports the development of services that will reduce the impact of problem gambling. Enhances the effectiveness and efficiency of its member organizations through support, information dissemination, and adherence to professional standards.

11945 ■ Council on Compulsive Gambling of New Jersey (CCGNJ)
3635 Quakerbridge Rd., Ste.7
Hamilton, NJ 08619
Ph: (609)588-5515
E-mail: ccgnj@800gambler.org
URL: http://www.800gambler.org
Contact: Edward Looney, Exec. Dir.
Founded: 1983. **Members:** 8,500. **Membership Dues:** individual, $25 (annual). **Staff:** 7. **Budget:** $500,000. **Description:** Recovering gamblers; health, law, and education professionals; other interested persons. Seeks to provide information, training, education, and referrals nationwide on the treatment of compulsive gambling. Sponsors training programs for counselors and health service professionals involved in the rehabilitation of compulsive gamblers. Promotes the certification of counselors and the development of residential and outpatient treatment programs. Conducts research. **Awards:** Educational Award. **Frequency:** annual. **Type:** recognition ● Governmental Award. **Frequency:** annual. **Type:** recognition ● Person of the Year. **Frequency:** annual. **Type:** recognition ● Volunteer Award. **Frequency:** annual. **Type:** recognition. **Computer Services:** database ● mailing lists ● online services. **Telecommunication Services:** phone referral service, (800)GAM-BLER, provides assistance and referrals for those who either are or maybe being effected by compulsive gambling. **Publications:** Ad Journal, annual. Included as part of awards banquet. **Advertising:** accepted ● The Council Connection, 2-3/year. Newsletter. **Price:** included in membership dues. **Advertising:** accepted ● Brochure (in English and Spanish). Offers information on adolescent, senior citizen, women, and employee assistance programs. **Conventions/Meetings:** periodic Compulsive Gambling - seminar and lecture (exhibits) ● annual Statewide Conference on Compulsive Gambling (exhibits) - usually September, in New Jersey.

11946 ■ Gam-Anon International Service Office (GAM-ANON)
PO Box 157
Whitestone, NY 11357
Ph: (718)352-1671
Fax: (718)746-2571
E-mail: gamanonoffice1@aol.com
URL: http://www.gam-anon.org
Contact: Regina Kaplan, Exec. Sec.
Founded: 1960. **National Groups:** 500. **Languages:** English, Spanish. **Multinational. Description:** Represents husbands, wives, relatives, and close friends of compulsive gamblers. Seeks to help members better understand the compulsive gambler and learn to cope with the problems involved. Conducts regularly scheduled meetings throughout the world to allow members to share experiences, strength, and hope, recover from the effects of compulsive gambling, and achieve a normal way of thinking and living. Maintains speakers' bureau. Sponsors social activities. Conducts open, topic, recognition, and special focus meetings. **Libraries: Type:** not open to the public. **Holdings:** 12; books, periodicals. **Subjects:** compulsive gambling, the effects of compulsive gambling on the loved ones, 12 steps recovery, starting a meeting. **Computer Services:** Information services, about organization, international meeting schedule. **Publications:** Gam-A-News, quarterly. Newsletter. Contains financial reports, information and letters. **Price:** $16.00 ● Also publishes Gam-Anon Way of Life, Living With the Gambling Problem, Games Compulsive Gamblers and We Play, For the Parents, and other

books and booklets to help the meetings and individual members learn about compulsive gambling, and the Gam-Anon recovery program. **Conventions/Meetings:** annual conference.

11947 ■ Gamblers Anonymous (GA)
PO Box 17173
Los Angeles, CA 90017
Ph: (213)386-8789
Fax: (213)386-0030
E-mail: isomain@gamblersanonymous.org
URL: http://www.gamblersanonymous.org
Contact: Karen H., Exec. Sec.
Founded: 1957. **National Groups:** 1,250. **Description:** Men and women who have joined together in order to stop gambling and to help other compulsive gamblers do the same; is self-supporting, declines outside contributions, and neither opposes nor endorses outside causes. **Divisions:** International Service Office. **Programs:** Recovery; Unity. **Publications:** Lifelines Bulletin, monthly. **Price:** $18.00/year in U.S.; $50.00/year outside U.S. **Circulation:** 7,500 ● Books ● Pamphlets ● Videos ● Also publishes pamphlets on compulsive gambling and the nature of GA fellowship. **Conventions/Meetings:** semiannual conference.

11948 ■ National Council on Problem Gambling (NCPG)
216 G St. NE, Ste.200
Washington, DC 20002
Ph: (202)547-9204
Free: (800)522-4700
Fax: (202)547-9206
E-mail: ncpg@ncpgambling.org
URL: http://www.ncpgambling.org
Contact: Keith S. Whyte, Exec. Dir.
Founded: 1972. **Members:** 400. **Membership Dues:** individual, $75 (annual) ● corporate, $5,000 (annual) ● supporter, $25 ● contributor, $250 ● silver, $500 ● gold, $1,000 ● platinum, $2,500. **Staff:** 4. **Budget:** $400,000. **State Groups:** 33. **Description:** Professionals in health, education, and law; recovering gamblers; supportive citizens. Advocates for programs and services to assist problem gamblers and their families. Makes referrals for compulsive gamblers and their families; seeks to stimulate the concern of the medical profession, educators, legislators, and the criminal justice system. Conducts training programs for professionals and information programs to encourage business management, educators, and the public to become aware of and to understand compulsive gambling. Compiles statistics; maintains speakers' bureau. Administers national 24 hour toll-free helpline for individuals with gambling problems. **Computer Services:** Online services, listing of gambling counselors. **Formerly:** (1989) National Council on Compulsive Gambling. **Publications:** Journal on Gambling Studies. **Price:** $22.00 plus shipping and handling ● National Council on Problem Gambling—Newsletter, quarterly. Includes book reviews and calendar of events. **Price:** included in membership dues ● Problem Gamblers and their Finances: A Guide for Treatment Professionals. Book. **Price:** free. Alternate Formats: online ● Annual Report. **Conventions/Meetings:** annual conference and seminar, dedicated to problem gambling.

Gay/Lesbian

11949 ■ Alliance for Full Acceptance (AFFA)
PO Box 22088
Charleston, SC 29413
Ph: (843)883-0343
Fax: (843)723-3859
E-mail: info@affa-sc.org
URL: http://www.affa-sc.org
Contact: Warren Redman-Gress, Exec. Dir.
Membership Dues: student, special circumstances, $20 (annual) ● individual, $75 (annual) ● cohabitating partner of an individual, $50 (annual) ● business, $250 (annual). **Description:** Seeks to eliminate prejudice and secure social justice and civil rights for gay, lesbian, bisexual and transgender

people. Provides education and information to individuals wishing to learn more about sexual orientation. Provides a forum for public officials, religious, business and community leaders to share information and engage in dialogue. Educates and supports parents of gay and lesbian children in order to decrease suicide rate among gay children. **Publications:** Coming Out and Internalized Homophobia. Article. Alternate Formats: online ● Religion and Homosexuality. Article. Alternate Formats: online ● Sexual and Gender Orientation. Article. Alternate Formats: online.

11950 ■ American Library Association/Gay, Lesbian, Bisexual and Transgendered Round Table (ALA/GLBTRT)
c/o Norman Eriksen, Asst. Division Mgr.
Brooklyn Public Lib.
Brooklyn, NY 11238
Ph: (718)230-2716
Free: (800)545-2433
Fax: (718)230-2064
E-mail: n.eriksen@brooklynpubliclibrary.org
URL: http://www.ala.org/ala/glbtrt/welcomeglbtround.htm
Contact: Norman Eriksen, Asst. Division Mgr.
Founded: 1970. **Members:** 532. **Description:** Promotes gay, lesbian, bisexual and transgendered professionals. **Awards:** Stonewell Book Award. **Frequency:** annual. **Type:** recognition. **Recipient:** for literature and non-fiction books relating to the gay experience. **Committees:** Book Award; Breakfast Planning; External Relations; Fundraising; Nominating; Program Planning; Website. **Formerly:** (1979) Task Force on Gay Liberation; (1987) Gay Task Force of ALA; (1994) Gay and Lesbian Task Force. **Publications:** GLBTRT Newsletter, quarterly. Contains information about GLBT issues in libraries. **Price:** $10.00/year. ISSN: 1533-7219. **Circulation:** 550. Alternate Formats: online. **Conventions/Meetings:** semiannual meeting, held in conjunction with American Library Association Conferences (exhibits).

11951 ■ American Veterans for Equal Rights (AVER)
PO Box 97
Plainville, IL 62365-0097
Ph: (773)752-0058
Fax: (773)752-0058
E-mail: president@aver.us
URL: http://www.glbva.org
Contact: A.J. Rogue, Natl.Pres./Newsletter Ed.
Founded: 1990. **Membership Dues:** individual, $25 (annual) ● corporate/organizational sponsor, $50 (annual) ● life, $500. **Regional Groups:** 11. **Description:** Dedicated to serving gay, lesbian, bisexual and transgender veterans and active duty personnel, "challenging the discriminatory policies of the Department of Defense," eliminating Uniform code of Military Justice restrictions on private, adult consensual sexual activities, and working on issues of importance to veterans, especially gay, lesbian, bisexual, and transgender veterans. **Libraries: Type:** open to the public. **Holdings:** artwork. **Subjects:** gays, veterans. **Awards:** Happy Warrior Service Award. **Frequency:** annual. **Type:** recognition. **Formerly:** (2002) Gay, Lesbian, and Bisexual Veterans of America. **Publications:** The Forward Observer, quarterly. Newsletter. **Price:** $25.00 for nonmembers; free for members ● Local chapter newsletters: Chicago - Vet Pride; Palm Springs - Gay Guidon; Houston - Present Arms; Denver - The Quarter Deck; San Antonio - Front and Center; Los Angeles - Aware; Albuquerque - High Desert Signals. **Conventions/Meetings:** annual convention and conference, wall of fame (exhibits).

11952 ■ Association for Gay, Lesbian, and Bisexual Issues in Counseling (AGLBIC)
c/o Brian Dew, PhD, Pres.
640 Glen Iris Dr., No. 510
Georgia State Univ.
Atlanta, GA 30308
Ph: (404)651-3409
Fax: (404)651-1109

E-mail: bdew@gsu.edu
URL: http://www.aglbic.org
Contact: Brian Dew PhD, Pres.
Founded: 1974. **Members:** 260. **Membership Dues:** professional, $151 (annual) ● student, new professional, retired, $85 (annual) ● regular, $151 (annual). **Description:** Counselors, personnel and guidance workers concerned with lesbian and gay issues. Seeks to eliminate discrimination against and stereotyping of gay and lesbian individuals, particularly gay counselors. Works to educate heterosexual counselors on how to overcome homophobia and to best help homosexual clients. Provides a referral network and support for gay counselors and administrators; encourages objective research on gay issues. Organizational affiliate of the American Counseling Association. **Awards:** AGLBIC Service Award. **Frequency:** annual. **Type:** recognition. **Recipient:** for the meritorious service of a distinguished member ● Joe Norton Award. **Frequency:** annual. **Type:** recognition. **Recipient:** for the meritorious service of a distinguished ally. **Formerly:** (1978) Caucus of Gay Counselors; (1986) National Caucus of Gay and Lesbian Counselors; (1988) Association for Gay and Lesbian Issues in Counseling. **Publications:** *The Journal of GLBT Issues in Counseling*, quarterly ● Handbook. Alternate Formats: online ● Newsletter, quarterly. **Price:** by subscription only. **Circulation:** 260. **Advertising:** accepted. Alternate Formats: online ● Also publishes annotated bibliography of basic resources for counselors working with gay, lesbian, and bisexual clients. **Conventions/Meetings:** annual meeting, held in conjunction with American Counseling Association (exhibits).

11953 ■ Association of Gay and Lesbian Psychiatrists (AGLP)
4514 Chester Ave.
Philadelphia, PA 19143-3707
Ph: (215)222-2800
Fax: (215)222-3881
E-mail: rharker@aglp.org
URL: http://www.aglp.org
Contact: Roy Harker, Exec. Dir.
Founded: 1975. **Members:** 600. **Membership Dues:** regular, associate, $225 (annual) ● ally, international, early career, $100 (annual) ● sponsor, $300 (annual) ● patron, $500 (annual) ● founder, $1,000 (annual) ● resident, $45 (annual) ● medical student, $15 (annual). **Staff:** 1. **Budget:** $100,000. **Description:** Psychiatrists, psychiatrists in training, other mental health professionals promoting concerns of lesbian, gay, bisexual, and transgendered (LGBT) people within the psychiatric community. Maintains speakers' bureau. speakers' bureau; presents papers and panels. **Awards: Type:** recognition. **Computer Services:** database ● mailing lists ● online services. **Committees:** Education; Issues. **Affiliated With:** American Psychiatric Association. **Formerly:** (1979) Gay, Lesbian, and Bisexual Caucus of the American Psychiatric Association; (1980) Gay Caucus of Members of the American Psychiatric Association; (1985) Caucus of Gay, Lesbian, and Bisexual Members of the American Psychiatric Association. **Publications:** *Journal of Gay & Lesbian Psychotherapy*, quarterly. **Price:** included in membership dues ● *Newsletter of the Association of Gay and Lesbian Psychiatrists*, quarterly. Includes book reviews, calendar of events, and obituaries. **Price:** included in membership dues; $40.00 /year for nonmembers. **Circulation:** 625. **Advertising:** accepted. Alternate Formats: online ● Papers. **Conventions/Meetings:** annual convention and workshop, held in conjunction with APA (exhibits) - May-June ● annual meeting - always fall, usually Washington, DC ● annual meeting - in San Francisco, CA ● seminar (exhibits).

11954 ■ Bay Area Physicians for Human Rights (BAPHR)
PO Box 14188
San Francisco, CA 94114-0188
Ph: (415)558-9353
Fax: (413)556-4700
URL: http://www.baphr.org
Contact: Willis Navarro MD, Contact
Founded: 1977. **Members:** 350. **Membership Dues:** friend (non-doctors), health care professional, $60

(annual) ● resident, $25 (annual). **Budget:** $50,000. **Description:** Graduates of and students in approved schools of medicine and osteopathy; dentist and podiatrists. Aims to: improve the quality of medical care for gay and lesbian patients; educate physicians, both gay and nongay, in the special problems of gay and lesbian patients; educate the public about health care needs of the homosexual; maintain liaison with public officials about gay and lesbian health concerns; offer the gay and lesbian physician support through social functions and consciousness-raising groups. Sponsors research into medical problems and issues which are of special interest to homosexual patients. Provides medical and physician referral service and monthly educational programs; operates speakers' bureau; compiles statistics. **Awards: Type:** recognition. **Conventions/Meetings:** annual conference and symposium (exhibits).

11955 ■ Bi Women's Cultural Alliance (BWCA)
PO Box 2254
Washington, DC 20013-2254
Ph: (202)828-3065
E-mail: biwca@tripod.net
URL: http://biwca.tripod.com
Description: Offers social activities for bisexual females and bi-friendly lesbian and heterosexual women.

11956 ■ BiNet USA
4201 Wilson Blvd., No. 110, Box 311
Arlington, VA 22203-1859
Free: (800)585-9368
E-mail: binetusa@yahoo.com
URL: http://www.binetusa.org
Contact: Luigi Ferrer, Pres.
Founded: 1990. **Membership Dues:** limited income/ student, $20 (annual) ● regular, $35 (annual). **Description:** Promotes media advocacy and education to bisexuals and the general public. Facilitates the development of bisexual communities. Increases the accuracy and depth of public debate on issues of sexuality. Encourages individuals to feel proud of their bisexuality. **Computer Services:** Mailing lists, of members ● online services, discussion group. **Telecommunication Services:** electronic mail, binetusa-subscribe@yahoogroups.com.

11957 ■ Center for Lesbian and Gay Studies (CLAGS)
Graduate Center
City Univ. of New York, Rm. 7115
365 Fifth Ave.
New York, NY 10016
Ph: (212)817-1955
Fax: (212)817-2985
E-mail: clags@gc.cuny.edu
URL: http://web.gc.cuny.edu/clags
Contact: Paisley Currah, Exec. Dir.
Founded: 1991. **Members:** 3,000. **Membership Dues:** individual, $35 (annual) ● student, $10 (annual). **Staff:** 4. **Budget:** $175,000. **Description:** Promotes gay/lesbian studies at the University level. Encourages the development of scholarship, courses, and degree programs in gay/lesbian studies; works to recognize the contributions of lesbians and gay men in the arts and sciences. Maintains speakers' bureau and lesbian/gay collection at The Mina Rees Library of The Graduate School, City University of New York. **Libraries: Type:** open to the public. **Subjects:** homosexuality. **Awards:** CLAGS Fellowship. **Frequency:** annual. **Type:** fellowship. **Recipient:** for research in LGBT studies ● CLAGS Student Paper Awards. **Type:** monetary. **Recipient:** for best papers written by CUNY graduates and SUNY or CUNY undergraduates related to lesbian, gay, transgender, bisexual, or queer experiences ● CLAGS Student Travel Award. **Frequency:** semiannual. **Type:** monetary ● Martin Duberman Award. **Frequency:** annual. **Type:** monetary. **Recipient:** for scholarly research in LGBT studies ● Paul Monette-Roger Horwitz Dissertation Prize. **Type:** monetary. **Recipient:** for dissertation ● Sylvia Rivera Award in

Transgender Studies. **Type:** monetary. **Recipient:** for best book or article in transgender research. **Computer Services:** database ● mailing lists. **Publications:** *CLAGS News*, semiannual. Newsletter. **Conventions/Meetings:** periodic conference ● monthly meeting - always first Wednesday.

11958 ■ COLAGE
1550 Bryant St., Ste.830
San Francisco, CA 94103
Ph: (415)861-5437
Fax: (415)255-8345
E-mail: colage@colage.org
URL: http://www.colage.org
Contact: Beth Teper, Exec. Dir.
Founded: 1990. **Members:** 7,000. **Membership Dues:** individual, $35 (annual) ● family/household, $60 (annual). **Staff:** 4. **Budget:** $250,000. **Local Groups:** 30. **Description:** Children of lesbian, gay, or transgender parents. Provides support and advocacy for members. Makes available children's services; maintains speakers' bureau; compiles statistics. **Libraries: Type:** lending. **Holdings:** 50. **Subjects:** parenting, GLBT issues. **Awards:** Lee Dubin Memorial Scholarship. **Frequency:** annual. **Type:** monetary. **Recipient:** for children of GLBT parent. **Computer Services:** database, email chat lists ● mailing lists, of members ● online services, publication. **Committees:** Scholarship. **Formerly:** Children of Lesbians and Gays Everywhere. **Publications:** *Just for Us*, quarterly. Newsletter. **Circulation:** 2,000. Also Cited As: *JFU*. **Conventions/Meetings:** annual Family Week - conference (exhibits).

11959 ■ Columbia Queer Alliance (CQA)
c/o NYU Office of LGBT Student Services
Kimmel Ctr.
60 Washington Sq. S, Ste.602
New York, NY 10012
E-mail: shc2107@columbia.edu
URL: http://www.columbia.edu/cu/lbgc
Contact: Sydney Cochran, Pres.
Founded: 1967. **Members:** 100. **Budget:** $1,500. **Description:** Gay, lesbian, and bisexual students, faculty, and staff of Columbia University. Attempts to present as complete a view as possible of the contemporary social, educational, and political gay experience. Aims to: create a gay community at Columbia that will enable its members to relate to each other as people in an unoppressive atmosphere; promote among homosexuals, bisexuals, and heterosexuals alike an enlightened understanding of homosexuality free of the taboos, misconceptions, and stigmatization of a sexist society; fight against the oppression of gay persons, in and out of Columbia. Sponsors discussions as well as many social activities for gay people on campus. Conducts dances to bring together the gay youth of New York City and surrounding areas. Distributes literature to educate the public. Maintains speakers' bureau, biographical archives, and library of 300 volumes on gay life. Compiles statistics. **Libraries: Type:** not open to the public. **Holdings:** 300. **Computer Services:** Mailing lists. **Telecommunication Services:** electronic mail, majordomo@columbia.edu. **Formerly:** (1985) Gay People at Columbia; (1989) Columbia Gay and Lesbian Alliance; (1998) Lesbian Bisexual Gay Coalition. **Supersedes:** (1970) Student Homophile League. **Conventions/Meetings:** weekly meeting.

11960 ■ Community United Against Violence (CUAV)
170 A Capp St.
San Francisco, CA 94110
Ph: (415)777-5500
Fax: (415)777-5565
E-mail: info@cuav.org
URL: http://www.cuav.org
Contact: Andy Wong, Contact
Description: Works to end violence against and within the lesbian, gay, bisexual, transgender and queer/questioning (LGBTQ) communities. Provides free counseling, legal advocacy, and emergency assistance to survivors of domestic violence, hate violence and sexual assault. Uses education as a

violence prevention tool through the speaker's bureau, the youth program and the domestic violence prevention program. **Telecommunication Services:** 24-hour hotline, support line, (415)333-HELP. **Programs:** Domestic Violence; Youth. **Projects:** Hate Violence Advocacy.

11961 ■ Evergreen International

307 W 200 S, Ste.4006
Salt Lake City, UT 84101
Ph: (801)363-3837
Free: (800)391-1000
E-mail: info@evergreeninternational.org
URL: http://www.evergreeninternational.org
Contact: David Pruden, Exec. Dir.

Founded: 1989. **Members:** 2,000. **Membership Dues:** $25 (annual). **Staff:** 2. **Budget:** $150,000. **Regional Groups:** 26. **Languages:** English, Spanish. **Multinational. Description:** Heterosexuals and friends dedicated to helping individuals who desire to change their same-sex orientation. While the group does not condemn homosexuals, members encourage adoption of a heterosexual lifestyle. Promotes reevaluation of the idea that homosexuals cannot change their sexual orientation. Works to clarify issues of identity confusion and same sex attraction; acts as a liaison between available resources and individuals in need of educational and emotional support. Conducts educational programs. Maintains Speaker's Bureau. **Libraries: Type:** reference. **Holdings:** 250; audio recordings, books, clippings, video recordings. **Subjects:** homosexuality, identity, sexual addiction. **Awards: Type:** recognition. **Recipient:** for service to organization. **Subgroups:** The Center for Gender Affirmative Therapy. **Formerly:** Crossroads; (1992) Evergreen Foundation. **Publications:** *Journey*, quarterly. Newsletter. Contains articles and information on group activities. **Price:** included in membership dues. **Circulation:** 800 ● *Resource List*. Bibliography. Lists books, videos, pamphlets, and other publications on overcoming homosexuality. **Price:** included in membership dues. **Circulation:** 1,000. **Conventions/Meetings:** annual conference (exhibits) ● quarterly seminar.

11962 ■ Family Pride Coalition (FPC)

PO Box 65327
Washington, DC 20035-5327
Ph: (202)331-5015
Fax: (202)331-0080
E-mail: info@familypride.org
URL: http://www.familypride.org
Contact: Jennifer Chrisler, Exec. Dir.

Founded: 1979. **Members:** 17,000. **Membership Dues:** individual, family, $35 (annual). **Staff:** 8. **Budget:** $750,000. **Local Groups:** 151. **Description:** Aims to secure equality for lesbian, gay, bisexual and transgender parents and their families through advocacy, education and support. Strives to educate society about the families, supports passage of legislation created to eliminate discrimination due to sexual orientation, coordinates the establishment of local support groups for parents and children, conducts educational outreach programs to educate professionals and the public of the joys, challenges, and special concerns related to gay parenthood. Maintains speakers' bureau. **Libraries: Type:** reference. **Awards:** College Scholarship Fund. **Frequency:** annual. **Type:** scholarship. **Programs:** Children of Lesbians and Gays Everywhere. **Formerly:** Gay Fathers Coalition; (1986) Gay Fathers Coalition International; (1998) Gay and Lesbian Coalition International. **Publications:** *Opening Doors: Creating Policy Change to Include Our Families*. Booklet. Alternate Formats: online ● *Opening Doors: Lesbian and Gay Parents and Schools*. Booklet. Alternate Formats: online ● *Talking to Children About Our Families: Sexual Orientation and Gender Identity*. Booklet. **Price:** $4.00. Alternate Formats: online. **Conventions/Meetings:** annual Family Week in Provincetown - conference (exhibits).

11963 ■ Gay Asian Pacific Alliance (GAPA)

PO Box 421884
San Francisco, CA 94142-1884

E-mail: info@gapa.org
URL: http://gapa.org
Contact: Robert Bernardo, Co-Chm.

Founded: 1988. **Membership Dues:** student/senior (age 60 and above), $10 (annual) ● single, $20 (annual) ● couple/single household, $30 (annual). **Description:** Promotes gay and bisexual Asian/Pacific Islanders, focusing on sexual identity, racial and cultural bond, familial background and values. **Awards:** George Choy Memorial/Gay Asian Pacific Alliance Scholarship. **Type:** scholarship. **Recipient:** to an ardent activist who spoke out for queer APIs. **Computer Services:** Mailing lists, closet list ● mailing lists, open list. **Telecommunication Services:** electronic mail, robert@gapa.org. **Publications:** *Lavender Godzilla*, monthly. Newsletter. Contains articles and announcements. **Advertising:** accepted. Alternate Formats: online.

11964 ■ Gay Asian Pacific Support Network (GAPSN)

PO Box 461104
Los Angeles, CA 90046-1104
Ph: (213)368-6488
E-mail: gapsn@gapsn.org
URL: http://www.gapsn.org
Contact: Tim Chan, Chm.

Founded: 1984. **Membership Dues:** general/supporter for Asian Pacific Islander, $20 (annual) ● student, must be enrolled in 4-year college program, $10 (annual) ● star, $50 (annual) ● superstar, $100 (annual). **Multinational. Description:** Represents gay, bisexual, and transgender Asian Pacific Islander individuals. **Publications:** Newsletter. **Conventions/Meetings:** Socials - meeting.

11965 ■ Gay and Lesbian National Hotline (GLNH)

PMB No. 296
2261 Market St.
San Francisco, CA 94114
Ph: (415)355-0003
Free: (888)THE-GLNH
Fax: (415)552-5498
E-mail: info@glbtnationalhelpcenter.org
URL: http://www.glnh.org
Contact: Brad Becker, Exec. Dir.

Founded: 1995. **Members:** 75. **Description:** Provides nationwide peer counseling, information and referrals to gay, lesbian, bisexual and transgender community, and those with questions about these topics.

11966 ■ Gay Officers' Action League (GOAL)

PO Box 1774
New York, NY 10113
Ph: (212)NY1-GOAL
E-mail: goalny1@goalny.org
URL: http://www.goalny.org
Contact: George J. Farrugia Esq., Pres.

Founded: 1982. **Membership Dues:** criminal justice professional, associate, $25 (annual) ● life, $250. **Description:** Addresses the needs, issues, and concerns of gay and lesbian law enforcement personnel. Advocates for the rights of its members and assists them on matters of discrimination, harassment, and disparate treatment in the workplace. **Awards:** Annual Child's Scholarship. **Frequency:** annual. **Type:** scholarship. **Publications:** *GOAL Gazette*, 10/year. **Advertising:** accepted ● *GOAL NY*. Newsletter. Alternate Formats: online. **Conventions/Meetings:** monthly meeting - always second Tuesday.

11967 ■ HeartStrong

PO Box 2051
Seattle, WA 98111
Ph: (206)388-3894 (206)351-9993
E-mail: heartstrong@heartstrong.org
URL: http://www.heartstrong.org
Contact: Marc Adams, Exec. Dir.

Description: Provides outreach to gay, lesbian, bisexual, transgendered (GLBT) and other persons adversely affected by the influence of all denominations of religious educational institutions. Educates the public about the persecution of GLBTs in religious educational institutions. **Computer Services:** Online

services, HeartStrong News. **Telecommunication Services:** electronic mail, marcadams@heartstrong.org.

11968 ■ Heritage of Pride (HOP)

154 Christopher St., Ste.1D
New York, NY 10014
Ph: (212)807-7433 (212)807-7441
Fax: (212)807-7436
URL: http://www.hopinc.org
Contact: Phil Mannino, Co-Chm.

Founded: 1984. **Members:** 90. **Staff:** 1. **Budget:** $800,000. **Description:** Gay, lesbian, bisexual, transgender, and straight individuals working together to produce and organize the annual Gay and Lesbian Pride Events in New York City. Events include a march, rally, festival, and dance on the last 2 Sundays of every June. **Awards:** David Norrie Award. **Frequency:** annual. **Type:** trophy ● Pride Awards. **Frequency:** annual. **Type:** trophy. **Recipient:** volunteer based ● Spirit of Stonewall Award. **Frequency:** annual. **Type:** trophy. **Recipient:** to individual or organization advancing the cause for equality. **Computer Services:** Mailing lists, to members. **Boards:** Executive. **Committees:** Dance; H.R.; International Association of Gay and Lesbian Pride Organizers; March; Northeastern Regional Pride Conference; PrideFest; Rally. **Subgroups:** Fundraising/Development; Media; Outreach; Volunteer/Membership. **Formerly:** (1985) Christopher Street Liberation Day Committee. **Publications:** *Lavender Line*, quarterly. Newsletter. **Price:** free. **Circulation:** 3,000. **Advertising:** accepted. **Conventions/Meetings:** monthly general assembly, committee chairs present reports, and discussions of major organization-wide policies - every 2nd Monday, except May and June.

11969 ■ Hetrick-Martin Institute (HMI)

740 Broadway, 8th Fl.
New York, NY 10003
Ph: (212)674-2400 (212)674-8695
Fax: (212)674-8650
E-mail: info@hmi.org
URL: http://www.hmi.org
Contact: David K. Mensah, Exec. Dir.

Founded: 1979. **Staff:** 45. **Budget:** $4,000,000. **Languages:** English, Spanish. **Description:** Informs and educates the public and youth service agencies about the needs of gay and lesbian youth. Coordinates existing services, and provides direct service to gay and lesbian youth, including group and individual counseling and referral, outreach services to homeless youth, and education on human sexuality and AIDS. Helps for the development and sponsors the Harvey Milk School, a New York City high school for gay and lesbian students named after slain San Francisco, CA, city supervisor and gay activist Harvey Milk. Researches and disseminates information on youth sexuality and peer education. Sponsors the National Advocacy Coalition on Youth and Sexuality. **Libraries: Type:** reference. **Holdings:** 2,000; articles, books, periodicals. **Subjects:** homosexuality and young people, health, gender, education. **Awards:** Emery's. **Frequency:** annual. **Type:** recognition. **Divisions:** Housing/Transitional; Peer Education; Training; Youth Leadership Training and Placement. **Programs:** National Advocacy Coalition on Youth and Sexual Orientation. **Formerly:** (1987) Institute for the Protection of Lesbian and Gay Youth. **Publications:** *HMI Report Card*, quarterly. Newsletter. **Price:** free ● *Tales of the Closet*, periodic. Directory. Comic book series. ● *You Are Not Alone: National Directory of Lesbian, Gay, and Bisexual Youth Organization* ● Also publishes fact sheets on lesbian, gay, and bisexual youth.

11970 ■ Homosexual Information Center (HIC)

c/o Tangent Group
PO Box 310
Bell, CA 90201
Ph: (585)880-0831
URL: http://www.tangentgroup.org
Contact: Jim Schneider, Pres.

Founded: 1968. **Staff:** 3. **Description:** Educational service of the Tangent Group (see separate entry).

Consultants in the field of homosexuality. Provides speakers for college classes and civic and church groups. Broadcasts radio interviews and discussions with gays and lesbians and informed persons; counsels veterans on their rights in upgrading less-than-honorable discharges; helps with legal cases in instances where decisions may change present antisex laws; refers individuals with legal, medical, and other personal problems to sympathetic, qualified counselors, and agencies for help. Maintains 5500 volume library of books, periodicals, tapes, documents, and records on the gay movement. **Libraries: Type:** reference. **Holdings:** 5,500; books, periodicals. **Subjects:** gay movement. **Affiliated With:** Tangent Group. **Publications:** *A Few Doors West of Hope* ● *A Selected Bibliography of Homosexuality*, periodic ● *Directory of Homosexual Organizations and Publications: A Field Guide to the Homosexual Movement in the United States and Canada with Topical Index.* Includes listing of research centers. ● *Homosexual Information Center— Newsletter*, periodic. Contains articles on sexual freedom, freedom of the press, and civil rights. Includes book reviews. ● *Prostitution Is Legal* ● *Reader at Large* ● *Seeds of the American Sexual Revolution* ● Also publishes bibliographies and subject headings guides. **Conventions/Meetings:** annual meeting - always July, Los Angeles, CA.

11971 ■ Homosexuals Anonymous Fellowship Services (HAFS)
PO Box 7881
Reading, PA 19603-7881
Ph: (610)779-2500
Free: (800)288-HAFS
URL: http://www.ha-fs.org
Contact: John J., Service Coor.
Founded: 1980. **Members:** 400. **Staff:** 1. **Budget:** $85,000. **Local Groups:** 50. **Description:** Serves as a self-help group for individuals seeking "freedom from homosexuality." Seeks to help each other realize their true identity as part of "God's heterosexual creation." Offers support and guidance through weekly meeting; holds training sessions. **Publications:** *Experience, Strength and Hope.* Book. Contains explanatory articles on 14-step program. Alternate Formats: CD-ROM ● *HA News*, monthly. Newsletter. Includes directory. **Price:** free on request ● *Lord, Set Me Free!* (in English and Spanish). Book. Self-help workbook. Alternate Formats: CD-ROM ● *The Path to Freedom.* Video. Features explanation of HAFS' Program. ● Brochures ● Monographs. **Conventions/Meetings:** weekly Chapter Meeting ● annual conference, fellowship and informative speakers for interested persons ● Recovery Seminar, utilizes 14-step program and Christian ministry ● Training Seminar, helps interested parties start and maintain HA chapters.

11972 ■ Immigration Equality
40 Exchange Pl., 17th Fl.
New York, NY 10005
Ph: (212)714-2904
Fax: (212)714-2973
E-mail: info@immigrationequality.org
URL: http://www.immigrationequality.org
Contact: Ms. Rachel B. Tiven Esq., Exec. Dir.
Founded: 1994. **Members:** 10,000. **Membership Dues:** individual, $50 (annual) ● couple/family, $75 (annual) ● friend, $100 (annual) ● low income, $25 (annual). **Regional Groups:** 19. **Languages:** English, Spanish. **Description:** Advocates for equal immigration rights for lesbian, gay, bisexual, transgender and HIV-positive people. **Formerly:** (2004) Lesbian and Gay Immigration Rights Task Force. **Publications:** *Sexual Orientation Based Asylum Handbook.* Alternate Formats: online ● Brochures.

11973 ■ International Federation of Black Prides (IFBP)
PO Box 1301
Washington, DC 20013
E-mail: admin@ifbprides.org
URL: http://www.ifbprides.org
Contact: Earl Fowlkes, Pres./CEO
Founded: 1999. **Membership Dues:** regular, $100 (annual). **Multinational. Description:** Promotes a multinational network of LGBT/SGL (Lesbian, Gay, Bisexual, Transgender/Same Gender Loving) Prides and community-based organizations. Seeks to eliminate discrimination against gay and lesbian individuals. Provides support, mentoring, networking and technical assistance. Facilitates communication and cooperation among members.

11974 ■ International Gay and Lesbian Human Rights Commission (IGLHRC)
80 Maiden Ln., Ste.1505
New York, NY 10038
Ph: (212)268-8040 (212)430-6051
Fax: (212)430-6060
E-mail: iglhrc@iglhrc.org
URL: http://www.iglhrc.org
Contact: Paula Ettelbrick, Exec. Dir.
Founded: 1990. **Members:** 6,000. **Staff:** 9. **Budget:** $1,000,000. **Languages:** English, Russian, Spanish. **Description:** Works to secure the full enjoyment of human rights of all people and communities subject to discrimination and abuse on the basis of sexual orientation or expression, gender identity, and/or HIV status through advocacy, documentation, coalition building, public education, and technical assistance. **Libraries: Type:** reference. **Awards:** The Felipa Award. **Frequency:** annual. **Type:** recognition. **Recipient:** for LGBT and HIV positive activists from around the world. **Computer Services:** Mailing lists, Emergency Response Network Action Alert email. **Telecommunication Services:** electronic mail, pettelbrick@iglhrc.org. **Publications:** *Emergency Response Network* (in English and Spanish), weekly. Newsletter. **Price:** free. **Circulation:** 4,000. Alternate Formats: online ● *Human Rights Reports* ● *The Rights of Lesbians and Gay Men in the Russian Federation.* **Price:** $12.00/year, plus $3 shipping. **Circulation:** 1,000. **Conventions/Meetings:** periodic conference.

11975 ■ InterPride
c/o Southern Maine Pride
PO Box 9715
Portland, ME 04104-5015
Ph: (207)773-4188
E-mail: info@interpride.org
URL: http://www.interpride.org
Contact: Russell Murphy, Co-Pres.
Founded: 1982. **Members:** 350. **Membership Dues:** organization (with $100,000 or less annual gross income), $6-$125 (annual) ● organization (with more than $250,000 annual gross income), $218-$625 (annual). **Staff:** 1. **Budget:** $40,000. **Regional Groups:** 9. **State Groups:** 45. **Languages:** English, French, Spanish. **Multinational. Description:** Organizations involved in the organization of community lesbian and gay pride celebrations and activities. Promotes festivals celebrating the contributions of gay and lesbian people to their communities. Conducts charitable and educational programs; maintains speakers' bureau; operates museum and hall of fame. **Awards:** Conference Grant. **Frequency:** annual. **Type:** grant. **Recipient:** for qualified organizations. **Computer Services:** Electronic publishing, newsletter ● mailing lists, of members ● online services, publication. **Boards:** Directors. **Committees:** Regional Directors. **Formerly:** (2001) International Association of Lesbian/Gay Pride Coordinators. **Publications:** *Anomaly*, quarterly. Newsletter. Contains organizational and national news updates. **Price:** free for members. **Circulation:** 350. **Advertising:** accepted. Alternate Formats: online ● Newsletter, quarterly. Alternate Formats: online. **Conventions/Meetings:** annual IAL/GPC Pride Fest - conference and workshop, discussion groups, support groups (exhibits) - mid-October.

11976 ■ Lambda Legal Defense and Education Fund (LLDEF)
120 Wall St., Ste.1500
New York, NY 10005-3904
Ph: (212)809-8585
Fax: (212)809-0055
E-mail: members@lambdalegal.org
URL: http://www.lambdalegal.org
Contact: Kevin M. Cathcart, Exec. Dir.
Founded: 1973. **Members:** 22,000. **Membership Dues:** regular, $40 (annual). **Staff:** 80. **Budget:** $8,700,000. **Regional Groups:** 3. **Description:** Aims to defend the civil rights of lesbians, gay men, bisexuals, the transgendered and people with HIV or AIDS, in areas such as employment, housing, education, child custody, and the delivery of medical and social services. Engages in test case litigation as counsel or as "a friend of the court" to help inform the court of the civil rights and needs of lesbians, gay men, bisexuals, the transgendered and people with HIV or AIDS. Provides resources and assistance to attorneys working on behalf of gay clients. Maintains a national network of cooperating attorneys. Helps inform the gay community about its rights and recent legal developments. Educates the public and the legal community about issues and concerns of lesbians, gay men, bisexuals, the transgendered and people with HIV or AIDS. Operates speakers' bureau; sponsors seminars; compiles statistics. Maintains web site containing court decisions and copies of briefs and pleadings. **Awards:** Lambda Liberty Award. **Type:** recognition. **Recipient:** for service in the gay/lesbian community. **Programs:** Education; Legal. **Publications:** *Changing Lives, Changing Minds*, annual. Annual Report. Alternate Formats: online ● *Lamba Legal Video: 2005.* Alternate Formats: online ● *Lambda Update*, triennial. Newsletter. Reports on the court cases in which LLDEF is involved and issues of concern to the organization and its members. **Price:** $40.00. ISSN: 1058-949X. **Circulation:** 25,000. Alternate Formats: online ● Brochures, annual. Alternate Formats: online ● Booklets, annual. **Conventions/Meetings:** annual meeting.

11977 ■ Lesbian, Bisexual, Gay and Transgendered United Employees at AT&T (LEAGUE)
c/o Sheldon Hogueisson
555 S Executive Dr.
Brookfield, WI 53005
Ph: (703)691-5734
E-mail: attleague@aol.com
URL: http://www.league-att.org
Contact: Mr. Mark Carden, Natl. Co-Pres.
Founded: 1987. **Membership Dues:** individual, $15 (annual). **State Groups:** 10. **Description:** Individuals employed at or retired from AT&T or any of its subsidiaries. Fosters the value of mutual respect and appreciation of cultural differences among employees. Offers educational programs and support groups to address issues that affect lesbian, gay, and bisexual employees, and their friends and families. Acts as an information clearinghouse on homosexuality, bisexuality, and lesbian and gay issues. Provides referral services to support groups and community and service organizations. **Libraries: Type:** lending. **Holdings:** books, video recordings. **Telecommunication Services:** TDD, (800)855-2880. **Committees:** Benefits; Diversity; Education; Marketing; Professional Development. **Conventions/Meetings:** annual Professional Development Conference (exhibits).

11978 ■ Lesbian, Gay, Bisexual, and Transgender People in Medicine (LGBTPM)
c/o American Medical Student Association
1902 Assn. Dr.
Reston, VA 20191
Ph: (703)620-6600
Free: (800)767-2266
Fax: (703)620-5873
E-mail: bhurley@usc.edu
URL: http://www.amsa.org/advocacy/lgbtpm
Contact: Brian Hurley, Natl.Coor.
Founded: 1976. **Members:** 350. **Local Groups:** 35. **Description:** Advocacy Group of the American Medical Student Association. Physicians and physicians in training; others interested in gay/lesbian issues. Purposes are to improve the quality of health care for gay patients; to improve working conditions and professional status of gay health professionals and students. Administers educational workshops for

health professionals; designs training materials; conducts research on the health problems of gay people and surveys on admissions, hiring, and promotion policies of medical schools and hospitals; provides referrals; sponsors support groups for gay professionals to meet, socialize, and organize; presses for legislative and political action to end discrimination against gay people. Maintains speakers' bureau. **Affiliated With:** American Medical Student Association. **Formerly:** (1980) Gay People in Medicine; (1985) Lesbian and Gay People in Medicine; (2004) Lesbian, Gay and Bisexual People in Medicine. **Publications:** *LGBTPM Residency Survey*, biennial. Alternate Formats: online ● *Paint Your School Pink*. Handbook ● Newsletter, semiannual. **Conventions/Meetings:** annual conference (exhibits).

11979 ■ Lesbian Resource Center (LRC)
227 S Orcas St.
Seattle, WA 98108
Ph: (206)322-3953 (206)322-3965
Fax: (206)322-0586
E-mail: lrc@lrc.net
URL: http://www.lrc.net
Contact: Alex Miller, Sec.
Founded: 1971. **Staff:** 5. **Budget:** $225,000. **Description:** Provides classes, groups, workshops, and information on housing, employment, and lesbian community groups and events. Represents the lesbian community in areas of political and social concern. **Convention/Meeting:** none. **Libraries: Type:** open to the public; lending; reference. **Holdings:** 1,500; books, periodicals. **Subjects:** lesbian/bisexual women's interest, feminism. **Committees:** Scholarship. **Also Known As:** Pacific Women's Resources. **Formerly:** (1973) Gay Women's Alliance. **Publications:** *Lesbian Resource Center News*, monthly. Newspaper. Covers community and center events; includes calendar, editorials, news, and feature stories. **Price:** free; $35.00 /year for nonmembers. **Circulation:** 10,000. **Advertising:** accepted.

11980 ■ National Association of Social Workers National Committee on Lesbian, Gay and Bisexual Issues (NASW)
750 First St. NE, Ste.700
Washington, DC 20002-4241
Ph: (202)408-8600
Free: (800)742-4089
E-mail: membership@naswdc.org
URL: http://www.socialworkers.org/governance/cmtes/nclgbi.asp
Contact: Elizabeth J. Clark PhD, Exec. Dir.
Founded: 1976. **Members:** 5. **Staff:** 1. **State Groups:** 30. **Description:** A committee of the National Association of Social Workers. Seeks to ensure equal employment opportunities for lesbian, gay and bisexual individuals. Informs the NASW about: domestic, racial, and antigay violence; civil rights; family and primary associations. Encourages the NASW to support legislation, regulations, policies, judicial review, political action, and other activities that seek to establish and protect equal rights for all persons without regard to affectional and/or sexual orientation. Advises government bodies and political candidates regarding the needs and concerns of social workers and lesbian and gay people; reviews proposed legislation. **Libraries: Type:** by appointment only. **Formerly:** National Association of Social Workers Committee on Lesbian and Gay Issues; (1998) National Association of Social Workers-National Committee on Lesbian and Gay Issues. **Publications:** *Lesbian and Gay Issues: A Resource Manual*. **Conventions/Meetings:** annual conference and meeting.

11981 ■ National Center for Lesbian Rights (NCLR)
870 Market St., Ste.370
San Francisco, CA 94102
Ph: (415)392-6257
Fax: (415)392-8442

E-mail: info@nclrights.org
URL: http://www.nclrights.org
Contact: Kate Kendell Esq., Exec. Dir.
Founded: 1977. **Membership Dues:** student, low-income, $20 (annual) ● individual, $40 (annual) ● family, $65 (annual) ● sustaining, $100 (annual). **Staff:** 15. **Budget:** $2,400,000. **Regional Groups:** 2. **State Groups:** 1. **Languages:** English, Spanish. **Description:** A legal resource center specializing in sexual orientation discrimination cases, particularly those involving lesbians. Activities include: legal counseling and representation, community education, and technical assistance. Provides legal services to lesbian, gay and transgender youths, adults and elders on issues of custody and foster parenting, visitation rights second parent adoption. **Libraries: Type:** reference. **Holdings:** archival material, articles, books, clippings. **Subjects:** law. **Projects:** Elder Law; Family Law; Immigration/Asylum; Youth. **Formerly:** (1989) Lesbian Rights Project. **Publications:** *Lesbian Mother Litigation Manual* ● *Lesbians Choosing Motherhood: Legal Implications of Alternative Insemination & Reproductive Technologies* ● *Life Lines: Documents to Protect You and Your Family in Times of Trouble*. Alternate Formats: online ● *Recognizing Lesbian and Gay Families* ● *Recognizing Lesbian and Gay Families: Strategies for Obtaining Domestic Partner's Benefits* ● *Transgender Equality: A Handbook for Activists and Policymakers*. **Conventions/Meetings:** monthly Free Immigration Clinics - meeting - first Wednesday, in San Francisco ● Partnership Protection Custody Rights - workshop, on legal issues for lesbians.

11982 ■ National Coalition for LGBT Health
1407 S St. NW
Washington, DC 20009
Ph: (202)797-3516
Fax: (202)797-4430
E-mail: coalition@lgbthealth.net
URL: http://www.lgbthealth.net
Contact: Jay Laudato, Exec. Dir.
Membership Dues: individual, $50 (annual) ● organization (based on budget income), $250-$7,000 (annual). **Description:** Aims to improve the health and well-being of lesbian, gay, bisexual and transgender individuals through federal advocacy that is focused on research, policy, education and training. Increases knowledge regarding Lesbian, Gay, Bisexual and Transgender (LGBT) populations' health status, access to and utilization of health care and other health-related information. Increases LGBT participation in the formation of public and private sector policy regarding health and related issues. Eliminates disparities in health outcomes of LGBT populations and the community including differences that occur by gender, race, education, disability, nationality, geographic location, age, sexual orientation or gender identity.

11983 ■ National Coming Out Day (NCOD)
c/o Human Rights Campaign
1640 Rhode Island Ave. NW
Washington, DC 20036-3200
Ph: (202)628-4160
Free: (800)777-4723
Fax: (202)347-5323
E-mail: comingout@hrc.org
URL: http://www.hrc.org/comingout
Founded: 1988. **Staff:** 2. **Description:** A project of the Human Rights Campaign. Works to increase the gay/lesbian community's visibility and demonstrate its diversity by: Coordinating National Coming Out Day, an annual campaign taking place on October 11; encouraging gay and lesbian individuals to "come out" to friends, family, and coworkers; coordinating a national public relations campaign. Offers support and technical assistance to local gay/lesbian organizations. Makes available shirts, posters, and buttons to organizations for wholesale distribution and retail. Conducts national and local educational programs and activities; maintains speakers' bureau. **Libraries: Type:** reference. **Holdings:** clippings. **Subjects:** coming out for lesbians, gays, and bisexuals; gay, lesbian, and bisexual organizations and businesses. **Telecommunication Services:** TDD, (202)628-4169

● additional toll-free number, (800)866-6263. **Publications:** *Talk About It: A Coming Out Resource for GLBT Americans*, periodic. **Advertising:** accepted. **Conventions/Meetings:** annual meeting, celebration to begin a dialogue with non-gay America - every October 11th.

11984 ■ National Gay and Lesbian Task Force (NGLTF)
1325 Massachusetts Ave. NW, Ste.600
Washington, DC 20005
Ph: (202)393-5177 (202)639-6333
Fax: (202)393-2241
E-mail: thetaskforce@thetaskforce.org
URL: http://www.ngltf.org
Contact: Matt Foreman, Exec. Dir.
Founded: 1973. **Members:** 37,000. **Membership Dues:** individual, $40 (annual) ● student/senior/partially employed, $20 (annual) ● family, $75 (annual) ● advocate, $125 (annual) ● activist, $250 (annual) ● ambassador, $500 (annual) ● Leadership Council, $1,500 (annual). **Staff:** 35. **Budget:** $4,200,000. **Description:** Works to end violence and discrimination against gay, lesbian, bisexual, and transgendered people at the state, local, and federal level. Does grassroots organizing, training, and legislative advocacy. Monitors and tracks legislation in 50 states. Houses GLBT think tank producing research and analysis on GLBT issues. Maintains speakers' bureau. **Awards:** Leadership Award. **Frequency:** annual. **Type:** recognition. **Recipient:** to community leaders, allies and groups. **Councils:** Leadership. **Departments:** Media and Communications; Organizing and Training. **Projects:** Anti-Violence; Campus; Civil Rights; Legislative; Lesbian/Gay Families; Media; Privacy; Transgender Civil Rights. **Affiliated With:** International Lesbian and Gay Association. **Formerly:** National Gay Task Force; NGLTF Policy Institute. **Publications:** *Capital Gains and Losses: State by State Review of Gay, Lesbian, Bisexual, Transgender and HIV/AIDS Related Legislation in 1999*, annual. Book. **Price:** $10.00 ● *Creating Change*. Newsletter. Alternate Formats: online ● *Frontline*, quarterly. Newsletter. Alternate Formats: online ● *State Legislative Update: Review of State Legislation*, monthly. Newsletter ● *Task Force Report*, quarterly. Newsletter ● Reports, periodic. Covers policy on gay, lesbian, bisexual, and transgender issues. Alternate Formats: online. **Conventions/Meetings:** annual Creating Change Conference - 2008 Feb. 6-12, Detroit, MI ● semiannual National Policy Roundtable - meeting ● semiannual National Religious Leadership Roundtable - meeting.

11985 ■ NOLOSE - The National Organization for Lesbians of Size
PO Box 7522
Ann Arbor, MI 48107
Ph: (510)541-5948
E-mail: info@nolose.org
URL: http://www.nolose.org
Contact: Max Airborne, Pres.
Staff: 7. **Description:** Provides support for fat or fat-positive lesbians, bi-women, trans folks, and allies. **Publications:** Newsletter. **Conventions/Meetings:** conference.

11986 ■ ONE, Inc. (OI)
c/o Institute for the Study of Human Resources
PO Box 191728
Los Angeles, CA 90019-1028
Ph: (323)737-1066
Fax: (323)737-0212
E-mail: info@ishrdbaone.org
URL: http://www.ishrdbaone.org
Contact: Thomas Hunter Russell JD, Pres.
Founded: 1952. **Description:** Promotes, assists, encourages and fosters scientific research, study and investigation of male and female homosexuality and various other types of human behavior; to advance education, educational facilities and the training of persons for the aid and betterment of persons having behavioral patterns which may result in social disorientation; and to gather, analyze and evaluate from a unified point of view available data from the fields of anthropology, biology, medicine, psychology,

law, religion and other studies, and to generally do anything and everything necessary, expedient or incidental to the carrying of the above purpose. **Awards:** David Cameron Legal Research Award. **Frequency:** annual. **Type:** grant. **Recipient:** to scholars doing research and dissertations to benefit gay, lesbian, and transgender communities ● Dr. H. Hamilton Williams PhD Scholarship Award. **Type:** grant. **Recipient:** to scholars doing research and dissertations to benefit gay, lesbian, and transgender communities ● Hall Call Mattachine Scholar Award. **Type:** grant. **Recipient:** to scholars doing research and dissertations to benefit gay, lesbian, and transgender communities ● Howard Beck Scholar Award. **Type:** grant. **Recipient:** to scholars doing research and dissertations to benefit gay, lesbian, and transgender communities ● University Scholarships. **Frequency:** biennial. **Type:** scholarship. **Also Known As:** Institute for the Study of Human Resources. **Conventions/Meetings:** biennial seminar and symposium ● periodic seminar and symposium.

11987 ■ OutProud
369 3rd St., Ste.B-362
San Rafael, CA 94901-3581
E-mail: info@outproud.org
URL: http://www.outproud.org
Contact: Christopher A. Kryzan, Exec. Dir.
Founded: 1993. **Budget:** $10,000. **Description:** Provides education, advocacy, support and organizing resources for gay, lesbian, bisexual and transgender youth. **Libraries: Type:** reference. **Holdings:** books. **Subjects:** families, parents, youth, transgendered individuals. **Computer Services:** Online services, publication. **Formerly:** (2003) !Out Proud! The National Coalition for Gay, Lesbian, Bisexual and Transgender Youth.

11988 ■ Parents, Families, and Friends of Lesbians and Gays (PFLAG)
1726 M St. NW, Ste.400
Washington, DC 20036
Ph: (202)467-8180
Fax: (202)467-8194
E-mail: info@pflag.org
URL: http://www.pflag.org
Contact: Jody M. Huckaby, Exec. Dir.
Founded: 1981. **Members:** 200,000. **Membership Dues:** household, $35 (annual) ● individual household, $40 (annual). **Staff:** 17. **Budget:** $2,500,000. **Regional Groups:** 14. **Local Groups:** 425. **Languages:** English, Spanish. **Description:** Represents communities nationwide, promotes the health and well-being of gay, lesbian, bisexual, and transgendered persons, their family and friends through: support, to cope with an adverse society; education, to enlighten an ill-informed public; and advocacy; to end discrimination and to secure equal civil rights. Provides opportunity for dialogue about sexual orientation and gender identity, and acts to create a society that is healthy and respectful of human diversity. **Libraries: Type:** reference. **Subjects:** information for parents of gays and lesbians on youth issues, homosexuality and religion, biology. **Awards: Type:** recognition. **Formerly:** (1993) Parents and Friends of Lesbians and Gays. **Publications:** Be Yourself. Booklet. Features a coming-out guide for youth. ● Be Yourself: Q&A for Gay, Lesbian, and Bisexual Youth ● Beyond the Bible: Parents, Families, and Friends Talk About Religion and Homosexuality. Booklet ● Opening Straight Spouse's Closet. Booklet ● Our Daughters and Sons: Q&A for Parents of Gay, Lesbian, and Bisexual People. Booklet ● PFLAGpole Newsletter, quarterly. Covers regional and national news. ● Recommended Reading List ● "Respect All Youth" Issues Papers ● 10 Simple Things You Can Do to End Homophobia ● Audiotapes ● Videos. **Conventions/Meetings:** annual conference and regional meeting ● biennial convention ● annual international conference (exhibits) - always Labor Day weekend ● seminar and workshop.

11989 ■ Parents and Friends of Ex-Gays and Gays (P-FOX)
c/o Regina Griggs, Exec. Dir.
PO Box 561
Fort Belvoir, VA 22060-0561

Ph: (703)360-2225
E-mail: pfox@pfox.org
URL: http://www.pfox.org
Contact: Regina Griggs, Exec. Dir.
Founded: 1996. **Description:** Seeks to educate the public about "ex-gays, former lesbians and homosexuals". Conducts educational programs. **Publications:** Is Change Possible?. Brochure. Alternate Formats: online ● PFOXPRESS, bimonthly. Newsletter.

11990 ■ Rainbow Alliance of the Deaf (RAD)
c/o Steven Schumacher, Sec.
9804 Walker House Rd., No. 4
Montgomery Village, MD 20886-0506
E-mail: president@rad.org
URL: http://www.rad.org
Contact: Bob Donaldson, Pres.
Founded: 1977. **Members:** 500. **Membership Dues:** individual, $25 (annual) ● chapter, $150 (biennial). **Budget:** $2,500. **Regional Groups:** 2. **State Groups:** 24. **Local Groups:** 22. **Languages:** English, French, Spanish. **Description:** Seeks to foster the educational, economical and social welfare of deaf Lesbian, Gay, Bisexual, Transgender and Questioning (LGBTQ). Represents the interests and promotes the rights of deaf gay and lesbians. **Libraries: Type:** reference. **Subjects:** deaf gay, lesbians and bisexuals. **Committees;** Conference Co-Chairs; Deaf Glow Representative; Deaf Queer Resource Center; Historian; Lesbian Member at Large; Pageant Coordinator; RER Representative; Seniors; Webmaster. **Affiliated With:** National Association of the Deaf. **Conventions/Meetings:** biennial conference (exhibits).

11991 ■ Senior Action in a Gay Environment (SAGE)
305 7th Ave., 16th Fl.
New York, NY 10001
Ph: (212)741-2247
E-mail: info@sageusa.org
URL: http://www.sageusa.org
Contact: Michael Adams, Exec. Dir.
Founded: 1977. **Members:** 4,000. **Membership Dues:** individual, $35 (annual) ● family, $50 (annual) ● sponsor, $75 (annual) ● patron, $125 (annual). **Staff:** 7. **Budget:** $550,000. **Description:** Professional social workers and trained volunteers including doctors, lawyers, psychologists, gerontologists, and others dedicated to meeting the needs of older gays and lesbians and ending the isolation that has kept them separate from each other, other gays, and from the larger community. Centered in the New York City area, SAGE provides: information and referral in areas of legal matters, assessments, and friendly visitor homebound program; individual and group counseling, including bereavement services; social activities to reduce loneliness, rebuild relationships, and establish supportive connections with the gay and lesbian community. Provides in-service training for agency members and institutions serving older gays. Educates professionals and the public with regard to lesbian and gay aging. Sponsors AIDS Service Program for the Elderly. Conducts weekly workshops and training programs for volunteers and social service agencies interested in issues of lesbian and gay aging. Maintains speakers bureau; conducts research programs; compiles statistics. **Awards:** Lifetime Achievement Award. **Frequency:** annual. **Type:** recognition. **Recipient:** for achievement in gay and lesbian community. **Committees:** Assessors; Brunch; Cultural Diversity and Inclusion; Development; Friendly Visiting; Fundraising; Group Activities; Long Range Planning; Nominating; Public Information, Communication, and Education; Women's Special Events. **Departments:** Clinical and Social Services; Community Organizing and Caregiving Services; Development and Fundraising; Education and Advocacy; Group and Volunteer Services. **Publications:** SAGE Bulletin, monthly. **Price:** free for members. **Circulation:** 4,000. **Conventions/Meetings:** annual conference.

11992 ■ Tangent Group (TG)
PO Box 310
Bell, CA 90201
Ph: (585)880-0831
URL: http://www.tangentgroup.org
Contact: Jim Schneider, Pres.
Founded: 1965. **Members:** 20. **Description:** Supports the Homosexual Information Center by donations of money and time. Conducts charitable programs; maintains speakers' bureau. **Also Known As:** Tangents. **Publications:** Tangents Magazine, annual. Alternate Formats: online. **Conventions/Meetings:** annual meeting - always July, Los Angeles, CA.

11993 ■ Trikone
PO Box 14161
San Francisco, CA 94114
Ph: (415)487-8778
E-mail: trikone@trikone.org
URL: http://www.trikone.org
Founded: 1986. **Membership Dues:** subscriber in U.S. and Canada, $15 (annual) ● subscriber outside U.S. and Canada, $30 (annual) ● life, $700. **Description:** Participants are gay and lesbian persons living in Southern Asia or of Southern Asian descent and their friends. Support group for gay or lesbian persons from Southern Asia. Seeks to help participants come to terms with their sexual orientation. Networks with homosexual groups around the world. Compiles material for a gay/lesbian archives to document the history of homosexuality in the area. **Libraries: Type:** reference. **Holdings:** 13. **Subjects:** South Asian lesbian gay issues. **Awards:** Pink Peacock. **Type:** recognition. **Computer Services:** Mailing lists, of members. **Formerly:** (1987) Trikon. **Publications:** Trikon, quarterly. Magazine. Includes personal stories, interviews, news about gay and lesbian South Asians, letters, personal ads, and resource listings. **Price:** $12.95/year in North America; $24.95/year outside North America. ISSN: 1042-735X. **Circulation:** 6,400. **Advertising:** accepted. Alternate Formats: online ● Trikone Magazine December 2004: Touch of Pink, Touch of Blue. **Price:** $3.95. Alternate Formats: online ● Trikone Magazine June 2004: Bollywood Dreams. **Price:** $3.95. Alternate Formats: online ● Trikone Magazine March 2005: Out There: Who's Making Waves in the South Asian Queer Communities. **Price:** $3.95 ● Trikone Magazine September 2004: Immigration—Crossing Borders. **Price:** $3.95. Alternate Formats: online. **Conventions/Meetings:** DesiQ - convention - every 5-6 years. 2010 June 23-26, San Francisco, CA.

Genocide

11994 ■ Help Darfur Now (HDN)
PO Box 5062
Basking Ridge, NJ 07920-5062
Ph: (908)647-4198
E-mail: arielle@helpdarfurnow.org
URL: http://www.helpdarfurnow.org
Contact: Arielle Wisotsky, Co-Founder
Founded: 2005. **Multinational. Description:** Represents educators, parents, community leaders, and other individuals who are interested in helping victims of genocide in Darfur. Raises funds and awareness for the genocide in Darfur, Sudan. Provides information on issues concerning Darfur and its people.

Gerontology

11995 ■ Brookdale Foundation
950 3rd Ave., 19th Fl.
New York, NY 10022
Ph: (212)308-7355
Fax: (212)750-0132
E-mail: janetsainer@brookdalefoundation.org
URL: http://www.brookdalefoundation.org
Contact: Janet Sainier, Special Consultant
Description: Works to support the elderly. **Awards: Type:** grant. **Programs:** Brookdale Leadership in Ag-

ing Fellowship; Brookdale National Fellowship; The Group Respite; Relatives as Parents.

Grandparents

11996 ■ Foundation for Grandparenting (FG)
108 Farnham Rd.
Ojai, CA 93023
E-mail: gpfound@grandparenting.org
URL: http://www.grandparenting.org
Contact: Arthur Kornhaber MD, Founder/Pres.
Founded: 1980. **Description:** Dedicated to the betterment of society through intergenerational involvement. Seeks to increase public awareness of the importance of the grandparent/grandchild bond. Goal is to assure grandparents their rightful place in society through education, demonstration projects, researches, and support. Plans to develop grandparent programs in which elders visit youngsters in residential settings; to establish a national policy regarding grandparents' role in society; to serve as a central clearinghouse through the Grandparent Network; to organize a grandparent clinical project where grandparents can learn to help families in times of stress. Is working toward raising funds for a National Grandparent Center and the Centrum Project, a multigeneration elementary school and day care center where children, teachers, and elders work together. Sponsors grandparent/grandchild summer camp. Hopes to organize a grandparent conference and workshop and grandparents' day in schools. Is currently developing funding. Maintains speakers' bureau. **Publications:** *Vital Connections*, quarterly. Newsletter. **Price:** $20.00/year. **Circulation:** 10,000 ● Bibliography. Features annotated bibliography/filmography developed collectively with the Westchester Library System. ● Plans to compile a grandparent reading list. **Conventions/Meetings:** annual conference.

11997 ■ Grandparents as Parents (GAP)
22048 Sherman Way, Ste.217
Canoga Park, CA 91303
Ph: (562)421-7991 (818)789-1177
Fax: (818)264-0882
E-mail: madelyng@grandparentsasparents.com
URL: http://www.grandparentsasparents.com
Contact: Madelyn Gordon, Exec. Dir.
Founded: 1987. **Regional Groups:** 8. **Nonmembership. Description:** Seeks to "provide the foundation crucial to the development of the whole and healthy family environments, and to educate relative caregivers as to their rights and responsibilities". Operates psychological, emotional, and peer support groups for grandparents functioning as parents; networks with local child welfare and related agencies to assure public response to the needs of grandparents functioning as parents; provides counseling and referral services to children being raised by their grandparents. **Computer Services:** Mailing lists, of members. **Publications:** *Filling the GAP*, quarterly. Newsletter ● Book.

11998 ■ Grandparents Rights Organization (GRO)
100 W Long Lake Rd., Ste.250
Bloomfield Hills, MI 48304
Ph: (248)646-7177 (248)646-7191
Fax: (248)646-9722
E-mail: rsvlaw@aol.com
URL: http://grandparentsrights.org
Contact: Richard S. Victor, Exec. Dir.
Founded: 1984. **Members:** 1,000. **Membership Dues:** regular, $40 (annual). **Staff:** 4. **Description:** Conducts educational and advocacy activities aimed at preserving and fostering the child-grandparent relationship in cases where grandparents have been denied the right to visit their grandchildren for any reason. Conducts research programs; compiles statistics. **Publications:** *Grandparents Rights Organization Newsletter*, periodic. **Price:** included in membership dues.

Guardians

11999 ■ Guardian Association of Pinellas County (GAPC)
PO Box 1826
Pinellas Park, FL 33780
Ph: (727)323-9380
Fax: (727)323-7140
E-mail: info@guardianassociation.org
URL: http://www.guardianassociation.org
Contact: Patricia Hall, Exec. Dir.
Founded: 1977. **Members:** 300. **Membership Dues:** corporation, $50 (annual) ● individual, $35 (annual). **Description:** Legal guardians and others supportive of quality guardianship services. Educates legal guardians, professionals, and other individuals involved with guardianship issues. Serves on local and state legislative committees. Provides public speakers and informal recruitment services to assist the court and all those needing qualified guardians. Sponsors (with junior college) seminars and training classes that work to improve the guardianship system and set standards for guardians. GA operates in the state of Florida, where there is a high concentration of legal guardians. **Committees:** Education; Grievance and Review; Legislative; Public Relations; Speakers' Bureau; Standards and Ethics. **Also Known As:** Guardian Association of Pinellas County. **Publications:** *The Professional Guardian*, monthly. Newsletter. Includes court developments, legal and medical news, services available, meetings, and local happenings, legislation, etc. **Price:** included in membership dues. **Advertising:** accepted. **Conventions/Meetings:** annual Expo - seminar (exhibits).

Haiti

12000 ■ Mission to Haiti
PO Box 523157
Miami, FL 33152-3157
Ph: (305)823-7516
Fax: (305)362-4211
E-mail: info@missiontohaiti.org
URL: http://www.missiontohaiti.org
Contact: Bill Nealey Sr., Exec. Dir.
Founded: 1994. **Multinational. Description:** Brings volunteers to the field to serve the Haitian people through building projects, medical clinics and Bible schools for children. Distributes beans and rice to needy families in Haiti. Shares the Gospel and helps improve the daily lives of the Haitian people. **Publications:** *The Vision*, monthly. Newsletter. Alternate Formats: online.

Health

12001 ■ Circle of Health International (COHI)
PO Box 163323
Austin, TX 78716-3323
Ph: (512)517-3220
E-mail: info@cohintl.org
URL: http://www.cohintl.org
Contact: Sera Bonds, Exec. Dir./Founder
Multinational. Description: Empowers women in conflict and disaster zones worldwide. Balances the scales of access and equity through the provision of women's health services and training in conflict and post-conflict zones. Addresses literacy, basic public health care and women's issues, leadership development and sustainability. **Computer Services:** Mailing lists. **Publications:** *The Circle*. Newsletter. Alternate Formats: online.

12002 ■ National Latino Council on Alcohol and Tobacco Prevention (LCAT)
1616 P St. NW., Ste.430
Washington, DC 20036
Ph: (202)265-8054
Fax: (202)265-8056

E-mail: lcat@nlcatp.org
URL: http://www.nlcatp.org
Contact: Marilyn Aguirre-Molina EdD, Pres.
Founded: 1989. **Staff:** 5. **Description:** Seeks to combat alcohol and tobacco problems and their underlying causes in Latino communities. Reduces the harm caused by alcohol and tobacco in the Latino community through research, advocacy and policy analysis. Provides community education, training and information dissemination on alcohol and tobacco prevention. **Libraries: Type:** reference. **Holdings:** 1,500; articles, books, papers, periodicals, reports, video recordings. **Subjects:** alcohol, tobacco, gender issues. **Computer Services:** Information services, tobacco resources ● online services, national directory of professionals. **Programs:** Strengthening Hispanic/Latino Tobacco Prevention and Control. **Subgroups:** Speakers Bureau. **Publications:** *LCAT News*. Newsletter. Alternate Formats: online.

12003 ■ Partners in Health (PIH)
641 Huntington Ave., 1st Fl.
Boston, MA 02115
Ph: (617)432-5256
Fax: (617)432-5300
E-mail: info@pih.org
URL: http://www.pih.org
Contact: Ophelia Dahl, Pres./Exec. Dir.
Founded: 1987. **Multinational. Description:** Provides a preferential option for the poor in health care. Strives to bring the benefits of modern medical science to poor communities. **Libraries: Type:** reference. **Holdings:** articles, books. **Subjects:** patient stories. **Boards:** Advisory. **Publications:** *PIH Bulletin*, quarterly. Newsletter. Alternate Formats: online.

Health Care

12004 ■ Covering Kids and Families (CKF)
c/o Southern Institute on Children and Families
500 Taylor St., Ste.202
Columbia, SC 29201
Ph: (803)779-2607
Fax: (803)254-6301
E-mail: info@coveringkidsandfamilies.org
URL: http://coveringkidsandfamilies.org
Contact: Denise Crouch, Contact
Founded: 2002. **Members:** 5,500. **Description:** Aims to reduce the number of uninsured children and adults who are eligible but not enrolled in Medicaid and the State Children's Health Insurance program by conducting and coordinating outreach programs, simplifying enrollment and renewal processes and coordinating existing health care coverage programs.

12005 ■ National PACE Association (NPA)
801 N Fairfax St., Ste.309
Alexandria, VA 22314
Ph: (703)535-1565
Fax: (703)535-1566
E-mail: info@npaonline.org
URL: http://www.npaonline.org
Contact: Shawn Bloom, Pres./CEO
Founded: 1971. **Membership Dues:** exploring, technical assistance center, $2,650 (annual) ● prospective provider, capitated provider, $9,000 (annual) ● associate, $3,700 (annual). **Description:** Promotes the availability of healthcare services to older adults through the Program of All-inclusive Care for the Elderly (PACE) and similar care models. **Committees:** Audit; Awards; Education; Nominating; Primary Care; Public Policy; Research.

Health Education

12006 ■ Bill and Melinda Gates Foundation
PO Box 23350
Seattle, WA 98102
Ph: (206)709-3140 (206)709-3100
E-mail: info@gatesfoundation.org
URL: http://www.gatesfoundation.org
Description: Guided by the belief that every life has equal value, the foundation works to reduce inequi-

ties and improve lives around the world. In developing countries, it focuses on improving health, reducing extreme poverty, and increasing access to technology in public libraries. In the United States, the foundation seeks to ensure that all people have access to a great education and to technology in public libraries. In local region, it focuses on improving the lives of low-income families. **Awards: Type:** grant. **Programs:** Scholarship; U.S. Library. **Publications:** *Connections*, semiannual. Newsletter. Alternate Formats: online ● *Possibilities*. Newsletter. Alternate Formats: online ● *Sound Families*, quarterly. Newsletter. Alternate Formats: online ● Reports, annual.

Hearing Impaired

12007 ■ Global Deaf Connection (GDC)
2901 38th Ave. S
Minneapolis, MN 55406
Ph: (612)724-8565
Fax: (612)729-3839
E-mail: travel@deafconnection.org
URL: http://www.deafconnection.org
Contact: Mark Geiger, Pres.
Founded: 1996. **Multinational. Description:** Seeks to increase the social, economic and educational opportunities for deaf people in developing nations. Strives to close the gap between the number of deaf children enrolled in school and the number of deaf adults in the professional world. Develops self-sustaining cycles of deaf education and leadership skills through advocacy, multi-cultural exchange, college scholarships and mentor support. Aims to increase the social and economic self-sufficiency of deaf individuals.

Hispanic

12008 ■ Grand Council of Hispanic Societies in Public Service
PO Box 636, Stuyvesant Sta.
New York, NY 10009
Ph: (212)615-6625
Contact: Debra Martinez, Pres.
Founded: 1966. **Members:** 75,000. **Membership Dues:** hispanic fraternal group, $150 (annual). **State Groups:** 1. **Languages:** English, Spanish. **Description:** Umbrella organization for 22 Hispanic societies. Advocates affirmative action, equal employment, and economic opportunities for Hispanics. **Libraries: Type:** not open to the public. **Holdings:** business records, clippings. **Subjects:** organizing political efforts. **Awards:** Annual Scholarship. **Frequency:** annual. **Type:** scholarship. **Recipient:** for Hispanic college students who participate in civic work. **Computer Services:** Mailing lists. **Conventions/Meetings:** monthly meeting - third Thursday of the month in New York City; **Avg. Attendance:** 50.

12009 ■ Mexican-American Opportunity Foundation (MAOF)
401 N Garfield Ave.
Montebello, CA 90640
Ph: (323)890-9600 (323)890-3691
Fax: (323)890-9637
E-mail: maofinfo@maof.org
URL: http://www.maof.org
Contact: Martin Castro, Pres./CEO
Founded: 1962. **Staff:** 330. **Budget:** $15,000,000. **State Groups:** 220. **Description:** Seeks to create solutions to the needs and problems of Spanish-speaking and Hispanic Americans; conducts programs of benefit to all U.S. minorities. Activities include child care services, bilingual and bicultural development, training and assistance to senior citizens, apprenticeship preparation for women and minorities, home exterior painting and home repairs, employment services, educational and vocational training, counseling, information and referral for child care services, and musical entertainment. Operates 21 programs throughout the state of California. Compiles statistics. **Libraries: Type:** reference. **Hold-**

ings: 2,500. **Subjects:** bilingual and bicultural materials including audiovisual aids, primarily for preschool children head start program, and persons in child care development. **Awards:** Aztec Award. **Frequency:** annual. **Type:** recognition. **Recipient:** for individuals contributing to the cultural, social, and economic improvement of the Mexican-American community. **Telecommunication Services:** electronic mail, mcastro@maof.org ● electronic mail, crufino@maof.org. **Publications:** *Information and Referral Newsletter*, quarterly. Includes information on child care. ● Newsletter, annual. **Conventions/Meetings:** annual National Hispanic Women's Conference - meeting (exhibits) - always spring, Los Angeles, CA.

12010 ■ Mexican American Unity Council (MAUC)
2300 W Commerce St., Ste.200
San Antonio, TX 78207
Ph: (210)978-0500
Fax: (210)978-0547
E-mail: info@mauc.org
URL: http://www.mauc.org
Contact: Fernando S. Godinez, Pres./CEO
Founded: 1967. **Staff:** 43. **Budget:** $2,994,085. **Languages:** English, Spanish. **Description:** Works to improve opportunities and promote economic development in the low income Hispanic neighborhoods of San Antonio. Empowers the people to take control of their lives and their community.

12011 ■ National Council of La Raza (NCLR)
Raul Yzaguirre Bldg.
1126 16th St. NW
Washington, DC 20036
Ph: (202)785-1670
E-mail: pubs@nclr.org
URL: http://www.nclr.org
Contact: Janet Murguia, Pres./CEO
Founded: 1968. **Members:** 7,000. **Staff:** 60. **Budget:** $7,000,000. **Local Groups:** 160. **Description:** Serves as a national umbrella organization for civil rights and economic opportunities for Hispanics. Provides technical assistance to Hispanic community-based organizations in comprehensive community development, including economic development, housing, employment and training, business assistance, health, and other fields. Conducts research programs; compiles statistics; advocates on behalf of Hispanics. Offers private sector resource development training and board of directors training. Provides policy analysis. **Libraries: Type:** reference. **Subjects:** census information. **Awards:** Congressional Recognition Awards. **Frequency:** annual. **Type:** recognition. **Recipient:** for outstanding service to Hispanic community on tough policy issues affecting Hispanics ● NCLR Awards. **Frequency:** annual. **Type:** recognition. **Recipient:** for excellence in leadership communications, sports, and commitment and service to the Hispanic community. **Departments:** Public Information; Research, Advocacy, and Legislation; Special and International Projects; Technical Assistance and Constituency Support. **Formerly:** (1973) Southwest Council of La Raza. **Publications:** *Action Alerts*, periodic ● *Agenda*, quarterly. Magazine. Features information on issues affecting the Hispanic community. ● *Backgrounders, Issue Briefs*, periodic ● *Education Network News*, quarterly. Newsletter ● *Elderly Network News*, quarterly. Newsletter ● *Policy Analysis Monographs*, periodic ● *Poverty Network News*, quarterly. Newsletter ● *State of Hispanic America: Toward A Latino Anti-Poverty Agenda*, annual. Report. **Price:** $7.00. **Circulation:** 8,000 ● Handbooks ● Manuals ● Reports ● Also publishes statistical analyses and news releases. **Conventions/Meetings:** annual conference (exhibits) - always July ● seminar, proposal writing.

12012 ■ National Hispanic Employee Association (NHEA)
25A Crescent Dr., No. 312
Pleasant Hill, CA 94523
Ph: (202)842-4812

E-mail: mentor@mentores.org
URL: http://www.mentores.org
Contact: Louis A. Berrios, Chm.
Description: Promotes a national network of Hispanic employee associations that promotes career development through education, mentoring, and networking activities to advance the social and economic status of the U.S Hispanic community. **Publications:** Newsletter. Alternate Formats: online.

12013 ■ National Puerto Rican Forum (NPRF)
1910 Webster Ave.
Bronx, NY 10457
Ph: (718)466-3992
Free: (800)662-1220
Fax: (718)466-5262
E-mail: elopez@nprf.org
URL: http://www.nprf.org
Contact: Stephen Rosario, Chm.
Founded: 1957. **Staff:** 100. **Budget:** $8,500,000. **Regional Groups:** 2. **State Groups:** 2. **Languages:** English, Spanish. **Description:** Concerned with the overall improvement of Puerto Rican and Hispanic communities throughout the U.S. Seeks to identify the obstacles preventing the advancement of the Puerto Rican and Hispanic communities and to develop strategies to remove them. Designs and implements programs in areas of job counseling, training and placement, and English language skills, to deal effectively with the problems of Puerto Ricans and other Hispanics. Sponsors Career Services and Job Placement Program at the national level. Also provides specialized programs in New York, such as: Employment Placement Initiative, Access and Family Services in the schools, and job counseling. **Awards:** Si Se Puede Award. **Frequency:** annual. **Type:** recognition. **Recipient:** for outstanding Latino employees. **Computer Services:** Mailing lists. **Publications:** *El Foro*, quarterly. Magazine ● *New York City Metropolitan Area Vocational Resource Directory*, annual ● *Si Se Puede Journal* ● Annual Report. **Price:** free. **Advertising:** accepted. **Conventions/Meetings:** annual Latino Role Model Luncheon - meeting and conference ● periodic luncheon.

12014 ■ Puerto Rican Family Institute (PRFI)
145 W 15th St.
New York, NY 10011
Ph: (212)924-6320
Fax: (212)691-5635
E-mail: developmental@prfi.org
URL: http://www.prfi.org
Contact: Ms. Maria Elena Girone, Pres./CEO
Founded: 1960. **Staff:** 350. **Budget:** $23,000,000. **Languages:** English, Spanish. **Nonmembership. Description:** Aims to enhance the functioning and self-sufficiency of diverse marginalized communities, and to prevent family disintegration. Provides culturally sensitive services to all children, youth, adults and families, and respects all individual's ethnic, cultural and personal identities. Includes services such as: outpatient mental health treatment, child foster-placement preventive services, HIV/AIDS mental health treatment prevention and education, case management programs, residential care, crisis intervention and Head Start. Operates over 25 programs located through New York city, Jersey City, New Jersey and Puerto Rico. **Awards:** Community Excellence Awards. **Frequency:** annual. **Type:** recognition. **Recipient:** for service to Hispanic/Latino community. **Conventions/Meetings:** annual conference.

12015 ■ Secretariat for Hispanic Affairs, United States Conference of Catholic Bishops (SHA/USCCB)
3211 4th St. NE
Washington, DC 20017
Ph: (202)541-3150 (202)541-3000
Fax: (202)722-8717
E-mail: hispanicaffairs@usccb.org
URL: http://www.usccb.org/hispanicaffairs
Contact: Ronaldo M. Cruz, Exec. Dir.
Founded: 1945. **Languages:** English, Spanish. **Description:** Secretariat under the U.S. Conference of Catholic Bishops; assists Catholic dioceses in their

efforts to develop response to pastoral concerns of Hispanics in the U.S. **Absorbed:** Bishops' Committee for Migrant Workers. **Formerly:** Bishops' Committee for the Spanish Speaking; Division for the Spanish Speaking; Secretariat for the Spanish Speaking; (2000) Secretariat for Hispanic Affairs/National Conference of Catholic Bishops; (2002) United States Catholic Conference. **Publications:** *En Marcha* (in English and Spanish), quarterly. Newsletter. **Circulation:** 7,000. Alternate Formats: online ● *Hispanic Apostolate Diocesan Directors List*, annual. **Conventions/Meetings:** Bishops' Committee on Hispanic Affairs - conference - 3/year.

Home Care

12016 ■ God's Love We Deliver
166 Avenue of the Americas
New York, NY 10013
Ph: (212)294-8100
Fax: (212)294-8101
E-mail: info@glwd.org
URL: http://www.godslovewedeliver.org
Contact: Barbra Locker PhD, Sec.
Founded: 1985. **Staff:** 86. **Budget:** $7,770,736. **Languages:** English, Spanish. **Description:** Delivers nutritious meals to men, women, and children with AIDS. Provides free nutritional counseling to people living with HIV/AIDS and their care providers. **Committees:** Development. **Publications:** *Food for Thought*, 3/year. Newsletter.

12017 ■ Meals on Wheels Association of America (MOWAA)
203 S Union St.
Alexandria, VA 22314-3355
Ph: (703)548-5558
Fax: (703)548-8024
E-mail: mowaa@mowaa.org
URL: http://www.mowaa.org
Contact: Enid A. Borden, CEO
Founded: 1973. **Members:** 900. **Membership Dues:** general, $125 (annual) ● corporate, $200-$300 (annual) ● organization, $200 (annual) ● retiree, $35 (annual). **Staff:** 5. **Budget:** $400,000. **Description:** Agencies that provide home-delivered meals and/or meals in a congregate setting, and other health and social services such as transportation, recreation, nutrition education, information, referral, and case management. Promotes the improvement of the quality of life for the needy, particularly the elderly, disabled, and homebound. Delivers nutritionally balanced meals to disabled and homebound elderly persons, thereby reducing or eliminating the need for institutionalization and promoting independent and community-based living arrangements. Advocates community-based, home-delivered, and congregate meal programs; encourages and assists in establishing new programs; provides technical assistance to community meal programs and acts as a forum for exchange of information regarding home-delivered and congregate meal programs. **Awards:** Golden Meal Award. **Frequency:** periodic. **Type:** recognition. **Recipient:** for those who have done something on a national level affecting senior meal programs ● Mayors for Meals/March for Meals Campaign. **Frequency:** annual. **Type:** recognition. **Recipient:** for awareness on senior hunger ● **Type:** scholarship. **Committees:** Executive. **Subgroups:** Member Services; Operations; Public Policy. **Formerly:** (1976) National Association of Home Delivered and Congregate Meal Providers; (1999) National Association of Meal Programs. **Publications:** *MOWAA News*, quarterly. Newsletter. Contains substantive issues concern to elderly nutrition programs. **Price:** included in membership dues. **Advertising:** accepted ● Membership Directory. **Price:** included in membership dues, for members only. Alternate Formats: online. **Conventions/Meetings:** annual conference and seminar (exhibits).

Home Economics

12018 ■ American Association of Family and Consumer Sciences (AAFCS)
400 N Columbus St., Ste.202
Alexandria, VA 22314

Ph: (703)706-4600
Free: (800)424-8080
Fax: (703)706-4663
E-mail: staff@aafcs.org
URL: http://www.aafcs.org
Contact: Dixie R. Crase CFCS, Pres.-Elect
Founded: 1909. **Members:** 11,000. **Membership Dues:** active, associate, $135 (annual) ● retired professional, $65 (annual), ● undergraduate/graduate student, $60 (annual) ● new professional, $100 (annual) ● sustaining, $250 (annual). **Staff:** 12. **Budget:** $2,400,000. **State Groups:** 54. **Description:** Elementary, secondary, post-secondary and extension educators and administrators; other professionals in government, business and nonprofit sectors; and students preparing for the field. Works to improve the quality of individual and family life through programs that "educate, influence public policy, disseminate information and publish research findings". **Awards:** AAFCS Fellowships. **Frequency:** annual. **Type:** recognition. **Recipient:** to support graduate study in family and consumer sciences ● AAFCS Leaders Awards. **Frequency:** annual. **Type:** recognition. **Recipient:** to family and consumer sciences professionals who have made significant contributions to the field through involvement with AAFCS ● AAFCS New Achievers Awards. **Frequency:** annual. **Type:** recognition. **Recipient:** for emerging professionals who have exhibited the potential for making significant contributions in or through family and consumer sciences ● Borden Award. **Frequency:** annual. **Type:** recognition. **Recipient:** for a researcher in the field of nutrition and/or experimental foods who employs fundamental principles of research ● Massachusetts Avenue Building Assets Fund Grants Programs. **Frequency:** annual. **Type:** recognition. **Recipient:** for initiatives that enhance the well being of families, which support the program of AAFCS ● Nationally Family and Consumer Sciences Teacher of the Year. **Frequency:** annual. **Type:** recognition. **Recipient:** for outstanding educational programs, methods, techniques, and activities that provide the stimulus for and give visibility to family and consumer sciences elementary and secondary education ● **Type:** recognition. **Recipient:** for excellence in experimental foods and nutrition research ● Ruth O'Brien Project Grants. **Type:** recognition. **Recipient:** for individuals concerned with research and development in family and consumer sciences ● 21st Century Community Champion Award. **Frequency:** annual. **Type:** recognition. **Recipient:** to individuals or groups who promote the connection, create projects, and are identified as an effective voice. **Computer Services:** Mailing lists, available for purchase. **Divisions:** Apparel and Textiles; Art and Design; Communication; Education and Technology; Family Economics and Resource Management; Family Relations and Human Development; Housing and Environment; International; Nutrition, Health and Food Management. **Programs:** Certified in Family and Consumer Sciences. **Sections:** Business; Colleges, Universities and Research; Elementary, Secondary, and Adult Education; Extension; Home and Community; Human Services; Preprofessional/Graduate Student. **Formerly:** (1994) American Home Economics Association. **Publications:** *The FACS*. Newsletter. Alternate Formats: online ● *Family and Consumer Sciences Research Journal*, 5/year. Feature scholarly, refereed journal reports and records scientific methods and applications of family and consumer sciences research. **Price:** $30.00 for members; $54.00 for nonmembers individuals; $104.00 for nonmembers institutions. Also Cited As: *FCSRJ* ● *Higher Education Units*. Newsletter. Alternate Formats: online ● *In the Know*. Newsletter. Alternate Formats: online ● *Journal of Family and Consumer Sciences*, quarterly. Carries articles by AACS members and other professionals. **Price:** $140.00 /year for individuals in U.S.; $173.00 /year for institutions in U.S.; $194.00 /year for institutions outside U.S. **Circulation:** 12,000. **Advertising:** accepted. Also Cited As: *JFCS* ● *Products and Publications Catalog*, annual. Contains listing of periodicals, public policy references, publications and AAFCS/CFCS products. ● Also publishes pamphlets, leaflets, section and division newsletters, and reports. **Conventions/Meetings:** annual convention and work-

shop, professional and leadership development panels, workshops, networking, curriculum showcase, juried research reports, design showcase (exhibits) - June ● annual Leadership Conference - meeting - October.

Homeless

12019 ■ American Bar Association Commission on Homelessness and Poverty
740 15th St. NW
Washington, DC 20005-1022
Ph: (202)662-1694
Fax: (202)638-3844
E-mail: homeless@abanet.org
URL: http://www.abanet.org/homeless/home.html
Contact: Amy Horton-Newell, Dir.
Founded: 1991. **Members:** 15. **Staff:** 1. **Budget:** $80,000. **Description:** Assists state and local bar associations in the implementation and maintenance of programs for the homeless. Serves as an information clearinghouse of programs and resource materials on homelessness. Assists organizations in establishing programs designed to meet the needs of their community's homeless population. Offers testimonies and comments on legislation affecting the homeless. Participates in local and national conferences. Maintains speakers' bureau. Offers educational programs. **Formerly:** (1992) American Bar Association Representation of the Homeless Project. **Publications:** *Educating Children Without Housing*. Book. **Price:** $15.00 ● *The Homeless Court Program*. Book. **Price:** $15.00 ● *NIMBY: A Primer for Lawyers and Advocates*. Book. **Price:** $10.00 ● *Representing the Poor and Homeless*. Book. **Price:** $15.00 ● Also publishes annual listing of state and local bar association and law school homeless programs. **Conventions/Meetings:** quarterly meeting.

12020 ■ American Rescue Team International (ARTI)
PO Box 237
San Francisco, CA 94127
Ph: (415)533-2231
E-mail: amerrescue@aol.com
URL: http://www.amerrescue.org
Contact: Mr. Doug Copp, Rescue Chief/Exec. Dir.
Founded: 1986. **Members:** 40,000. **Multinational.** **Description:** Counsels homeless children, youths, and adults. Provides basic education and vocational skills to individuals in need. Sends educational materials to African communities. **Formerly:** American Knowledge Rescue. **Publications:** *The Triangle of Life*. Video. Alternate Formats: CD-ROM ● Videos. Alternate Formats: online ● Newsletter. Alternate Formats: online.

12021 ■ Community for Creative Non-Violence (CCNV)
425 2nd St. NW
Washington, DC 20001
Ph: (202)393-1909 (202)393-4409
Fax: (202)783-3254
E-mail: ccnv@erols.com
URL: http://users.erols.com/ccnv
Contact: Terri Bishop, Exec. Dir.
Founded: 1970. **Members:** 70. **Membership Dues:** corporate sponsor, $2,500 (annual) ● life, $1,000 ● patron, $500 (annual) ● community, $250 (annual) ● friend, $50 (annual). **Description:** Individuals working to combat homelessness and poverty in the U.S. Serves as a nonpartisan advocate to influence federal legislation relevant to the homeless; sponsors and participates in public demonstrations protesting homelessness. Operates Federal City Shelter, which provides social services including medical and mental health care, substance abuse rehabilitation, and recreational opportunities to 1500 homeless people in Washington, DC. **Publications:** *Housing and Homelessness: A Teaching Guide*. Book ● *Managing the Media: A Guide for Activists* ● Pamphlets.

12022 ■ End Homelessness Now
c/o Heather Guillen
PO Box 3374
Santa Clara, CA 95055
Fax: (805)772-4359
E-mail: heather@cybercsj.org
Contact: Heather Guillen, Contact
Description: Promotes awareness of social issues/ projects recognizing homelessness as a result of domestic violence, drugs, sexism, racism.

12023 ■ Family Promise
71 Summit Ave.
Summit, NJ 07901
Ph: (908)273-1100
Fax: (908)273-0030
E-mail: info@familypromise.org
URL: http://www.nihn.org
Contact: Cary R. Hardy Esq., Treas.
Founded: 1986. **Members:** 60,000. **Description:** Volunteers and congregations. Seeks to eradicate homelessness and improve the quality of life of homeless people. Provides shelter, meals, and comprehensive support to families without homes. Encourages religious congregations to establish "hospitality rooms" in their places of worship to temporarily house the homeless. Provides support and services to participating congregations including community needs assessments, educational and volunteer training programs, and technical assistance. Facilitates communication, cooperation, and networking among members. **Computer Services:** Online services, publications. **Additional Websites:** http://www.familypromise.org. **Formerly:** (2006) National Interfaith Hospitality Network. **Publications:** *Hospitality*, quarterly. Newsletter. Alternate Formats: online.

12024 ■ Hands of Mercy (HM)
PO Box 320735
Cocoa Beach, FL 32932-0735
Ph: (321)799-9445
URL: http://www.wego.org/pages/hands-of-mercy.cfm
Founded: 1987. **Staff:** 2. **Budget:** $56,000. **Nonmembership. Description:** Individuals organized to provide housing, food, and medical aid to homeless persons. Offers referral, job training, and placement services. **Convention/Meeting:** none. **Formerly:** America Individual and Group Home Health Care Association.

12025 ■ HELP USA
5 Hanover Sq.
New York, NY 10004
Ph: (212)400-7000
Fax: (212)400-7005
E-mail: info@helpusa.org
URL: http://www.helpusa.org
Contact: Mr. Larry Belinsky, Pres./CEO
Founded: 1986. **Nonmembership. Description:** Helps homeless individuals and others in need to become self-reliant.

12026 ■ Manna House
PO Box 675
Concordia, KS 66901
Ph: (785)243-4428
Fax: (785)243-4321
E-mail: retreatcenter@mannahouse.org
URL: http://www.mannahouse.org
Contact: Marcia Allen CSJ, Contact
Founded: 1967. **Members:** 6. **Description:** Provides advocacy services for the homeless and the poor. Offers shelters, soup kitchens, and extra care for convalescents. **Formerly:** (1998) Midtown Churches Community Association. **Publications:** *Midtown Caller*, quarterly. Newsletter.

12027 ■ National Alliance to End Homelessness (NAEH)
1518 K St. NW, Ste.410
Washington, DC 20005
Ph: (202)638-1526
Fax: (202)638-4664
E-mail: naeh@naeh.org
URL: http://www.endhomelessness.org
Contact: Churchill J. Gibson IV, Exec. Dir.
Founded: 1983. **Staff:** 10. **Description:** Works closely with the public, private, and non-profit sectors to develop and implement policies and programs that prevent and end homelessness and to help each sector fulfill its unique role in ending homelessness. Supports policies and programs that reduce homelessness; engages in research to analyze the nature of homelessness and the elements of successful program solutions; conducts educational programs. **Formerly:** (1984) National Citizens Committee for Food and Shelter; (1988) Committee for Food and Shelter. **Publications:** *Alliance Online News*, weekly. Newsletter. Provides information and links regarding new developments in federal programs and policy. Alternate Formats: online ● *Factsheets on Homelessness for Students*. Provides teachers, parents and students with information and research ideas on homelessness. Alternate Formats: online ● *Life Skills Manual*. Contains practical information for people trying to establish stable and independent lives. Alternate Formats: online ● *The Prevention of Homelessness*. Report. Discusses the nature of prevention programs and the major issues affecting the success of prevention. **Price:** $3.00 for alliance members; $5.00 for nonmembers. Alternate Formats: online ● *The Ten-Year Plan to End Homelessness*. Contains information on the practical steps necessary to prevent and end homelessness effectively. Alternate Formats: online ● *Turning the Financial Corner From Survival to Prosperity* ● *The Way Home: Ending Homelessness in America*. Highlights the solutions to homelessness. ● Annual Report, annual. Alternate Formats: online. **Conventions/Meetings:** annual conference, includes training institutes.

12028 ■ National Center for Homeless Education (NCHE)
PO Box 5367
Greensboro, NC 27435
Free: (800)755-3277
Fax: (336)315-7457
E-mail: homeless@serve.org
URL: http://www.serve.org/nche
Contact: Diana Bowman, Dir.
Staff: 4. **State Groups:** 54. **Description:** Aims to overcome barriers to education, strives to improve educational opportunities for homeless children and youth. **Telecommunication Services:** electronic mail, dbowman@serve.org ● additional toll-free number, toll-free helpline, (800)308-2145. **Publications:** *Increasing School Stability for Students Experiencing Homelessness: Overcoming Challenges to Providing Transportation to the School of Origin*. Monograph. Reviews provisions related to transportation to the school of origin and provides recommendations for implementing the transportation mandate. Alternate Formats: online ● *Parent Brochure* (in English and Spanish). Explains the educational rights of children and youth and inform parents about ways in which to support their children. Alternate Formats: online ● *The State Coordinator's Handbook*. Provides information and strategies compiled from State Coordinators across the country. Alternate Formats: online ● *Students on the Move: Reaching and Teaching Highly Mobile Children and Youth*. Handbook. Synthesizes research on the education of various subpopulations of students. Alternate Formats: online.

12029 ■ National Coalition for the Homeless (NCH)
2201 P St. NW
Washington, DC 20037-1033
Ph: (202)462-4822
Fax: (202)462-4823
E-mail: info@nationalhomeless.org
URL: http://www.nationalhomeless.org
Contact: Michael Stoops, Acting Exec. Dir.
Founded: 1984. **Members:** 12,000. **Membership Dues:** regular, $35 (annual) ● contributor, $50 (annual) ● student/low income, $15 (annual) ● friend, $100 (annual) ● sponsor, $250 (annual) ● benefactor, $500 (annual) ● organization (below $100,000 up to $1,500,000 annual budget), $65-$500. **Staff:** 7. **Budget:** $800,000. **State Groups:** 50. **Local Groups:** 500. **National Groups:** 100. **Description:** Advocates for education at all levels of society in order to identify and end the social and economic causes of homelessness; works to increase the capacity of local supportive housing and service providers to better meet the urgent needs of those families and individuals now homeless in their communities. Work focuses on five policy areas: civil rights of those who are without homes, housing that is affordable to those with the lowest incomes, accessible/comprehensive health care and other needed support services, and livable incomes that make it possible to afford the basic necessities of life, using litigation, lobbying, public education, policy analysis, community organizing, research and provision of technical assistance. **Awards:** Curtis/Gray Award. **Frequency:** annual. **Type:** recognition. **Recipient:** for homeless/formerly homeless person or homeless self-help group. **Computer Services:** Online services, public information and legislative updates. **Projects:** Hate Crimes/Violence Prevention; National Homeless Civil Rights Organizing. **Absorbed:** (1993) Homelessness Information Exchange. **Publications:** *Hate, Violence, and Death on Main Street USA: A Report on Hate Crimes And Violence Against People Experiencing Homelessness*, annual. Annual Report. **Price:** $10.00. Alternate Formats: online ● *NCH News*, monthly. Newsletter ● Directories. **Price:** $10.00. Alternate Formats: online ● Manuals. **Price:** $10.00. Alternate Formats: online ● Reports. Alternate Formats: online ● Papers. Alternate Formats: online. **Conventions/Meetings:** semiannual board meeting.

12030 ■ National Law Center on Homelessness and Poverty (NLCHP)
1411 K St. NW, Ste.1400
Washington, DC 20005
Ph: (202)638-2535
Fax: (202)628-2737
E-mail: nlchp@nlchp.org
URL: http://www.nlchp.org
Contact: Maria Foscarinis, Exec. Dir.
Founded: 1989. **Staff:** 11. **Budget:** $600,000. **Languages:** English, Spanish. **Description:** Seeks eliminate homelessness in the United States by addressing its underlying causes. Advocates for new public policies dealing with homelessness and its causes; seeks to insure that existing laws protecting the rights of the homeless are enforced to their fullest extent; promotes and conducts research on homelessness and poverty and their causes. Sponsors educational programs to raise public awareness of homelessness and poverty; serves as a forum for public discussion of homelessness, poverty, and related issues. Provides legal assistance to homeless people and mounts test cases to challenge statutes that criminalize homelessness. Lobbies for innovative programs to alleviate the plight of the homeless, including the conversion of unused military properties into dwellings. **Libraries:** Type: reference. **Subjects:** homelessness, poverty, legal. **Publications:** *In Just Times*, quarterly. Newsletter. **Circulation:** 5,000. **Conventions/Meetings:** quarterly board meeting.

12031 ■ National Resource Center on Homelessness and Mental Illness (NRCHMI)
c/o The CDM Group
7500 Old Georgetown Rd., Ste.900
Bethesda, MD 20814
Ph: (301)654-6740
Fax: (301)656-4012
E-mail: health@cdmgroup.com
URL: http://www.nrchmi.samhsa.gov
Founded: 1988. **Staff:** 6. **Description:** Serves as a center for technical assistance and information on the housing and service needs of the mentally ill homeless. Compiles annotated bibliographies and sponsors workshops and training events. **Libraries:** Type: reference. Holdings: 10,000. **Publications:** *Access*, periodic. Newsletter. Features articles on service delivery, housing, research and program evaluation, staff training, and federal, state and local initiatives. **Price:** free. **Circulation:** 7,500.

12032 ■ ReREAD
Address Unknown since 2007
Description: Seeks to increase literacy among the homeless. Collects and distributes periodicals to homeless shelters.

12033 ■ Tatry Housing Organization (THO)
603 S Ann St.
Baltimore, MD 21231
Ph: (410)342-7200 (410)276-8681
Fax: (410)276-1233
Contact: Mrs. Ivanna Zhyzko, Dir.
Founded: 1938. **Members:** 12,000. **Membership Dues:** $50 (annual). **Staff:** 3. **Budget:** $250,000. **Regional Groups:** 5. **State Groups:** 5. **Local Groups:** 5. **National Groups:** 15. **Languages:** English, Polish, Ukrainian. **Description:** Individuals and organizations. Seeks to improve the quality of life of homeless and mentally ill people of Slavic origin. Makes available programs and services; maintains six institutional houses. **Libraries: Type:** reference. **Holdings:** 5,000. **Subjects:** cultural. **Awards:** Annual Recognition Award. **Frequency:** annual. **Type:** recognition. **Conventions/Meetings:** monthly convention, cultural and economic issues.

Horse Racing

12034 ■ National Horsemen's Benevolent and Protective Association (HBPA)
Natl. Horse Center
Bldg. B, Ste.2
4063 Ironworks Pkwy.
Lexington, KY 40511-8905
Ph: (859)259-0451
Free: (866)245-1711
Fax: (859)259-0452
E-mail: racing@hbpa.org
URL: http://www.hbpa.org
Contact: Remi Bellocq, CEO
Founded: 1940. **Members:** 40,000. **Membership Dues:** associate, $100 (annual). **Description:** Represents owners, breeders, and trainers committed to betterment of thoroughbred horse racing. **Telecommunication Services:** electronic mail, rbellocq@hbpa.org. **Committees:** Audit; Investment; Nominating; Personnel; Planning; Special. **Programs:** Employee Assistance; Owners and Trainers Liability. **Publications:** *Horsemen's Journal*, quarterly. Features information that matters most to the Thoroughbred industry. **Price:** included in membership dues. Alternate Formats: online ● *Simulcast Directory* ● *Track Directory*.

Horses

12035 ■ Thoroughbred Adoption and Retirement Association (TARA)
Address Unknown since 2007
Description: Committed to assist and accredit groups that rehabilitate and place ex-racehorses.

Housing

12036 ■ American Association of Housing Educators (AAHE)
c/o Jean A. Memken, PhD, Exec. Dir.
5060 FCS Dept.
Illinois State Univ.
Normal, IL 61790-5060
Ph: (309)438-5802
E-mail: jmemken@rs6000.cmp.ilstu.edu
URL: http://www.extension.iastate.edu/Pages/housing/aahe-links.html
Contact: Jean A. Memken PhD, Exec. Dir.
Founded: 1965. **Members:** 200. **Membership Dues:** active, $85 (annual) ● library, $130 (annual) ● student, $35 (annual) ● life, $1,275. **Staff:** 2. **Description:** College teachers and researchers in various aspects of housing; government employees, including U.S. Department of Agriculture extension

workers; industry representatives; students. Affiliate group members are organizations with an interest in housing for American families; honorary members are leaders in housing education. Objectives are: to develop a better understanding of the role of housing in the well-being of people; to increase effectiveness of housing education at all levels; to optimize quality of housing environments; to coordinate efforts among professionals in housing and to develop their expertise; to disseminate information on current housing developments; to recruit students for advanced study of housing. Conducts research and specialized education programs. **Awards: Frequency:** annual. **Type:** recognition. **Recipient:** for best original paper on housing by student ● Tessie Agan Award. **Type:** scholarship. **Committees:** Academic; Extension; Research; Scholarship and Development. **Formerly:** (1965) Housing Conference to Improve Instruction. **Publications:** *AAHE Policy Handbook*. Alternate Formats: online ● *Developing Community Housing Needs Assessments and Strategies: A self-help Guidebook for Nonmetropolitan Communities*. Alternate Formats: online ● *Housing and Society*, 3/year. Journal. ISSN: 0888-2746 ● *In House*, 3/year. Newsletter ● Membership Directory, annual ● Proceedings, annual ● Also publishes annotated bibliography of journal and listing of graduate schools with housing education related programs. **Conventions/Meetings:** annual conference.

12037 ■ American Seniors Housing Association (ASHA)
5100 Wisconsin Ave. NW, Ste.307
Washington, DC 20016
Ph: (202)237-0900
Fax: (202)237-1616
E-mail: dschless@seniorshousing.org
URL: http://www.seniorshousing.org
Contact: David S. Schless, Pres.
Founded: 1991. **Members:** 250. **Membership Dues:** executive board, state association, $10,000 (annual) ● associate, $2,500 (annual) ● advisory committee, $5,000 (annual). **Staff:** 3. **Description:** Members are engaged in all aspects of the development and operation of housing for older adults, including construction, finance, and management of the housing. Represents the interests of most prominent firms participating in seniors housing and has played an integral role in seniors housing advocacy. Focuses on long-term care policy, state regulations, and other issues concerned with this topic. **Committees:** Senior Housing Political Action. **Publications:** *The Seniors Housing Construction Report*. Contains a summary of construction trends. **Price:** $75.00 for nonmembers; $50.00 for members ● *Seniors Housing Legal Notes*. Newsletter ● *Seniors Housing Research Notes*. Newsletter. Features in depth analysis on a specific topic. ● *Seniors Housing Statistical Handbook*. Features data and statistics of importance to senior housing industry. **Price:** $125.00 for nonmembers; $100.00 for members ● *Seniors Housing Update*. Newsletter. Features latest research findings and strategies. **Conventions/Meetings:** board meeting, for executive board members - 3/year ● annual meeting, for executive board, advisory committee and associate members - 2008 Jan. 14-15, Henderson, NV.

12038 ■ American Society of Roommate Services (ASRS)
c/o Ms. Susan Stein
5353 N Fed. Hwy., No. 212
Fort Lauderdale, FL 33308
Ph: (212)362-0162
E-mail: roommatebroker@saol.com
Contact: Michael Santomauro, Exec. Off.
Founded: 1979. **Members:** 2. **Staff:** 2. **Description:** Roommate-finding agencies. Major objective is to broaden, through the publicity of radio and talk shows, the concept of lower rental cost. To cut rental costs, members help individuals find roommates (20&percent; of the clientele are in the process of divorce). **Formerly:** (1981) National Roommate Association. **Publications:** *Ins and Outs of the Roommate Biz*, 3/year ● *Roommate Finding Service*. Manual.

12039 ■ Assisted Living Federation of America (ALFA)
1650 King St., Ste.602
Alexandria, VA 22314-2747
Ph: (703)894-1805
Fax: (703)894-1831
E-mail: info@alfa.org
URL: http://www.alfa.org
Contact: Evrett Benton, Chm.
Founded: 1990. **Members:** 6,000. **Membership Dues:** associate/industry partner, $595 (annual) ● associate/government agency, $100 (annual) ● international, $500 (annual). **Staff:** 12. **Budget:** $3,000,000. **State Groups:** 43. **Description:** Providers of assisted living, state associations of providers, and others interested or involved in the industry. Promotes the interests of the assisted living industry and works to enhance the quality of life for the population it serves. Provides a forum for assisted living providers to unite, exchange information, and interact. Encourages the development of high standards for the industry. Promotes the concept of assisted living facilities with public and private agencies and other professionals. Works to educate providers and the public and increase national awareness of assisted living. Sponsors speakers' bureau, conferences, educational opportunities, trade show, research & training products. **Libraries: Type:** not open to the public. **Holdings:** books, periodicals. **Subjects:** long-term care and assisted living. **Awards:** ALFA Hero Awards. **Frequency:** annual. **Type:** recognition. **Recipient:** for outstanding employees or volunteers of assisted living facilities ● ALFA Pioneer Award. **Frequency:** annual. **Type:** recognition. **Recipient:** for outstanding innovative state regulator ● Best of Home Architectural Design Award. **Frequency:** annual. **Type:** recognition. **Formerly:** (1997) Assisted Living Facilities Association of America. **Publications:** *ALFA Alert*, weekly. Describes current issues, programs, and services. **Price:** free for members. **Circulation:** 7,500. **Advertising:** accepted. Alternate Formats: online ● *ALFA Executive Portfolio: Inside the Minds of the Leaders in Assisted Living and Senior Housing*. Book. **Price:** $757.00 for members; $1,407.00 for nonmembers ● *Assisted Living Executive*, 9/year. Magazine. Includes stories on families involved in assisted living, along with coverage on issues such as regulation, financing, operations and care giving. **Price:** free for members; $10.00/back issue for nonmembers. **Circulation:** 15,000. **Advertising:** accepted ● *Guide to Choosing an Assisted Living Residence*. Brochure. **Price:** $36.00 for members; $71.00 for nonmembers. **Conventions/Meetings:** biennial conference (exhibits) - always spring and fall.

12040 ■ Builders Without Borders (BWB)
119 Main St.
Kingston, NM 88042
Ph: (505)895-5400
E-mail: mail@builderswithoutborders.org
URL: http://builderswithoutborders.org
Contact: Dr. Owen Geiger, Dir.
Founded: 1999. **Membership Dues:** contributor, $25 ● donor, $50 ● sponsor, $75 ● business, partner, $100 ● angel, $500. **Multinational. Description:** Forms partnerships with communities and organizations around the world to create affordable housing from local materials. Trains local population to provide housing for themselves. Advocates the use of straw, earth and other easily obtainable materials for the construction of homes. **Projects:** Bustan L'Shalom; Casas de la Cruz - Mexico; Mongolian Tour of the Southwest; Sacred Mountain Camp National Indian Youth Leadership. **Publications:** *The Art of Natural Building*. Handbook ● *The Last Straw*. Journal. Alternate Formats: online ● *Natural Building and Ecological Design, Educational Curriculum and Teachers Notes*. Handbook ● *Strawbale Emergency Shelter Plans*. Handbook ● Newsletter. Alternate Formats: online.

12041 ■ Community Economics, Inc. (CEI)
538 9th St., Ste.200
Oakland, CA 94607
Ph: (510)832-8300

Fax: (510)832-2227
E-mail: info@communityeconomics.org
URL: http://communityeconomics.org
Contact: Joel Rubenzahl, Dir.
Founded: 1973. **Staff:** 6. **Budget:** $500,000. **Description:** Provides technical assistance to community groups and local governments in areas of community development, housing, and real estate. Offers advice in the areas of financing, organization, and syndication of nonprofit and cooperatively owned housing. Involves in new construction, restoration, historic properties, mobile home parks, tenant conversion, and artists' live/work space. **Publications:** none. **Formed by Merger of:** (1978) Community Ownership Organizing Project.

12042 ■ Cooperative Housing Foundation (CHF)
8601 Georgia Ave., Ste.800
Silver Spring, MD 20910
Ph: (301)587-4700
Fax: (301)587-7315
E-mail: mailbox@chfhq.org
URL: http://www.chfhq.org
Contact: Michael E. Doyle, Pres./CEO
Founded: 1952. **Members:** 75. **Staff:** 200. **Languages:** Arabic, English, French, German, Polish, Romanian, Russian, Spanish. **Multinational. Description:** Leaders in housing cooperative, labor, business and civic organizations who are interested in improving the quality of housing and communities, especially for persons of modest income. Provides private-sector assistance directed at economic development, settlements and planning. Sponsors the development of cooperative and self-help housing. Strives to enable families to invest their own resources to improve their income situation and their living conditions; strengthens new capabilities of host governments and communities, donor agencies, small and medium-sized private businesses, and nongovernmental organizations. **Libraries: Type:** reference. **Holdings:** 3,500; monographs. **Also Known As:** (2005) CHF International. **Formerly:** (1981) Foundation for Cooperative Housing. **Publications:** *Building a Better World*, annual. Annual Report. Alternate Formats: online ● *CHF Newsbriefs*, quarterly. Newsletter. **Price:** free. ISSN: 0895-5735. **Circulation:** 5,000. Alternate Formats: online ● Brochures ● Also publishes case studies, fact sheets and technical manuals. **Conventions/Meetings:** annual meeting, for trustees.

12043 ■ Council for Affordable and Rural Housing (CARH)
1112 King St.
Alexandria, VA 22314-3022
Ph: (703)837-9001
Fax: (703)837-8467
E-mail: carh@carh.org
URL: http://www.carh.org
Contact: Colleen M. Fisher, Exec. Dir.
Founded: 1980. **Members:** 320. **Membership Dues:** basic/associate, $600 ● basic plus, $1,500 ● advisory trustee, $3,000. **Staff:** 4. **Budget:** $500,000. **Description:** Managers, developers, owners, syndicators, and suppliers of products and services of the affordable rural housing industry. Represents the interests of members before Congress, the White House, and relevant federal agencies. Works to maintain a tax environment conducive to the continued production of affordable housing. Conducts educational programs. **Libraries: Type:** reference; not open to the public. **Subjects:** rural housing, development, finance, management of affordable housing. **Awards:** Harry L. Tomlinson Award. **Frequency:** annual. **Type:** recognition. **Recipient:** for meritorious achievement in delivering affordable housing ● Member of the Year Award. **Frequency:** annual. **Type:** recognition. **Recipient:** to an outstanding member. **Computer Services:** Mailing lists, members only. **Formerly:** (1995) Council for Rural Housing and Development. **Publications:** *AN Express*, monthly. **Price:** $225.00 /year for members. Alternate Formats: online ● *Insights for On-Sites*, quarterly. Newsletter. Contains information pertaining to all management aspects. ● Brochure ● Alternate Formats: online ● Newsletter,

bimonthly. Contains industry-related articles. **Circulation:** 1,000. **Advertising:** accepted. Alternate Formats: online. **Conventions/Meetings:** semiannual meeting.

12044 ■ Enterprise Community Partners
10227 Wincopin Cir.
Columbia, MD 21044
Ph: (410)964-1230
Free: (800)624-4298
Fax: (410)964-1918
URL: http://www.enterprisefoundation.org
Contact: Doris W. Koo, Pres./CEO
Founded: 1982. **Staff:** 280. **Budget:** $18,000,000. **Local Groups:** 1,900. **Description:** Helps rebuild communities. Works with community based organizations and other partners to provide low-income people with affordable housing, safer streets and access to jobs and child care. **Libraries: Type:** open to the public. **Holdings:** 1,900. **Subjects:** social science, housing, urban development. **Awards:** Ellen Sulzberger Straus Leadership Award. **Frequency:** annual. **Type:** grant. **Recipient:** for a nonprofit leader ● Excellence in Urban Journalism Award. **Frequency:** annual. **Type:** monetary. **Recipient:** to professional journalists. **Computer Services:** Online services. **Divisions:** Community Services; Fundraising, Public Policy, and Communications; Housing Services; Research Evaluation and Documentation. **Formerly:** (2006) Enterprise Foundation. **Publications:** *Enterprise Annual Report* ● *Enterprise Quarterly*. Magazine. Contains information on housing and community development programs and financing. **Price:** free. **Circulation:** 12,000. **Advertising:** accepted. Also Cited As: *EQ*. **Conventions/Meetings:** annual conference, premier national conference for low-income housing and community development practitioners (exhibits) - usually October or November. 2007 Nov. 14-16, Cleveland, OH ● annual Ready, Work, Grow - conference, for workforce-development practitioners (exhibits) - usually in May.

12045 ■ Greener Pastures Institute (GPI)
c/o William L. Seavey, Dir.
PO Box 2916
Orcutt, CA 93457
Free: (800)688-6352
Fax: (805)938-1396
URL: http://mythbreakers.com/gpi
Contact: William L. Seavey, Dir.
Founded: 1983. **Members:** 1,000. **Membership Dues:** regular, $49 (annual). **Staff:** 2. **Budget:** $25,000. **Description:** Assists urban dwellers in relocating to more rural environments (mainly in the west). Organizes seminars and meetings; maintains speakers' bureau. **Libraries: Type:** open to the public; by appointment only. **Holdings:** 500. **Subjects:** relocation, population, alternative energy, rural living, urban living, demographics, real estate, quality of life. **Awards: Frequency:** annual. **Type:** grant. **Recipient:** for environmentally oriented home based businesses. **Publications:** *The Rural Property Investor*, quarterly. Newsletter. Features articles on alternative house building, off-grid living, telecommuting, home businesses, and small towns. **Price:** $28.00/ year. **Circulation:** 1,000. **Advertising:** accepted. **Conventions/Meetings:** periodic Greener Pastures Expo - conference and workshop.

12046 ■ Habitat for Humanity International (HFHI)
121 Habitat St.
Americus, GA 31709-3498
Ph: (229)924-6935
E-mail: publicinfo@habitat.org
URL: http://www.habitat.org
Contact: Millard Fuller, Pres./Founder
Founded: 1976. **Staff:** 450. **Budget:** $111,000,000. **Regional Groups:** 15. **Local Groups:** 1,470. **National Groups:** 348. **Multinational. Description:** Ecumenical Christian housing organization. Works in partnership with people in need throughout the world to build shelter that is sold to them at no profit through no-interest loans. Funds, building materials, and labor are donated by individuals, churches, corporations and other organizations that share the goal of

eliminating substandard housing in the world. Campus chapters department oversees projects at more than 1200 colleges and universities. Provides training for international partners. **Departments:** Construction and Environmental Resources. **Programs:** Global Village; Habitat for Humanity AmeriCorps; International Volunteer; RV Care-A-Vanner; Women Build; Youth. **Projects:** Jimmy Carter Work. **Formerly:** (1987) Habitat for Humanity. **Publications:** *A Simple, Decent Place to Live*. Book ● *Bokotola* ● *Community Self-Help Housing Manual* ● *The Excitement is Building* ● *Habitat World*, bimonthly. **Price:** free. ISSN: 0890-958X. **Circulation:** 1,005,000 ● *Kingdom Building* ● *Love in the Mortar Joints* ● *No More Shacks* ● *Theology of the Hammer* ● Audiotapes ● Brochures ● Videos.

12047 ■ Homeowners Against Deficient Dwellings (HADD)
c/o Nancy Seats, Pres.
410 S Geyer Rd.
Kirkwood, MO 63122
Ph: (314)909-1667
E-mail: nseats@aol.com
URL: http://www.hadd.com
Contact: Nancy Seats, Pres.

Description: Offers support and suggestions to assist consumers in making educated, informed decisions when buying a home or resolving the complicated issues with deficient homes. Promotes better building standards and practice. Educates the general public on how to avoid substandard, deficient housing and how to rectify current instances of substandard, deficient housing. Assists home buyers/owners in their pursuits of various remedies leading to the possible recovery of damages. **Computer Services:** Mailing lists, of members ● online services, message boards.

12048 ■ Housing Assistance Council (HAC)
1025 Vermont Ave. NW, Ste.606
Washington, DC 20005
Ph: (202)842-8600
Fax: (202)347-3441
E-mail: hac@ruralhome.org
URL: http://www.ruralhome.org
Contact: Moises Loza, Exec. Dir.
Founded: 1971. **Staff:** 51. **Regional Groups:** 4. **Languages:** English, Spanish. **Nonmembership. Description:** Works to increase the availability of decent and affordable housing for rural low-income people. Provides seed money loans, technical assistance, program and policy assistance, and training and information services to public and private organizations. Conducts analyses of rural housing and community development legislation and programs with federal agencies. Reviews state housing and community development policy, legislation, and organizational structures. Researches housing affordability, availability, and adequacy in rural areas. Equal opportunity lender. Compiles statistics. **Libraries: Type:** reference; by appointment only. **Holdings:** 1,500; books, periodicals, photographs, reports. **Subjects:** rural housing. **Awards:** Clay Cochran Award. **Frequency:** biennial. **Type:** recognition ● Skip Jason Award. **Frequency:** biennial. **Type:** recognition. **Computer Services:** Online services. **Divisions:** Finance and Administration; Loan Fund; Research and Information; Training and Technical Assistance. **Publications:** *HAC News*, biweekly. Newsletter. Features current events affecting rural housing nationwide. **Price:** free. ISSN: 1093-8036. **Circulation:** 5,000. Alternate Formats: online ● *Rural Voices*, quarterly. Magazine. **Price:** $12.00/year; $4.00 single copy. ISSN: 1093-8044. Alternate Formats: online ● *Taking Stock: Rural People, Poverty, and Housing at the Turn of the 21st Century*. Reports. **Price:** $26.00 print copy. Alternate Formats: online ● *Turning Challenges into Opportunities: Housing and Community Development Strategies in Rural Population Loss Counties*. Report. **Price:** $10.00 ● Monographs ● Also publishes analyses. **Conventions/Meetings:** biennial National Rural Housing Conference (exhibits) - December ● annual Rural Housing Training Workshops - seminar and workshop.

12049 ■ International Association for Housing Science (IAHS)
PO Box 340254
Coral Gables, FL 33134
Ph: (305)446-9462
Fax: (305)461-0921
E-mail: uraloktay@aol.com
URL: http://www.housingscience.org
Contact: Dr. Oktay Ural, Pres.
Founded: 1972. **Members:** 600. **Membership Dues:** individual, $75 (annual). **National Groups:** 5. **Multinational. Description:** Engineers, architects, lawyers, medical personnel, contractors, educators, sociologists, economists, and interior designers. Collects and disseminates information related to housing problems. Conducts seminars, conferences, and workshops. **Awards:** Distinction Award. **Frequency:** annual. **Type:** recognition. **Recipient:** for contributions to the field of housing. **Publications:** *IAHS World Congress Proceedings*, annual. **Circulation:** 1,000 ● *International Journal for Housing Science and Its Applications*, quarterly. Contains research reports. **Price:** included in membership dues; $300.00/year for institutions. ISSN: 0146-6518. **Circulation:** 1,000. **Advertising:** accepted ● Membership Directory, annual. **Conventions/Meetings:** annual World Congress on Housing (exhibits).

12050 ■ McAuley Institute
8380 Colesville Rd., Ste.300
Silver Spring, MD 20910
Ph: (301)587-0423
Fax: (301)587-0533
Contact: JoAnn Kane, Pres.
Founded: 1983. **Staff:** 32. **Budget:** $3,500,000. **Regional Groups:** 3. **Nonmembership. Description:** Open to all people who wish to join. Works to build affordable housing. Assists community-based nonprofits through loans and technical assistance. **Awards:** Courage in Community. **Frequency:** annual. **Type:** recognition. **Recipient:** to recognize outstanding contributions of women in housing and community development. **Publications:** *Housing Gazette*, quarterly. Journal. **Price:** $15.00. **Circulation:** 15,000. Alternate Formats: online. **Conventions/Meetings:** biennial National Women and Housing Conference, for community-based housing developers, primarily women (exhibits).

12051 ■ National Affordable Housing Network
PO Box 3706
Butte, MT 59702
Ph: (406)782-8145
Fax: (406)782-5168
E-mail: info@nahn.com
URL: http://www.nahn.com
Contact: Barbara Miller, Exec. Dir.
Founded: 1994. **Staff:** 3. **Budget:** $750,000. **Description:** Conducts research and demonstration projects to design safe, comfortable, affordable housing for disadvantaged families. Utilizes the collective experience of staff members to design and build homes that requires less energy, water, and natural resources. Provides technical support and education to non-profit housing organizations. Develops detailed, easy-to-follow house plans and graphics to allow volunteers and self-help builders to use new methods while sharply reducing or eliminating marginal costs. **Convention/Meeting:** none. **Libraries: Type:** reference. **Holdings:** artwork, books, business records, clippings, monographs, periodicals. **Subjects:** affordable housing, sustainable technologies. **Projects:** Central Butte Neighborhood Redevelopment; The High Performance Housing Partnership in Texas; Homes on the Richest Hill on Earth; Mutual Self-Help Housing. **Publications:** *Net Results*, quarterly. Newsletter ● *Publications Catalog*, annual.

12052 ■ National AIDS Housing Coalition (NAHC)
1518 K St. NW, Ste.410
Washington, DC 20005-1518
Ph: (202)347-0333
Fax: (202)347-3411

E-mail: nahc@nationalaidshousing.org
URL: http://www.nationalaidshousing.org
Contact: Nancy Bernstine, Exec. Dir.
Founded: 1994. **Membership Dues:** agency (based on budget), $100-$1,000 (annual) ● individual, $50-$250 (annual) ● corporate, $250-$1,000 (annual). **Description:** Advances the creation, development, management and growth of housing for persons living with HIV/AIDS. Educates legislators and public policy makers about the need for housing programs that assist persons living with HIV/AIDS. Encourages new initiatives and better coordination between federal agencies. **Publications:** Newsletter. Alternate Formats: online.

12053 ■ National Association of Housing Cooperatives (NAHC)
1707 H St. NW, Ste.201
Washington, DC 20006
Ph: (202)737-0797
Fax: (202)783-7869
E-mail: info@coophousing.org
URL: http://www.coophousing.org
Contact: Bill Magee, Chm.
Founded: 1950. **Members:** 1,000. **Membership Dues:** housing cooperative corporation (add 3.25/unit), $30 (annual) ● professional, organizational, $275 (annual). **Staff:** 5. **Budget:** $600,000. **Regional Groups:** 10. **Description:** Represents about 1,200,000 families. Sets standards; promotes development of housing cooperatives through research, education, and forums; Aids individuals and groups interested in forming housing cooperatives to find sources for technical advice and assistance. Covers topics such as management, energy conservation, board-member relations, development of community facilities, conversion from rental to cooperative home ownership, and community relations. **Awards:** Jerry Voorhis Award. **Frequency:** annual. **Type:** recognition. **Recipient:** for contribution to cooperative living. **Publications:** *Cooperative Housing Bulletin*, bimonthly ● *Cooperative Housing Journal*, annual. **Price:** $75.00/issue. **Circulation:** 1,500. **Advertising:** accepted ● Brochures ● Handbook. **Conventions/Meetings:** annual conference (exhibits).

12054 ■ National Center for Housing Management (NCHM)
12021 Sunset Hills Rd., Ste.210
Reston, VA 20190
Ph: (703)435-9393
Free: (800)368-5625
Fax: (703)435-9775
E-mail: service@nchm.org
URL: http://www.nchm.org
Contact: W. Glenn Stevens, Pres.
Founded: 1972. **Staff:** 31. **Description:** Purposes are to upgrade and professionalize the housing management industry through training, accreditation of firms, certification of individuals, research, technical assistance, and clearinghouse activities. Funded by performance contracts with federal, state, and local agencies, grants from foundations, and contracts with public and private management and mortgage servicing organizations. Provides training for all levels of housing management and currently awards certifications for occupancy specialists and maintenance managers. Offers technical assistance on compliance with the Fair Housing Act and Section 504 of the Rehabilitation Act of 1973. **Libraries: Type:** reference. **Holdings:** 1,000. **Awards:** Type: recognition. **Publications:** *Certified Manager of Housing* ● *Certified Manager of Maintenance* ● *Housing Management Quarterly*. Newsletter. Provides information on changes in housing regulations, training updates, and programs schedule. **Price:** $37.00. **Circulation:** 15,000. **Advertising:** accepted ● *HUD Handbook 4350.3: Occupancy Requirements of Subsidized Multifamily Housing Programs.* Alternate Formats: online ● *National Register*, annual. Directory. Lists certified professionals. **Price:** $27.95. **Circulation:** 10,000. Also Cited As: *Certified Occupancy Specialists* ● *Realistic Approaches to Drug and Alcohol Reduction Training Programs* ● *Tenant Integrity Program.* **Conventions/Meetings:** annual meeting - usually January, Washington, DC.

12055 ■ National Council on Agricultural Life and Labor Research Fund (NCALL)
363 Saulsbury Rd.
Dover, DE 19904
Ph: (302)678-9400
Fax: (302)678-9058
E-mail: info@ncall.org
URL: http://www.ncall.org
Contact: Joe L. Myer, Exec. Dir.
Founded: 1976. **Members:** 16. **Staff:** 20. **Budget:** $1,000,000. **Description:** Funded by grants and contracts, such as the U.S. Department of Labor and Rural Development to provide technical assistance to communities and non-profit groups interested in developing new or improving existing rural housing for low- and moderate-income families, particularly farmworkers. Agency primarily uses loan and grant authorities of the RD, the federal agency responsible for providing safe and sanitary rural housing. Aids communities in forming nonprofit housing development corporations that can sponsor RD financed housing. Provides homeownership counseling to low- and moderate-income individuals. Conducts seminars and offers training workshops. **Publications:** *The American Dream*, semiannual. Newsletter. Contains information for graduates who now own their own home. ● *NCALL News*, 3/year. Newsletter. Contains updates and information about the agency's housing efforts. **Circulation:** 1,100. Alternate Formats: online ● *Nonprofit Housing Handbook.* Describes the development process, typical obstacles and determining project feasibility. ● *Self-Helper*, quarterly. Newsletter. Contains information for self-help housing grantees and advocates. **Circulation:** 400. Alternate Formats: online ● Annual Report, annual. Highlights the status of the housing programs and the financial picture of the organization. Alternate Formats: online.

12056 ■ National Federation of Housing Counselors (NFHC)
Address Unknown since 2006
Founded: 1973. **Members:** 1,350. **Membership Dues:** individual, $35 (annual) ● organization, $50 (annual) ● staff, $125 (annual) ● affilate, $50 (annual). **Staff:** 2. **Budget:** $40,000. **Regional Groups:** 3. **State Groups:** 20. **Description:** Housing counselors, housing agency executives, and redevelopment officials; agencies on the state and municipal levels dealing with prepurchase, mortgage, tenant counseling, and financial/credit management. Works to secure safe, affordable, multifamily and single family housing for moderate- and low-income persons; promotes the exchange of information, resources, and techniques among members. Monitors actions of government, lenders, and other industries to assess the impact of their decisions and plans on low- and moderate-income families served by housing counselors. Acts as a clearinghouse of information about federal government activities, funding sources, and the most recent ideas in the mortgage lending industry; operates a certification program to encourage competence and to train housing counselors in the latest regulatory and market trends. Sponsors comprehensive housing counselor training sessions, mortgage default training, credit and information management programs, and energy conservation courses. Maintains speakers' bureau. **Libraries: Type:** not open to the public. **Holdings:** books. **Subjects:** housing counseling skills and techniques. **Awards:** Housing Counselor of the Year. **Frequency:** annual. **Type:** recognition. **Departments:** Education and Training; Legislative. **Divisions:** Certification. **Affiliated With:** National Low Income Housing Coalition. **Publications:** *Comprehensive Housing Counseling Reference Manual* ● *Housing Pipeline*, quarterly. Newsletter ● *Housing Summaries*, quarterly ● *The Pipeline*, 4/year. **Conventions/Meetings:** quarterly meeting (exhibits) ● annual Training Conference (exhibits) - always in June.

12057 ■ National Foundation of Manufactured Home Owners (NFMHO)
c/o Deborah Chapman, Chair
62 Hawthorne Cir.
Willow Street, PA 17584
Ph: (717)284-4520

Fax: (717)284-4520
E-mail: pamhoa@aol.com
URL: http://www.manhousingfoundation.org
Contact: Deborah Chapman, Chair
Founded: 1978. **State Groups:** 34. **Local Groups:** 1,080. **Description:** Represents 20,000,000 owners of mobile/manufactured homes. Serves as a unified national voice for mobile/manufactured homeowners and to improve communications among members, and research problems homeowners can experience. Maintains resources, include extensive collection of material, clearinghouse of information, especially on the purchase, set-up and maintenance of homes. **Awards:** Doris Levesque Award. **Frequency:** annual. **Type:** recognition ● Leonard G and Marie Wehrman Award. **Frequency:** annual. **Type:** recognition. **Formerly:** (1990) National Mobile/Manufactured Home Owners Foundation. **Supersedes:** Mobile Home Owners Federation; National Federation of Mobile Home Owners. **Publications:** *VOICE*, quarterly. Newsletter. Provides membership activity information. **Price:** free to any manufactured homeowner association. **Advertising:** accepted. **Conventions/Meetings:** annual meeting, varies on points of interest to manufactured housing/home living.

12058 ■ National Homeowners Association (NHA)
PO Box 221225
Chantilly, VA 20153
Ph: (703)581-1515
Fax: (703)581-1234.
Contact: John L. Weidlein, Pres.
Founded: 1975. **Staff:** 3. **Description:** Advocacy organization for individual homeowners. Promotes a political and economic climate favorable to American homeowners; provides legislative/regulatory liaison. Conducts political, educational, and consumer programs. Topics researched include: taxes, insurance, energy savings, home maintenance and repairs, mortgage and financing options, crime and safety precautions, and real estate practices. **Convention/Meeting:** none. **Publications:** *Homefront*, periodic. Newsletter.

12059 ■ National Housing Conference (NHC)
1801 K St. NW, Ste.M-100
Washington, DC 20006-1301
Ph: (202)466-2121
Fax: (202)466-2122
E-mail: cegan@nhc.org
URL: http://www.nhc.org
Contact: Conrad Egan, Pres./CEO
Founded: 1931. **Members:** 800. **Membership Dues:** subscriber, $550 ● friend, $1,650 ● supporter, $2,750 ● sustainer, $4,400 ● pacesetter, $5,500 ● retired individual, $100 ● sponsor, $1,000 ● patron, $20,000 ● benefactor, $30,000 ● Chairman's Circle, $50,000. **Staff:** 12. **Budget:** $2,000,000. **Description:** Housing authority officials, community development specialists, builders, bankers, lawyers, accountants, owners, residents, insurers, architects and planners, religious organizations, labor groups, and national housing and housing related organizations. Mobilizes support for effective programs in housing and community development as well as affordable and accessible housing for all Americans. Holds educational programs. **Awards:** **Type:** recognition. **Formerly:** National Public Housing Conference. **Publications:** Annual Report, annual. Alternate Formats: online. **Conventions/Meetings:** semiannual meeting (exhibits) - always fall.

12060 ■ National Housing Institute (NHI)
460 Bloomfield Ave., Ste.211
Montclair, NJ 07042-3552
Ph: (973)509-2888
Fax: (973)509-8005
E-mail: nhi@nhi.org
URL: http://www.nhi.org
Contact: Harold Simon, Exec. Dir.
Founded: 1975. **Staff:** 6. **Description:** Dedicated to community revitalization by empowering residents of low-income neighborhoods, strengthening the civil society, and enhancing the work of community building. Conducts research, acts as a resource center.

Formerly: Shelterforce Collective. **Publications:** *Shelterforce*, bimonthly. Magazine. Trade publication for community building professionals, covering theory, policy, and practice. **Price:** $18.00 /year for individuals; $30.00 /year for institutions and libraries. ISSN: 0885-9612. **Circulation:** 3,500. **Advertising:** accepted. Alternate Formats: online.

12061 ■ National Housing and Rehabilitation Association (NH&RA)
1400 16th St. NW, Ste.420
Washington, DC 20036-2244
Ph: (202)939-1750
Fax: (202)265-4435
E-mail: pbell@dworbell.com
URL: http://www.housingonline.com
Contact: Peter H. Bell, Exec. Dir.
Founded: 1970. **Members:** 390. **Membership Dues:** full, $1,650 (annual) ● associate, $1,100 (annual) ● public, $385 (annual). **Staff:** 9. **Budget:** $500,000. **Description:** Organizations and individuals in development, finance, construction, and property management fields who are committed to multi-family housing rehabilitation, new construction, and historic preservation effort; organizations and individuals in allied fields; city governments, local housing or community development agencies, state housing agencies, and other public bodies concerned with housing rehabilitation and new construction. Monitors all governmental policies affecting multi-family housing development and rehabilitation activity under federal housing programs. Informs members of congressional, HUD, IRS, state housing finance agency, and court actions. Conducts research on government incentives for rehabilitation. Comments on proposed governmental policies to ensure that the objectives of multi-family housing rehabilitation are advanced. Provides a forum for members to meet and speak with government officials on an informal basis. Operates speakers' bureau. **Libraries:** **Type:** reference. **Holdings:** audio recordings. **Computer Services:** Mailing lists. **Committees:** Congressional Relations; HUD Affairs; Tax and Finance Issues. **Formerly:** (1985) National Housing Rehabilitation Association. **Publications:** *First of the Month*, monthly. Bulletin. **Price:** included in membership dues ● *Housingonline Weekly*. Newsletter. **Price:** included in membership dues. Alternate Formats: online. **Conventions/Meetings:** annual Fall Multifamily Finance and Tax Credit Conference - meeting - always November, San Francisco, CA ● Fall Multifamily Finance Meeting - always November, Boston, MA ● Spring Forum - conference ● Summer Institute - conference - always August.

12062 ■ National Institute of Senior Housing (NISH)
c/o National Council on the Aging
1901 L St. NW, 4th Fl.
Washington, DC 20036
Ph: (202)479-1200
Free: (800)424-9046
Fax: (202)479-0735
E-mail: info@ncoa.org
URL: http://www.ncoa.org/content.cfm?sectionID=45
Contact: Mary H. Yearns PhD, Chair
Founded: 1979. **Members:** 725. **Membership Dues:** individual, $90 (annual) ● organization, $125 (annual). **Staff:** 1. **Description:** Organizations and individuals interested in the special housing needs of older adults. Works to organize and maintain a national response to the growing needs for affordable, decent housing and living arrangements for older adults, and serve individuals involved in providing senior housing. Promotes the development of community-based housing options for senior citizens. Provides a forum for the exchange of information and experience in the development and management of housing suitable for the elderly. Represents the needs and concerns of members to national, state, and local legislative bodies, to the Department of Housing and Urban Development, and to other agencies of the federal government. Serves as a clearinghouse on housing options for older adults. Maintains speakers' bureau and registry of experts in the senior housing field; provides information and referral services.

Libraries: **Type:** open to the public. **Subjects:** issues and topics relevant to aging. **Awards:** Bright Ideas in Housing. **Frequency:** annual. **Type:** monetary. **Recipient:** for creative ideas that enrich housing environment for seniors ● The Sid Spector Memorial Award for Excellence in Senior Housing Service. **Frequency:** annual. **Type:** recognition. **Recipient:** to an individual with outstanding accomplishments and achievements in the field. **Telecommunication Services:** electronic bulletin board, Aging Online ● electronic mail, yerns@iastate.edu. **Committees:** Conference and Training; Public Policy; Research and Development; Standing. **Affiliated With:** National Council on the Aging. **Publications:** *NCOA Networks*, bimonthly. Newspaper. Covers activities of NCOA constituent units, regulatory and judicial decisions affecting older persons, and significant field developments. **Price:** included in membership dues. ISSN: 1045-9073. **Circulation:** 7,000. **Advertising:** accepted ● *Perspective on Aging*, bimonthly. Journal. **Conventions/Meetings:** periodic symposium ● periodic workshop.

12063 ■ National Leased Housing Association (NLHA)
1900 L St. NW, Ste.300
Washington, DC 20036
Ph: (202)785-8888
Fax: (202)785-2008
E-mail: info@hudnlha.com
URL: http://www.hudnlha.com
Contact: Denise B. Muha, Exec. Dir.
Founded: 1972. **Members:** 650. **Membership Dues:** standard private, $1,000 (annual) ● affiliate private, $650 (annual) ● sustaining private, $2,500 (annual) ● large agency/non-profit public, $1,000 (annual) ● standard public, $500 (annual) ● sustaining public, $2,500 (annual). **Staff:** 5. **Description:** Public and private organizations and individuals concerned and involved with government-assisted housing programs. Informs members of program developments; represents members' interests before Congress and HUD. **Committees:** Developers; Housing Management; PHA Management; Syndicators. **Formerly:** (1974) Section 23 Leased Housing Association. **Publications:** *The Bulletin*, monthly. Newsletter. Provides an in depth analysis of the legislative and administrative developments. ● Bulletin, monthly ● Membership Directory, annual ● Also publishes deskbook and special mailings. **Conventions/Meetings:** annual meeting - always January and June ● seminar, for training and education.

12064 ■ National Low Income Housing Coalition (NLIHC)
727 15th St. NW, 6th Fl.
Washington, DC 20005
Ph: (202)662-1530
Fax: (202)393-1973
E-mail: sheila@nlihc.org
URL: http://www.nlihc.org
Contact: Sheila Crowley, Pres.
Founded: 1978. **Members:** 1,300. **Membership Dues:** low income (individual, student), $3 ● low income (resident association), $100 ● organization (250000 operating budget), $200 ● organization (250000-499999 budget), $350 ● organization (500000-999999 budget), $500 ● organization (one million to two million budget), $1,000-$2,000. **Staff:** 12. **Description:** Individuals and organizations concerned with improving and expanding low-income housing programs. Carries out a program of education, organization, and advocacy designed to provide decent housing, suitable environments, adequate neighborhoods, and freedom of housing choice for low-income people. Primary focus is on programs to meet housing needs of very low-income people, whose problems are most acute. Monitors low-income housing needs and programs and alerts members of actions to be taken. Develops policy positions and testifies and works with Congress and other government bodies to get them adopted. **Libraries:** **Type:** reference. **Subjects:** housing. **Absorbed:** Low Income Housing Information Service. **Supersedes:** Ad Hoc Low Income Housing Coalition. **Publications:** *A Report on State-Funded Rental As-*

sistance Programs: A Patchwork of Small Measures. Contains information on the characteristics and funding levels of rental assistance programs. **Price:** $15.00 for members; $25.00 for nonmembers ● *America's Neighbors: The Affordable Housing Crisis and the People it Affects*. Report. Contains data on the housing problems. Alternate Formats: online ● *Calls to Action*, periodic. Newsletter ● *Changing Priorities: The Federal Budget and Housing Assistance 1976-2005*. Report. Provides a history of funding for housing assistance. **Price:** $15.00 for members; $20.00 for nonmembers. Alternate Formats: online ● *Changing Priorities: The Federal Budget and Housing Assistance, 1976-2007*. Report. Provides an overview of the HUD budget trends from fiscal year 1976-2006. **Price:** $15.00 for members; $20.00 for nonmembers ● *Memo to Members*, weekly. Newsletter. **Price:** available to members only. **Circulation:** 1,300. Alternate Formats: online ● *NIMBY Report*, semiannual. Contains news about the NIMBY syndrome and the efforts being done to overcome it. **Price:** $10.00 for nonmembers; $5.00 for members. Alternate Formats: online ● *Out of Reach*, annual. Annual Report. Contains income and rental housing cost data for the fifty states. **Price:** $15.00 for members; $25.00 for nonmembers. Alternate Formats: online ● *Scarcity and Success: Perspective on Assisted Housing*. Report. Contains information about voucher use. **Price:** $15.00 for members; $25.00 for nonmembers. **Conventions/Meetings:** annual Housing Policy Conference and Lobby Day - meeting - always Washington, DC.

12065 ■ National Organization of African Americans in Housing (NOAAH)
507 Capitol Ct. NE, Ste.300
Washington, DC 20002
Ph: (202)544-1058
Fax: (202)544-1059
E-mail: adriannetodman@noaah.org
URL: http://www.noaah.org
Contact: Adrianne Todman, Pres.
Membership Dues: public housing authority, $750-$5,000 (annual) ● public or industry agency/corporation, $5,000 (annual) ● small business/consultant, $500 (annual) ● public housing resident organization, $175 (annual) ● individual, $125 (annual) ● public housing resident, $50 (annual) ● student, $25 (annual). **Description:** Improves the quality of housing services. Provides technical, operational and moral support to members. Offers opportunities for professional skills enhancement, resident training and economic development. Advocates for fair housing policies and programs. **Publications:** *NOAAH News*. Newsletter.

12066 ■ National Rural Housing Coalition (NRHC)
1250 Eye St. NW, Ste.902
Washington, DC 20005
Ph: (202)393-5229
Fax: (202)393-3034
E-mail: nrhc@nrhcweb.org
URL: http://www.nrhcweb.org
Contact: Claudia Shay, Pres.
Founded: 1970. **Membership Dues:** individual, $50 (annual) ● organization (with housing budget of $300,000 or less to $700,000), $250-$750 (annual) ● organization (with housing budget of $700,000 to $1,000,000 and above), $1,500-$2,000 (annual). **Description:** Advocates for improved government and private housing programs for people in small towns and rural areas. Develops informational and educational material; gives and coordinates testimony before congressional committees; seeks improved administrative procedures within the executive branch of the federal government. Lobbies for low-income rural housing and community facilities. **Publications:** *Action Letters*, periodic ● *Legislative Update*, biweekly, while Congress is in session. **Price:** $250.00/year. **Conventions/Meetings:** annual conference ● workshop.

12067 ■ National Shared Housing Resource Center (NSHRC)
c/o Laura Fanucchi, Treas.
364 S Railroad Ave.
San Mateo, CA 94401

Ph: (650)348-6660
Fax: (650)348-0284
E-mail: lfanucchi@hiphousing.org
URL: http://www.nationalsharedhousing.org
Contact: Laura Fanucchi, Treas.
Founded: 1981. **Members:** 300. **Membership Dues:** professional in shared housing or related field, $50 (annual) ● consumer, $20 (annual). **Description:** Aims to provide information, education, technical assistance, and research on shared housing. Provides speakers, technical assistance, consultations, and regional training workshops on planning and developing match-up and group residence programs; works toward removal of financial, regulatory, legislative, zoning, and other barriers inhibiting development of shared housing; provides legislative testimony. Makes available funds for the purchase and planting of trees. **Libraries: Type:** reference. **Awards:** Maggie Tree Award. **Type:** recognition. **Recipient:** for outstanding and creative shared housing program in the U.S. **Formerly:** (1984) Shared Housing Resource Center; (1988) National Shared Housing Resource Center. **Publications:** *Consumers Guide to Home Sharing*, published as needed. Book ● *Homesharing: Matching for Independence. A Planning Manual for Organizations*, published as needed ● *Shared Housing for Older People - A Planning Manual for Group Residences*, published as necessary ● *Shared Housing News*, biennial. Newsletter. **Conventions/Meetings:** annual conference.

12068 ■ Neighborhood Housing Services of America (NHSA)
1970 Broadway, Ste.470
Oakland, CA 94612
Ph: (510)832-5542
Fax: (510)444-3063
E-mail: info@nhsofamerica.org
URL: http://www.NHSAonline.org
Contact: Mary Lee Widener, Pres./CEO
Founded: 1974. **Nonmembership. Description:** Works to revitalize neighborhoods and strengthen communities across America. Collaborates with private sector institutional investors, philanthropic organizations, governmental entities, and NeighborWorks America to improve mortgage industry products and services for community initiatives. Provides affordable financing, services, and products that strengthen communities and improve lives for the long term.

12069 ■ NeighborWorks America
1325 G St. NW, Ste.800
Washington, DC 20005-3100
Ph: (202)220-2300
Free: (800)438-5547
Fax: (202)376-2600
E-mail: nti@nw.org
URL: http://www.nw.org
Contact: Kenneth D. Wade, CEO
Description: Provides financial support, technical assistance, and training for community-based revitalization efforts. Revitalizes older urban neighborhoods by mobilizing public, private, and community resources at the neighborhood level. Provides matching capital grants, operating subsidies, and technical services to mutual housing associations for the development, acquisition and rehabilitation of multi-family and single-family properties to ensure affordability by low- and moderate-income families. **Also Known As:** (2005) Neighborhood Reinvestment Corporation. **Publications:** *Bright Ideas*, quarterly. Magazine. Alternate Formats: online ● Annual Report, annual. Alternate Formats: online ● Newsletter, monthly. Alternate Formats: online.

12070 ■ Rebuilding Alliance
457 Kingsley Ave.
Palo Alto, CA 94301
Ph: (650)325-4663
Fax: (650)325-4667
E-mail: info@rebuildingalliance.org
URL: http://www.rebuildingalliance.org
Contact: Donna Baranski-Walker, Exec. Dir.
Founded: 2003. **Multinational. Description:** Lends support to Palestinian families in rebuilding homes

and schools during continuing occupation and siege. Educates the global community; raises funds and provides grants to Israeli and Palestinian NGOs who coordinate the rebuilding of demolished homes and schools. Selects precedent-building projects and defends them all the way up to the Israeli Supreme Court. Solicits amicus curae briefs for pivotal court cases to save homes, schools and towns from demolition.

12071 ■ Rebuilding Together
1536 Sixteenth St. NW
Washington, DC 20036-1402
Ph: (202)483-9083
Free: (800)4RE-HAB9
Fax: (202)483-9081
E-mail: info@rebuildingtogether.org
URL: http://www.rebuildingtogether.org
Founded: 1988. **Members:** 251. **Staff:** 17. **Budget:** $2,600,000. **Description:** Works in partnership with the community. Preserves and revitalizes houses and communities to ensure that low-income homeowners, particularly the elderly, disabled, and families with children, live in safety, warmth and independence. **Awards:** Community Builder Award. **Frequency:** annual. **Type:** recognition ● Exemplary Management. **Frequency:** annual. **Type:** recognition ● Spread the Spirit Award. **Frequency:** annual. **Type:** recognition. **Computer Services:** database ● mailing lists. **Formerly:** (2001) Christmas in April - U.S.A.; (2001) Rebuilding Together with Christmas in April - U.S.A. **Publications:** *Community Warehouses*. Brochure ● *Home Modifications*. Brochure ● *Homeowner Information*. Brochure ● *Homeowner Maintenance Workshops*. Brochure ● *Involving Youth*. Brochure ● Newsletter, semiannual ● Annual Report, annual. **Conventions/Meetings:** annual conference, workshops for affiliates.

12072 ■ Tile Partners for Humanity (TPFH)
3845 Holcomb Bridge Rd., Ste.400
Norcross, GA 30092
Ph: (770)416-0200
Fax: (770)209-0209
E-mail: ally@tpfh.com
URL: http://www.tpfh.com
Contact: Allyson Feritta, Exec. Dir.
Founded: 2002. **Multinational. Description:** Partners with Habitat for Humanity International to eliminate substandard housing around the world. Pledges to provide materials and labor for Habitat for Humanity projects. Supports programs that strengthen homes and communities around the world. **Affiliated With:** Habitat for Humanity International.

12073 ■ Urban Homesteading Assistance Board (UHAB)
120 Wall St., 20th Fl.
New York, NY 10005
Ph: (212)479-3300
Fax: (212)344-6457
E-mail: webmaster@uhab.org
URL: http://www.uhab.org
Contact: Andrew Reicher, Exec. Dir.
Founded: 1973. **Staff:** 30. **Budget:** $2,000,000. **Languages:** English, Russian, Spanish. **Description:** Assists low-income neighborhood housing groups and tenant organizations. Works to develop nonprofit, cooperative, resident-controlled housing. Provides technical assistance and services to low- and moderate-income families seeking self-help solutions to their housing needs; assists in developing and implementing sweat equity rehabilitation and homesteading projects throughout New York City. Offers management training and support to tenant groups who own and/or manage their own housing. Offers consulting services to community groups nationally and internationally on issues surrounding resident participation in housing. **Libraries: Type:** reference. **Holdings:** 1,000; books, clippings, periodicals. **Subjects:** housing, cooperative movement. **Publications:** *City Limits - The News Magazine of New York City Housing and Neighborhoods*, 10/year ● *Complete Training Catalogue*. Contains in-depth descriptions of courses offered to TTL buildings and HDFCs through UHAB's neighborhood centers. Alternate

Formats: online ● *Cooking and Building*. Book. Features recipes contributed by co-op residents, and friends and staff of UHAB. **Price:** $5.00 ● *Neighborhood Network Newsletter*, bimonthly. **Price:** free ● *Resource Directory of Vendors and Service Providers*. **Price:** free. Alternate Formats: online ● *Self Help In Our Own Words: 1974-1988*. Booklet. Features interviews of homesteaders and co-op residents. **Price:** $5.00. Alternate Formats: online ● *Self-Help Update*, 8/year. Contains information about cooperative management and ownership for limited equity cooperations. **Circulation:** 500 ● Manuals. Covers management, development, construction, cooperative ownership, and financial management. ● Pamphlets. **Conventions/Meetings:** annual conference (exhibits).

Human Development

12074 ■ Aloha International (AI)
PO Box 426
Volcano, HI 96785
Ph: (808)826-1643 (808)645-7007
Fax: (808)826-1963
E-mail: huna@huna.org
URL: http://huna.org
Contact: Serge Kahili King PhD, Contact
Founded: 1973. **Members:** 14,000. **Staff:** 5. **Description:** Nondenominational religious order of individuals dedicated to creating peace and environmental harmony through the use of Huna (Hawaiian word meaning "hidden" or "secret"). Huna is a system of psychology used to remedy emotional and physical problems based on the knowledge of how the physical, mental, and spiritual levels of consciousness function effectively when used properly. Conducts classes, courses, lectures, tour groups, seasonal celebrations, and workshops; administers training in Huna techniques to individuals, group leaders, and counselors; offers Hawaiian shaman training. Participates in spiritual healing; sponsors voluntary research projects; organizes spiritual cooperatives (kokuas). **Projects:** Aloha. **Formerly:** Huna International. **Publications:** *Aloha News*, semiannual. Newsletter. **Circulation:** 10,000. Alternate Formats: online ● *The Aloha Spirit*. Booklet. **Price:** free ● *Basic Huna*. Brochure. **Price:** $1.00/copy ● Also publishes catalog of publications and tools. **Conventions/Meetings:** annual Makahiki Festival - always Thanksgiving Day, in Kauai, HI.

12075 ■ American Men's Studies Association
22 East St.
Northampton, MA 01060
Ph: (336)323-2672
E-mail: amsamail@gmail.com
URL: http://www.mensstudies.org
Founded: 1991. **Members:** 150. **Membership Dues:** individual, $60 (annual) ● student, $45 (annual) ● friend of AMSA, $100 (annual) ● individual outside U.S., $70 ● student outside U.S., $55 (annual). **Description:** Men and women interested in men's studies. Defines men's studies as the analyses of male experiences as social-historical-cultural constructions. Provides a forum for exchanging information about theories of masculinity through teaching, research, and clinical practice. **Awards:** The Loren Frankel Scholarship Award. **Frequency:** annual. **Type:** monetary. **Recipient:** to the best student proposal accepted for presentation at the organization's annual conference. **Publications:** Brochure. **Conventions/Meetings:** annual conference (exhibits).

12076 ■ Be Somebody, Be Yourself Institute (BSBYI)
PO Box 416
Denver, CO 80201-0416
Ph: (303)575-5676
Fax: (303)575-1187
E-mail: mail@gumbomedia.com
Contact: A. Doyle, Founder
Founded: 1989. **Staff:** 1. **For-Profit. Description:** Promotes personal growth through development of individual gifts and talents. Assists individuals in identifying their areas of strengths and abilities; facilitates development of improved self-esteem among members. **Awards:** Be Somebody, Be Yourself Emergchant Award. **Frequency:** annual. **Type:** recognition. **Publications:** *Be Somebody Be Yourself Poetry Book One* ● *Be Somebody, Be Yourself Poetry Newsletter*, annual. Contains poems about developing one's personal gifts and talents. ISSN: 1053-6531. **Circulation:** 5,000 ● *Recycling Find, Seek and Sell Workbook*. **Conventions/Meetings:** Be Somebody Be Yourself - seminar and workshop, virtual workshop available online (exhibits).

12077 ■ Consciousness Research and Training Project (CRTP)
Address Unknown since 2007
Founded: 1980. **Members:** 850. **Staff:** 2. **Budget:** $30,000. **Regional Groups:** 4. **State Groups:** 5. **Local Groups:** 2. **National Groups:** 4. **Description:** Teaches, sponsors, and conducts research into the nature of human consciousness, parapsychology, paranormal healing, and newly recognized dimensions of human potential. Sponsors introductory level and advanced courses in paranormal healing and eclectic meditations. Studies and evaluates health regimens and therapies. **Libraries: Type:** reference. **Holdings:** 600; articles, audio recordings, books, periodicals, video recordings. **Subjects:** parapsychology, consciousness research, meditation, mysticism, spirituality, healing, hard sciences, physics, complementary, alternative and traditional medicine. **Special Interest Groups:** Healing and meditation. **Affiliated With:** American Society for Psychical Research; Association for Transpersonal Psychology; IONS - Institute of Noetic Sciences; Parapsychology Foundation. **Publications:** *Compendium of Newsletters 1989-2000, Edited*, annual, 1-2/year. Covers topics in parapsychology, consciousness, and complementary healing modalities and resources, training and research activities. **Price:** $25.00 each. **Circulation:** 850. **Advertising:** not accepted ● *Compendium of Newsletters, 1978-1989, Edited*, annual. Contains articles on consciousness, healing, human potentials and resources. **Price:** $25.00 each. **Circulation:** 850. **Advertising:** not accepted ● *Consciousness Research and Training Project—Newsletter*, 1-2/year. Covers topics in parapsychology, consciousness, and complementary healing modalities and resources, training and research activities. **Price:** included in membership dues. **Circulation:** 850 ● Also publishes various training materials. **Conventions/Meetings:** periodic LeShan Introductory and Advanced Healing Seminar, for training and practice in LeShan healing process and in depth introduction to the field, discussion, work with resource materials - October, May, April, November, and occasional other times, each 5 days long including east and west coast ● periodic meeting and workshop, to train individuals in the process, use, and practice of the LeShan method of healing - 5 days/residential ● periodic workshop and seminar, for practitioners of the LeShan healing practice and trained researchers.

12078 ■ Earthstewards Network (ESN)
Box 10697
Bainbridge Island, WA 98110
Ph: (206)842-7986
Free: (800)561-2909
Fax: (206)842-8918
E-mail: outreach@earthstewards.org
URL: http://www.earthstewards.org
Contact: Jerilyn Brusseau, Contact
Founded: 1980. **Members:** 800. **Membership Dues:** general, $40 (annual). **Multinational. Description:** Worldwide multicultural network dedicated to "inspiring and empowering ordinary people to stretch, grow and learn." Acts for conflict transformation and the creation of positive relationships bridging boundaries of gender, age, culture, race, nations and beliefs. Aims to develop and support simple, effective and innovative programs that create a more viable future at the personal, community and global levels. Had developed programs and projects in grassroots citizen diplomacy, environmental service, global networking, conflict resolution, and gender-to-gender communication. **Projects:** Caring Clowns International; Citizen Diplomacy Trips; Essential Peacemaking Women and Men; Peace Trees. **Publications:** *Essene Book of Days 2007*, annual. Journal. **Price:** $19.95 plus shipping and handling. **Advertising:** accepted ● *Warriors of the Heart*. Book. **Price:** $12.95 ● Newsletter, quarterly. **Price:** included in membership dues. **Conventions/Meetings:** annual European Gathering - conference, conference of European members ● seminar, on conflict resolution and effective gender communication ● annual US Gathering - conference, conference of US members and Canadians.

12079 ■ Feathered Pipe Foundation (FPF)
PO Box 1682
Helena, MT 59624
Ph: (406)442-8196
Fax: (406)442-8110
E-mail: fpranch@mt.net
URL: http://www.featheredpipe.com
Contact: India Supera, Exec. Dir.
Founded: 1975. **Members:** 300. **Staff:** 10. **Description:** Seeks to provide opportunities for people to become healthier in body, mind, and spirit. Sponsors retreats and training intensives year-round at Feathered Pipe Ranch near Helena, MT. Conducts educational seminars; sponsors educational tours throughout the world with leaders in the field of conscious evolution. Primary focus of the tours is experiential learning in places of pilgrimage and power centers such as India, Tibet and Nepal, the Great Pyramid in Egypt, and Machu Pichu in Peru. **Convention/Meeting:** none. **Formerly:** (1986) Holistic Life Foundation. **Publications:** *Circle*, 3/year. Newsletter. Includes information on seasonal events in and around Montana related to personal and community awakening and empowerment. **Price:** $10.00/year. **Advertising:** accepted.

12080 ■ The FORUM (TF)
PO Box 5915
Santa Fe, NM 87502
Ph: (505)983-7077
Contact: Carol Bell Knight, Dir.
Founded: 1970. **Members:** 100. **Staff:** 6. **Budget:** $32,000. **State Groups:** 2. **Local Groups:** 1. **Description:** Research, religious, and educational foundation engaged in the study and exploration of futuristic concepts for the upliftment and understanding of humanity. Investigates phenomena related to the physical, emotional, mental, and spiritual aspects of the individual. Holds classes, seminars, worship service, and retreats; offers counseling services and directions for participating in a new culture based upon caring and creativity. Maintains speakers' bureau. **Libraries: Type:** reference. **Holdings:** 900; archival material, books, periodicals. **Subjects:** multilevel consciousness, philosophy. **Computer Services:** database ● mailing lists. **Affiliated With:** IONS - Institute of Noetic Sciences. **Also Known As:** (1995) Forum Christian Fellowship of Light. **Publications:** *Forum of Cosmic Light*, monthly. **Advertising:** accepted ● *The Teachings of Acumana*. Books. A series of 6 books. **Conventions/Meetings:** annual Summer Solstice Gathering - conference, gathering of seekers from 8 countries.

12081 ■ Hanuman Foundation (HF)
223 N Guadalupe St.
Box 269
Santa Fe, NM 87501-1850
Ph: (505)982-1176
Fax: (505)982-1759
E-mail: hanuman1008@earthlink.net
Contact: Jai Lakshman, Pres.
Founded: 1974. **Description:** Aims to provide spiritual well-being in society through seed projects including work with the terminally ill and the Hanuman Tape Library, which produces and distributes books and tapes of meditation instructors, musicians, and singers. The Foundation is named for Hanuman, a monkey that was considered to be the perfect servant of God in ancient Indian tales.

12082 ■ Himalayan International Institute of Yoga Science and Philosophy of the U.S.A.
952 Bethany Tpke.
Honesdale, PA 18431-4194
Ph: (570)253-5551
Free: (800)822-4547
Fax: (570)253-9078
E-mail: info@himalayaninstitute.org
URL: http://www.himalayaninstitute.org
Contact: Pandit Rajmani Tigunait, Spiritual Head
Founded: 1971. **Members:** 1,500. **Membership Dues:** individual, $60 (annual) ● family, $80 (annual). **Staff:** 49. **Regional Groups:** 10. **Multinational. Description:** Aims to teach meditation, philosophy, and holistic health care based on a synthesis of Eastern and Western knowledge and techniques; benefit mankind and society. Offers programs on holistic health, yoga, meditation, Eastern philosophy, stress management and psychology. Maintains speakers' bureau. Has established the Himalayan Institute Teachers Association, which certifies yoga teachers. Holistic health services available through the Institute's Center for Health and Healing. Publishes over 80 titles and numerous educational audio and video products on similar topics. **Libraries: Type:** reference. **Holdings:** 10,000. **Subjects:** yoga science, meditation, holistic health. **Additional Websites:** http://www.yimag.org. **Departments:** Himalayan Institute Press. **Programs:** Herbal Apprenticeship; Residential; Self-Transformation. **Publications:** *Himalayan Institute Quarterly Guide to Programs.* Newsletter. Contains course descriptions and editorials on yoga related topics. **Price:** included in membership dues. ISSN: 0891-6144. **Circulation:** 35,000 ● *Yoga Joyful Living*, bimonthly. Magazine. **Price:** $3.50/issue; $17.99/year; $32.00/2 years. ISSN: 1055-7911. **Circulation:** 120,000. **Advertising:** accepted. **Conventions/Meetings:** weekly seminar.

12083 ■ HUNA Research (HUNA)
1760 Anna St.
Cape Girardeau, MO 63701-4504
Ph: (573)334-3478
E-mail: huna@mail.com
URL: http://www.huna-research.com
Contact: Ms. Amanda Lemonds, Office Mgr.
Founded: 1945. **Members:** 19,016. **Membership Dues:** individual in U.S., $35 (annual) ● overseas, first class, $45 (annual). **Staff:** 1. **Regional Groups:** 10. **State Groups:** 22. **Local Groups:** 163. **Languages:** English, German, Portuguese, Spanish. **Multinational. Description:** Represents teachers of Huna and others from the healing professions; individuals wishing to develop and improve their lives; others interested in Huna. (Huna is a system of psychology used by the Kahunas of ancient Hawaii to remedy emotional and physical problems. The system is based on the knowledge of how the physical, mental, and spiritual levels of consciousness function effectively when used properly.) Works to assist members and others in taking charge of their own destiny and making a better life for themselves and their friends. Offers self-development program and classes. Conducts research; sponsors Certified Huna Teacher Program. **Awards: Type:** recognition. **Recipient:** for Huna teachers and lecturers. **Committees:** Research Group; Teacher Certification; Telepathic Mutual Healing Group. **Also Known As:** The Huna Fellowship. **Publications:** *The Aka Cord*, 8/year. Newsletter. Contains information about group meetings, classes, seminars, research projects, books, and related activities of Huna Research. **Price:** included in membership dues. **Circulation:** 2,000 ● *The Huna Research Bulletin*, quarterly. Newsletter. Devotes to the distribution of information and instruction of Huna. Includes book reviews. **Price:** included in membership dues. **Circulation:** 2,000. Also Cited As: *The Huna Work* ● *Huna, The Ancient Religion of Positive Thinking*. Book ● *Recovering the Ancient Magic*. Book ● *Tarot Card Symbology*. Book. **Conventions/Meetings:** periodic lecture and workshop ● annual seminar (exhibits).

12084 ■ Institute of Cultural Affairs (ICA)
4750 N Sheridan Rd.
Chicago, IL 60640
Ph: (773)769-6363
Free: (800)742-4032
Fax: (773)769-1144
E-mail: chicago@ica-usa.org
URL: http://www.ica-usa.org
Contact: Carolyn Antenen, Pres.
Founded: 1973. **Members:** 1,500. **Staff:** 60. **Budget:** $5,000,000. **Regional Groups:** 4. **National Groups:** 35. **Description:** U.S. branch of the Institute of Cultural Affairs International. Global research, training, and demonstration group concerned with the human factor in world development. Activities are based on the belief that effective human development must be initiated on the local level. Major training and demonstration programs include community development and facilitation services and training programs in 35 nations. **Computer Services:** Mailing lists. **Formerly:** (1973) Ecumenical Institute. **Publications:** *The Art of Focused Conversation*. Booklets. **Price:** $21.95 ● *ICA Initiatives*, quarterly. Newsletter. Features news, program highlights and articles about how people use ICA's methods. Alternate Formats: online ● *IERD Project Directory* ● *Participation Works*. Series of 12 examples of ICA methods used from around the world. ● *Winning Through Participation; Art of focused Conversation*. Book ● Pamphlets ● Annual Report, annual. Alternate Formats: online. **Conventions/Meetings:** quadrennial conference, on global futures.

12085 ■ Institute for the Development of the Harmonious Human Being (IDHHB)
PO Box 370
Nevada City, CA 95959
Ph: (530)272-0180
Free: (800)869-0658
Fax: (530)272-0184
E-mail: contributions@idhhb.org
URL: http://www.idhhb.org
Contact: E.J. Gold, Founder
Founded: 1971. **Members:** 1,400. **Staff:** 30. **Budget:** $200,000. **Local Groups:** 35. **Languages:** English, French, German, Portuguese, Spanish. **Description:** Individuals and groups studying the ancient teachings of spiritual awakening and personal transformation. Seeks to provide public access to information about: Voluntary Evolution, a practical approach to spiritual work on the self; spiritual disciplines dating back to ancient cultures; objective art and iconography. The Labyrinth Readers Course fosters new attitudes toward death and dying; other educational programs include Gateways books and tapes, sacred theater and dance training, mask initiation workshops, and professional evolutionary marketing seminars. Provides consultants in publicity, lecturing, sacred theater and dance. Maintains publishing house, tape service, and support service for local chapters. Offers Zen Basics, a training course for essence attention on audiocassette. **Computer Services:** Mailing lists. **Telecommunication Services:** electronic mail, info@gatewaysbooksandtapes.com. **Publications:** *American Book of the Dead*. Contains practical instructions to guide readers along the labyrinthine voyage of spiritual transformation. **Price:** $15.95. **Circulation:** 125,000 ● *Angels Healing Journey*. Videos. **Price:** $19.95 ● *Character and Neurosis: An Integrative View*. Contains an explanation of the enneagram of personality types. **Price:** $24.95 ● *The Dream Assembly*. Book. Features the mystical tales set in the old world of the Hassidic masters. **Price:** $19.95 ● *Galaxy*, bimonthly. Magazine. Contains science fiction/fantasy short stories and novellas, as well as editorials, science column, and book reviews. ISSN: 1073-4422. **Circulation:** 5,000. **Advertising:** accepted ● *Gestalt Therapy: The Attitude and Practice of an Atheoretical Experientialism*. Book. Contains a collection of recent talks and essays reassessing Gestalt for the 90's. **Price:** $29.95 ● *The Hidden Work*. Book. Explains the inner meaning of rituals and shamanistic methods. **Price:** $15.95 ● *The Human Biological Machine as a Transformation Apparatus*. Book. Presents vital information for anyone on a spiritual path in a practical way. **Price:** $22.95. **Conventions/Meetings:** annual convention.

12086 ■ Institute for Individual and World Peace (IIWP)
2101 Wilshire Blvd., Ste.119
Santa Monica, CA 90403-5745
Ph: (310)315-3451
Free: (888)848-4497
Fax: (310)315-3452
E-mail: peace@iiwp.org
URL: http://www.iiwp.org
Contact: David Rogers, Contact
Founded: 1982. **Staff:** 6. **Budget:** $350,000. **Description:** Creates projects and events designed to bring people to a direct and personal experience of peace. (This is based on the tenet that "with a direct and personal experience of peace, we can more effectively assume our heritage as peacemakers on earth.") Sponsors workshops, seminars and meetings in support of greater understanding and world peace. **Formerly:** (1988) John Roger Foundation. **Publications:** *The Peaceful Times*, quarterly. Newsletter. **Price:** free. **Conventions/Meetings:** annual FTP Donor Seminar ● One Accord: The Process Toward Peace - workshop, for leaders and peacemakers.

12087 ■ Institute for Theological Encounter With Science and Technology (ITEST)
20 Archbishop May Dr.
St. Louis, MO 63119
Ph: (314)533-0349
E-mail: postigm@faithscience.org
URL: http://www.faithscience.org
Contact: Sister Marianne Postiglione, Acting Dir.
Founded: 1968. **Members:** 400. **Membership Dues:** individual, $50 (annual) ● student, $25 (annual) ● institutional, $125 (annual). **Staff:** 2. **Description:** Scientists, theologians, and academicians dedicated to an "interdisciplinary search for meaning in the context of revolutionary change." Concerned with "the opportunities and problems arising from our ability to control nature and ourselves;" goal is to involve religious, legal, political, and educational institutions in these "opportunities and problems." Conducts educational programs. **Libraries: Type:** reference. **Holdings:** 60. **Subjects:** science/technology as they relate to encounter with theology/faith. **Awards:** ITEST Award For Meritorious Service. **Type:** recognition. **Computer Services:** database, contains all proceedings from conferences and workshops. **Publications:** *Advances in Neuroscience: Implications for Christian Faith (2002)*. Proceedings ● *Biotechnology Patent Law and Theology (2005)*. Proceedings. Discusses on the implications of advances in biotechnology especially adult and embryonic stem cell research. ● *Christianity and the Human Body (1999)*. Book. Contains essay and discussion about the Christian theology of the human body. ● *Computers Artificial Intelligence and Virtual Reality (2004)*. Proceedings. Talks about the social, moral, philosophical, and theological implications of computers. **Price:** $19.95 ● *Creation and Evolution (1997)*. Book. Deals with the questions surrounding the topic of Creation and Evolution. ● *Genetics and Nutrition (2001)*. Book. Contains essay written by scientists, biotechnologists and a theologian examining various approaches to genetically modified food. ● *The Genome: Plant, Animal, Human (1999)*. Book. Explains the genetic advancement on plant, human and animal. ● *The Human Genome Project*. Book. Contains an explanation of the Christianity's interest on DNA and the Human Genome Initiative. ● *Institute for Theological Encounter With Science and Technology—Bulletin*, quarterly. **Price:** included in membership dues. **Circulation:** 800 ● *Institute for Theological Encounter With Science and Technology—Conference Proceeding*, semiannual. Proceedings. **Price:** included in membership dues; $6.00 /year for nonmembers ● *ITEST Bulletin*, quarterly. **Price:** included in membership dues. ISSN: 1073-5976 ● *ITEST Directory*, annual ● *Lights Breaking: A Journey Down the Byways of Genetic Engineering and Decision*. Video. Features the technological breakthrough in genetic engineering. **Price:** $14.95 ● *Patenting of Biological Entities (2000)*. Proceedings ● *The Science and Politics of Food* ● *Transfiguration: Elements of Science and Christian Faith (1992)*. Book ● *You See Lights Breaking Upon Us: Doctrinal Perspectives*

on Biological Advance. Book. Explores the beginning of scientific advancement using sacramental and covenantal doctrinal themes. **Price:** $15.95. **Conventions/Meetings:** semiannual conference and workshop.

12088 ■ International Society for a Complete Earth (ISCE)

PO Box 1952
Kapaa, HI 96746
Free: (808)245-3820
E-mail: director@hollow-earth.org
URL: http://www.hollow-earth.org
Contact: Danny L. Weiss, Dir.

Founded: 1977. **Members:** 1,000. **Staff:** 7. **National Groups:** 9. **Description:** Launches expeditions to either the North or South Poles and there enter "the inner world of the hollow earth." Postulates that these expeditions will prove that Admiral Richard Evelyn Byrd accidentally entered this world in 1947. Contends that (flying saucers) "flugelrads" emanate from this inner world and that powerful force have been suppressing truth for mankind making the world incomplete (hence the name of the organization), and that world peace will be realized only when finally joined with the advanced beings of the inner-earth. Has conducted expeditions to German Antarctica; engages in research. **Libraries: Type:** reference. **Holdings:** 5; books. **Subjects:** hollow earth, UFO, abductions. **Computer Services:** Mailing lists, current and potential members. **Committees:** Conventions. **Also Known As:** Hollow Earth. **Publications:** *A Flight to the Land Beyond the North Pole.* Booklet. **Advertising:** accepted. Also Cited As: *Is This the Missing Secret Diary of Admiral Richard Evelyn Byrd?* ● *ISCE Compendium: Books, Essays, Videos, and Things.* Catalogs ● *ISCE Quarterly.* Newsletter. **Price:** $25.00/year ● *Video Production: Journey to the Hollow Earth* ● Brochure.

12089 ■ Krishnamurti Foundation of America (KFA)

PO Box 1560
Ojai, CA 93024
Ph: (805)646-2726 (805)646-4773
Fax: (805)646-6674
E-mail: kfa@kfa.org
URL: http://www.kfa.org
Contact: Diane White, Contact

Founded: 1968. **Staff:** 60. **Budget:** $2,500,000. **Nonmembership. Description:** Disseminates information to individuals, organizations, libraries, and foundations with an interest in the teachings of J. Krishnamurti (1895-1986), author, educator, and philosopher. Has established the Oak Grove School in Ojai, CA for elementary and secondary students. **Libraries: Type:** reference; open to the public. **Holdings:** 1,500; archival material, audiovisuals, books. **Subjects:** J. Krishnamurti work. **Publications:** *Foundation Focus,* semiannual. Newsletter. Covers the activities of the Krishnamurti foundations and worldwide schools. Includes book reviews. **Circulation:** 20,000 ● *Krishnamurti Bulletin,* annual. Features unpublished materials from the archives. **Price:** free. **Circulation:** 1,000 ● Booklets, annual. Alternate Formats: online ● Books ● Pamphlets ● Also provides book reviews, calendar of events, and catalog online. **Conventions/Meetings:** annual seminar (exhibits) - first weekend of May ● semiannual workshop - February and October.

12090 ■ Mandala Society

PO Box 1233
Del Mar, CA 92014
Ph: (858)481-7751
E-mail: info@year2020vision.net
URL: http://www.year2020vision.net/mandala.htm
Contact: David J. Harris, Founder

Founded: 1972. **Staff:** 2. **Description:** Philosophical society concerned with creating environments that better integrate the body, mind, spirit and social conscience of the individual. Provides education, training and guidance and encourages others everywhere to focus on cooperation and abundance. **Libraries: Type:** reference. **Holdings:** 7. **Subjects:** personal and global transformation. **Publications:**

Chronicle of Holistic Health, periodic. Journal. **Price:** $108.00 plus shipping and handling.

12091 ■ Men's Resource Center (MRC)

12 SE 14th Ave.
Portland, OR 97214
Ph: (503)235-3433 (503)235-4050
Fax: (503)235-4762
E-mail: mensresourcecent@qwest.net
URL: http://www.portlandmrc.com
Contact: Roberto Olivero PhD, Contact

Founded: 1974. **Members:** 5. **Description:** Men committed to exploring and supporting antisexist attitudes and practices in themselves and in other men. Provides individual, couple, and group counseling. Problem-solving groups discuss men's issues, domestic violence, male survivors of sex abuse and sexual assault, and gay communities; offers consultation and professional training on these topics.

12092 ■ New Civilization Network (NCN)

PO Box 260433
Encino, CA 91316
Ph: (818)774-1462
E-mail: ffunch@newciv.org
URL: http://www.newciv.org
Contact: Flemming Funch, Founder

Founded: 1986. **Members:** 30. **Staff:** 3. **Budget:** $2,000. **Languages:** English, Esperanto, French, Polish, Spanish. **Description:** Promotes the development of "more loving, intelligent, and truly advanced civilizations." Seeks to attain higher levels of consciousness. Maintains speakers' bureau. Conducts charitable, educational, and research programs. Uses "Total Systems Approach" to develop repeatable social models, tested by volunteers in day-to-day operations. **Libraries: Type:** reference. **Holdings:** 200; books, periodicals. **Awards:** Best Ideas for New Civilizations Design. **Type:** recognition. **Computer Services:** Online services. **Divisions:** Finance; Food; Heath; Insurance; Learning; Retirement/Unemployment; Space/Facilities; Thinking. **Formerly:** (2005) New Civilization. **Publications:** *Progress Report,* quarterly. Reprint. **Price:** free. **Circulation:** 50. Alternate Formats: online ● Also offers various other publications. **Conventions/Meetings:** periodic meeting.

12093 ■ New Road Map Foundation (NRM)

PO Box 15320
Seattle, WA 98115
Ph: (206)527-0437
E-mail: newroadmap@igc.org
URL: http://www.newroadmap.org
Contact: Vicki Robin, Pres.

Founded: 1984. **Nonmembership. Description:** Provides educational programs designed to help individuals assume personal responsibility for their lives and make a meaningful contribution to the world. Teaches the 9-step program for saving money in the book Your Money or Your Life: provides related group study materials for use in the workplace, community education programs and churches. Provides financial assistance to related groups. Maintains speakers' bureau. **Publications:** *Group Study Guide for Use with Your Money or Your Life.* **Price:** $5.00 ● *Money and Spirit for Use with Your Money or Your Life.* **Price:** $5.00 ● *Study Guide for Contemporary Christians for Use with Your Money or Your Life.* **Price:** $5.00 ● *Transforming Your Relationship with Money and Achieving Financial Independence.* Includes audiocassette and workbook course. **Price:** $39.95 ● *Your Money or Your Life.* Book. Includes 9-step program for creating a low consumption, high fulfillment lifestyle. **Price:** $13.95.

12094 ■ Quartus Foundation for Spiritual Research (QFSR)

PO Box 1768
Boerne, TX 78006-6768
Ph: (830)249-3985
Fax: (830)249-3318

E-mail: quartus@quartus.org
URL: http://www.quartus.org
Contact: John Randolph Price, Chm.

Founded: 1981. **Members:** 3,000. **Staff:** 5. **Description:** Promotes spiritual research and communication on the reality and truth of the individual being. Works to expand the human mind to its "divine origin," affect a "measurable change in the collective consciousness of humanity," and assist in ushering in a new world of harmony and divine order. Conducts healing groups, seminars and daily worldwide meditations; sponsors World Healing Day. **Commissions:** Planetary Commission for Global Healing. **Publications:** *Quartus Report,* monthly. Newsletter. Includes articles on expanding consciousness, wisdom teaching, esoteric philosophy, and new thought psychology; provides news on member activities. **Price:** $25.00/year in U.S.; $35.00/year outside U.S. Alternate Formats: online. **Conventions/Meetings:** meeting - 4-6/year ● annual workshop, four-day mystery school.

12095 ■ Sacred Passage and the Way of Nature Fellowship

PO Box 3388
Tucson, AZ 85722-3388
Free: (877)818-1881
E-mail: info@sacredpassage.com
URL: http://www.sacredpassage.com
Contact: John P. Milton, Founder

Founded: 1987. **Members:** 1,100. **Staff:** 12. **Regional Groups:** 12. **Local Groups:** 144. **National Groups:** 4. **Languages:** English, Spanish. **Multinational. Description:** Promotes spiritual growth and ecological conservation through "solo vision quest" wilderness experiences, "Awareness Training" Intensives and meditation retreats. Maintains speakers' bureau. Conducts research, education, youth programs, and programs for civil and corporate leadership. **Libraries: Type:** reference. **Holdings:** 30,000; books, periodicals. **Subjects:** ecology, environment, spiritual growth. **Awards:** Gaia Award. **Frequency:** annual. **Type:** scholarship. **Recipient:** for major contributions in developing spiritual and sacred ecology perspectives. **Councils:** Sacred Land; Trust; The Way of Nature Fund. **Affiliated With:** Threshold. **Formerly:** (1998) Sacred Passage, NatureQuest. **Publications:** *Passages* (in English and Spanish), periodic. Journal. Shares articles, news, and stories on Sacred Ecology, Gaia, Meditation, and Awareness Training. **Price:** free. **Circulation:** 8,000. Alternate Formats: online ● *Sacred Land Trust.* Video. **Price:** $15.00 minimum donation ● *Sacred Passage and The Way of Nature Fellowship Brochure.* **Price:** $10.00 minimum donation. **Conventions/Meetings:** annual reunion.

12096 ■ Somatics Society (SS)

1516 Grant Ave., Ste.212
Novato, CA 94945
Ph: (415)892-0617
Fax: (415)892-4388
E-mail: info@somaticsed.com
URL: http://somaticsed.com/somSociety.html
Contact: Eleanor Criswell Hanna EdD, Dir.

Founded: 1981. **Members:** 1,000. **Membership Dues:** regular, $25 (annual) ● special (for those already subscribing to Somatics), $5. **For-Profit. Description:** Professionals and laypeople including educators, psychologists, researchers, dancers, health clinic personnel, chiropractors, doctors, and physical therapists. Promotes a philosophy of behavioral medicine, known as somatics. Fosters the belief that humans can enjoy healthy lives and treat and heal their own ailments through mind control techniques such as relaxation and concentration and other mind-over-body practices. Members sponsor classes and workshops. **Convention/Meeting:** none. **Publications:** *Somatics Magazine - Journal of the Mind/Body Arts and Sciences,* semiannual. Includes popular articles, theoretical studies, poetry, book reviews and research papers. **Price:** included in membership dues; $20.00 /year for individuals; $25.00 /year for institutions. ISSN: 0147-5231. **Circulation:** 1,200. **Advertising:** accepted ● Audiotapes ● Booklets.

12097 ■ The Stelle Group (TSG)
127 Sun St.
Stelle, IL 60919
Ph: (815)256-2200
Fax: (815)256-2220
E-mail: stellegroup@stelle.net
Contact: Carolyn Jacobson, Contact
Founded: 1963. **Members:** 15. **Staff:** 1. **State Groups:** 1. **Description:** Promotes spirituality; seeks to provide training in the Wisdom Teachings, within a supportive group context, as a group work. Training involves character development, meditation, expansion of consciousness, and creating an energy environment that supports the revelation of the Divine in all beings, through study, meditation, and service. programs. Maintains library. **Publications:** Also publishes catalog of books and monographs. **Conventions/Meetings:** quarterly meeting.

12098 ■ Teleos Institute (TI)
7119 E Shea Blvd., Ste.109
PMB 418
Scottsdale, AZ 85254
Ph: (480)948-1800
Fax: (480)948-1870
E-mail: teleosinst@aol.com
URL: http://www.consciousnesswork.com
Contact: Diane K. Pike, Co-Dir.
Founded: 1970. **Members:** 150. **Membership Dues:** non-voting sponsor, $50 (annual). **Staff:** 2. **Multinational. Description:** Those who "choose to know and dare to embody the Individualizing Process." Seeks to enable members to "replace belief with knowing." Offers classes, seminars, intensives, and travel in foreign countries on Journeys Into Self. Sponsors advanced work through the Theatre of Life, Life As a Waking Dream, and Energy Odysseys. **Also Known As:** Love Project. **Supersedes:** Bishop Pike Foundation. **Publications:** *Awakening to Wisdom.* Book. Presents an overview of the Wisdom Teachings. **Price:** $12.95 ● *Cosmic Unfoldment.* Book. Describes the various stages by which individuals awaken and recognize their inherent divinity. **Price:** $4.95 ● *Emerging,* semiannual. Magazine. Contains articles on personal growth, unconditional love, wisdom teachings, and creative self-expression. Includes calendar of events. **Price:** included in membership dues. ISSN: 0890-538X. **Circulation:** 300 ● *Four Paths To Union.* Book. Explains the individualized approach to the quest for meaning, for a worthy cause or leader. **Price:** $14.95 ● *House of Self.* Book ● *India Through Eyes of Love.* Book. Features a story of an adventure into the heart of Self while traveling for four weeks in India and Nepal. **Price:** $7.95 ● *The Love Principles.* Book. Contains practical examples of unconditional love. **Price:** $14.95 ● *The Love Project Way.* Book. Features the story of how The Love Project brought positive change in a Ghetto high school in Brooklyn, New York. **Price:** $10.95 ● *My Journey Into Self.* Book. **Price:** $9.95 ● *The Two.* Book.

12099 ■ Together, Inc. (TI)
c/o The Pin Man
PO Box 52817
Tulsa, OK 74152
Ph: (918)587-2405
Free: (800)282-0085
Fax: (918)382-0906
E-mail: pinrus@aol.com
URL: http://aquarius.lunarpages.com/~positi5/positivepins
Founded: 1973. **Staff:** 6. **Budget:** $600,000. **Regional Groups:** 6. **Description:** Assists people in making the transition from the disadvantaged to the mainstream sector of American life by strengthening the management of those agencies that serve them and by teaching mainstream Americans to facilitate the transition of the poor. Provides training to state and local governments, businesses, and community and volunteer organizations in planning, program design, community interaction, management and individual development, board and staff training, Equal Employment Opportunity system design, program assessment and evaluation, and conference and convention design. Maintains speakers' bureau.

Also Known As: Center for Individual and Community Development. **Publications:** *Affirmative Action Manual,* semiannual ● *Fund Raising Primer,* annual ● *What If - Community Education,* annual. **Conventions/Meetings:** annual conference (exhibits).

12100 ■ Unarius Academy of Science
145 S Magnolia Ave.
El Cajon, CA 92020-4522
Ph: (619)444-7062
Free: (800)475-7062
Fax: (619)444-9637
E-mail: uriel@unarius.org
URL: http://www.unarius.org
Contact: Carol Robinson, Admin. Coor.
Founded: 1954. **Members:** 3,900. **Membership Dues:** open, $50 (annual). **Staff:** 10. **Budget:** $100,000. **Regional Groups:** 4. **State Groups:** 3. **Local Groups:** 1. **Languages:** English, French, German, Italian. **Multinational. Description:** Promotes the teaching of past life therapy. Believes all humans have lived on other worlds in the past and will do so again; that humans draw on energies and experiences of past lives, but are unaware of doing so; because of this one functions at "half-potential" until psychic awareness is achieved. Works to liberate individuals from the "psychic amnesia" of the past. Maintains speaker's bureau; conducts classes. Sponsors research programs and annual interplanetary of light symposium. **Libraries: Type:** reference. **Holdings:** 133. **Subjects:** psychology, psycho-social, science, history, metaphysics, past life therapy, interdimensional science, UFO(s), extraterrestrials, poetry. **Departments:** Education/Teaching; Music and Art; National Public Access Productions; Television Broadcast; Television Production. **Subgroups:** Publications. **Also Known As:** Universal Articulate Interdimensional Understanding of Science; Unarius Educational Foundation. **Publications:** *Monographs on Galactic Intelligence.* Book ● *The Psychology of Consciousness, Lesson Course.* Book ● *UNARIUS Academy of Science Publications Catalogue.* Booklet ● *UNARIUS Cablevision Guide,* semiannual. Booklet. Contains listings of program and descriptions. **Price:** $1.00. **Circulation:** 500 ● *UNARIUS E-News,* 3/year. Newsletter. **Price:** $1.00. Alternate Formats: online. **Conventions/Meetings:** annual Interplanetary Conclave of Light Symposium - meeting, a preparation for the landing of advanced human beings on earth (exhibits) ● lecture and workshop (exhibits) - Sundays, Wednesdays, and Fridays.

12101 ■ World Peace One (WPI)
5100 Penn Ave., 3rd Fl.
Pittsburgh, PA 15224
Ph: (412)661-0805
E-mail: info@all-around.org
URL: http://www.missionball.org
Contact: Timothy L. Cimino, Exec. Dir.
Founded: 1988. **Members:** 12. **Membership Dues:** individual, $25 (annual) ● low income (less than $10,000), $10 (annual). **Staff:** 1. **Budget:** $2,000. **Local Groups:** 1. **Description:** Seeks to help people look at their lives and make changes that improve the quality of life for all through various programs. Programs integrate five areas: personal mission and fulfillment; increasing personal capacity; empowering others; creating a world-sustaining lifestyle; and inviting others to participate in continuing this "chain-reaction" process. **Additional Websites:** http://www.fellowshipofthedream.org, http://www.all-around.org, http://proofthroughthenight.org.

Human Rights

12102 ■ Bilateral Safety Corridor Coalition (BSCC)
1132 E Plaza Blvd., No. 203
National City, CA 91950
Ph: (619)336-0770
Fax: (619)336-0791

E-mail: mubava@msn.com
URL: http://www.bsccoalition.org
Contact: Marisa Ugarte Bava, Exec. Dir.
Founded: 2000. **Description:** Works to prevent and intervene in the commercial and sexual exploitation of women and children, while advocating for all exploited persons. **Telecommunication Services:** hotline, (619)666-2757. **Conventions/Meetings:** annual conference ● monthly meeting.

12103 ■ Center for Civil and Human Rights (CCHR)
Notre Dame Law School
301 Law School
Notre Dame, IN 46556
Ph: (574)631-8555
Fax: (574)631-8702
E-mail: cchr@nd.edu
URL: http://www.nd.edu/~cchr
Contact: Garth Meintjes, Assoc. Dir.
Founded: 1973. **Description:** Works to raise international awareness of important human rights issues and solutions. **Publications:** *Notre Dame Human Rights Advocate,* semiannual. Newsletter. Alternate Formats: online.

12104 ■ Coalition to Abolish Slavery and Trafficking (CAST)
5042 Wilshire Blvd., No. 586
Los Angeles, CA 90036
Ph: (213)365-1906
Fax: (213)365-5257
E-mail: info@castla.org
URL: http://www.castla.org
Contact: Kay Buck, Exec. Dir.
Founded: 1998. **Staff:** 16. **Description:** Assists persons trafficked for the purpose of forced labor and slavery-like practices and works towards ending all instances of such human rights violations. Provides social services and legal assistance to trafficking survivors. Promotes policy advocacy at the state and national levels. Conducts public education and training on human trafficking to other community-based organizations and law enforcement agencies. **Telecommunication Services:** electronic mail, kay@castla.org.

12105 ■ Free the Slaves
1012 14th St. NW, Ste.600
Washington, DC 20005
Ph: (202)638-1865
Free: (866)324-FREE
Fax: (202)638-0599
E-mail: info@freetheslaves.net
URL: http://www.freetheslaves.net
Contact: Jolene Smith, Exec. Dir.
Staff: 18. **Description:** Seeks to end slavery worldwide. **Libraries: Type:** reference. **Holdings:** films, reports. **Affiliated With:** Anti-Slavery International. **Formerly:** (2000) Anti-Slavery International. **Publications:** *Community Member Guide.* Booklet. Explains slavery and trafficking in the US and around the world. ● *Modern Slavery.* Video. Features stories from slavery. **Price:** $15.00 ● *Slavery: A Global Investigation.* Video. Exposes cases of slavery. **Price:** $20.00 ● *Understanding Global Slavery: A Reader.* Book. **Price:** $20.00.

12106 ■ Global Jewish Assistance and Relief Network (GJARN)
666 5th Ave., Ste.246
New York, NY 10103
Ph: (212)868-3636
Fax: (212)868-7878
E-mail: info@gjarn.org
URL: http://www.globaljewish.org
Contact: Rabbi Eliezer Avtzon, Exec. Dir./Founder
Founded: 1992. **Multinational. Description:** Solicits, collects and distributes humanitarian aid throughout the United States, Central and Eastern Europe, Asia and the Far East; maintains ongoing programs in Russia and Ukraine with occasional programs in most of the former Soviet Republics.

12107 ■ Human Rights in China (HRIC)
350 Fifth Ave., Ste.3311
New York, NY 10118
Ph: (212)239-4495
Fax: (212)239-2561
E-mail: hrichina@hrichina.org
URL: http://www.hrichina.org
Contact: Sharon Hom, Exec. Dir.

Founded: 1989. **Description:** Promotes universally recognized human rights and to advance the institutional protection of these rights in China; encourages victims of human rights abuses to seek redress under domestic law, and assists them in seeking international intervention when appropriate. **Computer Services:** database, political prisoners ● mailing lists. **Publications:** *China Rights Forum* (in Chinese and English), quarterly. Journal. **Price:** $50.00/year. ISSN: 1068-4166. Alternate Formats: online ● *Empty Promises: Human Rights Protections and China's Criminal Procedure Law*. Book ● *Hua Dianzi Bao* (in Chinese), weekly. Newsletter. Alternate Formats: online ● *Media Control in China*. Book. **Price:** $20.00/copy; $150.00 bulk rate (10 copies); $15.00/copy, after first 10 copies ● *Ren Yu Quan*, monthly. Journal ● Reports. **Price:** $8.00 for individuals; $10.00 for institutions. Alternate Formats: online ● Papers. Alternate Formats: online.

12108 ■ Huquqalinsan.org
955 Massachusetts Ave., No. 242
Cambridge, MA 02139
Ph: (617)588-0224
Fax: (617)588-0224
E-mail: info@mafqud.org
URL: http://www.huquqalinsan.org/en/intro.htm

Founded: 1993. **Description:** Advocates issues of human rights in Iraq. **Computer Services:** database, Mafqud. **Projects:** Mafqud.org. **Formerly:** Organization for Human Rights in Iraq. **Publications:** *Rights*, quarterly. Newsletter. Contains articles related to Iraqi human rights. **Conventions/Meetings:** symposium.

12109 ■ Institute for Humane Studies (IHS)
George Mason Univ.
3301 N Fairfax Dr., Ste.440
Arlington, VA 22201-4432
Ph: (703)993-4880
Free: (800)697-8799
Fax: (703)993-4890
E-mail: ihs@theihs.org
URL: http://www.theihs.org
Contact: Ms. Autumn Brookmire, Marketing Asst.

Founded: 1961. **Multinational. Description:** Serves as an organization that assists undergraduate and graduate students worldwide with an interest in individual liberty. Devoted to research and education in the conviction that greater understanding of human affairs and freedom will foster peace, prosperity, and social harmony. **Libraries: Type:** reference. **Holdings:** 11,000. **Subjects:** classical and liberal tradition. **Awards:** Charles G. Koch Outstanding IHS Alum Award. **Frequency:** annual. **Type:** recognition ● Charles G. Koch Summer Fellow Program. **Frequency:** annual. **Type:** fellowship ● Felix Morley Journalism Competition. **Frequency:** annual. **Type:** monetary ● Film and Fiction Scholarships. **Frequency:** annual. **Type:** scholarship ● Hayek Fund for Scholars. **Frequency:** periodic. **Type:** grant ● Humane Studies Fellowships. **Frequency:** annual. **Type:** scholarship ● Summer Graduate Research Fellowships. **Frequency:** annual. **Type:** fellowship ● Young Communicators Fund. **Frequency:** periodic. **Type:** grant.

12110 ■ International Justice and Human Rights, National Council of Churches of Christ USA
c/o NCC Communications Department
475 Riverside Dr., Ste.880
New York, NY 10115
Ph: (212)870-2227 (212)870-2025
Fax: (212)870-2030

E-mail: news@nccusa.org
URL: http://www.ncccusa.org
Contact: Rev. Robert W. Edgar, Gen. Sec.

Founded: 1970. **Members:** 30. **Budget:** $760,000. **Description:** Advocates for the rights of all people. **Commissions:** Education and Leadership Ministries; Faith and Order; Interfaith Relations; Justice and Advocacy. **Absorbed:** (1989) Committee on Christian Literature for Women and Children. **Formed by Merger of:** (1993) Intermedia; Human Rights and International Affairs. **Formerly:** (1998) World Community. **Publications:** *Church Bulletin Inserts*. Includes information for worship services, study groups and other gatherings. **Price:** free ● *EcuLink*, quarterly. Newsletter. Includes topics about developments in Christian education, faith and order discussions and peacemaking activities. **Price:** free ● *Friendship Press*. Catalog. Features articles of interest to adults, youth and children. Includes study guides to help educators plan their curricula. ● Yearbook, annual. Includes American and Canadian churches. **Price:** $50.00/copy.

12111 ■ Protection Project
c/o The Paul H. Nitze School of Advanced International Studies
The Johns Hopkins Univ.
1717 Massachusetts Ave. NW
Washington, DC 20036
Ph: (202)663-5894
Fax: (202)663-5899
E-mail: protection_project@jhu.edu
URL: http://www.protectionproject.org
Contact: Dr. Mohammed Mattar, Exec. Dir.

Staff: 6. **Description:** Promotes legal human rights; documents and disseminates information about the scope of issues involving trafficking of persons, especially women and children, focusing on national and international laws, case law, and implications of trafficking on U.S. and international foreign policy. **Computer Services:** database, law collection, comprehensive legal charts, maps, survivor stories, daily press, custom map generating capability. **Publications:** *Human Rights Report on Trafficking in Persons, Especially Women and Children*, annual.

12112 ■ Vietnam Human Rights Network
14550 Magnolia St., Ste.203
Westminster, CA 92683
Ph: (714)897-1950 (714)719-5220
E-mail: vnhrnet@vietnamhumanrights.net
URL: http://www.vietnamhumanrights.net
Contact: Mr. Nguyen Le, Chm./Pres.

Founded: 1997. **Members:** 174. **Staff:** 2. **Budget:** $50,000. **Regional Groups:** 17. **National Groups:** 5. **Languages:** English, Vietnamese. **Multinational. Description:** Promotes human rights, civil liberties and all other basic freedoms for Vietnamese people in Vietnam and around the world. **Awards:** The Vietnam Human Rights Award. **Frequency:** annual. **Type:** recognition. **Recipient:** for prominent human rights activists with outstanding contributions to the defense of Vietnamese people's human rights.

12113 ■ Women for Afghan Women (WAW)
32-17 Coll. Point Blvd., Rm. 206
Flushing, NY 11354
Ph: (718)321-2434
E-mail: office@womenforafghanwomen.org
URL: http://www.womenforafghanwomen.org
Contact: Fahima Vorgetts, Dir.

Founded: 2001. **Membership Dues:** supporting, $25 (annual). **Staff:** 3. **Budget:** $200,000. **Languages:** Dari, English, Farsi, Pashto. **Multinational. Description:** Committed in ensuring the human rights of Afghan women. **Publications:** *Women for Afghan Women: Shattering Myths and Claiming the Future*. Book. Presents a collection of essays by key Afghan and non-Afghan women engaged in the reconstruction of Afghanistan. ● Newsletter, quarterly. Alternate Formats: online. **Conventions/Meetings:** annual conference ● quarterly Cultural Empowerment Events - meeting ● monthly Forums - meeting.

12114 ■ Women's Alliance for Peace and Human Rights in Afghanistan (WAPHA)
PO Box 77057
Washington, DC 20013-7057
E-mail: info@wapha.org
URL: http://www.wapha.org
Contact: Zieba Shorish-Shamley PhD, Founder
Membership Dues: individual, $40 (annual) ● family, $75 (annual). **Multinational. Description:** Promotes peace and human rights for women and girls in Afghanistan.

12115 ■ World Organization for Human Rights USA
1725 K St. NW, Ste.610
Washington, DC 20006
Ph: (202)296-5702
Fax: (202)296-5704
E-mail: info@humanrightsusa.org
URL: http://www.humanrightsusa.org
Contact: Morton Skalar, Exec. Dir.

Founded: 1996. **Staff:** 8. **Description:** Works to prevent torture and other forms of cruel and inhumane treatment or punishment. **Programs:** Criminal Authority; Refugee and Asylum; United States Compliance with International Home Rights Standards. **Formerly:** (2006) World Organization Against Torture USA.

12116 ■ Youth for Human Rights International (YHRI)
PO Box 27306
Los Angeles, CA 90029
Ph: (323)663-5799
Fax: (323)663-2013
E-mail: info@youthforhumanrights.org
URL: http://www.youthforhumanrights.org
Contact: Mary Shuttleworth, Pres.

Founded: 2001. **Membership Dues:** basic, $40 ● contributing, $300 (annual) ● corporate, $500 (annual). **Multinational. Description:** Educates young people in the Universal Declaration of Human Rights. Works with human rights advocates, legislators, teachers, police and humanitarians. Encourages young people to learn and champion human rights. Raises human rights awareness through instructional tools and events. **Publications:** *UNITED*. Video ● *What Are Human Rights?* (in Arabic, Czech, Danish, Dutch, English, Finnish, French, German, Italian, Portuguese, Russian, and Swedish). Booklet. Alternate Formats: online.

Human Services

12117 ■ Elwyn
111 Elwyn Rd.
Elwyn, PA 19063
Ph: (610)891-2000
Fax: (610)891-2458
E-mail: info@elwyn.org
URL: http://www.elwyn.org
Contact: Sandra S. Cornelius PhD, Pres.

Founded: 1852. **Description:** Human services, especially children and adults with a wide range of physical, development, sensory (deafness, blindness), and emotional disabilities as well as those with mental illness, disabilities due to age, and the economically disadvantaged. Provides services such as education, rehabilitation, employment options, child welfare services, assisted living, respite care, campus and community therapeutic residential programs, and other supports for daily living.

12118 ■ Opportunity International-USA (OI)
2122 York Rd., Ste.340
Oak Brook, IL 60523
Ph: (630)242-4100
Free: (800)793-9455
Fax: (630)645-1458
E-mail: getinfo@opportunity.org
URL: http://www.opportunity.org
Contact: Laura Allen, Exec. Dir.

Founded: 1971. **Multinational. Description:** Maintains 42 banking and lending institutions in 27 countries that helps the world's poorest entrepreneurs with microcredit loans; 810,000 clients were served with a 98&percent; loan repayment rate, and approximately 8.1 million lives were supported through its network of financial institutions.

12119 ■ People Helping People (PHP)
c/o Andrea Clinton, Pres.
53 Watson Ave.
East Orange, NJ 07018
Ph: (973)676-4292
Fax: (973)443-2680
E-mail: teaclinton@aol.com
URL: http://hometown.aol.com/teaclinton/myhomepage/index.html
Contact: Andrea Clinton, Pres.
Founded: 1999. **Members:** 5. **Staff:** 5. **State Groups:** 1. **Description:** Aims to assist the community in the areas of, and promote self-sufficiency in: preventing homelessness; hunger and undernourishment; child education and after school programs; business training; drug/alcohol/nicotine intervention; job search; Big Sister/Big Brother and adult counseling; advocate against child/women abuse; and assist with entrepreneurship.

Humanities

12120 ■ Consortium of Humanities Centers and Institutes (CHCI)
c/o The Humanities Center
Harvard Univ.
Barker Ctr. 136
12 Quincy St.
Cambridge, MA 02138
Ph: (617)495-0738
Fax: (617)495-0730
E-mail: chci@fas.harvard.edu
URL: http://www.fas.harvard.edu/~chci
Contact: Marjorie Garber, Pres.
Founded: 1988. **Members:** 160. **Multinational. Description:** Institutes and centers. Strives to be a forum for discussion and information exchange among its members. Hosts the "Woodrow Wilson Postdoctoral Fellowships".

Hunger

12121 ■ Alliance to End Hunger (ATEH)
c/o Bread for the World Institute
50 F St. NW, No. 500
Washington, DC 20001
Ph: (202)639-9400
Free: (800)82-BREAD
Fax: (202)639-9401
E-mail: mfinberg@alliancetoendhunger.org
URL: http://www.alliancetoendhunger.org
Contact: Max Finberg, Dir.
Description: Seeks justice for the world's hungry by lobbying the nation's decision makers. **Projects:** Hunger Message. **Publications:** Paper. Contains mission paper.

12122 ■ America's Second Harvest (SH)
35 E Whacker Dr., No. 2000
Chicago, IL 60601
Ph: (312)263-2303
Free: (800)771-2303
URL: http://www.secondharvest.org
Contact: Vicki B. Escarra, Pres./CEO
Founded: 1979. **Members:** 200. **Staff:** 40. **Budget:** $8,000,000. **Regional Groups:** 3. **Languages:** English, Spanish. **Description:** Network of food banks that distribute millions of pounds of donated food and grocery products to the hungry through food pantries, soup kitchens, and homeless shelters. **Awards:** Hungers Hope. **Frequency:** annual. **Type:** monetary. **Recipient:** for excellence in foodbanking. **Formerly:** (1993) Second Harvest, The National Food Bank Network; (2004) Second Harvest. **Publications:** Update, quarterly. Magazine ● Annual Report. **Conventions/Meetings:** annual conference ● regional meeting - 3/year.

12123 ■ Educational Concerns for Hunger Organization (ECHO)
17391 Durrance Rd.
North Fort Myers, FL 33917
Ph: (239)543-3246
Fax: (239)543-5317
E-mail: echo@echonet.org
URL: http://www.echonet.org
Contact: Stan Doerr, Exec. Dir.
Founded: 1973. **Staff:** 20. **Budget:** $1,000,000. **Multinational. Description:** Works to fight world hunger by providing information, ideas, seeds, and training to missionaries and voluntary agencies involved in improving the efficiency of farming in the Third World. Trains prospective agricultural development workers; promotes exchange of information among organizations working with Third World farmers. Encourages university professors and students in the U.S. to conduct research on topics beneficial to subsistence farmers in various geographical regions. Maintains a seed bank for under-utilized food plant species; operates demonstration farm in North Ft. Myers, FL. **Libraries: Type:** reference. **Holdings:** 3,000; books, periodicals, video recordings. **Subjects:** agriculture, development. **Publications:** *ECHO Development Notes* (in English and Spanish), quarterly. Newsletter. Contains agricultural information for Third World farmers and development workers. **Price:** $10.00/year. **Circulation:** 4,000. Alternate Formats: online ● *ECHO News*, quarterly. Newsletter. **Price:** free for individuals in U.S. Alternate Formats: online. **Conventions/Meetings:** annual Agricultural Missions Conference - conference and workshop, with 3 full days of intense training, speakers from over 30 countries (exhibits) - mid-November.

12124 ■ Feeding Hungry Children International
PO Box 2300
Redlands, CA 92373-0761
Ph: (909)793-2009
Fax: (909)793-6880
E-mail: info@feedinghungrychildren.net
URL: http://www.feedinghungrychildren.net
Contact: Fred M. Johnson, Pres.
Multinational. Description: Represents the interests of individuals dedicated to fighting hunger. Provides food, shelter, medicine, education, counseling and other necessary care for needy children in Third World countries and in the US. Sponsors and assists trained national workers in their program services.

12125 ■ Food for the Hungry (FH)
1224 E Washington St.
Phoenix, AZ 85034-1102
Ph: (480)998-3100
Free: (800)248-6437
E-mail: webquestions@fh.org
URL: http://www.fh.org
Contact: Benjamin K. Homan, Pres.
Founded: 1971. **Staff:** 1,600. **Budget:** $52,000,000. **Description:** International relief and development agency of Christian motivation that helps the poor in 30 countries through integrated self-development and relief programs. Helps those affected by natural disasters such as floods, famines, and earthquakes, as well as those affected by war, hunger and poverty. Programs include child sponsorship, emergency relief and rehabilitation, community clean water projects, health education and intervention, agricultural development, income generation, skills training and education. Also works with churches and indigenous organizations to help them better serve the needs of people in their own communities. Mission opportunities are offered through the team's ministries and longer-term assignments are offered through the Hunger Corps program. **Publications:** *Feeding the Hungry*, monthly. Newsletter. Covers FH's programs. **Price:** free. ISSN: 9642-4557. **Circulation:** 6,000 ● Annual Report, annual. Alternate Formats: online.

12126 ■ Food Providers of America (FPOA)
PO Box 83775
Phoenix, AZ 85071
Ph: (602)241-2873

E-mail: info@foodproviders.org
URL: http://www.foodproviders.org
Contact: Kerry Ketchum, Pres.
Description: Supports, sponsors and coordinates the distribution of food commodities to Food Banks throughout the United States of America. Provides a transportation link between National food products donors and the independently operated Food Banks across the USA. Provides the general public with information about the availability of food commodities at member Food Banks.

12127 ■ Food Research and Action Center (FRAC)
1875 Connecticut Ave. NW, Ste.540
Washington, DC 20009-5728
Ph: (202)986-2200
Fax: (202)986-2525
E-mail: foodresearch@frac.org
URL: http://www.frac.org
Contact: James D. Weill, Pres.
Founded: 1970. **Staff:** 20. **Budget:** $1,900,000. **Description:** Renders technical assistance, training, research, information, and community organizing assistance to low-income organizations endeavoring to make federal food assistance programs more responsive to the acute needs of millions of hungry Americans. Seeks to enhance public awareness of problems of hunger and poverty. Researches, writes, and publishes analyses of federal food programs and offers strategies for local and statewide anti-hunger activities. Coordinates nationwide "Campaign to End Childhood Hunger" and "Building Blocks Project.". **Publications:** *FRAC Afterschool Guide: Nourish Their Bodies, Feed Their Minds.* Report. Alternate Formats: online ● *Hunger Doesn't Take A Vacation: A Status Report on the Summer Food Service Program for Children.* **Price:** $7.00. Alternate Formats: online ● *News Digest*, weekly. Newsletter. Highlights new information on hunger, nutrition, and poverty issues at FRAC, at USDA, etc. Alternate Formats: online ● *School Breakfast Scorecard: 2005.* Report. Alternate Formats: online ● *State of the States: A Profile of Food and Nutrition Programs Across the Nation (2005, 9th Ed.).* Report. **Price:** $20.00 ● *State of the States: A Profile of Food and Nutrition Programs Across the Nation (2004, 8th Ed.).* Report. **Price:** $20.00. Alternate Formats: online ● Also publishes annual School Breakfast and Summer Food "Score Cards," guides to the federal food assistance programs, analyses of President's budget proposals, annual poverty statistics, studies and reports on hunger and poverty, and weekly updates on federal nutrition programs. **Conventions/Meetings:** semiannual conference (exhibits).

12128 ■ Freedom from Hunger
1644 DaVinci Ct.
Davis, CA 95616
Ph: (530)758-6200
Free: (800)708-2555
Fax: (530)758-6241
E-mail: info@freefromhunger.org
URL: http://www.freefromhunger.org
Contact: Dr. Christopher Dunford, Pres.
Founded: 1946. **Staff:** 65. **Budget:** $4,000,000. **Languages:** English, French, Spanish. **Description:** Promotes "self-help for a hungry world." Works to build the capacity of individuals and communities to overcome the root causes of chronic hunger and malnutrition. Commits to have a major long-term impact on hunger by improving on the record of traditional development approaches. Provides women with the opportunities to invest in their own small businesses and to save for emergency needs. Educates the people on better health, nutrition and family planning, presented in the context of local beliefs and cultures. **Computer Services:** Mailing lists. **Departments:** CEO's Office; Programs Dept. **Programs:** Credit With Education. **Formed by Merger of:** (1979) Meals for Millions Foundation; American Freedom from Hunger Foundation. **Formerly:** Freedom from Hunger Foundation; (1988) Meals for Millions/Freedom from Hunger Foundation. **Publications:** *The Community Bank Learning Game.* Manual. Includes information on village based income

generation projects. **Price:** $7.50 plus postage ● *Conditions Under Which Credit and Savings Services Can be Effective Against Hunger and Malnutrition: A Literature Review and Analysis.* **Price:** free ● *Freedom from Hunger's New Credit-Led Approach to Alleviating Hunger: Is It Working?.* **Price:** free ● *Information Bulletin,* semiannual. Reports on progress and international development. **Price:** free ● Annual Report (in English and French), annual ● Newsletters. Alternate Formats: online.

12129 ■ MAZON
1990 S Bundy Dr., Ste.260
Los Angeles, CA 90025
Ph: (310)442-0020
Fax: (310)442-0030
E-mail: mazonmail@mazon.org
URL: http://www.mazon.org
Contact: Rabbi Arnold Rachlis, Chm.
Founded: 1985. **Staff:** 13. **Multinational. Description:** Aims to educate and raise the consciousness of the Jewish community regarding its obligation to alleviate hunger and its causes. **Computer Services:** Mailing lists. **Publications:** *MAZON eNews,* semiannual. Newsletter. Alternate Formats: online ● *MAZON News,* semiannual. Newsletter.

12130 ■ National Student Campaign Against Hunger and Homelessness (NSCAHH)
407 S Dearborn, Ste.701
Chicago, IL 60605
Ph: (312)291-0349
Free: (800)NO-HUNGR
Fax: (312)275-7150
E-mail: info@studentsagainsthunger.org
URL: http://www.studentsagainsthunger.org
Contact: Stacey Hafner, Organizing Dir.
Founded: 1985. **Members:** 600. **Staff:** 3. **Budget:** $95,000. **Description:** Colleges and high schools organized to educate students on and promote student interest in world and domestic hunger and homelessness. Offers site visits, phone consultations, and manuals to assist students in establishing and implementing programs to combat poverty. Sponsors international development projects in Africa, Asia, and Latin America. Promotes educational and community outreach programs. Provides professional on-site training. Maintains placement service and speakers' bureau. **Libraries: Type:** reference. **Subjects:** hunger, homelessness, volunteer opportunities. **Awards:** Hunger Cleanup Award. **Frequency:** annual. **Type:** recognition. **Recipient:** for schools performing the best in the Hunger Cleanup. **Computer Services:** Mailing lists, of members. **Programs:** Food Salvage; H and H Week; Hunger Cleanup; National Conference; Survey of Hunger and Homelessness; West Coast Summit. **Formerly:** (1989) National Student Campaign Against Hunger. **Publications:** *Advocacy Handbook.* Includes a list of more than 300 local and regional advocacy groups. Alternate Formats: online ● *Going Places,* periodic. Catalog. Lists internship, travel, and career opportunities. **Price:** $6.25 ● *Hunger Cleanup Manual.* Includes information on how to organize a successful Hunger Cleanup. Alternate Formats: online ● *Setting a New Course: Expanding Collegiate Curricula to Incorporate the Study of Hunger and Homelessness* ● *SPLASH Handbook* ● *Students Making a Difference,* semiannual. Newsletter. **Price:** $15.00/year. Circulation: 4,500. **Advertising:** accepted. **Conventions/Meetings:** annual conference - always October ● annual Leadership Conference (exhibits).

12131 ■ Presbyterian Hunger Program (PHP)
Presbyterian Church (U.S.A.)
100 Witherspoon St.
Louisville, KY 40202-1396
Free: (888)728-7228
Fax: (502)569-8963
E-mail: gpoyntz@ctr.pcusa.org
URL: http://www.pcusa.org/hunger
Contact: Ms. Georgetta Poyntz, Sr. Admin. Asst.
Founded: 1981. **Members:** 2,500,000. **Staff:** 8. **Budget:** $3,500,000. **Description:** Responds to hunger through direct food relief, development assistance, lifestyle integrity, public policy education, and educa-

tion. Works for environmental justice and homelessness. **Awards: Type:** grant. **Recipient:** for projects in the U.S. and worldwide. **Telecommunication Services:** additional toll-free number, (800)872-3283 ● additional toll-free number, (888)728-5832. **Programs:** The Campaign for Fair Food; Enough for Everyone; The Food and Faith Initiative; Joining Hands Against Hunger; Just Trade. **Subcommittees:** International Relief and Development; National Relief and Development/Education/Public Policy/Lifestyle. **Formed by Merger of:** Task Force on World Hunger/Presbyterian Church in the United States; Hunger Program Committee of the United Presbyterian Church of the United States of America in 1981. **Publications:** *PHP Annual Report,* annual. **Price:** free.

12132 ■ Senior Gleaners (SGI)
1951 Bell Ave.
Sacramento, CA 95838
Ph: (916)925-3240
Free: (800)585-1530
Fax: (916)568-1528
E-mail: sgi@seniorgleaners.org
URL: http://www.seniorgleaners.org
Contact: Jim Pitts, Pres.
Founded: 1976. **Members:** 1,000. **Membership Dues:** regular, $4 (monthly). **Staff:** 1,200. **Budget:** $2,000,000. **Description:** Works as a food bank in the U.S., operated by volunteer retired senior citizens who salvage edible but often unsalable foods. Collects what farmers and grocery stores cannot harvest or cannot sell, not only for themselves, but also to distribute to over 300 charitable organizations. **Publications:** *Gleanings,* quarterly. Newsletter. **Price:** free. **Circulation:** 2,000 ● Brochures. **Conventions/Meetings:** bimonthly general assembly, membership meeting.

12133 ■ Share Our Strength (SOS)
1730 M St. NW, Ste.700
Washington, DC 20036
Ph: (202)393-2925
Free: (800)969-4767
Fax: (202)347-5868
E-mail: info@strength.org
URL: http://www.strength.org
Contact: Bill Shore, Exec. Dir./Founder
Founded: 1984. **Members:** 10,000. **Staff:** 40. **Budget:** $14,000,000. **Description:** Chefs, restaurateurs, creative professionals, and interested volunteers. Seeks to alleviate hunger in the U.S. and around the world. Distributes grants to qualified hunger relief organizations, food assistance programs, and community development organizations. Maintains educational programs to increase public awareness, dispense information, and encourage creative solutions to hunger. Organizes volunteers to work directly with agencies serving people at risk of hunger and malnutrition in local communities. Holds fundraising benefits including Taste of the Nation, an annual food and wine tasting event held in approximately 100 cities across North America, and Writers Harvest, an annual literary reading conducted in bookstores and on college campuses. **Awards:** Humanitarian of the Year. **Frequency:** annual. **Type:** recognition. **Publications:** *50 State Survey of "Good Samaritan" Laws* ● *Frontier,* quarterly. Magazine. **Circulation:** 14,000. **Advertising:** accepted ● *SOS Gift Catalogue* ● *Table Talk,* monthly. Newsletter ● Also organizes and edits fiction anthologies and collections of original writings for publication. **Conventions/Meetings:** annual Conference of Leaders.

12134 ■ Trees for Life (TFL)
3006 W St. Louis St.
Wichita, KS 67203-5129
Ph: (316)945-6929
Free: (800)873-3736
Fax: (316)945-0909
E-mail: info@treesforlife.org
URL: http://www.treesforlife.org
Contact: David Kimble, Exec. Dir.
Founded: 1984. **Members:** 6,000. **Staff:** 12. **Budget:** $800,000. **Description:** Empowers people by demonstrating that in helping each other can unleash

extraordinary power that impacts people's lives. Enables people around the world to help plant fruit trees in developing countries. Activities include three elements: education, health and environment. Offers the Trees for Life Adventure, a program where US children can grow a tree from seed and learn about the world. **Computer Services:** Online services, link with appropriate groups. **Publications:** *Life Lines,* quarterly. Newsletter. Contains individual stories from field experiences. **Price:** free. **Circulation:** 12,000. Alternate Formats: online ● *Trees for Life Update,* periodic ● Reprints. Alternate Formats: online ● Book. Alternate Formats: online ● Brochure. Alternate Formats: online. **Conventions/Meetings:** quarterly board meeting - always April.

12135 ■ U.S. National Committee for World Food Day (USNCWFD)
2175 K St. NW
Washington, DC 20437
Ph: (202)653-2404
Fax: (202)653-5760
E-mail: patricia.young@fao.org
URL: http://www.worldfooddayusa.org
Contact: Patricia Young, Natl. Coor.
Founded: 1981. **Members:** 450. **Staff:** 1. **Budget:** $80,000. **National Groups:** 450. **Description:** Sponsors World Food Day every 16th day of October. The first World Food Day was in 1981 and is observed in 150 nations; it's supported by 450 national sponsoring organizations. Works to increase awareness, understanding and informed action on hunger issues. Conducts educational and charitable programs; compiles statistics. **Libraries: Type:** open to the public; by appointment only. **Subjects:** hunger, food security. **Computer Services:** Mailing lists, of members. **Additional Websites:** http://www.feedingminds.org. **Committees:** National Advisory. **Publications:** *Teleconference Study/Action Packet,* annual. **Price:** free. **Conventions/Meetings:** annual Advisory Committee - meeting.

12136 ■ U.S.A. Harvest (USAH)
PO Box 1628
Louisville, KY 40201-1628
Ph: (502)895-3924
E-mail: stan@usaharvest.com
URL: http://www.usaharvest.com
Contact: Stan Curtis, Founder
Founded: 1989. **Members:** 117,000. **Local Groups:** 4. **Description:** Collects and delivers restaurant, hotel, and caterers' leftovers to mission kitchens that feed the poor. Facilitates the establishment of local chapters; provides information and materials. **Computer Services:** Mailing lists. **Conventions/Meetings:** annual National Convention - convention and workshop.

Immigration

12137 ■ American Civic Association (ACA)
131 Front St.
Binghamton, NY 13905-3193
Ph: (607)723-9419
Fax: (607)723-0023
E-mail: americancivic@stny.rr.com
URL: http://www.unitedwaybroome.org
Contact: Fred Trzcinski, Exec. Dir.
Founded: 1939. **Members:** 750. **Membership Dues:** family, $15 (annual). **Staff:** 5. **Budget:** $180,000. **Languages:** Czech, English, French, Polish, Russian, Spanish, Ukrainian. **Description:** Organization established by naturalized citizens to assist foreign-born persons with problems occasioned by foreign birth. Encourages them to become American citizens, and to use the schools for learning the language; provides a common ground for the integration of new Americans into the life of the community and helps use their contributions for the benefit of their adopted country. **Affiliated With:** Immigration and Refugee Services of America. **Publications:** Newsletter, quarterly. **Conventions/Meetings:** annual meeting - always in Binghamton, NY.

12138 ■ Immigration and Refugee Services of America (IRSA)
c/o U.S. Committee for Refugees and Immigrants
1717 Massachusetts Ave. NW, 2nd Fl.
Washington, DC 20036
Ph: (202)347-3507
Fax: (202)347-3418
E-mail: irsa@irsa-uscr.org
URL: http://www.refugeesusa.org
Contact: Lavinia Limon, Pres.
Founded: 1958. **Staff:** 38. **Budget:** $21,179,769. **Multinational. Description:** Service organization that promotes cultural pluralism and assists refugees and immigrants in adjusting to American life and becoming fully participating citizens. Has member agencies, usually called International Institutes, in 36 cities that act as centers of service and fellowship for all nationalities. Advises its affiliated agencies on program and policy developments affecting the foreign born. Provides local agencies working with immigrants with information on and technical assistance in immigration, language training, social casework, and related service issues. Works to improve immigration and naturalization laws and practices. Cooperates with U.S. government in U.S. resettlement of refugees. **Affiliated With:** American Civic Association; International Institute of Wisconsin; United States Committee for Refugees and Immigrants. **Formed by Merger of:** Common Committee for American Unity; American Federation of International Institutes. **Publications:** *Refugee Reports*, monthly. Includes reports on conditions for refugees and internally displaced persons in 120 countries. **Price:** $55.00/year. **Advertising:** accepted ● *World Refugee Survey*, annual. Sponsorship is accepted. **Price:** $25.00/copy. Alternate Formats: CD-ROM. **Conventions/Meetings:** annual convention.

India

12139 ■ Help the Helpless
PO Box 270308
Vadnais Heights, MN 55127
Ph: (651)762-8857
Fax: (651)762-8857
E-mail: helpthehelpless@yahoo.com
URL: http://www.helpthehelpless.org
Contact: Fr. Robert Altier, Pres.
Description: Seeks to improve the life of extremely disabled Catholic children in India. **Projects:** St. Mary's School and Orphanage.

Indian

12140 ■ Indicorps
3418 Hwy. 6 S, Ste.B, No. 309
Houston, TX 77082
Ph: (646)240-4152
E-mail: info@indicorps.org
URL: http://www.indicorps.org
Founded: 2001. **Description:** Encourages people of Indian origin to participate in India's development. Promotes civic responsibility and helps strengthen potent leaders of Indian origin. Encourages the sharing of information and best practices for the development of India. **Publications:** Newsletter, semiannual. Alternate Formats: online.

Infants

12141 ■ FORMULA Inc.
Address Unknown since 2007
Founded: 1980. **Description:** To ensure the safety and nutritional completeness of all infant formulas. Gathers data from parents whose children have suffered learning disabilities, gross motor dysfunction, seizures, and other symptoms as a result of having been fed Neo-Mull-Soy or Cho-Free, infant formulas manufactured without chloride by the Syntex Corporation. Serves as an information center and communication link for concerned parents. Seeks to

ensure that affected children receive proper medical attention and that the federal government acts to prevent similar incidents. Has successfully worked toward the passage of the Infant Formula Act, which sets nutrient standards for all infant formula and requires routine testing by manufacturers to see that each formula meets those standards. **Publications:** none.

12142 ■ Human Lactation Center (HLC)
666 Sturges Hwy.
Westport, CT 06880
Ph: (203)259-5995
Fax: (203)259-7667
E-mail: danaraphael@earthlink.net
Contact: Dana Raphael PhD, Dir.
Founded: 1975. **Staff:** 6. **Languages:** English, French. **Nonmembership. Multinational. Description:** Dedicated to international education and research on lactation (breastfeeding). Current activities include: research into the long term effects of childhood sexual abuse on women's experience of pregnancy, labor, childbirth and lactation; effects of lactation as a factor that inhibits fertility; consultation for national and international government, industry, and medical institutions on food policy, indigenous weaning foods, and infant and maternal nutrition and feeding practices; design and management of conferences to encourage dialogue among professionals; cooperative meetings with health and family planning groups; development of methodology for use by researchers in anthropology, nutrition, and public health in field work on childbirth, effect of early child abuse on birth and lactation; breast milk and AIDS virus. **Libraries: Type:** reference. **Holdings:** 6,000; books, periodicals. **Publications:** *Only Mothers Know: Infant Feeding Practices in Traditional Cultures* ● *The Tender Gift: Breastfeeding*. **Conventions/Meetings:** conference - 3/year.

12143 ■ International Lactation Consultant Association (ILCA)
1500 Sunday Dr., Ste.102
Raleigh, NC 27607
Ph: (919)861-5577
Fax: (919)787-4916
E-mail: info@ilca.org
URL: http://www.ilca.org
Contact: Jim Smith, Exec. Dir.
Founded: 1985. **Members:** 4,600. **Membership Dues:** standard, $146 (annual) ● contributing professional, $178 (annual). **Regional Groups:** 62. **Description:** Lactation consultants, institutions, and health professionals from 20 countries interested in breastfeeding and lactation. Works to: establish and maintain quality educational and practice standards and ethical principles for lactation consultants; initiate and conduct continuing education and research in the field; promote work concerning lactation/breastfeeding issues; increase public and health care worker awareness of lactation and breastfeeding. Facilitates communication among members. Bestows ILCA Outstanding Achievement in Human Lactation Award. **Computer Services:** Mailing lists. **Committees:** Conference; Education; Executive; External Affairs; Finance; Membership; Nominating; Professional Practice; Public Relations; Publications; Research; Third Party Reimbursement. **Publications:** *Annual Syllabus of Conference*, annual ● *ILCA Globe*, bimonthly. Newsletter. **Price:** included in membership dues ● *ILCA Membership Directory*, annual ● *Journal of Human Lactation*, quarterly. Contains research and scientific articles, book reviews, association news, and film reviews. **Price:** included in membership dues. ISSN: 0890-3344. **Circulation:** 4,700. **Advertising:** accepted ● Also publishes journal supplements, recommendations, papers, and brochure. **Conventions/Meetings:** annual conference (exhibits).

12144 ■ La Leche League International (LLLI)
PO Box 4079
Schaumburg, IL 60168-4079
Ph: (847)519-7730
Free: (800)LALECHE
Fax: (847)519-0035

E-mail: llli@llli.org
URL: http://www.lalecheleague.org
Contact: Ms. Barbara Emanuel, Exec. Dir.
Founded: 1956. **Members:** 40,000. **Membership Dues:** individual, $40 (annual) ● alumnae association, $10 (annual) ● alumnae for retired, $46 (annual) ● family, $52 (annual) ● sustaining, $115 (annual). **Staff:** 42. **Budget:** $3,000,000. **State Groups:** 2,126. **Local Groups:** 3,000. **National Groups:** 5,146. **Languages:** English, Spanish. **Description:** Helps mothers worldwide to breastfeed through mother-to-mother support, encouragement, information, and education; promotes a better understanding of breastfeeding as an important element in the healthy development of the baby and mother. Provides support through informal discussions and individualized phone counseling. Maintains that breastfeeding infants will encourage closer family relationships. Has organized a professional advisory board and 550 breastfeeding resource centers in 48 countries. Supplies information through publications, telephone service, and correspondence. **Libraries: Type:** reference. **Holdings:** 15,000; archival material, audiovisuals, books, clippings, periodicals. **Subjects:** breastfeeding, related topics. **Computer Services:** Mailing lists ● online services, help forms, chats. **Telecommunication Services:** teletype, (847)592-7570. **Departments:** Medical Associates; Public Relations; Publications. **Divisions:** Eastern and Western; International. **Programs:** Peer Counselor. **Publications:** *Adventures in Tandem Nursing: Breastfeeding during Pregnancy & Beyond*. Book. **Price:** $15.00 ● *Becoming a Father*. Manual. Serves as a self-help parenting book. ● *Breastfeeding Abstracts*, quarterly. Newsletter. Emphasizes clinical applications; includes book reviews. **Price:** $12.50/year. ISSN: 0896-4572. **Circulation:** 1,200 ● *Breastfeeding Answer Book, 3rd Revised Edition*. **Price:** $68.00 ● *Breastfeeding Pure & Simple*. Book. **Price:** $8.00 ● *Breastfeeding Your Premature Baby, 2nd Revised Edition*. Book. **Price:** $6.00 ● *The Cuddlers*. Book. **Price:** $10.00 ● *Defining Your Own Success: Breastfeeding After Breast Reduction Surgery*. **Price:** $19.00 softcover; $21.00 hardcover ● *The Fussy Baby: How to Bring Out the Best in Your High Need Child*. Book. **Price:** $10.00 ● *Growing Together: A Parent's Guide to Baby's First Year*. Book. **Price:** $11.00 ● *How Weaning Happens*. Book. **Price:** $8.00 ● *La Leche League International Catalogue*, semiannual ● *Leaven*, bimonthly. **Advertising:** accepted ● *The LLLove Story*. Book. **Price:** $10.00 ● *Maggie's Weaning*. Book. **Price:** $7.00 ● *Michele the Nursing Toddler: A Story about Sharing Love*. Book. **Price:** $15.00 ● *Mothering Multiples*. Book. **Price:** $15.00 ● *Mothering Your Nursing Toddler*. Book. **Price:** $13.00 ● *Motherwise: 101 Tips for a New Mother*. Book. **Price:** $8.00 ● *New Beginnings*, bimonthly. Journal. Includes articles about breastfeeding, parenting, family life, and nutrition, and book reviews. **Price:** included in membership dues; $20.00 for nonmembers. ISSN: 8756-9981. **Circulation:** 30,000. **Advertising:** accepted. **Conventions/Meetings:** annual workshop.

12145 ■ National Abandoned Infants Assistance Resource Center (AIA)
Univ. of California, Berkeley
1950 Addison St., Ste.104, No. 7402
Berkeley, CA 94720-7402
Ph: (510)643-8390
Fax: (510)643-7019
E-mail: aia@berkeley.edu
URL: http://aia.berkeley.edu
Contact: Jeanne Pietrzak, Dir.
Founded: 1991. **Staff:** 5. **Description:** Seeks to improve social services for infants and children affected by drugs or HIV by providing training, technical assistance and information to professionals serving these families; conducts policy research. **Libraries: Type:** by appointment only; open to the public. **Holdings:** articles, audiovisuals, books, monographs, video recordings. **Subjects:** child welfare, substance abuse, HIV. **Computer Services:** Mailing lists, of members. **Telecommunication Services:** teleconference, with guest trainers. **Publications:** *Report to Congress: National Estimates on the Number of Boarder Babies, the Cost of their Care and the*

Number of Abandoned Infants. **Price:** free ● *The Source,* 3/year. Newsletter. Alternate Formats: online ● Articles. **Conventions/Meetings:** annual Teleconference Series.

12146 ■ Newborn Rights Society (NRS)

PO Box 48
St. Peters, PA 19470-0048
Ph: (610)323-6061 (610)547-6263
Contact: Paul Zimmer, Pres.
Founded: 1980. **Members:** 20. **Membership Dues:** $25 (annual). **Staff:** 1. **Languages:** English, German. **Multinational. Description:** Individuals interested in promoting the rights of newborn infants. Opposes "unnecessary medical procedures" such as circumcision of newborns. Disseminates information to physicians, childbirth educators, expectant parents, and activists. Compiles statistics; conducts children's services. Conducts research and educational programs; maintains speakers' bureau. **Libraries: Type:** reference. **Computer Services:** Mailing lists. **Formerly:** INTACT of Pennsylvania. **Publications:** Pamphlets. **Circulation:** 8,000. **Advertising:** accepted. **Conventions/Meetings:** annual meeting.

12147 ■ Nursing Mothers Counsel (NMC)

PO Box 50063
Palo Alto, CA 94303
Ph: (650)599-3669 (408)291-8008
Fax: (408)739-4169
URL: http://www.nursingmothers.org
Contact: Peggy Burgi, Treas.
Founded: 1955. **Members:** 206. **Membership Dues:** full, $25 (annual). **Budget:** $24,000. **Regional Groups:** 3. **Description:** Counseling members are mothers who have nursed a baby for at least six months, attended the orientation session, and completed additional reading on breastfeeding and related topics. Helps mothers enjoy a relaxed and happy relationship with their babies. Achieves this goal by giving breastfeeding information, providing support to breastfeeding mothers, and encouraging informational exchanges with medical professionals. Offers one-to-one counseling for breastfeeding mothers, primarily by telephone. Provides a hospital in-service program to visit new mothers. Maintains speakers' bureau. **Libraries: Type:** lending; not open to the public. **Holdings:** articles, books, periodicals. **Subjects:** breastfeeding, nutrition. **Publications:** *The Baby Who Won't Breastfeed.* Brochure ● *Inverted Nipples.* Brochure ● *Jaundice.* Brochure ● *Maintaining a Milk Supply for the Premature or Ill Infant* (in English and Spanish). Brochure ● *Manual Expression of Breastmilk.* Brochure ● *Nursing Mothers Counsel Manual of Breastfeeding.* **Price:** $14.00 ● *Nursing Twins.* Brochure ● *Proper Positioning Techniques for Breastfeeding.* Brochure ● *Treatment of Mastitis.* Brochure ● *The Working Nursing Mother* (in English and Spanish). Brochure ● Newsletter, quarterly.

International Development

12148 ■ Aid to Artisans (ATA)

331 Wethersfield Ave.
Hartford, CT 06114
Ph: (860)947-3344
Fax: (860)947-3350
E-mail: info@aidtoartisans.org
URL: http://www.aidtoartisans.org
Contact: David O'Connor, Pres.
Founded: 1976. **Members:** 400. **Membership Dues:** $50 (annual). **Staff:** 30. **Budget:** $7,500,000. **Languages:** English, French, Portuguese, Russian, Spanish. **Multinational. Description:** Offers practical assistance worldwide to artisans. Fosters artistic traditions and cultural vitality to improve livelihood and keep communities healthy, strong and growing. Works with its artisan partners to develop products with the appeal to compete successfully in new markets around the world and to improve their business skills so that the changes achieved are enduring. **Awards:** Aid to Artisans Award for Artisan Advocate. **Frequency:** annual. **Type:** recognition.

Recipient: for outstanding individuals and organizations that have championed artisan development in their lives and work ● Aid to Artisans Award for Innovation in Craft. **Frequency:** annual. **Type:** recognition. **Recipient:** for outstanding individuals and organizations that have championed artisan development in their lives and work ● Aid to Artisans Award for Preservation of Craft. **Frequency:** annual. **Type:** recognition. **Recipient:** for outstanding individuals and organizations that have championed artisan development in their lives and work. **Publications:** *Artisans of Haiti* (in English and French). Book. **Price:** $24.95. Also Cited As: *Artisanat D'Haiti* ● *Romanian Folk Art: A Guide to Living Traditions.* Book. **Price:** $19.95 ● Magazine, quarterly. Contains news and photographs of the ATA activities. **Price:** included in membership dues. Alternate Formats: online.

12149 ■ Alliance for Communities in Action

PO Box 30154
Bethesda, MD 20824
Ph: (301)229-7707
Fax: (301)229-0457
Contact: Richard Schopfer, Exec.Dir.
Founded: 1981. **Members:** 40. **Description:** Institutions and groups interested in Latin American development programs. Provides funding, supplies, and technical assistance to Latin American community-based organizations and grass roots groups such as cooperatives, neighborhood organizations, and church and women's groups. Facilitates twinning of local groups in the U.S. with similar groups in Latin America to foster exchange and bicultural understanding. Serves as intermediary in the fundraising efforts of Latin American organizations. Sponsors development programs through TECHO institute (housing programs), Food for Families (food production and nutrition programs), and Agua Pura (potable water programs); also sponsors health education and medical supply and clinic provision programs. **Publications:** *Alliance,* semiannual. Newsletter. Contains information on current events in Latin America, development issues, program development, and project updates.

12150 ■ Alliance for Southern African Progress (ASAP)

1424 31st Ave., Ste.3R
Astoria, NY 11106
Free: (877)375-5778
Fax: (877)375-5778
E-mail: newsroom@asap-alliance.org
URL: http://www.asap-alliance.org
Contact: Mr. Sean DeWitt, Exec. Dir.
Founded: 2002. **Multinational. Description:** Promotes freedom, development and growth in southern Africa. Aims to build links among southern African groups with intimate knowledge of local needs and the international community. **Computer Services:** Information services, Zimbabwe resources. **Projects:** Rubber Stamping for Change; Zimbabwe Freedom Fund; Zimposium Network.

12151 ■ American Committee for KEEP (ACK)

825 Green Bay Rd., Ste.122
Wilmette, IL 60091-2500
Ph: (847)853-2502
Fax: (847)853-8901
E-mail: ack@ackeep.org
URL: http://www.keep.or.jp/indexe.html
Contact: Mr. Randy Osborne, Pres.
Founded: 1950. **Staff:** 2. **Budget:** $280,000. **Languages:** English, Japanese. **Description:** Supports the agricultural, health, rural life training, and religious programs of KEEP (Kiyosato Educational Experiment Project) in Japan and its outreach development activities in Asia. Maintains Brian Kane Fellowship, an English teaching program in rural Japan, and Paul Rusch Memorial Scholarship at Rikkyo University, Tokyo. **Formerly:** American Committee for the Brotherhood of Saint Andrew in Japan. **Publications:** *Bulletin of the American Committee for KEEP,* 3/year. Newsletter. Contains information on projects and scholarships. **Price:** free. **Circulation:** 1,800. Alternate Formats: online ● *Paul Rusch - The Story of*

KEEP ● *Road to KEEP.* **Conventions/Meetings:** periodic meeting.

12152 ■ Ashoka: Innovators for the Public

1700 N More St., Ste.2000
Arlington, VA 22209
Ph: (703)527-8300
Fax: (703)527-8383
E-mail: info@ashoka.org
URL: http://www.ashoka.org
Contact: Bill Drayton, CEO/Chm.
Founded: 1980. **Members:** 1,400. **Staff:** 100. **Budget:** $15,000,000. **Multinational. Description:** Searches the world for leading social entrepreneurs - individuals with unprecedented ideas for change in their communities. Helps emerging social entrepreneurs by electing them to an international fellowship of their peers, and by providing significant financial support and an array of demand-driven, non-financial services. Aims to grow these entrepreneurs' enterprises and to help them collaborate with like-minded social innovators around the world. **Libraries: Type:** reference. **Awards:** Ashoka Fellowship. **Frequency:** semiannual. **Type:** fellowship. **Publications:** *Changemakers,* quarterly. Magazine. **Price:** $25.00/year. **Advertising:** accepted ● *Leading Social Entrepreneurs,* annual. Book. Profiles leading social entrepreneurs - Ashoka Fellows elected in a particular year worldwide. ● Also publishes brochures.

12153 ■ Association for India's Development (AID)

PO Box F
College Park, MD 20741-3005
Ph: (301)717-1059
Fax: (301)513-0565
E-mail: info@aidindia.org
URL: http://www.aidindia.org
Contact: Sudhakar Adivikolanu, Pres.
Founded: 1991. **Members:** 3,000. **Budget:** $100,000. **Description:** Individuals with an interest in international development and related issues. Promotes establishment of grass roots organizations to guide local development worldwide. Provides monetary and advisory support to local groups seeking to direct development; conducts educational and charitable programs; makes available children's services. **Computer Services:** database ● mailing lists, on AID projects and activities. **Publications:** *DISHAA,* quarterly. Newsletter. Contains inspirational articles and update of AID projects and activities. ● *This Month in AID,* monthly. Newsletter. Contains updates of AID projects and activities. **Price:** free for members and donors. **Circulation:** 3,000 ● Annual Report, annual. Alternate Formats: online. **Conventions/Meetings:** quarterly meeting (exhibits) ● weekly meeting, volunteers meet to accomplish various tasks of AID - every Saturday.

12154 ■ Caribbean-Central American Action (CCAA)

1818 N St. NW, Ste.310
Washington, DC 20036
Ph: (202)466-7464
Fax: (202)822-0075
E-mail: info@c-caa.org
URL: http://www.c-caa.org
Contact: Federico Sacasa, Pres.
Founded: 1980. **Members:** 98. **Membership Dues:** board in U.S., $10,000 (annual) ● region-based company, $5,000 (annual) ● corporate benefactor, $2,500 (annual) ● corporate contributor, $1,000 (annual) ● individual benefactor, $500 (annual) ● individual contributor, $250 (annual). **Staff:** 12. **Budget:** $3,000,000. **Multinational. Description:** Promotes private-sector-led economic development in the Caribbean Basin and throughout the hemisphere; facilitates trade and investment in the region by stimulating a constructive dialogue between the private and public sectors to improve the policy and regulatory environments for business on both international and local levels; conducts policy-oriented programs in sectors such as financial services, transportation, energy, agriculture, textiles, intellectual property rights, tourism, telecommunications, and information technology. **Libraries: Type:** reference.

Subjects: Caribbean countries. **Formerly:** (1990) Caribbean/Central American Action; (2003) Caribbean/Latin American Action. **Supersedes:** Committee for the Caribbean. **Publications:** *Caribbean Basin Profile*, annual. **Price:** $80.00 domestic; $100.00 international ● *CCAA Quarterly*. Newsletter. Alternate Formats: online. **Conventions/Meetings:** annual Miami Conference on the Caribbean Basin - in December.

12155 ■ Centre for Development and Population Activities (CEDPA)
1133 21st St. NW, Ste.800
Washington, DC 20036
Ph: (202)667-1142
Fax: (202)332-4496
E-mail: info@cedpa.org
URL: http://www.cedpa.org
Contact: Yolonda C. Richardson, Pres./CEO
Founded: 1975. **Nonmembership. Description:** Aims to empower women at all levels of society to be full partners in development. Operates offices in Egypt, Guatemala, India, Nepal, Nigeria, Senegal, Russia and South Africa and has forged partnerships with non-governmental organizations in more than 150 countries worldwide. Works hand-in-hand with international partners to bring about empowerment for women through programs in reproductive health and family planning, literacy and education, individual and institutional capacity building, micro-enterprise development and political participation. **Programs:** Training Program. **Projects:** ACCESS to Family Planning Through Women Managers Project; Better Life Options for Girls and Young Women; The Romania Project. **Publications:** *The CEDPA Network*, bimonthly. Newsletter. Provides regular and timely summaries of CEDPA's latest news and activities. **Price:** free. Alternate Formats: online ● *CEDPA/ Nigeria News*, quarterly. Newsletter. Features CEDPA/Nigeria's recent activities, projects and successes. **Price:** free. Alternate Formats: online ● *CEDPA Partners: Empowering Women*. Video. **Price:** $10.00 ● *Connect: A Newsletter for the CEDPA TAACS Community*. **Price:** free. Alternate Formats: online ● *Reports-in-Brief*. Reprint ● *Voices of Young Women* (in English, French, and Spanish). Video. **Price:** $10.00 ● Manuals (in English, French, and Spanish). Publishes 12 training manuals. ● Booklets. Publishes 11 special booklets. ● Annual Report, annual. **Price:** $1.00. Alternate Formats: online. **Conventions/Meetings:** workshop, offered in English, French, and Spanish.

12156 ■ China Connection (CC)
c/o Kathy Call, Founder/Exec. Dir.
458 S Pasadena Ave.
Pasadena, CA 91105-1838
Ph: (626)793-3737
Fax: (626)793-3362
E-mail: kathycall@sbcglobal.net
URL: http://www.chinaconnection.org
Contact: Kathy Call, Founder/Exec. Dir.
Founded: 1990. **Budget:** $350,000. **Nonmembership. Description:** Publicizes and interprets the work of the Protestant church in China and the Christian-initiated humanitarian Amity Foundation in Nanjing. Seeks to improve China's social development and international relations. Supports locally administered projects to improve the economic status of China's underclass. Offers training programs to rural doctors/ surgeons; provides assistance to the disabled and orphans; coordinates emergency relief efforts. **Boards:** Reference. **Publications:** *China Chronicles*, quarterly. Newsletter. Contains news of projects in China, information on Protestant Church in China, and news clips from China. **Price:** free. **Circulation:** 1,660.

12157 ■ Christian Reformed World Relief Committee (CRWRC)
2850 Kalamazoo Ave. SE
Grand Rapids, MI 49560
Ph: (616)241-1691 (616)726-1140
Free: (800)552-7972
Fax: (616)224-0806

E-mail: crwrc@crcna.org
URL: http://www.crwrc.org
Contact: Andrew Ryskamp, Dir.
Founded: 1962. **Staff:** 185. **Budget:** $13,145,914. **Multinational. Description:** Agency of the Christian Reformed Church. Administers worldwide relief and development work in 30 countries. Administers self-help programs with national partner agencies in the areas of food production, health care, literacy, income earning, and community and church leadership. Works cooperatively with national groups and other voluntary agencies in providing immediate and long-term disaster aid. Conducts annual hunger awareness week. **Programs:** Disaster Response Services; Free A Family. **Publications:** *Annual Progress Report*, annual. Annual Report ● Brochures ● Also publishes project materials. **Conventions/Meetings:** semiannual Delegate Meeting - always February and September.

12158 ■ Consultative Group on International Agricultural Research (CGIAR)
World Bank
MSN G6-601
1818 H St. NW
Washington, DC 20433
Ph: (202)473-8951
Fax: (202)473-8110
E-mail: cgiar@cgiar.org
URL: http://www.cgiar.org
Contact: Ren Wang, Dir.
Founded: 1971. **Members:** 58. **Budget:** $350,000,000. **Languages:** English, French, German, Japanese, Russian, Spanish. **Description:** Promotes sustainable agricultural development based on the environmentally sound management of natural resources. Confronts interrelated global issues of poverty, hunger, population growth, and environmental degradation in order to help increase food security and lower food prices, create employment and generate income for the rural poor, alleviate rural and urban poverty, protect and conserve the environment, stimulate development in the rest of the economy, and ensure overall prosperity through the stimulation of global trade and greater global political stability. Comprises of agricultural and social scientists who reviews scientific and technical aspects of all center programs and gives advice on emergent needs, priorities, and opportunities for research. **Libraries: Type:** open to the public. **Holdings:** 5,000. **Subjects:** agricultural research. **Computer Services:** database, CGIAR's Core Collection. **Publications:** *CGIAR Corporate Brochure* (in Arabic, Chinese, English, French, German, Japanese, Russian, and Spanish). Alternate Formats: online ● *CGIAR News*, quarterly. Newsletter ● Annual Report, annual. Alternate Formats: online ● Also publishes policy booklets and informational brochures. **Conventions/Meetings:** International Centers Week - meeting.

12159 ■ Counterpart International
1200 18th St. NW, Ste.1100
Washington, DC 20036
Ph: (202)296-9676
Fax: (202)296-9679
E-mail: communications@counterpart.org
URL: http://www.counterpart.org
Contact: Lelei LeLaulu, Pres./CEO
Founded: 1965. **Staff:** 300. **Budget:** $155,351,211. **State Groups:** 3. **Description:** Manages civic, social and economic development, and humanitarian relief projects with partner nongovernmental organizations (NGOs) in the South Pacific, Former Soviet Republics and Vietnam. **Libraries: Type:** reference. **Holdings:** 2,000; articles, books, periodicals. **Subjects:** international development, Pacific nations, third and second worlds. **Computer Services:** Online services. **Programs:** Civil Society; Economic Development; Environment and Conservation; Food Security and Sustainable Agriculture; Global Health and Nutrition; Humanitarian Assistance. **Projects:** Sri Lanka Redevelopment. **Formerly:** Foundation for the Peoples of the South Pacific; (1966) Foundation for Emerging Peoples; (1997) Counterpart Foundation. **Publications:** *Small Islands, Big Issues*. Book. **Price:** $20.00 ● *Volunteer Executive Service Team Reports*, an-

nual. Annual Report. **Price:** $10.00 ● Reports. Covers global programs. ● Annual Report, annual. Alternate Formats: online. **Conventions/Meetings:** periodic conference (exhibits).

12160 ■ FARMS International
PO Box 270
Knife River, MN 55609-0270
Ph: (218)834-2676
Free: (888)99-FARMS
Fax: (218)834-2676
E-mail: info@farmsinternational.com
URL: http://www.farmsinternational.com
Contact: Joseph E. Richter, Exec. Dir.
Founded: 1961. **Staff:** 3. **Budget:** $300,000. **National Groups:** 15. **Multinational. Description:** Works as a Christian ministry that serves the church by equipping families in poverty with the means for self-support; works through the local church, provides (micro-credit) loans, technical support for income-generating projects, and spiritual training for families to help families find a Biblical path out of poverty. **Formerly:** (1979) FARMS, Inc. **Publications:** *A Biblical Solution to Poverty*. Video ● *Agricultural Evangelism*, 9/year. Newsletter. **Price:** free. **Circulation:** 2,500. Alternate Formats: online ● *Fish Farming "How to Grow Fish in the Mountains"*. Book ● *Prayer Updates*, semiannual ● Annual Report, annual ● Brochures ● Also publishes flyers.

12161 ■ Grassroots International (GRI)
179 Boylston St., 4th Fl.
Boston, MA 02130
Ph: (617)524-1400
Fax: (617)524-5525
E-mail: info@grassrootsonline.org
URL: http://www.grassrootsonline.org
Contact: Nikhil Aziz, Exec. Dir.
Founded: 1983. **Staff:** 10. **Budget:** $2,500,000. **Multinational. Description:** Aims to fund community-based relief and development projects in Africa, Asia, Latin America, and the Middle East, and to provide educational and information programs in the U.S. on peace and justice issues. Assists local social change organizations in Eritrea, Brazil, the West Bank and Gaza, Haiti, Mexico, and the Philippines. Provides humanitarian assistance to people in Eritrea, Cuba, East Timor and Lebanon. Supports rehabilitation and development projects examining the causes of famine. Organizes forums and media outreach programs to schools; operates speakers' bureau. **Convention/Meeting:** none. **Libraries: Type:** reference. **Holdings:** 2,000; books, clippings, periodicals. **Subjects:** grassroots' program areas. **Publications:** *Grassroots International—Insights*, 3/year. Newsletter. Provides information on GRI's activities. **Price:** available to sustaining donors. **Circulation:** 3,500. Alternate Formats: online ● *Haiti's Piggy Bank: The Story of the Loss and Recovery of the Haitian Creole Pig*. Videos ● Also publishes program profiles, fact sheets, and news releases; disseminates slideshow.

12162 ■ Heifer Project International (HPI)
1 World Ave.
Little Rock, AR 72202
Free: (800)422-0474
URL: http://www.heifer.org
Contact: Jo Luck, Pres./CEO
Founded: 1944. **Staff:** 250. **Budget:** $47,602,227. **Languages:** English, Spanish. **Multinational. Description:** Serves as a nonsectarian, self-help organization that has helped more than four million families in need, providing more than twenty types of food and income-producing animals, and intensive training in animal management, environmentally-sound farming and community development in more than 50 countries and 38 states, currently. Passes the first offspring to another needy project partner by the recipients of livestock. Provides opportunities for global education to many individuals and groups whose generous gifts make the organization's work possible. **Libraries: Type:** reference. **Holdings:** archival material, books, business records, periodicals, photographs. **Subjects:** food production, social sciences, energy and resources, animal feed, veterinary medicine. **Computer Services:** database, of

donor, webpage with links. **Formerly:** Heifers for Relief. **Publications:** *Gift Catalog.* Alternate Formats: online ● *Heifer International Exchange Newsletter,* quarterly ● *Project Profiles.* Report. **Circulation:** 350,000 ● *Reed to Feed.* Book ● *World Ark.* Newsletter. **Circulation:** 350,000. Alternate Formats: online ● Manuals. Covers animal husbandry. **Conventions/Meetings:** festival, groundbreaking ceremony for New Heifer Global Village, new headquarters.

12163 ■ Institute of Caribbean Studies (ICS)
7306 Georgia Ave. NW
Washington, DC 20012
Ph: (202)829-1887
Fax: (202)829-1667
E-mail: ics@icsdc.org
Contact: Claire Nelson PhD, Founder/Pres.
Founded: 1993. **Membership Dues:** friend, $50 (annual) ● supporter, $100 (annual) ● patron, $250 (annual) ● corporate silver, $1,000 (annual) ● benefactor, $5,000 (annual). **Description:** Individuals and organizations with an interest in Caribbean cultures and history, and in the development of the region. Promotes improved social and economic well-being for the Caribbean-Americans. Conducts studies and develops programs to increase exchanges between the U.S. and the Caribbean. Facilitates communication among expatriate Caribbeans worldwide. Supports research and educational programs in areas including economic development, science and technology, education and health, and history, sociology, and culture. Makes available internships. **Awards:** Caribbean American Heritage Awards. **Frequency:** annual. **Type:** recognition. **Recipient:** for individuals who have made national/international impact. **Programs:** HIV/AIDS Awareness Campaign; National Caribbean American Heritage Month; U.S. Political Participation of Caribbean Immigrants. **Conventions/Meetings:** periodic seminar ● periodic workshop.

12164 ■ Institute for International Cooperation and Development (IICD)
PO Box 520
Williamstown, MA 01267
Ph: (413)441-5126 (413)458-9466
Fax: (413)458-3323
E-mail: info@iicd-volunteer.org
URL: http://www.iicd-volunteer.org
Contact: Jytte Martinussen, Educational Dir.
Founded: 1986. **Staff:** 10. **National Groups:** 2. **Languages:** English, Portuguese, Spanish. **Multinational. Description:** Promotes global understanding and international solidarity. Trains volunteers to work in community projects in Africa, India, and Latin America. **Publications:** *Experiences in Development,* quarterly. Newsletter. **Price:** free. **Advertising:** accepted.

12165 ■ Inter-American Parliamentary Group on Population and Development (IAPG)
420 Lexington Ave., Rm. 303
New York, NY 10170-0002
Ph: (646)240-4055
Fax: (646)227-0160
E-mail: info@iapg.org
URL: http://www.iapg.org
Contact: Carla Rivera-Avni, Exec. Coor.
Founded: 1982. **Staff:** 3. **National Groups:** 10. **Languages:** English, Spanish. **Description:** Legislators from North and South American and Caribbean countries that have elected representatives. Promotes improved quality of life in the Western Hemisphere. Encourages cooperation among parliamentarians through exchange of information on population and development; promotes awareness of the relationships between population growth and development, particularly among countries of the Western Hemisphere. Facilitates the formation of national committees of parliamentarians. Encourages the adoption of policies designed to improve the status of women, provide better protection of children, rationalize patterns of migration within and among countries, and integrate population considerations into development planning. Promotes education, especially of children, and rural development in countries relying primarily on agriculture. Supports research projects; provides

technical assistance. **Libraries: Type:** reference. **Subjects:** family planning, gender issues, migration, population in general. **Computer Services:** Mailing lists. **Also Known As:** Grupo Parlamentario Inter-Americano Sobre Poblacion y Desarrollo. **Publications:** *Family Planning and the Health of Mothers and Children* ● *High Infant Mortality and the Health of Street Children.* Report ● *International Conference of Parliamentarians on Gender, Population and Development* (in English, French, and Spanish). Report ● *Parliamentary Dialogue,* quarterly. Newsletter. Promotes women's human rights in the Americas. **Price:** free. Alternate Formats: online ● *Population Growth and the Environment* ● *Population Policy in Latin America and the Caribbean* ● *Women in Latin America and the Caribbean* (in English, Portuguese, and Spanish), bimonthly. Bulletin. **Conventions/Meetings:** periodic conference and regional meeting.

12166 ■ Interaction/American Council for Voluntary International Action (Interaction)
1400 16th St. NW, Ste.201
Washington, DC 20036
Ph: (202)667-8227
Fax: (202)667-8236
E-mail: ia@interaction.org
URL: http://www.interaction.org
Contact: Mr. Samuel A. Worthington, Pres./CEO
Founded: 1984. **Members:** 165. **Membership Dues:** nonprofit, $1,000 (annual). **Staff:** 30. **Description:** Represents more than 160 US-based private voluntary organizations engaged in disaster relief, sustainable development and refugee assistance in over 100 countries. **Commissions:** Advancement of Women. **Committees:** Development Policy and Practice; Disaster Response; Membership; Migration and Refugee Affairs; Public Policy; PVO Standards. **Publications:** *Diversity in Development - A Survey of PVO Assistance to Africa* ● *Member Profiles,* annual. Membership Directory ● *Monday Developments,* biweekly ● *PVO Standards.* Booklet ● Annual Report, annual. Alternate Formats: online. **Conventions/Meetings:** annual conference, brings together top leaders from the NGOs, government, and private sector for networking, skill-building, and information sharing (exhibits).

12167 ■ The International Foundation (TIF)
PO Box 69
Brookfield, WI 53008-0069
Free: (888)334-3327
URL: http://www.ifebp.org
Contact: Joseph A. Brislin, Pres./Chm.
Founded: 1948. **Staff:** 3. **Budget:** $1,500,000. **Description:** Supports agricultural, environmental, nutritional, medical, public health, educational, and cultural projects throughout the Third World. Encourages projects that will provide the greatest promise of solid accomplishment in preserving resources, expanding educational awareness, and providing health and medical services in foreign countries. **Awards: Frequency:** annual. **Type:** grant. **Committees:** Grants and Finance. **Formerly:** (1966) China International Foundation. **Conventions/Meetings:** quarterly meeting - always third Wednesday and Thursday of January, April, July, and October, New York City.

12168 ■ Just Act: Youth Action for Global Justice
3307-26th St.
San Francisco, CA 94110
Ph: (415)431-4204
Fax: (415)431-5953
E-mail: info@justact.org
Contact: Liz Suk, Exec.Dir.
Founded: 1983. **Members:** 2,000. **Membership Dues:** student, $15 (annual) ● individual, $25 (annual). **Staff:** 6. **Budget:** $300,000. **Regional Groups:** 35. **State Groups:** 8. **Local Groups:** 5. **National Groups:** 35. **Description:** Campus student organizations, primarily undergraduates, united to learn more about global development issues and help to alleviate hunger, disease, and poverty in the third World and in the U.S. Focuses efforts through four major programs: the Partnership in Development Program,

which allows American college students direct contact with communities in the Third World and allows them to help raise funds for specific village-based development projects overseas. The Chapter Outreach Program, which aims to increase public understanding and awareness of the problems facing Third World nations by sponsoring films/video library, seminars, conferences, and cultural events. Also sponsors Bike-Aid, a cross-country bicycle tour that conducts educational presentations and raises funds for overseas projects and intern stipends through pledge donations. Provides information about internships, research, projects, and paid and voluntary positions with development organizations worldwide. Maintains internships in national office. **Libraries: Type:** reference. **Holdings:** audiovisuals. **Subjects:** global development education. **Computer Services:** database ● mailing lists. **Formerly:** (1998) Overseas Development Network. **Publications:** *A Handbook for Creating Your Own Internship in International Development.* **Price:** $7.95 ● *Career Opportunities in International Development in Washington DC.* Catalog. Resource for students and job seekers looking for internships and work opportunities in DC based organizations. **Price:** $6.00 for students; $9.00 for nonstudents; $12.00 for institutions ● *Global Development Studies-Toward Curricular Change.* Newsletter. **Price:** $7.00 ● *Opportunities in Grassroots Development in California.* Catalog. A resource guide for individuals seeking practical experience in domestic and international development with California based organizations. **Price:** $7.00 for students; $10.00 for nonstudents; $15.00 for institutions. **Circulation:** 3,000. **Advertising:** accepted. **Conventions/Meetings:** annual Summer Leadership Conference (exhibits) - always August.

12169 ■ New Forests Project (NFP)
c/o International Center
731 8th St. SE
Washington, DC 20003
Ph: (202)547-3800
Fax: (202)546-4784
E-mail: etoledo@newforests.org
URL: http://www.newforestsproject.com
Contact: Mr. Erick Toledo, Dir.
Founded: 1981. **Members:** 10,000. **Membership Dues:** individual, $700,000 (annual). **Staff:** 4. **Budget:** $700,000. **Languages:** English, Spanish. **Multinational. Description:** Strives to protect, conserve and enhance the health of the Earth's ecosystem along with the people depending on them, by supporting integrated grassroots efforts in agroforestry, reforestation, protection of watersheds, water and sanitation and renewable energy initiatives. Provides nitrogen fixing tree seeds, technical assistance, and training materials to groups and individuals in developing countries interested in reforestation and water and sanitation projects. Sponsors international development training seminar/workshops and programs in agro-forestry, watershed protection, and renewable energy. **Libraries: Type:** reference. **Subjects:** natural resources, agricultural development. **Affiliated With:** International Center. **Formerly:** (1986) New Forests Fund. **Publications:** *New Forests News,* semiannual. Newsletter. **Price:** free for members. **Circulation:** 10,000 ● *Seeds of Hope Newsletter,* quarterly. Bulletin. **Circulation:** 4,000 ● Reports. Alternate Formats: online.

12170 ■ One Earth One Justice (OEOJ)
4343 Clairemont Mesa Blvd.
San Diego, CA 92117
Ph: (619)223-3482
E-mail: jeremy@oeoj.org
URL: http://www.oneearthonejustice.org
Contact: Jeremy Linneman, Exec. Dir.
Membership Dues: basic, $25 (annual). **Description:** Seeks to advance social, economic and environmental justice issues. Engages America's youth through progressive social media and grassroots education campaigns that focus on environmental and social crises. Works in close collaboration with other countries to promote sustainability and global justice.

12171 ■ OXFAM America

226 Causeway St., 5th Fl.
Boston, MA 02114-2206
Ph: (617)482-1211 (617)728-2408
Free: (800)77-OXFAM
Fax: (617)728-2594
E-mail: info@oxfamamerica.org
URL: http://www.oxfamamerica.org
Contact: Helen DaSilva, Press Off.
Founded: 1970. **Staff:** 100. **Budget:** $79,000,000.
Regional Groups: 7. **Languages:** English, Spanish.
Multinational. Description: Autonomous development and disaster assistance organization cooperating in a worldwide network known as Oxfam, a name derived from the Oxford Committee for Famine Relief, which began in England in 1942. Provides funds for self-help projects in the poorer countries of Asia, Africa, and the Americas. Emphasizes on promoting economic and food self-reliance. Responds to emergency needs of political and natural disaster refugees by funding food, water resources, and medical aid programs. Supports development programs that address underlying causes of such disasters. Educates U.S. public about root causes of hunger; advocates for policy changes. **Departments:** Education and Outreach; Overseas Program; Resource Development. **Publications:** Books ● Newsletter, 3/year ● Pamphlets ● Videos ● Annual Report, annual. Alternate Formats: online. **Conventions/Meetings:** annual International Oxfams Conference - meeting.

12172 ■ PACT

1200 18th St. NW, Ste.350
Washington, DC 20036
Ph: (202)466-5666
Fax: (202)466-5669
E-mail: pact@pacthq.org
URL: http://www.pactworld.org
Contact: Sarah Newhall, Pres./CEO
Founded: 1971. **Staff:** 40. **Budget:** $20,000,000.
Description: Serves as an international development organization. Believes that "the foundation of civil society is pluralism—where citizens acting together can express their interests, exchange information, strive for mutual goals and influence government." Seeks to strengthen the community-focused nonprofit sector worldwide. Works with strategic partners to identify and implement participatory development approaches which promote social, economic, political, and environmental justice. Focuses work on organizations that have local impact and global relevance, especially those groups dealing with microenterprise development, healthcare, AIDS treatment and prevention, child welfare, environmental protection, participatory governance, nonformal education, women's issues, and human rights. Offers program and management training and technical assistance. **Computer Services:** Mailing lists. **Programs:** Community REACH HIV/AIDS; Global Civil Society Strengthening Leader with Associates Award; Omega Initiative; WORTH Regional HIV/AIDS. **Formerly:** (1997) Private Agencies Collaborating Together. **Publications:** Annual Report, annual. **Price:** free. Alternate Formats: online ● Also publishes and distributes more than 400 publications.

12173 ■ Panos Institute (PANOS)

Webster House
1718 P St. NW, Ste.T-6
Washington, DC 20036
Ph: (202)429-0730 (202)429-0731
E-mail: washington@panoscaribbean.org
URL: http://www.panosinst.org
Contact: Melanie Beth Oliviero, Exec. Dir.
Founded: 1986. **Staff:** 12. **Budget:** $500,000. **Languages:** English, French, Spanish. **Multinational. Description:** Works with media and nongovernmental organizations (NGOs), especially in Latin America and the Caribbean, to raise public understanding of sustainable development. Conducts Regional Information Partnership Programs to improve the information capacities and networks of Third World journalists and NGOs and to encourage action on the environment. Produces and distributes Mi Tierra, a radio tape and script series on sustainable develop-

ment, case studies on community development, and AIDS media materials. Conducts research for briefing documents; sponsors media seminars and workshops; bestows fellowships; produces educational materials. **Libraries: Type:** open to the public. **Holdings:** 2,000. **Subjects:** AIDS environment, economic development, conflict, immigration, population, women issues. **Publications:** *Community and the Environment: Lessons from the Caribbean, 1994.* Journal. Includes 3 case studies. **Price:** $10.00 complete set; $3.95 each ● *Cronica Mensual* (in Spanish), monthly. Article. **Price:** free ● *El Peligo Oculto, 1996.* Book. Includes information about HIV/AIDS from the perspective of Central American women. **Price:** $14.95 ● *SIDAmerica* (in Spanish), quarterly. Contains syndicated feature articles focusing on information on HIV/AIDS in the Americas written by journalist in the south in Spanish. ● *We Speak For Ourselves: Population and Development* (in Spanish). **Price:** $6.95. **Conventions/Meetings:** workshop, for NGOs, journalists, and media managers - 6-8/year.

12174 ■ Restoration Project International (RPI)

74 Trinity Pl., Ste.606, Wall St.
New York, NY 10006
Ph: (212)566-4919
Fax: (212)566-4915
E-mail: nod@restoreanation.org
URL: http://bethatchange.org
Contact: Nod Dorcilien, Pres./Founder/Exec. Dir.
Founded: 2002. **Multinational. Description:** Seeks to improve the lives of Haitian children living in both Haiti and the Dominican Republic. Coordinates the distribution of basic materials and services including food, clothing, shelter, and access to education and medical services. Provides educational opportunities to the Haitian youth by establishing new schools in rural areas where access to education is limited.

12175 ■ Self Help International (SHI)

805 W Bremer Ave.
Waverly, IA 50677-2927
Ph: (319)352-4040
Fax: (319)352-4040
E-mail: selfhelp@dybb.com
URL: http://www.selfhelpinternational.org
Contact: Merry Fredrick, Exec. Dir.
Founded: 1959. **Staff:** 2. **Budget:** $140,000. **Multinational. Description:** Seeks to alleviate hunger by helping people to help themselves. **Formerly:** (1998) Self Help Foundation. **Publications:** *Self-Help Newsletter*, 3/year. **Circulation:** 2,000.

12176 ■ Seva Foundation (SF)

1786 5th St.
Berkeley, CA 94710
Ph: (510)845-7382
Free: (800)223-7382
Fax: (510)845-7410
E-mail: dmoses@seva.org
URL: http://www.seva.org
Contact: Deborah Moses, Interim Exec. Dir.
Founded: 1978. **Members:** 27,000. **Staff:** 16. **Budget:** $2,450,000. **Description:** Seva (a Sanskrit word for service) works to prevent blindness in India, Nepal, and Tibet; community development in Mexico and Guatemala; and provides diabetes treatment for Native Americans on reservations. Provides small grants for local projects that serve homelessness, youth at risk, and persons with HIV/AIDS. **Committees:** Compassionate Action; Environmental; Fundraising; Mayan Renewal/Guatemala and Chiapas; Native American Projects; Neighborhood Initiatives; Sight Restoration. **Publications:** *Epidemiology of Blindness in Nepal: Report of the 1981 Nepal Blindness Survey.* Book ● *Gift of Service Catalog*, annual. Describes gifts that individuals can give to support needy communities, including traditional gifts and gifts of training. **Price:** free. **Circulation:** 550,000. Alternate Formats: online ● *Seva Foundation—Progress Report*, annual. Includes achievements, goals, and financial statement. ● *Special Project Reports*, periodic ● *Spirit of Service*, semiannual. Newsletter. Reports on national and international

humanitarian activities. Includes project updates and annual gift catalog. **Price:** free. **Circulation:** 30,000. Alternate Formats: online.

12177 ■ Sierra Visions (SV)

PO Box 3271
Laurel, MD 20709-3271
Ph: (240)554-1555
Fax: (240)554-1555
E-mail: info@sierravisions.org
URL: http://www.sierravisions.org
Contact: Ms. C. Davis, Pres.
Membership Dues: student, contributing, $80 (annual) ● associate, founding, $120 (annual). **Multinational. Description:** Fosters social reform and economic development in Sierra Leone and West Africa. Promotes and develops educational programs which involve scholarships, internships, professional training, and other career development initiatives. Collaborates with various proactive public and private sector organizations, and individual volunteers in Sierra Leone to implement the Five-T model. **Awards:** Gift to Succeed Scholarship. **Frequency:** annual. **Type:** scholarship. **Recipient:** for students of Sierra Leone. **Publications:** *5T - Training Initiative: Brain Gain Training Program.* Brochure. Alternate Formats: online ● Newsletter. Alternate Formats: online.

12178 ■ Social Relief International

PO Box 540765
Omaha, NE 68154
Ph: (402)932-5556
E-mail: info@socialrelief.org
URL: http://www.socialrelief.org
Contact: Kodjogan Ezui MA, Pres./CEO
Founded: 2004. **Multinational. Description:** Promotes child welfare and social change in Africa. Works to provide services and develop programs to serve needy individuals, families and communities. Provides technical assistance, training and program development in integrated service systems for children and family welfare. Promotes health, human rights, education and social support for the young generation. **Publications:** Annual Report, annual.

12179 ■ Trickle Up Program (TUP)

104 W 27th St., 12th Fl.
New York, NY 10001-6210
Ph: (212)255-9980
Free: (866)246-9980
Fax: (212)255-9974
E-mail: info@trickleup.org
URL: http://www.trickleup.org
Contact: William M. Abrams, Pres.
Founded: 1979. **Staff:** 21. **Budget:** $3,100,000. **Languages:** English, French, Spanish. **Description:** Strives to create new opportunities for self-employment and economic and social well-being among the low-income populations of the world. Assists qualified groups of individuals in establishing profit-making microbusinesses by providing basic business training and awarding them conditional grants. Initiates over 90,000 businesses in 117 countries. Maintains speakers' bureau. Sponsors events and activities throughout the year. **Convention/Meeting:** none. **Committees:** Business Council; Development; Media; Technology; Young Associate Program. **Publications:** *Fact Sheet*, annual. **Price:** free. **Circulation:** 8,000 ● *Regional Country Reports*, annual ● Annual Report, annual. **Price:** $25.00. **Circulation:** 4,000. Alternate Formats: online ● Newsletter, 3/year. Includes statistics. **Circulation:** 11,000. Alternate Formats: online.

12180 ■ Visions in Action

2710 Ontario Rd. NW
Washington, DC 20009
Ph: (202)625-7402
Fax: (202)588-9344
E-mail: visions@visionsinaction.org
URL: http://www.visionsinaction.org
Contact: Shaun Skelton PhD, Dir./Founder
Founded: 1989. **Staff:** 23. **Budget:** $300,000. **Languages:** English, French, Spanish. **Description:** Recruits and places volunteers wishing to assist urban development and journalism projects in Burkina Faso,

South Africa, Uganda, Tanzania, Zimbabwe and Mexico. Supports development projects exemplified by a grassroots approach, reliance on volunteer assistance, and local community scope. Wastes in health, environment, social work, human rights, research, journalism and small business. **Awards:** Global Justice Award. **Frequency:** annual. **Type:** recognition. **Publications:** *Action Notes*, quarterly. Newsletter. **Circulation:** 5,000. **Conventions/Meetings:** annual Working For Global Justice - conference, showcases careers in international development (exhibits).

12181 ■ Volunteers in Technical Assistance (VITA)

1825 Connecticut Ave. NW, Ste.630
Washington, DC 20009
Ph: (202)293-4600
Fax: (202)293-4598
E-mail: info@enterpriseworks.org
URL: http://www.enterpriseworks.org
Contact: Vicki Tsiliopoulos, COO
Founded: 1960. **Members:** 4,500. **Staff:** 35. **Budget:** $5,000,000. **Languages:** English, French, Spanish. **Description:** Private organization that provides technical assistance to individuals and organizations in the U.S. and developing countries. Operates internationally with emphasis on helping local groups adapt, implement, and market technologies appropriate to given situations. Basic services include: response to technical inquiries; on-site consultations; projects with the private and public sectors; promotion of small and medium-scale businesses; training in manual and computerized information service management; and distribution of how-to publications. Technologies involved include agriculture and food processing, renewable energy applications, water supply and sanitation, low-cost construction, reforestation and soil conservation, and small business development. **Computer Services:** database ● mailing lists. **Formerly:** (1972) Volunteers for International Technical Assistance. **Publications:** Annual Report ● Also publishes over 200 technical handbooks in different languages, industrial profile, and technical paper series. **Conventions/Meetings:** annual seminar.

12182 ■ World Development Federation (WDF)

6625 The Corners Pkwy., Ste.200
Norcross, GA 30092-2901
Ph: (770)446-6996
Fax: (770)263-8825
E-mail: wdf@conway.com
URL: http://www.wdf.org
Contact: Laura Lyne, Program Dir.
Founded: 1991. **Staff:** 2. **Languages:** English, Spanish. **Description:** Represents corporations and other entities interested in promoting sound economic development worldwide. Holds meetings and discussion forums to stimulate a global view of billion-dollar projects and strategies, including consideration of economic, environmental, political, and technical considerations; does not promote finance or endorse specific projects. **Libraries: Type:** not open to the public. **Subjects:** publications literature. **Awards:** Distinguished Service Award. **Frequency:** annual. **Type:** recognition. **Recipient:** for service to WDF-selected by WDF Board. **Computer Services:** database, lists names of 2,000 largest private firms and public organizations worldwide ● database, lists status of 2,000 "global super projects". **Conventions/Meetings:** annual Global Super Projects Conference (exhibits).

International Health

12183 ■ Global Healing

PO Box 2166
Orinda, CA 94563
Ph: (925)327-7889
E-mail: mail@globalhealing.org
URL: http://www.globalhealing.org
Contact: Cynthia Basso Eaton, Pres.
Multinational. Description: Aims to strengthen and improve the health and education of developing

countries throughout the world by establishing modern healthcare programs. Strives to ensure that the implementation of its medical programs will help developing countries attain self-sufficiency. Works directly with local government officials, healthcare providers, educators, businesses, public institutions, and private citizens in the facilitation of its projects.

International Relations

12184 ■ Hungarian American Coalition

1120 Connecticut Ave. NW, Ste.280
Washington, DC 20036
Ph: (202)296-9505
Fax: (202)775-5175
E-mail: hac@hacusa.org
URL: http://www.hacusa.org
Contact: Maximilian Teleki, Pres.

Membership Dues: student, $25 (annual) ● individual, $50 (annual) ● family, $100 (annual) ● organizational, $200 (annual) ● individual sponsor, $250-$500 (annual) ● individual - patron; organization - sponsor, $501-$1,000 (annual) ● individual - benefactor; organization - patron, $1,000-$2,500 (annual) ● organization - benefactor, $2,501-$5,000 (annual). **Multinational. Description:** Identifies and promotes the interests of the Hungarian-American community. Fosters interest and appreciation of the history and culture of Hungary, including its literature, arts and scientific achievements. Protects and preserves the human and minority rights and cultural heritage of Hungarians throughout the world. **Awards:** Dr. Elemer Kiss Scholarship. **Frequency:** annual. **Type:** recognition. **Recipient:** for Hungarian students who wish to pursue studies in a US college or university. **Computer Services:** Information services, coalition's accomplishments ● information services, key issues. **Committees:** Executive; Nominating.

Internet

12185 ■ CyberAngels

PO Box 3171
Allentown, PA 18106
Ph: (610)377-2966
Fax: (610)482-9101
E-mail: katya@cyberangels.org
URL: http://www.cyberangels.org
Contact: Katya Gifford, Contact
Founded: 1995. **Description:** Seeks to prevent Internet users from becoming victims of online criminal activities. Helps victims trace, identify and persecute perpetrators of online crime. **Computer Services:** Information services, internet resources ● information services, online safety ● online services, classes. **Telecommunication Services:** electronic mail, memberhelp@cyberangels.org. **Programs:** Connect-Ed; CyberCrime Unit; Homefront; Internet 101.

Israel

12186 ■ All4Israel

53 Dewhurst St.
Staten Island, NY 10314
Free: (877)812-7162
E-mail: info@all4israel.org
URL: http://www.all4israel.org
Contact: Zalman Indig, Dir.
Multinational. Description: Provides a resource for donors and organizations looking for ways to help Israel and its needy citizens. Provides emergency help to families and the seriously injured with medical assistance. Leverages relationships with professionals to help victims get top medical care and legal assistance. Helps unemployed victims of terror and their families find good jobs. **Telecommunication Services:** electronic mail, zalman@all4israel.org.

12187 ■ American Committee for Shaare Zedek Hospital in Jerusalem (ACSZJ)

49 W 45th St., Ste.1100
New York, NY 10036
Ph: (212)354-8801
Free: (800)346-1592
Fax: (212)391-2674
E-mail: northeastregion@acsz.org
URL: http://www.acsz.org
Contact: Robert R. Frankel, Purchasing Dir.
Founded: 1955. **Staff:** 20. **Description:** Provides financial support to Shaare Zedek Hospital in Jerusalem, Israel. Fundraising activities include dinners, concerts, travel missions to Israel, and direct mail solicitations. Purchases medical equipment and supplies and finances new hospital departments. **Awards: Type:** recognition. **Publications:** *Heartbeat*, quarterly. Newsletter. **Conventions/Meetings:** symposium, on medical subjects and internal hospital affiliations.

12188 ■ American Physicians Fellowship for Medicine in Israel (APF)

2001 Beacon St., Ste.210
Boston, MA 02135
Ph: (617)232-5382
Fax: (617)739-2616
E-mail: info@apfmed.org
URL: http://www.apfmed.org
Contact: Ms. Carol Ghatan, Assoc. Dir.
Founded: 1950. **Members:** 5,000. **Membership Dues:** regular, $125 (annual) ● student, $18 (annual). **Staff:** 5. **Budget:** $800,000. **Description:** North American physicians whose goals are to foster and aid medical progress in Israel and internationally. Includes major activities such as: fellowship assistance for Israeli physicians; funding medical research projects; emergency medical volunteers for Israel; CME seminars in Israel and North America; excellence awards; intensive specialty training for Israeli nurses; and general assistance to Israel's medical institutions. **Awards:** Edward H. Kass Medical Research Award. **Frequency:** annual. **Type:** monetary. **Recipient:** for a young Israeli investigator ● Fellowship Grants. **Frequency:** annual. **Type:** grant ● Klitzberg Award for Oncology. **Frequency:** annual. **Type:** recognition ● Solomon Hirsh Nursing Award for Education in Canada. **Frequency:** annual. **Type:** fellowship. **Recipient:** for a registered nurse. **Computer Services:** Mailing lists. **Formerly:** (1979) American Physicians Fellowship for the Israel Medical Association. **Publications:** *APF News*, semiannual. Newsletter. Alternate Formats: online ● *Volunteer Newsletter*. Alternate Formats: online ● Brochure. Alternate Formats: online ● Also publishes multi-language medical dictionary and other books. **Conventions/Meetings:** Israel Medicine Annual Update - meeting - usually fall ● annual seminar.

12189 ■ Emunah of America

7 Penn Plz.
New York, NY 10001
Ph: (212)564-9045
Free: (800)368-6440
Fax: (212)643-9731
E-mail: info@emunah.org
URL: http://www.emunah.org
Contact: Shirley Singer, Contact
Founded: 1935. **Membership Dues:** individual, $25 (annual) ● life, $250. **Description:** Project of Emunah Women of America. Facilitates the "proper" integration of Ethiopian Jews into Israel's social, cultural, political, and religious life. Emphasizes the importance of retaining allegiance to religious values and warns against the over-secularization of Ethiopian Jews as they become accustomed to a new way of life in Israel. Includes current programs such as: day-care centers for Ethiopian children, volunteer and professional counseling for families through community centers and through absorption centers, religious guidance, social services, and "one-on-one" help with the problems confronting immigrants in a new society. (Absorption centers provide new clothes, food, and medical care to immigrant families). **Formerly:** (1999) Operation Joshua. **Publications:** *Emunah*. Magazine. Features insightful articles of interest

to Jewish families. **Price:** included in membership dues. Alternate Formats: online.

12190 ■ Israel Humanitarian Foundation (IHF)
276 5th Ave., Ste.404
New York, NY 10001
Ph: (212)683-5676
Free: (888)4345IHF
Fax: (212)213-9233
E-mail: regina@ihf.net
URL: http://www.ihf.net
Contact: Regina Gottfried, Natl. Exec. Dir.
Founded: 1960. **Members:** 8,000. **Staff:** 15. **Budget:** $4,300,000. **Regional Groups:** 3. **Description:** Provides assistance and support for medical, vocational, educational, and social service institutions in Israel and fosters and supports philanthropy and educational activities in the United States and Israel. **Awards:** Herbert A. Rothman Award. **Frequency:** annual. **Type:** recognition. **Recipient:** for service. **Formerly:** (1970) American Histadrut Development Foundation; (1998) Israel Histadrut Foundation. **Publications:** *Impact*, quarterly. Magazine. **Price:** free. Circulation: 4,500 ● Newsletter. Alternate Formats: online. **Conventions/Meetings:** semiannual conference and seminar.

12191 ■ Meals4Israel
11301 W Olympic Blvd., No. 580
Los Angeles, CA 90064
Free: (877)647-7235
Fax: (877)647-7235
E-mail: info@meals4israel.com
URL: http://www.meals4israel.com
Contact: David Suissa, Founder
Multinational. Description: Works to raise money for soup kitchens in Israel. Helps feed needy families across the country. Collects donations from individuals throughout the world and disperses the funds to the soup kitchens and food banks. **Publications:** Newsletter ● Brochure. Alternate Formats: online.

12192 ■ National Committee for Labor Israel (NCLI)
275 7th Ave., Rm. 1501
New York, NY 10001
Ph: (212)647-0300
Fax: (212)647-0308
E-mail: info.ncli@laborisrael.org
Contact: Jerry Goodman, Exec. Dir.
Founded: 1923. **Staff:** 3. **Budget:** $400,000. **Description:** Composed of affiliated organizations, trade unions, and individual supporters. Works to complete equality and integration of all citizens in Israeli society. Provides support and information services. Brings together people of all cultures in programs to improve understanding of issues in the Middle East. Supports the Histadrut - General Federation of Labor in Israel; cooperates with the Labor Party. Conducts public educational activities in the Jewish and non-Jewish communities, and among trade unions; distributes material; arranges cultural exchanges between Israeli and American groups. **Awards:** Isaiah Award. **Frequency:** annual. **Type:** recognition. **Recipient:** for service to the Jewish people and to Israel. **Affiliated With:** Conference of Presidents of Major American Jewish Organizations; Jewish Labor Committee; Labor Zionist Alliance; Workmen's Circle. **Also Known As:** Israel Histadrut Campaign. **Formerly:** National Committee for Labor Palestine; National Labor Committee for the Jewish Workers in Palestine. **Publications:** *WebNews*, monthly ● Also publishes occasional background reports.

12193 ■ PEF Israel Endowment Funds (PEF)
317 Madison Ave., Ste.607
New York, NY 10017
Ph: (212)599-1260
Fax: (212)599-5981
E-mail: pefisrael@aol.com
URL: http://www.pefisrael.org
Contact: B. Harrison Frankel, Pres.
Founded: 1922. **Staff:** 5. **Nonmembership. Description:** Provides charitable, scientific, educational, cultural, and social aid to institutions and organizations in Israel. Works to provide relief for and to

minister to needy persons in Israel; to support and maintain public hospitals and clinics; to assist all types of social service agencies; to help support and maintain various universities and other educational and religious institutions in Israel; and to promote scientific research. **Awards: Type:** grant. **Recipient:** to students in academic, vocational, and technical boarding and day schools for text books, writing materials, and school outings. **Publications:** Annual Report, annual.

12194 ■ United Charity Institutions of Jerusalem (UCI)
1467 48th St.
Brooklyn, NY 11219
Ph: (718)633-8469
Fax: (718)633-8478
Contact: Rabbi Zevulun Charlop, Chm.
Founded: 1903. **Description:** Raises funds for the maintenance of 13 institutions in Jerusalem such as libraries, schools, and free kitchens. **Publications:** *Jewish Daily Calendar*.

12195 ■ United Tiberias Institutions Relief Society (UTIRS)
Address Unknown since 2007
Founded: 1900. **Members:** 8,000. **Description:** To support the high school and college of Torah as well as the free kitchen in Tiberias, Israel.

Jewish

12196 ■ 92nd Street Y
1395 Lexington Ave.
New York, NY 10128
Ph: (212)415-5500 (212)415-5450
Fax: (212)828-3077
URL: http://www.92Y.org
Contact: Sol Adler, Exec. Dir.
Founded: 1874. **Staff:** 300. **Budget:** $45,000,000. **Languages:** English, French, Hebrew, Italian, Spanish, Yiddish. **Nonmembership. Description:** Jewish community and cultural center in New York serving the educational and recreational needs of more than 300,000 people each year. Maintains 8 program centers including: the School of the Arts, offering music, dance, and fine and applied arts classes; the Bronfman Center for Jewish Life which sponsors classes, workshops, and lectures; the Charles Simon Center for Adult Life and Learning, which offers lectures, adult education, tour and travel programs, singles events, a senior adult program and maintains the Buttenwieser Library, the de Hirsch Residence for adults, and archives; the Goldman Center for Youth and Family which includes a parenting center, preschool, kindergarten, and after school programs as well as summer camps for children, including disabled youngsters; the May Center for Health, Fitness and Sport, a gym and health facility; the Tisch Center for the Arts, offering classical music, jazz, and a renowned literary series; Makor/Steinhardt Center, offering the Makor Program for young adults and the Daytime at The Steinhardt Building Program for baby boomers, and the Milstein/Rosenthal Center for Media & Technology. **Libraries: Type:** reference; open to the public. **Holdings:** 30,000; books, periodicals. **Subjects:** Judaica, children, general literature. **Awards:** 92nd Street Y Global Citizenship Award. **Frequency:** annual. **Type:** recognition. **Publications:** *92nd Street Y Catalog*, 3/year. **Price:** free ● Annual Report, annual. Includes financial statements.

12197 ■ American Jewish Joint Distribution Committee (AJJDC)
711 3rd Ave., 10th Fl.
New York, NY 10017-4014
Ph: (212)687-6200
Fax: (212)370-5467
E-mail: info@jdc.org
URL: http://www.jdc.org
Contact: Steven Schwager, Exec. VP
Founded: 1914. **Staff:** 1,000. **Description:** Maintains health, welfare, assistance and social programs for needy Jews in nearly 60 countries in Asia, Africa,

Europe, the former Soviet Union, and Latin America. Provides funds for secular and religious education, feeding and medical programs, economic aid, summer camps, community development, manpower training, and aid to the aged and handicapped. Has JDC program in Israel that provides a broad range of services for the aged, disabled, and children/youth at risk, and participates with local agencies in developing health, welfare, and rehabilitation services, vocational training and placement, social integration, and community center programs. Is financially supported by Jewish federations and welfare funds through the United Jewish Communities (see separate entry). **Libraries: Type:** open to the public. **Awards:** JDC Boris Smolar Award. **Type:** recognition. **Recipient:** for excellence in journalism in Israeli-Diaspora relations ● JDC Herbert Katzki Award. **Type:** recognition. **Recipient:** for outstanding historical writing based on archival material ● Larry and Leonore Zusman JDC Prize. **Type:** recognition. **Recipient:** for individuals or staff in the innovation and implementation of social service programs in Israel ● Ralph I. Goldman Fellowship. **Type:** fellowship. **Recipient:** for excellence in the area of Jewish communal service. **Computer Services:** Mailing lists. **Affiliated With:** United Jewish Communities. **Also Known As:** Joint Distribution Committee. **Formed by Merger of:** (1914) American Jewish Relief Committee; (1914) Central Relief Committee; People's Relief Committee. **Formerly:** Joint Distribution Committee for Relief of Jewish War Sufferers. **Publications:** *American Jewish Joint Distribution Committee—Annual Report*. Provides information on the JDC, its programs, and countries where the organization operates. Includes budget information. **Price:** free ● Brochures. **Conventions/Meetings:** annual meeting.

12198 ■ American Jewish Society for Service (AJSS)
10319 Westlake Blvd., Ste.193
Bethesda, MD 20817
Ph: (240)205-5940
E-mail: info@ajss.org
URL: http://www.ajss.org
Contact: Rena Convissor, Exec. Dir.
Founded: 1950. **Members:** 2,400. **Staff:** 12. **Budget:** $225,000. **Regional Groups:** 3. **Description:** Conducts voluntary work service camps for youth (15 1/2-17 1/2 years). Sponsors charitable program. Conducts three teenage volunteer camps in three different locations each summer, provides service to the elderly, disabled and deprived. **Awards: Type:** scholarship. **Publications:** *Project Brochure*, annual ● Brochure, annual. Describes the 3 work projects of the past summer. **Price:** $2,800.00. **Conventions/Meetings:** annual Camper Orientation - reunion.

12199 ■ Association of Jewish Center Professionals (AJCP)
15 E 26th St.
New York, NY 10010-1579
Ph: (212)786-5154 (212)786-5155
Fax: (212)481-4174
E-mail: info@ajcp.org
URL: http://www.ajcp.org
Contact: Harvey Rosenzweig, Exec.Dir.
Founded: 1918. **Members:** 1,050. **Membership Dues:** alumni, retiree, $55 (annual) ● executive director, $260 (annual) ● management, $135 (annual) ● department head, $85 (annual) ● professional, $65 (annual) ● student, $35 (annual). **Staff:** 2. **Regional Groups:** 11. **Description:** Professional workers in Jewish community centers, camps, and youth groups; students in schools of social work. Provides opportunities for building Jewish communities. **Awards:** Professional of the Year Awards. **Frequency:** annual. **Type:** recognition. **Recipient:** for model excellent programs and professional leadership. **Committees:** Aging; Camping; Cultural Arts; International Projects; Jewish Education; Nursery School; Personnel Practices; Physical Education; Professional Education; Public Affairs; Research; Retirees. **Affiliated With:** Jewish Communal Service Association of North America. **Formerly:** (1970) National Association of Jewish Center Workers; (1989) Association of Jewish Center Workers. **Publications:** *Conference Papers*,

annual ● *Kesher*, quarterly. Newsletter. Includes articles on professional practice and reflections from the field. **Conventions/Meetings:** biennial meeting.

12200 ■ Association of Jewish Family and Children's Agencies (AJFCA)
620 Cranbury Rd., Ste.102
East Brunswick, NJ 08816
Ph: (732)432-7120
Free: (800)634-7346
Fax: (732)432-7127
E-mail: ajfca@ajfca.org
URL: http://ajfca.org
Contact: Bert J. Goldberg, Pres./CEO
Founded: 1972. **Members:** 145. **Staff:** 9. **Budget:** $900,000. **Description:** Serves Jewish family and children's agencies in the U.S. and Canada. Provides opportunities for the exchange of experiences among member agencies; collects data; issues reports; develops guidelines and statements; offers consultation on programs and administration. Provides its members with professional expertise in understanding current and emerging tends, problem solving around service delivery issues, recruitment of personnel, research and planning. Administers Elder Support Network. **Publications:** *Professional Opportunities Bulletin*, monthly. Alternate Formats: online ● *Tachlis*, quarterly. Newsletter. Alternate Formats: online ● Directory, annual. **Price:** included in membership dues. Alternate Formats: online ● Directories. Alternate Formats: online. **Conventions/Meetings:** annual conference ● annual meeting (exhibits).

12201 ■ The Blue Card (TBC)
171 Madison Ave., Rm. 1405
New York, NY 10016-5115
Ph: (212)239-2251
Fax: (212)594-6881
E-mail: info@bluecardfund.org
URL: http://www.bluecardfund.org
Contact: Sandra Wiesel, Exec. Dir.
Founded: 1940. **Members:** 33. **Staff:** 2. **Budget:** $500,000. **Languages:** English, German. **Description:** Upon referral of social service agencies, provides financial assistance helping Jews who immigrated to the U.S. from Central Europe because of Nazi persecution. Gives financial help to the aged, sick, and unemployed when no other source of aid is available. Provides referral service. **Publications:** *The Blue Card Calendar*, annual ● Annual Report, annual. **Price:** free. **Conventions/Meetings:** annual meeting - always early spring, New York City.

12202 ■ B'nai B'rith Senior Citizens Housing Committee (BBSCHC)
Address Unknown since 2007
Founded: 1968. **Members:** 40. **Staff:** 3. **Regional Groups:** 29. **Description:** Provides housing facilities in six countries for elderly and handicapped people with low incomes. Encourages independent living within a supportive community "where residents look to the future with dignity and confidence." Operates B'nai B'rith Senior Citizens Housing Network, comprising 49 apartment buildings serving over 5000 senior citizens. **Affiliated With:** B'nai B'rith International. **Formerly:** (1991) B'nai B'rith International Senior Citizens Housing Committee. **Publications:** *B'nai B'rith Senior Housing Network*, quarterly. Newsletter. **Advertising:** not accepted. **Conventions/Meetings:** annual National Conference on Senior Housing - conference and workshop.

12203 ■ Conference on Jewish Material Claims Against Germany
15 E 26th St., Rm. 906
New York, NY 10010
Ph: (646)536-9100
Fax: (212)679-2126
E-mail: info@claimscon.org
URL: http://www.claimscon.org
Contact: Gideon Taylor, Exec. VP
Founded: 1951. **Languages:** English, German, Hebrew, Russian, Yiddish. **Description:** Represents world Jewry in negotiations for compensation and restitution from Germany and Austria and other entities. Serves as an operating agency that administers compensation funds, recovers Jewish property and allocates funds to institutions that provide social welfare services to Holocaust survivors and preserve the memory and lessons of the Shoah. **Computer Services:** Mailing lists. **Publications:** *Annual Report: Special Update on Negotiations*, annual. Claims Conference Guide to compensation and restitution for Holocaust survivors. Alternate Formats: online ● Videos. Alternate Formats: online. **Conventions/Meetings:** biennial meeting.

12204 ■ Hebrew Immigrant Aid Society (HIAS)
333 7th Ave., 16th Fl.
New York, NY 10001
Ph: (212)967-4100
Free: (800)HIAS714
Fax: (212)967-4483
E-mail: info@hias.org
URL: http://www.hias.org
Contact: Gideon Aronoff, Pres./CEO
Founded: 1881. **Members:** 11,500. **Membership Dues:** individual, $50 (annual) ● family, $100 (annual). **Staff:** 100. **State Groups:** 200. **Languages:** English, Farsi, Russian, Spanish. **Description:** Assists refugees and migrants from Europe, North Africa, the Middle East, and other trouble areas resettle in the United States, Canada, Latin America, and Australia. Maintains offices and committees around the world to: help locate relatives and friends; prepare documents; arrange for transportation; provide reception and resettlement services. Is involved in assistance to refugees at the request of the U.S. government. Compiles statistics. **Libraries:** **Type:** reference. **Holdings:** biographical archives, photographs. **Awards: Type:** recognition ● **Type:** scholarship. **Committees:** Government Relations; Overseas Operations; Public Relations; Retirement; Scholarship; U.S. Operations. **Departments:** Field Services; Location; Post-Migration; Pre-Migration; Public Affairs; Refugee and Immigrant Services. **Also Known As:** HIAS. **Formed by Merger of:** Hebrew Sheltering and Immigrant Aid Society; Migration Department of the American Jewish Joint Distribution Committee; United Services for New Americans. **Formerly:** (1975) United HIAS Service. **Publications:** *Immigration At A Glance*. Brochures. Alternate Formats: online ● *Passages*, quarterly. Magazine. **Price:** free for members. **Circulation:** 20,000. **Advertising:** accepted. Alternate Formats: online ● Annual Report, annual. Alternate Formats: online. **Conventions/Meetings:** monthly board meeting.

12205 ■ Jewish Communal Service Association of North America (JCSA)
520 Eighth Ave.
New York, NY 10018
Ph: (212)532-0167
Fax: (212)532-1461
E-mail: info@jcsana.org
URL: http://www.jcsana.org
Contact: Ms. Brenda D. Gevertz, Exec. Dir.
Founded: 1899. **Members:** 3,700. **Membership Dues:** general, $75 (annual) ● transitional, retiree, $50 (annual) ● full-time student, $15 (annual) ● adjunct, $25 (annual) ● supporting, $125 (annual). **Staff:** 2. **Budget:** $250,000. **Local Groups:** 15. **Multinational. Description:** Professional-level forum for the discussion of opportunities and developments in various fields of Jewish community service. **Awards:** JCSA Young Professional Award. **Frequency:** annual. **Type:** grant. **Computer Services:** Mailing lists. **Committees:** Graduate Student Network; Networking Parents. **Formerly:** National Conference of Jewish Communal Service; (1992) Conference of Jewish Communal Service. **Publications:** *e-Newsletter*, monthly. **Price:** free. **Circulation:** 3,000. **Advertising:** accepted. Alternate Formats: online ● *Journal of Jewish Communal Service*, quarterly. Includes book reviews and abstracts. **Price:** $36.00/year. ISSN: 0022-2089. **Circulation:** 4,000. **Advertising:** accepted. Alternate Formats: microform ● *The Turbulent Decades - Jewish Communal Service in America, 1958-1978*. Book. **Conventions/Meetings:** annual meeting - usually May or June.

12206 ■ Jewish Community Centers Association of North America (JCCANA)
520 8th Ave.
New York, NY 10018
Ph: (212)532-4949
Free: (877)452-2237
Fax: (212)481-4174
E-mail: jccal@jcca.org
URL: http://www.jcca.org
Contact: Allan Finkelstein, Pres.
Founded: 1917. **Members:** 275. **Staff:** 65. **Budget:** $10,000,000. **Description:** Promotes the Jewish community center movement; aims to provide educational, cultural, social, Jewish identity building and recreational programs; fosters connections between North American Jews and Israel and world Jewry. Jewish military personnel and their dependents in the U.S. Armed Forces and Veterans Administration Hospitals through the JWB Jewish Chaplains Council. Operates research center; compiles statistics; maintains placement services for professional Jewish community center and YM and YWHA workers. Jewish military personnel and their dependents in the U.S. Armed Forces and Veterans Administration Hospitals through the JWB Jewish Chaplains Council. Operates research center; compiles statistics; maintains placement services for professional Jewish community center and YM and YWHA workers. **Computer Services:** Online services, bulletin board, email and chat system for JCC Professionals and Association. **Absorbed:** (1921) Council of Young Men's Hebrew and Kindred Associations. **Also Known As:** JCC Association. **Formerly:** (1977) National Jewish Welfare Board; (1990) JWB. **Publications:** *Beyond 2000 - A Plan for the Jewish Community Center Movement*. Video. Contains presentation of Allan Finkelstein about bringing the JCC movement into the next century. **Price:** $4.00 ● *Circle*, quarterly. Magazine. For lay leaders and professional staffs of JCCs. **Price:** included in membership dues; $50.00 /year for nonmembers. **Circulation:** 25,000 ● *Security and Media Relations Program*. Video. Features an overview of communicating with media after a crisis and establishing a security plan. **Price:** $4.00 ● Annual Report, annual ● Directories. Alternate Formats: online. **Conventions/Meetings:** biennial conference, leadership training conference (exhibits).

12207 ■ Jewish Council for Public Affairs (JCPA)
116 E 27th St.
New York, NY 10016-7322
Ph: (212)684-6950
Fax: (212)686-1353
E-mail: contactus@thejcpa.org
URL: http://www.jewishpublicaffairs.org
Contact: Mr. Steve Gutow, Exec. Dir.
Founded: 1944. **Members:** 136. **Staff:** 17. **Budget:** $1,800,000. **Local Groups:** 122. **National Groups:** 14. **Description:** National Jewish agencies (13) and local Jewish community relations councils (123) jointly developing policies such as: interpretation of Israel, oppression of Jews abroad, combating anti-Semitism, equal opportunity, equal rights, civil liberties, religious freedom, and other democratic practices. Encourages friendly relationships among groups. Conducts placement services for member agencies. **Task Forces:** Equal Opportunity and Social Justice; Israel; Jewish Security and Bill of Rights; World Jewry and International Human Rights. **Formerly:** National Committee Relations Advisory Council. **Publications:** *Directory of Constituent Organizations*, annual ● *JCPA Agenda for Public Affairs*, annual ● *JCPA Insider*, weekly. Newsletter. Alternate Formats: online. **Conventions/Meetings:** annual Plenary Session - conference.

12208 ■ Jewish Philanthropic Fund of 1933 (JPF)
570 7th Ave., Rm. 1102
New York, NY 10018
Ph: (212)921-3871
Fax: (212)575-1918
Contact: Raymond V.J. Schrag Esq., Pres.
Description: Charitable fund created by the American Federation of Jews From Central Europe. Provides

financial assistance to institutions and agencies of the Jewish emigre community which "fled Nazi oppression in German-speaking Central Europe" and established themselves in the United States. Offers support to organizations that provide social services, encourage cultural preservation of the German-Jewish heritage, and document the acculturation of German-speaking Jews in the U.S. and other countries. Seeks to supplement the financial resources of community service organizations such as Blue Card, the Leo Baeck Institute, and the Research Foundation for Jewish Immigration. JPF raises funds primarily through legacies and testamentary dispositions. **Affiliated With:** American Federation of Jews From Central Europe.

12209 ■ Machne Israel
770 Eastern Pkwy.
Brooklyn, NY 11213
Ph: (718)774-4000 (718)771-6729
Fax: (718)774-2718
E-mail: info@lubavitch.com
URL: http://www.lubavitch.com
Contact: Rabbi Yehuda Krinsky, Exec. Dir.
Founded: 1942. **Members:** 600,000. **Description:** Serves as a social service arm of the Lubavitch Movement. Aids Jewish and non-Jewish persons by material and spiritual means. Provides clubs for senior citizens; relieves the hungry and homeless; assists the sick in hospitals; cooperates in the establishment of drug rehabilitation centers; and engages in other community social services. **Affiliated With:** Lubavitch Women's Organization. **Conventions/Meetings:** periodic conference.

12210 ■ Mirrer Yeshiva Central Institute (MYCI)
1791-5 Ocean Pkwy.
Brooklyn, NY 11223
Ph: (718)645-0536
Fax: (718)645-9251
Contact: Rabbi Osher Kalmanowitz, Pres.
Founded: 1947. **Description:** Maintains rabbinical college, postgraduate school for Talmudic research, and an accredited high school. Conducts rescue, rehabilitation, and overseas activities to assist Jewish scholars and other Jews in distress around the world.

12211 ■ National Conference of Shomrim Societies (NCSS)
c/o Martin Turetzky, Treas.
264 E Broadway, No. C1905
New York, NY 10002
Ph: (212)777-7809
Fax: (212)447-1633
E-mail: treasurer@nationalshomrim.org
URL: http://www.nationalshomrim.org
Contact: Louis Weiser, Exec. VP
Founded: 1958. **Members:** 32. **Membership Dues:** regular, $50 (annual). **Staff:** 2. **Regional Groups:** 22. **Local Groups:** 10. **Description:** Charitable organization. Shomrim is a Hebrew term meaning "Watchmen". **Telecommunication Services:** electronic mail, execvp@nationalshomrim.org. **Conventions/Meetings:** annual convention - 2007 Dec. 13-17, Fort Lauderdale, FL.

12212 ■ New York Association for New Americans (NYANA)
2 Washington St.
New York, NY 10004
Ph: (212)425-2900
E-mail: customercare@nyana.org
URL: http://www.nyana.org
Contact: Michael Loeb, Chm.
Founded: 1949. **Budget:** $43,000,000. **Description:** Serves as Resettlement and rehabilitation agency for Jewish newcomers and other refugees in the Greater New York area. Aids more than 350,000 Jewish displaced persons from World War II, refugees from Hungary and Cuba, Jews exiled from Egypt following the Suez crisis, and refugees from the former Soviet Union and other countries in Europe, Southeast Asia, and the Middle East; more than 100,000 Jews from the Soviet Union and other Eastern European countries have been resettled in New York City. Provides

financial assistance for housing; maintenance, food, and other special needs; casework and vocational counseling; job placement and follow-up; career planning for professionals; retraining, educational counseling, and scholarship aid; English-language training and other vocational needs. Works with national, state, and city government agencies in facilitating the delivery of services to refugees; supported by funds from the United Jewish Appeal, the Greater New York Fund/United Way, and private foundation and government grants. **Libraries: Type:** reference. **Committees:** Casework; Community Services/Acculturation; Employment and Training; Health Care; Interagency; Legal; Public Policy; Public Relations; Resources Development; Scholarship; Special Events; Special Populations. **Divisions:** Employment and Training; Grants and Government; Immigrant Services; Management, Finance, and MIS; Social Services. **Programs:** Master of Social Work Internship; Masters of Counseling Internship. **Affiliated With:** United Jewish Appeal - Federation of Jewish Philanthropies of New York. **Publications:** *NYANA News*, quarterly. Newsletter ● Also publishes educational materials for immigrants and immigration service professionals. **Conventions/Meetings:** annual meeting - always May or June in New York City.

12213 ■ ORT America
75 Maiden Ln., 10th Fl.
New York, NY 10038
Ph: (212)505-7700
Free: (800)519-2678
Fax: (212)674-3057
E-mail: info@ortamerica.org
URL: http://www.ortamerica.org
Contact: Hope Kessler, Exec. Dir.
Founded: 1922. **Members:** 10,000. **Membership Dues:** single person, $36 (annual) ● two person, $72 (annual) ● contributor, $150-$250 (annual) ● life, $500 ● student at risk campaign, $550 (annual) ● golden circle, $1,000 (annual). **Staff:** 50. **Budget:** $12,000,000. **Description:** Raises funds to support the educational programs of ORT, from Israel and the former Soviet Union to Latin America and India in nearly 60 countries. Uses current technology to educate, train and provide students with the skills and knowledge necessary to earn a living, foster economic self-sufficiency and help them lead lives of dignity. **Awards:** American ORT Chapter of the Year. **Frequency:** annual. **Type:** recognition. **Recipient:** for outstanding membership and leadership development and fundraising ● Paul Bernick New Leadership. **Frequency:** annual. **Type:** recognition. **Recipient:** for emerging national leader ● Supporter of the Year. **Frequency:** annual. **Type:** recognition ● William Haber. **Frequency:** annual. **Type:** recognition. **Recipient:** for commitment and leadership in the organization ● Yitzah Rabin Award. **Type:** recognition. **Computer Services:** Mailing lists ● online services. **Formed by Merger of:** (2007) American ORT and Women's American ORT. **Formerly:** (1998) American Ort Federation. **Publications:** *American ORT Times*, quarterly. Newsletter. Contains updates on American ORT events, plus calendars. **Price:** free. **Circulation:** 5,000. Alternate Formats: online ● Annual Report, annual. Contains comprehensive report of educational operations in 50 countries. Includes program budget report. **Price:** free. **Circulation:** 8,000. **Conventions/Meetings:** annual conference.

12214 ■ Shomrim Society
c/o Murray Ellman, Financial Sec.
PO Box 598
Knickerbocker, NY 10002
Ph: (718)730-8914
E-mail: mail@nypdshomrim.org
URL: http://www.nypdshomrim.org
Contact: Stephen L. Herman, Pres.
Founded: 1924. **Members:** 3,000. **Membership Dues:** Jewish law enforcement officer, $20 (annual). **Description:** New York City police officers and civilian members of the service of the Jewish faith. Sponsors Passover charity program. Holds annual memorial service, spiritual breakfast, and parade. Provides death benefits for members. Maintains speakers' bureau and charitable programs. **Libraries: Type:**

not open to the public. **Holdings:** archival material. **Awards:** Asser Levy Award. **Frequency:** annual. **Type:** recognition ● Person of the Year. **Frequency:** annual. **Type:** recognition. **Recipient:** for individuals exemplifying the "noblest traditions of the Jewish faith and of our country" ● **Frequency:** annual. **Type:** scholarship. **Recipient:** for children and grandchildren of members. **Computer Services:** database, membership ● mailing lists. **Committees:** Awards; Cemetery; Civilian Affairs; Collation; Entertainment; Financial Advisory; Legal; Public Relations; Recruitment; Welfare. **Affiliated With:** Council of Jewish Organizations in Civil Service; National Conference of Shomrim Societies. **Publications:** *Shomrim News*, monthly. Bulletin. **Price:** free ● Newsletter. Alternate Formats: online. **Conventions/Meetings:** annual convention ● meeting - 10/year.

12215 ■ United Jewish Appeal - Federation of Jewish Philanthropies of New York (UJAFJP)
130 E 59th St.
New York, NY 10022
Ph: (212)980-1000 (212)836-1486
E-mail: contact@ujafedny.org
URL: http://www.ujafedny.org
Contact: Dr. John S. Ruskay, Exec. VP/CEO
Founded: 1986. **Staff:** 550. **Budget:** $30,000,000. **Description:** Federation of agencies that provide hospital, health, geriatric, vocational, family and child care services, and Jewish education to individuals in the greater New York area, Israel, and 34 countries. Conducts fundraising and communal planning programs; maintains biographical archives. **Awards:** Distinguished Communal Service Award. **Type:** recognition ● Hurowitz Award. **Type:** recognition ● Rose Zeitlin Goldstein Memorial Award. **Type:** recognition ● Tzedakah Award. **Type:** recognition. **Committees:** Allocations; Building Operations; Campaign Cabinet; Designated Organizations; Domestic Affairs Division; Endowments and Bequests; 59th Street. **Departments:** Camping Services; Community Centers; Housing and Neighborhood Preservation; Human Services; Jewish Education and Culture; Jewish Information and Referral Service; Lawyers Division; Long Island Division; Marketing and Communications; Medical and Geriatric Services; Metropolitan Division; Policy Research and Planning; Public and Community Affairs; Real Estate; Religious Affairs; Thrift Shops; Trades and Professions; Vanguard Club; Wall Street; Westchester Division; Wiener Education Center; Women's Campaign. **Formed by Merger of:** Federation of Jewish Charities in Brooklyn; Federation for the Support of Jewish Philanthropic Societies of New York; United Jewish Appeal of Greater New York; Federation of Jewish Philanthropies of Greater New York. **Publications:** *Jewish Information and Referral Service Directory*, annual. Lists Jewish and non-Jewish social service programs. **Price:** $30.00 /year for members; $40.00 /year for nonmembers ● *Quarterly Report*. Newsletter. Reports on organization's activities and achievements within the quarter. **Price:** free. **Circulation:** 7,500 ● *UJA - Federation Network Directory*, biennial. Includes lists of agency services. ● Annual Report, annual. **Price:** free. **Circulation:** 10,000. **Conventions/Meetings:** annual meeting - usually May, in New York City.

12216 ■ United Jewish Communities (UJC)
PO Box 30
New York, NY 10113
Ph: (212)284-6500
E-mail: info@ujc.org
URL: http://www.uja.com
Contact: Howard Rieger, Pres./CEO
Founded: 1939. **Staff:** 210. **Regional Groups:** 5. **Description:** Principal fundraising organization in the U.S. on behalf of Jewish needs overseas. Works in conjunction with the American Jewish Joint Distribution Committee and the United Israel Appeal to provide humanitarian programs and social services for Jews worldwide and in Israel. Conducts joint campaigns with existing local Jewish federations and welfare funds; functions independently in smaller communities. Develops national fundraising programs and campaign themes for use on regional and local levels; trains solicitors in fundraising campaign

techniques; recruits and develops leadership; holds conferences, workshops, and seminars; provides speakers to constituent communities to present the campaign case; conducts missions to Israel, Europe, Washington, DC, and New York City; sponsors traveling exhibitions and cultural programs. **Awards:** Adele Rosenwald Levy Award. **Type:** recognition. **Recipient:** for women's leadership ● Pinhas Sapir Award. **Type:** recognition. **Recipient:** for campaign excellence. **Formerly:** (2000) United Jewish Appeal. **Publications:** *Advanced Gift Manual* ● *Campaign Guide for Students* ● *How Your Contribution Helps* ● *UJA and You* ● *The Whole UJA Catalog* ● *Women's Division Chairman's Manual* ● Annual Report, annual. Alternate Formats: online.

Journalists

12217 ■ John S. and James L. Knight Foundation (KF)
Wachovia Financial Ctr., Ste.3300
200 S Biscayne Blvd.
Miami, FL 33131-2349
Ph: (305)908-2600
Fax: (305)908-2698
E-mail: web@knightfdn.org
URL: http://www.knightfdn.org
Contact: Mr. Alberto Ibarguen, Pres./CEO
Founded: 1950. **Staff:** 44. **Budget:** $95,000,000. **Nonmembership. Description:** Promotes excellence in journalism worldwide and invests in the vitality of 26 U.S. communities. **Libraries: Type:** not open to the public. **Awards: Type:** grant. **Commissions:** Knight Commission on Intercollegiate Athletics. **Funds:** National Venture. **Programs:** Community Partners; Journalism Initiatives. **Affiliated With:** Council on Foundations. **Also Known As:** (2006) Knight Brothers Foundation. **Publications:** *Knight Forum,* bimonthly. Magazine. Features stories about transformational grantmaking and issues related to journalism and communities. **Circulation:** 8,000. Alternate Formats: online ● *Knight Foundation Annual Report,* annual. Alternate Formats: online ● *News@Knight,* quarterly, every February, May, August, and November. Newsletters. **Circulation:** 8,000. Alternate Formats: online ● *Working@Knight,* monthly, issued at mid-month. Newsletters. **Circulation:** 3,000. Alternate Formats: online.

Korean

12218 ■ Young Koreans United (YKU)
2701A W Peterson Ave., Ste.102
Chicago, IL 60659
Ph: (773)506-9299
Fax: (773)506-9159
E-mail: chicago@ykuusa.org
URL: http://www.ykuusa.org
Contact: Cliff Lee, Pres.
Founded: 1984. **Languages:** English, Korean. **Multinational. Description:** Seeks to build a progressive voice in the Korean American community through education, action and grassroots organizing. Advocates for the civil rights of Korean Americans. Contributes to the movement for peace, justice and disarmament in the Korean peninsula. Advocates for just and peaceful policies towards Korea.

Land Control

12219 ■ Land Loss Fund (LLF)
PO Box 61
Tillery, NC 27887
E-mail: tillery@aol.com
URL: http://members.aol.com/tillery/llf.html
Founded: 1983. **Membership Dues:** active (family), $15 (annual) ● active (senior), $5 (annual) ● adult, $7 (annual) ● youth, $1 (annual) ● group, $25 (annual) ● individual support, $10 (annual). **Description:** Farmers, educators, social workers, businesspersons, and others concerned with family land

loss. Strives to improve the social, educational and economic welfare of those affected by continued loss of family owned land, particularly in rural African-American communities. Provides educational resources and technical assistance in management and financial record keeping, aids in finding legal options and assistance, develops diversification plans, and new management procedures. **Conventions/Meetings:** meeting.

Language

12220 ■ Media Access Group (MAG)
125 Western Ave.
Boston, MA 02134
Ph: (617)300-3600
Fax: (617)300-1020
E-mail: access@wgbh.org
URL: http://main.wgbh.org/wgbh/pages/mag
Contact: Tom Apone, Dir. of Operations
Founded: 1972. **Languages:** English, Spanish. **Description:** Provides the widest possible access to television and video for deaf and hard-of-hearing people. **Formerly:** (2002) Caption Center. **Publications:** *MAG Newsletter.*

Learning Disabled

12221 ■ Academic Language Therapy Association (ALTA)
14070 Proton Rd., Ste.100
LB 9
Dallas, TX 75244
Ph: (972)233-9107
Free: (866)283-7133
Fax: (972)490-4219
E-mail: helpline@altaread.org
URL: http://www.altaread.org
Contact: Jeanine Phillips, Sec.
Founded: 1986. **Members:** 750. **Membership Dues:** student, $30 (annual) ● active, $60 (annual) ● qualified instructor, $80 (annual). **Description:** Written-language professionals. Seeks to establish, maintain, and promote high standards of education, practice and conduct for the profession of academic language therapy. Provides services for children and adults who have problems with reading, writing and spelling. Conducts educational programs; provides referral services; sponsors annual spelling bee; maintains Speaker's Bureau. **Committees:** Continuing Education; Exhibits; Programs; Public Relations; Registration Exam; Telephone Helpline/Hopeline; Website; Website Helpline. **Publications:** *National Registry,* annual. Directory ● Bulletin, quarterly. Alternate Formats: online.

12222 ■ Academy of Learning and Developmental Disorders (ALDD)
Address Unknown since 2007
Founded: 1999. **Members:** 20. **Membership Dues:** associate, $175 (annual) ● fellow, plus one time processing fee of $175, $50 (annual). **Staff:** 5. **Budget:** $25,000. **Description:** Psychologists, educators, counselors, optometrists, psychiatrists, neurologists, and pediatricians. Sponsors educational programs; conducts examinations and confers certification upon qualified professionals treating people with learning and developmental disorders. **Computer Services:** Mailing lists.

12223 ■ Council for Learning Disabilities (CLD)
11184 Antioch Rd.
Overland Park, KS 66210
Ph: (913)491-1011
Fax: (913)491-1012
E-mail: lnease@cldinternational.org
URL: http://www.cldinternational.org
Contact: Linda Nease, Exec. Dir.
Founded: 1967. **Members:** 1,200. **Membership Dues:** national, $75 (annual) ● student, $35 (annual). **Staff:** 2. **State Groups:** 10. **Description:** Professionals interested in the study of learning disabilities.

Works to promote the education and general welfare of individuals having specific learning disabilities by: improving teacher preparation programs and local special education programs, and resolving important research issues. Sponsors educational sessions. **Awards: Type:** recognition. **Formerly:** (1981) Division for Children with Learning Disabilities. **Publications:** *Intervention in School and Clinic.* Journal. **Price:** included in membership dues ● *LD Forum Newsletter,* bimonthly. Alternate Formats: online ● *Learning Disability Quarterly.* Journal. **Price:** included in membership dues ● Papers. **Conventions/Meetings:** annual conference (exhibits) - always October.

12224 ■ Friends of LADDERS
PO Box 920025
Needham, MA 02492
Ph: (781)449-6074
E-mail: fol@ladders.org
URL: http://www.ladders.org/friends.php
Contact: Margaret L. Bauman, Contact

Description: Represents the interests of parents, civic leaders, businesspersons, professionals and other volunteers committed to raising funds to underwrite expansion projects. Provides educational and outreach forums for parents and professionals.

12225 ■ Learning Disabilities Association of America (LDA)
4156 Lib. Rd.
Pittsburgh, PA 15234-1349
Ph: (412)341-1515
Fax: (412)344-0224
E-mail: info@ldaamerica.org
URL: http://www.ldaamerica.org
Contact: Sheila Buckley, Exec. Dir.

Founded: 1963. **Members:** 40,000. **Membership Dues:** regular, $30 (annual) ● foreign, $45 (annual). **Staff:** 7. **Budget:** $900,000. **State Groups:** 43. **Local Groups:** 300. **Description:** Parents of children with learning disabilities; interested professionals. Works to "advance the education and general well-being of children with adequate intelligence who have learning disabilities arising from perceptual, conceptual, or subtle coordinative problems, sometimes accompanied by behavior difficulties." Disseminates information to the public; provides assistance to state and local groups. These affiliated groups carry out direct services to parents and children, including schools, camps, recreation programs, parent education, information services, and publication of books and pamphlets. Offers information and referral services. **Libraries: Type:** reference. **Holdings:** 300. **Subjects:** learning disabilities. **Awards:** Education of the Year. **Frequency:** annual. **Type:** recognition ● Scientist of the Year. **Frequency:** annual. **Type:** recognition ● Statesman of the Year. **Frequency:** annual. **Type:** recognition. **Additional Websites:** http://www.ldaamerica.us. **Committees:** Adult Issues; Advocacy; Educational; Legislative; Membership/Cultural Diversity; Mental Health. **Formerly:** (1963) Association for Children with Learning Disabilities; (1990) Association for Children and Adults with Learning Disabilities. **Publications:** *Advocacy Handbook: A Parent's Guide for Special Education.* **Price:** free for members; $10.00 plus $2 shipping and handling ● *LDA Newsbriefs,* bimonthly. Newsletter. Contains items of interest on learning disabilities. **Price:** $15.00/year. ISSN: 0739-909X. **Circulation:** 40,000. **Advertising:** accepted ● *Learning Disabilities: A Multidisciplinary Journal,* quarterly. **Price:** $30.00 /year for members in U.S.; $60.00 /year for nonmembers; $45.00 /year for members outside U.S. **Conventions/Meetings:** annual international conference (exhibits) - always February or March.

12226 ■ National Association for the Education of African American Children with Learning Disabilities (NAEAACLD)
PO Box 9521
Columbus, OH 43209
Ph: (614)237-6021
Fax: (614)238-0929

E-mail: info@aacld.org
URL: http://www.charityadvantage.com/aacld
Contact: Nancy R. Tidwell, Founder/Pres.
Founded: 1999. **Description:** Seeks to improve the quality of education for African American children. Increases awareness and understanding of the specific issues facing African American children with learning disabilities. **Computer Services:** Information services, learning disability resources ● mailing lists, of members ● online services, chat room ● online services, message board. **Publications:** *One Child at a Time. A Parent Handbook and Resource Directory for African American Families with Children Who Learn Differently.*

12227 ■ National Center for Learning Disabilities (NCLD)
381 Park Ave. S, Ste.1401
New York, NY 10016
Ph: (212)545-7510
Free: (888)575-7373
Fax: (212)545-9665
E-mail: cnugent@ncld.org
URL: http://www.ncld.org
Contact: Mr. James H. Wendorf, Exec. Dir.
Founded: 1977. **Staff:** 17. **Description:** Seeks to increase opportunities for all individuals with learning disabilities to achieve their potential. Accomplishes its mission by promoting public awareness and understanding, conducting educational programs and services that advance research-based knowledge and providing national leadership in shaping public policy. **Libraries: Type:** not open to the public. **Awards:** Anne Ford Scholarship. **Frequency:** annual. **Type:** scholarship. **Recipient:** to high school seniors ● Bill Ellis Teacher Preparation Award. **Frequency:** annual. **Type:** scholarship. **Recipient:** for excellence in teaching ● Pete & Carrie Rozelle Award. **Frequency:** annual. **Type:** scholarship. **Computer Services:** database, learning disability resources. **Formerly:** (1989) Foundation for Children with Learning Disabilities. **Publications:** *LD News,* monthly. Newsletter. Addresses issues about learning disabilities for parents, caregivers, educators, advocates and individuals with learning disabilities. Alternate Formats: online ● *Our World,* 3/year. Newsletter. **Price:** free. Alternate Formats: online ● Annual Report, annual. Alternate Formats: online ● Also free literature about learning disabilities. **Conventions/Meetings:** periodic seminar, on teacher training, legislative advocacy, and employing the learning disabled.

12228 ■ National Networker (NN)
Address Unknown since 2007
Founded: 1982. **Members:** 2,500. **Staff:** 13. **Budget:** $89,000. **Description:** Learning disabled adults; professionals and others interested in problems concerning LD. The term "learning disability" refers to a range of difficulties in acquiring, receiving, and storing information. Seeks to educate, compile statistics, and disseminate information about LD. **Computer Services:** database, local services and programs. **Formerly:** (1992) National Network of Learning Disabled Adults.

12229 ■ Schwab Learning - A Program of the Charles Schwab Foundation
1650 S Amphlett Blvd., Ste.300
San Mateo, CA 94402
Ph: (650)655-2410
Free: (800)230-0988
Fax: (650)655-2411
E-mail: marketing@schwablearning.org
URL: http://www.schwablearning.org
Contact: Charles R. Schwab, Chm.
Founded: 1988. **Members:** 4,000. **Staff:** 50. **Languages:** English, Spanish. **Description:** Seeks to raise awareness about learning differences and equip parents, teachers, and other professionals with the resources they need to improve the lives of children with learning differences. Offers one-on-one guidance services with LD consultants. **Libraries: Type:** reference. **Holdings:** 4,000; audiovisuals, books. **Subjects:** learning differences and related topics. **Computer Services:** database, resource center for

information on children with learning differences and AD/HD. **Formerly:** (1998) Parents Educational Resource Center; (2001) Schwab Foundation For Learning. **Publications:** *LD Matters,* quarterly. Newsletter. Features articles, pertinent information, and practical suggestions to assist students with learning differences. **Price:** free. **Circulation:** 25,000.

Legal Services

12230 ■ Legal Counsel for the Elderly (LCE)
601 E St. NW, Bldg. A, 4th Fl.
Washington, DC 20049
Ph: (202)434-2120
Free: (888)687-2277
Fax: (202)434-6464
E-mail: jmay@aarp.org
URL: http://www.uaelderlaw.org
Contact: Jan May, Dir.
Founded: 1975. **Nonmembership. Description:** Provides free legal services to Washington, DC residents aged 60 and older, with priority given to low income persons. Serves as the Long-Term Care Ombudsman for DC by advocating for residents of nursing homes and board and care homes. **Programs:** National Guardianship Monitoring; National Homestudy in Elderlaw; National Money Management; National Volunteer Lawyers Project. **Affiliated With:** AARP. **Publications:** *Do You Have Questions or Concerns About Nursing Homes?* (in English and Spanish). Brochure. Describes role that the DC Long Term Care Ombudsman Program plays in advocating for residents of long term care facilities and nursing homes. **Price:** free ● *Do You Know What LCE Can Do For You?* (in English and Spanish). Brochure. Informational brochure describing problems that LCE can help solve: going through red tape, going to court, getting benefits you are entitled to, etc. **Price:** free. **Conventions/Meetings:** annual National Aging and Law - conference (exhibits).

12231 ■ Legal Services for Children (LSC)
1254 Market St., 3rd Fl.
San Francisco, CA 94102
Ph: (415)863-3762
Fax: (415)863-7708
E-mail: shannan@lsc-sf.org
URL: http://www.lsc-sf.org
Contact: Shannan Wilber JD, Exec. Dir.
Founded: 1975. **Staff:** 17. **Budget:** $1,100,000. **Languages:** Chinese, English, Hindi, Mandarin Dialects, Punjabi, Spanish, Tagalog. **Description:** Comprehensive, cost-free law firm devoted exclusively to protecting the legal rights of teens, children, and infants who are residents of San Francisco, CA, and other Bay Area counties. Supported by private contributions and foundation grants, the firm is staffed by attorneys, social workers, social work student interns, law students, and support staff. Clients receive the team services of attorneys and social workers. Accepts referrals from all public and private youth-serving agencies as well as from individual adults and some clients are referred by friends. Represents minors in child abuse and status offense cases in the Juvenile Court, in administrative proceedings, and in other civil matters such as guardianships, mental health, and special education. Attempts to break the cycle of neglect to delinquency; offers solution-oriented advocacy with respect to school, health, financial, and housing problems; advocates concrete alternatives to delinquency recidivism, institutionalization, and incarceration and provides advocacy and support groups for children in HIV positive families. **Projects:** Dependency; Detained Immigrant Children; Education; Guardianship; HOPE; Model Standards; Partners for Prevention; Young Women's Empowerment. **Publications:** *California Guardianship Manual.* Contains a training guide for attorneys. ● *California Manual on Emancipation of Minors.* Serves as a self-help manual for minors. ● *Getting the Healthcare You Need.* Manual. Features minor consent services. ● *The Guardianship Pamphlet* (in Chinese, English, and Spanish). Written for minors and proposed guardians. ● *Legal Rights and Options of Runaways*

Teens: Runaway, Throwaway, Kickout. Manual. Written for minors and advocates. ● *Parents Bill of Rights.* Pamphlet. Serves as a guide to parents and students rights in school. ● *Safety First.* Pamphlet. Serves as a survival guide for lesbian, gay, bisexual, transgender, and questioning youth.

12232 ■ Legal Services for the Elderly (LSE)
130 W 42nd St., 17th Fl.
New York, NY 10036
Ph: (212)391-0120
Fax: (212)719-1939
Contact: Jonathan A. Weiss, Exec.Dir.
Founded: 1969. **Staff:** 5. **Languages:** English, French, Italian, Russian, Spanish. **Description:** Lawyers who advise on and litigate cases concerning problems of the elderly. Funded through the Legal Services Corporation in New York City, attorney fees, grants, and the state of New York. Conducts research, litigation, and educational programs. **Libraries: Type:** reference. **Holdings:** 5,000. **Subjects:** law, elderly. **Formerly:** (1970) Legal Services for the Elderly Poor. **Publications:** *Progress Report,* 2/year ● Articles ● Papers ● Reports. **Conventions/Meetings:** monthly SSI Median - workshop, about Medicare age discrimination.

12233 ■ Migrant Legal Action Program (MLAP)
1001 Connecticut Ave. NW, Ste.915
Washington, DC 20036
Ph: (202)775-7780
Fax: (202)775-7784
E-mail: mlap@mlap.org
URL: http://www.mlap.org
Contact: Roger C. Rosenthal, Exec. Dir.
Founded: 1970. **Staff:** 5. **Budget:** $200,000. **Languages:** English, French, Spanish. **Description:** Provides legal representation to indigent migrant and seasonal farm workers and support to farmworker service organizations and advocates. Works with local legal services lawyers, private attorneys and migrant service providers assisting economically deprived agricultural workers on issues of working conditions, education, housing, minimum wage, occupational safety, and health standards and benefits. Engages in administrative and legislative monitoring. **Libraries: Type:** reference. **Publications:** *Field Memo,* bimonthly. Newsletter. **Price:** $450.00/year. **Advertising:** accepted ● *Migrant Education News,* monthly. Newsletter. **Price:** $120.00. **Conventions/Meetings:** board meeting - 4/year.

12234 ■ National Coalition of Concerned Legal Professionals (NCCLP)
25 Chapel St., Ste.601
Brooklyn, NY 11201
Ph: (718)522-1619
Fax: (718)522-1619
Contact: Susan Prensky, Managing Coor.
Description: Volunteer lawyers, law students, paralegals and concerned residents working in their communities. Provides legal education and information to low-income workers; coordinates and conducts major civil rights litigation on behalf of this constituency through a team approach. Promotes equal access to justice for the growing number of Americans who otherwise cannot afford legal resource and due process. **Publications:** *Verdict,* quarterly. Magazine. **Price:** $30.00/year ● Verdict is a forum promoting involvement by legal professionals and others active in searching for legal and organizational solutions to the problems facing the low income communities. Verdict takes positions and provides analysis; it tells those in and around the legal profession how they can fight for equal justice.

Literacy

12235 ■ Rolling Readers
4007 Camino Del Rio S, Ste.203
San Diego, CA 92108
Ph: (619)516-4095
Fax: (619)516-4096

E-mail: admin@rollingreaders.org
URL: http://www.rollingreaders.org
Contact: Jane Hopkins, Pres.
Founded: 1991. **Staff:** 3. **State Groups:** 16. **Languages:** English, Spanish. **Description:** Represents volunteers who are promoting literacy to children and youth in distressed neighborhoods. **Publications:** *Read-Aloud Training Manual*, semiannual. Provides parents with resources and tips to stimulate their child's love of reading. Alternate Formats: online ● *Read-Aloud Training Video*.

Magicians

12236 ■ Magicians Without Borders
100 Geary Rd.
Lincoln, VT 05443
Ph: (802)453-5425
E-mail: verner@gmavt.net
URL: http://www.magicianswithoutborders.org
Contact: Tom Verner, Founder
Founded: 2001. **Multinational. Description:** Aims to bring love, laughter and magic to refugee and orphan children around the world. Performs magic shows for children in refugee camps, orphanages and hospitals in war-torn countries.

Marriage

12237 ■ Alliance for Marriage (AFM)
PO Box 2490
Merrifield, VA 22116-2490
Ph: (703)934-1212
Fax: (703)934-1211
E-mail: info@allianceformarriage.org
URL: http://www.allianceformarriage.org
Contact: Matt Daniels PhD, Pres.
Description: Married families. Promotes marriage and importance of building strong family bond. Discusses "the scourge of fatherless families and the benefits and positive effects of keeping a marriage together". Supports public policy and civil society reforms geared toward strengthening marriages.

12238 ■ Association for Couples in Marriage Enrichment (ACME)
PO Box 21374
Winston-Salem, NC 27120
Ph: (336)724-1526
Free: (800)634-8325
Fax: (336)721-4746
E-mail: acme@bettermarriages.org
URL: http://www.bettermarriages.org
Contact: Renee Colclough Hinson, Exec. Dir.
Founded: 1973. **Members:** 1,000. **Membership Dues:** individual, $40 (annual). **Staff:** 2. **Budget:** $200,000. **State Groups:** 40. **Local Groups:** 100. **Description:** Married couples united to promote and support effective community services to foster successful marriages; improve public acceptance and understanding of marriage as a relationship capable of fostering personal growth and mutual fulfillment; educate and assist married couples in seeking growth and enrichment in their marriages. Conducts marriage enrichment retreats and growth groups, marital communication training courses, enrichment programs, and basic and advanced training workshops. Grants certification to leader couples. **Awards: Frequency:** annual. **Type:** recognition. **Committees:** Selection; Training and Certification. **Publications:** *Marriage Enrichment*, bimonthly. Newsletter. **Conventions/Meetings:** periodic conference ● conference, at the state, regional, international, and national levels.

12239 ■ Marriage Equality USA (MEUSA)
4043 Piedmont Ave., No. 334
Oakland, CA 94611
Ph: (510)332-0973 (510)496-2700
Fax: (510)380-5200

E-mail: info@marriageequality.org
URL: http://www.marriageequality.org
Contact: Davina Kotulski, Exec. Dir.
Founded: 1998. **Membership Dues:** individual, $35 (annual) ● family, $60 (annual) ● contributor, $250 (annual) ● partner, $100 (annual) ● student/senior, $15 (annual). **State Groups:** 3. **Description:** Aims to secure the freedom and the right of same-sex couples to enter into a legally-recognized civil marriage. Educates people on same-sex marriage through speaking engagements, forums and outreach activities. **Computer Services:** Information services, marriage resources. **Telecommunication Services:** electronic mail, davina@marriageequality.org. **Publications:** *Engaged*. Newsletter. Alternate Formats: online.

12240 ■ National Marriage Encounter (NME)
c/o Jeannette Babcock, Business Admin.
3922 77th St.
Urbandale, IA 50322
Ph: (515)278-8458
Free: (800)367-0343
E-mail: nmebabcock@mcshsi.com
URL: http://www.marriage-encounter.org
Contact: Jeannette Babcock, Business Admin.
Founded: 1970. **Regional Groups:** 8. **Description:** Offers weekend retreat programs organized by married couples and a member of the clergy. Retreats are aimed at encouraging communication between married partners and emphasizing personal and religious growth. **Telecommunication Services:** electronic mail, emory78@comcast.net. **Publications:** Newsletter, quarterly. **Conventions/Meetings:** annual conference and workshop.

12241 ■ Straight Spouse Network (SSN)
c/o Amity Pierce Buxton, PhD, Exec. Dir.
33 Linda Ave., No. 2607
Oakland, CA 94611-4820
Ph: (510)595-1005
E-mail: dir@ssnetwk.org
URL: http://www.ssnetwk.org
Contact: Amity Pierce Buxton PhD, Exec. Dir.
Founded: 1992. **Members:** 5,000. **Staff:** 8. **Budget:** $125,000. **State Groups:** 50. **Local Groups:** 60. **National Groups:** 6. **Languages:** Chinese, English, French, Spanish. **Multinational. Description:** Provides personal support and resource information to straight spouses and mixed-orientation couples to help them cope constructively and heal, to build bridges of understanding between spouses and among family members, and to raise public awareness of issues families face when a spouse comes out. **Libraries: Type:** by appointment only. **Holdings:** 5. **Subjects:** straight spouse issues, mixed-orientation couples and their children. **Computer Services:** Mailing lists, subscription, on-line groups; AOL message board. **Councils:** Advisory. **Working Groups:** Communication; Education; Fundraising; Outreach; Public Relations; Technical. **Affiliated With:** Family Pride Coalition; Parents, Families, and Friends of Lesbians and Gays. **Formerly:** (1991) Straight Spouse Support Network. **Publications:** *News and Notes*, semiannual. Newsletter. Includes network news, poems, reflections and book reviews. **Price:** $10.00. **Circulation:** 2,000. **Advertising:** accepted. Alternate Formats: online. **Conventions/Meetings:** monthly meeting, for local groups; semistructured peer support ● bimonthly regional meeting, in Northwest, South, New England, Southeast, Midwest and Southwest.

12242 ■ Wives of Older Men (WOOM)
c/o Beliza Ann Furman, Founder
1029 Sycamore Ave.
Tinton Falls, NJ 07724
Ph: (732)747-5586
Fax: (732)389-0304
E-mail: info@beliza.com
URL: http://www.beliza.com
Contact: Beliza Ann Furman, Founder
Founded: 1988. **Members:** 450. **Staff:** 2. **For-Profit. Description:** Married or dating couples in which the man is eight or more years older than his partner. Acts as a networking clearinghouse to introduce

wives of older men to each other for the purposes of self-help and support. **Computer Services:** Mailing lists. **Publications:** *Test Driving Marriage*. Book ● *Younger Women, Older Men*. Book. **Price:** $22.00 ● Newsletter, bimonthly. Addresses concerns of age-disparate couples. **Price:** $35.00/year. **Circulation:** 500. **Advertising:** accepted.

12243 ■ Worldwide Marriage Encounter (WWME)
2210 E Highland Ave., Ste.106
San Bernardino, CA 92404-4666
Ph: (909)863-9963
Free: (800)795-5683
Fax: (909)863-9986
E-mail: office@wwme.org
URL: http://www.wwme.org
Contact: Ms. Sharon Brooks, Admin. Asst.
Founded: 1952. **Budget:** $400,000. **Regional Groups:** 16. **Description:** Conducts weekend events to help married couples examine their relationship with each other and with God; guidance is given by three married couples and a priest. **Conventions/Meetings:** biennial meeting.

Media

12244 ■ Media Research Center (MRC)
325 S Patrick St.
Alexandria, VA 22314-3580
Ph: (703)683-9733
Free: (800)672-1423
Fax: (703)683-9736
E-mail: mrc@mediaresearch.org
URL: http://www.mediaresearch.org
Contact: Brent Bozell III, Founder/Pres.
Founded: 1987. **Description:** Works to bring balance and responsibility to the media. Researches news and entertainment media. **Awards: Type:** recognition. **Additional Websites:** http://www.mrc.org. **Divisions:** News. **Programs:** Internship. **Projects:** Free Market. **Publications:** *CyberAlert*. Report. Alternate Formats: online ● *Flash*, monthly. Newsletter. ISSN: 1087-5077. Alternate Formats: online ● *Media Reality Check*, weekly. Report. Alternate Formats: online ● *Notable Quotables*, biweekly. Report.

Medical Aid

12245 ■ Angel Flight West (AFW)
3161 Donald Douglas Loop S
Santa Monica, CA 90405
Ph: (310)390-2958 (310)398-6123
Free: (888)4AN-ANGEL
Fax: (310)397-9636
E-mail: info@angelflight.org
URL: http://www.angelflight.org
Contact: Jim Weaver, Exec. Dir.
Founded: 1983. **Members:** 1,000. **Membership Dues:** initial fee, $50 ● individual, $35 (annual). **Languages:** English, Spanish. **Description:** Provides free transportation to medical treatment for persons who cannot afford public transportation or cannot tolerate it for health reasons. **Telecommunication Services:** electronic mail, jimw@angelflight.org ● hotline, (310)317-1000.

12246 ■ Assist International (AI)
PO Box 66396
Scotts Valley, CA 95067-6396
Ph: (831)438-4582
Fax: (831)439-9602
E-mail: assist@assistinternational.org
URL: http://www.assistintl.org
Contact: Robert J. Pagett, Pres./Founder
Founded: 1990. **Description:** Health care organizations. Procures used cardiac care monitoring systems and other medical equipment in the United States for distribution among underserved populations in the developing world. Distributes medical equipment, food, and other supplies in needy areas worldwide; involved in the building and provision for three

orphanages in Romania and Uganda. **Projects:** Bear Hug; Bundles of Hope; Family Villages; Medical; Romania Orphanage; Tsunami Relief Efforts. **Publications:** Annual Report, annual. Alternate Formats: online.

12247 ■ Blessings International (BI)
PO Box 35292
Tulsa, OK 74153-0292
Ph: (918)250-8101
Free: (877)250-8101
Fax: (918)250-1281
E-mail: info@blessing.org
URL: http://www.blessing.org
Contact: Harold C. Harder PhD, Pres.
Founded: 1981. **Staff:** 4. **Multinational. Description:** Serves as a source of pharmaceuticals, vitamins, and medical supplies for churches and nonprofit groups planning medical mission outreaches to developing nations; have helped in situations such as Hurricane Mitch in Central America, cyclone in Orissa, India, and flooding in Mozambique. Ongoing projects include partnering with clinics and hospitals in Liberia, Sierra Leone, Nigeria, Ghana, and Myanmar. **Publications:** *Blessings Report*, several times yearly. Newsletter. **Price:** available upon request ● *Pharmaceutical Bulletin for Medical Personnel Planning Medical Mission Trip* ● *Prayer Letter*, monthly.

12248 ■ Catholic Medical Mission Board (CMMB)
10 W 17th St.
New York, NY 10011-5765
Ph: (212)242-7757
Free: (800)678-5659
Fax: (212)807-9161
E-mail: info@cmmb.org
URL: http://www.cmmb.org
Contact: John F. Galbraith, Pres./CEO
Founded: 1928. **Staff:** 35. **Budget:** $6,960,000. **Multinational. Description:** Makes health care available to people in need through shipments of medicines and medical supplies, training programs, disease eradication programs, emergency assistance, and medical volunteer placements. **Libraries: Type:** reference. **Holdings:** archival material, business records, clippings. **Funds:** Tsunami Survivor Relief. **Programs:** Back to Haiti; Born to Live; Choose to Care; Lymphatic Filariasis Elimination; Medical Volunteer; Physicians on a Mission; TB-DOTS. **Publications:** *CMMB Today*, quarterly. Newsletter. Provides information on CMMB's programs. Features recipients of shipments and health care placement opportunities are features. **Price:** free. **Circulation:** 60,000. Alternate Formats: online ● Annual Report, annual. **Price:** free. Alternate Formats: online.

12249 ■ CHOSEN
3638 W 26th St.
Erie, PA 16506-2037
Ph: (814)833-3023
Fax: (814)833-4091
E-mail: rick@chosenmissionproject.org
URL: http://www.chosenmissionproject.org
Contact: Mr. Richard King, Exec. Dir.
Founded: 1969. **Members:** 160. **Staff:** 4. **Budget:** $1,000,000. **Description:** Interdenominational organization supporting overseas Christian medical mission work. Procures new and used medical equipment for mission hospitals in economically deprived nations; repairs and modifies equipment; prepares equipment for shipping. Provides training in infection control (operating room and sterile departments) and in the proper use and maintenance of equipment for all mission hospital staffs. **Libraries: Type:** reference. **Holdings:** books. **Subjects:** technical equipment and medical manuals. **Awards:** Volunteer of the Year Award. **Frequency:** annual. **Type:** recognition. **Also Known As:** Christian Hospitals Overseas Secure Equipment Needs. **Formerly:** (1988) CHOSEN Mission Project. **Publications:** *CHOSEN Mission Project Newsletter*, quarterly. **Price:** free. **Circulation:** 600. **Conventions/Meetings:** annual meeting - usually August.

12250 ■ Direct Relief International (DRI)
27 S La Patera Ln.
Santa Barbara, CA 93117
Ph: (805)964-4767
Free: (800)676-1638
Fax: (805)681-4838
E-mail: info@directrelief.org
URL: http://www.directrelief.org
Contact: Thomas Tighe, Pres./CEO
Founded: 1948. **Staff:** 30. **Budget:** $3,500,000. **Languages:** English, French, German, Greek, Spanish, Thai. **Nonmembership. Multinational. Description:** Donates contributed pharmaceuticals, medical supplies, and equipment to health facilities and locally coordinated health projects in medically underdeveloped areas of the world. Provides emergency assistance to refugees and other victims of natural disaster and civil strife. **Boards:** International Advisory. **Departments:** Programs; Resource Acquisition. **Formerly:** (1982) Direct Relief Foundation. **Publications:** *Program Reports*, periodic ● *Response*, 3/year. Newsletter ● Report, annual. Contains a summary of year's accomplishments with financial report included. **Price:** available upon request. Alternate Formats: online. **Conventions/Meetings:** quarterly board meeting ● meeting - spring/early summer ● annual Shareholders Meeting.

12251 ■ DOCARE International, N.F.P. (DI)
430 King Ave.
East Dundee, IL 60118
Ph: (847)836-8022
Fax: (847)836-8022
E-mail: ljense@midwestern.edu
URL: http://www.docareintl.org
Contact: Larry A. Jensen, Exec. Dir.
Founded: 1961. **Members:** 400. **Membership Dues:** regular, $25 (annual) ● family, $35 (annual) ● individual, sustaining, $250 (annual) ● student, $5 (annual) ● life, $250 ● intern or resident, $10 (annual). **Staff:** 1. **Multinational. Description:** Volunteer organization of medical doctors, osteopathic physicians, nurses, dentists, veterinarians, pharmacists, optometrists, podiatrists, and laypersons with special skills. Serves as a medical outreach program providing health care services to people in remote areas of Mexico, Central America, and the Caribbean. Works with those deprived of medical care due to terrain, language, and cultural barriers. Conducts two to three one-week medical missions per year to areas in need until physicians or health care specialists are provided by the host country government. **Awards:** Dr. Ernest A. Allaby Award. **Frequency:** periodic. **Type:** recognition. **Recipient:** for contributions of skills, service and dedication. **Committees:** Bylaws; Public Relations. **Affiliated With:** American Osteopathic Association. **Publications:** *DOCARE Flyer*, quarterly. Newsletter. Includes stories about members, meetings, planned missions, and election of officers. **Price:** included in membership dues. **Circulation:** 400. **Conventions/Meetings:** annual meeting and board meeting - always fall.

12252 ■ Doctor to Doctor (D2D)
1749 MLK Jr. Way
Berkeley, CA 94709
Ph: (510)548-5200
E-mail: dolgoff@d2d.org
URL: http://www.d2d.org
Contact: Dr. Bob Dolgoff, Pres.
Founded: 1994. **Staff:** 1. **Multinational. Description:** Provides assistance to medical professionals in underserved places around the world by sending books and medications to medical facilities in countries where such items are in short supply. Assists American health professionals who wish to travel as individuals or in a small group to countries interested in professional collaboration. **Computer Services:** Online services, slideshows.

12253 ■ Doctors for Artists (DFA)
57 W 57th St.
New York, NY 10019
Ph: (212)355-1950 (718)385-7373
Fax: (212)319-0782
Contact: Dr. Lambert Macias, Dir.
Founded: 1984. **Members:** 20. **Staff:** 1. **Description:** Doctors in New York directly or indirectly involved with the arts. Established to provide performing and visual artists with specialized health care at a reduced rate, and treatment especially sympathetic to their needs. Artists receive a 20&percent; discount on medical services, including office visits and surgery; membership is represented in some 23 areas of specialized medicine. Although there are no plans to expand outside New York, assistance is offered to individuals wishing to establish similar groups in other parts of the country. **Telecommunication Services:** phone referral service. **Conventions/Meetings:** annual conference.

12254 ■ Doctors of the World (DW)
80 Maiden Ln., Ste.607
New York, NY 10038
Ph: (212)226-9890
Free: (888)817-HELP
Fax: (212)226-7026
E-mail: info@dowusa.org
URL: http://www.doctorsoftheworld.org
Contact: Thomas J. Dougherty MPH, Exec. Dir.
Founded: 1990. **Staff:** 30. **Budget:** $3,800,000. **Multinational. Description:** Seeks to increase the availability and quality of health services around the world. Creates sustainable medical programs that promote and protect health and human rights in the United States and abroad; the organization has deployed volunteer medical professionals to over 25 countries throughout the world. **Committees:** Development and Communications; Program. **Councils:** Advisory. **Projects:** Children with Special Needs; Survivors of Gross Human Rights Abuses; TB and HIV/AIDS; Women's Health.

12255 ■ Doctors to the World (DTTW)
PO Box 370167
Denver, CO 80237
Ph: (303)758-5405
Fax: (303)758-4124
E-mail: dttw@juno.com
URL: http://www.dttw.org
Founded: 1980. **Members:** 2,800. **Membership Dues:** family - life, $150 ● student - life, $50. **Description:** Physicians, nurses, and technical and support professionals. Service organization dedicated to providing medical assistance to underprivileged and needy areas throughout the world. Provided emergency care for individuals involved in the 1988 earthquake in Armenia, the 1989 revolution in Romania, and the 1990 earthquake in Peru. Participated in relief efforts in Homestead, Florida, in 1989, during and after hurricane Hugo. Operates support facilities in West Indies, Netherlands Antilles, and Central and South America. Operates Street Smart program for inner city youths. Offers homeless individuals medical services, food, clothing, shelter, and aid in obtaining employment. Conducts speakers' bureau and educational programs. **Awards:** Doctors to the World Humanitarian Award. **Frequency:** semiannual. **Type:** recognition. **Computer Services:** database. **Divisions:** Dentists for the World; Health USA; Student Volunteers to the World; Volunteers to the World. **Programs:** Rotary Clubs Joint Venture; Volunteer Tour. **Publications:** *Doctors to the World Newsletter*, semiannual. **Price:** free. **Circulation:** 5,000. **Advertising:** accepted. **Conventions/Meetings:** periodic Smoking Cessation Course - seminar.

12256 ■ Flying Doctors of America (FDoA)
15 Medical Dr.
Cartersville, GA 30121
Ph: (770)386-5221
E-mail: flyingdoctors@aol.com
URL: http://www.fdoamerica.org
Contact: Allan Gathercoal D.D., Pres./Founder
Founded: 1990. **Members:** 7,000. **Staff:** 3. **Description:** The organization brings together physicians, dentists, PA's, NP's, RN's and pharmacists who volunteer their time to bring medical/dental care to developing countries throughout the world. These medical/dental teams bring hope and healing to

hundreds (sometimes thousands) of poor children, women and men. All of the missions are short-term (one or two weeks), professionally managed and affordable. Each team member makes a tax-deductible donation to the organization which is used to cover the cost of transportation, lodging and mission expenses. **Telecommunication Services:** electronic mail, pittsman54@aol.com.

12257 ■ Gift of Life International
475 Northern Blvd., Ste.25
Great Neck, NY 11021
Ph: (516)504-0830
Fax: (516)504-0828
E-mail: info@giftoflifeinternational.org
URL: http://www.giftoflifeinternational.org
Contact: Robert Donno, Chm.
Multinational. Description: Facilitates free medical services to children suffering from heart disease and other similar or allied diseases. Helps needy children receive corrective heart surgery at Gift of Life Participating Hospitals. **Computer Services:** Online services, bulletin board. **Telecommunication Services:** electronic mail, gwilliams@giftoflifeinternational.org. **Programs:** Save-A-Life.

12258 ■ Global Outreach Mission (GOM)
PO Box 2010
Buffalo, NY 14231-2010
Ph: (716)688-5048
Free: (866)483-5787
Fax: (716)688-5049
E-mail: gomhq1670@missiongo.org
URL: http://www.missiongo.org
Contact: Dr. Brian M. Albrecht, Pres.
Founded: 1950. **Members:** 4,564. **Budget:** $150,000. **Multinational. Description:** Seeks to share the Gospel through the medium of dentistry. Provides dental services and conducts dental education programs in undeveloped or rural areas and cities overseas coupled with "the good news of the Gospel". Trains dentists, dental assistants, laboratory technicians, and hygienists for overseas service in their Overseas Training Seminar. **Also Known As:** Worldwide Dental Health Service. **Formerly:** (1998) Missionary Dentists. **Publications:** *The Missionary Dentist*, quarterly. Newsletter. **Conventions/Meetings:** annual seminar.

12259 ■ Health Volunteers Overseas (HVO)
1900 L St. NW, Ste.310
Washington, DC 20036
Ph: (202)296-0928
Fax: (202)296-8018
E-mail: info@hvousa.org
URL: http://www.hvousa.org
Contact: Nancy Kelly, Exec. Dir.
Founded: 1986. **Members:** 2,200. **Staff:** 14. **Budget:** $1,000,000. **Description:** Physicians, dentists, nurses, and physical therapists. Works to improve health care in developing countries through the participation of trained health and medical volunteers. Programs include Anesthesia, Dentistry, Nursing, Oral and Maxillofacial Surgery, Internal Medicine, Orthopaedics, Dermatology, and Pediatrics and Physical Therapy. HVO has program sites in St. Lucia, Uganda, Guyana, India, Philippines, Malawi, Indonesia, South Africa, Vietnam, Kenya, Bhutan, Nicaragua, Costa Rica, Moldova, Honduras, Eritrea, and Cambodia. **Publications:** *A Guide to Volunteering Overseas.* Booklet. **Price:** $15.00 ● *The Net Connection*, monthly. Newsletter. Alternate Formats: online ● *The Volunteer Connection*, semiannual. Newsletter. Alternate Formats: online ● Annual Report. Alternate Formats: online.

12260 ■ Humanitarian Medical Relief (HMR)
Address Unknown since 2007
Description: Provides assistance to those without access to healthcare by establishing humanitarian clinics.

12261 ■ Liga International (LI)
1464 N Fitzgerald Hangar 2
Rialto, CA 92376
Ph: (909)875-6300
Fax: (909)875-6900
E-mail: liga@ligainternational.org
URL: http://www.ligainternational.org
Contact: J. Bruce Camino AIA, Pres.
Founded: 1948. **Members:** 700. **Membership Dues:** basic, $50 (annual) ● household, $75 (annual) ● student, $25 (annual) ● contributing, $200 (annual) ● silver, $500 ● gold, $1,000 ● President's Circle, $2,500 ● Chairman's Club, $5,000. **Staff:** 1. **Regional Groups:** 6. **State Groups:** 4. **Local Groups:** 5. **Languages:** English, Spanish. **Description:** Physicians, dentists, nurses, pilots, technicians, assistants, educators, and laypeople interested in providing medical and educational assistance to impoverished people of rural Mexico. Seeks to stimulate interest and support for establishing and maintaining educational, charitable, and medical programs among underprivileged inhabitants of Mexico; exchange scientific information between medical and educational groups. Sponsors monthly trips to clinics in Ocoroni, El Fuerte, San Blas, and El Carrizo in Sinaloa Mexico. Operates speakers' bureau. **Also Known As:** Flying Doctors of Mercy. **Publications:** *El Carrizo Report*, annual. Features clinic summary. ● *Liga High Flying Times*, quarterly. Newsletter ● Brochure. **Conventions/Meetings:** annual Fly-In - meeting ● annual meeting.

12262 ■ MADRE
121 W 27th St., Rm. 301
New York, NY 10001
Ph: (212)627-0444
Fax: (212)675-3704
E-mail: madre@madre.org
URL: http://www.madre.org
Contact: Vivian Stromberg, Exec. Dir.
Founded: 1983. **Members:** 23,000. **Membership Dues:** regular, $35 (annual). **Staff:** 10. **Languages:** English, Spanish. **Description:** Works in partnership with community-based women's groups worldwide to address issues of economic development, health, education, and other human rights. Provides resources, training, and support to enable sister organizations to meet concrete needs in their communities while working to shift the balance of power to promote long-term development and social justice. Delivers over 22 million dollars worth of support to community-based groups in Latin America, the Caribbean, the Middle East, Africa, the Balkans, South Asia, and the United States. **Publications:** Newsletter, quarterly. **Circulation:** 20,000 ● Brochures ● Also publishes fact sheets.

12263 ■ MediSend International
9244 Markville Dr.
Dallas, TX 75243
Ph: (214)575-5006
Fax: (214)570-9284
E-mail: info@medisend.org
URL: http://www.medisend.org
Contact: Nick Hallack, Pres./CEO
Multinational. Description: Provides medical aid and education to people in need in developing countries worldwide. Offers education programs and technical training to facilitate improvement in community healthcare conditions. Develops and manages long-term medical aid programs and emergency-disaster relief campaigns. **Awards:** Humanitarian Award. **Frequency:** annual. **Type:** recognition. **Recipient:** to an individual who has rendered exemplary service to humanitarian causes.

12264 ■ MedShare International
3240 Clifton Springs Rd.
Decatur, GA 30034
Ph: (770)323-5858
Fax: (770)323-4301
E-mail: info@medshare.org
URL: http://www.medshare.org
Contact: A.B. Short, CEO
Founded: 1998. **Multinational. Description:** Recycles surplus medical supplies and equipment for use by healthcare institutions in developing countries.

12265 ■ Mission Doctors Association (MDA)
3435 Wilshire Blvd., Ste.1035
Los Angeles, CA 90010
Ph: (213)368-1875
Fax: (213)368-1871
E-mail: missiondrs@earthlink.net
URL: http://www.missiondoctors.org
Contact: Ms. Elise Frederick, Exec. Dir.
Founded: 1959. **Staff:** 1. **Multinational. Description:** Recruits, trains, and supports volunteer Catholic physicians and sends them to serve in mission hospitals or clinics. Runs two programs: the traditional program is an overseas commitment of 3 years following a four-month formation program in Los Angeles and the other program which began in 1997 is for doctors seeking opportunities to serve 1-3 months. Doctors considering this short-term service are invited to attend a weekend retreat/seminar in Los Angeles. Doctors accepted in the program must display a genuine spirit of sacrifice and view their work in the context of a Catholic lay missionary. **Subgroups:** Mission Doctors Auxiliary. **Affiliated With:** Lay Mission-Helpers Association. **Publications:** *Heal the Sick*, quarterly. Newsletter. Includes letters from doctors serving in missions. **Price:** free. Alternate Formats: online. **Conventions/Meetings:** annual luncheon, with mass.

12266 ■ New Eyes for the Needy (NEN)
PO Box 332
Short Hills, NJ 07078
Ph: (973)376-4903
Fax: (973)376-3807
E-mail: neweyesfortheneedy@verizon.net
URL: http://www.neweyesfortheneedy.org
Contact: Pamela DePompo-Klein, Exec. Dir.
Founded: 1932. **Members:** 200. **Staff:** 2. **Description:** Provides new prescription eyeglasses for individuals in the United States to whom no other funds, public or private, are available. Tests and distributes reusable framed glasses to overseas missions and hospital clinics upon request. Funds are derived from the melt of precious metals found in jewelry and eyeglass frames donated to the organization and through contributions from individuals and grants.

12267 ■ Operation Smile (OSI)
6435 Tidewater Dr.
Norfolk, VA 23509
Ph: (757)321-7645
Free: (888)OPSMILE
Fax: (757)321-7660
URL: http://www.operationsmile.org
Contact: Howard J. Unger, Chm.
Founded: 1982. **Staff:** 70. **Budget:** $11,750,000. **Regional Groups:** 40. **Nonmembership. Description:** Private, nonprofit volunteer medical services organization providing reconstructive surgery and related health care to indigent children and young adults in developing countries and in the United States. Provides education and training around the world to physicians and other health care professionals to achieve long-term self-sufficiency. Brings together health professionals with the public and private sectors to provide voluntary care to improve the quality of life for the children, families and communities that share in the Operation Smile experience. By creating international partnerships, the organization "builds trust, bridges cultures and bestows dignity at home and abroad.". **Committees:** Team Selection. **Formerly:** (1993) Operation Smile; (2001) Operation Smile International. **Publications:** *Operation Smile Annual Report*, annual ● *Operation Smile Newsletter*, 3/year. Contains highlights of Operation Smile activities. **Price:** free to donors of $25 and up. Alternate Formats: online. **Conventions/Meetings:** annual International Student Leadership Conference ● semiannual Mission Training - workshop, includes student conference ● annual Physicians' Training Program - conference.

12268 ■ Operation U.S.A. (OpUSA)
3617 Hayden Ave., Ste.A
Culver City, CA 90232
Ph: (310)838-3455
Free: (800)678-7255

Fax: (310)838-3477
E-mail: info@opusa.org
URL: http://www.opusa.org
Contact: Richard M. Walden, Pres./CEO
Founded: 1979. **Staff:** 6. **Budget:** $1,100,000. **Languages:** English, French, Spanish. **Description:** Provides relief aid to crisis areas in the U.S. and worldwide; makes available financial and material support and technical to clinics, hospitals, and orphanages. Maintains speakers' bureau. **Awards:** President's Volunteer Action Award. **Type:** recognition. **Computer Services:** Mailing lists, of members. **Formerly:** (1988) Operation California. **Publications:** *OP USA Newsletter*, semiannual. **Price:** free. **Circulation:** 11,000.

12269 ■ Pan American Health and Education Foundation (PAHEF)
525 23rd St. NW
Washington, DC 20037
Ph: (202)974-3416
Fax: (202)974-3636
E-mail: info@pahef.org
URL: http://www.pahef.org
Contact: Ms. Jess Gersky, Exec. Dir.
Founded: 1968. **Staff:** 10. **Budget:** $3,000,000. **Description:** Works to improve the health of the people in Latin America and the Caribbean and to advance the objectives of the Pan American Health Organization/World Health Organization for the Region of the Americas. Makes project grants; administers a program of textbooks and training materials for medical, nursing, dental and veterinary students in 18 countries; recognizes excellence in health leadership through a program of four international awards; works cooperatively with organizations and governmental bodies which share the same objectives. **Awards:** Abraham Horwitz Award. **Frequency:** annual. **Type:** recognition. **Recipient:** for distinguished contributions to inter-American health ● Clarence Moore Award. **Frequency:** annual. **Type:** recognition. **Recipient:** for contributions to health by volunteers or volunteer organizations ● Fred Soper Award. **Frequency:** annual. **Type:** recognition. **Recipient:** for an outstanding journal article (Latin American Topic) ● Pedro Acha Award. **Frequency:** annual. **Type:** recognition. **Recipient:** for an outstanding undergraduate thesis (Latin American University). **Publications:** *Boletin de Medicamentos y Terapeutica* (in Spanish), quarterly. Bulletin. **Price:** free. ISSN: 0257-7836. **Circulation:** 30,000 ● Manuals. Provides information for primary health care workers.

12270 ■ Partnership for Quality Medical Donations (PQMD)
146 Koenig Rd.
Bernville, PA 19506
Ph: (732)739-5492
E-mail: jbrusso@pqmd.org
URL: http://www.pqmd.org
Contact: Elizabeth Scott, Exec. Dir.
Founded: 1996. **Members:** 25. **Multinational. Description:** Works to raise the standards of medical donations to meet the needs of underserved populations and disaster victims around the world. Develops and promotes sound donation practices by donor and recipient organizations. Represents the interests of members before national and international agencies responsible for policy formulation affecting medical product donations and distribution. Encourages the documentation and scholarly study of the health and socioeconomic impacts of the donation of health care products and services.

12271 ■ Project: Hearts and Minds (PHAM)
599 Crock Ln.
Howard, PA 16841
E-mail: dpd46@optonline.net
Contact: Ann L. Kelsey, Contact
Founded: 1992. **Description:** A project of Veterans for Peace. Collects surplus medical supplies and equipment for delivery to hospitals in Vietnam, Cambodia, and Cuba.

12272 ■ Rapha International (RI)
402 Blue Smoke Ct. W
Fort Worth, TX 76105
Ph: (817)536-3383
Fax: (817)536-3414
E-mail: lori.rapha@sbcglobal.net
URL: http://www.raphainternational.org
Contact: Lori Reynolds, Admin. Asst.
Founded: 1998. **Multinational. Description:** Provides help, training and lifestyle improvements for peoples around the world. Strives to collect, process, ship and make resources available where and when they are needed. Provides medical supplies and equipment to those in great need around the world. Responds to foreign emergencies.

12273 ■ Refugee Relief International (RRI)
2995 Woodside Rd., No. 400-244
Woodside, CA 94062
Ph: (925)734-0100
Fax: (925)734-0207
E-mail: info@refugeerelief.org
URL: http://www.refugeerelief.org
Contact: David G. Mohler MD, Pres.
Founded: 1982. **Budget:** $60,000. **Description:** Physicians, paramedics, and nurses with prior military experience. Provides medical and other help to refugees and other victims of war and oppression throughout the world. Major efforts have been in Central America, although significant contributions to multi-national, multi-agency relief efforts have been made in Afghanistan, Azerbaijan, and in support of the Karens in Burma. Transports and distributes medical supplies and equipment. Conducts classes on first aid, hygiene, public health and sanitation for indigenous paramedics, refugees and others. Performs surgery and direct medical care. **Absorbed:** (1994) Parachute Medical Rescue Service. **Conventions/Meetings:** annual meeting, meeting of the Board of Directors.

12274 ■ Rizal-MacArthur Memorial Foundation (RMMF)
756 N 35th St., Ste.201
Milwaukee, WI 53208
Ph: (414)229-4277
E-mail: rmmf@fcmail.com
URL: http://www.fortunecity.com/victorian/manet/465
Founded: 1966. **Multinational. Description:** Collects medical equipment, supplies, educational materials and myriad of other articles for shipment to the Philippines.

12275 ■ Task Force for Child Survival and Development (TFCSD)
750 Commerce Dr., Ste.400
Decatur, GA 30030
Ph: (404)371-0466
Free: (800)765-7173
Fax: (404)371-1087
E-mail: info@taskforce.org
URL: http://www.taskforce.org
Contact: Mark L. Rosenberg MPP, Exec. Dir.
Founded: 1984. **Staff:** 45. **Budget:** $43,200,000. **Multinational. Description:** Sponsors are United Nations Children's Fund, United Nations Development Programme, World Health Organization, Rockefeller Foundation, and The World Bank. Program portfolio includes: Public Health Informatics; Child Well-being; Injury Prevention (Global Road Traffic Safety); Collaboration; Drug Donation; Infectious Disease (Lymphatic Filariasis Support Center) and Polio.

12276 ■ VOSH International
c/o Charles H. Covington, Sr., Sec.-Treas.
111 Linda Ln.
Lake Mary, FL 32746-4208
Ph: (407)328-5825
Free: (877)VOSHERS
Fax: (407)302-6046
E-mail: ccovington@cfl.rr.com
URL: http://www.vosh.org
Contact: Charles H. Covington Sr., Sec.-Treas.
Founded: 1971. **Members:** 2,000. **Membership Dues:** individual, $30 (annual) ● school, $50 (annual) ● chapter, $100 (annual). **Staff:** 5. **State Groups:** 26. **National Groups:** 6. **Multinational. Description:** Optometrists, optometric students, opticians, and other interested individuals. Conducts missions to disadvantaged countries, mostly in the Caribbean, Central and South America, Africa, Asia, and Eastern Europe to provide free visual care to the needy. Members pay their own travel, food, and lodging expenses, establish temporary clinics, and examine and distribute eyeglasses to an average of 2500 patients during each one-week mission. (Glasses are donated by civic clubs, churches, private citizens, and optical companies.) The acronym in the name stands for Volunteer Optometric Services to Humanity. **Libraries: Type:** reference. **Subjects:** used and cataloged eyeglasses. **Affiliated With:** Lions Clubs International; World Council of Optometry; World Health Organization. **Also Known As:** Volunteer Optometric Services to Humanity/International. **Publications:** Brochure ● Newsletter, quarterly. **Circulation:** 550. Alternate Formats: online. **Conventions/Meetings:** annual meeting ● semiannual meeting.

12277 ■ World Medical Relief (WMR)
11745 Rosa Park Blvd.
Detroit, MI 48206-1270
Ph: (313)866-5333
Fax: (313)866-5588
E-mail: info@worldmedicalrelief.org
URL: http://www.worldmedicalrelief.com
Contact: Rita Montgomery Grezlik, Pres./CEO
Founded: 1953. **Staff:** 15. **Budget:** $1,197,020. **Description:** Nonsectarian, philanthropic organization contributing medical supplies and equipment for the care of the world's destitute sick. Donates instruments, equipment, and pharmaceuticals to the organization, which in turn sends them to relief agencies and charitable medical clinics and hospitals worldwide. Provides prescriptions and medical supplies to needy senior citizens in the Detroit, MI area. **Convention/Meeting:** none. **Publications:** *The Good Samaritan*, semiannual ● Annual Report, annual.

Men

12278 ■ National Compadres Network (NCN)
PO Box 2007
Santa Ana, CA 92707
Ph: (714)745-8718
E-mail: info@nationalcompadresnetwork.com
URL: http://www.nationalcompadresnetwork.com
Contact: Mr. Alejandro Moreno, Exec. Dir.
Founded: 1998. **Staff:** 4. **Regional Groups:** 9. **State Groups:** 5. **Languages:** English, Spanish. **Nonmembership. For-Profit. Description:** Works to help fathers and men develop closer and stronger relations with their children and families. Works to prevent domestic violence, teen pregnancy, and alcohol and drug abuse. Conducts workshops and conference keynoting.

Mental Health

12279 ■ ABIL - Agoraphobics Building Independent Lives
2501 Fox Harbor Ct.
Richmond, VA 23235-2829
Ph: (804)353-3964
Fax: (804)353-3687
E-mail: answers@anxietysupport.org
URL: http://www.anxietysupport.org
Contact: Sharon Ritter, Pres.
Founded: 1986. **Membership Dues:** general, $20 (annual) ● professional, $30 (annual). **Description:** Supports and advocates for people suffering from phobias, panic attacks and anxiety disorders. Facilitates the development of self-help groups. Establishes a national network for persons with panic disorders. Develops a strong link with the professional community to improve the quality of treatment available. Works to eliminate the stigma associated

with panic disorder. **Computer Services:** Information services, anxiety disorders facts and resources ● online services, message board. **Publications:** Newsletter, quarterly.

12280 ■ Depressives Anonymous: Recovery From Depression (DARFD)
4625 Douglas Ave.
Bronx, NY 10471
Ph: (718)796-0308
Fax: (718)796-0308
Contact: Dr. Louis DeRosis, Coor.
Founded: 1977. **Members:** 3,000. **Description:** Individuals suffering from depression or anxiety. A self-help organization which helps people deal with their anxiety or depression through weekly meeting and sharing of experiences. Conducts research; offers classes. Disseminates information. Interested people may send a SASE or ask for a collect call at the above number. **Publications:** Newsletter, 3-4/year ● Also publishes brochures and pamphlets.

12281 ■ Double Trouble in Recovery (DTR)
c/o Howie Vogle
PO Box 245055
Brooklyn, NY 11224
Ph: (718)373-2684
E-mail: hv613@aol.com
URL: http://www.doubletroubleinrecovery.org
Contact: Howie Vogle, Contact
Description: Offers twelve-step fellowship to men and women who share experiences, strengths, and hope in order to recover from particular addictions and manage mental disorder; also addresses problems and benefits associated with psychiatric medication. **Publications:** Brochure.

12282 ■ Emotions Anonymous International Service Center (EA)
PO Box 4245
2233 Univ. Ave. W, Ste.402
St. Paul, MN 55104-0245
Ph: (651)647-9712
Fax: (651)647-1593
E-mail: info@emotionsanonymous.org
URL: http://www.emotionsanonymous.org
Contact: Karen Mead, Exec. Dir.
Founded: 1971. **Members:** 5,000. **Staff:** 5. **Budget:** $196,900. **State Groups:** 35. **Local Groups:** 20. **National Groups:** 1,175. **Languages:** English, Spanish. **Description:** "Fellowship of men and women who share their experience, strength, and hope with each other, that they may solve their common problem and help others recover from emotional illness." Uses the Twelve Steps of Alcoholics Anonymous World Services (see separate entry), adapted to emotional problems. Disseminates literature and information; provides telephone referrals to worldwide chapters. **Telecommunication Services:** information service, chat loop and general information. **Publications:** *Emotions Anonymous*. Book. Available in both soft and hard cover editions. **Price:** $15.00. Alternate Formats: magnetic tape ● *It Works if You Work It*. Book. **Price:** $15.00 ● *The New Message*, quarterly. Magazine. Provides stories from EA members and their recovery through EA. ISSN: 1072-3765 ● *Today*. Book. **Conventions/Meetings:** annual convention - September ● retreat.

12283 ■ Federation of Families for Children's Mental Health (FFCMH)
9605 Medical Center Dr., Ste.280
Rockville, MD 20850
Ph: (240)403-1901
Fax: (240)403-1909
E-mail: ffcmh@ffcmh.org
URL: http://www.ffcmh.org
Contact: Sandra Spencer, Exec. Dir.
Founded: 1987. **Members:** 6,300. **Membership Dues:** individual, $20 (annual) ● family, $30 (annual) ● youth, $10 (annual) ● local chapter, along with application, $100 (annual) ● organizational partner with budget less than $500000, $150 (annual) ● organizational partner with budget greater than $500000, $250 (annual). **Staff:** 12. **Budget:** $1,000,000. **Regional Groups:** 125. **State Groups:** 27. **National Groups:**

125. **Languages:** English, Spanish. **Description:** Parents, children, and mental health and related professionals. Seeks to ensure the rights to full citizenship, support, and access to services for children and youth with mental disorders and their families. Provides leadership in the field of children's mental health care and services; works to address the needs of children and youth with emotional, behavioral, and mental disorders. Gathers and disseminates information on mental illness and mental health care and services; conducts educational and training programs; makes available support, referral, and transition services to children and youth with mental disorders and their families. Maintains speakers' bureau. **Libraries: Type:** reference. **Holdings:** books, periodicals. **Subjects:** mental illness, mental health care. **Awards:** Celebration of Youth Awards. **Frequency:** annual. **Type:** recognition ● Claiming Children Award. **Frequency:** annual. **Type:** recognition. **Recipient:** for family member of a child or youth with an emotional, behavioral, or mental disorder ● Karl Dennis Award. **Frequency:** annual. **Type:** recognition ● Making a Difference Award. **Frequency:** annual. **Type:** recognition. **Recipient:** for outstanding professional in the field of children's mental health. **Publications:** *Blamed and Ashamed*. Monograph. Alternate Formats: online ● *Claiming Children* (in English and Spanish), quarterly. Newsletter. **Circulation:** 5,000 ● *Family Guide to Systems of Care for Children with Mental Health Needs* (in English and Spanish). Booklet. Alternate Formats: online ● *Learning From Colleagues: Family/Professional Partnerships Moving Forward Together*. Monograph. Alternate Formats: online ● *Your Family and Managed Care*. Booklet. **Conventions/Meetings:** annual Families Deserve the Best.Promising Interventions and Best Practices for Serving Children with Mental Health Needs - conference (exhibits).

12284 ■ LifeWorks Institute (LWI)
33 Creekside Dr.
Wimberley, TX 78676
Ph: (512)423-5638
E-mail: duanne@thelifeworksinstitute.org
URL: http://www.thelifeworksinstitute.org
Contact: DuAnne Redus, Exec. Dir.
Founded: 1996. **Staff:** 5. **Description:** Provides books and services that will improve people's lives. Offers Books for Kids program that provides web-based services enabling people to find, participate in, and support books-for-kids organizations at the local, national and international level. **Publications:** Newsletter ● Brochure.

12285 ■ NADD - An Association for Persons with Developmental Disabilities and Mental Health Needs
c/o Dr. Robert J. Fletcher, CEO/Founder
132 Fair St.
Kingston, NY 12401-4802
Ph: (845)331-4336
Free: (800)331-5362
Fax: (845)331-4569
E-mail: info@thenadd.org
URL: http://www.thenadd.org
Contact: Dr. Robert J. Fletcher, CEO/Founder
Founded: 1983. **Members:** 1,300. **Membership Dues:** family, student, $49 (annual) ● individual, $98 (annual) ● organization, $450-$600 (annual) ● sustaining, $165 (annual). **Staff:** 4. **Budget:** $650,000. **State Groups:** 6. **Description:** People with developmental disabilities and mental health care needs; mental health professionals; other interested individuals. Promotes public and professional interest in developmental disability; seeks to improve access to mental health care. Supports research programs; facilitates exchange of information among mental health professionals and consumers; conducts advocacy to insure implementation of effective public mental health policies and legislation. Holds educational programs; maintains speakers' bureau. **Libraries: Type:** not open to the public. **Holdings:** 10; audio recordings, books, periodicals, video recordings. **Subjects:** counseling, diagnosis, family issues, research, training. **Awards:** Menolascino Award. **Frequency:** annual. **Type:** recognition ●

Merck Award. **Frequency:** annual. **Type:** monetary. **Computer Services:** Mailing lists, of members. **Formerly:** (1997) National Association for the Dually Diagnosed. **Publications:** *NADD Bulletin*, bimonthly. Journal. **Price:** included in membership dues. ISSN: 1065-2574. **Circulation:** 1,500. **Advertising:** accepted. Alternate Formats: online ● Also publishes books, audio tapes, video tapes, and training materials. **Conventions/Meetings:** annual conference (exhibits) ● annual trade show ● Visions of the Future of Our Field: Intellectual Disability and Mental Health - congress.

12286 ■ National Mental Health Consumers' Self-Help Clearinghouse (NMHCSHC)
1211 Chestnut St., Ste.1207
Philadelphia, PA 19107
Ph: (215)751-1810
Free: (800)553-4KEY
Fax: (215)636-6312
E-mail: info@mhselfhelp.org
URL: http://www.mhselfhelp.org
Contact: Joseph Rogers, Exec. Dir.
Founded: 1986. **Staff:** 8. **Budget:** $350,000. **Languages:** English, Spanish. **Description:** Serves mental health consumers/ex-patients and consumer/ex-patients, self-help groups, and consumer-run services. Provides technical assistance in the development of self-help projects, including advocacy groups, support groups, consumer-run services and self-advocacy efforts. Offers informational referrals, written material, and consulting services. **Libraries: Type:** open to the public. **Holdings:** articles, periodicals. **Subjects:** mental health, self-help, consumer movement organization. **Computer Services:** database, consumer self-help groups ● database, key contacts ● database, technical assistance providers. **Telecommunication Services:** teletype, (215)751-9655. **Publications:** *Advocacy and Recovery Using the Internet*. Contains suggestions for unlocking the Internet's potential. **Price:** $3.00. Alternate Formats: online ● *Art and Science of Writing Proposals That Win*. Explains how to write a grant proposal to obtain public or private grant money. **Price:** $5.00 ● *Consumer-Run Businesses and Services*. Covers planning and operational issues. **Price:** $5.00. Alternate Formats: online ● *Consumer-Run Drop-In Centers*. Examines the role and function of consumer-run drop-in centers, and advises consumers on planning and operating. **Price:** $3.00. Alternate Formats: online ● *Fighting Stigma* (in English and Spanish). Outlines public relation strategies for countering the stigma. **Price:** $1.00. Alternate Formats: online ● *History of the Consumer Movement*. Contains the growth of the movement from its beginning to the present day development. **Price:** $1.00. Alternate Formats: online ● *Key Update*, monthly. Newsletter. Provides news and notes on important mental issues. Alternate Formats: online ● *Organizing and Operating a Speakers Bureau*. Explains how consumers have joined together to form speakers' bureaus. **Price:** $1.00. Alternate Formats: online ● *Raising Money for a Self-Help/Advocacy Group*. Contains proven strategies to raise money. **Price:** $2.00. Alternate Formats: online ● *Self-Advocacy*. Offers inspiration and advice. **Price:** $5.00. Alternate Formats: online ● *Serving on Boards and Committees*. Explains how to become an effective member of a board or committee. **Price:** $3.00. Alternate Formats: online ● *Starting a Self-Help/Advocacy Group*. Contains tips on setting up a peer support group. **Price:** $2.00. Alternate Formats: online ● *Systems Advocacy*. Provides an overview of mental health issues and tactics for influencing policy. **Price:** $5.00. Alternate Formats: online. **Conventions/Meetings:** annual Alternatives Conference, for mental health consumers and ex-patient organizers and leaders.

12287 ■ Network Against Coercive Psychiatry (NACP)
c/o Seth Farber, PhD
172 W 79th St., No. 2E
New York, NY 10024
Ph: (212)560-7288

E-mail: seth17279@aol.com
URL: http://www.sethhfarber.com/work6.htm
Contact: Seth Farber PhD, Contact
Founded: 1989. **Staff:** 4. **Description:** Comprised of psychotherapists including psychiatrists, survivors of psychiatric incarceration, scholars and other concerned citizens. Promotes the idea of mental illness as a misleading and degrading metaphor. Works towards the possible development of a social movement against the mental health system. **Conventions/Meetings:** semiannual general assembly.

12288 ■ Obsessive-Compulsive Anonymous (OCA)
PO Box 215
New Hyde Park, NY 11040
Ph: (516)739-0662
E-mail: west24th@aol.com
URL: http://www.hometown.aol.com/west24th
Founded: 1988. **Members:** 1,000. **Staff:** 7. **Regional Groups:** 70. **National Groups:** 70. **Description:** Individuals suffering from obsessive-compulsive disorders. (OCD is characterized by recurrent unpleasant thoughts and/or repetitive, irrational mannerisms the sufferer feels compelled to perform.) Follows the 12-step method originated by Alcoholics Anonymous World Services to assist members in their recovery. **Publications:** *Obsessive Compulsive Anonymous Second Edition - 1999.* Book. **Price:** $19.00. ISSN: 0962-8066 ● *Obsessive Compulsive Disorder: A Survival Guide for Family and Friends.* **Price:** $9.95. ISSN: 0962-8066.

12289 ■ Reclamation Inc.
2502 Waterford Dr.
San Antonio, TX 78217
Ph: (210)822-3569
Contact: Don H. Culwell, Dir.
Founded: 1974. **Members:** 20. **Membership Dues:** $12 (annual). **Staff:** 1. **Budget:** $10,000. **Local Groups:** 1. **Description:** Former mental patients; interested others. Seeks to eliminate the stigma of mental illness and reclaim members' "human dignity." Serves as a voice for mental health patients in consumer, social, and political affairs. Helps members to live outside a hospital setting by providing assistance in the areas of resocialization, employment, and housing. Monitors media coverage; encourages "positive" presentations of mental health patients and increased coverage of mental health community service projects and events. **Libraries:** Type: reference. **Holdings:** 25; books. **Subjects:** literature written by mental patients. **Awards:** Reclamation Award. **Frequency:** periodic. **Type:** recognition. **Recipient:** for outstanding service towards the elimination of stigma. **Publications:** *Positive Visibility,* quarterly. Newsletter. **Price:** included in membership dues. **Circulation:** 200. **Conventions/Meetings:** annual conference (exhibits).

12290 ■ S.A.F.E. Alternatives
c/o Linden Oaks Hospital
852 S West St.
Naperville, IL 60540
Ph: (630)305-5500
Free: (800)DONT-CUT
E-mail: wladersafe@aol.com
URL: http://www.safe-alternatives.com
Contact: Karen Conterio, CEO/Co-Founder
Founded: 1984. **Local Groups:** 1. **Description:** Professional group assisting self-injurious individuals in the treatment of their addictive behavior patterns. Maintains speakers' bureau; compiles statistics. **Additional Websites:** http://www.selfinjury.com. **Formerly:** (1987) Self-Mutilators Support Group; (2003) SAFE - Self Abuse Finally Ends. **Publications:** *Bodily Harm.* Book. **Price:** $14.95.

12291 ■ Schizophrenics Anonymous (SA)
c/o National Schizophrenia Foundation
403 Seymour Ave., Ste.202
Lansing, MI 48933
Ph: (517)485-7168
Free: (800)482-9534
Fax: (517)485-7180

E-mail: inquiries@nsfoundation.org
URL: http://www.nsfoundation.org/sa
Contact: Eric Hufnagel, Pres./CEO
Founded: 1985. **Local Groups:** 150. **Description:** Self-help groups organized and run by people with schizophrenia or schizophrenia-related disorders. Offers fellowship, support and information; focuses on recovery, using a 6-step program, along with medication and professional help. Provides telephone network assistance in starting and maintaining groups. **Publications:** *SA Forum,* semiannual. Newsletter. Written for and by members. **Price:** $5.00. **Circulation:** 1,200. **Advertising:** accepted ● Also distributes guidelines for establishing SA groups. **Conventions/Meetings:** weekly meeting.

12292 ■ Sidran Institute for Traumatic Stress Education
200 E Joppa Rd., Ste.207
Baltimore, MD 21286
Ph: (410)825-8888
Free: (888)825-8249
Fax: (410)337-0747
E-mail: info@sidran.org
URL: http://www.sidran.org
Contact: Esther Giller, Pres./Dir.
Founded: 1986. **Staff:** 8. **Budget:** $400,000. **Nonmembership. Description:** Supports people with trauma-generated psychological disorders. Educates trauma survivors, their support people and caregivers through the development of programs, projects, and publications. Provides advocacy services; maintains speakers' bureau; information clearinghouse; professional training. **Libraries:** Type: reference; by appointment only. **Holdings:** 2,000; articles, audiovisuals, books, clippings, monographs, periodicals. **Subjects:** mental health, psychological trauma, advocacy, child abuse. **Computer Services:** database, PsychTrauma Infobase, contains resources and texts ● mailing lists, of members. **Formerly:** (2000) Sidran Foundation and Press; (2004) Sidran Traumatic Stress Foundation. **Publications:** *Sidran Bookshelf on Trauma and Dissociation,* annual. Catalog ● *Training Materials* ● *Workbooks* ● Books. Informs professionals and lay audiences about the mental health effects of extremely traumatic experiences. **Conventions/Meetings:** quarterly Risking Connection - workshop, psychological outcomes of severe childhood trauma.

Mentally Disabled

12293 ■ American Network of Community Options and Resources (ANCOR)
1101 King St., Ste.380
Alexandria, VA 22314
Ph: (703)535-7850
Fax: (703)535-7860
E-mail: ancor@ancor.org
URL: http://www.ancor.org
Contact: Renee L. Pietrangelo, CEO
Founded: 1970. **Members:** 700. **Membership Dues:** full (based on total operating expenses), $380-$9,500 (annual) ● associate, $150-$3,000 (annual) ● state provider association (based on annual operating expenses), $1,000-$6,000 (annual). **Staff:** 9. **Budget:** $900,000. **State Groups:** 29. **Description:** National network of private providers representing provider interests at the national level and offering leading edge professional development opportunities. Works "at the forefront of trends and developments relevant to supports and services for people with disabilities and is committed to anticipating changes affecting private providers". Represents 700 member agencies and state provider associations nationwide that collectively support more than 250,000 people with disabilities. **Libraries:** Type: not open to the public. **Holdings:** 350. **Subjects:** mental retardation, other disabilities. **Awards:** Type: recognition. **Divisions:** Information; Policy; Services. **Affiliated With:** American Association on Intellectual and Developmental Disabilities; Continuing Care Accreditation Commission; Council on Quality and Leadership; National Fire Protection Association. **Formerly:** (1987) Na-

tional Association of Private Residential Facilities for the Mentally Retarded; (1993) National Association of Private Residential Resources. **Publications:** *Advocacy for Change: A Manual for Organizing.* Features a broader look at advocacy and builds on the key concepts and theories of organizing. **Price:** $32.00 ● *Directory of Members,* annual. Membership Directory. **Price:** $25.00 ● *Legislative Alert,* periodic ● *LINKS,* 10/year. Newsletter. Provides information on leading practices and federal legislative and regulatory updates. Includes calendar of events, news of members, research news. **Price:** included in membership dues; $750.00 for nonmembers. **Circulation:** 2,500 ● *Wage and Hour Handbook.* Contains the latest rules and interpretations from the US Dept. of Labor relative to employment. **Price:** $45.00 for members; $65.00 for nonmembers. **Conventions/Meetings:** annual Governmental Activities Seminar (exhibits) - always September, Washington DC ● annual Winter Conference (exhibits) - always February or March.

12294 ■ Arc of the United States
1010 Wayne Ave., Ste.650
Silver Spring, MD 20910
Ph: (301)565-3842
Free: (800)433-5255
Fax: (301)565-5342
E-mail: info@thearc.org
URL: http://www.thearc.org
Contact: Sue Swenson, Exec. Dir.
Founded: 1950. **Members:** 140,000. **Staff:** 20. **State Groups:** 46. **Local Groups:** 100,000. **Description:** Parents, professional workers, and others interested in individuals with mental retardation. Works on local, state, and national levels to promote services, research, public understanding, and legislation for people with mental retardation and their families. Strives to include all children and adults with cognitive, intellectual and developmental disabilities in every community. **Awards:** Research Award. **Frequency:** annual. **Type:** monetary. **Recipient:** for an outstanding researcher. **Telecommunication Services:** TDD, (817)277-0553. **Formerly:** Association for Retarded Citizens; (1952) National Association of Parents and Friends of Mentally Retarded Children; (1974) National Association for Retarded Children; (1980) National Association for Retarded Citizens; (1991) Association for Retarded Citizens of the United States. **Publications:** *The Arc Now,* monthly ● *The ARC's Government Report,* semimonthly. **Price:** $72.00/year ● *InSight,* quarterly. Newspaper. **Price:** $15.00/year. **Conventions/Meetings:** annual convention (exhibits).

12295 ■ Association for Children with Down Syndrome (ACDS)
4 Fern Pl.
Plainview, NY 11803
Ph: (516)933-4700
Fax: (516)933-9524
E-mail: msmith@acds.org
URL: http://www.acds.org
Contact: Michael M. Smith, Exec. Dir.
Founded: 1966. **Members:** 1,000. **Staff:** 120. **Budget:** $4,000,000. **Languages:** English, Spanish. **Description:** Administers infant, toddler, and preschool programs in New York state and sibling programs. Offers recreational and socialization programs and support groups for children over 5 years of age through adulthood; parents of children with Down Syndrome; health and educational professionals. Acts as resource and information center about Down Syndrome. Works to maintain contact with the medical and health related community and with parents of children with Down Syndrome; attempts to dispel myths about the capabilities of children with Down Syndrome through Learning is Necessary to Care, an outreach program. Provides referral services; sponsors conferences and workshops; conducts research; compiles statistics, group homes for young adults with Down Syndrome and other developmental disabilities. **Libraries:** Type: reference. **Holdings:** 2,000; books, video recordings. **Awards:** Type: scholarship. **Recipient:** for high school students. **Committees:** Critical Issues. **Affiliated With:** Na-

tional Down Syndrome Congress; National Down Syndrome Society. **Formerly:** Association for Special Children. **Publications:** *Accent on ACDS*, quarterly. Newsletter. Features information on advocacy, law, reading materials, references and reviews, conferences, and association programs. Alternate Formats: online ● *Special Kids Make Special Friends*. Book ● Bibliography ● Journal, annual. **Advertising:** accepted ● Videos. **Conventions/Meetings:** periodic meeting.

12296 ■ Association of University Centers on Disabilities (AUCD)

1010 Wayne Ave., Ste.920
Silver Spring, MD 20910
Ph: (301)588-8252
Fax: (301)588-2842
E-mail: gjesien@aucd.org
URL: http://www.aucd.org
Contact: George S. Jesien PhD, Exec. Dir.

Founded: 1971. **Members:** 61. **Staff:** 11. **Budget:** $2,000,000. **Description:** University-based or affiliated clinical service and interdisciplinary training centers for graduate students and others interested in the field of mental retardation and other developmental disabilities. Provides: coordination of federal funding for programs; technical assistance to Congress; information exchange among members; educational activities about programs. Compiles statistics. **Computer Services:** database, information from member university affiliated programs ● mailing lists. **Telecommunication Services:** electronic bulletin board. **Committees:** Database; National Training Outreach; Research; Telecommunication; Training Directors Steering. **Councils:** Interdisciplinary. **Projects:** National Service Inclusion; Training Initiative. **Formerly:** (1975) Association of University Affiliated Facilities; (1983) American Association of University Affiliated Programs for the Developmentally Disabled; (2001) American Association of University Affiliated Programs for Persons With Developmental Disabilities. **Publications:** *Resource Directory*, annual. Alternate Formats: online ● Brochure. Alternate Formats: online ● Reprints. Alternate Formats: online. **Conventions/Meetings:** annual conference.

12297 ■ Best Buddies International (BBI)

100 SE Second St., Ste.2200
Miami, FL 33131
Ph: (305)374-2233
Free: (800)89-BUDDY
Fax: (305)374-5305
E-mail: lisaplante@bestbuddies.org
URL: http://www.bestbuddies.org
Contact: Lisa Plante, Admin. VP

Founded: 1989. **Members:** 40,000. **Staff:** 175. **Budget:** $18,000,000. **Regional Groups:** 17. **Local Groups:** 600. **Multinational. Description:** Individuals interested in the social well being of people with mental retardation. Promotes establishment of friendships between people with mental retardation and other members of the community. Conducts fundraising activities; sponsors volunteer campaigns; maintains art collection.

12298 ■ Bethesda Lutheran Homes and Services

600 Hoffman Dr.
Watertown, WI 53094
Ph: (920)261-3050
Free: (800)369-4636
Fax: (920)261-8441
E-mail: dgeske@blhs.org
URL: http://www.blhs.org
Contact: David Geske PhD, Pres./CEO

Founded: 1904. **Members:** 5,000. **Staff:** 1,103. **Budget:** $37,000,000. **Regional Groups:** 5. **State Groups:** 11. **Description:** Provides religious education, habilitation services, therapeutic services, vocational training, and residential care for 700 persons with mental retardation in Florida, Illinois, Indiana, Kansas, Maryland, Michigan, Missouri, Ohio, Texas and Wisconsin. Offers paid summer co-op positions in nursing, social work, psychology, special education, recreation, Christian education, video

media production and public relations. Provides free information and referral services nationwide for parents, pastor's teachers, advocates and mental retardation professionals. Operates a fully accessible camp on its Watertown, Wisconsin campus. Offers workshops for pastors, teachers, parents and mental retardation professionals. **Libraries: Type:** reference. **Holdings:** 5,000; books, monographs, periodicals, video recordings. **Subjects:** mental retardation, health science, disability/religious, training materials. **Awards:** Career Awareness Award. **Frequency:** annual. **Type:** monetary. **Recipient:** for high school age Lutheran students ● Developmental Disabilities Awareness Award. **Frequency:** annual. **Type:** recognition. **Recipient:** for students to promote their knowledge of careers in the field of developmental disabilities services ● Developmental Disabilities Scholastic Achievement Scholarship. **Frequency:** annual. **Type:** scholarship. **Recipient:** for Lutheran, College junior, Human Services, Special Education or MR/DD Profession, volunteer work in DD ● Nursing Scholastic Achievement Scholarship. **Frequency:** annual. **Type:** scholarship. **Recipient:** for Lutheran College Junior Nursing students who have earned 3.0 GPA, volunteer work in development disabilities. **Programs:** Advocate; Companionship for the Dying; Foster Grandparents; Trusted Loyal Companions. **Formerly:** (1995) Bethesda Lutheran Home and Services. **Publications:** *Behavior Treatment I and II*. Videos. Contains learner packet. **Price:** $65.00 each ● *Breakthrough*, quarterly. Newsletter. Includes religious special education and disability ministry news, feature stories, and 13 weekly Biblical curriculum guides. **Price:** free. **Circulation:** 6,000 ● *Developing a Response to Our Loving God*. Book. Contains curriculum for preconfirmation for persons with mental retardation. **Price:** $5.00 ● *Eating Skills*. Video. Includes manual and learner packet. **Price:** $65.00 ● *Interacting With People Who Are Mentally Retarded*. Pamphlet ● *The Latest Development*, bimonthly. Newsletter. Contains news and current events at Bethesda. Alternate Formats: online ● *Leisure Skills Training*. Video. Includes learner packet. **Price:** $65.00 ● *Opening the Door to Learning for People With Mental Retardation*. Pamphlet. **Price:** free ● *Parish Advocacy*. Video. **Price:** $10.00 ● *Sidelines*, bimonthly. Newsletter. Alternate Formats: online ● *Walking With Jesus: Daily Devotions for Group Homes, Volume I, II, III*. Books. Contains 365 devotions for each volume. **Price:** $13.00/volume. **Conventions/Meetings:** Religious: Ministry and Special Religious Education, Congregations That Care: Becoming Accessible - workshop, religious resources from many faith groups (exhibits) ● Secular: Environments of Quality, Administrative Issues, Teaching Community Skills, Redirecting Behaviors - workshop, staff training materials (exhibits) - 8/year.

12299 ■ Center for Family Support (CFS)

333 7th Ave., 9th Fl.
New York, NY 10001-5004
Ph: (212)629-7939
Fax: (212)239-2211
URL: http://www.cfsny.org
Contact: Helen Benjamin, Residence Mgr.

Founded: 1953. **Staff:** 700. **Budget:** $12,000,000. **Languages:** English, Russian, Spanish. **Description:** Provides services and advocacy to persons with developmental and related disabilities and their families. Provides In-Home Care, Service Coordination and other Family Support Services. Offers long-term residential care to developmentally disabled individuals who are ready to live apart from their families. Provides short term Emergency Home Care Services to the elderly in New York City. **Affiliated With:** United Way of America. **Formerly:** (1958) Parents With a Purpose; (1991) Retarded Infants Service.

12300 ■ Council on Quality and Leadership (CQL)

100 West Rd., Ste.406
Towson, MD 21204
Ph: (410)583-0060
Fax: (410)583-0063

E-mail: info@thecouncil.org
URL: http://www.thecouncil.org
Contact: James F. Gardner PhD, Pres./CEO

Founded: 1969. **Members:** 10. **Staff:** 80. **Budget:** $3,000,000. **Multinational. Description:** Offers person-centered solutions for organizations and systems supporting individuals with disabilities and mental illness by providing accreditation, monitoring, evaluation, training and consultation services. Many of the Council's standards have been enacted into federal and state legislation and have been recognized by state and federal courts as the optimal measure of service quality. The Council "was the first organization to define and measure quality in terms of responsiveness to people and was the first organization to develop a statistically valid, consistent measurement process with its Personal Outcome Measures." Currently partners with organizations and providers throughout the USA, Canada, England, Ireland and Australia. **Awards:** Award of Excellence. **Frequency:** annual. **Type:** recognition. **Recipient:** for exceptional level of service quality. **Affiliated With:** American Association on Intellectual and Developmental Disabilities; American Network of Community Options and Resources; Arc of the United States; Autism Society of America; Brain Injury Association of America; Epilepsy Foundation; National Alliance on Mental Illness. **Formerly:** (1976) Accreditation Council for Facilities for the Mentally Retarded; (1986) Accreditation Council for Services for Mentally Retarded and Other Developmentally Disabled Persons; (1991) Accreditation Council on Services for People with Developmental Disabilities; (1998) Accreditation Council on Services for People with Disabilities; (2002) Council on Quality and Leadership in Supports for People with Disabilities. **Publications:** *Accreditation: A Quality Review and Enhancement Process*. **Price:** $25.00 ● *Assessment Workbook*, quarterly. Manual. **Price:** $75.00 for 12 issues. **Circulation:** 10,000 ● *The CAPstone*, quarterly. Newsletter. **Circulation:** 10,000. Alternate Formats: online ● *Impact Series for Organizational Performance Improvement*. Manual. **Price:** $35.00 ● *The Personal Outcome Measures*. Manual. **Price:** $59.00. **Conventions/Meetings:** Leadership Conference ● annual Quality Consortium Conference (exhibits) - held in spring.

12301 ■ Differently Abled Proud People Exercising Rights (DAPPER)

PO Box 12013
San Luis Obispo, CA 93406
Ph: (805)602-0076
E-mail: bradleywins@yahoo.com
Contact: Bradley Thomas Horton, Founder/Pres.

Description: Advocates locally for people with brain tumors, brain injury, developmental difficulties, and any of these problems mixed with homelessness; is working to become a national organization.

12302 ■ Federation for Children with Special Needs (FCSN)

1135 Tremont St., Ste.420
Boston, MA 02120
Ph: (617)236-7210
Free: (800)331-0688
Fax: (617)572-2094
E-mail: fcsninfo@fcsn.org
URL: http://www.fcsn.org
Contact: Richard J. Robison, Exec. Dir.

Founded: 1974. **Staff:** 48. **Languages:** English, Portuguese, Spanish. **Description:** Coalition of parents' organizations acting on behalf of children and adults with disabilities. Provides information and workshops on special education laws and resources, and how to obtain related services. Operates projects that help to increase and encourage parent involvement in the health care of children with disabilities or chronic illnesses; projects are: Parent Training and Information Project (PTI), which provides workshops in basic rights, parent consultations, and training, and an information service. **Libraries: Type:** reference. **Holdings:** 1,000. **Computer Services:** database, family resource ● mailing lists, of members. **Programs:** Early Childhood; Education; Health. **Publications:** *Newsline* (in English, Portuguese, and Spanish), quarterly. Newsletter. **Advertising:** accepted. Alternate Formats: online ● List available on request. **Conventions/Meetings:** annual conference, with federation statewide conference (exhibits).

12303 ■ JARC
30301 Northwestern Hwy., Ste.100
Farmington Hills, MI 48334
Ph: (248)538-6611
Fax: (248)538-6615
E-mail: jarc@jarc.org
URL: http://www.jarc.org
Contact: Joyce Keller, Exec. Dir.
Founded: 1969. **Budget:** $7,500,000. **Description:** Jewish association providing residential care and support services to developmental disabled adults. Operates group homes that provide access to Jewish services, maintains kosher kitchens, and offers independent living programs. Provides support to families of children with any disability including respite care, case management, and social activities. **Divisions:** Frankel Residential Services; Shetzer Independent Living Services. **Programs:** Harris Children and Family Division; Maas Supported Independence. **Also Known As:** Jewish Association of Residential Care. **Formerly:** (1975) Parents Association for Jewish Residential Care; (1980) Association for Jewish Retarded; (1989) Jewish Association for Retarded Citizens. **Publications:** *From Our Home to Yours*, bimonthly. Newsletter. Alternate Formats: online ● Brochure. **Conventions/Meetings:** annual meeting.

12304 ■ Joseph P. Kennedy, Jr. Foundation
1133 19th St. NW, 12th Fl.
Washington, DC 20036-3604
Ph: (202)393-1250
Fax: (202)824-0351
E-mail: info@jpkf.org
URL: http://www.jpkf.org
Contact: Senator Edward M. Kennedy, Pres.
Founded: 1946. **Description:** Works to provide support for persons with mental retardation, both those born and unborn, and their families. Strives to improve the way society deals with mental retardation and works to identify and disseminate ways to prevent the causes of mental retardation.

12305 ■ Lifespire
Empire State Bldg.
350 5th Ave., Ste.301
New York, NY 10118
Ph: (212)741-0100
Fax: (212)242-0696
E-mail: info@lifespire.org
URL: http://www.lifespire.org
Contact: Mark van Voorst, Pres./CEO
Founded: 1951. **Members:** 200. **Membership Dues:** regular, $25 (annual). **Staff:** 1,300. **Budget:** $62,000,000. **Languages:** Chinese, English, Filipino, Russian, Spanish. **Description:** Offers professionally supervised programs for adults with mental retardation and developmental disabilities, including day habilitation, vocational rehabilitation, dual diagnosis programs, job placement, rehabilitation workshops, activities for daily living, day treatment, day training, supported work, and family support programs. Operates the Lubin Center for Independent Living, an apartment complex for gainfully employed adults capable of independent living. Operates community residences, supportive apartments and intermediate care facilities in the city of New York. Advocates for people with mental retardation and developmental disabilities in all phases of life and participation in community. Sponsors conferences and training regarding mental retardation and developmental disability. Maintains job placement service. Membership is open to professionals, parents, siblings and all others interested in adults with mental retardation and developmental disabilities. **Formerly:** (1964) Parents Association for Children with Retarded Mental Development; (2001) Association for Children with Retarded Mental Development. **Publications:** Brochures ● Directory, annual ● Newsletters ● Annual Report, annual ● Also publishes agency profile.

12306 ■ Little City Foundation (LCF)
1760 W Algonquin Rd.
Palatine, IL 60067
Ph: (847)358-5510
Fax: (847)358-5563
E-mail: people@littlecity.org
URL: http://www.littlecity.org
Contact: Mr. Shawn E. Jeffers, Exec. Dir.
Founded: 1959. **Members:** 3,000. **Staff:** 550. **Budget:** $25,000,000. **Description:** Provides state-of-the-art community based services and service coordination to help children and adults with mental retardation or other developmental, emotional, and behavioral challenges to lead meaningful, productive, and dignified lives. Includes services such as: housing, employment, recreation, foster care, adoption, home-based support, service coordination, media and studio arts, advocacy, and public education. **Additional Websites:** http://www.artistical.org. **Publications:** *Little City Network*, quarterly ● *Parent*. Newsletter ● *Volunteer*. Newsletter. **Conventions/Meetings:** annual Little City Invitational - competition ● annual Sports Dinner.

12307 ■ Mental Disability Rights International (MDRI)
1156 15th St. NW, Ste.1001
Washington, DC 20005
Ph: (202)296-0800
Fax: (202)728-3053
E-mail: mdri@mdri.org
URL: http://www.mdri.org
Contact: Eric Rosenthal, Founder/Exec. Dir.
Founded: 1993. **Multinational. Description:** Promotes the human rights and full participation in society of people with mental disabilities worldwide. Trains and supports advocates seeking legal and service system reform. Assists governments in developing laws and policies to promote community integration and human rights enforcement for people with mental disabilities. **Computer Services:** Mailing lists. **Projects:** Americas Advocacy Initiative; Initiative for Inclusion: Kosovo; Women's Rights Advocacy Initiative. **Publications:** *Children in Russia's Institutions: Human Rights and Opportunities for Reform* (in English and Russian). Book. Alternate Formats: online ● *Forgotten People*. Video. **Price:** $20.00 in VHS. Alternate Formats: online ● *Human Rights and Mental Health: Hungary*. Book. Alternate Formats: online ● *Human Rights and Mental Health in Peru* (in English and Spanish). Book. Alternate Formats: online ● *Not on the Agenda: Human Rights of People with Mental Disabilities in Kosovo* (in Albanian, English, and Serbian). Book. Alternate Formats: online.

12308 ■ National Association of Councils on Developmental Disabilities (NACCD)
225 Reinekers Ln., Ste.650-B
Alexandria, VA 22314
Ph: (703)739-4400
Fax: (703)739-6030
E-mail: info@nacdd.org
URL: http://www.nacdd.org
Contact: Karen Flippo, Exec. Dir.
Founded: 1975. **Members:** 40. **Staff:** 4. **Budget:** $300,000. **Description:** Promotes national policy which provides individuals with developmental disabilities the opportunity to make choices regarding the quality of their lives and be included in the community; and provides support and assistance to member Councils. **Libraries: Type:** reference. **Holdings:** archival material, books, business records, monographs, periodicals. **Committees:** Council Services; Public Policy. **Formerly:** (1978) National Conference on Developmental Disabilities; (2004) National Association of Developmental Disabilities Councils. **Publications:** *Council Chronicles*. Newsletter. Alternate Formats: online ● *Quiknews*, bimonthly. Newsletter. **Price:** available to members only. **Circulation:** 250 ● Monographs ● Reports ● Annual Report, annual. Alternate Formats: online. **Conventions/Meetings:** conference ● annual meeting - always October/November.

12309 ■ National Association of State Directors of Developmental Disabilities Services (NASDDDS)
113 Oronoco St.
Alexandria, VA 22314
Ph: (703)683-4202
Fax: (703)684-1395
E-mail: nthaler@nasddds.org
URL: http://www.nasddds.org
Contact: Nancy Thaler, Exec. Dir.
Founded: 1963. **Members:** 53. **Budget:** $458,400. **Description:** State administrative personnel working with programs in the field of mental retardation. Monitors and reports on administrative, legislative, and judicial activities and other events affecting mental retardation programs. Provides technical assistance services. **Committees:** Governmental Affairs. **Formerly:** (1977) National Association of Coordinators of State Programs for the Mentally Retarded. **Publications:** *Community Service Reporter*, monthly. Newsletter. Includes calendar of events, member news, and reports on association programs. **Price:** included in membership dues; $95.00 /year for nonmembers. **Circulation:** 900. Alternate Formats: online. Also Cited As: *CSR* ● *Federal Funding Inquiry*, periodic ● *Medicaid and Case Management for People with Developmental Disabilities: Options, Practices and Issues.* Report. Contains information on the approaches used by states to finance developmental disabilities case management services. **Price:** $25.00 ● *Medicaid and Systems Change: Finding the Fit.* Report. **Price:** $25.00 ● *Perspectives*, monthly. Newsletter. **Price:** $95.00/year. Alternate Formats: online ● *Understanding State Individual Budgeting Strategies.* Report. Summarizes the findings of a study on individualized funding methodologies used by state developmental disabilities services systems. **Price:** $30.00. **Conventions/Meetings:** annual meeting - always December, Washington, DC ● annual meeting - always April, Washington, DC.

12310 ■ National Down Syndrome Congress (NDSC)
1370 Center Dr., Ste.102
Atlanta, GA 30338
Ph: (770)604-9500
Free: (800)232-NDSC
Fax: (770)604-9898
E-mail: info@ndsccenter.org
URL: http://www.ndsccenter.org
Contact: David Tolleson, Exec. Dir.
Founded: 1973. **Members:** 10,000. **Membership Dues:** individual in U.S., $25 (annual) ● individual outside U.S., $35 (annual) ● affiliate, $50 (annual) ● non-affiliate, $75 (annual). **Staff:** 4. **Budget:** $600,000. **Local Groups:** 600. **Languages:** English, Spanish. **Description:** Families of individuals with Down Syndrome; educators, health professionals, and other interested individuals. Works to promote the welfare of persons with Down Syndrome (DS), a chromosomal disorder which occurs in approximately one in every 800 to 1,100 births and usually causes delays in physical and intellectual development; its exact cause is unknown. Promotes the belief that persons with DS have the right to a normal and dignified life, particularly in the areas of education, medical care, employment, and human services. Examines issues of social policy and conditions that limit the full growth and potential of children and adults with DS. Assists parents on possible solutions to the needs of the child with DS; coordinates efforts and activities of local parents' organizations. Acts as clearinghouse for information on DS. **Libraries: Type:** not open to the public. **Holdings:** 600. **Committees:** Adoption; Awards; Citizens; Education; Legislative Awareness; Media; Parent Group; Public Awareness; Research; Siblings. **Formerly:** (1983) Down's Syndrome Congress; (1984) National Down's Syndrome Congress. **Publications:** *Alpha Fetoprotein and Prenatal Screening*. Position statement. ● *Atlanto-Axial Instability*. Position statement. ● *Depression in Persons with Down Syndrome*. Position statement. ● *Doman-Delacato Treatment*. Position statement. ● *Down Syndrome* (in English and Spanish). Booklet ● *Down Syndrome News*, 10/year. Newsletter. Provides information on the educational, research, and service

programs of NDSC. Includes book and film reviews, calendar of events, and statistics. **Price:** $20.00/year. ISSN: 0161-0716 ● *Management of Challenging Behaviors.* Position statement. ● *Mega Vitamin Therapy.* Position statement. ● *Quality Education for Students with Down Syndrome.* Position statement. ● Articles ● Bibliography ● Films ● Journals ● Pamphlets. **Conventions/Meetings:** annual convention (exhibits).

12311 ■ New Avenues to Independence
c/o Debbie Dombek, Human Resources Asst.
17608 Euclid Ave.
Cleveland, OH 44112-1216
Ph: (216)481-1909 (216)481-1907
Free: (888)782-3588
Fax: (216)481-2050
E-mail: ddombek@newavenues.net
URL: http://www.newavenues.net
Contact: Thomas Lewins, Exec. Dir.
Founded: 1952. **Members:** 755. **Description:** Professional staff, volunteers, and family members. Strives to enhance the lives of individuals who have mental retardation/developmental disabilities (MR/DD). Provides services that enable individuals to live in a community setting of their choice. Assists individuals in their family homes, and developing homes in established communities where there are greater opportunities for individuals with disabilities to grow and to become more independent and productive members of society. Works with government agencies and committees to formulate policies and services that improve quality of life for all persons with MR/DD. **Libraries: Type:** reference; lending. **Holdings:** archival material, articles, books, business records, periodicals. **Subjects:** mental retardation, developmental disabilities, ICF/MR regulations, social services, training materials. **Formerly:** (2003) Parents Volunteer Association.

12312 ■ Parents of Down Syndrome (PODS)
PO Box 10416
Rockville, MD 20849
Ph: (301)916-4985
E-mail: information@podsmc.org
Contact: Karen O'Connor, Pres.
Founded: 1966. **Members:** 180. **Membership Dues:** family, $12 (annual). **Languages:** English, Portuguese, Spanish. **Description:** Parents of children with Down Syndrome. Activities include formal and informal meetings; parent-to-parent counseling; contacting new parents of children with Down Syndrome to offer support and information on community resources; providing information on doctors, hospitals, and professionals; promoting membership in The ARC/MC (see separate entry). Maintains speakers' bureau. **Libraries: Type:** reference. **Affiliated With:** Arc of the United States; National Down Syndrome Congress; National Down Syndrome Society. **Formerly:** (1975) Mothers of Young Mongoloids; (1993) Parents of Down Syndrome Children; (2000) Parents of Children with Down Syndrome. **Publications:** *Parents of Children with Down Syndrome,* quarterly. Newsletter ● *PODS Monthly Newsletter.* Highlights legislation, education, recreation, medical information relating to Down Syndrome. **Price:** free.

12313 ■ People First International (PF)
PO Box 12642
Salem, OR 97309
Ph: (503)362-0336
Fax: (503)587-0287
E-mail: people1@people1.org
URL: http://www.people1.org
Contact: Steven Kramer, Pres.
Founded: 1974. **Membership Dues:** regular, $1 (annual). **National Groups:** 4. **Languages:** English, German. **Multinational. Description:** Seeks to provide mentally retarded and developmentally disabled persons with training in leadership skills and advocacy. Offers consultation. Helps new groups get started. **Awards: Type:** recognition. **Publications:** *We Are People First.* Book ● Film ● Audiotapes ● Videos. **Conventions/Meetings:** periodic international conference ● workshop.

12314 ■ Pilot Parents of Southern Arizona (PPSA)
2600 N Wyatt Dr.
Tucson, AZ 85712
Ph: (520)324-3150
Free: (877)365-7220
Fax: (520)324-3152
E-mail: ppsa@pilotparents.org
URL: http://www.pilotparents.org
Contact: Lynn Kallis, Exec. Dir.
Founded: 1971. **Members:** 340. **Description:** Parents, professionals, and others concerned with providing emotional and peer support to new parents of children with special needs. Sponsors a parent-matching program which allows parents who have sufficient experience and training in the care of their own children to share their knowledge and expertise with parents of children recently diagnosed as disabled. Provides information concerning developmental disabilities, medical services, and supportive agencies within communities. Maintains speakers' bureau. Conducts educational programs. Although activities are conducted on a local level, program serves as a model for similar groups that are being organized throughout the U.S. **Libraries: Type:** reference. **Subjects:** mental retardation. **Awards: Type:** recognition. **Publications:** *The Gazette,* bimonthly. Newsletter ● *The Navigator,* quarterly. Newsletter. Alternate Formats: online. **Conventions/Meetings:** annual meeting.

12315 ■ Symbral Foundation (SF)
914 Silver Spring Ave., Ste.103
Silver Spring, MD 20910
Ph: (202)726-1444
Fax: (301)650-5729
Contact: Yvonne Mohammed, Pres.
Founded: 1983. **Members:** 9. **Membership Dues:** general, $50 (annual). **Staff:** 75. **Budget:** $1,000,000. **Description:** Provides special services including medical and residential assistance to mentally retarded individuals. Maintains speakers' bureau; plans to conduct workshops and provide children's services. Activities are currently restricted to the Washington, DC area, but SF plans to operate on a national level. **Conventions/Meetings:** annual meeting - always February or March.

12316 ■ Voice of the Retarded (VOR)
PO Box 1208
Rapid City, SD 57709
Ph: (605)399-1624
Free: (877)399-4867
Fax: (605)399-1631
E-mail: vor@compuserve.com
URL: http://www.vor.net
Contact: Mr. Geoffrey Dubrowsky, Exec. Dir.
Founded: 1983. **Membership Dues:** individual, $25 (annual) ● family organization, $150 (annual) ● professional, provider, $200 (annual). **Staff:** 2. **Budget:** $450,000. **State Groups:** 50. **Local Groups:** 140. **National Groups:** 5. **Description:** Families and friends of individuals with mental retardation and developmental disabilities; MR/DD, autism professionals and providers. Advocates for the general welfare of individuals with mental retardation and developmental disabilities by: working to improve care and services; monitoring related legislation; increasing public awareness of disability issues; providing resources to individuals, guardians, families, and public officials. Promotes freedom of choice and residential alternatives for persons with developmental disabilities. **Libraries: Type:** not open to the public. **Holdings:** periodicals. **Subjects:** mental retardation, healthcare, federal legislation. **Computer Services:** database, membership. **Publications:** *Office Bulletin,* monthly. **Price:** free for members ● Newsletter, quarterly ● VOR Weekly e-mail update. Free to members and interested individuals. Send subscription request to vor@compuserve.com. **Conventions/Meetings:** annual meeting and workshop, with presentations (exhibits).

12317 ■ Young Adult Institute/National Institute for People with Disabilities (YAI/NIPD)
460 W 34th St.
New York, NY 10001-2382
Ph: (212)273-6100 (212)273-6182
Fax: (212)629-4113
URL: http://www.yai.org
Contact: Joel M. Levy DSW, CEO
Founded: 1957. **Staff:** 3,300. **Budget:** $40,000,000. **Description:** Provides comprehensive programs that enable people with development disabilities, mental retardation, learning disabilities, emotional disturbance, or brain damage to progress from a state of isolation and dependency to a more productive, self-sufficient, and integrated role in society. Offering an alternative to institutionalization and focusing on the development of a series of supportive community services to maintain individuals' independence, individuality, inclusion and productivity within the community; seeking to prevent institutionalization by providing services in local communities to assist parents through family supports or waiver programs to help prevent out of home placement, supporting families in the community through primary health care for children and adults, certified home health care, specialty therapy services. **Formerly:** (1964) Young Adult Adjustment Center; (2000) Young Adult Institute and Workshop. **Publications:** *Model Programs and New Technologies for People With Disabilities.* **Conventions/Meetings:** annual conference (exhibits).

Migrant Workers

12318 ■ Association of Farmworker Opportunity Programs (AFOP)
1726 M St. NW, Ste.800
Washington, DC 20036
Ph: (202)826-6006
Fax: (202)826-6005
E-mail: afop@afop.org
URL: http://www.afop.org
Contact: Mr. David A. Strauss, Exec. Dir.
Founded: 1971. **Members:** 53. **Membership Dues:** organization-voting, $1,000 (annual) ● individual, $100 (annual) ● individual, $25 (annual) ● organization - nonvoting, $500 (annual). **Staff:** 10. **Budget:** $3,200,000. **State Groups:** 53. **Languages:** English, Spanish. **Description:** Represents farmworker organizations in 49 states and Puerto Rico that operate employment, training, educates on pesticide worker safety, and related supportive service programs for migrant and seasonal farmworkers. Manages the National Children in the Fields campaign to eliminate child labor in agriculture. Conducts research; issues policy statements and analyses on federal regulations and legislation affecting farmworkers. Provides consultation service; operates speakers' bureau; compiles statistics. Operates national direct AmeriCorps program in 20 states with 80 members. Maintains hall of fame. Manages national farmworkers database containing individual records on over 80,000 migrant and seasonal farmworkers. Maintains national library and photo gallery. **Libraries: Type:** not open to the public. **Holdings:** 20,000; articles, books, periodicals. **Subjects:** farmworkers, farmworker programs, related issues. **Awards: Type:** recognition. **Computer Services:** database ● mailing lists. **Programs:** Serving America's Farmworkers Everywhere. **Publications:** *A Taste of English.* **Price:** $125.00 1 teacher's manual and 5 student workbooks ● *AFOP Washington Newsline,* bimonthly. Newsletter. Informs members of issues pertaining to migrant and seasonal farmworkers and other rural poor; analysis of legislative and regulatory actions. **Price:** free to members; $295.00/year for nonmember organizations; $250.00/year for member organizations. **Advertising:** accepted ● *AmeriCorps. Reporter,* monthly. Newsletter. Informs AmeriCorps members of progress and success with providing pesticide worker safety training and education to farmworkers. ● *English for Farm Safety.* **Price:** $125.00 one teacher's manual and five student's workbooks ● *Farmworker Nutrition Education Resource Guide.* Directory. Lists farmworker service providers nationwide. **Price:** $10.00 ● *Radio Nutricion.* **Price:** $50.00; $25.00 for supplement ● *Radio Pesticides* (in English and Spanish). **Price:** $50.00 ● Annual Report, annual. **Conventions/Meetings:** an-

nual National Farmworker Policy Summit - conference (exhibits).

12319 ■ Farm Worker Health Services

1221 Massachusetts Ave. NW, Ste.5
Washington, DC 20005
Ph: (202)347-7377
Fax: (202)347-6385
E-mail: oscar@farmworkerhealth.org
URL: http://www.farmworkerhealth.org
Contact: Oscar C. Gomez, Exec. Dir.
Founded: 1970. **Staff:** 30. **Budget:** $1,000,000. **Languages:** English, Spanish. **Description:** Health and social care delivery system for migrant and seasonal farm workers and their families. Provides health and social services to migrant workers through outreach health and parahealth professionals associated with existing community health clinics/departments in Delaware, Florida, Georgia, Maine, Maryland, New York, New Jersey, North Carolina, Pennsylvania, South Carolina, Tennessee, Virginia, and West Virginia. Goals are: empowerment of migrant and seasonal farmworkers and their families through practical health and social education. Activities include: staff orientation; in-service education; community liaison work; health education and cultural awareness. Maintains placement service. **Awards:** Sr. Cecilia B. Abhold Award. **Frequency:** annual. **Type:** recognition. **Recipient:** for excellence in farmworker health outreach services. **Telecommunication Services:** electronic mail, mail@farmworkerhealth.org. **Formerly:** (1997) East Coast Migrant Health Project. **Publications:** *Farmworker Health Outreach Needs Assessment Report.* Contains information about community health outreach programs serving farmworkers. **Price:** $9.00 ● *Innovative Outreach,* annual. Report. Contains a collection of innovative farmworker health outreach program practices in U.S. **Price:** $7.00 ● *Outreach,* quarterly. Newsletter. **Price:** $2.50 ● *Outreach Reference Manual,* annual. Guidelines for conducting outreach and health education to farm workers. Extensive list of resources and organizations dealing with farmworkers. **Price:** $30.00. **Conventions/Meetings:** semiannual board meeting.

12320 ■ Farmworker Justice Fund (FJF)

1126 16th St. NW, Ste.270
Washington, DC 20036
Ph: (202)293-5420
Fax: (202)293-5427
URL: http://www.fwjustice.org
Contact: Bruce Goldstein, Exec. Dir.
Founded: 1981. **Staff:** 8. **Budget:** $500,000. **Description:** Attorneys and other individuals taking part in federal and state legislative, administrative, and judicial advocacy on behalf of migrant and seasonal farmworkers and their families. Purpose is to improve health, sanitary, and other living and working conditions experienced by seasonal farmworkers. Seeks improved wages, working conditions, occupational safety, health services, and adequate housing for farmworkers. Cooperates with organizations that provide assistance to farmworkers, particularly farm labor unions and legal services programs. Conducts research. **Programs:** HIV/AIDS Prevention; H2-A Temporary Foreign Agricultural Worker. **Publications:** *Farmworker Justice News,* semiannual. Newsletter. Features update on latest issues and projects. **Price:** free. **Circulation:** 2,500. Alternate Formats: online ● Also publishes books, monographs, and materials on the problems of agricultural workers. **Conventions/Meetings:** quarterly board meeting.

12321 ■ Interstate Migrant Education Council (IMEC)

1 Massachusetts Ave., Ste.700
Washington, DC 20001
Ph: (202)336-7078
Fax: (202)408-8062
E-mail: nancyw@ccsso.org
URL: http://www.migedimec.org
Contact: Ms. Nancy Wiehe, Sr. Proj. Assoc.
Founded: 1976. **Members:** 55. **Staff:** 2. **State Groups:** 19. **Description:** A project of the Education Commission of the States. Seeks to create awareness of the educational needs of migrant students among U.S. government, business, and educational leaders. Serves as a forum for the discussion and resolution of educational difficulties faced by migrant youth; facilitates interstate cooperation and encourages the sharing of model programs. Identifies obstacles faced by migrant students and develops solutions to educational problems posed by factors such as the students' mobility, intermittent attendance, and limited English proficiency. Coordinates activities with National Conference of State Legislatures, American Association of School Administrators, Council of Chief State School Officers, and other educational organizations. Serves as liaison between migrant education organizations and federal health, agriculture, labor, and Head Start agencies. Provides the U.S. Congress with data, testimony, and recommendations. Conducts research; disseminates results. Holds workshop and seminars. **Libraries: Type:** reference. **Affiliated With:** National Association of State Directors of Migrant Education. **Formerly:** (1983) Interstate Migrant Education Task Force. **Publications:** *Issugram,* periodic ● *Migrant Education: A Consolidated View* ● *News Report,* quarterly ● *Students of the Nation.* Brochure ● Annual Report, annual ● Directory, periodic ● Proceedings, 3/year. **Conventions/Meetings:** periodic meeting.

12322 ■ Los Ninos

287 G St.
Chula Vista, CA 91910
Ph: (619)426-9110 (619)434-6230
Free: (866)567-6466
Fax: (619)426-6664
E-mail: info@losninosinternational.org
URL: http://www.losninosinternational.org
Contact: Elisa Sabatini, Exec. Dir.
Founded: 1974. **Staff:** 7. **Budget:** $500,000. **Description:** Works to help communities organize nutrition, family gardens, tree-planting, and school ecology programs in Tijuana and Mexicali, Mexico. Provides weekend and weeklong educational field trips in Tijuana. **Convention/Meeting:** none. **Libraries: Type:** reference. **Publications:** *Border Connections,* quarterly. Newsletter. Alternate Formats: online ● *Nutricion Familiar.* Manual. Covers nutrition. ● *Tres Semillas Para Una Mejor Alimentation.* Manual. Covers agriculture.

12323 ■ Migrant Health Promotion

224 W Michigan Ave.
Saline, MI 48176
Ph: (734)944-0244
Free: (800)700-6927
Fax: (734)944-1405
E-mail: info@migranthealth.org
URL: http://www.migranthealth.org
Contact: Kimberly Kratz, Exec. Dir.
Founded: 1983. **Staff:** 30. **Budget:** $2,500,000. **Languages:** English, Spanish. **Description:** Implements community-based health education programs for migrant farm workers. **Libraries: Type:** reference. **Awards:** Sister Donna Zetah Education Fund. **Frequency:** annual. **Type:** scholarship. **Recipient:** for camp health aide. **Formerly:** National Migrant Workers Council; (1979) Sisters Concerned for the Rural Poor; (1997) National Migrant Workers Council; (1999) Midwest Migrant Health Information Office. **Publications:** *Camp Health Aide Manual* (in English and Spanish) ● *Directory for Migrant Health Services-Midwest Regional* (in English and Spanish), annual. **Price:** free. **Circulation:** 30,000. Alternate Formats: online. Also Cited As: *La Guia* ● *Health for the Nation's Harvesters: A History of the Migrant Health Program in its Economic and Social Setting* ● *La Esperanza* (in English and Spanish), 2-3/year. Newsletter. Contains health education tips, advocacy tools and networking opportunities for Promotores(as). Alternate Formats: online ● *Nuestra Salud (Our Health)* (in English and Spanish), annual. Videos. Features a two-part women's health video series. ● Brochures ● Annual Report, annual. Alternate Formats: online.

12324 ■ National Alliance for Migrant and Seasonal Farmworker Vocational Rehabilitation (NAMSFVR)

c/o Noemi Ortega, Pres.
105-B S 6th St.
Sunnyside, WA 98944
Ph: (509)837-2525
Fax: (509)837-7745
E-mail: noemi.ortega@wsmconline.org
URL: http://www.ccer.org/migrant/homemig.htm
Contact: Noemi Ortega, Pres.
Founded: 2001. **Description:** Seeks to enhance career, employment and other opportunities for Migrant and Seasonal Farmworkers with disabilities and their families. Promotes collaboration, coordination; and sharing of knowledge and resources among individuals and other entities with similar goals. Helps coordinate and facilitate vocational rehabilitation services for persons with disabilities and their families. Supports efforts to involve former or current Migrant and Seasonal Farmworkers as practitioners of Vocational Rehabilitation. **Publications:** Brochure. Alternate Formats: online.

12325 ■ National Association of State Directors of Migrant Education (NASDME)

c/o Shawn Cockrum, Pres.
1001 Connecticut Ave. NW, Ste.915
Washington, DC 20036
Ph: (202)775-7780
E-mail: mlap@mlap.org
URL: http://www.nasdme.org
Contact: Shawn Cockrum, Pres.
Founded: 1975. **Members:** 50. **Staff:** 3. **Description:** State directors of migrant education programs funded under Title One Part C, of the Elementary and Secondary Education Act. Purpose is to keep members informed and to establish program policy and direction. Fosters interstate coordination and cooperation among programs. Sponsors annual national conference. **Awards:** NASDME Award of Excellence. **Frequency:** annual. **Type:** recognition ● NASDME National Conferences Award. **Frequency:** annual. **Type:** recognition. **Committees:** Conference Coordinating; Finance. **Publications:** Also published Giving Migrant Students an Opportunity to Learn (1995). **Conventions/Meetings:** annual National Migrant Education Conference, professional development, training, coordination activities (exhibits) - spring.

12326 ■ National Committee on the Education of Migrant Children (of the National Child Labor Committee) (NCEMC)

1501 Broadway, Ste.1908
New York, NY 10036
Ph: (212)840-1801
Fax: (212)768-0963
E-mail: nclckapow@aol.com
Contact: Jeffrey Newman, Exec.Dir.
Founded: 1963. **Description:** Promotes special projects and programs for the education of the children of migrant agricultural workers. **Convention/Meeting:** none. **Absorbed:** Migrant Children's Fund.

12327 ■ National Farm Worker Ministry (NFWM)

438 N Skinker Blvd.
St. Louis, MO 63130
Ph: (314)726-6470
Fax: (314)726-6427
E-mail: vnesmith@nfwm.org
URL: http://www.nfwm.org
Contact: Virginia Nesmith, Exec. Dir.
Founded: 1971. **Members:** 40. **Staff:** 6. **Description:** Seeks to bring together persons and resources "committed to supporting the farm workers' nonviolent struggle for dignity and a measure of justice". Does not itself engage in organizing farm workers but works directly with and supports the United Farm Workers of America, Farm Labor Organizing Committee, the Farmworker Association of Florida, and the Northwest Treeplanters and Farm Workers United (see separate entries). **Computer Services:** Online services, announcement list. **Supersedes:** (1920)

Migrant Ministry. **Publications:** *NFWM News & Views*, semiannual. Newsletter. Provides information for "advocacy action on behalf of farmworkers". **Price:** free to those who contribute to the Ministry. **Circulation:** 10,000. Alternate Formats: online ● *Worship Resources on Farm Work Justice* (in English and Spanish). Booklet. Alternate Formats: online. **Conventions/Meetings:** semiannual board meeting.

Migration

12328 ■ International Social Service, United States of America Branch (ISS-USA)
207 E Redwood St., Ste.300
Baltimore, MD 21202
Ph: (443)451-1200
Fax: (443)451-1220
E-mail: iss-usa@iss-usa.org
URL: http://www.iss-usa.org
Contact: Ms. Julie Gilbert Rosicky, Exec. Dir.
Founded: 1924. **Staff:** 12. **Budget:** $100,000. **National Groups:** 150. **Languages:** English, French, Spanish. **Multinational. Description:** International social work agency assisting individuals, families, and children requiring casework counseling and other help because of problems related to family separation or migration across national boundaries. Gives service in problems such as custody and care of children, inter-country adoptions, migration, family reunions, health, rights to benefits, pensions, and socio-legal problems. Undertakes studies and assumes an advocate role on behalf of children in migration across national boundaries. **Libraries: Type:** not open to the public. **Committees:** Task Force on Unaccompanied Refugee Minors. **Formerly:** (2001) International Social Service, American Branch. **Publications:** *Children Abandoned: Guatemala's Young People and Their Search for a Future* (in English and Spanish). Report. Alternate Formats: online ● Annual Report, annual. Alternate Formats: online. **Conventions/Meetings:** annual meeting.

Military Families

12329 ■ Sons and Daughters In Touch (SDIT)
PO Box 1596
Arlington, VA 22210
Free: (800)984-9994
E-mail: tony@sdit.org
URL: http://www.sdit.org/member.htm
Contact: Tony Cordero, Chm.
Founded: 1990. **Membership Dues:** general/associate, $20-$25 (annual) ● contributing, $50 (annual) ● patron, $100 (annual) ● benefactor, $1,000 (annual). **Description:** Provides support to sons and daughters and other family members of those who died or remain missing as a result of the Vietnam war. Addresses highschool and college classes in hopes of providing education on the historical and emotional legacy of war. **Computer Services:** Mailing lists, of members ● online services, discussion group. **Publications:** *Legacies*, quarterly. Newsletter. Alternate Formats: online.

Mining

12330 ■ United States Mine Rescue Association (USMRA)
PO Box 1010
Uniontown, PA 15401
Ph: (724)366-5272
E-mail: usmra@usmra.com
URL: http://www.usmra.com
Contact: Vernon Demich, Pres.
Multinational. Description: Works to serve mining and mine rescue personnel around the world. Advocates for improved mine rescue training. Reports worldwide mine disasters from around the world.

Missing Children

12331 ■ Association of Missing and Exploited Children's Organizations (AMECO)
PO Box 19668
Alexandria, VA 22320-0668
Ph: (703)838-8379
Free: (877)263-2620
Fax: (703)549-3787
E-mail: info@amecoinc.org
URL: http://www.amecoinc.org
Contact: Ms. Wendy Jolley-Kabi, Natl. Coor.
Founded: 1994. **Membership Dues:** regular, $200 (annual). **Local Groups:** 38. **Multinational. Description:** Aims to build and nurture an association of credible, ethical and effective non-profit organizations that serve missing and exploited children and their families.

12332 ■ The Child Connection (TCC)
2210 Meadow Dr., Ste.28
Louisville, KY 40218
Ph: (502)459-6888
Fax: (502)459-8899
E-mail: childk-9@iglou.com
URL: http://www.childconnection.org
Contact: Keith Herron Sr., Search Coor.
Founded: 1992. **Multinational. Description:** Works to search for missing and exploited children throughout all of U.S. and Canada. Aids and assists local law enforcement and other federal agencies in the recovery of missing children. Acts as a liaison between law enforcement and parents. Aims to prevent child abductions through educational awareness. **Publications:** Newsletter.

12333 ■ Committee for Missing Children (CMC)
242 Stone Mountain St.
Lawrenceville, GA 30045
Ph: (678)376-6265
Free: (800)525-8204
Fax: (678)376-6268
E-mail: info@findthekids.org
URL: http://findthekids.org
Contact: David C. Thelen, CEO
Founded: 1991. **Multinational. Description:** Serves as a clearinghouse for information on missing and abducted children and the laws that govern the missing children field. Assists parents of missing and abducted children by providing the help they deserve and ensuring that their rights are protected. Distributes images of missing children in elementary schools throughout the USA. Provides a link among non-profit child-find organizations and Non Governmental Organizations (NGO's) throughout the world. **Telecommunication Services:** electronic mail, findthekids@compuserve.com. **Publications:** Newsletter. **Price:** free.

12334 ■ Polly Klaas Foundation (PKF)
PO Box 800
Petaluma, CA 94953
Ph: (707)769-1334 (707)769-4050
Free: (800)587-4357
Fax: (707)769-4019
E-mail: info@pollyklaas.org
URL: http://www.pollyklaas.org
Contact: Robert De Leo, Exec. Dir.
Founded: 1993. **Description:** Aims to educate the public on the prevention of child abduction and aid in the search for missing children; provides support for legislative and regulatory protection for children. **Additional Websites:** http://www.stopfamilyabductionsnow.org. **Projects:** Stop Family Abductions Now.

12335 ■ Take Root
PO Box 930
Kalama, WA 98625
Ph: (360)673-3720
Free: (800)ROOT-ORG
Fax: (360)673-3732

E-mail: contact_ed@takeroot.org
URL: http://www.takeroot.org
Contact: Liss Hart-Haviv, Exec. Dir.
Founded: 2002. **Members:** 40. **Description:** Provides peer support to victims of parental abductions. Advocates healing and continued research into the short and long term impacts of such abductions. Conducts emotional outreach programs to increase awareness of the impact of parental abduction on children and adults. **Publications:** *Seeds*. Newsletter. **Price:** free for members.

12336 ■ Team H.O.P.E (Help Offering Parents Empowerment)
310 Pensdale St.
Philadelphia, PA 19128
Free: (866)305-4653
URL: http://www.teamhope.org
Founded: 1998. **Staff:** 13. **Description:** Assists families with missing children by offering counsel, resources, empowerment and emotional support from a trained volunteer who has had or still has a missing child. Enhances the skills of volunteers and provides them with the tools needed to assist families with missing children. **Computer Services:** Information services, abductions, runaways and missing adult children resources ● online services, missing person identity.

Missing Persons

12337 ■ American Association for Lost Children (AAFLC)
539 Fred Rogers Dr.
Latrobe, PA 15650
Ph: (724)537-6970
Free: (800)375-5683
URL: http://www.aaflc.org
Contact: Mark R. Miller, Contact
Founded: 1987. **Staff:** 1. **Budget:** $100,000. **Description:** Aims to locate and return missing children. Conducts investigative work on behalf of parents, along with educating, counselling and encouraging the parents. Supporters are companies, businesses and individuals.

12338 ■ Doe Network
c/o Todd Matthews
121 Short St.
Livingston, TN 38570
Ph: (931)397-3893
Fax: (931)823-9821
E-mail: doenetadminteam@gmail.com
URL: http://www.doenetwork.org
Contact: Helene Wahlstrom, Admin./Webmaster
Founded: 2001. **Multinational. Description:** Addresses the issue of missing persons. Works to assist law enforcement in solving cases concerning unexplained disappearances and unidentified victims from North America, Australia and Europe. Cooperates with several missing person, law enforcement agencies and medical examiners.

12339 ■ International Federation of Family Associations of Missing Persons from Armed Conflicts (IFFAMPAC)
PO Box 6888
Rockford, IL 61125
Fax: (815)637-4259
E-mail: info@iffampac.org
URL: http://www.iffampac.org
Contact: Jane E. Durgom-Powers, Founder/Pres.
Founded: 2003. **Multinational. Description:** Aims to help and assist families in coping with the loss of family members due to armed conflict. Focuses on the surviving families of armed conflict who face social, economic, legal and cultural challenges concerning the issues of the missing and their families. Coordinates the securing of humanitarian aid to family members. Identifies and advocates improvements in local country laws to protect the rights of the family members of missing persons. Improves opportunities for economic assistance to the families.

12340 ■ Outpost for Hope
7405 Greenback Ln., No. 147
Citrus Heights, CA 95610-5603
Ph: (916)965-4673
E-mail: info@outpostforhope.org
URL: http://www.outpostforhope.org
Contact: Libba Phillips, Founder/CEO

Founded: 2001. **Description:** Advocates for under-represented missing and unidentified persons and their families. Assists families of missing loved ones. Provides awareness through education and support for families in their efforts to locate missing loved ones. **Telecommunication Services:** electronic mail, libbahope@yahoo.com.

12341 ■ Search Reports, Inc./Central Registry of the Missing
Address Unknown since 2007

Founded: 1980. **Staff:** 5. **Description:** Distributes publication containing missing persons flyers and detailed data on unidentified deceased individuals to 45,000 groups, including: municipal, county, state, and federal law enforcement agencies; medical facilities; social services agencies such as youth shelters, runaway homes, and counseling services. Objective is to locate missing persons including juvenile runaways, child victims of custodial snatchings, and missing adults. Participates in seminars; researches news media data; compiles statistics. Encourages local development of citizen volunteer rehabilitation and preventive programs. **Libraries: Type:** reference. **Holdings:** books, clippings. **Subjects:** missing persons, forensic anthropology and medicine. **Publications:** *National Missing Persons Report*, 3/year. Directory. Contains listing of missing persons cases with photographs, physical descriptions, medical data, and work and behavioral patterns. **Price:** included in membership dues. ISSN: 1041-3022. **Circulation:** 45,000. **Advertising:** not accepted.

Multiple Birth

12342 ■ National Organization of Mothers of Twins Clubs (NOMOTC)
PO Box 700860
Plymouth, MI 48170-0955
Ph: (248)231-4480
Free: (877)540-2200
E-mail: info@nomotc.org
URL: http://www.nomotc.org
Contact: Dawn Keller, Exec. Sec.

Founded: 1960. **Members:** 23,500. **Membership Dues:** individual affiliate in U.S., $40 (annual) ● individual affiliate outside U.S., $50 (annual) ● professional affiliate in U.S., $55 (annual) ● professional affiliate outside U.S., $80 (annual). **Staff:** 1. **Budget:** $325,000. **Local Groups:** 475. **Description:** Support group for parents of twins and higher order multiples promoting research and education. Cooperates and participates in medical and psychological research projects. **Libraries: Type:** reference. **Subjects:** twinning, bibliography, incidence of multiple births. **Publications:** *Bereavement*. Booklet. **Price:** included in membership dues; $8.00 for nonmembers ● *Higher Order Multiples*. Booklet. **Price:** included in membership dues ● *NOMOTC's Notebook*, bimonthly. Magazine. Contains articles about multiple births and women's issues. **Price:** $15.00 for nonmembers in U.S.; $25.00 for nonmembers outside U.S. ● *Placement of Multiple Birth Children in School*. Booklet. **Price:** included in membership dues ● *Twins to Quints*. Book. **Price:** $22.00 plus shipping and handling ● Annual Report, annual ● Reports. **Price:** included in membership dues ● Survey. **Price:** included in membership dues. **Conventions/Meetings:** annual convention.

12343 ■ The Triplet Connection (TTC)
PO Box 429
Spring City, UT 84662
Ph: (435)851-1105

Fax: (435)462-7466
URL: http://www.tripletconnection.org
Contact: Janet L. Bleyl, Founder/Pres.

Founded: 1983. **Members:** 20,000. **Membership Dues:** regular, in U.S., $25 (annual) ● regular, outside U.S., $29 (annual). **Staff:** 7. **Description:** Parents and expectant parents of triplets or larger multiple births. Works to help families prepare and deal with high-risk multiple pregnancy and birth, and aftermath of such births. Acts as support group for members. Provides information on issues of relevance, including breastfeeding and medical sources. Offers advice on prevention of premature birth. Reports on experiences of families of multiple births. Compiles statistics on multiple births, and makes data available to expectant parents and medical researchers. Maintains Tender Hearts, a group which offers support to families of multiple births who have lost one or more of their babies. **Awards:** Higher Order Multiples. **Frequency:** periodic. **Type:** recognition. **Boards:** Scientific Advisory. **Funds:** The Triplet Connection. **Publications:** *Exceptional Pregnancies - A Survival Guide to Parents Expecting Triplets or More*. Book. Contains help for parents expecting triplets or more. **Price:** $16.95 ● *Exceptional Pregnancies: A Survival Guide to Parents Expecting Twins*. Book. **Price:** $16.95 ● *The Triplet Connection—Newsletter*, quarterly. Reports on multiple pregnancy and the problems faced by the birth and care of these children. Includes medical updates. **Price:** $22.00/year in U.S.; $29.00/year outside U.S.; $20.00 multiple years in U.S.; $27.00 multiple years outside U.S. **Circulation:** 7,000. **Advertising:** accepted ● Articles ● Books. **Conventions/Meetings:** annual convention and workshop.

12344 ■ Twinless Twins Support Group International (TTSGI)
PO Box 980481
Ypsilanti, MI 48198-0481
Free: (888)205-8962
E-mail: contact@twinlesstwins.org
URL: http://www.twinlesstwins.org
Contact: Michelle Getchell, Exec. Dir.

Founded: 1986. **Members:** 2,200. **Membership Dues:** regular, $50 (annual). **Staff:** 4. **Budget:** $28,000. **Regional Groups:** 12. **Languages:** English, French, German, Spanish. **Multinational. Description:** Twins (all multiples) who have lost their twin (through death or disappearance) and others dealing with multiple birth losses. Seeks to help twins, whose twin has died, in dealing with their grief. Helps parents and siblings support the surviving twin in their family. **Libraries: Type:** reference. **Holdings:** 200; archival material, artwork, books, films, photographs, video recordings. **Subjects:** twins, multiple births, parenting, counseling. **Computer Services:** database, membership. **Formerly:** Twinless Twins Support Group. **Publications:** *Living Without Your Twin*. Book. **Price:** $18.95 ● *Twin Loss*. Book. **Price:** $18.95 ● *Twinless Times*, quarterly. Newsletter. Includes scientific articles, stories, book reviews, events and artwork. **Price:** included in membership dues. **Circulation:** 2,500. **Advertising:** accepted. **Conventions/Meetings:** annual conference, with lectures, group therapy and information for professionals (exhibits).

12345 ■ Twins Foundation (TF)
PO Box 6043
Providence, RI 02940-6043
Ph: (401)751-8946
Fax: (775)245-1480
E-mail: tf-inquiry1a@twinsfoundation.com
URL: http://www.twinsfoundation.com
Contact: Kay Cassill, Founding Pres.

Founded: 1983. **Members:** 2,045. **Membership Dues:** single (in U.S.), $25 (annual) ● twins joining together (in U.S.), $35 (annual) ● institutional (in U.S.), $55 (annual) ● single (international), $32 (annual) ● twins joining together (international), $42 (annual) ● institutional (international), $62 (annual). **Staff:** 3. **Description:** Serves as primary research information center on twins and other multiples. Provides support to the twins, their families, the media, medical, and social scientists and the general

public through publications, National Twin Registry and multi-media resource center. **Libraries: Type:** reference. **Holdings:** archival material, books, photographs. **Subjects:** twins, multiple births, statistics, celebrity multiple births. **Awards:** Hall of Fame. **Frequency:** periodic. **Type:** recognition. **Computer Services:** database, twin registry. **Publications:** *Cumulative Index of Twins Letter*, annual. **Price:** $25.00 in U.S., plus shipping and handling; $5.00 outside U.S., plus shipping and handling. ISSN: 0743-748X ● *On Twins & Language Idioglossia, Mutism & Other Problems*. Booklet. **Price:** $13.00 plus $3 for postage & handling ● *Research Update*. **Price:** $4.00/issue (plus $1 for shipping & handling); $7.00 back issues - domestic; $8.00 back issues - international ● *Should Twins Be Separated in School*. Booklet. Features the discussion of several adult pairs on their early school experiences. **Price:** $12.95 plus $3 for shipping & handling ● *Source Directory*. Booklet. Contains information on pre-birth, birth and early days with multiples as well as specific studies of twins and other multiples. **Price:** $12.95 plus $3 for shipping & handling ● *The Twins Letter*, quarterly. Newsletter. **Price:** included in membership dues; $25.00 /year for institutions; $10.00 for back issues. ISSN: 0743-748X. **Circulation:** 10,000 ● Brochures ● Also publishes fact sheets.

Music

12346 ■ Better World Chorus (BWC)
PO Box 20934
Park West Finance Sta.
New York, NY 10025
E-mail: info@betterworldchorus.org
URL: http://www.betterworldchorus.org

Description: "Seeks to enlist the nation's singers from full music spectrum (pop, hip hop, folk, country, rock, gospel, reggae, blues, heavy metal, etc.) to: join under one musical umbrella; to sing audience participation songs related to non-partisan efforts or charities for the common good that they already (or wish to) champion; and to urge their audiences to volunteer their services".

12347 ■ Early Childhood Music and Movement Association (ECMMA)
805 Mill Ave.
Snohomish, WA 98290
Ph: (360)568-5635
Fax: (360)568-5635
E-mail: adminoffice@ecmma.org
URL: http://www.ecmma.org
Contact: Victoria Stratton, Office Admin.

Membership Dues: full-time student in U.S., $25 (annual) ● retiree (65 and above) in U.S., $45 (annual) ● individual in U.S., $65 (annual) ● per 3 teachers in U.S., $180 (annual) ● full-time student outside U.S., $30 (annual) ● retiree outside U.S., $50 (annual) ● individual outside U.S., $70 (annual) ● supporting business, $325 (annual). **Description:** Advocates for music and movement experiences for children.

Musicians

12348 ■ Musicians' Assistance Program (MAP)
322 W 48th St.
New York, NY 10036
Ph: (212)397-4802
Fax: (212)245-6255
E-mail: map@local802afm.org
URL: http://www.local802afm.org/frames/fs_about.htm
Contact: Janet Becker PhD, Coor.

Description: Offers treatment program for music professionals to recover from alcohol and/or drug addictions. **Publications:** *Year End Clinical Report*, annual.

12349 ■ Musicians' Assistance Program Alumni Association

c/o MAP
817 Vine St., No. 219
Hollywood, CA 90038
Ph: (323)933-3197
Free: (888)627-6271
Fax: (323)993-3198
URL: http://www.map2000.org/alumni.html
Membership Dues: standard, $50 (annual) ● bronze, $100 (annual) ● silver, $500 (annual) ● gold, $1,000 (annual) ● platinum, $2,500 (annual). **Description:** Represents individuals, families and friends of musicians impacted by the Musicians Assistance Program (MAP).

12350 ■ Society of Singers (SOS)

15456 Ventura Blvd., Ste.304
Sherman Oaks, CA 91403
Ph: (818)995-7100
Free: (866)767-7671
Fax: (818)995-7466
E-mail: sos@singers.org
URL: http://www.singers.org
Contact: Jerry F. Sharell, Pres./CEO
Founded: 1984. **Members:** 1,000. **Membership Dues:** individual, $50 ● couple, $100. **Staff:** 5. **Regional Groups:** 1. **Multinational. Description:** Aids professional singers facing financial, medical, and other crises; promotes advancement of vocal arts with vocal arts scholarships to accredited universities. **Awards:** ELLA Award. **Frequency:** annual. **Type:** recognition. **Recipient:** for contribution to the music world. **Publications:** The Voice. Newsletter. Alternate Formats: online.

Native American

12351 ■ American Indian Liberation Crusade (AILC)

4009 S Halldale Ave.
Los Angeles, CA 90062-1851
Ph: (323)299-1810
E-mail: basil@indiancrusader.org
URL: http://www.indiancrusader.org
Contact: Basil M. Gaynor, Pres./Dir.
Founded: 1952. **Members:** 4,000. **Membership Dues:** donor, $25 (annual). **Staff:** 3. **Budget:** $20,000. **Regional Groups:** 1. **Description:** Publicizes the physical and spiritual needs of American Indians and appeals for funds. Supports missionaries on American Indian fields; sponsors summer Bible camps, Bible schools for children, and other charitable programs; provides emergency relief and holiday food distributions. **Publications:** Indian Crusader, quarterly. Newsletter. Covers programs, ministries, and projects of the association. **Price:** included in membership dues. **Circulation:** 8,000. **Conventions/Meetings:** annual board meeting - always February.

12352 ■ American Indian Youth Running Strong (AIYRS)

2550 Huntington Ave., Ste.200
Alexandria, VA 22303-1499
Ph: (703)317-9881
Fax: (703)317-9690
E-mail: info@indianyouth.org
URL: http://www.indianyouth.org
Contact: Lauren Haas Finkelstein, Exec. Dir.
Founded: 1986. **Staff:** 6. **Budget:** $1,200,000. **Description:** Works to help American Indian people meet daily survival needs while creating opportunities for self-sufficiency. Conducts housing, water resource development, domestic violence, organic farming and health care programs. Acts as a resource to preserve and promote Indian culture and values. Offers cultural and language preservation programs. Conducts athletic and recreational activities. Distributes grants nationwide to support infrastructural and cultural endeavors of grassroots American Indian. **Awards: Type:** grant. **Programs:** Culture and Language; Emergency Heat; Housing; Midwifery; Organic Gardens; Wells; Youth. **Formerly:** (1998) Running

Strong for American Indian Youth. **Publications:** Running Strong, quarterly. Newsletter. **Advertising:** accepted ● Annual Report, annual. **Circulation:** 5,000. Alternate Formats: online. **Conventions/Meetings:** quarterly board meeting.

12353 ■ Americans for Indian Opportunity (AIO)

1001 Marquette Ave. NW
Albuquerque, NM 87102
Ph: (505)842-8677
Fax: (505)842-8658
E-mail: aio@aio.org
URL: http://www.aio.org
Contact: Laura Harris, Exec. Dir.
Founded: 1970. **Staff:** 9. **Budget:** $500,000. **Description:** Serves as a catalyst for initiatives and opportunities for native peoples and tribal governments. Incorporates traditional tribal values to promote innovative problem solving, develop leadership, and create contemporary institutions for the new millennium. Implements the American Indian Ambassadors Program, and nurtures a new generation of Indian leaders. Partners with indigenous communities worldwide. **Computer Services:** database, Clearinghouse for Native related information ● mailing lists, American Indians. **Subgroups:** American Indian Ambassadors Program. **Publications:** The Ambassador, quarterly. Newsletter. Alternate Formats: online ● Core Cultural Values. Report ● Messing with Mother Nature Can Be Hazardous to Your Health. Report ● You Don't Have to Be Poor to Be Indian. **Conventions/Meetings:** periodic seminar ● periodic symposium.

12354 ■ First Nations Development Institute (FNDI)

703 3rd Ave., Ste.B
Longmont, CO 80501
Ph: (303)774-7836
Fax: (303)774-7841
E-mail: info@firstnations.org
URL: http://www.firstnations.org
Contact: Mike Roberts, Pres.
Founded: 1980. **Staff:** 20. **Budget:** $3,000,000. **Nonmembership. Description:** Aims to help Native American tribes achieve self-sufficiency using culturally appropriate development methods; promotes economic development and commercial enterprises of reservation-based Indian tribes and non-profit organizations through technical assistance, grants and loans. **Awards:** Eagle Staff Fund. **Type:** grant. **Recipient:** for Native American community based non-profit economic development projects. **Programs:** Grantmaking; Native Assets Research Center; Oweesta - Capital Management and Reservation Lending. **Formerly:** (1991) First Nations Financial Project. **Publications:** Twenty Year Report 1980-2000, annual. Annual Report. Includes a bound version of Timelines 1980-2000 brochure. Alternate Formats: online ● Also publishes resource documents.

12355 ■ Indian Youth of America (IYA)

PO Box 2786
Sioux City, IA 51106
Ph: (712)252-3230
Fax: (712)252-3712
Contact: Patricia Trudell Gordon, Exec.Dir.
Founded: 1978. **Members:** 7. **Staff:** 5. **Description:** Native American organization dedicated to improving the lives of Indian children. Works to provide opportunities and experiences that will aid Indian youth in their educational, career, cultural, and personal growth. Maintains an Indian Child Welfare Program, which attempts to prevent the distressful effects brought on by the breakup of Indian families. Goals of the program are: to inform families, social service agencies, and courts about the rights of Indian people under the Indian Child Welfare Act; to provide referral services to social service agencies in locating tribes and suitable placement for Indian children; to counsel Indian children and their parents and recruit Indian foster homes for Indian children. Sponsors a summer camp program, an after school Indian youth program, and an annual Christmas party for Indian children.

Maintains resource center. **Publications:** Brochure. **Conventions/Meetings:** meeting - 3/year.

12356 ■ Maniilaq Association (MA)

PO Box 256
Kotzebue, AK 99752
Ph: (907)442-7660
Free: (800)478-3312
Fax: (907)442-7830
E-mail: humanresources@maniilaq.org
URL: http://www.maniilaq.org
Contact: Helen A. Bolen, Pres.
Founded: 1966. **Members:** 6,500. **Budget:** $39,000,000. **Regional Groups:** 4. **Local Groups:** 13. **Description:** Tribal organization serving 12 Alaskan Eskimo villages ranging from 60 to 3,000 in population. Works to promote health and social welfare in the Northwest Arctic Borough region of Alaska; preserves and promotes health and social welfare in the Northwest Arctic Borough region of Alaska; preserves and promotes the Eskimo arts, customs, and language; seeks to advance language in all forms; works to stimulate economic activity and social understanding between natives and non-natives. Maintains group home, senior citizen center, nursing wing, social rehabilitation center, youth camp, medical center. Provides women's crisis program, pre-maternal home, and placement and children's services. **Awards: Type:** recognition. **Departments:** Health Services; Tribal Services. **Absorbed:** Kotzebue Area Health Corporation; (1975) Kotzebue Area Health Corp. **Formerly:** (1972) Northwest Alaska Native Association; (1981) Mauneluk Association. **Publications:** Maniilaq Directory, annual ● Northwest Arctic NUNA, 10/year. Newsletter. Includes local news and program information. **Price:** free. **Circulation:** 2,500. **Advertising:** accepted. Alternate Formats: online ● Annual Report, annual ● Also publishes books. **Conventions/Meetings:** annual meeting - always winter.

12357 ■ National Center for American Indian Enterprise Development (NCAIED)

953 E Juanita Ave.
Mesa, AZ 85204
Ph: (480)545-1298
Fax: (480)545-4208
E-mail: ken.robbins@ncaied.org
URL: http://www.ncaied.org
Contact: Kenneth Robbins, Pres./CEO
Founded: 1969. **Staff:** 25. **Budget:** $1,500,000. **Regional Groups:** 3. **National Groups:** 3. **Description:** Promotes business and economic development among American Indians and tribes. Offers business training services to American Indians who own or plan to start businesses in fields including manufacturing, service, construction, retailing, and wholesaling. Assists Indians and tribes in: developing management abilities; assessing operating costs; preparing finance proposals; obtaining financing, bonding, and insurance; controlling the business through effective accounting and information systems; negotiating contracts, leases, and purchases; and planning for future business growth. Provides services such as feasibility studies, site/location analysis, loan packaging, and promotion and fundraising campaigns. Sponsors Management Institute: Training for Indian Managers; conducts youth entrepreneurship programs. Operates the UIDA Group Inc., a development company. **Libraries: Type:** open to the public. **Holdings:** 2,000. **Subjects:** Indian economic development. **Awards:** American Indian Enterprise Award. **Frequency:** annual. **Type:** recognition. **Recipient:** to a corporate citizen with an outstanding commitment to the development and growth of American Indian owned businesses ● American Indian Fellowship in Business. **Type:** recognition. **Recipient:** to American Indian university students enrolled in business studies ● First American Leadership Awards. **Type:** recognition. **Recipient:** to outstanding American Indian leaders and supporters of the American Indian business endeavors ● Indian Progress in Business Achievement Award. **Frequency:** annual. **Type:** recognition. **Recipient:** to outstanding American Indian leaders and to those who support their economic and business development endeavors ●

Jay Silverheels Achievement Award. **Frequency:** annual. **Type:** recognition. **Recipient:** to an outstanding individual of American Indian descent ● **Frequency:** annual. **Type:** scholarship. **Recipient:** to American Indian college or graduate students majoring in business. **Computer Services:** database, Indian reservations and procurement opportunities. **Councils:** Private Industry Advisory. **Divisions:** Business and Economic Development Services; First American Center for Entrepreneurship; Management Services and Training. **Programs:** Community Economic Development; Financial Analysis. **Formerly:** (1989) United Indian Development Association. **Publications:** *Directory of American Indian Businesses*, annual. **Price:** $25.00. **Advertising:** accepted ● *Indian Business and Management*, quarterly. **Conventions/Meetings:** annual American Indian Procurement Conference ● annual competition, golf tournament ● Indian Business Trade Fair - trade show (exhibits) ● annual Indian Progress in Business Awards Banquet - banquet and trade show (exhibits) ● annual Reservation Economic Summit and Business Trade Fair - meeting ● seminar, training and business success ● workshop, for business and pre-business.

12358 ■ National Indian Health Board (NIHB)
101 Constitution Ave. NW, Ste.8-B02
Washington, DC 20001
Ph: (202)742-4262
Fax: (202)742-4285
E-mail: info@nihb.org
URL: http://www.nihb.org
Contact: Stacy A. Bohlen, Exec. Dir.
Founded: 1969. **Members:** 12. **Membership Dues:** individual, $150 (annual) ● non-profit, government, educational, $250 (annual) ● for profit organization, $500 (annual). **Staff:** 6. **Budget:** $425,000. **Regional Groups:** 12. **Description:** Indians of all tribes and natives of Alaskan villages. Advocates the improvement of health conditions which directly or indirectly affect American Indians and Alaskan Natives. Seeks to inform the public of the health condition of Native Americans; represents Indians and their interests. Conducts seminars and workshops on health subjects. Provides technical assistance to members and Indian organizations. **Awards: Type:** recognition. **Recipient:** for nominated individuals who have made significant contributions in the Indian health field. **Telecommunication Services:** electronic mail, jpetherick@nihb.org. **Committees:** Medicare and Medicaid Policy. **Programs:** Strengthening Tribal Management Capabilities in Health and Human Service Delivery. **Publications:** *Conference Report*, annual ● *Health Reporter*, quarterly. Newsletter. Alternate Formats: online ● *Washington Report*. Alternate Formats: online ● Handbook, annual ● Also publishes special reports on health issues and produces audiotapes. **Conventions/Meetings:** annual Consumer's Conference (exhibits).

12359 ■ Native American Community Board (NACB)
PO Box 572
Lake Andes, SD 57356-0572
Ph: (605)487-7072
Fax: (605)487-7964
E-mail: nativewoman@igc.apc.org
URL: http://www.nativeshop.org
Contact: Charon Asetoyer, Exec. Dir.
Founded: 1985. **Staff:** 12. **Budget:** $325,000. **Description:** Works toward the educational, social, and economic advancement of American Indians. Maintains Native American Women Health Education Resource Center, which provides self-help programs and workshops on issues such as fetal alcohol syndrome, AIDS awareness, family planning, domestic abuse and crisis, reproductive rights, and child development. Conducts adult education classes; offers support services to Native Americans seeking employment and educational opportunities. Conducts charitable programs; offers children's services; maintains speakers' bureau and placement service. Compiles statistics; is concerned with treaty and environmental issues involving Native Americans. **Awards:** NACB Scholarship. **Type:** scholarship. **Committees:** Political Action. **Funds:** Scholarship.

Projects: Women and Children in Alcohol. **Publications:** *Wicozanni-Wowapi*, quarterly. Newsletter ● Brochures ● Pamphlets. **Conventions/Meetings:** annual Native Women's Reproductive Rights Conference.

12360 ■ North American Alliance for the Advancement of Native Peoples
29780 Hwy. UU
Keytesville, MO 65261
E-mail: naaanp_ceo@msn.com
URL: http://n.a.a.a.n.p.tripod.com
Contact: Harriet L. Randall, CEO/Pres.
Multinational. Description: Promotes the unification of all Native American tribes and nations with equal treatment for all the peoples regardless of nation. Advances medical research and care, centering on Native American health issues. Fosters family care programs and rehabilitation programs for Native Americans.

12361 ■ United South and Eastern Tribes (USET)
711 Stewarts Ferry Pike, Ste.100
Nashville, TN 37214
Ph: (615)872-7900
Fax: (615)872-7417
E-mail: mcook@usetinc.org
URL: http://usetinc.org
Contact: Michael Cook, Exec. Dir.
Founded: 1969. **Members:** 23. **Staff:** 8. **Description:** Alliance of 23 Indian tribes: Alabama-Coushatta Tribe of Texas; Aroostook Band of Mic Macs; Eastern Band of Cherokee Indians; Chitimacha Tribe of Louisiana; Mississippi Band of Choctaw Indians; Coushatta Tribe of Louisiana; Poarch Band of Creek Indians; Houlton Band of Maliseet Indians; Mashantucket Pequot Indians of Connecticut; Miccosukee Tribe of Indians; Narragansett Indian Tribe; Passamaquoddy Tribe-Indian Township; Passamaquoddy Tribe-Pleasant Point; Penobscot Indian Nation; St. Regis Mohawk; Seminole Tribe of Florida; Seneca Nation of Indians; Tunica-Biloxi Tribe of Louisiana; Wampanoag Tribal Council of Gay Head; Oneida Nation of New York; Catawba Indian Nation; Jena Band of Choctaw Indians; and the Mohegan Tribe of Connecticut. Promotes strength in unity of American Indian tribes and assists tribes in dealing with relevant issues. Fosters better understanding with other races. **Awards:** none. **Awards:** United South and Eastern Tribes Scholarship Fund. **Frequency:** annual. **Type:** scholarship. **Recipient:** to enrolled members of member tribes. **Committees:** Commercial Law, Legislation and Economic Development; Culture and Heritage; Education; EMS and Fire Protection; Health; Housing; Natural Resources; Social Services; Taxation and Legislation; Transportation; Tribal Administration; Tribal Emergency Services; Tribal Justice. **Formerly:** (1978) United Southeastern Tribes. **Conventions/Meetings:** semiannual board meeting, with business/economic development expo (exhibits) ● periodic general assembly (exhibits).

Natural Disasters

12362 ■ GeoHazards International (GHI)
200 Town and Country Village
Palo Alto, CA 94301
Ph: (650)614-9050 (650)283-0343
Fax: (650)614-9051
E-mail: info@geohaz.org
URL: http://www.geohaz.org
Contact: Brian E. Tucker, Pres.
Founded: 1991. **Membership Dues:** student, $25-$30 (annual) ● regular, $100-$125 (annual) ● supporting, $150-$180 (annual) ● contributing, $500-$600 (annual) ● benefactor, $1,000 (annual) ● partner, $10,000 (annual) ● pillar, $50,000 (annual). **Staff:** 23. **Multinational. Description:** Seeks to reduce death and injury caused by earthquakes and other natural hazards in the world's most vulnerable communities. **Publications:** *Issues in Urban EQ Risk*. Book ● *Proyecto RADIUS*. Book ● *Quito Proyecto Para El Manejo*. Book. Alternate Formats: online ●

Seismic Hazard and Building Vulnerability. Book ● *Uses of Earthquake Damage Scenario*. Book. Alternate Formats: online.

Natural Family Planning

12363 ■ American Academy of Fertility Care Professionals (AAFCP)
11700 Studt Ave., Ste.C
St. Louis, MO 63131
Ph: (402)489-3733
Fax: (402)488-6525
E-mail: aafcp@aol.com
URL: http://www.aafcp.org
Contact: Angelique Garcia, Pres.
Founded: 1982. **Members:** 300. **Membership Dues:** active, organizational, $100 (annual) ● associate, $35 (annual) ● student, special, $25 (annual). **Budget:** $75,000. **Description:** Individuals who participate in natural family planning instruction. (Natural family planning refers to methods that do not employ contraceptive devices of any kind, using instead the natural phases of fertility.) Seeks to improve the quality of natural family planning services by establishing specific certification and accreditation requirements for teachers and educational programs. Conducts training programs throughout the U.S. Promotes public recognition and acceptance of natural family planning; disseminates information. **Awards: Type:** recognition. **Commissions:** Accredits; Certification; Service Program. **Committees:** Bylaws; Continuing Education; Ethics; Legislative; Membership; Public Relations; Publication; Science and Research. **Subcommittees:** Awards; Credentials. **Affiliated With:** American Society of Association Executives; Catholic Health Association of the United States. **Formerly:** (2003) American Academy of Natural Family Planning. **Publications:** *Academy Activity*, quarterly. Newsletter. **Advertising:** accepted ● *Certification Directory*, annual ● Membership Directory, annual. **Conventions/Meetings:** annual Business and Educational Conference (exhibits) - always July.

12364 ■ Billings Ovulation Method Association - USA (BOMA-USA)
PO Box 2135
St. Cloud, MN 56302
Ph: (651)699-8139
Fax: (320)654-6486
E-mail: info@boma-usa.org
URL: http://www.boma-usa.org
Contact: Sue Ek, Exec. Dir.
Founded: 1981. **Members:** 500. **Membership Dues:** individual, $30 (annual). **Staff:** 1. **Description:** Works to teach and promote the authentic Billings Ovulation Method in the U.S. by providing teacher training programs, referrals and materials approved by the world headquarters in Melbourne, Australia. **Libraries: Type:** reference. **Holdings:** 3,000; audio recordings, books, monographs, periodicals, video recordings. **Subjects:** natural family planning. **Computer Services:** Mailing lists, of members. **Publications:** *The Billings Method - Using the body's natural signal of fertility to achieve or avoid pregnancy*. Book. **Price:** $19.95, plus shipping and handling ● *The Billings Ovulation Method* (in English and Spanish). Booklet. **Price:** $3.00 plus postage ● *BOMA News*, quarterly. Newsletter. **Price:** included in membership dues. **Circulation:** 500 ● *Teacher's Directory*, semiannual. **Price:** $5.00 ● *Victoria Bulletin*, quarterly. **Price:** included in membership dues. **Conventions/Meetings:** semiannual conference, for NFP teachers and agency directors (exhibits).

12365 ■ Couple to Couple League (CCL)
PO Box 111184
Cincinnati, OH 45211-1184
Ph: (513)471-2000
Free: (800)745-8252
Fax: (513)557-2449
E-mail: ccli@ccli.org
URL: http://www.ccli.org
Contact: Andrew B. Alderson, Exec. Dir.
Founded: 1971. **Membership Dues:** individual, $29 (annual) ● foreign, $48 (annual). **Staff:** 33. **Local**

Groups: 450. **Languages:** Czech, English, French, Hungarian, Polish, Russian, Spanish. **Description:** Assists married and engaged couples interested in natural family planning (a method of spacing pregnancies through reliance on the woman's natural fertility cycle). Believes natural birth control strengthens family bonds and is healthier and more morally acceptable than artificial birth control devices. Sponsors local teaching groups where couples are taught basic natural family planning techniques. Provides special training program for those who wish to become CCL teaching couples. Promotes premarital chastity through speakers and materials. **Libraries: Type:** not open to the public. **Publications:** *The Art of Natural Family Planning* (in Czech, English, French, Hungarian, Polish, Russian, and Spanish). Book. **Price:** $19.95 ● *Breastfeeding and Natural Child Spacing* ● *CCL Family Foundations*, bimonthly. Magazine. **Price:** $38.00 in Canada and Mexico; $48.00 others. Alternate Formats: online ● *Fertility, Cycles and Nutrition* ● *Marriage is for Keeps*. Book ● *Marriage is for Keeps, Wedding Edition*. Book ● *Sex and the Marriage Covenant*. Book ● *Annual Report*, annual. Alternate Formats: online. **Conventions/Meetings:** biennial convention (exhibits).

12366 ■ Family of the Americas Foundation (FAF)
c/o Dallas Diocesan NFP Centers
321 Calumat Ave.
Dallas, TX 75211
Ph: (214)467-1966 (301)627-3346
Free: (800)443-3395
Fax: (214)528-1180
E-mail: family@upbeat.com
URL: http://www.familyplanning.net
Contact: Mercedes Wilson, Pres.
Founded: 1977. **Members:** 270. **Staff:** 5. **Description:** Promotes teaching of the Ovulation Method of birth regulation in which a woman is taught to recognize the fertile phase of her cycle by identifying the appearance of mucus secreted from the cervix. Maintains permanent teacher training centers; certifies instructors of the method. Conducts regional, national, and international workshops to present new scientific information concerning the method and to train new and existing teachers; assists in the planning and implementation of local workshops. Sponsors teacher training and preparation of instructional materials for developing countries. Holds conferences to educate the public about the use of natural family planning in developed and developing countries. Participates in conferences with medical, religious, government, and educational personnel. Assists parents in providing effective sex education for their children; teaches adolescents about fertility and the importance of accepting responsibility for their sexual behavior. Maintains library of natural family planning reference materials. Offers standard teacher certification programs for Master Teachers and Master Trainers. **Telecommunication Services:** electronic mail, familyplanning@yahoo.com. **Formerly:** (1982) World Organization of the Ovulation Method-Billings, U.S.A.; (2001) Family of the Americas. **Publications:** *Appreciating Your Fertility*. Video ● *Charting Coach*. Contains diskette for Windows or Macintosh. ● *If You Love Me.Show Me* (in English and Spanish). Video. Alternate Formats: CD-ROM ● *Love and Family: Raising a Traditional Family in a Secular World* (in English and Spanish). Book ● *Love and Fertility* (in English and Spanish). Video ● *Natural vs. Artificial* (in English and Spanish). Video ● *Nature's Method*. Alternate Formats: CD-ROM.

Neurological Disorders

12367 ■ Dementia Advocacy and Support Network International (DASNI)
PO Box 1645
Mariposa, CA 95338
E-mail: morrisff@aol.com
URL: http://www.dasninternational.org
Contact: Morris Friedell, Dir.
Founded: 2000. **Multinational**. **Description:** Encourages people with dementia to improve the quality of their own life by advocating for others. Promotes respect and dignity for persons with dementia. Provides a forum for the exchange of information. Encourages support mechanisms such as local groups, counseling groups and Internet linkages. Advocates for services for people with dementia. Empowers people with dementia to actively participate in their own care and treatment. **Publications:** Reports. Alternate Formats: online.

Nonprofit Organizations

12368 ■ HandsNet
PO Box 90477
San Jose, CA 95109
Fax: (408)904-4874
E-mail: info@handsnet.org
URL: http://www.handsnet.org
Contact: Michael Saunders, CEO
Founded: 1987. **Description:** Works for online information exchange among human services community. **Computer Services:** Online services, Web-Clipper. **Telecommunication Services:** electronic mail, help@handsnet.org ● electronic mail, editor@handsnet.org. **Programs:** Training. **Conventions/Meetings:** seminar ● workshop.

12369 ■ National Center on Nonprofit Enterprise (NCNE)
205 S Patrick St.
Alexandria, VA 22314
Ph: (703)548-7978 (757)214-5084
Fax: (501)637-2807
E-mail: ncne@nationalcne.org
URL: http://www.nationalcne.org
Contact: Richard Brewster, Exec. Dir.
Membership Dues: individual, $75 (annual) ● organization with a budget of $500,000, $250 (annual) ● organization with a budget of up to $5,000,000, $500 (annual) ● organization with a budget above $5,000,000, $750 (annual). **Staff:** 6. **Description:** Represents academic researchers, business leaders, consultants and non-profit practitioners supporting a comprehensive program of educational activities and services addressing economic and business decision-making issues facing the nonprofit sector. **Telecommunication Services:** electronic mail, richard@nationalcne.org. **Councils:** Business Advisory; Practice Advisory; Research Advisory. **Programs:** Site Visit. **Sections:** Institutional Consortium. **Publications:** *Nonprofit Quarterly*. Magazines. Provides with values-based management information and proven articles. **Price:** $49.00 per year; $98.00 per two-year; $14.95 per single issue. **Conventions/Meetings:** conference and seminar.

Nonviolence

12370 ■ Men Stopping Violence (MSV)
533 W Howard Ave., Ste.C
Decatur, GA 30030
Ph: (404)270-9894
Fax: (404)270-9895
E-mail: msv@menstoppingviolence.org
URL: http://www.menstoppingviolence.org
Contact: Shelley Serdahely, Exec. Dir.
Founded: 1982. **Description:** Works to dismantle belief systems, social structures and institutional practices that oppress women and children and dehumanize men. Provides training and consultation services. Educates the public in order to end men's violence against women. **Programs:** Development Internship; Public Policy Internship. **Projects:** Community Restoration.

Obesity

12371 ■ Council on Size and Weight Discrimination (CSWD)
PO Box 305
Mount Marion, NY 12456-0305
Ph: (845)679-1209
Fax: (845)679-1206
E-mail: info@cswd.org
URL: http://www.cswd.org
Contact: Ms. Miriam Berg, Pres.
Founded: 1991. **Nonmembership. Description:** Works to educate the public and influence the decision makers to end discrimination based on body size, shape, or weight. Counsels victims of weight discrimination. Promotes Health At Every Size, including nutrition and exercise for health rather than solely for the purposes of weight loss. Promotes the concept that strong, capable, attractive people come in all sizes. **Publications:** *Annotated Bibliography on Size Acceptance, Anti-Dieting, Eating Disorders, and Related Issues*. Book.

12372 ■ International Size Acceptance Association (ISAA)
PO Box 82126
Austin, TX 78758
Ph: (206)600-3089
E-mail: directisaa@gmail.com
URL: http://www.size-acceptance.org
Contact: Mr. Allen Steadham, Dir.
Founded: 1997. **Members:** 2,500. **Membership Dues:** regular, $20 (annual). **Multinational. Description:** Promotes size acceptance and helps end weight-based discrimination and bigotry. **Awards:** Size Friendly Business Award. **Frequency:** periodic. **Type:** recognition. **Recipient:** for businesses that promote self respect, fitness, and healthy food choices. **Publications:** *Without Measure*, 3/year. Magazine. **Price:** free online. Alternate Formats: online.

12373 ■ Largesse, the Network for Size Esteem
74 Woolsey St.
New Haven, CT 06513-3719
Ph: (203)499-4747
E-mail: largesse@eskimo.com
URL: http://www.largesse.net
Contact: Ms. Karen Stimson, Dir.
Founded: 1983. **Nonmembership. Multinational. Description:** An international clearinghouse for information on size diversity empowerment. Aims to create personal awareness and social change which promotes a positive image, health, and equal rights for people of size. **Libraries: Type:** reference. **Holdings:** articles, audiovisuals, clippings, papers, periodicals, photographs. **Subjects:** size esteem, size discrimination, health issues, body image, fat feminist herstory. **Computer Services:** Electronic publishing, online fat feminist archives. **Subgroups:** Largesse Presse.

12374 ■ National Association to Advance Fat Acceptance (NAAFA)
PO Box 22510
Oakland, CA 94609
Ph: (916)558-6880
Fax: (916)558-6881
E-mail: naafa@naafa.org
URL: http://www.naafa.org
Contact: Laura Wills, Sec.
Founded: 1969. **Members:** 3,000. **Membership Dues:** regular, $35 (annual) ● joint, $15 (annual) ● philanthropist, $500 (annual) ● benefactor, $250 (annual) ● supporting, $100 (annual) ● sustaining, $60 (annual) ● regular - outside North America, $50 (annual) ● student, senior, individual with limited income, $5-$15 (annual) ● auxiliary, $5 (annual). **Staff:** 2. **Budget:** $200,000. **Local Groups:** 40. **Description:** Aims to improve the quality of life for fat people. Encourages the average fat person to improve his/her low self-esteem. Members are both fat and thin; the latter group is composed mostly of husbands, wives, or supporters of fat people. Opposes discrimination against fat people, including discrimination in advertising, employment, fashion, medicine, insurance, social acceptance, the media, schooling, and public accommodations. Monitors legislative activity and litigation affecting fat people. Sponsors letter writing campaigns; through Fat Activist Task Force, also sponsors pen pals, and other programs. Operates sales department for books of interest to

members. Assists research programs. Maintains speakers' bureau and public education materials. **Awards:** Big Success: NAAFA Hall of Fame. **Type:** recognition. **Recipient:** for well-known fat personalities who have served as positive role models ● Distinguished Achievement Award. **Frequency:** annual. **Type:** recognition. **Recipient:** for work towards the betterment of fat people. **Computer Services:** Mailing lists. **Committees:** Activism; Employment; Health; Insurance; Legislative; Local Chapters; Pen Pal; Publicity; Research; Teen/Young Adult. **Subgroups:** Couples; Diabetics; Fat Men; Feminists; Lesbians/Bisexuals/Gays; Midsize Women; Military Issues; People with Sleep Apnea; Teenage; Women Size 48 and Larger. **Formerly:** (1989) National Association to Aid Fat Americans. **Publications:** *NAAFA Newsletter*, quarterly. Provides help in fighting discrimination on the basis of size in employment, medicine, insurance, social activities, media, and other areas. **Price:** included in membership dues. **Circulation:** 10,000. **Advertising:** accepted. **Conventions/Meetings:** annual conference and symposium (exhibits) - always mid-August.

12375 ■ O-Anon General Service Office (OGSO)

Address Unknown since 2006
Description: Families and friends of compulsive overeaters. Provides support groups that offer opportunities for the sharing of experiences and viewpoints. Purposes are to: offer comfort, hope, and friendship to families and friends of compulsive overeaters; learn to grow spiritually by working with the Twelve Steps, patterned after Alcoholics Anonymous World Services; give understanding and encouragement to the compulsive overeater. Works in cooperation with Overeaters Anonymous, but is not affiliated with that organization. **Publications:** Newsletter, 3-4/year. **Price:** $5.00/year. **Advertising:** not accepted. **Conventions/Meetings:** periodic retreat ● workshop.

12376 ■ Overeaters Anonymous World Service Office (OA WSO)

PO Box 44020
Rio Rancho, NM 87174-4020
Ph: (505)891-2664
Fax: (505)891-4320
E-mail: info@oa.org
URL: http://www.overeatersanonymous.org
Contact: Naomi Lippel, Managing Dir.
Founded: 1960. **Members:** 65,000. **Staff:** 13. **Budget:** $1,400,000. **Regional Groups:** 6,500. **Multinational. Description:** Individuals who have a desire to stop eating compulsively. Program is a twelve-step self-help fellowship patterned after that of Alcoholics Anonymous. **Libraries: Type:** reference. **Holdings:** audio recordings, books, video recordings. **Subjects:** stories of recovery from compulsive overeating, how to work the Twelve Steps. **Computer Services:** database, meeting locations worldwide ● information services, 15 questions to determine if you are a compulsive overeater ● online services, catalog for OA literature. **Additional Websites:** http://www.overeatersanonymous.com, http://www.oa.org. **Committees:** Institutions; International; Literature; Twelfth-Step-Within. **Publications:** *A Step Ahead*, quarterly. Newsletter. Sent to all OA groups. ● *Lifeline*, monthly. Magazine. Features stories of recovery written and submitted by OA members. **Price:** $15.00/year. ISSN: 1051-9467. **Circulation:** 10,000. ● Audiotapes ● Books ● Pamphlets ● Also publishes posters, wallet cards, and recovery medallions. **Conventions/Meetings:** meeting, for young people and newcomers ● annual World Service Business Conference, to elect trustees, amend bylaws, adopt new business policies, and provide information to delegates through presentations and workshops ● triennial World Service Convention.

12377 ■ TOPS Club (Take Off Pounds Sensibly)

4575 S 5th St.
Milwaukee, WI 53207
Ph: (414)482-4620
Free: (800)932-8677

E-mail: topsinteractive@tops.org
URL: http://www.tops.org
Contact: Barb Cady, Pres.
Founded: 1948. **Members:** 230,000. **Membership Dues:** in U.S., $24 (annual) ● in Canada, $30 (annual). **Staff:** 40. **Multinational. Description:** Weight control self-help association using group dynamics, competition, and recognition to help members lose weight. Advocates physician-approved individual programs, and physician-set weight goals. **Also Known As:** Take Off Pounds Sensibly; TOPS. **Publications:** *TOPS News*, monthly. Magazine. Contains member news, success stories, inspirational materials, features on diet-related subjects, chapter news, medical questions and answers. **Price:** included in membership dues. **Circulation:** 309,512 ● Also publishes monograph on nutrition and other membership literature. **Conventions/Meetings:** annual International Recognition Days - meeting.

Organizations

12378 ■ Advocacy Institute (AI)

1629 K St. NW, Ste.200
Washington, DC 20006-1629
Ph: (202)777-7575
Fax: (202)777-7577
E-mail: info@advocacy.org
URL: http://www.advocacy.org
Contact: Jerry Hauser, Pres./CEO
Founded: 1985. **Staff:** 16. **Budget:** $2,000,000. **Description:** Strengthens the capacity of social and economic justice advocates to influence and change public policy. Provides training and counseling to environmental, consumer, health, and other non-profit public interest organizations on how to deal effectively with public policy issues. **Awards:** Leadership for a Changing World. **Frequency:** annual. **Type:** recognition. **Recipient:** for advocates of public policy issues ● **Type:** monetary. **Recipient:** for leaders tackling tough community problems. **Telecommunication Services:** electronic bulletin board, health and smoking issues. **Publications:** *Going to the Well*. Video ● Newsletter. **Price:** $25.00. Alternate Formats: online ● Annual Report, annual. Alternate Formats: online.

12379 ■ BoardSource

1828 L St. NW, Ste.900
Washington, DC 20036-5114
Ph: (202)452-6262
Free: (800)883-6262
Fax: (202)452-6299
E-mail: mail@boardsource.org
URL: http://www.boardsource.org
Contact: Deborah S. Hechinger, Pres./CEO
Founded: 1988. **Members:** 13,000. **Membership Dues:** individual, $99 (annual). **Staff:** 38. **Budget:** $6,500,000. **Description:** Seeks to improve the effectiveness of non-profit organizations by strengthening their boards of directors. Provides solutions and tools to improve board performance. Facilitates development of knowledge about boards. **Libraries: Type:** not open to the public. **Holdings:** 900. **Subjects:** governance and management of non-profits. **Computer Services:** Online services, publication. **Telecommunication Services:** additional toll-free number, (877)892-6273. **Formerly:** (2002) National Center for Nonprofit Boards. **Publications:** *Board Member*, 10/year. Newsletter. **Price:** $68.00 /year for members. ISSN: 1058-5419. **Circulation:** 13,000. Alternate Formats: online ● *Nonprofit Board Answer Book* ● *Nonprofit Board Resource*. Catalog. Contains lists of publications. ● Annual Reports, annual. **Conventions/Meetings:** annual National Leadership Forum - conference (exhibits).

12380 ■ Council on Foundations (COF)

1828 L St. NW, Ste.300
Washington, DC 20036
Ph: (202)466-6512
Fax: (202)785-3926

E-mail: info@cof.org
URL: http://www.cof.org
Contact: Steve Gunderson, Pres./CEO
Founded: 1949. **Members:** 2,100. **Staff:** 100. **Budget:** $15,000,000. **Description:** Community, private, operating, and corporate grant making foundations; corporations with philanthropic programs. Provides consultative and other services to its membership. Sponsors meetings to enable grantmakers, trustees, officers, and executives to keep abreast of current trends in the field of philanthropy and to share experience in the administration of philanthropic funds. Through regular mailings, membership is kept informed of legislative and other developments in the philanthropic field. Sponsors research and educational programs. **Libraries: Type:** reference; not open to the public. **Awards:** Distinguished Grantmaker Award. **Frequency:** annual. **Type:** recognition. **Recipient:** for lifetime achievement in philanthropy ● Henry Hampton Awards. **Frequency:** annual. **Type:** recognition. **Recipient:** for outstanding documentary film or video ● Paul Ylvisaker Award for Public Policy Engagement. **Frequency:** annual. **Type:** recognition. **Recipient:** for outstanding work on public policy issues ● Robert W. Scrivner Award. **Frequency:** annual. **Type:** recognition. **Recipient:** for creativity in grantmaking ● Wilmer Shields Rich Award. **Frequency:** annual. **Type:** recognition. **Recipient:** for communications. **Committees:** Annual Conference; Communications; Community Foundations; Corporate Grant Making; Family Foundations; Inclusiveness; International; Legislation and Regulations; Management; Media and Public Affairs; Research. **Formerly:** National Committee on Foundations and Trusts for Community Welfare; National Council on Community Foundations. **Publications:** *Foundation News and Commentary*, bimonthly. Contains news and opinion on foundations. **Price:** $60.00/year. **Advertising:** accepted. Alternate Formats: online. **Conventions/Meetings:** annual Fall Conference for Community Foundations (exhibits) ● annual Family Foundations Conference ● annual Institute for New Grantmakers - conference.

12381 ■ Foundation Center (FC)

79 5th Ave.
New York, NY 10003-3076
Ph: (212)620-4230
Free: (800)424-9836
Fax: (212)807-3677
E-mail: feedback@foundationcenter.org
URL: http://www.fdncenter.org
Contact: Sara L. Engelhardt, Pres.
Founded: 1956. **Budget:** $8,200,000. **Description:** Acquires, organizes, and disseminates information about foundations and the grants they award; collects and makes available published information about the foundation field and about its relationships to government and society, including historical records and supporting references in related fields. Conducts a fee based Associates Program that provides special services, including answers to fundraising questions, photocopies by mail and custom computer searches. Sponsors orientations on foundation and funding research. Maintains research libraries in New York City, Washington, DC, San Francisco, CA, Cleveland, OH, and Atlanta, GA. Network of 240 cooperating collections providing free public access to information on foundations, with particular emphasis on service to the grant-seeking public. **Libraries: Type:** reference. **Awards: Type:** grant ● **Type:** grant. **Computer Services:** database, accessible through DIALOG. **Formerly:** (1968) Foundation Library Center. **Publications:** *AIDS Funding: A Guide to Funding* ● *Corporate Foundation Profiles*, annual. **Price:** $155.00 ● *Foundation Directory*, annual. Features detailed listings of more than 7900 largest U.S. foundations including contact person and financial data. **Price:** $215.00 for hard cover; $185.00 for soft cover ● *Foundation Grants Index*, annual. Lists foundation grants of $10,000 or more, including foundation name, grant recipient, grant amount, purpose, and duration. **Price:** $165.00 ● *Foundation Grants to Individuals*, periodic. Lists grants available to the individual. Arranged in categories such as scholarship and loans, fellowships, foreign grants,

and medical assistance. **Price:** $65.00 ● *Foundation 1,000*, annual. Directory. Provides detailed information on the nation's 1000 largest foundations. **Price:** $295.00/year ● *Foundations of the 1990s*. Directory. **Price:** $150.00 ● *Grant Guides*, annual. **Price:** $75.00 ● *Guide to U.S. Foundations, Their Trustees, Officers, and Donors*, annual. Directory. Lists grant-making foundations. **Price:** $215.00 ● *National Directory of Corporate Giving*. Offers authoritative information on over 2800 corporate philanthropic programs. **Price:** $225.00 ● *National Guide to Foundation Funding in Arts and Culture* ● *National Guide to Foundation Funding in Health*. **Price:** $150.00 ● *National Guide to Foundation Funding in Higher Education*. **Price:** $145.00 ● *National Guide to Funding in Aging*. **Price:** $95.00 ● *New York State Foundations: A Comprehensive Directory*, periodic. **Price:** $180.00 ● Bibliographies ● Books ● Brochures ● Annual Report, annual. Alternate Formats: online ● Newsletters. **Price:** free. **Conventions/Meetings:** periodic Proposal Writing Seminars, Meet the Grantmakers (exhibits).

12382 ■ International Society for Third-Sector Research (ISTR)
559 Wyman Park Bldg.
3400 N Charles St.
Baltimore, MD 21218-2688
Ph: (410)516-4678
Fax: (410)516-4870
E-mail: istr@jhu.edu
URL: http://www.istr.org
Contact: Margery Berg Daniels, Exec. Dir.
Founded: 1992. **Members:** 775. **Membership Dues:** individual (with journal), $100 (annual) ● individual (without journal), $85 (annual) ● student (with journal), $80 (annual) ● student (without journal), $35 (annual) ● institutional (with journal), $200 (annual) ● reduced (with journal), $25 (annual) ● individual sponsor (with journal), $150 (annual) ● supporting (with journal), $1,000 (annual). **Staff:** 2. **Regional Groups:** 4. **Multinational. Description:** Open to those with an interest in the study of nonprofit, charitable, and voluntary organizations. Promotes interdisciplinary study of nonprofit organizations. Serves as a forum for exchange of information among members; facilitates communication between members, policy makers, and the public. Maintains networks and affinity groups structured on geographic and thematic lines. Gathers and disseminates information on nonprofit organizations. Conducts educational programs. Holds biennial research conferences. **Computer Services:** Mailing lists ● online services, listserv. **Telecommunication Services:** electronic mail, istr-l@yorku.ca. **Subgroups:** African Research Network; Asia/Pacific Research Network; European Research Network; Latin America and the Caribbean Research Network. **Publications:** *Inside ISTR*, quarterly. Newsletter. **Price:** included in membership dues ● *VOLUNTAS*, quarterly. Journal ● Membership Directory, annual. Alternate Formats: online. **Conventions/Meetings:** biennial conference (exhibits).

12383 ■ Management Assistance Group (MAG)
1555 Connecticut Ave. NW, 3rd Fl.
Washington, DC 20036-1103
Ph: (202)659-1963
Fax: (202)659-3105
E-mail: mag@magmail.org
URL: http://www.managementassistance.org
Contact: Inca A. Mohamed, Exec. Dir.
Founded: 1972. **Staff:** 10. **Budget:** $500,000. **Description:** Counsels non-profit social-purpose groups about organizational, developmental or managerial problems. Helps to identify problem areas and to recommend changes. Writes articles and sponsors discussions and workshops on organizational development matters. **Formerly:** (1983) Planning and Management Assistance Project of the Center for Community Change.

12384 ■ National Black United Fund (NBUF)
40 Clinton St.
Newark, NJ 07102

Ph: (973)643-5122
Free: (800)223-0866
E-mail: nbuf@nbuf.org
URL: http://www.nbuf.org
Contact: William T. Merritt, Pres./CEO
Founded: 1972. **Members:** 80. **Staff:** 7. **Budget:** $700,000. **Regional Groups:** 13. **State Groups:** 10. **Local Groups:** 12. **National Groups:** 47. **Description:** Provides financial and technical support to projects serving the critical needs of black communities nationwide. Local affiliates and federations solicit funds through payroll deduction to support projects in the areas of education, health and human services, economic development, social justice, arts and culture, and emergency needs. Programs supported by NBUF emphasize self-help, volunteerism, and mutual aid. Founded and administers National Black United Federation of Charities and NBUF Community Economic Development Resource Center. Provides nonprofit advocacy program. **Committees:** Economic Market Development; International Task Force. **Publications:** *NBUF Board Training Guidebook: A Guide for Volunteer Board Members Who Join Community Non-Profit Organizations* ● *NBUF News and Notes*, semiannual. Newsletter ● Annual Report. **Conventions/Meetings:** annual Collaboration Networking & Partnering Conference, federation members, affiliates, and other nonprofit organizations - always June.

12385 ■ North Star Fund
520 8th Ave., 22nd Fl.
36th and 37th St.
New York, NY 10018
Ph: (212)620-9110
Fax: (212)620-8178
E-mail: info@northstarfund.org
URL: http://www.northstarfund.org
Contact: Hugh Hogan, Exec. Dir.
Founded: 1979. **Members:** 15. **Staff:** 5. **Regional Groups:** 14. **Languages:** English, Spanish. **Description:** Community-based alternative foundations providing grants to grass roots projects organizing for progressive social change. Sponsors a donor-advised program that bestows grants on a national basis. Offers services and occasional seminars for foundation donors on such topics as tax methods and implications of donating money for social change. Sponsors conferences and occasional retreats for wealthy individuals. **Libraries: Type:** reference. **Awards: Frequency:** annual. **Type:** grant. **Recipient:** to local activists and organizers. **Publications:** *North Star News*, annual. Newsletter. Alternate Formats: online ● *Robin Hood Was Right*. Book ● Annual Report, annual. Alternate Formats: online ● Catalog, annual. **Conventions/Meetings:** annual National Donor Conference - meeting.

12386 ■ Resource Development Services
Address Unknown since 2006
Founded: 1980. **Staff:** 2. **Nonmembership. Description:** Develops communication, financial planning, programming, promotional services, and resources for community, cultural, educational, and human services organizations. Convention/Meeting: none.

12387 ■ Social Contract Press
445 E Mitchell St.
Petoskey, MI 49770
Ph: (231)347-1171
Free: (800)352-4843
Fax: (231)347-1185
URL: http://www.thesocialcontract.com
Contact: Wayne Lutton PhD, Ed.
Founded: 1981. **Description:** Works as an umbrella foundation for projects that are primarily concerned with natural resource conservation, national unity maintenance, and problems faced by partially sighted people. Seeks to provide projects with a streamlined, efficient, and well-established administrative structure. Projects include: ProWild, which advocates native wildlife ranching as opposed to cattle ranching; Raptor Research, which sponsors field study of great birds of prey in the Upper Great Lakes region; U.S. Lighthouse for the Partially Sighted, which aids individuals with sight problems. **Formerly:** (1987)

U.S., Inc.; (2005) U.S. **Publications:** *The Social Contract*, quarterly. Journal. Addresses interrelated topics of environment, population control, and immigration reform. **Price:** $25.00/year in North America; $31.00/year outside North America. **Circulation:** 1,500.

Orthotics and Prosthetics

12388 ■ A Leg To Stand On (ALTSO)
267 Fifth Ave., Ste.301
New York, NY 10016
Ph: (212)683-8805
Fax: (212)683-8813
E-mail: info@altso.org
URL: http://www.altso.org
Contact: C. Mead Welles, Pres./Co-Founder
Multinational. Description: Works to help transform the lives of disabled children through the use of corrective surgery and the provision of prosthetic limbs. Seeks to provide access to education, work and community opportunities to disabled children. Aims to conduct community outreach, awareness campaigns and prosthetic/orthotic training. **Telecommunication Services:** electronic mail, mwelles@altso.org. **Publications:** Newsletter. Alternate Formats: online.

Parents

12389 ■ American Fathers Coalition (AFC)
c/o American Coalition for Fathers and Children
1718 M St. NW, Ste.187
Washington, DC 20036
Free: (800)978-3237
Fax: (703)442-5313
E-mail: info@acfc.org
URL: http://www.acfc.org
Contact: Dr. Stephen Baskerville, Pres.
Description: Federal lobbying arm of the American Coalition for Fathers and Children; promoting rights of fathers. **Affiliated With:** National Congress for Fathers and Children.

12390 ■ Association for Recognizing the Life of Stillborns (ARLS)
601 W Rand Rd., No. 102
Arlington Heights, IL 60004
Ph: (847)749-4258
E-mail: linpav100@yahoo.com
Contact: Linda Pavlak, Exec. Officer
Founded: 1983. **Description:** Offers Certificates of Life (for a fee) to parents who have experienced a miscarriage, stillbirth, or early infant death to serve as tangible evidence that their babies were once alive. Conventions/Meetings: none.

12391 ■ Attachment Parenting International (API)
PO Box 210208
Nashville, TN 37221
Ph: (615)298-4334
Fax: (615)646-7480
E-mail: info@attachmentparenting.org
URL: http://www.attachmentparenting.org
Contact: Lysa Parker MS, Exec. Dir./Co-Founder
Founded: 1994. **Membership Dues:** individual, family, $35 (annual) ● individual, family (in Canada, Australia, Belgium, Ireland, New Zealand and UK), $30 (annual) ● premium support, $75 (annual). **Languages:** English, Spanish. **Multinational. Description:** Promotes parenting practices that create strong and healthy emotional bonds between children and their parents. Helps to reduce or prevent child abuse, behavioral disorders, criminal acts and other serious social problems. Provides assistance in forming Attachment Parenting support groups. Seeks to strengthen family ties and increase awareness of the importance of secure attachment through research, education, advocacy and support. **Publications:** *Attachment Parenting: The Journal of Attachment Parenting International*, quarterly. Contains articles about all aspects of parenting. **Price:** included in membership dues. **Advertising:** accepted. Alternate Formats: online.

12392 ■ Bereavement Services

c/o Gundersen Lutheran Medical Foundation
1900 S Ave.
La Crosse, WI 54601
Ph: (608)775-4747
Free: (800)362-9567
Fax: (608)775-5137
E-mail: info@bereavementprograms.com

Founded: 1981. **Languages:** English, Spanish. **Description:** Seeks to promote bereavement care by developing and continually improving bereavement training and support materials and by providing respectful, compassionate care for those experiencing a loss. Provides resources specific to perinatal loss. **Formerly:** RTS Bereavement Services; (1992) Resolve Through Sharing. **Publications:** *Art of Compassionate Death Notification.* Manual. Kit includes facilitator manual, video, manuals and pocket cards for up to 20 participants. **Price:** $565.00 ● *Compassionate Bereavement Care: A Model for Program Growth.* Manual ● *RTS Connection,* quarterly. Newsletter. Provides information only for those who have completed RTS training. **Circulation:** 20,000. ● *When a Baby Dies.* Book ● *When a Baby Dies.* Video ● Brochures. Contains information on ectopic pregnancy, stillbirth, newborn death, fathers' grief, grandparents' grief, and children's grief. ● Booklet. Contains support materials for bereaved parents or health care professionals. **Price:** free.

12393 ■ Catholic Parents Network

4012 29th St.
Mount Rainier, MD 20712
Ph: (301)277-5674
E-mail: newwaysm@verizon.net
URL: http://www.newwaysministry.org
Contact: Frank Debernardo, Exec. Dir.

Founded: 1995. **Members:** 270. **Staff:** 3. **Regional Groups:** 11. **Description:** Catholic parents of gay and lesbian children. Exchanges information, sponsors and conducts yearly retreats, and provides counseling and consultation to individuals and groups regarding homosexuality and Catholicism. Offers educational programs and a speakers bureau. **Publications:** *Families Helping Families,* quarterly. Newsletter. **Price:** $5.00/year. **Circulation:** 300. **Conventions/Meetings:** annual workshop.

12394 ■ Center for Loss in Multiple Birth (CLIMB)

PO Box 91377
Anchorage, AK 99509
Ph: (907)222-5321
E-mail: climb@pobox.alaska.net
URL: http://www.climb-support.org
Contact: Jean Kollantai, Founder

Founded: 1987. **Members:** 750. **Budget:** $10,000. **Description:** Bereaved parents and others affected by multiple birth loss. Provides peer support for parents who have experienced the death of one or more twins or other multiple birth children during pregnancy, birth, infancy, or childhood. Promotes public awareness of the incidence of multiple birth loss and the needs of bereaved parents. Offers materials for professionals, twins clubs and loss support groups providing services to bereaved parents. Maintains collection of resources available on multiple birth loss; provides assistance to researchers and journalists. **Libraries: Type:** open to the public. **Holdings:** 150. **Subjects:** multiple birth loss. **Publications:** *Our Newsletter,* quarterly. Includes listings of resources available on multiple birth loss and names of parents who wish to share their experiences. **Circulation:** 800. **Advertising:** accepted ● Special issues and materials on specialized topics.

12395 ■ The Compassionate Friends (TCF)

PO Box 3696
Oak Brook, IL 60522-3696
Ph: (630)990-0010
Free: (877)969-0010
Fax: (630)990-0246

E-mail: nationaloffice@compassionatefriends.org
URL: http://www.compassionatefriends.org
Contact: Patricia Loder, Exec. Dir.

Founded: 1972. **Membership Dues:** chrysalis, $1,000 (annual) ● sustaining, $500 (annual) ● sponsoring, $300-$499 (annual) ● supporting, $100-$299 (annual) ● participating, $40-$99 (annual). **Staff:** 7. **Budget:** $594,200. **Local Groups:** 600. **Languages:** English, Spanish. **Description:** Provides support to families who have experienced the death of a child of any age, from any cause. **Libraries: Type:** reference. **Formerly:** Society of the Compassionate Friends. **Publications:** *We Need Not Walk Alone,* quarterly. Newsletter. **Price:** $20.00/year. **Circulation:** 5,500 ● Annual Report ● Audiotapes ● Pamphlets ● Videos. **Conventions/Meetings:** annual regional meeting, for bereaved families.

12396 ■ Depression After Delivery (DAD)

91 E Somerset St., Ste.C
Raritan, NJ 08869
Ph: (908)541-9712
Fax: (908)541-9713
E-mail: dadorg@earthlink.net
URL: http://www.depressionafterdelivery.com
Contact: Brenda Bredahl MA, Contact

Founded: 1985. **Members:** 350. **Membership Dues:** individual, $30 (annual) ● mental health professional and professional with MD, $125 (annual). **National Groups:** 40. **Description:** Women who have experienced postpartum adjustment problems, depression, or psychosis; professionals in the health care industry. Provides support to members and their families. Acts as a clearinghouse for information on postpartum depression and psychosis. Maintains referral service. **Publications:** *Heartstrings,* semiannual. Newsletter. **Price:** included in membership dues. **Conventions/Meetings:** annual meeting ● annual regional meeting.

12397 ■ Fairview Pregnancy and Newborn Loss Information (PILC)

Address Unknown since 2007

Founded: 1983. **Members:** 2,500. **Staff:** 3. **Budget:** $98,000. **Description:** Parents who have suffered a miscarriage, stillbirth, or infant death; concerned health care professionals and volunteers. Seeks to increase public awareness and establish a network of support for families affected by perinatal death. Provides referral services for parents who wish to contact support groups, counselors, or other couples who have also experienced a perinatal death. Offers assistance to speakers and workshop directors seeking to contact churches, schools, and service organizations interested in conducting perinatal bereavement assistance programs. Produces educational materials dealing with funeral arrangements, guidelines for the friends and families of bereaved parents, high-risk pregnancies, and the grief of surviving siblings. Offers perinatal bereavement seminars and consulting services. Maintains speakers' bureau. Sponsors annual Pregnancy and Infant Loss Awareness Month in October; distributes information packets. **Awards: Type:** recognition. **Formerly:** (2004) Pregnancy and Infant Loss Center. **Publications:** *Loving Arms Newsletter,* quarterly. Features articles, poems, and resources on miscarriage, stillbirth, and infant death. **Price:** included in membership dues. **Circulation:** 2,500. **Advertising:** not accepted. **Conventions/Meetings:** annual meeting and workshop (exhibits) - always April, Minneapolis, MN.

12398 ■ Family and Home Network

PO Box 545
Merrifield, VA 22116
Ph: (703)352-1072
Free: (866)352-1075
Fax: (703)352-1076
E-mail: fahn@familyandhome.org
URL: http://www.familyandhome.org
Contact: Cathy Myers, Exec. Dir.

Founded: 1984. **Members:** 10,000. **Membership Dues:** associate, $10-$500. **Staff:** 12. **Description:** Serves as a forum for the exchange of information among parents. Provides information at congressional hearings. Conducts research; compiles statistics; maintains speakers' bureau. Advocates for recognition of the critical importance of nurturing children and acknowledgment of the short and long-term benefits to society of parents sharing time with their children. **Committees:** Congressional Liaison; Development; Editorial; Marketing; Parenting Education; Public Relations; Research. **Formerly:** (2003) Mothers at Home. **Publications:** *Blow-Drying the Frog and Other Parenting Adventures.* Book. Contains comic, real stories of family life. **Price:** $12.00 plus shipping and handling ● *Discovering Motherhood.* Book. **Price:** $5.00/copy; $4.00 for two or more copies ● *Motherhood: Journey Into Love.* Book ● *Welcome Home,* monthly. Magazine. Aimed at affirming the important and valuable work of parents. **Price:** $22.00 in U.S.; $25.00 in Canada; $32.00 overseas.

12399 ■ Fatherhood Project (FP)

c/o Families and Work Institute
267 5th Ave., 2nd Fl.
New York, NY 10016
Ph: (212)465-2044
Free: (800)978-3237
Fax: (212)465-8637
E-mail: jlevine@familiesandwork.org
Contact: James A. Levine PhD, Dir.

Founded: 1981. **Description:** Seeks to encourage the development of new options for male involvement in child rearing. Examines aspects of male parenthood in the areas of employment, law, education, social and supportive services, and health. Conducts research on innovative programs and policies throughout the U.S. supporting men in nurturing roles. Conducts educational projects. **Publications:** *Fatherhood U.S.A..* Book.

12400 ■ First Sunday (FS)

c/o Pope John XXIII Hospitality House
1050 Porter St.
Detroit, MI 48226
Ph: (313)965-4451
Fax: (313)965-4453
Contact: Rev. Russell Kohler, Advisor

Founded: 1974. **Members:** 200. **Description:** Couples who have experienced the death of a child and who wish to join with other couples as they make their individual and family adjustments. Seeks to help couples understand their many grief reactions through meetings with psychiatric social workers, clergy, and physicians. Couples actively share their experiences with each other and in seminars for clergy, health professionals, and police personnel-in-training. Holds liturgy for families on the first Sunday of each month. Sends artists to terminally ill children's homes, nursing homes, and the hematology/oncology waiting room at Children's Hospital of Michigan. Has developed summer arts day camp St. Patricks retreat in Irish Hills, MI. Funds hospitality home for chemotherapy ambulatory patients as well as for relatives of the critically ill. Offers transportation to six area hospitals for stranded chemotherapy and dialysis patients. **Committees:** Counseling; Education; Liturgy.

12401 ■ Great Dads

PO Box 7537
Fairfax Station, VA 22039
Ph: (703)830-7500
Fax: (703)968-2811
URL: http://www.greatdads.org
Contact: Dr. Bob Harmin, Founder/Pres.

Description: Motivates fathers to turn their hearts to their children. Trains fathers to be great dads. **Publications:** *Great Dad,* quarterly. Newsletter. Includes seminar information and schedule of events. **Price:** $12.00 per issue. **Alternate Formats:** online.

12402 ■ Holistic Moms Network (HMN)

PO Box 408
Caldwell, NJ 07006
Free: (877)465-6667
E-mail: info@holisticmoms.org
URL: http://www.holisticmoms.org
Contact: Nancy Massotto, Chair/Exec. Dir./Founder

Founded: 2002. **Membership Dues:** individual, $35 (annual) ● family, $50 (annual). **Description:** "Aims to generate national awareness, education and support for holistic parenting, and to provide a nurturing, open-minded, and respectful community for parents to share these ideals. Encourages holistic moms (and dads)to find others with whom they can connect, and to continually educate themselves and their families about alternative health, mindful parenting, and natural healing. Works with moms to create local chapters in their communities that will provide them with a happy, healthy forum for their mothering styles, and will bring them together in an environment that respects and honors their lifestyle and parenting choices". **Programs:** Helping Moms In Need. **Publications:** *The Wise Mom*, quarterly. Newsletter. Contains information about holistic living and parenting. Alternate Formats: online.

12403 ■ National Association of At-Home Mothers (NAAHM)
406 E Buchanan Ave.
Fairfield, IA 52556
Ph: (515)472-3202
Fax: (515)469-3068
E-mail: webmaster@at-home-mothers.com
URL: http://www.athomemothers.com
Contact: Jeanette Lisefski, Founder
Founded: 1996. **Membership Dues:** $18 (annual). **Staff:** 5. **Description:** Provides information, services, support and encouragement to at-home mothers and those women who would like to become at-home mothers. Assists mothers with earning an income from home and flexible work opportunities. Offers help with increasing self-esteem and improving parenting skills. Currently Inactive. **Awards:** Start a Home Business Grant. **Frequency:** quarterly. **Type:** grant. **Publications:** *At-Home Mother*, quarterly. Magazine. **Advertising:** accepted ● *At-Home Motherhood Resource Catalog* ● *At-Home Mother's Info Guides*. Bulletins ● *At-Home Mother's NEws*, quarterly.

12404 ■ National Association of Entrepreneurial Parents (NAEP)
PO Box 320722
Fairfield, CT 06432
Ph: (203)371-6212
Fax: (203)371-6212
E-mail: members@en-parent.com
URL: http://www.en-parent.com/NAEP.htm
Contact: Lisa Roberts, Dir.
Founded: 1999. **Membership Dues:** life, $50. **Staff:** 1. **For-Profit. Description:** Parents with home-based business careers. Seeks to assist "parents who are looking to balance work and family on their own terms." Facilitates networking among entrepreneurial parents; provides ad opportunities for members; organizes support groups for members; makes available discount programs and services to members. Conducts home career counseling sessions. **Computer Services:** Mailing lists, of members. **Publications:** *The Entrepreneurial Parent*. Book ● *EPnews*, quarterly. Newsletter. Features success strategies for home-based professionals. **Circulation:** 2,000. **Advertising:** accepted. Alternate Formats: online ● *How to Raise a Family and a Career Under One Roof*. Book. Contains valuable insight and useful advice on launching and growing a home career side by side with a growing family. **Price:** $15.00. Alternate Formats: online ● *Membership Directory*, annual. **Price:** $15.00. Alternate Formats: online.

12405 ■ National Association of Mothers' Centers (NAMC)
64 Div. Ave., Ste.LL7
Levittown, NY 11756
Ph: (516)520-2929
Free: (800)645-3828
Fax: (516)520-1639
E-mail: info@motherscenter.org
URL: http://www.motherscenter.org
Contact: Linda Lisi Juergens, Exec. Dir.
Founded: 1975. **Members:** 3,000. **Staff:** 4. **Budget:** $207,000. **Local Groups:** 40. **Description:** Network of community centers. Addresses the isolation and stress of parenting. Provides an open forum for learning about child development and parenting. Creates an environment of inquiry and research regarding the needs and experiences of women and families. Validates and builds on participants' skills and talents. Offers on-site programming at corporations. A new initiative focuses on the economic impact of motherhood. **Additional Websites:** http://www.mothersoughttohaveequalrights.org, http://www.MOTHERS-BookBag.org. **Formerly:** Mothers' Center Development Project. **Publications:** *How to Start a Mothers' Center*. Handbook. Offers advice for starting a center. **Price:** $5.00 ● *Mothers' Center*. Manual ● *NAMC News*, quarterly. Newsletter. **Conventions/Meetings:** National Conference, with workshops and keynote (exhibits) - every 1-1/2 to 2 years ● annual Work/Life Conference, with workshops, keynote and panel - usually in Nassau/Suffolk County, NY.

12406 ■ National Foster Parent Association (NFPA)
7512 Stanich Ave., Ste.6
Gig Harbor, WA 98335
Ph: (253)853-4000
Free: (800)557-5238
Fax: (253)853-4001
E-mail: info@nfpainc.org
URL: http://www.nfpainc.org
Contact: Karen Jorgenson, Exec. Dir.
Founded: 1972. **Members:** 2,500. **Membership Dues:** regular, $35 (annual) ● local affiliate, $50 (annual) ● state affiliate, $75 (annual) ● agency, $100 (annual) ● life, $1,000. **Staff:** 6. **Budget:** $300,000. **Regional Groups:** 10. **State Groups:** 49. **Local Groups:** 65. **Languages:** English, Spanish. **Description:** Foster parents, child social service line workers and administrators, and citizen child-advocates; interested associations. Seeks to identify and advocate the needs of children in foster care and those who care for them. Offers technical assistance and organizational skills training to state and local foster parent associations. Works to improve the foster parenting image nationwide and educate the courts, legislators, and the public to the needs of children in the foster care system. Has established a communication network among child advocacy organizations and developed a model recruitment plan to promote organized recruitment, development, and retention of foster family homes. Informs foster parents of their legal rights; encourages mandatory parenting skills training and a minimum requirement of pre-service training for all foster parents. Maintains speakers' bureau. **Libraries:** Type: reference. **Subjects:** foster care. **Awards:** NFPA Scholarship Fund. **Frequency:** annual. **Type:** scholarship. **Recipient:** for birth, foster, adopted youth in foster homes. **Committees:** Education; Public Relations. **Projects:** Public Education. **Publications:** *National Foster Parent Association—National Advocate*, quarterly. Magazine. Covers foster care issues nationwide; includes legislative news, innovative programs, and personal articles by foster parents. **Price:** included in membership dues; $35.00 for nonmembers. **Circulation:** 2,500. **Advertising:** accepted ● Monographs ● Pamphlets ● Papers ● Reports. **Conventions/Meetings:** annual Education Conference - general assembly (exhibits) - always May.

12407 ■ National Infertility Network Exchange (NINE)
PO Box 204
East Meadow, NY 11554
Ph: (516)794-5772
Fax: (516)794-0008
E-mail: info@nine-infertility.org
URL: http://www.nine-infertility.org
Contact: Ilene Stargot, Pres.
Founded: 1988. **Membership Dues:** individual, $40 (annual). **Description:** Assists individuals and couples suffering from infertility. Supports the decision of legal and medical means to build families as well as the decision to remain childfree. Provides workshops in pursuing adoption. Offers educational programs and referral services; advocates on behalf of participants. Maintains Speaker's Bureau. Answers inquiries from national level. **Special Interest Groups:** Adoption; Childfree; Female Factor Infertility; Male Factor Infertility; Miscarriage; Multiple Loss; Unexplained Infertility. **Publications:** *News from NINE*, bimonthly. Newsletter. **Conventions/Meetings:** monthly meeting.

12408 ■ National Parenting Association (NPA)
1841 Broadway, Rm. 808
New York, NY 10023
Ph: (212)315-2333
Free: (800)709-8795
Fax: (212)315-2336
E-mail: info@parentsunite.org
Contact: Sylvia Ann Hewlett, Chair
Founded: 1993. **Membership Dues:** supporter, $25 (annual) ● contributor, $50 (annual) ● donor, $100 (annual) ● sponsor, $250 (annual) ● benefactor, $1,000 (annual) ● advocate, $500 (annual). **Description:** Works to make parenting a higher priority in our personal lives and on the public agenda through research, communications, and non-partisan advocacy. Committed to developing family friendly policies in workplaces and the wider community. **Computer Services:** Mailing lists. **Task Forces:** Parenting for the 21st Century. **Publications:** *High-Achieving Women, 2001*, periodic. Report. Survey of high-achieving women and sample of men. **Price:** $10.00 electronic; $20.00 paper ● *The Parent Vote*. Report. National survey of parents. Alternate Formats: online ● *Parents' Voice Issues Guide*, periodic. Handbook ● *Taking Parenting Public: The Case for a New Social Movement*. Book. **Price:** $22.95 ● *What Will Parents Vote For in New York?*, periodic. Report. Survey of New York State and New York City parents. Alternate Formats: online ● *What Will Parents Vote For?*, periodic. Report. **Conventions/Meetings:** annual board meeting.

12409 ■ National Parents Association (NPA)
Main Sta., Box 1993
Valparaiso, IN 46384-1993
E-mail: npa@bixxo.com
URL: http://www.bixxo.com/npa
Contact: Larry Evans, Contact
Founded: 1989. **Members:** 5,000. **Membership Dues:** regular, $12 (annual) ● low income household, $6 (annual). **Description:** Parents interested in sharing ideas on raising children. Conducts educational programs. **Awards:** Parent-of-the-Month. **Frequency:** monthly. **Type:** recognition. **Recipient:** for parents who have the best ideas on raising children. **Publications:** *Parent to Parent: Parents Club News*, bimonthly. Newsletter. **Price:** included in membership dues. ISSN: 1073-8665 ● *Raising Responsible Children*. Handbook. **Price:** $8.95 for members; $14.95 for nonmembers ● Bulletins.

12410 ■ Parents' Action For Children
1875 Connecticut Ave. NW, Ste.650
Washington, DC 20009
Ph: (202)238-4878
Fax: (202)986-2539
E-mail: info@parentsaction.org
URL: http://www.parentsaction.org
Contact: Norman Rosenberg, Pres./CEO
Founded: 1997. **Description:** Advances the interests of families and young children. Develops parent education materials and connects parents with one another. Fights for issues of early education, health care and high quality child care. **Formerly:** (2004) I Am Your Child Foundation. **Publications:** Newsletter. **Price:** free.

12411 ■ Parents' Choice Foundation (PCF)
201 W Padonia Rd., Ste.303
Timonium, MD 21093
Ph: (410)308-3858
Fax: (410)308-3877
E-mail: info@parents-choice.org
URL: http://www.parents-choice.org
Contact: Claire S. Green, Contact
Founded: 1978. **Membership Dues:** subscriber, $20 (annual). **Description:** Provides parents and professionals with a central source of information about videos, books, toys, games, music, television programs, movies, and computer software. Selections are made by parents, children, teachers, librarians,

and other experts. **Awards:** Parents' Choice Awards. **Frequency:** annual. **Type:** recognition. **Recipient:** for children's books, toys, records, movies, television, videos, magazines, and software. **Programs:** Reading is Power; What-Kids-Who-Don't-Like-To-Read-Like-To-Read. **Publications:** *Look to Learn* (in English and Spanish) ● *Parents' Choice*, quarterly. **Price:** $20.00/year; $28.00/2 years. **Advertising:** accepted ● *Parent's Choice Features*, monthly. Newsletter. Contains information on products, articles and announcements by the foundation sent via email. Alternate Formats: online ● *Read to Achieve* ● *What-Kids-Who-Don't-Like-To-Read, Like-To-Read.* Booklet.

12412 ■ Parents Helping Parents (PHP)

3041 Olcott St.
Santa Clara, CA 95054-3222
Ph: (408)727-5775
Fax: (408)727-0182
E-mail: info@php.com
URL: http://www.php.com
Contact: Mary Ellen Peterson, CEO

Founded: 1976. **Members:** 19,000. **Staff:** 45. **Budget:** $1,700,000. **Languages:** English, Filipino, Japanese, Spanish, Vietnamese. **Description:** Parents, professionals, lay counselors, families, and friends committed to alleviating the problems, hardships, and concerns of families with children having special needs, such as physical, mental, emotional, or learning disabilities; intensive nursery care; preemies; long-term, chronic, or terminal illness due to accident, birth defect, or illness. Helps children with special needs receive the care, services, education, love, hope, respect, and acceptance they deserve. Offers education, support, information, and training for parents to decrease isolation and increase a sense of personal control. Provides a forum for the discussion of financial, social, and emotional needs, ideas, and experiences. Keeps parents abreast of legislation laws affecting education for disabled children. Maintains speakers' bureau. **Libraries: Type:** lending. **Holdings:** 6,000; articles, books, video recordings. **Subjects:** welfare of children with disabilities and special education needs. **Divisions:** ADD and LD; Adult Children with Developmental Disability; ASD Biomedical; Autism and PDD; Autism Parent Club of San Benito County; Childhood Bipolar Disorder; Chinese Support and Information Group; Down Syndrome; Educational Advocacy Workshops; Families for Effective Autism Treatment; Feingold Diet; Integrated Playgroup; Japanese Speaking Support; Ketogenic Diet; Neurofibromatosis; Pediatric Oncology; Seizures Support Network Group; Sibling Workshops; Spanish-Speaking (Puedo); Vietnamese. **Programs:** CIRCLES: Intimacy and Relationships Education; Early Intervention; Kids on the Block Puppets; Siblings. **Publications:** *Communicating with Parents of Disabled.* Newsletter. **Price:** included in membership dues. **Circulation:** 4,000 ● *Special Addition.* Newsletter. Includes medical and legislative updates, division highlights, association news, and calendar of events. **Price:** included in membership dues; $10.00 /year for nonmembers. Alternate Formats: online ● *Steps to Starting Self-Help.* Manual ● *Visiting Parents.* Books. **Conventions/Meetings:** annual conference and symposium, held in conjunction with Tuberous Sclerosis meeting (exhibits) ● annual symposium (exhibits) - always October in San Jose, CA.

12413 ■ Parents of Murdered Children (POMC)

100 E 8th St., Ste.B-41
Cincinnati, OH 45202
Ph: (513)721-5683
Free: (888)818-POMC
Fax: (513)345-4489
E-mail: natlpomc@aol.com
URL: http://www.pomc.org
Contact: Nancy Ruhe, Exec. Dir.

Founded: 1978. **Members:** 100,000. **Staff:** 4. **Budget:** $200,000. **Description:** Self-help organization for anyone who has had a friend or family member murdered. Offers support and friendship to those who have experienced the violent death of a family member or friend; fosters their physical and emotional health; works to heighten society's awareness of the problems faced by those who survive a homicide victim. Provides information about the grieving process and the criminal justice system as it pertains to survivors of a homicide victim. Establishes self-help and support groups that meet on a regular basis. Distributes literature and provides guest speakers. Prevention programs to stop the violence. **Computer Services:** Information services, survivors of homicide victims can ask questions to experts ● information services, topic forum ● mailing lists. **Programs:** Big Turn Off; Murder is Not Entertainment Alert; Parole Block; Second Opinion Services. **Publications:** *Survivors*, 3/year. Newsletter. Includes schedule of parole hearings for prisoners serving homicide sentences. **Price:** $10.00/year in U.S.; $25.00/year outside U.S. **Conventions/Meetings:** annual meeting.

12414 ■ Parents of Premature Babies (Preemie-L)

21 Lansing Ln.
East Northport, NY 11731
E-mail: lmwill262@aol.com
URL: http://www.preemie-l.org/welcome.htm
Contact: Laura Williams, Contact

Founded: 1996. **Description:** Parents, families and caregivers of premature babies. Provides mentor programs, essays, advice, information, and discussion forums. Offers support while babies are in the hospital and beyond. Holds conferences. **Publications:** *The Early Edition.* Newsletter. Contains information about the association and its members.

12415 ■ Parents Rights Coalition (PRC)

PO Box 1612
Waltham, MA 02454
Ph: (781)899-4905
URL: http://www.parentsrightscoalition.org

Founded: 1994. **Description:** Protects the rights of parents and families in Massachusetts and around the country. Advocates for more legislative laws protecting the structure of the family. Promotes traditional family values and morals. **Computer Services:** Information services, news articles.

12416 ■ Parents Without Partners (PWP)

1650 S Dixie Hwy., Ste.510
Boca Raton, FL 33432
Ph: (561)391-8833
Free: (800)637-7974
Fax: (561)395-8557
E-mail: pwp@jti.net
URL: http://www.parentswithoutpartners.org
Contact: Ms. Kay Brewer, Intl. Website Liaison

Founded: 1957. **Members:** 20,000. **Membership Dues:** chapter, $20-$40 (annual) ● member at large, $40 (annual). **Staff:** 3. **Regional Groups:** 58. **Local Groups:** 300. **Description:** Custodial and noncustodial parents who are single by reason of widowhood, divorce, separation, or otherwise. To alleviate the problems of single parents in relation to the welfare and upbringing of their children and the acceptance into the general social order of single parents and their children. **Awards:** PWP International Scholarship. **Frequency:** annual. **Type:** recognition. **Recipient:** for a child of a member. **Committees:** Community Relations; Family and Youth; Legislative Affairs; Programs and Education; Scholarship. **Publications:** *PWP Gazette.* Newsletter. Alternate Formats: online ● *The Single Parent*, quarterly. Magazine. **Price:** included in membership dues; $15.00 /year for nonmembers; $18.00/year in Canada; $30.00/year outside North America. **Advertising:** accepted ● Bibliographies ● Brochures ● Manuals. **Conventions/Meetings:** annual convention - in July.

12417 ■ Postpartum Support International (PSI)

PO Box 60931
Santa Barbara, CA 93160
Ph: (805)967-7636
Free: (800)944-4773
Fax: (805)967-0608

E-mail: psioffice@postpartum.net
URL: http://www.postpartum.net
Contact: Susan Dowd Stone, Pres.

Founded: 1987. **Members:** 500. **Membership Dues:** individual, $40 (annual) ● support group, $60 (annual) ● professional, $100 (annual) ● institution, $250 (annual). **Staff:** 1. **Budget:** $101,400. **Multinational**. **Description:** Promotes public awareness about the mental health issues of childbearing. Encourages research and the formation of support groups; addresses legal and insurance coverage issues. Provides educational programs. Maintains speakers' bureau. **Libraries: Type:** reference. **Holdings:** 1,000; audiovisuals, books, clippings, periodicals. **Subjects:** postpartum mood and anxiety disorders. **Awards:** Jane Honikman Volunteer Award. **Frequency:** annual. **Type:** recognition. **Recipient:** for outstanding contributions to mental health of mothers ● Susan Hideman Memorial Research Award. **Frequency:** annual. **Type:** monetary. **Recipient:** to a member of PSI, graduate student, application process. **Subgroups:** Advocacy and Education; Legal Issues. **Affiliated With:** National Alliance on Mental Illness; World Federation for Mental Health. **Publications:** *PSI News*, quarterly. Newsletter. Contains association, research, and membership news. **Price:** included in membership dues. Alternate Formats: online. **Conventions/Meetings:** annual Overcoming Barriers to Mental Health Treatment in Childbearing Women - conference (exhibits).

12418 ■ SHARE-Pregnancy and Infant Loss Support

St. Joseph Hea. Center
300 1st Capitol Dr.
St. Charles, MO 63301-2893
Ph: (636)947-6164
Free: (800)821-6819
Fax: (636)947-7486
E-mail: share@nationalshareoffice.com
URL: http://www.nationalshareoffice.com
Contact: Catherine Lammert RN, Exec. Dir.

Founded: 1977. **Members:** 10,000. **Staff:** 6. **State Groups:** 55. **Local Groups:** 3. **National Groups:** 110. **Languages:** English, Spanish. **Description:** Serves those who are touched by the tragic death of a baby through pregnancy loss, stillbirth or in the first few months of life. Provides support toward positive resolution of grief experienced at the time and/or following the death of a baby, encompassing emotional, physical, spiritual and social healing as well as sustaining the family unit. Also provides information, education and resources on the needs and rights of bereaved parents and siblings. Objective is to aid those in the community, including family, friends, employers, members of the congregation, caregivers and others in their supportive role. Presentations on grief. Plans to offer computerized services. **Libraries: Type:** reference. **Holdings:** articles, books, periodicals, video recordings. **Subjects:** grief, newborn loss, adoption. **Computer Services:** database. **Committees:** Education; Fundraising; Outreach. **Formerly:** (1991) SHARE. **Publications:** *Angelic Presence: Short Stories of Solace and Hope after the Loss of a Baby.* Book. **Price:** $9.95 ● *Caring Notes*, quarterly. Newsletter. Offers information and counsel to group facilitators and other professionals in perinatal bereavement support. **Price:** $35.00/year. **Circulation:** 125 ● *International Perinatal Support Groups Listing*, periodic ● *Sharing*, bimonthly. Newsletter. Covers bereavement especially following miscarriage, ectopic pregnancy, stillbirth, or newborn death. Includes listing of books and other resources. **Price:** $25.00/year. **Circulation:** 2,000. **Advertising:** accepted ● *Sharing with Thumpy.* Book. A workbook. **Price:** $9.95 ● *Starting Your Own SHARE Group.* Book. **Price:** $30.00 ● *Thumpy's Story* (in English and Spanish). Audiotape ● *Thumpy's Story: A Story of Love and Grief Shared* (in English and Spanish). Book. **Price:** $7.95 ● *Thumpy's Story: A Story to Color.* Book. **Price:** $5.95. **Conventions/Meetings:** biennial conference (exhibits).

12419 ■ Single and Custodial Fathers Network (SCFN)

608 Hastings St.
Pittsburgh, PA 15206

Ph: (412)665-5940
Fax: (412)291-1771
E-mail: webmaster@scfn.org
URL: http://www.scfn.org
Contact: John R. Sims Jr., Founder/Pres./Exec.Dir.
Founded: 1991. **Membership Dues:** general, $50 (annual) ● supporting, $100 (annual) ● corporate/ sponsoring, $1,000 (annual) ● life, $500. **Multinational. Description:** Represents the interests of single and custodial fathers. Provides education, research and supportive services to single and custodial fathers throughout the world. Seeks to educate the general public, the legislative and judicial systems about the needs and abilities of single and custodial fathers.

12420 ■ Single Mothers By Choice (SMC)
PO Box 1642
New York, NY 10028
Ph: (212)988-0993
Fax: (212)988-0993
E-mail: smc-office@pipeline.com
URL: http://mattes.home.pipeline.com
Contact: Jane Mattes, Chair
Founded: 1981. **Members:** 2,000. **Membership Dues:** individual, $55 (annual). **Staff:** 2. **State Groups:** 20. **Description:** Primarily single professional women in their 30s and 40s who have either decided to have or are considering having children outside of marriage; also welcomes women who are considering adoption as single parents. Provides support for single mothers; disseminates information to women who choose to be single parents. Offers the opportunity for single women to discuss the problems and benefits of being a single parent. Conducts research programs. **Computer Services:** Information services, sibling registry to register half-siblings conceived by donor insemination ● mailing lists, 8 email lists available to members. **Committees:** Information. **Publications:** Newsletter, quarterly. **Price:** $25.00/year. **Circulation:** 2,500. **Advertising:** accepted ● Also disseminates literature packet of articles about single motherhood. **Conventions/ Meetings:** periodic meeting ● seminar ● workshop, for children.

12421 ■ Single Parent Resource Center (SPRC)
31 E 28th St., 2nd Fl.
New York, NY 10016-7923
Ph: (212)951-7030
Fax: (212)951-7037
E-mail: sjones532@aol.com
URL: http://singleparentusa.com
Contact: Suzanne Jones, Exec. Dir./CEO
Founded: 1979. **Staff:** 13. **Budget:** $900,000. **Description:** Aims to establish a network of local single parent groups so that such groups will have a collective political voice. **Formerly:** (1985) National Single Parent Coalition.

12422 ■ Toughlove International
PO Box 491670
Los Angeles, CA 90049-1670
E-mail: comments@toughlove.com
URL: http://www.toughlove.com
Contact: Igal Jonathan Feibush, CEO
Founded: 1977. **Members:** 16,471. **Membership Dues:** $5 (weekly). **Staff:** 4. **Budget:** $400,000. **Local Groups:** 550. **Languages:** English, French, Spanish. **Description:** A network of over 800 support groups for parents of children aged 8-50 with problems. Encourages parents to work together in the community to initiate and maintain positive behavior changes for children in trouble. Local support groups meet weekly; members volunteer to help other parents and kids with active support such as tutoring, driving to counseling, and negotiating living arrangements. Encourages alternatives to suspension for school discipline. Conducts regional workshops for parents and professionals interested in forming a local support group. Maintains Toughlove for Kids Program, which is designed to help children complete school. Operates speakers' bureau. Operates speakers' bureau. **Telecommunication Services:** electronic mail, ijfeibush@toughlove.com. **Boards:** Directors. **Formerly:** (1988) Toughlove. **Publications:** *Rep Rap*, monthly. Newsletter. Includes information for ToughLove representatives. ● *Toughlove, A Self-Help Manual for Kids in Trouble* ● *Toughlove, a Self-Help Manual for Parents Troubled by Teenage Behaviour* ● *Toughlove Cocaine for People Who Care About a Cocaine Abuser* ● *Toughlove for Nurses* ● *Toughlove for Teachers* ● *Toughlove Notes*, quarterly ● *Update to Group*, monthly. **Conventions/Meetings:** annual Representatives Conference and Training - convention ● periodic workshop.

12423 ■ UNITE
c/o Jeanes Hospital
7600 Central Ave.
Philadelphia, PA 19111-2442
Ph: (215)728-3777
Free: (888)48UNITE
E-mail: administrator@unitegriefsupport.org
URL: http://www.unitegriefsupport.org
Contact: Joanne Porreca, Admin.
Founded: 1975. **Members:** 250. **Membership Dues:** individual, family, $25 (annual). **Staff:** 1. **Budget:** $25,000. **Regional Groups:** 12. **Local Groups:** 12. **Description:** Self-help support group for those experiencing grief after miscarriage or infant death. Offers counseling and educational programs for hospital staff. **Libraries:** Type: lending; not open to the public. **Holdings:** articles, books. **Formerly:** (2005) United Grief Support. **Publications:** *Unite Notes*, quarterly. Newsletter. Includes articles and poetry on grieving and recovery. **Price:** included in membership dues. **Circulation:** 250. **Conventions/ Meetings:** annual conference (exhibits) ● workshop, for grief counselors and group felicitators.

Peace

12424 ■ Children of the Earth (COE)
26 Baycrest Dr.
South Burlington, VT 05403
Ph: (802)862-1936
E-mail: coevt@aol.com
URL: http://www.children-of-the-earth.org
Contact: Nina Lynn Meyerhof, Pres.
Multinational. Description: Promotes global consciousness and cooperation, multi-cultural understanding, spiritual values and social responsibilities on behalf of the children. Offers leadership programs focused on peace-making and peace-keeping skills for children and youth at home and abroad. **Computer Services:** Information services, peace medicine. **Projects:** Apeadu Children's Peace Center. **Formerly:** (2004) Partners in Peace.

12425 ■ Coexistence International (CI)
Mailstop 086
Waltham, MA 02454
Ph: (781)736-5017
Fax: (781)736-5014
E-mail: coexistenceinntl@brandeis.net
URL: http://www.brandeis.edu/coexistence
Contact: Cynthia E. Cohen, Exec. Dir.
Founded: 1996. **Multinational. Description:** Peace workers. Works to establish a world secure with differences between people. Promotes human interaction. **Computer Services:** Mailing lists ● online services, Coexistence Resource Center. **Programs:** Coexistence Education; Communicating Coexistence; Information Resource and Coexistence Networking; Post-Conflict Coexistence - The Practices and Policies of Coexistence Work. **Formerly:** (2007) The Coexistence Initiative. **Publications:** Annual Report, annual. Alternate Formats: online ● Reports. Alternate Formats: online.

12426 ■ Pathways To Peace (PTP)
PO Box 1057
Larkspur, CA 94977
Ph: (415)461-0500
Fax: (415)925-0330

E-mail: info@pathwaystopeace.org
URL: http://www.pathwaystopeace.org
Contact: Avon Mattison, Pres.
Founded: 1983. **Multinational. Description:** Promotes Peace-building practices at all levels. **Programs:** Pathways Consulting, Educating and Mentoring. **Projects:** Events With Peace Leaders; Institute for Peacebuilding; Olympian Initiative/Peace Is The Only Gold; Talking Matters Radio Show; "We the People" Initiative/International Day of Peace.

12427 ■ Play for Peace
1 E Superior St., Ste.304
Chicago, IL 60611
Ph: (773)275-0077
Fax: (773)275-3385
E-mail: info@playforpeace.org
URL: http://www.playforpeace.org
Contact: Michael Terrien, Co-Founder/Pres.
Founded: 1996. **Multinational. Description:** Seeks to prevent violence in conflict-torn areas by teaching people to live together, play together, and work together. Promotes positive relationships among the people of societies in conflict. Aims to build self-sustaining learning communities. Works to teach children, teens, and adults to trust and respect others, and to break down generations of cultural barriers.

12428 ■ Pups for Peace (PFP)
8424A Santa Monica Blvd., Ste.112
West Hollywood, CA 90069-4267
Free: (800)669-8930
E-mail: info@pupsforpeace.org
URL: http://www.pupsforpeace.org
Contact: Alyson Bernstein, Office Admin.
Founded: 2002. **Multinational. Description:** Works to reduce death and injury through the use of explosive-detection dogs to counter terrorism. Purchases and trains bomb-sniffing dogs to protect Israeli citizens. Collaborates with Israel's security forces to provide additional protective services for Israel's civilian population. **Publications:** *Pups For Peace News Bulletin*. Newsletter. Alternate Formats: online.

12429 ■ September Eleventh Families for Peaceful Tomorrows
PO Box 1818
Peter Stuyvesant Sta.
New York, NY 10009
Ph: (919)608-7322 (212)598-0970
E-mail: office@peacefultomorrows.org
URL: http://www.peacefultomorrows.org
Contact: David Potorti, Dir.
Description: Advocacy organization founded by family members of September 11th terrorist attack victims. Aims are: "to promote a safe, open dialogue on alternatives to war; to provide support and fellowship to others seeking peaceful and just responses to terrorism; to educate and raise the consciousness of the public on issues surrounding war and peace; to call attention to threats to civil liberties and other freedoms at home as a consequence of war; to promote U.S. foreign policy that places a priority on the principles of democracy and human rights; to encourage a multilateral use of sensible and appropriate means to bring those responsible for the September 11th attacks to justice in accordance with the principles of international law; to recognize the fellowship with people of all nationalities afflicted by violence and war, and to extend to them the same compassion from people around the world; and to demand a full, fair and open investigation into the September 11th attacks that took the lives of our loved ones.". **Telecommunication Services:** electronic mail, david@peacefultomorrows.org. **Publications:** Newsletter. Alternate Formats: online ● Brochure.

Pensions

12430 ■ Pension Research Council (PRC)
The Wharton School of the Univ. of Pennsylvania
3620 Locust Walk
3000 Steinberg Hall - Dietrich Hall
Philadelphia, PA 19104-6302

Ph: (215)898-7620
Fax: (215)573-3418
E-mail: prc@wharton.upenn.edu
URL: http://prc.wharton.upenn.edu/prc/prc.html
Contact: Dr. Olivia S. Mitchell, Exec. Dir.
Founded: 1952. **Members:** 20. **Membership Dues:** institution, $7,500 (annual) ● senior partner, $10,000 (annual). **Staff:** 2. **Budget:** $150,000. **Languages:** English, Portuguese, Spanish. **Description:** Sponsors nonpartisan, interdisciplinary research on the entire range of private and social retirement security and related benefit plans in the United States and around the world. Is affiliated with the Wharton School of the University of Pennsylvania, and is supported by contributions from industry, insurance companies, banks, and pension consultants. Conducts interpretive studies of broad scope. **Libraries: Type:** open to the public. **Holdings:** 18. **Subjects:** pensions, employee benefits, social security reform, retirement. **Publications:** *The Future of Pensions in the United States.* Proceedings. **Price:** $39.95 ● *Providing Health Care Benefits in Retirement.* Proceedings. **Price:** $39.95 ● *Securing Employer Based Pensions: An International Perspective.* Book. **Price:** $42.95 each ● *Social Security.* Book. **Price:** $59.95 ● Also publishes annual working papers. **Conventions/Meetings:** annual symposium and conference, on specific pension issue.

12431 ■ Pension Rights Center (PRC)
1350 Connecticut Ave. NW, Ste.206
Washington, DC 20036-1739
Ph: (202)296-3776
Fax: (202)833-2472
E-mail: pnsnrights@aol.com
URL: http://www.pensionrights.org
Contact: Karen W. Ferguson, Dir.
Founded: 1976. **Staff:** 9. **Description:** Consumer organization whose purpose is to protect and promote the pension rights of workers, retirees, and their families and to develop solutions to the nation's retirement income problems. **Publications:** *The Pension Book: What You Need to Know to Prepare for Retirement.* **Price:** $12.95. Also Cited As: *Pensions in Crisis: Why the System is Failing and How You Can Protect Yourself* ● *Pension Resources Guide for the Greater Washington, D.C. Area.* Handbook. Features answers to general questions about pension and pension rights. **Price:** $6.50 ● *Where to Look for Help with a Pension Problem.* Booklet. Lists government agencies, private organizations, and legal referral programs that provide assistance in pension cases. **Price:** $8.50 ● *Your Pension Rights at Divorce: What Women Need to Know.* Book. Explains what a wife facing divorce should know about her rights under social security, private pensions, military and federal government pensions. **Price:** $24.95 ● Newsletter. Alternate Formats: online ● Also publishes fact sheets and booklets on pension issues. **Conventions/Meetings:** conference ● Conversation on Coverage - meeting.

Personal Computers

12432 ■ E-quip Africa
PO Box 3178
Willmar, MN 56201-8178
Ph: (320)894-1680
E-mail: e-quipafrica@charter.net
URL: http://www.e-quipafrica.org
Contact: Doug Wilkowske, Contact
Multinational. Description: Collects obsolete computers (by US standards), learning tools and school supplies and distributes them to schools in Ghana. Fosters better understanding and working relationships between diverse cultures.

Personal Development

12433 ■ Career Gear
Natl. HQ
120 Broadway, 36th Fl.
New York, NY 10271

Ph: (212)577-6190
Fax: (212)577-6194
E-mail: info@careergear.org
URL: http://www.careergear.org
Contact: John Sanful, Managing Dir.
Description: Provides career and support services to men graduating from skill training programs. Provides clean, contemporary, interview-appropriate clothing for clients facing job interviews. Offers long-range support with monthly financial planning seminars, peer support groups, mentoring and parenting skill workshops and time-management classes. **Programs:** Alumni.

Pets

12434 ■ Association for Pet Loss and Bereavement (APLB)
PO Box 106
Brooklyn, NY 11230
Ph: (718)382-0690
E-mail: aplb@aplb.org
URL: http://www.aplb.org
Contact: Dr. Wallace Sife, Chm./Founder/Treas.
Founded: 1999. **Membership Dues:** basic, $25 (annual) ● senior basic, $20 (annual) ● basic and memorial, $50 (annual) ● senior basic and memorial, $40 (annual). **Multinational. Description:** Provides support services to people who have experienced pain and grief over the loss of an animal companion. Serves as a worldwide clearing house for all information on pet bereavement. Offers pet loss training programs and bereavement counselling services. **Telecommunication Services:** electronic mail, sife@aol.com. **Publications:** Newsletter, quarterly. **Price:** included in membership dues. Alternate Formats: online.

12435 ■ Missing Pet Partnership (MPP)
PO Box 2457
Clovis, CA 93613-2457
Ph: (559)292-4385
E-mail: info@lostapet.org
URL: http://www.lostapet.org
Contact: Kathy Albrecht, Founder
Description: Seeks to help owners recover their missing pets. Provides behavior-based recovery tips along with referrals to lost pet resources. Provides lost pet behavior and recovery training for the staff and volunteers of animal shelters, humane societies, rescue groups, and animal welfare associations.

Philanthropy

12436 ■ AAFRC Trust for Philanthropy
4700 W Lake Ave.
Glenview, IL 60025
Ph: (847)375-4709
Free: (800)462-2372
Fax: (866)607-0913
E-mail: info@aafrc.org
URL: http://www.aafrc.org
Contact: C. Ray Clements, Chm.
Founded: 1985. **Staff:** 3. **Budget:** $325,000. **Description:** A foundation created by American Association of Fund-Raising Counsel. Works to: conduct programs and studies that will increase public awareness and understanding of philanthropy and the role it plays in society; provide funding for research on philanthropy; promote initiation of similar programs by other agencies and associations. In conjunction with the American Association of Colleges, established a program to develop and conduct undergraduate college and university courses on philanthropy. Commissions studies on tax reform and other issues that affect philanthropy. Conducts educational programs on philanthropic trends and developments. **Awards:** John Grenzebach Award. **Frequency:** annual. **Type:** recognition. **Recipient:** for outstanding research in philanthropy for education. **Affiliated With:** American Association of Fundraising Counsel. **Publications:** *Giving USA*, annual. Report. **Price:**

$49.95. ISSN: 0436-0257 ● *Giving USA Update*, quarterly. Newsletter. **Price:** $85.00.

12437 ■ American Association of Grant Professionals (AAGP)
c/o Gail Vertz, Exec. Dir.
8200 State Ave., Ste.No. 105
Kansas City, KS 66112
Ph: (913)788-3000
Fax: (913)788-3398
E-mail: info@grantprofessionals.org
URL: http://www.grantprofessionals.org
Contact: Gail Vertz, Exec. Dir.
Founded: 1998. **Membership Dues:** regular, $125 (annual) ● legacy, $50 (annual) ● student, $75 (annual). **Description:** Serves as a resource for the practice of grantsmanship. Enhances the role of grant developers who work for public or private organizations. Promotes the public image of professional grant developers. Enhances grant developers' relationships with funders and employers. Provides educational opportunities. **Telecommunication Services:** electronic mail, executivedirector@grantprofessionals.org. **Publications:** *Take It for Granted*, quarterly. Newsletter. **Price:** free for members. Alternate Formats: online ● Journal, semiannual. Provides scholarly articles, in-depth grants practice pieces and website reviews. **Price:** free for members.

12438 ■ American Institute of Philanthropy (AIP)
PO Box 578460
Chicago, IL 60657
Ph: (773)529-2300
Fax: (773)529-0024
E-mail: aipmail@charitywatch.org
URL: http://www.charitywatch.org
Contact: Mr. Daniel Borochoff, Pres.
Founded: 1992. **Members:** 8,000. **Membership Dues:** individual, $40 (annual). **Staff:** 5. **Budget:** $300,000. **Description:** Acts as a charity watchdog and information service. Works to provide donors with ratings, advice, and other information on the financial and managerial practices of charities. Goals are to research and evaluate the efficiency, accountability, and governance of non-profit organizations; to educate the public on the importance of wise giving; to inform the public of wasteful or unethical practices and give recognition to highly effective and ethical charities; to advise members, and conduct investigations and evaluations of non-profits; to develop an interactive computer network providing charity information and to expand and redefine the organization's programs periodically to keep the contributor informed. Compiles statistics. Conducts educational and research programs. **Publications:** *Charity Rating Guide*, 3/year, March, July, November. Newsletter. Contains evaluations and ratings about 450 charities in 36 popular issue areas, donor alerts, and tips on wise giving. **Price:** included in membership dues ● *Charity Watchdog Report.* Contains updates on issues related to charitable giving.

12439 ■ Asian Americans/Pacific Islanders in Philanthropy (AAPIP)
200 Pine St., Ste.700
San Francisco, CA 94104
Ph: (415)273-2760
Fax: (415)273-2765
E-mail: aapip@aapip.org
URL: http://www.aapip.org
Contact: Peggy Saika, Pres./Exec. Dir.
Founded: 1990. **Membership Dues:** institutional, $1,000-$10,000 (annual) ● full, $100-$500 (annual) ● associate, $50-$100 (annual). **Local Groups:** 8. **Description:** Represents the interests of individuals dedicated to bridging philanthropy and Asian Pacific American (APA) communities. Seeks to increase the leadership and participation of APAs in the philanthropic sector. Connects philanthropy with APAs and other immigrant and refugee communities. Increases resources to underserved populations. **Telecommunication Services:** electronic mail, membership@aapip.org. **Publications:** *Flash*, quarterly. Bulletin ● Annual Report, annual. Alternate Formats: online.

12440 ■ Bread for the Journey International
267 Miller Ave.
Mill Valley, CA 94941
Ph: (415)383-4600
Fax: (415)383-3836
E-mail: bjourney@pacbell.net
URL: http://www.breadforthejourney.org
Contact: Marianna Cacciatore, Exec. Dir.
Local Groups: 19. **Multinational. Description:** Nurtures the natural generosity of ordinary people. Teaches the simple practice of neighborhood philanthropy. Encourages people to improve their communities.

12441 ■ Caring Voice Coalition (CVC)
PO Box 838
Quinton, VA 23141
Free: (888)267-1440
E-mail: info@caringvoice.org
URL: http://www.caringvoice.org
Contact: Ms. Pamela Harris, Pres.
Founded: 2003. **Nonmembership. Description:** Works to build relationships with charitable organizations founded to help individuals and families affected by serious chronic disorders and diseases. **Councils:** Professional Advisory. **Programs:** Compassionate Care; Insurance Reimbursement and Advocacy; Mentor Training; Peer Mentoring; Personal Support; Public Advocacy; Vital Relief.

12442 ■ Catholic Campaign for Human Development (CCHD)
3211 4th St. NE
Washington, DC 20017
Ph: (202)541-3210
Fax: (202)541-3329
E-mail: cchdpromo@usccb.org
URL: http://www.nccbuscc.org/cchd
Contact: Tim Collins, Exec. Dir.
Founded: 1970. **Staff:** 20. **Budget:** $10,000,000. **Description:** Aims to: raise money through a collection in Catholic churches, and allocate these funds to self-help projects sponsored by groups of poor and low-income persons; educate the non-poor community about causes of poverty and injustice. **Awards:** Cardinal Bernardin New Leadership Award. **Frequency:** annual. **Type:** recognition. **Recipient:** for individuals ages 18 to 30 who have demonstrated leadership against poverty and injustice in the United States ● Community Organizing Grant. **Frequency:** annual. **Type:** grant. **Recipient:** for organizations ● Economic Development Implementation Grant. **Frequency:** annual. **Type:** grant. **Recipient:** for organizations ● Economic Development Planning Grant. **Frequency:** annual. **Type:** grant. **Recipient:** for organizations. **Committees:** Bishops; National. **Programs:** Community Organizing Grants; Economic Development; Youth and Young Adult. **Formerly:** (1999) Campaign for Human Development. **Publications:** *The Feasibility Study: Will it Work?.* Booklet. Alternate Formats: online ● *Helping People Help Themselves,* quarterly. Newsletter. Alternate Formats: online ● *Planning to Succeed in Business.* Booklet. Alternate Formats: online ● *Strategic Planning: Which Way is Best?.* Booklet. Alternate Formats: online ● Annual Report, annual. Alternate Formats: online ● Also publishes catalog of materials and resources.

12443 ■ Committee to Encourage Corporate Philanthropy (CECP)
110 Wall St., Ste.2-1
New York, NY 10005
Ph: (212)825-1000
Fax: (212)825-1251
E-mail: info@corporatephilanthropy.org
URL: http://www.corphilanthropy.org
Contact: Charles Moore, Exec. Dir.
Description: Promotes corporate philanthropy. **Awards:** Excellence in Corporate Philanthropy Awards. **Frequency:** annual. **Type:** recognition. **Recipient:** to the company demonstrating outstanding CEO leadership, innovation, dedication to measurement, and partnership in corporate philanthropy. **Programs:** Internship; John C. Whitehead Education Leadership. **Publications:** *The Corporate Philanthro-*

pist, quarterly. Newsletter. Features best practices and perspectives on corporate philanthropy from CEO and industry leaders. Alternate Formats: online. Also Cited As: *New Century Philanthropy.*

12444 ■ Dyson Foundation (DF)
25 Halcyon Rd.
Millbrook, NY 12545-6137
Ph: (845)677-0644
Fax: (845)677-0650
E-mail: info@dyson.org
URL: http://www.dysonfoundation.org
Contact: Ms. Diana Gurieva, Exec. VP
Founded: 1957. **Description:** Works to support American family philanthropy. **Awards: Type:** grant. **Publications:** Annual Report, annual. Alternate Formats: online.

12445 ■ East West Education Development Foundation (EWF)
c/o East-West Ministries
4450 Sojourn Dr., Ste.100
Addison, TX 75001-5043
Ph: (214)265-8300
Fax: (214)265-8503
E-mail: info@eastwest.org
URL: http://www.eastwestministries.org
Contact: Alexander V. Randall, Contact
Founded: 1990. **Staff:** 6. **Nonmembership. Multinational. Description:** Seeks to recycle computers and give them to public service organizations in America and overseas. Refurbishes donated computers, adds parts as needed and builds complete computer systems. **Programs:** Business Training; Computers for Sarajevo; Democracy Development; PC's for Pistols. **Publications:** Brochure. **Conventions/Meetings:** trade show.

12446 ■ Forum of Regional Associations of Grantmakers
1111 19th St. NW, Ste.650
Washington, DC 20036
Ph: (202)467-1120 (202)467-1129
Fax: (202)467-0055
E-mail: info@givingforum.org
URL: http://www.givingforum.org
Contact: Ellen Barclay, Pres.
Members: 4,000. **Regional Groups:** 29. **Description:** Promotes philanthropy; works to connect grant making individuals and institutions to a local or regional source of support, collaboration and professional development. **Computer Services:** Mailing lists ● online services, listserv. **Telecommunication Services:** electronic mail, ebarclay@givingforum.org. **Committees:** New Ventures National Advisory. **Funds:** Peer Exchange. **Programs:** Guest Membership; New Ventures in Philanthropy. **Publications:** *A Plan of One's Own: A Women's Guide to Giving.* Booklet. **Price:** $25.00 for profit; $15.00 for non-profit ● *Forum Bits,* biweekly. Newsletter. Alternate Formats: online ● *Growing Giving.* Newsletter. Alternate Formats: online ● *Growing Philanthropy: A Resource Guide for Increasing Organized Philanthropy at the Regional Level.* Book. **Price:** $70.00 for profit; $55.00 non-profit ● *How Effective Nonprofits Work: A Guide for Donors, Board Members and Foundation Officers.* Book. **Price:** $30.00 for profit; $20.00 for non-profit. Alternate Formats: online ● *So You Want To Give.* Booklet. **Price:** $4.00 for profit plus shipping and handling; $2.50 for non-profit. Alternate Formats: online ● *Starting a Private Foundation.* Booklet. **Price:** $15.00 for profit; $10.00 for non-profit. **Conventions/Meetings:** conference and seminar ● meeting ● annual Staff Conference and CEO Summer Seminar.

12447 ■ G. Unger Vetlesen Foundation
One Rockefeller Plz., Ste.301
New York, NY 10020-2002
Ph: (212)586-0700
Fax: (212)245-1863
E-mail: info@monellvetlesen.org
URL: http://www.monellvetlesen.org
Contact: George Rowe Jr., Pres./Dir.
Multinational. Description: Works to support religious, charitable, scientific, literary, and educational efforts. **Awards: Type:** grant.

12448 ■ Gifts In Kind International (GIKA)
333 N Fairfax St.
Alexandria, VA 22314
Ph: (703)836-2121
Fax: (877)798-3192
E-mail: rwong@giftsinkind.org
URL: http://www.giftsinkind.org
Contact: Richard Wong, Pres./CEO
Founded: 1983. **Members:** 50,000. **Staff:** 44. **Budget:** $7,500,000. **Local Groups:** 50,000. **Description:** Encourages and assists businesses in donating products to voluntary human services and environmental organizations and arts and education programs. Promotes in-kind gift giving as an effective means for donors to manage inventory levels, increase productivity, lower storage costs, and receive tax credits. Identifies and selects recipients; administers details involving taxes and transportation to facilitate donating. Operates information clearinghouse. Distributes $600 Million in newly manufactured products annual top global network of 50,000 non-profit organizations. **Formerly:** (1989) Gifts In Kind; (1990) Gifts in Kind of America. **Publications:** *In-Kind Chronicle,* monthly. Newsletter ● Annual Report, annual. Alternate Formats: online ● Brochures.

12449 ■ Grantmakers in the Arts (GIA)
604 W Galer St.
Seattle, WA 98119-3253
Ph: (206)624-2312
Fax: (206)624-5568
E-mail: gia@giarts.org
URL: http://www.giarts.org
Contact: Anne Focke, Exec. Dir.
Founded: 1985. **Membership Dues:** full organization (based on current year arts grantmaking budget), $100-$1,000 (annual) ● individual, $100 (annual). **Description:** Increases the presence of arts philanthropy within the broader foundation and policy making communities. Promotes more meaningful support of arts and culture. Supports individual arts grantmakers in increasing their effectiveness and their capacity to meet their objectives. Strengthens the field of private sector arts grantmaking by improving communication, information exchange and peer learning within the field. **Publications:** *Grantmakers in the Arts Reader,* 3/year. Newsletter. Features articles on topics of interest to arts grantmakers. **Price:** included in membership dues; $24.00 others; $35.00 overseas ● Membership Directory, annual ● Proceedings, annual ● Bulletin.

12450 ■ Grantmakers for Children, Youth, and Families (GCYF)
8757 Georgia Ave., Ste.540
Silver Spring, MD 20910
Ph: (301)589-4293
Fax: (301)589-4289
E-mail: info@gcyf.org
URL: http://www.gcyf.org
Contact: Dr. Stephanie McGencey, Exec. Dir.
Founded: 1985. **Members:** 250. **Membership Dues:** less than $250000 institutional support, $500 ● $250000-$1000000 institutional support, $1,000 ● $1000000-$5000000 institutional support, $1,500 ● $5000000-$20000000 institutional support, $2,500 ● $20000000-$50000000 institutional support, $3,500 ● $5000000 or more institutional support, $5,000. **Staff:** 3. **Budget:** $439,789. **Description:** Represents foundations and corporate grant-makers. Acts as a network to exchange ideas on and improve programs for children and youth. **Awards:** Fred Rogers Leadership Award. **Frequency:** annual. **Type:** recognition. **Recipient:** for outstanding contributions in the field of philanthropy. **Computer Services:** database, membership ● mailing lists, of members (available to grant making community only). **Telecommunication Services:** electronic mail, smcgencey@gcyf.org. **Committees:** Building Constituencies for Children Learning Circle; Race, Class and Ethnicity in Grant Making Learning Circle; Trends, Traditions and the Future of Philanthropy Learning Circle. **Formerly:** (1991) Grantmakers for Children and Youth. **Publications:** *Insight,* periodic. Newsletter. **Price:** free for members. **Circulation:** 1,000. Alternate Formats: online ●

Papers. Alternate Formats: online. **Conventions/ Meetings:** annual conference.

12451 ■ Grantmakers Without Borders (Gw/oB)
PO Box 181282
Boston, MA 02118
Ph: (617)794-2253
Fax: (617)266-0497
E-mail: gwob@gwob.net
URL: http://www.internationaldonors.org
Contact: John Harvey, Exec. Dir.
Multinational. Description: Increases the strategic and compassionate funding for international societal change. Provides peer-to-peer support to individuals and institutions new to funding internationally. **Computer Services:** Information services, global social change philanthropy resources. **Committees:** Steering. **Publications:** *China Philanthropy News*, bi-weekly. Newsletter. Alternate Formats: online.

12452 ■ Independent Sector
1200 18th St. NW, Ste.200
Washington, DC 20036
Ph: (202)467-6100
Free: (888)860-8118
Fax: (202)467-6101
E-mail: info@independentsector.org
URL: http://www.independentsector.org
Contact: Diana Aviv, Pres./CEO
Founded: 1980. **Members:** 800. **Staff:** 35. **Budget:** $6,200,000. **Description:** Represents charities and foundations. Organizes corporate giving programs committed to advancement of the common good in America and around the world. Leads, strengthens, and mobilizes charitable community. **Awards:** John W. Gardner Leadership Award. **Frequency:** annual. **Type:** recognition. **Recipient:** for an individual working in or with the charitable community ● Leadership IS Award. **Frequency:** annual. **Type:** recognition. **Recipient:** for organizations that value and develop a culture of investing in the people of the independent sector ● Virginia A. Hodgkinson Research Prize. **Frequency:** annual. **Type:** recognition. **Recipient:** for outstanding published research. **Formed by Merger of:** Coalition of National Voluntary Organizations; National Council on Philanthropy. **Publications:** *Giving and Volunteering in the United States*, biennial ● *Memo to Members* ● *Nonprofit Almanac*, biennial ● *Sarbanes-Oxley Act & Implications for Nonprofit Organizations* ● Annual Report, annual. **Conventions/ Meetings:** annual meeting, for members - always October/November ● biennial Spring Research Forum - meeting.

12453 ■ International Corrugated Packaging Foundation (ICPF)
113 S West St.
Alexandria, VA 22314
Ph: (703)549-8580
Fax: (703)549-8670
E-mail: info@icpfbox.org
URL: http://www.icpfbox.org
Contact: Richard M. Flaherty, Pres.
Founded: 1985. **Multinational. Description:** Foundation established for philanthropy, education, and scholarship. Seeks to increase student interest in the corrugated packaging industry through asset donations and curriculum development to educational institutions. **Committees:** Asset Placement; Curriculum; Educational Outreach; Fund Raising; International Outreach; Web Page. **Subcommittees:** Investment; Recruiting. **Affiliated With:** International Corrugated Packaging Foundation. **Publications:** *ICPF Direct*, quarterly. **Advertising:** accepted ● Annual Report, annual. Alternate Formats: online. **Conventions/Meetings:** annual Corrugated Industry Briefing Video Teleconference - symposium.

12454 ■ Jessie Ball duPont Fund
One Independent Dr., Ste.1400
Jacksonville, FL 32202-0511
Ph: (904)353-0890
Free: (800)252-3452
Fax: (904)353-3870

E-mail: contactus@dupontfund.org
URL: http://www.dupontfund.org
Contact: Sherry P. Magill PhD, Pres.
Founded: 1976. **Members:** 4. **Staff:** 8. **Description:** Works to support philanthropic efforts with a special, though not exclusive, focus on the South. **Awards:** Frequency: quarterly. **Type:** grant ● Jessie Ball duPont Award. **Frequency:** annual. **Type:** recognition. **Recipient:** to an individual whose life work focuses on promoting justice, equality and compassion in their communities ● Jessie Ball duPont Fund Making A Difference Award. **Frequency:** annual. **Type:** recognition. **Recipient:** to an individual, group or institution for creating a program that meets a critical societal need ● Jessie Ball duPont Fund Turnaround Award. **Frequency:** annual. **Type:** recognition. **Recipient:** to an individual who has made a significant contribution to the health and relevance of an institution. **Telecommunication Services:** electronic mail, publications@ dupontfund.org. **Publications:** *Great Little Grants*, annual, spring. Alternate Formats: online ● *Investing in Our Future: A Southern Perspective*. Report. Contains information on the southern region of the United States. ● *Unfinished Business: Overcoming Racism, Poverty, and Inequality in the South*. Report. Contains information on a conference held in 1998 that focused on race and poverty in the American South. Alternate Formats: online ● Annual Reports, annual. Alternate Formats: online.

12455 ■ Kettering Family Foundation
2833 S Colorado Blvd.
Denver, CO 80222
E-mail: info@ketteringfamilyfoundation.org
URL: http://www.ketteringfamilyfoundation.org/main. html
Contact: Charles F. Kettering III, Pres.
Founded: 1955. **Description:** Works to support philanthropic endeavors. **Awards: Type:** grant.

12456 ■ Local Independent Charities of America (LIC)
Natl. HQ
21 Tamal Vista Blvd., Ste.209
Corte Madera, CA 94925
Free: (800)876-0413
Fax: (415)924-1379
E-mail: info@lic.org
URL: http://www.lic.org
Contact: Don McPartland, Pres.
Local Groups: 600. **Description:** Represents charities specializing in areas such as feeding the hungry, sheltering homeless, child protection, medical healing, and animal welfare. **Publications:** Report, annual. Alternate Formats: online.

12457 ■ Makassed Foundation of America (MFA)
3231 P St. NW, 2nd Fl.
Washington, DC 20007
Ph: (202)783-7979
Fax: (703)760-0076
E-mail: mfa@makassedfoundationofamerica.org
URL: http://www.makassedfoundationofamerica.org
Contact: Mr. Kamel Tabbara, Pres.
Founded: 1999. **Nonmembership. Multinational. Description:** Aims to expand humanitarian work through enhanced public awareness and philanthropy in the Americas. Promotes social well being and the improvement of the quality of life. Advances human development through projects related to children, women, education, health and the environment. **Computer Services:** Mailing lists. **Telecommunication Services:** electronic mail, info@makassedusa.org. **Publications:** Newsletter.

12458 ■ National Center for Charitable Statistics (NCCS)
c/o The Urban Institute
2100 M St. NW, 5th Fl.
Washington, DC 20037
Ph: (202)833-7200
Free: (866)518-3874
Fax: (202)833-6231

E-mail: nccs@ui.urban.org
URL: http://nccsdataweb.urban.org/FAQ/index.php- ?category=31
Contact: Thomas H. Pollak, Program Dir.
Founded: 1982. **Staff:** 10. **Budget:** $2,000,000. **Description:** Serves as a data repository for IRS FORM 990 information and statistics on non-profits. **Libraries: Type:** reference. **Computer Services:** custom tabulations and summaries ● database, 1,100,000 charitable organizations registered with the Internal Revenue Service ● database, surveys and IRS statistics ● mailing lists. **Publications:** *Non-Profit Almanac Profiles of Charitable Organizations*, biennial ● *Nonprofits and Government: Collaboration and Conflict*. Book. **Price:** $29.50 paper ● *Scope and Dimension of the Nonprofit Sector* ● Brochure. Contains information on NCCS activities and services.

12459 ■ National Committee for Responsive Philanthropy (NCRP)
2001 S St. NW, Ste.620
Washington, DC 20009
Ph: (202)387-9177
Fax: (202)332-5084
E-mail: info@ncrp.org
URL: http://www.ncrp.org
Contact: Aaron Dorfman, Exec. Dir.
Founded: 1976. **Members:** 250. **Membership Dues:** core individual, $50 (annual) ● core organization, $250 (annual) ● core foundation, $2,500 (annual). **Staff:** 7. **Budget:** $1,200,000. **Local Groups:** 80. **Description:** Represents low income, minorities, women, consumers, environmentalists, older Americans, youth, and others working for social change and the public interest who are concerned about the lack of philanthropic giving to organizations working for social change or progressive issues. Works with leaders in the philanthropic community and the recipients of philanthropic giving to increase public accountability by philanthropies. Works to increase access to philanthropy's monies for those groups representing "critical public needs." Initiates efforts to facilitate access to charity drives in the workplace. Is concerned with the giving patterns of private foundations, United Way, and corporations with philanthropic programs. Conducts research; compiles statistics; publicizes reports; organizes local alternatives to United Way. **Libraries: Type:** reference. **Holdings:** books, clippings, monographs, periodicals. **Subjects:** social justice philanthropy and general philanthropy. **Computer Services:** database, organizations, donor networks and affinity groups. **Committees:** Corporate; Policy; Workplace Fundraising. **Formerly:** (1978) Committee for Responsive Philanthropy. **Supersedes:** Donee Group. **Publications:** *Axis of Ideology*. Report. **Price:** $25.00 for nonmembers; $12.50 for members ● *Funding the Culture Wars*. Report. **Price:** $25.00 for nonmembers; $12.50 for members ● *Funding the Culture Wars: Philanthropy, Church and State*. Report. **Price:** $25.00 for nonmembers; $12.50 for members ● *Responsive Philanthropy*, quarterly. Newsletter. Reports on changes in and reform of private philanthropy, particularly to benefit social, economic, and political justice groups. **Price:** included in membership dues; $25.00 /year for nonmembers; $30.00 in Canada; $35.00 outside U.S. **Circulation:** 6,000. **Advertising:** accepted ● *Social Justice Philanthropy: The Latest Trend or a Lasting Lens for Grantmaking*. Report. **Price:** $20.00 for nonmembers; $10.00 for members ● Also publishes special research reports.

12460 ■ Native Americans in Philanthropy (NAP)
2801 21st Ave. S, Ste.132 D
Minneapolis, MN 55407
Ph: (612)724-8798
Fax: (612)879-0613
E-mail: info@nativephilanthropy.org
URL: http://www.nativephilanthropy.org
Contact: Joy Persall, Exec. Dir.
Founded: 1990. **Membership Dues:** general (individual), $120 (annual) ● affiliate (individual), $100 (annual) ● tribe/native (organization), $500-$25,000 (annual) ● sustaining (organization), $1,000-$5,000 (annual) ● institutional (organization), $5,001-

$25,000 (annual). **Description:** Advocates within the philanthropic community the promotion, development, effectiveness and growth of philanthropy in Native communities. **Awards:** The Flying Eagle Woman Award. **Type:** recognition. **Recipient:** to an indigenous person who has demonstrated indigenous thinking and philosophy ● Louis T. Delgado Distinguished Grantmaker Award. **Type:** recognition. **Recipient:** to individual who has advanced the role of philanthropy between native indigenous communities and mainstream philanthropy. **Publications:** *Circle of Giving*, quarterly. Newsletter. **Price:** included in membership dues. Alternate Formats: online ● Annual Report, annual. **Conventions/Meetings:** annual meeting, for members.

12461 ■ Neighborhood Funders Group (NFG)
1301 Connecticut Ave. NW
Washington, DC 20036
Ph: (202)833-4690
Fax: (202)833-4694
E-mail: nfg@nfg.org
URL: http://www.nfg.org
Contact: Spence Limbocker, Exec. Dir.
Founded: 1980. **Members:** 280. **Staff:** 4. **Budget:** $800,000. **Description:** Grantmaking institutions whose mission is to strengthen organized philanthropy to improve economic, social fabric of low-income urban neighborhoods, rural communities. Provides information, learning opportunities and other professional development activities to members and encourages the support of policies and practices that advance economic and social justice.

12462 ■ Philanthropy Roundtable
1150 17th St. NW, Ste.503
Washington, DC 20036
Ph: (202)822-8333
Fax: (202)822-8325
E-mail: main@philanthropyroundtable.org
URL: http://www.philanthropyroundtable.org
Contact: Adam Meyerson, Pres.
Founded: 1987. **Members:** 600. **Staff:** 6. **Budget:** $1,600,000. **Description:** Dedicated to serving donors' needs. Offers consulting and referral services on starting, restructuring, and administering giving programs, designed especially for individual donors and small foundations that have limited staff and resources. Helps Philanthropists ensure that their intentions will be adhered to with long-term administration of their trusts. **Telecommunication Services:** electronic mail, ameyerson@philanthropyroundtable.org. **Roundtables:** Education; Environmental. **Subgroups:** Affinity. **Formerly:** (1998) Philanthropic Roundtable. **Publications:** *Philanthropy*, bimonthly. Magazine. For the grant-making community. **Advertising:** accepted. Alternate Formats: online ● Books ● Monographs, prices vary. **Conventions/Meetings:** annual Excellence in Philanthropy - meeting.

12463 ■ Rockefeller Brothers Fund (RBF)
437 Madison Ave., 37th Fl.
New York, NY 10022-7001
Ph: (212)812-4200
Fax: (212)812-4299
E-mail: info@rbf.org
URL: http://www.rbf.org
Contact: Ms. Gail Fuller, Communications Off.
Founded: 1940. **Multinational. Description:** Promotes social change that helps build a more just, sustainable, and peaceful world. **Programs:** Democratic Practice; Human Advancement; Peace and Security; Sustainable Development. **Publications:** *Philanthropy for an Interdependent World*, annual. Annual Report ● *Program Guidelines*, periodic. Handbook. Alternate Formats: online ● *Statistical Review of RBF Operations*, annual. Report.

12464 ■ Rockefeller Family Fund
437 Madison Ave., 37th Fl.
New York, NY 10022
Ph: (212)812-4252
Fax: (212)812-4299

E-mail: mmccarthy@rffund.org
URL: http://www.rffund.org
Contact: Lee H. Wasserman, Dir.
Founded: 1967. **Staff:** 4. **Description:** Makes grants for advocacy work on public policy by environmental, political participation and reform, women's rights, and activist-oriented non-profit groups. **Sections:** Environmental Grantmakers Association. **Publications:** Annual Report, annual.

12465 ■ Surdna Foundation
330 Madison Ave., 30th Fl.
New York, NY 10017
Ph: (212)557-0010
E-mail: questions@surdna.org
URL: http://www.surdna.org
Contact: Edward Skloot, Pres.
Founded: 1917. **Members:** 15. **Staff:** 18. **Description:** Works to support philanthropic efforts. **Awards: Type:** grant. **Telecommunication Services:** electronic mail, request@surdna.org. **Publications:** *More Than Bit Players: How Information Technology Will Change the Ways Nonprofits and Foundations Work and Thrive in the Information Age*. Report ● Annual Report, annual. Alternate Formats: online.

12466 ■ Trull Foundation
404 4th St.
Palacios, TX 77465
Ph: (361)972-5241
Fax: (361)972-1109
E-mail: info@trullfoundation.org
URL: http://www.trullfoundation.org
Contact: E. Gail Purvis, Exec. Dir.
Founded: 1948. **Members:** 5. **Staff:** 2. **Regional Groups:** 1. **Description:** Works to support 501c3 nonprofit organizations with a concern for: The Palacios, Matagorda County area; children and families; drug and alcohol abuse programs; the Texas Gulf Coast environment. **Awards: Frequency:** monthly. **Type:** grant. **Publications:** Reprint, biennial. **Conventions/Meetings:** monthly meeting.

12467 ■ Twenty-First Century Foundation (21CF)
271 W 125th St., Ste.303
New York, NY 10027-4424
Ph: (212)662-3700
Fax: (212)662-6690
E-mail: info@21cf.org
URL: http://www.21cf.org
Contact: Erica Hunt, Pres.
Founded: 1971. **Staff:** 6. **Budget:** $500,000. **Description:** For the development of an endowment for the support of black charitable institutions. **Awards: Type:** grant. **Recipient:** for organizations actively involved in projects that focus in areas of education and economic development. **Computer Services:** Mailing lists. **Programs:** Black Men and Boys Initiative. **Publications:** *Time, Talent and Treasure: A Study of Black Philanthropy*. Report. Alternate Formats: online ● *Vision News*, semiannual. Newsletter. Alternate Formats: online. **Conventions/Meetings:** annual Black Philanthropic Leadership: Giving with Intention & Impact - meeting.

12468 ■ Women's Philanthropy Institute (WPI)
550 W North St., Ste.301
Indianapolis, IN 46202-3272
Ph: (317)274-4200 (317)278-8990
Fax: (317)684-8900
E-mail: wpiinfo@iupui.edu
URL: http://www.philanthropy.iupui.edu/Philanthropic-Services/WPI
Contact: Dr. Eugene R. Tempel, Exec. Dir.
Founded: 1997. **Description:** Philanthropists and philanthropy professionals. Seeks to "educate and advance women as major donors and volunteer leaders for nonprofit causes". Facilitates establishment of partnerships involving women and philanthropic organizations and professionals; conducts financial and philanthropic educational programs for women and courses for philanthropic organizations seeking to obtain greater support from women. **Telecommunication Services:** electronic mail, etempel@iu-

pui.edu. **Publications:** *WPINews*, quarterly. Newsletter. Features articles on issues and trends related to women and philanthropy. **Price:** $50.00/year.

Phobias

12469 ■ Agoraphobics In Motion (AIM)
1719 Crooks
Royal Oak, MI 48067
Ph: (248)547-0400
E-mail: anny@ameritech.net
URL: http://www.aim-hq.org
Contact: Mary Ann Gogoleski, Founder/Dir.
Founded: 1983. **Members:** 500. **Membership Dues:** donation, $5 (weekly). **Staff:** 2. **State Groups:** 7. **Local Groups:** 7. **National Groups:** 2. **Description:** Individuals suffering from any anxiety disorder. Offers support, behavioral/cognitive techniques, and the opportunity to share concerns and experiences. Maintains Speaker's Bureau. **Libraries: Type:** reference; open to the public. **Holdings:** audio recordings, books. **Awards:** Diamond Crystal Award. **Type:** grant ● Success Award. **Type:** grant. **Publications:** *AIM Workbook*. Contains support manual. **Price:** $15.00 ● *Expect a Miracle*. Book. **Price:** $15.00 plus shipping and handling ● *Jogging Your Spiritual Consciousness*. Pamphlet ● Video. **Price:** $10.00 ● Audiotapes. Covers seminars. ● Manual. Provides information on starting a group.

12470 ■ Anxiety Disorders Association of America (ADAA)
8730 Georgia Ave., Ste.600
Silver Spring, MD 20910
Ph: (240)485-1001
Fax: (240)485-1035
URL: http://www.adaa.org
Contact: Heather Murray, Business Mgr.
Founded: 1980. **Members:** 3,000. **Membership Dues:** student, $30 (annual) ● professional, $175 (annual). **Staff:** 8. **Budget:** $1,800,000. **Description:** Health professionals involved in the research and treatment of anxiety disorders, including phobias, panic disorder, post-traumatic stress disorder, generalized anxiety disorder, and obsessive/compulsive disorders; families of those suffering from an anxiety disorder; interested others. Purpose is to aid sufferers of such conditions and their families through educational and informational services and to facilitate research, progress in treatment, and public and professional education. Does not recommend any one approach to treatment, but believes numerous treatments need to be developed and made available and encourages individuals seeking treatment to learn about treatment options. Fosters local self-help groups; operates information clearinghouse. Works to remove the stigma of anxiety disorders. **Libraries: Type:** open to the public. **Holdings:** 125; articles, books, periodicals. **Subjects:** anxiety disorders. **Awards:** Career Development Travel Award. **Frequency:** annual. **Type:** recognition. **Recipient:** to professionals with interest in anxiety disorders ● Junior Faculty Research Grants. **Frequency:** annual. **Type:** grant. **Recipient:** to individuals with post-doctoral fellowship/post-residency research training ● Trainee Travel Awards. **Frequency:** annual. **Type:** scholarship. **Recipient:** for new professionals and graduate students. **Computer Services:** Mailing lists ● online services, bookstore. **Boards:** Clinical Advisory; Scientific Advisory. **Councils:** Corporate Advisory. **Programs:** Award. **Formerly:** (1990) Phobia Society of America. **Publications:** *AADA Reporter*, bimonthly. Newsletter. Covers scientific developments, association activities, and educational programs. **Price:** $30.00/year for consumers; $165.00/year for professionals. **Circulation:** 10,000. **Advertising:** accepted ● *ADAA Set of ID Brochures*. Contains information on anxiety disorders. ● *Conference Program*. Booklets ● *Help Yourself: A Guide to Organizing an Anxiety Disorder Self-Help Group*. Book ● *National Professional Membership Directory*, annual. National/international listings of ADAA professional members who are also researchers and treatment providers. ● Newsletters, 3/year. **Advertising:**

accepted. **Alternate Formats:** online ● Books ● Brochures ● Also publishes a pamphlet series on anxiety disorders, and booklets; makes available audiotapes of conference programs. **Conventions/ Meetings:** annual National Conference on Anxiety Disorders, with speakers (exhibits).

12471 ■ Anxiety Disorders Special Interest Group (ADSIG)
c/o Alicia E. Meuret, PhD, Treas.
Southern Methodist Univ.
Hyer Hall
6424 Hilltop Ln.
Dallas, TX 75205
E-mail: ameuret@smu.edu
URL: http://www.aabt-anxietysig.org
Contact: Alicia E. Meuret PhD, Treas.
Founded: 1982. **Members:** 150. **Description:** Represents psychologists, psychiatrists, social workers, and other individuals interested in treatment of anxiety disorders. Aims to increase knowledge and expertise and facilitate communication regarding research and treatment of phobias and related anxiety disorders. Conducts programs at professional meetings. **Publications:** none. **Libraries: Type:** reference. **Holdings:** biographical archives. **Computer Services:** Mailing lists, of members only. **Telecommunication Services:** electronic mail, aegrills@uh.edu. **Affiliated With:** Association for Behavioral and Cognitive Therapies. **Formerly:** (2000) Anxiety Disorder SIG. **Conventions/Meetings:** periodic symposium ● periodic workshop.

12472 ■ Anxiety and Phobia Program
Address Unknown since 2006
Founded: 1974. **Members:** 3,000. **State Groups:** 27. **Local Groups:** 15. **Description:** Individuals suffering from severe anxiety. Offers support through educational programs. Maintains speakers' bureau. **Formerly:** (1999) Agoraphobics Anonymous. **Publications:** *The Connection*, quarterly. Newsletter. **Price:** $25.00. **Advertising:** not accepted.

12473 ■ Anxiety and Phobia Treatment Center
White Plains Hosp.
Davis Ave. at E Post Rd.
White Plains, NY 10601
Ph: (914)681-1038
E-mail: questions@phobia-anxiety.org
URL: http://www.phobia-anxiety.org
Contact: Fredric J. Neuman MD, Dir.
Founded: 1971. **Staff:** 43. **Description:** Treatment groups for individuals suffering from phobias. Aims to help phobic people deal with their fears through "contextual therapy," a treatment and study of the phobia in the actual setting in which the phobic reactions occur. Conducts Intensive Course, Phobia Self-Help Groups, and 8-week Phobia Clinics; also provides individual treatment. Although presently local in scope, serves as model for similar groups throughout the U.S. **Telecommunication Services:** electronic mail, jchessa@wphospital.org. **Formerly:** Phobia Clinic; (1997) Anxiety and Phobia Clinic. **Publications:** *PM Newsletter*, bimonthly ● Articles. Alternate Formats: online ● Papers. **Conventions/ Meetings:** annual conference.

12474 ■ Fly Without Fear (FWF)
36 Meadow Rue Ln.
East Northport, NY 11731
Ph: (516)829-2900 (631)368-4244
Fax: (516)829-5920
E-mail: ccg368@aol.com
Contact: Carol Gross, Dir.
Founded: 1969. **Members:** 25. **Membership Dues:** regular (covers 3 meeting), $150 ● regular (per meeting, after 3 meetings), $40. **Staff:** 2. **Regional Groups:** 1. **Local Groups:** 1. **For-Profit. Description:** Persons who are "terrified of airplane travel." Sponsors talks with ground controllers and safety experts and visits to airports in an effort to help members overcome their phobia. Conducts "Seminar in the Sky" conditioning flights and lectures on fear of flying to clubs and organizations; has graduated thousands of members who now accept commercial

jetliners as a standard mode of transportation. **Also Known As:** Travel and Fly Without Fear. **Publications:** *Things That Go Bump on the Flight*. Provides a relaxation exercise script. **Price:** $10.00 will mail on request. **Conventions/Meetings:** weekly meeting - every Thursday evening at La Guardia Airport, New York City.

12475 ■ Pass-Group
6 Mahogany Dr.
Williamsville, NY 14221
Ph: (716)689-4399 (716)689-4475
Contact: Shirley Swede, Program Coor.
Founded: 1981. **Description:** Offers six weekly half-hour telephone sessions to help panic attack sufferers recover. **Publications:** *The Panic Attack Recovery Book*. Explains the cause and cure for panic attack.

12476 ■ TERRAP Programs
c/o LaFrance and Associates Counseling Services
PO Box 19
Hershey, PA 17033
Ph: (717)832-3347
E-mail: lafrance@terrap.com
URL: http://www.terrap.com
Contact: Joseph A. LaFrance MS, Dir./Owner
Founded: 1962. **Membership Dues:** $200 (annual). **For-Profit. Description:** Stands for Territorial Apprehensiveness and disseminates information concerning the recognition, causes, and treatment of anxieties, fears, and phobias, especially agoraphobia (the abnormal fear of traversing or of being in open spaces). Provides information and counseling for those with phobias who are trying to help themselves. Sponsors service centers where professional psychotherapists and counselors are trained in the TERRAP Method. **Affiliated With:** Anxiety Disorders Association of America. **Supersedes:** TERRAP. **Publications:** Manual ● Audiotapes. Includes home-study course. ● Booklets ● Monographs ● Pamphlets ● Videos. **Conventions/Meetings:** annual conference (exhibits) ● annual symposium and retreat.

Physically Impaired

12477 ■ Charlotte W. Newcombe Foundation
c/o Woodrow Wilson National Fellowship Foundation
PO Box 5281
Princeton, NJ 08543
Ph: (609)452-7007
Fax: (609)452-0066
E-mail: charlotte@woodrow.org
URL: http://www.woodrow.org/newcombe/index.php
Contact: Shelia Walker, Program Assoc.
Description: Works to provide funds for three scholarship programs for the physically disabled, women, and minority and disadvantaged students. **Awards: Type:** scholarship. **Additional Websites:** http://www.newcombefoundation.org.

Physicians

12478 ■ Adopt a Doctor
150 Chestnut St.
Providence, RI 02903
Ph: (401)454-4523
Free: (800)714-9343
E-mail: info@adoptadoctor.org
URL: http://www.adoptadoctor.org
Contact: Rajiv A. Kumar, Co-Founder/Chm./Exec. Dir.
Founded: 2003. **Multinational. Description:** Seeks to reverse the brain drain that is drawing experienced physicians away from the poorest countries in the world. Aspires to solve this problem of high turnover rates and unavailability of experienced physicians by providing financial aid and other critical resources to physicians already working in these poor countries. Aims to provide a worldwide network through which doctors can request resources directly from donors. Educates local residents about international health care issues and promotes civic involvement. **Tele-**

communication Services: electronic mail, rajiv@adoptadoctor.org. **Publications:** Newsletter, weekly. **Price:** free. **Alternate Formats:** online.

Play

12479 ■ KaBOOM!
4455 Connecticut Ave. NW, Ste.B100
Washington, DC 20008
Ph: (202)659-0215
E-mail: info@kaboom.org
URL: http://www.kaboom.org
Contact: Darrell Hammond, Founder/CEO
Founded: 1995. **Description:** Promotes safe and accessible playgrounds to America's children; links communities and corporations to build playgrounds. Sponsors the KaBOOM! Let Us Play Camp. **Publications:** *Playtime*. Newsletter. **Alternate Formats:** online ● Handbooks. **Conventions/Meetings:** annual Playground Institute - conference, provides training.

Police

12480 ■ Concerns of Police Survivors (COPS)
PO Box 3199
Camdenton, MO 65020
Ph: (573)346-4911
Fax: (573)346-1414
E-mail: cops@nationalcops.org
URL: http://www.nationalcops.org
Contact: Suzie Sawyer, Exec. Dir.
Founded: 1984. **Members:** 15,000. **Regional Groups:** 6. **State Groups:** 26. **Local Groups:** 19. **Description:** Assists in the rebuilding of the lives of surviving families of law enforcement officers killed in the line of duty as determined by Federal criteria. Provides training to law enforcement agencies on survivor victimization issues. Educates the public on the need to support the law enforcement profession and its survivors. **Publications:** *Support Services to Surviving Families of Line-of-Duty Death*. Handbook ● Newsletter, quarterly. Focuses on the special concerns of law enforcement surviving families. **Circulation:** 22,000 ● Newsletter, semiannual. Contains articles related to law enforcement. **Circulation:** 37,000.

Political Education

12481 ■ Kashmiri American Council (KAC)
733 15th St. NW, Ste.1100
Washington, DC 20005
Ph: (202)628-6789 (703)295-8682
Fax: (202)393-0062
E-mail: kac@kashmiri.com
URL: http://www.kashmiri.com
Contact: Dr. Ghulam-Nabi Fai, Exec. Dir.
Founded: 1990. **Members:** 32,000. **Membership Dues:** individual, $50 (annual). **Staff:** 5. **Budget:** $100,000. **Description:** Persons interested in the issue of Kashmiri independence. Dedicated to raise awareness in the United States of the Kashmiri independence movement and to the promotion of social contacts among families of Kashmiri ancestry, regardless of religious or political affiliations. **Libraries: Type:** by appointment only. **Holdings:** articles, clippings. **Subjects:** South Asia. **Conventions/Meetings:** annual convention.

Population

12482 ■ Anita Borg Institute for Women and Technology (ABI)
1501 Page Mill Rd., MS 1105
Palo Alto, CA 94304
Ph: (650)236-4756
Fax: (650)852-8172

E-mail: information@anitaborg.org
URL: http://www.anitaborg.org/index.php
Contact: Telle Whitney PhD, Pres./CEO
Founded: 1997. **Multinational. Description:** Promotes replacing current emphases in international population control programs with a feminist framework stressing education and male contraceptive techniques. Seeks to make women's rights a primary criterion for assessing potential population control strategies. **Awards:** Anita Borg Early Career Award. **Frequency:** annual. **Type:** recognition. **Recipient:** for a woman in computer science or engineering who has made significant research contributions. **Formerly:** (2001) Institute on Women and Technology. **Publications:** *The Spiral*. Newsletter. Alternate Formats: online ● *Taking Population Out of the Equation: Reformulating I=PAT*. Book.

12483 ■ Center for Communication Programs (CCP)
Johns Hopkins Bloomberg School of Public Hea.
111 Market Pl., Ste.310
Baltimore, MD 21202
Ph: (410)659-6300
Fax: (410)659-6266
E-mail: webmaster@jhuccp.org
URL: http://www.jhuccp.org
Contact: Prof. Jane T. Bertrand PhD, Dir.
Founded: 1988. **Staff:** 400. **Description:** Works to focus attention on the central role of communication in behavior change and to provide leadership in the field of health communication and behavior change. Is currently active in nearly 40 countries worldwide with a portfolio that includes reproductive health, family planning, HIV/AIDS, maternal health, child survival and democracy and governance. Aims to provide leadership in meeting the health challenges of the future through state-of-the-art communication strategies, institution-building, community mobilization, advocacy training, interdisciplinary research, and program evaluation. Major components include the Health Communication Partnership (HIP), Information and Knowledge for Optimal Health (INFO), the Zambia Integrated Health Package Communication and Community Partnership (ZIHPCOMM, 1998), and the Sustaining Technical Achievements in Reproductive Health/Family Planning Project in Indonesia (STARH, 2000). Through these major components and other privately and publicly funded projects, the center "has set international standards for health communication". **Computer Services:** database, POPLINE, bibliographic retrieval system available online or on CD-ROM. **Programs:** Core Initiative; Malawi's BRIDGE. **Projects:** Family Health and AIDS; Health Communications Partnership; Healthy Russia 2020; Information and Knowledge for Optimal Health; Maternal and Neonatal Health; Sustaining Technical Achievement in Reproductive Health/Family Planning. **Publications:** *Communication Impact!* ● *POPLINE Users' Guide* ● *Population Reports* (in Arabic, English, French, and Spanish), quarterly. Journal. Contains information on family planning, population, and related health issues. **Price:** free in developing countries. **Circulation:** 180,000 ● Papers, periodic. Contains occasional papers on various topics related to family planning, communication, and research. **Conventions/Meetings:** annual Advances in Health Communication and Advocacy - workshop.

12484 ■ Negative Population Growth (NPG)
2861 Duke St., Ste.36
Alexandria, VA 22314
Ph: (703)370-9510
Fax: (703)370-9514
E-mail: npg@npg.org
URL: http://www.npg.org
Contact: Donald Mann, Pres.
Founded: 1972. **Members:** 25,000. **Membership Dues:** regular, $30 (annual). **Staff:** 5. **Budget:** $600,000. **Description:** Individuals who believe that "a drastic reduction in total population size represents the only viable option consistent with human survival." Promotes a 50&percent; reduction in U.S. and total world population size over the next 90-100 years. Advocates that the birth rate be lowered by voluntary measures such as national population control pro-

grams, financial and tax incentives, and public education. Maintains speakers' bureau. **Publications:** *NPG Forum Series, The NPG Letter*, 3/year. Newsletter. Alternate Formats: online ● *Population Resource Outlook*, quarterly. Newsletter. Alternate Formats: online ● *Position Papers*. Alternate Formats: online ● *Special Reports*. Alternate Formats: online. **Conventions/Meetings:** annual meeting - always third Wednesday in November, New York City.

12485 ■ Office of Population Affairs Clearinghouse (OPA)
PO Box 30686
Bethesda, MD 20824
Free: (866)640-7827
Fax: (866)592-3299
E-mail: clearinghouse@dhhsopa.net
URL: http://opa.osophs.dhhs.gov/clearinghouse.html
Regional Groups: 10. **State Groups:** 51. **Languages:** English, Spanish. **Description:** Makes available educational pamphlets on abstinence, contraception, adolescent pregnancy and sexuality, sexually transmitted diseases (including HIV/AIDS), and other important aspects of reproductive health care and family planning to all requesters, including Title X grantees, individual consumers, educators, health care providers, and others. Most titles are available in English and Spanish; several pamphlets are written and designed specifically for adolescents. **Formerly:** Family Life Information Exchange.

12486 ■ Population Action International (PAI)
1300 19th St. NW, Ste.100
Washington, DC 20036-1613
Ph: (202)557-3400
Fax: (202)728-4177
E-mail: pai@popact.org
URL: http://www.populationaction.org
Contact: Amy Coen, Pres./CEO
Founded: 1965. **Staff:** 40. **Budget:** $3,200,000. **Description:** Seeks to advance policies and programs that slow population growth in order to enhance the quality of life for all ages. Advocates expansion of voluntary family planning, other reproductive health services, and educational and economic opportunities for girls and women. **Libraries: Type:** reference. **Holdings:** 7,000. **Subjects:** demography, family planning, status of women, environment. **Computer Services:** Information services, population issues. **Departments:** Public Policy and Strategic Initiatives; Research and Communications. **Programs:** International Advocacy. **Formerly:** (1993) Population Crisis Committee. **Publications:** *Analytical Studies* ● *Population and Environment Studies*, periodic.

12487 ■ Population Communication (PC)
1250 E Walnut St., Ste.220
Pasadena, CA 91106
Ph: (626)793-4750
Fax: (626)793-4791
E-mail: popcommla@aol.com
URL: http://www.novacancythemovie.com
Contact: Robert Gillespie, Pres.
Founded: 1977. **Staff:** 3. **Budget:** $550,000. **Multinational. Description:** Seeks to develop and implement a strategy for global population stabilization and provide population information to national and community leaders in developing countries. Aims to: encourage national leaders to take an active role in solving the population problem and to sign a statement on population stabilization; develop population stabilization policies. Conducts programs such as: providing motion picture and television script writers with comedic and dramatic concepts that focus on the problems of population growth, environmental deterioration, adolescent pregnancies, and depletion of fossil fuels; informing doctors and paramedics in underdeveloped countries of the latest birth control techniques and how to obtain the equipment and training to provide services; preparing reports and protocols for applying population-planning technology and outlining population stabilization policies. **Publications:** *Developing a Population Communications Program for National Leaders*. Manual ● *Explaining Contraceptive Methods*. Manual ● *No Vacancy*. Film. Features 90-minutes odyssey that explores family

planning programs and policies around the world. **Price:** $10.00 ● *No Vacancy: Global Responses to the Human Population Explosion*. Book. **Price:** $20.00 ● *Population and Survival: The Challenge in Five Countries* ● Reports ● Surveys.

12488 ■ Population Communications International (PCI)
777 United Nations Plz., 5th Fl.
44th St. at 1st Ave.
New York, NY 10017
Ph: (212)687-3366
Free: (877)724-7627
Fax: (212)661-4188
E-mail: info@population.org
URL: http://www.population.org
Contact: Michael Tatu Castlen, Exec. Dir.
Founded: 1985. **Members:** 24,000. **Membership Dues:** individual, $20 (annual). **Staff:** 22. **Budget:** $4,900,000. **Description:** Works worldwide in the fields of population, environment and development. Develops motivational communication campaigns on family planning and other population-related topics for use in countries with the highest population growth rates. Promotes increased individual understanding of the relationships between family size, the environment, and the health, happiness, and prosperity of individuals, families, and communities. Uses a broad, multi-media approach, including family planning soap operas, to promote family health, family planning, and the small family norm. **Awards:** Population/ Environment Award. **Frequency:** annual. **Type:** monetary. **Recipient:** for population/environment programs by environmental organizations. **Publications:** *Global Intersections*, monthly. Newsletter. Alternate Formats: online ● *Member News*, quarterly. Newsletter. Provides updates for members on PCI activities. **Price:** free, for members only. **Circulation:** 7,000 ● *On Air*, quarterly. Newsletter ● Annual Report, annual. Alternate Formats: online. **Conventions/Meetings:** quarterly board meeting ● NGO Committee on Population and Development - meeting - 3/year ● annual Soap Summit - meeting.

12489 ■ Population Connection
2120 L St. NW, Ste.500
Washington, DC 20037
Ph: (202)332-2200
Free: (800)POP-1956
Fax: (202)332-2302
E-mail: info@populationconnection.org
URL: http://www.populationconnection.org
Contact: John Seager, Pres./CEO
Founded: 1968. **Members:** 50,000. **Membership Dues:** individual, $25 (annual) ● student, $10 (annual). **Budget:** $3,000,000. **Local Groups:** 16. **Description:** Works to educate and motivate Americans to help meet global population challenge, and to mobilize support for the adoption of policies and programs necessary to stop global population growth. Participates in coalitions, influences governmental policies on the international, national, state, and local levels; works with the media; engages in teacher training and public education programs. Conducts research, interprets and applies the research of others. Maintains Speaker's Bureau; compiles statistics. **Libraries: Type:** reference. **Subjects:** reproductive health, environment, poverty, women's issues, population. **Departments:** Field Outreach and Education; Government Relations; Media and Public Information; Population Education. **Projects:** Activist Network; Activist Training and Education; Campus Organizing; Legislative Alert; Population Education Training and Population Education Trainers Network; Population Issues Forum; Roving Reporter; Speakers Network; Table Net. **Formerly:** (2002) Zero Population Growth - Seattle Chapter. **Publications:** *Children's Environmental Index* ● *Making a Difference* ● *Planning the Ideal Family: The Small Family Option* ● *The Reporter*. Magazine. Alternate Formats: online ● *Selected Resources on Population* ● *USA by Numbers: A Statistical Portrait of the United States* ● *World Population*. Video. **Price:** $20.00 ● Newsletter, bimonthly. Provides commentary concerning international and domestic population-related issues. **Price:** included in membership dues. ISSN: 0199-0071. **Cir-**

culation: 50,000 ● Annual Report, annual. Alternate Formats: online ● Brochures ● Also publishes educational, informational, and policy material. Conventions/Meetings: monthly meeting - always in Washington, DC.

12490 ■ Population Council
1 Dag Hammarskjold Plz.
New York, NY 10017
Ph: (212)339-0500
Fax: (212)755-6052
E-mail: pubinfo@popcouncil.org
URL: http://www.popcouncil.org
Contact: Mr. Peter G. Donaldson, Pres.
Founded: 1952. **Staff:** 550. **Budget:** $84,000,000. **Regional Groups:** 5. **National Groups:** 14. **Languages:** Arabic, English, French, Spanish. **Multinational. Description:** Seeks to improve the well-being and reproductive health of current and future generations around the world. Helps achieve a humane, equitable, and sustainable balance between people and resources. **Libraries: Type:** reference. **Holdings:** 25,000. **Subjects:** demography, family planning, women's studies developing countries. **Awards:** MEAWARDS. **Type:** recognition. **Recipient:** for Middle East research ● Navrongo Health Research Centre Fellowships, Ghana. **Type:** fellowship. **Recipient:** for research in public health ● Reproductive Biomedicine Postdoctoral Fellowships. **Type:** fellowship. **Recipient:** for research on biomedical sciences ● Social Science Fellowship. **Type:** fellowship. **Recipient:** for research in the social sciences ● Vietnam Fellowship. **Type:** fellowship. **Boards:** Institutional Review; Population and Development Review Advisory; Studies in Family Planning Advisory; Trustees. **Committees:** Fellowship; International Committee for Contraception Research; MEAwards Advisory; Quality, Calidad, Qualite Advisory Group; SEEDS Steering. **Divisions:** Center for Biomedical Research; Corporate Affairs; International Programs; Policy Research. **Programs:** Communication of Research Results; Contraceptive Development; Demographic Behavior; Family Planning; Fellowships; Frontiers Reproductive Health; Gender, Family and Development; Horizons (HIV/AIDS/RTIs Prevention and Care); Interrelationships between Population and Socioeconomic Change; Population Policy; Reproductive Health; Reproductive Physiology; Strengthening Professional Resources. **Publications:** *Momentum*, semiannual. Newsletter. Highlights Population Council news, research, and institutional activities in the fields of biomedicine, public health, and social science. ● *Population and Development Review*, quarterly. Journal. Covers the interrelationships between population and socio-economic change and related public policy issues. **Price:** free to professionals in developing countries; $36.00/year. ISSN: 0098-7921. **Circulation:** 5,500. Alternate Formats: microform ● *Population Briefs*, quarterly. Newsletter. Results of research by council scientists in biomedical sciences, public health, and social sciences. **Price:** free. ISSN: 1084-6786. **Circulation:** 5,000 ● *Population Council Annual Report*, annual. **Price:** free. ISSN: 0361-7858 ● *Studies in Family Planning*, quarterly. Journal. Covers family planning and related health and development issues; including such aspects as fertility regulation and contraceptive technology. **Price:** free to professionals in developing countries; $24.00/year. ISSN: 0039-3665. **Circulation:** 5,500. Alternate Formats: microform ● Books ● Proceedings. From conferences. ● Papers ● Pamphlets. **Conventions/Meetings:** conference.

12491 ■ Population-Environment Balance (PEB)
2000 P St. NW, Ste.600
Washington, DC 20036
Ph: (202)955-5700
Fax: (202)955-6161
E-mail: uspop@us.net
URL: http://www.balance.org
Founded: 1973. **Members:** 10,000. **Membership Dues:** regular, $35 ● advocate, $250 ● friend, $75. **Staff:** 5. **Budget:** $400,000. **Description:** Works to educate and impress upon the American public and policymakers the "adverse effects" of population

growth on the environment. Advocates population stabilization in the U.S; seeks reform to U.S. immigration policy. Promotes increased contraceptive research and availability. Sponsors education programs and media campaigns. **Convention/Meeting:** none. **Formerly:** (1985) Environmental Fund. **Publications:** *Balance Activist*, quarterly. Newsletter. Analyzes the consequence of U.S. population growth. Discusses opportunities for action. **Price:** included in membership dues. ISSN: 1083-3498. **Circulation:** 10,000 ● *Balance Data*. Provides in-depth analysis of the U.S. population issue. **Price:** included in membership dues.

12492 ■ Population Institute (PI)
107 2nd St. NE
Washington, DC 20002
Ph: (202)544-3300
Free: (800)787-0038
Fax: (202)544-0068
E-mail: web@populationinstitute.org
URL: http://www.populationinstitute.org
Contact: Hal Burdett, Dir.
Founded: 1969. **Members:** 81,000. **Membership Dues:** direct, $25 (annual). **Staff:** 16. **Budget:** $1,350,000. **For-Profit. Description:** U.S. members are doctors, lawyers, businessmen, educators, religious leaders, and other concerned individuals. Overseas members are those influential in their country's leadership structure and those working directly in the population/family planning field. Seeks to marshal public opinion on global overpopulation problems. Keeps members abreast of initiatives and developments to curb world over population. Conveys members' views on global population issues to their elected representatives on matters of major legislation. Sponsors educational programs. Maintains an accredited fellows program that sponsors 4-8 fellows per year and speakers' bureau. **Awards:** Media Excellence Award. **Frequency:** annual. **Type:** recognition. **Recipient:** for population coverage. **Computer Services:** Online services, population news. **Committees:** Bankers Who Care; Business Leaders Who Care; Doctors Who Care; Educators Who Care; Lawyers Who Care; Religious Leaders Who Care; Scientists Who Care. **Formerly:** (1970) Population Institute Advocates, Inc. **Publications:** *Popline* (in English, French, and Spanish), bimonthly. Newsletter. Focuses on policy, research, and demographic developments related to world population problems and issues. **Price:** $25.00/year. **Circulation:** 233,000. Alternate Formats: online ● *Towards the 21st Century*, quarterly. Monograph ● *World Population News Service*. **Conventions/Meetings:** annual Global Media Award Ceremony - conference, for excellence in population reporting and family planning study tours.

12493 ■ Population Resource Center (PRC)
1725 K St. NW, Ste.1102
Washington, DC 20006
Ph: (202)467-5030
Fax: (202)467-5034
E-mail: prc@prcdc.org
URL: http://www.prcdc.org
Contact: Jane S. De Lung, Pres.
Founded: 1975. **Staff:** 10. **Budget:** $600,000. **Description:** Promotes better understanding of and capacity to deal with the determinants and consequences of demographic change by providing a link between the population experts and policymakers in both the public and private sectors. Provides professional analyses of: relationship of demographic trends to employment and urban revitalization; women's roles and the family; needs of the elderly; corporate planning and policy; health care and social security; community development, immigration and international aid; resources and the environment. Prepares and conducts briefings, workshops, and policy discussions, commissions research on population-related topics for foundation, corporations, government, trade and professional associations, and other organizations. **Publications:** *Executive Summaries*, 10-15/year. Newsletter. Alternate Formats: online ● *PRC Focus*, semiannual. Annual Report. Alternate Formats: online ● Brochure.

Pornography

12494 ■ Anti-Child Pornography Organization (ACPO)
PO Box 22338
Eagan, MN 55122-0388
E-mail: dstead@antichildporn.org
URL: http://www.antichildporn.org
Contact: Doug Stead, Vice Chm.
Multinational. Description: Seeks to stop the sexual exploitation of children on the internet. Provides information to law enforcement authorities, including activity hot spots on the internet and the activities of online child pornographers. Addresses the issues of child pornography production and distribution via the internet, and the predatory use of the internet for the sexual abuse of children. **Awards:** ACPO Child Friendly Award. **Frequency:** annual. **Type:** recognition. **Recipient:** to individuals for their contributions to the health, safety, rights and education of the world's children. **Telecommunication Services:** electronic mail, donations@antichildporn.org ● electronic mail, liaisons@antichildporn.org ● electronic mail, press@antichildporn.org. **Publications:** Brochure. Alternate Formats: online ● Papers. Alternate Formats: online.

Post-Traumatic Stress

12495 ■ EMDR - Humanitarian Assistance Programs (EMDR HAP)
PO Box 6505
Hamden, CT 06517
Ph: (203)288-4450
Fax: (203)288-4060
E-mail: emdrhap@emdrhap.org
URL: http://www.emdrhap.org
Contact: Robert A. Gelbach PhD, Exec. Dir.
Founded: 1995. **Multinational. Description:** Represents individuals committed to relieving human suffering and preventing the after-effects of trauma and violence. Promotes recovery from traumatic stress through direct service and community-based training in EMDR for mental health workers all over the world. Provides training to mental health professionals serving traumatized communities worldwide. Promotes further research on trauma risk and recovery factors and treatment outcomes. **Publications:** *What's Happening Now*. Newsletter. Alternate Formats: online.

12496 ■ Gift From Within (GFW)
16 Cobb Hill Rd.
Camden, ME 04843
Ph: (207)236-8858
Fax: (207)236-2818
E-mail: joyceb3955@aol.com
URL: http://www.giftfromwithin.org
Contact: Joyce Boaz, Co-Founder/Exec. Dir.
Founded: 1993. **Multinational. Description:** Offers support and counseling to victims of post-traumatic stress disorder. Provides educational resources related to post-traumatic stress disorder. Maintains a roster of survivors who are willing to participate in an international network of peer support.

Poverty

12497 ■ Center for Community Change (CCC)
1536 U St. NW
Washington, DC 20009
Ph: (202)339-9300
Free: (877)777-1536
E-mail: info@communitychange.org
URL: http://www.communitychange.org
Contact: Deepak Bhargava, Exec. Dir.
Founded: 1968. **Staff:** 46. **Budget:** $4,500,000,000. **Description:** Assists community groups of urban and rural poor in making positive changes in their communities. Designs and delivers technical assistance to these community organizations, focuses attention on national issues dealing with human poverty, and

works to make government more responsive to the needs of the poor. Sponsors workshops. **Committees:** National Issues. **Projects:** Community Voting; Fair Immigration Reform Movement; Movement Vision; Native American; Transportation Equity; Voices For Change. **Absorbed:** Citizens Crusade Against Poverty. **Publications:** *Center for Community Change—Annual Report.* **Price:** available to members only ● *Citizen Action Guides,* periodic. Monographs ● *Community Change,* quarterly. Newsletter. Provides information on low-income housing, community and economic development, community reinvestment by banks, and government funding. **Price:** $20.00/year. **Circulation:** 2,000. Alternate Formats: online ● *CRA Report,* 2-3/year ● *Education Organizing,* quarterly. Newsletter. Alternate Formats: online ● *Friday Report,* semimonthly. Newsletter. Provides information about job training programs for Native Americans. **Price:** included in membership dues. **Circulation:** 200 ● *Housing Organizing.* Newsletter. Alternate Formats: online ● *Organizing for Neighborhood Development: A Handbook for Citizen Groups.* **Price:** $4.00 ● *Special Project Report,* periodic ● Also publishes research papers and reports.

12498 ■ Community Action Partnership
1140 Connecticut Ave.
Washington, DC 20036
Ph: (202)265-7546
Fax: (202)265-8850
E-mail: info@communityactionpartnership.com
URL: http://www.communityactionpartnership.com
Contact: Derrick Span, Natl. Pres.

Founded: 1971. **Members:** 800. **Staff:** 12. **Budget:** $2,000,000. **Description:** Represents community action agencies and their executive directors and board members and promotes a unified approach to solving the problems of poverty within the U.S. Provides training and program information and promote members' professional growth in the field of community development and stimulates the cultivation of expertise in operating community action programs as means to demonstrate progress toward eliminating the causes of poverty. Serves as an advocate of the poor at all levels of society and government; solicits, compiles, publishes, and distributes information on progress in individual and community development; informs members of legislation and administrative policy pertinent to their projects; transmits recommendations from members to governmental agencies; works as a problem solver in areas affecting community action agencies; makes presentations and recommendations of community development projects to interested groups and agencies; develops standards of excellence and recognizes exceptional performance in community action; accepts and administers grants and contracts for the purpose of conducting programs in furtherance of achieving the goals; and prepares research papers on issues dealing with poverty, youth and the elderly. **Awards:** Award for Excellence in Community Action. **Frequency:** annual. **Type:** recognition. **Recipient:** for successful completion of a rigorous self study and peer review evaluation demonstrating an ongoing commitment to quality and performance. **Commissions:** Award for Excellence. **Formerly:** (1984) National Community Action Agency Executive Directors Association; (1986) National Community Action Agency Directors Association; (2004) National Association of Community Action Agencies. **Publications:** *Directory of Community Action Agencies,* annual ● *The Promise,* quarterly. Magazine. **Price:** $50.00 /year for members. **Advertising:** accepted ● *Training Manual* ● *Welfare Reform Statement* ● Annual Report, annual. **Conventions/Meetings:** annual convention.

12499 ■ Economic Success Clearinghouse
c/o The Finance Project
1401 New York Ave. NW, Ste.800
Washington, DC 20005
Ph: (202)628-4200
Fax: (202)628-1293

E-mail: es@financeproject.org
URL: http://www.financeproject.org/irc/win.asp
Contact: Cheryl D. Hayes, Exec. Dir.

Description: Provides information to individuals and organizations on policy choices, practices, program and financial data, funding sources, federal and state legislation and plans, program and management tools, and technical assistance to develop and implement welfare reforms to reduce dependency and promote the well-being of children and families. Offers website with access to more than 9,000 links on more than 400 websites. Maintains a clearinghouse of welfare reform-related information, policy analysis, and technical assistance resources; maintains a database containing information on organizations, experts, publications, state and local initiatives, technical assistance service offerings, and Web sites. **Formerly:** (2006) Welfare Information Network. **Publications:** *Issue Notes.* Alternate Formats: online ● *Resources for Welfare Decisions.* Alternate Formats: online.

12500 ■ Food for the Poor (FFP)
6401 Lyons Rd., Dept. 9662
Coconut Creek, FL 33073
Ph: (954)427-2222
Free: (800)427-9104
Fax: (954)570-7654
E-mail: contactffp@foodforthepoor.org
URL: http://www.foodforthepoor.com
Contact: Mr. Robin G. Mahfood, Pres./CEO

Founded: 1982. **Members:** 520,000. **Staff:** 145. **Description:** Works to improve the health, economic, spiritual, and social conditions of the poor, primarily in the Caribbean and Latin America. Provides educational and charitable programs, Speaker's Bureau, and children's services. **Convention/Meeting:** none. **Awards:** Chalice Award. **Frequency:** annual. **Type:** recognition. **Recipient:** for 15 to 30 consistent donors. **Publications:** *Answering The Call,* quarterly. Newsletter ● Annual Report, annual.

12501 ■ Free Store/Food Bank (FS/FB)
1250 Tennessee Ave.
Cincinnati, OH 45229
Ph: (513)482-4500 (513)241-1064
Fax: (513)482-7532
E-mail: jmorrow@freestorefoodbank.org
URL: http://www.freestorefoodbank.org
Contact: John J. Young, CEO

Founded: 1971. **Members:** 550. **Staff:** 90. **Budget:** $2,000,000. **Regional Groups:** 19. **Description:** Seeks to help those in need, including poor people and victims of disasters and emergencies. Supplies food, clothing, beds, blankets, stoves, refrigerators, and space heaters to the needy. Attempts to raise levels of fixed income programs for the poor; monitors food stamp legislation; offers advocacy services on behalf of the poor. Works to educate government officials, business people, church members, and others about poverty, its causes, and its real costs to taxpayers. Operates regional food banks in southwestern Ohio, northern Kentucky, and southeastern Indiana. Facilitates legislative advocacy around food and nutrition issues. Compiles statistics. **Awards:** **Type:** recognition. **Computer Services:** Mailing lists ● online services, client data access system. **Committees:** Benefits; Marketing. **Divisions:** Direct Services; Food Bank; Prepared and Perishable Foods; Processing. **Affiliated With:** America's Second Harvest; United Way of America. **Formerly:** (1983) Free Store. **Publications:** *FoodBank Statement,* quarterly. **Conventions/Meetings:** semiannual meeting.

12502 ■ Friends of the Third World (FTW)
611 W Wayne St.
Fort Wayne, IN 46802-2167
Ph: (260)422-6821
Free: (800)401-2672
Fax: (260)422-6821
E-mail: fotw@igc.org
URL: http://www.friendsofthethirdworld.org
Contact: James F. Goetsch, Exec. Off.

Founded: 1972. **Members:** 600. **Membership Dues:** general, $10 (annual). **Staff:** 6. **Budget:** $500,000.

Local Groups: 6. **Languages:** English, French, Spanish. **Description:** Individuals in 40 countries concerned with voluntary action against poverty; organizations of low-income persons including handicraft cooperatives, neighborhood associations, and agencies working on the poverty issue. Aims to demonstrate the existence and viability of an alternative system of trade as an effective means to deal with poverty and unemployment. Educates the public regarding poverty-related problems and possible solutions. Provides information, consultation, and training skills for low-income persons in graphic arts/retail sales, building maintenance, bookkeeping, and management; also provides marketing assistance for handicrafts produced by low-income persons and groups. Distributes books on poverty-related topics and organizes educational activities. Operates technical assistance and resource center; conducts workshops. **Libraries:** Type: open to the public. **Holdings:** 600. **Subjects:** informational economics. **Committees:** Education Advisory; Handicrafts Marketing; Printing. **Divisions:** Cooperative Trading; Delta Communications Printing Cooperative; United States Union of Third World Shoppes; Whole World Books. **Projects:** Hunger Fund; Technical Assistance. **Formerly:** (1973) Young World Development Regional Center. **Publications:** *Alternative Trading News,* quarterly. Newsletter. Covers organization's activities. Includes produce profile, marketing reports, calendar of events, and resource list. **Price:** included in membership dues. **Circulation:** 10,000 ● *Book Catalog,* periodic ● Pamphlets. **Conventions/Meetings:** annual conference (exhibits).

12503 ■ Inter-Faith Community Services (IFCS)
3370 S Irving St.
Englewood, CO 80110-1816
Ph: (303)789-0501
E-mail: ifcs@ifcs.org
URL: http://www.ifcs.org
Contact: Sandra Blythe-Perry, Exec. Dir.

Founded: 1965. **Staff:** 12. **Budget:** $1,500,000. **Languages:** English, Spanish. **Description:** Acts as a community social services agency supported by the cities it serves, county commissioners, school districts, businesses, service clubs, churches and individuals in the community. Provides food and clothing banks, financial assistance to prevent homelessness - rent, mortgage and utility assistance; offers a career center to assist in finding employment, provides transportation assistance, assistance with birth certificates, prescriptions, recreation passes, hearing aid and glasses, case management, referrals and two transitional housing programs for formerly homeless families. Assists victims of crime, homebound seniors, provides financial assistance to schools throughout the state whose children cannot afford reduced-priced lunch so that no child will go hungry during the school day, sends low-income children to summer camp. Outfits children for the first day of school with new clothing, shoes, school supplies, backpacks, etc. Provides Thanksgiving baskets with everything needed for the holiday meal as well as an Adopt-A-Family Program for the December holidays. **Programs:** Clothing Bank; Food Bank; Gift of Hearing; Gift of Sight; Holiday Adopt-a-Family; Rental, Mortgage and Utility Assistance; Thanksgiving Baskets; Transitional Housing. **Formerly:** (1998) Inter-Faith Task Force; (2005) Inter-Faith Task Force for Community Services. **Publications:** Newsletter, 3/year ● Brochures.

12504 ■ Jewish Fund for Justice (JFJ)
New York Off.
330 7th Ave., Ste.1902
New York, NY 10001
Ph: (212)213-2113
Fax: (212)213-2233
E-mail: info@jewishjustice.org
URL: http://www.jewishjustice.org
Contact: Simon Greer, Pres./CEO

Founded: 1985. **Staff:** 12. **Budget:** $2,500,000. **Description:** Provides financial and technical assistance to grassroots community organizations combating the root causes of poverty on a nonsectarian basis. Acts as "a visible Jewish moral and religious presence in support of social and economic justice". Presents grants to various groups and causes, including low-income women in Central Harlem working for improved public housing, child care workers in Oakland seeking fair wages and working conditions, and immigrants and refugees in Chicago organizing for legal, educational, employment, and human rights. **Awards: Frequency:** semiannual. **Type:** grant. **Recipient:** for non-profit organizations ● **Frequency:** biennial. **Type:** monetary. **Computer Services:** database, fundraising and grantmaking. **Committees:** Advisory. **Affiliated With:** National Network of Grantmakers; Women and Philanthropy. **Publications:** *Justice, Justice Shalt Thou Pursue: American Jews Building Grassroots Partnerships for Social Change* ● Annual Report, annual. Alternate Formats: online.

12505 ▪ Manpower Demonstration Research Corporation (MDRC)

16 E 34th St., 19th Fl.
New York, NY 10016-4326
Ph: (212)532-3200
Fax: (212)684-0832
E-mail: information@mdrc.org
URL: http://www.mdrc.org
Contact: Gordon Berlin, Pres.

Founded: 1974. **Budget:** $35,000,000. **Multinational. Description:** Studies social policies affecting low-income families. **Computer Services:** Online services; InPractice. **Projects:** Devolution and Urban Change; Graduation Really Achieves Dreams; JobsPlus; Next Generation; Opening Doors. **Affiliated With:** Ford Foundation. **Publications:** Papers ● Articles. **Conventions/Meetings:** seminar.

12506 ▪ Mercy Corps

Dept. W
PO Box 2669
Portland, OR 97208-2669
Free: (800)292-3355
E-mail: cnelson@mercycorpsfield.org
URL: http://www.mercycorps.org
Contact: Neal Keny-Guyer, CEO

Founded: 1979. **Staff:** 2,000. **Budget:** $132,647,360. **Description:** Exists to alleviate suffering, poverty and oppression by helping people build secure, productive and just communities. Provides over $830 million in assistance to people in 80 nations since 1979; agency's programs currently reach over 6 million people in more than 39 countries, including the United States. More than 91 percent of the agency's resources are allocated to programs that directly assist those in need. **Awards:** Humanitarian of the Year. **Frequency:** annual. **Type:** recognition. **Recipient:** for individual who has made significant contributions to the poor. **Telecommunication Services:** additional toll-free number, (888)256-1900. **Affiliated With:** Pax World Service. **Formerly:** (1979) Save the Refugees Fund. **Publications:** *The Bridge.* Magazine. Contains issues related to civil society and development. ● *Mercy Report*, 5/year. Newsletter. **Price:** free. **Advertising:** accepted.

12507 ▪ Mission of Mercy

15475 Gleneagle Dr.
PO Box 62600
Colorado Springs, CO 80962
Ph: (719)481-0400
Free: (800)864-0200
Fax: (719)481-4649
E-mail: mominfo@mofm.org
URL: http://www.missionofmercy.org
Contact: Dr. Wayde I. Goodall, Exec. Dir.

Founded: 1954. **Staff:** 27. **Budget:** $14,000,000. **Multinational. Description:** Works to meet the physical and spiritual needs of children in poverty-stricken areas of the world. Provides support through food, education, medical aid, health screening, social development and hope in Christ. **Publications:** *Mercy Connections*, 3/year. Magazine. Contains updates on organization projects worldwide. **Price:** free. **Circulation:** 45,000. Alternate Formats: online.

12508 ▪ National Black Survival Fund (EBSF)

PO Box 3005
Lafayette, LA 70502-3005
Ph: (337)942-2392
Fax: (337)232-5094
E-mail: foundation_s@bellsouth.net
Contact: Lena Charles, Pres.

Founded: 1982. **Description:** A project of the Southern Development Foundation (see separate entry). Improves the ability of black and other minority poor to achieve economic progress through their own effort and initiative. Believes that the economic, cultural, and physical survival of the nation's black community is endangered due to the recession, discrimination, and the Reagan administration's cutbacks in social assistance programs. Seeks to maintain and increase support for programs that can avert the economic and human catastrophe the fund says will result if the opportunities offered to blacks are undermined by current assistance cutbacks. Maintains Food for Survival Program in which landowners and sharecroppers in Mississippi and Louisiana volunteer land, equipment, and labor to provide food and employment for needy families; Health Care for Survival Program, a cooperative low-cost health center in Mississippi; Jobs for Survival Program, which has assisted in providing jobs for black workers in Alabama in construction, farming, and community service. **Formerly:** Emergency Black Survival Fund. **Publications:** Brochures ● Pamphlets.

12509 ▪ Poverty and Race Research Action Council (PRRAC)

1015 15th St. NW, Ste.400
Washington, DC 20005
Ph: (202)906-8023
Fax: (202)842-2885
E-mail: info@prrac.org
URL: http://www.prrac.org
Contact: Philip Tegeler, Exec. Dir.

Founded: 1990. **Staff:** 3. **Nonmembership. Description:** Social science researchers and activists. Promotes social science research and advocacy "on the intersection of race and poverty". Works to develop and advocate a planned policy agenda to address poverty and race issues. **Awards: Type:** grant. **Publications:** *Add it Up: Using Research to Improve Education for Low-Income and Minority Students.* Handbook. **Price:** $5.00. Alternate Formats: online ● *Civil Best Practices in State Low Income Housing Tax Credit Plans.* Report ● *Fragmented: Improving Education for Mobile Students.* Handbook. **Price:** $5.00 ● *Poverty and Race*, bimonthly. Newsletter. Each issues lists 100-200 resources. **Price:** $25.00/year; $42.00/2 years. ISSN: 1075-3591. Alternate Formats: online ● *Report of the Third National Conference on Housing Mobility.*

12510 ▪ The Revitalization Corps (TRC)

PO Box 1625
Hartford, CT 06101
Ph: (860)249-7523
Contact: Edward T. Coll, Dir.

Founded: 1964. **Description:** Professional and nonprofessional volunteers of all ages. Seeks to bridge the gap between suburbia and the inner city, as well as between other divergent groups including blue and white collar workers and the younger and older generations. Encourages suburban families, college students, and others to become personally involved in the problems of the inner city and the war on poverty and a one-to-one tutoring program for underprivileged children. Acts as advocate for people dealing with the bureaucratic systems with regard to housing, jobs, and drug treatment.

12511 ▪ Southern Development Foundation (SDF)

1006 Surrey St.
Lafayette, LA 70501
Ph: (337)232-7672
Fax: (337)232-5094
Contact: Rev. A. J. McKnight CS, Founder

Founded: 1972. **Description:** Combats black poverty in the South and helps the poor achieve economic independence. Provides, through its affiliates, money

and technical assistance to limited resource co-ops and community controlled organizations. Promotes minority co-ops. Helps to form selfhelp projects. Sponsors National Black Survival Fund (see separate entry). **Affiliated With:** National Black Survival Fund. **Supersedes:** Southern Cooperative Development Fund. **Conventions/Meetings:** semiannual meeting - always February and July.

12512 ▪ Synergos Institute

51 Madison Ave., 21st Fl.
New York, NY 10010
Ph: (212)447-8111
Fax: (212)447-8119
E-mail: synergos@synergos.org
URL: http://www.synergos.org
Contact: Robert H. Dunn, Pres./CEO

Founded: 1986. **Staff:** 20. **Budget:** $3,205,000. **Languages:** English, Spanish. **Multinational. Description:** Works to bring diverse sectors of society together to find new, more effective ways to narrow the gap between rich and poor. Strengthens the role of philanthropy and citizen leadership in social development, with particular emphasis on countries in Africa, Asia, and Latin America. **Computer Services:** database, funders to Latin American organizations. **Publications:** *A Survey of Endowed Grantmaking Foundations in Africa, Asia, Eastern Europe, Latin America and the Caribbean.* Report. **Price:** $5.00 ● *Building Development Projects in Partnership with NGOs and Communities: An Action Agenda for Government Policymakers and Donors.* Report. **Price:** $5.00 ● *Community-Based Development Experience: Can It Be Replicated from South to North, and If So, How?.* Report. **Price:** $5.00 ● *Endowed National Community Development Foundations: A New Approach to Financing the Non-Profit Sector in African Countries.* Report. **Price:** $5.00 ● *Establishing Endowed National Foundation in Countries of the South.* Report. **Price:** $5.00 ● *Holding Together: Collaborations and Partnerships in the Real World.* Report. **Price:** $5.00 ● *How Community Development Foundations Can Help Strengthen Civil Society.* Report. **Price:** $5.00 ● *Informal Survey of Activities Being Conducted in Japan by U.S. Non-Profit Organizations Working on Environment and Conservation Issues.* **Price:** $5.00 ● *Multiparty Cooperation for Development in Asia.* Report. **Price:** $5.00 ● *Proposal to Promote Democracy and Community Self-Reliance in Twenty Countries by Establishing Endowed Private Development Foundations.* Report. **Price:** $5.00 ● *Sustaining Collaborative Problem Solving: Strategies from a Study in Six Asian Countries.* Report. **Price:** $5.00. **Conventions/Meetings:** annual University for a Night - meeting, with discussion of specific actions to address poverty issues - held in May.

12513 ▪ Union Settlement Association (US)

237 E 104th St.
New York, NY 10029
Ph: (212)828-6000 (212)828-6018
Fax: (212)828-6022
E-mail: epsimon@unionsett.org
URL: http://www.unionsettlement.org
Contact: Ellen P. Simon, Exec. Dir.

Founded: 1895. **Members:** 12,000. **Staff:** 500. **Budget:** $19,000,000. **Languages:** English, Spanish. **Description:** Privately sponsored social service agency that assists individuals of all ages in low income neighborhoods in East Harlem, NY. Has served as a pioneer and innovator in neighborhood social action. Maintains a community center providing adult and senior citizen programs, and recreational, educational, and counseling programs for families and youth; an adolescent resource center and a community garden; a teen drug prevention model program, teen parenting and pregnancy prevention; four senior centers offering hot meals and recreational and social services to residents in one of the first violence prevention program city-sponsored apartment houses for older citizens; and the James Weldon Johnson Family and Children's Counseling Center providing complete psychiatric and psychological services and AIDS services. Sponsors adult literacy courses as well as information and counseling services. Sponsors the East Harlem HIV Care Network. Maintains credit union that encourages thrift through systematic savings and provides low interest loans to members. Offers head start and day care services for children and a nutrition and counseling program for seniors. **Programs:** Childcare; Education; Settlement College Readiness; Youth at Union. **Publications:** Annual Report, annual.

12514 ■ Women in Community Service (WICS)
1900 N Beauregard St., Ste.103
Alexandria, VA 22311
Ph: (703)671-0500
Free: (800)442-9427
Fax: (703)671-4489
E-mail: wicsnatl@wics.org
URL: http://www.wics.org
Contact: Jacquelyn L. Lendsey, Pres./CEO
Founded: 1964. **Members:** 7,000. **Staff:** 150. **Budget:** $5,700,000. **Regional Groups:** 10. **Description:** Aims to reduce the number of young women living in poverty by promoting self-reliance and economic independence. Addresses issues surrounding employment, job training, welfare reform, poverty and cultural diversity. Provides annual volunteers and staff for helping more than 150,000 low-income women and young adults by giving support services, mentoring and workforce preparation programs nationwide. **Programs:** Women's; Youth. **Publications:** *A Partnership for Success.* Handbook ● *Homophobia Booklet* ● *Lifeskills Brochure* ● *Mentor Handbook* ● *Professionalizing Your Image.* Video ● *Sexual Harassment Booklet* ● *This is WICS*, quarterly. Magazine ● *Workplace Etiquette.* Booklet ● Brochure ● Annual Report, annual. Alternate Formats: online. **Conventions/Meetings:** triennial board meeting ● semiannual meeting.

12515 ■ World Concern (WC)
19303 Fremont Ave. N
Seattle, WA 98133
Ph: (206)546-7201
Free: (800)755-5022
Fax: (206)546-7269
E-mail: info@worldconcern.org
URL: http://www.worldconcern.org
Contact: Mr. David Eller, Intl. Operations Dir.
Founded: 1955. **Staff:** 25. **Budget:** $81,676,323. **Regional Groups:** 3. **Local Groups:** 1. **Multinational. Description:** Provides disaster response and community development programs to the world's poor in Africa, Asia and the Americas without regard to race, religion, ethnicity or gender. Has served 5.5 million people in 32 countries. Believes that life is full of promise that no place is too difficult and no person too hopeless to reach. Works to: provide life, opportunity and hope to suffering people around the world; bring hope and reconciliation; empowers women with children. Gives women opportunities to improve their lives through education, small business and agricultural training programs, and microloans. World Concern works closely with local communities to eliminate core causes of poverty, with an emphasis on livelihood training, literacy and education; access to clean water, food and health care; disaster assistance; and special initiatives. **Departments:** International Operations; Ministry Management; Resource Development; World Concern Development Organization. **Affiliated With:** CRISTA Ministries. **Publications:** *World Concern's*, quarterly. Newsletter. **Price:** free. **Circulation:** 25,000.

Pro-Life

12516 ■ Healing the Culture
PO Box 82842
Kenmore, WA 98028
Ph: (425)481-6563
E-mail: mail@healingtheculture.com
URL: http://www.healingtheculture.com
Contact: Robert J. Spitzer PhD, Chm./Co-Founder
Founded: 2003. **Description:** Seeks to build a pro-life culture by teaching people to uphold the intrinsic

dignity of every human person, and inspiring individuals to live for deeper meaning and purpose. Works to transform the way human culture views the dignity of each human person. Aims to educate agents of cultural change and professionals who are influential in shaping cultural attitudes, and who can positively influence the behavior of others.

Public Health

12517 ■ Medicine for Peace (MFP)
2732 Unicorn Ln. NW
Washington, DC 20015
Ph: (202)362-9121
Fax: (202)362-6797
E-mail: medforpeace@aol.com
URL: http://www.medicineforpeace.org
Contact: Michael V. Viola MD, Dir.
Multinational. Description: Provides medical care and humanitarian assistance to mothers and children who are victims of war. **Boards:** Advisory.

Rape

12518 ■ National Clearinghouse on Marital and Date Rape (NCMDR)
2325 Oak St.
Berkeley, CA 94708
Free: (800)656-4673
Fax: (510)524-7768
URL: http://members.aol.com/ncmdr/index.html
Contact: Laura X, Dir.
Founded: 1978. **Members:** 5,000. **Membership Dues:** individual, $15 (annual) ● group, $30 (annual). **Staff:** 10. **Budget:** $50,000. **Languages:** English, Spanish. **For-Profit. Description:** Students, attorneys, legislators, faculty members, rape crisis centers, shelters, and other social service groups. Operates as speaking/consulting business. Is presently launching a nation-wide call for members to help marital, cohabitant, and date rape victims and to stop the rape of potential victims by vigorously educating the public and by providing resources to battered women's shelters, crisis centers, district attorneys and legislators through media appearances and lectures at college campuses and conferences. Ultimate goal is to "make intimate relationships truly egalitarian". Holds training sessions and workshops. Provides fee-based phone consultation (at $7.50 per 15 minutes) and fee-based document search and delivery services for the media, prosecutors, expert witnesses, victim/witness advocates, legislators, police, rape crisis workers, battered women's shelter workers, students, writers and others. Offers sociological and law research on court cases and legislation; year round volunteer program and internship program for credit. Compiles statistics. Maintains speakers' bureau. **Convention/Meeting:** none. **Libraries: Type:** reference. **Holdings:** 40,000; archival material, articles, clippings. **Subjects:** sexual assault, domestic violence. **Additional Websites:** http://ncmdr.org. **Formerly:** (1969) Women's History Research Center. **Publications:** *Date Rape/Marital Rape Packet.* Contains state law charts, statistics, issues and services. **Price:** $10.00 ● *Marital Rape Victims Fight Back.* **Price:** $3.00 ● *Prosecution Statistics on Marital/Date/cohabitant Rape.* **Price:** $3.00 ● *Rideout Trial Pamphlet.* **Price:** $3.00 ● *State Law Chart on Marital/Date Rape.* Pamphlet. **Price:** $3.00 ● $30 detailed Law Packet on E-mail (7 sections).

12519 ■ Rape, Abuse and Incest National Network (RAINN)
2000 L St. NW, Ste.406
Washington, DC 20036
Ph: (202)544-1034
Free: (800)656-HOPE
Fax: (202)544-3556
E-mail: info@rainn.org
URL: http://www.rainn.org
Contact: Scott Berkowitz, Pres.
Founded: 1994. **Membership Dues:** supporter, $25 ● keyholder, $50 ● bronze keyholder, $100 ● silver

keyholder, $250 ● gold keyholder, $500 ● platinum keyholder, $1,000. **Description:** Provides support for victims of sexual assault. **Boards:** Advisory; Online Hotline Program Advisory; Programmatic Advisory.

12520 ■ Women for Women
4455 Connecticut Ave., Ste.200
Washington, DC 20008
Ph: (202)737-7705
Fax: (202)737-7709
E-mail: general@womenforwomen.org
URL: http://www.womenforwomen.org
Contact: Zainab Salbi, Pres./CEO
Founded: 1993. **Members:** 7,000. **Membership Dues:** individual, $27 (monthly). **Staff:** 18. **Budget:** $8,000,000. **Description:** Seeks to help women survivors of war in Bosnia and Rwanda, provides emotional and financial support to women by matching them with sponsors in the U.S. Sponsors write letter and send small monthly donations. Runs a microcredit lending program in Bosnia. Also provides education and training to women. Also runs a Global Voices program. **Computer Services:** Mailing lists, of members. **Formerly:** (1998) Women for Women in Bosnia. **Publications:** *Outreach*, bimonthly. Newsletter. Discusses women's issues and women involved in wars. **Price:** included in membership dues.

Recreation

12521 ■ American Association for Physical Activity and Recreation (AAPAR)
1900 Assn. Dr.
Reston, VA 20191-1598
Ph: (703)476-3470
Free: (800)213-7193
Fax: (703)476-9527
E-mail: aapar@aahperd.org
URL: http://www.aahperd.org/aapar
Contact: Ms. Mariah Burton Nelson, Exec. Dir.
Founded: 1938. **Members:** 8,000. **Membership Dues:** professional, $125 (annual) ● undergraduate/graduate student, $45 (annual). **Staff:** 4. **Budget:** $500,000. **Regional Groups:** 6. **State Groups:** 50. **Description:** Aims to promote and support education, physical activity, and recreation by developing quality programming and professional training; providing leadership opportunities; disseminating guidelines and standards; enhancing public understanding of the importance of leisure and recreation in maintaining a creative and healthy lifestyle. Goals and objectives are to serve as a forum for professionals, students and organizations to educate and exchange information and ideas on physical activity and recreation services; develop and promote professional standards for education, physical activity and recreation services; increase public awareness, understanding, appreciation, and support for lifelong education, physical activity and recreation services; encourage professional training for all with an interest in education, leisure and recreation services; advance, encourage, conduct and publish scientific knowledge and research in the field of education, physical activity, and recreation services. **Libraries: Type:** reference. **Awards:** Student Literary Award. **Frequency:** annual. **Type:** recognition. **Recipient:** for writing excellence of students studying parks, recreation, or leisure services courses. **Formed by Merger of:** (2005) American Association for Leisure and Recreation and American Association for Active Lifestyles and Fitness. **Formerly:** (1974) Recreation Division of the American Alliance for Health, Physical Education and Recreation. **Publications:** *AALReporter*, quarterly. Newsletter. **Circulation:** 2,300. **Advertising:** accepted ● *Journal of Physical Education, Recreation and Dance*, 9/year. Also Cited As: *JOPERD* ● *Leisure Today*, annual. Journal. **Conventions/Meetings:** annual convention (exhibits).

12522 ■ American Recreation Coalition (ARC)
1225 New York Ave. NW, Ste.450
Washington, DC 20005-6405
Ph: (202)682-9530

Fax: (202)682-9529
E-mail: arc@funoutdoors.com
URL: http://www.funoutdoors.com
Contact: Derrick A. Crandall, Pres.
Founded: 1979. **Members:** 100. **Staff:** 5. **Budget:** $800,000. **Description:** Businesses, recreation associations, and corporations interested in promoting a wide variety of recreational activities and providing information to government and the public about the value of recreation to American society and the economy. Objectives are to serve as an authoritative source of information about recreation and to act as the advocate for all types of recreation. Sponsors research studies on the effects of federal policy on recreation and public and private planning for resources designed to meet future recreational needs. Compiles statistics. Conducts recreation exchanges featuring key federal officials. **Publications:** *Outdoor Recreation in America,* annual. Surveys. Features surveys monitoring recreation participation and analysis of societal concerns. **Conventions/Meetings:** annual Great Outdoors Week - meeting, held during Great Outdoors Week in Washington, DC - June ● annual Partners Outdoors - meeting - held in January.

12523 ■ Break Away: The Alternative Break Connection
2451 Cumberland Pkwy., Ste.3124
Atlanta, GA 30339
Free: (800)903-0646
E-mail: breakaway@alternativebreaks.org
URL: http://www.alternativebreaks.org
Contact: Jill Piacitelli, Dir.
Founded: 1991. **Members:** 547. **Membership Dues:** individual, $25 (annual) ● community organization, $100 (annual) ● chapter, $150 (annual). **Staff:** 1. **Budget:** $100,000. **Description:** Schools, colleges and universities, community organizations, and individuals interested in alternatives to traditional spring break activities. Promotes participation by students in community service and experiential education programs during their breaks. Develops and disseminates alternative break program plans and guidelines; provides support and assistance to alternative break programs. Operates Alternative Break Citizenship Schools to teach students to enhance existing alternative break programs; conducts Site Leader Retreats to train alternative break program leaders. **Awards:** Curriculum Based Alternative Break of the Year. **Frequency:** annual. **Type:** recognition ● Host Agency of the Year. **Frequency:** annual. **Type:** recognition ● Program of the Year. **Frequency:** annual. **Type:** recognition. **Computer Services:** database, SiteBank. **Formerly:** (2002) Break Away. **Publications:** *Break Away: Hosting an Alternative Break.* Manual ● *Break Away: Organizing and Alternative Spring Break.* Manual ● *Connections,* quarterly. Newsletter. Contains news of community service projects and service-learning opportunities. **Price:** $20.00/year. **Circulation:** 2,100. **Advertising:** accepted ● *Curriculum Based Alternative Breaks.* Manual ● *Site Leader Survival Manual.* **Conventions/Meetings:** annual Alternative Break Citizenship School - meeting.

12524 ■ Employee Services Management Association
568 Spring Rd., Ste.D
Elmhurst, IL 60126-3896
Ph: (630)559-0020
Fax: (630)559-0025
E-mail: esmahq@esmassn.org
URL: http://www.esmassn.org
Contact: Jennifer Morgan, Pres.
Founded: 1941. **Members:** 2,000. **Membership Dues:** organizational, $210 (annual) ● national associate, $675 (annual) ● corporate, $400 (annual). **Staff:** 4. **Budget:** $750,000. **Local Groups:** 25. **Description:** Corporations and governmental agencies that sponsor recreation, fitness, and service programs for their employees; associate members are manufacturers and suppliers in the employee recreation market and distributors of consumer products and services. Serves as an information resource network for members nationwide. Implements and maintains

a diverse range of employee services; believes that employee services, as practical solutions to work/life issues, are essential to sound business management. Conducts programs that improves relations between employees and management, increases overall productivity, boosts morale, and reduces absenteeism and turnover. Covers the 10 Components of a Well-Rounded Employee Services Program such as employee stores, convenience services, recognition programs, recreation programs, travel services, and special events. **Libraries: Type:** open to the public. **Holdings:** 46. **Subjects:** employee stores, community services, convenience services, dependent care, recreation programs, recognition programs, special events, travel services, voluntary benefits, wellness, trends, research, work/life issues. **Awards:** Employer of the Year. **Frequency:** annual. **Type:** recognition. **Computer Services:** Online services, members-only section: benchmarking, membership directory, buyer's guide, chapter leaders toolbox, ESM Association Foundation Monographs. **Formerly:** (1982) National Industrial Recreation Association; (2000) National Employee Services and Recreation Association. **Publications:** *Employee Services Management,* bimonthly. Magazine. Contains trends, information and research on employee stores, community services, convenience services, dependent care, recreation programs, etc. **Price:** free for members. ISSN: 0744-3676. **Circulation:** 2,500. **Advertising:** accepted. Alternate Formats: diskette ● *ESM Association Buyer's Guide,* annual, updated online monthly. Directory. **Price:** available to members only. Alternate Formats: online ● *ESM Association Monographs,* biennial. **Price:** available to members only ● Membership Directory, annual, updated online monthly. **Price:** available to members only. **Advertising:** accepted. Alternate Formats: online. **Conventions/Meetings:** annual conference and trade show (exhibits).

12525 ■ Hostelling International-American Youth Hostels (HI-AYH)
8401 Colesville Rd., Ste.600
Silver Spring, MD 20910
Ph: (301)495-1240
Fax: (301)495-6697
E-mail: hostels@hiusa.org
URL: http://www.hiayh.org
Contact: Russell K. Hedge Jr., Exec. Dir./CEO
Founded: 1934. **Members:** 123,000. **Membership Dues:** adult (ages 18-54), $28 (annual) ● senior (age 55 and over), $18 (annual) ● life, $250. **Staff:** 50. **Budget:** $5,000,000. **Regional Groups:** 4. **State Groups:** 35. **Local Groups:** 35. **Description:** Provides inexpensive, educational, and environmentally respectful travel opportunities for all ages, especially for youth; promotes appreciation for cultural values of all societies. Maintains over 150 hostels in the U.S; belongs to a network of over 4000 hostels in over 70 countries. Conducts local programs working with school and youth groups in an effort to increase their range of experiences, while providing a convenient and economical base for field work and recreational activities. Regional councils sponsor bicycling hiking, skiing, sailing, and canoeing trips and instructional programs. **Computer Services:** database, membership list. **Additional Websites:** http://www.hiusa.org. **Affiliated With:** International Youth Hostel Federation. **Formerly:** (1992) American Youth Hostels. **Publications:** *Hostelling North America: The Official Guide to Hostels in Canada and the United States,* annual. **Price:** included in membership dues; $3.00 for nonmembers, plus shipping and handling. **Circulation:** 200,000. **Advertising:** accepted. **Conventions/Meetings:** annual National Council Meeting (exhibits) - the weekend before Thanksgiving.

12526 ■ International Family Recreation Association (IFRA)
PO Box 520
Gonzalez, FL 32560-0520
Ph: (850)937-8354
Free: (800)281-9186
E-mail: rltresource@spydee.net
Contact: K.W. Stephens, Exec. Off.
Founded: 1982. **Members:** 6,840. **Membership Dues:** individual/family, $49 (annual) ● commercial,

$100 (annual). **Staff:** 3. **Budget:** $90,000. **Regional Groups:** 7. **State Groups:** 2. **Local Groups:** 15. **For-Profit. Description:** Individual and commercial advocates of family recreation, leisure and travel. Supports recommendations and legislation advantageous to recreation, leisure, and travel. Promotes safety policies and public participation in family recreational, leisure, and travel activities. Encourages the conservation of natural resources. Reviews and evaluates products. Supports the Recreation Vehicle Industry Association (see separate entry). Sponsors workshops, leadership training, and volunteer instruction programs. Conducts rallies, caravans, tours, cruises, tournaments, and charitable and youth programs. Maintains speakers' bureau; compiles statistics. Provides consulting services to recreation, leisure and travel-type businesses (including manufacturers, dealers, campgrounds, resorts, parks international). **Awards:** Member of the Year Award. **Frequency:** annual. **Type:** recognition. **Committees:** Destination Location Development; International Operation. **Publications:** *On the Line.* **Price:** for commercial members only ● *Recreation Advisor,* 10/year. Newsletter. Tabloid covering the recreation, leisure, and travel industry. Includes association and legislative news, calendar of events, and membership profiles. **Price:** included in membership dues. **Circulation:** 28,500. **Advertising:** accepted ● *Update,* monthly. **Conventions/Meetings:** annual International Camping and RVing Rally (exhibits).

12527 ■ Prairie Club
c/o Jacquie Dziak
110 E Schiller, Ste.302
Elmhurst, IL 60126
Ph: (630)516-1277
Fax: (630)516-1278
E-mail: info@prairieclub.org
URL: http://www.prairieclub.org
Contact: Jacquie Dziak, Contact
Founded: 1908. **Members:** 812. **Membership Dues:** active (private club), $75 (annual). **Staff:** 1. **Description:** Individuals united for: the promotion of outdoor recreation in the form of walks, outings, camping, and canoeing; the establishment and maintenance of permanent and temporary camps; the encouragement of the love of nature; the dissemination of knowledge of the environment and the conservation of land, water, and wildlife. **Committees:** Conservation; Family Cottage; Farmhouse; Historical; Permanent Camps; Saturday Walks; Sunday Walks. **Funds:** Prairie Club Conservation and Education. **Publications:** *Business Directory,* annual. Alternate Formats: online ● *The Prairie Club Bulletin,* quarterly. **Price:** free for members; $15.00 /year for nonmembers; $3.00 each, for nonmembers. **Conventions/Meetings:** annual meeting - always Chicago, IL.

Recycling

12528 ■ Aircraft Fleet Recycling Association (AFRA)
735 15th St. NW, Ste.620
Washington, DC 20005
E-mail: martin.fraissignes@chateauroux-airport.com
URL: http://www.afraassociation.org
Contact: Martin Fraissignes, Exec. Dir.
Multinational. Description: Improves the aircraft industry sustainability by promoting safe and environmentally proactive management of the world's aging aircraft fleet. Promotes safe and economical return of aircraft to revenue service. Promotes return of engines and parts to the world fleet. **Telecommunication Services:** electronic mail, william.l.carberry@boeing.com.

Refugees

12529 ■ Afghan Community in America (ACA)
PO Box 73
Old Bethpage, NY 11804
Ph: (516)816-2525

Fax: (516)756-9236
E-mail: afghancommunity@msn.com
Contact: Habib Mayar, Chm.
Founded: 1980. **Staff:** 5. **Languages:** English, Pashto, Persian. **Description:** Volunteers from the Afghan community and others interested in and sympathetic to its goals. Works to increase public awareness of the current situation in Afghanistan through press releases, demonstrations, walks, and radio and television messages. Provides occasional assistance in employment, housing, funeral arrangements, and immigration matters. Sponsors weekly radio broadcasts in Pashto and Dari. **Libraries: Type:** open to the public. **Subjects:** religion, culture, history.

12530 ■ American Fund for Czechoslovak Relief (AFCR)
Bohemian Natl. Hall
321 E 73rd St.
New York, NY 10021
Ph: (212)452-3015
Fax: (212)452-2763
E-mail: afcr@centrum.cz
URL: http://www.afcr-nyc.org
Contact: Vojtech Jerabek, Pres.
Founded: 1948. **Staff:** 1. **Budget:** $220,000. **Description:** Aims to help Czechoslovak democratic refugees or Czechoslovak democratic persons and institutions in need in the U.S., Czechoslovakia and elsewhere. **Formerly:** (1998) American Fund for Czechoslovakl Refugees. **Conventions/Meetings:** annual board meeting.

12531 ■ American Jewish Philanthropic Fund (AJPF)
27 E 61st St., 2nd Fl.
New York, NY 10021
Ph: (212)755-5640 (212)722-4719
Fax: (212)996-6020
Contact: Charles J. Tanenbaum, Pres.
Founded: 1955. **Description:** Provides assistance to Jewish refugees and their families. **Formerly:** American Council for Judaism Philanthropic Fund.

12532 ■ American Near East Refugee Aid (ANERA)
1522 K St. NW, Ste.600
Washington, DC 20005
Ph: (202)842-2766
Fax: (202)682-1637
E-mail: philip@anera.org
URL: http://www.anera.org
Contact: Philip Davies, VP
Founded: 1968. **Members:** 25,000. **Staff:** 40. **Budget:** $15,000,000. **Multinational. Description:** Organizations associated with economic development and refugee relief; interested individuals. Works to provide assistance to Palestinians, Lebanese, Jordanians, and other needy individuals in the Middle East and to further American understanding of the Middle East. Sponsors rural and urban development projects through local institutions, and social projects in health and education; helps support agricultural cooperatives; provides donations of medical supplies; offers scholarship program; helps to provide education and skills training for men, women and children; sponsors literacy classes and job-training programs for adults. Conducts fundraising appeals for socioeconomic development and humanitarian relief; prepares and distributes information materials on the Middle East crisis. **Convention/Meeting:** none. **Computer Services:** Mailing lists. **Committees:** Projects. **Publications:** *ANERA Newsletter*, quarterly. **Price:** free. **Circulation:** 15,000. Alternate Formats: online ● Annual Report, annual. Alternate Formats: online.

12533 ■ American Refugee Committee (ARC)
430 Oak Grove St., Ste.204
Minneapolis, MN 55403
Ph: (612)872-7060
Free: (800)875-7060
Fax: (612)607-6499

E-mail: archq@archq.org
URL: http://www.arcrelief.org
Contact: Hugh Parmer, Pres.
Founded: 1978. **Staff:** 20. **Budget:** $27,000,000. **State Groups:** 1. **Local Groups:** 1. **Description:** Works for the survival, health and well-being of refugees, displaced persons and those at risk. Has staff that provides primary health care, job training, small loans, shelter repair, psychosocial and legal counseling and other services to nearly one million people in Asia, Africa and Europe. **Libraries: Type:** not open to the public. **Holdings:** 200; articles, books. **Subjects:** refugee health. **Publications:** *Bridges Newsletter*, 3/year ● Annual Report, annual. Alternate Formats: online.

12534 ■ Association of Cambodian Survivors of America (ACSA)
Address Unknown since 2007
Founded: 1981. **Members:** 100. **Staff:** 4. **Description:** Volunteer relief groups that provide assistance to Cambodian refugees in the U.S. and at the Kampuchean-Thai border. Provides counseling services and information referrals. **Convention/Meeting:** none.

12535 ■ Catholic Relief Services (U.S. Catholic Conference) (CRS-USCC)
PO Box 17090
Baltimore, MD 21203-7090
Ph: (410)625-2220
Free: (800)736-3467
Fax: (410)685-1635
E-mail: webmaster@crs.org
URL: http://www.crs.org
Contact: Kenneth F. Hackett, Pres./CEO
Founded: 1943. **Staff:** 4,000. **Budget:** $520,707,000. **Description:** Nonpolitical, nonevangelical, official overseas relief and self-help development agency of the American Catholic community. Conducts programs of disaster response, refugee relief and rehabilitation, social welfare services, and socio-economic development in 94 countries. Distributes food, clothing, and medicine. Stimulates and supports indigenous agencies engaged in welfare and development. **Additional Websites:** http://campus.crs.org. **Programs:** Called To Witness; Fair Trade; Frontiers of Justice; Operation Rice Bowl; Parish Homily; Work of Human Hands. **Projects:** School Connectivity. **Formerly:** Catholic Relief Services - National Catholic Welfare Conference; (1955) War Relief Services - National Catholic Welfare Conference. **Publications:** *Catholic Relief Services—Annual Report*. Contains balance sheet, financial statements, and highlights of activities and goals accomplished for preceding year. **Price:** free. **Circulation:** 20,000. Alternate Formats: online ● *Going Global with Youth Newsletter*, monthly. Alternate Formats: online ● *The Wooden Bell*, quarterly. Newsletter. For donors and other interested individuals covering CRS-USCC's worldwide humanitarian efforts. **Price:** free. **Circulation:** 175,000.

12536 ■ El Rescate
1501 W 8th St., Ste.100
Los Angeles, CA 90017
Ph: (213)387-3284
Fax: (213)387-9189
URL: http://www.elrescate.org/main.asp
Contact: Richard Mendez, Exec. Dir.
Founded: 1981. **Staff:** 15. **Budget:** $500,000. **Local Groups:** 1. **Languages:** English, Spanish. **Description:** Provides economic development initiatives, and social and legal assistance to Central American refugees, immigrants and other Latinos in southern California. Investigates and addresses problems of human rights in Central America and operates an emergency response system for human rights violations. The group's name, El Rescate, is Spanish for "The Rescue.". **Computer Services:** database, Human Rights Violations in El Salvador and fraudulent attorneys and notaries practicing in Los Angeles. **Publications:** *El Salvador - Human Rights Chronology*, monthly ● *The Jesuit Assassinations* ● *Labor Under Siege and Counterterrorism in Action* ● *The Writings of Ellacuria, Baro, and Montes.*

12537 ■ Ethiopian Community Development Council (ECDC)
901 S Highland St.
Arlington, VA 22204
Ph: (703)685-0510
Fax: (703)685-0529
E-mail: info@ecdcinternational.org
URL: http://www.ecdcinternational.org
Contact: Tsehaye Teferra PhD, Pres.
Founded: 1983. **Staff:** 39. **Languages:** Amharic, Arabic, English, Farsi, German, Italian, Russian, Somali, Spanish, Swahili, Tigrinya. **Description:** Promotes cultural, educational, and socio-economic development programs in the immigrant and refugee community. Provides local social and support services designed to help people build economically independent lives. Conducts national public education programs to expand awareness of the concerns and needs of African refugees and immigrants. Promotes support on issues of public policy affecting African refugees and immigrants. Enhances networking among African community organizations around the country and assists them in community development and organizational capacity-building activities. Acts as a national voluntary agency to resettle refugees from Africa, the Near East, Indochina and Europe through a network of affiliates around the U.S. **Divisions:** Bridges for Cross-Cultural Understanding; Health Education and Promotion; Microenterprise Development; National Refugee Network; Resettlement; Social Services. **Publications:** *A Selected Resource Guide of African Refugees* ● *African Refugee Network*. Newsletter ● *African Refugees: Human Dimension of the Continuing Crises in Africa.* Proceedings ● *African Refugees: Human Dimensions To A Global Crisis.* Proceedings ● *Assessing the Development Needs of Ethiopian Refugees in the United States* ● *Bridges for Cross-Cultural Understanding.* Newsletter ● *Health Needs Assessment of African-Born Residents in the Washington, DC Metropolitan Area.* Reprint ● Brochures ● Monographs. **Conventions/Meetings:** annual Conference on African Refugees.

12538 ■ FilmAid International (FAI)
24 E 23rd St., 3rd Fl.
New York, NY 10010
Ph: (212)529-1088
Fax: (212)529-1084
E-mail: info@filmaidinternational.org
URL: http://www.filmaid.org
Contact: Elizabeth Silkes, Exec. Dir.
Founded: 1999. **Staff:** 5. **Multinational. Description:** Seeks to address the problem of refugee despair and psychological trauma. Uses the power of film to break monotony and isolation. Screens educational films on topics central to the refugee experience. Raises awareness of the global refugee crisis. Provides employment, skills and training on basic filmmaking. Shows films that "feed the soul, spirit and imagination.". **Computer Services:** Mailing lists. **Committees:** Advisory. **Publications:** Newsletter. Alternate Formats: online.

12539 ■ International Rescue Committee - USA (IRC)
122 E 42nd St.
New York, NY 10168-1289
Ph: (212)551-3000
Free: (877)REF-UGEE
Fax: (212)551-3179
E-mail: info@theirc.org
URL: http://www.theIRC.org
Contact: George Rupp, Pres./CEO
Founded: 1933. **Staff:** 857. **Budget:** $156,000,000. **Description:** Nonsectarian, nonpartisan, voluntary agency founded at the request of Albert Einstein and supported by individuals, foundations, corporations, unions, and civic, educational, human rights, and community groups. Assists refugee victims of religious, political, and racial persecution, civil strife, famine, and war. Current programs are located in Africa, Asia, Europe, North America, and the Middle East. **Awards:** Corporate Responsibility Award. **Frequency:** annual. **Type:** recognition ● Freedom Award. **Frequency:** annual. **Type:** recognition.

Formed by Merger of: (1942) Emergency Rescue Committee; (1942) International Relief Association. **Publications:** *Flight - Refugees and the Quest for Freedom.* Book. **Price:** $22.00/copy ● *International Rescue Committee Annual Report,* annual. Reviews agency's refugee activities and the worldwide refugee situation. ● *IRC at Work,* quarterly. Newsletter. **Price:** free. **Circulation:** 70,000. **Conventions/Meetings:** bimonthly board meeting.

12540 ■ Iranian Refugees' Alliance (IRA)

Cooper Sta.
PO Box 316
New York, NY 10276-0316
Ph: (212)260-7460
Fax: (212)260-7460
E-mail: irainc@irainc.org
URL: http://www.irainc.org
Contact: Deljou Abadi, Dir.

Founded: 1993. **Multinational. Description:** Preserves and promotes the human and civil rights of Iranian refugees and asylum seekers worldwide. Monitors, documents and reports the worldwide situation of Iranian refugees and asylum seekers. Provides refugees with information on asylum matters and their legal rights, affidavits, documentation, referrals, translation and educational outreach. Supports newly arrived Iranian refugees in the US who face discrimination and/or disfranchisement.

12541 ■ Jesuit Refugee Service/U.S.A. (JRS/USA)

1616 P St. NW, Ste.300
Washington, DC 20036-1405
Ph: (202)462-0400
Fax: (202)328-9212
E-mail: usa@jrs.net
URL: http://www.jesref.org
Contact: Rev. Kenneth Gavin SJ, Dir.

Founded: 1983. **Staff:** 15. **Budget:** $800,000. **Languages:** English, French, Italian, Spanish. **Multinational. Description:** Primary objective is to send members of the Society of Jesus (Jesuits), religious women, and lay persons to provide direct services to refugees worldwide. Works to recruit Jesuits to the Apostolate, stress little-known concerns about refugees, and foster knowledge and understanding of refugees by Jesuits. Disseminates information about refugee-related subjects and reports on placements and on issues affecting refugees, including legislative, judicial, and regional activity in the U.S. and abroad. **Convention/Meeting:** none. **Publications:** *Servir* (in English, French, Italian, and Spanish), 3/year. Magazine. **Circulation:** 1,500.

12542 ■ Lutheran Immigration and Refugee Service (LIRS)

700 Light St.
Baltimore, MD 21230
Ph: (410)230-2700
Fax: (410)230-2890
E-mail: lirs@lirs.org
URL: http://www.lirs.org
Contact: Ralston H. Deffenbaugh Jr., Pres.

Founded: 1939. **Staff:** 70. **Budget:** $21,680,000. **Regional Groups:** 25. **Description:** Advocates for immigrants and refugees and asylum seekers; resettles refugees; trains and encourages Lutheran groups and others of goodwill in advocacy processes; provides services for refugee minors. **Subgroups:** First Asylum Concerns. **Formerly:** Lutheran Immigration Service. **Publications:** *Ambassador News,* quarterly. Newsletter. Provides information on activities and best practices for circle members. Alternate Formats: online ● *Bringing New Hope and New Life.* Brochure. Features an overview of the organization's mission and work. ● *FYI,* bimonthly. Newsletter. Alternate Formats: online ● *RefugeeWorks,* quarterly. Newsletter. Alternate Formats: online ● *The Way to Work.* Video. Features a 20-minute employment orientation video. **Price:** $15.00 ● Annual Report, annual. Alternate Formats: online ● Also publishes papers.

12543 ■ Pontifical Mission for Palestine (PMP)

c/o Catholic Near East Welfare Association
1011 1st Ave.
New York, NY 10022-4195
Ph: (212)826-1480
Free: (800)442-6392
Fax: (212)826-8979
E-mail: cnewa@cnewa.org
URL: http://www.cnewa.org
Contact: Msgr. Robert L. Stern, Sec. Gen.

Founded: 1949. **Staff:** 40. **Description:** Papal agency for humanitarian and charitable assistance. Provides aid to victims of conflict in the Middle East without regard to their national or religious affiliation. Encourages and supports programs providing relief, rehabilitation, and development in the Middle East. **Affiliated With:** Catholic Near East Welfare Association. **Publications:** *Catholic Near East Magazine,* bimonthly. Includes trip information. **Price:** $12.00/year. **Circulation:** 107,000 ● *Resource Guide.*

12544 ■ Rav Tov International Jewish Rescue Organization (RTIJRO)

500 Bedford Ave.
Brooklyn, NY 11211
Ph: (718)963-1991
Contact: Divid Niederman, Exec. Dir.

Founded: 1973. **Staff:** 40. **Description:** International network of offices that aids refugees who wish to immigrate to the U.S. or any other Western country. Provides financial assistance to immigrants until they become self-supporting; sponsors domestic assistance program. Assists with visa applications and housing once destination is reached; provides moral and religious support for those in transit and those who have reached destination; maintains employment service with direct job placement and on-the-job training; offers preschool, kindergarten, elementary school, and adult religious instruction; conducts English as a second language training program. **Formerly:** (1982) Rav Tov Committee to Aid New Immigrants. **Publications:** *Achievement Bulletin,* quarterly. **Conventions/Meetings:** annual meeting.

12545 ■ Refugees International (RI)

1705 N St. NW
Washington, DC 20036
Ph: (202)828-0110
Free: (800)733-8433
Fax: (202)828-0819
E-mail: ri@refintl.org
URL: http://www.refugeesinternational.org
Contact: Kenneth H. Bacon, Pres./CEO

Founded: 1979. **Staff:** 15. **Budget:** $2,000,000. **Languages:** English, French, Italian, Korean, Spanish, Thai. **Description:** Provides advocacy, information, public education, and community support to refugees and displaced persons worldwide. Through voluntary action, seeks alternative means of handling refugee migration and permanent resettlement. Operates emergency need assessment program. Works to assist and support existing refugee relief and resettlement programs. Monitors and reports on events pertaining to refugees. Fosters voluntary support in the form of funds, sponsorship of refugee families, letters urging governmental support, medical services, and relief for refugees around the world. **Publications:** *Acts of Betrayal: The Challenge of Protecting North Koreans in China,* periodic. Report. Features the harrowing circumstances under which North Koreans must live when they flee to China. ● *Lives on Hold: The Human Cost of Statelessness,* periodic. Report. Features the difficulties faced by an estimated 11 million individuals worldwide who have no citizenship or effective nationality. ● *Peacekeeping in West Africa: A Regional Report,* periodic. Features on the need to coordinate separate UN operations in Sierra Leone, Liberia and the Ivory Coast. ● *Refugee & Relief Alert,* biennial. Newsletter ● *RI Bulletin,* periodic ● Also publishes crisis generated press releases and annual report. **Conventions/Meetings:** periodic Burundi Policy Forum - meeting.

12546 ■ Rights Action/Guatemala Partners

PO Box 50887
Washington, DC 20091
Ph: (202)783-1123
Fax: (202)332-8672
E-mail: info@rightsaction.org
URL: http://www.rightsaction.org
Contact: Graham Russell, Dir.

Founded: 1993. **Staff:** 2. **Budget:** $850,000. **Languages:** English, Spanish. **Description:** Supports grassroots human rights and development in Central America and Southern Mexico by funding and supplying groups and individuals who train and organize rural villagers. Provides farming, sanitation, and entrepreneurial supplies and assistance. Works to raise awareness about Mexico and Central America in the U.S. Funds education, leadership development, and skills training programs. **Libraries: Type:** reference. **Formed by Merger of:** PEACE for Guatemala; Guatemala Health Rights Support Project. **Publications:** *Rights Action.* Newsletter. Alternate Formats: online ● Annual Report, annual ● Reports. Alternate Formats: online ● Articles. Alternate Formats: online.

12547 ■ Southeast Asia Resource Action Center (SEARAC)

1628 16th St. NW, 3rd Fl.
Washington, DC 20009-3099
Ph: (202)667-4690
Fax: (202)667-6449
E-mail: searac@searac.org
URL: http://www.searac.org
Contact: Phitsamay Sychitkokhong Uy, Chm.

Founded: 1979. **Staff:** 7. **Budget:** $900,000. **Languages:** English, Khmer, Laotian, Vietnamese. **Nonmembership. Description:** Aims to help refugee organizations initiate self-help projects in impacted local communities, to promote community development and economic advancement among Southeast Asian refugees and immigrants, to promote advocacy activities among target communities, and to represent southeast Asian Americans on the national level. Promotes refugee protection and human rights; serves as a clearinghouse for information on Southeast Asian refugees. Conducts research on the needs of, and issues affecting, Southeast Asian refugees. Produces a variety of reports on refugee-related issues such as health, employment, vocational training, social adjustment, information-referral, and outreach. Offers one-on-one technical assistance to refugee community organizations throughout the country. Projects in Vietnam were completed in Dec., 1998. **Divisions:** Advocacy and Public Education; Cultural Preservation; Leadership and Community Development. **Projects:** Serving Organizations that Assist Refugees; Southeast Asian Californian Healthy Elders Leadership; Student Action and Visibility Education; Voting Orientation Training and Empowerment. **Formerly:** Indochina Refugee Action Center; Indochina Resource Action Center. **Publications:** *The Bridge,* quarterly. Newsletters. Includes news, statistics, and information on community resources. **Price:** $25.00. ISSN: 1083-9208. **Circulation:** 750 ● *The Bridge.* Video. Explores the memories of the journeys by Southeast Asians to the US and their subsequent resettlement in American society. **Price:** $24.95. Alternate Formats: online ● *Directory of Southeast Asian American Community-Based Organizations.* Lists organizations that provide services to SEARAC. **Price:** $15.00. Alternate Formats: online ● *In Search of Asylum: Vietnamese Boat People in Hong Kong.* Includes photos and important reference material. **Price:** $5.00 ● *The Vietnamese American Community.* Contains statistical and political perspective. **Price:** $5.00. **Conventions/Meetings:** annual retreat, 4-5-day-long program of activities focused on enhancing leadership abilities.

12548 ■ Spanish Refugee Aid (SRA)

c/o International Rescue Committee
122 E 42nd St.
New York, NY 10168-1289
Ph: (212)551-3000
Fax: (212)551-3179

E-mail: margaret@theirc.org
URL: http://www.theirc.org
Contact: Margaret Childers, Dir.
Founded: 1953. **Staff:** 2. **Budget:** $120,000. **Languages:** English, French, Spanish. **Description:** A division of the International Rescue Committee (see separate entry). Collects and distributes funds for old, sick, and needy refugees of the Spanish Civil War. Provides help to Spanish refugees with special problems. Maintains sponsorship program. Aids the elderly in hospitals and homes. **Committees:** Advisory. **Affiliated With:** International Rescue Committee - USA. **Publications:** Newsletter, semiannual, always May and November. Contains report to contributions. **Circulation:** 1,200. Alternate Formats: online.

12549 ■ Tibetan Aid Project (TAP)
2910 San Pablo Ave.
Berkeley, CA 94702
Ph: (510)848-4238
Free: (800)338-4238
Fax: (510)548-2230
E-mail: tap@tibetanaidproject.org
URL: http://www.tibetanaidproject.org
Contact: Tarthang Tulku, Pres.
Founded: 1974. **Members:** 10,000. **Staff:** 2. **Budget:** $500,000. **Languages:** Dutch, English, German, Japanese, Portuguese. **Description:** A project of the Tibetan Nyingma Relief Foundation. Offers assistance to individuals in Tibet and Tibetan refugees in India, Nepal, Bhutan, and Sikkim. Sponsors relief distribution to monasteries, nunneries, and schools for support of religious and community activities. Ships hundreds of thousands of traditional Tibetan books and art prints to the refugee community each November. Raises funds to support production of sacred Tibetan texts. **Libraries: Type:** open to the public. **Subjects:** Tibet, China, culture, human rights. **Publications:** *Bodh Gaya World Peace Ceremony 1994.* Film. Covers Bodh Gaya Stupa history. **Price:** $10.00 ● *From the Roof of the World: Refugees of Tibet*, annual. Books ● *Is Tibet Forgotten.* Booklet. Features lively description of Tibetan Aid Project's undertakings from 1969 through the present. **Price:** $24.95 ● *Your Friends the Tibetan Refugees.* Book ● Brochures, annual. **Conventions/Meetings:** annual Bodh Gaya Peace Ceremony - meeting, 10-day prayer session for world peace - in January, always Bodh Gaya, India.

12550 ■ United States Catholic Conference/Migration and Refugee Services
3211 4th St. NE
Washington, DC 20017-1194
Ph: (202)541-3000
E-mail: mrs@usccb.org
URL: http://www.nccbuscc.org/mrs
Contact: Most Rev. Gerald Barnes, Chm.
Founded: 1920. **Staff:** 100. **Budget:** $32,000,000. **Description:** Public policy and social action office of the U.S. Catholic Conference, on matters of migration, refugee, and immigration. Provides program support and regional coordination for a network of 110 diocesan refugee resettlement offices. Office for the Pastoral Care of Migrants and Refugees provides the pastoral foundation for all MRS programs and assists the Bishops in encouraging the integration of immigrants, migrants, and refugees into the life and mission of the local Church. The Catholic Legal Immigration Network (CLINIC), a related organization, ensures that all newcomers have access to affordable immigration related services. **Formerly:** (1993) Migration and Refugee Services; (1994) U.S. Catholic Conference Migration and Refugee Services; (2003) United States Catholic Conference/Migration and Refugee Services. **Publications:** *MRS Annual Review*, annual ● *MRS Resettlement and Immigration Directory*, annual ● *Update*, monthly. Newsletter ● Papers. **Conventions/Meetings:** periodic conference.

12551 ■ USA for the United Nations High Commissioner for Refugees (USA FOR UNHCR)
1775 K St. NW, Ste.290
Washington, DC 20006

Ph: (202)296-1115
Free: (800)770-1100
Fax: (202)296-1081
E-mail: info@usaforunhcr.org
URL: http://www.unrefugees.org
Contact: Caryl Garcia, Exec. Dir.
Staff: 4. **Multinational. Description:** Raises consciousness of Americans about the work and accomplishments of the United Nations High Commissioner for Refugees. Provides food, water, shelter, medical and other types of assistance to refugees worldwide. Establishes an international presence in countries on the verge of serious conflict. **Computer Services:** Information services, refugee stories ● mailing lists, of members. **Committees:** Development; Program and Communications. **Projects:** Emergency Appeals; Health and Education; Human Rights and Protection. **Publications:** Newsletter. Alternate Formats: online.

Rehabilitation

12552 ■ American Friends of ALYN Hospital
51 E 42nd St., Ste.308
New York, NY 10017
Ph: (212)869-8085
Free: (877)568-3259
Fax: (212)768-0979
E-mail: friends@alynus.org
URL: http://www.alynus.org
Contact: Cathy M. Lanyard, Exec. Dir.
Multinational. Description: Supports the children of ALYN Hospital in Israel. Encourages people to help the children and adolescents who have sustained either temporary or permanent handicaps as a result of the homicide bombings in Israel. **Computer Services:** Information services, ALYN Hospital resources. **Programs:** Kids Helping Kids; Wheels of Love Bike Ride.

Relief

12553 ■ Adventist Development and Relief Agency International (ADRA)
12501 Old Columbia Pike
Silver Spring, MD 20904
Ph: (301)680-6380
Free: (800)424-2372
Fax: (301)680-6370
E-mail: terezabyrne1@cs.com
URL: http://www.adra.org
Contact: Charles Sandefur, Pres.
Founded: 1956. **Staff:** 5,000. **Regional Groups:** 9. **Multinational. Description:** Provides relief and development to mankind regardless of ethnic, political, or religious affiliation in more than 120 countries. Focuses on the areas of food security, economic development, primary health, disaster response and preparedness, and education. **Libraries: Type:** reference. **Computer Services:** Online services, CompuServe. **Affiliated With:** Interaction/American Council for Voluntary International Action. **Formerly:** (1956) Seventh-Day Adventist Welfare Services. **Supersedes:** Seventh-Day Adventist World Service. **Publications:** *ADRA Works*, quarterly. Newsletter. Features international news and feature stories of projects. **Price:** free ● Newsletter, quarterly ● Annual Report, annual. Alternate Formats: online.

12554 ■ Air Serv International
410 Rosedale Ct., Ste.190
Warrenton, VA 20186
Ph: (540)428-2323
Fax: (540)428-2326
E-mail: asi@airserv.org
URL: http://www.airserv.org
Contact: Christopher Johnson, Chm.
Founded: 1984. **Staff:** 85. **Budget:** $4,000,000. **Description:** Provides air transport of relief and development personnel, medicines, and cargo to countries devastated by war or natural disasters. Utilizes small, light aircraft to deliver supplies and personnel to restricted areas. Conducts charitable programs. Con-

vention/Meeting: none. **Libraries: Type:** reference. **Holdings:** audio recordings, books, periodicals, video recordings. **Subjects:** relief and community development, Third World countries. **Publications:** *Flight Plan*, quarterly. Newsletter. Alternate Formats: online.

12555 ■ American Belarussian Relief Organization (ABRO)
PO Box 365
Zebulon, NC 27597
Ph: (919)269-6033
Fax: (919)404-0274
E-mail: joe@abro.org
URL: http://www.abro.org
Contact: Joe Strong, Dir.
Founded: 1993. **Description:** Aims to assist children living in areas contaminated with radiation from the Chernobyl Nuclear Plant accident. Provides clean food and sanctuary in radiation-free environments. Offers medical evaluation and treatment.

12556 ■ American Jewish World Service (AJWS)
45 W 36th St., 10th Fl.
New York, NY 10018-7904
Ph: (212)792-2900
Free: (800)889-7146
Fax: (212)792-2930
E-mail: ajws@ajws.org
URL: http://www.ajws.org
Contact: Ruth W. Messinger, Pres.
Founded: 1985. **Members:** 30,000. **Staff:** 60. **Budget:** $11,000,000. **Description:** A Jewish-sponsored humanitarian and relief organization working on an exclusively non-sectarian basis in the developing world. Aims to provide the means for disadvantaged people particularly women and children and threatened minorities, to move toward self-sufficiency. The organization's Jewish Volunteer Corps sends professionals to work with non-governmental organizations for periods of one to nine months. **Computer Services:** database ● mailing lists. **Projects:** Civil Society; Economic Development; Education; Health; HIV/AIDS; Sustainable Agriculture; Women's Empowerment. **Publications:** *AJWS Reports*, 3/year. Newsletter. Includes update of programming and volunteer activities. **Advertising:** accepted ● *Congregational Bulletin*, quarterly. Newsletter ● *Global Citizen*, monthly. Newsletter. Alternate Formats: online ● Annual Report, annual. **Price:** free. Alternate Formats: online.

12557 ■ American Red Cross National Headquarters (ARC)
2025 E St. NW
Washington, DC 20006
Ph: (202)303-4498
Free: (800)REDCROSS
E-mail: info@usa.redcross.org
URL: http://www.redcross.org
Contact: John F. McGuire, Interim Pres./CEO
Founded: 1881. **Staff:** 28,323. **Budget:** $1,500,000,000. **Local Groups:** 2,658. **Description:** Operates under congressional charter and fulfills America's obligations under certain international treaties, the American Red Cross serves members of the armed forces and veterans and their families, aids disaster victims, and assists other Red Cross societies in times of emergency. Includes other activities such as: blood services; training of volunteers for chapters, hospitals, and other community agencies; community services; international activities; service opportunities for youth. Maintains 46 regional blood centers. Conducts research programs. Local chapters provide speakers. Is a member of International Federation of Red Cross and Red Crescent Societies. **Awards:** Ann Magnussen Award. **Frequency:** annual. **Type:** recognition. **Recipient:** to nurses for outstanding leadership and services in their communities ● Certificate of Merit. **Type:** recognition. **Recipient:** for saving a life ● Good Neighbor Award. **Type:** recognition. **Recipient:** to outside groups for significant efforts on behalf of humanity ● Harriman Award. **Type:** recognition. **Recipient:** for significant volunteer leadership ● **Type:** recognition. **Recipient:** for health and safety ● Tiffany Award. **Type:** recogni-

tion. **Recipient:** for outstanding staff contribution. **Affiliated With:** International Federation of Red Cross and Red Crescent Societies. **Formerly:** (1893) American Association of the Red Cross; (1978) American National Red Cross. **Publications:** Annual Report, annual. Alternate Formats: online ● Booklets. **Conventions/Meetings:** annual meeting.

12558 ■ American Red Cross Overseas Association (ARCOA)
200 S Lebanon Rd.
Loveland, OH 45140
Ph: (770)427-4943
URL: http://www.arcoa.org
Contact: Anita L. Wright, Pres.
Founded: 1949. **Members:** 950. **Membership Dues:** active, associate, $15 (annual) ● life, $200 ● contributing, $20 (annual) ● sustaining, $30 (annual). **Staff:** 1. **Budget:** $30,000. **Regional Groups:** 10. **State Groups:** 50. **Local Groups:** 10. **Description:** Former members of the American Red Cross who have served overseas. Seeks to: help renew and continue friendships made while serving overseas with the ARC, and maintain "the spirit which prompted that service". Contributes to international understanding. Provides community service. Holds annual memorial ceremony in conjunction with ARC. **Libraries: Type:** reference. **Holdings:** archival material, video recordings. **Awards:** International Humanity Award. **Frequency:** annual. **Type:** recognition. **Recipient:** for service over and beyond call of duty ● Mary Louise Dowling Leadership Enhancement. **Type:** grant. **Recipient:** for educational, training, and research purposes. **Computer Services:** Mailing lists. **Committees:** Humanity Award. **Affiliated With:** American Red Cross National Headquarters. **Formerly:** (1990) American Overseas Association. **Publications:** ARCOA Directory, biennial. **Price:** available to members only. **Circulation:** 950 ● Group Bulletin, periodic ● The Oversea'r, quarterly. Newsletter. Includes directory updates, new member information, interesting service experiences, recollections, photos, and obituaries. **Price:** included in membership dues. **Circulation:** 1,000 ● President's Bulletin to District Directors, periodic ● President's Letter, annual. **Conventions/Meetings:** semiannual board meeting - usually October and February ● annual convention - usually June.

12559 ■ American Red Magen David for Israel - American Friends of Magen David Adom (ARMDI)
888 7th Ave., Ste.403
New York, NY 10106
Ph: (212)757-1627
Free: (866)632-2763
Fax: (212)757-4662
E-mail: info@afmda.org
URL: http://www.afmda.org
Contact: Stuart A. Jackson, Chm.
Founded: 1941. **Members:** 125,000. **Staff:** 15. **Local Groups:** 167. **Description:** U.S. support arm for Magen David Adom (MDA), Israel's equivalent of the Red Cross Society. Supports the MDA emergency medical, ambulance, blood, and disaster services which benefit Israel's entire population. Uses contributions to: supply and equip ambulances, bloodmobiles, and cardiac rescue ambulances serving all hospitals and communities throughout Israel; provide supplies and equipment for the MDA Blood Bank and MDA Fractionation Institute, and for MDA's emergency medical clinics; provide education funds to train paramedics, laboratory technicians, and scientists. Raises funds from individual donors, ARMDI chapters, foundation grants, and legacy programs. Maintains speakers' bureau. **Awards: Type:** recognition ● **Type:** scholarship. **Also Known As:** Red Mogen David. **Publications:** Chapter News, semiannual. Newsletter ● Lifeline, semiannual. **Conventions/Meetings:** annual conference.

12560 ■ AmeriCares Foundation (AF)
88 Hamilton Ave.
Stamford, CT 06902
Ph: (203)658-9500
Free: (800)486-HELP

Fax: (203)327-5200
E-mail: info@americares.org
URL: http://www.americares.org
Contact: Candace Hanau, Sr. VP of Communications/Marketing
Founded: 1982. **Staff:** 70. **Budget:** $650,000,000. **Languages:** English, French, German, Russian, Spanish. **Multinational. Description:** Provides immediate response to emergency medical needs and supports long-term humanitarian assistance programs for people around the world, irrespective of race, creed or political persuasion. Donates more than $6 billion dollars in aid since it's founding. Runs three domestic programs: AmeriKids, AmeriCares Free Clinics and AmeriCares HomeFront that provide aid to those in the United States that are less fortunate. **Publications:** Annual Report ● Newsletter, quarterly.

12561 ■ Association for International Medical Study (AIMS)
Address Unknown since 2007
Founded: 1985. **Languages:** English, Portuguese, Spanish. **Description:** Provides group travel to international medical congresses and meetings. **Libraries: Type:** reference. **Subjects:** international medical events. **Formerly:** (2001) New Frontiers of Medicine. **Publications:** Yearbook of International Medical Congresses, periodic. Journal. Provides information about special travel tours to selected international medical congresses. **Price:** free. **Circulation:** 5,000. **Advertising:** not accepted. Alternate Formats: online.

12562 ■ Batey Relief Alliance (BRA)
PO Box 300565
Brooklyn, NY 11230-5656
Ph: (917)627-5026
E-mail: bra@bateyrelief.org
URL: http://www.bateyrelief.org
Contact: Ulrick Gaillard JD, Founder/CEO
Founded: 1997. **Multinational. Description:** Unites grassroots groups, faith-based organizations, government agencies, universities and the international community. Works to alleviate suffering, and save lives. Seeks to create a productive and self-sufficient environment, through health care and development programs, for economically disadvantaged children and their families in the Caribbean. Provides support and services to impoverished communities throughout the country. Endeavors to empower the weak and protect rights, without regard to race, sex, creed, religion, national origin, or social status. **Publications:** Newsletter. Alternate Formats: online.

12563 ■ Box Project (BP)
100 Bus. Center Dr., Ste.26
Ormond Beach, FL 32174
Ph: (386)677-8094
Free: (800)268-9928
Fax: (386)677-8617
E-mail: info@boxproject.org
URL: http://www.boxproject.org
Contact: Susan Patneaude, Exec. Dir.
Founded: 1962. **Members:** 8,200. **Membership Dues:** family sponsor, community center sponsor, holiday sponsor, team, $50 (annual) ● recipient, $10 (annual) ● corporate sponsor or partner, $500 (annual). **Staff:** 3. **Budget:** $215,000. **Description:** Encourages families and individuals living in rural poverty in America to become self-sufficient and overcome the cycle of poverty by offering them friendship, education, and material aid. **Awards: Type:** scholarship. **Recipient:** for eligible students preparing for college or vocational training. **Funds:** Educational; Emergency; School Supplies. **Programs:** Community Center Match; Family Match; Holiday Match. **Publications:** The Newsbox, quarterly. Newsletter. **Price:** included in membership dues. **Circulation:** 4,000. Alternate Formats: online ● Annual Report, annual. Alternate Formats: online.

12564 ■ Brother's Brother Foundation (BBF)
1200 Galveston Ave.
Pittsburgh, PA 15233-1604
Ph: (412)321-3160
Free: (800)732-0999

Fax: (412)321-3325
E-mail: mail@brothersbrother.org
URL: http://www.brothersbrother.org
Contact: Luke L. Hingson, Pres.
Founded: 1958. **Staff:** 13. **Budget:** $224,192,200. **Nonmembership. Multinational. Description:** Promotes international health and education through the efficient and effective distribution and provision of donated medical, educational and other resources. Works to connect people's resources with people's needs. **Formerly:** (1960) Operation Brother's Keeper. **Publications:** Field News, semiannual. Newsletter. **Price:** free ● Annual Report, annual. **Conventions/Meetings:** quarterly Trustee Meeting - board meeting.

12565 ■ CARE International USA
151 Ellis St. NE
Atlanta, GA 30303
Ph: (404)681-2552
Free: (800)521-CARE
Fax: (404)589-2651
E-mail: info@care.org
URL: http://www.care.org
Contact: Helene D. Gayle MD, Pres./CEO
Founded: 1945. **Staff:** 9,000. **Budget:** $454,000,000. **Multinational. Description:** International humanitarian organization managing poverty-fighting programs in some 70 developing countries. Seeks to empower families and communities through programs in agriculture and natural resource management, education, emergency relief, health, nutritional support, small enterprise development, and water and sanitation. Has more than 12,000 expert staff members worldwide, 98 percent of whom are from the country in which they work. Maintains volunteer committees in many U.S. cities as well as the CARE Action Network, a volunteer group mobilized to help influence U.S. government policies that affect the poor. Conducts works that are supported by individual, governments, foundations and corporations. Is originally founded to send CARE packages to survivors of World War II. **Libraries: Type:** not open to the public. **Holdings:** 5,000; periodicals, reports. **Subjects:** international development, advocacy, fundraising, health, HIV/AIDS. **Telecommunication Services:** additional toll-free number, (800)422-7385. **Formerly:** Cooperative for Assistance and Relief Everywhere; Cooperative for American Remittances Everywhere. **Publications:** CARE Briefs ● CARE World Report, quarterly. Newsletter ● ICare News. Newsletter. Alternate Formats: online ● What and Where of CARE ● Annual Report, annual. Alternate Formats: online.

12566 ■ Caritas Puerto Rico
PO Box 8812
San Juan, PR 00910-0812
Ph: (787)727-7373
Fax: (787)728-4100
E-mail: ssc@arqsj.org
URL: http://www.caritas.org
Contact: Msgr. Roberto O. Gonzales Nieves, Pres.
Description: Promotes awareness of and efforts to overcome world poverty, hunger, oppression, and injustice. Raises funds for international development education and relief and development aid. Conducts educational programs and projects addressing famine, health concerns, natural disasters, unemployment, and youth issues. Supports and evaluates government and private development and relief programs. **Telecommunication Services:** electronic mail, ameri12@aol.com.

12567 ■ Change for Good (CFG)
c/o UNICEF House
3 United Nations Plz.
New York, NY 10017
Ph: (212)326-7000
Fax: (212)887-7465
URL: http://www.unicef.org/corporate_partners/index_25030.html
Contact: Ann M. Veneman, Exec. Dir.
Founded: 1986. **Budget:** $40,000. **Description:** Solicits donation of foreign change and currency possessed by American overseas travelers who have

returned to the US. Converts donations to U.S. dollars and uses funds for projects that benefit local communities in the U.S. Promotes international friendship and understanding; seeks to find uses for seemingly useless things. Encourages interaction between varied groups and classes of people; conducts educational program; maintains speakers' bureau.

12568 ■ Christian Relief Services (CRS)
2550 Huntington Ave., Ste.200
Alexandria, VA 22303-1499
Ph: (703)317-9086
Free: (800)33-RELIEF
Fax: (703)317-9690
E-mail: info@christianrelief.org
URL: http://www.christianrelief.org
Contact: James J. O'Brien, Chm.
Founded: 1985. **Members:** 11. **Staff:** 152. **Budget:** $50,000,000. **Multinational. Description:** Assists needy children and their families in the United States and Africa. Distributes food and clothing and emergency assistance. Conducts water development and home repair programs, to individuals in need around the world and in communities throughout the United States. Has various long-term development programs designed to result in self-sufficiency among the participants. Operates over 4,675 units of affordable housing throughout the U.S. supporting low income working families, homeless families, the physically and mentally handicapped, and victims of domestic violence.

12569 ■ Church World Service (CWS)
PO Box 968
Elkhart, IN 46515
Ph: (574)264-3102
Free: (800)297-1516
Fax: (574)262-0966
E-mail: info@churchworldservice.org
URL: http://www.churchworldservice.org
Contact: Betty Voskuil, Chair
Founded: 1946. **Members:** 36. **Staff:** 288. **Budget:** $59,000,000. **Multinational. Description:** Serves as a relief, development and refugee assistance ministry of 36 Protestant, Orthodox and Anglican denominations. Works in partnership with indigenous organizations in more than 80 countries. Supports sustainable self-help development, meets emergency needs, aids refugees and helps address the root causes of poverty and powerlessness. **Affiliated With:** Church World Service, Immigration and Refugee Program; Interchurch Medical Assistance; National Council of Churches of Christ in the U.S.A. **Formerly:** (1967) Christian Rural Overseas Program; (1968) Church World Service Community Appeal; (1992) CROP. **Publications:** *Church World Service Annual Report*, annual ● *One Great Hour of Sharing Materials*, annual ● *Service*, semiannual. Magazine. Features articles on the work of the CWS. **Circulation:** 180,000 ● Films. **Conventions/Meetings:** semiannual board meeting.

12570 ■ CitiHope International
PO Box 38
143 Main St.
Andes, NY 13731
Ph: (845)676-4400
Fax: (845)676-3332
E-mail: info@citihope.org
URL: http://www.citihope.org
Contact: Paul S. Moore Sr., Pres./CEO
Founded: 1985. **Multinational. Description:** Provides Christian humanitarian aid and relief to the needy. Offers medical and food relief through its outreach programs. **Programs:** Food Relief; Medical Relief.

12571 ■ CityTeam Ministries
2304 Zanker Rd.
San Jose, CA 95131
Ph: (408)232-5600
Free: (888)CITYTEAM
Fax: (408)428-9505

E-mail: info@cityteam.org
URL: http://www.cityteam.org
Contact: Mr. Patrick J. Robertson, Pres.
Founded: 1957. **Staff:** 160. **Budget:** $14,000,000. **Local Groups:** 2. **Languages:** English, Spanish. **Description:** Works to provide disadvantaged people in the inner city with emergency services and spiritual guidance. Serves meals, provides shelter, distributes food boxes and household items, and administers medical assistance. Provides career counseling, job-training skills, and recovery programs for alcoholics and drug addicts. Creates youth club programs, offers winter and summer camp programs, and distributes Christmas toys. **Convention/Meeting:** none. **Formerly:** (1987) San Jose Rescue Mission. **Publications:** *CityTeam Report*, monthly. Newsletter. **Price:** free. **Circulation:** 20,000.

12572 ■ Concern America (CA)
PO Box 1790
2015 N Broadway Ave.
Santa Ana, CA 92702
Ph: (714)953-8575
Free: (800)266-2376
Fax: (714)953-1242
E-mail: concamerinc@earthlink.net
URL: http://www.concernamerica.org
Contact: Marianne Loewe, Exec. Dir.
Founded: 1969. **Staff:** 8. **Budget:** $1,000,000. **Regional Groups:** 4. **Description:** Provides training, technical and material support to people in underdeveloped countries. Also provides assistance in public health, nutrition, sanitation, and economic and agricultural development in an effort to foster ultimate self-reliance. Maintains volunteer groups that share professional skills in health, community organizing, and education with victims of natural disaster, forced migration, civil disruption, discrimination, and poverty. Volunteers serve in El Salvador, Guatemala, Honduras, Mexico, and Mozambique. Conducts educational programs in the U.S. to increase public awareness of the need for individual and group involvement in the elimination of poverty and social injustice in Third World countries. **Committees:** Field. **Programs:** Appropriate Technology; Community Health Worker; Literacy; Nutrition; Sanitation; Women's Training. **Publications:** *Concern America Newsletter*, quarterly. Reports on hunger relief and Third World development. **Price:** free. Alternate Formats: online ● *Crafts of Concern America*. Catalog. **Price:** free. Alternate Formats: online ● *Social Justice Education: With Eyes to See*. Newsletter. Focuses on a peace and justice concept, providing information, stories, classroom activities, and lists of resources relating to the concepts. **Price:** free. Alternate Formats: online ● Annual Report, annual.

12573 ■ Concern Worldwide (CW)
104 E 40th St., Ste.903
New York, NY 10016
Ph: (212)557-8000
Free: (800)59-CONCERN
Fax: (212)557-8004
URL: http://www.concernusa.org
Contact: Thomas J. Moran, Chm.
Multinational. Description: Individuals in the United States who provide volunteer support to relief and development organizations worldwide. Promotes more effective provision of relief to victims of disaster; seeks to ensure appropriate and sustainable economic development. Conducts programs in areas including water supply and sanitation, women's empowerment, health and nutrition, and education and training.

12574 ■ Covenant World Relief (CWR)
c/o Jim Sundholm, Dir.
Evangelical Covenant Church
5101 N Francisco Ave.
Chicago, IL 60625
Free: (800)338-4332
E-mail: resource.center@covchurch.org
URL: http://www.covchurch.org/cwr
Contact: Jim Sundholm, Dir.
Founded: 1946. **Multinational. Description:** Offers relief, rehabilitation, and development to the "poorest

of the poor" communities. **Publications:** *Reporter*. Newsletter. Alternate Formats: online.

12575 ■ Direct Aid International (DAI)
PO Box 394
Northfield, VT 05663
E-mail: hoffman@directaidinternational.org
URL: http://www.directaidinternational.org
Contact: Jonathan I. Hoffman, Founder/Dir.
Founded: 1999. **Multinational. Description:** Provides direct aid to people most isolated from other sources of assistance. Provides essential materials, project planning and implementation. Helps create an atmosphere of self-reliance and sustainability through community-based initiatives.

12576 ■ Doctors Without Borders USA (MSF-USA)
333 7th Ave., 2nd Fl.
New York, NY 10001-5004
Ph: (212)679-6800
Free: (888)392-0392
Fax: (212)679-7016
URL: http://www.doctorswithoutborders.org
Contact: Darin Portnoy MD, Pres.
Founded: 1971. **Members:** 250. **Staff:** 25. **Budget:** $25,000,000. **Description:** Medical and non-medical professionals. Provides assistance to victims of war, natural and man-made disasters, and epidemics, and to others who lack access to health care. Each year more than 2000 volunteers provide relief in more than 80 countries. **Also Known As:** Medecins Sans Frontieres. **Publications:** *Alert*, quarterly. Newsletter. Contains articles on the fields where Doctors Without Borders are active. **Price:** free. Alternate Formats: online ● *Populations in Dangers*, annual. Book. Contains a look at 5 situations of crisis and the humanitarian response. **Price:** $19.00. ISSN: 9780-9525 ● Annual Report, annual. Alternate Formats: online ● Reports. Alternate Formats: online.

12577 ■ Doctors Worldwide (DWW)
1S132 Summit Ave., No. 301
Oakbrook Terrace, IL 60181
Ph: (630)889-9513
Fax: (630)889-9511
E-mail: info-us@doctorsworldwide.org
URL: http://www.doctorsworldwide.org
Founded: 2000. **Multinational. Description:** Provides medical relief and aid to people who are victims of poverty, famine, disease, natural and man-made disasters, and civil wars. Works for the rehabilitation, reconstruction, and medical education through the help of local doctors and medical personnel, of societies no longer at war in re-establishing their health care systems. Provides medical education and training to local health care workers. **Computer Services:** Mailing lists, member e-group ● online services, photo gallery. **Projects:** Medical Education and Exchange; Mercedes Duksil Medical Center; Mother and Baby Clinic.

12578 ■ Episcopal Relief and Development (ERD)
815 2nd Ave.
New York, NY 10017
Free: (800)334-7626
Fax: (212)687-5302
E-mail: er-d@er-d.org
URL: http://www.er-d.org
Contact: Robert W. Radtke, Pres.
Founded: 1940. **Staff:** 5. **Description:** Relief and development arm of the Episcopal Church. Aims to provide relief of worldwide human suffering. Responds to natural disasters and other emergencies; communicates appeals for financial aid at times of emergencies; makes grants for relief, rehabilitation, and development. Provides follow-up response to crisis situations through rehabilitation grants. Bestows development grants that focus on such areas as: agricultural education; purchase of seeds and farming equipment; distribution of tools; well-digging projects; upgrading of livestock; funding for doctors, nurses, and nutritionists; elimination of the root causes of famine and disease. Works to alleviate drought conditions. Cooperates with Anglican as well

as ecumenical and private voluntary agencies. **Awards: Frequency:** biennial. **Type:** grant. **Telecommunication Services:** electronic mail, president@erd.org. **Committees:** Administration and Finance; Appeals and Communications; Grants. **Programs:** Honor/Memorial; Matching Gifts. **Affiliated With:** Interaction/American Council for Voluntary International Action; National Council of Churches of Christ in the U.S.A.; World Council of Churches. **Formerly:** (2001) Episcopal Church's Presiding Bishop's Fund for World Relief. **Publications:** *Builder's Stone*, quarterly. Newsletter ● *Update*, quarterly. Newsletter ● Newspaper, periodic.

12579 ■ Estonian Relief Committee (ERC)
Estonian House
243 E 34th St.
New York, NY 10016
Ph: (212)685-7467
URL: http://www.estonianhousenewyork.com
Contact: Endel Reinpold, Pres.
Founded: 1941. **Members:** 250. **Membership Dues:** $5 (annual). **Budget:** $100,000. **Languages:** English, Estonian. **Description:** Provides relief to distressed Estonians in any part of the world through funds for medicine, food, and clothing. Cooperates with government authorities on immigration matters. Obtains employment and other assurances in accordance with regulations of the Immigration and Nationality Act. **Publications:** none. **Awards: Type:** grant. **Recipient:** for Estonian Boy Scouts and Girl Scouts organizations in the U.S. **Conventions/Meetings:** annual general assembly - always in New York City.

12580 ■ Feed the Children (FTC)
PO Box 36
Oklahoma City, OK 73101-0036
Ph: (405)942-0228
Free: (800)627-4556
Fax: (405)945-4177
E-mail: ftc@feedthechildren.org
URL: http://www.feedthechildren.org
Contact: Larry W. Jones, Pres./Founder
Founded: 1979. **Description:** Provides food, clothing, medical equipment and other necessities to people who lack these essentials because of famine, drought, flood, war or other calamities. **Formerly:** (1964) Larry Jones Evangelistic Association; (1985) Larry Jones International Ministries. **Publications:** Newsletter, quarterly ● Annual Report, annual.

12581 ■ Food for Life Global (FFL)
PO Box 59037
Potomac, MD 20859
Ph: (301)987-5883
Free: (888)816-6977
E-mail: contact@ffl.org
URL: http://www.ffl.org
Contact: Paul Rodney Turner, Dir.
Founded: 1974. **Membership Dues:** supporter, $10 (annual) ● life, $1,008. **Multinational. Description:** Seeks to eradicate hunger and malnutrition by providing free vegetarian meals to the disadvantaged and the victims of disaster. Establishes centers that provide free and inexpensive vegetarian meals, counseling, health education, and living skills training.

12582 ■ Friends Disaster Service (FDS)
33937 US Rte. 30
Lisbon, OH 44432
Ph: (330)429-4292
Fax: (330)650-2919
E-mail: frndsds@localnet.com
Contact: William Lawson, Interim Dir.
Founded: 1974. **Description:** Volunteer group of individuals who work within the Quaker ethic to provide cleanup and restoration services to communities devastated by natural disasters. Priority is given to elderly, disabled, low-income, and uninsured individuals. Cooperates and networks with other relief agencies. **Publications:** Newsletter, periodic. **Conventions/Meetings:** annual meeting, includes fundraiser.

12583 ■ Global Action International (GAI)
PO Box 717
Carlsbad, CA 92018-0717
Ph: (760)438-3979
Fax: (760)602-0383
E-mail: globalactn@aol.com
URL: http://www.global-action.com
Contact: Rev. Dwaine Lee, Pres.
Description: Christians. Seeks to "meet the needs of a hurting world." Works with local, national, and international organizations to supply food, medical equipment and services, and relief supplies to the needy worldwide. Assists community development programs focusing on the needs of children; makes available emergency relief; conducts humanitarian and spiritual assistance programs.

12584 ■ Heart to Heart International (HHI)
401 S Claiborne, Ste.302
Olathe, KS 66062
Ph: (913)764-5200
Fax: (913)764-0809
E-mail: info@hearttoheart.org
URL: http://www.hearttoheart.org
Contact: Jon D. North, CEO
Founded: 1992. **Regional Groups:** 2. **Description:** Volunteers and organizations. Seeks to alleviate human suffering worldwide. Provides medical assistance and food to people living in impoverished areas; makes available emergency relief to victims of natural disasters and human conflicts; provides volunteer support to relief and development programs.

12585 ■ Humanity International (HI)
PO Box 8222
Gaithersburg, MD 20898
Free: (800)HUMANITY
E-mail: info@humanityinternational.org
URL: http://www.humanityinternational.org
Contact: Dr. Daniel J. Aulicino, Chm.
Founded: 1990. **Staff:** 10. **Description:** Works to provide humanitarian aid to developing countries and to restore respect for humanity worldwide, regardless of race, creed, color, nationality, sex, age, ethnicity, or religious or political affiliations. Offers food, clothing, shelter, medical assistance and basic education programs. Establishes people-to-people programs, eliminating the red tape of bureaucracy and politics. Is currently developing the International Diversified Bone Marrow Registry (IDBMR). **Computer Services:** database, International Diversified Bone Marrow Registry. **Telecommunication Services:** electronic bulletin board, fundraising information. **Programs:** International Diversified Bone Marrow Registry. **Publications:** *Humanity International: An Urgent Appeal to All Who Love Humanity*. Brochure ● *Operation Cure America*. Brochure ● *Operation Save Humanity*. Brochure. **Conventions/Meetings:** annual board meeting.

12586 ■ Indian Muslim Relief Committee of ISNA (IMRC)
1000 San Antonio Rd.
Palo Alto, CA 94303
Ph: (650)856-0440
Fax: (650)856-0444
E-mail: info@imrc.ws
URL: http://www.imrc.ws
Contact: Manzoor Ghori, Pres./Dir.
Founded: 1981. **Members:** 8,000. **Staff:** 2. **Budget:** $1,200,000. **Regional Groups:** 4. **State Groups:** 23. **Local Groups:** 40. **Languages:** English, Urdu. **Description:** Aids India's Muslims in achieving security, freedom, and equality their rights as citizens of India. Provides economic and educational assistance to Yateem/Miskeen children, immediate relief to those affected by natural disasters or to victims of communal violence, and to disseminate information about the Muslims of India. Provides educational charitable programs. Offers legal aid services. **Awards: Type:** grant ● **Type:** scholarship. **Affiliated With:** Islamic Society of North America. **Publications:** Annual Report, annual. **Circulation:** 10,000 ● Bulletin ● Newsletter ● Reports. **Conventions/Meetings:**

quarterly board meeting ● monthly conference ● annual regional meeting.

12587 ■ International Aid (IA)
17011 W Hickory
Spring Lake, MI 49456-9712
Ph: (616)846-7490
Free: (800)968-7490
Fax: (616)846-3842
E-mail: volunteer@internationalaid.org
URL: http://www.internationalaid.org
Contact: Rev. Myles D. Fish, Pres./CEO
Description: Works to provide goods and resources to Christians involved in relief and missionary activities.

12588 ■ International Medical Corps (IMC)
1919 Santa Monica Blvd., Ste.400
Santa Monica, CA 90404
Ph: (310)826-7800
Free: (800)481-4IMC
Fax: (310)442-6622
E-mail: imc@imcworldwide.org
URL: http://www.imcworldwide.org
Contact: Nancy A. Aossey, Pres./CEO
Founded: 1984. **Staff:** 4,000. **Budget:** $100,000,000. **Multinational. Description:** Staff and volunteers include physicians, surgeons, nurses, physician assistants and persons with expertise in administration, management, logistics and finances. Seeks to save lives, relieve suffering and improve the quality of life through health interventions and related activities that build local capacity in areas worldwide where few organizations dare to serve. Offers medical training and health care to local populations and medical assistance to people at highest risk, and with the flexibility to respond rapidly to emergency situations. Rehabilitates devastated health care systems and helps bring them back to self-reliance. **Formerly:** World Medical Corps. **Publications:** *On The Line*. Newsletter. **Price:** free. **Alternate Formats:** online ● Annual Report, annual. **Price:** free. **Alternate Formats:** online ● Also publishes fact sheet.

12589 ■ International Relief Teams (IRT)
4560 Alvarado Canyon Rd., Ste.2G
San Diego, CA 92120
Ph: (619)284-7979
Fax: (619)284-7938
E-mail: info@irteams.org
URL: http://www.irteams.org
Contact: Barry La Forgia, Exec. Dir.
Founded: 1988. **Multinational. Description:** Provides medical and non-medical assistance to victims of disaster and poverty worldwide. **Programs:** Disaster Relief; Medical Training; Public Health; Surgical Outreach. **Publications:** *TEAM News*, 3/year. Newsletter. **Alternate Formats:** online.

12590 ■ Islamic American Relief Agency (IARA)
PO Box 7084
Columbia, MO 65205
Free: (800)298-1199
Fax: (573)443-5975
E-mail: iara@iara-usa.org
Founded: 1989. **Multinational. Description:** Provides humanitarian assistance and relief to people, especially children who are victims of conflict and political instability in the middle east and other Islamic countries. **Projects:** Food Baskets; Iftar; Online Orphan Sponsorship.

12591 ■ Islamic Relief USA
PO Box 5640
Buena Park, CA 90622
Ph: (714)676-1300
Free: (888)479-4968
Fax: (714)676-1301
E-mail: info@irw.org
URL: http://www.irw.org
Contact: Ahmad El Bendary, Exec. Dir.
Founded: 1993. **National Groups:** 14. **Multinational. Description:** Establishes development projects to alleviate suffering, hunger, illiteracy and diseases worldwide. Provides rapid relief in the event

of man-made or natural disasters. **Computer Services:** Mailing lists. **Projects:** Development; Emergency Relief; Orphans; Seasonal.

12592 ■ Lalmba Association
7685 Quartz St.
Arvada, CO 80007
Ph: (303)420-1810
Fax: (303)467-1232
E-mail: lalmba@lalmba.org
URL: http://www.lalmba.org
Contact: Hugh Downey, Pres.
Founded: 1963. **Members:** 35. **Multinational. Description:** International relief organization working primarily in health related areas in Kenya, Ethiopia, and Eritrea. Coordinates and supports community programs that enable local people to assume responsibility for their own development. Places 5-15 volunteers in overseas assignments each year. **Publications:** *Hugh's News,* quarterly. Newsletter. **Conventions/Meetings:** periodic board meeting.

12593 ■ Life for Relief and Development (LIFE)
17300 W 10 Mile Rd.
Southfield, MI 48075
Ph: (248)424-7493
Free: (800)827-3543
Fax: (248)424-8325
E-mail: life@lifeusa.org
URL: http://www.lifeusa.org
Contact: Dr. Abdulwahab Asamarai, Chm.
Founded: 1992. **Regional Groups:** 1. **National Groups:** 5. **Multinational. Description:** Commits itself to alleviating human suffering around the world regardless of race, color, religion or cultural background. Offers humanitarian, health, educational services and programs in aiding refugees and victims of natural or man-made disasters. **Computer Services:** Information services, newsroom ● online services, media gallery. **Projects:** Adopt A Town; Handicapped; Orphan Sponsorship; Udhiah. **Affiliated With:** American Friends Service Committee; AmeriCares Foundation; Brother's Brother Foundation; Interaction/American Council for Voluntary International Action; United Nations Development Programme; U.S. Fund for UNICEF; Veterans for Peace. **Publications:** *Life Link.* Newsletter. Alternate Formats: online ● Annual Report, annual. Alternate Formats: online.

12594 ■ Mapendo International
153 Lowell St.
Somerville, MA 02143
Ph: (617)628-0182
E-mail: info@mapendo.org
URL: http://www.mapendo.org
Contact: Sasha Chanoff, Exec. Dir./Co-Founder
Multinational. Description: Identifies, protects and cares for people fleeing war and violence whose lives are in imminent danger. Works to fill the critical and unmet needs of people affected by war and conflict who have fallen through the net of humanitarian assistance in Africa. Strives to alleviate human suffering, to protect life and health, and to raise awareness for these people.

12595 ■ Mennonite Disaster Service (MDS)
1018 Main St.
Akron, PA 17501
Ph: (717)859-2210
Free: (800)241-8111
Fax: (717)859-4910
E-mail: mdsus@mds.mennonite.net
URL: http://www.mds.mennonite.net
Contact: Kevin King, Exec. Coor.
Founded: 1950. **Staff:** 6. **Regional Groups:** 5. **Local Groups:** 50. **Description:** Coordinates the organized response to disasters for the constituent churches of the Mennonite churches in North America. Responds, through local units, with personal services (cleanup, repair, rebuilding) in time of natural or man-made disasters. When need in a specific disaster is too large for a local unit, other units within the region or other regions assist. Participates in non-disaster types of programs, and helping in home

building in rural poverty areas. **Affiliated With:** Mennonite Central Committee. **Publications:** *Behind the Hammer,* quarterly. Newsletter. **Price:** free. Alternate Formats: online ● Annual Report, annual. Alternate Formats: online. **Conventions/Meetings:** annual conference - always February.

12596 ■ Mercy-USA for Aid and Development (M-USA)
44450 Pinetree Dr., Ste.201
Plymouth, MI 48170-3869
Ph: (734)454-0011
Free: (800)556-3729
Fax: (734)454-0303
E-mail: info@mercyusa.org
URL: http://www.mercyusa.org
Contact: Mr. Umar al-Qadi, Pres./CEO
Founded: 1986. **Multinational. Description:** Represents the interests of individuals dedicated to alleviating human suffering. Focuses on improving health and promoting economic and educational growth around the world. **Telecommunication Services:** electronic mail, mercyusa@mercyusa.org. **Publications:** *Mercy News,* periodic. Newsletter. Alternate Formats: online ● Annual Report, annual. Alternate Formats: online.

12597 ■ Mir Pace International
1173 Nantasket Ave., Unit C-6
Hull, MA 02045
Ph: (781)925-0090
Free: (877)925-0090
E-mail: info@mirpace.org
URL: http://www.mirpace.org
Contact: Eileen M. Weisslinger, Chair/Exec. Dir.
Multinational. Description: Provides worldwide humanitarian relief and development programs in order to reduce vulnerability, alleviate human suffering and restore the self-sufficiency and livelihoods of disaster-affected populations. Fosters cultural understanding and volunteerism through International High School Mission (IHSM) programs. **Computer Services:** Mailing lists. **Programs:** International High School Mission. **Publications:** Newsletter, semiannual. Alternate Formats: online.

12598 ■ National Relief Network (NRN)
PO Box 125
Greenville, MI 48838-0125
Ph: (616)225-2525
Free: (866)286-5868
Fax: (616)225-1934
E-mail: info@nrn.org
URL: http://www.nrn.org
Contact: Scott Harding, Exec. Dir.
Founded: 1995. **Description:** Brings large numbers of volunteers to state and federally declared disaster areas for the purpose of helping families in their efforts to rebuild their homes, their communities and their lives. Administrates volunteer relief programs for organizations such as churches, youth groups, corporations, colleges, universities and high schools.

12599 ■ National Voluntary Organizations Active in Disaster (NVOAD)
1720 I St. NW, Ste.700
Washington, DC 20006
Ph: (202)955-8396
Fax: (202)955-5079
E-mail: info@nvoad.org
URL: http://www.nvoad.org
Contact: Cheryl Guidry Tyiska, Interim Exec. Dir.
Founded: 1971. **Members:** 34. **Membership Dues:** small agency, $500 (annual) ● medium agency, $1,500 (annual) ● large agency, $2,500 (annual). **Staff:** 1. **Budget:** $200,000. **State Groups:** 52. **Local Groups:** 65. **National Groups:** 34. **Description:** Disaster response organizations dedicated to the commitment of personnel, funds, and equipment to meet the needs of people affected by disaster. Coordinates national and local voluntary organizations active in disaster service to ensure more effective service to people beset by disaster and prepares communities before disaster strikes. Encourages training programs to increase awareness and preparedness; coordinates training programs; reviews

pending disaster response legislation. **Committees:** Communications; Donated Goods; Emotional and Spiritual Care; Mass Care; Public Awareness; Recovery. **Affiliated With:** American Red Cross National Headquarters; Catholic Charities USA; Volunteers of America; World Vision. **Publications:** *National Directory,* periodic ● *NVOAD Letter,* 3/year. Newsletter ● *VOAD Organizational Manual.* Alternate Formats: online ● Annual Report, annual. Alternate Formats: online. **Conventions/Meetings:** annual conference ● annual Leadership Conference - meeting, membership meeting - always March.

12600 ■ Need
PO Box 54541
Phoenix, AZ 85078
Ph: (623)879-9676
Fax: (623)879-9674
Contact: Mrs. Dulal Borpujari, Pres.
Founded: 1985. **Staff:** 2. **Budget:** $380,000. **Description:** Provides disaster relief, food distribution, and medical and building supplies to needy areas of the world. Supports a school and health clinic in Calcutta, India; maintains charitable program; offers children's services. Provides development assistance; conducts educational programs. Activities conducted primarily in Southeast Asia. **Affiliated With:** Evangelical Council for Financial Accountability. **Conventions/Meetings:** semiannual board meeting.

12601 ■ Northwest Medical Teams International
PO Box 10
Portland, OR 97207-0010
Ph: (503)624-1000
Free: (800)959-4325
Fax: (503)624-1001
E-mail: info@nwmti.org
URL: http://www.nwmedicalteams.org
Contact: Barbara Agnew, Press Contact
Founded: 1979. **Staff:** 65. **Budget:** $113,700,000. **Nonmembership. Multinational. Description:** Aims to demonstrate the love of Christ to people affected by disaster, conflict and poverty. **Publications:** *Reaching Hands,* bimonthly. Newsletter. Updates from disaster and development projects around the world. **Price:** free. **Circulation:** 50,000 ● Annual Report, annual. **Conventions/Meetings:** semiannual board meeting.

12602 ■ Oxfam International Advocacy Office
1100 15th St. NW, Ste.600
Washington, DC 20005
Ph: (202)496-1170
Fax: (202)496-0128
E-mail: advocacy@oxfaminternational.org
URL: http://www.oxfam.org
Contact: Bernice Romero, Advocacy Dir.
Founded: 1995. **Multinational. Description:** International group of independent, non-governmental organizations dedicated to fighting poverty and injustice around the world. Has offices that are located in: America, Australia, Belgium, Canada and Quebec, Great Britain, Hong Kong, Ireland, The Netherlands, New Zealand and Spain.

12603 ■ Plenty International
PO Box 394
Summertown, TN 38483
Ph: (931)964-4323
Fax: (931)964-4864
E-mail: plenty@plenty.org
URL: http://www.plenty.org
Contact: Peter Schweitzer, Exec. Dir.
Founded: 1974. **Members:** 3,500. **Staff:** 6. **Budget:** $300,000. **Regional Groups:** 2. **Local Groups:** 3. **Multinational. Description:** Works to assist indigenous people around the world, while allowing them to maintain their cultural identity. Provides charitable relief and development organization based on the concept that "there's plenty for everyone - if we all share". Helps the needy provide themselves with adequate food, housing, clean water, and medical care; focuses on projects that help create self-sufficiency through appropriate training and development of life-supporting technologies. Current pro-

grams include soybean propagation and utilization, alternative energy sources, soy dairies, reforestation, human rights litigation, Caribbean basin small business development, and community development on U.S. Indian reservations. **Libraries: Type:** reference. **Holdings:** archival material, audiovisuals. **Computer Services:** Mailing lists. **Projects:** Caribbean; Central America; Mexico; USA. **Formerly:** (1984) Plenty; (1993) Plenty - U.S.A. **Publications:** *Climate in Crisis: The Greenhouse Effect and What We Can Do.* Book. Provides information on growing and using soybeans for food. ● *The Global Kitchen: A Collection of Vegetarian Recipes.* Book ● *Plenty Bulletin*, quarterly. **Price:** $10.00/year. Alternate Formats: online. **Conventions/Meetings:** semiannual meeting.

12604 ■ Relief Interactive (REACT)
9902 Chase Hill Ct.
Vienna, VA 22182
Ph: (703)585-3614
Fax: (703)321-7407
E-mail: contact@reliefinteractive.org
Contact: Dr. Brady Brown, Founder/Pres.
Founded: 1998. **Languages:** English, French, Spanish. **Multinational. Description:** Volunteers. Provides information and links to crisis-specific participants. Promotes public awareness.

12605 ■ Religious Freedom Coalition (RFC)
717 2nd St. NE, No. 3000
Washington, DC 20002
Ph: (202)543-0300
Fax: (202)543-8447
E-mail: support@rfcnet.org
URL: http://www.rfcnet.org
Contact: William J. Murray, Chm.
Founded: 1982. **Members:** 15,000. **Staff:** 6. **Budget:** $1,100,000. **Description:** Christian organization dedicated to the restoration of religious freedom in the United States as envisioned by the authors of the Constitution. Works on issues of religious freedom for Christians worldwide and supports Christian schools in Islamic areas. **Additional Websites:** http://pledgeundergod.org. **Doing business as:** (2000) William J. Murray Faith Foundation; (2000) William J. Murray Evangelistic Association. **Formerly:** (2000) MFM Publishing. **Publications:** *Chairman's Report*, monthly. Newsletter. Features moral and religious liberty issues facing the United States and Christians worldwide. **Price:** $25.00 suggested donation. **Circulation:** 20,000 ● *Weekly Legislative Update*. Bulletins. Contains updated legislative information from Capitol Hill. Alternate Formats: online.

12606 ■ RHEMA International (RI)
PO Box 82085
Rochester, MI 48308-2085
Ph: (248)652-2450
Free: (866)652-2450
Fax: (248)652-9894
E-mail: pgruits@rhemainternational.org
URL: http://www.rhemainternational.org
Contact: Dr. Patricia Beall Gruits, Chair/Founder
Founded: 1977. **Budget:** $200,000. **Description:** Represents individuals concerned about the quality of life in Haiti. Seeks to afford to Haitians the opportunity to live better lives by providing educational and medical services and establishing self-help programs. Operates medical and dental clinics; conducts paramedical training courses in areas including prenatal care and physical hygiene. Maintains Hope Academy International, which trains Haitians to organize medical, health education, and spiritual enlightenment programs for the benefit of rural villages. Accepts donated funds, equipment, and medicine; cooperates with other non-profit charities and organizations to distribute aid to needy Haitians. Conducts job training courses to teach young Haitians marketable skills. Offers seminars for pastors, ministers, and Christian educators. **Libraries: Type:** reference. **Holdings:** 1,000. **Also Known As:** Restoring Hope through Educational and Medical Aid. **Publications:** *Rhema Newsletter*, monthly. **Price:** free. **Circulation:** 8,000. Alternate Formats: online ● *Understanding God and His Covenants* (in

English, French, Russian, and Spanish) ● *Understanding the Master's Voice.* **Conventions/Meetings:** convention - 3/year, held in Haiti ● quarterly Missions Conference - board meeting (exhibits) - September ● semiannual seminar.

12607 ■ U.S.A. for Africa (USAFA)
5670 Wilshire Blvd., Ste.1450
Los Angeles, CA 90036
Ph: (323)954-3124
Fax: (323)857-0048
E-mail: info@usaforafrica.org
URL: http://www.usaforafrica.org
Contact: Marcia Thomas, Exec. Dir.
Founded: 1985. **Description:** Represents American rock, pop, and country recording artists who have pooled their resources to raise money for victims of famine in Africa. Arranged for 45 artists to record We Are the World, a song written by recording stars Michael Jackson and Lionel Richie for the cause, with all of the royalties to be used to aid famine victims. Funds will be used for: immediate food relief with emphasis on medical aid; agricultural development; long term community development programs; ten percent will be used to alleviate hunger in America. Produces a video for MTV (music television) and an hour-long video special. Additional funds for famine relief will be raised through voluntary donations, the sale of shirts, posters, sweatshirts, and videocassettes. **Also Known As:** United Support of Artists for Africa. **Formerly:** African Relief and Development Foundation. **Publications:** Annual Report.

12608 ■ Wings of Hope (WOH)
18590 Edison Ave.
Spirit of St. Louis Airport
Chesterfield, MO 63005
Ph: (636)537-1302
Free: (800)448-9487
Fax: (636)537-3139
E-mail: woh206@earthlink.net
URL: http://www.wings-of-hope.org
Contact: Sanford N. McDonnell, Chm.
Founded: 1962. **Members:** 1,365. **Membership Dues:** angel, $500 (annual) ● chief pilot, $250 (annual) ● pilot, $100 (annual) ● co-pilot, $50 (annual) ● crew chief, $25 (annual). **Staff:** 300. **Budget:** $715,000. **Description:** Enhances humanitarian aviation and radio communication service helping to bring equipment, training, and the services of hospitals, educators, missionaries, health, world-aid, and development groups to people in need in remote areas of the world. Enables volunteer professional pilots to fly in the bush; offers bush pilot training. Provides speakers' bureau. **Committees:** Finance; Flight Operation; Marketing; Operations. **Supersedes:** Turkhana Desert Fund. **Publications:** Newsletter, quarterly. Reports on organization field operations. **Price:** included in membership dues. **Circulation:** 3,000. Alternate Formats: online. **Conventions/Meetings:** quarterly board meeting.

12609 ■ World Community Chaplains (WCC)
24303 Woolsey Canyon Rd., No. 142
West Hills, CA 91304
Ph: (818)884-6568
Free: (888)884-6567
Fax: (818)884-6568
E-mail: info@cc-la.org
URL: http://www.worldcommunitychaplains.org
Contact: Barbara Jean, Exec. Dir.
Founded: 1978. **Members:** 111. **Staff:** 3. **Languages:** Arabic, English, French, Spanish. **Multinational. Description:** PTSD - Minimizing the Effects. Assessing urgent physical and mental health to provide urgently needed resources. Working to promote individual and community progress to limit PTSD, Post Traumatic Stress Disorder. Offering effective pastoral care for people experiencing war, disaster or crisis. Operating Health and Welfare Inquiry system. Maintains a central location during disaster to receive information regarding the health and whereabouts of loved ones after disaster. The website hosts a World Community Education forum for the dissemination of critical information. Informa-

tion will be updated to reflect immediate community needs. The website also includes special military options including a Military Memorial page and a Chapel. **Telecommunication Services:** electronic mail, ptsdchaplains@aol.com. **Programs:** Chapel of the Divine Heart; The Comfort Zone; Military Memorial; Moving On Seminar; World Community Education. **Formerly:** (2003) World Community Projects; (2006) World Community. **Publications:** *Disaster Book*, annual, or as needed. Magazines. Provides current stats and outstanding photographs of one major disaster and its effects on the world community. Alternate Formats: online ● Also publishes books and magazines and educational materials for projects in developing countries.

12610 ■ World Emergency Relief (WER)
PO Box 131570
Carlsbad, CA 92013
Ph: (760)930-8001
Free: (888)HUG-4-KID
Fax: (760)930-9085
E-mail: info@wer-us.org
URL: http://www.worldemergency.org
Contact: Joel MacCollam, Pres.
Founded: 1985. **Staff:** 11. **Budget:** $17,000,000. **Nonmembership. Multinational. Description:** Promotes micro-economic development and institutional advancement for Native Americans and underdeveloped countries. Provides domestic and international emergency relief and orphan support services. **Libraries: Type:** reference; not open to the public. **Holdings:** articles, clippings. **Subjects:** social and economic development. **Publications:** *World Report*, quarterly. Newsletter. **Circulation:** 28,000. **Conventions/Meetings:** quarterly board meeting.

12611 ■ World Mercy Fund (WMF)
PO Box 227
Waterford, VA 20197-0227
Ph: (540)882-3226
E-mail: info@worldmercyfund.ie
URL: http://www.worldmercyfund.ie
Contact: John Horl, Dir.
Founded: 1969. **Budget:** $13,000,000. **Multinational. Description:** Builds hospitals and provides medical facilities and water for less fortunate peoples of the world, particularly those in Africa. Provides hospitals and clinics in Africa that are equipped with mobile units. Promotes initiated projects to bring fresh water to places where it is most urgently needed. Conducts child and adult education programs in nutrition and agriculture; provides on-the-spot education in villages to raise the standard of food production. **Awards:** Primum Vivere Award. **Frequency:** annual. **Type:** recognition. **Conventions/Meetings:** annual meeting.

Religion

12612 ■ Interfaith Working Group (IWG)
PO Box 11706
Philadelphia, PA 19101
E-mail: info@iwgonline.org
URL: http://www.iwgonline.org
Contact: David Drum, Pres.
Budget: $5,000. **Description:** Committed to religious diversity and social issues, including equal rights for gay, lesbian, bisexual and transgender people, reproductive freedom, and separation of church and state.

12613 ■ Recovery from Mormonism
c/o Richard Packham
2145 Melton Rd.
Roseburg, OR 97470
Ph: (541)672-2360
E-mail: packham@teleport.com
URL: http://www.exmormon.org
Contact: Richard Packham, Contact
Description: Former members and those questioning their faith in the Church of Jesus Christ of Latter-day Saints. **Conventions/Meetings:** semiannual conference.

Rescue

12614 ■ American Rescue Dog Association (ARDA)
PO Box 613
Bristow, VA 20136
Fax: (715)545-2220
E-mail: information@ardainc.org
URL: http://www.ardainc.org
Contact: Penny G. Sullivan, VP

Founded: 1972. **Members:** 100. **State Groups:** 10. **Description:** Volunteer search and rescue dog units and their handlers in ten states and Canada. Provides, free of charge to requesting official agencies, German shepherd dogs and handlers skilled in searching for lost or missing persons and assisting with criminal investigations. Units participate in over 100 search missions annually. Provides instruction on search dogs and search management to official agencies, and educational programs to children's groups and civic organizations. Maintains tape and written materials on search procedures and management techniques for wilderness, avalanche, and disasters. Operates speakers' bureau. **Computer Services:** Online services, publication. **Publications:** ARDA News, 3-4/year. Newsletter. Alternate Formats: online ● Directory of Member Units, annual ● Search and Rescue Dogs: Training the K-9 Hero. Book. Includes information on selecting and training the search dog, scent theory, handler training, responding to search mission, specialized training. **Price:** $16.99/copy ● Reports. **Conventions/Meetings:** annual meeting.

12615 ■ Mountain Rescue Association (MRA)
c/o Monty Bell, Pres.
PO Box 880868
San Diego, CA 92168-0868
Ph: (619)884-9456
Fax: (619)374-7072
E-mail: ubs@att.net
URL: http://www.mra.org
Contact: Monty Bell, Pres.

Founded: 1958. **Members:** 2,500. **Budget:** $50,000. **Regional Groups:** 11. **Description:** Provides rescue and mountain safety education. Provides accreditation of rescue units both in and outside of the U.S. for wilderness searches and snow and ice rescues. **Awards:** MRA R&D Grant. **Frequency:** annual. **Type:** grant. **Recipient:** for research, development and testing of SAR systems and equipment. **Committees:** Accreditation; Awards and Recognition; Communications; Directory; Education; Medical; Public Affairs; Website. **Publications:** Blue Book, annual ● Annual Report, annual. Alternate Formats: online. **Conventions/Meetings:** annual workshop (exhibits).

12616 ■ National Association for Search and Rescue (NASAR)
PO Box 232020
Centreville, VA 20120-2020
Ph: (703)222-6277
Free: (877)893-0702
Fax: (703)222-6277
E-mail: info@nasar.org
URL: http://www.nasar.org
Contact: Kathy Miller, Pres.

Founded: 1974. **Members:** 7,000. **Membership Dues:** individual, $74 (annual) ● organization, $185 (annual) ● corporate, $285 (annual) ● 5-year extended organization, $760 ● life, $1,250 ● 10-year extended organization, $1,420 ● individual outside U.S., $101 (annual) ● organization outside U.S., $212 (annual) ● corporate outside U.S., $322 (annual) ● 5-year extended organization outside U.S., $787 ● 10-year extended organization outside U.S., $1,447. **Staff:** 7. **Budget:** $3,000,000. **Description:** Directors or coordinators of state and regional emergency rescue services; medical rescue, fire, and emergency personnel; organizations or associations involved in search, rescue, or survival activities; state rescue-related agencies. Promotes and develops search and rescue (SAR) and disaster response capabilities. Provides for liaison of state, federal, local, and private search and/or rescue groups. Conducts training

programs for SAR professionals; promotes the standardization of procedures. Sponsors survival education programs designed to help the public cope with disaster and emergency situations. **Libraries:** Type: reference. **Holdings:** 600; articles, books. **Subjects:** search and rescue, rescue medicine, climbing technique, disaster management. **Awards:** Frequency: annual. **Type:** recognition. **Recipient:** for individuals or groups making important contributions to the search and rescue field. **Computer Services:** Mailing lists. **Councils:** Canine; High Angle Rescue; SAR Advisory; Swift Water Rescue; Urbansar; Wilderness Medicine. **Formerly:** (1976) National Association of Search and Rescue Coordinators. **Publications:** Briefings, bimonthly. Newsletter. **Circulation:** 3,500. **Advertising:** accepted ● New Fundamentals of Search and Rescue. Book. Includes the latest information based on the most current land SAR research available. **Price:** $39.95 ● The Response. Journal. An academic peer-reviewed journal. **Advertising:** accepted ● Sar Dog Alert, bimonthly ● Magazine, quarterly. **Conventions/Meetings:** annual conference and trade show, educational (exhibits).

12617 ■ National Disaster Search Dog Foundation (NDSDF)
206 N Signal St., Ste.R
Ojai, CA 93023
Free: (888)4K9-HERO
E-mail: rescue@ndsdf.org
URL: http://www.ndsdf.org
Contact: Debra Tosch, Exec. Dir.

Founded: 1995. **Description:** Finds, trains and matches disaster search dogs to handlers, usually firemen. **Publications:** Newsletter, quarterly. Alternate Formats: online.

12618 ■ United States Lifesaving Association (USLA)
PO Box 322
Avon-by-the-Sea, NJ 07717
Free: (866)FOR-USLA
E-mail: president@usla.org
URL: http://www.usla.org
Contact: B. Chris Brewster, Pres.

Founded: 1964. **Members:** 6,000. **Membership Dues:** individual, $25 (annual). **Budget:** $50,000. **Regional Groups:** 7. **Local Groups:** 271. **Description:** Professional open water and surf lifeguards from lake, river, and ocean beaches; aquatic rescue personnel. Associate members are interested citizens or organizations, and patrons. Purposes are to: establish and maintain high standards of professional surf and open water lifesaving for maximizing public safety; educate the public in the area of beach safety; support the general improvement of lifesaving and humanitarian causes. Works toward establishing standards of rating and categorization of lifeguard systems and of drowning determinations. Provides consulting services to lifeguarding agencies, recreation departments, and governments. Sponsors programs for underprivileged youth and day programs for interested youth groups. Members attend seminars and symposia with all types of aquatic organizations including diving seminars, flood rescue seminars, paramedical seminars, and international lifeguard exchanges. Compiles statistics; sponsors competitions; operates speakers' bureau. **Awards:** Heroic Acts Award. **Frequency:** periodic. **Type:** recognition. **Recipient:** for non-lifeguard persons who perform heroic acts. **Committees:** Activities; Certification; Junior Lifeguard; Lifesaving Certification and Standards; Public Education; Research and Development. **Affiliated With:** National Association for Search and Rescue. **Formerly:** (1978) National Surf Life Saving Association of America; (2001) American Lifesaving Emergency Response Team. **Publications:** American Lifeguard Magazine, 3/year. **Price:** free for members; $12.00 /year for nonmembers. Alternate Formats: online ● Beach Directories, annual ● Emergency Services Directory, annual ● Lifesaving and Marine Safety ● Open Water Lifesaving - The United States Lifesaving Association Manual. Includes illustrations, and technical drawings along with official report forms useful to lifesavers. **Price:** $26.07 ● Safety Bookmarkers, annual ● U.S. Lifesav-

ing Magazine, quarterly. **Conventions/Meetings:** semiannual board meeting - always first week in May and last week in October.

Retirement

12619 ■ AARP
601 E St. NW
Washington, DC 20049
Free: (888)OUR-AARP
Fax: (202)434-2320
E-mail: member@aarp.org
URL: http://www.aarp.org
Contact: Bill Novelli, CEO

Founded: 1958. **Members:** 35,000,000. **Membership Dues:** individual, $12 (annual). **Staff:** 1,200. **Regional Groups:** 10. **Local Groups:** 3,600. **Languages:** English, Spanish. **Description:** Represents persons 50 years of age or older, working or retired. Seeks to improve every aspect of living for older people. Has targeted four areas of immediate concern: health care, women's initiative, worker equity, and minority affairs. Provides group health insurance program, discounts on auto rental and hotel rates, and a specially designed and priced motoring plan. Sponsors community service programs on crime prevention, defensive driving, and tax aid. Provides pre-retirement planning program; offers special services to retired teachers through National Retired Teachers Association. Sponsors mail order pharmacy services. **Libraries:** Type: reference. **Holdings:** 20,000. **Awards:** Type: grant. **Recipient:** to universities for gerontology research. **Computer Services:** database, AGELINE. **Absorbed:** (1984) Action for Independent Maturity. **Formerly:** American Association of Retired Persons. **Publications:** AARP News Bulletin, 11/year. Newsletter. **Price:** included in membership dues. ISSN: 0010-0200. **Circulation:** 22,100,000. **Advertising:** accepted. Alternate Formats: online ● The Magazine, biweekly. Newsletter. Includes news and guidance on health, travel, celebrities and food. Features insights and inspiration. Alternate Formats: online ● Modern Maturity, bimonthly. Magazine. Contains articles on careers, the workplace, science and health, investments, and personal relationships. **Price:** included in membership dues; $5.00 /year for nonmembers. **Circulation:** 22,400,000. **Advertising:** accepted ● Working Age, bimonthly. Newsletter. Includes research reports, case studies, legislative updates, and calendar of events. **Price:** free. ISSN: 0883-2714. **Circulation:** 9,000 ● Also publishes books on housing, health, exercise, retirement planning, money management, and travel and leisure. **Conventions/Meetings:** biennial meeting.

12620 ■ American Association of Retirement Communities (AARC)
Univ. of Oklahoma
1600 S Jenkins Ave.
Norman, OK 73072
Ph: (405)325-3489
E-mail: hollymills@ou.edu
URL: http://www.the-aarc.org
Contact: Pat Shaddix, Exec. Dir.

Founded: 1994. **Membership Dues:** individual, $50 (annual) ● business (with less than 100 employees), educational institution, professional association, $250 (annual) ● business (with more than 100 employees), organization (with more than 12,000 population), $350 (annual) ● organization (with less than 12,000 population), $250 (annual). **Staff:** 4. **Budget:** $100,000. **Description:** Works to promote retirement as an industry. Assists local officials in developing strategies to attract retirees to communities. Provides information about the retirement market and educates local officials on the economic benefits of retirees to a community. Facilitates planning for growth and the increased demand for services which accompany increased retiree population. **Libraries:** Type: not open to the public. **Holdings:** books, business records, clippings. **Awards:** Community of Distinction. **Frequency:** annual. **Type:** recognition. **Publications:** AARC Quarterly. Newsletter. **Circulation:**

7,000. **Advertising:** accepted. Alternate Formats: online. **Conventions/Meetings:** periodic board meeting ● annual conference.

12621 ■ Association of Retired Americans (ARA)

6505 E 82nd St., No. 130
Indianapolis, IN 46250
Free: (800)806-6160
Fax: (317)915-2510
E-mail: ara@ara-usa.org
URL: http://www.ara-usa.org
Contact: John K. Smith, Pres.

Founded: 1975. **Members:** 25,000. **Membership Dues:** regular, $30 (annual) ● life, $250. **Staff:** 4. **Budget:** $300,000. **Description:** Comprises senior Americans age 45 or older interested in enhancing their lives through group benefits. Aims to offer programs of high quality, low-cost benefits and services to members. Provides services such as discounts on prescriptions, eyeglasses, and hearing aids; low interest credit cards; discounts on lodging, car rental, tours, cruises, and airfare; insurance benefits including emergency air medical transportation. Assists governmental bodies and agencies with the development of programs and legislation which benefit and promotes the well-being of mature Americans. **Libraries: Type:** reference. **Holdings:** audiovisuals, books, clippings, periodicals. **Publications:** *Vintage Times*, quarterly. Magazine. **Advertising:** accepted. **Conventions/Meetings:** annual board meeting - always 4th Saturday in June.

12622 ■ Institute for Retired Professionals (IRP)

New School Univ.
66 W 12th St., Rm. 502
New York, NY 10011
Ph: (212)229-5682
Fax: (212)229-5679
E-mail: irp@newschool.edu
URL: http://www.nsu.newschool.edu/irp
Contact: Michael I. Markowitz, Dir.

Founded: 1962. **Members:** 286. **Membership Dues:** regular, $665 (annual) ● inactive, $15 ● alumni/life, $25. **Staff:** 3. **Budget:** $200,000. **Description:** Retired professionals including doctors, lawyers, dentists, teachers, business executives, artists, and others. Provides an intense learning program in which members are both teachers and students, utilizing the experience and talents of members while meeting their needs and interests. Conducts over 40 peer-learning groups. Aids colleges in forming peer-learning programs. **Libraries: Type:** reference. **Holdings:** archival material, audiovisuals, books, clippings, monographs, periodicals. **Awards:** Ira Weinblatt Award. **Frequency:** annual. **Type:** recognition. **Recipient:** for contribution to elder education. **Computer Services:** Mailing lists. **Committees:** Changing Eye and Ear; Cultural Events; Curriculum; Diversity; Orientation; Social; Travel. **Publications:** *IRP Newsletter*, monthly. Contains academic and social issues during the year. ● *IRP Observer*, weekly during academic year. Newsletter. Alternate Formats: online ● *IRP Voices*, annual. Journal. Contains fiction by members. **Price:** $3.75. **ISSN:** 1060-4770. **Circulation:** 4,000. **Advertising:** accepted ● Membership Directory, one per semester. Lists offerings. **Conventions/Meetings:** annual Anniversary Luncheon ● annual Art Show - luncheon ● annual Awards Luncheon.

12623 ■ Mennonite Association of Retired Persons (MARP)

771 Rte. 113
Souderton, PA 18964
Ph: (215)721-7730
Free: (866)721-7730
E-mail: marp-soop@juno.com
URL: http://marp.mennonite.net
Contact: Helen L. Lapp, Exec. Dir.

Founded: 1989. **Members:** 4,000. **Membership Dues:** individual, $20 (annual) ● two persons at the same address, $30 (annual) ● life (individual), $300. **Staff:** 1. **Description:** Retired persons of the Mennonite faith. Promotes an active and healthy life for

its members. **Publications:** *PAGES*, quarterly. Newsletter. **Circulation:** 4,500. Alternate Formats: online.

12624 ■ Setting Priorities for Retirement Years (SPRY)

3916 Rosemary St.
Chevy Chase, MD 20815
Ph: (301)656-3405
Fax: (301)656-6221
E-mail: morganr@spry.org
URL: http://www.spry.org
Contact: Dr. Russell E. Morgan Jr., Pres.

Description: Aims to help older adults plan for a healthy and financially secure future. Works with top organizations in the field on aging, disseminates information to consumers and conducts applied research.

Right to Life

12625 ■ American Center for Law and Justice (ACLJ)

PO Box 90555
Washington, DC 20090-0555
Ph: (757)226-2489
Free: (800)684-3110
Fax: (757)226-2836
URL: http://www.aclj.org
Contact: Jay Alan Sekulow, Chief Counsel

Founded: 1990. **Members:** 18. **Staff:** 40. **Budget:** $9,618,116. **Description:** A public interest law firm defending religious liberties. Protects all human life beginning at the time of conception. Offers educational programs. **Libraries: Type:** reference. **Subjects:** law. **Telecommunication Services:** additional toll-free number, petition call-in, (877)989-2255.

12626 ■ American Life League (ALL)

PO Box 1350
Stafford, VA 22555
Ph: (540)659-4171
Free: (888)546-2580
Fax: (540)659-2586
E-mail: info@all.org
URL: http://www.all.org
Contact: Judie Brown, Pres.

Founded: 1982. **Members:** 300,000. **Staff:** 55. **Budget:** $6,900,000. **Description:** Serves as a pro-life service organization providing educational materials, books, flyers, and programs for local, state, and national pro-life, pro-family organizations. Sponsors national pro-life meetings, training sessions, and seminars. Special fields of interest: abortion; euthanasia; organ transplantation; population; world hunger. Sponsored Coalition for Unborn Children project. Produces *Celebrate Life!* magazine. **Libraries: Type:** reference. **Holdings:** books, clippings, periodicals. **Formerly:** American Life Education and Research Trust. **Publications:** *All News*, bimonthly. Newsletter ● *Celebrate Life*, bimonthly. Magazine. **Price:** $12.95 ● *Communique*, periodic. Newsletter ● *Reality Check*, monthly. Newsletter.

12627 ■ American Victims of Abortion (AVA)

419 7th St. NW, Ste.500
Washington, DC 20004
E-mail: nrlc@nrlc.org
URL: http://www.nrlc.org/outreach/victims.html
Contact: Olivia Gans, Dir.

Founded: 1985. **State Groups:** 50. **National Groups:** 8. **Description:** Individuals who have been affected by abortion including mothers, fathers, grandparents, and other relatives, doctors, nurses, and counselors. Works to expose "the truth of abortion's tragedy" and increase public awareness of "Post-Abortion Syndrome," which the association says is the physical, psychological, and emotional trauma suffered by the "secondary victims" of abortions. Conducts public awareness campaigns, legislative initiatives, and judicial activities. Maintains counseling referral service and speakers' bureau; encourages further research of "Post-Abortion

Syndrome". **Publications:** Newsletter, quarterly. **Price:** free ● Brochures ● Pamphlets.

12628 ■ Americans United for Life (AUL)

310 S Peoria St., Ste.300
Chicago, IL 60607-3534
Ph: (312)492-7234
Fax: (312)492-7235
E-mail: info@aul.org
URL: http://www.unitedforlife.org
Contact: Clarke D. Forsythe, Pres.

Founded: 1971. **Staff:** 16. **Description:** Pro-life legal and educational organization concerned with protecting human life at all stages of development. Specializes in legislation, litigation, and education. Focuses on initiatives that will change public policy and opinion on sanctity of human life. Provides legal assistance to individuals and organizations challenging legal abortion and physician-assisted suicide. Educational efforts include quantitative research on the physical harm to women caused by abortion, and possible links between abortion and breast cancer. Serves pro-life legislators, lobbyists, and leaders at the state and national level. **Libraries: Type:** reference. **Awards:** David W. Louisell Internship. **Frequency:** annual. **Type:** recognition. **Recipient:** for a pro-life law student. **Publications:** *AUL Forum*, quarterly. Newsletter. Includes information for donors and constituents. **Circulation:** 17,000 ● *2004 State Report Cards*. Book. **Price:** $20.00. Alternate Formats: online ● *2003 Legislative Session*. Report. Alternate Formats: online. **Conventions/Meetings:** annual Legislator's Educational Conference.

12629 ■ Anglicans for Life

405 Frederick Ave.
Sewickley, PA 15143-1522
Ph: (412)749-0455
Free: (800)707-6635
Fax: (412)749-0422
E-mail: info@anglicansforlife.org
URL: http://www.noelforlife.org
Contact: Georgette Forney, Pres.

Founded: 1966. **Members:** 3,000. **Membership Dues:** individual, $20 (annual) ● family, $25 (annual). **Staff:** 2. **Budget:** $50,000. **Regional Groups:** 50. **Local Groups:** 54. **Description:** Anglicans organized to reaffirm their faith and reestablish moral responsibility in the Christian response to human life issues. Focuses on issues concerning the protection and enhancement of human existence in accordance with God's laws. Aims are: to offer education within the Church on the value, dignity, and sanctity of human life; to provide support for the church in teaching life issues; to offer viable alternatives to abortion; to disseminate information through educational programs of a religious, ethical, and scientific nature. Co-sponsors the National Silent No More Awareness Campaign that raises awareness about the aftereffects of abortion on women and society and offers help to those hurting. **Libraries: Type:** reference. **Subjects:** sanctity of life. **Computer Services:** Mailing lists. **Formerly:** (1983) Episcopalians for Life; (2006) National Organization of Episcopalians for Life. **Publications:** *The Noel News*, bimonthly. Newsletter. Includes calendar of events, member news and articles related to life/family issues. **Price:** included in membership dues. Alternate Formats: online ● *The Reality of Abortion-Reflections of My Journey*. Report. Includes the personal testimony of Georgette Forney's abortion experience, facts and studies. Alternate Formats: online ● Booklets ● Brochures.

12630 ■ Association for Interdisciplinary Research in Values and Social Change (AIRVSC)

419 7th St. NW, Ste.500
Washington, DC 20004
Ph: (202)626-8800
Fax: (202)347-6121
E-mail: nrlc@nrlc.org
URL: http://www.euthanasia.com/inter.html
Contact: Marie Hagan, Exec. Sec.

Founded: 1986. **Members:** 700. **Membership Dues:** voluntary, $25 (annual). **Staff:** 45. **Regional Groups:**

3,000. **State Groups:** 50. **Local Groups:** 3,000. **For-Profit. Description:** Professionals who oppose abortion. Serves as a forum for exchange of ideas and research on abortion. Acts as a clearinghouse for information on abortion and abortion's effects on society. Promotes the idea that abortion is detrimental to the American family network. **Libraries: Type:** open to the public. **Holdings:** 64. **Subjects:** post abortion syndrome. **Computer Services:** database ● mailing lists. **Additional Websites:** http://www.abortionresearch.us/home.html. **Affiliated With:** National Right to Life Educational Trust Fund. **Publications:** *Research Bulletin*, quarterly. Newsletter. **Price:** $25.00/year. **Circulation:** 700. **Conventions/Meetings:** annual convention, held in conjunction with the National Right to Life Convention (exhibits) - always June.

12631 ■ Baptists for Life (BFL)
PO Box 3158
Grand Rapids, MI 49501
Ph: (616)257-6800
Free: (800)968-6086
Fax: (616)257-6805
E-mail: b4life@bfl.org
URL: http://www.bfl.org
Contact: M. Thomas Lothamer, Exec. Dir.
Founded: 1984. **Staff:** 9. **Nonmembership. Multinational. Description:** Helps the Body of Christ articulate the biblical pro-life message in word and deed. Works alongside God's people through churches, pregnancy care centers, and missionaries, forming pro-life ministries that change lives. Creates materials and ministry opportunities toward the goal of establishing pro-life, evangelistic outreaches all over the world. **Awards:** Bernie Berg Memorial Celebration of Life Award. **Frequency:** annual. **Type:** recognition. **Recipient:** to outstanding service to or through pro-life ministry. **Publications:** *Biblical Bioethics Advisor*, 3/year. Journal. **Circulation:** 500. Alternate Formats: online ● *Life Matters*, 3/year. Bulletin. **Price:** $5.00. **Circulation:** 200. **Conventions/Meetings:** annual Pregnancy Care Center Leadership Summit - conference and workshop.

12632 ■ Birthright United States of America
PO Box 98363
Atlanta, GA 30359-2063
Free: (800)550-4900
E-mail: info@birthright.org
URL: http://www.birthright.org
Contact: Terry Weaver, Natl. Dir.
Founded: 1969. **Regional Groups:** 33. **National Groups:** 350. **Multinational. Description:** People interested in alternatives to abortion. Provides support to girls and women distressed by an unplanned pregnancy. Offers friendship and emotional support, free pregnancy tests, referrals for medical, legal, housing and financial assistance, referrals to social agencies and maternity and baby clothes.

12633 ■ Black Americans for Life (BAL)
512 10th St. NW
Washington, DC 20004
Ph: (202)378-8858
E-mail: nrlc@nrlc.org
URL: http://www.nrlc.org/bal
Contact: Day Gardner, Dir.
Description: Individuals working to educate the black community on pro-life and pro-family issues. Promotes alternatives to abortion for women with crisis pregnancies; strives to be a visible presence defending the rights of the unborn in the black community. Asserts that black women are twice as likely as white women to have abortions; believes that abortions are counterproductive to advances made through civil rights efforts. Provides information on resources and available speakers. **Affiliated With:** National Right to Life Committee. **Publications:** *Black Americans for Life-Uniting the Black Community for Life*, annual. Newsletter ● Fact sheets.

12634 ■ Catholics United for Life (CUL)
3050 Gap Knob Rd.
New Hope, KY 40052-6927
Free: (800)764-8444

E-mail: buffalo@mich.com
URL: http://cul.detmich.com
Contact: Dennis Musk, Treas.
Founded: 1975. **Description:** Disseminates information on Catholic moral and social teachings regarding family life, marriage, and the value of human life. Provides speakers to family life, pro-life, or natural family planning conventions; suggests alternatives to abortion; teaches techniques of Sidewalk Counseling, through which individuals conduct legal vigils outside of abortion centers. Maintains chapel and holds daily services; sponsors regional and local conferences. **Libraries: Type:** reference. **Holdings:** 10,000. **Subjects:** theology, history, papal teachings, hagiology (literature dealing with venerated persons or writings). **Subgroups:** Free Speech Advocates. **Publications:** Books ● Newsletter, quarterly ● Also publishes educational materials. **Conventions/Meetings:** conference.

12635 ■ Collegians Activated to Liberate Life (CALL)
PO Box 259806
Madison, WI 53725
Ph: (608)256-2255
E-mail: callnet@aol.com
URL: http://www.veraprise.com/call
Founded: 1991. **Description:** People interested in promoting pro-life beliefs. Promotes "passionate pro-life Christian beliefs within the community". Sponsors activities, fund-raisers and conferences.

12636 ■ Heartbeat International
665 E Dublin-Granville, Ste.440
Columbus, OH 43229-3245
Ph: (614)885-7577
Free: (888)550-7577
Fax: (614)885-8746
E-mail: support@heartbeatinternational.org
URL: http://www.heartbeatinternational.org
Contact: Peggy Hartshorn PhD, Pres.
Founded: 1971. **Members:** 700. **Membership Dues:** regular, in U.S., $170 (annual) ● regular, outside U.S., $65 (annual). **Staff:** 19. **Budget:** $1,200,000. **Multinational. Description:** Affiliates are service groups offering alternatives to abortion. Assists persons with problem pregnancies and offers non-abortion personal and practical services; rather than engage in legislative or judicial activities and/or lobbying, the groups develop programs to assist girls who may be contemplating abortion by offering emotional, medical, legal, and social and spiritual support. Helps start pregnancy help centers worldwide, provides training, consultation, and support to affiliates. **Awards:** Servant Leader Award. **Frequency:** annual. **Type:** recognition. **Computer Services:** database, life-affirming pregnancy services ● mailing lists. **Councils:** Consultants and Resource Persons; International Council of Advisors; President's. **Formerly:** (1975) Alternatives to Abortion; (1993) Alternatives to Abortion/Women's Health and Education Foundation. **Publications:** *Pulse*, quarterly. Newsletter. Includes regional reports, news bulletin updates, educational articles, and resource information. ISSN: 0194-8032. **Circulation:** 2,000. **Advertising:** accepted ● *World-Wide Directory Life-Affirming Pregnancy Services*, annual. **Price:** $15.00. **Advertising:** accepted. **Conventions/Meetings:** annual international conference and regional meeting (exhibits) - always fall.

12637 ■ Human Development Resource Council (HDRC)
5415 Sugarloaf Pkwy., Ste.2201
Lawrenceville, GA 30043
Ph: (770)513-0060
Free: (866)356-0859
Fax: (770)513-0057
URL: http://www.hdrc.org
Founded: 1985. **Members:** 2,000. **Staff:** 3. **Budget:** $200,000. **Local Groups:** 1. **Description:** Promotes public awareness education in fetal development, pregnancy, sexually transmitted diseases, abortion, post-abortion syndrome and pre-marital abstinence. Publishes print and audio materials. **Libraries: Type:** open to the public.

12638 ■ Human Life Foundation (HLF)
215 Lexington Ave.
New York, NY 10016
URL: http://www.humanlifereview.com
Founded: 1975. **Description:** Serves as a charitable and educational foundation. Produces publications addressing issues such as abortion, euthanasia, infanticide, and family concerns. Offers financial support to organizations that provide women with alternatives to abortion. **Publications:** *Human Life Review*, quarterly. Journal. Focuses on abortion and features articles on a variety of other life issues. **Price:** $20.00/year in U.S.; $25.00/year outside U.S. ISSN: 0097-9783. **Circulation:** 6,000 ● Books ● Pamphlets. Contains information on abortion, bioethics, and family issues.

12639 ■ Human Life International (HLI)
4 Family Life Ln.
Front Royal, VA 22630
Ph: (540)635-7884
Free: (800)549-LIFE
Fax: (540)622-6247
E-mail: hli@hli.org
URL: http://www.hli.org
Contact: Rev. Thomas J. Euteneuer STL, Pres.
Founded: 1972. **Staff:** 50. **National Groups:** 60. **Languages:** English, French, German, Italian, Polish, Russian, Spanish. **Multinational. Description:** Promotes and defends the sanctity of life and the dignity of the family through prayer, education and service. Fosters loyalty to the people and the magistrate of the Roman Catholic Church, while ecumenical in its work with people of all religions to promote the cause of life. **Libraries: Type:** reference; not open to the public. **Holdings:** 8,000; audiovisuals, books, periodicals. **Subjects:** pro-life, pro-family, Catholic faith issues. **Computer Services:** database ● mailing lists ● online services. **Publications:** *Call to Action or Call to Apostasy?*. Book ● *Escoge la Vida* (in Spanish), quarterly. Newsletter ● *The Facts of Life*. Book ● *Faithful for Life*. Book ● *HLI Reports*, monthly. Newsletter. **Conventions/Meetings:** periodic conference (exhibits) ● annual symposium.

12640 ■ Human Life International - Puerto Rico
c/o La Asociacion Pro Derechos de la Familia
PO Box 916
Guaynabo, PR 00970-0916
Ph: (787)447-0826 (787)619-3965
E-mail: vhicsjpr@prtc.net
URL: http://www.aprodefa.org
Contact: Mrs. Joan Bermudez, Exec. Dir.
Description: Promotes the sanctity of life and dignity of the family through prayer, education and support services. **Additional Websites:** http://www.hli.org/puerto_rico.html.

12641 ■ International Life Services (ILS)
c/o Life Org
941 S Johnson St.
Kennewick, WA 99336
Ph: (509)735-8518
E-mail: info@life.org
URL: http://www.life.org
Contact: John Moloney, Contact
Founded: 1985. **Staff:** 10. **Budget:** $200,000. **National Groups:** 27. **Description:** A Judeo-Christian oriented research and educational association. Works to promote the pro-life movement; fosters respect for human life from the moment of conception until natural death. Recognizes God as the legitimate power over life and death. Promotes alternatives to abortion and euthanasia including premarital chastity and natural family planning; recognizes the family as the cornerstone of Judeo-Christian society. Opposes school-based health clinics that make available to teenagers contraceptives and abortion information. Operates speakers' bureau; compiles statistics. **Libraries: Type:** reference. **Holdings:** articles. **Subjects:** pro-life education. **Divisions:** Counseling; Education. **Publications:** Also publishes teaching materials and audiovisual tapes.

12642 ■ Last Harvest Ministries (LHM)
PO Box 462192
Garland, TX 75046-2192
Ph: (214)703-0505
URL: http://www.lastharvest.org
Contact: Ken Freeman, Pres.
Founded: 1984. **Members:** 2,315. **Staff:** 6. **Budget:** $150,000. **Regional Groups:** 4. **Local Groups:** 315. **Languages:** English, Spanish. **Description:** Offers information, Biblical support, and referrals to women who have had or are considering abortions. Maintains speakers' bureau; produces radio programs. Operates Samaritan Springs, a recovery retreat center. **Computer Services:** database, locations of post-abortion recovery and support centers. **Also Known As:** National Christian Network. **Formerly:** (2005) Last Harvest. **Publications:** *Behind Closed Doors* ● *Free Me to Live* ● *Healing the Hurts of Abortion*. Book ● *Ministry Memo*, monthly. Newsletter. **Price:** free. **Circulation:** 500 ● *Rachel's Circle*, monthly. Newsletter. **Price:** free. **Circulation:** 100 ● *Restoration Notes*. **Conventions/Meetings:** bimonthly seminar.

12643 ■ Liberty Godparent Home (LGH)
PO Box 4199
Lynchburg, VA 24502
Ph: (434)845-3466 (434)845-5334
Free: (800)542-4453
Fax: (434)845-1751
E-mail: lifekeeper@godparent.org
URL: http://www.godparent.org
Contact: Ruby Caskey, Admissions Coor.
Founded: 1982. **Staff:** 19. **Description:** Offers an alternative to abortion by meeting the immediate and long-term needs of teens in crisis pregnancy situations. Aims "to change one life and save another through sharing the gospel of Jesus Christ" via the ministry's educational and outreach program. The program consists of three divisions: the Pregnancy Crisis Hotline, the Maternity Home and the Adoption Agency. Offers guidance in the establishment of local pregnancy crisis centers and maternity homes. **Formerly:** (1986) Save-A-Baby; (1992) Liberty Godparent Ministry. **Publications:** *Family Life Services*. Brochure ● Brochure. **Conventions/Meetings:** annual conference (exhibits).

12644 ■ Life Coalition International (LCI)
PO Box 360221
Melbourne, FL 32936-0221
Ph: (321)726-0444
E-mail: patatlci@yahoo.com
URL: http://www.lifecoalition.com
Contact: Keith Tucci, Contact
Description: All people interested in the pro-life movement. Seeks to stop abortion and the population control agenda. Supports local pastors and missionaries through education and pro-life educational materials. **Projects:** Chinese Refugees in Ecuador; Latvia Public School Teachers; Peru; Russia. **Publications:** Newsletter, monthly. Alternate Formats: online.

12645 ■ Life Decisions International (LDI)
PO Box 75161
Washington, DC 20013-0161
Ph: (540)631-0380
Fax: (703)222-4346
E-mail: ldi@fightpp.org
URL: http://www.fightpp.org
Contact: Douglas R. Scott, Pres./Co-Founder
Multinational. Description: Committed to challenging the agenda of Planned Parenthood worldwide. **Projects:** Celebrity Watch; Collegian Outreach; Community Action; Corporate Funding; Organization Watch; Planned Parenthood Challenge; Prayer; Teach. **Publications:** *The Boycott List*, annual ● *The Caleb Report*, bimonthly. Newsletter. Provides current information on Planned Parenthood's activities and on life issues in general. Alternate Formats: online ● *Special Reports*, quarterly. Alternate Formats: online.

12646 ■ Lutherans For Life (LFL)
1120 S G Ave.
Nevada, IA 50201-2774
Ph: (515)382-2077
Free: (888)364-LIFE
Fax: (515)382-3020
E-mail: info@lutheransforlife.org
URL: http://www.lutheransforlife.org
Contact: Rev. Dr. James I. Lamb, Exec. Dir.
Founded: 1978. **Members:** 2,900. **Staff:** 7. **State Groups:** 15. **Local Groups:** 155. **Description:** Pro-Life advocacy group. **Libraries:** Type: reference. Holdings: archival material, books. Subjects: abortion, post-abortion, chastity, euthanasia, assisted suicide, family living. **Awards:** Dominus Vitae. Frequency: annual. Type: recognition. Recipient: for notable, national contribution to pro-life cause. **Computer Services:** database ● mailing lists. **Committees:** Health Professional; Legal; Medical; Theological. **Publications:** *For Life*. Video. Features a 14-minute video sharing the positive Gospel-centered message of LFL. **Price:** free for members; $5.00 for nonmembers ● *Life Date*, quarterly. Newsletter. Reports on the care of children, unwed mothers, disabled persons, the poor, and the repressed. Covers issues such as abortion, adoption, euthanasia. **Price:** included in membership dues. **Circulation:** 27,000. Alternate Formats: online ● *Life Quotes*. Bulletin. Alternate Formats: online ● *Life Resource Catalog*. **Price:** free. Alternate Formats: online ● *UpDate/Directions*, quarterly. Newsletter. Alternate Formats: online ● Also publishes Bible studies and worship materials and tracts. **Conventions/Meetings:** annual convention (exhibits) ● seminar.

12647 ■ National Life Center
686 N Broad St.
Woodbury, NJ 08096
Ph: (856)848-1819
Free: (800)848-LOVE
Fax: (856)848-2380
E-mail: nlc1stway@snip.net
URL: http://www.nationallifecenter.com
Contact: Denise F. Cocciolone, Pres./Founder
Founded: 1970. **Members:** 3,000. **Membership Dues:** organizational affiliation, $100 (annual). **Staff:** 25. **Description:** Pregnancy service centers. Works to help pregnant women find alternatives to abortion. All are private and interdenominational, supported by contributions, and operated by volunteers. Provides pregnancy, medical, legal & shelter information; abortion information also available. Maintains speakers' bureau. **Subgroups:** 1st Way Life Center. **Publications:** *The National Pulse*, bimonthly. Newsletter. **Circulation:** 1,500. Also Cited As: *The Pulse* ● Also publishes books. **Conventions/Meetings:** annual general assembly and convention - always June.

12648 ■ National Right to Life Committee (NRLC)
512 10th St. NW
Washington, DC 20004
Ph: (202)626-8800
Fax: (202)347-3668
E-mail: nrlc@nrlc.org
URL: http://www.nrlc.org
Contact: Wanda Franz PhD, Pres.
Founded: 1973. **State Groups:** 50. **Local Groups:** 3,000. **Description:** Serves as national grass roots pro-life group committed to the protection of human life from abortion, euthanasia, and infanticide. Works through public education, outreach, citizen action, and legislation to restore and maintain legal protection for the lives of all defenseless human beings. Monitors and conducts research on relevant social, medical, and political events and trends, prepares pro-life responses for the press, lobbies congress, maintains speakers' bureau, and publishes a regular newspaper. Encourages and supports abortion alternatives such as adoption. Also works with state affiliates to develop new chapters and address relevant state legislation. **Libraries:** Type: reference. Holdings: 3,000; audiovisuals, books. **Subjects:** brochures, pamphlets. **Awards:** National Oratory Contest. Frequency: annual. Type: recognition. **Computer Services:** Online services. **Committees:** National Right to Life Political Action. **Departments:** Communications; Development; Education; Federal Legislation; Financial Services; Medical Ethics; News; State Legislation; State Organizational Development; Voter Identification. **Publications:** *National Right to Life News*, 18/year. Newspaper. **Price:** $16.00 regular subscription; $10.00 student subscription; $25.00 first class subscription; $28.00 outside U.S. ISSN: 0164-7415 ● Also publishes books and pamphlets. **Conventions/Meetings:** annual National Right to Life Convention (exhibits).

12649 ■ National Teens for Life (NTL)
419 7th St. NW, Ste.500
Washington, DC 20004
URL: http://www.nrlc.org/outreach/teens.html
Founded: 1985. **Description:** All people interested in the pro-life movement. Seeks to stop abortion and population control.

12650 ■ People for Life (PFL)
PO Box 1126
Erie, PA 16512
Ph: (814)459-1333 (814)882-1333
E-mail: office@peopleforlife.org
URL: http://www.peopleforlife.org
Founded: 1984. **Membership Dues:** student, senior, $5 (annual) ● individual, $10 (annual) ● family, $20 (annual) ● group, $25 (annual) ● patron, $50 (annual) ● benefactor, $100 (annual). **Description:** Grass-roots, pro-life organization. Coordinates National Forum for Human Life amendment. Involves research, education, advocacy and debate. Provides pro-life education and counseling to anyone experiencing crisis pregnancy or post-abortion problems. Creates, publishes, disseminates, collects, and organizes materials and information concerning abortion, post-abortion, post miscarriage, fetal tissue research, and human rights. Provides advisory services for individuals, groups, classes, and educators who have an interest in these areas. Maintains speaker's bureau. **Committees:** Library; Public Relations; Speakers' Bureau; Statistics. **Publications:** *Erie Echo*, bimonthly. Newsletter. Alternate Formats: online.

12651 ■ Presbyterians Pro-Life (PPL)
3942 Middle Rd.
Allison Park, PA 15101
Ph: (412)487-1990
Fax: (412)487-1994
E-mail: ppl@ppl.org
URL: http://www.ppl.org
Contact: Mrs. Marie Bowen, Exec. Dir.
Description: Represents lay and clergy members of the Presbyterian Church (USA) who are opposed to abortion. Works to protect human life from conception until natural death. Opposes abortion, infanticide, and euthanasia. Believes that a "return to the Biblical teaching concerning the sacred value of the family is essential to recovering respect for the sacred value of individual human lives". **Publications:** *Not My Own: Abortion and the Marks of the Church*. Book. **Price:** $10.00 ● *PPL News*, quarterly. Newsletter. Alternate Formats: online ● Brochures. Alternate Formats: online ● Booklets. Alternate Formats: online ● Pamphlets ● Videos.

12652 ■ Pro-Life Alliance of Gays and Lesbians (PLAGAL)
PO Box 16753
Alexandria, VA 22302-0753
Ph: (202)223-6697
E-mail: plagal@plagal.org
URL: http://www.plagal.org
Contact: Cecilia Brown, Pres.
Founded: 1990. **Members:** 800. **Membership Dues:** individual, $20 (annual). **Budget:** $3,500. **Description:** Women and men of varying sexual orientations, political affiliations, and geographic locations, committed to raising awareness of the pro-life ethic as consistent with the gay and lesbian struggle for human rights. **Formerly:** (1991) Gays Against Abortion. **Publications:** *PLAGAL Memorandum*, 5/year. Newsletter. **Price:** free. **Circulation:** 900. Alternate

Formats: online ● Brochures. Alternate Formats: online. **Conventions/Meetings:** annual meeting and conference.

12653 ■ Students for Life of America (SFL)
4141 N Henderson Rd., Ste.4
Arlington, VA 22203
Ph: (703)351-6280
Free: (866)582-6420
E-mail: info@studentsforlife.org
URL: http://www.aclife.org
Contact: Kristan Hawkins, Exec. Dir.
Founded: 1987. **Members:** 5,000. **Staff:** 10. **Budget:** $510,000. **State Groups:** 8. **Local Groups:** 345. **Description:** Students for Life of America actively educates pro-life college students about the issues of abortion, euthanasia, and infanticide. Identifies pro-life student leaders; equips college pro-lifers with the training, skills and resources to be effective and successful; and promotes student activity to other local, college and national groups. **Additional Websites:** http://www.studentsforlife.org. **Formerly:** (1987) Coalition of American Pro-Life University Students; (2006) American Collegians for Life. **Publications:** *SFLA Allies*, biweekly. Newsletter. Alternate Formats: online ● Also publishes project manuals. **Conventions/Meetings:** annual Pro-Life Leadership Training Conference - conference and seminar (exhibits).

12654 ■ U.S. Coalition for Life (USCL)
Box 315
Export, PA 15632
Ph: (412)327-7379
E-mail: tengel@bellatlantic.net
Contact: Randy V. Engel, Dir.
Founded: 1972. **Budget:** $5,000. **Description:** Serves as a pro-life research organization and clearinghouse on population control activities such as abortion, sterilization, contraception, eugenics, March of Dimes, sex initiation programs, and anti-life government family planning programs. Maintains international reprint service. **Committees:** Education; Inter-Liaison; Research. **Publications:** *Pro-Life Reporter*. Journal ● Monographs ● Reports. **Conventions/Meetings:** seminar.

12655 ■ Victims of Choice (VOC)
PO Box 815
Naperville, IL 60566-0815
Ph: (630)378-1680
Free: (888)267-3998
E-mail: web@victimsofchoice.com
URL: http://www.victimsofchoice.com
Contact: Elizabeth Verchio, Exec. Dir.
Founded: 1983. **Staff:** 1. **Budget:** $20,000. **Description:** Ministry promoting abortion awareness and education. Offers one-on-one counseling; provides peer clergy and therapist referrals; trains lay facilitators; conducts outreach programs; maintains speakers' bureau. Establishes local, independent abortion recovery centers in existing churches, women's centers, etc. Conducts "MOM's Day" (Memorial of Mourning) on the first Saturday of June. Assists in establishing local memorials. **Libraries: Type:** reference; by appointment only. **Holdings:** 40; articles, books, clippings, periodicals. **Subjects:** abortion recovery, physical and emotional healing. **Affiliated With:** American Life League. **Publications:** *Abortion Recovery Facilitator Guidebook*. **Price:** $60.00 ● *VOC Journal*. Newsletter ● Brochures. **Conventions/Meetings:** periodic Abortion Recovery - seminar.

12656 ■ Women Affirming Life (WAL)
PO Box 35532
Brighton, MA 02135
Ph: (617)254-2277
Fax: (617)254-2299
E-mail: mail@affirmlife.com
URL: http://www.affirmlife.com
Contact: Marianne Rea-Luthin, Exec. Dir.
Founded: 1990. **Membership Dues:** full, $25 (annual). **Description:** Catholic women affirming the right to life of the unborn. Seeks to motivate and equip women to serve as public witnesses in the enormous challenge to build a culture of life. Offers public witness by women in defense of the unborn and unwanted through personal commitment, educational efforts, prayer, and home and professional life.

12657 ■ Women Exploited by Abortion (WEBA)
Address Unknown since 2007
Founded: 1982. **Members:** 90,000. **Membership Dues:** individual, $10 (annual). **Staff:** 16. **Budget:** $1,200. **Regional Groups:** 135. **State Groups:** 45. **Local Groups:** 500. **National Groups:** 1. **Description:** Christian-oriented organization of women who have had abortions and regret their action; associate members are concerned individuals who have not had abortions. Provides support and counseling for women and men who suffer from emotional and physical problems as a result of their abortions. Offers counseling to pregnant women considering abortion; refers women who decide to have their babies to other groups that assist needy expectant mothers. Seeks to reeducate society about abortion and the effect it has on women. Provides speakers for pro-life groups, schools, churches, seminars, and television and radio programs. Conducts research; compiles statistics. **Libraries: Type:** reference. **Holdings:** 560; books, clippings. **Subjects:** abortion, post-abortion aftermath, adoption, medical, pregnancy, crisis pregnancy counseling, maternity homes, political action, legislation, legal (litigation), euthanasia. **Awards:** Outstanding WEBA Counselor. **Frequency:** bimonthly. **Type:** recognition. **Recipient:** to an excellent worker who goes out of his or her way to do his or her job. **Computer Services:** database ● mailing lists ● online services. **Publications:** *A Pro Life Manifesto*. Book. **Advertising:** not accepted ● *Aborted Women, Silent No More*. Book ● *Abortions's Second Victim*. Book ● *After an Abortion: Everything looks Different! Where Do You Go to Recover?*. Pamphlet ● *The Aftereffects of Abortion: Understanding the Risks*. Pamphlet ● *Before You Make the Decision*. Pamphlet ● *Beyond Choice; The Story No One Is Telling*. Book ● *Fight for the Life of Your Child Inside of You*. Pamphlet ● *Finding Peace After Abortion*. Book ● *Healing Post-Abortion Trauma: Help for Women Hurt by Abortion*. Book ● *Help for the Post-Abortion Woman*. Book ● *Helping Women Recover from Abortion*. Book ● *Joy Comes in the Mourning*. Pamphlet ● *Planned Un-Parenthood: Racism.Illusion.Lies*. Pamphlet ● *Post-Abortion Trauma: Learning the Truth and Telling the Truth*. Pamphlet ● *Reconciler*, bimonthly. Newsletter. Covers pro-life and post-abortion issues. **Price:** included in membership dues. **Advertising:** accepted. Alternate Formats: online ● *Surviving Abortion*. Booklet ● *Testimony of an Aborted Woman.Set Free*. Pamphlet ● *Tilly*. Book ● *Will I Cry Tomorrow*. Book ● *Women at Risk: Abortion and the High-Risk Patient*. Pamphlet ● *Women Exploited*. Book. **Conventions/Meetings:** seminar and meeting (exhibits) ● monthly support group meeting.

Runaways

12658 ■ Children of the Night (COTN)
14530 Sylvan St.
Van Nuys, CA 91411
Ph: (818)908-4474
Free: (800)551-1300
Fax: (818)908-1468
E-mail: llee@childrenofthenight.org
URL: http://www.childrenofthenight.org
Contact: Dr. Lois Lee, Pres./Founder
Founded: 1979. **Staff:** 24. **Budget:** $1,800,000. **Languages:** English, Spanish. **Description:** Dedicated to rescuing America's children from the ravages of prostitution. **Libraries: Type:** reference. **Holdings:** archival material. **Subjects:** child prostitution. **Publications:** Brochures.

12659 ■ Girls and Boys Town
14100 Crawford St.
Boys Town, NE 68010
Ph: (402)498-1300
Fax: (402)498-1348
E-mail: publicrelations@girlsandboystown.org
URL: http://www.girlsandboystown.org
Contact: Fr. Steven E. Boes, Natl. Exec. Dir.
Founded: 1917. **Description:** Provides treatment and care of needy, abused, abandoned and neglected girls and boys through its youth care and health care programs. Provides these children with a safe, caring, loving environment where they gain confidence to get better and learn skills to become productive citizens, combined with state-of- the-art treatment technology to help them heal and overcome the obstacles they face. Aims to "change the way America cares for her children and families through its programs by partnering with communities, schools and other child-care organizations, in order to meet the growing and more diverse needs of today's children and families across the country.". **Libraries: Type:** open to the public; reference. **Holdings:** archival material, clippings, papers, periodicals, photographs, video recordings. **Computer Services:** Online services. **Telecommunication Services:** electronic mail, hotline@girlsandboystown.org ● hotline, (800)448-3000. **Programs:** Common Sense Parenting; Common Sense Programming; Emergency Shelter/Emergency Short-Term Residential Services; Family Preservation Services; Research Institute for Child and Family Studies; Residential Services; Residential Treatment Center; Treatment Foster Family Services. **Publications:** *Boys Town Journal*, quarterly. Serves as a gracious communique to donors so that they may be further connected to the children they support across the country. Alternate Formats: online ● Annual Report, annual. Alternate Formats: online ● Books ● Videos.

12660 ■ National Network for Youth (NNY)
1319 F St. NW, Ste.401
Washington, DC 20004-1106
Ph: (202)783-7949
Fax: (202)783-7955
E-mail: info@nn4youth.org
URL: http://www.nn4youth.org
Contact: Victoria A. Wagner, CEO
Founded: 1974. **Members:** 850. **Membership Dues:** individual, $5 (annual) ● individual adult (over the age of 21), $60 (annual) ● associate, $250 (annual) ● association, coalition, $500-$750 (annual) ● organization, $250-$850 (annual). **Staff:** 7. **Budget:** $1,400,000. **Regional Groups:** 10. **State Groups:** 35. **Local Groups:** 400. **Languages:** English, Spanish. **Description:** Works to ensure that young people can be safe and grow up to lead healthy and productive lives. Engages in public education efforts, promotes youth/adult partnerships, and strives to strengthen staff and community-based organization capacity to provide effective programs and services to youth in high-risk situations. Provides training and technical assistance in a variety of areas including professional development of youth workers, youth leadership, peer education, HIV/AIDS and substance abuse prevention, grant writing, and community and youth development. The National Network for Youth is a sponsoring member of the Council on Accreditation of Services for Families and Children. **Libraries: Type:** reference. **Awards:** National Leadership Awards. **Frequency:** annual. **Type:** recognition. **Computer Services:** Mailing lists ● online services, YOUTHNET. **Telecommunication Services:** electronic bulletin board, youthnet. **Councils:** National Council of Youth Policy. **Also Known As:** National Network. **Publications:** *At a Glance*, monthly. Newsletter. Alternate Formats: online ● *Being an Effective Youth Advocate*. Booklet. Contains important information on youth strategies, working with the media, and cultivating community allies. **Price:** $10.00 for members; $15.00 for nonmembers ● *Doing What We Do Best: Guide to Replication of an Independent Living Project*. Outlines ways to develop a successful independent living program; includes project definition, implementation procedures, local reports, & resources. **Price:** $3.00 for members; $4.00 for nonmembers ● *Helping Them Do Their Best: Guide to Using Volunteers in Runaway Centers*. Describes the benefits and essential components of a successful volunteer program; includes volunteer profile and innovative program models. **Price:** $3.00

for members; $4.00 for nonmembers ● *Network News*, quarterly. Newsletter. Provides updates on youth issues from a national perspective; features columns written by youth, an issues forum, legislative updates, and resources. **Price:** free for members; $30.00 /year for nonmembers ● *Policy Reporter*, quarterly. Newsletter. Reports on and analyzes current legislation, federal policy, and court decisions that impact services to youth. **Price:** included in membership dues; $30.00 /year for nonmembers ● *Public Policy Update*, quarterly. Newsletter. Informs members about the latest public policy issues, legislation, and news affecting youth and service providers. Alternate Formats: online. **Conventions/Meetings:** annual conference and symposium ● quarterly National Council on Youth Policy - congress.

12661 ■ National Runaway Switchboard (NRS)
3080 N Lincoln Ave.
Chicago, IL 60657
Ph: (773)880-9860
Free: (800)344-2785
Fax: (773)929-5150
E-mail: info@nrscrisisline.org
URL: http://www.nrscrisisline.org
Contact: Gordon Vance, Program Dir.
Founded: 1971. **Staff:** 15. **Budget:** $1,000,000. **Regional Groups:** 140. **Description:** Maintains a 24-hour, toll-free national switchboard for runaways, families of runaways, and other troubled youth. Provides names and phone numbers of centers for shelter and other social services across the country, including counseling centers, referral lines, drug treatment facilities, and family planning services. Offers to relay messages between young people and their families if desired; can also set up conferences calls between youths and parents or agencies. The caller's confidentiality is maintained. Maintains speakers' bureau. Funded in part by the Family and Youth Services Bureau of the U.S. Department of Health and Human Services. Provides free bus ride home for qualified runaways and access to AT&T Language Line. **Computer Services:** database, referral agencies ● mailing lists. **Telecommunication Services:** hotline, (800)RUN-AWAY. **Programs:** Home Free; Kids Call; Runaway Prevention. **Publications:** *Front-Line*, quarterly. Newsletter. Contains statistical data and reports on activities. **Price:** free. Alternate Formats: online ● Brochure. Features detailed description of the National Runaway Switchboard services. **Price:** $8.00/100 copies; $35.00/500 copies. Alternate Formats: online ● Annual Report, annual. Alternate Formats: online.

Rural Development

12662 ■ Federation of Southern Cooperatives Land Assistance Fund (FSC/LAF)
2769 Church St.
East Point, GA 30344
Ph: (404)765-0991
Fax: (404)765-9178
E-mail: fsc@mindspring.com
URL: http://www.federationsoutherncoop.com
Contact: Ralph Paige, Exec. Dir.
Founded: 1967. **Members:** 12,000. **Membership Dues:** individual, $25 (annual) ● cooperative, $250 (annual) ● life, $500. **Staff:** 36. **Budget:** $1,800,000. **State Groups:** 9. **Description:** Cooperative associations chartered or doing business in the 17 southern states or the District of Columbia. Objectives are to assist people in building community-owned enterprises so they can control their own livelihood and to create housing, health care, and educational programs to complement economic development. Aids in the retention, acquisition, and development of black land holdings. Sponsors training programs in membership education, board responsibilities, management, and bookkeeping. Makes available to members full-time marketing specialists in both agricultural and handicraft production; also offers technical assistance in areas of accounting, establishing credit unions, consumer education, research in co-op expansion,

market and product development, and improvement of production techniques. Provides legal, technical, and limited financial assistance to black farmers and landowners throughout the Southeast. Operates the FSC Rural Training and Research Center in Sumter County, AL. Has established the "Forty Acres and a Mule" endowment fund for educational and social programs that have the potential to be self-supporting. Provides educational materials to member cooperatives. **Awards:** Julious Anderson Scholarship. **Frequency:** annual. **Type:** scholarship. **Recipient:** for children of members. **Computer Services:** database ● mailing lists. **Departments:** Communications; Credit Unions; Housing. **Programs:** Cooperative; Cooperative Business Development; Land Assistance Fund; Rural Training and Research Center. **Projects:** Small Farm and Sustainable Agriculture. **Formed by Merger of:** (1986) Emergency Land Fund; Federation of Southern Cooperatives. **Publications:** *Cooperatives: Alone One Person Can Do Little.* Brochure. Includes the co-op principles and a list of some types of co-ops. ● *FSC/LAF News*, quarterly. Newsletter. **Price:** free for members. **Advertising:** accepted ● *Membership Newsletter*, monthly ● *The Rural Agenda*, quarterly. Newsletter ● Booklets ● Annual Reports, annual. **Conventions/Meetings:** annual workshop and general assembly (exhibits) - always Epes, AL.

12663 ■ International Institute of Rural Reconstruction, U.S. Chapter (IIRR)
333 E 38th St., 6th Fl.
New York, NY 10016-2772
Ph: (212)880-9147
Fax: (212)880-9148
E-mail: nyc.office@iirr-us.org
URL: http://www.iirr.org
Contact: Susan L. Grove, Dir.
Founded: 1960. **Budget:** $2,000,000. **Description:** A private, international training and research institution, based in the Philippines. Aims to foster rural reconstruction and human development through continuing action research on the basic needs of peasant people in developing countries and evolving new and better approaches to meet those needs. Provides high-level leadership training in rural reconstruction techniques, an international extension of its work to stimulate national leaders to implement private rural reconstruction programs in their respective countries. Supports autonomous affiliated programs in the Philippines, India, Thailand, Guatemala, Colombia, and Ghana. **Convention/Meeting:** none. **Publications:** *A Manual for Field Workers* ● *An Experiment in Integrated Rural Development: The Mampong Valley Social Laboratory in Ghana* ● *Back to the Barrios* ● *Building Rural Communities: The Experiences of the Indian Rural Reconstruction Movement* ● *Doctor to the Barrios* ● *IIRR Report*, semiannual. Newsletter ● *International Sharing*, 3/year ● *My Friends in the Barrios* ● *Parables of the Barrios* ● *Rural Reconstruction and Development* ● *Rural Reconstruction Review*, annual ● *Tell the People* ● *Ting Hsien Experiment* ● Monographs ● Papers.

12664 ■ National Rural Water Association (NRWA)
2915 S 13th St.
Duncan, OK 73533
Ph: (580)252-0629
Fax: (580)255-4476
E-mail: info@nrwa.org
URL: http://nrwa.org
Contact: Rob Johnson, CEO
Founded: 1976. **Members:** 8,500. **Membership Dues:** individual, $25 (annual) ● associate, $400 (annual). **Staff:** 30. **Budget:** $36,000,000. **Description:** State rural water and waste water systems. Works to improve the quality of utility services for rural Americans while protecting the natural resources. Provides legislative and public relations support for the water system industry. Offers information outreach and technical training programs. **Libraries: Type:** reference. **Holdings:** archival material, books, periodicals. **Telecommunication Services:** electronic mail, nrwakc@nrwa.org. **Committees:** Insurance; Legislative; Regulatory; Retirement; Training

and Technical. **Publications:** *Rural Water Magazine*, quarterly. **Circulation:** 28,000. **Advertising:** accepted. **Conventions/Meetings:** annual Leadership Forum and Technology Exhibit Center - conference (exhibits) - always September or October.

12665 ■ REAP International
1109 31st St. NE
Cedar Rapids, IA 52402
Ph: (319)366-4230
Fax: (319)366-2209
E-mail: reap@reapintl.com
Contact: William Mueller, Dir.
Founded: 1991. **Multinational. Description:** Seeks to help stabilize villages in Russia with strategies to become self-sufficient and independent of the State system. Works with schools and other groups to bolster rural resources and adapt survival techniques learned in the US. Encourages sustainable approaches that do not damage the environment. **Computer Services:** Information services, Lake Baikal. **Programs:** Green Walk; Internship; School Exchanges; Travel; Volunteer; Youth Activity Center. **Publications:** *REAP*, semiannual. Newsletter. Alternate Formats: online.

12666 ■ World Sustainable Agriculture Association (WSAA)
8554 Melrose Ave.
West Hollywood, CA 90069
Ph: (310)657-7202
Fax: (310)657-3884
E-mail: pmadden1@aol.com
URL: http://www.bcca.org/services/lists/noble-creation/wsaa.html
Contact: J. Patrick Madden, Pres.
Founded: 1991. **Budget:** $408,000. **Description:** Promotes adoption of sustainable agriculture systems and policies worldwide.

Russian

12667 ■ International Foundation for Terror Act Victims
PO Box 444
Southampton, PA 18966
Ph: (321)213-0198
Fax: (206)333-0505
E-mail: president@moscowhelp.org
URL: http://www.moscowhelp.org
Contact: Andrew Mogilyansky, Chm./Founder
Founded: 2002. **Multinational. Description:** Helps children who were injured or orphaned as a result of the Beslan tragedy. Raises personal and corporate charitable donations to help the families of the Nord-Ost Theater Siege terror victims. **Computer Services:** Mailing lists, of members ● online services, forum.

Safety

12668 ■ AAA Foundation for Traffic Safety
607 14th St. NW, Ste.201
Washington, DC 20005
Ph: (202)638-5944
Fax: (202)638-5943
E-mail: info@aaafoundation.org
URL: http://www.aaafoundation.org/home/index.cfm
Contact: J. Peter Kissinger, Pres./CEO
Founded: 1947. **Staff:** 6. **Budget:** $2,800,000. **Description:** Works to save lives and reducing injuries by preventing traffic crashes. Sponsors research into factors that affect driving behavior, such as drowsiness, age, driving experience, illusion-producing pavement markings, driver distraction, road rage, and other issues. Produces and distributes safety videos, and research reports, brochures, and other information to inform drivers about safe behavior. **Awards: Frequency:** annual. **Type:** monetary. **Recipient:** for universities, colleges, and research agencies for traffic safety studies, including such subjects as drowsy driving, driver education, and pedestrian and bicycle safety. **Committees:** Research and

Development; Research Reports; Traffic Safety Statistics. **Projects:** Distracted Driving; Drowsy Driving; LCV Safety; Seated for Safety; Traffic Safety Education Materials for Spanish-Speaking Audiences. **Formerly:** CAA/AAA Foundation for Traffic Safety. **Publications:** *AAA Foundation E-Newsletter*, quarterly. Reports on traffic safety research and educational projects. **Price:** free ● *Driver-Zed*. Video. Teaches drivers to make safe choices in traffic. ● Also publishes catalog of traffic safety materials.

12669 ■ Advocates for Highway and Auto Safety

750 First St. NE, Ste.901
Washington, DC 20002
Ph: (202)408-1711
Fax: (202)408-1699
E-mail: advocates@saferoads.org
URL: http://www.saferoads.org
Contact: Judith Lee Stone, Pres.
Founded: 1989. **Description:** Consumer, safety, and law enforcement groups; insurance and agents organizations. Promotes effective highway safety legislation, standards, policies, and programs at the national and state levels to reduce deaths, injuries, and economic losses associated with motor vehicle crashes, fraud, and theft. Monitors state and national automotive safety legislation. Lobbies Congress. Bestows safety leadership awards. **Publications:** *The Safety Advocate*, periodic. Includes updates on local and national safety legislation.

12670 ■ Aircraft Recovery Association (ARA)

38 Riverside Dr.
Rockville Centre, NY 11570
Ph: (516)764-2978 (718)288-6806
Fax: (516)678-0180
Contact: Tony Ristuccia, Exec. Officer
Description: Gathers and examines disabled aircraft that have been involved in accidents or incidents.

12671 ■ American Association for Horsemanship Safety (AAHS)

PO Box 39
Fentress, TX 78622
Ph: (512)488-2220
Fax: (512)488-2319
E-mail: jzdawson@aol.com
URL: http://home.centurytel.net/jan_dawson/AAHS
Contact: Jan Dawson, Pres.
Membership Dues: individual, $25 (annual) ● riding instructor, $50 (annual) ● stable/camp/business, $100 (annual). **Description:** Promotes safe horsemanship skills through training and education. Offers systematic approach to teaching horsemanship safety. Provides information to the general public about safe horsemanship practices. **Computer Services:** Mailing lists. **Publications:** *Caution: Horses*, quarterly. Newsletter. Contains horsemanship safety and legal liability information. Alternate Formats: online.

12672 ■ American Association of Safety Councils (AASC)

c/o Toni Burrows, Pres.
770 S Military Trail
West Palm Beach, FL 33415
Ph: (561)689-4733
Fax: (561)683-1717
E-mail: toni@safetycouncilpbc.org
URL: http://www.safetycouncils.org
Contact: Toni Burrows, Pres.
Membership Dues: voting, $100 (annual) ● associate, $50 (annual). **Regional Groups:** 14. **State Groups:** 3. **Local Groups:** 5. **Multinational.** **Description:** Aims to reduce preventable injuries and fatalities. Provides education programs on driving safety, first aid and CPR, substance abuse, hazardous materials, confined space, flagging, forklift safety, and health.

12673 ■ American Avalanche Association (AAA)

c/o Mark Mueller, Exec. Dir.
PO Box 2831
Pagosa Springs, CO 81147

Ph: (970)946-0822
Fax: (970)731-2486
E-mail: aaa@avalanche.org
URL: http://www.americanavalancheassociation.org
Contact: Russ Johnson, Pres.
Membership Dues: professional, $40 (annual) ● affiliate, $35 (annual) ● subscriber, $20 (annual) ● life, $800. **Description:** Represents researchers, professional avalanche forecasters, snow safety officers, snow rangers, ski patrollers, technicians and specialists engaged in the study, forecasting, control and mitigation of snow avalanches. Promotes research about avalanche safety. Acts as a resource base for public awareness programs about avalanche hazards and safety measures. **Publications:** *The Avalanche Review*, quarterly. Journal. Alternate Formats: online.

12674 ■ American Highway Users Alliance (HwyUsers)

1101 14th St. NW, Ste.750
Washington, DC 20005
Ph: (202)857-1200
Fax: (202)857-1220
E-mail: info@highways.org
URL: http://www.highways.org
Contact: Greg Cohen PE, Pres./CEO
Founded: 1932. **Members:** 380. **Staff:** 4. **Description:** Broad-based consumers group for American motorists, truckers and businesses. Employs lobbying, media, communications and grassroots advocacy, promotes public policy that devotes highway use taxes to investments in safe and uncongested national highway systems. **Libraries: Type:** not open to the public. **Subjects:** highway safety, mobility, environmental issues, federal funding of highways. **Committees:** Executive; Policy and Government Affairs. **Publications:** *Driving Ahead*, bimonthly. Newsletters ● Also publishes special reports and legislative updates. **Conventions/Meetings:** annual meeting - always November.

12675 ■ Arts, Crafts and Theatre Safety

181 Thompson St., Ste.23
New York, NY 10012-2586
Ph: (212)777-0062
Fax: (212)673-4403
E-mail: actsnyc@cs.com
URL: http://www.artscraftstheatersafety.org
Contact: Monona Rossol, Pres.
Founded: 1987. **Staff:** 5. **Budget:** $200,000. **Nonmembership. Description:** Provides health, safety, and industrial hygiene services to the arts community. Maintains speakers' and consultants bureau. **Libraries: Type:** not open to the public; reference. **Subjects:** health, safety, industrial hygiene, dyes, pigments, metals, solvents, and other chemicals. **Awards:** Anna DeCarmel Grant. **Frequency:** annual. **Type:** grant. **Recipient:** for artists. **Publications:** *Acts-Facts*, monthly. Newsletter. Covers health, safety and regulatory information for people in the arts. **Price:** $20.00/year; $23.00 in Canada; $26.00/year overseas; $23.00/year in Mexico. ISSN: 1070-9274. **Circulation:** 1,000 ● Also publishes 65 technical data sheets, various subjects available.

12676 ■ Association for the Advancement of Automotive Medicine (AAAM)

PO Box 4176
Barrington, IL 60011-4176
Ph: (847)844-3880
Fax: (847)844-3884
E-mail: info@aaam.org
URL: http://www.carcrash.org
Contact: Irene Herzau, Admin. Dir.
Founded: 1957. **Members:** 650. **Membership Dues:** regular/associate in North America, $260 (annual) ● regular/associate outside North America, $295 (annual) ● family, $400 (annual) ● student, $35 (annual) ● life, $3,000 ● sustaining, $2,600 (annual). **Staff:** 5. **Budget:** $600,000. **Description:** Physicians and other professionals concerned with motor vehicle safety, design, and road engineering. Works to reduce the number of injuries and fatalities on the nation's highways by encouraging research on the effects of diseases, disabilities, and environmental factors on driver capabilities. Supports laws and

regulations to upgrade the standards for licensing drivers and research and development programs leading to improved bio-engineering of motor vehicles. Encourages the use of appropriate protective devices and disseminates new information in the field of traffic, vehicular, and pedestrian safety. Individual members conduct research programs. **Awards: Type:** recognition. **Recipient:** for individuals and societies for meritorious work in prevention of motor vehicle trauma ● Student Research Grant. **Frequency:** annual. **Type:** scholarship. **Recipient:** to graduate students for research in epidemiology, biomechanics and other areas of concern and interest of the association. **Computer Services:** Mailing lists. **Additional Websites:** http://www.aaam.org. **Committees:** Injury Scaling; Scientific Program. **Formerly:** (1987) American Association for Automotive Medicine. **Publications:** *Abbreviated Injury Scale*. Book. Provides researchers with a simple numerical method for ranking and comparing injuries by severity. **Price:** $160.00 in North America; $200.00 all others. Alternate Formats: CD-ROM ● *Booster Seats for Children*. Video. Emphasizes the importance of proper seat and belt fit as well as the need for booster seat use. **Price:** $25.00 in North America; $45.00 all others ● *Crash Prevention and Injury Control*, quarterly. Journal. Features papers relating to accidental injury and damage including pre and post-injury phases. **Price:** included in membership dues. ISSN: 0001-4575. **Circulation:** 1,200 ● *Head Mechanisms: The Need for an Angular Acceleration Criterion 1989*. Report. **Price:** $25.00 in North America; $35.00 all others ● *INROADS*, quarterly. Bulletin. Alternate Formats: online ● *Traffic Injury: The Medicine-Engineering Link*. Video. **Price:** $80.00 in North America; $90.00 all others ● Proceedings, annual. **Price:** $85.00 in North America; $100.00 other. Alternate Formats: CD-ROM. **Conventions/Meetings:** annual conference.

12677 ■ ATV Safety Institute/Division of Specialty Vehicle Institute of America (ASI)

2 Jenner St., Ste.150
Irvine, CA 92618-3806
Ph: (949)727-3727
Free: (800)887-2887
Fax: (949)727-4216
URL: http://www.atvsafety.org
Contact: Tim Buche, Pres.
Founded: 1988. **Members:** 8. **Description:** A division of Specialty Vehicle Institute of America. Promotes safe and responsible use of all-terrain vehicles (ATVs). Conducts rider safety programs and disseminates public information. **Affiliated With:** Specialty Vehicle Institute of America. **Publications:** *A Guide to Off-Highway Riding*. Video ● *Parents, Youngsters and ATVs*. Article ● *Tips and Practice Guide for the ATV Rider*. Article.

12678 ■ Aviation Safety Institute (ASI)

PO Box 690
Worthington, OH 43085
Ph: (614)885-4242
Fax: (614)793-1708
E-mail: 110364.3550@compuserve.com
URL: http://www.aviationsafetyinstitute.com
Contact: Charles Minshall, Special Projects Dir.
Founded: 1973. **Members:** 500. **Membership Dues:** regular, $25 (quarterly). **Staff:** 7. **Budget:** $400,000. **Description:** Acts as an independent party not aligned with industry or government to promote and improve aviation safety. Activities include: operating an anonymous hazard reporting system; conducting safety education programs and seminars; maintaining a computerized safety information system; performing safety audits and consulting services; conducting aircraft accident investigations and research projects on topics such as pilot and crew fatigue. Conducts research. **Libraries: Type:** open to the public. **Computer Services:** database, aviation safety hazards and accidents. **Publications:** *Aviation Safety Institute—Monitor*, quarterly. Newsletter. Reports on aviation safety, both civil and military. **Price:** free for members; $60.00 /year for nonmembers. **Circulation:** 1,400. Alternate Formats: online ●

Also publishes results of research projects and other safety-related information.

12679 ■ Bicycle Helmet Safety Institute (BHSI)
4611 7th St. S
Arlington, VA 22204-1419
Ph: (703)486-0100
E-mail: info@helmets.org
URL: http://www.helmets.org
Contact: Randy Swart, Dir.
Founded: 1989. **Staff:** 5. **Budget:** $12,000. **Languages:** English, French. **Description:** A national consumer-supported advocacy program of the Washington Area Bicyclist Association. Promotes the use of helmets for bicyclists. Disseminates information to the public and press. Works on the ASTM helmet standards committee. Compiles statistics. Sends Toolkit for Helmet Promotion Programs to teachers and others at no charge. **Libraries: Type:** reference. **Subjects:** helmets. **Additional Websites:** http://www.bhsi.org. **Supersedes:** Helmet Committee, Washington Area Bicyclist Association. **Publications:** *Consumers Guide to Bicycle Helmets.* Pamphlets ● *Helmet Update Newsletter*, periodic. **Price:** free. Alternate Formats: online ● *Toolkit for Helmet Promotion Programs*, periodic. Contains statistics, speakers' outline, sources, manual, and pamphlets. **Price:** free. Alternate Formats: online.

12680 ■ Boaters Against Drunk Driving (BADD)
344 Clayton Ave.
Battle Creek, MI 49017-5218
Ph: (269)963-7068
Fax: (269)963-7068
E-mail: safeboating@badd.org
URL: http://www.badd.org
Contact: Jim Carlin, Pres./Founder
Founded: 1989. **State Groups:** 38. **Description:** Creates public awareness of safe, sober and responsible boating. Reduces injury, death and property damage caused by intoxicated boaters and irresponsible boating. **Computer Services:** Information services, boating articles and resources ● information services, boating fatality statistics. **Projects:** Lighthouse of Law.

12681 ■ Center for Auto Safety (CAS)
1825 Connecticut Ave. NW, Ste.330
Washington, DC 20009-5708
Ph: (202)328-7700
E-mail: mbarclift@autosafety.org
URL: http://www.autosafety.org
Contact: Clarence M. Ditlow III, Exec. Dir.
Founded: 1970. **Members:** 20,000. **Membership Dues:** consumer, $20 (annual). **Staff:** 10. **Budget:** $700,000. **Description:** Seeks to "reduce the human and economic losses wrought by the automobile and the auto industry." As an auto and highway safety advocate, the center monitors government agencies charged with regulation of the industry, supports safety standards, participates in the rule-making procedures of the National Highway Traffic Safety Administration and the Federal Highway Administration, and occasionally institutes legal action. Collects literature and statistics on automobile safety and analyzes developments in the field. Letters are being coded by auto make, 2nd model, year. **Libraries: Type:** not open to the public. **Programs:** Safety Research Service; Vehicle Safety. **Publications:** *Annual Supplement to Automobile Design Liability*, annual. Supplements a reference book on automobile liability laws and consumer protection. ● *The Car Book*, annual. Features a guide to buying new and used cars. Covers crash safety, fuel economy, maintenance, insurance, child seat ratings, and state lemon laws. **Price:** $20.00/copy; $30.00 in Canada and outside U.S. Alternate Formats: online ● *Center for Auto Safety—Impact: A Journal of Safety News*, bimonthly. Newsletter. Provides information on automobile defects, product liability, recalls, secret warranties, federal investigations, and center automobile safety work. **Price:** $100.00/year in U.S.; $100.00/year outside U.S. ISSN: 0162-4989. **Circulation:** 1,000 ● *Children at Risk: Failure of the Federal Child*

Restraint Recall Program ● *Guide to Sources of Information on Auto Defects* ● *The Lemon Book*. Handbook. **Price:** $17.50 ● *Lemon Times*, quarterly. Newsletter. Covers center's actions and findings. Includes consumer success stories and annual report. **Price:** $20.00/year in U.S.; $25.00/year outside U.S. **Circulation:** 12,000. Alternate Formats: online ● *Little Secrets of the Auto Industry*. Book. Features a guide to finding and using secret warranties. **Price:** $17.50 ● *Sudden Acceleration*. Book. Tells about the serious defect of sudden acceleration. **Price:** $25.00 ● Reports. Alternate Formats: online ● Videos. **Conventions/Meetings:** annual meeting - always spring, Washington, DC.

12682 ■ Citizens for Roadside Safety
3300 Robinson Pike Rd.
Grandview, MO 64030
E-mail: roadsafety@kc.rr.com
URL: http://www.guardrail.org
Contact: Galen Bird, Pres.
Founded: 1992. **State Groups:** 4. **Description:** Promotes highway safety throughout the United States. Focuses on guardrails, rumble strips and other roadside hazards. **Computer Services:** Information services, road rage and aggressive driving definition. **Telecommunication Services:** electronic mail, guardrails@gmail.com.

12683 ■ Danny Foundation (DF)
1451 Danville Blvd., Ste.202
Alamo, CA 94507-1941
Ph: (925)314-8130 (925)314-8131
Free: (800)833-2669
Fax: (925)314-8133
E-mail: info@dannyfoundation.org
URL: http://www.dannyfoundation.org
Contact: Jack Walsh, Exec.Dir.
Founded: 1986. **Staff:** 3. **Description:** Educates the public about baby cribs and the nursery products industry. Conducts research and surveys; compiles statistics. Operates speakers' bureau; The foundation is named for Danny Lineweaver, the founders' son who was strangled and suffered massive brain damage when his T-shirt strap got caught on a crib post. **Formerly:** (1987) Danny Lineweaver Foundation. **Publications:** *Crib Notes*, quarterly ● *Is Your Crib Safe?*. Brochure. **Conventions/Meetings:** bimonthly board meeting.

12684 ■ driveAWARE
PO Box 2114
Warminster, PA 18974-2114
Ph: (215)674-0447
Free: (877)343-1919
E-mail: trafficsafetyfirst@comcast.net
URL: http://driveaware.info
Contact: John E. Langan, Pres.
Founded: 2003. **Description:** Seeks to improve overall traffic safety awareness and reduce traffic crashes through education, engineering and enforcement. Coordinates various support services for those affected by traffic crashes. **Telecommunication Services:** electronic mail, rauanheimo@usa.net. **Committees:** Education; Enforcement; Engineering; Legislative and Lobbying; Membership Development; Publicity Promotion and Marketing; Support Services.

12685 ■ Farm Safety 4 Just Kids (FS4JK)
11304 Aurora Ave.
Urbandale, IA 50322
Ph: (515)331-6506
Free: (800)423-5437
Fax: (515)331-2947
E-mail: fs4jk@fs4jk.org
URL: http://www.fs4jk.org
Contact: Marilyn Adams, Pres.
Founded: 1987. **Members:** 3,194. **Membership Dues:** individual, family, $25 (annual) ● business, organization, $50 (annual). **Staff:** 9. **National Groups:** 150. **Description:** Individuals, businesses, and organizations with an interest in the safety of children living on farms. Seeks to increase public awareness of hazards to children present on farms; empowers families to make their farms safe for children. Serves as a clearinghouse on farm safety; develops and distributes educational materials; spon-

sors local farm safety programs. **Awards:** Farm Family Incentive Grant. **Frequency:** periodic. **Type:** grant. **Recipient:** for individual or organization working in farm safety or a related field. **Publications:** *Farm Safety Game and Activity Book*. **Price:** $27.50 for members; $38.00 for nonmembers ● *Let's Do A Farm Safety Day Camp*. Manual. **Price:** $9.00 for members; $11.25 for nonmembers ● Brochures ● Articles. **Conventions/Meetings:** biennial conference.

12686 ■ Forest Products Safety Conference (FPSC)
Address Unknown since 2007
Founded: 1935. **Budget:** $60,000. **Description:** Employers in wood products industries in northwestern U.S. and western Canada; associations and other groups dealing with wood products are associate members. Promotes sound accident prevention methods, procedures, and objectives for wood products employers and employees by holding a yearly conference for presentation and discussion of safety techniques and training. Presents plaques for best safety performances, by classification. Compiles statistical records on accident frequencies. **Computer Services:** Mailing lists. **Divisions:** Factory (Wood); Hardboard and Particleboard; Logging; Plywood; Pulp and Paper; Sawmill; Shingle Mills; Veneer. **Formerly:** (1938) Western States Safety Conference; (1945) Western Safety Conference; (1951) Western Forest Products Safety Conference. **Publications:** *Conference Proceedings*, annual. **Conventions/Meetings:** annual conference (exhibits) - always April.

12687 ■ Foundation for Aquatic Injury Prevention
c/o Ronald R. Gilbert, Chm.
11230 White Lake Rd.
Fenton, MI 48430
Free: (800)342-0330
Fax: (810)714-0354
E-mail: ron@aquaticisf.org
URL: http://www.aquaticisf.org
Contact: Ronald R. Gilbert, Chm.
Founded: 1988. **Members:** 6. **Description:** Works to reduce the number of diving injuries, drownings and near-drownings. Conducts public educational programs on water safety; instituted a registry of aquatic injuries in Michigan to track trouble areas and focus educational efforts; provides a forum for victims to support each other; encourages exchange of information; compiles statistics. **Libraries: Type:** reference. **Subjects:** aquatic safety, spinal cord injury. **Formerly:** (2007) Aquatic Injury Safety Foundation.

12688 ■ Insurance Institute for Highway Safety (IIHS)
1005 N Glebe Rd., Ste.800
Arlington, VA 22201
Ph: (703)247-1500
Fax: (703)247-1588
E-mail: iihs@highwaysafety.org
URL: http://www.highwaysafety.org
Contact: Russ Rader, Media Relations Dir.
Founded: 1969. **Staff:** 60. **Description:** Supported by casualty insurance companies and trade associations such as American Insurers Highway Safety Alliance, American Insurance Highway Safety Association, and National Association of Independent Insurers Safety Association. Independent public service research and communications organization dedicated to reducing the losses of deaths, injuries, and property damage resulting from crashes on the nation's highways. **Libraries: Type:** reference. **Holdings:** 1,500. **Subjects:** auto safety. **Computer Services:** Mailing lists. **Additional Websites:** http://www.iihs.org. **Programs:** Crash Testing. **Publications:** *Shopping For a Safer Car*, annual. Lists specific models of cars and their safety features. **Price:** free. Alternate Formats: online ● *Status Report*, 10/year. Newsletter. Alternate Formats: online ● Bibliography ● Videos ● Also publishes fact sheets.

12689 ■ Inter-American Safety Council (IASC)
Address Unknown since 2007
Founded: 1938. **Members:** 3,200. **Staff:** 15. **Languages:** English, Portuguese, Spanish. **Description:**

A nongovernmental, privately supported, public service and educational organization dedicated to creating accident prevention and loss control awareness among the Spanish- and Portuguese-speaking people of the world. IASC services, publications, and educational materials are being used in industrial plants, insurance companies, government agencies, transportation companies, commercial operations, universities, and other institutions in 20 countries throughout Latin America, as well as Spain and Portugal. Offers correspondence courses, in-plant instruction, and training programs on accident prevention, health, and traffic safety. **Libraries: Type:** reference. **Holdings:** video recordings. **Subjects:** safety. **Also Known As:** Consejo Interamericano de Seguridad. **Publications:** *El Supervisor* (in English and Spanish), monthly. Magazine. Provides articles on how to obtain better communication with workers and greater production with more efficiency. **Price:** included in membership dues. **Advertising:** not accepted. Also Cited As: *The Supervisor* ● *Noticias de Seguridad* (in Spanish), monthly. Magazine. Covers organization and programs, loss control, hygiene and health, maintenance, fires and explosions, first aid, off-the-job and traffic safety. ● *Usted y su Familia* (in Spanish), quarterly. Newsletter. Covers health and off-the-job safety. **Advertising:** not accepted ● Also publishes translations of materials of U.S. accident prevention organizations. **Conventions/Meetings:** annual competition ● annual meeting - always March, New York.

12690 ■ International Society of Air Safety Investigators (ISASI)

107 E Holly Ave., Ste.11
Sterling, VA 20164
Ph: (703)430-9668
Fax: (703)430-4970
E-mail: isasi@erols.com
URL: http://www.isasi.org
Contact: Frank S. Del Gandio, Pres.
Founded: 1964. **Members:** 1,422. **Membership Dues:** individual, $60 (annual) ● corporate, $500 (annual). **Staff:** 1. **State Groups:** 9. **National Groups:** 6. **Description:** Specialists who investigate and define the causes of aircraft accidents; persons who have made outstanding contributions to the promotion of air safety are honorary members. Encourages improvement of air safety and investigative procedures worldwide. **Libraries: Type:** reference. **Awards:** Jerome F. Lederer Award. **Frequency:** annual. **Type:** recognition. **Recipient:** for outstanding lifetime contributions to technical excellence ● Rudolf Kapustin Memorial Scholarship. **Frequency:** annual. **Type:** scholarship. **Recipient:** for members. **Formerly:** (1978) Society of Air Safety Investigators. **Publications:** *The Forum*, quarterly. Journal. **Price:** $24.00/year ● *Membership Roster*, biennial. Membership Directory. **Conventions/Meetings:** annual meeting and seminar.

12691 ■ Kidpower Teenpower Fullpower International

PO Box 1212
Santa Cruz, CA 95061
Ph: (831)426-4407
Free: (800)467-6997
E-mail: safety@kidpower.org
URL: http://www.kidpower.org
Contact: Irene van der Zande, Co-Founder/Exec. Dir.
Founded: 1989. **Multinational. Description:** Helps people of all ages and abilities learn how to stay safe, act wisely and believe in themselves. Develops and offers community violence prevention and self esteem building services. Creates an international community of leaders who are dedicated to making high quality self-protection and confidence building programs widely accessible. **Publications:** *California Newsletter*, monthly. **Price:** free. Alternate Formats: online ● *International Newsletter*, monthly. **Price:** free. Alternate Formats: online ● *KIDPOWER Safety Plan Comic Book* (in English and Spanish). Contains cartoon-illustrated explanations for adults on how to introduce personal safety skills to younger children. **Price:** $6.00 English only; $8.00 English and Spanish.

12692 ■ Knights of Life Motorcycle Club (KLMC)

PO Box 96
Wharton, NJ 07885
E-mail: info@knightsoflife.org
URL: http://www.knightsoflife.org
Contact: Jeff Goldstein, Pres.
Founded: 1987. **Members:** 40. **Membership Dues:** full, supportive, $25 (annual) ● associate, $20 (annual) ● at large, $15 (annual). **Staff:** 10. **Budget:** $500. **State Groups:** 1. **Description:** Emergency medical care professionals who are motorcycling enthusiasts. Promotes motorcycle safety and a positive image of bikers. Provides first aid services to other motorcycle clubs; conducts CPR and first aid classes. Assists in the training of emergency medical personnel in the proper techniques of helmet removal. **Awards:** Brighter Image from American Motorcyclist American. **Frequency:** annual. **Type:** trophy. **Recipient:** for outstanding efforts in public image enhancement ● Hazel Kolb. **Frequency:** annual. **Type:** trophy. **Recipient:** for outstanding efforts in public image enhancement. **Telecommunication Services:** electronic mail, president@knightsoflife.org. **Publications:** *The Pulse*, bimonthly. Newsletter. **Price:** included in membership dues. ISSN: 1067-9731. **Advertising:** accepted. **Conventions/Meetings:** Motorcycle Injury Management - seminar (exhibits) ● Motorcycle Trauma Management - seminar, post-accident helmets, motorcycles, motorcycle clothing (exhibits).

12693 ■ Mothers Against Drunk Driving (MADD)

511 E John Carpenter Fwy., Ste.700
Irving, TX 75062
Ph: (214)744-6233
Free: (800)GET-MADD
Fax: (972)869-2206
E-mail: info@madd.org
URL: http://www.madd.org
Contact: Glynn Birch, Pres.
Founded: 1980. **Members:** 3,200,000. **Membership Dues:** individual, $20 (annual) ● corporate, $150 (annual) ● family, $40 (annual). **Staff:** 317. **Budget:** $43,000,000. **State Groups:** 37. **Local Groups:** 300. **Description:** Represents victims of drunk driving crashes; concerned citizens. Encourages citizen participation in working towards reform of the drunk driving problem and the prevention of underage drinking acts and providing materials for use in medical facilities, and health and driver education programs. Conducts a variety of programs for youth and in the schools. Supports Law Enforcement Programs and state and federal legislation for reform of laws on drunk driving; provides public education programs for encouraging more stringent laws requiring mandatory minimum punishment. Conducts research programs; maintains biographical archives and extensive library; sponsors competitions; compiles statistics; maintains speakers' bureau. Holds regional workshops. **Awards: Type:** recognition. **Departments:** Field Services; Human Resources; Legal; Marketing and Resource Development; Programs; Public Policy; Public Relations; Victim Services. **Formerly:** (1984) Mothers Against Drunk Drivers. **Publications:** *Closed Head Injury* (in English and Spanish). Brochure ● *Don't Call Me Lucky* (in English and Spanish). Brochure ● *Driven*, biennial. Magazine. Includes national activities, public policy initiatives, calendars and chapter events. **Circulation:** 1,000,000 ● *Drunk Driving: An Unacknowledged Form of Child Endangerment* ● *Financial Recovery After A Drunk Driving Crash*. Brochure ● *Helping Children Cope With Death* (in English and Spanish). Brochure ● *How You Can Help* ● *MADDvocate*, semiannual. Magazine. Includes victims' stories, legislative updates, feature editions. **Circulation:** 50,000. Alternate Formats: online ● *Men and Mourning* (in English and Spanish). Brochure ● *Selecting a Civil Attorney* (in English and Spanish). Brochure ● *Someone You Know Drinks and Drives* (in English and Spanish). Brochure ● *Straight Talk About Death for Teenagers* (in English and Spanish). Brochure ● *Track* ● *Victim Information* (in English and Spanish). Pamphlet ● *We Hurt Too: Guide for Adult Siblings* (in English and Spanish).

Brochure ● *Will It Always Feel This Way?* (in English and Spanish) ● *Your Grief: You're Not Going Crazy* (in English and Spanish). Brochure ● *You're Not Alone: MADD Can Help!* ● Also publishes books, brochures on drunk driving, and compendiums on public policy. Produces video-tapes and public service announcements. **Conventions/Meetings:** annual Candlelight Vigil - meeting ● annual conference (exhibits) ● meeting, for state organizations ● Safe & Sober Workshops ● Victim Advocacy Training - meeting.

12694 ■ National Association of Women Highway Safety Leaders (NAWHSL)

c/o Suzanna M. Tye, PhD, Pres.
6513 Golf Village St., No. 1
St. Thomas, VI 00802
Ph: (340)777-6278
E-mail: safety_leaders@yahoo.com
URL: http://www.nawhsl.org
Contact: Suzanna M. Tye PhD, Pres.
Founded: 1967. **Members:** 100. **Membership Dues:** associate and governor appointed, $25 (annual). **Budget:** $75,000. **Regional Groups:** 10. **State Groups:** 50. **Description:** Women and representatives of women's organizations with interests in traffic safety. Seeks to reduce traffic crashes, injuries, and deaths by encouraging each political subdivision to assume its responsibility for highway safety. Aims to promote uniformity in traffic safety programs and regulations within the 50 states, the District of Columbia, Puerto Rico, St. Thomas, St. Croix, and American Samoa. Conducts educational programs including seminars and workshops; maintains speakers' bureau. **Committees:** Alcohol/Drugs Countermeasures; Bicycle Safety; Child Passenger Safety Seat Usage; Highway Environment; Mature Driver; Safety Belt; School Bus Safety. **Publications:** *Buckle Up*. Brochure ● *NEWS*, quarterly. Newsletter. **Conventions/Meetings:** annual conference.

12695 ■ National Child Safety Council (NCSC)

PO Box 1368
Jackson, MI 49204
Ph: (517)764-6070
Fax: (517)764-3068
Contact: Barbara Handley Huggett, Dir. of Res. and Devel.
Founded: 1955. **Description:** Furnishes complete child safety education programs through local law enforcement agencies and schools. **Formerly:** (1955) Police Safety Service; (1967) Child Safety Council. **Conventions/Meetings:** annual meeting - always November. Jackson, MI.

12696 ■ National Commission Against Drunk Driving (NCADD)

8403 Colesville Rd., Ste.370
Silver Spring, MD 20910
Ph: (240)247-6004
Fax: (240)247-7012
E-mail: info@ncadd.com
URL: http://www.ncadd.com
Contact: Mr. Robert C. Stempel, Chm.
Founded: 1984. **Membership Dues:** senior citizen, $10 (annual) ● individual, $20 (annual) ● family, $50 (annual) ● organization/small business, $150 (annual) ● friend, $500 (annual) ● patron, $1,000 (annual) ● contributor, $2,500-$4,999 (annual) ● sustaining partner, $5,000-$9,999 (annual) ● associate partner, $14,999 (annual) ● full partner, $19,999 (annual) ● chairman's circle, $20,000 (annual). **Staff:** 3. **Budget:** $770,000. **Description:** Individuals and organizations concerned with increasing highway safety. Seeks to reduce the incidence of drunk driving and resulting accidents. Holds public hearings; coordinates implementation of recommendations by the Presidential Commission on Drunk Driving. Operates speakers' bureau; conducts educational programs; compiles statistics. **Awards:** NCADD Annual Awards. **Frequency:** annual. **Type:** recognition. **Departments:** Network of Employees for Traffic Safety. **Programs:** Motorcycle Safety; SoberRide. **Projects:** BAC Testing Group. **Publications:** *Intersections*, quarterly. Newsletter. **Price:** included in membership

dues. **Circulation:** 6,700. **Conventions/Meetings:** annual conference and luncheon - always December.

12697 ■ National Drowning Prevention Alliance (NDPA)
c/o Diane Holm, Pres.
Lee County Hea. Dept.
3920 Michigan Ave.
Fort Myers, FL 33916
Ph: (239)332-9590
Fax: (239)332-9605
E-mail: diane_holm@doh.state.fl.us
URL: http://www.ndpa.org
Contact: Diane Holm, Pres.
Founded: 2004. **Membership Dues:** general, $50 (annual) ● bronze, $500 (annual) ● silver, $1,000 (annual) ● gold, $2,500 (annual) ● platinum, $5,000 (annual). **Description:** Serves as the central source of information and referral on research, data, education, policy and promotion of drowning prevention. Seeks to reduce the incidence of toddler drowning in swimming pools and spas. Aims to be a catalyst in preventing drowning among children. **Publications:** Newsletter. Alternate Formats: online.

12698 ■ National Fire Protection Association (NFPA)
1 Batterymarch Park
Quincy, MA 02169-7471
Ph: (617)770-3000
Free: (800)344-3555
Fax: (617)770-0700
E-mail: custserv@nfpa.org
URL: http://www.nfpa.org
Contact: James M. Shannon, Pres.
Founded: 1896. **Members:** 74,000. **Membership Dues:** regular, $135 (annual). **Staff:** 300. **Budget:** $50,000,000. **Regional Groups:** 4. **Languages:** English, Spanish. **Description:** Represents individuals from the fire service, business and industry, health care, educational and other institutions, and individuals in the fields of insurance, government, architecture, and engineering. Develops, publishes, and disseminates standards. Conducts fire safety education programs for the general public. Provides information on fire protection, prevention, and suppression; compiles annual statistics on causes and occupancies of fires, fire deaths, and fire fighter casualties. Provides field service by specialists on electricity, flammable liquids and gases, and marine fire problems. Sponsors National Fire Prevention Week each October and public education campaigns featuring Sparky the Fire Dog. **Libraries:** **Type:** by appointment only. **Holdings:** 20,000. **Subjects:** fire science and other related topics. **Awards:** Paul C. Lamb Award. **Frequency:** annual. **Type:** recognition. **Recipient:** for outstanding contribution to development of fire safety standards. **Sections:** Architects, Engineers, and Building Officials; Aviation; Building and Life Safety; Education; Electrical; Fire Marshals; Fire Science and Technology Educators; Fire Service; Health Care; Industrial Fire Protection; Lodging Industry; Metro Chiefs; Rail Transportation; Research; Wildland Fire Management. **Affiliated With:** American National Standards Institute. **Publications:** *Fire Protection Handbook* ● *Fire Protection Reference Directory and Buyer's Guide,* annual. Provides information on products, manufacturers and sales office, and services in the field of fire protection. Includes list of trade names. **Price:** free for members; $25.00/copy for nonmembers. **Circulation:** 80,000. **Advertising:** accepted ● *Fire Technology,* quarterly. Serves as a professional journal for the fire safety practitioner and the fire safety researcher. Describes advances in fire technology. **Price:** $39.50/year. ISSN: 0015-2684. **Circulation:** 4,500. Alternate Formats: microform ● *Learn Not to Burn Curriculum* ● *National Fire Codes,* annual. Features a compilation of over 300 fire codes, standards, recommended practices, manuals, and guides on fire protection. **Price:** $759.00/12-volume set; $683.00 for members ● *National Fire Protection Association—Technical Committee Reports/Documentation,* semiannual. Includes committee reports and interim documents on the fire code and standards development process. ● *NFPA Journal,* bimonthly. Features technical,

scientific, and industrial applications of fire protection, suppression, investigations, and education, plus association's news. **Price:** included in membership dues. **Circulation:** 64,000. **Advertising:** accepted ● *NFPA News,* monthly. Newsletter. Features news, calendar of events and committee openings. **Price:** free. **Circulation:** 68,000. Alternate Formats: online ● Catalog, quarterly ● Yearbook ● Reports. **Conventions/Meetings:** annual meeting ● annual World Fire Safety Congress and Exposition - meeting (exhibits) - 2008 June 2-6, Las Vegas, NV.

12699 ■ National Institute for Farm Safety (NIFS)
c/o Chip Petrea, PhD, Interim Sec.
1304 W Pennsylvania Ave.
Urbana, IL 61801
Ph: (217)333-5035
E-mail: repetrea@uiuc.edu
URL: http://www.ag.ohio-state.edu/~agsafety/NIFS/nifs.htm
Contact: Chip Petrea PhD, Interim Sec.
Founded: 1962. **Members:** 204. **Membership Dues:** associate, $75 (annual) ● full, $100 (annual) ● student, $50 (annual). **Staff:** 1. **Description:** Represents professional agricultural safety and health specialists devoting their efforts toward an improved agricultural injury and illnesses record through education, engineering, and research in the U.S. and Canada. Endorses use of Slow Moving Vehicle emblem and roll-over protection structures throughout North America; has suggested use of hand signals for agricultural purposes. Contributes to the Cooperative Standards Program handled by the American Society of Agricultural Engineers; helps fund accident studies and encourages industry support and research. Holds annual institute. **Awards:** Maynard Coe Award. **Frequency:** annual. **Type:** recognition. **Recipient:** for professional achievement in farm safety ● NIFS President's Award. **Frequency:** annual. **Type:** recognition. **Recipient:** to members or non-members for service provided to the organization ● NIFS Research Award. **Frequency:** annual. **Type:** recognition. **Recipient:** for innovative work in agricultural health and safety that results in improved injury and illness prevention in agricultural workplaces ●. Prevention Award. **Frequency:** annual. **Type:** recognition. **Recipient:** for education/intervention activity demonstrating either new or more effective approaches to agricultural injury or illness prevention. **Committees:** Home, Farmstead, and Leisure Time; Rural Occupational Health; Tractor and Machinery; Traffic and Transportation. **Affiliated With:** American Society of Agricultural and Biological Engineers; National Safety Council. **Conventions/Meetings:** annual conference.

12700 ■ National Safe Boating Council (NSBC)
c/o Virgil Chambers, Exec. Dir.
PO Box 509
Bristow, VA 20136
Ph: (703)361-4294
Fax: (703)361-5294
E-mail: nsbcdirect@safeboatingcouncil.org
URL: http://www.safeboatingcouncil.org
Contact: Virgil Chambers, Exec. Dir.
Founded: 1958. **Members:** 350. **Membership Dues:** state, regional, $150 (annual) ● local, $50 (annual) ● national, $200 (annual) ● commercial, trade association, $300 (annual) ● sustaining, $500 (annual) ● patron, $1,000 (annual) ● individual, $35 (annual). **Staff:** 3. **Budget:** $300,000. **Description:** Coalition of U.S. and Canadian government agencies, national, regional and local volunteer organizations, and corporations concerned with promoting recreational boating safety and stimulating public education in boating safety habits and techniques. Major activity is observance of National Safe Boating Week every May. Compiles and distributes a promotion and publicity kit to help local organizations and field units of member organizations set up their program, secure promotional materials, and publicize the week. Compiles statistics. Produces public service announcements. **Libraries:** **Type:** reference. **Holdings:** 2. **Awards:** Boating Education Advancement Award.

Frequency: annual. **Type:** recognition. **Recipient:** for state/region, one national ● Boating Safety Hall of Fame. **Frequency:** annual. **Type:** recognition. **Recipient:** for individuals with exemplary leadership and outstanding service on behalf of safe boating and the council ● Boating Safety Youth Award. **Frequency:** annual. **Type:** recognition. **Recipient:** for individuals and organizations that have developed and successfully implemented innovative youth boating education programs ● Local RBS Grant. **Frequency:** annual. **Type:** grant. **Recipient:** for organizations ● Youth Program of Excellence. **Frequency:** annual. **Type:** monetary. **Computer Services:** Mailing lists ● online services, organization member link. **Programs:** Boating Education for people of All Abilities; Boating Safety Youth; Local Recreational Boating Safety Grant. **Formerly:** (1968) National Safe Boating Week Committee; (1974) National Safe Boating Committee. **Publications:** *Anchorline,* quarterly. Newsletter. **Price:** included in membership dues. Alternate Formats: online ● *Boating Safety Sidekicks.* Booklets. Series addresses boating and water safety issues for children. ● *Saved by the Jacket.* Booklet. Contains true accounts of the lives saved because a life jacket was worn. **Price:** $2.00. **Circulation:** 35,000. Alternate Formats: online ● Membership Directory. **Price:** included in membership dues. **Conventions/Meetings:** International Boating and Water Safety Summit - seminar and meeting, on boating education, held in conjunction with the Water Safety Congress and US Coast Guard (exhibits) - usually April ● annual meeting.

12701 ■ National Safe Workplace Institute/SafeSpaces.com (NSWI)
3008 Bishops Ridge Ct.
Monroe, NC 28110
Ph: (704)282-1111
Fax: (704)550-5857
E-mail: info@safespaces.com
URL: http://www.safespaces.com
Contact: Joseph A. Kinney, Pres.
Founded: 1987. **Membership Dues:** individual, corporate, $25 (annual). **Budget:** $200,000. **Description:** Provides research and education on issues related to occupational health and safety. Is concerned with safe and healthy work environments and workplace violence. Seeks to make workplace safety and health a priority. Monitors efforts of the public and private sectors in improving workplace safety. Conducts periodic studies of national and regional industry issues. **Libraries:** **Type:** not open to the public. **Holdings:** 2,500. **Awards:** Commitment to Life. **Frequency:** annual. **Type:** recognition. **Publications:** *Electronic Newsletter,* semimonthly. **Price:** $179.00/year. ISSN: 1074-7974. **Circulation:** 500. Alternate Formats: online ● Newsletter, monthly ● Also publishes national, regional, and state reports on occupational safety and health issues. **Conventions/Meetings:** periodic conference.

12702 ■ National Safety Council (NSC)
1121 Spring Lake Dr.
Itasca, IL 60143-3201
Ph: (630)285-1121
Free: (800)621-7619
Fax: (630)285-1315
E-mail: info@nsc.org
URL: http://www.nsc.org
Contact: Alan McMillan, Pres.
Founded: 1913. **Members:** 16,000. **Membership Dues:** student, $30 (annual) ● community service, $50 (annual) ● organization, $250-$325 (annual) ● international, $475 (annual). **Staff:** 270. **Budget:** $44,000,000. **Local Groups:** 45. **Description:** Promotes injury reduction by providing a forum for the exchange of safety and health ideas, techniques, and experiences and the discussion of injury prevention methods. Offers courses in first aid, occupational safety and traffic safety. Maintains extensive library on health and safety subjects. **Libraries:** **Type:** open to the public. **Holdings:** 162,000; articles, books, periodicals, reports. **Subjects:** occupational, traffic/transportation, general safety. **Awards:** Occupational Awards. **Frequency:** periodic. **Type:** recognition. **Divisions:** Agriculture; Business and Industry; Campus

Safety; Community Safety; Construction Safety; Highway Traffic Safety; Labor; Motor Transportation; State and Local Safety Organizations; Utilities; Youth Activities. **Publications:** *Accident Prevention Manual for Business and Industry.* Manuals. Contains 2 volume per set. ● *Family Safety and Health*, quarterly. Magazine. Covers off-the-job safety and health; designed to prevent traffic, recreational, and home accidents and promote health and fitness. ● *Injury Facts*, annual. Book. Contains data on unintentional injuries. **Price:** included in membership dues. Alternate Formats: CD-ROM ● *Safe Driver*, monthly ● *Safe Worker*, monthly ● *Safety and Health*, monthly. Magazine. Covers all aspects of occupational safety and health. Features: advertisers index; bibliography of safety literature; and calendar of events. ● *Traffic Safety*, monthly. Newsletter. Covers topics in highway safety of interest to professionals in official agencies, public support groups, and driver education. **Conventions/Meetings:** annual National Safety Congress and Exposition (exhibits).

12703 ■ National Safety Management Society (NSMS)
PO Box 4460
Walnut Creek, CA 94596-0460
Free: (800)321-2910
Fax: (573)441-1765
E-mail: nsmsinc@yahoo.com
URL: http://www.nsms.us
Contact: Dr. Jeffrey Chung PhD, Exec. Dir.
Founded: 1966. **Members:** 500. **Membership Dues:** individual, $70 (annual) ● affiliate/retired, student/associate, $35 (annual). **Budget:** $32,000. **Description:** Individuals with managerial responsibilities related to safety/loss control management, including professionals in the fields of education, medicine, computer technology, security, personnel, law, and other disciplines. Advances new concepts of accident prevention and loss control and promotes the role of safety management in the total management effort. Advises concentration in areas where a favorable cost/benefit return can be achieved with these new concepts while being cognizant of humanitarian considerations. Participates in local, state, and regional safety conferences; conducts regional management improvement and executive safety training seminars. **Awards:** Frank Bird Award. **Frequency:** periodic. **Type:** recognition. **Computer Services:** database ● mailing lists ● online services. **Publications:** *Digest*, monthly. Newsletter. Contains news by and for members. **Price:** included in membership dues. Alternate Formats: online ● *Journal of Safety Management*, quarterly ● Also contributes to *Occupational Hazards Magazine.* **Conventions/Meetings:** annual meeting, with speakers.

12704 ■ National Water Safety Congress (NWSC)
c/o Cecilia Duer, Exec. Dir.
PO Box 1632
Mentor, OH 44061
Ph: (440)209-9805
E-mail: director@watersafetycongress.org
URL: http://www.watersafetycongress.org
Contact: Cecilia Duer, Exec. Dir.
Founded: 1951. **Members:** 300. **Membership Dues:** individual, $25 (annual) ● organization, $50 (annual) ● sustaining, $200 (annual) ● corporate, $500 (annual) ● patron, $1,000 (annual). **Regional Groups:** 8. **Multinational. Description:** Represents individuals, business firms, state and federal agencies, and safety organizations. Seeks to instill safe attitudes and behavior in recreational users of the nation's waters and waterways. Promotes water safety through education programs, water safety demonstrations and programs offered by civic and sportsmen's clubs, and cooperative actions between agencies. Encourages the inclusion of water safety concerns in the planning, design, and construction of structures and facilities in and along waterways. Promotes the formation of local water safety councils and provides continuing support and assistance to them. **Awards:** Award of Merit. **Frequency:** annual. **Type:** recognition. **Recipient:** for outstanding effort to promote water safety ● Letter of Commendation. **Frequency:**

annual. **Type:** recognition. **Recipient:** for outstanding accomplishments ● National Award. **Frequency:** annual. **Type:** recognition. **Recipient:** for significant participation in the cause of water safety ● President's Award. **Frequency:** annual. **Type:** recognition. **Recipient:** for a board member who has made the greatest contribution. **Committees:** Awards; Grants; Partnership Liaison; Public Relations; Summit Advisory; Water Safety Standards. **Publications:** *Water Safety Journal*, quarterly. Alternate Formats: online. **Conventions/Meetings:** annual conference (exhibits) - always April ● annual seminar (exhibits).

12705 ■ National Whistleblower Center
PO Box 3768
Washington, DC 20027
Ph: (202)342-1903
Fax: (202)342-1904
E-mail: contact@whistleblowers.org
URL: http://www.whistleblowers.org
Contact: Mr. Stephen Kohn, Exec. Dir.
Founded: 1988. **Membership Dues:** $20 (annual). **Staff:** 6. **Description:** Promotes and supports the rights of employee whistleblowers, whose actions protect public health and safety and correct abuses of authority and waste. Publicizes significant cases and distributes information and educational materials on whistleblower rights and developments. Operates a national Attorney Referral Service. **Libraries: Type:** reference. **Holdings:** books, video recordings. **Awards:** Awards for Courage. **Frequency:** periodic. **Type:** recognition. **Committees:** National Advisory; Whistleblower Review Panel. **Publications:** *Blowing the Whistle: How to Protect Yourself and Win.* Video. **Price:** $50.00 attorney/institution; $25.00 layperson ● *Concepts and Procedures in Whistleblower Law.* Book. **Price:** $135.00 ● *Whistleblower Law.* Book. **Price:** $54.95 ● *The Whistleblower Litigation Handbook.* **Price:** $125.00 attorney/institution; $105.00 layperson ● Brochure ● Also publishes a publication list. **Conventions/Meetings:** periodic seminar and workshop.

12706 ■ Operation Lifesaver (OLI)
1420 King St., Ste.401
Alexandria, VA 22314
Ph: (703)739-0308 (703)739-0309
Free: (800)537-6224
Fax: (703)519-8267
E-mail: general@oli.org
URL: http://www.oli.org
Contact: Helen Sramek, Pres.
Founded: 1972. **Staff:** 6. **Budget:** $1,800,000. **Regional Groups:** 8. **State Groups:** 50. **National Groups:** 2. **Languages:** English, French, Spanish. **Multinational. Description:** Seeks to reduce the incidence of highway-rail grade-crossing collisions and pedestrian fatalities on railroad tracks and right-of-way in the U.S. and Canada (Grade-crossing collisions involve motor vehicles and trains at highway/railroad intersections.) Works to increase public awareness on the frequencies of grade-crossing collisions and to correct driver behavior to avoid collisions. Conducts educational programs; maintains speakers' bureau. Provides media information and public service announcements. **Libraries: Type:** reference. **Councils:** Program Development. **Publications:** *OL Report On-Line*, quarterly. Newsletter. **Price:** free. **Circulation:** 3,600. Alternate Formats: online ● Membership Directory, annual. **Conventions/Meetings:** biennial symposium (exhibits).

12707 ■ Parents Against Tired Truckers (PATT)
PO Box 209
Lisbon Falls, ME 04252-0209
Free: (888)353-4572
E-mail: patt@gwi.net
URL: http://www.patt.org
Contact: John Lannen, Exec. Dir.
Founded: 1994. **Description:** Seeks to save lives by reducing heavy truck crashes resulting from truck driver fatigue. Fosters changes that place the public's safety first. Provides support and information to truck crash victims and their families. Promotes public

education on fatigued driving. **Publications:** *The Truck Safety Advocate.* Newsletter. Alternate Formats: online.

12708 ■ Physicians for a Violence-Free Society (PVS)
1001 Potrero Blvd., Bldg. 1, Rm. 300
San Francisco, CA 94110
Ph: (415)621-3582
Fax: (415)621-3438
E-mail: pvs@pvs.org
URL: http://www.pvs.org
Contact: Leigh Marecek, Exec.Dir.
Founded: 1993. **Members:** 1,000. **Membership Dues:** $100 (annual). **Staff:** 4. **Budget:** $250,000. **Description:** Physicians, health care providers and concerned citizens. Works to engage physician, health care provider, and concerned citizen leadership in addressing interpersonal violence as a public health crisis. Encourages public awareness of the possibility of a violence-free society. Supports physicians and health care providers who care for victims of violence. Maintains slideshows on domestic violence. **Awards: Frequency:** annual. **Type:** recognition. **Recipient:** for people in the health care field who have done outstanding work in violence prevention. **Publications:** *Action Notes*, bimonthly. Newsletter. **Circulation:** 676 ● *Physicians Guide to Domestic Violence: How to ask the Right Questions and Recognize Abuse.* Manual. Written for physicians and other health professionals who care for victims of domestic violence. **Conventions/Meetings:** annual conference ● annual seminar, with leadership training.

12709 ■ Recording Artists, Actors and Athletes Against Drunk Driving (RADD)
4370 Tujunga Ave., Ste.235
Studio City, CA 91604
Ph: (818)752-7799
Fax: (818)752-7792
E-mail: robert.pineda@radd.org
URL: http://www.radd.org
Contact: Erin Dugan Meluso, Pres.
Founded: 1986. **Multinational. Description:** Works to save lives and reduce injuries and fatalities. Uses celebrity power to create a positive attitude toward road safety. Raises awareness of the importance of road safety. Promotes safe and sober driving. **Boards:** Entertainment Advisory. **Divisions:** Youth. **Programs:** Media Outreach; RADD Celebrities; RADD Kids for Safe and Healthy Choices; RADD Teens.

12710 ■ RID - U.S.A. (RID)
PO Box 520
Schenectady, NY 12301
Ph: (518)372-0034
Free: (888)283-5144
Fax: (518)370-4917
E-mail: dwi@rid-usa.org
URL: http://www.rid-usa.org
Contact: Doris Aiken, Pres./Founder
Founded: 1978. **Membership Dues:** individual, $20 (annual) ● senior/student, $10 (annual). **Staff:** 5. **Budget:** $100,000. **Regional Groups:** 4. **State Groups:** 41. **Local Groups:** 153. **Description:** Businesses, organizations, churches, educational agencies, victims, citizen activists, and others dedicated to removing intoxicated drivers from the road. Goals include: heightening public awareness of the effects drunken drivers have on society; encouraging the development of and public demand for passage of more effective laws dealing with drunk drivers; increasing public involvement; supporting victims of drunk drivers. Provides background information on court procedures; acts as liaison between victims and agencies, courts, coroners, district attorneys, and police. Holds victim witness panels for convicted drunk drivers. Conducts educational programs to discourage underage binge drinking and prevent alcohol poisoning. Compiles statistics; maintains speakers' bureau. Sponsors competitions, charitable programs, and youth services. **Libraries: Type:** reference. **Holdings:** 1,000; archival material, books. **Subjects:** DUI and alcohol abuse, underage drinking.

Awards: Humanitarian Award. **Frequency:** annual. **Type:** recognition. **Recipient:** for volunteer and professional activity that saves lives and prevents injury. **Computer Services:** database ● mailing lists. **Telecommunication Services:** hotline, Victims National Helpline, (518)393-HELP. **Committees:** Courtwatch; Education; Legislative; Media; Research; Victims Aid; Victims Witness Panel. **Divisions:** Victim Center; Youth. **Projects:** Friends. **Affiliated With:** Transportation Alternatives. **Also Known As:** Remove Intoxicated Drivers - United States of America. **Formerly:** (1978) RID - Capital Area. **Publications:** *Arive Alive.* Book ● *Citizen Activist Register,* semiannual. Directory. Lists association leaders geographically. **Price:** available to members only ● *History of RID.* Brochure. Preface to Arrive Alive. **Price:** free ● *How Can I Help.* Manual. **Price:** $5.00 ● *How to Hire a Lawyer.* Brochure. **Price:** free ● *Media Game & How to Play It.* Manual. **Price:** $13.00 plus shipping and handling ● *My Life as a Pit Bull.* Book. **Price:** $9.00 for members, plus shipping and handling ● *RID Action Newsletter,* semiannual. Includes chapter and national news. **Price:** $10.00/year. Alternate Formats: online ● *RID Directory,* annual. For chapter leaders only ● *RID In Action Bulletin,* bimonthly. **Price:** available to chapters only ● *RID Media Manual.* Features media game and how to play it. Contains many examples of volunteer activity. **Price:** $13.00 ● *Victims Aid Network: How Can I Help,* annual. **Price:** available to members only; $7.00 plus shipping and handling ● *Victims Memorial.* Booklet. **Price:** $7.00 plus shipping and handling ● *Victims' Rights.* Booklet. **Price:** $7.00 plus shipping and handling ● *Without Warning.* Video. Discusses alcohol poisoning and teen binge drinking. **Price:** $95.00 plus shipping and handling. **Conventions/Meetings:** Safe & Sober - conference (exhibits) ● monthly Victim Support & Group - support group meeting (exhibits) - every 2nd Wednesday ● workshop and conference, for media and victims.

12711 ■ Roadway Safety Foundation (RSF)
1101 14th St. NW, Ste.750
Washington, DC 20005
Ph: (202)857-1200
Fax: (202)857-1220
E-mail: cherylhollins@highways.org
URL: http://www.roadwaysafety.org
Founded: 1995. **Members:** 53. **Staff:** 2. **Description:** Develops programs, awareness campaigns, publications regarding roadway safety issues and countermeasures. **Affiliated With:** American Highway Users Alliance. **Formerly:** (1998) Automotive Safety Foundation. **Publications:** *Action Update,* quarterly. Updates members on activities. **Price:** included in membership dues ● *Roadway Safety Reporter,* quarterly. Newsletter. Includes grassroots report and technology column. **Price:** $100.00/year. Alternate Formats: online. **Conventions/Meetings:** annual Trustees Meeting - always fall.

12712 ■ School and Community Safety Society of America of the American Association for Active Lifestyles and Fitness (SCSSA)
c/o American Alliance for Health, Physical Education, Recreation & Dance
1900 Assn. Dr.
Reston, VA 20191-1598
Ph: (703)476-3400
Free: (800)213-7193
E-mail: aaalf@aahperd.org
URL: http://www.aahperd.org/aapar
Contact: JoAnne Owens-Nauslar, Pres.
Founded: 1974. **Members:** 500. **Membership Dues:** professional, $125 (annual) ● associate, $75 (annual) ● student, $45 (annual). **Staff:** 4. **Regional Groups:** 6. **Description:** Teachers and others professionally involved in the educational aspects of areas such as: traffic safety education; emergency preparedness; health education for injury control; safety program management; professional preparation in safety; athletics, physical education and recreational sports safety; safety curriculum development; safety research and development; school/community/senior citizen/handicapped safety programming. Encour-

ages the development of safety concepts and behaviors among its members; sponsors national conferences and safety programs. **Affiliated With:** American Alliance for Health, Physical Education, Recreation and Dance. **Formerly:** (1985) American School and Community Safety Association; (1991) The Safety Society. **Publications:** *Safety Notebook,* semiannual. Newsletter. Addresses safety in sport, physical education, and recreation. **Price:** $15.00. **Circulation:** 1,500. **Advertising:** accepted. **Conventions/Meetings:** annual American Alliance for Health, Physical Education, Recreation and Dance Convention - meeting (exhibits).

12713 ■ Seatbelt Law Opposition Forum
c/o William J. Holdorf, Dir.
5839 S Harlem Ave., No. 517
Chicago, IL 60638
E-mail: wholdorf@msn.com
URL: http://www.atch.com/abate/cdl/seatbeltlaws.html
Contact: William J. Holdorf, Dir.
Founded: 1985. **Description:** Distributes brochures and other publications arguing that mandatory seat belt laws are unnecessary, hazardous, and unconstitutional. Compiles research. **Publications:** *Proof of Danger.* Pamphlet ● *Seat Belt Laws are a Fraud.* Brochure ● *State Mandatory Seat Belt Laws are Wrong for America.* Brochure. Lists traffic accidents.

12714 ■ Sheet Metal Occupational Health Institute Trust (SMOHIT)
601 N Fairfax St., Ste.250
Alexandria, VA 22314
Ph: (703)739-7130
Fax: (703)739-7134
E-mail: gbatykefer@sheetmetal-iti.org
URL: http://www.smohit.org
Contact: Gary Batykefer, Admin.
Founded: 1986. **Members:** 145,000. **Staff:** 4. **Budget:** $2,000,000. **Regional Groups:** 9. **State Groups:** 50. **Description:** Joint labor management trust sponsored by the Sheet Metal Workers International Association and Sheet Metal and Air Conditioning Contractors National Association. Works to educate the sheet metal industry about hazardous materials; monitors and disseminates information about proposed state and federal occupational health regulations that will affect workers and the industry; fosters labor/management awareness of safety programs. Conducts medical screening. **Awards:** Hard Hat Hints Contest. **Frequency:** monthly. **Type:** recognition ● Safety Matters Award. **Frequency:** annual. **Type:** recognition. **Programs:** Asbestos Screening; Legal Referral; Medical & Scientific. **Formerly:** (2002) Sheet Metal Occupational Health Institute. **Publications:** *Safety Matters,* quarterly. Newsletter. Alternate Formats: online. **Conventions/Meetings:** periodic board meeting ● workshop.

12715 ■ Students Against Destructive Decisions, Students Against Drunk Driving (SADD)
255 Main St.
Marlborough, MA 01752
Free: (877)SADD-INC
Fax: (508)481-5759
E-mail: info@sadd.com
URL: http://www.sadd.org
Contact: Penelope Wells, Exec. Dir.
Founded: 1981. **State Groups:** 50. **Local Groups:** 25,000. **Description:** Students in middle and high school and college and concerned adults. Aims to end death and injury due to drinking and driving, underage drinking, and drug abuse among youth. Maintains speakers' bureau. **Awards:** Outstanding Contribution Awards. **Frequency:** annual. **Type:** recognition. **Recipient:** to individuals or groups who have made contribution that stands out in size, creativity, sacrifice or commitment to SADD ● Student of the Year. **Frequency:** annual. **Type:** recognition. **Recipient:** for students and members of Student Leadership Council. **Computer Services:** Mailing lists. **Committees:** Development. **Councils:** Student Leadership. **Programs:** Family Focus. **Formerly:** (1997) Students Against Drunk Driving. **Publications:**

Decisions, 3/year. Newsletter. Alternate Formats: online ● *SADD and the Athlete* ● *SADD in the College* ● *SADD in the High School* ● *SADD in the Junior High School* ● *SADD Update,* quarterly. Newsletter ● Audiotapes ● Books ● Videos ● Annual Report, annual. Alternate Formats: online. **Conventions/Meetings:** annual conference.

12716 ■ Traffic Records Committee (TRC)
c/o National Safety Council
1121 Spring Lake Dr.
Itasca, IL 60143-3201
Ph: (630)285-1121
Free: (800)621-7619
Fax: (630)285-1315
E-mail: info@nsc.org
URL: http://www.nsc.org
Contact: Alan C. McMillan, Pres./CEO
Founded: 1932. **Members:** 300. **Budget:** $65,000. **Description:** Assists and advises Highway Traffic Safety Division of the National Safety Council (see separate entry) in the development and implementation of council positions, programs, and activities. Purposes are to: develop, improve, and evaluate traffic records data systems; encourage the use of improved techniques and innovative procedures in the collection, storage, and use of traffic records data; coordinate traffic records system programs of the NSC, federal agencies, and other organizations for the benefit of state and local traffic records systems managers, including collectors and users of traffic records data. **Committees:** Standardizing Summaries; Standards. **Affiliated With:** National Safety Council. **Formerly:** Traffic Accident Data Committee; (1958) National Committee on Uniform Traffic Accidents Statistics; (1965) Committee on Uniform Traffic Accident Statistics; (1973) Traffic Accident Data Project Committee. **Publications:** *The Exchange,* 3/year. Newsletter. **Price:** free. **Circulation:** 500 ● *Forum Proceedings,* annual ● *Manual on Classification of Motor Vehicle Accidents* ● *Vehicle Damage Scale.* Paper. **Conventions/Meetings:** annual International Forum on Traffic Records Systems - conference and workshop (exhibits).

12717 ■ Veterans of Safety (VOS)
c/o Lyle M. Rice, Pres.
97141 Kapalama Dr.
Diamondhead, MS 39525
Ph: (228)586-9954
Fax: (228)586-1414
E-mail: info@vetsofsafety.org
URL: http://www.vetsofsafety.org
Contact: Lyle M. Rice, Pres.
Founded: 1941. **Members:** 1,805. **Local Groups:** 14. **Description:** Safety engineers with 15 or more years of professional safety experience; associate members are those with 10 or more years of experience. Seeks to promote safety in all fields. Includes activities such as: Most Precious Cargo Program, to improve school bus safety; Unified Emergency Telephone Numbers Program, to establish nationwide uniformity in emergency telephone numbers to contact fire, police, and medical aid. Promotes Have A Safe Day Program. Cosponsors professional paper award with American Society of Safety Engineers (see separate entry). Maintains museum and supports Safety and Health Hall of Fame. **Libraries:** Type: reference. **Subjects:** safety. **Awards:** Frequency: annual. **Type:** recognition. **Recipient:** for best technical safety papers published. **Publications:** Newsletter, bimonthly. **Conventions/Meetings:** annual meeting - always first day of National Safety Congress.

Scouting

12718 ■ Association of Baptists for Scouting (ABS)
c/o Boy Scouts of America
PO Box 152079
Irving, TX 75015-2079

E-mail: ebrown@calpha.com
URL: http://www.scouting.org/factsheets/02-647.html
Contact: Ed Brown, VP
Description: Baptists participating in Boy Scout programs. Promotes formation of scout troops in Baptist congregations. Recruits new scouts and adult leaders; facilitates formation of Baptist scout troops. **Awards:** ABS Good Shepherd Award. **Frequency:** annual. **Type:** recognition. **Recipient:** for adults ● ABS Unit Award of Excellence. **Frequency:** annual. **Type:** recognition.

12719 ■ Association of Girl Scout Executive Staff (AGSES)

1801 N Mill St., Ste.R
Naperville, IL 60563
Ph: (630)369-7781
Free: (888)817-8507
Fax: (630)369-3773
E-mail: sue@agses.org
URL: http://www.agses.org
Contact: Sue Peterson, Exec. Dir.
Founded: 1939. **Members:** 1,200. **Membership Dues:** active, $75 (annual) ● associate, $50 (annual) ● life, $750. **Budget:** $150,000. **Regional Groups:** 8. **Description:** Executive/management staff employed by local Girl Scout Councils and the Girl Scouts of the U.S.A. **Awards:** AGSES Hall of Fame. **Frequency:** triennial. **Type:** recognition. **Recipient:** for role models that embody AGSES values. **Affiliated With:** Girl Scouts of the U.S.A. **Formerly:** (1955) National Association of Girl Scout Executives; (1975) Association of Girl Scout Professional Workers. **Publications:** *Intercom*, quarterly. Newsletter. **Circulation:** 1,200. **Advertising:** accepted. Alternate Formats: online ● *Survey of Girl Scout Executives*. **Conventions/Meetings:** triennial meeting and convention (exhibits) ● semiannual meeting, on topics such as human relations, marketing, management, assertiveness training, supervision, fundraising, and pluralism.

12720 ■ Boy Scouts of America (BSA)

PO Box 152079
Irving, TX 75015-2079
Ph: (972)580-2000
Fax: (972)580-2502
URL: http://www.scouting.org
Contact: Roy Williams, Chief Scout Exec.
Founded: 1910. **Members:** 5,363,593. **Membership Dues:** regular, $10 (annual). **Staff:** 3,850. **Local Groups:** 310. **Description:** Tiger Cubs (age six); Cub Scouts (ages seven-ten); Boy Scouts (ages 11-18); Venturers (male and female, age 15-20); Lone Scouts; male and female adult leaders and volunteer workers. Educational program geared toward the character development, citizenship training, and mental and physical fitness of boys and young adults. Conducts studies on problems and needs of youth. Programs are offered through community-based religious, civic, and educational groups. Encourages in-school scouting and offers religious emblems created by major church denominations. Operates councils and districts in local communities; maintains museum; compiles statistics. **Awards:** Cub Scout Outdoor Activity Award. **Frequency:** annual. **Type:** recognition. **Recipient:** for Tiger Cubs, Wolf and Bear Cub Scouts and Webelos Scouts who completed the requirements for outdoor activity ● Distinguished Service Award. **Frequency:** annual. **Type:** recognition. **Recipient:** for distinguished service to youth ● Emergency Preparedness Award. **Frequency:** annual. **Type:** recognition. **Recipient:** for members who have fulfilled the requirements for emergency preparedness ● Hometown U.S.A. Award. **Frequency:** annual. **Type:** recognition. **Recipient:** for outstanding effort of scouts in the community ● Lifesaving or Meritorious Action Awards. **Frequency:** annual. **Type:** recognition. **Recipient:** for members who demonstrate heroism and risk their own life ● **Type:** scholarship. **Recipient:** to post high school students. **Affiliated With:** World Scout Bureau. **Publications:** *Boys' Life*, monthly. Magazine. Covers Boy Scout activities and other information of interest for Boy Scouts, Cub Scouts, and others between the ages of eight and eighteen. **Price:** $18.00/year (discount available to

members). ISSN: 0006-8608. **Circulation:** 1,400,000. **Advertising:** accepted ● *Scouting Magazine: A Family Magazine*, bimonthly. Contains information for adult leaders of BSA. Includes BSA memorabilia and family quiz. **Price:** included in membership dues. ISSN: 0036-9500. **Circulation:** 1,000,000. **Advertising:** accepted ● Annual Report, annual. Includes financial statements and balance sheet, statistics on membership units, BSA publication subscriptions, staff, and council, and notes. **Price:** free. **Circulation:** 5,000 ● Handbooks (in English, Laotian, Spanish, and Vietnamese) ● Manuals (in English, Laotian, Spanish, and Vietnamese) ● Pamphlets ● Also publishes more than 2,000 other BSA program items. **Conventions/Meetings:** competition ● biennial meeting.

12721 ■ Girl Scouts of the U.S.A. (GSUSA)

420 5th Ave.
New York, NY 10018-2798
Ph: (212)852-8000
Free: (800)478-7248
URL: http://www.girlscouts.org
Contact: Kathy Cloninger, CEO
Founded: 1912. **Members:** 3,800,000. **Membership Dues:** girl (ages 5 to 17)/adult (ages 18 and above), $10 (annual) ● life, $250. **Staff:** 450. **Local Groups:** 317. **Description:** Daisy Girl Scouts (ages 5-6 or grades K-1); Brownie Girl Scouts (ages 6-8 or grades 1-3); Junior Girl Scouts (ages 8-11 or grades 3-6); Cadette Girl Scouts (ages 11-14 or grades 6-9); Senior Girl Scouts (ages 14-17 or grades 9-12). Membership includes girls, adult volunteers, and professional workers. Promotes ethical code through the Girl Scout Promise and Law. Provides girls with opportunities to expand personal interests, learn new skills, and explore career possibilities as well as fun, friendship, and the power of girls together. Offers leadership training, international exchange programs, and conferences and workshops on topics ranging from management to sports. **Awards: Frequency:** annual. **Type:** recognition. **Affiliated With:** World Association of Girl Guides and Girl Scouts. **Publications:** *Girl Scout Research Institute Survey*, periodic. Contains data and statistical information on the social, physical, emotional issues facing girls today. ● *GSUSA News*, bimonthly. Newsletter. Covers Girl Scout-related items in the news, national and international highlights, programs, and national meetings. ● *LEADER*, quarterly. Magazine. Covers programs, troop activities, health and safety, and news about people and events in Girl Scouting/Girl Guiding. **Price:** included in membership dues. ISSN: 0017-0577 ● Annual Report, annual. Includes financial statements and membership statistics. **Conventions/Meetings:** triennial Policy Making Convention (exhibits).

12722 ■ Hungarian Scouts Association (HSA)

2850 State Rte. 23 N
Newfoundland, NJ 07435-1443
Ph: (973)208-0450
E-mail: kmcssz@aol.com
URL: http://www.kmcssz.org
Contact: Gabor Szorad, Gen. Sec.
Founded: 1945. **Membership Dues:** regular, $30 (annual). **Description:** Scouts of Hungarian descent. Aims to preserve Hungarian heritage and culture through scouting activities. Instructs on outdoor living and scouting skills; teaches moral and religious standards. Conducts leadership training program; compiles statistics; maintains museum. **Libraries: Type:** reference. **Holdings:** 5,000; books. **Subjects:** scouting subjects and the humanities. **Awards: Type:** recognition. **Publications:** *The History of Hungarian Scouting*. Book ● *Hungarian Boy Scout Association— Headquarters Bulletin* (in English and Hungarian), periodic. Newsletter. Contains information for association leaders covering official resolutions, decisions, regulations, orders, and declarations. **Price:** included in membership dues. **Circulation:** 2,000 ● *Hungarian Scout Magazine* (in English and Hungarian), semiannual. Contains information for children; covers scout meetings, jamborees, camping, hiking, scout skills, character building, sports, fiction, and humor. **Price:** included in membership dues. **Circula-**

tion: 2,000 ● *Kozponti Ertesito* (in English and Hungarian), semiannual. Proceedings ● *Scout Leaders Magazine* (in English and Hungarian), semiannual. Covers scout meetings, jamborees, camping, hiking, scout skills, character, building, sports, fiction, and humor. **Price:** included in membership dues. **Circulation:** 2,000 ● Handbooks. **Conventions/Meetings:** biennial conference (exhibits).

12723 ■ National Association of Presbyterian Scouters (NAPS)

c/o Programs of Religious Activities with Youth
8520 MacKenzie Rd.
St. Louis, MO 63123
Ph: (636)391-0734
E-mail: wray-diana@mindspring.com
URL: http://www.presbyterianscouters.org
Contact: Wray Johanning, Pres.
Founded: 1986. **Members:** 600. **Membership Dues:** individual, $20 (annual) ● life, $350. **Description:** Adult scouters and youths who are registered members of Boy Scouts of America and active members of a particular Presbyterian Congregation, Presbytery, or Synod. Promotes Presbyterian Congregations to participate in the Boy Scouts of America program. Encourages Presbyterian congregations to become charted partners of scouting troops; assists local councils of Boy Scouts of America in the promotion and chartering of scouting units in Presbyterian congregations. Promotes religious education. **Awards:** God and Country Program. **Type:** recognition. **Recipient:** for youths ● God and Service Award for Adults. **Type:** recognition. **Recipient:** for outstanding leadership at the local level. **Publications:** *The Presbyterian Scouter*, bimonthly. Newsletter. Contains information about NAPS and news items. **Price:** included in membership dues. Alternate Formats: online. **Conventions/Meetings:** annual convention (exhibits).

12724 ■ National Catholic Committee on Scouting (NCCS)

PO Box 152079
Irving, TX 75015-2079
Ph: (972)580-2114
E-mail: bbbtrcolt@aol.com
URL: http://www.nccs-bsa.org
Contact: Bray Barnes, Natl. Chm.
Founded: 1934. **Members:** 360,000. **Membership Dues:** regular, $35 (annual) ● life, $350. **Staff:** 2. **Budget:** $250,000. **Local Groups:** 178. **Description:** Functions on national and diocesan levels to advise national and local Boy Scouts of America (see separate entry) councils on principles and practices of the Catholic Church as they apply to the 11,000 Scout units in Catholic parishes. Promotes integration of Catholic teachings and practices in the program of scouting for Catholic youth and adults. Compiles statistics on scouting under Catholic auspices. **Awards:** Gold Medallion Award. **Frequency:** annual. **Type:** recognition. **Recipient:** for the outstanding Catholic Cub Scout Pack, Boy Scout Troop, and Venturing Crew in the 14 Episcopal Regions of the United States ● NCCS Award for Excellence. **Frequency:** biennial. **Type:** recognition. **Recipient:** for outstanding efforts of a diocese ● Silver St. George Adult Recognition Award. **Frequency:** annual. **Type:** recognition. **Recipient:** to dedicated members of a national organization. **Committees:** Religious Activities; Religious Emblems; Saint George Trek. **Programs:** Catholic Scouter Development and Training. **Formerly:** Bishops' Committee on Scouting; Catholic Committee on Scouting. **Publications:** *Bridge*, quarterly. Newsletter. **Circulation:** 1,000. Alternate Formats: online ● Handbook. Alternate Formats: online. **Conventions/Meetings:** biennial meeting - always spring, even-numbered years.

12725 ■ National Eagle Scout Association (NESA)

c/o Boy Scouts of America
1325 W Walnut Hill Ln.
PO Box 152079
Irving, TX 75015-2079
Ph: (972)580-2000

Fax: (972)580-2399
URL: http://www.nesa.org
Contact: Terry C. Lawson, Natl. Dir.
Founded: 1972. **Members:** 292,000. **Membership Dues:** regular, $25 (quinquennial) ● life, $180. **Staff:** 6. **Description:** Boy Scouts, Venturers, and adults who have attained the Eagle Scout rank and wish to give continued service to the Boy Scout movement and local communities. Emphasizes high ideals and standards of personal conduct; promotes leadership, fellowship, citizenship, and a spirit of service among all Scouts; encourages Scout advancement. **Convention/Meeting:** none. **Libraries: Type:** not open to the public. **Awards:** NESA Scholarships. **Frequency:** annual. **Type:** scholarship. **Recipient:** for Eagle Scouts graduating from high school. **Supersedes:** Knights of Dunamis. **Publications:** *Eagletter*, 3/year. Newsletter. Contains news of Eagle Scouts, including promotions, obituaries, etc. **Price:** included in membership dues. **Circulation:** 290,000.

12726 ■ National Jewish Committee on Scouting (NJCS)
PO Box 152079
Irving, TX 75015-2079
Ph: (610)356-5165
Fax: (610)356-6713
E-mail: peh51@aol.com
URL: http://www.jewishscouting.org
Contact: Rabbi Peter Hyman, Chm.
Founded: 1926. **Members:** 60. **Membership Dues:** regular, $25 (annual). **Staff:** 1. **Regional Groups:** 4. **State Groups:** 50. **Local Groups:** 150. **Description:** Assists national and local Jewish organizations interested in promoting and strengthening Jewish identities through Scouting programs. Advises Boy Scouts of America (see separate entry) on matters concerning religious policy. Prepares program material to meet the needs of the Jewish community. Assists local councils in organizing Jewish committees on Scouting. Administers by the Relationships Division of Boy Scouts of America. **Libraries: Type:** reference. **Awards:** Aleph Award for Webelos Scouts. **Type:** recognition. **Recipient:** for Jewish Cub Scouts (grades 3 to 5) ● Chester M. Vernon Memorial Eagle Scout Scholarship Program. **Frequency:** annual. **Type:** recognition. **Recipient:** to a youth Eagle Scout ● Etz Chaim Award for Venturer and older Boy Scouts in grades nine and above. **Type:** recognition. **Recipient:** for Jewish Boy Scouts ● Florence & Marvin Arkans Eagle Scout Scholarship. **Frequency:** annual. **Type:** recognition. **Recipient:** for graduating senior high school Eagle Scout ● Frank Weil Award. **Frequency:** annual. **Type:** scholarship. **Recipient:** for Eagle Scouts and graduating seniors ● Maccabee Award for Tiger Cubs. **Type:** recognition. **Recipient:** for Jewish Cub Scouts (grades 1 to 3) ● Ner Tamid Emblem for Boy Scouts and Venturers. **Type:** recognition. **Recipient:** for Jewish Boy Scouts ● Shofar Award. **Type:** recognition. **Recipient:** for adult volunteers. **Computer Services:** Mailing lists. **Affiliated With:** Boy Scouts of America. **Conventions/Meetings:** conference and workshop - 3/year usually February, June, and October.

12727 ■ National Jewish Girl Scout Committee (NJGSC)
33 Central Dr.
Bronxville, NY 10708-4603
Ph: (914)738-3986 (718)252-6072
E-mail: njgsc@aol.com
URL: http://www.njgsc.org
Contact: Adele Wasko, Field Chm.
Founded: 1972. **Members:** 100. **Description:** Purposes are to: promote Girl Scouting within the Jewish community; encourage participation in Jewish award programs and religious services; promote exchanges with the Israeli Boy and Girl Scout Federation; advise Girl Scouts of the U.S.A. on religious policy. **Awards: Type:** recognition ● **Type:** scholarship. **Recipient:** for Girl Scouts participating in the Summer Scouting in Israel exchange program. **Formerly:** (1995) National Jewish Girl Scout Committee of the Synagogue Council of American. **Publications:** *Craft Ideas for Jewish Holidays/More Ideas for Jewish Holidays*. Includes craft projects for Jewish Holidays.

Price: $3.00 ● Newsletter, semiannual. Covers the annual meeting and activities of the committee. Includes annual membership list. **Price:** included in membership dues ● Brochures ● Books. **Price:** $3.00 ● Also publishes guidelines for award programs. **Conventions/Meetings:** annual meeting - always October.

12728 ■ Order of the Arrow (OA)
1325 W Walnut Hill Ln.
PO Box 152079
Irving, TX 75015-2079
Ph: (972)580-2438
Fax: (972)580-2399
E-mail: webmaster@oa-bsa.org
URL: http://www.oa-bsa.org
Contact: Clyde M. Mayer, Dir.
Founded: 1915. **Members:** 183,000. **Membership Dues:** regular, $2 (annual). **Staff:** 4. **Regional Groups:** 4. **Local Groups:** 313. **Description:** Boy Scouts, Varsity Scouts, and adult scout leaders who are qualified as first class scouts and campers (15 or more days and nights of camping) and elected as honor campers by members of their own units. Promotes scout camping and provides for leadership development, membership extension, adventurous programming and service to scouting and the community. **Awards:** Distinguished Service Award. **Frequency:** biennial. **Type:** recognition ● Head Arrow Award. **Frequency:** biennial. **Type:** recognition ● Lifetime Achievement Award. **Frequency:** biennial. **Type:** recognition. **Committees:** Communication and Marketing; Finance; Leadership Development; Lodge Operations; National Events; Outdoor Program; Recognition and Awards; Section and Region Operations. **Councils:** Founders'. **Affiliated With:** Boy Scouts of America. **Formerly:** (1934) WWW Wimachtendienk, Wingolauchsik, Witahemui. **Publications:** *Ceremony for the Brotherhood*. Book ● *Ceremony for the Ordeal*. Book ● *Ceremony for the Vigil Honor*. Book ● *Guide for Officers and Advisers*. Book ● *National Bulletin*, quarterly. **Price:** $10.00 2-year subscription. Alternate Formats: online ● *2005 Lodge Program Resource Book*. Alternate Formats: online ● Handbooks. **Conventions/Meetings:** biennial meeting.

12729 ■ Scouting For All (S4A)
PO Box 2832
Petaluma, CA 94953-2832
Ph: (707)778-0564
E-mail: info@scoutingforall.org
URL: http://www.scoutingforall.org
Contact: Scott Cozza, Pres./Co-Founder
Membership Dues: individual, $20 (annual) ● limited income, $10 (annual) ● household, $40 (annual) ● benefactor, $50 (annual). **Staff:** 6. **Description:** Advocates for the restoration of the values of scouting as expressed and embodied in the Scout Oath and the Scout Law. Aims to influence the Boy Scouts of America (BSA) to serve and include as participating members all youth and adult leaders, regardless of their spiritual belief, gender or sexual orientation. **Publications:** Brochure. Alternate Formats: online.

Seamen

12730 ■ North American Maritime Ministry Association (NAMMA)
c/o Rev. Lloyd Burghart, Exec. Sec.
PO Box 2434
Niagara Falls, NY 14302
Ph: (905)892-8818
E-mail: namma@cogeco.ca
URL: http://www.namma.org
Contact: Rev. Lloyd Burghart, Exec. Sec.
Founded: 1932. **Members:** 100. **Membership Dues:** ministry (not affiliated with a dues-paying agency), $70 (annual) ● ministry (associated with a dues paying agency), $45 (annual) ● agency (with less than $250,000 annual budget), $250 (annual). **Staff:** 1. **Budget:** $50,000. **Regional Groups:** 5. **Local Groups:** 50. **Multinational. Description:** Spiritual and social welfare agencies from the U.S., Canada,

and the Caribbean providing facilities and services for merchant seafarers. Sponsors Chaplain Training School; operates placement service. Maintains archives; conducts research programs. **Awards:** Meritorious Service. **Frequency:** annual. **Type:** recognition. **Recipient:** for retired officers. **Formerly:** (1968) National Council of Seamen's Agencies; (1991) International Council of Seamen's Agencies. **Publications:** *Waterlines*, quarterly. Newsletter. Contains news of ministry to merchant seafarers. **Price:** free. **Circulation:** 700. **Advertising:** accepted. **Conventions/Meetings:** annual conference (exhibits).

12731 ■ United Seamen's Service (USS)
635 Fourth Ave., Ground Fl.
Brooklyn, NY 11232
Ph: (212)269-0711 (718)369-3818
E-mail: ussammla@ix.netcom.com
URL: http://www.uss-ammla.com
Contact: Talmage E. Simpkins, Pres.
Founded: 1942. **Membership Dues:** regular, $25 (annual) ● special, $50 (annual) ● sponsor, $100 (annual) ● patron, $300 (annual) ● benefactor, $500 (annual). **Staff:** 10. **Description:** Promotes the welfare of American seafarers and their dependents, seafarers of all nations, and other persons engaged in the maritime industry. Provides health, welfare, and recreation services to American merchant mariners and seafarers worldwide through a network of 10 overseas centers. Implements U.S. commitments to 1936 Geneva Resolutions; conducts hospital and shipboard visits; assists with detention, repatriation, legal aid, and liaison with local authorities; provides currency exchange, transfer of funds, postal, and phone and cable services; offers money orders, souvenirs, and food and beverages. **Libraries: Type:** not open to the public. **Holdings:** books, periodicals. **Awards:** Ocean Crew and Great Lake Crew Award of Merit. **Type:** recognition. **Recipient:** for contributions to AMMLA. **Affiliated With:** American Merchant Marine Library Association. **Publications:** *AOTOS Journal*, annual. Honors those who have contributed much to the maritime industry in the previous year. **Price:** free. **Circulation:** 800. **Advertising:** accepted ● *The Maritime Industrial Revolution* ● *The Modern Seafarer* ● *Symposia Reports*, periodic ● *USS Annual Reports*, semiannual. Newsletter. Reports on association and affiliate activities. **Price:** free. **Circulation:** 3,000 ● *USS Narrative Report*, quarterly. Newsletter. **Conventions/Meetings:** annual meeting - usually second Wednesday of May in New York City.

Security

12732 ■ International Association of Professional Protection Specialists (IAPPS)
5255 Stevens Creek Blvd., Ste.308
Santa Clara, CA 95051
Free: (888)671-6803
Fax: (888)671-6803
E-mail: membership@iapps.org
URL: http://www.iapps.org
Founded: 1990. **Membership Dues:** associate, $100 (annual) ● professional, $75 (annual) ● corporate, $1,500 (annual). **Multinational. Description:** Supports professional protectors. Facilitates access to contemporary and superior security training and education. **Publications:** *Intelligent Insight*. Newsletter. Alternate Formats: online.

Self Defense

12733 ■ American Women's Self-Defense Association (AWSDA)
713 N Wellwood Ave.
Lindenhurst, NY 11757
Ph: (631)225-6262
Free: (888)STOP-RAPE
Fax: (631)226-5454

E-mail: awsda@nvbb.net
URL: http://www.awsda.org
Contact: Paula McCallum, Exec. Dir.
Founded: 1990. **Membership Dues:** general, $45 (annual). **Multinational. Description:** Aims to end violence against women. Provides training programs and services designed to increase awareness of self defense and rape prevention. **Computer Services:** database, listing of international trainers by state and country. **Publications:** *The Fisted Rose*, quarterly. Newsletter. Contains self-defense articles. **Conventions/Meetings:** annual Self Defense Training - seminar.

12734 ■ Mothers Arms (MA)
4757 E Greenway Rd., 107B No. 124
Phoenix, AZ 85032
Free: (800)464-4840
E-mail: awadas@mothersarms.org
URL: http://www.mothersarms.org
Contact: Alicia A. Wadas, Pres./Founder
Founded: 2000. **Membership Dues:** family, $35 (annual) ● individual, $20 (annual) ● student, $15 (annual) ● organization, $250 (annual) ● family - life, $850 ● individual - life, $500 ● organization - life, $2,500. **Languages:** English, Spanish. **Description:** Promotes self-defense. Educates women on how to defend and protect themselves and their children from assault and aggression. Enables women to develop awareness of their surroundings, gain common-sense safety skills and use safety defense tools. Provides safety information, guidance and support to help women and their families stay safe and secure. **Libraries: Type:** reference. **Holdings:** books, software, video recordings. **Also Known As:** Safely in Mothers Arms. **Publications:** *The Sentinel*. Newsletter. Alternate Formats: online.

Selfhelp

12735 ■ Adult Children of Alcoholics World Service Organization (ACA WSO)
PO Box 3216
Torrance, CA 90510
Ph: (310)534-1815
E-mail: info@adultchildren.org
URL: http://www.adultchildren.org
Founded: 1987. **National Groups:** 551. **Multinational. Description:** Spiritually-based, 12-Step, 12-Tradition, support groups focused on understanding the specific behavior and attitude patterns developed while growing up in alcoholic or other dysfunctional environments. **Computer Services:** Online services. **Affiliated With:** Alcoholics Anonymous World Services. **Formerly:** Adult Children of Alcoholics, Central Service Board. **Publications:** *ComLine*, monthly. Newsletter. **Price:** $14.00/year ● *Operating Policies and Procedures Manual*. Alternate Formats: diskette ● Will publish a Handbook for the membership within the next few years; also various pieces of official literature. **Conventions/Meetings:** annual general assembly and meeting, with business meeting - every 4th weekend of April.

12736 ■ American Self-Help Group Clearinghouse
100 E Hanover Ave., Ste.202
Cedar Knolls, NJ 07927-2020
Ph: (973)326-6789
Free: (800)367-6274
Fax: (973)326-9467
E-mail: njshc@cybernex.net
URL: http://www.selfhelpgroups.org
Contact: Edward J. Madara, Dir.
Founded: 1986. **Staff:** 5. **Budget:** $120,000. **Non-membership. Description:** Seeks to provide individuals with information and contacts for all types of national self-help support groups. Offers information on state and local self-help clearinghouses; provides suggestions and models for creating local groups and national networks should none exist in certain areas. **Libraries: Type:** reference. **Holdings:** books, clippings. **Subjects:** mutual aid self-help groups. **Formerly:** (2000) American Self-Help Clearinghouse.

12737 ■ A.R.T.S. Anonymous
PO Box 230175
New York, NY 10023
Ph: (212)873-7075
E-mail: artsevents@earthlink.net
URL: http://www.arts-on-the-net.com/artsanonymous/index.html
Contact: Abigail Brown, Founder
Founded: 1984. **Members:** 1,200. **Staff:** 1. **Local Groups:** 50. **Languages:** Dutch, English, French. **Description:** Artists who share experiences with each other in order to draw out creativity. Adapts the 12 steps of Alcoholics Anonymous World Services to the goal of assisting others in achieving creative freedom. **Also Known As:** Artists Recovering Through the Twelve Steps. **Publications:** Articles, quarterly. **Price:** $1.50. **Conventions/Meetings:** annual convention, for members only - in May.

12738 ■ Clutterers Anonymous (CLA)
PO Box 91413
Los Angeles, CA 90009-1413
Ph: (310)281-6064
E-mail: clawso@hotmail.com
URL: http://www.clutterersanonymous.net
Description: Fellowship of individuals sharing experience, strength and hope to solve common problem of clutter and help others recover and bring more order to their lives. **Conventions/Meetings:** meeting.

12739 ■ Co-Dependents Anonymous (CoDA)
PO Box 33577
Phoenix, AZ 85067-3577
Ph: (602)277-7991
E-mail: outreach@coda.org
URL: http://www.codependents.org
Contact: David L., Chm.
Founded: 1986. **Members:** 50,000. **Staff:** 1. **Regional Groups:** 2. **State Groups:** 30. **Local Groups:** 25. **National Groups:** 300. **Multinational. Description:** Self-help group based on an adaptation of the 12-step program of Alcoholics Anonymous World Services. Conducts recovery program for co-dependents, nationally and worldwide. **Libraries: Type:** reference. **Additional Websites:** http://www.coda.org. **Publications:** *Co-NNECTIONS*, quarterly. Newsletter. **Price:** $8.00/year. Alternate Formats: online ● *CODA Book* ● *Listening and Sharing at a Meeting*. Pamphlet ● *Newcomers Handbook* ● *Welcome to CoDA*. Pamphlet ● *What is Co-Dependency*. Pamphlet ● Audiotapes. **Conventions/Meetings:** annual conference, state and regional delegates and board members meet - usually fall ● biennial convention - odd numbered years.

12740 ■ Debtors Anonymous (DA)
PO Box 920888
Needham, MA 02492-0009
Ph: (781)453-2743
Fax: (781)453-2745
E-mail: new@debtorsanonymous.org
URL: http://www.debtorsanonymous.org
Founded: 1976. **Staff:** 2. **Budget:** $125,000. **State Groups:** 26. **Local Groups:** 420. **Description:** Fellowship of men and women who share their experience, strength, and hope with each other that they may solve their common problem of compulsive debiting. Adapts the Twelve Steps and Twelve Traditions of Alcoholics Anonymous World Services for compulsive debtors. Establishes and coordinates self help support groups for people seeking to live without incurring unsecured debt. Helps members develop workable plans for long-term financial and lifestyle goals. **Boards:** General Service. **Publications:** *Communicating with Creditors*. Pamphlet ● *Debt Payment*. Pamphlet ● *The P.I Manual*. Alternate Formats: online ● *Pressure Groups and Pressure Meetings* ● *Ways and Means*, quarterly. Newsletter. **Price:** $8.00/year (1-4 subscriptions); $7.00/year (5-9 subscriptions); $6.00/year (10 or more subscriptions). Alternate Formats: online ● Books ● Pamphlets ● Brochures ● Handbooks. **Price:** $2.00 ● Book- "A Currency of Hope" published Spring 1999. **Conventions/Meetings:** annual conference.

12741 ■ Delancey Street Foundation (DSF)
600 Embarcadero
San Francisco, CA 94107
Ph: (415)957-9800
Fax: (415)512-5186
E-mail: rgarr@grass-roots.org
URL: http://www.grass-roots.org/usa/delancey.shtml
Contact: Dr. Mimi Halper Silbert PhD, Pres.
Founded: 1971. **Members:** 2,000. **State Groups:** 2. **National Groups:** 3. **Description:** Former convicts, substance abusers, and prostitutes. Self help organization providing educational and vocational training programs in California, New Mexico, New York, and North Carolina. Conducts charitable activities.

12742 ■ Deliver the Dream
3223 NW 10th Terr., Ste.602
Fort Lauderdale, FL 33309
Ph: (954)564-3512
Free: (888)687-3732
E-mail: contact@deliverthedream.org
URL: http://www.deliverthedream.org
Contact: Pat Moran, Founder/CEO
Founded: 1998. **Description:** Mountain retreat and enrichment center for families and individuals in crisis. Provides hiking, horseback riding and other outdoor activities to establish a supportive environment. **Computer Services:** Mailing lists, of members. **Publications:** *DreamNotes*, periodic. Bulletin. Contains the latest news from the organization. Alternate Formats: online ● *Mending Spirits*, quarterly. Newsletter.

12743 ■ Gainsharing Institute
937 N Ashland Ave.
Chicago, IL 60622
Ph: (773)661-9070
Fax: (773)661-1902
E-mail: pavgain@aol.com
Contact: Michael Pavilon, Pres.
Founded: 1987. **Members:** 50. **Membership Dues:** educational, $1,000 (annual). **Staff:** 3. **Budget:** $100,000. **Regional Groups:** 2. **Description:** Promotes reward and recognition system for employees that augments and/or replaces part of the monthly compensation; it is almost always coupled with a problem solving system. **Publications:** none. **Libraries: Type:** reference. **Holdings:** archival material. **Computer Services:** Mailing lists. **Telecommunication Services:** phone referral service, for programs, (700)THE-CLUB. **Formed by Merger of:** United Self-Help Success Clubs. **Conventions/Meetings:** periodic Gainsharing Fundamentals - seminar (exhibits).

12744 ■ ManKind Project (MKP)
PO Box 230
Malone, NY 12953-0230
Free: (800)870-4611
E-mail: administrator@mkp.org
URL: http://www.mkp.org
Contact: Drury Heffernan, Admin.
Founded: 1985. **Members:** 8,000. **Staff:** 25. **Budget:** $1,500,000. **Regional Groups:** 20. **Multinational. Description:** Seeks to help men reclaim their warrior masculine sides in order to reach a healthy balance between the individual and community. Conducts weekend trainings involving initiation, self-examination, and physical training activities. **Awards:** Network Scholarship. **Frequency:** periodic. **Type:** scholarship. **Computer Services:** Mailing lists, of members. **Telecommunication Services:** electronic mail, dhnwmtl@aol.com. **Publications:** Brochure. Alternate Formats: online. **Conventions/Meetings:** semiannual board meeting.

12745 ■ Marijuana Anonymous World Services (MA)
PO Box 2912
Van Nuys, CA 91404
Free: (800)766-6779
E-mail: office@marijuana-anonymous.org
URL: http://www.marijuana-anonymous.org
Multinational. Description: Individuals wishing to stop using marijuana. Strives to remain free from marijuana addiction; supports other users to help break their addiction, using the basic 12 Steps of

Recovery founded by Alcoholics Anonymous. **Computer Services:** Online services, penpal service. **Publications:** *A New Leaf.* Newsletter. **Price:** $15.00/year in U.S.; $20.00/year in Canada and Mexico; $25.00/year for overseas ● *Life With Hope: A Return to Living Through the 12 Steps and 12 Traditions of Marijuana Anonymous.* Book. **Price:** $9.00/copy. **Circulation:** 8,000 ● Manual. Contains MA policy on everything from meeting commitments to the election of delegates and trustees. **Price:** $10.00 each. **Conventions/Meetings:** meeting.

12746 ■ Messies Anonymous (MA)
5025 SW 114th Ave.
Miami, FL 33165
Ph: (305)271-8404
Fax: (786)243-2793
E-mail: nestbuilder@earthlink.net
URL: http://www.messies.com
Contact: Sandra Felton, Founder
Founded: 1980. **Members:** 15,000. **Languages:** English, German, Spanish. **For-Profit. Description:** Teaches chronically disorganized people, known as Messies, to become more organized. Endorses the Mt. Vernon Method of organizing: those organizing begin working in one corner of the house and continue through the house until they have reached the corner in which they began. Encourages use of the Flipper System: a series of flip cards containing chores, schedules, menus, and shopping needs. Helps individuals form self-help groups at the local level. Seeks to meet the needs of special groups such as elderly, men, people with ADD, teachers, and others. **Computer Services:** Online services, self help groups. **Affiliated With:** National Association of Professional Organizers. **Publications:** *Meditations for Messies.* Book. **Price:** $10.00 ● *Messie No More.* Book. **Price:** $12.99 retail; $11.50 silver anniversary special ● *Neat Mom, Messie Kids.* Book. **Price:** $11.99 retail; $10.50 silver anniversary special ● *The New Messies Manual.* **Price:** $12.99 retail; $11.50 silver anniversary special ● *When You Live With a Messie.* Book. **Price:** $6.99 ● Books ● Audiotapes ● Videos ● These books above have been translated into German and distributed in Germany. Also in Spanish. **Conventions/Meetings:** competition ● seminar, on housekeeping techniques ● workshop.

12747 ■ Molesters Anonymous (M.AN)
Address Unknown since 2007
Founded: 1986. **Members:** 1,000. **Staff:** 1. **Regional Groups:** 10. **Description:** Selfhelp group for child molesters. **Publications:** *M.AN Program.* Book ● *Self Help Counseling for Men Who Molest Children.* **Price:** $9.95. **Circulation:** 1,000. **Advertising:** not accepted.

12748 ■ National Association for Shoplifting Prevention (NASP)
380 N Broadway, Ste.306
Jericho, NY 11753
Ph: (516)932-0165
Free: (800)848-9595
Fax: (516)932-9393
E-mail: nasp@shopliftingprevention.org
URL: http://www.shopliftersalternative.org
Contact: Peter D. Berlin, Founder
Founded: 1989. **Membership Dues:** individual, $50 (annual) ● justice agency, $100 (annual) ● affiliate agency, $475 (annual) ● student, $25 (annual) ● government/non-profit agency, $185 (biennial). **Staff:** 15. **Languages:** English, Spanish. **Description:** Provides educational rehabilitation programs for juveniles and adults with shoplifting problems. Applies modern behavioral techniques to terminate stealing habits and convert shoplifters into honest consumers. Works with both individuals and the courts. Offers self-help groups and referral counseling treatment. Compiles statistics; conducts research. **Additional Websites:** http://www.shopliftingprevention.org. **Formerly:** Shoplifters Alternative; (1988) Shoplifters Anonymous International; (2005) Shoplifters Anonymous. **Publications:** *National Report on Shoplifting,* semiannual. Newsletter. Contains information for retailers and the

criminal justice system. **Price:** $30.00/2 years. **Circulation:** 35,000.

12749 ■ National Self-Help Clearinghouse (NSHC)
c/o Graduate School & University Center of the City University of New York
365 5th Ave., Ste.3300
New York, NY 10016
Ph: (212)817-1822
E-mail: info@selfhelpweb.org
URL: http://www.selfhelpweb.org
Contact: Frank Riessman, Dir.
Founded: 1976. **Staff:** 2. **Nonmembership. Description:** Clearinghouse on self-help groups; provides referral services. Conducts research and training activities. Maintains speakers' bureau. Conventions/Meetings: none. **Libraries: Type:** reference. **Holdings:** 200. **Subjects:** self-help, support groups. **Publications:** Books ● Brochures ● Manuals ● Reports.

12750 ■ Nicotine Anonymous World Services (NAWS)
419 Main St., PMB No. 370
Huntington Beach, CA 92648
Ph: (415)750-0328
E-mail: info@nicotine-anonymous.org
URL: http://nicotine-anonymous.org
Languages: English, French, German, Portuguese, Spanish. **Description:** Seeks to help individuals quit smoking and get free of nicotine; provides 12-step program of quitting nicotine use. **Publications:** *Seven Minutes,* quarterly. Newsletter. **Price:** $9.00/year in U.S.; $11.00/year in Canada; $14.00/year overseas ● Books ● Pamphlets. **Conventions/Meetings:** annual conference.

12751 ■ Protecting Adult Welfare (PAW)
c/o William Margold
17400 Marilla St.
Northridge, CA 91325
Ph: (818)998-5400
Free: (800)506-4999
Fax: (775)871-6544
E-mail: info@pawfoundation.org
URL: http://www.pawfoundation.org
Contact: Phillip Berman PhD, Chm.
Founded: 1995. **Description:** Seeks to utilize a network of telephone awareness help lines, peer counseling sessions, specialized enlightenment seminars and practical experience services. Offers educational, charitable, and research programs. Maintains a speakers bureau. **Formerly:** (1998) Protect Adult Welfare. **Publications:** *The PAW Report,* periodic. Bulletin. **Conventions/Meetings:** periodic conference.

12752 ■ Sex Workers Anonymous
3395 S Jones Blvd., Ste.217
Las Vegas, NV 89146-6729
Ph: (702)953-6024
E-mail: sexworkrecovery@yahoo.com
URL: http://sexworkersanonymouswso.com
Contact: Jody Williams, Contact
Founded: 1985. **Members:** 100,000. **Staff:** 1. **Description:** Men and women who have been involved in prostitution, phone sex, nude dancing, pornography, mistressing, or any other form of commercial sex activities. Offers members a 12-step program for recovery from prostitution. Provides support for members by discussing experiences and problems in person, through the mail, or over the phone. Maintains speakers' bureau. **Libraries: Type:** open to the public. **Holdings:** books, video recordings. **Subjects:** prostitution. **Awards:** Volunteer Award. **Type:** recognition. **Formerly:** (2002) Prostitutes Anonymous. **Publications:** *No Sale,* monthly. Newsletter ● *Sold Out.* Book. **Price:** $15.00 each (covers all shipping and handling); $10.00 each (if ordering 10 or more books) ● Videos.

12753 ■ SOL
PO Box 2276
North Canton, OH 44720
Ph: (330)497-9645

E-mail: sol_org@yahoo.com
Contact: David H. Ries, Contact
Founded: 1980. **Members:** 300. **Membership Dues:** individual, $15 (annual) ● sustaining, $25 (annual) ● supporting patron, $75 (annual). **Staff:** 18. **Description:** Individuals interested in taking charge of their lives, using discernment in decision-making and stress management through meditation. Encourages individuals to take personal responsibility for their lives. Offers training in meditation. Fosters the development of members' inner strength through participation in charitable activities. **Libraries: Type:** open to the public. **Holdings:** 100. **Subjects:** spiritual, metaphysical. **Formerly:** Sons of Light. **Publications:** *The Council I.* Video ● *The Council II.* Video ● *The Council on Genesis II, A Personal Revelation.* Book. **Price:** $5.00 plus shipping and handling ● *5 Steps to Spirituality.* Audiotape ● *Insights From The Council.* Book. **Price:** $5.00 plus shipping and handling ● *Life After Death, A New Revelation.* Book. **Price:** $14.95 plus shipping and handling ● *Life After Death, A New Revelation.* Audiotape. **Price:** $9.00 ● *The Living Fountain Meditation Tape.* Audiotape ● *Lost Parable.* Book. **Price:** $3.00 plus shipping and handling ● *Meditation Package: A Definitive Study.* Book. **Price:** $14.00 plus shipping and handling ● *On the Brink: The Coming of AIDS.* Book. **Price:** $5.00 plus shipping and handling ● *Promises, A Metaphysical Approach to Marriage and Parenting.* Book. **Price:** $6.00 plus shipping and handling ● *Spiritual Harvest.* Book. **Price:** $14.95 plus shipping and handling. **Conventions/Meetings:** annual Universal Being - conference and lecture, on holistic subjects (exhibits) - in October.

12754 ■ Workaholics Anonymous (WA)
World Ser. Org.
PO Box 289
Menlo Park, CA 94026-0289
Ph: (510)273-9253
E-mail: wso@workaholics-anonymous.org
URL: http://www.workaholics-anonymous.org
Founded: 1983. **Nonmembership. Multinational. Description:** Provides support, education, and recovery programs to workaholics, their families and friends. **Computer Services:** Mailing lists ● online services. **Publications:** *Living In Balance,* quarterly. Newsletter. Contains stories, member activities, meetings and world service offices. Alternate Formats: online. **Conventions/Meetings:** biennial conference (exhibits).

Service Clubs

12755 ■ Active 20-30 Association of U.S./Canada
915 L St., Ste.1000
Sacramento, CA 95814
Ph: (916)447-3217
Fax: (916)442-0382
E-mail: info@active20-30.com
URL: http://www.active20-30.com
Contact: Karen Roberts, Exec. Dir.
Founded: 1922. **Members:** 1,065. **Membership Dues:** with name badge, $30 (annual) ● without name badge, $25 (annual). **Staff:** 3. **Budget:** $120,000. **Regional Groups:** 3. **Local Groups:** 38. **Description:** Business and professional men and women between the ages of 20 and 40 interested in citizenship, fellowship, and community betterment. **Libraries: Type:** not open to the public. **Holdings:** 10. **Subjects:** membership recruitment/retention, club news, calendar. **Computer Services:** database ● mailing lists. **Committees:** National Board. **Formed by Merger of:** Active International; 20-30 International. **Formerly:** (1982) Active 20-30 International. **Publications:** *The Active Twenty-Thirtian,* quarterly. Newsletter. Covers leadership, conducting meetings, and volunteer activities. Includes annual directory and list of national officers. **Price:** included in membership dues. **Circulation:** 2,000. Alternate Formats: online ● *Active 20-30 Club Operations Manual.* Alternate Formats: online ● *Anniversary*

Video. **Price:** $12.00. **Conventions/Meetings:** annual convention - June-August.

12756 ■ Altrusa International (AI)
332 S Michigan Ave., Ste.1123
Chicago, IL 60604
Ph: (312)427-4410
Fax: (312)427-8521
E-mail: info@altrusa.com
URL: http://www.altrusa.com
Contact: Ms. Regina Baras, Exec. Dir.
Founded: 1917. **Members:** 17,500. **Membership Dues:** individual/reinstating, $45 (annual). **Staff:** 8. **Budget:** $849,400. **Regional Groups:** 15. **Description:** Represents executives and professionals organized to "help resolve civic and social welfare problems within the community and the world and promote international understanding". Designs and implements community service projects such as Action for Literacy. Supports the AI Foundation, which sponsors the Literacy and Community Service of local clubs. **Awards:** Community Leadership Award. **Frequency:** annual. **Type:** monetary. **Recipient:** for significant contributions to the community as volunteer leaders ● Dr. Nina Fay Calhoun International Relations Award. **Frequency:** annual. **Type:** monetary. **Recipient:** for outstanding club achievement in international relations ● Letha H. Brown Literacy Award. **Frequency:** annual. **Type:** monetary. **Recipient:** for established literacy projects ● Mamie L. Bass Service Award. **Frequency:** annual. **Type:** monetary. **Recipient:** for outstanding service in the community. **Telecommunication Services:** electronic mail, altrusa@altrusa.com. **Committees:** International Communications; International Service Program Development; Leadership Development. **Publications:** *International Altrusa Accent*, quarterly. Magazine. **Circulation:** 16,000 ● *International Altrusan*, quarterly. Newsletter. Alternate Formats: online. **Conventions/Meetings:** biennial convention (exhibits).

12757 ■ AMBUCS
PO Box 5127
High Point, NC 27262
Ph: (336)852-0052
Free: (800)838-1845
Fax: (336)852-6830
E-mail: ambucs@ambucs.org
URL: http://www.ambucs.org
Contact: J. Joseph Copeland, Exec. Dir.
Founded: 1922. **Members:** 6,000. **Staff:** 7. **Regional Groups:** 6. **Description:** Local service clubs. Dedicated to creating opportunities for independence for people with disabilities. Each chapter also adopts a major civic project to coincide with mission statement. **Awards:** AMBUCS Scholars. **Frequency:** annual. **Type:** scholarship. **Recipient:** for students entering the fields of speech and hearing, and physical and occupational therapy. **Computer Services:** database. **Formerly:** National Association of American Business Clubs. **Publications:** *AMBUC Leader*, monthly. Newsletter ● *National AMBUC Directory*, annual ● Magazine, quarterly ● Reports. Alternate Formats: online. **Conventions/Meetings:** annual convention (exhibits) - usually in July.

12758 ■ Assistance League (AL)
PO Box 6637
Burbank, CA 91510-6637
Ph: (818)846-3777
Fax: (818)846-3535
E-mail: info@assistanceleague.org
URL: http://www.assistanceleague.org
Contact: Judy Mullin, Pres.
Founded: 1935. **Members:** 24,000. **Membership Dues:** regular, $25 (annual). **Staff:** 7. **Budget:** $1,200,000. **Local Groups:** 116. **Description:** Aims to "act as a friend at any and all times to men, women and children in need of care, guidance and assistance, spiritually, materially and physically." Each chapter controls and administers at least one self-sustaining philanthropic project. Projects include boys' clubs, children's theatre guilds, clothing centers, day nurseries, dental centers, family services, geriatric programs, girls' clubs, centers for the hearing-, visually-, and speech-impaired, homemaker service, hospital equipment bank, toy loans, volunteer bureaus, well-baby clinics, and youth employment service. **Libraries:** **Type:** reference. **Holdings:** audiovisuals, books, business records, periodicals. **Formerly:** (2006) National Assistance League. **Publications:** *NewsLink*, semiannual. Newsletter. **Conventions/Meetings:** annual meeting - always October.

12759 ■ Carnegie Hero Fund Commission (CHFC)
425 6th Ave., Ste.1640
Pittsburgh, PA 15219-1823
Ph: (412)281-1302
Free: (800)447-8900
Fax: (412)281-5751
E-mail: carnegiehero@carnegiehero.org
URL: http://www.carnegiehero.org
Contact: Mark Laskow, Pres.
Founded: 1904. **Members:** 21. **Description:** Recognizes and rewards heroism voluntarily performed at risk of life by civilians in the U.S. and Canada in saving or attempting to save the lives of others; grants monetary assistance to persons disabled in such efforts or to the dependents of individuals who have lost their lives in such efforts. **Publications:** *imPULSE*, periodic. Newsletter. Alternate Formats: online ● Annual Report, annual.

12760 ■ Circle K International (CKI)
3636 Woodview Trace
Indianapolis, IN 46268-3196
Ph: (317)875-8755
Free: (800)549-2647
Fax: (317)879-0204
E-mail: cki@kiwanis.org
URL: http://www.circlek.org
Contact: Brian Egger, Pres.
Founded: 1955. **Members:** 12,500. **Membership Dues:** individual, $25 (annual). **Staff:** 2. **Budget:** $450,000. **Regional Groups:** 30. **Local Groups:** 550. **Description:** Organized by Kiwanis International. College students worldwide interested in serving others and developing friendships and leadership skills. Provides opportunities for responsible student action in meeting the needs of the campus and community. **Publications:** *Circle K Magazine*, 5/year. Covers general interest and organizational news. **Price:** included in membership dues. **Circulation:** 11,000. **Conventions/Meetings:** annual convention (exhibits).

12761 ■ Civitan International (CI)
PO Box 130744
Birmingham, AL 35213-0744
Ph: (205)591-8910
Free: (800)CIVITAN
Fax: (205)592-6307
E-mail: civitan@civitan.org
URL: http://www.civitan.org
Contact: W. John Rynearson CAE, Exec. VP
Founded: 1917. **Members:** 57,000. **Membership Dues:** civic club outside U.S. and Canada, individual, $12 (quarterly) ● associate, $36 (annual). **Staff:** 30. **Budget:** $4,400,000. **Description:** Service organization of business and professional men and women in 20 countries interested in promoting good citizenship on local, national, and international levels. Sponsors a Research Center at University of Alabama at Birmingham. **Libraries:** **Type:** reference. **Holdings:** artwork, books, clippings, periodicals. **Programs:** Aid to the Physically and Mentally Handicapped; Clergy Appreciation Week; Scholarships; Special Olympics. **Publications:** *Civitan International—Directory*, annual. **Price:** available to members only ● *Civitan Magazine*, quarterly. **Price:** $1.00/copy; $2.00 for members in U.S. and Canada; $8.00 for members outside North America; $6.00 for nonmembers. Alternate Formats: online ● *Countdown*, quarterly. Report ● *Member Resource Handbook*, periodic. Alternate Formats: online ● Brochure, periodic ● Annual Report, annual. **Conventions/Meetings:** annual meeting and convention (exhibits) - always June or July.

12762 ■ Cosmopolitan International (CI)
7341 W 80th St.
PO Box 4588
Overland Park, KS 66204
Ph: (913)648-4330
Free: (800)648-4331
Fax: (913)648-4630
E-mail: headquarters@cosmopolitan.org
URL: http://www.cosmopolitan.org
Contact: Kevin Harmon, Exec. Dir.
Founded: 1918. **Members:** 2,100. **Staff:** 3. **Budget:** $180,000. **State Groups:** 7. **Local Groups:** 70. **Multinational. Description:** Contributes to community well-being through charitable donations and volunteer service with special emphasis on supporting efforts to prevent and find a cure for diabetes. **Councils:** Columbia Diabetes Center Advisory. **Formerly:** International Federation of Cosmopolitan Clubs. **Publications:** *Cosmo Topics*, quarterly. Magazine. **Price:** $2.00/issue. Alternate Formats: online. **Conventions/Meetings:** annual conference and seminar - always July.

12763 ■ Federation of Woman's Exchanges (FWE)
Address Unknown since 2007
Founded: 1934. **Members:** 29. **Membership Dues:** $50 (annual). **Budget:** $1,500. **State Groups:** 16. **Description:** Groups known as Woman's Exchanges which operate voluntary nonprofit consignment shops. (Consignment shops provide a sales outlet for high-quality handcrafts and home-cooked foods; the profits from such shops are disbursed among other local voluntary nonprofit groups according to local needs.) Purposes are to: provide a market for handcrafted products; share information on effective shop management techniques; provide consultation to potential Woman's Exchanges; insure that the shops of prospective members are nonprofit and staffed by volunteers. **Publications:** *Directory of Exchanges*, annual. **Advertising:** not accepted. **Conventions/Meetings:** annual conference and luncheon (exhibits) - always first week in May.

12764 ■ Good Bears of the World (GBW)
PO Box 13097
Toledo, OH 43613
Ph: (419)531-5365
Free: (877)429-2327
Fax: (419)531-5365
E-mail: terrie.stong@goodbearsoftheworld.org
URL: http://www.goodbearsoftheworld.org
Contact: Terrie Stong, Chm./Exec. Dir.
Founded: 1969. **Members:** 3,000. **Membership Dues:** regular in U.S., $14 (annual) ● regular in Canada and Mexico, $18 (annual) ● regular foreign, $24 (annual) ● bearo in U.S., $150 (annual) ● bearo in Canada and Mexico, $175 (annual) ● bearo foreign, $250 (annual). **Staff:** 3. **Regional Groups:** 50. **Description:** Promoters and collectors of teddy bears in 10 countries. Distributes teddy bears to children in hospitals, battered and abused children, persons with AIDS or Alzheimer's, victims of violent crimes, and senior citizens in institutions. Upholds the teddy bear as a symbol of love and affection and believes teddy bears spread comfort to old and young people. Sponsors Good Bear Day on October 27, Theodore Roosevelt's birthday. (It was Roosevelt who inspired a toymaker to create the "teddy" bear when he refused to shoot a bear on a hunting trip in Mississippi in 1902.) **Publications:** *Bear Tracks*, quarterly. Journal. Provides information of interest to teddy bear collectors and aficionados. Contains update on den activities and articles on teddy bears. **Price:** included in membership dues. **Circulation:** 10,000. **Advertising:** accepted. **Conventions/Meetings:** annual Jubilee - meeting.

12765 ■ Good Fellows (Old Newsboys)
PO Box 44444
Detroit, MI 48244-0444
Ph: (586)775-6139
Fax: (586)775-6173

E-mail: sarigoodfellows@wowway.com
URL: http://www.oldnewsboysgoodfellows.org
Contact: Sari B. Klok, Dir.
Founded: 1914. **Members:** 350. **Membership Dues:** individual, $50 (annual). **Staff:** 1. **Budget:** $1,600,000. **Description:** Represents former newspaper carriers; although charitable work is carried on year-round, primary purpose is "A Christmas for Every Needy Child". Old Newsboys hawk papers on one specified day each year and all profits are used to achieve the group's purpose. Similar organizations now exist in other large cities in the United States, modeled after the Detroit Good Fellows. **Convention/Meeting:** none. **Publications:** none.

12766 ■ Gyro International (GI)
1019 Mentor Ave.
PO Box 489
Painesville, OH 44077-0489
Ph: (440)352-2501
Fax: (440)352-3882
E-mail: pat@gyro.org
URL: http://international.gyro.ws
Contact: Pat Swanson, Office Mgr.
Founded: 1912. **Members:** 5,000. **Staff:** 3. **Budget:** $200,000. **Regional Groups:** 9. **Local Groups:** 113. **Multinational. Description:** Serves as Federation of business and professional men's civic service clubs. **Awards:** Gyro Award of Merit. **Frequency:** annual. **Type:** recognition. **Recipient:** to a non-Gyro who has rendered exceptional service as a club president or district governor ● Gyro Honor Key. **Frequency:** annual. **Type:** recognition. **Recipient:** to a Gyro who has rendered special and/or distinguished service to the organization ● Gyro of the Year Award. **Frequency:** annual. **Type:** recognition. **Recipient:** to a Gyro who has rendered extraordinary service to the Gyro Fraternity in club and district affairs, promoted external and internal expansion, and has shown exceptional involvement in community, business or governmental activities ● Lifetime Achievement Award. **Frequency:** annual. **Type:** recognition. **Recipient:** to a Gyro who has unstintingly given off his time, efforts and love in perpetuating the Fraternity and all it stands for over the course of twenty years or more. **Formerly:** (1924) International Association of Gyro Clubs. **Publications:** GyroScope, quarterly. Magazine. Contains information on new members, district-wide events, and inter-club activities; also features listings of future conventions and meetings. **Price:** $2.00/year. ISSN: 0279-6694. **Circulation:** 5,600 ● Supply Catalog. **Conventions/Meetings:** annual convention ● annual International Interim - meeting - 2008 Jan. 22-27, Tucson, AZ.

12767 ■ Junior Chamber International (JCI)
15645 Olive Blvd.
Chesterfield, MO 63017
Ph: (636)449-3100
Free: (800)905-5499
Fax: (636)449-3107
E-mail: sg@jci.cc
URL: http://www.jci.cc
Contact: Edson A. Kodama, Sec. Gen.
Founded: 1944. **Members:** 200,000. **Membership Dues:** individual, $100 (annual). **Staff:** 20. **Budget:** $3,200. **Regional Groups:** 102. **State Groups:** 50. **Local Groups:** 7,500. **National Groups:** 102. **Languages:** Chinese, English, French, German, Japanese, Korean, Russian. **Description:** National Jaycee organizations representing 200,000 individuals between the ages of 18 and 40 dedicated to the principles of leadership training through community development. Sponsors a course on individual development; conducts charitable programs; sponsors competitions. Maintains program information library. **Awards:** Ten Outstanding Young Persons of the World. **Frequency:** annual. **Type:** recognition. **Formerly:** (1986) Jaycees International. **Publications:** JCI News, quarterly. Newsletter ● Directory, annual ● Proceedings, annual ● Also publishes pamphlets. **Conventions/Meetings:** quarterly conference ● annual congress.

12768 ■ Junior Optimist Octagon International (JOOI)
4494 Lindell Blvd.
St. Louis, MO 63108
Ph: (314)371-6000
Free: (800)500-8130
Fax: (314)371-6006
E-mail: youthclubs@optimist.org
URL: http://www.optimist.org/default.cfm?content=jooi/jooi.htm
Contact: Benny Ellerbe, Exec. Dir.
Founded: 1920. **Members:** 20,000. **Membership Dues:** club, individual, $46 (annual) ● life, $308. **Staff:** 2. **State Groups:** 52. **Local Groups:** 700. **Languages:** English, French. **Multinational. Description:** Represents boys and girls in grades six through nine throughout North America. Sponsored by Optimist International (see separate entry) and local Optimist Clubs in North America. Fosters adult/youth relationships. Conducts community-serving and citizenship-building activities. **Awards:** Advisor of Excellence. **Frequency:** annual. **Type:** recognition ● Club Project Awards. **Frequency:** annual. **Type:** recognition. **Recipient:** for the best project submitted by a JOOI club ● Honor Club Award/Distinguished Honor Club Award. **Frequency:** annual. **Type:** recognition. **Recipient:** for JOOI clubs that recruit new members, keep good records and conduct great volunteer projects ● JOOI President's Citation. **Frequency:** annual. **Type:** recognition. **Recipient:** for members who have gone all out to promote and support JOOI in their school and community ● Member of Excellence. **Frequency:** annual. **Type:** recognition. **Recipient:** for members who have shown dedication and involvement in community service ● Ruby Blair JOOI Member of the Year Award. **Frequency:** annual. **Type:** recognition. **Recipient:** for outstanding member of the JOOI organization. **Formerly:** (1998) Junior Optimist Clubs. **Publications:** New Club Building, periodic. Handbook. Contains successful guidelines. ● Sow the Seeds, periodic. Brochure. Includes information about the organization, truth about volunteers and reasons for sponsoring the club. ● Torch (in English and French), monthly. Newsletter. Includes club news, policies, and general interest articles. **Price:** included in membership dues. **Circulation:** 20,000. **Advertising:** accepted. Alternate Formats: online. **Conventions/Meetings:** annual convention (exhibits).

12769 ■ Key Club International (KCI)
3636 Woodview Trace
Indianapolis, IN 46268-3196
Ph: (317)875-8755
Free: (800)KIW-ANIS
Fax: (317)879-0204
E-mail: keyclub@kiwanis.org
URL: http://www.keyclub.org
Contact: Daniel P. Borba, Exec. Dir.
Founded: 1925. **Members:** 240,000. **Staff:** 12. **Regional Groups:** 32. **Local Groups:** 4,800. **Multinational. Description:** Represents secondary school students interested in service for others, good citizenship, and leadership training. Sponsored by Kiwanis International. **Awards:** Ag-Bag Scholarship. **Frequency:** annual. **Type:** scholarship. **Recipient:** to students involved in agriculture ● Cunat International Scholarship. **Frequency:** annual. **Type:** scholarship. **Recipient:** for members only ● David Hancock Memorial Scholarship. **Frequency:** annual. **Type:** scholarship. **Recipient:** for members only ● Himmel Scholarship. **Frequency:** annual. **Type:** scholarship. **Recipient:** for members only ● Key Club International Opportunities Fund Scholarship. **Frequency:** annual. **Type:** scholarship. **Recipient:** for members only ● Robert Thal Scholarship. **Frequency:** annual. **Type:** scholarship. **Recipient:** for members only ● Stephen Sapaugh Memorial Scholarship. **Frequency:** annual. **Type:** scholarship. **Recipient:** for members only ● Who's Who Scholarship. **Frequency:** annual. **Type:** scholarship. **Recipient:** to members who have received the Who's Who Among American High School Students recognition. **Committees:** Communications and Marketing; Executive; International Services; Member Services; Service Programming. **Affiliated With:** Kiwanis International. **Formerly:**

(1999) International KCI. **Publications:** Keynoter, 7/year. Magazine. **Price:** included in membership dues. **Advertising:** accepted. Alternate Formats: online. **Conventions/Meetings:** annual convention (exhibits).

12770 ■ Keyette International (KI)
Address Unknown since 2006
Founded: 1955. **Members:** 2,400. **Regional Groups:** 4. **Description:** Girls in grades 9 through 12 united for service to the community, school, and the sponsoring organization. Sponsors competitions. Conducts charitable program, specialized education, and children's services. **Awards:** Type: recognition. **Committees:** Projects (Welfare). **Publications:** Keyette Guide Book ● Keyzette, quarterly. **Advertising:** not accepted ● Brochure. **Conventions/Meetings:** annual conference - always April.

12771 ■ Kiwanis International (KI)
3636 Woodview Trace
Indianapolis, IN 46268-3196
Ph: (317)875-8755
Free: (800)549-2647
Fax: (317)879-0204
E-mail: kiwanismail@kiwanis.org
URL: http://www.kiwanis.org
Contact: Stephen K. Siemens, Pres.
Founded: 1915. **Members:** 288,702. **Membership Dues:** individual, $27 (annual). **Staff:** 140. **Budget:** $15,000,000. **Local Groups:** 8,600. **Languages:** Chinese, English, French, German, Italian, Spanish. **Multinational. Description:** Local clubs representing business and professional individuals in 89 countries and geographic regions. Seeks to: provide assistance to the young and elderly; develop community facilities; foster international understanding and goodwill. Sponsors Young Children: Priority One, a service program to benefit children up to age five. Sponsors Key Club International for high school students, Circle K International for college students, Builders Clubs for junior high school students, K-Kids for elementary school students, and Aktion clubs for handicapped adults. **Awards:** Kiwanis World Service Medal. **Frequency:** annual. **Type:** recognition. **Recipient:** for outstanding involvement in service to others, especially children, international in scope. **Publications:** Kiwanis, 10/year. Magazine. Reports on current Kiwanis activities and current issues in the news. **Price:** included in membership dues; $18.00 /year for nonmembers. ISSN: 0162-5276. **Circulation:** 241,000. **Advertising:** accepted. Alternate Formats: online ● Kiwanis International Directory, annual ● The Kiwanis Leader, bimonthly. Bulletin. **Price:** $2.50 in U.S. **Circulation:** 32,600. **Conventions/Meetings:** annual convention (exhibits) - 2008 June 25-28, Orlando, FL; 2009 June 24-27, Nashville, TN; 2010 June 23-26, Las Vegas, NV.

12772 ■ La Sertoma International
21710 S Race
Spring Hill, KS 66083
Ph: (913)686-3000
Fax: (913)686-3000
E-mail: lasertomahq@earthlink.net
URL: http://www.lasertoma.org
Contact: Pamela E. Martell, Exec. Sec.
Founded: 1929. **Members:** 695. **Membership Dues:** individual, $35 (annual). **Staff:** 1. **Budget:** $27,200. **Regional Groups:** 7. **State Groups:** 25. **Local Groups:** 70. **National Groups:** 3. **Languages:** English, Spanish. **Multinational. Description:** Serves as civic club of people who are interested in community service. Sponsors educational and philanthropic enterprises and endeavors, especially for youth in the field of civic responsibilities. Maintains International Scholarship and Memorial Fund Grant for young people. **Awards:** Else A. Neilsen Memorial Scholarship. **Frequency:** annual. **Type:** grant. **Recipient:** to the top rated S&M selectee ● Marguerite Leander Nursing Scholarship. **Frequency:** annual. **Type:** scholarship. **Recipient:** to a student pursuing higher education in the field of nursing ● Rose Runzler Memorial Scholarship Program. **Frequency:** annual. **Type:** scholarship. **Recipient:** for visually handicapped students who have completed or in the

process of completing a Bachelor's Degree and have declared intent to continue graduate study leading to professional competence ● Scholarship and Memorial Programs. **Frequency:** annual. **Type:** grant. **Recipient:** for students completing work on a graduate degree (Masters or PhD) as well as to high school graduates just entering college ● Undergraduate Scholarships. **Frequency:** annual. **Type:** scholarship ● Youth Service Award Programs. **Frequency:** annual. **Type:** recognition. **Recipient:** to young people who are setting a pattern of leadership and service in their local communities. **Formerly:** (1951) Co-Operettes. **Publications:** *In La Sertoma Circles*, 3/year. Newsletter. **Price:** included in membership dues. **Conventions/Meetings:** annual international conference (exhibits).

12773 ■ Links
1200 Massachusetts Ave. NW
Washington, DC 20005-4501
Ph: (202)842-8686
Free: (800)574-3720
Fax: (202)842-9098
E-mail: janet.walker@linksinc.org
URL: http://www.linksinc.org
Contact: Janet Baker Walker, Exec. Dir.
Founded: 1946. **Members:** 9,000. **Staff:** 8. **Budget:** $550,000. **Regional Groups:** 4. **State Groups:** 40. **Local Groups:** 254. **Description:** Organization of women committed to the community through educational, cultural, and civic activities. Provides enrichment experiences for those who are educationally disadvantaged and culturally deprived, and support for talented individuals. Sponsors charitable activities and a National Grant-In-Aid program. **Libraries:** **Type:** reference. **Holdings:** artwork, audiovisuals, books, clippings, monographs, periodicals. **Awards:** **Frequency:** biennial. **Type:** monetary ● **Frequency:** biennial. **Type:** recognition. **Programs:** The Arts; International Trends and Services; International Women's Decade; National Trends and Services; Services to Youth. **Publications:** *Link to Link*, quarterly. Newsletter ● *Links Directory*, quadrennial ● Brochure ● Journal, annual. **Conventions/Meetings:** biennial assembly (exhibits).

12774 ■ Lions Clubs International (LCI)
300 W 22nd St.
Oak Brook, IL 60523-8842
Ph: (630)571-5466
Fax: (630)571-1691
E-mail: newclubs@lionsclubs.org
URL: http://www.lionsclubs.org
Contact: Jimmy M. Ross, Intl. Pres.
Founded: 1917. **Members:** 1,400,000. **Membership Dues:** individual, $24 (annual). **Staff:** 280. **Budget:** $50,000,000. **Languages:** Chinese, English, Finnish, French, German, Italian, Japanese, Korean, Portuguese, Spanish, Swedish. **Multinational. Description:** Promotes local clubs representing business and professional men and women in 186 countries and geographic areas. Provides community service in order to increase international understanding and cooperation. Fosters awareness of environmental, social, and health related problems. Activities include: blindness prevention; work with the deaf; drug awareness programs; international youth camp programs; youth exchange. Maintains Leo Clubs (for young adults), and a Foundation for sight conservation and work with the blind. **Awards:** Membership Key Awards. **Frequency:** annual. **Type:** medal. **Recipient:** for Lions members who sponsor new members that have met the requirements for eligibility ● October Membership Growth Award Program. **Frequency:** annual. **Type:** medal. **Recipient:** for individual Lions members who sponsor one or more new members during the month of October. **Also Known As:** International Association of Lions Clubs. **Formerly:** (1979) Lions International. **Publications:** *Club Membership Chairman's Manual*. Includes guidelines to follow toward attaining membership growth and membership development and retention. ● *The Lion Magazine*, 10/year. Includes club service and association news, and articles of general interest. Available in 21 languages. **Price:** included in membership dues; $6.00 /year for nonmembers. ISSN: 0024-4163.

Circulation: 640,000. **Advertising:** accepted ● *Year Round Membership Program*. Brochure. Includes information about the program, advice and materials that will help bring in new members year-round. **Conventions/Meetings:** annual convention (exhibits) - always June/July. 2008 June 23-27, Bangkok, Thailand; 2009 July 6-10, Minneapolis, MN; 2010 June 28-July 2, Sydney, Australia.

12775 ■ National Association of Colored Women's Clubs (NACWC)
1601 R St. NW
Washington, DC 20009
Ph: (202)667-4080
Fax: (202)667-2574
E-mail: cearly@nacwcya.org
URL: http://www.nacwc.org
Contact: Carole A. Early, Sec.
Founded: 1896. **Members:** 45,000. **Staff:** 4. **State Groups:** 38. **Local Groups:** 1,000. **Description:** Federation of black women's clubs. Carries on program of civic service, education, social service, and philanthropy. Sponsors National Association of Youth Clubs. **Committees:** Home and Child; Legislation; Mother; Women in Industry; Young Adults. **Affiliated With:** National Association of Youth Clubs. **Formed by Merger of:** National Colored Women's League; National Federation of Afro-American Women. **Publications:** *National Notes*, quarterly. **Conventions/Meetings:** biennial meeting (exhibits).

12776 ■ National Association of Junior Auxiliaries (NAJA)
PO Box 1873
Greenville, MS 38702-1873
Ph: (662)332-3000
Fax: (662)332-3076
E-mail: najanet@bellsouth.net
URL: http://www.najanet.org
Contact: Mrs. Merrill Greenlee, Exec. Dir.
Founded: 1941. **Members:** 13,542. **Staff:** 5. **Regional Groups:** 6. **State Groups:** 8. **Local Groups:** 102. **Description:** Women over 21 years of age. Encourages women to become active and constructive participants in their communities, assume responsible leadership in meeting community problems, render charitable services which are beneficial to the general public, and cooperate with other organizations performing similar services. Offers children's services. **Libraries:** **Type:** reference. **Subjects:** family, children, youth. **Awards:** **Type:** scholarship. **Recipient:** for graduate work in fields that will directly benefit children. **Publications:** *Crownlet*, semiannual. Magazine. Covers association activities and projects; also contains articles on subjects pertaining to community services targeting children. **Price:** included in membership dues. **Advertising:** accepted ● *National Association of Junior Auxiliaries—Bulletin*, annual. Lists chapters, projects, members, award winners, and current officers; also includes annual meeting program and minutes. **Price:** included in membership dues. **Conventions/Meetings:** annual meeting (exhibits).

12777 ■ National Association of Negro Business and Professional Women's Clubs (NANBPWC)
1806 New Hampshire Ave. NW
Washington, DC 20009
Ph: (202)483-4206
E-mail: info@nanbpwc.org
URL: http://www.nanbpwc.org
Contact: Peola Smith-Smith, Natl. Pres.
Founded: 1935. **Members:** 10,000. **Staff:** 4. **Budget:** $500,000. **Regional Groups:** 7. **Local Groups:** 350. **Description:** Women actively engaged in a business or a profession who are committed to rendering service through club programs and activities. Seeks to direct the interest of business and professional women toward united action for improved social and civic conditions, and to provide enriching and ennobling experiences that will encourage freedom, dignity, self-respect, and self-reliance. Offers information and help regarding education, employment, health, housing, legislation, and problems of the aged and the disabled. Sponsors educational assistance

program, which includes local and national scholarships. Conducts consumer education and prison reform programs. Maintains youth department clubs. Provides placement services; operates speakers' bureau; compiles statistics. **Awards:** Sojourner Truth Award. **Type:** recognition. **Recipient:** for national and community service. **Computer Services:** database ● online services. **Committees:** Economic Development; Educational Assistance; International Affairs; Political and Legislative Action; Social Welfare and Health. **Councils:** Business Women's. **Affiliated With:** International Council of Women. **Publications:** *Convention Proceeding*, annual. Proceedings ● *President's Newsletter*, monthly ● *Program Idea Exchange*, bimonthly. Newsletter. Alternate Formats: online ● *Responsibility*, quarterly ● Directory, annual ● Newsletter. **Price:** available to members only. Alternate Formats: online ● Also publishes handbooks and manuals. **Conventions/Meetings:** annual convention (exhibits).

12778 ■ National Exchange Club (NEC)
3050 Central Ave.
Toledo, OH 43606-1700
Ph: (419)535-3232
Free: (800)924-2643
Fax: (419)535-1989
E-mail: info@nationalexchangeclub.org
URL: http://www.nationalexchangeclub.org
Contact: Christopher Rice, Exec. VP
Founded: 1911. **Members:** 32,000. **Membership Dues:** individual, $15 (quarterly). **Staff:** 29. **Budget:** $2,200,000. **Regional Groups:** 37. **Local Groups:** 922. **Description:** Business and professional men's and women's service clubs involved in child abuse prevention, crime prevention, good citizenship, youth, and community service. Sponsors Americanism, Youth and Community Service projects including the Freedom Shrine, "One Nation Under God," National Crime Prevention Week, and the National Exchange Club Foundation (see separate entry). **Awards:** National Youth of the Year Award. **Frequency:** annual. **Type:** recognition. **Affiliated With:** National Exchange Club Foundation. **Also Known As:** Exchange Clubs of America. **Publications:** *Exchange Today*, bimonthly. Magazine. **Price:** included in membership dues; $6.00 /year for nonmembers. ISSN: 0014-4487. **Circulation:** 32,000. **Advertising:** accepted. **Conventions/Meetings:** annual conference (exhibits).

12779 ■ National Pinochle Bugs Social and Civic Club
c/o Millie Boatright, Program Chair
5201 Arlington St.
Philadelphia, PA 19131
Ph: (215)477-3617
E-mail: publications@pinochlebugs.com
URL: http://www.pinochlebugs.com
Contact: Vivien H. Hansbury, Pres.
Founded: 1955. **Members:** 273. **Local Groups:** 21. **Description:** African American women. Promotes social and civic cooperation among various women's groups. Encourages social, economic, educational, and cultural advancement. Supports community projects. Maintains speakers' bureau and scrapbook. **Libraries:** **Type:** reference. **Holdings:** archival material. **Awards:** Mattie Taylor-Antoinette Bruce Scholarship Award. **Type:** scholarship. **Publications:** *The Beetle*, biennial. Magazine. Includes coverage of chapter activities and member profiles. ● *The Foundation: Mattie Taylor/Antoinette Bruce Scholarship Tournament* ● *Pinochle Bugs Social and Civic Club Brochure* ● *Who's Who Among Bugs: National Talent Bank*. **Conventions/Meetings:** annual board meeting ● annual convention (exhibits) - always last weekend of April.

12780 ■ NGA
822 Veterans Way
Warminster, PA 18974
Ph: (215)682-9183
Free: (866)295-9974
E-mail: nga@nga-inc.org
URL: http://www.nga-inc.org
Contact: Maureen Schmidt, Exec. Dir.
Founded: 1885. **Members:** 100,000. **Staff:** 5. **Budget:** $192,244. **Local Groups:** 42. **Description:** Pro-

vides volunteer groups that collect and distribute new clothes, household linens and toiletries locally to those in need through recognized community organizations and agencies. **Awards:** Marion S. Bettle National Award. **Frequency:** annual. **Type:** recognition. **Recipient:** for outstanding organizational leadership. **Affiliated With:** American Red Cross National Headquarters; Camp Fire USA; General Federation of Women's Clubs; Girl Scouts of the U.S.A.; National Grange; Salvation Army. **Formerly:** (1989) Needlework Guild of America. **Publications:** *NGA News*, quarterly. Newsletter. **Advertising:** accepted. Alternate Formats: online. **Conventions/Meetings:** periodic conference.

12781 ■ Optimist International
4494 Lindell Blvd.
St. Louis, MO 63108
Ph: (314)371-6000
Free: (800)500-8130
Fax: (314)371-6006
E-mail: membership@optimist.org
URL: http://www.optimist.org
Contact: Ronnie Dunn, Intl. Pres.
Founded: 1919. **Members:** 115,000. **Membership Dues:** tier 1, $47 (annual) ● tier 2, $35 (annual) ● tier 3, $24 (annual) ● life (in U.S.), $318. **Staff:** 45. **Budget:** $6,000,000. **Local Groups:** 3,500. **Languages:** English, French, Spanish. **Multinational. Description:** Volunteer Service clubs dedicated to youth and community service. Fosters the motto "Bringing Out the Best in Kids". Sponsors essay and speech contests, airbag safety education, safety on wheels, sports skills contests and junior golf. **Publications:** *The Optimist* (in English and French), quarterly. Magazine. **Circulation:** 100,000. **Advertising:** accepted. **Conventions/Meetings:** annual convention (exhibits).

12782 ■ Pilot International and Pilot International Foundation (PI - PIF)
PO Box 4844
Macon, GA 31208-4844
Ph: (478)477-1208
Fax: (478)477-6978
E-mail: peggy@pilothq.org
URL: http://www.pilotinternational.org
Contact: Peggy Davidson, Exec. Dir.
Founded: 1921. **Members:** 13,458. **Membership Dues:** regular, $40 (annual). **Staff:** 14. **Budget:** $1,800,000. **Regional Groups:** 20. **Local Groups:** 490. **National Groups:** 2. **Languages:** English, Japanese. **Description:** Civic service organization with clubs in 6 countries. Local clubs seek to improve civic, social, and commercial welfare of their communities. Sponsors Anchor Clubs for students. Established the Pilot International Foundation in 1975 to provide grants for club projects that benefit people with brain disorders such as mental illness, Alzheimer's disease, and Parkinson's disease. Promotes safety program. Introduced signature Brainminders program in 2002, teaching children how to protect their brain for life. Maintains liaison with United Nations, National Safety Council, National Organization on Disability, Brain Injury Association, National Mental Health Association, and the National Alliance for the Mentally Ill. **Boards:** Directors; Executive Committee; Trustees. **Affiliated With:** Alzheimer's Association; Mental Health America; National Safety Council; United Nations. **Publications:** *Pilot Log*, quarterly. Magazine. **Price:** $10.00/year. ISSN: 1045-179X. **Circulation:** 15,500. **Advertising:** accepted. Alternate Formats: online ● Directory, annual. **Price:** available to members only. **Conventions/Meetings:** annual convention and meeting (exhibits).

12783 ■ Quota International (QI)
c/o We Share Foundation
1420 21st St. NW
Washington, DC 20036
Ph: (202)331-9694
Fax: (202)331-4395
E-mail: staff@quota.org
URL: http://www.wesharefoundation.org
Contact: Kathleen Treiber CAE, Exec. Dir.
Founded: 1919. **Members:** 7,000. **Membership Dues:** individual, $45 (annual). **Staff:** 5. **Budget:**

$700,000. **Multinational. Description:** Business executives and professionals in 14 countries. Seeks to create a worldwide network of service and friendship in order to improve the quality of life. Espouses values such as the desire to serve country and community, a commitment to high ethical standards, and a belief in the worth of work and friendship. Supports service to speech and hearing-impaired persons and disadvantaged women and children. **Awards: Frequency:** periodic. **Type:** recognition. **Additional Websites:** http://www.quota.org. **Formerly:** Quota Club International. **Publications:** *Quotarian Magazine*, annual. **Advertising:** accepted. **Conventions/Meetings:** biennial convention - always July.

12784 ■ Rotary International (RI)
One Rotary Center
1560 Sherman Ave.
Evanston, IL 60201
Ph: (847)866-3000
Fax: (847)328-8554
E-mail: ers@rotaryintl.org
URL: http://www.rotary.org
Contact: Willaim Boyd, Pres.
Founded: 1905. **Members:** 1,227,545. **Membership Dues:** regular, $35 (annual). **Staff:** 495. **Multinational. Description:** Business and professional executives in 166 countries and additional 34 geographical regions. Undertakes community development programs; promotes high ethical standards in business and professions; fosters "international understanding, goodwill, and peace". Supports polio immunization campaigns. Maintains Rotary Foundation which offers scholarships to outstanding men and women, enabling them to study or teach in other countries. Organizes exchange programs for business and professional people. Administers Interact and Rotaract programs for youths. **Libraries: Type:** reference. **Holdings:** 35,000; photographs, video recordings. **Subjects:** Rotary philanthropic projects, activities, events worldwide. **Awards:** Rotary Award for World Understanding. **Frequency:** annual. **Type:** monetary. **Recipient:** for individuals or organizations exemplifying the ideals of Rotary. **Formerly:** (1910) National Association of Rotary Clubs; (1912) International Association of Rotary Clubs. **Publications:** *Convention Proceedings*, annual ● *Navigating the Global Network*, semiannual ● *The Rotarian*, monthly. **Circulation:** 520,271. **Advertising:** accepted ● *Rotary World*, quarterly. **Conventions/Meetings:** annual convention (exhibits).

12785 ■ Round-Table U.S.A. (RTUSA)
MD Financial Bank
303 E Wacker Dr.
Chicago, IL 60601
E-mail: rtusa@aol.com
URL: http://www.rt6usa.org
Contact: Anders Hjorth Agerskov, Treas.
Founded: 1922. **Members:** 300. **Membership Dues:** regular, $125 (annual). **Staff:** 1. **Description:** Men's and women's service clubs. Derives inspiration from the ideal of service celebrated in the legends of King Arthur. Works closely with young people in schools and colleges; organizes special programs for disabled and mentally retarded youth. **Awards: Type:** scholarship. **Recipient:** for student therapists training to work with the physically disabled. **Committees:** Scholarship. **Also Known As:** Loyal Knights of the Round Table. **Formerly:** (2003) Round-Table International. **Publications:** *Excalibur Magazine*, quarterly. **Conventions/Meetings:** International Oratorical Contest - competition, for high school students ● annual meeting - always June.

12786 ■ Ruritan National (RN)
PO Box 487
Dublin, VA 24084
Ph: (540)674-5431
Free: (877)787-8727
Fax: (540)674-2304
E-mail: office@ruritan.org
URL: http://www.ruritan.org
Contact: Michael Chrisley, Exec. Dir.
Founded: 1928. **Members:** 37,513. **Membership Dues:** individual, $40 (annual) ● life, $600. **Staff:** 13.

Budget: $1,167,000. **Regional Groups:** 1,420. **Description:** Nonpartisan, non-sectarian community service organization. Goals are: to create better understanding between rural and urban people, communities, and business; to aid in charitable work and disaster relief efforts; to promote industrial and agricultural growth and economic development. Funds the Ruritan National Foundation, a trust for the encouragement, promotion, and financing of charitable, educational, and benevolent activities. Offers educational loan program. **Awards: Type:** grant. **Committees:** Business and Professions; Citizenship and Patriotism; Environment; Human Development; Public Services; Social Concern; Transportation. **Publications:** *Ruritan*, quarterly. Magazine ● *Ruritan Newsletter*, monthly. **Price:** $12.00/year. **Advertising:** accepted. Alternate Formats: online. **Conventions/Meetings:** annual meeting (exhibits).

12787 ■ Sertoma International (SI)
1912 E Meyer Blvd.
Kansas City, MO 64132-1174
Ph: (816)333-8300
Free: (800)593-5646
Fax: (816)333-4320
E-mail: infosertoma@sertoma.org
URL: http://www.sertoma.org
Contact: Mr. Steven Murphy, Exec. Dir.
Founded: 1912. **Members:** 20,000. **Membership Dues:** individual, $46 (annual). **Staff:** 15. **Budget:** $1,600,000. **Local Groups:** 700. **Languages:** English, Spanish. **Description:** Civic service club of business and professional men and women in Canada, Mexico, and the United States. Aims to render "service to mankind" (phrase from which group's name is derived). Sponsors: Sertoma Foundation, which provides service to persons with communicative disorders; Hearing and Speech Services; Serteen and Collegiate Sertoma clubs. **Awards:** Sertoma International Service to Mankind Awards. **Frequency:** annual. **Type:** recognition. **Recipient:** for volunteer service by a non-Sertoma member. **Formerly:** (1950) Cooperative Club International. **Publications:** *Directory of Sertoma Clubs*, annual. **Price:** available to members only. **Circulation:** 2,000 ● *Sertoman*, quarterly. Magazine. Covers promotions, growth, fundraising, awards, and membership activities. Includes obituaries and statistics. **Price:** included in membership dues. ISSN: 0744-2807. **Circulation:** 26,000. **Advertising:** accepted. Alternate Formats: online. **Conventions/Meetings:** annual convention (exhibits).

12788 ■ Singles in Service (SIS)
c/o Hands on Sacramento
909 12th St., Ste.200
Sacramento, CA 95814
Ph: (916)447-7063
Fax: (916)447-7052
E-mail: info@handsonsacto.org
URL: http://www.handsonsacto.org
Contact: Kathy Chow, Dir., Hands on Sacramento
Founded: 1972. **Members:** 29. **Membership Dues:** regular, $25 (annual). **Staff:** 1. **Description:** Unmarried men and women (divorced, widowed, or single), ages 18 and over, dedicated to charitable projects, particularly those projects not already supported by public or private agencies or religious organizations. Intents to encourage singles to find local charitable projects and to pledge their effort and time for the completion of such tasks; membership requires either a pledge of 25 hours a year or a cash contribution. **Libraries: Type:** not open to the public. **Holdings:** 63. **Subjects:** spiritual. **Awards: Type:** grant. **Recipient:** for member projects. **Study Groups:** Spiritual. **Publications:** *Occasional Thoughts*, periodic. Newsletter. **Price:** included in membership dues. **Conventions/Meetings:** annual What is Community? - conference, communities past, present, and future.

12789 ■ Soroptimist International of the Americas (SIA)
1709 Spruce St.
Philadelphia, PA 19103-6103
Ph: (215)893-9000
Fax: (215)893-5200

E-mail: siahq@soroptimist.org
URL: http://www.soroptimist.org
Contact: Tes Choa, Pres.
Founded: 1921. **Members:** 48,000. **Membership Dues:** individual, $36 (annual). **Staff:** 20. **Budget:** $2,500,000. **Regional Groups:** 28. **Local Groups:** 1,500. **Multinational. Description:** Represents professional women and women business executives. **Libraries: Type:** open to the public. **Holdings:** books, periodicals. **Subjects:** organizational history, women in volunteerism. **Awards:** Making a Difference for Women. **Frequency:** annual. **Type:** grant. **Recipient:** for women who are working to improve the lives of women and girls through their personal or professional activities ● Violet Richardson Award. **Frequency:** annual. **Type:** recognition. **Recipient:** for individual girls who donated their time and energy to the community ● Women's Opportunity Awards. **Type:** grant. **Recipient:** for women who provided the primary source of financial support for their families. **Affiliated With:** Venture Clubs. **Formerly:** (1958) American Federation of Soroptimist Clubs; (1975) Soroptimist Federation of the Americas. **Publications:** *The Soroptimist of the Americas,* quarterly. Magazine. Includes program and technical notes and listings of new clubs and Training Awards Program winners. **Price:** included in membership dues. ISSN: 0097-9562. **Circulation:** 50,000. **Conventions/Meetings:** biennial convention (exhibits).

12790 ■ United Nations Women's Guild (UNWG)
1 UN Plz., DC-1, Rm. 0775
New York, NY 10017
Ph: (212)963-8279 (212)963-5333
Fax: (212)963-3121
E-mail: unwg@un.org
URL: http://www.un.org/other/unwg
Contact: Ms. Tsu-Wei Chang, Pres.
Founded: 1948. **Members:** 220. **Multinational. Description:** Female staff and wives of those employed by the UN and its specialized agencies; individuals who contribute services to the guild. Sends direct aid to underprivileged children worldwide. Works on projects involving institutions that provide assistance to young victims of poverty, disease, and war. Works with sister groups offering suggestions for projects or requesting aid in supporting their own local projects. Sponsors fundraising projects. **Affiliated With:** United Nations. **Publications:** *United Nations Women's Guild News Bulletin,* quarterly. Newsletter. Alternate Formats: online ● Report, annual. **Conventions/Meetings:** annual meeting - usually February/March, New York.

12791 ■ United States Women of Today (USWT)
728 Prospect St.
York, PA 17403-2426
E-mail: president@uswt.org
URL: http://www.uswt.org
Contact: Brenda Almoney, Pres.
Founded: 1985. **Members:** 3,600. **Description:** Represents individuals over the age of 18. Serves as community service organization; conducts charitable activities. Promotes the personal development of members through programs such as Focus on Women, Success Through Enthusiastic Participation, Effective Writing, and Effective Speaking. **Committees:** Bylaw Review; Dues Billing Contract; Elections; Extensions; External Bid Process Review; Future Directions; Marketing; Materials Review. **Publications:** Newsletter, monthly. **Conventions/Meetings:** semiannual meeting - always November and June.

12792 ■ Venture Clubs
c/o Soroptimist International of the Americas
1709 Spruce St.
Philadelphia, PA 19103-6103
Ph: (215)893-9000
Fax: (215)893-5200
E-mail: siahq@soroptimist.org
URL: http://www.soroptimistnwr.com/venture.htm
Founded: 1934. **Members:** 2,700. **State Groups:** 171. **Description:** Service club for business and professional young women through age 40 who are concerned about their community and desire to take an active part in its development. Seeks to encourage high ethical standards in business, outlook, and understanding through the study of other countries; sponsored by Soroptimist International of the Americas (see separate entry). **Publications:** none. **Awards:** Student Aid Award. **Type:** monetary. **Recipient:** to physically disabled individuals between ages 15 to 35. **Affiliated With:** Soroptimist International of the Americas. **Formerly:** (1969) American Council of Venture Clubs; (1975) Venture Club Council of the Americas; (2004) Venture Clubs of the Americas. **Conventions/Meetings:** annual conference.

12793 ■ Women in Show Business for Children (WiSB)
Address Unknown since 2007
Founded: 1961. **Members:** 100. **Membership Dues:** active, $50 (annual) ● affiliate, $100 (annual). **Regional Groups:** 1. **Description:** Women and men employed in the entertainment industry and allied fields. Raises funds to pay for reconstructive and restorative surgery for poor children who are not eligible for state or federal aid and/or insurance coverage. Also provides for equipment, supplies, therapy, counseling, training services, prosthetics, and other materials. **Awards:** Bella Rackoff Humanitarian Award. **Frequency:** annual. **Type:** recognition. **Recipient:** one who has given time, money & caring to children. **Formerly:** (1982) Girls Friday of Show Business. **Publications:** *The Bulletin,* monthly. Newsletter. **Price:** $6.00/year. **Circulation:** 500. **Advertising:** accepted. **Conventions/Meetings:** annual Celebrity Benefit Ball - meeting, with guest speakers - Los Angeles - **Avg. Attendance:** 500.

12794 ■ Youth Service America (YSA)
1101 15th St., Ste.200
Washington, DC 20005
Ph: (202)296-2992
E-mail: sculbertson@ysa.org
URL: http://www.ysa.org
Contact: Steven A. Culbertson, Pres./CEO
Founded: 1985. **Members:** 300. **Description:** Promotes and develops youth service programs in schools, colleges, and community based agencies. Seeks to organize and mobilize youth for community service. Sponsors annual National Youth Service Day, Working Group on Youth Service Policy. **Awards:** Harris Wofford Award. **Frequency:** annual. **Type:** recognition. **Recipient:** to individual, institution or organization that best exemplifies the spirit of service. **Absorbed:** (1985) Roosevelt Centennial Youth Project. **Publications:** *The Adventure of Adolescence: Middle School Students and Community Service* ● *Big Picture* ● *Spotlights on Service* ● *Streams,* monthly. Newsletter ● *Youth Serving the Young.* **Conventions/Meetings:** annual conference ● periodic conference.

12795 ■ Zonta International (ZI)
557 W Randolph St.
Chicago, IL 60661-2202
Ph: (312)930-5848
Fax: (312)930-0951
E-mail: zontaintl@zonta.org
URL: http://www.zonta.org
Contact: Janet Halstead, Exec. Dir.
Founded: 1919. **Members:** 32,000. **Staff:** 11. **Budget:** $1,800,000. **Local Groups:** 1,250. **Multinational. Description:** Serves as a global organization of executives and professionals working together to advance the status of women through service and advocacy. Coordinates service projects that provide educational scholarships for women, health improvement activities for women, prevention of violence against women, and income-generating projects for women, including cooperative projects with U.N. agencies; has consultative status with International Labor Organization, United Nations Educational, Scientific and Cultural Organization (UNESCO), United Nations Economic and Social Council (ECOSOC), UNICEF and UNIFEM; and participatory status with Council of Europe. Local club members conduct community projects to assist women. **Awards:** Amelia Earhart Fellowships. **Frequency:** annual. **Type:** fellowship. **Recipient:** for women doing post-graduate work in aerospace-related sciences and engineering ● International Service Project Grants. **Frequency:** biennial. **Type:** grant. **Recipient:** for cooperative projects with UN agencies and other NGOs to improve women's lives. **Committees:** Communications and Public Relations; Organization Membership and Classification; Status of Women Service; Strategies to Prevent Violence Against Women; United Nations; Z-Club. **Formerly:** (1930) Confederation of Zonta Clubs. **Publications:** *The Zontian,* quarterly. Magazine. **Price:** $8.50/year. ISSN: 0279-3229 ● Directory, annual. **Conventions/Meetings:** biennial convention - June/July in even numbered years.

Sex Addiction

12796 ■ International Service Organization - COSA (ISO-COSA)
PO Box 14537
Minneapolis, MN 55414
Ph: (763)537-6904
E-mail: info@cosa-recovery.org
URL: http://www.cosa-recovery.org
Founded: 1980. **Regional Groups:** 4. **State Groups:** 102. **National Groups:** 4. **Multinational. Description:** Promotes self help program for those involved in relationships with people who have compulsive sexual behavior. Makes use of the Twelve Steps of Alcoholics Anonymous World Services, adapted for sexual behavior. Offers informational and inspirational support. **Also Known As:** Co-Dependents of Sex Addicts. **Formerly:** (1999) NSO of COSA; (2005) COSA; (2006) National Service Organization - COSA. **Publications:** *Balance,* bimonthly. Newsletter. **Price:** $24.00/year ● *COSA.* Brochure ● *COSA Stories, Volume 1* ● *COSA Stories, Volume 2* ● *How to Start a Group* ● *Newcomer Welcome.* Booklet ● *Tools.* Brochure. **Conventions/Meetings:** annual conference and convention.

12797 ■ Sex Addicts Anonymous (SAA)
PO Box 70949
Houston, TX 77270
Ph: (713)869-4902
Free: (800)477-8191
E-mail: info@saa-recovery.org
URL: http://www.saa-recovery.org
Contact: Jerry B., Dir.
Founded: 1977. **Members:** 4,500. **Staff:** 1. **State Groups:** 50. **Local Groups:** 450. **Description:** A 12-step recovery program to stop addictive sexual behavior. **Publications:** *Literature Catalog* ● *The Plain Brown Rapper,* bimonthly. Newsletter. Contains stories from other sex addicts, poetry, and news of activities. **Price:** free. Alternate Formats: online ● Book. **Price:** $14.00 soft cover copy; $18.00 hard cover copy ● Pamphlets ● Booklets. **Price:** $2.50 ● Also publishes group guides. **Conventions/Meetings:** annual meeting.

12798 ■ Sex and Love Addicts Anonymous (SLAA)
1550 NE Loop 410, Ste.118
San Antonio, TX 78209
Ph: (210)828-7900
Fax: (210)828-7922
E-mail: info@slaafws.org
URL: http://www.slaafws.org
Contact: Ms. Terri Smythe, Exec. Dir.
Founded: 1976. **Staff:** 4. **National Groups:** 1,200. **Description:** Individuals recovering from a compulsive need for sex, a desperate attachment to one person, or other sexual or emotional obsessive-compulsive behavior. Functions as a support group to help members achieve comfortable, long-term sexual and emotional sobriety. Employs the 12 Steps of Alcoholics Anonymous World Services, adapted to sexual addiction. **Affiliated With:** Alcoholics Anonymous World Services. **Also Known As:** The Augustine Fellowship. **Publications:** *F.W.S. Newsletter,* quarterly ● *The Journal,* bimonthly. Magazine. Covers upcoming conferences and current events and

articles and poems submitted by members. **Price:** $18.00/year. **Circulation:** 650 ● Audiotapes ● Books. **Price:** $15.00 for softcover; $20.00 for hardcover ● Pamphlets. **Conventions/Meetings:** weekly meeting.

12799 ■ Sexaholics Anonymous (SA)
PO Box 3565
Brentwood, TN 37024
Ph: (615)370-6062
Free: (866)424-8777
Fax: (615)370-0882
E-mail: saico@sa.org
URL: http://www.sa.org
Contact: Kay Shotwell, Office Mgr.
Founded: 1979. **Members:** 8,000. **Budget:** $125,000. **Regional Groups:** 700. **Multinational.** **Description:** Individuals wishing to stop their sexually self-destructive thinking and behavior such as fantasy, pornography, adultery, masturbation, incest, or criminal sexual activity. Group believes that the sexaholic is addicted to lust and sex as others are to alcohol or drugs; this behavior is often followed by guilt, remorse, and depression, and may damage relationships with family and peers. Conducts programs based on the 12-step recovery program used in Alcoholics Anonymous to help members achieve "sexual sobriety". **Publications:** *Essay*, quarterly. Newsletter. **Price:** $10.00/year ● *Member Stories*. Book ● *Practical Guidelines for Group Recovery*. Brochure ● *Recovery Continues*. Book ● Book. **Conventions/Meetings:** semiannual meeting and international conference - always January and July.

Sexual Abuse

12800 ■ Incest Survivors Anonymous (ISA)
PO Box 17245
Long Beach, CA 90807-7245
Ph: (562)428-5599
E-mail: isa@lafn.org
Contact: Erin Marie Parkhurst, Founder/Dir.
Founded: 1980. **Languages:** English, Spanish. **Multinational. Description:** A spiritually-based self-help, mutual-help recovery program for men, women, and teens who are victims of incest or other forms of sexual abuse. Applies the adapted twelve-step and twelve-tradition programs of Alcoholics Anonymous World Service. Does not accept initiators of sexual abuse, professionals or students who are not victims, or victims who have become perpetrators. **Libraries: Type:** not open to the public. **Publications:** *The Cuddly News*, semiannual. Magazine ● *The Family Letter*, 3/year. **Price:** free ● *I.S.A. Talks to Friends, Survivors, and Professionals*. **Price:** $4.00 ● *The Nightmare of Incest*. **Price:** $4.00 ● *Welcome to the Newcomer*. **Price:** $4.00. **Conventions/Meetings:** weekly meeting.

12801 ■ Male Survivor: The National Organization Against Male Sexual Victimization (MS:NOMSV)
PMB 103
5505 Connecticut Ave. NW
Washington, DC 20015-2601
Free: (800)738-4181
E-mail: admin@malesurvivor.org
URL: http://www.malesurvivor.org
Contact: Murray Schane MD, Pres.
Founded: 1988. **Members:** 240. **Membership Dues:** individual (with gross annual income of $34,999 and below), $35 (annual) ● individual (with gross annual income of ranging from $35,000 to $69,999), $65 (annual) ● individual (with gross annual income of $70,000 and above), $100 (annual) ● non-profit organization, $125 (annual) ● for profit organization, $250 (annual). **Staff:** 1. **Budget:** $25,000. **National Groups:** 2. **Description:** Strives to prevent, treat, and eliminate all forms of sexual victimization of boys and men. **Awards:** Fay Honey Knopp. **Frequency:** biennial. **Type:** recognition. **Recipient:** for contribution to mission statement. **Computer Services:** Online services, membership chatroom - manned and unmanned. **Committees:** Member Services; Re-

search. **Subcommittees:** Diversity; Endowment Fund; Fundraising; Inter-organization Liaison; International Liaison; Resource Directory, **Formerly:** (2003) National Organization on Male Sexual Victimization. **Publications:** *Men Speak Out*, quarterly. Newsletter. Contains reports on Male Survivor activities and events. **Price:** free for members. **Circulation:** 250. **Advertising:** accepted ● *Professional Resource Directory*. Provides a directory of professionals wishing to offer services to male sexual abuse survivors. Alternate Formats: online ● Annual Report. **Conventions/Meetings:** semiannual International Conference on Male Sexual Victimization (exhibits).

12802 ■ Mothers Against Sexual Abuse (MASA)
PO Box 371
Huntersville, NC 28070
E-mail: masa@iofx.com
URL: http://www.againstsexualabuse.org
Contact: Claire R. Reeves CCDC, Pres.
Membership Dues: founding, $500 ● charter/professional, $100 ● family, $50 ● individual, $25 ● student, $15 ● life, $1,000. **Description:** Works to prevent child sexual abuse by increasing adult awareness. Connects victims with resources and supports legislation to protect children. Provides access to a network of professionals who aid in the recovery of abuse victims and their families. **Computer Services:** Information services, child sex abuse resources ● online services, chat.

12803 ■ Mothers Against Sexual Predators At Large (MASPAL)
PO Box 7247
Missoula, MT 59807-7247
E-mail: contact@maspal.org
URL: http://www.maspal.org
Contact: Ron Rea, Chm.
Description: Advocates for the protection of children from sexual predators. Works to help change legislative issues concerning the reintegration of sex offenders into society.

12804 ■ National Sexual Violence Resource Center (NSVRC)
123 N Enola Dr.
Enola, PA 17025
Ph: (717)909-0710
Free: (877)739-3895
Fax: (717)909-0714
E-mail: resources@nsvrc.org
URL: http://www.nsvrc.org
Contact: Karen Baker MSW, Dir.
Founded: 2000. **Staff:** 15. **Languages:** English, French, Italian, Spanish. **Nonmembership. Description:** Serves requesters from across the country, including advocates, health care providers, sexual assault response teams, and the general public. Provides resource, referral, and assistance. **Libraries: Type:** reference. **Holdings:** 12,000; articles, books, periodicals, reports, video recordings. **Subjects:** sexual violence. **Computer Services:** Online services, library, event posting, job posting, materials purchasing, calendar, resources, funding sources. **Telecommunication Services:** teletype, (717)909-0715. **Publications:** *The Resource*, semiannual, spring/summer and fall/winter. Newsletter. Contains information about sexual violence and current events. **Price:** free. Alternate Formats: online ● Booklet, annual. Contains information about sexual violence and current events. **Price:** free. Alternate Formats: online.

12805 ■ Parents United (PU)
615 15th St.
Modesto, CA 95354
Ph: (209)572-3446
Fax: (209)524-7780
E-mail: parentsu@ainet.com
URL: http://members.tripod.com/~Parents_United/Chapters/PUI.htm
Contact: Karen C. Cosner, Exec. Dir.
Founded: 1972. **Members:** 6,000. **Staff:** 2. **Budget:** $98,000. **Regional Groups:** 4. **Local Groups:** 55. **Languages:** English, Spanish. **Description:** Represents individuals and families who have experienced

child sexual molestation. Works to provide assistance to families affected by incest and other types of child sexual abuse by providing crisis and long-term support. Provides weekly professional counseling and conducts self-help type therapy groups; promotes self-awareness and responsibility to self, family, and community. Compiles information and arranges medical, vocational, and legal counseling for families. Encourages the affected child to meet with other children in self-help sessions for children ages five to 18, and Adults Molested as Children United (see separate entry). Works in conjunction with the Child Sexual Abuse Treatment Program, which provides coordination and professional counseling support. Conducts educational programs; maintains speakers' bureau. **Telecommunication Services:** 24-hour hotline, (408)279-1957. **Publications:** Also distributes tapes and printed materials. **Conventions/Meetings:** annual meeting.

12806 ■ Paul and Lisa Program (P&L)
PO Box 348
Westbrook, CT 06498
Ph: (860)767-7660
Free: (800)518-2238
Fax: (860)767-3122
E-mail: contact@paulandlisa.org
URL: http://www.paulandlisa.org
Contact: Bruce Lehman, Pres.
Founded: 1980. **Staff:** 8. **State Groups:** 2. **Description:** Serves as national program for the prevention and rehabilitation of sexually exploited youth and adults. Believes that "sexual abuse and exploitation of children and adults is a silent but virulent epidemic that must be brought to the attention of the public"; educates children, the public, and professionals in the dangers of Commercial Sexual Exploitation and the problems of sexual exploitation in children. Provides training for professionals through conferences, seminars, and workshops. Sponsors educational presentations to schools and private and civic clubs, religious organizations, business and industry associations, and concerned citizen action groups. Works with local, state, and federal officials in promoting laws dealing with the sexual exploitation of children. **Formerly:** (1982) Paul and Lisa Foundation. **Publications:** *Female Juvenile Prostitution: Problem and Response, National Center for Missing and Exploited Children* ● *Internet Safety Guide* ● *The P&L Connection*, quarterly. Newsletter. Includes calendar of events and profiles of volunteer activities. **Price:** free. **Circulation:** 2,600 ● *RISSK (Risk, Issues and Safety Strategies for Kids)*. Magazine.

12807 ■ People Against Rape (PAR)
2154 N Centre St., Ste.302-C
North Charleston, SC 29406
Ph: (843)745-0144
Free: (800)241-7273
Fax: (843)745-0119
E-mail: par@peopleagainstrape.org
URL: http://www.peopleagainstrape.org
Contact: Ms. Leslie E. Brown, Exec. Dir.
Founded: 1974. **Description:** Seeks to help teens and children avoid becoming the victims of sexual assault and rape by providing instruction in the basic principles of self-defense. Promotes self-esteem and motivation in teens through educational programs, offers substance abuse prevention programs, and teacher/parent training programs. Sponsors speakers' bureau; operates referral service. Provides experts to appear on television talk shows regarding rape, self defense, assertiveness training, and advice on parents on protecting children. **Telecommunication Services:** 24-hour hotline, rape crisis center, (800)241-7273. **Publications:** *Hands Off, I'm Special*, semiannual. Booklet. Includes information on rape, sexual assault, and defense techniques; educational packet for use in classroom. **Price:** $5.00 ● *My Power Book*. Booklet ● *Sexual Assault: How to Defend Yourself*. Book.

12808 ■ Survivor Connections (SC)
52 Lyndon Rd.
Cranston, RI 02905-1121
Ph: (401)941-2548

Fax: (401)941-2335
E-mail: survivorconnections@cox.net
URL: http://members.cox.net/survivorconnections
Contact: Mr. Francis L. Fitzpatrick, Founder
Founded: 1993. **Members:** 4,500. **Budget:** $10,000.
Description: Survivors of sexual assault and incest by clergy, family, ritual, youth leaders, and counselors. Seeks to provide communication and a support network for survivors. Encourages criminal prosecution and civil lawsuits. Conducts research on current sexual assault cases in the news. Provides educational programs. Compiles statistics; maintains Speaker's Bureau. **Libraries: Type:** reference. **Holdings:** audiovisuals, books, clippings, periodicals. **Subjects:** sexual assault. **Awards:** Dancing in the Streets. **Frequency:** annual. **Type:** recognition. **Recipient:** for effectiveness in preventing sexual abuse ● The Kathleen Guilfoyle Award. **Frequency:** periodic. **Type:** recognition. **Recipient:** to a supportive professional, or a supportive relative or friend of a survivor who has made a significant positive difference in the war against sexual abuse. **Computer Services:** database, connecting survivors of sexual assault, upon the request of the individuals desiring contact ● database, contains perpetrators reported by the victims, used solely to connect survivors for mutual support at their request. **Publications:** *The Survivor Activist*, periodic. Newsletter. Lists services for survivors of sexual assault. Contains items of interest. **Circulation:** 6,500. Alternate Formats: online. **Conventions/Meetings:** annual To Tell the Truth - meeting, with music - always fall ● periodic To Tell the Truth Conference and Awards Ceremony - conference and workshop (exhibits).

12809 ■ Survivors of Incest Anonymous (SIA)
c/o World Service Office
PO Box 190
Benson, MD 21018-0190
Ph: (410)893-3322
E-mail: feedback@siawso.org
URL: http://www.siawso.org
Contact: Linda L. Davis, Public Information Off.
Founded: 1982. **Members:** 100,000. **Staff:** 3. **Budget:** $20,000. **Local Groups:** 800. **National Groups:** 300. **Description:** Serves as a support group and self-help recovery program for any adult who was a victim of sexual abuse as a child. Follows a 12-step approach, modeled after the program espoused by Alcoholics Anonymous World Services, to assist members in their recovery. Sponsors educational programs; Maintains Speaker's Bureau. **Committees:** Literature; Public Information. **Absorbed:** (1987) Sexual Abuse Anonymous. **Publications:** *After-Effects of Repressed Satanic Cult Abuse.* Price: $1.25 plus shipping and handling ● *Autobiography Guide ● The Backlash: Obstacles to Being Believed.* Price: $2.75 plus shipping and handling ● *Bittersweet: a Pamphlet for Those in Other 12-Step Programs.* Price: $1.25 plus shipping and handling ● *Building From the Void: Survivors Frustrations with Parenting ● Characteristics of Survivors of Childhood Sexual Abuse ● The Confrontation.* Price: $1.50 plus shipping and handling ● *Criteria to Think About When Choosing a Therapist ● The Domino Effect: From Incest to a Cult and the Road to Recovery.* Price: $2.25 plus shipping and handling ● *The Effects of Child Sexual Abuse on the Adult Survivor ● Family Dynamics in an Incestuous Family ● Female Perpetrators ● First Step Inventory ● For Partners of Survivors: Comrades in Healing ● For the Male Survivor - I was a Victim Too ● Information Packet.* Includes 44 of the association's publications. **Price:** $25.00 plus shipping and handling ● *SIA Bulletin*, bimonthly. Directory ● *SIA World Service Bulletin*, bimonthly ● *Survivors of Incest Anonymous: Survivors Reaching Out to Survivors.* Brochure. Provides the group's definition of incest; explains the purpose of the group. ● *World Service Directory of SIA Meetings.* Price: $6.00 plus shipping and handling. **Conventions/Meetings:** periodic meeting.

12810 ■ VOICES in Action
8041 Hosbrook Rd., Ste.236
Cincinnati, OH 45236

Ph: (513)745-9555
Free: (800)786-4238
Fax: (513)745-9105
E-mail: voicesinaction@aol.com
URL: http://www.voices-action.org
Contact: Holly Sowels-Jenkins, Pres.
Founded: 1980. **Members:** 280. **Membership Dues:** individual, $35 (annual) ● additional household (same address), $5 (annual) ● life, $1,000 ● international, $45 (annual). **Staff:** 2. **Budget:** $75,000. **Multinational. Description:** Acronym means "Victims of Incest Can Emerge Survivors". Provides assistance to adult victims of child sexual abuse; seeks to help victims become survivors and create accurate public awareness of the prevalence of child sexual abuse, its impact, and ways in which it can be prevented or stopped through educational programs. **Committees:** Male Survivors; Ritual Abuse; Special Interest Groups; Volunteer. **Formerly:** (1982) Victims of Incest Concerned Effort; (1984) Victims of Incest Can Emerge; (1985) Victims of Incest Can Emerge Survivors. **Publications:** *The CHORUS*, bimonthly. Newsletter. **Price:** $10.00 for nonmembers. **Circulation:** 1,300 ● *How to Choose a Therapist.* Pamphlet ● *How to Confront Your Perpetrator: Living or Deceased.* Pamphlet ● *How to Start Your Own Self-Help Support Group.* Pamphlet ● *What Helps?.* Pamphlet. **Conventions/Meetings:** annual international conference (exhibits) - always July.

12811 ■ WINGS Foundation
8725 W 14th Ave., Ste.150
Lakewood, CO 80215
Ph: (303)238-8660
Free: (800)373-8671
E-mail: aguarnera@wingsfound.org
URL: http://www.wingsfound.org
Contact: Anne Guarnera MA, Exec. Dir.
Founded: 1982. **Description:** Volunteers, sexual abuse survivors. Strives to assist childhood sexual abuse survivors reduce the trauma of their abuse, improve their quality of life, and break the cycle of childhood sexual abuse. Hosts support groups. **Publications:** *On the Wings of Love.* Newsletter ● Handbook. **Price:** $25.00.

Sexual Freedom

12812 ■ Crossdressers International (CDI)
404 W 40th St.
New York, NY 10018
Ph: (212)564-4847
E-mail: info@cdinyc.org
URL: http://www.cdinyc.org
Contact: S. Kristine James, Dir.
Founded: 1990. **Members:** 101. **Membership Dues:** regular, $45 (annual). **Staff:** 2. **Budget:** $50,000. **State Groups:** 2. **Description:** Crossdressers. Promotes toleration of alternative lifestyles; seeks to educate the public regarding cross dressing. Conducts research, educational, and charitable programs; maintains speakers' bureau; makes available children's services. **Awards: Frequency:** periodic. **Type:** recognition. **Publications:** *CDI News*, monthly. Newsletter. **Price:** $25.00. **Circulation:** 150. **Advertising:** accepted. **Conventions/Meetings:** annual convention and board meeting - always April, New York City.

12813 ■ Gender Education and Advocacy (GEA)
PO Box 33724
Decatur, GA 30033-0724
E-mail: dallas@gender.org
URL: http://www.gender.org
Contact: Dallas Denny MA, Sec.
Founded: 1990. **Staff:** 5. **Budget:** $10,000. **Regional Groups:** 2. **Local Groups:** 1. **Nonmembership. Description:** Dedicated to improving the lives of all gender variant people regardless of sexual identities. **Libraries: Type:** reference. **Holdings:** 1,000. **Subjects:** transgender and transsexual issues. **Formerly:** (2000) American Educational Gender Information Service.

12814 ■ International Foundation for Gender Education (IFGE)
PO Box 540229
Waltham, MA 02454
Ph: (781)899-2212 (781)894-8340
Fax: (781)899-5703
E-mail: info@ifge.org
URL: http://www.ifge.org
Contact: Ms. Denise Leclair, Exec. Dir.
Founded: 1978. **Members:** 900. **Membership Dues:** subscriber, $36 (annual) ● student, $50 (annual) ● basic, $65 (annual) ● professional, $175 (annual) ● benefactor, $500 (annual) ● life, $2,500 ● supporting, $125 (annual). **Staff:** 5. **Budget:** $350,000. **Regional Groups:** 200. **Description:** Serves as an educational resource for the transgender, cross-dressing and transsexual community and those persons affected by or serving that community. Supports a communications network and mutual support system for transgender, cross-dressing and transsexual organizations and services worldwide. Administers the Foundation Trust Fund. Maintains Speaker's Bureau. **Libraries: Type:** reference. **Holdings:** 200; archival material, audiovisuals, books, clippings, monographs, periodicals. **Subjects:** cross dressing, sex reassignment, transgenderism. **Awards:** Conference Scholarship Funds. **Frequency:** annual. **Type:** scholarship ● Transgender Scholarship and Education Legacy Fund. **Frequency:** annual. **Type:** scholarship ● Trinity Award. **Frequency:** annual. **Type:** recognition. **Recipient:** for service to the community ● Virginia Prince Award. **Frequency:** annual. **Type:** recognition. **Recipient:** for service to the community. **Programs:** Female-to-Male Issues Conference; Mental Health Professional Conference; Transsexual Issues Conference. **Formerly:** (1987) Tiffany Club. **Publications:** *IFGE's Thread*, quarterly. Newsletter. **Price:** free. **Circulation:** 1,000. Alternate Formats: online ● *Legal Aspects of Transsexualism.* Book ● *Speakers Handbook ● Transgender Tapestry*, quarterly. Magazine. Includes editorials, entertainment news, personal listing directory, and updated organizations and services directory. **Price:** $12.00/copy; $40.00/year. ISSN: 0884-8749. **Circulation:** 10,000. **Advertising:** accepted ● *Wives and Partners.* Booklet. **Conventions/Meetings:** annual Coming Together - meeting (exhibits) - always spring.

12815 ■ International Sex Worker Foundation for Art, Culture and Education (ISWFACE)
8801 Cedros Ave., No. 7
Panorama City, CA 91402
Ph: (818)892-2029
Fax: (818)892-8109
E-mail: normaja@webuniverse.net
URL: http://www.iswface.org
Contact: Norma Jean Almodovar, Pres.
Founded: 1997. **Members:** 25,000. **Membership Dues:** regular, $100 (annual). **Multinational. Description:** Serves as an educational resource center for serious research and other information about prostitution and sex work, in order to provide the public with access to these academic reports and studies. Fosters, perpetuates and preserves an appreciation of the art and culture created by and about sex workers. Establishes and maintains a permanent collection of art (including, but not limited to, paintings, sculpture, photos, writing, etc.) and related archival materials created by and about sex workers, past and present, throughout the world, and provides for their display, both through regular exhibits and through the creation of a cyberspace museum. Educates the public about sex workers, their art and culture. Provides economic alternatives and opportunities for creative, artistic sex workers, to enable them to transition out of prostitution and into another profession if that is their goal. Contributes, or otherwise assists, corporations, organizations and institutions in the field of health care, law enforcement, and education through the dissemination of accurate, timely information relating to this important social and political issue. **Libraries: Type:** open to the public. **Holdings:** 450; articles, books, video recordings. **Subjects:** adult sexuality, prostitution, pornography. **Formerly:** (2004) Sex Worker Foundation for Art, Culture and Education. **Publications:**

Secretary's Report ● Newsletter, quarterly. **Conventions/Meetings:** annual board meeting - usually 2nd Sunday in September.

12816 ■ Intersex Society of North America (ISNA)
979 Golf Course Dr., No. 282
Rohnert Park, CA 94928
Fax: (801)348-5350
E-mail: info@isna.org
URL: http://www.isna.org/drupal/index.php
Contact: Cheryl Chase, Exec. Dir./Founder
Founded: 1993. **Staff:** 1. **Budget:** $100,000. **Languages:** English, Spanish. **Nonmembership. Multinational. Description:** Intersexual people born with mixed sex anatomy; individuals with an interest in intersexuality. Offers advocacy and policy around intersex issues; public and medical education campaigns. **Libraries: Type:** by appointment only; reference. **Holdings:** archival material, books, clippings, periodicals, video recordings. **Subjects:** intersexuality. **Also Known As:** ISNA. **Publications:** *The Child With an Intersex Condition: Total Patient Care.* Video. **Price:** $150.00 for institutions ● *Hermaphrodites Speak!.* Video. **Price:** $150.00 for institutions ● *Is It a Boy or a Girl?.* Video. **Price:** $150.00 for institutions ● *ISNA News,* quarterly. Newsletter. ISSN: 1084-5771. **Circulation:** 2,000. Alternate Formats: online ● *Yellow for Hermaphrodites: Mani's Story.* Video. **Conventions/Meetings:** semiannual conference.

12817 ■ Johns and Call Girls United Against Repression (JACGUAR)
Address Unknown since 2007
Founded: 1978. **Members:** 11. **Description:** Seeks to: dispel "the notion that there is anything reprehensible or immoral in being a prostitute whose customers are adults, or in being the customer of an adult prostitute"; instill in adult prostitutes and their adult customers a sense of self-respect. Works to legally safeguard civil rights and liberties of prostitutes and their customers, and to repeal laws criminalizing prostitution. Speaks out on public issues affecting prostitutes and their customers; testifies at legislative hearings; maintains speakers' bureau. Sponsors litigation challenging antiprostitution laws. **Conventions/Meetings:** annual meeting - always second Tuesday in August.

12818 ■ Lifestyles Organization
2641 W La Palma Ave., Ste.F
Anaheim, CA 92801
Ph: (714)821-9953
Free: (888)821-1235
Fax: (714)821-9919
E-mail: info@playcouples.com
URL: http://www.lifestyles.org/jos
Contact: Robert L. McGinley PhD, Chm./Co-Founder
Founded: 1973. **Members:** 40,000. **Membership Dues:** individual, $20 (annual). **Staff:** 9. **Budget:** $250,000. **For-Profit. Description:** Participants are persons living an alternative lifestyle. Holds seminars, workshops, and panel presentations on topics including ways of living, social recreation, marriage and other interpersonal relationships, swinging, communes, legal and medical aspects of human behavior, and human sexuality. Offers theme dances, periodic tours and special events. Conducts research programs. **Awards:** Lifestyles Awards of Recognition. **Frequency:** annual. **Type:** recognition. **Computer Services:** Mailing lists. **Formerly:** (1984) Society for the Study of Alternative Lifestyles. **Publications:** *Annual Program,* annual. Proceedings. **Price:** $5.00. **Advertising:** accepted ● *Lifestyles eNews.* Newsletter. Alternate Formats: online ● *Lifestyles Magazine,* 3/year ● *Playcouples Journal, Newsletter,* bimonthly. **Conventions/Meetings:** annual Lifestyles Convention, for couples (exhibits).

12819 ■ Loving More
PO Box 4358
Boulder, CO 80306-4358
Ph: (303)543-7540

E-mail: lovingmore@lovemore.com
URL: http://www.lovemore.com
Contact: Robyn Trask, Managing Dir.
Founded: 1984. **Members:** 1,500. **Membership Dues:** basic, $36 (annual) ● family, $75 (annual) ● supporter, $49 (annual) ● professional, $65 (annual) ● patron, $100 (annual) ● life, $1,000. **Description:** Promotes "loving more", which the organization characterizes as polyamory, group marriage, intimate networks, and expanded family. Provides a forum for exchange between members. Works to increase public awareness through media campaign and educational workshops and conferences. **Publications:** *Loving More Magazine,* quarterly. Features articles from people who are deeply involved in the poly lifestyle on the central issues of multi-partner relating topics. **Price:** $6.00 for members. ISSN: 1523-5858. **Circulation:** 1,500. **Advertising:** accepted ● *Loving More: The Polyfidelity Primer.* Book. **Conventions/Meetings:** annual conference, covers all aspects of responsible non-monogamy (exhibits) - summer ● retreat ● workshop.

12820 ■ NASCA International (NASCA)
PO Box 7128
Buena Park, CA 90622-7128
Ph: (714)229-4870
Fax: (714)821-9919
E-mail: nasca@nasca.com
URL: http://www.nasca.com
Contact: Tony Lanzaratta, Exec. Dir.
Founded: 1980. **Members:** 500. **Membership Dues:** individual/couple (in U.S., Canada and Mexico), $50 (annual) ● individual/couple (outside U.S., Canada and Mexico), $60 (annual) ● business associate, $75 (annual). **Staff:** 4. **Regional Groups:** 3. **Description:** Individuals, clubs, and organizations interested in the alternative lifestyle known as swinging (recreational social sex). Presents swinging as a viable lifestyle to the public. Objectives are to protect members of the swinging community against unfair or harmful business practices; to develop a set of standards and etiquette for swinging; to present swinging to the communications media in a non-explosive and factual manner; to encourage participation in swinging. Acts as a clearinghouse and resource center for the dissemination of social and sexual research data. Maintains speakers' bureau; compiles statistics. **Libraries: Type:** reference. **Holdings:** archival material. **Subjects:** swinging since 1969. **Awards: Type:** recognition. **Computer Services:** database, affiliate clubs. **Also Known As:** NASCA, Inc. **Formerly:** (2000) North American Swing Club Association. **Publications:** *Etiquette in Swinging.* Booklet. **Price:** $5.00 in U.S. ● *NASCA Inside Report,* bimonthly. Newsletter. **Price:** included in membership dues ● *NASCA International Swing Clubs and Publications Directory,* annual. **Price:** $19.95/copy. **Conventions/Meetings:** annual conference.

12821 ■ National Leather Association - International (NLA-I)
PO Box 423
Blacklick, OH 43004-0423
Ph: (780)454-1992
E-mail: info@ppfund.org
URL: http://www.nla-i.com
Contact: Jan Hall, Pres.
Founded: 1986. **Membership Dues:** individual, $20 (annual) ● commercial, affiliate, $50 (annual). **Description:** Individuals and organizations promoting the right of consenting adults to engage in nontraditional sexual practices, particularly those involving sadomasochism, leather, and fetishism. Seeks to establish and maintain a communication, education, and support network for members of the "leather/SM/fetish community" worldwide. Conducts political activism and public education to remove misconceptions about leather/SM/fetish behavior and protect the constitutional rights of members; supports and raises funds on behalf of individuals, organizations, and institutions that work for the decriminalization of all sexual acts between consenting adults. Conducts outreach programs for women, minorities, the physically challenged, and other groups that have traditionally been excluded from the Leather/SM/fetish com-

munity; works to preserve records of the history, traditions, and culture of individuals whose sexual practices involve leather, sadomasochism, and fetishism. Makes charitable contributions to AIDS and other service groups. Sponsors competitions. Holds workshops. **Awards:** Man of the Year Award. **Frequency:** annual. **Type:** recognition. **Recipient:** for outstanding contributions to the leather/sadoma sochistist/fetish community ● Woman of the Year Award. **Frequency:** annual. **Type:** recognition. **Recipient:** for outstanding contributions to the leather/sadoma sochistist/fetish community. **Formerly:** (2003) National Leather Association. **Publications:** *The Link.* Newsletter. Features calendar of events, NLA news, and relevant political information. **Price:** for members only. **Circulation:** 1,500. **Advertising:** accepted. **Conventions/Meetings:** annual Living in Leather Conference (exhibits) - always October.

12822 ■ North American Man/Boy Love Association (NAMBLA)
PO Box 174
New York, NY 10018
Ph: (212)631-1194
E-mail: peterherman@netzero.net
URL: http://www.nambla.org
Contact: Mr. Arnold Schoen, Contact
Founded: 1978. **Members:** 1,500. **Membership Dues:** individual in U.S. and Canada, $35 (annual) ● subscription and institution in U.S. and Canada, $40 (annual) ● outside U.S. and Canada, $50 (annual) ● supporting, $200 (annual) ● life, $1,000. **Budget:** $70,000. **Description:** Men, women, and youth. Promotes sexual freedom in all aspects, particularly in man/boy relationships. Opposes the oppression of men and boys involved in consensual sexual and emotional relationships. Opposes "age of consent laws and other restrictions which deny adults and youths the full enjoyment of their bodies and control over their own lives." Condemns sexual abuse and all forms of coercion. Calls for the gay and lesbian community to support gay youth because of the disassociation of the gay and lesbian community from gay youth. Maintains speakers' bureau; offers educational programs. **Publications:** *NAMBLA Bulletin,* periodic. Magazine. Includes news, opinion, photography, art, and short stories. **Price:** $10.95 for nonmembers, includes shipping; free for members. ISSN: 9100-2624. **Circulation:** 2,200. **Advertising:** accepted. Alternate Formats: CD-ROM ● *NAMBLA Updates,* quarterly. Newsletters. **Price:** $3.00 for nonmembers, includes shipping; free for members ● *Topics,* periodic. Booklet. Monographs on various relevant topics. **Price:** $10.95 for nonmembers, includes shipping; free for members. **Circulation:** 2,000. **Conventions/Meetings:** annual conference.

12823 ■ Renaissance Transgender Association
987 Old Eagle School Rd., Ste.719
Wayne, PA 19087
Ph: (610)975-9119
Free: (866)481-7366
E-mail: info@ren.org
URL: http://www.ren.org
Contact: Rev. Kaye S. Fox, Exec. Dir.
Founded: 1987. **Members:** 450. **Staff:** 1. **Budget:** $20,000. **Local Groups:** 16. **Description:** Transvestites, transsexuals, and individuals interested in transgender behavior. Provides support and information about gender issues. Educates professionals and the general public about transgender behavior and people who exhibit such behavior. Operates speakers' bureau for college and university lectures. Sponsors Pen Pal Project for members unable to attend meetings. Facilitates formation of local chapters. **Libraries: Type:** reference. **Holdings:** 150; books. **Subjects:** transgender issues. **Formerly:** (2001) Renaissance Education Association. **Publications:** *Aids and HIV Safety and Ethics.* Pamphlet ● *The Matter of Children.* Pamphlet ● *Myths and Misconceptions About Crossdressing.* Pamphlet ● *Partners: Spouses and Significant Others.* Pamphlet ● *Reasons for Male to Female Crossdressing.* Pamphlet ● *Renaissance News and Views,* monthly. Newsletter. Features chapter activities and current transgender

issues. **Price:** $36.00/year ● *Telling the Children: A Transsexuals Commentary.* Pamphlet ● *Transgender Community News and Views*, monthly. Magazine. **Price:** $45.00/year ● *Understanding Transsexualism.*

12824 ■ Sacred Space Institute
PO Box 4322
San Rafael, CA 94913
Ph: (415)507-1739 (415)456-0100
E-mail: info@lovewithoutlimits.com
URL: http://www.lovewithoutlimits.com
Contact: Ms. Carolena Fleishman, Dir.
Founded: 1985. **Members:** 500. **Membership Dues:** low income, $30 (annual) ● individual, $49 (annual) ● family, $75 (annual) ● life, $1,000. **Regional Groups:** 23. **Description:** Serves as a resource for people who are living or are exploring ethical multipartner relationships. Provides access to a network that links up people and organizations isolated by the social stigma which has kept many polyamorous people in the closet. Acts as a research and seminar company to investigate alternatives to the nuclear family and to provide information on new paradigm relationships for TV and radio talk shows and at conferences across the country. Offers seminars and training in sexual healing and tantric sexuality. **Libraries: Type:** reference. **Holdings:** 100; archival material, audiovisuals, books, periodicals. **Subjects:** polylove, sacred sex, future of the family. **Awards:** Poly Love Song Contest. **Frequency:** periodic. **Type:** monetary. **Recipient:** for the songwriter or performing artist whose work best promotes ethical and responsible sexual love and intimacy among three or more partners. **Additional Websites:** http://www.sacredspaceinstitute.com. **Formerly:** (1988) Intinet; (1995) Intinet Resource Center; (1997) Abundant Love Institute. **Publications:** *Love Without Limits.* Book. **Price:** $16.00 plus shipping and handling ($4) ● *The New Love Without Limits.* Book ● *Polyamory.* Book. **Conventions/Meetings:** annual Celebration of Eros - conference (exhibits) ● Love Without Limits - workshop, for people interested in exploring polyamory.

12825 ■ Society for the Second Self (SSS)
c/o Jane Ellen Fairfax, Chair
PO Box 980638
Houston, TX 77098-0638
Ph: (713)349-8969
E-mail: info@tri-ess.org
URL: http://www.tri-ess.org
Contact: Jane Ellen Fairfax, Chair
Founded: 1976. **Members:** 1,400. **Membership Dues:** individual, $42 (annual) ● couple, $57 (annual). **Staff:** 20. **Budget:** $40,000. **Local Groups:** 38. **Description:** Heterosexual crossdressers who are not transsexuals, fetishists, or sadomasochists; interested spouses. Encourages members to live happy and well adjusted lives as crossdressers and accept their desire to dress in women's clothes. Conducts public education programs on the true nature of crossdressing. Functions as a network for communication among members; local groups conduct regular support group meetings and social gathering. Maintains speakers' bureau. **Telecommunication Services:** electronic mail, jeftris@aol.com. **Also Known As:** Tri-Ess Sorority. **Formed by Merger of:** (1976) Mamselle Sorority; (1976) Phi Pi Epsilon. **Publications:** *Mirror*, quarterly. Magazine. **Circulation:** 1,400. **Advertising:** accepted ● *The Sweetheart Connection*, quarterly. Newsletter. Designed for spouses and partners. ● Directory, annual. Contains pictures and members' profiles. **Price:** available to members only. **Conventions/Meetings:** annual Holiday en Femme - convention (exhibits) - always November ● annual Spouses' and Partners' International Conference for Education (SPICE) - workshop - always July.

12826 ■ World Professional Association for Transgender Health (HBIGDA)
1300 S Second St., Ste.180
Minneapolis, MN 55454
Ph: (612)624-9397
Fax: (612)624-9541

E-mail: hbigda@hbigda.org
URL: http://www.wpath.org
Contact: Bean Robinson PhD, Exec. Dir.
Founded: 1994. **Members:** 500. **Membership Dues:** full, supporting, $110 (annual) ● emeritus, $70 (annual) ● student, $55 (annual). **Description:** Mental health providers, psychotherapists, psychologists, psychiatrists, reconstructive surgeons, plastic surgeons, general surgeons, and endocrinologists specializing in "standards of care" for gender dysphoric individuals. Maintains a geographic locator file and information service for transsexuals/gender dysphoric individuals seeking mental health providers, reconstructive surgeons, and endocrinologists. Maintains Speaker's Bureau. **Libraries: Type:** reference. **Holdings:** business records, clippings. **Subjects:** hormonal reassignment, genital reassignment, transsexual "standards of care". **Committees:** Advocacy and Liaison; Archives; By-Laws; Child and Adolescent; Ethics; Intersex; Legal Issues; Newsletter; Standards of Care Revision; STD and Blood-Borne Infections; Symposium; Transgender Medicine and Research Discussion; Website. **Formerly:** (2003) National Harry Benjamin Gender Dysphoria Association; (2007) Harry Benjamin International Gender Dysphoria Association. **Publications:** Newsletter, semiannual ● Membership Directory, annual. **Price:** $10.00 for nonmembers; free for members. **Conventions/Meetings:** biennial symposium - 2007 Sept. 5-8, Chicago, IL.

Shortness

12827 ■ Billy Barty Foundation (BBF)
929 W Olive Ave., Ste.C
Burbank, CA 91506
Ph: (818)953-5410
E-mail: billybarty@myself.com
URL: http://www.rth.org/bbf
Contact: Chuck Cerbello, Pres.
Founded: 1975. **Budget:** $50,000. **Description:** Provides medical, educational, vocational, social, and psychological support for people less than 4'10" tall. Advises on issues concerning adoption, public education on dwarfism, and legal aid. Assists individuals in living independently by supplying information on adapting automobiles and homes for use by little people and providing information on clothing and shoe stores offering small sizes. Promotes Billy Barty Collection of furniture designed for use by little people. Sponsors sports teams and annual golf tournament in California; offers placement and children's services; maintains Speaker's Bureau. Conducts charitable program; compiles statistics. **Libraries: Type:** reference. **Awards:** BBF Scholarship Fund. **Frequency:** annual. **Type:** scholarship. **Recipient:** for college student who has medical form of dwarfism ● **Type:** recognition. **Committees:** Adoption; Educational; Grant Research; Medical Research. **Affiliated With:** Little People of America. **Also Known As:** Billy Barty Foundation for Little People. **Publications:** *My Child is a Dwarf.* Book ● Newsletter, quarterly ● Pamphlets. **Conventions/Meetings:** quarterly board meeting (exhibits).

12828 ■ Little People of America (LPA)
5289 NE Elam Young Pkwy., Ste.F-100
Hillsboro, OR 97124
Ph: (503)846-1562
Free: (888)LPA-2001
Fax: (503)846-1590
E-mail: info@lpaonline.org
URL: http://www.lpaonline.org
Contact: Lois Gerage-Lamb, Pres.
Founded: 1957. **Members:** 24,616. **Membership Dues:** household, $50 (annual) ● life, $500 ● senior (65 years and older), $10 (annual). **Staff:** 1. **Budget:** $63,771. **Regional Groups:** 14. **Local Groups:** 54. **Languages:** English, Spanish. **Description:** Assists those who have a diagnosis of dwarfism with their physical and developmental concerns resulting from short stature. Offers information on employment, education, disability rights, adoption of short statured children, medical issues, clothing, adaptive devices,

and parenting tips. Provides information through hundreds of dedicated volunteers throughout the U.S. as well as through a national newsletter. Gives opportunities for social interaction at chapter, district, regional meetings, national conferences, and participation in athletic events. Provides educational scholarships, medical assistance grants, access to medical advisory board, and funds for publications and other projects. **Libraries: Type:** reference. **Holdings:** 4; archival material. **Subjects:** health, medicine, social. **Awards:** Distinguished Service Award. **Frequency:** annual. **Type:** recognition. **Recipient:** for service and outstanding contributions to LPA. **Computer Services:** database ● mailing lists, available to officers only. **Committees:** Adoption; Advocacy; ANSI Delegate; Conference Review; Development, Fundraising and Grant Writing; Dwarf Artist Coalition; Dwarf Athletic Association of America; Education; Employment; Export; Historian; International; Medical Board; Parent's; Public Relations; Scholarships; Teen-Age; Young Adult. **Absorbed:** (1998) Short Stature Foundation. **Publications:** *It's a Whole New View* (in English and Spanish), quinquennial. Booklet. Provides information for new parents with a child who has a leading form of dwarfism. **Price:** free for new applicants with dwarf child—$1.50/ex. Also Cited As: *Una Perspectives Totalmente Distinta* ● *LPA Today*, quarterly. Newsletter. Includes medical information, book reviews, personal stories, and meeting calendar. **Price:** included in membership dues. **Circulation:** 8,612. **Advertising:** accepted ● Brochure. **Price:** free ● Annual Report, annual. Alternate Formats: online. **Conventions/Meetings:** annual conference, art and products geared for the short-statured; talent; fashion (exhibits) - always July ● semiannual regional meeting - spring and fall.

Singles

12829 ■ American Singles Golf Association (ASGA)
PO Box 848
Pineville, NC 28134
Ph: (704)889-4600
Free: (888)GOLFMATE
Fax: (704)889-4607
E-mail: asganational@aol.com
URL: http://www.singlesgolf.com
Contact: Thomas A. Alsop, Founder/CEO
Founded: 1996. **Members:** 4,000. **Membership Dues:** individual, $70 (annual). **Staff:** 7. **Budget:** $750,000. **Local Groups:** 65. **Description:** Single, divorced, or separated individuals who play golf. Promotes fun and fellowship among members. Encourages tournament play. Sponsors educational and charitable programs; conducts competitions, and multi-chapter golf weekends. **Awards:** Lifetime Membership. **Frequency:** periodic. **Type:** recognition. **Publications:** *American Single Golfer*, monthly. Newsletter. **Price:** included in membership dues. **Circulation:** 4,000. **Advertising:** accepted.

12830 ■ National Association of Single People (NASP)
380 E Yale Loop
Irvine, CA 92614
Ph: (714)756-1000 (949)559-1800
E-mail: erbgroup10@aol.com
Contact: Richard Baron, Exec. Dir.
Founded: 1992. **Members:** 10,000. **Membership Dues:** individual, $24 (annual). **Staff:** 4. **Description:** Promotes improvement of benefits and representation for single community. Conducts educational and research programs; maintains speakers' bureau. Operates Political Action. **Awards:** Member of the Year. **Frequency:** annual. **Type:** recognition. **Publications:** *Single People*, bimonthly. Magazine. **Circulation:** 10,000. **Advertising:** accepted. Alternate Formats: CD-ROM; online; magnetic tape. **Conventions/Meetings:** annual convention (exhibits).

12831 ■ National Organization of Single Mothers (NOSM)
PO Box 68
Midland, NC 28107
URL: http://www.singlemothers.org
Contact: Andrea Engber, Dir./Founder
Founded: 1991. **Members:** 2,000. **Membership Dues:** best bet, $39 (annual) ● regular, $19 (annual)

● regular, $35 (biennial). **Regional Groups:** 2. **Description:** Offers support to single mothers. **Libraries: Type:** lending; reference. **Holdings:** archival material, articles, books, periodicals. **Subjects:** single parenting. **Awards:** Complete Single Mother Award. **Frequency:** annual. **Type:** recognition. **Recipient:** for single moms.

Social Change

12832 ■ Justice Studies Association (JSA)
Mohawk Valley Community Coll.
Social Science/Criminal Justice Dept.
Utica, NY 13501
Ph: (315)792-5653
Fax: (315)792-5666
E-mail: bquist@mvcc.edu
URL: http://www.justicestudies.org
Contact: Susan Krumholz, Pres.
Founded: 1998. **Membership Dues:** regular (based on income range), $38-$78 (annual) ● student, $38 (annual) ● unemployed, $28 (annual) ● institutional, $130 (annual) ● corporate, $300 (annual) ● life, $400. **Description:** Fosters progressive writing, research and practice in all areas of criminal, social and restorative justice. Represents the interests of scholars from all academic disciplines and fields of endeavor as well as activists and practitioners of justice from around the globe. Seeks to explore and develop social arrangements and ways of life that promote justice without violence. **Awards:** JSA Social Activist Award. **Frequency:** annual. **Type:** recognition. **Recipient:** for a social activist who lives in the city and/or in environs where the annual conference is held ● Noam Chomsky Award. **Frequency:** annual. **Type:** recognition. **Recipient:** for an individual who has the commitment to scholarly/intellectual activities related to justice. **Publications:** Contemporary Justice Review, quarterly. Journal. **Price:** 62.00 /year for individuals; 154.00 /year for institutions; $74.00 /year for individuals; $256.00 /year for institutions. Also Cited As: CJR ● Justitia, annual. Newsletter. **Price:** included in membership dues. Alternate Formats: online.

Social Issues

12833 ■ Ambrose Monell Foundation
One Rockefeller Plz., Ste.301
New York, NY 10020-2002
Ph: (212)586-0700
Fax: (212)245-1863
E-mail: info@monellvetlesen.org
URL: http://www.monellvetlesen.org
Contact: Maurizio J. Morello, Sec./Asst. Treas.
Multinational. Description: Strives to promote religious, charitable, scientific, literary, and educational causes. **Awards: Type:** grant.

12834 ■ Brecht Forum
451 West St.
New York, NY 10014
Ph: (212)242-4201
E-mail: info@brechtforum.org
URL: http://www.brechtforum.org
Contact: Liz Mestres, Exec. Dir.
Membership Dues: subscriber, $15 (monthly). **Staff:** 2. **Multinational. Description:** Works for fundamental social change and a new culture that puts human needs first. **Conventions/Meetings:** lecture ● seminar ● workshop.

12835 ■ Center for the American Founding (CAF)
Address Unknown since 2006
Founded: 1996. **Members:** 2,100. **Staff:** 4. **Budget:** $300,000. **Languages:** English, French, German, Hungarian. **Description:** Individuals with an interest in what the center believes are the founding principles of the American republic: "the Rule of Law, Individual Rights, the security of Property, and the same American Identity for all its citizens." Conducts advocacy and educational activities. **Libraries: Type:**

reference; by appointment only. **Holdings:** 1,500; clippings. **Subjects:** public policy, American Founding philosophy. **Awards:** Constitutional Compass. **Frequency:** periodic. **Type:** recognition. **Recipient:** for commitment to America's founding principles. **Computer Services:** Mailing lists. **Publications:** America on My Mind, weekly. Articles. Nationally syndicated column. ● America on My Mind. Book ● America's 30 Years War, periodic. Book ● The Vazsonyi Analysis, periodic. Newsletter. **Conventions/Meetings:** Four Points of the Compass - meeting ● quarterly meeting, panel discussion ● quarterly Social Justice - meeting, panel discussion.

12836 ■ Center for Human Services (CHS)
7200 Wisconsin Ave., Ste.600
Bethesda, MD 20814
Ph: (301)654-8338
Fax: (301)941-8427
E-mail: webmaster@urc-chs.com
URL: http://www.urc-chs.com
Contact: David D. Nicholas MD, Sr. VP/Dir. of Quality Assurance Proj.
Founded: 1968. **Staff:** 150. **Languages:** English, French. **Description:** Provides technical assistance to government, industry, and human service agencies in areas of training, human resource management, leadership and management development, health education, quality assurance, communications, and international development. Assists organizations in enhancing productivity and competitiveness by developing bias-free selection tests, performance appraisals, certification procedures, and job design and redesign. Makes available development services including organizational diagnosis, systems analysis and intervention, change and total quality management, strategic planning, team building, and management coaching and counseling. Conducts training programs in labor-management relations, behavioral leadership, sexual harassment protection, and equal opportunity and affirmative action programs. Holds health education programs in areas including smoking cessation, stress management, and alcohol and drug abuse; and international health education programs in family planning, child survival, and health care management. Develops curricula and training materials including computer-based programs and simulations, seminars, self-paced courses, and audio and videotapes. **Publications:** Mande. Magazine. Contains information about health and monthly celebrations.

12837 ■ Charles Stewart Mott Foundation
Mott Found. Bldg.
503 S Saginaw St., Ste.1200
Flint, MI 48502-1851
Ph: (810)238-5651
Fax: (810)766-1753
E-mail: info@mott.org
URL: http://www.mott.org
Contact: William S. White, Pres./CEO
Founded: 1926. **Nonmembership. Description:** Strives to support efforts that promote a just, equitable, and sustainable society. **Awards: Type:** grant. **Publications:** Mott Mosaic, periodic. Magazine. Alternate Formats: online ● Annual Report, annual. Alternate Formats: online.

12838 ■ Compton Foundation
255 Shoreline Dr., Ste.540
Redwood City, CA 94065
Ph: (650)508-1181
Fax: (650)508-1191
URL: http://www.comptonfoundation.org
Contact: Edith T. Eddy, Exec. Dir.
Founded: 1946. **Multinational. Description:** Strives to support welfare, social justice, and the arts in communities.

12839 ■ Doris Duke Charitable Foundation (DDCF)
Off. of Grants Admin.
650 Fifth Ave., 19th Fl.
New York, NY 10019
Ph: (212)974-7000
Fax: (212)974-7590

E-mail: webmaster@ddcf.org
URL: http://www.ddcf.org
Contact: Joan E. Spero, Pres.
Founded: 1996. **Staff:** 32. **Description:** Strives to improve the quality of life by nurturing the arts, protecting and restoring the environment, seeking cures for disease, and protecting children from neglect and abuse. **Awards: Type:** grant. **Programs:** Child Abuse Prevention; Environment; Medical Research; Performing Arts.

12840 ■ Dudley Foundation
609 N Shore Dr.
Bellingham, WA 98226-4414
Ph: (360)671-8251
E-mail: dudleyfdn@yahoo.com
URL: http://www.dudleyfoundation.org
Contact: Rick Dudley, Pres.
Founded: 1990. **Description:** Provides grants to organizations that strive to promote awareness on human overpopulation, wanton consumption of resources, ecological degradation, and intolerance; applications for funding are by invitation only. **Awards: Frequency:** annual. **Type:** grant.

12841 ■ Edward E. Ford Foundation
66 Pearl St., Ste.322
Portland, ME 04101
Ph: (207)774-2346
Fax: (207)774-2348
E-mail: info@eeford.org
URL: http://www.eeford.org
Contact: Robert W. Hallett, Exec. Dir.
Founded: 1957. **Multinational. Description:** Works to support organizations that strengthen democratic values, reduce poverty and injustice, promote international cooperation, and advance human achievement. **Publications:** Win Win. Report. Contains information on companies that invest in low-income U.S. communities.

12842 ■ Fuller Foundation
c/o John T. Bottomley, Exec. Dir.
PO Box 479
Rye Beach, NH 03871
Ph: (603)964-6998
E-mail: atfuller@aol.com
URL: http://www.fullerfoundation.org
Contact: John T. Bottomley, Exec. Dir.
Description: Strives to support non-profit agencies that improve the quality of life for people, animals, and the environment.

12843 ■ Geraldine R. Dodge Foundation
163 Madison Ave.
PO Box 1239
Morristown, NJ 07962-1239
Ph: (973)540-8442
Fax: (973)540-1211
E-mail: info@grdodge.org
URL: http://www.grdodge.org
Contact: David Grant, Pres./CEO
Founded: 1974. **Description:** Strives to promote and encourage educational, cultural, social, and environmental values that contribute to making society humane and more livable. **Programs:** Dodge Poetry. **Publications:** Reports.

12844 ■ Hearst Foundation
90 New Montgomery St., Ste.1212
San Francisco, CA 94105
Ph: (415)543-0400 (415)543-6033
Fax: (415)348-0887
E-mail: journalism@hearstfdn.org
URL: http://www.hearstfdn.org
Contact: Paul Dinovitz, Dir.
Founded: 1945. **Description:** Works to support nonprofit organizations. **Awards:** Grant. **Type:** recognition.

12845 ■ Heartland Institute
19 S LaSalle St., Ste.903
Chicago, IL 60603
Ph: (312)377-4000
Fax: (312)377-5000

E-mail: think@heartland.org
URL: http://www.heartland.org
Contact: Joseph L. Bast, Pres./CEO
Founded: 1984. **Membership Dues:** basic, $29 (annual) ● sponsor, $49 (annual) ● premium, $99 (annual). **Staff:** 14. **Description:** Works to build social movements in order to empower individuals, through ideas such as "parental choice in education, choice and personal responsibility in health care, market-based approaches to environmental protection, privatization of public services, and deregulation in areas where property rights and markets do a better job than government bureaucracies". **Boards:** Legislative Advisors; Policy Advisors. **Conventions/Meetings:** quarterly board meeting.

12846 ■ Ittleson Foundation
15 E 67th St.
New York, NY 10021
Ph: (212)794-2008
URL: http://www.ittlesonfoundation.org
Contact: Anthony C. Wood, Exec. Dir.
Founded: 1932. **Description:** Works to provide resources for non-profit organizations focused on AIDS, environmental issues, and mental health. **Awards: Type:** grant.

12847 ■ Kresge Foundation
3215 W Big Beaver Rd.
Troy, MI 48084
Ph: (248)643-9630
Fax: (248)643-0588
E-mail: info@kresge.org
URL: http://www.kresge.org
Contact: Rip Rapson, Pres./CEO
Founded: 1924. **Staff:** 28. **Multinational. Description:** Strives to strengthen the capacity of charitable organizations through grantmaking programs. Hosts information workshops. **Programs:** Bricks and Mortar; Scientific Equipment. **Publications:** Annual Report, annual. Alternate Formats: online.

12848 ■ L. Mike Association (LMA)
Address Unknown since 2007
Founded: 1998. **Membership Dues:** active, $20 (annual). **Description:** Currently Inactive. Investigative clearinghouse dealing with bigotry and hate to help eliminate them. Individuals who harbor feelings of racial hatred or bigotry. Seeks to help members manage their hate through application of a 12-step program similar to that operated by Alcoholics Anonymous World Services. Although L. Mike recommends the Bigots Anonymous and Big-Anon programs, it is not associated with them or AA. **Publications:** Trouble Spots, The L. Mike Update, semiannual. Newsletter.

12849 ■ Nathan Cummings Foundation (NCF)
475 10th Ave., 14th Fl.
New York, NY 10018-9715
Ph: (212)787-7300
Fax: (212)787-7377
E-mail: info@nathancummings.org
URL: http://www.nathancummings.org
Contact: Lance E. Lindblom, Pres./CEO
Description: Seeks to build a society that values nature and protects ecological balance for future generations, to promote humane health care, and foster arts to enrich communities. **Programs:** Arts and Culture; Environment/Contemplative Practice; Health; Jewish Life. **Publications:** Annual Report.

12850 ■ National Science and Technology Education Partnership (NSTEP)
2500 Wilson Blvd., Ste.300
Arlington, VA 22201-3834
Ph: (703)907-7400 (703)907-7050
Fax: (703)907-7401
E-mail: bwortmann@nationalstep.org
URL: http://www.nationalstep.org
Contact: John Clough, Interim Exec. Dir.
Founded: 1975. **Staff:** 20. **Budget:** $1,800,000. **Description:** Aims to encourage electronics industry firms to participate in programs that help solve social problems and increase employment opportunities for minority youth and disabled people in the electronics

industry. Participates in private and governmental planning and policy-making boards, councils, and advisory groups. Sponsors: the Rehabilitation Engineering Center to improve the technology and marketability of devices to aid disabled people; Project With Industry to help place disabled persons in competitive employment. Offers training programs for minority youth and disabled people interested in electronics. Conducts demonstrations and research. Awards scholarships to disabled youths studying in a technical field; presents awards to companies and individuals making significant contributions to EIF programs. **Libraries: Type:** reference. **Holdings:** 4,000. **Programs:** Electronic Service Technicians Training. **Affiliated With:** Electronic Industries Alliance. **Formerly:** Electronic Industries Foundation. **Conventions/Meetings:** periodic board meeting.

12851 ■ Needmor Fund
42 S St. Clair St.
Toledo, OH 43602
Ph: (419)255-5560
URL: http://fdncenter.org/grantmaker/needmor
Founded: 1956. **Description:** Family members. Works to promote social issues. **Awards: Type:** grant.

12852 ■ Norman Foundation
147 E 48th St.
New York, NY 10017
Ph: (212)230-9830
Fax: (212)230-9849
E-mail: info@normanfdn.org
URL: http://www.normanfdn.org
Contact: June Makela, Program Dir.
Description: Strives to support charitable organizations. **Awards: Type:** grant.

12853 ■ Pew Charitable Trusts
2005 Market St., Ste.1700
Philadelphia, PA 19103-7077
Ph: (215)575-9050 (215)575-4700
Fax: (215)575-4939
E-mail: info@pewtrusts.org
URL: http://www.pewtrusts.org
Contact: Rebecca W. Rimel, Pres./CEO
Founded: 1948. **Staff:** 140. **Budget:** $140,000,000. **Description:** Strives to support non-profit activities in the areas of culture, education, the environment, health and human services, public policy, and religion. **Libraries: Type:** not open to the public. **Holdings:** 2,800. **Subjects:** culture, education, health, philanthropy, religion, public policy. **Awards: Type:** grant. **Funds:** Culture Program; Education Program; Environment Program; Health and Human Services Program; Venture. **Programs:** Public Policy; Religion. **Publications:** Trust, quarterly. Magazine. **Price:** free. ISSN: 1540-4587. Alternate Formats: online.

12854 ■ Preservation Institute
2140 Shattuck Ave., Ste.2122
Berkeley, CA 94704
Ph: (510)848-7827
E-mail: preserve@preservenet.com
URL: http://www.preservenet.com
Description: Works to develop new politics related to emerging technology and focuses on the natural and social environment. **Publications:** The End of Economic Growth. Booklet. Contains information on study done relating to economic growth. **Price:** $9.95/copy.

12855 ■ Public Welfare Foundation
1200 U St. NW
Washington, DC 20009-4443
Ph: (202)965-1800
Fax: (202)265-8851
E-mail: reviewcommittee@publicwelfare.org
URL: http://www.publicwelfare.org
Founded: 1947. **Description:** Works to support organizations that help people overcome barriers to full participation in society. **Awards: Type:** grant ● **Type:** recognition. **Telecommunication Services:** electronic mail, lk@publicwelfare.org. **Publications:** Annual Report, annual. Alternate Formats: online.

12856 ■ Samuel H. Kress Foundation
174 E 80th St.
New York, NY 10021
Ph: (212)861-4993
Fax: (212)628-3146
E-mail: lisa@shkf.org
URL: http://www.kressfoundation.org
Contact: Lisa M. Ackerman, Exec. VP
Founded: 1929. **Staff:** 6. **Budget:** $5,000,000. **Description:** Seeks to advance the history, conservation and enjoyment of the vast heritage of European art, architecture and archaeology from antiquity to the 19th Century. **Awards:** The Care and Presentation of European Art. **Frequency:** annual. **Type:** grant. **Recipient:** for the documentation, care and display of European art and architecture ● Kress Conservation Fellowships. **Frequency:** annual. **Type:** fellowship. **Recipient:** for individuals who have completed an M.A. degree in art conservation ● Kress Curatorial Fellowships. **Frequency:** annual. **Type:** fellowship. **Recipient:** for individuals who have completed a PhD in the history of European art ● Kress Fellowships in Art History at Foreign Institutions. **Frequency:** annual. **Type:** fellowship. **Recipient:** for pre-doctoral candidates in the history of art ● The Practice of Art History and Conservation. **Frequency:** annual. **Type:** grant. **Recipient:** for trained professionals.

12857 ■ Social Choice for Social Change: Campaign for a New TIAA-CREF
Box 135
Manchester Coll.
North Manchester, IN 46962
Ph: (260)982-5346 (260)982-5009
Fax: (260)982-5043
E-mail: njwollman@manchester.edu
URL: http://www.manchester.edu/links/socialchoice-forsocialchange
Contact: Neil Wollman, Co-Chm.
Founded: 1996. **Members:** 400. **Staff:** 2. **Budget:** $1,000. **Local Groups:** 1. **Description:** College faculty. Seeks to persuade TIAA-CREF, the largest private pension system in the world, to begin "positive investing" of pension funds. Aims to acquire the 5&percent;-10&percent; of assets in the Social Choice Account, a socially responsible fund, to be invested in companies that are models of social and environmental responsibility. **Formerly:** (2004) Graduation Pledge of Social and Environmental Responsibility. **Publications:** Brochure.

12858 ■ Society for the Study of Social Problems (SSSP)
901 McClung Tower
Univ. of Tennessee
Knoxville, TN 37996-0490
Ph: (865)974-7026
Fax: (865)689-1534
E-mail: tomhood@utk.edu
URL: http://www.sssp1.org
Contact: Thomas C. Hood, Exec. Off.
Founded: 1951. **Members:** 1,800. **Membership Dues:** student, unemployed, $20 (annual) ● first time professional, $35 (annual) ● professional (based on gross annual income), $50-$135 (annual) ● departmental, $60 (annual) ● sustaining, $1,200 (annual). **Staff:** 2. **Budget:** $460,000. **Description:** An interdisciplinary community of scholars, activists, practitioners, and students endeavoring to create greater social justice through social research. Members are often social scientists working in colleges and universities, in non-profit organizations and in other applied and policy settings. **Awards:** C. Wright Mills Award. **Frequency:** annual. **Type:** recognition. **Recipient:** for outstanding book on social problems ● Lee-Founders Award. **Type:** recognition. **Recipient:** for lifetime achievement ● Racial/Ethnic Minority Graduate Scholarship. **Frequency:** annual. **Type:** scholarship. **Recipient:** to a sociology graduate student ● Social Action Award. **Frequency:** annual. **Type:** recognition. **Recipient:** to an organization in the city or area where the annual meeting is held. **Computer Services:** Mailing lists. **Divisions:** Community Research and Development; Conflict, Social Action, and Change; Crime and Juvenile Delinquency;

Drinking and Drugs; Educational Problems; Environment and Technology; Family; Global; Health, Health Policy, and Health Services; Institutional Ethnography; Labor Studies; Law and Society; Mental Health; Poverty, Class, and Inequality; Racial and Ethnical Minorities; Sexual Behavior, Politics, and Communities; Social Problems Theory; Sociology and Social Welfare; Teaching Social Problems; Youth, Aging, and the Life Course. **Publications:** *Anthologies of Articles from Social Problems*, periodic. Monographs ● *Social Problems*, quarterly. Journal. Contains scholarly studies of social problems. Includes annual index. **Price:** included in membership dues; $55.00 /year for institutions. ISSN: 0037-7791. **Circulation:** 4,000. **Advertising:** accepted ● Membership Directory, monthly. Alternate Formats: online ● Newsletter, 3/year. **Conventions/Meetings:** annual meeting, with workshops and presentations of research (exhibits).

12859 ■ Training for Change (TFC)

1501 Cherry St.
Philadelphia, PA 19102-1403
Ph: (215)241-7035
Fax: (215)241-7252
E-mail: peacelearn@igc.org
URL: http://www.trainingforchange.org
Contact: George Lakey, Exec. Dir.
Founded: 1992. **Budget:** $150,000. **For-Profit. Multinational. Description:** Works for democratic, nonviolent social change through training. **Conventions/Meetings:** workshop, with training skills.

12860 ■ Unitarian Universalist Association of Congregations (UUA)

25 Beacon St.
Boston, MA 02108
Ph: (617)742-2100 (617)948-4652
Free: (888)792-5885
E-mail: info@uua.org
URL: http://www.uua.org
Contact: Rev. William G. Sinkford, Pres.
Founded: 1961. **Members:** 220,000. **Staff:** 200. **Budget:** $22,000,000. **Regional Groups:** 23. **Local Groups:** 989. **Description:** Liberal religious movement. Priorities include reproductive rights, affirmative action, comprehensive nuclear test ban treaty, racial justice, civil rights, and religious liberties. **Awards:** Bennett. **Frequency:** annual. **Type:** recognition. **Recipient:** for congregation that has done exemplary work in social justice ● Stewardship Sermon. **Frequency:** annual. **Type:** recognition. **Recipient:** for professional religious leaders. **Formerly:** (1983) Unitarian Universalist Association - Washington Office for Social Concern; (1998) Unitarian Universalist Association of Congregations- Washington Office for Social Justice; (2002) Unitarian Universalist Association of Congregations - Washington Office for Faith in Action. **Publications:** *Action Alerts*, periodic. Newsletter. **Circulation:** 700. Alternate Formats: online ● *Faith in Action*, semiannual. Newsletter. **Circulation:** 3,000 ● *Interconnections*, quarterly. Newsletter ● *The UU World*, bimonthly. Newsletter. **Circulation:** 3,000. **Conventions/Meetings:** annual general assembly - always June ● biennial National Public Policy and Advocacy Conference - always Washington, DC ● seminar and workshop, at district conferences and summer institutes.

Social Justice

12861 ■ National Organizers Alliance (NOA)

2307 Martin Luther King Jr. Ave. SE
Washington, DC 20020
Ph: (202)543-6603
Fax: (202)543-2462
E-mail: patrick@noacentral.org
URL: http://noacentral.org
Contact: Patrick Masterson, Exec. Dir.
Founded: 1993. **Description:** Works to advance progressive organizing for social, economic and environmental justice and to sustain, support and nurture people of all ages. Represents the interests of organizers who are responsible for building a defined constituency through leadership develop-

ment, collective action and development of democratic structures. **Publications:** *Practicing What We Preach*. Report. Reflects the contributions of members around the country. **Price:** $15.00/issue.

12862 ■ Resource Generation (RG)

511 Ave. of the Americas, No. 183
New York, NY 10011
E-mail: info@resourcegeneration.org
URL: http://www.resourcegeneration.org
Contact: Taij Kumarie Moteelall, Exec. Dir.
Members: 500. **Description:** Works with young people with financial wealth committed to social change and economic justice. **Computer Services:** Mailing lists. **Telecommunication Services:** electronic mail, taij@resourcegeneration.org. **Programs:** Class and Activism Workshop; Creating Change Through Family Philanthropy; Fellowship; Money and Giving Across Generations Workshop; Philanthropology. **Publications:** *Money Talks, So Can We.* **Conventions/Meetings:** dinner ● annual Making Money Make Change - meeting ● workshop.

Social Sciences

12863 ■ Social Policy Action Network (SPAN)

Address Unknown since 2007
Members: 1,000. **Description:** Promotes social policy issues, including welfare reform, fatherhood, teen pregnancy and parenting, early childhood education and care.

Social Service

12864 ■ Charities Aid Foundation America (CAF)

King St. Sta.
1800 Diagonal Rd., Ste.150
Alexandria, VA 22314-2840
Ph: (703)549-8931
Fax: (703)549-8934
E-mail: info@cafamerica.org
URL: http://www.cafonline.org
Contact: Dr. Susan Saxon-Harrold, CEO
Founded: 1974. **Staff:** 300. **Multinational. Description:** Strives to do all in its power to ensure charitable giving to all charities. Distributes money for charitable purposes. **Additional Websites:** http://www2.cafonline.org/cafamerica. **Formerly:** (2004) Charities Aid Foundation.

12865 ■ Global Family

PO Box 90710
Santa Barbara, CA 93190
Ph: (805)892-2864
Free: (888)977-5888
Fax: (805)892-2860
E-mail: connect@globalfamily.net
URL: http://www.globalfamily.net
Contact: Carolyn Anderson, Co-Dir.
Founded: 1986. **Membership Dues:** regular (contribution), $33 (annual). **Local Groups:** 1. **National Groups:** 40. **Multinational. Description:** Fosters environmental and social awareness for permaculture and environmental sustainability. Provides social and humanitarian services through outreach programs. **Libraries: Type:** reference. **Subjects:** inspiration. **Programs:** Field Team Outreach; Global Youth Network Outreach; United Nations Outreach; Youth and Family Outreach. **Publications:** *The Co-Creators*. Handbook. Contains specific tools and experiential exercises for life purposes. ● Newsletter, quarterly. Alternate Formats: online ● Brochure. Features the work and activities of Global Family. Alternate Formats: online.

12866 ■ Healing Hands International (HHI)

455 McNally Dr.
Nashville, TN 37211
Ph: (615)832-2000
Fax: (615)832-2002

E-mail: ghurst@hhi-aid.org
URL: http://www.hhi-aid.org
Contact: Dr. Randy Steger, Pres.
Founded: 1994. **Multinational. Description:** Provides humanitarian aid. Increases awareness of worldwide medical and humanitarian needs. Distributes medical, agricultural and educational aids. **Projects:** Disaster Response; Drip Irrigation Kits; Gift of Hope; Magi.

12867 ■ LearnWell Resources

PO Box 944
Camino, CA 95709
Ph: (530)644-2123
E-mail: edu@learnwell.org
URL: http://www.learnwell.org
Contact: Rudolf E. Klimes PhD, Pres./CEO
Founded: 1994. **Members:** 95. **Staff:** 3. **Budget:** $30,000. **Description:** Works to provide learning improvement opportunities to underserved children and youth. Sponsors DrugFree USA, a drug prevention program for children, and the Education Exchange on the website. Provides online continuing education, certificate and college credit aimed at advancing health and interpersonal skills through education and outreach. **Libraries: Type:** open to the public; reference. **Holdings:** books, periodicals. **Awards: Type:** grant ● **Type:** recognition. **Recipient:** for innovative, effective learning-improvements undertakings. **Computer Services:** database, courses over the internet ● online services, continuing education courses; courses for the gifted and talented. **Additional Websites:** http://www.ce5.com, http://www.forgiver.net. **Divisions:** DrugFree USA; LearnWell Continuing Education Center; LearnWell Forgiveness Center; LearnWell Outreach Center. **Publications:** *Learn in Brain-friendly Ways; How to Succeed With Quality Learning Skills*. Book. **Price:** $9.95. Alternate Formats: online ● *Stories That Teach: An Oral Approach to Learning English, Basic Level.* Book. **Price:** $9.95. Alternate Formats: online. **Conventions/Meetings:** semiannual workshop.

12868 ■ Lotus Outreach (LO)

PO Box 1184
Cathedral City, CA 92235
Ph: (760)342-1487
Fax: (760)342-1487
E-mail: info@lotusoutreach.org
URL: http://www.lotusoutreach.org
Contact: Kathryn Meeske, Pres.
Founded: 1993. **Multinational. Description:** Works with communities to develop initiatives and create programs in the areas of educational development, community development and health services. Strives to educate children and build sustainable community programs. **Telecommunication Services:** electronic mail, kathryn.meeske@lotusoutreach.org. **Publications:** Annual Report, annual. Alternate Formats: online.

12869 ■ Planet Aid

One Cross St.
Holliston, MA 01746
Ph: (508)893-0644
Fax: (508)893-0641
E-mail: info@planetaid.org
URL: http://www.planetaid.org
Founded: 1997. **Staff:** 3. **Multinational. Description:** Provides emergency and disaster relief to victims of war, hunger, natural disasters, atomic accidents, plagues and other catastrophes. Works to preserve the natural habitat of the Earth by implementing environmental protection projects. **Telecommunication Services:** electronic mail, fredolsson@planetaid.org ● electronic mail, volunteer@planetaid.org. **Projects:** Child Aid; Humana People to People; Teacher Training; Total Control of the Epidemic. **Publications:** Annual Report. Alternate Formats: online.

12870 ■ Technical Assistance Collaborative (TAC)

535 Boylston St., Ste.1301
Boston, MA 02116
Ph: (617)266-5657
Fax: (617)266-4343

E-mail: info@tacinc.org
URL: http://www.tacinc.org
Contact: Stephen L. Day, Exec. Dir./Co-Founder
Founded: 1992. **Staff:** 11. **Description:** Works to achieve positive outcomes on behalf of people with disabilities, people who are homeless and people with other special needs. Provides information, capacity building, and technical expertise to organizations and policymakers in the areas of mental health, substance abuse, human services, and affordable housing. Supports the efforts of public and non-profit agencies to successfully plan and implement the design, financing and management of public sector human services, mental health, substance abuse and health care strategies.

12871 ■ Welfare Made A Difference National Campaign (WMAD)
Address Unknown since 2006
Founded: 1999. **Members:** 150. **Description:** Coalition of more than eighty organizations committed to reshaping public perception and policy relating to welfare. **Affiliated With:** Church Women United.

12872 ■ Welfare to Work Partnership
1129 20th St. NW, Ste.800
Washington, DC 20036
Ph: (202)955-3005
Fax: (202)955-1087
E-mail: info@welfaretowork.org
Contact: Rodney J. Carroll, Pres./CEO
Description: Provides solutions to companies through hiring welfare recipients, unemployed, or low-income workers.

Social Welfare

12873 ■ Airline Ambassadors International (AAI)
PO Box 459
Moss Beach, CA 94038
Ph: (650)728-7844
Free: (866)264-3586
Fax: (650)728-7855
E-mail: president@airlineamb.org
URL: http://www.airlineamb.org
Contact: Nancy Rivard, Pres./Founder
Founded: 1996. **Regional Groups:** 1. **Local Groups:** 12. **Multinational. Description:** Network of airline employees and others who help children in need. Provides ordinary people the opportunity to travel and make a difference. Provides humanitarian aid to orphanages, clinics and remote communities. **Affiliated With:** United Nations.

12874 ■ American Friends Service Committee (AFSC)
1501 Cherry St.
Philadelphia, PA 19102
Ph: (215)241-7000
Free: (800)558-AFSC
Fax: (215)241-7275
E-mail: afscinfo@afsc.org
URL: http://www.afsc.org
Contact: Mary Ellen McNish, Gen. Sec.
Founded: 1917. **Staff:** 340. **Budget:** $41,255,000. **Regional Groups:** 9. **Multinational. Description:** Founded by and related to the Religious Society of Friends (Quakers); supported and staffed by individuals sharing basic values regardless of religious affiliation. Attempts to relieve human suffering and find new approaches to world peace and social justice through nonviolence. Work in 22 countries and 43 areas of the United States includes development and refugee relief, peace education, and community organizing. Conducts programs with U.S. communities on the problems of minority groups such as housing, employment, and denial of legal rights. Maintains Washington, DC, office to present AFSC experience and perspectives to policymakers. Seeks to build informed public resistance to militarism and the military-industrial complex. Programs are multiracial, nondenominational, and international. **Divisions:** Community Relations Unit; International Programs;

Peace Building Unit. **Projects:** Peace Response. **Publications:** *Quaker Action*, 3/year. Newsletter. **Price:** $10.00/year. **Circulation:** 75,000. Alternate Formats: microform ● Annual Report, annual. Contains program activities and financial summary. **Price:** free ● Also publishes program literature; prepares video materials on current world problems. **Conventions/Meetings:** annual Public Gathering - general assembly (exhibits) - 2007 Nov. 3, Philadelphia, PA - **Avg. Attendance:** 700.

12875 ■ American Humane Association (AHA)
63 Inverness Dr. E
Englewood, CO 80112-5117
Ph: (303)792-9900
Free: (800)227-4645
Fax: (303)792-5333
E-mail: publicpolicy@americanhumane.org
URL: http://www.americanhumane.org
Contact: Marie Belew Wheatley, Pres./CEO
Founded: 1877. **Members:** 60,000. **Membership Dues:** individual, $59 (annual) ● agency, $119 (annual). **Staff:** 50. **Budget:** $9,000,000. **Description:** Represents agencies and individuals seeking to prevent cruelty to children and animals. Provides materials on animal care and child abuse and neglect. Offers training for animal care/control agencies and to child protective services personnel. Promotes solutions to pet overpopulation. Encourages effective response systems for abused and neglected children. Provides lobbies for animal welfare and child welfare at federal, state, and local levels. Maintains resource centers with information on animal welfare issues and child abuse. Operates speakers' bureau and referral service and monitors treatment of animals in movie and television productions. **Programs:** Animal Welfare; Child Welfare. **Publications:** *Child Protection Leader*, bimonthly. Presents timely information on significant issues related to the protection of children and strengthening of families. **Price:** included in membership dues ● *Protecting Animals*, quarterly. Journal. **Price:** included in membership dues. Alternate Formats: online ● *Protecting Children*. Journal. **Price:** included in membership dues. **Conventions/Meetings:** annual meeting (exhibits) - usually October.

12876 ■ American Institute for Public Service (AIPS)
100 W 10th St., Ste.215
Wilmington, DE 19801-1665
Ph: (302)622-9101
Fax: (302)622-9108
E-mail: s.beard@jeffersonawards.org
URL: http://www.aips.org
Contact: Sam Beard, Pres./CEO
Founded: 1972. **Staff:** 10. **Description:** Seeks to honor public service and community volunteerism on the national and local levels. Confers Jefferson Awards annually for Public Service in U.S. Supreme Court. **Convention/Meeting:** none. **Awards:** Jefferson Award. **Frequency:** annual. **Type:** recognition. **Recipient:** for individuals ● S. Roger Horchow. **Frequency:** annual. **Type:** recognition. **Recipient:** for private citizens ● Samuel S. Beard. **Frequency:** annual. **Type:** recognition. **Recipient:** for an individual below 35 years old ● U.S. Senator John Heinz. **Frequency:** annual. **Type:** recognition. **Recipient:** for an elected or appointed official. **Publications:** *American Institute for Public Service Newsletter*, 1-2/year ● *Directory of Local Sponsors*, annual.

12877 ■ American Public Human Services Association (APHSA)
810 1st St. NE, Ste.500
Washington, DC 20002
Ph: (202)682-0100
Fax: (202)289-6555
E-mail: pubs@aphsa.org
URL: http://www.aphsa.org
Contact: Jerry W. Friedman, Exec. Dir.
Founded: 1930. **Members:** 4,000. **Membership Dues:** regular individual, $66 (annual) ● sustaining, $77 (annual) ● Century Club, $103 (annual) ● associate, $360 (annual) ● retiree, $15 (annual) ●

student, $18 (annual). **Staff:** 55. **Budget:** $5,500,000. **Description:** Public human service agencies, their professional staff members, and others interested in public human services. Works to develop, promote and implement human service policies that improve the health and well-being of families, children and adults. **Awards:** Leadership in Human Services. **Frequency:** periodic. **Type:** recognition. **Computer Services:** database. **Subgroups:** National Council of Local Human Service Administrators; National Council of State Human Service Administrators. **Affiliated With:** American Association of Food Stamp Directors; American Public Human Services Association - Information Systems Management; Association of Administrators of the Interstate Compact on the Placement of Children; Center for Workers with Disabilities; National Association of Public Child Welfare Administrators; National Association of State Medicaid Directors; National Staff Development and Training Association. **Formerly:** (1998) American Public Welfare Association. **Publications:** *Policy and Practice of Public Human Services*, quarterly. Journal. Contains articles, research reports, and book reviews. **Price:** $75.00 /year for nonmembers; $64.00 /year for members; $95.00/year international. ISSN: 1520-801X. **Circulation:** 5,500. **Advertising:** accepted. Alternate Formats: online. Also Cited As: *Public Welfare* ● *Public Human Services Directory*, annual. Describes public human service programs and agencies in the United States. Lists contacts, phone and fax numbers, email addresses and Web sites, etc. **Price:** $99.00 /year for members; $115.00 /year for nonmembers; $150.00/year international. ISSN: 1521-1320. **Circulation:** 5,000. **Advertising:** accepted. Alternate Formats: online ● *This Week in Washington*, weekly. Newsletter. Summarizes congressional action on human service issues. **Price:** $110.00 /year for members; $120.00 /year for nonmembers; $150.00/year international. ISSN: 0743-2437. **Circulation:** 600 ● *W-Memo*, bimonthly. Bulletin. Analyzes congressional and federal agency action affecting human service programs. **Price:** $90.00 /year for members; $100.00 /year for nonmembers; $120.00/year international. ISSN: 0163-8300. **Circulation:** 1,000. **Conventions/Meetings:** meeting - 3/year.

12878 ■ American Public Human Services Association - Information Systems Management (APHSA-ISM)
c/o Marquett Youngblood, Chm.
Oklahoma Dept. of Human Services
2400 N Lincoln Blvd.
Oklahoma City, OK 73105
Ph: (405)521-6602
Fax: (405)521-6868
E-mail: marq.youngblood@okdhs.org
URL: http://www.aphsa-ism.org
Contact: Marquett Youngblood, Chm.
Members: 550. **Staff:** 1. **Description:** Information systems managers from state and local human service agencies. Serves as a network for exchange of information on technical matters and policy issues. Conducts training program; exchanges information with federal agencies. **Affiliated With:** American Public Human Services Association. **Formerly:** (2001) American Association of Public Welfare Information Systems Management. **Conventions/Meetings:** annual conference (exhibits).

12879 ■ American Rescue Workers (ARW)
25 Ross St.
Williamsport, PA 17701
Ph: (570)323-8693
Fax: (570)323-8694
E-mail: arwus@arwus.com
URL: http://www.arwus.com
Contact: Claude S. Astin Jr., Commander-in-Chief
Founded: 1884. **Description:** Religious social service organization motivated by the love of God and a practical concern for the needs of humanity. Has established a program to provide spiritual and material aid to all levels of societies in need, regardless of race, creed, age, sex, or color. **Awards:** Paul E. Martin Scholarship. **Frequency:** annual. **Type:** scholarship. **Recipient:** for a Mission/Ministerial/

Christian Service student in a Bible College with Christian character, maturity and positive social adjustment. **Boards:** Local Advisory; National Managers. **Departments:** Rehabilitation. **Formerly:** (1884) Salvation Army; (1913) American Salvation Army. **Publications:** *The Rescue Herald*, quarterly. Magazine. Alternate Formats: online. **Conventions/Meetings:** annual meeting, national field council - always 3rd week of June ● annual retreat, for officers.

12880 ■ American Society for Kurds (ASK)
227 N Bronough St., Ste.1001
Tallahassee, FL 32301
E-mail: info@askurds.org
URL: http://www.askurds.org
Contact: Dr. Salah Aziz, Pres.
Founded: 1997. **Multinational. Description:** Aims to encourage, establish and nourish constructive relationships and cooperation between Americans and Kurds. Conducts humanitarian projects to assist Kurds. **Computer Services:** Information services, human rights resources. **Telecommunication Services:** electronic mail, askurds@yahoo.com. **Programs:** Health; Internship; Nutrition. **Publications:** Newsletter. Alternate Formats: online.

12881 ■ Association of Gospel Rescue Missions (AGRM)
1045 Swift Ave.
North Kansas City, MO 64116
Ph: (816)471-8020
Free: (800)624-5156
Fax: (816)471-3718
E-mail: agrm@agrm.org
URL: http://www.agrm.org
Contact: Rev. Stephen E. Burger, Exec. Dir.
Founded: 1913. **Members:** 1,000. **Membership Dues:** individual, organization (based on budget), $50 (annual). **Staff:** 12. **Budget:** $1,200,000. **Regional Groups:** 9. **Description:** Rescue ministry executives and staff, and concerned individuals in 6 countries. Promotes rescue mission work for all persons experiencing crisis. Aims to sponsor coffeehouses for youths, emergency shelters for men and women, women with children, and families, day camps, resident camps, and wilderness camps for inner-city children, cafeterias for low-income persons. Serves meals and provide sleeping space to individuals in need. Sponsors long-term residential programs offering addiction recovery, education and employment services, and assistance to the elderly and mentally ill. Maintains speakers' bureau; offers placement service; compiles statistics. Rescue College is the accredited online distance learning program of the organization. **Libraries:** Type: reference. **Holdings:** 1,741. **Subjects:** homelessness, urban ministry, alcohol and drug assistance. **Awards:** President Citation of Merit. **Frequency:** periodic. **Type:** recognition ● Rescuer Award. **Frequency:** periodic. **Type:** recognition. **Recipient:** to supporters who have given exceptional volunteer service. **Committees:** Convention; Expansion; Program Services. **Programs:** Alcoholics Victorious; Certification; The Great Thanksgiving Banquet; Rescue College; Short Term Urban Missions Directory. **Affiliated With:** Christian Management Association; Evangelical Council for Financial Accountability. **Formerly:** (2000) International Union of Gospel Missions. **Publications:** *AGRM Directory*, biennial ● *How to Have a Better Board of Directors*. Directory ● *Membership and Resource Directory*. Journal ● *RESCUE*, bimonthly. Newsletter. Includes instructional articles for rescue ministry personnel. **Price:** free. **Circulation:** 4,500 ● *Rescue Happenings*, monthly. Survey. Covers IUGM activities; includes calendar of events. **Price:** free. **Circulation:** 1,200. Alternate Formats: online ● *Rescue Mission Salary Survey*. Manual ● *Sample Staff Policy Manual* ● Surveys. **Conventions/Meetings:** annual convention (exhibits).

12882 ■ Carrie Estelle Doheny Foundation
707 Wilshire Blvd., Ste.4960
Los Angeles, CA 90017
Ph: (213)488-1122
Fax: (213)488-1544

E-mail: doheny@dohenyfoundation.org
URL: http://www.dohenyfoundation.org
Contact: Robert A. Smith III, Pres.
Founded: 1949. **Staff:** 4. **Description:** Supports organizations that deal with education, health, social welfare, medicine and religion. **Awards:** Type: grant. **Programs:** Imagining Tomorrow Pico Aliso Community Teen Outreach.

12883 ■ Catholic Central Union of America (CCUA)
3835 Westminster Pl.
St. Louis, MO 63108
Ph: (314)371-1653
Fax: (314)371-0889
E-mail: centbur@juno.com
URL: http://www.socialjusticereview.org
Contact: Rev. John H. Miller CSC, Dir.
Founded: 1855. **Members:** 1,000. **Membership Dues:** individual, $25 (annual). **Staff:** 3. **Budget:** $85,000. **State Groups:** 3. **Local Groups:** 119. **Description:** Individual Catholic men and affiliated societies interested in Catholic social action as promulgated by Papal Encyclicals and current studies. Headquarters, publications office, library, and programs maintained by Central Bureau, Catholic Central Union of America (see separate entry). **Libraries:** Type: open to the public. **Holdings:** 250,000. **Subjects:** history, philosophy, theology. **Committees:** Scholars for Social Justice; Social Action. **Sections:** Charitable; Educational; Political Economy; Public Relations; Religious; Sociological. **Affiliated With:** Central Bureau, Catholic Central Union of America. **Formerly:** (1956) Catholic Central Verein of America. **Publications:** *Social Justice Review*, bimonthly. Journal. **Price:** $20.00 /year for nonmembers in U.S.; included in membership dues; $23.00 /year for nonmembers outside U.S. ISSN: 0037-7767. **Circulation:** 4,800 ● Also publishes 14 books. **Conventions/Meetings:** annual conference.

12884 ■ Catholic Charities USA (CCUSA)
1731 King St.
Alexandria, VA 22314
Ph: (703)549-1390
Fax: (703)549-1656
E-mail: info@catholiccharitiesusa.org
URL: http://www.catholiccharitiesusa.org
Contact: Rev. Larry Snyder, Pres.
Founded: 1910. **Members:** 4,633. **Membership Dues:** individual/parish social ministry, $25 (annual) ● century club/parish, $100 (annual) ● aging/children, youth and family service/health and behavioral health care, $50 (annual) ● emergency services/management and administration, $35 (annual) ● development and communication/housing and community development, $30 (annual). **Staff:** 43. **Budget:** $2,819,000. **Description:** Local Catholic agencies in the U.S. Maintains consulting and information service; promotes research; maintains interest in broad social problems including welfare, teen pregnancy, child hunger and care for the elderly and coordinates Catholic responses to disasters in the United States. **Committees:** Residential Child Care and Services; Social Policy; Women. **Formerly:** National Conference of Catholic Charities. **Publications:** *Charities USA*, quarterly. Magazine. **Price:** $25.00. ISSN: 0364-0760. **Circulation:** 3,500. **Advertising:** accepted ● *Directory of Diocesan Agencies of Catholic Charities in the U.S., Puerto Rico and Canada*, biennial ● *Publications List*, annual. **Conventions/Meetings:** annual conference - 2007 Sept. 13-16, Cincinnati, OH ● annual Leadership Institute - seminar, integrates leadership and management training with theological and spiritual instruction - 2008 June 7-14, Raleigh, NC ● annual meeting - always fall.

12885 ■ Christian Foundation for Children and Aging (CFCA)
1 Elmwood Ave.
Kansas City, KS 66103
Ph: (913)384-6500
Free: (800)875-6564
Fax: (913)384-2211

E-mail: mail@cfcausa.org
URL: http://www.cfcausa.org
Contact: Robert K. Hentzen, Pres./Co-Founder
Founded: 1981. **Members:** 190,000. **Membership Dues:** sponsorship, $20 (monthly). **Staff:** 89. **Budget:** $50,000,000. **Languages:** English, Spanish. **Multinational. Description:** Seeks to advance the physical, mental, spiritual, and social welfare of the economically disadvantaged, especially children and aging persons in developing countries. Provides financial support and correspond with individuals in need; volunteers help provide social services, including medical, educational, and nutritional programs. Provides Christian Education and guidance. Conducts orientation program for volunteers and Mission Awareness trips to Mexico and Central America, India, Africa and Philippines. **Libraries:** Type: reference. **Holdings:** 50; books, video recordings. **Subjects:** theology, international activity. **Awards:** Pilgrimage of Faith. **Frequency:** annual. **Type:** recognition. **Recipient:** for dedication of individual and organization. **Computer Services:** database ● online services. **Affiliated With:** Catholic Network of Volunteer Service; Catholic Press Association; International Catholic Stewardship Council; United States Catholic Mission Association. **Formerly:** (1987) Christian Foundation for Children. **Publications:** *CFCA Spirit*, quarterly. Newsletter. Alternate Formats: online ● *CFCA Update*, monthly. Newsletter. Alternate Formats: online ● *Country Report*, periodic ● *Project Perspectives*, quarterly. Newsletter. Alternate Formats: online ● *Sacred Ground* (in English and Spanish), 3/year. Magazine. Contains news of sponsorship and mission activity. **Circulation:** 190,000. Alternate Formats: online. **Conventions/Meetings:** annual Spring Preachers Conference - meeting.

12886 ■ Coalition for Economic Survival (CES)
514 Shatto Pl., Ste.270
Los Angeles, CA 90020
Ph: (213)252-4411
Fax: (213)252-4422
E-mail: contactces@earthlink.net
URL: http://www.cesinaction.org
Contact: Larry Gross, Exec. Dir.
Founded: 1973. **Members:** 5,000. **Membership Dues:** regular, $15 (annual) ● fixed income, $10 (annual) ● supporting, $25 (annual) ● contributor, $50 (annual) ● donor, $100 (annual). **Staff:** 7. **Languages:** English, Korean, Spanish. **Description:** Addresses the economic concerns of senior citizens and low-income families, especially issues dealing with rent control, tenants' rights, and affordable housing. Conducts tenants' rights clinic and organizes tenant unions to empower tenants to fight against increases, displacement, and obtain needed repairs; disseminates information. **Publications:** *Gone, But Not Forgotten*. Video. Documents a struggle against displacement due to redevelopment, linking it to LA's redevelopment history. ● *Mark to Market Tenant Outreach Brochure* (in English and Spanish). Brochures. Alternate Formats: online ● *Organizing Times*, quarterly. Newsletter. **Circulation:** 5,000. Alternate Formats: online ● Bulletin, periodic. **Conventions/Meetings:** seminar ● workshop.

12887 ■ Coalition on Human Needs (CHN)
1120 Connecticut Ave. NW, Ste.910
Washington, DC 20036
Ph: (202)223-2532
Fax: (202)223-2538
E-mail: info@chn.org
URL: http://www.chn.org
Contact: Deborah Weinstein, Exec. Dir.
Founded: 1981. **Members:** 100. **Staff:** 3. **Budget:** $400,000. **National Groups:** 100. **Description:** National advocacy organizations working in areas such as federal budget and tax policy, low wage employment, and welfare policy. Works for adequate federal funding for human needs and income maintenance programs. Promotes public policies which address the needs of low-income and other vulnerable populations. Publishes legislative update on issues affecting low-income Americans. **Computer Services:** Mailing

lists ● online services, electronic newsletter, legislative updates, issue briefs, article, calendar. **Committees:** Legislative; Program. **Working Groups:** Welfare. **Affiliated With:** Center for Community Change. **Formerly:** (1982) Ad Hoc Coalition on Block Grants; (1987) Coalition on Block Grants and Human Needs. **Publications:** *The Human Needs Report*, biweekly, when Congress is in session. Legislative update on human needs issues. ● *Issue Briefs*.

12888 ■ Coleman Foundation
651 W Washington, Ste.306
Chicago, IL 60661
Ph: (312)902-7120
Fax: (312)902-7124
E-mail: info@colemanfoundation.org
URL: http://www.colemanfoundation.org
Contact: Michael W. Hennessy, Pres./CEO

Founded: 1951. **Description:** Strives to support entrepreneurship, cancer research, housing and education for the handicapped, and diverse educational programs. **Awards:** Entrepreneur Excellence in Teaching. **Frequency:** annual. **Type:** grant. **Programs:** Cancer Care; Disability Services; Education; Entrepreneurship.

12889 ■ Conrad N. Hilton Foundation (CNHF)
100 W Liberty St., Ste.840
Reno, NV 89501
E-mail: cnhf@hiltonfoundation.org
URL: http://www.hiltonfoundation.org
Contact: Steven M. Hilton, Chm./Pres./CEO

Founded: 1944. **Description:** Works to alleviate human suffering, targeting specific program areas described on the foundation's website. The foundation generally does not accept unsolicited proposals. **Awards:** Conrad N. Hilton Humanitarian Prize. **Type:** recognition ● **Type:** grant. **Publications:** Annual Reports, annual. Alternate Formats: online.

12890 ■ Council on Accreditation (COA)
120 Wall St., 11th Fl.
New York, NY 10005-3902
Ph: (212)797-3000
Free: (866)262-8088
Fax: (212)797-1428
E-mail: coainfo@coanet.org
URL: http://www.coanet.org
Contact: Richard Klarberg, Pres./CEO

Founded: 1977. **Staff:** 60. **Multinational. Description:** Serves in partners with human service organizations worldwide to improve service delivery outcomes by developing, applying, and promoting accreditation standards. In addition to standards for private social service and behavioral health care organizations, it has developed separate business lines for public agencies, opioid treatment programs, employee assistance programs, and financial management/debt counseling services. Over 1,500 organizations-voluntary, public and proprietary, local and statewide, large and small-have either successfully achieved accreditation or are currently engaged in the process. **Awards:** Agency Accreditation. **Type:** recognition. **Recipient:** for those who meet the standards that are applicable ● Healthy Families America Program Certification. **Type:** recognition. **Recipient:** for those who meet the standards that are applicable. **Additional Websites:** http://www.coastandards.org. **Divisions:** Accreditation Programs; Peer Services; Public Agency and Government Relations; Standards Development; Training. **Affiliated With:** Alliance for Children and Families; American Association of Children's Residential Centers; Catholic Charities USA; Child Welfare League of America; Foster Family-Based Treatment Association; National Alliance on Mental Illness; National Association for Children's Behavioral Health; National Council for Adoption; National Foundation for Credit Counseling; National Network for Youth; Prevent Child Abuse. **Formerly:** (2001) Council on Accreditation of Services for Families and Children. **Publications:** *COA Accreditation Policies and Procedures* ● *8th Edition Standards for Private Organizations*. Manual ● *8th Edition Standards for Public Organizations*. Manual.

12891 ■ Council for Health and Human Services Ministries, United Church of Christ (CHHSM)
700 Prospect Ave.
Cleveland, OH 44115
Ph: (216)736-2251
Free: (866)822-8224
Fax: (216)736-2251
E-mail: sickbert@chhsm.org
URL: http://www.chhsm.org
Contact: Bryan W. Sickbert, Pres./CEO

Founded: 1939. **Members:** 329. **Staff:** 5. **Budget:** $750,000. **Description:** Health and human service institutions related to the United Church of Christ. Seeks to study, plan, and implement a program in health and human services; assist members in developing and providing quality services and in financing institutional and non-institutional health and human service ministries; stimulate awareness of and support for these programs; inform the UCC of policies that affect the needs, problems, and conditions of patients; cooperate with interdenominational agencies and others in the field. Maintains placement service and hall of fame. Compiles statistics; provides specialized education programs. **Awards:** Employee of the Year. **Frequency:** annual. **Type:** recognition ● Executive of the Year. **Frequency:** annual. **Type:** recognition ● Innovative Program. **Frequency:** annual. **Type:** fellowship. **Recipient:** for hospital administration for UCC ordained clergy ● Julius Varwing Award. **Frequency:** annual. **Type:** recognition ● Retiring Administration. **Frequency:** annual. **Type:** recognition ● Volunteer of the Year. **Frequency:** annual. **Type:** recognition. **Computer Services:** database, membership ● mailing lists. **Committees:** Awards; Leadership Resource; Public Policy; Public Relations; Wellness. **Divisions:** Aging; Children and Youth; Community Centers; Developmentally Disabled; Hospitals; Specialized Housing. **Formerly:** (1961) Commission on Benevolent Institutions; (1983) Council for Health and Welfare Services, United Church of Christ; (1993) Council for Health and Human Services. **Publications:** *CHHSM News*, monthly. Newsletter. Alternate Formats: online ● *Diakonie Newsletter*, quarterly. Alternate Formats: online ● *Directory of Services*, biennial. Contains listing of UCC Chaplains in Health Care and CHHSM Organizations. **Price:** $2.50. **Circulation:** 1,200. Alternate Formats: microform ● *Employment Opportunities*, monthly ● *President's Newsletter*, 2-3/year ● Annual Report, annual. Alternate Formats: online. **Conventions/Meetings:** annual general assembly (exhibits) - always February or March.

12892 ■ CRISTA Ministries (CRISTA)
19303 Fremont Ave. N
Seattle, WA 98133
Ph: (206)546-7200
E-mail: info@crista.net
URL: http://www.crista.org
Contact: Bob Lonac, Pres./CEO

Founded: 1948. **Staff:** 1,400. **Budget:** $70,000,000. **Description:** Christian service organization composed of 10 outreach ministries devoted to serving human needs. Offers services and programs for youth, the elderly, the impoverished, and the troubled. Maintains camps, schools for preschool through 12th grade, an athletic program, and an apartment complex and nursing home for senior citizens. Offers individual and family counseling services. Provides information and support for Christian missionaries on overseas assignments. Works for Third World relief and development; provides inspirational radio programming. Sponsors retreats and seminars; offers adoption and foster care services and educational programs for street kids. **Convention/Meeting:** none. **Divisions:** Broadcasting; Camps and Conferences; Counseling; Intercristo; Kings Schools; New Hope Child and Family Services; Seattle Urban Academy; Senior Community; Women's Ministries; World Concern (see separate entry). **Formerly:** (1979) King's Garden. **Publications:** Brochures.

12893 ■ Cuban American National Council (CNC)
1223 SW 4th St.
Miami, FL 33135
Ph: (305)642-3484
Fax: (305)642-9122
E-mail: csantana@cnc.org
URL: http://www.cnc.org
Contact: Maria Cristina Santana, Board Liaison/Event Coor.

Founded: 1972. **Staff:** 100. **Budget:** $5,992,200. **Languages:** English, French, Spanish. **Description:** Aims to identify the socioeconomic needs of the Cuban population in the U.S. and to promote needed human services. Services the needy through research and human services while advocating on behalf of Hispanics and other minority groups. **Libraries: Type:** open to the public. **Holdings:** 500; archival material. **Subjects:** population and economic data. **Awards:** Community Service Award. **Frequency:** biennial. **Type:** recognition. **Recipient:** for distinguished community service. **Computer Services:** database. **Telecommunication Services:** electronic mail, gmd@cnc.org. **Departments:** Accounting. **Programs:** Alpha; Centers for Hispanic Educational Progress; CreditSmart Espanol; Hispanic Leadership Training; Latin American Studies; Latino Technology Network; Youth Opportunity Center. **Projects:** Cuba Solidarity. **Formerly:** (1987) Cuban National Planning Council. **Publications:** *The Council Letter*, quarterly. Newsletter. **Price:** $10.00. Alternate Formats: online ● *The Cubanization and Hispanicization of Metropolitan Miami*. **Price:** $5.00 ● *Ethnic Block Voting and Polarization in Miami*. **Price:** $4.00 ● *Ethnic Segregation in Greater Miami: 1980-1990*. **Price:** $5.00 ● *Freedom of Speech in Miami*. **Price:** $4.00 ● *Housing Needs of the Hispanic Elderly in Greater Miami*. **Price:** $4.00 ● *Laws and Politics in Florida's Redistricting*. **Price:** $4.00 ● *Miami Mosaic: Ethnic Relations in Dade County*. **Price:** $4.00 ● *Miami's Latin Businesses*. **Price:** $4.00 ● *Recommendations for the United States Government Measurements of Race and Ethnicity*. **Price:** $3.00 ● Pamphlets ● Book ● Monographs. **Conventions/Meetings:** biennial conference (exhibits) - May.

12894 ■ Evangelical Lutheran Good Samaritan Society (ELGSS)
PO Box 5038
Sioux Falls, SD 57117-5038
Ph: (605)362-3100
E-mail: moreinfo@good-sam.com
URL: http://www.good-sam.com
Contact: David J. Horazdovsky, Pres.

Founded: 1922. **Staff:** 24,000. **State Groups:** 25. **Description:** Owns, operates, and manages 240 Christian institutions in 25 states, including nursing homes with levels of care ranging from senior living to skilled nursing. Provides each center with computerized accounting, comparative data, administrator and staff training programs, a regional director, special purchasing agreements, life enrichment programming, emergency financial backing, and specialists in other fields. Conducts meetings to provide administrators with credits for continuing education. **Libraries: Type:** reference. **Holdings:** 400; books. **Subjects:** nursing home care. **Publications:** *Donor eNewsletter*, weekly. Features articles on Social Security, Healthcare, Washington events and other timely information. **Price:** free. Alternate Formats: online ● *The Good Samaritan*, quarterly ● Directory, periodic. **Conventions/Meetings:** annual meeting (exhibits).

12895 ■ First Foundations
c/o Dick Jensen, Pres.
PO Box 991
Travelers Rest, SC 29690
Ph: (864)834-2300
Fax: (864)834-2300
E-mail: ffi113@bellsouth.net
Contact: Dick Jensen, Pres.

Founded: 1986. **Description:** Charitable organization supported by donations of individuals and corporations. Researches and reports on the societal foundations of family, government, and religion. **Also Known As:** Faith and Freedom International. **Publications:** *The Billy Pulpits*. Book. Chronicles the careers of Billy Sunday and Billy Graham. ● *Dedication Music*. Video. Highlights of 2001 organ concert by Dr. Don Hustad. ● *Life or Death?*. Pamphlet ● *Man of Law and Grace*. Video. Features interview with Attorney Hickman Ewing. ● *Pearl Survivors*. Book. Contains eyewitness stories from Pearl Harbor veterans. ● *Pocket Edition of the Declaration of Independence*. Book ● *Pocket Edition of the U.S. Constitution*. Book ● *The U.S. Constitution*. Audiotape ● *Why Christmas?*. Pamphlet.

12896 ■ Generations United (GU)
1333 H St. NW, Ste.500W
Washington, DC 20005
Ph: (202)289-3979
Fax: (202)289-3952
E-mail: gu@gu.org
URL: http://www.gu.org
Contact: Ms. Donna M. Butts, Exec. Dir.
Founded: 1986. **Members:** 287. **Membership Dues:** individual, $50 (annual) ● student, retired, $25 (annual) ● sustaining, $100 (annual). **Staff:** 7. **Budget:** $700,000. **Description:** Seeks to: increase public awareness of issues faced by Americans of all ages; participate in endeavors that unite differing generations in community service; unite members at the local, state, and national levels to support key public policies affecting all generations; produce and disseminate materials that demonstrate the value of intergenerational cooperation. Facilitates unity and cooperation among members. Promotes: access to services for grandparents and relatives raising children; quality public education; access to health care for all Americans; a humane welfare system of public assistance that encourages its beneficiaries to develop new job skills; dependable and affordable day care for children and dependent adults; strengthened programs that assist the needy. **Libraries: Type:** open to the public. **Awards:** Leadership Awards. **Frequency:** biennial. **Type:** recognition ● Ossofsky Award. **Frequency:** biennial. **Type:** recognition. **Recipient:** for lifetime achievement in support of children, youth and the elderly. **Computer Services:** database, online directory with over 400 intergenerational programs from across the united states and the world. **Publications:** *Together*, 3/year. Magazine. Includes information about intergenerational programs, policies, resources, initiative updates, and the latest news from the field. **Price:** free. **Circulation:** 10,000. **Advertising:** accepted ● *Young and Old Serving Together: Meeting Community Needs Through Intergenerational Partnerships*. Book. **Price:** $18.00 ● Also publishes fact sheets. **Conventions/Meetings:** semiannual conference (exhibits).

12897 ■ International Relief Friendship Foundation (IRFF)
30 Seminary Dr., No. 228
Barrytown, NY 12507
Ph: (917)319-6802 (917)319-6202
Fax: (845)758-4509
E-mail: executivedirector@irff.org
URL: http://www.irff.org
Contact: Mr. Ichinori Tsumagari, Exec. Dir.
Founded: 1976. **Staff:** 5. **Budget:** $1,000,000. **State Groups:** 3. **National Groups:** 80. **Description:** Seeks to address the problems of sickness, poverty, illiteracy, and other forms of human suffering. Supports programs that encourage the active participation of the intended beneficiaries. Operates programs in agricultural and technical training, education - both youth and adult literacy, health education/support, direct relief aid, and interreligious youth service programs. Cooperates Religious Youth Service, a service learning program for young people of all faiths to work together in needy communities. Special projects are Africa Rising and Friendship Americas. Projects running in Bulgaria, Croatia, Moldova, Albania, Russia, Ghana, Ivory Coast, Mali, Rwanda, Cameroon, Nigeria, Peru, Brazil, Honduras, Guatemala, Dominican Republic, Bangladesh, India, Sri Lanka, Uganda, and Haiti. Has sponsored two international conferences on Development in the Millennium. **Additional Websites:** http://www.irff-europe.org. **Telecommunication Services:** electronic mail, irffint@aol.com. **Formerly:** World Relief Friendship Foundation. **Publications:** *East-West Perspec-*

tive (in English and German) ● *Frontiers in Development*, periodic. Newsletter. **Price:** free.

12898 ■ Jesuit Social and International Ministries
1616 P St. NW, Ste.300
Washington, DC 20036-1420
Ph: (202)462-0400
Fax: (202)328-9212
Founded: 1972. **Staff:** 4. **Description:** Aims to: represent the Jesuit concern for social justice; coordinate social justice efforts in Jesuit sponsored industries throughout the U.S; coordinate efforts of and provide resource services to 10 regional U.S. Jesuit Provinces; provide legislative advocacy on issues of social justice concern. **Formerly:** (1981) Jesuit Office of Social Ministry; (2000) National Office of Jesuit Social Ministries. **Conventions/Meetings:** semiannual board meeting.

12899 ■ Ladies of Charity of the United States of America (LCUSA)
PO Box 31697
St. Louis, MO 63131
Ph: (816)942-5622
Fax: (816)942-8654
E-mail: lcstlouis@aol.com
URL: http://www.famvin.org/LCUSA
Contact: Margaret Hanson, Pres.
Founded: 1960. **Members:** 1,300. **Staff:** 1. **Budget:** $45,000. **Regional Groups:** 5. **Local Groups:** 78. **Description:** Local autonomous associations operating under the auspices of the Roman Catholic church. Gives personal service and pastoral care to the poor, the sick, the elderly, and youth wherever and whenever necessary. Conducts national and regional workshops. **Committees:** Concentrated Act of Charity (Indian Missions); Extension; Project Special Care (Resettlement); Service to the Aging; Spiritual Renewal; Youth. **Affiliated With:** Catholic Charities USA; National Council of Catholic Women. **Formerly:** (1991) Association of Ladies of Charity of the U.S. **Publications:** *Servicette*, quarterly. Newsletter. **Price:** $5.00/year. **Circulation:** 15,000 ● Brochures ● Manual. **Conventions/Meetings:** annual conference and meeting.

12900 ■ Louis and Harold Price Foundation
1371 Hecla Dr., Ste.B-1
Louisville, CO 80027-2318
Ph: (303)665-9201
Fax: (303)665-1027
E-mail: grantinquiry@pricefoundation.org
URL: http://www.pricefoundation.org
Contact: Timothy A. Jones, Pres.
Founded: 1951. **Staff:** 4. **Description:** Promotes social welfare in the areas of education, health, and human social services, particularly entrepreneurial studies conducted at institutes of higher learning. **Awards: Type:** grant. **Recipient:** to tax exempt organizations. **Telecommunication Services:** electronic mail, tjones@pricefoundation.org.

12901 ■ Magic Johnson Foundation
9100 Wilshire Blvd., Ste.700 E
Beverly Hills, CA 90212
Ph: (310)246-4400
Fax: (310)246-1106
URL: http://www.magicjohnson.org
Contact: Towalame Q. Austin, Exec. VP
Founded: 1991. **Description:** Dedicated to a positive future of children; supports community based organizations that deal with educational, health and social programs for America's youth. **Awards: Type:** grant. **Recipient:** to community-based organizations.

12902 ■ National Alliance for Hispanic Health
1501 16th St. NW
Washington, DC 20036
Ph: (202)387-5000
E-mail: alliance@hispanichealth.org
URL: http://www.hispanichealth.org
Contact: Jane L. Delgado PhD, Pres./CEO
Founded: 1973. **Members:** 1,000. **Membership Dues:** regular, $75 ● student, senior, $25. **Staff:** 32. **Budget:** $3,400,000. **Languages:** English, Spanish.

Description: Aims to improve the health and well-being of Hispanics. Delivers services to over 12 million people annually. Informs and mobilizes consumers; supports providers in the delivery of quality care; promotes appropriate use of technology; improves the science base for accurate decision making; and promotes philanthropy. Provides key leadership and advocacy to ensure accountability in these priority areas. Constituents are its members, Hispanic consumers and greater society. **Telecommunication Services:** hotline, National Hispanic Prenatal Helpline, (800)504-7081 ● hotline, Su Familia: The National Hispanic Family Health Helpline, (866)SU-FAMILIA. **Programs:** Hispanic Health Insurance Agenda; Hispanic Health Needs Assessment; Juntos Contra la Diabetes/United Against Diabetes; Juntos Executive Briefings; Limited English Proficiency Leadership Network; Mental Health Outreach and Crisis Prevention Project; Moving Forward: CHIP for Hispanic Children; National Colorectal Cancer Outreach and Education Project; National Hispanic Digital Community; National Hispanic Environmental Health Education Network; National Hispanic Leadership Network for Tobacco Control; Nuestros Tesoros (Our Treasures); Patient Safety Institute; Proyecto Ciencia: Project Science; Stage HIV/AIDS Prevention and Education; Towards Feeling Good; Vacunas para la familia: Immunization for All Ages. **Formerly:** (1976) Coalition of Spanish Speaking Mental Health Organizations; (2001) National Coalition of Hispanic Health and Human Services Organizations. **Publications:** *Salud, National Guide to Total Health*. Book ● Bibliographies ● Manuals ● Papers ● Report, annual ● Videos.

12903 ■ National Benevolent Association of the Christian Church (NBA)
149 Weldon Pkwy., Ste.115
Maryland Heights, MO 63043-3103
Ph: (314)993-9000
Fax: (314)993-9018
E-mail: nba@nbacares.org
URL: http://www.nbacares.org
Contact: Dennis Hagemann, Pres./CEO
Founded: 1887. **Staff:** 3,608. **Budget:** $150,000,000. **Local Groups:** 88. **Languages:** English, Spanish. **Description:** Division of Social and Health Services of the Christian Church (Disciples of Christ). Cares for older adults, children, youth, families, children and adults with mental retardation. Services are provided through over 100 facilities or programs in 22 states offering residential living and independent retirement living, nursing care, treatment centers for children who are emotionally disturbed, crisis intervention centers for children, foster care and adoption, single parent training programs, sheltered workshops, and day-care centers. Maintains liaison with interfaith and professional organizations concerned with children, older adults, and mentally retarded individuals. **Libraries: Type:** not open to the public. **Computer Services:** database. **Also Known As:** National Benevolent Association; The Other "NBA". **Publications:** *The Bugle*, monthly. Newsletter ● *Family Talk*, semiannual. Journal. Alternate Formats: CD-ROM; online ● Brochures ● Monographs ● Videos. **Conventions/Meetings:** annual conference.

12904 ■ National Council of Local Public Human Service Administrators (NCLPWA)
c/o American Public Human Services Association
810 1st St. NE, Ste.500
Washington, DC 20002
Ph: (202)682-0100
Fax: (202)289-6555
URL: http://www.aphsa.org
Contact: Dan Engstrom, Chm.
Founded: 1940. **Members:** 150. **Staff:** 1. **Description:** Administrators of local public human service agencies who are members of the American Public Welfare Association (see separate entry). Objectives are to positively influence the development of national policies and programs affecting local public human service administration and promote the professional interests, competence, and leadership of local public welfare administrators. **Publications:** none. **For-**

merly: (2004) National Council of Local Public Welfare Administrators. **Conventions/Meetings:** meeting - 3/year.

12905 ■ National Council of State Human Service Administrators (NCSHSA)

c/o American Public Human Services Association
810 1st St. NE, Ste.500
Washington, DC 20002
Ph: (202)682-0100
Fax: (202)289-6555
URL: http://www.aphsa.org
Contact: Cari DeSantis, Chair

Founded: 1939. **Members:** 700. **Description:** Chief executives, managers, and staff aides of state public welfare agencies. Provides a forum for state public welfare administrators to discuss and develop positions on national policy issues affecting state welfare programs and to exchange information on state management practices and experiences. **Committees:** Children, Family, and Adult Services; Economic Security; Education, Training, and Employment; Health Care; Information Systems; Quality Control. **Formerly:** (1984) National Council of State Public Welfare Administrators. **Conventions/Meetings:** quarterly meeting.

12906 ■ National Staff Development and Training Association (NSDTA)

c/o Dee Gross, Conference Coor.
Amer. Public Human Services Assn.
810 First St. NE, Ste.500
Washington, DC 20002-4207
Ph: (202)682-0100
Fax: (202)289-6555
E-mail: dgross@aphsa.org
URL: http://nsdta.aphsa.org
Contact: Dee Gross, Conference Coor.

Founded: 1983. **Members:** 100. **Description:** Social welfare workers engaged in staff development and training. Attempts to: support people in the field; influence welfare policy-making on the national level; form a network of contacts for members. Provides technical assistance. Maintains speakers' bureau; offers placement services. **Awards:** Distinguished Service in Training. **Frequency:** annual. **Type:** recognition. **Recipient:** for individual who demonstrates evidence of outstanding skills as trainer ● Joan Carrera Memorial Scholarships. **Frequency:** annual. **Type:** scholarship. **Recipient:** for human services trainers and training management staff members ● Lifetime Achievement. **Frequency:** annual. **Type:** recognition. **Recipient:** for individual who has significant contribution to the profession in terms of leadership, new ideas, and education ● Quality Award. **Frequency:** annual. **Type:** recognition. **Recipient:** for a training agency or training program. **Affiliated With:** American Public Human Services Association. **Publications:** *Training and Development in Human Services.* Journal. **Price:** $25.00 ● Membership Directory, annual. Includes titles, addresses, program responsibilities, and names by state. ● Newsletter, 3/year. **Conventions/Meetings:** annual Professional Development Institute - meeting.

12907 ■ Opportunities Industrialization Centers International (OICI)

240 W Tulpehocken St.
Philadelphia, PA 19144
Ph: (215)842-0220
Fax: (215)849-7033
E-mail: info@oici.org
URL: http://www.oicinternational.org
Contact: Dr. Edmund D. Cooke Jr., Chm.

Founded: 1964. **Members:** 46. **National Groups:** 18. **Multinational. Description:** Works to improve the lives of the underprivileged in developing nations. Promotes human resource development through career development, small business support, and post-war rehabilitation services. **Programs:** Food Security.

12908 ■ Pakistan Welfare Organization (PWO)

PO Box 20328
Houston, TX 77025-0328
Ph: (713)851-0834

Fax: (713)783-5519
E-mail: info@pakistanwelfare.org
URL: http://pakistanwelfare.org
Contact: Aeta Moin, Dir.

Founded: 2003. **Multinational. Description:** Encourages the Pakistani youth to contribute towards the well-being of Pakistan. Locates small organizations and provides them with funds to disperse among their projects. Holds awareness programs to educate Pakistanis on social behavior. Establishes health facilities that provide free dispensaries and emergency services. **Computer Services:** Information services, Pakistan resources. **Projects:** Al-Burooj; Al-Burooj Asthma Clinic and Elderly Care; Al-Wahab.

12909 ■ People's Involvement Corporation (PIC)

Address Unknown since 2007
Founded: 1968. **Staff:** 20. **Description:** Community development organization working to improve the economic and physical well being of underprivileged individuals nationwide. Provides educational programs to enable individuals to make use of government programs for which they qualify. Offers food, clothing, and furniture to underprivileged individuals free of charge. **Convention/Meeting:** none. **Publications:** *PIC Quarterly Newsletter.*

12910 ■ Presbyterian Health, Education and Welfare Association (PHEWA)

c/o Rev. Nancy K. Troy, Exec. Dir.
100 Witherspoon St., No. 4617
Louisville, KY 40202
Ph: (502)569-5800
Free: (888)728-7228
Fax: (502)569-8034
E-mail: ntroy@ctr.pcusa.org
URL: http://www.pcusa.org/phewa
Contact: Rev. Nancy K. Troy, Exec. Dir.

Founded: 1955. **Members:** 1,500. **Membership Dues:** individual, $35 (annual) ● retired, student or low income, $10 (annual) ● congregation, $110 (annual) ● family group, $110 (annual) ● agency, $150 (annual) ● governing body, $250 (annual) ● life, $525. **Staff:** 4. **Regional Groups:** 100. **National Groups:** 10. **Description:** Health, education, and welfare agencies and programs related to the Presbyterian Church, U.S.A; individuals with a variety of professional skills who are concerned about issues in the health, education, and welfare fields. Among member agencies are hospital and health services, community centers, and neighborhood houses. Coordinates HEW programming; establishes standards for the effectiveness of services; organizes social action and research; provides consultative services to community ministries; prepares and distributes materials on critical issues. Maintains library of periodicals from government, religious, social, welfare, and other agencies. **Awards:** John Park Lee Award. **Frequency:** semiannual. **Type:** recognition. **Recipient:** for a Presbyterian who has done exemplary work in social welfare ● Rodney T. Martin Award. **Frequency:** semiannual. **Type:** recognition. **Divisions:** Alcohol and Other Drug Abuse; Child Advocacy; Community Ministries; Disabilities; Health; HIV/AIDS Ministries; Reproductive Options; Serious Mental Illness; Specialized Ministries; Urban Pastors and Congregations. **Formerly:** (1969) National Presbyterian Health and Welfare Association; (1979) United Presbyterian Health, Education and Welfare Association. **Publications:** *Directory of Presbyterian Related Agencies,* periodic ● *PHEWA Newsletter,* quarterly ● Annual Report, annual. **Conventions/Meetings:** biennial conference.

12911 ■ Rainbow/PUSH Coalition (RPC)

930 E 50th St.
Chicago, IL 60615-2702
Ph: (773)373-3366
Fax: (773)373-3571
URL: http://www.rainbowpush.org
Contact: Rev. Jessie Jackson, Founder/Pres.

Founded: 1971. **Membership Dues:** general, $35 (annual) ● senior, $15 (annual) ● student, $15 (annual) ● trade bureau business (with sales of over

$1,500,000/year), $2,500 (annual) ● trade bureau business (with sales of $1,000,000 to $1,500,000/year), $1,000 (annual) ● trade bureau business (with sales of $500,000 to $999,000/year), $500 (annual) ● trade bureau business (with sales of less than $500,000/year), $300 (annual). **Staff:** 10. **Budget:** $300,000. **Local Groups:** 50. **Description:** National and international human rights organization and movement directed toward educational and economic equity and parity for all, particularly black, Hispanic, and poor people. Seeks to create an ethical atmosphere; encourages self and community motivation and social responsibility. Uses research, education, negotiation, and direct action to achieve its goals. Sponsors Push for Excellence Program to aid the nation's public schools and restore academic excellence and discipline. Conducts conferences; maintains tape and speech library; operates speakers' bureau. (PUSH stands for People United to Serve Humanity.). **Libraries: Type:** open to the public. **Holdings:** 300. **Subjects:** civil rights. **Departments:** Communications; Community Action; Economic Development; National Director's Office; National President's Office; Political Education; Research. **Formerly:** (2002) Operation PUSH. **Publications:** *The Push Magazine,* quarterly ● *The Voice of Excellence,* bimonthly. Newspaper. **Conventions/Meetings:** annual meeting.

12912 ■ Right Turn, International (RTI)

4520 Ashland City Hwy.
PO Box 280735
Nashville, TN 37228-0735
Ph: (334)727-5372
Fax: (334)727-5204
E-mail: clgpgt@bellsouth.net
URL: http://www.clgpgt.org
Contact: Dr. Meharry H. Lewis PhD, Exec. Dir.

Founded: 1924. **Local Groups:** 20. **Description:** Outreach and benevolent arm of the United Churches of the Living God, the Pillar and Ground of the Truth, Inc. Seeks to help the needy, rejected, neglected, and downcast of the society; encourages the errant to "turn right and go straight." Provides food and material assistance for the homeless and others in need. Offers seminars on the hazards of drugs, addiction, and delinquency. **Telecommunication Services:** electronic mail, meharrylew@usa.net. **Departments:** Juvenile; Mature Adult; Senior Citizen; Young Adult. **Publications:** *RTI News and Views,* bimonthly. Newsletter. **Conventions/Meetings:** annual general assembly - always last week of July in Nashville, TN.

12913 ■ Salvation Army (SA)

PO Box 269
615 Slaters Ln.
Alexandria, VA 22313
Ph: (703)684-5500
Free: (800)SAL-ARMY
Fax: (703)684-3478
E-mail: sa_information@usn.salvationarmy.org
URL: http://www.salvationarmyusa.org
Contact: Commissioner Israel L. Gaither, Natl. Commander

Founded: 1865. **Members:** 454,982. **Staff:** 40,519. **Budget:** $1,354,000. **Regional Groups:** 4. **State Groups:** 41. **Local Groups:** 1,743. **Languages:** Cantonese, Chamorro, English, Japanese, Korean, Laotian, Mandarin Dialects, Pohnpeian, Portuguese, Russian, Spanish, Tagalog. **Description:** Commissioned officers are ordained ministers devoting full time to religious and social welfare activities; members of local church or corps community centers are known as soldiers. An international Christian religious and charitable movement, organized on a paramilitary pattern, dedicated to meeting the physical, spiritual, and emotional needs of mankind. Work is carried out through local centers of operation which include adult rehabilitation centers, clinics, outpatient programs for unwed mothers, recreation centers, camping programs for children and adults, senior and children's day care, senior housing and activity centers, and emergency feeding and shelter stations; and through service extension units located in communities not supporting a full Salvation Army program, which extend aid in emergencies. Maintains speakers' bureau and 40 divisions; compiles statistics. Offers placement and referral services at local level. Provides officers' training schools. **Libraries: Type:** reference; by appointment only. **Holdings:** 5,000; archival material. **Subjects:** historical publications, posters, documents and records. **Publications:** *War Cry*, biweekly. Magazine. Features articles on Christian topics; includes association news and Bible studies. **Price:** $26.00/year. ISSN: 0043-0234. **Circulation:** 400,000 ● *What Is The Salvation Army?.* Booklet ● *Women's Ministry Resources*, annual. Contains weekly in-house programs for women, including ideas for decorations, games, refreshments, and devotionals. **Price:** $9.00/year. **Circulation:** 7,500 ● *Young Salvationist*, 10/year. Magazine. Covers issues confronting teenagers from a Christian perspective. **Price:** $4.00/year. ISSN: 0746-861X. **Circulation:** 50,000 ● Annual Report. Alternate Formats: online. **Conventions/Meetings:** National Advisory Board Meeting - 3/year ● triennial National Advisory Organization Conference ● periodic National Forum - meeting.

12914 ■ Samuel Rubin Foundation
c/o Ms. Lauranne Jones, Grants Admin.
777 United Nations Plz.
New York, NY 10017-3521
Ph: (212)697-8945
Fax: (212)682-0886
E-mail: lauranne@igc.org
URL: http://www.samuelrubinfoundation.org
Contact: Ms. Lauranne Jones, Grants Admin.
Nonmembership. Multinational. Description: Works to support social, economic, political, civil, and cultural rights for everyone. **Awards: Type:** grant.

12915 ■ Scherman Foundation
16 E 52nd St., Ste.601
New York, NY 10022-5306
Ph: (212)832-3086
Fax: (212)838-0154
E-mail: info@scherman.org
URL: http://www.scherman.org
Contact: Sandra Silverman, Pres./Exec. Dir.
Founded: 1941. **Description:** Works to support nonprofit organizations that are focused on the environment, disarmament and peace, reproductive rights and family planning, human rights, and social welfare. **Awards: Type:** recognition. **Publications:** Annual Report, annual. Alternate Formats: online.

12916 ■ Society of St. Vincent de Paul Council of the U.S. (SVDP)
58 Progress Pkwy.
Maryland Heights, MO 63043-3706
Ph: (314)576-3993
Fax: (314)576-6755
E-mail: usacouncil@svdpusa.org
URL: http://www.svdpusa.org
Contact: Roger Playwin, Natl. Exec. Dir.
Founded: 1833. **Members:** 120,000. **Staff:** 10. **Budget:** $3,706,459. **Regional Groups:** 8. **Local Groups:** 4,400. **Description:** Offers tangible assistance to those in need, and spiritual services through prayer and person-to-person contact. **Libraries: Type:** reference. **Holdings:** 500. **Subjects:** St. Vincent de Paul, Blessed Frederic Ozanam, St. Louise de Marillac, Blessed Rosalie Rendu, Society of St. Vincent de Paul, Vincentian spirituality. **Committees:** Cause of Ozanam; Communications; Development; Disaster; Finance and Governance; Stores; Vincentian Formation; Vincentian Services; Voice of the Poor; Youth. **Formerly:** (1989) Superior Council of U.S. Society of St. Vincent de Paul. **Publications:** *Consolidated Annual Report*, annual. **Circulation:** 70,000 ● *Ozanam News*, quarterly. Magazine. Covers the activities and projects of the society and its members. **Price:** free. **Circulation:** 59,000. Alternate Formats: online ● Survey. **Conventions/Meetings:** annual conference, with business meeting, workshops for leadership/members.

12917 ■ Travelers Aid International
1612 K St. NW, Ste.206
Washington, DC 20006
Ph: (202)546-1127
Fax: (202)546-9112
E-mail: info@travelersaid.org
URL: http://www.travelersaid.org
Contact: Ray Flynt, Pres.
Founded: 1984. **Members:** 54. **Staff:** 17. **Budget:** $1,150,000. **Description:** Agencies providing travelers aid services, primarily to persons in transition. Promotes policies and services that meet emergency needs; provides assistance and encourages self-sufficiency for those who have experienced problems related to homelessness, mobility, rejection, relocation, or lack of resources. Conducts research; compiles statistics. Also operates local Washington Travelers Aid programs. **Computer Services:** database, membership service statistics. **Councils:** Professional. **Formerly:** (2000) National Organization of Travelers Aid Societies. **Publications:** *TAI Directory of Programs and Services*, annual.

12918 ■ Volunteers of America
1660 Duke St.
Alexandria, VA 22314
Ph: (703)341-5000
Free: (800)899-0089
Fax: (703)341-7000
E-mail: info@voa.org
URL: http://www.voa.org
Contact: Charles W. Gould, Pres./CEO
Founded: 1896. **Staff:** 15,000. **Local Groups:** 38. **Description:** Works as a national, non-profit, faith-based organization that helps others rebuild their lives and reach their full potential by providing thousands of human service programs, and many opportunities for individual and community involvement. **Libraries: Type:** reference. **Subjects:** human services. **Awards:** Annie E. Casey Foundation Family Strengthening Awards. **Frequency:** annual. **Type:** recognition ● Ballington and Maud Booth Award. **Frequency:** annual. **Type:** recognition: for distinguished service to humanity ● Empathy Award. **Frequency:** annual. **Type:** recognition ● Innovation Awards. **Frequency:** annual. **Type:** recognition ● Major League Baseball Players Grant. **Frequency:** annual. **Type:** grant ● Maud Booth Correctional Service Award. **Frequency:** annual. **Type:** recognition ● National Endowment Funds. **Frequency:** annual. **Type:** grant ● Outstanding Community Service Award. **Frequency:** annual. **Type:** recognition. **Divisions:** National Housing and Health Services. **Publications:** *The Gazette*, quarterly. **Circulation:** 15,000 ● *Spirit*, quarterly. Magazine. **Price:** $8.00/year. **Circulation:** 21,000. Alternate Formats: online ● Annual Report, annual. Alternate Formats: online. **Conventions/Meetings:** annual assembly.

12919 ■ Welfare Research, Inc. (WRI)
112 State St.
Albany, NY 12207
Ph: (518)432-2563
Fax: (518)432-2564
E-mail: administration@welfareresearch.org
URL: http://www.welfareresearch.org
Contact: Rebecca McBride, Ed.
Founded: 1967. **Staff:** 30. **Budget:** $3,000,000. **Description:** A consulting organization aimed at improving social service agencies operations and services. Provides research, evaluation, training, and technical and management assistance to the human services community. Conducts policy studies in child welfare, adolescent health, teen pregnancy, employment for welfare recipients, and service needs of refugees. Emphasis is on training needs of minority community agencies and staff of mental health and long term care facilities. Operates orientation program for public employees. **Publications:** *Adoption Recruitment Brochure*. Describes New York's children awaiting adoption, adoptive families and services available for children, birth parents and adoptive parents. ● *Congregate Care Health Services Manual*. Presents policies and procedures related to intake, health care maintenance and emergencies. **Price:** $9.00 ● *Foster Care Team Manual for Niagara County*. Contains information on placement, family court and day-to-day foster parent activities. **Price:** $10.00 ● *New York State Foster Parent Manual*. Contains information

reflecting current policy, regulations and practices in foster care. **Price:** free ● *When your Child is in Foster Care: A Handbook for Parents*. Provides information on the rights and responsibilities of parents.

12920 ■ William and Flora Hewlett Foundation
2121 Sand Hill Rd.
Menlo Park, CA 94025
Ph: (650)234-4500
Fax: (650)234-4501
E-mail: info@hewlett.org
URL: http://www.hewlett.org
Contact: Paul Brest, Pres.
Founded: 1966. **Staff:** 49. **Description:** Works to support activities in education, performing arts, population, environment, conflict resolution, family and community development, and U.S.-Latin American relations. **Awards: Type:** grant. **Publications:** Annual Reports, annual. Alternate Formats: online ● Newsletter, quarterly. Alternate Formats: online.

12921 ■ Windward Foundation
55 Windward Ln.
Klickitat, WA 98628
Ph: (509)369-2000
E-mail: windward@gorge.net
URL: http://www.windward.org
Contact: T. Brooks Landers, Sec.
Founded: 1976. **Members:** 21. **Staff:** 3. **Budget:** $50,000. **Description:** Promotes self-reliance among homeless persons, single parents, and senior citizens through remedial work and hands-on programs. Focuses on food, communication, and personal growth. Bestows scholarships; conducts research. **Libraries: Type:** reference. **Holdings:** archival material, books, periodicals. **Subjects:** self-reliance skills and crafts. **Publications:** *Notes From Windward*, annual. Newsletter. **Price:** $15.00/year. **Circulation:** 100. Alternate Formats: online. **Conventions/Meetings:** seminar - 5/year.

12922 ■ World Technical Volunteers (WTV)
17482 Isle Royale Terr.
Dumfries, VA 22026
Ph: (703)220-4606
Fax: (703)441-1022
E-mail: wtv@worldtechnical.org
URL: http://www.worldtechnical.org
Contact: Philip Darko, Pres./CEO
Multinational. Description: Strives to provide quality technical programs in poor and underserved communities around the world to improve their health and livelihood. Helps reduce the vulnerability of the poor to AIDS and other related diseases. Helps poor communities gain access to basic amenities. Assists communities in responding to new ideas and technology. **Publications:** *VillageTek*, monthly. Newsletter.

12923 ■ Zarrow Families Foundation
401 S Boston Ave., Ste.900
Tulsa, OK 74103-4012
Ph: (918)295-8004
Fax: (918)295-8049
E-mail: jgillert@zarrow.com
URL: http://www.zarrow.com
Contact: Jeanne Gillert, Grants Mgr.
Description: Works to support education, social services, Jewish causes, health programs, medical research, mental health programs. **Awards: Type:** grant.

Social Work

12924 ■ Association for Community Organization and Social Administration (ACOSA)
20560 Bensley Ave.
Lynwood, IL 60411
Ph: (708)757-4187
Fax: (708)757-4234

E-mail: akj@uic.edu
URL: http://www.acosa.org
Contact: Alice K. Johnson, Coor., Operations & Administration
Founded: 1987. **Members:** 400. **Membership Dues:** regular, $75 (annual) ● sponsor, $100 (annual) ● institutional, $300 (annual) ● student, $35 (annual). **Staff:** 1. **Budget:** $40,000. **Regional Groups:** 7. **Description:** Strengthens community organization and social administration; a membership organization for community organizers, activists, nonprofit administrators, community builders, policy practitioners, students and professors. **Awards:** Emerging Scholar/Career Achievement/Student/Practitioner. **Frequency:** annual. **Type:** recognition. **Recipient:** for achievement in community organization and social administration. **Computer Services:** database ● mailing lists ● online services. **Telecommunication Services:** electronic mail, billb@en.com. **Publications:** *ACOSA Update*, quarterly. Newsletter. **Price:** included in membership dues. **Circulation:** 600. **Advertising:** accepted. Alternate Formats: online ● *Journal of Community Practice*, quarterly. **Price:** included in membership dues. Also Cited As: *JCP*. **Conventions/Meetings:** annual symposium, held in conjunction with APM of CSWE (exhibits).

12925 ■ Association of Oncology Social Work (AOSW)
100 N 20th St., 4th Fl.
Philadelphia, PA 19103
Ph: (215)599-6093
Fax: (215)545-8107
E-mail: info@aosw.org
URL: http://www.aosw.org
Contact: Kimberly Barrio Lawson MSW, Pres.
Founded: 1984. **Members:** 900. **Membership Dues:** full, $125 (annual) ● retired, full time student, $95 (annual). **Regional Groups:** 5. **Description:** Promotes excellence in psychosocial care of persons with cancer, their families and caregivers. **Awards:** Leadership in Oncology Social Work. **Frequency:** annual. **Type:** recognition. **Recipient:** for an AOSW member ● Neuro-Oncology Social Work of the Year Award. **Frequency:** annual. **Type:** recognition. **Recipient:** to a hospital based oncology social worker who provides innovative and compassionate services to brain tumor patients and their families ● Oncology Social Worker of the Year. **Frequency:** annual. **Type:** recognition. **Recipient:** for an AOSW member. **Computer Services:** Mailing lists, of members. **Special Interest Groups:** AIDS; Ambulance Care/Fee for Service; Blood and Marrow Transplant; BMT; Brain Tumor; Children and Cancer; Complementary/Alternative Medicine; Computing; Diversity; End of Life Care; Pain and Palliative Care; Spirituality. **Formerly:** (1993) National Association of Oncology Social Workers. **Publications:** *AOSW News*, 3/year. Newsletter. Includes career opportunity listings and meeting announcements. **Price:** included in membership dues. **Circulation:** 1,000. **Advertising:** accepted ● *Journal of Psychosocial Oncology*, quarterly. Includes camera-ready artwork. **Price:** included in membership dues. **Circulation:** 2,000. **Advertising:** accepted ● Membership Directory ● Also publishes *Social Worker Standards of Practice* and *BMT Directory*. Tools for the practice evaluation of oncology social work. **Conventions/Meetings:** annual conference (exhibits).

12926 ■ Association of Social Work Boards (ASWB)
400 S Ridge Pkwy., Ste.B
Culpeper, VA 22701
Ph: (540)829-6880
Free: (800)225-6880
Fax: (540)829-0142
E-mail: info@aswb.org
URL: http://www.aswb.org
Contact: Donna DeAngelis ACSW, Exec. Dir.
Founded: 1979. **Members:** 52. **Staff:** 20. **Budget:** $4,000,000. **Description:** State boards and authorities empowered to regulate the practice of social work within their own jurisdictions. Seeks to protect the recipient of social work service and promote confidence in and accountability of the social work profes-

sion by establishing national regulatory standards for the practice of professional social work. Works to facilitate communication and the exchange of information concerning the regulation of social workers; promote the standardization of credential assessment by encouraging collaborative efforts by states to develop compatible standards and procedures for regulation; provide guidance and education on regulation of the practice of social work to legal bodies, regulatory agencies, and other groups concerned with the protection of the public; offer assistance in fulfilling statutory, public, and ethical obligations in legal regulation and enforcement. Provides uniform examinations to state boards and agencies to enable them to evaluate qualifications for social work credentials. Promotes research on matters regarding legal regulations; has established the American Foundation for Research and Consumer Education in Social Work Regulation to research the ramifications of licensing, explore ethical issues raised by professional regulation, and educate the public in what constitutes good social work practice. **Awards:** Board Administrator Award. **Frequency:** annual. **Type:** recognition. **Recipient:** to two staff members of boards for their contributions to their individual boards ● Sunny Andrews Award. **Frequency:** annual. **Type:** recognition. **Recipient:** for volunteer members of social work regulatory boards. **Committees:** Approved Continuing Education; Bylaws and Resolutions; Discipline and Regulatory Standards; Examination; Nominating; Program and Education. **Formerly:** (2003) American Association of State Social Work Boards. **Publications:** *Association News*, bimonthly. Newsletter. Includes association and state legislative information; contains calendar of events. **Advertising:** accepted. Alternate Formats: online ● *Reciprocity and Endorsement in Social Work Licensure*. Report ● Also publishes examination study guides and continuing education tapes. **Conventions/Meetings:** semiannual Delegate Assembly - always in the spring and fall.

12927 ■ Clinical Social Work Federation (CSWF)
PO Box 3740
Arlington, VA 22203
Ph: (703)522-3866
Free: (800)270-9739
Fax: (703)522-9441
E-mail: nfscswlo@aol.com
URL: http://www.cswf.org
Contact: Richard P. Yanes, Exec.Dir.
Founded: 1971. **Members:** 9,000. **Staff:** 2. **State Groups:** 31. **Description:** State societies of clinical social work united to provide a vehicle for states and/or regional societies to share concerns common to clinical social work, develop consensual solutions to problems beyond the jurisdiction of any single society, and carry out appropriate courses of action. **Committees:** Clinical Social Work Education; Licensure/Vendorship/Marketing; National Advocacy; Professional Standards. **Formerly:** (1976) National Federation of Clinical Social Workers; (1998) National Federation of Societies for Clinical Social Work. **Publications:** *Access*, semiannual. Newsletter. **Advertising:** accepted. Alternate Formats: online ● *Clinical Social Work Journal*, quarterly ● *National News*, quarterly ● *Progress Report*, semiannual. Newsletter. Includes book reviews and legislative updates. **Price:** included in membership dues; $25.00 /year for nonmembers. **Circulation:** 11,000. **Advertising:** accepted. **Conventions/Meetings:** semiannual board meeting - usually May and October ● convention and conference.

12928 ■ Council of International Programs USA (CIPUSA)
1700 E 13th St., Ste.4ME
Cleveland, OH 44114-3241
Ph: (216)566-1088
Fax: (216)566-1490
E-mail: info@cipusa.org
URL: http://www.cipusa.org
Contact: Lisa L. Purdy, Pres./CEO
Founded: 1955. **Staff:** 3. **Budget:** $300,000. **National Groups:** 8. **Nonmembership. Multinational.**

Description: Funded by governments, corporations, foundations, and community sources. Conducts educational and cultural training exchanges for professionals in the fields of architecture, business, communications, commerce, education, special education, engineering, finance, health, information technology, law, library science, management, public administration, social work, and social sciences. Programs include practical training, orientation, evaluation, predeparture preparation, and cultural and educational opportunities. **Telecommunication Services:** electronic mail, lisapurdy@cipusa.org. **Programs:** Community Leadership; Core; Custom; Global Partners. **Formerly:** (1998) Council of International Programs. **Publications:** *Directory of Former Participants*, periodic. **Conventions/Meetings:** biennial International Conference of Alumni.

12929 ■ Employee Assistance Professionals Association (EAPA)
4350 N Fairfax Dr., Ste.410
Arlington, VA 22203
Ph: (703)387-1000
Fax: (703)522-4585
E-mail: info@eap-association.org
URL: http://www.eap-association.com
Contact: John Maynard PhD, CEO
Founded: 1971. **Members:** 7,000. **Membership Dues:** individual in U.S., associate in U.S., $135 (annual) ● organizational individual in U.S., organizational associate in U.S., $242 (annual) ● student in U.S., retired individual in U.S., $47 (annual) ● individual outside U.S., associate outside U.S., $89 (annual) ● organizational individual outside U.S., organizational associate outside U.S., $175 (annual) ● student outside U.S., $40 (annual) ● affiliate outside U.S., $25 (annual). **Budget:** $2,500,000. **Regional Groups:** 10. **Local Groups:** 105. **Description:** Persons employed in the development or operation of employee assistance programs (EAPs) and/or services as administrators, consultants, or motivational advisors; persons with an interest in the field; individuals enrolled in courses leading to degrees in employee assistance-related disciplines; firms, institutions, and associations. Encourages the systematic development of employee assistance programs. Serves as an advocate with the public and private sectors for the support and development of the EAP movement. Conducts research and educational programs; offers certification; compiles statistics. **Libraries:** Type: reference. **Holdings:** 2,090. **Subjects:** EAP specific concerns. **Awards:** Type: recognition. **Computer Services:** Mailing lists. **Committees:** Accreditation; Benefits; Bylaws; Consultants; Development; Education and Training; Ethics; Legislative and Public Policy; Research; Standards; Treatment; Women's Issues. **Also Known As:** (1993) EAPA. **Formerly:** (1989) Association of Labor-Management Administrators and Consultants on Alcoholism. **Publications:** *EAP Exchange*, monthly ● *EAPA Directory of EAP Consultants*, biennial ● *Focus Papers*, periodic ● *Member Resource Directory*, annual. Membership Directory. Alternate Formats: online ● *Publications Catalog*. Books. **Circulation:** 10,000 ● Brochures ● Newsletter. **Conventions/Meetings:** annual conference (exhibits).

12930 ■ National Association of Black Social Workers (NABSW)
2305 Martin Luther King Ave. SE
Washington, DC 20020-5813
Ph: (202)678-4570
Fax: (202)678-4572
E-mail: nabsw.harambee@verizon.net
URL: http://www.nabsw.org
Contact: Gloria Batiste-Roberts D.PH, Pres.
Founded: 1968. **Members:** 7,000. **Staff:** 7. **Budget:** $1,400,000. **State Groups:** 43. **Local Groups:** 115. **Description:** Works to promote African American human service workers. Provides a forum for the exchange of ideas; offers services and programs to improve welfare services in African American communities; advocates for legislation to preserve and strengthen African American families; conducts educational and research programs. **Awards:** Cenie J. Williams Tuition. **Frequency:** annual. **Type:**

scholarship ● Distinguished Individual Service Award. **Frequency:** annual. **Type:** recognition ● Emma and Meloid Algood Scholarship. **Frequency:** annual. **Type:** scholarship ● Guynn Family Book Scholarship. **Frequency:** annual. **Type:** scholarship ● Nia Award. **Frequency:** annual. **Type:** recognition ● Presidential Award. **Frequency:** annual. **Type:** recognition. **Recipient:** for chapter that has added the most members ● Selena Brown Book. **Frequency:** annual. **Type:** scholarship ● Ujima Award. **Frequency:** annual. **Type:** recognition. **Task Forces:** Civil Liberties; Family; Health Wellness; Youth. **Publications:** *Kinship Care.* Paper. Alternate Formats: online ● *Preserving the Black Family Beyond the Rhetoric.* Paper ● *Welfare Reform.* Paper. Alternate Formats: online. **Conventions/Meetings:** annual conference and board meeting ● semiannual Making a Difference: Implementing Effective African-centered Social Work Policies & Practices - conference.

12931 ■ National Association of Puerto Rican Hispanic Social Workers (NAPRHSW)

PO Box 651
Brentwood, NY 11717
Ph: (631)864-1536
Fax: (631)864-1536
E-mail: naprhsw@aol.com
URL: http://www.naprhsw.org
Contact: Luis Valenzuela PhD, Pres.
Founded: 1983. **Members:** 400. **Membership Dues:** regular, $50 (annual) ● senior, $35 (annual) ● student, $20 (annual) ● corporate, $250 (annual). **Description:** Promotes professional development of Hispanic social workers. Creates standards and enforces a Code of Ethics for social work practice. Lobbies to influence legislation on social work issues. Conducts educational and credentialing programs. **Awards:** Social Worker of the Year. **Frequency:** annual. **Type:** monetary. **Recipient:** for MSW student. **Publications:** *NAPRHSW Newsletter,* 3/year. Journal. **Advertising:** accepted ● Journal, periodic. **Conventions/Meetings:** periodic conference, with scholarship fundraisers.

12932 ■ National Association of Social Workers (NASW)

750 First St. NE, Ste.700
Washington, DC 20002-4241
Ph: (202)408-8600
Free: (800)638-8799
Fax: (202)336-8313
E-mail: info@naswdc.org
URL: http://www.naswdc.org
Contact: Elvira Craig de Silva, Pres.
Founded: 1955. **Members:** 150,000. **Membership Dues:** regular, $125-$190 (annual) ● student, $48 (annual) ● associate, $151 (annual) ● doctoral student, $143 (annual). **Staff:** 120. **Budget:** $18,000,000. **State Groups:** 55. **Description:** Regular members are persons who hold a minimum of a baccalaureate degree in social work. Associate members are persons engaged in social work who have a baccalaureate degree in another field. Student members are persons enrolled in accredited (by the Council on Social Work Education) graduate or undergraduate social work programs. Works to create professional standards for social work practice; advocate sound public social policies through political and legislative action; provide a wide range of membership services, including continuing education opportunities and an extensive professional program. Operates National Center for Social Policy and Practice. Conducts research; compiles statistics. **Libraries: Type:** reference. **Holdings:** 1,000; periodicals. **Subjects:** social work. **Awards:** National Public Citizen of the Year. **Type:** recognition ● National Social Worker of the Year. **Type:** recognition. **Computer Services:** database, social work abstracts ● mailing lists. **Committees:** PANELS; Peace and Justice; Racial and Ethnic Diversity; Women's Issues. **Absorbed:** (1994) National Center for Social Policy and Practice. **Formed by Merger of:** American Association of Group Workers; American Association of Medical Social Workers; American Association of Psychiatric Social Workers; American Association of Social Workers; Association for the Study of Com-

munity Organization; National Association of School Social Workers; Social Work Research Group. **Publications:** *Children and Schools: A Journal of Social Work Practice,* quarterly. Focuses on problems encountered by social workers and educators in schools. Includes information on new developments, practices, and programs. **Price:** $54.00 /year for members; $89.00 /year for nonmembers; $37.00/year for student members; $125.00 /year for libraries and institutions. ISSN: 1532-8759. **Circulation:** 2,300. **Advertising:** accepted. Alternate Formats: microform ● *Encyclopedia of Social Work,* every 10 years. Book. **Price:** $159.00. Alternate Formats: CD-ROM ● *Health and Social Work,* quarterly. Journal. Gives information on improving social work practice for physical and mental health personnel. Includes legislation updates and innovative practices. **Price:** $54.00 for members; $89.00 /year for nonmembers; $37.00/year for student members; $125.00 /year for libraries and institutions. ISSN: 0360-7283. **Circulation:** 4,000. **Advertising:** accepted. Alternate Formats: microform ● *NASW News,* 10/year. Newspaper. Reports on developments in the profession. Includes updates on social policy developments in such areas as child welfare, Medicaid, AIDS, and housing. **Price:** included in membership dues; $33.00 /year for nonmembers; $8.00/copy for nonmembers. ISSN: 0027-6022. **Advertising:** accepted. Alternate Formats: microform ● *Professional Writing for the Human Services* ● *Social Work,* quarterly. Journal. Covers social work and social welfare. Examines current social problems such as child abuse, homelessness, working parents, and women's roles. **Price:** free for members; $129.00 /year for libraries and institutions; $89.00 /year for nonmembers; $37.00/year for student members. ISSN: 0037-8046. **Circulation:** 150,000. **Advertising:** accepted. Alternate Formats: microform ● *Social Work Abstracts,* quarterly. Journal. **Price:** $89.00 /year for nonmembers; $37.00/year for student members; $129.00 /year for libraries and institutions. ISSN: 1070-5317. **Advertising:** accepted ● *Social Work Almanac* ● *The Social Work Dictionary* ● *Social Work Research,* quarterly. Journal. Provides over 500 abstracts from 300 journals on social work and related fields. Includes original research articles and research methods. **Price:** $54.00 /year for members; $89.00 /year for nonmembers; $37.00/year for student members; $125.00 /year for libraries and institutions. ISSN: 1070-5309. **Circulation:** 2,200. **Advertising:** accepted. Alternate Formats: microform. **Conventions/Meetings:** triennial Delegate Assembly - conference (exhibits).

12933 ■ National Network for Social Work Managers (NNSWM)

c/o Jane Addams College of Social Work
M/C 309
1040 W Harrison St.
Chicago, IL 60607-7129
Ph: (312)413-2302
Fax: (312)996-2770
E-mail: info@socialworkmanager.org
URL: http://www.socialworkmanager.org
Contact: Glynne Gervais, Exec. Dir.
Founded: 1985. **Members:** 250. **Membership Dues:** individual, $130 (annual) ● student, retiree, $55 (annual) ● organizational, $95 (annual) ● international, $145 (annual) ● organization (varies on organization's budget), $500-$2,000 (annual). **Staff:** 2. **Budget:** $40,000. **Description:** Enhances and promotes effective and values-based social work management. Recognizes outstanding practitioners through it's annual exemplar awards program and lifetime achievement awards program; certifies qualified social work managers (CSWM credential); develops and disseminates standards for social work leadership and management; holds national and regional training and conferences offered through the Institute of the National Network and the training arm of the organization; publishes a scholarly journal, an electronic newsletter and a website to disseminate information on best practices in social work management. **Awards:** Chauncey Alexander Lifetime Achievement Award in Social Work Management. **Frequency:** annual. **Type:** recognition. **Recipient:** for an outstanding social work manager ● Exemplar Award. **Fre-

quency:** annual. **Type:** recognition. **Recipient:** for an effective social work manager ● National Management Excellence Award for Social Work Executives and Managers. **Type:** recognition. **Computer Services:** Mailing lists, of members. **Publications:** *Administration in Social Work,* quarterly. Journal. **Price:** included in membership dues ● *Social Work Executive,* quarterly. Newsletter. Provides information on the national management of social policies; includes conference and member information. **Price:** included in membership dues. **Advertising:** accepted ● Membership Directory, annual. **Price:** included in membership dues. Alternate Formats: online. **Conventions/Meetings:** annual National Management Institute - meeting - sometimes held twice per year ● periodic Regional Training - seminar, upon request.

12934 ■ North American Association of Christians in Social Work (NACSW)

PO Box 121
Botsford, CT 06404-0121
Ph: (203)270-8780
Free: (888)426-4712
Fax: (203)270-8780
E-mail: info@nacsw.org
URL: http://www.nacsw.org
Contact: Rick Chamiec-Case, Exec. Dir.
Founded: 1954. **Members:** 2,000. **Membership Dues:** student, $23 (annual) ● regular, $75 (annual). **Staff:** 3. **State Groups:** 5. **Local Groups:** 3. **Multinational. Description:** Professional social workers and related professionals, students, interested individuals. Supports the integration of Christian faith and professional social work practice in the lives of its members, the profession and the church, promoting love and justice in social service and social reform. Provides opportunities for Christian fellowship, education and service opportunities; articulates informed Christian voice on social welfare practice and policy to the social work profession; provides professional understanding and help for the social ministry of the church; and promotes social welfare services and policies in society that bring about greater justice and meet basic human needs. **Libraries: Type:** reference. **Awards:** Distinguish Service to Social Work. **Frequency:** annual. **Type:** recognition ● Distinguished Service to Social Welfare. **Frequency:** annual. **Type:** recognition. **Recipient:** for distinguished service. **Computer Services:** Mailing lists, labels. **Formerly:** Evangelical Social Work Conference; (1984) National Association of Christians in Social Work. **Publications:** *A Christian Response to Domestic Violence: A Reconciliation Model for Social Workers.* Monograph. **Price:** $10.00. ISSN: 8756-5013. **Advertising:** accepted ● *Catalyst,* bimonthly. Newsletter. Examines the relationship between churches and social work. Reports on association activities; includes calendar of events and chapter news. **Price:** included in membership dues. **Circulation:** 1,500. **Advertising:** accepted ● *Christianity and Social Work: Readings on the Integration of Christian Faith and Social Work Practice.* Book. **Price:** $23.00 ● *Hearts Strangely Warmed: A Reflection on Biblical Passages Relevant to Social Work* ● *Integrating Faith and Practice: A History of the North American Association of Christians in Social Work.* Monograph ● *So You Want to Be a Social Worker: A Primer for the Christian Student.* Journal. **Price:** $10.00 ● *Social Work and Christianity,* semiannual. Monograph. Contributes to the "growth of social workers in the Christian faith." Includes book reviews. **Price:** included in membership dues; $25.00 /year for institutions in U.S.; $27.00 /year for institutions outside U.S. ISSN: 0737-5778. **Circulation:** 1,500 ● *Spirit-Led Helping: A Model for Evangelical Social Work Counseling.* Monograph. **Price:** $10.00. **Conventions/Meetings:** Convention and Training Conference - workshop (exhibits) - always October.

12935 ■ Society for Social Work Leadership in Health Care (SSWLHC)

100 N 20th St., 4th Fl.
Philadelphia, PA 19103
Ph: (215)599-6134
Free: (866)237-9542
Fax: (215)564-2175

E-mail: lgroff@fernley.com
URL: http://www.sswlhc.org
Contact: Lindsay Groff, Exec. Dir.
Founded: 1965. **Members:** 1,300. **Membership Dues:** full, management, $125 (annual) ● direct patient care, transitional, emeritus, faculty, student, $70 ● associate, $150. **Staff:** 5. **Budget:** $650,000. **State Groups:** 50. **Description:** Social work administrators, leaders, consultants, and educators working in health care; students with an interest in health care social work administration. Fosters communication among members. Conducts educational programs; makes available discounts and other services to members; educational programs award continuing education units. **Awards:** Ida M. Cannon Healthcare Social Work Leader of the Year. **Frequency:** annual. **Type:** recognition. **Computer Services:** database ● mailing lists. **Telecommunication Services:** electronic mail, pjones@ascensionhealth.org. **Funds:** Kermit B. Nash Memorial. **Programs:** Mentoring. **Subgroups:** Advocacy; Chapter Relations; Continuing Education; Information Management; Interorganizational Networks; Nominating; Publications. **Formerly:** (1998) Society for Social Work Administration in Health Care. **Publications:** *Conference Proceedings.* Features highlights of the National Society Conference. **Price:** $25.00 for members; $30.00 for nonmembers ● *Emerging Opportunities for Social Work in the Health Care Continuum: Selected Proceedings of the 38th Annual Educational Conference.* Book. Contains clinical insights. **Price:** $25.00 for members; $30.00 for nonmembers ● *The Premiere Society for Social Work Professionals in Health Care.* Brochure. Alternate Formats: online ● *Social Work Leader,* 8/year. Newsletter. **Price:** free, for members only. **Circulation:** 1,500. **Advertising:** accepted ● Membership Directory. Alternate Formats: online ● Monographs. **Price:** $15.00 for members; $20.00 for nonmembers. **Conventions/Meetings:** annual convention (exhibits) ● annual Social Work in Health Care: Our Next 100 Years - conference.

12936 ■ We Care America (WCA)
44180 Riverside Pkwy., Ste.201
Lansdowne, VA 20176
Ph: (703)554-8600
Fax: (703)554-8630
E-mail: info@wecareamerica.org
Contact: Tom Knox, Chm.
Description: Helps the community of faith build greater capacity to serve those in need through strategic partnerships with government, corporations and other faith-based organizations, leadership training, leveraging resources and volunteerism. Engages in advocacy and public policy that benefit the poor and the hurting. **Computer Services:** none. **Divisions:** National Grant Center; We Care For Youth. **Publications:** *The Advocate,* monthly. Newsletter. Alternate Formats: online ● Articles. Alternate Formats: online.

Speech and Hearing

12937 ■ VOICES Association
11132 S Freeman Ave., Ste.C
Inglewood, CA 90304
Ph: (310)910-3555
Fax: (310)695-7420
E-mail: voices_inc@comcast.net
URL: http://www.4voices.org
Contact: Tamara Hill, Co-Founder
Description: Improves the lives of children with speech and other communication disorders and their families through community education, parental advocacy and family support. Develops and enhances the awareness of and educates communities about the needs of children with communication disorders. Provides a forum for parents and professionals to receive information, support and resources. **Publications:** *VOICES Magazine Online: The Virtual Speech and Language Magazine.* Alternate Formats: online.

Student Services

12938 ■ National Council for Support of Disability Issues (NCSD)
Mountain Rd.
Haymarket, VA 20169

Ph: (703)753-9148
E-mail: tflink@ncsd.org
URL: http://www.ncsd.org
Contact: Trisha Flink, Sec./Exec. Dir.
Founded: 1995. **Description:** Works to strengthen legal rights and remedies, build networks among student groups, and expand education opportunities for students with disabilities. **Awards:** Scholarships. **Type:** scholarship. **Computer Services:** Mailing lists ● online services, forum. **Committees:** At Large; Fundraising; Legal; Special Projects. **Projects:** The Able Crew; People Resources. **Formerly:** (2005) National Coalition for Students with Disabilities. **Publications:** *Parent Handbook.* Alternate Formats: online ● Newsletter. Alternate Formats: online ● Articles ● Survey.

Substance Abuse

12939 ■ Addiction Research and Treatment Corporation (ARTC)
22 Chapel St.
Brooklyn, NY 11201
Ph: (718)260-2900
Fax: (718)875-2817
E-mail: info@artcny.org
URL: http://www.Artcny.org
Contact: Dr. Beny J. Primm MD, Exec. Dir.
Founded: 1969. **Members:** 250. **Staff:** 250. **Budget:** $16,000,000. **Languages:** English, Spanish. **Description:** Operates a multi-modality drug treatment program with ten ambulatory treatment clinics and a Vocational Evaluation Center. Funded by the state of New York Substance Abuse Services and third party reimbursements. Treatments employed are primarily detoxification, methadone maintenance, and drug-free services. Other services include: individual counseling, group therapy, job development, vocational counseling, mental health care, and recreation. Participates in national research programs. Sponsors substance abuse and AIDS research projects. Maintains speakers' bureau. **Convention/Meeting:** none. **Additional Websites:** http://www.uriny.org, http://www.ndvl.org. **Publications:** Articles ● Publishes abstracts.

12940 ■ Al-Anon Family Group Headquarters, World Service Office (AFG)
1600 Corporate Landing Pkwy.
Virginia Beach, VA 23454-5617
Ph: (757)563-1600
Free: (888)4AL-ANON
Fax: (757)563-1655
E-mail: wso@al-anon.org
URL: http://www.al-anon.alateen.org
Contact: Richard L. Buchanan, Exec. Dir.
Founded: 1951. **Staff:** 52. **Budget:** $4,400,000. **Regional Groups:** 26,000. **National Groups:** 24,000. **Languages:** English, French, Spanish. **Description:** Offers a twelve-step program for the relatives and friends of individuals with an alcohol problem. Operates Alateen for members 12-18 years of age whose lives have been adversely affected by someone else's drinking problem, usually by parents. **Committees:** Alateen; Archives; French and Spanish Services; Group Services; Institutions; International; Literature; Public Outreach. **Publications:** *Al-Anon/Alateen Member Survey,* triennial. Contains a survey from its members in the US and Canada. ● *Al-Anon Family Group Headquarters—The Forum: A Meeting in My Pocket,* monthly. Magazine. Includes calendar of events; written by Al-Anon members. **Price:** $10.00/year. ISSN: 0194-8121. **Circulation:** 54,000. Alternate Formats: online ● *Al-Anon Speaks Out,* semiannual. Newsletter. Informs the professional community regarding alcohol abuse. **Price:** free. Alternate Formats: online ● *Alateen Talk,* bimonthly. Newsletter. Contains written and artistic contributions from Alateen members. Includes articles written by adult Alateen sponsors and coordinators. **Price:** included in Alateen Group Registration; $2.50 /year for individuals. **Circulation:** 8,000 ● *Loner's Letter*

Box, bimonthly. Newsletter. **Price:** available to members only ● Also publishes leaflets, pamphlets, and books.

12941 ■ Alateen
1600 Corporate Landing Pkwy.
Virginia Beach, VA 23454-5617
Ph: (757)563-1600
Free: (888)425-2666
Fax: (757)563-1655
E-mail: wso@al-anon.org
URL: http://www.al-anon.alateen.org
Contact: Barbara Older, Assoc. Dir.
Founded: 1957. **Staff:** 56. **Budget:** $5,000,000. **National Groups:** 1,100. **Languages:** English, French, Spanish. **Multinational. Description:** Individuals ages 12-18 who have been adversely affected by a relative or friend with an alcohol problem. **Affiliated With:** Al-Anon Family Group Headquarters, World Service Office. **Publications:** *Alateen Talk,* quarterly. Newsletter. ISSN: 1054-1411. **Circulation:** 6,500.

12942 ■ Alcohol and Drug Problems Association of North America (ADPA)
307 N Main
St. Charles, MO 63301
Ph: (314)589-6702
Fax: (314)940-2358
E-mail: annsu@ipinc.net
URL: http://www.adpana.com
Contact: Ann Uhler, Vice Chair
Founded: 1949. **Members:** 1,325. **Staff:** 3. **Budget:** $360,000. **Description:** Individuals (1100), official state or provincial alcoholism program members (75), and other alcoholism and/or drug agencies and institutions (150). Seeks to facilitate governmental and professional activities in the fields of alcoholism, alcohol-related problems, and drug abuse by exchange of information, promotion of legislation and standards which will contribute to the care and control of alcoholism, and research and cooperation. Maintains continuing education program and placement service. **Awards: Frequency:** annual. **Type:** recognition. **Councils:** Agencies; Individuals; State Authorities. **Formerly:** (1956) National States Conference on Alcoholism; (1972) North American Association of Alcoholism Programs. **Publications:** *ADPA Professional,* bimonthly. Newsletter. Includes book reviews, calendar of events, educational opportunities on public policy concerning drug and alcohol abuse. **Price:** included in membership dues ● *Special Reports,* periodic. **Conventions/Meetings:** annual conference (exhibits).

12943 ■ Alcohol Research Information Service (ARIS)
430 Lanthrop St.
Lansing, MI 48912
Ph: (517)485-9900
Fax: (517)485-1928
E-mail: alcoholresearch@ameritech.net
URL: http://www.mondaymorningreport.org
Founded: 1931. **Staff:** 2. **Budget:** $60,000. **Non-membership. Description:** Individual and corporate contributors. Collects, correlates, and disseminates information regarding alcohol and alcoholic products, their manufacture, sale, and use for beverage, industrial, or other purposes, and their relation to the health and well-being of the people of the United States. Operates clearinghouse for information on alcohol, drugs, and compulsive and problem gambling. Compiles statistics. **Convention/Meeting:** none. **Libraries: Type:** reference. **Holdings:** 1,000. **Subjects:** alcohol consumption, alcohol problems, drug abuse. **Formerly:** (1984) American Business Men's Research Foundation. **Publications:** *Monday Morning Report,* bimonthly. Newsletter. **Price:** $100.00 first class mail. ISSN: 0891-8651. **Circulation:** 500 ● Also provides teaching materials for elementary and secondary school levels, and adults.

12944 ■ Alcoholics Anonymous World Services (AA)
PO Box 459
New York, NY 10163
Ph: (212)870-3400

Fax: (212)870-3003
URL: http://www.aa.org
Founded: 1935. **Description:** Individuals recovering from alcoholism. Maintains that members can solve their common problem and help others achieve sobriety through a twelve step program that includes sharing their experience, strength, and hope with each other. Self-supported through members' contributions, not an allied with any sect, denomination, political organization, or institution and does not endorse nor oppose any cause. **Telecommunication Services:** teletype, (212)870-3199. **Publications:** *AA Comes of Age* ● *Alcoholics Anonymous* ● *As Bill Sees It* ● *Dr. Bob and the Good Oldtimers* ● *Pass it On* ● *Twelve Steps and Twelve Traditions*. **Conventions/Meetings:** quinquennial international conference.

12945 ■ American College of Addiction Treatment Administrators (ACATA)
c/o Ronald J. Hunsicker, Pres./CEO
313 W Liberty St., Ste.129
Lancaster, PA 17603-2748
Ph: (717)392-8480
Fax: (717)392-8481
E-mail: rhunsicker@naatp.org
URL: http://www.naatp.org
Contact: Ronald J. Hunsicker, Pres./CEO
Founded: 1984. **Members:** 250. **Membership Dues:** professional, $100 (annual). **Staff:** 2. **Budget:** $60,000. **Description:** Administrators of addiction treatment facilities. Promotes educational and professional standards in the field of addiction treatment administration. Encourages continuing education and training of members. Recognizes individuals who have provided outstanding service in the field. Seeks to educate members and the public on issues surrounding the administration of treatment programs. Sponsors workshops. **Awards:** ACATA Administrator of the Year. **Frequency:** annual. **Type:** recognition. **Recipient:** nomination and selection committee. **Committees:** Awards; Credentials; Professional Development. **Publications:** *Visions*, monthly. Newsletter. **Conventions/Meetings:** annual meeting.

12946 ■ American Council on Alcohol Problems (ACAP)
2376 Lakeside Dr.
Birmingham, AL 35244
Ph: (205)989-8177
E-mail: dliacap@aol.com
Contact: Dr. D.L. Ireland, Contact
Founded: 1895. **Staff:** 3. **Budget:** $26,000. **Description:** Federation of 36 state affiliates and 22 denominational judicatories; 1000 associate members. Seeks long-range solutions to the problems posed by alcohol. Employs educational, and legislative approaches for the prevention of alcoholism and other alcohol-related problems. Coordinates the work of state affiliates who carry on their programs under provisions of the 21st Amendment, putting alcohol control largely at state level. Denominations channel their cooperative social concerns through elected directors who guide the program and activities. **Libraries:** Type: reference. **Holdings:** 1,200; audiovisuals, books, business records, clippings, monographs, periodicals. **Subjects:** alcohol, drugs. **Awards:** Clarence True Wilson Christian Leadership Award. **Frequency:** annual. **Type:** recognition. **Recipient:** for church leaders who made an outstanding contribution to the cause of promoting temperance and abstinence ● National Distinguished Service Award. **Frequency:** annual. **Type:** recognition. **Recipient:** for national agency or organization that made outstanding contribution to the cause of promoting temperance and abstinence ● William N. Plymat Temperance Award. **Frequency:** annual. **Type:** recognition. **Recipient:** for an individual who has made outstanding contribution to the cause of promoting temperance and abstinence. **Departments:** Educational; Legislative. **Formerly:** (1948) Anti-Saloon League of America; (1950) Temperance League of America; (1964) National Temperance League. **Publications:** *The American Issue*, quarterly. Newsletter. **Circulation:** 1,000 ● Directory, annual. **Conventions/Meetings:** annual meeting.

12947 ■ American Council on Alcoholism (ACA)
1000 E Indian School Rd.
Phoenix, AZ 85014
Free: (800)527-5344
Fax: (602)264-7403
E-mail: info@aca-usa.org
URL: http://www.aca-usa.org
Contact: Lloyd Vacovsky, Exec. Dir.
Founded: 1953. **Members:** 400. **Membership Dues:** individual, $25 (annual). **Staff:** 1. **Description:** Works to educate the public about the effects of alcohol, alcoholism, alcohol abuse, and the need for prompt, effective, affordable, and available treatment. **Libraries:** Type: reference. **Subjects:** alcoholism, alcohol abuse. **Formerly:** Maryland Society on Alcoholism; (1974) Baltimore Area Council on Alcoholism. **Publications:** *Frequently Asked Questions About Alcoholism* ● *Recovery*, quarterly. Newsletter. Publicizes issues concerning alcoholism; promotes the understanding that alcoholism is a treatable disease; contains research results. **Price:** included in membership dues. **Circulation:** 3,000. **Advertising:** accepted ● *Teenage Drinking*.

12948 ■ American Council for Drug Education (ACDE)
164 W 74th St.
New York, NY 10023
Ph: (646)505-2060
Free: (800)488-DRUG
Fax: (212)595-2553
E-mail: acde@phoenixhouse.org
URL: http://www.acde.org
Contact: Naomi Weinstein, Exec. Dir.
Founded: 1977. **Staff:** 4. **Languages:** English, Spanish. **Nonmembership. Description:** Doctors, mental health counselors, teachers, clergymen, policymakers, school librarians, parent groups, industry leaders, and concerned individuals. Disseminates information and research on all drugs of abuse. Makes available resource information kits that include both written and audiovisual materials. Provides prevention materials to colleges and high schools. **Libraries:** Type: not open to the public. **Subjects:** substance abuse, drugs, treatment, referral, prevention, addiction. **Awards:** Type: recognition. **Computer Services:** Information services. **Additional Websites:** http://www.drughelp.org, http://www.factsontap.org. **Boards:** Scientific Advisory. **Committees:** General Advisory. **Affiliated With:** Phoenix House. **Formerly:** (1983) American Council on Marijuana and Other Psychoactive Drugs. **Publications:** *Free Catalog*. For parents, children, schools, and other professionals. ● Brochures (in English and Spanish) ● Handbooks.

12949 ■ American Outreach Association (AOA)
5490 Delhart Rd., Ste.205
Galax, VA 24333
Ph: (276)236-5934
E-mail: info@americanoutreach.org
URL: http://www.americanoutreach.org
Contact: Charles Prusch, Pres.
Founded: 1989. **Membership Dues:** corporate sponsor (minimum), $75 (annual) ● individual, $25 (annual). **Regional Groups:** 5. **Languages:** English, French, Spanish. **Description:** Collects and disseminates information on subjects such as alcoholism, drug abuse, inhalants, and smoking to the public. Organizes community awareness activities and presentations. Reviews drug policies, programs, and educational material. Assists business and industry in establishing drug-free work environments. Sponsors Project HOLD, a program that fosters a change of attitudes, values, and behaviors in the home away from drug abuse. Operates placement service; maintains speakers' bureau. **Libraries:** Type: reference. **Holdings:** 500; artwork, books, clippings, monographs, periodicals. **Subjects:** drugs, alcohol, smoking, inhalants. **Publications:** *AOA Newsletter*, semiannual. ● *Health Watch*, quarterly. Newsletter. **Circulation:** 5,000. **Advertising:** accepted ● *Mommy, What are Drugs?* ● *Mommy What are Inhalants?* ● *Mommy,*

What is Alcohol? ● *Mommy, What is Smoking?* ● *Mother Earth, What is Cultural Diversity?*. **Conventions/Meetings:** annual board meeting - always October, in Colorado Springs, CO.

12950 ■ Association of Halfway House Alcoholism Programs of North America (AHHAP)
860 N Center St.
Mesa, AZ 85201
Ph: (480)610-8300
Free: (800)861-0599
Fax: (480)834-5372
E-mail: ahhap@aol.com
URL: http://www.ahhap.org
Contact: Jason Conrad, Pres.
Founded: 1965. **Members:** 450. **Membership Dues:** new, $100 (annual) ● individual, $25 (annual). **Staff:** 1. **Regional Groups:** 13. **State Groups:** 50. **Description:** Halfway house corporations, staff, board members, and individuals closely related to the halfway house movement. Educates and serves halfway house programs through technical assistance, consultant services, workshops, conferences, and related services. Operates placement service. Disseminates information and materials. **Computer Services:** database ● mailing lists. **Publications:** *Communications and Services Newsletter*, quarterly ● *Conference Proceedings*, annual ● Membership Directory, annual. **Conventions/Meetings:** annual conference, with training (exhibits).

12951 ■ Association of Recovering Motorcyclists (ARM)
1503 Market St.
La Crosse, WI 54601
E-mail: armintl86@aol.com
URL: http://arm-intl.com
Contact: Jerry Scudder, Pres.
Founded: 1985. **Members:** 500. **Budget:** $20,000. **State Groups:** 44. **For-Profit. Description:** Support group for motorcyclists who are recovering from alcohol or drug addiction. Helps members enjoy the hobby of motorcycling; tries to eliminate the notion of motorcycling as a negative lifestyle. Sponsors motorcycle runs, picnics, and dances. Operates speakers' bureau. **Publications:** Newsletter, quarterly. **Price:** included in membership dues; free for inmates. **Circulation:** 500. **Advertising:** accepted ● Directory, periodic. **Conventions/Meetings:** annual board meeting - always second weekend of February ● annual Campout - meeting (exhibits) ● annual International Picnic - held in June or July.

12952 ■ BACCHUS Network
PO Box 100430
Denver, CO 80250-0430
Ph: (303)871-0901
Fax: (303)871-0907
E-mail: admin@bacchusnetwork.org
URL: http://www.bacchusgamma.org
Contact: Drew Hunter MPA, Pres./CEO
Founded: 1975. **Members:** 24,500. **Staff:** 6. **Budget:** $1,200,000. **Regional Groups:** 13. **State Groups:** 49. **Local Groups:** 750. **National Groups:** 3. **Multinational. Description:** Students, advisors, faculty, and staff of colleges and universities in the U.S., Canada, and Mexico. Aims to deliver alcohol abuse prevention and health education to college students and their communities. Promotes responsible decisions and healthy lifestyles and discourages irresponsible or illegal use of alcohol. Encourages year-round prevention and education programs and activities. Operates: Project GAMMA (Greeks Advocating Mature Management of Alcohol), a cooperative effort between BACCHUS and national Greek-letter organizations to increase undergraduate participation in alcohol education programs; National Collegiate Alcohol Awareness Week; and Safe Spring Break. Offers the Certified Peer Educator Training Program, a skill-based training curriculum for students. (BACCHUS is the acronym for Boost Alcohol Consciousness Concerning the Health of University Students and the name of the Roman god of wine.). **Awards:** Chapter of the Year. **Frequency:** annual. **Type:** recognition ● Individual Awards. **Frequency:**

annual. **Type:** recognition. **Recipient:** for students and advisors who have gone above and beyond the call of duty to motivate and educate the student body and campus community ● Outstanding Advisor Awards. **Frequency:** annual. **Type:** recognition. **Recipient:** for outstanding advisor ● Outstanding Alumni Awards. **Frequency:** annual. **Type:** recognition. **Recipient:** for individuals who have served as peer educators or affiliate advisors in the past ● Outstanding Impaired Driving Prevention Programming. **Frequency:** annual. **Type:** recognition. **Recipient:** for peer education affiliate ● Outstanding Network Affiliates. **Frequency:** annual. **Type:** recognition. **Recipient:** for network affiliates ● Outstanding Program/Event. **Frequency:** annual. **Type:** recognition. **Recipient:** for outstanding program/event ● Outstanding Student Awards. **Frequency:** annual. **Type:** recognition. **Recipient:** for students. **Additional Websites:** http://www.friendsdrivesober.org. **Committees:** Nominating; Steering; Student Advisory. **Formerly:** (1993) BACCHUS of the U.S.; (2005) BACCHUS and Gamma Peer Education Network. **Publications:** *The BACCHUS Beat*, monthly. Newsletter. **Price:** free for members. **Circulation:** 2,800 ● *CPE Training Series* ● Catalog. Lists educational materials. ● Newsletter, 10/year ● Pamphlets ● Videos. **Conventions/Meetings:** annual General Assembly - conference (exhibits) - always November.

12953 ■ Calix Society (CS)
2555 Hazelwood Ave.
St. Paul, MN 55109-2030
Ph: (651)773-3117
Free: (800)398-0524
Fax: (651)777-3069
E-mail: calix@usfamily.net
URL: http://www.calixsociety.org
Contact: Jim Billigmeier, Pres.
Founded: 1947. **Members:** 3,000. **Membership Dues:** regular, $15 (annual). **Staff:** 1. **State Groups:** 14. **Local Groups:** 22. **Multinational. Description:** Catholic alcoholics who are maintaining sobriety through their own participation in Alcoholics Anonymous. Non-Catholic alcoholics and interested individuals are welcome. Promotes total abstinence for Catholic alcoholics and encourages their spiritual development. ("Calix" means "chalice" in Latin and refers to the society's belief in "substituting the cup that sanctifies for the cup that stupefies"). **Libraries: Type:** reference. **Subjects:** recovery from alcoholism. **Publications:** *Calix and the Twelve Steps*. Book. **Price:** $7.00 ● *The Chalice*, bimonthly. Newsletter. Contains contributed stories regarding spiritual and physical recovery. Includes book reviews, obituaries, research reports, and statistics. **Price:** $15.00/year. **Circulation:** 1,200 ● *Directory of Calix Units in the U.S. and Canada*, periodic ● *The Light of Faith*. Book. **Price:** $7.00 ● *What and Why*. Brochure. **Price:** $30.00 each ● Pamphlets. **Price:** $3.00/set. **Conventions/Meetings:** annual meeting, with books and literature (exhibits) - August.

12954 ■ Children of Alcoholics Foundation (COAF)
164 W 74th St.
New York, NY 10023-2301
Ph: (646)505-2060
Fax: (212)595-2553
E-mail: nweinstein@phoenixhouse.org
URL: http://www.coaf.org
Contact: Naomi Weinstein, Dir.
Founded: 1982. **Staff:** 6. **Description:** Seeks to educate the public and professionals about children of substance abusers and the effects of parental substance abuse, and stimulate interest in seeking solutions to their problems. Promotes research, educational and informational programs, and public discussion on alcoholism, substance abuse, and its effects on children; disseminates reports and research results; investigates the effectiveness of public policies, programs, and laws; encourages participation and assists government and community agencies in providing assistance to children of substance abusers and seeking solutions to the problems of these children. Facilitates research and educational and informational programs on other aspects of child-

hood, the parent-child relationship, physiological and psychological aspects of human development, child abuse and neglect, and substance abuse of other psychoactive substances. **Telecommunication Services:** electronic mail, coaf@phoenixhouse.org. **Affiliated With:** American Council for Drug Education; Phoenix House. **Publications:** *Free Catalog*.

12955 ■ Christian Addiction Rehabilitation Association (CARA)
c/o Heather Rice
Whosoever Gospel Mission
101 E Chelten Ave.
Philadelphia, PA 19144
Ph: (215)438-3094
E-mail: agrm@agrm.org
URL: http://www.iugm.org/cara.html
Contact: Heather Rice, Contact
Founded: 1967. **Members:** 48. **Membership Dues:** regular, $20 (annual). **Budget:** $2,000. **Description:** Provides support and serves as a clearinghouse of information for individuals involved in ministry to addicts. Conducts two conferences per year. **Affiliated With:** Association of Gospel Rescue Missions. **Formerly:** Christian Alcoholic Rehabilitation Association. **Publications:** Newsletter, monthly. **Price:** included in membership dues. **Conventions/Meetings:** semiannual conference.

12956 ■ Citizens Against Drug Impaired Drivers (CANDID)
PO Box 249
Thiensville, WI 53092
Ph: (414)352-2043
Free: (800)929-9077
Fax: (414)352-7080
E-mail: candid@candid.org
Contact: Karen Tarney, Founder
Membership Dues: individual, $25 (annual) ● family, $40 (annual) ● sustaining, $250 (annual) ● patron, $1,000 (annual) ● corporate, $500 (annual). **Description:** Seeks to reduce injuries caused by drug-impaired drivers. Increases the awareness of the risks involved when driving under the influence of illicit prescription or over-the-counter drugs. **Computer Services:** Information services, drug and driving resources ● online services, discussion forum. **Councils:** Corporate Advisory. **Programs:** Speaker's Bureau. **Publications:** Newsletter.

12957 ■ Co-Anon Family Groups
PO Box 12722
Tucson, AZ 85732-2722
Ph: (520)513-5028
Free: (800)898-9985
E-mail: info@co-anon.org
URL: http://co-anon.org
Founded: 1985. **National Groups:** 28. **Description:** Spouses, relatives, and friends of people who are chemically dependent. Seeks to help individuals affected by another's cocaine addiction by applying the Twelve Steps and Twelve Traditions of Co-Anon Family Groups. Assists in the formation of local Co-Anon groups. **Publications:** Brochure. **Conventions/Meetings:** support group meeting.

12958 ■ Cocaine Anonymous World Services (CAWS)
PO Box 2000
Los Angeles, CA 90049-8000
Ph: (310)559-5833
Free: (800)347-8998
Fax: (310)559-2554
E-mail: cawso@ca.org
URL: http://www.ca.org
Contact: Patty Flanagan, Dir. of Operations
Founded: 1982. **Members:** 15,000. **Staff:** 9. **Budget:** $433,370. **Regional Groups:** 2,000. **Languages:** English, French, Spanish. **Description:** Represents men and women who state a desire to stop using cocaine, including crack cocaine, as well as other mind-altering substances. Applies the Alcoholics Anonymous World Services' 12-step approach to persons addicted to cocaine. **Committees:** Hospitals and Institutions; Public Information. **Publications:** *A Guide to the Twelve Steps*. Pamphlet ● *A Higher

Power*. Pamphlet ● *And All Other Mind Altering Substances*. Pamphlet ● *Choosing Your Sponsor* (in English, French, and Spanish). Pamphlet ● *Crack*. Pamphlet ● *The First 30 Days*. Pamphlet ● *Home Group*. Pamphlet ● *Hope, Faith, and Courage*. Book. **Price:** $12.95 hard cover; $9.95 soft cover ● *The Newsgram*, quarterly. Newsletter. **Price:** $10.00/year. **Circulation:** 40,000. Alternate Formats: online ● *Self Test for Cocaine Addiction*. Pamphlet ● *Tips on Staying Clean and Sober*. Pamphlet ● *To the Newcomer*. Pamphlet ● *Tools of Recovery*. Pamphlet ● *Unity*. Pamphlet ● *What Is C.A.?*. Pamphlet. **Conventions/Meetings:** annual Global Awakening - convention, fund raiser - every May.

12959 ■ Community Anti-Drug Coalitions of America (CADCA)
625 Slaters Ln., Ste.300
Alexandria, VA 22314-1176
Ph: (703)706-0560
Free: (800)54-CADCA
Fax: (703)706-0565
E-mail: info@cadca.org
URL: http://cadca.org
Contact: Arthur T. Dean, Chm.
Founded: 1992. **Members:** 5,000. **Membership Dues:** sustaining (national organization/state association/federal organization), $2,500 (annual) ● special interest group, $500 (annual) ● professional individual, $50 (annual) ● coalition, community based organization (based on annual budget), $200-$500 (annual). **Staff:** 30. **State Groups:** 35. **Local Groups:** 5,000. **Languages:** English, French, Portuguese, Spanish. **Description:** Represents coalitions working to make America's communities safe, healthy and drug-free. **Publications:** *Coalitions*, quarterly. Newsletter. **Circulation:** 10,000. Alternate Formats: online. **Conventions/Meetings:** conference (exhibits) ● annual National Leadership Forum - meeting.

12960 ■ D.A.R.E. America
PO Box 512090
Los Angeles, CA 90051-0090
Ph: (310)215-0575
Free: (800)223-DARE
Fax: (310)215-0180
E-mail: webmaster@dare.com
URL: http://www.dare.com
Contact: Charlie Parsons, Pres./CEO
Description: Seeks to provide students with a knowledge base on the effects of drug abuse that go beyond the physical ramifications and extend to emotional, social, and economic aspects of life. Aims to build decision-making and problem solving skills and strategies to help students make informed decisions and resist drug use, peer pressure, and violence. Provides students with alternatives to drug use. Sponsors National D.A.R.E. Day. **Awards:** D.A.R.E. America Scholarship Winner. **Frequency:** annual. **Type:** scholarship. **Recipient:** for the most outstanding student ● D.A.R.E. Educator of The Year. **Frequency:** annual. **Type:** recognition. **Recipient:** for the best educator ● D.A.R.E. Officer Of The Year. **Frequency:** annual. **Type:** recognition. **Recipient:** for the best officer ● DEA/D.A.R.E. Law Enforcement Executive of the Year. **Frequency:** annual. **Type:** recognition. **Recipient:** for the best law enforcement executive ● Lifetime Achievement Award. **Frequency:** annual. **Type:** recognition. **Recipient:** for the most dedicated member. **Publications:** *Keeping Kids Drug Free: The Official Parents' Guide*. Book. **Conventions/Meetings:** conference and workshop.

12961 ■ Do It Now Foundation (DINF)
PO Box 27568
Tempe, AZ 85285-7568
Ph: (480)736-0599
Fax: (480)736-0771
E-mail: info@doitnow.org
URL: http://www.doitnow.org
Contact: James D. Parker, Exec. Dir.
Founded: 1968. **Members:** 40. **Membership Dues:** request/invitation, $20 (annual). **Staff:** 5. **Budget:** $500,000. **Languages:** English, Spanish. **Description:** Works to provide factual information to students and adults about prescription drugs, over-the-counter

drugs, street drugs, alcohol, eating disorders, AIDS, and related health issues. Assists organizations engaged in alcohol and drug abuse education. **Libraries: Type:** reference. **Holdings:** 5,000; books, periodicals, reports. **Subjects:** health and well-being. **Computer Services:** Online services, library information and referrals. **Publications:** Publishes educational materials; offers pamphlets, posters, books, and radio public service tapes in Spanish and English.

12962 ■ Drug and Alcohol Testing Industry Association (DATIA)

1325 G St. NW, Ste.500, No. 5001
Washington, DC 20005
Free: (800)355-1257
Fax: (202)315-3579
E-mail: info@datia.org
URL: http://www.datia.org
Contact: Laura Shelton, Exec. Dir.
Founded: 1995. **Members:** 1,300. **Membership Dues:** regular, $195 (annual) ● corporate, $500 (annual) ● sustaining corporate, $1,500 (annual). **Description:** Drug and alcohol service providers including collection sites, laboratories, consortiums/TPA's, MRO's and testing equipment manufacturers. **Computer Services:** database, nationwide regional certified professional collector trainer. **Programs:** Accredited Specimen Collection Facility; Professional Liability Insurance. **Publications:** *DATIA's Newsletter*, bimonthly. Alternate Formats: online ● *eNews-weekly*. Newsletter. Contains current information on issues and activities in the industry. Alternate Formats: online ● *Membership Brochure*. Alternate Formats: online ● *Red Book*. Contains updated regulatory information critical to the industry. **Price:** $99.00/year with monthly update subscription ● Membership Directory. Alternate Formats: online.

12963 ■ Dual Disorders Anonymous

PO Box 681264
Schaumburg, IL 60168-1264
Ph: (847)490-9379
E-mail: ddapat@aol.com
Contact: Pat Kent, Pres.
Founded: 1982. **Members:** 500. **Staff:** 4. **Regional Groups:** 3. **State Groups:** 1. **Local Groups:** 21. **National Groups:** 20. **Description:** Individuals with alcohol or drug addictions as well as mental or emotional disorders. Provides support group opportunities to emotionally or mentally disordered alcoholics and addicts; conducts volunteer programs for dually diagnosed patients. Utilizes the 12-step method of self-help. **Libraries: Type:** reference. **Subjects:** depression, manic depression, panic attacks. **Publications:** Booklet ● Brochures. Includes a beginner's kit. **Conventions/Meetings:** annual dinner ● annual picnic.

12964 ■ Entertainment Industries Council (EIC)

c/o Government Relations and Administration
1760 Reston Pkwy., Ste.415
Reston, VA 20190-3360
Ph: (703)481-1414
Fax: (703)481-1418
E-mail: eic@eiconline.org
URL: http://eiconline.org
Contact: Brian L. Dyak, Pres./CEO/Co-Founder
Founded: 1983. **Members:** 130. **Staff:** 14. **Budget:** $2,500,000. **Description:** Aims to utilize the power and influence of the entertainment industry in a national campaign to combat and deglamorize substance abuse, especially among young people. Seeks to identify, provide celebrity role models for young people, and increase youth awareness of drug abuse through television, radio, music, and motion pictures. Develops projects to aid in eliminating substance abuse problems within the entertainment industry. Conducts seminars, training sessions on drug abuse prevention, radio interview series, television specials, outreach programs, and employee assistance and fundraising programs. Collects and disseminates information on progress made by the entertainment industry in drug abuse prevention. **Awards:** Prism Awards. **Frequency:** annual. **Type:**

recognition ● Prism Generation Next. **Frequency:** annual. **Type:** scholarship. **Computer Services:** Mailing lists. **Programs:** First Draft. **Publications:** *Profile*, monthly. Alternate Formats: online ● *Spotlight on Depiction*, annual ● Annual Report, annual.

12965 ■ Ethos Foundation (EF)

312 S Washington St., Ste.3-A
Alexandria, VA 22314
Ph: (703)535-6800
Fax: (703)535-6999
E-mail: drphilbrennan@aol.com
Contact: Philip I. Brennan PhD, Administrator
Founded: 1978. **Staff:** 35. **Budget:** $1,000,000. **Regional Groups:** 1. **Languages:** English, Spanish. **Description:** Provides counseling, education, and rehabilitation services and crisis intervention in the area of mental health and substance abuse. Conducts training programs for counselors, physicians, clergy, social workers, and employees; offers programs for hospitals, federal and local governments, and the private and public sectors. Cooperates with criminal justice departments. Conducts research. Sponsors workshops and seminars. Maintains speakers' bureau; compiles statistics. (Ethos is the Greek word for sentiment, values, and moral nature.) Publications: none. **Also Known As:** Ethos Group - Infant, Child, Adolescent and Family Therapy Centers.

12966 ■ Families Anonymous (FA)

PO Box 3475
Culver City, CA 90231-3475
Ph: (310)815-8010
Free: (800)736-9805
Fax: (310)815-9682
E-mail: famanon@familiesanonymous.org
URL: http://www.familiesanonymous.org
Contact: Don S., Chm.
Founded: 1971. **Staff:** 1. **National Groups:** 300. **Languages:** English, Greek, Hungarian, Indian Dialects, Portuguese, Spanish. **Multinational. Description:** Twelve-step support groups of parents, relatives, and friends concerned about drug abuse, alcoholism, or related behavioral problems. Self-supported, self-help modeled after Al-Anon Family Groups and Alcoholics Anonymous programs (see separate entries). Assists families in overcoming over-protectiveness of substance abusers and developing a better understanding of their problems, thereby improving interfamily relationships. Aids in establishing community meetings; makes referrals to other agencies. Can provide speakers on request. **Libraries: Type:** reference. **Holdings:** archival material, audio recordings. **Subjects:** personal recovery issues for growth, change, enabling, rescuing, recovery, co-dependency. **Computer Services:** database, member groups. **Committees:** Ad-Hoc; Standing. **Publications:** *Today A Better Way* (in Bengali, English, Greek, Italian, Portuguese, and Spanish). Book. Serves as a daily thought book, written entirely by the fellowship. **Price:** $9.00/copy. **Circulation:** 60,000. Also Cited As: *TABW* ● *The Twelve Step Rag: For Relatives and Friends Concerned about the Use of Drugs or Related Behavioral Problems*, bimonthly. Newsletter. Contains articles, poetry and organizational information. **Price:** free to FA groups; $4.50 /year for individuals; $8.50/2 years; $12.00/3 years. **Circulation:** 2,200 ● Catalog ● Directory, periodic ● Pamphlets ● Publishes over 80 items of literature for member inspiration and recovery. Prices vary by size and pages. **Conventions/Meetings:** annual convention and general assembly, with new articles of literature (exhibits) - Memorial Day weekend in conjunction with annual convention at Lexington, KY.

12967 ■ Families Worldwide

5248 Pinemont Dr., Ste.C-190
Salt Lake City, UT 84123
Ph: (801)268-6461
Fax: (801)268-6471
E-mail: bstone81@comcast.net
URL: http://www.fww.org
Contact: Brad C. Stone, Chm.
Founded: 1972. **Staff:** 5. **Budget:** $100,000. **Description:** Strengthens family bonds through pro-

grams that promote well-researched wellness skills and traditional family values. The program can be used in alcohol/substance abuse prevention with at-risk families and also in bolstering stronger families. Volunteers work as facilitators in presenting the program to families, school, civic and church groups, and other community organizations. Conducts workshops for family care professional. Currently developing chapters to extend outreach and a family center program which will strengthen families and provide humanitarian services. **Libraries: Type:** not open to the public. **Holdings:** 75; books, periodicals, video recordings. **Computer Services:** database. **Programs:** Solutions for Families. **Formerly:** (1997) The Cottage Program International, Inc. **Publications:** *Solutions for Families*. Book. Offers ways to strengthen family relationships. Alternate Formats: online.

12968 ■ Family Council on Drug Awareness (FCDA)

c/o Mikki Norris
PO Box 1716
El Cerrito, CA 94530
Ph: (510)215-8326
Fax: (510)234-4460
E-mail: chris@fcda.org
URL: http://www.fcda.org
Contact: Chris Conrad, Dir.
Founded: 1989. **Description:** Promotes "legal reforms that recognize human rights, encourage responsible behavior, separate cannabis from hard drugs, and protect children from the unregulated and indiscriminate market of illegal drugs." Serves as an information clearinghouse on medical marijuana, illegal substances and drug law reform; distributes educational materials and supports 18 years as the legal age of consent for cannabis use. **Libraries: Type:** reference. **Holdings:** archival material, articles, clippings. **Subjects:** drug education, drug law reform. **Additional Websites:** http://www.equalrights4all.org. **Publications:** *The Drug War: How Much Longer Will This Scene be Accepted?*. Brochure ● *Marijuana and The Bible*. Brochure ● *10 Things Every Parent, Teacher and Teenager Should Know About Marijuana*. Brochure ● Annual Report, annual. Features the State Attorney General's advisory report on marijuana and drugs.

12969 ■ Friendly Hand Foundation (FHF)

347 S Normandie Ave.
Los Angeles, CA 90020
Ph: (213)389-9964
Fax: (213)389-9747
E-mail: friendlyhouse@sbcglobal.net
URL: http://www.friendlyhouse.net
Contact: Peggy Albrecht, Exec. Dir.
Founded: 1951. **Budget:** $175,000. **Description:** Operates Friendly House, a home to aid in the recovery of alcoholic women. Provides a home-like setting, love and understanding, and the companionship of individuals in similar situations to women recovering from alcohol dependence. Not officially affiliated with Alcoholics Anonymous World Services, but women in the home learn the principles of AA as part of group and individual therapy; the average stay at Friendly House is four weeks. Supported by contributions and through projects undertaken by affiliated groups of alcoholic and nonalcoholic women in California (known as Sweet Hearts and Grateful Hearts).

12970 ■ Hazelden Foundation (HF)

PO Box 11-C03
Center City, MN 55012-0011
Ph: (651)213-4200
Free: (800)257-7810
Fax: (651)213-4411
E-mail: info@hazelden.org
URL: http://www.hazelden.org
Contact: Ellen L. Breyer, Pres./CEO
Founded: 1949. **Description:** Provides treatment, recovery, education, and professional services for chemical dependency and other addictive behaviors. Operates: Hazelden Foundation Center, a treatment center; Fellowship Club in New York, St. Paul and

West Palm Beach, Florida, an intermediate care facility; Hazelden Center for Youth and Families for adolescents and young adults; Hazelden Renewal Center for individuals recovering from addictive behaviors and their families; Hanley-Hazelden Center in West Palm Beach, Florida, for inpatient and outpatient treatment; Provides: aftercare therapy; counselor training; 5-7 day, live-in family program that acquaints relatives and other associates of chemically-dependent individuals with problems of chemical dependency; continuing education programs for professionals; and communities. **Committees:** Educational Materials; Planning Treatment, Public Policy. **Programs:** Chemical Dependency Counselor Training; Chemical Dependency Studies; Clergy Training; Continuing Education; Health Promotion; Professional and Community Educator. **Affiliated With:** Alcohol and Drug Problems Association of North America; Association for Clinical Pastoral Education; Continuing Care Accreditation Commission; Joint Commission on Accreditation of Healthcare Organizations. **Publications:** Hazelden Voice, semiannual. Newsletter. Provides information on health and recovery from addictive behavior. **Circulation:** 45,000 ● Publishing Catalog, monthly ● Books ● Pamphlets ● Makes available educational and audiovisual materials.

12971 ■ Health Connection

55 W Oak Ridge Dr.
Hagerstown, MD 21740
Ph: (301)393-3270
Free: (800)548-8700
Fax: (888)294-8405
E-mail: sales@healthconnection.org
URL: http://www.healthconnection.org
Contact: Larry Macomber, Supervisor
Founded: 1954. **Staff:** 3. **Description:** Promotes nationwide education for the prevention of drug addiction and alcoholism through direct mailings of materials to schools, churches, and civic organizations. Participates, through exhibits, in conferences and conventions of teachers and school personnel. **Libraries: Type:** reference. **Holdings:** archival material, audiovisuals, books, business records, periodicals. **Subjects:** drug prevention and health education. **Formerly:** (1993) Narcotics Education. **Publications:** Listen, monthly. Magazine ● Teaching Guide to Winner Magazine, 9/year ● Winner, 9/year. Magazine ● Catalog, annual ● Books ● Films ● Pamphlets ● Reprints ● Videos ● Also publishes teaching aids, posters, and filmstrips. Distributes puppets/puppet programs.

12972 ■ Impaired Physician Program (IPP)

c/o Talbott Recovery Campus
5448 Yorketowne Dr.
Atlanta, GA 30349
Ph: (770)994-0185
Free: (800)445-4232
Fax: (770)994-2024
URL: http://www.talbottcampus.com
Contact: Benjamin H. Underwood, CEO
Founded: 1975. **Staff:** 5. **Description:** Provides assistance to physicians, other health professionals, and their spouses with problems such as alcoholism, substance abuse, or codependence; seeks to locate and identify persons in need of help and to provide assistance. Conducts in-and-outpatient treatment programs. Offers counseling; maintains advocacy program to assist physicians and other health professionals in re-entering their profession. Maintains speakers' bureau. **Conventions/Meetings:** quarterly meeting ● annual retreat ● monthly seminar.

12973 ■ Institute for a Drug-Free Workplace

8614 Westwood Center Dr., Ste.950
Vienna, VA 22182
Ph: (703)288-4300 (703)821-2189
Fax: (703)506-0064
E-mail: debernam@jacksonlewis.com
URL: http://www.drugfreeworkplace.org
Contact: Mark A. de Bernardo, Exec. Dir.
Founded: 1989. **Members:** 90. **Membership Dues:** board, $10,000 (annual) ● corporate, $2,500 (annual) ● nonprofit organization, $500 (annual). **Staff:**

10. **Budget:** $1,000,000. **Description:** Businesses, organizations, and individuals united to preserve the rights of employers and employees involved in corporate drug abuse prevention programs. Seeks to influence public policy pertaining to drug-abuse prevention in the workplace. Conducts surveys. **Publications:** Avoiding Legal Liability: The 25 Most Common Employer Mistakes in Addressing Drug Abuse. Book. **Price:** $40.00 ● Does Drug Testing Work?. Book. **Price:** $36.00 ● Drug and Alcohol Abuse Prevention and the ADA: An Employer's Guide. Book. **Price:** $32.00 ● Drug Testing in the Workplace: Basic Issues, Answers, and Options for Employees. Booklet. **Price:** $4.50 ● Employee Assistance Programs: An Employer's Development and Implementation Guide. Booklet. **Price:** $4.50 ● Employee Drug Education and Awareness and Supervisor Training: An Employer's Development and Implementation Guide. Booklet. **Price:** $4.50 ● Guide to Dangerous Drugs. Booklet. **Price:** $2.40 ● Guide to State and Federal Drug Testing Laws, annual. Book. **Price:** $345.00 ● International Guide to Workplace Substance Abuse Prevention. Book. **Price:** $80.00 ● Policy on Drug and Alcohol Abuse Prevention: An Employer's Development and Implementation Guide. Booklet. **Price:** $4.50 ● What Every Employee Should Know About Alcohol Abuse: Answer to 25 Good Questions. Booklet. **Price:** $2.30. **Conventions/Meetings:** annual meeting - always September.

12974 ■ Institute on Global Drug Policy (IGDP)

c/o Drug Free America Foundation, Inc.
2600 9th St. N, Ste.200
St. Petersburg, FL 33704-2744
Ph: (727)828-0211
Fax: (727)828-0212
E-mail: evoth@storntvail.org
URL: http://www.dfaf.org/globaldrugpolicy.php
Contact: Eric A. Voth MD, Chm.
Founded: 2000. **Members:** 40. **Description:** Works to develop effective international policies and strategies to discourage drug use and legalization of illicit drugs. Disseminates accurate scientific information on drugs. **Publications:** none. **Convention/Meeting:** none. **Additional Websites:** http://www.globaldrugpolicy.org. **Formerly:** (2004) International Drug Strategy Institute.

12975 ■ Institute for Integral Development (IID)

PO Box 2172
Colorado Springs, CO 80901
Ph: (719)634-7943
Free: (800)544-9562
Fax: (719)630-7025
E-mail: iidevo@aol.com
URL: http://www.institutefortraining.com
Contact: Dan Barmettler MA, Founder/Dir.
Founded: 1977. **Description:** Provides a forum for discussion of issues pertaining to alcoholism and other addictions; seeks to train educators, medical professionals, and mental health practitioners in understanding and assisting addicted individuals. Sponsors seminars and workshops; provides educational audiotapes; offers consulting services. Maintains speakers' bureau; operates small library. **Publications:** none. **Computer Services:** Mailing lists, of members. **Committees:** Continuing Education. **Conventions/Meetings:** annual Conference on Addictions (exhibits) ● annual Institute on Alcoholism and Drug Dependence - meeting ● annual MNM Training Institute on Addictions - meeting ● annual National Conference of Adult Children of Dysfunctional Families ● periodic regional meeting.

12976 ■ Inter-Association Task Force on Alcohol and Other Substance Abuse Issues (IATF)

c/o Dr. Herbert Songer, VP for Student Affairs
Forts Hays State Univ.
600 Park St.
Hays, KS 67601-4099
Ph: (785)628-4277
Fax: (785)628-4113

E-mail: hsonger@fhsu.edu
URL: http://www.iatf.org
Contact: Dr. Herbert Songer, VP for Student Affairs
Founded: 1983. **Members:** 20. **Description:** Associations of college professionals and student leaders. Aims to enhance the development and implementation of alcohol and other substance abuse education activities in institutions of higher education throughout the U.S. and to encourage collaboration among professionals and student associations. Sponsors National Collegiate Alcohol Awareness Week and National Collegiate Health and Wellness Week. **Awards:** Outstanding Campus Prevention Programs. **Frequency:** annual. **Type:** recognition. **Recipient:** for NCAAW campus programs. **Formerly:** Inter-Association Task Force on Alcohol Issues; (2002) Inter-Association Task Force on Campus Alcohol and Other Substance Abuse Issues. **Publications:** First National Conference on Alcohol Policy Initiatives. Proceedings ● Guidelines for Marketing of Alcohol Beverage on Campus. Pamphlet ● National Collegiate Alcohol Awareness Week Mailing Handbook. **Conventions/Meetings:** annual Lifeskills Conference.

12977 ■ International Commission for the Prevention of Alcoholism and Drug Dependency (ICPA)

12501 Old Columbia Pike
Silver Spring, MD 20904
Ph: (301)680-6719
E-mail: the_icpa@hotmail.com
URL: http://www.health20-20.org/icpa.htm
Contact: Dr. Peter N. Landless, Exec. Dir.
Founded: 1952. **Description:** Representatives of national public health committees and other individuals interested in the physical and social effects of alcoholism and drug dependency. Fosters the scientific study of alcohol and drugs, their effects on the physical, mental, and moral powers of the individual, and their effects on social, economic, political, and religious life. Encourages preventive education; disseminates information on drug and alcohol abuse. Serves as a liaison with similar groups around the world. Sponsors exchange and research programs. Conducts film shows, forums, and radio and television events. **Libraries: Type:** reference. **Subjects:** alcohol, tobacco, drugs. **Telecommunication Services:** electronic mail, landlessp@gc.adventist.org. **Formerly:** (1982) International Commission for the Prevention of Alcoholism. **Publications:** ICPA Dispatch, periodic ● ICPA Reporter, quarterly. Bulletin. Describes worldwide activities of ICPA and local communities. Alternate Formats: online. **Conventions/Meetings:** seminar ● triennial World Prevention Congress.

12978 ■ International Doctors in Alcoholics Anonymous (IDAA)

c/o Gordon L. Hyde, MD, Exec. Dir.
3311 Brookhill Cir.
Lexington, KY 40502
Ph: (859)277-9379
Fax: (859)278-6128
URL: http://www.idaa.org
Contact: Gordon L. Hyde MD, Exec. Dir.
Founded: 1949. **Members:** 4,700. **Multinational.** **Description:** Doctorate level health care professionals interested in Alcoholics Anonymous. Seeks to exchange knowledge and experience in the recovery from and management of alcoholism for members and persons who fall within their sphere of influence. Supports AA-type group activities. **Libraries: Type:** reference; not open to the public. **Committees:** Administrative; Site Selection; Steering. **Funds:** General; Luke Reed Memorial; Scholarship. **Publications:** International Doctors in Alcoholics Anonymous—Newsletter, semiannual. **Price:** included in membership dues. Alternate Formats: online ● Letter, semiannual. **Conventions/Meetings:** annual meeting and conference, with speakers - 2008 Aug. 6-10, Portland, OR; 2009 July 29-Aug. 2, San Antonio, TX.

12979 ■ International Lawyers in Alcoholics Anonymous (ILAA)
c/o Eli Gauna, Sec.
14123 Victory Blvd.
Van Nuys, CA 91401
E-mail: secretary@ilaa.org
URL: http://www.ilaa.org
Contact: Eli Gauna, Sec.
Founded: 1975. **Members:** 1,300. **Multinational.**
Description: Alcoholic lawyers who are seeking sobriety through their affiliation with Alcoholics Anonymous World Services (see separate entry). Seeks to: spread the message of AA to alcoholic attorneys; work to educate the judiciary and lawyers on the problem of alcoholism; support attorneys in their recovery. **Publications:** Newsletter, 3-4/year. **Circulation:** 1,300. **Conventions/Meetings:** annual meeting (exhibits) - usually second weekend of September.

12980 ■ Jewish Alcoholics, Chemically Dependent Persons and Significant Others (JACS)
120 W 57th St.
New York, NY 10019
Ph: (212)397-4197
Fax: (212)399-3525
E-mail: jacs@jacsweb.org
URL: http://www.jacsweb.org
Contact: Ms. Sharon Darack, Programs Dir.
Founded: 1979. **Members:** 1,000. **Membership Dues:** individual, $36 (annual) ● family, $72 (annual) ● professional, $75 (annual) ● institutional, $100 (annual). **Staff:** 2. **State Groups:** 28. **Description:** Jewish alcoholics and addicts, family members, and concerned friends. Acts as an additional resource to promote and enhance recovery from chemical dependency. Provides research and information on chemical addiction in the Jewish community. Maintains Speaker's Bureau. **Libraries:** Type: reference; by appointment only. **Holdings:** 100; articles, audiovisuals, clippings. **Subjects:** addiction in Jewish community. **Awards:** Retreat Scholarships. **Frequency:** semiannual. **Type:** scholarship. **Recipient:** for recovering alcoholics, addicts and family members in financial need. **Computer Services:** database. **Committees:** Event. **Councils:** Governing; JACS. **Publications:** JACS Journal, annual. **Circulation:** 3,000 ● JACS Newsletter, monthly. **Price:** free. **Circulation:** 1,000. **Conventions/Meetings:** semiannual retreat, spiritual weekend for recovering Jewish alcoholics, addicts and family members ● annual Spiritual Day - meeting.

12981 ■ Luz Social Services
2797 N Introspect Dr.
Tucson, AZ 85745
Ph: (520)882-6216
Fax: (520)623-9291
E-mail: luz@luzsocialservices.org
Contact: Dr. Pepe Barron, CEO
Founded: 1989. **Members:** 18. **Staff:** 7. **Languages:** English, Spanish. **Description:** Assists with family issues, specifically substance abuse. Maintains a Speaker's Bureau. Conducts research and educational programs. **Libraries:** Type: reference. **Publications:** Adelante Juntos Coalition, monthly. Newsletter. **Conventions/Meetings:** annual conference ● monthly meeting.

12982 ■ Narcotic Educational Foundation of America (NEFA)
28245 Ave. Crocker, Ste.230
Santa Clarita, CA 91355-1201
Ph: (661)775-6960
Free: (877)775-6272
Fax: (661)775-1648
E-mail: lwhite@cnoa.org
URL: http://www.cnoa.org/NEFA.htm
Contact: Lorraine White, Exec. Sec.
Founded: 1924. **Description:** Conducts an education program revealing the dangers that result from the illicit and abusive use of narcotics and dangerous drugs, so that youth and adults will be protected from both mental and physical drug dependency and harm. **Publications:** Alcohol-A Potent Drug. Pamphlet ● Am I Addicted or Dependent?. Pamphlet ● Designer

Drugs: The Analog Game. Pamphlet ● The Heroin Story. Pamphlet ● Huffing: Inhalants. Pamphlet ● Lysergic Acid Diethylamide: Is it a Dream or Nightmare?. Pamphlet ● The PCP Story. Pamphlet ● Rohypnol: The Date Rape Drug. Pamphlet ● Speed: Amphetamines. Pamphlet ● The Story of Cocaine. Pamphlet ● Tobacco: Smoke or Chew. Pamphlet ● Understanding Anabolic Steroids. Pamphlet ● Use of Marijuana as a Medicine. Pamphlet ● Valium and Other Depressants. Pamphlet ● What About Marijuana?. Pamphlet.

12983 ■ Narcotics Anonymous (NA)
c/o World Service Office
PO Box 9999
Van Nuys, CA 91409
Ph: (818)773-9999
Fax: (818)700-0700
E-mail: fsmail@na.org
URL: http://www.na.org
Contact: Jeff Gershoff, Service Coor.
Founded: 1953. **Members:** 500,000. **Staff:** 48. **Budget:** $6,400,000. **Regional Groups:** 105. **State Groups:** 50. **Local Groups:** 27,400. **Languages:** Arabic, English, French, German, Hebrew, Italian, Japanese, Norwegian, Portuguese, Spanish, Swedish. **Description:** Aims to recover addicts throughout the world, works to offer help to fellow addicts seeking recovery. Meets regularly to facilitate and stabilize their recovery. Uses 12-step program adapted from Alcoholics Anonymous to aid in the recovery process. **Libraries:** Type: not open to the public. **Holdings:** 4; articles, periodicals. **Publications:** A Guide to Public Information. Handbook. **Price:** $4.20 ● Introductory Guide to NA. Booklet. **Price:** $1.70 ● It Works: How and Why. Book. Contains guide to NA primary principles. **Price:** $7.70 hardcover casebound ● Just For Today: Daily Meditations for Recovering Addicts. Book ● NA Update. Newsletter. Alternate Formats: online ● The NA Way Magazine: The International Journal of the Fellowship of Narcotics Anonymous, quarterly. Recounts experiences of members during their recoveries. Includes calendar of events and annual index. **Price:** free. ISSN: 0896-9116. Alternate Formats: online ● Bulletins. Alternate Formats: online. **Conventions/Meetings:** annual convention, celebration of NA recovery - usually Labor Day weekend.

12984 ■ National Asian Pacific American Families Against Substance Abuse (NAPAFASA)
340 E Second St., Ste.409
Los Angeles, CA 90012
Ph: (213)625-5795
Fax: (213)625-5796
E-mail: napafasa@napafasa.org
URL: http://www.napafasa.org
Contact: Emilie G. Dearing RN, Chair
Founded: 1988. **Membership Dues:** individual, $25 (annual) ● limited income, $15 (annual) ● organization (based on annual budget), $100-$1,000 (annual). **National Groups:** 200. **Description:** Represents AAPI and human service organizations. Works to involve service providers, families, and youth to reach API communities in the promotion of health, social justice and the reduction of substance abuse and related problems. Special projects offer organizations technical assistance, training, program planning and clinical training.

12985 ■ National Association of Addiction Treatment Providers (NAATP)
313 W Liberty St., Ste.129
Lancaster, PA 17603-2748
Ph: (717)392-8480
Fax: (717)392-8481
E-mail: rhunsicker@naatp.org
URL: http://www.naatp.org
Contact: Ronald J. Hunsicker, Pres./CEO
Founded: 1978. **Members:** 210. **Membership Dues:** associate, $600 (annual) ● less than 1.5 million gross charges to greater than 35 million gross charges, $750-$10,000 (annual). **Staff:** 2. **Budget:** $200,000. **State Groups:** 12. **Description:** Corporate and private institutional alcohol and/or drug dependency

treatment facilities. Promotes awareness of chemical dependency as a treatable disease; advocates high standards of health care in substance abuse treatment facilities. Encourages member education. Maintains contact with U.S. Congress and state and local governments. Serves in an advisory capacity to the Joint Commission on Accreditation of Healthcare Organizations and to the Commission on Accreditation of Rehabilitation Facilities (see separate entries). Compiles statistics on chemical dependency treatment and recovery. **Libraries:** Type: reference. **Awards:** Nelson J. Bradley Life Time Achievement Award. **Frequency:** annual. **Type:** recognition. **Recipient:** for lifelong achievements of individuals ● Outstanding Service Award. **Frequency:** annual. **Type:** recognition. **Computer Services:** Mailing lists. **Committees:** Ethics; Reimbursement; Research. **Affiliated With:** Continuing Care Accreditation Commission; Joint Commission on Accreditation of Healthcare Organizations. **Formerly:** (1987) National Association of Alcoholism Treatment Programs. **Publications:** Benchmark Survey, annual. Alternate Formats: online ● NAATP Visions, 10/year. Newsletter. **Price:** free, for members only. **Circulation:** 1,500. **Advertising:** accepted. Alternate Formats: online ● Annual Report, annual. Alternate Formats: online. **Conventions/Meetings:** annual Addiction Treatment Leadership Conference (exhibits) ● regional meeting and seminar ● seminar, on marketing, management, and reimbursement.

12986 ■ National Association of Athletes Against Drugs (NAAAD)
2481 Pacific Ave., Ste.C
Long Beach, CA 90806-2953
Ph: (562)989-9692 (562)424-6542
Fax: (562)426-9863
E-mail: educat2100@aol.com
Contact: Elliott Smith, Chm.
Founded: 1992. **Members:** 1,293. **Staff:** 5. **Regional Groups:** 3. **Description:** Professional athletes in motor sports. Promotes use of the fame enjoyed by racing drivers to deter youth from substance abuse. Seeks to increase participation by African-Americans in professional motor sports. Conducts educational programs; participates in charitable activities; makes available children's services; compiles statistics; maintains speakers' bureau. **Libraries:** Type: reference. **Holdings:** articles. **Subjects:** minorities in motor sports, substance abuse. **Also Known As:** (2006) Athletes Against Drugs. **Publications:** The Informer, periodic. Newsletter. **Price:** free for members. **Circulation:** 1,283. **Conventions/Meetings:** quarterly board meeting.

12987 ■ National Association for Children of Alcoholics (NACoA)
11426 Rockville Pike, Ste.100
Rockville, MD 20852
Ph: (301)468-0985
Free: (888)554-2627
Fax: (301)468-0987
E-mail: nacoa@nacoa.org
URL: http://www.nacoa.org
Contact: Sis Wenger, Pres./CEO
Founded: 1983. **Members:** 4,000. **Membership Dues:** individual, $50. **Staff:** 6. **Budget:** $150,000. **Description:** Authors, educators, physicians, psychologists, therapists, parents of children of alcoholics and the children of alcoholics. Supports and serves as a resource for individuals of all age groups who are COAs. Aims to increase public and professional awareness and recognition of the special needs of children of alcoholics; to provide leadership in public policy at the national, state, and local level; to act as an informational and educational resource to academic and other community systems; to create networks that facilitate the exchange of information and resources; to initiate and advance professional knowledge and understanding; to advocate for accessible programs and services. Compiles statistics; conducts educational programs. **Libraries:** Type: reference. **Subjects:** children of alcoholics. **Awards:** Margaret Cork Award. **Frequency:** annual. **Type:** recognition. **Publications:** Children of Alcoholics: Selected Readings, Vol. II. Book ● Kit for Early Child-

hood *Professionals.* Booklet. **Price:** $8.50 ● *Kit for Educators.* Booklet. **Price:** $8.50 ● *Kit for Kids.* Booklet. **Price:** $1.00 ● *Kit for Parents.* Booklet. Offers facts about alcoholism, encouraging parents to support their children and get help for themselves and their spouses. **Price:** $5.00 ● *NACoA Network,* bimonthly. Newsletter. **Price:** $20.00. Alternate Formats: online ● *Poor Jennifer: She's Always Losing Her Hat.* Video ● Annual Report, annual. Alternate Formats: online ● Also makes available posters, videos, booklets, brochures.

12988 ■ National Association on Drug Abuse Problems (NADAP)
355 Lexington Ave.
New York, NY 10017
Ph: (212)986-1170
Fax: (212)697-2939
E-mail: info@nadap.com
URL: http://www.nadap.org
Contact: John Darin, Pres.
Founded: 1971. **Staff:** 35. **Budget:** $2,500,000. **Description:** Serves as an information clearinghouse and referral bureau for corporations and local communities interested in prevention of substance abuse and treatment of substance abusers. Provides resources to local communities seeking to combat drug and alcohol abuse; corporate services for employers interested in creating a drug-free workplace. Makes available vocational education services including training in job hunting, job interview workshops, training programs for substance abuse treatment professionals, and individual consultations for recovering substance abusers seeking to return to the job market. Provides placement services; has conducted surveys on the employability of rehabilitated drug users and found that former addicts perform comparably with others hired for similar jobs. Operates Neighborhood Prevention Network, through which local communities develop parent support groups and youth peer leadership groups dedicated to combating drug and alcohol abuse. Maintains speakers' bureau. **Departments:** AIDS Services; Community Services; Information Clearinghouse and Referral Bureau; Neighborhood Prevention Network; Research; Vocational Education and Placement Services; Workplace Services. **Formed by Merger of:** National Association for the Prevention of Addiction to Narcotics; Institute for the Advancement of Criminal Justice; Provide Addict Care Today. **Publications:** *Conference Proceedings,* biennial ● *NADAP News/Report,* quarterly. Newsletter. Covers current issues in the field of substance abuse. **Price:** free. **Circulation:** 7,500. **Advertising:** accepted ● Reports.

12989 ■ National Association of Lesbian/Gay Addiction Professionals (NALGAP)
901 N Washington St., Ste.600
Alexandria, VA 22314
Ph: (703)465-0539
E-mail: joecd1@aol.com
URL: http://www.nalgap.org
Contact: Joseph M. Amico, Pres.
Founded: 1979. **Members:** 95. **Membership Dues:** individual, $35 (annual) ● agency, $50 (annual). **Budget:** $50,000. **Description:** Doctors, nurses, social workers, psychologists, certified counselors, and other professionals who work with gay, lesbian, transgendered, and bisexual alcoholics and addicts; drug, alcohol, and gay agencies, organizations, and institutes. Provides a network for support and communication among professionals working with chemically dependent gay, lesbian, and bisexual people. Seeks to educate members of organizations and agencies about gay, lesbian, and bisexual people and addiction; assure that workshops, seminars, conferences, and publications that deal with addiction address the special needs and problems of gay, lesbian, and bisexual people and their families; coordinates services provided by educators and training personnel who are available to help others in the addiction field to better serve gay and lesbian clients. Acts as a clearinghouse for resource and research information in the field of addiction as it pertains to homosexuality; provides referral information about

gay, lesbian, and bisexual groups of Alcoholics Anonymous World Services; develops and distributes a list of resource facilities for gay, lesbian, and bisexual alcoholics, addicts and their family and friends. Maintains a training and Speaker's Bureau. **Libraries: Type:** reference. **Subjects:** gay, lesbian, bisexual, transgender, addiction. **Awards: Frequency:** periodic. **Type:** recognition. **Computer Services:** Mailing lists. **Committees:** Education; Legislative/Public Policy. **Task Forces:** AIDS. **Formerly:** (1984) National Association of Gay Alcoholism Professionals; (1997) National Association of Lesbian/Gay Alcoholism Professionals. **Publications:** *The NALGAP Annotated Bibliography: Alcoholism, Substance Abuse, and Lesbians/Gay Men.* Book ● *NALGAP Reporter,* semiannual. Newsletter. Includes book reviews. ● *National Directory of Facilities and Services for Lesbian and Gay Alcoholics,* periodic ● Newsletter, quarterly. **Price:** free for members. **Advertising:** accepted ● Monographs. **Conventions/Meetings:** annual conference (exhibits).

12990 ■ National Association of State Alcohol and Drug Abuse Directors (NASADAD)
1025 Connecticut Ave. NW, Ste.605
Washington, DC 20036
Ph: (202)293-0090
Fax: (202)293-1250
E-mail: dcoffice@nasadad.org
URL: http://www.nasadad.org
Contact: Lewis Gallant PhD, Exec. Dir.
Founded: 1971. **Members:** 61. **Staff:** 11. **Budget:** $1,300,000. **Regional Groups:** 10. **Description:** Supports the development of effective alcohol and other drug abuse prevention and treatment programs throughout every state. Works to promote the establishment of national standards for quality assurance, outcomes and performance; and to facilitate the transition of research and knowledge into practice and to identify problems and issues that merit further study and research. **Awards: Type:** recognition. **Formerly:** (1978) National Association of State Drug Abuse Program Coordinators. **Conventions/Meetings:** annual meeting, policy, programs implementation, and association business meetings (exhibits) - usually first full week in June.

12991 ■ National Black Alcoholism and Addiction Council (NBAC)
5104 N Orange Blossom Trail, Ste.111
Orlando, FL 32810-1013
Ph: (407)532-2747
Free: (877)NBAC-ORG
Fax: (407)532-2815
E-mail: mail@nbacinc.org
URL: http://www.nbacinc.org
Contact: Dr. John Robertson, Exec. Dir.
Founded: 1978. **Members:** 1,050. **Membership Dues:** regular, $45 (annual) ● special (unemployed/full time student/senior citizen over 65), $25 (annual). **Staff:** 2. **Budget:** $85,000. **Description:** Individuals concerned about alcoholism among black Americans. Works to support and initiate activities that will improve alcoholism treatment services and lead to the prevention of alcoholism in the black community. Provides training on how to treat black alcoholics from a cultural perspective. Bestows political and service awards. Maintains biographical archives. Compiles statistics concerning alcoholism among blacks. **Committees:** Education, Research, and Training; Public Policy. **Formerly:** (1998) National Black Alcoholism Council. **Publications:** *Model for Working With Children of Alcoholic and Drug Addicted Parents* ● *National News and Views,* semiannual ● *Treatment of Black Alcoholics.* **Conventions/Meetings:** annual Black Alcoholism Institute - meeting ● annual conference.

12992 ■ National Catholic Council on Alcoholism and Related Drug Problems (NCCA)
1601 Joslyn Rd.
Lake Orion, MI 48360
Ph: (248)391-4445
Free: (800)626-6910

Fax: (248)391-4445
E-mail: ncca@guesthouse.org
URL: http://www.nccatoday.org
Contact: Mr. Richard G. Thibodeau, Exec. Dir.
Founded: 1949. **Members:** 300. **Membership Dues:** individual, $50 (annual) ● student/retiree, $25 (annual) ● patron, $100 (annual) ● parish/group, $250 (annual). **Staff:** 1. **Budget:** $85,000. **Multinational.** **Description:** Promotes and educates about adequate treatment for clergy and religious laymen and women suffering from alcoholism and drug dependency through consultation and supportive services. Cooperates with treatment programs for the spiritual, physical, and mental rehabilitation of alcoholics and drug dependent persons, especially with Alcoholics Anonymous World Services. Promotes pastoral ministry to alcoholics and their families. Educates Catholics, especially priests and religious men and women in pastoral ministries, on alcohol and alcohol problems as well as the use and abuse of alcohol and drugs. Sponsors workshops; conducts alcohol and drug abuse education programs in houses of formation and seminaries. Maintains speakers' bureau. **Libraries: Type:** reference. **Holdings:** 200. **Subjects:** alcoholism, addiction, treatment. **Awards:** Honorary Membership. **Type:** recognition. **Recipient:** for longtime association. **Computer Services:** Mailing lists. **Telecommunication Services:** electronic mail, nccanow@nlci.com. **Boards:** Directors. **Committees:** Publications. **Formerly:** National Clergy Conference on Alcoholism; (1988) National Clergy Council on Alcoholism and Related Drug Problems. **Publications:** *Alcoholism A Source Book for the Priest-Reprint of 1960 Edition in 1998.* **Price:** included in membership dues ● *The Best of the Blue Book Vol. II 1960-1997 published 1999.* **Price:** included in membership dues ● *The Blue Book,* annual. Includes proceedings of annual symposium. **Price:** $15.00 donation. **Circulation:** 2,000. Alternate Formats: online ● *Hope Journal Series for Teens.* **Price:** included in membership dues ● *NCCA Today,* quarterly. Newsletter. **Price:** included in membership dues ● *Prayers for Addicted Persons and Their Loved Ones.* Booklet. **Price:** included in membership dues. **Conventions/Meetings:** annual symposium.

12993 ■ National Committee for the Prevention of Alcoholism and Drug Dependency (NCPADD)
c/o International Commission for the Prevention of Alcoholism and Drug Dependency
12501 Old Columbia Pike
Silver Spring, MD 20904-6600
Ph: (301)680-6719
Fax: (301)680-6707
E-mail: the_icpa@hotmail.com
URL: http://www.health20-20.org
Contact: Dr. Peter N. Landless, Exec. Dir.
Founded: 1950. **Staff:** 50. **Staff:** 2. **Regional Groups:** 60. **National Groups:** 60. **Multinational.** **Description:** Health officials, physicians, educators, social workers, youth leaders, clergymen, temperance leaders, businessmen, judges, and others. Aims to further the study of the effects of alcohol and other drugs on the physical, mental and moral powers of the individual citizen and on the social, economic, political, and religious life of the nation. Fosters nationwide educational program through films, lectures, forums, radio, and television programs. **Affiliated With:** International Commission for the Prevention of Alcoholism and Drug Dependency. **Formerly:** National Committee for the Prevention of Alcoholism. **Publications:** *ICPA Reporter,* quarterly. Bulletin. Describes worldwide activities of ICPA and local communities. **Price:** included in membership dues. Alternate Formats: online. **Conventions/Meetings:** meeting and workshop - 2-4/year ● annual seminar.

12994 ■ National Council on Alcoholism and Drug Dependence (NCADD)
244 E 58th St., 4th Fl.
New York, NY 10022
Ph: (212)269-7797
Free: (800)622-2255
Fax: (212)269-7510

E-mail: national@ncadd.org
URL: http://www.ncadd.org
Contact: Mrs. Marty Mann, Founder
Founded: 1944. **Staff:** 10. **Budget:** $1,000,000. **State Groups:** 11. **Local Groups:** 90. **Description:** Works for the prevention and treatment of alcoholism and other drug dependence through programs of public education, information, and public policy advocacy. Sponsors National Alcohol Awareness Month each April. **Awards:** Gold Key Award. **Frequency:** annual. **Type:** recognition. **Recipient:** for major contributions to the field and organization ● Humanitarian Award. **Type:** recognition. **Recipient:** for private citizens; for contributions to the field of alcoholism ● Marty Mann Founder's Award. **Type:** recognition. **Recipient:** for individuals of national prominence in the field of alcoholism ● R. Brinkley Smithers Award. **Type:** recognition. **Recipient:** for an individual who made significant contributions of time, financial support and volunteer recruitment to the mission of NCADD ● Silver Key. **Type:** recognition. **Recipient:** for outstanding individuals who made contributions to the work of NCADD at national level. **Computer Services:** Mailing lists. **Departments:** Development; Public Information; Public Policy. **Formerly:** (1949) National Committee for Education on Alcoholism; (1955) National Committee on Alcoholism; (1990) National Council on Alcoholism. **Publications:** *NCADD Amethyst*, quarterly. Newsletter. Serves as an "Alcohol Alert" keeping readers updated with the latest research from National Institute on Alcohol Abuse and Alcoholism. **Price:** $50.00. **Circulation:** 2,000 ● *NCADD Washington Report*, monthly. Newsletter. Presents reports on Washington issues related to alcoholism/drug dependence. **Price:** $97.00/year; $174.00/2 years; $259.00/3 years. **Circulation:** 350 ● *Resource and Referral Guide*, annual ● *What Are the Signs of Alcoholism?*. Brochure ● *What Can You Do About Someone Else's Drinking?*. Brochure ● *Whos' Got the Power? You . or Drugs?*. Pamphlets ● Annual Report. **Conventions/Meetings:** annual Conference of Affiliates - usually October/November.

12995 ■ National Families in Action (NFIA)
2957 Clairmont Rd., Ste.150
Atlanta, GA 30329
Ph: (404)248-9676
Fax: (404)248-1312
E-mail: nfia@nationalfamilies.org
URL: http://www.nationalfamilies.org
Contact: Sue Rusche, Pres./CEO
Founded: 1977. **Staff:** 9. **Budget:** $1,300,000. **State Groups:** 9. **Description:** Parents and other adults concerned about preventing drug abuse. Seeks to: educate parents, children, and the community about the use of drugs; counteract social pressures that condone and promote drug use; stop drug use. Worked for passage of statewide drug paraphernalia statutes. Collects and disseminates information about the effects of drugs. Maintains Drug Information Center, which contains more than 500,000 documents, studies, books, brochures, and films and videos relating to drug abuse. Operates after-school program for parents and youth. **Libraries: Type:** reference. **Holdings:** 500,000; archival material, audiovisuals, books, clippings, monographs, periodicals. **Subjects:** drug use. **Computer Services:** database. **Formerly:** (1982) DeKalb Families in Action; (1983) Families in Action; (1984) Families in Action Drug Information Center; (1990) Families in Action National Drug Information Center. **Publications:** *Crack Update*. Brochure. Describes the effects of this highly addictive form of cocaine. **Price:** $35.00/100 copies ● *False Messengers: How Addictive Drugs Change the Brain*. Book ● *Guide to the Legalization Movement and How You Can Stop It*. Book. **Price:** $15.00 ● *12 Reasons Not to Legalize Drugs*. Article. **Price:** $15.00/100 copies ● *12 Tips for Helping Your Children Stay Drug-Free* (in English and Spanish). Article. **Price:** $15.00/100 copies ● *You Have the Right to Know Curriculum Series*. Books. **Price:** $10.00/each ● Annual Report, annual. Alternate Formats: online ● Also publishes Inhalant Update. **Conventions/Meetings:** quarterly Parent Leader Certification - meeting ● workshop - 5-day basic training.

12996 ■ National Family Partnership (NFP)
c/o Informed Families Education Center
2490 Coral Way, Ste.501
Miami, FL 33145
Ph: (305)856-4886
Free: (800)705-8997
Fax: (305)856-4815
E-mail: ireyes@informedfamilies.org
URL: http://www.nfp.org
Contact: Ileana Reyes, Contact
Founded: 1980. **Members:** 65. **Regional Groups:** 32. **State Groups:** 22. **Description:** Provides services, resources, and drug prevention programs for local parent and youth groups across the country. Sponsors Annual Red Ribbon Celebration in October; serves as a clearinghouse for state and federal legislation. **Awards:** Camarena Award. **Frequency:** annual. **Type:** recognition. **Recipient:** for leadership in substance abuse prevention. **Computer Services:** database, membership. **Additional Websites:** http://www.redribbon.org. **Committees:** Communication Network; Legislative; Red Ribbon. **Formerly:** National Federation of Parents for Drug-Free Youth. **Publications:** *NFP Update*, quarterly. Newsletter. **Price:** $25.00 /year for individuals; $100.00/year for groups. **Circulation:** 1,500 ● Manuals.

12997 ■ New Hope Foundation
PO Box 66
Marlboro, NJ 07746
Ph: (732)946-3030
Fax: (732)946-3507
E-mail: info@newhopefoundation.org
URL: http://www.newhopefoundation.org
Contact: Tony Comerford PhD, Pres./CEO
Description: Private citizens, businesses, and organizations. Strives to serve those in need of treatment of alcoholism, drug addition, and gambling. Offers both inpatient and outpatient services.

12998 ■ Partnership for a Drug-Free America
405 Lexington Ave., Ste.1601
New York, NY 10174
Ph: (212)922-1560 (212)973-3517
Free: (888)575-3115
Fax: (212)922-1570
E-mail: webmail@drugfree.org
URL: http://www.drugfree.org
Contact: Mr. Stephen J. Pasierb, Pres./CEO
Founded: 1986. **Members:** 2,500. **Description:** Represents the advertising, production, and communications industries. Seeks to utilize the creative skills of members to change social attitudes towards illegal drugs. Works to evoke a social revulsion to what the group views as current public acceptance and complacency toward illegal drugs. Focuses on advertising campaigns and strategies that will "unsell" illegal drugs, "de-normalize" drug usage in the U.S., and reinforce positive factors of life without drugs. Conducts research evaluation program to assess attitudinal changes of targeted groups toward illegal drugs, monitor usage trends, and evaluate the effectiveness of these advertisements. **Committees:** Review. **Programs:** Attitudinal Tracking Research. **Task Forces:** Black; Business; Healthcare Professional; Hispanic. **Formerly:** (1990) Media-Advertising Partnership for a Drug-Free America. **Publications:** *Partnership for a Drug-Free America Newsletter*, quarterly ● Bulletin, periodic. Alternate Formats: online. **Conventions/Meetings:** monthly board meeting.

12999 ■ Phoenix House
164 W 74th St.
New York, NY 10023
Ph: (212)595-5810
Free: (800)HELP-111
Fax: (212)496-6035
E-mail: phcomm@phoenixhouse.org
URL: http://www.phoenixhouse.org
Contact: Mitchell S. Rosenthal MD, Pres.
Founded: 1967. **Members:** 760. **Budget:** $50,000,000. **Description:** Provides substance abuse treatment, education and prevention services. Operates more than 100 programs in nine states. Works to heal families, strengthen communities, and

save lives. Offers short-term outpatient and in-patient adult drug treatment. Conducts adult and adolescent drug education workshops in public and private schools, corporations and other workplaces. **Affiliated With:** American Council for Drug Education; Children of Alcoholics Foundation. **Formerly:** (2000) Phoenix House Foundation. **Publications:** *Phoenix House News*, quarterly. Newsletter. **Price:** free ● Brochures ● Pamphlets ● Annual Report, annual.

13000 ■ Pill Addicts Anonymous (PAA)
947 Amity St.
Reading, PA 19604
Ph: (215)372-1128 (610)374-7430
Contact: Richard L. Linderman, Contact
Founded: 1979. **Members:** 10. **State Groups:** 2. **Local Groups:** 2. **Description:** Individuals who wish to recover from pill and drug addiction. Provides support through group sessions. **Publications:** Pamphlets. Help for active addicts. **Price:** free. **Conventions/Meetings:** weekly Just For Today Group - support group meeting, open discussion about pill addiction - on Friday. Wyomissing, PA - **Avg. Attendance:** 12.

13001 ■ Pills Anonymous (PA)
c/o CFR
2740 Grant St.
Concord, CA 94520
E-mail: info@pillsanonymous.net
URL: http://www.pillsanonymous.net
Founded: 1975. **Local Groups:** 3. **Description:** Persons addicted to drugs including tranquilizers, stimulants, analgesics, sedatives, cocaine, and marijuana. Applies the Alcoholics Anonymous World Services' (see separate entry) 12-step approach to persons dependent on addictive drugs. Provides emotional support to members, many of whom became addicted after using the drugs for legitimate reasons (for example, to alleviate the chronic pain of migraine headaches or arthritis) and teaches them methods of coping with pain that do not require drugs. **Affiliated With:** Alcoholics Anonymous World Services. **Formerly:** (1984) Pills Anonymous; (1992) Drugs Anonymous.

13002 ■ PRIDE Youth Programs (PYP)
4684 S Evergreen
Newaygo, MI 49337
Free: (800)668-9277
Fax: (231)652-2461
E-mail: info@prideyouthprograms.org
URL: http://www.prideyouthprograms.org
Contact: Jay DeWispelaere, Pres./CEO
Founded: 1977. **Staff:** 25. **Description:** Parents, youth groups, educators, law enforcement officials, community groups, and corporations. Promotes drug abuse prevention through education. Provides current research information on drug abuse and facilitates the organization of parent peer groups, parent-school teams, and community action groups to reduce adolescent drug abuse. Gathers and disseminates information on the latest medical and scientific findings on the effects of drugs on youth, current patterns of drug and alcohol use among youth, social and cultural pressures that encourage youth to use drugs, and institutional and legal efforts being made to prevent drug abuse, reduce drug supplies, and prosecute drug traffickers. Conducts the PRIDE Community Action Plan to assist communities in establishing an effective drug abuse program and the PRIDE's Parent Training Program to assist concerned parents. Offers America's PRIDE, Club-PRIDE, and PRIDE Junior youth programs. Develops workplace drug training programs for corporations. Sponsors the annual PRIDE World Drug Conference, which seeks to bring parents, youth, and the public into contact with scientists, physicians, and policy-makers dealing with adolescent drug abuse; also sponsors a series of one-day conferences for local community teams who are trained to return to their neighborhoods to organize workshops. Operates speakers' bureau; conducts educational programs and children's services; compiles statistics. Maintains library. **Libraries: Type:** reference. **Holdings:** books, reports. **Formerly:** (1982) Parent Resources and

Information on Drug Education. **Publications:** *PRIDE Quarterly.* Newsletter. Discusses the legal, pharmacological, psychological, social, cultural, and physiological effects of adolescent drug use. Includes overviews. **Price:** $25.00/year. **Circulation:** 3,100 ● *PYP Times.* Newsletter. Alternate Formats: online ● Also publishes books and pamphlets. **Conventions/Meetings:** annual World Drug Conference, largest youth/adult conference focusing on drug prevention (exhibits) - always spring.

13003 ■ Project Renewal
200 Varick St.
New York, NY 10014
Ph: (212)620-0340
E-mail: kristinf@projectrenewal.org
URL: http://www.projectrenewal.org
Contact: Edward I. Geffner, Pres./CEO
Founded: 1967. **Staff:** 325. **Budget:** $25,000,000. **Description:** Provides care for homeless adults in New York City. Funded by the New York City Department of Mental Health, Mental Retardation and Alcoholism Services, the U.S. Department of Housing and Urban Development, the New York State Office of Mental Health, the New York State Department of Homeless Services, the New York City Human Resources Administrative Division of AIDS Service, the New York State Office of Alcoholism and Substance Abuse Services, private individuals, and corporations and foundations. Main components of the program are: a 48-bed alcohol detoxification facility for homeless male alcoholics; a 150-person alcoholism outpatient clinic for sober homeless alcoholics; a 20-person, year-long program offering therapy and work rehabilitation for homeless alcoholics and other substance abusers; Midtown Outreach Program, which sends medical and outreach teams to homeless people on the streets and in shelters. Offers training, job placement, and permanent supported housing. **Programs:** Arts; Comprehensive Outreach; Culinary Arts Training; In Homes Now; MedVan; Parole Support and Treatment; Shelter Outreach. **Projects:** Shelter Assessment and Referral. **Formerly:** (1995) Manhattan Bowery Corporation.

13004 ■ Recovered Alcoholic Clergy Association (RACA)
c/o Christ Church Episcopal
2000 S Maryland Pkwy.
Las Vegas, NV 89104-3200
Ph: (702)735-7655
E-mail: pc@petercourtney.net
URL: http://racapecusa.org
Contact: Fr. Peter Courtney, Dir.
Founded: 1968. **Members:** 350. **Staff:** 1. **Budget:** $4,000. **Local Groups:** 100. **National Groups:** 2. **Description:** Clergy in the Episcopal Church orders and persons attending or teaching at Episcopal seminaries who have drinking problems. Recommends alcohol addiction treatment centers for members; trains individuals involved in confronting persons with drinking problems. Seeks to provide moral support to members; provides guidance to the families and/or colleagues of problem drinkers; maintains speakers' bureau. **Affiliated With:** Recovery Ministries. **Publications:** *No foolin,* monthly. Newsletter. **Circulation:** 350 ● Directory, annual ● Pamphlets. **Conventions/Meetings:** annual conference.

13005 ■ Recovery Ministries (RM)
PO Box 115
Cloverdale, IN 46120
Ph: (317)797-3813
E-mail: info@recoveryministries.com
URL: http://www.recoveryministries.com
Contact: Virginia M. King, Exec. Dir.
Founded: 1982. **Members:** 600. **Membership Dues:**. individual, $35 (annual) ● parish, $75 (annual) ● diocese/institution, $150 (annual) ● family, $50 (annual). **Budget:** $86,000. **Description:** A network of individuals, parishes, and Episcopal Church diocesan committees addressing the issue of alcohol and drug use and addiction. Seeks to involve the Episcopal Church in alcohol and other drug addiction issues.

Serves as a resource clearinghouse. Sponsors annual Alcohol-Drug Awareness Sunday to provide information to congregations. **Awards:** Russell Horton Award. **Frequency:** annual. **Type:** recognition ● Samuel Shoemaker Award. **Frequency:** annual. **Type:** recognition ● Vicki Vincent Memorial Award. **Frequency:** annual. **Type:** recognition. **Computer Services:** database ● mailing lists. **Formerly:** (1997) National Episcopal Coalition on Alcohol and Drugs. **Publications:** *Alcohol-Drug Awareness Sunday Information Packet,* annual. Includes educational material. **Price:** $6.00. **Circulation:** 2,000 ● *The NE-CAD News,* quarterly. **Price:** available to members only. **Circulation:** 600 ● Brochures ● Newsletter. **Conventions/Meetings:** annual meeting, provides assistance for diocesan programs.

13006 ■ Remembering ADAM
PO Box 665
Hastings, PA 16646
Free: (877)767-2326
E-mail: contact@rememberingadam.org
URL: http://www.rememberingadam.org
Contact: Deborah A. Fowler, Pres.
Founded: 1999. **Members:** 16. **Description:** Serves as a substance abuse prevention education organization. Educates children, adults, and communities on the dangers of alcohol and illicit drugs. Develops a volunteer drug screening program, which is currently running at several schools; this program promotes positive reinforcement for those children who choose to be drug free as well as a drug free lifestyle and healthy choices. **Awards:** The Gobbel Award. **Frequency:** annual. **Type:** recognition. **Recipient:** for visionary and victims advocate individuals.

13007 ■ Secular Organizations for Sobriety (SOS)
4773 Hollywood Blvd.
Hollywood, CA 90027
Ph: (323)666-4295
Fax: (323)666-4271
E-mail: sos@cfiwest.org
URL: http://www.cfiwest.org/sos/index.htm
Contact: James R. Christopher, Founder
Founded: 1986. **Members:** 20,000. **Description:** Recovering alcoholics and drug addicts; families and friends of alcoholics or drug addicts. Serves as a support system free of any religious or spiritual undercurrent; believes sobriety is a process of personal responsibility. Espouses "a healthy skepticism" and encourages self-reliance and free thought. Maintains speakers' bureau. Compiles statistics. **Libraries:** Type: reference. **Holdings:** archival material. **Publications:** *Save Our Selves,* quarterly. Newsletter. Also Cited As: *SOS National Newsletter; SOS Newsletter.*

13008 ■ Therapeutic Communities of America (TCA)
1601 Connecticut Ave. NW, Ste.803
Washington, DC 20009
Ph: (202)296-3503
Fax: (202)518-5475
E-mail: tca.office@verizon.net
URL: http://therapeuticcommunitiesofamerica.org
Contact: Linda Hay Crawford, Exec. Dir.
Founded: 1975. **Members:** 500. **Description:** Represents substance abuse treatment programs. **Committees:** Clinical Practice and Research; Criminal Justice; Membership; Public Information; Public Policy; Standards. **Publications:** *Data Bank Updates,* periodic ● *Legislative Updates,* periodic ● *TCA News,* 3/year. Newsletter ● Monographs ● Proceedings. **Conventions/Meetings:** meeting - 3/year.

13009 ■ Triangle Club
2030 P St. NW
Washington, DC 20036
Ph: (202)659-8641
E-mail: theclub@triangleclub.org
URL: http://www.triangleclub.org
Contact: Bill A., Pres.
Founded: 1980. **Members:** 1,000. **Membership Dues:** voluntary, $100 (annual). **Staff:** 1. **Description:** Regular groups of Alcoholics Anonymous World

Services specifically composed of gays and lesbians. Aims to serve the gay and lesbian members of AA and to provide advice and support to other members of AA. Works for unity and service with AA for the betterment of the gay and lesbian members and AA; advocates freedom in communication as an important aid to recovery. Provides alcoholism professionals with information about gay and lesbian AA groups for use in counseling lesbian and gay alcoholics. Assists in the exchange of recorded tapes of lesbian and gay AA speakers. **Libraries:** Type: open to the public. **Holdings:** 100; books. **Subjects:** recovery. **Committees:** Group Needs; Lesbian Outreach; Literature; Loners; Public Information. **Formerly:** International Advisory Council for Homosexual Men and Women in Alcoholics Anonymous. **Publications:** *World Directory of Gay/Lesbian Groups of Alcoholics Anonymous,* annual ● Newsletter, quarterly ● Also publishes calendar of events and pamphlet. **Conventions/Meetings:** semiannual meeting.

13010 ■ Women for Sobriety (WFS)
PO Box 618
Quakertown, PA 18951-0618
Ph: (215)536-8026
Fax: (215)538-9026
E-mail: newlife@nni.com
URL: http://www.womenforsobriety.org
Contact: Becky Fenner, Dir.
Founded: 1976. **Members:** 75,000. **Staff:** 5. **Budget:** $130,000. **National Groups:** 200. **Description:** Self-help groups of women alcoholics who use the New Life Program. Based on abstinence, comprised of Thirteen Statements of Acceptance that when used consistently, will provide each woman with a new way of life through a new way of thinking. Recovery starts with coping first but then moves on to meeting and overcoming challenges and a whole change in attitude and approach to each day. Recognizes differences between male and female alcoholics in the method of successful recovery. Small groups organize and meet independently. Huge selection of recovery related books and literature through on-line bookstore. **Programs:** Men for Sobriety. **Publications:** *Sobering Thoughts,* monthly. Newsletter. Contains calendar of events, research updates, membership articles, and news on WFS meetings. **Price:** $14.95/year. ISSN: 1071-4111. **Circulation:** 1,500 ● Also publishes the Women for Sobriety tapes, workbooks, booklets, and videos. **Conventions/Meetings:** annual DeSales University Summer Conference, includes emotional growth and empowerment workshops for members - always June ● seminar ● workshop.

13011 ■ Women's Drug Research Project (WDR)
Address Unknown since 2007
Founded: 1973. **Description:** Has investigated differences in the needs and problems of men and women entering drug abuse treatment programs. Studied two outpatient methadone programs and two residential therapeutic communities, which were established to gather new information about women addicts, their needs, and possible methods for meeting those needs. Also collected data from 20 programs in five cities for studies on treatment organization and psychosocial characteristics of addicts. **Convention/Meeting:** none.

Suicide

13012 ■ American Association of Suicidology (AAS)
5221 Wisconsin Ave. NW
Washington, DC 20015
Ph: (202)237-2280
Free: (800)273-TALK
Fax: (202)237-2282
E-mail: info@suicidology.org
URL: http://www.suicidology.org
Contact: James J. Mazza PhD, Pres.
Founded: 1968. **Members:** 1,100. **Membership Dues:** individual/family, $150 (annual) ● student/

volunteer, $38 (annual) ● organization, $200-$660 (annual). **Staff:** 5. **Budget:** $400,000. **Regional Groups:** 5. **Description:** Psychologists, psychiatrists, social workers, nurses, health educators, physicians, directors of suicide prevention centers, clergy, and others from various disciplines and fields of experience who share a common interest in the advancement of studies of suicide prevention and life-threatening behavior. Seeks to recognize and encourage suicidology (the study of suicide, suicide prevention, and related phenomena of self-destruction). Advances education, disseminates information through programs and publications, and cooperates with other organizations in suicidology. **Computer Services:** Mailing lists. **Publications:** *AAS Membership Roster*, periodic. Membership Directory. Arranged by state and region. **Price:** $10.00/copy ● *Directory of Survivors of Suicide Support Groups*, periodic. **Price:** $10.00 ● *Newslink*, quarterly. Newsletter. Includes association news and calendar of events. **Price:** included in membership dues. **Circulation:** 1,100. **Advertising:** accepted. Alternate Formats: online. Also Cited As: *American Association of Suicidology—Newslink* ● *Proceedings of Annual Meeting*. **Price:** $30.00 ● *Suicide and Life-Threatening Behavior*, quarterly. Journal. **Price:** available to members only. ISSN: 0363-0234. **Advertising:** accepted. Alternate Formats: online ● *Surviving Suicide*, quarterly. Newsletter. **Price:** $20.00/year. Alternate Formats: online. **Conventions/Meetings:** annual Healing After Suicide Conference (exhibits) - always April/May.

13013 ■ American Foundation for Suicide Prevention (AFSP)
120 Wall St., 22nd Fl.
New York, NY 10005
Ph: (212)363-3500
Free: (888)333-AFSP
Fax: (212)363-6237
E-mail: inquiry@afsp.org
URL: http://www.afsp.org
Contact: Robert Gebbia, Exec. Dir.
Founded: 1987. **Staff:** 29. **Regional Groups:** 20. **Nonmembership. Description:** Dedicated to funding research, developing prevention initiatives and offering educational programs and conferences for survivors, mental health professionals, physicians and the public. The Foundation's activities include: supporting research projects that help further the understanding and treatment of depression and the prevention of suicide; providing information and education about depression and suicide; promoting professional education for the recognition and treatment of depressed and suicidal individuals; publicizing the magnitude of the problems of depression and suicide and the need for research, prevention and treatment; and supporting programs for suicide survivor treatment, research and education. **Awards:** Distinguished Investigator Award. **Frequency:** annual. **Type:** grant. **Recipient:** to investigators at the level of associate professor or higher with an established record of research and publication on suicide ● Pilot Grant. **Frequency:** 3/year. **Type:** grant. **Recipient:** to investigators at any level ● Post Doctoral Research Fellowship. **Frequency:** annual. **Type:** fellowship. **Recipient:** for full time research by an investigator who has received a PhD degree within the previous 3 years but has not had 3 years of fellowship support ● Standard Research Award. **Frequency:** annual. **Type:** grant. **Recipient:** to individual investigators at any level ● Young Investigator Award. **Frequency:** annual. **Type:** grant. **Recipient:** to investigators at the level of assistant professor or lower. **Formerly:** (1998) Maryland Suicide Foundation. **Publications:** *Lifesavers*, quarterly. Newsletter. **Price:** included in membership dues - **Conventions/Meetings:** annual Lifesavers Dinner - always May ● annual National Survivors of Suicide Day Conference, healing conference for those grieving the loss of a friend or loved one to suicide - every Saturday before Thanksgiving.

13014 ■ Heartbeat
PO Box 16985
Colorado Springs, CO 80935
Ph: (719)596-2575 (719)593-8680

E-mail: archlj@msn.com
URL: http://www.heartbeatsurvivorsaftersuicide.org
Contact: LaRita Archibald, Founder/Dir.
Founded: 1980. **Staff:** 1. **Description:** Persons who have lost a loved one due to suicide. Provides an atmosphere whereby grieving participants receive support, understanding, direction, and encouragement from those who have successfully resolved their grief. Offers "postvention" education program aimed at preventing the suicide of survivors. Maintains speakers' bureau. **Libraries: Type:** reference. **Affiliated With:** American Association of Suicidology. **Formerly:** Heartbeat/Survivors After Suicide. **Publications:** *Forming Heartbeat Chapters*. Manual. **Conventions/Meetings:** biennial Healing after Suicide - conference ● monthly support group meeting.

13015 ■ National Organization for People of Color Against Suicide (NOPCAS)
4715 Sargent Rd. NE
Washington, DC 20017
Ph: (202)549-6039
Free: (866)899-5317
Fax: (866)899-5317
E-mail: info@nopcas.org
URL: http://www.nopcas.com
Contact: Donna Holland Barnes PhD, Pres.
Description: Aims to stop suicide in minority communities. Improves the knowledge of counselors and educators on suicidology. Provides insight on depression and other mental disorders. Shares information on suicide prevention and intervention. **Computer Services:** Information services, suicide resources. **Telecommunication Services:** hotline, suicide crisis assistance, (800)784-2433 ● hotline, suicide crisis assistance, (800)273-TALK. **Boards:** Scientific and Research Advisory. **Task Forces:** Cultural Difference.

13016 ■ Organization for Attempters and Survivors of Suicide in Interfaith Services (OASSIS)
211 Russell Ave., Apt. 71
Gaithersburg, MD 20877
Ph: (240)361-3171
Fax: (240)361-3183
E-mail: jamestclemons@aol.com
URL: http://www.oassis.org
Contact: James T. Clemons PhD, Founder/Pres.
Founded: 1997. **Description:** Works to prevent suicide. Increases suicide awareness and removes the stigma on attempters and survivors. Provides support, consultative services, training and educational programs. **Publications:** *Enriching Lives*, once or twice a year. Newsletter.

13017 ■ Ray of Hope (ROH)
2778 Snapfinger Rd.
Decatur, GA 30034
Ph: (770)696-5100
Fax: (770)696-5111
E-mail: kingdominfo@rayofhope.org
URL: http://www.rayofhope.org
Contact: Dr. Cynthia L. Hale, Sr. Pastor
Founded: 1977. **Members:** 25. **Staff:** 2. **Regional Groups:** 13. **State Groups:** 2. **Local Groups:** 1. **National Groups:** 10. **Description:** Self-help organization offering support for coping with suicide, loss, and grief. Organizes suicide survivor support groups. Offers training courses and consultation on bereavement and suicide postvention. Telephone counseling (pre-arranged). **Libraries: Type:** reference. **Subjects:** loss, grief, after suicide. **Publications:** *After Suicide: A Unique Grief Process*. Booklet. **Price:** $5.95 plus $1.50 first book and $.25 each addition ● *Life After Suicide: A Ray of Hope for Those Left Behind*. Book. Serves as a guide for suicide survivor's bereavement process. **Price:** $27.95 plus $3 postage and $.50 each additional book ● *Survivorship After Suicide*. Video. **Price:** $35.00 postage included. **Conventions/Meetings:** periodic After Suicide: A Ray of Hope/Healing in the Heartland - workshop.

13018 ■ Suicide Prevention Action Network USA (SPAN USA)
1025 Vermont Ave. NW, Ste.1066
Washington, DC 20005
Ph: (202)449-3600
Fax: (202)449-3601
E-mail: info@spanusa.org
URL: http://www.spanusa.org
Contact: Jerry Reed, Exec. Dir.
Founded: 1996. **Membership Dues:** individual, $25 (annual) ● family, $35 (annual) ● student/senior, $15 (annual) ● organization, $150 (annual). **Description:** Works to increase awareness of the toll of suicide in the nation. Advances public policies that help prevent suicide. Develops political will to ensure that government effectively addresses the problem of suicide. **Awards:** The Elsie and Jerry Weyrauch Award. **Frequency:** annual. **Type:** recognition. **Recipient:** to an individual who has made significant contributions to suicide prevention at the national level ● SPAN USA Allies for Action Award. **Frequency:** annual. **Type:** recognition. **Recipient:** to individual(s) who has made significant contributions to SPAN USA to help achieve its mission. **Computer Services:** Information services, suicide prevention and survivor resources. **Publications:** *The Network News*, quarterly. Newsletter.

Support Groups

13019 ■ Because I Love You: The Parent Support Group (BILY)
PO Box 2062
Winnetka, CA 91396-2062
Ph: (818)884-8242
E-mail: bily1982@aol.com
URL: http://www.becauseiloveyou.org
Contact: Dennis Poncher, Founder/Dir.
Founded: 1982. **Description:** Seeks to support parents of troubled children with behavioral problems such as substance abuse, attitude, school attendance, physical/verbal abuse, running away, and curfew. **Libraries: Type:** reference. **Subjects:** family problems, prohibited drugs, vices, disorders/disabilities. **Programs:** Youth. **Publications:** Books.

13020 ■ GriefNet
PO Box 3272
Ann Arbor, MI 48106-3272
Fax: (734)761-1960
E-mail: cendra@griefnet.org
URL: http://www.griefnet.org
Contact: Cendra Lynn PhD, Dir./Founder
Members: 47. **Description:** Supports persons dealing with grief, death and major loss. **Libraries: Type:** open to the public. **Holdings:** articles, books. **Subjects:** grief, bereavement. **Also Known As:** Rivendell Resources.

13021 ■ National Organization For Empowering Caregivers (NOFEC)
425 W 23rd St., Ste.9B
New York, NY 10011
Ph: (212)807-1204
Fax: (212)645-5143
E-mail: info@nofec.org
URL: http://www.nofec.org
Contact: Gail R. Mitchell, Exec. Dir./Pres.
Membership Dues: individual, $20 (annual) ● individual outside U.S., $25 (annual) ● professional, $35 (annual) ● silver benefactor, $500 (annual) ● gold benefactor, $1,000 (annual). **Multinational. Description:** Promotes public awareness of the realities of caregiving. Provides assistance, education, support and referrals to informal family caregivers. **Computer Services:** database, resources. **Telecommunication Services:** electronic mail, membership@nofec.org ● electronic mail, services@nofec.org.

13022 ■ S.M.A.R.T. (Secretive Societies, Mind Control and Ritual Abuse)
PO Box 1295
Easthampton, MA 01027

E-mail: smartnews@aol.com
URL: http://members.aol.com/SMARTNEWS/index2.html
Description: Promotes awareness of connections between secretive organizations, ritual abuse and mind control; seeks to end ritual abuse. **Affiliated With:** Survivorship. **Publications:** *Seventh Annual Ritual Abuse, Secretive Organizations and Mind Control Conference.* Audiotape ● Newsletter, bimonthly. **Price:** $12.00/year in U.S.; $18.00 in Canada and Mexico; $27.00 international. Alternate Formats: online. **Conventions/Meetings:** annual conference.

Surrogate Parenthood

13023 ■ Center for Surrogate Parenting (CSP)
West Coast Off.
15821 Ventura Blvd., Ste.675
Encino, CA 91436
Ph: (818)788-8288
Fax: (818)981-8287
E-mail: centersp@aol.com
URL: http://www.creatingfamilies.com
Contact: Joanne Bubrick, Program Admin.
Founded: 1980. **Members:** 2,000. **Staff:** 14. **State Groups:** 2. **For-Profit. Multinational. Description:** Attorneys and psychologists who are experts in the field of surrogate parenting, an alternative method of childbearing employed when a woman is unable to conceive a child. Works to disseminate current and accurate information on the legal, moral, ethical, and psychological aspects of surrogate parenting. Advises legislators and establishes ethical and procedural guidelines regarding new laws protecting those involved. Conducts research; maintains speaker's bureau; sponsors radio and television interviews. **Formerly:** (1986) Surrogate Parent Foundation.

13024 ■ Donors' Offspring (DO)
Address Unknown since 2007
Founded: 1981. **Description:** Selfhelp support group for individuals involved in artificial fertilization, including donors, recipients, surrogate parents, offspring, parents of donor or recipient, and fertility experts and professionals. Assists in locating individual medical histories. Operates referral service and speakers' bureau. Offers educational and research programs; provides children's services and peer counseling. Conducts lobbying activities; compiles statistics. **Libraries: Type:** reference. **Holdings:** archival material, audiovisuals, books, business records, clippings, periodicals. **Computer Services:** database. **Telecommunication Services:** electronic bulletin board ● phone referral service. **Committees:** Donors' Network; Donors' Offspring Registry; Helping Offspring Pursue Ethics; Parents Network; Political Action. **Publications:** *Donors' Offspring,* quarterly. Newsletter. Contains personal stories, search ads, and book reviews. **Price:** $10.00/year. **Advertising:** accepted. **Conventions/Meetings:** monthly conference, meets by conference phone call - last Wednesday of each month.

13025 ■ Organization of Parents Through Surrogacy (OPTS)
PO Box 611
Gurnee, IL 60031
Ph: (847)782-0224
E-mail: bzager@msn.com
URL: http://www.opts.com
Contact: Shirley Zager, Dir.
Founded: 1987. **Members:** 1,500. **Membership Dues:** professional, $100 (annual) ● individual, couple, international, surrogate mother, $50 (annual). **Regional Groups:** 4. **Description:** Parents of children born through assisted reproductive technologies; lawyers, doctors, and social workers involved in the infertility field; surrogate mothers. Provides support services for families created through surrogate parenting. Advocates the right to choose assisted reproductive technology. Offers information and referrals to infertile couples. Advocates for positive legisla-

tion concerning surrogacy. Coordinates Phone Friends Network, a nonprofessional informational/emotional support service for members. Also an e-mail chat group (on-line). **Libraries: Type:** not open to the public. **Holdings:** 50. **Subjects:** surrogate parenting, other reproductive technologies. **Computer Services:** Online services, member newsgroup. **Publications:** *OPTS News,* annual. Newsletter. Includes information on current issues and provides format for sharing of personal experiences. **Circulation:** 2,000. Alternate Formats: online. **Conventions/Meetings:** bimonthly regional meeting - always held concurrently in Northern and Southern CA and the Chicago, Newark, and Boston areas.

Tallness

13026 ■ Tall Clubs International (TCI)
PMB 400 W 3 St. D156
Santa Rosa, CA 95401
Free: (888)468-2552
E-mail: admin@tall.org
URL: http://www.tall.org
Contact: Fred T. Heater, Pres.
Founded: 1938. **Members:** 4,200. **Membership Dues:** social, $30 (annual). **Staff:** 7. **Budget:** $10,000. **National Groups:** 69. **Multinational. Description:** Represents women 5'10" or taller and men 6'2" and taller. Promotes "tall awareness" and the happiness and welfare of tall people. Encourages tall people to be undeterred in perspective on life and activities because of height. Seeks to educate the public to the needs and problems of tall people, such as obtaining clothes, accommodations, and facilities of suitable size and convenience. Fosters friendship, companionship, and the exchange of information and ideas among members. Sponsors charitable programs. **Libraries: Type:** reference. **Holdings:** archival material, periodicals. **Awards:** Man of the Year. **Frequency:** annual. **Type:** recognition. **Recipient:** for male ● Miss Tall International. **Frequency:** annual. **Type:** recognition ● TCI Scholarship Award. **Frequency:** annual. **Type:** scholarship. **Recipient:** for tall students who are under 21 years of age ● Woman of the Year. **Frequency:** annual. **Type:** recognition. **Recipient:** for female. **Affiliated With:** National Marfan Foundation. **Formerly:** (1966) American Affiliation of Tall Clubs. **Publications:** *Tall Topix,* annual. Journal. **Price:** available to members only. **Advertising:** accepted ● *There Ought to be a Club for Tall People.* Book ● Newsletter, monthly. Contains executive club minutes. **Price:** free for members. **Circulation:** 4,200. **Advertising:** accepted. Alternate Formats: online ● Directory, periodic. **Conventions/Meetings:** annual convention ● annual meeting.

Technology

13027 ■ SIMPUTER (USA)
Hickory Grove Bus. Park
6630-J E Harris Blvd.
Charlotte, NC 28215
Ph: (704)535-4774
Fax: (704)567-2534
E-mail: anything@simputerusa.org
URL: http://www.simputerusa.org
Contact: Roger Deora, Pres.
Description: Provides access to computer technology. Offers positive option for disposal of no longer needed cell phones and computer equipment. Collects cell phones and computer equipment donated by businesses and individuals. Provides computers, training, office equipment and other technical support to non-profits in need. **Telecommunication Services:** electronic mail, roselynl@simputerusa.org ● electronic mail, rdeora@simputerusa.org.

Technology Education

13028 ■ SeniorNet
900 Lafayette St., Ste.604
Santa Clara, CA 95050

Ph: (408)615-0699
Free: (800)747-6848
Fax: (408)615-0928
E-mail: kfabos@hq.seniornet.org
URL: http://www.seniornet.org
Contact: Kristin Fabos, Exec. Dir.
Founded: 1986. **Membership Dues:** individual, $40 (annual) ● individual, $60 (biennial) ● individual, $85 (triennial). **Multinational. Description:** Represents the interests of computer-using adults, aged 50 and older. Provides older adults with education for and access to computer technologies to enhance their lives and share their knowledge and wisdom. Collaborates on research on older adults and technology. Teaches older adults to use computers and communications technologies to accomplish a variety of tasks. **Telecommunication Services:** electronic mail, members@hq.seniornet.org. **Publications:** *Newsline,* quarterly. Newsletter. Contains news about the organization and technologies that would be useful for older adults. Alternate Formats: online ● Annual Report, annual. Alternate Formats: online.

Temperance

13029 ■ American Health and Temperance Association (AHTA)
c/o Dr. DeWitt S. Williams, Dir.
12501 Old Columbia Pike
Silver Spring, MD 20902
Ph: (301)680-6733
Fax: (301)680-6464
E-mail: dewitt.williams@nad.adventist.org
URL: http://www.nadhealthministries.org
Contact: Dr. DeWitt S. Williams, Dir.
Founded: 1826. **Members:** 622,000. **Staff:** 14. **Regional Groups:** 9. **State Groups:** 58. **Local Groups:** 300. **Description:** Seeks to publicize, through popular education, the effects of alcoholic beverages, tobacco, and narcotics; foster health; promote an alcohol and drug-free way of life. Conducts research programs and offers children's services. Maintains speakers' bureau. **Convention/Meeting:** none. **Libraries: Type:** reference. **Holdings:** 300. **Committees:** Education; Promotion. **Formerly:** American Health and Temperance Society; (1982) American Temperance Society. **Publications:** *Health Connection Catalog,* annual. **Price:** free. **Advertising:** accepted ● *Listen,* monthly ● *Vibrant Life,* bimonthly ● *Winner,* 9/year.

13030 ■ International Health and Temperance Association (IHTA)
12501 Old Columbia Pike
Silver Spring, MD 20904
Ph: (301)680-6702 (301)680-6707
Fax: (301)680-6707
URL: http://www.health20-20.org
Contact: Dr. Peter Landless, Assoc. Dir.
Founded: 1947. **Members:** 650,000. **Staff:** 2. **Regional Groups:** 68. **State Groups:** 20. **Local Groups:** 2. **Multinational. Description:** Seeks to "enlighten the public concerning the harmful effects of alcohol, tobacco, and narcotics and to mount an educational campaign to solve these problems." Promotes principles of health and temperance. **Libraries: Type:** reference. **Holdings:** 3,200; books. **Subjects:** health and temperance, drugs and abuse. **Computer Services:** Mailing lists. **Affiliated With:** International Commission for the Prevention of Alcoholism and Drug Dependency. **Formerly:** (1982) International Temperance Association. **Publications:** *Listen,* monthly. **Conventions/Meetings:** quinquennial meeting.

13031 ■ National Temperance and Prohibition Council (NTPC)
PO Box 532
Richardson, TX 75083-0532
Ph: (972)235-4960 (517)321-2012
Fax: (972)690-4189

E-mail: unalcohol@aol.com
Contact: Howard Lydick, Pres.
Founded: 1913. **Members:** 53. **Membership Dues:** organization, $25 (annual). **Description:** National temperance, prohibition or reform groups, and religious denominations; represents an estimated 10,000,000 individuals. Coordinates efforts by member organizations to promote total abstinence for the individual and prohibition for the nation. The council works for the passage of legislation, especially at the national level, which will restrict the advertising, distribution, and sale of alcoholic beverages. **Publications:** none. **Committees:** Legislative; Resolutions. **Conventions/Meetings:** annual conference (exhibits) - always March.

13032 ■ National Woman's Christian Temperance Union (WCTU)

c/o Frances Williard Memorial Library Archives
1730 Chicago Ave.
Evanston, IL 60201-4585
Ph: (847)864-1397
Fax: (847)864-9497
E-mail: donwert@msn.com
URL: http://www.wctu.org
Contact: Rita Kaye Wert, Pres.
Founded: 1874. **Members:** 5,000. **Membership Dues:** regular, $10 (annual). **Staff:** 4. **Budget:** $250,000. **State Groups:** 35. **Local Groups:** 500. **Description:** Nonpartisan, interdenominational Christian women dedicated to educating America's youth about the harmful effects of alcohol, illegal drugs, and tobacco on the human body and American society. Seeks to build sentiment for total abstinence through teaching the effects of alcohol on the mental, moral, social, spiritual and physical well-being of the individual and the nation. Promotes essay, poster, picture coloring, and speech medal contests as well as intercollegiate oratorical contests on alcohol and related problems; produces literature on temperance for use in schools and churches; sponsors total abstinence training camps for children and youth; makes available research materials to professionals and students. Research and educational programs deal with such topics as alcohol and traffic accidents; consumer expenditures; teenage drinking; per capita consumption of alcohol; economic aspects; tobacco and health; gambling; illegal drugs; and pornography. Sponsors Youth Temperance Council (ages 13-21) and Loyal Temperance Legion (ages 6-12). Maintains Frances E. Willard Home as a museum and maintains Frances Willard Memorial Library. **Libraries: Type:** reference. **Holdings:** 5,000. **Subjects:** alcohol, narcotics, tobacco, gambling, prohibition, women's movement. **Awards:** Annie Wittenmyer White Ribbon Award. **Type:** recognition. **Recipient:** for significant contribution to the cause of the organization. **Departments:** Christian Outreach; Education; Home Protection; Legislation/Citizenship; Public Relations; Social Service. **Publications:** *Promoter*, quarterly. Newsletter. Contains samples of new literature. **Price:** $2.50. **Circulation:** 550 ● *The Union Signal*, quarterly. Journal. Includes factual timely articles on alcohol, tobacco and illegal drugs. **Price:** $8.00/year. ISSN: 0041-7033. **Circulation:** 550. **Conventions/Meetings:** annual convention and lecture (exhibits) - always August.

Thanatology

13033 ■ Americans for Better Care of the Dying

1700 Diagonal Rd., Ste.635
Alexandria, VA 22314
Ph: (703)647-8505
Fax: (703)837-1233
E-mail: info@abcd-caring.org
URL: http://www.abcd-caring.org
Contact: Atty. Charles Sabatino Esq., Dir.
Founded: 1997. **Members:** 150. **Staff:** 1. **Description:** Strives to improve the experience of the last phase of life for all Americans. Advocates the interest of patients and families. Works to improve communication between providers and patients.

13034 ■ Center for Death Education and Bioethics (CDEB)

c/o Gerry Cox, PhD, Dir.
Univ. of Wisconsin - La Crosse
SOC/ARC Dept. - 435 NH
1725 State St.
La Crosse, WI 54601-3742
Ph: (608)785-6784
Fax: (608)785-8486
E-mail: cdeb@uwlax.edu
URL: http://www.uwlax.edu/sociology/cde&b
Contact: Gerry Cox PhD, Dir.
Founded: 1969. **Staff:** 3. **Description:** Pioneering program in death education designed to bring recent and relevant ideas, information, and insights concerning death to the public. Sponsors original research into grief and bereavement as well as studies of attitudes and responses to death and dying. Conducts television, newspaper, college and university classes, symposia, and workshops for care-giving professions. Provides research opportunities for graduate and undergraduate students and speakers for regional and national conclaves. **Formerly:** (1999) Center for Death Education and Research. **Publications:** *Illness, Crises and Loss*, quarterly. Journal. ISSN: 1054-1373.

13035 ■ International Institute for the Study of Death (IISD)

1000 Island Blvd., No. 512
Aventura, FL 33160
Ph: (305)936-1408
Fax: (305)936-1408
E-mail: srf5@juno.com
Contact: Arthur S. Berger, Dir.
Founded: 1985. **Members:** 85. **Description:** Investigative body of cross-cultural and interdisciplinary scholars and scientists interested in issues raised by death and dying. Seeks to nurture dialogue between academics in religion, nursing, medicine, philosophy, psychology, and parapsychology regarding the areas of death and dying. Hopes to develop new methods of thinking and investigation in the subjects of death and dying. Facilitates exchange of ideas with members. **Affiliated With:** Survival Research Foundation. **Formerly:** (1986) International Institute for the Study of Death and Immortality.

13036 ■ Living/Dying Project (L/DP)

PO Box 357
Fairfax, CA 94978-0357
Ph: (415)456-3915
E-mail: info@livingdying.org
URL: http://www.livingdying.org
Contact: Dr. Dale Borglum, Exec. Dir.
Founded: 1977. **Staff:** 2. **Budget:** $60,000. **Regional Groups:** 2. **Description:** Seeks to "consciously and compassionately explore life through the mirror of the dying process." Provides local telephone and mail counseling services and outreach services to terminally ill patients. Provides training for health care professionals and the general public around North America. Maintains speakers' bureau. **Publications:** Newsletter, periodic. **Conventions/Meetings:** workshop.

13037 ■ William Wendt Center for Loss and Healing

4201 Connecticut Ave. NW, Ste.300
Washington, DC 20008
Ph: (202)624-0010
Fax: (202)624-0062
E-mail: info@wendtcenter.org
URL: http://www.wendtcenter.org
Contact: Ms. Susan Ley, Exec. Dir.
Founded: 1975. **Members:** 1,000. **Staff:** 19. **Description:** Nondenominational organization that provides information, individual and group counseling, and support to individuals of all ages, families, and organizations affected by life-threatening illness or loss or death. Sponsors program, which provides consultative, curriculum, and training resources for state, district, and school administrators, psychologists, counselors, teachers, caregivers, partners, health care professionals, and parents; courses and programs for students in public and private schools;

crisis intervention at the time of a death or other traumatic event, which affects students and coworkers and affected family members. Curriculum topics include personal loss experience, suicide, HIV/AIDS, children, communication, and grief and bereavement. Conducts educational workshops on death and dying for clergy, laypersons, students and professional caregivers. Maintains Friends Program where professionally trained volunteers provide emotional and practical support to individuals who are coping with life-threatening illnesses or problems related to grief, separation, and loss. Makes available a list of educational materials including audiotapes, books, literature, and video tapes for educational purposes. **Libraries: Type:** reference. **Holdings:** 500. **Formerly:** (1978) Saint Francis Burial and Counseling Society; (1999) St. Francis Center. **Publications:** *Centering*, quarterly. Newsletter. **Price:** free. **Circulation:** 5,500. **Conventions/Meetings:** biennial conference - always fall in Washington, DC Metro area.

Therapy

13038 ■ Create A Smile Dental Foundation (CASDF)

607 W Idaho Ave.
Carterville, IL 62918
Ph: (618)985-4964
E-mail: jflora1947@yahoo.com
URL: http://www.casdf.net
Contact: John Flora Sr., Pres./Founder
Founded: 2003. **Members:** 180. **Membership Dues:** non-working people, $15 (annual). **Description:** Provides dental care funding for people who do not have dental insurance especially those in the low-income group, both children and adults. Raises funds, gives free toothpastes and toothbrushes, and sponsor health fairs. **Divisions:** Training Center.

13039 ■ People, Animals, Nature (PAN)

1820 Princeton Cir.
Naperville, IL 60565
E-mail: pan@pan-inc.org
URL: http://www.pan-inc.org
Contact: Debbie Coultis, Founder/Pres./CEO
Founded: 1995. **Membership Dues:** US resident, $30 (annual) ● non-US resident, $35 (annual). **Description:** Seeks to improve the safety and quality of clinical practice in the field of animal assisted therapy. Disseminates information about the vital linkages between healthy human growth, development and education and contact with animals and natural environments. **Programs:** Certificate; Master's. **Publications:** *Kids and Animals: A Healing Partnership*. Video ● *Safe Pets Program, Animals Can Be Victims Of Domestic Violence Too*. Video ● Newsletter. Contains articles of interest to members.

Toxic Exposure

13040 ■ Alliance for Healthy Homes

PO Box 75941
Washington, DC 20013
Ph: (202)543-1147
Fax: (202)543-4466
E-mail: afhh@afhh.org
URL: http://www.afhh.org
Contact: Robert Zdenek, Exec. Dir.
Founded: 1990. **Staff:** 14. **Budget:** $1,300,000. **Description:** Public interest organization dedicated to the elimination of childhood lead poisoning. Seeks to inform health professionals, the general public, and policy makers of the hazards posed by lead and the need for prevention of lead poisoning. Works to strengthen federal policies and programs developing cost-effective strategies for protecting children and targeting resources where most needed and ensuring the development of a national infrastructure for reducing lead hazards. Strives to accelerate national action by keeping pressure on federal agencies, overcoming private sector obstacles, and mobilizing other resources. Conducts lobbying activities. **Committees:** Technical Advisory. **Formerly:** (2004) Alli-

ance to End Childhood Lead Poisoning. **Publications:** *Alliance Alert*, bimonthly. Newsletter. Contains an update on important national developments related to lead poisoning prevention. **Price:** $350.00. **Circulation:** 3,000 ● Brochures ● Also publishes technical, policy, and program guides. **Conventions/Meetings:** conference.

13041 ■ Asbestos Litigation Group (ALG)
5113 Southwest Pkwy., No. 285
Austin, TX 78735
Free: (800)443-1757
E-mail: inquiry@motleyrice.com
URL: http://www.motleyrice.com
Contact: Ronald Motley, Pres.
Founded: 1979. **Members:** 150. **Description:** Comprised of lawyers representing litigants in asbestos-related disease cases throughout the U.S. **Additional Websites:** http://www.asbestoslitigationgroup.com. **Conventions/Meetings:** semiannual meeting.

13042 ■ Beyond Pesticides - National Coalition Against the Misuse of Pesticides (NCAMP)
701 E St. SE, Ste.200
Washington, DC 20003
Ph: (202)543-5450
Fax: (202)543-4791
E-mail: info@beyondpesticides.org
URL: http://www.beyondpesticides.org
Contact: Jay Feldman, Exec. Dir.
Founded: 1981. **Members:** 1,400. **Membership Dues:** individual, $25 (annual) ● low income, $15 (annual) ● all-volunteer organization, $30 (annual) ● public interest organization, $50 (annual) ● corporate, $100 (annual). **Staff:** 5. **Budget:** $400,000. **Description:** Individuals and consumer, environmental, farming, health, labor, and church organizations concerned with pesticide hazards and safety. Seeks to advance national and international awareness of public health, environmental, and economic problems caused by pesticides; to protect individuals exposed to pesticides. Works to improve legislation, regulation, and enforcement affecting pesticide use and to stress a systematic approach emphasizing preventive public health measures to control pesticides from production through use and disposal. Promotes alternatives to pesticide use such as integrated pest management, which ensures reduced soil and water contamination and lower residues in food. Stresses that these alternatives will reduce environmental damage, ease economic burdens, and improve the general health of the public. Collects and disseminates information and monitors governmental activities. **Libraries: Type:** reference. **Holdings:** 2,000. **Formerly:** (2001) National Coalition Against the Misuse of Pesticides. **Publications:** *Legislative Alerts*, periodic ● *Pest Control Without Toxic Chemicals*. Brochure. **Price:** $2.00 ● *Pesticide Safety: Myths and Facts*. Pamphlet ● *Pesticides and You*, quarterly. Newsletter. **Price:** included in membership dues. Alternate Formats: online ● *Poison Poles: Their Toxic Trail and the Safer Alternatives*. Report. **Price:** $22.00 ● *Publications List* ● *Safety at Home: A Guide to the Hazards of Lawn and Garden Pesticides*. Report. **Price:** $11.00 ● *Technical Report*, monthly. Provides the most current information on pesticide issues. **Price:** $50.00 ● *Unnecessary Risks*. Report. **Price:** $10.00 ● Reports ● Brochures. **Price:** $2.00. **Conventions/Meetings:** annual conference and workshop (exhibits) - always March/April, in Washington, DC or California.

13043 ■ Black Lung Association (BLA)
c/o Bill Bailey
PO Box 872
Crab Orchard, WV 25827
Ph: (304)252-9654
E-mail: webmaster@chaos.x-philes.com
URL: http://chaos.x-philes.com/home/blacklung/index.html
Contact: Bill Bailey, Contact
Founded: 1968. **Members:** 73,000. **Regional Groups:** 14. **State Groups:** 7. **Local Groups:** 2. **Description:** Working miners, disabled miners, and friends. Objectives are to promote safer working

conditions for coal miners and just compensation for disabled miners. Strives for increases in: mine health and safety standards; state and federal benefits for victims of black lung (pneumoconiosis), and other chronic respiratory and pulmonary diseases caused by coal dust; Social Security disability insurance benefits; workmen's compensation; hospitalization and pension benefits for disabled miners and the widows and orphans of miners who have died as a result of their occupation. Attempts to secure better political representation for miners. Maintains speakers' bureau; compiles statistics; conducts research programs. **Awards: Type:** recognition. **Affiliated With:** United Mine Workers of America. **Publications:** *Black Bulletin*, biweekly ● *Federal Black Lung Journal*, bimonthly ● *United Mine Workers Journal*, periodic ● Directory, biennial ● Newsletter, monthly.

13044 ■ CURE Formaldehyde Poisoning Association (CURE)
9255 Lynnwood Rd.
Waconia, MN 55387
Ph: (952)442-4665
Contact: Connie Smrecek, Exec. Officer
Founded: 1980. **Description:** Individuals, health professionals, and attorneys who share an interest in the toxic effects of formaldehyde. Seeks to educate health and legal professionals concerning problems caused by formaldehyde. Lobbies on matters relating to formaldehyde. Conducts seminars. CURE is an acronym for Citizens United to Reduce Emissions (of Formaldehyde Poisoning Association). **Formerly:** Save Us From Formaldehyde Environmental Repercussions; (1985) SUFFER. **Publications:** *Environmental Guardian*, 4/year. **Conventions/Meetings:** annual meeting.

13045 ■ Hawaii Heptachlor Research and Education Foundation (HHR&EF)
c/o Sherry P. Broder, Esq., Attorney-at-Law
841 Bishop St., Ste.800
Honolulu, HI 96813
Ph: (808)589-2963
Fax: (808)531-8411
E-mail: info@heptachlor.org
Contact: Willis Butler MD, Pres./Dir.
Founded: 1987. **Members:** 7. **Staff:** 1. **Budget:** $85,000. **Description:** Promotes public health and safety through medical and scientific research, and public education programs concerning the effects of pesticides and other toxic substances such as heptachlor, a chlorinated hydrocarbon pesticide. Conducts educational projects. **Libraries: Type:** reference; open to the public. **Awards: Type:** grant. **Recipient:** for medical monitoring and research projects. **Computer Services:** database, references to heptachlor and other organochlorinated pesticides and their effects on animals and humans. **Programs:** Hawaii Heptachlor Health Effects Research Program. **Conventions/Meetings:** annual meeting, review of research projects funded by the foundation.

13046 ■ National Institute for Chemical Studies (NICS)
2300 MacCorkle Ave. SE
Charleston, WV 25304
Ph: (304)346-6264
Fax: (304)346-6349
E-mail: nicsinfo@nicsinfo.org
URL: http://www.nicsinfo.org
Contact: Deepay Mukerjee, Pres./CEO
Founded: 1985. **Staff:** 4. **Description:** Participants include representatives of the chemical industry, people living adjacent to chemical plants (plant neighbors), emergency responders, and other interested individuals. Serves as liaison between the chemical industry and the public. Conducts research on environmental and chemical safety issues and shares results with the public and all stakeholders. Provides training on variety of relevant topics; sponsors conferences. Provides services nationally. **Conventions/Meetings:** periodic conference.

13047 ■ National Pesticide Information Center (NPIC)
Oregon State Univ.
333 Weniger Hall
Corvallis, OR 97331-8574
Free: (800)858-7378

Fax: (541)737-0761
E-mail: npic@ace.orst.edu
URL: http://npic.orst.edu
Contact: Dr. Terry Miller, Dir.
Staff: 12. **Languages:** English, Spanish. **Description:** Provides information on a wide variety of pesticide-related topics, including pesticide product information, information on the recognition and management of pesticide poisonings, toxicology, environmental chemistry, referrals for laboratory analyses, investigation of pesticide incidents, emergency treatment information, safety information, health and environmental effects, and clean-up and disposal procedures. **Libraries: Type:** reference. **Subjects:** toxicology, pesticides, agricultural chemicals, food safety. **Computer Services:** database, environmental and chemical properties ● database, health information ● database, product, label and MSDS. **Telecommunication Services:** TDD, (541)-737-1197. **Formerly:** National Pesticide Information Clearinghouse; National Pesticide Telecommunications Network. **Publications:** Brochure. Alternate Formats: online ● Annual Report, annual. Alternate Formats: online.

13048 ■ Northwest Coalition for Alternatives to Pesticides (NCAP)
PO Box 1393
Eugene, OR 97440-1393
Ph: (541)344-5044
Fax: (541)344-6923
E-mail: info@pesticide.org
URL: http://www.pesticide.org
Contact: Norma Grier, Exec. Dir.
Founded: 1977. **Members:** 2,000. **Membership Dues:** basic, $25 (annual) ● associate, $50 (annual) ● sustaining, $100 (annual) ● limited income, $15 (annual) ● advocate, $75 (annual) ● benefactor, $500 (annual). **Staff:** 9. **Description:** Works to protect people and the environment by advancing healthy solutions to pest problems. **Libraries: Type:** reference; open to the public. **Holdings:** articles, books, clippings, periodicals. **Subjects:** pesticides, alternatives to pesticides, sustainable agriculture, inert ingredients, pesticide-free parks, organic food in schools. **Telecommunication Services:** electronic mail, ngrier@pesticide.org. **Publications:** *Journal of Pesticide Reform*, quarterly. **Price:** free for members; $5.00 for each back issue; $15.00 for a complete volume of back issues; $25.00 /year for nonmembers. ISSN: 0893-357X. **Circulation:** 1,800 ● Brochures ● Brochure ● Reports. **Conventions/Meetings:** annual board meeting and meeting ● annual meeting.

13049 ■ Pesticide Action Network North America Regional Center (PANNA RC)
49 Powell St., Ste.500
San Francisco, CA 94102
Ph: (415)981-1771
Fax: (415)981-1991
E-mail: panna@panna.org
URL: http://www.panna.org
Contact: Monica Moore, Co-Dir./Program Dir.
Founded: 1984. **Membership Dues:** basic, $35 (annual). **Staff:** 17. **Budget:** $672,000. **Languages:** English, French, Spanish, Thai. **Description:** Part of an international coalition of citizens' groups and individuals who advocate adoption of ecologically sound practices in place of pesticide use. **Libraries: Type:** open to the public. **Holdings:** 4,000; articles, audio recordings, books, reports. **Subjects:** toxicology, health, environment, developing countries, alternatives, IPM, biotechnology, legislation, labor, pest management, industry profiles, online information, food security, pesticides. **Computer Services:** database, PESTIS: contains pesticide reform-related material generated by NGOs ● online services, PAN-UPS, a weekly pesticide-related news service. **Telecommunication Services:** electronic mail, mhm@panna.org. **Formerly:** (1989) Pesticide Education and Action Project. **Publications:** *Alternatives to Methyl Bromide: Excerpts from the U.N. Methyl Bromide Technical Options Committee Assessment 1995* (in English and Spanish). **Price:** $5.00 ● *Demise of the Dirty Dozen Chart*. Gives registration status of 18 hazardous pesticides in over 75 countries. **Price:**

$3.00 ● *Dirty Dozen Fact Sheets* (in English and Spanish). Contains updated summaries of the health and environmental effects of the Dirty Dozen pesticides. **Price:** $5.00 ● *Global Pesticide Campaigner*, quarterly. Includes features on the pesticide industry, sustainable agriculture, and other related topics globally. **Price:** $35.00/year. **ISSN:** 1055-548X. **Circulation:** 4,000. **Booklets** ● **Manuals** ● **Publishes** additional books not listed here. List available. **Conventions/Meetings:** semiannual board meeting, includes steering committee ● periodic conference.

13050 ■ Rachel Carson Council (RCC)

PO Box 10779
Silver Spring, MD 20914-0779
Ph: (301)593-7507
Fax: (301)593-6251
E-mail: rccouncil@aol.com
URL: http://members.aol.com/rccouncil/ourpage
Contact: Dr. Diana Post VMD, Exec. Dir.

Founded: 1965. **Membership Dues:** associate, $25 (annual). **Staff:** 3. **Budget:** $100,000. **Description:** Seeks to inform and advise people and institutions about the effects of pesticides that threaten the health, welfare, and survival of living organisms and biological systems. Promotes alternative, environmentally benign pest management strategies to encourage healthier life styles. Fosters a sense of wonder and respect towards nature. **Libraries: Type:** reference; lending. **Holdings:** 700; audio recordings, books, periodicals, video recordings. **Subjects:** environmental contamination, pesticides, alternative pest control methods. **Computer Services:** database, pesticides. **Programs:** Green Mantle; Resource Center; Wildlife Resource. **Formerly:** (1979) Rachel Carson Trust for the Living Environment. **Publications:** *Basic Guide to Pesticides.* Book. Alternate Formats: online ● *Cancer and Pesticides.* Booklet ● *EcoHeal Integrated Pest Management (IPM) for Outdoors.* Booklet ● *Health-Based Integrated Pest Management (IPM) for Indoors.* Booklet ● *Least Toxic Freshwater Mosquito Control.* Booklet ● *Out of Control: Pesticides Adrift.* Booklet ● *Parkinson's and Pesticides.* Booklet ● *Pesticides and the West Nile Virus in Maryland.* Booklet ● *Pesticides, People and Nature.* Journal. **Price:** $72.00 /year for individuals; $180.00 /year for institutions ● *RCC News*, annual. Newsletter. Includes articles on the effects of pesticides. **Conventions/Meetings:** semiannual workshop, for the general public.

13051 ■ Tobacco Control Resource Center (TCRC)

102 The Fenway
Cushing Hall, Ste.117
Boston, MA 02115
Ph: (617)373-2026
Fax: (617)373-3672
E-mail: r.daynard@neu.edu
URL: http://www.tobacco.neu.edu
Contact: Prof. Richard A. Daynard PhD, Pres.

Founded: 1979. **Staff:** 18. **Description:** Brings together doctors, lawyers, public health officials, and academics. Encourages product liability suits against the tobacco products marketers in order to: compensate victims of tobacco-related diseases and injuries such as cancer or burns; discourage smoking among teenagers; publicize the effects of smoking on health. Works for an end to the "disinformation campaign" of the tobacco companies in their understating of the dangers of tobacco. Acts as information clearinghouse. **Projects:** Endgame; Internet; Massachusetts Coalition for a Healthy Future; NCI; Tobacco Products Liability. **Publications:** *Tobacco on Trial*, 8/year. Newsletter. Covers related liability cases against tobacco companies. **Price:** $35.00 /year for individuals; $95.00 /year for institutions. **Circulation:** 300. Alternate Formats: diskette ● *The Tobacco Products Liability Reporter.* Journal. Features an accurate chronicle of tobacco litigation, including key opinions and litigation documents. **Conventions/Meetings:** annual conference and seminar, gathering of lawyers, scientists, politicians, physicians, and activists interested in tobacco control.

13052 ■ White Lung Association (WLA)

PO Box 1483
Baltimore, MD 21203-1483
Ph: (410)243-5864
E-mail: jfite@whitelung.org
URL: http://www.whitelung.org
Contact: James Fite, Natl. Sec.

Founded: 1979. **Members:** 30,000. **Membership Dues:** individual, $20 (annual) ● life, $100. **Staff:** 4. **Budget:** $110,000. **Multinational. Description:** A self-help organization for those with conditions associated with exposure to asbestos. Serves as a clearinghouse providing information on legal and medical assistance to asbestos victims and interested persons. Conducts investigations of suspected contamination. Maintains speakers' bureau; conducts charitable programs to ban asbestos use. **Libraries: Type:** by appointment only. **Holdings:** 15,000. **Subjects:** asbestos. **Departments:** Asbestos Abatement; Inspection. **Publications:** *Asbestos Watch*, monthly. Newsletter. **Price:** $35.00 each. **Circulation:** 600. Alternate Formats: online. **Conventions/Meetings:** semiannual board meeting (exhibits) - always January and July ● periodic conference and seminar.

Transgender

13053 ■ National Transgender Advocacy Coalition (NTAC)

PO Box 76027
Washington, DC 20013
Ph: (978)373-8898
E-mail: ntac@comcast.net
URL: http://www.ntac.org
Contact: Vanessa Edwards Foster, Dir.

Founded: 1999. **Description:** Serves as political advocacy working to establish and maintain rights of all transgendered, intersexed, and gender-variant people to live and work without fear of violence or discrimination.

Transportation

13054 ■ Association for Commuter Transportation (ACT)

1444 I St. NW, Ste.700
Washington, DC 20005
Ph: (202)712-9021
E-mail: info@actweb.org
URL: http://www.actweb.org
Contact: Jon W. Martz, Pres./Chm.

Founded: 1976. **Members:** 1,000. **Membership Dues:** organization, $575 (annual) ● individual, $375 (annual). **Staff:** 4. **Budget:** $600,000. **Regional Groups:** 15. **Multinational. Description:** Employers; transportation, energy, ride-sharing, relocation, and development planners and engineers; government representatives; academic and corporate researchers; interested individuals. Promotes alternatives to the solo commute to increase mobility, reduce congestion, and improve air quality. **Computer Services:** database. **Telecommunication Services:** electronic mail, jon.martz@vpsiinc.com. **Committees:** Membership; National Conference; Professional Development. **Councils:** Commuter Choice; Public Policy; Telework; University; Van Pool. **Absorbed:** (1985) Association of Ridesharing Professionals. **Formerly:** (1984) National Association of Van Pool Operators. **Publications:** *Membership Brochure.* Alternate Formats: online ● *TDM Review*, quarterly. Journal. **Price:** included in membership dues; $45.00 /year for nonmembers. **Advertising:** accepted ● *TDM Tool Kit.* **Price:** $40.00 for members; $75.00 for nonmembers ● *TMA Directory: Directory of Transportation Management Associations*, periodic. Indexed by organization and state. **Price:** $25.00 for members; $50.00 for nonmembers. **Advertising:** accepted ● *TMA Handbook.* Contains information needed at various stages in a TMA's life cycle. **Price:** $30.00 for members; $50.00 for nonmembers. **Conventions/Meetings:** annual conference (exhibits) ● semiannual TMA Summit - conference.

13055 ■ Association for Safe International Road Travel (ASIRT)

11769 Gainsborough Rd.
Potomac, MD 20854
Ph: (301)983-5252
Fax: (301)983-3663
E-mail: asirt@asirt.org
URL: http://www.asirt.org
Contact: Rochelle Sobel, Pres.

Founded: 1995. **Members:** 400. **Membership Dues:** global traveler (individual), $100 (annual) ● travel smart (individual), $50 (annual) ● travel safe (individual), $35 (annual) ● vanguard (organization), $500 (annual) ● trendsetter (organization), $250 (annual) ● protector (corporate), $5,000 (annual) ● guardian (corporate), $2,500 (annual) ● advocate (corporate), $1,000 (annual). **Multinational. Description:** Promotes road safety through education and advocacy. Collects and analyzes data on road safety worldwide; serves as an information resource; advances legislation designed to reduce traffic fatalities; encourages safe driving habits; promotes rigorous enforcement of traffic regulations; advocates travel to countries with acceptable road safety records. Maintains Speaker's Bureau. **Computer Services:** database, international road statistics ● online services. **Publications:** Brochure ● Newsletter. **Conventions/Meetings:** monthly meeting - always third Sunday.

13056 ■ Bicycle Network (BN)

PO Box 8194
Philadelphia, PA 19101
Ph: (215)222-1253
Fax: (215)222-1253
E-mail: cyclerecycle@hotmail.com
Contact: John Dowlin, Ed.

Founded: 1976. **Members:** 500. **Languages:** English, French, Spanish. **Description:** Advocates the bicycle as a healthful, low-cost, and energy efficient means of transportation. Seeks to demonstrate the practical importance of bicycle transit and pedal technology worldwide. Works for the "velorution" on a global basis. (According to the network, "velorution" is the French-Canadian word for "bicycle revolution.") Disseminates information. Addresses issues such as: safe and practical cycling facilities (parking, commuting, and transport); cyclist education; bicycle integration with public transportation; the role of the bicycle in developing countries. **Libraries: Type:** reference. **Holdings:** 800. **Subjects:** sustainable transportation, pedal technology. **Absorbed:** (1993) The Spokespeople. **Publications:** *Cycle and Recycle* (in English, French, and Spanish), annual. Features a reusable wall calendar. **Price:** $11.00 1-3 copies; $12.00 1-3 copies in Canada; $10.00 4-9 copies; $11.00 4-9 copies in Canada. **Circulation:** 6,000 ● *Network News: The Bicycle Network's Clipping Service*, quarterly. Includes monitoring world bicycle news between 1979-99 and complete set of back issues 1-80. Back issues available to libraries and collectors. **Price:** $6.00 for 10 or more copies; $10.00 for 10 or more copies in Canada; $95.00 plus shipping and handling. **Circulation:** 6,000. **Conventions/Meetings:** annual conference and seminar ● seminar ● workshop.

13057 ■ Coalition Against Bigger Trucks (CABT)

901 N Pitt St., Ste.310
Alexandria, VA 22314
Ph: (703)535-3131
Free: (888)CAB-T123
Fax: (703)535-3322
E-mail: info@cabt.org
URL: http://www.cabt.org

Description: Individuals and organizations. Opposes use of longer and heavier trucks on public roads. Conducts grass roots campaigns to insure more effective regulation of truck transport; works to improve the safety of public roads and highways; sponsors educational programs; lobbies government agencies on highway safety and trucking regulation issues. **Publications:** Newsletter. Alternate Formats: online.

13058 ■ International Bicycle Fund (IBF)

4887 Columbia Dr. S
Seattle, WA 98108-1919
Ph: (206)767-0848

Fax: (206)767-0848
E-mail: ibike@ibike.org
URL: http://www.ibike.org.
Contact: David Mozer, Dir.
Founded: 1984. **Staff:** 1. **Budget:** $35,000. **Non-membership. Multinational. Description:** Promotes transportation by bicycle. In Africa, promotes bicycle transportation as a means of reducing urban pollution and traffic congestion, increasing efficiency and productivity, and encouraging responsible urban planning and rural development. In the U.S., stresses safety issues and the economic and environmental advantages of bicycle transportation. Sponsors Bicycle Africa, an educational travel program to further international understanding. Conducts workshops on bicycle safety education. Makes available slide/lecture presentations on bicycle transportation planning, economic development, international studies, and bicycle safety. **Convention/Meeting:** none. **Awards:** Student Bicycle Essay Contest. **Frequency:** annual. **Type:** monetary. **Recipient:** for best essay in age group. **Publications:** *Bicycle and Development.* Report ● *Bicycle Helmets.* Brochure. **Price:** $1.00 ● *Bicycle Safety: What Every Parent Should Know.* Brochure. **Price:** $1.00 ● *Bicycling in Africa.* Book. **Price:** $14.95 ● *Bicyclist's Dilemma in African Cities.* Report. **Price:** $3.00 ● *Flying With Your Bicycles.* Features a summary of baggage regulations for bicycles on 40 major airlines. Provides hints and strategies for packing and flying with a bike. **Price:** $4.00 ● *IBF Bike Trailer: Assembly Instructions.* Report. **Price:** $5.00 ● *Language in Cross-Cultural Understanding.* Report. **Price:** $3.00 ● *Selecting and Repairing A Bicycle for Travel in Remote Areas.* Report. **Price:** $5.00 ● *Share the Trail.* Brochure. **Price:** $1.00 ● *Survey of Baggage of Regulations for Bicycles.* Report. **Price:** $5.00 ● *Transportation, Bicycles and Development In Africa.* Report. **Price:** $3.00 ● *Transportation Patterns in Nairobi.* Report. **Price:** $3.00.

13059 ■ National Association of Transit Consumer Organizations (NATCO)
Address Unknown since 2007
Founded: 1981. **Members:** 50. **Staff:** 2. **Local Groups:** 37. **Description:** Transit consumer and environmental organizations; appointed advisory committees reporting to transit operating authorities; other organizations supporting citizen participation for improved mass transit. Seeks to maintain and improve urban transit services. Provides information to members on transit consumer advocacy, and serves as a national spokesperson for transit users to Congress and regulatory agencies. Works for the continuance of federal and local funding for public transit; improves and increases public participation in mass transit by encouraging appropriate regulations requiring public hearings and advisory councils; increases public recognition of mass transit; encourages innovative transportation techniques in the planning, construction, scheduling, operation, and funding of transit services. Maintains 100 volume library and speakers' bureau. Conducts research programs. **Computer Services:** directory ● membership list, subject to members' authorization ● Mailing lists, upon request. **Also Known As:** Transit Advocacy. **Publications:** *For the Ride,* periodic. Newsletter. Includes information on transit consumer activities and legislative issues. **Advertising:** not accepted ● *Listing of Major U.S. Transit Modes* ● Directory, annual. **Advertising:** not accepted. **Conventions/Meetings:** annual meeting.

13060 ■ National Motorists Association (NMA)
402 W 2nd St.
Waunakee, WI 53597
Ph: (608)849-6000
Free: (800)882-2785
Fax: (608)849-8697
E-mail: nma@motorists.org
URL: http://www.motorists.org
Contact: James J. Baxter, Pres.
Founded: 1982. **Members:** 6,500. **Membership Dues:** individual, $35 (annual) ● family, $45 (annual) ● business, $75 (annual). **Staff:** 5. **State Groups:**

50. **For-Profit. Description:** Works to protect the rights of motorists; enhance personal mobility; implement rational traffic laws; and improve driver skills and driver courtesy. Supports physical improvements in the highway environment; the return of integrity to user fee taxation and expenditures; speed limits that are set according to sound engineering principles; and the elimination of "speed traps", arbitrary and abusive insurance company practices and discriminatory traffic regulations. Seeks to find ways to improve driver education and accommodation of the physically impaired. Contracts a lobbyist and compiles driver-related statistics. Includes additional benefits to members such as: "special alerts" free information from experts on numerous topics, and ticket fighting assistance. **Libraries: Type:** reference. **Holdings:** 100. **Subjects:** all motorist issues. **Additional Websites:** http://www.speedtrap.org, http://www.roadblock.org. **Programs:** Attorney Referral; Traffic Justice. **Formerly:** (1987) Citizens Coalition for Rational Traffic Laws; (1990) Citizens for Rational Traffic Laws. **Publications:** *Driving Freedoms,* bimonthly. Newsletter. Contains information on traffic laws, motorist issues and rights as a driver. **Price:** included in membership dues. **Circulation:** 6,800. **Advertising:** accepted. Alternate Formats: online ● *Guerilla Ticket Fighter.* Audiotapes. **Price:** $19.95 plus shipping and handling.

Travel

13061 ■ Delta Teen-Lift (DTL)
c/o Delta Sigma Theta Sorority, Inc.
1707 New Hampshire Ave. NW
Washington, DC 20009
Ph: (202)986-2400
Fax: (202)986-2513
E-mail: dstemail@deltasigmatheta.org
URL: http://www.deltasigmatheta.org
Contact: Louise A. Rice PhD, Pres.
Founded: 1963. **Members:** 185,000. **Regional Groups:** 7. **Local Groups:** 800. **Description:** Sponsored by Delta Sigma Theta to raise the aspirations of disadvantaged teenagers by providing travel experiences which would combine first-hand information on educational opportunities and facilities, contact with persons in diversified occupations, and an opportunity to meet and talk with people who have made outstanding contributions to public and private enterprises; Teen-Lift is an organized tour that takes selected young people on trips to educational, business, and cultural centers in metropolitan areas. Provides financial assistance to cover costs of tours. National pilot program encourages the local Delta Sigma Theta chapters to organize and sponsor Teen-Lifts in their areas. **Commissions:** Arts and Letters; Social Action. **Publications:** *Delta,* periodic. Newsletter ● *Delta Journal,* periodic. **Conventions/Meetings:** biennial meeting (exhibits) ● biennial regional meeting.

13062 ■ Federation of American Consumers and Travelers (FACT)
PO Box 104
Edwardsville, IL 62025
Ph: (618)656-0454
Free: (800)872-3228
Fax: (618)656-5369
E-mail: cservice@usafact.org
URL: http://usafact.org
Contact: Vicki Rolens, Managing Dir.
Founded: 1984. **Members:** 1,000,000. **Membership Dues:** regular, $36 (annual). **Description:** Individuals organized to obtain lower prices for merchandise, consumer services, and travel. Disseminates consumer information to members; monitors legislation affecting consumers; conducts educational programs. Provides assistance to members affected by federally-declared disasters. **Libraries: Type:** reference. **Subjects:** money matters, nutrition, childcare, medicine and health, federal programs, travel, insurance tips, energy efficiency, how to prepare for a natural disaster. **Awards:** Classroom and Community Grant Programs. **Frequency:** quarterly. **Type:** grant.

Recipient: for schools at classroom level and communities ● Continuing Education Scholarships. **Frequency:** annual. **Type:** scholarship. **Formed by Merger of:** (1984) Association of American Consumers; National Consumers Council. **Publications:** *FACTFINDER,* quarterly. Newsletter. Covers consumer affairs including information on goods and services, health and safety, insurance, and helpful hints. Contains statistics. **Price:** free.

13063 ■ International Association for Medical Assistance to Travellers (IAMAT)
1623 Military Rd., No. 279
Niagara Falls, NY 14304-1745
Ph: (716)754-4883
Fax: (519)836-3412
E-mail: info@iamat.org
URL: http://www.iamat.org
Contact: Mrs. M.A. Uffer-Marcolongo, Pres.
Founded: 1960. **Members:** 9,500,000. **Staff:** 15. **Multinational. Description:** Serves as division of the Foundation for the Support of International Medical Training. Seeks to make competent medical care available to the traveller around the world by doctors who usually speak English or French and have had medical training in Europe or North America. **Publications:** *Be Aware of Schistosomiasis* ● *Directory of Participating Physicians and Medical Institutions Abroad,* annual ● *How to Protect Yourself Against Malaria* ● *When Hiking Through Latin America, Be Alert to Chagas' Disease.* Pamphlet ● *World Immunization Chart,* annual. Pamphlet. Contains the required and recommended immunizations. ● *World Malaria Risk Chart.* Pamphlet ● *World Schistosomiasis Risk.* Pamphlet ● Also issues world climate charts, world malaria risk chart, world immunization chart, and world schistosomiasis risk chart, be aware of schistosomiasis.

13064 ■ Motorist Information and Services Association (MISA)
229 Madrona Ave. SE
Salem, OR 97302
Ph: (503)373-0864 (503)373-1042
Fax: (503)378-6282
E-mail: info@misaonline.org
URL: http://www.misaonline.org
Contact: Cheryl Gribskov, Exec. Dir.
Founded: 1988. **Members:** 125. **Membership Dues:** government agency, employee, $100 (annual) ● business, association, $250 (annual) ● individual, $125 (annual). **Staff:** 2. **Budget:** $10,000. **National Groups:** 2. **Description:** State transportation and tourism officials and public and private sector travel service providers. Works to improve the effectiveness of informational road signs; seeks to develop alternative means of communicating information to motorists, such as radio loop systems, emergency call box systems, and rest area information programs. **Libraries: Type:** open to the public. **Holdings:** 100; periodicals. **Subjects:** highway signing, tourism. **Computer Services:** database ● online services. **Committees:** Research. **Publications:** *MISA Messenger,* quarterly. Newsletter. Forum for government transportation and tourism agencies and private motorist information providers. **Price:** included in membership dues. **Circulation:** 500. **Advertising:** accepted. **Conventions/Meetings:** annual conference (exhibits) - always in the fall.

13065 ■ Travel Information Service/MossRehab ResourceNet (TIS)
c/o MossRehab Hospital
1200 W Tabor Rd.
Philadelphia, PA 19141-3019
Ph: (215)456-9900
Free: (800)CALL-MOSS
E-mail: staff1@mossresourcenet.org
URL: http://www.mossresourcenet.org/travel.htm
Description: Provides information services by telephone for travelers with physical disabilities on the accessibility of transportation, tourist sites, and accommodations. A division of the Moss Regional Resource and Information Center for individuals with Disabilities. **Telecommunication Services:** teletype, (215)456-9602.

Trucking

13066 ■ Loved Ones and Drivers Support (LOADS)
PO Box 544
Plover, WI 54467-0544
E-mail: support@loads.org
URL: http://www.loads.org
Contact: Kathy Harders, Founder
Founded: 1992. **Description:** Seeks to better the lives of people associated with long-distance trucking relationships. Works to increase the public awareness and advocate for improved relationships with all that are associated with long-distance relationships. Offers support, education, comfort and understanding to those in a trucking relationship.

Unemployment

13067 ■ UWC - Strategic Services on Unemployment and Workers' Compensation (UWC)
1331 Pennsylvania Ave. NW, Ste.600
Washington, DC 20004
Ph: (202)637-3464
Fax: (202)783-1616
E-mail: info@uwcstrategy.org
URL: http://www.uwcstrategy.org
Contact: Douglas J. Holmes, Pres.
Founded: 1933. **Members:** 238. **Staff:** 3. **Description:** Works to serve the business community by promoting Unemployment Insurance (UI) and Workers' Compensation (WC) programs that provide fair benefits to workers at affordable cost to employers and the community. **Awards:** Unemployment Insurance Awards. **Frequency:** annual. **Type:** recognition. **Formerly:** (2003) Strategic Services on Unemployment and Workers' Compensation and the National Foundation for UC & WC. **Publications:** *Highlights of State Unemployment Compensation Laws,* annual. Book. **Conventions/Meetings:** annual Fall Forum for Staff Association Executives - meeting ● annual National Unemployment Insurance Issues Conference, focusing on current issues in public policy and practices relating to UI/ES system - spring.

Urban Affairs

13068 ■ International Healthy Cities Foundation (IHCF)
555 12th St., 10th Fl.
Oakland, CA 94607
Ph: (510)642-1715
Fax: (510)643-6981
E-mail: hcities@uclink4.berkeley.edu
URL: http://www.healthycities.org
Contact: Leonard Duhl MD, Contact
Founded: 1985. **Multinational. Description:** Promotes community ownership of actions to solve quality of life problems. Assists communities in developing their capacities based on their strengths and potentials. Facilitates linkages among people, issues, and resources in order to support the development of "Healthy Cities" initiatives. **Computer Services:** database ● information services.

Vegetarianism

13069 ■ Compassionate Cooks
PO Box 18512
Oakland, CA 94619
Ph: (510)531-2665
E-mail: info@compassionatecooks.com
URL: http://www.compassionatecooks.com
Membership Dues: supporting, $30 (annual) ● sustaining, $60 (annual). **Description:** Seeks to empower people to make informed food choices. Aims to debunk myths about vegetarianism through cooking classes, nutrition workshops, supermarket tours and a cooking DVD. **Computer Services:** data-

base, recipes ● information services, vegetarian resources ● mailing lists.

Veterans

13070 ■ Help Hospitalized Veterans (HHV)
36585 Penfield Ln.
Winchester, CA 92596
Ph: (951)926-4500
Fax: (951)926-3569
E-mail: hhv@hhv.org
URL: http://www.hhv.org
Contact: Mike Lynch, Exec. Dir.
Founded: 1970. **Staff:** 43. **Description:** Seeks to improve the welfare and morale of hospitalized veterans and aid in their mental and physical rehabilitation. Provides arts and crafts materials in kit form to recreation therapy, occupational therapy, and voluntary service departments and wards of Department of Veterans Affairs Medical Centers, state Veterans Nursing Homes, and military hospitals. **Publications:** Newsletter. Alternate Formats: online ● Annual Report, annual.

13071 ■ National Association of Atomic Veterans (NAAV)
11214 Sageland
Houston, TX 77089
Ph: (281)481-1357
E-mail: cmdr@naav.com
URL: http://www.naav.com
Contact: R.J. Ritter, Natl. Commander
Founded: 1979. **Members:** 5,000. **Membership Dues:** regular, $20 (annual) ● life, $200. **Staff:** 7. **Budget:** $45,000. **State Groups:** 40. **Description:** Veterans of U.S. nuclear weapons testing and Nagasaki/Hiroshima occupation forces who now have cancer or other diseases believed to be radiation-related; their widows and interested persons. Works to assure veterans and widows that such diseases are recognized as service-related illnesses and assist in obtaining proper medical attention, compensation, and other benefits through the Veterans Administration. Participates in related legislative activities. **Computer Services:** Online services, data system for Atomic Veteran status information, branch of service, including name, address, nuclear test and number of tests participated in. **Affiliated With:** Disabled American Veterans. **Absorbed:** (1983) Committee for U.S. Veterans of Hiroshima and Nagasaki. **Publications:** *Atomic Veterans News,* quarterly. Newsletter. **Circulation:** 5,000. Alternate Formats: online. **Conventions/Meetings:** annual meeting.

13072 ■ National Association of State Veterans Homes (NASVH)
5211 Auth Rd.
Suitland, MD 20746
Ph: (301)899-7908
Fax: (301)899-8186
E-mail: info@nasvh.org
URL: http://www.nasvh.org
Contact: Mr. Bryan Batulis, Pres.
Founded: 1953. **Members:** 110. **Budget:** $90,000. **State Groups:** 46. **Description:** Represents state supported veterans' homes. Seeks to maintain high standards of domiciliary, nursing home, and hospital care for veterans and eligible family members. Provides a clearinghouse for techniques and expertise in veteran care and in the management of these institutions. Represents the veterans' needs before Congress and the Veterans Administration. Encourages continued federal financial support for building state facilities and for providing care for veterans currently living in state homes. Works to sustain current veterans' benefits. Assists other states in establishing homes. Compiles statistics. **Committees:** Legislative; Veterans Administration Liaison. **Publications:** *LINK,* quarterly ● Directory, annual. **Conventions/Meetings:** annual conference.

13073 ■ National Veterans Outreach Program (NVOP)
c/o American GI Forum
5038 W 127th St.
Alsip, IL 60803

Ph: (708)371-9800
Fax: (708)371-1150
Contact: James Jazo, Pres./CEO
Founded: 1972. **Staff:** 50. **Budget:** $3,000,000. **For-Profit. Description:** A program sponsored by the American G.I. Forum of United States (see separate entry) funded by local, state, and national government contracts. Provides services to the economically disadvantaged, recently separated veterans (within the last 48 months), and Vietnam era veterans. Counsels veterans in making a smooth transition to the civilian community and mobilizes and coordinates all available resources serving veterans. Provides family counseling to Vietnam veterans who served in or near Vietnam between 1961-1972. Works with the private sector and local, state, and national employment services in order to place the economically disadvantaged and veterans in meaningful jobs. Offers V.A. benefit counseling and outreach follow-up and referral, including field counseling, home contacts, public service announcements, and street leaflet distribution. **Affiliated With:** American GI Forum of United States. **Conventions/Meetings:** annual American GI Forum National Conference (exhibits) - always August.

13074 ■ National Veterans Services Fund (NVSF)
PO Box 2465
Darien, CT 06820-0465
Ph: (203)656-0003
Free: (800)521-0198
Fax: (203)656-1957
E-mail: natvetsvc@nvsf.org
URL: http://www.nvsf.org
Contact: Phil Kraft, Pres.
Founded: 1978. **Staff:** 3. **State Groups:** 1. **Non-membership. Description:** Educates and informs the public about the needs of veterans and their families, primarily concerning the Agent Orange and Gulf War Illness issues; to assess the needs and provide limited assistance, relief and referrals to appropriate agencies using programs that combine family-guided case management (service coordination) and advocacy assistance while building social and community support. Administers a national hotline for veterans and their families. Strives to create partnerships with other agencies that make it possible to secure services and equipment at reduced rates or at no cost for families in need. Gives free educational materials including brochures. **Divisions:** Counseling; Medical. **Funds:** Assistance. **Programs:** Independence Technology. **Formerly:** (1983) Agent Orange Victims International.

13075 ■ Tee it up for the Troops
2422 E 117th St., No. 102
Burnsville, MN 55337
Ph: (952)646-2490
E-mail: info@teeitupforthetroops.com
URL: http://www.teeitupforthetroops.com
Contact: James Ball, Pres./Dir.
Description: Helps support the fallen and disabled members of the Armed Forces and their families. Honors and recognizes the needs of all military veterans who have served the nation. Facilitates cooperation and communication among members.

13076 ■ Veterans Education Project (VEP)
PO Box 416
Amherst, MA 01004
Ph: (413)253-4947
E-mail: vep@vetsed.org
URL: http://www.vetsed.org
Contact: Keith D. Snyder, Pres.
Founded: 1982. **Description:** Informs veterans, including those with less than honorable discharges and those who are incarcerated, of their rights to veterans' benefits. Does not represent individual veterans. **Publications:** Also publishes self-help guides.

13077 ■ VietNow National (VN)
1835 Broadway
Rockford, IL 61104
Ph: (815)227-5100
Free: (800)837-8669

E-mail: vnnatl@inwave.com
URL: http://www.vietnow.com
Contact: Rich Sanders, Pres.
Founded: 1980. **Members:** 3,000. **Membership Dues:** full, associate, $15 (annual) ● life, $150. **Staff:** 1. **Local Groups:** 20. **Description:** Veterans (1957-present); interested civilians and other veterans are associate members. Aims to provide a forum through which veterans can help other veterans with problems such as drug abuse, delayed stress syndrome, unemployment, and health problems related to Agent Orange exposure. Attempts to educate the public about those missing in action and prisoners of war who have still not been accounted for. Conducts educational and charitable programs; maintains speaker's bureau and 15 standing committees. **Libraries: Type:** reference. **Holdings:** books, periodicals. **Awards:** VietNow National Scholarship. **Frequency:** annual. **Type:** scholarship. **Recipient:** for children of a full member. **Formerly:** (1992) VietNow. **Publications:** *VietNow Magazine*, quarterly. **Circulation:** 20,000. Alternate Formats: online. **Conventions/Meetings:** monthly board meeting ● annual convention - always May.

Victims

13078 ■ American Society of Victimology (ASV)
c/o Division of Continuing Education
Washburn Univ.
1700 SW Coll. Ave.
Topeka, KS 66621
Ph: (785)231-1010 (203)932-7041
Fax: (785)231-1028
E-mail: mgaboury@newhaven.edu
URL: http://www.american-society-victimology.us
Contact: Mario Gaboury, Pres.
Founded: 2003. **Membership Dues:** individual, $60 (annual) ● institutional, $180 (annual) ● student, $30 (annual) ● life, $300. **Description:** Serves as an American forum for victimologists and as the national voice of academicians and practitioners on all topics related to victimoloy. Provides leadership in the field of victimological education and training. Addresses the needs of victims through research, education and service. **Publications:** Proceedings. **Price:** included in membership dues.

13079 ■ Center for Victims of Torture (CVT)
717 E River Rd.
Minneapolis, MN 55455
Ph: (612)436-4800
Fax: (612)626-2600
E-mail: cvt@cvt.org
URL: http://www.cvt.org
Contact: Douglas A. Johnson MPPM, Exec. Dir.
Founded: 1985. **Multinational. Description:** Provides direct care and rehabilitation services to survivors of politically-motivated torture and their families. Also offers training to health care providers, educators, and social workers; performs torture treatment and human rights research. **Awards:** Eclipse Award. **Frequency:** annual. **Type:** recognition. **Recipient:** to an individual who has given extraordinary service on behalf of torture survivors. **Computer Services:** Mailing lists. **Programs:** Circle of Hope. **Projects:** CVT-Oxford Methodologies Workshop; Former Client Survey; International Capacity-Building; Life Events Measure; Measures of Adaptation; National Capacity-Building; War Problems and Well-being Interviews. **Publications:** *New Neighbors, Hidden Scars*. Handbook. **Price:** $10.00 plus shipping and handling. Alternate Formats: online ● *Resource Manual For Teachers*. Alternate Formats: online ● *Storycloth*, quarterly. Newsletter. **Price:** free for members. Alternate Formats: online ● Bibliography. Alternate Formats: online ● Report.

13080 ■ Institute for Victims of Trauma (IVT)
6801 Market Square Dr.
McLean, VA 22101
Ph: (703)847-8456
Fax: (703)847-0470

E-mail: ivt@microneil.com
Contact: Leila F. Dane PhD, Exec. Dir.
Founded: 1987. **Staff:** 2. **Languages:** English, French. **Description:** Professionals specializing in post-traumatic stress, crisis intervention, and the study of terrorism; a nonpolitical group assisting direct victims of terrorism, accidents, and natural and man-made disasters, as well as victims' families, friends, and associates. Works to respond forcefully, effectively, and quickly to the increasing incidence of stress disorders resulting from the experiences of victims. Protects and promotes victims' health, welfare, and human rights. Provides professional and paraprofessional training in crisis intervention, emergency services, diagnosis and treatment, and counseling; offers services and assistance to organizations whose activities may be susceptible to incidents involving terrorism. Acts as a liaison with governmental and nongovernmental organizations and institutions; operates referral service and Speaker's Bureau. Offers graduate and undergraduate level internships. Conducts research. **Libraries: Type:** reference. **Subjects:** traumatic stress, victimology, terrorism, community violence. **Awards: Frequency:** biennial. **Type:** monetary. **Recipient:** for services in the spirit of the resolution on mental health services to victims of community violence. **Computer Services:** Online services. **Boards:** Advisory. **Affiliated With:** World Federation for Mental Health. **Formerly:** (1989) Institute for Victims of Terrorism. **Publications:** *1994 Conference on Building Tolerance for Diversity*. Proceedings. **Conventions/Meetings:** semiannual conference.

13081 ■ Life After Assault League (LAAL)
1336 W Lindbergh St.
Appleton, WI 54914
Ph: (920)739-4489
Fax: (920)739-1990
Contact: Kay Zibolsky, Founder
Founded: 1986. **Members:** 20,000. **Staff:** 10. **Description:** Christian individuals. Seeks to improve the quality of life and assist in the healing process of victims of sexual assault. Provides counseling and support to assault victims; conducts educational programs and lectures; Jesus Christ centered. **Libraries: Type:** by appointment only. **Holdings:** books. **Subjects:** sexual assault. **Publications:** *Healing Hidden Hurts*. Book. Contains the testimony of LAAL founder and information regarding sexual assault. **Price:** $7.00/copy.

13082 ■ National Association of Crime Victim Compensation Boards (NACVCB)
PO Box 16003
Alexandria, VA 22302
Ph: (703)780-3200
Fax: (703)313-0546
E-mail: nacvcb@nacvcb.org
URL: http://nacvcb.org
Contact: Dan Eddy, Exec. Dir.
Founded: 1978. **Members:** 52. **Description:** State crime victim compensation programs. Objectives are: to develop better methods of administering existing programs; to enhance public awareness of programs for crime victims; to foster the exchange of ideas and experience between agencies that deal with crime victims; to coordinate claim verification for crime victims who are injured in another state; to form liaisons with other victim-oriented groups; to encourage appropriate state and federal legislation relative to crime victims. Operates speakers' bureau. **Libraries: Type:** reference. **Publications:** Directory, periodic ● Newsletter, quarterly. **Price:** $25.00/year. **Circulation:** 750. **Conventions/Meetings:** annual conference and seminar.

13083 ■ National Association of State VOCAL Organizations (NASVO)
Address Unknown since 2007
Founded: 1984. **Members:** 7,000. **Membership Dues:** chapter, $100 (annual) ● individual, $25 (annual). **Staff:** 5. **Budget:** $30,000. **Regional Groups:** 5. **State Groups:** 115. **Local Groups:** 5. **National Groups:** 11. **Languages:** English, Spanish. **Description:** National association of state and local support

groups for men and women who feel they have been unjustly harmed by existing child abuse laws. (VOCAL stands for Victims of Child Abuse Laws.) Promotes legislation that would allow prosecution of individuals who make false child abuse reports; seeks to reform existing laws regarding child abuse. Conducts public education about problems arising from existing child abuse statutes. Maintains speakers' bureau. Provides charitable programs; compiles statistics. **Libraries: Type:** reference. **Holdings:** 5,000. **Subjects:** child abuse, neglect, statistical research; law: family, civil, criminal; evidence, police procedure, medical, mental health. **Awards: Type:** recognition. **Computer Services:** Online services. **Committees:** Political Action. **Affiliated With:** Children's Rights of America. **Publications:** *Corrupted Innocence: The Making of False Accusations*. Video. Provides a history & overview of child protection, problems and stats. **Price:** $10.00. **Circulation:** 250. **Advertising:** not accepted ● *False Accusations of Child Abuse in Divorce/Custody Disputes - NASVO News*. Newsletter. **Price:** $25.00/year. **Circulation:** 40,000. **Advertising:** accepted. Alternate Formats: online ● *Teacher's Facts Brochure* ● *Valuing the American Family: Overview of Child Protection - Problems & Solutions*. Brochure ● *Vocal's Fact Sheet* ● *Vocal's To-Do's and Not-To-Do's When Falsely Accused*. **Conventions/Meetings:** annual Issues of Child Abuse - convention (exhibits) - usually September or October; **Avg. Attendance:** 500.

13084 ■ National Center for Victims of Crime (NCVC)
2000 M St. NW, Ste.480
Washington, DC 20036-3398
Ph: (202)467-8700
Free: (800)FYI-CALL
Fax: (202)467-8701
E-mail: gethelp@ncvc.org
URL: http://www.ncvc.org
Contact: Mary Lou Leary, Exec. Dir.
Founded: 1985. **Members:** 1,800. **Membership Dues:** regular, $75 (annual) ● regular plus, $150 (annual). **Staff:** 40. **Budget:** $3,900,000. **Description:** Aims to function as a national resource center to seek redress for injustices done to crime victims. Promotes public awareness, judicial responsiveness, and social service referrals for crime victims. Compiles statistics on crime and victimization; maintains toll-free information and referral line. Offers national referrals for crime victims to attorneys for civil cases. Provides education through conferences, workshops, seminars, and videocassettes for victims and victims' rights attorneys and organizations. Offers resources for the development of community-based programs for victims of violent crimes; sponsors intern program for students of criminal justice and sociology. **Libraries: Type:** reference. **Holdings:** books. **Subjects:** victim services, victimology, criminal justice. **Computer Services:** database, civil litigation (9,000 annotated cases) ● database, victim's rights issues, state and federal legislation, 30,000 statutes. **Telecommunication Services:** teletype, (800)211-7996. **Committees:** Parallel Justice; Stalking Resource Center. **Projects:** Dating Violence Resource Center/ Teen Victim. **Sections:** Civil Justice; Public Affairs and Legislation; Resource Library and Database; Victim Services. **Formerly:** (1988) Sunny Von Bulow National Victim Advocacy Center. **Publications:** *Networks*, quarterly. Magazine. Contains articles on emerging trends, legislation, key court decisions, innovative programs, and new resources. **Price:** included in membership dues; $5.00 for nonmembers. Alternate Formats: online ● *Pipeline*, quarterly. Newsletter. Focuses exclusively on current victim legislation in Congress and across the 50 states. **Conventions/Meetings:** annual National Conference ● quarterly Training Institute - workshop.

13085 ■ National Child Abuse Defense and Resource Center (NCADRC)
PO Box 638
Holland, OH 43528
Ph: (419)865-0513
Fax: (419)865-0526

E-mail: ncadrc@aol.com
URL: http://www.falseallegation.org/index.shtml
Contact: Kimberly A. Hart, Exec. Dir.
Founded: 1986. **Description:** Provides assistance to individuals who feel they have been falsely accused of child abuse or neglect. Serves as a network for mental health professionals who research child abuse issues. Conducts children's services; maintains speaker's bureau. Compiles statistics. **Libraries: Type:** reference. **Holdings:** 10,000. **Subjects:** psychiatric, psychological, legal materials on child abuse. **Publications:** *Guilty Until Proven Innocent: A Manual for Surviving False Allegations of Child Abuse.* **Price:** $30.50. **Conventions/Meetings:** annual Defending Child Abuse Allegations: The Law, The Science, The Myths, The Reality - conference (exhibits).

13086 ■ National Coalition of Homicide Survivors (NCHS)
c/o Pima County Attorney
32 N Stone, 11th Fl.
Tucson, AZ 85701
Ph: (520)740-5729
Fax: (520)740-5642
E-mail: survivor@pcao.co.pima.az.us
URL: http://www.mivictims.org/nchs
Contact: Gail Leland, Pres.
Founded: 1998. **Description:** Facilitates communication among individuals, professionals and organizations who share an interest in the concerns of homicide survivors. Seeks to share information, resources and ideas, to improve support and victim assistance services to homicide survivors. Conducts regional meetings, conferences and outreach programs for survivors, professionals and organizations. **Telecommunication Services:** hotline, helpline, (520)881-1794.

13087 ■ National Organization for Victim Assistance (NOVA)
510 King St., Ste.424
Alexandria, VA 22314
Ph: (703)535-6682
Free: (800)TRY-NOVA
Fax: (703)535-5500
URL: http://www.trynova.org
Contact: Jeannette M. Adkins, Exec. Dir.
Founded: 1975. **Members:** 5,500. **Membership Dues:** individual, $50 (annual) ● agency, $200 (annual) ● senior/student, $35 (annual) ● sustaining, $100 (annual) ● life, $500 ● patron, $200 (annual) ● individual, outside U.S., $65 (annual) ● life, outside U.S., $650. **Staff:** 8. **Description:** Victim counselors, district attorneys, police officials, mental health professionals, judges, crisis intervention specialists, domestic violence and rape crisis workers, former victims, and others whose purpose is "to express forcefully the victims' claims, too long ignored, for decency, compassion, and justice; to press those claims for the victims of crime and also for the victims of other stark misfortunes; and to ensure that victims' rights are honored by government officials and all others who can aid in the victims' relief and recovery." Offers technical counsel, referral services, and victim assistance training programs; also provides services to victims directly. Serves as clearinghouse on state and federal legislation. Maintains speakers' bureau; conducts educational activities. Sponsors Regional Victim Assistance Training Program and National Victim Rights Week. Compiles statistics. Has established network of service providers to foster communications. **Libraries: Type:** reference. **Awards:** Donald E. Santarelli Public Policy Award. **Frequency:** annual. **Type:** recognition. **Recipient:** to an individual who has demonstrated outstanding public policy leadership ● Edith Surgan Victim Activist Award. **Frequency:** annual. **Type:** recognition. **Recipient:** to victims or survivors who have demonstrated a lifetime commitment to promote rights and services that help change the victims' lives ● George M. Donnelly Crisis Responder of the Year Award. **Frequency:** annual. **Type:** recognition. **Recipient:** to a NOVA affiliated state or local crisis response team ● H. John Heinz III Federal Public Service Award. **Frequency:** annual. **Type:** recognition. **Recipient:** to an individual

working in the federal government who helped in the development of the victim's movement ● John J.P. Dussich Founders Award. **Frequency:** annual. **Type:** recognition. **Recipient:** to the member of the Board of Directors or individual who has devoted extraordinary time, resources, and efforts for the organization ● Margery Fry Victim Service Practitioner Award. **Frequency:** annual. **Type:** recognition. **Recipient:** to an individual who adheres to the highest standard in providing quality victim services ● Marlene A. Young Leadership Award. **Frequency:** annual. **Type:** recognition. **Recipient:** for an individual who has demonstrated leadership in promoting the provision of victims' rights and services ● Morton Bard Allied Professional Award. **Frequency:** annual. **Type:** recognition. **Recipient:** to individual who has developed innovations that helped victims ● **Frequency:** annual. **Type:** recognition. **Recipient:** for outstanding contributions and services ● Stephen Schafer Research Award. **Frequency:** annual. **Type:** recognition. **Recipient:** to an individual with substantial contribution in the field of research ● Tadini Bacigalupi Program of Distinction Award. **Frequency:** annual. **Type:** recognition. **Recipient:** for innovation in service, longevity of the program and use of volunteers ● Volunteer of the Year Award. **Frequency:** annual. **Type:** recognition. **Recipient:** to an individual who has made contributions in the field of crisis response. **Committees:** Domestic Violence; Elderly Victimization; Judiciary; Juvenile Victimization; Law Enforcement; Legislation and Litigation; Minority Victims; Network; Office on Victims; Probation and Parole; Prosecution; Reparations; Sexual Assault; Victim Rights. **Divisions:** Field Services; Resource Development; Victim Services. **Publications:** *Coping with the Iraq/Kuwait Crisis.* Handbook. Alternate Formats: online ● *National Organization for Victim Assistance—Newsletter*, monthly. Includes book reviews, calendar of events, and legislative and research updates. **Price:** included in membership dues; $1.00 for nonmembers ● *Program Directory*, annual ● *Victim Assistance Programs and Resources*, annual. Lists 8000 programs and resources, compensation programs, crisis centers, and incest and abuse centers. **Price:** $22.50 for members; $27.50 for nonmembers ● *Victim Rights and Services: A Legislative Directory*, periodic. Provides state-by-state victim laws and legislation. **Price:** $22.50 for members; $27.50 for nonmembers ● *Victim Rights Campaign*, annual ● *Victim Services System: A Guide to Action* ● Also makes available Victim Rights Week kits. **Conventions/Meetings:** annual Victim Assistance Conference (exhibits).

13088 ■ No Greater Love (NGL)
1750 New York Ave. NW, Ste.1971
Washington, DC 20006
Ph: (202)637-0776
Fax: (202)637-0776
E-mail: remembrance@ngl.org
URL: http://www.ngl.org
Contact: Benjamin Barbin, Communications/Activities Mgr.
Founded: 1971. **Staff:** 5. **Budget:** $1,000,000. **Description:** Provides annual programs of remembrance and care for families of those who died in the service of the U.S. or were victims of terrorism. Conducts humanitarian and educational programs. Functions as a support group for families of hostages. Promoted yellow ribbon pin campaign during the Iran hostage crisis. **Convention/Meeting:** none. **Publications:** Brochure.

13089 ■ September 11th Families' Association
c/o 9-11 Widows and Victims' Families Association
22 Cortlandt St., 20th Fl.
New York, NY 10007
Ph: (212)422-3520
E-mail: donate@911families.org
URL: http://www.911families.org
Contact: Jennifer Adams, Exec. Dir.
Description: Aims to support victims of terrorism. Provides peer support, communication, and representation. Seeks to unite the September 11th community and share resources for long-term recovery.

13090 ■ Survivors Network of Those Abused by Priests (SNAP)
PO Box 6416
Chicago, IL 60680
Ph: (312)409-2720
Free: (877)762-7432
E-mail: snapblaine@hotmail.com
URL: http://www.survivorsnetwork.org
Contact: Barbara Blaine, Pres.
Members: 6,500. **Membership Dues:** survivor, family member or support person, $25 (annual) ● survivor on limited income, $15 (annual) ● associate, $100 (annual). **State Groups:** 60. **Description:** Individuals who have been victims of abuse and exploitation by members of the clergy, their family members and supporters. Gathers and disseminates statistics. Operates Speaker's Bureau. **Computer Services:** database. **Additional Websites:** http://SNAPnetwork.org. **Publications:** *SNAP News*, quarterly. Newsletter. **Price:** free. **Conventions/Meetings:** quarterly meeting.

13091 ■ Victims of Crime and Leniency (VOCAL)
111 N St. Andrews St.
Dothan, AL 36303
Ph: (334)242-7197 (334)279-8300
Free: (866)31-VOCAL
Fax: (334)834-5645
E-mail: joyce@vocalonline.org
URL: http://www.vocalonline.org
Contact: Joyce Miller, Contact
Founded: 1982. **Members:** 2,500. **Membership Dues:** family, $25 (annual) ● agency and organization, $40 (annual). **Staff:** 3. **State Groups:** 13. **Description:** Individuals and their family members who have been victims of crime; businesses and agencies; concerned individuals. Seeks to ensure that a crime victim's rights are recognized and protected. Believes that the U.S. justice system goes to great lengths to protect the rights of criminals while discounting those of the victim. Discourages the commutation of sentences through parole and "good time," an arrangement where inmates' sentences may be shortened two days for every one day served without violation of prison conduct regulations. Promotes recognition of the third week in April as Victim's Rights Week. Introduces and supports 14 victim's rights bills, including the Victim's Bill of Rights that provides for considerations to the victim guaranteed by law such as notification prior to the release of prisoners convicted of crimes perpetrated against them. Maintains speakers' bureau. **Awards: Type:** recognition. **Telecommunication Services:** 24-hour hotline, crisis helpline, (800)239-3219. **Committees:** Chapter Development; Legislative; Publicity. **Affiliated With:** National Center for Victims of Crime. **Publications:** *VOCAL Voice*, quarterly. Newsletter. **Conventions/Meetings:** semiannual conference.

Violence

13092 ■ Communities Against Violence Network (CAVNET)
c/o Marc Dubin, Founder/Exec. Dir.
2711 Ordway St. NW, No. 111
Washington, DC 20008
E-mail: mdubin@pobox.com
URL: http://www.cavnet2.org
Contact: Marc Dubin, Founder/Exec. Dir.
Membership Dues: member who wants to receive the emails from the listserve, $50 (annual) ● individual/organization (ability to access non-public areas of the website/database), $100 (annual) ● charter, $150 (annual). **Multinational. Description:** Professionals addressing domestic violence, sexual assault, rape, incest, stalking, youth violence, youth suicide, criminal victimization of people with disabilities. **Computer Services:** database, information and resources. **Telecommunication Services:** teleconference, paltalk program. **Subgroups:** Speaker's Bureau. **Publications:** Directory. Features issues about abuse and violence in society. Alternate Formats: online.

13093 ■ Mothers Against Violence in America
105 14th Ave., Ste.2A
Seattle, WA 98122
Ph: (206)323-2303
Free: (800)897-7697
Fax: (206)323-2132
E-mail: info@mavia.org
Contact: Pamela Eakes, Pres.
Founded: 1994. **Membership Dues:** supporter, $25
● cherub, $50 ● angel, $100 ● business/organization/other, $150. **Description:** Prevents violence by and against children through education, outreach and advocacy. Encourages individuals to take personal responsibility for creating safe communities and schools. **Awards:** Community Catalyst Award. **Frequency:** annual. **Type:** recognition. **Computer Services:** Information services, violence-related literature. **Programs:** Educational Outreach; Gun Violence Prevention Education; Public Policy; Students Against Violence Everywhere; Youth Recognition Program. **Publications:** Brochure. Alternate Formats: online.

13094 ■ Stop the Violence, Face The Music (STV)
723 Casino Center Blvd., 2nd Fl.
Las Vegas, NV 89101-6716
Free: (800)732-6366
Fax: (877)707-3417
E-mail: admin@stv.net
URL: http://www.stv.net
Founded: 1992. **Multinational. Description:** Counteracts the negative influences affecting the youth. Provides counselling and messages for anti-violence, crime, and substance abuse through the use of educational programs, music, public service ads, and television campaigns. **Libraries: Type:** reference. **Holdings:** articles, audio recordings, reports, video recordings. **Subjects:** child psychology, non-violence, U.S. demographics. **Computer Services:** database, counsellor directory ● information services, facts and statistics, public service announcements ● online services, online store. **Telecommunication Services:** hotline, free counselling services, (888)647-STOP. **Councils:** Advisory. **Programs:** Jeff Gaia Choices for Life Workshop. **Projects:** Drama Presentation; Internet Assignment for Students. **Publications:** *Teenagers Guide to Surviving the Teenage Years.* Book. Contains a collection of real life stories that cover issues such as peer pressure, violence, prostitution, and sex. **Price:** free ● Brochures. Alternate Formats: online.

13095 ■ Survivorship
PMB 139
3181 Mission St.
San Francisco, CA 94110
E-mail: info@survivorship.org
URL: http://www.survivorship.org
Contact: Jeannie Riseman, Ed.
Membership Dues: regular, in U.S., $30 (annual) ● regular, in Canada, $36 (annual) ● regular, outside U.S. and Canada, $42 (annual) ● internet, $25 (annual). **Multinational. Description:** Supports adult survivors of ritualized abuse (defined as the abuse of children and non-consenting adults in the name of an ideology or belief system). **Telecommunication Services:** electronic bulletin board, password-protected. **Publications:** *Monthly Notes.* Newsletter. Contains short articles dealing with after-affects of ritualistic abuse. ● Newsletter, quarterly. Contains stories, artwork, poetry and book and movie reviews. **Conventions/Meetings:** Conferences on Ritualistic Abuse, for survivors of ritualistic abuse and professionals; with speakers, workshops, panel discussions, small group discussions, art gallery - 2-3/year.

Visually Impaired

13096 ■ Clearer Vision Ministries (CVM)
PO Box 2085
Sanford, FL 32772-2085
Ph: (352)475-2742
E-mail: cvminc@clearervisionministries.org
URL: http://www.clearervisionministries.org
Contact: Rev. Sam Thompson, Founder/Pres.
Founded: 1979. **Staff:** 2. **Budget:** $65,000. **Nonmembership. Multinational. Description:** Serves as nondenominational organization dedicated to providing services for print impaired persons. Provides awareness and education for communities and churches and quality Christian materials on cassette for those with a visual or physical disability. **Libraries: Type:** lending. **Holdings:** 147; audio recordings, books, periodicals. **Subjects:** inspirational materials. **Publications:** *South Truth Magazine,* bimonthly. Features a collection of interviews, music, stories, and Bible studies. **Circulation:** 100. **Advertising:** accepted ● *Visionary Voice,* bimonthly. Newsletter. Contains current news of ministry. **Circulation:** 600.

13097 ■ Helping Hands for the Blind (HHB)
20734-C Devonshire St.
Chatsworth, CA 91311
Ph: (818)341-8217
Free: (877)422-0300
Fax: (818)341-8217
E-mail: boacosta@pacbell.net
URL: http://helpinghands4theblind.com
Contact: Robert J. Acosta, Pres./Founder
Founded: 1990. **Description:** Promotes social, economic and educational opportunities for the blind. Works to provide assistance to blind persons. Addresses the concerns of the blind. Provides financial grants to blind students and travel assistance for blind persons. Conducts special programs specifically designed for the blind.

13098 ■ National Church Conference of the Blind
PO Box 163
Denver, CO 80201
Ph: (303)455-3430
E-mail: care@careministries.org
URL: http://www.thenccb.com
Contact: B.J. LeJeune, Contact
Description: Represents blind Christians united to address accessibility issues; encourages members in faith. **Conventions/Meetings:** annual meeting.

13099 ■ Unite for Sight
31 Brookwood Dr.
Newtown, CT 06470
E-mail: jstaple@uniteforsight.org
URL: http://www.uniteforsight.org
Contact: Jennifer Staple, Pres./CEO
Founded: 2000. **State Groups:** 23. **Local Groups:** 90. **National Groups:** 12. **Multinational. Description:** Empowers communities to improve eye health. Eliminates preventable blindness. Provides eye care and eye health education to medically underserved communities. **Awards:** Volunteer of the Year. **Frequency:** annual. **Type:** recognition. **Recipient:** for remarkable contribution in providing eye care services to communities. **Computer Services:** Mailing lists ● online services, eye health course. **Boards:** Medical Advisory. **Programs:** Microedit and Microenterprise; Refugee Camp; Vision Screening and Vision Education. **Publications:** Brochure. **Circulation:** 20,000. Alternate Formats: online.

Voluntarism

13100 ■ American Society of Directors of Volunteer Services (ASDVS)
One N Franklin, Ste.2800
Chicago, IL 60606
Ph: (312)422-3938
Fax: (312)422-4579
E-mail: aharris@aha.org
URL: http://www.asdvs.org
Contact: Audrey Harris, Exec. Dir.
Founded: 1968. **Members:** 1,200. **Membership Dues:** regular, $125 (annual) ● emeritus, $67 (annual) ● allied, $190 (annual). **Staff:** 1. **Budget:** $490,000. **Regional Groups:** 2. **State Groups:** 49. **Local Groups:** 3. **Description:** Members are persons who are employed or recognized by the administration of a health care institution as having major or continuing responsibility for managing and coordinating the volunteer services program within that institution and who are eligible for personal membership in the American Hospital Association (see separate entry). Purposes are: to develop the knowledge and increase the competence of the individual member; to provide a means of intercommunication for directors of volunteer services and health care institutions; to conduct periodical surveys; to provide consultation and guidance on matters relating to health care volunteer services management; to establish and maintain professional standards and ethics; to cooperate with appropriate organizations in activities relating to volunteer services management that will be beneficial to the society; to cooperate with institutions of higher education in the development of programs in volunteer services management. Offers course on basic principles of volunteer services management. **Awards:** Volunteer Leader. **Frequency:** annual. **Type:** recognition. **Recipient:** for national leader/celebrity who has made major contributions to healthcare issues/volunteerism. **Computer Services:** Mailing lists. **Additional Websites:** http://www.todaysvolunteer.org. **Committees:** Affiliations; Professional Development; Publicity. **Programs:** Professional Achievement. **Affiliated With:** American Hospital Association. **Publications:** *Membership Roster,* annual. Membership Directory ● *Partners in Community Health,* quarterly. Newsletter. **Price:** $20.00 /year for nonmembers ● *Volunteer Services Administration,* bimonthly. Newsletter ● *Volunteer Services Department in a Health Care Institution.* **Conventions/Meetings:** annual Leadership Training Conference (exhibits).

13101 ■ AmeriCorps VISTA
1201 New York Ave. NW
Washington, DC 20005
Ph: (202)606-5000 (202)606-3472
Free: (800)942-2677
Fax: (202)565-2789
E-mail: questions@americorps.org
URL: http://www.americorps.org
Contact: Rosetta Freeman-Busby, Dir.
Founded: 1965. **Members:** 6,082. **Staff:** 17. **Budget:** $73,000,000. **Regional Groups:** 5. **Description:** National volunteer assistance program administered by the Corporation for National Service, an independent government agency. Individuals committed to improving the self-sufficiency of low-income communities. Members are assigned to local sponsors in the U.S., Puerto Rico, the Virgin Islands, and Guam, and are provided with health insurance, a basic subsistence allowance or education award, and a stipend upon completion of service. They live and work among the poor and share their skills and experiences in topics including: education and literacy, technology, welfare-to-work, mentoring, tutoring, neighborhood revitalization, and economic development. Members must be U.S. citizens or permanent residents and be at least 18 years old. Conducts orientation and training sessions for volunteers. **Convention/Meeting:** none. **Telecommunication Services:** electronic mail, rm-busby@cns.gov ● TDD, (800)833-3722. **Formerly:** (2000) Volunteers in Service to America.

13102 ■ Amigos de las Americas (AMIGOS)
5618 Star Ln.
Houston, TX 77057
Ph: (713)782-5290
Free: (800)231-7796
Fax: (713)782-9267
E-mail: info@amigoslink.org
URL: http://www.amigoslink.org
Contact: Emily Untermeyer MPH, Exec. Dir./Pres.
Founded: 1965. **Staff:** 25. **Budget:** $2,600,000. **State Groups:** 18. **Languages:** English, Portuguese, Spanish. **Multinational. Description:** Aims to build partnerships to empower young leaders, advance community development, and strengthen multicultural understanding in the Americas. Trains high school and college age students for community service, exploration and learning. Offers summer programs in Mexico, Honduras, Nicaragua, Costa

Rica, Dominican Republic, Paraguay, Panama, and Brazil. **Committees:** Communications; Development; Field Program; Gift Acceptance; Recruiting; Safety; Training. **Affiliated With:** Council on Standards for International Educational Travel; Global Health Council; Independent Sector. **Publications:** *Resource*, semiannual ● *Volunteer Directory*, annual ● Annual Report, annual ● Newsletter. Alternate Formats: online ● Also publishes fact sheet and brochure. **Conventions/Meetings:** annual workshop.

13103 ■ Amizade Global Service-Learning and Volunteer Programs
PO Box 110107
Pittsburgh, PA 15232
Ph: (412)441-6655
Free: (888)973-4443
Fax: (757)257-8358
E-mail: volunteer@amizade.org
URL: http://www.amizade.org
Contact: Michael Sandy, Exec. Dir.
Founded: 1994. **Staff:** 8. **Budget:** $380,000. **Non-membership.** **Multinational.** **Description:** Encourages intercultural exploration and understanding through community-driven, service-learning courses and volunteer programs. **Libraries: Type:** not open to the public. **Holdings:** books, periodicals. **Subjects:** intercultural service-learning. **Computer Services:** Mailing lists. **Additional Websites:** http://www.globalservicelearning.org. **Publications:** *Amizade Update*, monthly. Newsletter. **Price:** free. **Circulation:** 4,000. Alternate Formats: online.

13104 ■ Association of Junior Leagues International (AJLI)
80 Maiden Ln., Ste.305
New York, NY 10038
Ph: (212)951-8300 (212)951-8322
Fax: (212)481-7196
E-mail: info@ajli.org
URL: http://www.ajli.org
Contact: Susan Danish, Exec. Dir.
Founded: 1921. **Members:** 195,000. **Regional Groups:** 294. **Description:** Works to serve the Junior Leagues in developing the potential of women, promoting volunteerism and improving communities. Provides leadership and organizational development to Leagues; provides networking and partnership opportunities; and offers educational and training programs. **Libraries: Type:** not open to the public. **Holdings:** books, periodicals. **Computer Services:** database ● mailing lists ● online services. **Telecommunication Services:** electronic bulletin board ● electronic mail, sdanish@ajli.org. **Publications:** *Celebration Cookbook*. Contains most requested recipes. ● *Centennial Cookbook*. Contains most treasured recipes. ● *The Junior League at Home.* Book. Features meals and menus for everyday and special occasions. **Conventions/Meetings:** board meeting and conference.

13105 ■ Association for Research on Nonprofit Organizations and Voluntary Action (ARNOVA)
340 W Michigan St., Canal Level Ste.A
Indianapolis, IN 46202-3272
Ph: (317)684-2120
Fax: (317)684-2128
E-mail: tjeavons@arnova.org
URL: http://www.arnova.org
Contact: Thomas Jeavons, Exec. Dir.
Founded: 1971. **Members:** 1,341. **Membership Dues:** individual, $110 (annual) ● institution, $250 (annual) ● full-time student, $45 (annual) ● part-time student, retiree, $70 (annual) ● supporting, $500 (annual). **Staff:** 4. **Budget:** $650,000. **Multinational.** **Description:** Scholars and professionals interested and/or engaged in research, scholarship, or programs related to non-profit organizations, voluntary action, philanthropy, or citizen participation. This includes social movements, interest groups, consumer groups, political participation, community development, and religious organizations. Stimulates, coordinates, and aids the efforts of those engaged in voluntary action research, scholarship, and professional activity; makes the results of that research, scholarship, and

action more readily available both to fellow professionals and scholars and to leaders of and participants in voluntary associations and voluntary action agencies; fosters the dissemination and application of knowledge about voluntary action in order to enhance the quality of life and the general welfare of citizens and communities. **Libraries: Type:** reference. **Holdings:** 28. **Awards:** Book Award. **Frequency:** annual. **Type:** monetary ● Distinguished Achievement and Leadership in Non-profit and Voluntary Action Research Award. **Frequency:** annual. **Type:** monetary ● Outstanding NVSQ Article. **Frequency:** annual. **Type:** monetary ● Outstanding PhD Thesis. **Frequency:** annual. **Type:** monetary. **Committees:** Information and Membership; Nominations; Publications; Research; Resource Development. **Sections:** Community and Grassroots; Social Entrepreneurship and Enterprise; Teaching; Theories, Issues and Boundaries. **Affiliated With:** American Association for the Advancement of Science. **Formerly:** (1990) Association of Voluntary Action Scholars. **Publications:** *ARNOVA Abstracts*, quarterly. Bibliographies. Lists latest journal and magazine publications on philanthropy, voluntary action and non-profit studies. **Price:** $1.00 for nonmembers; free for members. **Circulation:** 1,200. Alternate Formats: online ● *ARNOVA News*, quarterly. Newsletter. Includes articles, research summaries, general information, book reviews and calendar of events. **Price:** included in membership dues. **Advertising:** accepted ● *Nonprofit and Voluntary Sector Quarterly*. Journal. **Price:** included in membership dues. ISSN: 0094-0607. **Advertising:** accepted. Also Cited As: *NVSQ* ● *Occasional Paper Series*, periodic, published every other year or less. Papers. **Price:** $25.00. **Conventions/Meetings:** annual conference, with more than 400 academic papers presented (exhibits).

13106 ■ Brethren Volunteer Service (BVS)
1451 Dundee Ave.
Elgin, IL 60120
Ph: (847)742-5100
Free: (800)323-8039
Fax: (847)742-0278
E-mail: bvs_gb@brethren.org
URL: http://www.brethren.org/genbd/bvs
Contact: Dan McFadden, Dir.
Founded: 1948. **Members:** 125. **Staff:** 6. **Budget:** $230,000. **Description:** People 21 years of age and over with a college degree for overseas projects, individuals 18 years of age and over quality for domestic projects. A full-time volunteer service program of the Church of the Brethren. Goals are advocating justice, peacemaking, and serving basic human needs and maintaining the integrity of creation. Volunteers serve 1 year in the U.S. or 2 years overseas. The range of projects includes children, youth, senior citizens, community services, farmworkers, disabled workers, homeless, prisoners and the prison system, hunger, peace, domestic violence, housing, health care, and camping and development ministries. Volunteers receive room and board, medical expenses, and a monthly allowance. **Awards:** Americorp Education Awards. **Frequency:** periodic. **Type:** monetary. **Recipient:** for U.S. projects. **Publications:** *Brethren Volunteer Service—Project Book*, annual. Directory. Lists available volunteer positions; includes description of requirements and duties. ● *BVS Brochure* ● *Needed: A Few Good Servants.* Video ● *Volunteer*, semiannual. Newsletter. Contains accounts of the experiences of BVS volunteers in various international and social causes. **Price:** free. Alternate Formats: online. **Conventions/Meetings:** annual conference ● quarterly meeting, for orientation.

13107 ■ Business Volunteers Unlimited (BVU)
200 Public Sq., Ste.2650
Cleveland, OH 44114-2383
Ph: (216)736-7711
Fax: (216)736-7710
E-mail: bvu@businessvolunteers.org
URL: http://www.businessvolunteers.org
Contact: Brian F. Broadbent, Pres./CEO
Description: Works to promote effective volunteerism and strong leadership. Provides consulting,

education and volunteer referral services to nonprofit and businesses. Trains business executives for leadership roles on nonprofit boards.

13108 ■ Council of Religious Volunteer Agencies (CRVA)
c/o Dan McFadden, Dir.
Brethren Volunteer Ser.
1451 Dundee Ave.
Elgin, IL 60120
Ph: (847)742-5100
Free: (800)323-8039
Fax: (847)742-0278
E-mail: dmcfadden_gb@brethren.org
URL: http://www.religiousvolunteers.org
Contact: Dan McFadden, Dir.
Founded: 1946. **Members:** 35. **Membership Dues:** organization, $100 (annual). **Description:** Works as a broad, faith-based coalition of North American organizations (promoters, planners, users) of voluntary service; members include local, community-based organizations using small numbers of volunteers and national agencies placing thousands of volunteers annually. **Formerly:** (1970) Commission on Youth Service Projects; (1991) Commission on Voluntary Service and Action; (2000) Council of Religious Volunteer Agencies; (2003) Global Mission Service. **Publications:** *Volunteer!*, semiannual. Newsletter. Contains information on volunteer opportunities. **Conventions/Meetings:** semiannual meeting and workshop - April and October.

13109 ■ Global Service Corps (GSC)
300 Broadway, Ste.28
San Francisco, CA 94133-3312
Ph: (415)788-3666
Fax: (415)788-7324
E-mail: gsc@earthisland.org
URL: http://www.globalservicecorps.org
Contact: Rick Lathrop, Founder/Exec. Dir.
Founded: 1992. **Multinational.** **Description:** Provides volunteer opportunities for people to live and work in developing countries. Provides community development services to developing countries, particularly in Tanzania and Thailand. **Programs:** Buddhist Immersion; Education; Fellowship; Health Care; HIV/AIDS Prevention; International Health Internship; Sustainable Agriculture. **Publications:** Newsletter. Alternate Formats: online.

13110 ■ Globe Aware
7232 Fisher Rd.
Dallas, TX 75214-1917
Ph: (214)823-0083
Free: (877)588-4562
Fax: (214)823-0084
E-mail: info@globeaware.org
URL: http://www.globeaware.org
Multinational. **Description:** Promotes cultural awareness and sustainability through its volunteer vacation programs. Provides community services in Europe and Asia. **Computer Services:** Mailing lists, of members.

13111 ■ Good Shepherd Volunteers (GSV)
337 E 17th St.
New York, NY 10003
Ph: (212)475-4245
Free: (888)668-6478
Fax: (212)979-8604
E-mail: gsv@goodsheperds.org
URL: http://www.gsvolunteers.org
Contact: Michele G. Gilfillan, Dir.
Founded: 1992. **Multinational.** **Description:** Assists individuals who have experienced injustice, oppression, and alienation due to life circumstances or unjust social structures. **Additional Websites:** http://www.goodshepherdvolunteers.org. **Publications:** Newsletter, quarterly. Alternate Formats: online.

13112 ■ Holiday Project (THP)
21 Eagle St.
Iselin, NJ 08830
Ph: (732)527-0737
Fax: (570)828-2493

E-mail: holidayproject@comcast.net
URL: http://www.holiday-project.org
Contact: Bobby Anderson, Contact
Founded: 1980. **Staff:** 1. **Budget:** $30,000. **Local Groups:** 24. **Description:** Promotes the importance of contribution by visiting with people confined to institutions during the holidays. Volunteers visit public and private institutions such as hospitals, nursing homes, institutions for the mentally retarded, orphanages, juvenile detention homes, institutions for the handicapped, prisons, and homes for battered women. Small gifts are brought for each individual visited. Raises funds to further its charitable purposes. **Computer Services:** Online services, benefice data entry, ICA. **Projects:** Adopt A Home. **Formerly:** (1980) Holiday Hospital Project. **Publications:** *The Holiday Spirit,* quarterly. Newsletter. **Price:** free. **Circulation:** 350. Alternate Formats: online. **Conventions/Meetings:** annual conference ● regional meeting and convention - at least once a year.

13113 ■ International Association for Volunteer Effort (IAVE)
c/o Civil Society Consulting Group, LLC
805 15th St. NW, Ste.100
Washington, DC 20005
Ph: (202)628-4360
E-mail: membership@iave.org
URL: http://www.iave.org
Contact: Mary Ripley, Founding Pres.
Founded: 1970. **Members:** 1,800. **Membership Dues:** individual, $40 (annual) ● organization, $125 (annual) ● corporate, $1,000 (annual) ● youth (under age 25), $25 (annual) ● soft currency country, $15 (annual). **Staff:** 1. **Budget:** $180,000. **Multinational. Description:** Individuals and organizations interested in action through voluntary commitment to human service. Maintains an international network to encourage volunteer program development and promote understanding through volunteer effort.

13114 ■ International Volunteer Program (IVP)
678 13th St., Ste.100
Oakland, CA 94612
Ph: (510)433-0414
Free: (866)614-3438
Fax: (510)433-0419
URL: http://www.ivpsf.org
Contact: Allison Phillips, Program Mgr.
Founded: 1991. **Multinational. Description:** Promotes volunteerism in Europe and the United States, to enhance cultural understanding. **Projects:** Camp for the Visually Impaired; Children's Camp for Domestic Violence Victims; HIV/AIDS; Intergenerational Assistance; Non-profit Publishing; Northern England Children's Camp; Northern Ireland Conservation.

13115 ■ International Volunteer Programs Association (IVPA)
c/o Foundation of Sustainable Development
870 Market St., Ste.321
San Francisco, CA 94102
Ph: (201)221-4105
E-mail: international_ivpa@yahoo.com
URL: http://www.volunteerinternational.org
Membership Dues: organization, $75-$150 (annual). **Description:** Encourages excellence and responsibility in the field of international volunteerism. **Computer Services:** Online services, INTVOL listserv ● online services, listserv email discussion group. **Publications:** *International Volunteer Opportunities.* Brochure ● *Volunteer International News* email, bimonthly. Newsletter. Alternate Formats: online ● Directory. **Conventions/Meetings:** Community Service Around the World Conference & Expo (exhibits) ● roundtable ● workshop.

13116 ■ Kids Korps USA
265 Santa Helena, Ste.130
Solana Beach, CA 92075
Ph: (858)259-3602
Fax: (858)259-3603

E-mail: info@kidskorps.org
URL: http://www.kidskorps.org
Contact: Joani Wafer, Founder/CEO
Founded: 1995. **Members:** 2,775. **Membership Dues:** life, $250 ● individual, $20 (annual) ● family, $45 (annual). **Staff:** 4. **Budget:** $500,000. **Regional Groups:** 2. **State Groups:** 2. **Local Groups:** 20. **Description:** Represents children 5 to 18 years of age. Provides opportunities for children to partake in charitable and environmental activities. Offers training and resources. **Awards:** Presidential Student Service. **Frequency:** annual. **Type:** recognition. **Recipient:** for school colleges and community organizations for their outstanding community service. **Affiliated With:** California Association of Nonprofits. **Publications:** Newsletter. Alternate Formats: online.

13117 ■ National Human Services Assembly
1319 F St. NW, Ste.402
Washington, DC 20004
Ph: (202)347-2080
Fax: (202)393-4517
E-mail: nassembly@nassembly.org
URL: http://www.nassembly.org
Contact: Irv Katz, Pres./CEO
Founded: 1923. **Members:** 70. **Staff:** 8. **Budget:** $1,000,000. **National Groups:** 70. **Description:** Convenes member networks in collaborative strategies to improve human services policy and service delivery in the U.S. Association of national nonprofit health and human service organizations bound by a common concern for the effective delivery of health and human services to the American people, especially those in need. Builds capacity of its member organizations by providing an opportunity for members to network with one another and exchange ideas and information about issues, trends and innovations relevant to managing and governing national health and human services organizations. Supported by dues paid by member organizations. Some projects are funded by private foundations. **Awards:** Award for Excellence in National Board Leadership. **Frequency:** annual. **Type:** recognition. **Recipient:** for a volunteer board member of a national nonprofit health and human services organization ● Award for Excellence in National Executive Leadership. **Frequency:** annual. **Type:** recognition. **Recipient:** for a chief professional officer of a national nonprofit health and human services organization. **Additional Websites:** http://www.nydic.org. **Councils:** National Collaboration for Youth. **Subcommittees:** Charting the Future of Youth Development Professionals; Program Support Group. **Subgroups:** Washington Support Group. **Affiliated With:** AARP; Alliance for Children and Families; Alliance of Information and Referral Systems; American Association of Homes and Services for the Aging; American Camp Association; American Cancer Society; American Heart Association; America's Promise - The Alliance for Youth; Association of Jewish Family and Children's Agencies; Association of Junior Leagues International; Big Brothers Big Sisters of America; Boy Scouts of America; Boys and Girls Clubs of America; Camp Fire USA; Child Welfare League of America; Coalition for Juvenile Justice; Communities in Schools; Council on Accreditation; Friends of the Children; Generations United; Girl Scouts of the U.S.A.; Girls Inc.; Hostelling International-American Youth Hostels; I Have a Dream Foundation; Joint Action in Community Service; KaBOOM!; Lutheran Services in America; Mental Health America; National 4-H Council; National Alliance for Hispanic Health; National Association for Parents of Children With Visual Impairments; National Benevolent Association of the Christian Church; National Center for Missing and Exploited Children; National Center for Tobacco-Free Kids; National Council on the Aging; National Crime Prevention Council; National Foundation of Dentistry for the Handicapped; National Industries for the Blind; National Network for Youth; National Urban League; National Youth Employment Coalition; Points of Light Foundation; Salvation Army; Save the Children; Street Law; Travelers Aid International; United Jewish Communities; United Neighborhood Centers of America; United Seamen's Service; United Way of America; Volunteers of America; Women in Com-

munity Service; YMCA of the USA; Young Women's Christian Association of the United States of America YWCA of the U.S.A.; Youth Crime Watch of America; Youth Service America. **Formerly:** (1945) National Social Work Council; (1967) National Social Welfare Assembly; (1973) National Assembly for Social Policy and Development; (1999) National Assembly of National Voluntary Health and Social Welfare Organizations; (2000) National Collaboration for Youth; (2001) National Assembly of National Health and Social Welfare Organizations; (2004) National Assembly of Health and Human Service Organizations. **Publications:** *Community Collaborations Manual* ● *Salary and Benefits Survey of National Voluntary Human Service Organizations.* Book. **Conventions/Meetings:** annual Leadership Retreat - always fall ● meeting.

13118 ■ Points of Light Foundation
1400 I St. NW, Ste.800
Washington, DC 20005-2208
Ph: (202)729-8000
Free: (800)750-7653
Fax: (202)729-8100
E-mail: info@pointsoflight.org
URL: http://www.pointsoflight.org
Contact: Robert K. Goodwin, Pres./CEO
Founded: 1990. **Staff:** 60. **Local Groups:** 500. **Description:** Works to engage more people in volunteer community service to help solve serious social problems. Assists organizations in reinforcing, expanding, and improving the effectiveness of their volunteer activities. Maintains a network of 500 affiliated Volunteer Centers. Provides technical assistance and training to Volunteer Centers, and corporations, with employee volunteer programs, and nonprofit organizations. Sponsors National Volunteer Week and President's Service Awards. **Awards:** Award for Excellence in Workplace Volunteer Programs. **Frequency:** annual. **Type:** recognition. **Recipient:** for overall employee/retiree volunteer effort ● Community Leadership Award. **Frequency:** annual. **Type:** recognition. **Recipient:** to the outstanding citizen volunteer in the community ● Daily Points of Light Awards. **Frequency:** weekly. **Type:** recognition. **Recipient:** to the best volunteer ● George Bush Corporate Leadership Award. **Frequency:** annual. **Type:** recognition. **Recipient:** for corporate leader who supports the involvement of his/her company's employees as volunteers ● George W. Romney Citizen Volunteer Award. **Type:** recognition. **Recipient:** for excellence in the Volunteer Center core competencies ● Lenore and George W. Romney Citizen Volunteer Award. **Frequency:** annual. **Type:** recognition. **Recipient:** to a person who best exemplifies those qualities demonstrated by Lenore and Romney ● National Family Volunteer Award. **Frequency:** annual. **Type:** recognition. **Recipient:** for outstanding family volunteering activities ● Volunteer Center Communications Excellence Awards. **Type:** recognition. **Recipient:** for excellence in communication efforts. **Computer Services:** Mailing lists. **Programs:** Disaster Preparedness and Volunteers; Earned Income Tax Credit Initiative; Family Strengthening and Neighborhood Transformation; FamilyCares; 50 Volunteering Initiative; International Youth Hall of Fame; MissionFish; Points of Light Youth Leadership Institute. **Absorbed:** (1984) Association of Volunteer Bureaus; (1991) National Volunteer Center. **Formed by Merger of:** National Information Center on Volunteerism; National Center for Voluntary Action. **Publications:** *News From the Points of Light Foundation,* monthly. Newsletter. **Price:** included in membership dues. **Circulation:** 3,000 ● *To The Point,* bimonthly. Newsletter. Features news, highlights and updates on the latest initiatives and programs of the foundation. Alternate Formats: online ● *Volunteer Action Leadership,* quarterly. Magazine. Provides information on key aspects of volunteer administration. Includes calendar of events, research reports, and resource listings. **Price:** included in membership dues; $25.00 /year for nonmembers. **Circulation:** 6,500. **Advertising:** accepted ● *Volunteer Marketplace Catalog of Publications and Specialty Items,* annual. **Conventions/Meetings:** annual National Community Service Conference (exhibits).

13119 ■ Retired and Senior Volunteer Program (RSVP)
c/o Corporation for National and Community Service
1201 New York Ave. NW
Washington, DC 20525
Ph: (202)606-5000
Free: (800)424-8867
E-mail: help@joinseniorservice.org
URL: http://www.seniorcorps.gov/about/programs/
rsvp.asp
Contact: David Eisner, CEO
Founded: 1971. **Members:** 485,000. **Budget:** $47,700,000. **Local Groups:** 764. **Languages:** English, Spanish. **Description:** A program administered by The Corporation for National Service, a part of the federal government. Represents volunteers of at least 55 years of age from all socioeconomic levels and educational backgrounds who are willing and able to perform services on a regular basis. Brings persons of retirement age more fully into community life through volunteer services that vary according to their preference and community needs. Projects are planned, organized, and operated at the local level, and settings include schools, courts, health care, rehabilitation, day care, youth, and other community centers. Supports activities such as management consultation for nonprofit service agencies, telephone reassurance programs, and intergenerational projects. **Awards:** RSVP. **Type:** grant. **Telecommunication Services:** teletype, (202)606-3472. **Publications:** Brochure, periodic. Gives overview of the Program. **Price:** free for members. **Conventions/Meetings:** periodic conference, for training and technical assistance (exhibits).

13120 ■ SCI - International Voluntary Service (SCI/IVS-USA)
5505 Walnut Level Rd.
Crozet, VA 22932
Ph: (206)350-6585
Fax: (206)350-6585
E-mail: sciinfo@sci-ivs.org
URL: http://www.sci-ivs.org
Contact: Andrea Stanton, Dir.
Founded: 1920. **Members:** 250. **Membership Dues:** general, $35 (annual). **Description:** American branch of Service Civil International, a part of an international voluntary work camp organization that came into being after World War I and now functions in 36 countries. Aims: "to render constructive civilian service to society through voluntary manual labor and social welfare work; to bring together people of all backgrounds to work for better understanding, reconciliation, and peace by helping underprivileged communities and groups; to demonstrate the effectiveness of a voluntary reconstructive corps as an alternative to armed force in the resolution of social and international conflict". The organization has no political or religious affiliations and is open to anyone regardless of national and racial origin or beliefs "who works to promote self-help through deeds, not words." Projects include: service in economically deprived areas; community peace work; environmental and manual camps; work and study camps; East-West work camps; work with refugees; emergency camps. National branches of SCI design their own programs according to local needs, but all camps are international. In the U.S., programs are organized by former volunteers and others. Programs have been carried out from California to New York. Workcamps are usually 2-3 weeks. **Formerly:** (1966) International Voluntary Service; (1984) Service Civil International - United States of America. **Publications:** *Service Civil International - U.S.A.—Workcamp Listing*, annual, in April. Directory. Lists international voluntary workcamps sponsored by Service Civil International. Also lists projected camps and workcamp reviews. **Price:** $5.00 ● *Workcamp News*, semiannual. Newsletter. **Conventions/Meetings:** annual meeting - always fall ● National Committee Meeting - always spring.

13121 ■ Senior Companion Program (SCP)
c/o Corporation for National & Community Service
1201 New York Ave. NW
Washington, DC 20525

Ph: (202)606-5000
Free: (800)424-8867
E-mail: help@joinseniorservice.org
URL: http://www.seniorcorps.gov/for_individuals/
ready/index.asp
Contact: David Eisner, CEO
Founded: 1974. **Members:** 7,800. **Budget:** $26,692,000. **Description:** Administered by ACTION, an independent government agency. Offers volunteer opportunities for low-income persons age 60 and over to establish a one-to-one relationship with other older persons, particularly the frail elderly in their homes, in an effort to delay or prevent institutionalization. Provides services to the elderly in institutions in an attempt to render them capable of returning to community life. Volunteers serve through health and social services agencies dealing with mental health, acute care, substance abuse, care of the terminally ill, and respite. **Convention/Meeting:** none. **Publications:** *SCP Address Book*, biennial. Directory.

13122 ■ TECH CORPS
199 Forest St.
Marlborough, MA 01752
Ph: (703)357-3055
E-mail: info@techcorps.org
URL: http://www.techcorps.org
Contact: Allan Jones, Exec. Dir.
Founded: 1995. **Staff:** 6. **State Groups:** 50. **Description:** Technology volunteers dedicated to helping improve K-12 education through the effective integration of technology into the learning environment. Recruits, places, and supports volunteers from the technology community who advise and assist schools in the introduction and integration of new technologies into the educational system. Volunteers provide assistance with local planning, technical support and advice, staff training, mentoring, and classroom interactions. Provides state organizations with a model for implementation which includes training and materials to guide the formation of an effective state chapter; guidance is also provided in how schools can screen volunteers, develop in-depth project lists, nurture volunteer participation, set appropriate volunteer expectations, and successfully match volunteer expertise with school needs. Additional resources provided to schools include webTeacher, on online Internet tutorial, and tech4schools, an online mentoring initiative providing technical support to remote schools nationwide. **Awards:** Leadership in Technology Awards. **Frequency:** annual. **Type:** recognition. **Recipient:** for private sector leaders in educational technology. **Computer Services:** database, for Tech Corps members only. **Conventions/Meetings:** annual State Directors Meeting, three-day working session - fall.

13123 ■ Volunteers in Asia (VIA)
965 Mission St., Ste.751
San Francisco, CA 94103
Ph: (415)904-8033
Fax: (415)618-0509
E-mail: info@viaprograms.org
URL: http://www.viaprograms.org
Contact: Ms. Diane Nguyen, Outreach Coor.
Founded: 1963. **Staff:** 10. **Budget:** $1,200,000. **Nonmembership. Multinational. Description:** Volunteers serve either summer or one or two-year term as English teachers or English resource persons for local NGOs in China, Vietnam, Indonesia, Myanmar, Laos, and Thailand. Stanford Programs (formerly TPE) hosts Asian students for spring break, summer, and intermittent year long programs in American culture, language, and society as well as medical ethics, environmentalism, and socially responsible business. **Programs:** Asia; Stanford. **Publications:** *Lorena Stoves*. Book. **Price:** $4.00 each, plus shipping and handling; $7.04 for California residents (with 8.25&percent; sales tax) ● *Staying Healthy in Asia, Africa, and Latin America*. Book. Serves as a health manual for travelers which is updated every two years. **Price:** $11.95 each, plus shipping and handling; $15.64 for California residents (with 8.25&percent; sales tax) ● *Transcultural Study Guide*. Book.

Price: $7.95 each, plus shipping and handling; $10.77 for California residents (with 8.25&percent; sales tax).

13124 ■ Volunteers in Overseas Cooperative Assistance - USA (VOCA)
50 F St. NW, Ste.1175
Washington, DC 20001
Ph: (202)383-4961
Fax: (202)383-7204
E-mail: webmaster@acdivoca.org
URL: http://www.acdivoca.org
Contact: Carl Leonard, Pres./CEO
Founded: 1970. **Budget:** $3,100,000. **Languages:** Armenian, English, Polish, Russian. **Description:** National volunteer organizations in central and eastern Europe and the former Soviet Union. Seeks to enhance economic opportunity and contribute to the development of democratic institutions worldwide. Recruits volunteers in the U.S. to provide technical assistance and professional support to health and community development organizations operating agricultural and rural cooperative programs. **Publications:** *World Report*, quarterly. Magazine. **Price:** free ● Annual Report, annual. **Price:** free. Alternate Formats: online.

13125 ■ Winant and Clayton Volunteers (WCV)
109 E 50th St.
New York, NY 10022
Ph: (212)378-0271
Fax: (212)378-0281
E-mail: info@winantclaytonvolunteer.org
URL: http://www.winantclaytonvolunteer.org
Contact: Nanette Rousseau, Contact
Founded: 1948. **Members:** 1,000. **Staff:** 1. **Description:** U.S. citizens 18 years of age or older who volunteer at community social service organizations in Great Britain. Volunteers assist in community agencies, youth clubs, programs for the elderly, mental health centers, and people with AIDS. Seeks to recruit men and women in the U.S. to serve as Winant volunteers for nine weeks (June through mid-August). The Winant volunteers pay their own grouprate (organized by New York office) transportation to and from England, but receive free room and a food stipend while they volunteer. Offers an opportunity to see England from inside and develop an understanding of a different culture. At the same time, the U.S. hosts 20 Clayton volunteers (British counterparts) performing similar services in the United States. Named for John Gilbert Winant, U.S. Ambassador to England, 1941-46, and The Rev. Dr. P.B. (Tubby) Clayton, Chaplain to the Queen Mother. **Committees:** Clayton; Hospitality; Recruiting; Selection; Winant. **Formerly:** (1963) League of Winant Volunteers. **Publications:** Newsletter, semiannual ● Also publishes booklet on the volunteers. **Conventions/Meetings:** monthly board meeting.

Water

13126 ■ Healing Waters International (HWI)
534 Commons Dr.
Golden, CO 80401
Ph: (303)526-7278
Fax: (303)526-7288
E-mail: eanderson@healingwatersintl.org
URL: http://www.healingwatersintl.org
Contact: Ed Anderson, Exec. Dir.
Founded: 1999. **Multinational. Description:** Works to reduce water-related illness and death in developing countries by building self-sustaining projects that make safe drinking water accessible to the poor. Partners with churches to bring physical, social and spiritual healing, and safe and affordable drinking water to impoverished communities throughout the world. Builds water purification systems and recruits U.S. organizations to sponsor those systems. **Publications:** *HWI News*. Newsletter. Alternate Formats: online ● Report. Alternate Formats: online.

13127 ■ Water Missions International (WMI)
PO Box 31258
Charleston, SC 29417
Ph: (843)769-7395
Fax: (843)763-6082
E-mail: info@watermissions.org
URL: http://www.watermissions.org
Contact: George C. Greene III, Co-Founder/Chief Technical Off.
Multinational. Description: Provides access to safe water and an opportunity to learn about the Christian faith to people in need throughout the world. Serves the water and sanitation needs of developing countries and disaster areas. Uses low maintenance, appropriate water technologies for drinking water treatment and distribution, wastewater management and storm weather control. **Telecommunication Services:** electronic mail, ggreeneiii@watermissions.org.

13128 ■ WaterPartners International
PO Box 22680
Kansas City, MO 64113-0680
Ph: (913)312-8600
E-mail: info@water.org
URL: http://www.water.org
Contact: Gary White, Exec. Dir.
Founded: 1990. **Staff:** 9. **Multinational. Description:** Provides clean drinking water to communities in developing countries. Creates global awareness of water supply crisis. Helps people develop accessible, sustainable, and community-level water supplies. **Computer Services:** Online services, discussion group. **Projects:** Community Participation; Construction and Maintenance; Health Education and Sanitation; Watersource Protection. **Publications:** *From the Field*, quarterly. Newsletter ● Newsletter. Alternate Formats: online.

Weather

13129 ■ National Association of Storm Chasers and Spotters (NASCAS)
c/o Weatherstock Inc.
PO Box 31808
Tucson, AZ 85751
E-mail: storm@weatherstock.com
URL: http://www.chasingstorms.com
Contact: Jeff Carter, Dir.
Founded: 1999. **Description:** Provides accurate safety and educational information to the public, educators, media, government officials, students and to those who pursue severe weather. **Computer Services:** Information services, resources for educators and students. **Projects:** Emergency Storm Spotters Fund. **Publications:** *How To Survive Any Storm*. Manual. Contains information on how to survive severe weather conditions. **Price:** included in professional and corporate membership.

Widowhood

13130 ■ AARP Grief and Loss Program
601 E St. NW
Washington, DC 20049
Free: (888)687-2277
E-mail: griefandloss@aarp.org
URL: http://www.aarp.org/families/grief_loss
Contact: Bill Novelli, CEO
Founded: 1973. **Staff:** 7. **Local Groups:** 230. **Languages:** Chinese, English, Spanish. **Description:** Provides resources and information on grief and loss issues, as well as technical assistance in the development of local community bereavement programs. Provides widowed volunteers to assist new widows and widowers cope with the change. **Affiliated With:** AARP. **Formerly:** (1998) Widowed Persons Service. **Publications:** *Directory of Services for the Widowed in the U.S. and Canada*, periodic ● *Final Details: A Guide for Survivors* (in English and Spanish). Brochure. Contains information on making decisions and taking action in the first few months after death. ● *On Being Alone* (in English and Spanish). Booklet.

Provides a comprehensive guide for recently widowed men and women. **Conventions/Meetings:** regional meeting.

Women

13131 ■ About-Face
PO Box 77665
San Francisco, CA 94107
Ph: (415)436-0212
E-mail: info@about-face.org
URL: http://www.about-face.org
Contact: Kathy Bruin, Founder
Founded: 1995. **Staff:** 10. **Description:** Media literacy organization focused on the mass media impact on the physical, mental and emotional well-being of women and girls.

13132 ■ Afghan Women's Association International (AWAI)
PO Box 637
Fremont, CA 94537-0637
Ph: (510)574-2182 (510)574-2180
Fax: (510)574-2185
E-mail: afghancoal@aol.com
URL: http://awai.org
Contact: Rona Popal, Exec. Dir.
Founded: 1992. **Multinational. Description:** Aims to defend the rights of Afghan women. Raises awareness of women's issues in Afghanistan. Provides assistance and basic human services to Afghan women and refugee camps in Pakistan. **Telecommunication Services:** electronic mail, awai@aol.org.

13133 ■ All India Women's Conference - North America (AIWCNA)
86-42 Midland Pkwy.
Jamaica Estate
Jamaica, NY 11432
Ph: (718)523-7668
E-mail: sacharya@netzero.net
Contact: Sudha Acharya, Contact
Languages: English, Hindi. **Description:** Individuals and organizations. Seeks to ensure equal rights and social justice for women; promotes increased economic self-sufficiency for women in developing areas. Conducts vocational training programs; provides support and assistance to women wishing to create microenterprises or other business ventures; identifies and disseminates appropriate technologies.

13134 ■ Alliance of American and Russian Women (AARW)
Address Unknown since 2007
Budget: $300,000. **Languages:** English, Russian. **Description:** Assists Russian women to make the transition to a market economy. Provides networking opportunities and assistance to businesswomen in Russia and the United States. Provides mentoring, cultural information, professional training, business development and support.

13135 ■ Arab Women's Solidarity Association (AWSA)
c/o Rabab Abdulhadi, Rep.
New York Univ.
Center for the Stud. of Gender and Sexuality
285 Mercer St., 3rd Fl., Rm. 307
New York, NY 10003-6653
Ph: (212)992-9543
Fax: (212)995-4433
E-mail: awsa_sc@yahoo.com
URL: http://www.awsa.net
Contact: Rabab Abdulhadi, Rep.
Founded: 1982. **Languages:** Arabic, English. **Description:** Arab women. Works to enhance the economic, legal, and social status of Arab women worldwide. Conducts research on human rights, religious, and other issues confronting Arab women.

13136 ■ Black, Indian, Hispanic, and Asian Women in Action (BIHA)
1830 James Ave. N
Minneapolis, MN 55417
Ph: (612)521-2986
Fax: (612)529-6745
E-mail: info@biha.org
URL: http://www.biha.org
Contact: Alice O. Lynch, Exec.Dir.
Founded: 1983. **Members:** 200. **Staff:** 3. **Budget:** $200,000. **Description:** Strives to empower Black, Indian, Hispanic, and Asian women through implementation of educational projects. Acts as an advocate for women of color in the areas of family violence, chemical dependence, education, and physical and mental health. Works for social change, the health of the family and advancement of socioeconomic status. **Libraries: Type:** open to the public. **Holdings:** 200. **Subjects:** battering, sexual abuse, child abuse, racism. **Awards:** Women of Color Recognition Award. **Frequency:** annual. **Type:** recognition. **Recipient:** for women of color volunteering or working in their communities. **Publications:** *Unison*, quarterly. Newsletter. Covers issues of concern for women of color. **Price:** free. **Circulation:** 1,000. **Conventions/Meetings:** annual Recognition Celebration - meeting - always March 1st.

13137 ■ Black Women Organized for Educational Development (BWOED)
c/o Black Women Organized for Political Action
449 15th St., 3rd Fl.
Oakland, CA 94612
Ph: (510)763-9523
Fax: (510)763-4327
E-mail: blkwopa@aol.com
URL: http://www.bwopa.org/programs/bwoed.htm
Contact: LaNiece Jones, Exec. Dir.
Founded: 1984. **Staff:** 5. **Description:** Fosters self-sufficiency in and encourages empowerment of low-income and socially disadvantaged women by establishing and maintaining programs that improve their social and economic well-being. Sponsors mentor program for junior high-age young women in low-income urban areas; offers support groups. Maintains Black Women's Resource Center, an information and referral service for African American women and youth. **Awards: Type:** scholarship. **Publications:** *BWOED Newsletter*, quarterly. **Conventions/Meetings:** seminar and workshop - 8-10/year.

13138 ■ Black Women in Sisterhood for Action (BISA)
PO Box 1592
Washington, DC 20013
Ph: (202)543-6013
Fax: (202)543-5719
E-mail: info@bisa-hq.org
URL: http://www.bisa-hq.org
Contact: Verna S. Cook PhD, Natl. Pres.
Founded: 1980. **Description:** Promotes alternative strategies for educational and career development for black women; provides support and social assistance to senior black women in the community; disseminates information; provides leadership, role models, and mentors to young people. Provides management and leadership skills training, networking, team building, communication techniques, and image building. **Awards:** BISA Scholarship. **Type:** scholarship. **Recipient:** to 15 historically black colleges and universities in America. **Committees:** Calendar; Executive; Finance; Membership; Newsletter; Program; Scholarship; Senior Partners; Travel. **Programs:** Community Outreach for Exchange of Information and Sharing of Resources; Distinguished Black Women Network; Educational and Career Development for Members; Scholarship Assistance for Young High School Graduates; Senior Partners for Elderly Women in the Community; Travel/Study of Africa for Members and Invited Guests. **Publications:** *The Black Woman*, quarterly. Newsletter ● *Distinguished Black Women*, quinquennial. Book. **Conventions/Meetings:** annual Back to College Brunch - luncheon - held in August ● annual dinner, scholarship - held in January ● annual Distinguished Black Women Exhibit - specialty show - held in Febru-

ary ● annual Gala to Salute Distinguished Black Women - conference - held in April ● annual Pre-Thanksgiving Dinner Program for Senior Partners, for seniors and their guests - held in November ● annual workshop, for program planning by members - held in August.

13139 ■ Black Women United for Action (BWUFA)
6551 Loisdale Ct., Ste.400
Springfield, VA 22150
Ph: (703)922-5757
Fax: (703)922-7681
E-mail: info@bwufa.org
URL: http://www.bwufa.org
Contact: Sheila Coates, Pres.
Founded: 1985. **Membership Dues:** general, $35 (annual). **Multinational. Description:** Aims to increase the visibility and involvement of the African-American family. Advocates the concerns of women and improves the lives of impoverished, vulnerable families through a self-sufficiency and empowerment approach. Seeks to provide a variety of community programs and support services to create positive change. **Publications:** *BWUFA News.* Annual Report. **Price:** included in membership dues. Alternate Formats: online ● Newsletter, monthly. **Price:** included in membership dues.

13140 ■ Dress for Success Worldwide
32 E 31st St., 7th Fl.
New York, NY 10016
Ph: (212)532-1922
Fax: (212)684-9563
E-mail: worldwide@dressforsuccess.org
URL: http://www.dressforsuccess.org
Contact: Joi Gordon, CEO
Founded: 1996. **Multinational. Description:** Seeks to advance low-income women's economic and social development. Encourages self-sufficiency through career development and employment retention. Provides programs that help economically disadvantaged women acquire jobs, retain their new positions and succeed in the mainstream workplace. Each client receives one suit when there is a job interview and a second suit when finally gets the job. **Computer Services:** Information services, interview tips. **Telecommunication Services:** electronic mail, joi@dressforsuccess.org. **Subgroups:** Professional Women's. **Affiliated With:** Dress for Success of Louisville; Dress for Success, Northwest Minnesota.

13141 ■ Feminist Center for Human Growth and Development (FCHGD)
c/o Charlotte Schwab, PhD, Exec. Dir.
14719C Canalview Dr.
Delray Beach, FL 33484
Ph: (561)638-4757
E-mail: drschwab@drcharlotteschwab.com
URL: http://www.drcharlotteschwab.com
Contact: Charlotte Schwab PhD, Exec. Dir.
Founded: 1976. **Description:** Provides resources, information, and referral support system for people who need personal or career counseling. Aims to formulate a "new theory of personality development that will help to free women and men from the social, political and cultural limitations that now form the basis of existing psychological theories." Conducts nonsexist and feminist lectures, panels, and counseling. Sponsors participatory and experiential workshops and groups on such topics as relationships, self-identity, self-esteem, goal setting, risk taking, networking, assertiveness, and positive communication. Offers a nonsexist therapy-training program for human resources personnel and others interested in counseling women and men. **Publications:** *A Model for Effective Positive Communication* ● *A Model for Positive Self Identity and Self Defined Success.*

13142 ■ Hope International (HI)
215 W Sycamore St.
PO Box 1211
Kokomo, IN 46903-1211
Ph: (765)457-3373
Free: (800)968-5541
Fax: (317)456-3121
E-mail: tltaylor@hopeintl.org
URL: http://www.hopeinternational.net
Contact: Timothy Lee Taylor Jr., Contact
Founded: 1987. **Staff:** 5. **Languages:** Arabic, English, Spanish. **Multinational. Description:** Development organization. Promotes increased participation by women in economic development programs. Provides technical, financial, and administrative assistance to selected development projects and microenterprises. Emphasizes issues related to Sudanese refugees in USA and Horn of Africa. **Projects:** Adoption; Orphanage. **Also Known As:** Analytical Development. **Formerly:** (2003) Pacific Rim Consortium. **Conventions/Meetings:** periodic conference.

13143 ■ International Wages for Housework Campaign
c/o Crossroads Women's Centre
PO Box 86681
Los Angeles, CA 90086-0681
Ph: (323)292-7405
Fax: (323)292-7405
E-mail: la@crossroadswomen.net
URL: http://www.allwomencount.net
Founded: 1972. **Regional Groups:** 9. **State Groups:** 3. **Multinational. Description:** A multi-racial grassroots network of women campaigning for compensation for housework through governments. Asserts that women's unpaid work is the foundation of every nation's economy and should be measured and valued in national statistics. Supports diverting money used in military spending into welfare, social security, healthcare and other social programs. **Libraries: Type:** reference; open to the public. **Holdings:** audiovisuals, clippings. **Subjects:** women's waged and unwaged work, welfare, prostitution, women's rights, ecology, peace, lesbian and gay rights, immigration controls. **Formerly:** (2004) Wages for Housework Campaign. **Publications:** *Black Women and the Peace Movement.* Book. **Price:** $8.00 ● *Black Women: Bringing It All Back Home.* Book. **Price:** $7.00 ● *The Disinherited Family.* Book. **Price:** $14.00 ● *The Global Kitchen.* Pamphlet. **Price:** $10.00 ● *Journey with the Revolution.* Video. **Price:** EUR 8.00; EUR 12.00 solidary; EUR 30.00 in behalf of institution ● *La Cocina Global.* Pamphlet. **Price:** $7.00 ● *The Ladies & The Mammies: Jane Austen and Jean Rhys.* Book. **Price:** $8.00 ● *Marx and Feminism.* Pamphlet. **Price:** $4.00 ● *The Milk of Human Kindness: A Global Fact Sheet on the Economic Value of Breastfeeding.* Book. **Price:** $14.95 ● *The Power of Women and the Subversion of the Community.* Book. **Price:** $6.00 ● *Rape in the Media: Submission to the National Heritage Committee Inquiry into Privacy and Media Intrusion.* Pamphlet. **Price:** $4.00 ● *The Rapist Who Pays the Rent: Women's Case of Changing the Law on Rape.* Book. **Price:** $6.00 ● *The Sans-Papiers.* Pamphlet. **Price:** $4.00 ● *Strangers and Sisters: Women, Race & Immigration.* Book. **Price:** $10.00 ● *Wages for Housework Campaign Catalogue,* periodic. **Price:** free. **Conventions/Meetings:** biennial conference ● quarterly meeting.

13144 ■ International Women's Forum (IWF)
2120 L St. NW, Ste.460
Washington, DC 20037
Ph: (202)387-1010
Fax: (202)387-1009
E-mail: iwf@iwforum.org
URL: http://iwforum.browsermedia.com
Contact: Lillie Richardella, CEO
Founded: 1982. **Members:** 29. **Languages:** English, French, Italian, Spanish. **Description:** Domestic and international women's networks that seek to bring together women of influence and achievement and allow them to share ideas, experiences, and resources, and to solidify relationships that can enhance their effectiveness. Each state or local network is autonomous and may have different goals. **Awards:** International Hall of Fame Award. **Frequency:** annual. **Type:** recognition. **Recipient:** for women in leadership. **Formerly:** (1987) National Women's Forum. **Publications:** *Connection,* periodic. Newsletter. **Price:** included in membership dues.

Conventions/Meetings: annual meeting - 2008 Oct. 15-17, Pittsburgh, PA.

13145 ■ Jewish Women's Coalition
Address Unknown since 2007
Founded: 1996. **Members:** 950. **Membership Dues:** individual, ($36 (annual) ● contributing, $54 (annual) ● sustaining, $99 (annual) ● patron, $118 (periodic) ● Jewish Women Leaders online, $18 (annual). **Description:** Fosters the elimination of all forms of discrimination, especially against Jewish women. **Computer Services:** Online services, weekly email messages to 1000 leaders. **Boards:** Advisory. **Councils:** Public Policy. **Projects:** Coalition-Building; Jewish Women Leaders Online; Kol Isha, Voices of Women; Women's International Newsgathering Service. **Publications:** Directories, periodic. **Advertising:** accepted ● Manuals, periodic. **Advertising:** accepted. **Conventions/Meetings:** workshop, at conferences of member organizations (exhibits).

13146 ■ National Institute of Womanhood
6917 Arlington Rd., Ste.302
Bethesda, MD 20814-6300
Ph: (301)654-1014
Fax: (301)654-4131
Contact: Cecilia A. Royals, Pres.
Founded: 1991. **Membership Dues:** senior and student, $15 (annual) ● regular, $25 (annual). **Description:** Acts as a clearinghouse for information on women's issues. Promotes self-development for women. Offers educational and research programs. **Publications:** *NIW Newsletter,* quarterly. **Conventions/Meetings:** annual conference.

13147 ■ National Network to End Violence Against Immigrant Women
c/o Family Violence Prevention Fund
383 Rhode Island St., Ste.304
San Francisco, CA 94103
Ph: (415)252-8900
Fax: (415)252-8991
E-mail: monica@endabuse.org
URL: http://www.immigrantwomennetwork.org
Contact: Monica Arenas, Contact
Founded: 1992. **Description:** Seeks to eliminate all forms of oppression and discrimination against immigrant women facing violence. Works with diverse immigrant communities to prevent violence against women. Increases public awareness, education and understanding of issues around violence against immigrant women. **Telecommunication Services:** electronic mail, leni@endabuse.org.

13148 ■ The Nurturing Network (TNN)
Development Off.
PO Box 1489
White Salmon, WA 98672
Ph: (509)493-4026
Free: (800)TNN-4MOM
Fax: (509)493-4027
E-mail: tnn@nurturingnetwork.org
URL: http://www.nurturingnetwork.org
Contact: Mary Cunningham Agee, Pres./Founder
Founded: 1985. **Members:** 42,000. **Staff:** 6. **Description:** Represents network of volunteers who provide practical support for college and working women facing unplanned pregnancies. Offers counseling, medical services, nurturing homes, employment, and assistance with financial and educational issues. Makes available referrals for legal assistance, adoption, and support services for over 17000 mothers and their children. **Publications:** *Heart to Heart,* semiannual. Newsletter. **Price:** free. Alternate Formats: online.

13149 ■ Older Women's League (OWL)
3300 N Fairfax Dr., Ste.218
Arlington, VA 22201
Ph: (703)812-7990
Free: (800)825-3695
Fax: (703)812-0687

E-mail: owlinfo@owl-national.org
URL: http://www.owl-national.org
Contact: Laurie Young PhD, Exec. Dir.

Founded: 1980. **Members:** 15,000. **Membership Dues:** individual, $25 (annual). **Staff:** 11. **Budget:** $1,000,000. **Local Groups:** 68. **Description:** Middle-aged and older women; persons of any age who support issues of concern to mid-life and older women. Primary issues include access to health care insurance, support for family caregivers, reform of social security, access to jobs and pensions for older women, effects of budget cuts on women, and maintaining self-sufficiency throughout life. Operates speakers' bureau; prepares educational materials; compiles statistics. **Awards:** Type: recognition. **Publications:** *A Matter of Life and Death.* Video ● *Gray Papers* ● *Model State Bills* ● *Older Women and Job Discrimination* ● *OWL OBSERVER*, quarterly. Newsletter. Provides membership activity information. **Price:** included in membership dues ● *Status Report*, annual. **Conventions/Meetings:** biennial meeting.

13150 ■ Power for Women
28 E Jackson Blvd., Ste.1900
Chicago, IL 60604
Ph: (312)957-0195
Fax: (312)957-0196
E-mail: powerforwomen@hotmail.com
URL: http://www.powerforwomen.org
Contact: A. Hartman, Pres.

Founded: 1976. **Members:** 300. **Membership Dues:** associate, $20 (annual). **Description:** Women's self-defense organization. Seeks to prevent violence against women. Teaches self-defense techniques to women of all ages through both public and private sector classes. **Formerly:** (2003) Chimera Educational Foundation. **Publications:** *Chimera Newsletter*, periodic. Includes instructor profiles, book, television, and movie reviews, and consumer self-defense product test results. ● Annual Report, annual. **Conventions/Meetings:** seminar ● workshop.

13151 ■ Pride Program
4123 E Lake St.
Minneapolis, MN 55406-2028
Ph: (612)728-2062 (612)729-0340
Free: (888)PRIDE-99
E-mail: pride@fscmn.org
URL: http://www.fcsmn.org/PRIDE/index.html
Contact: Artika Roller, Program Supervisor

Founded: 1978. **Staff:** 6. **Description:** A program of Family and Children's Service of the Minneapolis Metro Area. Works to help women and teenage girls who have been used in prostitution, while promoting societal change to stop the perpetuation of commercial sexual exploitation. Services include: PRIDE groups, information and referral, transitional housing, teenPRIDE for girls, advocacy services, court intervention, 24-hour crisis line, child care, crisis intervention, and individual support. Conducts community education and public speaking on the issues of prostitution and working with survivors. **Publications:** none. **Libraries:** Type: reference. **Holdings:** audiovisuals, books, clippings. **Subjects:** violence against women, women's issues.

13152 ■ Real Foundation
550 Hinesburg Rd.
South Burlington, VT 05403
Ph: (802)846-7871
URL: http://www.therealfoundation.com
Contact: Kathy O'Brien, Dir./Pres.

Description: Committed to helping women discover internal strength and self-confidence in order to succeed in life through counseling and special projects such as adventure experiences. **Awards:** Type: grant. **Publications:** Newsletter.

13153 ■ Solace International
408 E Camino Limon Verde
Sahuarita, AZ 85629-8748
Ph: (520)393-8776

E-mail: info@solaceinternational.org
URL: http://solaceinternational.org
Contact: Nathaniel York, Exec. Dir.

Founded: 2002. **Multinational. Description:** Seeks to provide additional income and status to women. Provides opportunities for girls to advance to higher education and professional careers. Responds to the needs of women in Afghanistan with education and home-based industries. Creates community partnerships to establish self-sustainable economic development in emerging nations. Builds schools for girls in northern Afghanistan. Provides a market for traditional crafts. **Libraries:** Type: reference. **Holdings:** photographs. **Telecommunication Services:** electronic mail, nate@solaceinternational.org ● electronic mail, donations@solaceinternational.org.

13154 ■ Step Up Women's Network
3540 Wilshire Blvd., Ste.502
Los Angeles, CA 90010
Ph: (213)382-9161
Fax: (213)559-0595
E-mail: dcarrig@suwn.org
URL: http://www.stepupwomensnetwork.org
Contact: Danielle Carrig, Exec. Dir.

Founded: 1998. **Members:** 3,500. **Membership Dues:** individual in Chicago, $40-$1,000 (annual) ● individual in Los Angeles, $40-$1,500 (annual) ● individual in New York, $40-$2,500 (annual) ● corporate, $25,000 (annual). **Description:** Encourages strengthening of community resources for women and girls. Raises funds for women's health and critical issues. Ensures that women and girls are equipped with the tools they need to create a better future. **Awards:** Inspiration Awards. **Frequency:** annual. Type: recognition. **Recipient:** for women who embody the spirit of Step Up through their philanthropic impact in the lives of women and girls. **Publications:** Newsletter, biweekly. Contains updates on the organization's activities and programs. **Price:** included in membership dues. Alternate Formats: online ● Newsletter, monthly. **Price:** included in membership dues. Alternate Formats: online.

13155 ■ United Nations Division for the Advancement of Women (DAW)
2 United Nations Plz., DC2-12th Fl.
New York, NY 10017
Fax: (212)963-3463
E-mail: daw@un.org
URL: http://www.un.org/womenwatch/daw
Contact: Ms. Carolyn Hannan, Dir.

Founded: 1946. **Languages:** Arabic, Chinese, English, French, Russian, Spanish. **Description:** Focuses on the economic, political, and social status of women. Promotes increased participation of women in society; seeks to protect and expand the legal rights of women. Conducts research; gathers and disseminates information. **Publications:** *Handbook for Parliamentarians* (in Arabic, Chinese, English, French, Russian, and Spanish). **Price:** $18.95 each. **Conventions/Meetings:** annual World Conference on Women - meeting.

13156 ■ We Are AWARE
PO Box 242
Bedford, MA 01730-0242
Ph: (781)893-0500
Free: (877)672-9273
E-mail: info@aware.org
URL: http://www.aware.org
Contact: Lyn Bates, VP

Founded: 1990. **Description:** Seeks to reduce violence against women by teaching women about effective self-protection. Stresses the concepts of choice and empowerment, with the philosophy that individuals should be armed with courage, determination, spirit, and knowledge, whether or not one is armed with anything else. Advocates self-protection methods incorporating a range of weapons, recognizing that firearms are not the solution for every situation. Makes referrals and acts as information clearinghouse. Offers courses taught by certified instructors in the use of firearms, temporarily disabling aerosols, and in general personal protection. Provides special services for individuals at high risk, such as stalking

victims. **Also Known As:** AWARE; Arming Women Against Rape and Endangerment.

13157 ■ Women in Crisis (WIC)
360 W 125th St., No. 11
New York, NY 10027
Ph: (212)665-2020 (212)665-2021
Fax: (212)665-2022
E-mail: diane.nash@palladiainc.org
URL: http://www.palladiainc.org
Contact: Diane Nash, Supervisor

Founded: 1979. **Staff:** 2. **Description:** National conference participants concerned with the plight of "women in crisis," including victims of sexual discrimination and poverty, battered wives, rape and incest victims, women offenders, and female drug abusers and alcoholics. Focuses efforts on women and work, mental health, women in leadership positions, drugs and alcohol, and justice. Seeks to create a network of professionals in these areas. **Awards:** Type: recognition. **Committees:** Alcohol; Drugs; Justice Task Forces; Mental Health. **Conventions/Meetings:** annual conference.

13158 ■ Women in Informal Employment: Globalizing and Organizing (WIEGO)
Harvard Univ.
79 John F. Kennedy St.
Cambridge, MA 02138
Ph: (617)496-1310
Fax: (617)496-2828
E-mail: wiego@ksg.harvard.edu
URL: http://www.wiego.org
Contact: Elena Patino, Mgr.

Founded: 1997. **Languages:** English, Spanish. **Description:** Represents institutions and women workers. Seeks to formulate and promote policies that will directly benefit women in informal employment. **Programs:** Global Markets; Organization and Representation; Social Protection; Statistics; Urban Policies. **Publications:** *WIEGO E-Newsletter*. Alternate Formats: online ● Annual Report, annual. Alternate Formats: online ● Brochure. Alternate Formats: online.

13159 ■ Women, Ink
777 United Nations Plz.
New York, NY 10017
Ph: (212)687-8633
Fax: (212)661-2704
E-mail: marywong@womenink.org
URL: http://www.womenink.org
Contact: Mary Wong, Sales Mgr.

Founded: 1992. **Staff:** 4. **Description:** A project of the International Women's Tribune Centre. Works to increase awareness of issues affecting the well-being of women worldwide. Conducts research and educational programs; develops, markets, and distributes resources on women and development. **Publications:** *Booklink*, monthly. Bulletin. Alternate Formats: online ● Books ● Reports.

13160 ■ Women in Progress
PO Box 18323
Minneapolis, MN 55418
Free: (800)338-3032
Fax: (612)781-0450
E-mail: info@womeninprogress.org
URL: http://www.womeninprogress.org
Contact: Renae Adam, Exec. Dir.

Founded: 2002. **Staff:** 2. **Nonmembership. Multinational. Description:** Strives to alleviate poverty by increasing opportunity for African American women entrepreneurs. **Awards:** Internships. Type: fellowship. **Recipient:** to students.

13161 ■ Women in Transition (WIT)
21 S 12th St., 6th Fl.
Philadelphia, PA 19107
Ph: (215)564-5301
Free: (866)SAF-E014
Fax: (215)564-5723

E-mail: witinfo@womenintransitioninc.org
URL: http://www.womenintransitioninc.org
Contact: Roberta L. Hacker, Exec. Dir.
Founded: 1971. **Staff:** 14. **Budget:** $550,000. **Description:** Offers support groups for women endangered by domestic violence and/or substance abuse. Provides outreach, assessment, and referrals to abused women and to women with drug and/or alcohol addiction; makes available individual and group counseling. Offers consultation and training to mental health and social service agency personnel. Maintains speakers' bureau. **Telecommunication Services:** 24-hour hotline, (215)751-1111. **Publications:** *Transitions*, quarterly. Newsletter. Alternate Formats: online ● *Volunteer Newsletter*, annual. Annual Report. Alternate Formats: online.

13162 ■ Women of the World (WOW)
7908 NW Pleasant Ford
Kansas City, MO 64152
Ph: (816)746-6869
E-mail: questions@wownow.org
URL: http://www.wownow.org
Contact: Lynn Hinkle, Pres./Founder
Founded: 1993. **Multinational. Description:** Individuals interested in the leadership skills of women. Promotes development of women's unique leadership abilities worldwide, and to broaden the influence of women in community decision-making. Prepares and distributes leadership training materials for women of all cultural backgrounds; serves as a clearinghouse on women and leadership; operates Native American Women's Leadership Project and Native American Youth Initiative. Provides clothing and other assistance to economically disadvantaged people worldwide. **Projects:** Afghanistan; Native American Women's Leadership. **Publications:** Newsletter. Alternate Formats: online.

13163 ■ Women's Freedom Network (WFN)
4410 Massachusetts Ave. NW, Ste.179
Washington, DC 20016
Ph: (202)885-6245
Free: (800)575-3313
E-mail: wfn@american.edu
URL: http://www.womensfreedom.org
Contact: Rita J. Simon, Pres.
Founded: 1993. **Members:** 1,200. **Staff:** 3. **Description:** Seeks alternatives to both extremist ideological feminism and anti-feminist traditionalism. Seeks to give both sexes the tools to make informed choices and take responsibility for the consequences. **Publications:** *The Women's Freedom Network Newsletter*, bimonthly. Alternate Formats: online ● Books ● Papers. Alternate Formats: online. **Conventions/Meetings:** conference.

13164 ■ Women's Funding Network (WFN)
1375 Sutter St., Ste.406
San Francisco, CA 94109
Ph: (415)441-0706
Fax: (415)441-0827
E-mail: info@wfnet.org
URL: http://www.wfnet.org
Contact: Ms. Cynthia Schmae, COO
Founded: 1985. **Members:** 67. **Staff:** 4. **Description:** Serves as a worldwide partnership of women's funds, donors, and allies committed to social justice. Seeks to ensure that women's funds are recognized as the "investment of choice" for people who value the full participation of women and girls as key to strong, equitable, and sustainable communities and societies. Supports the solutions of women and girls through local, national and international grants. Advances the movement by supporting funds through innovative programs and capacity-building expertise. **Formerly:** (1995) National Network of Women's Funds. **Publications:** *Donor Circles: Launching and Leveraging Shared Giving*. Report. Alternate Formats: online ● *Making a Difference: New Wealth, Women & Philanthropy*. Report. Alternate Formats: online ● Annual Reports, annual. Alternate Formats: online. **Conventions/Meetings:** annual conference.

13165 ■ Women's International Center (WIC)
PO Box 880736
San Diego, CA 92168-0736
Ph: (619)295-6446
Fax: (619)296-1633
E-mail: info@wic.org
URL: http://www.wic.org
Contact: Gloria J. Lane PhD, Pres./Founder
Founded: 1982. **Membership Dues:** regular, $40 (annual). **Description:** Individuals interested in the "enduring contributions to humanity" of women. Seeks to "acknowledge, honor, and encourage women". Operates: Women's International Institute, which offers educational programs on the social, political, and economic contributions of women to society; and O[Wo]men's International Center, which displays the enduring works of women. Sponsors Operation Greatness, which donates low water tree seedlings to environmentally minded individuals and organizations. Maintains Sistership Fund, which offers financial assistance to young women wishing to attend the Living Legacy Awards ceremonies. **Awards:** Living Legacy Awards. **Frequency:** annual. **Type:** recognition. **Recipient:** for individuals who have made outstanding contributions to humanity. **Publications:** *Living Legacy International Cookbook*. **Price:** $20.00.

13166 ■ Women's Learning Partnership for Rights, Development, and Peace (WLP)
4343 Montgomery Ave., Ste.201
Bethesda, MD 20814
Ph: (301)654-2774
Fax: (301)654-2775
E-mail: wlp@learningpartnership.org
URL: http://learningpartnership.org
Contact: Mahnaz Afkhami, Pres./CEO
Multinational. Description: Empowers women and girls in the Global South to re-imagine and restructure their roles in their families, communities and societies. Forms partnerships with women's NGOs in the Global South to collaborate on rights, development and peace education. Advances sustainable development and the equitable distribution of resources to women and women's organizations. **Publications:** *eNews*, quarterly. Newsletter. Alternate Formats: online ● Annual Report. Alternate Formats: online.

13167 ■ Women's Services Worldwide (WSW)
PO Box 136
Frazier Park, CA 93225
Ph: (661)361-1177
E-mail: anodyne911@hotmail.com
Contact: Dr. Kate Alexander, Pres./CEO
Founded: 1955. **Membership Dues:** general, $12 (annual). **Languages:** Chinese, English, French, Italian, Japanese. **For-Profit. Multinational. Description:** Individuals and organizations. Seeks to improve the quality of life of women worldwide. Provides assistance to women, including legal services in child support and stalking cases, secretarial and information services, credit, and political advocacy and action campaigns. Conducts environmental protection activities; sponsors research and educational programs; makes available children's services; maintains museum and hall of fame; participates in charitable initiatives; compiles statistics; offers retreats in Maine and Missouri. **Libraries: Type:** open to the public; reference. **Holdings:** archival material, books, clippings, periodicals. **Subjects:** women's issues. **Awards:** Glenayre. **Frequency:** periodic. **Type:** recognition. **Recipient:** to individuals and organizations helping women ● **Frequency:** periodic. **Type:** monetary ● Two White Wolves Awards. **Frequency:** periodic. **Type:** fellowship. **Recipient:** for members or their children. **Computer Services:** database ● mailing lists ● online services ● record retrieval services. **Telecommunication Services:** 24-hour hotline, (818)753-3348. **Publications:** *William Wallace Worldwide*, monthly. Newsletter. **Price:** included in membership dues. **Advertising:** accepted ● Journal, periodic ● Directory, periodic ● Brochure ● Bulletin. **Conventions/Meetings:** periodic board meeting ● periodic conference ● periodic convention ● periodic trade show.

13168 ■ Women's World Banking - USA (WWB)
8 W 40th St., 9th Fl.
New York, NY 10018
Ph: (212)768-8513
Fax: (212)768-8519
E-mail: wwb@swwb.org
URL: http://www.swwb.org
Contact: Ms. Mary Ellen Iskenderian, Pres./CEO
Founded: 1979. **Members:** 49. **Staff:** 30. **Budget:** $8,000,000. **Languages:** English, French, Spanish. **Multinational. Description:** Aims to expand low-income women's economic assets, participation and power by opening access to finance, information and markets. Provides and organizes support to affiliates who in turn offer direct services to low-income women. Builds learning and change networks comprised of leading microfinance institutions and banks. Works with policy makers to build financial systems that work for the "poor majority". Seeks to create an environment that will help a low income woman build her business, improve her living conditions, keep her family well-fed and healthy, educate her children, develop respect at home and in her community, and secure a political voice. **Libraries: Type:** open to the public. **Publications:** *Global Network for Banking Innovation*. Bulletin. Alternate Formats: online ● *What Works*, periodic. Newsletter ● Manuals. **Conventions/Meetings:** annual Global Meeting - conference.

Women's Rights

13169 ■ Alliance for Women's Equality (AWE)
25 Washington St., 4th Fl.
Brooklyn, NY 11201
Ph: (718)237-8761
E-mail: info@womensequality.org
URL: http://www.womensequality.org
Contact: Erin Michelson, Founder/Pres.
Founded: 2002. **Description:** Seeks to advance gender equality and helps build sustainable organization that protects and promotes women's and girls' rights. Conducts independent research on nonprofit sustainability issues. Hosts public education and outreach programs. **Publications:** *Equality Update*, quarterly. Newsletter. Alternate Formats: online.

13170 ■ Black Women's Agenda (BWA)
1090 Vermont Ave. NW, Ste.800
Washington, DC 20005
Ph: (202)216-5797
Fax: (202)408-9888
URL: http://www.blackwomensagenda.org
Contact: Ms. Sonia R. Jarvis Esq., Pres.
Founded: 1977. **Description:** Promotes education and advocates for the rights of Black women. **Publications:** *BWA Report*, quarterly. Newsletter.

13171 ■ Shared Hope International (SHI)
PO Box 65337
Vancouver, WA 98665
Ph: (360)693-8100 (703)351-8062
Free: (866)HER-LIFE
Fax: (360)695-9489
E-mail: savelives@sharedhope.org
URL: http://www.sharedhope.org
Contact: Linda Smith, Founder
Founded: 1998. **Multinational. Description:** Commits to rescue and restore women and children in crisis; aims to prevent and eradicate sex trafficking and slavery. **Publications:** Report, annual ● Newsletter. Alternate Formats: online.

Workers

13172 ■ Coalition of Immokalee Workers (CIW)
PO Box 603
Immokalee, FL 34143
Ph: (239)657-8311
Fax: (239)657-5055

E-mail: workers@ciw-online.org

URL: http://www.ciw-online.org

Founded: 1993. **Members:** 2,500. **Description:** Represents immigrants working in low-wage jobs throughout the state of Florida; launches boycotts against corporations to improve wages and working conditions for immigrant workers. **Computer Services:** Mailing lists, listserv. **Publications:** Videos ● Audiotapes ● Reports. Alternate Formats: online.

World War II

13173 ■ Global Alliance for Preserving the History of WWII in Asia (GA)

PO Box 1478

Cupertino, CA 95015-1478

E-mail: gainfo@global-alliance.net

URL: http://www.global-alliance.net

Founded: 1994. **Members:** 40. **Multinational.** **Description:** Works to preserve the historical truth of the Asia-Pacific War (1931-1945). **Telecommunication Services:** electronic mail, gainfo@gainfo.org. **Conventions/Meetings:** biennial conference.

YMCA

13174 ■ Association of YMCA Professionals (AYP)

12 Broad St., Ste.2-1

Westerly, RI 02891

Ph: (401)604-0034

Fax: (401)604-0036

E-mail: john@aypymca.org

URL: http://www.aypymca.org

Contact: Mr. John B. Coduri, Natl. Exec. Dir./CEO

Founded: 1871. **Members:** 6,500. **Membership Dues:** individual, $125 (annual). **Staff:** 3. **Regional Groups:** 7. **Local Groups:** 36. **Description:** Professional organization of YMCA directors in the U.S. Develops professional skills, leadership, and bonds of fellowship. **Sections:** Physical Education and Retired. **Formerly:** Association of Secretaries, Young Men's Christian Associations of North America; (2002) Association of Professional Directors, Young Men's Christian Associations in the United States; (2005) Association of Professional Directors of YM-CAs in the United States. **Publications:** *Perspective*, 8/year. Journal. **Advertising:** accepted. **Conventions/Meetings:** annual meeting (exhibits).

13175 ■ North American YMCA Development Organization (NAYDO)

c/o Mary Zoller

21 Chateau Trianon

Kenner, LA 70065

Ph: (504)464-7845

Fax: (504)464-6718

E-mail: info@naydo.org

URL: http://www.naydo.org

Contact: Merv Bennett, Chm.

Membership Dues: new, $175 ● association (based on association budget), $200-$1,250 (annual). **Multinational. Description:** Strengthens the financial development of YMCA. Supports the integration of philanthropy into all aspects of YMCA work in North America. **Libraries: Type:** reference. **Awards:** Excellence in Fundraising Eagle Award. **Frequency:** annual. **Type:** recognition. **Recipient:** for outstanding work in financial development. **Computer Services:** Online services, e-mail discussion group. **Publications:** Newsletter. Alternate Formats: online. **Conventions/Meetings:** annual conference.

13176 ■ YMCA International Branch

5 W 63rd St., 2nd Fl.

New York, NY 10023

Ph: (212)727-8800

Free: (888)477-9622

Fax: (212)727-8814

E-mail: ips@ymcanyc.org

URL: http://www.internationalymca.org

Contact: Alice L. Mairs, Exec. Dir.

Founded: 1911. **Members:** 20. **Budget:** $2,000,000. **Multinational. Description:** International program run through YMCA of Greater New York, on behalf of the YMCA of the USA. Aims to assist international students and sponsored visitors who have come to the U.S. for study or purposeful, short-term travel. Serves all students, scholars,, and trainees from abroad as the designated agency for their reception at 12 international airports in the U.S. Plans educational tours within the U.S. for individuals and groups. **Convention/Meeting:** none. **Awards: Frequency:** annual. **Type:** scholarship. **Recipient:** for participants in YMCA International Camp Counselor Program. **Committees:** International Advisory. **Programs:** Arrivals Service; Educational Travel; International Camp Counselor (inbound and outbound); Multinational Leadership Training. **Formerly:** YMCA International Student Services; (1998) YMCA International Program Services. **Publications:** *IPS News*, semiannual. **Price:** free. **Circulation:** 5,000 ● Brochures ● Handbooks ● Newsletter. Alternate Formats: online.

13177 ■ YMCA of the USA

c/o Association Advancement

101 N Wacker Dr.

Chicago, IL 60606

Ph: (312)977-0031

Free: (800)872-9622

Fax: (312)977-9063

E-mail: fulfillment@ymca.net

URL: http://www.ymca.net

Contact: Mr. Neil Nicoll, Pres./CEO

Founded: 1851. **Members:** 13,509,199. **Staff:** 9,692. **Budget:** $1,762,514,148. **Description:** A volunteer movement characterized by local program control designed to meet the community needs of people of all ages, races, religions, abilities, and incomes. Focuses on nurturing the healthy development of children, promoting positive behavior in teens, and strengthening families. Provides group activities, facilities for physical and health education and training, youth sports activities, aquatics instruction, camping, parent-child programs, child care, and counseling. Works to address a diversity of social issues through innovative programs in juvenile justice, international exchange and education, job training, relief work, and environmental action. Each YMCA functions independently to meet the needs of the community it serves. Maintains placement service and hall of fame. Compiles statistics. A member of World Alliance of Young Men's Christian Associations. **Libraries: Type:** reference. **Awards: Type:** recognition. **Absorbed:** (2003) YMCA International. **Also Known As:** Young Men's Christian Associations of the United States of America. **Publications:** *Discovery YMCA*, quarterly. Magazine. **Advertising:** accepted ● *Executive Notes*, bimonthly ● *Program Notes*, quarterly ● *Property Management News*, quarterly ● *Risk Report*, quarterly ● *Yearbook and Official Roster* ● *YMCA Directory*, annual ● Annual Report, annual ● Books ● Manuals ● Pamphlets. **Conventions/Meetings:** general assembly - every 4-5 years ● biennial meeting (exhibits).

13178 ■ Y's Men International, U.S. Area

c/o Rob Wilby, Pres.

1165 Concord Dr.

Haddonfield, NJ 08033-3502

E-mail: ihq@ysmen.org

URL: http://www.ysmen.org

Contact: Rob Wilby, Pres.

Founded: 1922. **Members:** 2,200. **Regional Groups:** 9. **Local Groups:** 140. **Description:** Serves as a service club for the Young Men's Christian Associations of the United States of America. Raises funds, operates youth camps, and engages in other activities in support of local YMCA clubs and youth. Conducts regional training programs. **Awards: Type:** recognition. **Recipient:** for club achievements and to outstanding YMCA professionals. **Additional Websites:** http://www.ysmenusa.com. **Funds:** Brotherhood; Time of Fast. **Programs:** International Brother Club; Short Term Exchange; Youth Educational

Exchange. **Projects:** Time of Fast. **Publications:** *Y's Alliance*, quarterly. Newsletter. Features membership activities. **Price:** included in membership dues. **Circulation:** 10,000. **Conventions/Meetings:** biennial convention (exhibits).

Youth

13179 ■ Allied Youth and Family Counseling Center (AYFCC)

8204 Elm Brook Dr.

Dallas, TX 75247

Ph: (214)943-1044

Fax: (214)361-7501

Contact: Kathie H. Higgins, Dir.

Founded: 1931. **Description:** An outpatient counseling program for youth and their families. Services include treatment for alcohol and drug abuse, marriage and family counseling, psychological testing, and insurance coverage. Sponsors education program. **Formerly:** Allied Youth.

13180 ■ American Association of Children's Residential Centers (AACRC)

11700 W Lake Park Dr.

Milwaukee, WI 53224

Free: (877)332-2272

Fax: (877)362-2272

E-mail: mskarich@alliance1.org

URL: http://www.aacrc-dc.org

Contact: Maggie Skarich, Natl. Coor.

Founded: 1956. **Members:** 400. **Membership Dues:** agency, $950 (annual) ● individual, $95 (annual) ● student, $20 (annual). **Budget:** $200,000. **Description:** Multidisciplinary mental health professionals involved in treatment services for emotionally disturbed children; agencies meeting quality standards of residential care. Promotes high standards and advances the concepts and methods of residential treatment; encourages public and government understanding of basic concepts and practices in residential treatment. Represents children and families before standard-setting and rate-setting bodies; participates in programs of education, training, and research in the field of residential treatment, and offers children's services and continuing education credit programs. Maintains speakers' bureau and placement service. **Libraries: Type:** reference. **Holdings:** clippings, periodicals. **Subjects:** children's mental health. **Awards:** Albert E. Trieschman Award. **Frequency:** annual. **Type:** recognition. **Publications:** *Contributions to Residential Treatment*, annual. Proceedings. Contains papers presented at AACRC annual meeting. Topics include research, protocols, treatment, and quality assurance. **Price:** included in membership dues; $20.00 for nonmembers. **Circulation:** 200. **Advertising:** accepted ● *Journal of Residential Treatment for Children and Youth*, quarterly. Includes book reviews, children's writings, poetry, research summaries, and scientific papers. **Price:** included in membership dues. ISSN: 0731-7123. **Advertising:** accepted ● *Residential Treatment Newsletter*, bimonthly. Reports on residential issues relating to children's mental health. Covers research, treatment, government programs, and AACRC news. **Price:** included in membership dues. **Circulation:** 350. **Advertising:** accepted ● Membership Directory, annual. Includes costs, location, staffing patterns, treatment philosophy, and accreditations. **Price:** $20.00/year. **Conventions/Meetings:** annual conference (exhibits) - always October.

13181 ■ American Youth Policy Forum (AYPF)

1836 Jefferson Pl. NW

Washington, DC 20036

Ph: (202)775-9731

Fax: (202)775-9733

E-mail: aypf@aypf.org

URL: http://www.aypf.org

Contact: Betsy Brand, Dir.

Founded: 1993. **Description:** Works to improve opportunities, services and life prospects for youth; provides training for policy makers and practitioners at all levels. **Publications:** *Finding Common Ground: Service-Learning and Education Reform.* Report. **Price:** $10.00. Alternate Formats: online ● *Higher Learning = Higher Earnings.* Booklet. For students in middle and high school needing guidance in decision-making for their future. **Price:** $2.00. Alternate Formats: online ● *Lessons Learned: What the WAY Program Can Teach Us About Program Replication.* Paper. **Price:** $3.00. Alternate Formats: online ● *Restoring the Balance Between Academics and Civic Engagements in Public Schools.* Report. **Price:** $5.00 plus shipping and handling. Alternate Formats: online ● *Twenty-Five Years of Educating Children with Disabilities: The Good News and the Work Ahead.* Highlights statistics showing progress in educating disabled children. **Price:** $4.00. Alternate Formats: online.

13182 ■ American Youth Work Center (AYWC)
1200 17th St. NW, 4th Fl.
Washington, DC 20036
Ph: (202)785-0764
E-mail: info@youthtoday.org
URL: http://www.youthtoday.org
Contact: Bill Treanor, Exec. Dir.
Founded: 1984. **Members:** 25. **Membership Dues:** regular, $1,000 (annual). **Staff:** 10. **Budget:** $2,000,000. **Description:** Represents the interests of community-based youth service programs, including group homes, runaway programs, counseling centers, hot lines, multi-purpose programs, youth employment programs, and delinquency treatment and prevention programs. Assists youth service programs through training, seminars, technical assistance, conferences, legislative information, and research. Acts as an advocate for youth programs; monitors Congress and federal agencies. Coordinates international exchange programs for youth workers. **Publications:** *Adolescent Life Stress as a Predictor of Alcohol and/or Runaway Behavior* ● *American Directory of Youth Work Educators and Trainers* ● *Barriers to Developing Comprehensive and Effective Youth Services* ● *Kids and Guns* ● *National Directory of Runaway Programs* ● *Youth Today: The Newspaper on Youth Work*, 10/year. Contains issues of child advocacy, juvenile justice, youth development and health, after school programs and other issues. **Price:** $24.50/year. **Circulation:** 15,331. **Advertising:** accepted. **Conventions/Meetings:** annual meeting.

13183 ■ America's Promise - The Alliance for Youth
909 N Washington St., Ste.400
Alexandria, VA 22314-1556
Ph: (703)684-4500
Free: (888)55Y-OUTH
Fax: (703)535-3900
E-mail: webmaster@americaspromise.org
URL: http://www.americaspromise.org
Contact: Marguerite W. Kondracke, Pres./CEO
Founded: 1997. **Members:** 500. **Languages:** English, Spanish. **Description:** Works to strengthen the character and competence of youth by fulfilling Five Promises for young people. **Computer Services:** database, Great Ideas ● mailing lists, young leaders listserv. **Publications:** *America's Promise Email Bulletin*, weekly. Alternate Formats: online ● *The Promise Letter*, quarterly. Newsletter. Alternate Formats: online.

13184 ■ Boys and Girls Clubs of America (BGCA)
1275 Peachtree St. NE
Atlanta, GA 30309-3506
Ph: (404)487-5700
Free: (800)854-CLUB
Fax: (404)487-5825
E-mail: info@bgca.org
URL: http://www.bgca.org
Contact: Roxanne Spillett, Pres./CEO
Founded: 1906. **Members:** 3,600,000. **Local Groups:** 3,300. **Description:** Serves as a youth development organization comprised of a network of more than 3,300 neighborhood-based facilities offering services to more than 3.6 million disadvantaged

youth. Promotes the health, social, educational, vocational, and character development of youth. Provides club, known as the "Positive Place for Kids" that conducts a variety of guidance activities every afternoon and evening. Provides programs that emphasize on: drug and alcohol prevention, delinquency intervention, health and fitness, career exploration, educational enhancement, and leadership development. **Awards: Frequency:** annual. **Type:** recognition. **Formerly:** (1906) Boys' Club Federation of America; (1991) Boys Clubs of America. **Publications:** *Connections*, quarterly. Magazine ● Annual Report, annual ● Also publishes pamphlets, manuals, guidebooks, and booklets. **Conventions/Meetings:** annual conference (exhibits) - usually May.

13185 ■ Boys Hope Girls Hope
12120 Bridgeton Square Dr.
Bridgeton, MO 63044-2607
Ph: (314)298-1250
Free: (877)878-HOPE
Fax: (314)298-1251
E-mail: hope@bhgh.org
URL: http://www.boyshopegirlshope.org
Contact: Peggy Slater, Dir. of Organizational Advancement
Founded: 1975. **Staff:** 21. **Budget:** $1,900,000. **Local Groups:** 16. **National Groups:** 3. **Nonmembership. Multinational. Description:** Long-term residential and educational program. Provides stable homes, college preparatory education, family support, counseling, and referral services to children who are in need of a long-term, alternative living arrangement. **Affiliated With:** Boys Hope Girls Hope of Chicago; Boys Hope Girls Hope of San Francisco Bay Area. **Formerly:** (2000) Boys Hope.

13186 ■ Boys Town Jerusalem Foundation of America (BTJFOA)
12 W 31st St., Ste.300
New York, NY 10001
Ph: (212)244-2766
Free: (800)4MY-BOYS
Fax: (212)244-2052
E-mail: btjny@compuserve.com
URL: http://www.boystownjerusalem.com
Contact: Rabbi Ronald L. Gray, Exec. VP
Founded: 1948. **Description:** Provides financial support for growth and maintenance of Boys Town Jerusalem, Israel, which provides academic, religious, and technological training to over 1000 students at the junior and senior high school levels and offers a college of applied engineering. Raises funds, conducts a public relations program, and purchases technological equipment for the school. **Supersedes:** American Friends of Boys Town Jerusalem. **Publications:** *Boys Town Jerusalem Newsbriefs*, annual.

13187 ■ Boys' Towns of Italy (BTI)
250 E 63rd St., Ste.204
New York, NY 10021
Ph: (212)980-8770
Fax: (212)644-0766
E-mail: office@btiofny.org
URL: http://www.boystown.it
Contact: Grace M. Iannuzzi, Dir.
Founded: 1945. **Description:** Serves as an American agency that raises funds to establish and sustain child-care facilities in Italy and the U.S. Sponsors Boys' Town of Rome, Girls' Town of Rome, and International Center for Youth Studies, specializing in education for responsibility through self-government. **Formerly:** American Relief for Italy. **Publications:** *News*, monthly.

13188 ■ Camp Fire USA
1100 Walnut St., Ste.1900
Kansas City, MO 64106-2197
Ph: (816)285-2010
Fax: (816)285-9444
E-mail: info@campfireusa.org
URL: http://www.campfireusa.org
Contact: Jill Pasewalk, Natl. CEO
Founded: 1910. **Members:** 735,000. **Staff:** 30. **Local Groups:** 121. **Languages:** English, Spanish. **De-

scription:** Provides all-inclusive, coeducational programs in hundreds of communities across the United States. Provides outcome-based programs including youth leadership, self-reliance, camping and environmental education and child care. Aims to build caring, confident youth and future leaders. **Awards:** Camp Fire USA Wohelo Award. **Frequency:** annual. **Type:** recognition. **Recipient:** for high school juniors and seniors whose works focus on leadership, teaching, service, and advocacy. **Formerly:** (1910) Camp Fire Girls; (1989) Camp Fire Boys and Girls. **Publications:** *Camp Fire USA Annual Report*, annual, usually fall. Includes the corporate year's accomplishments and financial statements. **Price:** $1.00. Alternate Formats: online ● *Letters from the Heart: A Celebration of Letters to Absolutely Incredible Kids.* Book. **Conventions/Meetings:** annual conference, provides training opportunities for council executives, Board chairs, program and other lead staff and youth leaders.

13189 ■ Campaign For Our Children (CFOC)
c/o Hal Donofrio, Pres./CEO
One N Charles St., Ste.1100
Baltimore, MD 21201
Ph: (410)576-9015
Fax: (410)752-7075
E-mail: hal@cfoc.org
URL: http://www.cfoc.org
Contact: Bronwyn Mayden MSW, Consultant
Founded: 1987. **Staff:** 5. **Languages:** English, Spanish. **Description:** Promotes healthy and responsible sexual decisions among early-adolescent youth. Provides support system. **Computer Services:** Mailing lists, of members. **Programs:** Marriage Works USA.

13190 ■ Carnegie Council on Adolescent Development (CCAD)
PO Box 753
Waldorf, MD 20604
Free: (800)998-2269
URL: http://www.carnegie.org/sub/research/adol
Contact: Vartan Gregorian, Pres.
Founded: 1986. **Staff:** 8. **Description:** A program of Carnegie Corporation of New York. Works to "place the challenges of the adolescent years higher on the nation's agenda." Provides information to the general public on the risks and opportunities of the adolescent years; generates support for measures that facilitate the critical transition into adulthood. **Libraries: Type:** not open to the public. **Holdings:** 1,000. **Subjects:** adolescence, health, education, public policy. **Publications:** *A Matter of Time: Risk and Opportunity in the Nonschool Hours.* Book ● *Carnegie Council on Adolescent Development Working Papers*, periodic ● *Fateful Choices: Healthy Youth for the 21st Century.* Book ● *Preventing Abuse of Drugs, Alcohol, and Tobacco by Adolescents.* Book ● *Risk Taking in Adolescence: A Decision-Making Perspective.* Book ● *Turning Points: Preparing American Youth for the 21st Century.* Book ● Papers.

13191 ■ Children's Friendship Project for Northern Ireland (CFPNI)
c/o Glenn A. Martinsen, Treas.
7 Old Manchester Rd.
Derry, NH 03038-7312
Ph: (603)432-4301
Fax: (603)437-6543
E-mail: president@cfpni.org
URL: http://www.cfpni.org
Contact: Christine Robidoux, Pres.
Founded: 1987. **Members:** 5,000. **State Groups:** 28. **Description:** Promotes increased understanding and tolerance among the youth of Northern Ireland. Sponsors a summer program which pairs Catholic and Protestant youths between the ages of 15-18 for a four-week stay with a host family in the United States. Organizes ongoing activities in Northern Ireland for former participants. Conducts fundraising activities to corn cost of trainport activities. **Publications:** *CFPNI Cookbook.* Contains over 100 recipes from Northern Ireland and USA. **Price:** $15.00/copy (shipping included) ● *Host Family.* Handbook. Alternate Formats: online ● *National Newsletter*,

quarterly. **Price:** free. **Circulation:** 2,200. Alternate Formats: online ● Books ● Brochures. **Conventions/Meetings:** annual board meeting and reunion - always last weekend of October, in Dungannon Co. Tyrone, Northern Ireland.

13192 ■ CityKids Foundation (CKF)
57 Leonard St.
New York, NY 10013
Ph: (212)925-3320
Fax: (212)925-0128
E-mail: info@citykids.com
URL: http://www.citykids.com
Contact: Elizabeth Sak, Pres.
Founded: 1985. **Members:** 300. **Staff:** 21. **Budget:** $1,200,000. **Languages:** English, Spanish. **Description:** Designs and organizes youth initiative programs including: City Kids Coalition, which works with multiracial teenagers from schools and youth groups to organize projects and events; CityKids Speak, an annual event that provides a platform for young people to express themselves on youth issues. Collaborates with professionals to provide social services and job training. Conducts workshops. Conducts programs in the New York City and New Haven, CT area, but plans to expand activities internationally. **Computer Services:** Mailing lists. **Telecommunication Services:** electronic mail, sak@citykids.com. **Programs:** Bridgebuilder Initiative; CityKids in Action; CityKids Repertory Company; CK101; Coalition; New Works Lab; Support Services; Youth Leadership Conferences. **Projects:** International Youth Exchange; Peer Leadership Training. **Formerly:** (1989) Network International. **Publications:** *City Kids Speak on Prejudice.* Book ● *City Kids Speak on Relationships.* Book ● *Kayla's Story.* Video. **Price:** $79.00 plus shipping and handling and taxes ● *Monthly Letter.* Newsletter.

13193 ■ Coalition for Positive Sexuality (CPS)
PO Box 77212
Washington, DC 20013-8212
Ph: (773)604-1654
URL: http://www.positive.org
Contact: Jeanette May, Founding Member
Founded: 1992. **Members:** 10. **Languages:** English, Spanish. **Description:** Provides complete and honest sex education to teens. **Computer Services:** Online services, Let's Talk, Talk Back. **Publications:** *Just Say Yes* (in English and Spanish). Booklet. Contains information about teen sex education, with annual updates. Alternate Formats: online.

13194 ■ Covenant House (CH)
5 Penn Plz.
New York, NY 10108
Ph: (212)727-4000
Free: (800)388-3888
Fax: (212)727-4992
E-mail: info@covenanthouseny.org
URL: http://www.covenanthouse.org
Contact: Mr. William J. Montgoris, Chm.
Founded: 1972. **Staff:** 1,250. **Budget:** $69,000,000. **Regional Groups:** 14. **Multinational. Description:** Crisis center providing immediate, short-term care for runaway and homeless youth under 21 years of age, including counseling, food, shelter, clothing, medical treatment, and legal assistance. Operates transitional living programs for homeless youth, young mothers and their children. Operates short-term substance abuse intervention program. Maintains speakers' bureau. **Computer Services:** Mailing lists. **Telecommunication Services:** hotline, crisis counseling, (800)999-9999. **Programs:** Aftercare; Mother/Child; Substance Abuse. **Publications:** *The Covenant House Beacon,* monthly. Newsletter. Alternate Formats: online ● Annual Report, annual. Alternate Formats: online.

13195 ■ Direction Sports (DS)
Address Unknown since 2007
Founded: 1968. **Members:** 17,000. **Staff:** 4. **Budget:** $100,000. **State Groups:** 7. **Local Groups:** 2. **Languages:** English, Spanish. **Description:** Designs, tests, and operates methods of peer-run educational/recreational programming to enhance learning skills, motivation to learn, and self-esteem. The programs are designed to be operated by community teenagers, including gang members and drop-outs, who work under the mentorship of college students. They are paid minimum wage and instruct the communities children, ages 7 to 12, including: 30-minute reading and math lessons, called "chalk talks," which are designed to teach academic skills; an hour of team practice in a seasonal sport; a 30-minute group discussion session emphasizing values. Sponsors team competitions weekly. Maintains speakers' bureau. Trains and awards older youth as peer instructors. Schools, recreation departments, and youth-serving organizations such as YMCAs and Boys Clubs can purchase curriculum, program materials, and training and evaluation systems from DS. A video containing clips from some of the fourteen network and International television shows can be purchased. **Publications:** *Direction Sports—Newsletter,* semiannual. **Price:** $6.00/year. **Circulation:** 10,000. **Advertising:** not accepted ● Also makes available videotapes from network television coverage. **Conventions/Meetings:** After School Peer Power - meeting and seminar, provide training and materials in each city.

13196 ■ Families, 4-H, and Nutrition
Cooperative State Res. Educ. and Extension Ser.
1400 Independence Ave. SW, Stop 2225
Washington, DC 20250-2225
Ph: (202)720-2908
Fax: (202)720-9366
E-mail: mgray@csrees.usda.gov
URL: http://www.csrees.usda.gov/about/offices/f4hn.html
Contact: Mary McPhail Gray PhD, Deputy Admin.
Founded: 1900. **Members:** 6,834,338. **Description:** Youth, primarily nine to 19 years old, in rural and urban areas of 3150 counties in the United States, the District of Columbia, Puerto Rico, Guam, Virgin Islands, American Samoa, Micronesia, and Northern Marianas. Serves as a youth education program of the Cooperative Extension System. Volunteer adult and junior leaders guide the program with the help of the U.S. Department of Agriculture and participating governments. Assists youths in acquiring knowledge, developing life skills, and forming attitudes that will enable them to become self-directing, contributing members of society. **Affiliated With:** American Humanics; National 4-H Council. **Formerly:** 4-H Program and Youth Development. **Conventions/Meetings:** annual National 4-H Congress ● annual National 4-H Week - meeting.

13197 ■ Fresh Lifelines for Youth (FLY)
120 W Mission St.
San Jose, CA 95110
Ph: (408)263-2630
E-mail: christa@flyprogram.org
URL: http://www.flyprogram.org
Contact: Christa Gannon, Exec. Dir.
Founded: 1998. **Description:** Advocates for reduction of juvenile crime and incarceration through legal education, mentoring and peer leadership services. Educates disadvantaged and at-risk youth to help them become more responsible, accountable and capable of making healthier lifestyle choices. Helps teens in trouble learn to make healthy decisions. Provides graduates the opportunity to advance to a leadership program where they have the chance to use their knowledge and skills to help other teens in trouble.

13198 ■ Friends for Youth (FFY)
1741 Broadway
Redwood City, CA 94063
Ph: (650)368-4444
Fax: (650)368-4467
E-mail: info@mentoringinstitute.org
URL: http://www.homestead.com/prosites-ffy
Contact: Becky Cooper, Exec. Dir.
Founded: 1979. **Description:** Works to support youth in need through mentoring and Mentoring Institute. **Publications:** Annual Report, annual. Alternate Formats: online. **Conventions/Meetings:** conference.

13199 ■ Girls Inc.
120 Wall St.
New York, NY 10005-3902
Ph: (212)509-2000
Free: (800)374-4475
Fax: (212)509-8708
E-mail: nrc@girls-inc.org
URL: http://www.girlsinc.org
Contact: Joyce M. Roche, Pres./CEO
Founded: 1945. **Members:** 130. **Budget:** $9,800,000. **Regional Groups:** 4. **Local Groups:** 130. **Description:** Works to inspire girls to be strong, smart, and bold; aims to respond to the changing needs of girls and their communities through programs and advocacy that empower girls to reach full potential and to understand, value, and assert their rights. **Libraries: Type:** reference. **Holdings:** 6,000; articles, periodicals, video recordings. **Subjects:** gender equity for girls. **Computer Services:** database. **Programs:** Discovery; Economic Literacy; Friendly PEERsuasion; Media Literacy; Operation Smart; Preventing Adolescent Pregnancy; Project Bold; Sporting Chance. **Formerly:** (1990) Girls Clubs of America. **Publications:** *Annual Report,* annual. Provides information of the club's financial status. **Price:** free. Alternate Formats: online ● *Girls Ink,* quarterly. Newsletter. Provides information of interest to young girls and women including teen pregnancy and drug abuse. Includes calendar of events. **Price:** free ● *Publications Catalogue.* **Conventions/Meetings:** biennial conference - always April ● meeting - always fall.

13200 ■ I Have a Dream Foundation
330 7th Ave., 20th Fl.
New York, NY 10001-5010
Ph: (212)293-5480
Fax: (212)293-5478
E-mail: info@ihad.org
URL: http://www.ihad.org
Contact: Ms. Kara Forte, Interim Pres./CEO
Founded: 1985. **Members:** 75. **Staff:** 11. **Budget:** $1,500,000. **Local Groups:** 196. **Description:** Works to help children from low income areas reach their education and career goals by providing a long-term program of mentoring, tutoring, and enrichment with an assured opportunity for higher education. **Publications:** *Dreamer Digest,* semiannual. Newsletter. Provides news and announcements. **Circulation:** 2,500. Alternate Formats: online ● Annual Report. Alternate Formats: online.

13201 ■ Indify
3418 Hwy. 6 S, Ste.B, No. 309
Houston, TX 77082
E-mail: info@indify.org
URL: http://www.indify.org
Description: Seeks to empower the new generation of Indian-Americans as they strive to create their identity in the United States. Creates experiences and opportunities that encourage Indian-Americans to strengthen themselves and to actively contribute to the world around them. Develops programs to encourage leadership and build strong community identity and unity. **Publications:** Newsletter, semiannual. Alternate Formats: online.

13202 ■ Institute in Basic Life Principles (IBLP)
Box 1
Oak Brook, IL 60522-3001
Ph: (630)323-9800
Free: (800)398-1290
E-mail: info@iblp.org
URL: http://www.iblp.org
Contact: Bill Gothard, Pres.
Founded: 1961. **Staff:** 150. **Languages:** Chinese, English, Russian, Spanish. **Description:** Conducts seminars for parents and youth on how to apply 7 universal, non-optional principles of life. Sponsors a curriculum designed for parents to use in educating their sons and daughters at home and through ap-

prenticeship training. Conducts specialized seminars for corporate leaders, medical doctors, and vocational groups. **Formerly:** (1964) Campus Teens; (1992) Institute in Basic Youth Conflicts.

13203 ■ International Youth Foundation (IYF)
32 South St., Ste.500
Baltimore, MD 21202
Ph: (410)951-1500
Fax: (410)347-1188
E-mail: youth@iyfnet.org
URL: http://www.iyfnet.org
Contact: William S. Reese, Pres./CEO

Founded: 1990. **Staff:** 30. **Budget:** $15,236,659. **Description:** Dedicated to the positive development of children and youth between the ages of 5 and 20. Strives to build a global network of independent youth foundations; seeks to increase international philanthropy; conducts educational programs. **Computer Services:** database ● mailing lists. **Publications:** *Perspectives on Children and Youth.* Newsletter ● Brochure.

13204 ■ Jackie Robinson Foundation (JRF)
3 W 35th St., 11th Fl.
New York, NY 10001-2204
Ph: (212)290-8600
Fax: (212)290-8081
E-mail: general@jackierobinson.org
URL: http://www.jackierobinson.org
Contact: Della Britton Baeza, Pres./CEO

Founded: 1973. **Staff:** 8. **Budget:** $1,200,000. **Regional Groups:** 6. **Description:** Seeks to develop the leadership and achievement potential of minority and urban youth. Founded by the friends and family of Jackie Robinson (1919-72), the first black athlete to play major league baseball. Trains minority and poor youths for sports management careers. Provides counseling, support, and placement services. Awards full college scholarships to promising minority students. Maintains collection of Jackie Robinson memorabilia; has produced a national touring exhibit of archival materials pertaining to Robinson. **Libraries:** Type: reference. **Awards:** Robie Award for Achievement in Industry. **Frequency:** annual. **Type:** recognition. **Recipient:** to an individual who has devoted a lifetime to the promotion of social justice and human dignity ● Robie Award Humanitarianism. **Frequency:** annual. **Type:** recognition. **Recipient:** to an individual who has devoted a lifetime to the promotion of social justice and human dignity. **Computer Services:** database. **Committees:** Regional Scholarship Selection. **Programs:** Education and Leadership Development. **Publications:** *Fastball.* Newsletter. Alternate Formats: online ● *Jackie Robinson Foundation Awards Dinner Journal,* annual. Describes foundation programs and services; includes profiles of award recipients and scholarship sponsors. **Circulation:** 1,300. **Advertising:** accepted ● *Jackie Robinson Foundation Newsletter,* semiannual. Includes program updates and volunteer profiles. **Circulation:** 2,500 ● *Scholarship Student Handbook* ● Annual Report, annual. Alternate Formats: online ● Also publishes concert program. **Conventions/Meetings:** annual dinner - always New York City ● annual Jazz Concert - meeting - always Norwalk, CT.

13205 ■ Jewish Board of Family and Children's Services/Youth Counseling League Division (JBFCS)
120 W 57th St.
New York, NY 10019
Ph: (212)582-9100
Free: (888)523-2769
E-mail: admin@jbfcs.org
URL: http://www.jbfcs.org
Contact: Laura Curchack, Dir.

Languages: English, Spanish. **Description:** An outpatient mental health clinic for troubled adolescents and young adults ages 12 to 21 offering short- and long-term individual, group, and family therapy.

13206 ■ Levitt Foundation
c/o The Philanthropic Group
630 Fifth Ave., 20th Fl.
New York, NY 10111
Ph: (212)501-7785
Fax: (212)501-7788
E-mail: bgreenberg@philanthropicgroup.com
URL: http://foundationcenter.org/grantmaker/levitt
Contact: Barbara R. Greenberg, Contact
Founded: 1949. **Budget:** $700,000. **Description:** Strives to fund youth-based programs that build youth confidence, self-esteem, citizenship skills, and leadership abilities.

13207 ■ National 4-H Council (N4-HC)
7100 Connecticut Ave.
Chevy Chase, MD 20815
Ph: (301)961-2800
E-mail: info@fourhcouncil.edu
URL: http://www.fourhcouncil.edu
Contact: Donald T. Floyd Jr., Pres./CEO
Founded: 1976. **Staff:** 150. **Budget:** $17,000,000. **Nonmembership. Description:** Works to advance the youth development movement to build a world in which youth and adults learn, grow and work together as catalysts for positive change. Operates National 4-H Center, a conference facility. **Awards:** Lifetime Volunteer Award. **Frequency:** annual. **Type:** recognition. **Recipient:** for individual who has spent 10 or more years volunteering for 4-H ● **Frequency:** annual. **Type:** recognition. **Recipient:** for youth led proposals related to community improvements performed by youth-adult partnership teams. **Programs:** Citizenship Washington Focus; Community ATV Safety; 4-H Afterschool; Lawn and Garden Safety Education; Rural Youth Development; Wonders of Washington; Workforce Preparation. **Formed by Merger of:** National 4-H Foundation of America; National 4-H Service Committee. **Publications:** *National 4-H Council Annual Report,* annual. Alternate Formats: online ● *Supply Source Book,* annual. Catalog. Contains curricula and 4-H recognition items for purchase. **Price:** free. **Advertising:** accepted. Alternate Formats: online.

13208 ■ National Association of Extension 4-H Agents (NAE4-HA)
1800 Camden Rd., Ste.107, No. 213
Charlotte, NC 28203
Ph: (704)333-3234
E-mail: 4h@themanagementoffice.com
URL: http://www.nae4ha.org
Contact: Clyde Jackson, Pres.

Founded: 1946. **Members:** 3,452. **Membership Dues:** individual, $65 (annual) ● life, $195. **Budget:** $250,000. **Regional Groups:** 4. **State Groups:** 50. **Description:** Professional extension 4-H and youth personnel. Presents professional improvement scholarships and grants to members. Conducts educational programs. **Awards:** NAE4-HA Communicator Awards. **Type:** recognition. **Recipient:** for members ● **Type:** recognition. **Recipient:** for outstanding service and excellence in programming. **Computer Services:** Mailing lists ● online services, membership records. **Committees:** News and Views; Policy and Resolutions; Professional Improvement; Public Relations and Information; Strategic Planning, Nomination and Member Recognition. **Formerly:** National Association of County Club Agents; (1969) National Association of County 4-H Club Agents. **Publications:** *National Association of Extension 4-H Agents—Membership Report,* annual. Directory. Lists all members, with statistical facts on membership. **Price:** free for members and selected professionals; $4.00 for nonmembers ● *National Association of Extension 4-H Agents—News and Views,* quarterly. Newsletter. Contains professional improvements and association activities. Includes calendar of events. **Price:** included in membership dues; $20.00 /year for nonmembers. **Circulation:** 3,400. **Advertising:** accepted ● *Summary of Annual Professional Improvement Conference.* Includes information on current professional and youth issues, research reports, committee work, and commercial exhibits. **Conventions/Meetings:** annual conference (exhibits) - always November.

13209 ■ National Association of Police Athletic Leagues
658 W Indiantown Rd., Ste.201
Jupiter, FL 33458
Ph: (561)745-5535
Fax: (561)745-3147
E-mail: copnkid@nationalpal.org
URL: http://www.nationalpal.org
Contact: Mr. Mike Dillhyon, Exec. Dir.
Founded: 1944. **Members:** 350. **Membership Dues:** regular, $400 (annual). **Staff:** 6. **Budget:** $750,000. **Description:** Local police athletic leagues; individuals and corporations. A crime prevention program that relies on athletics and recreational activities to create a bond between police officers and community youths that will contribute to the positive prevention of juvenile delinquency while fostering a strong, positive attitude toward police officers. Focuses on the problems of crime and delinquency and on ways to reduce juvenile restlessness. Works to create a series of national youth leagues and to develop new programs and materials. Seeks interaction at state, regional, and national levels with civic and other sports organizations. Offers insurance coverage and a group purchasing program. Conducts research and development programs and national tournaments in basketball, baseball, boxing, ice hockey, and girls' softball. Compiles statistics. **Awards: Type:** recognition. **Also Known As:** National PAL; National Police Athletic League. **Publications:** *Cops n' Kids Chronicles,* quarterly. Newsletter. Provides latest information on sports, fundraising, advertising programs, events, tournaments, and success stories of the league. **Price:** free. **Circulation:** 22,000. **Advertising:** accepted ● *National PAL E-News,* monthly. Newsletter. Contains information about the new programs and opportunities of the association. Alternate Formats: online. **Conventions/Meetings:** annual conference and seminar (exhibits) - May or June ● annual show and general assembly (exhibits).

13210 ■ National Association of Service and Conservation Corps (NASCC)
666 11th St. NW, Ste.1000
Washington, DC 20001
Ph: (202)737-6272
Fax: (202)737-6277
E-mail: sprouty@nascc.org
URL: http://www.nascc.org
Contact: Sally Prouty, Pres.
Founded: 1985. **Members:** 106. **Staff:** 7. **Description:** Acts as a leader of the national corps community providing growth, quality and sustainability of corps. Aims to provide high-quality corps serving every community. **Publications:** *Conservation and Service Corps Profiles,* annual. **Circulation:** 500. Alternate Formats: online ● *Crew Supervisor Training Manual.* Alternate Formats: online ● *NASCC News,* quarterly. Newsletter. Contains corps profiles and calendar of events. **Price:** $25.00/year. **Circulation:** 500 ● *Tools for the Environment.* Manual. Alternate Formats: online ● *Wellness Guide.* Manual ● Also publishes occasional technical resource papers. **Conventions/Meetings:** annual Corps Forum - meeting (exhibits) ● workshop - 20/year.

13211 ■ National Association of Youth Clubs (NAYC)
c/o National Association of Colored Women's Clubs
1601 R St. NW
Washington, DC 20009
Ph: (202)667-4080
Fax: (202)667-2574
E-mail: cearly@nacwcya.org
URL: http://www.nacwc.org/programs/youth.php
Contact: Carole A. Early, Headquarters Sec.
Founded: 1930. **Membership Dues:** regular, $60 (annual) ● associate, $100 (annual) ● life, $500. **Description:** Sponsored by National Association of Colored Women's Clubs. Black youth, ages 6-18. Promotes the moral, mental, and material development of members; fosters positive attitudes toward health, beauty, love, home, and service among members. **Departments:** Arts and Crafts; Business; Education; Fine Arts; Industrial; Interracial; Music; Peace. **Sections:** Band; Better Homes; Camp; Com-

munity Projects; Domestic Science; Dramatics; Drum Corps; Games; Hikes; Interior Decorating; Literature; Music; Negro History; Orchestra; Pageantry; Painting; Physical Education; Rug Making. **Affiliated With:** National Association of Colored Women's Clubs. **Formerly:** (1992) National Association of Girls Clubs. **Conventions/Meetings:** biennial meeting.

13212 ■ National Campaign to Prevent Teen Pregnancy
1776 Massachusetts Ave. NW, Ste.200
Washington, DC 20036
Ph: (202)478-8500
Fax: (202)478-8588
E-mail: campaign@teenpregnancy.org
URL: http://www.teenpregnancy.org
Contact: Sarah S. Brown, Dir.
Founded: 1996. **Languages:** English, Spanish. **Description:** Works to improve the well being of children, youth, and families by reducing teen pregnancy. **Computer Services:** Mailing lists, notification network ● mailing lists, youth network. **Task Forces:** Effective Programs and Research; Media; Religion, Public Values and Public Policy; State and Local Action. **Publications:** *Campaign Update*, quarterly. Newsletter. Alternate Formats: online ● *Partners in Progress.* Offers ways the education community can help prevent teen pregnancy. **Price:** free. Alternate Formats: online ● *Playing Catch-Up: How Children Born to Teen Mothers Fare.* Report. **Price:** $10.00. Alternate Formats: online ● *Talking Back: Ten Things Teen Wants Adults to Know About Teen Pregnancy.* Brochure. **Price:** $1.00/copy, for 1-100 copies. Alternate Formats: online.

13213 ■ National Child Labor Committee (NCLC)
1501 Broadway, Ste.1908
New York, NY 10036
Ph: (212)840-1801
Fax: (212)768-0963
E-mail: nclckapow@aol.com
URL: http://www.kapow.org/nclc.htm
Contact: Jeffrey Newman, Exec. Dir.
Founded: 1904. **Members:** 8,000. **Staff:** 9. **Budget:** $1,229,500. **Description:** Parent organization of National Committee on Employment of Youth and National Committee on the Education of Migrant Children. Provides direct and technical assistance to programs on youth-related issues, particularly education, job training, and employment. **Awards:** Lewis Hine Award. **Frequency:** annual. **Type:** recognition. **Recipient:** to ten individuals for service contribution to children and youth. **Programs:** Kids and the Power of Work. **Publications:** Numerous publications to cooperative education, work experience education programs, and manuals for supervisors of young workers. **Conventions/Meetings:** semiannual board meeting - always New York City.

13214 ■ National Consortium on Alternatives for Youth at Risk
Address Unknown since 2006
Founded: 1989. **Staff:** 2. **Budget:** $120,000. **Description:** Works to research and disseminate information on the needs of youth and on programs that meet these needs. Researches alternatives for youth-at-risk; surveys programs to validate success; acquaints practitioners with alternative programs; educates the public on the needs of youth-at-risk. **Libraries:** Type: reference; by appointment only. **Holdings:** articles, audiovisuals, books, clippings, monographs. **Subjects:** juvenile justice, children, education, outdoor education, alternative programs, violence, women, drugs. **Computer Services:** database, alternative programs. **Publications:** *Green Sheet/Mailing*, monthly. Newsletter. **Advertising:** not accepted. **Conventions/Meetings:** quarterly board meeting (exhibits) - Sarasota, FL.

13215 ■ National Fellowship of Child Care Executives (NFCCE)
c/o Michael H. Danjczek, Exec. Sec.
113 Geneva Rd.
New Bern, NC 28562

E-mail: mike@danjczek.com
URL: http://www.nfcce.org
Contact: Michael H. Danjczek, Exec. Sec.
Founded: 1954. **Members:** 60. **Membership Dues:** residential child care, $250 (annual). **Description:** Executives of child welfare homes including boys' ranches and farms, girls' homes, and religious and private nonprofit agency institutions. Holds conferences to exchange information on topics such as child care, management of homes, public relations, current issues, and fundraising. **Formerly:** (1981) National Association of Homes for Boys. **Publications:** *That You May Know*, biennial. Newsletter. **Conventions/Meetings:** annual conference (exhibits) - usually June.

13216 ■ National Organizations for Youth Safety (NOYS)
c/o Sandy Spavone, Exec. Dir.
7371 Atlas Walk Way, No. 109
Gainesville, VA 20155
Ph: (703)981-0264
Fax: (703)754-8262
E-mail: sspavone@noys.org
URL: http://www.noys.org
Contact: Sandy Spavone, Exec. Dir.
Founded: 1994. **Description:** Promotes youth empowerment and leadership. Builds partnerships that save lives, prevent injuries and enhance safe and healthy lifestyles among all youth. **Publications:** *NOYS Noise.* Newsletter. Alternate Formats: online ● *Speak Out and Make NOYS.* Brochure.

13217 ■ National Tots and Teens
PO Box 1517
Washington, DC 20012
Ph: (202)723-5680
Free: (877)424-5999
E-mail: rozwilcots@cd.com
URL: http://prlewis0001.tripod.com/totsandteenspg-county/index.html
Contact: Rosalyn L. Wilcots, Pres.
Founded: 1952. **Members:** 400. **Regional Groups:** 3. **Local Groups:** 20. **Description:** Comprises of families—parents/guardians and youth who believe that the family unit is the most important setting for influencing positive pursuits and for instilling values that produce full and effective participants in society. Sponsors programs that are educational, foster civic responsibility, broaden appreciation of different cultural heritages, and promote wholesome social development. Provides programs that focus on leadership and civic responsibility. **Awards:** **Frequency:** annual. **Type:** recognition. **Recipient:** for one of America's foremost fundraising organizations for education ● **Type:** scholarship. **Publications:** Newsletter, periodic. **Advertising:** accepted. **Conventions/Meetings:** semiannual Youth Mixer - meeting - always August and April.

13218 ■ National Young Adult Association (NYAA)
938 E Swan Creek Rd.
Box 283
Fort Washington, MD 20744
E-mail: nyaa@calltohumanity.org
URL: http://www.calltohumanity.org
Contact: Khalil Abdur-Rashid, Pres.
Founded: 1998. **Multinational. Description:** Strengthens, nurtures and supports the life skills of young adults globally. Provides leadership, training and development for young adults. Utilizes Islamic principles such as faith, service, tolerance, leadership, patience, and ethical strategies. Seeks to organize and implement activities and services that dignify the skills, talent and contributions of young adults.

13219 ■ National Youth Advocacy Coalition (NYAC)
1638 R St. NW, Ste.300
Washington, DC 20009
Ph: (202)319-7596
Free: (800)541-6922
Fax: (202)319-7365

E-mail: nyac@nyacyouth.org
URL: http://www.nyacyouth.org
Contact: Craig Bowman, Exec. Dir.
Founded: 1993. **Members:** 127. **Staff:** 7. **Budget:** $1,700,000. **Description:** Young people, youth-service providers, researchers, and other advocates. Advocates for and with young people who are lesbian, gay, bisexual, and/or transgender. **Awards:** Youth Scholarships. **Frequency:** annual. **Type:** scholarship. **Recipient:** to young people currently living in United States. **Computer Services:** Mailing lists. **Telecommunication Services:** teletype, (202)-319-9513. **Publications:** *Generation Out*, quarterly. Newsletter. Alternate Formats: online ● *Youth Connections*, biennial. Contains resource guide. Alternate Formats: online. **Conventions/Meetings:** annual National Youth Summit - conference, skills building, networking, training, and health conference for LG-BTG youth and their service providers - summer.

13220 ■ National Youth Employment Coalition (NYEC)
1836 Jefferson Pl. NW
Washington, DC 20036
Ph: (202)659-1064
Fax: (202)659-0339
E-mail: nyec@nyec.org
URL: http://www.nyec.org
Contact: Ms. Mala Thakur, Exec. Dir.
Founded: 1979. **Members:** 153. **Membership Dues:** subscriber, $50 (annual) ● organization (based on annual budget), $350-$850 (annual) ● contributing, $1,000 (annual) ● affiliate, $200 (annual). **Staff:** 9. **Budget:** $1,300,000. **State Groups:** 3. **Local Groups:** 85. **National Groups:** 26. **Description:** A network of over 180 community-based organizations, research organizations, public interest groups, policy analysis organizations, and others dedicated to promoting improved policies and practices related to youth employment/development, to help youth succeed in becoming lifelong learners, productive workers and self-sufficient citizens. **Libraries:** Type: reference. **Projects:** Education Initiatives; Equip 3; Indicators of Youth Economic Achievement; Institutional Racism; New Leaders Academy/WIA Leaders Academy; PEPNet; Workforce and Youth Development for Young Offenders; Youth With Disabilities. **Publications:** *Making Sense of Federal Job Training Policy for Youth and Adults Volume II: Expert Recommendations to Create a Unified System.* Book ● *Making Sense of Federal Job Training Policy: 24 Expert Recommendations to Create a Comprehensive and Unified Federal Job Training System.* Book ● *NYEC Youth Notes*, monthly. Newsletter. Includes statistics. **Price:** free for members. **Circulation:** 300 ● *PEP-NET: Lessons Learned from 51 Effective Youth Employment Initiatives*, annual. Book. **Price:** free ● *Toward A National Youth Development System: How We Can Better Serve Youth At Risk.* **Conventions/Meetings:** annual retreat.

13221 ■ Network of Iranian American Society (NIAS)
14252 Culver Dr., No. 406
Irvine, CA 92604
E-mail: niasinfo@niasnet.org
URL: http://www.niasnet.org
Contact: Foroogh Gomarooni, Dir. of Social Affairs
Membership Dues: student, $20 (annual) ● regular, $30 (annual) ● silver, $75 (annual) ● gold, $100 (annual) ● platinum/business, $500 (annual). **Description:** Represents the interests of young Iranian-Americans dedicated to humanitarian and cultural events. Seeks to achieve self growth and self education and advance the humanitarian cause within the Iranian community through networking, social events, financial sponsorships and professional guidance. **Conventions/Meetings:** monthly meeting - every first Tuesday.

13222 ■ Nongovernmental Organizations Committee on Youth
c/o Conference of NGOs
777 United Nations Plz., 6th Fl.
New York, NY 10017
Ph: (212)986-8557

Fax: (212)986-0821
E-mail: congony@ngocongo.org
URL: http://www.ngocongo.org
Contact: Anita Thomas, Coor.

Description: United Nations nongovernmental organizations with a concern for youth. Acts as a liaison between the U.N. and various youth-oriented organizations. **Formerly:** (1998) United Nations Headquarters Nongovernmental Organizations Committee on Youth. **Conventions/Meetings:** monthly meeting.

13223 ■ Ophelia Project
718 Nevada Dr.
Erie, PA 16505
Ph: (814)456-5437
Free: (888)256-5437
Fax: (814)455-2090
E-mail: ophelia@opheliaproject.org
URL: http://www.opheliaproject.org
Contact: Mary Baird, Pres./CEO

Founded: 1997. **Membership Dues:** individual, $30 ● supporting, $50-$5,000 ● corporate, $1,000-$10,000. **Multinational. Description:** Increases parental and community support for adolescent girls. Raises awareness about relational aggression. Provides educational resources and programs. Advocates for healthy youth throughout the United States and Canada. **Computer Services:** Information services, relational aggression resources ● mailing lists ● online services, message board. **Programs:** Creating a Safe School. **Publications:** Newsletter, monthly. **Price:** included in membership dues.

13224 ■ Polish-American-Jewish Alliance for Youth Action (PAJA)
1131 Univ. Blvd. W, No. 1116
Silver Spring, MD 20902
Ph: (301)681-5322
E-mail: youthunderstanding@hotmail.com
URL: http://www.polishandjewishyouth.org
Contact: Dennis Misler, Pres.

Multinational. Description: Aims to create learning and interaction opportunities for young people in the United States and Poland. Promotes the development of youth infrastructure that implements sharing, education and community activities. Facilitates the implementation of educational curricula in American and Polish public and parochial schools that focus on the history of prejudice, anti-Semitism and anti-Polish sentiments.

13225 ■ Prepare Tomorrow's Parents
454 NE 3rd St.
Boca Raton, FL 33432
Ph: (561)620-0256
Free: (888)727-3687
Fax: (561)391-9711
E-mail: info@preparetomorrowsparents.org
URL: http://www.parentingproject.org
Contact: Suzy Garfinkle Chevrier, Pres./Founder

Founded: 1995. **Description:** Works to bring parenting, empathy and nurturing skills education to all school age children and teens. Raises public awareness of parenting education for young people through the media and in presentations. Increases nurturing and relationship skills to improve the quality of parenting in the next generation. Seeks to include parenting education as an essential part of the elementary and secondary school curriculum. Assists and encourages initiatives, strategic partnerships and staff development to implement the teaching of parenting skills to children. **Additional Websites:** http://www.preparetomorrowsparents.org. **Publications:** Brochure. Alternate Formats: online.

13226 ■ Reviving Baseball in Inner Cities (RBI)
c/o MLB Advanced Media, L.P.
75 Ninth Ave., 5th Fl.
New York, NY 10011
Free: (866)800-1275

E-mail: rbi@mlb.com
Contact: Thomas C. Brasuell, Community Affairs VP
Founded: 1989. **Local Groups:** 186. **Description:** Works to provide youths in disadvantaged urban areas opportunities to participate in activities that foster athletic and academic growth. Promotes the formation of RBI programs in inner cities to promote the sport of baseball and girls softball in order to instill self-esteem, team spirit and academic and community involvement in youth. **Publications:** RBI Newsletter, semiannual. **Conventions/Meetings:** annual World Series - competition.

13227 ■ Robert F. Kennedy Memorial (RFKM)
1367 Connecticut Ave. NW, Ste.200
Washington, DC 20036
Ph: (202)463-7575
Fax: (202)463-6606
E-mail: info@rfkmemorial.org
URL: http://www.rfkmemorial.org
Contact: Jennifer Jones, Development Off.

Founded: 1968. **Membership Dues:** associate, $35 (annual) ● supporter, $100 (annual) ● contributor, $500 (annual) ● friend, $1,000 (annual) ● patron, $5,000 (annual). **Description:** A "living memorial" established to promote Robert Kennedy's ideals of civic responsibility and social conscience, the importance of the power of communities and community involvement, and the pursuit of social justice and human rights for all people at home and abroad. Programs and activities include: Center for Human Rights and National Youth Project. **Awards:** RFK Book Awards. **Frequency:** annual. **Type:** recognition. **Recipient:** to the author whose work most faithfully and forcefully reflects Robert Kennedy's concern for the poor and the powerless ● RFK Human Rights Award. **Frequency:** annual. **Type:** recognition. **Recipient:** to an individual or group fighting oppression and striving for freedom ● RFK Journalism Award. **Frequency:** annual. **Type:** recognition. **Recipient:** to recognize outstanding print and broadcast media coverage of the disadvantaged and neglected in American society. **Computer Services:** Mailing lists. **Publications:** Currents, quarterly. Newsletter.

13228 ■ Society for Research on Adolescence (SRA)
3131 S State St., Ste.302
Ann Arbor, MI 48108-1623
Ph: (734)998-6567
Fax: (734)998-9586
E-mail: socresadol@umich.edu
URL: http://www.s-r-a.org
Contact: Vonnie McLoyd, Pres.

Founded: 1984. **Members:** 1,100. **Membership Dues:** full, $105 (annual) ● new professional, emeritus, $75 (annual) ● student, $53 (annual) ● student (non-journal), $35 (annual). **Staff:** 4. **Description:** Social science researchers. Promotes the study and understanding of adolescence through research. Disseminates research findings and information. **Awards:** Hershel D. Thornburg Dissertation Award. **Frequency:** biennial. **Type:** recognition. **Recipient:** for research on adolescence ● John P. Hill Memorial Award. **Frequency:** biennial. **Type:** recognition. **Recipient:** for excellence in theory development and research on adolescence ● Roberta Grodberg Simmons Prize Lecture. **Frequency:** biennial. **Type:** monetary. **Recipient:** for a distinguished speaker who represents Roberta's commitment to interdisciplinary and theoretically sound empirical work ● Social Policy Award. **Frequency:** biennial. **Type:** recognition. **Committees:** Awards. **Formerly:** Search Institute. **Publications:** Journal of Research on Adolescence, quarterly. Contains research papers on empirical studies and theoretical issues. **Price:** included in membership dues. ISSN: 1050-8392. **Circulation:** 1,200. **Conventions/Meetings:** biennial conference (exhibits).

13229 ■ Subud Youth Association (SYA)
14019 NE 8th St., Ste.A
Bellevue, WA 98007
Ph: (425)643-1904
Fax: (425)643-2725

E-mail: subudusa@subudusa.org
URL: http://www.subudusa.org
Contact: Melinda Wallis, Office Mgr.

Founded: 1963. **Local Groups:** 56. **Description:** Individuals who belong to Subud U.S.A. Sponsors camps and programs for young people. **Affiliated With:** Subud United States of America. **Conventions/Meetings:** annual workshop (exhibits) - every July 4th weekend.

13230 ■ SustainUS
3300 16th St. NW, Unit No. 617
Washington, DC 20010
E-mail: lauren@sustainus.org
URL: http://www.sustainus.org
Contact: Lauren Inouye, Chair

Founded: 2001. **Description:** Aims to advance sustainable development and youth empowerment in the United States. Works to build a future in which all people recognize the inherent equality and interdependence of social, economic, and environmental sustainability. Educates peers and communities to advocate for a sustainable future and development. **Telecommunication Services:** electronic mail, kai@sustainus.org.

13231 ■ Theta Rho Girls' Club (TRGC)
422 Trade St.
Winston-Salem, NC 27101-2830
Ph: (336)725-5955
Free: (800)235-8358
Fax: (336)722-7317
E-mail: ioofthesgl@bellsouth.net
URL: http://www.ioof.org
Contact: R. Kenneth Babb, Sec.

Founded: 1931. **Members:** 1,027. **Staff:** 6. **State Groups:** 28. **Local Groups:** 74. **Description:** Girls between the ages of 8 and 18. Promotes citizenship and strength in character through "friendship, love, and truth." Teaches members "happiness through service". **Awards:** Advisor of the Year. **Frequency:** annual. **Type:** recognition ● Irene Meigs Community Service Award. **Frequency:** annual. **Type:** recognition. **Publications:** Youth Reporter, quarterly. Newsletter. Contains activities schedule and report and information on Annual International Youth Day. **Price:** $3.00. **Circulation:** 500. **Conventions/Meetings:** annual Youth Day - conference (exhibits).

13232 ■ Youth Crime Watch of America (YCWA)
9200 S Dadeland Blvd., Ste.417
Miami, FL 33156
Ph: (305)670-2409
Fax: (305)670-3805
E-mail: ycwa@ycwa.org
URL: http://www.ycwa.org
Contact: Cmdr. (Ret.) Gerald A. Rudoff, Chm.

Founded: 1979. **Membership Dues:** life, $198 ● youth, $10 (annual) ● individual, $25 (annual) ● school/community site, $150 (annual) ● corporate, $500 (annual). **Description:** Seeks to empower youth to participate in addressing issues in their schools, neighborhoods, public housing sites, and recreational centers and parks; assists students to organize programs; strives to provide a drug-free environment for youth; instills positive values, citizenship, and self-confidence. **Publications:** Annual Report, annual. Alternate Formats: online ● Handbooks ● Videos ● Manuals.

13233 ■ Youth Development International (YDI)
PO Box 178408
San Diego, CA 92177-8408
Ph: (858)292-5683
Fax: (858)292-9197
E-mail: 1800hithome@horizonsd.org
URL: http://members.aol.com/garnierlaw/YDIprof.html
Contact: Mike MacIntosh, Pres.

Founded: 1959. **Description:** Provides a 24-hour hotline to offer spiritual, emotional, and physical help to hurting youth across America. Conducts Thanksgiving and Christmas outreach program that provides clothing, food, and letters of encouragement to children in local shelters and detention centers.

Maintains listings of shelters and churches throughout the U.S. **Telecommunication Services:** hotline, provides counseling and referrals to shelters for runaways nationwide, (800)HIT-HOME. **Affiliated With:** National Network for Youth. **Publications:** *Heartline*, monthly. Newsletter.

13234 ■ Youth Impact International (YII)
124 Mt. Auburn St.
Univ. Pl.,
Harvard Sq., Ste.200 N
Cambridge, MA 02138-5700
Ph: (617)520-6610
Free: (800)478-7051
Fax: (617)547-1431
E-mail: info@youthimpactint.org
URL: http://www.youthimpactint.org
Contact: Bryan Acheampong, Exec. Dir.
Founded: 1999. **Multinational. Description:** Serves as an umbrella organization that supports youth groups and organizations, helping them to be more effective while setting the structure for wider cooperation among community-based youth organizations. **Programs:** AIDS-Scare; Global Citizens. **Projects:** International Science Frontier.

13235 ■ Youth Law Center
200 Pine St., Ste.300
San Francisco, CA 94104
Ph: (415)543-3379
Fax: (415)956-9022
E-mail: info@ylc.org
URL: http://www.ylc.org
Contact: Carole Shauffer, Exec. Dir.
Founded: 1978. **Staff:** 12. **Budget:** $3,600,000. **Nonmembership. Description:** Committed to the belief that "every child has a right to a permanent home and family". Works to protect children from abuse and neglect in the foster care and juvenile justice systems. **Computer Services:** database. **Publications:** *Building Blocks for Youth*. Report ● *The Inmate Exception and its impact on Health Care Services for Children in Out-of-Home Care in California* ● *Youth Rights* ● Annual Report.

13236 ■ Youth Organizations U.S.A. (YOUSA)
12 Tenafly Rd.
Englewood, NJ 07631
Ph: (201)894-1866
Fax: (201)894-5117
E-mail: agarf8730@aol.com
Contact: Anne M. Garfield, Pres./CEO
Founded: 1981. **Staff:** 2. **Budget:** $25,000. **Local Groups:** 1. **Description:** Provides programs that increase intellectual skills through homework-help and computer technology, develops performing arts both drama and dance to counteract misbehavior that leads to crime and/or abuse of alcohol, tobacco and other drugs. **Computer Services:** training for

adults and children. **Committees:** County Coalitions. **Conventions/Meetings:** board meeting - always June ● Concert In Dance - show.

13237 ■ Youth to Youth International (Y2Y)
547 E 11th Ave.
Columbus, OH 43221
Ph: (614)224-4506
Fax: (614)224-8451
E-mail: y2y@y2yint.com
URL: http://www.y2yint.com
Contact: Robert E. Sweet, Pres.
Founded: 1982. **State Groups:** 35. **National Groups:** 13. **Multinational. Description:** Teens helping other teens choose and maintain a drug-free lifestyle. **Boards:** Youth Advisory. **Divisions:** Speakers' Bureau. **Programs:** Junior Youth to Youth. **Publications:** *Adult Advisor News*, monthly. Newsletter ● *The Drug Free Teen Scene*. Newsletter. Alternate Formats: online ● *Network News*, monthly. Newsletter. Focuses on the happenings of Youth to Youth clubs around the world. Alternate Formats: online. **Conventions/Meetings:** annual conference - summer ● annual conference, Eastern States - July, Rhode Island ● annual conference, Western States ● annual international conference - held in Ohio ● annual regional meeting - held in California and Rhode Island ● Winners Choice Camps for 7th Graders - meeting.

13238 ■ YouthBuild USA
58 Day St.
Somerville, MA 02144
Ph: (617)623-9900
Fax: (617)623-4331
E-mail: info@youthbuild.org
URL: http://www.youthbuild.org
Contact: Suzanne Fitzgerald, Pres.
Founded: 1990. **Description:** Unemployed and out-of-school young adults ages 16-24. Strives to help young people recognize that they can have control over their future. Provides community service programs, an alternative school as well as job training and pre-apprenticeship programs. **Publications:** *YouthBuild Bulletin*. Newsletter. Alternate Formats: online ● *Youthbuild Innovations*. Newsletter. Contains information from conference activities and discussions among YouthBuild practitioners. Alternate Formats: online ● Annual Report, annual. Alternate Formats: online ● Brochure. Alternate Formats: online.

YWCA

13239 ■ Young Women's Christian Association - Puerto Rico
(Asociacion Cristiana Femenina)
PO Box 10111
San Juan, PR 00908

Ph: (787)724-1037
Fax: (787)724-1037
E-mail: ywca_puerto_rico@yahoo.com
URL: http://www.worldywca.info/index.php/ywca/world_ywca/national_ywcas
Contact: Jane L. Wolfe, Pres.
Description: Promotes the development of young women in Puerto Rico. Upholds Christian beliefs and values in its programs. Works to instill self-worth and self-esteem in young women.

13240 ■ Young Women's Christian Association of the United States of America YWCA of the U.S.A.
1015 18th St. NW, Ste.1100
Washington, DC 20036-5271
Ph: (202)467-0801
Fax: (202)467-0802
E-mail: info@ywca.org
URL: http://www.ywca.org
Contact: Dr. Lorraine Cole, CEO
Founded: 1858. **Staff:** 21,000. **Regional Groups:** 3. **Local Groups:** 446. **Description:** Women girls and their families who participate in service programs of health education, recreation, clubs and classes, and counseling and assistance to girls and women in the areas of employment, education, human sexuality, self improvement, voluntarism, citizenship, emotional and physical health, and juvenile justice. Seeks to make contributions to peace, justice, freedom, and dignity for all people; works toward the empowerment of women and the elimination of racism. Conducts international advocacy program on human rights and on peace and development. Sponsors national advocacy programs on: international peace and justice; economic and social justice; improved environmental quality; individual rights and liberties. Local units include 309 community YWCA's, 4 student associations. Men and boys participate in YWCA activities as associates or registrants. Maintains archives; compiles statistics. Maintains library of 8,000 books, pamphlets, and periodicals on contemporary American women and their concerns. **Awards:** Tribute to Women in Industry Award. **Type:** recognition. **Computer Services:** database, contains local YWCAs. **Divisions:** Business Support Services; Communications/Public Relations; Data Center/Research; Executive Office; Field Services; Finance; Financial Development; Leadership Development; MIS; National Personnel Services; National Support; Program Services; Services to Student Associations. **Affiliated With:** World Young Women's Christian Association. **Publications:** *YWCA*. **Price:** free ● *YWCA of the U.S.A.—Directory*, triennial. **Price:** available to member YWCAs only ● Annual Report, annual. Alternate Formats: online ● Also publishes public policy bulletin, informational and instructional brochures, promotion packets, financial administration and development materials, manuals and guides. **Conventions/Meetings:** triennial meeting.

Abortion

13241 ■ Clinicians for Choice (CFC)
c/o National Abortion Federation
1755 Massachusetts Ave. NW, Ste.600
Washington, DC 20036
Ph: (202)667-5881
Fax: (202)667-5890
E-mail: cfc@prochoice.org
Founded: 1997. **Members:** 4,000. **Multinational.**
Description: Promotes reproductive choice as an essential part of women's health. **Publications:** Newsletters.

13242 ■ National Coalition of Abortion Providers (NCAP)
1718 Connecticut Ave., Ste.700
Washington, DC 20009
Ph: (202)319-0055
Fax: (202)785-3849
E-mail: info@ncap.com
URL: http://www.ncap.com
Contact: Steven Emmert, Exec. Dir.
Founded: 1990. **Members:** 150. **Description:** Represents the political, business and networking needs of independent abortion providers.

Accounting

13243 ■ National CPA Health Care Advisors Association (HCAA)
1 Valmont Plz., 4th Fl.
Omaha, NE 68154
Ph: (402)778-7922
Free: (888)475-4476
Fax: (402)778-7931
E-mail: info@hcaa.com
URL: http://www.hcaa.com
Contact: Nancy Drennen, Exec. Dir.
Founded: 1992. **Members:** 51. **Membership Dues:** firm, $1,500 (annual). **Staff:** 4. **Description:** Certified public accountant (CPA) firms providing financial and consulting services to health care professionals. Seeks to enhance members' ability to serve the health care industry. Facilitates resource sharing and the establishment of joint ventures among members; provides marketing services to members; conducts industry surveys; sponsors continuing professional development and training courses. **Publications:** *Practice Management Advisor*, quarterly. Newsletter. A customizable newsletter for clients of members. Alternate Formats: online; diskette ● Brochure. Alternate Formats: online ● Bulletin. Alternate Formats: online. **Conventions/Meetings:** semiannual conference, educational and networking (exhibits).

Accreditation

13244 ■ Certification of Disability Management Specialists Commission (CDMSC)
300 N Martingale Rd., Ste.460
Schaumburg, IL 60173
Ph: (847)944-1335
Fax: (847)944-1346
E-mail: info@cdms.org
URL: http://www.cdms.org
Contact: Pam Caggianelli, Chair
Description: Promotes disability management specialists through certification program. **Publications:** *CDMS Commission Update.* Newsletter. Alternate Formats: online.

13245 ■ Commission on Accreditation of Ambulance Services (CAAS)
1926 Waukegan Rd., Ste.1
Glenview, IL 60025-1770
Ph: (847)657-6828
Fax: (847)657-6825
E-mail: meredithh@tcag.com
URL: http://www.caas.org
Contact: Meredith Hellestrae, Exec. Dir.
Description: Promotes quality patient care in U.S. medical transportation system.

13246 ■ Healthcare Quality Certification Board (HQCB)
PO Box 19604
Lenexa, KS 66285-9604
Ph: (913)599-4173
Free: (800)346-4722
Fax: (913)599-5340
E-mail: info@cphq.org
URL: http://www.cphq.org
Contact: Jerrie Lynn Kind, Exec. Dir.
Founded: 1984. **Description:** Promotes healthcare quality through certification, including quality management, quality improvement, case/care/disease utilization management, and risk management. **Affiliated With:** National Association for Healthcare Quality. **Publications:** *CPHQ News.* Newsletter. Alternate Formats: online.

13247 ■ National Board of Surgical Technology and Surgical Assisting (NBSTSA)
6 W Dry Creek Cir., Ste.100
Littleton, CO 80120
Free: (800)707-0057
Fax: (303)325-2536
E-mail: mail@nbstsa.org
URL: http://www.lcc-st.org
Contact: Sandy Edwards, Pres.
Founded: 1974. **Description:** Works as the certifying agency for surgical technologists. **Formerly:** (2006) Liaison Council on Certification for the Surgical Technologist.

Acid Maltase Deficiency

13248 ■ Acid Maltase Deficiency Association (AMDA)
PO Box 700248
San Antonio, TX 78270-0248
Ph: (210)494-6144
Fax: (210)490-7161
E-mail: tianrama@aol.com
URL: http://www.amda-pompe.org
Contact: Marylyn House, Contact
Founded: 1995. **Members:** 500. **Description:** Promotes awareness of Acid Maltase Deficiency, also known as Pompe's Disease; assists in funding research. **Programs:** Genzyme Pompe; Late-Onset Expanded Access. **Publications:** Newsletter. **Conventions/Meetings:** annual Patient Conference.

Acupuncture

13249 ■ Acupuncturists Without Borders (AWB)
37 Kelly Lynn Dr.
Sandia Park, NM 87047
Ph: (505)991-0112
E-mail: info@acuwithoutborders.org
URL: http://www.acuwithoutborders.org
Contact: Diana Fried MA, Exec. Dir.
Founded: 2005. **Multinational. Description:** Seeks to alleviate the suffering of people worldwide in urban and rural communities in need and to support self-empowerment through community acupuncture treatment and training. Provides services and training in local communities. Develops and implements acupuncture based programs that help facilitate community and personal healing in the face of large-scale traumatic events and their aftermath. **Telecommunication Services:** electronic mail, acuwithoutborders@simplelists.com. **Publications:** Newsletter. Alternate Formats: online.

13250 ■ Society for Acupuncture Research (SAR)
c/o Richard Harris, PhD
PO Box 385
Ann Arbor, MI 48106
E-mail: info@acupunctureresearch.org
URL: http://www.acupunctureresearch.org
Contact: Richard Harris PhD, Contact
Founded: 1993. **Membership Dues:** institutional affiliate, $500 (annual) ● professional affiliate, $100 (annual) ● student affiliate, $50 (annual). **Multinational. Description:** Seeks to elevate the standards of education and practice of acupuncture and Oriental medicine. Promotes, advances and disseminates scientific inquiry into Oriental medicine systems, which include acupuncture, herbal therapy and other modalities. Stimulates scholarship in acupuncture and Oriental medicine. **Awards:** Young Investigator Awards. **Frequency:** periodic. **Type:** grant. **Recipient:** for the best research presentations by a student or post-doctoral fellow in acupuncture and Oriental medicine. **Telecommunication Services:** electronic mail, rharris@acupunctureresearch.org. **Publications:** *Journal of Alternative and Complementary Medicine*, 10/year. Includes observational and analytical reports on treatments outside the realm of allopathic medicine. **Price:** $263.00 /year for individuals in U.S. (print and online); $285.00 /year for individuals outside U.S. (print and online); $597.00 /year for

institutions in U.S. (print and online); $700.00 /year for institutions outside U.S. (print and online). ISSN: 1075-5535. **Advertising:** accepted. **Alternate Formats:** online. **Conventions/Meetings:** annual conference, with symposium - 2007 Nov. 8-11, Baltimore, MD.

Aerospace Medicine

13251 ■ Aerospace Medical Association (ASMA)
320 S Henry St.
Alexandria, VA 22314-3579
Ph: (703)739-2240
Fax: (703)739-9652
E-mail: rrayman@asma.org
URL: http://www.asma.org
Contact: Russell B. Rayman MD, Exec. Dir./Sec.-Treas.
Founded: 1929. **Members:** 3,300. **Membership Dues:** regular, $235 (annual) ● student, resident in U.S., $122 (annual) ● resident outside U.S. (with rapid journal delivery), $280 (annual) ● regular, spouse (with one journal), $290 (annual) ● life, $3,525 ● technician, $125 (annual). **Staff:** 6. **Budget:** $1,000,000. **Description:** Medical and scientific personnel engaged in clinical, operational, and research activities in aviation, space, and environmental medicine. Sponsors continuing professional education programs. **Awards:** Boothby-Edwards Award. **Frequency:** annual. **Type:** recognition. **Recipient:** for outstanding research and/or clinical practice directed at the promotion of health and prevention of disease in professional airline pilots ● Eric Liljencrantz Award. **Frequency:** annual. **Type:** recognition. **Recipient:** for an educator in aerospace medicine ● Harry G. Moseley Award. **Frequency:** annual. **Type:** recognition. **Recipient:** for outstanding contribution to flight safety ● Louis H. Bauer Founders Award. **Frequency:** annual. **Type:** recognition. **Recipient:** for significant contribution in aerospace medicine ● Mary T. Klinker Award. **Frequency:** annual. **Type:** recognition. **Recipient:** for significant contribution in aerospace evacuation ● Theodore C. Lyster Award. **Frequency:** annual. **Type:** recognition. **Recipient:** for outstanding achievement in the general field of aerospace medicine. **Committees:** Aerospace Human Factors; Air Transport Medicine; Annual Scientific Meeting Chairs; Aviation Safety; Education and Training; History and Archives; Resolutions; Science and Technology. **Formerly:** (1959) Aero Medical Association. **Publications:** *Aviation, Space, and Environmental Medicine*, monthly. Journal. Covers the medical aspects of survival in aviation, space, and undersea exploration. Includes annual index, book reviews and meetings calendar. **Price:** included in membership dues; $205.00 /year for institutions in U.S.; $185.00 /year for nonmembers in U.S. ISSN: 0095-6562. **Circulation:** 4,000. **Advertising:** accepted. **Alternate Formats:** microform ● *Aviation, Space and Environmental Medicine*, annual. Membership Directory ● *Scientific Abstracts*, annual. **Conventions/Meetings:** annual Scientific Meeting - convention, with technical and scientific exhibits (exhibits).

13252 ■ Airlines Medical Directors Association (AMDA)
c/o Ralph G. Fennell, MD
United Airlines Medical
Denver Intl. Airport
Denver, CO 80249-6363
Ph: (303)348-4300
Fax: (303)348-4338
Contact: Dr. Ralph G. Fennell MD, Sec.Dir.
Founded: 1946. **Members:** 130. **Membership Dues:** active, $25 (annual) ● associate, $25 (annual). **Description:** Physicians employed by, or consulting to, commerical airlines. **Conventions/Meetings:** annual meeting, held in conjunction with Aerospace Medical Association (exhibits) - always May.

13253 ■ Civil Aviation Medical Association (CAMA)
PO Box 23864
Oklahoma City, OK 73123-2864

Ph: (405)840-0199
Fax: (405)848-1053
E-mail: jimlharris@aol.com
URL: http://www.civilavmed.com
Contact: David Bryman DO, Pres.
Founded: 1948. **Members:** 800. **Membership Dues:** regular, $100 (annual). **Staff:** 1. **Budget:** $100,000. **Multinational. Description:** Aviation medical examiners, physicians who are pilots, aviation medical educators, flight instructors, fixed base operators, NASA physicians, and airline medical department physicians. Purposes are to: ascertain the basic mental and physical requirements of civil airmen and the proper methods for the physical assessment of airmen engaged in civil aviation; review continuously the scientific status of civil aviation medicine and advance and disseminate the information by which civil aviation medicine safeguards public safety; sponsor basic and advanced training in civil aviation medicine; foster international fellowship among members, allied medical and technical groups, and students of aviation medicine; unite the designated civil aviation medical examiners of the world into an effective medical body dedicated to the promotion and practice of aviation safety for the public benefit. Maintains speakers' bureau; compiles statistics. **Libraries: Type:** not open to the public. **Awards:** Audie and Bernice Davis Award. **Frequency:** annual. **Type:** recognition ● Bird Award. **Frequency:** annual. **Type:** recognition. **Recipient:** for an aircrew member, conceptual aeromedical technologist, legislator, or physician ● President's Award. **Type:** recognition. **Recipient:** for an individual who has helped the President and has provided exemplary service to CAMA ● Tamisiea Award. **Frequency:** annual. **Type:** recognition. **Recipient:** to an aviation medical examiner or individual who has made outstanding contributions to the art and science of aviation medicine. **Affiliated With:** Aerospace Medical Association. **Formerly:** (1955) Airline Medical Examiners Association. **Publications:** *FlightPhysician*, bimonthly. Newsletter. Covers membership activities. Contains meetings calendar and promotion of members and medical information on all topics relative to aviation medicine. **Price:** $5.00/issue. **Circulation:** 850. **Advertising:** accepted. **Alternate Formats:** online. **Conventions/Meetings:** annual conference and symposium, with scientific equipment (exhibits) - 2007 Oct. 10-14, San Diego, CA - **Avg. Attendance:** 200.

13254 ■ International Association of Military Flight Surgeon-Pilots (IAMFSP)
c/o Dave Hiland, VP
Navy Environmental Hea. Ctr.
620 John Paul Jones Cir., Ste.1100
Portsmouth, VA 23708-2103
E-mail: webmaster@iamfsp.net
URL: http://iamfsp.net
Contact: Dwight Holland, Pres.
Membership Dues: general, $15 (annual). **Multinational. Description:** Promotes the advancement of military aviation. Increases the understanding of the physical, pathological or psychological factors associated with flight environment. **Computer Services:** Mailing lists ● online services, discussion forum through Yahoo groups. **Publications:** Newsletter, semiannual. **Alternate Formats:** online.

13255 ■ National Association of Air Medical Communication Specialists (NAACS)
PO Box 121822
Nashville, TN 37212-1822
Free: (877)396-2227
Fax: (866)869-9462
E-mail: looperdon@air-evac.com
URL: http://www.naacs.org
Contact: Don Looper, Pres.
Founded: 1989. **Members:** 300. **Membership Dues:** active, $30 (annual) ● associate/program, $25 (annual). **Staff:** 13. **Description:** Air medical communications specialists. Promotes professional advancement of members. Represents members at the national level; formulates standards of ethics and practice in air medical communications; sponsors educational and training programs. **Affiliated With:**

Air and Surface Transport Nurses Association; National EMS Pilots Association; National Flight Paramedics Association. **Publications:** *NAACS Newsletter*, quarterly. **Advertising:** accepted ● *NAACS Training Manual*. **Conventions/Meetings:** annual Air Medical Transport Conference (exhibits).

13256 ■ Society of United States Air Force Flight Surgeons (SoUSAFFS)
PO Box 35387
Brooks City Base, TX 78235
Ph: (210)975-2109
Fax: (210)536-2017
E-mail: cheryl.lowry@brooks.af.mil
URL: http://www.sousaffs.org
Contact: Major Cheryl Lowry, Exec. Off.
Founded: 1960. **Members:** 650. **Membership Dues:** regular, $20 (annual) ● life, $200. **Staff:** 5. **Budget:** $15,000. **Description:** Flight surgeons who are members of the Aerospace Medical Association (see separate entry) and who are currently serving on active duty with or have retired from the United States Air Force, or are serving in the Air Force Reserve or Air National Guard. Fosters advancement of aerospace medicine throughout the Air Force and encourages the clinical, laboratory, flight line, and in-flight investigation of medical problems in Air Force flying, missile, and space operations. **Awards:** George E. Schafer Award. **Frequency:** annual. **Type:** recognition. **Recipient:** for a United States Air Force Medical Corps officer ● Howard R. Unger Award. **Frequency:** annual. **Type:** recognition. **Recipient:** for the best publication of the year ● Julian E. Ward Award. **Frequency:** annual. **Type:** recognition. **Recipient:** for the most distinguished resident in aerospace medicine ● Malcolm C. Grow Award. **Frequency:** annual. **Type:** recognition. **Recipient:** for an outstanding flight surgeon of the year ● Olson-Wegner Award. **Frequency:** annual. **Type:** recognition. **Recipient:** for an aeromedical enlisted personnel. **Affiliated With:** Aerospace Medical Association. **Publications:** *Aircraft Mishap Investigation Handbook* ● *Flight Surgeon's Checklist*. Book ● *Flightlines*, quarterly. Newsletter. **Price:** included in membership dues; $15.00 /year for nonmembers. **Conventions/Meetings:** annual conference, held in conjunction with ASMA - always May.

13257 ■ Society of U.S. Naval Flight Surgeons (SUSNFS)
PO Box 33008
Pensacola, FL 32508-3008
Ph: (850)452-2257
E-mail: mark.edwards1@navy.mil
URL: http://www.aerospacemed.org
Contact: Capt. Mark Edwards, Pres.
Founded: 1976. **Membership Dues:** regular, $20 (annual) ● life, $300 (annual). **Description:** Committed to advancement of the science, art, and practice of aerospace medicine and mission of the U.S. Navy. **Awards:** Aerospace Medicine Technician of the Year. **Frequency:** annual. **Type:** recognition. **Recipient:** for AVT with exceptional professional growth ● Ashton Graybiel Award. **Frequency:** annual. **Type:** recognition. **Recipient:** for outstanding contributions to the medical literature ● Bruce Jackson Memorial Reserve Flight Surgeon Award. **Frequency:** annual. **Type:** recognition. **Recipient:** for outstanding contributions to the practice of aerospace medicine ● Richard E. Luehrs Memorial Award. **Frequency:** annual. **Type:** recognition. **Recipient:** for outstanding performance.

Aging

13258 ■ International Society for Aging and Physical Activity (ISAPA)
c/o Wojtek Chodzko-Zajko, PhD, Pres.
Dept. of Kinesiology
Univ. of Illinois at Urbana-Champaign
Louise Freer Hall
906 S Goodwin Ave.
Urbana, IL 61801
Ph: (217)244-0823

Fax: (217)244-7322
E-mail: wojtek@zajko.org
URL: http://www.isapa.org
Contact: Wojtek Chodzko-Zajko PhD, Pres.
Multinational. Description: Promotes physical activity, exercise science, and fitness in the health and well being of older persons. Promotes international initiatives in research, clinical practice, and public policy in the areas of aging and physical activity. Serves as a liaison between various international, national, and regional professional groups with an interest in activity and aging. Provides information about aging and physical activity. **Publications:** *Journal of Aging and Physical Activity.* Examines the dynamic relationship between physical activity and the aging process. **Price:** $77.00 /year for individuals (print and online); $308.00 /year for institutions (print and online); $52.00 per year for student (print and online). ISSN: 1063-8652. Alternate Formats: online. Also Cited As: *JAPA* ● Newsletter, semiannual.

AIDS

13259 ■ Aggressive Aids Prevention
PO Box 26227
San Francisco, CA 94126
Ph: (415)255-6022
Fax: (415)267-6980
E-mail: media@aggressive.org
URL: http://www.aggressive.org
Contact: Devin Kordt-Thomas, Pres./Founding Dir.
Founded: 1998. **Membership Dues:** individual, $15 (annual). **Description:** Promotes HIV/AIDS awareness. Provides information, materials and education. **Computer Services:** Mailing lists.

13260 ■ Aid for AIDS (AFA)
c/o Britanny Nuttal
515 Greenwich St., Ste.No. 506
New York, NY 10013
Ph: (212)337-8043
Fax: (212)337-8045
E-mail: usa@aidforaids.org
URL: http://www.aidforaids.org
Contact: Maria Eugenia Maury Arria, Pres.
Founded: 1996. **Staff:** 10. **Multinational. Description:** Improves the quality of life of people living with HIV/AIDS in Latin America and the Caribbean. Empowers HIV/AIDS patients and their caregivers by providing access to medications, medical monitoring and treatment/prevention education. Promotes leadership and capacity building. **Boards:** Medical Advisory. **Committees:** Honorary Advisory. **Programs:** AIDS Treatment Access.

13261 ■ AIDS Alliance for Children, Youth and Families
1600 K St. NW, Ste.200
Washington, DC 20006
Ph: (202)785-3564
Free: (800)917-AIDS
Fax: (202)785-3579
E-mail: info@aids-alliance.org
URL: http://www.aids-alliance.org
Contact: David C. Harvey, Exec. Dir.
Members: 550. **Description:** Advocates for children, youth, families living with, and/or affected by, or at risk for HIV and AIDS.

13262 ■ AIDS Clinical Trials Group (ACTG)
c/o Dr. Yvette Delph, MD, Operations Center Dir.
8757 Georgia Ave., Ste.1200
Silver Spring, MD 20910
Ph: (301)628-3338
Fax: (301)628-3302
E-mail: ydelph@s-3.com
URL: http://aactg.org
Contact: Dr. Yvette Delph MD, Operations Center Dir.
Founded: 1987. **Multinational. Description:** Serves as federal government-funded program of the National Institutes of Health. Conducts HIV/AIDS treatment research. Seeks to enroll HIV-infected individuals in AIDS treatment research trials in the U.S. and

worldwide. **Awards:** Constance B. Wofsy Women's Health Investigator. **Frequency:** annual. **Type:** recognition. **Recipient:** for an investigator who contributed in the research of HIV-infected women ● John Carey Young Investigator. **Frequency:** annual. **Type:** recognition. **Recipient:** for an individual who exemplifies the ideals of AACTG. **Committees:** Laboratory Technologist; Network Community Advisory Board; Resource; Scientific; Site Management and Clinical Care; Women's Health.

13263 ■ AIDS Empowerment and Treatment International (AIDSETI)
PO Box 27143
Washington, DC 20038-7143
Ph: (202)518-0402
Fax: (202)518-5202
E-mail: asall@aidseti.org
URL: http://www.aidseti.org
Contact: Dr. Francoise Ndayishimiye, Pres.
Staff: 2. **National Groups:** 13. **Multinational. Description:** Aims to expand access to HIV/AIDS treatment in resource-poor countries. Empowers associations of people living with HIV/AIDS, along with their doctors and counselors, with knowledge, financial and pharmaceutical resources to run their own holistic HIV treatment programs. **Committees:** Finances; Information Management; Medical; Pharmaceutical; Training. **Projects:** Data Collection; Save the Activist; Scaling Up Access to Treatment. **Publications:** *Progress.* Reports.

13264 ■ AIDS, Medicine and Miracles (AMM)
3288 21st St., No. 201
San Francisco, CA 94110-2423
Ph: (415)252-7111
Free: (800)875-8770
Fax: (415)252-7117
E-mail: amm@aidsmedicineandmiracles.org
URL: http://www.csd.net/~amm
Contact: Mr. Skip Rosenthal, Co-Chair
Founded: 1987. **Staff:** 2. **Description:** Promotes the well-being of people afflicted with AIDS. Provides educational programs that support the mind, body and spirit of AIDS victims. Offers medical and complementary therapies and psychosocial and spiritual opportunities. **Computer Services:** Information services, resources on AIDS and HIV ● online services, message board. **Programs:** AM&M Retreats; HIV Positive Youth; One Day Initiatives. **Subgroups:** Miracle Club. **Publications:** *AM&M Matters,* biennial. Newsletter. Alternate Formats: online.

13265 ■ AIDS Research Alliance (ARA)
621-A N San Vicente Blvd.
West Hollywood, CA 90069
Ph: (310)358-2423 (310)358-2429
Fax: (310)358-2431
E-mail: info@aidsresearch.org
URL: http://www.aidsresearch.org
Contact: Carolyn Carlburg JD, CEO
Languages: English, Spanish. **Description:** Promotes HIV/AIDS research. **Boards:** Institutional Review. **Committees:** Medical Executive. **Programs:** Priority Notification. **Publications:** *Searchlight.* Magazine. Highlights emerging issues related to HIV/AIDS research. Alternate Formats: online ● *Spotlight,* semiannual. Magazine. Serves as companion magazine to Searchlight. Alternate Formats: online ● Annual Report, annual. Alternate Formats: online.

13266 ■ AIDS Resource Foundation for Children (ARFC)
182 Roseville Ave.
Newark, NJ 07107-1619
Ph: (973)483-4250
Fax: (973)483-1998
E-mail: info@aidsresource.org
URL: http://www.aidsresource.org
Contact: Terrence P. Zealand, Exec. Dir.
Founded: 1985. **Staff:** 85. **Languages:** English, Spanish. **Description:** Operates homes for children ages birth thru 12 years of age with HIV, AIDS, or AIDS-Related Complex (ARC) medically fragile (ie: cerebral palsy, mentally retarded, etc.) who are well enough to be released from the hospital

but are in need of foster care placement or respite care; provides support services to families coping with AIDS or related diseases. Operates foster parent recruitment, training, and support programs; collects and distributes toys and clothing. Sponsors summer camp for families. Conducts HIV training workshops, community outreach programs, and agency networking; maintains Speaker's Bureau. Provides referrals, bereavement counseling, and emergency assistance. Acts as a model program for transitional foster homes nationwide. **Also Known As:** St. Clare's Home for Children; St. Clare's Home Properties. **Publications:** Newsletter, periodic. Alternate Formats: online.

13267 ■ AIDSinfo
PO Box 6303
Rockville, MD 20849-6303
Ph: (301)519-0459
Free: (800)448-0440
Fax: (301)519-6616
E-mail: contactus@aidsinfo.nih.gov
URL: http://www.aidsinfo.nih.gov
Languages: English, Spanish. **Description:** Provides bilingual health information regarding HIV/AIDS treatment options. **Libraries: Type:** reference. **Subjects:** federally approved HIV/AIDS treatment guidelines. **Computer Services:** database ● mailing lists ● online services. **Telecommunication Services:** TDD, (888)480-3739. **Formerly:** (2002) ACTIS/ATIS; (2004) HIV/AIDS Treatment Information Service. **Publications:** Newsletter. Contains new information on treatment guidelines, clinical trials, drugs, etc. ● Brochure. Alternate Formats: online.

13268 ■ American Academy of HIV Medicine (AAHIVM)
1705 DeSales St. NW, Ste.700
Washington, DC 20036
Ph: (202)659-0699
Free: (866)241-9601
Fax: (202)659-0976
E-mail: info@aahivm.org
URL: http://www.aahivm.org
Contact: Brian Hujdich, Interim Exec. Dir.
Members: 2,000. **Membership Dues:** individual, $175 (annual) ● student, $25 (annual). **Description:** Furthers HIV/AIDS care through advocacy and education. Seeks to support health care providers in HIV medicine and to ensure better care for those living with AIDS and HIV disease. **Telecommunication Services:** electronic mail, brian@aahivm.org.

13269 ■ American Foundation for AIDS Research (amfAR)
120 Wall St., 13th Fl.
New York, NY 10005-3908
Ph: (212)806-1600
Free: (800)39-AMFAR
Fax: (212)806-1601
E-mail: information@amfar.org
URL: http://www.amfar.org
Contact: William F. Zabel Esq., Sec.
Founded: 1985. **Staff:** 60. **Budget:** $18,000,000. **Regional Groups:** 2. **Multinational. Description:** Seeks to support AIDS research and prevention, treatment education, and advocacy of AIDS-related public policy. **Awards: Frequency:** periodic. **Type:** recognition. **Committees:** Scientific Advisory. **Formed by Merger of:** AIDS Medical Foundation; National AIDS Research Foundation. **Publications:** *amfAR e-News,* monthly. Newsletter. Contains updates on programs, activities, HIV/AIDS-related news, and resent fund-raising events. Alternate Formats: online ● *amfAR News,* semiannual. Newsletter. Provides updates on research, prevention, education, and policy initiatives. Alternate Formats: online ● *amfAR Treatment Insider* (in Chinese, English, French, and Spanish), bimonthly. Reprint ● *HIV/AIDS Treatment Directory,* semiannual. **Price:** free. ISSN: 0898-5030. **Circulation:** 50,000. Alternate Formats: online ● Bulletin, periodic. **Conventions/Meetings:** annual National HIV/AIDS Update Conference (NAUC) - convention.

13270 ■ American Institute for Teen AIDS Prevention
Address Unknown since 2007
Founded: 1987. **Description:** Provides HIV/STD education programs to schools and churches. Maintains speakers' bureau. Develops and distributes HIV/STD education materials. **Formerly:** American Institute for Teen Aids Prevention. **Publications:** *Developing Your Church AIDS Policy.* Book. Leads church leaders through the process of researching, drafting, and implementing an AIDS policy. **Price:** $8.00 ● *Don't Let AIDS Catch You!.* Brochure. HIV/AIDS education for teens. ● *Guide to Positive HIV/AIDS Education.* Book ● *It's Your Choice.* Video ● *Making Love without Doing It.* Brochure.

13271 ■ Association of Nurses in AIDS Care (ANAC)
3538 Ridgewood Rd.
Akron, OH 44333
Ph: (330)670-0101
Free: (800)260-6780
Fax: (330)670-0109
E-mail: anac@anacnet.org
URL: http://www.anacnet.org
Contact: Adele Webb, Exec. Dir.
Founded: 1987. **Members:** 2,800. **Membership Dues:** individual, affiliate, $70 (annual) ● associate, disable, $53 (annual) ● international, $80 (annual). **Staff:** 6. **Budget:** $1,000,000. **State Groups:** 52. **Description:** Nurses and other health care professionals involved in caring for people who are HIV-infected or have AIDS. Functions as a network and provides leadership and educational services for members. Promotes public awareness of AIDS issues; advocates for HIV-infected individuals. Plans to develop a national standard for care of people with AIDS. **Awards: Frequency:** annual. **Type:** monetary. **Computer Services:** Mailing lists. **Publications:** *ANACdotes*, quarterly. Newsletter ● *Journal of the Association of Nurses in AIDS Care*, bimonthly. **Advertising:** accepted ● Also publishes position papers. **Conventions/Meetings:** annual conference (exhibits).

13272 ■ Athletics and Entertainers for Kids (AEFK)
3337 Colorado St.
Long Beach, CA 90814
Ph: (562)438-5905
Free: (800)933-KIDS
Fax: (562)438-9175
E-mail: aefkoffice@aefk.org
URL: http://www.aefk.org
Contact: Elise Kim, Exec. Dir.
Founded: 1986. **Staff:** 5. **Budget:** $1,000,000. **State Groups:** 5. **Languages:** English, Spanish. **Description:** Participants include individuals and corporations concerned about children with catastrophic illnesses, particularly AIDS. Seeks to bring hope to seriously ill children. Provides services to children and their families including: counseling and referral services; community outings; educational rallies. Provides AIDS education and awareness programs and presentations. Conducts hospital and charitable programs; provides placement and children's services. Sponsored by Athletes and Entertainers for Kids. **Formerly:** (1998) Ryan White National Teen Education Program. **Publications:** *Financial Report*, annual ● *Heros*, quarterly. Newsletter. **Conventions/Meetings:** quarterly board meeting.

13273 ■ Balm in Gilead
130 W 42nd St., Ste.704
New York, NY 10036
Ph: (212)730-7381
Free: (888)225-6243
Fax: (212)730-2551
E-mail: info@balmingilead.org
URL: http://www.balmingilead.org
Contact: Pernessa C. Seele, Founder/CEO
Multinational. Description: Dedicated to stopping the spread of HIV/AIDS throughout the African Diaspora by building the capacity of faith communities to provide services, HIV/AIDS education and to build support networks for all people living with and af-

fected by HIV/AIDS. **Computer Services:** Online services, survey. **Programs:** Black Church HIV/AIDS Training Institute; Faith-Based HIV/AIDS National Technical Assistance. **Conventions/Meetings:** annual Black Church Week of Prayer for the Healing of AIDS - meeting ● conference ● annual National Certification and Capacity Building - conference.

13274 ■ Body Positive
250 W 57th St.
New York, NY 10107
Ph: (212)566-7333
Free: (800)566-6599
Fax: (212)566-4539
E-mail: bodypositive@bodypos.org
URL: http://www.thebody.com/bp/bp.html
Contact: Bonnie Goldman, Editorial Dir.
Founded: 1987. **Members:** 15,000. **Staff:** 26. **Budget:** $2,000,000. **Languages:** English, Spanish. **Description:** Provides support services for people who are HIV-infected or have AIDS, and their families and friends. Organizes seminars on treatment issues and socials. Provides outreach programs and recreational services. **Libraries: Type:** reference. **Publications:** *Positive Options.* Book. Contains information for people living with HIV/AIDS. ● *Resource Directory*, semiannual ● Newsletter (in English and Spanish), monthly. **Price:** $35.00 for individuals. **Circulation:** 200,000. **Advertising:** accepted.

13275 ■ CAVDA-Citizens AIDS Project (CAP)
800 W Central Rd., Ste.128
Mount Prospect, IL 60056
Ph: (847)398-3378
Fax: (847)398-7309
E-mail: cavdarx@earthlink.net
Contact: Howard A. Mirsky, Dir.
Founded: 1986. **Members:** 125. **Description:** A project of the Citizens Alliance for VD Awareness. Physicians, pharmacists, nurses, health professionals, and interested others. Seeks to provide information and educational programs to professionals and the public in order to dispel myths associated with sexually transmitted diseases and Acquired Immune Deficiency Syndrome. Conducts research programs and disseminates information and surveys through media and group presentations. Compiles statistics; maintains speakers' bureau. **Affiliated With:** Citizens Alliance for VD Awareness. **Publications:** *STD Spotlight*, quarterly. Newsletter. **Price:** $30.00/year. **Circulation:** 350. Also Cited As: *VD Spotlight* ● Pamphlets. **Conventions/Meetings:** conference - 2-3/year.

13276 ■ CDC National Prevention Information Network (CDC NPIN)
PO Box 6003
Rockville, MD 20849-6003
Ph: (301)588-1589
Free: (800)458-5231
Fax: (888)282-7681
E-mail: info@cdcnpin.org
URL: http://www.cdcnpin.org
Founded: 1987. **Languages:** English, Spanish. **Nonmembership. Multinational. Description:** Works as the U.S. reference, referral, and distribution service for information on HIV/AIDS, sexually transmitted diseases (STD's) and tuberculosis (TB) sponsored by the Centers for Disease Control and Prevention (CDC). Services are designed to facilitate the sharing of information and resources among people working in HIV, STD, and TB prevention, treatment, and support services. Bilingual staff is available to speak with callers and all calls are confidential. **Libraries: Type:** reference. **Holdings:** 18,000; archival material, audio recordings, books, periodicals, video recordings. **Computer Services:** database, information on educational materials and organizations pertaining to HIV/AIDS, STDs and TB. **Formerly:** (1991) National AIDS Information Clearinghouse; (1992) National AIDS Clearinghouse.

13277 ■ Gay Men's Health Crisis (GMHC)
119 W 24th St.
The Tisch Bldg.
New York, NY 10011-1913

Ph: (212)367-1000 (212)807-6655
Free: (800)243-7692
Fax: (212)367-1236
E-mail: lynns@gmhc.org
URL: http://www.gmhc.org
Contact: Lynn Schulman, Contact
Founded: 1982. **Members:** 14,000. **Staff:** 200. **Budget:** $21,000,000. **Languages:** English, Spanish. **Description:** Fosters national leadership in the fight against AIDS. Works to reduce the spread of HIV disease. Helps people with HIV maintain and improve their health and independence. Keeps the prevention, treatment and cure of HIV an urgent national and local priority. Provides services and programs to over 15,000 men, women and families that are living with or affected by HIV/AIDS in New York City. **Libraries: Type:** reference. **Holdings:** 200; books. **Subjects:** health issues and history relating to HIV/AIDS. **Telecommunication Services:** TDD, (212)645-7470. **Departments:** Client Services; Legal and Advocacy; Public Information; Public Policy; Testing and Consulting; Treatment Education; Volunteer. **Publications:** *Program Service News*, monthly. Newsletter ● *Treatment Issues*, monthly. Newsletter. **Price:** $55.00 individuals; $95.00 physicians/institutions/international. **Circulation:** 26,000 ● *The Volunteer*, bimonthly. Newsletter. Updates medical, clinical, political, and referral information on AIDS. Includes calendar of events. **Price:** free ● Catalog. Contains marketed education materials. ● Pamphlets. Contains prevention of AIDS materials. **Conventions/Meetings:** annual AIDS Walk New York - rally ● periodic lecture.

13278 ■ Global AIDS Alliance (GAA)
1413 K St. NW, 4th Fl.
Washington, DC 20005
Ph: (202)789-0432
Fax: (202)789-0715
E-mail: info@globalaidsalliance.org
URL: http://www.globalaidsalliance.org
Contact: Dr. Paul Zeitz, Exec. Dir.
Founded: 2001. **Description:** Aims to put an end to the global AIDS crisis through enhanced awareness, increased funding on research, and improved national policies. Evaluates data and formulates options for action in the fight against AIDS. Runs an intensive information campaign in support of other organizations, the media, and legislators. **Computer Services:** Information services, government documents, news. **Publications:** *Waves of Change.* Newsletter. Contains news, articles, interviews, and schedule of activities. Alternate Formats: online ● Annual Report, annual. Alternate Formats: online ● Reports. Alternate Formats: online ● Videos. Alternate Formats: online.

13279 ■ Global Strategies for HIV Prevention
104 Dominican Dr.
San Rafael, CA 94901
Ph: (415)451-1814
Fax: (415)456-2622
E-mail: globalhiv@aol.com
URL: http://www.globalstrategies.org
Contact: Dr. Arthur Ammann MD, Pres.
Multinational. Description: Implements strategies to prevent HIV infection. Maintains alliances with other organizations that work to alleviate the suffering of women and children. Provides education and care to HIV-infected mothers and children. **Computer Services:** Information services, resources on HIV/AIDS. **Programs:** Cradle of Life. **Publications:** Newsletter.

13280 ■ Haitian Coalition on AIDS (HCA)
c/o Haitian Centers Council
10 St. Pauls Pl. - Wing B, 5th Fl.
Brooklyn, NY 11226
Ph: (718)940-5200
Fax: (718)940-5296
E-mail: info@hccinc.org
URL: http://www.hccinc.org
Contact: Dr. Henry Frank, Exec. Dir.
Founded: 1983. **Members:** 70. **Budget:** $300,000. **Regional Groups:** 8. **State Groups:** 7. **Local Groups:** 6. **Description:** Community centers; professional groups of doctors, journalists, lawyers, nurses,

social workers, and civil rights and media representatives. Educates the public concerning what the coalition feels is the discriminatory classification of Haitians as an ethnonational group that runs a high risk of contracting AIDS. Seeks to heighten AIDS awareness within the Haitian community. Offers social services and placement for persons with AIDS; provides counseling to their families. Sponsors conferences and seminars at churches and universities. Compiles statistics; maintains speakers' bureau. **Libraries: Type:** reference. **Awards: Type:** recognition. **Computer Services:** database. **Conventions/Meetings:** semiannual meeting.

13281 ■ Health Education Resource Organization (HERO)
1734 Maryland Ave.
Baltimore, MD 21201
Ph: (410)685-1180
Fax: (410)685-3101
E-mail: lorte@hero-mcrc.org
URL: http://www.hero-mcrc.org
Contact: Leonardo R. Ortega MD, Exec. Dir./CEO
Founded: 1983. **Description:** Provides client care services and preventive education regarding AIDS to Maryland residents; disseminates information on AIDS prevention and treatment to interested individuals nationwide. Provides social service and mental health counseling, support groups, legal aid, emergency funding, referrals, and case management. **Subgroups:** Client Care; Education Services; Volunteer Services. **Also Known As:** HERO. **Publications:** Hero News, monthly. Newsletter ● Also produces a wide range of educational materials on AIDS prevention.

13282 ■ HIV Medicine Association (HIVMA)
66 Canal Center Plz., Ste.600
Alexandria, VA 22314
Ph: (703)299-1215 (703)299-0200
Fax: (703)299-0473
E-mail: hivma@idsociety.org
URL: http://www.idsociety.org/HIVMA_Template.cfm
Contact: Christine B. Lubinski, Exec. Dir.
Founded: 2000. **Members:** 2,500. **Membership Dues:** domestic, associate, $225 (annual) ● international (with subscription to print journal), $270 (annual) ● international (with subscription to electronic journal), $190 (annual) ● international (from developing nations with subscription to print journal), $105 (annual) ● international (from developing nations with subscription to electronic journal), $25 (annual). **State Groups:** 51. **National Groups:** 36. **Multinational. Description:** Represents interests of HIV patients by promoting quality in HIV care, advocates for policies in HIV care. **Libraries: Type:** reference. **Subjects:** HIV medicine. **Telecommunication Services:** electronic mail, mmazzotta@idsociety.org. **Affiliated With:** Infectious Diseases Society of America. **Publications:** Clinical Infectious Diseases, semimonthly. Journal. **Price:** $609.00 institutions in U.S.; $696.63 institutions in Canada; $140.00 individuals in U.S. (print and electronic); $194.80 individuals in Canada. Alternate Formats: online. Also Cited As: CID ● HIV Quality Care News, bimonthly. Newsletter. **Price:** included in membership dues. Alternate Formats: online ● Journal of Infectious Diseases, semimonthly. **Price:** $609.00 institutions in U.S.; $696.63 institutions in Canada; $140.00 individuals in U.S. (print and electronic); $194.80 individuals in Canada. Alternate Formats: online. Also Cited As: JID ● Member List. Directory. Compiled to assist individuals looking for an HIV medical provider. **Conventions/Meetings:** annual meeting.

13283 ■ International AIDS Society - USA (IAS-USA)
425 California St., Ste.1450
San Francisco, CA 94104-2120
Ph: (415)544-9400
Fax: (415)544-9401
E-mail: info2006@iasusa.org
URL: http://www.iasusa.org
Contact: Paul A. Volberding MD, Chm.
Founded: 1992. **Description:** Works to find a cure for HIV/AIDS through medical education programs

for physicians. **Publications:** Topics in HIV Medicine, 5-6/year. Newsletter. Features summaries of talks given at courses, highlights of scientific meetings, and review articles. **Circulation:** 12,000. Alternate Formats: online.

13284 ■ International AIDS Vaccine Initiative (IAVI)
New York Off.
110 William St., Fl. 27
New York, NY 10038-3901
Ph: (212)847-1111
Fax: (212)847-1112
E-mail: info@iavi.org
URL: http://www.iavi.org
Contact: Dr. Seth F. Berkley MD, Pres./CEO
Founded: 1996. **Multinational. Description:** Works to speed the development and distribution of preventive AIDS vaccines. **Computer Services:** database. **Committees:** Policy Advisory; Scientific Advisory. **Publications:** IAVI Report, bimonthly. Newsletter. Provides comprehensive coverage of the AIDS vaccine field. Alternate Formats: online ● Vax (in English, French, German, Portuguese, and Spanish), monthly. Bulletin. Contains AIDS vaccine research and news intended for non-technical readers. Alternate Formats: online ● Annual Report, annual. Alternate Formats: online ● Papers. Alternate Formats: online ● Reports. Alternate Formats: online.

13285 ■ International Partnership for Microbicides (IPM)
1010 Wayne Ave., Ste.1450
Silver Spring, MD 20910
Ph: (301)608-2221
Fax: (301)608-2241
E-mail: info@ipm-microbicides.org
URL: http://www.ipm-microbicides.org
Contact: Zeda F. Rosenberg, CEO
Founded: 2002. **Staff:** 26. **Languages:** English, French. **Multinational. Description:** Accelerates the discovery, development and accessibility of microbicides to prevent the transmission of HIV. Seeks to deliver safe and effective microbicides for women in developing countries. **Computer Services:** Information services, AIDS resources ● information services, microbicides resources. **Programs:** Research and Development. **Publications:** Brochure (in English, French, and Spanish). Alternate Formats: online ● Annual Report (in English and French), annual. Alternate Formats: online. **Conventions/Meetings:** biennial conference.

13286 ■ International Treatment Preparedness Coalition (ITPC)
c/o Collaborative Fund for HIV Treatment Preparedness
Tides Found.
40 Exchange Pl., Ste.1111
New York, NY 10005
Ph: (212)509-1049
Fax: (212)509-1059
E-mail: hunkhk@hotmail.com
URL: http://www.hivcollaborativefund.org
Contact: Susie Lim, Proj. Coor.
Founded: 2002. **Members:** 470. **Multinational. Description:** Represents the interests of people living with HIV/AIDS and their advocates. Advocates for universal and free access to treatment for AIDS for all HIV-infected individuals. **Telecommunication Services:** electronic mail, slim@tides.org. **Publications:** Papers. Alternate Formats: online.

13287 ■ Mothers' Voices
150 W Flagler St., Ste.1820
Miami, FL 33130
Ph: (305)347-5467
Fax: (305)377-3313
E-mail: voicessf@bellsouth.net
URL: http://www.mothersvoices.org
Contact: Todd Fogel, Pres.
Founded: 1991. **Staff:** 8. **Budget:** $650,000. **Regional Groups:** 5. **Description:** National, grassroots, non-profit organizations mobilizing mothers as AIDS and sexual health educators and advocates. Provides resources for mothers to educate their children

regarding sexuality and drug use, and how better understanding can help prevent HIV infection. **Awards:** Extraordinary Voices Award. **Type:** recognition. **Subgroups:** Expert Advisory. **Publications:** Comfort Foods from Mothers' Voices. Book. **Price:** $20.00 each ● Finding Our Voices: Talking With Our Children About Sexuality and AIDS. Handbook. **Price:** $5.00 each ● Newsletter, quarterly ● Brochure. Alternate Formats: online.

13288 ■ Names Project Foundation - AIDS Memorial Quilt (NPF)
637 Hoke St. NW
Atlanta, GA 30318-4315
Ph: (404)688-5500
Fax: (404)688-5552
E-mail: info@aidsquilt.org
URL: http://www.aidsquilt.org
Contact: Julie Rhoad, Exec. Dir.
Founded: 1987. **Staff:** 18. **Budget:** $2,600,000. **Local Groups:** 53. **National Groups:** 38. **Languages:** English, French, Italian, Spanish. **Description:** Promotes creation of AIDS Memorial Quilt as an "appropriate, compassionate response" to the AIDS epidemic. Goals of the project are to provide a creative means of remembrance and healing; to illustrate the enormity of the AIDS epidemic; to increase public awareness of AIDS; to assist with HIV prevention education; and to raise funds for community-based AIDS service organizations. The 25-acre quilt currently contains 43,000 panels from each of the 50 states and 39 foreign countries bearing the names of persons who have died as a result of AIDS. Among materials sewn into the panels are stuffed animals, merit badges, records, feather boas, and a baseball jersey. **Libraries: Type:** reference; open to the public. **Holdings:** archival material, audiovisuals, clippings. **Subjects:** AIDS memorial quilt. **Formerly:** Names Project. **Publications:** A Promise To Remember. Book ● Always Remember. Book ● eQuilt. Newsletter. Alternate Formats: online ● On Display, quarterly. Newsletter. **Circulation:** 50,000 ● The Quilt: Stories From the NAMES Project. Book ● Also publishes fact sheets, flyers, and press releases. **Conventions/Meetings:** annual Chapter Conference - meeting (exhibits) ● annual Unites States Conference on AIDS - convention, national HIV prevention/care services conference, co-sponsored with National Minority AIDS Council.

13289 ■ National AIDS Fund
729 15th St. NW, 9th Fl.
Washington, DC 20005-1511
Ph: (202)408-4848
Free: (888)234-AIDS
Fax: (202)408-1818
E-mail: info@aidsfund.org
URL: http://www.aidsfund.org
Contact: Kandy Ferree, Pres./CEO
Founded: 1988. **Members:** 200. **Membership Dues:** corporate, $1,000 (annual) ● pacesetter, $5,000 (annual) ● non-profit organization, $500 (annual). **Staff:** 14. **Budget:** $6,000,000. **State Groups:** 27. **Description:** Promotes leadership and generates resources for effective community responses to HIV/AIDS. **Libraries: Type:** reference; open to the public. **Holdings:** 700. **Subjects:** AIDS in the workplace. **Awards: Frequency:** annual. **Type:** scholarship. **Recipient:** for activists to participate in conference/training. **Formerly:** (1996) Rational Community AIDS Partnership. **Publications:** News from the National AIDS Fund, quarterly. Newsletter. Alternate Formats: online ● AIDS-in the workplace publications list available. **Conventions/Meetings:** annual meeting (exhibits).

13290 ■ National AIDS Treatment Advocacy Project (NATAP)
580 Broadway, Ste.1010
New York, NY 10012
Ph: (212)219-0106
Free: (888)26-NATAP
Fax: (212)219-8473
E-mail: info@natap.org
URL: http://www.natap.org
Contact: Jules Levin, Exec. Dir.
Membership Dues: individual, $25 (annual) ● corporate, $75 (annual). **Description:** Educates

individuals about HIV and Hepatitis treatments. Advocates on behalf of those living with HIV/AIDS and HCV. **Computer Services:** Information services, hepatitis resources. **Programs:** Community Treatment Education; National Education; Women's Programs. **Publications:** *The Hepatitis C and Hepatitis C Co-Infection Handbook* (in English and Spanish). Alternate Formats: online ● *NATAP Reports.* Newsletter. Provides the latest HIV and AIDS treatment information and research. **Price:** included in membership dues; $25.00 for nonmembers; $75.00 for institutions/physicians/corporate. **Circulation:** 17,000. Alternate Formats: online ● *What you need to know about HIV/HCV co-infection.* Brochure. **Conventions/Meetings:** monthly Treatment Training - meeting.

13291 ■ National Association of People With AIDS (NAPWA)
8401 Colesville Rd., Ste.750
Silver Spring, MD 20910
Ph: (240)247-0880
Fax: (240)247-0574
E-mail: info@napwa.org
URL: http://www.napwa.org
Contact: Frank Oldham Jr., Exec. Dir.
Founded: 1983. **Membership Dues:** health partner, $300 (annual) ● grassroot, $5-$34 (annual) ● premium, $35 (annual). **Staff:** 20. **Budget:** $2,000,000. **Description:** Serves as the collective voice and national consumer health education and advocacy resource for all people living with HIV disease in the United States. Advocates on behalf of all people living with HIV and AIDS in order to end the epidemic and the human suffering caused by HIV/AIDS. **Libraries: Type:** reference. **Holdings:** books, clippings, periodicals. **Subjects:** AIDS information, treatment, resources. **Awards:** Life Award. **Frequency:** annual. **Type:** recognition. **Recipient:** for major contributions to the fight to end AIDS. **Computer Services:** Mailing lists. **Telecommunication Services:** information service, AIDS fax on demand facts service, (202)789-2222. **Programs:** Leadership Development Initiative; National HIV Testing Day. **Publications:** *Active Voice,* quarterly. Provides information about healthcare and advocacy issues. **Price:** free. **Circulation:** 12,000. **Advertising:** accepted ● *An Ounce of Prevention.* Informs family members and caregivers about the prevention of further HIV infection. ● *Facts About AIDS.* Provides an introduction of HIV and related issues. ● *Living with HIV.* Provides information on resources for treatment and offers prevention against further infection. ● *Medical Alert,* quarterly. Identifies new approaches to treating HIV/AIDS, explains what new drugs are being tested and how they work, and provides treatment strategies. **Price:** free. **Circulation:** 45,000. **Advertising:** accepted ● *Positive Voice Update,* periodic. Newsletter. Alternate Formats: online. **Conventions/Meetings:** annual Staying Alive - conference (exhibits).

13292 ■ National Catholic AIDS Network (NCAN)
10 E Pearson St., 4th Fl.
Chicago, IL 60611-2052
Ph: (312)915-7790
Fax: (312)915-7793
E-mail: info@ncan.org
URL: http://www.ncan.org
Contact: Mr. Daniel T. Lunney, Exec. Dir.
Founded: 1989. **Members:** 4,500. **Membership Dues:** friend, $25 (annual) ● supporter, $50-$99 (annual) ● patron, $100-$249 (annual) ● sponsor, $250-$499 (annual) ● lumina, $1,000-$2,499 (annual) ● sustainer, $500-$999 (annual) ● benefactor, $2,500-$4,999 (annual) ● visionary, $5,000 (annual). **Staff:** 1. **Budget:** $300,000. **Regional Groups:** 5. **Description:** Provides support and exchange of information between Roman Catholic HIV/AIDS service workers and pastoral ministers. Disseminates educational materials on HIV/AIDS. **Awards:** Lumina Award. **Frequency:** annual. **Type:** recognition. **Recipient:** for creative and effective pastoral leadership in HIV/AIDS ministry ● **Frequency:** annual. **Type:** monetary. **Recipient:** for an individual with HIV from an economi-

cally impoverished area or service providers who qualify to attend annual ministry conference. **Computer Services:** database, call-in referrals. **Publications:** *Connections,* 3/year. Newsletter. **Price:** included in membership dues. **Circulation:** 4,000. **Advertising:** accepted. **Conventions/Meetings:** annual National Catholic HIV/AIDS Ministry Conference (exhibits).

13293 ■ National Minority AIDS Council (NMAC)
1931 13th St. NW
Washington, DC 20009
Ph: (202)483-6622
Fax: (202)483-1135
E-mail: info@nmac.org
URL: http://www.nmac.org
Contact: Paul A. Kawata, Exec. Dir.
Founded: 1986. **Members:** 480. **Membership Dues:** individual, $150 (annual) ● organization (based on the annual budget), $150-$1,200 (annual). **Staff:** 20. **Budget:** $12,000,000. **Regional Groups:** 2. **State Groups:** 20. **Local Groups:** 160. **Description:** Public health departments and AIDS service organizations. Serves as a clearinghouse of information on AIDS as it affects minority communities in the U.S. Facilitates discussion among national minority organizations about AIDS. Maintains Project Health, Education, and AIDS Leadership, which provides computer usage, strategic planning, financial management, and volunteer program development assistance to AIDS service organizations, and Project Volunteer Information, Technical Assistance, and Leadership, which provides technical assistance in volunteer program development and maintenance. Conducts training conferences. Offers educational and research programs; compiles statistics. Maintains speakers' bureau. **Libraries: Type:** reference. **Holdings:** reports. **Awards: Type:** recognition ● **Type:** scholarship. **Publications:** *Computer Technical Assistance Manual* ● *Leadership Reprint Series,* quarterly. Includes information on strategies for addressing HIV/AIDS and scientific updates. ● *Legislative Update,* bimonthly ● *Lifeline.* Newsletter. Alternate Formats: online ● *NMAC HEALer,* bimonthly. Includes updates on projects, community needs, and statistics. ● *NMAC Update,* bimonthly. Newsletter. Includes association information and coverage of HIV/AIDS issues. ● *Technical Assistance Manual for Volunteer Program Development* ● *Technical Assistance Newsletter,* bimonthly. **Circulation:** 1,300. **Conventions/Meetings:** annual National Skills Building Conference (exhibits).

13294 ■ National Pediatric and Family HIV Resource Center (NPHRC)
Univ. of Medicine & Dentistry of New Jersey
30 Bergen St., ADMC No. 4
Newark, NJ 07103
Ph: (973)972-0410
Free: (800)362-0071
Fax: (973)972-0399
E-mail: ortegaes@umdnj.edu
URL: http://www.thebody.com/nphrc/nphrcpage.html
Founded: 1990. **Description:** Provides education, consultation, technical assistance and training for health and social service professionals caring for children, adolescents, and families with HIV and AIDS.

13295 ■ Pediatric AIDS Foundation
2950 31st St., No. 125
Santa Monica, CA 90405
Ph: (310)314-1459
Free: (888)499-HOPE
Fax: (310)314-1469
E-mail: info@pedaids.org
URL: http://www.pedaids.org
Contact: Pamela W. Barnes, Pres./CEO
Founded: 1988. **Staff:** 26. **Budget:** $13,500,000. **Description:** Confronts medical problems unique to children infected with HIV/AIDS, and focuses on finding medical answers that will bring hope. Identifies and funds critically needed pediatric AIDS research worldwide. Provides funds to hospitals around the country that serve children with HIV/AIDS through an

Emergency Assistance Program. Encourages students to enter the field of pediatric AIDS through a Student Intern Award Program. Develops and distributes national Parent Education Program for parents of elementary and pre-school age children. **Awards:** Elizabeth Glaser Scientist Award. **Frequency:** annual. **Type:** recognition. **Recipient:** for scientists ● International Leadership Awards. **Frequency:** annual. **Type:** grant. **Recipient:** for researchers ● International Scholar Award. **Frequency:** annual. **Type:** fellowship. **Recipient:** for clinicians and scientists. **Programs:** HIV/AIDS: A Challenge to Us All; Project HEART. **Projects:** Call to Action. **Publications:** Annual Report, annual. **Conventions/Meetings:** workshop.

13296 ■ Project Inform (PI)
205 13th St., Ste.2001
San Francisco, CA 94103
Ph: (415)558-9051
Free: (800)822-7422
Fax: (415)558-0684
E-mail: web@projectinform.org
URL: http://www.projectinform.org
Contact: Glen Tanking, Admin. Dir.
Founded: 1985. **Members:** 70,000. **Staff:** 19. **Budget:** $1,800,000. **Languages:** English, Spanish. **Description:** Provides an information clearinghouse and hotline giving updated information on drug treatments for persons with AIDS or the Human Immunodeficiency Virus. Disseminates information on organizations through which the drug treatments can be obtained. Works to speed up research process and focus on promising new treatments. **Publications:** *PI Perspective* (in English and Spanish), semiannual. Journal. Contains HIV treatment information and focuses on advocacy issues. **Price:** free. **Circulation:** 60,000. Alternate Formats: online ● Also publishes information packet and fact sheets on treatments and standards of care. **Conventions/Meetings:** periodic Town Meeting, provides information on new and updated HIV/AIDS treatment developments and current research.

13297 ■ San Francisco AIDS Foundation (SFAF)
995 Market St., Ste.200
San Francisco, CA 94103
Ph: (415)487-3000
Free: (800)367-AIDS
Fax: (415)487-3009
E-mail: feedback@staf.org
URL: http://www.sfaf.org
Contact: Mark Cloutier, Exec. Dir.
Founded: 1982. **Staff:** 60. **Budget:** $26,600,000. **Languages:** English, Filipino, Spanish. **Description:** Regional organization whose goals are to educate the public on the prevention of AIDS and to make various social service programs accessible to people with AIDS. Provides community forums; develops and distributes educational materials. Provides assistance to people with AIDS in obtaining emergency housing, social security and veterans' benefits, medical and insurance benefits, and legal referral services. Works with legislators, corporations, public health coalitions, activists, and the media to advance public health policy and improve media coverage. Maintains speakers' bureau. **Telecommunication Services:** TDD, (888)225-2437. **Formerly:** AIDS/Kaposi's Sarcoma Research and Education Foundation. **Publications:** *Bulletin of Experimental Treatments for AIDS* (in English and Spanish), quarterly. Covers AIDS-related diseases, research, care, treatment, and clinical trials. **Price:** free for individuals and institutions. **Circulation:** 27,000 ● *HIV Policy Watch,* monthly. Bulletin. Contains brief updates on ongoing HIV policy issues. **Circulation:** 1,200. Alternate Formats: online ● *OUT-Reach,* 3/year. Newspaper. Features concise articles on a wide range of HIV/AIDS topics. Alternate Formats: online ● Booklets ● Brochures ● Videos ● Also distributes AIDS educational materials. **Conventions/Meetings:** quarterly board meeting.

13298 ■ Student Global AIDS Campaign (SGAC)
c/o Global Justice
1225 Connecticut Ave. NW, Ste.401
Washington, DC 20036

Ph: (202)296-6727
Fax: (202)296-6728
E-mail: info@fightglobalaids.org
URL: http://www.fightglobalaids.org
Contact: Healy Thompson, Natl. Coor.

Founded: 2001. **Local Groups:** 75. **Description:** Aims to bring an end to AIDS in the US and around the world through education, informed advocacy, media work, and direct action. Seeks increased funding for AIDS programs, access to medication, and full debt cancellation for people living with AIDS. Serves as a network of students and youth organizations committed to the global fight against AIDS. **Computer Services:** Information services, facts and figures about AIDS ● mailing lists, of members. **Committees:** Steering. **Projects:** G8 Youth Initiative. **Working Groups:** Drop the Debt; 04.Stop.AIDS; Gender and AIDS; Policy - Congress and the White House; Trade and Treatment Access; Treat your Workers/Multi-National Corporations. **Publications:** *Christian AIDS Brochure.* Alternate Formats: online ● *Summer Advocacy Guide.* Handbook. Alternate Formats: online.

13299 ■ Transatlantic Partners Against AIDS (TPAA)
165 Broadway, 36th Fl.
New York, NY 10006
Ph: (212)584-1680
Fax: (212)584-1699
E-mail: info@tpaa.net
URL: http://www.tpaa.net
Contact: John E. Tedstrom, Founder

Founded: 2003. **Multinational. Description:** Seeks to improve the lives of people living with HIV/AIDS by promoting sound policies concerning access to treatment, care and support. Works to reduce the stigma of HIV/AIDS and ensure the human rights and civil liberties of those infected with HIV. Leverages the political, civic, scientific, and economic resources of North American, European, and Eurasian partners to combat the spread of HIV/AIDS in Russia, Ukraine and neighboring countries. **Awards:** Kaiser/TPAA Journalism Fellowships. **Frequency:** annual. **Type:** fellowship. **Recipient:** for Russian and Ukrainian journalists pursuing specific reporting projects related to HIV/AIDS. **Publications:** *HIV/AIDS, Law and Human Rights: A Handbook for Russian Legislators.* Alternate Formats: online ● *TPAA Newsletter.* Alternate Formats: online ● Annual Report, annual. Alternate Formats: online ● Reports. Alternate Formats: online.

13300 ■ Treatment Action Group (TAG)
611 Broadway, Ste.608
New York, NY 10012
Ph: (212)253-7922
Fax: (212)253-7923
E-mail: tagnyc@verizon.net
URL: http://www.aidsinfonyc.org/tag
Contact: Mr. Mark Harrington, Exec. Dir.

Founded: 1992. **Members:** 50. **Staff:** 5. **Budget:** $750,000. **Description:** Individuals who are HIV positive and individuals interested in AIDS treatment research. Promotes AIDS research; advocates for research and treatment. Conducts educational programs. Issues publications. Publishes monographs. **Awards:** Research in Action Awards. **Frequency:** annual. **Type:** recognition. **Recipient:** for outstanding individuals in the area of advocacy, science, and industry. **Publications:** *Tagline* (in English and Spanish), periodic. Newsletter. Features AIDS research and policy. **Price:** $30.00 /year for individuals; $50.00 /year for institutions. **Circulation:** 5,000. Alternate Formats: online ● Also publishes various reports on AIDS research and treatments.

13301 ■ Women Alive Coalition
1566 Burnside Ave.
Los Angeles, CA 90019
Ph: (323)965-1564
Free: (800)554-4876
Fax: (323)965-9886

E-mail: info@women-alive.org
URL: http://www.women-alive.org
Contact: Carrie Broadus, Exec. Dir.

Founded: 1991. **Description:** Sets the standards of quality care for women with HIV/AIDS. Challenges national policies on the treatment and prevention of HIV/AIDS, thus affecting world policy. Provides community leadership and mentors other women to become effective advocates. Combats stigma and eliminates isolation. Generates treatment research for women with HIV infection. **Telecommunication Services:** electronic mail, carrie@women-alive.org. **Publications:** *Women Alive Newsletter,* quarterly. Alternate Formats: online.

13302 ■ Women Organized to Respond to Life-Threatening Diseases (WORLD)
414 13th St., 2nd Fl.
Oakland, CA 94612-2603
Ph: (510)986-0340
Fax: (510)986-0341
E-mail: info@womenhiv.org
URL: http://www.womenhiv.org
Contact: Rebecca Denison, Founder

Founded: 1991. **Members:** 12,000. **Staff:** 12. **Budget:** $400,000. **Languages:** English, Spanish. **Multinational. Description:** An empowerment organization by and for women infected or affected by the HIV virus. Offers support and information to women who have AIDS and HIV. Offers retreats and educational classes. Maintains speaker's bureau. **Also Known As:** WORLD. **Publications:** Newsletter, monthly. Contains personal testimonies of infected women; medical and political information. Features easy-to-understand women specific HIV/AIDS treatment. **Circulation:** 12,000. **Advertising:** accepted.

Alcohol

13303 ■ Century Council
1310 G St. NW, Ste.600
Washington, DC 20005
Ph: (202)637-0077
Fax: (202)637-0079
E-mail: kimball@centurycouncil.org
URL: http://www.centurycouncil.org
Contact: Susan Molinari, Chair

Founded: 1991. **Languages:** English, Spanish. **Description:** Promotes responsible decision-making about the use or non-use of alcoholic beverages; fights drunk driving and underage drinking.

Allergy

13304 ■ American Academy of Allergy, Asthma and Immunology (AAAAI)
555 E Wells St., Ste.1100
Milwaukee, WI 53202-3823
Ph: (414)272-6071
Free: (800)822-2762
Fax: (414)272-6070
E-mail: info@aaaai.org
URL: http://www.aaaai.org
Contact: Amber Johnson, Membership Asst.

Founded: 1943. **Members:** 6,200. **Membership Dues:** regular, fellow (domestic), $350 (annual) ● regular, fellow (international), $263 (annual) ● allied health, $50 (annual). **Staff:** 40. **Budget:** $6,000,000. **Languages:** English, Spanish. **Description:** Professional society of physicians specializing in allergy and allergic diseases. Sponsors annual two-day postgraduate course and three-day scientific session. Conducts research and educational programs. Maintains speakers' bureau; operates placement service; compiles statistics. **Libraries: Type:** reference. **Awards: Frequency:** annual. **Type:** grant ● **Type:** recognition. **Recipient:** for research. **Committees:** Audiovisual and Media; Awards, Memorials, and Commemorative Lectureships; Continuing Medical Education; Liaison; Military Allergy; Postgraduate Education; Practice Standards; Public Education; Related Organizations; Undergraduate and Graduate Education. **Councils:** Physician's

Public Services; Professional Education; Research. **Formed by Merger of:** American Association for the Study of Allergy; Association for the Study of Asthma and Allied Conditions. **Formerly:** (1982) American Academy of Allergy. **Publications:** *AAAAI Tips Brochure* (in English and Spanish). Brochures. **Price:** $40.00/copy (up to 99 brochures); $30.00/copy (100-999 brochures); $20.00/copy (1000 brochures); $15.00/copy (over 5000 brochures). Alternate Formats: online ● *Allergy & Asthma Advocate,* quarterly. Newsletter. Alternate Formats: online ● *Allergy Report* ● *American Academy of Allergy Asthma and Immunology—Abstract Book,* annual. Journal. Contains abstracts of papers presented at annual meeting. **Price:** $30.00/copy. **Advertising:** accepted ● *American Academy of Allergy, Asthma and Immunology—Academy News,* bimonthly. Newspaper. **Price:** included in membership dues. **Circulation:** 10,000. **Advertising:** accepted ● *American Academy of Allergy, Asthma and Immunology—Membership Directory,* biennial. **Price:** included in membership dues; $200.00/copy for nonmembers ● *Journal of Allergy and Clinical Immunology,* monthly. **Price:** included in membership dues. **Advertising:** accepted. **Conventions/Meetings:** annual meeting (exhibits) - 2008 Mar. 14-18, Philadelphia, PA; 2009 Mar. 13-17, Washington, DC.

13305 ■ American Academy of Otolaryngic Allergy and Foundation (AAOF)
1990 M St. NW, Ste.680
Washington, DC 20036
Ph: (202)955-5010
Fax: (202)955-5016
E-mail: info@aaoaf.org
URL: http://www.aaoaf.org
Contact: Jami Lucas, Exec. Dir.

Founded: 1941. **Members:** 2,300. **Staff:** 7. **Description:** Otolaryngologists who are interested in the study, research, and practice of otolaryngic allergy. Offers research fellowship in allergy related to the head and neck. Sponsors scientific meetings and continuing medical education programs. **Awards:** Research Grant. **Frequency:** annual. **Type:** grant. **Recipient:** for studies that are of clinical interest to the members and utilize AAOA techniques. **Committees:** Public Education; Research; Scientific Affairs. **Formerly:** American Society of Ophthalmologic and Otolaryngologic Allergy. **Publications:** *AAOA News,* quarterly. Newsletter. **Price:** free. **Circulation:** 11,000. **Advertising:** accepted ● Directory, annual. **Conventions/Meetings:** annual meeting (exhibits).

13306 ■ American Association of Certified Allergists (AACA)
85 W Algonquin Rd., Ste.550
Arlington Heights, IL 60005
Ph: (847)427-8111
Fax: (847)427-1294
Contact: Richard Slawny, Exec.Dir.

Founded: 1968. **Members:** 510. **Membership Dues:** $75 (annual). **Staff:** 2. **Budget:** $30,000. **Description:** Physicians specializing in allergy and clinical immunology. Objectives are to: improve expertise in allergy treatment; disseminate information pertaining to undergraduate and graduate education in allergology; promote improved standards for the practice and teaching of allergy; exchange information between physicians facing similar problems under different circumstances. **Publications:** Newsletter, 3/year. **Price:** included in membership dues. **Circulation:** 500. **Conventions/Meetings:** annual conference and symposium.

13307 ■ American Board of Allergy and Immunology (ABAI)
111 S Independence Mall E, Ste.701
Philadelphia, PA 19106-2512
Ph: (215)592-9466
Free: (866)264-5568
Fax: (215)592-9411
E-mail: abai@abai.org
URL: http://www.abai.org
Contact: David B. Peden, Chm.

Founded: 1971. **Members:** 5,110. **Staff:** 3. **Description:** Examining and credentialing body whose primary function is to establish qualifications and examine physician candidates who meet the requirements for training and experience and grant certification to those who pass the examination. Does not recommend specialists and cannot offer advice on individual allergic or immunologic problems. Member board of the American Board of Medical Specialties and conjoint board of the American Board of Internal Medicine and the American Board of Pediatrics. **Affiliated With:** American Academy of Allergy, Asthma and Immunology; American Academy of Pediatrics; American Board of Internal Medicine; American Board of Pediatrics; American College of Allergy, Asthma and Immunology; American Medical Association; Clinical Immunology Society. **Publications:** Newsletters, annual. **Price:** free. **Circulation:** 5,000. Alternate Formats: online. **Conventions/Meetings:** semiannual board meeting.

13308 ■ American College of Allergy, Asthma and Immunology (ACAAI)
85 W Algonquin Rd., Ste.550
Arlington Heights, IL 60005-4425
Ph: (847)427-1200
Fax: (847)427-1294
E-mail: mail@acaai.org
URL: http://www.acaai.org
Contact: Daniel Ein, Pres.
Founded: 1942. **Members:** 4,900. **Membership Dues:** fellow, $50 (annual) ● regular/scientific, $25 (annual). **Staff:** 12. **Budget:** $6,000,000. **Description:** Practicing allergists, educators, researchers, and clinical immunologists united to: encourage the study, improve the practice, and advance the cause of clinical immunology and allergy; promote association of and highest possible standards among medical scientists and physicians specializing in clinical immunology and in research, teaching, and treatment of allergy; promote dissemination of information regarding clinical immunology and allergy. Maintains a special program for allergy assistants such as nurses, technologists, and clinic aides of lectures, conferences, seminars, participatory workshops, peer-group discussions, poster programs, and technical and scientific exhibits. **Awards: Type:** recognition. **Recipient:** for selected fellows in clinical immunology and allergy and in specialized continuing medical education. **Computer Services:** database ● mailing lists ● online services. **Committees:** Adverse Reactions to Foods; Aerobiology; Allied Health Professionals; Annual Program; Asthma and Respiratory Disease. **Councils:** Communications; Professional Education; Scientific. **Affiliated With:** American Board of Allergy and Immunology. **Formed by Merger of:** American College of Allergists; American Association for Clinical Immunology and Allergy. **Formerly:** (1996) American College of Allergy and Immunology. **Publications:** ACAAI News, bimonthly. Newsletter. Alternate formats: online ● Annals of Allergy, Asthma and Immunology, monthly. Journal. Includes original articles by experts in the field, abstracts, reviews, and editorials. **Price:** $50.00 /year for individuals; $75.00 /year for institutions; $78.00/ year outside U.S. ISSN: 0003-4738. **Circulation:** 5,500. **Advertising:** accepted ● Membership Directory, biennial. **Conventions/Meetings:** annual meeting and lecture, with continuing medical education course (exhibits) - 2007 Nov. 9-14, Dallas, TX - **Avg. Attendance:** 2000; 2008 Nov. 7-12, Seattle, WA; 2009 Nov. 6-11, Miami Beach, FL.

13309 ■ American Latex Allergy Association
PO Box 198
Slinger, WI 53086
Ph: (262)677-9707
Free: (888)972-5378
Fax: (262)677-2808
E-mail: alert@latexallergyresources.org
URL: http://www.latexallergyresources.org
Contact: Sue Lockwood CST, Exec. Dir.
Founded: 1993. **Members:** 4,000. **Membership Dues:** basic, $25 (annual) ● professional, $65 (annual) ● international (basic), $35 (annual) ● international (professional), $75 (annual). **Description:** Creates awareness of latex allergy through education. Provides support to individuals who have been

diagnosed with latex allergy. Minimizes latex exposure in the workplace. Promotes research on latex allergy. **Computer Services:** Information services, latex facts and resources. **Publications:** The ALERT, quarterly. Newsletter. **Price:** included in membership dues. Alternate Formats: online.

13310 ■ Asthma and Allergy Foundation of America (AAFA)
1233 20th St. NW, Ste.402
Washington, DC 20036
Free: (800)7ASTHMA
E-mail: aafawa@aafawa.org
URL: http://www.aafawa.org
Contact: Penny Nelson, Exec. Dir.
Founded: 1953. **Membership Dues:** individual, family, $25 (annual) ● patron, $495 (annual) ● limited income, $15 (annual) ● sustaining, $60 (annual) ● professional, $100 (annual) ● sponsor, $125 (annual) ● benefactor, $245 (annual). **Staff:** 15. **Budget:** $2,574,000. **Regional Groups:** 12. **Description:** Works to find a cure for and controlling asthma and allergic diseases. Serves the estimated 50 million Americans with asthma and allergic diseases through the support of research, patient and public education programs, public and governmental advocacy, and a nationwide network of chapters and education/support groups. **Libraries: Type:** reference. **Awards:** Investigator Grants. **Frequency:** annual. **Type:** grant. **Recipient:** for researchers referred by NIH. **Formerly:** (1957) American Foundation for Allergic Diseases; (1978) Allergy Foundation of America. **Publications:** Advance, bimonthly. Newsletter ● Also publishes educational pamphlets.

13311 ■ Environmental Research Foundation (ERF)
PO Box 160
New Brunswick, NJ 08903-0160
Ph: (732)828-9995
Free: (888)272-2435
Fax: (732)791-4603
E-mail: erf@rachel.org
URL: http://www.drrapp.com
Contact: Rachel Carson, Contact
Founded: 1980. **Description:** Seeks to enhance public awareness of allergies, their symptoms, and remedies; fosters research in allergy. Produces and distributes teaching aids; participates in allergy teaching programs and seminars worldwide. Maintains speakers' bureau. **Libraries: Type:** reference. **Holdings:** audiovisuals, books. **Additional Websites:** http://www.rachel.org. **Formerly:** (2004) Practical Allergy Research Foundation. **Publications:** Allergies and Your Family. Book ● Allergies Do Alter Activities and Behavior. Video ● Environmentally Sick Schools. Video ● The Impossible Child. Book ● Impossible Child or Allergic Child? (in English and Spanish). Video ● Is This Your Child?. Book ● Is This Your Child's World?. Book ● Our Toxic World A Wake Up Call. Book ● Recognize and Manage Your Allergies. Book ● Why An Environmentally Clean Classroom?. Video ● Why Some Children Can't Learn or Behave. Video ● Audiotapes ● Catalog. **Conventions/Meetings:** annual meeting - always in Buffalo, NY.

13312 ■ Food Allergy and Anaphylaxis Network (FAAN)
11781 Lee Jackson Hwy., Ste.160
Fairfax, VA 22033-3309
Ph: (703)691-3179
Free: (800)929-4040
Fax: (703)691-2713
E-mail: faan@foodallergy.org
URL: http://www.foodallergy.org
Contact: Lauren Lawson, Public Relations Mgr.
Founded: 1991. **Members:** 30,000. **Membership Dues:** individual, $30 (annual) ● health care professional, $100 (annual) ● corporation, $500 (annual). **Staff:** 20. **Description:** Individuals with food allergies; health care professionals with an interest in allergology. Aims to raise public awareness, to provide advocacy and education, and to advance research on behalf of all those affected by food allergies and anaphylaxis. Provides information about food allergy and educational resources to patients, their families,

schools, health professionals, pharmaceutical companies, the food industry, and government officials. Sponsors awareness programs such as Food Allergy Awareness Week and Food Allergy Conferences as well as fundraising walks across the country. **Awards:** Food Allergy & Anaphylaxis Network Research Grant. **Frequency:** annual. **Type:** grant ● Founders Award. **Frequency:** annual. **Type:** recognition. **Recipient:** for individuals who have made a broad impact on food allergy issues ● Mariel C. Furlong Award for Making a Difference. **Frequency:** annual. **Type:** recognition. **Recipient:** for outstanding service and contribution by individuals or organizations who have addressed the needs of individuals with food allergies. **Formerly:** (2001) Food Allergy Network. **Publications:** Food Allergy News, bimonthly. Newsletter. ISSN: 1075-4318. **Circulation:** 25,000 ● Food Allergy News for Kids, bimonthly. Newsletter.

13313 ■ International Correspondence Society of Allergists and Clinical Immunologists (ICSA)
6806 W 83rd St.
Overland Park, KS 66204
Ph: (913)469-4043
Fax: (913)469-6580
E-mail: allergylink@kc.rr.com
Contact: Dr. Jeremy E. Baptist PhD, Exec. Dir.
Founded: 1936. **Members:** 204. **Membership Dues:** individual, $35 (annual). **Staff:** 1. **Description:** Physicians who specialize in research and treatment of allergies. Exchanges of technical information and experiences are conducted via letters. **Formerly:** (1995) International Correspondence Society of Allergists. **Publications:** Allergy Letters, monthly. Newsletter. Includes case reports, comments, questions and answers, and related material. **Price:** included in membership dues. **Circulation:** 250.

13314 ■ Joint Council of Allergy, Asthma and Immunology (JCAAI)
50 N Brockway, Ste.3-3
Palatine, IL 60067
Ph: (847)934-1918
Fax: (847)934-1820
E-mail: info@jcaai.org
URL: http://www.jcaai.org
Contact: Robert A. Nathan MD, Pres.
Founded: 1975. **Members:** 2,350. **Membership Dues:** individual, $150 (annual). **Staff:** 3. **Description:** Physicians specializing in allergy or clinical immunology. Members must belong to the American Academy of Allergy and Immunology or the American College of Allergy and Immunology (see separate entries). Serves as political and socioeconomic arm for these sponsoring organizations. **Committees:** Allergist in Multi-Speciality; Clinical Research; CPT Coding; Government Relations; Managed Care; Training Program Liaison; Website Monitoring. **Formerly:** (1977) Joint Council of Socio Economics of Allergy. **Publications:** JCAAI Reports, periodic. Newsletter. **Conventions/Meetings:** annual meeting.

13315 ■ Kids With Food Allergies
73 Old Dublin Pike, Ste.10, No. 163
Doylestown, PA 18901
Ph: (215)230-5394
Fax: (215)340-7674
E-mail: info@kidswithfoodallergies.org
URL: http://www.kidswithfoodallergies.org
Contact: Lynda Mitchell, Pres.
Members: 7,000. **Membership Dues:** family, $25 (annual). **Description:** Aims to enhance the quality of life of children with food allergies. Seeks to improve food allergy management strategies through exchange of information. Provides various programs and services that will allow parents to connect with one another for social and emotional support. Supports public health, awareness, advocacy, and research initiatives about food allergies and anaphylaxis. **Telecommunication Services:** electronic mail, webmaster@kidswithfoodallergies.org. **Publications:** Kids with Food Allergies e-news, monthly. Newsletter. Includes recipes, food ideas and other articles relat-

ing to food allergies. **Price:** free. Alternate Formats: online ● Brochure. **Price:** free. Alternate Formats: online.

13316 ■ Pan-American Allergy Society (PAAS)
PO Box 700587
San Antonio, TX 78270-0587
Ph: (210)495-9853
Fax: (210)495-9852
E-mail: panamallergy@sbcglobal.net
URL: http://www.paas.org
Contact: Ann Brey, Exec. Dir.
Founded: 1956. **Members:** 400. **Membership Dues:** regular, $300 (annual). **Staff:** 1. **Budget:** $200,000. **Description:** Physicians who include allergy diagnosis and management in their practice. Serves as a forum for physicians who actively participate in the diagnosis and treatment of allergic disorders. Seeks to provide a means of social communication among members, thereby promoting inter-specialty cooperation and an increase in individual excellence. Sponsors continuing medical education programs annually. **Computer Services:** database, on members and their practices. **Formerly:** (1976) Gulf Coast Allergy Study Group. **Publications:** Newsletter, semiannual ● Membership Directory, biennial. **Price:** $5.00 hard copy. **Conventions/Meetings:** semiannual Current Methods of Diagnosis & Treatment of Allergy & Immunology - seminar, training course in diagnosis and treatment of allergic disorders (exhibits) - always March and August.

13317 ■ World Allergy Organization (WAO)
555 E Wells St., Ste.1100
Milwaukee, WI 53202-3823
Ph: (414)276-1791
Fax: (414)276-3349
E-mail: info@worldallergy.org
URL: http://www.worldallergy.org
Contact: Charu Malik, Exec. Dir.
Founded: 1951. **Members:** 38,000. **Staff:** 6. **Budget:** $1,500,000. **Regional Groups:** 4. **National Groups:** 52. **Description:** Umbrella organization for 56 international allergy associations representing 38,000 health professionals. **Awards:** Student Grants. **Frequency:** biennial. **Type:** monetary. **Recipient:** for aspiring allergists. **Committees:** Bylaws; Communication; Nomenclature and Review; Research; Specialty. **Programs:** Global Resources in Allergy; World Allergy Forum. **Projects:** Prevention of Allergy and Asthma. **Formerly:** (1980) International Association of Allergology; (2002) International Association of Allergology and Clinical Immunology. **Publications:** *Allergy and Clinical Immunology International,* bimonthly. Journal. Includes research updates. **Price:** $136.00 /year for members; $125.00/year for member societies. **Circulation:** 20,000. **Advertising:** accepted. Also Cited As: *ACI International.* **Conventions/Meetings:** biennial International Congress of Allergology and Clinical Immunology, pharmaceutical companies (exhibits) - 2007 Dec. 2-6, Bangkok, Thailand.

Alternative Lifestyles

13318 ■ Everyday Ayurveda
PO Box 681
Cedar Ridge, CA 95924
Ph: (530)470-9789
E-mail: everydayayurveda@hotmail.com
URL: http://www.everydayayurveda.org
Contact: Mary Thompson CAS, Exec. Dir./Founder
Membership Dues: dragonfly, $10 (annual) ● sunrise, $25 (annual) ● lotus, $60 (annual). **Description:** Introduces the art of Ayurvedic living to modern-day Americans in ways that will be accessible, affordable and adaptable to their lives. Creates a supportive, non-competitive network of Ayurvedic teachers and practitioners willing to work together to advance the spread of Ayurveda in their communities. **Computer Services:** Information services, Ayurveda resources. **Publications:** Newsletter, quarterly.

Alternative Medicine

13319 ■ Acupuncture and Oriental Medicine Alliance
PO Box 738
Gig Harbor, WA 98335
Ph: (253)238-8134 (253)238-8133
Free: (866)698-8994
Fax: (866)698-8994
E-mail: info@aomalliance.com
URL: http://www.aomalliance.org
Contact: Michael McCoy PhD, Exec. Dir.
Founded: 1994. **Members:** 1,600. **Membership Dues:** practitioner, $175 (annual) ● associate, $75 (annual) ● student, $25 (annual) ● consumer, acudetox specialist, $30 (annual) ● corporate (pearl), $1,000 (annual) ● corporate (jade), $2,000 (annual) ● corporate (phoenix), $3,500 (annual) ● corporate (dragon), $5,000 (annual). **Staff:** 4. **Budget:** $350,000. **Description:** Works to the advancement of acupuncture and Oriental medicine. **Also Known As:** AOMAlliance. **Publications:** *Acupuncture and Oriental Medicine.* Brochure. Provides an overview of acupuncture and oriental medicine. **Price:** $23.00 for members (for 100 brochures); $35.00 for nonmembers (for 100 brochures) ● *Chinese Herbal Medicine.* Brochure. Provides an overview of Chinese herbal medicine. **Price:** $23.00 for members (for 100 brochures); $35.00 for nonmembers (for 100 brochures) ● *The Forum,* quarterly. Newsletter. **Circulation:** 13,500. **Advertising:** accepted. Alternate Formats: online ● *Safety Record of Acupuncture.* Report. Summarizes the remarkable safety record of acupuncture for the last 25 years. **Price:** $2.00 for members; $3.00 for nonmembers. **Conventions/Meetings:** annual conference and workshop, includes continuing education (exhibits).

13320 ■ Alexander Technique International (ATI)
c/o Nicole Rosenberg, Admin. Asst.
1692 Massachusetts Ave., 3rd Fl.
Cambridge, MA 02138
Ph: (617)497-5151
Free: (888)668-8996
Fax: (617)497-2615
E-mail: ati-usa@ati-net.com
URL: http://www.ati-net.com
Contact: Nicole Rosenberg, Admin. Asst.
Members: 320. **Membership Dues:** general, $60 (annual) ● trainee, $30 (annual) ● teaching, sponsoring, $135 (annual). **National Groups:** 13. **Multinational. Description:** Worldwide organization of Alexander technique teachers, students and supporters of the technique, created to promote and advance the work discovered by F.M. Alexander. Alexander technique is a bodywork described as a preventative technique which can improve health and overcome present harmful habits that cause unnecessary stress and restrict physical and mental capabilities. **Publications:** Books ● Videos.

13321 ■ Alliance for Alternatives in Healthcare (AAH)
PO Box 730605
San Jose, CA 95173
Ph: (408)223-1787
Free: (800)331-2713
Fax: (208)567-2507
E-mail: healthyins@aol.com
URL: http://www.alternativeinsurance.com
Contact: Steven S. Gorman, Pres./CEO
Founded: 1983. **Members:** 1,500. **Staff:** 4. **Description:** Holistic physicians; employers; interested individuals. Seeks to enhance public recognition of holistic, homeopathic, naturopathic, chiropractic, and acupuncture treatments. (Holistic medicine focuses on the treatment of the entire body, rather than on any one organ or system; homeopathic medicine treats diseases by administering minute quantities of a substance that would produce the disease's symptoms in a healthy person; naturopathic medicine avoids the use of surgery and drugs, focusing instead on natural agents, such as sunshine and fresh air, or on physical means, such as manipulation or acupunc-

ture.) Encourages health insurance systems to cover holistic, homeopathic, and naturopathic treatments in their policies. Attends exhibitions to disseminate information on holistic, homeopathic, and naturopathic medicine to health care providers and the public. Offers group medical, dental, and vision plans to members. Manages network of holistic and natural providers who offer discounts to subscribers of the Holistic Health Network. **Convention/Meeting:** none. **Formerly:** Alternative Health Insurance Services; (1989) Natural Marketing Association. **Publications:** *Natural Marketing News,* periodic ● *Press Releases,* periodic.

13322 ■ Alternative Health Professionals Association (AHPA)
PO Box P
Aiken, SC 29802
Ph: (803)278-1002
E-mail: ahpa1@aol.com
URL: http://www.geocities.com/Athens/4024
Contact: Judi Byers, Contact
Membership Dues: professional, $75 (annual) ● active, $55 (annual) ● student, $25 (annual) ● vendor, $45 (annual). **Description:** Helps individuals in creating and maintaining a strong and balanced physical body and mind. Informs the public on possible alternative options to health care. Encourages health care practitioners to share their experiences and knowledge on alternative health concerns. **Telecommunication Services:** electronic mail, phoenixe@phoenixe.net. **Subgroups:** Speaker's Bureau. **Publications:** Membership Directory, quarterly ● Newsletter, quarterly. Features timely articles and latest research and discoveries.

13323 ■ American Academy of Acupuncture and Oriental Medicine (AAAOM)
1925 W County Rd., B2
Roseville, MN 55113
Ph: (651)631-0204 (651)631-0216
E-mail: webmaster@aaaom.org
URL: http://www.aaaom.org
Contact: Changzhen Gong PhD, Pres.
Description: Seeks to advance acupuncture and oriental medicine. **Conventions/Meetings:** conference.

13324 ■ American Academy of Alternative Medicine (AAAM)
Address Unknown since 2007
Founded: 1984. **Members:** 800. **Membership Dues:** ordinary, $275 (annual) ● fellow, $370 (annual). **Staff:** 5. **National Groups:** 2. **Description:** Advocates of alternative medicine. Promotes increased reliance on alternative treatments by professionals. Conducts research; sponsors training programs for health care professionals wishing to make use of alternative therapies. Conducts continuing education leading to American Board of Alternative Medicine Certification for members. **Libraries: Type:** by appointment only. **Holdings:** 250; books, clippings, periodicals. **Subjects:** alternative medicine, medical and non-medical. **Awards:** Fellow of the American College of Alternative Medicine. **Frequency:** monthly. **Type:** fellowship. **Recipient:** for interest in alternative medicine and contribution to the field, direct patient care, and/or research ● **Frequency:** monthly. **Type:** recognition ● **Frequency:** monthly. **Type:** recognition. **Computer Services:** Mailing lists. **Divisions:** International; Regional. **Affiliated With:** American Board of Alternative Medicine. **Publications:** *Restricted,* periodic. Newsletter. **Price:** free for members. **Circulation:** 900. **Advertising:** accepted. Also Cited As: *AAA Newsletter.* **Conventions/Meetings:** annual Themes in Alternative Medicine - convention (exhibits).

13325 ■ American Alternative Medical Association (AAMA)
2200 Market St., Ste.329
Galveston, TX 77550-1530
Ph: (409)621-2600
Free: (888)764-2237
Fax: (775)703-5334

E-mail: office@joinaama.com
URL: http://www.joinaama.com
Contact: Donald A. Rosenthal MD, Exec. Dir.
Founded: 1990. **Membership Dues:** life, $260. **Description:** Fosters unity among "grassroots practitioners" and those with advanced academic credentials. Educates the public that good health can be obtained without the use of drugs. Encourages improved public awareness of the benefits of alternative health care. **Computer Services:** database, school listings. **Affiliated With:** American Association of Drugless Practitioners.

13326 ■ American Apitherapy Society (AAS)
4835 Van Nuys Blvd. 100
Sherman Oaks, CA 91403
Ph: (818)501-0446
Fax: (818)995-9334
E-mail: info@apitherapy.org
URL: http://www.apitherapy.org
Contact: Dr. Andrew Kochan MD, Pres.
Founded: 1989. **Members:** 800. **Membership Dues:** basic, $45 (annual) ● health care professional, $60 (annual) ● organization, $100 (annual). **Staff:** 2. **Budget:** $50,000. **Regional Groups:** 9. **Description:** Beekeepers, physicians, scientists, and others interested in apitherapy, the therapeutic use of honeybee products. Purpose is to collect and disseminate information in the field and to provide a forum for researchers to present the results of their work. Encourages investigation of hive products in order to provide a scientific foundation for their curative properties and use in human medicine. Seeks to prove the effectiveness of bee venom in treating inflammatory diseases such as arthritis and rheumatism. Gains funding for clinical laboratory studies through contributions. Supports selected research and fundraising projects for the investigation of apiotherapeutic agents. Compiles statistics. **Libraries: Type:** reference. **Holdings:** 500; archival material, audiovisuals, books, periodicals. **Subjects:** therapeutic uses of honeybee products and honeybee venom. **Computer Services:** Mailing lists, of members. **Formerly:** (1989) North American Apio-Therapy Society. **Publications:** *Journal of the American Apitherapy Society*, quarterly. **Price:** free with membership; $6.00/copy for nonmembers. **Circulation:** 1,000. **Advertising:** accepted ● Brochures. Contains information on bee venom, honey, pollen, and beeswax. ● Journal, annual. **Conventions/Meetings:** annual Charles Mraz Apitherapy Course - conference and symposium, with hands-on teaching (exhibits).

13327 ■ American Association of Drugless Practitioners (AADP)
2200 Market St., Ste.329
Galveston, TX 77550-1530
Ph: (409)621-2600
Free: (888)764-AADP
Fax: (775)703-5334
E-mail: join@aadp.net
URL: http://www.aadp.net
Contact: Donald A. Rosenthal MD, Exec. Dir.
Founded: 1990. **Members:** 1,000. **Membership Dues:** regular, $260. **Staff:** 20. **Description:** Health care professionals including physicians, chiropractors, nurses, and herbalists. Promotes drugless health care and the professional advancement of members. Serves as a clearinghouse on drugless health care; sponsors educational and training programs for health care professionals interested in drugless practice. Conducts examinations and bestows certification upon qualified drugless practitioners.

13328 ■ American Board of Alternative Medicine (ABAM)
c/o Dr. B. Alli
PO Box 24224
Detroit, MI 48224-0224
Ph: (313)882-0641
Contact: Dr. B. Alli, Contact
Founded: 1994. **Members:** 1,800. **Membership Dues:** ordinary, $375 (annual) ● diplomate/fellow, $500 (annual). **Staff:** 5. **Budget:** $127,000. **Description:** Practitioners of alternative medicine. Promotes

increased use of alternative treatments including mind-body intervention, bioelectromagnetic therapy, and herbal medicines. Conducts research and educational programs; maintains hall of fame. **Libraries: Type:** not open to the public. **Holdings:** 5,000; books, clippings, periodicals. **Subjects:** alternative medicine. **Awards:** FABLM. **Frequency:** periodic. **Type:** fellowship. **Recipient:** to former members. **Computer Services:** Mailing lists. **Publications:** *Newsletter of the American Board of Alternative Medicine*, periodic. **Price:** $120.00 free, for members only. **Advertising:** accepted. **Conventions/Meetings:** semiannual meeting.

13329 ■ American Center for the Alexander Technique (ACAT)
39 W 14th St., Rm. 507
New York, NY 10011
Ph: (212)633-2229
Fax: (212)633-2239
E-mail: acat@acatnyc.org
URL: http://www.acatnyc.org
Contact: Joan Frost, Training Dir.
Founded: 1964. **Members:** 200. **Staff:** 4. **Budget:** $190,000. **Description:** Promotes the Alexander Technique, an educational technique that enables individuals to use their bodies with ease, grace, flexibility, and freedom from strain in any physical activity. Formed to assure further development of the technique in this country and to maintain its standards. Answers requests for information and refers interested people to certified teachers. Sponsors Teacher Certification Program consisting of 1600 hours over nine ten-week terms, the last a teaching apprenticeship, to certify students who have demonstrated, to the satisfaction of the faculty, a high standard both of teaching skills and of personal use. **Libraries: Type:** not open to the public. **Holdings:** 200. **Subjects:** Alexander Technique. **Publications:** *ACAT News*, periodic. Newsletter ● *Annual Certified Member/Teacher List*, annual. Membership Directory. **Conventions/Meetings:** annual meeting.

13330 ■ American Manual Medicine Association (AMMA)
c/o Marie A. Ruberto, Managing Dir.
1845 Lakeshore Dr., Ste.7
Muskegon, MI 49441
Free: (888)375-7245
Fax: (231)755-2963
E-mail: info@americanmanualmedicine.com
URL: http://www.americanmanualmedicine.com
Contact: Marie A. Ruberto, Managing Dir.
Membership Dues: professional, $300 (annual) ● associate (student), $225 (annual). **Description:** Promotes manual therapy as an allied health care profession. Seeks to advance the practice of manual therapy and manual acupuncture through professional standards, education and testing. Offers training to clinicians in order for them to provide quality medical care to patients. Provides National Board Certification Diplomate status to qualified members. **Publications:** Journal, 3/year. Provides official information on the development of the manual therapy profession. **Price:** $245.00 /year for institutions; $195.00 /year for individuals; $155.00/year for student.

13331 ■ American Polarity Therapy Association (APTA)
122 N Elm St., Ste.512
Greensboro, NC 27401
Ph: (336)574-1121
Fax: (336)574-1151
E-mail: aptaoffices@polaritytherapy.org
URL: http://www.polaritytherapy.org
Contact: Ellie Simmons RPP, Exec. Dir.
Founded: 1984. **Members:** 1,200. **Membership Dues:** general, $66 (annual) ● international, $53 (annual) ● student, $44 (annual). **Staff:** 5. **Budget:** $250,000. **State Groups:** 6. **Description:** Dedicated to the advancement of polarity therapy. (Polarity therapy is a non-diagnostic holistic health system supplementing and supporting medical treatment. Polarity techniques include bodywork, diet, exercise and self awareness for health maintenance.) Devel-

ops and disseminates educational and support materials; registers practitioners; holds competitions. **Awards:** Dr. Stone Award. **Frequency:** annual. **Type:** monetary. **Committees:** Awards; Course Approval; Education; Ethics; International Issues; Planning; Public Relations; Research. **Publications:** *Energy*, quarterly. Newsletter. **Price:** included in membership dues. **Advertising:** accepted ● Books. **Conventions/Meetings:** annual conference (exhibits) ● semiannual regional meeting (exhibits).

13332 ■ American Qigong Association (AQA)
117 Topaz Way
San Francisco, CA 94131
Ph: (415)285-9400
Fax: (415)647-5745
E-mail: eastwestqi@aol.com
URL: http://www.eastwestqi.com/aqa
Contact: V. Kay Lahdenpera RN, Exec. Dir.
Members: 723. **Membership Dues:** individual, $150 (annual) ● senior, student, $100 (annual). **Description:** Promotes the principles and practices of Qigong. Brings together scientists, professionals, institutions and lay people to promote research and education in the areas of Qigong. Provides professional visibility for Qigong practitioners. Supports Qigong professionals in establishing general acceptance and recognition within the medical and scientific community. Acts as an information clearinghouse for Qigong and reference for services for individual clients, masters and teachers.

13333 ■ American Reflexology Certification Board (ARCB)
PO Box 740879
Arvada, CO 80006-0879
Ph: (303)933-6921
Fax: (303)904-0460
E-mail: info@arcb.net
URL: http://www.arcb.net
Contact: George S. Balut, Pres.
Founded: 1992. **Nonmembership. Description:** Works to protect the public; promotes advancement of field through recognition of competent reflexologists meeting national standards; provides National Board Certified Reflexologist certification. **Computer Services:** Online services, practitioner referral. **Publications:** *Reflexology Today*, semiannual. Newsletter. Keeps members updated on latest information. **Circulation:** 1,000. **Advertising:** accepted.

13334 ■ American Reiki Master Association (ARMA)
c/o Cheri L. Robertson, Pres.
PO Box 130
Lake City, FL 32056-0130
Ph: (904)755-9638
E-mail: american_reiki@yahoo.com
URL: http://members.atlantic.net/~arma
Contact: Cheri L. Robertson, Pres.
Description: Promotes the Reiki therapy technique as a method of natural healing; offers training and certification.

13335 ■ American Society for the Alexander Technique (AMSAT)
PO Box 60008
Florence, MA 01062-0008
Ph: (413)584-2359
Free: (800)473-0620
Fax: (413)584-3097
E-mail: info@amsat.ws
URL: http://www.amsat.ws
Contact: Ralph Zito, Chm.
Founded: 1987. **Members:** 600. **Membership Dues:** associate, student trainee, non-practicing teacher, international (non-voting), resident/non-resident teacher (voting), $60-$500 (annual). **Staff:** 3. **Description:** Individuals who have completed a three-year training course and have been certified by the society; students currently enrolled in an approved AmSAT teacher training course. Promotes and trains teachers of the Alexander Technique. Created by Australian actor F. M. Alexander (1863-1955), the technique employs reeducation of habitual movement patterns so the body is used efficiently with the least

amount of "wear and tear." Seeks to: promote proficiency, knowledge, and skill in the field of psycho-physical reeducation; encourage education and study in the Alexander Technique; approve the establishment and continuation of teacher training courses. Promotes communication and the interchange of skills and information between the society and other organizations of teachers in the Alexander Technique; works to achieve reciprocal memberships between such organizations. Promotes and conducts research. Compiles information regarding teacher members and members of affiliated societies and disseminates this information to the public. Maintains speakers' bureau. **Libraries: Type:** not open to the public. **Holdings:** articles. **Computer Services:** database ● information services, referral. **Committees:** Credentials; Ethics; Friends of the Society; Fundraising; Professional Conduct; Publicity. **Publications:** *AMSAT News*, quarterly. Newsletter. **Price:** included in membership dues. **Circulation:** 700. **Advertising:** accepted ● *List of Certified Training Courses*, annual. Directory ● *Teaching Members List*, annual. Directory. **Conventions/Meetings:** annual meeting, with workshops ● annual Teacher Refresher Course - meeting ● workshop.

13336 ■ American Society of Alternative Therapists (ASAT)
PO Box 703
Rockport, MA 01966
Ph: (978)281-4400
Fax: (978)282-1144
E-mail: asat@asat.org
URL: http://www.asat.org
Contact: Dr. Martin Hart, Pres.
Founded: 1990. **Members:** 1,700. **Membership Dues:** registered affiliate, \$85 (annual) ● lay affiliate, \$55 (annual). **Staff:** 55. **Description:** CORE counselors. Seeks to advance CORE counseling training and services; promotes continuing professional development of members. Conducts educational programs to raise public awareness and acceptance of CORE counseling methods; sponsors training programs for CORE counselors; holds examinations and bestows CORE counseling certification upon qualified individuals; establishes and monitors CORE counseling guidelines.

13337 ■ Archaeus Project (AP)
PO Box 7079
Kamuela, HI 96743
E-mail: dstillings@archaeusproject.com
URL: http://www.archaeusproject.com
Contact: Dennis Stillings, Ed.
Founded: 1981. **Staff:** 3. **Budget:** \$239,000. **Languages:** English, French, German. **Description:** Business, medical, academic, and engineering professionals, scientists, psychologists, psi researchers, and interested others. Investigates the effects of ordinary and altered states of consciousness on conditions of health and disease; studies the relationships between the mind, body, and matter, and the implications of these relationships for medicine. Sponsors lecture series, seminars, and workshops; conducts cyberphysiology (science of self-regulation in physiology) research. **Libraries: Type:** reference. **Holdings:** 2,500; artwork, audio recordings, books, periodicals. **Subjects:** alternative medicine, anomalies, bioelectromagnetics, parapsychology, holistic health, Jungian psychology, Hawaiian. **Publications:** *Healing Island*, quarterly. Journal. Contains items on health care, health care costs, and the integration of alternative with mainstream medicine, Hawaii as a health/healing destination. **Price:** free on request. ISSN: 0895-125X ● *Project 2010*. Monograph ● *Tape Catalog*. **Conventions/Meetings:** Healing Island Conference - congress (exhibits) - every 3-4 years.

13338 ■ Association for Holotropic Breathwork International (AHBI)
8987 E Tanque Verde Rd., No. 110
Tucson, AZ 85749
Ph: (520)760-7446
Fax: (520)760-2335

E-mail: office@breathwork.com
URL: http://www.breathwork.com
Contact: Ted Riskin, Pres.
Membership Dues: professional, \$65 (annual) ● general, \$45 (annual) ● donation, \$10 (annual) ● friend of AHBI, \$100 (annual) ● professional couple, \$80 (annual) ● general couple, \$55 (annual). **Multinational. Description:** Works to preserve and enhance the principles of holotropic breathwork. **Publications:** *The Inner Door*, quarterly. **Price:** included in membership dues. ISSN: 1524-623X. **Conventions/Meetings:** conference.

13339 ■ Citizens for Health
2104 Stevens Ave. S
Minneapolis, MN 55404
Ph: (612)879-7585
E-mail: info@citizens.org
URL: http://www.citizens.org
Contact: Ana Micka, Pres./CEO
Founded: 1992. **Membership Dues:** individual (minimum), \$19 (annual). **Local Groups:** 150. **Description:** Works to protect and expand consumers' natural health choices. Initiates and monitors legislation with the goal of ensuring access to health information and the freedom to choose from a broad range of health options. **Publications:** *Action Alert*, periodic. Bulletin ● *The Natural Activist*, bimonthly. Newsletter. **Price:** included in membership dues.

13340 ■ Committee for Freedom of Choice in Medicine (CFCM)
Address Unknown since 2007
Founded: 1972. **Members:** 30,000. **Staff:** 5. **Local Groups:** 30. **Description:** Purpose is to support freedom of choice for any therapy which shows clear evidence of efficacy and to prohibit the interference of government or any third party in the relationship between an informed patient and his or her physician. Activities include publishing information to keep members apprised of the latest developments in research and treatment, directing people with questions concerning alternative therapy to physicians in their areas, maintaining an information service for physicians interested in expanding their knowledge of metabolic/nutritional treatment, and providing educational exhibits for programs and seminars being conducted by various medical groups. Conducts research; compiles statistics on people with degenerative diseases who have been treated with metabolic therapy. Operates speakers' bureau. **Formerly:** (1985) Committee for Freedom of Choice in Cancer Therapy. **Publications:** *Choice Magazine*, quarterly. Includes science corner and heart, cancer, drug, and court watch sections. **Price:** included in membership dues ● Audiotapes ● Books ● Brochures ● Pamphlets ● Reprints ● Videos. **Conventions/Meetings:** annual meeting ● symposium, on alternative therapies to educate the public and the medical profession about new discoveries in the treatment of degenerative disease.

13341 ■ Complementary Alternative Medical Association (CAMA)
PO Box 373478
Decatur, GA 30037
E-mail: cama@camaweb.org
URL: http://www.camaweb.org
Contact: Marge Roberts, Pres.
Founded: 1996. **Membership Dues:** supporter (single, couple, student), \$20-\$50 (annual) ● professional, \$100 (annual) ● corporate, \$250-\$10,000 (annual). **Description:** Educates consumers, practitioners and policy makers on complementary/ alternative medicine with an emphasis on natural healing and health. Advances the practice of complementary/alternative medicine. Provides health care services to the public. **Libraries: Type:** reference. **Holdings:** articles. **Subjects:** cancer, infectious disease, public policy, traditional Chinese medicine. **Computer Services:** database, lists of practitioners ● mailing lists, of members. **Telecommunication Services:** electronic mail, msmarge@camaweb.org. **Publications:** *Choices*, monthly. Newsletter. Alternate Formats: online.

13342 ■ Complementary Medicine Association (CMA)
c/o Mary Wolken-Rodriguez, Exec. Dir.
4649 E Malvern St.
Tucson, AZ 85711-4249
Ph: (520)323-6291
Fax: (520)323-0264
E-mail: compmeded@aol.com
Contact: Mary Wolken-Rodriguez, Exec. Dir.
Founded: 1990. **Members:** 80. **Staff:** 1. **Description:** Fosters and teaches cost effective and natural systems of medicine to professionals and the public. Focuses on homeopathic, herbal medicines, kinesiology and learning/memory improvement for the learning and traumatically injured individual. **Libraries: Type:** reference. **Holdings:** 300; books. **Subjects:** holistic medicine. **Awards:** Special Needs Family Education Fund. **Frequency:** 7/year. **Type:** monetary. **Recipient:** for individuals who need financial help for energetic kinesiology work. **Computer Services:** database. **Telecommunication Services:** information service, journal articles and other energetic medicine classes and services. **Publications:** *Complementary Health Online*, 2-3/year. Journal. Holistic scientific publication. Alternate Formats: online.

13343 ■ Dinshah Health Society (DHS)
PO Box 707
Malaga, NJ 08328-0707
Ph: (856)692-4686
Fax: (856)696-7890
E-mail: dinshahhealth@aol.com
URL: http://www.dinshahhealth.org
Contact: Darius Dinshah, Pres.
Founded: 1975. **Members:** 3,149. **Membership Dues:** individual, \$3 (annual). **Staff:** 3. **Multinational. Description:** Health professionals and other interested individuals who use and promote chromopathy as a therapy. Chromopathy, or color therapy, involves the use of projected colors of light to treat specific health problems. Seeks to stimulate interest in and knowledge of chromopathy and other lesser-known therapies. **Publications:** *Let There Be Light*. Book. **Price:** \$15.00. Also Cited As: *Es Werde Licht* ● *Spectro-Chrome Metry Ency*, new editions when needed. Book. Contains information about the theory and development of Spectro-Chrome. **Price:** \$14.00 ● Newsletter, quarterly. **Price:** \$3.00. **Circulation:** 4,500. **Conventions/Meetings:** annual convention - usually November.

13344 ■ Gerson Institute (GI)
1572 Second Ave.
San Diego, CA 92101
Ph: (619)685-5353
Free: (888)4-GERSON
Fax: (619)685-5363
E-mail: info@gerson.org
URL: http://www.gerson.org
Contact: Anita Wilson, Exec. Dir.
Founded: 1977. **Members:** 1,000. **Membership Dues:** in U.S., \$30 (annual) ● outside U.S., \$35 (annual) ● individual, \$50-\$99 (annual) ● supporting, \$100-\$249 (annual) ● donor, \$250-\$499 (annual) ● patron, \$500-\$999 (annual) ● benefactor, \$1,000-\$2,499 (annual). **Staff:** 9. **Budget:** \$800,000. **Languages:** English, French, German, Spanish. **Multinational. Description:** Individuals interested in health information. Aims to educate the public on nutritional health and to disseminate information about the Gerson therapy for healing. (The Gerson therapy was developed by Max Gerson, MD, and seeks to prevent disease as well as to restore the natural healing mechanism in patients suffering from cancer and other degenerative diseases without the use of standard toxic therapies. Therapy includes a detoxification program to help the body eliminate toxins and waste materials that interfere with metabolism and healing and an intensive nutrition program.) Makes referrals to Gerson licensed clinics in Mexico, Big Bear, CA and Hawaii, and soon opening in Tokyo, Japan; assists and trains physicians who want to learn the Gerson therapy. Presents lectures on health; conducts medical and nutritional research. **Libraries: Type:** by appointment only. **Holdings:** 30; archival material, articles, audio recordings, books,

films, video recordings. **Subjects:** Gerson Therapy, nutrition, alternative medicine, natural healing. **Publications:** *A Cancer Therapy - Results of 50 Cases* (in English, German, Japanese, and Romanian). Includes historical reviews and therapy details. **Price:** $25.00/year in U.S.; $30.00/year outside U.S. ● *Censored for Curing Cancer* ● *Gerson Healing Newsletter*, bimonthly. **Price:** included in membership dues. **Circulation:** 1,000. **Advertising:** accepted ● *The Gerson Therapy*. Book. **Price:** $17.00.

13345 ■ Guild for Structural Integration (GSI)
PO Box 1559
Boulder, CO 80306
Ph: (303)447-0122
Free: (800)447-0150
Fax: (303)447-0108
E-mail: gsi@rolfguild.org
URL: http://www.rolfguild.org
Contact: Richard Stenstadvold, Pres.
Founded: 1989. **Membership Dues:** subscriber, $100 (annual). **Description:** Dedicated to the teaching of Dr. Ida P. Rolf, a ten-session sequence of structural, fascial and educational goals establishing order in human structures. **Publications:** *Guild Online.* Newsletter. Provides exchange of information. Alternate Formats: online ● Catalog.

13346 ■ Herbalists Without Borders
153 S Allen St.
State College, PA 16801
E-mail: info@herbalistswithoutborders.org
URL: http://www.herbalistswithoutborders.org
Contact: Jennifer Chesworth, Managing Dir.
Membership Dues: individual, $35 (annual) ● student, $25 (annual) ● non-profit, educational organization, $75 (annual) ● business, $150 (annual) ● benefactor, $2,500 (periodic) ● life, $1,000. **Multinational. Description:** Provides health care to underserved communities. Works with small farmers, women's groups and conservation organizations in promoting the health and well-being of communities. Encourages reforestation projects worldwide. **Programs:** Botanical Gardens and Seed Banks; Clinical Services; Education; Fair Botanical Trade; Phytomediation; Publications; Reforestation. **Publications:** *Herbal Sojournal*, semiannual. **Price:** included in membership dues; $12.00 /year for nonmembers. **Advertising:** accepted. Alternate Formats: online. **Conventions/Meetings:** annual meeting.

13347 ■ Institute for Traditional Medicine and Preventive Health Care (ITM)
2017 SE Hawthorne Blvd.
Portland, OR 97214
Ph: (503)233-4907
Fax: (503)233-1017
E-mail: itm@itmonline.org
URL: http://www.itmonline.org
Contact: Subhuti Dharmananda PhD, Dir.
Founded: 1979. **Membership Dues:** group, $30 (annual). **Staff:** 24. **Multinational. Description:** Helps people seeking traditional medicine knowledge and services by clarifying the nature of traditional medicine and demonstrating how it can be utilized in the modern setting. Provides educational materials and articles on traditional medicine and related topics. Conducts background research in traditional medicine including journal searches in China and computer searches in the US. Provides especially designed herbal formulations for use in clinics and practitioners who read institutes literature. **Computer Services:** database, traditional medicine ● information services, herbal formulas, famous Chinese Physicians of the past, five organ networks ● mailing lists, of traditional medicine articles ● online services, practitioner list, acupuncture schools and veterinarian guide. **Projects:** Immune Enhancement. **Publications:** *A Bag of Pearls*. Handbook. Serves as a guide for practitioners and other traditional medicine herb specialists. **Price:** $20.00 plus shipping and handling ● *Internet Journal of the Institute for Traditional Medicine*. Contains manuscripts and articles relevant to traditional medicine and to its practitioners. Alternate Formats: online.

13348 ■ International Aromatherapy and Herb Association (IAHA)
c/o Jeffrey Schiller, Pres.
3541 W Acapulco Ln.
Phoenix, AZ 85053
Ph: (602)938-4439
E-mail: jeffreys@aztec.asu.edu
URL: http://www.aromaherbshow.com
Contact: Jeffrey Schiller, Pres.
Founded: 1996. **Members:** 300. **Membership Dues:** general, $15 (annual). **Staff:** 15. **Description:** Represents people interested in aromatherapy, herbs and natural health. **Additional Websites:** http://www.aztecfreenet.org/makingscents. **Publications:** *Making Scents*, semiannual. Magazine. Includes articles of interest, resource lists, and book and product reviews. **Price:** included in membership dues. **Circulation:** 500. **Advertising:** accepted. **Conventions/Meetings:** annual Aroma Herb Show - convention and trade show (exhibits) - winter.

13349 ■ International Association of Reiki Professionals (IARP)
PO Box 6182
Nashua, NH 03063-6182
Ph: (603)881-8838
Fax: (603)882-9088
E-mail: info@iarp.org
URL: http://www.iarp.org
Founded: 1997. **Membership Dues:** professional - with insurance, $249 (annual) ● professional - with insurance, $498 (biennial) ● associate, $85 (annual) ● associate, $150 (biennial) ● associate, $225 (triennial). **Multinational. Description:** Provides a forum to encourage support, partnership, cooperation and connection among Reiki masters and practitioners throughout the world. Partners with medical and healing profession communities in raising public awareness of Reiki. Promotes personal and spiritual growth as well as professional development. **Computer Services:** database, searchable list of Reiki professionals ● information services, Reiki resources. **Programs:** Certificate Service. **Publications:** *The Reiki Times*, quarterly. Newsletter. **Price:** included in membership dues.

13350 ■ International Association of Structural Integrators (IASI)
PO Box 8664
Missoula, MT 59807
Ph: (406)543-4856
Free: (877)843-4274
URL: http://www.theiasi.org
Contact: Buddy Frank, Contact
Membership Dues: professional in U.S., $150 (annual) ● professional outside U.S., $100 (annual) ● student, friend, $50 (annual). **Multinational. Description:** Aims to uphold the standards of practice and quality of work which embodies the profession of structural integration. Supports research on the effects and benefits of structural integration. Provides appropriate legislative support and continuing educational opportunities for its members. **Publications:** *Yearbook of Structural Integration*, annual. **Price:** included in membership dues ● Newsletter. **Price:** included in membership dues. Alternate Formats: online.

13351 ■ International Society for Complementary Medicine Research (ISCMR)
715 E Huron St., Ste.2E
Ann Arbor, MI 48104-1555
Ph: (734)998-9553
Fax: (734)998-7720
E-mail: info@iscmr.org
URL: http://www.iscmr.org
Contact: George Lewith, Pres.
Founded: 2003. **Membership Dues:** professional, practitioner, $80 (annual) ● student, resident, fellow, emeritus, retired, $40 (annual) ● low income, $25 (annual) ● sustaining, $150-$1,000 (annual). **Multinational. Description:** Fosters complementary and integrative medicine research. Provides a platform for knowledge and information exchange to enhance international communication and collaboration. Facilitates communication and collaboration among

researchers and practitioners with an interest in research. **Telecommunication Services:** electronic mail, gl3@soton.ac.uk. **Publications:** *Journal of Alternative and Complementary Medicine*, 10/year. Contains observational and analytical reports on treatments outside the realm of allopathic medicine. **Price:** $263.00 personal (print and online in U.S.); $285.00 personal (print and online outside U.S.); $597.00 institutional (print and online in U.S.); $700.00 institutional (print and online outside U.S.). ISSN: 1075-5535. Alternate Formats: online. Also Cited As: *JACM* ● Newsletter, quarterly. **Price:** included in membership dues. Alternate Formats: online ● Brochure. Alternate Formats: online. **Conventions/Meetings:** annual conference - 2008 Mar. 29-31, Sydney, NW, Australia.

13352 ■ International Yan Xin Qigong Association (IYXQA)
PO Box 1332
Church Sta.
New York, NY 10008-1332
E-mail: info@yanxinqigong.net
URL: http://www.yanxinqigong.net
Contact: Dr. Xin Yan, Contact
Founded: 1991. **Multinational. Description:** Promotes the learning, understanding and practice of Yan Xin Qigong (a method for healing and fitness). Aims to bring health, well-being, peace and harmony to humankind. Works with people from all walks of life.

13353 ■ National Association of Alternative Medicines (NAAM)
PO Box 35215
Chicago, IL 60707-0215
Ph: (708)453-0080
Fax: (708)453-0083
E-mail: naam@rentamark.com
Contact: L. Stollen, Contact
Founded: 1975. **Members:** 69,071. **Membership Dues:** individual, $25 (annual) ● business, $100 (annual) ● corporate sponsor, $250 (annual). **Staff:** 100. **Description:** Practitioners of alternative medical specialties. Seeks to increase members' public visibility and professional influence. Provides member education; also provides trademark licensing and product and service endorsement services to support members' activities. Serves as a major platform for professional advancement and knowledge. **Libraries:** Type: not open to the public. **Holdings:** 12,500. **Subjects:** alternative medicines. **Awards:** Alternative Medicine Award of the Year. **Frequency:** annual. **Type:** recognition. **Computer Services:** Mailing lists, product endorsements ● online services, ad banner (468x60 pixel) advertising opportunity. **Also Known As:** (2000) American Alternative Medicine Association. **Publications:** *NAAM Journal*, monthly: Contains articles submitted by authors via email. **Circulation:** 200,000. **Advertising:** accepted. Alternate Formats: online. **Conventions/Meetings:** annual convention.

13354 ■ National Ayurvedic Medical Association (NAMA)
620 Cabrillo Ave.
Santa Cruz, CA 95065
E-mail: info@ayurveda-nama.org
URL: http://www.ayurveda-nama.org
Contact: Cynthia Copple, Pres.
Membership Dues: general, $50 (annual) ● student, $25 (annual) ● life, $500 ● benefactor (bronze level), $100 (annual) ● benefactor (silver level), $500 (annual) ● benefactor (gold level), $1,000 (annual) ● benefactor (platinum level), $5,000 (annual) ● educator, $75 (annual) ● practitioner, $150 (annual). **Description:** Represents the interests of the Ayurvedic profession. Aims to preserve, protect, improve, and promote the philosophy, knowledge, science and practice of Ayurveda. Maintains the professional competency and licensing of Ayurveda through enhancement of knowledge, practice and application of Ayurvedic profession. Encourages the public to appreciate and accept Ayurveda. **Computer Services:** Mailing lists, of members. **Conventions/Meetings:** annual Rejuvenation, Ayurveda and Yoga in the Desert - conference.

13355 ■ National Center for Complementary and Alternative Medicine (NCCAM)
PO Box 7923
Gaithersburg, MD 20898-7923
Ph: (301)519-3153
Free: (888)644-6226
Fax: (866)464-3616
E-mail: info@nccam.nih.gov
URL: http://nccam.nih.gov
Contact: Dr. Ruth L. Kirschstein MD, Acting Dir.
Founded: 1998. **Staff:** 90. **Languages:** English, Spanish. **Nonmembership. Description:** Committed to exploring complementary and alternative healing practices, including but not limited to acupuncture, herbs, homeopathy, therapeutic massage, and traditional oriental medicine; trains CAM researchers; conducts biomedical research; disseminates information. Programs focus on evaluating the safety and efficacy of natural products, supporting pharmacological studies to determine potential interactive effects with standard treatment medications, evaluates CAM practices such as acupuncture and chiropractic. **Awards:** National Research Service Award Institutional Training Grants. **Type:** grant. **Recipient:** for eligible institutions, to develop or enhance research training in specified areas of biomedical and behavioral research. **Computer Services:** database, AM database of CHID ● database, CAM on PubMed. **Telecommunication Services:** TDD, (866)464-3615. **Committees:** Trans-Agency CAM Coordinating. **Councils:** Program Advisory. **Programs:** Extramural Research; Intramural Research Training; Liaison with CAM Stakeholders; Public Information Clearinghouse; Scientific Databases. **Publications:** *Complementary and Alternative Medicine at the NIH*, quarterly. Newsletter. Features CAM updates, NIH research news, and information from the NCCAM. **Price:** free. Alternate Formats: online. **Conventions/Meetings:** conference, with educational programs ● meeting, town meetings ● workshop.

13356 ■ National Qigong (Chi Kung) Association (NQA)
PO Box 252
Lakeland, MN 55043
Free: (888)815-1893
E-mail: info@nqa.org
URL: http://www.nqa.org
Contact: Michael DeMolina, Chm.
Membership Dues: general, $50 (annual) ● practitioner, $100 (annual) ● professional, $150 (annual) ● healing wave supporter, $30 (annual). **Description:** Promotes the principles and practices of Qigong on self-healing and spiritual self-development. Integrates medical Qigong in the health care community. Improves the practice and understanding of Qigong. **Computer Services:** database, directory of qigong teachers ● information services, qigong resources ● mailing lists. **Committees:** Communication; Education; Events; Healing Wave; Public Relations; Qigong in School; Strategic Planning; Travel. **Publications:** *The Journal of Qigong in America*, quarterly. **Advertising:** accepted ● *Qi Mail*, bimonthly. Newsletter. Alternate Formats: online.

13357 ■ North American Tang Shou Tao Association (NATSTA)
PO Box 36235
Tucson, AZ 85740
Ph: (520)498-0678
E-mail: natsta2@earthlink.net
URL: http://www.natsta.org
Contact: Dr. Vince Black, Founder
Founded: 1990. **Members:** 350. **Description:** Seeks to build a community of individuals dedicated to the research, practice, preservation and dissemination of the traditional Chinese internal arts, both martial and medical. Develops qualified instructors and practitioners to provide the highest level of competence in the practice, understanding and teaching of the traditional Chinese internal martial arts and medical arts. Provides opportunities for students and instructors to meet, exchange information, train together and expand the community of dedicated practitioners.

13358 ■ Physicians' Association for Anthroposophical Medicine (PAAM)
1923 Geddes Ave.
Ann Arbor, MI 48104-1797
Ph: (734)930-9462
Fax: (734)662-1727
E-mail: paam@anthroposophy.org
URL: http://www.paam.net
Contact: Christian Wessling MD, Pres.
Founded: 1981. **Members:** 70. **Membership Dues:** regular (MD, DO), $350 (annual) ● retired/provisional, $125 (annual) ● international/advocate, $125 (annual) ● student, $40 (annual). **Staff:** 1. **Description:** Physicians promoting the use and learning of anthroposophical medicine. Sponsors educational programs. **Libraries:** Type: not open to the public. **Holdings:** 10,000. **Publications:** *Directory of Physicians*, biennial. **Price:** free ● *PAAM Newsletter*, biennial. **Conventions/Meetings:** annual conference - always June.

13359 ■ QiGong Research Society (QRS)
3201 Rte. 38, Ste.201
Mount Laurel, NJ 08054
Ph: (856)234-3056
E-mail: faxiang@aol.com
URL: http://www.qigongresearchsociety.com
Contact: Master FaXiang Hou, Dir.
Description: Promotes the principles and practices of QiGong. Improves the practice and understanding of QiGong therapy. Integrates medical QiGong in the health care community. Conducts QiGong classes.

13360 ■ The Radiance Technique International Association (TRTIA)
PO Box 40570
St. Petersburg, FL 33743-0570
Fax: (727)347-2106
E-mail: trtia@aol.com
URL: http://www.trtia.org
Contact: Shoshana Shay, Asst. Dir.
Founded: 1980. **Membership Dues:** regular, $50 (annual). **Multinational. Description:** Protects and preserves the science known as The Radiance Technique (R), an Authentic Reiki(R) "science of universal energy which harmonizes and aligns the mind-body-spirit dynamic." Provides a network for those interested in The Radiance Technique(R). Maintains speakers' bureau. Compiles statistics and conducts research on experiences with The Radiance Technique(R). Creates and promotes Radiant Peace Projects. **Awards:** Peace Education Awards. **Frequency:** annual. **Type:** monetary. **Recipient:** for elementary-school children writing on the selected theme about peace ● Peace Profiles. **Type:** recognition. **Recipient:** for people and organizations who have made a definite contribution towards peace locally or globally. **Computer Services:** Mailing lists. **Additional Websites:** http://www.radiantpeace.org. **Projects:** Experiential Data Collection; TRT and Stress Management for Staff in an Assisted-Living Facility; TRT and the Quality of Life for Women over 40; TRT and the Quality of Life for Women over 75. **Formerly:** (1980) American Reiki Association; (1987) American/International Reiki Association; (1997) Radiance Technique Association International; (1998) Radiance Technique and Radiant Peace Association International. **Publications:** *The Expanded Reference Manual of The Radiance Technique, Authentic Reiki*. Contains an A-Z reference manual. **Price:** $26.95 ● *The Radiance Technique and Managing Stress*. Book. Contains information about TRT and managing stress factors in your life. **Price:** $16.00 regular; $14.40 for supporters; $12.80 for friends; $12.00 for contributors ● *The 'Reiki' Factor in The Radiance Technique*. Book. Contains sharing of hundreds who have used this technique. **Price:** $19.95 regular; $17.95 for supporters; $15.96 for friends; $14.96 for contributors ● *TRTIA Journal* (in English, German, Italian, and Spanish), 3/year. Newsletter. **Price:** included in membership dues. ISSN: 1040-5836. **Circulation:** 4,000. **Advertising:** accepted.

13361 ■ Radix Institute (RI)
3212 Monte Vista NE
Albuquerque, NM 87106-2120
Free: (888)777-2349
E-mail: information@radix.org
URL: http://www.radix.org
Contact: Becky Bosch, Training Dir.
Founded: 1963. **Members:** 60. **Staff:** 11. **Description:** Works to the study of the creative process in nature as described by Wilhelm Reich. Offers classes, workshops, and individual sessions in "Education in Feeling". Conducts teacher training and programs for professionals and research on the nature of the Radix training and programs for professionals and research on the nature of the Radix. **Formerly:** Interscience Research Institute. **Publications:** *Journal of the Radix Teachers Association*, annual. **Price:** free ● *The Radix Journal*, biennial. **Price:** $26.00 /year for individuals ● *Radix Newsletter*, 3/year ● Also publishes books and a newsletter. **Conventions/Meetings:** annual conference - first weekend in March.

13362 ■ Reflexology Association of America (RAA)
PO Box 26744
Columbus, OH 43226-0744
Ph: (740)657-1695
Fax: (740)657-1695
E-mail: inforaa@reflexology-usa.org
URL: http://www.reflexology-usa.org
Contact: Opal Knowles, Pres.
Founded: 1995. **Members:** 500. **Membership Dues:** professional (individual), $75 (annual) ● benefactor (office, school, business, state association), student of reflexology, $50 (annual). **State Groups:** 20. **Multinational. Description:** Promotes and supports reflexology ("the systematic, manual stimulation of the reflex maps located on the feet, hands and outer ears that resemble a shape of the human body"). **Telecommunication Services:** electronic mail, raapres@reflexology-usa.org. **Committees:** Conference; Delegate; Education; Legislation/Law; Member Benefit; Newsletter; Public Relations; Web Site. **Affiliated With:** American Reflexology Certification Board. **Publications:** *Conference 2004 Transcript*. Proceedings ● *Guidelines to Setting up a Reflexology Association*. Booklet ● *How do Reflexologists Earn a Living?*. Booklet ● *Reflexology Across America*, quarterly. Newsletter. Disseminates information about reflexology. **Price:** included in membership dues. **Advertising:** accepted. Alternate Formats: online ● *State Leadership Training Manual*. Booklet ● *State Organizational Development Guidelines*. Booklet. **Conventions/Meetings:** biennial conference.

13363 ■ Reiki Alliance
204 N Chestnut St.
Kellogg, ID 83837
Ph: (208)783-3535
Fax: (208)783-4848
E-mail: internationaloffice@reikialliance.com
URL: http://www.reikialliance.com
Contact: Marvin Kelsey, Exec. Dir.
Founded: 1983. **Members:** 750. **Membership Dues:** professional, $200 (annual). **Staff:** 8. **Budget:** $350,000. **Languages:** Dutch, English, Finnish, French, German, Italian, Portuguese, Russian, Spanish. **Multinational. Description:** Teachers of Reiki, the Usui System of Reiki Healing. Supports teachers of the Usui System Of Reiki Healing in 40 countries. Promotes exchange among teachers and students; provides member referrals; supports workshops for additional teacher training. Sponsors annual Global Gathering. **Libraries:** Type: reference. **Holdings:** archival material, books, clippings, periodicals. **Subjects:** Usui System of Natural Healing. **Computer Services:** database, referrals ● mailing lists, of members. **Boards:** Arbitration. **Publications:** *Reiki Alliance Membership Newsletter* (in Dutch, English, French, German, Italian, and Spanish), 3/year. **Price:** included in membership dues. **Circulation:** 750 ● *Student Book*. **Conventions/Meetings:** annual Global Gathering - festival.

13364 ■ Rolf Institute of Structural Integration (RISI)
5055 Chaparral Ct., Ste.103
Boulder, CO 80301
Ph: (303)449-5903
Free: (800)530-8875
Fax: (303)449-5978
E-mail: info@rolf.org
URL: http://www.rolf.org
Contact: Heidi Hauge, Office Mgr.
Founded: 1971. **Members:** 1,550. **Membership Dues:** inactive (rolfing and practitioner), $100 (annual) ● limited (rolfing and practitioner), $225 (annual) ● rolfing practitioner, $450 (annual). **Staff:** 8. **Description:** Aims to: train and certify Rolfers and Movement Practitioners; serve the professional needs of members; inform the public about the benefits of Rolfing and Rolfing Movement Integration. (Rolfing is a technique devised by Dr. Ida P. Rolf, an American biochemist, for reordering the body to bring its major segments toward a vertical alignment.) Conducts research activities; maintains speaker's bureau. **Libraries: Type:** reference. **Computer Services:** database, of members ● online services. **Formerly:** (1975) Ida P. Rolf Foundation for Structural Integration; (2006) Rolf Institute. **Publications:** *Expressive Movement* ● *Healing Through Touch* ● *Ida Rolf Talks* ● *Rolfing: Establishing the Natural Alignment* ● *The Rolfing Experience* ● *Rolfing Stories of Personal Empowerment* ● *Structural Integration: The Journal of the Rolf Institute*, quarterly. **Price:** available to members only ● Books ● Films ● Pamphlets ● Reprints ● Videos. **Conventions/Meetings:** biennial meeting - every August in Colorado.

13365 ■ Sound Healers Association (SHA)
PO Box 2240
Boulder, CO 80306
Ph: (303)443-8181
Free: (800)246-9764
Fax: (303)443-6023
E-mail: info@healingsounds.com
URL: http://www.healingsounds.com/sha-about.asp
Contact: Jonathan Goldman, Dir.
Founded: 1982. **Membership Dues:** regular, $25 (annual). **Description:** Promotes research and awareness for the use of sound and music as therapeutic and transformational modalities for healing. **Additional Websites:** http://www.soundhealersassociation.org. **Publications:** Membership Directory. **Price:** included in membership dues ● Newsletter. Features articles and announcements of workshops and concerts related to sound, music and well-being. **Conventions/Meetings:** Concerts - workshop ● Healing Sounds Seminars - meeting, with guest lecturers ● lecture ● seminar.

13366 ■ Touch for Health Kinesiology Association (TFHKA)
PO Box 392
New Carlisle, OH 45344-0392
Ph: (937)845-3404
Free: (800)466-8342
Fax: (937)845-3909
E-mail: admin@tfhka.org
URL: http://www.tfhka.org
Contact: Robert Aboulache, Pres.
Founded: 1974. **Members:** 1,500. **Membership Dues:** basic, $25 (annual) ● associate, $100 (annual) ● organizational, $175 (annual) ● professional instructor, $150 (annual) ● life, $1,250. **Staff:** 3. **Budget:** $150,000. **Description:** International network of independent instructors. Promotes techniques for restoring natural energies and improving postural balance through muscle testing using applied kinesiology and acupressure points to improve muscle function and balance the body's energy. Stimulates trained professionals to utilize natural health care research techniques with laypeople and their associates, and disseminates information on research plans, methodology, and results of self-development programs in health care, both mental and physical. Increases the level of professional confidence and keeps interested instructors, trainers, laypeople, and those in the health care profession regularly and reliably informed on development in natural health care.

Libraries: Type: reference. **Holdings:** 100. **Subjects:** alternative health practices. **Awards:** Weissenberg Scholarship Fund. **Frequency:** periodic. **Type:** scholarship. **Recipient:** for students with financial restraints. **Computer Services:** database, referrals; promotional materials. **Telecommunication Services:** electronic mail, tfhka@sbcglobal.net. **Formerly:** (1990) Touch for Health Foundation; (1993) Touch for Health Association of America; (1998) Touch for Health Association. **Publications:** *Annual Conference Journal*, annual. Contains compilation of papers presented at the annual meeting. **Price:** $15.00. **Circulation:** 1,000 ● *Keeping in Touch*, quarterly. Newsletter. Includes coverage of research developments, book reviews, calendar of events tips for professionals, anecdotal reports, news of upcoming events. **Price:** $250.00 full page; $150.00 1/2 page; $75.00 1/4 page; $35.00 business card ● *Touch for Health Association Directory*, annual. Membership Directory. **Price:** $125.00 full page; $75.00 1/2 page; $50.00 1/4 page; $35.00 business card. **Circulation:** 1,000 ● *Touch for Health Book* (in English, French, German, Italian, Spanish, and Swedish). Features photographs and illustrations. **Price:** $28.95 for regular edition; $40.99 for Spanish edition. **Circulation:** 500,000 ● *Touch for Health in Practice*, monthly. Newsletter. **Price:** included in membership dues ● *Touch for Health Reference Chart*. **Price:** $35.95 ● *Touch for Health Reference Folio*. Booklet. **Price:** $23.95 full size; $19.95 pocket size. **Conventions/Meetings:** annual Energy Medicine - conference and meeting, alternative health practices (exhibits) ● seminar, with keynote speeches.

13367 ■ United Plant Savers (UpS)
PO Box 400
East Barre, VT 05649
Ph: (802)476-6467
Fax: (802)476-3722
E-mail: info@unitedplantsavers.org
URL: http://unitedplantsavers.org
Contact: Betzy Bancroft, Office Mgr.
Membership Dues: individual, $35 (annual) ● corporation, $200 (annual) ● educational institution, non-profit organization, $50 (annual) ● life, $1,000. **Multinational. Description:** Protects the native medicinal plants of United States and Canada. Ensures the renewable supply of medicinal plants. Establishes independent medical plant sanctuaries. Provides research and education on native medicinal plant preservation. **Computer Services:** Online services, discussion forum. **Telecommunication Services:** electronic mail, plants@unitedplantsavers.org. **Publications:** Newsletter ● Bulletin. Alternate Formats: online.

13368 ■ United States Trager Association (USTA)
PO Box 1009
Burton, OH 44021
Ph: (440)834-0308
Fax: (440)834-0365
E-mail: info@trager-us.org
URL: http://www.trager-us.org
Contact: Patricia Riley, Pres.
Description: Supports the use and recognition of the Trager Approach and Mentastics movement education in the United States. Enforces professional standards of practice and instruction in accordance with the standards of Trager International. Develops, coordinates and regulates the teaching of The Trager Approach and Mentastics movement education in the USA.

13369 ■ Upledger Institute (UI)
11211 Prosperity Farms Rd., Ste.D-325
Palm Beach Gardens, FL 33410
Ph: (561)622-4334 (561)622-4706
Free: (800)233-5880
Fax: (561)622-4771
E-mail: upledger@upledger.com
URL: http://www.upledger.com
Contact: John Matthew Upledger, CEO
Founded: 1985. **Staff:** 2,070. **Multinational. Description:** Promotes complementary health care; provides educational and training courses to osteo-

pathic physicians, medical doctors, dentists, nurses, doctors of Chiropractic, doctors of Oriental medicine, naturopathic physicians, psychiatric specialists, psychologists, physical therapists, occupational therapists, speech therapists, massage therapists, acupuncturists, and other professional bodyworkers. Maintains speakers' bureau. **Computer Services:** Electronic publishing, important news and information sent via email to members. **Publications:** *UI Date*, semiannual. Newsletter. **Circulation:** 45,000. **Advertising:** accepted. Alternate Formats: online ● *Upta-Date*, annual. Newsletter. **Circulation:** 3,000. **Conventions/Meetings:** semiannual Beyond the Dura - conference.

13370 ■ Worldwide Aquatic Bodywork Association (WABA)
PO Box 1817
Middletown, CA 95461
Ph: (707)928-5860
Fax: (707)317-0052
E-mail: info@waba.edu
URL: http://www.waba.edu
Contact: Andre Schaart, Chm.
Nonmembership. Description: Promotes the study, practice, and teaching of Watsu and aquatic bodywork; maintains the Registry of the Worldwide Water Family. **Publications:** *WABA Logbook*. Alternate Formats: online.

Alzheimer's Disease

13371 ■ Alzheimer's Association (ADRDA)
225 N Michigan Ave., 17th Fl.
Chicago, IL 60601-7633
Ph: (312)335-8700
Free: (800)272-3900
Fax: (866)699-1246
E-mail: info@alz.org
URL: http://www.alz.org
Contact: Sheldon Goldberg, Pres./CEO
Founded: 1980. **Staff:** 220. **Budget:** $65,500,000. **Local Groups:** 83. **Languages:** English, Spanish. **Nonmembership. Description:** Promotes research to find the cause, treatment, and cure for the disease; provides educational programs for the public, media, and health care and medical professionals; represents the continuing care needs of the affected population before government and social service agencies. Seeks to destroy the myth that what were once called "senile behaviors" are a natural part of aging. Works to develop family support systems for relatives of persons with the disease. Sponsors educational forums; operates speakers' bureau. Compiles statistics. **Libraries: Type:** reference. **Holdings:** 5,000; audiovisuals, books, periodicals. **Subjects:** Alzheimer's disease, related disorders, caregiving. **Awards: Frequency:** annual. **Type:** grant. **Recipient:** for research. **Telecommunication Services:** TDD, (866)403-3073. **Councils:** Medical and Scientific Advisory. **Programs:** Research Grants. **Formerly:** (1989) Alzheimer's Disease and Related Disorders Association. **Publications:** *Advances*, quarterly. Newsletter. Covers stories and developments of interest to patients with Alzheimer's disease and related disorders, and their families and friends. **Price:** free. **Circulation:** 300,000. Also Cited As: *AD Newsletter* ● *Alzheimer's and Dementia: The Journal of the Alzheimer's Association*, quarterly. Presents original, peer-reviewed, basic and clinical research advances in Alzheimer's Disease. ● Brochures ● Also publishes a variety of fact sheets, video kits, and patient care publications. **Conventions/Meetings:** annual Education Conference ● biennial Research Conference - always July.

13372 ■ Alzheimer's Foundation of America (AFA)
322 Eighth Ave., 6th Fl.
New York, NY 10001
Free: (866)232-8484
Fax: (646)638-1546

E-mail: info@alzfdn.org
URL: http://www.alzfdn.org
Contact: Eric J. Hall, CEO
Founded: 2002. **Description:** Provides optimal care and services to individuals confronting dementia, their caregivers and families, in order to improve quality of life. **Divisions:** Dementia Care Professionals of America. **Programs:** Teens for Alzheimer's Awareness. **Publications:** *AFA Voices*, quarterly. Newsletter. Contains information about AFA activities and events. Alternate Formats: online ● Magazine, quarterly. **Price:** free for caregivers. **Advertising:** accepted. Alternate Formats: online. **Conventions/Meetings:** conference ● workshop.

Ambulatory Care

13373 ■ Accreditation Association for Ambulatory Health Care (AAAHC)
5200 Old Orchard Rd., Ste.200
Skokie, IL 60077
Ph: (847)853-6060
Fax: (847)853-9028
E-mail: info@aaahc.org
URL: http://www.aaahc.org
Contact: John E. Burke PhD, Exec. Dir./CEO
Founded: 1979. **Members:** 16. **Membership Dues:** regular, $6,000 (annual). **Staff:** 23. **Budget:** $4,300,000. **Description:** Operates a voluntary, peer-based accreditation and consulting program for ambulatory health care organizations as a means of assisting them in efficiently providing a high level of care for patients. Distributes free lists of accredited organizations. **Libraries: Type:** not open to the public. **Awards:** President's Award. **Frequency:** annual. **Type:** recognition. **Recipient:** for service and quality standards in health care. **Programs:** Achieving Accreditation. **Affiliated With:** American Academy of Cosmetic Surgery; American Academy of Dental Group Practice; American Academy of Facial Plastic and Reconstructive Surgery; American Association of Oral and Maxillofacial Surgeons; American College Health Association; American College of Occupational and Environmental Medicine; American Society for Dermatologic Surgery; Association of Freestanding Radiation Oncology Centers; Federated Ambulatory Surgery Association; Medical Group Management Association; National Association of Community Health Centers; Outpatient Ophthalmic Surgery Society. **Publications:** *AAAHC Update*, quarterly. Newsletter. Alternate Formats: online ● *Accreditation Handbook for Ambulatory Health Care*, biennial. Features standards for accreditation of ambulatory health care centers. Includes subject index. **Price:** $135.00/copy prepaid ● Also publishes related survey materials. **Conventions/Meetings:** semiannual board meeting.

13374 ■ American Board of Urgent Care Medicine (ABUCM)
2813 S Hiawassee Rd., Ste.206
Orlando, FL 32835
Ph: (407)521-5789
Fax: (407)521-5790
E-mail: info@ambulatorymedicine.com
URL: http://www.urgentcaremedicine.org
Contact: Franz Ritucci Jr., Pres.
Founded: 1997. **Membership Dues:** physician, $295 (annual) ● physician assistant/nurse practitioner, $175 (annual). **Staff:** 5. **Languages:** English, Italian, Spanish. **Description:** Represents licensed practitioners advancing the profession of Ambulatory Care/Acute Care Medicine by elevating standards through education, basic and advanced training, and board certification. Contributes to the field in the areas of professional growth, scientific and medical research, and medical education, to improve the overall quality of medical care. **Libraries: Type:** not open to the public. **Subjects:** ambulatory medicine. **Awards: Frequency:** annual. **Type:** recognition. **Formerly:** (2005) American Academy of Ambulatory Care. **Publications:** *Ambulatory Medicine Today*, quarterly. Newsletter. Features current issues and relevant reviews on ambulatory medicine. **Price:** included in member-

ship dues. **Advertising:** accepted. Alternate Formats: online. Also Cited As: *AMT*. **Conventions/Meetings:** annual Ambulatory Care Today and Tomorrow (ACTT) - conference.

13375 ■ North American Association for Ambulatory Urgent Care
c/o Yvette Harvieux
600 S Hwy. 169, Ste.1585
Minneapolis, MN 55426
Free: (866)793-1396
Fax: (952)767-0008
E-mail: yvetteh@nafac.com
URL: http://www.nafac.com
Contact: Yvette Harvieux, Contact
Founded: 1981. **Members:** 200. **Membership Dues:** individual, $150 (annual) ● corporate, retail, $250 (annual). **Staff:** 2. **Budget:** $75,000. **Description:** Governing body for urgent care in North America. Represents hospital, corporate, and independently owned ambulatory urgent care centers. Seeks to: establish operational standards for such centers; in order for members to provide lower cost and more convenient outpatient urgent medical care; make the public aware of the concept of ambulatory urgent care centers and their usefulness in problem-based and episodic care. Cooperates with medical organizations; conducts public relations activities and studies on the industry as well as education programs and business support services. **Additional Websites:** http://www.urgentcare.org. **Boards:** Editorial Advisory. **Formerly:** (1981) National Association of Centers for Urgent Treatment; (1984) National Association of Freestanding Emergency Centers; (2000) National Association for Ambulatory Care Medicine; (2002) North American Association of Urgent Care Medicine.

13376 ■ North American Primary Care Research Group (NAPCRG)
11400 Tomahawk Creek Pkwy.
Leawood, KS 66211-2672
Ph: (913)906-6000
Free: (800)274-2237
Fax: (913)906-6096
E-mail: napcrg@stfm.org
URL: http://www.napcrg.org
Contact: Stacy Brungardt, Exec. Dir.
Founded: 1972. **Members:** 775. **Membership Dues:** physician, $195 (annual) ● non-physician, $130 (annual) ● fellow, student, resident, $65 (annual). **Staff:** 4. **Budget:** $400,000. **Multinational. Description:** Physicians and other individuals interested in primary care research. (Primary care is the type of medicine practiced by physicians who do not require patient referrals from other physicians.) Promotes research on primary care topics. Maintains 11 special interest groups including: Ambulatory Sentinel Practice; Clinical Decision Making; Health Status Group. Disseminates information and serves as a forum for exchange of ideas on research projects. **Awards:** Maurice Wood Award for Lifetime Contribution to Primary Care Research. **Frequency:** annual. **Type:** recognition. **Recipient:** to an individual who has made an outstanding contribution to primary care research and related fields ● **Type:** recognition. **Computer Services:** Online services. **Publications:** *Glossary of Primary Care Terms* ● *Process Classification for Family Care* ● Newsletter, quarterly. **Advertising:** accepted ● Proceedings ● Reports. **Conventions/Meetings:** annual conference - always fall.

13377 ■ Urgent Care Association of America (UCAOA)
4019 Quail Briar Dr.
Valrico, FL 33594
Ph: (813)239-6429
Free: (877)698-2262
Fax: (813)662-5560
E-mail: info@ucaoa.org
URL: http://www.ucaoa.org
Contact: William E. Meadows III, Pres.
Membership Dues: individual, $150 (annual) ● corporate (based on the number of clinics), $225-$375 (annual). **Description:** Represents the interests of urgent care centers that provide alternatives to

emergency departments. Encourages and facilitates the development of urgent care centers and the urgent care industry. Provides a forum for urgent care centers to join together and develop resources, improve standards of care, share best practices and voice their collective concerns. **Telecommunication Services:** electronic mail, bburress@ucaoa.org. **Publications:** *Urgent Care News*. Newsletter. Alternate Formats: online.

Amyotrophic Lateral Sclerosis

13378 ■ ALS March of Faces
4594 Ashton Ct.
Naples, FL 34112-8822
Ph: (239)404-9409
Free: (877)884-4798
Fax: (239)417-0790
E-mail: alsmof@march-of-faces.org
URL: http://www.march-of-faces.org
Contact: Terry Frank, Sec.-Treas.
Description: Promotes public awareness of Amyotrophic Lateral Sclerosis (ALS), or Lou Gehrig's Disease. Hosts fundraisers. **Computer Services:** Mailing lists. **Telecommunication Services:** electronic mail, terry@march-of-faces.org. **Publications:** *Brick by Brick*. Newsletter.

Anatomy

13379 ■ American Association of Anatomists (AAA)
9650 Rockville Pike
Bethesda, MD 20814-3998
Ph: (301)634-7910
Fax: (301)634-7965
E-mail: exec@anatomy.org
URL: http://www.anatomy.org
Contact: Andrea Pendleton, Exec. Dir.
Founded: 1888. **Members:** 2,500. **Membership Dues:** regular, international, $130 (annual) ● student, $30 (annual) ● postdoctoral, $45 (annual). **Staff:** 4. **Multinational. Description:** Represents biomedical researchers and educators focusing on anatomical form and function. Focuses on imaging, cell biology, genetics, molecular development, endocrinology, histology, neuroscience, forensics, microscopy, physical anthropology, and other areas. Promotes the three-dimensional understanding of structure as it relates to development and function, from molecule to organism through research and education. **Publications:** *AAA Newsletter*, quarterly. **Price:** included in membership dues. **Circulation:** 2,000. **Advertising:** accepted. Alternate Formats: online ● *Anatomical Record*, monthly. Journal ● *Developmental Dynamics*, monthly. Journal ● *Directory, Departments of Anatomy, U.S. and Canada*. Alternate Formats: online ● *New Anatomist*, bimonthly. **Conventions/Meetings:** annual conference (exhibits) - in April/May.

13380 ■ American Association of Clinical Anatomists (AACA)
c/o Brian R. MacPherson, PhD, Sec:
Anatomy and Neurobiology
Univ. of Kentucky Coll. of Medicine
MN225 Chandler Medical Ctr.
Lexington, KY 40536-0298
Ph: (859)323-5539
Fax: (859)323-5946
E-mail: brmacp@uky.edu
URL: http://www.clinicalanatomy.org
Contact: Prof. Thomas H. Quinn PhD, Pres.
Membership Dues: regular, $125 (annual) ● associate, affiliate, $40 (annual) ● senior, $75 (annual). **Description:** Strives to advance science and art of clinical anatomy; encourages research and publication in the field and maintains high standards in teaching anatomy. **Publications:** *Clinical Anatomy*. Journal. Provides a medium for the exchange of current information between anatomists and clinicians. **Conventions/Meetings:** annual meeting - 2008 July, Toronto, ON, Canada.

13381 ■ Pan American Association of Anatomy
Address Unknown since 2007
Founded: 1966. **Membership Dues:** founding, $30 (annual) ● full, $30 (annual) ● associate, $30 (annual) ● honorary, $30 (annual). **Multinational. Description:** Anatomists. Seeks to stimulate the development and promotion of the Morphological Sciences on the American Continent. Facilitates scientific exchange and friendship among members. **Publications:** Newsletter. **Conventions/Meetings:** biennial congress.

Anesthesiology

13382 ■ American Academy of Anesthesiologist Assistants (AAAA)
PO Box 13978
Tallahassee, FL 32317
Ph: (850)656-8848
Free: (866)328-5858
Fax: (850)656-3038
E-mail: info@anesthetist.org
URL: http://www.anesthetist.org
Contact: Susan Cabrera, Exec. Dir.
Founded: 1975. **Members:** 412. **Membership Dues:** fellow, associate, $350 (annual) ● student, $60 (annual) ● physician affiliate, $150 (annual). **Staff:** 5. **Description:** Represents active anesthesiologist assistants who have graduated from an accredited training program and full-time students currently enrolled in an accredited program. Establishes and maintains the standards of the profession. Fosters and encourages continuing education and research. Sponsors educational meetings for graduates and student anesthesiologist assistants. **Computer Services:** database ● mailing lists. **Committees:** Legislative. **Publications:** The Anesthesia Record, 5/year. Newsletter. **Price:** included in membership dues. **Advertising:** accepted ● Membership Directory. **Conventions/Meetings:** annual conference, those offering products and services to AA's (exhibits).

13383 ■ American Board of Anesthesiology (ABA)
4101 Lake Boone Trail, Ste.510
Raleigh, NC 27607-7506
Ph: (919)881-2570
Fax: (919)881-2575
E-mail: president@theaba.org
Contact: Francis P. Hughes PhD, Exec. Dir.
Founded: 1937. **Members:** 12. **Staff:** 23. **Description:** Seeks to elevate and maintain the standards of the practice of anesthesiology and to establish criteria of fitness for the designation of a certified specialist in this field. Advises the Accreditation Council for Graduate Medical Education concerning training of individuals seeking certification. Arranges and conducts examinations to determine whether physicians who apply meet its standards; issues certificates to those who meet the required standards. **Publications:** ABA News. Newsletter. Alternate Formats: online ● Booklet of Information, annual. Describes the examination system and the policies and regulations governing the board's examination and certification process. **Price:** free. Alternate Formats: online. Also Cited As: BOI. **Conventions/Meetings:** semiannual meeting.

13384 ■ American Osteopathic College of Anesthesiologists (AOCA)
6500 NW Tower Dr., Ste.103
Kansas City, MO 64151-4414
Ph: (816)584-2622
Free: (800)842-2622
Fax: (816)584-2620
E-mail: osteoanest@aol.com
URL: http://www.aocaonline.org
Contact: Joseph R.N. Thomas D.O., Pres.
Founded: 1952. **Members:** 500. **Budget:** $100,000. **Description:** Members of American Osteopathic Association (see separate entry) who are engaged in the practice of anesthesiology. **Formerly:** (1952) American Osteopathic Society of Anesthesiologists.

Publications: Membership Directory, annual ● Newsletter, 3/year. **Conventions/Meetings:** annual meeting (exhibits) ● annual seminar - midyear.

13385 ■ American Society for Advancement of Anesthesia and Sedation in Dentistry (ASAAD)
6 E Union Ave.
Bound Brook, NJ 08805
Ph: (732)469-9050
Fax: (732)271-1985
E-mail: info@sedation4dentists.com
URL: http://www.sedation4dentists.net
Contact: Dr. David Crystal DDS, Exec. Sec.
Founded: 1925. **Members:** 200. **Membership Dues:** $195 (annual). **Multinational. Description:** Dentists and physicians interested in dental anesthesia. Studies new anesthetics and chemicals; researches pain control methods. Organized and sponsored international congresses on modern pain control in dentistry in Latin America, Europe, and Japan. Advances education opportunities for dentists using sedation and anesthesia. Maintains speakers' bureau. **Libraries: Type:** reference; not open to the public. **Holdings:** 23; periodicals. **Subjects:** pain control. **Awards:** Fellowship Award - Hillel Feldman Award. **Frequency:** annual. **Type:** fellowship. **Recipient:** for efforts to improve the delivery of dentistry and the elimination of pain. **Computer Services:** database ● mailing lists. **Committees:** Continuing Education; Research. **Affiliated With:** American Dental Association. **Formerly:** (1975) American Society for Advancement of General Anesthesia in Dentistry; (2001) American Society for Advancement of Anesthesia in Dentistry. **Publications:** Modern Anesthesia in Dentistry. Book. **Advertising:** accepted ● Modern Dental Anesthesia. Book ● Modern Pain Control, biennial ● Pain Control in Dentistry, semiannual. Journal. Covers and promotes the use of dental anesthesia. **Price:** included in membership dues. ISSN: 0164-1700. **Circulation:** 450. **Advertising:** accepted. Also Cited As: American Society for the Advancement of Anesthesia in Dentistry—Proceedings ● Transcripts, semiannual. **Conventions/Meetings:** annual conference and symposium ● triennial convention ● periodic seminar and symposium, continuing education.

13386 ■ American Society of Anesthesiologists (ASA)
520 N Northwest Hwy.
Park Ridge, IL 60068-2573
Ph: (847)825-5586
Fax: (847)825-1692
E-mail: mail@asahq.org
URL: http://www.asahq.org
Contact: Ronald A. Burns, Exec. Dir.
Founded: 1905. **Members:** 38,000. **Membership Dues:** active, $450 (annual) ● affiliate, $225 (annual) ● resident, educational student, $25 (annual) ● medical student, $10 (annual) ● educational, $225 (annual). **Staff:** 53. **Budget:** $20,000,000. **State Groups:** 50. **Description:** Professional society of physicians specializing or interested in anesthesiology. Seeks "to develop and further the specialty of anesthesiology for the general elevation of the standards of medical practice". Encourages education, research, and scientific progress in anesthesiology. Conducts refresher courses and other postgraduate educational activities. Maintains placement service. **Libraries: Type:** open to the public. **Holdings:** 9,000; articles, books, periodicals. **Subjects:** anesthesia. **Sections:** Clinical Care; Education and Research; Representation. **Formerly:** (1911) Long Island Society of Anesthetists; (1936) New York Society of Anesthetists; (1945) American Society of Anesthetists. **Publications:** Anesthesiology, monthly. Journal. **Price:** $301.00 /year for individuals; $553.00 /year for institutions. **Circulation:** 38,000. ● ASA Newsletter, monthly. Reports on the educational and scientific work of ASA. Contains calendar of events. **Price:** included in membership dues; $36.00 /year for nonmembers. **Circulation:** 38,500 ● Refresher Courses in Anesthesiology, annual. Booklet. **Price:** $49.00 for 2003 volume. **Conventions/Meetings:** annual meeting

(exhibits) - always October. 2007 Oct. 13-17, San Francisco, CA; 2008 Oct. 18-22, Orlando, FL.

13387 ■ American Society of Critical Care Anesthesiologists (ASCCA)
520 N Northwest Hwy.
Park Ridge, IL 60068-2573
Ph: (847)825-5586
Fax: (847)825-5658
E-mail: ascca@asahq.org
URL: http://www.ascca.org
Contact: Gerald A. Maccioli MD, Pres.
Founded: 1986. **Members:** 400. **Membership Dues:** active (physician member of ASA), affiliate (physician nonmember of ASA), $150 (annual) ● educational, $50 (annual) ● international, $100 (annual). **Description:** Provides for the specialized needs of intensivists as well as the broader needs of practicing anesthesiologists. **Publications:** The Interchange, quarterly. Newsletter. Disseminates thought and information about various topics including historical aspects of anesthesiology, ethically controversial issues, and surveys. ● Membership Directory. **Conventions/Meetings:** annual meeting, with breakfast panel - 2007 Oct. 12, San Francisco, CA; 2008 Oct. 17, Orlando, FL.

13388 ■ American Society of Regional Anesthesia and Pain Medicine (ASRA)
520 N Northwest Hwy.
Park Ridge, IL 60068-2573
Ph: (847)825-7246
E-mail: asra@asahq.org
URL: http://www.asra.com
Contact: F. Michael Ferrante MD, Pres.
Founded: 1975. **Members:** 7,400. **Membership Dues:** active, in U.S., $195 (annual) ● associate outside U.S., affiliate, $95 (annual) ● resident/fellow, $25 (annual). **Staff:** 4. **Budget:** $1,000,000. **Multinational. Description:** Physicians and research PhD's. Conducts educational workshops. Sponsors annual refresher course. **Awards:** Gaston Labat Award. **Frequency:** annual. **Type:** recognition. **Recipient:** for an individual with outstanding contributions to the development, teaching and practice of regional anesthesia ● John J. Bonica Award. **Frequency:** annual. **Type:** recognition. **Recipient:** for an individual with contributions to the development, teaching and practice of pain medicine. **Computer Services:** Mailing lists. **Formerly:** (2002) American Society of Regional Anesthesia and Pain Practice. **Publications:** ASRA Newsletter, quarterly. **Price:** included in membership dues. **Circulation:** 9,000. Alternate Formats: online ● 1997 Annual Meeting Syllabus. Book. **Price:** $20.00 in U.S. and Canada; $35.00 outside U.S. and Canada ● Regional Anesthesia and Pain Medicine, bimonthly. Journal. **Price:** included in membership dues. **Circulation:** 9,000. **Advertising:** accepted ● 2003 Annual Spring Meeting and Workshops Syllabus. Book. **Price:** $50.00 in U.S. and Canada; $65.00 outside U.S. and Canada ● 2002 Annual Fall Pain Meeting and Workshops Syllabus. Book. Contains workshops/master classes, basic science/clinical translations sessions and poster presentations. **Price:** $45.00 in U.S. and Canada; $60.00 outside U.S. and Canada ● 2002 Annual Spring Meeting and Workshops Syllabus. Book. **Price:** $45.00 in U.S. and Canada; $60.00 outside U.S. and Canada. **Conventions/Meetings:** annual meeting and workshop (exhibits).

13389 ■ Anesthesia Awareness Campaign
PO Box 8592
Reston, VA 20195-2492
Ph: (703)437-7327
E-mail: anesawareness@aol.com
URL: http://www.anesthesiaawareness.com
Contact: Carol Weihrer, Pres./Founder
Founded: 1998. **Description:** Aims to prevent patients from experiencing anesthesia awareness and its consequences through education, prevention, and empowerment by replacing ignorance or fear with knowledge. Addresses the concerns of awareness victims. Facilitates cooperation and communication among members.

13390 ■ Anesthesia History Association (AHA)

200 Medical Arts Bldg.
200 Delafield Ave., Ste.2070
Pittsburgh, PA 15215
Ph: (412)784-5343
Fax: (412)784-5350
E-mail: copedk@anes.upmc.edu
URL: http://www.anes.uab.edu/anesthesia_history_association.htm
Contact: Douglas Bacon MD, Pres.
Founded: 1982. **Membership Dues:** library, student, senior (retired), $60 (annual) ● regular, $100 (annual). **Description:** Promotes, stimulates, and encourages research, study, interest, and writing in the history of anesthesia and its relationship to allied medical services. Supports and cooperates with local, national, and international organizations having similar purposes. **Awards:** David M. Little Prize. **Frequency:** annual. **Type:** recognition. **Recipient:** for the best work of anesthesia history published in English ● Resident Essay Contest. **Frequency:** annual. **Type:** monetary. **Recipient:** for written works related to the history of anesthesia, pain management or critical care. **Publications:** *Bulletin of Anesthesia History*, quarterly. Journal. Alternate Formats: online ● Articles. Alternate Formats: online. **Conventions/Meetings:** annual meeting.

13391 ■ Anesthesia Patient Safety Foundation (APSF)

8007 S Meridian St., Bldg. 1, Ste.2
Indianapolis, IN 46217-2922
Fax: (317)888-1482
E-mail: apsfoffice@aol.com
URL: http://www.apsf.org
Contact: Deanna M. Walker, Exec. Sec.
Founded: 1984. **Membership Dues:** founding, $400,000 ● sponsor, $749. **Description:** Promotes safer anesthesia, fosters investigations to provide understanding of preventable anesthetic injuries. **Awards: Type:** grant. **Telecommunication Services:** electronic mail, stoelting@apsf.org. **Publications:** *Anesthesia Patient Safety, A Modern History*. Book. Contains substantive articles from the APSF Newsletter. **Price:** $25.00 includes postage ● Newsletter, quarterly. Contains information on issues pertaining to anesthesia safety.

13392 ■ Association of University Anesthesiologists (AUA)

520 N Northwest Hwy.
Park Ridge, IL 60068-2573
Ph: (847)825-5586
Fax: (847)825-5658
E-mail: aua@asahq.org
URL: http://www.auahq.org
Contact: Roberta L. Hines MD, Pres.
Founded: 1953. **Members:** 700. **Description:** Academic anesthesiologists from medical school faculties. Encourages members to pursue original investigations in the clinic and the laboratory; develops methods of teaching anesthesiology. **Boards:** Educational Advisory; Scientific Advisory. **Formerly:** (1990) Association of University Anesthetists. **Publications:** Directory, annual. **Conventions/Meetings:** annual meeting - always May or April. 2008 May 16-18, Chapel Hill, NC.

13393 ■ Association of Veterans Affairs Anesthesiologists (AVAA)

c/o Prof. Martin J. London, MD, Pres.
4150 Clement St.
San Francisco, CA 94121
E-mail: getinfo@vaanes.org
URL: http://www.vaanes.org
Contact: Prof. Martin J. London MD, Pres.
Founded: 1991. **Membership Dues:** regular, $35 (annual). **Description:** Advances the practice of anesthesiology in the Department of Veterans Affairs. Represents members on important clinical, administrative, and educational issues. Works collaboratively with the American Society of Anesthesiologists and other organizations to further the education and knowledge in the field. **Computer Services:** database, membership directory ● information services,

educational resources ● online services, clinical forums. **Committees:** Field Advisory. **Publications:** Reports. Alternate Formats: online. **Conventions/Meetings:** annual meeting.

13394 ■ Dannemiller Memorial Educational Foundation (DMEF)

5711 Northwest Pkwy.
San Antonio, TX 78249
Ph: (210)641-8311
Free: (800)328-2308
Fax: (210)641-8329
E-mail: editor@dannemiller.com
URL: http://www.dannemiller.com
Contact: Ron M. Pobuda, Pres.
Founded: 1971. **Members:** 30. **Staff:** 14. **Budget:** $1,750,000. **For-Profit. Description:** Conducts annual Anesthesia Review Course, in June for MD anesthesiologists and in the fall for nurse anesthesiologists, and review course of current concepts in anesthesiology. Sponsors weekend anesthesia and pain management meetings. **Libraries: Type:** not open to the public. **Subjects:** anesthesiology and pain management. **Awards:** Dannemiller Memorial Lecture Award. **Frequency:** annual. **Type:** recognition. **Computer Services:** Online services. **Committees:** CRNA Advisory; Education; Medical Specialty Review. **Formerly:** (1984) Society of Air Force Anesthesiologists. **Publications:** *Anesthesia File*, monthly. Journal. Contains abstracted articles on anesthesia. **Price:** $290.00 /year for institutions in U.S.; $250.00 /year for individuals in U.S.; $325.00 /year for institutions outside U.S.; $325.00 /year for individuals outside U.S. **Circulation:** 550. **Conventions/Meetings:** annual Anesthesiology Review Course - conference (exhibits).

13395 ■ International Anesthesia Research Society (IARS)

2 Summit Park Dr., Ste.140
Cleveland, OH 44131-2571
Ph: (216)642-1124
Fax: (216)642-1127
E-mail: iarshq@iars.org
URL: http://www.iars.org
Contact: Anne F. Maggiore, Exec. Dir.
Founded: 1922. **Members:** 15,000. **Membership Dues:** individual, $140 (annual) ● joint, $210 (annual) ● associate educational, $75 (annual). **Staff:** 9. **Multinational. Description:** Anesthesiologists and other doctors of medicine and dentistry interested in the specialty of anesthesiology; associate members are registered nurses, physician assistants, and respiratory therapists. Fosters progress and research in all phases of anesthesiology. **Awards:** Clinical Scholar Research Award. **Frequency:** annual. **Type:** monetary. **Recipient:** for members ● Frontiers in Anesthesia Research Award. **Frequency:** biennial. **Type:** monetary. **Recipient:** for members ● Teaching Recognition Award. **Frequency:** annual. **Type:** monetary. **Recipient:** for member with outstanding teaching skills. **Affiliated With:** Society of Cardiovascular Anesthesiologists. **Publications:** *Anesthesia and Analgesia*, monthly. Journal. Contains research articles and clinical reports on anesthesia and anesthesia-related subjects. Includes book reviews and employment listings. **Price:** $120.00 /year for members; $440.00/year for nonmember institutions. ISSN: 0003-2999. **Circulation:** 21,000. **Advertising:** accepted. Alternate Formats: microform. Also Cited As: *A & A.* **Conventions/Meetings:** annual Clinical and Scientific Congress, research presentations, clinical review, and update (exhibits).

13396 ■ International Society for Anaesthetic Pharmacology (ISAP)

2 Summit Park Dr., No. 140
Cleveland, OH 44131-2571
Ph: (216)447-7862
Fax: (216)642-1127
E-mail: isaphq@isaponline.org
URL: http://www.isaponline.org
Contact: Steven L. Shafer MD, Pres.
Membership Dues: regular, $50 (annual). **Multinational. Description:** Promotes the study of anaesthetic pharmacology. Encourages high ethical and

professional standards by fostering and encouraging research, education and scientific progress in anaesthetic pharmacology. Publishes and disseminates information about the role of anaesthetic pharmacology. Supports the development and promotion of policies and programs of other professional organizations regarding anaesthetic pharmacology. **Conventions/Meetings:** annual meeting.

13397 ■ International Trauma Anesthesia and Critical Care Society (ITACCS)

PO Box 4826
Baltimore, MD 21211
Fax: (410)235-8084
E-mail: traumacaremail@aol.com
URL: http://www.itaccs.com
Contact: Christopher M. Grande MD, Exec. Dir.
Founded: 1988. **Members:** 2,000. **Membership Dues:** in-training, $40 (annual) ● full, $100 (annual) ● corporate, $1,000 (annual). **Multinational. Description:** Healthcare professionals involved in trauma and critical care anesthesiology. Works to gain recognition for trauma anesthesiology as a discipline within anesthesiology and critical care medicine. Promotes cooperation and information sharing among healthcare professionals. Sponsors seminars and workshops; conducts research and educational programs; provides children's services; holds competitions; maintains speakers' bureau and placement service. **Libraries: Type:** reference. **Holdings:** artwork, audio recordings, books, clippings, monographs, periodicals. **Subjects:** trauma anesthesia, critical care. **Awards:** ITACCS Research Award. **Frequency:** annual. **Type:** grant. **Recipient:** for investigators who seek to obtain further support for the continuation of their projects. **Committees:** Critical Care; Developing Nations Program; Disaster and Mass Casualty; Military Intensive Care and Trauma Anesthesia Consortium; Pediatric Trauma; Prehospital and EMS; Special Equipment and Techniques for Trauma. **Subcommittees:** Biotechnology. **Also Known As:** Trauma Care International. **Publications:** *Textbook of Trauma Anesthesia and Critical Care* (in English and Spanish) ● *Trauma Care Journal*, biennial. Magazine. **Price:** free. **Circulation:** 10,000. **Advertising:** accepted. Alternate Formats: online ● Books ● Monographs. **Conventions/Meetings:** Trauma, Anesthesia and Critical Care - symposium (exhibits).

13398 ■ Navy Anesthesia Society (NAS)

c/o LCDR David G. Elkins, Sec.
Dept. of Anesthesiology
Naval Medical Ctr.
34800 Bob Wilson Dr.
San Diego, CA 92134-5000
Ph: (619)532-8943
Fax: (619)532-8945
E-mail: elkinsdave@aol.com
URL: http://www.geocities.com/Vienna/2209/nas.html
Contact: LCDR David G. Elkins, Sec.
Founded: 1988. **Members:** 400. **Membership Dues:** regular, $25 (annual). **Multinational. Description:** Military physicians and nurse anesthetists. Committed to the delivery of anesthesia and critical care services, trauma care and combat casualty transport in a military environment, including natural or man-made disasters and in under-developed countries. **Publications:** *NAS Newsletter*, quarterly. **Conventions/Meetings:** annual meeting and banquet ● annual symposium.

13399 ■ Society for Ambulatory Anesthesia (SAMBA)

520 N Northwest Hwy.
Park Ridge, IL 60068-2573
Ph: (847)825-5586
Fax: (847)825-5658
E-mail: samba@asahq.org
URL: http://www.sambahq.org
Contact: Walter G. Maurer MD, Pres.
Founded: 1985. **Members:** 2,000. **Membership Dues:** individual, $150 (annual) ● international, $25 (annual). **Description:** Works to advance the study and growth of ambulatory anesthesia. Encourages high ethical and professional standards. Supports

research, education and scientific progress in ambulatory anesthesia. **Awards:** Outcomes Research Award. **Type:** monetary. **Recipient:** for high quality research in ambulatory anesthesia ● Resident Travel Awards. **Frequency:** annual. **Type:** grant. **Recipient:** for anesthesiology residents ● SAMBA Distinguished Service Awards. **Frequency:** annual. **Type:** recognition. **Recipient:** for outstanding achievement in ambulatory anesthesia. **Publications:** *Anesthesia and Analgesia*. Journal. Price: $85.00/year ● *SAMBA Talks*. Newsletter. Alternate Formats: online. **Conventions/Meetings:** annual meeting ● workshop.

13400 ■ Society of Cardiovascular Anesthesiologists (SCA)

2209 Dickens Rd.
Richmond, VA 23230-2005
Ph: (804)282-0084
Fax: (804)282-0090
E-mail: sca@societyhq.com
URL: http://www.scahq.org
Contact: Christina Mora Mangano MD, Pres.
Founded: 1977. **Members:** 7,000. **Membership Dues:** active/associate, $175 (annual) ● SCA/IARS joint, $210 (annual) ● resident/fellow, $75 (annual). **Staff:** 16. **Budget:** $1,000,000. **Description:** Anesthesiologists who specialize in cardiovascular surgical conditions. Works to further medical education of cardiovascular anesthesiologists. Establishes goals and objectives for education of trainees in cardiovascular anesthesia; promotes personnel exchange between the U.S. and other countries; reviews related literature; maintains workshops; conducts research competitions. Sponsors Anesthesia Grand Rounds: Case Presentations, as a section of the annual meeting. **Awards:** Research Starter Grant. **Frequency:** annual. **Type:** monetary. **Recipient:** for a SCA member. **Computer Services:** Mailing lists. **Committees:** Allied Health Liaison; Bylaws; Education; Ethics; Governmental Affairs; International; Newsletter; Nominating; Publications; Research; Scientific Program. **Publications:** *Anesthesia and Analgesia*, monthly. Journal. Includes peer-reviewed, original clinical and research articles. **Price:** $421.00 for nonmembers; included in membership dues. ISSN: 0003-2999. **Circulation:** 30,000. **Advertising:** accepted. Alternate Formats: online ● *Society of Cardiovascular Anesthesiologists—Newsletter*, bimonthly. Contains discussions of major issues within the cardiovascular anesthesiology field and reviews of related literature being published. **Price:** included in membership dues. **Circulation:** 7,000. Alternate Formats: online ● Also publishes monographs. **Conventions/Meetings:** annual Comprehensive Review and TEE Update - meeting - always February in San Diego, CA. 2008 Feb. 10-16, San Diego, CA; 2009 Feb. 8-14, San Diego, CA ● annual meeting and workshop (exhibits) ● annual Update on Cardiopulmonary Bypass - meeting (exhibits) - always March. 2008 Mar. 9-15, Whistler, BC, Canada.

13401 ■ Society for Education in Anesthesia (SEA)

520 N Northwest Hwy.
Park Ridge, IL 60068-2573
Ph: (847)825-5586
Fax: (847)825-5658
E-mail: sea@asahq.org
URL: http://www.seahq.org
Contact: Nicole C. Bradle, Exec. Dir.
Founded: 1984. **Membership Dues:** active, $195 (annual) ● international, $30 (annual) ● resident, $15 (annual). **Description:** Represents anesthesiology educators. Works to improve skills in anesthesia education. Offers an online discussion forum. **Awards:** Ronald L. Katz Traveling Fellowship. **Frequency:** annual. **Type:** fellowship. **Recipient:** for senior anesthesia residents and fellows interested in spending 3 to 4 weeks teaching anesthesia students in a developing country. **Telecommunication Services:** electronic mail, n.bradle@asahq.org. **Committees:** Education Resources; Educational Meetings; Faculty Development; Fundraising; Info Technology; JEPM; Med Student Curriculum; Nominations. **Publications:** *Journal of Education in Perioperative Medicine*, quarterly. Provides educationally

important material to perioperative physicians. Alternate Formats: online. **Conventions/Meetings:** annual meeting and workshop - always fall.

13402 ■ Society for Pediatric Anesthesia (SPA)

2209 Dickens Rd.
Richmond, VA 23230-2005
Ph: (804)282-9780
Fax: (804)282-0090
E-mail: spa@societyhq.com
URL: http://www.pedsanesthesia.org
Contact: Francis X. McGowan Jr., Pres.
Membership Dues: active, affiliate, $125 (annual) ● international, $50 (annual) ● resident, $75 (annual). **Description:** Works to foster quality anesthesia and preoperative care, and to alleviate pain in children. **Publications:** Newsletter, quarterly. Alternate Formats: online.

13403 ■ Society for Technology in Anesthesia (STA)

2 Summit Park Dr., Ste.140
Cleveland, OH 44131
Ph: (216)447-7864
Fax: (216)642-1127
E-mail: stahq@anestech.org
URL: http://www.anestech.org
Contact: Anne Maggiore, Exec. Dir.
Membership Dues: regular, $100 (annual) ● silver (entrepreneur class), $1,000 (annual) ● gold (entrepreneur class), $2,000 (annual) ● silver (corporate), $5,000 (annual) ● gold (corporate), $7,500 (annual) ● platinum (corporate), $10,000 (annual). **Multinational. Description:** Represents physicians, engineers, students and others with an interest in anesthesia-related technologies. Aims to improve the quality of patient care by improving technology and its application. Promotes education and research. **Awards:** Best Abstract Awards. **Frequency:** annual. **Type:** recognition. **Recipient:** to the authors of the best technology-related abstracts ● J.S. Gravenstein Award. **Frequency:** annual. **Type:** recognition. **Recipient:** for lifetime achievement in the area of technology in anesthesia ● Research Grants. **Frequency:** annual. **Type:** grant. **Recipient:** for research directed towards technologies used in anesthesia. **Affiliated With:** International Anesthesia Research Society. **Publications:** *Anesthesia & Analgesia*, monthly. Journal. **Price:** $85.00 /year for members. Alternate Formats: online ● *Interface*, quarterly. Newsletter. Contains technology, computing and simulation technical articles. **Price:** included in membership dues. Alternate Formats: online.

Animal Research

13404 ■ American Association for Laboratory Animal Science (AALAS)

9190 Crestwyn Hills Dr.
Memphis, TN 38125-8538
Ph: (901)754-8620
Fax: (901)753-0046
E-mail: info@aalas.org
URL: http://www.aalas.org
Contact: Ann Tourigny Turner PhD, Exec. Dir.
Founded: 1950. **Members:** 12,000. **Membership Dues:** commercial, $600 (annual) ● institutional, $450 (annual) ● affiliate, $250 (annual) ● individual in U.S., $35-$180 (annual) ● individual in Canada and Mexico, $40-$195 (annual) ● individual international, $45-$220 (annual). **Staff:** 30. **Budget:** $4,500,000. **Regional Groups:** 8. **Local Groups:** 48. **Description:** Persons and institutions professionally concerned with the production, use, care, and study of laboratory animals. Serves as clearinghouse for collection and exchange of information on all phases of laboratory animal care and management and on the care, use, and procurement of laboratory animals used in biomedical research. Conducts examinations and certification through its Animal Technician Certification Program. **Awards:** Bhatt Young Investigator Award. **Frequency:** annual. **Type:** recognition. **Recipient:** for outstanding young scien-

tist with significant role to the field of laboratory animal science and comparative medicine ● Cohen Award. **Frequency:** annual. **Type:** recognition. **Recipient:** for individual with outstanding achievements in animal welfare improvement ● Collins Award. **Frequency:** annual. **Type:** recognition. **Recipient:** for individuals with outstanding contributions in the field of laboratory animal training ● Garvey Award. **Frequency:** annual. **Type:** recognition. **Recipient:** for research and education ● Griffin Award. **Frequency:** annual. **Type:** recognition. **Recipient:** for individual with outstanding accomplishment in the improvement of care, quality, and environment of animals used in biologic and medical research ● Nathan R. Brewer Scientific Achievement Award. **Frequency:** annual. **Type:** recognition. **Recipient:** for members of professional scientific societies with contributions to the fields of laboratory animal science, animal or comparative medicine ● Technician of the Year Award. **Frequency:** annual. **Type:** recognition. **Recipient:** for laboratory animal technician ● Technician Publication Award. **Frequency:** annual. **Type:** recognition. **Recipient:** for technician and technologist. **Formerly:** (1967) Animal Care Panel. **Publications:** *AALAS in Action*, bimonthly. Newsletter. **Price:** included in membership dues. Alternate Formats: online ● *American Association for Laboratory Animal Science— Reference Directory*, annual. Membership Directory. Contains alphabetically and geographically arranged list of names. **Price:** included in membership dues. **Circulation:** 5,500. **Advertising:** accepted ● *Comparative Medicine*, bimonthly. Journal. Covers comparative and experimental medicine related to laboratory animal science. **Price:** $180.00 /year for nonmembers in U.S.; $195.00 /year for nonmembers in Canada and Mexico; $220.00 /year for nonmembers international; included in membership dues. **Circulation:** 3,300. **Advertising:** accepted. Alternate Formats: online ● *Journal of the American Association for Laboratory Animal Science*, bimonthly. Contains refereed papers covering topics in laboratory animal science; covers association activities. **Price:** included in membership dues; $180.00 /year for nonmembers in U.S.; $195.00 /year for nonmembers in Canada and Mexico; $220.00 /year for nonmembers international. ISSN: 1559-6109. **Circulation:** 5,500. **Advertising:** accepted ● *Tech Talk*, bimonthly. Journal. **Price:** $180.00 /year for nonmembers in U.S.; $195.00 /year for nonmembers in Canada and Mexico; $220.00 /year for nonmembers international; included in membership dues ● Also publishes educational materials. **Conventions/Meetings:** annual convention and meeting (exhibits) - 2007 Oct. 14-18, Charlotte, NC; 2008 Nov. 9-13, Indianapolis, IN.

13405 ■ Americans for Medical Progress Educational Foundation (AMPEF)

908 King St., Ste.301
Alexandria, VA 22314
Ph: (703)836-9595
Fax: (703)836-9594
E-mail: info@amprogress.org
URL: http://www.amprogress.org
Contact: Jacqueline Calnan MPA, Pres.
Founded: 1990. **Members:** 3,000. **Staff:** 4. **Budget:** $500,000. **Description:** Works to ensure the public supports the role of animals in medical research. Supports scientists' ability to search for cures and treatments for injury, illness, and disease. **Libraries: Type:** reference. **Holdings:** archival material, books, clippings, periodicals. **Awards:** Albert B. Sabin Heroes of Science Award. **Frequency:** semiannual. **Type:** recognition. **Recipient:** for advancements in scientific research. **Absorbed:** (1995) Americans for Medical Progress. **Publications:** *News and Notes*, quarterly. Newsletter. **Price:** included in membership dues ● Brochures ● Also, publishes biomedical research fact sheets and other educational materials.

13406 ■ Association for Assessment and Accreditation of Laboratory Animal Care International (AAALAC)

5283 Corporate Dr., Ste.203
Frederick, MD 21703
Ph: (301)696-9626

Fax: (301)696-9627
E-mail: accredit@aaalac.org
URL: http://www.aaalac.org
Contact: Dr. John G. Miller DVM, Exec. Dir.
Founded: 1965. **Members:** 65. **Staff:** 9. **Description:** Promotes the humane treatment of animals in science through a voluntary accreditation program; more than 600 institutions around the world have earned the association's International Accreditation, demonstrating their commitment to responsible animal care and use. **Councils:** Accreditation. **Formerly:** American Association for Accreditation of Laboratory Animal Care. **Publications:** *AAALAC Connection*, quarterly. Newsletter. Alternate Formats: online. **Conventions/Meetings:** annual board meeting and meeting.

13407 ■ Foundation for Biomedical Research (FBR)
818 Connecticut Ave. NW, Ste.900
Washington, DC 20006
Ph: (202)457-0654
Fax: (202)457-0659
E-mail: info@fbresearch.org
URL: http://www.fbresearch.org
Contact: Ms. Frankie L. Trull, Pres.
Founded: 1981. **Staff:** 5. **Budget:** $1,100,000. **Description:** Individuals and organizations supporting humane animal research. Serves as public information and education program on what the foundation sees as the necessary and important role of laboratory animals in biomedical research and testing. Maintains speakers' bureau and public relations program. **Convention/Meeting:** none. **Awards:** De-Bakey Journalism Award. **Frequency:** annual. **Type:** recognition. **Recipient:** for an individual with public understanding, respect, appreciation and support to animals in medical and scientific research. **Publications:** *Bleeding Heart, Broken Promises*. Booklet. Contains Hollywood's conflicting support for disease research and animal rights. **Price:** $3.00 ● *Caring for Life*. Video. Shows daily routine of two veterinary technicians, focusing on humane care and treatment of laboratory animals. **Price:** $15.00 ● *Exploring the Mysteries of Aging*. Booklet. Outlines the contributions of animal research to the health of aging population. **Price:** $2.00 1-5 pieces; $1.50 6-99 pieces; $1.00 100 or more ● *Fact vs. Myth*. Brochure. Alternate Formats: online ● *FBRoadcast*, bimonthly. Newsletter. Includes foundation news and calendar of events. **Price:** free. Also Cited As: *FBR Newsletter* ● *Hope!*. Film ● *Science Action*. Video. Tells the story of two scientists who takes a young boy and his sister on an adventure through time and space. **Price:** $20.00 ● *Waiting for a Cure*. Video. Profiles advances in spinal cord and injury research in rats. **Price:** $15.00 ● *Why I Should Stay Awake in Science Class*. Video.

13408 ■ Incurably Ill for Animal Research (IIFAR)
2510 Champion Way
Lansing, MI 48910
Ph: (517)887-1141
Fax: (517)887-1710
E-mail: info@iifar.org
URL: http://www.iifar.org
Contact: Gregory A. Maas, CEO
Founded: 1985. **Members:** 2,500. **Membership Dues:** individual, $25 (annual) ● supporting, $50 (annual) ● century club, $100 (annual) ● gold club, $250 (annual) ● contributing, $500 (annual). **Staff:** 1. **Budget:** $100,000. **Local Groups:** 18. **Description:** Persons who have health problems and interested individuals who are concerned that animal research for medical purposes will be stopped or severely limited due to the efforts of animal rights activists. Supports the use of animals for the purpose of medical research, teaching, and testing. Seeks to educate the public regarding the role animals serve in biomedical research and improving human and animal health. Maintains Speaker's Bureau. **Libraries:** Type: reference. **Holdings:** clippings. **Awards:** Dr. Louis J. Kettel Memorial Award. **Frequency:** annual. **Type:** recognition ● Richard Simpson Memorial Award. **Frequency:** annual. **Type:** recognition. **Publi-**

cations: *Have You Benefited?*. Brochure ● *How Can You Show Your Support?*. Brochure ● *IIFAR Update*, monthly. Newsletter. Includes local chapter news and information on legislation and the activities of animal rights activists. ● *IIFARsighted Report*, quarterly ● *Why Should You Care?*. Brochure ● Also distributes educational literature and student information packets. **Conventions/Meetings:** annual board meeting ● annual symposium.

13409 ■ Institute for Laboratory Animal Research (ILAR)
500 Fifth St. NW
Washington, DC 20001
Ph: (202)334-2590
Fax: (202)334-1687
E-mail: jzurlo@nas.edu
URL: http://dels.nas.edu/ilar_n/ilarhome/index.shtml
Contact: Joanne Zurlo PhD, Dir.
Founded: 1952. **Membership Dues:** individual in U.S., $60 (annual) ● individual outside U.S., $75 (annual) ● institutional in U.S., $550 (annual) ● institutional outside U.S., $600 (annual) ● supporting institution in U.S., $1,100 (annual) ● supporting institution outside U.S., $1,200 (annual) ● student in U.S., $25 (annual) ● student outside U.S., $35 (annual). **Staff:** 5. **Description:** Organized under the auspices of the National Academy of Sciences (see separate entry). Acts in an advisory capacity to the federal government, upon request, and to other public and private agencies. Maintains website to address inquiries concerning animal models for biomedical research, location of unique animal colonies, and non-animal alternatives. Committees develop guidelines on breeding, conservation, and humane care and use of animals, including species-specific documents on dogs, nonhuman primates, and rodents. Prepares documents on guidelines and policy issues of biotechnology and use of animals in precollege education, facilities, disease prevention, and other topics in laboratory animal science. Sources of financial support include government agencies and private organizations. **Libraries:** Type: reference. **Holdings:** books, periodicals. **Subjects:** laboratory animal science and medicine, zoology, pathology, other medical topics. **Formerly:** (1997) Institute of Laboratory Animal Resources. **Publications:** *Guide for the Care and Use of Laboratory Animals*. Book ● *ILAR e-Journal*, quarterly. Expands Journal content with pertinent online only articles. **Price:** $8.00 each. ISSN: 1930-6180. Alternate Formats: online. Also Cited As: *Agricola, Embase, Medline, Thomson ISI* ● Journal, quarterly. **Price:** $30.00 for nonmembers; $15.00 for members. ISSN: 1084-2020. **Circulation:** 1,100. Alternate Formats: online ● Proceedings ● Reports. Includes laboratory animal management documents. **Conventions/Meetings:** annual conference, forum for discussion of laboratory animal problems.

13410 ■ Laboratory Animal Management Association (LAMA)
7500 Flying Cloud Dr., Ste.900
Eden Prairie, MN 55344
Ph: (952)253-6235
Fax: (952)835-4774
E-mail: kknapp@lama-online.org
URL: http://www.lama-online.org
Contact: Regina Correa-Murphy, Pres.
Founded: 1984. **Members:** 435. **Membership Dues:** domestic, $50 (annual) ● outside U.S., $60 (annual) ● institution, $250 (annual). **Staff:** 1. **Budget:** $170,000. **Regional Groups:** 3. **Description:** Laboratory animal facility managers. Seeks to evaluate and update basic and advanced management techniques and to educate laboratory animal facility managers. Makes available resource material; coordinates exchange programs for management personnel. Offers consulting on management techniques. **Awards:** Charles River Medallion. **Type:** monetary. **Recipient:** for distinguished contributions to the field by an administrator/manager who is a current member of LAMA and engaged in laboratory animal management ● LAMA Foundation Award. **Type:** monetary. **Recipient:** to qualified members within laboratory animal management for the further-

ance of his or her education in the field ● U. Kristina Stephens Award. **Type:** monetary. **Recipient:** to a LAMA member for outstanding and exceptional service to LAMA. **Formerly:** Laboratory Animal Managers Association. **Publications:** *LAMA Lines*, bimonthly. Article. Includes branch news and employment opportunities' list. **Price:** included in membership dues. **Circulation:** 500. **Advertising:** accepted ● *Lama Review*, quarterly. Journal ● Membership Directory, annual. **Conventions/Meetings:** annual Educational Program - seminar and workshop, includes tour of facilities and/or manufacturing plants - usually the Sunday before the AALAS meeting at the same location ● annual meeting, with educational seminar ● annual Mid-Year Forum - meeting and seminar, includes tour of facilities and/or manufacturing plants - usually early summer.

13411 ■ National Association for Biomedical Research (NABR)
818 Connecticut Ave. NW, Ste.900
Washington, DC 20006
Ph: (202)857-0540
Fax: (202)659-1902
E-mail: info@nabr.org
URL: http://www.nabr.org
Contact: Ms. Mary F. Hanley, Exec. VP
Founded: 1979. **Members:** 400. **Staff:** 5. **Budget:** $700,000. **Description:** Universities, medical and veterinary schools, teaching hospitals, professional societies, voluntary health agencies, pharmaceutical companies and other research-related firms that use laboratory animals for biomedical research, education, and testing. Monitors and, when appropriate, attempts to influence legislation and regulations on behalf of members who are dependent on animals for biomedical research, education, and testing. **Affiliated With:** Foundation for Biomedical Research. **Formed by Merger of:** National Society for Medical Research; Association for Biomedical Research. **Publications:** *NABR Alert*, 6-10/year. Newsletter. Covers regulatory and legislative action related to the use of animals in biomedical research, research, and testing. **Price:** included in membership dues. **Circulation:** 2,500 ● *NABR Update*, 48/year. Bulletin. Covers national, state, and local regulatory and legislative activities affecting biomedical research. **Price:** included in membership dues. **Circulation:** 2,500 ● Annual Report, annual. Describes the previous year's activities. **Price:** included in membership dues. **Circulation:** 2,500. **Conventions/Meetings:** annual conference.

13412 ■ Nature of Wellness
PO Box 10400
Glendale, CA 91209-3400
Ph: (818)790-6384
Fax: (818)790-9660
E-mail: info@animalresearch.org
Multinational. Description: Seeks to inform the public about medical and scientific invalidity of animal experimentation and testing; investigates the impact of reliance by the medical/pharmaceutical/petrochemical industry on animal experimentation (in biomedical research) and animal testing (to assess the safety of drugs, pesticides and other chemicals) has on the health care system, environment and economy.

Animal Welfare

13413 ■ American Association of Human-Animal Bond Veterinarians (AAH-ABV)
c/o Dr. Thomas Krall, DVM, Treas.
PO Box 13489
St. Petersburg, FL 33733-3489
E-mail: info@aah-abv.org
URL: http://www.aahabv.org
Contact: Dr. Thomas Krall DVM, Treas.
Founded: 1993. **Membership Dues:** veterinarian, associate, $35 (annual) ● student, $10 (annual). **Description:** Strives to enhance the ability of veterinarians to create a positive and ethical relationship

between people, animals and the environment. Raises veterinary awareness and advances scientific progress in the area of human-animal bond. Furthers educational opportunities in the human-animal bond through training programs and curriculum development in veterinary colleges and schools of veterinary technology. Encourages the development of continuing education for veterinarians, veterinary technicians and veterinary staff. **Publications:** Newsletter. **Price:** included in membership dues. Alternate Formats: online.

Animals

13414 ■ International Alliance for Animal Therapy and Healing (IAATH)
c/o Maryann Adams
PO Box 1255
Winters, CA 95694
Ph: (530)795-5040
E-mail: info@iaath.com
URL: http://www.iaath.com
Contact: Maryann Adams, Contact
Founded: 1999. **Membership Dues:** friend, $20 ● practitioner, $45 (annual) ● business, organizational, group, $250 (annual) ● benefactor, $500 (annual). **Multinational. Description:** Seeks to continue the development of education, communication, support and opportunities for all those interested in animal health care. Ensures that animal guardians (owners) have choices and take part in their animal's health care. Provides a network for sharing research, education and information. **Computer Services:** Information services, treatments and therapies.

Aphasia

13415 ■ Academy of Aphasia (AA)
c/o Executive Administrative Services
PO Box 26532
Minneapolis, MN 55426
Ph: (952)920-0484
Fax: (952)920-6098
E-mail: contact@academyofaphasia.org
URL: http://www.academyofaphasia.org
Contact: Frances Laven, Dir.
Founded: 1962. **Members:** 189. **Description:** Neurologists, psychologists, linguists, speech pathologists, and others specializing in aphasia (impairment of language caused by focal brain damage). Seeks to encourage research and promote communication among the scientific disciplines that can contribute to the understanding of aphasia. **Publications:** none. **Committees:** Scientific Affairs. **Conventions/Meetings:** annual meeting - always October.

13416 ■ National Aphasia Association (NAA)
7 Dey St., Ste.600
New York, NY 10007
Free: (800)922-4622
Fax: (212)267-2812
E-mail: naa@aphasia.org
URL: http://www.aphasia.org
Contact: Barbara C. Martin, Pres.
Founded: 1987. **Membership Dues:** sponsor, $25 (annual). **Staff:** 2. **Description:** Works to promote the care, rehabilitation and quality of life of individuals with aphasia, a speech and language disorder caused by stroke, head trauma or other neurological conditions. Conducts public and professional education programs; facilitates the development of community programs to meet the needs of people with aphasia and their families; and provides referrals to professionals. **Publications:** *Aphasia Community Group Manual.* Contains information to aid in the establishment of new support groups. **Price:** $32.95 personal subscription, plus shipping and handling; $52.95 professional subscription, plus shipping and handling ● *Listing of Aphasia Community Groups.* Directory. **Price:** $2.75/copy ● *National Aphasia Association Newsletter*, monthly. **Price:** $1.

00. Alternate Formats: online ● *News Bulletin.* Alternate Formats: online ● *Videotape of 3 Community Groups.* **Price:** $10.00. **Conventions/Meetings:** biennial Speaking Out - conference, for people with aphasia, family members, and rehabilitation professionals - always first week of June.

Apheresis

13417 ■ American Society for Apheresis (ASFA)
c/o Mark Brecher
Univ. of NC Hospitals
Chapel Hill, NC 27599
E-mail: asfa@azstarnet.com
URL: http://www.apheresis.org
Contact: Mark Brecher, Pres.
Founded: 1981. **Members:** 800. **Membership Dues:** allied health professional/physician in training, $55-$120 (annual) ● physician/PhD/corporate supplier employee, $125-$145 (annual). **Staff:** 5. **Budget:** $100,000. **Description:** Physicians, nurses, technologists, scientists, and other allied health professionals active in the field of apheresis, the separation and removal of components from blood. Aims to: promote training and research in apheresis therapy for patients; improve the care and management of apheresis donors; encourage the use of apheresis technology; assist in forming standards and regulations in the field of apheresis. Provides opportunity for the exchange of experiences and opinions through discussions, presentations, and publications; offers consulting on problems in the practice of apheresis. Conducts studies and courses. Plans to establish a central registry of apheresis information. **Libraries: Type:** reference. **Holdings:** video recordings. **Subjects:** apheresis. **Awards:** Allied Health Award. **Frequency:** annual. **Type:** recognition. **Recipient:** for outstanding members ● Junior Investigator Award. **Frequency:** annual. **Type:** recognition. **Recipient:** for outstanding members. **Publications:** *Journal of Clinical Apheresis*, quarterly. **Price:** $124.00/year. ISSN: 0733-2459. **Advertising:** accepted. Alternate Formats: online ● Newsletter, periodic. **Advertising:** accepted. **Conventions/Meetings:** annual meeting and trade show, with 10x10 industry-related booths (exhibits).

Art

13418 ■ Association of Medical Illustrators (AMI)
PO Box 1897
Lawrence, KS 66044
Free: (866)393-4264
Fax: (785)843-1274
E-mail: hq@ami.org
URL: http://www.ami.org
Contact: Ms. Vanessa Reilly, Exec. Dir.
Founded: 1945. **Members:** 800. **Membership Dues:** student, $85 (annual) ● associate, professional, $230 (annual). **Staff:** 5. **Budget:** $250,000. **Multinational. Description:** Represents medical illustrators and individuals engaged in related pursuits. Promotes the study and encourages the advancement of medical illustration and allied fields of visual education. Works to advance medical education and to promote understanding and cooperation with medical and related professions; accredits six postgraduate medical illustration programs. Offers continuing education program; provides professional certification; compiles statistics. **Libraries: Type:** reference. **Holdings:** archival material. **Committees:** Accreditation; Certification; Education; Workshops. **Publications:** *Journal of Biocommunication*, quarterly ● *Medical Illustration Sourcebook*, annual ● Directory, annual ● Newsletter, bimonthly. **Conventions/Meetings:** annual meeting and workshop (exhibits).

13419 ■ Foundation for Hospital Art
120 Stonemist Ct.
Roswell, GA 30076
Ph: (770)645-1717

Fax: (770)645-1720
E-mail: johnfeight@hospitalart.org
URL: http://www.hospitalart.org
Contact: John Feight, Founder/Exec. Dir.
Founded: 1984. **Staff:** 2. **Multinational. Description:** Dedicated to involving patients and volunteers to create colorful, soothing artwork donated to hospitals to help soften the stressful hospital experience. **Publications:** *Hospital Art*, annual. Newsletter. Alternate Formats: online. **Conventions/Meetings:** PaintFest - meeting.

Art Therapy

13420 ■ Arts in Therapy Network (AiT)
c/o The Arts We Need
PO Box 2652
New York, NY 10009
Free: (800)586-TAWN
Fax: (646)390-3596
E-mail: info@theartsweneed.org
URL: http://www.artsintherapy.com
Contact: Chriss Berk MA, Founder/CEO
Members: 3,400. **Multinational. Description:** Promotes the practice of Creative Arts Therapy. Provides an online community for Creative Arts Therapists (CAT) and those who are interested in the Healing Arts. Facilitates cooperation and communication among members. **Telecommunication Services:** electronic mail, chriss@artsintherapy.com.

13421 ■ The Arts We Need (TAWN)
PO Box 2652
New York, NY 10009
Free: (800)586-TAWN
Fax: (646)390-3596
E-mail: info@theartsweneed.org
URL: http://www.theartsweneed.org
Contact: Chriss Berk MA, Founder/CEO
Founded: 2001. **Description:** Provides Creative Arts Therapy and related arts programs to people with special needs. Ensures that people with special needs are recognized for their creative ability. Assists programs that are either attempting to start an arts program or improve upon an existing program. **Telecommunication Services:** additional toll-free number, (888)799-9147.

13422 ■ International Association for Voice Movement Therapy (IAVMT)
912 Hunters Ln.
Oreland, PA 19075
Ph: (267)625-5451
E-mail: info@iavmt.org
URL: http://www.iavmt.org
Contact: Deborah Crane, Pres./Treas.
Multinational. Description: Promotes the practice of voice movement therapy. Facilitates a forum for the exchange of ideas, information and experience. Provides professional and political representation of Voice Movement Therapy (VMT) practitioners.

13423 ■ International Expressive Arts Therapy Association (IEATA)
PO Box 320399
San Francisco, CA 94132-0399
Ph: (415)522-8959
E-mail: ieata@ieata.org
URL: http://www.ieata.org
Contact: Maria Gonzalez-Blue MA, Exec. Co-Chair
Membership Dues: professional, honorary, $85 (annual) ● supporting, $65 (annual) ● supporting (with lower/limited income), student, intern, $40 (annual). **Multinational. Description:** Seeks to improve the standards of practice for expressive arts professionals worldwide. Aims to increase professional recognition of the expressive arts. Supports an integrative approach to psychotherapy, education and the community arts. Promotes research and publication in the field of expressive arts. **Telecommunication Services:** electronic mail, maria@ieata.org. **Publications:** Newsletter, semiannual. **Advertising:** accepted. **Conventions/Meetings:** annual Expressive

Arts and the Earth: Ancient Mountains, Whispering Waters, Sacred Stone - conference.

Artificial Organs

13424 ■ Tissue Banks International (TBI)
815 Park Ave.
Baltimore, MD 21201
Ph: (410)752-3800
Free: (800)756-4TBI
Fax: (410)783-0183
E-mail: tdevens@tbionline.org
URL: http://www.tbionline.org
Contact: Gerald J. Cole, Pres./CEO
Founded: 1962. **Members:** 76. **Multinational.** **Description:** Represents medical eye and tissue banks. Provides eye tissue for sight-restoring corneal transplant surgery. Distributes bone, skin, and other soft tissues. Assists members with operational areas. Provides grants for research into the causes and cures of blindness. Disseminates information on eye, tissue, and organ donation. Conducts educational and charitable programs. **Awards: Type:** grant. **Publications:** Brochure.

Arts

13425 ■ Society for the Arts in Healthcare (SAH)
2437 15th St. NW
Washington, DC 20009
Ph: (202)299-9770
Fax: (202)299-9887
E-mail: mail@thesah.org
URL: http://www.thesah.org
Contact: Gay Hanna, Exec. Dir.
Founded: 1991. **Membership Dues:** organizational, $250 (annual) ● organizational affiliate, $35 (annual) ● individual, $100 (annual) ● student, $35 (annual). **Multinational. Description:** Promotes the incorporation of the arts as an integral component of healthcare. Demonstrates the valuable role of the arts in enhancing the healing process. Provides resources and education to healthcare and arts professionals. Encourages and supports research and investigation into the beneficial effects of the arts in healthcare. **Committees:** Education/Research; Fundraising; PR/Marketing; Travelling Exhibits. **Programs:** Arts in Healing. **Publications:** SAH News, semiannual. Newsletter.

Assyrian

13426 ■ Assyrian Medical Society (AMS)
c/o Samir Johna, MD, Pres.
1616 W Olive Ave.
Redlands, CA 92373
E-mail: s.johna@verizon.net
Contact: Samir Johna MD, Pres.
Membership Dues: physician, dentist, $100 (annual) ● non-physician, $50 (annual) ● nurse/technician, resident, $25 (annual). **Multinational. Description:** Serves physicians and other health professionals interested in advancing and sharing their expertise all over the world. Seeks to educate and stimulate interest in all aspects of medicine and health related sciences. Fosters health education among Assyrians and promotes the use of Assyrian language in health education. Provides a source of health education to the Assyrian community.

Audiology

13427 ■ National Association of Future Doctors of Audiology (NAFDA)
c/o Vicky Moore, Treas.
8264 Deerbrook Cir.
Sarasota, FL 34238
Ph: (817)403-8575

E-mail: nafda@nafda.org
URL: http://www.nafda.org
Contact: Elizabeth Gray, Pres.
Founded: 1998. **Membership Dues:** regular, $30 (annual). **Description:** Audiology students. Provides forum on national, state and regional issues of concern to the Doctor of Audiology students, including opportunity to travel internationally to offer audiologic healthcare to underprivileged nations. **Telecommunication Services:** electronic mail, president@nafda.org ● electronic mail, treasurer@nafda.org. **Conventions/Meetings:** annual conference.

Autism

13428 ■ Autism Network International (ANI)
PO Box 35448
Syracuse, NY 13235-0448
Ph: (315)476-2462
Fax: (315)425-1978
E-mail: ani@autistics.org
URL: http://ani.autistics.org
Contact: Jim Sinclair, Coor.
Founded: 1992. **Members:** 400. **Multinational. Description:** Autistic-run self-help and advocacy organization for autistic individuals. Seeks to provide a forum for autistic people to share information and tips for coping and problem-solving; advocates for appropriate services and civil rights for all autistic people at all levels of functioning. Provides information and referrals for parents and teachers of autistic people; sponsors group lobbying and educational campaigns. Serves as a support group. **Computer Services:** Mailing lists.

13429 ■ The Autism Research Foundation (TARF)
c/o Moss-Rosene Lab
715 Albany St., W701
Boston, MA 02118
Ph: (617)414-7012
Fax: (617)414-7207
E-mail: tarf@ladders.org
URL: http://www.ladders.org/tarf
Contact: Daniel Paik, Proj. Mgr./Coor.
Founded: 1990. **Description:** Works to research the neurological underpinnings of autism and other related developmental brain disorders. **Conventions/Meetings:** annual conference.

13430 ■ Autism Research Institute (ARI)
4182 Adams Ave.
San Diego, CA 92116
Ph: (619)281-7165
Fax: (619)563-6840
E-mail: media@autismresearchinstitute.com
URL: http://www.autismwebsite.com/ari/index.htm
Contact: Matt Kabler, Contact
Founded: 1967. **Multinational. Description:** Works to conduct and disseminate research on the causes of autism and methods of preventing, diagnosing and treating autism and other severe behavioral disorders of childhood. **Computer Services:** Mailing lists. **Publications:** Autism: Effective Biomedical Treatments. Manual. **Price:** $30.00 ● The Autism Research Review International, quarterly. Newsletter. **Price:** $18.00/year ● Vitamin B6 and Magnesium in Treatment of Autism. Video. **Price:** $16.00.

13431 ■ Autism Services Center (ASC)
The Keith Albee Bldg.
929 4th Ave.
PO Box 507
Huntington, WV 25710-0507
Ph: (304)525-8014
Fax: (304)525-8026
URL: http://www.autismservicescenter.org
Contact: Ruth C. Sullivan PhD, Exec. Dir.
Founded: 1979. **Staff:** 220. **Description:** Service agency for individuals with autism and other developmental disabilities, and their families. (Autism is a disorder of communication and behavior, which often manifests itself in social isolation, severe language deficiency, and compulsive insistence on routine and ritual in daily activities.) Assists families and agencies attempting to meet the unique needs of individuals with autism and other developmental disabilities; makes available technical assistance in designing programs. Provides supervised apartments, group homes, respite services, independent living services, and job-coached employment. Conducts workshops and consulting in autism. Disseminates information regarding autism and its treatment. **Libraries: Type:** reference. **Holdings:** articles. **Subjects:** court case briefs, legal materials related to autism. **Projects:** Apartment Living; Autism Group Home; Case Management Services; Monitored Employment; Respite Services. **Formerly:** (1993) National Autism Hotline.

13432 ■ Autism Society of America (ASA)
7910 Woodmont Ave., Ste.300
Bethesda, MD 20814-3067
Ph: (301)657-0881
Free: (800)328-8476
Fax: (301)657-0869
E-mail: info@autism-society.org
URL: http://www.autism-society.org
Contact: Lee Grossman, Pres./CEO
Founded: 1965. **Members:** 60,000. **Membership Dues:** individual, $30 (annual) ● outside U.S., $50 (annual) ● family, $40 (annual) ● agency, $500 (annual) ● life, $1,500 ● professional, $100 (annual). **Staff:** 14. **Budget:** $1,500,000. **Local Groups:** 200. **Description:** Parents, teachers, psychologists, speech therapists, pediatricians, neurologists, and others interested in the welfare of children with severe disorders of communication and behavior. Informs the public of the symptoms and problems of children and adults with autism; promotes better understanding of the condition in general; aids physicians in making earlier and more accurate diagnoses. Commits in the alleviation of this disorder through support of research, public and professional education, and development of habilitative services. Sponsors two mail-order bookstores with over 100 titles on autism. **Awards:** Autism Professional of the Year. **Frequency:** annual. **Type:** recognition. **Recipient:** to a psychologist, psychiatrist or other physician, educator, speech-language therapist, social worker, and researcher in the autism field ● Chapter of the Year. **Frequency:** annual. **Type:** recognition ● Collins. **Frequency:** annual. **Type:** scholarship. **Recipient:** to a person doing graduate study in autism ● Corporate Recognition Award. **Frequency:** annual. **Type:** recognition. **Recipient:** to a firm with full participation to individual with autism in the community ● Eden Service Charles H. Hoens, Jr., Scholar Program. **Frequency:** annual. **Type:** scholarship. **Recipient:** to an individual with autism ● Outstanding Individual with Autism of the Year. **Frequency:** annual. **Type:** recognition. **Recipient:** to a person with autism who excelled in one or more areas of life experiences ● Parent/s of the Year. **Frequency:** annual. **Type:** recognition. **Recipient:** for a parent with unusual dedication or effort to an individual with autism ● Volunteer of the Year. **Frequency:** annual. **Type:** recognition. **Recipient:** to members with positive influence to lives of individuals, parents, and professionals. **Computer Services:** Online services, includes referral service. **Committees:** Advocacy; Education; Government Affairs; Information and Referral; International; Research. **Formerly:** (1981) National Society for Autistic Children; (1987) NSAC, The National Society for Autistic Children and Adults with Autism. **Publications:** The Autism Advocate, quarterly. Magazine. Promotes better understanding of autism by informing the public of the symptoms and problems of children and adults with autism. **Price:** included in membership dues. ISSN: 0047-9101. **Circulation:** 60,000. **Advertising:** accepted. Alternate Formats: online ● National Conference on Autism Spectrum Disorder, annual. Proceedings ● Reprints ● Newsletter. **Price:** free. Alternate Formats: online. **Conventions/Meetings:** annual National Conference on Autism Spectrum Disorders (exhibits) - always July.

13433 ■ Autism Speaks
2 Park Ave., 11th Fl.
New York, NY 10016
Ph: (212)252-8584

Fax: (212)252-8676
E-mail: contactus@autismspeaks.org
URL: http://www.autismspeaks.org
Contact: Mark Roithmayr, Pres.
Founded: 2005. **Description:** Aims to change the future for all who struggle with Autism Spectrum Disorders (ASD). Supports and funds global biomedical research focuses in the causes, prevention, treatments and cure for autism. Raises public awareness about autism and its effects on families and communities. **Awards:** Research and Fellowship Award. **Frequency:** annual. **Type:** grant. **Recipient:** for autism research projects, fellowships, and collaborative programs.

13434 ■ Global Autism Project
6910 Roosevelt Way NE, No. 201
Seattle, WA 98115
Ph: (206)850-9265
E-mail: information@globalautismproject.org
URL: http://www.globalautismproject.org
Contact: Molly Ola Pinney, Founder/Dir.
Founded: 2003. **Multinational. Description:** Seeks to address the needs of children with autism in developing countries. Cooperates with local individuals currently providing services. Conducts family and community education through workshops and hands on training. Aims to teach parents how to effectively work with their own children. **Telecommunication Services:** electronic mail, molly@globalautism-project.org.

13435 ■ National Alliance for Autism Research (NAAR)
99 Wall St., Res. Park
Princeton, NJ 08540
Ph: (609)430-9160
Free: (888)777-NAAR
Fax: (609)430-9163
E-mail: naar@naar.org
URL: http://www.autismwalk.org
Contact: Glenn R. Tringali, CEO
Founded: 1994. **Staff:** 20. **Budget:** $250,000. **Regional Groups:** 6. **Description:** Dedicated to finding the causes, prevention, effective treatment and, ultimately, cure of the autism spectrum disorders. **Awards:** Collaborative Programs. **Type:** recognition ● **Frequency:** annual. **Type:** fellowship. **Recipient:** for mentor-based fellowships ● London Award. **Frequency:** annual. **Type:** recognition. **Recipient:** to an extraordinary member who has contributed for the good of the organization ● Pilot Study. **Type:** grant. **Computer Services:** Information services ● online services. **Telecommunication Services:** electronic mail, autismwalk@naar.org. **Boards:** Honorary; Scientific Advisory; Trustees. **Programs:** Autism Tissue; Training in Autism Research. **Projects:** Autism Genome; Exploring the Genetic Roots of Autism; Identifying Early Markers of Autism: A Study of Infant Siblings. **Publications:** *NAARRATIVE*, quarterly. Newsletter. Features autism research articles. **Circulation:** 35,000. Alternate Formats: online. **Conventions/Meetings:** periodic meeting, parent conferences ● periodic workshop.

13436 ■ National Autism Association (NAA)
1330 W Schatz Rd.
Nixa, MO 65714
Free: (866)622-6733
E-mail: naa@nationalautism.org
URL: http://www.nationalautismassociation.org
Contact: Rita Cave Shreffler, Exec. Dir.
Founded: 2003. **Membership Dues:** individual, $35 (annual) ● family, $60 (annual) ● international, $30 (annual) ● student, $20 (annual) ● professional, $75 (annual). **Description:** Promotes public and professional awareness of autism spectrum disorders. Aims to further the advancement of preventive studies, therapy and research of autism spectrum disorders. Works in partnership with other organizations dedicated to breaking down the barriers currently standing against those with autism spectrum disorders. **Telecommunication Services:** electronic mail, rita@nationalautism.org. **Publications:** *NAA News & Views*, bimonthly. Newsletter. Alternate Formats: online.

13437 ■ Organization for Autism Research (OAR)
2000 N 14th St., Ste.480
Arlington, VA 22201
Ph: (703)243-9710
Free: (866)366-9710
E-mail: oar@researchautism.org
URL: http://www.researchautism.org
Contact: Michael V. Maloney, Exec. Dir.
Founded: 2001. **Description:** Promotes autism research and disseminates information to the autism community. Examines issues and challenges that children and adults with autism and their families face everyday. Funds pilot studies and targeted research within specific modalities and issues affecting the autism community. **Awards:** Research Grants. **Frequency:** annual. **Type:** grant. **Recipient:** for researchers and graduate students conducting autism research in support of an advanced degree. **Telecommunication Services:** electronic mail, mmaloney@researchautism.org. **Publications:** *An Educator's Guide to Asperger Syndrome.* Book. Provides guidelines for meeting the needs of the student with Asperger Syndrome. Alternate Formats: online ● *An Educator's Guide to Autism.* Book. Provides parents, teachers and education professionals with a plan for teaching a child with autism. Alternate Formats: online ● *The OARacle*, monthly. Newsletter. Alternate Formats: online ● Annual Report, annual. Alternate Formats: online.

Autoimmune Disorders

13438 ■ Churg Strauss Syndrome Association (CSSA)
PO Box 671
Southampton, MA 01073-0671
Ph: (413)862-3636
E-mail: support@cssassociation.org
URL: http://www.cssassociation.org
Contact: Jane Dion, Co-Dir.
Founded: 2004. **Description:** Represents medical professionals and concerned individuals dedicated to the identification, treatment, and cure of Churg Strauss Syndrome. Promotes and supports research to improve treatment and find a cure for Churg Strauss Syndrome and related vasculitic diseases. Promotes public awareness through seminars and workshops, publicity campaigns, education and literature. **Computer Services:** Information services, Churg Strauss Syndrome facts.

13439 ■ Platelet Disorder Support Association (PDSA)
PO Box 61533
Potomac, MD 20859
Ph: (301)770-6636
Free: (877)528-3538
Fax: (301)770-6638
E-mail: pdsa@pdsa.org
URL: http://www.pdsa.org
Contact: Joan Young, Pres.
Founded: 1998. **Membership Dues:** regular, $25 (annual) ● friend, $50 (annual) ● contributor, $100 (annual) ● associate, $250 (annual). **Description:** Provides online and printed information that enhances knowledge of idiopathic thrombocytopenic purpura (ITP) and other platelet disorders. Encourages patient involvement in treatment and lifestyle decisions. Assists and encourages research in the treatment of ITP and other platelet disorders. **Publications:** *Platelet News*, quarterly. Newsletter. Includes helpful articles, news, book reviews, and interviews written by physicians, nurses, and individuals. **Price:** included in membership dues. Alternate Formats: online.

Aviation

13440 ■ Flying Physicians Association (FPA)
PO Box 677427
Orlando, FL 32867
Ph: (407)568-0655

Fax: (407)568-0654
E-mail: pnodecker@fpadrs.org
URL: http://www.fpadrs.org
Contact: Stephen Towle MD, Pres.
Founded: 1954. **Members:** 1,200. **Membership Dues:** physician active military, $225 (annual) ● intern/resident/fellow/associate, $125 (annual) ● emeritus, $180 (annual) ● physician, $300 (annual) ● corporation, $1,500 (annual). **Regional Groups:** 5. **Description:** Represents doctors of medicine who have a current pilot certificate and are members of an ethical medical organization. Promotes the interests of medicine in aviation, safety, and education. **Awards:** Airman of the Year Award. **Frequency:** annual. **Type:** recognition ● Co-Pilot of the Year. **Frequency:** annual. **Type:** recognition. **Computer Services:** Mailing lists. **Committees:** Aviation Legislation; Awards; Continuing Medical Education; Human Factors; Medical Advisory; Safety; Samaritan. **Publications:** *The Flying Physician*, quarterly. Magazine. Covers medical and aviation topics. Includes association activities, book reviews, and calendar. **Price:** included in membership dues; $50.00 /year for nonmembers. **Circulation:** 5,000. **Advertising:** accepted ● *Flying Physicians Association—Bulletin*, monthly. Newsletter. Highlights the activities of the members. **Price:** included in membership dues. **Advertising:** accepted ● *Flying Physicians Association—Directory*, annual. **Price:** included in membership dues. **Advertising:** accepted ● Annual Report, annual. Alternate Formats: online. **Conventions/Meetings:** annual seminar (exhibits).

Behavioral Medicine

13441 ■ Academy of Behavioral Medicine Research (ABMR)
c/o Dr. Philip McCabe, Sec.
Dept. of Psychology
Univ. of Miami
PO Box 248185
Coral Gables, FL 33124-0751
Ph: (305)284-5507
Fax: (305)284-3402
E-mail: pmccabe@miami.edu
URL: http://www.academyofbmr.org
Contact: Kathleen Light PhD, Pres.
Founded: 1978. **Members:** 275. **Membership Dues:** fellow, $60 (annual). **Description:** Individuals actively involved in research in more than one aspect of biobehavioral science, and who have been published in refereed journals relevant to the field. Seeks to foster the integration of research in biomedical and behavioral science; identify current and future areas of research in the field; provide a multidisciplinary forum for review of research findings and assessment of applicability of such findings to prevention, diagnosis, and treatment of and rehabilitation from illness; serve as a technical and educational resource for academic, governmental, and public bodies. Promotes research and professional standards within the field. Assists in developing guidelines for research training in behavioral medicine. **Awards:** Neal E. Miller Award. **Frequency:** annual. **Type:** recognition ● President's Award. **Frequency:** annual. **Type:** recognition. **Committees:** Liaison; Program; Training. **Publications:** *AMBR Membership Directory*, periodic ● *Experimental Foundations of Behavioral Medicine*, annual ● *Perspectives on Behavioral Medicine*, annual. **Conventions/Meetings:** competition ● annual conference (exhibits) ● annual meeting - always June.

13442 ■ Association for Behavioral and Cognitive Therapies (ABCT)
305 7th Ave., 16th Fl.
New York, NY 10001-6008
Ph: (212)647-1890
Fax: (212)647-1865
E-mail: mjeimer@aabt.org
URL: http://www.aabt.org
Contact: Mary Jane Eimer CAE, Exec. Dir.
Founded: 1966. **Members:** 4,500. **Membership Dues:** student, $49 (annual) ● full/associate, $199

(annual) ● professional, $149 (annual). **Staff:** 10. **Budget:** $1,000,000. **Description:** Psychologists primarily, but also psychiatrists, social workers, counselors, physicians, dentists, nurses, students, and other professionals interested in the issues, problems, and development of the field of behavior therapy and cognitive behavior therapy, with specific emphasis on research and clinical applications. Sponsors training programs and lectures for professionals; maintains speakers' bureau; handles referrals for the public to locate behavior therapists in their area; facilitates communication between behavior therapists interested in specific problems or information. Local affiliates hold training meetings, workshops, seminars, case demonstrations, and discussion groups. **Libraries: Type:** by appointment only. **Holdings:** books, periodicals. **Subjects:** behavior therapy and cognitive behavior therapy. **Awards:** Career/ Lifetime Achievement. **Frequency:** annual. **Type:** recognition ●. Distinguished Friend to Behavior Therapy. **Frequency:** annual. **Type:** recognition ● Distinguished/Outstanding Contribution by an Individual for Education/Training. **Frequency:** triennial. **Type:** recognition ● Elsie Ramos Awards. **Frequency:** annual. **Type:** recognition. **Recipient:** for the best student poster submitted at annual convention ● Outstanding Training Program. **Frequency:** annual. **Type:** recognition ● President's New Researcher Award. **Frequency:** annual. **Type:** recognition ● Virginia A. Roswell Student Dissertation Award. **Frequency:** annual. **Type:** monetary. **Computer Services:** Mailing lists. **Committees:** Academic and Training Issues; Awards and Recognition; Continuing Education; International Associates; Program; Public Education; Research Agenda; Student Membership. **Special Interest Groups:** Addictive Disorders; Aging Issues. **Formerly:** (1968) Association for Advancement of the Behavioral Therapies; (2006) Association for Advancement of Behavior Therapy. **Publications:** *The Behavior Therapist*, 10/year. Newsletter. Reports the latest research and includes book reviews, association news, professionals and legislative issues reports, training updates, job listings. **Price:** included in membership dues; $60.00 /year for nonmembers. ISSN: 0278-8403. **Circulation:** 5,400. **Advertising:** accepted ● *Behavior Therapy*, quarterly. Journal. Devoted to the application of behavioral and cognitive sciences to clinical problems. **Price:** $75.00 /year for nonmembers; $145.00 /year for institutions. ISSN: 0005-7894. **Circulation:** 3,350. **Advertising:** accepted ● *Cognitive and Behavioral Practice*, quarterly. Journal. Integrates behavior therapy principles and research with clinical practice techniques. **Price:** $75.00 /year for nonmembers; $145.00 /year for institutions. ISSN: 1077-7229. **Circulation:** 3,200. **Advertising:** accepted ● *Directory of Graduate Training in Behavior Therapy and Experimental-Clinical Psychology*, biennial. Lists over 300 psychology, special education, and counseling programs that offer training in behavior therapy. **Price:** $20.00 for members; $25.00 for nonmembers ● *Directory of Psychology Internships: Programs Offering Behavioral Training*, periodic. Contains information on admission requirements, application deadlines, and program structure; statistics. **Price:** $20.00 for members; $25.00 for nonmembers ● Videos. For training purposes. **Price:** included in membership dues; $50.00 for nonmembers. **Circulation:** 5,500 ● Also publishes a series of Fact Sheets to educate lay audiences about a variety of psychological disorders, including panic attacks, obsessive-compulsive disorder, post-traumatic stress syndrome, depression, eating disorders, and more. Call for a complete list of available titles. **Conventions/Meetings:** annual conference, offers pre-convention fundamentals courses, professional seminars and institutes (exhibits) - always November.

13443 ■ Devereux National
PO Box 638
Villanova, PA 19085
Ph: (610)520-3000
Free: (800)345-1292
URL: http://www.devereux.org
Contact: Robert Q. Kreider, Pres./CEO
State Groups: 13. **Description:** Provides services to children, adults, and families with special needs such as behavioral, psychological, intellectual or neurological impairments to foster human potential and contribute to health, social, psychological, and educational well-being. **Projects:** Devereux ERate. **Publications:** Annual Report, annual ● Newsletter, monthly. Alternate Formats: online ● Also publishes a guide entitled Facts and Figures.

13444 ■ Institute for the Advancement of Human Behavior (IAHB)
4370 Alpine Rd., Ste.209
Portola Valley, CA 94028
Ph: (650)851-8411
Free: (800)258-8411
Fax: (650)851-0406
E-mail: staff@iahb.org
URL: http://www.iahb.org
Contact: Gerry Piaget, Pres.
Founded: 1977. **Staff:** 8. **Description:** Continuing educational organization for health care professionals. Provides training opportunities in behavioral topics such as: anxiety, depression, trauma, PTSD, couples therapy, treating difficult patients, and spirituality and psychotherapy. **Also Known As:** Institute for Behavioral Healthcare. **Publications:** Audiotapes, periodic. **Conventions/Meetings:** annual conference (exhibits) ● periodic seminar ● periodic workshop, on behavioral topics.

13445 ■ Mental Health Corporations of America (MHCA)
1876-A Eider Ct.
Tallahassee, FL 32308
Ph: (850)942-4900
Fax: (850)942-0560
E-mail: heveyd@mhca.com
URL: http://www.mhca.com
Contact: Don Hevey, Pres./CEO
Description: Behavioral healthcare organizations. Strives to enhance the business performance of members, while preserving its social mission. **Publications:** *Executive Report*, quarterly. Newsletter. Alternate Formats: online.

13446 ■ Mental Research Institute (MRI)
555 Middlefield Rd.
Palo Alto, CA 94301
Ph: (650)321-3055
Fax: (650)321-3785
E-mail: mri@mri.org
URL: http://www.mri.org
Contact: Mary McCusker, Exec. Dir.
Founded: 1959. **Staff:** 30. **Budget:** $350,000. **Languages:** English, French, German, Italian, Spanish. **Description:** Psychiatrists, psychologists, and licensed therapists skilled in the disciplines related to the behavioral sciences. Conducts research, training, and service programs in the field of human behavior, with special emphasis on the family as a social unit. (Research programs are primarily funded by foundation grants and private donations.) Offers short-term residency programs, and short- and long-term workshops on family therapy, brief therapy, communication, and related subjects. Operates family-oriented and brief therapy-oriented sliding scale fee clinic, which also serves as a training and research base. Maintains speakers' bureau. Focuses on longitudinal study of families of alcoholics, youth, violence, bullying, and pain management research programs. **Libraries: Type:** reference. **Holdings:** 1,500; articles, biographical archives, books, periodicals, reports. **Subjects:** human interaction, family and individual psychology, psychiatry, anthropology, behavioral sciences. **Committees:** Clinic; Research; Training. **Conventions/Meetings:** International Symposium.

13447 ■ National Association of Therapeutic Schools and Programs (NATSAP)
126 N Marina
Prescott, AZ 86301
Ph: (928)443-9505
Fax: (928)443-9507
E-mail: info@natsap.org
URL: http://www.natsap.org
Contact: Jan Moss, Exec. Dir.
Founded: 1999. **Membership Dues:** general, $1,100 (annual). **Description:** Provides therapeutic and educational services to children, adolescents and young adults with emotional and behavioral difficulties. Promotes the healthy growth, learning, motivation and personal well-being of therapeutic program participants. **Computer Services:** database, program directory. **Programs:** Emotional Growth School; Home-Based Residential; Outdoor Therapeutic School; Residential Treatment Center; Therapeutic Boarding School; Transitional Independent Living; Wilderness. **Publications:** *National Association of Therapeutic Schools and Programs Directory*, annual, published in April. Contains residential placement alternatives for young people. Alternate Formats: online ● *NATSAP News*. Newsletter. Alternate Formats: online ● Journal. **Price:** $20.00. Alternate Formats: online. **Conventions/Meetings:** annual conference, with paper presentation.

13448 ■ National Institute for Clinical Application of Behavioral Medicine (NICABM)
PO Box 523
Mansfield Center, CT 06250
Ph: (860)456-1153
Free: (800)743-2226
Fax: (860)423-4512
E-mail: information@nicabm.com
URL: http://www.nicabm.com
Contact: Ruth M. Buczynski PhD, Pres.
Founded: 1987. **Description:** Works to provide information to behavioral health professionals. Conducts educational programs. **Telecommunication Services:** electronic mail, audiostore@nicabm. com ● electronic mail, discussion@nicabm.com. **Publications:** Newsletter, quarterly ● Audiotapes. **Conventions/Meetings:** annual Psychology of Health Immunity and Disease - conference, clinical application of PNI and the mind/body connection.

13449 ■ Society of Behavioral Medicine (SBM)
555 E Wells St., Ste.1100
Milwaukee, WI 53202-3823
Ph: (414)918-3156
Fax: (414)276-3349
E-mail: info@sbm.org
URL: http://www.sbm.org
Contact: Ms. Tara Withington, Exec. Dir.
Founded: 1978. **Members:** 2,300. **Membership Dues:** full/associate, $190 (annual) ● transitional/ retired, $150 (annual) ● student/trainee, $80 (annual). **Staff:** 4. **Budget:** $400,000. **Description:** Behavioral and biomedical researchers and clinicians studying health promotion and disease prevention, with primary focus on the interactions between health and behavior. Seeks to function as a forum for the exchange of ideas and information between health care providers and basic scientists and medical researchers. Gathers and disseminates information to members and the public; conducts educational programs for health care professionals; works to integrate behavioral and biomedical research. **Awards:** Distinguished Scientist Award. **Frequency:** annual. **Type:** monetary. **Recipient:** for individuals who have achieved great scholarly distinction ● Early Career Investigator Award. **Frequency:** annual. **Type:** monetary. **Recipient:** for career achievement and review of a representative published paper ● Outstanding Dissertation Award. **Frequency:** annual. **Type:** monetary. **Recipient:** for student members of the society who have successfully defended his/her dissertation over the past year ● SBM Distinguished Mentor Award. **Frequency:** annual. **Type:** monetary. **Recipient:** for outstanding service as a mentor, in the clinical/professional arena for the clinical mentor award, and in research endeavors for the research mentor award. **Publications:** *Annals of Behavioral Medicine*, quarterly. Journal. Features comprehensive area reviews of topics affecting biobehavioral research and practice; also contains abstracts of recent articles in the field. **Price:** included in membership dues; $145.00 for nonmembers in U.S.; $175.00 for

nonmembers outside U.S. ISSN: 0883-6612. **Circulation:** 3,200. Alternate Formats: online ● *Annual Meeting Proceedings.* Serves as a supplement to *Annals of Behavioral Medicine.* ● *Education and Training Directory.* Alternate Formats: online ● *SBM Outlook,* 3/year. Newsletter. **Advertising:** accepted. Alternate Formats: online ● Membership Directory, biennial. Alternate Formats: online. **Conventions/Meetings:** annual meeting (exhibits) - always spring. 2008 Mar. 26-29, San Diego, CA.

13450 ■ Society for Behavioral Neuroendocrinology (SBN)
c/o Geert De Vries, Pres.
Univ. of Massachusetts
Center for Neuroendocrine Stud.
Amherst, MA 01003-7720
E-mail: gjd@cns.umass.edu
URL: http://www.sbn.org
Contact: Geert De Vries, Pres.
Membership Dues: regular, emeritus, associate, $50 (annual) ● student, $25 (annual). **Description:** Promotes the field of neuroendocrinology. **Computer Services:** Mailing lists, of members. **Committees:** Awards; Education; Program. **Publications:** *Hormones and Behavior.* Journal. **Price:** included in membership dues (electronic version); $78.00 paper version; $53.00 paper version for student members. Alternate Formats: online. **Conventions/Meetings:** annual meeting.

13451 ■ Society for the Study of Ingestive Behavior (SSIB)
c/o Marianne Van Wagner, Exec. Coor.
8181 Tezel Rd., No. 10269
San Antonio, TX 78250
Ph: (830)796-9393
Free: (866)377-4416
Fax: (830)796-9394
E-mail: ssib@ssib.org
URL: http://www.ssib.org
Contact: Hans-Rudolf Berthoud PhD, Pres.
Membership Dues: regular, $65 (annual) ● student, $10 (annual). **Description:** Advances the scientific research on food and fluid intake and its associated biological, psychological and social processes. Provides a multi-disciplinary environment for the free exchange of ideas and information. Serves as a resource for scientific expertise and education on topics related to the study of ingestive behavior. **Awards:** Alan N. Epstein Research Award. **Frequency:** annual. **Type:** monetary. **Recipient:** for research related to ingestive behavior ● Distinguished Career Award. **Frequency:** annual. **Type:** monetary. **Recipient:** for contributions to the understanding of ingestive behavior. **Committees:** Animal Care; Intersociety Relations; Long Range Planning; New Investigator; Nominations; Program; Publications; Special Appointments. **Publications:** *Intake,* semiannual. Newsletter. Alternate Formats: online.

13452 ■ United States of America Transactional Analysis Association (USATAA)
4810 Sutcliff Ave.
San Jose, CA 95118-2341
Ph: (408)723-8231
Fax: (408)723-8235
E-mail: info@usataa.org
URL: http://www.usataa.org
Contact: Dianne Maki, Gen. Coor.
Membership Dues: general, $35 (annual). **Regional Groups:** 6. **Description:** Utilizes transactional analysis in organizational, educational, and clinical settings and for personal growth. Creates options for problem solving, healing, and living well. **Computer Services:** database, professional listings ● information services, transactional analysis perspective. **Affiliated With:** International Transactional Analysis Association. **Publications:** Newsletter. Alternate Formats: online. **Conventions/Meetings:** annual conference, with speakers; paper presentations.

Behavioral Sciences

13453 ■ American Association of Behavioral Therapists (BT)
PO Box 1737
Ormond Beach, FL 32175-1737
Ph: (386)767-4060
Fax: (386)767-4060
E-mail: dallen50@aol.com
URL: http://www.btherapy.org
Contact: Dan J. Allen PhD, Contact
Founded: 1987. **Members:** 1,156. **Budget:** $25,000. **Description:** Professionals from the fields of mental health counseling, marriage/family counseling, biofeedback therapy, hypnotherapy, medicine, psychology, pastoral counseling, alcohol/drug counseling, and others disciplined and experienced in the use of the behavioral sciences. Promotes the profession and role of the behavioral therapist. Encourages the sharing of ideas and information among the various disciplines of behavioral therapists. Reports on skill improvements, member articles, new research, business improvements, and skills to help market a successful practice. Maintains national registry of members for referrals. **Publications:** *National Directory of Behavioral Therapists,* annual ● *Special Reports* ● *The Therapist Report,* quarterly. Newsletter. Provides information on therapy techniques, career opportunities, research, and skills updates. **Price:** included in membership dues. **Circulation:** 1,156.

Behcet's Syndrome

13454 ■ American Behcet's Disease Association (ABDA)
PO Box 19952
Amarillo, TX 79114-9952
Free: (800)7BEHCETS
Fax: (480)247-5377
E-mail: cfornabio@behcets.com
URL: http://www.behcets.com
Contact: Catherine Fornabaio, Pres./Dir. of Fundraising
Founded: 1986. **Members:** 1,000. **Membership Dues:** individual, $35 (annual) ● sustaining, $50 (annual) ● sponsoring, $75 (annual) ● patron, $100 (annual) ● life, $2,000. **Budget:** $40,000. **Local Groups:** 25. **Languages:** English, Spanish. **Description:** Gathers statistics on people with Behcet's syndrome; educates the public and medical community about the disease. (Behcet's syndrome is characterized by painful oral ulcers which often resolve spontaneously, but recur at unpredictable intervals. Other symptoms include recurring genital lesions, skin lesions, blurred vision, pain and redness of the eyes, and nervous system abnormalities. The disease is most common among young adults, and methods of treatment are varied and controversial.) Conducts educational programs; maintains speakers' bureau. **Boards:** Medical Advisory. **Formerly:** (1995) American Behcet's Association. **Supersedes:** American Behcet's Foundation. **Publications:** *ABDA Flame,* biennial. Newsletter. Contains news on research projects, treatments, patients, and organizational activities. **Price:** $35.00. **Circulation:** 1,000 ● *Basic Information on Behcet's Disease.* Brochure. Contains pain-free way to educate family, friends, partners or healthcare providers on the basic of Behcet's. **Price:** $5.00 ● *Behcet's Disease.* Book. **Price:** $35.00 ● *Behcet's Disease: A Contemporary Synopsis.* Book. Contains comprehensive and concise information about Behcet's. **Price:** $33.00 ● *Behcet's Disease and Your Eyes.* Brochure ● *Behcet's Disease and Your Nervous System.* Brochure ● *Behcet's Disease: What You Should Know.* Brochure ● *Only Hope.* Brochure ● *You are not alone: 15 People with Behcet's.* Book. **Price:** $18.00. **Conventions/Meetings:** biennial Patient/Family Conference.

Beverages

13455 ■ Caffeine Awareness Alliance (CAA)
32 Saddleview Dr.
Royersford, PA 19468
E-mail: info@caffeineawareness.org
URL: http://www.caffeineawareness.org
Contact: Marina Kushner, Founder
Founded: 2003. **Description:** Raises public awareness of caffeine intoxication through education and advocacy. Supports research focusing on caffeine. Works with policy makers on federal, state and local initiatives. **Computer Services:** Information services, facts about caffeine.

Biochemistry

13456 ■ National Academy of Clinical Biochemistry (NACB)
2101 L St. NW, Ste.202
Washington, DC 20037
Ph: (202)857-0717
Fax: (202)887-5093
URL: http://www.nacb.org
Contact: Catherine A. Hammett-Stabler, Pres.
Founded: 1976. **Membership Dues:** individual, $60 (annual). **Description:** Strives to advance the science and practice of clinical laboratory medicine through research, education, and professional development. **Awards:** Fellowships, **Type:** grant ● George Grannis Award for Excellence in Research and Scientific Publication. **Frequency:** annual. **Type:** monetary. **Recipient:** for a young investigator who has demonstrated excellence in research and scientific publication ● NACB Distinguished Scientist Award. **Frequency:** annual. **Type:** monetary. **Recipient:** for an individual who has demonstrated significant research in the field of clinical biochemistry ● Professor Alvin Dubin Award. **Frequency:** annual. **Type:** monetary. **Recipient:** for a current or past member of the Academy who has made noteworthy contributions to NACB. **Committees:** Awards; By-laws; Education and Scientific Affairs; Fundraising; Liaisons to Other Organizations; Membership; Nominating; Publications. **Publications:** *Laboratory Medicine Practice Guidelines.* Monograph. **Price:** $20.00/copy ● *News & Views.* Newsletter. Alternate Formats: online ● Monographs. **Price:** $20.00/copy. **Conventions/Meetings:** annual meeting ● workshop.

Biofeedback

13457 ■ Association for Applied Psychophysiology and Biofeedback (AAPB)
10200 W 44th Ave., Ste.304
Wheat Ridge, CO 80033
Ph: (303)422-8436
Free: (800)477-8892
Fax: (303)422-8894
E-mail: aapb@resourcenter.com
URL: http://www.aapb.org
Contact: Francine Butler PhD, Exec. Dir.
Founded: 1969. **Members:** 2,000. **Membership Dues:** individual, associate, $165 (annual) ● corporate, $630 (annual) ● student, $55 (annual) ● friend, $315 (annual) ● supporting, $500 (annual) ● corresponding, $63 (annual). **Staff:** 3. **Budget:** $500,000. **State Groups:** 35. **Description:** Persons interested in the "interrelationship of external feedback systems, states of consciousness, and the physiological mechanisms involved." Promotes rapid interchange of ideas and information among members. Offers Continuing Education Training Programs. Maintains numerous committees. **Awards:** AAPB Foundation Award. **Type:** recognition ● Distinguished Scientist Award. **Type:** recognition ● Mary Brazier Scholarship. **Type:** monetary ● Student Travel Scholarship. **Type:** monetary. **Formerly:** (1976) Biofeedback Research Society; (1988) Biofeedback Society of America. **Publications:** *Applied Psychophysiology and Biofeedback,* quarterly. Journal. Contains conceptual and theoretical articles and evaluative reviews. **Price:** included in membership dues. **Circulation:** 2,000. **Advertising:** accepted. Alternate Formats: online. Also Cited As: *Biofeedback and Self-Regulation* ● *Biofeedback News* magazine, quarterly. Newsletter. **Price:** included in membership dues. ISSN: 1081-5937. **Circulation:** 2,100. Alternate Formats: online. **Conventions/Meetings:** annual conference and meeting (exhibits) - always March or April.

13458 ■ Biofeedback Certification Institute of America (BCIA)
10200 W 44th Ave., Ste.310
Wheat Ridge, CO 80033-2840
Ph: (303)420-2902
Fax: (303)422-8894
E-mail: bcia@resourcenter.com
URL: http://www.bcia.org
Contact: Ms. Judy Crawford, Dir. of Certification
Founded: 1981. **Description:** Aims to establish and maintain professional standards for the provision of biofeedback services and to certify those who meet the standards. **Programs:** EEG Biofeedback Certification; General Biofeedback Certification; Pelvic Muscle Dysfunction Biofeedback.

Birth Defects

13459 ■ Birth Defect Research for Children (BDRC)
800 Celebration Ave., Ste.225
Celebration, FL 34747
Ph: (407)566-8304
E-mail: staff@birthdefects.org
URL: http://www.birthdefects.org
Contact: Betty Mekdeci, Exec. Dir.
Founded: 1982. **Staff:** 3. **Budget:** $150,000. **Description:** Provides information about specific birth defects, its causes and treatment to parents and expectant parents, support group referrals and parent matching services. Also provides information about environmental exposures that may be associated with birth defects; to study these exposures further, sponsors the National Birth Defect Registry, a research project that collects data on all kinds of birth defects and prenatal/preconceptual exposures of mothers and fathers. **Libraries: Type:** not open to the public. **Subjects:** birth defects. **Computer Services:** database, National Birth Defect Registry and Parent Matching. **Projects:** National Birth Defect Registry; Parent Matching. **Formerly:** (1982) Association of Benedictin Children; (2000) Association of Birth Defect Children. **Publications:** *Birth Defect Fact Sheets.* Offers diagnosis, treatment, and support group information. ● *Birth Defects News*, monthly. Newsletter. Includes parent-to-parent column and a birth defects registry. **Price:** free. **Circulation:** 10,000. **Advertising:** accepted. Alternate Formats: online ● *Special Reports.* Reports on important environmental birth defect issues. Alternate Formats: online ● *Why My Child?*. Videos.

13460 ■ CHERUBS - Association of Congenital Diaphragmatic Hernia Research, Advocacy and Support
270 Coley Rd.
Henderson, NC 27537
Ph: (252)492-9066 (252)492-6003
Free: (866)603-1944
Fax: (815)425-9155
E-mail: info@cherubs-cdh.org
URL: http://www.cherubs-cdh.org
Contact: Dawn M. Torrence, Founder/Pres.
Founded: 1995. **Members:** 650. **State Groups:** 50. **National Groups:** 27. **Multinational. Description:** Parents, grandparents, foster parents, pediatric surgeons, genetic counselors, pediatricians, nurses, ECMO directors, respiratory therapists, and epidemiologists. Helps families of children born with Congenital Diaphragmatic Hernia (CDH); promotes research into possible causes and better treatments. **Publications:** *Silver Lining*, quarterly. Newsletter. Contains stories of cherubs and medical information. **Price:** $20.00/year. Alternate Formats: online.

13461 ■ Cornelia de Lange Syndrome Foundation (CdLSF)
302 W Main St., No. 100
Avon, CT 06001
Ph: (860)676-8166 (860)676-8255
Free: (800)223-8355
Fax: (860)676-8337
E-mail: info@cdlsusa.org
URL: http://www.cdlsusa.org
Contact: Julie Mairano, Exec. Dir.
Founded: 1977. **Members:** 5,000. **Membership Dues:** family, professional, $25 (annual). **Staff:** 9. **Budget:** $300,000. **Description:** Seeks to ensure early and accurate diagnosis of the syndrome and to enable families, friends, and professionals to make informed decisions and plans for the affected person. Provides updates on the medical aspects of CdLS and responds to correspondences and members' inquiries on an individual basis. Supports research programs. **Libraries: Type:** not open to the public. **Holdings:** 94; articles. **Subjects:** behavior, dental, education, emotional, eyes, ears, GI, genetics, growth and development, siblings, information update, speech and language, puberty, special interest. **Telecommunication Services:** electronic mail, director@cdlsusa.org. **Formerly:** (1981) Cornelia de Lange Parents Group. **Publications:** *CdLS Foundation - Album*, periodic. Yearbook. Lists families and professionals interested in providing mutual support. **Price:** $25.00. **Circulation:** 5,000 ● *Facing the Challenges: A Parent's Guide to CdLS.* Book ● *Facts about Cornelia de Lange Syndrome.* Pamphlet ● *Reaching Out*, bimonthly. Newsletter. Provides articles of general interest dealing with the complexities of raising a handicapped child. Includes medical column. **Circulation:** 5,000 ● Videos. **Conventions/Meetings:** annual international conference (exhibits) ● annual meeting.

13462 ■ Klippel-Trenaunay Support Group (KTSG)
5404 Dundee Rd.
Edina, MN 55436
Ph: (952)925-2596 (623)975-6902
Fax: (612)925-4708
E-mail: ktnewmembers@gmail.com
URL: http://www.k-t.org
Contact: Judy Vessey, Dir.
Founded: 1986. **Members:** 600. **Languages:** English, Spanish. **Description:** Support group for individuals affected by Klippel-Trenaunay Syndrome and their families. (Klippel-Trenaunay Syndrome is a congenital malformation of the extremities and is characterized by birth marks the color of port wine, excessive growth of the soft tissue and bone, and varicose veins. The cause is presently unknown but believed to be either genetic or the result of an intrauterine insult occurring between the third and sixth week of gestation.) Acts as a clearinghouse of information and correspondence between members. **Libraries: Type:** reference. **Subjects:** medical literature pertaining to Klippel-Trenaunay Syndrome. **Also Known As:** K-T Support Group. **Publications:** *KLIPnotes—K-T Newsletter*, quarterly. Annual Reports. **Conventions/Meetings:** biennial conference.

13463 ■ March of Dimes Birth Defects Foundation (MDBDF)
1275 Mamaroneck Ave.
White Plains, NY 10605
Ph: (914)997-4488
E-mail: newsletter@marchofdimes.com
URL: http://www.marchofdimes.com
Contact: Dr. Jennifer L. Howse, Pres.
Founded: 1938. **Regional Groups:** 3. **State Groups:** 54. **Languages:** English, Spanish. **Description:** Founded by President Franklin D. Roosevelt as the National Foundation for Infantile Paralysis. Promotes prevention of birth defects by focusing on maternal and child health issues including low birthweight, infant mortality, prenatal care, and maternal substance abuse. Offers public and professional health education and community service programs to improve maternal and newborn health. Works with other national and local organizations to initiate and implement community programs of prenatal care education and service. Operates the Pregnancy and Newborn Health Education Center which provides information on pregnancy, birth defects, genetic disorders and related topics. Develops and distributes educational materials for health professionals and the public. **Libraries: Type:** not open to the public. **Awards: Type:** grant. **Recipient:** to hospitals and universities for clinical research ● **Type:** grant. **Recipient:** for professionals concerned with prevention of birth defects ● **Type:** grant. **Recipient:** for improved perinatal and genetic services ● **Type:** monetary. **Recipient:** for promising young scientists and medical students. **Formerly:** (1958) National Foundation for Infantile Paralysis; (1979) National Foundation - March of Dimes. **Publications:** *Miracles*, monthly. Newsletter. Alternate Formats: online. **Conventions/Meetings:** periodic conference ● symposium.

13464 ■ National Birth Defects Prevention Network (NBDPN)
c/o Prof. Lowell E. Sever, PhD
Convener, Intl. & Family Hea.
Univ. of Texas School of Public Hea.
1200 Herman Pressler, Ste.E1023
Houston, TX 77030
Ph: (404)498-3918 (770)488-3550
Fax: (713)599-9406
E-mail: cmai@cdc.gov
URL: http://www.nbdpn.org
Contact: Cara Mai, Contact
Description: Committed to the prevention of birth defects in the U.S. **Computer Services:** database, surveillance listserv. **Committees:** Annual Meeting; Data; Education & Outreach; Publications & Communications. **Publications:** *Congenital Malformations Surveillance Report* ● *Folic Acid Surveys* ● *HIPAA Awareness for Birth Defect Surveillance Systems.* Journal ● Newsletters, semiannual. **Conventions/Meetings:** annual meeting.

13465 ■ Organization of Teratology Information Services (OTIS)
Univ. of Arizona
Drachman Hall
PO Box 210202
Tucson, AZ 85721-0202
Ph: (520)626-3547
Free: (866)626-6847
E-mail: otispregnancy@pharmacy.arizona.edu
URL: http://www.otispregnancy.org
Contact: Sharon Voyer Lavigne, Pres.
Founded: 1990. **Members:** 70. **Membership Dues:** individual (non-voting), $75 (annual) ● individual (voting), $100 (annual). **State Groups:** 23. **Description:** Provides information on teratology; teratology is the study of agents used during pregnancy and their potential effects on the developing baby. **Projects:** Accutane and Pregnancy; Asthma Medications and Pregnancy; Autoimmune Diseases in Pregnancy. **Publications:** *Fact Sheets*, annual. Report. Alternate Formats: online ● Annual Report, annual. Alternate Formats: online. **Conventions/Meetings:** annual Educational Conference - always April or June.

13466 ■ Rubinstein-Taybi Parent Group U.S.A. (RTSPG)
c/o Ms. Lorrie Baxter, Coor.
PO Box 146
Smith Center, KS 66967
Ph: (785)697-2989
Free: (888)447-2989
E-mail: lbaxter@ruraltel.net
URL: http://www.rubinstein-taybi.org
Contact: Ms. Lorrie Baxter, Coor.
Founded: 1984. **Members:** 425. **Description:** Families with children diagnosed with Rubinstein-Taybi Syndrome. Provides information and support. **Computer Services:** Mailing lists, of members. **Special Interest Groups:** Special Friends Foundation. **Also Known As:** RTS Parent Group U.S.A. **Publications:** *Rubinstein-Taybi Syndrome.* Brochure. **Conventions/Meetings:** quinquennial International Family Conference-Rubinstein-Taybi Syndrome (exhibits).

Blind

13467 ■ Sea to See Project
Sixty Mt. Vernon St.
Boston, MA 02108

E-mail: tom@seatosee.org
URL: http://www.seatosee.org
Contact: Thomas J. Livelli Jr., Pres./CEO
Founded: 2001. **Description:** Works to prevent and correct blindness in children so that they may lead independent and productive lives. Provides eye screening, vision rehabilitation, education and advocacy for children who are blind or have severely impaired vision. Teaches basic eye care and hygiene to children and funds eye screening and rehabilitation programs. Fosters an awareness of blindness as an avoidable and curable affliction.

Blood

13468 ■ American Association of Blood Banks (AABB)
8101 Glenbrook Rd.
Bethesda, MD 20814-2749
Ph: (301)907-6977
Fax: (301)907-6895
E-mail: aabb@aabb.org
URL: http://www.aabb.org
Contact: Jennifer Garfinkel, Public Relations Dir.
Founded: 1947. **Members:** 11,500. **Membership Dues:** physician, $218 (annual) ● healthcare professional, physician in residency, $108 (annual) ● institutional, $950 (annual) ● affiliate, $1,000 (annual) ● corporate affiliate, $1,700 (annual). **Staff:** 70. **Budget:** $14,000,000. **Description:** Represents an international association of blood banks, including hospital and community blood centers, transfusion and transplantation medicine. Supports activities related to transfusion and transplantation medicine. Supports high standards of medical, technical, and administrative performance, scientific investigation, clinical application and education. Encourages the voluntary donation of blood and other tissues and organs through education, public information and research. Member facilities are responsible for collecting virtually all of the nation's blood supply and transfusing more than 80 percent. **Computer Services:** database ● mailing lists ● online services. **Publications:** *AABB News*, 11/year. Magazine. Includes calendar of events, employment listings, and government affairs update. **Price:** included in membership dues. ISSN: 8756-6095. **Circulation:** 11,500. **Advertising:** accepted. Alternate Formats: online ● *AABB Weekly Report*. Newsletter. Covers scientific, legislative, and regulatory events affecting blood banking and transfusion medicine. **Price:** $179.00 /year for members; $299.00 /year for nonmembers. ISSN: 0747-2420. **Circulation:** 1,400 ● *American Association of Blood Banks—Membership Directory*, biennial. Lists institutional and individual members in alphabetical and geographic order. **Price:** included in membership dues. Alternate Formats: online ● *Directory of Community Blood Centers*, biennial. **Price:** $70.00 for participating members; $90.00 for nonmembers. **Circulation:** 1,000 ● *Regulatory Update*. Newsletter. **Price:** $178.00 for members; $278.00 for nonmembers ● *Standards for Blood Banks and Transfusion Services*, every 18 months. **Price:** $85.00 for members; $123.00 for nonmembers. **Circulation:** 35,000 ● *Technical Manual*, triennial. **Price:** $114.00 for members; $179.00 for nonmembers; $99.00 for students. **Circulation:** 35,000 ● *Transfusion*, monthly. Journal. Presents scientific, technical, and administrative papers relating to the field of blood banking. Includes advertisers' index and convention abstract. **Price:** $210.00 /year for members; $378.00 /year for nonmembers. ISSN: 0041-1132. **Circulation:** 12,800. **Advertising:** accepted. Alternate Formats: online ● Books ● Monographs ● Annual Report, annual. Alternate Formats: online. **Conventions/Meetings:** annual meeting and symposium (exhibits) ● annual meeting (exhibits) - 2007 Oct. 20-23, Anaheim, CA; 2008 Oct. 4-7, Montreal, QC, Canada.

13469 ■ America's Blood Centers (ABC)
725 15th St. NW, Ste.700
Washington, DC 20005
Ph: (202)393-5725
Free: (888)USB-LOOD

Fax: (202)393-1282
E-mail: abc@americasblood.org
URL: http://www.americasblood.org
Contact: Donald Doddridge, Pres.
Founded: 1962. **Members:** 75. **Staff:** 17. **Budget:** $2,800,000. **Description:** Federally licensed blood centers serving defined geographic areas that collectively provide about half of the nation's volunteer donor blood supply. Ensures an optimal supply of blood, blood components, and blood derivatives and the development of a comprehensive range of the highest quality blood services to meet the needs of the American people. Compiles data and statistics; conducts research concerning organizational, administrative, fiscal, and operational phases of blood banking; establishes liaison and conducts cooperative activities of all kinds with national, regional, and local associations, groups, and organizations having a relationship of any kind to the drawing, processing, storing, or distribution of blood. **Committees:** Donor Resources; Group Services; Scientific, Medical, and Technical. **Formerly:** (1971) Community Blood Bank Council; (1998) Council of Community Blood Centers. **Publications:** *ABC Blood Bulletin*, quarterly. Journal. Contains issues in blood banking. Alternate Formats: online ● *ABC Brochure*. Alternate Formats: online ● *ABC Membership Directory*, semiannual ● *ABC Newsletter*, weekly. Includes calendar of events and list of employment opportunities. **Price:** free for members; $492.00 /year for nonmembers, in North America; $588.00 /year for nonmembers, outside North America; $348.00 /year for nonmembers, email. **Circulation:** 1,000. **Advertising:** accepted ● *Blood Counts*, periodic. Reports. Contains reports on financial and operational topics affecting the nonprofit blood center community. Alternate Formats: online ● Annual Report, annual. Alternate Formats: online ● Papers. Alternate Formats: online. **Conventions/Meetings:** annual conference and symposium - February.

13470 ■ Cord Blood Donor Foundation (CBDF)
1200 Bayhill Dr., Ste.301
San Bruno, CA 94066
Ph: (650)635-1452
Fax: (650)635-1428
E-mail: information@cordblooddonor.org
URL: http://www.cordblooddonor.org
Contact: Gloria J. Ochoa, Pres./Exec. Dir.
Description: Promotes education awareness and further research in the use of cord blood stem cells. (Cord blood is blood that remains in the umbilical cord and placenta following birth. Cord blood stem cells are used to treat life-threatening diseases including leukemia, other cancers, and blood and immune disorders).

13471 ■ International Society of Radiolabeled Blood Elements (ISORBE)
c/o Prof. Christopher J. Palestro, Pres.
Chief Division of Nuclear Medicine
Long Island Jewish Medical Center
270-05 76th Ave.
New Hyde Park, NY 11040
E-mail: palestro@lij.edu
Contact: Prof. Christopher J. Palestro, Pres.
Founded: 1990. **Members:** 201. **Membership Dues:** regular, $50 (annual) ● student, $20 (annual). **Staff:** 1. **State Groups:** 28. **Multinational**. **Description:** Scientists working in the field of labeled blood cells. Seeks to promote the study of radio-labeled blood elements. Protects archives and promotes standardization. **Libraries: Type:** reference. **Holdings:** articles, audiovisuals, books, periodicals. **Subjects:** inflammation, infection, atherosclerosis, use of any labeled blood elements. **Awards:** ISORBE Young Investigator. **Frequency:** annual. **Type:** monetary. **Recipient:** for young investigator aged 35 years or younger for his/her innovative, unpublished year-long research project.

13472 ■ National Blood Foundation (NBF)
8101 Glenbrook Rd.
Bethesda, MD 20814-2749
Ph: (301)215-6552 (301)215-6575

Fax: (301)907-6895
E-mail: nbf@aabb.org
URL: http://www.aabb.org/content/programs_and_services/national_blood_foundation
Contact: Marc Pearce, Division Dir.
Founded: 1983. **Staff:** 3. **Description:** Promotes the safety and adequacy of America's blood supply by supporting research and education for blood banking and transfusion medicine. **Awards:** Scientific Research Grants Program. **Frequency:** annual. **Type:** grant. **Recipient:** to new investigators and innovative projects with the potential to have a practical impact on patients and donors in transfusion medicine. **Telecommunication Services:** electronic mail, marc_p@aabb.org. **Conventions/Meetings:** annual Leadership Forum - meeting.

13473 ■ Plasma Protein Therapeutics Association (PPTA)
147 Old Solomons Island Rd., Ste.100
Annapolis, MD 21401
Ph: (410)263-8296
Fax: (410)263-2298
E-mail: ppta@pptaglobal.org
URL: http://www.pptaglobal.org
Contact: Jan M. Bult, Pres.
Founded: 1992. **Members:** 6. **Staff:** 33. **Description:** Works for consensus development of industry-wide initiatives and primary advocate for the world's leading producers of plasma-based and recombinant analog therapeutics. **Programs:** International Quality Plasma; Quality Standards of Excellence Assurance and Leadership. **Absorbed:** (2002) American Blood Resources Association. **Publications:** *The Source*. Magazine. Alternate Formats: online.

13474 ■ USBloodDonors.org
c/o Pat Boone Foundation
9220 Sunset Blvd., Ste.310
Los Angeles, CA 90069
E-mail: admin@usblooddonors.org
URL: http://usblooddonors.org
Contact: Tammie Reber, Contact
Description: Establishes and maintains national register so blood, organ, tissue and other life-giving services can be donated. **Telecommunication Services:** electronic mail, feedback@usblooddonors.org.

Body Therapy

13475 ■ Society of Ortho-Bionomy International
5335 N Tacoma St., Ste.21G
Indianapolis, IN 46220
Ph: (317)536-0064
Free: (800)809-3747
Fax: (317)536-0065
E-mail: office@ortho-bionomy.org
URL: http://www.ortho-bionomy.org
Contact: Ms. Danyell Wiley, Office Admin.
Founded: 1985. **Members:** 600. **Membership Dues:** student, $55 (annual) ● associate, $85 (annual) ● practitioner, $135 (annual). **Staff:** 3. **Multinational**. **Description:** Promotes the practice, advancement and evolvement of Ortho-Bionomy, a gentle and effective form of bodywork that works with the patterns in the body to alleviate pain and stress. Fosters awareness of Ortho-Bionomy. Provides professional services and support for society members. Encourages the creative expression of Ortho-Bionomy as an art. **Computer Services:** Information services, ortho-bionomy resources. **Programs:** Registered Advanced Practitioner; Registered Basic Practitioner. **Publications:** *Ortho-Bionomy News*, quarterly. Newsletter. **Price:** $25.00 /year for nonmembers. **Advertising:** accepted. **Conventions/Meetings:** annual conference.

Bone

13476 ■ American Bone Marrow Donor Registry (ABMDR)
PO Box 8841
Mandeville, LA 70470-8841

Ph: (985)626-1749
Free: (800)745-2452
Fax: (985)626-7414
E-mail: jakabmdr@bellsouth.net
URL: http://www.abmdr.org
Contact: Joan Keller MT, Headquarters Dir.
Founded: 1984. **Members:** 60,000. **Staff:** 7. **Description:** Educates, tests, enrolls potential marrow donors for matching against patients who are viable candidates for marrow transplant; enrolls donors as individuals or at scheduled marrow donor drives; supports donors throughout marrow donation process; maintains ethnically diverse donor panel; conducts searches requested by physicians or transplant centers for patients in need of marrow transplant; strives to contain costs to patients; serves as resource center for patient. **Libraries: Type:** reference. **Holdings:** video recordings. **Divisions:** Marrow Donor Services; Patient Advocacy. **Also Known As:** (2005) Bone Marrow Donor Registry-American.

13477 ■ Bone Marrow Foundation (BMF)
337 E 88th St., Ste.1B
New York, NY 10128
Ph: (212)838-3029
Free: (800)365-1336
E-mail: info@bonemarrow.org
URL: http://www.bonemarrow.org
Contact: Christina Merrill, Exec. Dir.
Founded: 1992. **Staff:** 4. **Description:** Works to improve quality of life for bone marrow and stem cell transplant patients and their families through financial aid, education, and emotional support. **Awards:** Patient Aid. **Type:** monetary.

13478 ■ Caitlin Raymond International Registry (CRIR)
UMass Memorial Medical Center
55 Lake Ave. N
Worcester, MA 01655
Ph: (508)334-8969
Free: (800)726-2824
Fax: (508)334-8972
E-mail: info@crir.org
URL: http://www.crir.org
Contact: Joanne Raymond, Exec. Dir.
Founded: 1986. **Multinational. Description:** Serves as a comprehensive resource for patients and physicians conducting a search for unrelated bone marrow or cord blood donor.

13479 ■ Center for International Blood and Marrow Transplant Research (CIBMTR)
Hea. Policy Inst.
Medical Coll. of Wisconsin
PO Box 26509
Milwaukee, WI 53226
Ph: (414)456-8325
Fax: (414)456-6530
E-mail: cibmtr-contact@nmdp.org
URL: http://www.cibmtr.org
Contact: Jeffrey W. Chell MD, Exec. Dir.
Founded: 1972. **Members:** 400. **Staff:** 50. **Description:** Voluntary organizations of basic and clinical scientists. Works to address important issues in blood and marrow transplantation. Gathers information on results of blood and marrow transplants. Uses information to guide clinical decisions and identify the most effective treatment strategies for individual patients based on a number of variables including age, disease type and stage, prior treatment, etc. **Formerly:** (2005) International Bone Marrow Transplant Registry. **Publications:** *CIBMTR Newsletter*, semiannual. Alternate Formats: online. **Conventions/Meetings:** annual meeting.

Breast Diseases

13480 ■ American Society of Breast Disease (ASBD)
PO Box 140186
Dallas, TX 75214
Ph: (214)368-6836
Fax: (214)368-5719

E-mail: info@asbd.org
URL: http://www.asbd.org
Contact: Brooke Breslow, Exec. Dir.
Founded: 1976. **Members:** 1,100. **Membership Dues:** individual professional, $195 (annual) ● allied health professional, $100 (annual). **Staff:** 2. **Multinational. Description:** Advocates an interdisciplinary team approach to breast health management and promotes breast disease prevention, early detection, treatment and research. Provides a forum among professionals for sharing current information on breast disease; presents understandable, timely and authoritative information regarding breast health to the general public; offers training and professional development programs; supports a national breast disease research agenda; and creates a community for healthcare professionals committed to a multidisciplinary team approach to breast health management. **Computer Services:** database, consensus statements and practice guidelines on breast cancer and disease ● electronic publishing, newsletter and symposium proceedings. **Formerly:** (1994) Society for the Study of Breast Disease. **Publications:** *ASBD Advisor*, quarterly. Newsletter ● *ASBD Membership Directory*, annual. **Price:** $1.00 for nonmembers; free for members ● *Breast Diseases: A Yearbook Quarterly*. **Price:** $1.00 for nonmembers; free for members ● *Breast Healthcare Update*, periodic. Newsletter. **Price:** $1.00 for nonmembers; free for members ● *The Breast Journal*, bimonthly. **Price:** $1.00 for nonmembers; free for members. **Conventions/Meetings:** annual symposium, exhibits and posters (exhibits) - usually April.

13481 ■ National Consortium of Breast Centers (NCBC)
PO Box 1334
Warsaw, IN 46581-1334
Ph: (574)267-8058
Fax: (574)267-8268
E-mail: wiggins@breastcare.org
URL: http://www.breastcare.org
Contact: Deb Wiggins, Exec. Dir.
Founded: 1985. **Membership Dues:** business, medical organization, government facility and individual, $250 (annual) ● associate, $90 (annual) ● independent professional, $195 (annual) ● corporate, $500 (annual). **Description:** Represents breast professionals, breast centers, providers of services to care providers and corporations that supply equipment and pharmaceuticals to care providers. **Additional Websites:** http://www.ncbcinc.org. **Publications:** *Breast Center Bulletin*. Newsletter. **Conventions/Meetings:** annual Multidisciplinary Breast Conference (exhibits).

Breastfeeding

13482 ■ International Board of Lactation Consultant Examiners (IBLCE)
7245 Arlington Blvd., Ste.200
Falls Church, VA 22042-3217
Ph: (703)560-7330
Fax: (703)560-7332
E-mail: iblce@iblce.org
URL: http://www.iblce.org
Contact: Roberta Hewat PhD, Chair
Founded: 1985. **Multinational. Description:** Works as certifying board for lactation consultants; offers exams in eight languages.

13483 ■ International Society for Research in Human Milk and Lactation (ISRHML)
c/o Dr. Frank R. Greer, MD, Sec.-Treas.
Meriter Hosp.
Perinatal Center
202 S Park St.
Madison, WI 53715
Ph: (608)262-6561
Fax: (608)267-6377
E-mail: frgreer@facstaff.wisc.edu
URL: http://www.isrhml.org.umu.se
Contact: Dr. Frank R. Greer MD, Sec.-Treas.
Founded: 1984. **Members:** 260. **Membership Dues:** full, $75 (annual) ● associate, $30 (annual). **Description:** Promotes research and dissemination of findings in the field of human milk and lactation. Establishes liaisons with government agencies, public health authorities, industry, and other organizations; provides listserver for communication of information among members. **Awards:** Ehrlich-Koldovsky Award. **Type:** recognition. **Recipient:** for outstanding young investigators ● Macy-Gyorgy Award. **Type:** recognition. **Recipient:** for outstanding and original scientific contributions to the study of human milk and lactation. **Computer Services:** Mailing lists. **Publications:** *Protecting Infants Through Human Milk*, biennial. Proceedings. Contains conference proceedings. ● Monographs. **Conventions/Meetings:** biennial international conference - 2008 Jan. 31-Feb. 5, Perth, WA, Australia ● annual symposium and meeting - 2008 Apr. 5-9, San Diego, CA.

13484 ■ National Alliance for Breastfeeding Advocacy (NABA)
c/o Marsha Walker, RN, Exec. Dir.
254 Conant Rd.
Weston, MA 02493-1756
E-mail: marsha@naba-breastfeeding.org
URL: http://www.naba-breastfeeding.org
Contact: Marsha Walker RN, Exec. Dir.
Founded: 1995. **Description:** Promotes breastfeeding as a public health issue. Coordinate efforts by organizations, agencies, institutions, and individuals towards the development of strategic plans, policies, and goals for breastfeeding reform. **Publications:** *Abreast of Our Times*, quarterly. Newsletter. **Price:** $30.00 /year for members ● *Action Packet*. **Price:** $20.00 ● *Baby Friendly Hospital Initiative*. **Price:** $35.00 ● *Baby Friendly: The Whole Story*. Film. **Price:** $60.00 ● *Breastfeeding Timeline*. Article. **Price:** free. Alternate Formats: online ● *Growing the Breastfeeding Friendly Community*. Booklet. **Price:** $20.00 ● *Minority Report of the Expert Work Group*. **Price:** $15.00 ● *US Breastfeeding Report Card*. **Price:** free.

Bronchoesophagology

13485 ■ American Broncho-Esophagological Association (ABEA)
c/o Dr. Peter J. Koltai, MD, Sec.
Div. of Pediatric Otolaryngology
Stanford Univ. School of Medicine
801 Welch Rd.
Stanford, CA 94305
E-mail: pkoltai@ohns.stanford.edu
URL: http://www.rothschilddesign.com/abea/website/
index.html
Contact: Dr. Peter J. Koltai MD, Sec.
Founded: 1917. **Members:** 386. **Staff:** 1. **Description:** Professional society of otolaryngologists, chest specialists, thoracic surgeons, and gastroenterologists engaged in the practice of bronchoesophagology (diseases and injuries of the respiratory system and upper digestive tract). Conducts program on study of foreign bodies. **Awards:** Broyles-Maloney Award. **Frequency:** annual. **Type:** monetary. **Recipient:** for outstanding manuscripts, a thesis, or accomplishments in endoscopy, bronchology, esophagology, laryngology, and related science ● Seymour R. Cohen Award for Pediatric Laryngology Broncho-Esophagology. **Frequency:** annual. **Type:** monetary. **Recipient:** for the resident, fellow, or practicing physician who submits the best original paper in either basic research or clinical investigation in pediatric laryngology and bronchoesophagology ● Steven Dean Gray Resident Research Award. **Frequency:** annual. **Type:** monetary. **Recipient:** for the best original paper on research in clinical bronchoesophagology, physiology, or pathology of the larynx, tracheobronchial tree, or esophagus written by a resident or fellow in training. **Committees:** Awards and Thesis; Difficult Airway; Foreign Body and Accidents; International Relations; New Technology; Oncology; Pharyngeal and Esophageal; Research and Education. **Affiliated With:** American Academy of Otolaryngology - Head and Neck Surgery. **Formerly:** (1928) American Bronchoscopic Society. **Pub-**

lications: *Annals of Otology, Rhinology and Laryngology.* Proceedings ● *Transactions,* annual. **Conventions/Meetings:** annual meeting (exhibits).

13486 ■ International Bronchoesophagological Society (IBES)

Mayo Clinic Arizona
13400 E Shea Blvd.
Scottsdale, AZ 85259
Ph: (480)301-8000 (480)301-9692
Fax: (480)301-4869
E-mail: helmers.richard@mayo.edu
Contact: Dr. Richard A. Helmers MD, Exec. Sec.-Treas.

Founded: 1951. **Members:** 600. **Membership Dues:** in U.S., $25 (annual). **Multinational. Description:** Represents endoscopists from varying disciplines. Fosters advances in laryngology, bronchoscopy, upper gastrointestinal endoscopy, diagnostic techniques, and endoscopic therapy. Encourages exchange of ideas; conducts original investigations and research. **Affiliated With:** American Broncho-Esophagological Association; American College of Chest Physicians; American Society for Gastrointestinal Endoscopy. **Conventions/Meetings:** biennial World Congress on Bronchoesophagology (exhibits) ● biennial World Posters Congress of Bronchoesophagology - lecture (exhibits).

Burns

13487 ■ Alisa Ann Ruch Burn Foundation (AARBF)

Southern CA Off.
2501 W Burbank Blvd., Ste.201
Burbank, CA 91505
Ph: (818)848-0223
Free: (800)242-BURN
Fax: (818)848-0269
E-mail: corozco@aarbf.org
URL: http://www.aarbf.org

Founded: 1971. **Description:** Works to enhance the lives of burn survivors. Promotes burn prevention. Coordinates with Fire Departments and Burn Units throughout California. **Awards:** Bridge-To-Life Scholarship. **Type:** scholarship. **Recipient:** for high school graduates who will pursue education at the university. **Computer Services:** Mailing lists. **Telecommunication Services:** information service, survivor assistance line, (800)755-BURN. **Funds:** Bridge-To-Life Scholarship. **Programs:** Back-To-School; Champ Camp; Family Camp; Firefighters in Safety Education; Juvenile Firesetters Intervention Training; Protect Your Child; Young Adult Summit. **Publications:** Newsletter, quarterly. Alternate Formats: online. **Conventions/Meetings:** Adult Survivor Family Camp - workshop ● conference ● Young Adult Summit - meeting.

13488 ■ American Burn Association (ABA)

625 N Michigan Ave., Ste.2550
Chicago, IL 60611
Ph: (312)642-9260
Free: (800)548-2876
Fax: (312)642-9130
E-mail: info@ameriburn.org
URL: http://www.ameriburn.org
Contact: Dr. David Greenhalgh MD, Pres.

Founded: 1967. **Members:** 3,500. **Membership Dues:** physician in U.S. and Canada, $300 (annual) ● resident, nurse, other non-physician in U.S. and Canada, $125 (annual) ● medical/other student in U.S. and Canada, $65 (annual) ● physician outside U.S. and Canada, $320 (annual) ● resident, nurse, other non-physician outside U.S. and Canada, $145 (annual) ● medical/other student outside U.S. and Canada, $85 (annual). **Description:** Physicians, nurses, physical therapists, occupational therapists, dietitians, biomedical engineers, social service workers, and researchers interested in the care of burn injuries. Promotes the improvement of the care and treatment of burns, which includes a program of prevention of burn injuries. Sponsors visiting professorship, education, and awards. **Awards:** Burn

Prevention Award. **Frequency:** annual. **Type:** recognition. **Recipient:** for contributions having worldwide, nationwide, or statewide impact ● Carl A. Moyer Resident Award. **Type:** monetary. **Recipient:** for the best paper submitted by a medical doctor who has not yet completed his/her formal training ● Curtis P. Artz Distinguished Service Award. **Frequency:** annual. **Type:** monetary. **Recipient:** for a nonphysician member of the ABA for his/her outstanding contributions in the burn field ● Education Exchange Program. **Type:** grant. **Recipient:** for OTs, PTs, RNs, and other non-physician individuals to visit another (or other) burn center ● Everett Idris Evans Memorial Lecture Award. **Type:** monetary. **Recipient:** for an outstanding scientist in the burn field outside the U.S. ● Harvey Stuart Allen Distinguished Service Award. **Type:** monetary. **Recipient:** for an outstanding U.S. scientist for his/her contributions in the burn field ● International Association of Fire Fighters Burn Foundation Research Grant. **Type:** grant. **Recipient:** for burn-injury related research ● President's Continuing Education Grant. **Frequency:** annual. **Type:** grant. **Recipient:** for an ABA member other than a physician who has made significant contributions to the care of burned patients ● Robert A. Lindberg Award. **Type:** monetary. **Recipient:** for the best scientific paper submitted by a non-physician ● Traveling Fellowship Award. **Frequency:** annual. **Type:** fellowship. **Recipient:** for a physician or postdoctoral fellow who has given evidence of a continuing interest and productivity in the field of burn care, teaching, and/or research ● Visiting Professor Program. **Type:** monetary. **Recipient:** for a physician, educator, or specialist to visit a specified school, hospital, or community and present his/her expertise in the burn field. **Computer Services:** Mailing lists, of members. **Committees:** ABLS Advisory; Archives; Audit; Awards; Burn Prevention; Burn Registry; Education; Ethical Issues; Exhibitor Advisory; Federal Issues; Government Affairs; Membership Advisory; Organization and Delivery of Burn Care; Program; Regionalization; Rehabilitation; Research; Verification. **Publications:** *ABA Education Resource Manual.* **Price:** included in membership dues. Alternate Formats: online ● *American Burn Association—Book of Abstracts,* annual. Journal. **Price:** included in membership dues; $15.00/copy, for nonmembers. **Circulation:** 5,000 ● *Burn Care Services in North America,* annual. Directory. Lists specialized burn care facilities in the United States and Canada. **Price:** included in membership dues; $300.00/copy, for nonmembers. **Circulation:** 5,000 ● *Journal of Burn Care and Rehabilitation,* bimonthly. Covers burn injuries and their treatment. Includes a list of employment opportunities, research reports, and statistics. **Price:** included in membership dues; $120.00 /year for nonmembers; $214.00 /year for institutions. ISSN: 0273-8481. **Circulation:** 5,000. **Advertising:** accepted ● *National Burn Repository 2002 Report.* **Price:** $400.00 for nonmembers ● *Proceedings of the ABA Annual Meeting,* annual. **Price:** $200.00/issue ● Membership Directory, annual. **Price:** included in membership dues. **Circulation:** 5,000. Alternate Formats: online ● Newsletter. **Price:** included in membership dues. **Conventions/Meetings:** annual meeting, scientific (exhibits) ● seminar and regional meeting.

13489 ■ Burns United Support Groups (BUSG)

PO Box 36416
Detroit, MI 48236
Ph: (313)881-5577
E-mail: burnsunited@hotmail.com
Contact: Donna Schneck, Exec. Off.

Founded: 1986. **Members:** 150. **Membership Dues:** $15 (annual). **Staff:** 3. **Regional Groups:** 4. **State Groups:** 4. **Local Groups:** 3. **National Groups:** 2. **Description:** Burn survivors and their families. Provides support services and information on burn care and prevention. Conducts educational programs and children's services. Operates Speaker's Bureau. **Libraries: Type:** open to the public. **Holdings:** 50. **Subjects:** burn care, surgery. **Affiliated With:** American Burn Association; Phoenix Society for Burn Survivors. **Publications:** Newsletter.

13490 ■ International Society for Burn Injuries (ISBI)

c/o Dr. Ronald Tompkins, MD, Treas.
Massachusetts Gen. Hosp.
55 Fruit St.
Boston, MA 02114-2621
Ph: (617)726-3447
Fax: (617)367-8936
E-mail: rtompkins@partners.org
URL: http://www.worldburn.org
Contact: Dr. Ronald Tompkins MD, Treas.

Founded: 1965. **Members:** 1,740. **Membership Dues:** physician, PhD, individual (high income country), $50-$100 (annual) ● physician, PhD, individual (low income country), $30-$50 (annual). **Multinational. Description:** Physicians, surgeons, nurses, scientists, and other interested medical and non-medical personnel who are engaged in the care and research of burns. Seeks to disseminate knowledge and stimulate prevention in the field of burns. Promotes and coordinates scientific, clinical, and social research in burns; promotes first aid, nursing, and other types of education in all phases of burn care. **Libraries: Type:** not open to the public. **Awards:** Tanner-Vandeput-Boswick Prize. **Frequency:** quadrennial. **Type:** recognition. **Recipient:** for individuals who have made outstanding contributions to any aspect of burn management ● Tanner-Vandeput Prize for Burn Research. **Frequency:** quadrennial. **Type:** recognition. **Recipient:** for the individual who has made the greatest contribution to burn research. **Computer Services:** Mailing lists. **Telecommunication Services:** electronic mail, sd.mackie@wxs.nl. **Committees:** Burn Care; Disaster Planning; Industry; Lab Services; Nursing; Prevention; Rehabilitation; Research; Web. **Publications:** *BURNS,* 8/year. Journal. **Price:** included in membership dues. **Circulation:** 2,500. **Advertising:** accepted ● Membership Directory, annual. **Conventions/Meetings:** biennial Congress on Burn Injuries (exhibits) ● periodic regional meeting ● periodic seminar.

13491 ■ National Burn Victim Foundation (NBVF)

Address Unknown since 2007

Founded: 1974. **Membership Dues:** public, $25 (annual) ● professional, $25. **Staff:** 4. **Budget:** $300,000. **Regional Groups:** 2. **State Groups:** 1. **National Groups:** 1. **Languages:** English, Spanish. **Description:** Supporters are physicians specializing in burn treatment and care, fire services prevention personnel, nurses, communications experts, health and chemical industry representatives, and others interested in burn treatment and care. Maintains 24-hour emergency burn referral service. Conducts medical emergency burn care seminars and workshops for physicians, nurses, EMTs, and emergency rescue personnel. Operates Medical Disaster Response System, which utilizes private helicopters for transporting medical teams to disaster sites where large numbers of survivors have been tramatized. Collects burn data from New Jersey hospitals daily. Program currently provides direct professional services in New Jersey and information and referral services nationally. Offers consultation and evaluation services to the Division of Youth and Family Services and law enforcement agencies in cases involving suspected child abuse or neglect by burning. Presents burn awareness and prevention programs to schools, civic organizations, and day-care centers. Maintains speakers' bureau; conducts specialized education, children's services, and research programs; compiles statistics. **Libraries: Type:** open to the public. **Holdings:** 300. **Subjects:** burns, research. **Awards:** Humanitarian, Leadership, Appreciation. **Frequency:** annual. **Type:** recognition. **Recipient:** self sacrifice to help another cause or person. **Computer Services:** database. **Committees:** Urban Burn. **Publications:** *Burn Awareness.* Pamphlets ● *Child Abuse? Think Again.* Video. **Price:** $125.00. **Advertising:** not accepted ● *Disaster Medical Response.* Video. **Price:** $29.95. **Advertising:** not accepted ● *General Burn Awareness.* Video ● *Training Professionals - Child Abuse/Neglect Investigation.* Video ● Also publishes The Use of Forensics in the Investgation of Burn Injuries. **Conventions/ Meetings:** Child Abuse? Think Again - conference and workshop, with forensics - 4/year.

13492 ■ Phoenix Society for Burn Survivors (PSBS)

1835 R W Berends Dr. SW
Grand Rapids, MI 49519-4955
Ph: (616)458-2773
Free: (800)888-2876
Fax: (616)458-2831
E-mail: info@phoenix-society.org
URL: http://www.phoenix-society.org
Contact: Amy Acton RN, Exec. Dir.
Founded: 1977. **Members:** 7,500. **Membership Dues:** burn survivor, $25 (annual) ● associate, $50 (annual) ● professional, $100 (annual) ● institutional, $150 (annual). **Staff:** 1. **Budget:** $104,000. **Local Groups:** 340. **Description:** Serves as self-help service organization for burn survivors and their families. Works to ease the psychosocial adjustment of severely burned and disfigured persons during and after hospitalization so they may return to normal and satisfactory lives within their communities; former burn survivors work as volunteers on a one-to-one basis with other burn survivors and their families. Offers a training program for volunteers; seeks to educate the public about the nature and problems of disfigurement; discourages concealment of disfigurement, which the society believes compounds the difficulty of adjustment; conducts research on psychological ramifications of burn disfigurement and disseminates information on burns and trauma and their treatment. Conducts school programs for burned children returning to classes. **Libraries:** Type: reference. **Holdings:** 100; audiovisuals, books. **Subjects:** burn recovery. **Formerly:** (1991) Phoenix Center. **Publications:** *Burn Support News*, quarterly. Newsletter. **Circulation:** 8,000. Alternate Formats: online. **Conventions/Meetings:** annual World Burn Congress (exhibits).

Cancer

13493 ■ African American Breast Cancer Alliance (AABCA)

PO Box 8981
Minneapolis, MN 55408
Ph: (612)825-3675
Fax: (612)827-2977
E-mail: aabcainc@yahoo.com
URL: http://www.geocities.com/aabcainc
Contact: R. Berry, Pres.
Founded: 1990. **Description:** Helps Black women, people of color, families and communities to cope with breast cancer. Sponsors a breast cancer support group for patients and survivors at various stages of their experiences; addresses the specific needs of Black women diagnosed with breast cancer; also sponsors celebrations and health events for survivors, families, friends, and communities. **Publications:** *Being There!*. Brochure. Contains advice to empower women to take charge of their health and care of their lives by becoming more informed about breast cancer. **Price:** $2.50/pack of 25, plus shipping and handling.

13494 ■ Alliance for Childhood Cancer (ACC)

c/o Jay Ingram
1900 Duke St., Ste.200
Alexandria, VA 22314
Ph: (703)299-1050
Fax: (703)684-8364
URL: http://www.allianceforchildhoodcancer.org
Contact: Jay Ingram, Contact
Founded: 2001. **Description:** Addresses the needs of childhood cancer survivors. Advocates for programs and policies that ensure access to and insurance coverage for long-term follow-up care. Raises public awareness on childhood cancer. Provides a forum for national patient advocacy groups and medical and scientific organizations for the exchange of information and collaboration on efforts concerning the prevention, diagnosis and treatment of cancer.

13495 ■ Alliance for Lung Cancer Advocacy, Support and Education (ALCASE)

888 16th St. NW, Ste.800
Washington, DC 20006
Ph: (202)463-2080
Free: (800)298-2436
Fax: (202)463-2038
E-mail: info@alcase.org
Contact: Cynthia M. Langhorne, Exec.Dir.
Founded: 1995. **Members:** 35,000. **Membership Dues:** individual, $25 (annual). **Staff:** 9. **Budget:** $750,000. **Description:** Helps people living with or at risk of lung cancer on a worldwide basis. **Affiliated With:** American Cancer Society. **Formerly:** (1998) Spirit and Breath. **Publications:** *Information for the Asking*. Booklet. Increases communication between survivors and their healthcare team. **Price:** free ● *The Lung Cancer Manual*. Contains information on lung cancer treatments, diagnosis and staging, complementary medicine, financial issues and end-of-life issues. **Price:** free ● *Lung Cancer Resource Guide*. Booklet. Includes list of organizations, programs, and other services for people living with lung cancer. **Price:** free ● *Spirit and Breath*, quarterly. Newsletter. Provides information on new treatments, patient profiles, symptom management and advocacy issues. **Price:** free. Alternate Formats: online.

13496 ■ American Association for Cancer Education (AACE)

c/o Paula Brown, Exec. Asst.
San Diego Hospice and Palliative Care
4311 3rd Ave.
San Diego, CA 92103-1407
Ph: (619)278-6164
Fax: (619)298-7027
E-mail: pbrown@sdhospice.org
URL: http://www.aaceonline.com
Contact: Paula Brown, Exec. Asst.
Founded: 1947. **Members:** 550. **Membership Dues:** regular, $150 (annual). **Description:** Physicians, dentists, nurses, health educators, social workers, and occupational therapists; others interested in cancer education. Provides a forum for individuals concerned with the study and improvement of cancer education focusing on prevention, early detection, treatment, and rehabilitation. **Awards:** Margaret Hay Edwards Achievement Medal. **Frequency:** annual. **Type:** medal. **Committees:** Advisory; Archives/ Historian; Basic Science; Bylaws; Dental; Editorial; Education Evaluation; Gynecologic; Medical; Nominating; Nursing; Palliative Oncology; Pathology; Pediatric; Preventive Oncology; Professional Education in the Community; Program; Psychosocial; Radiation; Surgical. **Sections:** Cancer Education Evaluation and Methods; Cancer Prevention Education. **Supersedes:** Cancer Coordinators. **Publications:** *Journal of Cancer Education*, quarterly. **Price:** $95.00 for members; $195.00 for institutions and libraries. ISSN: 0885-8195. **Circulation:** 800. **Advertising:** accepted ● Membership Directory, annual. **Conventions/Meetings:** annual conference (exhibits).

13497 ■ American Brachytherapy Society (ABS)

12100 Sunset Hills Rd., Ste.130
Reston, VA 20190
Ph: (703)234-4078
Fax: (703)435-4390
E-mail: rguggolz@drohanmgmt.com
URL: http://www.americanbrachytherapy.org
Contact: Rick Guggolz, Exec. Dir.
Founded: 1978. **Members:** 1,000. **Membership Dues:** regular, $180 (annual) ● associate, $100 (annual). **Budget:** $400,000. **Description:** Strives to provide insight and research into the use of brachytherapy in malignant and benign conditions. **Publications:** *Brachytherapy*, quarterly. Journal. Contains articles on the techniques and clinical applications of interstitial radiation and other related information. ● Newsletter, quarterly. **Conventions/Meetings:** annual conference (exhibits).

13498 ■ American Brain Tumor Association (ABTA)

2720 River Rd.
Des Plaines, IL 60018
Ph: (847)827-9910
Fax: (847)827-9918
E-mail: info@abta.org
URL: http://hope.abta.org/site/PageServer
Contact: Naomi L. Berkowitz, Exec. Dir.
Founded: 1973. **Staff:** 15. **Budget:** $2,225,000. **Description:** Seeks to eliminate brain tumors through research and meet the needs of brain tumor patients and their families. **Libraries:** Type: reference. **Holdings:** 40. **Awards:** Basic Research Fellowships. **Frequency:** annual. **Type:** fellowship. **Recipient:** for talented scientists ● Research Awards for Post-Doctorates. **Frequency:** annual. **Type:** fellowship. **Recipient:** for post-doctoral candidates whose intent is to pursue a career in brain tumor research. **Telecommunication Services:** information service, patient line, (800)886-2282. **Councils:** Scientific Advisory. **Departments:** Social Work. **Formerly:** (1992) Association for Brain Tumor Research. **Publications:** *Building Knowledge* (in English and Spanish). Booklets. Consists of: A Brain Tumor-Sharing Hope (also in Spanish); Dictionary for Brain Tumor Patients; Living with a Brain Tumor; A Primer of Brain Tumors. **Price:** free. Alternate Formats: online ● *Connections - A Pen Pal Program*. Pamphlet ● *Focusing on Treatment*. Pamphlets. Includes: Gene Therapy; Radiation Therapy of Brain Tumors: A Basic Guide; Stereotactic Radiosurgery. Alternate Formats: online ● *Focusing on Tumors*. Pamphlets. Features Ependymoma, Glioblastoma Multiforme and Anaplastic Astrocytoma, Medullobblastoma, Meningioma, Metastatic Tumors and Oligodendroglioma. Alternate Formats: online ● *For and About Children Series*. Pamphlets. Titles include: Alex's Journey: The Story of a Child with a Brain Tumor for ages 9-13, video and booklet format; When Your Child Returns to School. ● *Message Line*, triennial. Newsletter. Alternate Formats: online. **Conventions/Meetings:** annual Fellows Meeting - May ● meeting, town hall meetings for patients - 3/year ● annual regional meeting, for patients.

13499 ■ American Cancer Society (ACS)

PO Box 22718
Oklahoma City, OK 73123-1718
Free: (800)ACS-2345
URL: http://www.cancer.org
Contact: Anne Isenhower, Natl. Dir.
Founded: 1913. **Staff:** 450. **Regional Groups:** 17. **Local Groups:** 3,400. **Description:** Serves as a nationwide, community-based, voluntary health organization dedicated to eliminating cancer as a major health problem by preventing cancer, saving lives and diminishing suffering from cancer, through research, education, advocacy, and service. **Libraries:** Type: reference. **Awards:** Lane Adams Award. **Frequency:** annual. **Type:** recognition. **Recipient:** for individuals who demonstrate excellence in caring for people with cancer ● Medal of Honor. **Frequency:** annual. **Type:** recognition. **Committees:** Professional Education; Public Information; Public Issues; Research and Clinical Investigation; Service and Rehabilitation; Tobacco and Cancer. **Programs:** Ostomy Rehabilitation. **Absorbed:** (1969) Reach to Recovery Foundation. **Formerly:** (1944) American Society for the Control Cancer. **Publications:** *CA-A Cancer Journal for Clinicians*, bimonthly. Covers cancer treatment, prevention, and diagnosis. **Price:** free for health professionals. ISSN: 0007-9235. **Circulation:** 400,000. **Advertising:** accepted. Alternate Formats: microform ● *Cancer*, semimonthly. Journal. Covers cancer prevention, research, diagnosis, and treatment. Includes proceedings supplement covering ACS conferences. **Price:** $219.00 /year for individuals; $437.00 /year for institutions. ISSN: 0008-543X. **Circulation:** 20,000. **Advertising:** accepted ● *Cancer Facts and Figures*, annual. Report. Provides statistical information on the major sites of cancer including incidence, mortality and survival rates, and risk factors. **Price:** free. **Circulation:** 500,000 ● Annual Report. **Price:** free. **Circulation:** 100,000. Alternate Formats: online.

13500 ■ American Institute for Cancer Research (AICR)
1759 R St. NW
Washington, DC 20009
Ph: (202)328-7744
Free: (800)843-8114
Fax: (202)328-7226
E-mail: aicrweb@aicr.org
URL: http://www.aicr.org
Founded: 1983. **Staff:** 98. **Budget:** $38,009,176. **Description:** Fosters research on diet, nutrition and cancer prevention and educates the public about the results. **Awards:** AICR Research Grants. **Frequency:** semiannual. **Type:** grant. **Publications:** Newsletter, quarterly. **Price:** free. **Circulation:** 1,600,000. Alternate Formats: online. **Conventions/Meetings:** annual conference.

13501 ■ Association of American Cancer Institutes (AACI)
200 Lothrop St.
Iroquois Bldg., Ste.308
Pittsburgh, PA 15213
Ph: (412)647-6111 (412)647-2076
Fax: (412)647-3659
E-mail: mail@aaci-cancer.org
URL: http://www.aaci-cancer.org
Contact: Barbara Duffy Stewart, Exec. Dir.
Founded: 1959. **Members:** 85. **Membership Dues:** individual, $5,000 (annual). **Budget:** $130,000. **Description:** Directors of cancer centers. Informs members of important legislative and program developments in the field. Promotes discussion among cancer center leadership throughout the world; fosters collaboration between members on research, education, and service programs; works to further educational and training opportunities in related biomedical sciences; advises federal, state, and local governments, and private and civic organizations concerning cancer research and related health topics. **Formerly:** (1968) Association of Cancer Institute Directors. **Publications:** AACI Newsletter, periodic. **Price:** free. **Conventions/Meetings:** annual meeting - June and October.

13502 ■ Association of Cancer Executives (ACE)
c/o Brian J. Mandrier, Exec. Dir.
1255 Twenty-Third St. NW
Washington, DC 20037-1174
Ph: (202)521-1886
Fax: (202)833-3636
E-mail: bmandrier@cancerexecutives.org
URL: http://www.cancerexecutives.org
Contact: Brian J. Mandrier, Exec. Dir.
Membership Dues: delegate, $195 (annual) ● corporate, $400 (annual) ● associate, physician director, $150 (annual). **Description:** Promotes the advancement of professional standing and personal achievement in oncology management, research, strategic planning and program development. **Telecommunication Services:** electronic mail, egundersen@cancerexecutives.org. **Publications:** ACE Update, bimonthly. Newsletter. **Price:** included in membership dues. Alternate Formats: online. **Conventions/Meetings:** annual meeting.

13503 ■ Association of Cancer Online Resources (ACOR)
173 Duane St., Ste.3A
New York, NY 10013-3334
Ph: (212)226-5525
E-mail: webfeedback@acor.org
URL: http://www.acor.org/about/about.html
Description: Provides information and support cancer patients and those who care for them through creation and maintenance of cancer-related Internet mailing lists and Web-based resources. **Computer Services:** Bibliographic search, cancer ● database, cancer facts collection ● information services, NCI what you need to know series. **Publications:** Abstracts. Contains abstracts of new knowledge about cancer, treatment, side effects and more. Alternate Formats: online.

13504 ■ Association of Community Cancer Centers (ACCC)
11600 Nebel St., Ste.201
Rockville, MD 20852
Ph: (301)984-9496
Fax: (301)770-1949
E-mail: info@accc-cancer.org
URL: http://www.accc-cancer.org
Contact: James C. Chingos MD, Pres.
Founded: 1974. **Members:** 6,000. **Membership Dues:** general, $110 (annual) ● institution, group practice, $1,045 (annual) ● sustaining, $5,500 (annual). **Staff:** 20. **State Groups:** 23. **Description:** Institutions (680) and 23 state oncology societies involved in the provision of community cancer care. Fosters communication among providers of community cancer care; seeks to improve the quality of care available to cancer patients in community settings; encourages clinical research utilizing the community as a setting. **Libraries: Type:** reference. **Holdings:** books, periodicals. **Awards:** Clinical Research Award. **Frequency:** annual. **Type:** recognition. **Recipient:** for contribution to the field of community cancer care. **Committees:** Community Research/CCOP; Government Affairs; Medical Directors; Nursing; Practice Administrators; Program Administrators; Radiation Oncology; Reimbursement; Standards. **Publications:** Community Cancer Programs in the U.S., annual. Serves as a reference guide to freestanding and hospital-based cancer programs. **Price:** $50.00 non-profit organizations; $150.00 others. Advertising: accepted. Alternate Formats: CD-ROM ● Compendia-Based Drug Bulletin, quarterly ● Critical Pathways, periodic ● Oncology Issues, bimonthly. Journal. Provides information on community cancer programs for association members, who are physicians, nurses, social workers, and other health professionals. **Price:** $60.00/year. **Circulation:** 18,000 ● Standards for Cancer Programs, periodic. **Conventions/Meetings:** annual conference, oncology-related products and services (exhibits) - always March ● annual National Oncology Economics Conference (exhibits) - usually September or October. 2007 Oct. 3-6, Dallas, TX; 2008 Sept. 17-20, San Francisco, CA; 2009 Sept. 22-25, Minneapolis, MN.

13505 ■ Association for Research of Childhood Cancer (AROCC)
PO Box 251
Buffalo, NY 14225-0251
Ph: (716)681-4433
E-mail: president@arocc.org
URL: http://www.arocc.org
Contact: Anne O'Donnell, Pres.
Founded: 1971. **Members:** 1,000. **Regional Groups:** 2. **Description:** Parents who have lost children to various pediatric cancers; persons supporting cancer research. Seeks to fund the expansion and continuation of research in pediatric cancer centers and to provide seed money for pilot projects in cancer research. Offers support to parents of children with cancer. Bestows research and clinical investigation grants; offers research and medical student fellowships. **Computer Services:** database ● mailing lists. **Boards:** Community Advisory; Medical/Scientific Advisory. **Publications:** AROCC—Newsletter, quarterly. Contains book reviews, donations list, and memorial list. **Price:** included in membership dues. **Circulation:** 1,000. Alternate Formats: online ● Parent/Child Handbook. **Conventions/Meetings:** bimonthly board meeting.

13506 ■ Bladder Cancer Advocacy Network (BCAN)
PO Box 341105
Bethesda, MD 20827
Ph: (301)469-6865
Fax: (301)469-7526
E-mail: info@bcan.org
URL: http://www.bcan.org
Contact: Diane Zipursky Quale, Dir./Pres./Co-Founder
Founded: 2005. **Description:** Raises awareness of bladder cancer among the general public and the medical community. Advocates for the allotment of additional governmental and private funds for research in the diagnosis, treatment and cure of bladder cancer. Works with and provides financial assistance and grants to individuals, corporations, and health and medical institutions for bladder cancer research. **Publications:** Outlook, quarterly. Newsletter. Alternate Formats: online.

13507 ■ Boarding for Breast Cancer Foundation (B4BC)
6230 Wilshire Blvd., No. 179
Los Angeles, CA 90048
Ph: (323)571-2197 (323)467-2663
E-mail: email@b4bc.org
URL: http://www.b4bc.org
Contact: Lisa Hudson, Co-Founder
Founded: 1996. **Description:** Youth promoting breast cancer education, awareness, and fundraising.

13508 ■ Breast Cancer Action (BCA)
55 New Montgomery St., Ste.323
San Francisco, CA 94105
Ph: (415)243-9301
Free: (877)278-6722
Fax: (415)243-3996
E-mail: info@bcaction.org
URL: http://www.bcaction.org
Contact: Barbara Brenner, Exec. Dir.
Founded: 1990. **Members:** 12,000. **Membership Dues:** individual, $50 (annual). **Staff:** 9. **Budget:** $795,000. **Regional Groups:** 1. **Description:** Women living with breast cancer. Seeks to carry "the voices of people affected by breast cancer to inspire and compel the changes necessary to end the breast cancer epidemic." Monitors and publicizes developments in breast cancer detection and treatment; sponsors lobbying programs; advocates for increased access to breast cancer screening and treatment services; facilitates environmental protection initiatives; works to ensure accurate reporting of breast cancer issues in public media. **Libraries: Type:** lending; reference. **Holdings:** books, clippings, periodicals. **Subjects:** breast cancer. **Additional Websites:** http://www.thinkbeforeyoupink.org. **Programs:** The Breast Cancer Puzzle Project; Follow the Money/Think Before You Pink; Stop Cancer Where It Starts. **Publications:** Breast Cancer Action Newsletter (in English and Spanish), bimonthly. Contains information on developments in treatment, research, detection and politics of breast-cancer. **Price:** $35.00/year. **ISSN:** 1088-386X. **Circulation:** 7,000. Alternate Formats: online ● Spanish Newsletter, quarterly. **Conventions/Meetings:** annual Town Meeting for Breast Cancer Activists - conference and workshop, organizing meeting.

13509 ■ C3: Colorectal Cancer Coalition
4301 Connecticut Ave. NW, Ste.404
Washington, DC 20008
Ph: (202)244-2906
E-mail: info@fightcolorectalcancer.org
URL: http://www.fightcolorectalcancer.org
Contact: Nancy Roach, Founder/Pres./Chair
Description: Furthers research to improve the screening, diagnosis and treatment of colorectal cancer. Advocates for policy decisions that make the most effective colorectal cancer prevention and treatment available to the public. Increases awareness that colorectal cancer is preventable, treatable and beatable. **Telecommunication Services:** electronic mail, nancy.roach@fightcolorectalcancer.org. **Publications:** Momentum, quarterly. Newsletter.

13510 ■ Cancer Care (CC)
275 7th Ave.
New York, NY 10001-6708
Ph: (212)712-8400 (212)712-8080
Free: (800)813-4673
Fax: (212)712-8495
E-mail: info@cancercare.org
URL: http://www.cancercare.org
Contact: Diane Blum MSW, Exec. Dir.
Founded: 1944. **Members:** 90,000. **Staff:** 113. **Budget:** $16,500,000. **Languages:** English, Spanish. **Description:** Provides emotional support, information

and practical help to people with cancer, and their loved ones; has assisted over two million people nationwide through telephone counseling, referral services, teleconference programs, office-based services, and via the Internet. All services are provided free of charge and are available to people of all ages, with all types of cancer, at any stage of the disease. All services, including cancer awareness initiatives, extend also to family members, caregivers and professionals. **Formerly:** (1986) National Cancer Foundation; (1991) National Cancer Care Foundation. **Publications:** *Cancer Care News*, 3/year. Newsletter. Provides articles about CancerCare programs, helpful tips for coping with cancer, and lists of telephone education workshops and support groups. Alternate Formats: online ● *Community News*, quarterly. Newsletter. Alternate Formats: online ● *Connect*. Booklets ● Annual Report, annual. **Price:** free ● Also publishes symposia proceedings, social research studies, professional papers, and brochures; distributes films and videotapes.

13511 ■ Cancer Control Society (CCS)
2043 N Berendo St.
Los Angeles, CA 90027
Ph: (323)663-7801
Fax: (323)663-7757
E-mail: cancercontrol@cox.net
URL: http://www.cancercontrolsociety.com
Contact: Norman Fritz, Pres.
Founded: 1973. **Members:** 5,000. **Staff:** 3. **Description:** Educates the public and professionals on the prevention and control of cancer and other diseases through nutrition, tests, and nontoxic alternative therapies, such as Laetrile, Gerson, Hoxsey, Vaccines, Oxygen, Enzymes, Wheat Grass, Electro-Magnetic and supplements including Mega-Vitamins and Minerals, Detoxification and Nutrition, and DMSO and Chelation Therapy. Provides information through a 12-hour telephone hot line, direct mail, doctor and patient lists, memberships, conventions, videos, cancer clinic tours, and Cancer Book House. **Awards:** Humanitarian Award. **Frequency:** annual. **Type:** recognition. **Publications:** *Cancer Book House List*, biennial ● *Cancer Control Journal*, periodic. Reports on one specific cancer-related topic in each issue. **Price:** included in membership dues. **Circulation:** 20,000 ● *Doctor and Clinic Directory*, bimonthly ● *Patient Directory*, bimonthly. **Conventions/Meetings:** annual Cancer Convention - meeting (exhibits) - always Labor Day weekend in Los Angeles, CA.

13512 ■ Cancer Federation
PO Box 1298
Banning, CA 92220-0009
Ph: (951)849-4325
Fax: (951)849-0156
E-mail: info@cancerfed.org
URL: http://www.cancerfed.com
Contact: John Steinbacher, Exec. Dir./Founder
Founded: 1977. **Members:** 1,500. **Membership Dues:** general, $20 (annual) ● life, $150. **Staff:** 4. **Budget:** $600,000. **Description:** Physicians, scientists, nurses, and laymen (both cancer patients and nonpatients). Promotes research and education in the field of cancer immunology. Seeks to discover appropriate cancer therapies using natural biological modifiers. Funds research at major centers throughout the U.S., including the University of California (Riverside and Santa Barbara), University of Hawaii, and University of Pittsburgh, on biological modifiers, such as lymphokines; killer cells; Interleukin I and II; diet; and psychological aspects of cancer. Compiles statistics; conducts research and education in cancer therapy, including vaccines, and in psychological programming for patients. Offers counseling program for cancer patients and their families. Sponsors public medical conferences and in-service courses for nurses on the psychology of cancer, and research projects at many universities and hospitals in the field of immunology. Sponsors charitable program. **Libraries: Type:** reference. **Holdings:** 500. **Awards: Frequency:** annual. **Type:** scholarship. **Recipient:** for high school and college seniors in the field of microbiology ● Science, Communication, and Service Awards. **Frequency:** annual. **Type:** recognition. **Pub-**

lications: *Challenge of the Cancer Federation*, quarterly. Newsletter. Provides general information on cancer research and treatments. Contains information on federation activities and book reviews. **Price:** included in membership dues. **Circulation:** 2,000. **Advertising:** accepted ● Audiotapes ● Booklets ● Books ● Monographs ● Videos. **Conventions/Meetings:** annual meeting.

13513 ■ Cancer Hope Network
2 North Rd., Ste.A
Chester, NJ 07930
Ph: (908)879-4039
Free: (877)HOPE-NET
Fax: (908)879-6518
E-mail: info@cancerhopenetwork.org
URL: http://www.cancerhopenetwork.org
Contact: Wanda Diak, Managing Dir./COO
Founded: 1981. **Staff:** 8. **Budget:** $550,000. **Nonmembership. Description:** Offers emotional support and encouragement to cancer patients and caregivers. Patients are matched with survivors of the same cancer, treatment and side effects, as well as by age and gender. Support provided via telephone by more than 325 trained support volunteers. **Libraries: Type:** reference. **Holdings:** archival material, articles, books, business records, clippings. **Subjects:** cancer. **Awards:** Flame of Courage Award. **Frequency:** annual. **Type:** recognition. **Recipient:** to an individual who has made a significant difference in a cancer patient's life or has shown courage in the face of his/her own cancer. **Formerly:** CHEMOcare. **Publications:** *Cancer Hope Network News*, semiannual. Newsletter. **Price:** free. **Circulation:** 5,000.

13514 ■ Cancer Information Service (CIS)
c/o National Cancer Institute
6116 Executive Blvd., Ste.3036 A
MSC 8322
Bethesda, MD 20892-8322
Free: (800)4-CANCER
E-mail: cancer.gov_staff@mail.nih.gov
URL: http://www.cancer.gov
Contact: Mary Anne Bright, Program Dir.
Founded: 1975. **Nonmembership. Description:** Funded by the National Cancer Institute. Provides information about cancer causes, prevention, detection, diagnosis, rehabilitation, and research. Provides technical assistance to state and regional organizations conducting cancer education activities. Serves the entire United States, Puerto Rico, the U.S. Virgin Islands and the Pacific territories through a network of regional offices. **Telecommunication Services:** TDD, (800)332-8615.

13515 ■ Cancer Prevention Coalition (CPC)
c/o Dr. Samuel S. Epstein, MD, Chm./Founder
Univ. of Illinois at Chicago
Scholarship of Public Hea., MC 922
2121 W Taylor St.
Chicago, IL 60612
Ph: (312)996-2297
Fax: (312)413-9898
E-mail: epstein@uic.edu
URL: http://www.preventcancer.com
Contact: Dr. Samuel S. Epstein MD, Chm./Founder
Founded: 1994. **Membership Dues:** basic, $35 (annual) ● family, $75 (annual) ● local office director, $100 (annual) ● professional, executive, $100-$1,000 (annual) ● benefactor, corporate, $1,000 (annual). **Multinational. Description:** Represents independent experts in cancer prevention and public health, citizen activists and representatives of organized labor, public interest, environmental and women's health groups. Raises public awareness of the importance of early cancer detection. Works to reduce cancer rates through a comprehensive strategy of outreach, public education, advocacy and public policy initiatives.

13516 ■ Cancer Quality Alliance (CQA)
1900 Duke St., Ste.200
Alexandria, VA 22314
Ph: (703)299-1050
Fax: (703)684-8364

E-mail: cancerquality@asco.org
URL: http://www.cancerqualityalliance.org
Contact: Patricia Ganz, Co-Chair
Description: Seeks to improve the quality of care provided to cancer patients. Fosters collaboration among stakeholders who are committed to cancer care quality improvement. Encourages the implementation of practical programs to improve quality of care. Seeks to become a national voice for quality of cancer care.

13517 ■ Cancer Research and Prevention Foundation (CRPF)
1600 Duke St., Ste.500
Alexandria, VA 22314
Ph: (703)836-4412
Free: (800)227-2732
Fax: (703)836-4413
E-mail: info@preventcancer.org
URL: http://www.preventcancer.org
Contact: Carolyn Aldige, Pres./Founder
Founded: 1985. **Description:** Represents foundations, individuals, and companies. Aims to prevent cancer through research and education. Publishes educational materials. **Awards: Type:** fellowship ● **Type:** grant. **Publications:** *In the News*, biweekly. Newsletter. Contains information of interest to cancer community. Alternate Formats: online.

13518 ■ Candlelighters Childhood Cancer Foundation (CCCF)
PO Box 498
Kensington, MD 20895-0498
Ph: (301)962-3520
Free: (800)366-2223
Fax: (301)962-3521
E-mail: staff@candlelighters.org
URL: http://www.candlelighters.org
Contact: Ruth Hoffman, Exec. Dir.
Founded: 1970. **Members:** 100,000. **Staff:** 2. **Budget:** $300,000. **Local Groups:** 400. **Description:** Educates, supports, serves and advocates for children and adolescents with cancer, their family members, survivors of childhood cancer, and professionals who work with them. Coordinates a network of more than 400 peer support groups and contacts for parents of children/adolescents with cancer. Offers newsletters, other publications, literature and searches. Makes referrals to volunteers who can assist with health insurance problems, second opinions, and employment issues. Local groups offer meetings at which parents share information and emotional support and hear speakers. Referrals for parent-to-parent visitation, transportation, blood or wig banks, speakers' bureaus, meetings for young people, and bereavement groups. Named for the Chinese proverb, "It is better to light one candle than to curse the darkness". **Libraries: Type:** open to the public. **Holdings:** 1,200; articles, books, video recordings. **Subjects:** childhood cancers, treatments, family and child health, disabilities. **Awards:** Candlelighters Group Awards. **Frequency:** annual. **Type:** recognition. **Programs:** Vehicle Donation. **Formerly:** (1984) Candlelighters Foundation. **Publications:** *The Candlelighters Guide to Bone Marrow Transplants in Children*. Handbook. **Price:** $7.50 others; free to families of children with cancer ● *CCCF Bibliography and Resource Guide*, annual. Contains annotated reviews of books, articles, pamphlets, and videos. **Price:** $5.00 in U.S.; $8.00 in Canada and Mexico; $12.00 all other countries; free for families of children with cancer. **Circulation:** 5,000 ● *CCCF Quarterly Newsletter*. Contains articles, poetry, and reviews pertaining to living with and treating childhood cancer. **Price:** free to families/health education professionals. **Circulation:** 40,000 ● *CCCF Youth Newsletter*. **Price:** included in membership dues ● *Educating the Child with Cancer*. Handbook. **Price:** $7.50 others; free for families of children with cancer ● *Know Before You Go*. Handbook ● *The Phoenix*, periodic. Newsletter. For adult survivors of childhood cancer. ● *You Are Not Alone*. Handbook. Alternate Formats: online ● Journal, quarterly. Alternate Formats: online ● Also publishes basic family library, publications list, guide to the Americans with Disabilities Act, camp list, and

wish fulfillment organizations list. **Conventions/ Meetings:** periodic meeting.

13519 ■ Carcinoid Cancer Foundation (CCF)
333 Mamaroneck Ave., No. 492
White Plains, NY 10605
Ph: (914)683-1001
Free: (888)722-3132
Fax: (914)683-0183
E-mail: carcinoid@optonline.net
URL: http://www.carcinoid.org
Contact: Monica Warner, Dir. of Development/ Research Coor.
Founded: 1968. **Staff:** 8. **Languages:** Chinese, Dutch, English, German, Swedish. **Multinational. Description:** Promotes and conducts research and education on carcinoid tumors and related neuroendocrine tumors (NETs). Provides information for the general public and health care professionals regarding special carcinoid-neuroendocrine related research, diagnosis and treatment options. Announces special events/conferences. Provides information about national and international specialists and support groups. Provides webcasts and transcripts of lectures from carcinoid/NETs conferences. Sponsors annual research awards. **Libraries: Type:** reference. **Holdings:** articles. **Awards: Frequency:** periodic. **Type:** recognition. **Recipient:** for promising research related to neuroendocrine tumors in genetics, diagnosis and treatment development ● **Frequency:** biennial. **Type:** scholarship. **Recipient:** for promising research related to neuroendocrine tumors: genetics, diagnostic and treatment development.

13520 ■ Children's Cause for Cancer Advocacy (CCCA)
1010 Wayne Ave., Ste.770
Silver Spring, MD 20910
Ph: (301)562-2765
Fax: (301)565-9670
E-mail: questions@childrenscause.org
URL: http://www.childrenscause.org
Contact: Susan L. Weiner PhD, Founder
Founded: 1999. **Description:** Works to stimulate drug discovery and development for childhood cancers. Encourages research on cancer and the expansion of resources for such endeavor. Addresses the social, emotional and rehabilitatory needs of cancer survivors. **Libraries: Type:** reference. **Holdings:** papers. **Publications:** *The Next Step*, quarterly. Newsletter. Contains news about cancer victims and survivors. Includes updates on ongoing research on different types of cancer. Alternate Formats: online.

13521 ■ Children's Leukemia Research Association (NLA)
585 Stewart Ave., Ste.18
Garden City, NY 11530
Ph: (516)222-1944
Fax: (516)222-0457
E-mail: info@childrensleukemia.org
URL: http://www.childrensleukemia.org
Contact: Peter H. Wiernik, Chm.
Founded: 1965. **Staff:** 3. **Description:** Promotes leukemia research and public awareness of the disease. Provides financial aid to leukemia patients and their families, based on need. **Awards: Frequency:** annual. **Type:** grant. **Recipient:** for research ● **Type:** recognition. **Committees:** Medical Advisory; Patient Aid. **Formerly:** (1994) National Leukemia Association. **Conventions/Meetings:** annual meeting.

13522 ■ Coalition of Cancer Cooperative Groups
1818 Market St., No. 1100
Philadelphia, PA 19103
Ph: (215)789-3600
Free: (877)520-4457
Fax: (215)789-3655
E-mail: info@cancertrialshelp.org
URL: http://www.cancertrialshelp.org
Contact: Robert L. Comis MD, Pres./Chm.
Founded: 1997. **Membership Dues:** institution (cancer care provider), $2,500 (annual). **Description:** Seeks to improve the quality of life and survival

of cancer patients through increased participation in cancer clinical trials. Works to address issues facing cooperative groups, such as improvement of clinical trials experience, regulatory requirements, and provision of professional support services. Provides programs and information for physicians, patient advocate groups and patients designed to increase awareness of, and participation in, cancer clinical trials. **Telecommunication Services:** additional toll-free number, (866)772-9897. **Publications:** *Clinical Trial Matters.* Newsletter. Alternate Formats: online ● Brochures. Alternate Formats: online ● Surveys. Alternate Formats: online ● Annual Report, annual. Alternate Formats: online ● Articles. Alternate Formats: online.

13523 ■ Colorectal Cancer Network (CCN)
PO Box 182
Kensington, MD 20895-0182
Ph: (301)879-1500
Fax: (301)879-1901
E-mail: ccnetwork@colorectal-cancer.net
URL: http://www.colorectal-cancer.net
Contact: Louise Bates, Chair/Pres.
Membership Dues: individual, $15 (annual) ● corporate, $1,000 (annual) ● corporate partner, $15,000 (annual). **Description:** Works to eliminates colorectal cancer. Provides support to patients on treatment and management of colorectal cancer. **Awards:** King and Queen of Colon Cancer Prevention. **Frequency:** annual. **Type:** recognition ● Marshall Kragen Above and Beyond Award. **Frequency:** annual. **Type:** recognition. **Recipient:** for best patient advocacy ● Ninety in Nine Awards. **Type:** recognition. **Recipient:** for significant contribution in the field of colorectal cancer. **Computer Services:** Information services, colorectal cancer resources ● mailing lists, listserv ● online services, message board. **Boards:** Science Medical Advisory. **Programs:** One Step. **Projects:** Genomics. **Affiliated With:** Digestive Disease National Coalition; Genetic Alliance; National Coalition for Cancer Survivorship. **Publications:** Journals. Alternate Formats: online.

13524 ■ Concern Foundation
8383 Wilshire Blvd., Ste.337
Beverly Hills, CA 90211
Ph: (323)852-9844
Free: (800)867-2279
Fax: (323)852-9873
E-mail: info@concernfoundation.org
URL: http://www.concernfoundation.org
Contact: Steve R. Freed, Chm.
Founded: 1968. **Membership Dues:** regular, $50 (annual) ● active, $100 (annual) ● contributing, $200 (annual) ● family, $1,200 (annual) ● research sponsor, $2,500 (annual) ● gold sponsor, $5,000 (annual) ● hall of fame sponsor, $12,000 (annual). **Description:** Strives to raise funds for basic cancer research. **Awards: Type:** grant. **Recipient:** to independent investigators ● Concern Foundation Grants. **Divisions:** Cancer Immunology Research Foundation. **Programs:** Tribute. **Publications:** Newsletter, quarterly. Alternate Formats: online. **Conventions/Meetings:** annual Block Party.

13525 ■ Corporate Angel Network (CAN)
Westchester County Airport
One Loop Rd.
White Plains, NY 10604-1215
Ph: (914)328-1313
Free: (866)328-1313
Fax: (914)328-3938
E-mail: info@corpangelnetwork.org
URL: http://www.corpangelnetwork.org
Contact: Bonnie LeVar, Exec. Dir.
Founded: 1981. **Members:** 500. **Staff:** 6. **Budget:** $300,000. **Description:** Arranges free air transportation for cancer patients traveling to and from recognized cancer treatment centers, using empty seats on corporate aircraft. All ambulatory cancer patients and bone marrow donors not needing onboard care are eligible. **Libraries: Type:** reference. **Publications:** *FlightLines*, quarterly. Newsletter. Alternate Formats: online.

13526 ■ Cure Research Foundation
PO Box 3782
Westlake Village, CA 91359
Ph: (805)498-0185
Free: (800)282-2873
Fax: (805)498-4868
E-mail: ccf@cancure.org
URL: http://www.cancure.org
Contact: G. Edward Griffin, Pres./Exec. Dir.
Founded: 1976. **Description:** Dedicated to research and treatment in alternative cancer therapies, particularly non-drug therapies. Provides individuals with information about the availability of treatments, doctors and clinics and assists them in gathering the information they need to make the best decision for their particular situation. Also offers counseling (where funding permits) for AIDS, Alzheimer's disease, arthritis, diabetes, heart and circulatory disorders, neurological disorders, and pathogen-related diseases. **Libraries: Type:** open to the public. **Holdings:** archival material, audio recordings, books, papers, video recordings. **Subjects:** cancer.

13527 ■ Damon Runyon Cancer Research Foundation
675 3rd Ave., 25th Fl.
New York, NY 10017
Ph: (212)455-0500
Free: (888)722-6237
Fax: (212)455-0509
URL: http://www.cancerresearchfund.org
Contact: Lorraine W. Egan, Exec. Dir.
Founded: 1946. **Staff:** 13. **Budget:** $13,200,000. **Description:** Aims to advance cancer research through the funding of initial postdoctoral fellowships and junior faculty awards nationwide. Raises monies through the Fund's Broadway Tickets theater service and the solicitation of individuals, foundations and corporations. **Awards:** Clinical Investigator Award. **Frequency:** annual. **Type:** recognition ● Damon Runyon Scholar Award. **Frequency:** annual. **Type:** scholarship ● Damon Runyon-Walter Winchell Post Doctoral Fellowship. **Type:** fellowship. **Formerly:** Damon Runyon Foundation for Cancer Research; (1973) Damon Runyon Memorial Fund for Cancer Research; (1988) Damon Runyon - Walter Winchell Cancer Fund; (1993) Damon Runyon - Walter Winchell Cancer Research Fund. **Publications:** Annual Report, annual ● Brochures ● Newsletter, 3/year. **Conventions/Meetings:** periodic Former Fellows Symposium, with leading scientists' presentations on advances in cancer research (exhibits).

13528 ■ Dana-Farber Cancer Institute (DFCI)
44 Binney St.
Boston, MA 02115
Ph: (617)632-3000 (617)632-3301
Free: (866)408-3324
Fax: (617)632-4421
E-mail: dana-farbercontactus@dfci.harvard.edu
URL: http://www.dfci.harvard.edu
Contact: Dr. Edward J. Benz Jr., Pres./CEO
Founded: 1947. **Membership Dues:** individual, $50 (annual) ● family, $75 (annual) ● life (individual), $250 ● life (family), $350. **Description:** Physicians and scientists. Disseminates innovative patient therapies and scientific discoveries worldwide to aid the fight against cancer and AIDS. Works to provide compassionate care and support to both children and adults with cancer, AIDS, and related diseases. **Publications:** *Impact.* Newsletter. Highlights the fundraising activities of the Institute and the Jimmy Fund. Alternate Formats: online ● *Inside the Institute*, semimonthly. Newspaper. Alternate Formats: online ● *Side-By-Side*, quarterly. Newsletter. Alternate Formats: online.

13529 ■ DES Action, U.S.A.
158 S Stanwood Rd.
Columbus, OH 43209
Free: (800)337-9288
E-mail: desaction@columbus.rr.com
URL: http://www.desaction.org
Contact: Ms. Frances Howell, Exec. Dir.
Founded: 1977. **Members:** 3,000. **Membership Dues:** individual, $40 (annual). **Staff:** 1. **Budget:**

$98,000. **Languages:** English, Spanish. **Description:** DES-exposed persons and others "working to try to ameliorate the problems caused by DES". DES (diethylstilbestrol) is a synthetic estrogen in use since 1938 and often prescribed for prevention of miscarriage, diabetes during pregnancy, difficulty in conceiving, staining during pregnancy, and cessation of premature labor. It has since been found that, in some cases, daughters born to women taking DES in the first five months of pregnancy have developed cervical and vaginal abnormalities, a very small percentage of which have resulted in cancer, and a greater number of DES daughters experience problems with pregnancies, including seven times the rate of tubal pregnancy and twice the rate of miscarriage. DES mothers have a higher risk of breast cancer. Aims to reach DES-exposed persons and to stress to them the need for medical attention and monitoring; to educate professionals and the public. **Formerly:** (1986) DES Action, National. **Publications:** *DES Action Voice: A Focus on Diethylstilbestrol Exposure*, quarterly. Newsletter. Includes medical question and answer column; book reviews; legislation and litigation news; conference reports. **Price:** $35.00/year. ISSN: 1522-0389. **Circulation:** 3,000 ● Also publishes fact sheets, booklets and doctor referral sheet.

13530 ■ Esophageal Cancer Awareness Association (ECAA)
PO Box 3842
Ithaca, NY 14852-3842
Ph: (607)257-1141
Free: (866)370-3222
E-mail: rstienmier@ecaware.org
URL: http://www.ecaware.org
Contact: Richard H. Stienmier, Pres.
Founded: 2001. **Membership Dues:** regular, $25 (annual). **Description:** Seeks to increase public awareness of esophageal cancer. Strives to raise funds for research into the causes, treatments and outcome of esophageal cancer. Helps patients, survivors and caregivers to deal more effectively with the uncertainties of the disease and its consequences.

13531 ■ Facing Our Risk of Cancer Empowered (FORCE)
16057 Tampa Palms Blvd. W
PMB No. 373
Tampa, FL 33647
Ph: (954)255-8732
Free: (866)288-7475
Fax: (954)827-2200
E-mail: info@facingourrisk.org
URL: http://www.facingourrisk.org
Contact: Sue Friedman, Chair
Description: Provides women with resources to determine the high risk for breast and ovarian cancer due to genetic predisposition, family history or other factors. Provides information and support for women and families about options for managing and living with these risk factors. Represents the concerns and interests of the high-risk constituency to the cancer advocacy community, scientific and medical community, legislative community, and general public. **Publications:** *Joining FORCEs*, quarterly. Newsletter ● Brochures. Alternate Formats: online.

13532 ■ Foundation for Advancement in Cancer Therapy (FACT)
PO Box 1242
Old Chelsea Sta.
New York, NY 10113
Ph: (212)741-2790
URL: http://www.fact-ltd.org
Contact: Ruth Sackman, Pres.
Founded: 1971. **Members:** 2,500. **Membership Dues:** regular, $10 (annual). **Staff:** 3. **Budget:** $80,000. **Regional Groups:** 1. **Description:** Believes that cancer is a symptom of imbalance in body chemistry; thus, to control the disease, not only must any tumors be destroyed, but the body must also be regenerated through the "total person approach" which emphasizes nutrition, detoxification, and mind-body cohesion. Asserts the right of the public to be

informed of the "nontoxic biological" adjuncts and alternatives to surgery, chemotherapy, and radiotherapy, but cautions that patients be discriminating; disseminates information concerning only those preventive schemes and nontoxic therapies that have been verified as "safe" by long-term clinical tests; does not intend to discredit traditional therapies, but to complement them; works cooperatively with established practitioners and institutions. Seeks the elimination of carcinogens from the environment; supports cancer and nutrition research and compiles statistics; maintains speakers' bureau. **Libraries: Type:** not open to the public. **Formerly:** (1988) Foundation for Alternative Cancer Therapies. **Publications:** *Cancer Forum*, bimonthly. Magazine. **Price:** included in membership dues. **Circulation:** 2,000 ● *Cancer Program at Tallmogarden*. Audiotape. **Price:** $5.00.

13533 ■ Friends of the Jose Carreras International Leukemia Foundation (FJCILF)
PO Box 19024
Seattle, WA 98109-1024
Ph: (206)667-7108
Fax: (206)667-6124
E-mail: friendsjc@carrerasfoundation.org
URL: http://www.carrerasfoundation.org
Contact: Ms. Karen Carbonneau, Admin.
Founded: 1990. **Staff:** 1. **Nonmembership. Description:** Raises money to fund annual fellowship awards focused on research into the treatment and cure of leukemia and hematologic diseases. **Awards:** E.D. Thomas Post Doctoral Fellowship. **Frequency:** annual. **Type:** fellowship. **Recipient:** for young investigators less than 10 years post their first doctoral degree, supporting research into the diagnosis, prevention and cure of leukemia and related hematological malignancies. **Publications:** *Friends to Friends*, periodic. Newsletters.

13534 ■ Gilda Radner Familial Ovarian Cancer Registry
Roswell Park Cancer Inst.
Elm & Carlton Sts.
Buffalo, NY 14263-0001
Ph: (716)845-4503
Free: (800)682-7426
Fax: (716)845-8266
E-mail: gradner@roswellpark.org
URL: http://www.ovariancancer.com
Contact: Cathy Fahey BS, Operations Mgr.
Founded: 1981. **Multinational. Description:** Committed to the identification of new genes associated with familial ovarian cancer, thereby improving genetic and psychosocial counseling for individuals and families. Characterizes lifestyle choices (i.e., oral contraceptive use, hormone replacement therapy, number of pregnancies) that reduce ovarian cancer risk in women who may be susceptible to the disease. Strives for better methods for detecting ovarian cancer, for reliable predictive testing for cancer predisposition and prevention.

13535 ■ Gilda's Club
322 8th Ave., Ste.1402
New York, NY 10001
Ph: (917)305-1200
Free: (888)GILDA-4-U
Fax: (917)305-0549
E-mail: info@gildasclub.org
URL: http://www.gildasclub.org
Contact: Ms. Vivien Hoexter, CEO
Founded: 1991. **Members:** 30,000. **Regional Groups:** 27. **Languages:** English, Spanish. **Multinational. Description:** Provides places where people with cancer and their families and friends join with others to build social and emotional support as a supplement to medical care. Offers free program consists of The Basic III: I, Support and Networking groups; II, lectures and workshops; and III, social activities. **Computer Services:** database, resource directory ● information services, cancer resources.

13536 ■ Haitian American Association Against Cancer (HAAAC)
225 NE 34th St., Ste.208
Miami, FL 33137
Ph: (305)572-1825
Fax: (305)572-1827
E-mail: info@haaac.org
URL: http://www.haaac.org
Contact: Jacques-Albert Calixte, Pres.
Founded: 1997. **Membership Dues:** corporate, $250 (annual) ● small business, $150 (annual) ● organization (non-profit), $75 (annual) ● individual, $50 (annual) ● student, $20 (annual). **Description:** Provides information on detection services of cancer to the public, particularly Haitians and Haitian-Americans who are uninsured and/or not being served. Serves as a support center for cancer survivors, particularly Haitians and Haitian-Americans, who are suffering from the emotional stress of cancer. Offers counseling, community outreach, and support groups. **Publications:** Pamphlets (in Creole and English). Provides alternative information in the fight against cancer. ● Videos (in Creole and English). Provides alternatives in the crusade against cancer. Alternate Formats: diskette. **Conventions/Meetings:** workshop, health fairs.

13537 ■ Hereditary Colon Cancer Association (HCCA)
3601 N 4th Ave., Ste.201
Sioux Falls, SD 57104
Free: (800)264-6783
E-mail: info@hereditarycc.org
URL: http://www.hereditarycc.org
Contact: Carolyn Cole, Pres.
Description: Promotes awareness, education, and prevention of hereditary colon cancer. Promotes and funds research to find better treatments for those who have hereditary colon cancer. **Publications:** *Prevention Advocate*. Newsletter. Alternate Formats: online.

13538 ■ Intercultural Cancer Council (ICC)
6655 Travis, Ste.322
Houston, TX 77030-1312
Ph: (713)798-4617
Fax: (713)798-6222
E-mail: info@iccnetwork.org
URL: http://iccnetwork.org
Contact: Stephen P. Jiang, Chm.
Membership Dues: individual, $99 (annual) ● corporate, $279 (annual) ● educational, $89 (annual). **Regional Groups:** 8. **Multinational. Description:** Seeks to provide services, programs and research about health care system and cancer related studies to racial and ethnic minorities as well as to medically underserved populations in United States and its associated territories. **Computer Services:** Information services, cancer fact sheets, health and human resources ● mailing lists, of members. **Publications:** *Cancer Fact Sheet* ● Articles. Contains information on cancer and its intercultural experiences. Alternate Formats: online. **Conventions/Meetings:** biennial symposium, discussion of cancer related problem, issues and solutions.

13539 ■ International Association of Cancer Victors and Friends (IACVF)
20111 Canyon View Dr., No. 277
Santa Clarita, CA 91351
Ph: (661)251-1082
E-mail: babed@netzero.net
URL: http://www.cancervictors.net
Contact: C. McKenna, Coor.
Founded: 1963. **Members:** 4,000. **Membership Dues:** regular, gift, $25 (annual) ● sustaining, $100 (annual) ● life, $300 ● perpetual, $1,000. **Staff:** 2. **Budget:** $50,000. **Regional Groups:** 13. **State Groups:** 2. **National Groups:** 10. **Description:** Encourages independent research on cancer therapies and disseminates information on "nontoxic" chemotherapies. Works directly with cancer patients providing one-on-one services. Offers educational programs on topics including carcinogens in air, food, and water and nutrition in relation to cancer. **Libraries: Type:** reference. **Holdings:** 4; archival material, artwork,

books, business records, clippings, periodicals. **Subjects:** cancer research. **Awards:** Cecile Pollack Hoffman Memorial Award. **Frequency:** annual. **Type:** recognition. **Recipient:** to an individual who exemplifies the ideas of Cecile Pollack Hoffman ● Distinguished Service Award. **Frequency:** annual. **Type:** recognition. **Recipient:** to an individual who has given the most important service voluntarily to the association ● Humanitarian Award. **Frequency:** annual. **Type:** recognition. **Recipient:** for exceptional service in science, medicine or humanities. **Formerly:** (1985) International Association of Cancer Victims and Friends. **Publications:** *Cancer Victors Journal*, quarterly. Provides news on non-toxic cancer treatments and breakthroughs in cancer research; includes studies on carcinogenic conditions. **Price:** included in membership dues. ISSN: 0891-0766. **Circulation:** 5,000. **Advertising:** accepted ● Audiotapes. **Advertising:** accepted ● Books ● Pamphlets ● Reprints. **Conventions/Meetings:** annual meeting and seminar ● regional meeting.

13540 ■ International Association for the Study of Lung Cancer (IASLC)
c/o Pia Hirsch
PO Box 6511
Aurora, CO 80045-0511
Ph: (303)724-3155
Fax: (303)724-3162
E-mail: pia.hirsch@iaslc.org
URL: http://www.iaslc.org
Contact: Pia Hirsch, Contact
Founded: 1972. **Members:** 2,000. **Membership Dues:** regular, $150 (annual). **Multinational. Description:** Promotes the study of the etiology, epidemiology, prevention, diagnosis, treatment and all other aspects of lung cancer, and to disseminate information about lung cancer to members of the association, the medical community, and the public. **Publications:** Newsletter, monthly. Contains news and upcoming events. Alternate Formats: online.

13541 ■ International Myeloma Foundation (IMF)
12650 Riverside Dr., Ste.206
North Hollywood, CA 91607-3421
Ph: (818)487-7455
Free: (800)452-CURE
Fax: (818)487-7454
E-mail: theimf@myeloma.org
URL: http://www.myeloma.org
Contact: Susie Novis, Pres.
Founded: 1990. **Members:** 95,000. **Staff:** 13. **Local Groups:** 57. **Languages:** Chinese, Danish, English, French, Italian, Japanese, Korean, Polish, Portuguese, Russian, Spanish, Turkish. **Multinational. Description:** Promotes education, treatment and research of multiple myeloma (a little-known cancer of the bone marrow.) Provides a variety of patient and physician education and support programs and services. **Awards:** Brian D. Novis Research Grant. **Frequency:** annual. **Type:** grant. **Recipient:** for a doctor or researcher who is actively working on multiple myeloma ● Junior and Senior Grants. **Type:** grant. **Telecommunication Services:** electronic mail, snovis@myeloma.org. **Publications:** *A Concise Review of the Disease and Treatment Options*. Book. **Price:** free. Alternate Formats: online ● *Myeloma Minute*, weekly. Newsletter. **Price:** free. Alternate Formats: online ● *Myeloma Today*, bimonthly. Newsletter. **Price:** free for U.S. subscribers; $15.00 for international subscribers. Alternate Formats: online ● *Patient Handbook*. **Price:** free. Alternate Formats: online ● *So You're Considering..* Brochure ● Booklets. **Price:** free. Alternate Formats: online. **Conventions/Meetings:** biennial conference, for physicians ● semiannual Patient & Family Seminar, for patients and family members.

13542 ■ International Oncology Study Group (IOSG)
Address Unknown since 2006
Founded: 1993. **Members:** 170. **Multinational. Description:** Promotes clinical therapeutic research in order to improve the prognosis for patients with cancer. **Publications:** *IOSG Update*. Newsletter.

13543 ■ International Psycho-Oncology Society (IPOS)
c/o Custom Management Group
2365 Hunters Way
Charlottesville, VA 22911
Ph: (434)293-5350
Fax: (434)977-1856
E-mail: info@ipos-society.org
URL: http://www.ipos-society.org
Contact: Ms. Elliott Graham, Exec. Dir.
Founded: 1984. **Members:** 200. **Membership Dues:** active, associate - developing nation, $75 (annual) ● member-in-training - developing nation, $45 (annual) ● active, associate, $95 (annual) ● member-in-training, $55 (annual). **Staff:** 1. **Budget:** $50,000. **Multinational. Description:** Fosters international multidisciplinary communication about clinical, educational and research issues that relate to the subspecialty of psycho-oncology and two primary psychosocial dimensions of cancer: response of patients, families and staff to cancer and its treatment at all stages; and psychological, social and behavioral factors that influence tumor progression and survival. Represents over two hundred members from thirty-eight countries: these include, but are not limited to, physicians, social workers, nurses, psychologists, rehabilitation specialists, epidemiologists, social scientists and educators. **Awards:** Bernard Fox Award. **Frequency:** annual. **Type:** recognition. **Recipient:** to an IPOS or community member who has made an outstanding contribution (practice, education, research, and leadership) to the field of psychosocial oncology ● Hiroomi Kawano New Investigator Award. **Frequency:** annual. **Type:** recognition. **Recipient:** to a new investigator for outstanding research contributions in psychosocial oncology ● Sutherland Award and Memorial Lecture. **Frequency:** annual. **Type:** recognition. **Recipient:** to an individual for lifetime achievement in the field of psychosocial oncology. **Computer Services:** Information services ● online services, lectures, webcasts ● online services, listserv. **Committees:** Education. **Affiliated With:** International Union Against Cancer. **Publications:** Membership Directory. Alternate Formats: online. **Conventions/Meetings:** annual World Congress of Psycho-Oncology - 2008 June 9-13, Madrid, Spain.

13544 ■ International Society for Biological Therapy of Cancer (ISBTC)
555 E Wells St., Ste.1100
Milwaukee, WI 53202-3823
Ph: (414)271-2456
Fax: (414)276-3349
E-mail: info@isbtc.org
URL: http://www.isbtc.org
Contact: Ulrich Keilholz MD, Pres.
Founded: 1984. **Members:** 500. **Membership Dues:** fellow, regular, affiliate, $195 (annual) ● student, $50 (annual) ● associate, $140 (annual) ● corporate, $275 (annual). **Staff:** 5. **Multinational. Description:** Represents physicians, researchers and others in the national and international medical field who are committed to investigating, developing and utilizing biological therapy for the treatment of malignant diseases. Provides a forum for the international community of researchers and clinicians who work with biological approaches to cancer therapy to share and discuss their work. **Awards:** Presidential Awards. **Frequency:** annual. **Type:** recognition. **Computer Services:** database, membership directory. **Committees:** Collaborations; Constitution and Bylaws; Development; Public Relations, Publications and Communications. **Formerly:** (2002) Society for Biological Therapy. **Publications:** *Journal of Immunotherapy*, bimonthly. Features articles on immunomodulators, lymphokines, antibodies, cells and cell products in cancer biology and therapy. **Price:** included in membership dues. ISSN: 1524-9557. **Advertising:** accepted. **Conventions/Meetings:** annual meeting.

13545 ■ Kidney Cancer Association (KCA)
1234 Sherman Ave., Ste.203
Evanston, IL 60202-1375
Ph: (847)332-1051
Free: (800)850-9132

Fax: (847)332-2978
E-mail: office@curekidneycancer.org
URL: http://www.curekidneycancer.org
Contact: William P. Bro, Pres.
Founded: 1990. **Membership Dues:** individual, $200 (annual). **Description:** Provides a broad range of services related to kidney cancer, including patient meetings, annual convention for patients and doctors, sponsors research and advocates for changes. **Publications:** *Kidney Cancer Journal*, quarterly. Alternate Formats: online ● Annual Report, annual. Alternate Formats: online ● Videos. **Conventions/Meetings:** annual convention.

13546 ■ Leukemia and Lymphoma Society
1311 Mamaroneck Ave.
White Plains, NY 10605
Ph: (914)949-5213
Free: (800)955-4572
Fax: (914)949-6691
E-mail: infocenter@leukemia-lymphoma.org
URL: http://www.lls.org
Contact: Dwayne Howell PhD, Pres./CEO
Founded: 1949. **Staff:** 375. **State Groups:** 64. **Languages:** English, Spanish. **Nonmembership. Description:** Works to cure leukemia, lymphoma, and myeloma; seeks to improve the quality of life of patients and their families. Sponsors medical symposia and research; provides financial aid for patients; provides free information, support groups, teleconferences, and Web conferences for patients and families. **Libraries:** **Type:** reference; not open to the public. **Holdings:** 300; books, clippings, reports. **Subjects:** myeloma, leukemia, lymphomas, Hodgkin's disease. **Awards:** Specialized Center of Research Grant. **Type:** grant ● Translational Research PRG. **Type:** grant. **Committees:** Communications; Development; Medical; Patient Aid; Professional Education; Scientific. **Formerly:** (1955) Robert Roesler de Villiers Foundation; (2000) Leukemia Society of America. **Publications:** *Educational Literature*. Brochures. Provides information about leukemia, lymphoma, myeloma, etc. **Price:** free. Alternate Formats: online ● *The Leukemia & Lymphoma Society—Newsline*, quarterly. Newsletter. Provides information on advances in the research into leukemia, lymphoma, Hodgkin Disease and Myeloma. Includes research updates. **Price:** free. **Circulation:** 77,000. **Conventions/Meetings:** annual meeting and symposium (exhibits) - always October.

13547 ■ Life Raft Group (LRG)
40 Galesi Dr.
Wayne, NJ 07470
Ph: (973)837-9092
Fax: (973)837-9095
E-mail: liferaft@liferaftgroup.org
URL: http://www.liferaftgroup.org
Contact: Norman Scherzer, Exec. Dir.
Founded: 2002. **Members:** 500. **Staff:** 7. **Budget:** $1,470,000. **Regional Groups:** 19. **State Groups:** 7. **Multinational. Description:** Provides support, through information, education and research to patients with a rare cancer called GIST (Gastrointestinal Stromal Tumor). **Computer Services:** database, to assist patients in finding area doctors ● information services. **Additional Websites:** http://www.globalgist.org. **Publications:** Newsletter, monthly. Alternate Formats: online.

13548 ■ Lung Cancer Alliance (LCA)
888 16th St. NW, Ste.800
Washington, DC 20006
Ph: (202)463-2080
Free: (800)298-2436
E-mail: info@lungcanceralliance.org
URL: http://www.lungcanceralliance.org
Contact: Laurie Fenton, Pres.
Founded: 2001. **Staff:** 5. **Description:** Advocates for people living with lung cancer or those at risk for the disease. Educates policy leaders and the public of the need for lung cancer research. Offers patient education and support for lung cancer patients. **Computer Services:** Information services, lung cancer resources ● mailing lists. **Boards:** Medical Advisory.

Programs: Phone Buddy. **Publications:** *Spirit and Breath*, quarterly. Newsletter. Alternate Formats: on-line.

13549 ■ Lymphoma Research Foundation (LRF)

8800 Venice Blvd., Ste.207
Los Angeles, CA 90034
Ph: (310)204-7040 (212)349-2910
Free: (800)500-9976
Fax: (310)204-7043
E-mail: lrf@lymphoma.org
URL: http://www.lymphoma.org
Contact: Suzanne Bliss, Exec. Dir.
Founded: 2001. **Staff:** 20. **Budget:** $5,000,000. **State Groups:** 20. **Languages:** English, Spanish. **Description:** Provides support and information for lymphoma patients and their families regarding diagnosis, treatments, clinical trials, support services, literature, and physician referrals. Serves patients with a buddy support program. Supports lymphoma specific education for both patients and healthcare professionals. Promotes advocacy; funds research. **Awards:** Clinical Investigator Career Development Award. **Frequency:** annual. **Type:** grant. **Recipient:** for fellows and scientists ● Fellowship Awards. **Frequency:** annual. **Type:** grant. **Recipient:** for fellows and scientists. **Additional Websites:** http://www.lymphomafocus.org. **Boards:** Scientific Advisory. **Programs:** Clinical Research; Fellowship Research; Lymphoma Support Network; Patient Aid Grant. **Formed by Merger of:** (2002) Cure For Lymphoma Foundation; (2002) Lymphoma Research Foundation of America. **Publications:** *Lymphoma Today*, quarterly. Newsletter. Provides information about lymphoma and the Foundation, as well as current events. **Circulation:** 80,000. Alternate Formats: online ● Booklets. **Conventions/Meetings:** annual Educational Forum on Lymphoma - meeting (exhibits) - always October.

13550 ■ Make Today Count (MTC)

1235 E Cherokee St.
Springfield, MO 65804-2203
Ph: (417)820-2588
Fax: (417)820-2587
E-mail: czimmerman@sprg.mercy.com
Contact: Connie Zimmerman, Exec. Dir.
Founded: 1974. **Members:** 5,000. **Staff:** 3. **Local Groups:** 200. **Description:** Cancer patients and others with life-threatening illnesses, and their immediate families. Works to bring members and their neighbors together to discuss openly the false implications and the realities of life-threatening diseases. Takes a positive approach to the problems of serious illness in order to lessen the emotional trauma for all concerned. Assists professionals in communicating with and meeting the needs of seriously ill patients. Maintains speakers' bureau and referral service; plans educational programs, films, and tapes. **Publications:** *Chapter Directory*, annual ● *Make Today Count Newsletter*, bimonthly. Offers emotional support to people with cancer or other life-threatening illnesses, and to their family members, friends, and professionals. **Price:** $10.00/year ● *Make Today Count - Until Tomorrow Comes*. **Conventions/Meetings:** annual meeting (exhibits).

13551 ■ Melanoma Research Foundation (MRF)

24 Old Georgetown Rd.
Princeton, NJ 08540
Free: (800)MRF-1290
Fax: (732)821-5955
E-mail: wrmarsch@earthlink.net
URL: http://www.melanoma.org
Contact: William Marsch, Program Dir.
Founded: 1996. **Members:** 500. **Budget:** $700,000. **Description:** Committed to finding a cure for melanoma through research, education and advocacy. **Awards:** **Frequency:** annual. **Type:** grant. **Recipient:** to researchers. **Computer Services:** Information services, melanoma resources. **Programs:** Miles for Melanoma. **Publications:** Newsletter, quarterly. **Circulation:** 9,500. Alternate Formats: online ● Brochure. Alternate Formats: online.

13552 ■ Men Against Breast Cancer (MABC)

PO Box 150
Adamstown, MD 21710-0150
Free: (866)547-6222
Fax: (301)874-8657
E-mail: info@menagainstbreastcancer.org
URL: http://www.menagainstbreastcancer.org
Contact: Marc Heyison, Pres./Co-Founder
Membership Dues: $35 (annual). **Description:** Strives to eradicate breast cancer as a life-threatening disease by mobilizing and supporting men as active participants in the fight against the disease. **Telecommunication Services:** electronic mail, marc@menagainstbreastcancer.org.

13553 ■ Mothers Supporting Daughters with Breast Cancer (MSDBC)

c/o Charmayne Dierker, Pres.
25235 Foxchase Dr.
Chestertown, MD 21620
Ph: (410)778-1982
Fax: (410)778-1411
E-mail: msdbc@verizon.net
URL: http://www.mothersdaughters.org
Contact: Charmayne Dierker, Pres.
Founded: 1995. **Budget:** $10,000. **Multinational. Description:** Assists mothers of daughters with breast cancer. Provides basic medical information about breast cancer as a disease and the various treatments that patients may receive. Offers a local, regional, and national communication network for mothers and daughters. Works to offer emotional support to mothers of daughters newly-diagnosed with breast cancer. **Libraries: Type:** reference. **Subjects:** breast cancer. **Publications:** *Daughter's Brochure*. Provides information about the difficulties a mother may be experiencing and how to help. **Price:** free ● *Mother's Handbook*. Prepared for mothers who have had a daughter diagnosed with breast cancer. Provides a list of free resources. ● *MSDBC—Tells of Services (Caring, Supportive, Involved)*, biennial. Brochure.

13554 ■ Multiple Myeloma Research Foundation (MMRF)

383 Main Ave., 5th Fl.
Norwalk, CT 06851
Ph: (203)229-0464
E-mail: info@themmrf.org
URL: http://www.multiplemyeloma.org
Contact: Kathy Giusti, Founder/CEO
Founded: 1998. **Multinational. Description:** Strives to find a cure for multiple myeloma. **Awards:** Fellows' Grant. **Frequency:** annual. **Type:** grant. **Recipient:** for researchers entering the field of multiple myeloma ● Senior Research Grant. **Frequency:** annual. **Type:** grant. **Recipient:** for investigators with an interest in myeloma. **Computer Services:** Information services, myeloma resources. **Publications:** *Myeloma Focus*, quarterly. Newsletter. Alternate Formats: online. **Conventions/Meetings:** symposium.

13555 ■ National Alliance of Breast Cancer Organizations (NABCO)

Address Unknown since 2007
Founded: 1986. **Membership Dues:** individual, $50 (annual) ● nonprofit organization, $100 (annual) ● corporate, $200 (annual). **Staff:** 11. **Budget:** $2,500,000. **Description:** The National Alliance of Breast Cancer Organization (NABCO) is the leading non-profit information and education resource on breast cancer in the U.S. NABCO provides information to medical professionals and their organizations and to patients and their families, and advocates for beneficial regulatory change and legislation. With public and corporate partners, NABCO has collaborated on programs that have reached a national audience, heightening public awareness and connecting women with needed services. Services are free of charge. **Libraries: Type:** not open to the public. **Subjects:** breast cancer. **Awards:** Within Our Reach (a NABCO program). **Frequency:** annual. **Type:** grant. **Recipient:** for community programs serving poor and medically underserved women. **Publications:** *NABCO News*, quarterly. Newsletter.

Monitors developments relating to breast cancer. **Price:** included in membership dues. **Advertising:** not accepted ● *NABCO's Breast Cancer Resource List*, annual. Contains information on materials and organizations that provide information about breast cancer. **Price:** included in membership dues. ISSN: 1526-5803.

13556 ■ National Black Leadership Initiative on Cancer (NBLIC)

c/o Robin Mitchell, Research Specialist
311 SPWH m/c 922
2121 W Taylor St.
Chicago, IL 60612
Ph: (312)996-8046
Fax: (312)996-0064
E-mail: bird@uic.edu
URL: http://ness2.uic.edu/UI-Service/programs/UIC168.html
Contact: Robin Mitchell, Research Specialist
Founded: 1994. **Members:** 36. **Regional Groups:** 44. **State Groups:** 1. **Local Groups:** 1. **Description:** Represents African-Americans and health care professionals concerned with the prevention, diagnosis, and treatment of people with cancer, particularly those of African-American descent. Seeks to facilitate "closing the gap in cancer incidence and mortality and increasing survival from cancer" by increasing awareness among African-Americans of cancer and its prevention and treatment. Conducts educational programs to develop volunteer leaders in African-American communities, with emphasis on increasing understanding of breast, colorectal, and prostate cancer and the role played by diet in their prevention. **Libraries: Type:** reference. **Holdings:** video recordings. **Subjects:** cancer, health. **Awards: Frequency:** periodic. **Type:** scholarship. **Publications:** Newsletter, monthly. **Conventions/Meetings:** annual regional meeting.

13557 ■ National Breast Cancer Coalition (NBCC)

1101 17th St. NW, Ste.1300
Washington, DC 20036
Ph: (202)296-7477
Free: (800)622-2838
Fax: (202)265-6854
URL: http://www.stopbreastcancer.org
Contact: Frances M. Visco, Pres.
Founded: 1991. **Members:** 60,000. **Membership Dues:** individual, $35 (annual) ● group, organization, $100 (annual) ● President's Council, $1,000 (annual). **Staff:** 34. **Description:** Promotes research into the cause of, optimal treatments and cure for breast cancer, aims to improve coordination and distribution of research funds and recruitment and training of scientists; strives to improve access to breast cancer screening, diagnosis, treatment and care for all women, particularly the underserved and uninsured, through legislation and change in regulation and delivery of breast health care; dedicated to increasing involvement and influence of those living with breast cancer in the areas of legislation, regulatory processes and all aspects of clinical trial design, including access to clinical trials; advocacy activities; formulated national action plan on breast cancer, to which the Clinton Administration committed in 1993. Operates: Aspen Project, which brings together industrial, scientific, governmental, and consumer representatives to develop innovative approaches to the prevention and treatment of breast cancer; Project LEAD, which trains grass roots advocates to influence public policies affecting people with breast cancer; Clinical Trials Project, which trains members to collaborate with scientific and industrial organizations to expedite clinical trials of breast cancer drugs and treatments. **Programs:** Clinical Trials Initiative; Environmental Initiative; International Initiative; Quality Care Initiative. **Projects:** Aspen; LEAD. **Publications:** *Call to Action*, quarterly. Newsletter. **Price:** included in membership dues. **Circulation:** 60,000. Alternate Formats: online ● *Powerful Voices*, annual. Annual Report. Alternate Formats: online. **Conventions/Meetings:** annual Advocacy Training Conference - spring, Washington, DC ● periodic international conference ● periodic Media Workshop.

13558 ■ National Cervical Cancer Coalition (NCCC)

7247 Hayvenhurst Ave., Ste.A-7
Van Nuys, CA 91406
Ph: (818)909-3849
Free: (800)685-5531
Fax: (818)780-8199
E-mail: info@nccc-online.org
URL: http://www.nccc-online.org
Contact: Ms. Sarina Araujo, Exec. Dir.
Founded: 1995. **Languages:** English, Spanish. **Description:** Grass roots campaign educating the public about cervical cancer prevention, outreach, screening, treatment, and follow-up. **Awards:** Focus Award. **Type:** recognition. **Recipient:** to web sites. **Telecommunication Services:** electronic mail, nccc@nccc-online.org. **Publications:** *Extraordinary Moments*. Newsletter. Alternate Formats: online. **Conventions/Meetings:** conference.

13559 ■ National Childhood Cancer Foundation (NCCF)

4600 E West Highway, Ste.600
Bethesda, MD 20814-3457
Ph: (626)447-1674
Free: (800)458-6223
Fax: (626)447-1675
E-mail: info@curesearch.org
URL: http://www.curesearch.org
Contact: Paul T. Burke, Pres./CEO
Description: Physician-scientists. Supports a network of childhood cancer treatment and research institutions caring for infants, children, teens and young adults. **Awards:** Foundation Fellowship Program. **Type:** fellowship. **Recipient:** for young physicians. **Formerly:** (2002) National Childhood Cancer Foundation; (2003) Foundation for the Children's Oncology Group. **Publications:** *Childhood Cancerline*, published several times a year. Newsletter. Alternate Formats: online.

13560 ■ National Children's Cancer Society (NCCS)

1015 Locust, Ste.600
St. Louis, MO 63101
Ph: (314)241-1600
Free: (800)532-6459
Fax: (314)241-1996
E-mail: krudd@children-cancer.org
URL: http://www.nationalchildrenscancersociety.com
Contact: Mark Stolze, Pres./CEO
Founded: 1987. **Description:** Aims to improve the quality of life for children with cancer. Strives to reduce risk of cancer in children by promoting children's health through financial and in kind assistance, advocacy, support services, education and prevention programs. **Computer Services:** Online services, message board. **Telecommunication Services:** electronic mail, pfs@children-cancer.org. **Programs:** Global Outreach; Vending Outreach. **Publications:** *Patient and Family Services*, quarterly. Newsletter ● Annual Report, annual.

13561 ■ National Coalition for Cancer Survivorship (NCCS)

1010 Wayne Ave., Ste.770
Silver Spring, MD 20910
Ph: (301)650-9127
Free: (877)622-7937
Fax: (301)565-9670
E-mail: info@canceradvocacy.org
URL: http://www.canceradvocacy.org
Contact: Ellen L. Stovall, Pres./CEO
Founded: 1986. **Staff:** 14. **Budget:** $2,500,000. **Regional Groups:** 7. **Description:** Advocates for quality of cancer care for all Americans. Provides leadership in public policy. Empowers and educates those dealing with cancer. **Awards:** NCCS Logan Award for Service to Survivorship. **Frequency:** annual. **Type:** recognition. **Recipient:** for an outstanding individual who has worked on his/her own or through an organization or institution on behalf of cancer survivors and has shown exemplary leadership ● NCCS Public Service Leadership Award. **Frequency:** annual. **Type:** recognition. **Recipient:** for public service figure who has worked on behalf of cancer

survivors ● NCCS Spingarn Writer's Award. **Frequency:** annual. **Type:** recognition. **Recipient:** for an outstanding author writing on the subject of survivorship. **Computer Services:** Information services, list of organizations concerned with survivorship. **Committees:** Book Mart; Development; Public Policy; Research; Technical Assistance. **Programs:** Cancer Advocacy Now!; Cancer Keys; Cancer Survival Toolbox; Everyday Heroes; Town Hall. **Task Forces:** Outreach to Underserved Populations. **Affiliated With:** Candlelighters Childhood Cancer Foundation; Make Today Count; Oncology Nursing Society. **Publications:** *Advocacy. Authenticity. Passion.*, annual. Annual Report. Alternate Formats: online ● *Charting the Journey: An Almanac of Resources for Cancer Survivors*. Book. Contains information on health insurance, communicating with family and friends, dealing with loss, advocating for yourself, and job discrimination. **Price:** $6.25 ● *InterActions*, quarterly. Newsletter. Gives updates on the association and in the cancer community. Alternate Formats: online ● *NCCS Networker*, quarterly. Newsletter. News and articles on cancer survivorship, interviews, and reviews. **Price:** included in membership dues. **Circulation:** 8,000 ● *Survivors*. Book ● *Teamwork: The Cancer Patient's Guide to Talking With Your Doctor*. Booklet ● *What Cancer Survivors Need to Know About Health Insurance*. Booklet ● Also publishes many booklets on cancer-related topics.

13562 ■ National Comprehensive Cancer Network (NCCN)

500 Old York Rd., Ste.250
Jenkintown, PA 19046
Ph: (215)690-0300
Free: (888)909-6226
Fax: (215)690-0280
URL: http://www.nccn.org
Contact: Kim Schwalje, Contact
Founded: 1995. **Members:** 19. **Description:** Acts as an authoritative source of information to help patients and health professionals make informed decisions about cancer care. Develops, updates, and disseminates a complete library of clinical practice guidelines through the collective expertise of member institutions. These guidelines are the standard for clinical policy in oncology; programs emphasize improving the quality, effectiveness, and efficiency of oncology practice. **Projects:** Oncology Outcomes. **Publications:** *The Complete Library of Practice Guidelines in Oncology*, annual. Alternate Formats: CD-ROM; online ● *Journal of the National Comprehensive Cancer Network*, bimonthly. **Price:** $399.00 /year for individuals in U.S.; $499.00 /year for individuals outside U.S.; $599.00 /year for institutions in U.S.; $699.00 /year for institutions outside U.S. ISSN: 1540-1405. **Advertising:** accepted. Alternate Formats: online. Also Cited As: *JNCCN*. **Conventions/Meetings:** annual Practice Guidelines and Outcomes Data in Oncology - meeting (exhibits).

13563 ■ National Lung Cancer Partnership

222 N Midvale Blvd., Ste.6
Madison, WI 53705
Ph: (608)233-7905
Fax: (608)233-7893
E-mail: info@nationallungcancerpartnership.org
URL: http://www.nationallungcancerpartnership.org
Contact: Regina Vidaver PhD, Exec. Dir.
Founded: 2001. **Membership Dues:** full, $75 (annual). **Description:** Seeks to decrease deaths due to lung cancer. Raises awareness of lung cancer. Increases funding for lung cancer research. Supports research in sex differences in lung cancer. Encourages professionals, particularly women, to be successful in lung cancer research, treatment and care. **Computer Services:** Information services, lung cancer resources. **Committees:** Awareness; Professional Development; Public Policy; Science and Research. **Formerly:** (2006) Women Against Lung Cancer.

13564 ■ National Ovarian Cancer Coalition (NOCC)

500 NE Spanish River Blvd., Ste.8
Boca Raton, FL 33431

Ph: (561)393-0005
Free: (888)OVARIAN
Fax: (561)393-7275
E-mail: nocc@ovarian.org
URL: http://64.132.170.241/newnocc/updateie.asp
Contact: Suzy Lockwood-Rayermann PhD, Chair
Founded: 1995. **Members:** 16,000. **Staff:** 5. **Budget:** $350,000. **State Groups:** 25. **Description:** Individuals with ovarian cancer and their families; health care professionals treating people with ovarian cancer. Seeks to advance the prevention, diagnosis, and treatment of ovarian cancer. Serves as a clearinghouse on ovarian cancer; provides support and services to members; conducts educational programs. **Libraries:** Type: open to the public; lending; reference. **Holdings:** audio recordings, books, business records, periodicals, video recordings. **Subjects:** ovarian cancer. **Awards:** Research Fund. **Frequency:** annual. **Type:** grant.

13565 ■ National Prostate Cancer Coalition (NPCC)

1154 15th St. NW
Washington, DC 20005
Ph: (202)463-9455
Free: (888)245-9455
Fax: (202)463-9456
E-mail: info@fightprostatecancer.org
URL: http://www.pcacoalition.org
Contact: Richard Atkins MD, CEO
Founded: 1996. **Staff:** 12. **Description:** Sets the standards for rapidly reducing the burden of prostate cancer on American men and their families through awareness, outreach and advocacy. Strives to educate every American about the risk of prostate cancer, the importance of early detection and the research funding needed to beat the disease. Works with government officials to increase federal funding for prostate cancer research. **Computer Services:** Information services, prostate cancer resources. **Programs:** Drive Against Prostate Cancer. **Publications:** *Aware*, weekly. Newsletter. Contains information about prostate cancer. **Price:** free. Alternate Formats: online.

13566 ■ Native American Cancer Research (NACR)

3022 S Nova Rd.
Pine, CO 80470-7830
Ph: (303)838-9359
Free: (800)537-8295
Fax: (303)838-7629
E-mail: contact05@natamcancer.org
URL: http://natamcancer.org
Contact: Linda Burhansstipanov PhD, Pres./Exec. Dir.
Founded: 1999. **Description:** Strives to reduce Native American cancer incidence and mortality, and to increase survival from cancer among Native Americans; implements cancer primary prevention, secondary prevention, risk reduction, screening (early detection), education, training, research, diagnoses, control, treatment, support, quality of life, and/or studies of cancer among Native Americans. **Publications:** *Native American Cancer Research Program Newsletter*, 3/year. Informs native and non-natives of Native American cancer prevention and control. **Conventions/Meetings:** National Native American Cancer Survivors/Thrivers Conference ● workshop.

13567 ■ North American Association of Central Cancer Registries

2121 W White Oaks Dr., Ste.C
Springfield, IL 62704-7412
Ph: (217)698-0800
Fax: (217)698-0188
E-mail: hhowe@naaccr.org
URL: http://www.naaccr.org
Contact: Holly L. Howe PhD, Exec. Dir.
Founded: 1987. **Members:** 147. **Membership Dues:** individual, $125 (annual) ● full, $375 (annual) ● sustaining nonprofit, $500 (annual) ● basic sponsoring, $2,000 (annual) ● sustaining for profit, $1,000 (annual). **Staff:** 10. **Multinational. Description:** Cancer registries, government agencies, professional associations, and private groups interested in enhanc-

ing the quality and use of cancer registry data. Seeks to advance the use of cancer registration techniques in cancer control and epidemiological research, public health programs, and patient care. **Awards:** Calum S. Muir Memorial Award. **Frequency:** annual. **Type:** recognition. **Recipient:** for individual who has made substantive and outstanding contributions in cancer registration ● Constance L. Percy Award for Distinguished Service. **Frequency:** annual. **Type:** recognition. **Recipient:** for member who has demonstrated outstanding volunteer service to the association. **Also Known As:** NAACCR. **Publications:** *CINA*, annual. Monograph. Features cancer incidence and mortality statistics. ● *NAACCR Narrative*, quarterly. Newsletter. Alternate Formats: online. **Conventions/Meetings:** annual meeting and workshop (exhibits).

13568 ■ North American Brain Tumor Coalition (NABTC)
c/o Elizabeth Goss, Esq., Counsel
1 Metro Ctr.
700 12th St. NW, Ste.900
Washington, DC 20005
Ph: (202)508-4670
Fax: (202)508-4650
E-mail: egoss@ropesgray.com
URL: http://www.nabraintumor.org
Contact: Elizabeth Goss Esq., Counsel
Founded: 1993. **Description:** Dedicated to eradicating brain tumors; promotes awareness, research, access to specialized care and other issues affecting brain tumor patients. Sponsors Brain Tumor Action Week in U.S., Brain Tumor Action Month, Canada. **Publications:** *The Faces of Brain Tumors*, annual. Book. Alternate Formats: online ● Papers, annual. Alternate Formats: online ● Reports. Alternate Formats: online.

13569 ■ Ovarian Cancer National Alliance
910 17th St. NW, Ste.1190
Washington, DC 20006
Ph: (202)331-1332
Free: (866)399-6262
Fax: (202)331-2292
E-mail: ocna@ovariancancer.org
URL: http://www.ovariancancer.org
Contact: Sherry Salway Black, Exec. Dir.
Founded: 1997. **Staff:** 4. **Budget:** $375,000. **Description:** Works to promote knowledge about breast cancer. Aims to establish a coordinated national effort to place ovarian cancer education, policy and research issues prominently on the agendas of national policy makers and women's health care leaders. **Computer Services:** Information services, ovarian cancer resources. **Telecommunication Services:** electronic mail, sflynn@ovariancancer.org. **Publications:** *OC Connection*, quarterly. Newsletter. Alternate Formats: online.

13570 ■ Patient Advocates for Advanced Cancer Treatments (PAACT)
1143 Parmelee NW
PO Box 141695
Grand Rapids, MI 49504
Ph: (616)453-1477
Fax: (616)453-1846
E-mail: paact@paactusa.org
URL: http://www.paactusa.org
Contact: Janet E. Ney, Pres./Chair
Founded: 1984. **Members:** 36,000. **Membership Dues:** patient/advocate, $50 (annual) ● professional, $100 (annual) ● donor, $500 (annual) ● corporation/sponsor, $1,000 (annual). **Staff:** 3. **Description:** Prostate cancer patients and physicians. Engages in advocacy activities. Provides educational materials to those with prostate cancer. Conducts protocol studies and research. **Libraries: Type:** reference. **Holdings:** audiovisuals, books, clippings, periodicals. **Subjects:** prostate cancer. **Awards:** Certificate of Appreciation. **Frequency:** periodic. **Type:** recognition. **Recipient:** for individuals who have made significant contributions to the study and treatment of prostate cancer. **Computer Services:** database, PDQ, contains cancer literature. **Telecommunication Services:** information service. **Publications:** *Financial Summary Report*. Alternate Formats: online

● *Prostate Cancer Communication*, quarterly. Newsletter. **Circulation:** 27,750. Alternate Formats: online
● *Prostate Cancer Report*.

13571 ■ Pediatric Brain Tumor Foundation of the United States (PBTF)
302 Ridgefield Ct.
Asheville, NC 28806
Ph: (828)665-6891
Free: (800)253-6530
Fax: (828)665-6894
E-mail: pbtfus@pbtfus.org
URL: http://www.pbtfus.org
Contact: Mike Traynor, Pres.
Founded: 1991. **Description:** Seeks to find the cause and cure of brain tumors in children. Supports medical research; promotes public awareness of the disease; aids in early detection and treatment of childhood brain tumors. **Awards:** Peter Steck Memorial Research Award & Lecture. **Frequency:** annual. **Type:** monetary. **Recipient:** for exceptional individuals in the field of pediatric brain tumor research. **Publications:** *International Neuro-Oncology Journal*.

13572 ■ People Against Cancer (PAC)
604 East St.
PO Box 10
Otho, IA 50569
Ph: (515)972-4444
Fax: (515)972-4415
E-mail: info@peopleagainstcancer.net
URL: http://www.peopleagainstcancer.net
Contact: Frank D. Wiewel, Contact
Founded: 1985. **Members:** 2,000. **Membership Dues:** individual, $35 (annual) ● sustaining, $450 (annual) ● benefactor, $500 (annual) ● foreign, $50 (annual) ● founding, $1,000 (annual) ● Golden Circle patron, $10,000 (annual) ● patron, $5,000 (annual) ● supporting, $100 (annual). **Staff:** 5. **Budget:** $300,000. **Description:** Promotes research into alternative cancer therapy and prevention. Conducts educational, charitable, and research programs; finds members the best cancer treatment. **Libraries: Type:** reference. **Holdings:** 4,000; books, periodicals. **Subjects:** alternative medicine. **Computer Services:** database ● record retrieval services. **Publications:** *Options*, quarterly. Newsletter ● Bulletin ● Directory.

13573 ■ Pregnant With Cancer Network (PWCN)
PO Box 1243
Buffalo, NY 14220
Free: (800)743-4471
E-mail: info@pregnantwithcancer.org
URL: http://www.pregnantwithcancer.org
Contact: Christine M. Bradford, Exec. Dir.
Founded: 1997. **Description:** Provides hope, encouragement and support to women who are diagnosed with cancer while pregnant. Seeks to connect pregnant women with cancer with other women who had the same type of cancer while pregnant. Trains survivors who experienced the same fate through its volunteer certification program. Offers a network of resources to serve pregnant women with cancer. **Publications:** *Hopeline*, quarterly. Newsletter. Features news and inspirational articles dealing with issues of pregnancy and cancer. Alternate Formats: online ● Annual Report, annual. Alternate Formats: online.

13574 ■ R.A. Bloch Cancer Foundation
One H&R Block Way
Kansas City, MO 64105
Ph: (816)854-5050
Free: (800)433-0464
Fax: (816)854-8024
E-mail: hotline@hrbloch.com
URL: http://www.blochcancer.org
Contact: Vangie Rich, Admin.
Founded: 1980. **Members:** 500. **Staff:** 2. **Languages:** English, Spanish. **Description:** Sponsors the Cancer Hot Line, a support group that matches cancer patients with volunteers who are survivors of the same type of cancer. Offers resource information. Provides articles, programs and projects for cancer patients. **Libraries: Type:** reference. **Holdings:**

audiovisuals, books, periodicals. **Subjects:** cancer. **Formerly:** (1989) Cancer Connection. **Publications:** *Cancer. . .There's Hope*. Book. Alternate Formats: online ● *Cancer Hot Line News*, quarterly. Newsletter ● *Fighting Cancer* (in English and Spanish). Book. Alternate Formats: online ● *Guide for Cancer Supporters*. Book. Alternate Formats: online. **Conventions/Meetings:** annual Fighting Cancer Rally - meeting - always 1st Sunday of June in Kansas City, MO.

13575 ■ Reach to Recovery
c/o American Cancer Society
PO Box 22718
Oklahoma City, OK 73123-1718
Free: (800)ACS-2345
URL: http://www.cancer.org/docroot/ESN/content/
ESN_3_1x_Reach_to_Recovery_5.asp
Founded: 1952. **Members:** 17,000. **Languages:** Chinese, English, Spanish. **Description:** Serves as a peer support program for people with a personal concern about breast cancer; sponsored by the American Cancer Society. Provides support and information for people and help them meet the physical, emotional and cosmetic needs related to their disease and its treatment; patient and volunteer may meet face to face or by telephone. Volunteers are able to provide support and up-to-date information, including literature for spouses, partners, children, other loved ones, and friends. **Awards:** Terese Lasser. **Frequency:** annual. **Type:** recognition. **Recipient:** for outstanding service to Reach to Recovery Program. **Publications:** *Reach to Recovery Program*. Brochure.

13576 ■ Retinoblastoma International (RBI)
4650 Sunset Blvd., MS No. 88
Los Angeles, CA 90027
Ph: (323)669-2299
Fax: (323)660-8541
E-mail: info@retinoblastoma.net
URL: http://www.retinoblastoma.net
Contact: Christina Saffran Ashford, Pres.
Founded: 1998. **Multinational. Description:** Aims to eradicate retinoblastoma and its ensuing complications through education and research. Raises public awareness of retinoblastoma and infant retinal cancer. Supports programs promoting early diagnosis of retinoblastoma. Seeks to improve the quality of treatment of the disease. **Publications:** Brochure. Alternate Formats: online.

13577 ■ Rose Kushner Breast Cancer Advisory Center (RKBCAC)
PO Box 757
Palos Verdes Estates, CA 90274
Fax: (301)897-3444
E-mail: lkkushner@yahoo.com
Contact: Mr. Harvey D. Kushner, Exec. Dir.
Founded: 1975. **Staff:** 2. **Description:** Information service for people, mostly women concerned about or with breast cancer. Provides information to public, patients and physicians concerning current knowledge about breast cancer detection, diagnosis, treatment and follow-up. **Formerly:** Breast Cancer Advisory Center; (1991) Women's Breast Cancer Advisory Center; (1991) Women's Breast Cancer Advisory Center. **Publications:** *If You've Thought About Breast Cancer by Rose Kushner*, biennial. Booklet. **Price:** free.

13578 ■ Sarcoma Alliance
775 E Blithedale, No. 334
Mill Valley, CA 94941
Ph: (415)381-7236
Fax: (415)381-7235
E-mail: info@sarcomaalliance.org
URL: http://www.sarcomaalliance.org
Contact: Jennifer Henerlau, Contact
Founded: 1999. **Staff:** 1. **Description:** Works to guide, educate, and support adults with sarcomas and their family, friends, and caregivers. **Publications:** *Sarcoma Alliance News*, biennial. Newsletter. Alternate Formats: online.

13579 ■ Sharsheret

1086 Teaneck Rd., Ste.3A
Teaneck, NJ 07666
Free: (866)474-2774
Fax: (973)438-7810
E-mail: info@sharsheret.org
URL: http://www.sharsheret.org
Contact: Rochelle Shoretz, Exec. Dir.

Founded: 2001. **Description:** Provides culturally sensitive support to young Jewish women who are newly diagnosed with breast cancer as well as to those facing the risk of developing breast cancer. Offers related resources for Jewish communities and health care organizations. Educates the health care community and the Jewish community about the unique concerns of Jewish women facing breast cancer. Addresses the unique concerns of younger women facing breast cancer through programs that address their quality of life. **Publications:** Newsletter, annual. Alternate Formats: online ● Newsletter, bimonthly. Alternate Formats: online.

13580 ■ Sisters Network (SNI)

8787 Woodway Dr., Ste.4206
Houston, TX 77063
Ph: (713)781-0255
Free: (866)781-1808
Fax: (713)780-8998
E-mail: infonet@sistersnetworkinc.org
URL: http://sistersnetworkinc.org
Contact: Karen E. Jackson, Founder/CEO

Founded: 1994. **Members:** 3,000. **Membership Dues:** individual, $50 (annual) ● physician, $100 (annual) ● church/group, $250 (annual) ● medical/healthcare organization, $350 (annual) ● corporation, $500 (annual). **Staff:** 4. **Budget:** $750,000. **Description:** Serves as national African-American breast cancer survivorship organization. Promotes improved breast health among African-American women; seeks to reduce the incidence of breast cancer. Gathers and disseminates information on breast cancer prevention and self detection; provides emotional and psychological support to African-American women with breast cancer; supports breast cancer research initiatives and advocacy training. **Awards:** **Frequency:** annual. **Type:** recognition. **Committees:** Medical Advisors. **Publications:** Newsletter, periodic. **Conventions/Meetings:** annual National African-American Breast Cancer Conference.

13581 ■ Skin Cancer Foundation (SCF)

245 5th Ave., Ste.1403
New York, NY 10016
Ph: (212)725-5176
Free: (800)SKIN-490
Fax: (212)725-5751
E-mail: info@skincancer.org
URL: http://www.skincancer.org
Contact: Perry Robins MD, Pres.

Founded: 1977. **Membership Dues:** affiliate, $350 (annual) ● fellow, $500 (annual) ● Medical Council, $1,000 (annual) ● Amonette Circle, $5,000 (annual). **Staff:** 20. **Budget:** $2,000,000. **Description:** Sponsors medical symposia and public education programs on the prevention and early recognition of skin cancer. Grants its Seal of Recommendation to sunscreen products that meet the criteria and standards established by the organization as effective aids in the prevention of sun-induced damage to the skin. **Awards:** Excellence in Media Award of The Skin Cancer Foundation. **Frequency:** annual. **Type:** recognition. **Recipient:** for editor of a magazine that has furthered the mission of the foundation in its editorial content ● Frederic E. Mohs Memorial Award. **Frequency:** annual. **Type:** grant. **Recipient:** for qualified researchers and institutions ● Henry W. Menn Memorial Award. **Frequency:** annual. **Type:** recognition. **Recipient:** for researchers ● The Henry W. Shotmeyer Award. **Frequency:** annual. **Type:** recognition. **Boards:** Cosmetic Industry. **Committees:** Communications; Grants Review; Melanoma; Photobiology; Public Information. **Councils:** Advisory; Corporate; Corporate Leadership; Fellows; Honorary Associates; International Advisory; Medical; President. **Formerly:** (1978) National Skin Cancer Foundation. **Publications:** Flash! Hot News About You and

the Sun. Newsletter. **Price:** $5.00 ● Melanoma Letter, quarterly. Newsletter. Contains articles and commentary on advances in the prevention and treatment of skin cancer. **Price:** $30.00/year (minimum donation) ● News from The International Alliance Against Skin Cancer. Newsletter. Alternate Formats: online ● Play It Safe In The Sun. Book. **Price:** $10.50 ● Skin Cancer Foundation Journal, annual. Contains short articles on the prevention, early detection, and treatment of skin cancer. Includes publications list. **Price:** $8.00/copy. **Circulation:** 30,000. **Advertising:** accepted ● Sun and Skin News, quarterly. Newsletter. Provides practical advice on the prevention, treatment, and early detection of skin cancer. Includes research updates. **Price:** $30.00/year (minimum donation). **Circulation:** 60,000 ● Sun Sense: A Complete Guide to Prevention, Early Detection and Treatment of Skin Cancer. Book. **Price:** $14.95 for members ● Understanding Melanoma: What You Need To Know. Book. **Price:** $14.95 for members ● Worldwide Melanoma Update. Newsletter. Contains articles from a vast array of the scientific and medical publications throughout the world. **Price:** $6.00 for members ● Also publishes posters, charts, sun protection guidelines, slide sets, audiovisuals, CD-ROM materials and brochures. **Conventions/Meetings:** annual Mohs Surgery Conference, interactive discussion on latest topics and approaches on how to prevent, detect and treat skin cancer by faculty members and distinguished panel quests - always January or February ● biennial World Congress on Cancers of the Skin.

13582 ■ Sun Safety Alliance (SSA)

c/o Phil Schneider, Exec. Dir.
413 N Lee St.
Alexandria, VA 22314
Ph: (703)837-4202
E-mail: pschneider@sunsafetyalliance.org
URL: http://www.sunsafetyalliance.org
Contact: Phil Schneider, Exec. Dir.

Description: Represents the interests of individuals dedicated to the task of reducing the incidence of skin cancer in America. Improves public awareness of the importance of sun care safety, especially for children. Encourages the public to take action to protect themselves and their families from the dangers of the sun. Strives to eliminate skin cancer due to sun exposure.

13583 ■ Support for People with Oral and Head and Neck Cancer (SPOHNC)

PO Box 53
Locust Valley, NY 11560-0053
Free: (800)377-0928
Fax: (516)671-8794
E-mail: info@spohnc.org
URL: http://www.spohnc.org
Contact: Nancy E. Leupold, Founder/Pres.

Founded: 1991. **Membership Dues:** individual, $25 (annual) ● family/foreign, $30 (annual). **Description:** Raises awareness of oral and head and neck cancer. Provides current information for oral and head and neck cancer patients who are trying to gain a better understanding of their illness and their lives. Addresses and promotes physical, emotional, medical and humanistic needs of patients. **Publications:** News From SPOHNC, 9/year. Newsletter. Contains medical information and issues related to oral and head and neck cancer. **Price:** included in membership dues ● Brochure. Provides information about the basic objectives of SPOHNC's program and a listing of its services.

13584 ■ Susan G. Komen Breast Cancer Foundation (SGKF)

5005 LBJ Fwy., Ste.250
Dallas, TX 75244
Ph: (972)855-1600
Free: (800)IM-AWARE
Fax: (972)855-1605
E-mail: info@komen.org
URL: http://www.komen.org
Contact: Patrice Tosi, Acting CEO

Founded: 1982. **Members:** 75,000. **Staff:** 100. **National Groups:** 118. **Languages:** English, Spanish.

Multinational. **Description:** Breast cancer patients, health care professionals, and other interested individuals. Works to: increase the recovery and survival rates of breast cancer patients; heighten public awareness of the risks of breast cancer and the need for early detection. Establishes breast screening and training in self-examination procedures; provides funding through grants for research and screening programs. Sponsors educational programs and competitions. Maintains speakers' bureau. **Awards:** College Scholarship Award. **Frequency:** annual. **Type:** scholarship. **Recipient:** for high school seniors who have lost a parent due to breast cancer ● **Frequency:** annual. **Type:** fellowship ● **Frequency:** annual. **Type:** grant. **Recipient:** for individuals who have potentials of having an impact on breast cancer. **Councils:** Komen Million Dollar. **Programs:** Interdisciplinary Breast Fellowship. **Formerly:** (1989) Susan G. Komen Foundation. **Publications:** Frontline, quarterly. Newsletter. Highlights current breast cancer issues and Komen events. **Price:** free. **Circulation:** 500,000. Alternate Formats: online ● Komenlink, monthly. Newsletter. Includes timely information about breast health, breast cancer and the Foundation's program. **Price:** free. Alternate Formats: online ● Annual Report, annual. Alternate Formats: online. **Conventions/Meetings:** annual Mission Conference - meeting ● periodic Race for the Cure - meeting and symposium.

13585 ■ Us TOO International

5003 Fairview Ave.
Downers Grove, IL 60515
Ph: (630)795-1002
Free: (800)808-7866
Fax: (630)795-1602
E-mail: ustoo@ustoo.org
URL: http://www.ustoo.org
Contact: Thomas Kirk, Pres./CEO

Founded: 1990. **Description:** Strives to enhance the quality of life of individuals affected by prostate cancer. Develops new programs and materials on the latest treatment and diagnostic strategies available for patients. Advocates for increased funding for early detection, diagnosis, treatment and research of prostate cancer. Provides prostate cancer education to minorities, underserved communities and those in the rural areas. **Telecommunication Services:** electronic mail, tom@ustoo.org. **Publications:** Hot-Sheets, monthly. Newsletter. **Price:** $35.00/year. Alternate Formats: online ● Brochure. Alternate Formats: online.

13586 ■ William H. Donner Foundation

60 E 42nd St., Ste.1560
New York, NY 10165
Ph: (212)949-0404 (212)949-5213
Fax: (212)949-6022
E-mail: dfeeney@donner.org
URL: http://www.donner.org
Contact: Deborah Donner, Pres.

Founded: 1961. **Description:** Strives to fund thoughtful and creative medical-related projects. **Awards:** **Type:** grant.

13587 ■ Women's Cancer Network (WCN)

230 W Monroe, Ste.2528
Chicago, IL 60606
Ph: (312)578-1439
Fax: (312)578-9769
E-mail: info@thegcf.org
URL: http://www.wcn.org

Description: Disseminates information about various types of gynecologic cancer. Educates women on the prevention and treatment of cancer.

13588 ■ Y-ME National Breast Cancer Organization (Y-ME)

212 W Van Buren St., Ste.1000
Chicago, IL 60607
Ph: (312)986-8338
Free: (800)221-2141
Fax: (312)294-8597

E-mail: contact@y-me.org
URL: http://www.y-me.org
Contact: Margaret C. Kirk, CEO
Founded: 1978. **Staff:** 80. **Budget:** $10,000,000.
Regional Groups: 13. **State Groups:** 13. **Local Groups:** 13. **Languages:** English, Spanish. **Description:** Aims to ensure, through information, empowerment and peer support, that no one faces breast cancer alone. Has 24-hour hotline staffed entirely by trained breast cancer survivors. Provides services such as support groups, early detection workshops, wigs and prostheses for women with limited resources, and advocacy on breast cancer related policies in their respective communities. **Computer Services:** Information services, breast cancer information. **Telecommunication Services:** 24-hour hotline, (800)986-9505, Spanish. **Affiliated With:** Y-ME of Connecticut; Y-Me National.Breast Cancer Organization, Rocky Mountain Affiliate; Y-ME Northern California Affiliate. **Formerly:** (1989) Y-Me Breast Cancer Support; (1994) Y-Me National Organization for Breast Cancer Information and Support.

13589 ■ Young Survival Coalition (YSC)
61 Broadway, Ste.2235
New York, NY 10006
Ph: (646)257-3000
Fax: (646)257-3030
E-mail: info@youngsurvival.org
URL: http://www.youngsurvival.org
Contact: Michele Przypyszny, Exec. Dir./CEO
Founded: 1998. **Members:** 13,000. **Multinational.**
Description: Promotes awareness of the concerns and issues that are unique to young women with breast cancer. Seeks to educate and persuade the medical, research, breast cancer and legislative communities to address breast cancer in women who are less than 40 years old. Serves as a point of contact for young women living with breast cancer. **Telecommunication Services:** electronic mail, michelep@ youngsurvival.org. **Publications:** *Young Perspective,* quarterly. Newsletter. Alternate Formats: online ● *YSC Weekly.* Newsletter. Alternate Formats: online.

Cardiology

13590 ■ Adult Congenital Heart Association (ACHA)
6757 Greene St., Ste.335
Philadelphia, PA 19119
Ph: (215)849-1260
Free: (888)921-2242
Fax: (215)849-1261
E-mail: info@achaheart.org
URL: http://www.achaheart.org
Contact: Ms. Amy Verstappen, Pres.
Membership Dues: individual, $25 (annual) ● professional, hospital, $50 (annual) ● supporting, $50 (annual) ● corporate, $75 (annual) ● sustaining, $100 (annual). **Description:** Seeks to improve the quality of life of adults with congenital heart defects through education, outreach, advocacy, and research. **Computer Services:** Information services, congenital heart disease facts and resources ● mailing lists, of members ● online services, message board. **Publications:** *Heart Matters,* 3/year. Newsletter. Alternate Formats: online.

13591 ■ Alliance of Cardiovascular Professionals (ACVP)
PO Box 2007
Midlothian, VA 23113
Ph: (804)632-0078 (804)639-9213
Fax: (804)639-9212
E-mail: peggymcelgunn@comcast.net
Contact: Peggy McElgunn, Exec. Dir.
Founded: 1967. **Members:** 3,200. **Membership Dues:** cardiovascular or pulmonary specialist, $85 (annual) ● manager, $105 (annual). **Staff:** 3. **Budget:** $250,000. **Description:** Strives to meet educational needs. Develops programs to meet those needs. Provides a structure to offer the cardiovascular and pulmonary technology professional a key to the future as a valuable member of the medical team. Seeks

advancement for members through communication and education. Provides coordinated programs to orient the newer professional to his field and continuing educational opportunities for technologist personnel; has established guidelines for educational programs in the hospital and university setting. Works with educators and physicians to provide basic, advanced, and in-service programs for technologists. Sponsors registration and certification programs which provide technology professionals with further opportunity to clarify their level of expertise. Compiles statistics. **Awards: Frequency:** annual. **Type:** recognition. **Recipient:** for outstanding service and contributions to society. **Computer Services:** Mailing lists, member's continuing education transcripts ● mailing lists, of members. **Formed by Merger of:** (1993) National Society for Cardiovascular Technology; (1995) ASCP; (1995) Society for Cardiovascular Management; National Society for Pulmonary Technology; American College of Cardiovascular Invasive Specialists. **Formerly:** (1980) National Society of Cardiopulmonary Technologists; (1986) National Society for Cardiopulmonary Technology; (1988) National Alliance of Cardiovascular Technologists; (1989) American Cardiology Technologists Association; (1998) American Society of Cardiovascular Professionals/Society for Cardiovascular Management. **Publications:** *ACP Membership Directory,* annual. Arranged alphabetically; includes field specialty, geographical location, and chapter affiliation. **Price:** included in membership dues; $55.00 /year for nonmembers. **Circulation:** 3,000. **Advertising:** accepted ● *Beat Goes On* ● *CP Digest,* bimonthly. Newsletter. Includes employment opportunity listings, legislative reports, and new member information. **Price:** included in membership dues; $55.00 /year for nonmembers. **Circulation:** 3,000. **Advertising:** accepted ● *Heart to Heart* ● *Pulmonary News,* quarterly. **Circulation:** 3,000. **Advertising:** accepted ● *Strategies* ● Books ● Monographs. **Conventions/Meetings:** annual Cardiovascular Management Conference - conference and meeting (exhibits).

13592 ■ American Association of Cardiovascular and Pulmonary Rehabilitation (AACVPR)
401 N Michigan Ave., Ste.2200
Chicago, IL 60611-4267
Ph: (312)321-5146
Fax: (312)527-6635
E-mail: aacvpr@aacvpr.org
URL: http://www.aacvpr.org
Contact: Jody R. Heggestad-Hereford PhD, Pres.
Founded: 1985. **Members:** 3,000. **Membership Dues:** individual, associate, $150 (annual) ● student, $75 (annual). **Staff:** 7. **Budget:** $2,000,000. **Description:** Allied health professionals involved in the field of cardiovascular and pulmonary rehabilitation. Fosters the improvement of clinical practice in CVPR; promotes scientific CVPR research; seeks the advancement of CVPR education for health care professionals and the public. **Awards: Type:** recognition. **Computer Services:** Mailing lists. **Publications:** *AACVPR Directory,* annual ● *Directory of Cardiovascular and Pulmonary Rehabilitation Programs,* annual ● *Journal of Cardiopulmonary Rehabilitation,* bimonthly. Provides theoretical and practical information on cardiovascular and pulmonary rehabilitation. Includes reviews and calendar of events. **Price:** included in membership dues; $120.00 /year for nonmembers. ISSN: 0883-9212. **Circulation:** 8,000. **Advertising:** accepted ● *News and Views of AACVPR,* monthly. Newsletter. **Conventions/Meetings:** annual meeting, brings the latest information regarding advances and new challenges in rehabilitation (exhibits) - 2007 Oct. 18-21, Salt Lake City, UT.

13593 ■ American Board of Cardiovascular Perfusion (ABCP)
207 N 25th Ave.
Hattiesburg, MS 39401
Ph: (601)582-2227
Fax: (601)582-2271

E-mail: abcp@abcp.org
URL: http://www.abcp.org
Contact: Dr. Beth A. Richmond PhD, Exec. Co-Dir.
Founded: 1975. **Members:** 3,682. **Description:** Certified clinical perfusionists. Seeks to protect the public through the establishment and maintenance of standards in the field. Has established qualifications for examination and procedures for recertification. Administers annual board examinations. **Publications:** *Booklet of Information.* Provides information about the ABCP examination process, applying for certification and recertification and requirements for continuing education. Alternate Formats: online.

13594 ■ American College of Cardiology (ACC)
2400 North St. NW
Washington, DC 20037-1153
Ph: (202)375-6601
Free: (800)253-4636
Fax: (202)375-7000
E-mail: cthompso@acc.org
URL: http://www.acc.org
Contact: Carolyn G. Thompson, Assoc. Dir.
Founded: 1949. **Members:** 28,000. **Membership Dues:** fellow, associate fellow, $530 (annual) ● in-training, $175 (annual). **Staff:** 201. **Budget:** $30,000,000. **State Groups:** 39. **Description:** Professional society of physicians, surgeons, and scientists specializing in cardiology (heart) and cardiovascular (circulatory) diseases. Operates Heart House Learning Center. Maintains numerous committees. **Libraries: Type:** reference. **Holdings:** 2,000. **Subjects:** medical. **Awards:** ACC W. Proctor Harvey MD Young Teacher Awards. **Frequency:** annual. **Type:** recognition. **Recipient:** to young members of the college who have distinguished themselves by their dedication and skill in teaching ● Distinguished Fellowship Award. **Frequency:** annual. **Type:** recognition. **Recipient:** for an individual with meritorious service to the college and whose activities are considered to qualify him/her as a role model for others ● Distinguished Scientist Award. **Frequency:** annual. **Type:** recognition. **Recipient:** to a fellow of the college who has made major scientific contributions to the advancement of scientific knowledge in the field of cardiovascular disease ● Distinguished Service Award. **Frequency:** annual. **Type:** recognition. **Recipient:** to certain individuals, who by individual efforts has made profound contributions to medicine and/or the delivery of health care ● Douglas P. Zipes Distinguished Young Scientist Award. **Frequency:** annual. **Type:** monetary. **Recipient:** for a young scientist who has made outstanding contributions to the field of cardiovascular medicine and who has amassed an impressive body of scientific research in either the clinical or basic domain ● Gifted Teacher Award. **Frequency:** annual. **Type:** recognition. **Recipient:** to a fellow of the college who has demonstrated innovative, outstanding teaching characteristics and compassionate qualities and because of these attributes, has made major contributions to the field of cardiovascular medicine ● Honorary Fellowship Award. **Frequency:** annual. **Type:** recognition. **Recipient:** for a distinguished physician or scientist who is not a member of the college and who would not otherwise have routinely had an opportunity to pursue fellowship in the college, but whose professional performance warrants recognition by the college ● International Service Award. **Frequency:** annual. **Type:** recognition. **Recipient:** for an individual who, through his or her outstanding contributions to cardiovascular medicine and science, has significantly enhanced cardiovascular care throughout the world ● Master of American College of Cardiology. **Frequency:** annual. **Type:** recognition. **Recipient:** to a dedicated fellow of the college for more than fifteen years. **Computer Services:** Mailing lists, of rental. **Committees:** ACC/AHA Task Force on Practice Guidelines; Advocacy; Bylaws; Cardiac Catheterization and Intervention; Cardiovascular Imaging; Clinical Electrophysiology; Congenital Heart Disease and Pediatric Cardiology; Development. **Publications:** *ACC Current Journal Review,* bimonthly. Provides abstracts and reviews of pertinent clinical articles. **Price:** included in membership dues;

$105.00 for individuals; $185.00 for institutions; $60.00 for interns. ISSN: 1062-1458. **Circulation:** 24,000. **Advertising:** accepted ● *ACCEL*, monthly. Journal. On audiocassette. Contains 15 to 20 interviews with leaders in the field of cardiovascular medicine. **Price:** $165.00 /year for members; $200.00 /year for nonmembers. **Circulation:** 7,000 ● *Affiliates in Training*, bimonthly. Newsletter. Provides information of the association pertinent to the Affiliate-In-Training category. Includes list of employment opportunities. **Price:** included in membership dues; $20.00 /year for nonmembers. **Circulation:** 4,500 ● *Cardiology*, monthly. Newsletter. Contains information on clinical cardiology practice. Covers health care issues, legislative and socioeconomic activities, education opportunities. **Price:** included in membership dues; $59.00/year. **Circulation:** 24,500 ● *Journal of the American College of Cardiology*, monthly. Covers original clinical and experimental papers on cardiovascular disease featuring reports on medical and surgical therapy, and other subjects. **Price:** included in membership dues; $152.00/year for nonmember individuals; $236.00 /year for institutions; $92.00/year for interns, residents, health professionals. ISSN: 0735-1097. **Circulation:** 31,000. **Advertising:** accepted. Alternate Formats: microform; online; CD-ROM ● Also publishes self-study materials. **Conventions/Meetings:** annual assembly (exhibits).

13595 ■ American College of Chest Physicians (ACCP)

3300 Dundee Rd.
Northbrook, IL 60062
Ph: (847)498-1400
Free: (800)343-ACCP
Fax: (847)498-5460
E-mail: accp@chestnet.org
URL: http://www.chestnet.org
Contact: Alvin Lever, Exec. VP/CEO

Founded: 1935. **Members:** 16,000. **Membership Dues:** affiliate, allied, $60 (annual). **Staff:** 79. **Budget:** $13,000,000. **Description:** Serves as a professional society of physicians and surgeons specializing in diseases of the chest (heart and lungs). Promotes undergraduate and postgraduate medical education and research in the field. Sponsors forums. Maintains placement service; conducts educational programs. **Libraries: Type:** reference. **Holdings:** archival material, periodicals. **Awards:** Governor's Community Service Award. **Frequency:** annual. **Type:** grant. **Recipient:** to a member serving community needs ● **Type:** recognition ● **Type:** scholarship. **Computer Services:** Online services, book review service and CME's. **Committees:** Political Action. **Publications:** *American College of Chest Physicians Membership Directory*, annual. Lists members in geographical order and by specialty. **Price:** included in membership dues. **Circulation:** 15,000. **Advertising:** accepted ● *Chest: The Pulmonary and Critical Care Journal*, monthly. Presents clinical investigations and case reports in cardiopulmonary medical and surgical specialties. Contains author and subject indexes. **Price:** included in membership dues; $144.00 /year for nonmembers; $186.00 /year for institutions. ISSN: 0012-3692. **Circulation:** 23,000. **Advertising:** accepted ● Books ● Brochures. Includes topics on smoking and health, bronchitis, and asthma. ● Also publishes self-teaching series on pulmonary and critical care medicine. **Conventions/Meetings:** annual CHEST - assembly (exhibits) - always October/November ● seminar.

13596 ■ American Heart Association (AHA)

7272 Greenville Ave.
Dallas, TX 75231
Ph: (301)223-2307
Free: (800)242-8721
Fax: (214)706-1191
E-mail: aharesume@heart.org
URL: http://www.americanheart.org
Contact: Raymond Gibbons MD, Pres.

Founded: 1924. **Members:** 26,000. **Staff:** 500. **Budget:** $252,000,000. **Regional Groups:** 15. **State Groups:** 56. **Description:** Physicians, scientists, and laypersons. Supports research, education, and community service programs with the objective of reduc-

ing premature death and disability from cardiovascular diseases and stroke; coordinates the efforts of physicians, nurses, health professionals, and others engaged in the fight against heart and circulatory disease. Supports entirely by voluntary contributions of the public, principally during the Heart Campaign held in February. **Libraries: Type:** not open to the public; reference. **Holdings:** 2,000; books, periodicals, reports. **Subjects:** cardiology, business, philanthropy, patient education. **Computer Services:** Online services, publication. **Councils:** Arteriosclerosis; Basic Science; Cardiopulmonary Diseases; Cardiovascular Disease in the Young; Cardiovascular Nursing; Cardiovascular Radiology; Cardiovascular Surgery; Circulation; Clinical Cardiology; Epidemiology; High Blood Pressure Research; Kidney in Cardiovascular Disease; Stroke; Thrombosis. **Divisions:** Medical. **Absorbed:** (1983) Intersociety Commission for Heart Disease Resources; (1993) Courage Stroke Network. **Publications:** *Arteriosclerosis, Thrombosis, and Vascular Biology*, monthly. Journal. Contains findings of basic and clinical research related to vascular biology and related topics. **Price:** $227.00 /year for individuals; $363.00 /year for institutions. ISSN: 1079-5642. **Circulation:** 3,200. **Advertising:** accepted. Alternate Formats: microform; online; CD-ROM ● *Circulation*, weekly. Journal. Covers clinical research, including clinical studies and trials, and advances in cardiovascular medicine. **Price:** $223.00 /year for individuals; $396.00 /year for institutions. ISSN: 0009-7322. **Circulation:** 26,500. **Advertising:** accepted. Alternate Formats: microform; online; CD-ROM ● *Circulation Research*, biweekly. Journal. Covers basic cardiovascular research in the areas of biology, biochemistry, biophysics, microbiology, cellular biology, genetics, molecular biology. **Price:** $267.00 /year for individuals; $487.00 /year for institutions. **Circulation:** 4,000. **Advertising:** accepted. Alternate Formats: microform; online; CD-ROM ● *Council Connections*, quarterly. Newsletter. Contains information of interest to each of the 13 councils and three Interdisciplinary Working Groups. Alternate Formats: online ● *Currents in Emergency Cardiac Care*, quarterly. Newsletter. Offers scientific information about ideas, development, and trends in emergency cardiac care. **Price:** free. ISSN: 1054-917X. **Circulation:** 25,000 ● *Hypertension*, monthly. Journal. Reports clinical and laboratory investigations in blood pressure regulation and pathophysiological mechanisms underlying the hypertensive diseases. **Price:** $213.00 /year for individuals; $302.00 /year for institutions. ISSN: 0194-911X. **Circulation:** 44,000. **Advertising:** accepted. Alternate Formats: microform; online; CD-ROM ● *Stroke—A Journal of Cerebral Circulation*, monthly. Provides information on the prevention, diagnosis, treatment, and rehabilitation of cerebrovascular disease. **Price:** $213.00 /year for individuals; $299.00 /year for institutions. ISSN: 0039-2499. **Circulation:** 8,100. **Advertising:** accepted. Alternate Formats: microform; CD-ROM; online. **Conventions/Meetings:** annual assembly, for delegates - always November ● annual Science Writers Forum - meeting - always January ● annual Scientific Session - meeting (exhibits).

13597 ■ American Society of Echocardiography (ASE)

1500 Sunday Dr., Ste.102
Raleigh, NC 27607
Ph: (919)861-5574
Fax: (919)787-4916
E-mail: rwiegerink@asecho.org
URL: http://www.asecho.org
Contact: Robin Wiegerink MNPL, Exec. Dir.

Founded: 1975. **Members:** 11,000. **Membership Dues:** Mexico physician, physical scientist, lab manager - in U.S. and Canada, $175 (annual) ● Mexico sonographer, nurse, medical student, resident, sonographer student - in U.S. and Canada, $75 (annual) ● Mexico physician, physical scientist, lab manager - outside U.S. and Canada, $140 (annual) ● Mexico sonographer, nurse, medical student, resident, sonographer student - outside U.S. and Canada, $95 (annual) ● first time medical/sonographer student - in U.S., Canada, and Mexico, $55 (annual) ● first time medical/sonographer student -

international, $75 (annual). **Staff:** 14. **Multinational**. **Description:** Physicians and sonographers specializing in ultrasound heart and vascular imaging and diagnosis. Promotes excellence in the ultrasonic examination of the heart and assists in establishing standards for education of physicians and cardiac-sonographers in cardiovascular ultrasound. Sponsors educational activities including distribution of self-testing materials, continuing education calendar, and annual scientific sessions. Maintains liaison with governmental agencies and other professional groups. **Awards:** Distinguished Sonographer Teacher Award. **Frequency:** annual. **Type:** recognition. **Recipient:** to sonographer members, who exemplify teaching expertise in echocardiography, act as mentors for students and fellow sonographers, and serve as role models for future cardiac sonographers ● Excellence in Teaching in Pediatrics. **Frequency:** annual. **Type:** recognition. **Recipient:** for a sonographer or a physician with exceptional commitment and skill in teaching pediatric echocardiography ● Meritorious Service Award. **Type:** recognition. **Recipient:** for individuals who have made extraordinary contributions to the society in time and talent ● Pediatric Founders Award. **Frequency:** annual. **Type:** recognition. **Recipient:** to a member of the pediatric echocardiography community for service to the field of echocardiography ● Research Awards. **Frequency:** annual. **Type:** recognition ● Richard Popp Excellence in Teaching Award. **Frequency:** annual. **Type:** recognition. **Recipient:** to young physicians who epitomize the ideal qualities possessed by a mentor and role model ● Sonographer Scholarships. **Frequency:** annual. **Type:** scholarship. **Recipient:** for students enrolled in a cardiac ultrasound program accredited by CAAHEP in the U.S. or by an equivalent Canadian ultrasound program ● Young Investigator Award. **Frequency:** annual. **Type:** monetary. **Recipient:** for young investigators who present their work during the opening plenary session of the annual meeting. **Computer Services:** database ● mailing lists. **Committees:** Continuing Education; Development; Legislative and Regulatory; Local Society Relations; Nomenclature and Standards; Outcomes Research; Physician Training and Education; Professional Ethics and Practice; Public Relations; Research; Scientific Program; Sonographer Education and Training. **Publications:** *American Society of Echocardiography Standards Documents*, periodic ● *Journal of the American Society of Echocardiography*, monthly. For physicians and sonographers covering echocardiography. Includes legislative and membership updates. **Price:** included in membership dues. Alternate Formats: online ● *Membership Directory*, biennial ● Also publishes standards documents and number news briefs. **Conventions/Meetings:** annual Scientific Session - conference, applications and advances in Echocardiography (exhibits) - 2008 June 8-11, Toronto, ON, Canada.

13598 ■ American Society of Nuclear Cardiology (ASNC)

4550 Montgomery Ave., Ste.780 N
Bethesda, MD 20814-3304
Ph: (301)215-7575
Fax: (301)215-7113
E-mail: admin@asnc.org
URL: http://www.asnc.org
Contact: Steve Carter, Exec. Dir.

Founded: 1993. **Members:** 4,100. **Membership Dues:** associate, $95 (annual) ● full international, $200 (annual) ● technologist, $75 (annual) ● full domestic, $220 (annual). **Staff:** 5. **Budget:** $1,500,000. **Regional Groups:** 28. **Description:** Physicians, scientists, technologist, biomedical engineers, and health care workers. Seeks to foster optimal delivery of nuclear cardiology services and promote research. Provides continuing medical education opportunities; establishes guidelines and standards for training and practice; provides information on licensure requirements. **Awards:** ASNC/Amersham Clinical Research in Nuclear Cardiology. **Frequency:** annual. **Type:** grant. **Computer Services:** Mailing lists. **Telecommunication Services:** electronic bulletin board ● teleconference. **Committees:** Annual Meeting Organizing; Communications; Education; Ethics; Government Relations; Nominating; Quality Assurance; Service Awards. **Publications:** *Journal of Nuclear Cardiology*, bimonthly. **Price:** $205.00 /year for individuals in U.S.; $250.00 /year for individuals outside U.S.; $90.00/year for students in U.S.; $111.00/year for students outside U.S. Alternate Formats: online ● Membership Directory, biennial ● Newsletter, monthly. **Conventions/Meetings:** biennial International Conference in Nuclear Cardiology - meeting - in April ● annual symposium - 2007 Sept. 6-9, San Diego, CA; 2008 Sept. 11-14, Boston, MA; 2009 Oct. 1-4, Minneapolis, MN.

13599 ■ Association of Black Cardiologists (ABC)
5355 Hunter Rd.
Atlanta, GA 30349
Ph: (404)201-6600
Free: (800)753-9222
Fax: (404)201-6601
E-mail: abcardio@abcardio.org
URL: http://www.abcardio.org
Contact: B. Waine Kong PhD, CEO
Founded: 1974. **Members:** 800. **Membership Dues:** regular, $350 (annual) ● associate, $175 (annual) ● cardiologist in training, $88 (annual) ● student, $50 (annual) ● institutional, $1,000 (annual) ● life, $5,250 ● industry partner, $15,000 (annual) ● community health advocate (individual), $35 (annual) ● community health advocate (church), $100 (annual). **Staff:** 14. **Budget:** $4,000,000. **Description:** Physicians and other health professionals interested in lowering mortality and morbidity resulting from cardiovascular diseases. Seeks to improve prevention and treatment of cardiovascular diseases. Conducts educational and research programs; maintains speakers' bureau. **Awards:** Dr. Daniel D. Savage Memorial Scientific Award. **Frequency:** annual. **Type:** recognition. **Recipient:** for scientific achievement in cardiovascular disease research ● Dr. Herbert Nickins Epidemiology Award. **Frequency:** annual. **Type:** recognition. **Recipient:** for outstanding contribution to the promotion and reduction of cardiovascular risks for minority populations ● Dr. Jay Brown Medical C.I.T. Abstract Ward. **Frequency:** annual. **Type:** recognition. **Recipient:** to a leading cardiologist-in-training for the best abstract presentation delivered at the ABC Annual Scientific Sessions ● Dr. Richard Allen Williams Scholarship. **Frequency:** annual. **Type:** scholarship. **Recipient:** for medical students pursuing a career in cardiology ● Dr. Walter M. Booker Sr. Health Promotion Award. **Frequency:** annual. **Type:** recognition. **Recipient:** for an individual who has pioneered programs and innovative thinking that improve the health status in African-American communities ● Fourth Year Cardiology Subspecialty Fellowship Award. **Frequency:** annual. **Type:** scholarship. **Recipient:** for a minority cardiology fellow to fund fourth year training to universities with electrophysiology and interventional subspecialty training programs. **Publications:** *The Digest of Urban Cardiology*, periodic. Journal. Price: included in membership dues. ISSN: 1096-3863. Circulation: 30,000. Advertising: accepted ● Newsletter, quarterly. **Price:** free. **Conventions/Meetings:** annual Congress on the Treatment of Cardiovascular Disease in African Americans ● annual meeting, scientific sessions (exhibits) ● annual Walter M. Booker, Jr. Memorial Symposium.

13600 ■ Association for Eradication of Heart Attack (AEHA)
2472 Bolsover St., No. 439
Houston, TX 77005
Ph: (713)529-4484
Free: (877)742-7311
Fax: (713)529-4494
E-mail: info@aeha.org
URL: http://www.aeha.org
Contact: Dr. Morteza Naghavi MD, Founder
Founded: 2001. **Description:** Seeks to end the threat and complications of heart attack. Advances the science and the practice of heart attack prevention, detection and treatment. Raises public awareness and understanding of the disease and its devastating effects. Organizes the SHAPE-a-thon, a fun walk/run event. **Publications:** *Daily VP Watch.* Newsletter ● *Weekly VP Watch.* Newsletter.

13601 ■ Association of Physician Assistants in Cardiovascular Surgery (APACVS)
PO Box 4834
Englewood, CO 80155
Ph: (303)221-5651
Free: (877)221-5651
Fax: (303)771-2550
E-mail: carol@goddardassociates.com
URL: http://www.apacvs.org
Contact: Carol A. Goddard, Exec. Dir.
Founded: 1981. **Members:** 650. **Membership Dues:** fellow, $165 (annual) ● student, $25 (annual). **Staff:** 4. **Budget:** $100,000. **Description:** Represents physician assistants who work with cardiovascular surgeons. Assists in defining the role of physician assistants in the field of cardiovascular surgery through educational forums. **Awards:** APACUS Student Scholarship. **Frequency:** annual. **Type:** scholarship. **Computer Services:** Mailing lists. **Publications:** *CardioVision*, quarterly. Newsletter. **Advertising:** accepted ● *Salary and Benefits Survey*, annual ● Membership Directory, annual. **Conventions/Meetings:** annual meeting (exhibits).

13602 ■ Association of Professors of Cardiology (APC)
2400 N St. NW
Washington, DC 20037
Ph: (202)375-6191
Fax: (202)375-6839
URL: http://www.cardiologyprofessors.org
Contact: William Grossman MD, Pres.
Founded: 1990. **Members:** 115. **Membership Dues:** individual, $350 (annual). **Staff:** 2. **Budget:** $40,000. **Description:** Directors or acting directors of divisions of cardiology in accredited medical schools in the U.S. and Puerto Rico. Conducts educational and scientific programs with respect to cardiology. **Publications:** none. **Conventions/Meetings:** annual meeting.

13603 ■ Cardiac Arrhythmias Research and Education Foundation (CARE)
PO Box 369
Duvall, WA 98019
Ph: (425)788-1987
Free: (800)404-9500
Fax: (425)788-1927
E-mail: care@longqt.org
URL: http://www.longqt.org
Contact: Robert J. Myerburg MD, Pres.
Founded: 1995. **Staff:** 3. **Budget:** $250,000. **Non-membership. Description:** Dedicated to research and education about cardiac arrhythmias that cause sudden death. **Awards:** C.A.R.E. Foundation Career Development Award. **Frequency:** periodic. **Type:** grant. **Recipient:** for investigators working on mechanisms, therapy and prevention of arrhythmias and sudden death. **Also Known As:** Care Foundation. **Publications:** Newsletter, semiannual. Alternate Formats: online. **Conventions/Meetings:** Scientific Advisory Board Meeting.

13604 ■ Cardiovascular Credentialing International (CCI)
1500 Sunday Dr., Ste.102
Raleigh, NC 27607
Ph: (919)861-4539
Free: (800)326-0268
Fax: (919)787-4916
E-mail: director@cci-online.org
URL: http://www.cci-online.org
Contact: Aaron White, Exec. Dir.
Founded: 1988. **Members:** 26,000. **Membership Dues:** individual, $25 (annual). **Staff:** 5. **Budget:** $650,000. **Multinational. Description:** Cardiovascular technologists involved in the allied health professions. Conducts testing of allied health professionals throughout the U.S. and Canada. Provides study guides and reliability and validity testing. Compiles statistics. **Awards:** Art Hagan Award. **Type:** recognition. **Computer Services:** database, medical technology questions ● online services, services. **Commit-** tees: Editorial; Examination; Marketing. **Affiliated With:** Alliance of Cardiovascular Professionals; American College of Chest Physicians; American Society of Echocardiography. **Formed by Merger of:** National Board of Cardiovascular Technology; Cardiovascular Credentialing International. **Formerly:** (1984) National Board for Cardiopulmonary Credentialing; (1986) National Board for Cardiovascular and Pulmonary Credentialing; (1991) Cardiovascular Credentialing International/Board of Cardiovascular Technology. **Publications:** *Pulse*, quarterly. Newsletter. Contains information for Level II registered cardiovascular technologists. **Price:** included in membership dues; $25.00 /year for nonmembers. **Advertising:** accepted ● Directory, biennial. **Conventions/Meetings:** annual meeting.

13605 ■ Children's HeartLink (CHL)
5075 Arcadia Ave.
Minneapolis, MN 55436
Ph: (952)928-4860
Free: (888)928-6678
Fax: (952)928-4859
E-mail: elizabeth@childrensheartlink.org
URL: http://www.childrensheartlink.org
Contact: Elizabeth Bickel, Pres.
Founded: 1969. **Staff:** 9. **Budget:** $2,020,000. **Regional Groups:** 1. **Description:** Medical charity and service agency. Advocates the prevention and treatment of heart disease in needy children throughout the world; helps selected developing countries expand and improve their cardiac services for children. Provides: treatment for needy children with heart disease; support for rheumatic fever prevention programs; education and training opportunities for foreign physicians, nurses, and other medical professionals; technical advice and problem-solving assistance; medical equipment and supplies. Organizes fund-raising events. **Awards:** Outstanding Philanthropist and Volunteer. **Frequency:** annual. **Type:** recognition. **Recipient:** for an outstanding supporter of CHL initiatives through financial contributions or volunteer service. **Formerly:** (1994) Children's Heart Fund. **Publications:** *Heartbeat*, 3/year. Newsletter. **Price:** free. **Circulation:** 6,500. Alternate Formats: online ● Annual Report, annual. Contains key facts and provides a comprehensive overview of Children's HeartLink. Alternate Formats: online. **Conventions/Meetings:** annual Costa Rica/Minnesota Medical Conference (exhibits).

13606 ■ Congenital Heart Defects Awareness (CHDA)
1996 Hartford Tpke.
North Haven, CT 06473
Ph: (203)234-1371
Fax: (203)234-1067
E-mail: info@chdawareness.org
URL: http://www.chdawareness.org
Contact: Jeanne Imperati, Contact
Founded: 2000. **Description:** Represents the interests of individuals dedicated to meeting the needs of the families and individuals affected by congenital heart defects (CHD). Provides support and resources to families affected by CHD. Advances the awareness and treatment of congenital heart defects through education, information exchange and research. **Telecommunication Services:** electronic mail, jeanne@chdawareness.org.

13607 ■ Congenital Heart Information Network (CHIN)
First Fl., 600 N 3rd St.
Philadelphia, PA 19123-2902
Ph: (215)627-4034
Fax: (215)627-4036
E-mail: mb@tchin.org
URL: http://www.tchin.org
Contact: Mona Barmash, Pres.
Membership Dues: individual/family, $20 (annual) ● health professional, $35 (annual) ● donor, $50 (annual) ● sponsor, $100 (annual) ● benefactor, $250 (annual). **Multinational. Description:** Provides information, support services and resources to families of children with congenital heart defects and acquired heart disease, adults with congenital heart

defects, and the professionals who work with them. Provides financial assistance to families in crisis. Funds local affiliated support groups and sponsors an international CHD Awareness Campaign. **Publications:** Newsletter, semiannual. Features photos from events, articles, and news from members, support groups and organizations throughout the world. **Price:** included in membership dues ● Brochure. Includes information about CHIN's programs and services.

13608 ■ Council on Arteriosclerosis, Thrombosis and Vascular Biology of the American Heart Association (ATVB)

c/o American Heart Association National Center
7272 Greenville Ave.
Dallas, TX 75231
Ph: (214)706-1293
Free: (800)242-8721
Fax: (214)373-0268
E-mail: alan.daugherty@uky.edu
URL: http://www.americanheart.org/presenter.jhtml?identifier=1201
Contact: Alan Daugherty PhD, Chm.
Founded: 1946. **Members:** 1,014. **Membership Dues:** premium professional, $150 (annual). **Staff:** 7. **Description:** Serves as professional society of physicians and others interested in cardiovascular diseases, especially arteriosclerosis (hardening of the arteries). **Awards:** ATVB Merit Awards for Young Investigators. **Frequency:** annual. **Type:** recognition. **Recipient:** for predoctoral students ● Irvine H. Page Arteriosclerosis Research Award for Young Investigators. **Frequency:** annual. **Type:** recognition. **Recipient:** for talented young people to continue careers in arteriosclerosis research ● Jeffrey M. Hoeg Arteriosclerosis Award for Basic Science and Clinical Research. **Frequency:** annual. **Type:** recognition. **Recipient:** for outstanding contribution on pathophysiology of artherosclerosis ● Junior Investigator Award for Women. **Frequency:** annual. **Type:** recognition. **Recipient:** for excellent research conducted by women. **Committees:** Vascular Lesions. **Formerly:** (1959) American Society for the Study of Arteriosclerosis; (1997) Council on Arteriosclerosis of the American Heart Association. **Publications:** *Arteriosclerosis and Thrombosis - A Journal of Vascular Biology*, bimonthly ● Newsletter, semiannual. **Conventions/Meetings:** annual conference (exhibits) ● periodic meeting, scientific sessions.

13609 ■ Donald W. Reynolds Foundation

1701 Village Center Cir.
Las Vegas, NV 89134
Ph: (702)804-6000
Fax: (702)804-6099
E-mail: generalquestions@dwrf.org
URL: http://www.dwreynolds.org
Contact: Steven L. Anderson, Pres.
Description: Works to provide support for cardiovascular clinical research, aging, and quality of life programs. **Awards: Frequency:** annual. **Type:** grant. **Recipient:** to universities devoted to developing new ways to fight heart disease ● **Frequency:** annual. **Type:** grant. **Recipient:** to universities devoted to improving the training of physicians in geriatrics. **Programs:** Community Services Center. **Publications:** Annual Report, annual. Alternate Formats: online.

13610 ■ Heart Care International

139 E Putnam Ave.
Greenwich, CT 06830
Ph: (203)552-5343
Fax: (203)552-5344
E-mail: info@heartcareintl.org
URL: http://www.heartcareintl.org
Contact: Robert Michler MD, Chm./Founder
Multinational. Description: Provides open heart surgery for poor children and young adults in developing countries. Conducts annual mission trips of volunteer doctors to selected countries where the operation will be performed. Trains local health care professionals in the medical and surgical management of heart disease, enabling them to provide heart care within their own community. **Committees:** Auxiliary. **Publications:** Newsletter. Alternate Formats: online ● Brochure. Alternate Formats: online.

13611 ■ Heart Disease Research Foundation (HDRF)

50 Court St.
Brooklyn, NY 11201
Ph: (718)649-6210
Fax: (718)649-6210
Contact: Dr. Yoshiaki Omura M.D., Dir., Med. Research
Founded: 1962. **Staff:** 24. **Description:** Promotes research aimed at the prevention, early diagnosis, and treatment of cardiovascular disease and related medico-social problems. Supports and conducts research, both basic and clinical, in the early diagnosis, prevention, and treatment of cardiovascular diseases using a multidisciplinary approach. Studies include the effects of acupuncture and electrotherapeutics on blood chemistry and the cardiovascular system, the clinical applications of these methods, and the noninvasive early diagnostic methods of cardiovascular diseases. Sponsors postgraduate continuing medical educational courses for physicians, dentists, and medical researchers. Conducts public education programs on the heart and heart disease. Answers questions from the public and professionals; supplies available educational information on cardiovascular diseases and research. **Divisions:** Medical Advisory Board; Scientific Advisory Board.

13612 ■ Heart Failure Society of America (HFSA)

c/o Cheryl Yano, Exec. Dir.
Court Intl. - Ste.240 S
2550 Univ. Ave. W
St. Paul, MN 55114
Ph: (651)642-1633
Fax: (651)642-1502
E-mail: info@hfsa.org
URL: http://www.hfsa.org
Contact: Gary S. Francis MD, Pres.
Membership Dues: full-voting, $150 (annual) ● trainee, $35 (annual). **Description:** Enhances quality and duration of life of individuals with heart diseases. Encourages primary and secondary preventive measures to reduce the incidence of heart failure. Provides a forum for all those interested in heart function, heart failure, congestive heart failure research and patient care. **Publications:** *The Journal of Cardiac Failure*, bimonthly. **Price:** free for members ● Newsletter, quarterly. **Price:** free for members.

13613 ■ Heart Rhythm Society

1400 K St. NW, Ste.500
Washington, DC 20005
Ph: (202)464-3400
Fax: (202)464-3401
E-mail: info@hrsonline.org
URL: http://www.hrsonline.org
Contact: James Youngblood, CEO
Founded: 1979. **Members:** 3,500. **Membership Dues:** physician, industry, $425 (annual) ● scientist, $210 (annual) ● allied professional, $150 (annual) ● fellow physician, $475 (annual) ● international, $325 (annual) ● fellow allied, $200 (annual) ● fellow scientist, $260 (annual). **Staff:** 38. **Budget:** $4,000,000. **Multinational. Description:** Physicians, scientists, and allied professionals throughout the world dedicated to the study and management or cardiac arrhythmias. Improves the care of patients by promoting research, education and training, and providing leadership towards optimal health care policies and standards. **Awards:** Distinguished Scientist Award. **Frequency:** annual. **Type:** recognition ● Distinguished Service Award. **Frequency:** annual. **Type:** recognition ● Distinguished Teacher Award. **Frequency:** annual. **Type:** recognition ● Multiple Fellowships. **Frequency:** annual. **Type:** fellowship. **Recipient:** for cardiac pacing and electrophysiology ● Pioneer in Cardiac Pacing and EP Award. **Frequency:** annual. **Type:** recognition ● Young Investigator Award. **Type:** recognition. **Recipient:** for original clinical investigation or basic research in the area of cardiac and/or cardiac electrophysiology. **Computer Services:** database, membership list ● mailing lists, of members. **Committees:** Clinically Associated Professionals; Continuing Medical Educa-

tion; Endowment; Fellowship; Government Relations; Policy. **Formerly:** (2003) North American Society of Pacing and Electrophysiology; (2004) North American Society of Pacing and Electrophysiology/Heart Rhythm Association. **Publications:** *Heart Rhythm*, monthly. Journal. Contains important science developments in the field of arrhythmias and cardiovascular electrophysiology. **Advertising:** accepted ● *Journal of Cardiovascular Electrophysiology*, monthly ● *NASPE News*, 5/year. Newsletter. Covers membership activities. Includes calendar of events and information updates. ● *North American Society of Pacing and Electrophysiology Annual Scientific Session Program.* Paper ● *PACE: The Journal of Pacing and Clinical Electrophysiology*, monthly ● Brochure ● Membership Directory, annual. Includes geographic index. **Conventions/Meetings:** annual Scientific Session - meeting (exhibits).

13614 ■ Indo-American Society of Interventional Cardiology (ISIC)

185 Shore Dr. S
Miami, FL 33131
Ph: (305)285-4171
E-mail: mehtas@bellsouth.net
Contact: Sameer Mehta, Pres.
Founded: 2002. **Members:** 1,500. **Multinational. Description:** Upholds the practice of Interventional Cardiology. Conducts research at premier cardiology institutions in the country. Brings together a large group of physicians committed to providing educational, research and training benefits for its members and for the Indian community.

13615 ■ InterAmerican Heart Foundation (IAHF)

7272 Greenville Ave.
Dallas, TX 75231-4596
Ph: (214)706-1301
Fax: (214)706-1211
E-mail: iahf@interamericanheart.org
URL: http://www.iahf.org
Contact: Beatriz Marcet Champagne PhD, Exec. Dir.
Founded: 1992. **Members:** 31. **Languages:** English, Portuguese, Spanish. **Multinational. Description:** Works to reduce disability and death from cardiovascular diseases and stroke in the Americas. Promotes the growth and development of foundations that will take active roles in public education, professional education, public advocacy, and fund raising. Fosters partnerships between health professionals, business, industry, and other sectors of society for the accomplishment of its mission and goals. **Telecommunication Services:** electronic mail, beatriz.champagne@interamericanheart.org. **Formerly:** International Cardiology Foundation; (1998) Interamerican Heart Cardiology Foundation. **Publications:** *Heart of the Americas* (in English and Spanish), quarterly. Newsletter. **Price:** free. **Circulation:** 4,000. **Conventions/Meetings:** biennial Foundations Program - meeting (exhibits).

13616 ■ International Atherosclerosis Society (IAS)

c/o Ann Stephens Jackson, MBA, Exec.Dir.
6550 Fannin, Mail Stop A-601
Houston, TX 77030
Ph: (713)797-9620
Fax: (713)797-9507
E-mail: info@athero.org
URL: http://www.athero.org
Contact: Ann Stephens Jackson MBA, Exec.Dir.
Founded: 1979. **Members:** 9,500. **Membership Dues:** individual, $10 (annual). **Staff:** 3. **National Groups:** 36. **Multinational. Description:** Scientists and other professionals involved in research in the field of atherosclerosis; corporations and firms supporting its aims. Promotes the advancement of science, research, and teaching in the field of atherosclerosis throughout the world. (Atherosclerosis is a form of arteriosclerosis characterized by the deposition of fatty substances in and fibrosis of the inner layer of the arteries.) Advocates an interdisciplinary approach to the study of atherosclerosis and related diseases. Facilitates international communication and exchange of knowledge among scientists in the field.

Assists in the organization of exchange visits among scientists at various research centers. Fosters and encourages young researchers by arranging contacts, and offering travel support to world gatherings in the field. Coordinates activities in atherosclerosis research., **Libraries: Type:** reference. **Holdings:** periodicals. **Awards: Type:** scholarship ● Visiting Fellowship Award. **Frequency:** semiannual. **Type:** fellowship. **Computer Services:** Mailing lists. **Telecommunication Services:** electronic mail, ias@bcm.tmc.edu. **Committees:** Education; Fellows; Scientific Program; Strategic and Long-Range Planning. **Publications:** *Atherosclerosis*, monthly. Journal. **Price:** $214.00 for members ● *Proceedings of Symposia*, triennial ● *Roster of Member Societies*. Membership Directory ● Newsletter, semiannual. **Conventions/Meetings:** triennial International Symposium on Atherosclerosis - congress and symposium, exhibits on lipoproteins and apoliproteins, molecular genetics, cell biology, epidemiology and prevention, nutrition, drug treatment, diabetes, diagnostic and clinical aspects and growth factors (exhibits).

13617 ■ International Bundle Branch Block Association (IBBBA)
6631 W 83rd St.
Los Angeles, CA 90045-2899
Ph: (310)670-9132
Contact: Rita Kurtz Lewis, Exec.Dir.
Founded: 1979. **Description:** Individuals with bundle branch block (BBB), concerned professionals, and laypersons. (BBB is a rare heart condition caused by an "electrical malfunction".) Objectives are: to increase public awareness of BBB; to disseminate information on the disease; to answer inquiries of members; to serve as a forum for sharing information and experiences; to maintain a bank of information to aid professional research on BBB. Compiles statistics. Plans to conduct specialized education and research programs. **Libraries: Type:** reference. **Holdings:** archival material. **Publications:** *Heartbeat*, quarterly. Newsletter. Provides professional replies to readers' medical questions, reprints from other publications, and names and addresses of members. **Price:** included in membership dues. **Advertising:** accepted. **Conventions/Meetings:** periodic conference ● quarterly symposium.

13618 ■ International Society for Adult Congenital Cardiac Disease (ISACCD)
1500 Sunday Dr., Ste.102
Raleigh, NC 27607
Ph: (919)861-5578
Fax: (919)787-4916
E-mail: info@isaccd.org
URL: http://www.isaccd.org
Contact: Jack M. Colman MD, Pres.
Founded: 1992. **Members:** 200. **Membership Dues:** in-training, $35 (annual) ● professional, $60 (annual) ● physician, surgeon, $95 (annual). **Description:** Seeks to achieve and promote excellence in the care of adolescents and adults with congenital cardiac disease. **Committees:** Executive; Membership; Project. **Publications:** *ISACCD Update*, quarterly. Newsletter. Alternate Formats: online. **Conventions/Meetings:** semiannual meeting - always March, November.

13619 ■ International Society for Computerized Electrocardiology (ISCE)
11495 Emmanuel Way, No. 518
Solomons, MD 20688-3031
Ph: (301)855-1004 (410)394-3216
Fax: (410)394-3219
E-mail: isceoffice@comcast.net
URL: http://www.isce.org
Contact: Martha R. Horton, Exec. Admin.
Membership Dues: regular, in U.S. and Canada (with journal), $250 (annual) ● country (with journal), $295 (annual) ● country (without journal), $95 (annual). **Multinational. Description:** Promotes advancement of the science of electrocardiology. **Awards:** Jos Willems Young Investigators Award. **Frequency:** annual. **Type:** recognition. **Publications:** *Journal of Electrocardiology*, quarterly. **Conventions/Meetings:** lecture ● meeting, satellite meetings ●

annual Research and Technology Transfer in Computerized Electrocardiology - conference ● seminar.

13620 ■ International Society for Minimally Invasive Cardiothoracic Surgery (ISMICS)
900 Cummings Ctr., Ste.221-U
Beverly, MA 01915
Ph: (978)927-8330
Fax: (978)524-8890
URL: http://www.ismics.org
Contact: Randall K. Wolf MD, Pres.
Founded: 1997. **Members:** 600. **Membership Dues:** active, $200 (annual) ● fellow, resident, medical student, $100 (annual). **Description:** Works with patient outcomes, new technologies and techniques, and progressive development of less invasive forms of heart surgery. **Committees:** Ad Hoc Publications; By-Laws; Development; Local Arrangements; Nominating; Program. **Formerly:** (2004) International Society for Minimally Invasive Cardiac Surgery. **Publications:** *The Heart Surgery Forum*. Journal. Alternate Formats: online ● *Innovations*. Journal. Contains articles about developments in the treatment of cardio thoracic and vascular disease. **Conventions/Meetings:** annual meeting (exhibits).

13621 ■ Kids With Heart National Association for Children's Heart Disorders
PO Box 12504
Green Bay, WI 54307-2504
Free: (800)538-5390
E-mail: michelle@kidswithheart.org
URL: http://www.kidswithheart.org
Contact: Michelle Rintamaki BA, Pres.
Founded: 1985. **Description:** Improves the quality of life of children living with congenital heart defects and their families by providing support, information and education. Assists in finding a cause, cure and prevention of congenital heart defects. **Computer Services:** Online services, CHD Book Store. **Publications:** *Helping Enhance Awareness and Research Together*. Newsletter. Alternate Formats: online.

13622 ■ Mended Hearts, Inc. (MHI)
7272 Greenville Ave.
Dallas, TX 75231-4596
Ph: (214)360-6149
Free: (888)HEART-99
Fax: (214)360-6145
E-mail: info@mendedhearts.org
URL: http://www.mendedhearts.org
Contact: Cathy Clapp, Exec. Asst.
Founded: 1951. **Members:** 25,000. **Membership Dues:** individual in U.S., $17 (annual) ● family in U.S., $24 (annual) ● individual outside U.S., $22 (annual) ● family outside U.S., $32 (annual) ● life (individual), $150 ● life (family), $210. **Local Groups:** 285. **Description:** Persons who have heart disease; their families and friends. Works to: provide advice, encouragement, and services to heart disease patients and to their families and caregivers; establish programs of assistance to surgeons, physicians, and hospitals. Assists in research programs designed to benefit heart patients. **Awards:** Dwight Emary Harken Award. **Frequency:** biennial. **Type:** recognition. **Recipient:** for excellence in cardiovascular medicine. **Telecommunication Services:** electronic mail, cathy.clapp@heart.org. **Programs:** Mended Little Hearts. **Affiliated With:** American Heart Association. **Formerly:** (1955) Mended Hearts Club. **Publications:** *Heartbeat*, quarterly. Magazine. Features health tips, research updates, success stories and news on chapters. **Price:** free for members; $10.00 for nonmembers. **Advertising:** accepted. **Conventions/Meetings:** annual conference.

13623 ■ Michael E. DeBakey International Surgical Society (MEDISS)
c/o Kenneth L. Mattox, MD, Sec.-Treas.
1 Baylor Plz.
Houston, TX 77030
Ph: (713)798-4557
Fax: (713)796-9605

E-mail: mediss04@aol.com
URL: http://www.mediss.org
Contact: Renat Akchurin, Pres.
Founded: 1976. **Members:** 684. **Membership Dues:** active, $40 (annual). **Staff:** 3. **Multinational. Description:** Physicians organized to encourage, advance, and promote scientific research relating to the treatment of general vascular, cardiac and cardiovascular defects and diseases through general vascular and cardiovascular surgery. **Awards:** Fellowship Award. **Frequency:** annual. **Type:** fellowship. **Recipient:** for young surgeons, allowing them to study experimental and clinical cardiovascular surgery ● **Frequency:** annual. **Type:** recognition. **Formerly:** (1983) Michael E. DeBakey International Cardiovascular Society. **Conventions/Meetings:** biennial conference, with scientific symposium (exhibits).

13624 ■ National Heart Council (NHC)
c/o National Emergency Medicine Association
306 W Joppa Rd.
Baltimore, MD 21204-4048
Ph: (410)494-0300
Fax: (410)494-0725
E-mail: info@nemahealth.org
URL: http://www.nemahealth.org/programs/nhc
Contact: Howard H. Farrington, Pres.
Founded: 1982. **Staff:** 6. **Description:** A project of the National Emergency Medicine Association. Seeks to further advances made in the field of emergency medicine, particularly as related to heart trauma. **Convention/Meeting:** none. **Awards: Frequency:** annual. **Type:** grant. **Recipient:** to organizations and individuals for conducting research, meetings, or other activities that gather and disseminate information on traumatic medicine, particularly cardiac disorders. **Formerly:** (1994) National Heart Research. **Publications:** *Heart Research Newsletter*, quarterly ● Also publishes guides, reports, and brochures; plans to produce videotapes on first aid for household accidents, heart attacks, and choking.

13625 ■ National Heart Savers Association (NHSA)
c/o America Heart Association
16817 Holmes Cir.
Omaha, NE 68135-1455
Ph: (402)398-1993
Fax: (402)398-1994
E-mail: nhsa@aol.com
URL: http://www.americanheart.org
Contact: Phil Sokolof, Pres.
Founded: 1985. **Description:** Promotes cardiac health care by informing the public of the dangers of a high-cholesterol diet. Conducts public cholesterol screening program; secured congressional designation of September as National Cholesterol Education Month. Has been successful in persuading major food processing and fast food restaurants companies to stop using palm and coconut oil, lard, and beef tallow, which are high in saturated fats, as ingredients in prepared foods. Promotes nutrition education in public schools and lobbies for more healthful school lunches. **Convention/Meeting:** none. **Publications:** Books ● Pamphlets.

13626 ■ North American Society for Cardiac Imaging (NASCI)
1500 Sunday Dr., Ste.102
Raleigh, NC 27607
Ph: (919)861-4544
Fax: (919)787-4916
E-mail: robin@administrare.com
URL: http://www.nasci.org
Contact: Dave Feild, Exec. Dir.
Founded: 1973. **Members:** 350. **Membership Dues:** student, $60 (annual) ● regular, $160 (annual). **Budget:** $100,000. **Multinational. Description:** Represents individuals engaged in the practice and advancement of cardiac and vascular imaging are active members; medical students, other individuals, and corporations with an interest in cardiac imaging are sponsors. Seeks to advance the practice of cardiac imaging and to develop improved medical imaging technologies. Serves as a forum for the

exchange of information among individuals and corporations with an interest in cardiac imaging; sponsors educational programs; maintains Research and Education Fund. **Awards:** AHA Council of Cardiovascular Radiology. **Frequency:** annual. **Type:** grant ● Berlex Poster Awards. **Frequency:** annual. **Type:** grant ● Young Investigator's Awards. **Frequency:** annual. **Type:** grant. **Recipient:** for top oral presentation of participating trainees. **Publications:** *International Journal of Cardiovascular Imaging*, bimonthly. **Price:** included in membership dues; $562.00 for nonmembers, paper and online. Alternate Formats: online ● *NASCI Beat*, semiannual. Newsletter. Alternate Formats: online ● Membership Directory, annual. **Conventions/Meetings:** annual meeting.

13627 ■ Peripheral Arterial Disease Coalition
1075 S Yukon St., Ste.320
Lakewood, CO 80226
Ph: (301)524-1535
Free: (866)723-4636
Fax: (303)989-0200
E-mail: info@padcoalition.org
URL: http://www.padcoalition.org
Contact: Gwen Twillman, Exec. Dir.
Founded: 2004. **Description:** Raises public and health professional awareness of lower extremity Peripheral Arterial Disease (P.A.D.). Seeks to improve the prevention, early detection, treatment and rehabilitation of people with P.A.D. Creates a public and health professional education campaign to improve vascular disease awareness. **Publications:** Newsletter. Alternate Formats: online.

13628 ■ Peruvian Heart Association (PHA)
PO Box 797
Fabens, TX 79838
Ph: (915)764-4321
E-mail: victorbarahona43@hotmail.com
URL: http://www.peru-heart.org
Contact: Victoria A. Sanchez, Pres.
Founded: 1993. **Members:** 50. **Membership Dues:** active, $10 (annual). **Staff:** 3. **Regional Groups:** 6. **Languages:** English, Spanish. **Description:** Peruvian physicians, nurses, and other health care professionals specializing in cardiology that are devoted to research, training, teaching, and patient care. Offers continuing education courses for Peruvian physicians, enabling them to fulfill coursework required by Peruvian law for continuance of medical practice. Provides community health care information to residents of Lima, Peru concerning heart attacks, high blood pressure, cholesterol, diabetes, diet, and exercise. Provides printed information and speakers on health care. Also provides information to U.S. doctors who wish to study and assist with Peruvian health care. Offers Program of Basic Cardiac Life Support-Plus, and Advanced Cardiac Life Support-Plus. **Publications:** *Advanced Cardiac Life Support.* Book ● *Basic Cardiac Life Support for the Community.* Book ● *Basic Cardiac Life Support - Plus.* Book ● *Management of the Politrauma Patient.* Book. **Conventions/Meetings:** annual meeting (exhibits) - always last week in April ● periodic Resuscitation Course - meeting, in all parts of Peru.

13629 ■ Society for Cardiac Angiography and Interventions (SCAI)
2400 N St. NW
Washington, DC 20037-1153
Ph: (202)375-6195
Free: (800)992-7224
Fax: (202)375-6837
E-mail: info@scai.org
URL: http://www.scai.org
Contact: Norm Linsky, Exec. Dir.
Founded: 1978. **Members:** 2,000. **Membership Dues:** fellow in U.S. and Canada, $475 ● international, fellow outside U.S. and Canada, $335 ● international associate, $100. **Staff:** 4. **Budget:** $550,000. **Description:** Angiographers united to foster excellence in the field of cardiac catheterization, especially coronary arteriography and interventional angiography. (Angiography involves injecting substances opaque to radiation into blood vessels so

that diagnostic X-rays of those blood vessels may be made.) Conducts clinical research. **Awards:** BRACCO/SCA&I Fellowship Award. **Frequency:** annual. **Type:** fellowship. **Committees:** Cardiovascular Laboratory Technologists Standards; Continuing Medical Education; Credentials; Industry Relations; Interventional Cardiology; Laboratory Standards; Laboratory Survey; Pediatric Cardiology; Registry; Training and Education. **Publications:** *Catheterization and Cardiovascular Interventions*, monthly. Journal. **Price:** free for members ● *News Highlights*, bimonthly. Newsletter. Includes calendar of events and committee reports. **Price:** free. Alternate Formats: online. **Conventions/Meetings:** annual Scientific Sessions - meeting and symposium (exhibits) - always May.

13630 ■ Society for Cardiovascular Pathology (SCVP)
c/o Dr. Peter G. Anderson, Treas.
UAB Pathology, UH 213
1670 Univ. Blvd.
Birmingham, AL 35294-0019
Ph: (205)934-2414
Fax: (205)975-5697
E-mail: pga@uab.edu
URL: http://scvp.net
Contact: Dr. Peter G. Anderson, Treas.
Founded: 1985. **Members:** 200. **Membership Dues:** full, in U.S. and Canada, $150 (annual) ● full, outside U.S. and Canada, $160 (annual) ● trainee, in U.S. and Canada, $65 (annual) ● trainee, outside U.S. and Canada, $70 (annual). **Multinational. Description:** Authorities in the field of cardiovascular pathology. Seeks to advance the study of cardiovascular disorders. **Awards:** Cardiovascular Pathology Achievement Award. **Frequency:** annual. **Type:** recognition ● Young Investigator Award. **Frequency:** annual. **Type:** recognition. **Telecommunication Services:** electronic mail, webmaster@scvp.net. **Publications:** *Cardiovascular Pathology*, bimonthly. Journal. Supports the scholarly activities of the SCVP. **Conventions/Meetings:** annual meeting ● annual symposium - usually in March.

13631 ■ Society for Clinical Vascular Surgery (SCVS)
900 Cummings Ctr., No. 221-U
Beverly, MA 01915
Ph: (978)927-8330
Fax: (978)524-8890
E-mail: scvs@prri.com
URL: http://scvs.vascularweb.org
Contact: O. William Brown MD, Pres.
Founded: 1969. **Members:** 986. **Membership Dues:** active, $175 (annual). **Description:** Represents academic and community vascular surgeons. Promotes vascular surgery in the U.S. **Awards:** William J. von Liebig Foundation Award for Excellence in Vascular Surgical Research. **Frequency:** annual. **Type:** scholarship. **Recipient:** to individuals early in their training to pursue a career in research. **Publications:** *Journal of Vascular Surgery*, monthly. **Price:** included in membership dues. Alternate Formats: online. **Conventions/Meetings:** annual symposium (exhibits).

13632 ■ Society of Geriatric Cardiology (SGC)
Heart House
2400 N St. NW, 2nd Fl.
Washington, DC 20036
Ph: (202)375-6199
Fax: (202)375-6839
E-mail: sgcadmin@sgcard.org
URL: http://www.sgcard.org
Contact: Ebony Thomas-Blackmon, Mgr.
Founded: 1986. **Members:** 500. **Membership Dues:** trainee/associate, $50 (annual) ● regular, $95 (annual) ● fellowship, $150 (annual). **Staff:** 1. **Budget:** $200,000. **Description:** Geriatric cardiologists and physicians in related fields are fellows; medical practitioners certified in specialties other than geriatrics or cardiologists are members; other individuals with an interest in geriatric cardiology are nonphysician members. Works to improve the clinical

and therapeutic management of older individuals with cardiovascular disease; encourages use of preventive measures to avert the onset of cardiovascular aging and disease. Promotes more effective public policy and education regarding cardiac health. Conducts educational programs for physicians, other health care professionals, and the public. Supports research into cardiovascular aging and diseases relevant to older people. Serves as a clearinghouse on geriatric cardiology. Sponsors competitions. **Awards:** Merck Geriatric Cardiology Award. **Frequency:** annual. **Type:** grant. **Recipient:** for applicant reviewed by Research Committee. **Committees:** Development and Endowment; International Affairs; Long Range Planning; Membership and Credentials; Nominating and Awards; Nursing; Publications. **Formerly:** (1999) Council on Geriatric Cardiology. **Publications:** *American Journal of Geriatric Cardiology*, bimonthly. ISSN: 1076-7460. **Circulation:** 20,000. **Advertising:** accepted ● *News Brief*, 3/year. Newsletter. **Conventions/Meetings:** annual Scientific Session - meeting and seminar.

13633 ■ Society of Invasive Cardiovascular Professionals (SICP)
1500 Sunday Dr., Ste.102
Raleigh, NC 27607-5151
Ph: (919)861-4546
Fax: (919)787-4916
E-mail: director@sicp.com
URL: http://www.sicp.com
Contact: Nicole Shore, Exec. Dir.
Founded: 1993. **Members:** 700. **Membership Dues:** group, $230 (annual) ● individual, professional, $65 (annual). **Staff:** 2. **Description:** Cardiac catheterization laboratory personnel. Supports the highest quality of patient care. Serves as a forum for exchange of information among members. Defines core curricula for cardiovascular professionals; makes available educational opportunities to members; establishes standards of ethics and practice for the field. Facilitates cardiovascular research. **Computer Services:** Mailing lists. **Committees:** Educational. **Publications:** *Cath-Lab Digest*, monthly. Journal. **Price:** included in membership dues. **Circulation:** 16,000 ● *Journal of Invasive Cardiology*, monthly. **Conventions/Meetings:** annual meeting ● periodic regional meeting and symposium (exhibits).

13634 ■ WomenHeart: National Coalition for Women with Heart Disease
818 18th St. NW, Ste.930
Washington, DC 20006
Ph: (202)728-7199
Fax: (202)728-7238
E-mail: mail@womenheart.org
URL: http://www.womenheart.org
Contact: Nancy Loving, Co-Founder/Exec. Dir.
Founded: 2000. **Description:** Seeks to improve the quality of life of American women living with heart disease. Promotes early diagnosis and proper treatment of women living with heart disease. Improves the knowledge, attitudes and practices of health care professionals in the diagnosis and treatment of heart disease. Supports medical research into the causes, diagnosis, progression and treatment of heart disease. **Computer Services:** Information services, heart disease resources ● online services, bulletin board. **Boards:** Scientific Advisory. **Committees:** Corporate Advisory. **Programs:** Red Bag of Courage. **Publications:** Newsletter, quarterly ● Newsletter, monthly. Alternate Formats: online.

13635 ■ World Council for Cardiovascular and Pulmonary Rehabilitation (WCCPR)
c/o Susan Rees, Office Staff
2810 Crossroads Dr., Ste.3800
Madison, WI 53718
Ph: (608)443-2468
Fax: (608)443-2474
E-mail: srees@reesgroupinc.com
URL: http://www.wccpr.org
Contact: Susan Rees, Office Staff
Founded: 1994. **Multinational. Description:** Advances the profession of cardiovascular and pulmonary rehabilitation around the world. Encourages

rehabilitation-related research that will enhance the health and personal welfare of patients. Enhances international communication among members and provides professional educational opportunities. Provides a forum for information exchange.

Cardio-Pulmonary

13636 ■ National Alliance for Thrombosis and Thrombophilia (NATT)
PO Box 66018
Washington, DC 20035-6018
Ph: (860)376-3250
E-mail: nattinfo@yahoo.com
URL: http://www.nattinfo.org
Contact: Tom Hogan, Sec.
Founded: 2003. **Description:** Addresses major treatment issues to prevent thrombosis and its complications. Assists in establishing guidelines for prevention, treatment, and management. Encourages activities to increase the number of specialists in thrombosis and thrombophilia.

13637 ■ National Emphysema Foundation (NEF)
128 East Ave.
Norwalk, CT 06851
Ph: (203)866-5000
Fax: (203)286-1105
E-mail: nefsupport@sbcglobal.net
URL: http://emphysemafoundation.org
Contact: Sreedhar Nair MD, Pres.
Founded: 1971. **Description:** Aims to improve the quality of life for those with emphysema, asthma, and related diseases. **Additional Websites:** http://www.nef-usa.org, http://www.emphysemafoundation.org.

Cardiovascular Disease

13638 ■ Sudden Cardiac Arrest Association (SCAA)
1133 Connecticut Ave. NW, 11th Fl.
Washington, DC 20036
Ph: (202)719-8909
Free: (866)972-7222
Fax: (202)719-8983
E-mail: info@suddencardiacarrest.org
URL: http://www.early-defib.org
Contact: Diane M. Canova, Exec. Dir.
Founded: 2005. **Description:** Seeks to prevent loss of life from Sudden Cardiac Arrest (SCA). Raises awareness and understanding of SCA. Promotes solutions to prevent sudden cardiac death. Increases public access to defibrillation, CPR, and other SCA therapies. **Publications:** Brochure. Alternate Formats: online.

Cerebral Palsy

13639 ■ American Academy for Cerebral Palsy and Developmental Medicine (AACPDM)
555 E Wells St., Ste.1100
Milwaukee, WI 53202
Ph: (414)918-3014
Fax: (414)276-2146
E-mail: info@aacpdm.org
URL: http://www.aacpdm.org/index?service=page/Home
Contact: Sheril B. King, Exec. Dir.
Founded: 1947. **Members:** 1,600. **Membership Dues:** fellow, $230 (annual) ● international corresponding, student, resident, trainee, $35 (annual). **Staff:** 3. **Budget:** $250,000. **Description:** Professional organization of physicians, PhDs, and allied health care individuals concerned with diagnosis, care, treatment, and research of cerebral palsy and developmental disorders. **Awards:** Richmond Cerebral Palsy Award. **Frequency:** annual. **Type:** recognition. **Computer Services:** Mailing lists, available to educational programs only. **Committees:** Audiovi-

sual; Continuing Education; Research; Scientific Program. **Formerly:** (1976) American Academy for Cerebral Palsy. **Publications:** AACPDM News, biennial. Newsletter. Includes academy news. **Price:** included in membership dues. **Circulation:** 1,600. **Advertising:** accepted ● Journal of Developmental Medicine and Child Neurology, monthly ● Membership Roster, annual. Membership Directory. **Conventions/Meetings:** annual meeting (exhibits).

13640 ■ United Cerebral Palsy Associations (UCP)
1660 L St. NW, Ste.700
Washington, DC 20036
Ph: (202)776-0406 (202)973-7197
Free: (800)872-5827
Fax: (202)776-0414
E-mail: info@ucp.org
URL: http://www.ucp.org
Contact: Stephen Bennett, Pres./CEO
Founded: 1955. **Staff:** 30. **Budget:** $1,500,000. **Description:** Serves as a source of information on cerebral palsy. Works to advocate for the rights of persons with any disability. Advances the independence, productivity and full citizenship of people with disabilities through an affiliate network. **Councils:** Research Advisory. **Formerly:** (2005) United Cerebral Palsy Research and Educational Foundation. **Publications:** Research Fact Sheets, monthly ● Also publishes medical directors' reports and a foundation brochure. **Conventions/Meetings:** semiannual board meeting.

Chemistry

13641 ■ American Association for Clinical Chemistry (AACC)
1850 K St. NW, Ste.625
Washington, DC 20006
Ph: (202)857-0717
Free: (800)892-1400
Fax: (202)887-5093
E-mail: custserv@aacc.org
URL: http://www.aacc.org
Contact: Richard Flaherty, Exec. VP
Founded: 1948. **Members:** 10,000. **Membership Dues:** professional, $185 (annual) ● affiliate, $110 (annual) ● student associate, $25 (annual). **Staff:** 55. **Budget:** $13,000,000. **Local Groups:** 22. **Multinational. Description:** Clinical laboratory scientists and others engaged in the practice of clinical laboratory science in independent laboratories, hospitals, and allied institutions. Sponsors education programs; publishes books. **Awards:** AACC Lectureship Award. **Frequency:** annual. **Type:** recognition ● The Edwin F. Ullman Award. **Frequency:** annual. **Type:** recognition ● International Travel Fellowship Award. **Frequency:** annual. **Type:** fellowship ● Outstanding Contributions in Education. **Frequency:** annual. **Type:** recognition. **Recipient:** for contributions to education ● Outstanding Contributions Through Service to the Profession of Clinical Chemistry. **Frequency:** annual. **Type:** recognition. **Recipient:** for outstanding services to the profession ● Outstanding Contributions to Clinical Chemistry. **Frequency:** annual. **Type:** recognition. **Recipient:** for outstanding contributions to clinical chemistry ● Outstanding Scientific Achievements by a Young Investigator. **Frequency:** annual. **Type:** recognition ● Sigi Ziering Award for Outstanding Contribution for a Publication in the Journal Clinical Chemistry. **Frequency:** annual. **Type:** recognition. **Commissions:** Program Coordinating. **Committees:** Awards; Government Affairs; International Affairs. **Divisions:** Animal Clinical Chemistry; Clinical and Diagnostic Immunology; Critical and Point-of-Care Testing; History of Clinical Chemistry; Industry; Laboratory Information Systems and Medical Informatics; Lipoproteins and Vascular Diseases; Management Sciences; Molecular Pathology; Nutrition; Pediatric and Maternal-Fetal; TDM and Clinical Toxicology. **Formerly:** (1976) American Association of Clinical Chemists. **Publications:** Clinical Chemistry Journal, monthly ● Clinical Laboratory News, monthly. Newsletter ● Clinical Laboratory

Strategies, monthly ● Annual Report, annual ● Books ● Membership Directory. **Price:** included in membership dues. Alternate Formats: online. **Conventions/Meetings:** annual conference ● annual Clinical Laboratory Exposition - meeting (exhibits) - 2008 July 27-31, Washington, DC; 2009 July 19-23, Chicago, IL; 2010 July 25-29, Anaheim, CA.

13642 ■ Association for Chemoreception Sciences (AChemS)
5841 Cedar Lake Rd.
Minneapolis, MN 55416
Ph: (952)646-2035
Fax: (952)545-6073
E-mail: info@achems.org
URL: http://achems.org
Contact: Diego Restrepo, Pres.
Founded: 1979. **Members:** 700. **Membership Dues:** regular (with on-line subscription), $138 (annual) ● student and emeritus (with on-line subscription), $78 (annual). **Multinational. Description:** Research scientists, experimental psychologists, and industrial researchers. Works to study chemoreception (the physiological reception of chemical stimuli) by the senses of taste and smell. Conducts research on the differences in human and animal perception of chemical stimuli in taste and smell. Offers seminars, fellowships, and workshops. Maintains placement service. **Computer Services:** Mailing lists. **Publications:** Chemical Senses Journal. **Price:** included in membership dues ● Newsletter, biennial. Alternate Formats: online. **Conventions/Meetings:** annual meeting and conference (exhibits) - always April, in Sarasota, FL.

13643 ■ Histochemical Society (HCS)
Univ. Sta.
PO Box 85630
Seattle, WA 98145-1630
Ph: (206)616-5278
Fax: (206)616-5842
E-mail: mail@histochemicalsociety.org
URL: http://www.histochemicalsociety.org
Contact: William L. Stahl, Exec. Dir.
Founded: 1950. **Members:** 450. **Membership Dues:** associate, regular, $50 (annual) ● student, $20 (annual) ● associate, regular (international airmail), $140 (annual) ● student (international airmail), $110 (annual). **Staff:** 3. **Budget:** $250,000. **Description:** Represents physicians and scientists who employ histochemical and cytochemical techniques in their research. **Awards:** Lillie Award. **Frequency:** annual. **Type:** recognition. **Recipient:** for outstanding young histochemist ● Vector Award. **Type:** recognition. **Recipient:** for outstanding young histochemist. **Publications:** The Journal of Histochemistry and Cytochemistry, monthly. ISSN: 0022-1554. **Circulation:** 800. **Advertising:** accepted ● Newsletter, semiannual. **Conventions/Meetings:** annual meeting - 2008 Apr. 5-9, San Diego, CA.

13644 ■ National Registry of Certified Chemists (NRCC)
c/o Gilbert E. Smith, PhD, Exec. Dir.
927 S Walter Reed Dr., No. 11
Arlington, VA 22204
Ph: (703)979-9001
E-mail: nrcc6@aol.com
URL: http://www.nrcc6.org
Contact: Gilbert E. Smith PhD, Exec. Dir.
Founded: 1967. **Members:** 500. **Staff:** 1. **Budget:** $55,000. **Description:** Certifies programs for chemical hygiene officers, clinical chemists, clinical chemistry technologists, environmental analytical chemists, environmental analytical technicians, and toxicological chemists based on education, experience, and examination. **Committees:** Credentials; Examinations. **Formerly:** (2001) National Registry in Clinical Chemistry. **Publications:** Directory, annual.

Child Development

13645 ■ American Hyperlexia Association (AHA)
195 W Spangler, Ste.B
Elmhurst, IL 60126

Ph: (630)415-2212
Fax: (630)530-5909
E-mail: president@hyperlexia.org
URL: http://www.hyperlexia.org
Membership Dues: in U.S. and Canada, $25 (annual) ● outside U.S. and Canada, $35 (annual). **Description:** Dedicated to advancement of education and general welfare of children with hyperlexia. **Publications:** Newsletter, quarterly. **Price:** included in membership dues.

13646 ■ Developmental Delay Resources (DDR)
5801 Beacon St.
Pittsburgh, PA 15217
Free: (800)497-0944
Fax: (412)422-1374
E-mail: devdelay@mindspring.com
URL: http://www.devdelay.org
Contact: Patricia Lemer, Exec. Dir.
Founded: 1998. **Membership Dues:** student, retiree, $25 (annual) ● family, $50 (annual) ● professional, $90 (annual) ● organization, $150 (annual) ● educator, $60 (annual) ● sponsor, $250-$999 (annual). **Description:** Meets needs of families with children with developmental delays in sensory motor, language, social, and emotional areas. **Libraries: Type:** reference. **Computer Services:** database. **Formerly:** (1998) Developmental Delay Registry. **Publications:** *The Digest of Volume 1-7 of the DDR Newsletter New Developments.* Indexed by subject and name. ● *Networking Directory,* annual. **Price:** included in membership dues. **Advertising:** accepted ● *New Developments,* quarterly. Newsletter. **Price:** included in membership dues. **Conventions/Meetings:** lecture ● seminar ● workshop.

13647 ■ First Signs
PO Box 358
Merrimac, MA 01860
Ph: (978)346-4380
Fax: (978)346-4638
E-mail: info@firstsigns.org
URL: http://www.firstsigns.org
Contact: Nancy D. Wiseman, Pres./Treas.
Founded: 1998. **Description:** Educates parents and pediatric professionals about the early warning signs of autism and other developmental disorders. Promotes awareness of the aspects of development: social, emotional and communication. Improves screening and referral practices to lower the age at which young children are identified with autism and other developmental disorders.

13648 ■ National Association for Child Development (NACD)
549 25th St.
Ogden, UT 84401
Ph: (801)621-8606
Fax: (801)621-8389
E-mail: info@nacd.org
URL: http://www.nacd.org
Contact: Elizabeth B. Severino MD, Medical Dir.
Founded: 1979. **Staff:** 9. **Multinational. Description:** Helps children and adults reach full potential through specific home neurodevelopmental programs. **Publications:** *The Efficacy of the NACD Program.* Article. Alternate Formats: online ● *Journal of the National Academy for Child Development,* periodic. Contains articles about the aspects of human development. ● *NACD Neuroeducational Model Program.* Article. Alternate Formats: online.

13649 ■ Zero to Three: National Center for Infants, Toddlers and Families
2000 M St. NW, Ste.200
Washington, DC 20036
Ph: (202)638-1144
Free: (800)899-4301
Fax: (202)638-0851
E-mail: 0to3@presswarehouse.com
URL: http://www.zerotothree.org
Contact: Matthew E. Melmed JD, Exec. Dir.
Founded: 1977. **Staff:** 65. **Budget:** $8,000,000. **Description:** Professionals and researchers in the health care industry, policymakers, and parents work-

ing to improve the healthy physical, cognitive and social development of infants, toddlers, and their families. Members share their expertise about infants, toddlers, and their families. Sponsors training and technical assistance activities. **Awards:** Dolley Madison Award for Outstanding Contributions. **Frequency:** biennial. **Type:** recognition ● Sally Provence Award for Excellence. **Type:** recognition. **Recipient:** for individuals whose work demonstrates qualities essential to effective practice. **Computer Services:** Mailing lists, available to appropriate organizations, rental $110/thousand names. **Formerly:** (1992) National Center for Clinical Infant Programs; (2001) National Center for Infants, Toddlers and Families. **Publications:** *Zero to Three,* bimonthly. Journal. Includes research and practice reports, book and video reviews, calendar of events, funding source information, and lists of training opportunities. **Price:** $78.00/year in U.S.; $138.00/2 years outside U.S.; $94.00/year outside U.S. ISSN: 0736-8086. **Circulation:** 7,400. **Conventions/Meetings:** annual National Training Institutes - meeting (exhibits) - held first weekend every December, even years in Washington, DC, odd years various locations ● seminar.

Child Health

13650 ■ Action for Healthy Kids (AFHK)
4711 W Golf Rd., Ste.625
Skokie, IL 60076
Free: (800)416-5136
E-mail: info@actionforhealthykids.org
URL: http://www.actionforhealthykids.org
Contact: Alicia Moaq-Stahlberg MS, Exec. Dir.
Founded: 2002. **Staff:** 9. **Description:** Seeks to address the epidemic of overweight and obesity resulting from children's poor nutrition and sedentary lifestyles. Educates administrators, teachers, children and parents about how nutrition and physical activity impact children's health and academic achievement. **Publications:** Reports, periodic.

13651 ■ ALSAC/Saint Jude Children's Research Hospital
332 N Lauderdale
Memphis, TN 38105
Ph: (901)495-3300
Free: (800)822-6344
Fax: (901)578-2803
E-mail: info@stjude.org
URL: http://www.stjude.org
Contact: Marlo Thomas, Natl. Outreach Dir.
Founded: 1957. **Budget:** $365,000,000. **Multinational. Description:** Finds cure for childhood catastrophic diseases through research and treatment. ALSAC, the fund-raising arm of St. Jude, was organized through the auspices of Danny Thomas, television and theatre personality, to raise the necessary funds to operate and maintain the organization. **Awards: Type:** recognition. **Formerly:** (1972) Aiding Leukemia Stricken American Children. **Publications:** *ALSAC News,* quarterly. Newspaper. Informs members of St. Jude Hospital activities and ALSAC fundraising programs. Covers regional news. **Price:** included in membership dues. **Circulation:** 6,500. **Conventions/Meetings:** annual meeting.

13652 ■ Association of Maternal and Child Health Programs (AMCHP)
1220 19th St. NW, Ste.801
Washington, DC 20036
Ph: (202)775-0436
Fax: (202)775-0061
E-mail: info@amchp.org
URL: http://www.amchp.org
Contact: Barbara Laur, Interim CEO
Founded: 1944. **Members:** 450. **Membership Dues:** regular, individual associate, $110 (annual) ● organization, $770 (annual). **Staff:** 26. **Budget:** $3,000,000. **Description:** Individuals responsible for or involved in the Administration of state and territorial maternal and child health programs and programs for children with special health care needs. Seeks to: inform public and private sector decision makers of the

health care needs of mothers and children; develop and recommend maternal and child health policies and programs; develop coalitions with other interested organizations. Promotes exchange of ideas and experiences among members; studies and reports on the health of and services for mothers and children; develops models and standards for and provides technical assistance to maternal and child health programs. **Committees:** Data and Assessment; Policy and Program Development; Service Delivery and Finance System. **Affiliated With:** Association of State and Territorial Health Officials. **Formerly:** Association of State and Territorial Maternal and Child Health and Crippled Children's Directors. **Publications:** *Abstinence Education in the States: Implementation of the 1996 Abstinence Education Law* ● *AMCHP Updates,* bimonthly. Newsletter. **Price:** included in membership dues. **Circulation:** 500 ● *Caring for Mothers and Children: A Report of a Survey of 1987 State MCH Program Activities* ● *Dedicated to Care for Children: A Report on States Use of OBRA 1986 Earmarked Title V Funds* ● *Home Visiting: An Effective Strategy for Improving the Health of Mothers and Children* ● *The Impact of the State Child Health Insurance Program (CHIP) on Title V Children with Special Health Care Needs Programs* ● *Smoking Cessation Makes Cents: The Cost-Effectiveness of Tobacco Interventions* ● Magazines ● Proceedings ● Reports ● Also publishes cost-based reimbursement studies and health care reform studies. **Conventions/Meetings:** annual Evaluating Outcomes: Paving the Road to a Healthier Tomorrow - conference.

13653 ■ Brain Tumor Foundation for Children (BTFC)
6065 Roswell Rd. NE, Ste.505
Atlanta, GA 30328
Ph: (404)252-4107
Fax: (404)252-4108
E-mail: btfc@bellsouth.net
URL: http://www.braintumorkids.org
Contact: Mary Campbell, Exec. Dir.
Founded: 1983. **Description:** Provides support to families of children with brain tumors and promotes public education and awareness of the disease. **Libraries: Type:** not open to the public. **Holdings:** audio recordings, books. **Subjects:** brain tumors. **Awards: Type:** scholarship. **Recipient:** to graduate nursing students in pediatric oncology. **Publications:** *Butterfly Bulletin,* quarterly. Newsletter. Alternate Formats: online ● *Coloring Book* ● *News Views,* bimonthly. Newsletter. Provides information for families. **Conventions/Meetings:** monthly WACKY (Wild and Crazy Kourageous Youth) - meeting, support group for brain tumor patients 13 and older.

13654 ■ Child Health Foundation (CHF)
10630 Little Patuxent Pkwy., Ste.126
Columbia, MD 21044
Ph: (410)992-5512
Fax: (410)992-5641
E-mail: contact@childhealthfoundation.org
URL: http://www.childhealthfoundation.org
Contact: R. Bradley Sack, Pres.
Founded: 1985. **Staff:** 2. **Budget:** $100,000. **Languages:** English, French, Portuguese, Spanish. **Description:** Addresses significant health issues of children and families, primarily in developing countries and medically underserved populations in the U.S. Focuses on diarrheal diseases, related social and medical problems of malnutrition, and poverty. Develops and encourages use of simple, low-cost technologies. Conducts health programs in research training in oral rehydration therapies, nutrition, breastfeeding and other low-cost approaches to better health. Operates programs to strengthen research capabilities of institutions in developing countries to enable them to develop and perform research on diseases most prevalent in their own countries. Conducts educational training programs and workshops for: volunteers in disease prevention and simple treatments effective in rural and urban areas. Conducts charitable activities; maintains Speaker's Bureau. **Computer Services:** database. **Affiliated With:** Save the Children. **Formerly:** International Child Health Foundation; (1994) International Child

Health Foundation. **Publications:** *Cereal-Based Oral Rehydration Therapy Symposium Proceedings.* Journal ● *Child Health Foundation Newsletter,* quarterly. Includes research summaries and foundation information. ● *Food-based Oral Rehydration Therapy Report* ● *Proper Nutrition and Hygiene* ● *Training Manual for Treatment and Prevention of Childhood Diarrhea with Oral Rehydration Therapy* ● Annual Report, annual.

13655 ■ Child Life Council (CLC)
11820 Parklawn Dr., Ste.240
Rockville, MD 20852-2529
Ph: (301)881-7090
Free: (800)CLC-4515
Fax: (301)881-7092
E-mail: clcstaff@childlife.org
URL: http://www.childlife.org
Contact: Eric K. Munn, Pres.
Founded: 1982. **Members:** 2,200. **Membership Dues:** student, $45 (annual) ● associate, $80 (annual) ● active (professional), $90 (annual) ● corporate, $300 (annual) ● life, $1,000. **Staff:** 5. **Budget:** $500,000. **Multinational. Description:** Professional organization representing child life personnel, patient activities specialists, and students in the field. Promotes psychological well-being and optimum development of children, adolescents, and their families in health care settings. Works to minimize the stress and anxiety of illness and hospitalization. Addresses professional issues such as program standards, competencies, and core curriculum. Provides resources and conducts research and educational programs. Offers a Job Bank Service listing employment openings. **Awards: Type:** recognition. **Computer Services:** Mailing lists. **Committees:** Bulletin; Certification; Conference Planning; Diversity; Education; History; Nominating; Public Relations; Publications; Research; Technology. **Formerly:** (1975) Child Life Specialist Committee; (1979) Child Life Activity Study Section; (1982) Child Life Task Force. **Publications:** *Child Life Council Bulletin,* quarterly. **Advertising:** accepted ● *Child Life in Hospitals: Theory and Practice.* **Price:** $60.00 for nonmembers; $48.00 for members ● *Child Life Programs,* biennial. Directory ● *Official Documents of the Child Life Council* ● *Program Review Guidelines* ● *Psychosocial Care of Children in Hospitals: A Clinical Practice Manual.* **Conventions/Meetings:** annual Conference on Professional Issues, provides goods and services used by child life professionals (exhibits) - 2008 May 22-25, San Diego, CA.

13656 ■ Children's Brain Tumor Foundation (CBTF)
274 Madison Ave., Ste.1004
New York, NY 10016
Ph: (212)448-9494
Free: (866)228-HOPE
Fax: (212)448-1022
E-mail: info@cbtf.org
URL: http://www.cbtf.org
Contact: Judy Hurley, Exec. Dir.
Founded: 1988. **Staff:** 4. **Description:** Works to improve the outlook for children with brain and spinal cord tumors. Raises funds for research; provides counseling, education and support services for families and survivors. **Awards: Type:** fellowship. **Recipient:** for young physicians studying pediatric neurooncology ● Quality of Life Grant. **Frequency:** annual. **Type:** grant. **Recipient:** for research scientists. **Computer Services:** Mailing lists ● online services. **Publications:** *A Resource Guide for Parents of Children with Brain and Spinal Cord Tumors* (in English and Spanish). Booklet. Contains technical and practical information for parents. **Price:** free. Alternate Formats: online ● *The Challenge,* semiannual. Newsletter. Alternate Formats: online. **Conventions/Meetings:** board meeting.

13657 ■ Children's Health Environmental Coalition (CHEC)
12300 Wilshire Blvd., Ste.410
Los Angeles, CA 90025
Ph: (310)820-2030
Fax: (310)820-2070

E-mail: chec@checnet.org
URL: http://www.checnet.org
Contact: Nancy Gould Chuda, Pres./Co-Founder
Membership Dues: regular, $25 (annual) ● friend, $50 (annual) ● patron, $100 (annual) ● benefactor, $500 (annual). **Description:** Educates the public, specifically parents and caregivers, about environmental toxins that affect children's health. Promotes the right of consumers to know what is in their air, food, water and commercial products. Encourages the public to adopt safer products and practices. Works to change government and corporate policies to protect children from environmental hazards. **Publications:** *CHEC Health eNews,* monthly. Newsletter. Alternate Formats: online ● *CHEC Report,* quarterly. Newsletter. **Price:** included in membership dues ● *Household Detective.* Handbook. Contains information about threats to children's health and less toxic product alternatives.

13658 ■ Children's Health Fund (CHF)
215 W 125th St., Ste.301
New York, NY 10027
Ph: (212)535-9400
E-mail: dev@childrenshealthfund.org
URL: http://www.childrenshealthfund.org
Contact: Irwin Redlener MD, Co-Founder/Pres.
Founded: 1987. **Staff:** 12. **Budget:** $5,183,076. **Languages:** English, Spanish. **Description:** Supports pediatric programs for children who are homeless, poor, or have no other access to medical care. Maintains Children's Health Projects in urban and rural areas throughout the United States. Provides mobile medical units in order to bring health care to underserved children. **Computer Services:** database. **Telecommunication Services:** electronic mail, iredlener@chfund.org. **Projects:** Arkansas Children's Health; Austin Children's Health; Chicago Children's Health; Dallas Children's Health; Idaho Children's Health; Long Island Children's Health; Los Angeles Children's Health; Mississippi Children's Health. **Publications:** *The Children's Health Fund News.* Newsletter. Alternate Formats: online.

13659 ■ Children's Medical Ministries (CMM)
PO Box 3382
Crofton, MD 21114
Ph: (301)261-3211
Fax: (410)721-4647
E-mail: childmed@olg.com
URL: http://www.childmed.org
Contact: Rachel Brunk, Sec.
Founded: 1988. **Members:** 700. **Staff:** 700. **Description:** Works to serve the poor and needy children by offering health care, nutritional support, and dental care. **Programs:** Children's Health Education; King's Kid Vitamin. **Publications:** *Beauty for Ashes,* quarterly. Newsletter. Alternate Formats: online.

13660 ■ Children's Organ Transplant Association (COTA)
2501 COTA Dr.
Bloomington, IN 47403
Free: (800)366-2682
Fax: (812)336-8885
E-mail: cota@cota.org
URL: http://www.cota.org
Contact: Richard E. Lofgren, Pres./CEO
Founded: 1986. **Members:** 700. **Staff:** 9. **Budget:** $1,500,000. **Description:** Works to ensure that no U.S. child is ever denied a life-saving transplant, or access to a transplant waiting list, due solely to lack of funds; promotes organ donations and provides public education on all aspects of the organ donation process. **Publications:** *Life-Giving Report,* quarterly. Newsletter. Alternate Formats: online.

13661 ■ CityMatch
c/o Magda G. Peck, ScD, CEO/Sr. Advisor
Dept. of Pediatrics
982170 Nebraska Medical Ctr.
Omaha, NE 68198-2170
Ph: (402)561-7500
Fax: (402)561-7525

E-mail: citymch@unmc.edu
URL: http://www.citymatch.org
Contact: Magda G. Peck ScD, CEO/Sr. Advisor
Founded: 1988. **Members:** 142. **Staff:** 9. **Budget:** $500,000. **Regional Groups:** 10. **Local Groups:** 11. **National Groups:** 11. **Description:** City and county health departments, leaders representing urban communities in the United States, and interested others. Seeks to provide optimal health care for children and families in urban areas. Gives particular attention to increasing racial disparities in infant mortality, inadequate access to prenatal care, substance abuse in pregnancy, and interpersonal violence. Provides children's services; compiles statistics. **Libraries: Type:** not open to the public. **Holdings:** articles, audiovisuals, books, papers, periodicals. **Subjects:** maternal, child health issues. **Computer Services:** database. **Publications:** *CityLights,* quarterly. Newsletter. **Circulation:** 2,000. Alternate Formats: online ● *Technical Reports* ● *What Works: 1990 Urban MCH Programs.* Directory. Includes maternal and child health programs in major urban health departments. **Conventions/Meetings:** annual board meeting - always in May or June at Omaha, NE ● annual conference - always in September.

13662 ■ Docs for Tots (DFT)
2000 M St. NW, Ste.201
Washington, DC 20036
Ph: (202)296-2131
Fax: (202)638-0851
E-mail: dft@docsfortots.org
URL: http://www.docsfortots.org
Contact: George L. Askew MD, Founder/Exec. Dir.
Founded: 2003. **Members:** 734. **Description:** Aims to develop, support and grow a nationwide network of doctors who are able to respond to the requests of child advocacy organizations. Seeks to increase the civic involvement of doctors through advocacy of programs and policies that will improve the health and development of infants, toddlers and preschoolers. Provides advocacy toolkits for doctors. **Publications:** Newsletter, bimonthly. Alternate Formats: online.

13663 ■ Every Child By Two (ECBT)
666 11th St. NW, Ste.202
Washington, DC 20001-4542
Ph: (202)783-7034
Fax: (202)783-7042
E-mail: info@ecbt.org
URL: http://www.ecbt.org
Contact: Amy Pisani MS, Exec. Dir.
Founded: 1981. **Staff:** 4. **Description:** Campaigns for early immunization. Visits health departments, hospitals, and schools nationwide to promote timely immunizations. Works to raise awareness and foster a systematic way to ensure the health of all America's children. Targets community leaders of service organizations for assistance. Compiles statistics. Sponsors educational programs and children's services. **Awards: Frequency:** annual. **Type:** recognition. **Telecommunication Services:** electronic mail, amyp@ecbt.org. **Publications:** Newsletter, bimonthly. **Circulation:** 5,000. Alternate Formats: online. **Conventions/Meetings:** annual conference (exhibits).

13664 ■ Family Voices (FV)
2340 Alamo SE, Ste.102
Albuquerque, NM 87106
Ph: (505)872-4774
Free: (888)835-5669
Fax: (505)872-4780
E-mail: kidshealth@familyvoices.org
URL: http://www.familyvoices.org
Contact: Jennifer M. Cernoch PhD, Exec. Dir.
Members: 40,000. **Description:** Advocates for children with special health needs. **Publications:** *Friday's Child,* weekly. Newsletter. Contains information for existing and emerging family leaders on topics such as leadership, mentoring, partnership, and team building. **Price:** free for members. Alternate Formats: online.

13665 ■ Gift from the Heart Foundation
2653 N Narragansett Ave.
Chicago, IL 60639
Ph: (773)237-4800
Fax: (773)237-1221
E-mail: giftheart@sbcglobal.net
URL: http://www.promograph.com/giftfromtheheart
Contact: Krystyna B. Pasek, Pres.
Founded: 1988. **Staff:** 2. **Budget:** $250,000. **Local Groups:** 1. **Languages:** English, Polish, Russian. **Description:** Works to assist seriously ill children around the world by obtaining information regarding medical care. Provides food, lodging, transportation, and interpreters for children and their accompanying parents. Purchases rehabilitation equipment. Provides charitable programs and various social activities. **Awards:** Merit Award. **Type:** recognition. **Recipient:** for voluntary service. **Computer Services:** database, donors, sponsors, and contributors listing ● mailing lists, contacting donors, sponsors and contributors. **Formerly:** (1992) Dar Serca. **Publications:** *Gift from the Heart Foundation's Newsletter*, quarterly. Alternate Formats: online ● Brochure (in English and Polish), triennial. **Price:** free. **Circulation:** 5,000 ● Annual Report, annual. **Conventions/Meetings:** monthly board meeting - every first Tuesday.

13666 ■ Group B Strep Association (GBSA)
PO Box 16515
Chapel Hill, NC 27516
E-mail: bstrep@mindspring.com
URL: http://www.groupbstrep.org
Contact: Gina Burns, Pres.
Founded: 1990. **Members:** 3,000. **Staff:** 2. **Description:** Seeks to educate the public about Group B Strep (GBS) infections during pregnancy. Promotes screening of mothers and the development of a vaccine. Seeks to control the disease, which is a leading cause of life-threatening infections in newborns. Acts as a support group; provides educational programs. **Publications:** *GBSA Public Education Packet* ● Also provides medical contacts and legislation information. **Conventions/Meetings:** annual meeting.

13667 ■ International Society on Infant Studies (ISIS)
c/o Lawrence Erlbaum Associates, Inc.
10 Indus. Ave.
Mahwah, NJ 07430
E-mail: journals@erlbaum.com
URL: http://www.isisweb.org
Contact: Leslie B. Cohen, Pres.
Membership Dues: regular, $60 (annual) ● student, $40 (annual) ● spouse, $20 (annual) ● editor, $20 (annual). **Multinational. Description:** Promotes and disseminates research regarding the development of infants. **Computer Services:** Mailing lists. **Publications:** *Conference Abstracts* ● *Infancy*, bimonthly. Journal. Features latest research and theory in infant development. **Price:** included in membership dues ● Newsletter, periodic. Alternate Formats: online. **Conventions/Meetings:** biennial conference ● meeting.

13668 ■ KDWB Variety Family Center
Div. of Gen. Pediatrics & Adolescent Hea.
Univ. of Minnesota Gateway
200 Oak St. SE
Minneapolis, MN 55455-2002
Ph: (612)626-3087
Free: (800)276-8642
Fax: (612)624-0997
E-mail: instihd@tc.umn.edu
URL: http://www.geneticalliance.org
Contact: Elizabeth Latts, Research Coor.
Description: Provides family-centered services that promote physical, emotional, psychological and social health and well-being for children and youth at risk, including children and youth with disabilities. **Libraries: Type:** open to the public. **Holdings:** books, periodicals. **Subjects:** children and youth with disabilities. **Additional Websites:** http://allaboutkids. umn.edu/kdwbvfc/index.htm. **Telecommunication Services:** hotline, (612)624-3939. **Departments:** Behavioral Pediatrics; FAS Network; General Academic Pediatrics; Parents-as-Teachers; Pediatric Psychol-

ogy; STAR Center for Family Health. **Projects:** U Special Kids. **Publications:** *Health Issues*, periodic. Newsletter. Details the most current thinking on resilience, cross-cultural differences, and caregiving of children at risk in the society. **Circulation:** 15,000. Alternate Formats: online ● Report, periodic ● Monograph, periodic.

13669 ■ Klingenstein Third Generation Foundation (KTGF)
787 Seventh Ave., 6th Fl.
New York, NY 10019-6016
Ph: (212)492-6179
Fax: (212)492-7007
E-mail: sally@ktgf.org
URL: http://www.ktgf.org
Contact: Sally Klingenstein Martell, Exec. Dir.
Founded: 1983. **Members:** 7. **Staff:** 2. **Description:** Strives to improve the lives of families afflicted by clinical depressions; addresses childhood and adolescent depression as well as Attention Deficit/Hyperactivity Disorder. **Awards:** Post-doctoral ADHD Research Fellowship. **Frequency:** annual. **Type:** fellowship. **Recipient:** to organizations or programs which address childhood and adolescent ADHD ● Post-doctoral Depression Research Fellowship. **Frequency:** annual. **Type:** fellowship. **Recipient:** to organizations or programs focusing in the areas of childhood/adolescent depression.

13670 ■ MAGIC Foundation (MAGIC)
6645 W North Ave.
Oak Park, IL 60302
Ph: (708)383-0808
Free: (800)3MA-GIC3
Fax: (708)383-0899
E-mail: info@magicfoundation.org
URL: http://www.magicfoundation.org
Contact: Mary Andrews, CEO/Chair
Founded: 1989. **Members:** 10,000. **Membership Dues:** grandparent, $30 (annual) ● family, $50-$100 (annual) ● professional sponsor, $100 (annual) ● corporate sponsor, $1,000 (annual) ● Circle of Friends, $35-$49 (annual) ● regular, in Canada, $40-$59 (annual) ● overseas, $45-$69 (annual) ● visionary, $101-$250 (annual) ● platinum, $251-$500 (annual) ● life, $5,000. **Staff:** 5. **Budget:** $300,000. **Local Groups:** 16. **Description:** Provides support and assistance to families of children with physical growth related disorders. Sponsors educational programs, family networking, and Pen Pal for the Kids service. Maintains speakers' bureau. **Libraries: Type:** reference. **Holdings:** articles, periodicals. **Subjects:** growth disorders in children. **Awards:** Magic Kiss. **Frequency:** annual. **Type:** recognition. **Computer Services:** database, for parents/professionals; includes references of organizations and medical specialists. **Divisions:** Adult Growth Hormone Deficiency; Congenital Adrenal Hyperplasia; Growth Hormone Deficiency; McCune-Albright Syndrome; Panhypopituitarism; Precocious Puberty; Rare Disorders; Russell Silver Syndrome; Septo Optic Dysplasia; Thyroid Disorders; Turner Syndrome. **Formerly:** Major Aspects of Growth in Children Foundation; (2003) MAGIC Foundation for Children's Growth. **Publications:** *MAGIC Touch*, quarterly. Newsletter. **Price:** included in membership dues. **Advertising:** accepted ● Brochures. **Conventions/Meetings:** annual convention (exhibits) - always July.

13671 ■ Mothers Against Munchausen Syndrome by Proxy Allegations (MAMA)
1407 Ranch Dr.
Senatobia, MS 38668
Fax: (662)562-6669
E-mail: juliep@msbp.com
URL: http://www.msbp.com
Contact: Julie Patrick, Contact
Multinational. Description: Dedicated to ending accusations against parents from Munchausen Syndrome by Proxy (MSBP) allegations.

13672 ■ National Center for Education in Maternal and Child Health (NCEMCH)
Georgetown Univ.
PO Box 571272
Washington, DC 20057-1272

Ph: (202)784-9770
Fax: (202)784-9777
E-mail: mchlibrary@ncemch.org
URL: http://www.ncemch.org
Contact: Prof. Rochelle Mayer EdD, Dir.
Founded: 1982. **Staff:** 15. **Nonmembership. Description:** Multidisciplinary collection in fields such as pediatrics, public health, law, public policy, social work, psychology, behavioral health, nutrition, nursing, child development, education, communications, library science, and systems technology. Work with a broad range of public and private organizations to develop comprehensive program initiatives to advance the health of children and families. **Libraries: Type:** by appointment only. **Committees:** Education; Policy; Recruitment; Research.

13673 ■ National Initiative for Children's Healthcare Quality (NICHQ)
20 Univ. Rd., 7th Fl.
Cambridge, MA 02138
Ph: (617)301-4900
Free: (866)787-0832
Fax: (617)301-4899
E-mail: info@nichq.org
URL: http://www.nichq.org
Contact: Charles J. Homer MD, CEO/Co-Founder
Founded: 1999. **Description:** Seeks to improve the quality of health-care provided to children. Calls attention to the need for better children's health-care, and spreads stories of success that demonstrate that care can be improved to produce better outcomes. Provides tools and methods to improve systems of care.

13674 ■ National Institute of Child Health and Human Development (NICHD)
PO Box 3006
Rockville, MD 20847
Free: (800)370-2943
Fax: (301)496-7101
E-mail: nichdinformationresourcecenter@mail.nih. gov
URL: http://www.nichd.nih.gov
Nonmembership. Description: Part of the National Institutes of Health, a component of the U.S. Department of Health and Human Services. Has primary responsibility for conducting and supporting basic and clinical research in the biomedical, behavioral, and social sciences relating to child and maternal health, in medical rehabilitation, and in the reproductive sciences such as reproductive biology.

13675 ■ National Vaccine Information Center (NVIC)
204 Mill St., Ste.B1
Vienna, VA 22180
Ph: (703)938-3783 (703)938-0342
Free: (800)909-SHOT
Fax: (703)938-5768
E-mail: info@909shot.com
URL: http://www.909shot.com
Contact: Kathryn Williams, VP/Dir.
Founded: 1982. **Members:** 40,000. **Membership Dues:** individual, $25 (annual) ● family, $40 (annual) ● professional, $125 (annual) ● activist, $250 (annual) ● sponsor, $500 (annual) ● patron, $1,000 (annual). **Staff:** 6. **Budget:** $500,000. **Description:** Parents of children who have had reactions to or been injured by vaccines; individuals interested in working to reform the vaccine system. Disseminates information concerning vaccines to parents and doctors in order to assure safer administration of vaccines. Promotes the development of safer vaccines. Refers parents of vaccine-injured children to doctors, lawyers, and other parents for support services. Maintains speakers' bureau; compiles statistics. **Also Known As:** Dissatisfied Parents Together. **Publications:** *The Compensation System and How It Works*. **Price:** $5.00 ● *Law Firm Directory* ● *The Vaccine Reaction*, quarterly. Newsletter. **Price:** included in membership dues. **Conventions/Meetings:** annual International Public Conference on Vaccination - general assembly (exhibits).

13676 ■ Shriners Hospitals for Children (SHC)
c/o Shriners International Headquarters
2900 Rocky Point Dr.
Tampa, FL 33607-1460
Ph: (813)281-0300
Free: (800)237-5055
URL: http://www.shrinershq.org/hospitals/_hospitals_for_children
Contact: Ralph W. Semb, Chm.
Founded: 1922. **Members:** 22. **Staff:** 7,000. **Budget:** $540,000,000. **Description:** Represents orthopedic hospitals (19) and burn hospitals (4) founded by and affiliated with the Imperial Council of the Ancient Arabic Order of the Nobles of the Mystic Shrine for North America. Provides no-cost orthopedic and burn care to children under 18 years of age. Maintains the Shriners Hospitals for Children Endowment Fund. Conducts research; compiles statistics. **Awards:** **Type:** recognition. **Telecommunication Services:** additional toll-free number, (800)361-7256, in Canada. **Committees:** Special Study. **Councils:** Imperial. **Funds:** Pooled Income. **Programs:** Donor Recognition. **Publications:** *Between Us*, 3/year. Magazine. **Price:** free. **Circulation:** 18,000 ● *Imperial Council of the Ancient Arabic Order of the Nobles of the Mystic Shrine for North America* ● Booklet ● Brochures ● Pamphlets ● Also publishes fact sheets. **Conventions/Meetings:** annual conference and seminar.

13677 ■ Society for Adolescent Medicine (SAM)
1916 Copper Oaks Cir.
Blue Springs, MO 64015
Ph: (816)224-8010
Fax: (816)224-8009
E-mail: sam@adolescenthealth.org
URL: http://www.adolescenthealth.org
Contact: Edie Moore, Exec. Dir.
Founded: 1968. **Members:** 1,300. **Membership Dues:** doctorate level, $250 (annual) ● non-doctorate level, $200 (annual) ● affiliate, $55-$125 (annual). **Staff:** 3. **Regional Groups:** 17. **Description:** Physicians, psychologists, social workers, psychiatrists, nurses, and other health care professionals. Goals are: to improve the quality of health cares for adolescents; to encourage the investigation of normal growth and development during adolescence and of those diseases that affect adolescents; to stimulate the creation of health services for adolescents; to increase communication among health care professionals who care for adolescents; to foster and improve the quality of training of those individuals providing health care to adolescents. Seeks to: offer opportunities for discussion of teaching, research, and other common problems, through which coordinated efforts can be made toward their solution; publish and disseminate information related to adolescent medicine; identify, investigate, and list opportunities for careers in adolescent medicine; help plan and coordinate professional educational programs in the health care of the adolescent. Conducts research programs. **Awards:** Career Development Award in Adolescent Health. **Frequency:** annual. **Type:** recognition ● Diabetes. **Type:** recognition ● Innovative Approaches to Adolescent Health Care. **Frequency:** annual. **Type:** recognition ● New Investigator. **Frequency:** annual. **Type:** recognition ● Outstanding Achievement in Adolescent Medicine. **Frequency:** annual. **Type:** recognition ● Regional Chapter. **Type:** recognition ● Visiting Professor in Adolescent Medicine. **Frequency:** annual. **Type:** recognition ● Visiting Professor in Adolescent Research. **Frequency:** annual. **Type:** recognition. **Committees:** Abstract Review; Adolescent Clinical Services; Advocacy; Awards; Communications; Credentials Review; Information Technology; Multidisciplinary Grants; Research; Vaccination of Adolescents. **Publications:** *Journal of Adolescent Health*, monthly. Contains articles on study results of the anthropology, biochemistry, endocrinology, physiology and psychology. **Price:** included in membership dues; $199.00 /year for nonmembers; $475.00 /year for institutions. ISSN: 0197-0070. **Advertising:** accepted. **Conventions/Meetings:** annual meeting -

always March. 2008 Mar. 26-29, Greensboro, NC; 2009 Mar. 25-28, Los Angeles, CA.

Child Welfare

13678 ■ CURE International
701 Bosler Ave.
Lemoyne, PA 17043
Ph: (717)730-6706
Free: (866)730-2873
E-mail: info@cureinternational.org
URL: http://www.cureinternational.org
Contact: C. Scott Harrison MD, Pres./CEO
Founded: 1996. **Staff:** 700. **Languages:** English, Spanish. **Nonmembership. Multinational. Description:** Establishes and operates specialty teaching hospitals in the developing world for the physical and spiritual healing for disabled children and their families. **Programs:** Prayer Partner. **Publications:** *Cure for Life*, quarterly. Newsletter. Alternate Formats: online.

13679 ■ Ray Helfer Society
c/o Kent P. Hymel, MD, VP
Inova Fairfax Hosp. for Children
The Pediatric FACT Center
3300 Gallows Rd.
Falls Church, VA 22042-3300
Ph: (703)970-2630
Fax: (703)970-2620
E-mail: kent.hymel@inova.com
URL: http://helfersociety.org
Contact: Kent P. Hymel MD, VP
Founded: 1999. **Description:** Represents physicians seeking to provide leadership to enhance the prevention, diagnosis, and treatment of child abuse and neglect. Promotes education and training in the medical aspect of child abuse and neglect. Advocates for improved resources for research, clinical practice and education. Develops collaborative relationships with other professional organizations. Emphasizes the importance of the field of child abuse and neglect within medicine. **Telecommunication Services:** electronic mail, drunyan@med.unc.edu.

Childbirth

13680 ■ Association of Labor Assistants and Childbirth Educators (ALACE)
PO Box 390436
Cambridge, MA 02139
Ph: (617)441-2500
Free: (888)222-5223
Fax: (617)441-3167
E-mail: info@alace.org
URL: http://www.alace.org
Contact: DeeDee Lafayette, Exec. Dir.
Founded: 1994. **Members:** 900. **Membership Dues:** regular, in U.S., $20 (annual) ● regular, in Canada and Mexico, $23 (annual) ● international, $25 (annual). **Staff:** 10. **Budget:** $250,000. **Multinational. Description:** Provides pregnant women with information and alternatives for childbirth. **Computer Services:** Mailing lists. **Publications:** *Active Birth: The New Approach to Giving Birth Naturally*. Book. Features exercises and positions enabling the mother to be the active giver of birth. **Price:** $14.95 with 10&percent; discount on members, plus shipping and handling ● *Birthing from Within*. Book. Contains information about pregnancy and birth. **Price:** $19.95 with 10&percent; discount on members, plus shipping and handling ● *Special Delivery*, quarterly. Journal. Provides information on pregnancy and birth, midwifery, women's health issues, breastfeeding, parenting, childbirth education, and labor assisting. **Price:** included in membership dues; $4.00 for nonmembers, sample issue. ISSN: 1083-5008. **Circulation:** 1,000. **Advertising:** accepted. Alternate Formats: online. **Conventions/Meetings:** Labor Assistant/Birth Doula Training - workshop.

13681 ■ Association of Nurse Advocates for Childbirth Solutions (ANACS)
916 Daleview Dr.
Silver Spring, MD 20901
Ph: (301)434-5546
Fax: (301)434-5972
E-mail: info@anacs.org
URL: http://www.anacs.org
Membership Dues: student, $10 (annual) ● supporting institution, $100 ● MD, APN, CNM, midwife, $50 ● nurse, $35 ● other childbirth professional, $30 ● parent, $25. **Description:** Empowers nurses to advance evidence-based practices that facilitate improvements in maternity nursing services. Advocates for recognition of birth as a normal process. Supports groups and individuals who have similar philosophies through professional collegiality and mentorship. **Programs:** Mother-Friendly Nurse Recognition. **Projects:** Nurse/Doula Alliance; Nursing Student Outreach. **Publications:** *What Every Pregnant Woman Needs to Know About Caesarean Section*. Booklet. Contains information about Caesarean section childbirth. Alternate Formats: online.

13682 ■ Association for Pre- and Perinatal Psychology and Health (APPPAH)
PO Box 1398
Forestville, CA 95436
Ph: (707)887-2838
Fax: (707)887-2838
E-mail: apppah@aol.com
URL: http://www.birthpsychology.com/apppah
Contact: Maureen Wolfe CNM, Exec. Dir.
Founded: 1983. **Membership Dues:** within North and South America, $95 (annual) ● outside North and South America, $120 (annual) ● student, $60 (annual). **Description:** Serves as a forum for individuals interested in psychological dimensions of prenatal and perinatal experiences. **Affiliated With:** International Society of Prenatal and Perinatal Psychology and Medicine. **Publications:** *One Hundred Books*, annual. Contains list of publications and videos about childbirth and related topics. **Price:** included in membership dues; $6.00 printed copy for nonmembers. Alternate Formats: online ● *Prenatal and Perinatal Psychology and Health*, quarterly. Journal. Contains articles on the psychological aspects of prenatal and perinatal experiences. ● Newsletter, quarterly. **Price:** included in membership dues.

13683 ■ Childbirth and Postpartum Professional Association (CAPPA)
PO Box 491448
Lawrenceville, GA 30049
Free: (888)MY-CAPPA
Fax: (770)932-7281
E-mail: info@cappa.net
URL: http://www.cappa.net
Contact: Donna M. Johnson, Exec. Dir.
Founded: 1998. **Membership Dues:** general, $45 (annual). **Multinational. Description:** Trains doulas and childbirth educators. Supports women in their choices for childbirth. Educates health care providers and the public on the benefits of having doulas during and after childbirth. **Awards:** **Frequency:** annual. **Type:** grant. **Computer Services:** database, membership directory ● information services, childbirth, partum and lactation resources ● mailing lists, of members. **Programs:** Childbirth Education; Labor Doula; Lactation Education; Postpartum Doula. **Publications:** Newsletter, quarterly. **Conventions/Meetings:** annual international conference, with speaker (exhibits).

13684 ■ Citizens for Midwifery (CfM)
PO Box 82227
Athens, GA 30608-2227
Free: (888)CFM-4880
E-mail: info@cfmidwifery.org
Contact: Susan Hodges, Pres.
Founded: 1996. **Membership Dues:** student, $20 (annual) ● suggested, $30 (annual) ● supporter, $50 (annual) ● best friend, $100 (annual) ● guardian angel, $500 (annual) ● international student, $30 (annual) ● international suggested, $40 (annual) ● international supporter, $60 (annual) ● international

best friend, $110 (annual) ● international guardian angel, $510 (annual). **Description:** Works to ensure that the Midwives Model of Care is available to all childbearing women and recognized as best care for pregnancy and birth; endorses Mother-Friendly Childbirth Initiative. **Publications:** *CFM Brochure.* **Price:** free for members ● *Citizens for Midwifery News,* quarterly. Newsletter. **Price:** included in membership dues; $20.00 for nonmembers ● *Midwives Model of Care Brochure.* **Price:** free for members. Alternate Formats: online.

13685 ■ North American Registry of Midwives (NARM)
5257 Rosestone Dr.
Lilburn, GA 30047
Free: (888)842-4784
E-mail: info@narm.org
URL: http://www.narm.org
Contact: Debbie Pulley, Contact
Founded: 1987. **Description:** Establishes and administers certification for the credential "Certified Professional Midwife" (CPM). Identifies standards and practices that reflect the excellence and diversity of the independent midwifery community in order to set the standard for North American midwifery. **Publications:** *Candidate Information Bulletin.* Alternate Formats: online ● *Certified Professional Midwives.* Brochure. **Price:** $11.00 for 25 brochures; $20.00 for 50 brochures; $37.00 for 100 brochures. Alternate Formats: online ● *How To Become a CPM.* Booklet. Alternate Formats: online ● *North America Registry of Midwives News.* Newsletter. Alternate Formats: online ● *The Practice of Midwifery.* Paper. Alternate Formats: online. **Conventions/Meetings:** workshop.

13686 ■ Waterbirth International
PO Box 1400
Wilsonville, OR 97070
Ph: (503)673-0026
Free: (800)641-2229
Fax: (503)673-0029
E-mail: barbara@waterbirth.org
URL: http://www.waterbirth.org
Contact: Barbara Harper, Dir./Founder
Founded: 1988. **Membership Dues:** contributing, $35 (annual) ● professional, $75 (annual) ● corporate, $180 (annual). **Staff:** 10. **Multinational. Description:** Advocates for maternity care reform. Helps parents and practitioners institute policies for the use of warm water immersion during labor. Strives to alter the current technological dependency, excessive drug use and rising Cesarean rate. Educates medical professionals and the public on the benefits of natural childbirth. **Computer Services:** Bibliographic search, lists of published paper and books on waterbirth ● database, referral directory. **Publications:** Newsletter, quarterly. **Price:** included in membership dues. Alternate Formats: online.

Chinese

13687 ■ Federation of Chinese American and Chinese Canadian Medical Societies (FCMS)
c/o Chinese Hospital
835 Jackson St., Ste.304
San Francisco, CA 94133
Ph: (415)421-4240
Fax: (415)421-4242
E-mail: contact@fcmsdocs.org
URL: http://www.fcmsdocs.org
Contact: Sun-Hoo Foo MD, Chm.
Founded: 1991. **Membership Dues:** individual, $25 (annual) ● organization (based on number of members), $250-$2,000 (annual). **Multinational. Description:** Promotes the health status of the Chinese communities in North America through education and advocacy. Advances medical knowledge and education with emphasis on aspects related to the Chinese. Supports and facilitates collaboration in research and data collection. Promotes the scientific association of medical societies of health professionals of Chinese descent in North America. **Publications:** Newsletter. **Price:** included in membership dues ● Booklet.

Alternate Formats: online ● Brochures. **Conventions/Meetings:** biennial conference - 2008 Sept. 27-28, Toronto, ON, Canada.

Chiropractic

13688 ■ Academy of Upper Cervical Chiropractic Organizations (AUCCO)
1400 Court St.
Clearwater, FL 33756
E-mail: auccoweb@yahoo.com
URL: http://www.aucco.org
Contact: Richard G. Cockwill, Pres.
Membership Dues: regular (full privileges and voting), $100 (annual) ● student (Chiropractic student and doctor having graduated within 2 years, full privileges and voting), $25 (annual) ● member at large (access privileges, non-voting), $25 (annual). **Description:** Chiropractors and chiropractic organizations. Fosters and promotes information about atlas subluxation complex; disseminates information in order to preserve the science of upper cervical adjustment; provides resources and health tips. **Publications:** Newsletter. Contains information of interest to members. **Conventions/Meetings:** conference ● meeting and seminar.

13689 ■ American Board of Chiropractic Independent Examiners (ABCIE)
3343 Montrose Ave.
Laureldale, PA 19605
Ph: (610)929-9882
Fax: (610)929-9882
E-mail: docjoe1313@aol.com
Membership Dues: regular, $50 (annual). **Description:** Dedicated to providing a forum for Doctors of Chiropractic to network and share information. Membership qualifications are: Doctor of Chiropractic degree; five years of clinical experience in the treatment, assessment or representation of chiropractic patients; 300 post graduate continuing education hours, in the following classes: orthopedics, neurology, radiology, physical diagnosis, rehabilitation, occupational, physiological therapeutics, sports, pediatrics, ergonomics, physical therapy, athletic trainer, and chiropractic physical diagnosis and examination; 10 hours for each year in practice (counts towards 300 hours); three names/addresses/telephone numbers of references; personal resume; high moral character; no criminal convictions/no present state board/legal sanctions; national examination must be passed with a score of 75&percent;. Members must adhere to local, state and federal laws and regulations which apply to the practice of chiropractic, must pay annual dues, and attend annual ABCIE seminar. **Conventions/Meetings:** annual seminar.

13690 ■ American Chiropractic Association (ACA)
1701 Clarendon Blvd.
Arlington, VA 22209
Ph: (703)276-8800
Free: (800)986-4636
Fax: (703)243-2593
E-mail: memberinfo@acatoday.org
URL: http://www.amerchiro.org
Contact: Kevin P. Corcoran CAE, Exec. VP
Founded: 1930. **Members:** 18,000. **Membership Dues:** general, supporting, $600 (annual) ● family/sustaining, $300 (annual) ● associate, international, $150 (annual) ● retired, $90 (annual) ● disable, $60 (annual) ● life, $300 ● Governor's Advisory Cabinet, $1,200 (annual) ● senior, $360 (annual) ● chiropractic assistant, $30 (annual) ● student (one time), $30. **Staff:** 40. **Budget:** $6,000,000. **Description:** Enhances the philosophy, science, and art of chiropractic, and the professional welfare of individuals in the field. Promotes legislation defining chiropractic health care and improves the public's awareness and utilization of chiropractic. Conducts chiropractic survey and statistical study; maintains library. Sponsors Correct Posture Week in May and Spinal Health Month in October. Chiropractic colleges have student groups. **Awards: Frequency:** periodic. **Type:** scholarship.

Recipient: to students at chiropractic colleges. **Absorbed:** (1962) National Council of Chiropractic Hospital and Sanitaria. **Formerly:** (1963) National Chiropractic Association. **Publications:** *ACA/Today,* monthly. Newsletter. Covers the issues facing the profession and the association. **Price:** included in membership dues. **Circulation:** 21,000 ● *American Chiropractic Association Membership Directory,* annual ● *Journal of the American Chiropractic Association,* monthly. Provides information on the progress of chiropractic procedures and research, and developments in other fields of interest to chiropractors. **Price:** included in membership dues; $3.00/year for students; $80.00 /year for nonmembers. ISSN: 0744-9984. **Advertising:** accepted ● Newspaper, monthly. **Conventions/Meetings:** annual meeting (exhibits) - always August or September.

13691 ■ American Chiropractic Association Council on Sports Injuries and Physical Fitness (ACBSP)
c/o ACA Sports Council
PO Box 400
Norwalk, IA 50211
Ph: (515)981-9340
Free: (800)261-1495
Fax: (515)981-9427
E-mail: gypsydoc@bellsouth.net
URL: http://www.acasc.org
Contact: Jeffrey Solomon DC, Pres.
Membership Dues: student, $55 (annual) ● supporting, vender, faculty/retired, international, $95 (annual) ● network, $150 (annual). **Description:** Active chiropractors. Promotes the treatment of athletes; works closely with athletic organizations and health professionals to promote better understanding of chiropractic care as valuable in athletic training and treatment. **Committees:** Allied Health and Program Development; By-laws; Education/ACBSP; Electronic Communications; Grants/Research; Managed Care; Nominating; Public Relations. **Publications:** *Sports Talk,* quarterly. Journal. Features articles written by members of the Sports Council, news releases, as well as information relating to Sports Council activities. Alternate Formats: online ● Brochure. **Price:** $8.00 for members (per pack of 25 brochures); $15.00 for nonmembers (per pack of 25 brochures).

13692 ■ American Chiropractic College of Radiology (ACCR)
PO Box 3053
La Habra, CA 90632-3053
Ph: (562)947-8755
E-mail: dacbr219@hotmail.com
URL: http://www.dacbr.com
Contact: J. Todd Krudsen DC, Sec.-Treas.
Membership Dues: general, $200 (annual) ● international, $50 (annual). **Description:** Seeks to educate the chiropractic and health care communities. **Committees:** Academic Radiologists; Annual Meeting; Appeals; Credentialing; Nominating; Practice Guideline; Professional Practice. **Councils:** Diagnostic Imaging. **Conventions/Meetings:** annual symposium ● annual workshop.

13693 ■ American College of Chiropractic Consultants (ACCC)
28 E Jackson Bldg., 10th Fl., Ste.1020
Chicago, IL 60604
Ph: (708)895-3141
Fax: (708)895-2268
E-mail: accc@essex1.com
URL: http://www.accc-chiro.com
Contact: Jeffrey Cates DC, Chm.
Founded: 1980. **Membership Dues:** general, $250 (annual). **Description:** Independent contractors providing advisory consulting services to insurance carriers and health care organizations, and other entities sponsoring chiropractic benefits. Promotes adherence to high standards of ethics and practice among chiropractors. Establishes chiropractic standards and conducts certification examinations; sponsors continuing professional development courses for chiropractors. **Conventions/Meetings:** annual conference - always fall.

13694 ■ American College of Chiropractic Orthopedists (ACCO)
c/o Dr. William Valusek, Treas.
1030 Broadway
El Centro, CA 92243
Ph: (760)352-1452
Fax: (760)352-3966
E-mail: wvalusek@accoweb.org
URL: http://www.accoweb.org
Contact: Dr. William Valusek, Treas.
Founded: 1964. **Members:** 730. **Membership Dues:** full, $125 (annual) ● associate, $110 (annual) ● supporting, $90 (annual) ● student, faculty, $25 (annual). **Budget:** $100,000. **Multinational. Description:** Certified (426) and non-certified (304) chiropractic orthopedists; students enrolled in a postgraduate chiropractic orthopedic program (100). Seeks to establish and maintain optimal educational and clinical standards within the field of chiropractic orthopedics. Sponsors educational programs. **Awards:** F. Maynard Lipe Scholarship Award. **Frequency:** annual. **Type:** scholarship. **Recipient:** for college students enrolled in their 5th term or later of Chiropractic College education. **Boards:** Executive. **Committees:** Convention; Education. **Also Known As:** American College of Chiropractic Specialists. **Publications:** *Journal of the American College of Chiropractic Orthopedists*, semiannual. **Price:** available to members only. **Advertising:** accepted ● Membership Directory, annual. **Advertising:** accepted ● Also publishes orthopedic and neurologic tests booklets. **Conventions/Meetings:** annual seminar, clinical update (exhibits) ● periodic symposium, clinical.

13695 ■ Association of Chiropractic Colleges (ACC)
c/o David S. O'Bryon, CAE, Exec. Dir.
4424 Montgomery Ave., Ste.102
Bethesda, MD 20814
Ph: (301)652-5066
Fax: (301)913-9146
E-mail: info@chirocolleges.org
URL: http://www.chirocolleges.org
Contact: David S. O'Bryon CAE, Exec. Dir.
Founded: 1977. **Members:** 19. **Budget:** $600,000. **Multinational. Description:** Presidents of chiropractic colleges that are members of the Council on Chiropractic Education. Aims to provide a cooperative base that assists members in the search for and promotion of the practices and concepts most effective in the academic and continuing education of doctors of chiropractic. Serves as a clearinghouse for information related to opportunities and advancement in research as they affect chiropractic education and health care. Seeks to enhance services to the consumer of chiropractic education and to the public. **Awards:** Student Scholarships in Chiropractic. **Frequency:** annual. **Type:** scholarship. **Committees:** Demographic; Ethics. **Affiliated With:** Council on Chiropractic Education. **Formerly:** (1985) Association of Chiropractic College Presidents. **Publications:** *Journal of Chiropractic Education*, semiannual. **Conventions/Meetings:** annual Chiropractic Educational Conference - always 3rd weekend of March.

13696 ■ Association for the History of Chiropractic (AHC)
c/o Ms. Glenda Wiese, PhD, Exec. Dir.
1000 Brady St.
Davenport, IA 52803
Ph: (563)884-5894
Fax: (563)884-5267
E-mail: wiese_g@palmer.edu
URL: http://www.historyofchiropractic.org
Contact: Ms. Glenda Wiese PhD, Exec. Dir.
Founded: 1980. **Members:** 340. **Membership Dues:** regular, $75 (annual) ● regular outside North America, $85 (annual) ● institutional, $150 (annual) ● life, $750 ● student, $30 (annual) ● senior, $60 (annual). **Staff:** 1. **Budget:** $25,000. **National Groups:** 2. **Multinational. Description:** Represents chiropractors, students, educators, writers, chiropractic colleges and organizations. Researches and records the history of the chiropractic profession and disseminates information on the subject. Maintains speakers' bureau. **Libraries: Type:** reference. **Holdings:** 22;

archival material. **Subjects:** chiropractic history. **Awards:** Lee Homewood Chiropractic Heritage. **Frequency:** annual. **Type:** recognition. **Recipient:** to a pioneer in chiropractic. **Boards:** Directors. **Affiliated With:** Association for the History of Chiropractic. **Publications:** *AHC Bulletin*, 3/year. Newsletter. **Price:** included in membership dues ● *Association for the History of Chiropractic Membership Directory*, periodic. Includes association bylaws. **Price:** available to members only ● *Chiropractic History: The Archives and Journal of the Association of the History of Chiropractic*, semiannual. Magazine. Includes association news. **Price:** included in membership dues; $35.00 for nonmembers. ISSN: 0736-4377. **Advertising:** accepted ● *Style Manual for Authors*. **Conventions/Meetings:** annual conference, on chiropractic history.

13697 ■ Blair Chiropractic Society
c/o Dr. John Hilpisch, Pres.
8603 34th St. N
Lake Elmo, MN 55042
Ph: (651)748-5731
E-mail: holdingat6@aol.com
URL: http://www.blairchiropractic.com
Contact: Dr. John Hilpisch, Pres.
Founded: 1986. **Membership Dues:** doctor of chiropractic, $100 (annual). **Description:** Represents practitioners using the Blair method of upper cervical chiropractic. **Awards:** Beatrice K. Blair Scholarship. **Frequency:** annual. **Type:** scholarship. **Recipient:** for chiropractic students ● Blair Chiropractor of the Year. **Frequency:** annual. **Type:** recognition. **Recipient:** for members. **Committees:** Blair Scholarship; Conference; Equipment; Instruction and Technique; Patient Education; Publications; Research. **Councils:** Chiropractic Practice. **Publications:** *Convergence*. Newsletter ● *The Green Booklets*. Alternate Formats: online. **Conventions/Meetings:** seminar, in primary, intermediate, and advanced Blair Technique.

13698 ■ ChiroFeed International
Address Unknown since 2007
Founded: 1998. **Multinational. Description:** Chiropractors. Provide chiropractic exams and care to underprivileged people.

13699 ■ Congress of Chiropractic State Associations (COCSA)
PO Box 2054
Lexington, SC 29071
Ph: (803)356-6809
Fax: (803)356-6826
E-mail: cocsa@sc.rr.com
URL: http://www.cocsa.org
Contact: Dr. Stephen Simonetti, Pres.
Founded: 1968. **Members:** 69. **Membership Dues:** regular, $300 (annual) ● associate, supporting, $200 (annual). **Staff:** 2. **Budget:** $150,000. **Regional Groups:** 5. **State Groups:** 54. **National Groups:** 8. **Description:** State chiropractic associations. Seeks to "provide an apolitical forum for the promotion and advancement of the chiropractic profession". Works to advance the study, teaching, and practice of chiropractic and natural health; serves as a clearinghouse on problems facing the chiropractic profession; provides support and services to members. **Conventions/Meetings:** annual convention and congress, minimal table tops - usually first or second weekend in November. 2007 Nov. 8-11, Nashville, TN.

13700 ■ Council on Chiropractic Education (CCE)
8049 N 85th Way
Scottsdale, AZ 85258-4321
Ph: (480)443-8877
Fax: (480)483-7333
E-mail: cce@cce-usa.org
URL: http://www.cce-usa.org
Contact: Martha S. O'Connor PhD, Exec. Dir.
Founded: 1971. **Members:** 13. **Staff:** 3. **Budget:** $800,000. **Description:** Advocates high standards in chiropractic education; establishes criteria of institutional excellence for educating chiropractic physicians; acts as national accrediting agency for chiropractic colleges. Conducts workshops for college

teams, consultants, and chiropractic college staffs. **Commissions:** Accreditation. **Committees:** Accreditation of Graduate Education; Nominating; Review. **Publications:** *Commission on Accreditation Manual* ● *Standards for Doctor of Chiropractic Programs and Requirements for Institutional Status*, semiannual ● Newsletter, periodic ● Also publishes pamphlets, news releases, and lists of institutions conforming to its standards and policies. **Conventions/Meetings:** annual meeting (exhibits).

13701 ■ Council of Chiropractic Physiological Therapeutics and Rehabilitation (CCPT)
c/o Dr. Don Fedoryk, Pres.
312 Courtyard Dr.
Hillsborough, NJ 08844
E-mail: rehabdc18@aol.com
URL: http://www.ccptr.org
Contact: Dr. Don Fedoryk, Pres.
Founded: 1920. **Members:** 200. **Membership Dues:** regular, $100 (annual). **Staff:** 3. **Description:** Chiropractors who use physiotherapy and rehabilitation in their practice and are dedicated to furthering the extended use of physiotherapy in the chiropractic field. **Affiliated With:** American Chiropractic Association. **Formerly:** (1985) American Council on Chiropractic Physiotherapy. **Publications:** *Physiotherapy Briefs*, periodic. **Conventions/Meetings:** semiannual conference - always March and September.

13702 ■ Federation of Chiropractic Licensing Boards (FCLB)
5401 W 10th St., Ste.101
Greeley, CO 80634-4400
Ph: (970)356-3500
Fax: (970)356-3599
E-mail: info@fclb.org
URL: http://www.fclb.org
Contact: Donna M. Liewer, Exec. Dir.
Founded: 1926. **Nonmembership. Multinational. Description:** Aims to protect the public by promoting excellence in chiropractic regulation. **Computer Services:** database. **Publications:** *Chiropractic Licensure and Practice Statistics*, annual. Directory. **Price:** $75.00 plus shipping and handling. Alternate Formats: online. **Conventions/Meetings:** annual conference ● meeting, district meetings.

13703 ■ Federation of Straight Chiropractors and Organizations (FSCO)
2276 Wassergass Rd.
Hellertown, PA 18055
Ph: (610)838-3030
Free: (800)521-9856
Fax: (610)838-3031
E-mail: fsco@straightchiropractic.com
URL: http://www.straightchiropractic.com
Contact: Renee Hillman, Admin. Asst.
Founded: 1978. **Members:** 600. **Membership Dues:** ruling, $25-$100 (quarterly) ● ruling, $100-$400 (annual) ● faculty-DC, $50 (quarterly) ● faculty-DC, $200 (annual) ● student, entire course of study, $50 ● retired DC, $50 (quarterly) ● retired DC, $200 (annual) ● 1st DC spouse (full), $400 (annual) ● 2nd DC spouse (half), $200 (annual) ● non-DC, faculty, Chiropractic assistant, straight Chiropractic supporter, $50 (annual) ● international, $50 (annual) ● vendor, $150 (annual). **Staff:** 1. **Budget:** $150,000. **State Groups:** 5. **Description:** Individuals and organizations in the chiropractic field. Promotes the practice of straight (traditional) chiropractic. Conducts lobbying and educational programs. **Awards:** Triune Award. **Frequency:** annual. **Type:** recognition. **Formerly:** Federation of Straight Chiropractic Organizations. **Publications:** *FSCO Insider*, bimonthly. Newsletter. Reports on current organization news and professional information. **Circulation:** 2,000 ● *President's Update*, bimonthly. **Circulation:** 1,200. **Conventions/Meetings:** annual board meeting ● semiannual seminar, educational (exhibits).

13704 ■ Flying Chiropractors Association (FCA)
2001 Bridgeway St.
Sausalito, CA 94965
Ph: (415)332-4304

Fax: (415)332-6055
Contact: Dr. Dwight A. Shaneyfelt, Contact
Founded: 1968. **Members:** 300. **Regional Groups:** 9. **Description:** Flying chiropractic physicians. Objectives are to: promote fellowship; seek designation as aviation medical examiners (doctors who examine pilots for their licensure); promote aviation safety. Conducts seminars. **Computer Services:** database ● electronic publishing. **Publications:** *D.C. Flyer*, quarterly. **Conventions/Meetings:** annual Fly-In AOPA Expo - meeting, held in conjunction with the Airplane Owners and Pilots Association (exhibits).

13705 ■ Foundation for the Advancement of Chiropractic Tenets and Science (FACTS)

c/o International Chiropractors Association
1110 N Glebe Rd., Ste.650
Arlington, VA 22201
Ph: (703)528-5000
Free: (800)423-4690
Fax: (703)528-5023
E-mail: chiro@chiropractic.org
URL: http://www.chiropractic.org
Contact: Ronald Hendrickson, Exec. Dir.

Founded: 1972. **Description:** Works to improve the human health through understanding and development of new chiropractic information. Offers financial aid for education and research programs in colleges and independent institutions; supports chiropractic research program at University of Colorado in Boulder. Conducts extensive survey of the chiropractic profession for the federal government. **Awards: Type:** recognition. **Affiliated With:** International Chiropractors Association. **Formerly:** International Chiropractors Research Foundation. **Publications:** *Chiropractic Health Care.* **Conventions/Meetings:** annual meeting.

13706 ■ Foundation for Chiropractic Education and Research (FCER)

PO Box 400
Norwalk, IA 50211-0400
Ph: (515)981-9888
Free: (800)622-6309
Fax: (515)981-9427
E-mail: fcer@fcer.org
URL: http://www.fcer.org
Contact: DeAnna L. Beck, Exec. Dir.

Founded: 1944. **Members:** 3,000. **Membership Dues:** advocate, $154 (annual) ● benefactor, $200 (annual) ● patron, $500 (annual). **Staff:** 12. **Budget:** $3,000,000. **Description:** Chiropractors and laymen. Provides funding for scientific research and research training that will "enhance the knowledge and practice of chiropractic as a conservative approach to health care restoration, maintenance, and disease prevention". **Awards: Type:** fellowship. **Recipient:** for post doctorate students ● **Type:** grant. **Recipient:** for research in clinical science ● **Type:** grant. **Recipient:** for dissertations in biomechanics and public health. **Committees:** Communications; Development; Education; Research. **Affiliated With:** American Chiropractic Association. **Formerly:** (1958) Chiropractic Research Foundation; (1967) Foundation for Accredited Chiropractic Education. **Publications:** *Chiropractic Healthways Newsletter*, bimonthly. Promotes health and fitness. Includes research updates. **Price:** $14.95/year. **Circulation:** 125,000. **Advertising:** accepted ● *Foundation for Chiropractic Education and Research—Advance*, quarterly. Magazine. Contains information about foundation activities. **Price:** free. **Circulation:** 20,000. **Advertising:** accepted ● Also publishes pamphlets. **Conventions/Meetings:** annual International Conference on Spinal Manipulation - meeting (exhibits) ● annual meeting.

13707 ■ Gonstead Clinical Studies Society (GCSS)

900 17th Ave.
Santa Cruz, CA 95062
Free: (888)556-4277
Fax: (831)476-1873

E-mail: michele4gcss@aol.com
URL: http://www.gonstead.com
Contact: Dr. Jeanne Taylor, Pres.
Founded: 1979. **Membership Dues:** general, $125 (annual) ● retired, lay, $50 (annual). **Description:** Promotes awareness of the Gonstead System of chiropractic and its record of safety and effectiveness in correcting vertebral subluxation.

13708 ■ International Academy of Olympic Chiropractic Officers (IAOCO)

c/o Dr. Stephen J. Press, Chm.
546 Broad Ave.
Englewood, NJ 07631
Ph: (201)569-1444
E-mail: admin@iaoco.org
URL: http://www.iaoco.org
Contact: Dr. Stephen J. Press, Chm.
Founded: 1987. **Members:** 75. **Staff:** 4. **Languages:** English, French, Russian, Spanish. **Multinational. Description:** Serves as honorary society for doctors of chiropractic who have been officially accredited as team doctors in the Olympic games. **Awards:** Gold Member. **Frequency:** biennial. **Type:** recognition. **Recipient:** for Olympic team doctor invited by National Olympic Committee ● Silver Member. **Frequency:** biennial. **Type:** recognition. **Recipient:** for chiropractic doctors who have served in regional games or attended the Olympic games to work at the general polyclinic, FICS, WOA delegations, or as NGB doctors accredited other than through invitation by the NOC itself.

13709 ■ International Chiropractic Pediatric Association (ICPA)

327 N Middletown Rd.
Media, PA 19063
Ph: (610)565-2360
Free: (800)670-KIDS
Fax: (610)565-3567
E-mail: info@icpa4kids.com
URL: http://www.icpa4kids.com
Contact: Dr. Jeanne Ohm, Exec. Coor.
Founded: 1997. **Members:** 2,000. **Membership Dues:** chiropractor, $195 (annual) ● chiropractor, outside U.S. and Canada, $145 (annual) ● chiropractor, first year, $95 (annual) ● married couple, $245 (annual) ● student, $55 (annual). **Staff:** 5. **Multinational. Description:** Chiropractors and chiropractic students with an interest in the treatment of pediatric patients. Seeks to advance the study, teaching, and practice of pediatric chiropractic; promotes continuing professional development of members. Serves as a clearinghouse on pediatric health; sponsors research and educational programs; formulates standards of practice for pediatric chiropractic and conducts certification examinations. **Additional Websites:** http://www.icpa4kids.org. **Publications:** *Pathways*, quarterly. Newsletter. Contains informative articles for parents, educators, practitioners and other interested readers in the lay population. **Price:** included in membership dues. Alternate Formats: online.

13710 ■ International Chiropractors Association (ICA)

1110 N Glebe Rd., Ste.650
Arlington, VA 22201
Ph: (703)528-5000
Free: (800)423-4690
Fax: (703)528-5023
E-mail: chiro@chiropractic.org
URL: http://www.chiropractic.org
Contact: Dr. John Maltby, Pres.
Founded: 1926. **Members:** 8,000. **Membership Dues:** student (one-time fee), $30 ● faculty, $110-$300 (annual) ● lay, $85 (annual). **Staff:** 17. **Budget:** $2,900,000. **Description:** Professional society of chiropractors, chiropractic educators, students, and laypersons. Sponsors professional development programs and practice management seminars. **Awards:** Chiropractor of the Year Award. **Frequency:** annual. **Type:** recognition. **Computer Services:** Mailing lists. **Committees:** Education; Ethics and Standards; Health Planning; Insurance Review; International Chiropractors Political Action; International Development; Labor and Industrial Relations; Legal

Affairs; Medicare and National Health Action; Student Recruitment; Technical Publications Review; Veterans Affairs. **Affiliated With:** Council on Chiropractic Education; Foundation for the Advancement of Chiropractic Tenets and Science. **Formerly:** (1941) Chiropractic Health Bureau. **Publications:** *Congressional Directory*, annual ● *ICA Today*, bimonthly. Newsletter. Covers membership and association activities; includes legislative information and research updates. **Price:** included in membership dues. **Circulation:** 8,000 ● *International Chiropractors Association Membership Directory*, annual ● *International Review of Chiropractic*, bimonthly ● Also publishes materials on patient education. **Conventions/Meetings:** annual Natural Fitness - symposium (exhibits) - held in conjunction with the Arnold Schwarzenegger Fitness Weekend in Columbus, OH.

13711 ■ National Association for Chiropractic Medicine (NACM)

15427 Baybrook Dr.
Houston, TX 77062
Ph: (281)280-8262
Fax: (281)280-8262
E-mail: ron1slaughter@hotmail.com
URL: http://www.chiromed.org
Membership Dues: licensed, practicing chiropractor, $100 (annual). **Description:** Works to make professional manipulative procedures a regular part of mainstream healthcare delivery. **Publications:** Newsletter, quarterly. Notifies members of conferences and continuing education.

13712 ■ National Board of Chiropractic Examiners (NBCE)

901 54th Ave.
Greeley, CO 80634
Ph: (970)356-9100
E-mail: nbce@nbce.org
URL: http://www.nbce.org
Contact: Horace C. Elliott, Exec. VP
Founded: 1963. **Description:** Develops, administers and scores examinations taken by applicants for chiropractic licensure by experienced practitioners seeking reciprocity, endorsement or relicensure. **Telecommunication Services:** electronic mail, elliott@nbce. org. **Publications:** *Job Analysis of Chiropractic 2005*. Report. Includes a summary of chiropractic efficacy research from around the world. **Price:** $25.00/report, includes shipping ● *NBCE Journal* ● *Studies on Chiropractic*. Brochure. Contains studies and official inquiries regarding the efficacy, appropriateness and cost effectiveness of chiropractic health care. **Price:** $20.00/100 brochures, includes shipping.

13713 ■ National Board of Forensic Chiropractors (NBOFC)

Address Unknown since 2007
Founded: 1996. **Staff:** 2. **Budget:** $10,000. **Non-membership. For-Profit. Description:** Training association of examiners, scientists and professionals dedicated to orderly analysis, investigation and examination to obtain the truth, then provide expert opinion. **Publications:** Newsletter.

13714 ■ National Upper Cervical Chiropractic Association (NUCCA)

c/o Ms. Lesley Louvar, Exec. Dir.
2608 W Kenosha St., Ste.224
Broken Arrow, OK 74012-8952
Free: (800)541-5799
Fax: (800)541-5799
E-mail: frontdesk@nucca.org
URL: http://www.nucca.org
Contact: Ms. Lesley Louvar, Exec. Dir.
Founded: 1966. **Members:** 400. **Membership Dues:** active, in practice more than 2 years, $600 (quarterly) ● active, 1st and 2nd year doctor, $300 (quarterly) ● student, $50 (annual) ● retired, $300 (annual) ● life, $12,000 ● academic, $300 (quarterly). **Staff:** 2. **Budget:** $125,000. **Multinational. Description:** Promotes chiropractic, especially the NUCCA technique; seeks to improve the art of chiropractic; promotes education; sponsors studies. **Computer Services:** Online services. **Additional Websites:** http://nucca. com. **Publications:** *NUCCA News*, semiannual.

Newsletter. **Conventions/Meetings:** annual conference, continuing educational credit classes and certification training (exhibits) - always spring and fall.

13715 ■ Sacro Occipital Research Society International (SORSI)

PO Box 24361
Overland Park, KS 66283
Ph: (516)338-1973
Free: (888)245-1011
Fax: (516)338-1971
E-mail: cbinyon@kc.rr.com
URL: http://www.sorsi.com
Contact: Dr. Suzanne A. Seekins, Pres.

Founded: 1957. **Membership Dues:** chiropractic assistant, $35 (annual) ● student, $50 (annual) ● regular doctor, $175 (annual) ● first year doctor, $75 ● life, $1,750. **Multinational. Description:** Chiropractors in 6 countries. Promotes exchange and cooperation; conducts research; provides specialized education. **Absorbed:** (1982) International Craniopathic Society. **Formerly:** (1978) Sacro Occipital Research Society. **Publications:** *The Communicator.* Journal.

13716 ■ Society of Chiropractic Orthospinology

c/o Dr. Kirk Eriksen, Pres.
2500 Flowers Chapel Rd.
Dothan, AL 36305
Ph: (334)793-7992
Fax: (334)792-0210
E-mail: info@orthospinology.org
URL: http://www.orthospinology.org
Contact: Dr. Kirk Eriksen, Pres.

Multinational. Description: Represents doctors, student doctors, and patients. Promotes the Chiropractic approach for a healthy lifestyle; aims to increase understanding of the Orthospinology method. **Boards:** Advisory. **Publications:** *New Patient Booklets.* Price: $1.35/copy. **Conventions/Meetings:** seminar.

13717 ■ Victims of Chiropractic (VOC)

10049 San Juan Ct.
Fountain Valley, CA 92708
Ph: (714)962-8683
E-mail: debunker4@yahoo.com
URL: http://www.quackwatch.org/01QuackeryRelatedTopics/chirovic.html
Contact: Mr. Donald Paulin, Contact

Founded: 1991. **Description:** Support network and clearinghouse for chiropractic hazards and shortcomings.

13718 ■ Women's Auxiliary of the ICA (WAICA)

c/o International Chiropractors Association
1110 N Glebe Rd., Ste.650
Arlington, VA 22201
Ph: (703)528-5000
Free: (800)423-4690
Fax: (703)528-5023
E-mail: chiro@chiropractic.org
URL: http://www.chiropractic.org
Contact: Dr. DeeDee Humber, Pres.

Founded: 1951. **Members:** 500. **Description:** Women chiropractors; wives, daughters, and mothers of chiropractors who are members of the International Chiropractors Association. Promotes and educates the public about chiropractice. Grants scholarships to chiropractic students. Supports charitable programs. **Publications:** *Membership Roster,* biennial. Membership Directory ● Newsletter, quarterly. **Conventions/Meetings:** annual meeting, in conjunction with ICA.

13719 ■ World Chiropractic Alliance (WCA)

2950 N Dobson Rd., Ste.1
Chandler, AZ 85224
Ph: (480)786-9235
Free: (800)347-1011
Fax: (480)732-9313

E-mail: comments@worldchiropracticalliance.org
URL: http://www.worldchiropracticalliance.org
Contact: Dr. Terry A. Rondberg, Pres.

Founded: 1989. **Membership Dues:** doctor of chiropractic in U.S., $99 (quarterly) ● doctor of chiropractic in U.S., $396 (annual) ● doctor of chiropractic outside U.S. and Canada, $99 (semiannual) ● doctor of chiropractic outside U.S. and Canada, $198 (annual) ● chiropractic student, $30 (annual) ● full time faculty in chiropractic college, $99 (annual). **Multinational. Description:** Works to protect and strengthen chiropractic around the world. **Libraries:** Type: reference. **Holdings:** video recordings. **Subjects:** chiropractic. **Councils:** Addictionology; Children's Health; Chiropractic Advocacy; Chiropractic Clinical Science; Chiropractic Mentoring; Family Practice; International Chiropractic Law; Women's Health. **Publications:** *The Chiropractic Journal.* Newspaper. Features segments of the chiropractic profession. ● *Position Papers* ● *WCAnews/Health Watch,* weekly. Newsletter. Provides reports on scientific and medical research exposing the dangers of medical therapies and procedures. Alternate Formats: online ● Books.

Clinical Studies

13720 ■ American Clinical and Climatological Association (ACCA)

c/o Dr. Robert G. Luke, MD, Pres.
231 Albert Sabin Way, M.L. 0557
Cincinnati, OH 45267-0557
Ph: (513)558-0325
Fax: (513)558-0852
E-mail: robert.luke@uc.edu
URL: http://www.accasociety.org
Contact: Dr. Robert G. Luke MD, Pres.

Founded: 1884. **Members:** 375. **Description:** Represents internists interested in the clinical study of disease. **Publications:** *Transactions,* annual. **Conventions/Meetings:** annual meeting - 2007 Oct. 18-21, Tucson, AZ; 2008 Oct. 16-19, Ponte Vedra Beach, FL; 2009 Oct. 15-18, Hot Springs, VA.

13721 ■ American Federation for Medical Research (AFMR)

900 Cummings Ctr., Ste.221-U
Beverly, MA 01915
Ph: (978)927-8330
Fax: (978)524-8890
E-mail: afmr@prri.com
URL: http://www.afmr.org
Contact: Jim C. Oates MD, Pres.

Founded: 1940. **Members:** 2,500. **Membership Dues:** active, $195 (annual) ● associate, $90 (annual) ● emeritus, in U.S., $60 (annual) ● emeritus, in Canada and Mexico, $95 (annual) ● emeritus, non-North American, $105 (annual). **Regional Groups:** 4. **Local Groups:** 19. **Description:** Provides a forum for young clinical scientists (under 43); promotes and encourages original research in clinical and laboratory medicine. Offers specialized education program; maintains information services on membership status, files, and National Abstracting Processing. Annual scientific program presents sections on: Cardiovascular; Dermatology; Endocrinology; Gastroenterology; Genetics; Hematology; Immunology and Connective Tissue; Infectious Disease; Metabolism; Neoplastic Disease; Patient Care; Pulmonary; Renal and Electrolytes. **Formerly:** (1998) American Federation for Clinical Research. **Publications:** *Journal of Investigative Medicine,* bimonthly ● Newsletter. Alternate Formats: online. **Conventions/Meetings:** annual conference (exhibits).

13722 ■ American Society for Clinical Investigation (ASCI)

35 Res. Dr., Ste.300
Ann Arbor, MI 48103
Ph: (734)222-6050
Fax: (734)222-6058
E-mail: asci@the-jci.org
URL: http://www.asci-jci.org
Contact: Dr. Charles Sawyers, Pres.

Founded: 1909. **Members:** 2,600. **Membership Dues:** active, $90 (annual). **Staff:** 2. **Budget:**

$2,000,000. **Description:** Physician scientists with meritorious original clinical investigations. Active members are doctors under age 50; senior members are those over age 50. Promotes cultivation of clinical research by methods of natural sciences, correlation of science with the art of medical practice, encouragement of scientific investigation by medical practitioners, and publication of papers on the methods and results of clinical research. **Awards:** ASCI Award. **Frequency:** annual. **Type:** monetary. **Recipient:** to a society member, under 56 years of age. **Affiliated With:** Federation of American Societies for Experimental Biology. **Publications:** *Journal of Clinical Investigation,* biweekly. **Circulation:** 10,000. **Advertising:** accepted. Alternate Formats: online ● Newsletter, quarterly. **Conventions/Meetings:** annual conference.

13723 ■ Association of Clinical Research Organizations (ACRO)

c/o Douglas Peddicord, PhD, Exec. Dir.
227 Massachusetts Ave. NE, Ste.300
Washington, DC 20002
Ph: (202)543-4018
Fax: (202)543-5327
E-mail: info@acrohealth.org
URL: http://www.acrohealth.org
Contact: Douglas Peddicord PhD, Exec. Dir.

Membership Dues: regular, $100,000 (annual) ● associate, $25,000 (annual). **Description:** Fosters continued advancement of medical product development worldwide and an environment in which laws, regulations and public policies benefit members, customers, and patients. **Publications:** *Analysis & Perspective: Contract Research Organizations* ● *Sponsorship, Authorship, and Accountability.* **Conventions/Meetings:** annual Partnerships with CROs - conference, with keynote addresses and presentations.

13724 ■ Association of Clinical Scientists

PO Box 1287
Middlebury, VT 05753
Ph: (802)462-2507
Fax: (802)462-2673
E-mail: info@clinicalscience.org
URL: http://www.clinicalscience.org
Contact: F. William Sunderman Jr., Sec.-Treas.

Founded: 1949. **Members:** 500. **Membership Dues:** regular, $170 (annual). **Staff:** 1. **Budget:** $100,000. **Description:** Professional society of physicians and scientists working in various fields of laboratory medicine. Seeks to promote education and research in clinical science by practical methods; maintain and improve the accuracy of measurements in clinical laboratories and promote uniformity in clinical laboratory procedures; encourage cooperation between physicians and non-physicians concerned with the application of scientific methods to medical practice. **Committees:** Scientific Council. **Sections:** Cell and Tissue Pathology; Clinical Biochemistry and Biotechnology; Clinical Immunology and Microbiology; Clinical Molecular Biology and Genetics; Clinical Science in Practice; Environmental and Occupational Health; Hematology and Transfusion Medicine; Therapeutics and Toxicology. **Affiliated With:** American Association for the Advancement of Science. **Formerly:** (1956) Clinical Science Club. **Publications:** *Annals of Clinical and Laboratory Science,* quarterly. Journal. Features a scientific, peer-reviewed journal. **Price:** included in membership dues; $130.00 /year for nonmembers. ISSN: 0091-7370. **Circulation:** 750. **Advertising:** accepted ● *Clinical Science Trumpet,* bimonthly. Newsletter ● Membership Directory, annual. **Conventions/Meetings:** semiannual conference ● annual meeting - 2008 May 14-18, Los Angeles, CA ● seminar.

13725 ■ Central Society for Clinical Research (CSCR)

555 E Wells St., Ste.1100
Milwaukee, WI 53202-3823
Ph: (414)273-2209
Fax: (414)276-2146

E-mail: cscr@execinc.com
URL: http://www.cscr.com
Contact: James B. Martins MD, Pres.
Founded: 1928. **Members:** 1,294. **Membership Dues:** active, $110 (annual). **Staff:** 1. **Budget:** $100,000. **Description:** Individuals who have accomplished a meritorious original investigation in the clinical or allied sciences of medicine and who enjoy an unimpeachable moral standing in the profession. Objectives are: the advancement of medical science; the cultivation of clinical research; the correlation of science with the art of medical practice; the encouragement of scientific investigation by the medical practitioner; the diffusion of a scientific spirit among the members of the society; the sponsorship of scientific meetings; the publication of papers on the methods and results of clinical research. **Telecommunication Services:** electronic mail, james-martins@uiowa.edu. **Publications:** *Journal of Laboratory and Clinical Medicine*, monthly. Delivers clinical investigation and research articles to physicians, academic clinician-scientists and laboratory consultants. Alternate Formats: online ● *Roster*, quinquennial. Membership Directory. **Conventions/Meetings:** annual meeting - always in Chicago, IL.

13726 ■ Clinical Magnetic Resonance Society (CMRS)
5620 W Sligh Ave.
Tampa, FL 33634-4490
Ph: (813)806-1080
Free: (888)350-CMRS
Fax: (813)806-1081
E-mail: information@cmrs.com
URL: http://www.cmrs.com
Contact: Ms. D. Beth Lewis, Exec.Dir.
Founded: 1995. **Members:** 1,000. **Membership Dues:** physician, scientist, $195 (annual) ● credentialed, $250 (semiannual) ● technologist, resident, fellow, $75 (annual). **Description:** Offers experience-based credentialing for physicians who practice MRI. Provides a forum for networking among members. Defines procedure protocols and safety information. **Libraries:** Type: not open to the public. **Subjects:** magnetic resonance imaging. **Awards:** Frequency: annual. Type: recognition ● **Frequency:** annual. Type: scholarship. **Recipient:** for physicians in training. **Computer Services:** database, membership database; available to members only ● online services, discussion board ● online services, protocol database. **Publications:** *CMRS Vision*, quarterly. Newsletter. Contains information on new developments in magnetic resonance imaging. **Price:** included in membership dues. **Circulation:** 1,500. **Advertising:** accepted. **Conventions/Meetings:** annual meeting and conference, with educational programs for physicians and technologists (exhibits) - always June.

13727 ■ Foundation for Advances in Medicine and Science (FAMS)
PO Box 485
Mahwah, NJ 07430-0485
Ph: (201)818-1010
Free: (800)443-0263
Fax: (201)818-0086
E-mail: scanning@fams.org
URL: http://www.fams.org
Contact: Tony Bourgholtzer, Board Chm.
Founded: 1981. **Members:** 400. **Membership Dues:** individual sponsor, $200 (annual) ● individual, $50 (annual) ● student, $30 (annual) ● corporate, $1,000 (annual). **Staff:** 10. **Multinational. Description:** Clinical cardiologists, scientists, and scanning electron microscopists. Disseminates resource information in clinical medicine and science. Funds research projects. **Computer Services:** Mailing lists, available in scanning microscopy and applications. **Conventions/Meetings:** annual international conference.

13728 ■ Global Perioperative Research Organization (GPRO)
PO Box 17969
Durham, NC 27715
Free: (866)536-0568
Fax: (919)668-7153

E-mail: info@gpro.org
URL: http://www.gpro.org
Contact: Mark F. Newman MD, Dir.
Description: Develops and shares knowledge that improves the care of perioperative patients around the world through clinical research. Provides scientific leadership in the conduct of clinical research and advancement of clinical research methodology. Provides a full range of clinical research services to pharmaceutical, medical device, and biotechnology industry in compliance with worldwide regulatory standards. **Computer Services:** Information services, online presentations. **Committees:** Steering; Subspecialty. **Affiliated With:** International Anesthesia Research Society. **Publications:** *Global News*, quarterly. Newsletter. Alternate Formats: online.

13729 ■ Society of Clinical Research Associates (SoCRA)
530 W Butler Ave., Ste.109
Chalfont, PA 18914
Ph: (215)822-8644
Free: (800)762-7292
Fax: (215)822-8633
E-mail: socramail@aol.com
URL: http://www.socra.org
Contact: Joanne Goldberg MSc, Sec.
Members: 8,700. **Membership Dues:** regular, $75 (annual). **Multinational. Description:** Promotes excellence in the field of clinical trials. Represents and furthers the education and information exchange among clinical research professionals. Provides training and certification to clinical research professionals to enhance their professionalism. **Publications:** *SoCRA Source*, quarterly. Journal. Publishes regulatory, scientific and technical articles. **Circulation:** 6,300. **Advertising:** accepted ● Brochure. Alternate Formats: online ● Membership Directory. Alternate Formats: online.

13730 ■ Society for Clinical Trials (SCT)
600 Wyndhurst Ave., Ste.112
Baltimore, MD 21210
Ph: (410)433-4722
Fax: (410)435-8631
E-mail: sctbalt@aol.com
URL: http://www.sctweb.org
Contact: James Neaton, Pres.
Founded: 1978. **Members:** 1,450. **Membership Dues:** student, $50 (annual) ● full, $110 (annual). **Multinational. Description:** Represents the interests of persons with training and expertise in behavioral science, bioethics, biostatistics, computer science, dentistry, epidemiology, law, management, medicine, nursing and pharmacology. Promotes the development and dissemination of knowledge about the design and conduct of clinical trials and other research employing similar methods. **Committees:** Development; Education; Nominating; Policy; Program; Publications; Student Scholarship. **Publications:** *Clinical Trials*, bimonthly. Journal. ISSN: 1740-7745. Alternate Formats: online ● *SCT Newsletter*, semiannual, published in March and October. Alternate Formats: online. **Conventions/Meetings:** annual meeting (exhibits) - 2008 May 18-21, St. Louis, MO.

Coma

13731 ■ Coma Recovery Association (CRA)
8300 Republic Airport, Ste.106
Farmingdale, NY 11735
Ph: (631)756-1826
Fax: (631)756-1827
E-mail: inquiry@comarecovery.org
URL: http://www.comarecovery.org
Founded: 1980. **Members:** 1,056. **Membership Dues:** standard, $15 (annual) ● professional, $50 (annual). **Staff:** 3. **Budget:** $45,000. **Regional Groups:** 1. **State Groups:** 2. **Local Groups:** 1. **For-Profit. Description:** Coma and head injury survivors and their families; medical professionals; interested persons. Aims to provide support to and assist families of coma and head injury survivors. Provides

information and referrals regarding treatment, rehabilitation, and socialization options. Represents the common needs of families and patients before legislative bodies. **Publications:** *Coma Recovery Association Newsletter*, quarterly. **Price:** included in membership dues. **Circulation:** 1,200. **Advertising:** accepted. **Conventions/Meetings:** monthly support group meeting (exhibits) ● annual symposium (exhibits).

Communications

13732 ■ Association of Biomedical Communications Directors (ABCD)
c/o Manny Bekier, Dir.
SUNY Downstate Medical Ctr.
450 Clarkson Ave.
Brooklyn, NY 11203
Ph: (718)270-7551
Fax: (718)270-7549
E-mail: mbekier@downstate.edu
URL: http://www.abcdirectors.org
Contact: Manny Bekier, Dir.
Founded: 1974. **Members:** 87. **Membership Dues:** active, $110 (annual) ● associate, $50 (annual). **Description:** Individuals with common managerial concerns in health science communications, such as persons with direct administrative responsibility for operations of a biomedical communications facility in a school or academic health science center. Provides a forum for the sharing and dissemination of information, materials, and ideas. Promotes research and education in administrative practices with regard to health sciences communications. Works to develop information materials such as surveys and profiles helpful in the management of biomedical communications. **Publications:** *ABCD Exchange*, quarterly. Newsletter ● *Journal of Biocommunication*, quarterly. Provides objective and useful information to the biocommunication community. Alternate Formats: online. Also Cited As: *JBC* ● *Report of Annual Survey of Biomedical Communication Directors* ● Membership Directory, annual. **Conventions/Meetings:** annual conference ● seminar ● workshop.

13733 ■ BioCommunications Association (BCA)
220 Southwind Ln.
Hillsborough, NC 27278
Ph: (919)245-0906
Fax: (919)245-0906
E-mail: office@bca.org
URL: http://www.bca.org
Contact: Nancy Hurtgen, Central Office Admin.
Founded: 1931. **Members:** 250. **Membership Dues:** $100 (annual). **Staff:** 1. **Local Groups:** 29. **Multinational. Description:** Photographers, technicians, doctors, scientists, educators, and individuals concerned with photography in the health sciences and related fields. Seeks to advance the techniques of biophotography and biomedical communications through meetings, seminars, and workshops. **Boards:** Board of Governors. **Formerly:** (2001) Biological Photographic Association. **Publications:** *Journal of Biocommunication*, 3/year. Published jointly with three other associations. Alternate Formats: online. **Conventions/Meetings:** annual Bio-Comm - meeting (exhibits).

13734 ■ Health Science Communications Association (HeSCA)
39 Wedgewood Dr., Ste.A
Jewett City, CT 06351-2420
Ph: (860)376-5915
Fax: (860)376-6621
E-mail: hesca@hesca.org
URL: http://www.hesca.org
Contact: Ronald Sokolowski, Exec. Dir.
Founded: 1959. **Members:** 400. **Membership Dues:** individual, $150 (annual) ● student, $75 (annual) ● retiree, $90 (annual) ● institutional, $195 (annual) ● sustaining, $1,000 (annual). **Staff:** 2. **Budget:** $190,000. **Regional Groups:** 9. **Description:** Media managers, graphic artists, biomedical librarians,

producers, faculty members of health science and veterinary medicine schools, health professional organizations, and industry representatives. Acts as a clearinghouse for information used by professionals engaged in health science communications. Coordinates Media Festivals Program that recognizes outstanding media productions in the health sciences. Offers placement service. **Awards:** Distinguished Achievement Award. **Frequency:** annual. **Type:** recognition. **Recipient:** to individuals and organizations who have accomplished significant goals over a period of time and whose cumulative achievements are notable ● Distinguished Service Award. **Frequency:** annual. **Type:** recognition. **Recipient:** to HeSCA members who have demonstrated an outstanding level of service in a variety of areas over a long period of time ● Golden Raster Award. **Frequency:** annual. **Type:** recognition. **Recipient:** to individuals who have provided stability and inspiration to the organization through imaginative leadership and unswerving service ● HeSCA/JBC Literary Award. **Frequency:** annual. **Type:** recognition. **Recipient:** to the best Journal of Biocommunication article of the year by a HeSCA member. **Committees:** Awards; Education; Ethics; Evaluation; International; Regional Activities. **Affiliated With:** Association of Biomedical Communications Directors. **Formerly:** (1972) Council on Medical Television. **Publications:** *Feedback*, 5/year. Newsletter. Provides members with information on the field of biocommunications and on work of colleagues. Includes employment listings and regional news. **Price:** included in membership dues; $30.00 /year for nonmembers. Alternate Formats: online ● *Health Sciences Communications Association—Who's Who*, annual. Membership Directory. **Price:** included in membership dues. **Advertising:** accepted ● *HESCA Learning Resources Center Catalog*, annual ● *Journal of Biocommunication*, quarterly. Includes abstracts of biocommunication literature, gallery of medical art, and video and other media reviews. **Price:** included in membership dues; $25.00 /year for nonmembers; $28.00 /year for institutions; $20.00/year for students. ISSN: 0094-2499. Also Cited As: *JBC* ● *Patient Education Sourcebook* ● Brochures ● Monographs ● Also publishes indexes; distributes audiovisual materials. **Conventions/Meetings:** competition ● annual conference (exhibits) ● workshop.

Compensation Medicine

13735 ■ American Academy of Disability Evaluating Physicians (AADEP)
150 N Wacker Dr., Ste.1420
Chicago, IL 60606
Ph: (312)658-1171
Free: (800)456-6095
Fax: (312)658-1175
E-mail: aadep@aadep.org
URL: http://www.aadep.org
Contact: Sandra L. Yost, Exec. Dir.

Founded: 1987. **Members:** 1,300. **Membership Dues:** associate, $295 (annual) ● life, $4,500. **Staff:** 6. **Budget:** $1,200,000. **Description:** Physicians. Seeks to provide graduate and continuing medical education programs to qualify doctors of medicine and doctors of osteopathy to meet the needs of the public in the practice of the medical science of disability evaluation as well as disability consultation. Works to develop educational programs and training programs in disability evaluation and disability consultation for health care professionals. Fosters and develops the medical science of disability evaluation. Sponsors research programs. Establishes standards for physicians in the practice of disability evaluation and disability consultation. **Awards:** Fellowship. **Frequency:** semiannual. **Type:** recognition. **Recipient:** for a fellow who earns high points. **Computer Services:** Mailing lists. **Publications:** *AADEP Disability*, quarterly. Newsletter. **Price:** $100.00 /year for individuals; $120.00 /year for institutions; $25.00 plus shipping and handling. ISSN: 1047-1448 ● *AMA Guides, 5th Edition*. Book. **Price:** $138.13 plus shipping and handling ● *Disability*, quarterly. Journal.

Papers pertaining to information useful to physicians' disability arena. **Price:** $100.00 /year for individuals; $120.00 /year for institutions; $140.00 /year for individuals (foreign); $160.00 /year for institutions (foreign). **Circulation:** 2,500. **Advertising:** accepted ● Membership Directory, annual. **Price:** $106.25 plus shipping and handling. **Circulation:** 1,500. **Conventions/Meetings:** periodic A New Approach to AMA Guides Training Course - seminar ● periodic Advanced Course - seminar ● Advanced Short Course - seminar ● Advanced Skills Development - seminar ● periodic Comprehensive Training Program - meeting, co-sponsored by University of Cincinnati ● periodic International Congress on Disability in the Workplace, co-sponsored by University of Cincinnati ● Medical Evidence: Controversies & Challenges in Workers' Compensation - conference, with Impairment Rating Course ● periodic Scientific Session and Business Meeting (exhibits).

13736 ■ National Association of Disability Examiners (NADE)
c/o C.J. August, Sec.
25 Milton Loop
Los Lunas, NM 87031
Ph: (505)841-5679
Fax: (505)841-5743
E-mail: charles.schimmels@ssa.gov
URL: http://www.nade.org
Contact: Chuck Schimmmels, Pres.

Founded: 1963. **Members:** 1,700. **Membership Dues:** full, associate, $50 (annual) ● full support staff, retiree, $25 (annual) ● corporate, $200 (annual). **Budget:** $95,000. **Regional Groups:** 7. **Local Groups:** 56. **Description:** Disability claims examiners, attorneys, and physicians involved in determining the eligibility of applicants for social security benefits based on disability. Seeks to foster, promote, and participate in activities designed to improve the documentation of applications for disability insurance benefits and the evaluation of medical and/or vocational information obtained in connection with such applications. Works for the exchange of technical information, ideas, and philosophies. **Awards:** Charles O. Blalock Award. **Type:** recognition. **Recipient:** for outstanding contribution to the advancement of the association ● Examiner of the Year Award. **Frequency:** annual. **Type:** recognition ● **Type:** recognition. **Recipient:** for outstanding state agency supervisor, support staff member, and state unit. **Committees:** Awards and Citations; Certification; Continuing Education; Legislative. **Publications:** *NADE Advocate*, bimonthly. Newsletter. Includes listings of newly-certified examiners. **Price:** included in membership dues. **Advertising:** accepted ● Directory, annual. **Conventions/Meetings:** annual conference (exhibits) - usually September or October. 2008 Sept. 15-18, Nashville, TN ● regional meeting - during spring. 2008 May 14-16, Annapolis, MD.

Consciousness Studies

13737 ■ International Society for the Study of Subtle Energies and Energy Medicine (ISSSEEM)
c/o C. Penny Hiernu, CEO
11005 Ralston Rd., Ste.100D
Arvada, CO 80004
Ph: (303)425-4625
Fax: (303)425-4685
E-mail: issseem2@comcast.net
URL: http://www.issseem.org
Contact: C. Penny Hiernu, CEO

Founded: 1989. **Members:** 1,450. **Membership Dues:** professional/associate, $75 (annual) ● professional/associate (international), $84 (annual) ● senior/student/limited income, $45 (annual) ● senior/student/limited income (international), $54 (annual) ● institutional, $200 (annual) ● institutional (international), $229 (annual). **Staff:** 4. **Budget:** $250,000. **Description:** Individuals interested in the study of human capacities and the role of consciousness in nature. Offers educational programs. **Libraries:** **Type:** reference; not open to the public. **Holdings:**

13; articles, books, clippings, periodicals. **Subjects:** consciousness studies, energy medicine. **Awards:** Alyce and Elmer E. Green Award. **Frequency:** annual. **Type:** recognition. **Computer Services:** database. **Publications:** *Bridges*, quarterly. Magazine. Written for clinicians. **Price:** $50.00. **Circulation:** 1,400 ● *Subtle Energies and Energy Medicine*, 3/year. Journal. **Price:** $50.00 for members in U.S.; $68.00 for members outside U.S.; $60.00 for nonmembers in U.S.; $78.00 for nonmembers outside U.S. ISSN: 1099-6591. **Circulation:** 1,200. Alternate Formats: online. **Conventions/Meetings:** annual Return of the Sacred Science: Celebrating the Mysteries of Healing - conference - always June.

Consulting

13738 ■ National Association of Healthcare Consultants
1255 23rd St. NW, Ste.200
Washington, DC 20037-1174
Ph: (202)452-8282
Fax: (202)833-3636
E-mail: consultants@healthcon.org
Contact: Brian J. Mandrier, Exec. Dir.

Founded: 1994. **Members:** 350. **Membership Dues:** individual, $475 (annual). **Staff:** 3. **Budget:** $300,000. **Description:** Consultants who "provide ethical, confidential, and professional advice to the healthcare industry". Promotes professional development of members; works to improve the standard of healthcare consulting services. Facilitates exchange of information among members; conducts educational and training programs; encourages members to attain Certified Healthcare Business Consultant (CHBC) status. Compiles statistics; makes available legal and marketing advice; provides group purchasing discount programs to members; maintains speakers' bureau. **Publications:** *Hot Topics*, periodic. Newsletter. **Price:** included in membership dues ● *Medical and Dental Income and Expenses Averages*, annual. Report. **Price:** $495.00 for members (full report); $795.00 for nonmembers (full report); $99.00 for members (single specialty report); $249.00 for nonmembers (single specialty report) ● *Update*, periodic. Newsletter. **Price:** included in membership dues ● Membership Directory. **Conventions/Meetings:** annual HealthCon - conference and trade show - every June ● periodic regional meeting.

Contact Lenses

13739 ■ Contact Lens Council (CLC)
8201 Corporate Dr., Ste.850
Landover, MD 20785
Ph: (301)459-2618
Free: (800)884-4CLC
Fax: (301)459-1802
E-mail: clc@thecli.com
Contact: Mr. Ed Schilling, Dir.

Description: Works to promote the safe use of contact lenses and provides opportunities for both current and prospective contact lens consumers to learn about the variety of lens options available to meet their vision and lifestyle needs.

Cosmetic Surgery

13740 ■ American Academy of Cosmetic Surgery (AACS)
737 N Michigan Ave., Ste.2100
Chicago, IL 60611-5405
Ph: (312)981-6760
E-mail: info@cosmeticsurgery.org
URL: http://www.cosmeticsurgery.org
Contact: Jeffrey P. Knezovich, Exec. VP

Founded: 1985. **Members:** 1,400. **Staff:** 10. **Budget:** $2,500,000. **Description:** Licensed cosmetic surgeons. Seeks to encourage high-quality cosmetic medical and dental care; provides continuing education for cosmetic surgeons; promotes research.

Compiles statistics. Maintains hall of fame and speakers' bureau. **Libraries: Type:** reference. **Holdings:** archival material. **Awards: Type:** recognition. **Computer Services:** Mailing lists. **Formed by Merger of:** American Association of Cosmetic Surgeons; American Society of Cosmetic Surgeon. **Publications:** *American Journal of Cosmetic Surgery*, quarterly. **Price:** $110.00 in U.S.; $130.00 outside U.S. ISSN: 0748-8068. **Advertising:** accepted ● *Membership Roster*, annual. Membership Directory ● *Newsline*, bimonthly. Newsletter. **Conventions/Meetings:** annual Scientific Meeting (exhibits) - 2008 Jan. 17-20, Orlando, FL; 2009 Jan. 15-18, Phoenix, AZ ● periodic World Congress on Liposuction Surgery (exhibits).

13741 ■ American Academy of Facial Plastic and Reconstructive Surgery (AAFPRS)
310 S Henry St.
Alexandria, VA 22314
Ph: (703)299-9291
Free: (800)332-FACE
Fax: (703)299-8898
E-mail: info@aafprs.org
URL: http://www.aafrs.org
Contact: Stephen C. Duffy, Exec. VP
Founded: 1964. **Members:** 2,600. **Membership Dues:** regular, $625 (annual) ● fellow, $675 (annual) ● international, $195 (annual). **Staff:** 14. **Budget:** $3,000,000. **Description:** Physicians specializing in facial plastic surgery. Promotes research and study in the field. Maintains speakers' bureau. Conducts educational and charitable programs; compiles statistics. **Libraries: Type:** reference. **Holdings:** 200; video recordings. **Subjects:** cosmetic, reconstructive and trauma surgery. **Awards:** Ben Shuster Memorial. **Frequency:** annual. **Type:** monetary. **Recipient:** for the most outstanding research paper by a resident or fellow in training on any clinical work or research in facial plastic and reconstructive surgery delivered at a national meeting (or its equivalent) between March 1 and February 28 ● Bernstein Award. **Frequency:** annual. **Type:** grant. **Recipient:** for an AAFPRS fellow member who is conducting original research which will advance facial plastic and reconstructive surgery ● Community Service. **Frequency:** annual. **Type:** recognition. **Recipient:** for any member who has distinguished himself/herself by providing and/or making possible free medical service to the poor in his/her community ● F. Mark Rafaty Memorial. **Frequency:** annual. **Type:** recognition. **Recipient:** for any member who has made outstanding contributions to facial plastic and reconstructive surgery ● Investigator Development Award. **Frequency:** annual. **Type:** grant. **Recipient:** for AAFPRS member who is conducting significant clinical or laboratory research and for the training of resident surgeons in research ● Ira Tresley Research Award. **Frequency:** annual. **Type:** monetary. **Recipient:** for the best original research in facial plastic surgery by an AAFPRS member who has been board certified for at least three years ● John Dickinson Teacher. **Frequency:** annual. **Type:** recognition. **Recipient:** to a fellow member for sharing knowledge about facial plastic surgery with the effective use of audiovisuals over a number of years ● John Orlando Roe. **Frequency:** annual. **Type:** monetary. **Recipient:** for the graduate fellow who submits the best scholarly paper written during fellowship ● Resident Research Award. **Frequency:** annual. **Type:** grant. **Recipient:** for residents who are AAFPRS members ● Sir Harold Delf Gillies. **Frequency:** annual. **Type:** monetary. **Recipient:** for the graduate fellow who submits the best research paper written during fellowship ● William Wright. **Frequency:** annual. **Type:** recognition. **Recipient:** for a member who has made outstanding contributions to facial plastic and reconstructive surgery. **Computer Services:** Mailing lists, of members names and addresses available for sale for approved uses. **Formed by Merger of:** (1964) American Otorhinologic Society for Plastic Surgery; American Society of Facial Plastic Surgery. **Publications:** *The Face Book* ● *The Face Book Speakers Kit* ● *Face Facts*, quarterly ● *Facial Plastic Surgery Patient Information Series*. Brochures. Features 12 different brochures about facial plastic surgery procedures. ● *Facial Plastic Surgery Today*, quarterly. Newsletter.

Circulation: 1,000 ● *Facial Plastic Times*, monthly. Newsletter. Includes calendar of events and book reviews. **Price:** available to members only. **Circulation:** 3,000. **Advertising:** accepted ● Membership Directory, annual. Includes buyers' guide. **Price:** $35.00/copy for members; $80.00/copy for nonmembers. **Advertising:** accepted ● Monographs ● Videos. **Conventions/Meetings:** semiannual Scientific Meetings - symposium and seminar (exhibits) - usually May and September ● workshop.

13742 ■ American Academy of Micropigmentation (AAM)
c/o Charles S. Zwerling, MD, Chm.
2709 Medical Off. Pl.
Goldsboro, NC 27534
Ph: (919)736-3937
Fax: (919)735-3701
E-mail: zwerling@micropigmentation.org
URL: http://www.micropigmentation.org
Contact: Charles S. Zwerling MD, Chm.
Founded: 1992. **Membership Dues:** executive, instructor, vendor, $250 (annual) ● student, $100 (annual) ● international, active, fellow, $200 (annual) ● associate, $175 (annual). **Description:** Promotes excellence in micropigmentation. Seeks to improve the quality of the permanent makeup profession. Guides and promotes appropriate legislation for self-direction for all practitioners in each State. Fosters and encourages continuous learning and professional development. **Publications:** *Handy Guide to Permanent Makeup* (in English and Spanish). Pamphlet. Alternate Formats: online. Also Cited As: *La Guia A Maquillaje Permanente*.

13743 ■ American Association of Plastic Surgeons (AAPS)
900 Cummings Ctr., Ste.221-U
Beverly, MA 01915
Ph: (978)927-8330
Fax: (978)524-8890
E-mail: executivesecretary@aaps1921.org
URL: http://www.aaps1921.org
Contact: Dr. Susan E. Mackinnon, Pres.
Founded: 1921. **Members:** 425. **Staff:** 1. **Budget:** $140,000. **Description:** Professional society of plastic surgeons. Advances the science and art of plastic surgery through surgical education, research, scientific presentations, and professional interaction. **Awards:** Clinician of the Year. **Frequency:** annual. **Type:** recognition. **Recipient:** for remarkable clinical achievement in the field ● Honorary Award. **Frequency:** annual. **Type:** recognition. **Recipient:** for outstanding contributions in medicine and surgery ● James Barrett Brown Award. **Frequency:** annual. **Type:** recognition. **Recipient:** for best scientific publication. **Committees:** Academic Scholar; Awards; Communications; Constitution and Bylaws; Ethics; Local Arrangements; Research and Education; Scientific. **Formerly:** (1942) American Association of Oral and Plastic Surgeons. **Publications:** Newsletter, periodic. **Conventions/Meetings:** annual meeting - always April or May.

13744 ■ American Board of Plastic Surgery (ABPS)
7 Penn Center, Ste.400
1635 Market St.
Philadelphia, PA 19103-2204
Ph: (215)587-9322
Fax: (215)587-9622
E-mail: info@abplsurg.org
URL: http://www.abplsurg.org
Contact: Dr. R. Barrett Noone, Exec. Dir.
Founded: 1937. **Members:** 20. **Staff:** 4. **Description:** Certification board established to investigate the qualifications of, administer examinations to, and certify as diplomates medical doctors specializing in the entire field of plastic and reconstructive surgery. **Affiliated With:** American Board of Medical Specialties. **Publications:** *Booklet of Information*, annual.

13745 ■ American Society for Aesthetic Plastic Surgery (ASAPS)
11081 Winners Cir.
Los Alamitos, CA 90720-2813
Ph: (212)921-0500
Free: (888)272-7711

Fax: (212)921-0011
E-mail: media@surgery.org
URL: http://www.surgery.org
Contact: Sue Dykema, Deputy Exec. Dir.
Founded: 1964. **Members:** 2,250. **Staff:** 30. **Budget:** $4,650,000. **Description:** Board-certified plastic surgeons. Provides continuing education to members in the area of aesthetic plastic surgery, through presentation of papers, study sessions, and scientific sessions. Provides speakers; conducts research programs. **Awards:** Journalistic Achievement Award. **Frequency:** annual. **Type:** recognition. **Commissions:** Administrative; Communications; Education. **Committees:** Intranet Steering; Patient Safety Steering. **Councils:** Judicial. **Publications:** *Aesthetic Society News*, quarterly. Newsletter. **Advertising:** accepted ● *Aesthetic Surgery Journal*, bimonthly. Reviews developments in the field and research results; includes society news. **Price:** included in membership dues. **Circulation:** 5,000. **Conventions/Meetings:** annual meeting (exhibits).

13746 ■ American Society of Ophthalmic Plastic and Reconstructive Surgery (ASOPRS)
222 S Westmonte Dr., Ste.101
Altamonte Springs, FL 32714
Ph: (407)774-7880
Fax: (407)774-6440
E-mail: asoprs@kmgnet.com
URL: http://www.asoprs.org
Contact: Ms. Barbara Beatty, Exec. Dir.
Founded: 1969. **Members:** 500. **Multinational. Description:** Physicians specializing in ophthalmic plastic and reconstructive surgery. Seeks to "advance education, research, and the quality of clinical practice in the fields of plastic and reconstructive surgery involving the eyelids, orbits, and lacrimal system". Facilitates exchange of information among members; conducts fellowship training programs. **Awards:** ASOPRS Thesis Award. **Frequency:** annual. **Type:** recognition. **Recipient:** for the best thesis. **Publications:** *Ophthalmic Plastic and Reconstructive Surgery*. Journal ● *Spring Meeting Registration*. Brochure ● Newsletter. **Conventions/Meetings:** annual symposium.

13747 ■ American Society of Plastic Surgeons (ASPS)
444 E Algonquin Rd.
Arlington Heights, IL 60005
Ph: (847)228-9900
Free: (888)4-PLASTIC
Fax: (847)228-9131
E-mail: media@plasticsurgery.org
URL: http://www.plasticsurgery.org
Contact: Roxanne Guy MD, Pres.
Founded: 1931. **Members:** 5,000. **Membership Dues:** individual, $760 (annual). **Staff:** 70. **Budget:** $15,000,000. **Regional Groups:** 29. **State Groups:** 35. **Description:** Plastic surgeons. Dedicated to quality patient care and to maintain professional and ethical standards through education, research, and advocacy of socioeconomic and other professional activities. **Libraries: Type:** not open to the public. **Holdings:** 600. **Subjects:** plastic and reconstructive surgery. **Awards:** Circle of Excellence Media Awards. **Frequency:** annual. **Type:** monetary. **Recipient:** for newspapers, magazines, radio, television, news services, and news web sites. **Formerly:** ASPRS - American Society of Plastic and Reconstructive Surgery. **Publications:** *Plastic and Reconstructive Surgery*, monthly. Journal. Includes research reports and book reviews. **Price:** included in membership dues; $420.00 for nonmembers. **Circulation:** 12,300. **Advertising:** accepted. Alternate Formats: online. **Conventions/Meetings:** annual Scientific Meeting.

13748 ■ American Society of Plastic Surgeons and Plastic Surgery Education Foundation (ASPS)
444 E Algonquin Rd.
Arlington Heights, IL 60005
Ph: (847)228-9900
Free: (888)4-PLASTIC
Fax: (847)228-9131

E-mail: registration@plasticsurgery.org
URL: http://www.plasticsurgery.org
Contact: Bruce L. Cunningham MD, Pres. **Founded:** 1931. **Members:** 5,000. **Membership Dues:** regular, $870 (annual). **Staff:** 90. **Budget:** $15,000,000. **Regional Groups:** 29. **State Groups:** 35. **Description:** Professional society of plastic surgeons. Works in cooperation with the Plastic Surgery Educational Foundation to promote optimal care for plastic surgery patients through research, service, and education activities. Sponsors public/ patient education program, clinical symposia, and professional development workshops. Acts as a liaison between members and government and medical organizations. Conducts charitable activities; maintains speakers' bureau; compiles statistics. **Libraries: Type:** not open to the public. **Holdings:** 465; books, periodicals, video recordings. **Subjects:** plastic and reconstructive surgery. **Awards:** Circle of Excellence Journalism Award. **Frequency:** annual. **Type:** monetary. **Recipient:** for newspapers, wire services, magazines, radio, or TV. **Computer Services:** Mailing lists. **Telecommunication Services:** phone referral service, patient referral service, (800)- 635-0635. **Formerly:** (2000) American Society of Plastic and Reconstructive Surgeons. **Publications:** *American Society of Plastic and Reconstructive Surgeons Combined Roster*, annual. Directory. Lists administrative, member alpha/geo, bylaws and related organization. **Price:** free for members (first copy); $35.00 additional copies for members; $750.00 for nonmembers. **Circulation:** 6,000. **Advertising:** accepted. Alternate Formats: online. Also Cited As: *ASPRS/PSEF Combined Roster* ● *Journal of Plastic and Reconstructive Surgery*, monthly. Includes research reports and book reviews. **Price:** free for members; $554.00 /year for nonmembers, in U.S.; $690.00 /year for institutions, in U.S.; $724.00 /year for nonmembers, outside U.S. ISSN: 0032-1052. **Circulation:** 12,300. **Advertising:** accepted ● *Plastic Surgery News*, monthly. Newsletter. Includes information on employment opportunities and current events. **Price:** free for members; $75.00 for nonmembers. **Circulation:** 5,800. **Advertising:** accepted. **Conventions/Meetings:** annual Scientific Meeting (exhibits).

13749 ■ Association of Academic Chairmen of Plastic Surgery (AACPS)

c/o Peggy O'Carroll, Admin. Mgr.
444 E Algonquin Rd.
Arlington Heights, IL 60005
Free: (800)526-9884
Fax: (847)228-7099
E-mail: po@plasticsurgery.org
URL: http://www.aacplasticsurgery.org
Contact: Peggy O'Carroll, Admin. Mgr. **Founded:** 1985. **Members:** 270. **Membership Dues:** active, $250 (annual) ● associate, $75 (annual). **Staff:** 1. **Description:** Chairmen of plastic and reconstructive surgery education and residency programs. Seeks to advance the study and teaching of plastic and reconstructive surgery. Facilitates establishment of graduate medical education and residency programs in plastic and reconstructive surgery. Conducts educational programs. **Computer Services:** Mailing lists, of members. **Conventions/Meetings:** semiannual board meeting ● semiannual convention ● annual retreat.

13750 ■ International Confederation for Plastic, Reconstructive and Aesthetic Surgery (IPRAS)

4 Executive Park Dr.
Albany, NY 12203
Ph: (518)438-1434
Fax: (518)489-1205
E-mail: ipras@sover.net
URL: http://www.ipras.org
Contact: Dr. Marita Eisenmann-Klein, Gen. Sec. **Founded:** 1955. **Members:** 91. **Staff:** 2. **Budget:** $125,000. **Regional Groups:** 3. **National Groups:** 91. **Languages:** English, French, German, Spanish. **Multinational. Description:** National associations representing 13,000 plastic surgeons. Promotes plastic surgery both clinically and scientifically. Encourages closer relationships between interna-

tional members and direct contact between national societies. Disseminates information on developments in other countries. Seeks to widen the scope of understanding and knowledge in the field and reinforce the worldwide fraternity of plastic surgeons. **Computer Services:** database, of membership. **Committees:** Educational Programs; Electronic Communication; Evaluation of Biomaterial; Finance/ Bylaws; Medical Liability; Projects in Developing Countries; Publications and Video Library; Quality Assurance of Plastic Surgery Units; Relationship with Multi-Disciplinary International Society; Relationship with Other Specialties Performing Aesthetic Surgery; Worldwide Harmonization in Training. **Divisions:** Aesthetic Plastic Surgery; Craniomaxillofacial Surgery; Hand Surgery; Microsurgery. **Publications:** *GlobalPlast*. Newsletter. **Price:** free for members. **Circulation:** 11,000. Alternate Formats: online. **Conventions/Meetings:** quadrennial meeting and congress (exhibits).

13751 ■ International Society of Cosmetic and Laser Surgeons (ISCLS)

2563 Capital Medical Blvd.
Tallahassee, FL 32308
Ph: (850)531-8374
Free: (866)604-7257
Fax: (850)531-8344
E-mail: info@iscls.org
URL: http://www.iscls.org
Contact: Mark S. Nestor MD, Pres. **Membership Dues:** physician, scientist, $250 (annual) ● resident, fellow, $100 (annual) ● associate, $125 (annual). **Multinational. Description:** Aims to advance the study and practice of cosmetic laser surgery. Seeks to provide high quality education on all facets of cosmetic laser surgery to physicians, scientists, and trained staff. Offers in-depth scientific programs that address the educational needs, medical procedures, and controversial issues in the field of cosmetic laser surgery. **Awards:** Abstract Presentation Award. **Frequency:** annual. **Type:** monetary. **Recipient:** for the best oral abstract presentation about cosmetic laser surgery ● Cosmetic Laser Surgery Research Grant. **Frequency:** annual. **Type:** grant. **Recipient:** for innovative basic and clinical research projects with specific relevance to cosmetic laser surgery. **Publications:** *Journal of Cosmetic and Laser Therapy*, quarterly. Covers cosmetic and dermatological topics, with emphasis on the application of cosmetic laser and light therapies on the skin. **Price:** included in membership dues; $165.00 /year for nonmembers; $435.00 /year for institutions (print); $413.00 /year for institutions (online). ISSN: 1476- 4172 ● Membership Directory, biennial. Includes a listing of officers, trustees, and committees, by-laws, and information on upcoming symposiums. ● Brochure. Contains membership information and profile about the society. Alternate Formats: online.

13752 ■ Interplast

857 Maude Ave.
Mountain View, CA 94043
Ph: (650)962-0123
Free: (888)467-5278
Fax: (650)962-1619
E-mail: info@interplast.org
URL: http://www.interplast.org
Contact: Susan W. Hayes, Pres./CEO **Founded:** 1969. **Staff:** 20. **Budget:** $3,300,000. **Description:** Provides free reconstructive plastic surgery in developing countries, makes a direct and profound difference in the lives of 3000 children each year who suffer physically or emotionally from a congenital deformity or injury. Works in partnership with volunteers and overseas medical colleagues to educate and empower local communities so that medical access continues year-round. **Awards:** Medical Scholar Program. **Frequency:** annual. **Type:** scholarship. **Recipient:** for foreign medical personnel. **Telecommunication Services:** electronic mail, ipnews@interplast.org. **Publications:** *Healing Hands*, semiannual. Newsletter. Highlights photos and stories of programs. **Price:** free. **Circulation:** 10,000. Alternate Formats: online ● Annual Report. **Conventions/Meetings:** annual meeting.

13753 ■ Plastic Surgery Administrative Association (PSAA)

6324 Fairview Ave. N
Crystal, MN 55428
Free: (800)373-0302
E-mail: jddeiter@comcast.net
URL: http://www.plasticadmin.org
Contact: John Deiter, Pres. **Founded:** 1975. **Membership Dues:** individual, $130 (annual). **Description:** Represents plastic surgery administrators in all practices areas, including solo, group, academic, and surgi-center environments. Promotes the professional development of managers of plastic surgery practices; provides resources in order to achieve competency and efficiency; advocates for members on issues that affect the delivery of plastic surgery care; provides platform for networking. **Publications:** *Administrator Review*, quarterly. Newsletter. Contains product information, clinical and administrative updates, and organization activities. **Price:** included in membership dues. **Conventions/Meetings:** annual symposium, held in conjunction with the annual meeting of the American Society of Plastic Surgeons - held in the fall.

13754 ■ Plastic Surgery Educational Foundation (PSEF)

444 E Algonquin Rd.
Arlington Heights, IL 60005
Ph: (847)228-9900
Free: (888)4PLASTIC
E-mail: registration@plasticsurgery.org
URL: http://www.plasticsurgery.org
Contact: Brian M. Kinney MD, Pres. **Founded:** 1948. **Members:** 4,500. **Staff:** 67. **Budget:** $1,100,000. **Description:** Plastic and reconstructive surgeons. Seeks to identify and respond to the educational needs of members and their patients. Sponsors regional and national demonstrations, lectures, educational seminars, symposia, and workshops focusing on plastic surgery techniques and procedures. Conducts annual in-service and self-assessment examinations dealing with topics such as aesthetic and breast surgery, hand and extremities, integument, maxillofacial surgery, and pediatric plastic surgery. Administers Visiting Professors Program; compiles statistics; sponsors charitable programs. **Libraries: Type:** reference. **Holdings:** 465; books, periodicals, video recordings. **Subjects:** congenital deformities, flaps, head and neck, reconstructive, trauma. **Awards: Type:** scholarship. **Recipient:** in basic science, clinical research, and senior categories. **Telecommunication Services:** teleconference, covers plastic surgical education. **Affiliated With:** American Society of Plastic Surgeons and Plastic Surgery Education Foundation. **Formerly:** (1981) Education Foundation of American Society of Plastic and Reconstructive Surgeons. **Publications:** *Journal of Plastic and Reconstructive Surgery*, monthly. Includes research reports and book reviews. **Price:** $554.00 /year for nonmembers, in U.S.; $690.00 /year for institutions, in U.S.; $724.00 /year for nonmembers, outside U.S.; $864.00 /year for institutions, outside U.S. ISSN: 0032-1052. **Circulation:** 12,300. **Advertising:** accepted ● *Plastic Surgery News*, monthly. Newsletter. Includes information on employment opportunities and current events. **Price:** free for members; $75.00 for nonmembers. **Circulation:** 5,800. **Advertising:** accepted ● Booklets. **Conventions/Meetings:** annual Scientific Meeting (exhibits).

13755 ■ Plastic Surgery Research Council (PSRC)

45 Lyme Rd., Ste.304
Hanover, NH 03755
Ph: (603)643-2325
Fax: (603)643-1444
E-mail: psrc@sover.net
URL: http://www.ps-rc.org
Contact: Ms. Lori Maville, Membership Services Mgr. **Founded:** 1955. **Members:** 586. **Membership Dues:** active, $225 (annual) ● associate, $100 (annual) ● resident, $50 (annual). **Staff:** 3. **Budget:** $100,000. **Multinational. Description:** Fosters fundamental research in the fields of plastic and reconstructive

surgery. **Awards:** Crikelair. **Frequency:** annual. **Type:** recognition. **Recipient:** for best presentation by a high school or college student at annual meeting ● Gingrass. **Frequency:** annual. **Type:** recognition. **Recipient:** for best presentation by a medical student or non-plastic surgery resident at annual meeting ● Shenaq. **Frequency:** annual. **Type:** recognition. **Recipient:** for best presentation by a graduate of a foreign medical school (non-US or Canadian) at annual meeting ● Snyder. **Frequency:** annual. **Type:** recognition. **Recipient:** for best presentation by a plastic surgery resident or fellow at annual meeting. **Publications:** *Plastic and Reconstructive Surgery*, 14/year. Journal. **Price:** $516.00 /year for individuals; $642.00 /year for institutions; $262.00 for in-training. ISSN: 0032-1052. **Advertising:** accepted. Also Cited As: *White Journal*. **Conventions/Meetings:** annual conference, scientific/professional (exhibits) - always in spring. 2008 May 28-31, Springfield, IL - **Avg. Attendance:** 350.

Counseling

13756 ■ American Association of State Counseling Boards (AASCB)
5999 Stevenson Ave.
Alexandria, VA 22304
Ph: (703)212-2239
Fax: (703)212-4884
E-mail: aascbinfo@counseling.org
URL: http://www.aascb.org
Contact: Veronica Skoranski, Exec. Dir.
Founded: 1986. **Members:** 150. **Membership Dues:** state board, $400 (annual) ● individual, $25 (annual) ● organizational affiliate, $300 (annual). **State Groups:** 48. **Description:** Dedicated to the concept that individuals who have demonstrated competence to render counseling services are entitled to be licensed, certified or registered as counselors by member boards. **Computer Services:** Mailing lists. **Commissions:** Communication; Consultation; Public Protection; Research; Standards. **Divisions:** Delegate Assembly. **Publications:** *The Liaison*, bimonthly. Newsletter. **Price:** included in membership dues. **Advertising:** accepted. Alternate Formats: online ● *Policy and Procedures Manual*. Alternate Formats: online ● Proceedings. Alternate Formats: online. **Conventions/Meetings:** annual conference (exhibits) - 2008 Jan. 10-12, New Orleans, LA ● annual meeting.

Craniofacial Abnormalities

13757 ■ American Cleft Palate-Craniofacial Association (ACPA)
1504 E Franklin St., Ste.102
Chapel Hill, NC 27514-2820
Ph: (919)933-9044
Fax: (919)933-9604
E-mail: info@acpa-cpf.org
URL: http://www.acpa-cpf.org
Contact: Ms. Nancy C. Smythe, Exec. Dir.
Founded: 1943. **Members:** 2,700. **Membership Dues:** active, associate, $150 (annual) ● student, $75 (annual). **Staff:** 5. **Budget:** $500,000. **Languages:** English, Spanish. **Description:** Physicians, dentists, speech pathologists, audiologists, surgeons, psychologists, nurses and others surgeons actively engaged in the care of individuals with cleft lip and palate and associated craniofacial anomalies. Works to extend and improve the understanding of the scientific and clinical problems involved in the habilitation of patients with cleft lip and palate, and to stimulate professional and public interest in the field. Conducts educational programs. **Awards:** Distinguished Service Award. **Frequency:** annual. **Type:** recognition. **Recipient:** for exceptional service and contribution to the ACPA ● Honors Award. **Frequency:** annual. **Type:** recognition. **Recipient:** for outstanding achievement in the field. **Committees:** Education; Government Affairs; Honors and Awards; International Relations; Journal Policy; Research; Team Standards. **Affiliated With:** Cleft Palate Foun-

dation. **Formerly:** American Association for Cleft Palate Rehabilitation; (1949) American Academy of Cleft Palate Prosthesis; (1988) American Cleft Palate Association. **Publications:** *American Cleft Palate-Craniofacial Association Membership and Team Directory*, annual. Membership Directory. **Price:** available to members only. **Circulation:** 2,500 ● *American Cleft Palate-Craniofacial Association Newsletter*, quarterly. **Price:** included in membership dues. **Circulation:** 2,500. **Advertising:** accepted ● *Cleft Palate-Craniofacial Journal*, bimonthly. Includes research reports, book reviews, and commentaries. **Price:** included in membership dues; $110.00 /year for nonmembers; $145.00 /year for institutions. **Circulation:** 4,000. **Advertising:** accepted. **Conventions/Meetings:** annual meeting (exhibits) - 2008 Apr. 14-19, Philadelphia, PA ● symposium.

13758 ■ Center for Craniofacial Development and Disorders (CCDD)
733 N Broadway, Ste.411, Rm. 419
Baltimore, MD 21205
Ph: (410)955-4160
Fax: (410)502-5677
E-mail: ejabs1@jhem.jhmi.edu
URL: http://www.hopkinsmedicine.org/craniofacial
Contact: Ethylin Wang Jabs MD, Dir.
Founded: 1994. **Description:** Seeks to increase understanding of normal and abnormal craniofacial development, including cleft lip and palate, craniosynostosis, Apert and Crouzon syndromes. **Publications:** Brochures. **Conventions/Meetings:** symposium.

13759 ■ Children's Craniofacial Association (CCA)
13140 Coit Rd., Ste.307
Dallas, TX 75240
Ph: (214)570-9099
Free: (800)535-3643
Fax: (214)570-8811
E-mail: contactcca@ccakids.com
URL: http://www.ccakids.com
Contact: Rose Seitz, Chair
Founded: 1989. **Budget:** $400,000. **Description:** Participants include craniofacial surgeons and others wishing to aid individuals with craniofacial deformities. Promotes increased awareness of craniofacial deformities and their treatment among health care professionals and the public. Provides financial assistance to craniofacially deformed patients for costs related to treatment such as food, travel and lodging. Functions as a networking and referral service for patients. Makes referrals to qualified centers. Conducts craniofacial family workshops. **Additional Websites:** http://www.ccakids.org. **Formerly:** (1992) International Craniofacial Foundations. **Publications:** *CCAnetwork*, quarterly. Newsletter. Contains information on the latest craniofacial treatment. Alternate Formats: online ● Booklets. Provides information on craniofacial conditions and their treatment. ● Films ● Videos ● Also publishes materials for health care professionals, government officials, and parents of craniofacially deformed children. **Conventions/Meetings:** regional meeting and conference, for craniofacial families ● annual retreat.

13760 ■ Cleft Palate Foundation (CPF)
1504 E Franklin St., Ste.102
Chapel Hill, NC 27514-2820
Ph: (919)933-9044
Free: (800)242-5338
Fax: (919)933-9604
E-mail: info@cleftline.org
URL: http://www.cleftline.org
Contact: Nancy C. Smythe, Exec. Dir.
Founded: 1973. **Staff:** 4. **Budget:** $100,000. **Languages:** English, Spanish. **Description:** Enhances the quality of life for individuals with facial birth defects through education, research support, and facilitation of family-centered care. Provides research programs and information services. **Awards:** Parent-Patient Leadership Award. **Frequency:** annual. **Type:** monetary. **Recipient:** for outstanding contribution by individual or parent affected by facial birth defects. **Telecommunication Services:** electronic mail, ns-

mythe@acpa-cpf.org. **Funds:** CLEFTLINE Annual. **Affiliated With:** American Cleft Palate-Craniofacial Association. **Formerly:** (2000) American Cleft Palate Educational Foundation. **Publications:** *As You Get Older: Information for the Teenager Born with a Cleft Lip and/or Palate*. Booklet. **Price:** $2.00 each ● *Audiovisual and Supplemental Resource Catalog* ● *Cleft Lip and Cleft Palate: The First Four Years* (in English and Spanish). Booklet. **Price:** $2.00 ● *Cleft Lip and Cleft Palate - The School-Aged Child* (in English and Spanish). Booklet. **Price:** $2.00 ● *Cleft Lip and Palate: The Adult Patient*. Booklet ● *Cleft Palate and Hearing Loss*. Booklet ● *Cleft Palate-Craniofacial Journal*, bimonthly ● *Cleft Surgery* (in English and Spanish). Booklet ● *Feeding an Infant with a Cleft* (in English and Spanish). Booklet ● *For Parents of Newborn Babies with Cleft Lip/Palate* (in English and Spanish). Brochure ● *The Genetics of Cleft Lip and Palate: Information for Families*. Booklet. **Price:** $2.00 ● *Hemangiomas and Vascular Malformations*. Booklet ● *Information About Choosing a Cleft Palate or Craniofacial Team*. **Price:** free ● *Information About Crouzon's Disease*. **Price:** free ● *Information About Dental Care*. **Price:** free ● *Information About Financial Assistance*. **Price:** free ● *Information About Pierre Robin Malformation Sequence*. **Price:** free ● *Information About Submucous Cleft Palate*. **Price:** free ● *Information About Teacher Collins Syndrome*. **Price:** free ● *Information About Treatment for Adults with Cleft Lip and Palate*. **Price:** free. **Conventions/Meetings:** semiannual board meeting ● annual Parent-Patient Conference.

13761 ■ Craniofacial Foundation of America (CFA)
975 E 3rd St., Box 269
Chattanooga, TN 37403
Ph: (423)778-9192
Free: (800)418-3223
Fax: (423)778-8172
E-mail: info@craniofacialfoundation.org
URL: http://www.craniofacialfoundation.org
Contact: Terri Farmer, Exec. Dir.
Founded: 1989. **Description:** Dedicated to improving the lives of patients suffering from birth defects, tumors and trauma-related injuries affecting the shape and appearance of the face and skull.

13762 ■ Craniosynostosis and Positional Plagiocephaly Support (CAPPS)
6905 Xandu Ct.
Fredericksburg, VA 22407-2580
E-mail: cappsorg@aol.com
URL: http://www.cappskids.org
Contact: Jennifer Pitchke, Pres./Founder
Founded: 1999. **Description:** Provides support and information to families with children suffering from craniosynostosis and positional plagiocephaly. Aims to increase awareness through education, and ensures proper diagnosis and appropriate treatment for children afflicted with these conditions.

13763 ■ FACES: The National Craniofacial Association
PO Box 11082
Chattanooga, TN 37401
Free: (800)332-2373
E-mail: faces@faces-cranio.org
URL: http://www.faces-cranio.org
Founded: 1969. **Staff:** 3. **Budget:** $150,000. **Description:** Provides financial assistance for travel expenses to individuals with severe facial deformities resulting from congenital defects or accidents. Provides a resource file of available treatment centers, support groups, and general information concerning severe facial deformities. Is currently involved in an extensive fundraising campaign in order to increase awareness of the organization and to broaden its base of support. **Committees:** Client Review. **Formerly:** (1977) Debbie Fox Foundation for Treatment of Cranio-Facial Deformities; (1985) Debbie Fox Foundation; (1998) National Association for the Craniofacially Handicapped. **Publications:** *FACES*, quarterly. Newsletter. Provides information and support for craniofacially handicapped persons. Includes updates on clients and medical updates.

Price: free. **Circulation:** 15,000. **Advertising:** accepted ● *FACES Brochure.* Provides information on the organization. ● *So Brightly Within.* Video. **Price:** $20.00 donation. **Conventions/Meetings:** bimonthly board meeting.

13764 ■ Forward Face
317 E 34th St., Ste.901A
New York, NY 10016
Ph: (212)684-5860
Fax: (212)684-5864
E-mail: info@forwardface.org
URL: http://www.forwardface.org
Contact: Camille Walsh, Asst. Exec. Dir.
Founded: 1978. **Members:** 1,100. **Membership Dues:** individual, $30 (annual) ● life, $500 ● individual, $50 (biennial). **Staff:** 2. **State Groups:** 1. **Description:** Individuals with craniofacial disorders, their families and friends, and health care professionals. Provides medical, psychological, and financial support services. Facilitates communication and cooperation between patients and health care professionals; operates referral service. Offers workshops; conducts networking activities and children's services; also includes a support group, Inner Faces, specifically for teenagers and young adults; activities include communications workshops theatre productions and social functions. Operates family assistance fund to assist families with expenses not covered by insurance, such as lodging and transportation. **Libraries: Type:** reference. **Awards:** Forward Face. **Frequency:** annual. **Type:** scholarship. **Recipient:** for members ● The John McNeil Burns Scholarship. **Frequency:** annual. **Type:** scholarship. **Recipient:** for educational purposes. **Computer Services:** database ● mailing lists ● online services. **Committees:** Education; Networking/Outreach; Public Relations. **Affiliated With:** National Foundation for Facial Reconstruction. **Publications:** *Face Facts.* Videos ● *Forward Face Newsletter,* quarterly. **Price:** $20.00/year ● Brochures, quarterly. **Price:** included in membership dues. **Circulation:** 1,000 ● *My Face,* book about a child with Mobius Syndrome. **Conventions/Meetings:** quarterly Educational Forums - conference and workshop - fall/spring.

13765 ■ Freeman-Sheldon Parent Support Group (FSPSG)
509 Northmont Way
Salt Lake City, UT 84103
Ph: (801)364-7060
E-mail: fspsg@mail.burgoyne.com
URL: http://www.fspsg.org
Contact: Joyce Dolcourt, Exec. Dir.
Founded: 1982. **Members:** 150. **Staff:** 1. **Budget:** $1,000. **Multinational. Description:** Families affected by Freeman-Sheldon Syndrome; interested health professionals. (Freeman-Sheldon Syndrome, also known as Whistling Face Syndrome and Cranio-Carpo-Tarsal Dysplasia, is a disorder characterized by a flat, stiff, immobile face with excessively bulging cheeks, resembling that seen when whistling; retarded growth, flexion contraction of the fingers and thumbs, walking difficulties, and speech impairment may also be experienced. The syndrome is believed to be transmitted genetically.) Compiles information on the growth and development of individuals with Freeman-Sheldon Syndrome; disseminates information for parents of afflicted children. Operates referral services; promotes medical research. **Libraries: Type:** reference. **Subjects:** medical information. **Computer Services:** database, contains medical literature accessible through MEDLINE. **Affiliated With:** National Organization for Rare Disorders. **Publications:** Newsletter, annual. Updates members on research and news. **Circulation:** 225 ● Also publishes brochures. Bibliography of Medical Literature on Freeman-Sheldon syndrome.

13766 ■ Let's Face It USA (LFASU)
Univ. of Michigan
School of Dentistry
Dentistry Lib.
1011 North Univ.
Ann Arbor, MI 48109-1078

E-mail: faceit@umich.edu
URL: http://www.dent.umich.edu/faceit
Contact: Betsy Wilson, Founder/Dir.
Founded: 1987. **Staff:** 5. **Budget:** $30,000. **Description:** Provides information and support for people who have or who care for those with facial disfigurement. Website and annual publication with over 150 resources for professionals and families. Links to all related networks for specific conditions i.e. Genetic Disorders, Burns, Cancer, etc. **Publications:** *Resources for People with Facial Difference,* semiannual. Booklet. **Circulation:** 3,000.

13767 ■ National Foundation for Facial Reconstruction (NFFR)
317 E 34th St., Rm. 901
New York, NY 10016
Ph: (212)263-6656
Fax: (212)263-7534
E-mail: info@nffr.org
URL: http://www.nffr.org
Contact: Whitney Burnett, Exec. Dir.
Founded: 1951. **Staff:** 3. **Budget:** $1,300,000. **Description:** Assists individuals with a craniofacial deformity. Supports the treatment and rehabilitation efforts of the Institute of Reconstructive Plastic Surgery at New York University Medical center. Assists in patient care, research, the training and education of personnel engaged in reconstructive plastic surgery, conducts public education campaigns that promote national awareness of the problems of facial deformities and available treatment methods, and initiates and stimulates research. **Formerly:** (1986) Society for the Rehabilitation of the Facially Disfigured. **Publications:** Newsletter, annual. Reports on the rehabilitation of individuals with facial disfigurement. Includes case histories and research updates. **Price:** free. **Circulation:** 3,000.

13768 ■ Society of Craniofacial Genetics
c/o Virginia Kimonis, MD, Past Pres.
Children's Hosp.
300 Longwood Ave., Fegan 10
Boston, MA 02115
Ph: (617)355-4697
Fax: (617)730-0466
E-mail: vkimonis@uci.edu
URL: http://www.craniofacialgenetics.org
Contact: Virginia Kimonis MD, Past Pres.
Founded: 1975. **Membership Dues:** individual, $40 (annual). **Description:** Promotes education, research, and communication in normal and abnormal development of craniofacies. **Publications:** Newsletter. **Conventions/Meetings:** annual meeting and symposium.

13769 ■ Society for Craniofacial Morphometry
c/o Dr. Curtis K. Deutsch
Shriver Center
Harvard Medical School
200 Trapelo Rd.
Waltham, MA 02452-6332
Ph: (781)642-0163
Fax: (781)642-0196
E-mail: cdeutsch@shriver.org
URL: http://www.geocities.com/ResearchTriangle/Campus/7556/main.html
Contact: Dr. Curtis K. Deutsch, Contact
Description: Investigators and clinicians interested in measurements of normal craniofacial morphology and the methods to define dysmorphology of the head and face. **Telecommunication Services:** electronic mail, cdeutsch@bwh.harvard.edu. **Conventions/Meetings:** workshop.

13770 ■ Treacher Collins Foundation (TCF)
PO Box 683
Norwich, VT 05055-0683
Ph: (802)649-3050
Free: (800)TCF-2055
E-mail: hopecharkins@hotmail.com
Contact: Hope Charkins M.S.W., Exec.Dir.
Founded: 1988. **Staff:** 1. **Description:** Families, individuals, and professionals interested in developing and sharing knowledge about Treacher Collins

Syndrome and related conditions. (Treacher Collins Syndrome, also known as Franceschetti-Klein Syndrome, is a rare genetic condition involving underdevelopment of the structures of the head and face.) Promotes research to improve the quality of life of individuals with Treacher Collins Syndrome. Provides networking and support. Operates referral and resource listing service. **Libraries: Type:** reference. **Holdings:** audiovisuals, biographical archives, periodicals. **Subjects:** Treacher Collins Syndrome. **Divisions:** Cranofacial Advisory Board. **Formerly:** Treacher Collins Family Network. **Publications:** *Adults with Treacher Collins Syndrome Talk About Their Lives.* Video ● *American Resource List* ● *First Things First: Early Issues for Children with Treacher Collins Syndrome.* Video ● *Genetic Update: Treacher Collins Syndrome.* Offers information about the discovery of the gene which causes Treacher Collins; diagnostic and pre-natal testing; and TCF position on the discovery. ● *The Genetics of Treacher Collins Syndrome.* Video ● *Parents Talk About Treacher Collins Syndrome.* Video ● *The Psycho/Social Implications of Treacher Collins Syndrome.* Video ● *Rare Should Not Mean Alone.* Video. Covers Treacher Collins syndrome and the services of the foundation. ● *The Surgical Creation of an Ear.* Video ● *Terminology List* ● *Treacher Collins Syndrome - An Overview.* Booklet ● *Treacher Collins Syndrome: Nutrition, Feeding, and Eating.* Booklet ● Newsletter, annual. **Price:** donations accepted. **Circulation:** 500 ● Pamphlet ● Also publishes a networking list. **Conventions/Meetings:** periodic meeting.

13771 ■ World Craniofacial Foundation
7777 Forest Ln., Ste.C-621
PO Box 515838
Dallas, TX 75251-5838
Ph: (972)566-6669
Free: (800)533-3315
Fax: (972)566-3850
E-mail: worldcf@worldnet.att.net
URL: http://www.worldcf.org
Contact: Kenneth E. Salyer MD, Chm.
Description: Committed to helping children obtain craniofacial surgery. **Publications:** *Reflections,* quarterly. Newsletter. **Alternate Formats:** online.

Craniosacral Therapy

13772 ■ Craniosacral Therapy Association of North America (CSTA/NA)
c/o Clare Bonser, Admin. Dir.
852 Don Diego Ave.
Santa Fe, NM 87505
Ph: (505)820-1335
Fax: (505)820-1335
E-mail: info@craniosacraltherapy.org
URL: http://www.craniosacraltherapy.org
Contact: Michael Boxhall, Dir.
Founded: 1998. **Membership Dues:** graduate in U.S., $120 (annual) ● graduate in Canada, C$140 (annual) ● student in U.S., $50 (annual) ● student in Canada, C$65 (annual) ● associate in U.S., $75 (annual) ● associate in Canada, C$90 (annual) ● corporate/business in U.S., $250 (annual) ● corporate/business in Canada, C$330 (annual). **Multinational. Description:** Seeks to preserve the integrity of craniosacral therapy in relationship to "Breath of Life", promotes standards of biodynamic craniosacral therapy. **Telecommunication Services:** electronic mail, mboxhall@stillness.co.uk. **Publications:** Newsletter. **Conventions/Meetings:** conference.

Critical Care

13773 ■ Neurocritical Care Society (NCS)
5841 Cedar Lake Rd., Ste.204
Minneapolis, MN 55416
Ph: (952)646-2034
Fax: (952)545-6073

E-mail: info@neurocriticalcare.org
URL: http://www.neurocriticalcare.org
Contact: Michael N. Diringer MD, Pres.
Founded: 2002. **Membership Dues:** trainee, $100 (annual) ● affiliated, $150 (annual) ● physician, $250 (annual). **Multinational. Description:** Seeks to improve outcomes for patients with life-threatening neurological illnesses. Strives to identify and implement best medical practices for acute neurological disorders. Provides a forum for communication, collaboration, and exchange of ideas between physicians and allied health care professionals within different specialties. Fosters clinical, experimental, and outcomes research focused on developing medical and surgical interventions for acute neurological disorders. Develops standards for advanced fellowship training, program accreditation, and physician certification in the subspecialty of neurological intensive care. **Telecommunication Services:** electronic mail, diringerm@neuro.wustl.edu. **Publications:** *Currents*, quarterly. Newsletter. Provides information on key activities of the society. **Advertising:** accepted. Alternate Formats: online.

13774 ■ Society of Critical Care Medicine (SCCM)
701 Lee St., Ste.200
Des Plaines, IL 60016
Ph: (847)827-6869
Fax: (847)827-6886
E-mail: info@sccm.org
URL: http://www.sccm.org
Contact: David Julian Martin CAE, CEO/Exec. VP
Founded: 1970. **Members:** 13,000. **Membership Dues:** resident, fellow, $70 (annual) ● nurse, allied health professional, $120 (annual) ● outside U.S., $240 (annual) ● physician, $325 (annual). **Staff:** 50. **Budget:** $11,000,000. **Regional Groups:** 14. **Languages:** English, Spanish. **Multinational. Description:** Consists of physicians, nurses, scientists, technicians, respiratory therapists, engineers, pharmacists, physician's assistants and others involved in the field of critical care medicine. Aims to improve care for acute life-threatening illnesses and injuries; promote development of optimal care facilities; guarantee high educational standards in critical care medicine. Initiated self-assessment testing program in an effort to establish core curriculum and assist physicians in self-evaluation and established American College of Critical Care Medicine in 1988. **Awards:** American College of Critical Care Medicine Distinguished Investigator Award. **Frequency:** annual. **Type:** recognition. **Recipient:** for meritorious and pioneering research of an SCCM established clinical investigator ● Christer Grenvik Memorial Award. **Frequency:** annual. **Type:** monetary. **Recipient:** to an SCCM member who has promoted the ethical and humane delivery of critical care medicine ● ICU Design Citation. **Frequency:** annual. **Type:** recognition. **Recipient:** for a critical care unit that combines functional ICU design with the humanitarian delivery of critical care ● In-Training Award. **Frequency:** annual. **Type:** monetary. **Recipient:** for an author participating in critical care fellowship training program or who has completed a program not more than a year before the annual symposium ● Norma J. Shoemaker Award. **Frequency:** annual. **Type:** monetary. **Recipient:** to a nurse member, who demonstrates excellence in clinical practice, education, and/or administration ● Norma J. Shoemaker Grant. **Frequency:** annual. **Type:** grant. **Recipient:** for nursing research ● Shubin-Weil Award for Excellence. **Frequency:** annual. **Type:** recognition. **Recipient:** for outstanding clinician/teacher and a role model of excellence in teaching and the ethical practice of critical care medicine ● Young Investigator's Award. **Type:** recognition. **Divisions:** Education; Health Care Policy; Research. **Sections:** Anesthesiology; Clinical Pharmacology and Pharmacy; Emergency Medicine; In-Training; Industry and Technology; Neuroscience; Nursing; Osteopathic Medicine; Pediatrics; Physicians Assistants; Respiratory Care; Surgery; Uniformed Services. **Task Forces:** Cost Containment; Disaster Assistance; Distribution of ICU Resources; Ethics; Guidelines; ICU Management; Technology Assessment. **Publications:** *Critical Care*

Medicine, monthly. Journal. **Price:** $130.00 for nonmembers. ISSN: 0090-3493. **Circulation:** 15,000. **Advertising:** accepted ● *Critical Connections*, bimonthly. Newsletter. **Circulation:** 10,000. **Advertising:** accepted ● *Pediatric Critical Care Medicine*, bimonthly. Journal. **Advertising:** accepted. Alternate Formats: online. **Conventions/Meetings:** annual conference ● annual Critical Care Congress - meeting (exhibits) ● annual Critical Care Refresher Course - meeting ● annual Current Concepts in Pediatric Care - meeting ● annual Multidisciplinary Critical Care Board Review Course - meeting.

Cryonics

13775 ■ Alcor Life Extension Foundation (ALEF)
7895 E Acoma Dr., Ste.110
Scottsdale, AZ 85260-6916
Ph: (480)905-1906
Free: (877)462-5267
Fax: (480)922-9027
E-mail: stevevs@alcor.org
URL: http://www.alcor.org
Contact: Stephen Van Sickle, Exec. Dir.
Founded: 1972. **Members:** 820. **Membership Dues:** regular, $398 (annual) ● full-time student, additional family, $199 (annual) ● minor family, $100 (annual). **Staff:** 11. **Budget:** $1,100,000. **Regional Groups:** 10. **Multinational. Description:** Individuals who have made anatomical donation for purpose of being cryonically suspended. Seeks to extend lives of its members; currently 47 members in suspension. **Libraries: Type:** reference. **Holdings:** archival material. **Computer Services:** Information services, cryonics facts and resources ● online services, library. **Telecommunication Services:** electronic mail, dbora@alcor.org ● electronic mail, diane@alcor.org ● 24-hour hotline, emergency, (800)367-2228. **Committees:** Medical Advisory; Scientific Advisory. **Also Known As:** Alcor Foundation. **Publications:** *Alcor Life Extension Foundation: An Introduction*, biennial. Booklet. Covers cryonics, life extension, and immortality. **Price:** $8.95/year in U.S.; $20.00/year in Canada and Mexico; $25.00 other countries. ISSN: 1054-4305. **Circulation:** 1,000. **Advertising:** accepted ● *Alcor News*, periodic. Newsletter. **Price:** free. Alternate Formats: online ● *ALCOR: Reaching for Tomorrow*, quarterly. Magazine. Covers cryonics, life extension, and immortality. **Price:** $35.00/year in U.S.; $35.00/year in Canada and Mexico; $35.00/year in all other countries. ISSN: 1054-4305. **Circulation:** 1,000. **Advertising:** accepted ● *Cryonics*, bimonthly. Magazine. **Price:** included in membership dues; $35.00 /year for nonmembers. Alternate Formats: online ● Brochures. **Conventions/Meetings:** biennial Advancing Cryonics Technology Festival ● seminar.

13776 ■ American Cryonics Society (ACS)
PO Box 1509
Cupertino, CA 95015
Ph: (408)446-9001
Free: (800)523-2001
Fax: (801)720-9001
E-mail: cryonics@americancryonics.org
URL: http://www.americancryonics.org
Contact: Edgar Swank, Pres.
Founded: 1969. **Members:** 500. **Membership Dues:** student/associate in U.S. and Canada, $55 (annual) ● full, $378 (annual) ● lifeplus plan, $1,000 ● associate outside U.S. and Canada, $96 (annual). **Staff:** 2. **Budget:** $20,000. **Languages:** Chinese, English, French, German, Italian, Portuguese, Spanish. **Multinational. Description:** Individuals interested in life extension through cryonics (the practice of freezing a clinically dead human in hopes of bringing the person back to life when resuscitation or reconstruction is possible). Promotes education and provides information about cryonic suspension, suspended animation, and low-temperature medicine. Enables individuals to arrange for their own cryonic suspension. Sponsors research into suspended animation, life extension sciences, and low temperature medicine. Conducts

programs to freeze tissue samples from endangered species for possible future cloning. Maintains library; operates speakers' bureau; conducts charitable programs. **Libraries: Type:** open to the public. **Holdings:** 400; articles, books, papers, periodicals, video recordings. **Subjects:** life extension, cryonics, biostasis, suspended animation, science fiction. **Telecommunication Services:** electronic mail, cryonics@jps.net. **Committees:** Suspension Funds Management. **Affiliated With:** Immortalist Society. **Formerly:** (1985) Bay Area Cryonics Society. **Publications:** *American Cryonics*, semiannual. Journal. Features synopsis of research, national news and editorials affecting cryonics field. **Circulation:** 500. **Advertising:** accepted. Also Cited As: *ACS Digest* ● *American Cryonics News*, bimonthly. Newsletter. Covers cryonics and life extension. Includes calendar of events and research reports. **Price:** included in membership dues; $35.00 /year for nonmembers ● *The Immortalist*, monthly. Contains articles on cryonics, health, aging research, and science. **Circulation:** 400. **Conventions/Meetings:** annual Board of Governors Election and General Meeting, cryonic suspension training, association business.

13777 ■ Life Extension Society (LES)
990 N Powhatan St.
Arlington, VA 22205
Ph: (202)483-1760
E-mail: kfl071f@keithlynch.net
URL: http://keithlynch.net/les/index.html
Contact: Ronald Havelock, Pres.
Founded: 1992. **Members:** 25. **Membership Dues:** regular, $20 (annual). **Budget:** $1,500. **Description:** Individuals interested in life extension through nutritional supplementation or cryogenic preservation of remains. Provides educational materials; finances cryogenic training and equipment. Maintains speakers' bureau; conducts educational and research programs. **Publications:** *Life Extension Society News*, quarterly. Newsletter. Contains news of life extension and cryonics developments in the Mid-Atlantic. **Price:** $10.00/year. **Circulation:** 40. Alternate Formats: online. **Conventions/Meetings:** monthly board meeting and seminar.

Cytology

13778 ■ American Society of Cytopathology (ASC)
400 W 9th St., Ste.201
Wilmington, DE 19801
Ph: (302)429-8802
Fax: (302)429-8807
E-mail: asc@cytopathology.org
URL: http://www.cytopathology.org
Contact: Elizabeth A. Jenkins, Exec. Dir.
Founded: 1951. **Members:** 3,500. **Membership Dues:** medical, $248 (annual) ● junior medical, $90 (annual) ● scientist, cytotechnologist, $75 (annual) ● voting cytotechnologist, $95 (annual) ● affiliate, $45 (annual). **Staff:** 6. **Budget:** $1,000,000. **Description:** Physicians, cytotechnologists and scientists dedicated to the cytologic method of diagnostic pathology. **Awards:** Papanicoluau Award. **Frequency:** annual. **Type:** monetary. **Recipient:** for a cytopathologist selected by committee. **Computer Services:** database ● mailing lists. **Boards:** Foundation. **Committees:** Advocacy; Awards; Bylaws; Ethics and Conduct; Long Range Planning; Nominating; Public Information; Scientific Program. **Formerly:** Inter-Society Cytology Council; American Society of Cytology. **Publications:** *Annual Meeting Abstract Book*. Alternate Formats: online ● *The ASC Bulletin*, bimonthly. **Price:** included in membership dues. **Advertising:** accepted ● *Cancer Cytopathology*, bimonthly. Journal ● *Consider a Career in Cytotechnology*. Brochure ● Annual Report, annual. Alternate Formats: online. **Conventions/Meetings:** seminar ● workshop ● annual Scientific Meeting - conference (exhibits) - 2007 Nov. 2-7, Houston, TX; 2008 Nov. 7-12, Orlando, FL; 2009 Nov. 13-18, Denver, CO.

13779 ■ American Society for Cytotechnology (ASCT)
1500 Sunday Dr., Ste.102
Raleigh, NC 27607
Ph: (919)861-5571
Free: (800)948-3947
Fax: (919)787-4916
E-mail: info@asct.com
URL: http://www.asct.com
Contact: Kalyani Naik, Pres.
Founded: 1979. **Members:** 1,500. **Membership Dues:** general/associate, $50 (annual) ● student, $20 (annual). **Staff:** 3. **Regional Groups:** 10. **Description:** Cytotechnologists (technologists trained in the identification of cells and cellular abnormalities such as cancer), students of cytotechnology, and medical doctors in the field of cytopathology. Seeks to: enhance the role of the cytotechnologist in the health care system; stimulate communication and cooperation among cytotechnologists and other health professionals; inform members of current legislative and legal issues pertaining to the profession of cytotechnology and other related professions; support and promote educational opportunities. Urges participation in educational programs available through the American Society of Cytopathology (see separate entry). **Computer Services:** Mailing lists. **Committees:** Annual Meeting; Bylaws/Historical; Education; Legal Counsel; Legislative Consultant; Long Range Planning; Professional Stand/Practice; Public Relations; Publications. **Publications:** ASCT News, 8/year. Newsletter. Covers educational, legislative, and other developments affecting the profession. Includes book reviews, calendar of events and employment listings. **Price:** available to members only. **Advertising:** accepted. **Conventions/Meetings:** annual conference (exhibits) - usually spring.

13780 ■ International Federation of Societies for Histochemistry and Cytochemistry (IFSHC)
c/o Denis G. Baskin, PhD, Pres.
PO Box 357420
Seattle, WA 98195-9420
Ph: (206)616-5894
Fax: (206)616-5842
E-mail: baskindg@u.washington.edu
URL: http://www.ifshc.org
Contact: Denis G. Baskin PhD, Pres.
Founded: 1960. **Members:** 22. **Staff:** 5. **National Groups:** 22. **Languages:** Chinese, English, French, German, Italian, Japanese, Russian, Spanish. **Multinational. Description:** Members are national societies for histochemistry and cytochemistry. Seeks to promote communication and cooperation among scientists throughout the world and to establish histochemistry and cytochemistry institutes. Promotes histochemistry and cytochemistry as basic, independent sciences and advocates their teaching in universities. Appoints committees for the study of scientific matters requiring international collaboration. Sponsors International Congresses of Histochemistry and Cytochemistry every four years. **Awards:** David Glick Lectureship. **Frequency:** quadrennial. **Type:** scholarship. **Recipient:** for significant contribution to histochemistry ● Paul Nakane Prize. **Frequency:** quadrennial. **Type:** monetary. **Recipient:** for outstanding international contributions in the field of histochemistry and cytochemistry ● Young Histochemist Awards. **Frequency:** quadrennial. **Type:** monetary. **Recipient:** for new investigators from societies with paid-up dues to travel to International Congress of Histochemistry and Cytochemistry. **Publications:** Proceedings, quadrennial. **Advertising:** accepted. **Conventions/Meetings:** quadrennial International Congress of Histochemistry and Cytochemistry (exhibits) ● periodic symposium.

Data Processing

13781 ■ American Medical Informatics Association (AMIA)
4915 St. Elmo Ave., Ste.401
Bethesda, MD 20814
Ph: (301)657-1291

Fax: (301)657-1296
E-mail: mail@amia.org
URL: http://www.amia.org
Contact: Karen Greenwood, Exec. VP
Founded: 1990. **Members:** 3,200. **Membership Dues:** regular, $250 (annual) ● retired, $100 (annual) ● student, $35 (annual) ● institutional, $450 (annual) ● affiliate, $75 (annual). **Staff:** 12. **Budget:** $2,500,000. **Description:** Medical personnel, physicians, physical scientists, engineers, data processors, researchers, educators, hospital administrators, nurses, medical record administrators, and computer professionals. Objectives are: to apply advanced systems and information technologies to scientific, literary, and educational activities; to promote excellence in health care; to promote patient care, teaching, research, and health administration. **Awards: Frequency:** annual. **Type:** recognition. **Computer Services:** Mailing lists. **Working Groups:** Anesthesiology/Critical Care and Emergency Medicine; Automated Encoding/Electronic Patient Records; Clinical Computing; Computerized Medical Records; Dental Informatics; Education; Family Practice/Primary Care; Hospital/Medical Information Systems; Medical Imaging Systems; Nursing Informatics; Prevention and Health Evaluation Informatics; Student. **Formed by Merger of:** (1990) American Association for Medical Systems and Informatics; American College of Medical Informatics; Symposium on Computer Applications in Medical Care. **Publications:** Journal of the American Medical Informatics Association, bimonthly. Alternate Formats: online ● Proceedings of Annual Symposium, annual. Book. Contains abstracts of sessions of the association's annual symposium. **Price:** $95.00 plus shipping and handling. **Conventions/Meetings:** annual Biomedical & Health Informatics: From Foundation to Applications - symposium (exhibits).

13782 ■ Health Industry Business Communications Council (HIBCC)
2525 E Arizona Biltmore Cir., Ste.127
Phoenix, AZ 85016
Ph: (602)381-1091
Fax: (602)381-1093
E-mail: info@hibcc.org
URL: http://www.hibcc.org
Contact: Robert A. Hankin PhD, Pres./CEO
Founded: 1983. **Members:** 1,000. **Membership Dues:** corresponding, $150 (annual) ● corporate, $2,500 (annual). **Staff:** 7. **Budget:** $1,000,000. **Description:** Individuals and companies in the health care industry. Aims to improve the quality and economic efficiency of health care by instituting and overseeing a uniform system of computer bar coding (for identification of health care equipment) and by promoting the use of this and other automated technologies in the health care industry. **Formerly:** (1987) Health Industry Bar Code Council. **Publications:** Health Industry Lines, quarterly. Newsletter. **Price:** included in membership dues. **Circulation:** 1,600. **Advertising:** accepted. Alternate Formats: online ● HIN 101: A Quick Guide to Using the Health Industry Number System. Brochure. Alternate Formats: online ● Standards, periodic ● UPNs and Bar Code Labeling. Brochure. Alternate Formats: online ● Papers. Alternate Formats: online. **Conventions/Meetings:** annual conference (exhibits).

Death and Dying

13783 ■ Palliative Care Policy Center (PCPC)
RAND Hea.
1200 S Hayes St., Ste.6402
Arlington, VA 22202-5050
Ph: (703)413-1100
Fax: (703)413-8111
E-mail: info@medicaring.org
URL: http://www.medicaring.org
Contact: Anne Wilkinson PhD, Dir.
Description: Works to create quality improvement projects in end of life care, called MediCaring. **Affiliated With:** Americans for Better Care of the Dying; Institute for Healthcare Improvement. **Formerly:** Cen-

ter to Improve Care of the Dying; (2006) Washington Home Center for Palliative Care Studies. **Publications:** Brochure.

13784 ■ Rallying Points
Address Unknown since 2007
Description: Works to assist community-based coalitions in improving care and caring for those nearing the end of life. **Publications:** Survey report. **Conventions/Meetings:** annual conference.

Dentistry

13785 ■ Academy of Dental Materials (ADM)
21 Grouse Terr.
Lake Oswego, OR 97035
Ph: (503)636-0861
Fax: (503)675-2738
E-mail: admtreas@comcast.net
URL: http://www.academydentalmaterials.org
Contact: Thomas Hilton, Treas.
Founded: 1940. **Members:** 350. **Membership Dues:** regular, fellow, student, $175 (annual). **Budget:** $80,000. **Description:** Active members are licensed dentists, members of academic institutions, industrial employees, and individuals active or interested in dental materials. Coordinates activities relating to the use of dental materials. **Awards:** Academy of Dental Materials Founder's Award. **Frequency:** annual. **Type:** medal. **Recipient:** for individuals who have provided meritorious service to the academy ● Academy of Dental Materials Students Awards. **Frequency:** annual. **Type:** recognition. **Recipient:** for outstanding students or student researchers in the field of dental materials ● Paffenbager Research Award. **Frequency:** annual. **Type:** recognition. **Recipient:** for the best student research paper presented at the meeting. **Formerly:** (1983) American Academy for Plastics Research in Dentistry. **Publications:** ADM Newsletter, 3/year ● Dental Materials, bimonthly. Journal. Covers scientific research. **Price:** included in membership dues; $195.00 for nonmembers. ISSN: 0109-5641. **Circulation:** 900. **Advertising:** accepted. Alternate Formats: microform ● Transactions of the Academy of Dental Materials ● Directory, periodic. **Conventions/Meetings:** annual conference, dental products/equipment and research equipment (exhibits) ● annual meeting and seminar.

13786 ■ Academy of Dentistry International (ADI)
3813 Gordon Creek Dr.
Hicksville, OH 43526
Ph: (419)542-0101
Fax: (419)542-6883
E-mail: rramus@bright.net
URL: http://www.adint.org
Contact: Robert L. Ramus DDS, Exec. Dir.
Founded: 1974. **Members:** 2,700. **Membership Dues:** active, retired, distinguished, honorary, $80 (annual). **Staff:** 2. **Budget:** $130,000. **Regional Groups:** 10. **State Groups:** 4. **National Groups:** 55. **Description:** Dentists; membership by invitation only. Works to further dentistry and the prevention of dental diseases worldwide. Disseminates and promotes the exchange of scientific information and fosters research. **Awards:** Award of Distinction. **Frequency:** annual. **Type:** recognition. **Recipient:** for individuals who distinguished themselves in the field of continuing dental education ● **Type:** fellowship. **Recipient:** for an individual who has made outstanding contributions to his/her community and to the advancement of the dental profession ● Hillenbrand Award. **Frequency:** annual. **Type:** recognition. **Recipient:** for an individual who has demonstrated exceptional devotion to the affairs of the academy ● Humanitarian Award. **Frequency:** annual. **Type:** recognition. **Recipient:** for individuals who have significant contributions to the enhancement of the quality of life and human condition ● International Dentist of the Year. **Frequency:** annual. **Type:** recognition. **Recipient:** for individuals who exemplify international leadership. **Councils:** Executive. **Publications:** International Communicator, semiannual. Newsletter. **Price:**

included in membership dues. ISSN: 1057-5237. **Circulation:** 2,600. **Conventions/Meetings:** annual Continuing Education - symposium ● annual Convocation - assembly, induction of new fellows and honoring awardees ● annual Orientation - seminar.

13787 ■ Academy of General Dentistry (AGD)

211 E Chicago Ave., Ste.900
Chicago, IL 60611-1999
Ph: (312)440-4300 (312)440-4308
Free: (888)243-3368
Fax: (312)440-0559
E-mail: msc@agd.org
URL: http://www.agd.org
Contact: Bruce DeGinder DDS, Pres.
Founded: 1952. **Members:** 37,000. **Membership Dues:** active/associate, $334 (annual) ● affiliate, $167 (annual) ● student, $15 (annual) ● graduate, $67-$267 (annual) ● resident, $67 (annual). **Staff:** 85. **Budget:** $10,000,000. **Regional Groups:** 20. **State Groups:** 62. **Local Groups:** 35. **Description:** Seeks to serve the needs and represent the interest of general dentists. Fosters their dentists' continued proficiency through quality continuing dental education to better serves the public. **Awards:** Distinguished Service Award. **Frequency:** annual. **Type:** recognition. **Publications:** *AGD Impact*, 11/year. Magazine. Covers issues, legislation, and trends that affect the practice and role of dentistry in the health care community. **Price:** included in membership dues; $25.00 /year for nonmembers. ISSN: 0194-729X. **Circulation:** 36,000. **Advertising:** accepted ● *Dentalnotes*, quarterly. Newsletter. Provides information on the latest dental issues and trends; intended for the national media and to be displayed in dentists' reception areas. **Price:** $20.00 /year for members; $40.00 /year for nonmembers. **Circulation:** 540 ● *General Dentistry*, bimonthly. Journal. Provides research and clinical reports for the continuing education of general dentists. Contains advertisers' index, book reviews, and quizzes. **Price:** included in membership dues; $30.00 /year for nonmembers. ISSN: 0363-6771. **Circulation:** 65,000. **Advertising:** accepted. Alternate Formats: microform. **Conventions/Meetings:** annual meeting (exhibits) - 2008 July 16-20, Orlando, FL.

13788 ■ Academy for Implants and Transplants (AIT)

2250 Clarenden Blvd.
Arlington, VA 22201
Ph: (703)841-0300
Fax: (703)841-1570
URL: http://www.ada.org/ada/organizations
Contact: Dr. Anthony J. Viscido, Sec.-Treas.
Founded: 1972. **Members:** 180. **Membership Dues:** regular, $150 (annual). **Regional Groups:** 15. **Description:** Represents the interests of dentists united to motivate and assist men and women in the general practice of dentistry in the field of implants and transplants. Encourages and promotes the art and science of implant and transplant dentistry. Assists in research in the fields of implant and transplant dentistry. Conducts seminars. Teaches implantology. **Libraries: Type:** not open to the public. **Subjects:** implant and transplant dentistry. **Awards:** Honorary Fellowship. **Frequency:** periodic. **Type:** fellowship. **Recipient:** for qualified dental educators and leaders in implantology ● **Frequency:** annual. **Type:** recognition. **Computer Services:** Mailing lists. **Publications:** *Implant Update*, quarterly. Newsletter. Discusses developments in the field of implant and transplant dentistry. **Price:** included in membership dues. **Circulation:** 268 ● Journal, periodic. **Conventions/Meetings:** annual convention (exhibits).

13789 ■ Academy of Laser Dentistry (ALD)

PO Box 8667
Coral Springs, FL 33075
Ph: (954)346-3776
Free: (877)527-3776
Fax: (954)757-2598
E-mail: memberservices@laserdentistry.org
URL: http://www.laserdentistry.org
Contact: Gail S. Siminovsky, Exec. Dir.
Founded: 1993. **Members:** 1,200. **Membership Dues:** active, institutional, $395 (annual) ● affiliate,

non-practicing, associate individual, $150 (annual) ● student, $50 (annual). **Staff:** 5. **National Groups:** 5. **Description:** Dentists, hygienists, dental academicians and researchers, and corporate laser and laser accessory dental vendors. Promotes clinical education, research, and development of standards and guidelines for the safe and ethical use of dental laser technology. Conducts educational programs. Provides certification. **Awards: Frequency:** annual. **Type:** recognition. **Formed by Merger of:** American Academy of Laser Dentistry. **Publications:** *Lightwaves*, quarterly. Newsletter. **Price:** included in membership dues ● *Wavelengths*, quarterly. Journal. Contains clinical case studies, industry and academy news. **Price:** included in membership dues. **Advertising:** accepted ● Directory. **Price:** included in membership dues. **Conventions/Meetings:** annual conference, with dental industry vendors (exhibits).

13790 ■ Academy of Operative Dentistry (AOD)

c/o Dr. Gregory E. Smith, Sec.
PO Box 14996
Gainesville, FL 32604-2996
E-mail: greg679@cox.net
URL: http://operativedentistry.com
Contact: Dr. Gregory E. Smith, Sec.
Founded: 1972. **Members:** 1,000. **Membership Dues:** active, $130 (annual). **Budget:** $100,000. **Description:** Dentists and persons in allied industries. Seeks to ensure quality in all of operative dentistry, teaching, service and research. **Libraries: Type:** reference. **Awards:** Award of Excellence. **Frequency:** annual. **Type:** recognition. **Recipient:** for teaching and service to the academy ● Buocore Memorial Lecture. **Frequency:** annual. **Type:** recognition ● Hollenback Prize. **Frequency:** annual. **Type:** recognition. **Recipient:** for contributions to operative dentistry by a dentist and by a dental student. **Publications:** *Membership Roster*, periodic. Membership Directory ● *Operative Dentistry*, bimonthly. Journal. **Conventions/Meetings:** seminar ● annual meeting - 2008 Feb. 13-15, Chicago, IL; 2009 Feb. 25-27, Chicago, IL; 2010 Feb. 17-19, Chicago, IL.

13791 ■ Academy of Oral Dynamics (AOD)

134 E Church Rd.
Elkins Park, PA 19027-2208
Ph: (215)635-2336
URL: http://www.ada.org/ada/organizations
Contact: Dr. Richard B. Bradway, Pres.
Founded: 1950. **Members:** 75. **Membership Dues:** associate, $15 (annual) ● active, $25 (annual). **Languages:** English, Japanese. **Description:** Represents dentists. Promotes the study of oral dynamics, especially as it applies to the use of natural teeth in restoring and maintaining a healthy, functioning mouth; disseminates information gained through research. Conducts educational programs. **Publications:** none. **Libraries: Type:** reference. **Subjects:** case histories, records developing. **Committees:** Clinic; Nomenclature; Scientific Investigation. **Formerly:** (1950) International Academy of Oral Dynamics. **Conventions/Meetings:** annual Membership and Scientific Presentation - meeting, held in conjunction with the District of Columbia Dental Society Spring Meeting.

13792 ■ Academy of Osseointegration (AO)

85 W Algonquin Rd., Ste.550
Arlington Heights, IL 60005
Ph: (847)439-1919
Free: (800)656-7736
Fax: (847)439-1569
E-mail: academy@osseo.org
URL: http://www.osseo.org
Contact: Kevin P. Smith, Exec. Dir.
Founded: 1987. **Members:** 4,500. **Membership Dues:** affiliate/active, $355 (annual) ● student, $75 (annual). **Staff:** 8. **Budget:** $2,200,000. **Description:** Works for the advancement of osseointegration among dentists, physicians and related professionals. Conducts research and educational programs; disseminates information to the public and medical agencies; provides a forum for interdisciplinary discussions. **Libraries: Type:** not open to the public.

Holdings: audiovisuals. **Subjects:** implantology, osseointegration. **Awards:** Osseointegration Foundation Implant Research Grant. **Frequency:** annual. **Type:** grant ● Osseointegration Foundation Patient Care Grants. **Type:** grant. **Computer Services:** database, IMIS ● mailing lists ● online services. **Publications:** *Academy News*, bimonthly. Newsletter. **Advertising:** accepted ● *International Journal of Oral & Maxillofacial Implants*, bimonthly. Includes current information related to the management of patients utilizing implant modalities. **Price:** $118.00 in U.S.; $158.00 outside U.S. ISSN: 0882-2786. **Circulation:** 7,200. **Advertising:** accepted. Alternate Formats: CD-ROM. **Conventions/Meetings:** annual conference, scientific and research presentations, table clinics, poster sessions (exhibits).

13793 ■ Alliance of the American Dental Association (AADA)

211 E Chicago Ave., Ste.730
Chicago, IL 60611
Ph: (312)440-2865
Free: (800)621-8099
Fax: (312)440-2587
E-mail: aada@allianceada.org
URL: http://www.allianceada.org
Contact: Krystine Hansen, Exec. Dir.
Founded: 1955. **Members:** 12,000. **Membership Dues:** individual, $50 (annual) ● student spouse, $5 (annual) ● spouse, $23 (annual). **Staff:** 2. **Budget:** $300,000. **State Groups:** 32. **Local Groups:** 160. **Description:** Spouses of dentists. Promotes public dental health and creates public awareness of dentistry. Conducts preventive dental health education programs and assists organized dentistry in encouraging state and national legislation that benefits the public and dentistry. Maintains legislative projects and leadership skill development. **Libraries: Type:** reference. **Subjects:** dental health education. **Awards:** American Dental Political Action Committee Award. **Frequency:** annual. **Type:** monetary. **Recipient:** for outstanding work in the four categories of political action ● Beulah K. Spencer New Member Service Award. **Frequency:** annual. **Type:** recognition. **Recipient:** for outstanding contributions to the community ● Dental Health Education Awards. **Frequency:** annual. **Type:** monetary. **Recipient:** for outstanding work in the five categories of dental health education ● Legislative Awards. **Frequency:** annual. **Type:** monetary. **Recipient:** for component and constituent legislative activities ● Membership Awards. **Frequency:** annual. **Type:** monetary. **Recipient:** for components' and constituents' recruitment efforts ● Newsletter Awards. **Frequency:** annual. **Type:** monetary. **Recipient:** for component and constituent publications ● Public Relations Awards. **Frequency:** annual. **Type:** monetary. **Recipient:** for components' and constituents' public relations efforts ● Student Spouse Awards. **Frequency:** annual. **Type:** monetary. **Recipient:** for student spouse members ● Thelma J. Neff Distinguished Service Award. **Frequency:** annual. **Type:** recognition. **Recipient:** for outstanding contributions to the community. **Formerly:** Auxiliary to the American Dental Association; (1982) Women's Auxiliary to the American Dental Association. **Publications:** *Key*, quarterly. Newsletter. Serves as the main conduit of information from the Alliance to its members. ISSN: 1075-9794. **Circulation:** 12,000. **Advertising:** accepted. **Conventions/Meetings:** annual convention - 2008 Oct. 15-19, San Antonio, TX; 2009 Sept. 29-Oct. 4, Honolulu, HI ● annual Leadership Conference, with educational conference - 2008 Apr. 16-19, St. Louis, MO ● annual meeting.

13794 ■ American Academy of Cosmetic Dentistry (AACD)

5401 World Dairy Dr.
Madison, WI 53718
Ph: (608)222-8583
Free: (800)543-9220
Fax: (608)222-9540
E-mail: info@aacd.com
URL: http://www.aacd.com
Contact: Mr. Robert A. Hall CAE, Exec. Dir.
Founded: 1984. **Members:** 6,300. **Membership Dues:** student, $20 (annual) ● resident, hygienist,

recent graduate dentist, dental assistant, $95 (annual) ● full-time faculty, $115 (annual) ● doctor, laboratory technician/owner, supporting, $395 (annual) ● corporate gold, $2,500 (annual). **Staff:** 18. **Budget:** $5,000,000. **Description:** Cosmetic dentists. Seeks to advance the study, teaching, and practice of cosmetic dentistry. Facilitates exchange of information among members; conducts educational programs. **Computer Services:** Mailing lists, of members for rental. **Publications:** *Journal of Cosmetic Dentistry*, quarterly. Contains articles on clinical advice and practice development. **Price:** $25.00 for nonmembers; free for members. **Circulation:** 6,500. **Advertising:** accepted. Also Cited As: *JCD*. **Conventions/Meetings:** annual conference (exhibits).

13795 ■ American Academy of Dental Group Practice (AADGP)
2525 E Arizona Biltmore Cir., Ste.127
Phoenix, AZ 85016
Ph: (602)381-1185
Fax: (602)381-1093
E-mail: info@aadgp.org
URL: http://www.aadgp.org
Contact: Dr. Alan Slutsky, Pres.

Founded: 1973. **Members:** 2,000. **Membership Dues:** group/individual, $150 (annual) ● government/educational organization, $100 (annual) ● corporate/associate, $500 (annual). **Staff:** 2. **Budget:** $500,000. **Description:** Active dentists and dental group practices. Purpose is to improve the level of dental service provided by members through exchanging and expanding of ideas and techniques for patient treatment and practice administration. Promotes group practice and research; accumulates and disseminates information; seeks to achieve the proper recognition for the aims and goals of group practice. Helps support an accreditation program as a system of voluntary peer review. **Publications:** *AADGP Contact*, quarterly. Newsletter. **Price:** included in membership dues. **Circulation:** 1,500. **Advertising:** accepted ● Membership Directory, annual. **Price:** $50.00/copy. **Conventions/Meetings:** annual conference (exhibits).

13796 ■ American Academy of Dental Practice Administration (AADPA)
c/o Kathleen S. Uebel, Exec. Dir.
1063 Whippoorwill Ln.
Palatine, IL 60067-7064
Ph: (847)934-4404
Fax: (847)934-4410
E-mail: executivedirector@aadpa.org
URL: http://www.aadpa.org
Contact: Kathleen S. Uebel, Exec. Dir.

Founded: 1956. **Members:** 250. **Description:** Professional society of dentists interested in efficient administration of dental practice. Offers educational programs. **Publications:** *American Academy of Dental Practice Administration—Communicator*, 3/year. Newsletter ● *American Academy of Dental Practice Administration—Roster*, annual. Directory ● *Essay Tapes*, annual. **Type:** annual meeting (exhibits).

13797 ■ American Academy of Esthetic Dentistry (AAED)
737 N Michigan Ave., Ste.2100
Chicago, IL 60611
Ph: (312)981-6770
Fax: (312)981-6787
E-mail: info@estheticacademy.org
URL: http://www.estheticacademy.org
Contact: Mr. Joseph Jackson, Exec. Dir.

Founded: 1975. **Members:** 138. **Membership Dues:** associate and active, $1,200 (annual). **Staff:** 5. **Description:** Aims to promote the integration of dental esthetics into the total spectrum of oral health care and provide a leadership role for the profession by defining the highest interdisciplinary clinical, scientific, artistic and ethical standards through research, publications and educational presentations. **Awards:** AAED Research Grant. **Frequency:** annual. **Type:** grant. **Publications:** *Journal of Esthetic and Restorative Dentistry*, bimonthly. **Advertising:** accepted.

Conventions/Meetings: annual convention and meeting, for all dental professionals.

13798 ■ American Academy of Fixed Prosthodontics (AAFP)
PO Box 1409
Bodega Bay, CA 94923-1409
Ph: (707)875-3040
Free: (800)860-5633
Fax: (707)875-2927
E-mail: secaafp@comcast.net
URL: http://www.fixedprosthodontics.org
Contact: Dr. Robert S. Staffanou, Sec.

Founded: 1951. **Members:** 584. **Membership Dues:** active in Canada, $500 (annual) ● active in U.S., $449 (annual) ● active outside U.S. and Canada, $501 (annual). **Staff:** 2. **Budget:** $320,000. **Multinational. Description:** Dentists. Provides 2-day professional continuing education course in the specialty of fixed prosthodontics. **Libraries: Type:** not open to the public. **Awards:** Baker Teaching Award. **Frequency:** annual. **Type:** recognition. **Recipient:** for outstanding achievement in the art and science of fixed prosthodontic ● Moulton Achievement Award. **Type:** recognition ● Tylman Research Grants (prosthodontic residents). **Frequency:** annual. **Type:** monetary. **Recipient:** for graduate students studying in the specialty of prosthodontics. **Telecommunication Services:** information service, (866)254-0280. **Committees:** Baker Teaching Award; Budget & Finance; Bylaws; Credentials; Editor; Ethics; Exhibits; Future Planning; Future Planning and Policy; Historical; Information Technology; Local Announcements; Moulton Award; Program; Publicity & Communications; Research; Table Clinics; Tylman Award. **Formerly:** (1991) American Academy of Crown and Bridge Prosthodontics. **Publications:** *Journal of Prosthetic Dentistry*, monthly. **Price:** included in membership dues ● *Meeting Program/Directory*, annual ● Newsletter, semiannual. **Price:** included in membership dues. **Circulation:** 600. **Conventions/Meetings:** annual meeting (exhibits) - always February ● annual Scientific Session - lecture.

13799 ■ American Academy of Gnathologic Orthopedics (AAGO)
Box 687
Arnold, CA 95223
Free: (800)510-AAGO
Fax: (209)795-1610
E-mail: info@aago.com
URL: http://www.aago.com
Contact: Ms. Jennifer Menafee, Sec.

Founded: 1970. **Members:** 700. **Membership Dues:** regular, $350 (annual). **Staff:** 1. **Budget:** $50,000. **Regional Groups:** 9. **State Groups:** 16. **Description:** Dentists dealing with the prevention or correction of malocclusion and bony malformation of the jaw and face. Conducts activities in the fields of maxillofacial orthopedics/orthodontics and preventative and corrective orthodontics. **Libraries: Type:** reference. **Holdings:** books, clippings, periodicals. **Awards:** Wiebrecht Award. **Type:** recognition. **Committees:** Certified Member Examination; Documentation. **Publications:** *American Academy of Gnathologic Orthopedics—Journal*, quarterly. Includes scientific articles and case reports on orthodontic treatment. **Price:** $80.00 in U.S., plus postage; $85.00 in Canada; $100.00 outside U.S. and Canada. ISSN: 0886-1064. **Circulation:** 400. **Advertising:** accepted ● *American Academy of Gnathologic Orthopedics—Membership Roster*, annual. Membership Directory. **Price:** included in membership dues. **Circulation:** 400 ● Articles. Contains information on the Crozat Method. **Conventions/Meetings:** annual conference (exhibits).

13800 ■ American Academy of Gold Foil Operators (AAGFO)
c/o Dr. David F. Bridgeman, Pres.
701 N Main St.
New Martinsville, WV 26155
Ph: (740)483-9096

E-mail: dbnbigvl@orvis.net
URL: http://www.goldfoil.org
Contact: Dr. David F. Bridgeman, Pres.

Founded: 1952. **Members:** 285. **Membership Dues:** individual, $60 (annual). **Staff:** 1. **Description:** Dentists who perform restorative procedures utilizing gold foil, cast gold, and the rubber dam. Formulates and applies new ideas for research on gold restorations and the rubber dam; encourages members of the dental profession and research institutions in the armed forces, government, dental schools, and private enterprise to study gold restorations and rubber dam procedures. Presents chair demonstrations at dental schools. **Awards:** Distinguished Member. **Frequency:** annual. **Type:** recognition. **Recipient:** for member service ● Outstanding Clinician Award. **Frequency:** annual. **Type:** recognition. **Recipient:** for a younger member who displays special clinical or didactic skills ● Student Achievement Award. **Frequency:** annual. **Type:** recognition. **Recipient:** to outstanding graduating dental students for proficiency in gold foil and cast gold procedures. **Committees:** Constitution and Bylaws; Education and Clinical Seminars; Literature and Research; Nominating; Public Relations; Scientific Sessions. **Publications:** *Gold Leaf*, semiannual ● *Journal of Operative Dentistry*, bimonthly ● Directory, biennial ● Also prepares slides, charts, models, and written materials. **Conventions/Meetings:** annual lecture and meeting, for dental instrument manufacturers (exhibits).

13801 ■ American Academy of the History of Dentistry (AAHD)
c/o Marc B. Ehrlich, DMD, Sec.-Treas.
1371 Beacon St.
Brookline, MA 02446
Ph: (617)566-2734
E-mail: info@histden.org
URL: http://www.histden.org
Contact: Marc B. Ehrlich DMD, Sec.-Treas.

Founded: 1951. **Members:** 300. **Membership Dues:** regular in U.S., $65 (annual) ● regular in Canada and Mexico, $70 (annual) ● regular (other countries), $75 (annual). **Budget:** $10,000. **Regional Groups:** 1. **Description:** Seeks to stimulate interest, study, and research in the history of dentistry and promote the teaching of dental history. **Libraries: Type:** reference. **Holdings:** 600; papers. **Subjects:** general history, dentistry, medicine, artifacts. **Awards:** Bremner Award. **Frequency:** annual. **Type:** monetary. **Recipient:** for dental students only. **Committees:** Bremner Student Awards for Historical Essays; Hayden-Harris Award; Teaching Dental History and Ethics. **Publications:** *Journal of the History of Dentistry*, 3/year. Includes articles on the history of dentistry, book reviews, and 5 year cumulative index. **Price:** $55.00/year for nonmembers; included in membership dues. ISSN: 0007-5132. **Circulation:** 750. **Advertising:** accepted. **Conventions/Meetings:** annual meeting and conference.

13802 ■ American Academy of Implant Dentistry (AAID)
211 E Chicago Ave., Ste.750
Chicago, IL 60611
Ph: (312)335-1550
Free: (877)335-2243
Fax: (312)335-9090
E-mail: aaid@aaid-implant.org
URL: http://www.aaid-implant.org
Contact: J. Vincent Shuck, Exec. Dir.

Founded: 1951. **Members:** 2,200. **Membership Dues:** general, $295 (annual) ● student/resident, $50 (annual). **Staff:** 6. **Budget:** $1,100,000. **Regional Groups:** 4. **Description:** Works to further scientific research and development in the field of implantology. **Awards: Type:** recognition. **Recipient:** for three separate research achievements. **Telecommunication Services:** electronic mail, jvshuck@aaid.com. **Formerly:** American Academy of Implant Dentures. **Publications:** *AAIDNEWS*, quarterly. Newsletter. Includes news and calendar updates of Academy events. **Price:** free for members. **Circulation:** 2,500. **Advertising:** accepted ● *Journal of Oral Implantology*, bimonthly. Contains original manuscripts, clinical presentations, research annotations, and educational reports pertinent to dental studies. **Price:** included in membership dues; $75.00 /year for nonmembers; $100.00 /year for libraries, corporations, and institutes. **Advertising:** accepted ● Directory, annual. Contains geographically and alphabetically arranged information. **Price:** free for members. **Circulation:** 2,500. **Conventions/Meetings:** annual conference and workshop (exhibits) - always fall ● annual meeting (exhibits) - 2007 Nov. 7-11, Hollywood, FL; 2008 Oct. 29-Nov. 2, San Diego, CA; 2009 Nov. 10-15, New Orleans, LA; 2010 Oct. 20-24, Boston, MA.

13803 ■ American Academy of Implant Prosthodontics (AAIP)
709 Haddonfield-Berlin Rd.
Voorhees, NJ 08043
Ph: (856)782-3990
Fax: (856)782-3775
E-mail: piezoklein@wanadoo.fr
URL: http://perso.orange.fr/piezoklein
Contact: J. Makzoume, Gen. Sec.
Founded: 1982. **Members:** 1,500. **Membership Dues:** active, fellow, master, associate, $225 (annual) ● international, $250 (annual). **Staff:** 2. **Budget:** $100,000. **Regional Groups:** 1. **Local Groups:** 1. **National Groups:** 8. **Multinational. Description:** Experts in dental implantology; dental school professors, clinicians, and researchers. Encourages continuing education, advancement, and research in implant dentistry; believes that prosthodontics and implantology education and research should take place in academic institutions. Promotes the surgical insertion of dental implants and the design and insertion of prosthodontic devices to replace missing teeth. Emphasizes research on the construction and maintenance of fixed and removable prostheses. Conducts continuing education courses in conjunction with dental schools. Maintains speakers' bureau and small library. **Awards:** Fagan Personality Award. **Frequency:** annual. **Type:** recognition. **Study Groups:** South Jersey Implant. **Publications:** *The Dental Implant - Clinical and Biological Response of Oral Tissues.* Book ● *Implant Prosthodontics - Surgical and Prosthetic Techniques for Dental Implants,* periodic. Membership Directory ● *Journal of Oral Implantology,* bimonthly ● Membership Directory, periodic ● Newsletter, 3/year. **Conventions/Meetings:** annual IMPLANTS - meeting (exhibits).

13804 ■ American Academy of Maxillofacial Prosthetics (AAMP)
c/o Dr. Steven P. Haug, Exec. Sec.
1121 W Michigan St.
Indianapolis, IN 46202
Ph: (317)274-5571
Fax: (317)278-2818
E-mail: sphaug@iupui.edu
URL: http://www.maxillofacialprosth.org/home.htm
Contact: Dr. Steven P. Haug, Exec. Sec.
Founded: 1953. **Members:** 267. **Membership Dues:** $324 (annual). **Description:** Represents dentists specializing in maxillofacial prosthetics. **Awards:** Poster Award Competition. **Frequency:** annual. **Type:** monetary. **Recipient:** for residents and recent graduates ● Travel. **Frequency:** annual. **Type:** grant. **Recipient:** for residents and recent graduates. **Committees:** Auditing; Ethics and Medico-legal; Federal Services; Historical and Archives; Insurance/Oral Health; International Relations; Prosthodontic Examiner Nominating; Research. **Publications:** *Journal of Prosthetic Dentistry,* monthly. **Conventions/Meetings:** annual conference.

13805 ■ American Academy of Oral and Maxillofacial Radiology (AAOMR)
PO Box 1010
Evans, GA 30809-1010
Ph: (706)721-2607
Fax: (706)721-6276
E-mail: mshrout@mail.mcg.edu
URL: http://www.aaomr.org
Contact: Dr. Michael Shrout, Exec. Dir.
Founded: 1949. **Members:** 400. **Membership Dues:** active, $220 (annual) ● associate, $177 (annual) ● affiliate, $162 (annual) ● corporate (sustaining), $1,500 (annual) ● corporate (participating), $500 (an-

nual) ● corporate (sponsor), $1,000 (annual). **Budget:** $75,500. **Description:** Dentists and other professionals who specialize in oral and maxillofacial radiology in clinical practice, teaching or research. Serves as authoritative body on radiation hygiene and hazards for the American Dental Association (see separate entry). **Awards:** Albert G. Richards Graduate Student Research Grant. **Frequency:** annual. **Type:** monetary. **Recipient:** for applied research in radiology ● Charles R. Morris Student Research Award. **Frequency:** annual. **Type:** monetary ● Howard R. Raper Oral and Maxillofacial Radiology Award. **Frequency:** annual. **Type:** monetary. **Recipient:** for academic achievement in graduate studies and potential for a career in academia ● Radiology Centennial Scholarship. **Frequency:** annual. **Type:** monetary. **Recipient:** for performance during first year of graduate study ● Student Award. **Type:** recognition. **Recipient:** for senior dental students for achievement in oral and maxillofacial radiology ● William H. Rollins Award. **Frequency:** annual. **Type:** monetary. **Recipient:** for basic research in radiology. **Formerly:** (1951) American Academy of Oral Roentgenology; (1967) American Academy of Dental Radiology. **Publications:** *Oral and Maxillofacial Radiology Section of Oral Surgery, Oral Medicine, Oral Pathology, Oral Radiology, and Endodontics,* monthly. Journal. **Price:** included in membership dues for active members; $52.00 corporate, associate, affiliate, student, life ● *Roster of Membership,* annual. Membership Directory ● Newsletter, quarterly. Features news, president's messages, and announcements. **Price:** free. **Circulation:** 600. Alternate Formats: online. **Conventions/Meetings:** annual meeting, continuing education, scientific sessions (3), special focus group seminars, committee meetings, executive council meetings, business meeting (exhibits) - 2007 Nov. 28-Dec. 2, Chicago, IL - **Avg. Attendance:** 120; 2008 Oct. 29-Nov. 2, Pittsburgh, PA - **Avg. Attendance:** 120.

13806 ■ American Academy of Oral Medicine (AAOM)
PO Box 2016
Edmonds, WA 98020-9516
Ph: (425)778-6162
Fax: (425)771-9588
E-mail: info@aaom.com
URL: http://www.aaom.com
Contact: Nelson L. Rhodus DMD, Pres.
Founded: 1945. **Members:** 800. **Membership Dues:** active, $275 (annual) ● associate, $120 (annual). **Staff:** 1. **Budget:** $30,000. **Regional Groups:** 4. **Description:** Dental educators, specialists, general dentists, and physicians interested in the study of the oral health care of medically compromised patients and the nonsurgical management of medically related diseases and disorders affecting the maxillofacial region. Promotes an improved quality of life for people with oral and maxillofacial diseases and disorders; fosters better scientific understanding between the fields of dentistry and medicine. Maintains speakers' bureau; offers continuing education lectures and seminars. **Awards:** Lester Burket Award. **Frequency:** annual. **Type:** recognition. **Recipient:** for research in oral medicine by an oral medicine graduate student ● Samuel Charles Miller Award. **Frequency:** annual. **Type:** recognition. **Recipient:** for lecture presented on original work in oral medicine. **Publications:** *AAOM News,* semiannual. Newsletter. **Circulation:** 1,000. **Advertising:** accepted ● *The Clinician's Guide to Oral Health in Geriatric Patients.* Monograph. Provides oral health care for the older adult. **Price:** $29.95 in U.S.; $37.95 in Canada. **Circulation:** 1,000. **Advertising:** accepted ● *The Clinician's Guide to the Treatment of the Medically-Complex Dental Patients.* Monograph. Provides dental practitioners with a user-friendly reference for managing the complex dental patient. **Price:** $29.95 in U.S.; $37.95 in Canada. **Advertising:** accepted ● *The Clinician's Guide to Treatment of Common Oral Conditions* (in English and Spanish), every 3-5 years. Monograph. Provides quick reference to the etiologic factors, clinical description, and patient education of the more common oral conditions. **Price:** $29.95 in U.S.; $37.95 in Canada. **Advertising:** accepted ●

The Clinician's Guide to Treatment of HIV-infected Patients, periodic. Monograph. Assists oral health workers in obtaining information essential to their becoming an integral part of the treatment team for HIV-infected persons. **Price:** included in membership dues; $24.95 /year for nonmembers in U.S.; $27.95 /year for nonmembers in Canada. **Advertising:** accepted ● *Diagnosis and Treatment of Chronic Orofacial Pain.* Manual. Provides an aid for general dentists for the diagnosis and treatment of oral and facial pain. **Price:** $24.95 in U.S.; $27.95 in Canada. **Advertising:** accepted ● *Oral Surgery, Oral Medicine, Oral Pathology, Oral Radiology and Endodontics.* Journal. **Conventions/Meetings:** annual meeting and lecture.

13807 ■ American Academy of Orofacial Pain (AAOP)
19 Mantua Rd.
Mount Royal, NJ 08061
Ph: (856)423-3629
Fax: (856)423-3420
E-mail: aaopco@talley.com
URL: http://www.aaop.org
Contact: Peter M. Baragona DMD, Chm.
Founded: 1975. **Members:** 330. **Staff:** 1. **Budget:** $100,000. **Description:** Medical and dental doctors. Seeks to further knowledge of Orofacial Pain and Temporomandibular Disorders. Maintains patient referral program. **Awards:** Student Dental Award. **Frequency:** annual. **Type:** recognition. **Telecommunication Services:** electronic mail, pbarag0517@aol.com. **Formerly:** (1979) American Academy of Craniomandibular Orthopedics; (1992) American Academy of Craniomandibular Disorders. **Publications:** *Journal of Orofacial Pain,* quarterly. **Price:** included in membership dues ● *Orofacial Pain: Guidelines for Classification, Assessment, and Management.* Book. **Price:** $28.00 for members ● *Temporomandibular Disorders: Guidelines for Classification, Assessment, and Management.* **Conventions/Meetings:** annual conference (exhibits).

13808 ■ American Academy of Orthodontics for the General Practitioner (AAOGP)
9701 Wesley St., Ste.202
Greenville, TX 75402
Free: (800)634-2027
Fax: (888)634-2028
E-mail: cborde9321@aol.com
URL: http://www.academygportho.com
Contact: Cynthia Bordelon, Dir.
Founded: 1959. **Members:** 250. **Staff:** 1. **Regional Groups:** 2. **State Groups:** 5. **Description:** Licensed dentists. Provides dentists in general practice with an organization through which they can augment their basic knowledge and training in orthodontics. Offers continuing education courses for dentists and auxiliary personnel; sponsors seminars. Provides facilities and audiovisual material for its affiliated study clubs. **Affiliated With:** American Society for the Study of Orthodontics. **Publications:** *American Academy of Orthodontics for the General Practitioner—Continuing Education,* annual. Brochure. Lists AAOGP-sponsored continuing education courses, seminars, and meetings for the coming year. **Price:** free. **Advertising:** accepted ● *International Journal of Orthodontics,* semiannual. **Conventions/Meetings:** annual seminar (exhibits).

13809 ■ American Academy of Pediatric Dentistry (AAPD)
211 E Chicago Ave., Ste.700
Chicago, IL 60611-2663
Ph: (312)337-2169
Fax: (312)337-6329
E-mail: aapdinfo@aapd.org
URL: http://www.aapd.org
Contact: Dr. John S. Rutkauskas DDS, Exec. Dir.
Founded: 1947. **Members:** 6,400. **Membership Dues:** active, $590 (annual) ● associate/affiliate/friend, $295 (annual) ● international, $330 (annual) ● predoctoral student, $27 (annual) ● life, $275 ● allied, $145 (annual). **Staff:** 17. **Budget:** $3,000,000. **Regional Groups:** 6. **Description:** Professional society of dentists whose practice is limited to children; teachers and researchers in pediatric

dentistry. Seeks to advance the specialty of pediatric dentistry through practice, education, and research. Sponsors graduate student pediatric dentistry award program. **Awards:** Foundation Research Award. **Frequency:** annual. **Type:** monetary. **Recipient:** for a clinician, researcher or academician in pediatric dentistry ● Manuel M. Album Award. **Frequency:** annual. **Type:** recognition. **Recipient:** for individuals or organizations ● Merle C. Hunter Leadership Award. **Frequency:** annual. **Type:** recognition. **Recipient:** for volunteers ● OMNII Pediatric Dentistry Postdoctoral Fellowship. **Frequency:** annual. **Type:** fellowship. **Recipient:** for pediatric dentistry postdoctoral student/resident ● Pediatric Dentist of the Year. **Frequency:** annual. **Type:** recognition. **Recipient:** for pediatric dentists ● Ralph E. McDonald Award. **Frequency:** annual. **Type:** monetary. **Recipient:** for outstanding research project. **Formerly:** (1984) American Academy of Pedodontics. **Publications:** *American Academy of Pediatric Dentistry—Membership Roster*, annual. Membership Directory. **Circulation:** 5,600. **Advertising:** accepted ● *American Academy of Pediatric Dentistry—Today*, bimonthly. Newsletter. Includes employment listings, meetings calendar, research updates, and obituaries. **Price:** included in membership dues. **Circulation:** 5,600. **Advertising:** accepted ● *The Journal of Dentistry for Children*, 3/year. Covers a wide range of topics related to the clinical care of children. **Price:** $75.00 /year for individuals in U.S.; $110.00 /year for individuals outside U.S.; $90.00 /year for institutions in U.S.; $150.00 /year for institutions outside U.S. ISSN: 0022-0353. **Advertising:** accepted ● *Pediatric Dentistry*, bimonthly. Journal. Includes employment listings and conference proceedings. **Price:** included in membership dues; $132.00 /year for nonmembers; $192.00 /year for institutions; $25.00/issue for nonmembers. ISSN: 0164-1263. **Circulation:** 4,900. **Advertising:** accepted ● Pamphlets. **Conventions/Meetings:** annual meeting (exhibits) - always May. 2008 May 22-26, Washington, DC; 2009 May 21-25, Honolulu, HI; 2010 May 27-31, Chicago, IL.

13810 ■ American Academy of Periodontology (AAP)
737 N Michigan Ave., Ste.800
Chicago, IL 60611-6660
Ph: (312)787-5518
Free: (800)282-4867
Fax: (312)787-3670
E-mail: abperio@msn.com
URL: http://www.perio.org
Contact: Dr. Gerald M. Bowers, Exec. Dir.
Founded: 1914. **Members:** 8,000. **Membership Dues:** active, $793 (annual) ● associate, $282 (annual) ● international, $322 (annual) ● life (active), $397 ● retired, $74 (annual) ● student, $107 (annual). **Staff:** 40. **Budget:** $10,000,000. **Description:** Serves as professional society of dentists specializing in the prevention, diagnosis, and treatment of diseases affecting the gums and supporting structures of the teeth and in the placement and maintenance of dental implants. **Awards:** **Type:** recognition. **Absorbed:** (1967) American Society of Periodontists. **Publications:** *AAP News*, quarterly. Newsletter. Contains a variety of important information on upcoming Academy activities such as the annual meeting and new product launches. **Price:** included in membership dues. **Advertising:** accepted ● *AAP Product Catalog*. Contains information about periodontal diseases. **Price:** $10.00/100 copies for members; $23.00/100 copies for nonmembers ● *Annals of Periodontology*, annual. Journal ● *Journal of Periodontology*, monthly. **Price:** $195.00 /year for individuals in U.S. and Canada; $235.00 /year for individuals outside U.S. and Canada; $435.00 /year for institutions in U.S. and Canada; $515.00 /year for institutions outside U.S. and Canada. **Advertising:** accepted. Alternate Formats: online ● Membership Directory, annual. Contains referral phonebook. **Advertising:** accepted. **Conventions/Meetings:** annual meeting (exhibits) - 2007 Oct. 27-30, WASHINGTON, DC; 2008 Sept. 6-9, Seattle, WA; 2009 Sept. 12-15, Boston, MA.

13811 ■ American Academy of Restorative Dentistry (AARD)
c/o CityStar Group, Inc.
PO Box 26385
Colorado Springs, CO 80936

Ph: (719)559-1945
Fax: (719)623-0387
E-mail: admin@restorativeacademy.com
URL: http://www.restorativeacademy.com
Contact: Dr. Edward P. Allen, Pres.
Founded: 1921. **Members:** 285. **Budget:** $45,000. **Description:** Represents professional society of dentists practicing restorative dentistry, and educators interested in dentistry as it applies to treatment of the natural teeth to restore and maintain a healthy functioning mouth as part of a healthy body. **Additional Websites:** http://aard.citystar.biz/contact. **Committees:** ADA Liaison; Arrangements; Clinic; Foundation; Photo Poster; Reception; Scientific Investigation. **Formerly:** (1928) American Society of Dental Ceramics. **Publications:** *Journal of Prosthetic Dentistry*, periodic ● *Roster*, annual. Membership Directory. **Conventions/Meetings:** annual meeting and symposium - always February, Chicago, IL.

13812 ■ American Association for Community Dental Programs (AACDP)
635 W 7th St., Ste.309
Cincinnati, OH 45203
Ph: (513)621-0248
Fax: (513)621-0288
E-mail: info@aacdp.com
URL: http://www.aacdp.com
Contact: Jackie Campbell, Contact
Founded: 1983. **Members:** 200. **Membership Dues:** individual, $30 (annual) ● organization/agency, $100 (annual). **Staff:** 1. **Budget:** $10,000. **Description:** Community dental programs. Provides or arranges for dental care for people with specific needs, including financial hardships, disabilities, and medical complications. **Publications:** *AACDP Newsletter*. **Conventions/Meetings:** annual conference.

13813 ■ American Association of Dental Examiners (AADE)
211 E Chicago Ave., Ste.760
Chicago, IL 60611
Ph: (312)440-7464
Fax: (312)440-3525
E-mail: info@aadexam.org
URL: http://www.aadexam.org
Contact: Ms. Molly Nadler, Exec. Dir.
Founded: 1882. **Members:** 850. **Membership Dues:** agency, $1,600 (annual) ● specialty board, $1,300 (annual) ● active, individual active, $215 (annual) ● associate, educator, $80 (annual) ● life, $1,500. **Staff:** 3. **Budget:** $200,000. **Description:** Present and past members of state dental examining boards and board administrators. Assists member agencies with problems related to state dental board examinations and licensure, and enforcement of the state dental practice act. Conducts research; compiles statistics. **Awards:** Citizen of the Year. **Frequency:** annual. **Type:** recognition. **Commissions:** Dental Accreditation. **Committees:** Clearinghouse; Wildfire. **Councils:** Dental Education and Licensure. **Formerly:** National Association of Dental Examiners. **Publications:** *Advocacy Relations*. Manual. Contains compilation of policies and position papers of various organizations. **Price:** $25.00 for members; $35.00 for nonmembers ● *The Bulletin*, quarterly. Newsletter. Contains information that is relevant to the both dental boards and to the citizens of the states the boards serve. **Price:** included in membership dues; $75.00 for nonmembers ● *Composite - 17th Edition*. Handbook. Details the structure, licensure and disciplinary activities of all state dental boards. **Price:** $50.00 for members; $75.00 for nonmembers ● Proceedings, annual. **Conventions/Meetings:** semiannual meeting - always March. 2008 Mar. 10, Chicago, IL ● annual meeting - 2007 Sept. 25-26, San Francisco, CA.

13814 ■ American Association for Dental Research (AADR)
1619 Duke St.
Alexandria, VA 22314-3406
Ph: (703)548-0066
Fax: (703)548-1883

E-mail: research@iadr.org
URL: http://www.iadr.org
Contact: Christopher H. Fox, Exec. Dir.
Founded: 1972. **Members:** 4,500. **Membership Dues:** individual, $204 (annual) ● student, $47 (annual). **Staff:** 17. **Budget:** $3,000,000. **Regional Groups:** 40. **Description:** A division of the International Association for Dental Research (see separate entry). Dentists, researchers, dental schools, and dental products manufacturing companies. Seeks to promote better dental health and research activities. Presents current research information at annual meeting. Sponsors competitions; sponsors seminars. **Awards:** David B. Scott. **Frequency:** annual. **Type:** fellowship. **Recipient:** to a dental student in one IADR division ● Distinguished Scientist Award. **Frequency:** triennial. **Type:** monetary. **Recipient:** for an outstanding scientific achievement ● Student Research Fellowship. **Frequency:** annual. **Type:** monetary. **Recipient:** to the best research proposal. **Committees:** Ad Hoc; Annual Session; National Oral Health Advocacy; Science Information. **Affiliated With:** International Association for Dental Research. **Publications:** *Advances in Dental Research*, periodic. Journal. Provides a forum for detailed exploration and timely discussion of significant research developments in the sciences relevant to dentistry. **Price:** $25.00 for members; $40.00 for nonmembers ● *Journal of Dental Research*, monthly. Provides information on all sciences relevant to dentistry and to the oral cavity and associated structures in health and disease. **Price:** $82.00 /year for members; $37.00/year for student members; $432.00 /year for institutions. ISSN: 0022-0345. **Circulation:** 6,500. **Advertising:** accepted. Alternate Formats: online. **Conventions/Meetings:** annual convention and meeting (exhibits) - usually March. 2008 Apr. 2-5, Dallas, TX; 2009 Apr. 1-4, Miami, FL; 2010 Mar. 3-6, Washington, DC.

13815 ■ American Association of Endodontists (AAE)
211 E Chicago Ave., Ste.1100
Chicago, IL 60611-2691
Ph: (312)266-7255
Free: (800)872-3636
Fax: (312)266-9867
E-mail: info@aae.org
URL: http://www.aae.org
Contact: James M. Drinan, Exec. Dir.
Founded: 1943. **Members:** 6,500. **Membership Dues:** active, $285-$570 (annual) ● associate, educator, $143-$285 (annual) ● student, $50 (annual) ● auxiliary, $35 (annual). **Staff:** 25. **Budget:** $4,000,000. **Description:** Endodontic specialists and other interested professionals. (Endodontics is a branch of dentistry that deals with the soft tissues inside the tooth.) Seeks to promote the exchange of ideas, to stimulate research, and to encourage the highest standard of quality care in the practice of endodontics. **Libraries:** **Type:** not open to the public. **Awards:** Edgar D. Coolidge Award. **Frequency:** annual. **Type:** recognition ● Edward M. Osetek Educator Award. **Frequency:** annual. **Type:** recognition ● Louis I. Grossman Award. **Frequency:** annual. **Type:** recognition ● Ralph F. Sommer Award. **Frequency:** annual. **Type:** recognition. **Computer Services:** Mailing lists, of members. **Committees:** Clinical Practice; Constitutions and Bylaws; Continuing Education; Dental Benefits; Editorial Board; Educational Affairs; Governmental Affairs and Federal Dental Health Services; Honors and Awards; International Relations; Membership Insurance; Membership Services; Nominating; Peer Review and Ethics; Professional Standards; Public and Professional Affairs; Research and Scientific Affairs; Student and New Practitioner. **Publications:** *Appropriateness of Care and Quality Assurance Guidelines* ● *Communique*, quarterly. Newsletter ● *Endodontics: Colleagues for Excellence*, semiannual. Newsletter. Addresses clinical topics related to endodontics. Alternate Formats: online ● *Glossary: Contemporary Terminology for Endodontics* ● *Journal of Endodontics*, monthly. **Advertising:** accepted ● *Tooth Pain Guide*. Brochure ● *Your Guide to Cracked Teeth*. Brochure ● *Your Guide to Dental Benefits*. Brochure ● *Your Guide to Endodontic Re-*

treatment. Brochure ● *Your Guide to Endodontic Surgery.* Brochure ● *Your Guide to Endodontic Treatment* (in English and Spanish). Brochure ● Membership Directory, annual ● Brochure. **Conventions/Meetings:** annual convention (exhibits) - 2008 Apr. 9-12, Vancouver, BC, Canada; 2009 Apr. 29-May 2, Orlando, FL; 2010 Apr. 14-17, San Diego, CA.

13816 ■ American Association for Functional Orthodontics (AAFO)
106 S Kent St.
Winchester, VA 22601
Ph: (540)662-2200
Free: (800)441-3850
Fax: (540)665-8910
E-mail: aafo@verizon.net
URL: http://www.aafo.org
Contact: Rachele M. Riley, Contact
Founded: 1981. **Members:** 1,800. **Membership Dues:** individual, $325 (annual). **Staff:** 4. **Budget:** $450,000. **For-Profit. Description:** Represents dentists involved in orthodontic malocclusions and temporomandibular joint dysfunctions by utilization of functional appliances. Facilitates exchange of information and case reports on current developments in this type of treatment. Sponsors seminars; offers members discounts on accredited seminars sponsored by other organizations. **Libraries: Type:** reference. **Holdings:** 17. **Awards:** AAFO Clinician of the Year. **Frequency:** annual. **Type:** recognition. **Recipient:** to the clinician who exhibited knowledge, innovation and active participation in the field of functional orthodontics. **Formerly:** (1984) Northern Virginia Functional Jaw Study Club; (1985) American Association of Functional Orthodontists. **Publications:** *Functional Orthodontist: A Journal of Functional Jaw Orthopedics,* quarterly. Includes accredited course listings and new product information. **Price:** included in membership dues; $125.00 /year for nonmembers. ISSN: 8756-3150. **Circulation:** 7,000. **Advertising:** accepted. Alternate Formats: CD-ROM ● Membership Directory, annual. Provides contact information of members around the world. **Price:** included in membership dues. **Conventions/Meetings:** annual conference, orthodontic labs (exhibits).

13817 ■ American Association of Hospital Dentists (AAHD)
c/o Special Care Dentistry Association
401 N Michigan Ave., Ste.2200
Chicago, IL 60611
Ph: (312)527-6764
Fax: (312)673-6663
E-mail: scda@scdaonline.org
URL: http://www.scdaonline.org
Contact: James J. Balija CAE, Exec. Dir.
Founded: 1927. **Members:** 500. **Membership Dues:** individual, dentist, $165 (annual). **Staff:** 3. **Description:** Directors and staff members of dental departments in hospitals. Promotes dental education programs in hospitals. Offers examinations. **Awards:** Lawrence J. Chasko Award. **Frequency:** annual. **Type:** recognition. **Recipient:** for service to hospital dentistry. **Formerly:** American Association of Hospital Dental Chiefs. **Publications:** *InterFace.* Newsletter. **Price:** included in membership dues. ISSN: 0887-6304. **Advertising:** accepted ● *Oral Facial Emergencies* ● *Oral Medicine in Hospital Practice* ● *Special Care in Dentistry,* bimonthly. **Conventions/Meetings:** annual meeting (exhibits) - always spring, Chicago, IL.

13818 ■ American Association of Orthodontists (AAO)
401 N Lindbergh Blvd.
St. Louis, MO 63141-7816
Ph: (314)993-1700
Fax: (314)997-1745
E-mail: info@aaortho.org
URL: http://www.braces.org
Contact: Chris Vranas, Exec. Dir.
Founded: 1900. **Members:** 15,000. **Staff:** 49. **Budget:** $12,000,000. **Regional Groups:** 8. **State Groups:** 59. **Multinational. Description:** Serves as professional organization for educationally qualified orthodontists. Aims to advance the art and science of

orthodontics; to encourage and sponsor research; to strive for and maintain the highest standards of excellence in orthodontic education and practice; and to make significant contributions to the health of the public. **Libraries: Type:** reference; not open to the public. **Holdings:** 10,000; archival material, articles, audiovisuals, books, papers, periodicals. **Subjects:** orthodontics, dentistry. **Awards:** James E. Brophy AAO Distinguished Service Award. **Frequency:** annual. **Type:** recognition. **Recipient:** for individuals with outstanding achievements in the art and science of orthodontics. **Telecommunication Services:** phone referral service, for USA or Canadian consumers seeking an orthodontist, (800)STRAIGHT. **Councils:** Communications; Governmental Affairs; Information Technology; Insurance; Membership, Ethics, and Judicial Concerns; New and Younger Members; Orthodontic Education; Orthodontic Health Care; Orthodontic Practice; Scientific Affairs. **Formerly:** American Society of Orthodontists. **Publications:** *American Association of Orthodontists Membership Directory,* biennial. **Price:** $55.00 for members; $110.00 for nonmembers. **Advertising:** accepted ● *American Journal of Orthodontics and Dentofacial Orthopedics,* monthly. **Price:** included in membership dues. **Advertising:** accepted ● *The Bulletin,* 7/year. Newsletters. Contains information on the organization and its members. **Circulation:** 15,000. **Advertising:** accepted. Alternate Formats: online ● Also publishes administration guide kits. **Conventions/Meetings:** annual convention, with exhibitors of orthodontic products and services (exhibits).

13819 ■ American Association of Public Health Dentistry (AAPHD)
PO Box 7536
Springfield, IL 62791-7536
Ph: (217)391-0218
Fax: (217)793-0041
E-mail: natoff@aaphd.org
URL: http://www.aaphd.org
Contact: Pamela J. Tolson CAE, Exec. Dir.
Founded: 1937. **Members:** 900. **Membership Dues:** regular, affiliate, corporate, $100 (annual) ● contributing, $125 (annual) ● sustaining, $150 (annual) ● sponsoring, $200 (annual) ● associate, $80 (annual) ● full time student, $40 (annual) ● life, $75. **Staff:** 3. **Budget:** $250,000. **Description:** Professional society of dentists, dental hygienists, health educators, and others actively engaged in dental public health. Sponsors competitions. **Awards:** Distinguished Service Award. **Frequency:** annual. **Type:** recognition. **Recipient:** for individuals with excellent service to public health dentistry ● Student Merit Award for Outstanding Achievement In Community Dentistry International. **Frequency:** annual. **Type:** recognition. **Recipient:** for dental public health contributions of an individual outside USA. **Committees:** Annual Program; Diversity; Education; International Relations; Oral Health and Policy; Public Policy and Advocacy; Science; Workforce Development. **Affiliated With:** American Dental Association. **Formerly:** (1983) American Association of Public Health Dentists. **Publications:** *American Association of Public Health Dentistry—Communique,* quarterly. Newsletter. **Price:** included in membership dues; $25.00 /year for nonmembers. **Circulation:** 900. **Advertising:** accepted ● *Journal of Public Health Dentistry,* quarterly. Covers fluoridation, sealants, demographics, and utilization of dental services. Includes research reports and book reviews. **Price:** included in membership dues; $180.00 /year for nonmembers in U.S.; $210.00 /year for nonmembers outside U.S. ISSN: 0022-4006. **Circulation:** 1,500. **Advertising:** accepted. **Conventions/Meetings:** annual National Oral Health Conference (exhibits) - April/May.

13820 ■ American Association of Women Dentists (AAWD)
216 W Jackson Blvd., Ste.625
Chicago, IL 60606
Free: (800)920-2293
Fax: (312)750-1203
E-mail: info@aawd.org
URL: http://www.aawd.org
Contact: Lanette Sikes DDS, Pres.
Founded: 1921. **Membership Dues:** active/associate/affiliate/international, $185 (annual) ● active

(federal service), $99 (annual) ● active (1st year after graduation)/postgraduate student/dental office team, $95 (annual) ● student, $45 (annual) ● corporate benefactor, $1,000 (annual). **Staff:** 5. **Budget:** $250,000. **Regional Groups:** 17. **Description:** Dental students or dentists who are interested in dentistry and advancing women in dentistry. Dedicates itself to enhancing and promoting unique participation and leadership for women in organized dentistry. **Awards:** Colgate-Palmolive Research Award. **Frequency:** annual. **Type:** recognition. **Recipient:** for juniors or seniors in dental school achieving academic excellence and research. **Computer Services:** Mailing lists, of members by roster. **Formerly:** (1978) Association of American Women Dentists. **Publications:** *AAWD Membership Directory,* annual. **Advertising:** accepted ● *The Chronicle/Women's Dental Journal,* bimonthly. Includes member activities at the local and national level, scientific and technical news, upcoming events and a list of various jobs. **Price:** included in membership dues; $30.00 /year for nonmembers. **Circulation:** 19,000. **Advertising:** accepted. **Conventions/Meetings:** annual conference (exhibits) - held in spring.

13821 ■ American Board of Dental Public Health (ABDPH)
c/o E. Joseph Alderman, DDS, Exec. Sec.
827 Brookridge Dr. NE
Atlanta, GA 30306-3618
Ph: (404)876-3530
E-mail: abdph@comcast.net
URL: http://www.aaphd.org
Contact: E. Joseph Alderman DDS, Exec. Sec.
Founded: 1950. **Members:** 5. **Membership Dues:** regular, affiliate, corporate, $100 (annual) ● contributing, $125 (annual) ● sustaining, $150 (annual) ● sponsoring, $200 (annual) ● associate, $80 (annual) ● student, $40 (annual) ● life, $75. **Staff:** 1. **Description:** Investigates the qualifications of, administers examinations to, and certifies as diplomates, dentists specializing in dental public health. Sponsored by American Association of Public Health Dentistry (see separate entry). **Affiliated With:** American Association of Public Health Dentistry. **Publications:** *ABDPH Membership Directory,* triennial ● Newsletter, annual ● Brochure, periodic. Contains information about the organization. **Conventions/Meetings:** annual Board Examination and Meeting.

13822 ■ American Board of Endodontics (ABE)
211 E Chicago Ave., Ste.1100
Chicago, IL 60611-2691
Ph: (312)266-7255 (312)266-7310
Free: (800)872-3636
Fax: (312)266-9867
E-mail: abe@aae.org
URL: http://www.aae.org/certboard
Contact: Dr. Keith V. Krell, Pres.
Founded: 1956. **Staff:** 1. **Description:** Dentists who have successfully completed study and training in an advanced endodontics education program that is accredited by the Commission on Dental Accreditation of the American Dental Association (see separate entry). Primary objective is to protect the public by raising the standards of endodontic practice and requiring candidates for diplomate status to show strong evidence of specialized skills and knowledge in endodontics. Administers examinations and certifies dentists who successfully complete the examinations. **Publications:** *Membership Roster,* annual. Directory. Published in conjunction with American Association of Endodontists. **Conventions/Meetings:** semiannual meeting - always April and November ● annual Written Exam - meeting - always November, Chicago, IL.

13823 ■ American Board of Family Dentistry (ABFD)
1501 Camp Mohave Rd., No. 1
Fort Mohave, AZ 86426
E-mail: info@theabfd.com
URL: http://www.theabfd.com
Contact: Mark Collins, Contact
Founded: 2002. **Description:** Promotes the science and art of family dentistry. Strives to ensure that there

are enough highly trained family dentists and auxiliary personnel who are capable of providing quality dental care to patients. Grants credentials to dentists for their achievements and contributions to family dentistry. **Telecommunication Services:** electronic mail, dentist1@ctaz.com.

13824 ■ American Board of Operative Dentistry (ABOD)
c/o Clyde Roggenkamp, DDS, Sec.-Treas.
LLU School of Dentistry
Loma Linda, CA 92350
Ph: (909)558-4640
Fax: (909)558-0253
E-mail: croggenkamp@llu.edu
URL: http://operativedentistry.com/american.html
Contact: Clyde Roggenkamp DDS, Sec.-Treas.
Founded: 1980. **Members:** 51. **Membership Dues:** active, $115 (annual). **Budget:** $5,000. **Description:** Promotes greater excellence and advanced knowledge in the practice of operative dentistry. **Programs:** Certification. **Conventions/Meetings:** annual board meeting (exhibits).

13825 ■ American Board of Orthodontics (ABO)
401 N Lindbergh Blvd., Ste.308
St. Louis, MO 63141-7839
Ph: (314)432-6130
Fax: (314)432-8170
E-mail: info@americanboardortho.com
URL: http://www.americanboardortho.com
Contact: Christine L. Eisenmayer, Exec. Sec.
Founded: 1929. **Staff:** 5. **Regional Groups:** 8. **Description:** Investigates the qualifications of, administers examinations to, and certifies as diplomats dentists specializing in orthodontics (prevention and correction of irregularities and faulty positions of the teeth). Sponsored by the American Association of Orthodontists (see separate entry). **Awards:** Albert H. Ketcham Memorial Award. **Frequency:** annual. **Type:** recognition. **Recipient:** for an individual who has made a notable contribution to the science and art of orthodontics ● Dale B. Wade Award of Clinical Excellence. **Frequency:** annual. **Type:** recognition. **Recipient:** to a senior clinician who has demonstrated exceptional dedication to orthodontics through clinical excellence and/or devoted teaching in the image of Dr. Wade ● Earl E. and Wilma S. Shepard Distinguished Service Award. **Frequency:** annual. **Type:** recognition. **Recipient:** to an individual for outstanding dedication and advancement of the ideals and mission of The American Board of Orthodontics ● Special Recognition Award. **Frequency:** periodic. **Type:** recognition. **Recipient:** for persons who have boosted the prestige of the ABO. **Computer Services:** Online services, directory of diplomates. **Affiliated With:** American Association of Orthodontists. **Formerly:** (1938) American Board of Orthodontia. **Conventions/Meetings:** annual meeting, with examination (exhibits).

13826 ■ American Board of Periodontology (ABP)
4157 Mountain Rd.
PBN 249
Pasadena, MD 21122
Ph: (410)437-3749
Fax: (410)437-4021
E-mail: abperio@msn.com
URL: http://www.perio.org/amboard/amboard.html
Contact: Dr. Gerald M. Bowers DDS, Exec. Dir.
Founded: 1939. **Members:** 1,500. **Membership Dues:** active, $793 (annual) ● associate, $282 (annual) ● international, $322 (annual). **Staff:** 2. **Description:** Conducts examinations to determine the qualifications and competence of periodontists who voluntarily apply for certification as diplomates in the field of periodontology. Maintains registry of holders of diplomate certificates. **Affiliated With:** American Academy of Periodontology. **Conventions/Meetings:** annual meeting, with examination.

13827 ■ American Board of Prosthodontics (ABP)
PO Box 271894
West Hartford, CT 06127-1894
Ph: (860)679-2649
Fax: (860)679-1370
E-mail: ttaylor@nso.uchc.edu
URL: http://www.prosthodontics.org/abp
Contact: Dr. Thomas D. Taylor, Exec. Dir.
Founded: 1946. **Members:** 1,018. **Staff:** 1. **Budget:** $100,000. **Description:** Seeks to advance the science and art of prosthodontics by encouraging its study and improving its practice. Certifies dentists who specialize in the field of fixed, removable, and maxillofacial prosthodontics. Approved by the American Dental Association (see separate entry) and the Council on Dental Education. **Publications:** Guidelines for the Certification Process. Manual. Includes the mission statement, goals, and history of the association. **Conventions/Meetings:** semiannual meeting - usually January or February and June.

13828 ■ American Central European Dental Institute (ACEDI)
60 Fed. St.
Boston, MA 02110-2510
Ph: (617)423-6165
Fax: (617)426-0006
E-mail: info@watkinosorio.com
Contact: Dr. Arnold Watkin, Chm.
Founded: 1991. **Members:** 2. **Membership Dues:** $100 (annual). **Staff:** 3. **Budget:** $100,000. **Languages:** Czech, English, French, Lithuanian, Polish, Russian, Spanish. **Description:** Dentists and others serving in capacities related to the dental profession. Seeks to advance standards in the profession of dentistry. Conducts educational programs; maintains Speaker's Bureau. **Libraries:** Type: open to the public. **Computer Services:** database ● mailing lists. **Publications:** Newsletter, annual. **Conventions/Meetings:** quarterly symposium (exhibits).

13829 ■ American College of Dentists (ACD)
839J Quince Orchard Blvd.
Gaithersburg, MD 20878-1614
Ph: (301)977-3223
Fax: (301)977-3330
E-mail: office@acd.org
URL: http://acd.org
Contact: Dr. Stephen A. Ralls, Exec. Dir.
Founded: 1920. **Members:** 7,000. **Staff:** 6. **Budget:** $1,000,000. **Regional Groups:** 8. **State Groups:** 48. **Description:** Dentists and others serving in capacities related to the dental profession. Seeks to advance the standards of the profession of dentistry. Conducts educational and research programs. Maintains speakers bureau and charitable programs. **Libraries:** Type: reference. **Holdings:** archival material, artwork, books, clippings, monographs, periodicals. **Subjects:** dentistry. **Awards:** Award of Merit. **Frequency:** annual. **Type:** recognition. **Recipient:** to individual other than a fellow who has made a unique contribution or given exceptional service to the profession ● Ethics and Professionalism Award. **Frequency:** annual. **Type:** recognition. **Recipient:** for exceptional contributions by individuals or organizations in the promotion of ethics or professionalism in dentistry ● Honorary Fellowship. **Frequency:** annual. **Type:** recognition. **Recipient:** to non-dentist professionals who have significantly shown exceptional leadership ● Lifetime Achievement Award. **Frequency:** annual. **Type:** recognition. **Recipient:** for individuals who have been fellows for 50 years ● Outstanding Service Award. **Frequency:** annual. **Type:** recognition. **Recipient:** for exceptional support of the College to the profession, community, or humanity ● Section Achievement Award. **Frequency:** annual. **Type:** recognition. **Recipient:** to college section having effective projects and activities ● Section Newsletter Award. **Frequency:** annual. **Type:** recognition. **Recipient:** to an outstanding newsletter of a college section ● William John Gies Award. **Frequency:** annual. **Type:** recognition. **Recipient:** for exceptional service in the areas of professional and community activity. **Publications:** American College of Dentists Fellowship Guide 2004-2005, periodic.

Directory. Contains general information and bylaws. ● American College of Dentists News and Views, quarterly. Newsletter. **Price:** included in membership dues. **Circulation:** 6,500 ● Ethics Handbook for Dentists, periodic. Contains information for graduating and practicing dentists. Alternate Formats: online ● Information Brochure, periodic. Contains general information. ● Journal of the American College of Dentists, quarterly. Includes news and research reports. **Price:** included in membership dues; $40.00 /year for nonmembers in U.S. and Canada; $60.00 /year for nonmembers outside U.S. and Canada; $10.00/copy for nonmembers. ISSN: 0002-7979. **Circulation:** 5,000. **Conventions/Meetings:** annual meeting, held in conjunction with American Dental Association - 2007 Sept. 26-27, San Francisco, CA.

13830 ■ American College of Prosthodontists (ACP)
211 E Chicago Ave., Ste.1000
Chicago, IL 60611
Ph: (312)573-1260
Free: (800)378-1260
Fax: (312)573-1257
E-mail: acp@prosthodontics.org
URL: http://www.prosthodontics.org
Contact: Nancy Chandler, Exec. Dir.
Founded: 1970. **Members:** 2,800. **Membership Dues:** student, $75 (annual) ● active, life, $301 ● individual/fellow, $602 (annual) ● dental technician, $200 (annual) ● individual/fellow, life, $150. **Staff:** 9. **Budget:** $1,600,000. **Regional Groups:** 40. **State Groups:** 50. **Description:** Dentists specializing in prosthetics who are either board certified, board eligible, or under training in approved graduate or residency programs. Seeks to improve prosthodontic treatment for patients by encouraging educational activities designed to bring new ideas, techniques, and research into clinical practice. Sponsors annual prosthodontic research competition. **Libraries:** Type: reference. **Holdings:** periodicals. **Subjects:** prosthodontics. **Awards:** ACP Education Foundation Scholarship. **Frequency:** annual. **Type:** scholarship ● Fellowship Grants. **Frequency:** annual. **Type:** grant. **Computer Services:** database, members. **Committees:** Education and Advancement; Private Practice; Prosthetic Dental Care Programs; Prosthodontic Nomenclature; Public and Professional Relations; Research; Sections. **Affiliated With:** American Board of Prosthodontics; American Dental Association. **Publications:** Journal of Prosthodontics, quarterly. **Advertising:** accepted ● Journal of Prosthodontics—Clinical Journal. Articles ● The Messenger, quarterly. Newsletter. Delivers timely and relevant exposes, information on the College's current activities and future events. **Price:** included in membership dues. ISSN: 0736-346X. **Circulation:** 2,300. **Advertising:** accepted ● Also publishes study guide. **Conventions/Meetings:** annual Session - conference (exhibits) - always fall. 2007 Oct. 31-Nov. 3, Scottsdale, AZ - **Avg. Attendance:** 1000; 2008 Oct. 29-Nov. 1, Nashville, TN - **Avg. Attendance:** 1000.

13831 ■ American Dental Assistants Association (ADAA)
35 E Wacker Dr., Ste.1730
Chicago, IL 60601-2211
Ph: (312)541-1550
Fax: (312)541-1496
E-mail: lsepin@adaa1.com
URL: http://www.dentalassistant.org
Contact: Lawrence H. Sepin, Exec. Dir.
Founded: 1923. **Members:** 15,000. **Membership Dues:** individual, $105 (annual) ● student, $25 (annual). **Staff:** 10. **Budget:** $1,250,000. **State Groups:** 50. **Local Groups:** 125. **Description:** Individuals employed as dental assistants in dental offices, clinics, hospitals, or institutions; instructors of dental assistants; dental students. Sponsors workshops and seminars; maintains governmental liaison. Offers group insurance; maintains scholarship trust fund. Dental Assisting National Board (see separate entry) examines members who are candidates for title of Certified Dental Assistant. **Awards:** Recognition of Excellence Award. **Frequency:** annual. **Type:** recog-

nition. **Recipient:** for contributions to the profession or the Association. **Computer Services:** Mailing lists, of members. **Committees:** Community Involvement; Education; Judicial; Legislation; Relief. **Publications:** *The Dental Assistant*, bimonthly. Journal. Features articles pertaining to dental assisting. **Price:** included in membership dues; \$20.00 /year for nonmembers; \$10.00/copy for nonmembers. ISSN: 0011-8508. **Circulation:** 16,000. **Advertising:** accepted ● Also publishes educational materials. **Conventions/Meetings:** annual conference and general assembly, meets in conjunction with Academy of General Dentistry (exhibits) - always July or August.

13832 ■ American Dental Association (ADA)
211 E Chicago Ave.
Chicago, IL 60611-2678
Ph: (312)440-2500
Fax: (312)440-2800
E-mail: publicinfo@ada.org
URL: http://www.ada.org
Contact: James Bramson, Exec. Dir.
Founded: 1859. **Members:** 153,000. **Staff:** 380. **Budget:** \$72,000,000. **State Groups:** 54. **Local Groups:** 535. **Description:** Professional society of dentists. Encourages the improvement of the health of the public and promotes the art and science of dentistry in matters of legislation and regulations. Inspects and accredits dental schools and schools for dental hygienists, assistants, and laboratory technicians. Conducts research programs at ADA Foundation Research Institute. Produces most of the dental health education material used in the U.S. Sponsors National Children's Dental Health Month and Give Kids a Smile Day. Compiles statistics on personnel, practice, and dental care needs and attitudes of patients with regard to dental health. Sponsors 13 councils. **Libraries:** Type: reference; open to the public. **Holdings:** 40,000; archival material, books, periodicals. **Subjects:** dentistry, oral health, biographical records of U.S. dentists, published and original documentary material of historical interest to the profession. **Absorbed:** (1897) Southern Dental Association. **Formerly:** (1922) National Dental Association. **Publications:** *ADA News*, biweekly. Newspaper. **Price:** \$64.00 for nonmembers. ISSN: 0895-2930. **Circulation:** 148,000. **Advertising:** accepted ● *Journal of the American Dental Association*, monthly. **Price:** \$116.00 for nonmembers. ISSN: 0002-8177. **Circulation:** 136,000. **Advertising:** accepted. **Conventions/Meetings:** Annual Session - convention and general assembly, includes scientific sessions, continuing education, technical exhibits, and the house of delegates (exhibits) - usually in October.

13833 ■ American Dental Hygienists' Association (ADHA)
444 N Michigan Ave., Ste.3400
Chicago, IL 60611
Ph: (312)440-8911 (312)440-8900
Free: (800)243-ADHA
Fax: (312)467-1806
E-mail: mail@adha.net
URL: http://www.adha.org
Contact: Ann Battrell RDH, Exec. Dir.
Founded: 1923. **Members:** 35,000. **Membership Dues:** national, \$170 (annual) ● student, \$45 (annual). **Staff:** 40. **Budget:** \$6,000,000. **Regional Groups:** 12. **State Groups:** 53. **Local Groups:** 360. **Description:** Professional organization of licensed dental hygienists possessing a degree or certificate in dental hygiene granted by an accredited school of dental hygiene. Makes available scholarships, research grants, and continuing education programs. Maintains accrediting service through the American Dental Association's Commission on Dental Accreditation. Compiles statistics. **Awards:** Type: recognition. **Computer Services:** Mailing lists, of members. **Committees:** Education; Member Services; National Boards; Public Relations; Regulation and Practice; Research; Scholarship. **Divisions:** Communications; Finance and MIS; Government Affairs; Professional Development. **Publications:** *Access*, 10/year. Magazine. Covers current dental hygiene topics, regulatory and legislative develop-

ments, and association news. Includes membership profiles. **Price:** included in membership dues; \$48.00 /year for nonmembers; \$85.00/2 years; \$120.00/3 years. **Circulation:** 30,000. **Advertising:** accepted ● *Journal of Dental Hygiene*, quarterly. Includes association news, book reviews, abstracts, government news, and information on research and new products. **Price:** included in membership dues; \$45.00 /year for nonmembers; \$65.00/2 years; \$90.00/3 years. ISSN: 0091-3979. **Circulation:** 30,000. **Advertising:** accepted. Alternate Formats: microform. **Conventions/Meetings:** annual meeting (exhibits) - 2008 June 18-25, Albuquerque, NM; 2009 June 16-24, Washington, DC.

13834 ■ American Dental Society of Anesthesiology (ADSA)
211 E Chicago Ave., Ste.780
Chicago, IL 60611
Free: (877)255-3742
E-mail: jnjcarl@cetlink.net
URL: http://www.adsahome.org
Contact: Joseph E. Carlisle DMD, Pres.
Founded: 1953. **Members:** 3,200. **Membership Dues:** individual, \$175 (annual) ● non-dentist/foreign dentist, \$87 (annual) ● student/resident, \$26 (annual). **Staff:** 2. **Budget:** \$350,000. **State Groups:** 21. **Description:** Dentists and physicians. Encourages study and progress in dental anesthesiology. **Awards:** Heidbrink Award. **Frequency:** annual. **Type:** recognition ● Qualification for Use of General Anesthetic Fellowship. **Type:** fellowship ● **Type:** recognition. **Recipient:** to senior dental students for outstanding service in dental anesthesiology. **Committees:** Advanced Education; Continuing Education. **Publications:** *ADSA Directory*, annual. Membership Directory. Alternate Formats: online ● *Anesthesia Progress*, quarterly. Journal. **Price:** included in membership dues; \$35.00 /year for nonmembers; \$55.00 /year for institutions ● *The Pulse*, bimonthly. Newsletter. Includes society news, calendar of events, and research updates. **Price:** included in membership dues; \$5.00 /year for nonmembers. ISSN: 0274-9793. **Circulation:** 4,000. **Conventions/Meetings:** annual competition, essay contest for matriculated dental students (exhibits) ● annual meeting (exhibits).

13835 ■ American Endodontic Society (AES)
265 N Main St.
Glen Ellyn, IL 60137
Ph: (773)519-4879
Fax: (630)858-0525
E-mail: n2dontics@aol.com
URL: http://www.aesoc.com
Contact: Dr. Mark Piacine, Pres.
Founded: 1969. **Members:** 10,000. **Membership Dues:** dentist/active, \$195 (annual) ● auxiliary/student, allied, dentist/retired, \$50 (annual). **Staff:** 2. **Description:** Dentists. Promotes and provides educational and scientific information on simplified root canal therapy for the general practitioner. Conducts research programs. **Awards:** Fellowship of the Society. **Type:** fellowship ● Mastership of the Society. **Type:** recognition. **Publications:** *Hotline*, periodic. Article ● Newsletter, quarterly. Contains society news, member profiles, and instructional articles. Alternate Formats: online. **Conventions/Meetings:** annual meeting ● seminar.

13836 ■ American Equilibration Society (AES)
207 E Ohio St., Ste.399
Chicago, IL 60611
Free: (888)865-7778
E-mail: exec@aes-tmj.org
URL: http://www.occlusion-tmj.org
Contact: Dr. Ransom R. Altman, Pres.
Founded: 1955. **Members:** 1,100. **Membership Dues:** individual, \$650 (annual). **Budget:** \$75,000. **Description:** Dentists, orthodontists, oral surgeons, and physicians interested in study and proficiency in the diagnosis and treatment of occlusal and temporomandibular joint disorders. Deals with the diagnosis and treatment of diseases of dental occlusion and disorders of the Temporomandibular Joint (TMJ) and

associated muscles. **Awards:** Student Recognition Certificate. **Frequency:** annual. **Type:** recognition. **Recipient:** to outstanding graduating students. **Committees:** Research. **Publications:** *American Equilibration Society Newsletter*, 3/year. **Price:** included in membership dues ● *Roster*, annual. Directory ● *TMJ Update*, bimonthly. Newsletter. **Price:** included in membership dues; \$69.00 /year for nonmembers. **Conventions/Meetings:** annual international conference (exhibits) - always February, in Chicago, IL.

13837 ■ American Independent Dentist's Association (AIDA)
c/o K. Randall Groh, DDS, Acting Chm.
336 Alhambra Cir.
Coral Gables, FL 33134
Ph: (305)442-1177
E-mail: feeforserv@aol.com
URL: http://www.dentalbeacon.org
Contact: K. Randall Groh DDS, Acting Chm.
Membership Dues: regular, \$200 (annual) ● student, \$50 (annual) ● first year dentist, \$100. **Description:** Promotes traditional fee-for-service dentistry as an option that requires representation at all levels of organized dentistry and civil government.

13838 ■ American Institute of Oral Biology (AIOB)
PO Box 7184
Loma Linda, CA 92354-7184
Ph: (909)558-4671
Fax: (909)558-0285
E-mail: jbarrientos@sd.llu.edu
URL: http://www.theaiob.org
Contact: June J. Barrientos, Exec. Sec.
Founded: 1943. **Members:** 150. **Membership Dues:** individual, \$325 (annual). **Staff:** 1. **Description:** Represent dental and medical health professionals united for continuing education. Conducts lectures. **Publications:** *AIOB Proceedings Manual*, annual. **Price:** \$75.00/copy. ISSN: 0098-6119. **Conventions/Meetings:** annual seminar and meeting - always October, Palm Springs, CA.

13839 ■ American Orthodontic Society (AOS)
11884 Greenville Ave., Ste.112
Dallas, TX 75243-3537
Free: (800)448-1601
E-mail: aos@orthodontics.com
URL: http://www.orthodontics.com
Contact: Tom Chapman, Exec. Dir.
Founded: 1974. **Members:** 1,900. **Membership Dues:** individual, \$195 (annual). **Staff:** 4. **Budget:** \$900,000. **Description:** General and pediatric dentists. Objectives are: to make orthodontic information readily available to any ethical dentist; to zealously protect the right of members to pursue orthodontic knowledge; to keep a watchful eye on third party services and government programs. Offers courses in orthodontic techniques. Conducts educational programs. **Libraries:** Type: reference. **Holdings:** 1,000; audiovisuals. **Subjects:** orthodontics. **Awards:** Dr. Richard L. Moore Distinguished Service Award. **Frequency:** annual. **Type:** recognition. **Recipient:** for outstanding contribution to organized dentistry in the field of orthodontics. **Computer Services:** Mailing lists, referrals, directory. **Publications:** *American Orthodontic Society Newsletter*, quarterly. Provides information on the society's seminars and conventions and news of interest to members. **Price:** included in membership dues. **Circulation:** 4,000 ● *American Orthodontic Society Technique Directory*, biennial. Membership Directory. Lists members by city and state; includes the type of orthodontic technique used by listee. **Price:** \$150.00/year. **Advertising:** accepted ● Brochures. **Conventions/Meetings:** annual convention, held in conjunction with International Association of Orthodontics (exhibits) - usually September.

13840 ■ American Prosthodontic Society (APS)
426 Hudson St.
Hackensack, NJ 07601
Ph: (201)440-7699
Free: (877)499-3500

Fax: (201)440-7963
E-mail: aps@prostho.org
URL: http://www.prostho.org
Contact: Carol Bensky, Sec.
Founded: 1928. **Members:** 800. **Membership Dues:** active, $410-$455 (annual) ● associate, $300-$335 (annual) ● active, life, $251. **Staff:** 1. **Budget:** $150,000. **Description:** Dentists interested in the discipline of prosthodontics (the art and science of replacing missing teeth and supporting structures). **Awards:** APS Achievement Award. **Frequency:** annual. **Type:** recognition. **Recipient:** for prosthodontists who have made outstanding contributions worldwide to prosthodontics ● Kenneth D. Rudd Award. **Frequency:** annual. **Type:** recognition. **Recipient:** to a dental technologist who has made a significant contribution to the advancement of the dentist dental laboratory technologist team concept. **Publications:** *Journal of Prosthetic Dentistry,* monthly. Published in conjunction with 21 other prosthodontic organizations. **Price:** included in membership dues. **Conventions/Meetings:** annual Scientific Meeting, dentists and CDTs interested in prosthodontics (exhibits).

13841 ■ American Society for Dental Aesthetics (ASDA)
635 Madison Ave.
New York, NY 10022
Ph: (212)751-3263
Free: (888)988-ASDA
Fax: (212)755-3263
E-mail: info@asdatoday.com
URL: http://www.asdatoday.com
Contact: Irwin Smigel DDS, Pres.
Founded: 1978. **Members:** 175. **Membership Dues:** honorary, $350 (annual). **Staff:** 3. **Multinational. Description:** Represents accredited dentists practicing aesthetic concepts in dentistry, including porcelain lamination (a technique where porcelain veneer is chemically fused to teeth to lengthen them, close spaces, or recontour the entire mouth); dentists must have 5 years experience and submit 5 "before and after" photos of their work in aesthetic dentistry to qualify for membership. Promotes development, research, and teaching of aesthetic concepts in dentistry. Seeks for the expansion of aesthetic dentistry concepts in other states and abroad. Sponsors educational programs on tooth and crown repair, aesthetic fillings, orthodontics, periodontics, implantology, and other topics. **Awards:** **Frequency:** annual. **Type:** fellowship. **Recipient:** for a member who has helped in the advancement and development of aesthetic dentistry. **Computer Services:** database. **Publications:** *ASDA Today,* semiannual. Journal. Promotes development, teaching and research of aesthetic dentistry. **Price:** free. **Circulation:** 8,000. **Advertising:** accepted. **Conventions/Meetings:** annual International Conference on Aesthetic Dentistry - seminar, with lectures and participation workshops (exhibits).

13842 ■ American Society of Dentist Anesthesiologists (ASDA)
c/o Dr. Lee Lichtenstein, Treas.
723 N Beers St.
Holmdel, NJ 07733
Ph: (732)739-3337
Fax: (732)739-6288
E-mail: lml@netlabs.net
URL: http://www.asdahq.org
Contact: Dr. Lee Lichtenstein, Treas.
Membership Dues: active/associate, $100 ● resident/student, $35. **Description:** Strives to make the full spectrum of anesthesia care available to dental patients; train dentists in anesthesia care. **Conventions/Meetings:** annual Scientific Session - meeting.

13843 ■ American Society of Forensic Odontology (ASFO)
PO Box 156
Eastport, ID 83826
Fax: (250)426-2354

E-mail: asfoadmin@xplornet.com
URL: http://www.asfo.org
Contact: Dr. Ben Gibson DDS, Exec. Dir.
Founded: 1970. **Members:** 900. **Membership Dues:** regular, $75 (annual) ● student, $15 (annual). **Staff:** 1. **Regional Groups:** 1. **Multinational. Description:** Individuals interested in furthering the field of forensic dentistry. Conducts research and specialized education programs. **Libraries: Type:** reference. **Committees:** Research Grants Awards Review. **Publications:** *Digital Analysis of Bite Mark Evidence, 2nd Edition.* Book. Contains guide to bite mark analysis using computer imaging. Alternate Formats: CD-ROM ● *Forensic Dental Evidence.* Book. Contains excellent introduction text for dentists and law enforcement personnel. ● *Forensic Pathology.* Book. Contains superb introduction to forensic pathology. **Price:** $25.95/copy ● *Forensic Radiology.* Book. Includes chapter by Dr. David Sweet on bite marks and Dr. Mark Bernstein on identifications. **Price:** $99.95/copy (plus 4.99 sourcing fee) ● *The Manual of Forensic Odontology, Third Edition.* Covers all aspects of odontology including identification, bite marks, abuse, ageing, evidence collection and court presentation. **Price:** $53.00/copy, for members; $79.00/copy, for nonmembers ● Newsletter, 3/year. **Conventions/Meetings:** annual conference, in conjunction with the American Academy of Forensic Sciences.

13844 ■ American Society of Master Dental Technologists (ASMDT)
146-21 13th Ave.
Whitestone, NY 11357-2420
Ph: (718)746-8355 (718)347-1239
Fax: (718)746-8355
E-mail: valleluia@nyc.rr.com
URL: http://www.asmdt.com
Contact: Sue Heppenheimer, Exec. Dir.
Founded: 1976. **Members:** 125. **Membership Dues:** individual, $100 (annual). **Staff:** 2. **Description:** Represents dental lab technicians. Aims to upgrade dental technology. Seeks to provide educational resources such as texts, instructors, and guidance for technicians interested in becoming master dental technologists. Conducts associate and master level courses in conjunction with New York University School of Dentistry, Dept. of Continuing Education. **Awards:** Irving Sutla Award. **Frequency:** annual. **Type:** monetary. **Recipient:** for best tooth carving ● NGS (Northeastern Grathological Society) Award. **Frequency:** annual. **Type:** monetary. **Recipient:** for best student in courses. **Committees:** Educational; Publicity. **Conventions/Meetings:** annual Exposition - meeting ● semiannual meeting (exhibits).

13845 ■ American Society for the Study of Orthodontics (ASSO)
70-15 164th St.
Flushing, NY 11365
Ph: (718)591-6411
Fax: (718)591-5424
E-mail: mblochdds@yahoo.com
Contact: Dr. Milton Bloch, Pres.
Founded: 1945. **Members:** 100. **Membership Dues:** regular, $75 (annual). **Description:** Members of the American Dental Association (see separate entry) or other societies, with special interest in orthodontics but not limited to those who practice in the field. Purposes are to: preserve the highest ideals in orthodontics and in dentistry; encourage and assist the diffusion of orthodontic knowledge to all dentists who include orthodontics as an integral part of their health service or limit their practice to orthodontics; institute an intensive program of fundamental and advanced studies and guidance for its members in theoretical, didactic, and applied orthodontics; encourage the orthodontic departments of university dental schools to provide both short and extended courses in orthodontics; to establish discussion and clinical study groups throughout the U.S. Conducts lectures, panel discussions, postgraduate seminars, table clinics, and consultation service. **Formerly:** (1962) New York Society for the Study of Orthodontics. **Publications:** *ASSO Newsletter,* quarterly ● *International Journal of Orthodontics,* 3/year. **Con-**

ventions/Meetings: annual meeting - always November, New York City ● annual meeting and symposium.

13846 ■ Association of Managed Care Dentists (AMCD)
1223 Wilshire Blvd., Ste.483
Santa Monica, CA 90403
Ph: (310)453-3439
Fax: (310)453-7895
E-mail: bonnie4098@aol.com
URL: http://www.amcd.org
Contact: John J. Maguire DDS, Pres.
Membership Dues: recent graduate/additional dentist or staff from same office, $95 (annual) ● dentist/administrator, $150 (annual) ● affiliate, $250 (annual). **Description:** Dentists participating in managed dental care programs. Seeks to advance the provision of managed dental care. Serves as liaison linking members with government agencies and dental plan administrators; sponsors educational programs. **Formerly:** (2000) Association of Managed Care Providers. **Publications:** *News Flash,* periodic. Newsletter. **Conventions/Meetings:** annual symposium.

13847 ■ Association of State and Territorial Dental Directors (ASTDD)
105 Westerly Rd.
New Bern, NC 28560
Ph: (252)637-6333
Fax: (252)637-3343
E-mail: dperkins@astdd.org
URL: http://www.astdd.org
Contact: M. Dean Perkins DDS, Exec. Dir.
Founded: 1948. **Members:** 54. **Membership Dues:** regular, $100 (annual) ● associate, $50 (annual). **Description:** Represents directors and staff of state public health agency programs for oral health. Formulates and promotes the establishment of sound national dental public health policy and assists state dental programs in the development and implementation of programs and policies for the prevention of oral diseases. **Publications:** *Oral Health Matters,* periodic. Newsletter. **Conventions/Meetings:** annual National Oral Health Conference.

13848 ■ Christian Dental Society (CDS)
PO Box 296
Sumner, IA 50674
Ph: (563)578-8887
Fax: (563)578-8887
E-mail: cdssent@iowatelecom.net
URL: http://www.christiandental.org
Contact: Jodi Yarbro DDS, Pres.
Founded: 1962. **Members:** 900. **Membership Dues:** active, $150 (annual) ● life, $1,500. **Staff:** 2. **Description:** Encourages dentists to donate their professional services to Christian schools, clinics, and hospitals. Cooperates with churches, volunteer agencies, and service organizations to provide volunteers, equipment, and supplies. Maintains speakers' bureau. **Affiliated With:** American Dental Association. **Formerly:** (1962) Presbyterian Missionary Committee. **Publications:** *CDS News Update,* monthly. Newsletter ● *CDS Newsletter,* quarterly. **Circulation:** 3,000. **Advertising:** accepted ● *Portable Mission Dentistry.* Book. **Conventions/Meetings:** annual Family and Staff Retreat - meeting, offers continuing education credits.

13849 ■ Clinical Research Associates (CRA)
3707 N Canyon Rd., Ste.6
Provo, UT 84604
Ph: (801)226-2121
Fax: (801)226-4726
E-mail: cra@cranews.com
URL: http://www.cranews.com
Contact: Jennifer Bushman, Marketing Coor.
Founded: 1976. **Description:** Provides dental product evaluation through testing of all types of dental products. **Publications:** *Dental Hygiene,* bimonthly. Newsletter. Features non-biased dental research. **Price:** $25.00. Alternate Formats: online ● Newsletter, monthly. Serves as a product and technique guide for dental clinicians. **Price:** $65.00. Alternate Formats: online.

13850 ■ College of Diplomates of the American Board of Orthodontics (CDABO)
3260 Upper Bottom Rd.
St. Charles, MO 63303
Ph: (636)922-5551
Fax: (636)244-1650
E-mail: cdabo@charter.net
URL: http://www.cdabo.org
Contact: Karen Seiler, Exec. Dir.
Founded: 1979. **Members:** 1,732. **Membership Dues:** orthodontist, $50 (annual). **Staff:** 2. **Budget:** $275,000. **Description:** Members are diplomates of the American Board of Orthodontics who pass qualifying examinations. Promotes self-evaluation and ongoing professional improvement among orthodontists. Conducts seminars. **Affiliated With:** American Board of Orthodontics. **Publications:** *The Diplomate*, semiannual. Newsletter. **Price:** free, for members only. **Conventions/Meetings:** annual meeting - always July.

13851 ■ Dental Anthropology Association (DAA)
c/o Edward F. Harris, Ed.
Univ. of Tennessee
Coll. of Dentistry
870 Union Ave.
Memphis, TN 38163
E-mail: eharris@utmem.edu
URL: http://monkey.sbs.ohio-state.edu/DAA/index.htm
Contact: Edward F. Harris, Ed.
Membership Dues: regular, $20 (annual) ● student, $10 (annual). **Description:** Promotes scientific research on the dental evolution and variation in the oral health and dental morphology of modern and ancient human populations. **Awards:** Albert A. Dahlberg Award. **Frequency:** annual. **Type:** recognition. **Recipient:** to the best student paper submitted to the association. **Publications:** *Dental Anthropology*, 3/year. Journal. **Price:** included in membership dues.

13852 ■ Dental Assisting National Board (DANB)
444 N Michigan Ave., Ste.900
Chicago, IL 60611
Ph: (312)642-3368
Free: (800)FOR-DANB
Fax: (312)642-1475
E-mail: danbmail@danb.org
URL: http://www.danb.org
Contact: Cynthia C. Durley MEd, Exec. Dir.
Founded: 1948. **Staff:** 21. **Budget:** $1,000,000. **Description:** Certifying agency that administers examinations to dental assistants. **Formerly:** Certifying Board of the American Dental Assistants Association. **Publications:** *DANB's State Fact Booklet*, annual. Provides valuable dental assisting information.

13853 ■ Dental Health International (DHI)
847 S Milledge Ave.
Athens, GA 30605
Ph: (706)546-1716
Fax: (706)546-1715
E-mail: bsdds@bellsouth.net
Contact: Barry Simmons DDS, Pres.
Founded: 1973. **Staff:** 1. **Description:** Dentists, dental hygienists, dental technicians, and the International Association of Dental Students. Purposes are to promote dental health programs in developing countries; to provide general dental care using portable modular dental units in areas without electricity or water. Utilizes minimal fee structure to support projects; professionals in the field of dentistry donate their services for a period of 3 months. Volunteer dentists and dental technicians collect permanent non-obsolete dental equipment in their local areas and rendezvous with the equipment in the host country and assist with the installation of it. Serves "pro-United States" countries.

13854 ■ Flying Dentists Association (FDA)
10032 Wind Hill Dr.
Greenville, IN 47124-9673
Ph: (812)923-2100
Fax: (812)923-2900

E-mail: jsalis913@aol.com
URL: http://www.flyingdentists.org
Contact: Ms. Judy Salisbury, Exec. Dir.
Founded: 1960. **Members:** 400. **Membership Dues:** active, $90 (annual). **Staff:** 1. **Budget:** $121,000. **Regional Groups:** 4. **Description:** Members are dentists who have or have had an active aircraft pilot's license. Makes use of private air travel in conducting their dental practice. **Libraries:** Type: not open to the public. **Holdings:** periodicals. **Subjects:** association newsletters. **Computer Services:** database, iMIS. **Publications:** *FDA Newsletter*, monthly, except July ● *Flight Watch*, annual, July. Magazine. **Circulation:** 400. **Conventions/Meetings:** annual convention, business meeting, board meeting, continuing education, exhibits, networking, adult and children's social activities (exhibits) - usually June or July.

13855 ■ Friends of the National Institute of Dental and Craniofacial Research (FNIDCR)
11101 Georgia Ave., Ste.324
Silver Spring, MD 20902
Ph: (301)946-9444
E-mail: alec@fnidcr.org
URL: http://www.fnidcr.org
Contact: Alec J. Stone, Exec. Dir.
Founded: 1998. **Members:** 250. **Membership Dues:** corporate (regular), $3,000 (annual) ● corporate (contributor), $5,000 (annual) ● corporate (sponsor), $10,000 (annual) ● corporate (patron), $25,000 (annual) ● institutional (sponsor), $2,000 (annual) ● institutional (patron), $5,000 (annual) ● individual, $50 (annual) ● individual (corporate), $100 (annual) ● individual (sponsor), $250 (annual) ● individual (patron), $1,000 (annual). **Staff:** 2. **Budget:** $250,000. **Description:** Individuals, institutions, and corporations with an interest in dental research. Believes that dental, oral and craniofacial health are of critical importance to the well-being of society. **Awards:** Lifetime Achievement Award. **Frequency:** annual. **Type:** recognition ● Patient Advocacy Award. **Frequency:** annual. **Type:** recognition. **Publications:** *Online Update!*, monthly. Newsletter. Alternate Formats: online ● *Update!*, semiannual. Newsletter. **Conventions/Meetings:** annual Gala Awards Dinner.

13856 ■ Hispanic Dental Association (HDA)
1224 Centre W, Ste.400B
Springfield, IL 62704
Ph: (217)793-0035
Free: (800)852-7921
Fax: (217)793-0041
E-mail: hispanicdental@hdassoc.org
URL: http://www.hdassoc.org
Contact: Becky Jeppesen, Exec. Dir.
Founded: 1990. **Members:** 2,500. **Membership Dues:** dental professional, organization, $125 (annual) ● retired, $60 (annual) ● international, $30 (annual). **Staff:** 4. **Budget:** $200,000. **Regional Groups:** 31. **Description:** Provides leadership and represents professionals who share a common commitment to improve the oral health of the Hispanic community. **Awards:** HDA Foundation. **Type:** scholarship. **Recipient:** for entry level dental school students, and other programs. **Publications:** *HDA News & Reports*, quarterly. Newsletter. **Circulation:** 15,000. **Advertising:** accepted. **Conventions/Meetings:** annual meeting (exhibits).

13857 ■ Holistic Dental Association (HDA)
PO Box 151444
San Diego, CA 92175
Ph: (619)923-3120
Fax: (619)615-2228
E-mail: info@holisticdental.org
URL: http://www.holisticdental.org
Contact: Sandra Orion, Exec. Dir.
Founded: 1980. **Members:** 200. **Membership Dues:** dental practitioner, $295 (annual) ● dental student, $50 (annual) ● other, $125 (annual). **Staff:** 1. **Description:** Dentists, chiropractors, dental hygienists, physical therapists, and medical doctors. Goals are: to provide a holistic approach to better dental care for patients; to expand techniques, medications, and philosophies that pertain to extractions, anesthetics,

fillings, crowns, and orthodontics. Encourages use of homeopathic medications, acupuncture, cranial osteopathy, nutritional techniques, and physical therapy in treating patients in addition to conventional treatments. Sponsors training and educational seminars. **Formerly:** Holistic Dental Association International. **Publications:** *Communicator*, quarterly. Journal. Includes calendar of events and research updates. **Price:** included in membership dues. **Circulation:** 200. **Advertising:** accepted. **Conventions/Meetings:** annual Dental Materials Summit - symposium.

13858 ■ Indian Dental Association, U.S.A. (IDA-USA)
146-02 89th Ave.
Jamaica, NY 11435
Ph: (718)639-0192 (718)523-8438
Fax: (718)639-8122
URL: http://www.ida-usa.org
Contact: Dr. Daljeet S. Sidhu, Pres.
Founded: 1983. **Members:** 345. **Membership Dues:** life, $250 ● regular, $50 (annual) ● student, $10 (annual). **Staff:** 1. **State Groups:** 5. **Description:** Represents dentists in the U.S. who are of Asian-Indian descent. Seeks to further the professional education of members. Conducts social events. **Publications:** *IDA Newsletter*, monthly. **Conventions/Meetings:** annual meeting.

13859 ■ International Academy of Gnathology-American Section (IAG)
3868 Riviera Dr., Ste.3B
San Diego, CA 92109-6351
Ph: (858)273-9263
Fax: (858)274-9587
E-mail: jimbenson_99@yahoo.com
URL: http://www.gnathologyusa.org
Contact: Dr. James Benson, Sec.-Treas.
Founded: 1964. **Members:** 200. **Membership Dues:** general, $200 (annual) ● retired, full-time teaching, $125 (annual). **Staff:** 2. **Description:** Dentists and educators interested in the science of gnathology. (Gnathology is the science that treats the biology of chewing and the jaws and cheeks as related to the rest of the body.) Areas of concern include morphology, anatomy, psychology, physiology, pathology, and therapy of the mouth. **Awards:** McCullum Award. **Frequency:** biennial. **Type:** recognition. **Computer Services:** database. **Publications:** *The Gnathology Gnews*. Newsletter. **Conventions/Meetings:** biennial meeting - 2007 Oct. 17-20, Coronado, CA.

13860 ■ International Academy of Myodontics (IAM)
c/o Dr. Harry N. Cooperman, DDS, Pres.
777 Ferry Rd. P-6
Doylestown, PA 18901
Ph: (215)345-1149
Fax: (215)609-2588
E-mail: myodont@comcat.com
URL: http://www.myodontics.com/IAM/IAM-cooperman.hp/index.html
Contact: Dr. Harry N. Cooperman DDS, Pres.
Founded: 1970. **Members:** 1,100. **Regional Groups:** 2. **Description:** Dentists who specialize in the treatment of head and neck syndromes that cause dental or oral malfunction. Works with physicians and dentists in the field of myodontics, especially those working on the treatment of Cooperman-Muira Syndrome, also known as uvula-tongue malposture syndrome. **Conventions/Meetings:** annual meeting.

13861 ■ International Academy of Oral Medicine and Toxicology (IAOMT)
8297 Champions Gate Blvd., No. 193
Champions Gate, FL 33896
Ph: (863)420-6373
Fax: (863)419-8136
E-mail: info@iaomt.org
Contact: Kym Smith, Exec. Dir.
Founded: 1984. **Members:** 1,000. **Membership Dues:** initial, $350. **Staff:** 1. **National Groups:** 11. **Multinational. Description:** Dentists, physicians, and medical scientists. Encourages, sponsors, and

disseminates scientific research on the biocompatibility of materials used in dentistry. Offers educational programs; maintains speaker's bureau. **Libraries: Type:** reference; not open to the public. **Subjects:** materials used in dentistry. **Awards:** Fellow. **Type:** fellowship. **Recipient:** for education and attendance. **Computer Services:** Online services, forums. **Committees:** Education; Liaison; Protocol. **Publications:** *Bio-Probe Newsletter,* bimonthly. Features review of scientific literature and legislative activities. **Price:** included in membership dues ● *IN-VIVO,* quarterly. Newsletter. Contains information about activities and accomplishments of Academy members and important events of interest to Academy members. **Price:** included in membership dues ● Membership Directory. Contains member information indexed alphabetically and geographically. **Conventions/Meetings:** annual meeting - every September ● regional meeting ● semiannual seminar, scientific symposium (exhibits) - 2007 Sept. 7-8, Las Vegas, NV.

13862 ■ International Association for Dental Research (IADR)
1619 Duke St.
Alexandria, VA 22314-3406
Ph: (703)548-0066
Fax: (703)548-1883
E-mail: research@iadr.org
URL: http://www.iadr.com
Contact: Christopher H. Fox, Exec. Dir.
Founded: 1920. **Members:** 10,000. **Membership Dues:** individual, $50 (annual). **Staff:** 17. **Budget:** $2,500,000. **Regional Groups:** 20. **Description:** Individuals engaged or interested in advancing research in the various aspects of dental and related sciences. **Awards:** Edward H. Hatton Award. **Type:** recognition. **Recipient:** for winners of Junior Investigators competition ● H. Trendley Dean Memorial Award. **Type:** monetary. **Recipient:** for research in epidemiology and public health ● Young Investigator Award. **Type:** monetary. **Recipient:** for basic research in all dental research disciplines. **Subgroups:** Behavioral Sciences; Cariology Research; Craniofacial Biology; Dental Anesthesiology Research; Dental Materials; Diagnostic Systems; Education Research; Geriatrics; Implantology; Microbiology and Immunology; Mineralized Tissue; Neuroscience; Nutrition Research; Oral and Maxillofacial Surgery; Oral Health Research; Oral Medicine and Pathology; Periodontics; Pharmacology, Therapeutics and Toxicology; Pulp Biology; Salivary Research. **Publications:** *Abstracts, A Special Issue of Journal of Dental Research,* quarterly ● *Advances in Dental Research,* periodic. Journal. Covers developments in dental research and the chemistry, biology, and function of the oral cavity. Also includes conference proceedings. **Circulation:** 1,100. **Advertising:** accepted. Alternate Formats: online ● *Critical Reviews in Oral Biology and Medicine,* bimonthly. Alternate Formats: online ● *Journal of Dental Research,* monthly. Disseminates new information and knowledge on all sciences relevant to dentistry, the oral cavity, and associated structures in health and disease. Alternate Formats: online. **Conventions/Meetings:** annual general assembly (exhibits) - 2008 July 2-5, Toronto, ON, Canada; 2009 Apr. 1-4, Miami, FL ● annual meeting (exhibits).

13863 ■ International Association for Orthodontics (IAO)
750 N Lincoln Memorial Dr., Ste.422
Milwaukee, WI 53202
Ph: (414)272-2757
Free: (800)447-8770
Fax: (414)272-2754
E-mail: worldheadquarters@iaortho.org
URL: http://www.iaortho.org
Contact: Detlef B. Moore, Exec. Dir.
Founded: 1961. **Members:** 3,600. **Membership Dues:** developed country, $239 (annual) ● developing country, $106 (annual). **Staff:** 3. **Budget:** $500,000. **Regional Groups:** 15. **Local Groups:** 80. **Multinational. Description:** Dentists. Promotes the study and dissemination of information on the cause, control, treatment, and prevention of malocclusion of the teeth; facilitates exchange of ideas and experiences, based on a biomechanical approach, between

the various fields of dentistry related to orthodontics. **Libraries: Type:** not open to the public. **Holdings:** 150; video recordings. **Subjects:** orthodontics. **Awards:** Pinsker Award. **Frequency:** annual. **Type:** recognition. **Recipient:** for members of IAO with outstanding contributions to the profession. **Computer Services:** database ● information services ● mailing lists, labels. **Committees:** Dental Care; Peer Review; Postgraduate Education; Study Club. **Formerly:** International Academy of Orthodontics. **Publications:** *IAO Straight Talk,* quarterly. Newsletter. Provides information on membership activities. **Price:** included in membership dues; $15.00 /year for nonmembers. **Circulation:** 3,600 ● *International Association of Orthodontics—Directory of Members,* annual. **Price:** included in membership dues; $150.00 for nonmembers. **Circulation:** 3,600 ● *International Journal of Orthodontics,* quarterly. Contains clinical articles on orthodontics, self-assessment, troubleshooting, and new products. **Price:** $40.00/year. ISSN: 1048-1990. **Circulation:** 4,000. **Advertising:** accepted. **Conventions/Meetings:** annual meeting, with technical and services exhibits (exhibits) - usually April.

13864 ■ International College of Dentists (ICD)
51 Monroe St., Ste.1400
Rockville, MD 20850-2408
Ph: (301)251-8861
Fax: (301)738-9143
E-mail: reg-sg@icd.org
URL: http://www.icd.org
Contact: Donald E. Johnson, Pres.
Founded: 1928. **Members:** 9,200. **Membership Dues:** fellow, $115 (annual). **Staff:** 3. **Budget:** $700,000. **Description:** Dentists who have made outstanding contributions to the profession. Acclaims meritorious service to dentistry; fosters growth and diffusion of dental information; upholds high standards in dental education. Supports the Dental Career Option Seminar for Students. Promotes continuing education through the International Clinicians Program. Operates charitable programs. **Libraries: Type:** reference. **Holdings:** 45; audiovisuals. **Awards:** Dental Journalism Award. **Frequency:** annual. **Type:** recognition ● **Frequency:** annual. **Type:** recognition. **Recipient:** to outstanding graduate students at each U.S. dental school. **Publications:** *Globe,* annual. Journal ● *Key,* annual. Magazine ● *Keynotes,* semiannual. Newsletter ● *Roster,* periodic. Membership Directory. **Conventions/Meetings:** annual meeting.

13865 ■ International College of Prosthodontists (ICP)
PO Box 99119
San Diego, CA 92109
Ph: (858)270-1814
Fax: (858)272-7687
E-mail: icp@icp-org.com
URL: http://www.icp-org.com
Contact: Mr. Eben Yancey, Exec. Dir.
Members: 750. **Membership Dues:** constituent/affiliate, $195 (annual) ● affiliate student, $85 (annual). **Staff:** 2. **Multinational. Description:** Prosthodontists. Works to make the services of prosthodontists better understood by the patients. Advances the specialty of prosthodontists globally. **Awards:** Young Prosthodontists Award. **Frequency:** biennial. **Type:** monetary. **Committees:** Ambassadorial; Constitution and By-laws; Education and Research; Nominating; Professional Relations; Scientific; Sponsorship. **Publications:** *The International Journal of Prosthodontics,* bimonthly. **Price:** included in membership dues. **Advertising:** accepted ● Newsletter. Alternate Formats: online. **Conventions/Meetings:** biennial conference - held every odd numbered year. 2007 Sept. 5-8, Fukuoka, Japan.

13866 ■ International Congress of Oral Implantologists (ICOI)
248 Lorraine Ave., Ste.3
Upper Montclair, NJ 07043
Ph: (973)783-6300
Free: (800)442-0525

Fax: (973)783-1175
E-mail: icoi@dentalimplants.com
URL: http://www.icoi.org
Contact: R. Craig Johnson, Exec. Dir.
Founded: 1975. **Members:** 7,500. **Membership Dues:** dental practitioner, $350 (annual) ● full-time university faculty, military, $200 (annual) ● laboratory technician, research or industry personnel, recent graduate, $150 (annual) ● pre-doctoral or graduate student, $100 (annual) ● international, $275 (annual). **Staff:** 7. **Budget:** $2,000,000. **Description:** Dentists and oral surgeons dedicated to the teaching of and research in oral implantology (branch of dentistry dealing with dental implants placed into or on top of the jaw bone). Offers fellowship, mastership, and diplomate certification programs. Compiles statistics and maintains registry of current research in the field. Sponsors classes, seminars, and workshops at universities, hospitals, and societies worldwide. Provides consultation and patient information/referral services. **Computer Services:** Mailing lists, of members. **Committees:** Diplomate; Fellowship. **Departments:** Professional Services. **Formerly:** (1976) International College of Oral Implantologists. **Publications:** *Implant Dentistry,* quarterly. Journal. Includes scientific manuscripts, new product reports, membership updates, and calendar of seminars. **Price:** included in membership dues; $200.00 for nonmembers in U.S.; $246.00 for nonmembers outside U.S. ISSN: 0190-2024. **Circulation:** 9,000. **Advertising:** accepted ● *International Magazine of Oral Implantology,* quarterly. Journal. Includes society news from around the world, new product information, clinical care studies. **Price:** included in membership dues. **Circulation:** 10,000. **Advertising:** accepted ● Membership Directory, annual. **Conventions/Meetings:** annual symposium ● annual World Congress.

13867 ■ International Dental Health Foundation (IDHF)
2414 Black Cap Ln., Ste.L-1
Reston, VA 20191
Ph: (703)860-9244
Free: (800)368-3396
Fax: (703)860-9245
E-mail: idhf@aol.com
Contact: Patricia L. Cartwright, Exec.Dir.
Founded: 1981. **Members:** 450. **Membership Dues:** professional, dentist, $125 (annual) ● lay member, $10 (annual). **Staff:** 2. **Description:** Dentists, dental hygienists, and other dental professionals. Advocates a method of treating periodontal disease that de-emphasizes cleaning and surgery and instead concentrates on eliminating the disease-causing bacteria. **Publications:** *Annotations,* bimonthly. Newsletter. **Price:** included in membership dues. **Circulation:** 450 ● *Seminar Brochures* ● Brochures. **Conventions/Meetings:** annual conference ● periodic seminar.

13868 ■ International Federation of Esthetic Dentistry (IFED)
c/o Dan Nathanson, VP
Boston Univ.
100 E Newton St.
Boston, MA 02118
Ph: (617)638-5590
Fax: (617)638-5591
E-mail: dnathanson@rcn.com
URL: http://www.ifed.org
Contact: Dan Nathanson, VP
Founded: 1994. **Multinational. Description:** Aims to advance the science and art of esthetic dentistry. Seeks to contribute to the progress and development of worldwide esthetic and oral health and to enhance communication between members. Encourages countries to establish an academy of esthetic dentistry. Assists in the coordination of international and national meetings on esthetic dentistry. **Publications:** Newsletter. Alternate Formats: online ● Articles. Alternate Formats: online.

13869 ■ National Association of Dental Assistants (NADA)
900 S Washington St., No. G-13
Falls Church, VA 22046
Ph: (703)237-8616

Fax: (703)533-1153

Contact: R. Ludeman, Dir.

Founded: 1974. **Members:** 6,000. **Membership Dues:** $30 (annual). **Staff:** 4. **Budget:** $100,000. **Description:** Professional dental auxiliaries. Seeks to: bring added stature and purpose to the profession through continuing education; make available to dental assistants, the special benefits normally limited to members of specialized professional and fraternal groups. **Awards: Frequency:** annual. **Type:** scholarship. **Publications:** *Communication in the Workplace* ● *Dental Assistant Salary Survey*, biennial ● *The Explorer*, 11/year. Newsletter. Includes job exchange. **Price:** included in membership dues; $20.00 /year for nonmembers. ISSN: 0894-7929. **Circulation:** 6,000. **Advertising:** accepted ● *Infection Control* ● *Mercury Poisoning* ● *Radiology*.

13870 ■ National Association of Dental Laboratories (NADL)

325 John Knox Rd., No. L103

Tallahassee, FL 32303

Ph: (850)205-5626

Free: (800)950-1150

Fax: (850)222-0053

E-mail: nadl@nadl.org

URL: http://www.nadl.org

Contact: Bennett Napier CAE, Co-Exec. Dir.

Founded: 1951. **Members:** 2,900. **Membership Dues:** laboratory, supplier, educator, $300 (annual) ● component, $400 (annual) ● technician, $70 (annual). **Staff:** 5. **Budget:** $2,000,000. **State Groups:** 45. **Description:** Represents 2,900 commercial dental laboratories, manufacturers/suppliers and educators serving the dental profession. Develops criteria for ethical dental laboratories. Offers business and personal insurance programs, Hazardous Materials Training Program, and an infectious disease prevention training program, business management and technical education programs. Compiles statistics; conducts educational and charitable programs. **Libraries: Type:** reference. **Holdings:** video recordings. **Subjects:** technical and management information. **Awards:** Educator of the Year Award. **Frequency:** annual. **Type:** recognition. **Computer Services:** Mailing lists, cheshire or pressure sensitive labels, computer disk. **Committees:** Budget and Finance; Business Management. **Affiliated With:** National Board for Certification in Dental Laboratory Technology. **Formed by Merger of:** American Dental Laboratory Association; Dental Laboratory Institute of American. **Formerly:** National Association of Certified Dental Laboratories. **Publications:** *The Journal of Dental Technology*, 9/year. Magazine. **Price:** $65.00 for members in U.S.; $100.00 for members outside U.S.; $8.00/copy. ISSN: 0746-8962. **Circulation:** 18,000. **Advertising:** accepted ● *Leadership Newsletter*, periodic ● *Managing for Profit*. Book ● Also publishes standardized accounting system and makes available videotapes. **Conventions/Meetings:** annual Vision 21 - conference, with training in personnel, marketing and sales, and personal experience in large laboratory management.

13871 ■ National Association of Seventh-day Adventist Dentists (NASDAD)

PO Box 101

Loma Linda, CA 92354

Ph: (909)558-8187

Fax: (909)558-0209

E-mail: nasdad@llu.edu

URL: http://www.llu.edu/llu/dentistry/nasdad/index.html

Contact: Mark Lund DDS, Exec. Dir.

Founded: 1944. **Members:** 600. **Membership Dues:** DDS, $85 (annual) ● RDH, $42 (annual). **Regional Groups:** 11. **Description:** Promotes the interests and businesses of dentists who are Seventh Day Adventists. **Additional Websites:** http://nasdad.org. **Affiliated With:** American Dental Association. **Publications:** *NASDAD News*. Newsletter. Alternate Formats: online ● *SDA Dentist*, annual ● Newsletter, quarterly. **Conventions/Meetings:** annual meeting - usually October.

13872 ■ National Board for Certification in Dental Laboratory Technology (NBC)

325 John Knox Rd., No. L103

Tallahassee, FL 32303

Ph: (850)205-5627

Free: (800)684-5310

Fax: (850)222-0053

E-mail: certification@nadl.org

URL: http://www.nbccert.org

Contact: Lance Rodan, Dir. of Certification

Founded: 1956. **Members:** 7,000. **Staff:** 4. **Budget:** $1,000,000. **Description:** Certifies dental laboratory technicians and dental laboratories, including commercial, private, and dental or dental technology schools. Purpose is the certification and recognition of dental technicians who demonstrate knowledge and practical skills in the field of dental technology and for dental laboratories that demonstrate and document compliance with standards set by the industry for laboratory facilities, technical resources, safety, prevention of cross-contamination, and competence of personnel. **Libraries: Type:** not open to the public. **Awards:** Certified Dental Laboratory. **Frequency:** annual. **Type:** recognition. **Recipient:** for meeting published standards ● Certified Dental Technicians. **Type:** recognition. **Recipient:** for meeting published standards. **Computer Services:** database, available for educational use only ● mailing lists, available for educational use only. **Affiliated With:** National Association of Dental Laboratories. **Publications:** *Certified Mail*, periodic. Newsletter. **Circulation:** 600 ● *Who's Who in the Dental Laboratory Industry*, annual. Directory. **Price:** free. **Circulation:** 14,000. **Advertising:** accepted. Alternate Formats: online. **Conventions/Meetings:** semiannual board meeting - March and August.

13873 ■ National Board for Certification in Dental Technology (NBC)

325 John Knox Rd., No. L103

Tallahassee, FL 32303

Ph: (850)205-5627

Free: (800)684-5310

Fax: (850)222-0053

E-mail: lance@nbccert.org

URL: http://www.nbccert.org

Contact: Bart T. Donnell CDT, Chm.

Founded: 1958. **Members:** 10,000. **Membership Dues:** certificant, $120 (annual). **Staff:** 7. **Budget:** $1,000,000. **Description:** Certifies dental technicians with formal education in dental technology and a minimum of three years' experience who have passed written and practical exams administered by the NBC. Provides continuing education to certificants and recognizes competent dental technicians. Certifies dental laboratories that meet published standards for personnel, facility and infection control practice. **Awards:** Certified Dental Laboratory. **Frequency:** annual. **Type:** recognition. **Recipient:** to dental laboratories for meeting the published standards ● Certified Dental Technician. **Type:** recognition. **Recipient:** for meeting published standards. **Computer Services:** database, available for educational use only ● mailing lists, available for educational use only. **Affiliated With:** National Association of Dental Laboratories. **Publications:** *Who's Who in the Dental Laboratory Industry*, annual. Directory. **Price:** free. **Circulation:** 14,000. **Advertising:** accepted. Alternate Formats: online. **Conventions/Meetings:** semiannual board meeting - March and August.

13874 ■ National Dental Assistants Association (NDA)

c/o National Dental Association

3517 16th St. NW

Washington, DC 20010

Ph: (202)939-9796 (202)588-1697

Fax: (202)588-1244

E-mail: rsjohns@ndaonline.org

URL: http://www.ndaonline.org

Contact: Robert S. Johns, Exec. Dir.

Members: 500. **Membership Dues:** active, $463 (annual) ● faculty, active military, $338 (annual) ● life, $163. **Description:** An auxiliary of the National Dental Association (see separate entry). Works to encourage education and certification among dental assistants. Conducts clinics and workshops to further the education of members. Bestows annual Humanitarian Award; offers scholarships. **Telecommunication Services:** electronic mail, admin@ndaonline.org. **Committees:** Education; Legislation. **Publications:** *NDAA Journal*, annual. **Conventions/Meetings:** annual meeting.

13875 ■ National Dental Association (NDA)

3517 16th St. NW

Washington, DC 20010

Ph: (202)588-1697

Free: (877)628-3368

Fax: (202)588-1244

E-mail: admin@ndaonline.org

URL: http://www.ndaonline.org

Contact: Robert S. Johns, Exec. Dir.

Founded: 1913. **Members:** 7,000. **Membership Dues:** active, $395 (annual) ● faculty, active military, $270 (annual) ● 2005 graduate, $200 (annual) ● 2006 graduate, $125 (annual) ● resident, $75 (annual). **Staff:** 3. **Budget:** $1,000,000. **Regional Groups:** 6. **State Groups:** 15. **Local Groups:** 48. **Description:** Professional society for dentists. Aims to provide quality dental care to the unserved and underserved public and promote knowledge of the art and science of dentistry. Advocates the inclusion of dental care services in health care programs on local, state, and national levels. Fosters the integration of minority dental health care providers in the profession, and promotes dentistry as a viable career for minorities through support programs. Conducts research programs. Group is distinct from the former name of the American Dental Association. **Awards: Type:** recognition ● **Type:** scholarship. **Recipient:** to minorities for dentistry careers. **Computer Services:** database ● mailing lists. **Affiliated With:** National Dental Assistants Association; National Dental Hygienists' Association. **Absorbed:** Tri-State Dental Association. **Formerly:** (1932) Interstate Dental Association. **Publications:** *Flossline*, bimonthly. Newsletter. Contains educational news. **Price:** included in membership dues. **Circulation:** 5,000. **Advertising:** accepted ● *NDA Journal*, quarterly. **Conventions/Meetings:** annual conference and workshop, on technical and scientific topics (exhibits) - always last weekend of July or first week in August ● annual convention.

13876 ■ National Dental EDI Council (NDEDIC)

2020 W Indian School Rd., Ste.F44

Phoenix, AZ 85015-5040

Ph: (602)266-7740

Fax: (602)277-6798

E-mail: ndedic@ndedic.org

URL: http://www.ndedic.org

Contact: Carol L. Watkins CAE, Exec. Dir.

Founded: 1992. **Membership Dues:** corporate A, $1,500 (annual) ● corporate B, $995 (annual) ● corporate C, individual, $450 (annual) ● non-profit organization, dental school, government, $180 (annual) ● dental association, $25 (annual). **Staff:** 2. **Budget:** $140,000. **Description:** Works to unite all stakeholders in advancing the value and utilization of electronic connectivity in the dental community. **Awards:** Benjamin D. Ward Award. **Frequency:** annual. **Type:** recognition. **Recipient:** to an individual who has made an outstanding job in the dental industry. **Publications:** *Compendium of Current Issues in Dental EDI*, annual. Alternate Formats: CD-ROM ● *Council Byte*, quarterly. Newsletter. **Conventions/Meetings:** annual conference (exhibits).

13877 ■ National Dental Hygienists' Association (NDHA)

PO Box 22463

Tampa, FL 33622

Free: (800)234-1096

E-mail: forndha@aol.com

URL: http://ndhaonline.org

Contact: Gennette Robinson RDH, Pres.

Founded: 1932. **Members:** 100. **Membership Dues:** dental hygienist, $150 (annual) ● undergraduate dental hygiene student, $35 (annual) ● retired, $75 (annual). **Budget:** $50,000. **State Groups:** 10. **Description:** Minority dental hygienists. Cultivates and promotes the art and science of dental hygiene and enhances the professional image of dental hygienists. Attempts to meet the needs of society through educational, political, and social activities while giving the minority dental hygienist a voice in shaping the profession. Encourages cooperation and mutual support among minority professionals. Seeks to increase opportunities for continuing education and employment in the field of dental hygiene. Works to improve individual and community dental health. Sponsors annual seminar, fundraising events, and scholarship programs; participates in career orientation programs; counsels and assists students applying for or enrolled in dental hygiene programs. Maintains liaison with American Dental Hygienists' Association. **Awards:** NDHA Scholarship. **Frequency:** annual. **Type:** scholarship. **Recipient:** for an African American individual. **Boards:** Trustees. **Publications:** The Lore, quarterly. Newsletter. Covers information relative to NDHA and Dental Hygiene Activities. **Circulation:** 500. **Advertising:** accepted. **Conventions/Meetings:** annual conference and convention, in conjunction with the National Dental Association (exhibits) - every July/August.

13878 ■ National Denturist Association (NDA)

PO Box 308
Towanda, PA 18848
Ph: (570)265-0238
Free: (888)599-7958
Fax: (570)265-0239
E-mail: denture@sosbbs.com
URL: http://www.nationaldenturist.com
Contact: Austin Carbone, Pres.

Founded: 1975. **Members:** 350. **Membership Dues:** individual, $650 (annual) ● group (per number of members in group), $150 (annual). **Staff:** 1. **Budget:** $40,000. **Regional Groups:** 8. **State Groups:** 22. **Description:** Denturists and other dental professionals. Promotes recognition and authorization of the profession of denturism. Conducts research regarding law pertaining to the dental profession and to the profession and practice of denturism. Offers seminars for continuing education requirements. Compiles statistics. Provides political action counseling and organizing guidance. **Awards: Type:** recognition. **Subgroups:** Education; Ethics; Legislation; Public Relations. **Affiliated With:** International Federation of Denturists. **Publications:** NDA Denturist News, quarterly. Newsletter. Contains educational and business management articles and political reports. Includes new product information and legal news. **Price:** included in membership dues or free upon request. **Circulation:** 1,000. **Advertising:** accepted. **Conventions/Meetings:** semiannual convention (exhibits) - spring and fall.

13879 ■ National Foundation of Dentistry for the Handicapped (NFDH)

1800 15th St., Ste.100
Denver, CO 80202
Ph: (303)534-5360
Fax: (303)534-5290
E-mail: fleviton@nfdh.org
URL: http://www.nfdh.org
Contact: Larry Coffee DDS, Pres./CEO

Founded: 1974. **Staff:** 52. **Budget:** $9,000,000. **State Groups:** 29. **Nonmembership. Description:** Promotes preventive dentistry for handicapped individuals in order to reduce dental disease. Sponsors Campaign of Concern and Donated Dental Services program, which enlists the cooperation of members of the dental profession, special education personnel, disabled individuals and their parents, counselors, and civic organizations in helping developmentally disabled people enjoy good dental health. These programs currently serve 23,841 people in 29 states. Conducts preventive health education through in-service training for members of participating special education schools, sheltered workshops, day centers, and group/nursing homes; teaches handicapped individuals how to maintain their own oral hygiene and provides them with dental supplies; evaluates the oral health status of each participant;

suggests dentists who will accept handicapped patients if such a referral is desired. Sponsors Donated Dental Services Programs, which match indigent, elderly, and handicapped individuals with volunteer dentists. Operates a portable dental treatment system for the homebound, nursing home residents, and the developmentally disabled that is currently in use in Denver, CO, Newark, NJ, and Chicago, IL; has assisted in developing similar programs in Detroit, MI and Houston, TX. **Convention/Meeting:** none. **Affiliated With:** American Dental Association; Oral Health America. **Publications:** Guidelines for Dental Programs in Institutions for Developmentally Disabled Persons ● Guidelines for Using Fluorides Among Handicapped Persons ● Special Smiles, periodic ● Annual Report, annual ● Also distributes audiovisual and written materials on dentistry for the handicapped.

13880 ■ National Institute of Dental and Craniofacial Research (NIDCR)

c/o National Institutes of Health
45 Center Dr., MSC-6400
Bethesda, MD 20892
Ph: (301)496-4261 (301)480-4098
E-mail: nidcrinfo@mail.nih.gov
URL: http://www.nidcr.nih.gov
Contact: Lawrence A. Tabak DDS, Dir.

Description: Aims to improve oral, dental, and craniofacial health through research, research training, and the dissemination of health information.

13881 ■ National Oral Health Information Clearinghouse (NOHIC)

1 NOHIC Way
Bethesda, MD 20892-3500
Ph: (301)402-7364
Fax: (301)480-4098
E-mail: nidcrinfo@mail.nih.gov
URL: http://www.nidcr.nih.gov

Founded: 1994. **Nonmembership. Description:** Serves as resource for patients, health professionals, and the public seeking information on the oral health of special care patients, including people with genetic or systemic disorders that compromise oral health, people whose medical treatment causes oral problems, and people with mental or physical disabilities that make good oral hygiene practices difficult. Materials are available for viewing and ordering online, free of charge. **Libraries: Type:** not open to the public; reference. **Holdings:** 2,000; books, periodicals. **Subjects:** oral health, special care. **Computer Services:** Information services, offers professional and patient education materials through an online order form. **Affiliated With:** National Institute of Dental and Craniofacial Research. **Publications:** Also distributes other publications on special care topics, oral health care, oral cancer, smokeless tobacco, dry mouth, and oral complications of cancer treatment.

13882 ■ Organization for Safety and Asepsis Procedures (OSAP)

PO Box 6297
Annapolis, MD 21401
Ph: (410)571-0003
Free: (800)298-6727
Fax: (410)571-0028
E-mail: office@osap.org
URL: http://www.osap.org
Contact: Therese M. Long, Exec. Dir.

Founded: 1984. **Members:** 1,300. **Membership Dues:** regular, in U.S., $100 (annual) ● regular, outside U.S., $150 (annual) ● full time student, $25 (annual) ● corporate, $1,895 (annual). **Staff:** 4. **Languages:** English, Spanish. **Description:** Academicians, health care practitioners and dental industry representatives. Works to maximize problem solving of difficult dental infection control issues. **Awards: Frequency:** annual. **Type:** grant. **Computer Services:** database, membership and member services. **Telecommunication Services:** electronic mail, tlong@osap.org. **Publications:** Infection Control in Practice, 8/year. Newsletter. **Price:** included in membership dues; $50.00 for nonmembers. **Circula-**

tion: 1,300. Alternate Formats: online. **Conventions/Meetings:** annual conference and symposium (exhibits).

13883 ■ Orthodontic Education and Research Foundation (OERF)

3320 Rutger St.
St. Louis, MO 63104-1008
Ph: (314)977-8366
Fax: (314)977-8364
Contact: Becky Moscal, Office Mgr.

Founded: 1957. **Members:** 500. **Staff:** 1. **Description:** Orthodontists. Promotes research; conducts continuing education programs, seminars, and clinical and professional training. **Awards: Type:** recognition. **Publications:** OERF Journal, annual. Proceedings. Includes new members listing. **Price:** included in membership dues ● OERF Newsletter, annual. **Conventions/Meetings:** annual symposium - always February.

13884 ■ Pierre Fauchard Academy (PFA)

PO Box 3718
Mesquite, NV 89024-3718
Ph: (702)345-4450
Free: (800)232-0099
Fax: (702)345-4462
E-mail: rkozal@aol.com
URL: http://www.fauchard.org
Contact: Dr. William J. Winspear, Pres.

Founded: 1936. **Members:** 7,000. **Membership Dues:** individual, $110 (annual). **Staff:** 2. **Budget:** $250,000. **Regional Groups:** 10. **State Groups:** 50. **Local Groups:** 5. **Languages:** English, French, German, Italian, Portuguese, Spanish. **Description:** Dentists "of high standards and leadership" who are nominated to the academy by state or section chairmen. Objectives are to educate dentists by providing literature on developments and opinions in dentistry; promote continuing education for all members of the dental profession; facilitate the exchange of knowledge among dentists; foster contact between dentistry leaders and those who seek advice on scientific, technical, or economic subjects; encourage advancement of professional and scientific standards; further the improvement of oral health of the public through prevention, therapy, and restoration; emphasize professional responsibility to the public. Sponsors annual Memorial Lecture honoring a past leader of dentistry. The academy is named for Pierre Fauchard (1678-1761), a French dentist who pioneered modern dental practice and dental education. **Libraries: Type:** open to the public. **Holdings:** articles. **Subjects:** dental health services. **Awards:** Dental Trade and Industry Award of Recognition. **Frequency:** annual. **Type:** recognition. **Recipient:** for an outstanding leader in the field of dentistry ● Elmer S. Best Memorial Award. **Frequency:** annual. **Type:** recognition. **Recipient:** to members of the dental profession from outside the United States who have made distinguished contributions of international significance to dentistry ● Fauchard Gold Medal. **Frequency:** annual. **Type:** recognition. **Recipient:** to a person who has made outstanding contributions to the progress and standing of the dental profession. **Computer Services:** database ● mailing lists. **Telecommunication Services:** electronic mail, pfajdk@aol.com. **Publications:** Dental Abstracts, bimonthly. **Price:** $25.00 /year for individuals. **Circulation:** 7,000. **Advertising:** accepted ● Dental World, bimonthly. Newsletter. Includes member news, meeting announcements, abstracts, book reviews, and editorials. Alternate Formats: online. Also Cited As: PFA Newsletter ● Leadership Manual of the PFA ● Legacy, The Dental Profession. Book ● The Life and Times of Pierre Fauchard. Book. Alternate Formats: online ● Membership Directory. Alternate Formats: online. **Conventions/Meetings:** semiannual board meeting.

13885 ■ Special Care Dentistry (SCD)

401 N Michigan Ave., Ste.2200
Chicago, IL 60611
Ph: (312)527-6764
Fax: (312)673-6663

E-mail: scda@scdaonline.org
URL: http://www.scdaonline.org
Contact: Kristen Smith CAE, Exec. Dir.
Founded: 1987. **Members:** 1,600. **Membership Dues:** dentist, doctoral degree, $180 (annual) ● hygienist/manager/assistant, $90 (annual) ● dental resident, $55 (annual) ● dental hygiene student, $45 (annual) ● advocate/supporting, $90 (annual) ● retired, $30 (annual) ● foreign dentist, $215 (annual). **Staff:** 3. **Budget:** $400,000. **National Groups:** 3. **Description:** Dentists, hygienists, and lay public interested in special care dentistry. Seeks to improve the quality of oral health for persons with special needs; offers fellowships in hospital care dentistry, geriatric care dentistry, and disability care dentistry. Conducts educational programs. **Computer Services:** Mailing lists. **Telecommunication Services:** electronic mail, mulligan@usc.edu. **Committees:** Education and Networking; Policy and Advocacy; SCD Structural. **Subgroups:** Academy of Dentistry for Persons with Disabilities; American Association of Hospital Dentists; American Society Geriatric Dentistry. **Absorbed:** (2001) American Society for Geriatric Dentistry; (2001) American Association of Hospital Dentists; (2001) Academy of Dentistry for Persons with Disabilities. **Formerly:** (2001) Federation of Special Care Organizations in Dentistry. **Publications:** *Oral Facial Emergencies.* Book ● *Oral Medicine in Hospital Practice.* Book ● *Special Care in Dentistry,* bimonthly. Journal. Features information on practice and patient care, trends, policy changes, and calendar of events. **Price:** $150.00/year in U.S.; $180.00/year outside U.S. **Advertising:** accepted. **Conventions/Meetings:** annual meeting ● annual National Conference on Special Care Issues in Dentistry - convention (exhibits).

13886 ■ Western Society of Periodontology (WSP)
PO Box 458
Artesia, CA 90702
Ph: (562)493-4080
Free: (800)367-8386
Fax: (562)493-4340
E-mail: wsperio@aol.com
URL: http://www.wsperio.com
Contact: Kathleen Stambaugh DDS, Pres.
Founded: 1953. **Membership Dues:** active, $165 (annual) ● associate, $150 (annual) ● non-resident, $125 (annual) ● affiliate, $90 (annual) ● student, $25 (annual). **Regional Groups:** 5. **Multinational.** **Description:** Promotes the science and art of periodontology. **Programs:** Study Clubs. **Publications:** *The Journal of The Western Society of Periodontology,* quarterly. Provides literature reviews, original articles, and abstracts related to periodontology. ● Newsletter, quarterly. Contains reviews of the association's continuing education courses. **Conventions/Meetings:** annual meeting - mid-winter ● annual Scientific Session - meeting - spring.

13887 ■ World Federation of Orthodontists (WFO)
401 N Lindbergh Blvd.
St. Louis, MO 63141-7816
Ph: (314)993-1700
Fax: (314)993-5208
E-mail: wfo@wfo.org
URL: http://www.wfo.org
Contact: Athanasios E. Athanasiou DDS, Pres.
Founded: 1995. **Members:** 6,448. **Membership Dues:** fellow, $160 (quinquennial) ● affiliate, $50. **Staff:** 1. **Description:** Orthodontic specialists. Encourages high standards in orthodontics and promotes research in the field. **Publications:** *WFO Gazette,* semiannual. Newspaper. **Price:** included in membership dues. **Circulation:** 6,000. **Advertising:** accepted. Alternate Formats: online. **Conventions/Meetings:** quinquennial Council and International Orthodontic Congress - convention, continuing education - 2010 Feb. 5-11, Sydney, NW, Australia.

Dermatology

13888 ■ American Academy of Dermatology (AAD)
PO Box 4014
Schaumburg, IL 60168-4014

Ph: (847)240-1280
Free: (866)503-SKIN
Fax: (847)240-1859
E-mail: mrc@aad.org
URL: http://www.aad.org
Contact: Diane R. Baker MD, Pres.
Founded: 1938. **Members:** 14,000. **Membership Dues:** fellow/associate/affiliate/adjunct - veterinarian/corporate individual, $750 (annual) ● international fellow, $375 (annual) ● adjunct - PhD/scientist, $450 (annual). **Staff:** 120. **Multinational. Description:** Professional society of medical doctors specializing in skin diseases. Provides educational opportunities through meetings and publications. Provides support to members' practices. Promotes dermatologists as experts in treating skin, hair, and nail conditions. Maintains liaison with Congress, Federal agencies, State legislatures and State agencies. **Libraries:** Type: reference. **Computer Services:** Online services, DERM/INFONET. **Formerly:** American Academy of Dermatology and Syphilology. **Publications:** *Derm Coding Consult,* quarterly. Newsletter. Features the latest information on accurate diagnostic and procedural coding. Alternate Formats: online ● *Dermatology Insights,* semiannual. Magazine. **Price:** free. Alternate Formats: online ● *Dermatology World,* monthly. Magazine. Reports on timely news and actions of the Academy. ● *Dialogues in Dermatology,* monthly. Audiotapes ● *Journal of the American Academy of Dermatology,* monthly. **Conventions/Meetings:** annual Academy - meeting - summer ● annual meeting.

13889 ■ American Board of Dermatology (ABD)
Henry Ford Hea. Sys.
1 Ford Pl.
Detroit, MI 48202-3450
Ph: (313)874-1088 (313)874-1089
Fax: (313)872-3221
E-mail: abderm@hfhs.org
URL: http://www.abderm.org
Contact: Antoinette F. Hood MD, Exec. Dir.
Founded: 1932. **Staff:** 5. **Nonmembership. Description:** Serves as examining and certifying body. Seeks to assure provision of competent care for patients with cutaneous diseases, via capable board representation. Establishes requirements of postdoctoral training. Creates and conducts annual comprehensive examination to determine the competence of physicians who meet the requirements for examination by the board. Issues appropriate certificate to those who satisfactorily complete examination; member of American Board of Medical Specialties. **Affiliated With:** American Board of Medical Specialties. **Publications:** *Booklet of Information,* annual. Describes requirements for certification. **Price:** free.

13890 ■ American Contact Dermatitis Society (ACDS)
138 Palm Coast Pkwy. NE, No. 333
Palm Coast, FL 32137
Ph: (386)437-4405
Fax: (386)437-4427
E-mail: info@contactderm.org
URL: http://www.contactderm.org
Contact: Kathryn A. Zug MD, Pres.
Founded: 1989. **Members:** 500. **Membership Dues:** fellow, affiliate, associate, resident, $250 (annual). **Staff:** 6. **Description:** Promotes information about contact dermatitis and occupational skin disease. **Awards:** ACDS Mentoring Award. **Type:** recognition. **Recipient:** to medical residents and fellows ● Alexander A. Fisher Research Award. **Type:** monetary. **Recipient:** to resident or medical student ● Clinical Research Fellows. **Frequency:** annual. **Type:** monetary ● Howard Maibach Travel Award. **Frequency:** annual. **Type:** monetary. **Recipient:** to investigators outside U.S. **Publications:** *Dermatitis,* quarterly. Journal. **Price:** included in membership dues; $331.00 /year for nonmembers; $75.00/copy for nonmembers. **Conventions/Meetings:** annual meeting.

13891 ■ American Dermatological Association (ADA)
c/o Julie Odessky, Exec. Mgr.
PO Box 551301
Davie, FL 33355
Ph: (954)452-1113
Fax: (305)945-7063
E-mail: ameriderm1930@aol.com
URL: http://www.amer-derm-assn.org
Contact: Darrell Rigel MD, Pres.
Founded: 1876. **Members:** 350. **Budget:** $50,000. **Description:** Professional society of physicians specializing in dermatology. Promotes teaching, practice, and research in dermatology. **Conventions/Meetings:** annual Scientific Meeting.

13892 ■ American Hair Loss Council (AHLC)
30 S Main St.
Shenandoah, PA 17976-2331
Ph: (412)765-3666
Fax: (412)765-3669
E-mail: info@ahlc.org
URL: http://www.ahlc.org
Contact: Susan Kettering, Exec. Dir.
Founded: 1985. **Members:** 420. **Membership Dues:** general, $375 (annual). **Staff:** 2. **Budget:** $200,000. **Description:** Dermatologists, plastic surgeons, cosmetologists, barbers, and interested others. Provides nonbiased information regarding treatments for hair loss in both men and women. Facilitates communication and information exchange between professionals in different areas of specialization. Conducts educational programs; compiles statistics. **Libraries:** Type: reference. **Awards:** Volunteer of the Year and The Community Service Award. **Frequency:** annual. **Type:** recognition. **Boards:** Directors. **Publications:** *AHLC News,* quarterly. Brochures. Contains association and industry news. **Price:** free for members. **Advertising:** accepted. **Conventions/Meetings:** annual symposium, includes major manufacturers (exhibits).

13893 ■ American Osteopathic College of Dermatology (AOCD)
PO Box 7525
Kirksville, MO 63501
Ph: (660)665-2184
Free: (800)449-2623
Fax: (660)627-2623
E-mail: info@aocd.org
URL: http://www.aocd.org
Contact: Rebecca A. Mansfield, Exec. Dir.
Founded: 1958. **Members:** 300. **Membership Dues:** resident, $75 (annual) ● fellow, associate, affiliate, $300 (annual) ● student, $25 (annual). **Staff:** 2. **Description:** Members of the osteopathic profession certified or involved in dermatology. Conducts specialized education programs. **Telecommunication Services:** electronic mail, execdirector@aocd.org. **Committees:** AAD Liaison; Awards; Bylaws; Convention; Editorial/Public Relations; Education Evaluating; Ethics; Fellowship. **Publications:** *Journal of the American Osteopathic College of Dermatology.* Alternate Formats: online ● Membership Directory, annual. **Price:** free. **Advertising:** accepted ● Newsletter, quarterly. **Price:** included in membership dues. **Conventions/Meetings:** annual convention, held in conjunction with American Osteopathic Association (exhibits) - always October ● annual meeting, with scientific seminar (exhibits) - January-April.

13894 ■ American Skin Association (ASA)
346 Park Ave. S
New York, NY 10010
Ph: (212)889-4858
Free: (800)499-SKIN
Fax: (212)889-4959
E-mail: info@americanskin.org
URL: http://www.americanskin.org
Contact: George W. Hambrick Jr., Pres./Founder
Founded: 1987. **Members:** 200. **Membership Dues:** individual, $25 (annual). **Staff:** 2. **Budget:** $700,000. **Description:** Supports research on all skin diseases. Promotes public education on prevention and treatment of skin disorders. Created School Skin Health Education Program, K-12, with the New York Acad-

emy of Medicine. **Awards:** Research Achievement Awards. **Frequency:** annual. **Type:** recognition. **Recipient:** for original research in psoriasis, vitiligo, pigment cell biology, autoimmune/inflammatory skin disorders and skin cancer/melanoma ● Research Grants. **Frequency:** annual. **Type:** grant. **Recipient:** for dermatology research on psoriasis, melanoma/skin cancer, vitiligo, childhood diseases/disfigurement, autoimmune, and inflammatory diseases ● Research Scholar Awards. **Frequency:** annual. **Type:** grant. **Recipient:** to young research investigators. **Publications:** *Childhood Skin Diseases*. Brochure ● *Healthy Skin and Gardening*. Brochure ● *Melanoma*. Brochure ● *Outdoor Sports and Your Skin*. Brochure ● *Skin Facts*, quarterly. Newsletter. **Circulation:** 8,000 ● *The Sun, Your Skin, and Your Health*. Brochure ● *Your Newborn's Skin and the Sun*. Brochure. **Conventions/Meetings:** annual meeting, for members and directors - March/April.

13895 ■ American Society for Dermatologic Surgery (ASDS)
5550 Meadowbrook Dr., Ste.120
Rolling Meadows, IL 60008
Ph: (847)956-0900
Fax: (847)956-0999
E-mail: info@asds.net
URL: http://www.asds.net
Contact: Alastair Carruthers MD, Pres.
Founded: 1970. **Members:** 4,100. **Membership Dues:** fellow, associate, affiliate, $400 (annual) ● fellow in-training program, $35 (annual). **Description:** Physicians specializing in dermatologic surgery. Maintains the highest possible standards in medical education, clinical practice and patient care. Seeks to promote high standards in allied health professions and services as they relate to dermatology. **Awards:** Award for Distinguished Service. **Frequency:** annual. **Type:** recognition. **Recipient:** for significant contributions in furthering the goals of the society through education and/or research. **Publications:** *Dermatologic Surgery Journal*, monthly. **Price:** included in membership dues. **Advertising:** accepted. Alternate Formats: online ● *Roster*, biennial. Membership Directory. **Conventions/Meetings:** annual Clinical and Scientific Meeting - conference (exhibits) - always fall.

13896 ■ American Society of Dermatology (ASD)
2721 Capital Ave.
Sacramento, CA 95816-6004
Ph: (916)446-5054
Fax: (916)446-0500
E-mail: jeremy@aapsonline.org
URL: http://www.asd.org
Contact: M. John Hanni Jr., Exec. Dir.
Founded: 1992. **Membership Dues:** fellow, associate, affiliate, corporate, $275 (annual) ● student, $12 (annual) ● resident, $31 (annual). **Description:** Dermatologists. Committed to make dermatology care available to everyone in the U.S. **Publications:** *Front Line*. Newsletter. Alternate Formats: online ● Audiotapes, annual. **Price:** $10.00 each; $100.00/set ● Videos, annual. **Price:** $20.00 each; $225.00/set.

13897 ■ American Society of Dermatopathology (ASDP)
60 Revere Dr., Ste.500
Northbrook, IL 60062
Ph: (847)400-5820
Fax: (847)480-9282
E-mail: info@asdp.org
URL: http://www.asdp.org
Contact: James W. Patterson MD, Pres.
Founded: 1962. **Members:** 1,024. **Membership Dues:** fellow, associate, $250 (annual) ● nonresident associate, retired, $100 (annual). **Staff:** 2. **Description:** Seeks to improve the quality of dermatopathology (the study of abnormal skin conditions, especially the structural and functional changes produced by disease). Aids in the dissemination of information. Encourages continuing education and research. **Awards:** ASDP Research Grant. **Frequency:** annual. **Type:** recognition. **Recipient:** administered through Dermatology Foundation ●

Founders' Award. **Frequency:** annual. **Type:** recognition. **Recipient:** to individuals who have made outstanding original contributions to the field of dermatopathology ● Walter R. Nickel Award. **Frequency:** annual. **Type:** recognition. **Recipient:** to individuals who have made outstanding contributions in teaching dermatopathology. **Computer Services:** Mailing lists. **Committees:** Continuing Education and Research; Dermpath Fellowship Training Directors' Ad Hoc; Peer Review; Program. **Programs:** Quality Assurance and Laboratory Proficiency. **Publications:** *Journal of Cutaneous Pathology*, monthly. **Price:** $396.00/year for individuals in America; $822.00 /year for institutions in America; EUR 354.00 /year for individuals in Europe; EUR 489.00 /year for institutions in Europe. ISSN: 0303-6987. **Circulation:** 1,769. **Advertising:** accepted. Alternate Formats: online ● Membership Directory, semiannual. Alternate Formats: online. **Conventions/Meetings:** annual conference, scientific meeting (exhibits).

13898 ■ Dermatology Foundation (DF)
1560 Sherman Ave., Ste.870
Evanston, IL 60201-4808
Ph: (847)328-2256
Fax: (847)328-0509
E-mail: dfgen@dermatologyfoundation.org
URL: http://dermatologyfoundation.org
Contact: Sandra Rahn Benz, Exec. Dir.
Founded: 1964. **Members:** 3,300. **Staff:** 4. **Budget:** $450,000. **Description:** Members of national and regional dermatological societies; board-certified dermatologists. Raises funds for the control of skin diseases through research, improved education, and better patient care. Stimulates interest of graduate physicians in academic dermatology. Supports basic and clinical investigations. **Awards:** Clark W. Finnerud Award. **Frequency:** annual. **Type:** recognition. **Recipient:** for an outstanding clinician and teacher in dermatology ● Physician Scientist Career Development Award. **Frequency:** annual. **Type:** monetary. **Recipient:** for a clinically-oriented investigator in the early stages of his/her academic career ● Practitioner of the Year Award. **Frequency:** annual. **Type:** recognition ● Women's Health Research Career Development Award. **Frequency:** annual. **Type:** monetary. **Recipient:** for a strong commitment to skin research. **Committees:** Medical and Scientific. **Publications:** *Dermatology Focus*, quarterly. Newsletter. Covers membership activities. Includes research articles and lists recipients of foundation awards, fellowships and grants. Alternate Formats: online ● *Progress in Dermatology*, quarterly. Bulletin. Contains research reports. **Price:** included in membership dues ● *Stewardship Report*, annual. Annual Report. **Price:** free. **Conventions/Meetings:** annual meeting.

13899 ■ Dystrophic Epidermolysis Bullosa Research Association of America (DEBRA)
5 W 36th St., Ste.404
New York, NY 10018
Ph: (212)868-1573
Free: (866)332-7276
Fax: (212)868-9296
E-mail: staff@debra.org
URL: http://www.debra.org
Contact: Ms. Suzanne Cohen, Exec. Dir.
Founded: 1979. **Staff:** 4. **Budget:** $750,000. **State Groups:** 3. **Nonmembership. Description:** Aims to find a cure for Epidermolysis Bullosa and to improve the health and well being of all individuals and families in the United States affected by all forms of the disorder. Offers program of patient services including two Nurse Educators, a national physician referral service, free emergency supplies and financial assistance, a network of regional support groups and an informational website. Promotes and supports an extensive international scientific research effort. **Awards:** DEBRA International Research Grant. **Frequency:** semiannual. **Type:** grant. **Recipient:** for scientific and clinical research into the causes and manifestations of and treatments for epidermolysis bullosa. **Also Known As:** DEBRA of America. **Publications:** *Currents*, quarterly. Newsletters. Contains information on how to live with EB, research updates,

patient questions, and events coverage. **Circulation:** 8,500. **Advertising:** accepted. Alternate Formats: online. **Conventions/Meetings:** semiannual conference.

13900 ■ Foundation for Ichthyosis and Related Skin Types (FIRST)
1364 Welsh Rd., G2
North Wales, PA 19454
Ph: (215)619-0670
Fax: (215)619-0780
E-mail: info@scalyskin.org
URL: http://www.scalyskin.org
Contact: Jean R. Pickford, Exec. Dir.
Founded: 1981. **Members:** 3,300. **Membership Dues:** individual, $40 (annual) ● family, $50 (annual) ● sponsor, $100 (annual) ● patron, $250 (annual) ● benefactor, $500 (annual) ● grand benefactor, $1,000 (annual). **Staff:** 3. **Budget:** $250,000. **Regional Groups:** 10. **Description:** Helps individuals and families affected with ichthyosis. Offers information and education to both lay and professional communities. Advocates the political and healthcare arenas. Produces and distributes publications and resources that contain reliable information regarding ichthyosis. **Libraries: Type:** reference. **Holdings:** archival material, audiovisuals, books, clippings, monographs, periodicals. **Subjects:** ichthyosis, rare diseases. **Awards:** Dermatology Foundation. **Frequency:** annual. **Type:** monetary. **Computer Services:** database. **Telecommunication Services:** electronic mail, jpickford@scalyskin.org. **Boards:** Medical Advisory; Medical Editors. **Formerly:** (1986) National Ichthyosis Foundation. **Publications:** *A Handbook for Teachers of Children with Ichthyosis*. Serves as a tool for parents to help make the transition to the school environment for children with ichthyosis. **Price:** $5.00 ● *Butterflies: The Children of Ichthyosis*. Video ● *Ichthyosis: An Overview*. **Price:** free for members; $1.00 for nonmembers ● *Ichthyosis Focus*, quarterly. Newsletter. Features medical news, tips for day-to-day coping, and correspondence column for members who would like to exchange letters. **Price:** free for members. **Circulation:** 3,600 ● *Ichthyosis: The Genetics of Its Inheritance*. Booklet. Features description of the genetic inheritance patterns for the different forms of ichthyosis. **Price:** free for members; $1.00 for nonmembers ● *Release The Butterfly: A Handbook for Parents and Caregivers of Children with Ichthyosis*. Covers care, medication, therapy, and nutrition for child with ichthyosis. **Price:** $5.00. **Conventions/Meetings:** biennial National Family Conference (exhibits).

13901 ■ International Academy of Cosmetic Dermatology
c/o Larry Millikan, MD, Sec.-Treas.
Dept. of Dermatology and Cutaneous Biology
Jefferson Medical Coll.
233 S 10th St., Ste.450
Philadelphia, PA 19107
Ph: (215)503-5786
Fax: (215)503-5788
E-mail: eileen.oshaughnessy@jefferson.edu
URL: http://www.dermato.med.br/iacd
Contact: Eileen O'Shaughnessy, Contact
Founded: 1995. **Members:** 300. **Membership Dues:** individual, $195 (annual) ● corporate-platinum, $2,500 (annual) ● corporate-gold, $1,000 (annual) ● corporate-silver, $500 (annual). **Regional Groups:** 6. **Description:** Represents cosmetic dermatologists. **Awards:** Van Scott Lecture. **Frequency:** annual. **Type:** recognition. **Computer Services:** Mailing lists. **Telecommunication Services:** electronic mail, iacd@dermato.med.br. **Committees:** Organizing. **Publications:** *Clinics in Dermatology*. Journal ● *SkinMed*, bimonthly. Journal. Features articles, original papers, and case studies concerning clinical aspects of dermatology. **Price:** $90.00 /year for individuals in U.S.; $105.00 /year for institutions in U.S.; $105.00 /year for individuals outside U.S.; $120.00 /year for institutions outside U.S. **Circulation:** 28,000. **Advertising:** accepted. Alternate Formats: online ● Newsletter. Alternate Formats: online. **Conventions/Meetings:** Derm Party ● annual meeting ● World Congress, with plenary sessions.

13902 ■ International Federation of Psoriasis Associations (IFPA)
c/o Gail Zimmerman, Pres./CEO
6600 SW 92nd, Ste.300
Portland, OR 97223-7195
Ph: (503)244-7404
Fax: (503)245-0626
E-mail: getinfo@ifpa-pso.org
URL: http://www.ifpa-pso.org
Contact: Gail Zimmerman, Pres./CEO
Founded: 1968. **Members:** 22. **Membership Dues:** general (based on the number of active members), $25-$2,500 (annual). **Budget:** $33,000. **Description:** Represents psoriasis associations worldwide. Works with members to improve the lives people who live with psoriasis and psoriatic arthritis. **Libraries: Type:** reference. **Holdings:** periodicals. **Subjects:** medical and personal histories of psoriasis patients. **Computer Services:** Online services, Internet. **Additional Websites:** http://www.psoriasis.org. **Formerly:** (2000) National Psoriasis Foundation. **Publications:** *IFPA Newsletter*, monthly. Contains valuable information about psoriasis treatments and research. **Price:** included in membership dues. Alternate Formats: online ● *International Federation of Psoriasis Associations - Worldwide Unity for People Living with Psoriasis & Psoriatic Arthritis*. Pamphlet. **Conventions/Meetings:** annual International Psoriasis Conference ● annual World Psoriasis Conference - symposium.

13903 ■ International Society for Dermatologic Surgery (ISDS)
c/o Perry Robins, MD, Founder/Pres.
530 1st Ave.
New York, NY 10016
Ph: (212)686-4663
Fax: (212)686-5842
E-mail: info@isdsworld.org
URL: http://www.isdsworld.org
Contact: Perry Robins MD, Founder/Pres.
Founded: 1976. **Members:** 1,200. **Membership Dues:** professional, $100 (annual). **Description:** Dermatologists, otolaryngologists, plastic surgeons, and skin surgery specialists. Works to promote high standards of patient care; provides for continuing education and research in dermatologic surgery; encourages public interest in the field. Provides a forum for the exchange of ideas and methodology in dermatologic surgery and related basic sciences. **Awards:** Perry Robins Scholarship Award. **Frequency:** annual. **Type:** recognition. **Recipient:** to dermatologists who are completing residency in dermatology. **Publications:** *ISDS Envoy*. Newsletter. Alternate Formats: online ● Directory, annual. **Conventions/Meetings:** annual congress (exhibits).

13904 ■ International Society of Dermatology (ISD)
138 Palm Coast Pkwy. NE, No. 333
Palm Coast, FL 32137
Ph: (386)437-4405
Fax: (386)437-4427
E-mail: info@intsocdermatol.org
URL: http://www.intsocdermatol.org
Contact: Torello Lotti MD, Sec. Gen.
Founded: 1957. **Members:** 2,000. **Membership Dues:** associate, $65 (annual) ● regular, $100 (annual) ● individual sponsoring, $250 (annual) ● bronze (institution/corporate), $500 (annual) ● silver (institution/corporate), $1,000 (annual) ● gold (institution/corporate), $2,500 (annual) ● platinum (institution/corporate), $5,000 (annual). **Staff:** 2. **Budget:** $125,000. **Multinational. Description:** Dermatologists and general physicians. Promotes interest, education, and research in dermatology with international meetings, publications and scholarships. **Committees:** Communications. **Councils:** Advisory. **Formerly:** (1984) International Society of Tropical Dermatology; (1997) International Society of Dermatology: Tropical, Geographic, and Ecologic. **Publications:** *International Journal of Dermatology*, monthly. **Price:** included in membership dues; $277.00 /year for individuals. **Advertising:** accepted. **Conventions/Meetings:** quinquennial International World Congress of Dermatology (exhibits) ● quinquennial seminar.

13905 ■ Medical Dermatology Society (MDS)
820 W Superior Ave., Ste.700
Cleveland, OH 44113-1807
Ph: (216)579-9300
Fax: (216)579-9333
E-mail: hollis@meddermsociety.org
URL: http://www.meddermsociety.org
Contact: Jeffrey Callen MD, Pres.
Founded: 1994. **Members:** 78. **Membership Dues:** regular, $50 (annual) ● sustaining, $200 (annual). **Description:** Promotes patient-centered research in adult dermatology. (Medical dermatology refers to cutaneous changes that are associated with systemic disease processes and/or are potentially disabling or fatal).

13906 ■ National Association for Pseudoxanthoma Elasticum (NAPE)
8760 Manchester Rd.
St. Louis, MO 63144-2724
Ph: (314)962-0100
Fax: (314)962-0100
E-mail: napestlouis@sbcglobal.net
URL: http://www.pxenape.org
Contact: Frances Benham PhD, Pres.
Founded: 1989. **Members:** 625. **Staff:** 1. **Budget:** $30,000. **Description:** People who have Pseudoxanthoma Elasticum (PXE), as well as interested others (Pseudoxanthoma elasticum is a rare connective tissue disorder that can affect eyes, skin, and organs). Provides educational information about PXE. Compiles statistics. Serves to unite PXE patients and others who have the disease. Maintains database of patients with PXE. **Libraries: Type:** reference. **Holdings:** periodicals. **Subjects:** PXE newsletters published since 1993. **Awards: Type:** monetary. **Recipient:** to finance low vision devices for affected members. **Computer Services:** Mailing lists, not available to the general public. **Boards:** Directors; Medical Advisory. **Formerly:** (1999) NAPE, Inc. **Publications:** *PXE Awareness*, semiannual. Newsletter. Contains current treatment, research and legislative information. **Circulation:** 625. Alternate Formats: online; magnetic tape. **Conventions/Meetings:** annual board meeting (exhibits) ● annual meeting.

13907 ■ National Eczema Association (NEA)
4460 Redwood Hwy., Ste.16-D
San Rafael, CA 94903-1953
Ph: (415)499-3474
Free: (800)818-7546
Fax: (415)472-5345
E-mail: info@nationaleczema.org
URL: http://www.nationaleczema.org
Founded: 1988. **Members:** 35,000. **Staff:** 3. **Description:** Works to raise awareness of the inflammatory condition of the skin called eczema. Provides patient and provider education materials. Supports research. **Libraries: Type:** reference; open to the public. **Formerly:** (1997) Eczema Association for Science and Education; (2006) National Eczema Association for Science and Education. **Publications:** *The Advocate*, quarterly. Newsletter. Contains eczema related news and letters from patients and family members. **Price:** included in membership dues. **Circulation:** 9,500. **Advertising:** accepted ● Brochures ● Videos.

13908 ■ National Psoriasis Foundation/USA (NPF)
6600 SW 92nd Ave., Ste.300
Portland, OR 97223-7195
Ph: (503)244-7404
Free: (800)723-9166
Fax: (503)245-0626
E-mail: getinfo@psoriasis.org
URL: http://www.psoriasis.org
Contact: Gail M. Zimmerman, Pres./CEO
Founded: 1968. **Membership Dues:** professional, $95 (annual) ● international, $125 (annual). **Description:** People who have psoriasis and psoriatic arthritis, their family members, friends, physicians, nurses, researchers and corporations. United to improve the quality of life for people who have psoriasis and psoriatic arthritis, to educate the public about psoriasis, and to support research. **Publica-**

tions: *Psoriasis Advance*, bimonthly. Magazine. **Price:** included in membership dues ● *Psoriasis Forum*. Newsletter. Features reports on new and updated psoriasis treatments, new drug approvals, and insurance problems. Alternate Formats: online.

13909 ■ National Rosacea Society
800 S Northwest Hwy., Ste.200
Barrington, IL 60010
Fax: (847)382-5567
E-mail: rosaceas@aol.com
URL: http://www.rosacea.org
Contact: Samuel Huff, Exec. Dir.
Founded: 1997. **Description:** Aims to improve the lives of people with Rosacea by raising awareness, providing public health information and supporting research on this widespread but little-known disorder. **Awards:** Medical and Scientific Grants for Research. **Frequency:** annual. **Type:** grant. **Telecommunication Services:** information service, (888)NO-BLUSH, for requesting materials and services. **Publications:** *Rosacea Review*, 3-4/year. Newsletter. **Circulation:** 150,000.

13910 ■ National Vitiligo Foundation (NVF)
76 Garden Rd.
Columbus, OH 43214
Ph: (614)261-8145 (614)288-5105
Fax: (614)261-1254
E-mail: info@nvfi.org
URL: http://www.vitiligofoundation.org
Contact: James J. Nordlund MD, Chm.
Founded: 1985. **Members:** 25,000. **Membership Dues:** general, $40 (annual). **Staff:** 1. **Regional Groups:** 11. **Languages:** English, Spanish. **Description:** Doctors and patients; contributors and supporters. Provides information and counseling to vitiligo patients and their families. (Vitiligo is a skin disease that destroys pigment cells causing smooth, white-colored patches of skin.) Seeks to increase awareness and concern for the vitiligo patient. Raises funds for scientific and clinical research on the cause, treatment, and cure of vitiligo. **Convention/Meeting:** none. **Publications:** *Handbook for Patients* ● *Handbook for Physicians* ● *Handbook for Schools* ● *Vitiligo*, semiannual. Newsletter ● *Vitiligo Bulletin*, quarterly. Newsletter. **Price:** $10.00 for North American citizens; $20.00 for other country. Alternate Formats: online ● Brochures.

13911 ■ North American Clinical Dermatologic Society (NACDS)
c/o Judith A. Koperski, MD, Membership Chair
Dermatologic Medical Gp. of North County
9850 Genesee Ave., Ste.530
La Jolla, CA 92037
Ph: (858)558-0677
Fax: (858)558-3077
E-mail: jakoperski@yahoo.com
URL: http://www.nacds.com
Contact: Judith A. Koperski MD, Membership Chair
Founded: 1959. **Members:** 210. **Membership Dues:** dermatologist, $175 (annual). **Budget:** $200,000. **Multinational. Description:** Dermatologists practicing primarily in the U.S. and Canada and leaders of dermatology throughout the world. Promotes the interchange of information and research. **Awards:** Dermatology Resident Research Award. **Frequency:** annual. **Type:** recognition. **Recipient:** for best manuscript of dermatology research performed as resident. **Publications:** *Program*, annual. **Conventions/Meetings:** Scientific Meeting.

13912 ■ Pacific Dermatologic Association (PDA)
100 Meadowcreek Dr., Ste.150
Corte Madera, CA 94925
Ph: (415)927-5729
Fax: (415)927-5726
E-mail: pda@hp-assoc.com
URL: http://www.pacificderm.org
Contact: Margaret Wong, Exec. Dir.
Founded: 1948. **Members:** 800. **Membership Dues:** fellow, associate, affiliate, $150 (annual). **Staff:** 2. **Budget:** $250,000. **Regional Groups:** 1. **Description:** Represents dermatologists united to provide

opportunities for exchange of information and advancement of knowledge of dermatology and syphilology among physicians within the Pacific Rim. Conducts specialized education programs; sponsors competitions. **Awards:** Victor D. Newcomer Award. **Frequency:** annual. **Type:** monetary. **Recipient:** to physicians currently enrolled in a graduate dermatologic training program. **Committees:** Budget Review; Clinicopathologic; Communications; Education and Program; Ervin Epstein Lecturer; Meeting Site Selection; Nominating; Recognitions. **Conventions/Meetings:** annual meeting (exhibits) - 2008 Aug. 6-10, San Francisco, CA - **Avg. Attendance:** 250.

13913 ■ Society for Investigative Dermatology (SID)
820 W Superior Ave., 7th Fl.
Cleveland, OH 44113-1807
Ph: (216)579-9300
Fax: (216)579-9333
E-mail: sid@sidnet.org
URL: http://www.sidnet.org
Contact: Amy Paller MD, Pres.
Founded: 1938. **Members:** 2,300. **Membership Dues:** resident, fellow, $70 (annual) ● joint, $100 (annual) ● active, sustaining, $220 (annual) ● patron, $350 (annual). **Staff:** 10. **Budget:** $1,500,000. **Description:** Advances and promotes the sciences relevant to skin health and disease through education, advocacy and scholarly exchange of scientific information. Provides educational programs and services. **Libraries: Type:** reference. **Holdings:** archival material, business records, periodicals. **Subjects:** dermatology. **Awards:** Albert Kligman Travel Fellowship. **Frequency:** annual. **Type:** fellowship. **Recipient:** for young investigators ● Stephen Rothman Award. **Frequency:** annual. **Type:** recognition. **Recipient:** for distinguished contribution to research dermatology. **Computer Services:** database, membership. **Publications:** *Journal of Investigative Dermatology*, monthly. **Price:** included in membership dues. Alternate Formats: online. Also Cited As: *JID* ● *SID News*, quarterly. Newsletter. **Price:** included in membership dues. **Conventions/Meetings:** annual meeting and conference (exhibits) - usually in May.

13914 ■ Society for Pediatric Dermatology (SPD)
8365 Keystone Crossing, Ste.107
Indianapolis, IN 46240
Ph: (317)202-0224
Fax: (317)202-9841
E-mail: spd@hp-assoc.com
URL: http://www.pedsderm.net
Contact: Lawrence Eichenfield MD, Ed.
Founded: 1975. **Members:** 500. **Staff:** 1. **Description:** Pediatricians, dermatologists, pediatric or dermatologic house officers, manufacturers of children's skin products, and researchers in biomedicine with studies in pediatric dermatology. Conducts research programs. **Awards: Type:** recognition. **Publications:** *Society for Pediatric Dermatology—Newsletter*, quarterly. Reviews current publications in the field of pediatric dermatology; includes reviews in the areas of allergy and immunology, genetics and syndromes. **Price:** included in membership dues. **Circulation:** 500. **Conventions/Meetings:** annual conference ● annual meeting.

13915 ■ Women's Dermatologic Society (WDS)
575 Market St., Ste.2125
San Francisco, CA 94105
Ph: (415)927-5727
Fax: (415)927-5726
E-mail: wds@womensderm.org
URL: http://www.womensderm.org
Contact: Kerry G. Parker CAE, Exec. Dir.
Membership Dues: general, $100 (annual). **Multinational. Description:** Dermatology professionals promoting women in dermatology. Conducts mentoring program; provides networking opportunities. **Publications:** Newsletter, quarterly. Alternate Formats: online. **Conventions/Meetings:** annual meeting - 2008 Feb. 1-6, San Antonio, TX; 2009 Mar. 9-11, San Francisco, CA.

Diabetes

13916 ■ American Association of Diabetes Educators (AADE)
100 W Monroe St., Ste.400
Chicago, IL 60603-1901
Free: (800)338-3633
Fax: (312)424-2427
E-mail: aade@aadenet.org
URL: http://www.aadenet.org
Contact: Donna M. Rice RN, Pres.
Founded: 1973. **Members:** 10,000. **Membership Dues:** student, retired, $70 (annual) ● active, associate, $125 (annual). **Staff:** 24. **Budget:** $6,300,000. **Local Groups:** 105. **Description:** Nurses, dietitians, social workers, physicians, pharmacists, podiatrists, and others involved in teaching diabetes self-management to diabetics. Purposes are: to provide educational opportunities for the professional growth and development of members; to promote the development of quality diabetes education for the diabetic consumer; to foster communication and cooperation among individuals and organizations involved in diabetes patient education. Offers continuing education programs for diabetes educators. **Awards:** Diabetes Educator of the Year. **Frequency:** annual. **Type:** recognition. **Committees:** Cultural; Public Affairs; Reimbursement. **Publications:** *AADE Member Resource Guide*, annual. Membership Directory ● *Core Curriculum for Diabetes Education* ● *The Diabetes Educator*, bimonthly. Journal. Contains original articles from all disciplines regarding diabetes and diabetes patient education. Includes advertisers index and book reviews. **Price:** included in membership dues; $90.00 /year for nonmembers; $155.00 /year for institutions. ISSN: 0145-7217. **Circulation:** 15,000. **Advertising:** accepted. Alternate Formats: online. Also Cited As: *TDE* ● *e-FYI*, quarterly. Newsletter. Includes calendar of events, and articles on diabetes education and practice. **Price:** included in membership dues. **Circulation:** 11,000 ● Also publishes position statements and various guidelines for diabetes education. **Conventions/Meetings:** annual meeting and show, with educational program (exhibits) - always August.

13917 ■ American Diabetes Association (ADA)
1701 N Beauregard St.
Alexandria, VA 22311
Free: (800)806-7801
Fax: (703)549-1500
E-mail: askada@diabetes.org
URL: http://www.diabetes.org
Founded: 1940. **Members:** 280,000. **Membership Dues:** regular, $28 (annual) ● professional (Cat I), $125 (annual) ● professional (Cat II), $75 (annual). **Staff:** 829. **Budget:** $88,000,000. **State Groups:** 53. **Local Groups:** 800. **Languages:** English, Spanish. **Description:** Physicians, laypersons, and health professionals interested in diabetes mellitus. Promotes research, information and advocacy to find a prevention and cure for diabetes and to improve the lives of all people with diabetes. Promotes public awareness of diabetes as a serious disease. Conducts educational programs and provides information to people with diabetes and the health professionals who care for them. Administers research grants. **Libraries: Type:** reference. **Holdings:** books, software, video recordings. **Subjects:** medical management, self-care, coping, meal planning, cooking. **Awards:** Career Development Award. **Frequency:** semiannual. **Type:** grant. **Recipient:** for promising new investigator who holds an assistant professor or justified equivalent academic position within his/her institution ● Clinical Research Grant. **Frequency:** semiannual. **Type:** grant. **Recipient:** for investigators whose studies directly involve humans and focus on human subjects in which the effect of a change in the individual's external or internal environment is evaluated ● Lions Sight First Retinopathy Research Award. **Frequency:** annual. **Type:** grant. **Recipient:** for clinical or applied research in diabetic retinopathy ● Medical Student Diabetes Research Fellowships. **Frequency:** annual. **Type:** fellowship. **Recipient:** for

medical students to conduct a 3 to 6 months diabetes research project ● Mentor-Based Postdoctoral Fellowships. **Frequency:** annual. **Type:** fellowship. **Recipient:** for established diabetes investigators to provide stipend support of postdoctoral fellows who will train with them in diabetes research ● Research Award. **Frequency:** semiannual. **Type:** grant. **Recipient:** for investigators who are conducting studies in diabetes research. **Computer Services:** Mailing lists. **Telecommunication Services:** additional toll-free number, (800)342-2383. **Councils:** Behavioral Medicine and Psychology; Clinical Endocrinology, Diabetes, and Metabolism; Complications; Diabetes in Pregnancy; Diabetes in Youth; Education; Epidemiology and Statistics; Exercise; Footcare; Healthcare Delivery and Public Health; Molecular, Cellular, and Biochemical Aspects of Diabetes; Nutritional Science and Metabolism; Provisional Council on Immunology, Immunogenetics, & Transplantation. **Publications:** *Clinical Diabetes*, bimonthly. Newsletter. Provides current scientific information about diabetes and its treatment to the primary care provider. **Price:** $15.00 /year for members; $30.00 /year for nonmembers; $40.00 /year for institutions. **Circulation:** 50,000. **Advertising:** accepted ● *Diabetes*, monthly. Contains original research papers on the physiology and pathophysiology of diabetes mellitus and related disorders. **Price:** $75.00 /year for members; $135.00 /year for nonmembers; $200.00 /year for institutions. ISSN: 0012-1797. **Circulation:** 7,000. **Advertising:** accepted. Alternate Formats: microform; online ● *Diabetes Care*, monthly. Journal. Covers original clinical research and commentaries primarily directed toward improving the medical management of people with diabetes mellitus. **Price:** $75.00 /year for members; $100.00 /year for nonmembers; $150.00 /year for institutions. ISSN: 0149-5992. **Circulation:** 11,000. **Advertising:** accepted. Alternate Formats: online ● *Diabetes Forecast*, monthly. Magazine. Provides information about diabetes, self-care exercise, diet, travel, and personal development. **Price:** included in membership dues. ISSN: 0095-8301. **Circulation:** 280,000. **Advertising:** accepted ● *Diabetes Reviews*, quarterly. Journal. Provides comprehensive reviews of basic science and clinical issues in diabetes. **Price:** $45.00 /year for members; $85.00 /year for nonmembers; $125.00 /year for institutions. **Circulation:** 4,000. **Advertising:** accepted ● *Diabetes Spectrum: From Research to Practice*, quarterly. Journal. **Price:** included in membership dues; $45.00 /year for nonmembers. **Circulation:** 6,000. **Advertising:** accepted ● Videos ● Publishes a catalog of publications available. **Conventions/Meetings:** annual conference and meeting, with scientific sessions (exhibits).

13918 ■ American Youth Understanding Diabetes Abroad (AYUDA)
1700 N Moore St., Ste.2000
Arlington, VA 22209
Ph: (703)527-3860
Fax: (703)527-8383
E-mail: info@ayudainc.net
URL: http://www.ayudainc.net
Contact: Jesse Fuchs-Simon, Pres./Co-Founder
Founded: 1994. **Staff:** 2. **Multinational. Description:** Promotes sustainable development for diabetes communities. Raises international awareness of diabetes communities. Creates and strengthens self-sustaining local and national diabetes organizations throughout the Americas. Empowers youth with diabetes to develop and lead educational, medical, recreational and advocacy programs. **Programs:** Campo Amigo; Leadership. **Publications:** Newsletter.

13919 ■ Charles Ray III Diabetes Association
PO Box 792
Apex, NC 27502
Ph: (919)303-6949
Fax: (919)303-6949
E-mail: chuck@charlesray.g12.com
URL: http://www.charlesray.g12.com
Contact: Charles Ray III, Pres./CEO/Founder
Founded: 1998. **Multinational. Description:** Seeks to improve the quality of life of individuals with

diabetes all over the world by providing equipment and encouragement to those in need. Encourages people with diabetes to take control of their health. Provides medical devices and supplies to those unable to afford the cost.

13920 ■ Diabetes Action Research and Education Foundation
426 C St. NE
Washington, DC 20002
Ph: (202)333-4520
Fax: (202)558-5240
E-mail: info@diabetesaction.org
URL: http://www.diabetesaction.org
Contact: Patricia A. Faulkner, Chair
Founded: 1990. **Description:** Works to improve quality of life for those affected by diabetes and its complications. **Awards: Frequency:** annual. **Type:** grant. **Recipient:** to medical experts and researchers. **Subgroups:** Diabetes Action Team. **Publications:** *Diabetes Action*, monthly. Newsletter. Alternate Formats: online ● *Managing Your Diabetes: Basics and Beyond.* Booklet. **Price:** free.

13921 ■ Diabetes Exercise and Sports Association (DESA)
8001 Montcastle Dr.
Nashville, TN 37221
Free: (800)898-4322
Fax: (615)673-2077
E-mail: desa@diabetes-exercise.org
URL: http://www.diabetes-exercise.org
Contact: Paula Harper RN, Pres./Founder
Founded: 1985. **Members:** 3,500. **Membership Dues:** general, $20 (annual) ● professional, $30 (annual) ● youth (ages 9-18), $10 (annual). **Staff:** 2. **Budget:** $50,000. **Regional Groups:** 12. **Languages:** Catalan, Danish, English, French, German, Greek, Italian, Spanish. **Description:** Individuals with diabetes and healthcare professionals. Promotes the participation of individuals with diabetes in sports activities. Provides a network and support group for athletes with diabetes. Conducts educational programs to increase self care skills for individuals with diabetes and counseling skills for healthcare professionals. Offers blood sugar screenings; sponsors volunteer services and speakers' bureau. Conducts children's services. **Libraries: Type:** reference. **Holdings:** audio recordings, books, clippings, periodicals, video recordings. **Subjects:** diabetes, exercise. **Awards:** Lew Harper Memorial Youth Award. **Frequency:** annual. **Type:** recognition. **Recipient:** to young members for athletic and scholastic achievement ● Lifescan Prize for Athletic Achievement. **Frequency:** annual. **Type:** monetary. **Recipient:** for athletic achievements, potential for further success in endeavors potential for grant to assist in goal. **Formerly:** International Diabetic Athletes Association. **Publications:** *Challenge*, quarterly. Newsletter. Contains inspiring stories of success with diabetes and exercise. **Price:** included in membership dues. **Circulation:** 2,000. **Advertising:** accepted. Alternate Formats: online ● *Get Ready-Get Set-Go.* Pamphlet. **Conventions/Meetings:** annual Bike Ride - meeting ● annual Exercise for Diabetes: Good Medicine - conference (exhibits).

13922 ■ Diabetes Research Institute Foundation (DRIF)
3440 Hollywood Blvd., Ste.100
Hollywood, FL 33021
Ph: (954)964-4040
Free: (800)321-3437
Fax: (954)964-7036
E-mail: info@drif.org
URL: http://www.diabetesresearch.org
Contact: Robert A. Pearlman, Pres./CEO
Founded: 1971. **Members:** 10,000. **Membership Dues:** friend, $50-$499 (annual) ● partner, $500-$999 (annual) ● President's Circle, $1,000 (annual). **Staff:** 15. **Regional Groups:** 2. **Description:** Works to improve the quality of life for individuals with diabetes and to find a cure for diabetes. Acts as an information clearinghouse. Offers referral services. Fosters research on diabetes. Conducts educational programs; maintains speaker's bureau. Compiles

statistics. **Libraries: Type:** reference. **Holdings:** articles, audiovisuals, books, clippings, periodicals. **Awards: Type:** recognition. **Publications:** *Focus*, 3/year. Newsletter. Covers foundation events, research news, and donor profiles. **Price:** included in membership dues. **Circulation:** 15,000 ● Annual Report, annual. **Conventions/Meetings:** annual A World of Hope Conference - meeting and conference, an interactive educational conference on cure-focused research (exhibits).

13923 ■ Insulin-Free World Foundation (IFW)
677 Craig Rd., Ste.105
St. Louis, MO 63141-7115
Ph: (314)991-8004
Free: (888)746-4439
Fax: (314)991-2276
E-mail: diabetesportal@sbcglobal.net
Contact: Deb Butterfield, Founder/Exec.Dir.
Founded: 1996. **Multinational. Description:** Facilitates the exchange of information in the diabetes community. Corresponds with diabetes researchers and clinicians at 200 prominent academic institutions. Gathers research articles, facts and statistics, scientific abstracts, human-interest stories, insurance advice, pharmaceutical counsel, and as much information as possible about advances in insulin-free treatments and cures for diabetes. This information is redistributed through InsulinFree.org, Insulin-Free Times, on-line interviews through its sister-site, Diabetes Station, and other publications. Has created the "definitive on-line directory of pancreas and islet transplant specialists". **Computer Services:** database, referral resources ● information services, directory of pancreas and islet transplant specialists and cure-focused information. **Publications:** *Insulin-Free Times* (in English and Italian), quarterly. Magazine. Integrates information about advances toward curing diabetes. **Price:** free. **Advertising:** accepted. Alternate Formats: online ● *Showdown with Diabetes.* Book. **Price:** $7.50.

13924 ■ Joslin Diabetes Center (JDC)
One Joslin Pl.
Boston, MA 02215
Ph: (617)732-2400 (617)732-2415
Free: (800)JOSLIN-1
Fax: (617)732-2562
E-mail: diabetes@joslin.harvard.edu
URL: http://www.joslin.org
Contact: C. Ronald Kahn MD, Pres./Dir.
Founded: 1898. **Staff:** 500. **Budget:** $70,000,000. **Nonmembership. Description:** Conducts clinical programs such as the Diabetes Outpatient Intensive Treatment (DO IT) Program, a three and a half day program designed to instruct and empower people with diabetes to better manage the disease; other clinical services include internal medicine/endocrinology, ophthalmology, nephrology, pediatric endocrinology, pregnancy, mental health, nutrition and exercise physiology. Maintains affiliated treatment facilities in the Boston area and at prestigious hospitals from Florida to Washington state. Offers a disease management program as well as educational programs for health professionals, patients and corporations. **Libraries: Type:** reference. **Holdings:** 2,000. **Subjects:** diabetes. **Committees:** Drugs; Research. **Divisions:** Education; Elliott P. Joslin Research Laboratory; Joslin Clinic; Youth. **Formed by Merger of:** Diabetes Foundation; Joslin Clinic. **Formerly:** (1981) Joslin Diabetes Foundation. **Publications:** *Joslin Magazine*, quarterly. Provides information on diet, education, and research; also covers the activities of the center. **Price:** included in membership dues. **Circulation:** 20,000 ● *Joslin News Today.* Newsletter. **Circulation:** 30,000. Alternate Formats: online ● Annual Report, annual. Alternate Formats: online ● Books ● Videos. **Conventions/Meetings:** periodic board meeting.

13925 ■ Juvenile Diabetes Research Foundation International (JDRF)
120 Wall St., 19th Fl.
New York, NY 10005-4001
Ph: (212)785-9500
Free: (800)533-CURE

Fax: (212)785-9595
E-mail: info@jdrf.org
URL: http://www.jdrf.org
Contact: Arnold Donald, Pres./CEO
Founded: 1970. **Members:** 40,000. **Membership Dues:** individual, $25 (annual). **Staff:** 376. **Regional Groups:** 100. **Languages:** English, Spanish. **Multinational. Description:** Works to find a cure for diabetes and its complications through the support of research. Sponsors international workshops and conferences for biomedical researchers. Offers support groups and other activities for families affected by diabetes. **Libraries: Type:** reference. **Holdings:** books. **Subjects:** juvenile diabetes. **Awards: Type:** fellowship. **Recipient:** for research ● **Type:** grant ● **Frequency:** annual. **Type:** recognition. **Recipient:** for scientific and humanitarian achievements, and for public service. **Formerly:** (1983) Juvenile Diabetes Foundation. **Publications:** *Countdown*, quarterly. Magazine. Covers diabetes treatment and research. **Price:** included in membership dues. **Advertising:** accepted ● *Countdown for Kids*, quarterly. Magazine. **Price:** included in membership dues ● *JDRF Research E-Newsletter*, monthly. Alternate Formats: online ● *Matthew Takes His Shot.* **Price:** $13.95 for nonmembers; $11.16 for members ● *Sugar was My Best Food: Diabetes and Me.* Book. **Price:** $12.95 for nonmembers; $10.36 for members ● Also publishes pamphlets and brochures for diabetics, families, medical personnel, and teachers; produces videotapes. **Conventions/Meetings:** annual meeting (exhibits) - always June.

13926 ■ National Certification Board for Diabetes Educators (NCBDE)
330 E Algonquin Rd., Ste.4
Arlington Heights, IL 60005
Ph: (847)228-9795
Fax: (847)228-8469
E-mail: info@ncbde.org
URL: http://www.ncbde.org
Contact: Fern Vining, Chair
Founded: 1986. **Description:** Provides certification to qualified health professionals in diabetes education; promotes excellence in the profession. **Publications:** Newsletter.

13927 ■ National Diabetes Information Clearinghouse (NDIC)
1 Info. Way
Bethesda, MD 20892-3560
Ph: (301)654-3327
Free: (800)860-8747
Fax: (703)738-4929
E-mail: ndic@info.niddk.nih.gov
URL: http://www.diabetes.niddk.nih.gov
Founded: 1978. **Description:** Works to increase knowledge and understanding about diabetes among patients, health care professions, general public. **Computer Services:** database, Combined Health Information ● database, Diabetes subfile. **Publications:** Booklets. Contains information on all aspects of diabetes. Alternate Formats: online ● Brochures. Contains information on all aspects of diabetes. Alternate Formats: online.

13928 ■ Taking Control of Your Diabetes (TCOYD)
1110 Camino Del Mar, Ste.B
Del Mar, CA 92014
Ph: (858)755-5683
Free: (800)998-2693
Fax: (858)755-6854
E-mail: info@tcoyd.org
URL: http://www.tcoyd.org
Contact: Steven V. Edelman MD, Founder/Dir.
Founded: 1995. **Membership Dues:** regular, $35 (annual). **Languages:** English, Spanish. **Description:** Aims to educate and motivate people with diabetes and their loved ones. Empowers the people who are living with diabetes to take a more active role in their condition to live healthier, happier and more productive lives. Strives to improve the practice of diabetes care throughout the country. **Publications:** *MyTCOYD Newsletter*, quarterly. **Price:** included in membership dues ● Book. **Price:** $18.50

each, plus shipping and handling ● Video. Alternate Formats: online.

Disabilities

13929 ■ National Special Needs Network Foundation (NSNNF)
c/o Jeffrey H. Minde, Pres.
4613 N Univ. Dr., No. 242
Coral Springs, FL 33067
Ph: (954)345-6465
Fax: (954)345-6465
E-mail: jhmnetwork@bellsouth.net
URL: http://www.nsnn.com
Contact: Jeffrey H. Minde, Pres.

Description: Special needs professionals. Aims to provide the finest and most complete special needs support services in America, including individuals and families with developmental and acquired disabilities, mental illnesses, and chronic medical conditions. **Formerly:** (2003) National Special Needs Network.

13930 ■ NRH Center for Health and Disability Research (NHR-CHDR)
c/o National Rehabilitation Hospital
102 Irving St. NW
Washington, DC 20010
Ph: (202)466-1900 (202)877-1000
Fax: (202)466-1911
URL: http://www.nrhrehab.org/researchhome.cfm
Contact: Susan E. Palsbo PhD, Dir.

Founded: 1985. **Description:** Provides health and disability research.

Disabled

13931 ■ Ambucs Resource Center
PO Box 5127
High Point, NC 27262
Ph: (336)852-0052
Free: (800)838-1845
Fax: (336)852-6830
E-mail: joec@ambucs.org
URL: http://www.ambucs.org/resourcecenter.aspx
Contact: J. Joseph Copeland, Exec. Dir.

Founded: 1922. **Members:** 5,600. **Staff:** 7. **Description:** Works to create independence and opportunities for people with disabilities. Conducts service projects designed to give children with disabilities their first set of wheels. **Awards:** AMBUCS Scholars. **Frequency:** annual. **Type:** scholarship. **Recipient:** for PT, OT, Speech or Audiology students in junior year or higher. **Publications:** AMBUC Magazine, quarterly. **Conventions/Meetings:** annual conference.

13932 ■ American Association on Health and Disability (AAHD)
110 N Washington St., Ste.340
Rockville, MD 20850
Ph: (301)545-6140
Fax: (301)545-6144
E-mail: contact@aahd.us
URL: http://www.aahd.us
Contact: Ronald G. Blankenbaker MD, Pres.

Membership Dues: organization, $250 (annual) ● individual, $50 (annual) ● consumer, $10 (annual). **Description:** Advances health and wellness initiatives for people with disabilities through research, education, public awareness and advocacy. Prevents additional health complications in people with disabilities. Identifies effective intervention strategies to reduce the incidence of secondary conditions and the health disparities between people with disabilities and the general population. **Computer Services:** Information services, health and disability resources. **Programs:** Health Promotion and Wellness. **Publications:** Health and Disability News, quarterly. Newsletter. Alternate Formats: online.

13933 ■ Amputee Coalition of America (ACA)
900 E Hill Ave., Ste.285
Knoxville, TN 37915-2568
Ph: (865)524-8772
Free: (888)AMP-KNOW
Fax: (865)525-7917
E-mail: acainfo@amputee-coalition.org
URL: http://www.amputee-coalition.org
Contact: Paddy Rossbach RN, Pres./CEO

Founded: 1989. **Membership Dues:** corporate, $1,200 (annual) ● facility, $375 (biennial) ● facility, $200 (annual) ● disability organization, $100 (annual) ● support group, professional, $75 (annual) ● individual, amputee, family, caregiver, $30 (annual). **Staff:** 25. **Budget:** $2,500,000. **Languages:** English, Spanish. **Description:** Information resource center and cooperative program of the Centers for Disease Control and Prevention. Serves people who have limb differences, their families, and friends, healthcare providers, and the general public. Provides information on adapting to limb loss, directs referrals to groups/agencies and programs. Offers informative resources, technical assistance and education for consumer and professional groups. **Libraries: Type:** reference. **Holdings:** 5,000; articles, audiovisuals, books, clippings, monographs, periodicals. **Subjects:** limb loss, secondary conditions. **Awards:** Most Distinguished Role Model. **Frequency:** annual. **Type:** recognition. **Recipient:** for a person who exemplifies living life to the fullest with disability ● Professional Achievement. **Frequency:** annual. **Type:** recognition. **Recipient:** for a professional who has made a great impact on amputees ● Volunteer of the Year. **Frequency:** annual. **Type:** recognition. **Recipient:** for a person who has made a personal contribution of time and talent to ACA. **Publications:** First Step - A Guide For Adapting To Limb Loss, biennial. Magazine. **Circulation:** 100,000. **Advertising:** accepted ● inMotion, bimonthly. Magazine ● Books ● Videos. **Conventions/Meetings:** annual meeting and seminar.

13934 ■ Association of Assistive Technology Act Programs (ATAP)
c/o Deborah Buck, Exec. Dir.
PO Box 32
Delmar, NY 12054
Ph: (518)439-1263
Fax: (518)439-3451
E-mail: dvbuck@verizon.net
URL: http://www.ataporg.org
Contact: Deborah Buck, Exec. Dir.

Founded: 1997. **Description:** Promotes the collaboration of Assistive Technology (AT) Programs with persons with disabilities, providers, industry, advocates and others at the state and national level. Increases the availability and utilization of accessible Information Technology (IT) and AT devices and services for all individuals with disabilities in the United States and territories. Enhances AT programs in implementing the Assistive Technology Act.

13935 ■ Challenged America
c/o Disabled Businesspersons Association
3590 Camino del Rio N
San Diego, CA 92108
Ph: (619)594-8805
E-mail: ahoy@challengedamerica.org
URL: http://www.challengedamerica.org
Contact: Mr. Urban Miyares, Volunteer Dir.

Founded: 1990. **Nonmembership. Multinational. Description:** Seeks to enhance the lives of disabled veterans, children and adults with disabilities and their loved ones through sailing programs and innovative technology designed to advance rehabilitation and increase successful mainstream outcomes. **Publications:** Newsletter, monthly.

13936 ■ Disability International Foundation (DIF)
Address Unknown since 2007

Description: Fosters progress for the inclusion of people with disabilities, including children, youth and adults. **Publications:** Building the Network For Community Based Aquatic Therapy From Trauma To Independence. Survey. Alternate Formats: online.

13937 ■ Global Applied Disability Research and Information Network (GLADNET)
c/o Susanne M. Bruyere, Chair
Cornell Univ.
School of Indus. and Labor Relations
201 ILR Extension Bldg.
Ithaca, NY 14853-3901
Ph: (607)255-7727
Fax: (607)255-2763
E-mail: info@gladnet.org
URL: http://www.gladnet.org
Contact: Susanne M. Bruyere, Chair

Founded: 1997. **Membership Dues:** regular (with 15 or fewer members), $200 (annual) ● organization (with more than 15 members), $5,000 (annual). **Multinational. Description:** Brings together research centers, universities, enterprises, government departments, trade unions, and organizations of and for persons with disabilities. Advances employment and training opportunities for persons with disabilities. Promotes disability policy and program reform for working age persons with disabilities. **Telecommunication Services:** electronic mail, smb23@cornell.edu. **Publications:** Annual Report, annual. Alternate Formats: online.

13938 ■ International Association of Assistance Dog Partners (IAADP)
c/o Editor/Information and Advocacy Center
38691 Filly Dr.
Sterling Heights, MI 48310
Ph: (586)826-3938
E-mail: iaadp@aol.com
URL: http://www.iaadp.org
Contact: Ed Eames PhD, Pres.

Founded: 1993. **Membership Dues:** friend, $20 (annual) ● provider, $25 (annual) ● benefactor, $50 (annual) ● partner, $20 (annual). **Description:** Represents and advocates for disabled persons partnered with guide, hearing and service dogs. **Publications:** Access and Education. Brochure ● Partner's Forum Newsletter, quarterly. **Conventions/Meetings:** annual conference.

13939 ■ International Association for Disability and Oral Health (IADH)
c/o Dr. Daniel E. Jolly
Ohio State Univ. Coll. of Dentistry
305 W 12th Ave.
PO Box 182357
Columbus, OH 43218-2357
Ph: (614)292-1232
Fax: (614)292-4522
E-mail: jolly.4@osu.edu
URL: http://www.iadh.org
Contact: Dr. Jun Nunn, Sec.-Treas.

Founded: 1971. **Multinational. Description:** Aims to improve access to, and the quality of, oral health for individuals with disabilities. **Formerly:** International Association of Dentistry for the Handicapped. **Publications:** IADH News, quarterly. Alternate Formats: online ● International Journal of Disability and Oral Health. Alternate Formats: online. **Conventions/Meetings:** annual congress.

13940 ■ National Association for the Dually Diagnosed (NADD)
132 Fair St.
Kingston, NY 12401
Ph: (845)331-4336
Free: (800)331-5362
Fax: (845)331-4569
E-mail: info@thenadd.org
URL: http://www.thenadd.org
Contact: Dr. Robert J. Fletcher, Founder/Exec. Dir.

Founded: 1983. **Members:** 1,500. **Membership Dues:** individual, $98 (annual) ● family, student, $49 (annual) ● sustaining, $165 (annual) ● organization, $450-$600 (annual). **Staff:** 4. **Budget:** $533,000. **State Groups:** 6. **Multinational. Description:** Promotes understanding of and services for individuals with developmental disabilities and mental health needs. **Libraries: Type:** reference. **Holdings:** books, periodicals. **Subjects:** mental health in persons with mental retardation. **Awards:** Menolascino Award for Excellence. **Frequency:** annual. **Type:** scholarship.

Recipient: for significant advances in understanding and knowledge in the field of dual diagnosis ● Serena Merck Memorial Award. **Frequency:** annual. **Type:** recognition. **Recipient:** for individual who demonstrated outstanding leadership in the provision of services to individuals who have mental retardation and mental health needs. **Publications:** Bulletin, bimonthly ● Books ● Audiotapes. **Conventions/Meetings:** annual conference (exhibits).

13941 ■ National Center for the Dissemination of Disability Research (NCDDR)

c/o Southwest Educational Development Laboratory
211 E 7th St., Ste.448
Austin, TX 78701-3253
Ph: (512)476-6861
Free: (800)266-1832
Fax: (512)476-2286
E-mail: ncddr@sedl.org
URL: http://www.ncddr.org

Founded: 1995. **Languages:** English, Spanish. **Description:** Promotes disability research and dissemination of research results. **Computer Services:** Information services, NCDDR Alerts. **Publications:** Focus: Technical Brief, quarterly. Monographs. Alternate Formats: online ● Shaping Excellence through Research. Brochure. Describes the way NCDDR works with NIDRR grantees and stakeholders in disability research. Alternate Formats: online ● Technical Assistance Resources for NIDRR Grantees. Booklets. Outlines the technical assistance and training opportunities, consultation services, and resources offered by NIDRR Grantees by the NCDDR. Alternate Formats: online.

13942 ■ National Parent Network on Disabilities (NPND)

Address Unknown since 2007

Description: Families caring for people with special health care needs and developmental disabilities. Dedicated to empowering parents. Sponsors relays, leadership exchanges, weekly newsletter, legislative updates. **Publications:** Friday Facts, weekly. Newsletter.

13943 ■ PACER Center - Parent Advocacy Coalition for Educational Rights

8161 Normandale Blvd.
Minneapolis, MN 55437
Ph: (952)838-9000
Free: (800)537-2237
Fax: (952)838-0199
E-mail: pacer@pacer.org
URL: http://www.pacer.org
Contact: Paula F. Goldberg, Exec. Dir.

Founded: 1977. **Description:** Parents of children and youth with disabilities working to enhance the quality of life of children and young adults with disabilities and their families. **Telecommunication Services:** TDD, (952)838-0190. **Departments:** Health Information and Advocacy Center; Minnesota Parent Center. **Programs:** Count Me In; Early Childhood; Emotional/Behavioral Disorders; Juvenile Justice; Let's Prevent Abuse; Parents Helping Parents; Simon Technology Center; Surrogate/Foster Parents. **Projects:** American Indian Parent Network; Grandparent to Grandparent; KITE; Multicultural Services; PRIDE; SWIFT. **Publications:** A Little Help Along the Way. Brochure ● A Road Map for the Journey: Information to Gather. Brochure ● Activities That Help Your Child Learn (age 4 to 5). Brochure ● Adele Faber Workshop Tips. Brochure ● Ausentismo (Spanish Truancy). Brochure ● Catalog of Publications ● Parent Connection. Newsletter ● Articles.

13944 ■ World Association of Persons with disAbilities (WAPD)

5016 Alan Ln.
Oklahoma City, OK 73135
Ph: (405)672-4440
Fax: (405)672-4441

E-mail: webmaster@wapd.org
URL: http://www.wapd.org
Contact: Thomas J. Mecke, Pres.

Membership Dues: regular or sponsor, $20 (annual) ● life, $250 ● corporate/business (bronze), $1,200 (annual) ● corporate/business (silver), $2,500 (annual) ● corporate/business (gold), $5,000 (annual) ● corporate/business (platinum), $10,000 (annual) ● corporate/business (diamond), $20,000 (annual). **Description:** Seeks to advance the interests of persons with disabilities at national, state, local, and home levels. **Projects:** Credit Unions; Disabled Equipment; Employment; Entrepreneurship; Insurance; Networking; Telephone System; Working at Home. **Sections:** Speakers' Bureau. **Publications:** eWorld Media, weekly. Newsletter. Alternate Formats: online.

13945 ■ World Committee on Disability

910 16th St. NW, Ste.600
Washington, DC 20006
Ph: (202)293-5960
Fax: (202)293-7999
E-mail: ability@nod.org
URL: http://www.worldcommitteeondisability.org
Contact: Ms. Mary E. Dolan-Hogrefe, Dir.

Founded: 1985. **Multinational. Description:** Works to strengthen the work of the United Nations in implementing worldwide the U.N. World Programme of Action Concerning Disabled Persons. A program of the National Organization on Disability. **Awards:** Franklin Delano Roosevelt International Disability Award. **Frequency:** annual. **Type:** recognition. **Recipient:** to a nation making noteworthy progress toward the implementation of the World Programme of Action Concerning Disabled Persons. **Telecommunication Services:** TDD, (202)293-5968. **Affiliated With:** National Organization on Disability.

Disease

13946 ■ American Lyme Disease Foundation (ALDF)

PO Box 466
Lyme, CT 06371
Free: (800)876-LYME
E-mail: inquire@aldf.com
URL: http://www.aldf.com
Contact: David L. Weld, Exec. Dir.

Founded: 1990. **Membership Dues:** regular, $20 (annual). **Staff:** 2. **Budget:** $350,000. **Languages:** English, Spanish. **Description:** Health care professionals and other individuals with an interest in Lyme Disease, a disorder transmitted to humans by the deer tick. Works to control the spread of Lyme Disease, and to improve treatments for the disorder. Maintains physician referral service; produces educational materials and conducts public and professional education programs; supports Lyme Disease research. **Awards:** Research Fund. **Frequency:** annual. **Type:** monetary. **Recipient:** for prevention and control of tick-borne diseases. **Publications:** Newsletter, periodic. **Price:** included in membership dues. **Advertising:** accepted ● Video. Serves as a reference material for use in schools, libraries, and camps.

13947 ■ Amyloidosis Support Network (ASN)

1490 Herndon Ln.
Marietta, GA 30062
Ph: (770)977-1500
Free: (800)689-1238
E-mail: info@amyloidosis.org
URL: http://www.amyloidosis.org
Contact: Dennis Krysmalski, Pres./Founder

Founded: 1999. **Description:** Improves the survivability and quality of life of patients. Provides medical and emotional support to patients and caregivers. Raises public awareness of amyloidosis and its effects. Encourages the medical field to learn more about the diagnosis and treatment of amyloidosis. **Publications:** Brochure (in English and Spanish). Alternate Formats: online ● Annual Report, annual. Alternate Formats: online.

13948 ■ Association for the Bladder Exstrophy Community (ABC)

3075 First St.
La Salle, MI 48145
Ph: (734)243-9912
Free: (866)300-2222
Fax: (734)243-9912
E-mail: admin@bladderexstrophy.com
URL: http://www.bladderexstrophy.com
Contact: Cindy Buckley, Exec. Dir.

Founded: 1991. **Membership Dues:** family, patron, $25 (annual) ● professional, $55 (annual) ● institutional, hospital, $250 (annual). **Multinational. Description:** Provides assistance to patients affected with bladder exstrophy and their families. Raises public awareness and understanding of the medical and psychosocial issues of exstrophy. Conducts support group meetings to allow interaction among patients, their families and guest speakers. **Publications:** ABC Update, quarterly. Newsletter. **Price:** included in membership dues. Alternate Formats: online ● Living with Bladder Exstrophy. Book. Provides insight into many issues facing the family and individual living with bladder exstrophy. **Price:** included in membership dues; $55.00 for nonmembers.

13949 ■ Ataxia Telangiectasia Children's Project

668 S Military Trail
Deerfield Beach, FL 33442-3023
Ph: (954)481-6611
Free: (800)543-5728
Fax: (954)725-1153
E-mail: info@atcp.org
URL: http://www.atcp.org
Contact: Brad Margus, Pres.

Founded: 1993. **Description:** Supports laboratory research to accelerate the discovery of a cure or possible therapies for Ataxia Telangiectasia; develops and maintains international registry of A-T patients; supports and oversees clinical center and information clearinghouse; maintains a tissue/cell bank; develops quantitative endpoints for measuring the rate and severity of the symptoms of A-T. **Awards:** Frequency: periodic. **Type:** grant. **Recipient:** for scientists doing research on Ataxia Telangiectasia. **Computer Services:** Information services, Ataxia Telangiectasia resources. **Publications:** Newsletter. Alternate Formats: online.

13950 ■ Brain Tumor Society (BTS)

124 Watertown St., Ste.3H
Watertown, MA 02472
Ph: (617)924-9997
Free: (800)770-8287
Fax: (617)924-9998
E-mail: info@tbts.org
URL: http://www.tbts.org
Contact: Mr. N. Paul Ton That, Interim. Dir.

Founded: 1989. **Staff:** 8. **Budget:** $2,400,000. **Description:** Strives to improve the quality of life of brain tumor patients by providing support for them and their families. Raises funds for research in order to find a cure for brain tumors. **Awards:** Research Grant Awards. **Frequency:** annual. **Type:** grant. **Recipient:** for scientific research relevant to brain tumors. **Telecommunication Services:** information service, counseling by a licensed social worker and referrals to other support services. **Publications:** Color Me Hope. Serves as a resource guide for patients and families. **Price:** free. **Circulation:** 30,000. Alternate Formats: online ● Heads Up. Newsletter. **Price:** free. **Circulation:** 30,000. Alternate Formats: online. **Conventions/Meetings:** biennial Symposium for Patients, Families, and Professionals (exhibits).

13951 ■ CCHS Family Network

c/o Mary Vanderlaan, Founder/Dir.
71 Maple St.
Oneonta, NY 13820
Ph: (607)432-8872
Fax: (607)431-4351

E-mail: vanderlaanm@hartwick.edu
URL: http://www.cchsnetwork.org
Contact: Mary Vanderlaan, Founder/Dir.
Founded: 1990. **Members:** 300. **Description:** Seeks to provide support to families with a CCHS child. Supports CCHS research; shares information on ventilation methods and technologies and home care issues; collects data on CCHS. **Publications:** *CCHS Family Newsletter*, 3/year. Shares news on research/ technology development and family stories. **Circulation:** 350. **Conventions/Meetings:** triennial conference, family education ● biennial Family Conference, family education (exhibits) - always in June.

13952 ■ CFIDS Association of America
PO Box 220398
Charlotte, NC 28222-0398
Ph: (704)365-2343
Free: (800)442-3437
Fax: (704)365-9755
E-mail: cfids@cfids.org
URL: http://www.cfids.org
Contact: K. Kimberly McCleary, Pres./CEO
Founded: 1987. **Members:** 23,000. **Membership Dues:** regular, in U.S., $35 (annual) ● regular, in Canada, $45 (annual) ● regular, outside U.S. and Canada, $60 (annual). **Staff:** 13. **Budget:** $1,500,000. **Description:** Individuals with chronic fatigue and immune dysfunction syndrome (chronic viral illness associated with dysfunction of the immune system; formerly called chronic Epstein-Barr virus); doctors, nurses, and government officials. Advocates continued research into the cause and cure of the syndrome. Funds pilot medical research projects. **Awards: Type:** grant. **Recipient:** for research. **Formerly:** (1994) CFIDS Association. **Publications:** *The CFIDS Chronicle*, quarterly. Journal. Contains research and medical articles, advocacy efforts reports, practical tips on living with CFIDS and book and media reviews. **Price:** included in membership dues. **Circulation:** 15,000. **Advertising:** accepted. Alternate Formats: online ● *Research Review*, semiannual. **Price:** included in membership dues; $3.50 for nonmembers. Alternate Formats: online ● Also publishes patient guide and other educational materials.

13953 ■ Childhood Brain Tumor Foundation (CBTF)
20312 Watkins Meadow Dr.
Germantown, MD 20876
Ph: (301)515-2900
Free: (877)217-4166
E-mail: cbtf@childhoodbraintumor.org
URL: http://www.childhoodbraintumor.org
Contact: Jeanne Young, Pres.
Founded: 1994. **Description:** Strives to raise funds for scientific research and public awareness of brain tumors in children; works to improve prognosis and quality of life. **Awards: Frequency:** annual. **Type:** grant. **Programs:** Childhood Cancer Ombudsman. **Publications:** *The Neurotransmitter*, triennial. Newsletter. Contains educational articles, personal stories and updates. **Conventions/Meetings:** semiannual Family Retreat Weekend.

13954 ■ Chronic Granulomatous Disease Association
c/o Mary Hurley, Pres.
2616 Monterey Rd.
San Marino, CA 91108-1646
Ph: (626)441-4118
E-mail: cgda@socal.rr.com
URL: http://home.socal.rr.com/cgda
Contact: Mary Hurley, Pres.
Founded: 1982. **Languages:** English, Spanish. **Multinational. Description:** Seeks to improve the quality of life of people with Chronic Granulomatous Disease (CGD) and their families (CGD is characterized by the presence of multiple granulomas, or nodular inflammatory lesions). Provides support and services to people with CGD; assists in the formation of support networks for people with CGD; maintains international registry of CGD patients; compiles statistics. **Libraries: Type:** reference. **Holdings:** 1,000; articles. **Subjects:** chronic granulomatous

disease. **Computer Services:** database, people with CGD, physicians treating CGD ● mailing lists ● online services. **Publications:** Newsletter, semiannual. **Price:** free. **Circulation:** 1,000. Alternate Formats: online ● Brochures.

13955 ■ Chronic Syndrome Support Association (CSSA)
801 Riverside Dr.
Lumberton, NC 28358-4625
E-mail: nsolo@cssa-inc.org
URL: http://www.cssa-inc.org
Contact: Nancy Solo, Founder
Founded: 1997. **Description:** Seeks to educate the general public and health care professionals about the causes, symptoms, and effects of chronic immunological and neurological disorders. Supports research on these illnesses and other related diseases. Provides resources on chronic syndrome disorders and health related issues. **Publications:** Pamphlet (in Danish, English, French, and Spanish). Contains information on chronic immunological and neurological disorders and other related illnesses. Alternate Formats: online.

13956 ■ Disease Management Association of America (DMAA)
701 Pennsylvania Ave. NW, Ste.700
Washington, DC 20004
Ph: (202)737-5980
Fax: (202)478-5113
E-mail: dmaa@dmaa.org
URL: http://www.dmaa.org
Contact: Tracey Moorhead, Exec. Dir.
Founded: 1999. **Membership Dues:** health plan and integrated delivery system (based on company's revenue), $2,500-$10,000 (annual) ● DMO, DM vendor and consultant, pharmaceutical organization (based on company's revenue), $2,500-$50,000 (annual) ● partner, $1,500 (annual) ● gold partner, $3,000 (annual) ● government employee, full-time academician, $350 (annual) ● allied health professional, $150 (annual) ● international organization, $1,250 (annual). **Multinational. Description:** Disease management through standardization of definitions, program components, outcome measures; promotes public awareness of importance of disease management to enhance health. **Libraries: Type:** reference. **Holdings:** 200; audio recordings. **Awards:** Excellence Awards. **Frequency:** annual. **Type:** recognition. **Recipient:** for individuals and organizations who are contributing to the science of DMAA's industry. **Computer Services:** Online services, DM directory. **Committees:** Governmental Affairs and Health Policy; Program Planning; Quality and Research. **Publications:** *Disease Management*, quarterly. Journal. **Price:** included in membership dues. **Advertising:** accepted. Alternate Formats: online ● *DMAA e-News*, weekly. Newsletter. Features developments on health care policy, financial earnings, contract announcements and corporate acquisitions. Alternate Formats: online. **Conventions/Meetings:** annual Disease Management Leadership Forum - conference and workshop, with awards, keynote speakers, scientific posters (exhibits).

13957 ■ The Erythromelalgia Association (TEA)
200 Old Castle Ln.
Wallingford, PA 19086
E-mail: memberservices@erythromelalgia.org
URL: http://www.erythromelalgia.org/tea/skins/cms
Contact: Beth Coimbra, Pres.
Founded: 1999. **Members:** 500. **Membership Dues:** regular (donation), $20 (annual). **Description:** Promotes understanding of the symptoms and conditions of erythromelalgia. Provides emotional support to individuals diagnosed with erythromelalgia. Works closely with medical organizations involved in finding new treatments for erythromelalgia sufferers. **Computer Services:** Information services, erythromelalgia resources. **Committees:** Medical Advisory. **Publications:** *FootSteps*, quarterly. Newsletter. Alternate Formats: online.

13958 ■ Friends of Celiac Disease Research
Address Unknown since 2006
Founded: 1999. **Staff:** 2. **Nonmembership. Description:** Devoted to assisting people with celiac disease and dermatitis herpetiformis; supports research and education. **Committees:** Benefit.

13959 ■ Independent Citizens Research Foundation for the Study of Degenerative Diseases (ICRFSDD)
13 Mountain Rd.
Irvington, NY 10533-1405
Ph: (914)591-8837
Fax: (914)591-7090
Contact: Mark Bereday, Exec.Dir.
Founded: 1957. **Description:** Individuals united to seek and publish information of aid to those affected by degenerative diseases. Makes available in bulletin form documented information on the multiple and contributing causes of degenerative diseases, testing procedures for their early detection, and possible approaches to therapy and prevention. Seeks out factors in the environment that are detrimental to health. Supports research on calibrated transcutaneous electric nerve stimulation and preventive medicine techniques. Maintains 400 volume library on maintenance of health and prevention of disease. Seeks out factors in the environment that are detrimental to health. **Publications:** Newsletter, bimonthly ● Also publishes authorized transcripts of radio lectures on nutrition.

13960 ■ Inflammation Research Association (IRA)
c/o William M. Selig, PhD, Pres.
CombinatoRx, Inc.
245 First St.
Cambridge, MA 02142
Ph: (617)301-7225
E-mail: wselig@combinatorx.com
URL: http://www.inflammationresearch.org
Contact: William M. Selig PhD, Pres.
Founded: 1970. **Description:** Brings together scientists with an interest in inflammation research. Encourages the communication and discussion of science. **Awards:** C. Gordon Van Arman Scholarship Awards. **Frequency:** biennial. **Type:** recognition. **Recipient:** for research in inflammation. **Publications:** *IRA Newsletter*, quarterly. Exchanges information between the association and its members. ● *Official Journal: Inflammation Research*. **Conventions/Meetings:** annual conference, focuses on new therapies for allergy and inflammatory diseases ● semiannual conference ● biennial international conference ● monthly meeting - usually at the New York Academy of Sciences.

13961 ■ Inflammatory Skin Disease Institute (ISDI)
PO Box 1074
Newport News, VA 23601
Ph: (757)223-0795
Free: (800)484-6800
Fax: (757)595-1842
E-mail: ladonna.williams@isdionline.org
URL: http://www.isdionline.org
Contact: LaDonna Williams, Exec. Dir.
Founded: 2000. **Members:** 60. **Description:** Provides helpful information about inflammatory skin diseases through education, research, and patient advocacy. **Computer Services:** Mailing lists, pen pal/email buddy list for patient networking. **Publications:** Newsletter, quarterly ● Pamphlets. Provides patient education information.

13962 ■ International Association for Chronic Fatigue Syndrome (IACFS)
27 N Wacker Dr., Ste.416
Chicago, IL 60606
Ph: (847)258-7248
Fax: (847)579-0975

E-mail: admin@iacfs.net
URL: http://www.iacfs.net
Contact: Nancy G. Klimas MD, Pres.
Founded: 1992. **Members:** 500. **Membership Dues:** regular, $100 (annual) ● support group, $200 (annual) ● life, $1,000. **Staff:** 2. **Multinational. Description:** Research scientists, physicians and other health care professionals, and institutions with an interest in chronic fatigue syndrome (CFS). Seeks to advance the diagnosis and treatment of CFS. Facilitates exchange of information among members; sponsors research; serves as a clearinghouse on CFS diagnosis and patient care. Maintains speakers' bureau. **Libraries: Type:** not open to the public. **Awards:** Junior Investigator Award. **Frequency:** biennial. **Type:** monetary ● Rudy Perpich Award. **Frequency:** biennial. **Type:** monetary ● (2005) American Association for Chronic Fatigue Syndrome. **Publications:** Newsletter, quarterly. Alternate Formats: online ● Position papers and conference proceedings. **Conventions/Meetings:** biennial meeting and conference (exhibits) ● biennial meeting.

13963 ■ International Lyme and Associated Diseases Society (ILADS)

PO Box 341461
Bethesda, MD 20827-1461
Ph: (301)263-1080
Fax: (301)263-0776
E-mail: lymedocs@aol.com
URL: http://www.ilads.org
Contact: Barbara L. Buchman, Exec. Dir.
Membership Dues: student, $100 (annual) ● professional, affiliate, $150 (annual) ● regular, sustaining, $200 (annual) ● corporate, $1,000 (annual). **Multinational. Description:** Represents individuals dedicated to the diagnosis and appropriate treatment of Lyme and its associated diseases. Promotes understanding of these diseases through research and education. Supports physicians and other health care professionals dedicated to advancing the standards of care for Lyme and its associated diseases. **Publications:** *What Psychiatrists Should Know About Lyme Disease.* Brochure. Alternate Formats: online ● *What You Need to Know About ILADS and Lyme Disease.* Brochure. Alternate Formats: online ● Papers. Contains information about Lyme disease and other related issues. Alternate Formats: online ● Articles. Alternate Formats: online. **Conventions/Meetings:** annual meeting - 2007 Oct. 27-28, Newton, MA.

13964 ■ International Pemphigus Foundation (IPF)

1540 River Park Dr., Ste.208
Sacramento, CA 95815
Ph: (916)922-1298
Fax: (916)922-1458
E-mail: pemphigus@pemphigus.org
URL: http://www.pemphigus.org
Contact: Ms. Janet Segall, Interim Exec. Dir.
Founded: 1994. **Staff:** 3. **Budget:** $160,000. **Description:** Provides information and support for people living with pemphigus and their families, friends, and the general public. Provides general support and counseling for those in need, raises funds for research. **Affiliated With:** National Health Council. **Formerly:** (2003) National Pemphigus Foundation. **Publications:** Newsletter, quarterly. **Conventions/Meetings:** annual Patient/Doctor Meeting.

13965 ■ International Society for Disease Surveillance (ISDS)

136 Harrison Ave.
Boston, MA 02111
E-mail: info@syndromic.org
URL: http://www.syndromic.org
Contact: David L. Buckeridge MD, Contact
Founded: 2005. **Membership Dues:** student, $25 (annual) ● regular, $100 (annual). **Multinational. Description:** Improves population health by advancing the field of disease surveillance. Provides educational and scientific forums for epidemiologists, informaticists, public health practitioners, health care providers, and statisticians. Explores and addresses population health monitoring across institutional and

professional boundaries. **Publications:** *Advances in Disease Surveillance.* Journal. Alternate Formats: online. **Conventions/Meetings:** annual conference - 2007 Oct. 10-12, Indianapolis, IN.

13966 ■ LAM Foundation

10105 Beacon Hills Dr.
Cincinnati, OH 45241
Ph: (513)777-6889
Fax: (513)777-4109
E-mail: lam@one.net
URL: http://www.thelamfoundation.org
Contact: Sue Byrnes, Exec. Dir.
Founded: 1995. **Description:** Works to find a cure for LAM (lymphangioleimyomatosis), a progressive, fatal lung disease that affects women. Provides information and support; conducts education programs; promotes and funds clinical research; sponsors a tissue bank; supports a national registry of LAM patients. **Awards: Type:** fellowship. **Computer Services:** database. **Boards:** Scientific Advisory. **Publications:** *The Breath of Hope.* Newsletter ● *Facts About Lymphangioleiomyomatosis,* periodic. Booklet ● *LAM and Other Diseases Characterized by Smooth Muscle Proliferation.* Book. **Price:** $225.00 for non-subscribers; $135.00 for subscribers ● *The LAM Handbook.* **Price:** $10.00 for patients. Alternate Formats: online ● *Personal Journeys with LAM.* Booklet.

13967 ■ Lyme Disease Association (LDA)

PO Box 1438
Jackson, NJ 08527
Free: (888)366-6611
Fax: (732)938-7215
E-mail: lymeliter@aol.com
URL: http://www.lymediseaseassociation.org
Contact: Patricia Smith, Pres.
Description: Represents the interests of individuals dedicated to Lyme disease education, prevention, raising monies for research and patient support. Works to raise the standard of care available to people with Lyme Disease through education, research and policy development. Provides free literature, information line and doctor referrals. **Publications:** *ABC's of Lyme Disease.* Brochure. Alternate Formats: online ● *Lyme-R-Primer.* Brochure. Alternate Formats: online ● Books.

13968 ■ Lyme Disease Foundation (LDF)

PO Box 332
Tolland, CT 06084-0332
Ph: (860)870-0070
Free: (800)886-LYME
Fax: (860)870-0080
E-mail: info@lyme.org
URL: http://www.lyme.org
Contact: John F. Anderson PhD, Dir.
Founded: 1988. **Staff:** 4. **Budget:** $400,000. **Local Groups:** 200. **Description:** Seeks to educate medical professionals and the public about Lyme Borreliosis (Lyme disease), which is spread to humans by ticks with symptoms including rashes, joint swelling and pain, fever, severe headaches, and heart arrhythmia. Provides treatment protocols, diagnostic guidelines, and photographic case histories. Assists in the formation of support groups; offers referral service; maintains speakers' bureau. Sponsors medical seminars; provides videotape and slide programs; conducts research. Maintains registry of infected pregnant women and congenital cases. Works in cooperation with Congress, Centers for Disease Control, and National Institutes of Health. **Formerly:** (1992) Lyme Borreliosis Foundation. **Publications:** *Journal of Spirochetal and Tick Bourne Disease,* quarterly. **Price:** $75.00/year. ISSN: 1060-0051. **Circulation:** 500. **Advertising:** accepted ● *Lymelight,* quarterly. Newsletter. **Price:** $30.00/year. **Advertising:** accepted. Alternate Formats: online ● Pamphlets. **Conventions/Meetings:** annual International Scientific Conference - meeting ● semiannual Medical Conference (exhibits).

13969 ■ The Mastocytosis Society (TMS)

c/o Regina Rentz, Treas.
PO Box 511
Plainville, CT 06062
Ph: (413)862-4556
E-mail: jbar5@verizon.net
URL: http://tmsforacure.org
Contact: Rita Barlow, Chair
Founded: 1995. **Membership Dues:** family, $35 (annual). **Multinational. Description:** Provides support to individuals suffering from mastocytosis, a proliferation of mast cells in skin and/or body organs. **Publications:** *Mastocytosis Chronicles.* Newsletter. Produced by patients for patients. **Price:** included in membership dues. Alternate Formats: online. **Conventions/Meetings:** annual conference.

13970 ■ Mesothelioma Applied Research Foundation (MARF)

3944 State St., Ste.340
Santa Barbara, CA 93105
Ph: (805)563-8400
Free: (877)363-6376
Fax: (805)563-8411
E-mail: info@marf.org
URL: http://www.marf.org
Contact: Chris Hahn, Exec. Dir.
Founded: 1999. **Staff:** 3. **Description:** Works to eliminate mesothelioma as a life-ending disease. **Awards:** Mesothelioma Therapy Research Grant. **Type:** grant. **Recipient:** for funding of innovative mesothelioma treatment projects. **Publications:** Brochure.

13971 ■ Mitochondria Research Society (MRS)

PO Box 1952
Buffalo, NY 14221-1952
Ph: (716)845-8017 (716)907-4349
Fax: (716)845-1047
E-mail: keshav@mitoresearch.org
URL: http://www.mitoresearch.org
Contact: Keshav K. Singh PhD, Founder
Membership Dues: regular, $50 (annual) ● individual sponsor, $100 (annual) ● company sponsor, $1,000 (annual) ● sustaining sponsor, $5,000 (annual). **Multinational. Description:** Represents scientists and physicians. Committed to finding a cure for mitochondrial diseases; promotes research on basic science of mitochondria, mitochondrial pathogenesis, prevention, diagnosis and treatment throughout the world; fosters public education, training and provides a platform for communication and dissemination of knowledge among scientists, physicians and others interested in mitochondria. **Publications:** *Mitochondria Matters,* semiannual. Newsletter. Includes highlights of research, products, new developments in prevention, diagnosis and treatment of diseases associated with mitochondria. **Price:** included in membership dues ● *Mitochondrion.* Journal. **Price:** included in membership dues. **Conventions/Meetings:** meeting and workshop.

13972 ■ Multiple Sclerosis Association of America (MSAA)

706 Haddonfield Rd.
Cherry Hill, NJ 08002-2652
Ph: (856)488-4500
Free: (800)532-7667
Fax: (856)661-9797
E-mail: webmaster@msaa.com
URL: http://www.msaa.com
Contact: Douglas G. Franklin, Pres./CEO
Founded: 1970. **Members:** 31,000. **Membership Dues:** individual/patient, $25 (annual). **Staff:** 45. **Budget:** $19,500,000. **Regional Groups:** 5. **Description:** Works to fulfill the daily needs of multiple sclerosis patients. Provides patient support, counseling, local transportation, therapeutic equipment, and MRI scans for initial diagnosis and barrier-free housing. Conducts public education programs and symptom relief therapy research. **Telecommunication Services:** electronic mail, msaa@msassociation.org. **Publications:** *All About Multiple Sclerosis.* Booklet ● *The Motivator,* quarterly. Magazine. **Price:** free. **Circulation:** 31,000. **Advertising:** accepted. Alternate

Formats: online ● *Multiple Sclerosis Association of America Programs and Service Guide*. Booklet. **Conventions/Meetings:** quarterly board meeting - always third Thursday.

13973 ■ National Brachial Plexus-Erb's Palsy Association

Address Unknown since 2007
Founded: 1995. **Members:** 1,000. **Description:** Serves as a resource, information, and support center for the disease Brachial Plexus-Erb's Palsy. **Computer Services:** database ● mailing lists. **Publications:** *BPI News*, quarterly. Newsletter.

13974 ■ National Chronic Fatigue Syndrome and Fibromyalgia Association (NCFSFA)

PO Box 18426
Kansas City, MO 64133-8426
Ph: (816)737-1343
E-mail: information@ncfsfa.org
URL: http://www.ncfsfa.org
Contact: Orvalene Prewitt, Contact
Founded: 1985. **Members:** 2,000. **Membership Dues:** individual in U.S., $25 (annual) ● individual outside U.S., $35 (annual). **Staff:** 2. **Budget:** $15,000. **Regional Groups:** 2. **State Groups:** 14. **Local Groups:** 400. **Description:** Educates and informs the public about the nature and impact of Chronic Fatigue Syndrome and Fibromyalgia. Chronic Fatigue Syndrome, also known as Chronic Epstein-Barr Virus Syndrome, is characterized by persistent, recurring feelings of general weakness; other symptoms include sore throat, unexplained muscle pain, new headaches, devastating fatigue, impaired memory or concentration, tender lymph nodes, unrefreshing sleep and post-exertion malaise. Fibromyalgia is characterized as pain, generally felt all over, and can be compounded by fatigue, sleep disturbances, changes in mood, headaches and gastrointestinal problems. Sponsors educational programs. Maintains speakers' bureau. **Libraries: Type:** reference. **Subjects:** health and wellness. **Awards:** Research Grant. **Frequency:** annual. **Type:** grant. **Formerly:** (1985) National Chronic Epstein-Barr Virus Association; (1993) National Chronic Fatigue Syndrome Association. **Publications:** *A Guide for Physicians When Considering a Diagnosis of Chronic Fatigue Syndrome in Children*. Brochure. Alternate Formats: online ● *A School's Guide for Students with CFS*. Brochure. Alternate Formats: online ● *CFS: Addressing the Realities of a Chronic Illness*. Video. Includes educational information. ● *CFS and School Success*. Brochure. Alternate Formats: online ● *CFS in the Workplace*. Brochure. Alternate Formats: online ● *CFS: Thief of Vitality*. Brochure. Alternate Formats: online ● *Chronic Fatigue Syndrome*. Bibliography ● *Coping Skills*. Brochure ● *Free Health Information from the National Institutes of Health*. Brochure ● *Heart of America News*, quarterly. Newsletter. **Price:** free for members ● *How to be a Phone Contact Packet* ● *How to Start a Support Group Packet* ● *Neuro-Psychological Rehabilitation Techniques*. Brochure ● *Patient Information Packet* ● *Physician Information Packet* ● *Social Security Disability Benefits*. Brochure. Alternate Formats: online ● *Understanding the Emotions Surrounding CFS*. Brochure. Alternate Formats: online. **Conventions/ Meetings:** annual Chronic Fatigue Syndrome Awareness - meeting (exhibits) - always in March ● monthly meeting, support group meetings - every 2nd Saturday.

13975 ■ National Dysautonomia Research Foundation (NDRF)

PO Box 301
Red Wing, MN 55066-0301
Ph: (651)267-0525
Fax: (651)267-0524
E-mail: ndrf@ndrf.org
URL: http://www.ndrf.org
Description: Seeks to assist individuals afflicted with various forms of dysautonomia. **Computer Services:** database, clinical research. **Publications:** *NDRF Chat*. Newsletter. Alternate Formats: online ● *The NDRF Handbook for Patients with Dysautonomias*. Provides information on the autonomous nervous

system, dysautonomias and issues concerning patients with dysautonomia. **Price:** $27.95 ● *NDRF 2000 Conference Video Tape Set*. **Price:** $24.95.

13976 ■ National Hydrocephalus Foundation (NHF)

12413 Centralia Rd.
Lakewood, CA 90715-1623
Ph: (562)924-6666
Free: (888)857-3434
Fax: (562)924-6666
E-mail: hydrobrat@earthlink.net
URL: http://www.nhfonline.org
Contact: Debbi Fields, Exec. Dir.
Founded: 1979. **Members:** 350. **Membership Dues:** patient, family, caregiver, $35 (annual). **Staff:** 6. **Budget:** $15,000. **Regional Groups:** 1. **State Groups:** 1. **Local Groups:** 1. **National Groups:** 2. **Multinational. Description:** Works to assemble, disseminate, and research information about hydrocephalus, its treatments and outcomes, to families in need. Provides physician referrals, peer contact with another family or individual. **Libraries: Type:** lending; reference. **Holdings:** 300; archival material, articles, books, business records, papers, periodicals. **Subjects:** types of hydrocephalus, help sheets. **Computer Services:** Mailing lists, of members. **Publications:** *For Adults with Hydrocephalus*, biennial. Brochure. Provides information for teens through senior adults who have hydrocephalus. **Price:** free ● *For Parents of Children with Hydrocephalus* (in English and Spanish), biennial. Brochure. Provides information to parents about their child's hydrocephalus. **Price:** included in membership dues; $35.00 for nonmembers ● *Life-Line*, quarterly. Newsletter. Contains current medical information, feature story on an individual with hydrocephalus, Internet references, and more. **Price:** included in membership dues. **Circulation:** 350 ● *Living with Hydrocephalus- Adult Guide* ● Booklet. Includes several different help sheets with various situations to help and educate parents. **Price:** free for members; $1.00 for nonmembers. **Conventions/Meetings:** meeting, with professional lectures ● quarterly Support Group Meetings - assembly.

13977 ■ National Meningitis Association (NMA)

738 Robinson Farms Dr.
Marietta, GA 30068
Free: (866)366-3662
Fax: (877)703-6096
E-mail: support@nmaus.org
URL: http://www.nmaus.org
Contact: Candie Benn, Co-Founder
Founded: 2002. **Description:** Educates families, medical professionals and the public about the dangers of meningitis and prevention approaches to the disease. Increases protection from meningitis and meningococcal disease. Supports research and development of improved meningitis vaccines and treatments for patients stricken by meningitis. **Computer Services:** Information services, meningitis resources ● mailing lists. **Programs:** Mothers on Meningitis; Parent and Teacher Awareness; Summer Sleep-away Camp; Together Educating About Meningitis; Vaccination. **Publications:** Brochure. Alternate Formats: online.

13978 ■ National Organization for Rare Disorders (NORD)

PO Box 1968
Danbury, CT 06813-1968
Ph: (203)744-0100
Free: (800)999-6673
Fax: (203)798-2291
E-mail: orphan@rarediseases.org
URL: http://www.rarediseases.org
Contact: Ms. Abbey Meyers, Pres.
Founded: 1983. **Members:** 65,000. **Membership Dues:** individual, $30 (annual) ● friend, $50 (annual) ● contributing, $100 (annual) ● professional colleague, $75 (annual) ● organization (with operating budget of $50,001 to $2,000,000), $150-$700 (annual) ● organization (with operating budget of over $2,000,001), $900 (annual). **Staff:** 44. **National**

Groups: 130. **Description:** Doctors, professionals, academics, voluntary health organizations, and individuals interested in rare disorders. Serves as a clearinghouse for information concerning rare disorders. Objectives are: to monitor the Orphan Drug Act; to link individuals with rare disorders together for mutual support; to stimulate research on rare diseases; to foster communication among voluntary agencies, health-related industries, and government bodies. (Orphan drugs are used in the treatment of rare disorders. Since their use is not widespread, most drug companies cannot expect to profit from the development and manufacture of these drugs. The Orphan Drug Act gives financial assistance and tax incentives to drug companies that develop these drugs.) Provides information on rare disorders and referrals to organizations. **Libraries: Type:** reference; not open to the public. **Awards:** NORD Research Grant. **Frequency:** biennial. **Type:** grant. **Recipient:** to scientists for clinical research on new treatments for rare diseases ● **Frequency:** annual. **Type:** recognition. **Recipient:** to individuals and corporations for outstanding service in health or orphan drug development. **Computer Services:** database, organizational ● database, orphan drug ● database, rare disease ● online services, rare disease. **Telecommunication Services:** TDD, (203)797-9590. **Councils:** Research Advisory. **Publications:** *NORD On-Line Bulletin*, 3/year. Newsletter. Updates service for voluntary health agency members on legislation and other issues related to orphan drugs and diseases. Includes meeting schedule. **Price:** included in membership dues. **Circulation:** 285 ● *NORD Resource Guide*. Book. Lists national support groups and foundations that serve the needs of people with rare disorders and disabilities. **Price:** $57.00/copy in U.S., plus shipping and handling; $62.00/copy in Canada, plus shipping and handling; $70.00/copy outside U.S. and Canada, plus shipping and handling ● *Orphan Disease Update*, 3/year, every spring, summer, and fall. Newsletter. Updates information on orphan diseases and orphan drug research; discusses legislative issues related to health. **Price:** included in membership dues. **Circulation:** 65,000 ● *Physician Guide to Rare Diseases*. Book ● Annual Report, annual. Highlights and shows the sources of NORD's funding and how funds are disbursed. **Price:** free upon request. **Conventions/Meetings:** annual Patient/Family Conference (exhibits) - in autumn ● annual Tribute Banquet - meeting and dinner, with awards - always spring in Washington, DC.

13979 ■ National Tuberculosis Controllers Association (NTCA)

2452 Spring Rd. SE
Smyrna, GA 30080
Free: (877)503-0806
E-mail: jbernardo@lung.bmc.bu.edu
URL: http://www.ntca-tb.org
Contact: Carol Pozsik RN, Exec. Dir.
Founded: 1995. **Members:** 459. **Membership Dues:** active, $75 (annual) ● associate, nursing associate, $40 (annual). **Staff:** 2. **Budget:** $200,000. **Description:** Seeks to provide a collective voice for TB controllers to advance and advocate for tuberculosis control and elimination activities in the U.S. Advocates for policies and laws to advance tuberculosis control and elimination at the sate, local, and territorial levels. **Telecommunication Services:** electronic mail, jim_ cobb@doh.state.fl.us. **Publications:** *The Red Snapper Review*, quarterly. Newsletter. Contains organizational and scientific news. **Price:** included in membership dues. **Circulation:** 300. Alternate Formats: online. **Conventions/Meetings:** annual conference and board meeting.

13980 ■ Nevus Outreach

600 SE Delaware Ave., Ste.200
Bartlesville, OK 74003
Ph: (918)331-0595
Free: (877)426-3887
Fax: (281)417-4020
E-mail: mark@nevus.org
URL: http://www.nevus.org
Contact: Mark Beckwith, Exec. Dir.
Description: Works to find a cure for Giant Nevi and Neurocutaneous Melanosis. **Computer Services:**

Online services, chat rooms, message boards, email discussion group. **Committees:** Professional Advisory. **Publications:** *Nevus News*, semiannual. Newsletter. Contains up-to-date information about current research. **Advertising:** accepted. Alternate Formats: online. **Conventions/Meetings:** international conference.

13981 ■ Parkinson's Action Network (PAN)
1025 Vermont Ave. NW, Ste.1120
Washington, DC 20005
Ph: (202)638-4101
Free: (800)850-4726
Fax: (202)638-7257
E-mail: info@parkinsonsaction.org
URL: http://www.parkinsonsaction.org
Contact: Amy L. Comstock Esq., CEO
Description: Serves as the voice of people with Parkinson's disease. Advocates awareness through education and interaction with the Parkinson's community, scientists, policy and opinion leaders, as well as the public at large. Encourages increased and accelerated investment of public resources to ease the burden and fight for a cure for Parkinson's disease. **Awards:** Buddy Levenson Award. **Frequency:** annual. **Type:** recognition. **Recipient:** for individuals who exhibited enduring spirit by making extraordinary contributions despite suffering from Parkinson's disease ● Morris K. Udall Awards. **Frequency:** annual. **Type:** recognition. **Recipient:** for public figures who emulate the characteristics of former representative Morris K. Udall who advocated for Parkinson's disease. **Computer Services:** database ● information services ● online services, multimedia Parkinson's library. **Programs:** Grassroots. **Working Groups:** Caucus on Parkinson's Disease. **Publications:** *Action Reporter*, quarterly. Newsletter. Alternate Formats: online ● *Giving A Voice to Parkinson's*. Handbook. Alternate Formats: online. **Conventions/Meetings:** annual dinner.

13982 ■ Society for Progressive Supranuclear Palsy (SPSP)
Executive Plz. III
11350 McCormick Rd., Ste.906
Hunt Valley, MD 21031
Ph: (410)785-7004
Free: (800)457-4777
Fax: (410)785-7009
E-mail: info@curepsp.org
URL: http://www.psp.org
Contact: Richard G. Zyne, Pres./CEO
Founded: 1990. **Staff:** 9. **Budget:** $1,200,000. **State Groups:** 60. **Description:** Works to provide help and support to persons with Progressive Supranuclear Palsy (PSP), a degenerative brain disorder. Sponsors medical research; educates physicians, persons with PSP and their families on the disease and care; provides advocacy and support, support groups, symposiums and videos. **Libraries: Type:** reference. **Holdings:** articles, clippings. **Subjects:** research on PSP. **Awards:** Dudley Moore Research Fund. **Type:** recognition ● Eloise Troxel Memorial Grant and Fellowship. **Frequency:** annual. **Type:** recognition ● Erwin and Pearl Poizner Research Fund. **Type:** recognition. **Publications:** *The PSP Advocate*, quarterly. Newsletter. **Circulation:** 19,000. Alternate Formats: online. **Conventions/Meetings:** biennial conference (exhibits).

Donors

13983 ■ Association of Organ Procurement Organizations (AOPO)
1364 Beverly Rd., Ste.100
McLean, VA 22101
Ph: (703)556-4242
Fax: (703)556-4852
E-mail: aopo@aopo.org
URL: http://www.aopo.org
Contact: Paul M. Schwab, Exec. Dir.
Founded: 1984. **Members:** 59. **Staff:** 3. **Budget:** $650,000. **Description:** Works to represent and serve organ procurement organizations to maximize

the availability of organs and tissues and enhance the quality and effectiveness of the donation process. Establishes organizational and ethical standards for OPOs; offers accreditation; provides status reports of federal legislative activities; disseminates information on federal policies and technical advancements; conducts educational programs. **Committees:** Data & Information Management; Legislative and Government Affairs. **Councils:** Hospital Development; Medical Directors. **Publications:** *AOPO Update*, monthly. Newsletter. **Advertising:** accepted. Alternate Formats: online ● Membership Directory. **Conventions/Meetings:** Director's Workshop ● annual meeting (exhibits) ● annual Organ Donation - congress - 2007 Nov. 11-14, Philadelphia, PA.

13984 ■ Eye Bank Association of America (EBAA)
1015 18th St. NW, Ste.1010
Washington, DC 20036
Ph: (202)775-4999
Fax: (202)429-6036
E-mail: info@restoresight.org
URL: http://www.restoresight.org
Contact: Patricia Aiken-O'Neill Esq., Pres./CEO
Founded: 1961. **Members:** 109. **Membership Dues:** regular, $100 (annual) ● sponsoring organization, $2,000 (annual). **Staff:** 8. **Budget:** $1,000,000. **Description:** Eye banks working to restore sight through the promotion and advancement of eye banking. Makes possible over 46,000 corneal transplants annually. Establishes standards for the procurement and distribution of eyes and corneal tissue. Offers training and certification programs for eye banking personnel. Compiles statistics; maintains speakers' bureau. Conducts research and educational programs. **Libraries: Type:** reference. **Holdings:** 20; audiovisuals. **Awards:** Gift of Sight Award. **Frequency:** annual. **Type:** recognition ● Heise Award. **Frequency:** annual. **Type:** recognition ● Paton Award. **Frequency:** annual. **Type:** recognition ● Scientific Award. **Frequency:** annual. **Type:** grant. **Subgroups:** Paton Society. **Publications:** *Eye Bank Association of America—Eye Bank Statistics Report*, annual. Annual Report. Includes statistics on eye donations and corneal transplants. **Price:** $10.00 for members; $35.00 for nonmembers ● *Eye Bank Association of America—Insight*, periodic. Newsletter. Contains association and industry news. **Circulation:** 600 ● *Eye Bank Association of America—Membership Directory*, annual. Lists member eye banks; listed geographically by state. **Price:** free for members; $15.00 for nonmembers - refill; $40.00 for nonmembers - binder with refill. **Advertising:** accepted ● *Guidelines and Resources for Successful Public and Professional Relations and Development ● Medical Standards*. Manual. **Price:** $27.50 for members; $150.00 for nonmembers ● *Procedures Manual*. **Price:** $65.00 for members; $150.00 for nonmembers. **Conventions/Meetings:** annual Educational Conference ● annual meeting.

13985 ■ Eye-Bank for Sight Restoration (EBSR)
120 Wall St., 3rd Fl.
New York, NY 10005-3902
Ph: (212)742-9000
Fax: (212)269-3139
E-mail: info@ebsr.org
URL: http://www.eyedonation.org
Contact: Marilyn L. Castaldi, Pres.
Founded: 1944. **Staff:** 25. **Budget:** $3,400,000. **Languages:** English, Spanish. **Nonmembership.** **Description:** Collects, processes and distributes ocular tissue for transplantation, research and medical education. Provides public and professional education to encourage eye donation. Promotes research in the causes, treatment and cure of eye diseases. **Libraries: Type:** reference. **Holdings:** audiovisuals, books, periodicals. **Subjects:** ophthalmology, eye-banks. **Awards:** Man/Woman of Vision. **Frequency:** annual. **Type:** recognition. **Recipient:** for a corporate or civic leader who has played a major role in volunteer community activities. **Computer Services:** database ● mailing lists. **Departments:** Business Administration; Development; Ocular Laboratory;

Professional Education; Public Relations. **Publications:** *Eye-Bank for Sight Restoration—Eye to Eye*, 3/year. Newsletter. Includes annual report. **Price:** free. **Circulation:** 25,000.

13986 ■ LifeBanc
20600 Chagrin Blvd., Ste.350
Cleveland, OH 44122
Ph: (216)752-5433
Free: (888)558-5433
Fax: (216)751-4204
E-mail: info@lifebanc.org
URL: http://www.lifebanc.org
Contact: Debbie May-Johnson, Exec. Dir.
Founded: 1986. **Staff:** 54. **Description:** Responsible for all aspects of the organ and tissue donation process, as well as public and professional education programs, and bereavement services for donor families. Mission is to increase organ and tissue donation for those awaiting transplant, to provide community and professional education to people of all ages about the need for, and the benefits of, organ and tissue donation, and to respect and support those individuals and families whose generosity and compassion make it possible to improve and save the lives of others. **Affiliated With:** Association of Organ Procurement Organizations; United Network for Organ Sharing. **Supersedes:** Organ Recovery. **Publications:** Pamphlets.

13987 ■ The Living Bank International (TLBI)
PO Box 6725
Houston, TX 77265-6725
Ph: (713)528-2971
Free: (800)528-2971
Fax: (713)961-0979
E-mail: info@livingbank.org
URL: http://www.livingbank.org
Contact: Lisa Whitaker, Pres./CEO
Founded: 1968. **Members:** 1,850,000. **Staff:** 8. **Budget:** $1,200,000. **Languages:** English, Spanish. **Description:** Open to anyone who wishes to donate organs and/or tissues at time of death. Provides a centralized registry for people who want to donate organs/tissues at the time of death. Those interested in becoming donors can request donor registration forms on which they specify which organs and/or tissues they will donate and any limitations or special wishes. Document must be signed by two witnesses. Donors receive an organ donor card which is carried by the individual at all times and which indicates that the person is registered with The Living Bank. If death is imminent or has occurred, The Living Bank is notified and one of their staff members refers the situation to the closest organ procurement organization or other appropriate agency. The organ procurement organization makes the decision regarding what can and cannot be used for transplant. The major types of transplants that are currently being performed include cornea, skin, heart, liver, kidney, intestine, pancreas, and lung transplants. For individuals wishing to donate their whole bodies for anatomical research and study, they should contact The Living Bank for information on how to register with the nearest medical school. Due to many of the body donor programs being full, many medical schools now require that you be pre-registered. Operates speakers' bureau in communities throughout the country. **Libraries: Type:** reference. **Computer Services:** database, centralized registry of potential organ, tissue, and whole body donors ● online services, membership list. **Formerly:** (2001) The Living Bank. **Publications:** *Bank Account*, semiannual. Newsletter. Includes news updates on advances in the fields of organ donation and transplantation. **Price:** free. **Circulation:** 200,000 ● Brochures ● Also publishes educational and informational materials.

13988 ■ National Marrow Donor Program (NMDP)
3001 Broadway St. NE, Ste.500
Minneapolis, MN 55413-1753
Ph: (612)627-5800 (612)627-8140
Free: (800)627-7692
URL: http://www.marrow.org
Contact: Jeffrey W. Chell MD, CEO
Founded: 1986. **Members:** 468. **Staff:** 345. **Budget:** $107,000,000. **Languages:** Chinese, English, Japa-

nese, Korean, Spanish, Vietnamese. **Multinational. Description:** Facilitates unrelated donor stem cell transplants for patients with life-threatening blood diseases who do not have matching donors in their families. Facilitates more than 150 transplants each month. Provides a single point of access for all sources of blood stem cells used in transplantation: marrow, peripheral blood, and umbilical cord blood. The Registry is able to search its own database and provides physicians with information on multiple stem cell sources for life-saving transplants. Has recruited a diverse Registry of approximately four million potential volunteer marrow and blood stem cell donors, provided transplants to more than 15,000 patients, developed education and recruitment initiatives to increase the diversity of the Registry, increased the number of minority patients receiving transplant each year, developed patient advocacy services, established a system of listing cord blood units within its own national Registry. Materials are available free of charge for both potential donors and patients. There is access to interpreters in over 141 languages for these materials. **Libraries: Type:** reference. **Holdings:** audiovisuals, clippings. **Awards:** Admiral Zumwalt Corporate Award. **Frequency:** annual. **Type:** recognition. **Recipient:** for consistent donor awareness support by sponsoring projects and educational initiatives ● Allison Atlas Award. **Frequency:** annual. **Type:** recognition. **Recipient:** for outstanding commitment to the donor recruitment process ● C.W. Bill Young Congressional Award. **Frequency:** annual. **Type:** recognition. **Recipient:** for outstanding support through legislative initiatives ● Excellence in Local Media Award. **Frequency:** annual. **Type:** recognition. **Recipient:** for a journalist or media organization that has developed story on marrow transplantation awareness ● Grant Hartley Diversity Award. **Frequency:** annual. **Type:** recognition. **Recipient:** for leadership recruitment efforts to further diversify registry of marrow donors ● Heroes Award. **Frequency:** annual. **Type:** recognition. **Recipient:** for any member who performed a single, extraordinary act that demonstrates a dedicated commitment to the NMDP ● Lt. General Frank Petersen Award. **Frequency:** annual. **Type:** recognition. **Recipient:** for individual or group who showed support to NMDP by working with minority communities ● Medical Professional Education Award. **Frequency:** periodic. **Type:** recognition. **Recipient:** for a person or group who made medical innovations on marrow and blood cell transplantation ● Trailblazer Award. **Frequency:** annual. **Type:** recognition. **Recipient:** for terrific team leadership in developing/implementing innovative marrow related programming. **Telecommunication Services:** hotline, (800)526-7809. **Formerly:** National Bone Marrow Donor Registry. **Publications:** *Biennial Report of the National Bone Marrow Donor Registry.* Contains an overview of the NMDP and its centers. ● *Marrow Messenger,* annual. Newsletter. Contains information on donor search process, donor and patient stories and NMDP initiatives. **Circulation:** 3,800,000 ● *Medical Professionals' Guide to Unrelated Donor Stem Cell Transplants.* Alternate Formats: online ● *The Missing Piece,* annual. Brochure. **Circulation:** 1,000,000 ● *NMDP Research Program.* Brochure. Provides information on blood stem research project. **Conventions/Meetings:** annual meeting, for all participating centers in the NMDP network (exhibits).

Drug Rehabilitation

13989 ■ National Alliance of Methadone Advocates (NAMA)
435 2nd Ave.
New York, NY 10010
Ph: (212)595-6262
Fax: (212)595-6262
E-mail: nama.president@verizon.net
URL: http://www.methadone.org
Contact: Joycelyn Woods, Pres.
Founded: 1988. **Members:** 15,000. **Membership Dues:** individual, $25 (annual) ● institutional, $110 (annual). **Staff:** 1. **Budget:** $5,000. **Regional**

Groups: 5. **State Groups:** 20. **Local Groups:** 35. **National Groups:** 12. **Languages:** Danish, English, Italian, Spanish, Swedish. **Multinational. Description:** Methadone maintenance patients and supporters of methadone maintenance treatment. Promotes quality methadone maintenance treatment as the most effective modality for the treatment of opiate addiction. **Awards:** Advocate of the Year. **Frequency:** periodic. **Type:** recognition. **Recipient:** to a NAMA chapter that has done something exceptional ● Certified Methadone Advocate. **Frequency:** 3/year. **Type:** recognition. **Recipient:** to a member who has successfully undergone training and passed the test ● Honorary Methadone Patient. **Frequency:** periodic. **Type:** recognition. **Recipient:** to professionals working in the field who have demonstrated a commitment that is beyond what would be expected of them in providing quality treatment ● Lifetime Achievement. **Frequency:** periodic. **Type:** recognition. **Recipient:** to NAMA chapters that have provided outstanding work ● National Methadone Conference. **Frequency:** periodic. **Type:** scholarship. **Recipient:** to patient or family member interested in methadone advocacy. **Committees:** Gay/Lesbian; Hepatitis C; Training. **Publications:** *Manual Series - Starting A Methadone Advocacy Group.* Manuals. **Price:** $10.00. Alternate Formats: online ● *NAMA Advocate,* quarterly. Newsletter. **Price:** free. **Circulation:** 10,000. **Advertising:** accepted. Alternate Formats: online ● Educational Series - 2.00 each.

Dyslexia

13990 ■ Dyslexia Research Institute (DRI)
5746 Centerville Rd.
Tallahassee, FL 32309
Ph: (850)893-2216
Fax: (850)893-2440
E-mail: dri@dyslexia-add.org
URL: http://www.dyslexia-add.org
Contact: Patricia K. Hardman PhD, Dir.
Founded: 1975. **Description:** Works to change the perception of learning differences, specifically in the area of dyslexia and attention deficit disorders (ADD). **Conventions/Meetings:** seminar and workshop.

13991 ■ International Dyslexia Association (IDA)
40 York Rd., 4th Fl.
Baltimore, MD 21204-5202
Ph: (410)296-0232
Free: (800)ABC-D123
Fax: (410)321-5069
E-mail: info@interdys.org
URL: http://www.interdys.org
Contact: Megan P. Cohen MPA, Exec. Dir.
Founded: 1949. **Members:** 13,000. **Membership Dues:** regular, $70 (annual) ● college student, $40 (annual) ● retired, $45 (annual) ● sustaining, $150 (annual) ● supporting, $300 (annual) ● family, $110 (annual) ● life, $2,000 ● institutional (non-profit only), $395 (annual) ● corporate level I, $295 (annual) ● corporate level II, $795 (annual). **Staff:** 17. **Budget:** $2,000,000. **Regional Groups:** 44. **Description:** Offers free information to the public and referrals for diagnosis and treatment. Membership includes professionals in the fields of neurology, pediatrics, psychiatry, education, social work, and psychology; parents; other persons interested in the study, treatment, and prevention of the problems of specific language disability, often called developmental dyslexia or simply dyslexia. Provides a focal point for activities and ideas generated in various fields as they relate to problems of language development and learning. Establishes in memory of Dr. Samuel T. Orton, a pioneer in the field of dyslexia. Disseminates materials. Offers support groups. Presents seminars and conferences around the U.S. Advocates for appropriate educational policies. **Libraries: Type:** reference. **Holdings:** 200; books, video recordings. **Subjects:** learning disability, dyslexia, ADD. **Awards:** Margaret Byrd Rawson Lifetime Achievement Award. **Frequency:** annual. **Type:** recognition. **Recipient:** to an individual whose work embodies Rawson's com-

passion, leadership, commitment to excellence, and fervent advocacy for people with dyslexia ● Pinnacle Award. **Frequency:** annual. **Type:** recognition ● Samuel T. Orton Award. **Frequency:** annual. **Type:** recognition. **Recipient:** for outstanding contribution to the understanding of the treatment of dyslexia. **Computer Services:** database, referral for services ● mailing lists. **Formerly:** (1981) Orton Society; (1998) Orton Dyslexia Society. **Publications:** *Annals of Dyslexia,* annual. Journal. Features current research on dyslexia. **Price:** included in membership dues; $35.00 for nonmembers. ISSN: 0736-9387. **Circulation:** 15,000. ● *Orton Emeritus Series.* Monographs ● *Perspectives,* quarterly. Magazine ● Also issues reprints of papers. **Conventions/Meetings:** annual international conference, for schools, product manufacturers, service providers and publishers (exhibits) - usually October or November. 2007 Nov. 14-17, Dallas, TX; 2008 Oct. 29-Nov. 1, Seattle, WA ● annual workshop.

Eating Disorders

13992 ■ Academy for Eating Disorders (AED)
60 Revere Dr., Ste.500
Northbrook, IL 60062-1577
Ph: (847)498-4274
Fax: (847)480-9282
E-mail: info@aedweb.org
URL: http://www.aedweb.org
Contact: Eric van Furth PhD, Pres.
Founded: 1993. **Members:** 1,000. **Membership Dues:** regular/affiliate/fellow (low income; with subscription), $135 (annual) ● regular/affiliate/fellow (upper middle income; with subscription), $175 (annual) ● regular/affiliate/fellow (high income; with subscription), $235 (annual) ● student (low and upper middle income; with subscription), $110 (annual) ● student (high income; with subscription), $140 (annual). **Multinational. Description:** Focuses on eating disorders research and treatment, particularly anorexia nervosa, bulimia nervosa, binge eating disorder, and related disorders. Promotes effective treatment and care to patients; develops and advances primary and secondary preventions; disseminates information; advocates on behalf of patients, the public and eating disorder professionals; and assists in developing guidelines for training, practice and professionals within the field. **Computer Services:** Mailing lists, of members. **Telecommunication Services:** electronic mail, evanfurth@tiscali.nl. **Publications:** *AED Newsletter,* quarterly. Features eating disorders research and treatment information. **Advertising:** accepted. Alternate Formats: online ● *International Journal of Eating Disorders,* 8/year. Alternate Formats: online ● Brochures. Alternate Formats: online ● Audiotapes. **Conventions/Meetings:** annual international conference (exhibits) - 2008 May 14-17, Seattle, WA.

13993 ■ Alliance for Eating Disorders Awareness
PO Box 13155
North Palm Beach, FL 33408-3155
Ph: (561)841-0900
Free: (866)662-1235
Fax: (561)841-0972
E-mail: info@eatingdisorderinfo.org
URL: http://www.eatingdisorderinfo.org
Contact: Johanna Kandel, Founder/Exec. Dir.
Founded: 2000. **Description:** Aims to improve the intervention, education and support for people affected by eating disorders. Seeks to establish programs across the nation that allow children and young adults the opportunity to learn about eating disorders and the positive effects of a healthy body image. Provides educational information to parents and caregivers about the dangers and consequences of anorexia, bulimia and other related disorders.

13994 ■ Anorexia Nervosa and Related Eating Disorders (ANRED)
PO Box 5102
Eugene, OR 97405
Ph: (541)344-1144
Free: (800)931-2237

E-mail: jarinor@rio.com
URL: http://www.anred.com
Contact: Dr. J. Bradley Rubel, Pres.
Founded: 1979. **Multinational. Description:** Provides information about anorexia nervosa, bulimia, binge eating disorder, and other lesser known eating disorders. **Computer Services:** Information services, free online information about anorexia nervosa, bulimia and binge eating disorder. **Publications:** Pamphlets ● Also publishes resource material and fact sheets. **Conventions/Meetings:** annual meeting - always September or October, Eugene, OR.

13995 ■ Eating Disorders Coalition for Research, Policy and Action (EDC)
611 Pennsylvania Ave. SE, No. 423
Washington, DC 20003-4303
Ph: (202)543-9570
Fax: (202)543-9570
E-mail: manager@eatingdisorderscoalition.org
URL: http://www.eatingdisorderscoalition.org
Contact: Marc Lerro, Exec. Dir.
Founded: 2000. **Members:** 1,000. **Membership Dues:** coalition, $500 (annual) ● public policy, $1,000 (annual) ● executive leadership, $5,000 (annual) ● legislative leadership, $2,500 (annual). **Staff:** 3. **Budget:** $100,000. **Regional Groups:** 5. **Local Groups:** 10. **National Groups:** 15. **Description:** Seeks to advance federal recognition of eating disorders as a public health priority. **Libraries: Type:** by appointment only. **Holdings:** 100; books, reports. **Subjects:** eating disorders, public policy. **Computer Services:** Electronic publishing ● information services ● mailing lists. **Affiliated With:** International Association of Eating Disorders Professionals; National Eating Disorders Association. **Publications:** *Briefing Sheets*, biennial. Bulletin. Summarizes research and outlines problems associated with eating disorders. **Price:** $1.00. Alternate Formats: online ● *Report on Congressional Sponsorships*, annual. **Price:** $1.00. Alternate Formats: online. Also Cited As: *Congressional Report Card*.

13996 ■ International Association of Eating Disorders Professionals (IAEDP)
PO Box 1295
Pekin, IL 61555-1295
Ph: (309)346-3341
Free: (800)800-8126
Fax: (309)346-2874
E-mail: iaedpmembers@earthlink.com
URL: http://www.iaedp.com
Contact: Bonnie Harken, Managing Dir.
Founded: 1985. **Members:** 800. **Membership Dues:** individual, $195 (annual) ● organization, $1,500 (annual) ● student, $75 (annual). **Staff:** 4. **Description:** Eating disorders counselors, specialists, and associates. Establishes and develops curricula; operates and implements a system for certifying eating disorders specialists and associates; provides public education and information on eating disorders. Offers professional consulting and assistance to the medical community, hospitals, courts, law enforcement agencies, schools, churches, and social welfare agencies. Facilitates networking among members; makes available employment opportunity information. Sponsors workshops; maintains speakers' bureau. symposia. **Computer Services:** database ● mailing lists. **Committees:** Certification. **Publications:** *Clinical Quorum*. **Price:** included in membership dues. **Advertising:** accepted ● *Connections*, quarterly. Newsletter. Alternate Formats: online ● Bulletin, monthly. Contains association news and activities and certification update. **Price:** included in membership dues. **Advertising:** accepted ● Also publishes certification manual and curriculum for higher education. **Conventions/Meetings:** annual International Eating Disorders Symposium (exhibits) - 2008 Apr. 3-6, Orlando, FL.

13997 ■ National Association of Anorexia Nervosa and Associated Disorders (ANAD)
PO Box 7
Highland Park, IL 60035
Ph: (847)831-3438
Fax: (847)433-4632

E-mail: anad20@aol.com
URL: http://www.anad.org
Contact: Vivian Hanson Meehan RN, Pres./Founder
Founded: 1976. **Membership Dues:** friend, $30 (annual) ● supporter, $50 (annual) ● partner, $100 (annual). **Staff:** 10. **Budget:** $425,000. **National Groups:** 350. **Description:** Individuals with eating disorders, their families, health professionals, and others interested in the problems of anorexia, bulimia and binge-eating disorder. Maintains chapters in 45 states, Canada, South Africa, Ghana, France, Italy, Puerto Rico, Argentina, England, Slovenia, Ireland, Switzerland, Colombia, Spain and Germany. Aims to: seek a better understanding of, prevent, and cure eating disorders; educate the public and health professionals on illnesses relating to eating disorders and methods of treatment. Encourages and promotes research on the cause of eating disorders, methods of prevention, types of treatment and their effectiveness, and basic facts about victims. Acts as a resource center, compiling and providing information about eating disorders. **Libraries: Type:** reference. **Holdings:** 500; articles, books, papers. **Subjects:** anorexia nervosa, bulimia nervosa, binge eating disorder, compulsive exercise, obesity, self-motivation. **Awards:** ANAD Award. **Frequency:** annual. **Type:** recognition. **Formerly:** (1976) Anorexia Nervosa and Associated Disorders. **Publications:** *Working Together*, quarterly. Newsletter. **Price:** included in membership dues. **Circulation:** 15,000. **Conventions/Meetings:** biennial conference (exhibits).

13998 ■ National Eating Disorders Association (NEDA)
603 Stewart St., Ste.803
Seattle, WA 98101
Ph: (206)382-3587
Free: (800)931-2237
Fax: (206)829-8501
E-mail: info@nationaleatingdisorders.org
URL: http://www.nationaleatingdisorders.org
Contact: Barbara Reid, Office Mgr.
Founded: 2001. **Members:** 3,500. **Membership Dues:** student, $20 (annual) ● supporter, $35 (annual) ● friend, $50 (annual) ● activist, $75 (annual) ● guardian, $150 (annual) ● ambassador, $250 (annual) ● professional individual, $100 (annual) ● professional organization, $200 (annual) ● premiere professional, $500 (annual). **Staff:** 10. **Budget:** $1,600,000. **Description:** Provides educational programming, prevention efforts, research, advocacy, treatment and outreach for those suffering from eating disorders such as anorexia and bulimia. Sponsors National Eating Disorders Awareness Week, celebrated in fifty states. Distributes educational brochures, sponsors a Prevention Puppet Project designed to teach elementary school children about health, self-esteem and body image. Created the GO GIRLS! program, designed to help high school girls learn more about body image and the role that the media plays in the way they feel about themselves and their bodies. Runs a national media advocacy campaign. **Awards:** Lori Irving Memorial Research Grant. **Frequency:** annual. **Type:** grant. **Recipient:** for early prevention researchers. **Formed by Merger of:** (2001) American Anorexia Bulimia Association; (2001) National Eating Disorders Organization. **Formerly:** (1980) Anorexia Nervosa Aid Society; (1983) American Anorexia Bulimia Association; (2001) Eating Disorders Awareness and Prevention, Inc. **Publications:** *Body Thieves*. Book. Covers obesity myths, barriers from being physically active and strategies for integrating physical activity into girls' lives. **Price:** $20.00 ● *BodyTalk 3*. Video. Features body acceptance issues for 6 to 9 year old girls and boys. **Price:** $125.00 ● *BodyTalk 2: It's a New Language*. Video. Features a body examination-body acceptance for 8 to 11 year old girls and boys. **Price:** $125.00 ● *Fed Up*. Book. Contains eating disorders information and prevention on college campuses. **Price:** $3.50 ● *Outlook*, 3/year. Newsletter ● *When Girls Feel Fat: Helping Girls Through Adolescence*. Book. Talks about female development, promotion of healthy body image and self-esteem and the prevention of eating disorder to everyone. **Price:** $12.00 ● Brochures. Includes four different brochures on eating disorders.

Price: $12.00. **Conventions/Meetings:** annual conference, for families, educators and professionals (exhibits).

Editors

13999 ■ World Association of Medical Editors (WAME)
c/o Margaret A. Winker, MD, VP
515 N State St.
Chicago, IL 60610
Ph: (312)464-2486
Fax: (312)464-5824
E-mail: margaret.winker@jama-archives.org
URL: http://www.wame.org
Contact: Margaret A. Winker MD, VP
Founded: 1995. **Members:** 1,199. **National Groups:** 82. **Multinational. Description:** Promotes professionalism in medical editing through education, self-criticism and self regulation. Encourages research on the principles and practices of medical editing. Improves public health by providing quality medical care. **Computer Services:** Online services, listserv discussions. **Committees:** Editorial Policy; Education; Ethics.

Electricity

14000 ■ Lightning Strike and Electric Shock Survivors International (LSESSI)
PO Box 1156
Jacksonville, NC 28541-1156
Ph: (910)346-4708
Fax: (910)346-4708
E-mail: lightning1@ec.rr.com
URL: http://www.lightning-strike.org
Contact: Mr. Steve Marshburn Sr., Exec. Pres.
Founded: 1989. **Members:** 1,382. **Membership Dues:** survivor, lightning or electrical; family member of survivor or non-survivor; medical professional, $25 (annual) ● survivor and family member of survivor (includes entire household), $35 (annual) ● legal professional, $50 (annual). **Staff:** 2. **Budget:** $5,000,000. **State Groups:** 1. **Multinational. Description:** Provides support for lightning strike and electric shock survivors, family members of survivors and families of non-survivors. **Libraries: Type:** reference. **Subjects:** members' stories, ER treatment, legal information. **Awards:** Man and Woman of the Year. **Frequency:** annual. **Type:** recognition. **Recipient:** for dedication and contributions to the organization. **Telecommunication Services:** electronic mail, smarshburnsr@yahoo.com. **Also Known As:** LS ESSI, Inc.; Lightning Strike and Electric Shock Victims. **Publications:** *After Effects "Study"*. Shows the percentages of members injured by lightning and electricity. **Price:** $25.00 ● *Hit and Miss Newsletter*, quarterly ● *Life After Shock*. Book. Includes fifty-eight members telling their personal stories. **Price:** $23.00 ● *Life After Shock, Vol. II*. Book. Contains the stories of 49 members. **Price:** $23.00 ● Brochure. Features survivor application, non-victim application, calling card, daily diary, return envelope, and information. **Price:** free. **Conventions/Meetings:** annual conference.

Electroencephalography

14001 ■ American Board of Registration of EEG and EP Technologists (ABRET)
1904 Croydon Dr.
Springfield, IL 62703
Ph: (217)553-3758
Fax: (217)585-6663
E-mail: abreteo@aol.com
URL: http://www.abret.org
Contact: Janice Walbert, Exec. Dir.
Founded: 1964. **Staff:** 1. **Description:** Determines the competency of Electroneurodiagnostic Technologists through administration of written and oral examinations. **Convention/Meeting:** none. **Affiliated**

With: American Clinical Neurophysiology Society; American Society of Electroneurodiagnostic Technologists. **Formerly:** (1992) American Board of Registration of EEG Technologists.

14002 ■ American Clinical Neurophysiology Society (ACNS)

PO Box 30
Bloomfield, CT 06002
Ph: (860)243-3977
Fax: (860)286-0787
E-mail: info@acns.org
URL: http://www.acns.org
Contact: Mark A. Ross MD, Pres.
Founded: 1946. **Members:** 1,450. **Membership Dues:** regular, in U.S., $250 (annual) ● junior, $76 (annual) ● corresponding, outside North America, $135 (annual) ● regular, outside U.S., $220 (annual). **Description:** Professional society of electroencephalographers and neurophysiologists. Offers clinical course annually. Provides continuing education to its members and others interested in clinical neurophysiology. **Telecommunication Services:** electronic mail, acns@ssmgt.com. **Committees:** Continuing Education; Evoked Potentials; Fellowship; Guidelines in EEG; Infectious Diseases; Laboratory Accreditation; Medical Instrumentation; Practice of EEG; Research; Training. **Formerly:** (1997) American Electroencephalographic Society. **Publications:** *Journal of Clinical Neurophysiology*, bimonthly. **Advertising:** accepted ● Books, annual. **Conventions/Meetings:** annual convention (exhibits).

14003 ■ American Society of Electroneurodiagnostic Technologists (ASET)

6501 E Commerce Ave., Ste.120
Kansas City, MO 64120
Ph: (816)931-1120
Fax: (816)931-1145
E-mail: info@aset.org
URL: http://www.aset.org
Contact: Sheila R. Navis CAE, Exec. Dir.
Founded: 1959. **Members:** 2,750. **Membership Dues:** student, $40 (annual) ● active, $80 (annual) ● associate, $90 (annual) ● institutional, $350 (annual). **Staff:** 6. **Budget:** $800,000. **Description:** Persons engaged in clinical electroencephalographic (EEG) technology, evoked potential responses, nerve conduction studies, and polysomnography (sleep studies). Works for the advancement of electroneurodiagnostic technology education and practice standards. **Libraries: Type:** not open to the public. **Awards:** Maureen Berkeley Memorial Award. **Frequency:** annual. **Type:** recognition. **Recipient:** for the best article by an EEG technologist published in the *American Journal of Electroneurodiagnostic Technology* ● **Frequency:** quarterly. **Type:** scholarship. **Recipient:** to members for expenses in attending the annual meeting and short courses. **Computer Services:** Mailing lists. **Committees:** Academic Advisory; Continuing Education; Editorial Advisory; Education; Governmental Advocacy; Joint Review; Nominating; Program Planning; Scholarships & Awards. **Subcommittees:** Special Lectures. **Affiliated With:** American Clinical Neurophysiology Society. **Formerly:** (1985) American Society of Electroencephalographic Technologists. **Publications:** *ASET Newsletter*, quarterly. Includes calendar of events, local, state, and regional society news and workshop and seminar news. **Price:** included in membership dues. ISSN: 0886-5620. **Circulation:** 2,600. **Advertising:** accepted ● *Journal of Electroneurodiagnostic Technology*, quarterly. Covers EEG, evoked potentials, polysomnography, nerve conduction, and related electroneurodiagnostics. **Price:** included in membership dues; $50.00 /year for nonmembers in U.S.; $60.00 /year for nonmembers outside U.S.; $90.00 /year for libraries and institutions in U.S. ISSN: 1086-508X. **Circulation:** 3,500. **Advertising:** accepted. Also Cited As: *American Journal of EEG Technology ● Who's Who in Electroneurodiagnostics—Membership Directory*, annual. Provides product listings for suppliers. Contains member listings that are arranged alphabetically and geographically. **Price:** included in membership dues. **Advertising:** accepted ● Monographs. Provides information on selected END technology and related

management subjects. ● Books ● Also publishes study materials and guides. **Conventions/Meetings:** annual convention, with short courses (exhibits) ● quarterly Short Courses - workshop, two-day classes on END specialties.

Electrolysis

14004 ■ American Electrology Association (AEA)

c/o Patsy Kirby, CPE, Exec. Dir.
PO Box 687
Bodega Bay, CA 94923
Ph: (707)875-9135
Fax: (707)875-3340
E-mail: infoaea@electrology.com
URL: http://www.electrology.com
Contact: Patsy Kirby CPE, Exec. Dir.
Founded: 1958. **Members:** 2,000. **Membership Dues:** regular, $165 (annual). **Staff:** 1. **Budget:** $250,000. **State Groups:** 26. **National Groups:** 2. **Description:** Electrologists united for education, professional advancement, and protection of public welfare. Promotes uniform legislative standards throughout the states. Coordinates efforts of affiliated associations in dealing with problems of national scope. Sponsors the International Board of Electrologist Certification and Council on Accreditation of Electrology Schools/Programs. Maintains referral, reference, advisory, and consulting services. **Committees:** Certification; Legislation; Office of Continuing Education; Public Relations; Regulatory. **Councils:** Education. **Formerly:** (1986) American Electrolysis Association. **Publications:** *American Electrology Association—Roster*, annual. Membership Directory. Includes modalities used; arranged geographically. **Price:** included in membership dues. **Advertising:** accepted ● *Electrology World*, 3/year. Newsletter. Includes calendar of events. **Price:** available to members only. **Circulation:** 2,000. **Advertising:** accepted ● *Infection Control Standards for the Practice of Electrology ● Journal of the American Electrology Association*, semiannual. Includes case studies. **Price:** $10.00/issue. **Circulation:** 2,000. **Advertising:** accepted ● *Medical/Professional News*, semiannual. Newsletter ● Brochures. **Conventions/Meetings:** annual conference (exhibits) ● seminar ● workshop.

14005 ■ International Guild of Hair Removal Specialists (IGHRS)

1918 Bethel Rd.
Columbus, OH 43220
Ph: (614)457-0448
Free: (800)830-3247
Fax: (614)457-6884
E-mail: vickie@aboutface-ctc.com
Contact: Vickie L. Mickey, Pres.
Founded: 1978. **Members:** 2,200. **Membership Dues:** regular, in U.S., $99 (annual) ● regular, outside U.S., $110 (annual) ● regular, in Canada, $104 (annual) ● student (first year only), $60 ● school, manufacturer, $385 (annual) ● combined school/manufacturer, $660 (annual). **Budget:** $100,000. **Regional Groups:** 5. **For-Profit. Description:** Electrologists; electrology schools; manufacturers and suppliers of electrolysis equipment. Works to improve the image of electrolysis and promote it as an acceptable allied health profession. Promotes licensing of electrologists. Provides referral service. Conducts seminars. **Libraries: Type:** reference. **Holdings:** audio recordings. **Awards:** Dr. Charles Michel Award. **Frequency:** annual. **Type:** recognition. **Committees:** Review. **Formerly:** (2005) International Guild of Professional Electrologists. **Publications:** *A Complete Guide to Hair Removal* (in English and Spanish). Brochure. **Advertising:** accepted ● *A Doctor Answers Questions About Hair Removal*. Brochure ● *Consumer Health Guidelines*. Brochure ● *Everything You Ever Wanted to Know About Hair Removal But Were Afraid to Ask*. Brochure ● *International Directory*, annual ● *Physical Methods for the Management of Hirsutism*. Brochure ● *Professional Insider*. Newsletter. **Advertising:** accepted. Alternate

Formats: online ● *Selecting an Electrologist: Thermolysis for Permanent Hair Removal*. Brochure ● Newsletter, quarterly. Includes biennial conference reports. **Price:** free for members. **Circulation:** 5,000. **Conventions/Meetings:** annual conference, electrology supplies and equipment (exhibits).

14006 ■ Society for Clinical and Medical Hair Removal (SCMHR)

2810 Crossroads Dr., Ste.3800
Madison, WI 53718
Ph: (608)443-2470
Fax: (608)443-2474
E-mail: homeoffice@scmhr.org
URL: http://www.scmhr.org
Contact: Lisa M. Nelson, Exec. Sec.
Founded: 1985. **Members:** 300. **Membership Dues:** regular, in U.S., $145 (annual) ● regular, outside U.S., $90 (annual). **Regional Groups:** 10. **Multinational. Description:** Professional society of electrologists (persons engaged in the removal of superfluous hair by galvanic blend or short wave methods for cosmetic and medical purposes). Conducts continuing education and leadership development seminars. **Awards:** Dr. Bordier Award. **Frequency:** annual. **Type:** recognition. **Recipient:** for service to the profession. **Formed by Merger of:** Electrolysis Society of America; National Electrolysis Organization. **Formerly:** (2002) Society of Clinical and Medical Electrologists. **Publications:** *Perspectives*, periodic. Article ● *SCME Directory of Membership*, annual. Membership Directory ● *SCME Newsletter*, quarterly. **Conventions/Meetings:** annual conference (exhibits).

Electromedicine

14007 ■ National Institute of Electromedical Information (NIEI)

PO Box 4633
Bay Terrace, NY 11360-4633
Ph: (718)849-1044
Fax: (718)849-6523
E-mail: sniei@aol.com
URL: http://www.niei.org
Contact: Dr. Stanley H. Kornhauser PhD, Pres.
Founded: 1984. **Members:** 1,494. **Membership Dues:** regular, $60 (annual) ● charter, $250 ● life, $1,000 ● sponsoring, $5,000 ● student, $30 (annual) ● institutional, corporate, $80 (annual). **Staff:** 28. **Budget:** $100,000. **Description:** Health care practitioners, medical educators, research scientists, and electromedical device manufacturers. Disseminates information on research, case histories, new and proposed theories, and clinical applications of electromedicine to professionals, laypersons, federal agencies, U.S. industry, and universities. (Electromedicine deals with the application of diagnostic, monitoring and prosthetic electromedical devices used in research and clinical settings as well as the application of therapeutic electric currents in the prevention and treatment of diseases.) Supports the development of programs and materials for the preparation of those studying electromedicine; fosters the establishment of programs and creation of partnerships that provide resource-sharing networks and professional linkage among clinicians, researchers, colleges and universities, health care institutions, electromedical equipment manufacturers, and other scientific and educational organizations. Encourages exchange of information through an interdisciplinary forum between researchers and clinicians and advises and coordinates matters of mutual interest between members and other organizations. Enhances the career awareness of secondary or post-secondary students in the emerging fields of electromedical technology. Funds, when available, research and educational projects. Reviews standards and certification systems for determining the efficacy of electromedical devices. Offers seminars and tutorials. Maintains consulting service and speakers' bureau; compiles statistics. **Awards: Type:** fellowship ● **Type:** recognition. **Sections:** Biotechnology and Electromedical Devices; Electromedical Technol-

ogy Development; Health Education Awareness and Medical Screening Programs; Information and Reference Services; Pain Management and Rehabilitation; Psychobiological Diagnosis Research and Treatment; Stress and Electromedicine. **Affiliated With:** American Academy of Anti-Aging Medicine; National Health Council. **Publications:** *American Journal of Electromedicine (AJE).* Includes case studies, original research documentation, interviews etc. ISSN: 1520-8427. **Circulation:** 100,000. **Advertising:** accepted ● *National Institute of Electromedical Information—Membership Directory,* annual. **Price:** included in membership dues. **Advertising:** accepted ● Books ● Bulletin, periodic ● Proceedings, periodic ● Also publishes book reviews and educational materials. **Conventions/Meetings:** annual International Conference on Anti-Aging Medicine and Biomedical Technology - congress (exhibits) ● periodic seminar ● symposium ● workshop.

Emergency Aid

14008 ■ American Ambulance Association (AAA)
8201 Greensboro Dr., Ste.300
McLean, VA 22102
Ph: (703)610-9018
Free: (800)523-4447
Fax: (703)610-9005
E-mail: jpmpartlon@mohawkambulance.com
URL: http://www.the-aaa.org
Contact: Bob Garner, Pres.
Founded: 1979. **Membership Dues:** active, $8,135 (annual) ● associate, $749 (annual) ● affiliate, $1,128 (annual) ● individual, $272 (annual) ● state association, $267 (annual). **Budget:** $350,000. **Description:** Represents private suppliers of ambulance service. Aims to: aid in developing private enterprise prehospital emergency medical treatment and medical transportation services as a viable cost-effective alternative to publicly-operated services; promote improved patient care; develop efficient medical transportation at a reasonable cost; improve personnel and equipment standards; work with organizations offering medical transportation; encourage high standards of ethics and conduct. Acts as an information clearinghouse; informs members of developments in the industry. Offers advice on federal statutes and regulations related to the medical transportation industry, such as insurance and antitrust regulations. Holds four regional seminars per year on topics such as training requirements, insurance systems, medicare reimbursement, and local, state, and federal legislation and regulations. Conducts quarterly emergency medical services management seminar. **Formed by Merger of:** Ambulance Association of America; National Ambulance and Medical Services Association. **Formerly:** (1978) Ambulance and Medical Service Association of America. **Publications:** *Ambulance Service Journal,* quarterly. Includes book reviews and legislative reports. **Price:** free for members; $25.00 for nonmembers. **Circulation:** 5,000. **Advertising:** accepted. **Conventions/Meetings:** annual meeting (exhibits).

14009 ■ Angel Flight America (AFA)
4300 Westgrove Dr.
Addison, TX 75001
Ph: (214)234-8458
Free: (877)858-7788
Fax: (214)234-8459
E-mail: execdir@angelflightamerica.org
URL: http://www.angelflightamerica.org
Contact: Theresa Dorre, Exec. Dir.
Founded: 2003. **Regional Groups:** 6. **Description:** Voluntary association of pilots who donate their time, skills, fuel, and aircraft to fly medical missions. Provides free air transportation for financially needy patients who require specialized treatment at medical facilities far from their homes. **Telecommunication Services:** additional toll-free number, (877)621-7177. **Formerly:** (2003) AirLifeLine. **Publications:** *Pilot and Patient,* quarterly. Newsletter. Includes Victory Roll, a list of volunteer pilots who have flown medical mis-

sions and stories of patients. **Price:** free. **Circulation:** 15,000 ● *Skylines,* 3/year. Newsletter. Provides information on the program and on aviation in general. **Circulation:** 1,120 ● Membership Directory, 3/year. **Circulation:** 1,120.

14010 ■ Association of Air Medical Services (AAMS)
526 King St., Ste.415
Alexandria, VA 22314-3143
Ph: (703)836-8732
Fax: (703)836-8920
E-mail: information@aams.org
URL: http://www.aams.org
Contact: Dawn M. Mancuso CAE, Exec. Dir.
Founded: 1980. **Members:** 400. **Membership Dues:** personal, $94 (annual) ● associate, $1,200 (annual) ● affiliate (based on number of employees), $250-$1,000 (annual) ● regular (based on type and number of vehicles), $600-$4,800 (annual). **Staff:** 8. **Budget:** $1,800,000. **Regional Groups:** 10. **Multinational. Description:** Air medical transport providers; manufacturers and distributors of air medical transport equipment and supplies. Provides quality medical care during rapid air transport. Seeks to develop standards for aircraft configuration, minimum professional and educational requirements for personnel on board, medical and communications equipment, and operations. **Awards:** Barbara A. Hess Award. **Frequency:** annual. **Type:** recognition ● Crew Member of the Year. **Frequency:** annual. **Type:** recognition ● Fixed Wing Safety. **Frequency:** annual. **Type:** recognition ● Fixed Wing Scholarship. **Frequency:** annual. **Type:** recognition ● Jim Charlson. **Frequency:** annual. **Type:** recognition ● Marriott-Carlson. **Frequency:** annual. **Type:** recognition ● Program Director of the Year. **Frequency:** annual. **Type:** recognition ● Program of the Year. **Frequency:** annual. **Type:** recognition. **Computer Services:** Mailing lists. **Committees:** Conference Education; Critical Care Ground; Education and Publications; Finance and Reimbursement; Fixed Wing; Government Relations; Member Services; Membership/Communications; Nominating; Quality Management/Standards; Research; Safety. **Formerly:** (1988) American Society of Hospital-Based Emergency Air Medical Services. **Publications:** *AAMS Resource Guide,* annual. Membership Directory. Contains information on association and its products and services. **Price:** free for members ● *Air Medical Journal,* bimonthly. Magazine. Published in conjunction with several other associations. **Price:** included in membership dues. **Advertising:** accepted. Alternate Formats: online ● *Capitol Watch,* periodic. Newsletter. Provides members legislative and regulatory related information. Alternate Formats: online ● *News and Views,* monthly. Newsletter. Contains association activity updates, community and member news, crew fitness and survival, editorials and classifieds. Alternate Formats: online ● *On The Fly,* monthly. Newsletter. Compiles news stories on aviation safety and patient safety issues. Alternate Formats: online. **Conventions/Meetings:** annual Air Medical Transport Conference, held in conjunction with ASTNA, NFPA, NEMSPA, AMPA, and NAACS (exhibits) - 2007 Sept. 17-19, Tampa, FL; 2008 Oct. 20-22, Minneapolis, MN.

14011 ■ Doctors for Disaster Preparedness (DDP)
1601 N Tucson Blvd., Ste.No. 9
Tucson, AZ 85716
Ph: (520)325-2680
E-mail: jersnav@mindspring.com
URL: http://www.oism.org/ddp
Contact: Jane M. Orient MD, Pres.
Founded: 1982. **Members:** 200. **Membership Dues:** associate, $20 (annual) ● professional, $50 (annual). **Description:** Doctors, health professionals, medical students and interested individuals. Prepares physicians, health professionals, personnel, and the public for medical response in the case of natural or human-caused disaster. Seeks to prevent human suffering and death resulting from any catastrophe. Believes that "there is no disaster so great - including nuclear war - that the medical profession is not obliged to care for the survivors". Promotes accurate risk as-

sessment. Supports civil defense measures; maintains no position on specific military or foreign policy measures, weapons systems, or arms control. Sponsors lectures for health professionals, government leaders, and the public concerning disaster preparedness. Compiles statistics; maintains speakers' bureau. **Publications:** *Civil Defense Perspectives,* bimonthly. Newsletter. **Price:** included in membership dues. **Circulation:** 1,200 ● Newsletter, bimonthly. **Price:** included in membership dues. **Circulation:** 1,200 ● Reprints. Consists of literature related to disaster preparedness. Alternate Formats: CD-ROM. **Conventions/Meetings:** annual conference and seminar (exhibits).

14012 ■ International Rescue and Emergency Care Association (IRECA)
PO Box 431000
Minneapolis, MN 55443
Ph: (301)741-0455
Free: (800)85-IRECA
E-mail: rescuer@ireca.org
URL: http://www.ireca.org
Contact: Randy Tanner, Pres.
Founded: 1948. **Members:** 3,000. **Membership Dues:** individual, $30 (annual) ● senior, youth, $20 (annual) ● organization, $100 (annual) ● sustaining, bronze, $250 (annual) ● sustaining, silver, $500 (annual) ● sustaining, gold, $1,000 (annual). **Staff:** 1. **Local Groups:** 500. **Multinational. Description:** Organized volunteers and paid industrial rescue and emergency squads, ambulance and first aid crews, fire departments, military personnel, and other units equipped with rescue equipment and emergency care supplies which can be carried in mobile units; county, state, and other associations and individuals interested in rescue and emergency patient care. Works to cooperate in, foster, and conduct research designed to advance the science and art of rescue and emergency care and to encourage standardization of practice and equipment. Sponsors seminars. **Awards:** Max Spray Award. **Frequency:** annual. **Type:** recognition. **Recipient:** for a member who has demonstrated commitment to serving the association. **Telecommunication Services:** electronic mail, rtanner@ireca.org. **Committees:** Awards; Credentials; Education; Emergency Care Contest; EMT Contest; Rescue Contest; Technical. **Formerly:** (1978) International Rescue and First Aid Association. **Publications:** *International Rescuer,* quarterly. Newsletter. Alternate Formats: online ● Also publishes and endorses the publication of emergency care and rescue training information. **Conventions/Meetings:** annual conference (exhibits).

14013 ■ International Society of First Responders (ISOFR)
128 E 6th St.
Cincinnati, OH 45202
Ph: (513)333-7800
E-mail: info@isofr.org
URL: http://www.isofr.com
Contact: Keith Engel, Contact
Members: 1,915. **Multinational. Description:** Empowers and equips First Responders to better serve and protect their communities with the right tools, techniques and training. Focuses on the issues of training, education, best practices and shared experiences facing First Responders concerning Homeland Security. Consolidates and integrates best practice responses to Weapons of Mass Destruction (WMD) events among all First Responders. **Publications:** *The Responder.* Newsletter. **Price:** free for members. Alternate Formats: online.

14014 ■ MedicAlert Foundation International (MAFI)
2323 Colorado Ave.
Turlock, CA 95382
Ph: (209)668-3333
Free: (888)633-4298
Fax: (209)669-2450
E-mail: customer_service@medicalert.org
URL: http://www.medicalert.org/home/Homegradient.aspx
Contact: Paul Kortschak, Pres./CEO
Founded: 1956. **Members:** 4,000,000. **Membership Dues:** regular, $16 (annual). **Staff:** 142. **Multina-**

tional. **Description:** Provides medical information service that protects and saves lives. Enables members to manage their personal health records while maintaining security, privacy and confidentiality. Conducts continuous public and professional education program. **Telecommunication Services:** 24-hour hotline, customer support, (800)ID-ALERT. **Publications:** *MedicAlert News*, semiannual. Newsletter. **Price:** free for members. **Conventions/Meetings:** board meeting - 3/year.

14015 ■ Miracle Flights for Kids
2756 N Green Valley Pkwy., No. 115
Green Valley, NV 89014-2120
Ph: (702)261-0494
Free: (800)FLY-1711
Fax: (702)261-0497
E-mail: info@miracleflights.org
URL: http://www.miracleflights.org
Contact: Ann McGee, Natl. Pres.
Founded: 1985. **Members:** 500. **Staff:** 13. **Budget:** $4,100,000. **Description:** Provides free air transportation to families who are unable to get to medical treatment centers far from home. **Awards:** Award of Gratitude. **Frequency:** periodic. **Type:** recognition. **Recipient:** for outstanding community service. **Telecommunication Services:** electronic mail, amcgee@miracleflights.org. **Formerly:** (1998) The Angel Planes. **Publications:** Newsletter, quarterly. Includes safety and pilot news, flight updates, fundraising news, and news about flights. **Price:** free. **Advertising:** accepted.

14016 ■ National Association of First Responders (AAFAR-NAFR)
5334 Armadillo Ave.
Orange Beach, AL 36561-4211
Ph: (251)981-3383 (251)979-6592
Contact: Henry Weir Jr., Pres.
Founded: 1984. **Members:** 4,019. **Membership Dues:** individual, $40 (annual). **Staff:** 28. **Budget:** $265,000. **Regional Groups:** 99. **State Groups:** 201. **Local Groups:** 307. **National Groups:** 598. **Description:** Emergency medical responders who have had 40 hours of training. (EMRs, or first responders, arrive on the scene of a medical emergency and administer assistance prior to the arrival of paramedics or emergency medical technicians.) Provides a forum for exchange of ideas and medical information among EMRs. Offers a national certification program for first responders and educational and research programs. Maintains placement services and speakers' bureau. **Libraries: Type:** reference. **Holdings:** 15,018. **Awards:** President's Award. **Frequency:** annual. **Type:** recognition. **Recipient:** to EMT, 1st responder, medical professionals. **Computer Services:** Mailing lists. **Formerly:** (1989) American Association of First Responders. **Publications:** *National EMR Responder*, monthly. Newsletter. **Price:** included in membership dues. **Circulation:** 3,000. **Conventions/Meetings:** annual First Response - conference (exhibits) ● annual National First Response Seminar - regional meeting (exhibits) ● symposium.

14017 ■ National Emergency Number Association (NENA)
4350 N Fairfax Dr., Ste.750
Arlington, VA 22203-1695
Ph: (703)812-4600
Free: (800)332-3911
Fax: (703)812-4675
E-mail: rmartin@nena.org
URL: http://www.nena9-1-1.org
Contact: Robert L. Martin ENP, Exec. Dir.
Founded: 1982. **Members:** 7,500. **Membership Dues:** public sector, government (voting), $120 (annual) ● private sector, commercial (voting), $150 (annual) ● associate, emergency dispatcher, $75 (annual). **Staff:** 17. **Local Groups:** 46. **Description:** Fosters the technical advancement, availability, and implementation of a universal emergency telephone number system. Promotes research, planning, training, and education. **Publications:** *ENP Magazine*, 10/year. Covers many issues of the association. **Advertising:** accepted. Also Cited As: *Emergency Number Professional* ● *NENA NEWS e-blast*, bi-

weekly. Newsletter. Provides regional information. **Advertising:** accepted. **Conventions/Meetings:** annual conference and trade show (exhibits) - always June.

14018 ■ National EMS Pilots Association (NEMSPA)
526 King St., Ste.415
Alexandria, VA 22314-3143
Ph: (703)836-8930
Fax: (703)836-8920
E-mail: vicky_spediacci@mediplane.com
Founded: 1988. **Members:** 250. **Membership Dues:** active/affiliate in U.S., $38 (annual) ● corporate sponsor, junior corporate sponsor, $250 (annual) ● active/affiliate outside U.S., $55 (annual) ● senior corporate sponsor, $500 (annual) ● corporate benefactor, $1,000 (annual). **Description:** Pilots in the air medical industry and interested individuals. Works to help the air medical industry prosper safely and enhance the delivery of health care. Facilitates the exchange of information; evaluates new equipment; conducts educational programs; monitors governmental organizations; supports research; offers legal assistance. **Libraries: Type:** not open to the public. **Holdings:** articles, periodicals. **Subjects:** EMS, pilots. **Awards:** EMS Pilot of the Year. **Frequency:** annual. **Type:** scholarship. **Computer Services:** Mailing lists. **Telecommunication Services:** electronic bulletin board, (417)782-6909 ● electronic mail, president@nemspa.org. **Publications:** *Air Medical Journal*, bimonthly. Magazine. **Advertising:** accepted. Alternate Formats: online ● *AirNet*, quarterly. Newsletter. Alternate Formats: online. **Conventions/Meetings:** annual Air Medical Transport Conference (exhibits).

Emergency Medicine

14019 ■ American Academy of Emergency Medicine (AAEM)
555 E Wells St., Ste.1100
Milwaukee, WI 53202-3823
Ph: (414)276-7390
Free: (800)884-AAEM
Fax: (414)276-3349
E-mail: info@aaem.org
URL: http://www.aaem.org
Contact: Kay Whalen, Exec.Dir.
Founded: 1993. **Members:** 5,000. **Membership Dues:** resident, student, $50 (annual) ● emeritus, associate, $250 (annual) ● fellow, full voting, $345 (annual). **Staff:** 6. **Budget:** $1,500,000. **State Groups:** 11. **Description:** Board certified physicians specializing in emergency medicine or pediatric emergency medicine; medical students and residents. Promotes "unencumbered access to quality emergency care provided by a specialist in emergency medicine" for every individual. Seeks to advance the study and profession of emergency medicine. Represents members' economic and professional interests; supports growth of medical residency and graduate medical education programs; works to create a professional and legal environment conducive to the delivery of quality emergency medical care. **Awards:** David K. Wagner Award. **Frequency:** annual. **Type:** recognition ● James Keaney Award. **Type:** recognition ● Peter Rosen Award. **Type:** recognition ● Program Director of the Year. **Frequency:** annual. **Type:** recognition ● Resident/Fellow of the Year. **Frequency:** annual. **Type:** recognition ● Young Educator. **Type:** recognition. **Computer Services:** database ● online services. **Additional Websites:** http://www.911emergency.org. **Committees:** Academic Affairs; Bylaws/Policy; Communications; Education; EM Practice; EMS; Ethics; Finance. **Publications:** *Common Sense*, bimonthly. Newsletter. **Price:** included in membership dues. **Circulation:** 3,500. **Advertising:** accepted. Alternate Formats: online ● *Journal of Emergency Medicine*, 8/year. Features original contributions of interest to both the academic and practicing emergency physician. **Price:** included in membership dues. **Conventions/Meetings:** annual Scientific Assembly (exhibits).

14020 ■ American Association of Women Emergency Physicians (AAWEP)
c/o American College of Emergency Physicians
PO Box 619911
Dallas, TX 75261-9911
Ph: (972)550-0911
Free: (800)798-1822
Fax: (972)580-2816
E-mail: aawep.section@acep.org
URL: http://www.acep.org/webportal/membercenter/
sections/aawep
Contact: Lily C. Conrad MD, Chair
Founded: 1983. **Members:** 400. **Membership Dues:** active, $35 (annual) ● medical student, general medical officer, additional, $20 (annual). **Staff:** 3. **Budget:** $200,000. **Description:** Women engaged in the practice of emergency medicine. Promotes professional advancement of members. Provides support and guidance to female emergency physicians; conducts leadership skills development programs for female emergency physicians, residents, and medical students. Maintains speakers' bureau. **Awards:** Trish Blair Leadership Services Awards. **Frequency:** annual. **Type:** recognition. **Recipient:** for women emergency physicians. **Computer Services:** Online services. **Committees:** Education; Fundraising. **Publications:** *Epic Quarterly Newsletter*, periodic. Directory ● Newsletter, periodic. **Conventions/Meetings:** annual Leadership Conference ● quarterly Long Range Planning Conference.

14021 ■ American Board of Emergency Medicine (ABEM)
3000 Coolidge Rd.
East Lansing, MI 48823-6319
Ph: (517)332-4800
Fax: (517)332-2234
E-mail: abem@abem.org
URL: http://www.abem.org
Contact: Mary Ann Reinhart PhD, Exec. Dir.
Founded: 1976. **Staff:** 28. **Description:** Seeks to: improve the quality of emergency medical care; establish and maintain high standards of excellence in the specialty of emergency medicine and its approved subspecialties; improve medical education and facilities for training emergency physicians and sub specialist in approved ABEM subspecialties; evaluate specialists in emergency medicine and sub-specialist in approved ABEM subspecialties applying for continuous certification and recertification; serve the public, physicians, hospitals, and medical schools by furnishing lists of those diplomates certified by ABEM. **Committees:** Academic Affairs; Credentials; Executive Finance; Nominating; Research; Test Administration; Test Development. **Publications:** *ABEM Memo*, semiannual. Newsletter. For diplomates and organizations associated with ABEM. Alternate Formats: online ● *ABEM Policies and Procedures*, annual. Booklet. **Price:** free ● Annual Report. Includes summary of current year's events and activities, volunteers, and exam statistics. Alternate Formats: online.

14022 ■ American College of Emergency Physicians (ACEP)
1125 Executive Cir.
Irving, TX 75038-2522
Ph: (972)550-0911
Free: (800)798-1822
Fax: (972)580-2816
E-mail: execdirector@acep.org
URL: http://www.acep.org
Contact: Dean Wilkerson, Exec. Dir.
Founded: 1968. **Members:** 23,600. **Membership Dues:** individual, $515 (annual). **Staff:** 98. **Budget:** $18,500. **State Groups:** 53. **Description:** Supports quality emergency medical care and promotes the interests of emergency physicians. Represents more than 22,000 members and is the emergency medicine specialty society recognized by organized medicine. **Awards: Type:** recognition. **Committees:** Academic Affairs; Bylaws; Clinical Policies; Coding & Nomenclature; Educational Meetings; Emergency Medical Services; Emergency Medicine Practice; Ethics; Federal Government Affairs; Medical Legal; Membership; National Chapter Relations; Pediatric Emer-

gency Medicine; Public Health; Public Relations; Reimbursement; Research; Scientific Review; State Legislative/Regulatory; Trauma Care/Injury Control. **Publications:** *ACEP News*, monthly. Newsletter. Discusses socioeconomic issues affecting emergency medicine. **Price:** included in membership dues; $20.00 /year for nonmembers. **Circulation:** 20,000. **Advertising:** accepted ● *Annals of Emergency Medicine*, monthly. Journal. Covers emergency medicine and emergency health services. Includes abstracts of emergency medical literature, book reviews, and calendar of events. **Price:** included in membership dues. ISSN: 0196-0644. **Circulation:** 25,000. **Advertising:** accepted. Alternate Formats: microform; online ● *Foresight*, 3/year. Newsletter. Covers emergency medicine risk management. ● *Physicians Evaluation and Education Review* ● Also publishes a home study series, and reference manuals on diagnosis and procedure coding, quality assurance, independent contractor status, EMS medical direction, working with managed care plans, patient transfer, risk management, developing and negotiating contracts, and advanced pediatric life support. **Conventions/Meetings:** annual Scientific Assembly - meeting (exhibits).

14023 ■ American College of Osteopathic Emergency Physicians (ACOEP)
142 E Ontario St., Ste.1250
Chicago, IL 60611
Ph: (312)587-3709
Free: (800)521-3709
Fax: (312)587-9951
E-mail: janwachtler@acoep.org
URL: http://www.acoep.org
Contact: Janice Wachtler, Exec. Dir.

Founded: 1975. **Members:** 2,000. **Membership Dues:** active, $450 (annual). **Staff:** 4. **Budget:** $1,000,000. **Description:** Provides and evaluates postdoctoral and continuing education for osteopathic emergency physicians; encourages and implements the training of emergency physicians; promotes the coordination of community emergency care facilities and personnel. Sponsors Emergency Medicine CME Program for Accreditation. Conducts research and educational programs. Maintains speakers' bureau. **Awards:** Fellowship. **Frequency:** annual. **Type:** recognition. **Recipient:** to physicians who have met specific criteria for recognition as a fellow of the American College of Osteopathic Emergency Physicians ● Resident Research Award. **Frequency:** annual. **Type:** monetary. **Computer Services:** database, members ● mailing lists, of members. **Committees:** Communications and Publications; Continuing Medical Education; Education; EMS; Governmental Affairs; Graduate Medical Education; Membership and Credentials; Pediatric Emergency Medicine; Practice Management; Program Directors; Research; Resident Chapter; Student Chapter; Undergraduate Education. **Affiliated With:** American Osteopathic Board of Emergency Medicine. **Publications:** *The Pulse*, quarterly. Newsletter. **Price:** included in membership dues; $25.00 /year for nonmembers. **Circulation:** 2,500. **Advertising:** accepted. Alternate Formats: online. **Conventions/Meetings:** annual COLA Essentials - seminar, a program exploring various aspects of the curriculum of emergency medicine (exhibits) - every winter. 2008 Feb. 5-9, Marco Island, FL ● annual Emergency Medicine: An Intense Review - seminar, an intense board preparatory course for written certification exams in emergency medicine (exhibits) - every winter. 2008 Jan. 9-14, Chicago, IL ● semiannual Oral Board Review - seminar, preparatory course for the oral board portion of the certification process in emergency medicine - 2008 May 2-3, Chicago, IL; 2008 Sept. 14-15, Chicago, IL ● annual seminar, with update and information on emergency physicians on current trends in the specialty of emergency medicine (exhibits) - every spring ● annual seminar, held in conjunction with American Osteopathic Association Convention and Scientific seminar - every fall.

14024 ■ American Osteopathic Board of Emergency Medicine (AOBEM)
c/o Josette M. Fleming, Mgr.
142 E Ontario St.
Chicago, IL 60611

Ph: (312)335-1065
Fax: (312)335-5489
E-mail: aobem@aol.com
URL: http://www.aobem.org
Contact: Susan Hinchliffe DO, Chair

Founded: 1980. **Members:** 9. **Staff:** 1. **Budget:** $75,000. **Description:** Seeks to improve the quality of emergency medical care. Establishes and maintains high standards of excellence in the specialty of emergency medicine. Improves medical education and facilities for training emergency physicians. Evaluates specialists in emergency medicine applying for certification and recertification. Serves the public, physicians, hospitality, and medical schools by furnishing lists of medical schools and diplomates certified by the board. **Telecommunication Services:** electronic mail, jfleming@aobem.org. **Committees:** Credentials; Examination. **Affiliated With:** American College of Osteopathic Emergency Physicians; American Osteopathic Association. **Publications:** *American Osteopathic Association Yearbook and Directory of Osteopathic Physicians.*

14025 ■ Association of Emergency Physicians (AEP)
911 Whitewater Dr.
Mars, PA 16046
Ph: (724)772-1818
Free: (866)772-1818
Fax: (724)772-1818
E-mail: aep@aep.org
URL: http://www.aep.org
Contact: Janis R. Deitch MLS, Exec. Dir.

Founded: 1991. **Membership Dues:** regular, $250 (annual) ● associate, $125 (annual) ● honorary life, $2,500. **Description:** Represents emergency physicians who practice clinical emergency medicine.

14026 ■ Emergency Department Practice Management Association (EDPMA)
8405 Greensboro Dr., Ste.800
McLean, VA 22102
Ph: (703)506-3292
Fax: (703)506-3266
E-mail: info@edpma.org
URL: http://www.edpma.com
Contact: John Lyman MD, Chm.

Founded: 1997. **Membership Dues:** physician group, staffing company, $1,000-$40,000 (annual) ● billing company, supporting organization, $1,000-$10,000 (annual) ● affiliate, $1,000 (annual). **Description:** Represents emergency department physician groups, physician staffing organization, supplier, vendor, and consultant organizations serving emergency departments. **Task Forces:** Documentation Guidelines; EMTALA/Prudent Layperson; Practice Expense; Provider Enrollment/Reassignment.

14027 ■ Emergency Medicine Foundation (EMF)
PO Box 619911
Dallas, TX 75261-9911
Ph: (972)550-0911
Free: (800)798-1822
Fax: (972)580-2816
E-mail: rheard@emfoundation.org
URL: http://www.acep.org/emf
Contact: Robert Heard CAE, Exec. Dir.

Founded: 1972. **Staff:** 1. **Description:** Board of trustees is composed of representatives of American College of Emergency Physicians, Emergency Medicine Residents' Association, Emergency Nurses Association, Society for Academic Emergency Medicine (see separate entries). Promotes and provides improved education and research in the field of emergency medicine in order to improve the availability and quality of emergency medical treatment. Conducts research programs. Funds hypothesis-based emergency medical research. **Conventions/Meetings:** board meeting, for the Board of Trustees - 3/year.

14028 ■ Emergency Medicine Residents' Association (EMRA)
1125 Executive Cir.
Irving, TX 75038-2522
Ph: (972)550-0920
Free: (800)798-1822
Fax: (972)580-2829
E-mail: emra@emra.org
URL: http://www.emra.org
Contact: Michele Byers CAE, Exec. Dir.

Founded: 1974. **Members:** 6,000. **Staff:** 3. **Budget:** $500,000. **Description:** Physicians enrolled in emergency medicine residency training programs; medical students. Purposes are to provide a unified voice for emergency medicine residents and encourage high standards in training and education for emergency physicians. Encourages research to improve emergency medicine education; promotes community, state, and national representation for emergency medicine in organized and academic medicine. **Awards:** Academic Excellence. **Frequency:** annual. **Type:** recognition ● Clinical Excellence. **Frequency:** annual. **Type:** recognition ● Excellence in Teaching. **Frequency:** annual. **Type:** recognition ● J. D'Orta Award/Health Policy and Community Service. **Frequency:** annual. **Type:** recognition ● Jean Hollister Award for EMS. **Frequency:** annual. **Type:** recognition ● Leadership. **Frequency:** annual. **Type:** recognition. **Computer Services:** database, job search ● mailing lists, labels. **Telecommunication Services:** electronic mail, mbyers@emra.org. **Committees:** Education; Legislative Affairs; Policy. **Publications:** *Career Development Guide* ● *EM Resident*, bimonthly. Newsletter. Focuses on issues such as residency issues, utilization of emergency department services, and educational opportunities. **Price:** included in membership dues. **Circulation:** 5,000. **Advertising:** accepted ● *Emergency Medicine in Focus: A Handbook for Medical Students and Prospective Residents* ● *EMRA Job Catalog*, annual ● *Outpatient Guide to Antibiotics*. **Conventions/Meetings:** semiannual Business Meeting, held in conjunction with Society for Academic Emergency Medicine in spring and held in conjunction with American College of Emergency Physicians in fall ● annual meeting.

14029 ■ Emergency Nurses Association (ENA)
915 Lee St.
Des Plaines, IL 60016-6569
Ph: (847)460-4095
Free: (800)900-9659
Fax: (847)460-4006
E-mail: enainfo@ena.org
URL: http://www.ena.org
Contact: David Westman MBA, Exec. Dir.

Founded: 1970. **Members:** 23,000. **Membership Dues:** individual, $96 (annual) ● life, $1,200 ● nursing student (NSNA member), $36 (annual) ● affiliate, $57 (annual) ● international, $86 (annual) ● nursing student, $48 (annual). **Staff:** 50. **Budget:** $10,000,000. **State Groups:** 50. **Local Groups:** 150. **Description:** Registered nurses, licensed practical nurses, and licensed vocational nurses; emergency medical technicians or nurses and members of allied health fields engaged or interested in emergency patient care. Aims to promote emergency nursing and to establish standards in the field; to work with other health-related organizations toward the improvement of emergency care; to serve as a resource for emergency nursing education and research. Seeks to identify and address emergency nursing issues. Disseminates educational and research information in the field. Sponsors: Emergency Nursing Core Curriculum; Standards of Emergency Nursing Practice; Emergency Nursing Pediatric Course; Trauma Nursing Core Course; Concepts in Advanced Trauma Nursing Course. **Awards:** **Frequency:** annual. **Type:** grant ● **Frequency:** annual. **Type:** recognition. **Recipient:** for contributions of members ● **Frequency:** annual. **Type:** scholarship. **Computer Services:** Mailing lists. **Telecommunication Services:** electronic mail, execoffice@ena.org ● additional toll-free number, (800)243-8362. **Committees:** Education; Government Affairs; Nursing

Practice; Research; Scientific Assembly. **Departments:** Communication; Education; Executive Office; Financial Services; Marketing; Meeting Services; Nursing Resources; Professional Services; Research; Trauma and Pediatrics. **Formerly:** (1974) National Emergency Department Nurses Association; (1984) Emergency Department Nurses Association. **Publications:** *CEN Review Manual* ● *Connection,* 10/year. Newsletter. Provides current information on association activities and emergency nursing issues. **Price:** included in membership dues. **Advertising:** accepted ● *Disaster Management and Response,* quarterly. Journal. Focuses on health care management issues. **Advertising:** accepted ● *Emergency Nursing Core Curriculum* ● *Emergency Nursing Scope of Practice* ● *International Journal of Trauma Nursing,* quarterly ● *Journal of Emergency Nursing,* bimonthly. **Advertising:** accepted ● *Leadership and Clinical Monograph Series* ● *NewsBytes,* monthly. Newsletter. Alternate Formats: online ● *Standards of Emergency Nursing Practice* ● *Triage: Meeting the Challenge.* **Conventions/Meetings:** annual Leadership Challenge - convention, with courses and information sessions (exhibits) - always February. 2008 Feb. 28-Mar. 2, Honolulu, HI ● annual meeting, includes general and scientific assembly (exhibits) - usually September. 2007 Sept. 26-29, Salt lake City, UT; 2008 Sept. 24-27, Minneapolis, MN; 2009 Oct. 7-10, Baltimore, MD.

14030 ■ National Association of Emergency Medical Technicians (NAEMT)
PO Box 1400
Clinton, MS 39060-1400
Ph: (601)924-7744
Free: (800)34N-AEMT
Fax: (601)924-7325
E-mail: info@naemt.org
URL: http://www.naemt.org
Contact: Mr. Jerry Johnston, Pres.
Founded: 1975. **Members:** 24,000. **Membership Dues:** individual, $40 (annual) ● squad, $300 (annual) ● student, $25 (annual) ● military, state affiliate, $30 (annual). **Staff:** 5. **Budget:** $1,000,000. **State Groups:** 24. **Multinational. Description:** Represents and supports EMTS, paramedics and other professionals working in pre-hospital emergency medicine working in all sectors of EMS, including government third-service agencies, fire departments, hospital-based ambulance services, private companies, industrial, special operations settings, and in the military. Acts as a voice for EMS personnel in Washington, DC regarding decisions affecting EMS; speaks on behalf of all EMS providers; representatives sit on boards, associations, expert panels, and commissions to ensure that EMS is represented in decisions affecting health care and public safety; works on behalf of members in the areas of compensation and recognition, recruitment and retention, safety, and education and training. **Libraries: Type:** reference. **Awards: Type:** recognition. **Divisions:** Industrial; Instructor/Coordinator; International EMS; Military; National EMS Chiefs, Officers and Administrators; Paramedic; Special Operation. **Publications:** *NAEMT News,* quarterly. Newsletter. **Price:** free, for members only. **Advertising:** accepted. **Conventions/Meetings:** annual meeting, with pre-conference workshops.

14031 ■ National Association of EMS Physicians (NAEMSP)
PO Box 15945-281
Lenexa, KS 66285-5945
Ph: (913)895-4611
Free: (800)228-3677
Fax: (913)895-4672
E-mail: info-naemsp@goamp.com
URL: http://www.naemsp.org
Contact: Jerrie Lynn Kind, Exec. Dir.
Founded: 1984. **Members:** 1,480. **Membership Dues:** physician, $275 (annual) ● professional, fellow, international, $135 (annual) ● resident, $105 (annual) ● medical student, $75 (annual). **Staff:** 4. **Description:** Medical directors responsible for emergency medical services (EMS) programs throughout the United States; other physicians and nonphysician dedicated to out-of-hospital emergency care. (Most physicians within this organization are medically-legally responsible for the provision of out-of-hospital emergency care.) Strives to foster excellence and provide medical leadership so that all individuals and communities receive quality out-of-hospital emergency medical services. Works to develop guidelines and strategies to reduce and prevent discomfort, disability, and death in the community; define roles, responsibility, authority, and accountability of EMS physicians; promote communication and cooperation among EMS professionals; define the unique body of medical knowledge of pre-hospital and disaster medicine; promote cost-effective programs and interventions that optimize patient outcomes; advocate or initiate public policy for optimal emergency medical care; encourage and support quality EMS research. Provides forums for definition and debate of EMS issues. Encourages and promotes career development, career longevity, and professional well-being of EMS professionals. Defines and promotes ethical principles in the delivery of out-of-hospital emergency care. **Publications:** *EMS Medical Directors' Handbook* ● *NAEMSP Newsletter,* bimonthly. Alternate Formats: online ● *Prehospital Emergency Care,* quarterly. Journal. **Price:** $147.00 /year for institutions; $107.00 /year for individuals. ISSN: 1090-3127 ● *Prehospital Systems and Medical Oversight.* Book. **Price:** $75.00 for members; $90.00 for nonmembers ● *Quality Management in Prehospital Care.* Book. **Conventions/Meetings:** semiannual conference and workshop (exhibits) ● annual meeting (exhibits).

14032 ■ National Association of State EMS Directors (NASEMSD)
201 Park Washington Ct.
Falls Church, VA 22046-4527
Ph: (703)538-1799
Fax: (703)241-5603
E-mail: info@nasemsd.org
URL: http://www.nasemsd.org
Contact: Elizabeth B. Armstrong CAE, Exec. Dir.
Founded: 1981. **Members:** 56. **Membership Dues:** associate, $225 (annual) ● state EMS director, $450 (annual) ● corporate, $1,000 (annual) ● sponsor, $3,500 (annual). **Staff:** 1. **Budget:** $110,000. **Regional Groups:** 4. **Description:** Provides vision and leadership in the development and improvement of EMS systems and national EMS policy. **Libraries: Type:** reference. **Computer Services:** database, state statistics on EMS ● mailing lists, 25,000 ambulance services. **Committees:** Data; Government Affairs; Telecommunications. **Publications:** *EMS Office, Structure, and Functioning.* **Price:** $35.00 ● *EMT Certification, Licensing, and Reciprocity Requirements.* **Price:** $25.00 ● *Training and Certification of EMS Personnel.* **Price:** $50.00 ● *Trauma Center Designation Survey.* **Price:** $28.00 ● Annual Report, annual. Alternate Formats: online. **Conventions/Meetings:** annual meeting (exhibits).

14033 ■ National Collegiate EMS Foundation (NCEMSF)
PO Box 93
West Sand Lake, NY 12196
Ph: (208)728-7342
Fax: (208)728-7342
E-mail: info@ncemsf.org
URL: http://www.ncemsf.org
Contact: George J. Koenig, Pres.
Founded: 1993. **Members:** 600. **Membership Dues:** institutional, $25 (annual) ● student, $10 (annual) ● non-student, $20 (annual) ● life, student, $75 ● life, non-student, $150. **Staff:** 1. **Regional Groups:** 12. **Local Groups:** 200. **Description:** Committed to the advancement of existing emergency response groups, assists in the development of new response groups on college and university campuses. **Awards:** Campus EMS Provider of the Year. **Frequency:** annual. **Type:** recognition. **Recipient:** for outstanding leadership to a campus-based EMS organization ● Collegiate EMS Web Site of the Year. **Frequency:** annual. **Type:** recognition. **Recipient:** for campus EMS group's efforts to create and maintain a useful and aesthetically pleasing web site ● Outstanding Collegiate EMS Advisor of the Year. **Frequency:** annual. **Type:** recognition. **Recipient:** for a faculty advisor or college administrator who has given a significant amount of time and effort to the organization ● Outstanding Collegiate EMS Organization of the Year. **Frequency:** annual. **Type:** recognition. **Recipient:** for an individual who has demonstrated outstanding service to his/her campus ● Striving for Excellence. **Frequency:** annual. **Type:** recognition. **Computer Services:** database, collegiate EMS organizations ● online services, directory of collegiate EMS groups, library of SOPs, links ● online services, e-discussion. **Publications:** *Campus EMS Directory,* semiannual. Lists of campus EMS organizations. **Advertising:** accepted. Alternate Formats: online ● *NCEMSF News,* quarterly. Newsletter. Contains information for and about campus-based EMS. Alternate Formats: online. **Conventions/Meetings:** annual conference and workshop, with roundtable discussions (exhibits) - usually February.

14034 ■ National Emergency Equipment Dealers Association (NEEDA)
c/o Kenton H. Pattie, Exec. Dir.
8421 Frost Way
Annandale, VA 22003
Ph: (703)280-4622
Fax: (703)280-0942
E-mail: kentonp1@aol.com
URL: http://www.needa.org
Contact: Kenton H. Pattie, Exec. Dir.
Founded: 1996. **Members:** 88. **Membership Dues:** fire, rescue, emergency medical service, public safety dealer and distributor, $500 (annual). **Staff:** 1. **Budget:** $20,000. **Description:** Preserves and strengthens the free market systems for dealers through advocacy, information, and training. Assists dealers to profitably deliver high quality products and support to the nation's emergency services. **Publications:** *NEEDA Newsletter.* Contains information on the association and its members. **Price:** $100.00/year. **Circulation:** 780. **Advertising:** accepted. Alternate Formats: online. **Conventions/Meetings:** annual conference and meeting (exhibits) - always in March or August.

14035 ■ National Emergency Medicine Association (NEMA)
306 W Joppa Rd.
Baltimore, MD 21204-4048
Ph: (410)494-0300 (410)494-0724
Free: (800)332-NEMA
Fax: (410)494-0725
E-mail: info@nmahealth.org
URL: http://www.nemahealth.org
Contact: Howard H. Farrington, Pres.
Founded: 1982. **Members:** 5,000. **Staff:** 9. **Description:** Seeks to prevent trauma and improve emergency medical care nationwide. Concerned with: promoting lifestyles that reduce the likelihood of trauma; educating the public on how to help a trauma victim before emergency personnel arrive; ensuring that trained emergency personnel have the necessary resources to effectively do their jobs; promoting effective treatment and care of trauma victims at hospitals and trauma centers; ensuring the availability of proper services and facilities to the recovering trauma victim. Provides The Heart of the Matter, an educational radio program, to more than 250 radio stations nationwide. Maintains speakers' bureau; offers grants; provides direct-mail program focusing on heart disease prevention. **Convention/Meeting:** none. **Councils:** National Alzheimer's; National Heart; National Stroke. **Programs:** Grants; Kids Do Matter; Senior Life. **Publications:** *A Guide to the Emergency Room* ● *Heart of the Matter* ● *Heartlines,* quarterly. Newsletter ● *How to Survive Trauma.*

14036 ■ National Flight Paramedics Association (NFPA)
c/o International Association of Flight Paramedics
4835 Riveredge Cove
Snellville, GA 30039
Ph: (770)979-6372
Free: (800)367-0382
Fax: (770)979-6500

E-mail: m.newman@flightparamedic.org
URL: http://www.flightparamedic.org
Contact: Monica Newman, Account Exec.
Founded: 1986. **Members:** 950. **Membership Dues:**
active or associate, $60 (annual) ● international, $65
(annual). **Staff:** 1. **Description:** Flight paramedics.
Promotes education, professionalism, and communication within the emergency medical service
community. **Awards:** Tim Hynes Award. **Frequency:**
annual. **Type:** recognition. **Recipient:** to a member
who has made significant contributions to the profession. **Computer Services:** database ● mailing lists.
Affiliated With: Air and Surface Transport Nurses
Association. **Publications:** *Air Medical Journal*,
semimonthly. **Price:** included in membership dues.
Circulation: 4,000. **Advertising:** accepted ● *Flight
Paramedic News*, quarterly. Newsletter. **Price:**
included in membership dues. **Circulation:** 1,000.
Advertising: accepted. **Conventions/Meetings:** an-
nual Air Medical Transport Conference, in conjunc-
tion with Association of Air Medical Services, Air and
Surface Transport Nurses Association, National EMS
Pilots Association, and the Air Medicine Physician
Association (exhibits) ● annual Critical Care Trans-
port Medicine Conference, in conjunction with As-
sociation of Air Medical Services, Air and Surface
Transport Nurses Association, National EMS Pilots
Association, and the Air Medicine Physician Association (exhibits).

**14037 ■ National Native American EMS
Association (NNAEMSA)**
c/o Chebon Tiger
PO Box 80
Maricopa, AZ 85239
Ph: (602)361-2099
Fax: (520)568-0023
E-mail: nnaemsa@earthlink.net
Contact: Mr. Charles Kmet, Exec.Dir.
Membership Dues: active, $25 (annual) ● associ-
ate, $15 (annual). **Description:** Represents and
promotes first responders, emergency medical techni-
cians, emergency nurses, and emergency physicians
of Native American descent. **Publications:** Newslet-
ter. Alternate Formats: online ● Reports. **Conven-
tions/Meetings:** annual Educational Conference.

**14038 ■ National Registry of Emergency
Medical Technicians (NREMT)**
Rocco V. Morando Bldg.
6610 Busch Blvd.
PO Box 29233
Columbus, OH 43229
Ph: (614)888-4484
Fax: (614)888-8920
E-mail: webmaster@nremt.org
URL: http://www.nremt.org
Contact: Sandy Bogucki MD, Chair
Founded: 1970. **Members:** 170,000. **Staff:** 23. **Description:** Promotes the improved delivery of emergency medical services by: assisting in the development and evaluation of educational programs to train
emergency medical technicians; establishing qualifications for eligibility to apply for registration; preparing and conducting examinations designed to assure
the competency of emergency medical technicians
and paramedics; establishing a system for biennial
registration; establishing procedures for revocation of
certificates of registration for cause; maintaining a
directory of registered emergency medical technicians. **Formerly:** (1973) Registry of Emergency Medical Technicians - Ambulance. **Publications:** *The Registry*, annual. Newsletter. Informs on association
activities. Alternate Formats: online ● Annual Report,
annual. Alternate Formats: online. **Conventions/
Meetings:** annual meeting - always third Wednesday
in November.

**14039 ■ Residency Review Committee for
Emergency Medicine (RRCEM)**
c/o Accreditation Council for Graduate Medical
  Education
515 N State St., Ste.2000
Chicago, IL 60610
Ph: (312)755-5000 (312)755-5027
Fax: (312)755-7498

E-mail: lds@acgme.org
URL: http://www.acgme.org
Contact: Dr. Larry Sulton, Exec. Dir.
Founded: 1982. **Members:** 12. **Staff:** 2. **Descrip-
tion:** Representatives from the American College of
Emergency Physicians, the American Board of
Emergency Medicine, Council on Medical Education
of the American Medical Association, and the Emergency Medicine Residents' Association (see separate
entries). Accredits residency training programs in
emergency medicine. **Affiliated With:** American
Board of Emergency Medicine; American College of
Emergency Physicians; Council on Medical Education of the American Medical Association; Emergency
Medicine Residents' Association. **Supersedes:** Liaison Endorsement Committee. **Publications:** *Directory of Graduate Medical Education Programs*, annual. **Conventions/Meetings:** semiannual meeting.

**14040 ■ Society for Academic Emergency
Medicine (SAEM)**
901 N Washington Ave.
Lansing, MI 48906-5137
Ph: (517)485-5484
Fax: (517)485-0801
E-mail: saem@saem.org
URL: http://www.saem.org
Founded: 1989. **Members:** 5,000. **Membership
Dues:** active, $365 (annual) ● associate, $350 (annual) ● resident, fellow, $90 (annual) ● interest group,
$25 (annual) ● medical student, $75 (annual). **Staff:**
5. **Budget:** $1,000,000. **Description:** Physicians
teaching emergency medicine, emergency medicine
residents, and non-physicians teaching emergency
care. Seeks to: educate teachers of emergency
medicine and encourage its development as an
academic discipline; apply sound educational principles, thus improving the quality of teaching in the
field; promote research in educational methods and
clinical procedures. Provides a forum for the exchange of ideas and information. Promotes improved
emergency patient care through more direct involvement of teachers and consumers in the needs assessment, planning, and implementation of projects
and programs. Sponsors educational workshops;
conducts lectures. **Awards:** Excellence in Emergency
Medicine Award. **Frequency:** annual. **Type:** recognition. **Recipient:** for senior medical student who
demonstrated excellence in emergency medicine ●
Hal Jayne Academic Excellence Award. **Frequency:**
annual. **Type:** recognition. **Recipient:** for outstanding
contributions to emergency medicine through research, education and scholarly accomplishments ●
Institutional Research Training Grant. **Frequency:**
annual. **Type:** grant. **Recipient:** to an academic
emergency medicine program to train a research fellow ● Leadership Award. **Frequency:** annual. **Type:**
recognition. **Recipient:** for exceptional leadership in
academic emergency medicine ● Scholarly Sabbatical Grant. **Frequency:** annual. **Type:** grant. **Recipient:** to an individual emergency medicine academician ● Young Investigator Award. **Frequency:** annual. **Type:** recognition. **Recipient:** for young
investigators who demonstrated promise and distinction. **Affiliated With:** American College of Emergency
Physicians; Association of American Medical Colleges. **Formed by Merger of:** (1989) Society of
Teachers of Emergency Medicine; University Association for Emergency Medicine. **Publications:** *Academic Emergency Medicine*, monthly. Journal. Publishes information relevant to the practice, educational
advancements, and investigation of emergency
medicine. **Advertising:** accepted ● Newsletter,
bimonthly. Promotes research and education in
emergency medicine. **Price:** included in membership
dues. **Circulation:** 5,000. **Advertising:** accepted.
Alternate Formats: online. **Conventions/Meetings:**
annual meeting - 2008 May 29-June 1, Washington,
DC; 2009 May 14-17, New Orleans, LA; 2010 June
3-6, Phoenix, AZ.

**14041 ■ State EMS Training Coordinators
Council of NASEMSO**
c/o Beth Armstrong, Exec. Dir.
201 Park Washington Ct.
Falls Church, VA 22046-4513

Ph: (703)538-1794
Fax: (703)241-5603
E-mail: robinson@nasemso.org
URL: http://www.nasemso.org
Contact: Ms. Kathy Robinson, Program Mgr.
Founded: 1977. **Members:** 56. **Membership Dues:**
associate council, $225 (annual). **Staff:** 1. **Descrip-
tion:** Individuals employed by state-level emergency
medical services agencies who are responsible for
coordination or supervision of EMS training programs.
Promotes the responsible movement of emergency
medical technicians (EMTs) throughout the nation
through standardization of policies related, but not
limited to, curriculum, certification, recertification,
revocation, and reciprocity. Seeks to further develop
the public recognition and trust of the emergency
medical technician as a health care professional.
Formerly: (2006) National Council of State Emergency Medical Services Training Coordinators. **Con-
ventions/Meetings:** annual conference (exhibits) ●
annual meeting - 2007 Oct. 29-31, Minneapolis, MN.

Emergency Services

14042 ■ ComCARE Alliance
1701 K St. NW, Ste.400
Washington, DC 20006
Ph: (202)429-0574
Fax: (202)296-2962
E-mail: info@comcare.org
URL: http://www.comcare.org
Contact: David Aylward, Sec.
Founded: 1998. **Members:** 90. **Staff:** 12. **Description:** Emergency doctors and nurses, state and local
public safety officials, departments of transportation,
citizen organizations, wireless transportation and
technology companies committed to improving
emergency communications and response. **Publications:** *ComCARE Insider*, monthly. Newsletter.

**14043 ■ Committee on Accreditation of
Medical Transport Systems (CAMTS)**
PO Box 130
Sandy Springs, SC 29677
Ph: (864)287-4177
Fax: (864)287-4251
E-mail: efrazer@camts.org
URL: http://www.camts.org
Contact: Eileen Frazer, Exec. Dir.
Founded: 1990. **Members:** 16. **Membership Dues:**
application fee, $500. **Staff:** 3. **Multinational. De-
scription:** Works to improve patient care and safety
for air medical and ground critical care services.
Publications: Annual Report, annual. **Conventions/
Meetings:** periodic board meeting - 3/year.

**14044 ■ National Academies of Emergency
Dispatch (NAED)**
139 E South Temple, Ste.200
Salt Lake City, UT 84111
Ph: (801)359-6916
Free: (800)960-6236
Fax: (801)359-0996
E-mail: scott.freitag@emergencydispatch.org
URL: http://www.emergencydispatch.org
Contact: Scott Freitag, Pres.
Founded: 1988. **Members:** 33,000. **Membership
Dues:** associate/executive, $19 (annual) ● associ-
ate/executive, $35 (biennial) ● associate/executive,
$49 (triennial). **Multinational. Description:** Works to
advance public-safety emergency telecommunica-
tions professionals to ensure quality emergency,
health and social services. **Boards:** Accreditation; Al-
liance; Certification. **Councils:** Curriculum; Research;
Standards. **Formerly:** (2006) National Academy of
Emergency Medical Dispatch. **Publications:** *National
Journal for Emergency Dispatch*, quarterly. Journals.
Conventions/Meetings: annual conference.

14045 ■ Skyaid Organization
8800 SE 45th St.
Mercer Island, WA 98040
Ph: (206)498-6004

E-mail: hlahore@skyaid.org
URL: http://www.skyaid.org
Contact: Henry Lahore, Chm.
Founded: 2000. **Multinational. Description:** Strives to provide quick aid for sudden cardiac arrests, heart attacks, strokes, fires and accidents. **Additional Websites:** http://www.respectrfid.com.

Endocrinology

14046 ■ American Association of Clinical Endocrinologists (AACE)
245 Riverside Ave., Ste.200
Jacksonville, FL 32202
Ph: (904)353-7878
Free: (800)393-2223
Fax: (904)353-8185
E-mail: smerritt@aace.com
URL: http://www.aace.com
Contact: Richard Hellman, Pres.
Founded: 1991. **Members:** 4,000. **Membership Dues:** active, $150 (annual) ● international, $150 ● first year in practice/retired, $75. **Staff:** 21. **Description:** Clinical endocrinologists and physicians with special education in diabetes, osteoporosis, thyroid illness, lipid-cholesterol problems, reproductive disorders, obesity and nutrition. Seeks to enhance the practice of clinical endocrinology. **Awards:** Eugene T. Davidson, MD, Distinguished Service Award. **Frequency:** annual. **Type:** recognition. **Recipient:** to a non-physician for outstanding contribution to advancing AACE mission. **Computer Services:** Mailing lists. **Committees:** Annual Meeting Clinical Congress Program; Clinical Research; Coding; Continuing Medical Education Accreditation; Educational Initiatives; Endocrine Surgery; Endocrine Training Support; Ethical Affairs. **Publications:** *AACE Endocrine Coding Manual.* Includes endocrine-specific codes. **Price:** $145.00 for members; $165.00 for nonmembers ● *Endocrine Practice,* bimonthly. Journal. Features peer reviewed scientific articles on clinical endocrinology. **Price:** $175.00 /year for nonmembers in U.S.; $400.00 /year for institutions in U.S.; $500.00 /year for institutions outside U.S.; $350.00 /year for nonmembers outside U.S. ISSN: 1530-891. **Circulation:** 3,400. **Advertising:** accepted. Alternate Formats: online ● *The First Messenger,* bimonthly. Newsletter. **Advertising:** accepted ● Brochures. Alternate Formats: online. **Conventions/Meetings:** annual congress (exhibits).

14047 ■ Association of Program Directors in Endocrinology, Diabetes and Metabolism (APDEM)
8401 Connecticut Ave., Ste.900
Chevy Chase, MD 20815
Ph: (301)941-0243
Fax: (301)941-0259
E-mail: staff@apdem.org
URL: http://www.apdem.org
Contact: Nancy T. Chill, Admin.
Founded: 1996. **Members:** 160. **Membership Dues:** individual, $150 (annual). **Staff:** 2. **Budget:** $250,000. **Description:** Aims to benefit and aid the education, research and patient care missions of subspecialty training programs in endocrinology, diabetes and metabolism. Supports new initiative in educational and public research and patient care. **Computer Services:** database ● online services. **Telecommunication Services:** electronic mail, nchill@endo-society.org. **Formerly:** (2002) Association of Program Directors in Endocrinology and Metabolism. **Conventions/Meetings:** annual meeting.

14048 ■ Cushing's Support and Research Foundation (CSRF)
65 E India Row, Ste.22B
Boston, MA 02110
Ph: (617)723-3674
Fax: (617)723-3674
E-mail: cushinfo@csrf.net
URL: http://www.csrf.net
Contact: Louise Pace, Founding Pres.
Founded: 1995. **Members:** 500. **Membership Dues:** basic, $30 (annual) ● friend, $50 (annual) ● sponsor,

$100 (annual) ● donor, $500 (annual) ● benefactor, $1,000 (annual). **Description:** Provides information and support for Cushing's Disease and Cushing's Syndrome patients and their families; increases awareness, educates the public about Cushing's Disease and Cushing's Syndrome; provides information and support to health care professionals; raises and distribute funds for Cushing's Disease and Cushing's Syndrome research. **Computer Services:** database, Cushing's doctors. **Boards:** Medical Advisory. **Affiliated With:** National Organization for Rare Disorders. **Publications:** Newsletter, quarterly. **Price:** $20.00 for members. **Advertising:** accepted.

14049 ■ Endocrine Fellows Foundation (EFF)
5959 W Century Blvd., Ste.550
Los Angeles, CA 90045
Free: (877)877-6515
E-mail: endocrinefellows@sbcglobal.net
URL: http://www.endocrinefellows.org
Contact: Marilyn Fishman, Exec. Dir.
Founded: 1990. **Description:** Endocrine fellows. Provides support to endocrine fellows in education, research grant funding and career guidance. Also, works to provide both fellows and endocrinology professionals with cutting-edge research results on developments in the fields of endocrinology, metabolism and diabetology. **Libraries: Type:** open to the public; reference. **Holdings:** video recordings. **Awards:** Research Grant. **Frequency:** annual. **Type:** grant. **Recipient:** for first or second year fellows engaged in significant research. **Publications:** *EndoTrends.* Newsletter. Contains scientific abstracts, patient case studies, grant information, medical meetings calendar and other information for endocrine fellows. Alternate Formats: online.

14050 ■ Endocrine Nurses Society (ENS)
PO Box 211068
Milwaukee, WI 53221
Ph: (414)727-7422
Fax: (414)727-7422
E-mail: ens@endo-nurses.org
URL: http://www.endo-nurses.org
Contact: Michel Martin, Pres.
Membership Dues: full, associate, $75 (annual) ● optional, $140 (biennial). **Description:** Promotes excellence in the clinical care of patients through the advancement of the science and art of endocrine nursing. Supports professional development and facilitates communication among endocrine nurses. Provides educational forums. Supports nursing research on health topics related to endocrine disorders. **Programs:** ENS Preceptor. **Task Forces:** Osteoporosis Education; Thyroid Hormone Therapy. **Publications:** Newsletter, quarterly. Alternate Formats: online.

14051 ■ Endocrine Society
8401 Connecticut Ave., Ste.900
Chevy Chase, MD 20815-5817
Ph: (301)941-0200
Free: (888)363-6274
Fax: (301)941-0259
E-mail: societyservices@endo-society.org
URL: http://www.endo-society.org
Contact: Leonard Wartofsky MD, Pres.
Founded: 1916. **Members:** 8,000. **Membership Dues:** active, in U.S., $266 (annual) ● associate, outside U.S., $205 (annual) ● fellow/student associate, $20 (annual) ● active, outside U.S., $334 (annual) ● associate, in U.S., $190 (annual) ● active/associate (developing countries), $84 (annual). **Staff:** 26. **Budget:** $10,000,000. **Multinational. Description:** Promotes excellence in research, education, and clinical practice in endocrinology and related disciplines. Maintains placement service. **Awards:** Distinguished Educator Award. **Frequency:** annual. **Type:** recognition. **Recipient:** for achievement as educator ● Endocrine Society Laureate Award. **Frequency:** annual. **Type:** recognition. **Recipient:** for work of distinction in endocrinology ● Ernst Oppenheimer Award. **Frequency:** annual. **Type:** recognition. **Recipient:** for young educator in basic or clinical endocrinology ● Fred Conrad Koch Award. **Frequency:** annual. **Type:** recognition. **Recipient:**

for exceptional contribution to endocrinology. **Formerly:** Association for Study of Internal Secretions. **Publications:** *Endocrine News,* monthly. Magazine. Includes calendar of events and listing of honors and awards recipients; legislative issues and clinical practice column. **Price:** included in membership dues. **Advertising:** accepted ● *Endocrine Reviews,* bimonthly. Journal. Covers clinical and experimental endocrinology; readers are encouraged to suggest prospective authors and to submit their own manuscripts. **Price:** $92.00 /year for members in U.S.; $270.00 /year for nonmembers in U.S.; $465.00 /year for institutions in U.S.; $174.00/year for those in training in U.S. ISSN: 0163-769X. **Advertising:** accepted. Alternate Formats: online ● *Endocrinology,* monthly. Journal. Covers current biomedical research for basic scientists. **Price:** $137.00 /year for members in U.S.; $447.00 /year for nonmembers in U.S.; $967.00 /year for institutions in U.S.; $258.00/year for those in training in U.S. ISSN: 0013-7227. **Advertising:** accepted. Alternate Formats: online ● *Journal of Clinical Endocrinology and Metabolism,* monthly. Provides current information on the clinical applications of endocrine research for internists, pediatricians, and practicing obstetricians. **Price:** $137.00 /year for members in U.S.; $428.00 /year for nonmembers in U.S.; $769.00 /year for institutions in U.S.; $233.00/year for those in training in U.S. ISSN: 0021-972X. **Advertising:** accepted. Alternate Formats: online ● *Molecular Endocrinology,* monthly. Journal. Covers the molecular mechanisms of cellular regulation and hormone action. **Price:** $137.00 /year for members in U.S.; $402.00 /year for nonmembers in U.S.; $691.00 /year for institutions in U.S.; $226.00/year for those in training in U.S. ISSN: 0888-8809. **Advertising:** accepted. Alternate Formats: online. **Conventions/Meetings:** annual Clinical Endocrinology Update - convention (exhibits) ● annual ENDO - meeting (exhibits) - 2008 June 15-18, San Francisco, CA; 2009 June 10-13, Washington, DC; 2010 June 19-22, San Diego, CA.

14052 ■ Hypoparathyroidism Association
2835 Salmon St.
Idaho Falls, ID 83406
Ph: (208)524-3857
E-mail: hpth@hpth.org
URL: http://www.hypoparathyroidism.org
Contact: James Sanders, Pres.
Members: 2,299. **Regional Groups:** 3. **Multinational. Description:** Seeks to improve the lives of people affected with all forms of Hypoparathyroidism by maintaining a worldwide network of family support groups. Raises public and professional awareness on this rare medical disorder. Provides an online forum for its members to exchange information concerning issues relevant to Hypoparathyroidism. **Publications:** Newsletter, quarterly. Alternate Formats: online. **Conventions/Meetings:** annual meeting - held each August in Idaho Falls, Idaho.

14053 ■ International Hyperhidrosis Society (IHHS)
520 Walnut St., Ste.1160
Philadelphia, PA 19106
Ph: (215)351-9050
E-mail: info@sweathelp.org
URL: http://www.sweathelp.org
Contact: Lisa J. Pieretti, Exec. Dir.
Founded: 2003. **Languages:** English, German, Italian, Portuguese, Spanish. **Multinational. Description:** Promotes hyperhidrosis research. Strives to improve the lives of people affected with hyperhidrosis. Raises public awareness and understanding of the effects of this medical condition. Advocates for patient access to effective medication. **Publications:** *SweatSolutions,* monthly. Newsletter. Alternate Formats: online ● *Understanding Excessive Sweating: The help you need to live the life you deserve* (in English, Italian, and Spanish). Brochure. Provides current and objective information about hyperhidrosis.

14054 ■ National Adrenal Diseases Foundation (NADF)
505 Northern Blvd., Ste.200
Great Neck, NY 11021

Ph: (516)487-4992

Fax: (516)829-5710

E-mail: nadfmail@aol.com

URL: http://www.medhelp.org/nadf

Contact: Ms. Melanie Wong, Exec. Dir.

Founded: 1985. **Members:** 400. **Membership Dues:** patient (with adrenal disease), family, caregiver, $25 (annual). **Staff:** 1. **Regional Groups:** 29. **Description:** Individuals with adrenal diseases, especially Addison's disease, and their families; physicians. Seeks to provide a national self-help network for educational and emotional support for patients and their families. **Libraries: Type:** reference. **Holdings:** archival material, articles, papers, periodicals, reports. **Subjects:** adrenal disease, coping with illness. **Formerly:** (1991) National Addison's Disease Foundation. **Publications:** *Addison's Disease: The Facts You Need to Know.* Pamphlet ● *Congenital Adrenal Hyperplasia: The Facts You Need to Know.* Pamphlet ● *Cushing's Disease: The Facts You Need to Know.* Pamphlet ● *Emergency Care Instruction Sheet and Cover Letter* ● *Emergency Care Wallet Card* ● *Hyperaldosteronism: The Facts You Need to Know.* Pamphlet ● *NADF News,* quarterly. Newsletter. **Price:** $25.00/year. **Circulation:** 900. **Advertising:** accepted ● *Replacement Hormone Level Quick Reference Sheet* ● Also publishes educational materials. **Conventions/Meetings:** periodic seminar ● support group meeting.

14055 ■ Women in Endocrinology (WE)

c/o Carolyn L. Smith, PhD, Communications Committee Chair

Dept. of Molecular and Cellular Biology

Baylor Coll. of Medicine

One Baylor Plz.

Houston, TX 77030-3411

Ph: (713)798-6235

Fax: (713)790-1275

E-mail: carolyns@bcm.tmc.edu

URL: http://www.women-in-endo.org/Pages/index.shtml

Contact: Carolyn L. Smith PhD, Communications Committee Chair

Founded: 1976. **Membership Dues:** in training, $10 (annual) ● full, $40 (annual). **Description:** Women employed in the field of endocrinology; female endocrinology students and residents. Promotes "professional development and advancement of women in the field of endocrinology." Facilitates exchange of information among members; conducts educational programs. **Awards:** Abstract Awards. **Frequency:** annual. **Type:** recognition. **Recipient:** to new faculty, postdoctoral trainees, and senior graduate students in recognition of meritorious abstracts ● WE Mentor Award. **Frequency:** annual. **Type:** recognition. **Recipient:** for outstanding scientists who have played an important role in mentoring women endocrinologists. **Committees:** Awards; Communications; Development; Mentoring; Nominating; Program. **Publications:** Newsletter. **Price:** included in membership dues. **Conventions/Meetings:** annual dinner and meeting ● annual executive committee meeting.

Environmental Health

14056 ■ American Academy of Environmental Medicine (AAEM)

7701 E Kellogg Dr., Ste.625

Wichita, KS 67207-1705

Ph: (316)684-5500

Fax: (313)684-5709

E-mail: administrator@aaem.com

URL: http://www.aaem.com

Contact: De Rodgers, Exec. Dir.

Founded: 1965. **Members:** 400. **Membership Dues:** domestic, $430 (annual) ● international, professional/associate, affiliate, $285 (annual) ● medical student/intern or resident, $95 (annual) ● corporate, $1,000 (annual). **Staff:** 4. **Budget:** $160,000. **Multinational. Description:** Physicians, and others interested in the clinical aspect of environmental medicine. Supports physicians and other professionals in serving the public through education about the interactions

between humans and their environment. **Awards:** Carleton Lee Award. **Frequency:** annual. **Type:** recognition. **Recipient:** for dedication in expanding the knowledge of the Environmental Medicine ● Herbert J. Rinkel Award. **Frequency:** annual. **Type:** recognition. **Recipient:** for excellent contribution in teaching Environmental Medicine ● Jonathan Forman Award. **Frequency:** annual. **Type:** recognition. **Recipient:** for an individual who has made an outstanding contribution to clinical ecology. **Computer Services:** database, member information ● mailing lists. **Formerly:** (1984) Society for Clinical Ecology. **Publications:** *Environmental Physician,* quarterly. Newsletter ● *Journal of Nutritional and Environmental Medicine,* quarterly. **Conventions/Meetings:** annual conference, scientific meeting (exhibits) - always fall ● annual meeting, to educate physicians, nurses, and technicians in the basic techniques of environmental medicine and to keep members abreast of current advances in the field - always spring.

14057 ■ American Environmental Health Foundation (AEHF)

8345 Walnut Hill Ln., Ste.225

Dallas, TX 75231

Ph: (214)361-9515

Free: (800)428-2343

Fax: (214)361-2534

E-mail: aehf@aehf.com

URL: http://www.aehf.com

Contact: William J. Rea MD, Founder

Founded: 1975. **Description:** Provides research and education into chemical sensitivity. **Conventions/Meetings:** annual symposium.

14058 ■ Center for Health and the Global Environment

Harvard Medical School

401 Park Dr., 2nd Fl.

Boston, MA 02115

Ph: (617)384-8530

Fax: (617)384-8585

E-mail: chge@hms.harvard.edu

URL: http://www.med.harvard.edu/chge/the-center.html

Contact: Tracy Sachs MA, Admin. Dir.

Founded: 1996. **Nonmembership. Multinational. Description:** Promotes human health consequences of global environmental change. **Publications:** *Biodiversity: Its Importance to Human Health.* Report. Alternate Formats: online ● *Biological and Physical Signs of Climate Change: Focus on Mosquito-Borne Diseases.* Report ● *The Bulletin.* Provides the latest information on timely topics related to human health and global environmental change. Alternate Formats: online ● *Climate Change and U.S. Agriculture: The Impacts of Warming and Extreme Weather Events on Productivity, Plant Diseases, and Pests.* Report ● *Environment and Health: Species Loss and Ecosystem Disruption - the Implications for Human Health.* Report ● *Is Global Warming Harmful to Health?.* Report ● *Marine Ecosystems: Emerging Diseases as Indicators of Change.* Report ● *Oil: A Life Cycle Analysis of its Health and Environmental Impacts.* Report. Alternate Formats: online. **Conventions/Meetings:** seminar.

14059 ■ Children's Environmental Health Network (CEHN)

110 Maryland Ave. NE, Ste.505

Washington, DC 20002

Ph: (202)543-4033

Fax: (202)543-8797

E-mail: cehn@cehn.org

URL: http://www.cehn.org

Contact: Nsedu Obot Witherspoon, Exec. Dir.

Description: Promotes the development of sound public health and child-focused national policy for children affected by exposures to environmental hazards. **Computer Services:** database, lists of scientists and health professionals ● online services, listservs. **Telecommunication Services:** electronic mail, nobot@cehn.org.

14060 ■ Human Ecology Action League (HEAL)

PO Box 29629

Atlanta, GA 30359-0629

Ph: (404)248-1898

Fax: (404)248-0162

E-mail: healnatnl@aol.com

URL: http://members.aol.com/HEALNatnl

Contact: Bryan Welch, Contact

Founded: 1977. **Members:** 10,000. **Membership Dues:** in U.S., $26 (annual) ● in Canada, $32 (annual) ● outside U.S. and Canada, $38 (annual). **Staff:** 2. **Local Groups:** 50. **Description:** Individuals and organizations interested in the study of human ecology and multiple chemical sensitivities, specifically how human health may be affected by synthetic and natural substances in the environment. Seeks to collect and disseminate information on human ecology and ecological illness to persons suffering from such illness, and to government agencies scientists, and health care professionals; to raise public awareness about potential dangers from substances in the environment. **Convention/Meeting:** none. **Computer Services:** database. **Committees:** Action; Fundraising; Public Education. **Projects:** HEAL Chapters and Regional Support Service. **Publications:** *Directory of HEAL Members in the Healthcare Professions.* **Price:** $15.00 for members; $30.00 for nonmembers ● *Fragrance and Health.* Book. **Price:** $12.00 for members; $24.00 for nonmembers ● *HEAL's Service List* ● *Human Ecologist,* quarterly, March, June, September, December. Journal. Includes association news, book and video reviews, environmental health tips for children, and pesticide update. **Price:** $26.00/copy for nonmembers; $20.00/year for low-income individuals; $32.00 in Canada; $38.00 foreign. **Circulation:** 4,000. **Advertising:** accepted ● Brochures. Explains chemical sensitivities.

14061 ■ International Board of Environmental Medicine (IBEM)

65 Wehrle Dr.

Cheektowaga, NY 14225

Ph: (716)837-1320 (716)833-2214

Fax: (716)833-2244

E-mail: aehcwny@juno.com

Contact: Dr. Kalpana Patel, Pres.

Founded: 1988. **Members:** 110. **Membership Dues:** $1,000 (annual). **Staff:** 1. **Budget:** $25,000. **Description:** An accrediting agency for physicians and osteopaths working in related environmental professions. Examines licensed practitioners, facilities, and relevant training programs. Offers programs to evaluate qualifications of healthcare professionals, their training programs, and those facilities offering special types of treatment. Plans and supervises accrediting examinations. **Awards:** President's Award. **Frequency:** annual. **Type:** recognition. **Recipient:** for exceptional abilities. **Publications:** *Register of the International Board of Environmental Medicine,* annual. Directory. Contains names of diplomates. **Price:** $25.00. **Conventions/Meetings:** annual meeting.

14062 ■ National Center for Environmental Health Strategies (NCEHS)

c/o Mary Lamielle, Exec. Dir.

1100 Rural Ave.

Voorhees, NJ 08043

Ph: (856)429-5358

E-mail: info@ncehs.org

URL: http://www.ncehs.org

Contact: Mary Lamielle, Exec. Dir.

Founded: 1986. **Members:** 2,000. **Staff:** 2. **Description:** Persons with environmental illnesses, including those with chemical sensitivity disorders; medical, legal, and scientific professionals; government agencies; environmentalists; interested others. Promotes public awareness of health problems caused by chemical and environmental pollutants, focusing on chemical sensitivity disorders. Testifies before government agencies on behalf of persons with such health problems. Encourages the development and implementation of programs and policies aimed at assisting victims of pollutants and preventing future public health problems. Conducts educational programs and research. Gathers information and compiles statistics on indoor and outdoor pollutants, less-toxic products, pesticides, natural foods, and environmental disabilities, including alternative employment, workplace accommodations, social security disability and workmen's compensation, and housing. Maintains speakers' bureau. Provides advocacy and technical, referral, and children's services. Acts as a clearinghouse. **Libraries: Type:** reference. **Formerly:** (1989) Environmental Health Association of New Jersey. **Publications:** *Chemical Sensitivity: A Report to the New Jersey Department of Health* ● *The Delicate Balance*, quarterly. Newsletter. Covers issues related to indoor contaminants, outdoor toxins, legislative and policy updates, research summaries, information on consumer products. **Price:** included in membership dues; $15.00 /year for nonmembers. ISSN: 1045-2036. **Circulation:** 4,000 ● Also publishes reports, bibliographies, information packets, and books.

14063 ■ National Environmental Health Association (NEHA)
720 S Colorado Blvd., Ste.1000-N
Denver, CO 80246-1926
Ph: (303)756-9090
Fax: (303)691-9490
E-mail: staff@neha.org
URL: http://www.neha.org
Contact: Nelson E. Fabian, Exec. Dir.
Founded: 1937. **Members:** 5,100. **Membership Dues:** student, retired, $25 (annual) ● regular, $95 (annual) ● sustaining, $425 (annual) ● institutional/educational, $175 (annual) ● international, $125 (annual). **Staff:** 26. **Budget:** $2,500,000. **Regional Groups:** 10. **State Groups:** 50. **Local Groups:** 3. **National Groups:** 3. **Description:** Represents all professionals in environmental health and protection, including Registered Sanitarians, Registered Environmental Health Specialists, Registered Environmental Technicians, Certified Environmental Health Technicians, Registered Hazardous Substances Professionals and Registered Hazardous Substances Specialists. Advances the environmental health and protection profession for the purpose of providing a healthful environment for all. Provides educational materials, publications, credentials and meetings to members and non-member professionals who strive to improve the environment. **Libraries: Type:** reference. **Holdings:** 1,000; archival material. **Subjects:** environmental health and protection. **Awards:** NEHA/AAS Scholarship Award. **Frequency:** annual. **Type:** recognition. **Recipient:** for undergraduate or graduate students in environmental health science or public health ● Walter S. Mangold Award. **Frequency:** annual. **Type:** recognition. **Recipient:** for contribution to preservation of environment. **Computer Services:** database ● mailing lists. **Sections:** Air, Land and Water Quality; Counter-Bioterrorism; Emerging Pathogens; Environmental Justice; Environmental Management; Food; GIS; Hazardous Waste/Toxic Substances; Injury Prevention and Occupational Health; International Environmental Health; Noise Control; On-site Wastewater Management; Vector Control; Zoonotic Diseases. **Affiliated With:** National Association of Noise Control Officials; National Conference of Local Environmental Health Administrators. **Formerly:** (1937) California Association of Sanitarians; (1970) National Association of Sanitarians. **Publications:** *Journal of Environmental Health*, 10/year. **Price:** $135.00/year in U.S.; $160.00/year outside U.S. ISSN: 0022-0892. **Circulation:** 7,000. **Advertising:** accepted. Alternate Formats: microform. Also Cited As: *JEH* ● *National Environmental Health Association—Membership Directory*, annual. Alternate Formats: diskette. **Conventions/Meetings:** annual Educational Conference and Exhibition - conference and workshop, education training, business meetings, credentialing seminars, workshops (exhibits) - always June/July.

14064 ■ National Environmental Health Science and Protection Accreditation Council (EHAC)
2632 SE 25th Ave., Ste.D
Portland, OR 97202
Ph: (503)235-6047
Fax: (503)235-7300
E-mail: ehacinfo@aehap.org
URL: http://ehacoffice.org
Contact: Randall K. Bentley, Chm.
Founded: 1969. **Members:** 28. **Description:** Purposes are: to establish a system for accreditation of environmental health curricula and related procedures; to accredit and carry out other responsibilities as may be essential to the accreditation of academic programs leading to baccalaureate and graduate degrees in environmental health. Assumes responsibility for all functions, related records, and correspondence pertaining to accreditation of environmental health curricula. Renders advice and counsel to institutions in the development of curricula and the conduct of educational programs in the environmental health sciences. Acts as clearinghouse for reports and information pertaining to the environmental health accreditation process and activities. **Sections:** Graduate; Undergraduate. **Formerly:** National Accreditation Council for Environmental Health Curricula; (1993) National Accreditation Council for Environmental Health Science and Protection; (1998) National Environmental Health Science and Protection Accreditation Council; (2005) Environmental Health Accreditation Council. **Conventions/Meetings:** annual Business Meeting - conference, held in conjunction with National Environmental Health Association (exhibits) - always the third week of June.

14065 ■ National Foundation for the Chemically Hypersensitive (NFCH)
Address Unknown since 2006
Founded: 1986. **Members:** 16,000. **Membership Dues:** open, $20 (annual). **Staff:** 3. **Budget:** $14,000. **Regional Groups:** 40. **State Groups:** 40. **Description:** Individuals suffering from chemical hypersensitivity, their families, and friends; health care professionals; interested others. Promotes public awareness of chemical hypersensitivity disorders, such as multiple chemical sensitivities, environmental illness, food intolerance, total allergy syndrome, candida, and chronic fatigue. Disseminates information on symptoms of chemical hypersensitivity and the potential sources of exposure to the toxic substances that can result in hypersensitivity. Facilitates networking among those afflicted with chemical hypersensitivity. Compiles case histories and statistics; conducts research and educational programs; operates health care and legal referral services. Provides assistance in handling Social Security and worker's compensation claims and locating low-cost housing resources. Maintains speakers' bureau. **Convention/Meeting:** none. **Libraries: Type:** reference. **Awards: Type:** recognition.

14066 ■ Protect All Children's Environment (PACE)
c/o E.M.T. O'nan, Dir.
396 Sugar Cove Rd.
Marion, NC 28752
Ph: (828)724-4221
Fax: (828)724-4177
E-mail: pace@mcdowell.main.nc.us
URL: http://www.main.nc.us/pace
Contact: E.M.T. O'nan, Dir.
Founded: 1987. **Description:** Provides support to persons poisoned by the pesticide Chlordane. **Computer Services:** Information services, child health ● information services, chlordane resources ● information services, pesticides.

14067 ■ Society of Environmental Toxicology and Chemistry (SETAC)
1010 N 12th Ave.
Pensacola, FL 32501-3370
Ph: (850)469-1500
Fax: (850)469-9778
E-mail: setac@setac.org
URL: http://www.setac.org
Contact: G. Allen Burton, Pres.
Founded: 1979. **Members:** 5,000. **Membership Dues:** regular, associate, $140 (annual) ● student, $40 (annual) ● recent graduate, $80 (annual) ● senior, $70 (annual) ● multiple year, $345 (annual) ● developing country, $25 (annual). **Staff:** 12. **Budget:** $2,300,000. **Regional Groups:** 16. **Description:** Professionals in the fields of chemistry, toxicology, biology, and ecology; atmospheric, health, and earth sciences; and environmental engineering. Promotes the use of multidisciplinary approaches to examine the impacts of chemicals and technology on the environment. Strives to balance the interests of academia, business, and government. Conducts workshops and symposia on research topics of interest to members. **Libraries: Type:** reference. **Holdings:** 100; archival material, audio recordings, books, business records, clippings, periodicals. **Subjects:** environmental toxicology, chemistry, engineering, risk assessment. **Awards:** ET&C Best Student Paper Award. **Frequency:** annual. **Type:** recognition. **Recipient:** to the best published student paper during the past year ● Eugene Kenaga Membership Award. **Frequency:** annual. **Type:** recognition. **Recipient:** to a member who has been instrumental in the developing and working with the society's membership at either the national or chapter level ● Founders Award. **Frequency:** annual. **Type:** recognition. **Recipient:** for outstanding career with clearly identifiable contributions in the environmental sciences consistent with the goals of SETAC ● Government Service Award. **Frequency:** annual. **Type:** recognition. **Recipient:** for scientist or scientific organization ● Herb Ward Exceptional Service Award. **Frequency:** annual. **Type:** recognition. **Recipient:** to an individual who has performed long term and exceptionally high quality service for SETAC ● President Citations. **Frequency:** annual. **Type:** recognition. **Recipient:** for individuals who have worked behind the scenes to promote and support the activities of the society ● Procter & Gamble Fellowship for Doctoral Research in Educational Science. **Frequency:** annual. **Type:** scholarship. **Recipient:** for pursuit of a PhD degree in environmental toxicology, chemistry, or related disciplines ● Rachel Carson Award. **Frequency:** periodic. **Type:** recognition. **Recipient:** for substantially increasing public awareness and understanding of critical environmental issues ● SETAC/EA Engineering Jeff Black Award. **Frequency:** annual. **Type:** fellowship. **Recipient:** for master's level students ● SETAC/ICA Chris Lee Award for Metals Research. **Frequency:** annual. **Type:** recognition. **Recipient:** to a graduate student or recent graduate who has focused on research related to the fate and/or effects of metal in the environment ● SETAC/Menzie Cura Environmental Education Award. **Frequency:** annual. **Type:** recognition. **Recipient:** for individuals, organizations, or corporations making significant contribution to environmental education ● SETAC/Roy F. Weston Award. **Frequency:** annual. **Type:** recognition. **Recipient:** for individuals under the age of 35, selection based on the significance of contribution of published papers to the field of environmental chemistry. **Computer Services:** database, member ● mailing lists. **Committees:** Awards and Fellowships; Development; Elections/Nominations; International Programs; Liaison; Long-Range Planning; Meetings; Public Relations. **Publications:** *Asia/Pacific Bulletin*. Alternate Formats: online ● *Environmental Toxicology and Chemistry*, monthly. Journal. Contains peer-reviewed research papers. **Price:** included in membership dues; $640.00 /year for institutions. ISSN: 1552-8618. **Circulation:** 4,600. **Advertising:** accepted. Alternate Formats: online ● *Integrated Environmental Assessment and Management*, quarterly. Journal. **Price:** included in membership dues. ISSN: 1551-3793. Alternate Formats: online ● *Life-Cycle Assessment Data Quality: A Conceptual Framework*. Report ● *Radiotelemetry Applications for Wildlife Toxicology Field Studies*. Book ● *SETAC Globe*, bimonthly. Newsletter. Highlights environmental topics, SETAC activities, employment activities, and meetings of interest. **Price:** included in membership dues. **Advertising:** accepted ● Membership Directory, annual. Lists addresses and specialties of members. **Price:** available to members only ● Books ● Papers ● Publishes various technical and informal reports. **Conventions/Meetings:** annual meeting (exhibits) - 2007 Nov. 11-15, Milwaukee, WI; 2008 Nov. 16-20, Tampa, FL; 2009 Nov. 20-24, New Orleans, LA.

14068 ■ Society for Human Ecology (SHE)
c/o Ms. Barbara Carter, Exec. Asst.
Coll. of the Atlantic
105 Eden St.
Bar Harbor, ME 04609

Ph: (207)288-5015
Fax: (207)288-3780
E-mail: carter@coa.edu
URL: http://www.societyforhumanecology.org
Contact: Ms. Barbara Carter, Exec. Asst.
Founded: 1981. **Members:** 150. **Membership Dues:** regular, $60 (annual) ● student, retired and individual from developing country, $30 (annual) ● contributing, $150 (annual) ● sustaining, $1,000 (annual). **Multinational. Description:** Educators, health practitioners, scientists, and other professionals in 30 countries studying human ecology and its applications. Focuses attention on the consequences of human action on manufactured, natural, and social environments. Promotes interdisciplinary collaboration; facilitates the exchange of information; identifies problems and recommends solutions from an ecological perspective. Conducts workshops and symposia. Participates in human ecology consortium. Organization is distinct from the International Organization for Human Ecology, formerly known as the Society for Human Ecology. **Working Groups:** Education; Health; Modeling; Planning; Theory. **Affiliated With:** Commonwealth Human Ecology Council; Ecological Society of America; International Association for Impact Assessment. **Publications:** *Human Ecology: A Gathering of Perspectives.* Proceedings. Contains proceedings from SHE's First International Conference, held in 1985. ● *Human Ecology and Decision Making: An International and Interdisciplinary Collaboration* ● *Human Ecology Bulletin,* semiannual ● *Human Ecology—Coming of Age: An International Overview.* Proceedings. Contains proceedings of the symposium organized at the International Congress of Ecology in 1990. ● *Human Ecology: Crossing Boundaries.* Papers. Selected papers from the 6th conference of SHE. ● *Human Ecology: Research and Applications.* Proceedings. Contains proceedings from SHE's Second International Conference, held in 1988. ● *Human Ecology Review,* semiannual. Journal. **Price:** $75.00 for institution; $40.00 single issue. ISSN: 1074-4827 ● *Human Ecology: Steps to the Future.* Proceedings. Contains proceedings from SHE's Third International Conference. ● *Human Ecology: Strategies for the Future.* Papers. Selected papers from the 4th conference of the SHE, held in 1990. ● *International Directory of Human Ecologists,* periodic. Lists over 700 human ecologists worldwide, with descriptions of their work, research, and activities; includes addresses and phone numbers. **Conventions/Meetings:** annual Interdisciplinary Integration and Practice: Reconciling Humans and Nature - conference.

Epidemiology

14069 ■ Aeras Global TB Vaccine Foundation
1405 Res. Blvd.
Rockville, MD 20850
Ph: (301)547-2900
Fax: (301)547-2901
E-mail: info@aeras.org
URL: http://www.aeras.org
Contact: Jerald C. Sadoff MD, Pres./CEO
Founded: 1997. **Staff:** 9. **Budget:** $5,000,000. **Description:** Represents researchers. Serves as a resource for the Tuberculosis Research Community to help identify and develop concepts and tools for controlling the global epidemic.

14070 ■ American College of Epidemiology (ACE)
1500 Sunday Dr., Ste.102
Raleigh, NC 27607
Ph: (919)861-5573
Fax: (919)787-4916
E-mail: pkralka@olsonmgmt.com
URL: http://www.acepidemiology2.org
Contact: Peter Kralka, Exec. Dir.
Founded: 1979. **Members:** 960. **Staff:** 3. **Budget:** $180,000. **Description:** Medical professionals involved in the field of epidemiology. Promotes education in the practice of epidemiology and maintains professional standards in the field. Relates epidemiological issues to public policy. **Awards:** Abraham Lil-

ienfeld Award. **Frequency:** annual. **Type:** recognition. **Recipient:** to a distinguished epidemiologist ● Student Prize Paper Award. **Frequency:** annual. **Type:** recognition. **Recipient:** for outstanding scientific contribution by a student of epidemiology. **Telecommunication Services:** electronic mail, fkenan@firstpointresources.com. **Committees:** Admissions; Awards; Communications; Education; Ethics and Standards of Practice; Minority Affairs; Nominating; Policy. **Publications:** *Annals of Epidemiology,* monthly ● Newsletter, quarterly. **Conventions/Meetings:** annual meeting (exhibits) ● semiannual seminar.

14071 ■ Council of State and Territorial Epidemiologists (CSTE)
2872 Woodcock Blvd., Ste.303
Atlanta, GA 30341
Ph: (770)458-3811
Fax: (770)458-8516
E-mail: pmcconnon@cste.org
URL: http://www.cste.org
Contact: Pat McConnon, Exec. Dir.
Founded: 1951. **Members:** 850. **Membership Dues:** individual active/associate, $40 (annual) ● student, $25 (annual). **Staff:** 20. **Budget:** $3,500,000. **Regional Groups:** 4. **Description:** State epidemiologists. Works to establish closer working relationships among members; consults with and advises appropriate disciplines in other health agencies; provides technical advice and assistance to the Association of State and Territorial Health Officials (see separate entry); works closely with Centers for Disease Control on epidemiology, surveillance, and prevention activities. **Awards:** Pumphandle Award. **Frequency:** annual. **Type:** recognition. **Recipient:** for outstanding contribution in the field of Applied Epidemiology. **Computer Services:** Mailing lists. **Committees:** Chronic Disease; Environmental/Occupational/Injury; Executive; Infectious Disease. **Affiliated With:** Association of State and Territorial Health Officials. **Formerly:** (1986) Conference of State and Territorial Epidemiologists. **Publications:** *CSTE Update,* quarterly. Newsletter. **Conventions/Meetings:** annual conference (exhibits).

14072 ■ International Clinical Epidemiology Network (INCLEN)
1420 Walnut St., Ste.411
Philadelphia, PA 19102-4003
Ph: (215)222-7700
Fax: (215)222-7741
E-mail: inclen@inclen.org
URL: http://www.inclen.org
Contact: Dr. Narendra Arora, Exec. Dir.
Founded: 1980. **Members:** 1,400. **Membership Dues:** institution (for developed countries), $200 (annual) ● institution (for developing countries), $100 (annual). **Multinational. Description:** Represents physicians, statisticians, social scientists. Seeks to improve the health of individuals. Promotes clinical practice, research, and medical education. **Publications:** *INCLEN Monograph Series,* periodic. **Price:** included in membership dues; $4.00 for nonmembers ● *INCLEN News,* semiannual. Newsletter. Highlights research interests and accomplishments of members around the globe. **Price:** included in membership dues. Alternate Formats: online ● Brochure. Alternate Formats: online ● Membership Directory, annual. Contains names, specialties and contact information of members. **Price:** included in membership dues.

14073 ■ International Genetic Epidemiology Society (IGES)
c/o Michael A. Province, Sec.-Treas.
Washington Univ. School of Medicine
Div. of Biostatistics, Box 8067
660 S Euclid Ave.
St. Louis, MO 63108
Ph: (314)362-3616
Fax: (314)362-2693
E-mail: mike@wubios.wustl.edu
URL: http://www.biostat.wustl.edu/~genetics/iges
Contact: Michael A. Province, Sec.-Treas.
Founded: 1992. **Multinational. Description:** Promotes the study of genetic epidemiology and statisti-

cal genetics. Seeks to further the development of the methodology to permit studies in health and disease and the application of these approaches in human populations. Fosters continuing education and outreach to the scientific community about the discipline, analytical methods and software used in genetic epidemiology. **Awards:** James V. Neel Young Investigator Award. **Frequency:** annual. **Type:** recognition. **Recipient:** for best platform presentation by a young investigator (postdoctoral) at the IGES meeting ● Roger W. Williams Award. **Frequency:** annual. **Type:** recognition. **Recipient:** for best platform presentation by a graduate student (predoctoral) at the IGES meeting. **Telecommunication Services:** electronic mail, jeanne@wustl.edu. **Publications:** *Genetic Epidemiology.* Journal ● Newsletter. Alternate Formats: online ● Membership Directory. **Price:** for members only.

14074 ■ Society for Epidemiologic Research (SER)
PO Box 990
Clearfield, UT 84089
Ph: (801)525-0231
Fax: (801)774-9211
E-mail: membership@epiresearch.org
URL: http://www.epiresearch.org
Contact: Joseph L. Lyon MD, Sec.-Treas.
Founded: 1968. **Members:** 2,500. **Membership Dues:** regular, $145 (annual) ● student (with journal), $80 (annual) ● student (without journal), $50 (annual). **Staff:** 1. **Budget:** $50,000. **Description:** Epidemiologists, researchers, public health administrators, educators, mathematicians, statisticians, and others interested in epidemiological research. Stimulates scientific interest in and promotes the exchange of information about epidemiological research. **Awards:** Abraham Lilienfeld Prize Paper. **Frequency:** annual. **Type:** recognition. **Recipient:** for students ● John Cassel Memorial Lecture. **Frequency:** semiannual. **Type:** recognition. **Subgroups:** Student Caucus. **Publications:** *American Journal of Epidemiology,* bimonthly. Includes research reports and reviews, computer programs for epidemiologists, and annual meeting abstracts. **Price:** $190.00/year. **Circulation:** 4,000. **Advertising:** accepted. Also Cited As: *AJE* ● *Society for Epidemiologic Research—Membership Directory,* every 3-5 years ● *Society for Epidemiologic Research—Newsletter,* semiannual. Alternate Formats: online. **Conventions/Meetings:** annual conference (exhibits) ● workshop, for students.

14075 ■ Society for Healthcare Epidemiology of America (SHEA)
66 Canal Center Plz., Ste.600
Alexandria, VA 22314
Ph: (703)684-1006
Fax: (703)684-1009
E-mail: info@shea-online.org
URL: http://www.shea-online.org
Contact: Victoria Fraser MD, Pres.
Founded: 1980. **Members:** 1,100. **Membership Dues:** fellow, $150 (annual) ● associate, $100 (annual) ● training, $75 (annual) ● corporate, $175 (annual) ● emeritus, $100 (annual). **Staff:** 3. **Description:** Fosters the development and application of the science of healthcare epidemiology (broadly defined as any activity designed to study and/or improve outcomes in any type of healthcare institution or setting). **Formerly:** Society of Hospital Epidemiologists of America; (2000) Society of Healthcare Epidemiologists of America. **Publications:** *Infection Control and Hospital Epidemiology,* monthly. Journal. **Price:** included in membership dues. **Advertising:** accepted. Alternate Formats: online. **Conventions/Meetings:** annual meeting (exhibits) - 2008 Apr. 5-8, Orlando, FL - **Avg. Attendance:** 1100; 2009 Apr. 4-7, San Diego, CA; 2010 Mar. 18-21, Atlanta, GA.

Epilepsy

14076 ■ American Epilepsy Society (AES)
342 N Main St.
West Hartford, CT 06117-2507
Ph: (860)586-7505

Fax: (860)586-7550
E-mail: info@aesnet.org
URL: http://www.aesnet.org
Contact: M. Suzanne C. Berry CAE, Exec. Dir.
Founded: 1936. **Members:** 3,200. **Membership Dues:** corresponding (with Epilepsia subscription), $220 (annual) ● corresponding (without Epilepsia subscription), $145 (annual) ● active, corporate/associate, $200 (annual) ● junior (with Epilepsia subscription), $150 (annual) ● junior (without Epilepsia subscription), $75 (annual) ● allied health professional (without Epilepsia subscription), $115 (annual). **Staff:** 15. **Budget:** $500,000. **Description:** Clinicians, scientists investigating basic and clinical aspects of epilepsy, and related professional workers with an active interest in seizure disorders. Seeks to promote interdisciplinary communication, scientific investigation and exchange of clinical information about epilepsy. Works to prevent and treat epilepsy. **Awards:** AES Service Award. **Frequency:** annual. **Type:** recognition. **Recipient:** for outstanding service in the field of epilepsy ● Epilepsy Research Awards Program. **Frequency:** annual. **Type:** recognition. **Recipient:** to encourage and reward clincial and basic science investigators whose research contributes importantly to understanding and conquering epilepsy ● J. Kiffin Penry Award. **Frequency:** annual. **Type:** recognition. **Recipient:** for excellence in epilepsy care ● William G. Lennox Award. **Frequency:** annual. **Type:** recognition. **Recipient:** for senior members of the society with remarkable contributions in the field. **Computer Services:** Mailing lists, of members. **Affiliated With:** Epilepsy Foundation. **Formerly:** (1959) American League Against Epilepsy. **Publications:** *AES News.* Newsletter. Alternate Formats: online ● *Epilepsia,* monthly. Journal. Published in conjunction with the International League Against Epilepsy. **Price:** included in membership dues. **Advertising:** accepted ● *Epilepsy Currents,* 5/year, Journals. Contains original articles on areas of current interest. **Price:** included in membership dues. **Advertising:** accepted. Alternate Formats: online ● Also publishes Epilepsy Research incorporating the Journal of Epilepsy. **Conventions/Meetings:** annual conference, scientific meeting providing continuing medical education (exhibits) - 2007 Nov. 30-Dec. 4, Philadelphia, PA - **Avg. Attendance:** 4000; 2008 Dec. 5-9, Seattle, WA - **Avg. Attendance:** 4000; 2009 Dec. 4-8, Boston, MA - **Avg. Attendance:** 4000.

14077 ■ Epilepsy Foundation
8301 Professional Pl.
Landover, MD 20785-2223
Ph: (301)459-3700
Free: (800)332-1000
Fax: (301)577-2684
E-mail: postmaster@efa.org
URL: http://www.epilepsyfoundation.org
Contact: Eric R. Hargis, Pres./CEO
Founded: 1967. **Members:** 16,000. **Membership Dues:** full, $25 (annual). **Staff:** 71. **Budget:** $12,000,000. **Local Groups:** 60. **Languages:** English, Spanish. **Description:** Serves as the "focal point for the fight against epilepsy in the United States." Augmented by 60 affiliates in the U.S. committed to preventing and controlling epilepsy and improving the lives of those who have it. Provides federal government liaison. Supports medical, social, rehabilitational, legal, employment, and information, education, and advocacy programs. Sponsors research in causes of epilepsy, prevention, psychosocial needs, and improved methods of treatment. Provides research and training grants and fellowships to students and professionals. Provides assistance and counseling for epilepsy patients and their families through local organizations and the National Information Center on Epilepsy. Conducts Annual projects such as the National Epilepsy Month (November), School Alert (a national educational program for schools), selection of the Epilepsy Poster Child, and a continuing professional and public education and information program. Maintains a resource center. Provides members with access to mail order pharmacy program. Compiles statistics; maintains placement program. **Libraries:** Type: refer-

ence. **Holdings:** 2,000. **Subjects:** research, psychoscience, issuing, epidemiology, etiology, genetics, epilepsy, disability, seizure disorders. **Awards:** Frequency: annual. **Type:** grant. **Recipient:** for epilepsy research. **Telecommunication Services:** additional toll-free number, (800)213-5821. **Affiliated With:** National Health Council. **Formed by Merger of:** Epilepsy Foundation and Epilepsy Association of America. **Publications:** *Between Us,* bimonthly. Magazine. Alternate Formats: online ● *EpilepsyUSA,* bimonthly. Magazine. Contains news about epilepsy and seizure disorder. **Price:** $15.00. Alternate Formats: online ● *Kids News,* quarterly. Magazine ● Newsletter, quarterly ● Also publishes pamphlets and makes available audiovisual material and informational/educational pieces for diversified audiences. **Conventions/Meetings:** annual conference, professional and consumer education and leadership enhancement (exhibits).

14078 ■ Epilepsy Therapy Development Project
11921 Freedom Dr., Ste.730
Reston, VA 20190
Ph: (703)437-4250
Fax: (703)437-4288
E-mail: epilepsycure@aol.com
URL: http://www.epilepsytdp.org
Contact: William E. Braunlich, Pres.
Founded: 2002. **Description:** Advances new treatments for people living with epilepsy. Supports research in both academic and industry settings through direct grants and participation in the Partnership for Research in Pediatric Epilepsy. Facilitates the interchange of ideas and coordinates research agendas through the sponsorship of scientific meetings and workshops.

Family Medicine

14079 ■ American Academy of Family Physicians (AAFP)
PO Box 11210
Shawnee Mission, KS 66207-1210
Ph: (913)906-6000
Free: (800)274-2237
E-mail: fp@aafp.org
URL: http://www.aafp.org
Contact: Douglas E. Henley MD, Exec. VP
Founded: 1947. **Members:** 93,500. **Membership Dues:** resident, $25 (annual) ● active, $310 (annual) ● supporting, $260 (annual) ● international, $110 (annual) ● inactive, $50 (annual) ● life, $50. **Staff:** 420. **Budget:** $62,000,000. **State Groups:** 55. **Local Groups:** 200. **Description:** Serves as a professional society of family physicians who provide continuing comprehensive care to patients. **Libraries:** Type: not open to the public. **Holdings:** books. **Subjects:** medicine. **Awards:** Award for Excellence in Graduate Medical Education. **Frequency:** annual. **Type:** recognition. **Recipient:** for leadership, patient care and aptitude ● Distinguished Service Award. **Frequency:** annual. **Type:** recognition. **Recipient:** for dedication in family medicine. **Computer Services:** Mailing lists. **Committees:** Chapter Affairs; Clinical Policies and Research; Continuing Medical Education; Finance and Insurance; Health Care Services; Legislation and Governmental Affairs; Membership and Member Services; Public Health; Quality and Scope of Practice; Resident and Student Affairs; Rural Health; Scientific Program; Special Constituencies. **Divisions:** Administration; Communications; Education; Research and Information Services; Scientific Activities; Socioeconomic. **Formerly:** (1971) American Academy of General Practice. **Publications:** *American Family Physician,* semimonthly. Journal. Includes book reviews, newsletter, calendar of events, and therapeutic, product, and subject indexes. **Price:** $150.00 /year for individuals and physicians in U.S.; $232.00 /year for individuals and physicians outside U.S.; $199.00 /year for institutions in U.S.; $11.00 each, for back issues. ISSN: 1532-0650. **Circulation:** 150,000. **Advertising:** accepted. Alternate Formats: CD-ROM. Also Cited As: *AFP* ●

Annals of Family Medicine, bimonthly. Journal. Seeks to identify and address important questions in health and the provision of patient-centered, prioritized, high-quality health care. **Price:** $45.00/year for students and healthcare professionals; $125.00 /year for individuals and physicians; $175.00 /year for institutions in U.S.; $205.00 /year for institutions in Canada. **Advertising:** accepted ● *Family Practice Management,* 10/year. Journal. Covers practice management and socioeconomic issues. **Price:** $150.00 /year for individuals and physicians in U.S.; $232.00 /year for individuals and physicians outside U.S.; $199.00 /year for institutions in U.S.; $239.00 /year for institutions outside U.S. ISSN: 1531-1929 ● *Obesity Management,* bimonthly. Journal. Provides clinical strategies for management of overweight and obese patients. **Price:** $94.00 for nonmembers outside U.S.; $68.00 for members outside U.S.; $79.00 for nonmembers in U.S.; $58.00 for members in U.S. ● Annual Report. **Conventions/Meetings:** annual National Conference of Family Practice Residents/Students, for family practice residents and students (exhibits) ● annual Scientific Assembly - meeting, includes scientific assembly (exhibits).

14080 ■ American Board of Family Medicine (ABFM)
2228 Young Dr.
Lexington, KY 40505-4294
Ph: (859)269-5626
Free: (888)995-5700
Fax: (859)335-7501
E-mail: help@theabfm.org
URL: http://www.theabfm.org
Contact: James C. Puffer MD, Pres./CEO
Founded: 1969. **Staff:** 24. **Description:** Certifying board for physicians specializing in family practice. Conducts certification/recertification examinations. **Formerly:** (2005) American Board of Family Practice. **Publications:** *Journal of the American Board of Family Practice,* bimonthly. **Price:** $120.00 for institutions; $150.00 for institutions outside U.S. ISSN: 0893-8652. **Circulation:** 55,000. **Advertising:** accepted. Alternate Formats: online ● *The Phoenix,* semiannual. Newsletter. Alternate Formats: online.

14081 ■ Family and Health Section of the National Council on Family Relations (FHS)
c/o B. Jan McCulloch, Section Sec.-Treas.
290D McNeal Hall
1985 Buford Ave.
St. Paul, MN 55108-6134
Ph: (612)624-1208
E-mail: jmccullo@umn.edu
URL: http://www.ncfr.org/member/sections/family-health/home.asp
Contact: Sharon A. Denham, Section Chair
Founded: 1984. **Members:** 345. **Description:** A section of the National Council on Family Relations (see separate entry). Health and education professionals. Serves as a forum for all professionals involved in interdisciplinary work in the family and health fields. Presents clinical research and educational programs at NCFR conferences. **Awards:** Student/New Professional Award. **Frequency:** annual. **Type:** recognition. **Recipient:** for outstanding paper from student or new professional that is submitted and accepted for presentation at the annual conference. **Subgroups:** Chronic Illness and Disability. **Affiliated With:** National Council on Family Relations. **Formerly:** (1991) Family and Health Section. **Publications:** *Family Health News,* periodic. Newsletter. **Conventions/Meetings:** annual conference (exhibits) - always November.

14082 ■ Interstate Postgraduate Medical Association of North America (IPMANA)
PO Box 5474
Madison, WI 53705
Ph: (608)231-9045
Fax: (877)292-4489
E-mail: info@ipmameded.org
URL: http://www.ipmameded.org
Contact: Mary W. Ales, Exec. Dir.
Founded: 1916. **Staff:** 3. **Budget:** $250,000. **Description:** Presents an annual four-day teaching

program to provide a systematic update for family physicians, internists and allied health professionals working in the primary care office setting. Other educational opportunities are available online. **Publications:** none. **Awards: Type:** recognition. **Conventions/Meetings:** annual convention (exhibits) - 2007 Nov. 4-7, Savannah, GA - **Avg. Attendance:** 500.

14083 ■ Society of Teachers of Family Medicine (STFM)
11400 Tomahawk Creek Pkwy., Ste.540
Leawood, KS 66211
Ph: (913)906-6000 (713)798-7744
Free: (800)274-2237
Fax: (913)906-6096
E-mail: stfmoffice@stfm.org
URL: http://www.stfm.org
Contact: Stacy Brungardt, Deputy Exec. Dir.
Founded: 1967. **Members:** 5,000. **Membership Dues:** active physician, $235 (annual) ● non-physician, $175 (annual) ● associate, $105 (annual) ● fellow, $80 (annual) ● resident, $60 (annual) ● student, $25 (annual). **Staff:** 17. **Budget:** $2,200,000. **Multinational. Description:** Physicians involved in teaching or promoting family medicine; individuals in related fields. Promotes public welfare by maintaining and improving standards and practices of medical service, especially in the field of family medicine. Promotes these objectives by: supporting and expressing the tenets of family medicine as an academic discipline; maintaining and continually improving the quality of instructional and scientific skills and knowledge in the field of family medicine; providing a forum for the interchange of experience and ideas among its members and other interested persons; and encouraging research and teaching in family medicine. **Libraries: Type:** reference. **Subjects:** behavioral science, career development; clinical, family systems, geriatrics, humanities, patient education, practice management, research, sports medicine, teaching. **Committees:** Communications; Education; Legislative Affairs; Membership; Program; Research. **Publications:** *Family Medicine*, monthly. Journal. Includes annual index, book reviews, and employment opportunities. **Price:** included in membership dues; $12.50/copy for nonmembers; $88.00 /year for nonmembers; $120.00 /year for institutions. ISSN: 0742-3225. **Circulation:** 5,000. **Advertising:** accepted. Alternate Formats: online. Also Cited As: *Family Medicine Teacher ● STFM Messenger*, monthly. Newsletter. Covers general information related to family medicine issues. Includes research and education columns. **Price:** included in membership dues. **Circulation:** 5,000. **Advertising:** accepted ● Monographs. **Conventions/Meetings:** annual conference ● annual Conference on Families & Health ● annual Conference on Practice Improvement ● annual Forum for Behavioral Science in Family Medicine - conference ● annual Predoctoral Education Conference.

Fertility

14084 ■ American Fertility Association (AFA)
305 Madison Ave., Ste.449
New York, NY 10165
Free: (888)917-3777
Fax: (718)601-7722
E-mail: info@theafa.org
URL: http://www.theafa.org
Contact: Pamela Madsen, Exec. Dir.
Founded: 1999. **Members:** 30,000. **Description:** Educates the public about reproductive disease, and supports families struggling with infertility and adoption. Provides services designed to help people gather information about medical treatments, options, coping techniques, legal and insurance issues, and other concerns. Increases awareness of the medical and social issues on reproductive health and infertility, as well as prevention efforts that target young people to help them make informed choices about their sexual and reproductive lives. **Computer Services:** database ● information services, physician and therapist referral network ● online services,

forums about fertility and reproductive health. **Subgroups:** Coaching; Support. **Formerly:** (2004) American Infertility Association. **Publications:** *In Focus*. Magazine. Alternate Formats: online ● *Insurance Handbook*. Alternate Formats: online ● Newsletter, monthly. Alternate Formats: online ● Directory. Alternate Formats: online.

14085 ■ American Society for Reproductive Medicine (ASRM)
1209 Montgomery Hwy.
Birmingham, AL 35216-2809
Ph: (205)978-5000
Fax: (205)978-5005
E-mail: asrm@asrm.org
URL: http://www.asrm.org
Contact: Dr. Robert W. Rebar MD, Exec. Dir.
Founded: 1944. **Members:** 10,500. **Membership Dues:** active, doctoral level, $250 (annual) ● physician, doctorate, $250 (annual) ● allied health professional, non-doctoral level, $125 (annual). **Staff:** 25. **Multinational. Description:** Gynecologists, obstetricians, urologists, reproductive endocrinologists, veterinarians, research workers, and others interested in reproductive health in humans and animals. Seeks to extend knowledge of all aspects of fertility and problems of infertility and mammalian reproduction; provides a rostrum for the presentation of scientific studies dealing with these subjects. Offers patient resource information. **Formerly:** American Fertility Society; (1966) American Society for the Study of Sterility. **Publications:** *ASRM News*, quarterly. Newsletter. Contains meeting announcements and patient information pertinent to members. **Price:** included in membership dues ● *Fertility and Sterility*, monthly. Journal. Includes book reviews and announcements of meetings, courses, services, and employment opportunities. **Price:** included in membership dues. ISSN: 0015-0282. **Circulation:** 14,500. **Advertising:** accepted. Alternate Formats: online ● *Menopausal Medicine*, quarterly. Newsletter ● *Sexuality, Reproduction and Menopause*, quarterly. Journal ● Also publishes syllabi used for postgraduate courses. **Conventions/Meetings:** annual Scientific and Postgraduate - meeting (exhibits).

14086 ■ Fertile Hope
PO Box 624
New York, NY 10014
Free: (888)994-HOPE
E-mail: feedback@fertilehope.org
URL: http://www.fertilehope.org
Contact: Lindsay Nohr Beck, Exec. Dir./Founder
Founded: 2001. **Description:** Provides reproductive information, support and hope to cancer patients whose medical treatments present the risk of infertility. Offers programs and services that increase awareness of fertility risks and preservation options. Provides credible and accurate educational resources and fertility preservation financial assistance options. Makes fertility preservation treatments available to patients regardless of economic status. Helps patients cope with family planning issues.

14087 ■ Fertility Research Foundation (FRF)
877 Park Ave.
New York, NY 10021
Ph: (212)744-5500
Fax: (212)744-6536
E-mail: info@frfbaby.com
URL: http://www.frfbaby.com
Contact: Masood A. Khatamee MD, Exec. Dir.
Founded: 1962. **Members:** 500. **Membership Dues:** $200 (annual). **Staff:** 4. **Budget:** $85,000. **Languages:** English, Farsi, Spanish, Urdu. **Description:** Specializes in human reproduction. Provides therapeutic, diagnostic, and consultation service for childless couples. Conducts comprehensive infertility surveys which include: endoscopy, sperm antibodies determination, bacteriological assessment, endocrine studies, laboratory facilities for complete hormone assays, surgical correction of genital diseases, artificial donor insemination, and ovulation induction. Maintains research projects in human reproduction pertaining to: the study of influence of mycoplasma on infertility; the relationship of prostaglandins and

infertility; the study of genetic defects and dermatoglyphics; immunology research; sperm physiology and migration; ovum transplantation. Conducts educational programs for practicing physicians, residents, and medical students in infertility and education of the public about the human reproductive processes. **Libraries: Type:** not open to the public. **Holdings:** reports. **Formerly:** (1967) New York Fertility Institute; (1981) New York Fertility Research Foundation. **Publications:** *Fertility Sourcebook*. **Conventions/Meetings:** annual World Conference on Prevention of Human Infertility (exhibits).

14088 ■ International Council on Infertility Information Dissemination (INCIID)
PO Box 6836
Arlington, VA 22206
Ph: (703)379-9178
Fax: (703)379-1593
E-mail: inciidinfo@inciid.org
URL: http://www.inciid.org
Contact: Nancy Hemenway, Exec. Dir.
Founded: 1995. **Membership Dues:** professional, $395 (annual) ● corporate, $3,000 (annual) ● consumer e-member, $5 (annual) ● friend, $25 (annual) ● consumer-bronze, $55 (annual) ● consumer-silver, $250 (annual) ● consumer-gold, $500 (annual) ● consumer platinum, corresponding, $2,500 (annual). **Multinational. Description:** Helps individuals and couples explore their family-building options by providing current information and immediate support regarding the diagnosis, treatment and prevention of infertility and pregnancy loss. Offers guidance to those considering adoption or childfree lifestyles. **Computer Services:** database, geographic directory of professional members ● information services, news articles ● online services, forum, polls, surveys and chatroom. **Boards:** Advisory. **Programs:** Emilie's Legacy; From INCIID the Heart; Outcome Based Reporting System. **Publications:** *Insights*, 8/year. Newsletter. **Circulation:** 20,000.

14089 ■ Reproductive Toxicology Center (RTC)
7831 Woodmont Ave., Ste.375
Bethesda, MD 20814
Ph: (301)514-3081
Fax: (301)907-6827
E-mail: reprotox@reprotox.org
URL: http://reprotox.org
Contact: Kay Padgett, Admin.
Founded: 1981. **Membership Dues:** individual health care provider, $199 (annual) ● group (2 to 8 health care professionals), $499 (annual) ● institutional, $999 (annual). **Staff:** 5. **Multinational. Description:** Works to gather and disseminate information on the effects of the chemical and physical environment on human fertility, pregnancy, and fetal development. Provides members with information from the most relevant articles in the field. **Convention/Meeting:** none. **Computer Services:** database, REPROTOX, provides summaries on more than 4,000 agents ● online services. **Publications:** *Reprotox In a Nutshell*, quarterly. Newsletter. Alternate Formats: online.

14090 ■ Resolve, The National Infertility Association
7910 Woodmont Ave., Ste.1350
Bethesda, MD 20814
Ph: (301)652-8585
Free: (888)623-0744
Fax: (301)652-9375
E-mail: info@resolve.org
URL: http://www.resolve.org
Contact: Mr. Joseph C. Isaacs, Pres./CEO
Founded: 1974. **Members:** 15,000. **Membership Dues:** basic, $55 (annual) ● professional, $150 (annual). **Staff:** 17. **Budget:** $1,000,000. **Local Groups:** 56. **National Groups:** 50. **Description:** Persons with problems of infertility and associated professionals who work with infertile couples such as adoption workers, physicians, and counselors. Seeks to provide "timely, compassionate support and information to people who are experiencing infertility, and to increase awareness of infertility issues." Offers

information, referral, and support to persons with problems of infertility; conducts issue advocacy and public education programs. **Awards:** Barbara Eck Menning Award. **Frequency:** annual. **Type:** recognition. **Recipient:** for achievement in the field of fertility. **Formerly:** (1999) RESOLVE. **Publications:** *Family Building Magazine*, quarterly. Provides information on medical, emotional, and legislative issues, and upcoming conferences. Includes book reviews, research reports, and letters. **Price:** included in membership dues; $5.00/issue for nonmembers. **Circulation:** 16,000. **Advertising:** accepted ● *Resolving Infertility*. Book ● Bibliography ● Brochure ● Also publishes fact sheets and briefs. **Conventions/Meetings:** annual Resolve National Meeting - conference, infertility related resources (exhibits) ● periodic symposium.

Fibromyalgia

14091 ■ American Fibromyalgia Syndrome Association (AFSA)
6380 E Tanque Verde, Ste.D
Tucson, AZ 85715
Ph: (520)733-1570
Fax: (520)290-5550
E-mail: kthorson@afsafund.org
URL: http://www.afsafund.org
Contact: Kristin Thorson, Pres.
Founded: 1994. **Description:** Dedicated to research, education and patient advocacy for Fibromyalgia Syndrome (FMS) and Chronic Fatigue Syndrome (CFS). Provides phone service "warm line" for patients and physicians. Sponsors information booths at major medical conferences. **Awards:** Research Grant Award. **Frequency:** annual. **Type:** grant. **Recipient:** for pharmacological interventions or studies that can lead to novel pharmacological agents. **Publications:** *AFSA Update*. Newsletter. Alternate Formats: online.

14092 ■ Fibromyalgia Network
PO Box 31750
Tucson, AZ 85751
Ph: (520)290-5508
Free: (800)853-2929
Fax: (520)290-5550
E-mail: info@fmnetnews.com
URL: http://www.fmnetnews.com
Founded: 1988. **Members:** 16,000. **Membership Dues:** regular, $28 (annual). **Staff:** 6. **For-Profit. Multinational. Description:** Provides materials on fibromyalgia and chronic fatigue syndrome. **Publications:** Newsletter, quarterly. Features coping techniques, medical journal listings, conference news, interviews with experts, drug updates, and non-drug treatments. **Price:** $25.00 in U.S.; $27.00 in Canada; $30.00 outside North America.

14093 ■ National Fibromyalgia Association (NFA)
2200 N Glassell St., Ste.A
Orange, CA 92865
Ph: (714)921-0150
Fax: (714)921-6920
E-mail: nfa@fmaware.org
URL: http://fmaware.org
Contact: Lynne Matallana, Dir.
Founded: 1997. **Description:** Promotes programs dedicated to improving the quality of life for individuals with fibromyalgia by increasing awareness of the disease in the public, media, governmental, and medical communities. **Computer Services:** Information services, fibromyalgia resources. **Telecommunication Services:** electronic mail, ssquires@fmaware.org. **Formerly:** National Fibromyalgia Awareness Campaign. **Publications:** *Fibromyalgia AWARE*, 3/year. Magazine. Contains comprehensive resource to improve the quality of life of those affected by fibromyalgia and overlapping conditions. **Price:** $35.00 three issues, in U.S.; $45.00 three issues, in Canada; $60.00 three issues, overseas ● *Fibromyalgia Online*, monthly. Newsletter. Contains fibromyalgia information resource. **Price:** free.

Alternate Formats: online. **Conventions/Meetings:** annual Fibromyalgia Awareness Day - meeting - always May 12.

14094 ■ National Fibromyalgia Partnership (NFP)
PO Box 160
Linden, VA 22642-0160
Free: (866)725-4404
Fax: (866)666-2727
E-mail: mail@fmpartnership.org
URL: http://www.fmpartnership.org
Contact: Russell Rothenberg MD, Chm.
Founded: 1992. **Membership Dues:** regular, in U.S., Canada and Mexico, $25 (annual) ● elsewhere, $30 (annual). **Description:** Provides medically accurate and current information on symptoms, diagnosis, treatment, and research on fibromyalgia. **Boards:** Medical Advisory. **Formerly:** Fibromyalgia Association of Greater Washington. **Publications:** *Fibromyalgia Frontiers*, quarterly. Journal. Features medically accurate articles. **Price:** included in membership dues ● *FM Monograph*. Booklet. Provides resource information on fibromyalgia. **Price:** included in membership dues. **Conventions/Meetings:** conference ● seminar.

Food

14095 ■ Partnership for Food Safety Education (PFSE)
655 15th St. NW, 7th Fl.
Washington, DC 20005
Ph: (202)220-0651
E-mail: info@fightbac.org
URL: http://www.fightbac.org
Contact: Shelley Feist, Exec. Dir.
Founded: 1997. **Members:** 20. **Languages:** English, Spanish. **Description:** Educates the public about safe food handling to reduce foodborne illness. **Telecommunication Services:** electronic mail, sfeist@fightbac.org.

Forensic Medicine

14096 ■ American Board of Forensic Anthropology (ABFA)
c/o Elizabeth A. Murray, PhD, Sec.
Coll. of Mount St. Joseph
Dept. of Biology
5701 Delhi Rd.
Cincinnati, OH 45233-1670
Ph: (513)244-4948
E-mail: elizabeth_murray@mail.msj.edu
URL: http://www.csuchico.edu/anth/ABFA
Contact: Elizabeth A. Murray PhD, Sec.
Founded: 1977. **Members:** 50. **Description:** Board for certification of physical anthropologists who wish to become forensic anthropologists. (Forensic anthropology refers to application of the science of physical anthropology in assistance of law enforcement agencies; forensic anthropologists identify and glean information from human remains.) Promotes improvement in the practice of forensic anthropology and encourages adherence to high standards in the field. Conducts written and practical examinations for prospective forensic anthropologists; awards certificates of qualification. Compiles statistics. **Committees:** Ethics; Examinations. **Affiliated With:** American Academy of Forensic Sciences. **Publications:** *Diplomates, American Board of Forensic Anthropology Directory*, annual. Contains listings of current diplomates in forensic anthropology. **Conventions/Meetings:** annual board meeting.

14097 ■ American Board of Forensic Odontology (ABFO)
c/o The Forensic Sciences Foundation
PO Box 669
Colorado Springs, CO 80901-0669
Ph: (719)636-1100
Fax: (719)636-1993

E-mail: frnscdds@aol.com
URL: http://www.abfo.org
Contact: Jack Kenney DDS, Pres.
Founded: 1976. **Description:** Works to establish, enhance, and revise as necessary, the standards of qualifications for those practicing forensic odontology and certify qualified specialists. **Conventions/Meetings:** annual meeting.

14098 ■ Milton Helpern Institute of Forensic Medicine (MHIFM)
Address Unknown since 2006
Founded: 1968. **Members:** 405. **Description:** Operated by New York University and the city of New York to strengthen teaching and research in forensic medicine and forensic pathology. Trains postgraduate students; sponsors symposia, seminars, lectures, and courses; conducts research projects and undertakes investigations and related studies of sudden, suspicious, and violent deaths. Maintains Milton Helpern Library of Legal Medicine. **Libraries: Type:** reference. **Holdings:** 100. **Subjects:** crime, criminology, forensic science, forensic medicine, forensic pathology, toxicology. **Formerly:** (1978) Institute of Forensic Medicine.

Forensic Sciences

14099 ■ American College of Forensic Psychology (ACFP)
PO Box 5870
Balboa Island
Newport Beach, CA 92662
Ph: (949)673-7773
Fax: (949)673-7710
E-mail: psychlaw@sover.net
URL: http://www.forensicpsychology.org
Contact: Debbie Miller, Exec. Dir.
Founded: 1983. **Membership Dues:** college, $210 (annual). **Description:** Offers continuing education to psychologists. Keeps forensic psychologists updated on important issues that lie within the interface of psychology and law. **Computer Services:** database, directory of forensic psychologists ● mailing lists, of members. **Boards:** Advisory. **Publications:** *American Journal of Forensic Psychology*, quarterly. Features issues on forensic skills and practices. **Price:** free for members. Alternate Formats: online.

Friedreich's Ataxia

14100 ■ Friedreich's Ataxia Research Alliance (FARA)
PO Box 1537
Springfield, VA 22151
Ph: (703)426-1576
Fax: (703)413-4467
E-mail: fara@faresearchalliance.org
URL: http://www.faresearchalliance.org
Contact: Ronald J. Bartek, Pres./Dir./Co-Founder
Founded: 1998. **Description:** Supports scientific research leading to treatments and cure for Friedreich's ataxia. Promotes scientific biomedical research and the collaborative exchange of information within the scientific community. Serves as a patient advocacy group to educate the public, elected representatives, and other government officials regarding Friedreich's ataxia and the importance of funding biomedical research. Works with government entities and the other organizations that support scientific research aimed at treatments for Friedreich's ataxia. **Publications:** Newsletter. Alternate Formats: online.

Gases

14101 ■ National Home Oxygen Patients Association (NHOPA)
8618 Westwood Center Dr., Ste.210
Vienna, VA 22182-2222
Free: (888)646-7244

E-mail: execoffice@homeoxygen.org
URL: http://www.homeoxygen.org
Contact: Phillip Porte, Exec. Dir.
Membership Dues: oxygen user, $15 (annual) ● field professional, $25 (annual) ● individual, $50 (annual) ● corporate, $100 (annual). **Description:** Aims to improve the lives of people who require supplementary oxygen on a regular basis. Serves as a clearinghouse of information regarding supplementary oxygen. Encourages its members to contact state and federal policy makers to provide appropriate patient input into the development of health policies that affect patients who require supplementary oxygen. Aims to conduct its own research pertaining to oxygen therapy. **Telecommunication Services:** electronic mail, phil@grqconsulting.com. **Publications:** *Airline Travel with Oxygen.* Brochure. Includes updates on specific airline requirements. **Price:** included in membership dues. Alternate Formats: online ● *News from NHOPA*, monthly. Newsletter. Contains information about the activities of the association and health and travel tips. **Price:** included in membership dues. Alternate Formats: online.

Gastroenterology

14102 ■ American College of Gastroenterology (ACG)
PO Box 342260
Bethesda, MD 20827-2260
Ph: (301)263-9000
E-mail: mediaonly@acg.gi.org
URL: http://www.acg.gi.org
Contact: David A. Johnson MD, Pres.
Founded: 1932. **Members:** 7,000. **Membership Dues:** resident/trainee, $25 (annual) ● regular, fellow, $250 (annual) ● international, $150 (annual). **Staff:** 10. **Multinational. Description:** Professional society of physicians and surgeons specializing in diseases and disorders of the gastrointestinal tract and accessory organs of digestion, including disorders due to nutrition. **Libraries: Type:** reference. **Holdings:** reports. **Formerly:** (1934) Society for the Advancement of Gastroenterology; (1954) National Gastroenterological Association. **Publications:** *American Journal of Gastroenterology*, monthly. **Price:** free for members; $305.00 /year for individuals in U.S.; $215.00/year for students in U.S. **Advertising:** accepted. Alternate Formats: online ● *Natural Clinical Practice and Gastroenterology and Hepatology*, monthly. Journal. **Price:** $129.00 /year for individuals in North America and $750.00 /year for institutions in North America. **Conventions/Meetings:** annual meeting, includes postgraduate course (exhibits) - always October. 2007 Oct. 12-17, Philadelphia, PA; 2008 Oct. 3-8, Orlando, FL; 2009 Oct. 23-28, San Diego, CA.

14103 ■ American Gastroenterological Association (AGA)
4930 Del Ray Ave.
Bethesda, MD 20814
Ph: (301)654-2055
Fax: (301)654-5920
E-mail: member@gastro.org
URL: http://www.gastro.org
Contact: Robert B. Greenberg JD, Exec. VP
Founded: 1897. **Members:** 13,500. **Membership Dues:** trainee (free in the first year), $95 (annual) ● physician/scientist in U.S., Canada and Mexico, $345 (annual) ● physician/scientist international, $400 (annual) ● GI mid-level provider, $215 (annual) ● GI nurse/allied health professional, $175 (annual) ● GI practice manager/administrator, $100-$150 (annual) ● corporate, $300 (annual). **Staff:** 70. **Budget:** $15,000,000. **Description:** Physicians of internal medicine certified in gastroenterology; radiologists, pathologists, surgeons, and physiologists with special interest and competency in gastroenterology. Studies normal and abnormal conditions of the digestive organs and problems connected with their metabolism; conducts scientific research; offers placement services. **Libraries: Type:** reference. **Holdings:** archival material, books, periodicals, reports.

Awards: Astra Zeneca Fellowship/Faculty Transition. **Frequency:** annual. **Type:** monetary. **Recipient:** for advanced fellow, usually in second full research year ● Castell. **Frequency:** annual. **Type:** recognition ● Centecor. **Frequency:** annual. **Type:** recognition ● Elsevier Research Initiative Award. **Type:** monetary. **Recipient:** for junior faculty, senior faculty, or established investigator ● Fiterman Clinical Research Award. **Frequency:** annual. **Type:** monetary. **Recipient:** for senior faculty or established investigator by nomination ● Funderberg Scholar Award. **Type:** monetary. **Recipient:** for junior faculty, senior faculty, or established investigator ● Research Scholar Award. **Frequency:** annual. **Type:** monetary. **Recipient:** for junior faculty ● Roche Junior Faculty. **Frequency:** annual. **Type:** recognition. **Recipient:** to young investigators ● Solray Award for Clinical Research in IBS/Motility. **Frequency:** annual. **Type:** monetary ● Student Research Fellowship Award. **Frequency:** annual. **Type:** fellowship. **Recipient:** for high school undergraduate, medical, and graduate students. **Computer Services:** Mailing lists. **Committees:** Audit; Clinical Practice and Economics; Education and Training; Ethics; Future Trends; International; Public Affairs and Advocacy; Research Policy. **Publications:** *AGA Perspective*, bimonthly. Magazine. Tackles controversial issues in the field of gastroenterology. **Price:** included in membership dues. ISSN: 1554-3366. **Advertising:** accepted. Alternate Formats: online ● *Clinical Gastroenterology and Hepatology*, monthly. Journal. Contains original research and solicited review articles. **Price:** $189.00 /year for individuals, plus shipping and handling; $95.00/year for students, plus shipping and handling; $323.00 /year for institutions in U.S.; $371.00 /year for institutions outside U.S. **Advertising:** accepted ● *eDigest*, weekly. Newsletter. Provides latest news in gastroenterology. **Advertising:** accepted. Alternate Formats: online ● *Gastroenterology*, monthly. Journal. **Price:** $383.00 /year for individuals, plus shipping and handling; $679.00 /year for institutions in U.S.; $864.00 /year for institutions outside U.S.; $143.00/ year for students, plus shipping and handling. ISSN: 0016-5085. **Circulation:** 18,000. **Advertising:** accepted ● *GI Practice Management News*, monthly. Newsletter. Provides members with current information about coding changes and government regulations and advice on how to successfully manage a practice. **Price:** free for members ● *Perspective*, bimonthly. Magazine. Offers late-breaking news, tips and practical information on healthy living through good digestive health and proper nutrition. **Price:** free for members; $19.95 /year for nonmembers. **Advertising:** accepted. **Conventions/Meetings:** annual Digestive Disease Week - meeting (exhibits).

14104 ■ American Motility Society (AMS)
45685 Harmony Ln.
Belleville, MI 48111
Ph: (734)699-1130
Fax: (734)699-1136
E-mail: admin@motilitysociety.org
URL: http://www.motilitysociety.org
Contact: Henry P. Parkman MD, Pres.
Founded: 1980. **Members:** 220. **Membership Dues:** trainee, $50 (annual) ● non-trainee, $125 (annual). **Description:** Professionals interested in the study of gastrointestinal (GI) motility. Promotes basic science and clinical research on the neural, humoral, and paracrine control of GI tract motility in health and disease. **Libraries: Type:** open to the public. **Holdings:** reports. **Committees:** Clinical Practice; Education; External Advisory; Fundraising; Investment; Nominating; Public Relations; Research. **Publications:** *Neurogastroenterology and Motility*. Magazine. **Price:** free for members ● *The Recorder*. Newsletter. **Price:** free for members. **Conventions/Meetings:** biennial symposium and conference.

14105 ■ American Partnership for Eosinophilic Disorders (APFED)
3419 Whispering Way Dr.
Richmond, TX 77469
Ph: (713)498-8216
E-mail: mail@apfed.org
URL: http://www.apfed.org
Contact: Elizabeth Mays, Pres./Founder
Founded: 2001. **Membership Dues:** household in U.S., $30 (annual) ● household in Canada, $45 (an-

nual) ● household - Europe, Australia, $55 (annual) ● professional affiliate in U.S., $100 (annual) ● professional affiliate in Canada, $125 (annual) ● professional affiliate - Europe, Australia, $150 (annual). **Description:** Offers support to patients and families coping with eosinophilic disorders. Creates awareness and understanding of eosinophilic disorders. Strives to raise funds in support of research concerning eosinophilic disorders. **Publications:** *EOSolutions*, quarterly. Newsletter. **Price:** included in membership dues.

14106 ■ American Society for Gastrointestinal Endoscopy (ASGE)
1520 Kensington Rd., Ste.202
Oak Brook, IL 60523
Ph: (630)573-0600
Free: (866)353-ASGE
Fax: (630)573-0691
E-mail: info@asge.org
URL: http://www.asge.org
Contact: Grace H. Elta MD, Exec. Dir.
Founded: 1941. **Members:** 7,500. **Membership Dues:** active, $270 (annual) ● international, $215 (annual) ● trainee, $25 (annual) ● associate, $40 (annual) ● affiliate, $250 (annual). **Staff:** 14. **Description:** Gastroenterologists, internists, and surgeons who perform gastroscopic, esophagoscopic, coloscopic, and peritoneoscopic examinations. Works to further the knowledge of digestive disease by endoscopic methods (visual inspection of the intestinal tract). **Libraries: Type:** reference. **Holdings:** reports. **Awards:** ASGE/ComEd Award. **Frequency:** annual. **Type:** recognition. **Recipient:** for outstanding manuscript ● ASGE Distinguished Educator Award. **Frequency:** annual. **Type:** recognition. **Recipient:** for an individual who has contributed to the teaching of endoscopy ● ASGE/Don Wilson Award. **Frequency:** annual. **Type:** recognition ● ASGE Master Endoscopist Award. **Frequency:** annual. **Type:** recognition ● Distinguished Service Award. **Frequency:** annual. **Type:** recognition. **Recipient:** for individuals who have unique contributions to the society and gastrointestinal endoscopy ● Endoscopic Career Development. **Frequency:** annual. **Type:** recognition. **Recipient:** for an individual who enhances the career development of investigators in endoscopy ● Endoscopic Research Award. **Frequency:** annual. **Type:** recognition. **Recipient:** for individuals who aim to foster research in gastrointestinal endoscopy ● Schindler Award. **Frequency:** annual. **Type:** recognition. **Recipient:** for an individual who has contributed the most to gastrointestinal endoscopy during the previous year. **Special Interest Groups:** Ambulatory Endoscopy Centers; Capsule Endoscopy; Endoscopic Ultrasound; Enteral Nutrition; Invention Innovation; Photodynamic Therapy. **Formerly:** American Gastroscopic Club; American Gastroscopic Society. **Publications:** *ASGE News*, bimonthly. Magazine. Includes member and specialty news. **Price:** included in membership dues. ISSN: 0016-5107. **Circulation:** 6,900. **Advertising:** accepted. Alternate Formats: online ● *Gastrointestinal Endoscopy*, bimonthly. Journal. Includes index, book reviews, case reports, and new materials and methods. **Price:** included in membership dues. ISSN: 0016-5107. **Advertising:** accepted. **Conventions/Meetings:** annual meeting (exhibits) - held during Digestive Disease Week in May ● annual Postgraduate Course - meeting.

14107 ■ Association of Gastrointestinal Motility Disorders (AGMD)
12 Roberts Dr.
Bedford, MA 01730
Ph: (781)275-1300
Fax: (781)275-1304
E-mail: gimotility@msn.com
URL: http://www.agmd-gimotility.org
Contact: Mary-Angela DeGrazia-DiTucci, Pres./CEO
Founded: 1991. **Members:** 550. **Membership Dues:** individual in U.S., $35 (annual) ● professional in U.S., $45 (annual) ● individual outside U.S., $42 (annual) ● professional outside U.S., $52 (annual). **Multinational. Description:** Serves as an integral educational resource concerning digestive motility disor-

ders. Also functions as an important information base for members of the medical community. **Libraries: Type:** lending; reference. **Holdings:** articles. **Computer Services:** database, background information regarding AGMD members who are interested in networking with other members. **Affiliated With:** Digestive Disease National Coalition; National Digestive Diseases Information Clearinghouse; National Organization for Rare Disorders. **Formerly:** (2000) American Society of Adults with Pseudo-Obstruction. **Publications:** *AGMD Beacon,* quarterly. Newsletter. Updates members about organization and medical alerts. **Price:** included in membership dues. **Advertising:** accepted ● *AGMD Digestive Motility Forum.* Newsletter. Includes a compilation of articles submitted by AGMD General members. ● *AGMD Digestive Motility Symposium Program Book and Course Materials,* annual. **Price:** $20.00. **Advertising:** accepted ● *AGMD GI Compass,* quarterly. Contains forum of articles by physicians, scientists and general members. **Price:** included in membership dues. **Advertising:** accepted ● *AGMD Search and Research,* quarterly. Newsletter. Poses questions from members and provides responses. ● Also publishes educational materials concerning digestive motility disorders and diseases. **Conventions/Meetings:** annual AGMD Digestive Motility Disorders Symposium, patients, physicians, nurses, pharmaceutical, and other members of the medical/scientific communities (exhibits).

14108 ■ Bockus International Society of Gastroenterology (BISG)
c/o David E. Bernstein, MD, Treas.
North Shore Univ. Hosp.
300 Community Dr.
Manhasset, NY 11030
Ph: (516)562-4281
Fax: (516)562-2683
E-mail: deberns@banet.net
URL: http://www.bockus.org
Contact: Michael V. Sivak Jr., Pres.
Founded: 1958. **Members:** 440. **Budget:** $5,000. **Multinational. Description:** Physicians in 22 countries specializing in gastroenterology (the study of the anatomy, physiology, and pathology of the stomach and intestines). Furthers scientific advances in gastroenterology worldwide. (The society is named for noted gastroenterologist H.L. Bockus of Philadelphia, PA.). **Committees:** Postgraduate Courses; Research. **Publications:** Proceedings, biennial. **Conventions/Meetings:** annual conference ● biennial Scientific Congress.

14109 ■ Celiac Disease Foundation (CDF)
13251 Ventura Blvd., No. 1
Studio City, CA 91604
Ph: (818)990-2354
Fax: (818)990-2379
E-mail: cdf@celiac.org
URL: http://www.celiac.org
Contact: Elaine Monarch, Exec. Dir.
Founded: 1990. **Membership Dues:** individual, $35 (annual). **Staff:** 2. **Languages:** English, Spanish. **Description:** Provides services and support for persons with Celiac Disease/Dermatitis Herpetiformis (CD/DH) through programs of education advocacy, and research; telephone information and referral services; medical advisory board; and special educational seminars and general meetings. (CD is a digestive disorder found in genetically susceptible individuals, in which the surface of the small intestine is damaged by the ingestion of food products containing proteins commonly known as gluten. Toxic glutens are found in all forms of wheat, rye, barley, and possibly oats.). **Libraries: Type:** reference. **Holdings:** clippings, periodicals. **Subjects:** celiac disease, dermatitis herpetiformis. **Publications:** *Celiac Disease Foundation Newsletter,* quarterly. Includes information about the disease, treatment, nutrition, food and drug updates, support articles, and recipes. **Price:** included in membership dues. **Advertising:** accepted. **Conventions/Meetings:** annual meeting, with specialized food vendors (exhibits) - every November.

14110 ■ Celiac Sprue Association/United States of America (CSA/USA)
PO Box 31700
Omaha, NE 68131-0700
Ph: (402)558-0600
Free: (877)CSA-4CSA
Fax: (402)643-4108
E-mail: celiacs@csaceliacs.org
URL: http://www.csaceliacs.org
Contact: Mary A. Schluckebier, Exec. Dir.
Founded: 1977. **Members:** 9,143. **Membership Dues:** individual, $33 (annual). **Staff:** 9. **Budget:** $700,000. **State Groups:** 10. **Local Groups:** 98. **Languages:** English, Spanish. **Description:** Individuals with the conditions of celiac sprue and dermatitis herpetiformis; parents of celiac children. (Celiac sprue is a genetic disorder resulting in digestive malabsorption of the protein portion of wheat, rye, and other cereal grains, causing symptoms such as intestinal lesions, diarrhea, vomiting, weight loss, and abdominal discomfort; dermatitis herpetiformis is a gluten-related skin disorder. Successful treatment usually calls for removing all gluten-containing cereal grains and their derivatives from the diet.) Serves as a vehicle for the provision of mutual support groups and facilitates interaction with other organizations involved in digestive disorders. Encourages and supports research on celiac disease. Disseminates educational materials on gluten-free foods and research on results; exchanges information on maintaining a gluten-free diet. **Libraries: Type:** reference. **Subjects:** celiac disease and dermatitis herpetiformis. **Formerly:** (1979) Midwestern Celiac Sprue Association. **Publications:** *Cookbooks for Diets Free of Cereal Grains* ● *Lifeline,* quarterly. Newsletter. Contains information, recipes, human-interest articles and other items of interest to those with CD/DH. **Price:** included in membership dues. **Circulation:** 10,000 ● Brochures ● Pamphlets. **Conventions/Meetings:** annual conference (exhibits) ● regional meeting.

14111 ■ Crohn's and Colitis Foundation of America (CCFA)
386 Park Ave. S, 17th Fl.
New York, NY 10016-8804
Ph: (212)685-3440
Free: (800)932-2423
Fax: (212)779-4098
E-mail: info@ccfa.org
URL: http://www.ccfa.org
Founded: 1967. **Members:** 60,000. **Membership Dues:** individual, $30 (annual) ● family, $60 (annual) ● supporter, $100 (annual) ● contributor, $250 (annual) ● patron, $500 (annual) ● benefactor, $1,000 (annual) ● premier physician, $400 (annual) ● participating physician, $300 (annual) ● healthcare professional, $150 (annual) ● group (minimum due: 250/professional), $1,000 (annual). **Staff:** 140. **Budget:** $25,000,000. **State Groups:** 42. **Local Groups:** 300. **Languages:** English, Spanish. **Description:** Supports research to find the cause and cure of Crohn's Disease (ileitis) and ulcerative colitis. Provides educational programs for patients, physicians, and the public, support groups, chapter newsletters, a national magazine, informational brochures and books, professional medical forums, and research publications, and a website. **Awards:** Research Fellowship. **Frequency:** semiannual. **Type:** fellowship. **Recipient:** for training ● Research Grant. **Frequency:** semiannual. **Type:** grant. **Recipient:** for research. **Computer Services:** database ● mailing lists. **Telecommunication Services:** hotline, (800)-343-3637, for request of free brochures about IBD and information about CCFA. **Committees:** Government Affairs; Grants Review; Professional and Patient Education; Research Initiatives; Research Training Awards; Scientific Advisory. **Formerly:** (1969) Foundation for Ileitis and Colitis; (1992) National Foundation for Ileitis and Colitis. **Publications:** *Inflammatory Bowel Diseases,* quarterly. Journal. **Price:** included in membership dues ● *Take Charge,* quarterly. Magazine. **Price:** included in membership dues ● *Under the Microscope,* semiannual. Newsletter. **Price:** included in membership dues ● Books. **Conventions/Meetings:** periodic conference ● workshop.

14112 ■ Cyclic Vomiting Syndrome Association (CVSA)
3585 Cedar Hill Rd. NW
Canal Winchester, OH 43110
Ph: (614)837-2586
Fax: (614)837-2586
E-mail: cvsa@cvsaonline.org
URL: http://www.cvsaonline.org
Founded: 1993. **Members:** 2,000. **Staff:** 1. **Languages:** English, French, German, Japanese, Spanish. **Multinational. Description:** Raises awareness and provides education and support to those affected by cyclic vomiting syndrome, abdominal migraine and related disorders while advocating for and funding research. CVS is an unexplained, often misdiagnosed disorder of children and adults. The condition is characterized by recurrent, prolonged attacks of severe nausea, vomiting and prostration with no apparent cause. Vomiting occurs at frequent intervals (5-10 times per hour at its peak) for hours up to 10 days (1-4 most common). The person returns to their normal health between episodes. **Computer Services:** database ● mailing lists ● online services. **Formerly:** (1999) Cyclic Vomiting Syndrome Association. **Publications:** Newsletter, quarterly. **Price:** available to members only.

14113 ■ Digestive Disease National Coalition (DDNC)
507 Capitol Ct. NE, Ste.200
Washington, DC 20002
Ph: (202)544-7497
Fax: (202)546-7105
E-mail: vyas@hmcw.org
URL: http://www.ddnc.org
Contact: Maurice Cerulli MD, Pres.
Founded: 1978. **Members:** 30. **Description:** Lay and professional medical organizations concerned with digestive diseases. Objectives are to: inform the public and the health care community about digestive diseases and related nutrition; seek federal funding for research, education, and training. Represents members' interests regarding federal and state legislation that affects digestive diseases research, health care, and education. **Formerly:** (1986) Coalition of Digestive Disease Organizations. **Conventions/Meetings:** semiannual meeting.

14114 ■ Foundation for Digestive Health and Nutrition (FDHN)
4930 Del Ray Ave.
Bethesda, MD 20814-3015
Ph: (301)222-4002
Free: (866)337-3346
Fax: (301)222-4010
E-mail: info@fdhn.org
URL: http://www.fdhn.org
Contact: James W. Freston MD, Chm.
Founded: 2001. **Staff:** 5. **Description:** Aims to be the largest source of funds for research and public education in digestive diseases. **Awards:** Bernard L. Schwartz Designated Research Award in Pancreatic Cancer. **Frequency:** annual. **Type:** grant. **Recipient:** for young investigators conducting pancreatic cancer research ● Designated Research Award in Research Related to Pancreatitis. **Frequency:** annual. **Type:** grant. **Recipient:** for young investigators conducting research with a focus in pancreatic disease ● Jon I. Isenberg International Research Scholar Award. **Frequency:** annual. **Type:** grant. **Recipient:** for young investigators outside US who want to perform GI-related research at an American institution under the tutelage of an AGA member ● TAP Endowed Designated Research Award in Acid-Related Diseases. **Frequency:** annual. **Type:** grant. **Recipient:** for young investigators conducting acid-related research. **Affiliated With:** American Gastroenterological Association. **Formerly:** (2001) American Digestive Health Foundation.

14115 ■ Gastro-Intestinal Research Foundation (GIRF)
70 E Lake St., Ste.1015
Chicago, IL 60601
Ph: (312)332-1350
Fax: (312)332-4757

E-mail: girf@girf.org
URL: http://www.girf.org
Contact: Joseph B. Kirsner MD, Contact

Founded: 1967. **Description:** Represents physician-clinicians and physician-scientists. Strives to solve the problems of digestive diseases. **Boards:** Associates; Women's. **Publications:** Newsletter, annual. Alternate Formats: online.

14116 ■ International Foundation for Functional Gastrointestinal Disorders (IFFGD)

PO Box 170864
Milwaukee, WI 53217
Ph: (414)964-1799
Free: (888)964-2001
Fax: (414)964-7176
E-mail: iffgd@iffgd.org
URL: http://www.iffgd.org
Contact: Ms. Audra Baade, Managing Ed.

Founded: 1991. **Description:** Informs, assists and supports people affected by gastrointestinal disorders. **Libraries: Type:** reference. **Holdings:** 120; articles. **Subjects:** irritable bowel syndrome, functional diarrhea, functional constipation, bloating and gas, abdominal, pelvic floor, or anorectal pain, esophageal disorders and GERD, gastroduodenal disorders, anorectal disorders, incontinence. **Awards:** Research Awards. **Frequency:** biennial. **Type:** recognition. **Recipient:** to active investigators who have a record of research interest in basic mechanism or clinical aspects of functional gastrointestinal and motility disorders. **Additional Websites:** http://www.aboutibs.org, http://www.aboutgerd.org. **Absorbed:** (2002) American Pseudo-Obstruction and Hirschsprung's Disease Society. **Publications:** *Digestive Health Matters*, quarterly. Offers state-of-the-art information about functional GI disorders.

14117 ■ International Society for Digestive Surgery (ISDS)

Univ. of Washington Medical Center
Box 356410, BB487
Seattle, WA 98195-6410
Ph: (206)543-3106
Fax: (206)685-6912
E-mail: pellegri@u.washington.edu
URL: http://www.isds-cicd.org
Contact: Carlos A. Pellegrini MD, Past Pres.

Founded: 1969. **Members:** 1,205. **Description:** Presents current information to the medical world concerning advances in gastrointestinal surgery, permits the free exchange of new knowledge, allows comparison of experiences, stimulates clinical studies, seeks improved diagnostic and therapeutic measures. **Publications:** *Digestive Surgery*, bimonthly. Journal. Contains information concerned with diseases of the alimentary tract. ● *Journal of Gastrointestinal Surgery*, 08Y. Helps the surgeon with the latest developments in gastrointestinal surgery. **Price:** $179.00/year. ISSN: 1091-255X. **Conventions/Meetings:** annual World Congress of Digestive Surgery.

14118 ■ Intestinal Disease Foundation

Address Unknown since 2007

Founded: 1986. **Members:** 1,200. **Membership Dues:** individual, $25 (annual) ● professional, $100 (annual). **Staff:** 2. **Budget:** $125,000. **Local Groups:** 1. **Description:** Works to improve the quality of life of adults and children affected by chronic digestive illness through information, guidance and support. These illnesses include inflammatory bowel disease (Crohn's disease and ulcerative colitis), diverticular disease, short-bowel syndrome, irritable bowel syndrome (IBS) and other functional gastrointestinal disorders. **Publications:** *Intestinal Fortitude*, quarterly. Newsletter. Provides most current information on medical and surgical treatments, coping techniques, and inspiration for living better with chronic illness. **Price:** free, for members only. **Circulation:** 3,000. **Advertising:** not accepted. **Conventions/Meetings:** quarterly seminar (exhibits).

14119 ■ National Digestive Diseases Information Clearinghouse (NDDIC)

2 Info. Way
Bethesda, MD 20892-3570
Free: (800)891-5389
Fax: (703)738-4929
E-mail: nddic@info.niddk.nih.gov
URL: http://digestive.niddk.nih.gov
Contact: Kathy Kranzfelder, Dir.

Founded: 1980. **Languages:** English, Spanish. **Non-membership. Description:** An information and referral service of the National Institute of Diabetes and Digestive and Kidney Diseases. Serves as a central information resource on the prevention and management of digestive diseases. Responds to written inquiries, develops and distributes publications about digestive diseases, and provides referrals to digestive disease organizations, including support groups. Maintains a database of patient and professional education materials, from which literature searches are generated. Provides bulk orders of publications to health and information professionals planning patient health education programs. **Convention/Meeting:** none. **Libraries: Type:** reference. **Holdings:** articles, audio recordings, video recordings. **Also Known As:** Digestive Diseases Clearinghouse. **Formerly:** (1985) National Digestive Diseases Education and Information Clearinghouse. **Publications:** *Age Page: Constipation* ● *Cirrhosis of the Liver* ● *Constipation* ● *Crohn's Disease* ● *Digestive Diseases Statistics* ● *Diverticulosis and Diverticulitis* ● *Facts and Fallacies About Digestive Diseases* ● *Gallstones* ● *Gas in the Digestive Tract* ● *Gastroesophageal Reflux Disease (Hiatal Hernia and Heartburn)* ● *Harmful Effects of Medicines on the Adult Digestive System* ● *Hemorrhoids* ● *Irritable Bowel Syndrome* ● *Lactose Intolerance* ● *Pancreatitis* ● *Smoking and Your Digestive System* ● *Stomach and Duodenal Ulcers* ● *Ulcerative Colitis* ● *Your Digestive System and How it Works*.

14120 ■ National Heartburn Alliance (NHA)

303 E Wacker Dr., Ste.440
Chicago, IL 60601
Free: (877)471-2081
E-mail: nhbainformation@heartburnalliance.org
URL: http://www.heartburnalliance.org
Contact: Timothy R. Covington MS, Chm.-Elect

Description: Aims to improve the quality of life of heartburn sufferers. Provides education about the causes and effects of heartburn. Develops and implements consumer outreach programs that reduce educational gaps. Raises the level of awareness and understanding of heartburn issues with the general public. **Publications:** *Get Heartburn Smart*. Brochure. Contains valuable self-care strategies. Alternate Formats: online ● Newsletter. **Price:** free. Alternate Formats: online.

14121 ■ North American Society for Pediatric Gastroenterology, Hepatology and Nutrition (NASPGHAN)

PO Box 6
Flourtown, PA 19031
Ph: (215)233-0808
Fax: (215)233-3918
E-mail: naspghan@naspghan.org
URL: http://www.naspghan.org
Contact: Margaret Stallings, Exec. Dir.

Founded: 1970. **Members:** 1,150. **Staff:** 3. **Description:** Aims to be a world leader in advancing the science and clinical practice of Pediatric Gastroenterology, Hepatology and Nutrition in health and disease. Strives to improve the care of infants, children and adolescents with digestive disorders by promoting advances in clinical care, research and education. Specializes in the care of children with chronic abdominal pain, diarrhea, constipation, vomiting, bleeding from the GI tract, inflammatory bowel disease, liver diseases, diseases of the pancreas, poor weight gain and nutritional problems by pediatric gastroenterologists. Works on: improving the digestive health and nutrition of children worldwide and particularly in North America; fostering dialogue and research on pertinent issues that impact the pediatric gastroenterology patient and their family; providing

opportunities for clinicians and researchers to gain knowledge of the scientific advances in the field; and disseminating scientific information in order to improve clinical outcomes and advance the practice of the field. **Awards: Type:** recognition ● Young Investigator. **Frequency:** annual. **Type:** recognition. **Recipient:** for submission of research abstract to annual meeting. **Committees:** Clinical Practice; Endoscopy and Procedure; Fellows; Hepatology; Nutrition; Public Education; Research; Training. **Formerly:** (1988) North American Society for Pediatric Gastroenterology. **Publications:** *Journal of Pediatric Gastroenterology and Nutrition*, 10/year. **Price:** $440.00 /year for individuals; $869.00 /year for institutions in U.S.; $928.00 /year for institutions outside U.S.; $230.00/ year for on-training. ISSN: 0277-2116 ● *NASPGHAN Newsletter*, quarterly ● Membership Directory, annual. **Conventions/Meetings:** annual conference (exhibits).

14122 ■ Paratuberculosis Awareness and Research Association (PARA)

PO Box 16219
Temple Terrace, FL 33687-6219
E-mail: nasers@mail.ucf.edu
URL: http://www.crohns.org
Contact: Dr. Saleh A. Naser, Contact

Founded: 1997. **Multinational. Description:** Seeks to eliminate Crohn's disease. Raises awareness of the disease caused by mycobacterium avium subspecies paratuberculosis (MAP). Addresses the control and eradication of paratuberculosis. Encourages government and medical research groups to make funding available for research on the role of MAP in Crohn's disease. Promotes clinical trials of therapy against mycobacterium avium subspecies paratuberculosis (MAP) as treatment for Crohn's disease.

14123 ■ Pediatric/Adolescent Gastroesophageal Reflux Association (PAGER)

PO Box 486
Buckeystown, MD 21717-0486
Ph: (301)601-9541
E-mail: gergroup@aol.com
URL: http://www.reflux.org
Contact: Beth Anderson, Exec. Dir.

Founded: 1992. **Members:** 5,000. **Staff:** 2. **Multinational. Description:** Seeks to gather and disseminate information on pediatric gastroesophageal reflux (GER) and related disorders; provides educational and emotional support to patients with GER, their families, and professionals; promotes awareness of GER within the medical community and the general public; promotes research into the causes, treatments and eventual cure for pediatric GER. **Publications:** *Reflux Digest*, quarterly. Newsletter. Includes research updates, practical information, family stories. **Price:** included in membership dues. ISSN: 1088-4939. **Advertising:** accepted. Alternate Formats: online.

14124 ■ Pull-thru Network (PTN)

2312 Savoy St.
Hoover, AL 35226-1528
Ph: (205)978-2930
E-mail: info@pullthrough.org
URL: http://www.pullthrough.org

Founded: 1988. **Members:** 550. **Membership Dues:** family, $30 (annual) ● professional, $100 (annual). **Staff:** 1. **Description:** Families, individuals, and professionals dedicated to children born with congenital defects of the lower intestine. Provides support to parents of children who've had or will have a "pull-through" type of surgery to correct a congenital defect such as imperforate anus, or Hirschsprung's disease, or any other conditions that may require an ostomy or cause bladder or bowel incontinence. Conducts educational programs. Affiliated with the United Ostomy Association. **Computer Services:** database, assisting members with networking based on a variety of criteria (diagnoses, child's age or gender, geographic area, etc.) ● online services, e-mail support group (listserv); message board and chat room on website. **Publications:** *Pull-Thru Network News*, quarterly. Newsletter. **Conventions/Meetings:** periodic regional meeting.

14125 ■ Society of American Gastrointestinal and Endoscopic Surgeons (SAGES)
11300 W Olympic Blvd., Ste.600
Los Angeles, CA 90064
Ph: (310)437-0544
Fax: (310)437-0585
E-mail: sagesweb@sages.org
URL: http://www.sages.org
Contact: Sallie Matthews, Exec. Dir.
Founded: 1980. **Members:** 5,000. **Membership Dues:** active, $250 (annual) ● candidate, $60 (annual) ● international, $250 (annual). **Staff:** 14. **Budget:** $2,500,000. **Multinational. Description:** Surgeons who perform gastrointestinal endoscopy and laparoscopy. Promotes the concepts of gastrointestinal endoscopy as an integral part of surgery and encourages academic, clinical, and research achievements in the field. Establishes standards of training and practice and guidelines for privileging. Provides a forum for the exchange of ideas on gastrointestinal endoscopy and related sciences. Conducts scientific studies. **Libraries: Type:** reference. **Holdings:** books, video recordings. **Computer Services:** Mailing lists, service. **Committees:** Awards; Bariatric; By-Laws; Continuing Education; Development; Educational Resources; Ethics; Finance; Flexible Endoscopy; Guidelines; International Relations; Legislative Review; Membership; Nominating; Program; Public Information; Publications; Research; Resident Education; Technology Assessment. **Publications:** *Surgical Endoscopy*, monthly. Journal. Contains information on Surgical Endoscopy. **Price:** $135.00/year. ISSN: 0930-2794. **Advertising:** accepted ● Also publishes numerous guidelines on Gastrointestinal Endoscopic Surgery, privileging and standards of practice. **Conventions/Meetings:** annual conference (exhibits) - March or April. 2008 Apr. 9-12, Philadelphia, PA - **Avg. Attendance:** 1500; 2009 Apr. 22-25, Phoenix, AZ - **Avg. Attendance:** 1500.

14126 ■ Society of Gastroenterology Nurses and Associates (SGNA)
3943 Paysphere Cir.
Chicago, IL 60674
Ph: (312)321-5165
Free: (800)245-7462
Fax: (312)673-6694
E-mail: sgna@smithbucklin.com
URL: http://www.sgna.org
Contact: Mary Beth Hepp, Exec. Dir.
Founded: 1974. **Members:** 6,000. **Membership Dues:** voting, $105 (annual) ● non-voting, $90 (annual). **Staff:** 12. **Regional Groups:** 60. **Description:** Aims to unite personnel engaged in the field of gastroenterology/endoscopy in order to promote the highest professional standards for gastroenterology nurses and associates. Conducts national and regional educational courses and research programs. Cooperates with other professional associations, hospitals, universities, industries, technical societies, research organizations, and governmental agencies. **Awards:** Distinguished Service Award. **Frequency:** annual. **Type:** recognition. **Recipient:** for significant contributions to the association ● Gabriele Schindler Clinical Excellence Award. **Frequency:** annual. **Type:** recognition. **Recipient:** for contributions in direct patient care ● Outstanding Regional Society Award. **Frequency:** annual. **Type:** recognition. **Recipient:** for most active and dynamic regional society ● Regional Society Member of the Year Award. **Frequency:** annual. **Type:** recognition. **Recipient:** for a member who has made positive impact. **Committees:** Education; Practice. **Formerly:** (1989) Society of Gastrointestinal Assistants. **Publications:** *Gastroenterology Nursing*, bimonthly. Journal. Includes subject and author indexes, book reviews, new product information. **Price:** $52.00 /year for individuals; $80.00 /year for institutions; $25.00/year for students; $15.00/copy. ISSN: 0744-1128. **Advertising:** accepted. Alternate Formats: microform ● *Gastroenterology Nursing - A Core Curriculum* ● *Job Description Handbook* ● *Manual of Gastrointestinal Procedures* ● *Pediatric Supplement* ● *Pulmonary*

Supplement ● *SGNA News*, bimonthly. Newsletter. Contains regional directory, regional news, and articles on research and finance. **Price:** free for members. **Conventions/Meetings:** annual meeting (exhibits).

Gay/Lesbian

14127 ■ Fenway Community Health Center
7 Haviland St.
Boston, MA 02115-2608
Ph: (617)267-0900
Free: (888)242-0900
E-mail: information@fenwayhealth.org
URL: http://www.fenwayhealth.org
Contact: Stephen L. Boswell MD, Pres./CEO
Description: Strives to treat every client as a whole and unique person to receive the best health care available, including HIV prevention, treatment, and research; women's health, particularly understanding the needs of lesbians; and the health care needs of gays and lesbians.

14128 ■ Gay and Lesbian Medical Association (GLMA)
459 Fulton St., Ste.107
San Francisco, CA 94102
Ph: (415)255-4547
Fax: (415)255-4784
E-mail: info@glma.org
URL: http://www.glma.org
Contact: Joel Ginsberg JD/MBA, Interim Exec. Dir.
Founded: 1981. **Members:** 2,000. **Membership Dues:** independent practitioner, $295 (annual) ● household, $500 (annual) ● mid-level provider, $200 (annual) ● health-related professional, $150 (annual) ● first year practitioner, $100 (annual) ● student, friend, $40 (annual) ● retired, disabled, $75 (annual). **Staff:** 10. **Budget:** $1,200,000. **Description:** Health-care professionals. Seeks elimination of discrimination on the basis of gender identity and sexual orientation in the health profession; promotes unprejudiced medical care for LGBT patients through advocacy and education. Maintains a referral and support program for HIV infected health care workers. Sponsors annual continuing medical education (CME, CEU) symposium on LGBT issues. Offers support to lesbian, gay, bisexual, and transgendered health care workers; encourages research into the health needs of gays and lesbians. Maintains liaison with medical schools and other organizations concerning needs of gay patients and professionals; fosters communication and cooperation among members and other groups and individuals supportive of gay and lesbian physicians. Sponsors Lesbian Health Fund for researching lesbian health needs. **Libraries: Type:** reference. **Holdings:** biographical archives, reports. **Awards:** Achievement Awards. **Frequency:** annual. **Type:** recognition. **Computer Services:** Online services, National Health Care Referral Service. **Telecommunication Services:** electronic mail, jginsberg@glma.org. **Task Forces:** AIDS; Lesbian Health Research. **Formerly:** American Association of Physicians for Human Rights. **Publications:** *GLMA Report*, quarterly. Newsletter. Covers the activities of the association, the medical community, and the public regarding lesbian and gay health issues. **Price:** free, for members only. **Circulation:** 4,000. **Advertising:** accepted. **Conventions/Meetings:** annual conference and symposium.

14129 ■ Lesbian Health Fund (LHF)
c/o Gay and Lesbian Medical Association
459 Fulton St., Ste.107
San Francisco, CA 94102
Ph: (415)255-4547
Fax: (415)255-4784
E-mail: info@glma.org
URL: http://www.glma.org
Contact: Jason Schneider MD, Pres.-Elect
Founded: 1992. **Multinational. Description:** Works to recognize the unique healthcare needs of lesbians; and seeks to strengthen the health of lesbians and their families through health and medical research

grants and education. **Awards:** Lesbian Health Research Grant. **Frequency:** semiannual. **Type:** grant. **Affiliated With:** Gay and Lesbian Medical Association.

14130 ■ Mautner Project for Lesbian Health
1707 L St. NW, Ste.230
Washington, DC 20036
Ph: (202)332-5536
Free: (866)628-8637
Fax: (202)332-0662
E-mail: mautner@mautnerproject.org
URL: http://www.mautnerproject.org/home/index.cfm
Contact: Kathleen DeBold, Exec. Dir.
Founded: 1990. **Members:** 12,000. **Staff:** 11. **Budget:** $1,185,700. **Description:** Improves the health of lesbians and their families through advocacy, research, and direct services, and envisions a health-care system guided by social justice and responsiveness to the needs of all people. **Programs:** Advocacy; Family Services; Outreach and Health Education; Research; Resources and Referrals; Support Services; Training and Technical Assistance. **Formerly:** (2004) Mautner Project for Lesbians with Cancer. **Publications:** Newsletter, quarterly. **Price:** free. Alternate Formats: online ● Booklets. **Conventions/Meetings:** annual Gala, Dinner, Dance and Auction.

14131 ■ National Association for Research and Therapy of Homosexuality (NARTH)
16633 Ventura Blvd., Ste.1340
Encino, CA 91436-1801
Ph: (818)789-4440
Fax: (818)786-6452
E-mail: nationalarth@yahoo.com
URL: http://www.narth.com
Contact: Joseph J. Nicolosi PhD, Pres.
Founded: 1992. **Members:** 1,000. **Membership Dues:** student (add $15 for foreign), $10 (annual) ● general/research/academic/clinical (add $15 for foreign), $50 (annual) ● organizational (add $15 for foreign), $100 (annual). **Staff:** 3. **Budget:** $150,000. **Description:** Mental health care providers, religious leaders, educators, and other individuals with an interest in the study of homosexuality. Investigates the causes and treatment of homosexuality, conducts research and educational programs, and maintains referral service for individuals seeking therapy to overcome homosexuality. **Libraries: Type:** reference; not open to the public. **Holdings:** 500. **Subjects:** homosexuality. **Awards:** Fellow of NARTH. **Frequency:** annual. **Type:** fellowship. **Recipient:** for significant contributions to the understanding of homosexuality from a psychological and/or scientific point of view ● Freud Award. **Type:** recognition. **Formerly:** (2003) National Association for the Research and Treatment of Homosexuality. **Publications:** *Collected Conference Papers*, annual. Proceedings. **Price:** $15.00 ● *NARTH Bulletin*, 3/year. Magazine. **Price:** $5.00 for nonmembers; included in membership dues. **Circulation:** 1,000 ● *NARTH's "Understanding Homosexuality"*. Booklet. **Conventions/Meetings:** annual conference.

Genetic Disorders

14132 ■ A-T Medical Research Foundation (A-TMRF)
5241 Round Meadow Rd.
Hidden Hills, CA 91302
Ph: (818)703-0151 (818)704-8146
Fax: (818)703-8310
E-mail: becca4435@aol.com
URL: http://www.gspartners.com
Contact: George A. Smith, Pres.
Founded: 1989. **Budget:** $300,000. **Description:** Works to fund medical research to find a cure for Ataxia-Telangiectasia (A-T), a degenerative genetic disease of the nervous system. Sponsors pioneering research as well as advanced work. **Libraries: Type:** reference. **Holdings:** articles, clippings. **Subjects:** ataxia-telangiectasia research. **Awards: Type:** grant. **Recipient:** to support research. **Additional Websites:** http://www.pathology.ucla.edu/department/per-

dir/people/faculty/gatti/gatfound.htm.. **Publications:** Newsletter, annual. **Circulation:** 3,000. Alternate Formats: online. **Conventions/Meetings:** workshop - every 3 to 4 years.

14133 ■ Aicardi Syndrome Newsletter

c/o Denise Park Parsons
1510 Polo Fields Ct.
Louisville, KY 40245
Ph: (502)244-9152
E-mail: newsletter@aicardisyndrome.org
URL: http://www.aicardisyndrome.org
Contact: Denise Park Parsons, Contact

Founded: 1983. **Members:** 200. **Membership Dues:** family, $25 (annual). **Staff:** 2. **Regional Groups:** 6. **National Groups:** 5. **Multinational. Description:** Families with daughters affected by Aicardi Syndrome (Aicardi Syndrome is a rare genetic disorder affecting females only; and characterized by absence of the corpus callosum,. and retinal lesions, seizures, and mental retardation. Provides information, research opportunities, networking, and communication. Acts as a reference and resource contact for medical, educational, and professional organizations. Conducts research programs. **Libraries: Type:** not open to the public; reference. **Holdings:** articles, books, business records, clippings, periodicals. **Subjects:** Aicardi syndrome and other disability/rare disorders. **Affiliated With:** National Organization for Rare Disorders. **Publications:** *ASN Brief,* bimonthly. Newsletter ● Brochure ● Directory. **Conventions/Meetings:** biennial Aicardi Syndrome Family Conference, for families with affected daughters (exhibits).

14134 ■ Alagille Syndrome Alliance (ASA)

c/o Cindy L. Hahn, Pres.
10500 SW Starr Dr.
Tualatin, OR 97062
Ph: (503)885-0455
E-mail: alagille@alagille.org
URL: http://www.alagille.org
Contact: Cindy L. Hahn, Pres.

Founded: 1993. **Nonmembership. Description:** Works to provide a support network for family, friends and healthcare providers as well as children and adults with Alagille Syndrome, a liver disorder affecting the bile ducts and/or the pulmonary arteries, heart and lungs, spinal column, eyes, facial features and less frequently, the pancreas, renal system and arteries in the brain. **Computer Services:** database, parent to parent matching ● mailing lists. **Publications:** *Fact Sheet* ● *Links4Life,* quarterly. Newsletter. **Circulation:** 700 ● Brochure. **Conventions/Meetings:** triennial International Symposium on Alagille Syndrome - conference.

14135 ■ Alpha 1 Foundation

2937 SW 27th Ave., Ste.302
Miami, FL 33133
,Ph: (305)567-9888
Free: (877)228-7321
Fax: (305)567-1317
E-mail: rplant@alphaone.org
URL: http://www.alphaone.org
Contact: John W. Walsh, Pres./CEO

Founded: 1995. **Languages:** English, German, Spanish. **Description:** Strives to provide leadership and resources that will result in increased research, improved health, worldwide detection and a cure for Alpha1-Antitrypsin Deficiency (Alpha-1). Supports research for the cure of Alpha-1 through grant award programs, research registry, DNA and tissue bank, and various programs.

14136 ■ Alstrom Syndrome International (ASI)

14 Whitney Farm Rd.
Mount Desert, ME 04660
Ph: (207)288-6385 (207)244-7043
Free: (800)371-3628
Fax: (207)288-6078

E-mail: jdm@jax.org
URL: http://www.jax.org/alstrom
Contact: Jan D. Marshall, Chm.

Founded: 1995. **Staff:** 10. **Budget:** $90,000. **Languages:** English, French, Italian, Portuguese, Spanish. **Nonmembership. Multinational. Description:** Individuals with Alstrom's syndrome (a genetic disorder resulting in multiple organ failures) and their families; health care professionals with an interest in the syndrome and its diagnosis and treatment. Seeks to improve the quality of life of people with Alstrom's syndrome. Serves as a clearinghouse on the syndrome and its treatment; functions as a support group for people with Alstrom's syndrome and their families. Encourages and fosters genetic and clinical research on Alstrom Syndrome. **Libraries: Type:** not open to the public. **Holdings:** 100. **Subjects:** Alstrom Syndrome. **Computer Services:** database. **Affiliated With:** Genetic Alliance; National Organization for Rare Disorders. **Formerly:** (2002) International Society for Alstrom Syndrome Families. **Publications:** *The Alstrom Syndrome Handbook* ● *The Alstrom Syndrome Newsletter,* 3/year. **Conventions/Meetings:** Family Conference ● Scientific Congress.

14137 ■ Beckwith-Wiedemann Support Network (BWSN)

c/o Bruce Beckwith, MD
88 Brookside
Missoula, MT 59802
E-mail: bwsn@beckwith-weidemann.org
URL: http://www.beckwith-wiedemann.org
Contact: Bruce Beckwith MD, Contact

Founded: 1989. **Members:** 500. **Membership Dues:** individual, $20 (annual). **Staff:** 4. **Description:** Patients with Beckwith-Wiedemann Syndrome and their families; health care professionals; interested others. Works to provide information and peer support to individuals and families affected by Beckwith-Wiedemann Syndrome (BWS). (BWS is a congenital growth-related disorder. Patients are at risk for developing hypoglycemia and various tumors.) Seeks to increase public and professional awareness of BWS. Encourages research on the cause, early detection, and treatment of BWS as well as Simpson Golabi-Belomel Syndrome. **Computer Services:** database, for matching families with children who have BWS. **Publications:** *Beckwith Wiedemann Support Network Newsletter,* 3/year. **Price:** included in membership dues ● *Family Directory for Parent Members* ● *What Is Beckwith-Wiedemann Syndrome.* Brochure. **Conventions/Meetings:** biennial conference - usually in June.

14138 ■ Chromosome 9P Network (9P)

PO Box 54
Stanley, ID 83278-0054
Ph: (435)574-1121
E-mail: pduffy006@verizon.net
URL: http://www.9pminus.org
Contact: Beverly Udell, Contact

Founded: 1984. **Members:** 210. **Budget:** $40,000. **Multinational. Description:** Parents and caregivers of children that have Monosomy 9P (also known as 9P-; Alfi's Syndrome; Ring 9; 9PDeletion; Trisomy 9P). Monosomy 9P is a rare chromosome disorder in which a piece of the 9th chromosome pair is broken off. It results in mental retardation,. low muscle tone, possible physical deformities, and sometimes triganocephaly of the forehead. Acts as a clearinghouse for information on the disorder. Offers support to families. Maintains a roster of families having a child with Monosomy 9P. Partakes in research, and holds an annual conference. **Formerly:** (1999) Support Groups for Monosomy 9P. **Publications:** Newsletter, quarterly ● Brochures. **Conventions/Meetings:** annual Family Gathering - meeting, researchers (exhibits).

14139 ■ Chromosome 18 Registry and Research Society

7155 Oakridge Dr.
San Antonio, TX 78229
Ph: (210)657-4968
Fax: (210)657-4968

E-mail: office@chromosome18.org
URL: http://www.chromosome18.org
Contact: Claudia Traa, Exec. Dir.

Founded: 1990. **Members:** 500. **Membership Dues:** regular, in U.S., $20 (annual) ● regular, outside U.S., $25 (annual). **Staff:** 2. **Regional Groups:** 12. **Multinational. Description:** Individuals with the chromosome 18 disorder, their families, and physicians. (Chromosome 18 anomalies cover a wide range of disorders, including: Trisomy 18, 18q-, 18p-, and Ring 18.) Aims to: locate persons with chromosome 18 anomalies; educate the families, as well as the public about the prognoses and treatments of these disorders; encourage, conduct, and publish research into areas that impact these families; and link affected families and their physicians to the research community. Offers educational programs. **Publications:** *Chromosome 18 Communique,* quarterly. Newsletter ● Brochure. **Conventions/Meetings:** annual conference.

14140 ■ Chromosome Deletion Outreach (CDO)

PO Box 724
Boca Raton, FL 33429-0724
Ph: (561)395-4252
E-mail: info@chromodisorder.org
URL: http://www.chromodisorder.org
Contact: Linda Sorg, Pres.

Founded: 1992. **Members:** 2,000. **Multinational. Description:** Promotes research and understanding of chromosome disorders, including partial duplications (trisomies), inversions, translocations, rings and sex chromosome disorders; provides support to families of children born with these rare disorders; gathers and disseminates information; promotes research and a positive community understanding of these disorders. **Libraries: Type:** open to the public. **Holdings:** articles. **Subjects:** rare chromo disorders. **Computer Services:** Mailing lists. **Telecommunication Services:** electronic bulletin board. **Publications:** Newsletter, quarterly. Contains articles submitted by members and a column offering advice from doctors. **Price:** free for members; $10.00 /year for nonmembers. **Circulation:** 500. Alternate Formats: online.

14141 ■ Coalition For Heritable Disorders Of Connective Tissue (CHDCT)

4301 Connecticut Ave. NW, Ste.404
Washington, DC 20008
Ph: (202)362-9599
Fax: (202)966-8553
E-mail: chdct@pxe.org
URL: http://www.chdct.org
Contact: Sharon Terry MA, Co-Pres.

Founded: 1989. **Description:** Strives to bring about greater awareness of heritable disorders of connective tissue in the medical professions and in the public; encourages teaching about these conditions in medical schools; encourages the training of health practitioners to identify, diagnose and treat various heritable connective tissue disorders; fosters research.

14142 ■ Coffin-Lowry Syndrome Foundation (CLSF)

3045 255th Ave. SE
Sammamish, WA 98075
Ph: (425)427-0939
E-mail: clsfoundation@yahoo.com
URL: http://www.clsf.info
Contact: Mary Hoffman, Chair

Founded: 1991. **Multinational. Description:** Serves as a clearinghouse for information on Coffin-Lowry Syndrome. (CLS is an inherited syndrome causing retardation, developmental delay, dysmorphic features, and skeletal anomalies.) Offers support services for families dealing with CLS. **Libraries: Type:** reference. **Computer Services:** database ● mailing lists. **Publications:** *CLSF News,* monthly. Newsletter. **Price:** free.

14143 ■ Cri du Chat Syndrome Mutual Help Group
c/o Dr. Robert F. Clarke, PhD
10640 SW 129th Ct.
Miami, FL 33186
Ph: (305)382-1952
Fax: (305)382-1952
Contact: Dr. Robert F. Clarke PhD, Contact
Founded: 1997. **Membership Dues:** $15 (annual). **Staff:** 5. **Budget:** $500. **Regional Groups:** 12. **State Groups:** 1. **Local Groups:** 1. **Languages:** English, Spanish. **Description:** Family members of people with Cri du Chat Syndrome, a genetic disorder usually resulting in profound mental retardation. Promotes understanding of the syndrome and its manifestations. Facilitates communication and mutual support among members; conducts educational programs; makes available children's services. **Libraries: Type:** not open to the public. **Holdings:** books, periodicals. **Subjects:** Cri du Chat Syndrome. **Publications:** *Cri du Chat Newsletter*, periodic. **Price:** included in membership dues.

14144 ■ Disorders of Chromosome 16 Foundation (DOC16)
c/o Alex Schaeffel
331 Haddon Cir.
Vernon Hills, IL 60061
E-mail: danalex@avalon.net
URL: http://www.trisomy16.org
Contact: Karen Lange MS, Pres.
Multinational. Description: Promotes research into Disorders of Chromosome 16 and provides information on abnormalities; offers information, education, and support to families of children living with the disorder and to expectant parents confronting a similar diagnosis; serves as a resource aiding families, friends, caregivers, and medical professionals in their supportive roles. Provides referrals and a database of registered families. **Publications:** Newsletter, quarterly.

14145 ■ Fanconi Anemia Research Fund (FARF)
1801 Willamette St., Ste.200
Eugene, OR 97401
Ph: (541)687-4658
Free: (888)326-2664
Fax: (541)687-0548
E-mail: info@fanconi.org
URL: http://www.fanconi.org
Contact: Mary Ellen Eiler, Exec. Dir.
Founded: 1989. **Members:** 2,000. **Staff:** 4. **Budget:** $1,100,000. **National Groups:** 13. **Languages:** English, Spanish. **Description:** Aims to find effective treatments and a cure for Fanconi anemia and to provide education and support services to affected families worldwide. **Awards: Type:** grant. **Boards:** Directors; Scientific Advisory. **Formerly:** (1989) Fanconi's Anemia Support Group. **Publications:** *FA Family Directory*, annual. **Price:** $5.00 in U.S.; $7.00 all other countries ● *FA Family Newsletter*, semiannual. Alternate Formats: online ● *Fanconi Anemia: A Handbook for Families and Their Physicians* (in English, French, and Spanish). Alternate Formats: online ● *Fanconi Anemia Standards for Clinical Care*. Handbook. Alternate Formats: online ● *Science Letter*, periodic. Newsletter. **Conventions/Meetings:** annual Family Meeting ● annual Scientific Symposium.

14146 ■ Floating Harbor Syndrome Support Group of North America
160 Guild St. NE
Grand Rapids, MI 49505
E-mail: floatingharbor@sbcglobal.net
URL: http://www.geocities.com/floatingharbor@sbcglobal.net/floating_harbor.html
Contact: Deana Swanson, Contact
Multinational. Description: Provides information about the Floating Harbor Syndrome. Seeks to help others find a diagnosis and treatment for the syndrome. Offers support and solutions in dealing with kids who have Floating Harbor Syndrome. **Telecommunication Services:** electronic mail, floatingharbor@sbcglobal.com.

14147 ■ Foundation for Nager and Miller Syndromes (FNMS)
c/o DeDe Van Quill, Dir.
13210 SE 342nd St.
Auburn, WA 98092
Ph: (253)333-1483
Free: (800)507-3667
Fax: (253)288-7679
E-mail: ddfnms@aol.com
URL: http://www.fnms.net
Contact: DeDe Van Quill, Dir.
Founded: 1989. **Membership Dues:** family, $10 (annual). **Staff:** 2. **Description:** Families affected by Nager or Miller Syndromes, and interested individuals. (Nager syndrome is characterized by underdevelopment of the cheeks and lower jaw, and other craniofacial abnormalities; Miller syndrome is characterized by limb anomalies and craniofacial deformities including cleft palate and slanted lower eyelids.) Provides support to those affected by these rare genetic conditions. Seeks to increase awareness of the syndromes, and disseminates information to professionals, laypeople, and hospitals. Encourages the development of research and diagnostic testing procedures. Meetings/conventions usually held biannually. **Libraries: Type:** lending. **Holdings:** 55; archival material, articles, audio recordings, books, video recordings. **Subjects:** medical information, syndrome specific information, self esteem, bullying-teasing, inspiration, education, coping. **Telecommunication Services:** electronic bulletin board, membership may post messages and questions for review. **Publications:** *All About Us*, annual. Newsletter. Includes resource list, helpful hints, biographical information, research updates, articles on Nager/Miller Syndromes, and book reviews. **Price:** free. **Circulation:** 960. **Advertising:** accepted. Alternate Formats: online.

14148 ■ Hermansky-Pudlak Syndrome Network
1 South Rd.
Oyster Bay, NY 11771-1905
Ph: (516)922-3440
Free: (800)789-9HPS
Fax: (516)922-4022
E-mail: hpsnet@worldnet.att.net
URL: http://www.hpsnetwork.org
Contact: Donna Jean Appell, Founder/Pres.
Founded: 1992. **Languages:** English, Spanish. **Multinational. Description:** Networks individuals, families, and doctors for the purpose of education and research into Hermansky-Pudlak Syndrome, a genetic metabolic disorder causing albinism, visual impairment, platelet dysfunction, pulmonary fibrosis, inflammatory bowel disease, and kidney disease. **Additional Websites:** http://www.hermansky-pudlak.org. **Conventions/Meetings:** annual Family Conference.

14149 ■ HHT Foundation International
PO Box 329
Monkton, MD 21111
Ph: (410)357-9932
Free: (800)448-6389
Fax: (410)357-9931
E-mail: hhtinfo@hht.org
URL: http://www.hht.org
Contact: Ms. Marianne Clancy, Exec. Dir.
Founded: 1991. **Members:** 300. **Membership Dues:** donor, $45 ● friend, $50 ● supporter, $75 ● sponsor, $100 ● patron, $250 ● benefactor, $500 ● President's Club, $1,000 ● Doctor's Circle, $5,000. **Regional Groups:** 3. **State Groups:** 3. **Description:** Patients and their families; physicians, counselors, and health administrators; interested others. Promotes research into the treatment, causes, and cure of Hereditary Hemorrhagic Telangiectasia (HHT), also known as Osler-Weber-Rendu Syndrome. A rare genetic blood vessel disorder, HHT causes malformations of arteries and veins; hemorrhaging from the nose and intestine is also common. Malformations in the lungs cause shortness of breath, stroke, and brain abscess. Provides information exchange. Raises funds for research and patient service programs. Sponsors support groups. **Publications:** *Direct Connection*.

Newsletter. Alternate Formats: online ● *HHT Newsletter*, quarterly ● *Our Blood Vessels*. Pamphlet ● Brochures ● Newsletter, semiannual. **Conventions/Meetings:** annual conference.

14150 ■ Incontinentia Pigmenti International Foundation (IPIF)
c/o Susanne Bross Emmerich, Founder/Exec. Dir.
30 E 72nd St.
New York, NY 10021
Ph: (212)452-1231
Fax: (212)452-1406
E-mail: ipif@ipif.org
URL: http://imgen.bcm.tmc.edu/IPIF
Contact: Susanne Bross Emmerich, Founder/Exec. Dir.
Founded: 1995. **Languages:** Dutch, English, French, Italian, Portuguese, Spanish. **Multinational. Description:** Patients, physicians, educators, parents, relatives, volunteers. Strives to support research, education and funding for Incontinentia Pigmenti; provides family support and education; seeks to develop accurate and safe prenatal diagnostic testing; and develop database to assess clinical variation, natural history, and prognostic indicators. **Computer Services:** Information services, Incontinentia Pigmenti resources. **Affiliated With:** Genetic Alliance; National Organization for Rare Disorders. **Formerly:** (2003) National Incontinentia Pigmenti Foundation. **Publications:** Newsletter, annual. Alternate Formats: online ● Reports.

14151 ■ International Federation of Marfan Syndrome Organizations (IFMSO)
c/o National Marfan Foundation
22 Manhassett Ave.
Port Washington, NY 11050
E-mail: cilla71@aol.com
URL: http://www.marfanworld.org
Contact: Priscilla Ciccariello, Pres.
Founded: 1992. **Multinational. Description:** Shares current information about the Marfan syndrome worldwide. Facilitates international communication among medical professionals and the general public. Establishes standards for diagnosis and treatment of the Marfan syndrome. Supports and fosters research throughout the world. Facilitates communication with research centers and researchers worldwide. **Publications:** *Marfanworld E-News*. Newsletter. Alternate Formats: online.

14152 ■ International Fibrodysplasia Ossificans Progressiva Association (IFOPA)
PO Box 196217
Winter Springs, FL 32719-6217
Ph: (407)365-4194
Fax: (407)365-3213
E-mail: together@ifopa.org
URL: http://www.ifopa.org
Contact: Linda Daugherty, Exec. Dir.
Founded: 1988. **Members:** 387. **Membership Dues:** general, $25 (annual). **Staff:** 4. **Budget:** $50,000. **Description:** Individuals affected by FOP, their families and friends, and health care professionals. (FOP, also known as fibrodysplasia ossificans progressiva, is a rare genetic disorder in which normal bone is produced in abnormal locations, causing joints to become rigid and immobile. Onset usually occurs during childhood and may eventuate in the complete immobilization of nearly every joint in the body. The cause is currently unknown.) Provides support services to those affected by FOP, including medical resources. Encourages and funds medical research into causes of FOP and other bone-related disorders; promotes public education regarding the disorder and its effects. Facilitates communication among those affected by FOP. **Libraries: Type:** reference. **Committees:** Finance; Fundraising; International; LIFE: Living Independently with Full Equality; Membership; Patient Needs; Publication and Communication; Resource Center. **Also Known As:** International FOP Association. **Publications:** *FOP Connection*, quarterly. Newsletter. Including articles on daily coping skills new members, research updates. **Price:** included in membership dues. **Circulation:** 300. **Advertising:** accepted.

14153 ■ International Society for Mannosidosis and Related Diseases (ISMRD)
c/o Terri Klein, Exec. Dir.
PO Box 328
Dexter, MI 48130
Ph: (734)449-1190
Fax: (734)449-9038
E-mail: info@mannosidosis.org
URL: http://www.mannosidosis.org
Contact: Paul Murphy, Treas.

Founded: 1999. **Multinational. Description:** Advocates for families affected by Oligosaccharide Storage Disease. **Programs:** Parent Matching. **Publications:** *Pathways*, quarterly. Newsletter. **Price:** free for members ● Brochures. **Conventions/Meetings:** Family Conferences.

14154 ■ Joubert Syndrome Foundation and Related Cerebellar Disorders
6931 S Carlinda Ave.
Columbia, MD 21046
Ph: (410)997-8084
Fax: (410)992-9184
E-mail: joubertduquette@comcast.net
URL: http://www.joubertsyndrome.org
Contact: Cheryl Duquette, Co-Founder/Pres.

Founded: 1992. **Members:** 375. **Membership Dues:** family, $35 (annual) ● international, $40 (annual). **Regional Groups:** 7. **Description:** Serves as a support and information exchange group for families of people afflicted with Joubert's Syndrome, a genetically transmitted syndrome in which the cerebellar vermis, a section of the brain controlling balance and coordination, is partially or completely missing. Brain stem abnormality causes problems with breathing and eye movements. Physical manifestations of JS include disturbances in breathing patterns, ataxia (unsteadiness), abnormal eye movements, hypotonia, and possible mental retardation. Promotes continuing education for medical professionals. **Libraries: Type:** reference. **Holdings:** articles. **Subjects:** Joubert Syndrome. **Formerly:** (1999) Joubert Syndrome Parents in Touch Network; (2005) Joubert Syndrome Foundation. **Publications:** *Rainbow*, quarterly. Newsletter. **Price:** $35.00 in U.S.; $40.00 outside U.S. ● *Registry of Families.* **Conventions/Meetings:** biennial convention and conference.

14155 ■ Late-Onset Tay-Sachs Foundation (LOTSF)
Address Unknown since 2007

Description: Devoted to research and treatment of Late-onset Tay-Sachs disease, including clinical symptoms, molecular basis of the disease, and pattern of inheritance. **Publications:** *Horizon.* Newsletter.

14156 ■ Laurence-Moon-Bardet-Biedl Syndrome Network (LMBBSN)
c/o Mary Morris
15205 W Port Royale Lane Ave.
Surprise, AZ 85379-7011
E-mail: josiahsmom@hotmail.com
URL: http://mlmorris.com/lmbbs
Contact: Mary Morris, Contact

Founded: 1984. **Description:** Provides a network for individuals with Laurence-Moon-Bardet-Biedl syndrome, a genetic disorder. (Persons with LMBBS suffer from general developmental delay and exhibit symptoms of retinitis pigmentosa, a degenerative eye disease; hypogenitalism; polydactyly; obesity.). **Also Known As:** Laurence-Moon-Biedl Syndrome Network; LMBS Network. **Publications:** *LMBBS Network News*, periodic. Newsletter. Includes list of member families. Alternate Formats: online.

14157 ■ Lowe Syndrome Association (LSA)
18919 Voss Rd.
Dallas, TX 75287
Ph: (612)869-5693
Fax: (612)866-3222

E-mail: info@lowesyndrome.org
URL: http://www.lowesyndrome.org
Contact: Debbie Jacobs, Pres.

Founded: 1983. **Members:** 550. **Description:** Parents, friends, and relatives of individuals with Lowe syndrome; medical, educational, and social service professionals and agencies. Fosters communication among families; provides medical and educational information; promotes a better understanding of Lowe syndrome; supports and encourages medical research. **Libraries: Type:** reference. **Holdings:** reports. **Awards:** Medical Research Grant. **Frequency:** annual. **Type:** monetary. **Recipient:** to further the understanding of Lowe syndrome or lead to better treatments. **Publications:** *Living with Lowe Syndrome ● On the Beam*, 3/year. Newsletter. Provides useful information for families affected by Lowe syndrome. **Price:** included in membership dues. ISSN: 0740-218X. **Circulation:** 400. **Conventions/Meetings:** biennial International Conference on Lowe Syndrome.

14158 ■ Make Early Diagnosis to Prevent Early Death (MEDPED)
Univ. of Utah
School of Medicine
410 Chipeta Way, Rm. 161
Salt Lake City, UT 84108
Ph: (801)581-8720
Free: (888)244-2465
Fax: (801)585-9462
E-mail: stacey.larrinaga-shum@hsc.utah.edu
URL: http://www.medped.org
Contact: Stacey Larrinaga-Shum, Program Mgr.

Founded: 1989. **Multinational. Description:** Promotes early diagnosis, proper treatment, and prevention of premature deaths for people with inherited cholesterol disorders, specifically Familial Hypercholesterolemia (FH). **Formerly:** (2003) MedPed. **Publications:** Newsletter, semiannual.

14159 ■ Malignant Hyperthermia Association of the United States (MHAUS)
11 E State St.
PO Box 1069
Sherburne, NY 13460
Ph: (607)674-7901
Free: (800)644-9737
Fax: (607)674-7910
E-mail: info@mhaus.org
URL: http://www.mhaus.org
Contact: Dianne M. Daugherty, Exec. Dir.

Founded: 1981. **Members:** 2,500. **Membership Dues:** individual, $35 (annual). **Staff:** 5. **Budget:** $600,000. **Languages:** English, Spanish. **Description:** Malignant Hyperthermia (MH) susceptible patients and health care providers. MH is a genetically transmitted, often fatal, muscular disorder triggered in susceptible individuals by certain general anesthetic agents. Aims to save lives by making information about MH available. Discusses problems that confront families affected by MH. Funds research on the causes, detection, and management of MH. Disseminates research information. **Computer Services:** Information services, patient center ● information services, professional's center ● online services, brochure list ● online services, eShop ● online services, message board. **Councils:** Professional Advisory. **Publications:** *The Communicator*, quarterly. Newsletter. Contains MH updates for MHS patients and medical professionals. **Price:** $35.00/ year. **Circulation:** 2,500. Alternate Formats: online ● *Emergency Treatment for MH ● Malignant Hyperthermia, Four Cases (for medical professionals).* Video ● *Malignant Hyperthermia, Knowing Your Role (for medical professionals).* Video ● *Managing MH - Clinical Updates.* Pamphlet ● *MH Procedural Manuals.* Covers hospital and ambulatory versions with video. ● *Preventing MH - An Anesthesia Protocol.* Pamphlet ● *Testing for Susceptibility to MH.* Pamphlet ● *Understanding MH.* Booklet. **Conventions/Meetings:** semiannual regional meeting.

14160 ■ MHE Coalition
8838 Holly Ln.
Olmsted Falls, OH 44138
Ph: (440)235-6325 (440)427-9032

Fax: (440)427-9032
E-mail: chelez1@aol.com
URL: http://www.mhecoalition.org
Contact: Chele Zelina, Pres.

Founded: 2000. **Members:** 1,000. **Multinational. Description:** Dedicated to finding the causes, treatments and ultimately the cure for Multiple Hereditary Exostoses, and to providing support and information to health care providers, researchers, and individuals and families living with this rare genetic bone disease. **Libraries: Type:** reference. **Additional Websites:** http://www.mheandme.com. **Publications:** *MHE Coalition Newsletter*, semiannual.

14161 ■ Michael Fund/International Foundation for Genetic Research (MF/IFGR)
4371 Northern Pike
Monroeville, PA 15146-2837
Ph: (412)374-0111
URL: http://www.michaelfund.org
Contact: Randy Engel, Exec. Dir.

Founded: 1978. **Budget:** $65,000. **Description:** Intertwines the funding of scientific research on Down's Syndrome and related genetic disorders with a pro-life philosophy. Supports research on prevention, cure, or reduction of the effects of Down's Syndrome; enlists support from professionals; and advocates working in this field. Opposes intrauterine detection and abortion of the affected unborn as well as deliberate euthanasia of children and adults with birth defects. Aims to make research findings available to others conducting similar research and to advocate and encourage efforts to improve the care, treatment, education, evaluation and habilitation of children and adults with mental and physical handicaps, to the benefit of their families and communities. **Publications:** *Friends of the Michael Fund Newsletter*, semiannual. Contains topics on eugenics, genetics, and prenatal diagnosis.

14162 ■ National Foundation for Ectodermal Dysplasias (NFED)
410 E Main St.
Box 114
Mascoutah, IL 62258
Ph: (618)566-2020
Fax: (618)566-4718
E-mail: info@nfed.org
URL: http://www.nfed.org
Contact: Mary Kaye Richter, Exec. Dir.

Founded: 1981. **Members:** 4,300. **Staff:** 8. **Budget:** $1,000,000. **Languages:** English, French, Italian, Spanish. **Description:** Families of ectodermal dysplasia patients and the medical community. (Ectodermal dysplasia is a genetic birth defect usually resulting in an abnormal development of the outer layer of cells in the embryo. The disorder may be characterized by absent or poorly functioning sweat glands, sparse hair follicles, abnormal hair texture, absence of hair and skin oils, disfigured finger and toe nails, hearing or sight deficiencies, abnormalities of the limbs and cleft palate. With proper medical care, ED patients can live fairly normal lives.) Locates patients and provides them with support and information. Assists the medical community in acquiring the necessary information for treating an ED patient, locates treatment facilities and provides referral services. Makes funds available to qualified applicants for dental and other necessary care. Conducts educational meetings and assists with research projects. Provides children's services; compiles statistics. Supports researchers financially and through access to patients when approved. **Awards:** Kenneth S. Brown, MD Research Award. **Frequency:** periodic. **Type:** recognition. **Recipient:** for outstanding research with history of research and results applicable to ED ● Outstanding Service Award. **Type:** recognition ● Research Awards. **Frequency:** annual. **Type:** monetary. **Recipient:** for outstanding research with history of research and results applicable to ED. **Computer Services:** database, patient information. **Committees:** Dental; Dermatology; Ear, Nose, and Throat; Syndrome Identification. **Publications:** *A Multi-Syndrome Guide to ED.* Booklet ● *A Skin Guide to Ectodermal Dysplasia.* Booklet ● *Dental Guide to the Ectodermal Dysplasia.* Booklet ● *The Educator,* bimonthly. Newsletter. **Price:** $25.00/year ● *Evan's New Teeth.* Booklet ● *Eye, Ear, Nose and Throat Guide to the Ectodermal Dysplasias.* Booklet ● *Family Guide to the Ectodermal Dysplasias.* Booklet ● Bibliography. Includes citations of Ectodermal Dysplasias articles. **Price:** $15.00/item, plus shipping and handling. **Conventions/Meetings:** annual conference - always summer ● workshop and regional meeting - 3/year.

14163 ▪ National Fragile X Foundation (NFXF)
PO Box 190488
San Francisco, CA 94119
Ph: (925)938-9300
Free: (800)688-8765
Fax: (925)938-9315
E-mail: natlfx@fragilex.org
URL: http://www.FragileX.org
Contact: Robert M. Miller, Exec. Dir.
Founded: 1984. **Members:** 1,000. **Membership Dues:** basic, $25 (annual). **Staff:** 7. **Budget:** $1,000,000. **State Groups:** 70. **Description:** Unites Fragile X community to enrich lives through educational and emotional support, promote public and professional awareness, and advance research toward improved treatments and a cure for Fragile X Syndrome. (Fragile X syndrome is the most common inherited form of learning disabilities and mental retardation known. Inherited in an X-linked fashion, Fragile X Syndrome can cause intellectual and cognitive deficits ranging from subtle learning disabilities and a normal IQ, to severe mental retardation and autistic behaviors). **Libraries: Type:** reference. **Publications:** *The National Fragile X Foundation Quarterly.* Journal. Contains articles on research, behavior and therapy; success stories and legislative advocacy. **Price:** $25.00/year. **Circulation:** 3,500. Alternate Formats: online ● *10th International Fragile X Conference Proceedings 2006,* biennial. Features articles, abstracts and handouts. Alternate Formats: online ● Annual Report, annual. Alternate Formats: online ● Books ● Also publishes family and professional information packets and special topic pamphlets. **Conventions/Meetings:** biennial international conference.

14164 ▪ National Incontinentia Pigmenti Foundation (NIPF)
c/o Susanne Bross Emmerich, Exec. Dir.
30 E 72nd St., 16th Fl.
New York, NY 10021
Ph: (212)452-1231
Fax: (212)452-1406
E-mail: ipif@ipif.org
URL: http://imgen.bcm.tmc.edu/IPIF/NIPFjoin.htm
Contact: Susanne Bross Emmerich, Exec. Dir.
Description: Offers support to individuals and families affected by incontinentia pigmenti. **Publications:** Newsletter.

14165 ▪ Neurofibromatosis (NF)
PO Box 18246
Minneapolis, MN 55418
Ph: (301)918-4600
Free: (800)942-6825
Fax: (301)918-0009
E-mail: nfinfo@nfinc.org
URL: http://www.nfinc.org
Contact: Miguel Lessing, Pres.
Founded: 1988. **Membership Dues:** organization, $25 (annual). **Staff:** 2. **Budget:** $125,000. **Regional Groups:** 9. **Description:** Organizations providing support for individuals with neurofibromatosis (NF) and their families, physicians, and other health care providers. (NF is a genetic neurological disorder that can cause tumors to form on nerves and is linked to learning disabilities, hearing loss, vision impairment, epilepsy, and cancer.) Increases public awareness through information dissemination; informs federal, state, and local legislators of the needs of families. Promotes, supports, and funds medical, clinical, educational, and sociological research that addresses the need to diagnose, treat, cure, and prevent NF. Identifies local support and peer counseling groups; offers referrals to medical resources and scientifically-

evaluated research. Participates in networking of voluntary health organizations. **Libraries: Type:** not open to the public. **Holdings:** archival material. **Subjects:** neurofibromatosis, genetics, proteus syndrome. **Awards:** NF Inc. Scholar. **Frequency:** annual. **Type:** monetary. **Recipient:** for contribution to the NF cause. **Committees:** Advocacy; Education; International Liaison; Medicine; Military; Support. **Publications:** *Neurofibromatosis Ink,* semiannual. Newsletter. Includes research summaries, reports, chapter news, and symposia information, bibliography, fundraising activities. Alternate Formats: online ● *Understanding Neurofibromatosis: An Introduction for Patients and Parents.* Booklets. **Price:** $3.00 for each multiple copy. **Conventions/Meetings:** annual symposium.

14166 ▪ Organic Acidemia Association (OAA)
c/o Kathy Stagni, Exec. Dir.
13210 35th Ave. N
Plymouth, MN 55441-2227
Ph: (763)559-1797
Free: (866)539-4060
Fax: (866)539-4060
E-mail: oaanews@aol.com
URL: http://www.mmaresearch.com
Contact: Kathy Stagni, Exec. Dir.
Founded: 1982. **Members:** 900. **Membership Dues:** regular, in U.S., $25 (annual) ● regular, outside U.S., $35 (annual). **Description:** Dietitians, researchers, and geneticists; clinics; parents and relatives of children suffering from organic acidemia disorders. (Organic acidemia is a class of genetic metabolic disorders that lead to cellular enzyme deficiencies and require restricted diets.) Fosters communication among parents and professionals; acts as support group. **Computer Services:** Online services, Parent to Parent Matching; listserv for families AND professionals. **Additional Websites:** http://www.ivaresearch.org, http://www.paresearch.org, http://www.oaanews.org. **Funds:** OAA/IVA Research; OAA/MMA Research; OAA/PA Research. **Affiliated With:** Genetic Alliance; National Healthy Mothers, Healthy Babies Coalition; National Organization for Rare Disorders. **Publications:** *Organic Acidemia Association Newsletter,* 3/year. **Price:** $25.00/year in U.S.; $35.00/year outside U.S. **Conventions/Meetings:** biennial conference.

14167 ▪ Pierre Robin Network
3604 Biscayne St.
Quincy, IL 62305
E-mail: info@pierrerobin.org
URL: http://www.pierrerobin.org
Contact: Nancy Barry, Founder/Pres.
Founded: 1999. **Multinational. Description:** Provides support to individuals afflicted with Pierre Robin Sequence (PRS) and their families. Strives to improve the quality of life of patients suffering from PRS. Facilitates the exchange of information among members. **Telecommunication Services:** electronic mail, nancy@pierrerobin.org ● electronic mail, webmaster@pierrerobin.org.

14168 ▪ Prader-Willi Foundation
Address Unknown since 2007
Founded: 1994. **Staff:** 2. **Description:** Devoted to serving individuals with Prader-Willi Syndrome. Provides information on subjects related to Prader-Willi Syndrome. Finances related projects such as residential development, family support, behavioral research, and awareness. Works with other Prader-Willi organizations. **Awards: Type:** grant. **Recipient:** for other Prader-Willi organizations for development and publication. **Publications:** *Moris A. Angulo, MD Prader-Willi Syndrom: A Guide for Families & Others* (in English and Spanish) ● *News & Notes,* quarterly. Newsletter. **Price:** free. **Advertising:** not accepted.

14169 ▪ Prader-Willi Syndrome Association (U.S.A.) (PWSAUSA)
5700 Midnight Pass Rd., Ste.6
Sarasota, FL 34242
Ph: (941)312-0400
Free: (800)926-4797
Fax: (941)312-0142

E-mail: national@pwsausa.org
URL: http://www.pwsausa.org
Contact: Janalee Heinemann, Exec. Dir.
Founded: 1975. **Members:** 3,000. **Membership Dues:** individual in U.S., $30 (annual) ● individual outside U.S., professional/organization in U.S., $40 (annual) ● family in U.S., $35 (annual) ● family outside U.S., $45 (annual) ● professional/organization outside U.S., $50 (annual) ● professional/organization in U.S., $40 (annual) ● auxiliary in U.S., $15 (annual) ● auxiliary outside U.S., $25 (annual). **Staff:** 4. **Budget:** $575,000. **State Groups:** 34. **Languages:** English, Spanish. **Description:** Parents, physicians, educators, dieticians, group homes, and others interested in the Prader-Willi Syndrome, the most common known genetic cause of morbid obesity in children. (The significant manifestations of the syndrome are obesity, short stature, lack of muscle tone, hypogonadism, and central nervous system performance dysfunction). Works to provide a forum for communication about the syndrome, particularly the means to cope with it; to promote research and the establishment of treatment facilities. **Libraries: Type:** reference. **Holdings:** books, clippings, periodicals. **Subjects:** genetics, PWS, behavior management, diet. **Computer Services:** database. **Formerly:** (1977) Prader-Willi Syndrome Parents and Friends; (1992) Prader-Willi Syndrome Association; (1998) Prader-Willi Syndrome Association U.S.A.; (2002) PWSA USA. **Publications:** *Gathered View,* bimonthly. Newsletter. Provides information on education, learning problems, and new resources for individuals with PWS. Includes book reviews and research updates. **Price:** included in membership dues. **Circulation:** 2,300. **Advertising:** accepted ● *Management of Prader-Willi Syndrome.* Book ● Handbooks ● Books. Features topics about Prader-Willi Syndrome and other related topics. ● Also publishes information packets and produces videos. **Conventions/Meetings:** triennial international conference ● annual meeting (exhibits) - usually July.

14170 ▪ PRISMS: Parents and Researchers Interested In Smith-Magenis Syndrome
PO Box 741914
Dallas, TX 75374-1914
Ph: (972)231-0035
Fax: (413)826-6539
E-mail: info@prisms.org
URL: http://www.prisms.org
Contact: Randy Beall, Pres.
Founded: 1993. **Membership Dues:** SMS parent/primary caregiver, relative/friend, teacher, physician/health professional, $30 (annual) ● geneticist/genetic counselor, $50 (annual) ● international (additional fee), $5. **Multinational. Description:** Provides information and support to families of persons with Smith-Magenis Syndrome (SMS). Fosters partnerships with professionals to increase awareness and understanding of SMS. **Computer Services:** Information services, SMS facts and resources ● mailing lists ● online services, discussion forum. **Programs:** Parent-to-Parent. **Publications:** *Spectrum,* 2-3/year. Newsletter. **Price:** included in membership dues ● Annual Report, annual. Alternate Formats: online.

14171 ▪ Progressive Osseous Heteroplasia Association (POHA)
33 Stonehearth Sq.
Indian Head Park, IL 60525
Ph: (708)246-9410
Fax: (708)246-9410
E-mail: info@pohdisease.org
URL: http://www.pohdisease.org
Contact: Fred B. Gardner, Exec. Dir./Treas.
Founded: 1995. **Description:** Promotes public awareness of Progressive Osseous Heteroplasia (POH). Supports research to identify the cause of POH. Develops effective treatments for those with POH. **Boards:** Medical Advisory. **Projects:** POH Collaborative Research. **Publications:** Annual Report, annual. Alternate Formats: online.

14172 ▪ Prune Belly Syndrome Network (PBSN)
PO Box 154
Beloit, WI 53512-0154

E-mail: kwalker@prunebelly.org
URL: http://www.prunebelly.org
Contact: Kurt Walker, Pres.
Founded: 1996. **Multinational. Description:** Provides support for those who have Prune Belly Syndrome, their families, friends and the healthcare professionals who treat them. Educates the medical community about Prune Belly Syndrome. **Computer Services:** Information services, prune belly syndrome resources ● online services, forum. **Telecommunication Services:** electronic mail, fwalker@prunebelly.org ● electronic mail, lbrokus@prunebelly.org. **Publications:** Brochure (in English and Spanish).

14173 ■ PXE International
4301 Connecticut Ave. NW, Ste.404
Washington, DC 20008-2369
Ph: (202)362-9599
Fax: (202)966-8553
E-mail: info@pxe.org
URL: http://www.pxe.org
Contact: Patrick F. Terry, Pres.
Founded: 1995. **Members:** 4,000. **Staff:** 5. **Budget:** $150,000. **Regional Groups:** 20. **National Groups:** 22. **Multinational. Description:** Supports those affected by Pseudoxanthomas elasticum (PXE) and research into its causes, treatments, and cure. (Pseudoxanthomas elasticum is a heritable connective tissue disorder causing calcification of connective tissue, potentially affecting the skin, arteries, gastrointestinal tissue, and the retina.) Provides information and support to patients, their families, and clinicians on diagnosis, effects, and treatment. Through a consortium of researchers worldwide, supports research by providing to researchers monetary grants and samples from its confidential Blood and Tissue Bank. Initiates and conducts epidemiological studies and other research. **Libraries: Type:** reference. **Holdings:** audio recordings, papers, reports, video recordings. **Subjects:** PXE, extracellular matrix, membrane transport proteins. **Awards:** Excellence in PXE Research. **Frequency:** annual. **Type:** recognition. **Recipient:** for special contributions to PXE research ● **Frequency:** periodic. **Type:** grant. **Computer Services:** Mailing lists, of members ● online services, registry for patient database. **Boards:** Medical Advisory. **Committees:** Research Grant. **Publications:** MemberGram, quarterly. Newsletter. Contains PXE information; patient group and organization's activities; research updates; profiles of patients, volunteers, and researchers. **Circulation:** 5,000. **Advertising:** accepted. Alternate Formats: online ● Bulletin, periodic. **Conventions/Meetings:** biennial conference (exhibits) ● periodic meeting.

14174 ■ Share and Care Cockayne Syndrome Network
PO Box 570618
Dallas, TX 75357
Ph: (214)728-2679
E-mail: j93082@aol.com
URL: http://www.cockayne-syndrome.org
Contact: Jackie Clark, Contact
Founded: 1993. **Members:** 1,500. **Membership Dues:** family, professional, $25 (annual). **Staff:** 1. **Languages:** English, French, Japanese, Portuguese, Spanish. **Description:** Professionals and families. Works to provide information on Cockayne Syndrome, a rare form of dwarfism, to help parents and doctors to make informed decisions in the care of these children. Provides support for families; encourages research. **Committees:** Care Givers Support; Family Support/Update; PR/Education; Sibling Support. **Publications:** Aftercare. Newsletter. Contains obituaries past and current and anniversary of death notice. ● Cockayne's Syndrome. Handbook. Alternate Formats: online ● Sibling. Newsletter. Alternate Formats: online ● Brochure, quarterly. Features research updates and articles on individual children. **Circulation:** 400. **Conventions/Meetings:** annual retreat, for children and parents.

14175 ■ Shwachman Diamond America (SDA)
931-B S Main St., No. 332
Kernersville, NC 27284
Ph: (336)423-8158

E-mail: sdaboard@shwachmandiamondamerica.org
URL: http://www.shwachmandiamondamerica.org
Contact: Pattie Curran, Dir.
Description: Provides support to person with Shwachman-Diamond Syndrome and their families; funds and promotes research. Is not affiliated with Shwachman-Diamond Syndrome International. **Computer Services:** Mailing lists, of members. **Telecommunication Services:** electronic mail, shwachman-syndrome-subscribe@yahoogroups.com.

14176 ■ Sotos Syndrome Support Association (SSSA)
PO Box 4626
Wheaton, IL 60189
Ph: (630)682-8815
Free: (888)246-7772
E-mail: president@sotossyndrome.org
URL: http://www.well.com/user/sssa
Contact: Joanne Weick, Pres.
Founded: 1984. **Members:** 300. **Membership Dues:** regular, $25 (annual). **Multinational. Description:** Health care professionals and families of children with Sotos Syndrome. (Sotos Syndrome, also known as Cerebral Giantism, is a genetic disorder resulting in exceptional and rapid growth in the first five years, mental retardation, and speech and coordination impairments.) Works to disseminate information to families of children diagnosed with Sotos Syndrome. Forms support groups. Provides referral and networking services. **Libraries: Type:** reference. **Publications:** SSSA Notes, quarterly. Newsletter. Includes question and answer section, doctor's column, news updates, and comments from parents. **Price:** included in membership dues ● Brochure. **Conventions/Meetings:** annual conference.

14177 ■ Stickler Involved People (SIP)
15 Angelina Dr.
Augusta, KS 67010
Ph: (316)775-2993
E-mail: sip@sticklers.org
URL: http://www.sticklers.org
Contact: Pat Houchin, Coor.
Founded: 1995. **Membership Dues:** regular, $10 (annual). **Multinational. Description:** Works to diagnose and treat Stickler Syndrome; provides support, medical information, and offers ways in which to cope. **Awards:** Dr. Gunnar B. Stickler Scholarship. **Frequency:** annual. **Type:** scholarship. **Recipient:** to high school senior with Stickler Syndrome diagnosis. **Computer Services:** Mailing lists ● online services. **Affiliated With:** National Organization for Rare Disorders. **Publications:** Stickler - The Elusive Syndrome, quarterly. Book. **Price:** $29.00 ● Newsletter, quarterly. **Price:** included in membership dues. Alternate Formats: online. **Conventions/Meetings:** annual conference.

14178 ■ Sudden Arrhythmia Death Syndromes Foundation (SADS)
508 E South Temple, Ste.20
Salt Lake City, UT 84102-1013
Ph: (801)531-0937
Free: (800)STOP-SAD
Fax: (801)531-0945
E-mail: sads@sads.org
URL: http://www.sads.org
Contact: Alice Lara, Exec. Dir.
Founded: 1991. **Members:** 29,000. **Staff:** 3. **Budget:** $300,000. **Regional Groups:** 4. **Languages:** Chinese, English, Italian, Spanish. **Description:** Seeks to identify, help diagnose and help treat children and young adults who are genetically predisposed to sudden death by cardia arrhythmias. Supports patients, families and physicians dealing with Long QT Syndrome (LQTS) and other sudden death syndromes; educates medical personnel and the public about cardiac arrhythmias; supports genetic research; links individuals with similar concerns for support; and establishes support groups. **Libraries: Type:** open to the public. **Holdings:** 110. **Computer Services:** database ● mailing lists ● online services. **Telecommunication Services:** electronic mail, alice@sads.org. **Programs:** Advocacy/Research; Patient Support Services; Physician and Health Professional Educa-

tion; Public Awareness. **Affiliated With:** Genetic Alliance. **Publications:** Acquired Long QT Syndrome. Brochure ● Inherited Long QT Syndrome. Brochure ● SADS Foundation Brochure. Alternate Formats: online ● SADS Foundation News, triennial. Newsletter. **Circulation:** 10,000. Alternate Formats: online ● Newsletter. Alternate Formats: online ● Annual Report, annual. Alternate Formats: online. **Conventions/Meetings:** annual conference.

14179 ■ Support Organization for Trisomy 18, 13, and Related Disorders (SOFT)
c/o Barb VanHerreweghe, Pres.
2982 S Union St.
Rochester, NY 14624
Ph: (585)594-4621
Free: (800)716-SOFT
E-mail: barbsoft@rochester.rr.com
URL: http://www.trisomy.org
Contact: Barb VanHerreweghe, Pres.
Founded: 1979. **Members:** 2,100. **Membership Dues:** family in U.S., $25 (annual) ● family in Canada, $35 (annual) ● medical professional in U.S., $30 (annual) ● medical professional in Canada, $40 (annual). **State Groups:** 50. **Local Groups:** 1. **Languages:** English, Spanish. **Description:** Families, friends, and professionals involved with children born with Trisomy 18 or Trisomy 13. (Trisomy 18 and 13 are genetic disorders in which there are three no. 18 or no. 13 chromosomes rather than the usual two.) Offers support, understanding, and encouragement to families of affected individuals. Provides the public with information on these conditions and birth defects in general. Makes available to families and professionals a file of medical information. Participate in workshops, seminars, lectures, and group studies at universities and hospitals. Conducts surveys and compiles statistics about medical treatment and problems. Maintains speakers' bureau and placement service. **Libraries: Type:** reference. **Holdings:** photographs. **Awards:** Kari Deanne Holladay SOFT Service Award. **Frequency:** annual. **Type:** recognition. **Computer Services:** database ● mailing lists. **Committees:** Conference; Family Support; Fundraising; International Affairs; Legislative/Legal; Professional Advisory; Public Awareness/Community Relations. **Publications:** Care of Infant & Child with T18 & T13. Book. **Price:** $10.95 each ● SOFT Times, 4-6/year. Newsletter. Includes organization news, family forum and other related articles. **Price:** included in membership dues ● Trisomy 18 - A Book for Families. **Price:** $10.95 ● Trisomy 13 - A Guidebook for Families. **Price:** $10.95 ● Brochures. **Conventions/Meetings:** annual conference (exhibits).

14180 ■ Turner Syndrome Society of the U.S. (TSS US)
14450 T.C. Jester, Ste.260
Houston, TX 77014
Ph: (832)249-9988
Free: (800)365-9944
Fax: (832)249-9987
E-mail: tssus@turnersyndrome.org
URL: http://www.turnersyndrome.org
Contact: Barbara Flink, Pres.
Founded: 1987. **Members:** 7,000. **Membership Dues:** individual, $45 (annual) ● family outside U.S., $65 (annual) ● professional, $75 (annual). **Staff:** 2. **Local Groups:** 36. **Languages:** English, Spanish. **Description:** Persons suffering from Turner syndrome; families of persons with the syndrome; health care professionals. (TS is a genetic disorder affecting females, causing short stature and cardiac, kidney and spatial motor perception problems. TS can result in infertility and incomplete sexual maturation.) Seeks to increase public awareness of the medical and sociopsychological effects TS has on patients. Maintains speakers' bureau. **Libraries: Type:** reference. **Holdings:** clippings, monographs. **Computer Services:** database, health professionals referral ● mailing lists. **Publications:** Chapter and Support Group Handbook. Alternate Formats: online ● Turner Syndrome. Brochure ● Turner Syndrome: A Guide for Families (in English and Spanish). Booklet ● Videos ● Newsletter, quarterly. Alternate Formats: online ● Membership Directory. Alternate Formats: online ● Journals.

Alternate Formats: online ● Brochure (in English and Spanish). Alternate Formats: online ● Articles. Alternate Formats: online. Conventions/Meetings: annual conference, includes age appropriate sessions for children 5 years and up, pre-teens, teens and adults.

14181 ■ Velo-Cardio-Facial Syndrome (VCFS)
PO Box 874
Milltown, NJ 08850
Ph: (732)238-8803
Free: (866)VCF-SEF5
Fax: (732)238-8803
E-mail: info@vcfsef.org
URL: http://www.vcfsef.org
Contact: Karen J. Golding-Kushner PhD, Exec. Dir.
Members: 1,300. **Membership Dues:** single, $40 (annual) ● family, $50 (annual) ● student, $20 (annual). **Multinational. Description:** Aims to educate the lay and professional public, offer family programs, provide parent-to-parent networking; promotes the diagnosis and treatment of individuals with VCF; distributes educational materials about Velo-Cardio-Facial (also known as Shprintzen Syndrome, Di-George Sequence, and Catch 22); and distributes questionnaire regarding the medical diagnosis and management of individuals with this disorder. **Awards:** Caitlin Lynch Memorial Fund Award. **Frequency:** annual. **Type:** scholarship ● Tony Lipson Memorial Fund Award. **Frequency:** annual. **Type:** monetary. **Recipient:** for members from Australia to attend annual meetings. **Publications:** Newsletter, periodic. Alternate Formats: online. **Conventions/Meetings:** annual conference.

14182 ■ VHL Family Alliance (VHLFA)
2001 Beacon St., Ste.208
Boston, MA 02135-7787
Ph: (617)277-5667
Free: (800)767-4845
Fax: (858)712-8712
E-mail: info@vhl.org
URL: http://www.vhl.org
Contact: Joyce Graff, Exec. Dir.
Founded: 1993. **Members:** 14,000. **Membership Dues:** basic, in U.S., $25 (annual) ● basic, outside U.S., $35 (annual) ● corporate, $100 (annual) ● sustaining, $250 (annual) ● Lindau Society, $1,000 (annual). **Staff:** 1. **Budget:** $220,000. **State Groups:** 29. **National Groups:** 11. **Languages:** Croatian, Dutch, English, French, German, Hungarian, Italian, Swedish, Turkish. **Description:** Patients affected by Von Hippel-Lindau Disease; their families; medical professionals; interested others. Von Hippel-Lindau Disease is a genetic disorder involving abnormal growth forming "knots" of blood vessels in the retina, brain, or spinal cord areas. These knots are hemangiomas, a kind of tumor. Promotes education of the medical community, patients, and the general public about the disease. Provides an international support network to families affected by VHL. Conducts research and educational programs; funds research on VHL; maintains speakers' bureau. **Libraries: Type:** open to the public. **Holdings:** articles. **Subjects:** aspects of VHL. **Awards:** Minster Volunteer Award. **Frequency:** annual. **Type:** recognition ● Research Award. **Frequency:** annual. **Type:** grant. **Recipient:** for a proposal approved by research board. **Computer Services:** Online services, publication. **Boards:** Medical Advisory; Research Advisory. **Committees:** Chapters; Clinical Care; Dialysis and Transplant; Professional Education. **Affiliated With:** Genetic Alliance; National Organization for Rare Disorders. **Also Known As:** Von Hippel-Lindau Family Alliance. **Publications:** *VHL Family Forum* (in English and German), quarterly. Newsletter. Contains the latest information on VHL, research into the disease, and support network information. **Price:** included in membership dues. ISSN: 1066-4130. **Circulation:** 6,000. **Advertising:** accepted. Alternate Formats: online ● *VHL Patient Handbook* (in English, French, German, Italian, Japanese, and Spanish). Booklet ● *What is VHL?* (in English, French, German, Italian, and Spanish). Brochures. **Price:** $2.00 for 25 copies ● *Your Family Health Tree* (in English,

Italian, and Spanish). Booklet. **Conventions/Meetings:** annual conference, for patients and providers (exhibits).

14183 ■ Williams Syndrome Association (WSA)
PO Box 297
Clawson, MI 48017-0297
Ph: (248)244-2229
Free: (800)806-1871
Fax: (248)244-2230
E-mail: info@williams-syndrome.org
URL: http://www.williams-syndrome.org
Contact: Terry Monkaba, Exec. Dir.
Founded: 1982. **Members:** 8,000. **Membership Dues:** regular, in U.S., $20 (annual) ● regular, in Canada, $25 (annual) ● international, $35 (annual). **Staff:** 2. **Budget:** $300,000. **Regional Groups:** 11. **State Groups:** 50. **Languages:** English, Japanese, Spanish. **Description:** Individuals with Williams Syndrome and their families; medical and health care professionals; educators. (Williams Syndrome is characterized by similar facial features, low birth weight, heart disorders, hearing sensitivity, talkative personality, mild to severe learning disabilities, and developmental delays.) Provides support and assistance to families with a WS child. Conducts networking in the medical, scientific, educational, and professional communities for referral and study of newly-diagnosed WS individuals. Encourages medical behavior and supports research into all aspects of the syndrome. Compiles statistics. **Libraries: Type:** reference. **Holdings:** 1,000; articles, audio recordings, video recordings. **Subjects:** William Syndrome. **Awards:** Chloe Reisig Music Scholarship. **Frequency:** annual. **Type:** scholarship. **Recipient:** for interest and ability in music and financial need ● **Type:** monetary ● Research Grant. **Frequency:** periodic. **Type:** grant. **Computer Services:** database, articles and information on Williams Syndrome. **Publications:** *Ben's Big Decision.* Book. Includes storybook and tape. **Price:** $19.95. Alternate Formats: magnetic tape ● *Facts Brochure.* Brochures. **Price:** free for members ● *Heart to Heart*, quarterly. Newsletter. Contains information on medical and educational interventions for WS and profiles of WS individuals. ● *Information for Teachers.* Handbook. Contains information for parents and professionals. **Price:** $7.00 ● *The Promenade: A Story about Adolescents with Williams Syndrome.* Book. Provides testing and evaluations for WSA. **Price:** $10.00 ● *Williams Syndrome Association National Newsletter*, quarterly. Includes research updates and parent and professional forums. **Price:** $20.00/year. **Conventions/Meetings:** biennial convention and workshop (exhibits) ● International Professional Symposium on WS.

14184 ■ Xeroderma Pigmentosum Society (XPS)
437 Snydertown Rd.
Craryville, NY 12521
Ph: (518)851-2612
Free: (877)XPS-CURE
Fax: (518)851-2612
E-mail: xps@xps.org
URL: http://www.xps.org
Contact: Prof. Caren Mahar, Contact
Founded: 1995. **Members:** 3,500. **Staff:** 1. **Budget:** $215,000. **Languages:** English, French, German, Italian, Norwegian, Portuguese, Spanish. **Multinational. Description:** Promotes understanding of xeroderma pigmentosum, a rare genetic defect in ultraviolet radiation induced DNA repair mechanisms, characterized by severe sensitivity to all sources of UV radiation (especially sunlight). Provide information, education, protection and advocacy. Promotes research for a cure. **Computer Services:** Information services, education and information on and about related disorders, protection, detection, treatments and services. **Divisions:** XP Retreat Center. **Sections:** Speaker's Bureau. **Publications:** *Understanding Xeroderma Pigmentosum.'* Pamphlet. Alternate Formats: online ● *XP Report*, periodic. Newsletter. Alternate Formats: online.

Genetics

14185 ■ American Board of Genetic Counseling (ABGC)
9650 Rockville Pike
Bethesda, MD 20814-3998
Ph: (301)634-7316
Fax: (301)634-7320
E-mail: abgc@genetics.faseb.org
URL: http://www.abgc.net
Contact: Sharon Robinson, Admin.
Founded: 1993. **Members:** 2,000. **Staff:** 2. **Description:** Comprises only of individuals who have passed the certification examination. Certifies individuals for the delivery of genetic counseling services and accredits genetic counseling master's degree granting programs. **Computer Services:** Mailing lists, certified Genetic Counselors.

14186 ■ American Board of Medical Genetics (ABMG)
9650 Rockville Pike
Bethesda, MD 20814-3998
Ph: (301)634-7315 (301)634-7316
Fax: (301)634-7320
E-mail: abmg@genetics.faseb.org
URL: http://www.abmg.org
Contact: Karla Matteson PhD, Exec. Dir.
Founded: 1981. **Members:** 2,000. **Staff:** 2. **Description:** Certifies individuals and accredits training programs in the field of human genetics. **Programs:** Medical Genetics Training.

14187 ■ American College of Medical Genetics (ACMG)
9650 Rockville Pike
Bethesda, MD 20814-3998
Ph: (301)634-7127
Fax: (301)634-7275
E-mail: acmg@acmg.net
URL: http://www.acmg.net
Contact: Michael S. Watson PhD, Exec. Dir.
Founded: 1991. **Members:** 1,385. **Membership Dues:** MD (AMA), $370 (annual) ● PhD (non-AMA), $470 (annual) ● MD (non-AMA), Canadian, $570 (annual) ● associate, affiliate, $170 (annual) ● candidate/ affiliate specialist/corresponding, $220 (annual) ● emeritus, $50 (annual) ● trainee, $100 (annual). **Staff:** 5. **Budget:** $2,100,000. **Description:** Physicians and others with an interest in genetics and the delivery of medical genetics services to the public. Works to insure the availability of genetic services without regard to considerations of race, gender, sexual orientation, disability, or ability to pay. Promotes and supports genetics research. Establishes and maintains scientific and professional standards for medical genetics education, research, and practice. Lobbies for effective and fair health policies and legislation; provides information and technical assistance to government agencies engaged in health care regulation or policy formation. Makes available continuing professional education programs; represents members' interests. Conducts advocacy campaigns for people with genetic problems; sponsors public education programs. **Publications:** *Genetics in Medicine; Standards and Guidelines*, monthly. Journal. **Price:** $85.00/copy; $204.00/year for in-training in U.S.; $444.00 /year for individuals in U.S.; $844.00 /year for institutions. **Advertising:** accepted. **Conventions/Meetings:** annual Clinical Genetics Meeting, joint clinical genetics meeting with March of Dimes (exhibits) - 2008 Mar. 13-16, Phoenix, AZ ● biennial Genetics Review Course - meeting, a review course for genetics professionals - odd years.

14188 ■ American Society of Gene Therapy (ASGT)
555 E Wells St., Ste.1100
Milwaukee, WI 53202
Ph: (414)278-1341
Fax: (414)276-3349

E-mail: info@asgt.org
URL: http://www.asgt.org
Contact: Elizabeth Dooley CAE, Exec. Dir.
Founded: 1996. **Members:** 3,000. **Membership Dues:** active, $220 (annual) ● associate, $75 (annual). **Staff:** 6. **Budget:** $1,400,000. **Multinational. Description:** Medical professional organization representing researchers and scientists dedicated to discovering new gene therapies. Commits to promote and foster exchange and dissemination of information and ideas related to gene therapy; encourages the general field of research involving gene therapy; promotes professional and public education in all areas of gene therapy. **Committees:** Cancer Gene Therapy; Clinical and Regulatory Affairs; Education; Ethics; Industrial Liaison; International; Program; Publications. **Publications:** *Molecular Therapy*, monthly. Journal. Contains scientifically meritorious papers on primary research and methodological advances in general areas of gene transfer, gene and cell therapy. **Circulation:** 2,000. **Advertising:** accepted. Alternate Formats: CD-ROM; online. **Conventions/Meetings:** annual meeting (exhibits).

14189 ■ American Society for Genomic Medicine (AS-GM)
The Stefan Univ.
PO Box 2946
La Jolla, CA 92038
E-mail: genomic-medicine@stefan-university.edu
Contact: Dr. V. Alexander Stefan PhD, Pres.
Founded: 1999. **Multinational. Description:** Seeks to advance development and diffusion of achievements in genomic medicine and pharmacogenomics worldwide. **Publications:** *Frontiers in Genomic Medicine*. Newsletter. ISSN: 1541-4728 ● Brochures. **Conventions/Meetings:** workshop ● annual World Congress on Genomic Medicine.

14190 ■ Association of Professors of Human and Medical Genetics (APHMG)
c/o Gerald Feldman, PhD, Pres.
Wayne State Univ. School of Medicine
Molecular Medicine and Genetics Dept.
540 E Canfield St.
3216 Scott Hall
Detroit, MI 48201-1928
Ph: (313)577-6298
Fax: (313)577-9137
E-mail: glfeldman@genetics.wayne.edu
URL: http://genetics.faseb.org/genetics/aphmg/aphmg1.htm
Contact: Gerald Feldman PhD, Pres.
Founded: 1995. **Description:** Promotes human and medical genetics educational programs in North American medical and graduate schools. Conducts academic activities and workshops that deal with medical genetics.

14191 ■ Behavior Genetics Association (BGA)
c/o Stacey Cherny
Inst. for Behavioral Genetics
447 UCB
Univ. of Colorado
Boulder, CO 80309-0447
E-mail: treasurer@bga.org
URL: http://www.bga.org
Contact: Stacey Cherny, Contact
Founded: 1971. **Members:** 400. **Membership Dues:** regular, $85 (annual) ● associate, $45 (annual). **Multinational. Description:** Individuals engaged in teaching or research in some area of behavior genetics. Purposes are: to promote the scientific study of the interrelationship of genetic mechanisms and human and animal behavior through sponsorship of scientific meetings, publications, and communications among and by members; to encourage and aid the education and training of research workers in the field of behavior genetics; to aid in public dissemination and interpretation of information concerning the interrelationship of genetics and behavior and its implications for health, human development, and education. **Telecommunication Services:** electronic bulletin board, BGA Net. **Committees:** Publications and Communications. **Publications:** *Behavior Genet-*

ics, bimonthly. Journal. Includes research reports. **Price:** included in membership dues; $240.00 /year for nonmembers in U.S.; $267.00 /year for nonmembers outside U.S. ISSN: 0001-8244. **Conventions/Meetings:** annual congress.

14192 ■ Genetics Policy Institute (GPI)
11924 Forest Hill Blvd., Ste.22
Wellington, FL 33414-6208
Free: (888)238-1423
Fax: (561)791-3889
E-mail: bernard@genpol.org
URL: http://www.genpol.org
Contact: Bernard Siegel JD, Founder/Exec. Dir.
Founded: 2003. **Multinational. Description:** Gathers and disseminates information pertaining to laws and regulations relating to human reproductive cloning, therapeutic cloning, and stem cell research. Educates the public about cloning issues. Prohibits human reproductive cloning. Advocates legislation to support and regulate stem cell research and therapeutic cloning research. **Boards:** Human Rights Legal Advisory; Science Advisory. **Subgroups:** Action Network.

14193 ■ International Federation of Human Genetics Societies
c/o Office of the Secretariat
9650 Rockville Pike
Bethesda, MD 20814-3998
Ph: (301)634-7300
Fax: (301)634-7079
E-mail: estrass@ashg.org
URL: http://www.ifhgs.org
Contact: Jose Maria Cantu, Pres.
Founded: 1996. **Multinational. Description:** Supports human genetics research and practice.

14194 ■ International Society of Nurses in Genetics (ISONG)
461 Cochran Rd.
Box 246
Pittsburgh, PA 15228
Ph: (412)344-1414
Fax: (412)344-0599
E-mail: isonghq@msn.com
URL: http://www.isong.org
Contact: Ms. Beth Kassalen, Exec. Dir.
Founded: 1988. **Members:** 300. **Membership Dues:** full, $100 (annual) ● student/retired, $75 (annual) ● affiliate, $75 (annual). **Staff:** 1. **Multinational. Description:** Represents case managers, administrators, coordinators of public and private programs, educators in the field of nursing and/or genetics, genetic counselors, researchers. Committed to incorporating the knowledge of human genetics into nursing practice, education and research activities. **Awards:** Research Award. **Frequency:** annual. **Type:** grant. **Publications:** Newsletter, 3/year ● Membership Directory. **Conventions/Meetings:** annual conference ● annual meeting.

14195 ■ International Society of Psychiatric Genetics (ISPG)
650 1st Ave., 5th Fl., Rm. 543
New York, NY 10016
Ph: (212)263-3420
Fax: (212)263-3407
E-mail: lynn.delisi@med.nyu.edu
URL: http://www.ispg.net
Contact: Prof. Dr. Lynn E. DeLisi, Sec.
Membership Dues: regular, $50 (annual) ● student, $30 (annual). **Multinational. Description:** Promotes and facilitates research in the genetics of psychiatric disorders, substance use disorders and allied traits. Strives for the highest ethical standards in research and the application of findings from genetic research in clinical psychiatric practice. Encourages the development of research methods and the comparability and replicability of such results. **Awards:** Lifetime Achievement Award. **Frequency:** annual. **Type:** recognition. **Recipient:** to a scientist who has made a major contribution to the advancement of the field of psychiatric genetics ● Theodore Reich Young Investigator Award. **Frequency:** annual. **Type:** recognition. **Recipient:** for published work on psychi-

atric genetics that is of exceptional merit. **Telecommunication Services:** electronic mail, delisi76@aol.com. **Conventions/Meetings:** annual congress (exhibits) - 2007 Oct. 7-11, New York, NY; 2008 Oct. 11-15, Osaka, Japan; 2009 Oct., San Diego, CA.

14196 ■ International Society for Stem Cell Research (ISSCR)
60 Revere Dr., Ste.500
Northbrook, IL 60062
Ph: (847)509-1944
Fax: (847)480-9282
E-mail: isscr@isscr.org
URL: http://www.isscr.org
Contact: Paul J. Simmons PhD, Pres.
Founded: 2002. **Membership Dues:** active, affiliate, $95 (annual) ● associate, $45 (annual) ● organization, $5,000 (annual). **Multinational. Description:** Promotes the exchange and dissemination of information and ideas relating to stem cells. Encourages research involving stem cells. Promotes professional and public education in all areas of stem cell research and application. **Committees:** Ethics; Government Affairs and Policy; Industry; International; Junior Investigators; Planning; Public Education; Publications. **Publications:** *The Pulse*, monthly. Newsletter. Provides news and information about stem cell research, scientific and industrial meetings, and related topics. **Price:** free. Alternate Formats: online. **Conventions/Meetings:** annual meeting.

14197 ■ Mountain States Genetics Network (MostGene)
c/o Joyce Hooker, Exec. Dir.
8129 W Fremont Ave.
Littleton, CO 80128
Ph: (303)978-0125
Fax: (303)948-1890
E-mail: mostgenes@msn.com
URL: http://www.mostgene.org
Contact: Joyce Hooker, Exec. Dir.
Founded: 1984. **Membership Dues:** professional, $50 (annual) ● general, $25 (annual) ● institution, $30-$40 (annual). **Description:** Advocates and supports education, awareness and access to medical genetics information. **Libraries: Type:** lending. **Holdings:** articles, audiovisuals, books. **Subjects:** genetics materials for schools, consumers, general public, health professionals. **Telecommunication Services:** electronic mail, joycehooker@mostgene.org. **Publications:** *Directory of Genetic Services*. Contains a list of service providers in the Mountain States region. Alternate Formats: online ● *FOLATE: For a healthy you - For a healthy baby* (in English and Spanish). Pamphlet. Alternate Formats: online ● *Genetic Drift*. Journal. Alternate Formats: online ● *Have We Gotten Too Big For Our Genes?*. Handbook. Alternate Formats: online ● *Learn About Genetic Services* ● *Multiple Marker Screening*. Pamphlet. Alternate Formats: online ● *Newborn Screening Practitioners*. Manual. Alternate Formats: online ● *Thinking About Pregnancy* (in English and Spanish). Pamphlet. Alternate Formats: online ● Newsletter. **Price:** included in membership dues. **Conventions/Meetings:** annual conference.

14198 ■ National Coalition for Health Professional Education in Genetics (NCHPEG)
2360 W Joppa Rd., Ste.320
Lutherville, MD 21093
Ph: (410)583-0600
Fax: (410)583-0520
E-mail: info@nchpeg.org
URL: http://www.nchpeg.org
Contact: Joseph D. McInerney, Exec. Dir.
Founded: 1996. **Description:** Promotes advances in health professional education and access to human genetics information.

14199 ■ National Society of Genetic Counselors (NSGC)
401 N Michigan Ave., Ste.2200
Chicago, IL 60611
Ph: (312)321-6834 (312)673-4880

Fax: (312)673-6972
E-mail: nsgc@nsgc.org
URL: http://www.nsgc.org
Contact: Ms. Kristen Smith, Exec. Dir.
Founded: 1979. **Members:** 2,200. **Membership Dues:** full, $175 (annual) ● associate, $150 (annual) ● student, $100 (annual). **Regional Groups:** 6. **Description:** Promotes the genetic counseling profession as a recognized and integral part of health care delivery, education, research and public policy. **Awards:** Jane Engelberg Memorial Fellowship. **Frequency:** annual. **Type:** monetary. **Recipient:** for full member, Board Certified, or Board Eligible Genetic Counselor ● Natalie Weissberger Paul National Achievement Award. **Frequency:** annual. **Type:** recognition ● Special Project Fund. **Frequency:** annual. **Type:** recognition. **Recipient:** for full or associate member. **Computer Services:** Online services, job connection service. **Committees:** Communications; Education; Genetic Services; Professional Issues; Social Issues. **Publications:** *Journal of Genetic Counseling*, bimonthly. **Price:** $75.00/volume, for members; $85.00/volume, for nonmembers. Alternate ·Formats: online ● *Perspectives in Genetic Counseling*, quarterly. Newsletter. **Price:** $25.00/year. **Conventions/Meetings:** annual conference (exhibits).

Gerontology

14200 ■ American Aging Association (AGE)
c/o The Sally Balin Medical Center
110 Chesley Dr.
Media, PA 19063
Ph: (610)627-2626
Fax: (610)565-9747
E-mail: ameraging@aol.com
URL: http://www.americanaging.org
Contact: Holly Van Remmen PhD, Pres.
Founded: 1970. **Members:** 500. **Membership Dues:** lay, student, $50 (annual) ● scientific, $110 (annual). **Staff:** 2. **Budget:** $80,000. **Multinational. Description:** Laymen and scientists primarily in the biomedical field. Dedicated to "helping people live better, longer" by promoting biomedical aging studies directed toward slowing down the aging process, informing the public of the progress of aging research and of practical means of achieving a long and healthy life, and increasing knowledge of gerontology among physicians and other health workers. **Awards:** Denham Harman Research Award. **Frequency:** annual. **Type:** recognition. **Recipient:** for a person who has made significant contributions to biomedical aging research ● Distinguished Achievement Award. **Frequency:** annual. **Type:** recognition. **Recipient:** to a senior citizen still working ● Walter R. Nicolai Award. **Frequency:** annual. **Type:** recognition. **Recipient:** for a graduate or medical student who has done research in the area of biomedical gerontology. **Committees:** Awards; Bylaws; Clinical Gerontology; Education; Fellowship; Nomination; Public Policy; Research. **Publications:** *Age News*, quarterly. Newsletter. **Price:** included in membership dues. **Advertising:** accepted. Alternate Formats: online ● *Journal of the American Aging Association*, quarterly. Covers biomedical aging research. **Price:** $278.00 /year for institutions. ISSN: 0161-9152. **Circulation:** 500. **Advertising:** accepted. **Conventions/Meetings:** annual Interventions in Aging and Age-related Disease: The Present and the Future - meeting (exhibits).

14201 ■ American Federation for Aging Research (AFAR)
55 W 39th St., 16th Fl.
New York, NY 10018
Ph: (212)703-9977
Free: (888)582-2327
Fax: (212)997-0330
E-mail: info@afar.org
URL: http://www.afar.org
Contact: Stephanie Lederman EdM, Exec. Dir.
Founded: 1981. **Staff:** 7. **Budget:** $10,000,000. **Regional Groups:** 3. **State Groups:** 3. **Description:** Physicians, scientists, and other individuals involved

or interested in research in aging and associated diseases. Purpose is to stimulate and fund research on aging. Facilitates communication among scientists in the field. Fosters public education regarding the need for support of related research. **Awards:** Ellison Medical Foundation/AFAR Senior Postdoctoral Fellows Research Program. **Frequency:** annual. **Type:** grant. **Recipient:** for the encouragement and advancement of the careers of postdoctoral fellows (both MDs and PhDs) in the fundamental mechanisms of aging fellows ● Glenn/AFAR Breakthroughs in Gerontology Awards. **Frequency:** annual. **Type:** grant. **Recipient:** for pilot research programs that may be of relatively high risk but which offer significant promise of yielding transforming discoveries in the fundamental biology of aging ● Irving Wright Distinguished Achievement Award. **Frequency:** annual. **Type:** recognition ● Medical Student Summer Research Training in Aging Program. **Frequency:** annual. **Type:** grant. **Recipient:** for medical student geriatric scholars program; provides short-term research training opportunities for medical students ● Merck/AFAR Fellows in Geriatric Clinical Pharmacology. **Frequency:** annual. **Type:** grant. **Recipient:** to an individual ● Paul Beeson Physician Faculty Scholar in Aging Research. **Type:** grant ● The Pfizer/ AFAR Innovations in Aging Research Award Program. **Frequency:** annual. **Type:** grant. **Recipient:** for promising junior faculty scientists who wish to start highly innovative projects on the basic biology of aging and its relationship to human disease ● **Type:** recognition. **Computer Services:** Information services ● mailing lists. **Committees:** National Scientific Advisory Council; Research. **Publications:** *AFAR Newsletter*, biennial. Includes profiles of members. **Price:** free ● *The Paul Besson Physician Faculty Scholars in Aging Research Report*, annual. Reprint. Contains scientific research projects of physician scientists. **Conventions/Meetings:** annual Grantee Conference, poster session (exhibits) ● periodic meeting ● periodic seminar.

14202 ■ American Foundation for Aging Research (AFAR)
North Carolina State Univ.
Biochemistry Dept.
128 Polk Hall
Campus Box 7622
Raleigh, NC 27695-7622
.Ph: (919)515-5679
Fax: (919)515-2047
E-mail: afar_office@ncsu.edu
URL: http://www.agingresearchfoundation.org
Contact: Dr. Paul F. Agris, Pres./Treas.
Founded: 1979. **Members:** 375. **Membership Dues:** individual, $30 (annual) ● corporate, institution, $100 (annual). **Staff:** 1. **Description:** Supports basic research and educational opportunities for the study of age-related diseases and the biology of aging. Supports projects emphasizing modern biological, genetic, biochemical, and biophysical techniques and approaches to the problems of age-associated diseases and the understanding of aging. **Awards:** AFAR Fellowship. **Frequency:** semiannual. **Type:** fellowship. **Recipient:** for graduate students ● Cecille Gould Memorial Fund for Cancer Research. **Frequency:** annual. **Type:** monetary ● GlaxoSmithKline Foundation of NC Fellowship. **Frequency:** 7/year. **Type:** monetary. **Recipient:** to students attending school in North Carolina for molecular, genetic or cellular research on aging or age related illnesses ● MaWren Wilson Fulton Memorial Scholarship. **Frequency:** annual. **Type:** scholarship. **Recipient:** for undergraduates. **Additional Websites:** http://www. AmericanAgingResearch.org. **Telecommunication Services:** electronic mail, afar_applications@ncsu. edu. **Publications:** *The Newsletter of the American Foundation for Aging Research*, quarterly. **Price:** included in membership dues. **Advertising:** accepted. Alternate Formats: online. **Conventions/ Meetings:** annual lecture.

14203 ■ American Geriatrics Society (AGS)
c/o The Empire State Building
350 5th Ave., Ste.801
New York, NY 10118

Ph: (212)308-1414
Free: (800)247-4779
Fax: (212)832-8646
E-mail: info@americangeriatrics.org
URL: http://www.americangeriatrics.org
Contact: Linda Hiddemen Barondess, Exec. VP
Founded: 1942. **Members:** 6,022. **Membership Dues:** physician, $260 (annual) ● health care professional, $210 (annual) ● associate resident/fellow/post graduate trainee, $75 (annual) ● student, $40 (annual). **Staff:** 21. **Budget:** $2,700,000. **Regional Groups:** 3. **State Groups:** 23. **Description:** Professional society of physicians and other health care professionals interested in problems of the aged. Encourages and promotes the study of geriatrics; stresses the importance of medical research in the field of aging. Conducts seminars. **Awards:** Clinical Investigation Award. **Frequency:** annual. **Type:** recognition. **Recipient:** for an outstanding investigator ● Dennis W. Jahnigen Memorial Award. **Frequency:** annual. **Type:** recognition. **Recipient:** for a member who has provided leadership to train students in geriatrics ● .Edward Henderson Student Award. **Frequency:** annual. **Type:** recognition. **Recipient:** for a medical student who has demonstrated excellence in geriatrics ● Milo D. Leavitt Student Award. **Frequency:** annual. **Type:** recognition ● Nascher/Manning Award. **Frequency:** biennial. **Type:** grant. **Recipient:** for excellence in clinical geriatrics ● Student Research Award. **Frequency:** annual. **Type:** grant. **Recipient:** for an outstanding student abstract. **Computer Services:** Mailing lists. **Boards:** Directors. **Committees:** Annual Meeting Program; Clinical Practice; Education; Ethics; Ethnogeriatrics; Nominations; Professional Education Executive; Public Policy; Research. **Councils:** State Affiliates. **Special Interest Groups:** Acute Hospital Care. **Publications:** *AGS Newsletter*, bimonthly. Includes information on public policy issues of concern to members, upcoming courses, events, publications, and annual meeting. **Price:** free. **Circulation:** 11,000. **Advertising:** accepted. Alternate Formats: online ● *Annals of Long-Term Care*, monthly. Journal. Contains articles, abstracts and meeting notices. **Price:** included in membership dues; $95.00 for nonmembers in U.S.; $145.00 for nonmembers outside U.S. ● *Clinical Geriatrics*. Journal. Focuses on clinical and practical issues related to the treatment and management of older patients. ● *Doorway Thoughts: Cross-Cultural Health Care for Older Adults*. Book. **Price:** $14.95 for members; $21.95 for nonmembers ● *Geriatrics Review Syllabus: A Core Curriculum in Geriatric Medicine* ● *Journal of the American Geriatrics Society*, monthly. Includes original articles, abstracts of geriatric literature, book reviews, employment listings, and notices of meetings, courses, and symposia. **Price:** included in membership dues; $290.00 /year for nonmembers (the Americas); EUR 377.00 /year for nonmembers (Europe); 251.00 /year for nonmembers (rest of the world). ISSN: 0002-8614. **Circulation:** 9,800. **Advertising:** accepted. **Conventions/Meetings:** annual meeting (exhibits) - in May. 2008 Apr. 30-May 4, Washington, DC.

14204 ■ Gerontological Society of America (GSA)
1030 15th St. NW, Ste.250
Washington, DC 20005
Ph: (202)842-1275
Fax: (202)842-1150
E-mail: geron@geron.org
URL: http://www.geron.org
Contact: Carol A. Schutz, Exec. Dir.
Founded: 1945. **Members:** 5,000. **Membership Dues:** regular, $135 (annual) ● regular student, $65 (annual) ● undergraduate student, $20 (annual) ● spouse, $35 (annual). **Staff:** 22. **Budget:** $5,000,000. **Description:** Physicians, physiologists, psychologists, anatomists, biochemists, sociologists, social workers, psychiatrists, pharmacologists, nurses, geneticists, zoologists, endocrinologists, economists, administrators, and other professionals interested in improving the well-being of older people by promoting scientific study of the aging process, publishing information for professionals about aging, and bringing together groups interested in aging research.

Encourages research and education on the aging process. **Libraries: Type:** not open to the public. **Awards:** Donald P. Kent Award. **Frequency:** annual. **Type:** recognition. **Recipient:** for a member who exemplifies the highest standards for professional leadership in gerontology ● **Type:** fellowship. **Recipient:** for applied gerontology ● Margaret M. Baltes Early Investigator Award. **Frequency:** annual. **Type:** recognition. **Recipient:** for outstanding early career contributions in behavioral and social gerontology ● Maxwell A. Pollack Award for Productive Aging. **Frequency:** annual. **Type:** recognition. **Recipient:** for individuals who are actively engaged in development of programs that demonstrate excellence in translating research into practical application ● PGC Polisher Research Institute Award. **Frequency:** annual. **Type:** recognition ● Robert W. Kleemeier Award. **Frequency:** annual. **Type:** recognition. **Recipient:** for outstanding research in gerontology. **Computer Services:** Information services ● mailing lists. **Telecommunication Services:** electronic mail, cschutz@geron.org. **Committees:** Humanities and Arts; Program; Public Policy. **Sections:** Behavioral and Social Sciences; Biological Sciences; Clinical Medicine; Emerging Scholar and Professional Organization; Social Research, Policy and Practice. **Formerly:** (1980) Gerontological Society. **Publications:** *Aging and Sensory Change: An Annotated Bibliography* ● *CommonStake* ● *The Gerontologist*, bimonthly. Journal. Includes book and media reviews and abstracts of papers to be presented at the annual meeting. **Price:** included in membership dues; $77.00 /year for nonmembers in U.S.; $241.00 /year for institutions in U.S.; $271.00 /year for institutions outside U.S. ISSN: 0016-9013. **Circulation:** 7,400. **Advertising:** accepted. Alternate Formats: microform ● *Gerontology News*, monthly. Newsletter. Includes employment listings, information on fellowship opportunities and new books, and conference calendar. **Price:** included in membership dues; $50.00 /year for nonmembers. **Circulation:** 5,200. **Advertising:** accepted. Alternate Formats: online ● *Journal of Gerontology - Series B*, bimonthly. **Price:** $73.00 /year for members; $85.00 /year for nonmembers; $292.00 /year for institutions in U.S. (print and online); $322.00 /year for institutions outside U.S. (print and online). ISSN: 1079-5014. **Circulation:** 6,000. **Advertising:** accepted. Alternate Formats: online ● *Journals of Gerontology - Series A*, monthly. Contains two individual journals entitled *Biological Sciences*, *Medical Sciences*. **Price:** included in membership dues; $161.00 /year for nonmembers in U.S.; $649.00 /year for institutions in U.S. (print and online); $709.00 /year for institutions outside U.S. (print and online). ISSN: 1079-5006. **Circulation:** 4,000. **Advertising:** accepted. Alternate Formats: microform; online ● Membership Directory, periodic. **Conventions/Meetings:** annual meeting (exhibits) - always November. 2007 Nov. 16-20, San Francisco, CA.

14205 ■ International Psychogeriatric Association (IPA)
550 Frontage Rd., Ste.3759
Northfield, IL 60093
Ph: (847)501-3310
Fax: (847)501-3317
E-mail: membership@ipa-online.org
URL: http://www.ipa-online.org
Contact: Ms. Susan Oster CAE, Exec. Dir.
Founded: 1981. **Members:** 1,500. **Membership Dues:** individual, $110 (annual) ● institution, $225 (annual). **Staff:** 6. **Budget:** $1,000,000. **Regional Groups:** 2. **Description:** Seeks to improve the mental health of the aging world population through information dissemination, research, professional development, advocacy and service development. Multidisciplinary health care professionals and scientists from 70 countries with an interest in the behavioral and biological aspects of mental in the elderly. Works to keep members abreast of developments in research and clinical practice in the field of geriatric mental health. **Awards:** IPA Research Award in Psychogeriatrics. **Frequency:** biennial. **Type:** monetary. **Recipient:** for the best original, unpublished research in the field of psychogeriatrics ● Luigi Amaducci Memorial Award. **Frequency:** biennial.

Type: recognition. **Recipient:** for a living physician, researcher or clinician whose research in neuroscience, particularly in neurodegenerative disorders, contributed to notable advancements. **Computer Services:** database, membership ● mailing lists. **Committees:** Cross-Cultural Research; Delivery of Geriatric Services; Pharmacy and Therapeutics; Spirituality and Aging; Stroke and Multi-Infarct Dementia. **Special Interest Groups:** Primary Care Physicians. **Task Forces:** Mood Disorder; Service Delivery. **Publications:** *International Psychogeriatrics*, quarterly. Journal. **Price:** available to members only ● *IPA Bulletin*, quarterly. Newsletter ● Books ● Pamphlets. **Conventions/Meetings:** biennial congress ● annual regional meeting - in odd years.

14206 ■ National Association of Health Care Assistants (NAHCA)
1201 L St. NW
Washington, DC 20005
Ph: (202)454-1288
Free: (800)784-6049
E-mail: lcantrell@nagna.org
URL: http://www.nahcacares.org
Contact: Lisa Cantrell, Pres./Co-Founder
Founded: 1995. **Members:** 30,000. **Membership Dues:** certified nurse assistant, $10 (monthly) ● associate, $6 (monthly) ● certified nurse assistant, $120 (annual) ● associate, $72 (annual). **Description:** Ensures the quality of care given to the elders living in nursing homes. Elevates the professional standing and performance of the caregivers. Provides training, programs and other related activities that contribute to the development of its members and the field. **Awards:** CNA Key to Quality Awards. **Frequency:** annual. **Type:** recognition. **Recipient:** to outstanding certified nursing assistants for their achievements and contributions in providing the highest quality care. **Formerly:** (2006) National Association of Geriatric Nursing Assistants. **Publications:** *CNA Today*, quarterly. Magazine. Contains information about certified nursing assistants and their role in long term care. **Price:** $10.00 /year for members; $15.00 /year for nonmembers. **Circulation:** 10,000. **Advertising:** accepted ● *NAGNA News*. Newsletter. **Price:** included in membership dues.

14207 ■ National Gerontological Nursing Association (NGNA)
7794 Grow Dr.
Pensacola, FL 32514
Ph: (850)473-1174
Free: (800)723-0560
Fax: (850)484-8762
E-mail: ngna@puetzamc.com
URL: http://www.ngna.org
Contact: Belinda E. Puetz PhD, Exec. Dir.
Founded: 1984. **Members:** 1,400. **Membership Dues:** active, associate, $95 (annual) ● nursing assistant, senior, $80 (annual) ● international, $115 (annual) ● corporate, institutional, $1,000 (annual) ● student, $50 (annual). **Local Groups:** 17. **Description:** Gerontological nurses. Seeks to effectively improve the care and well-being of older adults. Provides a forum in which gerontological nursing issues are identified and explored. Develops and supports educational programs for nurses, health providers, and the general public. Disseminates information. **Awards:** Innovations in Practice Award. **Frequency:** annual. **Type:** recognition ● Judith V. Braun Research Award. **Frequency:** annual. **Type:** recognition ● Mary Opal Wolanin Scholarship. **Frequency:** annual. **Type:** scholarship. **Recipient:** for nursing students. **Committees:** Chapter Development; Clinical Practice; Program Planning. **Publications:** *Geriatric Nursing*, bimonthly. Journal. **Price:** included in membership dues. **Advertising:** accepted ● *SIGN*, bimonthly. Newsletter. **Conventions/Meetings:** annual convention (exhibits) - 2007 Oct. 18-21, Orlando, FL.

14208 ■ National Institute on Aging (NIA)
31 Center Dr., MSC 2292
Bldg. 31, Rm. 5C27
Bethesda, MD 20892

Ph: (301)496-1752
Free: (800)222-4225
Fax: (301)496-1072
URL: http://www.nia.nih.gov
Contact: Dr. Richard J. Hodes, Dir.
Founded: 1974. **Description:** Aims to conduct and support biomedical, social, and behavioral research, training, health information dissemination, and other programs on aging processes, diseases, and the special problems and need of older people. **Computer Services:** Online services, information dissemination. **Councils:** National Advisory Council on Aging.

14209 ■ New England Gerontological Association (NEGA)
1 Cutts Rd.
Durham, NH 03824-3102
Ph: (603)868-5757
E-mail: genetsr@comcast.net
URL: http://www.negaonline.org
Contact: Dr. Eugene E. Tillock, Exec. Dir.
Founded: 1958. **Members:** 125. **Membership Dues:** professional, $25 (annual) ● institutional, $100 (annual). **Staff:** 1. **Budget:** $25,000. **Regional Groups:** 1. **Description:** Promotes the study of the aging process. Conducts educational programs in aging, health service administration and long-term care administration. Computer Assisted Home Study Programs for CEU credits are made available. **Libraries: Type:** reference. **Holdings:** 500; books, periodicals. **Subjects:** aging, long-term care. **Computer Services:** Mailing lists, of members. **Publications:** *Gerontology Topics*, quarterly. Newsletter. Alternate Formats: online. **Conventions/Meetings:** periodic board meeting ● semiannual conference.

Hair

14210 ■ American Board of Hair Restoration Surgery (ABHRS)
c/o The American Board of Hair Restoration
18525 S Torrence Ave.
Lansing, IL 60438
Ph: (708)474-2600
Fax: (708)474-6260
E-mail: abhrs@sbcglobal.net
URL: http://www.abhrs.com
Contact: Mr. Peter Canalia, Exec. Dir.
Founded: 1996. **Multinational. Description:** Grants certification to candidates who meet the highest standards of the medical profession in the field of hair restoration surgery. Establishes requirements for qualification of applicants.

14211 ■ American Hair Loss Association (AHLA)
23679 Calabasas Rd., No. 254
Calabasas, CA 91302-1502
E-mail: inquire@americanhairloss.org
URL: http://www.americanhairloss.org
Description: Promotes the professional and public awareness of hair loss and the disease's impact on people's lives. Encourages the advancement of scientific research in the field of hair loss and alopecia disorders. Assists individuals with hair loss in finding appropriate treatment and developing self-help skills. **Computer Services:** Information services, hair loss resources. **Telecommunication Services:** electronic mail, membership@americanhairloss.org. **Boards:** Scientific Advisory.

14212 ■ American Society of Hair Restoration Surgery (ASHRS)
c/o American Academy of Cosmetic Surgery
737 N Michigan Ave., Ste.2100
Chicago, IL 60611
Ph: (312)981-6760
Fax: (312)981-6787
E-mail: info@cosmeticsurgery.org
URL: http://www.cosmeticsurgery.org
Contact: Jeffrey P. Knezovich, Exec. VP
Founded: 1985. **Members:** 1,800. **Staff:** 8. **Budget:** $2,500,000. **Multinational. Description:** Dedicated

to fostering the growth and quality of hair restoration surgery worldwide; promotes exchange of information among surgeons and allied professionals in the area of hair restoration surgery; advances the latest scientific data and techniques in clinical practice. **Publications:** *American Journal of Cosmetic Surgery*, quarterly.

14213 ■ International Society of Hair Restoration Surgery (ISHRS)
13 S 2nd St.
Geneva, IL 60134
Ph: (630)262-5399
Free: (800)444-2737
Fax: (630)262-1520
E-mail: info@ishrs.org
URL: http://www.ishrs.org
Contact: Victoria Ceh MPA, Exec. Dir.
Founded: 1993. **Members:** 700. **Membership Dues:** physician, adjunct, $450 (annual) ● resident, $125 (annual) ● surgical assistant, $100 (annual). **Description:** Hair restoration specialists. Endeavors to advance the art and science of hair restoration. **Publications:** *Dermatologic Surgery*, monthly. Journal. **Price:** included in membership dues ● *Hair Transplant Forum International*, bimonthly. Newsletter. **Price:** included in membership dues.

Hand

14214 ■ American Association for Hand Surgery (AAHS)
20 N Michigan Ave., Ste.700
Chicago, IL 60602
Ph: (312)236-3307
Fax: (312)782-0553
E-mail: contact@handsurgery.org
URL: http://www.handsurgery.org
Contact: Ms. Laura Downes CAE, Exec. Dir.
Founded: 1970. **Members:** 1,100. **Membership Dues:** affiliate, $190 (annual) ● international, $165 (annual) ● active, $440 (annual). **Staff:** 4. **Budget:** $600,000. **Description:** Plastic, orthopedic, general surgeons, and physical and occupational therapists having a specific interest in hand surgery; individuals in the medical profession, basic sciences, or allied services interested in the improvement of hand surgery. Purpose is to advance hand surgery. Conducts symposia; offers specialized education. **Awards:** Research Grants. **Frequency:** annual. **Type:** grant. **Recipient:** based on proposal submission ● Vargas International Hand Therapist Teaching Award. **Frequency:** annual. **Type:** grant. **Recipient:** to a hand therapist. **Computer Services:** Mailing lists, of members. **Committees:** Education; Hand Therapy; Research Grants; Technology. **Publications:** *Annual Program*, annual. Proceedings. **Circulation:** 500. **Advertising:** accepted ● *Hand*, quarterly. Journal. **Circulation:** 1,000. **Advertising:** accepted. Alternate Formats: online ● *Hand Surgery Newsletter*, quarterly. **Price:** included in membership dues. Alternate Formats: online. **Conventions/Meetings:** annual meeting (exhibits) - 2008 Jan. 9-12, Beverly Hills, CA - **Avg. Attendance:** 500; 2009 Jan. 7-10, Wailea, HI - **Avg. Attendance:** 600.

14215 ■ American Foundation for Surgery of the Hand (AFSH)
6300 N River Rd., Ste.600
Rosemont, IL 60018-4256
Ph: (847)384-8300
Fax: (847)384-1435
E-mail: info@assh.org
URL: http://www.assh.org
Contact: Mark C. Anderson CAE, Exec. Dir.
Founded: 1986. **Membership Dues:** active, supporting, $530 (annual) ● senior, candidate, senior supporting, $300 (annual) ● international, $250 (annual) ● life (for 30 or more years active member), $300. **Staff:** 1. **Budget:** $400,000. **Description:** Aims to advance the science and practice of hand and upper extremity surgery through education, research and advocacy on behalf of patients and practitioners. Provides reliable and authoritative source of informa-

tion on all aspects of hand and upper extremity disorders for all audiences: surgeons, allied health professionals, government, business and industry, patients and the general public. **Awards: Type:** grant. **Recipient:** to medical, educational, research, and public education programs related to the field of hand and upper extremity surgery. **Telecommunication Services:** electronic mail, manderson@assh.org. **Programs:** International Scholarship. **Affiliated With:** American Society for Surgery of the Hand. **Publications:** Annual Report, annual. **Conventions/Meetings:** annual meeting - 2007 Sept. 27-29, Seattle, WA; 2008 Sept. 18-20, Chicago, IL; 2009 Sept. 3-5, San Francisco, CA; 2010 Oct. 7-9, Boston, MA.

14216 ■ American Society of Hand Therapists (ASHT)
401 N Michigan Ave.
Chicago, IL 60611-4267
Ph: (312)321-6866
Fax: (312)673-6670
E-mail: info@asht.org
URL: http://www.asht.org
Contact: Stacey L. Doyon, Pres.
Founded: 1977. **Members:** 2,700. **Membership Dues:** individual, $225 (annual) ● student, $45 (annual). **Staff:** 8. **Budget:** $1,200,000. **State Groups:** 14. **Description:** Registered and licensed occupational and physical therapists specializing in hand therapy and committed to excellence and professionalism in hand rehabilitation. Works to promote research, publish information, improve treatment techniques, and standardize hand evaluation and care. Fosters education and communication between therapists in the U.S. and abroad. Compiles statistics; conducts research and education programs and continuing education seminars. **Computer Services:** Mailing lists. **Boards:** Editorial Review. **Committees:** Certification; Clinical Assessment; Communications; Continuing Education; International Affairs; Practice Issues; Research. **Publications:** *ASHT Times*, bimonthly. Newsletter. **Price:** included in membership dues. **Advertising:** accepted. Alternate Formats: online ● *Journal of Hand Therapy*, quarterly. Includes original reports, clinical reviews, case studies, editorials, and book reviews. **Price:** included in membership dues. **Advertising:** accepted. Alternate Formats: online. **Conventions/Meetings:** annual meeting (exhibits) - 2007 Oct. 4-7, Phoenix, AZ.

14217 ■ American Society for Surgery of the Hand (ASSH)
6300 N River Rd., Ste.600
Rosemont, IL 60018
Ph: (847)384-8300
Fax: (847)384-1435
E-mail: info@assh.org
URL: http://www.assh.org
Contact: Mark C. Anderson CAE, Exec. Dir.
Founded: 1946. **Members:** 2,000. **Membership Dues:** active, supporting, $530 (annual) ● senior, candidate, senior supporting, $300 (annual) ● international, $250 (annual). **Staff:** 13. **Budget:** $5,000,000. **Description:** Surgeons specializing in surgery of the hand. Funds research in the field of hand surgery. Sponsors educational programs. Maintains a website that offers information on common hand problems. **Libraries: Type:** reference. **Holdings:** archival material, artwork, audiovisuals, books, periodicals. **Subjects:** hand surgery. **Awards: Type:** recognition. **Publications:** *American Foundation for Surgery of the Hand Brochure*. **Price:** free ● *Ganglion Cysts Brochure*. **Price:** $18.00 ● *Global Service Guide to Hand Surgery: 2003 Edition*. Book. **Price:** $80.00 ● *Hand Surgery Update 3*. Book. **Price:** $140.00 ● *ICD-9-CM Coding Book for Hand Surgery*. **Price:** $55.00 ● *The Journal of Hand Surgery*, bimonthly ● *On The Shoulders of Giants*. Book. **Price:** $25.00 ● *Self-assessment Examination in Hand Surgery*, annual. **Price:** $75.00. **Conventions/Meetings:** annual meeting (exhibits) - 2007 Sept. 27-29, Seattle, WA; 2008 Sept. 18-20, Chicago, IL.

14218 ■ Foundation for Hand Research and Education
c/o Indiana Hand Center
PO Box 80434
Indianapolis, IN 46280-0434

Ph: (317)875-9105 (317)471-4340
Free: (800)888-HAND
Fax: (317)471-4382
URL: http://www.indianahandcenter.com/center_foundation.html
Contact: Tony O'Connell MALS, Foundation Mgr.
Founded: 1988. **Staff:** 2. **Description:** Promotes the advancement of hand surgery and research. Aims to improve the quality of life of persons with injuries or disorders of the hands and upper extremities. Conducts educational programs. **Libraries: Type:** reference. **Holdings:** 1,000; audiovisuals, books, monographs, periodicals. **Subjects:** hand, wrist, elbow and shoulder surgery and rehabilitation. **Awards:** Research Grant. **Frequency:** annual. **Type:** grant. **Recipient:** for board certified hand surgeons engaged in research. **Computer Services:** database, information on hands and upper extremities. **Formerly:** Indiana Foundation for Hand Surgical Research. **Publications:** *Indiana Hand Center Newsletter*, 3/year. Features full color descriptions of hand surgery and rehabilitation. **Price:** $75.00/year. **ISSN:** 1072-3528. **Circulation:** 400. **Conventions/Meetings:** quarterly board meeting.

14219 ■ International Federation of Societies for Surgery of the Hand (IFSSH)
c/o Dr. James R. Urbaniak, MD, Sec. Gen.
PO Box 2912
Duke Univ. Medical Center
Durham, NC 27710
Ph: (919)684-5388
Fax: (919)681-7378
E-mail: urban006@mc.duke.edu
Contact: Dr. James R. Urbaniak MD, Sec. Gen.
Founded: 1966. **Members:** 5,000. **Membership Dues:** active, $10 (annual). **Staff:** 1. **Budget:** $40,000. **Regional Groups:** 48. **Multinational. Description:** Individuals involved in hand surgery. Coordinates activities by maintaining liaison among member societies; promotes the exchange of information; attempts to improve opportunities for study and observation on an international level. Establishes and recommends standards of nomenclature, classification of malformations, and disability evaluation; promotes a bibliography of world literature on surgery of the hand. Conducts scientific sessions; maintains committees to develop standards and agreements on special areas of hand surgery. **Libraries: Type:** reference. **Holdings:** archival material. **Awards:** Pioneer in Hand Surgery. **Frequency:** quinquennial. **Type:** recognition. **Publications:** *Terminology of Hand Surgery*, annual. Newsletter. **Conventions/Meetings:** triennial congress (exhibits).

Head Injury

14220 ■ Brain Injury Association of America (BIAA)
8201 Greensboro Dr., Ste.611
McLean, VA 22102
Ph: (703)761-0750
Free: (800)444-6443
Fax: (703)761-0755
E-mail: braininjuryinfo@biausa.org
URL: http://www.biausa.org
Contact: Mr. Greg Ayotte, Dir. of Consumer Services
Founded: 1980. **Members:** 41. **Staff:** 7. **Budget:** $2,000,000. **State Groups:** 41. **Local Groups:** 600. **Languages:** English, Spanish. **Description:** National organization working for and with people with brain injury and their families. Seeks to create a better future through brain injury prevention, research, education and advocacy. **Libraries: Type:** reference; by appointment only. **Holdings:** archival material, articles, periodicals, reports. **Subjects:** head injury, brain injury, rehabilitation, public policy. **Awards:** Founders Award. **Frequency:** annual. **Type:** recognition. **Recipient:** for outstanding contributions in building and strengthening the BIA, enabling it to fulfill its mission ● Jim and Sarah Brady Public Service Award. **Frequency:** annual. **Type:** recognition. **Recipient:** for an individual who has enhanced the understanding of brain injury through public service

and education at the national level ● Sheldon Berrol Clinical Service Award. **Frequency:** annual. **Type:** recognition. **Recipient:** for individual who, through clinical service, has made outstanding contributions to improving quality of care, professional training, and/or education ● Silvio O. Conte Award. **Frequency:** annual. **Type:** recognition. **Recipient:** for outstanding contributions in affecting national policy as it relates to brain injury ● William Fields Caveness Award. **Frequency:** annual. **Type:** monetary. **Recipient:** for an individual who, through research, has made outstanding contributions toward bettering the lives of persons who have sustained traumatic brain injuries ● Young Investigator Award. **Frequency:** annual. **Type:** recognition. **Recipient:** for an individual within five years of completing professional training. **Computer Services:** database ● mailing lists. **Formerly:** National Head Injury Foundation; (2002) Brain Injury Association. **Publications:** *Brain Injury Awareness Month Booklets.* Provides information and resources on "Living with Brain Injury". **Price:** $3.00/booklet ● *Brain Injury Awareness Presentation Kit.* Handbook. **Price:** $175.00 ● *National Directory of Rehabilitation Services,* annual. **Price:** $20.00. Alternate Formats: CD-ROM; online ● *TBI Challenge!,* quarterly. Newsletter. **Price:** $25.00/year. **Circulation:** 30,000. **Advertising:** accepted. Alternate Formats: online ● Annual Report, annual. Alternate Formats: online. **Conventions/Meetings:** annual conference and convention, latest technology/cutting edge research in the field, providers of quality brain injury services (exhibits).

14221 ■ National Association of State Head Injury Administrators (NASHIA)

4330 EW Hwy., Ste.301
Bethesda, MD 20814
Ph: (301)656-3500 (301)656-3145
Fax: (301)656-3530
E-mail: nashia@nashia.org
URL: http://www.nashia.org
Contact: Kenneth Currier, Exec. Dir.

Founded: 1995. **Membership Dues:** state agency, $450 (annual) ● individual, $175 (annual) ● supporting gold, $1,500 (annual) ● supporting silver, $1,000 (annual) ● supporting bronze, $500 (annual) ● associate, $100 (annual). **Description:** Assists state governments in promoting partnerships and building systems to meet the needs of individuals with brain injuries and their families. Serves as a source of professional education and training for state head injury officials. Promotes excellence in the practice of head injury rehabilitation, community support services and prevention programs. **Telecommunication Services:** electronic mail, khcurrier@nashia.org. **Publications:** *NASHIA News.* Newsletter. Alternate Formats: online.

Headache

14222 ■ American Council for Headache Education (ACHE)

19 Mantua Rd.
Mount Royal, NJ 08061
Ph: (856)423-0258
Free: (800)255-ACHE
Fax: (856)423-0082
E-mail: achehq@talley.com
URL: http://www.achenet.org
Contact: Linda McGillicuddy, Exec. Dir.

Founded: 1990. **Members:** 5,000. **Membership Dues:** regular, $20 (annual). **Budget:** $250,000. **Description:** Headache sufferers and physicians dedicated to advancing treatment and management of headache; promotes public awareness. **Libraries:** **Type:** reference. **Holdings:** books. **Computer Services:** database, ACHE physicians ● mailing lists. **Publications:** *Headache,* quarterly. Newsletter. Provides current information on new treatments and management strategies. **Price:** included in membership dues. **Circulation:** 10,000. Alternate Formats: online ● *Migraine: The Complete Guide.* Book.

14223 ■ American Headache Society (AHS)

19 Mantua Rd.
Mount Royal, NJ 08061
Ph: (856)423-0043
Fax: (856)423-0082
E-mail: ahshq@talley.com
URL: http://www.ahsnet.org
Contact: Linda McGillicuddy, Exec. Dir.

Founded: 1959. **Members:** 2,000. **Membership Dues:** active in U.S., $150 (annual) ● associate, $60 (annual) ● trainee, $50 (annual) ● active outside U.S., $170 (annual). **Budget:** $1,500,000. **Description:** Professional society of health care providers dedicated to the study and treatment of headache and face pain. Objectives are to promote the exchange of information and ideas concerning the causes and treatments of headache and related painful disorders, to educate physicians, health professionals and the public, and to encourage research. **Libraries:** **Type:** reference. **Holdings:** reports. **Awards:** American Council for Headache Education Lecture Award. **Frequency:** annual. **Type:** recognition. **Recipient:** for health professionals ● Arnold P. Friedman Distinguished Clinician Award. **Frequency:** annual. **Type:** recognition. **Recipient:** for distinguished clinicians ● Harold G. Wolff Lecture Award. **Frequency:** annual. **Type:** recognition. **Recipient:** to the author who has contributed the best original paper on headache, head or face pain, or the nature of pain itself ● John R. Graham Senior Clinician's Forum Award. **Frequency:** annual. **Type:** recognition. **Recipient:** for clinicians ● Kaplan Award. **Frequency:** annual. **Type:** recognition. **Recipient:** for health professional who has submitted the best abstract on chronic daily headache ● Seymour Solomon Presidential Lecture Award. **Frequency:** annual. **Type:** recognition. **Recipient:** for achievements in the field of headache. **Computer Services:** Mailing lists. **Councils:** American Council for Headache Education. **Special Interest Groups:** Academic Affairs; Cluster Headache; Complementary and Alternative Medicine; Disease Management; Pediatric-Adolescent Headache; Primary Care; Refractory Headache. **Formerly:** (2001) American Association for the Study of Headache. **Publications:** *Headache: The Journal of Head and Face Pain,* 10/year. Presents papers concerning basic research and clinical studies. Includes book reviews. **Price:** included in membership dues; $40.00/year for medical students, interns, and residents; $95.00 /year for nonmembers in U.S.; $110.00 /year for nonmembers outside U.S. ISSN: 0017-8748. **Circulation:** 2,550. **Advertising:** accepted. Alternate Formats: microform; online. **Conventions/Meetings:** annual Scientific Meeting (exhibits) - always June.

14224 ■ Migraine Awareness Group: A National Understanding for "Migraineurs" (MAGNUM)

113 S St. Asaph, Ste.300
Alexandria, VA 22314
Ph: (703)739-9384
Fax: (703)739-2432
E-mail: comments@migraines.org
URL: http://www.migraines.org
Contact: Michael John Coleman, Exec. Dir./Founder

Founded: 1994. **Description:** Works to bring public and governmental awareness to the medical seriousness of the migraine disease. Provides information and support to migraine sufferers and their families. **Computer Services:** Online services.

14225 ■ National Headache Foundation (NHF)

820 N Orleans St., Ste.217
Chicago, IL 60610-3498
Free: (888)NHF-5552
Fax: (773)525-7357
E-mail: info@headaches.org
URL: http://www.headaches.org
Contact: Seymore Diamond MD, Exec. Chm.

Founded: 1970. **Members:** 20,000. **Membership Dues:** individual, $20 (annual) ● associate, health-care professional, $60 (annual) ● physician, $100 (annual) ● corporate, $1,000 (annual). **Staff:** 7. **Budget:** $900,000. **Description:** Headache sufferers, physicians, health care professionals. Serves as an information resource to headache sufferers, their families, and the physicians who treat them. Promotes research into potential headache causes and treatments. Educates the public to the fact that headaches are a legitimate biological disease and sufferers need understanding and continuity of care. Disseminates free information on headache causes and treatments. Funds research. Operates network of local support groups. **Libraries:** **Type:** reference. **Holdings:** monographs, reports, video recordings. **Awards:** NHF Lectureship Award. **Frequency:** annual. **Type:** recognition. **Computer Services:** database, members and donors. **Committees:** Fellowship; Finance and Program; Fundraising; Newsletter; Personnel; Research. **Programs:** E-mail Pen Pal. **Formerly:** (1986) National Migraine Foundation. **Publications:** *About Headaches.* Pamphlet ● *The Headache Handbook* ● *How to Talk to Your Healthcare Provider About Headaches.* Brochure ● *NHF Head Lines,* bimonthly. Newsletter. Includes information on headache causes and treatments, foundation news, book reviews, research reports, support group updates, and reader Q&A. **Price:** included in membership dues; $20.00 /year for nonmembers. **Circulation:** 45,000 ● Headache: A Guide to Prevention and Treatment/A Patient's Guide to Migraine Prevention and Treatment/Headache Q & A. **Conventions/Meetings:** Educational Seminars ● seminar, for public and professional education.

Health

14226 ■ Academy Health Sciences

229 W 97th St.
New York, NY 10025
Ph: (212)932-2381
Fax: (212)932-1363
E-mail: naturaltherapy@pipeline.com
URL: http://www.naturaltherapy.org
Contact: Dr. Shoshana Margolin, Coor.

Founded: 1996. **Members:** 120. **Staff:** 4. **Description:** Arranges conferences where researchers and practitioners share innovative ideas on upgrading the skills of healthcare professionals. Conducts research and educational programs.

14227 ■ AcademyHealth

1801 K St. NW, No. 701-L
Washington, DC 20006
Ph: (202)292-6700
Fax: (202)292-6800
E-mail: info@academyhealth.org
URL: http://www.academyhealth.org
Contact: W. David Helms PhD, Pres./CEO

Founded: 1981. **Members:** 4,125. **Membership Dues:** regular, international, $150 (annual) ● student, $25 (annual) ● contributing affiliate, $10,000 ● supporting affiliate, $5,000 ● affiliate, $2,000. **Staff:** 50. **Budget:** $8,000,000. **Description:** Promotes interaction across the health research and policy arenas by bringing together a broad spectrum of players to share their perspectives, learn from each other and strengthen their working relationships. Convenes national scientific and health policy conferences; helps public and private policymakers transform research and policy into workable programs; educates policymakers, researchers, government officials, and business leaders; disseminates vital information through research syntheses, special report findings, newsletters and website; and conducts major programs that serve the research community, health policy leaders, and business and government decision-makers. **Computer Services:** Mailing lists. **Programs:** Commission on a High Performance Health System; Medicare's Future; State Coverage Initiatives. **Projects:** W.K. Kellogg Foundation Diversity in Health Services Research. **Formed by Merger of:** (2000) Association for Health Services Research; (2000) Alpha Center. **Formerly:** (2000) Academy for Health Services Research and Health Policy. **Publications:** *AcademyHealth Reports,* quarterly. Newsletter. Covers legislative news and association activities. Includes conference calendar, employment listings, and training opportunities. **Price:** included in membership dues. **Circulation:** 3,700. **Advertising:** accepted ● *Health Affairs*, bimonthly. Journal ● Annual Report, annual. Alternate Formats: online. **Conventions/Meetings:** annual Research Meeting (exhibits) - 2008 June 8-10, Washington, DC.

14228 ■ AHEAD-INC., African Health Education and Development
PO Box 600379
Dallas, TX 75206
Ph: (214)823-0007 (214)823-7666
Fax: (214)823-7373
E-mail: ad@aheadinc.com
URL: http://www.aheadinc.com
Contact: Dr. Richard O. Nwachukwu, Exec. Dir./ Founder
Founded: 1997. **Multinational. Description:** Offers health education and development in Africa in order to help its people become self-sufficient.

14229 ■ America on the Move Foundation (AOMF)
44 School St., Ste.325
Boston, MA 02108
Ph: (617)367-6894
Free: (800)807-0077
Fax: (617)367-6899
E-mail: sani@americaonthemove.org
URL: http://www.americaonthemove.org
Contact: Sani Liu, Admin. Coor.
Nonmembership. Description: Works to help individuals, families, and communities to make small, positive changes to improve their health and quality of life. Focuses on individuals and communities and strives to support healthy eating and active living habits in the society.

14230 ■ American Association for Klinefelter Syndrome Information and Support (AAKSIS)
c/o Roberta Rappaport, Founding Pres.
2945 W Farwell Ave.
Chicago, IL 60645-2925
Ph: (773)761-5298
Free: (888)466-5747
Fax: (773)761-5298
E-mail: ksinfo@aaksis.org
URL: http://www.aaksis.org
Contact: Roberta Rappaport, Founding Pres.
Founded: 1999. **Members:** 750. **Membership Dues:** general, $25 (annual). **Staff:** 3. **Budget:** $25,000. **Regional Groups:** 11. **Languages:** English, Spanish. **Description:** Volunteers, those affected by the genetic chromosomal condition and parents of those affected. Provides support, information and resources. Promotes public awareness. **Libraries: Type:** open to the public. **Holdings:** books. **Subjects:** Klinefelter Syndrome. **Awards:** AAKSIS Special Recognition Award. **Frequency:** annual. **Type:** recognition. **Computer Services:** database, information, support, resources ● mailing lists. **Affiliated With:** National Organization for Rare Disorders. **Also Known As:** AAKSIS. **Publications:** *KaleidoScope*, 3/year. Newsletter. Contains information, support, resources, and articles of interest on XXY/Klinefelter Syndrome. **Price:** included in membership dues. **Circulation:** 250. Alternate Formats: online. **Conventions/Meetings:** annual conference.

14231 ■ American Council on Science and Health (ACSH)
1995 Broadway, 2nd Fl.
New York, NY 10023-5882
Ph: (212)362-7044
Fax: (212)362-4919
E-mail: acsh@acsh.org
URL: http://www.acsh.org
Contact: Mr. Jeff Stier, Assoc. Dir.
Founded: 1978. **Members:** 2,000. **Membership Dues:** funder, $250-$100,000 (annual) ● individual, $50-$249 (annual). **Staff:** 12. **Budget:** $2,000,000. **Description:** Provides consumers with scientifically balanced evaluations of food, chemicals, the environment, and human health. Council personnel participate in government regulatory proceedings, congressional hearings, contribute op-ed pieces to major

newspapers, appear on radio and television programs, and public debates and forums. **Additional Websites:** http://healthfactsandfears.com. **Publications:** *ACSH in Action*, quarterly. Newsletter ● *Cigarettes: What the Warning Label Doesn't Tell You* ● *Drug-Supplement Interaction.* Brochure. **Price:** $1.00 ● *The Dry-Cleaning Chemical Perc.* Brochure. **Price:** $1.00 ● *Eggs.* Brochure. **Price:** $1.00 ● *Media Update*, semiannual ● *MMT's.* Brochure. **Price:** $1.00 ● *Olestra.* Brochure. **Price:** $1.00 ● *PCB's.* Brochure. **Price:** $1.00 ● *Pressure-Treated Wood.* Brochure. **Price:** $1.00 ● *The Role of Milk in Your Diet.* Brochure. **Price:** $1.00 ● Papers ● Reports. On health risks and benefits associated with public health and environmental issues. **Conventions/Meetings:** annual board meeting.

14232 ■ American Foundation for Health (AFH)
Address Unknown since 2006
Founded: 1979. **Members:** 17,000. **Staff:** 18. **Description:** Individuals interested in improving the delivery of health care services. Encourages recording of personal medical data. Conducts educational research projects and activities. **Publications:** *Health Features*, periodic. Newsletter. **Advertising:** not accepted. **Conventions/Meetings:** periodic conference.

14233 ■ American Health Care Association (AHCA)
1201 L St. NW
Washington, DC 20005
Ph: (202)842-4444
Fax: (202)842-3860
E-mail: update@ahca.org
URL: http://www.ahca.org
Contact: Dr. Hal Daub, Pres./CEO
Founded: 1949. **Members:** 12,000. **Staff:** 85. **Budget:** $15,000,000. **State Groups:** 50. **Description:** Federation of state associations of long-term health care facilities. Promotes standards for professionals in long-term health care delivery and quality care for patients and residents in a safe environment. Focuses on issues of availability, quality, affordability, and fair payment. Operates as liaison with governmental agencies, Congress, and professional associations. Compiles statistics. **Libraries: Type:** lending; reference; by appointment only. **Holdings:** audiovisuals, books, clippings, monographs, periodicals. **Subjects:** long-term care, nursing facilities, assisted living, subacute care. **Awards:** AHCA/NCAL Quality Award. **Frequency:** annual. **Type:** recognition. **Recipient:** to AHCA/NCAL-member facilities for applying continuous quality improvement principles ● James Durante Nurse Scholarship. **Frequency:** annual. **Type:** scholarship. **Recipient:** for nursing student working in a long-term care facility. **Committees:** Assisted Living; Ethics; Independent Owners; Life Safety; Medicaid; Medicare; Multifacility; Non-Proprietary; Political Action. **Departments:** Administrative Knowledge Management; Legislative; Membership; Professional Development; Public Relations; Regulatory; Sales and Marketing. **Absorbed:** (1984) National Council of Health Centers. **Formed by Merger of:** American Association of Nursing Homes; National Association of Registered Nursing Homes. **Formerly:** (1975) American Nursing Home Association. **Publications:** *AHCA Notes*, monthly. Newsletter. Covers legislation and regulations. **Price:** included in membership dues ● *Provider: For Long Term Care Professionals*, monthly. Magazine. Includes buyers' guide, news reports, advertisers' index, a listing of new products and services, and calendar of events. **Price:** free to long-term health care professionals; $48.00 /year for nonmembers and libraries. ISSN: 0360-4069. **Circulation:** 24,000. **Advertising:** accepted. Alternate Formats: microform ● Also produces audiovisual aids. **Conventions/Meetings:** annual conference, for long-term care professionals (exhibits) ● periodic conference ● seminar, for nursing home personnel ● annual convention - always October. 2007 Oct. 7-10, Boston, MA; 2008 Oct. 5-8, Nashville, TN; 2009 Oct. 4-7, Chicago, IL.

14234 ■ American Health Decisions (AHD)
The Hastings Center
21 Malcolm Gordon Rd.
Garrison, NY 10524

Ph: (845)424-0005 (845)424-4040
E-mail: jennings@thehastingscenter.org
URL: http://www.ahd.org
Contact: David Clarke, Chm.
Founded: 1989. **Members:** 13. **State Groups:** 13. **Description:** Confederation of state health decision programs. Assists in establishing public education programs about health care and policy; works to increase availability of quality medical care. Promotes personal autonomy on ethical issues, such as patients making the decision to refuse or accept treatment. Addresses problems arising from ethical conflicts over new medical technologies and disease prevention. Maintains research and educational programs; disseminates information.

14235 ■ American Health Planning Association (AHPA)
7245 Arlington Blvd., Ste.300
Falls Church, VA 22042
Ph: (703)573-3103
Fax: (703)573-3103
E-mail: info@ahpanet.org
URL: http://www.ahpanet.org
Contact: Karen Cameron MPH, Exec. Dir.
Founded: 1970. **Membership Dues:** individual-regular, $75 (annual) ● individual-supporting, affiliate-regular, $250 (annual) ● affiliate-supporting, organizational, $500 (annual) ● student, $25 (annual). **Description:** State and local health planning agencies and affiliated organizations and individuals. Conducts research; disseminates information; serves as clearinghouse for health planning activities and concepts; sponsors programs of technical assistance; provides continuing education. **Awards:** CHPPD Section Service Award. **Frequency:** annual. **Type:** recognition. **Recipient:** for a section member who has made a significant contribution to the sections' operations ● Henrik L. Blum Award. **Frequency:** annual. **Type:** recognition. **Recipient:** for excellence in health policy ● James R. Kimmey Award. **Frequency:** annual. **Type:** recognition. **Recipient:** for excellence in health planning practice. **Computer Services:** Mailing lists. **Formerly:** (1977) American Association for Comprehensive Health Planning. **Publications:** *Certificate of Need Regulation of Home Health and Hospice Services in the United States, 1996-2000.* Monograph ● *Certificate of Need Regulation of Nursing Home Services in the United States, 1996-2000.* Monograph ● *National Directory of Health Planning, Policy, and Regulatory Agencies*, annual. **Price:** $125.00 for nonmembers; included in membership dues ● *TODAY in Health Planning*, quarterly. Newsletter. **Price:** included in membership dues. **Conventions/Meetings:** conference and meeting.

14236 ■ American Hemochromatosis Society (AHS)
c/o Sandra Thomas, Pres./Founder
4044 W Lake Mary Blvd., Unit No. 104
PMB 416
Lake Mary, FL 32746-2012
Ph: (407)829-4488
Free: (888)655-4766
Fax: (407)333-1284
E-mail: mail@americanhs.org
URL: http://www.americanhs.org
Contact: Sandra Thomas, Pres./Founder
Membership Dues: general, $25 (annual). **Description:** Educates and supports victims of HFE-associated hereditary hemochromatosis (genetic iron overload) and their families. Educates the medical community on the latest research on the disease. Seeks to identify, through genetic testing, Americans who are unknowingly carrying gene mutations that put them at risk for hereditary hemochromatosis. **Computer Services:** Information services, hemochromatosis resources ● information services, resources for physicians ● online services, memorials. **Committees:** AHS Chapters; Legislative Affairs; Nursing Advisory. **Publications:** *The Blood Letter.* Newsletter.

14237 ■ Aneurysm Outreach Inc. (AOI)
17222 Hwy. 929
Prairieville, LA 70769
Ph: (225)622-1577 (225)622-2202

Fax: (225)622-1502
E-mail: aoi@alink.org
URL: http://www.alink.org
Contact: Sheila G. Arrington, Pres./Founder
Founded: 1999. **Staff:** 1. **Budget:** $50,000. **State Groups:** 1. **Nonmembership. Description:** Provides support network for those affected or at risk of abdominal aortic aneurysm and other aneurysms. Gives aneurysm research questionnaire at web site. Promotes public awareness about the silent threat of undiscovered aneurysms; plans to fund aneurysm research through advocacy and tax-deductible donations. Uses volunteers to coordinate a free abdominal aorta aneurysm screening program in Louisiana's major cities and participates in area health fairs. **Computer Services:** Information services, research connections, FAQ, physician referral.

14238 ■ Asian and Pacific Islander American Health Forum (APIAHF)
450 Sutter St., Ste.600
San Francisco, CA 94108
Ph: (415)954-9988
Fax: (415)954-9999
E-mail: healthinfo@apiahf.org
URL: http://www.apiahf.org
Contact: Dr. Ho L. Tran MD, Pres./CEO
Founded: 1986. **Members:** 350. **Membership Dues:** student/senior, $15 (annual) ● individual, $60 (annual) ● non-profit organization, $150 (annual) ● corporate, $1,500 (annual) ● individual, $150 (triennial). **Staff:** 17. **Budget:** $1,400,000. **Description:** Promotes policy, program, and research efforts for the improvement of health status of all Asian and Pacific Islander Americans. Examines and reviews the distribution of factors associated with health problems and issues facing Asian and Pacific Islander Americans, including infectious diseases, diabetes, hypertension, cancer, HIV/AIDS, substance abuse, and mental health disorders. Compiles statistics. **Libraries: Type:** reference. **Holdings:** articles, audiovisuals, books, clippings, monographs. **Programs:** API Center for Census Information and Services; API Health Information; API HIV Capacity-Building Assistance; Asian and Pacific Islander Chronic Disease; The Asian and Pacific Islander Institute on Domestic Violence. **Subgroups:** Asian and Pacific Islander Center for Census Information and Services; Asian and Pacific Islander Health Information Network; Asian and Pacific Islander Tobacco Education Network; Asian and Pacific Islander's California Action Network; California Multicultural Health Information Network; Empowerment Through Training and Technical Assistance. **Publications:** *AIDS Prevalence in US Asian and Pacific Islander Populations.* Bibliography. Contains analysis of data regarding the prevalence of the HIV virus and AIDS in Asian and Pacific Islander populations in the United States. ● *APIAHF Focus,* quarterly. Newsletter. **Circulation:** 500 ● *APITEN Newsletter.* **Circulation:** 500 ● *Confronting Critical Health Issues of Asian and Pacific Islander Americans.* Book ● *Youth Wire.* Newsletter. Alternate Formats: online. **Conventions/Meetings:** board meeting ● biennial conference.

14239 ■ Association of Academic Health Centers (AAHC)
1400 16th St. NW, Ste.720
Washington, DC 20036
Ph: (202)265-9600
Fax: (202)265-7514
E-mail: ahc@aahcdc.org
URL: http://www.aahcdc.org
Contact: Ms. Veronica Hardy, Admin. Asst.
Founded: 1969. **Members:** 102. **Staff:** 12. **Description:** Aims to improve health and well-being through the vigorous leadership of academic health centers. An academic health center is defined as an accredited, degree-granting institution of higher education that consists of a medical school (allopathic or osteopathic), one or more health professions schools and/or graduate programs, and an affiliated or owned relationship to a teaching hospital, health system, or other organized health care provider. Takes leadership in the areas of teaching, patient care, and

research as applied to educating the next generation of health professionals, providing comprehensive and advanced medical care, and discovering new knowledge and tools in the fight against disease. **Task Forces:** Executive Leadership Group for Senior Administrative and Fiscal Officers. **Working Groups:** Executive Leadership Group for the Forum on Regulation; Executive Leadership Group for Vice Presidents for Research; Executive Leadership Group of Senior Legal Counsel; The Policy Assembly; The Policy Network. **Formerly:** Academic Health Centers: Responses to the Malpractice Insurance Crisis. **Conventions/Meetings:** annual meeting.

14240 ■ Association for the Advancement of Wound Care (AAWC)
83 Gen. Warren Blvd., Ste.100
Malvern, PA 19355
Ph: (610)560-0484 (610)560-0500
Free: (866)AAWC-999
Fax: (610)560-0502
E-mail: info@aawcone.org
URL: http://www.aawcone.org
Contact: Tina Thomas, Exec.Dir.
Founded: 1995. **Members:** 1,600. **Membership Dues:** individual/clinician, $120 (annual) ● student/retiree, $50 (annual) ● organization/industry, $300 (annual) ● patient/caregiver, $25 (annual). **Staff:** 1. **Budget:** $100,000. **Description:** Works to advance the cause of wound care through education, research, clinical practice and public policy. Provides a forum for communication and partnership among all people involved in wound care. **Awards:** Distinguished Member Award. **Frequency:** annual. **Type:** recognition. **Recipient:** for excellence and dedicated service in the wound care arena. **Computer Services:** Mailing lists, of companies involved in wound care products; list for rent to those advertising for wound care seminars, conventions ● online services. **Publications:** *AAWC Newsletter,* quarterly. Contains updates on wound care. **Price:** free for members. **Circulation:** 1,600 ● *Ostomy/Wound Management,* monthly. Journal. **Price:** free for members. **Advertising:** accepted ● *Wound Care Clinic Directory,* annual. **Price:** free for members; $250.00 hard copy; $150.00 CD-ROM for members; $600.00 CD-ROM for nonmembers. Alternate Formats: CD-ROM ● *Wounds: A Compendium of Clinical Research and Practice,* bimonthly. Journal. **Price:** free for members. **Advertising:** accepted. **Conventions/Meetings:** annual Symposium on Advanced Wound Care - meeting (exhibits).

14241 ■ Association of International Health Researchers (AIHR)
2665 Pleasant Valley Rd.
Mobile, AL 36606
Ph: (251)473-3946
Fax: (251)478-0022
Contact: Dr. Roy E. Kadel, Pres.
Founded: 1982. **Members:** 123. **Regional Groups:** 5. **Description:** Individuals interested in quality health research. Works to: promote a better understanding of scientifically effective research techniques and methodologies; encourage interaction among individuals in international health research. Compiles statistics. **Libraries: Type:** reference. **Subjects:** research methodology, health care. **Committees:** Article Translation. **Conventions/Meetings:** competition ● annual conference and symposium (exhibits).

14242 ■ Benjamin Franklin Literary and Medical Society (BFLMS)
1100 Waterway Blvd.
Indianapolis, IN 46202
Ph: (317)634-1100 (317)636-8881
Free: (800)829-5576
E-mail: cservaasmd@aol.com
URL: http://www.satevepost.org
Contact: Dr. Cory SerVaas, Pres./CEO
Founded: 1976. **Members:** 2,300,000. **Staff:** 100. **Description:** Individuals, industries, and businesses united to support research and promote sciences, literature, and the arts in order to achieve greater public understanding of science and the humanities. Emphasizes on the dissemination of health, preven-

tive medicine, and nutrition information to the health community and the public. Advocates a preventive approach to health care including proper nutrition, daily exercise, and good health habits. Offers training in cardiopulmonary resuscitation and other life-saving skills; conducts health education programs. Operates the Children's Better Health Institute, which publishes material designed to educate children of preschool through elementary school levels on health, nutrition, safety, and exercise, and Medical Education and Research Foundation, which disseminates medical information in lay terms, covering concepts and developments in preventive medicine, safety procedures and techniques, health dangers, proper dietary habits, and reports on new and developing treatments and medications for cancer patients and techniques used for early detection of cancer. Sponsors the Saturday Evening Post Society which conducts national health surveys; publicizes advances in science, medicine, nutrition, and preventive medicine; funds research projects; and encourages commercial manufacturers to produce innovative health equipment. **Awards:** Tulip Time Scholarship Games. **Frequency:** annual. **Type:** scholarship. **Publications:** *Child Life,* 8/year. Magazine. Promotes reading and good health habits in children between the ages of seven and nine. Includes "Ask the Doctor" column, poems, and short stories. **Price:** $14.95/year. ISSN: 0009-3971. **Circulation:** 75,000. **Advertising:** accepted. Alternate Formats: microform ● *Children's Digest,* 8/year. Magazine. Promotes reading and good health habits in children between the ages of eight and ten. Includes book reviews. **Price:** $14.95/year. **Circulation:** 115,000. **Advertising:** accepted. Alternate Formats: microform ● *Children's Playmate,* 8/year. Magazine. Promotes reading and good health habits for children between the ages of five and seven. Includes book reviews. **Price:** $14.95/year. ISSN: 0009-4161. **Circulation:** 130,000. **Advertising:** accepted. Alternate Formats: microform ● *Humpty Dumpty,* 8/year. Magazine. Promotes reading and good health habits for children between the ages of four and six. **Price:** $14.95/year. ISSN: 0273-7590. **Circulation:** 260,000. **Advertising:** accepted. Alternate Formats: microform ● *Jack and Jill,* 8/year. Magazine. Promotes reading and good health habits for children between the ages of six and eight. **Price:** $14.95/year. ISSN: 0021-3829. **Circulation:** 340,000. **Advertising:** accepted. Alternate Formats: microform ● *Medical Update Newsletter,* monthly. Includes foundation news and research updates. **Price:** $12.00/year. **Circulation:** 25,000 ● *Saturday Evening Post,* bimonthly. Magazine ● *Turtle Magazine for Preschool Kids,* 8/year. Promotes reading and good health, safety, and nutrition habits for children between the ages of two and twelve. Includes book reviews. **Price:** $14.95/year. ISSN: 0191-3654. **Circulation:** 500,000. **Advertising:** accepted. Alternate Formats: microform. **Conventions/Meetings:** annual board meeting.

14243 ■ Center for Medical Consumers (CMC)
239 Thompson St.
New York, NY 10012
Ph: (212)674-7105
E-mail: medconsumers@earthlink.net
URL: http://www.medicalconsumers.org
Contact: Arthur Aaron Levin MPH, Dir.
Founded: 1976. **Staff:** 3. **Budget:** $105,000. **Description:** Serves as an advocacy group on health and medical information at the state and local legislative level. **Libraries: Type:** reference. **Holdings:** articles, periodicals. **Subjects:** medicine, health. **Committees:** FDA Drug Safety and Risk Management Advisory. **Formerly:** (1998) Center for Medical Consumers and Health Care Information. **Publications:** *HealthFacts,* monthly. Newsletter. Contains tips to determine the risks and effectiveness of common medical procedures. Presents all treatment options, including nonmedical. **Price:** $25.00/year in U.S.; $29.00/year in Canada and Mexico; $36.00/year outside U.S. ISSN: 0738-811X. **Circulation:** 13,000 ● Reports.

14244 ■ Christian Connections for International Health (CCIH)
c/o Ray Martin, Exec. Dir.
1817 Rupert St.
McLean, VA 22101

Ph: (703)556-0123 (703)989-4718
Fax: (703)917-4251
E-mail: ccihdirector@aol.com
URL: http://www.ccih.org
Contact: Ray Martin, Exec. Dir.
Founded: 1987. **Members:** 350. **Membership Dues:** organizational, $40-$750 (annual) ● affiliate, $40-$5,000 (annual) ● individual, $25-$50 (annual). **Staff:** 2. **Budget:** $110,000. **Multinational. Description:** Promotes international health and wholeness from a Christian perspective. Provides a forum for discussion, networking and fellowship to Christian organizations and individuals in the field of international health. **Computer Services:** Mailing lists, of members. **Publications:** CCIH Forum, periodic. Newsletter. Contains articles and resources about international health. Alternate Formats: online ● CCIH News, AIDS, ABCplus, and Hospitals, weekly. Bulletin. E-mail listservs on topics of interest to Christian professionals working in international health and AIDS. **Circulation:** 750. Alternate Formats: online. **Conventions/Meetings:** annual Global Missions Health Conference, co-sponsored by the Southeast Christian Church (exhibits).

14245 ■ Council on Certification of Health, Environmental and Safety Technologists (CCHEST)

208 Burwash Ave.
Savoy, IL 61874
Ph: (217)359-2686
Fax: (217)359-0055
E-mail: cchest@cchest.org
URL: http://www.cchest.org
Contact: Roger L. Brauer PhD, Exec. Dir.
Founded: 1985. **Members:** 2,800. **Staff:** 2. **Budget:** $200,000. **Description:** Grants certification to individuals involved in the field of safety; conducts research in evaluation of competency for those in the field of safety, health and environmental practice. **Libraries: Type:** reference. **Holdings:** 1,800; periodicals. **Subjects:** safety, health, environmental management and engineering, human resources development, training, professional conduct and ethics. **Telecommunication Services:** electronic mail, brauer@bcsp.org. **Affiliated With:** American Board of Industrial Hygiene; Board of Certified Safety Professionals. **Publications:** CCHEST Directory and International Registry, biennial. Lists all persons with CCHEST certifications. **Price:** free online; $100.00 CD-ROM. Alternate Formats: CD-ROM; online ● CCHEST Newsletter, annual. Describes financial activities of CCHEST. **Price:** free. **Circulation:** 3,000. Alternate Formats: online.

14246 ■ Council on Health Information and Education (CHIE)

2272 Colorado Blvd., No. 1228
Los Angeles, CA 90041
Fax: (323)344-8594
E-mail: jamkraut@earthlink.net
Contact: D. Andre, Dir.
Founded: 1978. **Description:** Promotes health and fitness of Americans through the dissemination of information on health care, nutrition, and exercise. Warns against fads in health and nutrition; conducts research on health and exercise products; reviews books on health, fitness, nutrition, sexuality, and sports. **Awards: Type:** recognition. **Publications:** Pamphlets.

14247 ■ Doctors Ought to Care (DOC)

Address Unknown since 2007
Founded: 1977. **Members:** 1,374. **Membership Dues:** student, $10 (annual) ● resident, $25 (annual) ● individual, $25 (annual) ● physician, $50 (annual) ● corporate, $1,000 (annual). **Staff:** 2. **Budget:** $100,000. **Local Groups:** 76. **Description:** A physician-led organization of medical students, teachers, parents, and other concerned individuals working to counteract the promotion of unhealthy products, primarily tobacco and alcohol. Works through school programs, health professionals' offices, hospitals, media, and Super Health 2000, a health promotion effort which attempts to counter the effects of advertising unhealthy products. Seeks to launch a broad

health promotion effort aimed at educating the public, particularly teenagers and children, on the "lethal" lifestyles of tobacco and alcohol use. Campaigns through television commercials, radio, sports events, posters and t-shirts, and its speakers' bureau to promote the image of good health through community-wide reinforcement of the positive role model of the health professional. Serves as a resource center on tobacco and alcohol issues. **Libraries: Type:** not open to the public. **Holdings:** 3,000,000; periodicals. **Subjects:** tobacco, alcohol industries. **Awards:** Alan M. Blum Award in Medical Activism. **Frequency:** annual. **Type:** recognition. **Publications:** The Journal of Medical Activism, quarterly. Newsletter. Fights advertising and promotion of unhealthy products by the tobacco and alcohol industry. Includes information on the pro-health community. **Price:** included in membership dues. **Circulation:** 3,000. **Advertising:** not accepted. **Conventions/Meetings:** annual conference (exhibits).

14248 ■ Federation of Associations of Regulatory Boards (FARB)

1603 Orrington Ave., Ste.2080
Evanston, IL 60201
Ph: (847)328-7909
Fax: (847)864-0588
E-mail: farb@farb.org
URL: http://www.farb.org
Contact: Vickie Sheets, Pres.
Founded: 1974. **Members:** 13. **Membership Dues:** full, $750 (annual) ● affiliate, $500 (annual) ● associate, $262 ● contributing, $1,000 (annual). **Staff:** 2. **Budget:** $75,000. **Description:** National associations of regulatory boards. United to exchange information and engage in programs and joint activities relating to the education and licensing of professionals and to cooperate in solving the mutual problems of members. Conducts attorney certification course. **Formerly:** (1985) Federation of Associations of Health Regulatory Boards. **Publications:** FARB Facts, periodic. **Conventions/Meetings:** annual meeting ● workshop, for attorney certification.

14249 ■ Foundation for Health (FFH)

337 East Ave.
Watertown, NY 13601-3829
Ph: (315)782-6664
Free: (800)724-7460
Fax: (315)782-6664
E-mail: geobonadio@westelcom.com
Contact: George Bonadio, Exec. Dir.
Founded: 1972. **Description:** Gathers and disseminates information regarding health; seeks to publicize "natural" laws of health in an effort to make excellent health and long, useful lives common throughout the world. Proclaims the simplicity and inexpensiveness of maintaining one's health in contrast to the complexity and expense of disease. Researches and develops nutrition and health related projects and programs. **Convention/Meeting:** none. **Libraries: Type:** reference. **Holdings:** 1,000; archival material, books, business records, clippings, monographs, periodicals. **Subjects:** health. **Publications:** Ask the Nutritionist, weekly. Newspaper ● Seven Disciplines of Health ● Also contributes weekly health column to newspapers; plans to publish book.

14250 ■ Gait and Clinical Movement Analysis Society (GCMAS)

c/o Sahar Hassani, MS
Shriners Hosp. for Children
2211 N Oak Park Ave.
Chicago, IL 60707-3392
Ph: (773)385-5457
Fax: (773)385-5459
E-mail: info@gcmas.net
URL: http://www.gcmas.net
Contact: Sahar Hassani MS, Contact
Membership Dues: regular, $150 (annual) ● student, affiliate, $60 (annual). **Description:** Aims to stimulate and advance scientific knowledge of gait and human movement analysis in both clinical and research settings. Promotes education, professional interaction, and exchange of ideas among members. Fosters interest in the study of the field of human motion

analysis. **Awards:** GCMAS Student Scholarship Program. **Frequency:** annual. **Type:** scholarship. **Recipient:** to students who show potential to advance the clinical and technical science of movement analysis. **Telecommunication Services:** electronic mail, sahar.hassani@gcmas.net. **Publications:** Gait and Posture, annual. Journal. **Price:** included in membership dues.

14251 ■ Global Lawyers and Physicians (GLP)

c/o Dept. of Health Law, Bioethics and Human Rights
Boston Univ. of Public Hea.
715 Albany St.
Boston, MA 02118
Ph: (617)638-4626
E-mail: annasgj@bu.edu
URL: http://www.glphr.org
Contact: George J. Annas J.D., Co-Founder
Founded: 1996. **Membership Dues:** student, $25 (annual) ● regular, $95 (annual) ● supporter, $150 (annual) ● sponsor, $200 (annual) ● benefactor, $2,000 (annual). **Multinational. Description:** Provides information and resources about human rights. Serves as a network and referral source for professionals working on health-related human rights issues. Provides support and assistance in developing, implementing and advocating policies and legal remedies that protect and enhance human rights in health. **Computer Services:** database, global policies on human cloning and germline engineering ● information services, health and human rights resources. **Boards:** Advisory. **Publications:** Reports.

14252 ■ Global Vaccine Awareness League (GVAL)

25422 Trabuco Rd., Ste.105-230
Lake Forest, CA 92630-2797
E-mail: michelle@gval.com
URL: http://www.gval.com
Contact: Ms. Michelle Helms-Gaddie, Founder
Founded: 1995. **Members:** 430. **Staff:** 6. **Description:** Disseminates information on the serious side effects of government sponsored vaccinations. Conducts educational programs; promotes parents right to choose whether or not to vaccinate their children; supports research; conducts fundraising events. **Publications:** Newsletter.

14253 ■ Guam Lytico and Bodig Association

PO Box 1458
Hagatna, GU 96932
Ph: (671)477-2293
Fax: (671)477-2294
E-mail: lytico@lycos.com
URL: http://lytico.tripod.com
Contact: Madeleine Z. Bordallo, Pres.
Founded: 1983. **Members:** 18. **Staff:** 1. **Description:** Provides supportive services and information to individuals stricken with disease.

14254 ■ Health and Development International (HDI)

c/o Michael Pajonk, Deputy Exec. Dir.
1001 Wenonah
Oak Park, IL 60304
Ph: (708)386-3688
Fax: (708)386-5802
E-mail: hdi@sbcglobal.net
URL: http://www.hdi.no
Contact: Michael Pajonk, Deputy Exec. Dir.
Multinational. Description: Works to free the world of guinea worm and lymphatic filariasis (elephantiasis). **Publications:** Annual Report, annual. Alternate Formats: online.

14255 ■ Health Education Council (HEC)

3950 Indus. Blvd., Ste.600
West Sacramento, CA 95691-6509
Ph: (916)556-3344
Free: (888)442-2836
Fax: (916)446-0427

E-mail: admin@healthedcouncil.org

URL: http://www.healthedcouncil.org

Founded: 1979. **Description:** Seeks to promote healthy communities. Conducts grant-funded health education programs targeting at-risk populations, specifically the medically underserved, diverse ethnic populations and other communities. **Programs:** Cancer Detection; Energize Nature's Way; 5-A-Day; Gold Country Regional Nutrition Collaborative; National African American Tobacco Education Network; National Network on Tobacco Prevention and Poverty; School Beverage; Youth Access to Produce. **Formerly:** (1991) Hypertension Council.

14256 ■ Health for Humanity (HH)

415 Linden Ave., Ste.B

Wilmette, IL 60091

Ph: (847)425-7900

E-mail: information@healthforhumanity.org

URL: http://www.healthforhumanity.org

Contact: May Khadem MD, Exec. Dir.

Founded: 1992. **Membership Dues:** regular, institution, $150 (annual) ● student, $25 (annual). **Multinational. Description:** Collaborates with local governmental and non-governmental organizations to improve capacity for blindness prevention, HIV/AIDS prevention, maternal and child health and youth wellness. Seeks to strengthen capacities for health development by applying universal moral principles and scientific strategies. **Projects:** Blindness Prevention; Domestic Wellness; HIV/AIDS Prevention; International Maternal and Child Health; International Physician Exchange; Youth Wellness. **Publications:** Newsletter. **Conventions/Meetings:** annual conference.

14257 ■ Health Information Resource Center (HIRC)

1850 W Winchester Rd., Ste.213

Libertyville, IL 60048

Ph: (847)816-8660

Free: (800)828-8225

Fax: (847)816-8662

E-mail: info@fitnessday.com

URL: http://www.healthawards.com

Contact: Patricia Henze, Exec. Dir.

Founded: 1993. **Membership Dues:** individual, $149 (annual) ● corporate, $295 (annual). **Staff:** 2. **For-Profit. Description:** Clearinghouse for consumer health information. Provides information and referral services to many organizations that use or produce consumer health information materials. Conducts market research. **Convention/Meeting:** none. **Libraries: Type:** not open to the public; by appointment only. **Holdings:** articles, audiovisuals, books, clippings, monographs, periodicals. **Subjects:** consumer health. **Awards:** National Health Information Awards. **Frequency:** annual. **Type:** recognition. **Recipient:** for the best consumer health information ● WWW Health Awards. **Frequency:** semiannual. **Type:** recognition. **Recipient:** for the best consumer health information on the web. **Computer Services:** Mailing lists, 20,000 names of consumer health promotion managers. **Additional Websites:** http://www.fitnessday.com. **Telecommunication Services:** electronic mail, healthprograms@aol.com. **Publications:** Consumer Health Information Online, annual. **Price:** $29.95. Alternate Formats: online ● Consumer Health Information: The Professional Guide to the Nations' Best Consumer Health Information Programs and Materials, annual ● Health and Medical Media '99, annual. Book. Contains health and medical media contacts. **Price:** $149.00 ● The Health Events Calendar, annual. Book. Contains planning guide to national health events. **Price:** $24.95/copy, plus shipping and handling.

14258 ■ Health Promotion Institute (HPI)

Address Unknown since 2007

Description: Provides health education, promotion, and disease prevention services to ethnically and culturally diverse communities. **Programs:** AIDS Quilt Panels; Computer & Internet Classes; Consultation; Dolls of Hope Campaign; Sister to Sister.

14259 ■ Imagine World Health (IWH)

105 E Dolphin Blvd.

Ponte Vedra Beach, FL 32082-1714

Ph: (904)285-0240

E-mail: imaginewldhealth@bellsouth.net

URL: http://www.imagineworldhealth.org

Contact: David Stearns, Founder

Founded: 1998. **Description:** Strives to educate and promote good health and fitness in mind, body and spirit.

14260 ■ International Association for Colon Hydrotherapy (I-ACT)

PO Box 461285

San Antonio, TX 78246-1285

Ph: (210)366-2888

Fax: (210)366-2999

E-mail: iact@healthy.net

URL: http://www.i-act.org

Contact: Barbara Chivvis, Pres.

Membership Dues: affiliate, $250 (annual) ● full, $150 (annual). **Multinational. Description:** Heightens awareness of the colon hydrotherapy profession. Ensures continuing and progressive education in the field of colon hydrotherapy. **Computer Services:** database, IACT recognized schools ● information services, colon hydrotherapy facts. **Publications:** Newsletter, quarterly.

14261 ■ International Health Evaluation Association (IHEA)

846 S Hotel St., Ste.301

Honolulu, HI 96813-2583

Ph: (808)524-4411

Fax: (808)524-5559

E-mail: administration@ihea.net

Contact: Vicki Shambaugh, Exec. VP

Founded: 1971. **Members:** 300. **Membership Dues:** corporate, $500 (annual) ● individual, $120 (annual). **Staff:** 2. **Budget:** $50,000. **Regional Groups:** 3. **Description:** Users, suppliers, and manufacturers of computer-based health evaluation systems including clinics, hospitals, physicians, medical students, and research institutions. Is dedicated to the improvement of health care through: the advancement of computer-based health testing and evaluation techniques; the refinement of associated data-processing systems and biomedical devices; the development of a low-cost, high-quality health programs. Believes the technique of computer-based health evaluation can be used in the areas of testing industrial workers and others exposed to environmental hazards, mandatory tests conducted by governmental agencies, and pre-admission hospital testing. Sponsors seminars on clinical preventive medicine for the discussion of medical results, operational techniques, new applications, and cost-effectiveness data. Conducts research; compiles statistics; maintains library; operates speakers' bureau. **Libraries: Type:** not open to the public. **Holdings:** 700. **Subjects:** preventive health care. **Computer Services:** database. **Committees:** Health Data Analysis. **Publications:** Proceedings of Annual Symposia (in English and Japanese), quarterly. **Price:** free. **Advertising:** accepted. Alternate Formats: CD-ROM ● Regional Newsletter, periodic ● Newsletter, quarterly. **Conventions/Meetings:** biennial conference and symposium ● biennial Special Convention - meeting.

14262 ■ International Medical Equipment Collaborative (IMEC)

1600 Osgood St., 30-1 Y-8

North Andover, MA 01845

Ph: (978)557-5510

Fax: (978)557-5525

E-mail: imec@imecamerica.org

URL: http://www.imecamerica.org

Contact: Tom Keefe, Pres.

Founded: 1995. **Multinational. Description:** Creates centers of health in the poorest countries around the world. Provides doctors and nurses with the medical tools to improve the delivery of vital health services. Distributes medical equipment, supplies and support services to doctors, nurses and technologists working in clinics and orphanages in under-

served locations worldwide. **Publications:** World News, monthly. Newsletter. Alternate Formats: online.

14263 ■ International Society of Regulatory Toxicology and Pharmacology (ISRTP)

6546 Belleview Dr.

Columbia, MD 21046-1054

Ph: (410)992-9083

Fax: (410)740-9181

E-mail: c.carr65@comcast.net

URL: http://www.isrtp.org

Contact: Sallie W. Carr, Exec. Sec.

Multinational. Description: Identifies and prioritizes scientific issues that would affect the development, modification or application of regulations affecting human health and safety and the environment. Provides an open public forum promoting the evaluation and application of sound toxicologic and pharmacologic science as a basis for developing new regulations or for modifying or applying existing regulations affecting human health and safety and the environment. **Awards:** International Achievement Award. **Frequency:** annual. **Type:** recognition. **Recipient:** to outstanding individuals in recognition of their contributions and achievements in the resolution of public environmental concern. **Telecommunication Services:** electronic mail, rtp-isrtp@erols.com. **Committees:** Financial; Public Awareness. **Publications:** Regulatory Toxicology and Pharmacology. Journal. **Price:** included in membership dues.

14264 ■ Josiah Macy, Jr. Foundation

44 E 64th St.

New York, NY 10021

Ph: (212)486-2424

Free: (800)521-0600

Fax: (212)644-0765

E-mail: jmacyinfo@josiahmacyfoundation.org

URL: http://www.josiahmacyfoundation.org

Contact: June E. Osborn MD, Pres.

Staff: 7. **Description:** Strives to promote public health awareness. **Publications:** Chairman's Summary of the Conference, Education for More Synergistic Practice of Medicine and Public Health. Proceedings. Contains information on conference.

14265 ■ Life Research Institute (LRI)

4279 Armand Dr.

Concord, CA 94521

URL: http://www.geocities.com/kekogut/about_lri/about_lri.html

Founded: 1993. **Description:** Works to save the lives and health of women, babies, and men by reducing the rate of promiscuity and abortion.

14266 ■ Lifegain Institute (LI)

151 Dunder Rd.

Burlington, VT 05401

Ph: (802)862-8855

Fax: (802)862-6389

E-mail: info@healthyculture.com

URL: http://www.healthyculture.com

Contact: Judd Allen PhD, Pres.

Founded: 1977. **Members:** 600. **Budget:** $50,000. **Description:** Represents people who work with health promotion programs in hospitals, corporations, colleges, and communities. Promotes healthy practices such as exercise, nutrition, safety, and the reduction or curtailment of smoking and alcohol consumption through health promotion programs that provide a supportive environment. Maintains speakers' bureau. Compiles data on improvements cultural support nationwide. **Libraries: Type:** reference. **Subjects:** health and lifestyle improvement. **Awards:** Robert F. Allen Scholarship Award. **Type:** scholarship. **Recipient:** for an individual who has made a unique contribution to culture change ● Robert F. Symbol of HOPE Award. **Frequency:** annual. **Type:** scholarship. **Recipient:** for health promotion contribution to underserved populations. **Affiliated With:** SHRM Global Forum. **Also Known As:** Human Resources Institute. **Publications:** American Journal of Health Promotion, quarterly ● Lifegain: A Culture-Based Approach to Positive Health. Book ● Lifegain Healthy Communities System ● Articles ● Also publishes support materials. **Conventions/Meetings:** annual conference.

14267 ■ National Association of Community Health Centers (NACHC)

7200 Wisconsin Ave., Ste.210
Bethesda, MD 20814
Ph: (301)347-0400
Fax: (301)347-0459
E-mail: contact@nachc.com
URL: http://www.nachc.com
Contact: Tom Van Coverden, Pres./CEO
Founded: 1970. **Members:** 1,000. **Membership Dues:** basic individual, $30 (annual) ● full individual, $65 (annual) ● associate, $750 (annual) ● corporate, $5,000 (annual) ● network associate, $2,500-$5,000 (annual) ● organizational, $20,000 (annual). **Staff:** 60. **Description:** Advocacy organization of ambulatory healthcare centers, administrators, clinicians, and consumers. Works to assure the continued growth and development of community-based healthcare delivery programs for medically underserved populations by providing technical assistance and education and training opportunities for health center staff and board members. Disseminates information and research data and provides representation in legislative and professional arenas. Sponsors educational institutes, workshops, and seminars throughout the year. **Libraries: Type:** reference. **Holdings:** archival material, reports. **Awards:** NACHC Awards of Excellence. **Frequency:** annual. **Type:** recognition. **Recipient:** for outstanding achievement in the community health field. **Committees:** Clinical Practice and Programs; Consumer/Board Member; Health Policy; Legislative. **Formerly:** National Association of Directors and Administrators; (1977) National Association of Neighborhood Health Centers. **Publications:** *Fraud and Abuse Manual - 2003.* **Price:** $99.00 for members; $150.00 for nonmembers ● *NACHC Community Health Forum,* bimonthly. Magazine. **Price:** $35.00/year. **Advertising:** accepted ● *Washington Update,* monthly. Newsletter. **Conventions/Meetings:** annual Community Health Institute - convention (exhibits) - 2008 Sept. 12-17, New Orleans, LA; 2009 Aug. 21-26, Chicago, IL ● annual Policy and Issues Forum - meeting - usually February or March. 2008 Mar. 11-16, Washington, DC; 2009 Mar. 23-28, Washington, DC.

14268 ■ National Association of Disability Evaluating Professionals (NADEP)

c/o Dr. Virgil R. May, III, Exec. Dir.
13801 Village Mill Dr., Ste.204
Midlothian, VA 23113
Ph: (804)378-7275
E-mail: mayrehab@att.net
URL: http://www.nadep.com
Contact: Dr. Virgil R. May III, Exec. Dir.
Founded: 1984. **Members:** 1,000. **Membership Dues:** professional, $150 (annual). **Staff:** 3. **For-Profit. Description:** Lawyers, doctors, psychologists, employers, and others interested or involved in disability claims process, evaluation, and case management. Provides a forum for the exchange of information. Serves as a training center which prepares health professionals to qualify for the Certified Disability Examiner credential offered by the Commission on Disability Examiner Certification. **Libraries: Type:** reference. **Holdings:** periodicals. **Subjects:** rehabilitation. **Awards:** NADEP Lifetime Achievement Award. **Frequency:** annual. **Type:** recognition ● NADEP Research Award. **Type:** recognition ● Robert Sandell Certification Award. **Frequency:** annual. **Type:** recognition. **Computer Services:** Mailing lists. **Formerly:** (1991) International Health Consultants. **Publications:** *Disability Evaluation and Rehabilitation Review,* quarterly. Newsletter. **Price:** included in membership dues. Alternate Formats: online ● *NADEP Guide to Functional Capacity Evaluation with Department Rating Applications Textbook.* **Price:** $140.00 for nonmembers; $120.00 for members. **Conventions/Meetings:** bimonthly conference.

14269 ■ National Association of Health Data Organizations (NAHDO)

448 E 400 S, Ste.301
Salt Lake City, UT 84111

Ph: (801)532-2299
Fax: (801)532-2228
E-mail: nahdoinfo@nahdo.org
URL: http://www.nahdo.org
Contact: Denise Love, Exec. Dir.
Founded: 1986. **Members:** 112. **Membership Dues:** corporate, other organization, $3,200 (annual) ● public organization, $2,500 (annual) ● individual, $500 (annual) ● student, $75 (annual). **Staff:** 6. **Description:** Members include state, federal, nonprofit and private health data organizations, employee benefits consultants, professional review organizations, data analysis firms, software vendors, and health services consultants, health care researchers, third-party payers, hospital associations, managed care organizations. Seeks to improve health care through the collection, dissemination, and application of health care data. Promotes public availability of and access to health data; supports use of health care data to guide formulation of health policy, purchasing, and establishment of needed health services. Sponsors educational programs, workshops, and seminars. Conducts surveys and comparative studies; maintains speakers' bureau. **Awards:** NAHDO Award of Excellence. **Frequency:** annual. **Type:** recognition ● NAHDO Best Practices Award. **Frequency:** annual. **Type:** recognition. **Boards:** Directors. **Committees:** Annual Program. **Publications:** *Inventory of Statewide Hospital Discharge Data Activities.* Manual. **Price:** $225.00. **Advertising:** accepted ● *NAHDO Annual Report,* annual. **Price:** free. Alternate Formats: online. **Conventions/Meetings:** annual Healthcare Quality and Accountability: Information Takes Center Stage - conference (exhibits).

14270 ■ National Association of Health Services Executives (NAHSE)

8630 Fenton St., Ste.126
Silver Spring, MD 20910
Ph: (202)628-3953
Fax: (301)588-0011
E-mail: nahsehq@nahse.org
URL: http://www.nahse.org
Contact: Mr. Christopher R. Mosley, Pres./CEO
Founded: 1968. **Members:** 500. **Membership Dues:** student, $50-$100 (annual) ● personal, $200 (annual) ● associate, $500 (annual). **Staff:** 6. **Budget:** $125,000. **Regional Groups:** 16. **Local Groups:** 7. **Description:** Black health care executive managers, planners, educators, advocates, providers, organizers, researchers, and consumers participating in academic ventures, educational forums, seminars, workshops, systems design, legislation, and other activities. Conducts National Work-Study Program and sponsors educational programs. **Awards:** Hall of Fame Award. **Frequency:** annual. **Type:** recognition. **Recipient:** for men and women with exceptional achievements and contributions in the field of health care ● NAHSE Scholarship. **Frequency:** annual. **Type:** scholarship. **Recipient:** for minority students pursuing careers in health care management or related fields ● Senior Healthcare Executive of the Year. **Frequency:** annual. **Type:** recognition. **Recipient:** for a member who has demonstrated leadership and vision ● Young Healthcare Executive of the Year. **Frequency:** annual. **Type:** recognition. **Recipient:** for a member who has demonstrated commitment to the development of young health professionals. **Telecommunication Services:** electronic mail, info@nahse.org. **Committees:** Awards; By-laws; CEO/Senior Executive Conference; Chapter Development; Education; Educational Conference Planning; NAHSE Foundation; Public Policy/Advocacy. **Affiliated With:** American College of Healthcare Executives; American Hospital Association; Association of University Programs in Health Administration. **Publications:** *NAHSE Notes,* quarterly. Newsletter. **Price:** free. **Circulation:** 1,000. **Advertising:** accepted. **Conventions/Meetings:** annual Educational Conference ● semiannual meeting.

14271 ■ National Association of Health Unit Coordinators (NAHUC)

1947 Madron Rd.
Rockford, IL 61107-1716

Ph: (815)633-4351
Free: (888)22-NAHUC
Fax: (815)633-4438
E-mail: office@nahuc.org
URL: http://www.nahuc.org
Contact: Ms. Kelly Lemanski, Pres.
Founded: 1980. **Members:** 1,900. **Membership Dues:** regular, $30 (annual) ● student, $20 (annual) ● retired, $15 (annual) ● institutional provider, $300 (annual). **Budget:** $170,000. **Regional Groups:** 6. **Local Groups:** 30. **Description:** Coordinators of non-clinical nursing unit activities; educators, supervisors, students, and graduates in the field. Promotes the professional practice of unit coordinating. Has established standards of practice defining the role and responsibilities of health unit coordinators in the non-clinical area of health care and ensuring delivery of quality patient care. Works to establish certification guidelines for individual practitioners with a goal of national certification. Seeks recognition of the change in job title from clerk to that of coordinator, which the group believes better describes the nature of the position. Promotes continuing education and research; endeavors to develop accreditation of educational programs and standards of education for job entry. Provides vocational information to prospective students in the field; recruits students into the profession. Represents members' interests before allied health professionals, educational institutions, governmental bodies, and the community. Sponsors regional workshops, seminars, and other educational programs; compiles statistics. Maintains certification board and speakers' bureau; offers annual national certification exam and annual educational conference. **Libraries: Type:** reference. **Holdings:** 50; audiovisuals. **Awards:** Certified Health Coordinator of the Year. **Frequency:** annual. **Type:** recognition. **Recipient:** to a member in good standing who practices personal and professional development through continuing education, is a role model for peers, and actively participates in the NAHUC on the local and national level ● Institution of the Year. **Frequency:** annual. **Type:** recognition. **Recipient:** to an institution that contributes to the recognition of the NAHUC and supports participation in the NAHUC ● Outstanding Individual of the Year. **Frequency:** annual. **Type:** recognition. **Recipient:** to an individual who has assisted or promoted the NAHUC. **Computer Services:** database ● mailing lists, membership information. **Boards:** Certification; Education. **Committees:** Archives; Awards; Bylaws/Policies; Chapters/State Associations; Ethics; Fiscal Affairs; Marketing/Public Relations; Program; Publication. **Formerly:** (1990) National Association of Health Unit Clerks-Coordinators. **Publications:** *Information Booklet,* annual. **Price:** $2.00. **Circulation:** 2,500 ● *National Association of Health Unit Coordinators— Coordinator,* quarterly. Newsletter. **Price:** included in membership dues; $15.00 /year for nonmembers. **Circulation:** 4,000. **Advertising:** accepted ● *National Association of Health Unit Coordinators - Education Program Procedure Guide.* Booklet. Provides information to assist in the development or evaluation of a formal educational program. **Price:** $30.00 for members; $50.00 for nonmembers ● *National Association of Health Unit Coordinators— Membership Directory,* annual. **Price:** $5.00 for members ● *Question & Answer Brochures.* **Conventions/Meetings:** semiannual board meeting ● annual conference (exhibits) ● semiannual symposium.

14272 ■ National Association of Healthcare Transport Management (NAHTM)

c/o Cathleen Thom, Sec.
PO Box 409
Twin Falls, ID 83303
Ph: (208)737-2929
E-mail: cathleent@mvrmc.org
URL: http://www.nahtm.org
Contact: Cathleen Thom, Sec.
Membership Dues: full, $125 (annual) ● associate, $75 (annual) ● corporate, $1,000 (annual). **Description:** Represents management personnel throughout the United States who are responsible for the transportation of patients in hospital settings. Provides members with the resources necessary for patient

transportation and related activities. Promotes relevant technological advances, current management and leadership philosophy. Develops and implements certification programs. **Computer Services:** Online services, discussion forums. **Publications:** Articles. Alternate Formats: online.

14273 ■ National Business Coalition on Health (NBCH)
1015 18th St. NW, Ste.730
Washington, DC 20036-5214
Ph: (202)775-9300
Fax: (202)775-1569
E-mail: awebber@nbch.org
URL: http://www.nbch.org
Contact: Andrew Webber, Pres./CEO
Founded: 1992. **Members:** 80. **Staff:** 4. **Description:** Employer-led coalitions that group-purchase health care benefits for employees and measure and improve health care quality. **Conventions/Meetings:** annual conference, focuses on a variety of industry experts (exhibits) - 2007 Nov. 11-13, Scottsdale, AZ.

14274 ■ National Center for Farmworker Health (NCFH)
1770 FM 967
Buda, TX 78610
Ph: (512)312-2700
Free: (800)531-5120
Fax: (512)312-2600
E-mail: info@ncfh.org
URL: http://www.ncfh.org
Contact: E. Roberta Ryder, CEO
Founded: 1975. **Staff:** 15. **Budget:** $1,000,000. **Languages:** English, Spanish. **Description:** Seeks to make quality primary health care accessible to migrant and seasonal farm workers. Supports the establishment of a national network of migrant health centers through the production, processing, and distribution of information, including information on health problems specific to one or more prevalent in the migrant community. Works to provide technical assistance for health development and research. Develops collaborative working relationship between agencies serving migrant farmworkers. Maintains job/resume bank, biographical archives, library and speakers' bureau. Operates placement service and compiles statistics. **Libraries: Type:** not open to the public. **Holdings:** 4,500. **Subjects:** migrant farmworkers, health. **Awards:** Migrant Health Scholarship. **Frequency:** annual. **Type:** scholarship. **Recipient:** for work in migrant health center. **Computer Services:** database, migrant health professionals. **Affiliated With:** National Association of Community Health Centers. **Formerly:** (1989) National Migrant Referral Project. **Publications:** *Migrant Health Newsline*, bimonthly. Newsletter. Includes clinical supplement. **Price:** free for members. **Circulation:** 4,000 ● *Migrant Health Referral Directory*, annual ● *Migrant Health Resource Catalog* ● Books ● Directory ● Videos. **Conventions/Meetings:** annual Migrant Health Conference (exhibits).

14275 ■ National Center for Health Education (NCHE)
375 Hudson St.
New York, NY 10014
Ph: (212)463-4053
Free: (800)551-3488
Fax: (212)463-4060
E-mail: nche@nche.org
URL: http://www.nche.org
Contact: Dr. John P. Allegrante, Pres./CEO
Founded: 1975. **Staff:** 10. **Budget:** $1,000,000. **Description:** Professionals promoting health education in schools, communities, and family settings. Aims to "extend the reach and power of education for health." Advocates health education and health promotion; builds coalitions of private and public sector groups; documents, develops, and disseminates model programs. Develops and manages Growing Healthy, a comprehensive school health education curriculum for kindergarten through grade six and "Starting Healthy" pre-kindergarten curriculum. **Supersedes:** Health Education Research Council. **Publications:** *Growing Healthy (K-6)*. Book. Contains school health

education. **Circulation:** 15,000 ● *Starting Healthy (Pre-K)*. Book. Contains school health education. **Circulation:** 15,000. **Conventions/Meetings:** periodic conference and seminar ● annual meeting, with forum.

14276 ■ National Coalition for Adult Immunization (NCAI)
4733 Bethesda Ave., Ste.750
Bethesda, MD 20814-5278
Ph: (301)656-0003
Fax: (301)907-0878
E-mail: ncai@nfid.org
Contact: David A. Neumann PhD, Dir.
Founded: 1988. **Members:** 126. **Staff:** 1. **Description:** Medical associations, advocacy groups, vaccine manufacturers, and government health agencies. Dedicated to promoting adolescent and adult immunization and to raise immunization levels in high-risk and other target groups. Promotes and supports National Adult Immunization Awareness Week and the objectives of the U.S. Healthy People 2010 initiative. Educates physicians and public on vaccines for diphtheria, hepatitis A and B, influenza, measles, mumps, pneumococcal pneumonia, rubella (German measles), tetanus, and chickenpox. **Publications:** *National Adult Immunization Awareness Week Campaign Kit*, annual. Fact sheets on vaccine-preventable diseases of adults and adolescents. **Circulation:** 1,200 ● *Resource Guide for Adolescent and Adult Immunization*, semiannual.

14277 ■ National Episcopal Health Ministries (NEHM)
6050 N Meridian St.
Indianapolis, IN 46208
Ph: (317)253-1277
Fax: (317)726-0569
E-mail: nehm@stpaulsindy.org
URL: http://www.episcopalhealthministries.org
Contact: Rita Goldenberg, Dir.
Founded: 1995. **Members:** 850. **Budget:** $90,000. **Regional Groups:** 8. **Description:** Promotes health ministry in Episcopal congregations. Provides assistance to the congregation to reclaim the Gospel imperative of health and wholeness. **Publications:** *Body and Soul*, quarterly. Newsletter. Alternate Formats: online.

14278 ■ National Free Clinic Foundation of America
c/o Estelle Nichols Avner, Exec.Dir.
1240 3rd St. SW
Roanoke, VA 24016
Ph: (540)344-8242
Fax: (540)342-0220
E-mail: freeclinic@mailcity.com
URL: http://www.freeclinic.net
Contact: Estelle Nichols Avner, Exec.Dir.
Founded: 1975. **Members:** 330. **Description:** Provides start up information, advice, and networking for free clinics. **Publications:** *How To Start A Free Clinic*. Manual. **Price:** free. Alternate Formats: online ● *National Directory of Free Clinics*. **Price:** free. Alternate Formats: online.

14279 ■ National Health Council (NHC)
1730 M St. NW, Ste.500
Washington, DC 20036
Ph: (202)785-3910
Fax: (202)785-5923
E-mail: info@nhcouncil.org
URL: http://www.nhcouncil.org
Contact: Myrl Weinberg, Pres.
Founded: 1920. **Members:** 115. **Staff:** 9. **Budget:** $1,200,000. **Description:** National association of voluntary and professional societies in the health field; national organizations and business groups with strong health interests. Seeks to improve the health of patients, particularly those with chronic diseases, through conferences, publications, policy briefings and special projects. Distributes printed material on health careers and related subjects. Promotes standardization of financial reporting for voluntary health groups. **Committees:** Forum Planning; Government Relations; Research Administrators. **Pro-**

grams: Voluntary Health Agency Development. **Publications:** *Council Currents*, bimonthly. Books. **Price:** free. **Circulation:** 3,800. Alternate Formats: diskette ● *Directory of Health Groups in Washington*. Contains contact information of more than 700 organizations. **Price:** $40.00 for members; $50.00 for nonmembers ● *Guide to America's Voluntary Health Agencies*. Directory ● *Standards of Accounting and Reporting for Voluntary Health and Welfare Organizations (The Black Book)*. **Price:** $44.00 for members; $55.00 for nonmembers ● *300 Ways to Put Your Talent to Work in the Health Field*. Book. **Price:** $15.00 for members; $18.00 for nonmembers.

14280 ■ National Health Federation (NHF)
PO Box 688
Monrovia, CA 91017
Ph: (626)357-2181
Fax: (626)303-0642
E-mail: contact-us@thenhf.com
URL: http://www.nationalhealthfederation.org
Contact: Scott Tips, Pres.
Founded: 1955. **Members:** 6,000. **Membership Dues:** regular, $36 (annual) ● life, $1,000 ● corporate, $200 (annual) ● international, sustaining, $100-$1,000 (annual) ● in Canada and Mexico, $48 (annual). **Staff:** 4. **Local Groups:** 123. **Description:** Persons interested in individual freedom of choice in matters relating to health. Represents belief "that organized medicine, the pharmaceutical industry, and other special interests have been responsible for many laws, rules, and regulations which very often better serve the interests of these groups than the interests of the American public." Seeks to serve as a "watch dog" and to institute corrective measures through investigation, education, legislation, and coordination of organizations with similar purposes. Supports research in areas such as laetrile testing; supports numerous educational foundation programs. Conducts lobbying activities. **Libraries: Type:** open to the public. **Holdings:** 25,000; articles, books, periodicals, video recordings. **Subjects:** alternative health and related laws. **Awards:** Fred Hart Health Freedom Award. **Frequency:** annual. **Type:** recognition. **Recipient:** for outstanding contributions to alternative health. **Computer Services:** database. **Absorbed:** (1976) National Committee Against Fluoridation. **Publications:** *Health Freedom News*, quarterly. Magazine. Covers topics such as the latest health threats, vaccinations, mercury fillings, legislative updates, fluoridation, and nutritional health products. **Price:** $5.00 plus shipping and handling. **Circulation:** 20,000. **Advertising:** accepted. **Conventions/Meetings:** Natural Health Show, includes natural health and fitness products and services (exhibits) - 6/year.

14281 ■ National Health Information Center (NHIC)
PO Box 1133
Washington, DC 20013-1133
Ph: (301)565-4167
Free: (800)336-4797
Fax: (301)984-4256
E-mail: info@nhic.org
URL: http://www.health.gov/nhic
Contact: Mr. Rachel Langston, Proj. Mgr.
Founded: 1979. **Languages:** English, Spanish. **Nonmembership. Description:** A health information referral service that links consumers and health professionals who have health questions with organizations best able to provide answers. Funded by the Office of Disease Prevention and Health Promotion, Public Health Service, U.S. Department of Health and Human Services. Maintains an online directory of more than 1,600 health-related organizations that can provide health information. These include Federal and State agencies, voluntary associations, self-help and support groups, trade associations and professional societies. Prints directories and resource guides on a variety of health topics. **Computer Services:** Online services, directory of more than 1,100 health-related organizations providing health information. **Additional Websites:** http://www.health-finder.gov. **Telecommunication Services:** electronic mail, healthfinder@nhic.org ● information service,

health information referral. **Formerly:** (1986) National Health Information Clearinghouse; (1987) ODPHP Health Information Center; (2005) ODPHP National Health Information Center. **Publications:** *Federal Health Information Centers and Clearinghouses*, annual ● *National Health Observances Calendar*, annual ● *Toll-Free Numbers for Health Information*, annual.

14282 ■ National Latina Health Network (NLHN)

2201 Wisconsin Ave. NW, Ste.340
Washington, DC 20007
Ph: (202)965-9633
Fax: (202)965-9636
E-mail: info@nlhn.net
URL: http://www.nlhn.net
Contact: Elena M. Alvarado, Pres./CEO

Members: 1,500. **Membership Dues:** student, mature citizen, $25 (annual) ● individual, $100 (annual) ● small business, $250 (annual) ● nonprofit organization (based on annual budget), $150-$500 (annual) ● corporate, $1,500 (annual). **Description:** Works to address critical health concerns affecting Latinas and their families. Educates communities to help close health care gaps. Promotes leadership, advocacy, community health partnerships and initiatives within the Latino communities. **Publications:** *Latinas: Partners for Health Partnership Directory.* Contains contact information for colleagues.

14283 ■ National Minority Health Association (NMHA)

10 E Baltimore St., Ste.1404
Baltimore, MD 21202
Free: (866)347-9959
Fax: (410)347-1542
E-mail: dldhri@aol.com
Contact: Dr. David Dalton, Chm.

Founded: 1987. **Members:** 53,000. **Membership Dues:** individual, $15 (annual) ● corporate, $150 (annual). **Staff:** 15. **Budget:** $32,000,000. **Regional Groups:** 5. **State Groups:** 27. **Local Groups:** 7. **Description:** Health care providers and associations, consumers, executives and administrators, educators, pharmaceutical and health insurance companies, and other corporations with an interest in health care. Seeks to identify and focus attention on the health needs of minorities. Promotes: more effective research in minority health issues; better training of health care practitioners; development of programs that encourage minorities to pursue careers in the health care industry and educate minority communities on the importance of good health. Initiates discussions with professional health organizations, academic institutions, state and federal governments, and health departments to develop strategies to improve the quality and availability of health care, health delivery systems, and health professionals to minority communities. Maintains Speaker's Bureau, conducts research and educational programs; sponsors children's programs; complies statistics. **Libraries: Type:** reference. **Awards:** National Health Achievement Award. **Frequency:** annual. **Type:** recognition. **Recipient:** for an individual or group that have made significant contributions in the area of minority health. **Computer Services:** database, clinical research, best practice, network links ● mailing lists. **Committees:** Awards; Communications; Education, Research, and Evaluation; Policy Development; Resource Development. **Publications:** *The National Minority Health Association News*, quarterly. **Conventions/Meetings:** annual Quality Healthcare for Culturally Diverse Populations - conference, individual programs and organizations, corporations, and government (exhibits).

14284 ■ National Organization for Competency Assurance (NOCA)

2025 M St. NW, Ste.800
Washington, DC 20036
Ph: (202)367-1165
Fax: (202)367-2165

E-mail: info@noca.org
URL: http://www.noca.org
Contact: Jim Kendzel, Exec. Dir.

Founded: 1977. **Members:** 300. **Membership Dues:** individual, $300 (annual) ● affiliate, $1,200 (annual) ● organizational, $600 (annual) ● sustaining, $2,500 (annual). **Staff:** 4. **Description:** Organizations conducting certification programs for occupations and professionals and trade associations representing these professionals. Seeks to increase public awareness, understanding, and acceptance of private sector credentialing as an alternative to licensure; promotes non-licensed but certified practitioners as a means to achieving high quality and cost containment. **Computer Services:** Mailing lists, of members. **Formerly:** (1989) National Commission for Health Certifying Agencies. **Publications:** *NOCA News*, quarterly. Newsletter. **Price:** $95.00 /year for non-members; included in membership dues. **Advertising:** accepted. **Conventions/Meetings:** annual Audio Seminar - always spring ● annual Educational Conference and Business Meeting - conference and meeting (exhibits) - held the week before Thanksgiving ● Seminar Series - 4-5/year.

14285 ■ Pan American Health Organization (PAHO)

525 23rd St. NW
Washington, DC 20037
Ph: (202)974-3000
Fax: (202)974-3663
E-mail: publinfo@paho.org
URL: http://www.paho.org
Contact: Dr. Mirta Roses Periago, Dir.

Founded: 1902. **Members:** 41. **Staff:** 1,100. **National Groups:** 35. **Languages:** English, Spanish. **Multinational. Description:** Governments of Western Hemisphere nations united to improve physical and mental health in the Americas. Coordinates regional activities combating disease including exchange of statistical and epidemiological information, development of local health services, and organization of disease control and eradication programs. Encourages development in health systems and technology; provides consulting services; conducts educational courses on public health topics including environmental health, food and nutrition, and tropical diseases. Has established Emergency Preparedness and Disaster Relief Coordination Program in order to increase the ability of health institutions to effectively handle emergencies. Operates the Natural Disaster Relief Voluntary Fund to support disaster relief activities. Maintains the Pan American Sanitary Bureau, the regional office for the Americas of the World Health Organization. Develops health documentaries and coordinates teleconferences. **Libraries: Type:** open to the public. **Holdings:** 20,000. **Subjects:** public health and related issues. **Awards: Type:** fellowship. **Recipient:** for training health services personnel. **Programs:** Publications. **Subcommittees:** Planning and Programming; Women, Health and Development. **Publications:** *Disaster Preparedness in the Americas*, quarterly. Newsletter. Covers disaster preparedness, mitigation, and management. **Price:** free. ISSN: 0251-4494 ● *EPI Newsletter*, bimonthly. Provides information on immunization programs in the Americas. Covers new technologies available for the execution of programs. **Price:** free for health workers. ISSN: 0251-4710 ● *Epidemiological* (in English and Spanish), bimonthly. Bulletin. Disseminates epidemiological information regarding communicable and noncommunicable diseases of public health importance. **Price:** free. ISSN: 0256-1859 ● *Health in the Americas*, quadrennial ● *Revista Panamericana de Salud Publica/Pan American Journal of Public Health* (in English, Portuguese, and Spanish), monthly. Serves as a reference source regarding health problems in the Americas and progress made toward solutions. Includes book reviews and results. **Price:** $75.00/year. ISSN: 1020-4989. **Circulation:** 15,000. Alternate Formats: online ● Manuals ● Monographs ● Reports ● Also publishes scientific books and technical paper. **Conventions/Meetings:** quadrennial Pan American Sanitary Conference - meeting.

14286 ■ Pan American Sanitary Bureau (PASB)

c/o Pan American Health Organization
525 23rd St. NW
Washington, DC 20037
Ph: (202)974-3000
Fax: (202)974-3663
URL: http://www.paho.org/english/paho/mission.htm
Contact: Dr. Mirta Roses Periago, Dir.

Multinational. Description: Improves and maintains a healthy environment for people of the Americas. Aims to develop a course on sustainable human development. Works as the Secretariat of the Pan American Health Organization. **Conventions/Meetings:** conference and meeting.

14287 ■ Partnership for Prevention

1015 18th St. NW, Ste.200
Washington, DC 20036
Ph: (202)833-0009
Fax: (202)833-0113
E-mail: info@prevent.org
URL: http://www.prevent.org
Contact: John M. Clymer, Pres.

Membership Dues: for-profit (based on gross annual revenues), $2,750-$11,000 (annual) ● state health agency, $110 (annual) ● non-profit (based on annual operating budget), $550-$5,500 (annual). **Staff:** 12. **Description:** Improves people's health by preventing diseases and injuries. Educates policy makers on disease prevention and health issues and strategies. **Computer Services:** Mailing lists, of members. **Projects:** Active Aging; Adult Immunization; Child Safety Seats; Chronic Disease Prevention; Genetics and Disease Prevention; Medicare-Health Promotion and Disease Prevention; Physical Activity; Tobacco Control and Prevention. **Publications:** *Comprehensive and Integrated Chronic Disease Prevention Action Planning.* Handbook. Alternate Formats: online.

14288 ■ Physicians Committee for Responsible Medicine (PCRM)

5100 Wisconsin Ave. NW, Ste.400
Washington, DC 20016
Ph: (202)686-2210
Fax: (202)686-2216
E-mail: pcrm@pcrm.org
URL: http://www.pcrm.org
Contact: Neal D. Barnard MD, Pres.

Founded: 1985. **Members:** 110,000. **Membership Dues:** supporter, $20 (annual) ● friend, $35 (annual) ● partner, $50 (annual) ● advocate, $100 (annual) ● fellow, $500 (annual). **Staff:** 25. **Budget:** $2,200,000. **Description:** Physicians, scientists, healthcare professionals, and interested others. Increases public awareness about the importance of preventive medicine and nutrition, and raises scientific and ethical questions pertaining to the use of humans and animals in medical research. Supports research into U.S. agricultural and public health policies. Promotes the New Four Food Groups, a no-cholesterol, low-fat alternative to U.S.D.A. dietary recommendations. Maintains the Gold Plan program, which includes information on low-fat, cholesterol-free entrees and nutrition for institutional food services. Offers fact sheets on nutrition, preventive medicine, and non-animal research topics. Maintains speakers' bureau. **Publications:** *Alternatives in Medical Education ● Best in the World (Cookbook).* **Price:** $11.95 ● *Eat Right, Live Longer.* **Price:** $13.00 ● *Food for Life.* **Price:** $14.00 ● *Foods That Fight Pain.* **Price:** $14.00 ● *Good Medicine*, quarterly. Magazine. Provides information about preventive medicine, nutrition, public health policy, medical/nutrition research updates, and AIDS research. **Price:** included in membership dues ● *PCRM Online*, monthly. Newsletter. Features nutrition and research updates. Alternate Formats: online ● *The Power of Your Plate.* **Price:** $12.95 each ● Brochures ● Also publishes fact sheets.

14289 ■ Planetree

130 Div. St.
Derby, CT 06418
Ph: (203)732-1365
Free: (866)732-1364

E-mail: planetree@planetree.org
URL: http://www.planetree.org
Contact: Susan Frampton PhD, Pres.
Founded: 1978. **Membership Dues:** friend, $100 (annual) ● partner, $500 (annual) ● sustainer, $1,000 (annual). **Description:** Promotes holistic approach to healing in all dimensions, including mental, emotional, spiritual and social, as well as physical; integrates complementary medical therapies such as mind/body medicine and therapeutic massage with conventional medical therapies. **Publications:** *PlaneTalk*, bi-monthly. Newsletter. Provides information on affiliates and other activities, summaries of current research, and interviews with leaders in patient-centered care. ● Brochure ● Video.

14290 ■ Premier Advocacy
444 N Capitol St. NW, Ste.625
Washington, DC 20001-1511
Ph: (202)393-0860
Fax: (202)393-6499
URL: http://www.premierinc.com
Contact: Barb Babauta, Mgr.
Founded: 1984. **Members:** 40. **Staff:** 12. **Description:** Sponsors educational programs for corporate officers and trustees of multi-hospital systems. Monitors, investigates, and develops policy positions on developments in the health care field. **Formed by Merger of:** Associated Health Systems; United Healthcare Systems. **Formerly:** Association AMHS Institute; (1988) American Healthcare Institute; (1998) AMHS Institute; (1999) Premier. **Publications:** *Washington Outlook*, biweekly. Newsletter. Alternate Formats: online. **Conventions/Meetings:** annual Governance Conference.

14291 ■ Project HOPE
255 Carter Hall Ln.
Millwood, VA 22646
Ph: (540)837-2100
Free: (800)544-HOPE
Fax: (540)837-1813
E-mail: hope@projecthope.org
URL: http://www.projecthope.org
Contact: Dr. John P. Howe III, Pres./CEO
Founded: 1958. **Multinational. Description:** Peacetime hospital ship conducting land-based medical training and health care education programs to advance healthcare globally. **Publications:** *Project HOPE Today*. Newsletter ● Annual Report, annual. Alternate Formats: online.

14292 ■ Regulatory Affairs Professionals Society (RAPS)
5635 Fishers Ln., Ste.550
Rockville, MD 20852
Ph: (301)770-2920
Fax: (301)770-2924
E-mail: raps@raps.org
URL: http://www.raps.org
Contact: Sherry Keramidas PhD, Exec. Dir.
Founded: 1976. **Members:** 10,000. **Membership Dues:** active, associate, $185 (annual) ● student, $65 (annual). **Staff:** 26. **Budget:** $5,000,000. **Multinational. Description:** Represents the regulatory affairs profession and the individuals who are part of this dynamic field. Includes health regulatory leaders of today and tomorrow in areas such as medical devices, pharmaceuticals, biologics, biotechnology and in vitro diagnostics. **Awards:** Leonard Stauffer Award. **Frequency:** annual. **Type:** recognition. **Recipient:** for exceptional contributions to mentoring, professional education development in the regulatory affairs ● New Professional Award. **Frequency:** annual. **Type:** recognition. **Recipient:** to professionals early in their careers for exceptional service in the profession and to RAPS, and special accomplishments in regulatory affairs ● Richard E. Greco Award. **Frequency:** annual. **Type:** recognition. **Recipient:** to outstanding leaders who have made significant contributions to the regulatory affairs profession and to RAPS and who show personal involvement and commitment in their personal lives ● Special Recognition Awards. **Frequency:** annual. **Type:** recognition. **Recipient:** for the unique and special contributions and achievements of individuals and organiza-

tions to advancing the quality of health and regulatory affairs. **Computer Services:** database, document catalog. **Committees:** Certification; Education; Publications. **Publications:** *RA News*. Newsletter ● *Regulatory Affairs Focus*, monthly. Magazine. Features articles, reports on global regulatory issues, and information about members, programs, activities. **Price:** included in membership dues. ISSN: 1097-2668. **Circulation:** 8,900. **Advertising:** accepted ● *RRC Document Catalog*. Contains extensive collection of complete-text regulations, guidance documents, publications, articles and reports focusing on global regulation. **Conventions/Meetings:** Best Practices in Biotherapeutics: The State of the Art - meeting ● annual conference (exhibits) ● Principles & Practices of US Regulatory Affairs - meeting ● Regulatory Strategy Workshop ● seminar.

14293 ■ Stratis Health
2901 Metro Dr., Ste.400
Bloomington, MN 55425-1525
Ph: (952)854-3306
Free: (877)787-2874
Fax: (952)853-8503
E-mail: info@stratishealth.org
URL: http://www.stratishealth.org
Contact: Jennifer Lundblad PhD, Pres./CEO
Founded: 1971. **Members:** 3,500. **Staff:** 60. **Budget:** $7,000,000. **Description:** Physicians interested in ensuring the availability of quality health care at reasonable costs. Evaluates health care services at hospitals, retirement homes, and other facilities. Develops health care standards for hospitals and offers consultation services to operators of health care facilities to improve efficiency in services. Conducts research and development on latest treatments and medical technologies. Tests new medical technologies. **Computer Services:** database. **Affiliated With:** American Health Quality Association. **Conventions/Meetings:** quarterly board meeting.

14294 ■ Tel-Med
Address Unknown since 2007
URL: http://www.tel-med.com
Founded: 1971. **Members:** 200. **Membership Dues:** program support, $80 (monthly). **Staff:** 3. **Languages:** English, Spanish. **For-Profit. Description:** Hospitals, medical societies, universities, medical centers, public libraries, and other organizations offering the Tel-Med program. Tel-Med is a library of three to five minute recorded health related messages created to be played over the telephone for public use, free of charge. Provides messages to communities; local libraries are established where individuals from the community can call to listen to messages. Operates as an information service intended to educate and assist in recognizing early signs of illness and is not designed to diagnose or treat medical problems. Scripts are written by medical professionals and examined by a team of physicians; messages are reviewed at least annually. Offers services and information on a wide range of medical subjects including alcoholism, arthritis, bee stings, cancer, diabetes, drug abuse, influenza, medical costs, mental health, nutrition, parenting, sex education, smoking, vasectomies, and vaginitis. **Libraries: Type:** not open to the public. **Holdings:** 650; audio recordings. **Committees:** Tape Development and Review. **Publications:** *Tel-Med Newsletter*, quarterly ● Annual Report, annual ● Brochures ● Also publishes tape listings and literature on implementation of the Tel-Med program. **Conventions/Meetings:** monthly conference.

14295 ■ United Methodist Association of Health and Welfare Ministries (UMA)
407 Corporate Center Dr., Ste.B
Vandalia, OH 45377
Ph: (937)415-3624
Free: (800)411-9901
Fax: (937)222-7364
E-mail: info@umassociation.org
URL: http://www.umassociation.org
Contact: Rev. Dr. Mearle L. Griffith, CEO/Pres.
Founded: 1940. **Members:** 400. **Membership Dues:** student, $30 (annual) ● retired, emeritus, $35 (an-

nual) ● associate, $45 (annual) ● affiliate, $80 (annual) ● community service ministry, $90 (annual) ● conference related unit, $170 (annual) ● organizational (based on previous year's expenses), $695-$4,675 (annual). **Staff:** 5. **Budget:** $850,000. **Description:** Offers communications and church relations guidance. Provides leadership development training for health and human service professionals in United Methodist related organizations and agencies. Develops ethical and theological statements on institutional care. Operates Educational Assessment Guidelines Leading Toward Excellence (EAGLE), a self-assessment and peer review accreditation program. Operates a Field Consultation Program; members may access skilled professionals to assist with governance questions. Offers audiovisual services to members. Administers the Order of Good Shepherds program designed to recognize ministry in the workplace by employees at member organizations. Maintains speakers' bureau; compiles statistics. **Awards: Frequency:** annual. **Type:** recognition. **Recipient:** to outstanding participants in various fields of health care and social service ministries. **Sections:** Chaplains; Children, Youth and Family Services; Community-Based Ministries; Conference Related Units; Hospitals and Health Systems; Ministries for Persons with Disabilities; Older Adult Ministries; Public Relations, Development, and Marketing; Trustees. **Formerly:** (1968) Board of Hospitals and Homes of The Methodist Church; (1972) Division of Health and Welfare Ministries of The United Methodist Church; (1983) National Association of Health and Welfare Ministries of The United Methodist Church. **Publications:** *Children, Youth, and Family Services Section Salary and Benefit Study* ● *National Directory of all United Methodist Related Health and Welfare Ministries*, annual. **Price:** $17.00 /year for members; $27.00 /year for nonmembers. **Circulation:** 400. **Advertising:** accepted ● *Older Adult Ministries Section Salary and Benefit Study*. **Conventions/Meetings:** annual Children, Youth and Family Services Section/Older Adult Ministries Section - workshop (exhibits) ● annual meeting and convention (exhibits) - always early March to mid-April.

14296 ■ Weight Watchers International (WWI)
11 Madison Ave.
New York, NY 10010
Ph: (212)589-2700
Free: (800)651-6000
Fax: (212)589-2600
E-mail: hr@weight-watchers.com
URL: http://www.weightwatchers.com
Contact: Linda Huett, CEO
Founded: 1963. **For-Profit. Description:** Promotes the Weight Watchers Program that includes a balanced diet, exercise and behavior modification. At weekly meetings, members learn how to modify current eating and exercise habits. Operates centers worldwide.

14297 ■ World Research Foundation (WRF)
41 Bell Rock Plz.
Sedona, AZ 86351
Ph: (928)284-3300
Fax: (928)284-3530
E-mail: info@wrf.org
URL: http://www.wrf.org
Contact: Laverne Boeckmann, Co-Founder
Founded: 1980. **Staff:** 25. **Languages:** English, German, Spanish. **Multinational. Description:** Informs the public of the latest developments in health and environmental issues. Provides health care professionals and the public with information on health tools and technologies currently available outside the U.S. but which have been overlooked or are unavailable in the U.S. Acts as a depository of public information. **Libraries: Type:** reference; open to the public. **Holdings:** 30,000; articles, books, periodicals. **Subjects:** health, environment. **Computer Services:** Information services, data searches in the field of health and environment from more than 100 countries. **Publications:** *World Research News*, quarterly. Newsletter ● Journal, quarterly. Contains traditional and nontraditional international health news. **Price:** $20.00. **Circulation:** 40,000 ● Proceedings, annual ● Reports.

Conventions/Meetings: annual Congress of Bio-Energetic Medicine, health technologies (exhibits).

Health Care

14298 ■ Access Project
89 South St., Ste.404
Lincoln Plz.
Boston, MA 02111
Ph: (617)654-9911
Fax: (617)654-9922
E-mail: info@accessproject.org
URL: http://www.accessproject.org
Contact: Cathy Dunham, Pres.
Description: Promotes social change and improved health, especially for vulnerable populations. **Publications:** Reports. Alternate Formats: online ● Manuals. Alternate Formats: online.

14299 ■ Alliance for Advancing Nonprofit Health Care
PO Box 41015
Washington, DC 20018
Free: (877)299-6497
E-mail: mcphersonbruce@aol.com
URL: http://www.nonprofithealthcare.org
Contact: Bruce McPherson, Exec. Dir.
Membership Dues: organization, $5,000 (annual).
Description: Seeks to protect and enhance the abilities of nonprofit healthcare organizations in serving society and their individual communities. Aims to bring balance to public policy discussions about nonprofit healthcare. Serves as the voice of nonprofit healthcare organizations through research, public education and advocacy. **Publications:** Newsletter, monthly. **Price:** included in membership dues ● Reports. Alternate Formats: online.

14300 ■ Alliance of Minority Medical Associations (AMMA)
1200 New Hampshire Ave. NW, Ste.575
Washington, DC 20036
Ph: (202)223-7560
Fax: (202)223-7567
URL: http://www.ammaonline.org
Contact: L. Natalie Carroll MD, Contact
Description: Aims to eliminate racial ethno-cultural disparities in health in the United States. Seeks to increase the quality of health care and access to health care for minority populations. Develops awareness, surveillance and treatment programs targeting major chronic diseases that impact racial/ethnic disparities in health. Promotes optimal health and wellness for all Americans through education, research and health policy. **Affiliated With:** Association of American Indian Physicians; National Medical Association.

14301 ■ American Association of Nurse Assessment Coordinators (AANAC)
1873 S Bellaire St., Ste.800
Denver, CO 80222
Ph: (303)758-7647
Free: (800)768-1880
Fax: (303)758-3588
E-mail: info@aanac.org
URL: http://www.aanac.org
Contact: Diane Carter, Pres./CEO
Founded: 1999. **Members:** 7,500. **Membership Dues:** individual, $110 (annual). **Staff:** 10. **Budget:** $1,700,000. **Description:** Represents registered nurses, licensed practical and vocational nurses, nurse assessment coordinators, administrators and other health care professionals committed to an interdisciplinary approach to resident care. Provides health care professionals with accurate and timely information, education, networking and advocacy related to clinical assessment, care planning and completion of federally mandated instruments. **Awards:** Administrator of the Year. **Frequency:** annual. **Type:** recognition. **Recipient:** for an administrator who has an outstanding performance for the year ● Nurse Assessment Coordinator of the Year. **Frequency:** annual. **Type:** recognition. **Recipient:** for a

member who has an outstanding contribution to the profession ● Outstanding Contributor to AANAC. **Frequency:** annual. **Type:** recognition. **Recipient:** for a member who has an outstanding contribution to AANAC. **Computer Services:** database, articles ● online services, discussion groups.

14302 ■ American College of Contingency Planners (ACCP)
701 Lee St., Ste.600
Des Plaines, IL 60016-4516
Ph: (847)759-8601
Fax: (847)759-8602
E-mail: info@aameda.org
URL: http://www.aameda.org/Specialtygroups/ACCP/
contingency.html
Contact: Stewart D. Smith, Pres.
Founded: 1998. **Membership Dues:** associate, $90 (annual) ● student, $45 (annual) ● regular, $195 (annual). **Description:** Supports health care planning professionals in contingency, emergency, and disaster response. **Programs:** The Seven Deadly Sins of Contingency Planning. **Publications:** Action Alerts ● Newsletters ● Reports. **Conventions/Meetings:** annual conference.

14303 ■ American College of Healthcare Architects (ACHA)
PO Box 14548
Lenexa, KS 66285-4548
Ph: (913)492-4307
Fax: (913)599-5340
E-mail: acha-info@goamp.com
URL: http://www.healtharchitects.org
Contact: Janene Dawson, Exec. Dir.
Founded: 1999. **Description:** Provides Board Certification for Architects practicing as healthcare specialists.

14304 ■ American College of Healthcare Information Administrators (ACHIA)
701 Lee St., Ste.600
Des Plaines, IL 60016-4516
Ph: (847)759-8601
Fax: (847)759-8602
E-mail: gregory.parish@verizon.net
URL: http://www.aameda.org
Contact: Gregory L. Parish, Pres.
Description: Promotes advancement of healthcare information administrators. **Publications:** Newsletter. Alternate Formats: online.

14305 ■ American Nutraceutical Association (ANA)
5120 Selkirk Dr., Ste.100
Birmingham, AL 35242
Ph: (205)980-5710
Free: (800)566-3622
Fax: (205)991-9302
E-mail: info@ana-jana.org
URL: http://www.ana-jana.org
Contact: Allen Montgomery, Exec. Dir.
Founded: 1997. **Membership Dues:** professional in U.S., $125 (annual) ● professional in Canada, $135 (annual) ● professional outside U.S. and Canada, $175 (annual) ● individual, consumer in U.S., $75 (annual). **Description:** Develops and provides educational materials and programs on nutraceuticals and nutrition for health care professionals, consumers and sales associates from nutraceutical companies. **Computer Services:** Information services, e-news; articles and clinical studies ● online services, shopping. **Programs:** Dietary Supplement Health and Education Act Home Study and Certification. **Publications:** Immune Response. Video. Describes the importance of a healthy and properly functioning immune system through detailed microscopic presentation of the human body. **Price:** $25.00 each ● JANA, quarterly. Journal. Serves as a guide to members on the current research in nutrition and nutraceuticals for the prevention and treatment of disease. **Price:** $36.00 each. Alternate Formats: CD-ROM ● Nutraceuticals and Medicine Conference Audio Tape Set. Audiotape. Provides a clinical approach to disease prevention and management through the use of specific nutraceuticals and micro-

nutrients. **Price:** $49.95 each ● Questioning Chemotherapy. Book. Probes the scientific and statistical advantages and disadvantages of chemotherapy. **Price:** $19.95 each ● Brochure. Alternate Formats: online.

14306 ■ American Society of Healthcare Publication Editors (ASHPE)
8870 Darrow Rd., Ste.F106-155
Twinsburg, OH 44087
Ph: (330)487-0344
Fax: (330)487-0530
E-mail: info@ashpe.org
URL: http://www.ashpe.org
Membership Dues: individual, $60 (annual) ● publication, $150 (annual) ● corporate, $240 (annual). **Description:** Works to enhance knowledge and skill of healthcare publication editors. **Awards:** Competition Awards. **Frequency:** annual. **Type:** recognition. **Recipient:** for excellence and achievement in the healthcare publication field. **Publications:** Editors' Salary Survey. **Price:** included in membership dues ● Outlook, quarterly. Newsletter. **Price:** included in membership dues.

14307 ■ America's Health Together (AHT)
3220 Ordway St. NW
Washington, DC 20008
Ph: (202)966-1138 (202)544-8455
Fax: (202)364-6929
E-mail: comments@healthtogether.org
URL: http://www.healthtogether.org
Contact: Margaret Heldring PhD, Pres./Founder
Description: Promotes access to essential and affordable healthcare services regardless of social and financial standing. **Committees:** Advisory. **Programs:** Facing Fear Together; Health and Social Justice; Health Care for Everyone.

14308 ■ Association of Clinicians for the Underserved (ACU)
1420 Spring Hill Rd., Ste.600
McLean, VA 22102
Ph: (703)442-5318
Fax: (703)749-5348
E-mail: acu@clinicians.org
URL: http://www.clinicians.org
Contact: Kathie Westpheling, Exec. Dir.
Founded: 1996. **Members:** 8,900. **Membership Dues:** sponsor, $2,500 ● organization, $500 ● clinic, $200 (annual) ● individual, $100 (annual) ● associate, $85 (annual) ● student, $65 (biennial). **Description:** Aims to improve the health of America's underserved populations. Serves as a forum for clinicians and other health workers to interact with other professionals. **Publications:** Newsletter, quarterly. Alternate Formats: online.

14309 ■ Association for Community Affiliated Plans (ACAP)
1400 Eye St. NW, Ste.330
Washington, DC 20005
Ph: (202)331-4601
Fax: (202)296-3526
E-mail: mmurray@communityplans.net
URL: http://www.ahcahp.org
Contact: Margaret A. Murray, Exec. Dir.
Description: Supports managed care plans that primarily serve the Medicaid and SCHIP populations and are owned by or affiliated with Community Health Centers (CHC). Improves the health of medically underserved populations through the development, survival, promotion and growth of CHC-affiliated health plans. **Publications:** Newsletter. Alternate Formats: online ● Annual Reports.

14310 ■ Association For Electronic Health Care Transactions (AFEHCT)
c/o Healthcare Information and Management Systems Society
230 E Ohio St., Ste.500
Chicago, IL 60611
Ph: (312)664-4467
Fax: (312)664-6143

E-mail: pmatthews@himss.org
URL: http://www.himss.org/ASP/topics_FocusDy-namic.asp?faid=170
Contact: Sheila Schweitzer, Chair
Founded: 1992. **Membership Dues:** individual, $250 (annual) ● not-for-profit corporation/organization, $750-$1,500 (annual) ● for profit corporation/organization, $500-$5,000 (annual). **Description:** Promotes the interchange of electronic health care information in an open and secure environment. Improves and reduces the cost of health care through the use of EDI. Furthers the use of standards and the application of health care information technology to the delivery, financing and administration of health care.

14311 ■ Center for Health Design
1850 Gateway Blvd., Ste.1083
Concord, CA 94520
Ph: (925)521-9404
Fax: (925)521-9405
E-mail: admin@healthdesign.org
URL: http://www.healthdesign.org
Contact: Debra J. Levin, Pres.
Founded: 1988. **Membership Dues:** student affiliate, $25 (annual) ● individual affiliate, $100-$400 (annual) ● professional affiliate, $500-$1,000 (annual) ● corporate affiliate (based on number of employees), $1,500-$5,000 (annual) ● affiliate partner, $15,000 (annual). **Description:** Works to create a future where healthcare environments enhance healing and promote well-being for patients, staff, and visitors through research, design, architecture. Conducts fundraisers. **Awards:** Changemaker Award. **Frequency:** annual. **Type:** recognition. **Recipient:** to an individual or organization that has demonstrated exceptional ability to make changes in healthcare facility design. **Councils:** Environmental Standards. **Projects:** Pebbie. **Publications:** *Enhancing the Quality of Health Care with the Built Environment: Through the Patient's Eye—Acute Care.* Video ● *Journal of Healthcare Design.* Contains a collection of proceedings from the Symposium on Healthcare Design. **Price:** $16.00 online, Vols. 1-10; $40.00 print, Vols. 9 & 10; $150.00 CD format, Vols. 1-10 ● *News From The Center.* Newsletter. Alternate Formats: online ● Reports. Alternate Formats: CD-ROM ● Magazine, 5/year. Provides latest trends and issues in healthcare building design and construction. **Conventions/Meetings:** semiannual Symposium on Healthcare Design - conference and seminar, with networking, products (exhibits).

14312 ■ Center for Patient Advocacy
Address Unknown since 2007
Description: Represents patients; dedicated to ensuring all Americans access to quality medical care.

14313 ■ Center for Studying Health System Change (HSC)
600 Maryland Ave. SW, Ste.550
Washington, DC 20024
Ph: (202)484-5261
Fax: (202)484-9258
E-mail: hscinfo@hschange.org
URL: http://www.hschange.org
Contact: Paul B. Ginsburg PhD, Pres.
Description: Works to inform health care decision makers about changes in health care system at local and national levels, and effects of such changes on people. **Telecommunication Services:** electronic mail, pginsburg@hschange.org. **Study Groups:** Community Tracking Study. **Publications:** *Data Bulletins.* Alternate Formats: online ● *Issue Briefs.* Alternate Formats: online ● Reports. Contains community and tracking reports. Alternate Formats: online ● Annual Reports, annual. Provides updates on HSC's activities and publications. Alternate Formats: online ● Articles. Alternate Formats: online.

14314 ■ Coalition for Healthcare Communication (CHC)
c/o John Kamp, Exec. Dir.
405 Lexington Ave.
New York, NY 10174-1801

Ph: (212)850-0708
E-mail: info@cohealthcom.org
URL: http://www.cohealthcom.org
Contact: John Kamp, Exec. Dir.
Founded: 1991. **Description:** Represents communications industry groups engaged in medical publishing, in the development of medical education materials, and in the dissemination of information concerning medical products and services. Seeks to defend the rights of medical professionals and consumers to receive appropriate health care information. Promotes the free flow of medical and other scientific information to professional care givers and the general public. **Libraries: Type:** reference. **Holdings:** articles, papers, reports. **Subjects:** healthcare communications, health economics. **Telecommunication Services:** electronic mail, jkamp@cohealthcom.org. **Publications:** *The Right to Know.* Brochure. Explains the role of medical marketing and its value to society. Alternate Formats: online ● Annual Report, annual. Alternate Formats: online.

14315 ■ Coalition for Healthcare eStandards (CHeS)
3300 Washtenaw Ave., Ste.222
Ann Arbor, MI 48104-4250
Ph: (734)677-3300
Fax: (734)677-6622
E-mail: info@chestandards.org
URL: http://www.chestandards.org
Contact: Mr. Mark McDougall, Exec. Dir.
Membership Dues: core, $36,000 (annual) ● affiliate, $500 (annual). **Description:** Promotes uniform industry data standards for healthcare supply chain transactions over the Internet. **Committees:** CID; Legal; Pharmacy eStandards; Product Taxonomy; Public Relations; UPN. **Conventions/Meetings:** board meeting.

14316 ■ Consumer Coalition for Quality Health Care
1101 Vermont Ave. NW, Ste.1001
Washington, DC 20005
Ph: (202)789-3606
Fax: (202)898-2389
E-mail: bwlind@erols.com
URL: http://www.consumers.org
Contact: Brian W. Lindberg, Exec. Dir.
Founded: 1993. **Description:** Consumer groups dedicated to protecting and improving quality of health care for all Americans. **Telecommunication Services:** hotline, Quality Watchline, (899)720-8090. **Projects:** Consumer Coalition's State Campaign. **Publications:** *The Quality Connection.* Newsletter. Contains information about the association. ● *White Papers.*

14317 ■ Council for Affordable Quality Healthcare (CAQH)
South Bldg., Ste.500
601 Pennsylvania Ave. NW
Washington, DC 20004
Ph: (202)861-1492
Fax: (202)861-1454
E-mail: info@caqh.org
URL: http://www.caqh.org
Contact: Robin J. Thomashauer, Exec. Dir.
Description: Acts as a catalyst for industry collaboration on initiatives that simplify healthcare administration. Strives to reduce costs and frustrations associated with healthcare administration. Facilitates administrative healthcare information exchange. Encourages administrative and clinical data integration. **Telecommunication Services:** electronic mail, rthomashauer@caqh.org. **Publications:** Annual Report. Alternate Formats: online ● Brochures. Alternate Formats: online.

14318 ■ Cross Cultural Health Care Program (CCHCP)
270 S Hanford St., Ste.208
Seattle, WA 98134
Ph: (206)860-0329 (206)860-0331
Fax: (206)860-0334

E-mail: resource@xculture.org
URL: http://www.xculture.org
Contact: Ira SenGupta MA, Exec. Dir.
Founded: 1992. **Description:** Committed to quality health care that is culturally and linguistically appropriate. **Libraries: Type:** reference; open to the public. **Subjects:** cross-cultural healthcare. **Computer Services:** Online services, library. **Programs:** Cultural Competency in a Major Medical Center; Death and Dying in Ethnic America; The Significance of Trained Medical Interpretation in Obstetrical Care; Standard of Best Cultural Competency Practices for Medicaid Managed Care Populations; Strengthening Children and Families in White Center; Washington State DOH: Cross Cultural Workshop on Tobacco. **Projects:** Cross Cultural Health and Nutrition Demonstration; Reflections on the CLAS Standards. **Publications:** *Bridging the Gap Interpreter Handbook.* **Price:** $50.00/copy ● *CCHCP's Community Profile Series.* Booklets. **Price:** $10.00/copy ● *Chronology of United States Immigration History 1790-1998.* **Price:** $10.00/copy ● *Constructing the Middle Ground: Cultural Competence in Medicaid Managed Care.* Book. **Price:** $45.00 book version; $25.00 CD version. Alternate Formats: CD-ROM ● *Death & Dying in Ethnic America.* Book. **Price:** $30.00/copy ● *Interpreter's Guide to Common Medications.* **Price:** $10.00/copy ● *Medical Glossaries.* **Price:** $10.00/copy ● *Medical Glossaries Expanded* ● *Medical Glossaries Expanded & Revised* ● *Survey of Interpreter Services Utilization.* **Price:** $10.00/copy ● *Voices of the Communities: Survey Highlights.* **Price:** $10.00/copy ● Videos ● Articles.

14319 ■ eHealth Initiative
818 Connecticut Ave. NW, Ste.500
Washington, DC 20006
Ph: (202)624-3270
Fax: (202)429-5553
E-mail: info@ehealthinitiative.org
URL: http://www.ehealthinitiative.org
Contact: Ann Barcome, Contact
Membership Dues: corporate, $2,500-$25,000 (annual). **Description:** Works to improve the quality, safety and efficiency of healthcare through information and information technology. **Publications:** Newsletter.

14320 ■ Esperanca
1911 W Earll Dr.
Phoenix, AZ 85015
Ph: (602)252-7772
Free: (888)701-5150
Fax: (602)340-9197
E-mail: info@esperanca.org
URL: http://esperanca.org
Contact: Raul Espericueta, Pres.
Founded: 1970. **Staff:** 6. **Budget:** $2,000,000. **Multinational. Description:** Helps improve the well-being of children and their families through public health programming and volunteer surgical missions. Encourages self-reliance in health, through prevention, training and treatment in the areas of greatest need throughout the world. **Programs:** Adopt-A-Clinic; Dental; Local Volunteer; Volunteer Surgical. **Subgroups:** Esperanca Women's Guild. **Publications:** Newsletter, monthly. Alternate Formats: online ● Annual Report, annual. Alternate Formats: online.

14321 ■ Ethiopian North American Health Professionals Association (ENAHPA)
6632 Telegraph Rd., Box 150
Bloomfield Hills, MI 48301
Ph: (248)858-6974
Fax: (248)858-6976
E-mail: enahpa1@aol.com
URL: http://www.enahpa.org
Contact: Dr. Ingida Asfaw MD, Pres./Founder
Founded: 1999. **Membership Dues:** medical/non-medical, $200 (annual) ● graduate/postgraduate, $100 (annual) ● student, $50 (annual) ● resident of Ethiopia, E$50 (annual) ● life, $900. **Description:** Promotes the specific healthcare needs of women and children in Ethiopia. Assists in delivery of medical and surgical services to Ethiopian adults.

14322 ■ Global Health Ministries (GHM)
7831 Hickory St. NE
Minneapolis, MN 55432-2500
Ph: (763)586-9590
Fax: (763)586-9591
E-mail: ghmoffice@cs.com
URL: http://www.ghm.org
Contact: Rev. Timon C. Iverson, Exec. Dir.
Founded: 1987. **Staff:** 3. **Budget:** $1,400,000. **Multinational. Description:** Provides Lutheran health care work overseas; gathers and sends medical supplies around the world, recruits health related personnel; funds training of national health care givers. **Publications:** *Global Health*, bimonthly. Newsletter. **Circulation:** 16,000. Alternate Formats: online ● Annual Report, annual.

14323 ■ Healing Touch International (HTI)
445 Union Blvd., Ste.105
Lakewood, CO 80228
Ph: (303)989-7982
Fax: (303)980-8683
E-mail: htiheal@aol.com
URL: http://www.healingtouch.net
Contact: Lisa Anselme, Exec. Dir.
Founded: 1996. **Members:** 3,000. **Membership Dues:** regular, $100 (annual). **Staff:** 5. **Multinational. Description:** Promotes the practice and teaching of Healing Touch. **Publications:** *Healing Touch*, bimonthly. Newsletter. **Price:** included in membership dues. **Conventions/Meetings:** annual Healing Touch: The Language of the Heart - meeting and workshop.

14324 ■ Health Care Compliance Association (HCCA)
5780 Lincoln Dr., Ste.120
Minneapolis, MN 55436
Free: (888)580-8373
Fax: (952)988-0146
E-mail: info@hcca-info.org
URL: http://www.hcca-info.org
Contact: Odell Guyton, Pres.
Founded: 1997. **Members:** 3,200. **Membership Dues:** individual, $295 (annual) ● corporate, $2,500 (annual). **Staff:** 10. **Budget:** $3,800,000. **Regional Groups:** 10. **Description:** Healthcare professionals involved in compliance in the health care industry. Promotes quality compliance programs in health care. Offers educational programs, professional network, and discussion groups. **Computer Services:** database ● mailing lists ● online services. **Boards:** Healthcare Compliance Certification. **Committees:** Compensation; Governance and Ethics; Nominating. **Publications:** *Compliance Today*, monthly. Magazine. **Price:** included in membership dues. **Advertising:** accepted. Alternate Formats: online ● *This Week in Corporate Compliance*, weekly. Newsletter. **Advertising:** accepted. Alternate Formats: online ● Annual Report, annual. Alternate Formats: online ● Brochure. Alternate Formats: online ● Surveys, annual. Alternate Formats: online ● Reports. Alternate Formats: online. **Conventions/Meetings:** annual Compliance Institute - conference and trade show (exhibits) ● bimonthly conference, specialty conferences ● regional meeting and conference - 10/year.

14325 ■ Health Care eBusiness Collaborative (HCEC)
1405 N Pierce St., Ste.100
Little Rock, AR 72207-5378
Ph: (501)661-9408
Free: (800)905-4583
Fax: (501)661-0507
E-mail: hcec@hcec.org
URL: http://www.hcec.org
Contact: Garren Hagemeier, Exec. Dir.
Members: 350. **Membership Dues:** provider facility owner, $650 (annual) ● provider group (base), $2,000 (annual) ● provider group affiliate, $800 (annual) ● trading partner (based on annual revenues), $770-$5,000 (annual). **Description:** Seeks to advance electronic business efficiencies in the health care industry. **Telecommunication Services:** electronic mail, garren@hcec.org. **Conventions/Meetings:** Economical EBusiness - workshop and seminar.

14326 ■ Health Care Without Harm (HCWH)
c/o Colleen Funkhouser
1901 N Moore St., Ste.509
Arlington, VA 22209
Ph: (703)243-0056
Fax: (703)243-4008
E-mail: info@hcwh.org
URL: http://www.noharm.org
Contact: Colleen Funkhouser, Contact
Founded: 1996. **Members:** 375. **Multinational. Description:** Seeks to change the health care industry to be ecologically sustainable and no longer a source of harm to public health and the environment, without compromising patient safety or care. **Libraries: Type:** reference. **Holdings:** clippings, reports. **Subjects:** chemical policy, electronics, healthy building, non-English document, cleaners and disinfectants, food, incineration, pesticides, waste minimization, dioxin, green purchasing, mercury, phthalates, worker safety.

14327 ■ Health Coalition on Liability and Access (HCLA)
PO Box 19008
Washington, DC 20036-9008
Ph: (202)293-4255
E-mail: media@hcla.org
URL: http://www.hcla.org
Contact: Christian Shalgian, Chm.
Description: Medical organizations. Aims to improve America's health care system through reform. **Libraries: Type:** reference. **Formerly:** (2003) Health Care Liability Alliance. **Publications:** *Issue Briefing*. Book.

14328 ■ Health Level Seven (HL7)
3300 Washtenaw Ave., Ste.227
Ann Arbor, MI 48104
Ph: (734)677-7777
Fax: (734)677-6622
E-mail: hq@hl7.org
URL: http://www.hl7.org
Contact: Mark McDougall, Exec. Dir.
Founded: 1987. **Membership Dues:** individual, $450 (annual) ● student, $125 (annual). **Description:** Provides standards for the exchange, management and integration of data that support clinical patient care and the management, delivery and evaluation of healthcare services. Creates flexible, cost effective approaches, standards, guidelines, methodologies, and related services for interoperability between healthcare information systems. **Telecommunication Services:** electronic mail, markmcd@hl7.org. **Committees:** Architectural Review Board; Clinical Decision Support; Control/Query; International Affiliates; Technical Steering. **Special Interest Groups:** Arden Syntax; Attachments; Clinical Guidelines; Imaging Integration; Java; Laboratory; Medication; Patient Safety. **Publications:** Newsletter. **Conventions/Meetings:** annual Plenary & Working Group Meeting.

14329 ■ Institute for Healthcare Improvement (IHI)
20 Univ. Rd., 7th Fl.
Cambridge, MA 02138
Ph: (617)301-4800
Free: (866)787-0831
Fax: (617)301-4848
E-mail: info@ihi.org
URL: http://www.ihi.org
Contact: Donald M. Berwick MD, Pres./CEO
Founded: 1991. **Description:** Committed to improving health by advancing quality and value of healthcare. **Programs:** Advanced Training; Collaborative Learning; Impact Network; Improvement Advisor Professional Development; 100K Lives Campaign; Patient Safety Officer Executive Development; Pursuing Perfection; Transforming Care at the Bedside. **Publications:** *Innovation Series*. Papers. Includes white papers to further quality and value of healthcare. Alternate Formats: online ● Annual Report, annual. Alternate Formats: online ● Brochure. Alternate Formats: online ● Books ● Audiotapes ● Videos. **Conventions/Meetings:** annual International Summit on Redesigning Hospital Care - conference ● annual International Summit on Redesigning the Clini-

cal Office Practice - conference ● annual National Forum on Quality Improvement in Healthcare - conference.

14330 ■ Institute for Safe Medication Practices (ISMP)
1800 Byberry Rd., Ste.810
Huntingdon Valley, PA 19006
Ph: (215)947-7797
Fax: (215)914-1492
E-mail: ismpinfo@ismp.org
URL: http://www.ismp.org
Contact: Michael R. Cohen RPh, Pres.
Description: Dedicated to the safe use of medications through improvements in drug distribution, naming, packaging, labeling, and delivery system design. **Awards:** Three Cheers Awards. **Frequency:** annual. **Type:** recognition. **Boards:** Advisory. **Publications:** *ISMP Medication Safety Alert! Acute Care Edition*, biweekly. Newsletter. Alternate Formats: online ● *ISMP Medication Safety Alert! Community/Ambulatory Edition*, monthly. Newsletter. Alternate Formats: online ● *ISMP Medication Safety Alert! Consumer Edition*. Newsletter ● *ISMP Medication Safety Alert! Nursing Edition*, monthly. Newsletter. **Conventions/Meetings:** annual dinner.

14331 ■ International Association of Healthcare Practitioners (IAHP)
11211 Prosperity Farms Rd., Ste.D-325
Palm Beach Gardens, FL 33410
Ph: (561)622-4334 (561)622-4706
Free: (800)311-9204
Fax: (561)622-4771
E-mail: iahp@iahp.com
URL: http://www.iahp.com
Contact: Kathy Woll, Dir.
Founded: 1996. **Members:** 50,000. **Membership Dues:** silver, $25 (annual) ● gold, $50 (annual) ● platinum, $125 (annual) ● silver, $100 (quinquennial) ● gold, $200 (quinquennial) ● platinum, $500 (quinquennial). **Staff:** 4. **Multinational. Description:** Osteopathic physicians, medical doctors, doctors of Chiropractic, doctors of Oriental medicine, naturopathic physicians, nurses, psychiatric specialists, psychologists, dentists, speech pathologists, physical acupuncturists, massage therapists and other professional bodyworkers. Offers innovative therapies and solutions in healthcare; provides a united voice to legislative bodies, insurance regulators, patients, clients and other healthcare providers. **Also Known As:** Upledger's International Association of Healthcare Practitioners. **Publications:** *IAHP Connections*, annual. Newsletter. **Price:** included in membership dues. Alternate Formats: online ● Directories, annual. Contains member listing. **Price:** $10.00. **Circulation:** 7,000. Alternate Formats: online; CD-ROM. **Conventions/Meetings:** seminar.

14332 ■ International Association for Human Caring (IAHC)
c/o Christine Filipovich, Admin.
2090 Linglestown Rd., Ste.107
Harrisburg, PA 17110
Ph: (717)703-0033
Fax: (717)234-6798
E-mail: pnrnr@aol.com
URL: http://www.humancaring.org
Contact: Gwen Sherwood PhD, Pres.
Founded: 1987. **Membership Dues:** individual, $85 (annual) ● student, retiree, $38 (annual) ● institutional, $210 (annual) ● contributor, $300 (annual) ● president's circle, $500 (annual) ● life, $2,000. **Multinational. Description:** Serves as an international, scholarly forum for all nurses interested in the advancement of the knowledge of human care and caring within the discipline of nursing. Identifies major philosophical, epistemological and professional dimensions of care and caring to advance the body of knowledge that constitutes nursing. **Awards:** Droesbeke Caring Award. **Frequency:** annual. **Type:** scholarship. **Recipient:** for support to a non-US undergraduate student attending the IAHC conference each year ● Leininger Award. **Frequency:** periodic. **Type:** monetary. **Recipient:** for nurse scholars who research care/caring as the essence of

nursing discipline ● Watson Scholarship. **Frequency:** annual. **Type:** scholarship. **Recipient:** for support to a nursing student attending the IAHC conference each year. **Computer Services:** Mailing lists, listserv. **Committees:** By-Laws; Conference; Continuing Education; Fundraising; Nominating; Publications; Research Grant; Scholarship. **Publications:** *International Journal for Human Caring*, 3/year. Serves as a scholarly publication for nurses to advance knowledge of care and caring. **Price:** $80.00 for nonmembers; $130.00 /year for institutions; $16.00 additional for foreign countries ● Newsletter. Alternate Formats: online. **Conventions/Meetings:** annual Reflection and Action - Promoting Harmony in Caring Environments - conference, with abstract presentations.

14333 ■ Jacobs Institute of Women's Health (JIWH)
2021 K St. NW, Ste.800
Washington, DC 20006
Ph: (202)530-2376
Fax: (202)296-0025
E-mail: whieditor@gwu.edu
URL: http://www.jiwh.org
Contact: Dr. Richard Mauery MS, Managing Dir.
Members: 2,000. **Membership Dues:** individual, $110 (annual) ● student, retired, disabled, $50 (annual) ● individual, $195 (biennial) ● organization, institutional, $255 (annual) ● organization, institutional, $495 (biennial). **Description:** Works to improve health care for women through research, dialogue, and education. **Publications:** *In Touch*, quarterly. Newsletter. **Price:** included in membership dues. Alternate Formats: online ● *Women's Health Data Book, 3rd Edition* ● *Women's Health Issue*, monthly. Journal. **Conventions/Meetings:** seminar and symposium.

14334 ■ Kaiser Family Foundation (KFF)
2400 Sand Hill Rd.
Menlo Park, CA 94025
Ph: (650)854-9400
Fax: (650)854-4800
URL: http://www.kff.org
Contact: Drew Altman PhD, Pres./CEO
Multinational. Description: Works to research and promote health care issues. Focuses on health policy, media and public education, and health and development in South Africa. **Additional Websites:** http://www.kaisernetwork.org. **Programs:** Health and Development in South Africa; Health Policy; Media and Public Education.

14335 ■ Leapfrog Group
c/o Academy Health
1801 K St. NW, Ste.701-L
Washington, DC 20006
Ph: (202)292-6711 (202)292-6713
Fax: (202)292-6813
E-mail: info@leapfroggroup.org
URL: http://www.leapfroggroup.org
Contact: Suzanne Delbanco PhD, CEO
Members: 135. **Staff:** 9. **Description:** Works to save lives and reduce preventable medical mistakes. Promotes high-value health care through incentives and rewards. **Telecommunication Services:** electronic mail, sdelbanco@leapfroggroup.org.

14336 ■ Medical Outcomes Trust
235 Wyman St., Ste.130
Waltham, MA 02451
Ph: (781)890-4884
Fax: (781)890-0922
E-mail: info@outcomes-trust.org
URL: http://www.outcomes-trust.org
Founded: 1992. **Description:** Works to advance universal adoption of health outcomes assessment in health care to improve value of health care services.

14337 ■ Medical Wings International (MWI)
PO Box 610542
Dallas, TX 75261
Ph: (817)467-5020
Fax: (817)467-5077

E-mail: info@medicalwings.org
URL: http://www.medicalwings.org
Contact: Glenda Johnson, Exec. Dir.
Founded: 1998. **Multinational. Description:** Provides basic medical, dental and eye care services to impoverished children and families around the world. Delivers life-saving medicines, medical equipment and supplies. Provides unique opportunities to increase understanding of the needs of people in the developing world. **Boards:** Advisory. **Programs:** Outreach; Youth.

14338 ■ Mobile Healthcare Alliance (MOHCA)
2100 M St. NW, 170-343
Washington, DC 20037
Ph: (202)452-0889
Fax: (202)659-2218
E-mail: ctessier@mohca.org
URL: http://www.mobilehealthcarealliance.org
Contact: Claudia Tessier, Exec. Dir.
Membership Dues: strategic, $20,000 (annual) ● institutional, $2,500 (annual) ● individual, $450 (annual). **Description:** Promotes mobile technologies to support delivery of quality health care.

14339 ■ Movement Disorder Society (MDS)
555 E Wells St., Ste.1100
Milwaukee, WI 53202-3823
Ph: (414)276-2145
Fax: (414)276-3349
E-mail: info@movementdisorders.org
URL: http://www.movementdisorders.org
Contact: Caley Kleczka, Exec. Dir.
Founded: 1985. **Members:** 1,746. **Membership Dues:** regular, $200 (annual) ● junior, $100 (annual) ● waived, $10 (annual). **Staff:** 7. **Multinational. Description:** Provides international forums and research to disseminate information on recent advances in clinical and basic science pertinent to movement disorders, enhance education of physicians and public, and enrich the quality of care to patients. **Awards:** Abstract Awards. **Frequency:** annual. **Type:** monetary ● Honorary Member Award. **Frequency:** annual. **Type:** grant. **Computer Services:** Mailing lists. **Publications:** *Movement Disorders*, monthly. Journal. Alternate Formats: online ● *Moving Along*, quarterly. Newsletter. Contains up-to-date information on new developments such as clinical trials, upcoming meetings, and policy issues. **Conventions/Meetings:** annual International Congress of Parkinson's Disease and Movement Disorders.

14340 ■ National Academies of Practice (NAP)
PO Box 1037
Edgewood, MD 21040
Ph: (410)676-3390
E-mail: naphdq@comcast.net
URL: http://www.napnet.us
Contact: Jane Williams Ball, Pres.
Founded: 1981. **Members:** 1,000. **Membership Dues:** general, $195 (annual). **Description:** Works to promote quality health care for all, through interdisciplinary practice, education, and research. **Awards:** Interdisciplinary Creativity in Practice & Education Award. **Type:** recognition ● Interdisciplinary Group Recognition Award. **Type:** recognition ● Nicholas Andrew Cummings Award. **Frequency:** annual. **Type:** recognition. **Recipient:** to an individual NAP distinguished practitioner ● Senator Daniel K. Inouye Award. **Type:** recognition. **Recipient:** to individuals with significant and enduring contributions to health. **Councils:** Dentistry; Medicine; Nursing; Optometry; Osteopathic Medicine; Pharmacy; Podiatric Medicine; Psychology. **Publications:** *National Academies of Practice Forum*. Journal. Includes interdisciplinary issues in health care. ● Papers ● Newsletter, quarterly. Alternate Formats: online. **Conventions/Meetings:** symposium.

14341 ■ National Academy for State Health Policy (NASHP)
50 Monument Sq., Ste.502
Portland, ME 04101
Ph: (207)874-6524
Fax: (207)874-6527

E-mail: info@nashp.org
URL: http://www.nashp.org
Contact: Alan Weil, Pres./Exec. Dir.
Staff: 21. **Description:** Works to help states achieve excellence in health policy and practice. **Committees:** Access for the Uninsured; Family and Community Health; Health Care Marketplace; Long-Term and Chronic Care; Managed Care and Purchasing Strategies. **Programs:** Flood Tide Forum; User Liaison. **Publications:** *Building a Pathway to Universal Coverage: How Do We Get From Here to There?*. Paper. Contains a summary of a discussion during the Flood Tide Forum. ● *Enhancing State and Local Capacity to Promote Healthy Weight in Children: Addressing Disparities in the Real World*. Report. Contains information to implement projects aimed at reducing disparities in childhood overweight. ● *ERISA Preemption Manual for State Health Policy Makers*. Features analysis and source materials related to the federal Employee Retirement Income Security Act of 1974 (ERISA). ● *The Health Coverage Tax Credit for Trade Dislocated Workers and Retirees: Lessons from Maine's Early Experience*. Paper. Contains details of the design and structure of the Health Coverage Tax Credit (HCTC). ● *Lessons from 25 Years of State Initiatives*. Paper. Contains examinations of state health policy reforms enacted over the past quarter century. ● Directory. Alternate Formats: online. **Conventions/Meetings:** annual State Health Policy Conference.

14342 ■ National Association of Specialty Health Organizations (NASHO)
222 S First St., Ste.303
Louisville, KY 40202
Ph: (502)403-1122
Fax: (502)403-1129
E-mail: jroberts@nasho.org
URL: http://www.nasho.org
Contact: Al Schubert, Chm.
Founded: 2003. **Description:** Aims to fully integrate specialty health organizations into the health care reimbursement model. Educates the public policy/regulatory arena on specialty health business practices. Promotes specialty health through strategic communications outlets. Supports professional growth of specialty health care through comprehensive educational programs. **Telecommunication Services:** electronic mail, pcoffey@nasho.org ● phone referral service, membership, (404)634-8911.

14343 ■ National Association for the Support of Long Term Care (NASL)
1321 Duke St., Ste.304
Alexandria, VA 22314
Ph: (703)549-8500
Fax: (703)549-8342
E-mail: clendenin@nasl.org
URL: http://www.nasl.org
Contact: Peter Clendenin, Exec. VP
Founded: 1989. **Membership Dues:** bronze, $3,850 ● silver, $7,425 ● gold, $14,300 ● board of governor, $25,000. **Description:** Long term care executives and businesses. Dedicated to providing a national communication forum and legislative and regulatory representation for the long term care industry. **Conventions/Meetings:** annual convention - always October ● semiannual Legislative and Regulatory Conference - January and April.

14344 ■ National Center for Assisted Living (NCAL)
1201 L St. NW
Washington, DC 20005
Ph: (202)842-4444
Free: (800)321-0343
Fax: (202)842-3860
URL: http://www.ncal.org
Contact: Bruce Yarwood, Pres./CEO
Description: Advocates for long-term care and assisted living issues. **Programs:** Caring For Our Caregivers. **Formerly:** American Health Care Association. **Publications:** *Assisted Living State Regulatory Review*. Report. Contains a state-by-state summary of assisted living regulations. Provides contact information for the state agency. Alternate Formats:

online ● *Focus*, monthly. Newsletter. Features the latest news, trends, regulatory activities and legislative developments relevant to the organization. ● *NCAL Connections*. Newsletter. Informs members about the organization and developing events in assisted living. Alternate Formats: online ● *Provider*. Magazine. Contains pragmatic hands-on guidance on assisted living issues. ● *Resident Assistant Newsletter*. **Conventions/Meetings:** annual convention.

14345 ■ National Coordinating Council for Medication Error Reporting and Prevention (NCC MERP)
c/o Deborah Nadzam, PhD, Chair
One Renaissance Blvd.
Oakbrook Terrace, IL 60181
Ph: (630)261-5048
E-mail: dnadzam@jrcinc.com
URL: http://www.nccmerp.org
Contact: Deborah Nadzam PhD, Chair
Founded: 1995. **Members:** 22. **Description:** Aims to maximize the safe use of medications amongst all stakeholders. Seeks to increase awareness of medication errors through open communication, promotion of medication error prevention strategies, and increased reporting. Advocates for a nationwide campaign of medication error reporting and prevention that will promote recommendations broadly to the academic community, national professional associations, managed care organizations, and third-party payers. **Telecommunication Services:** electronic mail, ddc@usp.org. **Publications:** *NCC MERP: The First Ten Years - Defining the Problem and Developing Solutions.* Report. Alternate Formats: online.

14346 ■ National Guideline Clearinghouse (NGC)
c/o Vivian Coates, Proj. Dir.
ECRI
5200 Butler Pike
Plymouth Meeting, PA 19462
E-mail: info@guideline.gov
URL: http://www.guideline.gov
Contact: Vivian Coates, Proj. Dir.
Description: Provides physicians, nurses, health professionals, healthcare providers, health plans, integrated delivery systems, purchasers detailed information on clinical practice guidelines. **Computer Services:** database, evidence-based clinical practice guidelines. **Publications:** Bibliographies. Covers development methodology, implementation, and use.

14347 ■ National Institute for Health Care Management Research and Educational Foundation (NIHCM Foundation)
1225 19th St. NW, Ste.710
Washington, DC 20036
Ph: (202)296-4426
Fax: (202)296-4319
E-mail: nihcm@nihcm.org
URL: http://www.nihcm.org
Contact: Nancy Chockley, Pres./CEO
Founded: 1993. **Description:** Conducts and disseminates research on health care issues; promotes innovation in health care delivery and management. **Awards:** General Health Research Awards. **Type:** monetary ● Journalism Award. **Type:** monetary. **Telecommunication Services:** electronic mail, nchockley@nihcm.org.

14348 ■ National Patient Safety Foundation (NPSF)
1120 MASS MoCA Way
North Adams, MA 01247
Ph: (413)663-8900
Fax: (413)663-8905
E-mail: info@npsf.org
URL: http://www.npsf.org
Contact: Diane C. Pinakiewicz MBA, Pres.
Membership Dues: charter, $10,000 (annual) ● partner, $1,500-$5,000 (annual). **Description:** Works to improve the safety of patients. **Telecommunication Services:** electronic mail, dpinakiewicz@npsf.org. **Publications:** *Journal of Patient Safety.* **Price:**

$168.00 /year for individuals; $248.00 /year for institutions ● Newsletters. Alternate Formats: online ● Annual Report, annual. Alternate Formats: online ● Reports. Alternate Formats: online ● Brochures. **Conventions/Meetings:** annual Patient Safety Congress.

14349 ■ National Pressure Ulcer Advisory Panel (NPUAP)
1255 23rd St. NW, Ste.200
Washington, DC 20037
Ph: (202)521-6789
Fax: (202)833-3636
E-mail: npuap@npuap.org
URL: http://www.npuap.org
Contact: David A. Saunders, Exec. Dir.
Founded: 1987. **Staff:** 2. **Budget:** $250,000. **Nonmembership. Description:** Works to prevent and manage pressure ulcers. Acts as information resource for health care professionals, government, public and health care agencies. Promotes research and legislative action. **Committees:** Education; Public Policy; Research. **Councils:** Corporate Advisory; Provider Advisory. **Projects:** Neonatal/Pediatric Task Force Initiative; Nutrition Initiative; Support Surfaces Initiative. **Publications:** *Inside the NPUAP*, quarterly. Newsletter. Alternate Formats: online ● Brochure. Alternate Formats: online ● Report ● Survey. **Conventions/Meetings:** biennial conference.

14350 ■ National Quality Forum (NQF)
601 13th St. NW, Ste.500 N
Washington, DC 20005
Ph: (202)783-1300
Fax: (202)783-3434
E-mail: info@qualityforum.org
URL: http://www.qualityforum.org
Contact: Janet Corrigan, Pres.
Description: Seeks to advance the science of quality measurement in health information systems. **Formed by Merger of:** (2005) National Quality Forum and National Committee for Quality Health Care. **Formerly:** (2005) National Forum for Health Care Quality Measurement and Reporting. **Publications:** *Information Technology & Healthcare: Proceedings of a Summit* ● Reports. **Conventions/Meetings:** board meeting ● workshop.

14351 ■ Partnership for Patient Safety (P4PS)
1 W Superior St., Ste.2410
Chicago, IL 60610
Ph: (312)274-9695
Fax: (312)274-9696
E-mail: mhatlie@p4ps.org
URL: http://www.p4ps.org
Contact: Martin J. Hatlie JD, Pres.
Founded: 2000. **Staff:** 2. **Budget:** $200,000. **Nonmembership. For-Profit. Description:** Represents people and organizations involved in health care. Strives to reduce the harm caused by healthcare errors. **Computer Services:** Mailing lists, of members. **Telecommunication Services:** electronic mail, info@p4ps.org.

14352 ■ Patient Advocate Foundation (PAF)
700 Thimble Shoals Blvd., Ste.200
Newport News, VA 23606
Free: (800)532-5274
Fax: (757)873-8999
E-mail: help@patientadvocate.org
URL: http://www.patientadvocate.org
Contact: Nancy Davenport-Ennis, CEO/Pres.
Founded: 1996. **Description:** Seeks to protect patients through mediation assuring access to care, maintenance of employment and preservation of financial stability. **Awards:** **Frequency:** annual. **Type:** scholarship. **Publications:** *First My Illness, Now Job Discrimination: Steps to Resolution* ● *Managed Care Answer Guide* ● *National Financial Resources Guidebook for Patients: A State by State Directory* ● *The Patient Pal* ● *Your Guide to the Appeals Process.*

14353 ■ Patient Safety Institute (PSI)
555 Republic Dr., Ste.200
Plano, TX 75074
Ph: (972)444-9800
Fax: (972)422-9134

E-mail: info@ptsafety.org
URL: http://www.ptsafety.org
Contact: Johnny Walker, CEO/Exec. Dir.
Founded: 2001. **Description:** Acts to combine technology with patient-provider relationships to improve care, decrease rate of medical errors and lower costs of healthcare.

14354 ■ P.U.L.S.E.
PO Box 353
Wantagh, NY 11793-0353
Ph: (516)579-4711
Free: (800)96-PULSE
Fax: (516)520-8105
E-mail: pulse516@aol.com
URL: http://pulseamerica.org
Contact: Ilene Corina, Co-Pres.
Description: Represents survivors and victims of medical errors, adverse events and substandard health care. Seeks to educate, advocate and offer support and work in joint cooperation with the medical, legislative and legal communities who support a zero-tolerance rate of medical error. **Telecommunication Services:** electronic mail, pulsecolo@yahoo.com. **Publications:** *Patient Fact Sheet* ● *Patient to Patient.* Newsletter.

14355 ■ SATELLIFE Global Health Information Network
30 California St.
Watertown, MA 02472
Ph: (617)926-9400
Fax: (617)926-1212
URL: http://www.satellife.org
Contact: Holly Ladd JD, Exec. Dir.
Founded: 1989. **Multinational. Description:** Strengthens the global health community by facilitating dialogue and disseminating relevant information on the world's most urgent health topics through the use of the Internet and other modern communication methods. Supports HealthNet knowledge networks in six countries, which provide a variety of services to their local health communities, including free or low-cost email, computer literacy training, health data collection and information resources. **Computer Services:** Information services, healthnet ● online services, discussion groups; getweb. **Councils:** International Advisory. **Publications:** *Healthnet News*, weekly. Newsletter. Features current, peer-reviewed, practical, clinical and research information. Alternate Formats: online ● *Healthnet News - AIDS*, bimonthly. Newsletter. Features current medical information about HIV/AIDS. Alternate Formats: online ● *Healthnet News - Community Health*, monthly. Newsletter. Features current, thematic public health information. Alternate Formats: online.

14356 ■ Society of Primary Care Policy Fellows (SPCPF)
1522 K St. NW, Ste.702
Washington, DC 20005
Ph: (202)289-7735
Fax: (202)289-8046
E-mail: primarycaresociety@primarycaresociety.org
URL: http://www.primarycaresociety.org
Contact: Gary Colangelo DDS, Pres.
Membership Dues: active, $100 (annual) ● associate, $80 (annual) ● sustaining, $150 (annual). **Description:** Aims to advance multi-disciplinary studies in the development of primary health care policy, development implementation, evaluation, and research. Seeks to address health issues affecting primary care policy. Promotes creativity and innovations in primary care. **Publications:** Papers. Alternate Formats: online.

14357 ■ Volunteers in Health Care (VIH)
111 Brewster St.
Pawtucket, RI 02860
Ph: (401)729-3284
Fax: (401)729-2955
E-mail: janet_walton@mhri.org
URL: http://www.volunteersinhealthcare.org
Contact: Janet Walton, Deputy Dir.
Founded: 1997. **Description:** Provides resources for organizations and clinicians caring for the unin-

sured, focusing on using volunteer clinicians to provide medical, dental and other healthcare services. **Awards:** Grants. **Type:** grant. **Computer Services:** Mailing lists. **Additional Websites:** http://www.rxassist.org. **Telecommunication Services:** electronic mail, info@volunteersinhealthcare.org. **Publications:** *Mailing List Survey* ● *Recruiting and Retaining Dental Volunteers.* Manual. Contains information on motivations and barriers for volunteering as well as recruitment and retention strategies. ● *Starting a Free Clinic.* Manual. Contains information such as checklist of steps to take, "how to" reports by those who have started such clinics, and sample job descriptions. ● *VIH Dental Survey* ● Newsletter. **Conventions/Meetings:** Getting Started: Enrolling Patients in Pharmaceutical Company Assistance Programs - workshop, teleworkshop.

14358 ■ Wellstart International

PO Box 80877
San Diego, CA 92138-0877
Ph: (619)295-5192
Fax: (619)574-8159
E-mail: info@wellstart.org
URL: http://www.wellstart.org
Contact: Audrey Naylor, CEO
Description: Seeks to advance the knowledge, skills, and ability of breastfeeding to health care providers in order to promote, protect, and support infant and maternal health and nutrition from conception through the completion of weaning.

14359 ■ Women in Health Care Management (WHCM)

84 Fenwick Rd.
Newton, MA 02468
E-mail: info@whcm.org
URL: http://www.whcm.org
Founded: 1977. **Members:** 350. **Membership Dues:** regular, $50 (annual). **Regional Groups:** 1. **Local Groups:** 1. **Description:** Represents professional women working in health care management. **Programs:** Job Bank. **Publications:** *Member Survey.* Alternate Formats: online ● Membership Directory, annual. **Price:** included in membership dues. **Conventions/Meetings:** annual meeting.

14360 ■ Wound Healing Society (WHS)

1133 W Morse Blvd., Ste.201
Winter Park, FL 32789
Ph: (407)647-8839
Fax: (407)629-2502
E-mail: president@woundheal.org
URL: http://www.woundheal.org
Contact: Ms. Kim O'Dell, Exec. Dir.
Founded: 1990. **Members:** 525. **Membership Dues:** active, $225 (annual) ● student/trainee, $60 (annual) ● senior/military/government, $125 (annual). **Multinational. Description:** Promotes scientific advances and education in the field of wound healing. **Awards:** Blue Ribbon Industrial Research and Development Award. **Frequency:** annual. **Type:** recognition. **Recipient:** for research and development team members who are working to show mechanisms of action or efficacy for their company's products ● Distinguished Service Award. **Frequency:** annual. **Type:** recognition. **Recipient:** for outstanding contributions to the growth and development of the organization ● Lifetime Achievement Award. **Frequency:** annual. **Type:** recognition. **Recipient:** for an individual who has provided leadership in the field of wound healing ● WHF 3M Young Investigator Fellowship Award. **Frequency:** annual. **Type:** monetary. **Recipient:** for young investigators or junior faculty who are pursuing a career in academic research in wound healing ● Young Investigator Award. **Frequency:** annual. **Type:** recognition. **Recipient:** for deserving young scientists in the wound healing field. **Committees:** Awards; Government Relations; Industry Advisory; Program. **Publications:** *Wound Repair and Regeneration,* bimonthly. Journal. Contains information on wound healing and tissue regeneration. **Price:** included in membership dues. Alternate Formats: online. **Conventions/Meetings:** annual meeting, for students of wound healing (new and seasoned) (exhibits).

Health Care Products

14361 ■ Advanced Medical Technology Association (AdvaMed)

701 Pennsylvania Ave. NW, Ste.800
Washington, DC 20004-2654
Ph: (202)783-8700
Fax: (202)783-8750
E-mail: info@advamed.org
URL: http://www.advamed.org
Contact: Stephen J. Ubl, Pres./CEO
Founded: 1974. **Members:** 1,500. **Membership Dues:** active, $650 (annual) ● associate-gold, $12,000 (annual) ● associate-platinum, $25,000 (annual). **Budget:** $13,500,000. **Description:** Represents domestic (including U.S. territories and possessions) manufacturers of medical devices, diagnostic products, and healthcare information systems. Develops programs and activities on economic, technical, medical, and scientific matters affecting the industry. Gathers and disseminates information concerning the United States and international developments in legislative, regulatory, scientific or standards-making areas. Conducts scientific and educational seminars and programs. **Libraries: Type:** open to the public. **Holdings:** archival material, reports. **Formed by Merger of:** (1974) Medical-Surgical Manufacturers Association; Health Industries Association. **Formerly:** (2001) Health Industry Manufacturers Association. **Publications:** *Health Industry Manufacturers Association—Directory,* annual. Covers issues facing the health industry. **Price:** free, for members only ● *In Brief,* monthly. Newsletter. **Price:** free, for members only. **Circulation:** 4,500 ● Manuals ● Proceedings ● Reports ● Also publishes a catalogue. **Conventions/Meetings:** annual meeting, for member CEOs and senior executives only - always March ● seminar - 20-25/year.

14362 ■ American Association for Homecare (AAHomecare)

2011 Crystal Dr., Ste.725
Arlington, VA 22202
Ph: (703)836-6263
Fax: (703)836-6730
E-mail: info@aahomecare.org
URL: http://www.aahomecare.org
Contact: Tyler Wilson, Pres./CEO
Founded: 2000. **Members:** 3,000. **Membership Dues:** regular (maximum), $93,000 (annual) ● associate (maximum), $5,400 (annual) ● state association, $500 (annual). **Staff:** 15. **Budget:** $2,700,000. **Regional Groups:** 2. **State Groups:** 22. **Description:** Represents all elements of home care; dedicated to advancing value and practice of quality health care services at home. **Awards:** Industry Achievement Awards. **Frequency:** annual. **Type:** recognition. **Computer Services:** Mailing lists, in label form or diskette in ASCII format. **Telecommunication Services:** electronic mail, tylerw@aahomecare.org. **Committees:** Education; Ethics; Legislative Policy; Membership/Marketing; Regulatory Affairs. **Task Forces:** Technology. **Formed by Merger of:** (1962) National Affiliation of Durable Medical Equipment Companies; Association of Independent Medical Equipment Suppliers. **Formerly:** (1994) National Association of Medical Equipment Suppliers; (2000) National Association for Medical Equipment Services. **Publications:** *AAHomecare Update,* weekly. Newsletter ● *Financial Performance Survey,* annual. Report. Helps in benchmarking the company's financial performance. **Price:** $300.00 for members; $450.00 for nonmembers ● *HME Answer Book,* quarterly. Manual. Provides information and guidance on Medicare coverage, billing and payment rules for DMEPOS claims processing under DMERCs. ● Also publishes press releases. **Conventions/Meetings:** annual Leadership Conference - conference and trade show (exhibits) - usually May ● Road Scholars Tour - conference - 2007 Oct. 29-30, San Diego, CA.

14363 ■ Center for Biologics Evaluation and Research (CBER)

Food and Drug Admin.
1401 Rockville Pike, Ste.200N
Rockville, MD 20852-1428
Ph: (301)827-1800
Free: (800)835-4709
Fax: (301)827-0440
E-mail: octma@cber.fda.gov
URL: http://www.fda.gov/cber
Contact: Jesse L. Goodman MD, Dir.
Description: Advances public health through innovated regulations that ensure safety, effectiveness, timely delivery to patients of biological products including blood, vaccines, tissue, allergenics, and biological therapeutics. **Publications:** *Centennial Book.* Alternate Formats: online ● *Cyber Vision,* quarterly. Newsletter. Alternate Formats: online ● Annual Report, annual. Alternate Formats: online. **Conventions/Meetings:** meeting ● workshop.

14364 ■ Health Industry Group Purchasing Association (HIGPA)

2025 M St. NW, Ste.800
Washington, DC 20036
Ph: (202)367-1162
Fax: (202)367-2162
E-mail: info@higpa.org
URL: http://www.higpa.org
Contact: Curtis Rooney, Pres.
Founded: 1990. **Membership Dues:** general, $5,300 (annual). **Description:** For-profit and not-for-profit corporations, purchasing groups, associations, multi hospital systems and health care provider alliances. **Awards:** Purchaser of the Year. **Frequency:** annual. **Type:** recognition. **Recipient:** to a member who participated actively in promoting HIGPA and the health care purchasing industry. **Publications:** *CapitoLine,* monthly. Newsletter. **Price:** included in membership dues.

14365 ■ Healthcare Manufacturers Marketing Council (HMMC)

1 Rebecca Ln.
Savannah, GA 31411
Ph: (912)598-1607
Fax: (912)598-7844
E-mail: hmmc@hmmc.com
URL: http://www.hmmc.com
Contact: Madeline Sandy, Exec. Admin.
Founded: 1986. **Membership Dues:** individual, corporate, $499 (annual). **Description:** Represents and promotes senior-level sales and marketing executives. **Conventions/Meetings:** semiannual conference, educational and networking meeting for members.

Health Education

14366 ■ Health Jam

221 E 122nd St., 5th Fl.
New York, NY 10035
Ph: (212)722-7987
Fax: (212)722-7252
E-mail: health@healthjam.org
URL: http://www.healthjam.org
Contact: Maribel Cruz, Exec. Dir.
Founded: 1995. **Multinational. Description:** Uses entertainment to arm children and families with the facts they need to make sensible lifestyle choices. Helps adolescents to increase their self-esteem and to learn how to avoid and cope with HIV and sexually transmitted infections, obesity, unplanned pregnancies, negative peer pressure, drugs, alcohol and relationship abuse. Collaborates with high-profile recording artists, actors, sports figures, radio personalities, community leaders, corporate executives, teachers, principals and trained health guest speakers to develop programs that educate adolescents.

Health Law

14367 ■ Hi-Ethics - Health Internet Ethics

c/o Alan Greene, Pres.
9000 Crow Canyon Rd., Ste.S220
Danville, CA 94506
Ph: (925)964-1793

E-mail: cgreene@drgreene.com
Contact: Alan Greene MD, Pres.
Founded: 2000. **Membership Dues:** general, $1,500 (quarterly). **Description:** Seeks to advance the Internet in order to improve consumers' health.

Health Plans

14368 ■ Academy of Managed Care Providers (AMCP)
1945 Palo Verde Ave., Ste.202
Long Beach, CA 90815-3445
Ph: (562)682-3559
Free: (800)297-2627
Fax: (562)799-3355
E-mail: members@academymcp.org
URL: http://www.academymcp.org
Contact: Dr. John K. Russell, Pres.
Founded: 1993. **Members:** 2,500. **Membership Dues:** general, affiliate, $175 (annual) ● corporate (Internet), $1,000 (annual) ● student (Internet), $35 (annual) ● general, affiliate (Internet), $125 (annual). **Description:** Clinicians and Managed Care Industry executives. Provides a multitude of services to members. Awards diplomate status to qualified members who meet criteria and pass written exam. **Computer Services:** database ● mailing lists. **Publications:** *Managed Care Times*, monthly. Newsletter. Contains update on all aspects of the healthcare industry. **Price:** included in membership dues.

14369 ■ Alliance of Community Health Plans (ACHP)
1729 H St. NW, Ste.400
Washington, DC 20006
Ph: (202)785-2247
Fax: (202)785-4060
E-mail: info@achp.org
URL: http://www.achp.org
Contact: Jack C. Ebeler, Pres./CEO
Founded: 1984. **Description:** Members are twenty-two not-for-profit and provider-based health plans, non-investor owned and provider-based, that serve more than 12 million Americans in 18 states and the District of Columbia. These plans have distinguished themselves through the National Committee for Quality Assurance accreditation, and with superior scores in both the Health Plan Data and Information Set and the Consumer Assessment of Health Plan Survey. Provides aid to contributing plans to enhance the well being of their members and their communities and promotes the improvement in health care services of member plans by supporting activities which focus on the achievement of the highest standards of health care delivery. **Formerly:** The HMO Group. **Publications:** *ACHP Bulletin*, monthly. Newsletter. Contains news about the organization's programs, policy advocacy and members. Alternate Formats: online.

14370 ■ American Accreditation Healthcare Commission (URAC)
1220 L St. NW, Ste.400
Washington, DC 20005
Ph: (202)216-9010
Fax: (202)216-9006
E-mail: communications@urac.org
URL: http://www.urac.org
Contact: Alan P. Spielman, Pres./CEO
Founded: 1990. **Members:** 300. **Staff:** 30. **Description:** Serves as an accreditation body for the managed health care industry. Seeks to establish and enforce standards for the managed care industry. Examines managed healthcare providers and bestows accreditation upon qualifying case management, health utilization management, health network, health plan, practitioner credentialing, credentials verification, workers' compensation utilization management, workers' compensation network, and health call center programs. **Publications:** *AccreditWatch*, quarterly. Newsletter. Helps keep accredited organizations, regulators, and others in the health and managed care industry informed about the latest events. Alternate Formats: online ● *Directory of Accredited*

Organizations, annual. **Price:** $39.00/copy ● *Models of Care: Case Studies of Healthcare Delivery Innovation*. Book. **Price:** $195.00/copy. **Conventions/Meetings:** annual Quality Summit and Exhibit - conference (exhibits).

14371 ■ American Association of Preferred Provider Organizations (AAPPO)
222 S First St., Ste.303
Louisville, KY 40202
Ph: (502)403-1122
Fax: (502)403-1129
E-mail: kgreenrose@aappo.org
URL: http://www.aappo.org
Contact: Karen Greenrose, Pres.
Founded: 1983. **Members:** 400. **Staff:** 4. **Regional Groups:** 1. **Description:** Seeks to advance the awareness of the benefits - greater access, choice and flexibility - that PPOs bring to American healthcare. Advocates solely on behalf of PPOs and their high quality, certified provider networks. Serves as a resource for its members and policymakers on issues surrounding the PPO industry. Facilitates initiatives to support the business needs of all PPOs and releases an assortment of information on many important topics impacting the PPO industry. Provides valuable benefits in the public policy, communications, education and marketing arenas. **Computer Services:** Online services, Market & Industry Trend Report, national PPO database and directory, publications, legislative tracking, education, position statements, guidelines. **Committees:** Business and Membership Development; Education Advisory; Medical Provider Affairs; Political Action; Public Policy; Rules, By-laws and Nominations. **Formerly:** (1999) Association of Managed Healthcare Organizations. **Publications:** *Online Directory of Operational PPOs*, annual. Provides a variety of search options to find the location, geographic coverage and specific details about any PPO nationwide. **Price:** free to organizational members; $750.00 for nonmembers. Alternate Formats: online ● *PPO Datasource*, annual. Directory. Includes executive contact information, office locations and other information relevant to the organization. **Price:** free for members; $750.00 /year for nonmembers ● *PPO Outlook Market & Industry Trend Report*, annual. Offers industry outlook, stakeholder perspectives, statistics, trends, and commentary on current industry challenges and future strategies. **Price:** free for members; $325.00 /year for nonmembers - hard copy; $295.00 /year for nonmembers - online. Alternate Formats: online. **Conventions/Meetings:** annual PPO Forum - conference (exhibits) - 2008 Jan. 27-29, Marco Island, FL ● annual Technology Forum - conference (exhibits).

14372 ■ American College of Managed Care Medicine (ACMCM)
PO Box 4765
Glen Allen, VA 23058-4765
Ph: (804)527-1906 (804)527-1905
Fax: (804)747-5316
E-mail: info@acmcm.org
Contact: Dr. W.C. Williams III, Pres.
Founded: 1995. **Members:** 2,000. **Membership Dues:** physician, $195 (annual) ● resident/student, $25 (annual) ● other professional, $250 (annual). **Description:** Physicians and other healthcare providers working for managed care organizations. Seeks to advance the effectiveness of managed care health services. Conducts continuing professional development courses for health care providers and prepares members for a managed care certificate examination; facilitates exchange of information among members; sponsors research; maintains speakers' bureau. **Libraries:** Type: reference. Holdings: monographs, periodicals. **Subjects:** managed care medicine. **Publications:** *American Journal of Integrated Health Care*, quarterly. **Circulation:** 25,000. **Advertising:** accepted ● *Journal of Managed Care Medicine*, annual. **Price:** $95.00 /year for individuals; $175.00/2 years for individuals. **Advertising:** accepted. **Conventions/Meetings:** semiannual conference - always spring and fall.

14373 ■ America's Health Insurance Plans (AHIP)
601 Pennsylvania Ave. NW, Ste.500
Washington, DC 20004
Ph: (202)778-3200
Fax: (202)331-7487
E-mail: ahip@ahip.org
URL: http://www.ahip.org
Contact: Michael E. Abbott, Pres./CEO
Founded: 1989. **Members:** 1,300. **Membership Dues:** student, $95 (annual) ● individual, $295 (annual) ● state association, $600 (annual) ● international organization/primary supporting, $4,000 (annual) ● premier supporting, $7,500 (annual). **Description:** Provides leadership role in driving high-quality, cost-effective, consumer-focused health care delivery systems. **Awards:** Innovation and Excellence Program. **Frequency:** annual. **Type:** recognition. **Recipient:** to member organizations for their leading practices and programs in the health insurance plan industry. **Formerly:** (2004) Employers' Managed Health Care Association. **Publications:** *AHIP Coverage*, bimonthly. Magazine. Provides timely analysis of what's new in the industry, highlighting what's important. **Price:** $60.00/year ● *The Employers' Guide to Medicare Managed Care in 1998 and Beyond*. Report.

14374 ■ Biotech Medical Management Association (BMMA)
10592 Perry Hwy., No. 300
Wexford, PA 15090
Free: (888)990-2662
Fax: (866)706-8622
E-mail: general@bmma.org
URL: http://www.bmma.org
Contact: Mark G. Fuller MD, Exec. Dir.
Founded: 1993. **Description:** Physicians and pharmacists involved in managed care insurance programs; insurance companies, pharmaceutical manufacturers, and other firms with an interest in managed care medicine; academic institutions, medical and insurance consultants, and health care representatives. Promotes establishment of national standards regulating medical and drug policies and the administration of medical and pharmacy benefits. Represents members before government agencies, industrial organizations, and the public; facilitates communication between biotechnology manufacturers and health care payers and providers; supports pharmaceutical research; conducts educational programs. **Awards:** BMMA Awards. **Frequency:** annual. **Type:** recognition. **Recipient:** to health plans and manufacturers for their contributions in the field. **Publications:** *Journal of the Biotech Medical Management Association*, quarterly. Dedicated to new developments in biotechnology. **Price:** $120.00/year. **Advertising:** accepted. **Conventions/Meetings:** semiannual conference, scientific presentation devoted to the developments in biotechnology.

14375 ■ Center for Medicare Advocacy
PO Box 350
Willimantic, CT 06226
Ph: (860)456-7790 (202)216-0028
Free: (800)262-4414
Fax: (860)456-2614
URL: http://www.medicareadvocacy.org
Contact: Judith Stein JD, Exec. Dir.
Founded: 1986. **Description:** Provides education, advocacy, legal assistance to help elders and people with disabilities obtain necessary healthcare. **Publications:** *Healthcare Rights Review*, quarterly. Newsletter. **Price:** $75.00/year.

14376 ■ Consumer Health Education Council (CHEC)
c/o Employee Benefit Research Institute
2121 K St. NW, Ste.600
Washington, DC 20037-1896
Ph: (202)775-6322
Fax: (202)775-6312

E-mail: checinfo@healthchec.org
URL: http://www.ebri.org/research/hrep
Contact: Dallas L. Salisbury, Chm.
Description: Seeks to reduce the number of uninsured Americans and improve public health.

14377 ■ Council for Affordable Health Insurance (CAHI)
127 S Peyton St., Ste.210
Alexandria, VA 22314
Ph: (703)836-6200
E-mail: mail@cahi.org
URL: http://www.cahi.org
Contact: Dr. Merrill Matthews Jr., Dir.
Founded: 1992. **Members:** 200. **Description:** Companies and individuals with an interest in the health care financing system in the United States. Promotes health care reforms that "preserve freedom of choice for individuals and encourage a competitive health care market". Devises model health care reform plans; conducts lobbying and advocacy campaigns; sponsors educational programs. **Publications:** *Access*, biweekly. Newsletter. **Price:** free for members. Alternate Formats: online ● *CAHI Annual Report*, annual. **Conventions/Meetings:** annual board meeting.

14378 ■ Delta Dental Plans Association (DDPA)
801 Ogden Ave.
Lisle, IL 60532
Ph: (630)964-2400
Free: (800)323-1743
Fax: (630)964-2494
E-mail: csi@deltadentalil.com
Contact: Kim Volk, Pres./CEO
Founded: 1965. **Members:** 30. **Staff:** 13. **Description:** Active state dental service corporations; state dental societies; foreign dental service plans. Seeks to increase the availability of dental service to the public by assisting and coordinating the activities of dental service corporations and helping them in the development of dental care programs for application to multistate and national accounts. A dental service corporation (or dental service plan) refers to a nonprofit corporation organized by the dental profession to provide prepaid dental care coverage to the public on a group basis. Maintains speakers' bureau; conducts specialized education programs; compiles statistics. Holds marketing, management, financial, and educational workshops, seminars, and conferences. **Committees:** Actuarial; Corporate Communications; Dental Policy; Dental Relations; Educations and Program Planning; Government Relations; Marketing/Communications; Operations and Technology. **Formerly:** National Association of Dental Service Plans. **Publications:** *The Communicator*, quarterly. Newsletter. Covers members' news. ● *Legal Briefs*, quarterly. Newsletter. Covers legislative issues. ● Also publishes educational and promotional literature. **Conventions/Meetings:** annual conference.

14379 ■ Health Benefits Coalition for Affordable Choice and Quality
1201 F St. NW, Ste.200
Washington, DC 20004
URL: http://www.hbcweb.com
Members: 3,000,000. **Description:** Employers providing health care coverage. Promotes affordable, quality health care, through broader coverage, choice and competition in the marketplace, rather than government mandates.

14380 ■ Institute for Health Policy Solutions (IHPS)
1444 I St. NW, Ste.900
Washington, DC 20005
Ph: (202)789-1491
Fax: (202)789-1879
E-mail: inquiries@ihps.org
URL: http://www.ihps.org
Contact: Richard E. Curtis, Pres.
Founded: 1992. **Description:** Seeks to develop and create solutions to health system problems related to access, cost and quality. **Programs:** Academy for Consumer-Choice Health Purchasing Groups; Local

Coverage. **Sections:** Resource Center. **Publications:** Reports. Alternate Formats: online.

14381 ■ ITEM Coalition
1875 Eye St. NW, 12th Fl.
Washington, DC 20006
Ph: (202)349-4260
Fax: (202)785-1756
E-mail: info@itemcoalition.org
URL: http://www.itemcoalition.org
Contact: Emily Neiderman, Contact
Description: Aims to raise awareness about devices, technologies and related services used to enhance the quality of life of people with disabilities and chronic conditions. Identifies barriers to such devices under Medicare and Medicaid and other health programs and plans. Builds support for broad-based legislative and regulatory changes to address the problems of inadequate access to assistive devices, technologies and related services.

14382 ■ National Association of State Comprehensive Health Insurance Plans (NASCHIP)
5775 Wayzata Blvd., Ste.910
St. Louis Park, MN 55416
Ph: (952)593-9609
Fax: (952)593-9673
E-mail: michelle@flcomphealth.org
URL: http://www.naschip.org
Contact: Michelle Robleto, Chair
Founded: 1993. **Description:** Seeks to enhance the ability of state comprehensive health insurance plans. Serves as a resource for potential new plans in other states. Provides educational opportunities and information for state high risk health insurance pools. **Publications:** *Comprehensive Health Insurance for High-risk Individuals: A State-by-State Analysis.* Book. Includes data on all existing state comprehensive health insurance plans. **Price:** $39.95/copy ● *NASCHIP News.* Newsletter. Contains news on the status of health insurance plans of the states. Alternate Formats: online.

14383 ■ National Association of State Medicaid Directors (NASMD)
810 1st St. NE, Ste.500
Washington, DC 20002-4207
Ph: (202)682-0100
Fax: (202)289-6555
E-mail: atrantham@aphsa.org
URL: http://www.nasmd.org
Contact: Ms. Nancy Atkins, Chair
Founded: 1979. **Members:** 55. **Description:** Representatives of state Medicaid agencies. Promotes effective and efficient management of federal and state health care programs. Facilitates communication and cooperation between state and federal Medicaid authorities; serves as a clearinghouse on Medicaid benefits. **Publications:** *Medicaid Management Institute Bulletin*, monthly. Includes update on federal legislative and regulatory activity that affects Medicaid. **Price:** free for members. **Conventions/Meetings:** annual conference.

14384 ■ Women in Managed Care (WIMC)
4435 Waterfront Dr., Ste.101
PO Box 6026
Glen Allen, VA 23058-6026
Ph: (804)527-1905
Fax: (804)747-5316
E-mail: info@namcp.com
URL: http://www.wimc.org
Contact: Alison Waters, Exec. Administrator
Founded: 1996. **Members:** 1,000. **Membership Dues:** student, $15 (annual) ● individual, $60 (annual). **Description:** Women working for managed care health services providers. Promotes professional advancement of members. Conducts research and educational programs. **Computer Services:** database ● mailing lists ● online services. **Publications:** *Women in Managed Care*, monthly. Newsletter. **Conventions/Meetings:** periodic regional meeting.

Health Professionals

14385 ■ American Academy of Professional Coders (AAPC)
2480 S 3850 W, Ste.B
Salt Lake City, UT 84120
Ph: (801)236-2200
Free: (800)626-2633
Fax: (801)236-2258
E-mail: info@aapc.com
URL: http://www.aapc.com
Contact: Ms. Traci Wood, Marketing Coor.
Founded: 1988. **Members:** 50,000. **Membership Dues:** individual, $120 (annual) ● student, $70 (annual) ● corporate, $500-$650 (annual) ● individual (international), $145 (annual) ● student (international), $85 (annual). **Staff:** 110. **State Groups:** 50. **Local Groups:** 449. **Description:** Works to elevate the standards of medical coding by providing ongoing education, certification, networking and recognition. Represents nearly 50,000 members worldwide. Promotes high standards of physician and outpatient facility coding through education and certification. **Libraries:** Type: reference. **Holdings:** archival material, articles, books, clippings, periodicals. **Subjects:** medical coding. **Awards:** Coder of the Year. **Frequency:** annual. **Type:** recognition. **Recipient:** for excellence in medical coding ● Networker of the Year. **Frequency:** annual. **Type:** recognition. **Recipient:** for connecting coders together for discussion leading to correct solutions of reimbursement problems. **Boards:** National Advisory. **Formerly:** (2001) American Academy of Procedural Coders. **Publications:** *ACADEMY CODING EDGE*, monthly. Magazine. **Price:** included in membership dues. **Circulation:** 55,000. **Advertising:** accepted. **Conventions/Meetings:** annual Coding Conference, with general speakers, specialty specific break-out sessions, networking (exhibits).

14386 ■ American Association of Medical Review Officers (AAMRO)
PO Box 12873
Research Triangle Park, NC 27709
Free: (800)489-1839
Fax: (919)490-1010
E-mail: cferrell@mindspring.com
URL: http://www.aamro.com
Description: Establishes national standards and certification for medical practitioners in the field of drug and alcohol testing. **Computer Services:** database, list of certified physicians ● information services, medical review resources. **Boards:** Advisory; Federal Advisory; Laboratory Director Advisory. **Programs:** Education. **Publications:** *MRO Alert*, 10/year. Journal. Alternate Formats: online.

14387 ■ American Medical Women's Association (AMWA)
211 N Union St., Ste.100
Alexandria, VA 22314
Ph: (703)838-0500
Free: (800)995-AMWA
Fax: (703)549-3864
E-mail: info@amwa-doc.org
URL: http://www.amwa-doc.org
Contact: Linda Hallman, Exec. Dir.
Founded: 1915. **Members:** 10,000. **Membership Dues:** circle of honor, $225 (annual) ● resident, life, $125 ● student, renewing, $50 (annual) ● regular, $150 (annual) ● student, graduating (one-time payment for students in their last year), $25 ● student, life, $75. **Budget:** $1,500,000. **Staff:** 10. **Regional Groups:** 4. **Local Groups:** 160. **Description:** Women holding a MD or DO degree from approved medical colleges; women interns, residents, and medical students. Promotes women's health issues in medical education and public policy. Seeks to find solutions to problems common to women studying or practicing medicine, such as career advancement and the integration of professional and family responsibilities. Provides student members with educational loans and personal counseling. Sponsors continuing medical education programs. **Awards:** Bertha Van-Hoosen Award. **Frequency:** annual. **Type:** recogni-

tion. **Recipient:** to a woman physician who has demonstrated exceptional leadership and service ● Carroll L. Birch Student Research Award. **Type:** recognition. **Recipient:** for a medical student writing the best scientific research paper ● Elizabeth Blackwell Medal. **Type:** recognition. **Recipient:** for a major contribution to medicine by a woman physician ● Glasgow-Rubin Student Achievement Certificates. **Type:** recognition. **Recipient:** for women medical students graduating at the top of their class. **Committees:** American Women's Hospital Service; Archives; Liaison With American Medical Association (see separate entry); Student Loans, Fellowships, and Grants; Women's Health. **Publications:** *Connections*, quarterly. Newsletter. Features timely commentary on the issues that matter most to women physicians. **Price:** included in membership dues. **Circulation:** 10,000. Alternate Formats: online ● *Newsflash*, weekly. Newsletter. Updates members on advocacy issues, along with health and professional information. **Conventions/Meetings:** annual conference ● annual Interim Meeting.

14388 ■ American Professional Practice Association (APPA)
Assn. Member Ser. Center
Hillsboro Executive Center N
350 Fairway Dr., Ste.200
Deerfield Beach, FL 33441-1834
Free: (800)221-2168
E-mail: membership@assnservices.com
URL: http://www.appa-assn.com
Contact: Marisol Dioses Jr., Mgr., Membership
  Services
Founded: 1963. **Members:** 70,000. **Membership Dues:** individual, $50 (annual) ● individual, $120 (triennial) ● life, $395. **Staff:** 15. **Description:** Provides physicians with economic benefits and financial services including the following: unsecured loan plans, mortgage loans, group insurance discounts, accounts receivable collections, office supplies, wealth protection and a vision and dental plan. **Publications:** *Association's Digest*, semiannual. Newsletter. Provides business advice on private practice; also covers APPA activities. **Price:** included in membership dues. **Circulation:** 19,000. **Advertising:** accepted.

14389 ■ Association of Family Practice Physician Assistants (AFPPA)
295 W Crossville Rd., Ste.130
Roswell, GA 30075
Ph: (770)640-7605
Free: (877)890-0181
Fax: (770)640-1095
E-mail: info@afppa.org
URL: http://www.afppa.org
Contact: Charles B. Dillehay MBA, Exec. Dir.
Membership Dues: fellow, $75-$85 (annual) ● fellow, $200 (triennial) ● life - fellow, $1,000 ● physician, associate, sustaining, $50 (annual) ● affiliate, $35 (annual) ● student, $25 (annual). **Description:** Promotes the educational and professional interests of family practice physician assistants (PAs) by promoting clinical and academic excellence. Provides a forum for assembling and distributing information. Seeks to provide a base for mentoring future PAs. Promotes relevant CME resources and employment information. **Awards:** Student Scholarship. **Frequency:** annual. **Type:** scholarship. **Recipient:** to first and second year physician assistant student members of AFPPA. **Committees:** Student Scholarship. **Affiliated With:** American Academy of Physician Assistants. **Publications:** *ADVANCE for Physician Assistants.* Magazine. **Price:** free for members. **Advertising:** accepted ● *Family Matters*, quarterly. Newsletter. **Price:** free for members.

14390 ■ Association of Hispanic Healthcare Executives (AHHE)
PO Box 230832
Ansonia Sta.
New York, NY 10023
Ph: (212)877-1615
Fax: (212)877-2406

E-mail: ahheinnyc@aol.com
URL: http://www.ahhe.org
Contact: George A. Zeppenfeldt-Cestero, Natl. Pres.
Founded: 1988. **Members:** 215. **Membership Dues:** individual, $75 (annual) ● student, senior, disabled person, $25 (annual) ● corporate charter, $3,000 (annual) ● affiliate for profit, $1,000-$2,500 (annual) ● affiliate non-profit, $750-$1,500 (annual) ● healthcare roundtable for-profit, $10,000 (annual) ● healthcare roundtable non-profit, $5,000 (annual). **Staff:** 1. **Budget:** $100,000. **Regional Groups:** 2. **State Groups:** 13. **Languages:** English, Spanish. **Description:** Seeks to foster programs and policies to increase presence of Hispanics in health administration professions. **Libraries:** **Type:** open to the public. **Holdings:** 2. **Subjects:** diversity and healthcare costs to small business. **Divisions:** National job bank. **Programs:** Mentorship; Summer Enrichment. **Publications:** Reports.

14391 ■ Center for Professional Well-Being (CWBP)
21 W Colony Pl., Ste.150
Durham, NC 27705
Ph: (919)489-9167
Fax: (919)419-0011
E-mail: cpwb@mindspring.com
URL: http://www.cpwb.org
Contact: Dr. John-Henry Pfifferling PhD, Dir./Founder
Founded: 1979. **Members:** 800. **Membership Dues:** full, professional, $55 (annual) ● student, intern, resident, retired professional, $15 (annual) ● practicewide, $100 (annual). **Staff:** 2. **Budget:** $160,000. **Regional Groups:** 1. **Description:** Serves health and other professional associations. Promotes the well-being of health professionals and their families through: preventive education on manifestations of disabilities; increased awareness about the stresses inherent in the system of providing health services; efforts to improve and maintain effectiveness. Conducts research and supports efforts to study the incidence and causes of professional impairment, with prevention as a goal. Maintains speakers' bureau; provides individual consulting and counseling. Offers workshops on The Joy of Medicine, Physician Burnout, and Preventive Malpractice Strategies; sponsors retreats, seminars, and lectures. **Libraries:** **Type:** reference. **Holdings:** 1,200; articles, books, video recordings. **Formerly:** (1993) Center for the Well-Being of Health Professionals. **Publications:** *Being Well: Bulletin of the Society for Professional Well-Being*, quarterly. Newsletter. **Price:** included in membership dues; $55.00 for nonmembers ● Booklets ● Monographs ● Videos. **Conventions/Meetings:** annual Networking Conference - meeting.

14392 ■ Center for the Well Being of Health Professionals
21 W Colony Pl., Ste.150
Durham, NC 27705-5589
Ph: (919)489-9167
Fax: (919)419-0011
E-mail: cpwb@mindspring.com
URL: http://www.cpwb.org
Contact: John-Henry Pfifferling PhD, Founder/Dir.
Description: Offers presentations on all areas relevant to professional well-being. Works to find a balance between personal and professional lives. **Conventions/Meetings:** conference.

14393 ■ Certification Board of Infection Control and Epidemiology (CBIC)
PO Box 19554
Lenexa, KS 66285-9554
Ph: (913)599-4174
Fax: (913)599-5340
E-mail: cbic-info@goamp.com
URL: http://cbic.org
Contact: Sheila O'Neal, Exec. Dir.
Founded: 1981. **Members:** 4,000. **Membership Dues:** initial certificant (examination fee), $295 (5/ year). **Multinational. Description:** Promotes certification process in infection control and applied epidemiology. **Awards:** Achievement Award. **Frequency:** annual. **Type:** recognition. **Recipient:** for individual certificants who have demonstrated the

highest level of professionalism, service to the profession and organization, educational achievements and promotion of certification ● Chapter of the Year Award. **Frequency:** annual. **Type:** recognition. **Recipient:** for APIC and CHICA chapters.

14394 ■ Commission for Case Manager Certification (CCMC)
300 N Martingale Rd., Ste.460
Schaumburg, IL 60173
Ph: (847)944-1330
Fax: (847)944-1346
E-mail: info@ccmcertification.org
URL: http://www.ccmcertification.org
Contact: Beverly Cunningham, Chair
Description: Promotes the case management industry through certification. **Publications:** *CCM Update.* Newsletter. Alternate Formats: online.

14395 ■ Institute for Diversity in Health Management
1 N Franklin, 30th Fl.
Chicago, IL 60606
Ph: (312)422-2630
Free: (800)233-0996
Fax: (312)895-2561
E-mail: fhobby@aha.org
URL: http://www.diversityconnection.org
Contact: Frederick D. Hobby, Pres./CEO
Founded: 1994. **Membership Dues:** hospital and health care organization, $425-$500 (annual) ● health consultant, supplier, vendor, $2,500 (annual). **Description:** Seeks to expand leadership opportunities to ethnic minorities in health services management. **Programs:** Residency/Fellowship; Scholarship Program Assistance; Summer Enrichment. **Affiliated With:** American Hospital Association. **Publications:** *Bridges*, quarterly. Newsletter. **Price:** $20.00. Alternate Formats: online.

14396 ■ International Academy of Health Care Professionals (IAHCP)
Address Unknown since 2007
Founded: 1984. **Members:** 6. **Staff:** 3. **Local Groups:** 1. **Description:** Nurses, psychologists, social workers, and medical and health care professionals. Provides for educational exchange among members. Offers research and educational materials to Third World health care institutions. **Libraries:** **Type:** reference. **Holdings:** books, periodicals. **Subjects:** medicine, psychology, health care issues. **Awards:** Diplomate-Health Care Professions. **Frequency:** biennial. **Type:** recognition. **Recipient:** for outstanding achievements in the health care field. **Publications:** *Membership Brochure* ● Newsletter, periodic. **Conventions/Meetings:** periodic executive committee meeting.

14397 ■ International Association of Sickle Cell Nurses And Physician Assistants (IASCNAPA)
c/o Jane Hennessy, RNCNP, MPH, Treas.
Hematology/Oncology Clinic
2525 Chicago Ave. S, Ste.4150
Minneapolis, MN 55404
Ph: (612)813-6998
Fax: (612)813-6325
E-mail: president@iascnapa.org
URL: http://www.iascnapa.org
Contact: Jackie Davis RN, Pres.
Founded: 1900. **Members:** 300. **Membership Dues:** full, $65 (annual) ● associate, $35 (annual) ● charter, $50 (annual). **Multinational. Description:** Strives to unite and organize sickle cell nurses and physician assistants throughout the world. Establishes guidelines for standards of nursing care for individuals with sickle cell disease. Seeks to develop an international certification system for professionals who provide care for patients with sickle cell disease. **Computer Services:** database, publications by members. **Telecommunication Services:** electronic mail, treasurer@iascnapa.org. **Committees:** Activities; Archives; Audit; Education; Nominating; Publication; Research; Scholarship. **Publications:** Newsletter.

14398 ■ National Arab American Medical Association (NAAMA)
801 S Adams Rd., Ste.208
Birmingham, MI 48009
Ph: (248)646-3661
Fax: (248)646-0617
E-mail: naama@naama.com
URL: http://www.naama.com
Contact: Dr. Mohammed Hammami, Exec. Dir.
Founded: 1974. **Members:** 2,500. **Membership Dues:** national, $150 (annual). **Staff:** 4. **State Groups:** 29. **Description:** Medical professionals of Arab descent. Fosters exchange of scientific information. Encourages continuing education for members. Provides financial and technical support for medical students and institutions in the United States and in Arab countries. Offers medical assistance to needy individuals of Arab descent. **Awards:** NAAMA Scholarship. **Frequency:** annual. **Type:** grant. **Recipient:** for medical students. **Subcommittees:** Auxiliary; Bylaws; Continuing Medical education; Foundation; Liaison to Arab America; Liaison to the Arab World; Membership. **Affiliated With:** American Medical Association. **Formerly:** (1997) Arab American Medical Association. **Publications:** *Al Hakeem* (in Arabic and English), 3/year. Newsletter. Contains medical and cultural articles. **Price:** included in membership dues; $12.00 /year for nonmembers. **Circulation:** 2,500. **Advertising:** accepted ● *NAAMA News*, quarterly. Newsletter. **Advertising:** accepted. Alternate Formats: online. **Conventions/Meetings:** annual International Medical Convention (exhibits) ● annual National Medical Convention (exhibits).

14399 ■ National Association of County Behavioral Health Directors (NACBHD)
c/o NACo
440 First St. NW, Ste.800
Washington, DC 20001
Ph: (202)661-8816
E-mail: mstaats@nacbhd.org
URL: http://www.nacbhd.org
Contact: Melissa Staats, Pres./CEO
Founded: 1996. **Members:** 325. **Membership Dues:** state association, associate (non-county authority), $375 (annual). **Staff:** 3. **Description:** County/local behavioral health authorities responsible for the planning and delivery of mental health, developmental disabilities and substance abuse services, and state's associations representing their interests. Promotes excellence in the delivery of county/local behavioral health services. **Computer Services:** Online services, e-newsletter, distribution list. **Affiliated With:** National Association of Counties. **Publications:** *NACBHD Bulletin*, bimonthly. Newsletter. Contains policy information, articles of interest on local programs, association announcements, and job bank. **Price:** free for members. **Circulation:** 350. **Advertising:** accepted. Alternate Formats: online. **Conventions/Meetings:** annual conference, policy-oriented; legislative and federal agency briefings; addressing critical county system concerns (exhibits) ● annual conference, legislative issues - last week of February, held in Washington, DC.

14400 ■ National Association for Direct Care Workers of Color (NADCWOC)
PO Box 3036
South Bend, IN 46619
Ph: (574)289-9326
Fax: (574)289-9326
E-mail: j.booker@directcareworkersofcolor.org
URL: http://www.directcareworkersofcolor.org
Contact: John Booker, Exec.Dir.
Founded: 2002. **Membership Dues:** direct-care worker, $10 (annual) ● associate, $50 (annual) ● corporate, $150 (annual). **Description:** Represents the interests of individuals committed to the advancement of all direct-care workers with an emphasis on minority direct-care professionals. Aims to deliver quality care and services to the elderly and disabled. Provides educational training and support services to all direct-care workers. Promotes public awareness of the value and challenges of all direct-care professionals. **Publications:** Newsletter, quarterly. **Price:** included in membership dues.

14401 ■ National Rural Recruitment and Retention Network (3R Net)
2004 King St.
La Crosse, WI 54601
Ph: (608)782-0660
Free: (800)787-2512
Fax: (608)687-3993
E-mail: info@3rnet.org
URL: http://www.3rnet.org
Contact: Mr. Tim Skinner MSEd, Exec. Dir.
Founded: 1995. **Members:** 43. **Staff:** 2. **State Groups:** 43. **Description:** Works to provide services that support statewide organizations that have common missions and grant support from across HRSA.

14402 ■ National Society of Certified Healthcare Business Consultants (NSCHBC)
12100 Sunset Hills Rd., Ste.130
Reston, VA 20190
Ph: (703)234-4099
Fax: (703)435-4390
E-mail: info@nschbc.org
URL: http://www.healthcon.org
Contact: Carol Wynne, Exec. Dir.
Founded: 2006. **Membership Dues:** regular, $625 (annual). **Description:** Advances the profession of healthcare business consultants through education, certification and professional interaction. Provides education and training to assist members in fulfilling the requirements of certification. **Publications:** Newsletter, bimonthly. Alternate Formats: online.

14403 ■ North American Taiwanese Medical Association (NATMA)
c/o Daniel C. Hsu, DMD, Pres.
7923 Garden Grove Blvd.
Garden Grove, CA 92841
Ph: (949)854-0539
Fax: (714)373-2659
E-mail: hsu0316@hotmail.com
URL: http://www.natma.org
Contact: Daniel C. Hsu DMD, Pres.
Founded: 1983. **Membership Dues:** medical/dental student, $10 (annual) ● physician/dentist, retired, $25 (annual) ● regular, $50 (annual) ● life (regular), $500 ● life (retired), $250. **Description:** Promotes Taiwanese cultural, educational exchange among medical and dental professionals. **Awards:** Dr. I-Yan Lin Memorial Lecture Award. **Type:** recognition. **Committees:** Membership; Publication. **Subcommittees:** Public Relations. **Conventions/Meetings:** annual meeting.

14404 ■ Scottsdale Institute (SI)
1660 Hwy. 100 S, Ste.306
Minneapolis, MN 55416
Ph: (952)545-5880
Fax: (952)545-6116
E-mail: scottsdale@scottsdaleinstitute.org
URL: http://www.scottsdaleinstitute.org
Contact: Stanley R. Nelson, Founder/Chm.
Founded: 1993. **Description:** Assist members in understanding and deploying strategic initiatives involving information management and process improvement in healthcare. **Formerly:** Center for Clinical Integration. **Publications:** *Information Edge*, monthly. Report. Executive review of the IT and redesign aspects of strategic issues. Alternate Formats: online ● *Program Brochure*. Alternate Formats: online. **Conventions/Meetings:** annual Executive Team Conference.

Health Services

14405 ■ American College Health Association (ACHA)
PO Box 28937
Baltimore, MD 21240-8937
Ph: (410)859-1500
Fax: (410)859-1510

E-mail: contact@acha.org
URL: http://www.acha.org
Contact: Col. Doyle E. Randol MS, Exec. Dir.
Founded: 1920. **Members:** 3,438. **Membership Dues:** regular (from a member institution), $140 (annual) ● associate, regular (from a nonmember institution), $170 (annual) ● student/emeritus, $35 (annual) ● student /emeritus (with journal), $80 (annual) ● institutional (base dues), $285 (annual) ● nonprofit sustaining, $300 (annual) ● for-profit sustaining, $1,650 (annual). **Staff:** 20. **Budget:** $2,000,000. **Regional Groups:** 6. **Local Groups:** 11. **Description:** Provides an organization in which institutions of higher education and interested individuals may work together to promote health in its broadest aspects for students and all other members of the college community. Offers continuing education programs for health professionals. Maintains placement listings for physicians and other personnel seeking positions in college health. Compiles statistics. Conducts seminars and training programs. **Awards:** ACHA Lifetime Achievement Award. **Frequency:** annual. **Type:** recognition. **Recipient:** to individuals who have provided outstanding service to ACHA ● Best Practices in College Health Award. **Frequency:** annual. **Type:** recognition. **Recipient:** for exemplary, innovative and inspirational practices in one of four major areas of college health ● Edward Hitchcock Award. **Frequency:** annual. **Type:** recognition. **Recipient:** for members who have made outstanding contributions to advancing the health of all college students ● Lewis Barbato Award. **Frequency:** annual. **Type:** recognition. **Recipient:** for students (members or nonmembers) who have made major contributions to college health ● Outstanding Research Publication Award. **Frequency:** annual. **Type:** recognition. **Recipient:** to members and individuals at member institutions who have published their research activities and therefore advanced the field of college health ● Ruth E. Boynton Award. **Frequency:** annual. **Type:** recognition. **Recipient:** for members who have provided distinguished service to the association. **Computer Services:** Online services, discussion forum. **Committees:** ACHA-NCHA Advisory; Advocacy; Alcohol and Other Drugs; Audit; Awards; Benchmarking Advisory; Campus Violence; Consultation Services Program Advisory; Continuing Education; Ethics; Ethnic Diversity; Fellows; GLBT Issues; HIPAA; National Health Objectives; Professional and Continuing Education; Program Planning; Resolutions; Standards of Practice for Health Promotion in Higher Education; STIs; Tobacco Prevention and Intervention; Vaccine Preventable Diseases; Volunteer Leadership Infrastructure Review. **Formerly:** American Student Health Association. **Publications:** *ACHA Action*, quarterly. Newsletter. Includes calendar of events, college health resource listings, annual report, and leadership directory. **Price:** included in membership dues. **Circulation:** 3,000 ● *Health Information Series*. Pamphlets ● *Journal of American College Health*, bimonthly. Publishes articles on student behaviors, mental health and healthcare policies, and includes a section for discussion of controversial issues. **Advertising:** accepted ● *Membership Profile Directory*, periodic ● Catalog. Lists publications. ● Monographs ● Reports ● Also publishes guidelines. **Conventions/Meetings:** annual meeting (exhibits) - 2008 June 3-7, Orlando, FL; 2009 May 26-30, San Francisco, CA ● seminar.

14406 ■ American Correctional Health Services Association (ACHSA)
250 Gatsby Pl.
Alpharetta, GA 30022-6161
Free: (877)918-1842
Fax: (770)650-5789
E-mail: admin@achsa.org
URL: http://www.achsa.org
Contact: Royanne Schissel RN, Pres.
Founded: 1975. **Members:** 1,100. **Membership Dues:** individual (national), $50 (annual) ● chapter, $15 (annual). **Staff:** 3. **Budget:** $250,000. **State Groups:** 8. **Description:** Represents individuals interested in improving the quality of correctional health services. Aims to promote the provision of health services to incarcerated persons consistent in

quality and quantity with acceptable health care practices. Promotes and encourages continuing education and provides technical and professional guidance for correctional health care personnel. Establishes a forum for the sharing and discussion of correctional health care issues. Conducts conferences on correctional health care management, nursing, mental health, juvenile corrections, dentistry and related subjects. Maintains placement service. **Awards:** Distinguished Service Award. **Frequency:** annual. **Type:** recognition. **Computer Services:** Mailing lists. **Telecommunication Services:** electronic mail, achsa@bellsouth.net ● electronic mail, president@achsa.org ● electronic mail, board@achsa.org. **Affiliated With:** American Correctional Association; American Jail Association. **Publications:** *CorHealth Journal*, quarterly. Newsletter. Includes book reviews, conference calendar, list of new members, and chapter news. **Price:** included in membership dues. **Circulation:** 1,600. **Advertising:** accepted ● Brochures. Provides information on policy matters. **Conventions/Meetings:** annual Multidisciplinary Training Conference (exhibits).

14407 ■ American International Health Alliance (AIHA)
1225 Eye St. NW, Ste.1000
Washington, DC 20005
Ph: (202)789-1136
Fax: (202)789-1277
E-mail: aiha@aiha.com
URL: http://www.aiha.com
Contact: James P. Smith MA, Exec. Dir./CEO
Founded: 1992. **Multinational. Description:** Institutional health care providers. Promotes increased availability of healthcare services in previously underserved areas worldwide. Creates partnerships between hospitals in the United States and their counterparts abroad to facilitate sharing of technology and expertise; sponsors educational programs; serves as a clearinghouse on international health issues and emerging medical technologies and practices. **Libraries: Type:** reference. **Holdings:** books, monographs, periodicals, reports. **Subjects:** health, medicine, information technology, international development. **Programs:** Community Leadership Development; Emergency and Disaster Medicine; Health Management Education; Healthcare Partnerships; Healthy Communities; Infection Control; Information and Communication Technology; Learning Resources Centers/Evidence-Based Practice. **Publications:** *CommonHealth* (in English and Russian), periodic. Journal. Focuses on topics of concern to healthcare providers/practitioners in the countries of the former Soviet Union and Central and Eastern Europe. **Price:** free. Alternate Formats: online ● *Connections*, monthly. Newsletter. Updates partners on the latest news and activities. Alternate Formats: online ● Brochure. Alternate Formats: online ● Booklets. Alternate Formats: online ● Reports, quarterly. Alternate Formats: online.

14408 ■ American Medical Group Association (AMGA)
1422 Duke St.
Alexandria, VA 22314-3403
Ph: (703)838-0033
Fax: (703)548-1890
E-mail: roconnor@amga.org
URL: http://www.amga.org
Contact: Dr. Donald W. Fisher CAE, Pres./CEO
Founded: 1950. **Members:** 300. **Membership Dues:** 3-50 full time equivalent physicians, $4,500 (annual) ● 51-150 full time equivalent physicians, $8,250 (annual) ● more than 150 full time equivalent physicians, $12,250 (annual). **Staff:** 27. **Budget:** $6,000,000. **Description:** Represents the interests of medical groups. Advocates for the medical groups and patients through innovation and information sharing, benchmarking, developing leadership, and improving patient care. Provides political advocacy, educational and networking programs and publications, benchmarking data services, and financial and operations assistance. **Libraries: Type:** reference. **Holdings:** archival material. **Awards:** Acclaim Award. **Frequency:** annual. **Type:** recognition. **Recipient:** for

physician-directed organizations that achieved exceptional results through quality and outcome improvement efforts ● Distinguished Corporate Partner Award. **Frequency:** annual. **Type:** recognition ● Models of Excellence in High Risk Patient Management. **Frequency:** annual. **Type:** recognition ● Preeminence Award. **Frequency:** annual. **Type:** recognition. **Computer Services:** database. **Committees:** Editorial Advisory; Education; Group Practice Political Action; Insurance; Membership and Public Relations; Public Policy. **Councils:** Accountable Physician Practices; CFO Leadership; CIO Leadership; COO/CAO Leadership; Human Resources Leadership; Marketing/Public Relations Leadership; Medical Director/CMO Leadership; Medical Group Attorneys; Medical Group Compliance Officers; President/Chair/CEO Leadership; Quality Improvement Leadership. **Formerly:** American Group Practice Association; (1974) American Association of Medical Clinics. **Publications:** *Group Practice Journal*, 10/year. Covers market trends, health care policy and legislation, and management topics affecting the medical profession. Includes advertiser index. **Price:** included in membership dues; $87.00 /year for nonmembers. ISSN: 0199-5103. **Circulation:** 60,000. **Advertising:** accepted. **Conventions/Meetings:** annual Learning from the Best! - conference, educational programming, networking and services with the medical elite.

14409 ■ American School Health Association (ASHA)
PO Box 708
7263 State Rte. 43
Kent, OH 44240
Ph: (330)678-1601
Fax: (330)678-4526
E-mail: asha@ashaweb.org
URL: http://www.ashaweb.org
Contact: Susan F. Wooley PhD, Exec. Dir.
Founded: 1927. **Members:** 2,000. **Membership Dues:** emeritus, student, $40 (annual) ● basic, $50 (annual) ● contributing, $175 (annual) ● professional, $110 (annual) ● life, $1,500 ● institutional, $295 (annual). **Staff:** 9. **Budget:** $1,000,000. **State Groups:** 12. **Description:** School physicians, school nurses, counsellors, nutritionists, psychologists, social workers, administrators, school health coordinators, health educators, and physical educators working in schools, professional preparation programs, public health, and community-based organizations. Promotes coordinated school health programs that include health education, health services, a healthful school environment, physical education, nutrition services, and psycho-social health services offered in schools collaboratively with families and other members of the community. Offers professional reference materials and professional development opportunities. Conducts pilot programs that inform materials development, provides technical assistance to school professionals, advocates for school health. **Libraries: Type:** not open to the public. **Awards:** ASHA Scholarship. **Frequency:** annual. **Type:** scholarship. **Recipient:** for college juniors, seniors, and graduate students majoring in health education, nursing, adolescent/pediatric medicine, or dentistry ● Distinguished Service Award. **Frequency:** annual. **Type:** recognition. **Recipient:** for outstanding contributions to the child health field through ASHA ● Student Research Grant. **Frequency:** annual. **Type:** grant. **Recipient:** for graduate and undergraduate students ● William A. Howe Award. **Frequency:** annual. **Type:** recognition. **Recipient:** for distinguished service in school health. **Councils:** Alcohol, Tobacco, and other Drugs; Early Childhood Education and Services; Food and Nutrition; Health Behaviors; Injury and Violence Prevention; International Health; Physical Education and Physical Activities; Research; School Health Instruction and Curriculum; Sexuality Education and Reproductive Health. **Sections:** Health Educators; Mental and Social Health Professionals; Physicians; School Coordinators; School Nurses. **Formerly:** (1936) American Association of School Physicians. **Publications:** *A Comprehensive Approach to Reduce Pregnancy & the Spread of HIV*. Book. **Price:** $29.00 for members; $25.00 for nonmembers ● *Building Ef-*

fective Coalitions to Prevent the Spread of HIV. Book. **Price:** $18.00 for nonmembers; $16.00 for members ● *Guide to Developing and Evaluating Medicine Education Programs*. **Price:** $7.00 for members; $10.00 for nonmembers ● *Guidelines for Protecting Confidential Student Health Information*. Book. **Price:** $13.00 for members; $19.00 for nonmembers ● *Health Counseling*. Book. **Price:** $14.00/issue ● *Health in Action*, quarterly. Booklet. Contains topics on diabetes, depression and other mood disorders, violence prevention, HIV prevention, transportation safety, asthma, etc. **Price:** $5.00/issue for members; $10.00/issue for nonmembers ● *Health is Academic: A Guide to Coordinated School Health Programs*. Book. **Price:** $24.00/issue ● *How Physicians Work & How to Work with Physicians*. Booklet. **Price:** $10.00 for members; $11.00 for nonmembers ● *Introductory Guide to Advocacy*. Booklet. **Price:** $10.00 for members; $15.00 for nonmembers ● *Journal of School Health*, 10/year. Includes articles, research papers, reports, commentaries, teaching techniques, and health service application. **Price:** included in membership dues; $250.00 /year for institutions; $270.00 /year for individuals outside U.S.; $11.00/ copy for nonmembers. ISSN: 0022-4391. **Circulation:** 7,200. **Advertising:** accepted. Alternate Formats: online ● *National Health Education Standards: Achieving Health Literacy*. Booklet. **Price:** $8.00/issue ● *The PULSE*, bimonthly. **Price:** included in membership dues. ISSN: 0022-4391. **Circulation:** 3,000. **Advertising:** accepted. Alternate Formats: online ● *The Role of the Nurse in the School Setting: A Historical Perspective*. Book. **Price:** $10.00 for members; $11.00 for nonmembers ● *Roll Up Both Sleeves: Vaccinating Students & Staff at School*. Book. Includes book and video. **Price:** $15.00/issue ● *School Health: Findings form Evaluated Programs, 2nd Ed.*. Book. **Price:** $16.00 for members; $18.00 for nonmembers ● *School Health in America*. Survey. **Price:** $18.00 for members; $20.00 for nonmembers ● *Scope & Standards of Professional School Nursing Practice*. Book. **Price:** $15.00/issue ● *Sexuality Education Within Comprehensive School Health Education*. Book. **Price:** $16.00 for members; $20.00 for nonmembers ● *Tell Me About AIDS*. Contains curricular materials for grades K-1, 2-3, 4-5, & 6. ● *Topical Packages of Articles From the Journal*, annual. Book. Book series, updated annually. **Price:** $16.00 for members; $22.00 for nonmembers. **Conventions/Meetings:** annual National School Health Conference, multi-discipline collaboration of research geared towards school-aged children's issues (exhibits) - 2008 Nov. 12-15, Tampa, FL.

14410 ■ Association of Asian Pacific Community Health Organizations (AAPCHO)
300 Frank H. Ogawa Plz., Ste.620
Oakland, CA 94612
Ph: (510)272-9536
Fax: (510)272-0817
E-mail: info@aapcho.org
URL: http://www.aapcho.org
Contact: Jeffrey B. Caballero, Exec. Dir.
Founded: 1987. **Members:** 14. **Membership Dues:** full, $2,500 (annual) ● associate, $500 (annual). **Staff:** 15. **Budget:** $1,200,000. **Languages:** Chinese, English, Hindi, Japanese, Korean, Laotian, Thai, Vietnamese. **Description:** Works to improve access to culturally and linguistically appropriate health care in order to improve the health status of Asians and Pacific Islanders with a special focus on the medically underserved. **Computer Services:** database, AAPI health data ● database, AAPI health literature ● mailing lists. **Telecommunication Services:** electronic mail, jeffc@aapcho.org. **Programs:** Capacity Building; Coalition Building; Disease Specific. **Publications:** *Hepatitis B*. Brochure ● *Midwest Conference Proceedings*. Contains detailed information from sessions held at the national conference in Illinois. Alternate Formats: online ● *Parent's Guide to Common Childhood Illnesses*. Brochure ● *Thalassemia Among Asians*. Brochure.

14411 ■ Association of Nutrition Services Agencies (ANSA)
1634 Eye St. NW, Ste.605
Washington, DC 20006

Ph: (202)737-1011
Fax: (202)737-1152
E-mail: fabdale@ansanutrition.org
URL: http://www.ansanutrition.org
Contact: Frank Abdale, Exec. Dir.
Founded: 1997. **Members:** 120. **Membership Dues:** organization (with under 1000000 budget), $200-$1,500 (annual) ● organization (with under 5000000 budget), $3,000-$6,000 (annual) ● organization (with over 5000000 budget), $7,500 (annual). **Staff:** 3. **Budget:** $500,000. **Multinational. Description:** Aims to strengthen the capability of community-based nutrition support programs for people living with AIDS and other critical illnesses. Provides various forums for information sharing and technical assistance. Negotiates on behalf of members for discounted prices on food, food containers, nutritional supplements and insurance. Advocates for the nutrition needs of people with HIV/AIDS and other critical illnesses and the issues of those who serve them. **Programs:** Tech Assistance. **Publications:** *Nutrition Guidelines for Agencies Providing Food to People Living with HIV Disease.* Handbook. Alternate Formats: online ● *Practical Abundance: A Comprehensive Guide to Fundraising and Development for Nonprofits.* Handbook. **Price:** $20.00 plus shipping and handling.

14412 ■ Clinical Directors Network (CDN)
5 W 37th St., 10th Fl.
New York, NY 10018
Ph: (212)382-0699
Fax: (212)382-0669
E-mail: info@cdnetwork.org
URL: http://www.cdnetwork.org
Contact: Jonathan N. Tobin PhD, Pres./CEO
Founded: 1985. **Members:** 15. **Membership Dues:** associate, supporting, $50 (annual) ● student, $25 (annual) ● active, $100 (annual). **Staff:** 40. **Budget:** $2,200,000. **Languages:** Creole, English, Spanish. **Description:** Provides clinical leaders and staff at community, migrant, HIV and homeless health centers with educational meetings and peer support activities. Improves access of minority communities to clinical research. **Programs:** Behavioral Medicine & Mental Health; Cancer Prevention & Control; Cardiovascular Disease; Clinical Informatics; Complementary/Alternative Therapies; HIV/AIDS; Immunization; Nutrition and Physical Activity; Oral Health; Pediatrics. **Publications:** Annual Report, annual. **Advertising:** accepted ● Brochure, annual ● Newsletters. **Conventions/Meetings:** annual Clinical Leadership Conference.

14413 ■ Filipino American Medical Inc. (FAMI)
PO Box 161
New York, NY 10101
Ph: (212)582-3304
E-mail: info@ifami.org
URL: http://www.ifami.org
Contact: Niles Perlas CRNA, Chair
Founded: 1999. **Membership Dues:** regular, $25 (annual) ● supporter, $200 (annual) ● patron, $250 (annual). **Multinational. Description:** Brings American and Filipino-American physicians and other medical professionals to the Philippines to serve the poor. Provides surgery and medical care for people in need. Conducts surgical and medical workshops for local medical professionals. Partners with local medical teams to maximize service to the poor.

14414 ■ Healthcare Leadership Council (HLC)
1001 Pennsylvania Ave. NW, Ste.550 S
Washington, DC 20004-2505
Ph: (202)452-8700
Fax: (202)296-9561
E-mail: mgrealy@hlc.org
URL: http://hlc.org
Contact: Mary R. Grealy, Pres.
Founded: 1988. **Description:** Health care industry executives. Promotes the advancement of a market-based health care system that values innovation and provides affordable, high-quality health care; presents its system idea to Congress, administration, media,

the research community and the public. **Publications:** Newsletter. Alternate Formats: online.

14415 ■ International Mobile Health Association (IMHA)
PO Box 7611
Huntington, WV 25777-7611
Ph: (228)238-9676 (304)633-1771
E-mail: lseim@chfund.org
URL: http://www.internationalmobilehealthassociation.org
Contact: Lynn Gardiner Seim RN, Pres.
Membership Dues: healthcare organization, $300 (annual) ● individual professional, $150 (annual) ● student, $75 (annual) ● associate, $500 (annual). **Multinational. Description:** Promotes the development, enhancement, and implementation of global mobile health services. Aims to increase public access to vital healthcare services, especially among underserved populations. Provides educational support services and networking opportunities for mobile health specialists. **Publications:** Newsletter. **Price:** included in membership dues. Alternate Formats: online ● Membership Directory. **Price:** included in membership dues.

14416 ■ Medical Benevolence Foundation (MBF)
PO Box 770636
Houston, TX 77215-0636
Free: (800)547-7627
E-mail: info@mbfoundation.org
URL: http://www.mbfoundation.org
Contact: Dr. Maria Zack, Pres.
Founded: 1963. **Staff:** 11. **Nonmembership. Multinational. Description:** Medical mission providing support for medical personnel, as well as equipment and financial aid to hospitals, medical outposts and clinics outside the U.S. **Funds:** Medical Assistance. **Projects:** C.U.R.E.; Community Health; Construction; Development and Training for Indigenous Personnel; Diseases of Poverty; Mission Hospitals and Clinics; Overseas Shipping of Supplies and Equipment Containers. **Publications:** *Mission Connection,* quarterly. Newsletter.

14417 ■ Microsoft Healthcare Users Group (MS-HUG)
230 E Ohio St., Ste.500
Chicago, IL 60611
Ph: (312)664-4467 (312)915-9245
Fax: (312)915-9209
E-mail: msuerth@himss.org
URL: http://www.mshug.org
Contact: Ike Ellison, Chm.
Membership Dues: regular in U.S. and Canada, international, $140 (annual) ● student, $30 (annual). **Description:** Serves as a forum for the exchange of ideas. Promotes learning, and sharing solutions for information systems using Microsoft technologies. Works to provide industry leadership, drive appropriate standards and develop associated requirements in support of healthcare solutions. **Awards:** Microsoft Clinic of the Year. **Frequency:** annual. **Type:** recognition. **Recipient:** to the clinic that applies innovative technology to improve patient care or practice efficiency ● Microsoft Clinician of the Year. **Frequency:** annual. **Type:** recognition. **Recipient:** to the clinician who applies innovative technology to improve patient care or clinician efficiency ● Microsoft Hospital of the Year. **Frequency:** annual. **Type:** recognition. **Recipient:** to the hospital that applies innovative technology to improve patient care or hospital efficiency.

14418 ■ National Association of Free Clinics (NAFC)
1140 19th St. NW, Ste.900
Washington, DC 20036
Ph: (202)223-5120 (202)223-5130
Fax: (202)223-5619
E-mail: bbeavers@freeclinics.us
URL: http://www.freeclinics.us
Contact: Bonnie A. Beavers, Exec. Dir.
Founded: 2001. **Membership Dues:** basic (based on current operating budget), $100-$3,000 (annual) ● associate - individual (based on membership level),

$100-$1,000 (annual) ● associate - corporate (maximum), $50,000 (annual) ● state association (per association member organization), $10 (annual). **Description:** Provides advocacy and service to free clinics throughout the United States of America. Monitors the national legislative and regulatory issues that affect the ability of free clinics to serve uninsured and underinsured patients. Seeks to educate the general public and health industry leaders about the free clinic industry and its significance.

14419 ■ National Association of Subacute and Post-Acute Care (NASPAC)
PO Box 65085
Washington, DC 20035
Ph: (202)429-2700
Free: (888)758-8970
Fax: (202)429-2701
E-mail: naspac@naspac.net
URL: http://www.naspac.net
Contact: Hon. Lyle Williams, Exec. Dir.
Founded: 1995. **Members:** 1,500. **Membership Dues:** individual, $225 (annual) ● institutional provider, $400 (annual) ● payor, $500 (annual) ● vendor, $1,000 (annual). **Staff:** 3. **Description:** Hospitals, nursing facilities, professionals and suppliers. Works to serve and represent the subacute and transitional healthcare industry. Provides information on subacute healthcare; promotes high level of ethics; develops standards. **Libraries: Type:** reference. **Holdings:** articles, periodicals. **Subjects:** health care. **Telecommunication Services:** electronic mail, lyle.williams@naspac.net. **Committees:** Clinical; Education; Government; Quality Analysis. **Formerly:** (2003) National Association of Subacute and Post Acute Care; (2006) National Subacute Care Association. **Publications:** *NSCA News,* quarterly. Newsletter. **Advertising:** accepted ● *Subacute Care,* quarterly. Journal. **Advertising:** accepted ● Also issues InfoFaxes and Government Affairs Updates. **Conventions/Meetings:** board meeting ● annual convention ● periodic seminar.

14420 ■ National Commission on Correctional Health Care (NCCHC)
1145 W Diversey Pkwy.
Chicago, IL 60614
Ph: (773)880-1460
Fax: (773)880-2424
E-mail: info@ncchc.org
URL: http://www.ncchc.org
Contact: Edward A. Harrison, Pres.
Founded: 1983. **Members:** 38. **Staff:** 16. **Budget:** $3,000,000. **Description:** Professional organizations in the fields of medical and health care. Works to improve the quality of and set standards for medical care in correctional institutions in the U.S. including prisons, jails, and detention and juvenile facilities. Acts as an accrediting body for such facilities; develops training programs and conducts seminars; provides technical assistance; organizes special task forces on issues such as suicide and AIDS; disseminates information. **Awards:** Bernard P. Harrison Award of Merit. **Frequency:** annual. **Type:** recognition. **Recipient:** for individual or group that has demonstrated excellence and service to the correctional health care field ● Facility of the Year. **Frequency:** annual. **Type:** recognition. **Recipient:** for excellence and professionalism in providing efficient and effective care of prisons, jails, juvenile detention and confinement facilities. **Computer Services:** Mailing lists. **Publications:** *CorrectCare,* quarterly. Journal. **Advertising:** accepted. Alternate Formats: online ● *Correctional Health Care: Guidelines for the Management of an Adequated Delivery System.* Manuals ● *Journal of Correctional Health Care,* quarterly. Contains articles on correctional health care topics including law, medicine, and ethics. **Price:** $30.00 /year for individuals; $65.00 /year for institutions. **ISSN:** 0731-8332. **Circulation:** 500. **Advertising:** accepted ● Films ● Monographs ● Proceedings. **Conventions/Meetings:** annual Updates in Correctional Health Care - conference (exhibits) - always spring and fall.

14421 ■ National Health Care for the Homeless Council (NHCHC)
PO Box 60427
Nashville, TN 37206-0427
Ph: (615)226-2292
Fax: (615)226-1656
E-mail: council@nhchc.org
URL: http://www.nhchc.org
Contact: Mr. John Lozier, Exec. Dir.

Members: 785. **Membership Dues:** practicing clinician, $35 (annual) ● student, $15 (annual). **Staff:** 9. **National Groups:** 64. **Description:** Agencies and clinicians with an interest in providing health care services to the homeless. Promotes increased availability of primary health care services to homeless people; seeks to prevent homelessness. Works to reform the U.S. health care system to best serve the needs of the homeless and indigent; cooperates with other organizations and agencies working to eradicate homelessness. Facilitates networking, information sharing, and peer support among members; conducts educational programs. **Awards:** Award for Outstanding Service. **Frequency:** annual. **Type:** recognition. **Publications:** *HCH Mobilizer*, annual. Newspaper. **Price:** $15.00. Alternate Formats: online ● *Healing Hands*. Newsletter. **Price:** $35.00. **Conventions/Meetings:** annual Health Care for the Homeless Policy Symposium - meeting.

14422 ■ Trinity Health International (THI)
34605 12 Mile Rd.
Farmington Hills, MI 48331
Fax: (248)489-6102
E-mail: international@trinity-health.org
URL: http://www.mercyinternational.com
Contact: David Vellinga, Pres.

Founded: 1981. **Languages:** Chichewa, English, French, Spanish. **Multinational. Description:** Offers quality health and professional services to the poor and disadvantaged. **Formerly:** (2005) Mercy International Health Services. **Publications:** *Trinity Health International Newsletter*.

14423 ■ Wellness Councils of America (WELCOA)
9802 Nicholas St., Ste.315
Omaha, NE 68114
Ph: (402)827-3590
Fax: (402)827-3594
E-mail: wellworkplace@welcoa.org
URL: http://www.welcoa.org
Contact: David Hunnicutt PhD, Pres.

Founded: 1987. **Members:** 500. **Membership Dues:** general, $365 (annual). **Staff:** 15. **Regional Groups:** 10. **Description:** Conducts health education at the workplace. Offers advisory services; maintains educational programs. **Awards:** Platinum Award. **Frequency:** annual. **Type:** recognition. **Recipient:** to organizations that have previously achieved a Gold Well Workplace designation ● The Well Workplace Award. **Frequency:** periodic. **Type:** recognition. **Publications:** *Absolute Advantage*, 10/year. Magazine. Contains tips, strategies, and insights from the nation's best minds in workplace wellness. **Price:** $89.00/year. Alternate Formats: online ● *The Well Workplace*, monthly. Newsletter. **Circulation:** 300,000 ● Reports. Contains information regarding worksite health programming. Alternate Formats: online ● Catalogs. Contains information on health and worksite wellness products. Alternate Formats: online.

Hearing Impaired

14424 ■ Academy of Dispensing Audiologists (ADA)
401 N Michigan Ave., Ste.2200
Chicago, IL 60611
Free: (866)493-5544
Fax: (312)673-6725

E-mail: info@audiologist.org
URL: http://www.audiologist.org
Contact: Dr. Craig Johnson AuD, Past Pres.

Founded: 1977. **Members:** 936. **Membership Dues:** fellow, $210 (annual) ● associate, $170 (annual) ● student, $25 (annual). **Description:** Individuals with graduate degrees in audiology who dispense hearing aids as part of a rehabilitative practice. Fosters and supports professional dispensing of hearing aids by qualified audiologists; encourages audiology training programs to include pertinent aspects of hearing aid dispensing in their curriculums; conducts seminars on the business aspects of the hearing aid industry. **Awards:** Joel Wernick Award. **Frequency:** annual. **Type:** recognition. **Recipient:** for outstanding educational contribution within the fields of audiology or hearing science. **Telecommunication Services:** electronic mail, cjohnson@audiologist.org. **Publications:** *Feedback Magazine*, quarterly. Includes book reviews and new members listing. **Price:** free. **Circulation:** 1,000. **Advertising:** accepted. **Conventions/Meetings:** annual conference - usually May ● annual convention (exhibits) - 2007 Oct. 10-13, Orlando, FL.

14425 ■ Academy of Rehabilitative Audiology (ARA)
PO Box 952
DeSoto, TX 75123-0952
Ph: (605)274-4629
Fax: (605)274-4616
E-mail: ara@audrehab.org
URL: http://www.audrehab.org
Contact: Gabrielle Saunders PhD, Pres.

Founded: 1966. **Members:** 400. **Membership Dues:** regular, $55 (annual) ● associate, $40 (annual) ● student, $20 (annual). **Staff:** 1. **Budget:** $45,000. **Multinational. Description:** Individuals who hold graduate degrees in audiology, language, or speech pathology, education of the deaf, or allied fields, and who have at least two years of post-degree involvement in rehabilitative or educational programs for the hearing impaired. Provides a forum for exchange of ideas in audiology; fosters professional education, research, and interest in programs for hearing handicapped persons. Maintains speakers' bureau. **Libraries: Type:** reference. **Holdings:** periodicals. **Subjects:** aural rehabilitation. **Awards:** Herbert J. Oyer Student Research Award. **Frequency:** annual. **Type:** recognition. **Recipient:** for students completing exemplary research and advances in the area of audiologic rehabilitation. **Computer Services:** Mailing lists. **Publications:** *ARA Membership Directory*, annual ● *Journal of the Academy of Rehabilitative Audiology*, annual. **Price:** $25.00/year. **Circulation:** 600. Alternate Formats: CD-ROM. Also Cited As: *JARA* ● Monograph of Academy of Rehabilitative Audiology, quinquennial. **Price:** $20.00. **Circulation:** 1,000. **Conventions/Meetings:** annual Summer Institute - conference (exhibits).

14426 ■ ADARA: Professionals Networking for Excellence in Service Delivery with Individuals who are Deaf or Hard of Hearing (ADARA)
PO Box 480
Myersville, MD 21773
Ph: (301)293-8969
Fax: (301)293-9698
E-mail: adaraorgn@aol.com
URL: http://www.adara.org
Contact: Steve Hamerdinger, Pres.

Founded: 1966. **Members:** 600. **Membership Dues:** regular/family, $55 (annual) ● regular, $105 (biennial) ● student/retired, $30 (annual) ● foreign, $75 (annual) ● organizational, $155 (annual). **Staff:** 1. **Budget:** $37,000. **State Groups:** 12. **Description:** Psychiatrists, mental health counselors, students, teachers, researchers, rehabilitation facility personnel, interpreters, speech therapists, social workers, doctors, and rehabilitation counselors who serve deaf and deaf-blind persons. Promotes the development and expansion of quality services to deaf and hard-of-hearing persons. Strives to bring about a better understanding of deaf, hard-of-hearing, and deaf-blind people as a whole by encouraging students, professionals, and laymen to develop more than a

superficial understanding of the needs and problems of this group, especially the problems related to communication techniques needed to work effectively with deaf, hard-of-hearing, and deaf-blind persons in human services or a rehabilitation setting. Encourages scientific research of the needs and problems engendered by deafness. Promotes and develops recruitment and training of professional workers with deaf, hard-of-hearing, and deaf-blind persons. Sponsors a professional publication for the promotion of inter- and intradisciplinary communication among professionals concerned with deaf adults and others interested in such activities. Cooperates with other organizations in promoting and encouraging legislation pertinent to the development of professional services and facilities for deaf, hard-of-hearing, and deaf-blind persons. **Libraries: Type:** reference. **Holdings:** archival material. **Awards:** Bellflasher Award. **Frequency:** biennial. **Type:** recognition. **Recipient:** for the person contributing the most in presentation or planning of the biennial conference ● Boyce R. Williams Award. **Frequency:** biennial. **Type:** recognition. **Recipient:** for meritorious service to deaf people ● Eugene W. Peterson Award. **Frequency:** biennial. **Type:** recognition. **Recipient:** to individuals who have demonstrated exemplary direct service provision in the rehabilitation of Deaf adults with additional handicapping conditions ● Frederick C. Schreiber Award. **Frequency:** biennial. **Type:** recognition. **Recipient:** to individuals who have outstanding contributions to ADARA ● Legislative Award. **Frequency:** biennial. **Type:** recognition. **Recipient:** to individuals who have demonstrated contributions related to legislative activities that benefit deaf, deafened, hard of hearing and deaf-blind individuals ● Outstanding JADARA Article Award. **Frequency:** biennial. **Type:** recognition. **Recipient:** for the author of the outstanding JADARA article recommended by the JADARA editor. **Computer Services:** database ● mailing lists, of members. **Sections:** Chemical Dependency; Deaf-Blind; Deaf Professional Forum; Mental Health Counseling; Placement; Post-Secondary Education; Research. **Formerly:** American Deafness and Rehabilitation Association; (2003) ADARA. **Publications:** *ADARA Update*, quarterly. Newsletter. Includes membership activities information, research reports, and lists of employment opportunities. **Price:** included in membership dues. **Circulation:** 600. **Advertising:** accepted ● *JADARA: A Journal for Professionals Networking for Excellence in Service Delivery with Individuals who are Deaf or Hard of Hearing*, 3/year. Provides research findings and information on new ideas within the field. Includes reviews of current literature. **Price:** included in membership dues; $60.00 /year for nonmembers in U.S.; $70.00 /year for nonmembers outside U.S. ISSN: 0899-9228. **Circulation:** 800. **Advertising:** accepted. Also Cited As: *Journal of Rehabilitation of the Deaf and Journal of American Deafness and Rehabilitation Association* ● Monographs. **Conventions/Meetings:** biennial conference (exhibits).

14427 ■ Alexander Graham Bell Association for the Deaf and Hard of Hearing (AG BELL)
3417 Volta Pl. NW
Washington, DC 20007
Ph: (202)337-5220
Fax: (202)337-8314
E-mail: info@agbell.org
URL: http://www.agbell.org
Contact: K. Todd Houston PhD, Exec. Dir./CEO

Founded: 1890. **Members:** 5,000. **Membership Dues:** premium, $50 (annual) ● standard, $40 (annual) ● household, $60 (annual) ● student/senior premium, $30 (annual) ● life, premium, $850. **Staff:** 20. **Budget:** $1,000,000. **Local Groups:** 32. **National Groups:** 35. **Multinational. Description:** Represents the interests of educators; parents of children with hearing loss, adults with hearing loss and hearing health professionals. Offers members a wide range of programs and services and provides to all inquirers information on a vast array of issues pertaining to hearing loss. Publishes books and provides financial aid to qualifying applicants for mainstreamed, auditory-based education at pre-school, school-age and university levels. Provides governmental and education advocacy services through its national office and state chapters, children's rights coordinators and international affiliates. **Awards:** College Scholarship Awards. **Frequency:** annual. **Type:** scholarship. **Recipient:** to qualified students with moderate to profound hearing loss to continue their education on undergraduate and graduate levels ● Early Hearing Detection and Intervention Award. **Frequency:** annual. **Type:** recognition. **Recipient:** for hospitals that provide exemplary service to families and children who are identified with hearing loss. **Telecommunication Services:** TDD, (202)337-5221. **Programs:** Children's Legal Advocacy; Leadership Enrichment Adventure; Leadership Opportunities for Teens; Public School Program Assistance. **Sections:** Deaf and Hard of Hearing; International Parents'; International Professional. **Formerly:** (1948) American Association to Promote the Teaching of Speech to the Deaf; (1953) Volta Speech Association for the Deaf; (2003) Alexander Graham Bell Association for the Deaf. **Publications:** *OK Kids* ● *The Volta Review*, bimonthly. Journal. Covers issues related to hearing impairment for teachers of the hearing impaired. **Price:** included in membership dues; $62.00 /year for institutions. ISSN: 0042-8639. **Circulation:** 5,500. **Advertising:** accepted ● *Volta Voices*, bimonthly. Magazine. Includes the latest research and updates in the field of oral deafness. **Advertising:** accepted ● Also publishes bibliographies, teachers' and clinicians' textbooks, lipreading books, and references; produces audiovisuals. **Conventions/Meetings:** biennial meeting (exhibits).

14428 ■ American Association of the Deaf-Blind (AADB)
8630 Fenton St., Ste.121
Silver Spring, MD 20910-4500
Ph: (301)495-4403
Fax: (301)495-4404
E-mail: info@aadb.org
URL: http://www.aadb.org
Contact: Ms. Elizabeth Spiers, Dir., Information Services

Founded: 1984. **Members:** 1,040. **Membership Dues:** active, associate, $20 (annual) ● organization, $50 (annual). **Staff:** 3. **Budget:** $200,000. **Description:** National consumer organization of, for and by deaf-blind Americans and their supporters. Ensures that all deaf-blind persons achieve their maximum potential, through increased independence, productivity, and integration into the community. **Libraries: Type:** reference. **Subjects:** deaf-blindness. **Awards:** Laura Bridgman Award. **Frequency:** annual. **Type:** recognition. **Recipient:** for leadership and independence. **Telecommunication Services:** TDD, (301)-495-4402. **Divisions:** Support Service Provider. **Projects:** Mentoring Pilot. **Formerly:** (1937) American League for Deaf-Blind. **Publications:** *Deaf-Blind American*, quarterly. Magazine. In large print and Braille. **Price:** $15.00. **Circulation:** 700. **Conventions/Meetings:** biennial convention, with educational, social and recreational opportunities (exhibits).

14429 ■ American Auditory Society (AAS)
352 Sundial Ridge Cir.
Dammeron Valley, UT 84783-5196
Ph: (435)574-0062
Fax: (435)574-0063
E-mail: amaudsoc@aol.com
URL: http://www.amauditorysoc.org
Contact: Wayne J. Staab PhD, Exec. Dir.

Founded: 1973. **Members:** 2,000. **Membership Dues:** regular/associate, $55 (annual) ● student/resident, $35 (annual). **Staff:** 2. **Budget:** $150,000. **Description:** Audiologists, otolaryngologists, scientists, hearing aid industry professionals, and educators of hearing impaired people; individuals involved in industries serving hearing impaired people, including the amplification systems industry. Works to increase knowledge and understanding of: the ear, hearing, and balance; disorders of the ear, hearing, and balance; prevention of these disorders; habilitation and rehabilitation of individuals with hearing and balance dysfunction. **Libraries: Type:** reference. **Holdings:** papers, periodicals. **Awards:** Carhart Memorial Lecturer. **Frequency:** annual. **Type:** mon-

etary. **Recipient:** for contribution to the goals of the society ● Lifetime Achievement Award. **Frequency:** periodic. **Type:** recognition. **Recipient:** for contributions to the discipline of hearing. **Computer Services:** Mailing lists. **Formerly:** (1982) American Audiology Society. **Publications:** *The Bulletin of the American Auditory Society*, 3/year. Newsletter. **Price:** included in membership dues. ISSN: 0196-0202. **Circulation:** 2,500. **Advertising:** accepted. Also Cited As: *Corti's Organ* ● *Ear and Hearing*, bimonthly. Journal. Includes periodic supplements. **Price:** included in membership dues; $114.00 for nonmember individuals; $214.00 for nonmember institutions ● *Peer Reviewed Clinical Research Publication*. **Price:** $77.00 personal in U.S.; $112.00 personal outside U.S.; $145.00 institution in U.S.; $180.00 institution outside U.S. **Conventions/Meetings:** annual Scientific Meeting - conference.

14430 ■ American Hearing Aid Associates (AHAA)
1380 Wilmington Pike
West Chester, PA 19382
Free: (800)984-3272
Fax: (610)455-3018
E-mail: webmaster@ahaanet.com
URL: http://www.ahaanet.com

Description: Aims to raise the quality of hearing health care throughout America through evaluation and upgrade of the educational standards and technical expertise of hearing aid associates. Increases awareness of hearing loss throughout the country. **Computer Services:** Information services, hearing loss facts and resources.

14431 ■ American Hearing Research Foundation (AHRF)
8 S Michigan Ave., Ste.814
Chicago, IL 60603-4539
Ph: (312)726-9670
Fax: (312)726-9695
E-mail: ahrf@american-hearing.org
URL: http://www.american-hearing.org
Contact: William L. Lederer, Exec. Dir.

Founded: 1956. **Members:** 1,585. **Staff:** 2. **Budget:** $180,000. **Description:** Works to encourage and support medical research, education, and public information concerning deafness and other hearing disorders. Produces scientific exhibits and film exhibits for professional and public audiences. **Libraries: Type:** reference. **Holdings:** audiovisuals. **Telecommunication Services:** electronic mail, blederer@american-hearing.org. **Committees:** Development; Education; Publicity; Research. **Publications:** *American Hearing Research Foundation Newsletter*, 3/year. Reviews developments in hearing research and education. **Price:** free. **Circulation:** 14,000 ● *Hearing Health*. Brochure ● *Progress Report*, semiannual ● Also publishes research papers. **Conventions/Meetings:** seminar ● symposium ● workshop.

14432 ■ American Sign Language Teachers Association (ASLTA)
PO Box 92445
Rochester, NY 14692
E-mail: info@aslta.org
URL: http://www.aslta.org
Contact: Glenna Ashton, Pres.

Members: 1,000. **Membership Dues:** supporting, $25 (annual) ● associate, $40 (annual) ● certified, $50 (annual) ● institutional, $150 (annual). **Regional Groups:** 33. **Description:** Represents and promotes American Sign Language and Deaf Studies teachers in the U.S. **Publications:** Newsletter, 3/year. **Price:** included in membership dues. **Conventions/Meetings:** annual conference - 2007 Oct. 25-27, Tampa, FL.

14433 ■ American Society for Deaf Children (ASDC)
3820 Hartzdale Dr.
Camp Hill, PA 17011
Ph: (717)703-0073
Free: (800)942-2732
Fax: (717)909-5599

E-mail: asdc@deafchildren.org
URL: http://www.deafchildren.org
Contact: Diana Poeppelmeyer, Exec. Sec.

Founded: 1967. **Membership Dues:** individual/family, $40 (annual) ● patron, $100 (annual) ● benefactor, $500 (annual) ● parent affiliate group, $75 (annual) ● library, $90 (annual) ● organizational/educational, $125 (annual) ● student, $25 (annual) ● life, $5,000. **Description:** Parents of deaf and hard of hearing children; researchers, professionals, and others interested in the welfare of deaf and hard of hearing children and their families. Seeks to provide parent-to-parent support to help improve the education, recreation, health, and employment opportunities of deaf and hard of hearing children and youth. Promotes "total communication" as a way of life for deaf and hard of hearing children and their families. Assists other organizations in locating parents for seminars, workshops, and learning sessions regarding parental needs and the education of deaf and hard of hearing children. Provides speakers for meetings, seminars, and conventions. **Boards:** Directors. **Formerly:** (1984) International Association of Parents of the Deaf. **Publications:** *The Endeavor*, quarterly. Newsletter. **Price:** included in membership dues. **Circulation:** 1,700. **Advertising:** accepted. **Conventions/Meetings:** biennial Bridging the Rivers of Change - convention.

14434 ■ Association of Late-Deafened Adults (ALDA)
8038 MacIntosh Ln.
Rockford, IL 61107
Ph: (815)332-1515
Free: (866)402-ALDA
E-mail: info@alda.org
URL: http://www.alda.org
Contact: Bernie Palmer, Pres.

Founded: 1987. **Members:** 1,500. **Membership Dues:** regular, $25 (annual) ● senior, $20 (annual) ● business, $40 (annual). **Regional Groups:** 25. **Description:** People who have become deaf adventitiously and rely on visual systems to communicate effectively. Provides information, support, and social opportunities through self-help groups, general membership meetings, and social events. Advocates for the needs of late-deafened people. Conducts and participates in surveys, workshops, and seminars on late-deafness. Maintains speakers' bureau and biographical archives. **Awards:** I. King Jordan Award. **Frequency:** annual. **Type:** recognition. **Telecommunication Services:** TDD, (708)358-0135. **Committees:** ALDAcon Planning; Bylaws; Development; International; Nominations; Outreach; Publications; Strategic Planning; Volunteers. **Publications:** *ALDA Biz*, semiannual, fall and spring. Newsletters. Contains board of directors and committees report. **Price:** included in membership dues. **Advertising:** accepted ● *ALDA News*, quarterly. Newsletter. Includes pen pal section. **Price:** included in membership dues. **Circulation:** 1,000. **Advertising:** accepted ● *Proceedings of ALDAcon*. Monograph. **Conventions/Meetings:** annual international conference, exhibitors, workshops, banquet, awards, social, self-help support groups, karaoke party (exhibits).

14435 ■ Association of Medical Professionals with Hearing Losses (AMPHL)
10708 Nestling Dr.
Miamisburg, OH 45342-0886
E-mail: secretary@amphl.org
URL: http://www.amphl.org
Contact: Candice A. Corriher DVM, Pres.

Founded: 1999. **Nonmembership. Multinational. Description:** Provides information, promotes advocacy and mentorship. Creates a network for individuals with hearing losses interested in or working in health care fields.

14436 ■ Better Hearing Institute (BHI)
515 King St., Ste.420
Alexandria, VA 22314
Ph: (703)684-3391

E-mail: mail@betterhearing.org
URL: http://www.betterhearing.org
Contact: Sergei Kochkin PhD, Exec. Dir.
Founded: 1973. **Description:** Professionals and others dedicated to helping persons with impaired hearing. Purpose is to inform the public about the nature of hearing loss and the available medical, surgical, rehabilitative, and amplification help. Methods of communication used include television and radio public service announcements, films, speakers' bureaus, booklets, editorial publicity, and exhibits. Produces general information and education kits of communication tools. Maintains telephone service that provides information on hearing loss and help to callers from anywhere in the United States and Canada. **Telecommunication Services:** information service, about hearing loss for the hearing impaired. **Publications:** *Your Guide to Better Hearing.* Booklet.

14437 ■ Child Aid
917 SW Oak St., Ste.301
Portland, OR 97205
Ph: (503)223-3008
Free: (888)881-8241
Fax: (503)223-3008
E-mail: info@child-aid.org
URL: http://www.child-aid.org
Contact: Richard T. Carroll PhD, CEO
Founded: 1988. **Staff:** 2. **Languages:** English, Spanish. **Description:** Individuals who volunteer to aid hearing impaired children in Mexico and Guatemala. Promotes increased access to audiological aids and services among Mexican, Guatemalan, and Turkish children. Provides audiological and educational services to indigent children with impaired hearing; provides funds and assistance to organizations pursuing similar goals; conducts fundraising programs; recruits and trains volunteers. Supports literacy, education and health programs in Latin America. **Formerly:** (2001) SoundAid. **Publications:** Newsletter. Alternate Formats: online ● Annual Report, annual.

14438 ■ Children of Deaf Adults (CODA)
PO Box 30715
Santa Barbara, CA 93130-0715
Ph: (805)682-0997
URL: http://www.coda-international.org
Contact: Millie Brother, Founder
Founded: 1983. **Members:** 500. **Membership Dues:** non-voting, $20 (annual) ● voting, $25 (annual) ● organization, $50 (annual). **Languages:** English, German, Japanese, Swedish. **Multinational. Description:** Hearing children of deaf parents who are interested in sharing experiences with others of similar backgrounds. Provides information to professional organizations, libraries, community agencies, researchers, and other interested persons. Acts upon issues regarding deafness; provides support to deaf parent/hearing child families. Serves as clearinghouse for deaf parent/hearing children families. **Libraries: Type:** reference. **Subjects:** hearing children of deaf parents. **Awards:** Millie Brother Scholarship. **Frequency:** annual. **Type:** scholarship. **Computer Services:** Mailing lists. **Publications:** *CODA Connection,* quarterly. Newsletter. For the adult hearing children of deaf parents. Reports on national and international meetings and resources. Includes association news. **Price:** included in membership dues. ISSN: 0885-7962. **Circulation:** 500 ● *Hearing Children/Deaf Parents.* Bibliography ● *Proceedings from Annual Conferences.* **Conventions/Meetings:** annual conference.

14439 ■ Cochlear Implant Association, Inc. (CIAI)
5335 Wisconsin Ave. NW, Ste.440
Washington, DC 20015-2052
Ph: (202)895-2781
Fax: (202)895-2782
E-mail: info@cici.org
URL: http://www.cici.org
Contact: Dr. Peg S. Williams, Exec. Dir.
Founded: 1981. **Members:** 3,100. **Membership Dues:** individual in U.S., $25 (annual) ● professional in U.S., $60 (annual) ● individual in Canada, $30

(annual) ● professional in Canada, $65 (annual) ● individual outside U.S. and Canada, $37 (annual) ● professional outside U.S. and Canada, $72 (annual). **Staff:** 1. **Budget:** $260,000. **Local Groups:** 38. **Description:** Cochlear implant users, candidates for cochlear implant, and their families and friends; health care professionals. Provides support services including advocacy for the hearing impaired. Promotes improved cochlear implant technology and research on hearing impairment. Serves as an information clearinghouse. Conducts educational programs and children's services; operates Speaker's Bureau. **Awards:** Dr. Bill House. **Frequency:** biennial. **Type:** monetary. **Recipient:** for a child who overcomes his/her hearing loss and shows good response to cochlear implant. **Publications:** *Contact,* quarterly. Magazine. Covers current research, legislation, insurance issues, association activities, and coping advice. **Price:** included in membership dues. ISSN: 1060-2496. **Circulation:** 1,500. **Advertising:** accepted. **Conventions/Meetings:** biennial competition and convention (exhibits) - always odd years.

14440 ■ Conference of Educational Administrators of Schools and Programs for the Deaf (CEASD)
c/o Joseph P. Finnegan, Jr., Exec. Dir.
PO Box 1778
St. Augustine, FL 32085-1778
Ph: (904)810-5200
Fax: (904)810-5525
E-mail: nationaloffice@ceasd.org
URL: http://www.ceasd.org
Contact: Joseph P. Finnegan Jr., Exec. Dir.
Founded: 1868. **Members:** 355. **Membership Dues:** educational program (based on size), $500-$900 (annual) ● administrative unit, $500 (annual) ● affiliate program, $225 (annual) ● independent associate, $75 (annual). **Staff:** 2. **Budget:** $90,000. **Description:** Executive heads of public, private, and denominational schools for the deaf in the U.S. and Canada. Coordinates research on the problems of deafness. Compiles statistics on pupils, teachers, and programs from schools for the deaf. **Awards:** Citation for Leadership and Service. **Frequency:** periodic. **Type:** recognition. **Recipient:** for retiring CEOs (superintendent, president, executive director, headmaster) of programs for the deaf/hard of hearing ● Edward Allen Fay Award. **Frequency:** periodic. **Type:** recognition. **Recipient:** for a significant publication related to deafness ● Robert R. Davila Award of Merit. **Frequency:** annual. **Type:** recognition. **Recipient:** for meritorious contributions in the field of deafness. **Committees:** Accreditation; Career Development; Career Education; Community Education for the Deaf; Deaf-Blind; Dormitory Counselors; Educational Research; Honors and Awards; Legislation; Multi-Handicapped; Parent Education; Post-Secondary Education; Public Relations; Time and Place. **Formerly:** Association of Superintendents and Principals of American Schools for the Deaf; (1980) Conference of Executives of American Schools for the Deaf; (2000) Conference of Educational Administrators Serving the Deaf. **Publications:** *American Annals of the Deaf,* 5/year ● *President's Update,* bimonthly. Newsletter. Alternate Formats: online. **Conventions/Meetings:** annual conference and workshop (exhibits).

14441 ■ Council of American Instructors of the Deaf (CAID)
PO Box 377
Bedford, TX 76095-0377
Ph: (817)354-8414
E-mail: caid@swbell.net
URL: http://www.caid.org
Contact: Helen Lovato, Office Mgr.
Founded: 1850. **Members:** 1,000. **Membership Dues:** full, $55 (annual). **Budget:** $80,000. **Description:** Professional organization of teachers, administrators, and professionals in allied fields related to education of the deaf and hard-of-hearing. Provides opportunities for a free interchange of views concerning methods and means of educating the deaf and hard-of-hearing. Promotes such education by the publication of reports, essays, and other information.

Develops more effective methods of teaching deaf and hard-of-hearing children. **Awards:** Educational Assistance Award. **Frequency:** biennial. **Type:** recognition ● Howard M. Quigley Award. **Type:** recognition ● Outstanding Teacher Award. **Frequency:** biennial. **Type:** recognition. **Committees:** Deaf and Hard of Hearing Alliance; Joint Annals Administrative. **Councils:** Education of the Deaf. **Special Interest Groups:** Deaf Studies; Mathematics Teachers; Program Supervisors/Coordinators/Consultants; Science and Technology; Success within the Mainstream; Teachers of English and Language Arts. **Also Known As:** American Instructors of the Deaf. **Formerly:** Convention of American Instructors of the Deaf. **Publications:** *American Annals of the Deaf,* quarterly. Journal. Includes scholarly articles on deafness. **Price:** included in membership dues; $50.00 /year for nonmembers. **Advertising:** accepted ● *News 'N' Notes,* quarterly. Newsletter. Includes articles on education of the deaf and organization activities. **Price:** free for members. **Advertising:** accepted ● *Reference Issue of the American Annals of the Deaf.* Directory ● Proceedings. **Conventions/Meetings:** biennial conference (exhibits).

14442 ■ Council on Education of the Deaf (CED)
c/o Dr. Roslyn Rosen, EdD, Exec. Dir.
Gallaudet Univ.
PO Box 2094
Washington, DC 20002-3695
Ph: (412)244-4216
Fax: (412)244-4223
E-mail: ced@gallaudet.edu
URL: http://www.deafed.net
Contact: Cathy Rhoten, Pres.
Founded: 1930. **Membership Dues:** certified teacher, $50 (quinquennial). **Staff:** 1. **Budget:** $35,000. **National Groups:** 6. **Description:** Representatives from the Alexander Graham Bell Association for the Deaf, the Conference of Educational Administrators Serving the Deaf, the Convention of American Instructors of the Deaf, Association of College Educators; Deaf and Hard of Hearing, National Association of the Deaf and The American Society for Deaf Children. Certifies teachers and accredits university teacher training programs specializing in deaf education and the related. Seeks to improve educational opportunities for deaf and hard of hearing children through cooperation in publication practices, liaison with lay and peripheral groups, teacher certification, public information, and research. Provides certification programs for educators and professionals. Establishes, evaluates, accredits, and maintains certification standards for teacher education programs. **Committees:** International Relations; Professional Preparation and Certification. **Publications:** *Certification Standards Document* ● *Standards for Evaluation of Programs.* **Conventions/Meetings:** semiannual meeting.

14443 ■ Deaf-REACH
3521 12th St. NE
Washington, DC 20017
Ph: (202)832-6681
Fax: (202)832-8454
E-mail: info@deafreach.org
URL: http://www.deaf-reach.org
Contact: Sarah Brown, Exec. Dir.
Founded: 1972. **Membership Dues:** associate, $10 ● active, $100 ● sustaining, $1,000. **Staff:** 28. **Budget:** $1,000,000. **Description:** Works to maximize the self-sufficiency of deaf people needing special services by providing referral, education, advocacy, counseling, and housing. Seeks to establish residential homes and provide psychological, physical, spiritual, and social aid to deaf persons with mental and emotional problems. Operates Otis House and Kearny House, group homes for mentally ill deaf persons, designed to help meet the residents' emotional and social needs and teach them independent living skills. Administers the Community Housing for the Hearing Impaired Program which also provides a group home. Offers in-take, referral, housing placement assistance, and personal counseling; provides day-programs for learning disabled, deaf adults.

Works in community advocacy for the mentally ill hearing impaired. **Programs:** Community Service Center; Deaf Horizons; HIV Prevention; Otis House. **Formerly:** (1990) National Health Care Foundation for the Deaf. **Publications:** Annual Report, annual. **Price:** free for members ● Brochure ● Newsletter, quarterly. Alternate Formats: online.

14444 ■ Deafness Research Foundation (DRF)

2801 M St. NW
Washington, DC 20007
Ph: (202)719-8088
Free: (866)454-3924
Fax: (202)338-8182
E-mail: info@drf.org
URL: http://www.drf.org
Contact: Mr. Steve Orr, Exec. Dir.
Founded: 1958. **Nonmembership. Description:** Participates in the National Temporal Bone and Balance Pathology Resource Registry Program of the National Institute on Deafness and Other Communication Disorders. Approximately 1000 physicians and other professionals in ear medicine and research and 52 medical societies underwrite the foundation's fundraising costs through membership in the Centurions of the Deafness Research Foundation; approximately 300 other interested individuals raise funds through membership in the Deafness Research Foundation Alliance. **Awards:** Otologic Fellowship. **Frequency:** annual. **Type:** fellowship. **Recipient:** for third-year medical students to allow research for one year ● Otologic Research Grant. **Frequency:** annual. **Type:** grant. **Recipient:** for 1-3 years of support to promising new research projects related to hearing disorders and ear diseases. **Telecommunication Services:** teletype, (888)435-6104. **Affiliated With:** NIDCD - National Temporal Bone, Hearing and Balance Pathology Resource Registry. **Publications:** *Cochlear Implant: A Primer for Parents.* Booklet ● *Deafness Research Foundation Annual Report.* **Price:** free ● *Hearing Health*, quarterly. Magazine. **Advertising:** accepted ● Brochures.

14445 ■ Dogs for the Deaf (DFD)

10175 Wheeler Rd.
Central Point, OR 97502
Ph: (541)826-9220
Free: (800)990-DOGS
Fax: (541)826-6696
E-mail: info@dogsforthedeaf.org
URL: http://www.dogsforthedeaf.org
Contact: Mrs. Robin Dickson, Pres./CEO
Founded: 1977. **Members:** 35,000. **Staff:** 18. **Budget:** $1,000,000. **Description:** Trains hearing dogs to alert deaf persons to certain sounds. Dogs are chosen from pet adoption shelters and assigned on the basis of a prioritized waiting list. They undergo four to five months of training during which they are taught to alert their masters to the sounds of alarm clocks, smoke alarms, doorbells, oven timers, crying babies, and telephones. Deaf or severely hearing-impaired persons are eligible to be recipients if they are old enough to assume responsibility for the care of the dog. When assigned, a trainer and the dog travel to the recipient's home for a week to teach the dog and recipient to work together. Costs of dog selection, veterinary care, housing, training, and placement are covered; recipients make a donation only if able. Trains individuals to be certified audio canine trainers. Has appeared on local and national television programs to present the hearing ear dog training process and the results of dog placement. **Convention/Meeting:** none. **Affiliated With:** Assistance Dogs International. **Publications:** *Canine Listener*, quarterly. Newsletter. Provides information on the Hearing Ear Dog Program for the deaf; includes profiles of dogs and owners. **Price:** free. **Circulation:** 35,000. Alternate Formats: online.

14446 ■ Educational Audiology Association (EAA)

13153 N Dale Mabry Hwy., Ste.105
Tampa, FL 33618-2410
Free: (800)460-7322
Fax: (813)968-3597

E-mail: eaa@l-tgraye.com
URL: http://www.edaud.org
Contact: Lois Kostroski, Exec. Dir.
Founded: 1984. **Members:** 1,020. **Membership Dues:** affiliate in North America, $75 (annual) ● foreign resident, $100 (annual) ● student, $40 (annual). **Staff:** 5. **Description:** Audiologists and others with an interest in the field. Promotes advancement in the field of audiology and its educational applications. Conducts educational programs. **Awards:** EAA Doctoral Scholarship. **Frequency:** annual. **Type:** scholarship. **Recipient:** for a member of the association practicing as an educational audiologist ● Fred Berg Award. **Frequency:** periodic. **Type:** recognition. **Recipient:** for an outstanding member of the association ● Noel D. Matkin Award. **Frequency:** annual. **Type:** recognition. **Recipient:** for practitioners and students who are members of the association. **Computer Services:** database ● mailing lists. **Formerly:** (1998) Educational Audiology Society. **Publications:** *Educational Audiology Review*, quarterly. Newsletter. Circulation: 900. **Advertising:** accepted ● *Journal of Educational Audiology*, annual. Includes membership directory. Circulation: 800. **Advertising:** accepted ● Membership Directory, annual. **Conventions/Meetings:** biennial conference.

14447 ■ HEAR Center (HEAR)

301 E Del Mar Blvd.
Pasadena, CA 91101
Ph: (626)796-2016
Fax: (626)796-2320
E-mail: auditory@hearcenter.org
URL: http://www.hearcenter.org
Contact: Josephine F. Wilson MA, Exec. Dir.
Founded: 1954. **Staff:** 10. **Budget:** $500,000. **Languages:** English, Spanish, Yiddish. **Nonmembership. Description:** Auditory and verbal program designed to help hearing-impaired children, infants, and adults lead normal and productive lives. Seeks to develop auditory techniques to aid people who have communication problems due to deafness; primary objectives include early identification of hearing loss in infants and children and early amplification. Operates a program involving: binaural hearing aids where appropriate; continuous exposure to sound; development of auditory perception; wide-range amplification; environmental stimulation. Provides services in: diagnosis and audiological evaluation; hearing aid evaluation and trial use; development of listening skills and articulation; speech therapy; hearing aid dispensing; parent counseling. **Awards:** Glen H. Bollinger Humanitarian Award. **Frequency:** periodic. **Type:** recognition. **Departments:** Audiology; Speech/Language Pathology. **Programs:** Community Outreach; Hearing Screening. **Formerly:** (1975) Hearing Education Through Auditory Research Foundation. **Publications:** *Conquering Childhood Deafness.* Book ● *Effectiveness of Early Detection and Auditory Stimulation on the Speech and Language of Hearing Impaired Children* ● *Hear: A Four Letter Word.* Book ● *HEAR Center Proceedings*, periodic ● *The Listener*, quarterly. Newsletter. Covers topics of interest to the hearing and speech impaired community, as well as services and activities of the center. **Price:** free. **Circulation:** 4,500. Alternate Formats: online. **Conventions/Meetings:** annual board meeting - always October or November.

14448 ■ Hear Now (HN)

c/o The Starkey Hearing Foundation
6700 Washington Ave. S
Eden Prairie, MN 55344-3405
Free: (800)648-HEAR
Fax: (952)947-4997
E-mail: nonprofit@starkey.com
URL: http://www.sotheworldmayhear.org
Contact: Joanita Stelter, Program Dir.
Founded: 1988. **Staff:** 12. **Budget:** $3,500,000. **Description:** Provides hearing aids for very low income hard of hearing individuals of all ages. Offers financial and fund raising assistance for hard of hearing and deaf individuals. Collects broken and used hearing aids through its HEAR-O Recycling Program to support assistance programs. Donates aids package in a

padded envelope or box and mail to the address listed above. All donations are tax deductible and acknowledgment letters will be sent to all known donors. Determining the value of the donation is the responsibility of the donor. **Awards:** Legacy Award. **Frequency:** annual. **Type:** recognition. **Recipient:** for individuals making significant contribution to deaf and hard of hearing individuals. **Computer Services:** Information services, National Hearing Assistance Directory - provides information throughout the country. **Publications:** Also publishes information packet.

14449 ■ Hearing Instrument Manufacturers' Software Association (HIMSA)

2550 Univ. Ave. W, Ste.241N
St. Paul, MN 55114
Ph: (651)644-2921
Free: (800)435-9246
Fax: (651)644-3046
E-mail: himsa@himsa.com
URL: http://www.himsa.com
Contact: Scott Peterson, Contact
Founded: 1993. **Multinational. Description:** Works to develop, market, and support NOAH, one standard for integrated hearing care software. **Telecommunication Services:** electronic mail, speterson@himsa.com. **Publications:** *HIMSA News* (in English, French, German, and Spanish), quarterly. Newsletter. Contains recent information on the organization and products. Alternate Formats: online.

14450 ■ Hearing Loss Association of America (HLAA)

7910 Woodmont Ave., Ste.1200
Bethesda, MD 20814
Ph: (301)657-2248
Fax: (301)913-9413
E-mail: info@hearingloss.org
URL: http://www.hearingloss.org
Contact: Mr. Terry Portis EdD, Exec. Dir.
Founded: 1979. **Members:** 10,000. **Membership Dues:** individual/couple/family, $25 (annual) ● student, $20 (annual) ● professional, $50 (annual). **Staff:** 10. **Budget:** $1,100,000. **Regional Groups:** 10. **State Groups:** 250. **Description:** Advocates for persons with hearing loss and their families; strives to open the world of communication to people with hearing loss by providing information, education, support and advocacy. **Awards:** Community Access. **Frequency:** annual. **Type:** recognition ● Community Awareness. **Frequency:** annual. **Type:** recognition ● Education Award. **Frequency:** annual. **Type:** recognition ● Employment Award. **Frequency:** annual. **Type:** recognition ● Group Development. **Frequency:** annual. **Type:** recognition ● Hospital Program Award. **Frequency:** periodic. **Type:** recognition ● Newsletter Award. **Frequency:** annual. **Type:** recognition ● Rocky Stone Humanitarian Award. **Frequency:** annual. **Type:** recognition. **Telecommunication Services:** teletype, (301)657-2249. **Also Known As:** SHHH. **Formerly:** (2005) Self Help for Hard of Hearing People. **Publications:** *E-News*, biweekly. Newsletter. **Advertising:** accepted. Alternate Formats: online ● *Hearing Loss*, bimonthly. Magazine ● Offers various publications on hearing loss, products, and related subjects. **Conventions/Meetings:** annual international conference (exhibits).

14451 ■ Helen Keller National Center for Deaf-Blind Youths and Adults (HKNC)

141 Middle Neck Rd.
Sands Point, NY 11050-1218
Ph: (516)944-8900
Fax: (516)944-8637
E-mail: hkncinfo@hknc.org
URL: http://www.hknc.org
Contact: Joseph J. McNulty, Exec. Dir.
Founded: 1969. **Staff:** 150. **Budget:** $10,000,000. **Regional Groups:** 10. **Languages:** English, Spanish. **Description:** Provides diagnostic evaluations, comprehensive vocational and personal adjustment training, job preparation and placement for adults who are deaf-blind from every state and territory. Includes field services such as: information, referral, advocacy, and technical assistance to professionals,

consumers, and families. Sponsors annual National Helen Keller Deaf-Blind Awareness Week. **Libraries: Type:** not open to the public. **Subjects:** deaf-blindness. **Computer Services:** Mailing lists, for information on congenital rubella syndrome. **Programs:** Affiliate; Community Services; Older Adult; PATH; Traditional. **Publications:** *Giving.* Newsletter. Alternate Formats: online ● *Guidelines for Helping Deaf-Blind Persons.* Brochure ● *HKNC Description of Services.* Booklet ● *Nat-Cent News,* periodic. Magazine ● *Older Adult Program.* Brochure ● Also publishes many other free materials about the annual Deaf-Blind Awareness week.

14452 ■ HIKE Fund

c/o Mrs. Shirley R. Terrill, Corresponding Sec.
10115 Cherryhill Pl.
Spring Hill, FL 34608-7116
Ph: (352)688-2579
Fax: (352)688-2579
E-mail: ceterrill1@aol.com
URL: http://www.missouriiojd.org/MO-HIKE/HIKE.htm
Contact: Mrs. Shirley R. Terrill, Corresponding Sec.
Founded: 1985. **Members:** 12. **Budget:** $200,000.
Description: Supported by the International Order of Job's Daughters. Works for complete equality and integration of the hearing impaired in society. Provides support and information services. Provides hearing devices for children (up to the age of 20) with financial need. **Awards:** The HIKE Fund. **Frequency:** monthly. **Type:** grant. **Additional Websites:** http://www.thehikefund.org. **Also Known As:** Hearing Impaired Kids Endowment Fund. **Conventions/Meetings:** semiannual board meeting (exhibits) - mid-year meeting in February, annual meeting in July/August.

14453 ■ International Hearing Dog, Inc. (IHDI)

5901 E 89th Ave.
Henderson, CO 80640
Ph: (303)287-3277
Fax: (303)287-3425
E-mail: ihdi@aol.com
URL: http://www.ihdi.org
Contact: Valerie Foss-Brugger, Pres.
Founded: 1979. **Staff:** 10. **Multinational. Description:** An independent organization formed to train and place dogs, free of cost, with the deaf. (Hearing dogs are trained to alert the hearing impaired to important sounds that occur in the owners' environment, such as a door knock or bell, a baby crying, a smoke alarm, an alarm clock, a telephone, a security buzzer, and other sounds which might indicate danger.) Presents public awareness demonstrations. **Formerly:** (1981) Hearing Dogs. **Publications:** *Paws for Silence,* 3/year. Newsletter. Reports on the group's current activities and includes stories about hearing dog recipients. **Price:** free. **Conventions/Meetings:** annual meeting.

14454 ■ International Hearing Society (IHS)

16880 Middlebelt Rd., Ste.4
Livonia, MI 48154-3374
Ph: (734)522-7200
Fax: (734)522-0200
E-mail: chelms@ihsinfo.org
URL: http://www.ihsinfo.org
Contact: Cindy J. Helms, Exec. Dir.
Founded: 1951. **Members:** 3,000. **Membership Dues:** board certified/audiologist/audioprosthologist/physician/provisional, $137 (annual) ● international, $125 (annual) ● industrial, $100 (annual) ● associate/affiliate, $50 (annual) ● student, $35 (annual). **Staff:** 12. **Budget:** $1,500,000. **State Groups:** 54. **Description:** Hearing aid specialists who test hearing for the selection, adaptation, fitting, adjusting, servicing, and sale of hearing aids. Members counsel the hearing impaired and instruct them in care and use of hearing aids. Activities include: administration of a qualification program for screening persons designated as Hearing Instrument Specialists; administration of a consumer information program; publication of information and research concerning hearing health care; establishment of standards of education, equipment, and techniques in the fitting of hearing aids; cooperation with other professional

organizations engaged in hearing health care; cooperation and consultation with government officials and agencies in the development of policies and legislation. Accredits seminars and workshops for the education of hearing aid specialists. Maintains the International Institute for Hearing Instruments Studies as the educational arm of the society. **Libraries: Type:** reference. **Awards: Type:** recognition. **Telecommunication Services:** hotline, Hearing Aid Helpline, (800)521-5247. **Committees:** Federal and State Affairs; The Hearing Professional; Marketing; National Board for Certification in Hearing Instrument Sciences; Public Relations; Standards. **Formerly:** (1966) Society of Hearing Aid Audiologists; (1990) National Hearing Aid Society. **Publications:** *The Hearing Professional,* bimonthly. Journal. Contains technical articles, business information, and news for hearing health professionals. Includes annual index, chapter news, and book reviews. **Price:** free for members; $45.00 /year for nonmembers ous; $35.00 /year for nonmembers in U.S. ISSN: 0004-7473. **Circulation:** 3,300. **Advertising:** accepted. Alternate Formats: microform ● *International Hearing Society-Professional Association of Hearing Instrument Specialists.* Brochures ● *World of Sound.* Pamphlets ● *Membership Directory,* annual. Includes supplemental directory of manufacturers, suppliers, hearing aid designers, and others; arranged geographically and alphabetically. ● Books ● Brochures ● Also publishes bylaws and code of ethics. **Conventions/Meetings:** annual conference and seminar, major manufacturers of hearing aids and equipment (exhibits).

14455 ■ John Tracy Clinic (JTC)

806 W Adams Blvd.
Los Angeles, CA 90007
Ph: (213)748-5481
Free: (800)522-4582
Fax: (213)749-1651
E-mail: jcooper@johntracyclinic.org
URL: http://www.jtc.org
Contact: Mr. Jack Cooper, Assoc. Dir. of Communications
Founded: 1942. **Staff:** 79. **Budget:** $5,000,000. **Languages:** English, Spanish. **Multinational. Description:** Provides worldwide services to families of young children with hearing loss. Provides audiological evaluation, parent education and counseling, parent/infant programs, parent-centered preschool, summer sessions and an international correspondence course in English and Spanish. Offers Master's Degree and credential program for graduate students seeking professional certification in auditory oral and auditory verbal, early childhood deaf education. **Telecommunication Services:** TDD, (213)747-2924. **Publications:** *The John Tracy Clinic Bulletin,* semiannual. Newsletter. Contains news of services, campaigns, and events. **Price:** free. **Circulation:** 12,000.

14456 ■ League for the Hard of Hearing

50 Broadway, 6th Fl.
New York, NY 10004
Ph: (917)305-7700
Fax: (917)305-7888
E-mail: info@lhh.org
URL: http://www.lhh.org
Contact: Laurie Hanin PhD, Exec. Dir.
Founded: 1910. **Description:** Strives to improve the lives of infants, children, and adults with all degrees of hearing loss. **Telecommunication Services:** TDD, (917)305-7999.

14457 ■ Model Secondary School for the Deaf (MSSD)

Gallaudet Univ.
800 Florida Ave. NE
Washington, DC 20002
Ph: (202)651-5031
Fax: (202)651-5109
E-mail: michael.peterson@gallaudet.edu
URL: http://clerccenter.gallaudet.edu/mssd
Contact: Michael Peterson, Admissions Coor.
Founded: 1969. **Description:** Authorized under Model Secondary School for the Deaf Act of 1966. An agreement between the Secretary of Health, Education, and Welfare and Gallaudet College

provided for the establishment of the school. Operation was initiated in September 1969, with the intent to provide an exemplary program of instruction and construction of a facility which would exhibit excellence in both architecture and design and would include all innovative auditory and visual devices necessary for education of the deaf. The school's primary service area includes deaf residents of the District of Columbia, Maryland, Virginia, West Virginia, Delaware, and Pennsylvania. Students from all other states may also be accepted as space is available. Additional criteria for admission, such as age level, degree of hearing loss, and previous educational attainment are included in the agreement. **Convention/Meeting:** none. **Libraries: Type:** reference. **Holdings:** 25,000; books, periodicals, software, video recordings. **Subjects:** deaf and sign language, Spanish, career resources, African-American collection, general non-fiction, fiction. **Programs:** Internship; Performing Arts; Software to Go. **Publications:** *Family Newsletter* ● *LRC Update,* monthly. Newsletter. **Price:** free. **Circulation:** 300 ● *Perspectives.* Magazine ● *Preview.* Magazine ● *SAERIE.* Magazine. Features literary works by students. ● Brochures.

14458 ■ National Association of the Deaf (NAD)

8630 Fenton St., Ste.820
Silver Spring, MD 20910-3819
Ph: (301)587-1788 (301)587-1789
Fax: (301)587-1791
E-mail: nadinfo@nad.org
URL: http://www.nad.org
Contact: Nancy J. Bloch, CEO
Founded: 1880. **Members:** 22,000. **Membership Dues:** regular, $40 (annual) ● senior (60 years old and above), student (ID required), $25 (annual) ● international, $60 (annual). **Staff:** 20. **State Groups:** 51. **Description:** Safeguards accessibility and civil rights of America's deaf population in areas of education, employment, healthcare, and telecommunications. **Committees:** Youth Relations Advisory. **Publications:** *NADmag,* bimonthly. Magazine. **Price:** included in membership dues. **Advertising:** accepted. **Conventions/Meetings:** biennial conference (exhibits) - always summer.

14459 ■ National Association of School Nurses for the Deaf (NASND)

c/o Virginia Muraoka-Meyer
CID
4560 Clayton Ave.
St. Louis, MO 63110
E-mail: drobarge@isd.k12.in.us
URL: http://www.nasnd.org
Contact: Virginia Muraoka-Meyer, Contact
Founded: 1992. **Membership Dues:** regular (nurse), $25 (annual) ● associate/retired nurse, $10 (annual) ● regular (nurse), $40 (biennial) ● associate/retired nurse, $15 (biennial). **Description:** Aims to enhance the quality of health education and services to deaf students. Fosters effective communication between school nurses and deaf students. Seeks to lessen workplace isolation by offering professional support and providing opportunities for its members to engage in networking activities. **Publications:** Newsletter, quarterly. Includes health articles. ● Brochure.

14460 ■ National Captioning Institute (NCI)

1900 Gallows Rd., Ste.3000
Vienna, VA 22182
Ph: (703)917-7600
Fax: (703)917-9853
E-mail: mpresswood@ncicap.org
URL: http://www.ncicap.org
Contact: Ms. Mary Presswood, Corporate Admin. Mgr.
Founded: 1979. **Staff:** 160. **Description:** Aims to caption television programs for the deaf and hard-of-hearing on behalf of public and commercial television broadcasters, cablecasters, and the home video industry. Makes available captioning services, making use of a "closed captioning" system that allows coded captions not visible on a normal television set to be decoded and made visible by the use of a

special adapter which may be attached to a television set. **Publications:** Newsletter, semiannual. Alternate Formats: online.

14461 ■ National Education for Assistance Dog Services (NEADS)
PO Box 213
West Boylston, MA 01583
Ph: (978)422-9064
Fax: (978)422-3255
E-mail: info@neads.org
URL: http://www.neads.org
Contact: Sheila O'Brien, Exec. Dir.
Founded: 1976. **Members:** 6,000. **Staff:** 21. **Budget:** $500,000. **Regional Groups:** 21. **State Groups:** 15. **Description:** Interested individuals, clubs, and organizations. Trains dogs to alert deaf or hearing impaired individuals to specific sounds of the environment; also trains dogs to help disabled individuals. After extensive screening, dogs are trained by a professional staff for three to five months, learning: basic obedience; how to respond to household and other sounds including alarm clocks, doorbells, smoke alarms, telephone, babies' crying, kettle whistles, oven timer, car horns, and sirens; how to perform assistance tasks such as pulling wheelchairs, using light switches, and retrieving articles from the floor or high shelves. Maintains speakers' bureau. **Computer Services:** Information services, assistance dogs facts and resources. **Programs:** Early Learning; Prison PUP Partnership. **Affiliated With:** American Humane Association; Assistance Dogs International; Delta Society; International Hearing Society. **Also Known As:** (2006) Dogs for Deaf and Disabled Americans. **Formerly:** New England Assistance Dog Service; (1989) Hearing Ear Dog Program; (1992) New England Assistance Dog Program. **Publications:** *Hearing Ear Dogs: A Sound Relationship.* Brochure ● *Help Make a Miracle—Participate in Our Puppy Program.* Brochure ● *NEADS Newsletter,* quarterly. Alternate Formats: online. Also Cited As: *Hearing Ear Dog Program Newsletter* ● *Service Dogs - Trained to Help the Physically Disabled.* Brochure ● *Sound Friendships - The Story of Willa and Her Hearing Ear Dog.* Book ● *Special Dogs for Special People.* Brochure. **Conventions/Meetings:** quarterly Graduation - meeting (exhibits).

14462 ■ National Family Association for Deaf-Blind (NFADB)
141 Middle Neck Rd.
Sands Point, NY 11050
Free: (800)255-0411
Fax: (516)883-9060
E-mail: nfadb@aol.com
URL: http://www.nfadb.org
Contact: Linda Syler, Pres.
Membership Dues: individual, $15 (annual) ● individual, $30 (triennial) ● life, $100. **Description:** Organization founded on the belief that individuals who are deaf-blind are valued members of society and are entitled to the same opportunities and choices as other members of the community. Runs a large national network of families who focus on issues surrounding deaf-blindness. Advocates for all persons who are deaf-blind of any chronological age and cognitive ability; supports national policy to benefit people who are deaf-blind; encourages the founding and strengthening of family organizations in each state dedicated to assisting families of persons who are deaf-blind; shares information related to deaf-blindness and provides resources and referrals; collaborates with professionals who work with persons who are deaf-blind.

14463 ■ National Hearing Conservation Association (NHCA)
7995 E Prentice Ave., Ste.100
Greenwood Village, CO 80111
Ph: (303)224-9022
Fax: (303)770-1614
E-mail: nhca@gwami.com
URL: http://www.hearingconservation.org
Contact: Karen Wojdyla, Exec. Dir.
Founded: 1976. **Members:** 480. **Staff:** 2. **Description:** Individuals holding advanced academic degrees

in a discipline involving hearing and hearing loss; professional service organizations engaged in industrial hearing conservation programs; companies that manufacture or sell occupational noise or hearing loss products. Promotes hearing conservation in all sectors of society. Encourages education and standards development among members and industrial groups; monitors legislation and regulatory activities related to hearing conservation. **Libraries: Type:** reference. **Holdings:** archival material. **Awards:** Hearing Conservation Award. **Frequency:** annual. **Type:** recognition ● Media Award. **Frequency:** annual. **Type:** recognition ● Michael Beall Threadgill Award. **Frequency:** annual. **Type:** recognition. **Computer Services:** database ● mailing lists. **Publications:** *NHCA Membership Directory,* annual. Lists members in alphabetical, geographical and categorical order. Includes consumer guide. **Price:** included in membership dues. **Circulation:** 450. **Advertising:** accepted ● *Resources in Hearing Conservation,* annual. Features a compilation of references and films listed in previous "Spectrum" issues. **Price:** included in membership dues; $20.00/issue. **Circulation:** 700 ● *Spectrum,* quarterly. Newsletter. Provides information on technology, research, practice, and federal and state legal and regulatory activities. Includes book reviews. **Price:** included in membership dues; $10.00/issue for nonmembers; $20.00 for supplements. **Circulation:** 500. **Advertising:** accepted.

14464 ■ National Institute on Deafness and Other Communication Disorders Information Clearinghouse
c/o National Institutes of Health
31 Center Dr., MSC 2320
Bethesda, MD 20892-2320
Free: (800)241-1044
Fax: (301)770-8977
E-mail: nidcdinfo@nidcd.nih.gov
URL: http://www.nidcd.nih.gov
Founded: 1988. **Description:** Disseminates information on the normal and disordered processes of hearing, balance, smell, taste, voice, speech, and language. **Computer Services:** database, combined health information. **Telecommunication Services:** TDD, (800)241-1055. **Formerly:** (1998) National Committee in Deafness and Other Communication Disorders. **Publications:** *Information Resources for Human Communication Disorders,* annual. Directory. Encourages networking among those with an interest in deafness and communication disorders. **Price:** free. Alternate Formats: online ● *NIDCD Inside.* Newsletter ● *NIDCD Publications List,* annual. Pamphlet.

14465 ■ National Service Dog Center (NSDC)
c/o Delta Society
875 124th Ave. NW, Ste.101
Bellevue, WA 98005
Ph: (425)226-7357
Fax: (425)235-1076
E-mail: info@deltasociety.org
URL: http://www.deltasociety.org
Contact: Lawrence J. Norvell, Pres./CEO
Founded: 1977. **Staff:** 1. **Description:** Serves as a program of the Delta Society. Provides service, dog education, advocacy and referral services. Promotes the health benefits of service animals for people with disabilities. **Libraries: Type:** reference. **Formerly:** (1983) Hearing Dog Program; (1987) Hearing Dog Project; (1989) National Center for Hearing Dog Information; (1993) Hearing Dog Resource Center. **Publications:** *Service Animal Resource Directory,* annual. Lists service dog training programs and information about selecting a supplier that best meets the consumer's needs. Alternate Formats: online ● *Service Dogs Welcome!.* Video.

14466 ■ Oral Hearing-Impaired Section (OHIS)
3417 Volta Pl. NW
Washington, DC 20007
Ph: (202)337-5220
Fax: (202)337-8314

E-mail: info@agbell.org
URL: http://www.agbell.org
Contact: K. Todd Houston PhD, Exec. Dir.
Founded: 1964. **Members:** 345. **Membership Dues:** regular, $50 (annual) ● student, $30 (annual). **Staff:** 1. **Local Groups:** 3. **Description:** Section of the Alexander Graham Bell Association for the Deaf (see separate entry). Persons who are deaf or hard of hearing predominantly use speech and lipreading work. Encourages deaf young people and their families to use speech, lipreading, and residual hearing. Participates in regional, national, and international conferences on deafness. Appears on television and radio programs to demonstrate communications skills. Seeks to dispel outmoded conceptions about deafness. Supports: richer educational opportunities for the hearing impaired; workshops and outings for deaf or hard of hearing children and their families and teachers; scholarship funds for qualified students with hearing impairments; improved methods for developing better speech, voice, lipreading, and auditory training techniques. **Awards:** OHIS Youth Achievement. **Frequency:** annual. **Type:** recognition. **Recipient:** for members. **Formerly:** (1988) Oral Deaf Adults Section. **Publications:** *Valta Voices OHIS Section,* bimonthly. Magazine. **Advertising:** accepted. **Conventions/Meetings:** biennial meeting.

14467 ■ Parents' Section of the Alexander Graham Bell Association for the Deaf and Hard of Hearing (AG Bell)
3417 Volta Pl. NW
Washington, DC 20007
Ph: (202)337-5220
Free: (866)337-5220
Fax: (202)337-8314
E-mail: jripper@agbell.org
URL: http://www.agbell.org
Contact: Mr. K. Todd Houston PhD, Exec. Dir./CEO
Founded: 1890. **Members:** 5,000. **Membership Dues:** standard, $40 (annual) ● premium, $50 (annual) ● household, $60 (annual) ● student, senior, $30 (annual). **Staff:** 23. **Budget:** $4,000,000. **State Groups:** 30. **Local Groups:** 28. **National Groups:** 3. **Description:** Resource, support network and advocate for listening, learning, talking and living independently with hearing loss. Promotes the use of spoken language and hearing technology through publications, outreach, training, scholarships and financial aid. **Libraries: Type:** by appointment only. **Holdings:** 12,000; archival material, biographical archives, books, monographs, periodicals, photographs. **Subjects:** deafness, hearing loss, auditory learning, spoken language, Auditory-Verbal therapy, speech pathology, audiology, deaf education, early intervention, cochlear implants, hearing aids, newborn hearing screening, auditory-oral therapy. **Awards:** Alexander Graham Bell Award of Distinction. **Frequency:** annual. **Type:** trophy. **Recipient:** to an individual or organization outside the field of education or rehabilitation of the hearing impaired for outstanding contributions to the field ● Arts and Sciences Financial Aid. **Frequency:** annual. **Type:** scholarship. **Recipient:** to students 6 to 19 years old diagnosed with moderate to profound hearing loss prior to learning, listening and talking ● Cochlear Implant Fellowship Award. **Frequency:** annual. **Type:** fellowship. **Recipient:** for professionals in the fields of audiology, speech-language pathology, auditory-verbal therapy and education ● College Scholarship Awards. **Frequency:** annual. **Type:** scholarship. **Recipient:** to students diagnosed with a moderate to profound hearing loss prior to learning, listening and talking and who are seeking to continue their undergraduate or graduate level education in any field of study ● Early Hearing Detection and Intervention (EHDI) Award. **Type:** recognition. **Recipient:** for hospitals that provide exemplary service to families and children who are screened, evaluated and identified with hearing loss ● Honors of the Association. **Frequency:** biennial. **Type:** trophy. **Recipient:** to an individual for their dedication to, and sustained efforts toward, the goals and purposes of the association and enhancing the lives of people with hearing loss ● International Voices for Deafness. **Frequency:** an-

nual. **Type:** trophy. **Recipient:** to an organization or individual based outside US and its territories for dedication to and sustained efforts to the betterment of the lives of people with hearing loss ● Parent-Infant Preschool Services. **Frequency:** annual. **Type:** scholarship. **Recipient:** to families of children under six years old who have a moderate to profound hearing loss prior to learning, listening and speaking ● School Age Financial Aid. **Frequency:** annual. **Type:** scholarship. **Recipient:** to students 6 to 21 years old diagnosed with a moderate to profound hearing loss prior to learning, listening and talking ● Volta Award. **Frequency:** annual. **Type:** trophy. **Recipient:** to organizations or individuals for increasing public awareness of the problems and potential of people with hearing loss. **Computer Services:** database, of articles from the membership magazine ● mailing lists, of members. **Telecommunication Services:** TDD, (202)337-5221. **Caucuses:** Public School Caucus. **Committees:** College Leadership. **Programs:** Children's Legal Advocacy; First Years Certificate in Auditory Learning; Parent Advocacy Training; Public School Program Assistance. **Special Interest Groups:** Deaf and Hard of Hearing Section; International Professional Section; Parent Section. **Formerly:** (1989) International Parents' Organization; (2003) Parents' Section of the Alexander Graham Bell Association for the Deaf. **Publications:** *The Volta Review*, 3/year. Journal. Features the latest research, current perspectives and case studies focused on hearing loss and spoken language. **Price:** $10.00 each; $62.00 includes Volta Voices; $24.95 each - monograph issues. ISSN: 0042-8639. **Circulation:** 4,000. **Advertising:** accepted ● *Volta Voices*, bimonthly. Magazine. **Price:** $7.50 each; $62.00 includes The Volta Review. ISSN: 1074-8016. **Circulation:** 5,000. **Advertising:** accepted. **Conventions/Meetings:** biennial convention, topics on deafness and hearing loss, hearing health, education, spoken language communication and related technologies (exhibits) - late June or early July, during even-numbered years. 2008 June 27-30, Milwaukee, WI - **Avg. Attendance:** 2250.

14468 ■ Phone-TTY
1246 Rte., 46 W
Parsippany, NJ 07054-2121
Ph: (973)229-6627
Free: (888)332-3889
Fax: (973)299-7768
E-mail: phonetty@aol.com
URL: http://www.phone-tty.com
Contact: Anna M. Terrazzino, Exec. Dir.
Founded: 1969. **Members:** 20. **Staff:** 5. **Budget:** $500,000. **Description:** Seeks to develop and promote better communication for the deaf using an ordinary telephone and current technology. Installs computerized phone-teletype equipment in the homes of individuals who are deaf, enabling these individuals to communicate with local police, hospitals, answering services, and news services, as well as members of the deaf community who have a PHONE-TTY in their homes. Researches, designs, manufactures, and distributes other communication devices for the deaf. Solicits grants and donations. **Telecommunication Services:** teletype, (973)299-6626. **Conventions/Meetings:** annual meeting (exhibits).

14469 ■ Registry of Interpreters for the Deaf (RID)
333 Commerce St.
Alexandria, VA 22314
Ph: (703)838-0030 (703)838-0459
Fax: (703)838-0454
E-mail: admin@rid.org
URL: http://www.rid.org
Contact: Clay Nettles, Exec. Dir.
Founded: 1964. **Members:** 10,300. **Membership Dues:** certified, $115 (annual) ● associate, $85 (annual) ● student, $25 (annual) ● supporting, $24 (annual) ● organization, $150 (annual). **Staff:** 11. **Budget:** $1,500,000. **Regional Groups:** 5. **State Groups:** 58. **Description:** Advocates sign language and oral interpreters program. Maintains 34 committees. Compiles statistics. **Awards:** Elizabeth Benson Scholarship. **Frequency:** annual. **Type:** scholarship.

Recipient: for a student member who has completed at least one semester of a related program. **Telecommunication Services:** teletype, (301)608-0562. **Programs:** Certification Maintenance Program; Ethical Practices System; National Testing System. **Formerly:** National Registry of Professional Interpreters and Translators for the Deaf. **Publications:** *Registry of Interpreters for the Deaf—Proceedings of National Conventions*, biennial. **Price:** $11.95/copy. **Advertising:** accepted ● *Views*, monthly ● Also publishes texts and other materials on interpretation, transliteration, and translation. **Conventions/Meetings:** biennial conference, includes educational workshops of interpreters (exhibits) ● workshop.

14470 ■ Signing Exact English Center for the Advancement of Deaf Children (SEE Center)
PO Box 1181
Los Alamitos, CA 90720
Ph: (562)430-1467
Fax: (562)795-6614
E-mail: seecenter@seecenter.org
URL: http://www.seecenter.org
Contact: Esther Zawolkow, Contact
Founded: 1984. **Description:** Works to promote early identification and intervention, to develop understanding of principles of signing, to provide information to parents on deafness and related topics and to foster the positive development of self concept in the deaf child. Conducts workshops, and sign skills evaluations. Provides introductory information. **Conventions/Meetings:** workshop.

14471 ■ Telecommunications for the Deaf and Hard of Hearing, Inc. (TDI)
8630 Fenton St., Ste.604
Silver Spring, MD 20910
Ph: (301)589-3786
Fax: (301)589-3797
E-mail: info@tdi-online.org
URL: http://www.tdi-online.org
Contact: Claude Stout, Exec. Dir.
Founded: 1968. **Members:** 30,000. **Membership Dues:** large business (with 15 or more employees), $75 (annual) ● small business (with less than 15 employees), government agency, $50 (annual) ● individual, household, $25 (annual). **Staff:** 7. **Budget:** $1,200,000. **Description:** Promotes equal access to telecommunications, media and information technology for individuals who are deaf, late-deafened, hard of hearing, or deaf-blind. Advocates for standards and compatibility for all telecommunication and media devices. Promotes closed captioning on television, cable, and the Internet. Sells International TTY Logo Decals to the public. Administers Community Emergency Preparedness Information Network (CEPIN) Project and develop disaster preparedness education programs for deaf and hard of hearing people. **Awards:** Andrew Saks Engineering Award. **Frequency:** biennial. **Type:** recognition. **Recipient:** for outstanding contributions in improving visual accessibility of information, entertainment, or telecommunications in the U.S. through efforts in design, electronics or engineering ● H. Latham Breunig Humanitarian Award. **Frequency:** biennial. **Type:** recognition. **Recipient:** for outstanding contributions to the program or activities of TDI ● I. Lee Brody Lifetime Achievement Award. **Frequency:** biennial. **Type:** recognition. **Recipient:** for individual who has devoted significant time and energy over an extended number of years in improving the visual accessibility of information, entertainment, or telecommunications in the U.S. ● James Marsters Promotion Award. **Frequency:** biennial. **Type:** recognition. **Recipient:** for outstanding contributions in improving visual accessibility of information, entertainment, or telecommunications in the U.S. through efforts in promotion, marketing or public relations ● Robert H. Weitbrecht Telecommunication Access Award. **Frequency:** biennial. **Type:** recognition. **Recipient:** for outstanding contributions by any means to improve the visual accessibility of information, entertainment, or telecommunications in U.S. **Computer Services:** Mailing lists, sell access to membership list by disseminating materials to deaf and hard of hearing people. **Additional Websites:** http://www.cepintdi.org. **Telecom-**

munication Services: electronic mail, execdir@tdi-online.org ● teletype, (301)589-3006. **Projects:** Community Emergency Preparedness Information Network. **Formerly:** (1980) Teletypewriters for the Deaf; (2000) Telecommunications for the Deaf, Inc.; (2004) TDI. **Publications:** *A Phone of Our Own - The Deaf Insurrection Against Ma Bell*. Book ● *The Blue Book - TDI National Directory of TTY Numbers*, annual. Contains directory and resource guide for deaf community. **Price:** $20.00. **Advertising:** accepted. Alternate Formats: online ● *The eBlue Book Online Directory*. Alternate Formats: online ● *Emergency Access Evaluation Kit*. Manual. Contains emergency personnel training for use of TTY's and dealing with deaf and hard of hearing callers. **Price:** $35.00 ● *Emergency Responders and the Deaf and Hard of Hearing Community: Taking the First Steps to Disaster Preparedness*. Manual. **Price:** $24.00 ● *GA & SK Etiquette*. Book ● *GA-SK Newsletter*, quarterly. **Advertising:** accepted ● *One Thing Led to the Next, The Real History of TTYs*. Book ● *Using Your TTY/TDD*. Video. **Price:** $34.95. **Conventions/Meetings:** biennial conference (exhibits) - always summer.

14472 ■ TRIPOD
1727 W Burbank Blvd.
Burbank, CA 91506
Ph: (818)972-2080
Fax: (818)972-2090
E-mail: info@tripod.org
Contact: Christopher W. Opie, Exec.Dir.
Founded: 1983. **Description:** Established a private/public partnership with Burbank Unified School District to assist individuals who are deaf or hard of hearing. Offers educational programs. **Awards:** Tripod Friends Award. **Frequency:** annual. **Type:** recognition. **Telecommunication Services:** phone referral service ● TDD, Grapevine hotline, (800)352-8888. **Publications:** *Language Says It All*. Videos ● *We Can Do Anything*. Video.

Heart Disease

14473 ■ Hypertrophic Cardiomyopathy Association (HCMA)
PO Box 306
Hibernia, NJ 07842
Ph: (973)983-7429
Fax: (973)983-7870
E-mail: support@4hcm.org
URL: http://www.4hcm.org
Contact: Lisa Salberg, Pres.
Founded: 1996. **Membership Dues:** regular, $50 (annual) ● overseas, $65 (annual). **Multinational**. **Description:** Provides information, support and advocacy for individuals with hypertrophic cardiomyopathy. Promotes education on symptoms of and treatment options for hypertrophic cardiomyopathy. Heightens awareness of sudden death and life threatening arrhythmia. **Computer Services:** Information services, hypertropic cardiomyopathy resources ● online services, message boards and chatroom. **Publications:** *Heart Link Online*. Newsletter. Alternate Formats: online.

Hematology

14474 ■ American Society of Hematology (ASH)
1900 M St. NW, Ste.200
Washington, DC 20036
Ph: (202)776-0544
Fax: (202)776-0545
E-mail: ash@hematology.org
URL: http://www.hematology.org
Contact: Martha Liggett, Exec. Dir.
Founded: 1958. **Members:** 10,000. **Membership Dues:** active, $225 (annual) ● international, $245 (annual) ● associate, $50 (annual). **Staff:** 45. **Description:** Hematologists (specialists in the study of blood) and other persons holding doctorate degrees with an interest in the field. Promotes exchange of

information and ideas related to blood and blood-forming tissues and investigation of hematologic problems. Offers educational programs. **Awards:** ASH Scholar Awards. **Frequency:** annual. **Type:** grant. **Recipient:** for research in the field of hematology ● Dameshek Prize. **Frequency:** annual. **Type:** recognition. **Recipient:** for outstanding contribution to hematology ● E. Donnall Thomas Lectureship. **Frequency:** annual. **Type:** recognition. **Recipient:** for notable scientific contributions in the field of hematology ● Stratton Medal. **Frequency:** annual. **Type:** recognition. **Computer Services:** Mailing lists. **Telecommunication Services:** electronic mail, mliggett@hematology.org. **Committees:** Education; Financial Affairs; Membership; Practice; Public Information; Publications; Training Programs. **Publications:** *Blood*, semimonthly. Journal ● *The Hematologist: ASH News & Reports*, 3/year. Newsletter ● *Meeting Program*, annual. **Conventions/Meetings:** annual meeting (exhibits).

14475 ■ American Society of Pediatric Hematology/Oncology (ASPHO)
4700 W Lake Ave.
Glenview, IL 60025-1485
Ph: (847)375-4716
Free: (877)734-9557
Fax: (877)734-9557
E-mail: info@aspho.org
URL: http://www.aspho.org
Contact: Cynthia Porter, Exec. Dir.
Founded: 1981. **Members:** 1,020. **Membership Dues:** active, $335 (annual) ● affiliate (without optional journal), $50 (annual) ● affiliate (with optional journal), $75 (annual) ● trainee, $115. **Budget:** $600,000. **Description:** Promotes optimal care of children and adolescents with blood disorders and cancer by advancing research, education, treatment and professional practice. Scientists, and others interested in comprehensive care or research in the field. Promotes the knowledge, understanding, and management of disorders of the blood and of cancer in children. Seeks improvements in the total care of children with these diseases through the fostering of education and all relevant clinical and basic research. Provides a forum for the exchange of ideas on issues in the field. Cooperates with other societies concerned with the field. **Awards:** Distinguished Career Award. **Frequency:** annual. **Type:** recognition. **Recipient:** for lifetime contributions to research treatment and training in pediatric hematology/oncology ● Young Investigator Awards. **Frequency:** annual. **Type:** recognition. **Recipient:** for outstanding research abstract submitted to annual meeting. **Computer Services:** Mailing lists. **Publications:** *Journal of Pediatric Hematology/Oncology*, 9/year. **Advertising:** accepted. Also Cited As: *American Journal of Pediatric Hematology/Oncology* ● *President's Letter*, bimonthly. Newsletter. Contains news of the society, members, and committees. Alternate Formats: online ● Membership Directory, annual. **Conventions/Meetings:** annual meeting (exhibits).

14476 ■ Aplastic Anemia and MDS International Foundation (AA&MDSIF)
PO Box 310
Churchton, MD 20733
Ph: (410)867-0242
Free: (800)747-2820
Fax: (410)867-0240
E-mail: help@aamds.org
URL: http://www.aamds.org/aplastic
Contact: Marilyn Baker MBS, Pres.
Founded: 1983. **Members:** 21,000. **Staff:** 9. **Languages:** English, French, German, Italian, Russian, Spanish. **Multinational. Description:** Serves as a resource for patient assistance, advocacy, and emotional support; provides educational materials and updated medical information; funds medical research to find effective treatments and cure for aplastic anemia, myelodysplastic syndromes, paroxysmal nocturnal hemoglobinuria, and related bone marrow failure diseases. **Libraries: Type:** open to the public. **Subjects:** Aplastic Anemia, Myelodysplastic Syndromes, Paroxysmal Nocturnal Hemoglobinuria, Acquired Bone Marrow Diseases. **Awards:** Es-

tablished Researcher Award. **Frequency:** annual. **Type:** monetary ● New Researcher Award. **Frequency:** annual. **Type:** monetary. **Computer Services:** database ● online services, publication. **Formerly:** (1999) Aplastic Anemia Foundation of America. **Publications:** *Aplastic Anemia Basic Explanations*, periodic. Describes the course of the disease and current treatment options. Includes glossary of medical terms. **Price:** free ● *eBulletin*, monthly. Bulletins. **Circulation:** 15,000. Alternate Formats: online ● *Families Coping With AA and MDS*. Brochure ● *Iron Overload Management*. Brochure ● *Managing Treatment Decisions*, periodic. **Price:** free ● *MDS Basic Explanations*, periodic. Describes the course of the disease and current treatment options. Includes glossary of medical terms. **Price:** free ● *PNH Basic Explanations*, periodic. Describes the course of the disease and current treatment options. Includes glossary of medical terms. **Price:** free ● Newsletter (in English and Spanish), quarterly. Provides information on aplastic and other bone marrow failure diseases. **Price:** free. **Circulation:** 20,000. Alternate Formats: online. **Conventions/Meetings:** annual Patient and Family Conference, for patients and their families.

14477 ■ Children's Blood Foundation (CBF)
111 W 57th St., Ste.420
New York, NY 10019
Ph: (212)297-4336
Fax: (212)888-7724
E-mail: info@childrensbloodfoundation.org
URL: http://www.childrensbloodfoundation.org
Contact: John Calicchio, Chm.
Founded: 1952. **Regional Groups:** 1. **Description:** Seeks to raise funds to combat diseases of the blood in children, such as Leukemia, Hemophilia, Thalassemia (Cooley's anemia), childhood cancers, sickle cell, and other anemias and diseases of the immune system, and AIDS. Supports a total patient care center in the New York Hospital-Cornell Medical Center, which includes diagnostic and treatment clinics, progressive research laboratories, and intensive training of physicians in the specialty of pediatric hematology/oncology. Sponsors specialized social events. **Awards:** Key of Life. **Frequency:** annual. **Type:** recognition. **Computer Services:** Mailing lists. **Programs:** Employer Matching Gift. **Publications:** *The Key*, semiannual. Newsletter.

14478 ■ Cooley's Anemia Foundation (CAF)
330 7th Ave., No. 900
New York, NY 10001
Free: (800)522-7222
Fax: (212)279-5999
E-mail: info@cooleysanemia.org
URL: http://www.cooleysanemia.org
Contact: Gina Cioffi, Natl. Exec. Dir.
Founded: 1954. **Members:** 8,000. **Staff:** 11. **State Groups:** 4. **Local Groups:** 6. **National Groups:** 16. **Languages:** Chinese, English, Italian, Polish, Spanish. **Description:** Works to advance the treatment and cure of Cooley's Anemia (also known as Thalassemia). Conducts national programs that provide medical research patient services, awareness and education. Sponsors the Thalassemia Action Group, a support group for patients and families. Provides information about the condition referrals to local medical sources, brochures, newsletters and other information. Provides medical supplies to patients in need, Anemia or other Thalassemias. Sponsors Thalassemia Action Group, a networking task force of young adult victims of Thalassemia. Operates speakers' bureau. Conducts blood drives. **Libraries: Type:** by appointment only. **Subjects:** Thalassemia Major, Intermedia, treatment and research. **Awards:** Fellowship Grant. **Frequency:** annual. **Type:** grant. **Recipient:** for fellowships and innovative and promising research projects ● Humanitarian Achievement. **Type:** recognition ● Patient Scholarship. **Frequency:** annual. **Type:** recognition. **Recipient:** for patients pursuing undergraduate and graduate degrees ● **Type:** recognition. **Recipient:** for scientific and humanitarian achievement. **Computer Services:** database, referral resources ● mailing lists. **Telecommunication Services:** electronic mail, g.cioffi@cooleysanemia.org. **Committees:** Medical Advisory;

Patient Services; Public Education. **Subgroups:** Thalassemia Action. **Formerly:** (1977) Cooley's Anemia Blood and Research Foundation for Children. **Publications:** *CAF Medical Update*, semiannual. Newsletter ● *Lifeline*, semiannual. Newsletter ● Annual Report, annual. Alternate Formats: online ● Also publishes "What is Thalassemia Trait?", "Desferal Q&A" and "What Is Cooley's Anemia?". **Conventions/Meetings:** annual Continuing Medical Education Meetings - spring ● annual Patient/Parent Conference, with display products and services for patients and families (exhibits) - in the spring.

14479 ■ Histiocytosis Association of America
332 N Broadway
Pitman, NJ 08071
Ph: (856)589-6606
Free: (800)548-2758
Fax: (856)589-6614
E-mail: jmt4histio@aol.com
URL: http://www.histio.org
Contact: Jeffrey M. Toughill, Pres.
Founded: 1985. **Members:** 5,200. **Staff:** 6. **Budget:** $850,000. **Description:** Patients, families, and friends of those suffering from histiocytic disorders; physicians, oncologists, and hematologists working in the field of histiocytosis research. (Histiocytosis is a rare disease that causes histiocytes, a type of white blood cell, to multiply and attack organs, body systems, or bones.) Works to provide support for patients and their families and friends. Funds research on the cause and treatment of histiocytosis. Acts as a referral service. Maintains speakers' bureau. **Libraries: Type:** reference. **Holdings:** photographs. **Awards:** Medical Research. **Frequency:** annual. **Type:** monetary. **Computer Services:** database. **Committees:** Association News; Lay Information; Live Conferences; Postings. **Formerly:** (1987) Histiocytosis-X Association of America. **Publications:** *The Facts About HLH/FHL*. Brochure. **Price:** free. Alternate Formats: online ● *The Facts about Langerhans Cell Histiocytosis* (in English and Spanish). Brochure. **Price:** free. Alternate Formats: online ● *The Facts about Langerhans Cell Histiocytosis and Diabetes Insipidus*. Brochure ● *Patient Directory*, periodic ● Newsletter, quarterly. Reports on histiocytosis patients, their families, physicians, researchers, and other interested parties. **Price:** free. **Circulation:** 5,200. **Conventions/Meetings:** periodic Parent, Patient, Physicians Support Meeting - regional meeting.

14480 ■ International Society of Blood Purification (ISBP)
c/o Prof. Thomas A. Golper, MD, Sec.
S-3303 MCN
Vanderbilt Univ. Medical Ctr.
1161 21st Ave. S
Nashville, TN 37232-2372
Ph: (615)343-2220
Fax: (615)343-7156
E-mail: thomas.golper@vanderbilt.edu
URL: http://www.isbp.org
Contact: Prof. Thomas A. Golper MD, Sec.
Founded: 1982. **Members:** 140. **Membership Dues:** regular, $125 (annual). **Multinational. Description:** Represents the interests of blood purification professionals dedicated to the development, improvement and dosing of extracorporeal and peritoneal treatment modalities of acute and terminal renal failure. Works on the new and future technologies and principles of blood purification and organ replacement. **Publications:** *Blood Purification*, bimonthly. Journal. **Price:** included in membership dues. ISSN: 0253-5068. Alternate Formats: online. **Conventions/Meetings:** annual meeting - 2007 Sept. 6-8, Prague, Czech Republic.

14481 ■ International Society for Experimental Hematology (ISEH)
2025 M St. NW, Ste.800
Washington, DC 20036-3309
Ph: (202)367-1183
Fax: (202)367-2183

E-mail: iseh@smithbucklin.com
URL: http://www.iseh.org
Contact: Patrice McKenney, Exec. Dir.
Founded: 1972. **Members:** 1,400. **Membership Dues:** active, $150 (annual) ● in-training, $55 (annual). **Staff:** 2. **Multinational. Description:** Scientists and health care professionals in the field of experimental hematology. Seeks to advance the science and practice of hematology; promotes professional development of members. Serves as a forum for the exchange of information on experimental hematology and related topics; sponsors research and educational programs. **Libraries: Type:** reference. **Holdings:** 13; periodicals. **Subjects:** experimental hematology. **Awards:** ISEH Honorary Metcalf Lecture and Award. **Frequency:** annual. **Type:** recognition. **Recipient:** to scientists for their outstanding contributions to the field ● ISEH Travel Grants. **Frequency:** annual. **Type:** grant. **Recipient:** to young investigators for their latest cutting edge research ● New Investigator Awards. **Frequency:** annual. **Type:** recognition. **Recipient:** to new investigators for their outstanding work. **Computer Services:** database ● mailing lists ● online services. **Telecommunication Services:** electronic mail, iseh@dc.sba.com. **Committees:** Nominating; Publications; Scientific Program. **Task Forces:** Emerging Leaders. **Publications:** *Experimental Hematology*, monthly. Journal. Features research reports, reviews, letters to the editor and abstracts of the annual meeting of the ISEH. **Price:** included in membership dues; $339.00 for nonmembers. ISSN: 0301-472X. **Advertising:** accepted ● Membership Directory, periodic. Alternate Formats: online. **Conventions/Meetings:** annual Scientific Meeting, poster sessions and company exhibits (exhibits).

14482 ■ International Society on Thrombosis and Haemostasis (ISTH)
932 ME Jones Bldg.
CB 7035
UNC Medical School
Chapel Hill, NC 27599-7035
Ph: (919)929-3807
Fax: (919)929-3935
E-mail: headquarters@isth.org
URL: http://www.med.unc.edu/isth
Contact: Cathy Cole, Exec. Sec.
Founded: 1969. **Members:** 2,800. **Membership Dues:** individual, $160 (annual). **Staff:** 5. **Multinational. Description:** Biomedical scientists in over 70 countries interested in thrombosis (the presence of a clot in a blood vessel) and haemostasis (the arrest of bleeding). Engages in research and education concerning thrombosis, haemostasis, blood clotting, and vascular biology. **Awards: Frequency:** biennial. **Type:** recognition. **Computer Services:** database, Factor IX ● database, mutations ● database, Protein S Deficiency: A Database of Mutations ● database, SSC VWF. **Committees:** Scientific; Scientific and Standardization. **Formerly:** (2002) International Society on Thrombosis and Haemostasis. **Publications:** *Journal of Thrombosis and Haemostasis*, monthly. ISSN: 1538-7933. **Advertising:** accepted. Alternate Formats: online. Also Cited As: *JTH* ● Abstracts of congressional proceedings and lectures published as special issues of journal, and annual reports of SSC Scientific subcommittees. **Conventions/Meetings:** biennial International Congress (exhibits) - 2009 July 11-18, Boston, MA; 2011 July 16-23, Kyoto, Japan ● annual Scientific and Standardization Committee - meeting.

14483 ■ National Anemia Action Council (NAAC)
555 E Wells St., Ste.1100
Milwaukee, WI 53202
Ph: (414)225-0138
Fax: (414)276-3349
E-mail: info@anemia.org
URL: http://www.anemia.org
Contact: Joan Geiger, Assoc. Exec. Dir.
Description: Raises awareness of health care professionals and the public regarding the prevalence, symptoms, consequences and undertreatment of anemia. Improves anemia identification, treatment

and patient outcomes. **Computer Services:** Information services, anemia facts and resources.

14484 ■ National Hemophilia Foundation (NHF)
116 W 32nd St., 11th Fl.
New York, NY 10001
Ph: (212)328-3700
Free: (800)42-HANDI
Fax: (212)328-3777
E-mail: handi@hemophilia.org
URL: http://www.hemophilia.org
Contact: Dr. Alan Kinniburgh PhD, CEO
Founded: 1948. **Members:** 1,500. **Membership Dues:** person with bleeding disorder, family, $25 (annual) ● researcher, physician, industry, $100 (annual) ● social worker, physical therapist, nurse, $50 (annual). **Staff:** 40. **Local Groups:** 48. **Description:** Consists of individuals with hemophilia, their families, medical and paramedical professionals, and other interested persons. (Hemophilia is a hereditary disease in which blood clotting is abnormally delayed.) Supports research through postgraduate fellowship program; disseminates literature for the public and medical and paramedical personnel. Conducts educational programs. Operates information center to provide research assistance, referrals, and comprehensive resources on hemophilia, HIV/AIDS, and related topics. Chapters help in blood recruitment drives and referral services for patients and sponsor summer camps for young people with hemophilia. Maintains library. **Awards:** Judith Graham Pool Fellowships. **Type:** fellowship. **Recipient:** for hemophilia research ● Kevin Child Scholarship. **Frequency:** annual. **Type:** scholarship. **Recipient:** to a qualified individual in memory of Kevin Child. **Councils:** Medical and Scientific Advisory. **Programs:** First Step; National Preventive. **Projects:** Red Flag. **Affiliated With:** World Federation of Hemophilia. **Formerly:** (1956) Hemophilia Foundation. **Publications:** *Directory of Hemophilia Treatment Centers*, periodic ● *HemAware*, bimonthly. Magazine. **Price:** free for members ● *HemAware Jr.*, bimonthly. Magazine. **Price:** free for members ● *NHF eNotes*, monthly. Newsletter. Alternate Formats: online. **Conventions/Meetings:** annual meeting (exhibits).

14485 ■ National Phlebotomy Association (NPA)
1901 Brightseat Rd.
Landover, MD 20785
Free: (866)329-9108
Fax: (301)386-4203
E-mail: naltphle@aol.com
URL: http://www.nationalphlebotomy.org
Contact: Diane Crawford, CEO
Founded: 1978. **Members:** 12,000. **Membership Dues:** certification, $100 (annual). **Regional Groups:** 10. **Description:** Offers educational programs for phlebotomists; to accredit phlebotomy programs; to give national certification examinations in phlebotomy at the request of approved program. (Phlebotomy is the collection of a blood specimen for analysis in the treatment of disease.) Conducts regional workshops and educational programs. Compiles statistics. **Publications:** *National Phlebotomy Association Certified Phlebotomists Registry*, periodic ● *Self Study Modules in Phlebotomy*. **Conventions/Meetings:** semiannual conference (exhibits).

14486 ■ Sickle Cell Disease Association of America (SCDAA)
231 E Baltimore St., Ste.800
Baltimore, MD 21202
Ph: (410)528-1555
Free: (800)421-8453
Fax: (410)528-1495
E-mail: scdaa@sicklecelldisease.org
URL: http://www.sicklecelldisease.org
Contact: Willarda V. Edwards MD, Pres./COO
Founded: 1971. **Members:** 65. **Membership Dues:** organization, $500 (annual). **Staff:** 6. **Budget:** $624,000. **Local Groups:** 86. **Description:** Community groups involved in sickle cell anemia programs throughout the U.S. Provides leadership on a national level in order to create awareness in all circles of the

negative impact of sickle cell anemia on the health and economic, social, and educational well-being of the individual and his/her family and to create awareness of the requirements for resolution. Prepares and distribute substantive educational materials. Develops and promotes implementation of service program standards that will be in the best interest of the affected population. Provides ongoing technical assistance to interested groups. Encourages adequate support for research. Operates Charles F. Whitten Sickle Cell Summer Research Apprenticeships, Roland J. Nyman Research Fund, and Rick Berry Fund. **Awards:** Kermit B. Nash Academic Scholarship. **Frequency:** annual. **Type:** scholarship. **Recipient:** for individuals with sickle cell disease ● **Type:** recognition. **Recipient:** for outstanding service ● SCDAA Post Doctoral Research Fellowship. **Frequency:** annual. **Type:** fellowship. **Recipient:** for young investigators in sickle cell disease related research. **Computer Services:** Mailing lists. **Committees:** Legislation; Public Relations; Scientific Advisory. **Formerly:** National Association for Sickle Cell Disease. **Publications:** *Comprehensive Guide to Sickle Cell Disease and SCDAA Services* ● *HELP, A Guide to Sickle Cell Disease Programs and Services*, periodic ● *SCD Parent/Teacher Guide* ● *Sickle Cell Disease Association of America Newsletter*, quarterly. **Price:** free ● *Sickle Cell Disease Association of America Viewpoint*, periodic ● *Sickle Cell Disease Fact Brochures* ● Brochures ● Pamphlets ● Annual Report, annual. Alternate Formats: online. **Conventions/Meetings:** annual convention (exhibits) - always October ● periodic Regional Educational Conference.

14487 ■ Society for the Advancement of Blood Management (SABM)
555 E Wells St., Ste.1100
Milwaukee, WI 53202-3823
Ph: (414)276-9339
Free: (800)823-8325
Fax: (414)276-3349
E-mail: info@sabm.org
URL: http://www.sabm.org
Contact: Robert J. Kopchinski, Exec. Dir.
Founded: 2001. **Membership Dues:** active (physician), $150 (annual) ● associate, affiliate, $100 (annual) ● student, $10 (annual) ● active - Latin America, $75 (annual) ● associate, affiliate - Latin America, $50 (annual) ● student - Latin America, $5 (annual). **Multinational. Description:** Aims to improve patient outcomes through optimal blood management, including appropriate provision and use of blood and blood products, and strategies to reduce or avoid transfusion. Works toward incorporating blood management modalities into clinical practice. Helps the public and medical communities to embrace the benefits of simple, safe, and effective blood management practices. Maintains speakers' bureau. **Libraries: Type:** reference. **Holdings:** articles. **Subjects:** blood management. **Awards:** SABM President's Award. **Frequency:** annual. **Type:** recognition. **Recipient:** for substantial contribution to the field of blood conservation and safety of blood supply or reduction of unnecessary transfusions. **Publications:** *Membership Brochure*. Alternate Formats: online ● *SABM Patient Information Brochure*. Promotes education about blood management, transfusion options, and strategies to minimize blood loss. Alternate Formats: online ● Newsletter. **Price:** for members. **Conventions/Meetings:** annual meeting - 2007 Sept. 7-9, Hollywood, CA.

Hemochromatosis

14488 ■ Hemochromatosis Foundation (HF)
Address Unknown since 2007
Founded: 1982. **Members:** 4,000. **Membership Dues:** in U.S., $35 (annual) ● outside U.S., $40 (annual). **Staff:** 2. **Budget:** $25,000. **Regional Groups:** 8. **State Groups:** 6. **Local Groups:** 4. **Description:** Physicians and other individuals concerned with hereditary hemochromatosis. (Hereditary hemochromatosis is a disorder of iron metabolism in which dietary iron absorption exceeds body needs. If not

diagnosed and treated, the accumulating iron may result in one or more complications: liver enlargement, heart irregularities and failure, diabetes and other hormonal deficiencies, arthritis, and early death.) Seeks to increase public and professional awareness of hereditary hemochromatosis and of the hazards of supplemental iron. Encourages routine use of screening tests by physicians, conducts screening studies of apparently healthy blood donors. Assists public, patients, families, and physicians with HH diagnosis, treatment, and genetic counseling and in forming regional support networks. Sponsors periodic teaching day for physicians and patients and their families. Conducts research programs. **Awards:** Marcel Simon Award. **Frequency:** biennial. **Type:** recognition. **Computer Services:** Mailing lists. **Telecommunication Services:** phone referral service, for patients requesting names of physicians and research centers concerned with HH. **Committees:** Fund-raising; Publicity. **Affiliated With:** Digestive Disease National Coalition; Genetic Alliance; National Organization for Rare Disorders. **Formerly:** (1992) Hemochromatosis Research Foundation. **Publications:** *Family Teaching Conference 1992 at Cleveland Clinic,* annual. Video ● *Hemochromatosis Awareness: A Quarterly Update on Hereditary and Acquired Iron-Overload.* Newsletter. Includes calendar of events and information on available services. **Price:** included in membership dues. ISSN: 0883-2285. **Advertising:** accepted ● Booklets. **Conventions/Meetings:** annual meeting ● biennial World Congress on Iron Metabolism of the International Bio-Iron Society - meeting, with podium presentations and poster sessions (exhibits).

14489 ■ Hemochromatosis Information Society
3017 Princeton Dr.
Plano, TX 75075
Ph: (214)893-6960
E-mail: info@hemoinfo.org
URL: http://www.hemoinfo.org
Contact: Jason P. Edwards, Pres./Chm.

Description: Strives to meet the needs of individuals diagnosed with hereditary hemochromatosis. Supports routine screening of patients for hereditary hemochromatosis to prevent adverse health effects and premature death. Raises public awareness of hereditary hemochromatosis. Provides information to patients and physicians concerning the disease.

Hepatology

14490 ■ American Association for the Study of Liver Diseases (AASLD)
1001 N Fairfax, Ste.400
Alexandria, VA 22314
Ph: (703)299-9766
Fax: (703)299-9622
E-mail: aasld@aasld.org
URL: http://www.aasld.org
Contact: Denise Davis, Asst. Dir.

Founded: 1950. **Members:** 2,400. **Membership Dues:** regular, $305 (annual) ● international, $340 (annual) ● associate, trainee in North America, $90 (annual) ● trainee international, $165 (annual). **Staff:** 18. **Budget:** $7,300,000. **Description:** Medical society focused solely on the science and practice of hepatology, promoting liver wellness and high-quality, cost-effective, compassionate care of patients with hepatobiliary diseases. **Computer Services:** Mailing lists. **Committees:** Education; Practice; Publications; Research; Surgery; Training and Workforce. **Publications:** *AASLD News,* bimonthly. Newsletter. Contains information about the activities of the association. **Price:** free for members. Alternate Formats: online ● *Hepatology,* monthly. Journal. Contains most cited reference on liver and biliary tract information. Also includes the latest research findings and relevant scientific data. **Circulation:** 10,000. **Advertising:** accepted. Alternate Formats: online ● *Liver Transplantation,* monthly. Journal. Alternate Formats: online. **Conventions/Meetings:** annual meeting (exhibits) ● symposium.

14491 ■ American Hepato-Pancreato-Biliary Association (AHPBA)
341 N Maitland Ave., Ste.130
Maitland, FL 32751
Ph: (407)647-8839
Fax: (407)629-2502
E-mail: kim@crowsegal.com
URL: http://www.ahpba.org
Contact: Kim O'Dell, Exec. Dir.

Founded: 1978. **Members:** 400. **Membership Dues:** active, $150 (annual) ● candidate, $110 (annual). **Multinational. Description:** Endoscopists, hepatologists, radiologists, and surgeons in 25 countries. Provides a forum for the presentation of papers concerning diagnostic and treatment modalities of lymphatic, pancreatic, and biliary disorders. Promotes exchange of ideas, reviews current standards of practice, and seeks to establish prospective controlled protocols in the field. Initiates research regarding factors involved in biliary, pancreatic, and liver diseases. **Formerly:** International Hepato-Biliary Pancreatic Association; (1988) International Biliary Association; (2003) International Hepato-Pancreato-Biliary Association. **Publications:** *Journal of Gastrointestinal Surgery,* monthly. **Conventions/Meetings:** biennial World Congress - congress and meeting (exhibits).

14492 ■ American Liver Foundation (ALF)
75 Maiden Ln., Ste.603
New York, NY 10038
Ph: (212)668-1000
Free: (800)GO-LIVER
Fax: (212)483-8179
E-mail: info@liverfoundation.org
URL: http://www.liverfoundation.org
Contact: Frederick G. Thompson, Pres./CEO

Founded: 1976. **Members:** 24,000. **Membership Dues:** associate, $25-$99 (annual) ● partner's circle, $100-$499 (annual) ● president's circle, $500-$999 (annual) ● chairman's circle, $1,000 (annual). **Staff:** 42. **Description:** Health agency working to fund research, promote the understanding and prevention of hepatitis and other liver diseases, and find cures for hepatitis and other liver diseases. Disseminates public and patient information on liver diseases, liver functions, and preventive measures. Provides information about support groups for liver disease patients and their families. Offers physician referral service. Sponsors seminars on disease diagnosis and management for physicians and other health professionals. Sponsors programs, which enables liver disease patients and concerned individuals to meet specialists and learn of recently developed information on treatment and research. Operates continuing organ donor awareness campaign in order to increase the number of organs available for transplant; monitors legislation (nationally and regionally) in areas affecting liver patients. Serves as trustee of funds raised to cover costs related to liver transplant surgery. Sponsors Corporate Wellness Program to provide information on liver disease for use in employee publications. **Awards:** AASLD Jan Albrecht Award. **Frequency:** annual. **Type:** recognition. **Recipient:** to individuals performing clinical research in a liver-related area who has shown commitment to excellence at an early stage of his/her research study ● AASLD Sheila Sherlock Awards. **Frequency:** annual. **Type:** recognition. **Recipient:** to individuals performing clinical and/or transitional research in a liver-related area ● Innovative Hepatology Seed Grant. **Frequency:** annual. **Type:** grant. **Recipient:** for the study of Hepatitis C ● Liver Scholar. **Frequency:** annual. **Type:** scholarship. **Recipient:** for students with continued involvement in liver research ● Postdoctoral Research Fellowship Award. **Frequency:** annual. **Type:** fellowship. **Recipient:** for individuals engaged in doctoral or postdoctoral liver disease research. **Telecommunication Services:** additional toll-free number, (800)4HEP-USA. **Publications:** *American Liver Foundation—Annual Report.* **Price:** free ● Also publishes brochures, leaflets, and information sheets. **Conventions/Meetings:** annual meeting - always October/November.

14493 ■ Children's Liver Association for Support Services (CLASS)
27023 McBean Pkwy., No. 126
Valencia, CA 91355

Ph: (661)263-9099
Free: (877)679-8256
Fax: (661)263-9099
E-mail: supportsrv@aol.com
URL: http://www.classkids.org
Contact: Diane Sumner, Pres.

Founded: 1995. **Description:** Offers emotional, educational and financial support to families coping with childhood liver disease and transplantation. Provides a telephone helpline to allow families, healthcare professionals, and caregivers to obtain free information about pediatric liver disease. Provides a source of financial aid for families of pediatric liver patients through its direct family support program. Serves as a resource for the medical community. **Publications:** *C.L.A.S.S. Notes,* quarterly. Newsletter. Features articles about various aspects of pediatric liver disease and transplantation. **Price:** free. Alternate Formats: online.

14494 ■ Crigler-Najjar Association (CNA)
c/o Cory Mauck, Dir.
3134 Bayberry St.
Wichita, KS 67226
Ph: (316)685-7477 (570)966-3814
E-mail: mauckc@msn.com
URL: http://www.criglernajjar.com
Contact: Katie Martin, Pres.

Founded: 2002. **Description:** Aims to improve the quality of life for persons living with Crigler-Najjar Syndrome. Increases awareness and understanding of this medical condition. Offers support, understanding, and compassion to children and young adults diagnosed with Crigler-Najjar Syndrome. Provides phototherapy equipment and medical supplies to families that cannot afford them. Assists its medical and scientific advisory board in medical research. Raises funds to find a cure for the disease. **Publications:** *Crigler-Najjar Family Newsletter.* Alternate Formats: online ● *God's Golden Children.* Book. Features stories of people afflicted with Crigler-Najjar syndrome. **Price:** $9.95/copy.

14495 ■ Frontline Hepatitis Awareness
701 W Elizabeth St., No. 54
Monroe, WA 98272
Ph: (360)805-1700
Free: (866)437-4646
E-mail: tara@frontline-hepatitis-awareness.com
URL: http://frontline-hepatitis-awareness.com
Contact: Sandra Tara Baldruf, Founder/Exec. Dir.

Description: Works to educate medical professionals and the general public about the hepatitis virus. Improves the quality of life of persons living with hepatitis. Promotes awareness of hepatitis through educational and outreach programs. **Publications:** *Frontline Hepatitis Beacon.* Newsletter. Alternate Formats: online.

14496 ■ Hepatitis C Association
1351 Cooper Rd.
Scotch Plains, NJ 07076-2844
Free: (866)437-4377
Fax: (908)561-4575
E-mail: info@hepcassoc.org
URL: http://www.hepcassoc.org
Contact: Susan Simon, Pres.

Description: Works to educate medical professionals and the general public about the Hepatitis C virus. Promotes awareness of Hepatitis C through educational programs and support materials. Provides emotional support to patients living with Hepatitis C. Strives to minimize the social and personal impact of Hepatitis C on the patient. **Publications:** *Hepatitis C Awareness.* Brochure ● Booklet.

14497 ■ Hepatitis C Caring Ambassadors Program (HCCAP)
PO Box 1748
Oregon City, OR 97045
Ph: (503)632-9032
Free: (877)828-3464

E-mail: lorren@hepcchallenge.org
URL: http://www.hepcchallenge.org
Contact: Lorren Sandt, Managing Ambassador
Founded: 1999. **Description:** Identifies the best possible treatment options for chronic Hepatitis C. Educates people about their treatment options. Helps people living with Hepatitis C to improve the quality of their lives. Provides insights toward identifying cures for Hepatitis C. **Publications:** *Hepatitis C Choices.* Book. Includes information about the treatment options used by people with Hepatitis C. **Price:** $19.95 each. Also Cited As: *Choices* ● Newsletter, monthly. Alternate Formats: online.

14498 ■ Hepatitis Foundation International (HFI)
504 Blick Dr.
Silver Spring, MD 20904-2901
Ph: (301)622-4200
Free: (800)891-0707
Fax: (301)622-4702
E-mail: hfi@comcast.net
URL: http://www.hepfi.org
Contact: Thelma King Thiel, Chair/CEO
Founded: 1994. **Members:** 50,000. **Staff:** 12. **Budget:** $1,200,000. **Local Groups:** 425. **Multinational.** **Description:** Individuals concerned about those with hepatitis. Provides education and information for distribution to the general public, patients, educators, and medical professionals about the diagnosis, treatment, and prevention of viral hepatitis. Maintains database of hepatitis support groups and website information. Conducts train-the-trainer programs for those interested in the topic. **Awards:** Career Development Award. **Frequency:** annual. **Type:** grant. **Recipient:** for epidemiology and outcomes research of viral hepatitis. **Publications:** *Hepatitis Alert,* quarterly. Newsletter. Contains current articles about the latest research and developments in combating viral hepatitis. **Price:** $20.00/year donation.

14499 ■ Hepatitis Resource Network (HRN)
400 E Pioneer Ave., Ste.102
Puyallup, WA 98372
Ph: (253)435-4582
Fax: (253)435-4584
E-mail: contact@h-r-n.org
URL: http://www.h-r-n.org
Contact: Lisa Ball RN, Exec. Dir.
Founded: 1997. **Description:** Seeks to increase the number of physicians and healthcare providers who treat and manage chronic viral hepatitis in patients with and without HIV co-infection. Provides physicians with educational resources and access to clinical trials. Improves the quality of life for persons living with chronic viral hepatitis.

14500 ■ Latino Organization for Liver Awareness (LOLA)
PO Box 842
Throggs Neck Sta.
Bronx, NY 10465
Ph: (718)892-8697
Free: (888)367-5652
Fax: (718)918-0527
URL: http://www.lola-national.org
Contact: Debbie Delgado-Vega, Founder/CEO
Founded: 1994. **Description:** Raises awareness of liver diseases. Provides prevention and education community outreach programs, treatment and referral services to Latino and American communities. Offers bilingual informational materials on liver transplantation. Encourages organ and tissue donation. **Publications:** Newsletter, quarterly.

14501 ■ National Association of Hepatitis Task Forces (NAHTF)
PO Box 66
Miller, NE 68858
Ph: (308)457-2641
Fax: (308)457-2641
E-mail: wmremak@yahoo.com
URL: http://www.nahtf.org
Contact: Bill Remak BSc, Sec.
Description: Provides support and networking for developing and existing community hepatitis task

forces. Improves the quality of life for persons living with hepatitis. Strives to minimize the social and personal impact of hepatitis on the patient.

14502 ■ National Hepatitis C Advocacy Council (NHCAC)
c/o Missouri Hepatitis C Alliance
10800 E Walnut Dr.
Centralia, MO 65240
Free: (877)737-4372
E-mail: president@hepcnetwork.org
URL: http://www.hepcnetwork.org
Contact: Lorren Sandt, Contact
Description: Serves as the voice for all people living with or affected by Hepatitis C. Seeks to promote ethical guidelines and improve the quality of services for people affected by Hepatitis C. Ensures that hepatitis public health policy is shaped to include funding for research and community based organizations. Advances issues of importance to all people affected by Hepatitis C. **Telecommunication Services:** electronic mail, lorren@hepcchallenge.org ● electronic mail, membership@hepcnetwork.org ● electronic mail, media@hepcnetwork.org ● electronic mail, legislative@hepcnetwork.org.

14503 ■ National Hepatitis C Coalition (NHCC)
PO Box 5058
Hemet, CA 92544
Ph: (951)658-4414
E-mail: mail@nationalhepatitis-c.org
URL: http://nationalhepatitis-c.org
Contact: Patty Krueger, Pres.
Founded: 1997. **Description:** Hepatitis C coalition of patients and families dedicated to providing education and support through online communications, Hepatitis C Hotline, and grassroots networks across America.

14504 ■ National Viral Hepatitis Roundtable (NVHR)
750 Commerce Dr., Ste.400
Decatur, GA 30030
Ph: (404)483-2826
Fax: (404)371-1087
E-mail: mconti@nvhr.org
URL: http://www.nvhr.org
Contact: Molli Conti, Chair
Founded: 2003. **Description:** Represents public, private and voluntary organizations dedicated to reducing the incidence of infection, morbidity and mortality from viral hepatitis in the United States through strategic planning, leadership, coordination, advocacy and research. Strives to minimize the social and personal impact of hepatitis C on the patient. Improves the quality of life for persons with chronic hepatitis and helps them participate in the management of their condition. Develops, implements and maintains a national strategy to eliminate viral hepatitis. **Publications:** *Eliminate Hepatitis: A Call to Action.* Report. Alternate Formats: online.

14505 ■ PBCers Organization
1430 Garden Rd.
Pearland, TX 77581
E-mail: executivecommittee@pbcers.org
URL: http://www.pbcers.org
Contact: Linie A. Moore, Pres./CEO/Founder
Founded: 1996. **Members:** 3,000. **Multinational.** **Description:** Aims to improve the quality of life for people affected with Primary Biliary Cirrhosis (PBC) and helps them cope with the disease. Provides education and support for family members and friends of people with PBC. Seeks to raise funds to support education and research that will lead to identifying a cure for PBC. Provides an online chatroom for its members to interact with one another and share information concerning PBC and other autoimmune liver diseases. **Telecommunication Services:** electronic mail, board@pbcers.org. **Publications:** *PBCers Meeting the Challenge,* quarterly. Newsletter. **Price:** $15.00 /year for members ● Videos. Features guest speaker presentations during

the past conferences. Alternate Formats: CD-ROM. **Conventions/Meetings:** annual PBC Mini-Conference.

Herbalism

14506 ■ American Herbalists Guild (AHG)
141 Nob Hill Rd.
Cheshire, CT 06410
Ph: (203)272-6731
Fax: (203)272-8550
E-mail: ahgoffice@earthlink.net
URL: http://www.americanherbalistsguild.com
Contact: Aviva Jill Romm CPM, Pres.
Founded: 1989. **Members:** 750. **Membership Dues:** student, $50 (annual) ● general, $60 (annual) ● professional, $120 (annual). **Staff:** 1. **State Groups:** 3. **Description:** Promotes research and education in the field of herbal medicine. Works to establish high standards for the professional practice of herbalism. Provides a forum for the exchange of information in the field. **Committees:** Admissions Review; Certification; Education; Legal; Media Response. **Publications:** *Directory of Herbal Education Programs.* **Price:** $7.95/copy ● *The Herbalist,* quarterly. Newsletter. **Circulation:** 750. **Advertising:** accepted ● *Recommended Reading List.* **Conventions/Meetings:** annual Herbal Symposium (exhibits).

14507 ■ Flower Essence Society (FES)
PO Box 459
Nevada City, CA 95959
Ph: (530)265-9163
Free: (800)736-9222
Fax: (530)265-0584
E-mail: mail@flowersociety.org
URL: http://www.flowersociety.org
Contact: Patricia A. Kaminski, Co-Dir.
Founded: 1979. **Members:** 5,000. **Membership Dues:** individual, $25 (annual) ● overseas, $30 (annual). **Staff:** 13. **Budget:** $500,000. **Multinational.** **Description:** Project of Earth-Spirit Inc. Health centers, holistic health practitioners, and interested individuals. Seeks to increase public awareness of Nature and the evolving spiritual relationship between human beings and the earth. Promotes the use of flower essences as catalysts to health and important tools "for personal and planetary evolution." Seeks to establish a worldwide network among health practitioners and others using flower essences. Encourages intuitive and scientific investigation of the essences and the creation of a center for educational and research programs. Organizes introductory weekends and annual week-long intensives for professional and lay health practitioners. Sponsors lectures and research, educational, and experimental activities on topics concerning scientific and spiritual approaches to nature, preparation and use of flower essences, practical skills for flower essence practitioners, and recent developments in the field. Maintains library and referral service. Conducts seven-day professional training seminar and wildflower preservation and naturalist program. **Awards: Frequency:** annual. **Type:** scholarship. **Recipient:** for certification program. **Computer Services:** database. **Committees:** Research. **Also Known As:** Earth-Spirit, Inc. **Publications:** *Flower Essence Repertory* (in English, French, German, Italian, and Spanish). Books. **Price:** $19.95 ● *Flower Essence Society—Members' Newsletter,* 1-2/year. Includes book reviews, calendar of events, and research updates. **Price:** included in membership dues. **Circulation:** 25,000 ● *Member E-Bulletin,* quarterly. Alternate Formats: online ● Also publishes informational flyer series. **Conventions/Meetings:** annual Flower Essence Practitioner's Training - workshop, includes wildflower and naturalist program - 7 days, always July.

14508 ■ North American College of Botanical Medicine
Address Unknown since 2007
Founded: 1996. **Staff:** 2. **Budget:** $100,000. **Description:** Dedicated to providing herbal education by training herbalists and providing information for

health care professionals and the community. **Libraries: Type:** reference; not open to the public. **Holdings:** audiovisuals, books, periodicals.

Hispanic

14509 ■ National Hispanic Medical Association (NHMA)
1411 K St. NW, Ste.1100
Washington, DC 20005
Ph: (202)628-5895
Fax: (202)628-5898
E-mail: nhma@nhmamd.org
URL: http://www.nhmamd.org
Contact: Elena Rios MD, Pres./CEO
Founded: 1994. **Members:** 1,000. **Membership Dues:** full, $150 (annual) ● associate, $40 (annual) ● student, $20 (annual). **Staff:** 5. **Budget:** $1,000,000. **Description:** Hispanic physicians. Works to improve health care for Hispanics and underserved populations. Promotes Hispanic health policy issues in relevant forums. Conducts continuing education programs. **Libraries: Type:** reference; not open to the public. **Holdings:** books, clippings, periodicals. **Programs:** Cultural Competence; Leadership Fellowship; NHTSA; Office on Women's Health; Redes En Accion; Residential Leadership. **Projects:** Commonwealth Fund. **Working Groups:** Hispanic Curriculum for NYC GME. **Publications:** *NHMA-NET*, periodic. Newsletter. Alternate Formats: online. **Conventions/Meetings:** annual conference ● annual meeting.

Holistic Medicine

14510 ■ Advocate Health Care (AHC)
2025 Windsor Dr.
Oak Brook, IL 60523
Ph: (630)572-9393 (630)990-5389
Free: (800)323-8622
Fax: (630)990-4752
E-mail: webmaster@advocatehealth.com
URL: http://www.advocatehealth.com
Founded: 1995. **Members:** 10. **Description:** Health care corporations. Promotes the philosophy that good health care involves an understanding of human ecology and must meet the emotional and spiritual as well as the physical needs of patients. (Human ecology is the "understanding and care of human beings as whole persons in light of their relationships to God, themselves, their families, and the society in which they live"). Supports the concept of holistic health care. Sponsors teaching programs at hospitals; maintains support groups. Sponsors the Park Ridge Center, an institute for the study of health, faith, and ethics; and Parkside Alcoholic Research Foundation, which studies the cause and course of alcoholism and substance abuse. Maintains speakers' bureau. **Libraries: Type:** reference. **Holdings:** audiovisuals, books, monographs, periodicals. **Subjects:** medicine, education. **Awards: Type:** recognition. **Telecommunication Services:** TDD, (630)990-4700. **Formed by Merger of:** Lutheran General Health System; EHS Health Care. **Publications:** *Human Ecology Booklet*, semiannual ● *Ounce of Prevention*, quarterly ● *Second Opinion: Health, Faith, and Ethics*, 3/year. Journal. **Price:** $35.00/year. ISSN: 0890-1570. **Circulation:** 2,500 ● *Senior Advocate Magazine*, bimonthly. Delivers news and features about health issues that matter most to people, from advances in medicine to ways to keep oneself fit and well. **Price:** free to seniors living in Chicagoland ● Annual Report ● Bulletin, bimonthly. **Conventions/Meetings:** workshop and seminar.

14511 ■ American CranioSacral Therapy Association (ACSTA)
c/o Upledger Institute
11211 Prosperity Farms Rd., Ste.D-325
Palm Beach Gardens, FL 33410
Ph: (561)622-4334

Fax: (561)622-4771
URL: http://www.acsta.com
Contact: John Matthew, Dir.
Membership Dues: individual, $25 (annual). **Description:** CranioSacral Therapy practitioners and proponents of the modality. Represents the CranioSacral Therapy profession; creates understanding and acceptance of CST within legislative, insurance, public, media, and medical arenas; supports educational and competency standards; monitors insurance and public policy.

14512 ■ American Holistic Health Association (AHHA)
PO Box 17400
Anaheim, CA 92817
Ph: (714)779-6152
E-mail: mail@ahha.org
URL: http://ahha.org
Contact: Ms. Suzan Walter, Pres.
Founded: 1989. **Membership Dues:** $100 (annual) ● $25 (annual) ● $50 (annual). **Nonmembership**. **Description:** Seeks to further the understanding of holistic health care, a concept that stresses the integration of physical, mental, emotional, and spiritual concerns with environmental harmony. **Boards:** Advisors.

14513 ■ American Holistic Medical Association (AHMA)
PO Box 2016
Edmonds, WA 98020
Ph: (425)967-0737
Fax: (425)771-9588
E-mail: ahma@holisticmedicine.org
URL: http://www.holisticmedicine.org
Contact: Dr. Lawrence B. Palevsky MD, Pres.
Founded: 1978. **Members:** 1,000. **Membership Dues:** active physician, $335 (annual) ● licensed healthcare practitioner, $185 (annual) ● retired healthcare practitioner, $150 (annual) ● resident, intern, $65 (annual) ● student, $30 (annual) ● supporting (from public), $50 (annual). **Staff:** 4. **Budget:** $400,000. **State Groups:** 32. **Description:** Represents healthcare practitioners who are interested in furthering the practice of holistic health care, a concept that stresses the integration of physical, mental, emotional, and spiritual concerns with environmental harmony. Advances personal and professional development for physicians and health care professionals in holistic medicine through education and fellowship. Acts as catalysts in the transformation of health care to a sustainable holistic system. Provides medical education. **Awards:** Norm Shealy Scholarship. **Frequency:** annual. **Type:** scholarship. **Recipient:** for student members to attend annual conference. **Computer Services:** Mailing lists, of members and potential members available for purchase for relevant medical education, conferences, and products ● online services, physician finder for members of the public to find holistic practitioners in their area. **Committees:** Conference; Education. **Publications:** *AHMA Member Directory*, annual. Membership Directory. **Price:** available to members only. **Advertising:** accepted. Alternate Formats: online ● *Members Brochures*. Alternate Formats: online ● *National Referral Directory of Holistic Practitioners*. **Price:** $15.00. Alternate Formats: online ● *Newsletter to Members*, quarterly. **Circulation:** 1,000. **Advertising:** accepted. Alternate Formats: online. **Conventions/Meetings:** annual conference, with 50 booths (exhibits).

14514 ■ American Holistic Nurses' Association (AHNA)
323 N San Francisco St., Ste.201
Flagstaff, AZ 86001
Ph: (928)526-2196
Free: (800)278-2462
Fax: (928)526-2752
E-mail: info@ahna.org
URL: http://www.ahna.org
Contact: Jeanne Crawford, Exec. Dir.
Founded: 1981. **Members:** 3,200. **Membership Dues:** individual, $125 (annual) ● student, $50 (annual) ● elder, $75 (annual). **Staff:** 6. **Budget:**

$100,000. **Regional Groups:** 100. **Local Groups:** 100. **Description:** Represents nurses and other individuals interested in holistically-oriented health care practices throughout the United States and the world. Supports the education of nurses, allied health practitioners, and the general public on health-related issues. Embraces nursing as a lifestyle and a profession and provides a means to create bonds within the nursing community. Recognizes that nurses must first heal themselves before they can facilitate the healing of others. **Awards:** Holistic Nurse of the Year. **Frequency:** annual. **Type:** recognition. **Computer Services:** Mailing lists. **Publications:** *Beginnings*, quarterly. Newsletter. Covers membership activities. Includes calendar of events, tape and book reviews, holistic modalities, legislative news and more. **Price:** included in membership dues; $32.00 /year for nonmembers. ISSN: 1071-2984. **Circulation:** 3,200. **Advertising:** accepted ● *Come Home to the Heart of Nursing*. Brochure ● *Journal of Holistic Nursing*, quarterly. Presents academic and scholarly works from the field of holistic nursing practice; includes research news. **Price:** included in membership dues; $69.00 /year for nonmembers; $270.00 /year for institutions. **Circulation:** 3,000 ● *Standards of Advanced Holistic Nursing Practice* ● *Standards of Practice* ● Also publishes membership directory and position statements. **Conventions/Meetings:** annual conference, includes speakers and workshops (exhibits).

14515 ■ Health Optimizing Institute (HOI)
PO Box 1233
Del Mar, CA 92014
Ph: (858)481-7751
E-mail: info@year2020vision.net
URL: http://www.year2020vision.net/hoi.htm
Contact: David J. Harris, Contact
Founded: 1978. **Staff:** 2. **Description:** Disseminates information on holistic and alternative health therapies aimed at building the human immune system and reversing the aging process. Conducts research and training programs in energy medicine. **Libraries: Type:** reference. **Holdings:** 10. **Subjects:** holistic health. **Formerly:** National Center for the Exploration of Human Potential. **Publications:** *Chronicle of Holistic Health*. Journal. **Price:** $108.00. **Conventions/Meetings:** periodic meeting.

14516 ■ International College of Applied Kinesiology - U.S.A. (ICAK-USA)
6405 Metcalf Ave., Ste.503
Shawnee Mission, KS 66202-3929
Ph: (913)384-5336
Fax: (913)384-5112
E-mail: info@icakusa.com
URL: http://www.icakusa.com
Contact: Terry Underwood, Exec. Dir.
Founded: 1975. **Members:** 700. **Membership Dues:** doctor, $400 (annual) ● student, $25 (annual) ● retired healthcare practitioner, $200 (annual). **Staff:** 8. **Multinational. Description:** Promotes the science of Applied Kinesiology. Applied Kinesiology is the system of evaluating the structural, chemical, and mental aspect of human health, involving muscle health, nutrition, manipulation, diet, acupressure, and exercise. Conducts educational programs, research programs, and training seminars. **Libraries: Type:** reference; not open to the public. **Subjects:** Applied Kinesiology. **Awards: Frequency:** annual. **Type:** scholarship. **Computer Services:** database ● mailing lists. **Publications:** *International Journal*, semiannual. **Advertising:** accepted ● *News Update*, quarterly. Newsletter. Features up-to-date developments in AK and College activities. **Price:** included in membership dues. **Advertising:** accepted ● Membership Directory, annual. **Price:** $16.00/issue. **Advertising:** accepted. **Conventions/Meetings:** annual conference and meeting (exhibits) ● semiannual regional meeting (exhibits).

14517 ■ Kundalini Research Network (KRN)
c/o Lawrence Edwards, PhD, VP
PO Box 215
Bedford Hills, NY 10507
Ph: (914)234-4800

E-mail: ledwards1@verizon.net
URL: http://www.kundalininet.org
Contact: Lawrence Edwards PhD, VP
Founded: 1990. **Multinational. Description:** Dedicated to expanding and sharing knowledge about Kundalini and related spiritual transformations of consciousness. Welcomes interested individuals from around the world. Not restricted to any religious tradition or spiritual discipline. Aims to establish a network of scientists, professionals and individuals interested in Kundalini research; to contact, establish and expand linkages with other groups and individuals who share an interest in Kundalini research; to share and exchange information; to encourage and collaborate in Kundalini research and resulting publications; and to disseminate information on Kundalini to health care professionals and others experiencing this process. **Publications:** Newsletter. **Conventions/Meetings:** annual Spirituality, Psychology and Healthcare: On Spiritual Emergence and Evolution - conference ● annual symposium, with lectures and workshops.

14518 ■ Life Resources Institute (LRI)
116 High St.
Ashland, OR 97520
Ph: (541)482-1289
Fax: (541)482-1289
E-mail: kabbott@life-resources.org
URL: http://www.life-resources.org
Contact: Cheryl Rawson, Exec. Dir.
Founded: 1997. **Members:** 36. **Staff:** 4. **Description:** Seeks to implement a holistic approach for conscious living through education, research and service via a new understanding in consciousness, one which is reliant on the principle of self-responsibility. Implementation of this mission will be accomplished through the formation of partnerships with individuals and other organizations that work at the most advanced frontiers of education, research, healthcare and environmental health. Focuses on creating a center of excellence for learning in areas that are key to its mission: experiential education, biological medicine, psychology of identity consciousness, and eco-development. **Libraries: Type:** lending; reference; by appointment only. **Holdings:** archival material, artwork, audiovisuals, books. **Subjects:** holistic health, biological medicine, consciousness, eco-development. **Formerly:** (2005) World Institute of Holistic Therapies.

14519 ■ National Association for Holistic Aromatherapy (NAHA)
3327 W Indian Trail Rd.
PMB 144
Spokane, WA 99208
Ph: (509)325-3419
Fax: (509)325-3479
E-mail: info@naha.org
URL: http://www.naha.org
Contact: Michele Miller, Pres.
Founded: 1990. **Members:** 1,600. **Membership Dues:** donor in U.S., $250 (annual) ● professional in U.S., $125 (annual) ● friend in U.S., $50 (annual) ● friend outside U.S., $75 (annual) ● professional outside U.S., $155 (annual) ● business in U.S., $150 (annual) ● business outside U.S., $180 (annual) ● donor outside U.S., $300 (annual) ● grand donor, $1,000 (annual). **Staff:** 1. **Budget:** $50,000. **Regional Groups:** 30. **National Groups:** 7. **Description:** Seeks to establish and promote the art and science of aromatherapy as a health care alternative. Works to elevate and maintain high standards of aromatherapy education. Works to raise public awareness of the benefits of aromatherapy. Fosters communication and exchange among members. Offers educational programs. Maintains speakers' bureau. **Libraries: Type:** reference; open to the public; by appointment only. **Holdings:** 25. **Subjects:** aromatherapy. **Awards:** Student Education Scholarship. **Frequency:** annual. **Type:** scholarship. **Computer Services:** database ● mailing lists. **Committees:** Advisory; Bylaws; Ethics; Safety. **Councils:** Aromatherapy Schools and Educators. **Publications:** *Aromatherapy Journal*, quarterly. **Price:** $35.00/year. **Circulation:** 2,000. **Advertising:** accepted ● *Online Membership*

and Practitioner Directory, annual. Alternate Formats: online. **Conventions/Meetings:** quarterly regional meeting ● annual World of Aromatherapy - conference and trade show, with board and general meeting.

14520 ■ Nurse Healers Professional Associates International (NH-PAI)
PO Box 158
Warnerville, NY 12187-0158
Fax: (509)693-7555
E-mail: nhpai@therapeutic-touch.org
URL: http://www.therapeutic-touch.org
Contact: Diane May RN, Coor.
Founded: 1977. **Members:** 700. **Membership Dues:** senior, student, international, $50 (annual) ● individual, $75 (annual) ● agency, $200 (annual) ● associate, $15 (annual). **Staff:** 1. **Budget:** $50,000. **Multinational. Description:** Official organization for Therapeutic Touch (TT). Healthcare professionals and lay persons united to promote a holistic approach to healing and health maintenance and nontraditional healing methods. Disseminates information on therapeutic touch. Maintains speakers' bureau; conducts research and educational programs for Therapeutic Touch. Sets standards and scope of practice for TT and recognition program for Qualified Therapeutic Touch teachers and practitioners. **Libraries: Type:** reference. **Holdings:** archival material. **Subjects:** therapeutic touch. **Awards:** Healer's Award. **Frequency:** annual. **Type:** monetary ● **Frequency:** annual. **Type:** scholarship. **Recipient:** for outstanding accomplishments in working for the advancement of complementary therapies and therapeutic touch through research, practice, education and/or publications. **Computer Services:** database, members. **Formerly:** (2002) Nurse Healers Professional Associates. **Publications:** *Cooperative Connection*, quarterly. Newsletter. Cooperative connection newsletter of the Nurse Healers Professional Associate International, Inc (NH-PAI). **Price:** $20.00/year in U.S.; $28.00/year outside U.S. ISSN: 1097-9522. **Advertising:** accepted. **Conventions/Meetings:** annual Healers Teaching Healers - conference (exhibits) - October or November.

14521 ■ Serendipity Association
c/o Dr. Doug Hemstreet, Chm.
4614 Edgeware Rd., No. 4
San Diego, CA 92116-4760
Ph: (619)284-2468
Fax: (619)284-2468
E-mail: serendipityassn@yahoo.com
Contact: Dr. Doug Hemstreet, Chm.
Founded: 1973. **Membership Dues:** individual, $45 ● couple, $55 ● student, $30. **Staff:** 1. **Budget:** $5,800. **Description:** Individuals and professionals interested in or working with holistic health care, world peace, and concepts involved with a "How to Make the World Work Project." Proposes reinventing the world to create a happy, healthy home for humanity, so that "all children everywhere are loved, housed, and well fed." Works to: reform educational system based on "correcting 14 vested Interest Distortions"; stop "government lies, deceit, and cover-ups in health, agriculture, education, defense, and waste." Promotes herbs, natural healing systems, and energy medicine for healing problems such as cancer and AIDS. Supports scientific research in the field of holistic medicine. Sponsors speakers and training programs. Offers consulting services on designing and starting Holistic Health Centers and for government and corporations on reducing health care costs. **Libraries: Type:** reference. **Holdings:** 2,400; books, periodicals. **Special Interest Groups:** BioElectronics; BioPhysics; Energy Medicine; Healing; Herbs; Psychotronics; Radionics; Support and Information Sharing; Training and Research. **Formerly:** (1999) Serendipity Association for Research and Implementation of Holistic Health and World Peace; (2003) Serendipity Association and How to Make the World Work Project. **Publications:** *Serendipity News*, semiannual. Newsletter. **Price:** included in membership dues. **Advertising:** accepted ● Also publishes library information packages ($45). **Conventions/Meetings:** workshop.

14522 ■ World Wide Essence Society (WWES)
PO Box 285
Concord, MA 01742
Ph: (978)369-8454
E-mail: wwes@essences.com
URL: http://www.essences.com/wwes
Contact: Deborah Bier PhD, Founder
Description: Represents educators, practitioners, manufacturers, and distributors of vibrational/flower essences for health. **Publications:** *Vibration Magazine*, quarterly. Journal. Contains information about all types of vibrational essences. Alternate Formats: online.

14523 ■ Zero Balancing Health Association (ZBHA)
Kings Contrivance Village Ctr.
8640 Guilford Rd., Ste.240
Columbia, MD 21046
Ph: (410)381-8956
Fax: (410)381-9634
E-mail: zbaoffice@zerobalancing.com
URL: http://www.zerobalancing.com
Contact: Cindi Pridgen, Exec. Dir.
Founded: 1991. **Members:** 800. **Membership Dues:** $125 (annual). **Multinational. Description:** Promotes the teaching and practice of Zero-Balancing, the hands-on body/mind system designed to align body energy with the body's physical structure; strives to relieve physical and mental symptoms and improve quality of life. Offers educational courses. **Study Groups:** ZB Study Group. **Affiliated With:** Upledger Institute. **Formerly:** (2005) Zero Balancing Association. **Publications:** *Interface*, quarterly. Newsletter. **Price:** free for members. Alternate Formats: online.

Home Care

14524 ■ American Academy of Home Care Physicians (AAHCP)
PO Box 1037
Edgewood, MD 21040-0337
Ph: (410)676-7966
Fax: (410)676-7980
E-mail: aahcp@comcast.net
URL: http://www.aahcp.org
Contact: Constance F. Row, Exec. Dir.
Membership Dues: physician in U.S., affiliate, corporate associate, $150 (annual) ● physician outside U.S., $165 (annual) ● group, $130 (annual) ● associate in U.S., $75 (annual) ● associate outside U.S., $90 (annual) ● resident, student, $50 (annual) ● corporate sponsor, $2,000 (annual). **Description:** Physicians, home care professionals and agencies, and student affiliates and corporate sponsors-members. Patient referral services. **Awards:** House Call Clinician of the Year. **Frequency:** annual. **Type:** recognition. **Recipient:** to outstanding practitioner ● Poster of the Year. **Frequency:** annual. **Type:** recognition. **Recipient:** for posters. **Computer Services:** database ● mailing lists. **Committees:** Public Policy; Research. **Publications:** *Frontiers*, bimonthly. Newsletter. **Price:** included in membership dues. **Advertising:** accepted ● *Home Care Bibliography*. **Price:** $25.00 CD-Rom, plus shipping and handling. Alternate Formats: CD-ROM ● Annual Report, annual. Alternate Formats: online ● Booklets. **Price:** $18.00 for members, plus shipping and handling; $25.00 for nonmembers, plus shipping and handling.

14525 ■ American Association for Continuity of Care (AACC)
PO Box 532
Dunedin, FL 34697
Ph: (727)738-1030 (727)410-8705
Fax: (727)738-8099
E-mail: phudsonsommers@ij.net
Contact: Pat Hudson-Sommers, Pres.
Founded: 1982. **Members:** 500. **Membership Dues:** general, $90 (annual). **Staff:** 1. **Budget:** $250,000. **Regional Groups:** 6. **Description:** Health care professionals involved in discharge planning, social

work, hospital administration, home care, long-term care, home health agencies, and continuity of care. Studies and researches issues; proposes and supports legislation concerning Medicare changes and home health care. **Awards:** Distinguished Service Award. **Frequency:** annual. **Type:** recognition ● Sarah Craig Leadership Award. **Frequency:** annual. **Type:** recognition. **Computer Services:** Mailing lists, labels (for a fee). **Committees:** Certification; Government Relations. **Publications:** *ACCESS*, bimonthly. Newsletter. Includes calendar of events, regional reports, member notes, and committee reports. **Price:** included in membership dues. **Circulation:** 700. **Advertising:** accepted ● *American Association for Continuity of Care—Membership Directory*, annual. Handbook. Contains membership directory, bylaws and historical information. **Price:** included in membership dues. **Advertising:** accepted. **Conventions/Meetings:** annual conference (exhibits).

14526 ■ Hospice Association of America (HAA)
228 Seventh St. SE
Washington, DC 20003
Ph: (202)546-4759
Fax: (202)547-9559
URL: http://www.nahc.org/haa
Contact: Susan Goldwater Levine, Exec. Dir.
Description: Home care, hospice and home care aide services. Works to heighten the public visibility of hospice services, to affect legislative and regulatory processes impinging on hospice services. Promotes hospice care as a viable component of the health care delivery system. Provides an organized and unified voice for hospice providers, to disseminate information and provides for the exchange of information, to collaborate with state organizations representing hospice interests and initiate, sponsor and promote research related to hospice services.

14527 ■ International Association for Hospice and Palliative Care (IAHPC)
5535 Memorial Dr., Ste.F
PMB 509
Houston, TX 77007
Ph: (936)321-9846
Free: (866)374-2472
Fax: (713)880-2948
E-mail: info@iahpc.com
URL: http://www.hospicecare.com
Contact: Liliana De Lima MHA, Exec. Dir.
Founded: 2000. **Members:** 400. **Membership Dues:** individual (based on annual earnings), $10-$115 (annual) ● life, $500. **Multinational. Description:** Promotes availability and access to high quality hospice and palliative care for patients and families in order to alleviate physical and psychosocial suffering associated with progressive, incurable illness throughout the world. Provides communication and education for patients, professionals, healthcare providers and policy makers. **Libraries:** Type: not open to the public. **Holdings:** 3,000; books. **Subjects:** palliative care, bereavement, nursing, ethical issues, end of life care, grief, pediatric palliative care, death and dying, psychosocial issues. **Awards:** Faculty Development Program. **Frequency:** semiannual. **Type:** grant. **Recipient:** for a full time physician or nurse to teach palliative care in an academic hospital or institution ● Individual Recognition Awards. **Frequency:** annual. **Type:** recognition ● Institutional Recognition Awards. **Frequency:** annual. **Type:** recognition ● Traveling Scholarships. **Frequency:** quarterly. **Type:** scholarship. **Recipient:** for palliative care and hospice leaders in their countries to attend a meeting, conference or teaching and training session in a highly recommended institution ● Traveling Teachers. **Frequency:** quarterly. **Type:** fellowship. **Recipient:** for individuals who want to spend time teaching hospice and palliative care in developing countries ● University Award. **Frequency:** annual. **Type:** recognition. **Recipient:** to a university which has adopted a palliative care curriculum and actively teaching palliative care to physicians and nurses. **Computer Services:** database, of palliative care centers, professionals and hospices around the world ● electronic publishing, guides and manuals which are available for free in the website ●

information services. **Publications:** Newsletter, monthly. **Price:** free. Alternate Formats: online.

14528 ■ National Alliance for Infusion Therapy (NAIT)
901 New York Ave. NW, 3rd Fl.
Washington, DC 20001
Ph: (202)347-0066
Fax: (202)624-7222
URL: http://www.pogolaw.com
Contact: Alan K. Parver, Managing Partner
Founded: 1991. **Members:** 20. **Description:** National health care providers and manufacturers. Promotes the appropriate use of infusion therapies (parenteral or enteral administration of drugs or nutrients) at home or in other alternate-site settings. Seeks to raise awareness of infusion therapies through educational and research programs. Works to influence public policy and private payer advocacy of infusion therapy. Establishes and disseminates guidelines for quality patient care. **Publications:** *Infusion News*, bimonthly. Newsletter. **Price:** free for members.

14529 ■ National Association for Home Care and Hospice (NAHC)
228 7th St. SE
Washington, DC 20003
Ph: (202)547-7424
Fax: (202)547-3540
E-mail: exec@nahc.org
URL: http://www.nahc.org
Contact: Val J. Halamandaris, Pres.
Founded: 1982. **Members:** 6,000. **Membership Dues:** provider, $500-$7,400 (annual) ● corporate, $8,500-$70,000 (annual) ● associate, $1,000 (annual). **Staff:** 65. **Budget:** $12,000,000. **Description:** Represents providers of home health care, hospice, and homemaker-home health aide services; interested individuals and organizations. Develops and promotes high standards of patient care in home care services. Seeks to affect legislative and regulatory processes concerning home care services; gathers and disseminates home care industry data; develops public relations strategies; works to increase political visibility of home care services. Provides legal and accounting consulting services; conducts market research and compiles statistics. Sponsors educational programs for organizations and individuals concerned with home care services. **Libraries:** Type: reference. **Holdings:** reports. **Awards:** Type: recognition. **Computer Services:** Mailing lists, home health care organizations. **Committees:** Congressional Action. **Formed by Merger of:** Council of Home Health Agencies/Community Health Services; National Association of Home Health Agencies. **Formerly:** (2005) National Association for Home Care. **Publications:** *Caring*, monthly. Magazine. **Price:** included in membership dues; $45.00 /year for nonmembers in U.S.; $65.00 /year for nonmembers outside U.S. ISSN: 0738-467X. **Circulation:** 6,000. **Advertising:** accepted. Also Cited As: *Home Health Review* ● *Homecare News*, monthly. Newspaper. Serves as an information exchange between state associations and providers/suppliers to the industry. **Price:** included in membership dues; $18.00 /year for nonmembers. ISSN: 0886-4951. **Circulation:** 15,000. **Advertising:** accepted ● *Hospice Forum*, biweekly. Newsletter. Covers legislative and regulatory issues related to the home health care industry. Contains employment opportunity listings. **Price:** included in membership dues; $105.00 /year for nonmembers. **Advertising:** accepted ● *NAHC Report*, weekly. Newsletter. Covers legislative and regulatory issues related to the home health care industry. Contains employment opportunity listings. **Price:** included in membership dues; $325.00 /year for nonmembers ● *National Home Care and Hospice Directory*, annual. **Conventions/Meetings:** annual Homemaker-Home Health Aide Conference ● annual Legislative and Regulatory Conference (exhibits) ● regional meeting (exhibits) ● annual trade show (exhibits).

14530 ■ National Family Caregivers Association (NFCA)
10400 Connecticut Ave., Ste.500
Kensington, MD 20895-3944

Ph: (301)942-6430
Free: (800)896-3650
Fax: (301)942-2302
E-mail: info@thefamilycaregiver.org
URL: http://www.thefamilycaregiver.org
Contact: Suzanne Geffen Mintz, Pres./Co-Founder
Founded: 1992. **Members:** 25,000. **Membership Dues:** individual professional, $40 (annual) ● organization, $60-$100 (annual) ● family, friend, former caregiver, $20 (annual). **Staff:** 4. **Description:** Individual caregivers, family friends, professionals, affiliated organizations, healthcare providers. Works to meet the needs of family caregivers and improve the caregivers quality of life. Offers educational materials for caregivers and health professionals; advocates for respite assistance and other resources for caregivers. Provides information and referrals. **Publications:** *Love, Honor, Value*. Book. **Price:** $11.20 for members; $14.95 for nonmembers ● *Take Care!*, quarterly. Newsletter. **Price:** included in membership dues; $1.50 for nonmembers. **Advertising:** accepted ● Brochure. **Conventions/Meetings:** quarterly board meeting.

14531 ■ National Private Duty Association (NPDA)
941 E 86th St., Ste.270
Indianapolis, IN 46240
Ph: (317)663-3637
Fax: (317)663-3640
E-mail: info@privatedutyhomecare.org
URL: http://www.privatedutyhomecare.org
Contact: Sheila McMackin, Pres.
Founded: 2002. **Members:** 600. **Membership Dues:** full, $395 (annual) ● branch office, $100 (annual) ● associate, $595 (annual). **Description:** Aims to uphold the industry standards for private duty home care. Fosters ethical business practices through the implementation of adopted ethical guidelines. Educates the public about the differences in private duty models. Develops core training and education programs pertaining to private duty home care. **Publications:** Newsletter, monthly. **Price:** included in membership dues.

14532 ■ Oley Foundation for Home Parenteral and Enteral Nutrition
214 Hun Memorial, MC-28
Albany Medical Ctr.
Albany, NY 12208-3478
Ph: (518)262-5079
Free: (800)776-OLEY
Fax: (518)262-5528
E-mail: bishopj@mail.amc.edu
URL: http://www.oley.org
Contact: Joan Bishop, Exec. Dir.
Founded: 1983. **Members:** 6,000. **Membership Dues:** voluntary, $20 (annual) ● professional, $40 (annual). **Staff:** 20. **National Groups:** 72. **Languages:** English, French, German, Spanish. **Description:** Provides information and psycho-social support for home nutrition support patients, their families, caregivers and professionals. Programs include: bi-monthly newsletter, national network of volunteers providing patient support, annual summer conference, regional meetings, toll-free patient-to-patient networking and information clearinghouse. Seeks to enrich and enhance the lives of those requiring home nutrition support through an outreach system of patient volunteers, educational meetings and clearinghouse activities. **Libraries:** Type: lending. **Holdings:** audiovisuals. **Awards:** Lifeline Letter. **Frequency:** annual. **Type:** recognition. **Publications:** *LifelineLetter*, bimonthly. Newsletter. Contains articles about medical advances and personal experiences. **Price:** included in membership dues; $40.00 /year for nonmembers. **Advertising:** accepted. Alternate Formats: online ● Brochures. **Conventions/Meetings:** annual Consumer/Clinician Conference (exhibits).

14533 ■ World Homecare and Hospice Organization (WHHO)
PO Box 91486
Washington, DC 20090
Ph: (202)547-7424

Fax: (202)547-3540
E-mail: whho@nahc.org
URL: http://www.whho.org
Contact: Ann Smith Gordon MBE, Chair
Membership Dues: individual, $150 (annual). **Multinational. Description:** Represents providers and organizations involved in delivering health, hospice, and social services. Raises global awareness about client-centered home care and hospice services. Formulates and advances the concept of an international clearinghouse as a forum for communication, business development, and information and technology sharing. **Affiliated With:** Canadian Home Care Association; National Association for Home Care and Hospice. **Publications:** *CARING.* Magazine. Offers coverage of global home care and hospice issues. **Price:** included in membership dues.

Homeopathy

14534 ■ American Institute of Homeopathy (AIH)
801 N Fairfax St., Ste.306
Alexandria, VA 22314
Free: (888)445-9988
Fax: (703)548-7792
E-mail: aih@homeopathyusa.org
URL: http://www.homeopathyusa.org
Contact: Bernardo Merizalde MD, Pres.
Founded: 1844. **Members:** 150. **Membership Dues:** regular/active, $250 (annual) ● active-in-training/associate/corresponding, $150 (annual) ● student, $20 (annual). **Staff:** 1. **Budget:** $60,000. **Description:** Represents professional society of medical doctors, osteopaths, dentists, advanced practice nurses and physicians' assistants practicing homeotherapeutics according to the three natural laws of cure propounded by German physician Samuel C. F. Hahnemann (1755-1843). Promotes research and quality homeopathic health care. **Computer Services:** database, indices and reprints of articles. **Publications:** *American Journal of Homeopathic Medicine*, quarterly. **Price:** $130.00 /year for institutions in U.S.; $55.00 /year for individuals in U.S.; $65.00 /year for individuals in Canada and Mexico; $80.00/year for other countries. **Circulation:** 700. **Advertising:** accepted. Also Cited As: *AJHM* ● *Homeopathy Notes*, monthly. Newsletter. **Conventions/Meetings:** annual conference (exhibits).

14535 ■ Homeopathic Nurses Association (HNA)
c/o Margaret Easter, Sec.-Treas.
8403 Tahona Dr.
Silver Spring, MD 20903
Free: (866)240-0495
Fax: (508)223-1801
E-mail: hnanurses@lycos.com
URL: http://hnanurses.tripod.com
Contact: Margaret Easter, Sec.-Treas.
Membership Dues: general, $40 (annual). **Multinational. Description:** Promotes and represents homeopathic nurses in the medical, nursing and homeopathic communities. Creates a recognized homeopathic specialty within the nursing profession. Promotes homeopathic education in nursing schools. **Publications:** Newsletters.

14536 ■ Homeopathic Pharmacopoeia of the U.S. (HPUS)
PO Box 2221
Southeastern, PA 19399-2221
Ph: (707)575-0955
Fax: (707)569-0955
E-mail: hpus@aol.com
URL: http://www.hpus.com
Contact: Andy P. Bormeth, Exec. Dir.
Founded: 1980. **Members:** 75. **Membership Dues:** associate, active, $100 (annual). **Description:** Prepares, publishes and distributes the Homeopathic Pharmacopoeia of the U.S. **Publications:** Booklets. **Conventions/Meetings:** annual convention.

14537 ■ Homeopaths Without Borders
c/o Joe Lillard, Treas.
33 Fairfax St.
Berkeley Springs, WV 25411
Ph: (304)258-2541
Free: (800)336-1695
E-mail: joelillard@homeopathyworks.com
URL: http://www.homeopathswithoutborders-na.org
Contact: Joe Lillard, Treas.
Membership Dues: student, $55 (annual) ● associate, $80 (annual) ● special friend, $150 (annual) ● student outside U.S. and Canada, $65 (annual) ● associate outside U.S. and Canada, $90 (annual) ● special friend outside U.S. and Canada, $160 (annual). **Description:** Homeopaths working in other countries to improve health. **Publications:** *The American Homeopath*, annual. Journal ● *NASH News*, quarterly. Newsletter. **Conventions/Meetings:** annual conference.

14538 ■ International Foundation for Homeopathy (IFH)
Address Unknown since 2007
URL: http://www.healthy.net/library/journals/resonance/editors.htm
Founded: 1978. **Members:** 2,000. **Membership Dues:** in U.S., $40 (annual) ● outside U.S., $50 (annual). **Staff:** 2. **Budget:** $200,000. **Description:** Medical professionals (700) and laypersons (1300) interested in homeopathy. Promotes homeopathy and provides the public with a better understanding of health and diseases through homeopathy. (The word "homeopathy" is taken from the Greek "homeos", meaning "similar", and "pathos", meaning "suffering." Homeopathy therefore means "to treat with something that produces an effect similar to the suffering.") Works to: increase public and professional education; promote acceptance and teaching of homeopathy in medical schools. Sponsors research; conducts annual courses for licensed medical professionals and serious students of homeopathy. Maintains referral service. **Formerly:** (1981) International Foundation for the Promotion of Homeopathy. **Publications:** *International Foundation for Homeopathy—Resonance*, bimonthly. Magazine. Contains information on case histories and clinical advances in research, medicine, and technology. Includes book reviews and calendar of events. **Price:** included in membership dues. **Circulation:** 2,200. **Advertising:** accepted ● *Proceedings of Professional Case Conference*, annual. Book. Contains presentation of cured cases. **Price:** $34.50. **Advertising:** not accepted. Alternate Formats: CD-ROM. **Conventions/Meetings:** annual meeting, professionals present cases (exhibits); **Avg. Attendance:** 150.

14539 ■ National Center for Homeopathy (NCH)
801 N Fairfax St., Ste.306
Alexandria, VA 22314
Ph: (703)548-7790
Free: (877)624-0613
Fax: (703)548-7792
E-mail: info@homeopathic.org
URL: http://www.homeopathic.org
Contact: Sharon Stevenson, Exec. Dir.
Founded: 1974. **Members:** 6,000. **Membership Dues:** regular in U.S. and Canada, $55 (annual) ● regular outside U.S. and Canada, family in U.S. and Canada, $75 (annual) ● family outside U.S. and Canada, $90 (annual). **Staff:** 6. **Budget:** $180,000. **Description:** Promotes the art of healing according to the natural laws of cure from a strictly homeopathic standpoint. Facilitates the study of homeopathy by the medical and allied health professions. Implements the study of homeopathic philosophy and principles among laypersons. Funds scientific research in the field. Sponsors introductory courses in homeopathy to licensed health care practitioners and laypersons; maintains speakers' bureau and library. **Libraries: Type:** reference. **Holdings:** articles, reports. **Telecommunication Services:** electronic mail, hoagland@nationalcenterforhomeopathy.org. **Divisions:** Education; Research. **Affiliated With:** American Institute of Homeopathy. **Publications:** *Homeopathy Today*, bimonthly. Newsletter. Covers membership

activities. Includes calendar of events, employment opportunity and new member listings, and book reviews. **Price:** included in membership dues; $55.00 for nonmembers in U.S.; $75.00 for nonmembers outside U.S. ISSN: 0886-1676. **Circulation:** 7,400. **Advertising:** accepted. Alternate Formats: online ● *Membership Directory and Homeopathic Resource Guide*, biennial. **Price:** $10.00. **Circulation:** 14,000 ● Brochures ● Pamphlets ● Reprints ● Also distributes Homeopathic Household Kit. **Conventions/Meetings:** annual conference.

14540 ■ North American Society of Homeopaths (NASH)
PO Box 450039
Sunrise, FL 33345-0039
Ph: (206)720-7000
Fax: (208)248-1942
E-mail: nashinfo@homeopathy.org
URL: http://www.homeopathy.org
Contact: Ms. Elizabeth Bonfig, Admin.
Membership Dues: student, $55 (annual) ● associate, $80 (annual) ● special friend, $150 (annual) ● student outside U.S. and Canada, $65 (annual) ● associate outside U.S. and Canada, $90 (annual) ● special friend outside U.S. and Canada, $160 (annual) ● registered, $250 (annual). **Description:** Promotes, represents and serves as the voice of all professional homeopaths in North America. Aims to develop and uphold the highest level of excellence in homeopathic practice while enhancing the role of the homeopathic profession as an integral part of health care delivery. **Publications:** *The American Homeopath*. Journal ● *NASH News*. Newsletter. **Conventions/Meetings:** annual conference.

Hospice

14541 ■ Acute Long Term Hospital Association (ALTHA)
c/o Jennifer Connors, Dir. of Communications
625 Slaters Ln., Ste.302
Alexandria, VA 22314
Ph: (703)518-9900
Fax: (703)518-9980
E-mail: william.walters@altha.org
URL: http://www.altha.org
Contact: William E. Walters, CEO
Members: 245. **Membership Dues:** bronze, $2,500 (annual) ● silver, $5,000 (annual) ● gold, $10,000 (annual). **Description:** Represents acute long-term care hospitals and their patients. **Publications:** *ALTHA Insights*. Journal. Features clinical, administrative and regulatory issues facing the LTACH industry. ● Newsletter, weekly. Features a summary of federal and state health care issues. **Conventions/Meetings:** Coding Seminar ● convention.

14542 ■ Children's Hospice International (CHI)
1101 King St., Ste.360
Alexandria, VA 22314
Ph: (703)684-0330
Free: (800)24-CHILD
Fax: (703)684-0226
E-mail: info@chionline.org
URL: http://www.chionline.org
Contact: Ann Armstrong Dailey, Founding Dir./CEO
Founded: 1983. **Members:** 700. **Membership Dues:** individual, professional, $80 (annual) ● institutional, $350 (annual). **Staff:** 4. **Budget:** $950,000. **Multinational. Description:** Represents physicians, nurses, teachers, social workers, clergy, psychologists, art and music occupational therapists, volunteers, and students who work or are interested in hospice programs. Aims to: promote hospice support through pediatric care facilities; encourage the inclusion of children in existing and developing hospices and home care programs; include hospice perspectives in all areas of pediatric care and education. Supports health care agencies that engage in the treatment of terminally ill children and their families. Disseminates information concerning support groups and research, education, and training programs. Involves an

interdisciplinary team of physicians, social workers, nurses, clergy, therapists, teachers and trained volunteers for children's hospice care while parents act as primary care-givers. **Publications:** *Approaching Grief.* Pamphlet ● *Home Care for Seriously Ill Children: A Manual for Parents* ● *Interdisciplinary Clinical Manual for Pediatric Hospice and Palliative Care* ● *Palliative Pain and Symptom Management for Children and Adolescents* ● *The Psychological Aspects of Pain and Symptom Management* ● Audiotapes ● Videos. **Conventions/Meetings:** conference.

14543 ■ Hospice Education Institute (HEI)

3 Unity Sq.
PO Box 98
Machiasport, ME 04655-0098
Ph: (207)255-8800
Free: (800)331-1620
Fax: (207)255-8008
E-mail: info@hospiceworld.com
URL: http://www.hospiceworld.org
Contact: Michal Galazka, Exec. Dir.
Founded: 1985. **Staff:** 7. **Nonmembership.** **Description:** Provides educational and informational services to health professionals and the public on subjects such as hospice and palliative care, death and dying, and bereavement counseling. Encourages educational exchange among hospice and palliative care professionals and volunteers. Offers advice and support to persons working to open local hospice programs. Organizes continuing education seminars on hospice care throughout the U.S. and abroad. **Computer Services:** database, worldwide hospice and palliative care programs. **Telecommunication Services:** information service. **Publications:** *Notes on Symptom Control in Hospice and Palliative Care.* Book. **Price:** $30.00 ● Booklets. **Conventions/Meetings:** annual Hospice & Palliative Care Seminar (exhibits).

14544 ■ Hospice Foundation of America (HFA)

1621 Connecticut Ave. NW, Ste.300
Washington, DC 20009
Free: (800)854-3402
Fax: (202)638-5312
E-mail: hfaoffice@hospicefoundation.org
URL: http://www.hospicefoundation.org
Contact: David Abrams, Pres./CEO
Founded: 1982. **Staff:** 7. **Budget:** $1,800,000. **Languages:** English, French, Italian, Spanish. **Nonmembership.** **Description:** Works to promote the philosophy and application of hospice care for terminally ill people and improve the American health system. Advocates the hospice concept of care; offers professional development and educational programs; sponsors research on ethical issues; participates in public policy initiatives; and provides technical assistance to hospices. **Libraries:** **Type:** reference. **Holdings:** 10. **Subjects:** grief and bereavement, pain, Alzheimer's disease, cancer. **Awards:** **Type:** grant. **Computer Services:** database ● online services, publication. **Telecommunication Services:** electronic mail, david@hospicefoundation.org. **Committees:** Education; Government Affairs; Insurance. **Publications:** *Choosing Hospice.* Booklet. Provides consumer information on hospices. **Price:** free. Alternate Formats: online ● *HFA E-Newsletter*, monthly. Alternate Formats: online ● *Hospice Care and the Military Family.* Brochure. Alternate Formats: online ● *Journeys*, monthly. Journal. **Price:** $12.00 /year for individuals ● *Volunteering in Hospice.* Booklet. **Price:** free ● Annual Report, annual. Alternate Formats: online ● Books ● Pamphlets. **Conventions/Meetings:** annual meeting, held in conjunction with NAHC (exhibits) ● annual meeting - always spring ● regional meeting.

14545 ■ National Hospice and Palliative Care Organization (NHPCO)

1700 Diagonal Rd., Ste.625
Alexandria, VA 22314-2848
Ph: (703)837-1500
Free: (800)658-8898
Fax: (703)837-1233

E-mail: nhpco_info@nhpco.org
URL: http://www.nhpco.org
Contact: J. Donald Schumacher Psy.D, Pres./CEO
Founded: 1978. **Members:** 6,500. **Membership Dues:** provider (minimum), $200 (annual) ● associate, $650 (annual) ● affiliate, $200 (annual). **Staff:** 27. **Budget:** $5,000,000. **State Groups:** 48. **Local Groups:** 2,600. **Description:** Represents hospice organizations and individuals interested in the promotion of the hospice concept and program of care. Promotes standards of care in program planning and implementation. Monitors health care legislation and regulation relevant to hospice care. Sponsors professional liaison and peer group networking. Collects data for demonstrating definitive national trends in the hospice movement. Compiles statistics. Conducts educational and training programs in numerous aspects of hospice care for administrators and caregivers. Maintains nonlending library of hospice-related books. Operates helpline to assist public in identifying hospice programs in their area. **Libraries:** **Type:** open to the public. **Holdings:** 3,000; audio recordings, books, periodicals, video recordings. **Subjects:** hospice, related topics, death, medicine. **Awards:** Award of Excellence. **Frequency:** annual. **Type:** recognition. **Recipient:** for best educational programs ● Champion Award. **Frequency:** annual. **Type:** recognition. **Recipient:** for corporation, foundation or individual who is a champion of the hospice movement ● Founder's Award. **Frequency:** annual. **Type:** recognition. **Recipient:** for person of national or international stature with longevity in the hospice movement showing tenacity and inspiration in the hospice movement ● Heart of Hospice. **Frequency:** annual. **Type:** recognition. **Recipient:** for NCHP member showing outstanding achievement in hospice. **Telecommunication Services:** electronic mail, dschumacher@nhpco.org. **Committees:** AIDS Resource; Council of States; Ethics; Personnel; Research; Standards and Accreditation. **Task Forces:** Access to Hospice Care by Minorities; Managed Care. **Formerly:** (2000) National Hospice Organization. **Publications:** *Journal of Pain and Symptom Management*, monthly. **Advertising:** accepted ● *NewsLine*, monthly. Newsletter. Contains information relevant to hospice and palliative care. **Price:** included in membership dues. **Advertising:** accepted. Alternate Formats: CD-ROM. **Conventions/Meetings:** annual Management and Leadership - conference (exhibits) ● annual meeting, on special topics (exhibits) ● annual symposium (exhibits).

14546 ■ National Institute for Jewish Hospice (NIJH)

732 Univ. St.
Valley Stream, NY 11581
Ph: (516)791-9888
Free: (800)446-4448
Fax: (516)791-6999
E-mail: info@nijh.org
URL: http://www.nijh.org
Contact: Shirley Lamm, Exec. Dir.
Founded: 1985. **Members:** 52,000. **Staff:** 8. **Description:** Individuals, business firms, and organizations concerned about terminally ill Jewish people. Serves as a resource center that seeks to help terminal patients and their families deal with their grief by providing information on traditional Jewish views on death, dying, and managing the loss of a loved one. Offers guidance and training to patients and interested hospice personnel, health care professionals, clergy, and family members who work with terminally ill Jewish people. Maintains speakers' bureau; conducts research programs. Jewish living will, booklets and tapes are available. Accreditation is given by training onsite at hospices. **Computer Services:** database ● mailing lists. **Telecommunication Services:** electronic mail, shirlamm@nijh.org. **Programs:** National Institute for Jewish Hospice Training and Accreditation. **Publications:** *At Bedside.* Booklet. **Price:** $3.00/copy ● *Caring for the Jewish Terminally Ill.* Booklet. **Price:** $3.00/copy ● *For Families of the Jewish Terminally Ill.* Booklet. **Price:** $3.00/copy ● *Hemlock Is Poison for Society* ● *How to Console.* Booklet. **Price:** $1.00/copy ● *Introduction to Jewish Hospice* ● *The Jewish Hospice Times.*

Newsletter. **Price:** free ● *The Jewish Living Will.* **Price:** $1.00/copy ● *The Jewish Orphaned Adult.* Booklet. **Price:** $3.00/copy ● *NIJH Hospice Training Manual.* **Price:** $18.00 ● *Realities of the Dying.* Booklet. **Price:** $3.00/copy ● *Self-Healing and Hospice Care.* Booklet. **Price:** $3.00/copy ● *The Spiritual Component Cannot Be Ignored.* Article. **Price:** $1.00/copy ● *Strategies for Jewish Care* ● *The Undying Hope.* Article. **Price:** $1.00/copy.

14547 ■ National Prison Hospice Association (NPHA)

PO Box 4623
Boulder, CO 80306-4623
Ph: (303)447-8051
E-mail: npha@npha.org
URL: http://www.npha.org
Contact: Fleet Maull, Founder/Dir.
Founded: 1991. **Staff:** 3. **Budget:** $75,000. **Regional Groups:** 4. **Description:** Promotes hospice care for terminally ill inmates and those facing the prospect of dying in prison. Assists corrections and hospice professionals in their continuing efforts to develop high quality patient care procedures and management programs. **Libraries:** **Type:** reference. **Holdings:** 7. **Subjects:** hospice care. **Computer Services:** Information services. **Publications:** *NPHA News*, annual. Newsletter. **Price:** free. **Circulation:** 2,500.

Hospital

14548 ■ Accrediting Commission on Education for Health Services Administration (ACEHSA)

Address Unknown since 2006
Founded: 1968. **Members:** 67. **Membership Dues:** not for profit Corp., $950. **Staff:** 3. **Budget:** $250,000. **Description:** Accredits graduate degree programs in health services administration, health planning, and health policy. Goal is the improvement of professional education. **Formerly:** (1976) Accrediting Commission on Graduate Education for Hospital Administration. **Publications:** *Official List of Accredited Programs*, semiannual. **Price:** free. **Advertising:** not accepted. **Conventions/Meetings:** semiannual meeting.

14549 ■ American Association of Eye and Ear Hospitals (AAEEH)

1100 Wilson Blvd., Ste.1200
Arlington, VA 22209
Ph: (703)243-8848
Fax: (703)243-8664
E-mail: rbetz@aaeeh.org
URL: http://www.aaeeh.org
Contact: Robert Betz PhD, Exec. Dir.
Founded: 1983. **Members:** 13. **Staff:** 4. **Multinational.** **Description:** Chief executive officers and administrators of eye and ear specialty hospitals. Seeks to advance, at the federal level, fair economic treatment for eye and ear specialty hospitals; to share business functions such as purchasing, planning, and information and data collection. Compiles statistics. **Publications:** *Washington Eyeline*, monthly. Newsletter. **Conventions/Meetings:** annual meeting.

14550 ■ American Association of Healthcare Consultants (AAHC)

5938 N Drake Ave.
Chicago, IL 60659
Free: (888)350-2242
Fax: (773)463-3552
E-mail: info@aahcmail.org
URL: http://www.aahc.net
Contact: Linda Campbell CAE, Exec. Dir.
Founded: 1949. **Members:** 100. **Membership Dues:** individual/associate, $325 (annual) ● firm, $1,795 (annual). **Staff:** 1. **Budget:** $100,000. **Description:** Represents professional association of individuals and firms exclusively devoted to health care consultation. Serves as a resource for health care providers; offers continuing education to members. Provides information concerning the role of health consulting. **Awards:** Chester A. Minkalis Award for Service. **Fre-**

quency: annual. **Type:** recognition. **Recipient:** for long-term service to health field, healthcare consulting and professional association. **Computer Services:** Mailing lists, labels. **Telecommunication Services:** electronic mail, webmaster@aahcmail.org. **Formerly:** (1984) American Association of Hospital Consultants. **Publications:** *Update*, quarterly. Newsletter. **Price:** included in membership dues. Alternate Formats: online ● Membership Directory, annual. **Price:** included in membership dues. **Circulation:** 18,000. **Conventions/Meetings** - annual conference, covers practice development - always fall ● annual Mid-year Conference - meeting, includes professional development program - in the spring.

14551 ■ American Association of Psychiatric Administrators (AAPA)
c/o Frances M. Bell, Exec. Dir.
PO Box 570218
Dallas, TX 75357-0218
Free: (800)650-5888
Fax: (972)613-5532
E-mail: frda1@airmail.net
URL: http://psychiatricadministrators.org
Contact: Frances M. Bell, Exec. Dir.
Founded: 1961. **Members:** 300. **Membership Dues:** individual, $75 (annual). **Staff:** 1. **Regional Groups:** 3. **State Groups:** 6. **Description:** Psychiatrists who occupy the position of chief administrative or clinical officer of a public or private neuropsychiatric hospital or clinic. Provides for the efficient consolidation and dissemination of information concerning the treatment, care, and rehabilitation of the mentally ill or handicapped; the effective application of training and research; and the development of the highest standards and qualifications for administrators of public neuropsychiatric hospitals. Conducts educational programs. Acts as a forum through which the common voice of the membership may be expressed and publicized. **Awards:** Outstanding Administrative Psychiatrist of North America. **Frequency:** annual. **Type:** recognition. **Committees:** Academic Psychiatry; Administration and Management Liaison; Bylaws; Ethics; Nominating; Public and Forensic Psychiatry. **Task Forces:** Continuing Education. **Affiliated With:** American Psychiatric Association; Institute on Psychiatric Services/American Psychiatric Association. **Formerly:** (1975) Association of Medical Superintendents of Mental Hospitals. **Publications:** *List of Members*, biennial. Membership Directory ● *Psychiatrist Administrator*, periodic. Journal. **Circulation:** 400. Alternate Formats: online ● Newsletter, quarterly. **Conventions/Meetings:** semiannual Educational and Business Meeting (exhibits).

14552 ■ American College of Healthcare Executives (ACHE)
1 N Franklin, Ste.1700
Chicago, IL 60606-4425
Ph: (312)424-2800
Fax: (312)424-0023
E-mail: geninfo@ache.org
URL: http://www.ache.org
Contact: Thomas C. Dolan PhD, Pres./CEO
Founded: 1933. **Members:** 30,000. **Membership Dues:** faculty associate, $115 (annual) ● member, international associate, $150 (annual) ● student associate, $75 (annual). **Staff:** 100. **Budget:** $16,000,000. **Local Groups:** 110. **Description:** Healthcare executives. Conducts credentialing and educational programs and an annual Congress on Healthcare Management. Conducts groundbreaking research and career development and public policy programs. Publishing division, Health Administration Press, publishes books and journals on health services management and textbooks for use in college and university courses. Works to improve the health status of society by advancing healthcare leadership management excellence. **Awards:** Affiliated Group Award. **Frequency:** annual. **Type:** recognition. **Recipient:** for one officially designated healthcare executive group or women's healthcare executive network ● Dean Conley Award. **Frequency:** annual. **Type:** recognition. **Recipient:** for the author of an outstanding article on an administrative theme ● Edgar C. Hayhow Award. **Frequency:**

annual. **Type:** recognition. **Recipient:** for the author of an outstanding article published in ACHE's quarterly journal ● Gold Medal Award. **Frequency:** annual. **Type:** recognition. **Recipient:** for an exceptional individual who exemplifies the highest standards and values of the healthcare profession ● Health Management Research Award. **Frequency:** annual. **Type:** recognition. **Recipient:** for a faculty research project ● Honorary Fellowship. **Frequency:** annual. **Type:** fellowship. **Recipient:** for distinguished leader who is not eligible to join ACHE ● James A. Hamilton Award for Book of the Year. **Frequency:** annual. **Type:** recognition. **Recipient:** for the author of a book with exceptional merit in the field of healthcare or general management ● Lifetime Service Award. **Frequency:** annual. **Type:** recognition. **Recipient:** for a healthcare executive who has made substantial contributions to ACHE ● Management Innovation Poster Session Award. **Frequency:** annual. **Type:** recognition. **Recipient:** for the originator(s) of a management innovation judged as the best innovation in the healthcare management field ● Robert S. Hudgens Memorial Award. **Frequency:** annual. **Type:** recognition. **Recipient:** for the young healthcare executive of the year ● Student Chapter Awards. **Frequency:** annual. **Type:** recognition. **Recipient:** for student chapters of ACHE that have demonstrated a commitment to promoting advancement in ACHE ● Student Essay Competition in Healthcare Management. **Frequency:** annual. **Type:** recognition. **Recipient:** for student essays. **Computer Services:** Online services, employment postings and members' resumes. **Divisions:** Administration; Communications and Marketing; Education; Health Administration Press; Healthcare Executive Career Resource Center; Management Information Systems; Regional Services; Research and Development. **Programs:** Leader to Leader. **Formerly:** (1985) American College of Hospital Administrators. **Publications:** *Frontiers of Health Services Management*, quarterly. Journal. Contains articles debating current healthcare topics and commentaries from outstanding scholars and practitioners in the field. **Price:** $85.00/year; $23.00/issue. ISSN: 0748-8157. **Circulation:** 800. Alternate Formats: microform ● *Healthcare Executive*, bimonthly. Magazine. Provides in-depth analysis of emerging trends in healthcare management and includes strategies for confronting healthcare management issues. **Price:** $118.00 /year for institutions outside U.S.; $65.00 /year for individuals in U.S.; $75.00 /year for individuals outside U.S. ISSN: 0883-5381. **Circulation:** 27,000. Alternate Formats: online ● *Journal of Healthcare Management*, bimonthly. Provides healthcare management research and articles on topics such as leadership and managed care. **Price:** $85.00/year outside U.S.; $75.00/year in U.S. ISSN: 1096-1092. **Circulation:** 30,000. **Advertising:** accepted ● Membership Directory. **Price:** free for members. Alternate Formats: online ● Also publishes case studies, books, journals, manuals, and newsletters; offers cassette tapes. **Conventions/Meetings:** annual Congress on Healthcare Leadership - meeting, provides more than 80 educational seminars, career development programs, and networking opportunities - always February or March, typically, Chicago, IL. 2008 Mar. 17-20, Chicago, IL ● annual meeting and general assembly.

14553 ■ American Hospital Association (AHA)
1 N Franklin
Chicago, IL 60606-3421
Ph: (312)422-3000
Fax: (312)422-4796
E-mail: ddavidson@aha.org
URL: http://www.aha.org
Contact: Richard Umbdenstock PhD, Pres.
Founded: 1898. **Members:** 54,500. **Membership Dues:** associate advantage, $10,000 (annual) ● associate, $2,950 (annual) ● international organization, degree-granting health education program, $500 (annual). **Staff:** 884. **Budget:** $79,000,000. **Description:** Represents health care provider organizations. Seeks to advance the health of individuals and communities. Leads, represents, and serves health care provider organizations that are accountable to the

community and committed to health improvement. **Awards:** **Type:** recognition. **Committees:** Institutional Practices. **Affiliated With:** American Organization of Nurse Executives; Health Research and Educational Trust. **Formerly:** (1906) Association of Hospital Superintendents of U.S. and Canada. **Publications:** *AHA News*, biweekly. Newsletter. **Price:** included in membership dues ● *AHA News Now*, daily. Newsletter. **Price:** included in membership dues. Alternate Formats: online ● *Guide to the Health Care Field*, annual. Handbook ● *Hospital Statistics*, annual. Handbook ● *Hospitals and Health Networks*, monthly. Magazine. **Conventions/Meetings:** annual meeting (exhibits).

14554 ■ American Society for Healthcare Central Service Professionals (ASHCSP)
1 N Franklin, No. 3100
Chicago, IL 60606
Ph: (312)422-3700 (312)422-3861
Fax: (312)422-4577
E-mail: ashcsp@aha.org
URL: http://www.ashcsp.org
Contact: Virginia Sylvestri, Exec. Dir.
Founded: 1967. **Members:** 1,000. **Membership Dues:** individual, $85 (annual). **Staff:** 2. **Budget:** $500,000. **Regional Groups:** 6. **State Groups:** 20. **Local Groups:** 48. **Description:** Represents managers, directors, technicians and supervisors of central service-supply distribution and sterile processing of medical devices and instrumentation. Provides education, publications and training. **Libraries: Type:** reference. **Holdings:** archival material. **Awards: Frequency:** annual. **Type:** recognition. **Computer Services:** Mailing lists. **Committees:** Advocacy; Affiliated Society Relations; Education; Membership/Marketing; Publications; Recognition. **Affiliated With:** American Hospital Association. **Formerly:** (1987) American Society for Hospital Central Service Personnel. **Publications:** *ASHCSP News*, quarterly. Newsletter. **Price:** available to members only. **Advertising:** accepted. Alternate Formats: CD-ROM; online; magnetic tape ● Also publishes technical materials and training manuals. **Conventions/Meetings:** annual conference (exhibits) - always fall.

14555 ■ American Society for Healthcare Engineering of the American Hospital Association (ASHE)
c/o American Hospital Association
One N Franklin, 28th Fl.
Chicago, IL 60606
Ph: (312)422-3800
Fax: (312)422-4571
E-mail: ashe@aha.org
URL: http://www.ashe.org
Contact: Mr. Albert J. Sunseri PhD, Exec. Dir.
Founded: 1962. **Members:** 7,300. **Membership Dues:** educator/student, $25 (annual) ● associate, $175 (annual) ● professional, $125 (annual). **Staff:** 16. **Budget:** $4,000,000. **Local Groups:** 75. **Multinational. Description:** Hospital engineers, facilities managers, directors of buildings and grounds, assistant administrators, directors of maintenance, directors of clinical engineering, design and construction professionals, and safety officers. Works to: promote better patient care by encouraging and assisting members to develop their knowledge and increase their competence in the field of facilities management; cooperate with hospitals and allied associations in matters pertaining to facilities management; bring about closer cooperation among members; provide contractors a medium for interchange of material relative to facilities management. Maintains library; conducts educational programs. Offers Actions for Professional Excellence Recognition Program and the Certified Healthcare Facility Manager (CHFM) Designation. **Libraries: Type:** by appointment only. **Holdings:** archival material, articles, books, monographs, papers, periodicals. **Awards:** Crystal Eagle and Regional Leader VISTA. **Frequency:** annual. **Type:** recognition. **Recipient:** for chapter professional and personal recognition. **Computer Services:** Mailing lists, of members. **Affiliated With:** American Hospital Association. **Formerly:** American Society for Hospital Engineering. **Publica-**

tions: *ASHE Fire, Electrical and Life Safety Compendium*. Book. **Price:** $65.00 for members; $85.00 for nonmembers ● *Emergency Management Handbook*. **Price:** $85.00 for members; $125.00 for nonmembers ● *The Guidelines for Design and Construction of Hospital and Health Care Facilities - 2001 Edition*. **Price:** $65.00 for members; $75.00 for nonmembers ● *Health Facilities Management Magazine*, monthly. Journal. Lists books, films, tapes, documents, and publications available from the society. **Price:** free. **Circulation:** 40,000. **Advertising:** accepted ● *Inside ASHE Magazine*, monthly. Journal. **Circulation:** 6,000. **Advertising:** accepted ● *Preparing for the Certified Healthcare Facility Manager Exam. A Compendium of Resources*. Book. **Price:** $75.00 for members, plus shipping and handling; $95.00 for nonmembers, plus shipping and handling ● Also publishes books. **Conventions/Meetings:** annual Planning Design and Construction Conference, with trade show (exhibits) - 2008 Mar. 10-13, Orlando, FL.

14556 ■ American Society for Healthcare Environmental Services of the American Hospital Association (ASHES)
1 N Franklin St., Ste.2800
Chicago, IL 60606
Ph: (312)422-3860 (312)422-3862
Fax: (312)422-4578
E-mail: ashes@aha.org
URL: http://www.ashes.org
Contact: Patti Costello, Exec. Dir.
Founded: 1986. **Members:** 1,800. **Membership Dues:** full (from an AHA member institution), $105 (annual) ● full (from a non-AHA member institution), $135 (annual) ● subscribing, $155 (annual) ● retired, full-time student, $67 (annual) ● associate, $135 (annual). **Staff:** 3. **Budget:** $750,000. **Regional Groups:** 16. **Multinational. Description:** Managers and directors of hospital environmental services, laundry and linen services, as well as housekeeping departments and waste management (non-hazardous and hazardous), in government or university settings. Provides a forum for discussion among members of common challenges, Professional development, and career advancement. Maintains liaison between members and governmental and standards setting bodies. Certified Healthcare Environmental Services Professional (CHESP) available through education and Examination. **Libraries: Type:** not open to the public. **Awards:** ASHES Recognition Program. **Frequency:** annual. **Type:** recognition ● Phoenix Award. **Type:** recognition ● Years of Service Award. **Frequency:** annual. **Type:** recognition. **Recipient:** for membership and at least 15 years of service. **Computer Services:** Mailing lists, labels. **Committees:** Advocacy; Affiliated Society Relations; Conference Planning; Education; Membership; Nominations; Publications; Web Site Recognition. **Affiliated With:** American Hospital Association. **Publications:** *Phoenix Newsletter*, quarterly. **Circulation:** 1,600. **Advertising:** accepted. Alternate Formats: online ● Multiple publications related to env. svc. and technical issues. **Conventions/Meetings:** annual conference (exhibits).

14557 ■ American Society for Healthcare Food Service Administrators (ASHFSA)
304 W Liberty St., Ste.201
Louisville, KY 40202
Free: (800)620-6422
Fax: (502)589-3602
E-mail: khoward@hqtrs.com
URL: http://www.ashfsa.org
Contact: Keith Howard, Exec. VP
Founded: 1967. **Members:** 1,200. **Membership Dues:** regular, $125 (annual) ● consultant, $145 (annual) ● business, $450 (annual) ● associate, $95 (annual) ● student, retired, $50 (annual). **Staff:** 4. **Local Groups:** 50. **Description:** Serves individuals with healthcare food service management responsibilities, educators, suppliers and consultants to the profession, is the driving force in the healthcare food service industry and provides healthcare professionals with the resources to compete and succeed. **Awards:** Bonnie Miller Continuing Education Award. **Frequency:** annual. **Type:** scholarship. **Recipient:**

for deserving individual in the field of food and nutrition services ● Chapter Leadership Award. **Frequency:** annual. **Type:** recognition. **Recipient:** for an outstanding local chapter ● Chip Off the Bloch Award. **Frequency:** annual. **Type:** recognition. **Recipient:** for excellence and innovation in food and nutrition services ● Jacques Bloch Award. **Frequency:** annual. **Type:** recognition. **Recipient:** for a member with remarkable contributions in food and nutrition service ● James C. Rose Publication Award. **Frequency:** annual. **Type:** recognition. **Recipient:** for a great food and nutrition publication ● Operator of the Year Award. **Frequency:** annual. **Type:** recognition. **Recipient:** for national members with excellent contributions in the organization. **Committees:** Education; Research and Development; Scholarship. **Formerly:** American Society for Hospital Food Service Administrators. **Publications:** *Food Service Manual for Health Care Institutions, 3rd Edition*. **Price:** $80.00 ● *Healthcare Food Service TRENDS*, quarterly. Magazine ● Also publishes food service reference works on administration, budgeting, cafeteria and financial management, and hospital food service system planning. **Conventions/Meetings:** annual conference and trade show (exhibits).

14558 ■ American Society for Healthcare Human Resources Administration (ASHHRA)
c/o American Hospital Association
1 N Franklin, 31st Fl.
Chicago, IL 60606
Ph: (312)422-3725
Fax: (312)422-4577
E-mail: ashhra@aha.org
URL: http://www.ashhra.org
Contact: Ms. Shirley Armistead, Proj. Specialist
Founded: 1964. **Members:** 2,400. **Membership Dues:** 1st individual, $125 (annual) ● 2nd individual, $95 (annual) ● consultant, $250 (annual) ● student/retired, $45 (annual). **Staff:** 4. **Budget:** $850,000. **Description:** Provides effective and continuous leadership in the field of health care human resources administration. Promotes cooperation with hospitals and allied associations in matters pertaining to hospital human resources administration. Works to further the professional and educational development of members. Encourages and assists local groups in chapter formation through regular programs and institutes on health care human resources issues. Offers placement service. **Awards:** Distinguished Service Chapter Press Award. **Type:** recognition. **Recipient:** for outstanding chapter contributors. **Computer Services:** Mailing lists. **Affiliated With:** American Hospital Association. **Publications:** *Directory of Health Care Human Resources Consultants*, annual ● *Hospitals*, bimonthly ● *The Pulse*, quarterly. Journal. Reports on professional ethics and legislative activity. Includes calendar of events and chapter and member news. **Price:** included in membership dues. **Circulation:** 2,400 ● *Roster of Membership*, annual. Membership Directory. **Conventions/Meetings:** annual conference (exhibits).

14559 ■ American Society for Healthcare Risk Management (ASHRM)
1 N Franklin St.
Chicago, IL 60606
Ph: (312)422-3980 (312)422-3989
Fax: (312)422-4580
E-mail: ashrm@aha.org
URL: http://www.ashrm.org
Contact: Elizabeth Summy, Exec. Dir.
Founded: 1980. **Members:** 4,600. **Membership Dues:** regular, $140 (annual) ● interest network, $25 (annual) ● student, retired person, $85 (annual). **Staff:** 8. **Budget:** $2,500,000. **State Groups:** 47. **Description:** Employees actively involved in the risk management functions of hospitals or other health care providers, and others involved in insurance, brokerage, and consulting. Purposes are to: promote professional development of hospital risk managers; provide educational resources and programs on healthcare risk management; address risk management issues affecting the health care industry, particularly patient safety and risk financing. **Awards:** Innovation and Research Awards. **Frequency:** an-

nual. **Type:** monetary. **Committees:** Annual Conference; Bylaws; Nominating; Professional Ethics. **Special Interest Groups:** Ambulatory Care; Behavioral Health; Compliance; Nursing. **Affiliated With:** American Hospital Association. **Publications:** *Forum*, bimonthly. Newsletter. Provides information about the association, its members and affiliated chapters. **Price:** included in membership dues. Alternate Formats: online ● *Journal of Healthcare Risk Management*, quarterly. Covers research, trends, and new developments in the field of healthcare risk management. Includes educational program calendar and legal update. **Price:** included in membership dues; $80.00 /year for nonmembers. **Circulation:** 4,500. **Advertising:** accepted. Alternate Formats: online. **Conventions/Meetings:** annual conference (exhibits).

14560 ■ American Women's Hospitals Service Committee of AMWA (AWHS/AMWA)
801 N Fairfax St., Ste.400
Alexandria, VA 22302
Ph: (703)838-0500
Fax: (703)549-3864
E-mail: info@amwa-doc.org
URL: http://www.amwa-doc.org
Contact: Roberta G. Rubin MD, Chair
Founded: 1917. **Description:** A project of the American Medical Women's Association Foundation. International philanthropic medical relief service that supports medical and hospital services conducted by women doctors and nurses for the care of the indigent sick and prevention of disease. Currently supports nine clinics in the U.S. and abroad, including Haiti and India. **Formerly:** (1959) American Women's Hospitals; (1982) American Women's Hospitals Service. **Conventions/Meetings:** semiannual meeting.

14561 ■ Association for Healthcare Philanthropy (AHP)
313 Park Ave., Ste.400
Falls Church, VA 22046
Ph: (703)532-6243
Fax: (703)532-7170
E-mail: ahp@ahp.org
URL: http://www.ahp.org
Contact: Dr. William C. McGinly PhD, Pres./CEO
Founded: 1967. **Members:** 3,400. **Membership Dues:** individual, $420 (annual) ● affiliate, $675 (annual) ● associate, $315 (annual) ● institutional (depends upon the number of development professionals), $954-$3,218 (annual). **Staff:** 13. **Budget:** $2,200,000. **Regional Groups:** 7. **Multinational. Description:** Represents persons employed by healthcare organizations in the field of healthcare resource development and fundraising; hospital administrators and trustees; hospitals; interested individuals. Purposes are: to create a cohesive body of healthcare development executives to advance the interests and knowledge of healthcare fund development; to encourage and stimulate better understanding of healthcare needs; to accomplish common goals through an exchange of ideas and information. Conducts educational programs. Holds regional seminars. Compiles statistics; conducts research; sponsors competitions. Maintains library. **Awards:** Harold J. Seymour Award. **Frequency:** annual. **Type:** recognition. **Recipient:** for individuals who have displayed outstanding commitment to the profession of philanthropy. **Computer Services:** Mailing lists. **Committees:** Education; Long-Range Planning; Nominating; Personnel. **Funds:** Pooled Income. **Programs:** Certified Fundraising Executive; Fellow Certification; Government Relations. **Formerly:** (1967) Developartners; (1991) National Association for Hospital Development. **Publications:** *AHP Development Primer Manual*. Includes sample materials used in development programs and foundations. **Price:** $140.00 for nonmembers; $70.00 for members ● *AHP E-Connect*, 8/year. Newsletter. **Price:** included in membership dues; $60.00 /year for nonmembers. Alternate Formats: online ● *Association for Healthcare Philanthropy—Directory*, annual. Lists members and allied firms. Includes calendar of events. **Price:** included in membership dues. **Circulation:** 3,400.

Advertising: accepted ● *Association for Healthcare Philanthropy—Journal*, semiannual. **Price:** included in membership dues; $50.00 /year for nonmembers. **Circulation:** 2,800. **Advertising:** accepted. Alternate Formats: online ● *Report on Giving.* **Price:** $150.00 for nonmembers; $100.00 for members. Alternate Formats: CD-ROM ● *Salary and Benefits* ● *Salary Report 2004.* Lists the low, mid and high salary ranges for defined positions in the health care fund-raising profession. **Price:** $25.00 for nonmembers; included in membership dues ● *Membership Directory*, annual. **Price:** included in membership dues. Alternate Formats: online ● *Brochures.* Alternate Formats: online ● *Books.* **Conventions/Meetings:** annual International Educational Conference (exhibits) - always September or October. 2007 Oct. 3-7, Philadelphia, PA; 2008 Sept. 24-28, Chicago, IL.

14562 ■ Association for Healthcare Resource and Materials Management (AHRMM)
c/o American Hospital Association
1 N Franklin
Chicago, IL 60606
Ph: (312)422-3840
Fax: (312)422-4573
E-mail: ahrmm@aha.org
URL: http://www.ahrmm.org
Contact: Deborah Sprindzunas, Exec. Dir.

Founded: 1962. **Members:** 2,950. **Membership Dues:** regular, $100 (annual) ● nonmember of American Hospital Association, $130 (annual) ● chief executive officer of nonmember institution, $140 (annual) ● student/retired, $66 (annual). **Staff:** 6. **Budget:** $1,700,000. **Local Groups:** 45. **Description:** Represents individuals active in the field of purchasing, inventory and distribution, and materials management as performed in hospitals, related patient care institutions, or government and voluntary Health organizations, and also individuals active in the areas of health care supply manufacturing, distributing, and consulting. Assists members with their responsibilities. Provides access to the latest ideas, methods, developments, information, and techniques in the field of hospital purchasing and materials management; establish associations with others in the profession. Provides recognition in the profession through participation in policy-making. Conducts certification program in health care management. **Awards:** Chapter of the Year Award. **Frequency:** annual. **Type:** recognition ● Leadership Award. **Frequency:** annual. **Type:** recognition. **Computer Services:** Mailing lists. **Committees:** Certification; Conflict of Interest; Education; Legislative Management; Marketing; Product Development; Sponsorship Issues. **Formerly:** (1976) American Society for Hospital Purchasing Agents; (1983) American Society for Hospital Purchasing and Materials Management; (1994) American Society for Hospital Materials Management; (1998) American Society for Healthcare Materials Management. **Publications:** *Association for Healthcare Resource & Materials Management—Conference Proceedings*, annual. Presents case studies. **Price:** $45.00 /year for members; $65.00 /year for nonmembers ● *Association for Healthcare Resource & Materials Management—Membership Roster*, annual. Membership Directory. **Price:** included in membership dues ● *Healthcare Resource & Materials Management News*, bimonthly. Newsletter. Contains reviews of educational programs, current legal and legislative problems, new resources and materials management techniques, and assoc. news. **Price:** included in membership dues. **Circulation:** 2,950. **Advertising:** accepted ● *Resource Catalog*, annual. **Conventions/Meetings:** annual conference (exhibits) ● Healthcare Supply Chain Technology Conference & Exhibition - meeting ● annual Leadership Training - conference.

14563 ■ Association for Hospital Medical Education (AHME)
109 Bush Creek Rd.
Irwin, PA 15642
Ph: (724)864-7321
Fax: (724)864-6153

E-mail: info@ahme.org
URL: http://ahme.org
Contact: Margie Kleppick, Exec. Dir.

Founded: 1956. **Members:** 683. **Membership Dues:** individual, $495 (annual) ● institutional, $1,500 (annual) ● associate, $50 (annual) ● sustaining, $1,000 (annual). **Staff:** 3. **Budget:** $420,000. **Description:** Dedicated to the comprehensive support of medical education professionals; supports continuum of medical education. **Awards:** John C. Leonard. **Type:** recognition. **Recipient:** selected by committee; to person who has made a significant contribution to the field of Graduate Medical Education Management. **Councils:** Administrative Directors of Medical Education; Continuing Medical Education; Medical Education Consortia; Transitional Year Program Directors. **Affiliated With:** Accreditation Council for Graduate Medical Education. **Formerly:** (1968) Association of Hospital Directors of Medical Education. **Publications:** *AHME Membership Directory*, annual. Serves as an information resource for members. **Price:** included in membership dues. Alternate Formats: online ● *AHME News*, semiannual. Newsletter. Provides updates on AHME's educational programs, council activities & related information about medical education. **Price:** included in membership dues. **Advertising:** accepted. Alternate Formats: online ● *Guide to Graduate Medical Education (Guide I and II).* Guide III will be posted online as articles become available. **Price:** included in membership dues; $50.00 for nonmembers ● *The Purple Book Online*, annual. Alternate Formats: online ● *Resource and Reference Center* ● *Transitional Year Program Directory*, annual. **Price:** included in membership dues. **Conventions/Meetings:** annual Fall Educational Institute - seminar, educational sessions on the continuum of medical education - in November ● annual Spring Educational Institute - seminar - in May ● workshop (exhibits) - 2-3/year.

14564 ■ Catholic Health Association of the United States (CHA)
4455 Woodson Rd.
St. Louis, MO 63134-3797
Ph: (314)427-2500
Fax: (314)427-0029
E-mail: webmaster@chausa.org
URL: http://www.chausa.org
Contact: Carol Keehan DC, Pres./CEO

Founded: 1915. **Members:** 2,000. **Staff:** 85. **Budget:** $15,000,000. **Description:** Aims to support the Catholic health ministry's pursuit of the strategic directions of mission, ethics and advocacy; improves the health status of communities; and creates quality and compassionate health care. **Libraries: Type:** not open to the public. **Holdings:** 2,500; books, periodicals. **Subjects:** healthcare, Catholicism. **Awards:** Achievement Citation Award. **Frequency:** annual. **Type:** recognition ● Lifetime Achievement Award. **Frequency:** annual. **Type:** recognition ● Mid-Career Award. **Frequency:** annual. **Type:** recognition ● Sr. Mary Concilia Moran Leadership Award. **Frequency:** annual. **Type:** recognition. **Committees:** Executive and Administrative Services; Planning and Policy Development; Public Policy and Advocacy; Sponsorship and Mission Services. **Formerly:** (1915) Catholic Hospital Association of U.S. and Canada; (1965) Catholic Hospital Association. **Publications:** *Catholic Health World*, bimonthly, except January and August. Newspaper. Reports on the health care ministry. Includes *Catholic Health Association Assembly.* **Price:** included in membership dues; $35.00 /year for nonmembers. ISSN: 8756-4068. **Circulation:** 11,500. **Advertising:** accepted ● *Health Progress*, bimonthly. Journal. Addresses the administrative, ethical, financial, legal, and political problems faced by Catholic health care administrators. **Price:** included in membership dues; $50.00 /year for nonmembers. ISSN: 0082-1577. **Circulation:** 12,000. **Advertising:** accepted. Alternate Formats: microform. **Conventions/Meetings:** annual Catholic Health Assembly.

14565 ■ Center to Advance Palliative Care (CAPC)
1255 5th Ave., Ste.C-2
New York, NY 10029-3852
Ph: (212)201-2670 (212)201-2683

E-mail: capc@mssm.edu
URL: http://www.capc.org
Contact: Carol E. Sieger JD, Deputy Dir.

Description: Acts as a resource for hospitals and health systems interested in developing palliative care programs. **Programs:** Building a Hospital-Based Palliative Care; Palliative Care Leadership Centers. **Publications:** *A Guide to Building a Hospital-Based Palliative Care Program.* Handbook. **Price:** $99.00/ copy ● *CAPC Manual* ● *The Case for Hospital-Based Palliative Care.* Brochure. Alternate Formats: online ● *Health Care Financing in the United States* ● *Hospital-Hospice Partnerships in Palliative Care.* Report. Alternate Formats: online ● *Palliative Care Academic Career Awards: A Public-Private Partnership to Improve Care for the Most Vulnerable.* Report ● *Palliative Care: An Opportunity for Medicare.* Alternate Formats: online ● *Planning a Hospital-Based Palliative Care Program.* Brochure. Alternate Formats: online ● *Pull Up Three Chairs: Teaching Palliative Care at Mount Sinai School of Medicine.* Video ● *2004 Crosswalk of JCAHO Standards and Palliative Care - with PC Policies, Procedures and Assessment Tools.* Alternate Formats: online. **Conventions/Meetings:** periodic Training Seminars.

14566 ■ College of Osteopathic Healthcare Executives (COHE)
c/o Wilson Chen, Treas.
3500 Camp Bowie
Box 300
Fort Worth, TX 76107
E-mail: jlin@hsc.unt.edu
URL: http://www.hsc.unt.edu/organizations/ache/
main.html
Contact: Rick Lin, Pres./CEO

Founded: 1954. **Members:** 124. **Membership Dues:** student chapter, $20 (annual) ● national, $40 (annual). **Description:** Executives and other employees of osteopathic hospitals. Encourages development of hospital administration. Sets criteria of competency and assists in educational programs. Contributes to the advancement of efficient hospital administration. **Awards:** CEO Award of Excellence. **Frequency:** annual. **Type:** recognition. **Recipient:** to individual for an outstanding contribution in the advancement of hospital administration ● Distinguished Service Award. **Frequency:** annual. **Type:** recognition. **Recipient:** for a person contributing to the advancement of hospital administration ● Senior Management Award. **Frequency:** annual. **Type:** recognition. **Recipient:** to individual for an outstanding contribution in the advancement of hospital administration. **Formerly:** (1986) American College of Osteopathic Hospital Administrators. **Publications:** *Osteopathic Membership Directory*, annual. **Advertising:** accepted ● *Osteopathic Progress*, bimonthly. Newsletter. **Price:** included in membership dues. **Conventions/Meetings:** annual conference, held in conjunction with Association of Osteopathic Directors and Medical Educators and the American Osteopathic Healthcare Association (exhibits).

14567 ■ Committee to Reduce Infection Deaths (RID)
1110 Park Ave.
New York, NY 10128
E-mail: info@hospitalinfection.org
URL: http://www.hospitalinfection.org
Contact: Dr. Betsy McCaughey PhD, Founder/Chair

Description: Aims to motivate hospitals to facilitate better infection control systems. Provides patients with information on how to protect themselves from the hazards of contracting an infection. Seeks to educate future doctors and nurses on the precautions needed to stop the spread of bacteria from one patient to another patient. Creates educational tools for medical and nursing schools. **Telecommunication Services:** electronic mail, betsymccaughey@ hospitalinfection.org.

14568 ■ Competency and Credentialing Institute (CCI)
2170 S Parker Rd., Ste.295
Denver, CO 80231
Ph: (303)369-9566
Free: (888)257-2667

Fax: (303)695-8464
E-mail: info@cc-institute.org
URL: http://www.certboard.org
Contact: Shannon S. Carter MA, CEO
Founded: 1979. **Members:** 30,000. **Staff:** 7. **Description:** Works to promote surgical services registered nurses. Offers certification programs for nurses practicing in the operating room and assist in surgeries. **Affiliated With:** Association of PeriOperative Registered Nurses. **Formerly:** (2001) National Certification Board Perioperative Nursing; (2005) Certification Board Perioperative Nursing. **Publications:** *CCI News*, semiannual. Newsletter. Contains information about CCI. Alternate Formats: online. **Conventions/Meetings:** triennial board meeting.

14569 ■ Council of Teaching Hospitals (COTH)
c/o Association of American Medical Colleges
2450 N St. NW
Washington, DC 20037-1126
Ph: (202)828-0400 (202)828-0491
Fax: (202)828-1125
E-mail: egreen@aamc.org
URL: http://www.aamc.org
Contact: Ephonia M. Green, Contact
Founded: 1965. **Members:** 400. **Membership Dues:** teaching hospital (individual, common/health system, multiple teaching hospitals), $15,495 (annual) ● Canadian, $3,730 (annual) ● federal, $7,455 (annual) ● corresponding, $3,730 (annual). **Staff:** 12. **Description:** Teaching hospitals. Provides activities and programs relating to specific problems and opportunities in medical school-affiliated or university-owned teaching hospitals. Distributes communications analyzing congressional activities, Executive Branch actions, court decisions affecting teaching hospitals, and teaching hospital reimbursement regulations; disseminates special interest bibliographies, surveys of house staff policies, comparative hospital financial data, and other materials. Appoints study groups and ad hoc advisory task forces. **Affiliated With:** Association of American Medical Colleges. **Publications:** *COTH Report*, 8-10/year. Newsletter. Reviews current federal and state legislation and general activities of the association and its affiliates. **Price:** $30.00/year. ISSN: 0146-2814 ● *Survey of House Staff Stipends, Benefits, and Funding*, annual. **Conventions/Meetings:** semiannual meeting - always spring and fall.

14570 ■ Council of Women's and Infants' Specialty Hospitals (CWISH)
c/o National Perinatal Information Center
144 Wayland Ave., Ste.300
Providence, RI 02906
Ph: (401)274-0650 (401)274-0758
E-mail: npic@npic.org
URL: http://www.cwish.org
Contact: Tricia Schmehl, Pres.
Founded: 1991. **Members:** 12. **Description:** Represents hospitals that specialize in providing services to women and infants. Seeks to improve the health services of hospitals. Fosters sharing of financial and operational data of hospitals that will help each member hospital to enhance their quality of service to their patients. **Telecommunication Services:** electronic mail, cwish_webmaster@cwish.org.

14571 ■ Federation of American Hospitals (FAH)
801 Pennsylvania Ave. NW, Ste.245
Washington, DC 20004-2604
Ph: (202)624-1500
Fax: (202)737-6462
E-mail: info@fah.org
URL: http://www.americashospitals.com
Contact: Charles N. Kahn III, Pres.
Founded: 1966. **Members:** 1,000. **Staff:** 20. **Budget:** $4,000,000. **Description:** Represents privately- or investor-owned (for-profit) hospitals. **Awards:** Individual of the Year Award. **Type:** recognition ● President's Achievement Award. **Type:** recognition. **Boards:** Exposition Advisory. **Committees:** Audit/Administrative Affairs; Federal Tax; Health Financing; Hospital Leadership; Legal and Operational Policy;

Legislative; Public Relations; Quality; Rural Hospital. **Task Forces:** Investor Relations. **Formerly:** (2001) Federation of American Health Systems. **Publications:** *Hospital Outlook*, bimonthly. Newsletter. Monitors health legislation, regulatory and reimbursement matters and developments in the health care industry. **Price:** included in membership dues; $150.00 /year for nonmembers. **Circulation:** 3,500. Alternate Formats: online ● Directory. **Price:** $85.00 for members; $125.00 for nonmembers. Alternate Formats: diskette. **Conventions/Meetings:** annual conference (exhibits) - 2008 Mar. 2-5, Washington, DC.

14572 ■ The Floating Hospital (TFH)
PO Box 3391
New York, NY 10163-3391
Ph: (212)514-7440
Fax: (718)784-0240
E-mail: info@thefloatinghospital.org
URL: http://www.thefloatinghospital.org
Contact: Sean T. Granahan Esq., Pres./Gen. Counsel
Founded: 1866. **Staff:** 88. **Budget:** $10,000,000. **Description:** Provides primary health care services to underserved New Yorkers. On a daily basis, provides acute care, physical exams, episodic care, and referrals to specialty and emergency care; delivers a unique blend of health care, health education, outreach, social services and advocacy to over 5 million individuals in the Greater New York area. Serves as citywide resource providing services to clients by responding quickly to the changing circumstances of New York's poorest citizens and remains responsive to their needs for assistance. Provides quality health care and quality of life for the most disadvantaged and destabilized children, families and single adults. **Awards:** Business Leadership Award. **Frequency:** annual. **Type:** recognition. **Recipient:** for outstanding business leaders. **Formerly:** (1980) St. John's Guild - The Floating Hospital.

14573 ■ Health Academy (HA)
c/o Public Relations Society of America
33 Maiden Ln., 11th Fl.
New York, NY 10038-5150
Ph: (212)460-1482
Fax: (212)995-0757
E-mail: alison.calvello@prsa.org
URL: http://www.healthacademy.prsa.org
Contact: Alison Calvello, Health Academy Liaison
Founded: 1989. **Members:** 788. **Membership Dues:** individual, $60 (annual). **Staff:** 1. **Description:** A professional section of the Public Relations Society of America. Senior public relations professionals working in hospitals, multi-hospital systems, medical and dental organizations, insurance companies and Health Maintenance Organizations, foundations, rehabilitation facilities, pharmaceutical firms, government health care units, or health education and research organizations; public relations consultants working in the health care industry. Seeks to enhance the quality and stature of health care public relations. Conducts professional development seminars. **Awards:** MacEachern Award. **Frequency:** annual. **Type:** recognition. **Recipient:** for excellence in health care public relations. **Telecommunication Services:** TDD, (212)254-9464. **Committees:** Awards; Communications; Diversity; Marketing; Nominations; Programming; Promotions; Sponsorship. **Formed by Merger of:** (1989) Hospital Academy; (1989) Health Section. **Publications:** *By-laws and Membership Directory*, annual. **Price:** included in membership dues. **Circulation:** 700. **Advertising:** accepted ● *Health Academy News*, bimonthly. Newsletter ● Monographs. **Conventions/Meetings:** annual conference, with table displays (exhibits) - always spring in Washington, DC ● annual MacEachern Awards Competition.

14574 ■ Health Research and Educational Trust (HRET)
c/o American Hospital Association
1 N Franklin, Ste.2800
Chicago, IL 60606
Ph: (312)422-2600

Fax: (312)422-4568
E-mail: ahaque@aha.org
URL: http://www.hret.org
Contact: Mr. Ahmed Haque, Web Mgr.
Founded: 1944. **Staff:** 25. **Budget:** $6,000,000. **Description:** Advances ideas and practices beneficial to health care practitioners, institutions, consumers and society at large. Principal activities focus on identifying, exploring, demonstrating and evaluating key strategic health care issues affecting innovative health care delivery systems, educating the field about the implications of changing health policies and developing strategies for community health improvement. **Awards:** Trust Award. **Frequency:** annual. **Type:** recognition. **Recipient:** to a health care leader who has exhibited visionary leadership trust that has been a hallmark of HRET for more than 60 years. **Affiliated With:** American Hospital Association. **Formerly:** (1959) Educational Trust of the American Hospital Association; (2002) Hospital Research and Educational Trust. **Publications:** *Health Services Research*, bimonthly ● Books ● Manuals ● Monographs. **Conventions/Meetings:** annual meeting.

14575 ■ Healthcare Information and Management Systems Society (HIMSS)
230 E Ohio St., Ste.500
Chicago, IL 60611-3270
Ph: (312)664-4467
Fax: (312)664-6143
E-mail: himss@himss.org
URL: http://www.himss.org
Contact: H. Stephen Lieber CAE, Pres./CEO
Founded: 1961. **Members:** 17,000. **Membership Dues:** individual, $140 (annual) ● student, $30 (annual) ● corporate gold, $7,500 (annual) ● corporate platinum, $13,000 (annual) ● corporate diamond, $25,000 (annual). **Staff:** 55. **Budget:** $14,000,000. **Regional Groups:** 40. **Description:** Represents persons who, by education and/or appropriate experience, are professionally qualified to engage in the analysis, design, and operation of health care information systems, management engineering, telecommunications, and clinical systems professions. Also, corporate members include companies with information technology solutions for health care organizations. Provides leadership in health care for the management of systems, information, and change, while striving for high quality, efficient and effective patient care through analysis and technology implementation. Maintains speakers' bureau. Offers placement service. **Libraries: Type:** reference. **Holdings:** audiovisuals, books, monographs, periodicals. **Subjects:** information systems, management engineering, clinical informatics, quality management, telecommunications. **Awards:** CEO IT Achievement Award. **Frequency:** annual. **Type:** recognition. **Recipient:** for healthcare industry chief executive officers who demonstrate leadership and commitment to using information technology to advance their healthcare organization's strategic goals ● CIO of the Year Award. **Frequency:** annual. **Type:** recognition. **Recipient:** for information technology integration executives ● Davies Awards of Excellence. **Frequency:** annual. **Type:** recognition. **Recipient:** to healthcare provider organizations that have successfully used EHR systems to improve healthcare delivery ● Healthcare Information Management Systems Scholarship. **Frequency:** annual. **Type:** scholarship. **Recipient:** to an undergraduate, Masters and PhD student enrolled in a program related to the healthcare information and management systems field ● Healthlink Informatics Scholarship. **Frequency:** annual. **Type:** scholarship. **Recipient:** to a student pursuing an advanced degree (Masters or PhD) in the field of healthcare informatics ● John E. Gall Award. **Frequency:** annual. **Type:** recognition ● MANI Scholarship. **Frequency:** annual. **Type:** scholarship. **Recipient:** to an individual pursuing a degree (undergraduate or higher) in the healthcare informatics field ● Richard P. Covert Scholarship. **Frequency:** annual. **Type:** scholarship. **Recipient:** for student member in field of study consistent with HIMSS service areas. **Computer Services:** Mailing lists, special interest group. **Committees:** Chapters;

Chapters Education; Membership Services; Nominating; Professional Development; Publications; Special Interests. **Absorbed:** (1984) Center for Hospital Management Engineering. **Formerly:** (1987) Hospital Management Systems Society. **Publications:** *Annual Conference*, annual. Proceedings. **Price:** $90.00 for members, CD; $135.00 for nonmembers, CD. **Circulation:** 17,000. Alternate Formats: CD-ROM ● *Compensation Survey*, annual. **Price:** included in membership dues. Alternate Formats: online ● *HIMSS E-News*, weekly. Newsletter. **Price:** included in membership dues. **Circulation:** 12,000. Alternate Formats: online ● *HIMSS PULSE on Public Policy*, bimonthly. Newsletter. **Price:** included in membership dues. Alternate Formats: online ● *Journal of Healthcare Information Management*, quarterly. Contains topics in the areas of clinical systems, information systems, management engineering and telecommunications in healthcare organizations. **Price:** $69.00 /year for individuals in U.S. and Canada; $104.00 /year for institutions, library, agency in U.S. and Canada; $109.00 /year for individuals outside U.S. and Canada; $144.00 /year for institutions, library, agency outside U.S. and Canada. **Circulation:** 12,000. Alternate Formats: online ● *Leadership Survey*, annual. **Price:** included in membership dues. Alternate Formats: online ● *Monographs*, periodic ● *Books*, periodic ● *Handbooks*, periodic. **Conventions/Meetings:** annual conference, educational (exhibits).

14576 ■ International Association of Healthcare Central Service Materiel Management (IAHCSMM)
213 W Inst. Pl., Ste.307
Chicago, IL 60610
Ph: (312)440-0078
Free: (800)962-8274
Fax: (312)440-9474
E-mail: mailbox@iahcsmm.org
URL: http://www.iahcsmm.com
Contact: Betty Hanna, Exec. Dir.
Founded: 1958. **Members:** 9,000. **Membership Dues:** active, associate, $40 (annual). **Staff:** 4. **Budget:** $500,000. **State Groups:** 35. **Description:** Represents professional personnel responsible for management and distribution of supplies from central service materiel management departments of a hospital. Works to improve the quality of central service materiel management departments in hospitals; share information and ideas; research Hospital central service materiel management methods and practices; conduct and promote continuing education programs. Sponsors management correspondence courses, technician training and materials management courses through Purdue University in Indiana. Establishes a certification program to recognize exceptional achievement. Maintains technician registry and placement service. Surveys salaries. Conducts research programs; compiles statistics. Maintains 23 committees. **Awards:** Cardinal Health. **Frequency:** annual. **Type:** recognition. **Recipient:** for members ● Golden Slipper Award for Service Excellence. **Frequency:** annual. **Type:** recognition. **Recipient:** for central service professionals ● IAHCSMM Cost Savers Award. **Frequency:** annual. **Type:** recognition. **Recipient:** to an individual who has creatively reduced cost in Central Supply or the Sterile Processing Department without terminating staff ● Purdue University Scholarship Awards. **Frequency:** annual. **Type:** scholarship. **Recipient:** to individuals who wish to continue their educational and individual growth ● Ruth Anne Brooks, RN, Past President's Award. **Frequency:** annual. **Type:** recognition. **Recipient:** for outstanding papers on the management of human resources, equipment, and supplies in the healthcare setting sponsored by Kimberly-Clark. **Computer Services:** Information services ● mailing lists. **Committees:** Awards; Bylaws; Conference Observers; Fellowship; Marketing; Nominating; Parliamentarian; Past Presidents Advisory. **Formerly:** (1969) National Association of Hospital Central Service Personnel; (1989) International Association of Hospital Central Service Management. **Publications:** *Central Service Technical Manual, 6th Edition*. **Price:** $50.00 ● *Communique*,

bimonthly. Newsletter. **Advertising:** accepted. Alternate Formats: online ● *Today's CS: Instrumental to Patient Care*. Video. **Price:** $7.95 ● Books ● Surveys. Alternate Formats: online ● Also publishes technical management and training manuals. **Conventions/Meetings:** competition ● annual meeting (exhibits) - always May and November. 2008 May 4-7, Reno, NV.

14577 ■ International Association for Healthcare Security and Safety (IAHSS)
PO Box 5038
Glendale Heights, IL 60139
Ph: (630)529-3913
Free: (888)353-0990
Fax: (630)529-4139
E-mail: info@iahss.org
URL: http://www.iahss.org
Contact: Thomas A. Smith CHPA, Pres.
Founded: 1968. **Members:** 1,700. **Membership Dues:** senior, $100 (annual) ● general, $175 (annual). **Regional Groups:** 17. **Local Groups:** 53. **Description:** Administrative and supervisory personnel in the field of hospital security and safety. Develops, promotes, and coordinates better security/safety programs in medical care facilities. Offers placement services; conducts specialized education programs. **Libraries: Type:** reference. **Subjects:** security-related. **Awards:** Elwood G. Near Presidential Award. **Frequency:** annual. **Type:** recognition. **Recipient:** to an individual or facility awarded by the association president, for outstanding service and support ● Lindberg Bell Award. **Frequency:** annual. **Type:** recognition. **Recipient:** to a facility that has demonstrated an outstanding healthcare security and/or safety program ● Medal of Valor Award. **Frequency:** annual. **Type:** medal. **Recipient:** to individuals for a selfless and/or courageous act taken at risk of their own lives with full awareness of the danger involved ● Outstanding Chapter Award. **Frequency:** annual. **Type:** recognition. **Recipient:** to the chapter showing the greatest initiative and/or innovation in promoting the healthcare security and safety profession ● Russell L. Colling Literary Award. **Frequency:** annual. **Type:** recognition. **Recipient:** for individuals who have made significant contributions to the healthcare security, safety, and/or risk management professions. **Committees:** Budget; Bylaws; Education; Liaison; Nominating; Relations; Research; Seminar. **Affiliated With:** American Hospital Association; National Crime Prevention Council. **Formerly:** (1990) International Association for Hospital Security. **Publications:** *Healthcare Protection Management*, semi-annual. Journal. **Price:** included in membership dues. **Advertising:** accepted. Alternate Formats: online ● Membership Directory, annual. **Price:** included in membership dues. Alternate Formats: online ● Newsletter, quarterly. **Price:** included in membership dues. **Conventions/Meetings:** annual meeting (exhibits).

14578 ■ Joint Commission on Accreditation of Healthcare Organizations (JCAHO)
One Renaissance Blvd.
Oakbrook Terrace, IL 60181
Ph: (630)792-5000
Fax: (630)792-5005
E-mail: doleary@jcaho.org
URL: http://www.jointcommission.org
Contact: Dennis S. O'Leary MD, Pres.
Founded: 1951. **Staff:** 1,000. **Budget:** $128,000,000. **Description:** Strives to improve the safety and quality of health care provided to the public through the provision of health care accreditation and related services that support performance improvement in health care organizations. Evaluates and accredits nearly 15,000 health care organizations and programs in the United States and other countries, including hospitals, networks, home care, long term care, assisted living, behavioral health care, laboratory and ambulatory care services. **Libraries: Type:** reference. **Awards:** Ernest A. Codman Award. **Frequency:** annual. **Type:** recognition. **Recipient:** for use of performance measures to achieve health care quality improvement ● John M. Eisenberg Award. **Frequency:** annual. **Type:** recognition. **Recipient:**

for contributions to patient safety and health care quality. **Divisions:** Accreditation and Certification Operations; Government Relations and External Affairs; Performance Measurement and Research; Standards and Survey Methods; Support Operations. **Subgroups:** Joint Commission International Center for Patient Safety; Joint Commission Resources. **Affiliated With:** American College of Physicians-American Society of Internal Medicine; American College of Surgeons; American Dental Association; American Hospital Association; American Medical Association. **Formerly:** (1987) Joint Commission on Accreditation of Hospitals. **Publications:** *Accreditation Manuals for all Programs* ● *Joint Commission Perspectives*, monthly. Newsletters. Alternate Formats: online ● *Journal on Patient Safety and Health Care Quality*, monthly. Journals. Alternate Formats: online ● *Perspectives on Patient Safety*, monthly. Newsletters. Alternate Formats: online ● *Sentinel Event Alert*, bimonthly. Newsletter ● *This Month*, monthly. Newsletter ● Also publishes educational materials, software, and videos. **Conventions/Meetings:** annual Ambulatory Care Conference (exhibits) ● annual National Conference on Quality and Safety in Health Care - meeting (exhibits).

14579 ■ National Association of Children's Hospitals and Related Institutions (NACHRI)
401 Wythe St.
Alexandria, VA 22314
Ph: (703)684-1355
Fax: (703)684-1589
E-mail: lmcandrews@nachri.org
URL: http://www.childrenshospitals.net
Contact: Lawrence A. McAndrews, Pres./CEO
Founded: 1968. **Members:** 204. **Staff:** 70. **Budget:** $13,000,000. **Description:** Children's hospitals and related institutions whose programs are clinical (as opposed to social or custodial). Aims to promote the quality of child health care through the dissemination of information and the promotion of research and education programs related to such care. Participates in related charitable, scientific, and educational endeavors. Conducts surveys and research; disseminates information; maintains computerized services. Compiles statistics. **Libraries: Type:** reference. **Committees:** Audit; Bylaws and Resolutions. **Councils:** Child Advocacy; Child Health and Financing; Education; Management Information Services; NACH Public Policy. **Publications:** *Children's Hospitals Today*, quarterly. Magazine. **Advertising:** accepted. **Conventions/Meetings:** annual meeting.

14580 ■ National Association of Healthcare Access Management (NAHAM)
2025 M St. NW, Ste.800
Washington, DC 20036
Ph: (202)367-1125
Fax: (202)367-2125
E-mail: info@naham.org
URL: http://www.naham.org
Contact: Steven C. Kemp, Exec. Dir.
Founded: 1974. **Members:** 1,100. **Membership Dues:** active, $165 (annual) ● business partner, $1,000 (annual). **Staff:** 3. **Budget:** $600,000. **Regional Groups:** 6. **Description:** Represents healthcare access managers united to improve patient care and community relations. Promotes professional recognition and provides educational resources for the healthcare patient access field. Serves as a central source of technical information on changes and trends in healthcare that affect patient access services. Advocates progressive changes in healthcare practices; provides information on admissions and registration procedures. **Awards:** Dale Williams Scholarship Award. **Frequency:** annual. **Type:** scholarship. **Recipient:** for individuals working in the field of patient access services ● Doris E. Gleason Publication Award. **Frequency:** annual. **Type:** recognition. **Recipient:** for members ● Marian Blankenship & Murray Rimmer Awards. **Frequency:** annual. **Type:** recognition. **Recipient:** to an individual who has made a significant contribution to the field of patient healthcare access. **Computer Services:** Mailing lists, for rent. **Telecommunication Services:** electronic bulletin board, access forum. **Committees:**

Accreditation; Communications and Publications; Education; Policy Development and Government Relations; Special Projects. **Programs:** Awards; Fellows. **Affiliated With:** American Hospital Association. **Formerly:** (1990) National Association of Hospital Admitting Managers. **Publications:** *Access Management Journal*, quarterly. Contains reports on trends affecting admissions, patient registration, and patient access; includes descriptions of techniques, systems, and services. **Price:** included in membership dues; $90.00 /year for nonmembers. ISSN: 0894-1068. **Circulation:** 1,600. **Advertising:** accepted. Alternate Formats: online. Also Cited As: *NAHAM Journal* ● *Connections*, bimonthly. Newsletter. Contains list of employment opportunities. **Price:** included in membership dues; $75.00 /year for nonmembers. Alternate Formats: online ● *Healthcare Access Associate Training Manual* ● *National Association of Healthcare Access Management—Membership Directory*, annual. **Price:** free, for members only. Alternate Formats: online. **Conventions/Meetings:** annual Educational Conference & Exposition (exhibits) - always spring.

14581 ■ National Association of Hospital Hospitality Houses (NAHHH)
PO Box 18087
Asheville, NC 28814-0087
Ph: (828)253-1188
Free: (800)542-9730
Fax: (828)253-8082
E-mail: helpinghomes@nahhh.org
URL: http://www.nahhh.org/index.php
Contact: Phyllis Youngberg, Pres.
Founded: 1986. **Members:** 175. **Membership Dues:** house, $425 (annual) ● provisional, affiliate, $275 (annual). **Staff:** 2. **Budget:** $64,000. **Regional Groups:** 10. **Description:** Hospitals, hospital hospitality houses (HHH), charitable foundations, and interested individuals. (Hospital hospitality houses are temporary residential facilities for patients and their families.) Provides assistance to members and offers information and guidance to those who wish to establish an HHH. Conducts educational programs; operates resource center and speaker's bureau; compiles statistics. **Libraries: Type:** not open to the public. **Subjects:** various aspects of operating HHH programs. **Awards: Frequency:** annual. **Type:** recognition. **Recipient:** for best brochure and newsletter. **Computer Services:** database ● mailing lists. **Publications:** *Inside Hospitality*, quarterly. Newsletter. **Price:** free. **Circulation:** 380 ● *National Association of Hospitality Houses: Home Away From Home*. Brochure. Sent to members, hospitals, and healthcare agencies. **Conventions/Meetings:** annual conference (exhibits).

14582 ■ National Association of Public Hospitals and Health Systems (NAPH)
1301 Pennsylvania Ave. NW, Ste.950
Washington, DC 20004
Ph: (202)585-0100 (202)585-0559
Fax: (202)585-0101
E-mail: info@naph.org
URL: http://www.naph.org
Contact: Christine Capito Burch, Exec. Dir.
Founded: 1980. **Members:** 70. **Membership Dues:** regular, $31,000 (annual). **Staff:** 23. **Budget:** $500,000. **Description:** Represents urban public hospitals. Promotes the development of federal, state, and local legislative and policy agendas for members. **Computer Services:** database. **Programs:** Health Policy Fellows; NAPH Fellows; Physician Leadership for Department Chiefs. **Formerly:** (1998) National Association of Public Hospitals. **Publications:** *Safety Net*, quarterly. Alternate Formats: online ● Newsletter, periodic ● Books. Alternate Formats: online ● Monographs. Alternate Formats: online ● Surveys. **Conventions/Meetings:** semiannual conference.

14583 ■ National Association of Urban Hospitals (NAUH)
21351 Gentry Dr., Ste.210
Sterling, VA 20166
Ph: (703)444-0989
Fax: (703)444-3029
E-mail: info@nauh.org
URL: http://www.nauh.org
Contact: John Day, Pres.
Founded: 1993. **Membership Dues:** full, $12,000 (annual) ● associate, $5,000 (annual). **Description:** Represents the federal policy interests of private, non-profit, urban hospitals in cities throughout the United States. Advocates adequate support and financing for the private, non-profit, urban safety-net hospitals that serve America's needy urban communities. **Publications:** *NAUH Update*. Newsletter ● Reports.

14584 ■ Section for Long Term Care and Rehabilitation
c/o American Hospital Association
1 N Franklin St.
Chicago, IL 60606
Ph: (312)422-3000
Fax: (312)422-4796
E-mail: ssonik@aha.org
URL: http://www.aha.org
Contact: Susanne Sonik, Dir.
Founded: 1984. **Members:** 2,900. **Staff:** 3. **Description:** Functions as part of the American Hospital Association. Promotes understanding of the health and continuing care needs of persons of all ages and issues pertinent to health care provider organizations. Seeks to improve continuity of care between acute, pre- and post-acute, and long-term services; supports efforts to improve health care delivery to chronically ill, elderly and disabled. **Supersedes:** Center for Rehabilitation Hospitals and Services. **Conventions/Meetings:** annual conference, held in conjunction with American Academy of Physical Medicine and Rehabilitation Annual Assembly.

14585 ■ Section for Metropolitan Hospitals (SMH)
c/o American Hospital Association
1 N Franklin St., Ste.27
Chicago, IL 60606
Ph: (312)422-3000
Fax: (312)422-4583
E-mail: jsupplitt@aha.org
URL: http://www.aha.org/aha/member-center/
constituency-sections/Metropolitan/callfornoms.html
Contact: John T. Supplitt, Sr. Dir.
Founded: 1984. **Members:** 1,365. **Staff:** 3. **Budget:** $239,000. **Description:** Promotes institutional members of the American Hospital Association (see separate entry) that are located within a metropolitan statistical area and/or provide a significant proportion of Medicare, Medicaid, and uncompensated care. Provides high volumes of ambulatory care; offer specialized services. Assists in the development and implementation of policies and programs to promote recognition, support, and growth for its members within the health care field. Serves as clearinghouse for metropolitan hospital delivery, finance, governance, management, and organizational issues. Compiles statistics; maintains databases; conducts forums. **Convention/Meeting:** none. **Committees:** Policy. **Supersedes:** Center for Urban Hospitals; Public-General Hospital Section.

14586 ■ Society for Healthcare Strategy and Market Development of the American Hospital Association (SHSMD)
1 N Franklin, 31st Fl.
Chicago, IL 60606
Ph: (312)422-3888 (312)422-3739
Fax: (312)422-4579
E-mail: stratsoc@aha.org
URL: http://www.stratsociety.org
Contact: Lauren Barnett, Exec. Dir.
Founded: 1996. **Members:** 3,500. **Membership Dues:** student, $85 (annual) ● full, $195 (annual). **Staff:** 7. **Budget:** $2,000,000. **Description:** Represents persons in hospitals, health systems and networks, managed care plans, ambulatory care and physician groups who are engaged in strategic planning, business development, marketing, or public relations activities. **Awards:** Award for Individual Excellence. **Frequency:** annual. **Type:** recognition. **Recipient:** for excellence in healthcare strategy

development and leadership in the healthcare field. **Computer Services:** Mailing lists ● online services, publication. **Committees:** Education; Newsletter; Professional Achievement; Research. **Affiliated With:** American Hospital Association. **Absorbed:** (1999) Society for Healthcare Planning and Marketing of the American Hospital Association. **Formerly:** (1984) American Society for Hospital Public Relations; (1990) American Society for Hospital Marketing and Public Relations; (1998) American Society for Healthcare Marketing and Public Relations. **Publications:** *Spectrum*, bimonthly. Newsletter. Includes calendar of events. **Price:** included in membership dues. **Circulation:** 4,000. Alternate Formats: online. **Conventions/Meetings:** annual Educational Conference (exhibits) - 2007 Oct. 3-6, Washington, DC; 2008 Sept. 17-20, San Francisco, CA.

14587 ■ Society of Hospital Medicine (SHM)
190 N Independence Mall W
Philadelphia, PA 19106-1508
Ph: (215)351-2742
Free: (800)843-3360
Fax: (215)351-2536
E-mail: customerservice@hospitalmedicine.org
URL: http://www.joinshm.org
Contact: Steven Poitras, Dir. of Business Operations
Founded: 1998. **Members:** 4,700. **Membership Dues:** physician, affiliate, allied health, $230 (annual) ● resident/fellow-in-training, $110 (annual). **Staff:** 14. **Local Groups:** 41. **Description:** Works to promote quality care for all hospitalized patients. Promotes excellence in the practice of hospital medicine through education, advocacy, and research. **Awards:** Award for Clinical Excellence. **Frequency:** annual. **Type:** recognition. **Recipient:** for outstanding contributions to patient care ● Award for Excellence in Teaching. **Frequency:** annual. **Type:** recognition. **Recipient:** for outstanding contributions in medical education administration ● Award for Outstanding Service in Hospital Medicine. **Frequency:** annual. **Type:** recognition. **Recipient:** for exceptional service in the discipline of Hospital Medicine ● Young Investigator's Award. **Type:** recognition. **Recipient:** for outstanding achievement as a researcher in the discipline of Hospital Medicine. **Computer Services:** Online services, resource rooms, career center, discussion forum. **Telecommunication Services:** electronic mail, membership@hospitalmedicine.org. **Formerly:** (2003) National Association of Inpatient Physicians. **Publications:** *The Hospitalist*, bimonthly. Newsletter. Forum for exchange of clinical and practice news. **Price:** included in membership dues. **Circulation:** 12,000. **Advertising:** accepted. Alternate Formats: online ● *Journal of Hospital Medicine*. **Circulation:** 10,000. **Advertising:** accepted. **Conventions/Meetings:** semiannual Leadership Academy - meeting (exhibits) ● annual meeting - 2008 Apr. 3-5, San Diego, CA; 2009 May 14-16, Chicago, IL.

14588 ■ Spirit of Women Hospital Network
1100 Republic Bldg.
25 W Prospect Ave.
Cleveland, OH 44115
Ph: (216)523-1300
Fax: (216)523-1811
E-mail: tabreu@mx.com
URL: http://www.spiritofwomen.com
Contact: Tanya Abreu, Natl. Program Dir./Pres.
Founded: 1998. **Membership Dues:** basic, $19 (annual) ● premier, $29 (annual). **Description:** Advances the cause and business of women's health. Partners with hospitals to provide programs and educational initiatives for women and their families. Helps to focus a hospital's community outreach and marketing efforts on the power of women as healthcare consumers and the positive business influence of engaged physicians and nurses. **Awards:** Spirit of Women Regional and National Awards. **Frequency:** annual. **Type:** recognition. **Recipient:** for ordinary women who do extraordinary things. **Additional Websites:** http://www.spiritofwomen.org. **Publications:** *Extend Your Reach*. Newsletter. Showcases strategies and network best practices. **Price:** included in membership dues ● *Spirit of Women*, quarterly.

Magazine. Inspires and empowers women to take control of all aspects of their lives. **Price:** included in membership dues; $9.95 for nonmembers (4 issues). **Advertising:** accepted. Alternate Formats: online. **Conventions/Meetings:** annual meeting.

14589 ■ Sustainable Hospitals Project (SHP)
Kitson 200, 1 Univ. Ave.
Lowell, MA 01854
Ph: (978)934-3386
E-mail: shp@uml.edu
URL: http://www.sustainablehospitals.org
Contact: Catherine Galligan MS, Mgr.
Description: Provides technical support to the healthcare industry for selecting products and work practices that eliminate or reduce occupational and environmental hazards, maintain quality patient care, and contain costs. **Libraries: Type:** reference. **Holdings:** books, periodicals, reports, video recordings. **Subjects:** healthcare product sources. **Boards:** Research Advisory. **Projects:** Pollution Prevention and Occupational Safety and Health.

14590 ■ Trinity Medical Center
4343 N Josey Ln.
Carrollton, TX 75010-4603
Ph: (972)492-1010 (972)394-2255
Free: (877)228-3638
Fax: (972)394-4783
URL: http://www.trinitymedicalcenter.com/CWSContent/trinitymedicalcenter
Contact: Craig Sims, Pres./CEO
Founded: 1985. **Members:** 110. **Description:** Represents hospitals sponsored by a Lutheran church or bearing the title Lutheran. Offers periodic grants for the advancement of health care chaplaincy programs. **Publications:** *Lutheran Health Resources Directory*, periodic ● Newsletter, quarterly. **Conventions/Meetings:** annual meeting, held in conjunction with Protestant Health and Human Services Assembly - always March.

14591 ■ VHA
220 E Las Colinas Blvd.
Irving, TX 75039-5503
Ph: (972)830-0000 (972)830-0626
Free: (800)842-5146
E-mail: lgentry@vha.com
URL: http://www.vha.com
Contact: Gerard Miller, Chm.
Founded: 1977. **Members:** 2,400. **Staff:** 1,000. **Regional Groups:** 22. **Description:** Health care alliance that represents 2,400 healthcare organizations nationwide, offering its members programs and services to help them improve their operational and clinical efficiency as well as community health. **Formerly:** (1995) Voluntary Hospitals of America. **Publications:** *Alliance*, monthly. Newsletter. Publishes programs, services and member activities. **Price:** available to members only ● Annual Report, annual. **Conventions/Meetings:** annual Leadership Conference (exhibits) - usually April.

14592 ■ Volunteer Trustees of Not-for-Profit Hospitals
818 18th St. NW, Ste.410
Washington, DC 20006
Ph: (202)659-0338
Fax: (202)659-0116
Contact: Linda B. Miller, Pres.
Founded: 1980. **Members:** 155. **Membership Dues:** sustaining, $5,000 (annual) ● affiliate, $500 (annual) ● associate, $95 (annual). **Staff:** 5. **State Groups:** 45. **Description:** Represents 155 not-for-profit hospitals and their voluntary governing boards. Aims to provide a trustee voice in policy-making and legislative activities. Develops a communications network among trustees in order to provide the highest quality medical care at the lowest possible price. Provides educational services to hospital governing boards. Facilitates accurate portrayal of not-for-profit hospitals in the media and Congress. Areas of concern include: Medicare; controlling hospital costs; strategic planning for the not-for-profit hospital community. Compiles information on governing boards. Conducts roundtables. **Committees:** Capital; Govern-

ment Relations; Policy and Planning; Public Relations. **Publications:** *The Sale and Conversion of Not-For-Profit Hospitals: A State-by-State Analysis of New Legislation.* Report. Alternate Formats: online. **Conventions/Meetings:** annual National Conference of Volunteer Trustees.

Human Life Issues

14593 ■ After Death Communication Research Foundation (ADCRF)
PO Box 23367
Federal Way, WA 98093
Fax: (253)568-7778
E-mail: adcrf@adcrf.org
URL: http://www.adcrf.org
Contact: Dr. Jeffrey P. Long, Contact
Description: Undertakes and publishes research committed to understanding the After Death Communication experience, defined as "a spontaneous experience of communication with a deceased friend or family member.". **Computer Services:** database, of publicly submitted AD experiences ● information services, after death experience resources ● online services, forum.

14594 ■ Near Death Experience Research Foundation (NDERF)
PO Box 23367
Federal Way, WA 98093
Fax: (253)568-7778
E-mail: nderf@nderf.org
URL: http://www.nderf.org
Contact: Dr. Jeffrey Long MD, Contact
Description: Promotes research and understanding into near death experiences; hosts the largest database to date in the world of published NDE accounts, supported by several languages. **Computer Services:** database, of written NDE experiences ● information services, NDE resources ● online services, chat ● online services, forums.

Hypertension

14595 ■ American Society of Hypertension (ASH)
148 Madison Ave., 5th Fl.
New York, NY 10016-6700
Ph: (212)696-9099
Fax: (212)696-0711
E-mail: ash@ash-us.org
URL: http://www.ash-us.org
Contact: Torry Mark Sansone, Exec. Dir.
Founded: 1985. **Members:** 4,000. **Membership Dues:** full, in U.S., $150 (annual) ● full, outside U.S., $175 (annual) ● training, $75 (annual). **Staff:** 14. **Regional Groups:** 6. **Multinational. Description:** Organizes and conducts educational activities designed to promote and encourage the development, advancement and exchange of scientific information in all aspects of research, diagnosis and treatment of hypertension and related cardiovascular diseases. **Libraries: Type:** not open to the public. **Awards:** ASH Distinguished Scientist Award. **Frequency:** annual. **Type:** recognition. **Recipient:** to individuals for outstanding achievements in the field of hypertension ● Recognition Awards Program. **Frequency:** annual. **Type:** recognition ● Young Scholars Award. **Frequency:** annual. **Type:** recognition. **Committees:** Chapter Relations; Corporate Affairs; Intersocietal Affairs; Membership; Membership, CME; Nominating; Public Policy; Scientific Awards. **Publications:** *Journal of Clinical Hypertension*, monthly. **Advertising:** accepted. Alternate Formats: online. Also Cited As: *JCH* ● Membership Directory. Alternate Formats: online. **Conventions/Meetings:** annual meeting (exhibits) - usually in New York City or San Francisco.

14596 ■ HELLP Syndrome Society
PO Box 44
Bethany, WV 26032

E-mail: hellp1995@aol.com
URL: http://www.hellpsyndrome.org
Contact: Steve Bohach, Co-Founder
Founded: 1995. **Multinational. Description:** Provides information, education, and support to individuals affected by HELLP Syndrome and their families. **Computer Services:** Online services, message board. **Publications:** Newsletter, monthly.

14597 ■ International Pediatric Hypertension Association (IPHA)
c/o Kathy Franco, Coor.
Univ. of Texas Houston Hea. Sci. Center
Dept. of Pediatrics/Div. of Nephrology and Hypertension
6431 Fannin St., MSB 3.124
Houston, TX 77030
Ph: (713)500-5113
Fax: (713)500-0525
E-mail: contact@pediatrichypertension.org
URL: http://www.pediatrichypertension.org
Contact: Dr. Joseph T. Flynn MD, Chm.
Multinational. Description: Fosters and maintains an open forum for pediatric hypertension healthcare professionals. Seeks to educate healthcare professionals and the general public about childhood hypertension. Participates in research initiatives that promote improved treatment of hypertensive patients. **Telecommunication Services:** electronic mail, jflynn@montefiore.org ● electronic mail, kathy.d.franco@uth.tmc.edu. **Publications:** *The IPHA Link.* Newsletter. Alternate Formats: online.

14598 ■ International Society of Hypertension (ISH)
2045 Manchester St. NE
Atlanta, GA 30324
Fax: (404)875-6334
E-mail: kermit-payne@ishib.org
Founded: 1966. **Multinational. Description:** Promotes the advancement of scientific knowledge in all aspects of research in hypertension and connected cardiovascular diseases.

14599 ■ International Society on Hypertension in Blacks (ISHIB)
100 Auburn Ave. NE, Ste.401
Atlanta, GA 30303
Ph: (404)880-0343
Fax: (404)880-0347
E-mail: inforequest@ishib.org
URL: http://www.ishib.org
Contact: Christopher T. Fitzpatrick, CEO
Founded: 1986. **Membership Dues:** practicing healthcare professional, $180 (annual) ● non-practicing healthcare professional, $150 (annual) ● life, $2,500. **Multinational. Description:** Aims to improve the health and life expectancy of ethnic minorities and eliminate racial and ethnic health disparities in cardiovascular disease through professional and public education, targeted clinical research, and facilitation of the delivery of higher quality cardiovascular health care. **Computer Services:** Mailing Services. **Telecommunication Services:** electronic mail, member@ishib.org. **Publications:** *Ethnicity & Disease*, quarterly. Journal. Offers reports, reviews and commentaries. **Price:** $115.00 for individuals in U.S. and Canada; $207.00 for institutions in U.S. and Canada; $145.00 for individuals outside U.S. and Canada; $237.00 for institutions outside U.S. and Canada ● *ISHIB Insider.* Newsletter. Alternate Formats: online ● Articles. **Price:** $6.00/reprint.

14600 ■ National Hypertension Association (NHA)
324 E 30th St.
New York, NY 10016
Ph: (212)889-3557
Fax: (212)447-7032
E-mail: nathypertension@aol.com
URL: http://www.nathypertension.org
Contact: William M. Manger MD, Chm.
Founded: 1977. **Membership Dues:** advisory board, $100. **Staff:** 5. **Budget:** $350,000. **Description:** Physicians, medical researchers, and business profes-

sionals dedicated to the prevention of the complications of hypertension. Seeks to combat hypertension by developing, directing, and implementing effective programs to educate physicians and the public about the severe, life-threatening dangers of this health disorder. Conducts research on the cause of hypertension through basic laboratory studies. Provides the public with basic information on hypertension; conducts hypertension and hypercholesterol detection programs. Offers medical consulting to those found to have high blood pressure or hypercholesterolemia. Develops educational materials and participates in radio and television programs. **Libraries: Type:** open to the public. **Subjects:** hypertension. **Awards:** National Hypertension Recognition Award. **Frequency:** periodic. **Type:** recognition. **Recipient:** for advancing the mission of NHA according to principles of Dr. Irving Page. **Boards:** Trustees. **Publications:** *Clinical and Experimental Pheochromocytoma*. Book ● *Hypertension and What You Can Do About It*, annual. Brochure. **Price:** $1.00. **Circulation:** 2,000 ● *News Report*, annual. Newsletter ● *100 Questions and Answers About Hypertension*. Book. Contains information on hypertension and the importance of controlling high blood pressure. **Price:** $14.95 ● Annual Report, annual. Features updates of the activities implemented to combat hypertension and reviews of history and mission of the association. ● Also publishes medical journal periodicals. **Conventions/Meetings:** annual seminar (exhibits) ● periodic symposium.

14601 ■ Pulmonary Hypertension Association (PHA)
801 Roeder Rd., Ste.400
Silver Spring, MD 20910
Ph: (301)565-3004
Free: (866)474-4742
Fax: (301)565-3994
E-mail: pha@phassociation.org
URL: http://www.phassociation.org
Contact: Mr. Rino Aldrighetti, Pres.
Founded: 1990. **Members:** 7,000. **Membership Dues:** individual, $15 (annual) ● family/non-MD medical professional section, $35 (annual) ● supporter, $60 (annual) ● leadership, $100 (annual) ● committee of 10, $1,000 (annual) ● physician/researcher section, $135 (annual). **Staff:** 23. **Budget:** $4,800,000. **Local Groups:** 140. **Description:** Patients with Pulmonary Hypertension (PH); families and physicians of patients; researchers. Provides fellowship and educational support for members and the public on PH, including current research and findings, early detection, resource organizations, organ transplantation, and support networks. Conducts support group meetings. Funds medical research. **Awards:** Outstanding Physician Award. **Frequency:** biennial. **Type:** recognition ● Outstanding Volunteer Award. **Frequency:** biennial. **Type:** recognition ● Research Fellowships. **Frequency:** annual. **Type:** monetary. **Recipient:** proposal. **Telecommunication Services:** electronic bulletin board, message boards ● hotline, (800)748-7274, patient-to-patient helpline. **Affiliated With:** National Organization for Rare Disorders. **Formerly:** (1998) United Patients Association for Pulmonary Hypertension. **Publications:** *Advances in Pulmonary Hypertension*, quarterly. Journal. **Price:** free. **Circulation:** 31,000 ● *Pathlight*, quarterly. Newsletter. **Price:** $25.00 for nonmembers; included in membership dues. **Circulation:** 5,000 ● *Patients Guide to Pulmonary Hypertension, 3rd Edition*. Book. **Price:** $25.00 for nonmembers; included in membership dues. **Circulation:** 5,000 ● *Persistent Voices*, semiannual. Newsletter. **Price:** free. **Circulation:** 5,000. Alternate Formats: online ● *PHA News*, biweekly. Newsletter. **Price:** free. **Circulation:** 5,000. Alternate Formats: online. **Conventions/Meetings:** biennial International Pulmonary Hypertension Conference (exhibits) ● biennial International Pulmonary Hypertension Conference - Scientific Sessions.

14602 ■ World Hypertension League (WHL)
c/o Claude Lenfant, MD, Pres.
PO Box 83027
Gaithersburg, MD 20883-3027
Ph: (301)926-1938

Fax: (301)869-3768
E-mail: lenfantc@prodigy.net
Contact: Claude Lenfant MD, Pres.
National Groups: 91. **Multinational. Description:** Federation of professional hypertension leagues, societies, and other national bodies. Liaises between member organizations; promotes internationally applicable methods and programs for hypertension control. **Publications:** Newsletter (in Chinese, English, Italian, and Portuguese), bimonthly. Discusses the activities of member organizations and cardiovascular-related topics. **Circulation:** 50,000. Alternate Formats: online ● Yearbook, biennial. Summarizes the activities of the WHL and its member organizations over 2 years.

Hypnosis

14603 ■ Academy of Scientific Hypnotherapy (ASH)
Address Unknown since 2007
Founded: 1977. **Members:** 250. **Membership Dues:** regular, $60 (annual) ● fellow, $120. **Staff:** 3. **Description:** Professionals in the healing arts who have been properly trained in hypnosis, and who are known to the academy to be ethical and of good professional reputation. The academy plans to fill the need for training programs, continuing education, and certification throughout the U.S. Maintains placement and referral service; compiles statistics. **Convention/Meeting:** none. **Libraries: Type:** reference. **Holdings:** 500; biographical archives. **Subjects:** hypnosis/hypnotherapy. **Committees:** Certification; Dental; Medical; Psychological. **Publications:** *Hypnotherapy in Review*, periodic. Newsletter. Reports on medical and psychological research in hypnotherapy. Includes book reviews. **Price:** included in membership dues. **Circulation:** 2,000. **Advertising:** not accepted ● Bulletin, periodic. **Advertising:** not accepted ● Monograph, periodic. **Price:** included in membership dues.

14604 ■ American Academy of Medical Hypnoanalysts (AAMH)
1022 Depot Hill Rd.
Broomfield, CO 80020
Free: (888)454-9766
Fax: (303)465-1260
E-mail: info@aamh.com
URL: http://www.aamh.com
Contact: Donald E. Hardy-Holley MA, Pres.
Founded: 1974. **Members:** 125. **Membership Dues:** clinical, $195 (annual) ● associate, $145 (annual) ● student, $95 (annual). **Staff:** 1. **Budget:** $50,000. **Regional Groups:** 8. **Description:** Medical doctors, doctors of osteopathy, psychologists, social workers, and professional counselors. Provides training in and promotes the use of medical hypnoanalysis. (Medical hypnoanalysis employs an analytic approach to resolving emotional disorders that is applied while the subject is hypnotized.) Conducts 3-month residency training programs. **Libraries: Type:** reference. **Holdings:** audiovisuals. **Subjects:** hypnoanalysis. **Publications:** Newsletter. Informs members on the latest updates of the organization. ● Membership Directory, annual. Contains alphabetic, geographic, clinical and associate listings of members. **Conventions/Meetings:** semiannual Advanced Topics in Hypnoanalysis - meeting ● annual conference.

14605 ■ American Association of Professional Hypnotherapists (AAPH)
4149-A El Camino Way
Palo Alto, CA 94306-4036
Ph: (650)323-3224
URL: http://www.aaph.org
Contact: Josie Hadley, Pres.
Founded: 1980. **Members:** 1,525. **Membership Dues:** individual, $55 (annual) ● individual, $85 (biennial) ● life, $295. **Staff:** 3. **For-Profit. Description:** Represents hypnotherapists, marriage and family therapists, psychologists, clinical social workers, physicians, pastoral counselors, and others trained and experienced in hypnosis therapy. Promotes

public awareness of hypnosis as applied to personal motivation and improvement, habit control, and assisting the healing process. Acts as forum for the exchange of ideas and techniques; encourages a high level of professional ethics; promotes positive image of hypnotherapy. **Libraries: Type:** reference. **Holdings:** periodicals. **Subjects:** hypnotherapy. **Computer Services:** Mailing lists. **Publications:** *Hypnotherapy Today*, quarterly. Newsletter. Covers techniques, new theories and innovations, case descriptions, and new uses of hypnotherapy. **Price:** included in membership dues. ISSN: 0882-8652. **Circulation:** 3,000. **Advertising:** accepted ● *National Register of Professional Hypnotherapists*, annual. Lists information by state and country. **Price:** included in membership dues. **Circulation:** 2,000.

14606 ■ American Board of Hypnotherapy (ABH)
4224 Waialae Ave., No. 347
Honolulu, HI 96816
Ph: (808)596-7765
Free: (888)823-4823
Fax: (808)596-7764
E-mail: info@hypnosis.com
URL: http://www.hypnosis.com
Contact: Dr. A.M. Krasner, Founder
Founded: 1982. **Members:** 4,000. **Membership Dues:** first year registration in U.S. and overseas, $85 ● renewal, in U.S. (plus 10 outside U.S.), $65 (annual). **Multinational. Description:** Provides registration and certification for qualified hypnotherapists. **Additional Websites:** http://www.abh-abnlp.com. **Publications:** Articles. **Conventions/Meetings:** annual convention.

14607 ■ American Board of Psychological Hypnosis (ABPH)
c/o Samuel M. Migdole, EdD, Pres.
North Shore Counseling Ctr.
23 Broadway
Beverly, MA 01915
Ph: (978)922-2280
Fax: (978)927-1758
E-mail: pres.abph@prodigy.net
Contact: Samuel M. Migdole EdD, Pres.
Founded: 1959. **Description:** Awards specialty diplomas to qualified licensed doctoral level psychologists in experimental and clinical hypnosis. Aims to raise the standards of individuals conducting research in hypnosis and those using it in clinical practice by requiring specialized training and experience in the field as evidenced by advanced educational credentials in psychology, published research, written and oral examinations, and recommendations of colleagues. **Formerly:** American Board of Examiners in Psychological Hypnosis; American Board of Professional Psychology in Hypnosis. **Conventions/Meetings:** annual meeting.

14608 ■ American Council of Hypnotist Examiners (ACHE)
700 S Central Ave.
Glendale, CA 91204
Ph: (818)242-1159
Fax: (818)247-9379
E-mail: hypnotismla@earthlink.net
URL: http://www.hypnotistexaminers.org
Contact: Gil Boyne, Exec. Dir.
Founded: 1980. **Members:** 8,200. **Membership Dues:** $50 (biennial). **Staff:** 5. **Budget:** $175,000. **Regional Groups:** 8. **State Groups:** 1. **Local Groups:** 1. **National Groups:** 4. **Description:** Educates, examines, and awards certification in the field of hypnotherapy. Maintains speakers' bureau. Sponsors educational programs. **Libraries: Type:** reference. **Holdings:** 4,400. **Subjects:** hypnotherapy, psychotherapy, healing, mind power. **Awards:** Leadership Award. **Frequency:** annual. **Type:** recognition ● Lifetime Achievement Award. **Frequency:** annual. **Type:** recognition ● Special Achievement Award. **Frequency:** annual. **Type:** recognition ● Unsung Hero Award. **Frequency:** annual. **Type:** recognition. **Computer Services:** Mailing lists. **Committees:** Credentials; Ethics; Specialized Education. **Also Known As:** Hypnotists Examining Council. **Publications:** *Ameri-*

can Hypnotherapy Report, annual. Contains news and information on the hypnotherapy profession. **Price:** included in membership dues. **Circulation:** 8,000 ● *Directory of Certified Members*, periodic. Membership Directory ● *International Hypnotherapy Report*, quarterly. Magazine. **Price:** free for members. **Circulation:** 8,000 ● Newsletter, periodic. **Price:** free for members. **Circulation:** 8,000. **Conventions/Meetings:** annual International Hypnotherapy Conference (exhibits).

14609 ■ American Guild of Hypnotherapists (AGH)

2200 Veterans Blvd., Ste.108
Kenner, LA 70062-4005
E-mail: drreg@hypnotherapistcollege.com
URL: http://www.hypnotherapistcollege.com/guild.
  html
Contact: Reg Sheldrick PhD, Pres.
Founded: 1975. **Members:** 685. **Membership Dues:** initial hypnotist, $50 ● renewal hypnotist, $35 (annual) ● hypnotherapist, $40 (annual). **Staff:** 2. **Description:** Represents hypnotherapists and professional hypnotists; mental health, medical, dental, and chiropractic professionals who use hypnosis in their practices. Offers home study course in hypnosis/hypnotherapy. Is approved by many state licensing boards as a provider of continuing education credit. **Divisions:** Law Enforcement Officers; Medical Professionals; Mental Health Professionals. **Publications:** *Journal of Hypnotherapy*, quarterly. **Circulation:** 1,500 ● Newsletter, periodic. **Conventions/Meetings:** seminar, for health professionals, law enforcement officers, counselors, and educators - always on weekends.

14610 ■ American Hypnosis Association (AHA)

c/o Hypnosis Motivation Institute .
18607 Ventura Blvd., Ste.310
Tarzana, CA 91356
Ph: (818)758-2747
Free: (800)479-9464
Fax: (818)344-2262
E-mail: info@hypnosismotivation.com
URL: http://www.hypnosis.edu
Contact: George Kappas, Pres.
Founded: 1972. **Members:** 1,000. **Membership Dues:** regular, $49 (annual). **Staff:** 4. **State Groups:** 2. **For-Profit. Description:** Professionals and para-professionals in hypnotherapy. Acts as a resource center for members. **Libraries: Type:** reference. **Holdings:** 100; video recordings. **Subjects:** topics related to hypnosis and alternative healing. **Computer Services:** database ● mailing lists ● online services. **Affiliated With:** Office and Professional Employees International Union. **Publications:** *American Hypnotherapist*, quarterly. Newsletter. **Conventions/Meetings:** monthly conference and lecture - every last Saturday ● quarterly meeting and lecture.

14611 ■ American Society of Clinical Hypnosis (ASCH)

140 N Bloomingdale Rd.
Bloomingdale, IL 60108-1017
Ph: (630)980-4740
Fax: (630)351-8490
E-mail: info@asch.net
URL: http://www.asch.net
Contact: Dana Downing, Member Services Mgr.
Founded: 1957. **Members:** 3,000. **Membership Dues:** associate, researcher, regular, $210 (annual) ● regular, in Canada, $185 (annual) ● resident, intern, $77-$90 (annual) ● student affiliate, $57-$70 (annual). **Staff:** 6. **Budget:** $800,000. **Regional Groups:** 36. **State Groups:** 17. **Local Groups:** 19. **Description:** Physicians, dentists, psychologists with doctoral or masters degrees, and clinical social workers and counselors, and nurses with master's degrees. Brings together professional people in medical, dental, and psychological fields using hypnosis; sets up standards of training; conducts teaching sessions and workshops at basic and advanced levels. Offers instruction on clinical hypnosis and various simple forms of psychotherapy and psychodynamics. Cooperates with all scientific disciplines with regard

to use of hypnosis. Maintains speakers' bureau. **Libraries: Type:** reference. **Holdings:** 150; audiovisuals. **Subjects:** hypnosis. **Awards:** Awards of Merit. **Frequency:** annual. **Type:** recognition. **Recipient:** for persons who have made exceptional and outstanding contributions to the society ● Irving Secter Awards. **Frequency:** annual. **Type:** recognition. **Recipient:** to individuals for substantial and material contributions to the society ● Presidential Awards. **Frequency:** annual. **Type:** recognition. **Recipient:** for persons with exemplary commitment to ASCH in leadership, volunteer and teaching capacities ● Thomas P. Wall, DMD, Award. **Frequency:** annual. **Type:** recognition. **Recipient:** for outstanding teachers of clinical hypnosis. **Computer Services:** database, journal search ● database, member referral ● mailing lists. **Committees:** Program. **Publications:** *American Journal of Clinical Hypnosis*, quarterly. Contains scientific articles and clinical case reports on hypnosis. **Price:** $62.50 /year for individuals; $125.00 /year for institutions. ISSN: 0002-9157. **Circulation:** 4,000. **Advertising:** accepted. Alternate Formats: online ● *American Society of Clinical Hypnosis—Newsletter*, quarterly. Promotes the acceptance of hypnosis as a tool in clinical medicine and scientific research. Includes member news and calendar of events. **Price:** included in membership dues. **Circulation:** 3,000. **Conventions/Meetings:** annual convention, features workshops and scientific symposia on clinical hypnosis - 2008 Mar. 7-11, Chicago, IL - **Avg. Attendance:** 400.

14612 ■ American Society of Clinical Hypnosis - Education and Research Foundation (ASCH-ERF)

140 N Bloomingdale Rd.
Bloomingdale, IL 60108-1017
Ph: (630)980-4740
Fax: (630)351-8490
E-mail: info@asch.net
URL: http://www.asch.net
Contact: Philip R. Appell PhD, Accreditation Committee Chm.
Founded: 1957. **Members:** 2,400. **Membership Dues:** regular, $160. **Staff:** 3. **Budget:** $114,000. **Description:** Teaching and research arm of the American Society of Clinical Hypnosis (see separate entry). Physicians, dentists, and psychologists. Underwrites workshops in the U.S. and Canada to train professionals in hypnosis and broaden their knowledge of psychotherapy. Basic section is designed to familiarize physicians, psychologists, and dentists with hypnosis and its applications to problems of the psychologically normal patient including preparation for childbirth, comfort in the dental chair, and other problems and complaints complicated by emotional conflicts, such as smoking and obesity. Advanced section deals with techniques that can be used in addition to hypnotherapy in treating patients. **Awards:** Mutter Foundation Tuition Grants. **Type:** grant. **Recipient:** for financial hardship students. **Committees:** Joint Committee on Education. **Affiliated With:** American Society of Clinical Hypnosis. **Formerly:** (1962) Seminars on Hypnosis Foundation. **Conventions/Meetings:** semiannual Clinical Hypnosis Workshops.

14613 ■ Institute for Research in Hypnosis and Psychotherapy (IRHP)

Address Unknown since 2006
Founded: 1954. **Membership Dues:** fellow/associate of the Morton Prince Mental Health Center, $150 (annual). **Staff:** 45. **Budget:** $250,000. **Description:** Psychologists, psychiatrists, physicians, and social workers trained in clinical hypnosis, hypnotherapy, and hypnoanalysis. Sponsors research in clinical and experimental hypnosis; offers postgraduate training in hypnosis and its applications; develops standards and procedures for advanced education in clinical and experimental hypnosis. Operates Morton Prince Centers, low-cost treatment centers for outpatients who cannot afford hypnotherapy or hypnoanalysis in private practice. Conducts consulting and educational training services. Compiles statistics; maintains databases and speakers' bureau. **Libraries: Type:** reference. **Holdings:** 1,400; archival material. **Sub-**

jects: hypnosis, hypnotherapy. **Awards:** Morton Prince Award. **Frequency:** annual. **Type:** fellowship. **Recipient:** for research in clinical hypnotherapy ● Prof. Marco Marchesan Award. **Type:** recognition. **Recipient:** for research in other institutions. **Divisions:** Forensic Hypnosis, Consulting and Research; Hypnoanalysis; Hypnotherapy. **Formerly:** (1982) Institute for Research in Hypnosis. **Conventions/Meetings:** periodic conference (exhibits) ● seminar ● workshop.

14614 ■ International Association of Counselors and Therapists (IACT)

RR No. 2, Box 2468
Laceyville, PA 18623
Ph: (570)869-1021
Fax: (570)869-1249
E-mail: iactnow@aol.com
URL: http://www.iact.org
Contact: Linda Otto, Exec. Dir.
Founded: 1990. **Members:** 7,000. **Membership Dues:** professional, $69 (annual). **Staff:** 4. **Budget:** $100,000. **Description:** Mental health professionals, medical professionals, social workers, clergy, educators, hypnotherapists, counselors, and individuals interested in the helping professions. Promotes enhanced professional image and prestige for complementary therapy. Provides a forum for exchange of information and ideas among practitioners of traditional and nontraditional therapies and methodologies; fosters unity among "grassroots" practitioners and those with advanced academic credentials. Facilitates the development of new therapy programs. Conducts educational, research, and charitable programs. Awards credits for continuing education. Maintains speakers' bureau and library; operates referral and placement services; compiles statistics. Assists in the development of local chapters. **Awards:** Therapist of the Year. **Frequency:** annual. **Type:** recognition. **Recipient:** nominated and voted on by local chapters. **Committees:** Political Action. **Publications:** *Unlimited Human!*, quarterly. Magazine. Includes health and wellness articles. **Price:** included in membership dues. **Circulation:** 10,000. **Advertising:** accepted. **Conventions/Meetings:** periodic conference and workshop, for professionals (exhibits).

14615 ■ International Medical and Dental Hypnotherapy Association (IMDHA)

Box 2468
Laceyville, PA 18623
Ph: (570)869-1021
Free: (800)553-6886
Fax: (570)869-1249
E-mail: info@imdha.com
URL: http://www.imdha.com
Contact: Linda Otto, Exec. Dir.
Founded: 1987. **Members:** 2,500. **Membership Dues:** initial certified, $155 ● renewal certified, $85 (annual) ● associate, $55 ● student in training, $35 (annual). **Staff:** 5. **State Groups:** 18. **Local Groups:** 2. **For-Profit. Multinational. Description:** Certified hypnotherapists; associate members are non-certified hypnotherapists and individuals interested in hypnosis. Hypnotherapists help to mentally prepare patients to deal with the stress and pain involved with medical and dental procedures. Offers certification courses. Maintains an International Referral Directory which lists certified members. Maintains speakers' bureau and library on hypnosis and mind development. Offers educational programs; has affiliate Hypnosis training schools, free Email Hypnosis and Holistic Living Journal written monthly. Offers Specialty Certifications to certified members at annual Educational Conference. **Libraries: Type:** not open to the public; by appointment only; reference. **Holdings:** 150; articles, audio recordings, books, periodicals, video recordings. **Subjects:** hypnosis, hypnotherapy, guided imagery, medical hypnosis, visualization, pain control, pediatric hypnosis, marketing, tapes, regression therapy, Ericksonian Hypnotherapy, Forensic Hypnosis, inductions. **Awards:** Diplomat. **Frequency:** annual. **Type:** recognition ● Fellow Award. **Frequency:** annual. **Type:** recognition ● Founders Award. **Frequency:** annual. **Type:** recogni-

tion ● Presidents Award. **Frequency:** annual. **Type:** recognition. **Recipient:** for research in hypnosis ● Service Awards (Team Work). **Frequency:** annual. **Type:** recognition. **Publications:** *Hypnosis and Holistic Health.* Journal. Alternate Formats: online ● *Subconsciously Speaking: You Can Change Your Life Through the Powers of Your Mind,* bimonthly. Newsletter. Contains articles of interest including hypnosis, imagery, holistic health, and consciousness. **Price:** \ included in membership dues; $14.00 /year for nonmembers in U.S. **Circulation:** 5,000 ● Articles. Alternate Formats: online. **Conventions/Meetings:** annual Hypnosis and Holistic Living - conference, hypnosis and healing (exhibits) - every fourth weekend of October.

14616 ■ National Board for Certified Clinical Hypnotherapists (NBCCH)

1110 Fidler Ln., Ste.1218
Silver Spring, MD 20910
Ph: (301)608-0123
Free: (800)449-8144
Fax: (301)588-9535
E-mail: admin@natboard.com
URL: http://www.natboard.com
Contact: Ron Klein, Exec. Dir. for Admin.
Founded: 1991. **Description:** Aims to professionalize the mental health specialty/sub-specialty of hypnotherapy, including addictions, counselors, marriage and family therapists, mental health counselors, pastoral counselors, psychiatric nurse, physicians, psychiatrists, psychologists, school counselors, and social workers; promotes standards for certification; sponsors educational activities; promotes public and professional awareness; sponsors scientific investigation into the uses of hypnotherapy. **Telecommunication Services:** electronic mail, interlink@natboard.com. **Publications:** *Interlink*, periodic. Newsletter. Alternate Formats: online.

14617 ■ National Guild of Hypnotists (NGH)

PO Box 308
Merrimack, NH 03054
Ph: (603)429-9438
Fax: (603)424-8066
E-mail: ngh@ngh.net
URL: http://www.ngh.net
Contact: Dr. Dwight F. Damon, Pres./Exec. Dir.
Founded: 1951. **Members:** 10,000. **Membership Dues:** professional (certified), $85-$95 (annual) ● regular (non-certified), $95 (annual) ● international, $105 (annual). **Staff:** 14. **State Groups:** 65. **Multinational. Description:** Aims to unite all persons sharing a professional interest in hypnotism. Seeks to establish standards for professional conduct; to increase members' knowledge in their respective areas of specialization; to improve members' professional skills; to enhance the quality of services provided to clients; to maintain standards and Code of Ethics; to encourage educational programs; to further the knowledge and understanding of hypnosis; to promote the acceptance of hypnosis; to stimulate scientific research in the field and dissemination of results; to cooperate with other professional societies that share mutual goals, ethics, and interests; to provide members with group benefits; to improve members' individual skills in the marketing of their services and management of their practices. Offers ongoing educational seminars and workshops, and certification program. Compiles statistics; conducts research programs. Provides an open forum for a free exchange of ideas concerning hypnotism. **Libraries: Type:** reference. **Holdings:** 1,000. **Subjects:** hypnosis, psychology, counseling. **Awards:** Charles C. Curtis Religion and Hypnosis Award. **Frequency:** annual. **Type:** recognition. **Recipient:** for a member voted by SIG of Clergy Hypnotherapists ● Charles Tebbetts Award. **Frequency:** annual. **Type:** recognition. **Recipient:** for educating the public about hypnosis and hypnotherapy ● Hypnosis Humanities Award. **Frequency:** annual. **Type:** recognition. **Recipient:** for a member voted by peer group nominations ● Hypnosis Research Award. **Frequency:** annual. **Type:** recognition. **Recipient:** for a research reported during a given year ● Member of the Year. **Frequency:** annual. **Type:** recognition. **Recipient:**

for a member voted by committee and peer group nominations ● Meritorious Service Award. **Frequency:** annual. **Type:** recognition. **Recipient:** for a member voted by committee and peer group nominations ● Ormond McGill Award. **Frequency:** annual. **Type:** recognition. **Recipient:** to the "most outstanding presenter" at the previous year's conference; nominated by conference attendees ● President's Award. **Frequency:** annual. **Type:** recognition. **Recipient:** for outstanding service to the profession and the Guild ● Rexford L. North Memorial Trophy. **Frequency:** annual. **Type:** trophy. **Recipient:** for a member selected by NGH president. **Computer Services:** database, new chapters and referrals. **Boards:** Advisory; Certification Examination. **Committees:** Awards and Honors; Conferences and Meetings; Continuing Education; Convention/Conference Adjunct Faculty Selections; Ethics; Info/Science/Education; Standards. **Departments:** Certified Instructor Development and Support. **Sections:** International Affairs. **Subgroups:** Clergy Hypnotherapists; Division de Hypnotizadores Hispanos. **Task Forces:** Governmental and Legislative. **Working Groups:** Contemporary History. **Formed by Merger of:** (1959) International Hypnological Association; (1990) Hypnosis Educational Council International; (1990) National Association of Clergy Hypnotherapists; (1996) National Board of Hypnosis Education & Certification. **Publications:** *Hypno-Gram*, quarterly. Newsletter. **Price:** included in membership dues. **Circulation:** 8,000. **Advertising:** accepted ● *Hypnosis Today*, annual. Magazine. **Price:** $4.95. **Advertising:** accepted ● *The Journal of Hypnotism*, quarterly. Magazine. **Price:** included in membership dues. **Advertising:** accepted ● *NGH Video Rental Library.* Videos ● Audiotapes ● Books. **Conventions/Meetings:** annual conference (exhibits) - always second weekend of August ● Continuing Education Workshops, for members and nonmembers - 12-15/year.

14618 ■ Society for Clinical and Experimental Hypnosis (SCEH)

221 Rivermoor St.
Boston, MA 02132
Ph: (617)469-1981
Fax: (617)469-1889
E-mail: sceh@mspp.edu
URL: http://www.sceh.us
Contact: Dean Abby, Exec. Dir.
Founded: 1949. **Members:** 400. **Membership Dues:** full, $129 (annual) ● student, $39 (annual). **Budget:** $175,000. **Description:** United States constituent society of the International Society of Hypnosis. Professional society of physicians, dentists, doctoral level psychologists, social workers, chiropractors, psychiatric nurses and other mental health and health professionals interested in research in hypnosis and its boundary areas as well as the therapeutic use of hypnosis in clinical practice. Encourages cooperation among professional and scientific disciplines in use of hypnosis; promotes educational standards; conducts introductory and advanced workshops and continuing education seminars in therapeutic hypnosis. **Awards: Frequency:** annual. **Type:** recognition. **Recipient:** for outstanding contributions in the field of clinical and experimental hypnosis. **Computer Services:** database, referrals. **Affiliated With:** American Association for the Advancement of Science; World Federation for Mental Health. **Publications:** *Focus*, quarterly. Newsletter. Contains research and clinical notes, society news, book reviews, and obituaries. **Price:** $11.00/year. ISSN: 0583-8975. **Circulation:** 950 ● *International Journal of Clinical and Experimental Hypnosis*, quarterly. Contains book reviews, statistics, and research and clinical reports. **Price:** included in membership dues; $49.00 /year for nonmembers. ISSN: 0020-7144. **Circulation:** 1,000. **Advertising:** accepted ● Membership Directory, periodic. **Conventions/Meetings:** annual Scientific Program - conference and workshop.

Hypoglycemia

14619 ■ HELP - Institute for Body Chemistry (HELP)

6 Mellon Terr.
Pittsburgh, PA 15206

Ph: (412)441-2909
E-mail: ekrimmel2@earthlink.net
URL: http://home.earthlink.net/~ekrimmel2
Contact: Ms. Patricia Krimmel, Dir.
Founded: 1979. **Members:** 2,500. **Staff:** 2. **Description:** Health professionals and interested individuals. Promotes public awareness of body chemistry problems within the context of general health. Seeks to collect, verify, and distribute information related to body chemistry especially hypoglycemia (low blood sugar), Celiac Disease, and cholesterol management. Conducts seminars regarding nutrition, exercise, life style, and emotional stability. Develops support groups and encourages communication among members. **Libraries: Type:** reference. **Publications:** *Cholesterol Control Handbook and Cookbook* ● *Low Blood Sugar Handbook* ● *Vital Health Facts and Composition of Foods.*

Immunology

14620 ■ American Association of Immunologists (AAI)

9650 Rockville Pike
Bethesda, MD 20814-3998
Ph: (301)634-7178
Fax: (301)634-7887
E-mail: infoaai@aai.org
URL: http://mercury.faseb.org/aai/default.asp
Contact: M. Michele Hogan PhD, Exec. Dir.
Founded: 1913. **Members:** 5,500. **Membership Dues:** regular, in U.S., $260 (annual) ● regular, in Canada, $367 (annual) ● regular, international, $360 (annual) ● trainee, in U.S., $64 (annual) ● trainee, in Canada, $165 (annual) ● trainee, international, $164 (annual). **Staff:** 17. **Budget:** $600,000. **Description:** Represents scientists engaged in immunological research including aspects of virology, bacteriology, biochemistry, genetics, and related disciplines. Advances knowledge of immunology and related disciplines and facilitate the interchange of information among investigators in various fields. Promotes interaction between laboratory investigators and clinicians. Conducts training courses, symposia, workshop, and lectures. Compiles statistics. **Awards:** AAI-BD Biosciences Investigator Award. **Frequency:** annual. **Type:** recognition. **Recipient:** to a member who received degree within 15 years of award ● AAI Excellence in Mentoring Award. **Frequency:** annual. **Type:** recognition. **Recipient:** to a member for his/her contributions to the profession through outstanding mentoring ● AAI-Huang Foundation Meritorious Career Award. **Frequency:** annual. **Type:** recognition. **Recipient:** to a mid-career scientist for outstanding research contributions to the field of immunology ● AAI-Huang Foundation Trainee Achievement Award. **Frequency:** annual. **Type:** recognition. **Recipient:** for promising trainees in the field of immunology ● AAI Junior Faculty Travel Awards. **Frequency:** annual. **Type:** recognition. **Recipient:** for young investigators ● AAI Minority Scientist Awards. **Frequency:** annual. **Type:** recognition. **Recipient:** for members ● Pfizer-Showell Travel Awards. **Frequency:** annual. **Type:** recognition. **Recipient:** for investigators. **Computer Services:** database ● mailing lists. **Committees:** Awards; Clinical Immunology; Education; Minority Affairs; Nominating; Program; Public Affairs; Publications; Status of Women; Veterinary Immunology. **Publications:** *AAI Newsletter*, bimonthly. **Price:** included in membership dues. Alternate Formats: online ● *Journal of Immunology*, semimonthly. Reports on original research efforts on cellular immunology; clinical immunology and immunopathology; cytokines, mediators, and regulatory molecules. **Price:** included in membership dues; $200.00 for nonmembers in U.S. ISSN: 0022-1767. **Circulation:** 10,000. **Advertising:** accepted. Alternate Formats: microform; online. **Conventions/Meetings:** annual Experimental Biology - meeting and conference, in conjunction with Federation of American Societies for Experimental Biology (exhibits).

14621 ■ American Autoimmune Related Diseases Association (AARDA)

22100 Gratiot Ave.
Eastpointe, MI 48021-2227

Ph: (586)776-3900
Free: (800)598-4668
Fax: (586)776-3903
E-mail: aarda@aarda.org
URL: http://www.aarda.org
Contact: Virginia Ladd RT, Pres./Exec.Dir.
Founded: 1991. **Members:** 4,000. **Membership Dues:** individual, $24 (annual) ● international, $34 (annual) ● organization/corporation, $100 (annual). **Staff:** 7. **Budget:** $500,000. **Description:** Promotes national focus and collaborative efforts among state and national volunteer health groups on autoimmunity, the major cause of serious chronic diseases. Offers research and educational programs; maintains speakers' bureau. **Awards: Type:** grant. **Recipient:** for non-profit organizations and foundations doing work on autoimmunity and basic autoimmunity research. **Computer Services:** Information services, autoimmune disease facts and resources ● mailing lists, advocacy notification ● online services, survey. **Affiliated With:** National Health Council; National Organization for Rare Disorders. **Publications:** *InFocus*, quarterly. Newsletter. Includes research updates and national autoimmune activities designed primarily for lay membership. **Price:** $24.00/year. **Circulation:** 5,000. **Conventions/Meetings:** periodic seminar, for the public (exhibits) ● periodic symposium, for physicians ● periodic workshop.

14622 ■ American Society for Histocompatibility and Immunogenetics (ASHI)
15000 Commerce Pkwy., Ste.C
Mount Laurel, NJ 08054
Ph: (856)638-0428
Fax: (856)439-0525
E-mail: info@ashi-hla.org
URL: http://www.ashi-hla.org
Contact: Kimberly Glenn, Exec. Dir.
Founded: 1972. **Members:** 1,000. **Membership Dues:** regular, full (non-doctoral), $100 (annual) ● associate, emeritus, $53 (annual) ● sustaining institution, $1,155 (annual) ● regular, institution, $630 (annual) ● regular, full (doctoral), $126 (annual) ● sustaining, full (doctoral), $230 (annual) ● sustaining, full (non-doctoral), $205 (annual). **Staff:** 7. **Budget:** $2,000,000. **Description:** Scientists, physicians, and technologists involved in research and clinical activities related to histocompatibility testing (a state of mutual tolerance that allows some tissues to be grafted effectively to others). Conducts proficiency testing and educational programs. Maintains liaison with regulatory agencies; offers placement services and laboratory accreditation. Has co-sponsored development of histocompatability specialist and laboratory certification program. **Awards:** Best Abstracts/ASHI Scholars/International Scholars Awards. **Frequency:** annual. **Type:** recognition. **Recipient:** for best abstracts presented at the annual meeting ● Distinguished Service Award. **Frequency:** annual. **Type:** recognition. **Recipient:** for colleagues who have contributed significantly to ASHI's heritage ● Outstanding Technologist Award. **Frequency:** annual. **Type:** recognition. **Recipient:** to a technologist who has provided outstanding contributions to the field of histocompatibility and immunogenetics ● Rose Payne Distinguished Scientist Award. **Frequency:** annual. **Type:** recognition. **Recipient:** for scientists ● Young Investigator Awards. **Frequency:** annual. **Type:** recognition. **Recipient:** to young investigators presenting noteworthy papers at the annual meeting. **Computer Services:** database, membership. **Committees:** Accreditation and Standards; External Affairs; Marketing and Public Relations; Membership Services; National Affairs/Public Policy; Nominations; Operations; Outstanding Technologist; Publications; Science and Education; Technologists' Affairs; Web. **Task Forces:** Strategic Planning. **Formerly:** American Association for Clinical Histocompatibility Testing. **Publications:** *ASHI Quarterly*. Newsletter. Includes calendar of events, employment listings, certification data, and notices of awards. **Price:** included in membership dues; $30.00/year for nonmembers. **Circulation:** 1,000. **Advertising:** accepted. Alternate Formats: online ● *Human Immunology*, monthly. Journal. Alternate Formats: online ●

Laboratory Procedure Manual. Covers laboratory procedures. **Price:** included in membership dues. Alternate Formats: CD-ROM ● Membership Directory, annual, published each spring. Includes names, postal and e-mail addresses, telephone numbers, and fax numbers of all members. **Price:** included in membership dues. Alternate Formats: online ● Papers ● Proceedings ● Brochures (in English and Spanish) ● Books ● Reprints. Alternate Formats: online ● Surveys. **Conventions/Meetings:** annual meeting (exhibits) - 2007 Oct. 8-12, Minneapolis, MN.

14623 ■ Association of Medical Laboratory Immunologists (AMLI)
c/o Maggie Fogel, Admin.
34 W 83rd St., Ste.R
New York, NY 10024
Ph: (212)873-2955
Fax: (212)873-2344
E-mail: maggie@maggiefogel.com
URL: http://www.amli.org
Contact: Barbara Detrick PhD, Pres.
Founded: 1987. **Membership Dues:** regular, $85 (annual) ● student, $25 (annual) ● corporate, $750 (annual) ● fellow, $120 (annual). **Description:** Aims to improve the practice of clinical immunology laboratory testing by encouraging education and training of all individuals in the organization, maximizing the quality of test procedures, promoting the exchange of information, supporting clinical research efforts and improving patient care. **Computer Services:** Information services, links, meetings, and related sites. **Committees:** Standards. **Publications:** *Clinical and Applied Immunology Reviews*, bimonthly. Journal. Presents timely peer reviewed articles and full length review format on all aspects of the immune system in healthy subjects and patients. **Price:** $480.00/year for institutions; $226.00/year for individuals. ISSN: 1529-1049. Also Cited As: *CAIR* ● *Clinical Diagnostic Immunology - Protocols in Quality Assurance and Standardization.* Book. **Conventions/Meetings:** annual meeting.

14624 ■ Clinical Immunology Society (CIS)
555 E Wells St., Ste.1100
Milwaukee, WI 53202-3823
Ph: (414)224-8095
Fax: (414)272-6070
E-mail: info@clinimmsoc.org
URL: http://www.clinimmsoc.org
Contact: George S. Eisenbarth MD, Pres.
Founded: 1986. **Members:** 840. **Membership Dues:** regular/associate, $150 (annual) ● trainee, $35 (annual) ● clinical, $150 (annual). **Staff:** 3. **Budget:** $300,000. **Description:** Investigators and clinicians concerned with immunologic diseases. Promotes research on: the causes and mechanisms of immunologic diseases; improved treatment, evaluation, and prevention of diseases related to immunity. Facilitates exchange of ideas and findings; fosters excellence in research and medical practice. Works to increase public awareness and knowledge of immunologically-mediated diseases. Conducts scientific, educational programs. **Awards:** CIS Science Recognition Award for New Investigators. **Frequency:** annual. **Type:** grant. **Recipient:** based on abstract submissions. **Computer Services:** Mailing lists. **Committees:** Clinical Laboratory Immunology; Communications; Development; Education; Financial; HIV; International; Membership; Nominations; Program; Public Policy; Publications. **Publications:** *Clinical Immunology*, monthly. Journal. **Price:** included in membership dues. **Circulation:** 1,920. **Conventions/Meetings:** annual Federation of Clinical Immunology Societies (FOCIS) - conference, scientific meeting.

14625 ■ Evans Syndrome Research and Support Group
1376 Presidential Hwy.
Jefferson, NH 03583
Fax: (603)586-7983
URL: http://www.evanssyndrome.org
Contact: Lou Addington, Pres./Founder
Founded: 1992. **Multinational. Description:** Provides mutual support and ongoing research for parents and concerned friends and caregivers of

children with Evans Syndrome. (Evans Syndrome is a rare autoimmune disease.) Facilitates networking and exchange of information. Distributes literature. Develops a group of interested physicians in immunology, genetics, and hematology/oncology. Works to formulate questions for caregivers/patients to ask their doctors. **Publications:** none. **Convention/ Meeting:** none. **Libraries: Type:** reference. **Holdings:** clippings, periodicals. **Subjects:** Evans Syndrome, Thrombocytopenia, Hemolytic Anemia.

14626 ■ Federation of Clinical Immunology Societies (FOCIS)
11950 W Lake Park Dr., Ste.320
Milwaukee, WI 53224
Ph: (414)359-1670
Fax: (414)359-1671
E-mail: info@focisnet.org
URL: http://www.focisnet.org
Contact: David Hafler MD, Chm.
Founded: 2003. **Members:** 28. **Staff:** 5. **Description:** Provides a scientific forum to foster the cross-disciplinary approach required to understand and treat immune-based diseases as the discipline of clinical immunology evolves. Seeks better understanding of the shared pathophysiological underpinnings of clinical immunology and the new therapeutic approaches suggested by these novel relationships, including the increasingly widespread use of biologics in therapy. Serves as a forum for education of trainees, physicians, patients and the public in the discipline of clinical immunology. **Committees:** Abstract Review; Steering. **Subgroups:** Centers of Excellence. **Affiliated With:** American Society for Blood and Marrow Transplantation; American Society for Histocompatibility and Immunogenetics; American Society of Transplantation; Clinical Immunology Society; International Cytokine Society; Society for Investigative Dermatology; Society for Mucosal Immunology; World Allergy Organization. **Publications:** Brochure. Alternate Formats: online.

14627 ■ Immune Deficiency Foundation (IDF)
40 W Chesapeake Ave., Ste.308
Towson, MD 21204
Ph: (410)321-6647
Free: (800)296-4433
Fax: (410)321-9165
E-mail: idf@primaryimmune.org
URL: http://www.primaryimmune.org
Contact: Logan Wilhelm, Admin. Asst.
Founded: 1980. **Members:** 11,500. **Staff:** 13. **State Groups:** 19. **Local Groups:** 14. **Description:** Immune deficiency patients, their families, and medical professionals. Promotes education and research in primary immune deficiency diseases. Holds medical symposia; bestows patient scholarship and research awards. **Awards:** Immune Deficiency Foundation Scholarship. **Frequency:** annual. **Type:** scholarship. **Recipient:** for primary immune deficiency diagnosis ● Novartis Fellowship. **Frequency:** annual. **Type:** fellowship. **Computer Services:** database ● mailing lists. **Publications:** *Guide for Nurses.* Alternate Formats: online ● *IDF Advocate*, quarterly. Newsletter. Contains announcements of patient scholarship and research awards. Includes health insurance information and calendar of events. **Price:** free. **Circulation:** 11,500. Alternate Formats: online ● *Our Immune System.* Book ● *Patient and Family Handbook* (in English, French, and Spanish). Alternate Formats: online ● *Primer for Physicians.* Alternate Formats: online. **Conventions/Meetings:** annual conference - always October or November.

14628 ■ Immunization Action Coalition (IAC)
1573 Selby Ave., Ste.234
St. Paul, MN 55104
Ph: (651)647-9009
Fax: (651)647-9131
E-mail: admin@immunize.org
URL: http://www.immunize.org
Contact: Deborah L. Wexler MD, Exec. Dir.
Founded: 1990. **Staff:** 7. **Budget:** $1,350,000. **Nonmembership. Description:** Works to increase immunization rates and prevent disease by creating and distributing educational materials for health

professionals and the public that enhances the delivery of safe and effective immunization services. Facilitates communication about the safety, efficacy, and use of vaccines within the broad immunization community of patients, parents, health care organizations, and government health agencies. **Libraries: Type:** reference. **Holdings:** articles, periodicals, photographs. **Subjects:** immunization resources. **Computer Services:** Online services, publication. **Programs:** Hepatitis B Coalition. **Publications:** *Hep Express*, monthly. Newsletter. Contains news service on viral hepatitis issues. **Price:** free. **Circulation:** 2,500. Alternate Formats: online. Also Cited As: *HEPX ● IAC Express*, weekly. Newsletter. Provides immunization news to health professionals and others interested in immunization issues. **Price:** free. **Circulation:** 22,000. Alternate Formats: online ● *Needle Tips and the Hepatitis B Coalition News*, semiannual. Newsletter. Discusses vaccine-preventable diseases and hepatitis B. **Price:** free. ISSN: 1525-7053. **Circulation:** 260,000. Alternate Formats: online ● *Vaccinate Adults*, semiannual. Newsletter. **Price:** free. ISSN: 1525-7061. **Circulation:** 260,000. Alternate Formats: online ● *Vaccinate Women*, annual. Newsletter. **Price:** free. ISSN: 1538-196X. **Circulation:** 40,000. Alternate Formats: online. **Conventions/Meetings:** conference.

14629 ■ International Complement Society (ICS)
c/o John D. Lambris, Pres.
401 Stellar Chance
Dept. of Pathology and Lab. Medicine
Univ. of Pennsylvania
Philadelphia, PA 19104
Ph: (215)746-5765
Fax: (215)573-8738
E-mail: info@complement.org
URL: http://www.complement.org
Contact: John D. Lambris, Pres.
Membership Dues: regular, $50 (annual) ● student, $30 (annual). **Multinational. Description:** Promotes advances of complement research and development through the encouragement of cooperative educational programs, clinical applications, and professional standards in the complement field. **Computer Services:** Online services, members' directory. **Committees:** Development; Nominating; Scientific Program.

14630 ■ Jeffrey Modell Foundation (JMF)
747 3rd Ave.
New York, NY 10017
Ph: (212)819-0200
Free: (866)INFO4PI
Fax: (212)764-4180
E-mail: info@jmfworld.org
URL: http://www.info4pi.org
Contact: Vicki Modell, Co-Founder
Description: Works on primary immune deficiency; including research, physician and patient education, patient support, and public awareness. **Additional Websites:** http://www.jmfworld.org. **Publications:** *Update*. Newsletter. Alternate Formats: online.

14631 ■ National Immunotherapy Cancer Research Foundation
PO Box 1027
Flemington, NJ 08822
Ph: (908)806-4300
Fax: (908)806-3548
Contact: Dale A. Facchina, Pres./CEO
Founded: 1990. **Description:** Promotes the use of immune system stimulation including vaccines, biological response modifiers, and other immuno-augmentative treatments as a cure for cancer. Raises funds for immunotherapy and immunology research in the prevention and treatment of cancer. **Publications:** none.

14632 ■ National Network for Immunization Information (NNII)
301 Univ. Blvd.
Galveston, TX 77555-0351
Ph: (409)772-0199
Fax: (409)747-4995

E-mail: nnii@i4ph.org
URL: http://www.immunizationinfo.org
Contact: Martin G. Myers MD, Exec.Dir./Ed.-in-Chief
Founded: 1999. **Staff:** 2. **Nonmembership. Description:** Provides current, science-based information to health care professionals, the media, policy makers, and the public, on issues and facts related to immunization. **Additional Websites:** http://www.i4ph.org. **Affiliated With:** American Academy of Family Physicians; American Academy of Pediatrics; American College of Obstetricians and Gynecologists; American Nurses Association; Infectious Diseases Society of America; National Association of Pediatric Nurse Practitioners; Society for Adolescent Medicine. **Publications:** *Are Vaccines Safe? Evaluating Information About Immunizations on the Internet*. Booklet. **Price:** $25.00/pack of 50 booklets ● *Know the Facts About Immunization ● National Network for Immunization Information Resource Kit* ● Brochure.

14633 ■ National Partnership for Immunization (NPI)
c/o National Immunization Program
Centers for Disease Control and Prevention
1600 Clifton Rd., Mailstop E-05
Atlanta, GA 30333
E-mail: npi@hmhb.org
URL: http://www.cdc.gov/nip/publications/default.htmbfp
Contact: Dena Penner, Program Mgr.
Founded: 2000. **Members:** 1,700. **Staff:** 4. **Description:** Encourages greater acceptance and use of immunization for people of all ages and cultures through partnerships with public and private organizations. Disseminates information about the importance of immunization in maintaining health and preventing disease to the public, the media, health care professionals, state and federal agencies, and members of local and state coalitions who work to assure that the benefits of immunization are available to all. **Awards:** Excellence in Immunization Awards. **Frequency:** annual. **Type:** recognition. **Publications:** *NPI Bulletin*, semiannual. Newsletter. **Price:** free. **Circulation:** 1,700. Alternate Formats: online ● *NPI VAXfacts*, monthly. Newsletter. Email newsletter. Alternate Formats: online ● *Reference Guide on Vaccines and Vaccine Safety*. Handbook. **Price:** $20.00. **Circulation:** 2,900. Alternate Formats: online. **Conventions/Meetings:** National Immunization Awareness Month - meeting - every August.

14634 ■ Society for Mucosal Immunology (SMI)
5272 River Rd., Ste.630
Bethesda, MD 20816
Ph: (301)718-6516
Fax: (301)656-0989
E-mail: smi@paimgmt.com
URL: http://www.socmucimm.org
Contact: Mark H. Epstein ScD, Exec. Dir.
Founded: 1987. **Members:** 700. **Staff:** 3. **Budget:** $400,000. **National Groups:** 37. **Multinational. Description:** Clinician-scientists and basic scientists comprised of immunologists, physicians, dentists, veterinarians, biochemists and others interested in the immunology of the gastrointestinal, respiratory and urogenital tracts, as well as the eye. Formed to advance research and education related to the field of mucosal immunology. **Telecommunication Services:** electronic mail, mepstein@paimgmt.com. **Publications:** *Mucosal Immunology Update*, quarterly. Journal. **Price:** included in membership dues. Alternate Formats: online. Also Cited As: *MIU*. **Conventions/Meetings:** triennial International Congress of Mucosal Immunology.

14635 ■ Think Twice Global Vaccine Institute
PO Box 9638
Santa Fe, NM 87504
Ph: (505)983-1856
E-mail: global@thinktwice.com
URL: http://thinktwice.com
Contact: Nathan Wright, Contact
Founded: 1996. **Nonmembership. For-Profit. Multinational. Description:** Provides parents and concerned individuals with educational resources to

make informed vaccine decisions. **Publications:** *Vaccines: Are They Really Safe and Effective?*. Book. **Price:** $12.95.

Infants

14636 ■ National Infant Torticollis Association (NITA)
200 Crestview Dr.
Springville, AL 35146
Ph: (205)467-0353
E-mail: info@infant-torticollis.org
URL: http://www.infant-torticollis.org
Contact: Jill Ramos, Exec. Dir.
Description: Acts as a source of information on torticollis for parents, families and healthcare professionals. Seeks to increase the desire within the medical community to conduct research on the disease. Encourages the establishment of a foundation to provide funding for medical research. Increases understanding and awareness of torticollis through education. **Telecommunication Services:** electronic mail, contactus@infant-torticollis.org. **Publications:** Brochure. Alternate Formats: online.

Infectious Diseases

14637 ■ American Sepsis Alliance (ASA)
c/o Dr. Carl Flatley, Chm., DDS
1865 Salem Ct.
Dunedin, FL 34698
Ph: (727)460-7765
Free: (866)ASA-8111
E-mail: flatc41@aol.com
URL: http://www.sepsisalliance.org
Contact: Dr. Carl Flatley DDS, Chm.
Membership Dues: general, $103. **Description:** Strives to increase awareness about sepsis. Promotes the need for early recognition, treatment options and proper treatment of sepsis. Creates more communication between health care givers, hospitals and the recipients of health care.

14638 ■ Association for Professionals in Infection Control and Epidemiology (APIC)
1275 K St. NW, Ste.1000
Washington, DC 20005-4006
Ph: (202)789-1890
Fax: (202)789-1899
E-mail: apicinfo@apic.org
URL: http://www.apic.org
Contact: Ms. Denise M. Murphy, Pres.
Founded: 1972. **Members:** 11,800. **Membership Dues:** active or associate in U.S. and Canada, Mexico, $163 (annual) ● active or associate outside U.S. and Canada, Mexico, $183 (annual) ● student in U.S., $80 (annual) ● student outside U.S., $95 (annual). **Staff:** 25. **State Groups:** 50. **Local Groups:** 112. **Description:** Physicians, microbiologists, nurses, epidemiologists, medical technicians, sanitarians, and pharmacists. Aims to improve patient care by improving the profession of infection control through the development of educational programs and standards. Promotes quality research and standardization of practices and procedures. Develops communications among members, and assesses and influences legislation related to the field. Conducts seminars at local level. **Libraries: Type:** not open to the public. **Committees:** Budget and Finance; Education; Exhibitor Advisory; Global Consensus II; Governmental Affairs; Guidelines; Information Technology Advisory; Member Services; Nominating; Policy and Bylaws. **Sections:** Ambulatory Care. **Task Forces:** Annual Conference; Corporate. **Formerly:** (1997) Association for Practitioners in Infection Control. **Publications:** *American Journal of Infection Control*, 8/year. Contains articles on infection control, epidemiology, infectious diseases, quality management, occupational health and disease prevention. **Price:** $99.00/year. ISSN: 0196-6553. **Circulation:** 13,930. Advertising: accepted. Alternate Formats: online. Also Cited As: *AJIC ● APIC News*, quarterly. Magazine. **Price:** included in membership dues.

Alternate Formats: online ● *Infection Connection*, quarterly. Newsletter. **Price:** $15.00. Alternate Formats: online. **Conventions/Meetings:** annual Advanced Practitioners Course - workshop ● Basic Training Course - workshop ● annual Educational Conference (exhibits).

14639 ■ Infectious Diseases Society of America (IDSA)
1300 Wilson Blvd., Ste.300
Arlington, VA 22209
Ph: (703)299-0200
Free: (888)844-IDSA
Fax: (703)299-0204
E-mail: info@idsociety.org
URL: http://www.idsociety.org
Contact: Henry Masur MD, Pres.

Founded: 1963. **Members:** 7,200. **Membership Dues:** domestic fellow, associate, $225 (annual) ● international fellow and associate, $270 (annual) ● domestic member-in-training, $115 (annual) ● international member-in-training, $160 (annual) ● international member-in-training, associate (from a developing nation), $105 (annual). **Staff:** 25. **Budget:** $5,000,000. **Description:** Physicians and microbiologists who have a career commitment to the field of infectious disease. Fosters research and training in the field. **Awards:** Bristol Award. **Type:** recognition ● Maxwell Finland Lectureship. **Frequency:** annual. **Type:** recognition ● Squibb Award. **Type:** recognition. **Publications:** *Clinical Infectious Diseases*, semimonthly. Journal. ISSN: 1058-4838. **Advertising:** accepted. Also Cited As: *CID* ● *Consult*, quarterly. Newsletter. **Price:** available to members only ● *Journal of Infectious Diseases*, semimonthly. ISSN: 0022-1899. Also Cited As: *JID* ● *Membership Roster*, triennial. Membership Directory. **Conventions/Meetings:** annual meeting - always September or October.

14640 ■ Infectious Diseases Society of America Emerging Infections Network (IDSA EIN)
c/o Susan Beekmann, RN, Program Coor.
Univ. of Iowa
Carver Coll. of Medicine
SW 34 GH
200 Hawkins Dr.
Iowa City, IA 52242
Ph: (319)384-8622
Free: (888)400-8387
Fax: (319)384-7208
E-mail: ein@uiowa.edu
URL: http://www.idsociety.org
Contact: Susan Beekmann RN, Program Coor.

Founded: 1995. **Multinational. Description:** Represents physicians specializing in adult and/or pediatric infectious diseases. **Committees:** Scientific Advisory. **Publications:** Reports ● Articles.

14641 ■ International Leptospirosis Society (ILS)
c/o Joe Vinetz, Sec.
Div. of Infectious Diseases
Univ. of California San Diego School of Medicine
9500 Gilman Dr., 0640
La Jolla, CA 92093-0640
Ph: (858)822-4469
Fax: (858)534-6020
E-mail: jvinetz@ucsd.edu
URL: http://www.med.monash.edu.au/microbiology/staff/adler/ils.html
Contact: Joe Vinetz, Sec.

Founded: 1994. **Multinational. Description:** Promotes knowledge on leptospirosis. Stimulates international leptospirosis research meetings worldwide through liaisons. Collaborates with other microbiological groups in leptospirosis and other fields of microbiology. Provides epidemiological information on leptospirosis to international and national health authorities. **Conventions/Meetings:** triennial meeting - 2007 Sept. 17-20, Quito, Ecuador.

14642 ■ International Society for Infectious Diseases (ISID)
1330 Beacon St., Ste.228
Brookline, MA 02446
Ph: (617)277-0551
Fax: (617)278-9113
E-mail: info@isid.org
URL: http://www.isid.org
Contact: Dr. Richard Wenzel, Pres.

Founded: 1986. **Members:** 20,000. **Multinational. Description:** Promotes research, prevention, and treatment of infectious diseases. Fosters partnerships for the control and cost-effective management of infectious diseases around the world. Enhances the professional development of individuals working in the field of infectious disease. **Publications:** *International Journal of Infectious Diseases*, bimonthly. Seeks to enhance the readers' understanding of the medical and cultural factors that affect infectious diseases. **Price:** free for members; $140.00 /year for nonmembers in U.S. and Canada; EUR 125.00 /year for nonmembers in Europe; 16,600.00 /year for nonmembers in Japan ● *ISID News*, quarterly. Newsletter. **Price:** free for members.

14643 ■ National Association on HIV Over Fifty (NAHOF)
23 Miner St.
Boston, MA 02215-3318
Ph: (617)233-7107
Fax: (617)262-5667
E-mail: jcampbell@hivoverfifty.org
URL: http://www.hivoverfifty.org
Contact: Jim Campbell, Pres.

Founded: 1995. **Membership Dues:** individual, $25 (annual) ● organization, $100 (annual). **Description:** Promotes the availability of education, prevention, service and health care programs for persons over age fifty affected by HIV. Seeks to address the issues of ageism in the community. Provides a forum for the exchange of information and issues on HIV. **Task Forces:** AIDS and Aging, Miami; AIDS and Aging, New Jersey; Boston Association on HIV over Fifty; Chicago Forum on HIV and Aging; Long Island Association on HIV over Fifty; Los Angeles Association on HIV over Fifty; New York Association on HIV over Fifty; Northern California Association on HIV over Fifty. **Publications:** *NAHOF Connection*, semiannual. Newsletter. Alternate Formats: online.

14644 ■ National Foundation for Infectious Diseases (NFID)
4733 Bethesda Ave., Ste.750
Bethesda, MD 20814
Ph: (301)656-0003
Fax: (301)907-0878
E-mail: info@nfid.org
URL: http://www.nfid.org
Contact: Carol J. Baker MD, Pres.

Founded: 1973. **Membership Dues:** supporting, $95 (annual). **Staff:** 9. **Budget:** $1,486,200. **Description:** Supports research into the causes and cures of infectious diseases; assists in the education of both professionals and the public in infectious diseases. Conducts programs in prevention of infectious diseases. **Libraries: Type:** reference. **Subjects:** infectious diseases. **Awards:** Jimmy & Rosalynn Carter Award for Humanitarian Contributions. **Frequency:** annual. **Type:** recognition. **Recipient:** for humanitarian contributions to the health of humankind ● Maxwell Finland Award for Scientific Achievement. **Frequency:** annual. **Type:** recognition. **Recipient:** for scientific achievements which contribute to improving medical research ● New Investigator Matching Grants. **Frequency:** annual. **Type:** grant ● NFID Postdoctoral Fellowships. **Frequency:** annual. **Type:** fellowship. **Recipient:** for physicians specializing in infectious diseases. **Computer Services:** Mailing lists. **Publications:** *Coccidiomycosis and Host-Fungus Interplay.* Proceedings ● *Double Helix*, quarterly. Newsletter. Reports on public welfare and support of research, education, and prevention of infectious disease. Monitors legislation. **Price:** free. **Circulation:** 8,000. Alternate Formats: online ● *National Foundation for Infectious Diseases—Annual Report* ● *Proceedings of the Fifth Symposium on*

Topics in Mycology: Host-Fungus Interplay. **Price:** $40.00/copy ● *Recognition and Management of Nursing Home Infections.*

14645 ■ Parents of Kids with Infectious Diseases (PKIDs)
PO Box 5666
Vancouver, WA 98668
Ph: (360)695-0293
Free: (877)557-5427
Fax: (360)695-6941
E-mail: pkids@pkids.org
URL: http://www.pkids.org
Contact: Trish Parnell, Exec. Dir.

Founded: 1996. **Description:** Assists the families of the children living with hepatitis, HIV/AIDS, or other chronic, viral infectious diseases with emotional, financial and informational support. Educates the public about infectious diseases, the methods of prevention and transmission, the advances in medicine, and the elimination of fear of those living with these diseases. Encourages global childhood immunizations, research to find cures for hepatitis B and C and HIV, and prevention of the spread of infectious disease through the education of kids and adults. **Publications:** *Pediatric Hepatitis Report* (in Chinese, English, Russian, and Spanish). Alternate Formats: online ● *Someone You Know Has Hepatitis B.* Brochure. Alternate Formats: online ● *Someone You Know Has Hepatitis C.* Brochure. Alternate Formats: online.

14646 ■ Pediatric Infectious Diseases Society (PIDS)
66 Canal Center Plz., Ste.600
Alexandria, VA 22314
Ph: (703)299-6764
Fax: (703)299-0473
E-mail: pids@idsociety.org
URL: http://www.pids.org
Contact: Terri Christene Phillips, Exec. Dir.

Membership Dues: regular, $210 (annual) ● first year out-of-fellowship, $115 (annual) ● emeritus, $119 (annual). **Multinational. Description:** Aims to advance the study of pediatric infectious diseases. Seeks to uphold the standards of professionalism in the field of pediatrics and its related disciplines. Ensures that issues concerning pediatric infectious diseases are considered and dealt with through collaborative projects with other medical associations. **Awards:** Fellowship Award. **Frequency:** annual. **Type:** fellowship. **Recipient:** for clinical research pertaining to different areas of pediatrics. **Publications:** *The Pediatric Infectious Disease Journal*, monthly. **Price:** $221.00 individual in U.S.; $274.00 individual outside U.S.; $496.00 institutional; $107.00 in-training. ISSN: 0891-3668. **Advertising:** accepted ● *Training Programs in Pediatric Infectious Diseases.* Directory. Alternate Formats: online.

Information Management

14647 ■ Association of Medical Directors of Information Systems (AMDIS)
PO Box 2934
Lake Almanor, CA 96137
Ph: (530)596-4477
Fax: (978)389-7729
E-mail: info@amdis.org
URL: http://www.amdis.org
Contact: Richard L. Rydell MBA, Pres./Exec. Dir.

Founded: 1997. **Membership Dues:** physician, $140 (annual) ● non-physician, $195 (annual). **Description:** Aims to advance the field of applied medical informatics and direct physician use of information technology. Seeks to improve the practice of medicine through proper application of advanced systems in technology. Promotes the education and professional development of physicians engaged in the practice of healthcare information technology. **Awards:** AMDIS Awards. **Frequency:** annual. **Type:** recognition. **Recipient:** for excellence and outstanding achievement in applied medical informatics. **Publications:** *The Informatics Review.* Journal. Contains reviews of articles about the latest developments in clinical informatics from leading medical and informatics journals. Alternate Formats: online. Also Cited As: *TIR* ● *The Physician-Computer Conundrum: Get Over It.* Book. Features case studies that show how other healthcare organizations achieved success. **Price:** $45.00 for members; $55.00 for nonmembers ● Articles. Alternate Formats: online.

Insurance

14648 ■ Association of Health Insurance Advisors (AHIA)
2901 Telestar Ct.
Falls Church, VA 22042-1205
Ph: (703)770-8200
Fax: (703)770-8201
E-mail: ahia@naifa.org
URL: http://www.ahia.net
Contact: Diane R. Boyle HIA, Exec. VP

Founded: 1990. **Members:** 5,000. **Membership Dues:** individual, $105 (annual). **Staff:** 75. **Description:** Insurance agents and advisors specializing in health, disability, long term care insurance and/or employee benefits. **Publications:** *AHIA Minute,* monthly, excluding the months of June, July and August. Newsletter. Provides information for local leaders to share on their meetings. Alternate Formats: online ● *Health Insurance Matters,* biweekly. Newsletter. **Price:** included in membership dues. Alternate Formats: online ● *Membership Marketing Matters,* monthly. Newsletter. Contains information on current membership marketing efforts at state and local levels.

14649 ■ Blue Cross and Blue Shield Association (BCBSA)
225 N Michigan Ave.
Chicago, IL 60611
Ph: (312)297-6000
Fax: (312)297-6609
E-mail: privacy@bcbsa.com
URL: http://www.bluecares.com
Contact: Scott P. Serota, Pres./CEO

Founded: 1982. **Description:** Local Blue Cross and Blue Shield Plans in the U.S., and other licensees in Europe, Japan, and Jamaica. Aims to promote the betterment of public health and security; to secure the widest public acceptance of voluntary non-profit, prepayment of health services; to provide services to Blue Cross and Blue Shield Plans and licensees. Contracts with federal government as administrative agency for federal health programs; sponsors and conducts programs on health care and prepayment issues. **Libraries: Type:** reference. **Holdings:** 16,000. **Formed by Merger of:** Blue Shield Association; Blue Cross Association. **Publications:** Also publishes reports and pamphlets.

14650 ■ Cover the Uninsured (CTU)
1010 Wisconsin Ave. NW, Ste.800
Washington, DC 20007
Ph: (202)572-2928
E-mail: info@covertheuninsured.org
URL: http://covertheuninsured.org

Members: 16. **Description:** Works to raise public awareness of the consequences of being uninsured.

14651 ■ MIB Group (MIB)
160 Univ. Ave.
Westwood, MA 02090-2307
Ph: (781)329-4500 (781)751-6003
E-mail: info@mib.com
URL: http://www.mib.com
Contact: Thomas M. West, Chm.

Founded: 1902. **Members:** 500. **Staff:** 200. **Description:** Life, health, and disability insurance companies. Seeks to reduce insurance fraud by providing member companies with information on previous claims. **Formerly:** (2004) Medical Information Bureau.

14652 ■ National Association of Dental Plans (NADP)
8111 Lyndon B. Johnson Fwy., Ste.935
Dallas, TX 75251-1347
Ph: (972)458-6998
Fax: (972)458-2258
E-mail: info@nadp.org
URL: http://www.nadp.org
Contact: Evelyn F. Ireland CAE, Exec. Dir./Pres.

Founded: 1989. **Members:** 100. **Staff:** 8. **Budget:** $1,000,000. **Description:** Dental HMO, PPOs and dental referral plans with Associate members that provide dental indemnity and dental practice management companies. Strives to improve consumer access to affordable quality dental care. **Publications:** *Data Reports,* quarterly. **Conventions/Meetings:** annual meeting (exhibits).

14653 ■ National Health Care Anti-Fraud Association (NHCAA)
1201 New York Ave. NW, Ste.1120
Washington, DC 20005-4006
Ph: (202)659-5955
Fax: (202)785-6764
E-mail: nhcaa@nhcaa.org
URL: http://www.nhcaa.org
Contact: Cynthia A. Lucas, Chair

Founded: 1985. **Members:** 910. **Membership Dues:** individual, $100 (annual) ● corporate (organization with business in one or more states), $6,500-$8,500 ● corporate (organization with nationwide business), $25,000. **Staff:** 6. **Budget:** $1,500,000. **Description:** Private insurance companies and public sector agencies that work against health insurance fraud. **Libraries: Type:** reference; lending; not open to the public. **Holdings:** audiovisuals, books, clippings, periodicals. **Subjects:** health care, anti-fraud investigations. **Awards:** Investigator of the Year. **Frequency:** annual. **Type:** recognition. **Computer Services:** Mailing lists, of members. **Telecommunication Services:** electronic mail, mcostello@nhcaa.org. **Publications:** *NHCAA Update,* quarterly. Newsletter. **Circulation:** 3,000 ● Annual Report, annual ● Reports ● Also makes available anti-fraud CDs. **Conventions/Meetings:** annual Training Conference - workshop (exhibits).

14654 ■ Physician Insurers Association of America (PIAA)
2275 Res. Blvd., Ste.250
Rockville, MD 20850
Ph: (301)947-9000
Fax: (301)947-9090
E-mail: ginnye@piaa.us
URL: http://www.piaa.us
Contact: Ginny Echeverria, Dir. of Business Development

Founded: 1977. **Members:** 60. **Membership Dues:** affiliate, $2,800 (annual). **Staff:** 14. **Budget:** $2,300,000. **Description:** Physician liability insurance companies, including domestic physician and dental liability insurers, international affiliates, and re-insurers. Seeks to further the best interests of member companies in areas related to physician liability insurance. Focuses on the availability and affordability of professional liability insurance and the effective delivery of quality healthcare. Conducts research and educational programs; monitors and advocates for legislation. **Libraries: Type:** reference; not open to the public. **Holdings:** archival material, business records. **Subjects:** member companies, annual reports, insurance filings. **Awards:** Peter Sweetland Award of Excellence. **Frequency:** annual. **Type:** recognition. **Recipient:** for board member or employee of member who exemplifies the spirit of Peter Sweetland, especially in the area of professional ethics. **Computer Services:** database, malpractice claims. **Publications:** *Newsbriefs,* weekly. Newsletter. Alternate Formats: online ● *The Physician Insurer,* quarterly. Magazine. **Price:** $45.00/year. **Circulation:** 1,500. **Advertising:** accepted ● *PIAA Membership Directory,* annual ● Also publishes studies of major liability concerns in the insurance industry, including issues related to treatment of breast, lung, and colon cancer; medication errors; and laparoscopy procedures. **Conventions/Meetings:** annual convention

and workshop (exhibits) - always May ● annual meeting, open to the public - 2008 May 14-18, Philadelphia, PA; 2009 May 13-16, Waikoloa, HI ● periodic workshop, for different functional areas in the medical malpractice insurance industry.

Internal Medicine

14655 ■ American Board of Internal Medicine (ABIM)
510 Walnut St., Ste.1700
Philadelphia, PA 19106-3699
Ph: (215)446-3500
Free: (800)441-2246
Fax: (215)446-3633
E-mail: request@abim.org
URL: http://www.abim.org
Contact: Ms. Christine K. Cassel MD, Pres.

Founded: 1936. **Staff:** 100. **Budget:** $18,000,000. **Nonmembership. Description:** Works as a certification board for doctors of internal medicine and the subspecialties of internal medicine. Assesses the qualifications of, and administers examinations to, general internists and sub-specialists. Certification is granted to those doctors meeting its standards of cognitive knowledge and clinical competence. Board members are elected from certified leaders in internal medicine. The board has certified approximately 150,000 internists and 65,000 sub-specialist diplomates and issued 15,000 recertification certificates. **Boards:** Cardiovascular Disease; Endocrinology and Metabolism; Gastroenterology; Hematology; Infectious Disease; Medical Oncology; Nephrology; Pulmonary Disease; Rheumatology. **Committees:** Adolescent Medicine; Critical Care Medicine; Geriatric Medicine; Sports Medicine; Transplantation Hepatology. **Publications:** *ABIM Perspectives,* quarterly. Newsletter. **Price:** free. **Circulation:** 160,000. Alternate Formats: online ● *Mini-CEX Brochure.* Alternate Formats: online ● *Policies and Information for Maintenance of Certification,* annual. **Price:** free. Alternate Formats: online ● *Policies and Procedures for Certification,* annual. **Price:** free. Alternate Formats: online ● *2005 Adolescent Medicine Maintenance of Certification Examination Information.* Booklet. Alternate Formats: online ● *2005 Sports Medicine Certification and Maintenance of Certification Examinations Information.* Booklet. Alternate Formats: online. **Conventions/Meetings:** quarterly Governing Board - meeting, closed meeting.

14656 ■ American College of Physicians-American Society of Internal Medicine (ACP-ASIM)
190 N Independence Mall W
Philadelphia, PA 19106-1572
Ph: (215)351-2600
Free: (800)523-1546
Fax: (215)351-2799
E-mail: custserv@acponline.org
URL: http://www.acponline.org
Contact: David C. Dale MD, Pres.

Founded: 1915. **Members:** 85,000. **Membership Dues:** regular, in U.S. (based on years out of medical school), $255-$425 (annual) ● regular, outside U.S. (based on years out of medical school), $99-$255 (annual) ● associate, fellowship trainee, $99 (annual) ● affiliate, $255 (annual). **Staff:** 250. **Description:** Professional society of medical doctors specializing in internal medicine and closely related specialties such as dermatology, neurology, psychiatry, cardiology, gastroenterology, and public health. Sponsors annual postgraduate courses for practicing physicians. Sponsors teaching and research scholarship competition. **Awards: Frequency:** annual. **Type:** recognition. **Formerly:** (2003) American College of Physicians. **Publications:** *ACP Journal Club,* bimonthly. Provides a brief commentary from a leading clinical expert. Alternate Formats: online ● *Annals of Internal Medicine,* biweekly. Journal. Delivers major review articles, incisive original research, topical clinical reviews, thought-provoking editorials, and much more. **Price:** $181.00 /year for individuals in U.S. and Canada; $126.00/year-medical school graduate in U.S. and Canada; $90.00/year-medical student member in U.S. and Canada; $15.00 each in U.S. and Canada. **ISSN:** 0003-4819. **Circulation:** 96,000. **Alternate Formats:** online ● *Medical Knowledge Self-Assessment*, triennial ● *Observer*, monthly. Journal ● Directory, periodic. **Conventions/Meetings:** annual Scientific Meeting.

14657 ■ Association of Program Directors in Internal Medicine (APDIM)

c/o Alliance for Academic Internal Medicine
2501 M St. NW, Ste.550
Washington, DC 20037-1325
Ph: (202)861-9351
Free: (800)622-4558
Fax: (202)861-9731
E-mail: apdim@im.org
URL: http://www.im.org/APDIM/About/default.htm
Contact: Deborah M. DeMarco MD, Pres.
Founded: 1977. **Members:** 1,641. **Membership Dues:** new residency program, $1,000 (annual) ● individual, $100 (annual). **Staff:** 4. **Budget:** $1,000,000. **Description:** Physicians in internal medicine including departmental chairmen and directors of internal medicine, directors of residency training programs, associate program directors, medical education directors, and chiefs of medical service. Advances medical education through assisting accredited hospital internal medicine residency training programs in the United States and Puerto Rico. Conducts annual course for chief residents and program directors. Offers consulting services. **Libraries: Type:** reference. **Holdings:** books, periodicals. **Awards:** Dema C. Daley Founders Award. **Frequency:** annual. **Type:** recognition. **Recipient:** for a member of the internal medicine community who is recognized nationally as an educator, innovator, and leader. **Computer Services:** database, membership ● mailing lists, of members. **Committees:** Accreditation; E-Services; Professional Development; Program Planning; Public Policy; Publications. **Task Forces:** Evaluation; Survey. **Publications:** *A Toolkit for Internal Medicine Education Programs.* Manual ● *Academic Internal Medicine Insight*, quarterly. Newsletter. Profiles successful residency programs and summarizes developments in the field of internal medicine. **Price:** included in membership dues. **Circulation:** 2,000 ● *APDIM Directory*, annual. Membership Directory. Alternate Formats: online ● *Careers in Internal Medicine*, quarterly. **Conventions/Meetings:** semiannual meeting (exhibits).

14658 ■ Clerkship Directors in Internal Medicine (CDIM)

2501 M St. NW, Ste.550
Washington, DC 20037-1325
Ph: (202)861-9351
Fax: (202)861-9731
E-mail: cdim@im.org
URL: http://www.im.org/CDIM
Contact: Paul A. Hemmer PhD, Pres.
Founded: 1989. **Members:** 369. **Membership Dues:** associate, individual, $100 (annual) ● institutional, $400 (annual). **Multinational. Description:** Promotes education in the core clerkship in internal medicine at accredited medical schools in the U.S., Puerto Rico, and Canada. **Awards:** CDIM Educational Research Award. **Frequency:** annual. **Type:** recognition. **Recipient:** to members who have greatly contributed to educational research ● CDIM Outstanding Educational Program Development Award. **Frequency:** annual. **Type:** recognition. **Recipient:** to members who have contributed to the development of an outstanding educational program ● CDIM Service Award. **Frequency:** annual. **Type:** recognition. **Recipient:** to members who have greatly contributed to the association. **Telecommunication Services:** electronic mail, mfelzjen@im.org. **Committees:** Curriculum; Educational; Publications; Research. **Publications:** *CDIM News* ● Membership Directory. Alternate Formats: online. **Conventions/Meetings:** annual meeting - 2007 Oct. 18-20, Pittsburgh, PA; 2008 Oct. 30-Nov. 2, Lake Buena Vista, FL.

14659 ■ National MedPeds Residents' Association (NMPRA)

c/o Cheryl Dempsey, Exec. Asst.
Dept. of Pediatrics
1430 Tulane Ave., SL-37
New Orleans, LA 70112

Fax: (240)209-2150
E-mail: nmpra@medpeds.org
URL: http://www.medpeds.org
Contact: Ranya Sweis, Pres.
Founded: 1987. **Members:** 1,200. **Membership Dues:** individual, $15 (annual) ● program, $150 (annual). **Staff:** 6. **Description:** Promotes the practice of MedPeds, combined internal medicine and pediatrics; educates and serves MedPeds residency and serves as a resource for medical students interested in MedPeds. **Awards:** Gary Onady Award. **Frequency:** annual. **Type:** recognition. **Recipient:** for contributions to NMPRA and/or Med-Peds at the national and regional level ● Howard Schubiner Award. **Frequency:** annual. **Type:** recognition. **Recipient:** for contributions to NMPRA and/or Med-Peds at the state and local level. **Publications:** *MedPeds News*, quarterly. Newsletter. Serves as a catalyst to increase communication between residents and residency programs in the combined field of medicine-pediatrics. **Price:** included in membership dues. **Conventions/Meetings:** annual meeting, held in conjunction with the American Academy of Pediatrics Meeting.

14660 ■ Society of General Internal Medicine (SGIM)

2501 M St. NW, Ste.575
Washington, DC 20037
Ph: (202)887-5150
Free: (800)822-3060
Fax: (202)887-5405
E-mail: karlsond@sgim.org
URL: http://www.sgim.org
Contact: David Karlson PhD, Exec. Dir.
Founded: 1978. **Members:** 3,000. **Membership Dues:** full, in U.S., $305 (annual) ● full, outside U.S. (with paper subscription to JGIM), $185 (annual) ● full, outside U.S. (with web access only to JGIM), $100 (annual) ● associate in U.S., $95 (annual) ● associate outside U.S. (with paper subscription to JGIM), $125 (annual). **Staff:** 11. **Budget:** $1,800,000. **Regional Groups:** 8. **Description:** Physicians combining clinical practice with research. Promotes improved patient care, research, and teaching in primary care and general internal medicine. Sponsors research and educational programs. **Awards:** Elnora M. Rhodes SGIM Service Award. **Frequency:** annual. **Type:** recognition. **Recipient:** for an individual who provides outstanding service to the society ● Herbert W. Nickens Award. **Frequency:** annual. **Type:** recognition. **Recipient:** for commitment to cultural diversity in medicine ● John M. Eisenberg National Award for Career Achievement in Medicine. **Frequency:** annual. **Type:** recognition. **Recipient:** for a senior member whose innovative research has changed patient care ● Lawrence S. Linn Awards. **Frequency:** annual. **Type:** recognition. **Recipient:** for young researchers and practitioners working to improve the quality of HIV/AIDS care ● Mid-Career Research Mentorship Award. **Frequency:** annual. **Type:** recognition. **Recipient:** for the mentoring activities of general medicine investigators ● National Award for Career Achievements in Medical Education. **Frequency:** annual. **Type:** recognition. **Recipient:** to an individual whose lifetime contributions have had a national impact on medical education ● National Awards for Scholarship in Medical Education. **Frequency:** annual. **Type:** recognition. **Recipient:** to individuals who have made major contributions to medical education in one of the following areas: scholarship in integration, educational methods/teaching, and clinical practice ● Outstanding Junior Investigator of the Year. **Frequency:** annual. **Type:** recognition. **Recipient:** for a junior investigator whose early career achievements have made a national impact on generalist medicine ● Robert J. Glaser Award. **Frequency:** annual. **Type:** recognition. **Recipient:** for an individual who has made exceptional contributions to generalism in medicine. **Computer Services:** Online services, publication. **Caucuses:** Women's. **Committees:** Career Satisfaction; Communications; Continuing Medical Education; Development; Education; Ethics; Finance; Health Policy; Minorities in Medicine; Research; Scientific Program. **Special Interest Groups:** Academic GIM

in Latin America; Anticoagulation/Thromboembolism; Clinician Examination Research; Ethics and Humanism; Faculty Development; Hospitalists; International Health; Medical Consultation; Medical Resident Clinic Directors; Primary Care Clinical Models; Primary Care Program Directors; Research in Careers; Social Responsibility; Specialty Referrals; Veterans Administration Prime Programs. **Task Forces:** AIDS; Clinician-Educators; Geriatrics; Health Promotion/Prevention; Managed Care; Substance Abuse. **Formerly:** (1987) Society for Research and Education in Primary Care Internal Medicine. **Publications:** *Directory of Primary Care Internal Medicine Residency Programs and Fellowship Training Programs*, annual. Contains descriptions of 146 primary care general internal medicine programs. Lists 60 fellowship programs in general internal medicine. **Advertising:** accepted. Alternate Formats: online ● *Journal of General Internal Medicine*, monthly. Contains articles, reports, clinical reviews, editorials, reflections about patient care, research, and teaching. Alternate Formats: online ● *SGIM Forum*, monthly. Newsletter. Contains issues about general internal medicine and the health care system at large. Alternate Formats: online. **Conventions/Meetings:** annual conference (exhibits) ● annual meeting - 2008 May 14-17, Pittsburgh, PA; 2009 May 13-16, Miami, FL.

International Health

14661 ■ African Medical and Research Foundation (AMREF USA)

19 W 44th St., Rm. 710
New York, NY 10036
Ph: (212)768-2440
Fax: (212)768-4230
E-mail: amrefusa@amrefusa.org
URL: http://www.amref.org
Contact: Lisa K. Meadowcroft, Exec. Dir.
Founded: 1957. **Regional Groups:** 11. **Description:** U.S. branch of the African Medical & Research Foundation. Voluntary organization providing medical services to aid and augment health programs in developing nations and in rural areas of East Africa. Attempts to reach isolated peoples and outlying medical facilities through a network of 100 two-way radios, clinic-equipped mobile units, and a "Flying Doctor Service." Undertakes research programs in the field of medicine and general health surveys. Designs and implements primary health care projects. Provides health education courses through its training center to train health educators and is implementing a program of continuing education for health workers. **Libraries: Type:** reference; not open to the public. **Holdings:** articles, books, periodicals. **Subjects:** international health issues, child survival, disaster relief, community health. **Computer Services:** Mailing lists. **Additional Websites:** http://www.usa.amref.org. **Telecommunication Services:** electronic mail, info@amrefusa.org. **Formerly:** African Research Foundation; (1973) African Medical and Research Foundation; (1981) International Medical and Research Foundation. **Publications:** *AFYA*, bimonthly. Journal ● *AMREFocus*, semiannual. Newsletter. Features AMREF USA events, general news and information. ● *Defender: Health Journal for Africa*, bimonthly ● *Rural Health Series*, periodic. **Conventions/Meetings:** annual meeting.

14662 ■ Aid for International Medicine (AIM)

PO Box 119
Rockland, DE 19732
Ph: (302)655-8290
Fax: (302)655-0487
Contact: Dr. John Levinson, Pres.
Founded: 1965. **Members:** 25. **Staff:** 3. **Regional Groups:** 2. **Description:** Extends medical help to areas where one or more members of the board have personally served and documented a need. Provides funding and/or materials to hospitals, medical schools, and orphanages in Asia, Africa, and the U.S. Has established medical textbook program which makes new books available to medical schools and

hospitals. **Conventions/Meetings:** semiannual board meeting ● annual meeting ● semiannual meeting.

14663 ■ American College of International Physicians (ACIP)
9323 Old Mt. Vernon Rd.
Alexandria, VA 22309
Ph: (703)221-1500
Fax: (703)221-1500
E-mail: walkwithgod@gmail.com
URL: http://acip.org
Contact: Alex Yadao MD, Chm./Pres.
Founded: 1975. **Members:** 1,200. **Membership Dues:** regular, $175 (annual) ● associate, $50 (annual) ● affiliate, student, $25 (annual) ● retired, $75 (annual). **Budget:** $150,000. **State Groups:** 8. **Description:** Physicians and surgeons interested in initiatives to promote national efforts in international health, education, research, training, and welfare. Promotes the betterment of the health of all people and seeks to advance the art and science of medicine. Emphasizes the international character of medicine and the education of international physicians. Seeks parity for foreign medical graduates. Supports relief programs to areas struck by natural calamities or epidemic diseases. **Awards:** Distinguished Fellowship Award. **Frequency:** annual. **Type:** recognition. **Committees:** Board Preparation; Geographic Medicine; International Health; Legal Action; National Health Issues; Political Action; Science and Research. **Absorbed:** National Association of Foreign Medical Graduates. **Publications:** *International Medical Journal*, semiannual. Newsletter ● *The International Physician*, quarterly. Newsletter. **Advertising:** accepted. **Conventions/Meetings:** annual Scientific Meeting and Convocation of Fellows - convention - usually late July.

14664 ■ American Medical Resources Foundation (AMRF)
PO Box 3609
Brockton, MA 02304-3609
Ph: (508)580-3301
Fax: (508)580-3306
E-mail: info@amrf.com
URL: http://www.amrf.com
Contact: Tom Magliochetti, Pres.
Founded: 1988. **Staff:** 5. **Budget:** $700,000. **Description:** Donates used, but fully functional, medical equipment to hospitals and clinics serving the poor in Third World and developing nations. The equipment is donated to AMRF by over 300 hospitals and industries in the U.S. and by private physicians and dentists. Donated equipment includes beds and patient transports; through monitors; x-rays; infant warmers; infant transformers; patient handling equipment; pulmonary, cardiac or ultrasonic diagnostic equipment; and diverse equipment for general and specialized use in prenatal, natal, pediatric and adult departments. Coordinates volunteer procedures and assists in the setting up and calibration of all equipment at the recipient hospitals. Provides training for the hospital biomedical technicians. **Libraries: Type:** reference. **Holdings:** 1,650. **Publications:** *AMRF News*, quarterly. Newsletter. **Circulation:** 4,000. Alternate Formats: online. **Conventions/Meetings:** quarterly board meeting.

14665 ■ BIO Ventures for Global Health (BVGH)
1225 Eye St. NW, Ste.1010
Washington, DC 20005
Ph: (202)312-9260
Fax: (202)962-9201
E-mail: info@bvgh.org
URL: http://www.bvgh.org
Contact: Christopher D. Earl, Pres./CEO
Founded: 2004. **Multinational. Description:** Aims to provide solutions to unmet medical needs in the developing world. Seeks to break down barriers that hinder industry involvement in global health product development and to catalyze new industry investment. Works to help companies build sound business strategies that can contribute to solving global health challenges. **Publications:** *Advance Market Commitments to Stimulate Industry Investment in Global Health Product Development*. Report. Alternate Formats: online ● *Making Markets for Vaccines: A Historic Call for Action*. Report. Alternate Formats: online ● *Tuberculosis Vaccines: The Case for Investment*. Report. Alternate Formats: online.

14666 ■ China Medical Board of New York (CMBNY)
c/o Institute for International Medical Education
750 Third Ave., 23rd Fl.
New York, NY 10017
Ph: (212)661-7375
Fax: (212)661-1177
E-mail: institute@iime.org
URL: http://www.iime.org
Contact: M. Roy Schwarz MD, Pres.
Founded: 1928. **Staff:** 5. **Multinational. Description:** Supports programs of medical, nursing and public health education and research. Assists institutions in East and Southeast Asia in improving the health levels and services in Asian societies. Improves the quality and increase the numbers of appropriate health practitioners in these societies. Provides programs in Korea, Taiwan, Hong Kong, Philippines, Thailand, Malaysia, Myanmar, Singapore, Indonesia, Mongolia, Vietnam, Laos and China. Supports the Peking Union Medical College, nationalized in 1949 by People's Republic of China. **Committees:** Advisory; Core; Member Index; Standard Setting; Steering. **Task Forces:** Assessment. **Publications:** Annual Report, annual. Includes list of grants and endowments made during year of report. **Price:** free. **Conventions/Meetings:** semiannual meeting - always June and December, New York City.

14667 ■ Foundation for the Support of International Medical Training (FSIMT)
c/o International Association for Medical Assistance to Travellers
1623 Military Rd., No. 279
Niagara Falls, NY 14304-1745
Ph: (716)754-4883
Fax: (519)836-3412
E-mail: info@iamat.org
URL: http://www.iamat.org
Contact: Mrs. M.A. Uffer, Pres.
Founded: 1960. **Members:** 6,000,000. **Staff:** 25. **Description:** Individuals and corporations organized to provide information regarding the availability of competent medical care overseas and information concerning sanitary conditions, health hazards, and climatic conditions in various parts of the world. Offers detailed guidance on vaccination and immunization requirements and tropical diseases. **Publications:** *Be Aware of Schistosomiasis* ● *How to Protect Yourself Against Malaria*, annual ● *Immunization Chart*, annual ● *Set of 24 World Climate Charts*, annual ● *Traveller Clinical Chart*, annual ● *When Hiking Through Latin America, Be Alert to Chagas' Disease*, annual ● *World Malaria Risk Chart*, annual ● *World Schistosomiasis Risk Chart*, annual ● Brochure, annual ● Directory, annual.

14668 ■ Global Health Action (GHA)
1902 Clairmont Rd.
Decatur, GA 30033
Ph: (404)634-5748
Fax: (404)634-9685
E-mail: gha@globalhealthaction.org
URL: http://www.globalhealthaction.org
Contact: Robin C. Davis RN, Exec. Dir.
Founded: 1972. **Staff:** 12. **Budget:** $1,021,000. **Languages:** English, French, Portuguese, Russian, Spanish. **Description:** Provides health education and leadership and management training for participants from more than 88 countries worldwide. Programs include: health management and leadership courses; community health worker, goat farmer, and maternal health training programs in Haiti; HIV/AIDS programs in Africa, China and India; U.S.-based community empowerment programs; organizational capacity building in Haiti and India; and custom-designed training courses and workshops held throughout the world. Participants include health and development professionals, community health workers and community health leaders from the U.S. and abroad.

Libraries: Type: reference; not open to the public. **Affiliated With:** Global Health Council. **Absorbed:** (2001) Institute for Development Training. **Formerly:** (1985) International Nursing Services Association; (1993) INSA, The International Service Association for Health. **Publications:** *A Great and Mighty Tree*. Video ● *Global Health Action Annual Report*, annual. Provides donor education and publicity. ● *Global Health Action General Brochure*, annual. Provides donor education and publicity. Alternate Formats: online ● *Global Health Action Newsletter*, semiannual. Primarily for donor education and publicity. Alternate Formats: online. **Conventions/Meetings:** annual meeting, includes graduation ceremony.

14669 ■ Global Health Council (GHC)
1111 19th St. NW, Ste.1120
Washington, DC 20036
Ph: (202)833-5900
Fax: (202)833-0075
E-mail: ghc@globalhealth.org
URL: http://www.globalhealth.org
Contact: Dr. Nils Daulaire, Pres./CEO
Founded: 1971. **Members:** 1,600. **Membership Dues:** health professional, $120 (annual) ● student, retiree, $60 (annual) ● organization (with annual budget of below $500000), $250 (annual) ● organization (with annual budget of $500000 to $49 million), $500-$3,000 (annual) ● organization (with annual budget of $50 million to over $500 million), $5,000-$10,000 (annual). **Staff:** 18. **Budget:** $1,200,000. **Languages:** English, French, Japanese, Nepali, Spanish. **Description:** Membership organization made up of private voluntary organizations, health and medical associations, universities, government agencies, foundations, corporations, consulting firms, and individuals interested in promoting greater and more effective U.S. participation in practical international health and development programs. Seeks to strengthen U.S. public and private sector participation in international health activities. Includes areas of concern such as: HIV/AIDS; women's health; improving primary healthcare worldwide; environmental health; population and family planning; tropical and preventive medicine; appropriate health technology. Supports improved health and development legislation. Conducts career service in conjunction with annual conference. **Libraries: Type:** reference. **Awards:** Best Practices in Global Health. **Frequency:** annual. **Type:** recognition. **Recipient:** for individuals who are dedicated to improving the health of disadvantaged populations ● Excellence in Media Award. **Frequency:** annual. **Type:** recognition. **Recipient:** for a journalist who has effectively captured the essence of a major issue in global health ● Gates Award for Global Health. **Type:** recognition. **Recipient:** for public service contribution to global health ● Jonathan Mann Award for Global Health and Human Rights. **Frequency:** annual. **Type:** recognition. **Recipient:** for a leading practitioner in health and human rights. **Committees:** Advocacy; Global AIDS Publications; Membership. **Formerly:** (1999) National Council for International Health. **Publications:** *AIDS Link*, bimonthly. Newsletter. Contains the latest global information on HIV/AIDS issues. **Advertising:** accepted ● *Career Network*, monthly. Bulletin. Contains listings of employment opportunities in International Health. **Circulation:** 400. **Advertising:** accepted ● *Directory of U.S.-Based Agencies Involved in International Health Assistance*, periodic. Lists geographical areas served and types of workers sought by U.S. health agencies. **Price:** $60.00 for nonmembers; $30.00 for members ● *Global Learning for Health*. Paper. **Price:** $16.95 for members; $26.95 for nonmembers ● *Healthlink*, 10/year. Contains information on international health policy issues and calendar of events. **Price:** available to members only. **Advertising:** accepted ● *NCIH Membership Directory*, periodic. Contains individual and organizational members with phone numbers and key contacts. ● *2003-2004 Global Health Directory*. **Price:** $25.00 for members; $50.00 for nonmembers, plus shipping and handling. Alternate Formats: online ● *2002-2003 Global AIDS Directory*. **Price:** $25.00 for members; $50.00 for nonmembers, plus shipping and handling. Alternate Formats: online ● Annual Report, annual.

Alternate Formats: online ● Reports. Alternate Formats: online. **Conventions/Meetings:** annual conference (exhibits) ● workshop and seminar, on HIV/AIDS strategies, careers in international health, and population issues.

14670 ■ Hesperian Foundation (HF)
1919 Addison St., Ste.304
Berkeley, CA 94704
Ph: (510)845-1447
Free: (888)729-1796
Fax: (510)845-9141
E-mail: hesperian@hesperian.org
URL: http://www.hesperian.org
Contact: Sarah Shannon, Exec. Dir.
Founded: 1973. **Staff:** 20. **Budget:** $1,800,000. **Languages:** English, Spanish. **Nonmembership. Multinational. Description:** Promotes good health in the developing world and in poor communities in the U.S. through community-based and informed self-care. Fosters constructive dialogue on health care and social change. Helps to launch Project Piaxtla, a health care network, and Project Projimo, a community-based rehabilitation center for spinal cord injuries, in Western Mexico. Focuses on publishing community self-help health care books that are used throughout the world. Analyzes and criticizes existing social, political, and economic systems that prevent the poor from obtaining adequate standards of life and health. Operates gratis book fund, in which Third World health care workers in the developing world receive Hesperian publications at no charge. **Libraries: Type:** reference. **Subjects:** health issues. **Publications:** *A Book for Midwives* (in English and Spanish). **Price:** $22.00 ● *Disabled Village Children* (in English and Spanish). Book. **Price:** $22.00 ● *Helping Children Who Are Blind* (in English and Spanish). Book. **Price:** $12.00 ● *Helping Health Workers Learn* (in English and Spanish). Book. **Price:** $20.00 ● *Where There Is No Dentist* (in English and Spanish). Book. **Price:** $12.00 ● *Where There Is No Doctor* (in English and Spanish). Book. **Price:** $17.00 ● *Where Women Have No Doctor* (in English and Spanish). Book. **Price:** $20.00 ● *The Women's Health Exchange* (in English and Spanish), quarterly. Newsletter. **Price:** free. **Conventions/Meetings:** seminar.

14671 ■ INMED Partnerships for Children (INMED)
45449 Severn Way, Ste.161
Sterling, VA 20166
Ph: (703)444-4477
Free: (800)521-1175
Fax: (703)444-4471
E-mail: contact@inmed.org
URL: http://www.inmed.org
Contact: Linda Pfeiffer PhD, Pres.
Founded: 1986. **Staff:** 35. **Budget:** $3,470,000. **Languages:** English, Portuguese, Spanish. **Nonmembership. Description:** Works to inspire communities and strengthen their capacity to support the development of healthy, educated children who have increased opportunities for the future. Toward that end, develops and implements family, school, and community health, social and educational programs; delivers culturally and linguistically appropriate training, technical assistance and education; provides nonprofit organizations and research institutions with procurement and consolidation services to help them obtain essential medicines, medical and laboratory supplies, equipment and other necessary materials; promotes and facilitates multi-sector cooperation to achieve international development goals; and pursues other social ventures that improve the health, lives and opportunities of children worldwide. **Formerly:** (2003) International Medical Services for Health.

14672 ■ Intermed International
420 Lexington Ave., Ste.2331
New York, NY 10170
Ph: (212)687-3620
Fax: (212)599-6137
E-mail: chaney@dooleyintermed.org
URL: http://www.dooleyintermed.org
Contact: Dr. Verne Chaney MD, Pres./Founder
Founded: 1961. **Staff:** 7. **Budget:** $500,000. **Description:** Assists Third World countries in the development of medical care systems through self-help projects in disease prevention, health education, personnel development, and research and medical aid to refugees. Presently operates programs in Laos, Honduras, Nepal, and Nicaragua. **Formerly:** Dooley Foundation/INTERMED; (1962) Dr. Thomas A. Dooley Foundation; (1978) Thomas A. Dooley Foundation; (1980) Thomas A. Dooley Foundation/INTERMED U.S.A. **Publications:** Brochure, annual. **Circulation:** 10,000 ● Journal, semiannual.

14673 ■ National Latina Health Organization (NLHO)
PO Box 7567
Oakland, CA 94601
Ph: (510)534-1362
Fax: (510)534-1364
E-mail: nlho@latinahealth.org
Contact: Luz Alvarez Martinez, Exec.Dir.
Founded: 1986. **Membership Dues:** low income/student, $15 (annual) ● general, $25 (annual) ● organization, $50 (annual). **Languages:** English, Spanish. **Description:** Puerto Rican, Chicana, Mexican, Cuban, Caribbean and South and Central American women. Works to increase awareness of health issues among Latin American women. Works to achieve bilingual access to quality health care and self-empowerment of Latinas through culturally sensitive educational programs, health advocacy, outreach, research, and the development of public policy. Cooperates with other organizations to defend reproductive rights, affordable birth control, sex education, prenatal care, and freedom from sterilization abuse. Offers technical training for community health facilitators. Organizes forums. **Libraries: Type:** open to the public. **Publications:** *Honoring Our Healers/Homenaje a Nuestras Curanderas.* Book ● Newsletter, periodic. Includes Latina health issues, legislation affecting Latinas, and calendar of events and activities on health and reproductive rights. **Conventions/Meetings:** conference.

14674 ■ People-to-People Health Foundation (HOPE)
Proj. HOPE Intl. HQ
255 Carter Hall Ln.
Millwood, VA 22646
Ph: (540)837-2100
Free: (800)544-HOPE
Fax: (540)837-1813
E-mail: hope@projecthope.org
URL: http://www.projecthope.org
Contact: Dr. John Howe III, Pres./CEO
Founded: 1958. **Staff:** 200. **Description:** Promotes better world health and understanding through the training of medical, nursing, dental, and allied health personnel in developing areas of the world. Operates the Center for Health Affairs, which provides research and policy analysis to help develop solutions to problems in worldwide health systems. Develops programs which include the use of volunteer doctors, nurses, and allied health professionals to teach modern techniques in health sciences education, health services delivery systems, health facilities management, and health-related humanitarian assistance. Has programs that are currently operating in 37 countries, located in Africa, Asia, Eastern Europe, and North, Central, and South America. **Boards:** Medical and Dental. **Also Known As:** Project HOPE. **Publications:** *Health Affairs*, quarterly. Journal. Covers domestic and international health policies; annual and five-year indexes available. **Price:** $122.00 /year for individuals in U.S. and Canada; $295.00 /year for institutions in U.S. and Canada; $162.00 /year for individuals outside U.S. and Canada; $335.00 /year for institutions outside U.S. and Canada. ISSN: 0278-2715. **Circulation:** 11,000. Alternate Formats: microform; online ● *HOPE News*, quarterly. Newsletter. Covers Project HOPE's international and domestic programs. Includes calendar of events and news of fundraising activities. **Price:** free. **Circulation:** 125,000 ● Annual Report, annual. Alternate Formats: online.

14675 ■ Project Concern International (PCI)
5151 Murphy Canyon Rd., Ste.320
San Diego, CA 92123
Ph: (858)279-9690
Free: (877)PCI-HOPE
Fax: (858)694-0294
E-mail: postmaster@projectconcern.org
URL: http://www.projectconcern.org
Contact: George Guimaraes, Pres./CEO
Founded: 1961. **Staff:** 550. **Budget:** $20,000,000. **Description:** Works with communities worldwide to ensure low-cost, basic health care for those most in need, particularly mothers and children. Provides education, training, and medical assistance to safeguard the world's impoverished children. Works with volunteers to prepare local communities to care for their own children with long-term, self-sustaining projects. Maintains programs in Bolivia, Guatemala, El Salvador, Ghana, Honduras, Mexico, Nicaragua, India, Indonesia, Zambia and the United States. **Formerly:** (1978) Project Concern, Inc. **Publications:** *Concern News*, quarterly. Newsletter. Includes news about the organization, special events and donors. **Price:** free. **Circulation:** 4,000 ● *Project Concern International—Annual Report.* Contains financial statements. **Price:** free. **Conventions/Meetings:** semiannual board meeting.

14676 ■ Tang Center for Herbal Medicine Research
Univ. of Chicago
Pritzer Scholarship of Medicine
Dept. of Anesthesia and Critical Care
5841 S Maryland Ave., MC 4028
Chicago, IL 60637
Ph: (773)834-2399 (773)702-4055
Fax: (773)834-0601
E-mail: tangcenter@dacc.uchicago.edu
URL: http://tangcenter.uchicago.edu
Contact: Dr. Chun-Su Yuan MD, Dir.
Founded: 1972. **Members:** 20. **Staff:** 4. **Budget:** $200,000. **Description:** Aims to advance international understanding between Asia and the West in the areas of science, medical systems, and health care delivery. Serves as a clearinghouse for international scholarly efforts in the comparative study of science and medicine. Provides consulting services and mediation of scientific and biomedical exchange with Asian countries. Assists in generating innovative curricula in medical education; translates contemporary and classical Asian scientific and medical literature; provides training for medical professionals in acupuncture therapeutics. **Libraries: Type:** reference. **Holdings:** 32; articles. **Subjects:** complementary and alternative medicine. **Sections:** Comparative Health-Care Delivery and Medical Education; Comparative Psychiatry and Mental Health. **Formerly:** (2004) Institute for Advanced Research in Asian Science and Medicine. **Publications:** *American Journal of Chinese Medicine*, bimonthly. Publishes original articles and essays related to traditional or ethnomedicine of all cultures. **Price:** $367.00 6 issues, for institution (electronic and print); $229.00 6 issues, for individual (print only). ISSN: 0192-415X. Also Cited As: *AJCM*. **Conventions/Meetings:** annual conference and seminar.

Iraq

14677 ■ Iraqi Medical Sciences Association (IMSA)
3912 Maple Hill E
West Bloomfield, MI 48323
Ph: (248)738-5995
Fax: (248)540-8982
E-mail: hashimalani@sbcglobal.net
URL: http://www.iraqimedical.com
Contact: Hashim Alani MD, VP
Founded: 2000. **Membership Dues:** associate, $25 (annual) ● active in training, $50 (annual) ● active, $100 (annual). **Multinational. Description:** Represents medical doctors, dentists, veterinarians and medical science professionals of Iraqi descent. Promotes scientific, social and cultural activities among its members. Seeks to "combat the negative image of the Iraqi people and present their true identity by means of their activities.".

Korean

14678 ■ Coalition for Healthy Korean Americans (COHKA)

c/o Koh Memorial Health Center
41 Montvale Ave., Ste.450
Stoneham, MA 02180
Ph: (781)438-6060
Fax: (781)438-6466
URL: http://www.bmc.org/physref/index.
asp?st=display_dept&dept_id=5
Description: Promotes better health through education. Health care services include cancer screening and dental care. Offers health insurance, HIV prevention, immunization, and smoking cessation programs.

Laboratory

14679 ■ American Association of Bioanalysts (AAB)

906 Olive St., Ste.1200
St. Louis, MO 63101-1434
Ph: (314)241-1445
Fax: (314)241-1449
E-mail: aab@aab.org
URL: http://www.aab.org
Contact: Mark S. Birenbaum PhD, Admin.
Founded: 1956. **Members:** 4,500. **Membership Dues:** owner/director, $225 (annual) ● manager/supervisor, $75 (annual) ● associate, $35-$75 (annual) ● affiliate, $100 (annual) ● supporting, $350 (annual) ● sustaining, $1,000 (annual). **Description:** Professional organization of directors, owners, managers, supervisors, technologists and technicians of bioanalytical clinical laboratories devoting their efforts to clinical laboratory procedure and testing. Sponsors Proficiency Testing Service open to individuals engaged in the clinical laboratory field. Provides specialized education and representation before federal and state legislatures and regulatory agencies. **Sections:** College of Reproductive Biology; Environmental Biology and Public Health; Executive Officers. **Affiliated With:** American Board of Bioanalysis. **Publications:** *AAB Bulletin*, quarterly. Newsletter. Provides latest information about the association. **Price:** included in membership dues ● *AAB Update*, periodic. Report. Provides latest legislative developments about CLIA and other regulations, Medicare reimbursement, and state licensure laws. **Price:** available to members only ● *Andrology and Embryology Review Course Manual*. Book. **Price:** $120.00 for members; $180.00 for nonmembers ● *General Knowledge for the Clinical Lab Director*. Book. **Price:** $60.00 for members; $90.00 for nonmembers ● *POLT*. Handbooks. **Price:** $19.95 for members; $24.95 for nonmembers ● *POLT Q&A*. Booklets. **Price:** $12.95 for members; $14.95 for nonmembers ● *QA Manual for POLs and Industries and Hospital Labs*. Book. **Price:** $34.95 for members; $49.95 for nonmembers. **Conventions/Meetings:** annual Meeting and Educational Conference, technical/managerial sessions for CLIN lab personnel (exhibits).

14680 ■ American Clinical Laboratory Association (ACLA)

1250 H St. NW, Ste.880
Washington, DC 20005
Ph: (202)637-9466
Fax: (202)637-2050
E-mail: info@clinical-labs.org
URL: http://www.clinical-labs.org
Contact: Alan Mertz, Pres.
Founded: 1971. **Description:** Corporations, partnerships, or individuals owning or controlling one or more independent clinical laboratory facilities operating for a profit and licensed under the Clinical Laboratories Improvement Act of 1967 or the Clinical Laboratories Improvement Amendment of 1988, or accredited by the Medicare program. Promotes the development of uniformly high quality laboratory testing; eliminates the present inequalities in the standards applied to different segments of the clinical laboratory market;

discourages the enactment of restrictive legislative or regulatory policies that may impede the free flow of commerce or operate to the detriment of the public. Examines federal and state health care and laboratory regulatory and legislative proposals and submits comments and opinions to the appropriate agencies or legislative bodies. **Committees:** Legislative and Regulatory. **Publications:** *Beltway Buzz*. Newsletter. Alternate Formats: online ● *Results*, monthly. Newsletter. Alternate Formats: online. **Conventions/Meetings:** annual meeting.

14681 ■ American Society for Clinical Laboratory Science (ASCLS)

6701 Democracy Blvd., Ste.300
Bethesda, MD 20817
Ph: (301)657-2768
Fax: (301)657-2909
E-mail: ascls@ascls.org
URL: http://www.ascls.org
Contact: Elissa Passiment EdM, Exec. VP
Founded: 1932. **Members:** 11,000. **Membership Dues:** professional I, $92 (annual) ● professional II, $70 (annual) ● collaborative, $40 (annual) ● student, $25 (annual). **Staff:** 4. **Budget:** $1,400,000. **Regional Groups:** 10. **State Groups:** 50. **Multinational. Description:** Primarily clinical laboratory personnel who have an associate or baccalaureate degree and clinical training and specialists who hold at least a master's degree in one of the major fields of clinical laboratory science such as bacteriology, mycology, or biochemistry; also includes technicians, specialists, and educators with limited certificates and students enrolled in approved programs of clinical laboratory studies and military medical technology schools. Promotes and maintains high standards in clinical laboratory methods and research and advances standards of education and training of personnel. Conducts educational program of seminars and workshops. Approves programs of continuing education and maintains records on participation in continuing education programs for members. **Awards:** ASCLS Education and Research Fund (E and R) Scholarship Program. **Frequency:** annual. **Type:** scholarship. **Recipient:** for training in clinical laboratory science; for students, practitioners and educators ● Education Scientific Assembly Student Paper Award. **Frequency:** annual. **Type:** recognition. **Recipient:** for best research papers and case studies of student. **Computer Services:** Mailing lists. **Telecommunication Services:** electronic mail, elissap@ascls.org. **Formerly:** American Society of Medical Technologists; (1936) American Society of Clinical Laboratory Technicians; (1993) American Society for Medical Technology. **Publications:** *ASCLS Today*, monthly. Newsletter. **Price:** included in membership dues. ISSN: 0895-3597. **Circulation:** 13,000. **Advertising:** accepted ● *Clinical Laboratory Science*, quarterly. Journal. **Price:** included in membership dues; $50.00 /year for individuals; $65.00/year for corporations; $100.00/year outside U.S. ISSN: 0894-959X. **Circulation:** 11,000. **Advertising:** accepted ● Books ● Brochures ● Manuals ● Videos. **Conventions/Meetings:** annual conference and meeting (exhibits).

14682 ■ Clinical Laboratory Management Association (CLMA)

989 Old Eagle School Rd., Ste.815
Wayne, PA 19087
Ph: (610)995-9580
Fax: (610)995-9568
E-mail: website@clma.org
URL: http://www.clma.org
Contact: Stephanie Robinson, Exec. Asst.
Founded: 1976. **Members:** 6,500. **Membership Dues:** regular, in North America, $145 (annual) ● regular, outside North America, $150 (annual) ● associate (student, pathology resident, retiree), $55 (annual). **Staff:** 24. **Budget:** $5,000,000. **Local Groups:** 103. **National Groups:** 90. **Description:** Individuals holding managerial or supervisory positions with clinical laboratories; persons engaged in education of such individuals; manufacturers or distributors of equipment or services to clinical laboratories. Objectives are: to enhance manage-

ment skills and promote more efficient and productive department operations; to further exchange of professional knowledge, new technology, and colleague experience; to encourage cooperation among those engaged in management or supervisory functions. Activities include: workshops, seminars, and expositions; dissemination of information about legislation and other topics. **Awards:** Chapter of the Year. **Frequency:** annual. **Type:** scholarship ● Educational Scholarship. **Frequency:** annual. **Type:** scholarship. **Committees:** Bylaws; Education Review and Selection; Exhibits Advisory; Health Care Policy; Industry Partners; Nominating. **Councils:** Quality Advisory. **Task Forces:** Advisory. **Formerly:** (1976) American Association of Clinical Laboratory Supervisors and Administrators. **Publications:** *Clinical Laboratory Management Association—Membership Directory*, annual. Lists members' names arranged alphabetically and geographically. **Circulation:** 5,000. Alternate Formats: online ● *Clinical Leadership Management Review*, bimonthly. Journal. Covers concepts and techniques of management and issues and trends in health care that affect the clinical laboratory. **Price:** included in membership dues; $150.00 /year for nonmembers. ISSN: 1527-3954. **Circulation:** 5,500. **Advertising:** accepted ● *CLMA Vantage Point*, monthly. Newsletter. Contains articles and regular columns on general management issues and specific topics relative to the clinical laboratory industry. **Price:** included in membership dues. **Circulation:** 5,000. **Advertising:** accepted. **Conventions/Meetings:** annual ThinkLab - conference (exhibits).

14683 ■ Clinical and Laboratory Standards Institute (CLSI)

940 W Valley Rd., Ste.1400
Wayne, PA 19087-1898
Ph: (610)688-0100
Free: (877)447-1888
Fax: (610)688-0700
E-mail: customerservice@clsi.org
URL: http://www.clsi.org
Founded: 1968. **Members:** 2,100. **Staff:** 24. **Budget:** $5,000,000. **Multinational. Description:** Government agencies, professional societies, clinical laboratories, and industrial firms with interests in medical testing. Purposes are to promote the development of national and international standards for medical testing and to provide a consensus mechanism for defining and resolving problems that influence the quality and cost of healthcare work performed. **Awards:** Russell J. Eilers Memorial Award. **Frequency:** annual. **Type:** recognition. **Recipient:** for outstanding contribution to voluntary consensus. **Affiliated With:** American National Standards Institute. **Formerly:** (1994) National Committee for Clinical Laboratory Standards; (1997) NCCLS: The Clinical Laboratory Standards Organization; (2000) National Committee for Clinical Laboratory Standards. **Publications:** Reports ● Videos ● Also publishes standards and guidelines and documents. **Conventions/Meetings:** annual international conference, addresses issues of foremost concern to the healthcare industry.

14684 ■ Clinical Ligand Assay Society (CLAS)

3139 S Wayne Rd.
Wayne, MI 48184
Ph: (734)722-6290
Fax: (734)722-7006
E-mail: clas@clas.org
URL: http://www.clas.org
Contact: Daisy McCann PhD, Exec. Dir.
Founded: 1976. **Members:** 400. **Membership Dues:** regular, $160 (annual) ● student, $25 (annual). **Staff:** 3. **Budget:** $250,000. **Regional Groups:** 12. **State Groups:** 8. **Description:** Seeks to establish and promote high standards in the science and application of ligand assay technology by encouraging research, education practitioners, and fostering communication and cooperation among individuals in laboratories in medicine, academia, and industry. Sponsors job placement service. **Awards:** CLAS Distinguished Scientist Award. **Frequency:** semiannual. **Type:** monetary. **Recipient:** for distinguished record in ligand assay technology ● Grafton Chase

Award. **Frequency:** annual. **Type:** recognition. **Recipient:** for a student or post-doctoral individual with excellent academic achievements related to ligand assays. **Computer Services:** Mailing lists. **Committees:** Certification; National Meeting; Publication and Education. **Formerly:** (1981) Clinical Radioassay Society. **Publications:** *CLAS News*, bimonthly. Newsletter. Alternate Formats: online ● *CLAS 25th Anniversary Commemorative Cookbook* ● *Ionizing Radiation Boon or Bane*. Book. **Price:** $39.95 plus shipping and handling ● *Journal of Clinical Ligand Assay*, quarterly. Contains reviews and articles on clinical ligand assay techniques. Includes bibliography of recent articles and manufacturers' directory. **Price:** included in membership dues. ISSN: 0736-4393. **Circulation:** 1,500. **Advertising:** accepted. Alternate Formats: CD-ROM; online ● *Laboratorian Desk Reference*. Manual. **Price:** included in membership dues ● Directory, biennial. **Advertising:** accepted ● Also publishes syllabi for annual meeting, and a newsletter. **Conventions/Meetings:** annual meeting and conference (exhibits) ● annual symposium and meeting (exhibits) ● periodic workshop.

Laser Medicine

14685 ■ American Society for Laser Medicine and Surgery (ASLMS)
2100 Stewart Ave., Ste.240
Wausau, WI 54401
Ph: (715)845-9283
Fax: (715)848-2493
E-mail: information@aslms.org
URL: http://www.aslms.org
Contact: Dianne Dalsky, Exec. Dir.
Founded: 1980. **Members:** 3,325. **Staff:** 5. **Description:** Physicians, physicists, and other scientists; nurses, dentists, podiatrists, veterinarians, and other paramedical personnel; technicians and commercial representatives concerned with the medical applications of lasers. Facilitates exchange of information concerning lasers. **Awards: Type:** grant. **Computer Services:** Online services, patient referrals, meeting registration, membership renewals, membership applications. **Divisions:** Biostimulation; Dermatology; General; GI/Endoscopy; Gynecology; Industrial; Laser Basic Science; Laser Biomedical Engineering; Laser Safety; Neurosurgery; New Devices; Nursing/Allied Health; Oncology; Ophthalmology; Oral and Maxillofacial; Orthopedic; Otolaryngology/Head and Neck; Plastic; Podiatry; Pulmonary; Surgery; Thoracic/Cardiovascular; Tissue Welding; Urology. **Publications:** *Lasers in Surgery and Medicine*, bimonthly. Journal. **Price:** included in membership dues. **Advertising:** accepted ● *Official ASLMS Newsletter*, periodic. **Conventions/Meetings:** annual conference (exhibits) - 2008 Apr. 2-6, Kissimmee, FL.

Learning Disabled

14686 ■ Nonverbal Learning Disorders Association (NLDA)
507 Hopmeadow St.
Simsbury, CT 06070
Ph: (860)658-5522
Fax: (860)658-6688
E-mail: info@nlda.org
URL: http://www.nlda.org
Contact: Patti Carrin, Pres.
Founded: 2000. **Members:** 3,000. **Membership Dues:** single, $50 (annual) ● professional/family, $75 (annual). **Multinational. Description:** Represents children and adults with Nonverbal Learning Disorders (NLD). Facilitates education, research and advocacy for children and adults who manifest disabilities associated with the syndrome of Nonverbal Learning Disorders. Strives to enhance the lives of all individuals with NLD by encouraging effective identification and intervention, fostering research, and protecting the rights of learning disabled individuals. **Telecommunication Services:** electronic mail, pcarrin@nlda.org. **Publications:** Newsletter, quarterly. Contains issues and research about nonverbal

learning disorders. **Price:** included in membership dues. Alternate Formats: online.

Legal

14687 ■ American Association of Legal Nurse Consultants (AALNC)
401 N Michigan Ave.
Chicago, IL 60611
Ph: (312)321-5177
Free: (877)402-2562
Fax: (312)673-6655
E-mail: info@aalnc.org
URL: http://www.aalnc.org
Contact: Ginger Varca, Pres.
Founded: 1989. **Members:** 3,600. **Membership Dues:** registered nurse (active or associate), $145 (annual) ● non-registered nurse (sustaining), $225 (annual). **State Groups:** 48. **Description:** Works for the professional enhancement and growth of registered nurses practicing in the specialty of legal nurse consulting. Acts as the pre-eminent resource for professionals with an interest in the legal nurse consulting arena including novice and veteran legal nurse consultants. Provides networking opportunities, educational advancement, professional development and supports certification through the American Legal Nurse Consultant Certification Board (ALNCCB). **Libraries: Type:** reference. **Holdings:** 30; archival material, articles, audio recordings, books, periodicals. **Subjects:** legal nurse consulting, medical record analysis, expert witnessing, business practices. **Awards:** Member of the Year Award. **Frequency:** annual. **Type:** recognition. **Recipient:** to an individual who has demonstrated career excellence, commitment to the association and service to the profession as a whole ● Volunteer of the Year Award. **Frequency:** annual. **Type:** recognition. **Recipient:** to an individual who has served on a committee or task force during the given year. **Computer Services:** Bibliographic search, public search engine, LNC locator ● mailing lists, of members. **Boards:** American Legal Nurse Consultant Certification. **Publications:** *Business Principles for Legal Nurse Consultants*. Book. **Price:** $70.00 ● *The Journal of Legal Nurse Consulting*, quarterly. Includes educational and legislative updates, and networking information. **Price:** free for members. **Circulation:** 3,700. **Advertising:** accepted ● *Legal Nurse Consulting: Principles and Practice*. Book. **Price:** $95.00 for members; $100.00 for nonmembers. **Conventions/Meetings:** annual conference and seminar, offers legal nurse consulting sessions, nursing contact hours and networking opportunities (exhibits).

14688 ■ American Association of Nurse Attorneys (TAANA)
PO Box 515
Columbus, OH 43216-0515
Free: (877)538-2262
Fax: (614)221-2335
E-mail: taana@taana.org
URL: http://www.taana.org
Contact: Janet K. Feldkamp, Pres.
Founded: 1982. **Members:** 400. **Membership Dues:** affiliate, first year post graduate, $90 (annual) ● fellow, $195 (annual) ● student, $25 (annual). **Local Groups:** 24. **Description:** Nurse attorneys, nurses in law school, and attorneys in nursing school. Aims to inform the public on matters of nursing, health care and law. Facilitates communication and information sharing between professional groups; establishes an employment network; assists new and potential nurse attorneys; develops the profession; promotes the image of nurse attorneys as experts and consultants in nursing and law. Maintains educational foundation. **Awards:** Cynthia Northrop Distinguished Service Award. **Frequency:** annual. **Type:** recognition. **Recipient:** for an individual member's leadership role in, and significant contributions to TAANA ● Outstanding Advocate Award. **Frequency:** annual. **Type:** recognition. **Recipient:** for an individual member's outstanding legal advocacy. **Computer Services:** Mailing lists. **Committees:** Awards; Convention Plan-

ning; Electronic Communication; Nominations and Elections. **Publications:** *Annual Meeting and Educational Conference Brochure*. Alternate Formats: online ● *Demonstrating Financial Responsibility in Nursing Practice*. Brochure. Contains information for nurses considering the purchase of professional liability insurance. **Price:** $2.00 ● *Inside TAANA*, 3/year. Newsletter. Contains reports from committees and chapters, legislative information, and member notes. **Price:** included in membership dues. **Circulation:** 625. **Advertising:** accepted ● *Journal of Nursing Law*, quarterly ● *Making the Transition: From Nursing to the Law* ● *Model Curriculum for Legal Content in Nursing Education* ● *On Becoming A Nurse Attorney*. **Conventions/Meetings:** annual Educational Symposium - conference (exhibits) ● seminar ● workshop.

14689 ■ American College of Legal Medicine (ACLM)
1111 N Plaza Dr., Ste.550
Schaumburg, IL 60173
Ph: (847)969-0283
Free: (800)433-9137
Fax: (847)517-7229
E-mail: info@aclm.org
URL: http://www.aclm.org
Contact: Bruce H. Seidberg MD, Pres.
Founded: 1960. **Members:** 1,450. **Membership Dues:** student, $35 (annual) ● regular, $190 (annual) ● fellow, $290 (annual). **Staff:** 4. **Budget:** $400,000. **Description:** Persons who hold degrees in medicine, dentistry, law and nursing. Promotes and advances the field of legal medicine or medical jurisprudence; arranges for meetings with medical, legal, and professional groups and legislative, judicial, and enforcement bodies interested in any province where law and medicine are contiguous; fosters and encourages centers for study and research in the field of legal medicine and publishes materials pertaining to legal medicine. **Awards:** Hirsh Award. **Frequency:** annual. **Type:** monetary. **Recipient:** to a dentistry, podiatry, nursing, pharmacy, health science or health care administration student for outstanding original paper on legal medicine ● Letourneau Award. **Frequency:** annual. **Type:** monetary. **Recipient:** to a law student for outstanding original paper on legal medicine ● Schwartz Award. **Frequency:** annual. **Type:** monetary. **Recipient:** to a medical student for outstanding original paper on legal medicine. **Computer Services:** database, membership application, upcoming meetings ● mailing lists. **Committees:** Bylaws; Education; Student Awards. **Publications:** *American College of Legal Medicine—Newsletter*, quarterly. Contains basic news and information of the College. **Price:** included in membership dues. **Circulation:** 1,500. Also Cited As: *Notes from the President* ● *College of Legal Medicine Membership Directory*, annual. **Price:** included in membership dues; $50.00/ copy for nonmembers. **Advertising:** accepted ● *Journal of Legal Medicine*, quarterly. Offers discussion of topics of interest in legal medicine, health law, food and drug law, and medicolegal research and education. **Price:** $299.00 /year for institutions; $160.00 /year for individuals ● *Legal Medicine*, bimonthly. Book. Contains legal implications of medical practice. **Price:** $179.00 retail ● *Legal Medicine Perspectives*, bimonthly. Report. Includes summaries of prominent cases and discussions of recent studies. **Price:** $78.00 /year for nonmembers; $50.00 /year for members. **Advertising:** accepted. Alternate Formats: online ● *Legal Medicine Q&A*, bimonthly. Report. Includes day-to-day medical legal concerns of the practicing physician. **Price:** $30.00 /year for nonmembers; $50.00/2 years for nonmembers. Alternate Formats: online ● *Medical Legal Lessons*, bimonthly. Report. Includes summaries of prominent cases and discussions of recent statutes. **Conventions/Meetings:** annual Conference on Legal Medicine (exhibits) - 2008 Feb. 28-Mar. 2, Houston, TX ● annual Mid-Year Educational Conference - meeting (exhibits) - 2007 Oct. 13-14, Chicago, IL.

14690 ■ American Society of Law, Medicine and Ethics (ASLME)
765 Commonwealth Ave., Ste.1634
Boston, MA 02215

Ph: (617)262-4990
Fax: (617)437-7596
E-mail: info@aslme.org
URL: http://www.aslme.org
Contact: Benjamin W. Moulton JD, Exec. Dir./Exec. VP

Founded: 1972. **Members:** 4,500. **Membership Dues:** doctoral, $230 (annual) ● institutional, $360 (annual) ● non-doctoral, allied health professional, $150 (annual) ● doctoral, $550 (triennial) ● institutional, $935 (triennial) ● non-doctoral, allied health professional, $355 (triennial) ● student, $90 (annual). **Staff:** 8. **Budget:** $1,000,000. **Description:** Physicians, attorneys, health care management executives, nurses, insurance company personnel, members of the judiciary, and others interested in medicolegal relations, health law, and ethics. Aims to provide opportunities for continuing education through publications, conferences, and information clearinghouse. Maintains speakers' bureau. **Libraries: Type:** reference. **Holdings:** 4,000; books, periodicals. **Subjects:** law, medicine, health care. **Awards:** Health Law Teachers Award. **Frequency:** annual. **Type:** recognition. **Recipient:** to leading health law professor in recognition of outstanding achievement in teaching and for publications. **Computer Services:** Mailing lists. **Formerly:** (1911) Massachusetts Society of Examining Physicians; (1973) Massachusetts Society of Law and Medicine; (1993) American Society of Law and Medicine. **Publications:** *American Journal of Law and Medicine*, quarterly. Contains annotations of recent court decisions, book releases, and student case and note section. **Price:** $250.00 /year for institutions; $140.00 /year for individuals. ISSN: 0098-8588. **Advertising:** accepted. Alternate Formats: microform ● *Journal of Law, Medicine and Ethics*, quarterly. Reports on medically related legal and social issues such as managed care, genetics, pain management, physician-assisted suicide. Peer reviewed. **Price:** $250.00 /year for institutions; $140.00 /year for individuals. ISSN: 1073-1105. **Advertising:** accepted. Alternate Formats: microform. **Conventions/Meetings:** annual meeting (exhibits).

14691 ■ American Society for Pharmacy Law (ASPL)
3085 Stevenson Dr., Ste.200
Springfield, IL 62703
Ph: (217)529-6948
E-mail: info@aspl.org
URL: http://www.aspl.org
Contact: Nathela Chatara, Exec. Dir.

Founded: 1974. **Members:** 400. **Membership Dues:** regular, $120 (annual) ● student, $40 (annual). **Staff:** 2. **Budget:** $65,000. **Description:** Pharmacists, lawyers, and students. Aims are to: further legal knowledge; communicate accurate legal information to pharmacists; foster knowledge and education pertaining to the rights and duties of pharmacists; distribute information of interest to members; provide a forum for exchange of information pertaining to pharmacy law. **Awards:** ASPL Legal Research Award. **Frequency:** annual. **Type:** recognition. **Recipient:** for scholarly legal writing on topics relevant to practicing pharmacists or attorneys ● Joseph L. Fink III Founders Award. **Frequency:** periodic. **Type:** recognition. **Recipient:** for sustained and outstanding service and contributions to the professions of pharmacy and law ● Larry Simonsmeizr Award. **Frequency:** annual. **Type:** monetary. **Recipient:** for best manuscript ● President's Award. **Type:** recognition. **Recipient:** for outstanding contributions to the field of pharmacy law. **Affiliated With:** American Pharmacists Association - Academy of Pharmacy Practice and Management; National Association of Boards of Pharmacy. **Publications:** *Rx Ipsa Loquitur*, bimonthly. Newsletter. Features recent court decisions, legislative and regulatory news, and other current pharmacy law news and articles. **Conventions/Meetings:** annual Developments in Pharmacy Law - seminar - always November ● annual National Pharmacy and other Organizations - meeting (exhibits) - always fall.

14692 ■ Children's Healthcare Is a Legal Duty (CHILD)
PO Box 2604
Sioux City, IA 51106

Ph: (712)948-3500
Fax: (712)948-3704
E-mail: childinc@netins.net
URL: http://www.childrenshealthcare.org
Contact: Dr. Rita Swan, Pres.

Founded: 1983. **Members:** 450. **Membership Dues:** individual, family, $35 (annual) ● overseas, $40 (annual). **Staff:** 1. **Description:** Advocates for the provision of healthcare for all children; opposes child abuse and neglect related to religious belief or cultural tradition; opposes religious exemptions from child health and safety laws. **Awards:** Imogene Temple Johnson Friend of Children Award. **Frequency:** annual. **Type:** recognition. **Recipient:** for successful lobbying against religious exemption laws. **Also Known As:** CHILD, Inc. **Publications:** *CHILD, Inc. Newsletter*, quarterly. **Price:** included in membership dues; $25.00 /year for nonmembers. **Circulation:** 500 ● *Children, Medicine, Religion and the Law*. Reprint. **Price:** $5.00 ● *Cry, the Beloved Children*. Booklet. **Price:** $2.00. **Conventions/Meetings:** annual support group meeting.

14693 ■ Society for Healthcare Consumer Advocacy of the American Hospital Association (SHCA AHA)
1 N Franklin/31N
Chicago, IL 60606
Ph: (312)422-3700
Fax: (312)422-4577
E-mail: shca@aha.org
URL: http://www.shca-aha.org
Contact: Lindsay Robinson, Exec. Dir.

Founded: 1972. **Members:** 960. **Membership Dues:** individual, $200 (annual) ● student, $75 (annual) ● associate, $200 (annual). **Staff:** 5. **Budget:** $330,000. **State Groups:** 31. **Description:** Advances the development of effective patient representative and advocacy programs in health care institutions. Conducts seminars and workshops. **Awards:** APEX Awards Program. **Frequency:** annual. **Type:** recognition. **Recipient:** for professionals having excellent achievement in the field of patient representation/consumer affairs ● Ruth Ravich Founder's Award. **Frequency:** annual. **Type:** recognition. **Recipient:** to an individual whose work supported the vision of the society. **Computer Services:** Mailing lists. **Affiliated With:** American Hospital Association. **Formerly:** (1981) Society of Patient Representatives; (1988) National Society of Patient Representatives of the American Hospital Association; (1998) National Society of Patient Representation and Consumer Affairs of the American Hospital Association. **Publications:** *Answering Your Call: A Guide for Living Your Deepest Purpose*, periodic. Book. Provides exercises that appeal to your practical side as well as inspirational examples from history and literature. ● *In The Name of the Patient*, periodic. Manual. Contains new chapters outlining resource services available to assist organizations in monitoring and developing patient relations. **Price:** $55.00 for members; $70.00 for nonmembers ● *In the Name of the Patient Chapter: Chapter on Disaster Readiness*, periodic. Manual. Contains chapter that deals with disaster readiness and many case studies. **Price:** $5.00 for members; $7.50 for nonmembers ● *Managing Patient Expectations: The Art of Finding and Keeping Loyal Patients*, periodic. Book. Contains realistic and cost-effective strategies for maintaining patient satisfaction, creating loyalty, and increasing referrals. ● *Membership Roster*, annual. Directory. **Advertising:** accepted ● *Resolving Patient Complaints: A Step-by-Step Guide to Effective Service Recovery*, periodic. Book. Contains a patient-oriented approach to complaint handling that can be used by all staff in an office, clinic, or system. **Price:** $82.95 ● *The Written Word: Guidelines for Responding in Writing to Patient Concerns*, periodic. Manual. Contains guideline information and samples of written responses to patient concerns. **Price:** $50.00 for members; $35.00 for nonmembers. Alternate Formats: CD-ROM. **Conventions/Meetings:** annual Transforming Healthcare by Transforming Service - conference (exhibits).

14694 ■ Society of Medical Jurisprudence (SMJ)
PO Box 1304
New York, NY 10008-1304

Ph: (212)473-0523
Contact: Lea Singer, Past Pres.

Founded: 1883. **Members:** 150. **Membership Dues:** lawyer and health professional, $50 (annual). **Description:** Lawyers, physicians, surgeons, health professionals, chemists, and law and medical school professors. Promotes the investigation, study, and advancement of medical jurisprudence and high standards of medical expert testimony. Sponsors individual lectures and serial presentations of medicolegal interest. **Committees:** Legislative; Liaison; Public Relations; Social Affairs. **Formerly:** (1883) Medico-Legal Society; (1891) Society of Medical Jurisprudence and State Medicine. **Publications:** *Ligature*, 9/year. Newsletter. Contains legislative and regulatory information. ● Directory ● Also plans to publish essays on current issues of medico-legal interest. **Conventions/Meetings:** monthly meeting.

Leprosy

14695 ■ American Leprosy Missions (ALM)
1 ALM Way
Greenville, SC 29601
Ph: (864)271-7040
Free: (800)543-3135
Fax: (864)271-7062
E-mail: amlep@leprosy.org
URL: http://www.leprosy.org
Contact: Christopher J. Doyle, Pres.

Founded: 1906. **Staff:** 25. **Description:** Provides medical, rehabilitative, and social care for people with leprosy, also known as Hansen's disease, in over 20 countries. Conducts specialized training for medical workers; supports medical and social rehabilitation; provides special literature on leprosy to medical personnel abroad. Sponsors research in the U.S., Brazil and India. Assists the national leprosy control programs of Brazil, Angola, Myanmar, Mexico and the Philippines. Provides management assistance for the International Journal of Leprosy. **Libraries: Type:** reference. **Holdings:** 500. **Subjects:** leprosy, health. **Publications:** *Word and Deed*, quarterly. Newsletter. Includes ALM news. **Price:** free ● Annual Reports, annual. Includes financial statements. Alternate Formats: online ● Brochure, annual. Contains information about leprosy. Alternate Formats: online.

14696 ■ Damien-Dutton Society for Leprosy Aid (DDSLA)
616 Bedford Ave.
Bellmore, NY 11710
Ph: (516)221-5829 (516)221-9588
Fax: (516)221-5909
URL: http://www.damien-duttonleprosysociety.org
Contact: Howard E. Crouch, Pres.

Founded: 1944. **Members:** 8,000. **Staff:** 6. **Budget:** $200,000. **Description:** Represents religious leaders and laypeople interested in aiding victims of Hansen's disease (leprosy). Provides relief, research, and recreation to victims of leprosy all over the world regardless of race, color, or creed. **Libraries: Type:** not open to the public. **Holdings:** articles. **Subjects:** Hansens disease. **Awards:** Damien Dutton Award. **Frequency:** annual. **Type:** recognition. **Recipient:** for a person or organization who has made a major contribution to leprosy research, treatment, rehabilitation, or philanthropy. **Computer Services:** Online services, information on leprosy and Damien-Dutton. **Formerly:** (1972) Damien-Dutton Society. **Publications:** *After Damien: Dutton*. Book ● *Brother Dutton of Molokai*. Book. Features heroes for young adults. **Price:** $10.95 ● *Damien-Dutton Call*, 3/year. Newsletter. **Price:** available to members only ● *Grace*. Book ● *Once Over and Lightly*. Book. Contains essays and editorials. **Price:** $12.00 ● *This One Is For Gussie*. Book. Features memoir of a nun in the modern world. **Price:** $18.75 ● *Two Hearts - One Fire*. Book. Contains personal encounters with leprosy. **Price:** $12.00 ● *Two Josephs on Molokai*. Book. Features story of a unique friendship. **Price:** $18.00. **Conventions/Meetings:** annual meeting - always in Bellmore, NY.

14697 ■ International Christian Leprosy Mission (ICLM)
PO Box 596
Forest Grove, OR 97116
Ph: (503)285-9098
Fax: (503)285-6535
E-mail: healinghands8414@aol.com
Contact: Dr. Daniel Pulliam, Dir.
Founded: 1943. **Members:** 12. **Staff:** 7. **Regional Groups:** 3. **Multinational. Description:** Carries on evangelical missionary work and assists in physical treatment of people with leprosy and their children. **Libraries: Type:** not open to the public. **Holdings:** 3,000. **Publications:** *Global Missions*, quarterly. Newsletter. **Price:** free. **Advertising:** accepted ● *ICLM Healing Hands*, monthly. Newsletter. **Price:** free. **Circulation:** 2,000. **Advertising:** accepted. **Conventions/Meetings:** annual board meeting.

14698 ■ Leonard Wood Memorial - American Leprosy Foundation (LWM)
11600 Nebel St., Ste.210
Rockville, MD 20852
Ph: (301)984-1336
Fax: (301)770-0580
E-mail: lwm-alf@erols.com
URL: http://users.erols.com/lwm-alf
Contact: Roland V. Cellona MD, Asst. Dir./Branch Chief
Founded: 1928. **Staff:** 37. **Budget:** $850,000. **Description:** Health and research foundation concerned with microbiological research of Hansen's Disease (leprosy), and other related diseases. Conducts research programs in the U.S. and the Philippines. Supports clinical and basic laboratory research and epidemiological surveys. Sponsors exchange programs. Conducts collaborative studies with the Philippine Leprosy Mission, Culion Foundation, Colorado State University, Rockefeller University, the Delta Primate Center, American Leprosy Missions, International Sasakawa Memorial Health Foundation, Damien-Dutton Society, World Health Organization, UCLA School of Medicine, Ethiopia, India, Korea. **Libraries: Type:** reference. **Committees:** Scientific Advisory Board/Board of Trustees. **Divisions:** Eversley Childs Sanitarium (Cebu, Philippines); Leonard Wood Memorial. **Also Known As:** American Leprosy Foundation. **Formerly:** (1978) Leonard Wood Memorial for the Eradication of Leprosy. **Publications:** Annual Report, annual. **Price:** free. **Conventions/Meetings:** board meeting - 3/year.

Licensing

14699 ■ National Association for Regulatory Administration (NARA)
910 Glen Falls Ct.
Newark, DE 19711
Ph: (302)234-4152
Fax: (302)234-4153
E-mail: pauline@naralicensing.org
URL: http://www.nara-licensing.org
Contact: Ms. Pauline Koch, Exec. Dir.
Founded: 1976. **Membership Dues:** regular (based on annual income), $35-$60 (annual) ● agency, $200 (annual). **Description:** Promotes human care licensing and regulation service related to mental illness, developmental disabilities and abuse of drugs and alcohol. Protects health, safety and well-being of children and adults. Provides leadership, education, collaboration and service. **Publications:** *The Licensing*, 3/year. Newsletter. Features articles, reports and reviews of current research and case law. **Price:** $40.00 /year for nonmembers; included in membership dues. Alternate Formats: online ● Membership Directory. **Conventions/Meetings:** annual seminar.

Linguistics

14700 ■ Society of Neuro-Linguistic Programming
c/o Bennett/Stellar University
6930 132nd St. SE
Snohomish, WA 98296
Ph: (206)444-4075
Free: (888)432-1122
Fax: (858)488-5369
E-mail: bestu@imagineit.org
URL: http://www.imagineit.org/NewSite/Home/About_
    Stellar/pg_Credentials.htm
Contact: Michael Bennett, Contact
Founded: 1978. **Multinational. Description:** Exerts quality control over training programs and services representing the model of neuro-linguistic programming.

Lupus Erythematosus

14701 ■ Alliance for Lupus Research (ALR)
28 W 44th St., Ste.1217
New York, NY 10036
Ph: (212)218-2840
Free: (800)867-1743
E-mail: info@lupusresearch.org
URL: http://www.lupusresearch.org
Contact: Robert Wood Johnson IV, Chm.
Founded: 1999. **Multinational. Description:** Seeks to prevent, find better treatments and cure systemic lupus erythematosus. Aims to improve the quality of life for people who live with this disease through fundraising, advocacy and research programs. Supports research into the cause, cure, treatment and prevention of systemic lupus erythematosus and its complications. Raises money for the support of scientists around the world. **Awards:** New Pilot Grant Program. **Frequency:** annual. **Type:** grant. **Recipient:** to fund research that is directly relevant to identifying the cause, cure and treatment of systemic lupus erythematosus and its complications ● Target Identification in Lupus (TIL) Grants. **Frequency:** biennial. **Type:** grant. **Recipient:** to highly meritorious and innovative research focused on the identification and scientific and/or clinical advancement of therapeutic targets. **Publications:** *Lupus Research Update*, quarterly. Newsletter. Alternate Formats: online ● Annual Report, annual. Alternate Formats: online.

14702 ■ Lupus Foundation of America (LFA)
2000 L St. NW, Ste.710
Washington, DC 20036
Ph: (202)349-1155
Free: (800)558-0121
Fax: (202)349-1156
E-mail: info@lupus.org
URL: http://www.lupus.org
Contact: Sandra C. Raymond, Pres./CEO
Founded: 1977. **Membership Dues:** $12 (annual). **Staff:** 12. **Budget:** $1,700,000. **Local Groups:** 94. **Languages:** English, Spanish. **Description:** Aims to find the causes and cure for lupus. Seeks to improve the diagnosis and treatment of lupus, increases awareness of lupus among the public and health professionals, helps individuals and families affected by the disease, and finds the causes and cure for lupus through research and advocacy. Lupus erythematosus is a non-contagious disease that may affect the skin alone or may manifest itself as a chronic, systemic, and inflammatory disease of the connective tissues. Assists lupus patients and their families, through chapters and patient support groups, to cope with the daily problems associated with lupus. Collects and distributes funds for research. Works to bring lupus to the attention of the public by encouraging the publication of articles on the disease by syndicated medical writers, national magazines, and newspapers, and by obtaining radio and television coverage. Has successfully worked for the establishment of an annual Lupus Awareness Month. Holds chapter meetings and occasional medical seminars. **Libraries: Type:** reference. **Holdings:** books. **Awards:** Student Finzi Fellowship Award. **Frequency:** annual. **Type:** fellowship. **Recipient:** to undergraduate, graduate and medical students that foster and support lupus through basic, clinical, and psychosocial research supervised by scientific investigators. **Committees:** Chapters; Governmental Affairs; Grants; Medical Advisory. **Publications:** *Lupus Erythematosus*. Pamphlet ● *Lupus News*, quar-

terly. Newsletter. Reports current research both directly and indirectly related to lupus. **Price:** free for members. **Advertising:** accepted ● Also publishes other informational materials in Braille and Spanish. **Conventions/Meetings:** annual conference and meeting (exhibits).

14703 ■ Lupus Information Network (LIN)
230 Ranch Dr.
Bridgeport, CT 06606-1747
Ph: (203)372-5795
Founded: 1985. **Nonmembership. Description:** Educators, medical professionals, and individuals suffering from systemic lupus erythematosus. (Systemic lupus erythematosus is a chronic inflammatory disease of the connective tissue that affects the skin, joints, kidneys, nervous system, and mucous membranes.) Seeks to foster better understanding of the disease among patients, educators, and professionals through the distribution of information, both orthodox and alternative. **Convention/Meeting:** none. **Libraries: Type:** reference. **Holdings:** 200. **Formerly:** (2001) Lupus Network. **Publications:** *Introduction to Lupus*. Brochure ● Pamphlets ● Reprints.

Lymphology

14704 ■ International Society of Lymphology (ISL)
c/o M.H. Witte, MD, Sec. Gen.
Univ. of Arizona
Coll. of Medicine
Dept. of Surgery
PO Box 245200
Tucson, AZ 85724-5200
Ph: (520)626-6118
Fax: (520)626-0822
E-mail: lymph@u.arizona.edu
URL: http://www.u.arizona.edu/~witte/ISL.htm
Contact: M.H. Witte MD, Sec. Gen.
Founded: 1966. **Members:** 385. **Membership Dues:** general, $120 (annual). **National Groups:** 9. **Multinational. Description:** Professionals active in the medical, biological, and technical sciences. Promotes the study of lymphology and seeks to advance and disseminate knowledge in the field. Activities include: stimulating and strengthening experimentation and clinical investigation in lymphology; establishing relations between researchers and clinicians in the different fields of lymphology; encouraging contact and exchange of ideas among members and national and international organizations. Organizes postgraduate courses. **Working Groups:** Complications of Lymphology; Endolymphatic Radiotherapy; Lymphology in Filariasis. **Publications:** *Lymphology*, quarterly. Journal. **Price:** $75.00 with 10&percent; discount for vendors. ISSN: 0024-7766 ● *Progress in Lymphology*, biennial. Proceedings. **Conventions/Meetings:** biennial International Congress of Lymphology (exhibits).

14705 ■ Lymphatic Research Foundation (LRF)
100 Forest Dr.
East Hills, NY 11548
Ph: (516)625-9675
Fax: (516)625-9410
E-mail: lrf@lymphaticresearch.org
URL: http://www.lymphaticresearch.org
Contact: Wendy Chaite Esq., Pres.
Founded: 1998. **Staff:** 2. **Description:** Health care professionals, scientists, and researchers with an interest in lymphatic diseases and related disorders. Seeks to advance the prevention, diagnosis, and treatment of lymphatic diseases. Serves as a clearinghouse on lymphatic research; facilitates exchange of information among members; advocates the creation of a nationally supported lymphatic research program; functions as a liaison linking public and private-sector lymphatic research institutions and programs. **Awards:** Andrew Moisoff Young Investigator Award. **Frequency:** periodic. **Type:** grant. **Recipient:** for lymphatic research. **Computer Services:**

database, investigator registry ● database, patient registry. **Boards:** Advisory; Directors; Scientific Advisory. **Publications:** *Lymphatic Research & Biology*, quarterly. Journal. **Price:** $163.00. ISSN: 1539-6851. **Advertising:** accepted. Alternate Formats: online. **Conventions/Meetings:** biennial Gordon Research Conference: Molecular Mechanisms in Lymphatic Function & Disease (exhibits).

14706 ■ National Lymphedema Network
1611 Telegraph Ave., Ste.1111
Oakland, CA 94612-2138
Ph: (510)208-3200
Free: (800)541-3259
Fax: (510)208-3110
E-mail: nln@lymphnet.org
URL: http://www.lymphnet.org
Contact: Saskia R.J. Thiadens RN, Exec. Dir.
Founded: 1988. **Members:** 2,800. **Membership Dues:** individual, $45 (annual) ● international, $80 (annual) ● institution, $200 (annual) ● individual, in Canada, $60 (annual). **Staff:** 5. **Budget:** $265,000. **Languages:** English, Russian. **Description:** Persons with lymphedema and their families, healthcare professionals. Provides education and support to patients, health care professionals and the general public by disseminating information on the prevention and management of primary and secondary lymphedema. Supports research into the causes and possible alternative treatments for this often-incapacitating condition. Offers referral service to medical facilities, helps locate support groups and sponsors research and educational programs. **Libraries: Type:** reference. **Awards:** National Lymphedema Day Award. **Frequency:** annual. **Type:** recognition. **Computer Services:** database. **Publications:** *NLN Newsletter*, quarterly. Features cutting-edge medical articles, features, and resource listings. **Circulation:** 5,000. **Advertising:** accepted ● *Resource Guide*. Contains list of treatment centers, health care professionals and suppliers, Support Groups, PenPals, and updates on professional training courses. **Conventions/Meetings:** conference, attended by over 500 health care professionals and patients ● biennial congress (exhibits) ● periodic workshop, for health care professionals and patients.

14707 ■ North American Vodder Association of Lymphatic Therapy (NAVALT)
c/o Bonnie Peterson, Membership Committee Chm.
833 Independence Dr.
Longmont, CO 80501
Ph: (303)702-0557
Free: (888)462-8258
Fax: (303)776-1891
E-mail: wellnessbp@earthlink.net
URL: http://www.navalt.org
Contact: Bonnie Peterson, Membership Committee Chm.
Membership Dues: active, $70 (annual) ● student, $40 (annual) ● associate, $35 (annual). **Multinational. Description:** Promotes the acceptance of Manual Lymph Drainage (MLD) throughout North America. Advances the Vodder method of MLD through quality of performance, education and research. Ensures high quality in the performance, knowledge and skills of its active therapists. Furthers the education of therapists, other health care professionals and the public in general. **Telecommunication Services:** electronic mail, info@navalt.org. **Publications:** *Lymphedema Brochure*. **Price:** $25.00 plus shipping and handling ● *MLD (Manual Lymph Drainage) Brochure*. **Price:** $25.00 plus shipping and handling ● Newsletter, quarterly. **Price:** included in membership dues. **Advertising:** accepted ● Articles. Alternate Formats: online.

Marijuana

14708 ■ American Alliance for Medical Cannabis (AAMC)
44500 Tide Ave.
Arch Cape, OR 97102
Ph: (503)436-1882

E-mail: info@letfreedomgrow.com
URL: http://www.letfreedomgrow.com
Contact: Dave Bishop, Natl. Dir.
Membership Dues: personal, $25 (annual) ● educational, $40 (annual) ● corporate, $100 (annual). **Description:** Represents the interests of health professionals, patients, educators, clergy, caregivers and community members. Focuses on patient advocacy, patient rights, and support. Identifies medical, social and legal resources for patients and caregivers. Provides technical assistance to patients and caregivers in the establishment of affordable home cannabis gardens. Identifies and assists in the provision of high quality medicinal cannabis seeds and clones for legitimate patient and caregiver gardens. **Telecommunication Services:** electronic mail, director@eldoradocountyaamc.com. **Publications:** Newsletter.

Martial Arts

14709 ■ International Federation of Martial Arts and Oriental Medicine (IFMAOM)
622 W Colorado St.
Glendale, CA 91204
Ph: (323)512-2538
E-mail: ajjif@yahoo.com
URL: http://www.ajjif.org/IFMAOMabout.htm
Contact: Grand Master Alexey Kunin, Pres.
Founded: 2000. **Membership Dues:** life, $100. **Multinational. Description:** Supports, recognizes and promotes the International Martial Arts and Oriental Healing Arts communities. Promotes the development of martial arts and healing arts and medicine in the world through mutual cooperation, friendship, education and training camps. Recognizes, supports and registers different styles of martial arts and healing arts, organizations, schools and clubs.

Massage

14710 ■ American Massage Therapy Association (AMTA)
500 Davis St., Ste.900
Evanston, IL 60201-4695
Ph: (847)864-0123
Free: (877)905-2700
Fax: (847)864-1178
E-mail: info@amtamassage.org
URL: http://www.amtamassage.org
Contact: Elizabeth Lucas CAE, Exec. Dir.
Founded: 1943. **Members:** 55,000. **Membership Dues:** professional, $235 (annual) ● student, $79 (annual) ● supporting, $99 (annual). **Staff:** 60. **State Groups:** 52. **Description:** Massage therapists and massage schools. Promotes standards for the profession, has a Code of Ethics, and supports chapter efforts for state regulation of massage. Sponsors National Massage Therapy Awareness Week to promote public education on the benefits of massage; offers educational literature. Supports research on the efficacy of massage. Offers free Find A Message Therapists National locator service to help consumers and healthcare professionals find qualified, professional massage therapists. **Libraries: Type:** reference. **Holdings:** archival material, clippings, periodicals. **Computer Services:** database, membership. **Telecommunication Services:** phone referral service, Massage Therapist Locator, (888)843-2682. **Formerly:** (1983) American Massage and Therapy Association. **Publications:** *AMTA's Find a Massage Therapist/Experience the Benefits of Massage.* Brochure ● *Hands On*, bimonthly. Newsletter. Features association and member news. **Price:** free for members. ISSN: 1073-9343. **Circulation:** 50,000 ● *Massage Therapy*. Brochure ● *Massage Therapy Journal*, quarterly. Contains scholarly articles on massage therapy. **Price:** $25.00/year in U.S.; $70.00/year outside U.S. ISSN: 0895-0814. **Circulation:** 64,000. **Advertising:** accepted ● *Sports Massage*. Brochure ● *Stress*. Brochure. **Conventions/Meetings:** annual convention and trade show, association business, educational workshops (exhibits) - always fall.

14711 ■ American Medical Massage Association (AMMA)
1845 Lakeshore Dr., Ste.7
Muskegon, MI 49441
Free: (888)375-7245
Fax: (231)755-2963
E-mail: info@americanmedicalmassage.com
URL: http://www.americanmedicalmassage.com
Contact: Dr. Marie A. Ruberto, Managing Dir.
Founded: 1998. **Membership Dues:** fellowship (without insurance), $100 ● professional (with insurance), $242 ● student (with insurance), $189. **Description:** Promotes manual medicine training within the allied health industry. **Conventions/Meetings:** seminar.

14712 ■ American Organization for Bodywork Therapies of Asia (AOBTA)
1010 Haddonfield-Berlin Rd., Ste.408
Voorhees, NJ 08043-3514
Ph: (856)782-1616
Fax: (856)782-1653
E-mail: office@aobta.org
URL: http://www.aobta.org
Contact: Debra Howard, Pres.
Founded: 1989. **Members:** 1,500. **Membership Dues:** student, $50 (annual) ● associate, $75 (annual) ● certified practitioner, $100 (annual) ● certified instructor, $150 (annual) ● school/program, $300 (annual). **Staff:** 3. **Budget:** $200,000. **Regional Groups:** 3. **State Groups:** 6. **Description:** Professional Asian Bodywork Therapy (ABT) practitioners, teachers, schools and programs; interested individuals. (Asian bodywork therapy is a form of therapeutic bodywork which utilizes theories and techniques directly and derived from ancient and tradtitional Chinese medicine, as well as evolving forms which stem from that 'root'. ABT focuses on balancing the Qi flow in the body, utilizing many techniques.) Identifies qualified practitioners; serves as a legal entity representing members when dealing with the government, especially in terms of establishing professional status. Sets educational standards for all styles of Asian bodywork including acupressure, Tuina, Amma, Chi Nei Tsang, Nuad bo Rarn, and Shiatsu, among others. Sponsors speakers' bureau; conducts educational programs. **Libraries: Type:** not open to the public. **Holdings:** articles, books, photographs. **Subjects:** Asian bodywork therapy, business practices, history of Asian medicines, Asian medicine. **Computer Services:** database. **Formerly:** (1990) American Shiatsu Association; (1991) American Association of Oriental Healing Arts; (2001) American Oriental Bodywork Therapy Association. **Publications:** *PULSE Newsletter*, quarterly. **Conventions/Meetings:** annual convention and workshop (exhibits) ● workshop.

14713 ■ Associated Bodywork and Massage Professionals (ABMP)
1271 Sugarbush Dr.
Evergreen, CO 80439-9766
Ph: (303)674-8478
Free: (800)458-2267
Fax: (800)667-8260
E-mail: expectmore@abmp.com
URL: http://www.abmp.com
Contact: Katie Armitage, Exec. Dir.
Founded: 1986. **Members:** 57,000. **Membership Dues:** professional or practitioner, $199 (annual) ● certified/skin care professional, $229 (annual) ● student, $49 (annual). **For-Profit. Description:** Professional massage therapists and bodyworkers, sports massage therapists, skin care professionals, reflexologists, energy practitioners, etc; massage therapy schools; affiliated organizations. Promotes massage and bodywork. Seeks to improve the image of massage therapy and bodywork, and to educate the public about its benefits. Fosters greater credibility and cooperation with the medical profession. Encourages ethical practices, high standards of professional conduct, and continuing education. Provides members with low-cost liability insurance coverage and product discounts. **Computer Services:** Information services, client referral services and employment information ● mailing lists, informa-

tional, advertising and regulatory issues. **Formerly:** (1988) Associated Professional Massage Therapists and Allied Health Practitioners International; (1990) Associated Professional Massage Therapists and Bodyworkers. **Publications:** *ABMP Massage Marketplace*, annual. Directory. **Advertising:** accepted ● *ABMP Successful Business Handbook*. Includes comprehensive information on starting a practice, managing financial health, good business basics, marketing and advertising. **Advertising:** accepted ● *ABMP Touch Resource Guide*. Directory. Serves as a reference for practicing professionals. **Advertising:** accepted ● *Body Sense*, biennial. Magazine. **Price:** $1.00/copy, for members. **Advertising:** accepted ● *Different Strokes*, bimonthly. Newsletter ● *Massage and Bodywork*, bimonthly. Magazine. **Price:** included in membership dues. **Circulation:** 110,000. **Advertising:** accepted ● *Skin Deep*, bimonthly. Newsletter. **Advertising:** accepted. **Conventions/Meetings:** annual School Issues Forum - meeting, for school owners, directors and teachers to gather and discuss subjects important to the profession.

14714 ■ Day-Break Geriatric Massage Institute

c/o Sharon Puszko, PhD, Dir./Owner
7434 King George Dr., Ste.A
Indianapolis, IN 46240
Ph: (317)722-9896
Fax: (317)722-0511
E-mail: spuszko@juno.com
URL: http://www.daybreak-massage.com
Contact: Sharon Puszko PhD, Dir./Owner
Founded: 1982. **Membership Dues:** life, $35. **Description:** Promotes geriatric massage to maintain health and regain physical capabilities that were thought permanently lost. **Publications:** Books ● Videos. **Conventions/Meetings:** seminar ● workshop.

14715 ■ Hospital-Based Massage Network (HBMN)

c/o Information for People
PO Box 1038
Olympia, WA 98507-1038
Ph: (360)754-9799
Free: (800)754-9790
Fax: (360)705-3864
E-mail: info@info4people.com
URL: http://secure.info4people.com/HBMN.php
Contact: Laura Koch, Founder/Dir.
Founded: 1995. **Multinational. Description:** Promotes integration of complementary health care into mainstream medicine supporting massage and touch therapists working with ill, recovering, elderly, hospitals, medical centers, and nursing homes. **Publications:** Books. **Price:** $69.95 for one book; $119.95 for 2 books; $169.95 for all 3 books.

14716 ■ International Association of Animal Massage and Bodywork (IAAMB)

3347 McGregor Ln.
Toledo, OH 43623
Ph: (419)727-6917
Free: (800)903-9350
Fax: (419)475-3539
E-mail: info@iaamb.org
URL: http://www.iaamb.org
Contact: Jonathan C. Rudinger, Pres.
Membership Dues: general, $75 (annual). **Multinational. Description:** Serves as a forum for animal massage and bodywork professionals to network and support each other. Aims to advance the field of animal massage and bodywork. **Computer Services:** database, member list. **Publications:** Newsletter, quarterly. Alternate Formats: online. **Conventions/Meetings:** annual conference.

14717 ■ International Association of Infant Massage (IAIM)

PO Box 6370
Ventura, CA 93006
Ph: (805)644-8524
Free: (800)248-5432
Fax: (805)830-1729

E-mail: iaim4us@aol.com
URL: http://www.iaim-us.com
Contact: Susan Campbell, CEO Admin./Finance
Founded: 1986. **Members:** 3,000. **Membership Dues:** student/CIMI involved, $85 (annual) ● supporting (non-IAIM instructor), $65 (annual). **Staff:** 3. **Multinational. Description:** Parents, caregivers. Works to promote nurturing touch, positive interactive contact, and communication through massage. Trains and certifies individuals to teach parents and caregivers to massage their babies. **Libraries: Type:** reference. **Holdings:** clippings. **Computer Services:** database, parent class referrals for certified instructors. **Additional Websites:** http://www.iaim.ws. **Committees:** Educational. **Also Known As:** (1986) International Association of Infant Massage Instructors. **Publications:** *Tender Loving Care*, semiannual. Newsletter. Features articles on infant massage. **Price:** included in membership dues. **Circulation:** 3,000. **Conventions/Meetings:** biennial conference (exhibits) ● annual conference.

14718 ■ International Massage Association (IMA)

PO Box 421
Warrenton, VA 20188-0421
Ph: (540)351-0800
Free: (800)933-7113
Fax: (540)351-0816
E-mail: info@imagroup.com
URL: http://www.holisticbenefits.com/ima/international-massage-association.html
Contact: Will Green, Pres.
Founded: 1994. **Members:** 60,000. **Membership Dues:** practicing/teaching, $199 (annual) ● associate, $149 (annual). **Staff:** 15. **Description:** Professional massage practitioners and massage schools. Promotes unification of massage practitioners, regardless of technique or training. Provides services to members including credit card merchant accounts, industry discounts, personal business assistance and free internet advertising. Makes available professional insurance policies and health care plan to members. **Publications:** *IMA Success*. Newsletter.

14719 ■ International Thai Therapists Association (ITTA)

PO Box 268
Grass Valley, CA 95945
Ph: (760)641-0756
E-mail: itta@core.com
URL: http://www.thaimassage.com/itta/ittaindex.html
Contact: Mr. Anthony B. James LMNT, Pres./Dir. of Education
Founded: 1992. **Members:** 400. **Membership Dues:** student, $14 (annual) ● associate, $19 (annual) ● certified Thai practitioner, $35 (annual) ● certified Thai therapist, $55 (annual) ● certified facilitator, $50 (annual) ● certified instructor, certified master practitioner, institutional and/or school, $100 (annual) ● certified instructor advanced, $150 (annual). **Staff:** 2. **Multinational. Description:** Promotes the needs and concerns of students, practitioners, teachers and schools of Nuat Thai and Thai Style therapeutic massage and bodywork. **Libraries: Type:** reference. **Holdings:** 20; books. **Subjects:** Thai massage. **Publications:** *ThaiMassage.com*. Contains articles on techniques, business practices, upcoming events and training. Alternate Formats: online.

14720 ■ National Certification Board for Therapeutic Massage and Bodywork (NCBTMB)

1901 S Meyers Rd., Ste.240
Oakbrook Terrace, IL 60181
Ph: (630)627-8000
Free: (800)296-0664
Fax: (866)402-1890
E-mail: info@ncbtmb.com
URL: http://www.ncbtmb.com
Contact: Donna Feeley, Chair
Description: Massage and bodywork practitioners. Formed to set standards of ethical and professional practice through a credible credentialing program. **Publications:** Newsletter, quarterly.

Medical

14721 ■ American Integrative Medical Association (AIMA)

PO Box 3204
Norfolk, VA 23514-3204
Ph: (757)623-1200
Free: (866)611-1200
E-mail: aima@aihcp-norfolkva.org
URL: http://aihcp-norfolkva.org/AIMA
Description: Serves as a professional certification and credentialing agency for medical practitioners of Integrative Medicine and Health Care. Enhances the public trust in the quality of complementary and alternative health care delivery in the US. Acts as a clearinghouse and registry for practitioners. Encourages and facilitates continuing education programs.

14722 ■ American Neuroendocrine Society (ANS)

c/o Dr. Susan Wray, Sec.
Cellular and Developmental Neurobiology Sect.
NIH, NINDS
Bldg. 35, Rm. 3A-1012
Bethesda, MD 20892
Ph: (301)496-8129
Fax: (301)496-8578
E-mail: swray@codon.nih.gov
URL: http://www.neuroendocrine.org
Contact: Jon E. Levine PhD, Pres.
Founded: 1996. **Membership Dues:** regular, $40 (annual) ● fellow, emeritus status, $20 (annual) ● student, $10 (annual) ● regular - with print and electronic newsletter subscription, $110 (annual) ● fellow - with print and electronic newsletter subscription, $80 (annual) ● student - with print and electronic newsletter subscription, $70 (annual) ● emeritus status - with print and electronic newsletter subscription, $90 (annual). **Description:** Promotes basic and applied research in all aspects of neuroendocrinology. Enhances the education and training of students and researchers in the field of neuroendocrinology. Fosters interdisciplinary communication. **Publications:** *Frontiers in Neuroendocrinology*. Newsletter.

14723 ■ American Surgical Hospital Association (ASHA)

910 E 20th St.
Sioux Falls, SD 57105
Ph: (605)275-5349
Fax: (605)731-2575
E-mail: info@surgicalhospital.org
URL: http://www.surgicalhospital.org
Contact: Ms. Molly Gutierrez JD, Exec. Dir.
Members: 78. **Membership Dues:** corporate gold, $6,000 (annual) ● associate, corporate bronze, $2,500 (annual) ● professional, $1,000 (annual) ● individual, $500 (annual) ● corporate platinum, $8,000 (annual) ● corporate silver, $4,500 (annual). **Description:** Promotes a common model of acute care surgical hospitals in the U.S. **Telecommunication Services:** electronic mail, lipomi@surgicalhospital.org. **Conventions/Meetings:** annual Legislative Conference and Capitol Hill Visits.

14724 ■ Association for Integrative Health Care Practitioners (AIHCP)

PO Box 3204
Norfolk, VA 23514-3204
Ph: (757)623-1200
Free: (866)611-1200
E-mail: adm@aihcp-norfolkva.org
URL: http://aihcp-norfolkva.org/AIHCP
Founded: 1998. **Membership Dues:** philanthropic, $1,000 ● collegiate/medical-clinical facility, $800 (annual) ● distributor, $600 (annual) ● professional/administrator/educator, $250 (annual) ● herbalist, $400 (annual) ● allied health care practitioner, $200 (annual) ● student, $110 (annual) ● retired practitioner, $100 (annual). **Description:** Represents the interests of practitioners, providers, administrators and educators of the complementary and alternative medical and health care profession. Aims to achieve professional practice independence and insurance reimbursement policies for practitioners and provid-

ers of integrative health care. **Publications:** Newsletter. **Price:** included in membership dues.

14725 ■ Association of Medical Device Reprocessors (AMDR)
1400 16th St. NW, Ste.400
Washington, DC 20036
Ph: (202)518-6796
Fax: (202)234-0399
E-mail: info@amdr.org
URL: http://www.amdr.org

Members: 3. **Description:** Promotes proper processing of medical devices labeled for single-use.

14726 ■ COLA
9881 Broken Land Pkwy., Ste.200
Columbia, MD 21046
Free: (800)981-9883
Fax: (410)381-8611
E-mail: info@cola.org
URL: http://www.cola.org
Contact: Dr. Mary E. Frank MD, Vice Chair

Founded: 1988. **Description:** Promotes quality in medicine and patient care through education, achievement and accreditation. **Publications:** *COLA Insights*, bimonthly. Newsletter. **Price:** $43.20 ● Manuals. **Conventions/Meetings:** conference ● seminar.

14727 ■ International Association of Medical Intuitives (IAMI)
c/o Charles Lightwalker, Treas.
PO Box 30752
Spokane, WA 99223-3021
E-mail: charleslightwalker@yahoo.com
URL: http://www.medical-intuitives.net
Contact: Charles Lightwalker, Treas.

Founded: 2002. **Membership Dues:** professional, $50 (annual) ● supporting, $35 (annual). **Multinational. Description:** Represents the medical intuition profession. Increases awareness of medical intuition within the health care industry and the society. **Computer Services:** Information services, medical intuition resources.

14728 ■ International Association for Medicinal Compliance (IAMC)
1441 Rhode Island Ave. NW, No. 601
Washington, DC 20005
E-mail: info@takeyourmedicine.org
URL: http://www.takeyourmedicine.org
Contact: Gunjan Koul, Program Dir.

Multinational. Description: Educates professionals, policymakers, media professionals and the public about the universal problem of medicinal compliance and how it is leading to higher health costs and lower productivity. **Computer Services:** Information services, medicinal compliance resources. **Telecommunication Services:** electronic mail, membership@takeyourmedicine.org.

14729 ■ Med Help International (MHI)
6300 N Wickham Rd., Ste.130
PMB No. 188
Melbourne, FL 32940
Ph: (321)259-7505
URL: http://www.medhelp.org
Contact: Cynthia Thompson, Pres./Co-Founder

Founded: 1994. **Description:** Provides online medical information on non-technical terminologies to help people understand their health conditions, and make informed choices about their health and path to recovery. **Computer Services:** database, health search engine ● online services, forums.

14730 ■ National Home Infusion Association (NHIA)
100 Daingerfield Rd.
Alexandria, VA 22314
Ph: (703)549-3740
Fax: (703)683-1484

E-mail: info@nhianet.org
URL: http://www.nhianet.org
Contact: Christopher Maksym PharmD, Pres.

Founded: 1991. **Membership Dues:** individual, $235 (annual) ● site, $470 (annual) ● student, $20 (annual) ● corporate, corporate provider (based on annual sales), $2,500-$10,000 (annual). **Description:** Represents and advances the interests of organizations and individuals who provide infusion and specialized pharmacy products and services to home-based patients. Seeks to enhance the business success of its members through the continued and focused development of a broad range of business tools and resources. Aims to create a favorable external environment that ensures appropriate differentiation of and reimbursement for infusion products and services. **Publications:** *Infusion*, bimonthly. Journal. Covers topics of interest to home infusion therapy professionals. ISSN: 1080-3858. **Advertising:** accepted. Alternate Formats: online ● Membership Directory. **Price:** included in membership dues. Alternate Formats: online ● Monographs. Alternate Formats: online.

Medical Administration

14731 ■ Academy for International Health Studies (AIHS)
273 Hebron Ave.
Glastonbury, CT 06033
Ph: (860)430-1388
Fax: (860)430-1420
E-mail: bruceapollack@aihs.com
URL: http://www.aihs.com
Contact: Bruce A. Pollack, Pres.

Founded: 1993. **Staff:** 10. **Multinational. Description:** Represents senior healthcare executives from multinational health industries including health plans, healthcare providers, medical device manufacturers, pharmaceutical companies, and information technology vendors. Seeks to improve understanding of the international healthcare market and the American health system. Brings together members for the discussion of matters of mutual concern; serves as a clearinghouse on the healthcare industries; organizes trade and study missions. Operates Mexico-U.S.A. CrossBorder Health Insurance Initiative, which assists in the development of commercially viable health insurance for Mexican nationals living in the United States. Maintains speakers' bureau; functions as the North American office of the International Federation of Health Funds. **Publications:** *Modern Healthcare International*, weekly. Magazine. **Conventions/Meetings:** annual International Summit - symposium.

14732 ■ American Academy of Medical Administrators (AAMA)
701 Lee St., Ste.600
Des Plaines, IL 60016-4516
Ph: (847)759-8601
Fax: (847)759-8602
E-mail: info@aameda.org
URL: http://www.aameda.org
Contact: Renee S. Schleicher CAE, Pres./CEO

Founded: 1957. **Members:** 2,500. **Membership Dues:** individual, $195 (annual) ● associate, $95 (annual) ● student, $45 (annual). **Staff:** 7. **Budget:** $1,000,000. **Regional Groups:** 7. **State Groups:** 50. **Description:** Serves healthcare management at all levels, within all types of healthcare organizations by providing solid solutions, unique connections, resources and professional recognition that healthcare professionals need to navigate today's complex healthcare environment and stay competitive. Has 7 specialty groups: American College of Cardiovascular Administrators; American College of Oncology Administrators; American College of Contingency Planners; Federal Sector; Small or Rural Healthcare; American College of Managed Care Administrators; and American College of Healthcare Information Administrators. **Awards:** Distinguished Service Award. **Frequency:** annual. **Type:** recognition ● Harry Shubin, MD Statesmen in Healthcare Administration. **Frequency:** annual. **Type:** recognition. **Re-**

cipient: for members or nonmembers who in at least 20 years of service have made significant innovative contribution to health care delivery ● Regional Director of the Year. **Frequency:** annual. **Type:** recognition ● State Director of the Year Award. **Frequency:** annual. **Type:** recognition. **Recipient:** for individuals who have contributed special services to the Academy through exceptional fulfillment of responsibilities ● William Newcomer Healthcare Executive of the Year Award. **Frequency:** annual. **Type:** recognition. **Recipient:** for outstanding executive performance in his/her organization. **Committees:** Awards; Credentials; Personnel and Public Relations; Strategic Planning. **Publications:** *American Academy of Medical Administrators—Executive*, quarterly. Newsletter. Covers membership activities. Includes triennial membership directory; also contains calendar of events, book reviews, and lists of new members. **Price:** included in membership dues; $60.00 /year for nonmembers. **Circulation:** 2,500. **Advertising:** accepted. Alternate Formats: online ● *Journal of Cardiovascular Management*, bimonthly ● *Journal of Oncology Management*, bimonthly. **Conventions/Meetings:** annual conference.

14733 ■ American Academy of Medical Administrators Research and Educational Foundation (AAMA)
701 Lee St., Ste.600
Des Plaines, IL 60016
Ph: (847)759-8601
Fax: (847)759-8602
E-mail: info@aameda.org
URL: http://www.aameda.org/aboutaama/aboutfoundation.html
Contact: Renee S. Schleicher CAE, Pres./CEO

Founded: 1976. **Membership Dues:** regular, $195 (annual) ● student, $45 (annual) ● associate, $95 (annual). **Staff:** 7. **Regional Groups:** 7. **State Groups:** 50. **Description:** Individuals with health care backgrounds. Conducts research in the health care field and seminars geared toward professional development. Maintains placement services. **Libraries: Type:** reference. **Holdings:** reports. **Publications:** *AAMA Executive*, quarterly. Newsletter. Covers management topics, industry trends, current developments in health care administration, and association news. Includes book reviews. **Price:** included in membership dues. **Advertising:** accepted. **Conventions/Meetings:** annual ACCA Cardiovascular Administrators' Leadership Conference (exhibits) - always November. 2008 Nov. 19-21, San Antonio, TX.

14734 ■ American Association of Healthcare Administrative Management (AAHAM)
11240 Waples Mill Rd., Ste.200
Fairfax, VA 22030
Ph: (703)281-4043
Fax: (703)359-7562
E-mail: moayad@aaham.org
URL: http://www.aaham.org
Contact: Sharon Rosenblatt Galler CMP, Exec. Dir.

Founded: 1968. **Members:** 2,600. **Membership Dues:** individual, $185 (annual). **Staff:** 5. **Budget:** $976,000. **State Groups:** 39. **Description:** Business offices, credit and collection managers, and admitting officers for hospitals, clinics, and other health care organizations. Educates members, exchanges information and techniques, and keeps members abreast of new regulations relating to their field. Seeks proper recognition for the financial aspect of hospital and clinic management. Offers certification program. Administers examinations in April and October for qualification as Certified Patient Account Manager (CPAM) and Certified Clinic Account Manager (CCAM). Maintains placement services; sponsors seminars and workshops on a local, regional, and national level. Operates speakers' bureau. **Awards:** **Type:** recognition. **Formerly:** (1981) American Guild of Patient Account Managers; (1999) American Guild of Patient Account Management. **Publications:** *Journal of Healthcare Administrative Management*, quarterly. Lists employment opportunities and includes industry news. **Price:** included in membership dues; $30.00 /year for nonmembers. **Circulation:**

3,500. **Advertising:** accepted. **Conventions/Meetings:** annual meeting (exhibits).

14735 ■ American Association of Integrated Healthcare Delivery Systems (AAIHDS)

4435 Waterfront Dr., Ste.101
PO Box 4913
Glen Allen, VA 23060
Ph: (804)747-5823
Fax: (804)747-5316
E-mail: bwilliams@aaihds.org
URL: http://www.aaihds.org
Contact: W.C. Williams III, Pres.
Founded: 1993. **Members:** 1,000. **Membership Dues:** individual, $275 (annual) ● sustaining, $5,000 ● participating, $2,500 ● contributing, $1,500 ● group, $750 (annual). **Staff:** 12. **Budget:** $500,000. **Description:** Works for the educational advancement of provider-based managed care professionals involved in integrated healthcare delivery. **Formerly:** (1998) American Association of Physician-Hospital Organizations. **Publications:** *Integrated Healthcare Delivery System*, quarterly. Newsletter. **Circulation:** 1,000. **Advertising:** accepted ● *Integrated Healthcare News*, quarterly. Newsletter. Alternate Formats: online. **Conventions/Meetings:** semiannual Advanced Managed Care for Hospital and Health System Managed Care Professionals - conference (exhibits) - always spring and fall.

14736 ■ American Association of Medical Audit Specialists (AAMAS)

PO Box 47609
San Antonio, TX 78265-8609
Ph: (210)590-2666
E-mail: info@aamas.org
URL: http://www.aamas.org
Contact: Ruth Gahan, Pres.
Members: 445. **Membership Dues:** general, $100 (annual). **Description:** Represents the interests of healthcare professionals from various health care reimbursement backgrounds dedicated to the advancement of the professional standard and ethical practices of the medical audit specialist. Aims to provide leadership in matters related to the practice of medical audit and its impact on the health care delivery system. Promotes public awareness of the rapidly changing and complex health care reimbursement environment. **Telecommunication Services:** electronic mail, ruth@aamas.org. **Publications:** *The Monitor*, quarterly. Newsletter. Contains important issues, information and other related matters about the association. **Price:** free for members. Alternate Formats: online.

14737 ■ American Association of Medical Billers (AAMB)

PO Box 44614
Los Angeles, CA 90044-0614
E-mail: aamb@aol.com
Contact: Willa Davis, Founder
Founded: 1996. **Description:** Promotes the medical billing profession. Aims to raise professional standards. **Awards:** Association awards. **Frequency:** annual. **Type:** recognition. **Recipient:** for medical biller and medical billing instructor. **Computer Services:** Online services, certification review, message boards, Career Enhancement Center. **Publications:** *Medical Billers Survey*, annual. **Conventions/Meetings:** annual Awards Dinner.

14738 ■ American College of Cardiovascular Administrators (ACCA)

c/o American Academy of Medical Administrators
701 Lee St., Ste.600
Des Plaines, IL 60016-4516
Ph: (847)759-8601
Fax: (847)759-8602
E-mail: info@aameda.org
URL: http://www.aameda.org
Contact: Ms. Marilyn M. Henry RN, Pres./CEO
Founded: 1986. **Members:** 900. **Membership Dues:** student, $45 (annual) ● associate, $95 (annual) ● individual, $195 (annual). **Staff:** 7. **Regional Groups:** 7. **State Groups:** 50. **Description:** A specialty college of the American Academy of Medical Administra-

tors. Upper and middle-level managers of health care professionals in the cardiovascular health care field; associate members are junior supervisors, salespersons, and individuals. Represents members within the medical industry; provides credentialing of cardiology administrators. Serves as a forum for the exchange of information. Conducts educational programs. **Awards:** Amersham Health Award for Excellence. **Frequency:** annual. **Type:** recognition. **Recipient:** for an individual or group who demonstrated outstanding lifetime achievements in cardiology ● Chairman's Award. **Frequency:** annual. **Type:** recognition. **Recipient:** for significant contributions to the strength and vitality of the academy and its services ● Charles U. Letourneau Student Research Paper of the Year. **Frequency:** annual. **Type:** recognition ● Distinguished Service Award. **Frequency:** annual. **Type:** recognition. **Recipient:** for service to the academy ● Faculty Publication of the Year. **Frequency:** annual. **Type:** recognition ● Healthcare Executive of the Year. **Frequency:** annual. **Type:** recognition. **Recipient:** for demonstrated outstanding executive performance in an organization with accomplishments revealing initiative, innovation, and performance results ● Honorary Fellowship. **Type:** recognition. **Recipient:** for outstanding contribution to the healthcare field ● Regional Director of the Year. **Frequency:** annual. **Type:** recognition. **Recipient:** for outstanding service to members and the academy through regional activities ● State Director of the Year. **Frequency:** annual. **Type:** recognition. **Recipient:** for exceptional fulfillment of director responsibilities ● Statesman in Healthcare Administration. **Frequency:** annual. **Type:** recognition. **Recipient:** for a healthcare professional who has made significant and innovative contributions to the aims of quality healthcare delivery. **Publications:** *Journal of Cardiovascular Management*, bimonthly. **Price:** included in membership dues. **Circulation:** 20,000. **Advertising:** accepted. Alternate Formats: online; CD-ROM; magnetic tape. **Conventions/Meetings:** annual conference (exhibits) ● annual National Cardiovascular Management Conferences - seminar and symposium, cardiovascular management (exhibits).

14739 ■ American College of Managed Care Administrators (ACMCA)

c/o American Academy of Medical Administrator
701 Lee St., No. 600
Des Plaines, IL 60016-4516
Ph: (847)759-8601
Fax: (847)759-8602
E-mail: montse.edie-korleski@peterson.af.mil
URL: http://www.aameda.org
Contact: Maj. Montserrat P. Edie-Korleski USAF, Pres.
Founded: 1994. **Members:** 600. **Membership Dues:** individual, first year, $145 ● fellow, individual, $180 (annual) ● regular, $190 (annual) ● associate, $90 (annual) ● student, $45 (annual). **Staff:** 7. **Regional Groups:** 7. **State Groups:** 50. **Description:** Serves as specialty college of the American Academy of Medical Administrators. Represents managers of professionals who are directly or indirectly providing managed healthcare. Works to promote the advancement of members' professional standing, education, and personal achievement and develop innovative concepts in managed care administration. Conducts an employment referral and educational programs. **Awards:** Chairman's Award. **Frequency:** annual. **Type:** recognition. **Recipient:** for significant contributions to the strength and vitality of the Academy and its services ● Charles U. Letourneau Student Research Paper of the Year. **Frequency:** annual. **Type:** recognition ● Distinguished Service Award. **Frequency:** annual. **Type:** recognition. **Recipient:** for service to the academy ● Faculty Publication of the Year. **Frequency:** annual. **Type:** recognition ● Healthcare Executive of the Year. **Frequency:** annual. **Type:** recognition. **Recipient:** for demonstrated outstanding executive performance in their organization with accomplishments revealing initiative, innovation, and performance results ● Honorary Fellowship. **Type:** fellowship. **Recipient:** for outstanding contribution to the healthcare field ● Regional Director of the Year. **Frequency:** annual. **Type:** recognition. **Recipi-**

ent: for outstanding service to members and the Academy through regional activities ● State Director of the Year. **Frequency:** annual. **Type:** recognition. **Recipient:** for exceptional fulfillment of director responsibilities ● Statesman in Healthcare Administration. **Frequency:** annual. **Type:** recognition. **Recipient:** to healthcare professional who has made significant, innovative contributions to the aims of quality healthcare delivery. **Publications:** *Executive*, bimonthly. Journal. **Conventions/Meetings:** annual conference and seminar (exhibits).

14740 ■ American College of Medical Practice Executives (ACMPE)

104 Inverness Terr. E
Englewood, CO 80112-5306
Ph: (303)799-1111
Free: (877)275-6462
Fax: (303)643-4439
E-mail: acmpe@mgma.com
URL: http://www.mgma.com/about/default.aspx?id=242
Contact: Sarah J. Holt PhD, Chair
Founded: 1956. **Members:** 5,000. **Membership Dues:** individual (nominee, certified member, fellow), $215 (annual). **Staff:** 9. **Budget:** $2,000,000. **Description:** Professional credentialing organization. Membership is drawn from Medical Group Management Association and beyond (see separate entry). Works to encourage medical group practice administrators to improve and maintain there proficiency and to provide appropriate recognition; to establish a program with uniform standards of admission, advancement, certification and fellowship in order to achieve the highest possible standards in the profession of medical group practice administration; to participate in the development of educational and research programs for the advancement of the profession; to inform the medical profession and the public of the value of trained and experienced men and women in the management of the administrative affairs of all forms of group practice; to instill in its membership a constant awareness of the high ideals and traditions of the medical profession and medical group administration so that its members will conduct themselves in such a manner as to augment those ideals and traditions. Conducts educational programs such as Management Education Programs and Group Practice Governance Leadership Institute. **Libraries:** Type: reference. **Holdings:** archival material, audiovisuals, books, clippings, periodicals. **Subjects:** medical group management. **Awards:** Edward B. Stevens Article Award. **Frequency:** annual. **Type:** recognition. **Recipient:** for a medical practice professional who has made a substantial contribution to the body of published literature ● Fred Graham Award for Innovation in Improving Community Health. **Frequency:** annual. **Type:** recognition. **Recipient:** to a medical group practice led by an ACMPE or MGMA member who has developed creative and innovative activities and solutions to advance the effectiveness of health care delivery and improved community health ● Harry J. Harwick Lifetime Achievement Award. **Frequency:** annual. **Type:** recognition. **Recipient:** for an outstanding health administration practitioner who has a lifetime achievement to medical practice management ● Medical Practice Executive Award. **Frequency:** annual. **Type:** recognition. **Recipient:** to a medical group practice executive affiliated with ACMPE or MGMA who has demonstrated within the last three years a noteworthy achievement of exceptional leadership and management proficiency ● Physician Executive Award. **Frequency:** annual. **Type:** recognition. **Recipient:** for a physician executive in a medical group practice led by an ACMPE or MGMA member, who has exhibited outstanding leadership to achieve exceptional medical group performance in the delivery of health care. **Committees:** Advancement; Examinations; Honors; Membership Development; Nominating; Professional Papers; Scholarship. **Formerly:** (1976) American College of Clinic Managers; (1993) American College of Medical Group Administrators. **Publications:** *College Review*, semiannual. Professional manuscripts submitted to the College for advancement to fellow status; arranged by subject and author. **Price:** $10.00/copy for

members; $16.00/copy for affiliates; $22.00/copy for nonmembers ● *Your Pathway to Excellence*. Brochure. Provides general information regarding ACMPE membership application. **Conventions/Meetings:** annual conference.

14741 ■ American College of Oncology Administrators (ACOA)

c/o American Academy of Medical Administrators
701 Lee St., Ste.600
Des Plaines, IL 60016-4516
Ph: (847)759-8601
Fax: (847)759-8602
E-mail: info@aameda.org
URL: http://www.aameda.org
Contact: Phyllis A. DeAntonio RN, Pres.
Founded: 1991. **Members:** 500. **Membership Dues:** individual, $190 (annual) ● associate, $90 (annual) ● student, $45 (annual). **Staff:** 7. **Regional Groups:** 7. **State Groups:** 50. **Description:** Serves as specialty College of the American Academy of Medical Administrators. Represents oncology administrators, managers, and consultants. Works to bring together all components of oncology management to develop creative strategies, quality programs, and sound evaluation mechanisms. Promotes advancement of members through continuing education and research in oncology management. Conducts educational programs. **Awards:** Chairman's Award. **Frequency:** annual. **Type:** recognition. **Recipient:** for significant contributions to the strength and vitality of the Academy and its services ● Charles U. Letourneau Student Research Paper of the Year. **Frequency:** annual. **Type:** recognition. **Recipient:** for outstanding services ● Distinguished Service Award. **Frequency:** annual. **Type:** recognition. **Recipient:** for service to the Academy ● Faculty Publication of the Year. **Frequency:** annual. **Type:** recognition ● Healthcare Executive of the Year. **Frequency:** annual. **Type:** recognition. **Recipient:** for demonstrated outstanding executive performance in the organization, with accomplishments revealing initiative, innovation, and performance results ● Honorary Fellowship. **Type:** fellowship. **Recipient:** for outstanding contribution to the healthcare field ● Regional Director of the Year. **Frequency:** annual. **Type:** recognition. **Recipient:** for outstanding service to members and the Academy through regional activities ● State Director of the Year. **Frequency:** annual. **Type:** recognition. **Recipient:** for exceptional fulfillment of director responsibilities ● Statesman in Healthcare Administration. **Frequency:** annual. **Type:** recognition. **Recipient:** to a healthcare professional who has made significant and innovative contributions to the aims of quality healthcare delivery. **Publications:** *Journal of Oncology Management*, bimonthly. Contains information and ideas for professionals involved in managing cancer programs. **Price:** included in membership dues. **Circulation:** 20,000. **Advertising:** accepted. **Conventions/Meetings:** annual conference and seminar (exhibits) ● annual symposium.

14742 ■ American College of Physician Executives (ACPE)

4890 W Kennedy Blvd., Ste.200
Tampa, FL 33609
Ph: (813)287-2000
Free: (800)562-8088
Fax: (813)287-8993
E-mail: acpe@acpe.org
URL: http://www.acpe.org
Contact: Roger S. Schenke, Exec. VP
Founded: 1974. **Members:** 9,000. **Membership Dues:** regular, $215 (annual). **Staff:** 23. **Budget:** $6,000,000. **Multinational. Description:** Physicians whose primary professional responsibility is in management. Provides for continuing education and certification of the physician executive and the advancement and recognition of the physician executive and the profession. Offers specialized career planning, counseling, recruitment and placement services, and research and information data on physician executives. **Libraries: Type:** not open to the public. **Holdings:** 250; books, periodicals. **Committees:** Certified Physician Executive; Diplomate; Distinguished Fellows; Fellows. **Absorbed:** (1989)

American Academy of Medical Directors. **Publications:** *American College of Physician Executives—Membership Registry*, annual. Membership Directory. **Price:** included in membership dues. **Circulation:** 9,000. Alternate Formats: online ● *The Ethics of the Ordinary in Healthcare: Concepts & Cases*. Book. **Price:** $52.00 for members; $57.00 for nonmembers ● *Fundamentals of Medical Management: A Guide for the Physician Executive*. Book. Includes discussion of organizational theory, effective communication, negotiating skills, conflict management, and organizational politics. **Price:** $48.00 for members; $58.00 for nonmembers ● *Get the Job You Want and the Money You're Worth, 2nd Edition*. Book. Presents a guide to successful opportunities. **Price:** $15.00 for members; $20.00 for nonmembers ● *The Higher Ground: Biomedical Ethics & the Physician Executive*. Book. **Price:** $10.00 for members; $55.00 for nonmembers ● *Hope for the Future: A Career Development Guide for Physician Executives*. Book. Provides a list of techniques for prospering in the environment in which health care organizations operate, audiotapes included. **Price:** $15.00 for members; $20.00 for nonmembers ● *The Leading Edge*. Magazine. Alternate Formats: online ● *Managed Care Ethics: Essays on the Impact of Managed Care on Traditional Medical Ethics*. Book. **Price:** $15.00 for members; $20.00 for nonmembers ● *Managing in an Academic Health Care Environment*. Book. Provides an overview of managing in this unique environment. **Price:** $20.00 for members; $35.00 for nonmembers ● *Mastering the Negotiation Process: A Practical Guide for the Healthcare Executive*. Book. **Price:** $40.00 for members; $55.00 for nonmembers ● *MD/MBA: Physicians on the New Frontier of Medical Management*. Book. Features a guide in assessing professional and personal strengths and more. **Price:** $30.00 for members; $45.00 for nonmembers ● *New Leadership in Health Care Management—The Physician Executive 2nd Edition*. Book. Outlines the knowledge base physician executives must master in order to effectively compete and succeed. **Price:** $15.00 for members; $20.00 for nonmembers ● *Physician Executive: Journal of Management*, bimonthly. Includes recurring columns on health economics and health law. **Price:** included in membership dues; $80.00 /year for nonmembers. **Circulation:** 10,000. **Advertising:** accepted. Also Cited As: *Medical Director* ● *Physician Executives: What, Why, How? 2nd Edition*. Book. Covers the responsibilities of the physician executive. **Price:** $20.00 for members; $30.00 for nonmembers ● *Physicians in Managed Care: A Career Guide*. Book. Presents topics written and edited by physicians who have made the transition into managed care. **Price:** $15.00 for members; $20.00 for nonmembers ● *The Shifting Sources of Power and Influence*. Monograph. Details how influence can be gained and used in the struggle for organizational power. **Price:** $20.95 for members; $25.95 for nonmembers ● *Top Docs: Managing the Search for Physician Leaders, 2nd Edition*. Monograph. Covers how to recruit physician leaders, what pitfalls to avoid, and when and how to use a recruiter. **Price:** $32.00 for members; $42.00 for nonmembers ● *Total Care Management: A Physician Executive's Guide to Medical Management for the 21st Century*. Book. Attempts to place the current health care delivery crisis into historical perspective. **Price:** $35.00 for members; $50.00 for nonmembers ● *Women in Medical Management*. Report. Provides information on current perceptions about women in medical management. **Price:** $30.00 for members; $38.00 for nonmembers ● *Women in Medicine & Management: A Mentoring Guide*. Book. Features individual accounts of entry into medicine by women executives. **Price:** $15.00 for members; $20.00 for nonmembers. **Circulation:** 11,500. Also Cited As: *Academy Digest*. **Conventions/Meetings:** lecture, multi-course CME - 3/year.

14743 ■ American Medical Billing Association (AMBA)

4297 Forrest Dr.
Sulphur, OK 73086
Ph: (580)622-2624
Fax: (580)622-5810

E-mail: larry@brightok.net
URL: http://www.ambanet.net/amba.htm
Contact: Cyndee Weston, Exec. Dir.
Founded: 1998. **Members:** 1,500. **Membership Dues:** individual, $99 (annual) ● business (with up to 3 members), $199 (annual). **Regional Groups:** 2. **Local Groups:** 5. **Description:** Promotes the medical billing profession; assists small and home medical billing professionals. **Computer Services:** Mailing lists, of members ● online services, training, bookstore, referrals, forums, roster listing, Medicare/DMERC information, free downloads, logos and artwork. **Committees:** Certification; Ethics and Conduct; HIPAA and Compliance. **Publications:** Brochure. **Conventions/Meetings:** annual conference (exhibits).

14744 ■ American Society of Ophthalmic Administrators (ASOA)

4000 Legato Rd., Ste.700
Fairfax, VA 22033
Ph: (703)591-2220 (703)591-2222
Free: (800)451-1339
Fax: (703)591-0614
E-mail: kkrzmarzick@asoa.org
URL: http://www.asoa.org
Contact: Karen Krzmarzick MEd, Sec.-Treas./Exec. Dir.
Founded: 1986. **Members:** 2,000. **Membership Dues:** administrator, $250 (annual). **Staff:** 21. **Budget:** $5,000,000. **Description:** Serves as a division of the American Society of Cataract and Refractive Surgery (see separate entry). Represents persons involved with the administration of an ophthalmic office or clinic. Facilitates the exchange of ideas and information in order to improve management practices and working conditions. Offers placement services. **Libraries: Type:** reference. **Holdings:** 4; books, clippings, periodicals. **Subjects:** ophthalmology, business and medical administration. **Awards:** William A. Rose Pinnacle Award. **Frequency:** annual. **Type:** monetary. **Recipient:** to ophthalmology practices demonstrating exemplary effort to eliminate potential abusive billing practices and maintains compliance with government regulations. **Computer Services:** Mailing lists ● online services. **Affiliated With:** American Society of Cataract and Refractive Surgery. **Publications:** *A Manager's Survival Guide to Employee Rights* ● *Administrative Eyecare*, quarterly. Magazine. **Price:** included in membership dues; $60.00 for nonmembers in U.S.; $100.00 for nonmembers outside U.S. ISSN: 1060-5991. **Circulation:** 8,000. **Advertising:** accepted ● *Effective Interviews for Every Situation* ● *Federal Employment Law*. **Price:** $95.00 for members; $125.00 for nonmembers ● *Guidebook to Medical Practice Finances Reporting* ● *Managed Care and Contracting*. Manual. **Price:** $150.00 for members; $225.00 for nonmembers ● *Marketing Ophthalmology* ● *Ophthalmic Practice Management I & II*. Alternate Formats: CD-ROM ● *Ophthalmic Regulatory Manual*. **Price:** $100.00 for members; $150.00 for nonmembers ● *Ophthalmic Reimbursement Manual*. **Price:** $90.00 for members; $145.00 for nonmembers ● *Performance Appraisals: The Latest Legal Nightmare*. **Conventions/Meetings:** annual Clinical & Surgical Staff Program - meeting and conference, with ophthalmic related exhibits in conjunction with ASCRS ● annual Congress on Ophthalmic Practice Management - congress and symposium, held in conjunction with ASCRS (exhibits).

14745 ■ Association of Family Medicine Residency Directors (AFMRD)

11400 Tomahawk Creek Pkwy., Ste.670
Leawood, KS 66211-2672
Ph: (913)906-6000
Free: (800)274-2237
Fax: (913)906-6105
E-mail: afmrd@aafp.org
URL: http://www.afmrd.org
Contact: Samuel M. Jones MD, Pres.
Founded: 1990. **Members:** 406. **Membership Dues:** individual, $350 (annual) ● associate, $175 (annual). **Staff:** 4. **Description:** Promotes excellence in family practice graduate education. Provides representation

for residency directors at a national level and provides a political voice for them in appropriate arenas. Promotes cooperation and communication between residency programs and different branches of the family practice specialty; dedicated to improving of education of family physicians. Provides a network for mutual assistance among family physicians and residency directors. **Computer Services:** Mailing lists, of members. **Formerly:** (2005) Association of Family Practice Residency Directors. **Publications:** *Highlights*, quarterly. Newsletter. **Price:** for members. **Circulation:** 406. **Advertising:** accepted. **Conventions/Meetings:** annual meeting and workshop, for directors of family practice residencies (exhibits) - always in Kansas City, MO.

14746 ■ Association of Family Practice Administrators (AFPA)
c/o Dawn Sexton, Exec. Sec.
11400 Tomahawk Creek Pkwy.
Leawood, KS 66211-2672
Free: (800)274-2237
Fax: (913)906-6092
E-mail: dsexton@aafp.org
URL: http://www.uams.edu/afpa/afpa1.htm
Contact: Dawn Sexton, Exec. Sec.
Founded: 1984. **Members:** 375. **Membership Dues:** individual, $150 (annual). **Staff:** 1. **Description:** Administrators and coordinators of family practice residency training programs. Promotes professionalism in family practice administration. Serves as a network for sharing of information and fellowship among members. Provides technical assistance to members; functions as a liaison to related professional organizations. **Committees:** Bylaws; Information Exchange; Marketing; Membership; Newsletter; Program; Strategic Planning. **Publications:** *Connections*, quarterly. Newsletter. **Advertising:** accepted. **Conventions/Meetings:** annual Rap Workshop - meeting (exhibits).

14747 ■ Association of Healthcare Internal Auditors (AHIA)
10200 W 44th Ave., Ste.304
Wheat Ridge, CO 80033
Ph: (303)327-7546
Free: (888)ASK-AHIA
Fax: (303)422-8894
E-mail: ahia@ahia.org
URL: http://www.ahia.org
Contact: Mr. David L. Stumph CAE, Exec. Dir.
Founded: 1981. **Members:** 1,000. **Membership Dues:** individual, $195 (annual) ● faculty, $75 (annual) ● student, $40 (annual) ● organization (based on the number of members), $11,315 (annual). **Staff:** 2. **Description:** Health care internal auditors and other interested individuals. Promotes cost containment and increased productivity in health care institutions through internal auditing. Serves as a forum for the exchange of experience, ideas, and information among members; provides continuing professional education courses and informs members of developments in health care internal auditing. Offers employment clearinghouse services. **Libraries: Type:** reference; not open to the public. **Subjects:** audit information. **Computer Services:** database. **Formerly:** (1989) Healthcare Internal Audit Group. **Publications:** *E-Perspective*, monthly. Newsletter. Contains information on auditing, compliance, and healthcare news. **Price:** included in membership dues. Alternate Formats: online ● *New Perspectives on Healthcare Auditing*, quarterly. Journal. Contains book reviews, audit findings, and local and regional group news. **Price:** included in membership dues; $60.00 /year for nonmembers. **Circulation:** 1,000. **Advertising:** accepted. **Conventions/Meetings:** annual conference and workshop (exhibits) - usually fall.

14748 ■ Association of Otolaryngology Administrators (AOA)
1844 Ardmore Blvd.
Pittsburgh, PA 15221
Ph: (412)243-5156
Fax: (412)243-5160

E-mail: aoa@oto-online.org
URL: http://www.oto-online.org
Contact: Ms. Robin Wagner, Exec. Dir.
Founded: 1983. **Members:** 1,000. **Membership Dues:** active, associate, $250 (annual). **Budget:** $300,000. **Regional Groups:** 6. **Description:** Persons employed in a managerial capacity for private or academic group medical practices specializing in otolaryngology (the study of the ear, nose, and throat). Seeks to: promote the concept of professional management in otolaryngology; provide a forum for interaction and exchange of information between otolaryngological managers; present educational programs. Maintains data exchange service for members researching specific topics. **Telecommunication Services:** electronic mail, jeicher@commonwealthent.com. **Boards:** Certification in Otolaryngology Practice Management Advisory. **Publications:** *Oto's Scope*, 3/year. **Conventions/Meetings:** annual meeting.

14749 ■ Case Management Society of America (CMSA)
6301 Ranch Dr.
Little Rock, AR 72223
Ph: (501)225-2229
Fax: (501)221-9068
E-mail: cmsa@cmsa.org
URL: http://www.cmsa.org
Contact: Cheri Lattimer RN, Exec. Dir.
Founded: 1990. **Members:** 7,500. **Membership Dues:** standard, $135 (annual) ● company, $675-$5,750 (annual) ● student, $85 (annual) ● military, $98 (annual) ● international, $170 (annual) ● corporate, $2,750-$5,500 (annual). **Staff:** 16. **Budget:** $2,500,000. **State Groups:** 1. **Local Groups:** 72. **Multinational. Description:** Case management and allied healthcare professionals. Offers members a voice in the future through opportunities for professional leadership and networking opportunities, case management legislative impact and visibility, publications, educational workshops, seminars, conferences, recognition and fellowship opportunities. **Awards:** CMSA Award of Excellence. **Frequency:** annual. **Type:** recognition. **Recipient:** to a practicing case manager who exemplifies the essence of CM ● CMSA Case Manager of the Year. **Frequency:** annual. **Type:** recognition. **Recipient:** to individuals whose notable contributions and exceptional dedication have provided a positive vision for the future of CM ● CMSA Chapter Excellence and Innovation Awards. **Frequency:** annual. **Type:** recognition. **Recipient:** for chapters that embody the mission of CMSA. **Computer Services:** database, list and labels, web server ● electronic publishing, e-newsletter ● mailing lists, of members ● online services, continuing education/web subscription. **Committees:** Case Manager of the Year; Center for Case Management Accountability; Health Policy; Nominations; Standards of Practice. **Programs:** Chapter Liability Insurance; Medical Case Management Liability Insurance; Seabury and Smith Life Disability. **Publications:** *ADVANCE For Providers of Post-Acute Care*. Magazine. Alternate Formats: online ● *The Case Manager*, bimonthly. Journal. **Price:** included in membership dues. **Circulation:** 26,000. **Advertising:** accepted. Alternate Formats: online ● *Case Report*, bimonthly. Newsletter. **Price:** included in membership dues. **Circulation:** 26,000. Alternate Formats: online ● *Chapter Dispatch*. Report. Alternate Formats: online ● *Standards of Practice*. **Price:** $25.00. Alternate Formats: online ● *Work For You*. Newsletter. **Price:** free. Alternate Formats: online ● Brochure, annual ● Membership Directory, annual. **Advertising:** accepted. Alternate Formats: online ● Survey. Alternate Formats: online ● Papers. **Conventions/Meetings:** Case Management - board meeting - 3/year ● annual conference (exhibits) - 2008 June 17-21, Orlando, FL.

14750 ■ Center for Research in Ambulatory Health Care Administration (CRAHCA)
104 Inverness Terr. E
Englewood, CO 80112-5306
Ph: (303)799-1111
Free: (877)275-6462

Fax: (303)643-4439
E-mail: comments@mgma.com
URL: http://www.mgma.com/research/index.cfm
Contact: Susan Turney MD, Chair
Founded: 1973. **Staff:** 9. **Budget:** $1,500,000. **Nonmembership. Description:** Seeks to advance the art and science of medical group practice management to improve the health of the communities. Aims to be the source of excellence and innovation in providing quality and timely services and resources for medical practice management and leadership. Develops and advances research-based knowledge in the field of ambulatory health care by improving education, management technology, publications, and database services. Research is directed toward health care economics, policy development and analysis, alternative organizational models for health care delivery, evaluation methodologies, models of provider team leadership, and the social aspects of health services organizations and the communities in which they serve. Research interests include provider reimbursement and the analysis of ambulatory health care and medical practice costs; the evolution and impact of integrated and managed care systems and the role of access and quality in the production and management of ambulatory care services will be examined; the impact of these areas on health system reform will be studied. **Libraries: Type:** reference. **Holdings:** archival material, audio recordings, books, clippings, monographs, periodicals. **Subjects:** group practice management. **Committees:** MGMA/CRAHCA Research. **Affiliated With:** American College of Medical Practice Executives; Medical Group Management Association. **Publications:** *Actuarial Issues in the Fee-for-Service/Prepaid Medical Group*. Book. **Price:** $32.00/copy ● *Case Management in Primary Care*. Manual. **Price:** $24.00/copy ● *Geriatric Collaborative Care Model*. Book. **Price:** $17.00/copy ● *Getting Started in Geriatrics*. Handbook. **Price:** $29.00/copy ● *Health Information Management Medical Record Processes in Group Practice*. Book. **Price:** $39.00/copy ● *Integrated Health Care*. Book. **Price:** $44.00/copy ● *Making Integrated Care Work*. Book. **Price:** $49.00/copy ● *Medical Group Practice Chart of Accounts*. Book. **Price:** $49.00/copy ● *Performance Efficiency Evaluation*, annual. Report. **Price:** $695.00/year ● *Prepare for Eldercare*. Handbook. **Price:** $14.00/copy ● *Quality Improvement*. Book. **Price:** $39.00/copy. **Conventions/Meetings:** annual conference (exhibits) - usually spring.

14751 ■ Dental Group Management Association (DGMA)
2525 E Arizona Biltmore Cir., Ste.127
Phoenix, AZ 85016
Ph: (602)381-8980
Fax: (602)381-1093
E-mail: dgma@aadgp.org
URL: http://www.dgma.org
Contact: Vincent Cardillo, Pres.
Founded: 1951. **Members:** 150. **Membership Dues:** regular, $75 (annual). **Description:** Represents dental group business managers and others interested in group practice management. **Publications:** *DGMA Communicator*, quarterly. Newsletter. Includes membership profiles. **Price:** free. **Circulation:** 200. **Advertising:** accepted. Alternate Formats: CD-ROM; online; diskette. Also Cited As: *The Communicator* ● Membership Directory, annual. Lists members by practice and by individual name. **Price:** $50.00 each. **Conventions/Meetings:** annual conference (exhibits) - always February in Hollywood, CA ● workshop.

14752 ■ Healthcare Financial Management Association (HFMA)
2 Westbrook Corporate Ctr., Ste.700
Westchester, IL 60154
Ph: (708)531-9600
Free: (800)252-4362
Fax: (708)531-0032
E-mail: memberservices@hfma.org
URL: http://www.hfma.org
Contact: Richard L. Clarke, Pres./CEO
Founded: 1946. **Members:** 34,000. **Membership Dues:** individual (based on the month joined), $41-$239 (annual). **Staff:** 80. **Budget:** $12,000,000. **State**

Groups: 70. **Description:** Financial management professionals employed by hospitals and long-term care facilities, public accounting and consulting firms, insurance companies, medical groups, managed care organizations, government agencies, and other organizations. Conducts conferences, including annual conference in late June and audio teleconferences. Publishes books on healthcare financial issues. A Fellowship in Healthcare Financial Management (FHFMA) as well as the Certified Healthcare Professional (CHFP) in Finance and Accounting, Financial Management of Physician Practices, Managed Care, and Patient Financial Services are offered. **Awards: Type:** recognition. **Recipient:** for individuals, chapters, and merit. **Committees:** Board of Examiners; Principles and Practices Board. **Divisions:** Operations; Support; Technical. **Formerly:** (1968) American Association of Hospital Accountants; (1982) Hospital Financial Management Association. **Publications:** *Executive Insights*, monthly. Newsletter. **Price:** $90.00 /year for members; $105.00 /year for nonmembers. **Circulation:** 2,000 ● *Healthcare Financial Management*, monthly. Magazine. Includes industry news, articles on financial management in all types of facilities across the healthcare continuum. **Price:** $82.00 /year for nonmembers. ISSN: 0735-0732. **Circulation:** 35,000.. **Advertising:** accepted. Alternate Formats: microform; online ● *Revenue Cycle Strategist*, monthly. Newsletter. **Price:** $95.00 /year for members; $165.00 /year for nonmembers ● Books ● Videos. **Conventions/Meetings:** annual convention, covers financial management techniques across the health care continuum (exhibits).

14753 ■ Institute of Certified Healthcare Business Consultants (ICHBC)

12100 Sunset Hills Rd., Ste.130
Reston, VA 20190
Ph: (703)234-4099
Fax: (703)435-4390
E-mail: info@ichbc.org
URL: http://www.ichbc.org
Contact: Carol Wynne, Exec. Dir.
Founded: 1975. **Members:** 295. **Membership Dues:** individual/professional society, $625 (annual). **Staff:** 3. **Description:** Represents individuals providing business advisory services to physicians, dentists, and other healthcare professionals. Maintains code of ethics, rules of professional conduct, and certification program; administers examination and conducts review course. (Membership by successful completion of certification examination only). **Telecommunication Services:** electronic mail, carol.wynne@nschbc.org. **Programs:** Continuing Education Accreditation Monitoring. **Formerly:** (1999) Institute of Certified Professional Business Consultants. **Publications:** *Institute of Certified Healthcare Business Consultants—Certified News*, quarterly. Newsletter. **Price:** available to members only. **Conventions/Meetings:** annual meeting.

14754 ■ Medical Group Management Association (MGMA)

104 Inverness Terr. E
Englewood, CO 80112-5306
Ph: (303)799-1111
Free: (877)275-6462
Fax: (303)643-4439
E-mail: service@mgma.com
URL: http://www.mgma.com
Contact: William F. Jessee MD, Pres./CEO
Founded: 1926. **Members:** 21,000. **Membership Dues:** regular, $355 (annual) ● full-time student, $65 (annual) ● faculty, $105 (annual). **Staff:** 150. **Regional Groups:** 4. **Description:** Represents professionals involved in the management of medical group practices and administration of other ambulatory healthcare facilities. Provides products and services that includes education, benchmarking, surveys, national advocacy and networking opportunities for members. **Libraries: Type:** reference. **Holdings:** 3,000; books, periodicals. **Subjects:** health administration, group practice, medical practice management, managed care, integration. **Committees:** Accreditation; Annual Conference; Center for Research; Ethics; Financial Management; Government Affairs;

Information Center; Learning and Networking Center; Marketing/Communications; Nominating; Specialty Assembly and Society; Survey Advisory. **Affiliated With:** American College of Medical Practice Executives. **Formerly:** (1946) Association of Clinic Managers; (1963) National Association of Clinical Managers. **Publications:** *Academic Practice Faculty Compensation and Production Survey Report*, annual. Contains a census of academic clinical science departments. **Price:** $225.00/copy for members; $275.00/copy for affiliates; $375.00/copy for nonmembers ● *Academic Practice Management Compensation Survey Report*, annual. Contains a census of academic clinical science departments and practice plans providing comparative information to academic medical practices. **Price:** $90.00/copy for members; $120.00/copy for affiliates; $150.00/copy for nonmembers ● *Ambulatory Surgery Center Performance Survey Report*, annual. Provides comparative measures to assess annual ambulatory surgery center (ASC) financial and operational results. **Price:** $90.00/copy for members; $120.00/copy for affiliates; $150.00/copy for nonmembers ● *Cost Survey Report*, annual. Covers every facet of medical group operating costs, enabling readers to right-size their practice. **Price:** $240.00/copy for members; $290.00/copy for affiliates; $450.00/copy for nonmembers ● *Management Services Organization Performance Survey Report*, annual. Provides comparative measures useful in benchmarking annual MSO corporate financial and operational results. **Price:** $240.00/copy for members; $290.00/copy for affiliates; $450.00/copy for nonmembers ● *Physician Compensation and Production Survey*, annual. Report ● *Star-Studded Service: 6 Steps to Winning Patient Satisfaction*. Book. Contains information about meeting the service expectations of patients and caregivers. **Price:** $51.30 for joint MGA-ACMPE; $57.00 for member; $68.00 for MGMA affiliate; $89.00 for nonmember. **Conventions/Meetings:** annual conference (exhibits) - in October.

14755 ■ NAMDRC

8618 Westwood Center Dr., Ste.210
Vienna, VA 22182-2222
Ph: (703)752-4359
Fax: (703)752-4360
E-mail: execoffice@namdrc.org
URL: http://www.namdrc.org
Contact: Phillip Porte, Exec. Dir.
Founded: 1977. **Members:** 600. **Membership Dues:** individual, $285 (annual) ● group, $710-$1,655 (annual). **Staff:** 2. **Budget:** $200,000. **Description:** Works to provide educational opportunities for pulmonologists and others involved in respiratory care. Interprets and advises on the changing healthcare delivery system and is a successful advocate on regulatory and legislative issues affecting pulmonary and critical care medicine. Offers educational programs, publications and assistance regarding coding issues and federal reimbursement policies. **Awards:** Jacob K. Javits Award for Public Service. **Frequency:** annual. **Type:** recognition. **Recipient:** for contributions to the prevention of lung disease. **Formerly:** (2003) National Association for Medical Direction of Respiratory Care; (2004) NAMDRC: Physician Advocacy for Excellence in the Delivery of Pulmonary and Critical Care. **Publications:** *Clinical and Management Quarterly*. Newsletter. **Advertising:** accepted. Alternate Formats: CD-ROM; online ● *Presidential Update*, biennial ● *Understanding Oxygen Therapy - A Patient Guide to Long Term Supplemental Oxygen*. Brochure. **Price:** $32.50 for members (50 copies); $42.50 for nonmembers (50 copies) ● *Washington Watchline*, monthly. Alternate Formats: online. **Conventions/Meetings:** annual Educational Conference - board meeting and conference ● annual Essentials in Pulmonary Medicine - convention.

14756 ■ National Association of County Health Facility Administrators (NACHFA)

c/o National Association of Counties
440 1st St. NW
Washington, DC 20001-2028
Ph: (202)942-4230
Fax: (202)942-4281

E-mail: jwilson@naco.org
URL: http://www.naco.org
Contact: Jennifer Wilson, Staff Liaison
Founded: 1977. **Members:** 250. **Staff:** 1. **Description:** Administrators of freestanding and hospital-based long-term care facilities owned and operated by county governments or city-county consolidations; elected local officials. Promotes interests of county long-term care facilities; offers guidance in relevant legislative and regulatory areas. Provides technical assistance; conducts training workshops. Compiles statistics on public policy changes, such as changes in the Medicaid program, which affect long-term care facilities. **Conventions/Meetings:** annual conference ● annual Health, Human Services & Workforce Conference - meeting, in conjunction with National Association of Counties.

14757 ■ National Association for Healthcare Recruitment (NAHCR)

1401 S Primrose Dr.
Orlando, FL 32806
Ph: (407)843-6981 (407)481-2893
Fax: (407)481-2825
E-mail: cathy@nahcr.com
URL: http://www.nahcr.com
Contact: Cathy Allman, Exec. Dir.
Founded: 1975. **Members:** 1,100. **Membership Dues:** active, $135 (annual) ● associate, $185 (annual) ● institution, $1,100 (annual). **Staff:** 3. **Regional Groups:** 57. **Local Groups:** 50. **Description:** Individuals employed directly by hospitals and other health care organizations which are involved in the practice of professional health care recruitment. Promotes sound principles of professional health care recruitment. Provides financial assistance to aid members in planning and implementing regional educational programs. Offers technical assistance and consultation services. Compiles statistics. **Awards:** Chapter Achievement Award. **Frequency:** annual. **Type:** recognition. **Recipient:** for local NAHCR chapters that have contributed to the national association, their community and their profession ● Distinguished Member Award. **Frequency:** annual. **Type:** recognition. **Recipient:** for individuals who have had active roles in NAHCR leadership for many years ● Jane Pauley Media Award. **Frequency:** annual. **Type:** recognition. **Computer Services:** Mailing lists, of members. **Committees:** Legislative; Marketing; Professional Issues. **Subgroups:** Allied Health Recruiters; Home Health Recruiters; Long-Term Care Recruiters; Physician Recruiters. **Formerly:** National Association of Nurse Recruiters; (1987) National Association of Healthcare Recruiters. **Publications:** *NAHCR Directions*, bimonthly. Newsletter. **Price:** $200.00/year. **Circulation:** 1,400. **Advertising:** accepted. Alternate Formats: CD-ROM; online ● *Recruiter's Handbook*. Serves as guides to health care recruitment competencies. **Price:** $150.00 for members; $300.00 for nonmembers ● *Trends Survey*, annual ● *Who's Who in Recruitment and Resources*, annual. Directory. **Conventions/Meetings:** annual Image - conference (exhibits) - 2008 July 21-26, Orlando, FL.

14758 ■ National Association Medical Staff Services (NAMSS)

2025 M St. NW, Ste.800
Washington, DC 20036
Ph: (202)367-1196
Fax: (202)367-2196
E-mail: info@namss.org
URL: http://www.namss.org
Contact: Carole La Pine, Pres.
Founded: 1971. **Members:** 4,000. **Membership Dues:** active, affiliate, $150 (annual). **Staff:** 3. **Budget:** $1,500,000. **Regional Groups:** 5. **State Groups:** 48. **Local Groups:** 32. **Description:** Individuals involved in the management and administration of healthcare provider services. Seeks to: enhance the knowledge and experience of medical staff services professionals; promote the certification of those involved in the profession. **Awards:** Golden Key Award. **Frequency:** annual. **Type:** recognition. **Recipient:** for outstanding contributions to the profession. **Computer Services:** database. **Boards:** Certi-

fication. **Councils:** Conference; Education; Membership and Communication; State Leadership. **Publications:** *Credentialing and Medical Staff Law* ● *Guidebook: Developing a Policy and Procedure Manual* ● *Medical Staff Leadership Orientation Manual* ● *NAMSS Membership Roster*, annual. Membership Directory ● *Synergy*, bimonthly. Magazine. **Price:** included in membership dues; $65.00 for nonmembers. **Advertising:** accepted. Alternate Formats: online ● Reports. **Conventions/Meetings:** annual conference (exhibits) - always fall.

14759 ■ National Renal Administrators Association (NRAA)
1904 Naomi Pl.
Prescott, AZ 86303-5061
Ph: (928)717-2772
Fax: (928)441-3857
E-mail: nraa@nraa.org
URL: http://www.nraa.org
Contact: Michael Paget, Exec. Dir.
Founded: 1977. **Members:** 700. **Membership Dues:** active, associate, $300 (annual) ● corporate, $1,000 (annual). **Staff:** 3. **Budget:** $500,000. **Description:** Represents administrative personnel involved with dialysis programs for patients suffering from kidney failure. Provides a vehicle for the development of educational and informational services for members. Maintains contact with health care facilities and government agencies. Operates placement service; compiles statistics; conducts political action committee. **Computer Services:** database, cost reports. **Publications:** *Renal Watch*, weekly. Newsletter. Alternate Formats: online. **Conventions/Meetings:** annual conference (exhibits) - always fall. 2007 Sept. 26-29, Huntington Beach, CA.

14760 ■ Professional Association of Health Care Office Management (PAHCOM)
461 E Ten Mile Rd.
Pensacola, FL 32534
Ph: (850)474-9460
Free: (800)451-9311
Fax: (850)474-6352
E-mail: richardb@pahcom.com
URL: http://www.pahcom.com
Contact: Richard Blanchette, Exec. Dir.
Founded: 1988. **Members:** 3,400. **Membership Dues:** active, $125 (annual) ● faculty/student, $85 (annual) ● corporate affiliate, $250 (annual). **Staff:** 6. **Budget:** $650,000. **Local Groups:** 40. **For-Profit. Description:** Office managers of group and solo medical practices. Operates certification program for health care office managers. **Libraries:** Type: not open to the public. **Awards:** Office Manager of the Year. **Frequency:** annual. **Type:** recognition. **Recipient:** for outstanding achievements. **Committees:** Awards; Corporate Advisory; Ethics; Hospitality; National Executive; Office Manager of the Year. **Formerly:** (2001) Professional Association of Health Care Office Managers. **Publications:** *Compliance Program Guide*. Manual ● *Medical Law and Ethics*. Manual ● *Medical Office Management*, bimonthly. Newsletter. Provides current event information. **Price:** free, for members only. ISSN: 0896-6583. **Circulation:** 7,000. **Advertising:** accepted ● *Personnel Management*. Manual. **Price:** $149.00 ● *Practice Enhancement*. Manual. **Price:** $119.00 ● *Revenue Management*. Manual. **Price:** $149.00. **Conventions/Meetings:** annual conference (exhibits).

14761 ■ Radiology Business Management Association (RBMA)
10300 Eaton Pl., Ste.460
Fairfax, VA 22030
Ph: (703)621-3355
Free: (888)224-7262
Fax: (703)621-3356
E-mail: info@rbma.org
URL: http://www.rbma.org
Contact: Gregory M. Kusiak MBA, Pres.
Founded: 1968. **Members:** 1,900. **Membership Dues:** active, $375 (annual) ● corporate, $1,050 (annual). **Staff:** 7. **Budget:** $2,000,000. **Regional Groups:** 4. **State Groups:** 50. **Local Groups:** 10. **Description:** Provides education, resources and

solutions to manage the business of radiology. Offers an online course in radiology coding. **Telecommunication Services:** electronic mail, gregory_kusiak@msn.com. **Committees:** Education and Conference; Information Development Membership; Publications. **Affiliated With:** American College of Radiology. **Formerly:** (1990) Radiologists Business Managers Association. **Publications:** *Radiology Business Management Association—Bulletin*, bimonthly. Newsletter. Covers organizational topics, industry trends, and legislative developments affecting the private practice of radiology; includes annual index. **Price:** included in membership dues; $100.00 /year for nonmembers. **Circulation:** 1,600. **Advertising:** accepted ● *Radiology Business Management Association—HIPAA Bulletin*, monthly. Serves as a radiology resource for education, implementation and compliance. ● *Radiology Business Management Association—Membership Directory*, annual ● Bulletin, bimonthly. Contains information about radiology business issues, association news and events and vendor advertisements promoting industry products and services. **Price:** $100.00 for members; $150.00 for nonmembers. **Conventions/Meetings:** periodic Radiology Coding, Radiology Billing, Physicians and Administrators - seminar, for continuing education ● semiannual Summit and Fall Educational Conference, educational sessions (exhibits) - always June and October.

14762 ■ Society of Medical-Dental Management Consultants (SMDMC)
125 Strafford Ave., Ste.300
Wayne, PA 19087-3318
Ph: (610)225-1990
Free: (800)826-2264
Fax: (610)687-7702
E-mail: patricia01@aol.com
URL: http://www.smdmc.org
Contact: Ms. Patricia M. Salmon CHBC, Exec.Sec.
Founded: 1968. **Members:** 60. **Membership Dues:** individual, $435 (annual). **Staff:** 2. **State Groups:** 50. **Description:** Professional medical and/or dental management consultants associated for educational and information sharing purposes. Objectives are to: advance the profession; share management techniques; improve individual skills; provide clients with competent and capable business management. Provides information on insurance and income tax. Conducts surveys; compiles statistics. **Awards: Frequency:** annual. **Type:** recognition. **Recipient:** for outstanding service. **Committees:** Constitution; Education; Planning; Projects. **Publications:** *Membership Roster*, annual. Membership Directory ● *SMD Statistics* ● *Society of Medical-Dental Management Consultants—Newsletter*, monthly. **Price:** included in membership dues. **Circulation:** 80. **Advertising:** accepted ● Bulletin. **Conventions/Meetings:** meeting (exhibits) - always June and fall ● annual meeting - always midwinter.

Medical Aid

14763 ■ International Medical Volunteers Association (IMVA)
PO Box 205
Woodville, MA 01784
Ph: (508)435-7377
Fax: (508)497-9568
E-mail: info@imva.org
URL: http://www.imva.org
Founded: 1996. **Multinational. Description:** Promotes, facilitates and supports voluntary medical activity through education and information exchange. Assists volunteer-seeking organizations in locating volunteers to work in their programs. Provides a forum for project cooperation, information, equipment and supply exchange.

14764 ■ Mercy Ships International Operations Center
PO Box 2020
Garden Valley, TX 75771-2020
Ph: (903)939-7000

Fax: (903)882-0336
E-mail: info@mercyships.org
URL: http://www.mercyships.org
Contact: Mr. Don Stephens, Founder/Pres.
Description: Brings hope and healing to the forgotten poor, mobilizing people and resources worldwide, and serving all people without regard for race, gender or religion. Has impacted over 5.5 million people; delivered more than $21 million of medical equipment, hospital supplies and medicines; completed close to 350 construction and agriculture projects including schools, clinics, orphanages and waterwells; and demonstrated the love of God to people in 95 ports in 53 developing nations.

14765 ■ Operation Rainbow
PMB 157
4200 Park Blvd.
Oakland, CA 94602
Ph: (510)273-2485
E-mail: laura@operationrainbow.org
URL: http://www.operationrainbow.org
Contact: Laura Escobosa, Dir.
Founded: 1978. **Description:** Provides free reconstructive surgery for children in medically underserved countries and throughout the United States.

14766 ■ Physicians for Peace (PFP)
229 W Bute St., Ste.200
Norfolk, VA 23510
Ph: (757)625-7569
Fax: (757)625-7680
E-mail: info@physiciansforpeace.org
URL: http://www.physiciansforpeace.org
Contact: Dr. Charles E. Horton, Founder/Chm.
Founded: 1989. **Multinational. Description:** Builds peace and international friendship in developing nations with unmet medical needs and scarce resources through medical education, training and clinical care. Teaches new skills to health care professionals in developing nations. Develops replicable and sustainable medical programs. Obtains and distributes contributions of medical supplies and equipment. Recruits health care providers to serve as volunteers throughout the world.

14767 ■ Recovered Medical Equipment for the Developing World (REMEDY)
PO Box 208051
New Haven, CT 06520-8051
Ph: (203)737-5356 (203)785-6750
Fax: (203)785-5241
E-mail: remedy@yale.edu
URL: http://www.remedyinc.org
Contact: Silvia Botero, Exec. Dir.
Founded: 1991. **Members:** 300. **Staff:** 3. **Budget:** $100,000. **Languages:** English, Spanish. **Multinational. Description:** Dedicated to achieving safe, efficient, and cost effective methods for recovering opened, but unused materials from hospital operating rooms. Provides teaching problem solving, and networking assistance. Sponsors the Medical Equipment Donation Agency (Med-Eq) program that links donors of medical equipment with receiving charitable organizations. **Publications:** *REMEDY Atlas*. Catalog ● *Remedy Newsletter*, semiannual. **Price:** free ● Video.

14768 ■ United Amputee Services Association (UASA)
PO Box 4277
Winter Park, FL 32793-4277
Ph: (407)359-5500
Fax: (407)359-8855
E-mail: uasa@oandp.com
URL: http://www.oandp.com/resources/organizations/uasa/index.htm
Founded: 1980. **Members:** 400. **Membership Dues:** regular, $20 (annual) ● professional, corporate, $50 (annual). **Staff:** 1. **Description:** Provides support and education to amputees and their families. **Libraries:** Type: open to the public. **Subjects:** amputees. **Computer Services:** database ● mailing lists. **Publications:** *A Survivor's Guide for the Recent Amputee* (in English and Spanish). Booklet. Provides pertinent information regarding amputation. **Price:** $5.50 each

(1 to 50 copies); $5.00 each (51 to 100 copies); $4.50 each (more than 101 copies) ● *Amputee Review*, quarterly. Newsletter. **Price:** included in membership dues. **Advertising:** accepted. **Conventions/Meetings:** monthly support group meeting - every second Friday in Orlando, FL.

Medical Assistants

14769 ■ American Association of Medical Assistants (AAMA)
20 N Wacker Dr., Ste.1575
Chicago, IL 60606
Ph: (312)899-1500
Free: (800)228-2262
Fax: (312)899-1259
E-mail: info@aama-ntl.org
URL: http://www.aama-ntl.org
Contact: Donald A. Balasa JD, Exec. Dir./Legal Counsel

Founded: 1956. **Members:** 20,000. **Membership Dues:** non-student (varies by state; includes national, state and local levels), $67-$97 (annual) ● student (varies by state; includes national, state and local levels), $20-$35 (annual). **Staff:** 21. **Budget:** $1,500,000. **State Groups:** 46. **Description:** Medical assistants are allied health professionals who work primarily in ambulatory (out patient) settings and perform clinical and administrative procedures. Activities include a certification program consisting of study and an examination, passage of which entitles the individual to become credentialed as a Certified Medical Assistant. Conducts accreditation of one and two-year programs in medical assisting in conjunction with the commission on Accreditation of Allied Health Education Programs. Provides assistance and information to institutions of higher learning desirous of initiating courses for medical assistants. Awards continuing education units for selected educational programs. **Libraries: Type:** reference. **Holdings:** books. **Awards:** Maxine Williams Scholarship. **Type:** scholarship. **Boards:** Certification; Continuing Education; Curriculum Review; Editorial. **Publications:** *Accounts Receivable and Collection for the Medical Practice*. **Price:** $20.00 for members; $30.00 for nonmembers ● *AIDS Concepts for Medical Assistants — Part I*. **Price:** $15.00 for members; $25.00 for nonmembers ● *Human Relations for the Medical Office*. **Price:** $30.00 for members; $50.00 for nonmembers ● *Law for the Medical Office*. **Price:** $30.00 for members; $50.00 for nonmembers ● *Managing Managed Care*. **Price:** $15.00 for members; $25.00 for nonmembers ● *Medical Office Management — Part I*. **Price:** $22.00 for members; $32.00 for nonmembers ● *PMA*, bimonthly. Journal. Includes association news, index of advertisers, continuing education articles, and calendar of events. **Price:** included in membership dues; $30.00 /year for nonmembers and students. ISSN: 0033-0140. **Circulation:** 14,000. **Advertising:** accepted ● *Urinalysis Today*. **Price:** $30.00 for members; $50.00 for nonmembers ● Brochures ● Pamphlets. **Conventions/Meetings:** annual convention, for medical assisting practitioners, educators and students; held in conjunction with the House of Delegates (exhibits) - 2007 Sept. 7-11, Louisville, KY; 2008 Oct. 17-21, Chicago, IL; 2009 Sept. 11-15, Houston, TX.

14770 ■ American Association for Medical Transcription (AAMT)
4230 Kiernan Ave., Ste.130
Modesto, CA 95356
Ph: (209)527-9620
Free: (800)982-2182
Fax: (209)527-9633
E-mail: aamt@aamt.org
URL: http://www.aamt.org
Contact: Kim Buchanan, Dir. of Credentialing and Education

Founded: 1978. **Members:** 7,000. **Membership Dues:** individual professional, $135 (annual) ● electronic, $75 (annual) ● student, $55 (annual) ● postgraduate, $85 (annual) ● corporate, $400 (annual) ● educational, $200 (annual) ● sustaining, $63

(annual). **Staff:** 20. **Budget:** $2,800,000. **State Groups:** 26. **Local Groups:** 86. **Description:** Medical transcriptionists, their supervisors, teachers and students of medical transcription, owners and managers of medical transcription services, and other interested health personnel. Provides information about the profession of medical transcription and gives continuing education for medical transcriptionists. Advocates professional recognition of medical transcriptionists in county, state, and national medical societies and in health care facilities nationwide. Sponsors voluntary certification/ credentialing program. Offers updates on developments in medicine and curricula, and on new transcription methods and equipment; sponsors and encourages research in the field. Establishes guidelines for education of medical transcriptionists. **Awards:** Chapter of the Year. **Frequency:** annual. **Type:** recognition ● CMT Key Award. **Frequency:** annual. **Type:** recognition ● Employer of the Year. **Frequency:** annual. **Type:** recognition ● The Marilyn Craddock Student of the Year. **Frequency:** annual. **Type:** recognition ● Practitioner of the Year. **Frequency:** annual. **Type:** recognition ● State/Regional Association of the Year. **Frequency:** annual. **Type:** recognition. **Computer Services:** Mailing lists, 32000 available names. **Sections:** Business Issues; Specialty. **Publications:** *The AAMT Book of Style for Medical Transcription, 2nd Edition*. **Price:** $79.00. Alternate Formats: CD-ROM ● *AAMT Insights*, monthly. Newsletter ● *Journal of the American Association for Medical Transcription*, bimonthly. Offers guidance in quality assurance for medical transcription, medical and non-medical educational articles, word lists, and technology updates. **Price:** included in membership dues; $62.49 for individuals in U.S.; $193.49 for institutions in U.S.; $140.49 for individuals outside U.S. ISSN: 0745-2624. **Circulation:** 10,000. **Advertising:** accepted ● *The Leading Edge*, monthly. Newsletter ● *Plexus*, bimonthly. Magazine. Contains articles on medical science, education and others. **Circulation:** 8,000. Alternate Formats: online. Also Cited As: *JAAMT* ● *Vitals*, weekly. Newsletter. Contains updates on the industry and strategic direction and initiatives of association. Alternate Formats: online ● Also publishes medical transcription modules and medical transcription video programs. **Conventions/Meetings:** annual convention (exhibits) - 2008 Aug. 6-9, Orlando, FL - **Avg. Attendance:** 1000.

14771 ■ American Registry of Medical Assistants (ARMA)
69 Southwick Rd.
Westfield, MA 01085-4729
Ph: (413)562-7336
Free: (800)527-2762
Fax: (413)562-9021
E-mail: arma@verizon.net
Contact: Annette H. Heyman RMA, Dir.

Founded: 1950. **Members:** 10,000. **Membership Dues:** $30 (annual). **Staff:** 8. **Languages:** English, Spanish. **Description:** Medical assistants who have completed an accredited medical assistant training course or who have trained with a physician for a minimum of three years. Objectives are to: establish and maintain high training standards for medical assistants; promote greater efficiency within the profession; raise awareness of medical assistants within the medical community. **Awards: Frequency:** annual. **Type:** recognition. **Recipient:** for 15, 20, and 35 years of service. **Publications:** *Registry Connection*, bimonthly. **Price:** included in registration fee.

14772 ■ American Society of Anesthesia Technologists and Technicians (ASATT)
55 Harristown Rd., 2nd Fl.
Glen Rock, NJ 07452
Ph: (201)652-6622
Fax: (201)447-3831
E-mail: asattinfo@aol.com
URL: http://www.asatt.org
Contact: Sheila Guston CAE, Exec. Dir.

Founded: 1989. **Members:** 1,900. **Membership Dues:** active, $50 (annual) ● regular, associate, physician, nurse, $60 (annual) ● institutional, corporate, $100 (annual) ● student, $35 (annual) ●

international, $70 (annual). **Staff:** 2. **Budget:** $150,000. **Regional Groups:** 7. **Description:** Anesthesia technicians and technologists, medical technology students, and other individuals, organizations, and corporations with an interest in the field of anesthesiology. Promotes continuing professional development of members. Conducts continuing educational programs for anesthesiology technicians and technologists; represents members' interests at the national level in the United States; and maintains certification program and develops standards of ethics and practice. **Publications:** *Sensor*, quarterly. Magazine. **Advertising:** accepted. Alternate Formats: CD-ROM ● Annual Report, annual. Alternate Formats: online ● Handbooks. Alternate Formats: online. **Conventions/Meetings:** annual conference, includes educational sessions (exhibits) - 2007 Oct., San Francisco, CA - **Avg. Attendance:** 250.

Medical Education

14773 ■ Alliance of Independent Academic Medical Centers (AIAMC)
401 N Michigan Ave., Ste.1200
Chicago, IL 60611
Ph: (312)836-3712
Fax: (312)988-7573
E-mail: kimberly@aiamc.org
URL: http://www.aiamc.org
Contact: Peter Coggan MD, Pres.

Founded: 1989. **Membership Dues:** health care system (for 1st hospital), single institution, $4,000 (annual). **Description:** Independent academic medical center that sponsor four or more accredited residency programs, supports an institutional research program, and serves as a major affiliate for a significant number of medical school student clerkships. Promotes the roles and contributions of independent academic medical centers, fosters professional collegiality among their leaders, and works with other professional organizations to achieve mutual goals.

14774 ■ American Academy of Medical Management (AAMM)
Crossville Commons
560 W Crossville Rd., Ste.103
Roswell, GA 30075
Ph: (770)649-7150
Fax: (770)649-7552
E-mail: webmaster@epracticemanagement.org
URL: http://www.epracticemanagement.org
Contact: Roger G. Bonds, Exec. Dir.

Founded: 1990. **Members:** 400. **Membership Dues:** individual, $378 (annual). **Staff:** 6. **Description:** Health care administrators with an interest in continuing professional development; continuing medical education programs. Seeks to increase the quality and availability of continuing medical education courses. Serves as a clearinghouse on continuing medical education; formulates model practice management and recruitment and physician employment contracts; sponsors fellowship and certification programs for continuing medical educators. **Libraries: Type:** open to the public. **Holdings:** books. **Subjects:** continuing medical education. **Awards:** Executive Fellowship in Practice Management. **Frequency:** monthly. **Type:** fellowship ● National Honors Program. **Frequency:** annual. **Type:** recognition. **Recipient:** for professionals of the year in the areas of medical staff development and practice management. **Formerly:** (2000) American College of Medical Staff Development; (2003) American College of Medical Practice Management. **Publications:** *Medical Staff Development Professional*, periodic. Journal. **Conventions/Meetings:** periodic conference ● periodic symposium.

14775 ■ Association of Native American Medical Students (ANAMS)
1225 Sovereign Row, Ste.103
Oklahoma City, OK 73108
Ph: (405)946-7072
Fax: (405)946-7651

E-mail: aaip@aaip.com
URL: http://www.aaip.org/programs/anams/anams.htm
Contact: Michael H. Arredondo, Pres.
Founded: 1975. **Membership Dues:** regular, $40. **Staff:** 19. **Description:** Committed to Native American medical students. **Telecommunication Services:** electronic mail, anams@aaip.com.

14776 ■ Association of Program Directors in Radiology (APDR)
820 Jorie Blvd.
Oak Brook, IL 60523
Ph: (630)368-3737
Fax: (630)571-7837
E-mail: apdr@rsna.org
URL: http://www.apdr.org
Contact: Lise Steg Thorsby, Account Exec.
Founded: 1993. **Members:** 457. **Membership Dues:** active, $190 (annual) ● coordinator, $75 (annual). **Description:** Directors, associate directors, assistant directors, and coordinators of medical residency and fellowship programs in radiology. Promotes the "advancement of the art and science of radiology." Facilitates communication and cooperation among members; sponsors research and educational programs. **Committees:** Awards; Education; Electronic Communications and Publications; Fellowship Issues; Nominating; Planning; Program; Rules. **Affiliated With:** Association of University Radiologists. **Conventions/Meetings:** annual meeting, in association with the Association of University Radiologists ● periodic seminar.

14777 ■ Boston International Foundation for Medical Education/Exchange
c/o Joseph J. Vitale, MD, Chm.
160 Heritage Ln.
Weymouth, MA 02189-1061
Ph: (617)414-4829 (781)337-3933
E-mail: jjvitale@bu.edu
URL: http://www.bifme.org
Contact: Joseph J. Vitale MD, Chm.
Founded: 1996. **Members:** 6. **Multinational. Description:** Supports senior medical students, medical and surgical residents and junior faculty from Harvard, Tufts and Boston University, who successfully completed a minimum two to six month elective at a foreign medical center acceptable to the respective medical school administration and the foundation. Support is intended to defray travel and living expenses. Believes this experience provides useful and practical insight into cultural, moral and ethnic perceptions of health care in multi-ethnic and multicultural society. **Libraries:** Type: reference. **Holdings:** archival material. **Subjects:** international health. **Awards:** Frequency: 3/year. Type: scholarship. Recipient: for 4th year medical student completing a 2 to 3 months overseas elective. **Formerly:** (2003) Boston International Foundation for Medical Exchange.

14778 ■ International Association of Medical Science Educators (IAMSE)
1 Crested Butte
Huntington, WV 25705
Ph: (304)733-1270
Fax: (304)733-6203
E-mail: admin@iamse.org
URL: http://www.iamse.org
Contact: Prof. E. Pat Finnerty PhD, Pres.
Founded: 1997. **Members:** 390. **Membership Dues:** individual (based on country's GNP per capita), $38-$115 (annual) ● institutional, $130-$425 (annual) ● student, $60 (annual). **Staff:** 1. **Description:** Strives to share experiences and strategies for teaching the fundamental sciences of medicine. **Computer Services:** Electronic publishing, for members. **Publications:** *Journal of the International Association of Medical Science Educators* (in English, French, and Spanish), semiannual. Includes articles about medical science. **Price:** included in membership dues. ISSN: 1550-8897. **Advertising:** accepted. Alternate Formats: online. Also Cited As: *JIAMSE.* **Conventions/Meetings:** annual meeting.

14779 ■ International Society for Medical Education - United States
Address Unknown since 2007
Founded: 1992. **Members:** 7. **Staff:** 400. **Budget:** $2,000,000. **Regional Groups:** 1. **National Groups:** 2. **Languages:** Hindi, Nepalese Dialects. **Multinational. Description:** Works to provide medical education and health care in under-developed and third-world countries by establishing medical schools and hospitals. Provides free medical education, and charity medical care. Establishes women's welfare centers. **Libraries:** Type: not open to the public. **Holdings:** 3,000. **Subjects:** medical. **Conventions/Meetings:** annual Medicine in India and Nepal, medical education program.

Medical Examiners

14780 ■ International Association of Coroners and Medical Examiners (IACME)
c/o Mr. John Fudenberg, Sec.
1704 Pinto Ln.
Las Vegas, NV 89106
Ph: (702)455-3385
Fax: (702)387-0092
E-mail: fud@co.clark.nv.us
URL: http://www.theiacme.com
Contact: Mr. John Fudenberg, Sec.
Founded: 1938. **Members:** 335. **Membership Dues:** regular, $100 (annual). **Staff:** 2. **Description:** Conducts educational seminar involving all aspects of death investigation such as pathology, autopsy, crime scene investigation, mass disasters and anthropology. Offers continuing medical education credit. **Awards:** Frequency: annual. Type: recognition. **Recipient:** for outstanding contributions. **Publications:** *RECAP,* quarterly. Newsletter. **Price:** included in membership dues. **Conventions/Meetings:** annual seminar - always June.

14781 ■ National Association of Medical Examiners (NAME)
430 Pryor St. SW
Atlanta, GA 30312
Ph: (404)730-4781
Fax: (404)730-4420
E-mail: denise.mcnally@thename.org
URL: http://www.thename.org
Contact: Denise McNally, Exec. Dir.
Founded: 1966. **Members:** 950. **Membership Dues:** active, $300 (annual) ● affiliate (with journal subscription), $200 (annual) ● affiliate (without journal subscription), $65 (annual) ● resident, $140 (annual). **Staff:** 1. **Description:** Medical examiners, pathologists, and other licensed physicians who have responsibilities in connection with the official investigation of sudden, suspicious, and violent deaths. Attempts to establish greater understanding and support for the medical examiner system among the public, government officials, and the medical and legal professions. Has established standards for inspection and accreditation of a modern medicolegal investigative system. **Publications:** *American Journal of Forensic Medicine and Pathology,* quarterly. **Price:** $337.00 /year for individuals; $584.00 /year for institutions; $190.00/year for in-training. ISSN: 0195-7910. **Advertising:** accepted. Alternate Formats: online. **Conventions/Meetings:** annual meeting, scientific session (exhibits).

14782 ■ National Board of Medical Examiners (NBME)
3750 Market St.
Philadelphia, PA 19104-3102
Ph: (215)590-9500 (215)590-9700
Fax: (215)590-9457
E-mail: webmail@nbme.org
URL: http://www.nbme.org
Contact: Donald E. Melnick MD, Pres.
Founded: 1915. **Members:** 75. **Staff:** 300. **Description:** Aims to prepare and administer qualifying examinations either independently or in conjunction with other organizations, of such high quality that legal agencies governing the practice of medicine

within each state may, in their discretion, grant a license without further examination for those who have successfully completed such examinations; to cooperate with and, where appropriate, to make its specialized services available to the examining boards of the states, specialty boards, and other organizations concerned with the education and qualification of personnel in the fields of health. **Libraries:** Type: not open to the public. **Holdings:** 2,300. **Awards:** John P. Hubbard Award. Frequency: annual. Type: recognition. Recipient: for contribution to assessment of professional competency ● Medical Education Research Fund. Frequency: annual. Type: grant. **Publications:** *NBME Examiner,* quarterly. Newsletter. Contains reports on new medical evaluation programs and new directions in the research and development of examinations. **Price:** free. **Circulation:** 65,000. Alternate Formats: online ● Annual Report, annual ● Also publishes information bulletins and policy statements. **Conventions/Meetings:** annual meeting - always spring, Philadelphia, PA.

Medical Identification

14783 ■ Surfer's Medical Association
PO Box 1210
Aptos, CA 95001
Ph: (831)684-0916
Fax: (831)684-0916
E-mail: smacentral@aol.com
URL: http://www.surfersmedicalassociation.org
Contact: Paula Smith, Exec. Dir.
Founded: 1986. **Members:** 1,000. **Membership Dues:** individual, charter, $100 (annual) ● individual, health professional, $50 (annual) ● individual, non-health professional, $35 (annual). **Regional Groups:** 2. **National Groups:** 2. **Multinational. Description:** Surfer-health professionals and surfers interested in the health and medical aspects of surfing. Works to educate surfers and medical practitioners on the unique health problems of surfers. Represents the sport of surfing in the fields of medicine and science and also works to preserve the environment of beaches and oceans. Established the first international network of surfing health professionals. Sponsors members' research in this field. **Awards:** Frequency: periodic. Type: scholarship. Recipient: to a Fijian village student. **Publications:** *Collected Surf Works,* 1-2/year. Book. Three volume set of articles and information on surfing and health. ● *Surfing Medicine.* Journal. Contains original articles, research reports, conference updates, etc. **Conventions/Meetings:** annual conference.

Medical Records

14784 ■ American Health Information Management Association (AHIMA)
233 N Michigan Ave., 21st Fl.
Chicago, IL 60601
Ph: (312)233-1100
Free: (800)335-5535
Fax: (312)233-1090
E-mail: info@ahima.org
URL: http://www.ahima.org
Contact: Bryon Pickard MBA, Pres.
Founded: 1928. **Members:** 40,000. **Membership Dues:** active, associate, $155 (annual) ● student, $35 (annual) ● new graduate, $100 (annual) ● senior, $60 (annual). **Staff:** 90. **Budget:** $12,000,000. **State Groups:** 52. **Description:** Registered record administrators; accredited record technicians with expertise in health information management, biostatistics, classification systems, and systems analysis. Sponsors Independent Study Programs in Medical Record Technology and coding. Conducts annual qualification examinations to credential medical record personnel as Registered Record Administrators (RRA), Accredited Record Technicians (ART) and Certified Coding Specialists (CCS). Maintains Foundation of Research and Education Library, Scholarships and loans. **Libraries:** Type: reference. **Hold-**

ings: 2,500. **Subjects:** medical records administration, coding, management. **Awards: Frequency:** annual. **Type:** recognition. **Computer Services:** database ● online services. **Divisions:** Business Services; Education/Certification; Independent Study; Marketing and Communications Services; Member and Volunteer Services; Practice Leadership; **Sections:** Ambulatory Care; Long Term Care; Mental Health; Physical Medicine and Rehabilitation; Quality Assurance. **Formerly:** (1928) American Association of Medical Record Librarians; (1938) Association of Record Librarians of North America; (1991) American Medical Records Association. **Publications:** *From the Couch: Official Newsletter of the Mental Health Record Section of the American Medical Record Association*, quarterly. **Price:** included in membership dues. **Circulation:** 800 ● *Journal of AHIMA*, 10/year. Contains articles on the theory, practice, and current issues in health information management. Includes book reviews and calendar of events. **Price:** $72.00. ISSN: 1060-5487. **Circulation:** 40,000. **Advertising:** accepted. Alternate Formats: online ● *Leader: AHIMA Volunteer*, quarterly. Newsletter. **Price:** included in membership dues ● *QA Section Connection*, bimonthly. Newsletter. Provides educational information on the management and methodology of health care quality assurance programs. Includes annual subject index. **Price:** included in membership dues. **Circulation:** 3,000 ● *Spectrum*, quarterly. Newsletter. **Price:** included in membership dues. **Circulation:** 1,400 ● Also publishes guides, workbooks, and other materials on medical record management and related subjects. **Conventions/Meetings:** annual meeting and convention (exhibits) - always October. 2007 Oct. 6-11, Philadelphia, PA - **Avg. Attendance:** 5000; 2008 Oct. 11-16, Seattle, WA; 2009 Oct. 3-8, Dallas, TX.

14785 ■ Medical Records Institute (MRI)
425 Boylston St., 4th Fl.
Boston, MA 02116-3315
Ph: (617)964-3923
Fax: (617)964-3926
E-mail: info@medrecinst.com
URL: http://www.medrecinst.com
Contact: Peter Waegemann, CEO
Founded: 1979. **Staff:** 5. **Budget:** $1,500,000. **For-Profit. Description:** Conducts research and education in the fields of medical documentation and computerization of patient information. Maintains committees and network groups. Compiles statistics. **Libraries: Type:** not open to the public. **Computer Services:** Mailing lists. **Committees:** Political Action. **Formerly:** (1988) Institute for Medical Record Economics. **Publications:** *Handbook of Optical Memory Systems*. **Price:** $100.50 ● *Toward An Electronic Patient Record*, 10/year. **Price:** $145.00. ISSN: 1063-973X. **Circulation:** 600 ● Proceedings. **Conventions/Meetings:** annual conference (exhibits) ● conference ● seminar.

Medical Research

14786 ■ Academy of Surgical Research (ASR)
7500 Flying Cloud Dr., Ste.900
Eden Prairie, MN 55344
Ph: (952)253-6240
Fax: (952)835-4774
E-mail: director@surgicalresearch.org
URL: http://www.surgicalresearch.org
Contact: Jacob T. Killinger, Sec.-Treas.
Founded: 1982. **Members:** 425. **Membership Dues:** individual, $200 (annual) ● associate, $100 (annual) ● institution, $495 (annual) ● corporate, $825 (annual). **Staff:** 15. **Description:** Individuals, organizations, and corporations with an interest in surgical research. Seeks to advance surgical techniques and equipment through improved research. Facilitates cooperation and exchange of information among members; and fosters interdisciplinary transfer of ideas to advance surgical research. **Awards:** Andreas von Recum Award. **Frequency:** annual. **Type:** monetary ● Barry Sauer Award. **Frequency:** annual.

Type: monetary. **Recipient:** to a student with the highest SRS exam score ● C. William Hall Outstanding Publication Award. **Frequency:** annual. **Type:** monetary. **Recipient:** for excellence in research endeavors ● C.William Hall Award. **Frequency:** annual. **Type:** trophy. **Recipient:** for excellence research endeavor in manuscripts ● Jacob Markowitz Award. **Frequency:** annual. **Type:** monetary. **Computer Services:** database ● mailing lists ● online services. **Affiliated With:** American Association for Laboratory Animal Science; Association for Assessment and Accreditation of Laboratory Animal Care International; National Association for Biomedical Research. **Publications:** *Journal of Investigative Surgery*, bimonthly. Discusses advances in surgical research techniques and education. **Price:** $29.95. ISSN: 0894-1939. **Circulation:** 500. **Advertising:** accepted.

14787 ■ American Health Assistance Foundation (AHAF)
22512 Gateway Center Dr.
Clarksburg, MD 20871-2005
Ph: (301)948-3244
Free: (800)437-2423
Fax: (301)258-9454
E-mail: sbarnhouse@ahaf.org
URL: http://www.ahaf.org
Contact: Ms. Sarah Barnhouse, Research Grants Coor.
Founded: 1973. **Staff:** 22. **Description:** Seeks to eradicate age-related and degenerative diseases by: facilitating research seeking causes, treatment and cures; promoting behavioral patterns in the public to combat Alzheimer's disease, glaucoma, and macular degeneration; and educating the public about these diseases. **Libraries: Type:** not open to the public. **Holdings:** 29; archival material, articles, books. **Subjects:** Alzheimer's disease, macular degeneration, glaucoma. **Awards:** Alzheimer's Disease Research Fellowship Award. **Type:** fellowship. **Recipient:** for research on the cause or treatment of Alzheimer's disease ● Alzheimer's Disease Research Pilot Award. **Frequency:** annual. **Type:** grant. **Recipient:** for research on the cause or treatment of Alzheimer's disease ● Alzheimer's Disease Research Standard Grant. **Frequency:** annual. **Type:** grant. **Recipient:** for research on the cause or treatment of Alzheimer's disease ● Macular Degeneration Research Grant. **Frequency:** annual. **Type:** grant. **Recipient:** for research on the cause or treatment of macular degeneration ● National Glaucoma Research Grant. **Frequency:** annual. **Type:** grant. **Recipient:** for research on the cause or treatment of glaucoma. **Programs:** Alzheimer's Disease Research; Macular Degeneration Research; National Glaucoma Research. **Publications:** *Alzheimer's Research Review*, quarterly. Newsletter. Updates the work of Alzheimer's disease researchers. Provides tips for families with members who have the disease. **Price:** free. Alternate Formats: online ● *Glaucoma Research News*, quarterly. Newsletters ● *Macular Research News*, quarterly. Newsletters.

14788 ■ Applied Research Ethics National Association (ARENA)
126 Brookline Ave., Ste.202
Boston, MA 02115-3920
Ph: (617)423-4112
Fax: (617)423-1185
E-mail: info@primr.org
URL: http://www.primr.org
Contact: Joan Rachlin, Exec. Dir.
Founded: 1986. **Members:** 1,500. **Membership Dues:** individual, $125 (annual). **Staff:** 2. **Regional Groups:** 6. **Description:** Professionals concerned with ethical issues related to humans and animal subject research. Promotes the protection of humans and the humane care and treatment of animals. Sponsors national and regional meetings, disseminates research information and assists with the development of regional networks. **Councils:** Certification of IRB Professionals. **Affiliated With:** Public Responsibility in Medicine and Research. **Conventions/Meetings:** annual conference (exhibits).

14789 ■ City of Hope National Medical Center (COH)
1500 E Duarte Rd.
Duarte, CA 91010
Ph: (626)359-8111 (626)256-4673
Free: (800)826-HOPE
E-mail: media@coh.org
URL: http://www.cityofhope.org
Contact: Michael A. Friedman MD, Pres./CEO
Founded: 1913. **Budget:** $312,100,000. **Nonmembership. Description:** Dedicated to the prevention and cure of cancer, diabetes, HIV/AIDS and other life-threatening diseases. Is guided by a "compassionate patient-centered philosophy". Has 244 chartered auxiliaries in 163 cities, donations from top corporations, national foundations, philanthropic agencies, industries, celebrities and individuals in every state of the nation. **Publications:** *City News*, quarterly. Magazine ● *eHope*, monthly. Newsletter. Alternate Formats: online. **Conventions/Meetings:** biennial meeting.

14790 ■ Coalition for the Advancement of Medical Research (CAMR)
2021 K St. NW, Ste.305
Washington, DC 20006
Ph: (202)293-2856
E-mail: camresearch@yahoo.com
URL: http://www.camradvocacy.org
Contact: Sean Tipton, Pres.
Founded: 2001. **Description:** Promotes the advancement of breakthrough research and technologies in regenerative medicine, including stem cell research and somatic cell nuclear transfer, to cure diseases. **Computer Services:** Information services. **Telecommunication Services:** electronic mail, 202-stipton@asrm-dc.org.

14791 ■ Committee for the Promotion of Medical Research
c/o NYU Medical Center
Dept. of Medicine
462 First Ave.
New York, NY 10016
Ph: (212)562-1000 (212)263-6394
URL: http://www.med.nyu.edu/medicine/research/resday-07-sponsor.html
Contact: Ellen M. Cosgrove, Exec. Sec.
Founded: 1944. **Staff:** 1. **Description:** Is concerned with the administration of medical research grants. **Convention/Meeting:** none.

14792 ■ Cornea Research Foundation of America
9002 N Meridian St., Ste.212
Indianapolis, IN 46260
Ph: (317)814-2993
Fax: (317)814-2806
E-mail: info@cornea.org
URL: http://www.cornea.org
Contact: Elaine Voci PhD, Development Dir.
Founded: 1988. **Description:** Works to restore and preserve vision through clinical research and educational programs that relate to eye disorders and corneal diseases. **Computer Services:** database, stores, tracks preoperative, surgical and postoperative statistics on transplants. **Publications:** *Visionary*, quarterly. Newsletter. Provides news and information to donors, patients, friends. ● Papers. **Conventions/Meetings:** annual Cornea Golf Classic - competition - always in Indianapolis, IN ● annual OD Seminar, with speaker.

14793 ■ Esther A. and Joseph Klingenstein Fund
787 7th Ave., 6th Fl.
New York, NY 10019-6016
Ph: (212)492-6181
Fax: (212)492-7007
E-mail: kathleen.pomerantz@klingenstein.com
URL: http://www.klingfund.org
Contact: Mr. John Klingenstein, Pres.
Founded: 1945. **Description:** Works to support neuroscience research, especially in the area of epilepsy, independent school education, separation of Church

and State, and animal-based research. **Awards:** Klingenstein Fellowship Awards in the Neurosciences. **Type:** fellowship. **Recipient:** for the most outstanding physician-scientist.

14794 ■ Howard Hughes Medical Institute (HHMI)
4000 Jones Bridge Rd.
Chevy Chase, MD 20815-6720
Ph: (301)215-8500
E-mail: webmaster@hhmi.org
URL: http://www.hhmi.org
Contact: Thomas R. Cech PhD, Pres.
Founded: 1953. **Multinational. Description:** Works to help enhance biomedical science education at all levels. Conducts research. **Awards: Frequency:** periodic. **Type:** grant. **Recipient:** to biomedical research institutions, universities and colleges which support science education programs at the pre-kindergarten to undergraduate levels ● HHMI Professor Award. **Frequency:** annual. **Type:** grant. **Recipient:** to professors nominated by their institutions.

14795 ■ International Society of Psychoneuroendocrinology (ISPNE)
c/o Alan F. Schatzberg, MD, Sec. Gen.
Dept. of Psychiatry and Behavioral Sciences
Stanford Univ. School of Medicine
401 Quarry Rd.
Stanford, CA 94305-5717
Ph: (650)723-6811
Fax: (650)498-5294
E-mail: afschatz@leland.stanford.edu
URL: http://www.ispne.org
Contact: Alan F. Schatzberg MD, Sec. Gen.
Founded: 1969. **Members:** 450. **Membership Dues:** professional, $175 (annual) ● student, $75 (annual). **Multinational. Description:** Promotes and disseminates knowledge on hormones, their interaction with the brain, body processes and behavior, as well as their clinical applications. Facilitates basic and clinical investigations in Psychoneuroendocrinology and integrates basic, clinical, and applied research in the field. Collaborates with investigators, clinicians, and organizations with mutual interest in the field. **Committees:** Journal and Publications; Nominating; Scientific. **Publications:** *Psychoneuroendocrinology.* Journal. Contains information on interrelated disciplines of psychology, neurobiology, endocrinology, immunology, neurology, and psychiatry. **Price:** included in membership dues. **Circulation:** 1,050.

14796 ■ Medical Research Modernization Committee (MRMC)
3200 Morley Rd.
Shaker Heights, OH 44122
Ph: (216)283-6702
Fax: (216)283-6702
E-mail: stkaufman@mindspring.com
URL: http://www.mrmcmed.org
Contact: Stephen R. Kaufman MD, Co-Chm.
Founded: 1987. **Members:** 100. **Membership Dues:** individual, $35 (annual). **Staff:** 1. **Budget:** $5,000. **Description:** Individuals, primarily scientists and clinicians, who evaluate the medical and/or scientific merit of research modalities in an effort to identify outdated research methods and to promote sensible, reliable, and efficient methods. Represents positions to the public, health care professionals, and government officials. Maintains speakers' bureau; distributes literature to the public. **Libraries: Type:** reference. **Holdings:** 250; periodicals. **Subjects:** animal and medical research. **Publications:** *A Critical Look at Animal Experimentation*, annual. Booklet. **Price:** free for members; $1.00/copy for nonmembers. **Circulation:** 20,000 ● *Aping Science: Summary.* Report ● *New: Science Watch.* Report ● *Of Pigs, Primates, and Plagues: Xenotransplantation Critique.* Report ● *Perspectives on Medical Research*, annual. Monograph. Includes essays and commentary. **Price:** $10.00 each - paperback copy; $16.00 each - hardback copy. ISSN: 1053-8984. **Circulation:** 1,500 ● *Shortcomings of AIDS-Related Animal Experimentation.* Report.

14797 ■ PanAmerican Society for Pigment Cell Research (PASPCR)
c/o Dr. Raymond E. Boissy, Sec.-Treas.
Dept. of Dermatology
Univ. of Cincinnati
231 Bethesda Ave.
Cincinnati, OH 45267-0592
Fax: (513)558-0198
E-mail: boissyre@ucmail.uc.edu
URL: http://paspcr.med.umn.edu
Contact: John Pawelek, Pres.
Founded: 1988. **Membership Dues:** regular, second membership, $77 (annual) ● student, $12 (annual). **Description:** Promotes pigment cell research. **Affiliated With:** European Society for Pigment Cell Research. **Publications:** *PASPCR Newsletter*, quarterly. Alternate Formats: online. **Conventions/Meetings:** annual meeting ● annual meeting.

14798 ■ Research! America
1101 King St., Ste.520
Alexandria, VA 22314-2960
Ph: (703)739-2577
Free: (800)366-2873
Fax: (703)739-2372
E-mail: info@researchamerica.org
URL: http://www.researchamerica.org
Contact: Mary Woolley, Pres./CEO
Founded: 1989. **Members:** 501. **Membership Dues:** institution (with less than $5 million research funding), $1,000 ● institution (with $5-$30 million research funding), $3,000 ● institution (with $30-$100 million research funding), $6,000 ● institution (with more than $100 million research funding), $7,500 ● business and industry (with no product and services), $600 ● business and industry (with less than $50 million annual sales), $1,800 ● business and industry (with $50-$500 million annual sales), $5,000 ● business and industry (with more than $500 million annual sales), $10,000 ● professional society (with less than 300 members), $250. **Staff:** 18. **Budget:** $4,000,000. **Description:** Academia, voluntary health organizations, professional and scientific societies, hospitals and independent research institutes, businesses and industries, and foundations and philanthropists. Works to increase public awareness of the benefits of medical and health research. Seeks to stimulate interest in medical research careers. Appeals to institutions and the government to provide essential funding for medical and health research. Engages in multimedia communications programs and serves as a clearinghouse and source of information to members, the media, the general public, and elected officials. Conducts public opinion polls and outreach programs; provides a unified link between citizens and local, state, and national opinion leaders and decision makers. **Awards:** Advocacy Awards. **Frequency:** annual. **Type:** recognition. **Recipient:** for outstanding advocacy for medical research ● Eugene Garfield Economic Impact on Medical Research Award. **Type:** recognition. **Committees:** Prevention Research Initiative Advisory; Scientific Advisory. **Publications:** *Membership Matters*, monthly. Newsletter. **Price:** included in membership dues. **Circulation:** 1,600 ● *Research Advocate*, monthly. Newsletter ● *Research! America Annual Report*, annual. Alternate Formats: online ● *Virtual News Stand*, monthly. Articles. Contains selected articles from The Research Advocate. Alternate Formats: online.

14799 ■ RGK Foundation
1301 W 25th St., Ste.300
Austin, TX 78705-4236
Ph: (512)474-9298
Fax: (512)474-7281
URL: http://www.rgkfoundation.org
Contact: Gregory A. Kozmetsky, Chm./Pres./Treas.
Founded: 1966. **Description:** Works to promote medical research. **Awards: Type:** grant.

14800 ■ Student Society for Stem Cell Research (SSSCR)
303 Bannockburn Ave.
Tampa, FL 33617
Ph: (813)368-8937

E-mail: info@ssscr.org
URL: http://www.ssscr.org
Contact: Marion J. Riggs, Founder
Founded: 2003. **Multinational. Description:** Promotes stem cell research by conducting education outreach to communities and disseminating petitions to world bodies about the importance of stem cell research. Serves as a forum of exchange and networking for undergraduates, students, researchers and young professionals around the world to discuss ways to alleviate and find a cure for the disease. **Publications:** Brochure. Contains information about the organization and stem cell education. Alternate Formats: online.

14801 ■ W.M. Keck Foundation
550 S Hope St., Ste.2500
Los Angeles, CA 90071
Ph: (213)680-3833
E-mail: info@wmkeck.org
URL: http://www.wmkeck.org
Contact: Robert A. Day, Pres./Chm./CEO
Founded: 1954. **Description:** Works to support medical research, science, and engineering. **Awards: Type:** grant.

Medical Specialties

14802 ■ American Association of Medical Dosimetrists (AAMD)
One Physics Ellipse
College Park, MD 20740
Ph: (301)209-3320
Fax: (301)209-3343
E-mail: aamd@aapm.org
URL: http://www.medicaldosimetry.org
Contact: Rudi J. Bertrand CMD, Pres.
Membership Dues: full, associate, $150 (annual) ● student, $50 (annual). **Multinational. Description:** Promotes and supports the medical dosimetry profession. **Awards:** Varian Award of Excellence. **Frequency:** annual. **Type:** grant. **Recipient:** for the recognition of contributions and achievements made in the field of Radiation Oncology Dosimetry. **Telecommunication Services:** electronic mail, aamd@medicaldosimetry.org. **Committees:** Administrative Conference; Awards; Education; Government Relations; Information Technology; Job Listing Service; Med Dos Human Resources; Protocol and Ethics. **Publications:** *Fanlines*, semiannual. Newsletter. Provides a forum for the Board of Directors and Committee Chairs to communicate with the membership. **Price:** included in membership dues ● *Medical Dosimetry*, quarterly. Journal. Features clinically related and continuing education articles, directed journal reading assessment, and upcoming events. **Price:** included in membership dues ● *Salary Survey* ● Membership Directory. **Conventions/Meetings:** annual meeting.

14803 ■ American Board of Medical Specialties (ABMS)
1007 Church St., Ste.404
Evanston, IL 60201-5913
Ph: (847)491-9091
Free: (866)ASK-ABMS
Fax: (847)328-3596
E-mail: info@abms.org
URL: http://www.abms.org
Contact: Stephen H. Miller MPH, Pres./CEO
Founded: 1933. **Members:** 32. **Staff:** 18. **Budget:** $2,500,000. **Description:** Primary medical specialty boards and conjoint boards; organizations with related interests are associate members. Acts as spokesman for approved medical specialty boards as a group; is actively concerned with the establishment, maintenance, and elevation of standards for the education and qualification of physicians recognized as specialists through the certification procedures of its members; cooperates with other groups concerned in establishing standards, policies, and procedures for ensuring the maintenance of continued competence of such physicians. Compiles statistics. **Libraries: Type:** reference. **Holdings:** archival material,

business records, monographs. **Subjects:** evaluation of physicians, graduate medical education. **Awards:** Distinguished Service Award. **Frequency:** annual. **Type:** recognition. **Recipient:** for individuals who have made significant contributions to the development, training, education and evaluation of physicians. **Computer Services:** database, certified medical specialists. **Committees:** Bylaws; Certification, Subcertification and Recertification; Competence. **Subgroups:** Finance; Nominating. **Supersedes:** Advisory Board for Medical Specialties. **Publications:** *ABMS Directory of Board Certified Medical Specialists,* annual. Contains four volumes listing over 500000 specialists certified by 24 U.S. medical specialty boards. Arranged by specialty, name, and location. **Price:** $525.00/copy; $1,200.00 CD-ROM. ISSN: 0884-1543. Alternate Formats: CD-ROM ● *ABMS Record,* quarterly. Newsletter. Reports on events related to medical certification and education. Includes meeting reports. **Price:** free ● *American Board of Medical Specialties - Annual Report and Reference Handbook,* annual. Serves as a guide to medical specialty boards and specialty certification. **Price:** $12.50. Alternate Formats: online ● Also publishes text publications on evaluating physicians. **Conventions/Meetings:** annual conference and general assembly - March, always Chicago, IL ● periodic conference ● annual Interim - conference, always Chicago, IL - usually in September.

14804 ■ American Society of Ocularists (ASO)
PO Box 608
Earlysville, VA 22936-0608
Ph: (434)973-4066
Free: (866)973-4066
E-mail: tzappone@ocularist.org
URL: http://www.ocularist.org
Contact: Ms. Toni Zappone, Exec. Dir.
Founded: 1957. **Description:** Technicians specializing in artificial eyes. Promotes research in the field of ophthalmic prosthetics and provides education and support members. **Publications:** *Journal of Ophthalmic Prosthetics,* annual. Features original articles containing clinical and research information for professionals who serve patients that have suffered eye loss. **Price:** $35.00 in North America; $45.00 outside North America. **Conventions/Meetings:** annual meeting - mid-year ● annual meeting - 2007 Oct. 19-24, Chicago, IL; 2008 Nov. 8-12, Atlanta, GA.

14805 ■ Certification Board for Sterile Processing and Distribution (CBSPD)
2 Indus. Park Rd., Ste.3
Alpha, NJ 08865
Ph: (908)454-9555
Free: (800)555-9765
Fax: (908)454-9554
E-mail: cbspd@att.net
URL: http://www.sterileprocessing.org
Contact: Nancy Chobin RN, Exec. Dir.
Founded: 1988. **Description:** Works to certify healthcare sterile processing and distribution personnel. **Formerly:** (2004) National Institute for the Certification of Healthcare Sterile Processing and Distribution Personnel.

14806 ■ Council of Medical Specialty Societies (CMSS)
51 Sherwood Terr., Ste.M
Lake Bluff, IL 60044-2232
Ph: (847)295-3456
Fax: (847)295-3759
E-mail: mailbox@cmss.org
URL: http://www.cmss.org
Contact: Walter J. McDonald MD, Exec. VP
Founded: 1965. **Members:** 20. **Membership Dues:** society, $3,750-$45,000 (annual). **Staff:** 4. **Budget:** $450,000. **Description:** National medical specialty societies representing 400,000 physicians. Improves the quality of medical care in the United States and fosters excellence in the education of physicians. Provides a forum for discussion by specialty societies of national issues affecting the practice and teaching of medicine. Promotes communication among specialty organizations involved in the principal disci-

plines of medicine. **Telecommunication Services:** electronic mail, wmcdonald@cmss.org. **Formerly:** Tri-College Council. **Conventions/Meetings:** semiannual meeting - usually March and November.

14807 ■ NIDCD - National Temporal Bone, Hearing and Balance Pathology Resource Registry (NTBR)
Massachusetts Eye and Ear Infirmary
243 Charles St.
Boston, MA 02114-3002
Ph: (617)573-3711
Free: (800)822-1327
Fax: (617)573-3838
E-mail: tbregistry@meei.harvard.edu
URL: http://www.tbregistry.org
Contact: Dr. Joseph B. Nadol Jr., Co-Dir.
Founded: 1960. **Staff:** 6. **Description:** Promotes research of hearing and balance disorders through the study of the temporal bone and related brain structures. Encourages individuals with hearing or balance disorders to bequeath their temporal bones to scientific research. Serves as a clearinghouse for information on temporal bone research. Develops strategies to conserve human temporal bone collections. Maintains a nationwide network to retrieve donated temporal bone and brain tissue. **Libraries: Type:** reference. **Holdings:** articles. **Subjects:** hearing disorders, hearing research. **Computer Services:** database, temporal bone specimens in U.S. **Telecommunication Services:** TDD, (617)573-3888 ● TDD, (888)561-3277. **Formerly:** (1992) National Temporal Bone Banks Program of The DRF; (1997) National Temporal Bone Registry; (1999) National Temporal Bone, Hearing and Balance Pathology Registry; (2003) National Temporal Bone, Hearing and Balance Pathology Resource Registry. **Publications:** *The Gift of Hearing, That Others May Hear.* Brochures ● *The Registry,* semiannual. Newsletter. Includes information about temporal bone research and donations. **Price:** free. **Circulation:** 20,000.

14808 ■ Periodic Paralysis Association (PPA)
1101 Douglas Dr.
Tracy, CA 95304-5879
Ph: (626)638-3326
E-mail: inquire@periodicparalysis.org
URL: http://www.periodicparalysis.org
Contact: Patrick E. Cochran PhD, Pres./Founder
Founded: 1997. **Description:** Offers information, support to those inflicted with periodic paralysis and brings awareness to the public of this disorder. **Libraries: Type:** reference. **Holdings:** video recordings. **Publications:** *PPA Communique.* Newsletter. Alternate Formats: online.

Medical Technology

14809 ■ Accreditation Review Committee on Education in Surgical Technology (ARC-ST)
6 W Dry Creek Cir., Ste.210
Littleton, CO 80120
Ph: (303)694-9262
Fax: (303)741-3655
E-mail: elaine.mcfarlane@arcst.org
URL: http://www.arcst.org
Contact: Ron Kruzel MA, Exec. Dir.
Founded: 1974. **Members:** 418. **Staff:** 4. **Description:** Reviews accreditation applications of surgical technology programs in hospitals, community colleges, technical schools, and universities and makes recommendations to the Commission on Accreditation of Allied Health Education Programs. Collaborates with American College of Surgeons, American Hospital Association, and the Association of Surgical Technologists. **Affiliated With:** American College of Surgeons; American Hospital Association; Association of Surgical Technologists. **Formerly:** (1987) Joint Review Committee on Education for the Surgical Technologist; (1990) Accreditation Review Committee for Educational Programs in Surgical Technology. **Publications:** *ARC-ST Communique,* quarterly. Newsletter ● *Surgical Technology: A Growing Career.* Brochure. Contains information on

careers in surgical technology, educational requirements, and a list of accredited programs. **Price:** free (first copy); $1.00/additional copy. **Conventions/ Meetings:** annual Instructors Workshop, for program inspectors - always spring ● semiannual meeting - always spring and fall.

14810 ■ Accrediting Bureau of Health Education Schools (ABHES)
7777 Leesburg Pike, Ste.314 N
Falls Church, VA 22043
Ph: (703)917-9503
Fax: (703)917-4109
E-mail: info@abhes.org
URL: http://www.abhes.org
Contact: Carol A. Moneymaker, Exec. Dir.
Founded: 1964. **Members:** 180. **Staff:** 5. **Budget:** $600,000. **Description:** Serves as a nationally recognized accrediting agency of health education institutions and schools conducting medical laboratory technician and medical assistant education programs. Establishes criteria and standards for the administration and operation of health education institutions. Seeks to enhance the profession through the improvement of schools, courses, and the competence of graduates. Schools must apply voluntarily for accreditation; once accredited, they must report to the bureau annually and be reexamined at least every 6 years. Has accredited 15 programs for medical laboratory technicians, 124 medical assistants, and 80 institutions of allied health. **Formerly:** Accrediting Bureau of Medical Laboratory Schools. **Publications:** *Accrediting Bureau of Health Education Schools—Directory of Accredited Schools and Programs,* annual. Lists education institutions and programs accredited by the commissioners of the ABHES. ● *Advantage,* quarterly. Newsletter. Includes calendar of events, news, lists personnel and commissioners. **Conventions/Meetings:** semiannual meeting, with school actions and policy discussion - May and November ● workshop, on accreditation, educational, and school operations.

14811 ■ American Academy of Anti-Aging Medicine (A4M)
c/o Dr. Ronald Klatz, Pres.
1510 W Montana St.
Chicago, IL 60614
Ph: (773)528-1000
Fax: (773)528-5390
E-mail: info@worldhealth.net
URL: http://www.worldhealth.net
Contact: Dr. Ronald Klatz, Pres.
Founded: 1993. **Members:** 11,500. **Membership Dues:** physician, $150 (annual) ● scientific/healthcare, $95 (annual) ● preferred general public, $89 (annual). **Description:** Dedicated to the advancement of technology to detect, prevent, and treat aging related disease and to promote research into methods to retard and optimize the human aging process. Also educates physicians, scientists and members of the public on anti-aging issues. Seeks to disseminate information concerning innovative science and research as well as treatment modalities designed to prolong human lifespan. **Libraries: Type:** reference. **Holdings:** articles, audio recordings, books, video recordings. **Subjects:** anti-aging. **Computer Services:** database ● mailing lists. **Publications:** *Anti-Aging Medical News,* quarterly. Newsletter. **Price:** included in membership dues ● *Bio Tech.* Newsletter. **Price:** included in membership dues. Alternate Formats: online ● *Report of the Medical Committee on Aging Research & Education,* quarterly. Newsletter. **Conventions/Meetings:** Anti-Aging Medicine and Biotechnology - congress, international scientific and medical conference - usually in December ● annual Office Based Anti-Aging Physician - seminar, scientific medical conference - usually in summer.

14812 ■ American Association of Bioanalysts Board of Registry (ABOR)
906 Olive St., Ste.1200
St. Louis, MO 63101-1434
Ph: (314)241-1445
Fax: (314)241-1449

E-mail: aab@aab.org
URL: http://www.aab.org
Contact: Mark S. Birenbaum PhD, Admin.
Founded: 1962. **Staff:** 5. **Description:** Autonomous certifying agency for medical technologists, laboratory technicians, and physician office laboratory technicians. Maintains Continuing Education for Professional Advancement (CEPA) program to approve and record continuing education unit credits. **Convention/Meeting:** none. **Formerly:** Accrediting Commission; (2000) Credentialing Commission.

14813 ■ American Medical Technologists (AMT)
10700 W Higgins Rd.
Rosemont, IL 60018
Ph: (847)823-5169
Free: (800)275-1268
Fax: (847)823-0458
URL: http://www.amt1.com
Contact: Christopher A. Damon JD, Exec. Dir.
Founded: 1939. **Members:** 35,000. **Staff:** 22. **Budget:** $3,000,000. **State Groups:** 38. **Description:** Represents medical technologists, medical laboratory technicians, medical assistants, medical administrative specialists, dental assistants, office laboratory technicians, phlebotomy technicians, laboratory consultants, and allied health instructors. Provides allied health professionals with professional certification services and membership programs to enhance their professional and personal growth. Aims to issue certification credentials to medical and dental assistants, clinical laboratory personnel, laboratory consultants, and allied health instructors. **Awards:** Distinguished Achievement. **Frequency:** annual. **Type:** recognition. **Recipient:** for involvement on state level ● Exceptional Merit. **Frequency:** annual. **Type:** recognition. **Recipient:** for involvement on national level ● Member and Student Writing. **Frequency:** annual. **Type:** recognition. **Recipient:** for essay and technical writing ● Order of the Golden Microscope. **Type:** recognition ● President's Award. **Frequency:** annual. **Type:** recognition. **Recipient:** for outstanding contribution/leadership skills to state society ● RMA Medallion of Merit. **Type:** recognition. **Recipient:** for an outstanding member ● RMA of the Year. **Frequency:** annual. **Type:** recognition. **Recipient:** for extraordinary service and contributions at all levels within AMT and to the medical assisting profession ● Technologist of the Year. **Frequency:** annual. **Type:** recognition. **Recipient:** for extraordinary service and contributions at all levels within AMT and to the laboratory profession. **Boards:** Directors. **Committees:** Education, Qualifications and Standards; Scientific Information Service; Vocational Guidance. **Publications:** *AMT Events and Continuing Education Supplement*, quarterly. Journal. Includes book reviews and legislative updates. **Price:** included in membership dues; $35.00 /year for nonmembers in U.S.; $45.00 /year for nonmembers outside U.S. ISSN: 0746-9217. **Circulation:** 25,000. **Advertising:** accepted. Alternate Formats: microform ● *Continuing Education Topics & Issues*, 3/year. Journal. **Price:** $50.00/year in U.S.; $60.00/year outside U.S. **Conventions/Meetings:** annual Educational and National Meeting - convention and meeting, educational sessions and business/town hall meeting, awards program five days long (exhibits) - always June or July.

14814 ■ American Registry of Radiologic Technologists (ARRT)
1255 Northland Dr.
St. Paul, MN 55120-1155
Ph: (651)687-0048
URL: http://www.arrt.org
Contact: Jerry B. Reid PhD, Exec. Dir.
Founded: 1922. **Members:** 250,000. **Membership Dues:** individual, $15 (annual). **Staff:** 45. **Description:** Radiologic technologist certification board that administers examinations, issues certificates of registration to radiographers, nuclear medicine technologists, and radiation therapists, and investigates the qualifications of practicing radiologic technologists. Governed by trustees appointed from American College of Radiology and American Society

of Radiologic Technologists. **Convention/Meeting:** none. **Formerly:** American Registry of X-Ray Technicians; (1936) American Registry of Radiological Technicians. **Publications:** *ARRT Annual Report*, annual. Alternate Formats: online ● *Educator Update*, semiannual, Newsletter.

14815 ■ American Society of Extra-Corporeal Technology (AmSECT)
2209 Dickens Rd.
Richmond, VA 23230-2005
Ph: (804)565-6363
Fax: (804)282-0090
E-mail: stewart@amsect.org
URL: http://www.amsect.org
Contact: Stewart Hinckley, Exec. Dir.
Founded: 1964. **Members:** 3,000. **Membership Dues:** active, $225 (annual) ● associate, $125 (annual) ● international, $90 (annual) ● clinical associate, autotransfusion, $75 (annual) ● student, $15 (annual). **Staff:** 5. **Budget:** $600,000. **Regional Groups:** 11. **Description:** Perfusionists, technologists, doctors, nurses, and others actively employed and using the applied skills relating to the practice of extracorporeal technology (involving heart-lung machines); student members. Disseminates information necessary to the proper practice of the technology. Conducts programs in continuing education and professional-public liaison and hands-on workshops. Maintains placement service. **Awards:** **Frequency:** annual. **Type:** recognition ● Research Grant Award. **Frequency:** annual. **Type:** grant ● **Type:** scholarship. **Computer Services:** Mailing lists. **Committees:** Education; Liaison. **Formerly:** (1968) American Society of Extracorporeal Circulation Technicians. **Publications:** *AMSECT Today*, 11/year. Magazine. Includes calendar of events, reading and employment opportunities lists, and reports of regional events. **Price:** included in membership dues; $55.00 /year for nonmembers. ISSN: 0747-3079. **Circulation:** 2,800. **Advertising:** accepted ● *Journal of Extra-Corporeal Technology*, quarterly. Covers dialysis, hemodynamics, organs and tissues , oxygenation, and research. Includes book reviews, case studies and membership directory. **Price:** included in membership dues; $70.00 /year for nonmembers. ISSN: 0022-1058. **Circulation:** 2,800 ● Also publishes self-study modules and monographs. **Conventions/Meetings:** annual international conference, with equipment used in operating room during open heart surgery (exhibits).

14816 ■ American Society for Mohs Histotechnology (ASMH)
555 E Wells St., Ste.1100
Milwaukee, WI 53202
Ph: (414)347-1103
Fax: (414)276-3349
URL: http://www.mohscollege.org/ASMH.htm
Contact: Cindy Rice HT, Pres.
Founded: 1995. **Membership Dues:** general, $125 (annual). **Description:** Encourages the professional growth and advancement of Mohs histotechnology practitioners. Promotes the exchange of ideas and knowledge significant to Mohs histotechnology. Assists in the establishment and mutual understanding of related societies. **Publications:** *ASMH Newsletter*, quarterly. Contains updates on the organization and recent articles about Mohs histotechnology. **Price:** included in membership dues. Alternate Formats: online.

14817 ■ American Society of Radiologic Technologists (ASRT)
15000 Central Ave. SE
Albuquerque, NM 87123-3909
Ph: (505)298-4500
Free: (800)444-2778
Fax: (505)298-5063
E-mail: customerinfo@asrt.org
URL: http://www.asrt.org
Contact: Cynthia K. Daniels, Pres.
Founded: 1920. **Members:** 120,000. **Membership Dues:** active/associate, $105 (annual) ● student, $30 (annual) ● retired, $52 (annual). **Staff:** 65. **Budget:** $10,000,000. **Regional Groups:** 10. **State Groups:**

50. **Description:** Serves as professional society of diagnostic radiography, radiation therapy, ultrasound, and nuclear medicine technologists. Advances the science of radiologic technology; establishes and maintains high standards of education; evaluates the quality of patient care; improves the welfare and socioeconomics of radiologic technologists. Operates ASRT Education and Research Foundation, which provides educational materials to radiologic technologists. **Awards:** Fellow American Society of Radiologic Technologists. **Frequency:** annual. **Type:** recognition. **Computer Services:** Mailing lists. **Formerly:** (1934) American Society of Radiographers; (1964) American Society of X-Ray Technicians. **Publications:** *ASRT Scanner*, monthly. Magazine. Includes calendar of events, member profiles, state affiliate news, educational opportunities, and research updates. **Price:** included in membership dues. ISSN: 0161-3863. **Circulation:** 85,000. **Advertising:** accepted ● *Radiation Therapist*, semiannual. Journal. **Price:** included in membership dues; $30.00 /year for nonmembers in U.S.; $60.00 /year for nonmembers outside U.S. **Circulation:** 13,000. **Advertising:** accepted ● *Radiologic Technology*, bimonthly. Journal. Includes advertisers and cumulative annual author and title indexes, book reviews, literature abstracts, and calendar of events. **Price:** $60.00 /year for individuals in U.S.; $90.00 /year for individuals outside U.S. ISSN: 0033-8397. **Circulation:** 100,000. **Conventions/Meetings:** annual conference (exhibits) ● annual Radiation Therapy Conference - conference and meeting, held in conjunction with American Society for Therapeutic Radiology and Oncology (exhibits) - 2007 Oct. 28-30, Los Angeles, CA.

14818 ■ Association for Education in Healthcare Information Technology
401 N Michigan Ave., Ste.2400
Chicago, IL 60611
Ph: (312)321-6839 (312)673-4770
Fax: (312)673-6721
E-mail: info@insight-net.org
URL: http://www.insight-net.org
Contact: Howard Fisher, Exec. Dir.
Membership Dues: individual, outsourced, consultant, $90 (annual) ● affiliate business partner, $1,500 (annual). **Description:** Employees, consultants in healthcare industry. Works to provide its members with information on the healthcare industry and related information technology issues. **Conventions/Meetings:** annual Insight Conference - lecture, with educators (exhibits).

14819 ■ Association of Surgical Technologists (AST)
6 W Dry Creek Cir.
Littleton, CO 80120
Ph: (303)694-9130
Free: (800)637-7433
Fax: (303)694-9169
E-mail: bteutsch@ast.org
URL: http://www.ast.org
Contact: William J. Teutsch, CEO
Founded: 1969. **Members:** 17,700. **Membership Dues:** active, associate, affiliate, $80 (annual) ● young professional, $65 (annual) ● retired/disabled, $45 (annual). **Staff:** 25. **Budget:** $980,000. **Description:** Individuals who have received specific education and training to deliver surgical patient care in the operating room. Membership categories are available for both certified and student surgical technologists. Emphasis is placed on encouraging members to participate actively in a continuing education program. Aims are: to study, discuss, and exchange knowledge, experience, and ideas in the field of surgical technology; to promote a high standard of surgical technology performance in the community for quality patient care; to stimulate interest in continuing education. Local groups sponsor workshops and institutes. Conducts research. **Awards:** AST Scholarship. **Frequency:** annual. **Type:** scholarship. **Recipient:** for students enrolled in CAAHEP accredited programs. **Computer Services:** Mailing lists. **Formerly:** (1978) Association of Operating Room Technicians. **Publications:** *AST Core Curriculum for Surgical First Assisting*. Book ● *AST Core Curriculum for Surgical Tech-*

nology. **Book. Price:** $125.00 ● *Identifying Surgical Instruments: A Training Manual.* Contains detailed illustration and information about surgical instruments. **Price:** $31.95 for members; $39.00 for nonmembers ● *The Surgical Technologist,* monthly. Journal. Covers surgical procedures and equipment, aseptic techniques, medical law, and legislation. Also includes association news, and annual subject index. **Price:** included in membership dues; $50.00 /year for nonmembers. **ISSN:** 0164-4238. **Circulation:** 18,000. **Advertising:** accepted ● *Surgical Technologist Certifying Exam Study Guide.* Book. **Price:** $45.00 ● *Surgical Technology for the Surgical Technologist: A Positive Care Approach.* Book. Includes detailed clinical information, strategies and instructions. **Price:** $72.00 for members; $77.00 for nonmembers. **Conventions/Meetings:** periodic competition ● annual conference, educational (exhibits) ● periodic seminar.

14820 ■ Board of Registered Polysomnographic Technologists (BRPT)
8201 Greensboro Dr., Ste.300
McLean, VA 22102
Ph: (703)610-9020
Fax: (703)610-9005
E-mail: info@brpt.org
URL: http://www.brpt.org
Contact: Bobby L. Stanley Jr., Exec. Dir.
Founded: 1978. **Multinational. Description:** Certifying board for the Registered Polysomnographic Technologist (RPSGT) credential, an internationally recognized credential earned by taking a rigorous exam, adhering to strict ethical standards and codes of conduct and requiring recertification every 5 years. Accredited by the National Commission of Certifying Agencies. **Affiliated With:** National Organization for Competency Assurance.

14821 ■ CuresNow
10100 Santa Monica Blvd., Ste.1300
Los Angeles, CA 90067
Ph: (323)660-6362
Free: (888)881-4009
Fax: (310)244-1480
E-mail: act@curesnow.org
URL: http://www.curesnow.org
Contact: Lucy Fisher, Contact
Description: Promotes scientific research in regenerative medicine to find cures for debilitating diseases such as heart disease, cancer, diabetes, Alzheimer's, Parkinson's, ALS, macular degeneration, spinal cord injury, multiple sclerosis, lupus, neurological diseases, autoimmune diseases and others.

14822 ■ ECRI
5200 Butler Pike
Plymouth Meeting, PA 19462-1298
Ph: (610)825-6000
Fax: (610)834-1275
E-mail: info@ecri.org
URL: http://www.ecri.org
Contact: Jeffrey C. Lerner PhD, Pres./CEO
Founded: 1955. **Members:** 5,000. **Staff:** 270. **Languages:** English, Spanish. **Multinational. Description:** Improves the safety, performance, reliability, and cost effectiveness of health care technology through research testing, and publication of results. Provides technical consulting and accident investigation and educational programs. Functions as a worldwide information clearinghouse for health care technology assessment and hazards and deficiencies in medical devices; sponsors seminars. Provides information and technical assistance for planning, procurement and management of medical equipment. Conducts research; compiles statistics and operates speakers' bureau. **Libraries:** Type: reference; not open to the public. **Holdings:** 5,000; archival material, articles, audio recordings, books, papers, reports. **Subjects:** health services research, health technology assessments, evidence reports, medical device evaluations, risk analyses, patient safety resources, environmental health and safety, clinical trials, healthcare standards, clinical guidelines. **Computer Services:** database, medical devices. **Telecommunication Services:** electronic mail, executiveadmins@ecri.org. **Formerly:** (1955) Graduate Pain Research

Foundation; (1968) Emergency Care Research Institute. **Publications:** *Health Devices Alerts,* weekly. **Price:** $3,345.00 ● *Health Devices Sourcebook & Sourcebase,* annual. Directory. **Price:** $695.00. Alternate Formats: online ● *Health Devices System,* monthly. Journal. **Price:** $3,895.00 for members. Alternate Formats: online ● *Health Technology Trends,* monthly. Newsletter. **Price:** $495.00. Alternate Formats: online ● *Healthcare Hazard Control System,* monthly. **Price:** $1,095.00 ● *Healthcare Hazard Management Monitor,* monthly. Newsletter. **Price:** $350.00 ● *Healthcare Product Comparison System,* monthly. **Price:** $2,095.00 ● *Healthcare Risk Control,* monthly. **Price:** $1,495.00 ● *Healthcare Standards Directory and HCS Online,* annual. Directories. Contains index of nearly 40,000 healthcare standards, guidelines, healthcare-related laws and regulations from nearly 1,500 issuing organizations. **Price:** $595.00. Alternate Formats: online ● *Operating Room Risk Management,* bimonthly. **Price:** $675.00 ● *Technology for Respiratory Therapy,* monthly. Newsletter. Evaluates medical devices and summarizes reported problems, hazards, and recalls. Includes research updates and health care technology abstracts. **Price:** $225.00/year.

14823 ■ Foundation for Informed Medical Decision Making (FIMDM)
40 Court St., Ste.200
Boston, MA 02108
Ph: (617)367-2000
Fax: (617)367-0315
E-mail: info@fimdm.org
URL: http://www.fimdm.org
Contact: Floyd J. Fowler Jr., Pres.
Founded: 1989. **Staff:** 2. **Description:** Gathers and contributes scientific research information for use in videotape programs on shared decision making topics. **Libraries:** Type: reference. **Holdings:** reports. **Awards:** Award for Excellence in Research. **Frequency:** annual. **Type:** recognition. **Recipient:** for outstanding research. **Publications:** Video ● Newsletter, quarterly. Includes programs update. Alternate Formats: online.

14824 ■ Health Technology Center
524 2nd St., 2nd Fl.
San Francisco, CA 94107
Ph: (415)537-6978
Fax: (415)537-6949
E-mail: jjanek@healthtech.org
URL: http://www.healthtech.org
Contact: Molly J. Coye MD, Founder/CEO
Founded: 2000. **Description:** Provides information and services to advance technologies that will impact healthcare delivery. **Working Groups:** Health Plan Initiatives; Hospital and Healthcare Environments of the Future; Information Technology; Regional Workforce. **Publications:** *Clinical Focus Reports* ● *High Impact Technology Reports.* Contains examinations of adoption scenarios and market and financial projections. ● *Technology Forecasts Reports.* Provides information on medical devices, biotechnology, pharmaceuticals and Information Technology. ● *Technology Planning Tools.* Reports.

14825 ■ International Association of Medical Equipment Remarketers and Servicers (IAMERS)
183 Lucy Ln.
Wylie, TX 75098-7244
Ph: (201)833-2021
Free: (877)304-2637
Fax: (201)833-2021
E-mail: info@iamers.org
URL: http://www.iamers.org
Contact: Diana Upton, Pres.
Founded: 1993. **Members:** 150. **Membership Dues:** voting, $500 (annual) ● associate, $250 (annual) ● affiliate, $850 (annual). **Staff:** 2. **Budget:** $200,000. **Description:** Dealers, lessors, refurbishers, and services of medical equipment. Promotes ethical business practices and delivers high quality previously owned medical equipment. Offers educational and research programs and maintains a speakers' bureau. **Libraries:** Type: reference; not open to the

public. **Holdings:** articles, clippings. **Awards: Type:** recognition. **Computer Services:** database ● mailing lists ● online services. **Formerly:** (2004) International Association of Medical Equipment Remarketers. **Publications:** Newsletter ● Directory ● Brochure. **Conventions/Meetings:** annual convention and conference ● periodic regional meeting.

14826 ■ Medical Image Perception Society (MIPS)
c/o Jannick Rolland, PhD
CREOL
Univ. Central Florida
4000 Central Florida Blvd.
Orlando, FL 32816-2700
Ph: (407)823-6870
E-mail: rolland@creol.ucf.edu
URL: http://www.mips.ws
Contact: Jannick Rolland PhD, Contact
Membership Dues: full, $50 (annual) ● in-training, $25 (annual). **Description:** Encourages and promotes medical image perception research and education. Establishes forums for the presentation of research and the dissemination of knowledge. Encourages the development of careers in medical image perception research. Promotes research and research funding for medical image perception research at the national level. Cooperates with other organizations whose purposes and goals include medical image perception research and related sciences. **Telecommunication Services:** electronic mail, krupinski@radiology.arizona.edu. **Publications:** Newsletter ● Proceedings. Alternate Formats: CD-ROM. **Conventions/Meetings:** biennial conference - 2007 Oct. 17-20, Iowa City, IA.

14827 ■ National Accrediting Agency for Clinical Laboratory Sciences (NAACLS)
8410 W Bryn Mawr Ave., Ste.670
Chicago, IL 60631
Ph: (773)714-8880
Fax: (773)714-8886
E-mail: info@naacls.org
URL: http://www.naacls.org
Contact: Shauna Anderson PhD, Pres.
Founded: 1973. **Members:** 695. **Staff:** 9. **Budget:** $1,000,000. **Description:** Independently accredits academic programs in hospitals, colleges, and universities for the following health professional classifications: Clinical Laboratory Scientist/Medical Technologist, Clinical Laboratory Technician/Medical laboratory Technician, Cytogenetic Technologist, Histologic Technician, Histotechnologist, Pathologists' Assistant. Independently approves academic programs in hospitals and colleges for the following: Phlebotomist, Clinical Assistant. Establishes standards for quality educational programs; determines if hospitals and colleges are maintaining standards through self-study and on-site visits. Provides workshops for program officials on self-study and accreditation. **Libraries:** Type: reference. **Computer Services:** Mailing lists. **Formerly:** (1973) Board of Schools of the ASCP. **Supersedes:** Board of Schools of Medical Technology. **Publications:** *Guide to Accreditation* ● *NAACLS News,* quarterly. Newsletter. Includes news related to clinical lab professions. **Price:** free to accredited program officials; $15.00 for non-accredited program officials. **Circulation:** 900 ● *NAACLS Program Approval Guide* ● *National Accrediting Agency for Clinical Laboratory Sciences—Annual Report* ● *National Accrediting Agency for Clinical Laboratory Sciences—Standards.* **Conventions/Meetings:** semiannual meeting - always April and September in Chicago, IL.

14828 ■ National Alliance for Health Information Technology
1 N Franklin St., 27th Fl.
Chicago, IL 60606
Ph: (312)422-2181
Fax: (312)422-2190
E-mail: info@nahit.org
URL: http://www.nahit.org
Contact: Scott Wallace, Pres./CEO
Members: 100. **Membership Dues:** care provider, $25,000 (annual) ● full-time physician, $2,500-

$10,000 (annual) ● others (based on revenues), $2,500-$50,000 (annual). **Description:** Works to advance the adoption and implementation of health-care information technology to achieve measurable improvements in patient safety, quality and efficiency. Accelerates the implementation of standards-based information technology to create a unified healthcare system. **Committees:** Technology Leadership.

14829 ■ National Association of Orthopaedic Technologists (NAOT)

8365 Keystone Crossing, Ste.107
Indianapolis, IN 46240
Ph: (317)205-9484
Fax: (317)205-9481
E-mail: naot@hp-assoc.com
URL: http://naot.org
Contact: Kent Lindeman, Exec. Dir.
Founded: 1982. **Members:** 1,100. **Membership Dues:** full, $75 (annual) ● student/associate, $30 (annual) ● military, $50 (annual). **Staff:** 3. **Regional Groups:** 4. **Local Groups:** 23. **Description:** Allied health assistants working with orthopedic patients. Promotes continued professional education of members and other orthopedic health care providers; administers certification examination. Seeks to enhance public understanding of orthopedics. Conducts seminars; compiles statistics. **Awards: Type:** recognition. **Computer Services:** Mailing lists, of continuing education students and members. **Publications:** *Journal of the National Association of Orthopaedic Technologists*, semiannual. Includes orthopaedic articles and case studies. **Circulation:** 1,000. **Advertising:** accepted. **Conventions/Meetings:** annual conference (exhibits) ● annual symposium.

14830 ■ National Credentialing Agency for Laboratory Personnel (NCA)

PO Box 15945-289
Lenexa, KS 66285
Ph: (913)438-5110
Fax: (913)599-5340
E-mail: nca-info@goamp.com
URL: http://www.nca-info.org
Contact: Louann Lawrence, Sec.-Treas.
Founded: 1977. **Members:** 65,000. **Staff:** 4. **Description:** Persons who direct, educate, supervise, or practice in clinical laboratory science. Assures the public and employers of the competence of clinical laboratory personnel; provides a mechanism for individuals demonstrating competency in the field to achieve career mobility. Develops and administers competency-based examinations for certification of clinical laboratory personnel; provides for periodic recertification by examination or through documentation of continuing education. Compiles statistics. **Councils:** Examination. **Affiliated With:** American Society for Clinical Laboratory Science; Association of Genetic Technologists. **Formerly:** (2001) National Certification Agency for Medical Lab Personnel. **Publications:** *Clipboard*, semiannual. Newsletter. **Conventions/Meetings:** annual board meeting.

14831 ■ National Society for Histotechnology (NSH)

4201 Northview Dr., Ste.502
Bowie, MD 20716-2673
Ph: (301)262-6221
Fax: (301)262-9188
E-mail: histo@nsh.org
URL: http://www.nsh.org
Contact: Vincent Della Speranza, Pres.
Founded: 1973. **Members:** 4,800. **Membership Dues:** professional, $60 (annual) ● student, $30 (annual). **Staff:** 5. **Regional Groups:** 9. **State Groups:** 42. **Description:** Histology laboratory technicians, pathologists, laboratory equipment manufacturers' representatives, and interested individuals. Encourages the professional growth and advancement of histoprofessionals and promotes the exchange of ideas and knowledge significant to histotechnology. Assists in the establishment and mutual understanding of related societies. Provides continuing education training courses. Investigates health hazards in the laboratory; ensures the safety of the laboratory; and participates in formulating federal laboratory

regulations. **Awards:** Histotechnologist of the Year Award. **Frequency:** annual. **Type:** recognition ● J.B. McCormick Award. **Frequency:** annual. **Type:** recognition ● Leica Leadership Awards. **Frequency:** annual. **Type:** recognition. **Recipient:** for management and teaching excellence ● Newsletter of the Year Award. **Frequency:** annual. **Type:** recognition ● Rosemary And Donald Ostermeier Memorial Award. **Frequency:** annual. **Type:** recognition. **Recipient:** for members who embody devotion in their profession ● **Type:** scholarship ● William J. Hacker Memorial Award. **Frequency:** annual. **Type:** recognition. **Recipient:** for best scientific paper. **Computer Services:** Mailing lists. **Committees:** Awards; Bylaws; Education; Employment; Health and Safety; Judicial; Public Relations; Quality Control. **Affiliated With:** American Society for Clinical Pathology. **Publications:** *Journal of Histotechnology*, quarterly. Includes anatomy, pathology, enzyme histochemistry, special stains, immunohistochemistry, cytology, and electron microscopy. **Price:** included in membership dues; $70.00 /year for nonmembers in U.S.; $110.00 /year for nonmembers outside U.S. ISSN: 0147-8885. **Circulation:** 5,200. **Advertising:** accepted ● *NSH In Action*, quarterly. Annual Report. **Price:** free for members ● *NSH in Action Newsletter*, quarterly ● Booklets. Pertains to careers. ● Also publishes training aids. **Conventions/Meetings:** annual conference and symposium (exhibits).

14832 ■ Society for Cardiovascular Magnetic Resonance (SCMR)

19 Mantua Rd.
Mount Royal, NJ 08061
Ph: (856)423-8955
Fax: (856)423-3420
E-mail: hq@scmr.org
URL: http://www.scmr.org
Contact: Deborah Berkowitz, Exec. Dir.
Founded: 1994. **Members:** 1,100. **Membership Dues:** regular/industrial, $225 (annual) ● associate/fellow/technologist, $60 (annual). **Multinational. Description:** Physicians and scientists with an interest in cardiovascular magnetic resonance imaging are members; physicians-in-training and doctoral candidates with an interest in the field are associates; medical technologists with at least two years of experience in cardiovascular magnetic resonance are technologist members; nonscientific professionals employed by companies engaged in magnetic resonance imaging are industrial members. Seeks to advance the practice of cardiovascular magnetic resonance; works to improve study and teaching in the field. Facilitates exchange of information among members and between members and physicians and scientists working in related fields. Conducts educational programs in the application of magnetic resonance imaging to cardiovascular conditions. Serves as a clearinghouse on cardiovascular magnetic resonance imaging; sets equipment standards; conducts multicenter trials to develop cardiovascular magnetic resonance imaging methods, clinical applications, and practice standards. **Computer Services:** Mailing lists. **Committees:** Annual Scientific Sessions; Clinical Practice; Clinical Trials; International; Nominating; Publications; Science; Technologist. **Publications:** *Journal for Cardiovascular Magnetic Resonance*, quarterly. Contains basic and clinical research articles, technical notes, review articles, and editorial commentary. **Advertising:** accepted. **Conventions/Meetings:** annual Scientific Sessions - meeting (exhibits) ● periodic seminar ● annual workshop.

14833 ■ Society for Simulation in Healthcare (SSH)

223 N Guadalupe St., PMB 300
Santa Fe, NM 87501
Ph: (505)983-4923
Fax: (505)983-5109
E-mail: info@ssih.org
URL: http://ssih.org
Contact: Beverlee Anderson, Exec. Dir.
Founded: 2004. **Members:** 1,000. **Membership Dues:** active, $125 (annual) ● retired, student, resident, $50 (annual). **Multinational. Description:**

Develops and fosters standards for simulation education and applications that affect health care practices. Stimulates and promotes the professional development of those individuals and institutions interested in simulation modalities and their applications. Fosters an international network of simulation educators. Serves as an international voice for medical simulation concerns. Advocates for improvement and availability of simulation based modalities for education and research. **Publications:** *Simulation in Healthcare*, quarterly. Journal. Includes original manuscripts, case studies, and brief reports. **Price:** included in membership dues. ISSN: 1559-2332. **Advertising:** accepted. Alternate Formats: online.

14834 ■ Society for Whole Body Autoradiography (SWBA)

c/o Alfred Lordi, Sec.
QPS, Quest Pharmaceutical Services
110 Executive Dr., Ste.7
Newark, DE 19702
Ph: (302)369-5204
Fax: (302)369-3753
E-mail: alfred.lordi@questpharm.com
URL: http://www.autoradiography.net
Contact: Eric Solon, Pres.
Founded: 1994. **Description:** Represents scientists dedicated to the utilization of autoradiographic techniques to study the distribution of radio labeled compounds in various preparations. Refines and implements autoradiography in academic and industrial research and development. Focuses on continued education and collaboration with other image-based and related science technologies.

Medicine

14835 ■ Academy of Molecular Imaging (AMI)

PO Box 951735
Los Angeles, CA 90095-1735
Ph: (310)267-2614
Fax: (310)267-2617
E-mail: ami@mednet.ucla.edu
URL: http://www.ami-imaging.org
Contact: Kim Pierce, Exec. Dir.
Membership Dues: physician, scientist, professional, administrator, $325 (annual) ● technologist, RN (practicing), government, emeritus, $170 (annual) ● institutional, $1,500 (annual) ● corporate council, $200,000 (annual) ● associate partner, $10,000 (annual) ● provider - minimum (based on number of scanners), $2,000 (annual) ● provider - maximum (based on number of scanners), $30,000 (annual). **Description:** Promotes molecular diagnostics and molecular therapies. **Councils:** Institute for Clinical PET; Institute for Molecular Imaging/Hires; Institute for Molecular Technologies; Society of Non-Invasive Imaging in Drug Development. **Publications:** *Molecular Imaging and Biology*, bimonthly. Journal. Contains information about various technologies of molecular imaging. ● Newsletter, quarterly. Alternate Formats: online. **Conventions/Meetings:** annual conference ● annual meeting.

14836 ■ Accreditation Council for Continuing Medical Education (ACCME)

515 N State St., Ste.2150
Chicago, IL 60610
Ph: (312)755-7401
Fax: (312)755-7496
E-mail: postmaster@accme.org
URL: http://www.accme.org
Contact: Murray Kopelow MD, Chief Exec.
Founded: 1981. **Staff:** 11. **Description:** Acts as an accrediting agency for sponsors of continuing medical education for physicians. Sponsoring participants are: American Board of Medical Specialties; American Hospital Association; American Medical Association; Association of American Medical Colleges; Association for Hospital Medical Education; Council of Medical Specialty Societies; Federation of State Medical Boards of the United States. **Publications:** none. **Convention/Meeting:** none. **Awards:** Rutledge W. Howard Awards. **Frequency:** periodic. **Type:** recogni-

tion. **Recipient:** for individual and organizational accomplishments ● Willard M. Duff Award. **Frequency:** periodic. **Type:** recognition. **Recipient:** for longtime volunteer service. **Affiliated With:** American Board of Medical Specialties; American Hospital Association; American Medical Association; Association of American Medical Colleges; Association for Hospital Medical Education; Council of Medical Specialty Societies; Federation of State Medical Boards of the United States. **Formerly:** Liaison Committee on Continuing Medical Education.

14837 ■ American Association of Integrative Medicine (AAIM)

2750 E Sunshine
Springfield, MO 65804
Ph: (417)881-9995
Free: (877)718-3053
Fax: (417)823-9959
E-mail: kelly@aaimedicine.com
URL: http://www.aaimedicine.com
Contact: Kelly Snider, Chief Association Off.

Founded: 2000. **Members:** 600. **Membership Dues:** regular, $150 (annual) ● student, $30 (annual) ● international, $175 (annual) ● international diplomate, $400 (annual) ● fellow, $445 (annual) ● international fellow, $470 (annual) ● life, $1,500 ● life, diplomate, $1,900 ● life, fellow, $2,150. **Staff:** 5. **Description:** Seeks to bring together health care providers of both traditional and nontraditional medicine, from varied backgrounds such as acupuncture, massage therapy, herbology, pain management, and pastoral counseling. **Publications:** Newsletter, monthly. **Conventions/Meetings:** annual trade show, with vendors who distribute medical or alternative medicine products.

14838 ■ American Association of Medical Society Executives (AAMSE)

555 E Wells St., Ste.1100
Milwaukee, WI 53202
Ph: (414)221-9275
Fax: (414)276-3349
E-mail: aamse@aamse.org
URL: http://www.aamse.org
Contact: Tricia Bork Canavan, Exec. Dir.

Founded: 1947. **Members:** 1,200. **Membership Dues:** active (first member; add $160 for each additional), $320 (annual) ● unemployed, $160 (annual) ● affiliate, $400 (annual). **Staff:** 4. **Budget:** $520,000. **Description:** Professional society of executives of national, state, regional, or county medical and specialty societies. Conducts continuing education seminars. Makes available management resources and operational evaluations. **Telecommunication Services:** electronic mail, tcanavan@aamse.org. **Formerly:** Medical Society Executives Association. **Publications:** Hotline, monthly. Newsletter ● Who's Who in Medical Society Management, annual. **Conventions/Meetings:** annual conference and meeting - always midsummer.

14839 ■ American Lebanese Medical Association (ALMA)

6302 Princeville Cir.
Huntington Beach, CA 92648
Ph: (714)960-0564
Fax: (714)960-7655
E-mail: paul@almamater.org
URL: http://www.almamater.org
Contact: Dr. Paul Wakim, Pres.

Founded: 1994. **Membership Dues:** active, $100 (annual) ● resident/intern, $50 (annual). **Description:** Health care professionals with Lebanese heritage, or with and interest in providing assistance to the people of Lebanon. Promotes increased access to improved health care for all religious and cultural communities in Lebanon. Fosters development of medical education institutions and health care facilities in Lebanon. Gathers and distributes Lebanese medical and scientific publications; conducts continuing professional education programs for members. Plans to operate library in conjunction with the Lebanese Medical Association. **Computer Services:** database, medical links, neuroscience sites,

neuroscience product information, Med Nexus ● mailing lists. **Conventions/Meetings:** annual convention.

14840 ■ American Medical Association (AMA)

515 N State St.
Chicago, IL 60610
Ph: (312)464-5000
Free: (800)621-8335
Fax: (312)464-4184
E-mail: msc@ama-assn.org
URL: http://www.ama-assn.org
Contact: William G. Plested III, Pres.

Founded: 1847. **Members:** 297,000. **Membership Dues:** regular, $420 (annual) ● second year in medical practice, $315 (annual) ● first year in medical practice, semi-retired, $210 (annual) ● military, $280 (annual) ● fully retired, $84 (annual) ● intern/resident/fellow, $45 (annual) ● intern/resident/fellow, $120 (triennial) ● intern/resident/fellow, $160 (quadrennial) ● medical student, $20 (annual) ● medical student, $38 (biennial) ● medical student, $54 (triennial) ● medical student, $68 (quadrennial). **State Groups:** 54. **Description:** Represents county medical societies and physicians. Disseminates scientific information to members and the public. Informs members on significant medical and health legislation on state and national levels and represents the profession before Congress and governmental agencies. Cooperates in setting standards for medical schools, hospitals, residency programs, and continuing medical education courses. Offers physician placement service and counseling on practice management problems. Operates library that lends material and provides specific medical information to physicians. Maintains Ad-hoc committees for such topics as health care planning and principles of medical ethics. **Awards:** AMA Foundation Excellence in Medicine Awards. **Frequency:** annual. **Type:** recognition. **Recipient:** for medical students, residents/fellows, and young physicians ● Community Service Award. **Frequency:** annual. **Type:** recognition. **Recipient:** for young physicians ● Nathan Davis Awards. **Frequency:** annual. **Type:** recognition. **Recipient:** to elected officials and career government employees for their outstanding endeavors that advance public health ● Nathan Davis International Awards. **Frequency:** annual. **Type:** recognition. **Recipient:** for physicians or health sector organizations that further health information and medical practice ● Physician's Recognition Award. **Frequency:** annual. **Type:** recognition. **Recipient:** for physicians who participate in continuing medical education. **Commissions:** Emergency Medical Services. **Councils:** Ethical and Judicial Affairs; Legislation; Long Range Planning and Development; Medical Education; Medical Service; Science and Public Health. **Absorbed:** (1994) American Association of Senior Physicians. **Publications:** American Medical News, weekly. Newspaper. Covers news and opinions on key issues of political, social, and economic significance concerning the practice and delivery of medical care. **Price:** included in membership dues; $99.00 /year for nonmembers; $49.50/year for medical students, interns, and residents. **Circulation:** 362,200 ● Archives of Dermatology, monthly. Journal. Includes book reviews, employment opportunity listings, annual index, and index of advertisers. **Price:** $67.50 /year for members; $135.00 /year for nonmembers; $67.50/year for residents and medical students. ISSN: 0003-987X. **Circulation:** 14,000. **Advertising:** accepted. Alternate Formats: online ● Archives of Family Medicine, monthly. Journal. Oriented to physicians in family and general practice. **Price:** $47.50 for members; $95.00 for nonmembers. **Circulation:** 83,000. **Advertising:** accepted ● Archives of General Psychiatry, monthly. Journal. Oriented toward the psychiatric clinician. Includes employment opportunity listings, book reviews, annual index, and index of advertisers. **Price:** $47.50 /year for members; $95.00 /year for nonmembers; $47.50/year for residents and medical students. ISSN: 0003-990X. **Circulation:** 27,500. **Advertising:** accepted. Alternate Formats: microform; online ● Archives of Internal Medicine, semimonthly. Journal. Oriented toward physicians in internal medicine. Includes employment opportunity listings, annual index, and index of advertisers. **Price:** $57.50

/year for members; $115.00 /year for nonmembers; $57.50/year for residents and medical students. ISSN: 0003-9926. **Circulation:** 87,000. **Advertising:** accepted. Alternate Formats: microform; online ● Archives of Neurology, monthly. Journal. Oriented toward the neurologic clinician. Includes employment opportunity listings, annual index, and index of advertisers. **Price:** $72.50 /year for members; $145.00 /year for nonmembers; $72.50/year for residents and medical students. ISSN: 0003-9942. **Circulation:** 12,500. **Advertising:** accepted. Alternate Formats: microform; online ● Archives of Ophthalmology, monthly. Journal. Includes employment opportunity listings, case reports, book reviews, annual index, and index of advertisers. **Price:** $55.00 /year for members; $110.00 /year for nonmembers; $55.00/year for residents and medical students. ISSN: 0003-9950. **Circulation:** 20,000. **Advertising:** accepted. Alternate Formats: microform; online ● Archives of Otolaryngology—Head and Neck Surgery, monthly. Journal. Oriented toward the otolaryngolic clinician. Includes employment opportunity listings, annual index, and index of advertisers. **Price:** $62.50 /year for members; $125.00 /year for nonmembers; $62.50/year for residents and medical students. ISSN: 0886-4470. **Circulation:** 12,000. **Advertising:** accepted. Alternate Formats: microform; online ● Archives of Pediatrics and Adolescent Medicine, monthly. Journal. Oriented toward the pediatric clinician. Includes book reviews, employment opportunity listings, annual index, and index of advertisers. **Price:** $50.00 /year for members; $100.00 /year for nonmembers; $50.00/year for residents and medical students. ISSN: 1072-4710. **Circulation:** 35,000. **Advertising:** accepted. Alternate Formats: microform; online. Also Cited As: American Journal of Diseases of Children ● Archives of Surgery, monthly. Journal. Oriented toward general surgeons. Includes employment opportunity listings, calendar of events, book reviews, index of advertisers, and annual index. **Price:** $50.00 /year for members; $100.00 /year for nonmembers; $50.00/year for medical students and residents. ISSN: 0004-0010. **Circulation:** 24,500. **Advertising:** accepted. Alternate Formats: microform; online ● Journal of the American Medical Association, weekly. Covers topics in general medicine; includes employment opportunity listings, book reviews, calendar of events, case reports, and obituaries. **Price:** included in membership dues; $120.00 /year for nonmembers; $60.00/year for medical students and residents. ISSN: 0098-7484. **Circulation:** 361,000. **Advertising:** accepted. Alternate Formats: online. Also Cited As: JAMA. **Conventions/Meetings:** semiannual meeting.

14841 ■ American Medical Association Alliance (AMAA)

515 N State St., 9th Fl.
Chicago, IL 60610
Ph: (312)464-4470
Free: (800)621-8835
Fax: (312)464-5020
E-mail: amaa@ama-assn.org
URL: http://www.ama-assn.org/ama/pub/category/2109.html
Contact: Linda Castilla, Contact

Founded: 1922. **Members:** 70,000. **Membership Dues:** individual, $45 (annual) ● student, $20 (annual) ● physician, $420 (annual). **Staff:** 15. **Budget:** $1,500,000. **State Groups:** 46. **Local Groups:** 815. **National Groups:** 100. **Description:** Physicians' spouses. Serves as the volunteer arm of the American Medical Association. Promotes the goals of the medical profession and works to meet public health needs. Raises more than $2 million annually for the American Medical Association Education and Research Foundation (see separate entry), which provides assistance to medical schools and students. Sponsors the Shape Up for Life Campaign, a nationwide auxiliary program to promote good health. Maintains Project Bank, an information clearinghouse of community projects initiated by auxiliaries across the country. Implements community health projects on such concerns as child abuse prevention, adolescent health, family violence, AIDS education, seatbelt usage, pre and postnatal care, drug abuse, suicide prevention, proper nutrition, drunk driving prevention, venereal disease awareness, and services to the aging. Works with the AMA to promote sound health legislation; conducts public education programs, letter-writing campaigns, and personal interviews with legislators involved in health matters. **Awards:** Health Awareness Promotion Award. **Frequency:** annual. **Type:** recognition. **Committees:** Health Promotion; Legislative Affairs. **Formerly:** (1975) Women's Auxiliary to the American Medical Association; (1993) American Medical Association Auxiliary. **Publications:** *AMA Alliance Today*, 3/year. Magazine. **Price:** included in membership dues ● *Facets Magazine*, bimonthly. Includes information on community health projects, public health issues, socioeconomic health care issues, and physician family concerns. **Price:** included in membership dues; $7.00 /year for nonmembers. ISSN: 0163-0512. **Circulation:** 80,000 ● *Horizons Newsletter*, bimonthly. Covers topics of concern to the families of resident physicians and medical students. **Price:** free to resident physicians and medical students. **Circulation:** 6,000 ● *Newsline*, bimonthly. Includes information on health periodicals and health projects. **Price:** included in membership dues. **Circulation:** 8,000. **Conventions/Meetings:** annual House of Delegates Meeting - always in Chicago, IL.

14842 ■ American Osler Society (AOS)
c/o Charles S. Bryan, MD, Sec.-Treas.
Univ. of South Carolina School of Medicine
Dept. of Medicine
2 Medical Park, Ste.502
Columbia, SC 29203
Ph: (803)540-1000
Fax: (803)540-1075
E-mail: cbryan@gw.mp.sc.edu
URL: http://www.americanosler.org
Contact: Charles S. Bryan MD, Sec.-Treas.
Founded: 1970. **Members:** 135. **Membership Dues:** active, emeritus, honorary, $100 (annual). **Staff:** 1. **Budget:** $60,000. **Description:** Physicians, librarians, and scientists united to further a humanistic approach to the study and practice of medicine as exemplified in the life work of Sir William Osler (1849-1919). **Libraries: Type:** reference. **Holdings:** archival material, books, periodicals. **Awards:** John P. McGovern Award. **Frequency:** annual. **Type:** recognition. **Recipient:** for distinguished leaders ● William B. Bean Student Research Award. **Frequency:** annual. **Type:** recognition. **Recipient:** for students in approved schools of medicine in United States and Canada. **Affiliated With:** American Association for the History of Medicine; American College of Physicians-American Society of Internal Medicine. **Publications:** *Osler Biographical Directory*, annual ● *The Persisting Osler*. Book ● *The Persisting Osler II*. Book ● Also publishes books on Sir William Osler, medical humanism, and the history of medicine. **Conventions/Meetings:** annual conference and meeting.

14843 ■ Americans for Free Choice in Medicine (AFCM)
1525 Superior Ave., Ste.101
Newport Beach, CA 92663
E-mail: mail@afcm.org
URL: http://www.afcm.org
Contact: Richard E. Ralston, Exec. Dir.
Founded: 1993. **Description:** Patients, Medicare recipients, physicians, nurses and health care professionals, insurance industry professionals, pharmacists and pharmaceutical industry professionals, financial services professionals, businessmen, employee benefits professionals, and hospital staff. Promotes the philosophy of individual rights, personal responsibility and free market economics in the health care industry. Sponsors educational programs, lectures and town hall meetings, as well as "The Andrew Lewis Show", a weekly radio show. **Publications:** *Pulse*, biweekly. Newsletter. Provides fast, relevant news about physicians, insurance, drugs, hospitals, HSAs, patients and the battle for individual rights in medicine. Alternate Formats: online.

14844 ■ Association of Haitian Physicians Abroad (AMHE)
1166 Eastern Pkwy.
Brooklyn, NY 11213

Ph: (718)245-1015
Fax: (718)735-8015
URL: http://www.amhe.org
Contact: Dr. Eric Jerome MD, Pres.
Founded: 1972. **Members:** 900. **Membership Dues:** regular, $250 (annual) ● life, $3,000. **Budget:** $35,000. **State Groups:** 8. **Description:** Represents Haitian doctors. Aims to unite Haitian doctors abroad and to organize professional activities among them. Provides charitable assistance to the Haitian community. Sponsors educational programs. **Computer Services:** Mailing lists. **Committees:** Community Relations; Scientific. **Programs:** Visiting Professor. **Task Forces:** Breast Cancer; HIV. **Formerly:** (1986) Haitian Medical Association Abroad. **Publications:** *Directory of Haitian Physicians in New York*, biennial ● *Journal des Medecins Haitien a l'Etranger*, bimonthly ● Also publishes educational materials. **Conventions/Meetings:** periodic conference ● annual meeting (exhibits).

14845 ■ Association of Telehealth Service Providers (ATSP)
4702 SW Scholls Ferry Rd., No. 400
Portland, OR 97225-2008
Ph: (503)922-0988
Free: (800)852-3591
Fax: (315)222-2402
E-mail: info@atsp.org
URL: http://www.atsp.org
Contact: Douglas Perednia MD, Pres.
Founded: 1996. **Membership Dues:** organization, $1,250 (annual) ● individual, $195 (annual). **Description:** Companies providing telemedical services. Seeks to advance the practice of telemedicine and to stimulate the development of more effective telemedical technologies. Provides educational, business leadership, and marketing services to members; facilitates networking among members; makes available discounts on products and services to members; represents members before government agencies, industry organizations, and the public. **Awards:** Special Achievement Telehealth Award. **Frequency:** annual. **Type:** recognition ● Telehealth Healthcare Providers Awards. **Frequency:** annual. **Type:** recognition. **Recipient:** to healthcare providers ● Telehealth Vendor Organizations Awards. **Frequency:** annual. **Type:** recognition. **Recipient:** to vendor organizations. **Computer Services:** Online services, ATSP Interlink. **Formerly:** (2004) Association of Telemedicine Service Providers. **Publications:** *ATSP Annual Survey*, annual ● *ATSP Newsletter*, 3/year. Alternate Formats: online ● *ATSP Telemedicine Telejournal*, bimonthly. Highlights audio teleconference with information on programs and organizations; access to archival material. Alternate Formats: online ● Membership Directory. Contains listing of organizations and companies in the telehealth industry. Alternate Formats: online. **Conventions/Meetings:** annual conference.

14846 ■ Auxiliary to the National Medical Association (ANMA)
1012 10th St. NW
Washington, DC 20001
Ph: (202)371-1674 (202)371-9008
Fax: (202)289-2662
E-mail: anmanationaloffice@earthlink.net
URL: http://www.anma-online.org
Contact: Dr. Beverly J. Anderson, Pres.
Founded: 1935. **Members:** 1,000. **Membership Dues:** regular, $100-$125 ● resident, intern spouse, physician, $50-$60. **Staff:** 1. **Regional Groups:** 6. **State Groups:** 14. **Local Groups:** 40. **Description:** Spouses of active members of the National Medical Association (see separate entry); widows and widowers of former members. Aims are to: create a greater interest in the NMA; assist and encourage the medical profession in its efforts to educate and serve the public in matters of sanitation and health; develop and promote a national program on health and education with subcategories in community needs, legislation, and human relations. Conducts workshops on teenage pregnancy, breast self-examinations, high blood pressure screening, and sickle cell anemia screening. Plans and implements an annual youth

forum under the auspices of the March of Dimes Birth Defects Foundation (see separate entry). **Libraries: Type:** reference. **Holdings:** archival material. **Awards:** Alma Wells Givens Scholarship. **Frequency:** annual. **Type:** scholarship. **Recipient:** to medical students ● Omega Mason Memorial Scholarship. **Type:** scholarship. **Recipient:** to outstanding student nurses. **Affiliated With:** American Cancer Society; National Association for the Advancement of Colored People. **Formerly:** (1975) Women's Auxiliary to the National Medical Association. **Publications:** Book. Covers standard procedures. ● Membership Directory, periodic. **Price:** available to members only ● Newsletter, quarterly. **Conventions/Meetings:** annual convention, held in conjunction with NMA (exhibits).

14847 ■ Bangladesh Medical Association of North America (BMANA)
4250 Hempstead Tpke., Ste.17
Bethpage, NY 11714-5707
Ph: (516)796-4245
Fax: (516)731-1683
E-mail: nhkhan@mail.com
URL: http://www.geocities.com/saabry/bmana.htm
Contact: Nazmul H. Khan MD, Sec.
Founded: 1982. **Members:** 1,000. **Staff:** 1. **Budget:** $100,000. **Regional Groups:** 5. **Description:** Physicians who are from Bangladesh or have graduated from a medical college in Bangladesh. Seeks to bring together and improve communication between physicians who are of Bangladeshi origin or have trained in Bangladesh, and are currently residents of the United States or Canada, and other physicians. Assists medical students and physicians in obtaining specialized medical training and in post-training job placement in North America. **Publications:** none. **Committees:** Advisory Committee for Residency Training; Education and Scientific Affairs; Fund Raising; Medical Relief; Research. **Conventions/Meetings:** annual meeting - always August or last weekend in July.

14848 ■ Chinese American Medical Society (CAMS)
c/o Dr. Hsueh-hwa Wang, MD, Exec. Dir.
281 Edgewood Ave.
Teaneck, NJ 07666
Ph: (201)833-1506
Fax: (201)833-8252
E-mail: hw5@columbia.edu
URL: http://www.camsociety.org
Contact: Pak Chung MD, Pres.
Founded: 1964. **Members:** 980. **Membership Dues:** regular, $200 (annual) ● resident, $25 (annual) ● life, $2,000. **Regional Groups:** 4. **Description:** Physicians of Chinese origin residing in the U.S. and Canada. Seeks to advance medical knowledge, scientific research, and interchange of information among members and to promote the health status of Chinese Americans. Conducts educational meetings; supports research. Maintains placement service. Sponsors limited charitable program. **Awards: Frequency:** annual. **Type:** scholarship ● Scientific Award. **Frequency:** annual. **Type:** recognition. **Recipient:** for member with highest scholastic achievements. **Committees:** Scholarship and Award. **Formerly:** (1985) American Chinese Medical Society. **Publications:** *Chinese American Medical Society—Newsletter*, 3-4/year. Includes membership news, announcements, and calendar of events. **Price:** included in membership dues. **Circulation:** 980. **Advertising:** accepted ● Membership Directory, annual. **Conventions/Meetings:** meeting, scientific (exhibits) ● annual meeting, scientific.

14849 ■ Consortium for Conservation Medicine (CCM)
460 W 34th St., Fl. 17
New York, NY 10001
Ph: (212)380-4473
Fax: (212)380-4475
E-mail: admin@conservationmedicine.org
URL: http://www.conservationmedicine.org
Contact: Dr. Peter Daszak, Exec. Dir.
Multinational. Description: Conducts research that involves animal extinction and biodiversity imbalance

to new pathogens and outbreaks of deadly diseases. Seeks to understand the link between anthropogenic environmental changes, the health of all species, and the conservation of biodiversity. **Projects:** Amphibian Declines; Avian Influenza; Global Hotspots; Nipah Virus; SARS; West Nile Virus; Wildlife Trade; Yellowstone to Yukon. **Affiliated With:** Wildlife Trust. **Publications:** *A DNA-Based Assay Identifies Batrachochytrium Dendrobatidis in Amphibians.* Report. Alternate Formats: online ● *Conservation Medicine: An Emerging Field.* Book. Alternate Formats: online ● *Conservation Medicine: Ecological Health in Practice.* Book ● *Experimental Evidence that the Bullfrog (Rana Catebiana) is a Potential Carrier of Chytridiomycosis, an Emerging Fungal Disease of Amphibians.* Report. Alternate Formats: online ● *West Nile Virus and Wildlife.* Journal. Alternate Formats: online.

14850 ■ Federation of State Medical Boards of the United States (FSMB)
PO Box 619850
Dallas, TX 75261-9850
Ph: (817)868-4000
Fax: (817)868-4099
E-mail: alpp@fsmb.org
URL: http://www.fsmb.org
Contact: James N. Thompson MD, Pres./CEO
Founded: 1912. **Members:** 70. **Membership Dues:** board, $2,000 (annual). **Staff:** 110. **Budget:** $12,000,000. **State Groups:** 69. **Multinational. Description:** Represents state medical examining and licensing boards (including fourteen osteopathic boards). **Libraries: Type:** reference. **Holdings:** 3,500; books, periodicals. **Subjects:** medical licensure and discipline. **Computer Services:** database, Board Action Data Bank. **Committees:** Board; Editorial; Special; USMLE. **Formed by Merger of:** (1912) American Confederation of Reciprocating, Examining and Licensing Medical Boards; American Confederation of State Medical Examining Boards. **Publications:** *Exchange,* biennial. Journal. Contains listing of MD and DO licensing requirements in each state of US. **Price:** $30.00 each volume; $50.00 for set of two volumes ● *FSMB NewsLine,* monthly. Newsletter. **Price:** $35.00/year; $4.00/copy ● *Journal of Medical Licensure and Discipline,* quarterly. **Price:** $70.00 /year for individuals; $140.00 /year for institutions ● Handbook, annual. **Price:** $15.00/copy. **Conventions/Meetings:** annual conference and meeting, includes educational presentations and convening of the House of Delegates - usually April. 2008 May 1-3, San Antonio, TX; 2009 Apr. 30-May 2, Washington, DC; 2010 Apr. 22-24, Chicago, IL.

14851 ■ Foundation for Innovation in Medicine (FIM)
411 North Ave. E
Cranford, NJ 07016
Ph: (908)272-2967
Fax: (908)272-4583
E-mail: fimdefelice@aol.com
URL: http://www.fimdefelice.org
Contact: Stephen L. DeFelice MD, Chm.
Founded: 1976. **Languages:** English, French, Italian. **Description:** Seeks to regenerate interest in medical discovery and innovation, which the foundation believes flourished in the U.S. in the 1940s and 1950s, but has since declined despite "vastly increased public and private expenditures in research and development". Intends to monitor the state of innovation by conducting seminars and conferences. Encourages clinical research on natural substances and substances with little commercial value. **Libraries: Type:** reference. **Holdings:** archival material, books, clippings. **Publications:** *From Oysters to Insulin: Nature and Medicine at Odds.* Book. **Price:** $15.95 ● *Nutraceutical White Paper.* **Price:** $10.00. **Conventions/Meetings:** semiannual Nutraceuticals - conference - always spring and fall.

14852 ■ Friends of the National Library of Medicine (FNLM)
2810 M St. NW
Washington, DC 20002
Ph: (202)719-8094
Fax: (202)338-8182

E-mail: info@fnlm.org
URL: http://www.fnlm.org
Contact: Rob Carter, Exec. Dir.
Founded: 1986. **Members:** 500. **Membership Dues:** patron, $10,000 (annual) ● sponsor, $5,000 (annual) ● contributor, $1,000 (annual) ● donor, $500 (annual) ● regular, $100 (annual). **Staff:** 3. **Description:** Seeks to improve health by increasing the use of the latest, most effective medical and scientific information by health care professionals, scientists, and the general public. Strives to educate the health, corporate, and public communities about the National Library of Medicine by building a coalition of financial and others supporters. **Publications:** Newsletter, monthly. **Price:** included in membership dues. **Conventions/Meetings:** annual Health Information Infrastructure - meeting.

14853 ■ Harvey Society (HS)
c/o Dr. Robert H. Singer, PhD, Sec.
Yeshiva Univ.
Golding Bldg., Rm. 601BA
1300 Morris Park Ave.
Bronx, NY 10461
Ph: (718)430-8646
Fax: (718)430-8697
E-mail: rhsinger@aecom.yu.edu
URL: http://www.harveysociety.org
Contact: Dr. Robert H. Singer PhD, Sec.
Founded: 1905. **Members:** 1,600. **Description:** Persons with a PhD or MD degree active or interested in making contributions to the literature of medical and biological science. Seeks to disseminate knowledge and promote the development of the biomedical sciences. Sponsors a series of public lectures delivered by leaders in the field. (Society is named after William Harvey (1578-1657), who identified the circulation of blood.). **Publications:** *Harvey Lectures,* annual. Book. Contains lectures given during the year. **Conventions/Meetings:** lecture - 8/year, always in New York City.

14854 ■ Healthcare Billing and Management Association (HBMA)
1540 S Coast Hwy., Ste.203
Laguna Beach, CA 92651
Free: (877)640-4262
Fax: (949)376-3456
E-mail: info@hbma.org
URL: http://www.hbma.org
Contact: Sanford J. Hill, Pres.
Founded: 1993. **Membership Dues:** principal (based on the number of employees), $600-$1,300 (annual) ● affiliate, vendor affiliate, $900 (annual) ● satellite officer, $250 (annual) ● associate, $150 (annual). **Staff:** 20. **Description:** Represents companies that provide third party medical billing services. **Publications:** *Billing,* monthly. Newsletter. Alternate Formats: online.

14855 ■ International Association for Dance Medicine and Science (IADMS)
1214 Univ. of Oregon
Dept. of Dance
Eugene, OR 97403-1214
Ph: (541)465-1763
Fax: (541)465-1763
E-mail: executivedirector@iadms.org
URL: http://www.iadms.org
Contact: Steven J. Chatfield PhD, Exec.Dir.
Founded: 1990. **Members:** 800. **Membership Dues:** physician, $85 (annual) ● dancer/student, $25 (annual) ● dance school/company, $100 (annual) ● educator, healthcare provider, $45 (annual) ● health care professional, $60 (annual) ● dance company director, $85 (annual). **Staff:** 3. **Budget:** $105,000. **Multinational. Description:** Serves as a forum for reeducation, promotion of research and public services in the field of dance medicine and science. Committed to providing continuing education for the dance and medical communities as well as the public regarding appropriate training for dance. Offers educational programs. **Computer Services:** Online services. **Publications:** *Annual Meeting Proceedings,* annual. Contains abstracts and summaries of presentations given at the IADMS Annual Meeting. ●

Dance Medicine Resource Guide. Directory. Contains information on health care professionals in the field of dance medicine. **Price:** $34.95 for nonmembers; $29.95 for members ● *The Dance Medicine/Science Bibliography.* Contains listing of all English language dance medicine articles (from 1975 to the present). **Price:** $42.95 for nonmembers; $35.00 for members ● *IADMS Newsletter,* quarterly. Offers information of recent activities both within the organization and the dance medicine field in general. ● *Journal of Dance Medicine/Science,* quarterly. Peer-reviewed medical journal. **Price:** $59.00 for individual subscription; $70.00 for library and institution; $49.00 for members; $59.00 for international members. **Conventions/Meetings:** annual conference and board meeting (exhibits).

14856 ■ International Society for Mountain Medicine (ISMM)
5390 N Acad. Blvd., Ste.310
Colorado Springs, CO 80918
Ph: (719)572-1372
Free: (800)967-7494
Fax: (719)572-1514
E-mail: membership@ismmed.org
URL: http://www.ismmed.org
Contact: Peter Hackett MD, Contact
Founded: 1985. **Members:** 450. **Membership Dues:** regular, $90 (annual) ● corresponding, $75 (annual) ● student, resident, $55 (annual). **Staff:** 1. **Multinational. Description:** Brings together scientists and physicians, and allied trade professionals interested in mountain medicine. Encourages research on all aspects of mountains, mountain people and mountaineers. **Awards:** ISMM Research Prize. **Frequency:** biennial. **Type:** monetary. **Recipient:** for scientific merit. **Publications:** *High Altitude Medicine and Biology,* quarterly. Journal. Provides information about high altitude/mountain physiology and clinical medicine. **Price:** included in membership dues. **Advertising:** accepted. Alternate Formats: online. **Conventions/Meetings:** biennial World Congress On Mountain Medicine - international conference and congress (exhibits).

14857 ■ International Society of Travel Medicine (ISTM)
PO Box 871089
Stone Mountain, GA 30087-0028
Ph: (770)736-7060
Fax: (770)736-6732
E-mail: istm@istm.org
URL: http://www.istm.org
Contact: Brenda Bagwell, Admin. Dir.
Members: 2,000. **Membership Dues:** individual, $125 (annual) ● individual, $250 (biennial) ● nurse, physician assistant, student, $75 (annual). **Multinational. Description:** Represents individuals committed to the promotion of healthy and safe travel. Advocates and facilitates education, service, and research activities in the field of travel medicine. Stimulates the professional advancement of travel medicine practice. Promotes development and evaluation of safe, effective, preventive and curative interventions. Fosters research in travel medicine. **Awards:** Research Grants. **Frequency:** annual. **Type:** grant. **Recipient:** for travel medicine researchers. **Publications:** *Journal of Travel Medicine,* bimonthly. Contains up-to-date research and peer-reviewed articles. **Price:** included in membership dues; $170.00 for nonmembers. Alternate Formats: online ● *NewsShare,* bimonthly. Newsletter. Contains news, views and notices for members. **Price:** included in membership dues. Alternate Formats: online.

14858 ■ Iranian American Medical Association (IAMA)
397 Haledon Ave.
Haledon, NJ 07508
Ph: (973)595-8888
Fax: (973)790-7755
E-mail: info@iama.org
URL: http://www.iama.org
Contact: Jasmin Moshirpur MD, Pres.
Multinational. Description: Disseminates medical knowledge to all members by means of journals,

meetings and continuous medical education. Encourages all members to seek further education in their respected fields. Promotes and maintains professional relationships among members in the US and in Iran. Provides financial assistance and guidance to Iranian students and students of Iranian descent studying in the field of medicine or allied medical sciences in the USA and Iran. Provides medical assistance to needy Iranians by establishing medical clinics in different states of the US. **Computer Services:** Information services, social and cultural resources ● online services, forums. **Boards:** Trustees. **Projects:** Bam. **Publications:** Bulletin, annual. Alternate Formats: online.

14859 ■ Korean-American Medical Association (KAMA)
40 Bennett Rd.
Englewood, NJ 07631-3306
Ph: (201)541-1345
Fax: (201)541-1344
E-mail: info@koreanama.org
URL: http://www.koreanama.org
Contact: Dr. Hoo Geun Chun, Pres.
Founded: 1974. **Members:** 4,300. **Membership Dues:** general, $50 (annual) ● life, $300. **Languages:** English, Korean. **Description:** Korean-American physicians. Purpose is to provide a social and scientific forum for the exchange of scholarly information among members and between Korean-Americans and Korean physicians. Plans to offer scholarship program and to form liaisons with other health care professional societies. **Formerly:** Korean-American Medical Association of America. **Publications:** KAMA News, 3/year. Newsletter. Alternate Formats: online ● Membership Directory, quinquennial. **Conventions/Meetings:** annual convention ● semiannual meeting - always summer and winter.

14860 ■ National Association of Residents and Interns (NARI)
Hillsboro Executive Center N
350 Fairway Dr., Ste.200
Deerfield Beach, FL 33441-1834
Ph: (954)571-1877
Free: (800)221-2168
Fax: (954)571-8582
E-mail: membership@assnservices.com
URL: http://www.nari-assn.com
Founded: 1959. **Members:** 40,000. **Membership Dues:** individual, $35 (annual) ● individual, $85 (triennial). **Staff:** 23. **Description:** Medical and dental students, interns, residents, and fellows. Contributes to the economic welfare of members through unsecured loan plans, affordable group insurance, group purchase discounts, and continuing medical education programs. **Computer Services:** database. **Publications:** Association's Digest, semiannual. Newsletter. Provides information on financial and business interests, industry news and member benefits. **Price:** free for members. **Circulation:** 18,000. **Advertising:** accepted.

14861 ■ National Medical Association (NMA)
1012 10th St. NW
Washington, DC 20001
Ph: (202)347-1895 (202)371-1674
Fax: (202)289-2662
E-mail: president@nmanet.org
URL: http://www.nmanet.org
Contact: Sandra L. Gadson MD, Pres.
Founded: 1895. **Members:** 4,000. **Membership Dues:** active, $255-$455 (annual) ● associate, $210 (annual) ● resident, fellow, $40 (annual) ● medical student, $20 (annual). **Staff:** 28. **Regional Groups:** 6. **State Groups:** 42. **Local Groups:** 93. **Description:** Serves as professional society of minority physicians. **Computer Services:** Mailing lists, for NMA regions and affiliates only. **Committees:** Liaison with ANMA and SNMA; Policy Implementation; Public Relations; Research and Development. **Councils:** Awards; Concerns of Women Physicians; Judicial; Maternal and Child Health; Medical Education and Hospitals; Medical Legislation; Scientific Assembly; Scientific Exhibits; Talent Recruitment, Retention and Financial Aid to Students. **Publications:** Journal of

the National Medical Association, monthly. Contains scientific articles. **Price:** $35.00. **Circulation:** 28,000. **Advertising:** accepted ● NMA News, quarterly. Newsletter. Contains medical and NMA news targeted to members. **Circulation:** 31,000. **Conventions/Meetings:** annual Convention and Scientific Assembly (exhibits).

14862 ■ Network for Continuing Medical Education (NCME)
1 Harmon Plz.
Secaucus, NJ 07094
Ph: (201)867-3550
Free: (800)223-0433
Fax: (201)867-2491
E-mail: info@ncme.com
URL: http://www.ncme.com
Contact: Paul Gersh, Pres.
Founded: 1965. **Members:** 800. **Staff:** 50. **For-Profit. Description:** Hospitals that subscribe to receive NCME services. Produces and distributes monthly course package including videotape, posters, program brochure, and workbook to members. Course packages cover the full spectrum of medical topics and are designed to provide category 1 continuing medical education credit to physicians. **Convention/Meeting:** none. **Publications:** Video Journal Dermatology, quarterly ● Video Journal Oncology, quarterly.

14863 ■ Royal Society of Medicine Foundation (RSMF)
207 E Westminster Rd., Ste.201
Lake Forest, IL 60045
Ph: (847)234-6382
Fax: (847)234-6511
E-mail: rsmfil@aol.com
URL: http://www.rsm.ac.uk
Contact: Dr. Richard S. Wilbur, Pres.
Founded: 1967. **Members:** 3,500. **Membership Dues:** fellow, $35 (annual). **Staff:** 2. **Description:** Serves as a forum for the discussion of topics relevant to the medical community in the U.S. and the United Kingdom. Sponsors conference series and exchange programs in conjunction with the Royal Society of Medicine. **Awards:** Hewitt. **Frequency:** semiannual. **Type:** monetary. **Recipient:** lifetime achievement. **Publications:** Digest, quarterly.

14864 ■ Society for Executive Leadership in Academic Medicine International (SELAM)
PO Box 72
Jenkintown, PA 19046
Ph: (215)842-6473
Fax: (215)842-1041
E-mail: selam@selaminternational.org
URL: http://selaminternational.org
Contact: Victoria C. Odhner, Admin.
Membership Dues: individual, $100 (annual) ● affiliate, $50 (annual) ● life, $2,500 ● institutional, $600 (annual). **Description:** Advocates for the advancement and promotion of women to executive positions in academic health professions. Supports programs designed for individuals interested in careers in academic medicine and dentistry. Promotes collaborations and networking among members and other organizations that share common goals. **Publications:** SELAM News, semiannual. Newsletter. Alternate Formats: online.

14865 ■ Society for Medical Decision Making (SMDM)
100 N 20th St., 4th Fl.
Philadelphia, PA 19103
Ph: (215)545-7697
Fax: (215)564-2175
E-mail: smdm-office@lists.smdm.org
URL: http://www.smdm.org
Contact: Angela Musial, Account Exec.
Founded: 1979. **Members:** 1,000. **Membership Dues:** regular, $205 (annual) ● trainee, emeritus, $120 (annual). **Staff:** 2. **Budget:** $400,000. **Description:** Individuals with an interest in "developing rational and systematic approaches" to medical decision making, including educators, clinicians, managers, and policy makers. Promotes improvement in all

aspects of medical decision making. Evaluates decision making applications and disseminates conclusions. Facilitates multi-disciplinary scholarship and research; conducts continuing professional education programs. **Awards:** Career Achievement Award. **Frequency:** annual. **Type:** recognition ● Distinguished Service Award. **Frequency:** annual. **Type:** recognition ● Lee B. Lusted Student Prizes. **Frequency:** annual. **Type:** grant. **Recipient:** for the outstanding research presented at SMDM annual meeting ● Outstanding Short Course. **Type:** recognition ● Young Investigator Award. **Frequency:** annual. **Type:** grant. **Special Interest Groups:** Decision Psychology; Disaster Simulation; Ethics Research; Medical Education; Medical Informatics; Pharmacoeconomics; Shared Decision Making. **Publications:** Medical Decision Making, bimonthly. Journal. ISSN: 0272-989X. **Advertising:** accepted ● Newsletter, quarterly. **Conventions/Meetings:** annual meeting, with continuing professional education programs (exhibits).

14866 ■ Society for Molecular Imaging (SMI)
PO Box 293878
Kerrville, TX 78029-3878
Ph: (830)257-0112
Fax: (830)257-0119
E-mail: cmetzger@molecularimaging.org
URL: http://www.molecularimaging.org
Contact: Charles Metzger, Exec. Dir.
Founded: 2000. **Membership Dues:** regular, $250 (annual) ● student, post-doc, fellow, $125 (annual). **Multinational. Description:** Advances the understanding of biology and medicine through noninvasive in vivo investigation of cellular molecular events involved in normal and pathologic processes. Fosters research and communication. Promotes education and advances the tools and applications of the field. **Awards:** SMI Achievement Award. **Frequency:** annual. **Type:** recognition. **Recipient:** to an individual who has made a fundamental discovery in the field of Molecular Imaging that has changed the direction of the field. **Publications:** Molecular Imaging, bimonthly. Journal. Publishes studies that combine recent advances in noninvasive imaging modalities with molecular and cellular biology. **Price:** included in membership dues. ISSN: 1535-3508. **Advertising:** accepted. Alternate Formats: online. **Conventions/Meetings:** annual conference, with symposium - 2007 Sept. 8-11, Providence, RI.

14867 ■ Ukrainian Medical Association of North America (UMANA)
2247 W Chicago Ave.
Chicago, IL 60622
Ph: (773)278-6962
E-mail: umana@umana.org
URL: http://www.umana.org
Contact: George Hrycelak MD, Exec. Dir.
Founded: 1950. **Members:** 1,000. **Membership Dues:** full, $175 (annual) ● emeritus/pharmacist/affiliate/associate, $100 (annual) ● resident, $75 (annual). **Staff:** 1. **Regional Groups:** 19. **Local Groups:** 1. **Languages:** English, Ukrainian. **Description:** Physicians, surgeons, dentists, and persons in related professions who are of Ukrainian descent. Provides assistance to members; sponsors lectures. Maintains placement service, museum, biographical and medical archives. **Libraries: Type:** by appointment only. **Holdings:** 1,800; articles, books, periodicals. **Subjects:** Ukrainian medicine. **Awards: Type:** recognition. **Committees:** Continuing Education. **Formerly:** American Ukrainian Medical Society. **Publications:** Journal of the Ukrainian Medical Association of North America (JUMANA) (in English and Ukrainian), quarterly. Contains medical research articles and news. **Price:** free for members; $25.00 each, for back issues. **Circulation:** 1,000 ● Newsletter to Membership, quarterly ● Umana News. Newsletter. Alternate Formats: online. **Conventions/Meetings:** biennial conference, scientific-continuing medical education (exhibits).

14868 ■ Vietnamese Medical Association of the U.S.A. (VMA-USA)
6255 Univ. Ave., Ste.A-2
San Diego, CA 92115
Ph: (619)583-0553

Fax: (619)583-5702
E-mail: totran10@yahoo.com
URL: http://vmausa.org
Contact: Ton Duy Tran MD, Pres.
Founded: 1989. **Members:** 498. **Membership Dues:** practicing, $80 (annual) ● resident, fellow, $25 (annual) ● life, $1,000. **Budget:** $36,000. **State Groups:** 10. **Languages:** English, Vietnamese. **Description:** Vietnamese-American medical professionals. Promotes mutual support and fellowship among its members, while fostering and maintaining medical ethics. Assures the provision of equal educational and professional opportunities for its members and the welfare of the general Vietnamese community. Supports and assists the Vietnamese victims of the Vietnamese communist regime. **Awards:** Pham Bieu Tam MD Award. **Frequency:** biennial. **Type:** monetary. **Recipient:** for contributions to the advancement of medical knowledge for the Vietnamese. **Also Known As:** Vietnamese American Medical Association. **Publications:** Newsletter, quarterly. Alternate Formats: online ● Magazine, annual. **Conventions/Meetings:** annual general assembly and convention.

14869 ■ Wilderness Medical Society (WMS)
PO Box 1897
Lawrence, KS 66044
Free: (800)627-0629
Fax: (785)843-1853
E-mail: wms@wms.org
URL: http://www.wms.org
Contact: Mr. Jason Gilbert, Mgr.
Founded: 1983. **Members:** 4,200. **Membership Dues:** doctoral, $160 (annual) ● non-doctoral, $100 (annual) ● resident, $75 (annual) ● student/friend, $50 (annual) ● doctoral, $640 (quinquennial) ● non-doctoral, $400 (quinquennial) ● life, $2,500 ● corporate, $1,200 (annual). **Staff:** 4. **Budget:** $900,000. **Description:** Regular membership for persons with advanced degrees in the biomedical or life sciences with an interest in the medical, behavioral, and life sciences aspects of wilderness environments. Aims to promote research and educational activities that increase scientific knowledge about human activities in wilderness environments; stimulate interest and research in health consequences of wilderness activities; serve as central information source. Areas of interest include treatment of accident victims and victims of bites and stings, exotic infectious diseases and toxic plants, desert survival, avalanche control, and search and rescue. **Awards:** Charles S. Houston Award. **Frequency:** annual. **Type:** recognition ● Member Award. **Frequency:** annual. **Type:** recognition ● Research Training Award. **Frequency:** annual. **Type:** recognition. **Committees:** Education Council. **Publications:** Wilderness and Environmental Medicine, quarterly. Journal. **Advertising:** accepted ● Wilderness Medicine, quarterly. Magazine. Features essays, humor, safety and fitness articles, news and announcements. **Advertising:** accepted. Alternate Formats: online ● Wilderness Medicine Letter, quarterly. Newsletter. **Price:** included in membership dues. **Circulation:** 4,200. **Advertising:** accepted. **Conventions/Meetings:** annual meeting, regarding travel and medicine ● annual Mountain and Wilderness Medicine - congress (exhibits) - 2007 Oct. 3-7, Aviemore, United Kingdom ● annual Winter Wilderness Medicine Conference (exhibits) - February.

Mental Health

14870 ■ American Association of Anger Management Providers (AAAMP)
12301 Wilshire Blvd., Ste.418
Brentwood, CA 94513
Ph: (310)207-3591
E-mail: georgeanderson@aol.com
URL: http://www.aaamp.org
Contact: George Anderson, Exec. Dir.
Membership Dues: general, $100 (annual) ● fellow, $150 (annual) ● diplomate, $200 (annual). **Description:** Represents the interests of anger management providers. Generates referrals for members. Promotes anger management as an area of specialization. **Computer Services:** database, list of providers ● database, news and articles. **Telecommunication Services:** electronic mail, membership@aaamp.org. **Publications:** Newsletter, monthly. Contains articles on various issues of interest.

14871 ■ American Association of Mental Health Professionals in Corrections (AAMHPC)
PO Box 160208
Sacramento, CA 95816-0208
Fax: (916)649-1080
E-mail: corrmentalhealth@aol.com
Contact: Prof. J.S. Zil MD, Natl. Pres.
Founded: 1940. **Members:** 2,000. **Membership Dues:** individual, fellow, $100 (annual). **Staff:** 2. **Budget:** $100,000. **Description:** Psychiatrists, psychologists, social workers, nurses, and other mental health professionals; individuals working in correctional settings. Fosters the progress of behavioral sciences related to corrections. Goals are: to improve the treatment, rehabilitation, and care of the mentally ill, mentally retarded, and emotionally disturbed; to promote research and professional education in psychiatry and allied fields in corrections; to advance standards of correctional services and facilities; to foster cooperation between individuals concerned with the medical, psychological, social, and legal aspects of corrections; to share knowledge with other medical practitioners, scientists, and the public. Conducts scientific meetings to contribute to the advancement of the therapeutic community in all its institutional settings, including correctional institutions, hospitals, churches, schools, industry, and the family. **Awards:** Presidential Award. **Frequency:** periodic. **Type:** recognition. **Recipient:** for special contributions to correctional research. **Formerly:** (1978) Medical Correctional Society of the American Correctional Association. **Publications:** Corrective and Social Psychiatry, quarterly. Journal. Includes book reviews, calendar of events, and research reports. **Price:** included in membership dues; $100.00/year for nonmembers. **Circulation:** 2,000. **Advertising:** accepted ● Papers. **Conventions/Meetings:** annual conference and symposium ● periodic regional meeting ● workshop, to assist other groups with staff education and analysis of program organization and development.

14872 ■ American College of Mental Health Administration (ACMHA)
7804 Lorma del Norte Rd. NE
Albuquerque, NM 87109
Ph: (505)822-5038
E-mail: executive.director@acmha.org
URL: http://www.acmha.org
Contact: Kris Ericson, Exec. Dir.
Founded: 1980. **Members:** 200. **Membership Dues:** individual, $250 (annual). **Staff:** 2. **Budget:** $75,000. **Description:** Mental health clinician administrators. **Awards:** Walter E. Barton Award. **Frequency:** annual. **Type:** recognition. **Recipient:** for contributions to the college and the field. **Computer Services:** Information services ● online services. **Publications:** Newsletter, quarterly. Includes organization news and critical essays. **Price:** $12.00/year. **Advertising:** accepted. **Conventions/Meetings:** annual Santa Fe Summit - conference.

14873 ■ American Mental Health Counselors Association (AMHCA)
801 N Fairfax, Ste.304
Alexandria, VA 22314
Ph: (703)548-6002
Free: (800)326-2642
Fax: (703)548-5233
E-mail: mhamilton@amhca.org
URL: http://www.amhca.org
Contact: W. Mark Hamilton PhD, Exec. Dir./CEO
Founded: 1976. **Members:** 5,500. **Membership Dues:** individual, $155 (annual) ● student or retired, $60 (annual). **Staff:** 5. **Budget:** $1,100,000. **State Groups:** 50. **Description:** Professional counselors employed in mental health services; students. Aims to: deliver quality mental health services to children, youth, adults, families, and organizations; improve the availability and quality of counseling services through licensure and certification, training standards, and consumer advocacy. Supports specialty and special interest networks. Fosters communication among members. A division of the American Counseling Association (see separate entry). **Libraries: Type:** not open to the public. **Holdings:** 100. **Subjects:** mental health. **Awards: Frequency:** annual. **Type:** recognition. **Computer Services:** database ● mailing lists. **Affiliated With:** American Counseling Association. **Publications:** Advocate, 11/year. Newsletter. Contains current information on the mental health profession. **Price:** included in membership dues; $25.00 for nonmembers. **Circulation:** 7,000. **Advertising:** accepted. Alternate Formats: diskette ● Journal of Mental Health Counseling, quarterly. **Advertising:** accepted ● Mental Health Connections. Brochures. Contains information on divorce, eating disorders, child abuse, parenting young children, handling conflict, caring for aging parents. **Conventions/Meetings:** annual National Leadership Conference, leadership training for presidents-elect and emerging state leaders (exhibits).

14874 ■ Armenian American Society for Studies on Stress and Genocide (AASSSG)
c/o Dr. Anie Kalayjian
139 Cedar St.
Cliffside Park, NJ 07010-1003
Ph: (201)941-2266
Fax: (201)941-5110
E-mail: akalayjian@meaningfulworld.com
URL: http://www.meaningfulworld.com/organizations.html1
Contact: Dr. Anie Kalayjian, Contact
Founded: 1988. **Membership Dues:** individual, $25 (annual). **Description:** Seeks to advance national and international understanding of the generational and intergenerational effects of traumatic experiences. Provides consultation to individuals and community groups. Educates the community about the impact of mass traumas. Fosters cooperation among allied groups.

14875 ■ Association of Behavioral Healthcare Management (ABHM)
c/o National Council for Community Behavioral Healthcare
12300 Twinbrook Pkwy., Ste.320
Rockville, MD 20852
Ph: (301)984-6200
Fax: (301)881-7159
E-mail: lindar@nccbh.org
Contact: Linda Rosenberg, Pres./CEO
Founded: 1959. **Members:** 500. **Membership Dues:** individual, $200 (annual) ● associate, $150 (annual). **Budget:** $107,500. **Description:** Administrators of services for the emotionally disturbed, mentally ill, mentally retarded, developmentally disabled, and those with problems of alcohol and substance abuse. Objectives are to: further the education of administrators; develop criteria for and certify the competence of administrators; promote adherence to a code of ethics. Aids in developing professional administrative skills and administration of services. Sponsors educational workshops. **Awards:** Piepenbrink Award. **Frequency:** annual. **Type:** recognition. **Formerly:** (1969) American Society of Mental Health Business Administrators; (1997) Association of Mental Heath Administrators. **Publications:** ABHM Leader, quarterly. Newsletter. Contains current news and information on mental health administration issues. **Price:** $90.00/year. **Circulation:** 1,100. **Advertising:** accepted ● Journal of Behavioral Health Services and Research, quarterly. Covers management practice, research, and policy issues in the mental health field. ISSN: 1094-3412. **Advertising:** accepted. **Conventions/Meetings:** annual meeting and convention (exhibits) ● annual regional meeting and seminar - always spring.

14876 ■ Association for Convulsive Therapy (ACT)
5454 Wisconsin Ave., Ste.1220
Chevy Chase, MD 20815
Ph: (301)951-7220

Fax: (301)299-4918
E-mail: bkillmeyer@triangleurology.com
URL: http://www.act-ect.org/act/index.php
Contact: Beth Killmeyer, Course Coor.
Founded: 1976. **Membership Dues:** regular, $285 (annual) ● overseas, $325 (annual) ● member-in-training, $100 (annual) ● regular (without Journal of ECT), $95 (annual). **Multinational. Description:** Promotes the safe, ethical and effective use of electroconvulsive therapy through education and scientific research. **Awards:** Young Investigator Award. **Frequency:** annual. **Type:** recognition. **Publications:** *Journal of ECT.* Covers all aspects of contemporary electroconvulsive therapy. **Price:** included in membership dues ● Newsletter, quarterly. **Price:** included in membership dues. **Conventions/Meetings:** annual meeting - 2008 May 4, WASHINGTON, DC; 2009 May 17, San Francisco, CA.

14877 ■ Black Mental Health Alliance (BMHA)
733 W 40th St., Ste.10
Baltimore, MD 21211
Ph: (410)338-2642
Fax: (410)338-1771
E-mail: tbryant@blackmentalhealth.org
URL: http://www.blackmentalhealth.org/default1.htm
Contact: Tracee E. Bryant, Exec. Dir.
Founded: 1984. **Members:** 250. **Membership Dues:** individual, $50 (annual) ● student/senior, $10 (annual) ● organization, $250 (annual) ● professional, $150 (annual) ● corporate, $1,000 (annual) ● life, $1,500. **Staff:** 7. **Budget:** $510,000. **Regional Groups:** 1. **State Groups:** 1. **Local Groups:** 1. **Description:** Seeks to increase clinicians, clergy, educators, and social service professionals awareness of African-Americans mental health needs and concerns on issues including stress, violence, racism, substance abuse, and parenting. Provides consultation, public information, and resource referrals. Conducts a public awareness campaign; educates the community about available resources; develops programs that benefit African-American children and families. Offers training to human service workers, teachers, police officers, and other service providers who work with culturally diverse populations. Maintains speakers' bureau. The support group provides emotional support, education and interaction for family members experiencing the stresses of caring for and/or living with a mentally ill relative. Provides a resource referral service; maintains an extensive list of African American mental health professionals who are sensitive to and appreciate cultural differences. Offers programs that invest in the needs of African American adult and adolescent females who are at risk of, or have, HIV or AIDS. Offers the "Free Yourself Stop Smoking and Prevention" program. **Libraries: Type:** reference. **Holdings:** 300; audio recordings, books, periodicals, video recordings. **Subjects:** mental health issues related to African-Americans and other ethnic groups. **Awards:** Addison Pope, MD Award. **Frequency:** annual. **Type:** trophy. **Recipient:** to a Mental Health Clinician ● Award of Special Recognition. **Type:** recognition. **Recipient:** for an outstanding contribution to BMHA ● Maxie T. Collier, MD Award. **Frequency:** annual. **Type:** recognition. **Recipient:** to a family member or consumer of mental health services ● Volunteer of the Year. **Type:** recognition. **Recipient:** for provision of resources, spirit of helping and sharing to enhance the programs and services of BMHA. **Computer Services:** Mailing lists, African-American health care providers. **Boards:** Circle of Friends; Directors. **Publications:** *Visions,* quarterly. Newsletter. Contains updates, information, employment opportunities, community service information, and calendar. **Price:** included in membership dues. **Advertising:** accepted. **Conventions/Meetings:** annual meeting and dinner (exhibits) - every December ● annual Optimal Mental Health for African American Families Conference (exhibits).

14878 ■ Center for Attitudinal Healing (CAH)
33 Buchanan Dr.
Sausalito, CA 94965
Ph: (415)331-6161
Fax: (415)331-4545

E-mail: home123@aol.com
URL: http://www.attitudinalhealing.org
Contact: Louise Franklin, Exec. Dir.
Founded: 1975. **Members:** 12,000. **Staff:** 10. **Budget:** $500,000. **Multinational. Description:** Nonsectarian organization established to supplement traditional health care by offering free services in attitudinal healing for both children and adults with life-threatening illnesses, loss, or other crises. (The concept of attitudinal healing is based on the belief that it is possible to choose peace rather than conflict, and love rather than fear; the center defines health as inner peace and healing as the process of letting go of fear.) Offers support groups and arranges home and hospital visits for children, youth, and adults. Offers volunteer training program. Maintains speakers' bureau; conducts educational programs and charitable activities. **Publications:** *Advice to Doctors and Other Big People.* Book ● *Another Look at the Rainbow.* Book ● *Rainbow Connection,* 3/year. Newsletter. **Circulation:** 8,000 ● *There is a Rainbow Behind Every Dark Cloud.* Book. **Conventions/Meetings:** Intro to Attitudinal Healing, Loss and Grief, Volunteer and Service Trainings - workshop - 5/year.

14879 ■ Center for Psychological and Spiritual Health (CPSH)
1453 Mission St.
San Francisco, CA 94109
Ph: (415)575-6299 (415)575-6234
E-mail: cpsh@ciis.edu
URL: http://www.cpsh.org
Contact: Christina Grot, Founder
Founded: 1980. **Members:** 10,000. **Membership Dues:** individual, $35 (annual). **Staff:** 3. **Description:** Seeks to develop an expanded model of mental health care to help people in crisis by using scientific and spiritual assistance. Operates an information and referral service. Offers educational programs. Maintains speakers' bureau. **Libraries: Type:** reference; not open to the public. **Holdings:** archival material, articles, books, periodicals. **Formerly:** (2003) Spiritual Emergence Network. **Publications:** *Spiritual Emergence Network Newsletter,* 2-3/year. **Circulation:** 3,000. **Advertising:** accepted ● *Spiritual Emergency.* Book ● Brochure. **Conventions/Meetings:** bimonthly board meeting ● annual conference.

14880 ■ Committee for Truth in Psychiatry (CTIP)
PO Box 1214
New York, NY 10003
Ph: (212)473-4786
E-mail: andrel@pie.org
URL: http://www.harborside.com/~equinox/ect.htm
Contact: Linda Andre, Dir.
Founded: 1984. **Members:** 500. **Description:** Former psychiatric patients who have had electroconvulsive therapy (ECT), working to bring about truthfully informed consent to shock treatment. Works to retain ECT's current FDA classification as a high-risk procedure. Has submitted a proposal to the Food and Drug Administration regarding a statement of information about ECT that would be given to patients before giving consent for treatment. Seeks endorsements for the CTIP statement. Has petitioned the FDA for an animal and human CAT scan study of ECT. Provides counseling for individuals/families facing a decision about ECT, or recovering from ECT. **Convention/Meeting:** none. **Publications:** *A Synopsis of the Conflict Over ECT at the FDA.* Pamphlet. **Price:** free ● *FDA's Regulatory Proceedings Concerning ECT.* Pamphlet. **Price:** free ● *Shockwaves,* quarterly. Newsletter. **Price:** $10.00/year for survivors and supporters; $5.00/year for low-income subscribers; $25.00/year for professionals, agencies, institutions. **Circulation:** 1,000 ● *What You Need to Know about ECT.* **Price:** free.

14881 ■ Depression and Bipolar Support Alliance (DBSA)
730 N Franklin, Ste.501
Chicago, IL 60610-7225
Ph: (312)642-0049
Free: (800)826-3632
Fax: (312)642-7243

E-mail: mheim@dbsalliance.org
URL: http://www.dbsalliance.org
Contact: Ms. Maria Heim, Public Relations Coor.
Founded: 1985. **Members:** 65,000. **Membership Dues:** individual, $20 (annual). **Staff:** 25. **State Groups:** 300. **Local Groups:** 1,003. **Description:** Seeks to educate patients, families, professionals, and the public concerning the nature of depression and bipolar disorder as treatable medical diseases; to foster self-help for patients and families; to eliminate discrimination and stigma; to improve access to care; and to advocate for research toward the elimination of these illnesses. **Awards:** Gerald Klerman Lifetime Research Award. **Frequency:** annual. **Type:** recognition. **Recipient:** for individuals advancing the treatment of depressive and bipolar illness. **Computer Services:** database ● online services, bipolar disorder and depression screening. **Boards:** Scientific Advisory. **Formerly:** (1978) Manic Depressive and Depressive Association; (2003) National Depressive and Manic Depressive Association. **Publications:** *A Guide to Depressive and Manic Depressive Illness: Diagnosis, Treatment and Support.* Pamphlet. Contains patient information on depression and bipolar illnesses. ● *Dark Glasses and Kaleidoscopes: Living with Manic Depression.* Video ● *Outreach,* quarterly. Newsletter. Includes book reviews, calendar of events, articles on research and treatment, consumer awareness, and advocacy. ● *The State of Depression in America.* Report. Alternate Formats: online. **Conventions/Meetings:** annual convention (exhibits) ● meeting.

14882 ■ Depression and Related Affective Disorders Association (DRADA)
c/o Organization Guidance Group, LLC
11616 Bedfordshire Ave.
Potomac, MD 20854
Ph: (301)294-6266
Free: (888)288-1104
E-mail: drada@jhmi.edu
URL: http://www.drada.org
Contact: John Ganoe, Exec. Dir.
Founded: 1986. **Members:** 1,300. **Membership Dues:** individual, $35 (annual) ● family, $50 (annual) ● organization, $150 (annual). **Staff:** 6. **Budget:** $210,000. **Description:** Individuals with affective disorders, their families and friends, and mental health professionals. (Affective disorders include depressive illnesses and manic-depression.) Provides support services including referrals, educational programs, networking, and consultation. Encourages and facilitates the formation of local support groups for those with affective disorders; provides training for support group leaders. Cosponsors with Johns Hopkins annual mood disorders symposium. Maintains speakers' bureau. **Libraries: Type:** not open to the public. **Holdings:** books, video recordings. **Subjects:** affective disorders and related topics. **Awards: Frequency:** annual. **Type:** scholarship. **Recipient:** to a research student. **Computer Services:** database. **Telecommunication Services:** electronic mail, crumbarger@ogg-inc.com. **Committees:** Education; Research; Support Services. **Publications:** *A Patients Perspective: Dick Cavett.* Video ● *A Patients Perspective: Mike Wallace.* Video ● *Day for Night: Recognizing Teenage Depression.* Video ● *Depressive Illness: What You Need to Know.* Video ● *Downtime: A Workplace Guide to Understanding Clinical Depression.* Video ● *DRADA Update,* bimonthly. Brochure. **Circulation:** 60,000 ● *Manual for Affective Disorder Support Groups* ● *Smooth Sailing,* quarterly. Newsletter. **Price:** included in membership dues. **Circulation:** 9,000. **Conventions/Meetings:** annual Mood Disorders Research and Education Symposium, with research/education (exhibits).

14883 ■ Families for Depression Awareness
395 Totten Pond Rd., Ste.404
Waltham, MA 02451
Ph: (781)890-0220
Fax: (781)890-2411
E-mail: info@familyaware.org
URL: http://www.familyaware.org
Contact: Julie Totten, Pres.
Founded: 2001. **Staff:** 1. **Description:** Helps families recognize and manage the various forms of depres-

sion and associated mood disorders. Reduces stigma associated with depressive disorders. **Computer Services:** Information services, depression resources ● mailing lists. **Boards:** Advisory. **Publications:** Brochure. **Price:** free for members.

14884 ■ Freedom From Fear (FFF)
308 Seaview Ave.
Staten Island, NY 10305
Ph: (718)351-1717
Fax: (718)980-5022
E-mail: help@freedomfromfear.org
URL: http://www.freedomfromfear.org
Contact: Mary Guardino, Founder/Exec. Dir.
Founded: 1984. **Languages:** English, Spanish. **Description:** Seeks to provide better understanding of the causes and treatments of anxiety and depressive disorders. **Programs:** Freedom From Fear Online Support; National College Mental Health; Sharon Davies Memorial Awards. **Publications:** *Freedom From Fear Survival.* Video. **Price:** $10.00. Alternate Formats: CD-ROM.

14885 ■ Global Alliance of Mental Illness Advocacy Networks (GAMIAN)
308 Seaview Ave.
Staten Island, NY 10305
Ph: (718)351-1717
Fax: (718)667-8893
E-mail: jcgamian@aol.com
URL: http://www.gamian.org
Contact: Jeanine Christiana, Contact
Founded: 1998. **Multinational. Description:** Fosters understanding on the prevalence and severity of mental illness through education and dissemination of information. Raises awareness of public policy issues related to mental illness and the implication of research findings. Facilitates and encourages individuals and groups to join together and engage themselves in advocacy action for people who are suffering from mental illness. **Publications:** Newsletter. **Price:** free for members ● Articles. Alternate Formats: online.

14886 ■ Institute for the Development of Emotional and Life Skills/National Institute of Relationship Enhancement (IDEALS/NIRE)
4400 East-West Hwy., Ste.28
Bethesda, MD 20814-4501
Ph: (301)986-1479
Free: (800)4FAMILIES
Fax: (301)680-3756
E-mail: niremd@nire.org
URL: http://www.nire.org
Contact: Dr. Bernard Guerney Jr., Founder/Dir.
Founded: 1972. **Members:** 12. **Staff:** 6. **Description:** Strives to develop and research effective programs for improving emotional and interpersonal skills and providing high-quality training and supervision for mental health professionals, managers, workers, and the public. Conducts training programs for professionals in the areas of mental health, health care, human services, education, and business; sponsors training programs for laypeople in the areas of improving interpersonal relations, problem solving, and effective functioning in family and in business settings. Offers programs for workers and managers in communication, goal planning, motivation, negotiation, stress and time management, personnel management, and supervision. **Convention/Meeting:** none. **Formerly:** (2000) Institute for the Development of Emotional and Life Skills. **Publications:** *A Scriptural Guide to a Fulfilling Marriage.* **Price:** $8.95 ● *Parenting: A Skills Training Manual.* **Price:** $9.95 ● *Relationship Skills Manual* ● Bibliography. Contains training programs, research articles, books and films.

14887 ■ Institute for Labor and Mental Health (ILMH)
3137 Telegraph Ave.
Oakland, CA 94609
Ph: (510)653-6166 (510)849-2212
Contact: Dr. Richard Epstein, Dir.
Founded: 1977. **Members:** 50. **Staff:** 6. **Description:** Purpose is to help working people with problems related to the workplace. Seeks to identify conditions

at work that cause stress; believes that education and communication about common work problems are the first steps in dealing with job stress. Assists unions in handling grievances and stress-related disabilities; provides counseling to union members and their families; offers legal and worker compensation assistance to working people. Provides consultation to government and businesses on ways to reduce stress. Develops ongoing stress programs; operates summer institute on occupational stress. **Committees:** Clinical Services; Education; Outreach; Research. **Publications:** *Occupational Stress,* bimonthly. Newsletter ● *Occupational Stress: A Union Based Approach* ● *Occupational Stress: The Inside Story* ● *Surplus Powerlessness.* Book ● Directory, periodic. **Conventions/Meetings:** annual conference - always June.

14888 ■ Institute for Mental Health Initiatives (IMHI)
2175 K St. NW, Ste.No. 700
Washington, DC 20037
Ph: (202)467-2285 (202)364-0402
Fax: (202)467-2289
E-mail: imhi-info@gwumc.edu
URL: http://www.gwumc.edu/sphhs
Contact: Prof. Suzanne Stutman MSW, Founding Exec. Dir.
Founded: 1982. **Staff:** 5. **Budget:** $400,000. **Description:** Uses a public health approach to promote mental health and prevent emotional disorders. Seeks to transform complex mental health concepts into positive models of human interaction. Gathers knowledge derived from clinical and research findings on good mental health, which it then adapts for use by the media, educators, health and mental health professionals, community leaders, and parents. Conducts meetings and workshops; consults with media professionals; creates training videos, discussion guides, and public service announcements. Works to influence perceptions and attitudes through the power of commercial mass media. **Libraries: Type:** reference. **Holdings:** archival material, audio recordings, books, video recordings. **Subjects:** mental health. **Programs:** Channeling Children's Anger; Channeling Parent's Anger. **Publications:** *Dialogue,* quarterly. Newsletter. Provides information on human emotions for media professionals. **Price:** $30.00. **Circulation:** 16,000 ● *Exploring First Feelings.* Video ● *Initiatives,* quarterly. Newsletter. Reports on current issues and new developments in mental health. ● *The Rethink Workout for Teens: Learning to Manage Anger.* Video ● *Take Another Look: Learning to Rethink Anger.* Video ● *The Violence Framework: Guidelines for Understanding, Reporting, and Portraying Violence.* Handbook ● *What Do You Tell the Children? How to Help Children Deal with Disasters.* Handbook. **Conventions/Meetings:** semiannual conference.

14889 ■ International Association of Transpersonal Therapists and Physicians (IATTP)
485 S Independence Blvd., Ste.111
Virginia Beach, VA 23452
Ph: (757)216-8096
Fax: (757)216-8101
E-mail: iattpmembers@aol.com
URL: http://iattp.org
Contact: Charisse Barksdale PhD, CEO/Co-Founder
Membership Dues: student, $45 (annual) ● professional, $75 (annual) ● life - professional, $700 ● instructor, $400 (annual). **Multinational. Description:** Provides training and continuing education to professionals who work with clients across all aspects of their lives. Provides a forum for professionals to share their knowledge and expertise in the field of transpersonal healthcare.

14890 ■ International Committee Against Mental Illness (ICAMI)
PO Box 1921
Grand Central Sta.
New York, NY 10163-1921
Ph: (212)263-6214
Fax: (212)263-5717

E-mail: rc31@nyu.edu
Contact: Dr. Robert Cancro, Pres.
Founded: 1958. **Multinational. Description:** Fosters psychosocial rehabilitation and mental health research, services, and information systems. Provides technical assistance to professional rehabilitation organizations in expanding or installing computer information systems in psychiatry and in planning workshops, symposia, and conferences. Organizes international consortium of voluntary agencies and rehabilitation groups. Conducts research; operates speakers' bureau. Works on projects in Colombia, Indonesia, Iran, Israel, Kuwait, Liberia, Nepal, Pakistan, and Yugoslavia. Serves as a direct outgrowth of a pioneering psychiatric treatment project in Haiti that is now operated by the Haitian government.

14891 ■ International Society for Mental Health Online (ISMHO)
c/o Patricia Kennington, PhD, Sec.-Treas.
388 Chester St. SE
Marietta, GA 30060-2086
Free: (888)875-3570
E-mail: ismho@ismho.org
URL: http://www.ismho.org
Contact: Patricia Kennington PhD, Sec.-Treas.
Founded: 1997. **Membership Dues:** individual, $25 (annual). **Multinational. Description:** Mental health professionals. Works to promote the understanding, use, and development of online communication, information and technology for the international mental health community. Hosts online discussion forums and annual dinners. **Computer Services:** Online services, forum.

14892 ■ International Society for the Study of Trauma and Dissociation (ISSTD)
8201 Greensboro Dr., Ste.300
McLean, VA 22102
Ph: (703)610-9037
Fax: (703)610-9005
E-mail: info@isst-d.org
URL: http://www.isst-d.org
Contact: Annita B. Jones PsyD, Sec.-Treas.
Founded: 1982. **Members:** 1,200. **Membership Dues:** regular, $149 (annual) ● student, affiliate, $80 (annual) ● retired, $69 (annual). **Staff:** 2. **Budget:** $300,000. **Description:** Promotes research and training in the identification and treatment of dissociative disorders. Supports international communications and cooperation among professional clinicians and investigators working in the field of dissociation. **Libraries: Type:** not open to the public. **Holdings:** 6. **Subjects:** dissociation. **Awards:** Cornelia Wilbur Award. **Frequency:** annual. **Type:** recognition. **Recipient:** for outstanding clinical contributions ● David Caul Award. **Frequency:** annual. **Type:** recognition. **Recipient:** for the best published or non-published paper, thesis, or conference abstract in the field of dissociation ● Media Award. **Frequency:** annual. **Type:** recognition. **Recipient:** for the best written media and best audiovisual media that deal with dissociation ● Morton Prince Award. **Frequency:** annual. **Type:** recognition. **Recipient:** for outstanding contributions in the area of dissociative disorders ● Pierre Janet Writing Award. **Frequency:** annual. **Type:** recognition. **Recipient:** for the best clinical, theoretical or research paper in the field of dissociative disorders within the past year ● President's Award. **Frequency:** annual. **Type:** recognition. **Recipient:** to an individual who has given outstanding service to the society. **Computer Services:** Mailing lists. **Committees:** Awards; Child and Adolescent; Components; Constitution; Critical Issues; Ethical Issues; Legal and Forensic Issues; Managed Care; Membership; Program; Research; Services; Standards of Practice; Women' Issues. **Formerly:** International Society for the Study of Multiple Personalities and Dissociation; (2006) International Society for the Study of Dissociation. **Publications:** *ISSD Membership Directory,* periodic. **Advertising:** accepted ● *ISSD News,* bimonthly. Newsletter. **Advertising:** accepted ● *The Journal of Trauma and Dissociation,* quarterly ● *Standards of Practice Guidelines for treating Dissociative Identity Disorder in Adults.* **Price:**

included in membership dues; $5.00/additional copy for members; $10.00 for nonmembers ● Bibliography. Alternate Formats: online ● Audiotapes ● Journals. **Conventions/Meetings:** annual international conference (exhibits) - 2007 Nov. 11-13, Baltimore, MD.

14893 ■ Mental Health America (MHA)
2000 N Beauregard St., 6th Fl.
Alexandria, VA 22311
Ph: (703)684-7722
Free: (800)969-NMHA
Fax: (703)684-5968
E-mail: infoctr@nmha.org
URL: http://www.mentalhealthamerica.net
Contact: David L. Shern PhD, CEO/Pres.
Founded: 1909. **Members:** 416,000. **Staff:** 60. **Regional Groups:** 320. **Description:** Addresses all aspects of mental health and mental illness and is dedicated to improving mental health, preventing mental disorders, and achieving victory over mental illnesses. Accomplishes its mission through advocacy, public education, research, and service in partnership with more than 340 affiliates across the country. **Awards:** Clifford W. Beers Award. **Frequency:** annual. **Type:** recognition ● Katherine Hamilton Volunteer of the Year Award. **Frequency:** annual. **Type:** recognition ● Media Award. **Frequency:** annual. **Type:** recognition ● William R. McAlpin Jr. Research Achievement. **Type:** recognition. **Computer Services:** database, Prevention Program ● database, Resource ● online services, Prevention Network. **Additional Websites:** http://www.mpoweryouth.org. **Absorbed:** National Organization for Mentally Ill Children. **Formed by Merger of:** National Committee for Mental Hygiene; National Mental Health Foundation; Psychiatric Foundation. **Formerly:** National Association for Mental Health; (1980) Mental Health Association; (2006) National Mental Health Association. **Publications:** *The Bell*, monthly. Newsletter. Includes association news, calendar of events, legislative news, mental health/health trends and research news. **Circulation:** 3,000 ● *Mental Health in the Headlines*, weekly. Newsletters ● *State Advocacy Update*, quarterly. Newsletters. **Conventions/Meetings:** annual Putting Research Into Practice - conference (exhibits) ● annual symposium.

14894 ■ Mental Health Workers Without Borders (MHWWB)
c/o Martin Gittelman
100 W 94th St.
New York, NY 10025
E-mail: mhwwb@mhwwb.org
URL: http://www.mhwwb.org
Contact: Martin Gittelman, Contact
Multinational. Description: Shares knowledge and ideas about psychosocial assistance for natural and man-made disasters, mental health and human rights, and treatment and psychosocial rehabilitation for people with severe mental illness. Encourages family and community-based psychosocial approaches to mental health problems, respectful of cultural variation, drawing on local resources and healing traditions. **Publications:** *Coping With Disaster: A Guidebook to Psychosocial Intervention* (in English and Spanish). Manual. Features expanded coverage of human sufferings. Alternate Formats: online ● *Humanitarian Companion*. Book. Contains guide for humanitarian aid workers.

14895 ■ NARSAD: Mental Health Research Association (NARSAD)
60 Cutter Mill Rd., Ste.404
Great Neck, NY 11021
Ph: (516)829-0091 (516)829-5576
Free: (800)829-8289
Fax: (516)487-6930
E-mail: info@narsad.org
URL: http://www.narsad.org
Contact: Constance E. Lieber, Pres./CEO
Founded: 1986. **Staff:** 15. **Budget:** $20,000,000. **Description:** Raises funds for research on schizophrenia, depression, and other mental illnesses. **Awards:** Independent Investigator Award. **Frequency:** annual. **Type:** grant. **Recipient:** for scientific research ● Lieber Prize. **Frequency:** annual. **Type:**

recognition. **Recipient:** for an established scientific investigator ● Young Investigator Award. **Frequency:** annual. **Type:** grant. **Recipient:** for scientific research. **Councils:** Scientific. **Programs:** Research Partners. **Affiliated With:** Depression and Bipolar Support Alliance; Mental Health America; National Alliance on Mental Illness. **Formerly:** (2006) National Alliance for Research on Schizophrenia and Depression. **Publications:** *NARSAD Research*, quarterly. Newsletter. Highlights current scientific research. **Circulation:** 100,000. Alternate Formats: online. **Conventions/Meetings:** annual symposium.

14896 ■ National Alliance on Mental Illness (NAMI)
Colonial Pl. Three
2107 Wilson Blvd., Ste.300
Arlington, VA 22201-3042
Ph: (703)524-7600
Free: (800)950-NAMI
Fax: (703)524-9094
E-mail: info@nami.org
URL: http://www.nami.org
Contact: Suzanne Vogel-Scibilia MD, Pres.
Founded: 1979. **Members:** 220,000. **Membership Dues:** individual (local, state, and national), professional, $35 (annual). **Staff:** 85. **Budget:** $9,000,000. **State Groups:** 52. **Local Groups:** 1,200. **Languages:** English, Spanish. **Description:** Improves the lives of children and adults with severe mental illness through support, education, research, and advocacy. Focuses on schizophrenia, bipolar disorder, major depression, and anxiety disorder. **Awards:** Anti-Discrimination Award. **Frequency:** annual. **Type:** recognition. **Recipient:** for public recognition ● Distinguished Award. **Frequency:** annual. **Type:** recognition. **Recipient:** for public recognition ● Exemplary Psychiatrist Awards. **Frequency:** annual. **Type:** recognition. **Recipient:** to a group of exemplary psychiatrists ● Media Award. **Frequency:** annual. **Type:** recognition. **Recipient:** for public recognition. **Telecommunication Services:** TDD, (703)516-7227. **Committees:** Legal Alliance; Legislation; Mentally Ill Children and Adolescents; Research; Veterans. **Councils:** Consumer. **Also Known As:** NAMI. **Formerly:** (2005) National Alliance for the Mentally Ill. **Publications:** *The Advocate*, quarterly. Magazine. **Price:** included in membership dues ● *Because Children Grow Up*, quarterly. Newsletter ● *Nami-E-News*, daily to weekly. Provides legislative policy updates online. Alternate Formats: online ● *Stigmabuster Alerts*, monthly. Report. Reports and recommends actions against prejudice and discrimination involving mental illness. ● Handbooks ● Brochures. **Conventions/Meetings:** annual convention (exhibits).

14897 ■ National Asian American Pacific Islander Mental Health Association (NAAPIMHA)
1215 19th St., Ste.A
Denver, CO 80202
Ph: (303)298-7910
Fax: (303)298-8081
E-mail: info@naapimha.org
URL: http://www.naapimha.org
Contact: DJ Ida PhD, Exec. Dir.
Founded: 2000. **Description:** Serves as the national voice to address the unique mental health issues of AAPI communities. Provides technical assistance and training to service providers, both professional and para-professional. Conducts research and evaluation on mental health issues.

14898 ■ National Association of Mental Health Planning and Advisory Councils (NAMHPAC)
2000 N Beauegard St., 6th Fl.
Alexandria, VA 22311
Ph: (703)797-2595
Fax: (703)684-5968
E-mail: judy@namhpac.org
URL: http://www.namhpac.org
Contact: Judy Stange PhD, Exec. Dir.
Founded: 1995. **Description:** Encourages planning and evaluating of mental health service delivery.

Advocates for adults with serious mental illnesses, children with severe disturbances and individuals with mental health needs. Provides technical support and opportunities for people to share information and ideas on mental health planning issues. **Computer Services:** Mailing lists ● online services, discussion forum. **Committees:** Public Policy. **Publications:** Brochure. Includes mental health issues and topics.

14899 ■ National Association for Rural Mental Health (NARMH)
300 33rd Ave. S, Ste.101
Waite Park, MN 56387
Ph: (320)202-1820
Free: (800)809-5879
Fax: (320)202-1833
E-mail: narmh@facts.ksu.edu
URL: http://www.narmh.org
Contact: Ms. Lu Ann Rice, Mgr.
Founded: 1977. **Members:** 500. **Membership Dues:** student, retired, consumer, $30 (annual) ● individual, $65 (annual) ● organizational, $175 (annual) ● large organization, $350 (annual) ● sponsor, $1,000 (annual). **Staff:** 1. **Description:** Mental health practitioners and administrators and others dedicated to improving mental health services in rural areas. Promotes effective rural mental health services. Promotes the use of services by rural community dwellers. **Awards:** Victor I. Howery Memorial Award and Going to Bat Award. **Frequency:** annual. **Type:** recognition. **Recipient:** for outstanding contributions in rural mental health. **Publications:** *Rural Mental Health*, quarterly. Newsletter. **Conventions/Meetings:** annual conference (exhibits) - usually summer.

14900 ■ National Association for Self Esteem (NASE)
PO Box 597
Fulton, MD 20759-0597
Free: (800)488-NASE
E-mail: sharon@sharonfountain.com
URL: http://www.self-esteem-nase.org
Contact: Sharon Fountain, Pres.
Founded: 1986. **Membership Dues:** student, $10 (annual) ● national, $20 (annual) ● supporting, $100 (annual). **Description:** Strives to integrate self-esteem within families, schools, and the workplace. **Publications:** *Self Esteem Today*. Newsletter.

14901 ■ National Association of State Mental Health Program Directors (NASMHPD)
66 Canal Center Plz., Ste.302
Alexandria, VA 22314
Ph: (703)739-9333
Fax: (703)548-9517
E-mail: bob.glover@nasmhpd.org
URL: http://www.nasmhpd.org
Contact: Dr. Robert W. Glover, Exec. Dir.
Founded: 1959. **Members:** 55. **Staff:** 19. **Description:** Promotes cooperation of state government agencies in delivery of services to people with severe mental illnesses; fosters the exchange of scientific and programmatic information in the administration of public mental health programs including treatment programs, community and hospital care of persons with mental illness, mental retardation, or substance abuse disorders. Monitors state and federal and congressional activities; gathers and analyzes information on organization, structure, funding, and programming of state government mental health programs. Operates under a cooperative agreement with the National Governors' Association (see separate entry). **Conventions/Meetings:** semiannual meeting - always July and December.

14902 ■ National Center for American Indian and Alaska Native Mental Health Research (NCAIANMHR)
UCDHSC Psychiatry Dept.
Nighthorse Campbell Native Hea. Bldg.
PO Box 6508, Mail Stop F800
Aurora, CO 80045-0508
Ph: (303)724-1414 (303)724-1482
Fax: (303)724-1474

E-mail: rhonda.dick@uchsc.edu
URL: http://www.uchsc.edu/ai/ncaianmhr/ncaianmhr_index.htm
Contact: Ms. Natasha Floersch, Journal Mgr.
Founded: 1987. **Staff:** 3. **Description:** Faculty, staff, and research associate in the mental health field. Conducts and supports research on management, prevention, and investigation of mental illness among Native Americans and Alaska Natives. Assists organizations in conducting and implementing mental health research. Disseminates information and statistics to public. **Libraries: Type:** reference. **Holdings:** 600; archival material, books, monographs, periodicals. **Subjects:** mental health. **Telecommunication Services:** electronic mail, aianp.journalmanager@uchsc.edu. **Publications:** *American Indian and Alaska Native Mental Health Research: The Journal of the National Center*, 3/year. Includes empirical research, case studies, unpublished dissertations, and articles on behavioral and social health sciences. **Price:** free online. ISSN: 1533-7731. Alternate Formats: online ● *Behavioral Health Issues Among American Indians and Alaska Natives: Explorations on the Frontiers of the Biobehavioral Sciences.* Monograph ● *Calling From the Rim: Suicidal Behavior Among American Indian and Alaska Native Adolescents.* Monograph. Alternate Formats: online ● *Mental Health Programs for American Indians: Their Logic, Structure and Function.* Monograph ● *New Directions in Prevention Among American Indian and Alaska Native Communities.* Monograph ● *The People Who Give More: Health and Mental Health Among the Contemporary Puyallup Indian Tribal Community.* Monograph. **Price:** $20.00. Alternate Formats: online.

14903 ■ National Coalition of Mental Health Professionals and Consumers (NCMHPC)
PO Box 438
Commack, NY 11725
Ph: (631)979-5307
Free: (866)826-2548
Fax: (631)979-5293
E-mail: ncmhpc@aol.com
URL: http://www.nomanagedcare.org
Contact: William MacGillivray PhD, Pres.
Founded: 1992. **Members:** 1,000. **Membership Dues:** professional, $100 (annual) ● consumer, student, $35 (annual) ● supporter, $35-$99 (annual) ● advocate, $100-$175 (annual) ● challenger, $176-$250 (annual) ● reformer, $251-$500 (annual) ● leader, $501-$1,000 (annual) ● champion, $1,001-$2,500 (annual) ● hero, $2,501-$5,000 (annual) ● super hero, $5,001-$10,000 (annual) ● angel, $10,000 (annual). **Budget:** $100,000. **Regional Groups:** 6. **State Groups:** 6. **Description:** Grassroots organization of mental health professionals, consumers and consumer advocates. Works to address the negative impact of managed care on patients and professionals in mental health care; promotes pro-patient, pro-quality alternatives that preserve a patient's right to choice, privacy, and control over treatment, expose abuses in managed care, bring about regulation and replacement of the managed care industry, and genuine system reforms that bring about affordable health care that is accessible by everyone. **Awards:** Karen Shore Mental Health Advocacy Award. **Frequency:** annual. **Type:** recognition. **Recipient:** for dedicated contribution to advocacy. **Computer Services:** database ● information services ● mailing lists ● online services. **Additional Websites:** http://www.thenationalcoalition.org. **Committees:** Social. **Publications:** *Coalition Report*, bimonthly. Newsletter. **Price:** included in membership dues. **Circulation:** 1,000. **Advertising:** accepted. Alternate Formats: online ● *Consumer Protection Manual.* **Price:** $14.00 for the first copy; $9.00 for each additional copy ● Articles. Alternate Formats: online. **Conventions/Meetings:** annual conference (exhibits).

14904 ■ National Coalition of Psychiatrists Against Motorcoach Therapy (NCPAMT)
c/o Dr. Anne Rose
4909 Briarwood Ave., No. 7
Royal Oak, MI 48073-1318
Contact: Jonathon Steele Ph.D., Exec.Dir.
Founded: 1985. **Members:** 430. **Description:** Psychiatrists, psychotherapists, psychologists, social workers, counselors, and mental health officials. Objective is to stop the practice of "Motorcoach Therapy," described by the coalition as the "escalating and unethical practice of procuring one-way bus fares for habitual and undesirable mental health patients" upon their release from local mental health facilities. Provides for information exchange; has launched an awareness campaign targeted primarily at mental health officials. **Convention/Meeting:** none.

14905 ■ National Council for Community Behavioral Healthcare (NCCBH)
12300 Twinbrook Pkwy., Ste.320
Rockville, MD 20852
Ph: (301)984-6200
Fax: (301)881-7159
E-mail: lindar@nccbh.org
URL: http://www.nccbh.org
Contact: Ms. Linda Rosenberg, Pres./CEO
Founded: 1969. **Members:** 1,200. **Staff:** 12. **Budget:** EUR 3,000,000. **State Groups:** 40. **Description:** Conducts educational programs. Maintains speakers' bureau. **Awards: Frequency:** annual. **Type:** recognition. **Computer Services:** Mailing lists, 2500 mental health agencies. **Formerly:** (1997) National Council on Community Mental Health Centers; (1999) National Community Mental Healthcare Council. **Publications:** *Letter from Linda*, monthly. Newsletter ● *National Council News*, 11/year. Newsletter. **Circulation:** 3,000. **Advertising:** accepted. **Conventions/Meetings:** annual conference (exhibits).

14906 ■ National Education Alliance for Borderline Personality Disorder (NEA-BPD)
PO Box 974
Rye, NY 10580
Ph: (914)835-9011
E-mail: neabpd@aol.com
URL: http://www.neabpd.org
Contact: Perry D. Hoffman PhD, Pres.
Founded: 2001. **Description:** Promotes medical research on borderline personality disorder (BPD). Provides educational materials and programs on BPD. Seeks to enhance the quality of life of those people affected by this mental illness. Raises public awareness on all aspects of BPD. **Awards:** Young Investigator's Award. **Frequency:** annual. **Type:** recognition. **Recipient:** for excellence in research on borderline personality disorder. **Publications:** *A BPD Brief.* Pamphlet. Provides an introductory overview of borderline personality disorder. Alternate Formats: online ● *NEA-BPD Update.* Newsletter. Alternate Formats: online ● *Perspectives on Borderline Personality Disorder.* Journal. Addresses the issues concerning borderline personality disorder. ● Articles. Alternate Formats: online.

14907 ■ National Foundation for Depressive Illness (NAFDI)
Address Unknown since 2007
URL: http://www.depression.org
Founded: 1983. **Membership Dues:** partner (base level), $25 (annual). **Staff:** 3. **Description:** Provides public and professional education and information on recent medical advances in affective mood disorders. Conducts seminars on affective disorders, pharmaceutical development, and disease-related loss of productivity. Maintains speakers' bureau. Provides support group and referral services to appropriate doctors. **Publications:** *NAFDI News*, quarterly. Newsletter. **Advertising:** not accepted ● *Now We Can Treat the Illness Called Depression* ● Brochures.

14908 ■ National Institute of Mental Health (NIMH)
6001 Executive Blvd., Rm. 8184
MSC 9663
Bethesda, MD 20892-9663
Ph: (301)443-4513
Free: (866)615-6464
Fax: (301)443-4279
E-mail: nimhinfo@nih.gov
URL: http://www.nimh.nih.gov
Nonmembership. Description: Conducts and supports mental health research. Distributes information about mental health and mental disorders. **Conventions/Meetings:** meeting ● symposium ● workshop.

14909 ■ National Latino Behavioral Health Association (NLBHA)
c/o A. Marie Sanchez, BSW, Exec. Dir.
PO Box 387
Berthoud, CO 80513
Ph: (970)532-7210
Fax: (970)532-7209
E-mail: marie.sanchez@prodigy.net
URL: http://www.nlbha.org
Contact: A. Marie Sanchez BSW, Exec. Dir.
Membership Dues: individual, mental health professional, $30 (annual) ● human services professional, other professional, $20 (annual) ● organization, $100 (annual) ● consumer, family member, student, $10 (annual). **Languages:** English, Spanish. **Description:** Provides national leadership for the advancement of Latino behavioral health services. Seeks to bring attention to the great disparities that exist in areas of access, utilization, practice-based research and adequately trained personnel.

14910 ■ National Stigma Clearinghouse
245 8th Ave., No. 213
New York, NY 10011
Ph: (212)255-4411
E-mail: stigmanet@webtv.net
URL: http://community-2.webtv.net/stigmanet
Description: Works to end exploitation of mental illness, encourage balanced portrayals of people with psychiatric vulnerabilities, promotes accuracy in using medical terms.

14911 ■ North American Society for Childhood Onset Schizophrenia (NASCOS)
88 Briarwood Dr. E
Berkeley Heights, NJ 07922
E-mail: info@nascos.org
URL: http://www.nascos.org
Contact: Karen Sniezek, Co-Dir.
Founded: 2004. **Description:** Provides web-based resources about childhood onset schizophrenia. Serves as a forum for families, caregivers, and medical professionals to interact and share their knowledge and information related to schizophrenia. **Computer Services:** Information services, readings in schizophrenia ● online services, knowledge base access.

14912 ■ Obsessive-Compulsive Foundation (OCF)
676 State St.
New Haven, CT 06511
Ph: (203)401-2070
Fax: (203)401-2076
E-mail: info@ocfoundation.org
URL: http://www.ocfoundation.org
Contact: Joy Kant, Pres.
Founded: 1986. **Members:** 11,000. **Membership Dues:** consumer or professional, $85 (annual) ● regular in U.S., $45 (annual) ● regular in Canada, $50 (annual) ● regular outside U.S. and Canada, $55 (annual) ● consumer or professional in Canada, $90 (annual) ● consumer or professional outside U.S. and Canada, $95 (annual) ● family, $65 (annual). **Staff:** 4. **Budget:** $1,000,000. **State Groups:** 9. **Languages:** English, Spanish. **Description:** Individuals with obsessive-compulsive disorders and their families and friends; professionals involved in the treatment of OCD. (OCD is often chronic and characterized by recurrent unpleasant thoughts and/or repetitive behaviors that the person feels driven to perform. Individuals with OCD realize their obsessions and compulsions are irrational or excessive, yet find they have no control over them. Individuals with OCD often become demoralized, depressed, and anxious.) Seeks to control and find a cure for OCD while improving the welfare of its individuals with OCD. Disseminates information on OCD and possible new therapies. Offers educational programs for professionals and the public. **Awards:** OCF Research Award. **Frequency:** annual. **Type:** recognition. **Recipient:** for research projects on any aspects of obsessive compulsive or its spectrum disorders.

Computer Services: database, membership list ● database, treatment providers list. **Boards:** OCD Scientific Advisory. **Divisions:** Behavior Therapy Institute. **Formerly:** (1988) Obsessive Compulsive Disorder Foundation. **Publications:** *Kidscope*, semiannual. Newsletter. Contains topics for children and teens with OCD. ● *OCD*. Brochure ● *OCD Newsletter*, bimonthly ● Also produces educational materials. **Conventions/Meetings:** annual conference (exhibits).

14913 ■ Psychiatric Rehabilitation Services (PRS)
500 W Annandale Rd.
Falls Church, VA 22046
Ph: (703)536-9000
Fax: (703)533-9858
E-mail: info@prsinc.org
URL: http://www.prsinc.org
Contact: Wendy Gradison, Pres./CEO
Founded: 1963. **Description:** Works to help people with serious mental illness develop the skills and resources to recover and live satisfying and more self-sufficient lives in the community. **Publications:** Newsletter. Alternate Formats: online.

14914 ■ Selective Mutism Foundation (SMF)
c/o Carolyn Miller, Co-Founder/Co-Dir.
PO Box 13133
Sissonville, WV 25360-0133
URL: http://selectivemutismfoundation.org
Contact: Carolyn Miller, Co-Founder/Co-Dir.
Founded: 1991. **Members:** 3,000. **Membership Dues:** regular, $25 (annual). **Staff:** 8. **Languages:** English, Portuguese. **Description:** Individuals and families affected by selective mutism, an inherited anxiety disorder in which children with normal language skills or deficient language skills are unable to speak in school or other social situations. (Selective mutism is often mistaken for normal shyness, and may go undetected for as long as two years). Promotes awareness and understanding of this condition. Encourages research and treatment. Maintains speakers' bureau. **Libraries: Type:** reference. **Subjects:** in-service/sensitivity training. **Formerly:** (1993) Foundation for Elective Mutism, Inc. **Publications:** *Characteristics of Selective Mutism*. Book. Includes pregnancy information, familial background, personal feelings of symptoms and associated behaviors. ● *Let's Talk*. Newsletter. **Price:** $35.00 plus shipping and handling (25 issues) ● *Selective Mutism, A Silent Cry for Help*. Brochure. **Price:** free. **Advertising:** accepted.

14915 ■ Suicide and Mental Health Association International (SMHAI)
PO Box 702
Sioux Falls, SD 57101-0702
E-mail: smhai@suicideandmentalhealthasso-
ciationinternational.org
URL: http://suicideandmentalhealthasso-
ciationinternational.org
Contact: Robert Roerich MD, Hd. of Mental Division
Founded: 1997. **Membership Dues:** organization, $250 (annual) ● professional, $75 (annual) ● associate, $50 (annual) ● survivor, $50 (annual). **Multinational. Description:** Prevents suicidal behavior and relieves its effects on people who may be affected by it. Monitors the progress of suicide prevention activities. Increases awareness of mental health issues. Provides comprehensive information on suicide and mental health. **Libraries: Type:** reference. **Holdings:** articles, papers, periodicals. **Subjects:** suicide, mental health. **Awards: Frequency:** periodic. **Type:** trophy. **Recipient:** for outstanding sites with medical or mental health content. **Computer Services:** Information services, mental health resources ● information services, suicide issues and facts ● online services, screening tools and tests. **Programs:** Website Award.

14916 ■ Treatment and Research Advancements Association for Personality Disorder (TARA APD)
23 Greene St., 3rd Fl.
New York, NY 10013
Ph: (212)966-6514
Free: (888)4TARA-APD

E-mail: taraapd@aol.com
URL: http://www.tara4bpd.org
Contact: Valerie Porr MA, Pres./Founder
Founded: 1994. **Membership Dues:** individual, $50 (annual) ● family, $75 (annual) ● professional, $100 (annual) ● patron, $200-$500 (annual) ● sponsor, $1,000 (annual) ● benefactor, $2,000 (annual). **Description:** Seeks to advance research into the causes and treatment of personality disorders. Promotes and encourages educational programs that will benefit health professionals and people with personality disorders. **Publications:** *Guidelines for Choosing a DBT Therapist*. Brochure.

14917 ■ Trichotillomania Learning Center (TLC)
303 Potrero St., Ste.51
Santa Cruz, CA 95060
Ph: (831)457-1004
Fax: (831)426-4383
E-mail: info@trich.org
URL: http://www.trich.org
Contact: Christina Pearson, Exec. Dir.
Founded: 1991. **Membership Dues:** renewal and basic, $45 (annual) ● new supporting, $75 (annual) ● new patron, $100 (annual) ● new professional, $120 (annual). **Description:** Offers support to compulsive hair-pullers, their families and friends, and medical and mental health professionals. **Computer Services:** Mailing lists, TLC email news. **Publications:** *In Touch*, quarterly. Newsletter. Contains personal essays, articles from treatment providers, research updates and TTM-related events. **Conventions/Meetings:** annual retreat.

14918 ■ World Federation for Mental Health (WFMH)
6564 Loisdale Ct., Ste.301
Springfield, VA 22150
Ph: (703)313-8680
Fax: (703)313-8683
E-mail: info@wfmh.com
URL: http://www.wfmh.org
Contact: Mr. Preston Garrison, CEO/Sec. Gen.
Founded: 1948. **Members:** 1,112. **Membership Dues:** individual, $35 (annual) ● affiliate organization, $50 (annual) ● voting organization, $100 (annual). **Staff:** 4. **Budget:** $450,000. **Regional Groups:** 9. **Multinational. Description:** Represents associations and individuals dedicated to achieving the highest level of public mental health. Conducts charitable, scientific, literary, and educational activities in the field of mental health. Organizes training programs. Sponsors World Mental Health Day. **Formerly:** (1948) International Committee for Mental Hygiene. **Publications:** Newsletter, quarterly. **Price:** free for members.

Mentally Disabled

14919 ■ Academy on Mental Retardation (AMR)
c/o Linda Hickson, PhD, Sec.
Box 223, Teachers Coll.
Columbia Univ.
New York, NY 10027
Ph: (212)678-3854
Fax: (212)678-4034
E-mail: lh76@columbia.edu
Contact: Linda Hickson PhD, Sec.
Founded: 1963. **Members:** 250. **Membership Dues:** individual, $50 (annual) ● student, $25 (annual). **Description:** Scientists actively engaged in research in any discipline relating to mental retardation; active membership is limited to scientists possessing a doctorate degree. Encourages and promotes investigative work in the clinical and experimental field of mental retardation; provides a forum for research workers in this field. Facilitates relations between various disciplines and stimulates cooperative research. Cooperates with national and international organizations and cosponsors colloquia, symposia, and other meetings. **Awards:** Career Scientist Award. **Frequency:** annual. **Type:** recognition. **Recipient:** to an individual who has a distinguished career in

research on mental retardation ● Dissertation Award. **Frequency:** annual. **Type:** recognition. **Recipient:** to one or more outstanding doctoral dissertations in the field of mental retardation. **Affiliated With:** American Association on Intellectual and Developmental Disabilities. **Formerly:** (2003) American Academy on Mental Retardation. **Publications:** Newsletter, semiannual. Alternate Formats: online. **Conventions/Meetings:** annual meeting.

14920 ■ American Association on Intellectual and Developmental Disabilities (AAIDD)
444 N Capitol St. NW, Ste.846
Washington, DC 20001-1512
Ph: (202)387-1968
Free: (800)424-3688
Fax: (202)387-2193
E-mail: dcroser@aamr.org
URL: http://www.aamr.org
Contact: Ms. M. Doreen Croser, Exec. Dir.
Founded: 1876. **Members:** 9,500. **Membership Dues:** active/active electronic, $150 (annual) ● active sustaining, $250 (annual) ● corporate active, $135 (annual) ● young professional/active retired/family member/self-advocate/joint, $75 (annual) ● corporate principal, $595 (annual) ● active student, $50 (annual). **Staff:** 10. **Budget:** $2,000,000. **Regional Groups:** 9. **State Groups:** 40. **Description:** Physicians, educators, administrators, social workers, psychologists, psychiatrists, students, and others interested in the general welfare of persons with mental retardation and the study of the cause, treatment, and prevention of mental retardation. Maintains 17 divisions and subdivisions. **Awards: Frequency:** annual. **Type:** recognition. **Computer Services:** Mailing lists. **Committees:** Awards and Fellowship; International Activities; Legal and Social Issues; Prevention; Special Courses. **Affiliated With:** Academy on Mental Retardation; International Association for the Scientific Study of Intellectual Disabilities; World Federation for Mental Health. **Formerly:** (1906) Association of Medical Officers of American Institutions of Idiotic and Feebleminded Children; (1933) American Association for the Study of the Feebleminded; (1987) American Association on Mental Deficiency; (2007) American Association on Mental Retardation. **Publications:** *American Journal of Mental Retardation* (in English, French, and Spanish), bimonthly. Contains research in the Biological Sciences. **Price:** $246.00 /year for institutions in U.S. (tier 1); $286.00 /year for institutions outside U.S. (tier 1); $283.00 /year for institutions in U.S. (tier 2); $323.00 /year for institutions outside U.S. (tier 2). ISSN: 0895-8017. **Circulation:** 10,000. **Advertising:** accepted. Also Cited As: *AJMR* ● *Innovations: A Research to Practice Series*, 3/year ● *Mental Retardation* (in English, French, and Spanish), bimonthly. Journal. Contains a journal of policy, practices, and perspectives. **Price:** $246.00 /year for institutions in U.S. (tier 1); $286.00 /year for institutions outside U.S. (tier 1); $283.00 /year for institutions in U.S. (tier 2); $323.00 /year for institutions outside U.S. (tier 2). ISSN: 0047-6765. **Circulation:** 10,000. **Advertising:** accepted. Also Cited As: *MR* ● *Mental Retardation: Definition, Classification, and Systems of Supports*. Manual. Contains terminology and classification in mental retardation. ● *News and Notes*, bimonthly. Newsletter. Alternate Formats: online ● Monograph ● Also publishes testing materials. **Conventions/Meetings:** annual meeting, products and services related to the field of mental retardation (exhibits) ● annual Public Policy Forum - meeting ● periodic regional meeting ● periodic seminar.

14921 ■ Association for the Help of Retarded Children (AHRC)
83 Maiden Ln.
New York, NY 10038
Ph: (212)780-2500
E-mail: sbstein@ahrcnyc.org
URL: http://www.ahrcnyc.org
Founded: 1949. **Members:** 12,000. **Membership Dues:** individual, $10 (annual) ● life, $200. **Staff:** 1,600. **Budget:** $100,000,000. **Description:** Developmentally disabled children and adults; their families; interested individuals. Provides support services,

training programs, clinics, schools, and residential facilities to the developmentally disabled. **Awards: Frequency:** annual. **Type:** scholarship. **Computer Services:** Online services, publication. **Telecommunication Services:** hotline, membership, (212)-895-3377. **Publications:** *The Chronicle*, 3/year. Magazine. **Price:** included in membership dues. **Circulation:** 12,000. Alternate Formats: online ● Reports, annual ● Bulletin.

14922 ■ National Association of Qualified Mental Retardation Professionals (NAQMRP)

100 N Gougar
Joliet, IL 60432
Ph: (815)485-6197
Fax: (815)485-5975
E-mail: hjanczak@trinity-services.org
URL: http://www.qmrp.org
Founded: 1996. **Membership Dues:** full, $50 (annual) ● student/affiliate, $25 (annual). **Description:** Promotes the interests of qualified mental retardation professionals in order to improve human welfare. **Conventions/Meetings:** annual conference.

Metabolic Disorders

14923 ■ Albinism World Alliance (AWA)

c/o National Organization for Albinism and Hypopigmentation
PO Box 959
East Hampstead, NH 03826-0959
Ph: (603)887-2310
Free: (800)473-2310
Fax: (800)648-2310
E-mail: awa@albinism.org
URL: http://www.albinism.org/awa.html
Contact: Jeannine Stearns, Chair
Founded: 1992. **Multinational. Description:** Albinism support groups in 15 countries. (Albinism is an inherited metabolic disorder that results in reduced pigment in the hair, eyes, and/or skin of those it affects; people with albinism also have impaired eye function including decreased visual acuity, involuntary eye movements, and increased sensitivity to light.) Fosters communication among albinism support groups, and promotes development of albinism support groups worldwide. Disseminates information. **Publications:** none. **Conventions/Meetings:** biennial meeting, held in conjunction with the National Organization for Albinism and Hypopigmentation National Conference.

14924 ■ American Porphyria Foundation (APF)

PO Box 22712
Houston, TX 77227
Ph: (713)266-9617
Free: (866)APF-3635
Fax: (713)840-9552
E-mail: porphyrus@aol.com
URL: http://www.porphyriafoundation.com
Contact: Desiree H. Lyon, Exec. Dir.
Founded: 1981. **Members:** 1,900. **Membership Dues:** in U.S., $30 (annual) ● outside U.S., $40 (annual). **Staff:** 2. **Budget:** $100,000. **Description:** Persons interested in advancing awareness and treatment of the porphyrias; affected patients. (Porphyria is a class of seven rare and usually inherited metabolic disorders of varying severity affecting the nervous system or the skin. It is characterized by a deficiency of an enzyme used in making heme a ring-shaped molecule called a porphyrin, which in turn is used in making hemoglobin. One of porphyria's recurrent though not requisite symptoms is purple-red urine.) Aims are to: provide financial support for researchers in porphyria; improve the diagnosis and treatment of porphyria through educational programs; locate porphyria patients. Maintains a lending library of videotapes, papers, and pamphlets. **Awards:** Research Grant. **Frequency:** annual. **Type:** grant. **Telecommunication Services:** electronic mail, lyonapf@aol.com. **Divisions:** Patient Education; Physician Education. **Publications:** *American Porphyria Foundation—Newsletter*, quarterly. Contains educational

information. **Price:** included in membership dues. **Circulation:** 1,000. **Advertising:** accepted. Alternate Formats: online ● *Porphyria, A Lyon's Share of Trouble.* Book. **Price:** $20.00 in U.S.; $30.00 outside U.S. ● Pamphlets ● Newsletter, bimonthly. Covers news in the world of porphyria. Alternate Formats: online ● Video. **Price:** $25.00 in U.S.; $30.00 outside U.S. ● Brochures ● Also compiles list of physicians with experience in treating porphyria. **Conventions/Meetings:** annual convention (exhibits) ● annual Physician Lecture Series and Symposium - lecture and symposium.

14925 ■ Association for Glycogen Storage Disease (AGSD)

PO Box 896
Durant, IA 52747
Ph: (563)785-6038
Fax: (563)785-6038
E-mail: maryc@agsdus.org
URL: http://www.agsdus.org
Contact: Hollie Swain, Pres.
Founded: 1979. **Members:** 400. **Membership Dues:** active, $20 (annual) ● associate, $15 (annual). **Description:** Individuals afflicted with glycogen storage disease; families of GSD sufferers; health care professionals. (GSD is a hereditary condition characterized by a lack of or deficiency in any of the enzymes used by the body to break down glycogen, resulting in hypoglycemia and related disorders, and requiring diet modifications and frequent or continual feeding, and in extreme cases resulting in death.) Acts as a forum for the discussion of GSD, its treatment, and the problems faced by parents raising children with GSD. Disseminates medical information; fosters communication between the families of GSD patients and health care professionals. Conducts fundraising drive. Aids members in obtaining equipment necessary for home care of GSD patients; provides referral services for individuals seeking GSD treatment facilities. **Awards:** AGSD Grant. **Frequency:** annual. **Type:** scholarship. **Recipient:** for work with GSD. **Publications:** *Could Someone You Know be Affected?*. Brochures. **Price:** free ● *Parent Handbook.* **Price:** $10.00 ● *The Ray*, quarterly. Newsletter. **Price:** free. **Circulation:** 900. **Conventions/Meetings:** annual conference.

14926 ■ Children's PKU Network (CPN)

3790 Via De La Valle, Ste.120
Del Mar, CA 92014
Ph: (858)509-0767
Free: (800)377-6677
Fax: (858)509-0768
E-mail: pkunetwork@aol.com
URL: http://www.pkunetwork.org
Founded: 1991. **Members:** 8. **Staff:** 1. **Budget:** $40,000. **Description:** Works to address the special needs of all people involved in the treatment of Phenylketonuria (PKU), a genetic metabolic disease whereby the body is unable to process the amino acid phenylalanine. Networks families and individuals with each other; provides discount dietary aids; offers financial assistance and support groups; provides crisis intervention; advocates mandatory guidelines for insurance carriers to cover expenses of medical food treatment of PKU individuals; conducts fundraisers; endows research benefiting PKU and other metabolic disorders. **Libraries: Type:** lending. **Holdings:** articles, video recordings. **Subjects:** PKU research, effects and treatment. **Awards:** Children's PKU Network Annual Scholarship. **Frequency:** annual. **Type:** scholarship. **Recipient:** students with PKU. **Councils:** Regional Coordinators. **Programs:** Crisis Intervention. **Publications:** *UPDATE*, semiannual. Newsletter. **Conventions/Meetings:** monthly board meeting - always second Wednesday.

14927 ■ Cystinosis Foundation (CF)

604 Vernon St.
Oakland, CA 94610
Ph: (559)222-7997
Free: (800)392-8458
Fax: (559)222-7997

E-mail: jean.cystinosis@sbcglobal.net
URL: http://www.cystinosisfoundation.org
Contact: Jean Hotz, Pres.
Founded: 1983. **Members:** 150. **Membership Dues:** individual, $20 ● family, $45 ● contributing, $100 ● professional, $250 ● patron, $500 ● life, $1,000 ● corporation, $2,000 ● Honor Circle, $5,000. **Budget:** $118,500. **Regional Groups:** 20. **Description:** Parents, relatives, and friends of cystinotic children; interested members of the medical community and the public. (Cystinosis is a genetic metabolic disease in which abnormal amounts of the amino acid cystine collect in the cells, leading to kidney failure.) Aims to increase public awareness about cystinosis; to act as a support group to parents of children with the disease; to raise funds for research. Maintains speakers' bureau. **Libraries: Type:** reference. **Holdings:** books, papers. **Subjects:** cystinosis. **Awards: Type:** grant. **Recipient:** for research ● Volunteer of the Year Award. **Type:** recognition. **Affiliated With:** National Organization for Rare Disorders. **Formerly:** Alliance of Genetic Support Groups; (1986) Cystinosis Foundation of California. **Publications:** *Cystinosis Foundation Newsletter*, quarterly ● *Facts About Cystinosis*. Brochure. Alternate Formats: online ● *National Directory of Information*, periodic. Contains information about physicians engaged in cystinosis research. ● *Directory*, periodic. Contains information about children with cystinosis. **Conventions/Meetings:** annual conference and symposium.

14928 ■ Cystinosis Research Network (CRN)

10 Pine Ave.
Burlington, MA 01803
Ph: (781)229-6182
Free: (866)276-3669
Fax: (781)229-6182
E-mail: crn@cystinosis.org
URL: http://www.cystinosis.org
Contact: Jose T. Morales, Pres.
Description: Seeks to discover improved treatments and a cure for cystinosis. Supports and advocates research on cystinosis. Provides family assistance through the establishment of support groups. Educates the public and medical communities about the symptoms and complications of cystinosis. **Awards:** CRN Scholarship. **Frequency:** annual. **Type:** scholarship. **Recipient:** to students who have demonstrated strong academic skills and excellent recommendations. **Publications:** *Cystinosis - Information for Medical Professionals*. Brochure. Alternate Formats: online ● Newsletter. Alternate Formats: online.

14929 ■ FOD Family Support Group

c/o Deb Lee Gould, MEd, Dir.
2041 Tomahawk
Okemos, MI 48864
Ph: (517)381-1940
E-mail: deb@fodsupport.org
URL: http://www.fodsupport.org
Contact: Deb Lee Gould MEd, Dir.
Founded: 1991. **Members:** 1,100. **Staff:** 1. **Budget:** $6,000. **Multinational. Description:** Seeks to provide emotional and practical support for families living with Fatty Oxidation Disorders (FODs), as well as interested professionals. **Computer Services:** Mailing lists, available only to FOD families and interested professionals. **Affiliated With:** Genetic Alliance. **Formerly:** MCAD Family Support Group. **Publications:** *FOD Communication Network*, semiannual. Newsletter. Contains medical and pharmaceutical updates, family stories, questions and answers; available in hardcopy. **Price:** free. **Circulation:** 1,100. Alternate Formats: online ● *FOD Family Support Group Brochure*. Alternate Formats: online. **Conventions/Meetings:** convention - every 18 months.

14930 ■ Iron Overload Diseases Association (IOD)

PO Box 15857
West Palm Beach, FL 33416-5857
Ph: (561)586-8246

E-mail: iod@ironoverload.org
URL: http://www.ironoverload.org
Contact: Roberta Crawford, Pres./Founder
Founded: 1980. **Members:** 8,000. **Membership Dues:** individual, $50-$499 (annual) ● sustaining, $500-$999 (annual) ● sponsor, $1,000-$4,999 (annual) ● patron, $5,000-$9,999 (annual) ● benefactor, $50,000 (annual). **Staff:** 5. **Budget:** $150,000. **Multinational. Description:** Physicians and patients. Serves hemochromatosis patients and families. Encourages research and public information. Develops a public relations plan, television interviews, and press releases. Sponsors screening programs and patient referral service. Prepares diagnosis sheets for doctors and medical schools. Authorities believe that five in 1000 carry both genes and that one in eight carries a single gene. Acts as a clearinghouse for doctors to call on for research materials. Sponsors fundraising program. Is also in the process of setting up an index of laboratory research in progress. Conducts programs; compiles statistics; maintains speakers' bureau; conducts research programs. **Libraries: Type:** reference. **Holdings:** 2; archival material, books. **Subjects:** medical literature, case histories. **Awards: Type:** grant. **Recipient:** for research. **Telecommunication Services:** phone referral service, physician referral and counseling. **Committees:** Public Health Education. **Publications:** *Ironic Blood*, bimonthly. Newsletter. Contains information on iron overload. **Price:** free. ISSN: 0895-7762. **Circulation:** 8,000. Alternate Formats: online ● *Overload: An Ironic Disease*. Booklet. **Conventions/Meetings:** annual Medical Symposium ● periodic workshop, for physicians, nurses, and the general public.

14931 ■ Maple Syrup Urine Family Support Group
82 Ravine Rd.
Powell, OH 43065
Ph: (740)548-4475
E-mail: dbulcher@aol.com
URL: http://www.msud-support.org
Contact: Sandra Bulcher, Dir.
Founded: 1982. **Members:** 600. **Membership Dues:** family with child with MSUD or any interested person, $10 (annual). **Description:** Those affected by Maple Syrup Urine Disease (MSUD) and their families; health care professionals, and other interested persons from the U.S. and other countries. (Maple Syrup Urine Disease usually occurs in infancy and is characterized by a strong odor of the urine, loss of sucking reflex, general listlessness, episodes of rigidity, and high-pitched crying. If undiagnosed, the condition can progress to seizures, coma and death. Symptoms sometimes do not occur for several months.) Gathers and distributes information on MSUD. Seeks to strengthen the liaison between families and health care professionals. Funds and encourages research and advocates newborn screening for MSUD. **Formerly:** Families with Maple Syrup Urine Disease; (2003) MSUD Family Support Group. **Publications:** *MSUD Brochure* ● *MSUD Newsletter*, semiannual ● Also publishes information packet. **Conventions/Meetings:** biennial symposium (exhibits) - usually summer.

14932 ■ National Center for the Study of Wilson's Disease (NCSWD)
Address Unknown since 2007
Founded: 1971. **Members:** 9. **Staff:** 6. **Description:** Performs and supports research concerning hereditary diseases of metal metabolism, in particular Wilson's disease and Menkes' disease. Seeks to increase doctors' awareness of these diseases. (Wilson's disease, named for S.A.K. Wilson, who discovered the disease and published his findings in 1912, is caused by a genetic defect that permits excessive amounts of copper to accumulate in the liver and brain. The disease is fatal if untreated, but, if detected early enough, can be completely suppressed.) Encompasses research, diagnostic, and treatment center for Wilson's disease. Compiles statistics. **Libraries: Type:** reference. **Holdings:** archival material. **Subjects:** Wilson's disease. **Formerly:** Foundation for the Study of Wilson's Disease. **Publications:** *What is Wilson's Disease?*. Brochure

● *Wilson's Disease, 1st Ed. 1984; 2nd Ed in preparation*. Monograph. **Advertising:** not accepted.

14933 ■ National Gaucher Foundation (NGF)
2227 Idlewood Rd., Ste.12
Tucker, GA 30084
Free: (800)504-3189
Fax: (770)934-2911
E-mail: ngf@gaucherdisease.org
URL: http://www.gaucherdisease.org
Contact: Rhonda P. Buyers, Exec. Dir.
Founded: 1984. **Members:** 1,000. **Membership Dues:** subscription, $35 (annual). **Staff:** 3. **Budget:** $600,000. **Regional Groups:** 2. **Local Groups:** 2. **Description:** Persons with Gaucher Disease; interested medical professionals and individuals. Gaucher Disease, one of the most common inherited metabolic disorders, is caused by an enzyme deficiency which renders the body unable to break down and dispose of complex lipids (fat-like substances). Sponsors direct funding of and support for research and clinical programs at medical centers in the U.S. and abroad to develop a cure and/or treatment for Gaucher Disease. Seeks to help persons with the disorder by providing them the opportunity to share experiences and feelings on a confidential, personal basis. Disseminates technical and nontechnical information concerning the disease. Advocates increased screening for carriers and availability of prenatal diagnosis for families at risk. **Libraries: Type:** reference. **Holdings:** archival material, artwork, audiovisuals, clippings, reports, video recordings. **Subjects:** Gaucher's disease, Ceredase/Cerezyme. **Awards: Type:** grant. **Computer Services:** Online services, publication. **Supersedes:** Gaucher Disease Registry. **Publications:** *Gaucher Disease Newsletter*, quarterly. Includes index, reprints of recent literature, legislative reports, and medical questions and answers. **Price:** included in membership dues. **Circulation:** 1,000. Alternate Formats: online. **Conventions/Meetings:** biennial conference.

14934 ■ National MPS Society
PO Box 736
Bangor, ME 04402-0736
Ph: (207)947-1445
Fax: (207)990-3074
E-mail: info@mpssociety.org
URL: http://www.mpssociety.org
Contact: Barbara Wedehase, Exec. Dir.
Founded: 1974. **Members:** 800. **Membership Dues:** family, $50 (annual) ● professional, $75 (annual) ● foreign, $80 (annual) ● corporate, $1,000 (annual). **Staff:** 3. **Budget:** $500,000. **Regional Groups:** 9. **Description:** Professionals and families devoted to educating the public and discovering and aiding families of MPS and ML children. Mucopolysaccharidoses (MPS) and mucolipidoses (ML) are extremely rare hereditary diseases caused by particular enzyme deficiencies and range in severity from strictly bone and joint involvement to massive complications in all organ systems. Helps to facilitate diagnosis and treatment through referrals to doctors and hospitals. Maintains parent referral service to direct families with newly diagnosed MPS and ML children to other members. **Libraries: Type:** reference. **Holdings:** articles, books. **Subjects:** mucopolysaccharidoses and related diseases. **Awards:** MPS and related disease research. **Frequency:** annual. **Type:** grant. **Recipient:** for individuals. **Formerly:** (1975) Parents for MPS; (1985) MPS Society. **Publications:** *Anesthesia*. Booklet ● *Courage*, quarterly. Newsletter ● *Education Strategies & Resources*. Booklet ● *Ethan's Feeling Switch*. Booklet. **Price:** $5.00 ● *Management of MPS & ML*. Booklet ● *ML II/III*. Booklet ● *MPS I*. Booklet ● *MPS II*. Booklet ● *MPS III*. Booklet ● *MPS IV*. Booklet ● *MPS VI*. Booklet. **Price:** $1.00 ● *MPS VII*. Booklet. **Conventions/Meetings:** annual MPS Society Family Conference - conference and symposium.

14935 ■ National Niemann Pick Disease Foundation (NNPDF)
PO Box 49
401 Madison Ave., Ste.B
Fort Atkinson, WI 53538

Ph: (920)563-0930
Free: (877)287-3672
Fax: (920)563-0931
E-mail: nnpdf@nndf.org
URL: http://www.nnpdf.org
Contact: Hunt Ozmer, Chm.
Founded: 1992. **Members:** 4,500. **Membership Dues:** individual/family, $20 (annual) ● friend, $50 (annual) ● contributor, $100 (annual) ● sponsor, $500 (annual) ● benefactor, $1,000 (annual). **Description:** Parents, medical and educational professionals, and friends. Works to promote medical research on Niemann-Pick Disease (NPD), a disorder which prevents metabolizing of the sphingomyelin lipid or cholesterol. Provides medical and educational information; offers support to families of children with NPD; facilitates genetic counseling for parents; supports legislation that affects patients and families with NPD; sponsors medical research. **Libraries: Type:** reference. **Holdings:** articles, periodicals. **Awards: Type:** grant. **Recipient:** for research of Niemann Pick Disease. **Publications:** *Niemann-Pick Newsletter*, quarterly. **Price:** free for members ● Directory. **Conventions/Meetings:** annual Family Conference - July or August.

14936 ■ National Organization for Albinism and Hypopigmentation (NOAH)
PO Box 959
East Hampstead, NH 03826-0959
Ph: (603)887-2310
Free: (800)473-2310
Fax: (800)648-2310
E-mail: webmaster@albinism.org
URL: http://www.albinism.org
Contact: Michael McGowan, Pres.
Founded: 1982. **Members:** 1,000. **Membership Dues:** individual, $20 (annual) ● family, $25 (annual) ● contributing, agency, $35 (annual) ● international, $30 (annual). **Regional Groups:** 40. **State Groups:** 21. **Description:** Individuals with albinism and their families; health care professionals; others interested in learning more about albinism. (Albinism is an inherited metabolic disorder that results in reduced pigment in the hair, eyes, and/or skin of those it affects; people with albinism also have impaired eye function including decreased visual acuity, involuntary eye movements, and increased sensitivity to light.) Seeks to educate the public, teachers, and health care professionals about albinism. Provides support to individuals with albinism and their families. Encourages research on the cause, results, and management of the disorder. **Libraries: Type:** reference. **Subjects:** albinism. **Committees:** Advocacy. **Projects:** Parent Book. **Subgroups:** Adults with Albinism; Ethnic Minorities; Hermansky-Pudlak Syndrome; Parents. **Affiliated With:** Hermansky-Pudlak Syndrome Network. **Publications:** *NOAH Information Bulletin*, periodic. Provides information on various aspects of albinism. ● *NOAH News*, quarterly. **Price:** $5.00 ● *The Student with Albinism in the Regular Classroom*. Book. **Conventions/Meetings:** biennial conference (exhibits).

14937 ■ Paget Foundation for Paget's Disease of Bone and Related Disorders (PDF)
120 Wall St., Ste.1602
New York, NY 10005-4001
Ph: (212)509-5335
Free: (800)23-PAGET
Fax: (212)509-8492
E-mail: pagetfdn@aol.com
URL: http://www.paget.org
Contact: Stanley Wallach, Pres.
Founded: 1978. **Staff:** 4. **Budget:** $600,000. **Languages:** English, French. **Description:** Patients and their families and friends; physicians; paramedical professionals interested in improving health care of persons suffering from Paget's disease, a chronic disorder which may result in enlarged, deformed, and fragile bones in one or more regions of the skeleton, fibrous dysplasia, and Primary Hyperparathyroidism (PHPT). Addresses related bone disorders such as fibrous dysplasia and both breast, prostate cancer hetastatic to bone. Conducts educational programs for patients, health care professionals, and the public;

provides patient assistance and research advocacy; maintains referral service for patients seeking physicians who specialize in treating Paget's disease and PHPT. **Committees:** Advisory Medical Panel. **Formerly:** (1992) Paget's Disease Foundation. **Publications:** *Q+A*. Brochures ● *Update*, 3/year. Newsletter. **Price:** free. **Circulation:** 30,000. **Conventions/ Meetings:** symposium - 2-3/year. 2007 Oct. 25-27, Philadelphia, PA.

14938 ■ Parents of Galactosemic Children (PGC)

c/o Michelle Fowler, Pres.
PO Box 2401
Mandeville, LA 70470
Ph: (985)875-3136
Free: (866)900-7421
Fax: (985)875-3136
E-mail: president@galactosemia.org
URL: http://www.galactosemia.org
Contact: Michelle Fowler, Pres.

Founded: 1985. **Members:** 1,200. **Staff:** 3. **Description:** Parents of children born with galactosemia, galactosemic adults, and family members and professionals of those affected by galactosemia. (Children with galactosemia are missing an enzyme in their body (liver) that metabolizes (breaks down) lactose and/or galactose into glucose. Some possible side affects include jaundice, an enlarged liver, cataracts, kidney failure, speech delays, fine and gross motor skill complications, tremors, and possibly even brain damage.) Run by volunteers that rely solely on donations in order to obtain financial support for galactosemia research professionals and reach as many families' possible affected by galactosemia. Offers support, educational programs, and other information to galactosemic families and interested professionals. Seeks ways for children and adults with galactosemia to live their lives to their fullest potential. Keeps in touch with one another through monthly e-mails. Maintains website that offers discussion forum and support. Publishes newsletters mailed twice a year. Conducts national conference held every two years. **Libraries: Type:** open to the public. **Holdings:** articles, books, periodicals, video recordings. **Publications:** *Galactosemia Newsletter*, semiannual. **Circulation:** 1,200. **Advertising:** accepted. **Conventions/Meetings:** semiannual Galactosemia Conference (exhibits).

14939 ■ Purine Research Society

c/o Tahma Metz, Exec. Dir.
5424 Beech Ave.
Bethesda, MD 20814-1730
Ph: (301)530-0354
Fax: (301)564-9597
E-mail: purine@erols.com
URL: http://www.purineresearchsociety.org
Contact: Tahma Metz, Exec. Dir.

Founded: 1986. **Membership Dues:** individual, $25 (annual). **Staff:** 1. **Description:** Supports DNA research, looking for mutations in DNA, both nuclear and mitochondrial that might cause autistic symptoms or autistic/epileptic symptoms in patients. Offers publications and reference information, including a purine-restricted diet. **Awards: Type:** grant. **Formerly:** (1995) Purine 24, Inc. **Publications:** Brochure. **Price:** free ● Bulletin. **Conventions/Meetings:** annual board meeting - in Washington, DC.

14940 ■ Syndrome X Association

PO Box 331
Munroe Falls, OH 44262
E-mail: info@syndromexassoc.org
URL: http://www.syndromexassoc.org
Contact: Lana W. Koehler BSEd, Founder/Pres./ Exec. Dir.

Founded: 2003. **Description:** Represents individuals dedicated to helping patients and their healthcare providers with early diagnosis and treatment of Metabolic Syndrome X (MSX). Seeks to understand this disease through education, information and research. Provides support and encouragement to those who have been diagnosed. **Telecommunication Services:** electronic mail, lanakoehler@syn-

dromexassoc.org. **Publications:** *XChanges*, bimonthly. Newsletter.

14941 ■ Wilson's Disease Association International (WDA)

1802 Brookside Dr.
Wooster, OH 44691
Ph: (330)264-1450
Free: (888)264-1450
Fax: (330)264-0974
E-mail: info@wilsonsdisease.org
URL: http://www.wilsonsdisease.org
Contact: Kimberly F. Symonds, Exec. Dir.

Founded: 1978. **Members:** 1,000. **Membership Dues:** basic, $35 (annual) ● basic plus, $60 (annual) ● silver, $120 (annual) ● gold, $250 (annual) ● copper, $1,000 (annual). **Staff:** 1. **Budget:** $36,000. **Local Groups:** 2. **Languages:** English, French, German, Portuguese, Spanish. **Multinational. Description:** Patients of Wilson's disease relatives and friends of patients; physicians and other health care professionals. (Wilson's disease, named for S.A.K. Wilson, a pioneer in the study of the disease, is a genetic nervous disorder in which excessive amounts of copper collect in the liver, brain, and kidneys.) Promotes and sponsors research regarding the cause, treatment, cure, and prevention of Wilson's and related diseases. Stresses the importance of public awareness, early diagnosis, and treatment. Provides financial aid and moral support to needy individuals and organizations sharing the association's goals; serves as liaison among members and cooperating organizations. **Libraries: Type:** reference. **Holdings:** 5. **Awards:** Morton and Henrietta Sellivan Professorship in Human Genetics. **Type:** recognition. **Recipient:** spontaneous with board approval. **Computer Services:** database ● mailing lists. **Publications:** *The Copper Connection*, quarterly. Newsletter. Includes research reports, member profiles, and book reviews. **Price:** included in membership dues. **Circulation:** 750. **Advertising:** accepted. Alternate Formats: online ● *Wilson's Disease: Questions and Answers*. Brochures ● Membership Directory, annual. **Price:** included in membership dues. **Circulation:** 200. **Advertising:** accepted ● Also publishes many other brochures on various aspects of Wilson's disease. **Conventions/Meetings:** annual meeting, topic development and education.

Military

14942 ■ Armed Forces Institute of Pathology (AFIP)

6825 16th St. NW
Washington, DC 20306-6000
Ph: (202)782-2882
E-mail: draleyd@afip.osd.mil
URL: http://www.afip.org
Contact: Col. Renata B. Greenspan MC, Dir.

Founded: 1862. **Members:** 842. **Budget:** $53,000,000. **Languages:** English, French, German, Spanish. **Description:** Chartered by the Department of Defense to: maintain a consultation service for the diagnosis of pathologic material; conduct experimental, statistical, and morphological research in pathology; provide instruction in advanced pathology and related subjects; prepare, procure, and duplicate teaching aids; operate the AFIP Repository and Research Services; maintain the National Museum of Health and Medicine and a Visual Information Service for the collection, preparation, duplication, reference, and filing of medical illustrative material. Sponsors a series of courses. **Libraries: Type:** reference; open to the public. **Subjects:** medicine, pathology. **Telecommunication Services:** electronic mail, greenspan@afip.osd.mil ● electronic mail, telepath@ afip.osd.mil. **Formerly:** (1949) Army Medical Museum. **Publications:** *AFIP Letter*, bimonthly. Newsletter. Third series, containing 30 separate fascicles, with international distribution. **Circulation:** 20,000 ● *Atlas of Tumor Pathology*. Book. **Price:** $120.00/copy. **Conventions/Meetings:** annual seminar and conference.

14943 ■ Army Nurse Corps Association (ANCA)

PO Box 39235
San Antonio, TX 78218-1235
Ph: (210)650-3534
Fax: (210)650-3494
E-mail: membership@e-anca.org
URL: http://e-anca.org
Contact: Ltc. Larry W. Moss, Pres.

Founded: 1977. **Members:** 2,100. **Membership Dues:** regular, $40 (biennial). **Description:** Army Nurse Corps officers from active, or retiree status or those serving honorably for shorter periods, or reserve duty. Provides educational and social opportunities for members; disseminates information to the public. Seeks to preserve history of the U.S. Army Nurse Corps. **Awards:** Army Nurse Corps Education Fund. **Type:** grant. **Recipient:** for baccalaureate or graduate nursing programs. **Formerly:** (2001) Retired Army Nurse Corps Association. **Publications:** *Connection*, quarterly. Newsletter. **Conventions/Meetings:** biennial congress and convention.

14944 ■ Association of Military Surgeons of the U.S. (AMSUS)

9320 Old Georgetown Rd.
Bethesda, MD 20814-1653
Ph: (301)897-8800
Free: (800)761-9320
Fax: (301)530-5446
E-mail: amsus@amsus.org
URL: http://www.amsus.org
Contact: Maj. Gen. George K. Anderson Ret., Exec. Dir.

Founded: 1891. **Members:** 12,000. **Membership Dues:** student, $17 (annual) ● regular, $50 (annual) ● life, $750. **Staff:** 10. **Local Groups:** 10. **Description:** Physicians, dentists, veterinarians, nurses, pharmacists, dietitians, therapists, and others of commissioned rank (or grades E5 through E9) or equivalent in the Army, Navy, Air Force, Public Health Service, and Veterans Administration; Reserve and National Guard officers are also eligible for membership. Advances all phases of federal medicine and allied sciences related to federal health services. Provides group insurance. **Libraries: Type:** reference. **Holdings:** articles, books. **Awards:** Capt. Carl A. Schlack Award. **Frequency:** annual. **Type:** recognition. **Recipient:** for contribution in dental education and research ● Lewis L. Seaman Enlisted Award. **Frequency:** annual. **Type:** recognition. **Recipient:** for outstanding accomplishments in advancing healthcare mission ● Major General Jerry Sanders Scholarship Program. **Frequency:** annual. **Type:** scholarship. **Recipient:** for those who are pursuing a healthcare related career ● Outstanding Federation Healthcare Executive Award. **Frequency:** annual. **Type:** recognition. **Recipient:** for outstanding senior healthcare executive officer. **Publications:** *Military Medicine*, monthly. Journal. Contains scientific papers, case reports, and editorials. **Price:** included in membership dues. Alternate Formats: online ● Newsletter, quarterly. Features legislative matters, health care news, news of members, meeting notices and other items of interest. **Price:** included in membership dues. Alternate Formats: online. **Conventions/Meetings:** annual convention (exhibits) - always November. 2007 Nov. 11-16, Salt Lake City, UT; 2008 Nov. 9-14, San Antonio, TX; 2009 Nov. 15-20, St. Louis, MO.

14945 ■ Society of Air Force Physicians (SAFP)

PO Box 64
Devine, TX 78016-0064
Ph: (830)665-4048
Fax: (830)665-9658
E-mail: safp2002@aol.com
URL: http://www.acponline.org/chapters/usaf
Contact: JoAnn Honn, Admin. Asst.

Founded: 1958. **Members:** 300. **Membership Dues:** individual, $20 (annual). **Staff:** 1. **Description:** Air Force internists, family practitioners, and specialists in emergency medicine, dermatology, allergy/immunology, and neurology. Seeks to foster advancement of the art and science of medicine in the Air

Force; encourage clinical and laboratory investigation; disseminate information. **Awards:** Grollman Award. **Frequency:** annual. **Type:** recognition ● Malcolm C. Grow Award. **Frequency:** annual. **Type:** recognition ● Resident Research Award. **Type:** recognition. **Affiliated With:** American College of Physicians-American Society of Internal Medicine. **Conventions/Meetings:** annual symposium, with scientific presentation (exhibits).

14946 ■ Society of Medical Consultants to the Armed Forces (SMCAF)
5 Southern Way
Fredericksburg, VA 22406
Ph: (540)548-2019
Fax: (540)361-2589
E-mail: margo@smcaf.org
URL: http://www.smcaf.org
Contact: Margo Cabrero, Exec. Dir.
Founded: 1946. **Members:** 716. **Membership Dues:** regular, $100 (annual). **Description:** Professional society of physicians and surgeons who have been in active military service and who have acted as consultants to the Surgeons General of the Army, Navy, or Air Force. Preserves and encourages the association of civilian consultants and military medical personnel and assists in the development and maintenance of the highest standards of medical practice in the Armed Forces. **Awards:** SMCAF Award. **Type:** recognition. **Recipient:** for a graduating student with highest level of academic performance. **Committees:** Archives and Medical History; Ethical Issues in Military Medicine; Legislative and Legal; Medical Education; Membership; Professional Services; Research and Development; Retention and Readiness. **Formerly:** Society of U.S. Medical Consultants in World War II. **Publications:** Directory, every 2-3 years ● Newsletter, 3/year. Alternate Formats: online. **Conventions/Meetings:** annual conference - always Bethesda, MD.

14947 ■ Society of Military Orthopaedic Surgeons (SOMOS)
c/o T.R.U.E. Research Foundation
8610 N New Braunfels Ave., Ste.705
San Antonio, TX 78217
Ph: (210)829-1239
Free: (888)329-1239
Fax: (210)829-5513
E-mail: j.bennett@truresearch.org
URL: http://www.truresearch.org/somos
Contact: Dr. James Rungee, Exec. Dir.
Founded: 1958. **Members:** 750. **Membership Dues:** staff/fellow/allied, $50 (annual) ● resident, $25 (annual). **Budget:** $40,000. **For-Profit. Description:** Orthopedic surgeons who have served in the active or reserve military. Seeks to stimulate scholarly contribution by military medical residents; act as clearinghouse; provides opportunities for consultation with and contributions of surgeons who are retired from the military; furthers the continuing education of orthopedic surgeons and residents. Presents scientific papers at annual meeting. **Awards:** Founders Award. **Frequency:** annual. **Type:** recognition ● Kirk Award. **Frequency:** annual. **Type:** recognition. **Telecommunication Services:** electronic mail, rungee@comcast.net. **Programs:** Military Orthopaedic Fellowship; Military Orthopaedic Residency. **Subgroups:** Collaborative Research. **Publications:** SOMOS Sentinel. Newsletter. Serves as a forum for members. Alternate Formats: online. **Conventions/Meetings:** annual meeting.

14948 ■ Society of Military Otolaryngologists - Head and Neck Surgeons (SMO-HNS)
c/o Sue Pearce, Admin. Sec.
9231 Shadow Lawn Cir.
Converse, TX 78109
Ph: (210)945-9006 (210)916-2367
Fax: (210)945-9024
E-mail: spearce@worldnet.att.net
Contact: Sue Pearce, Admin. Sec.
Founded: 1952. **Members:** 320. **Membership Dues:** $15 (annual). **Staff:** 1. **Description:** Otolaryngologists, head and neck surgeons and residents in training of the U.S. Army, Air Force, Navy, and former ac-

tive duty members. Purposes are to further the social and professional contacts of military otolaryngologists and to advance the science and art of the field. **Awards: Frequency:** annual. **Type:** recognition. **Recipient:** for military residents for the best papers ● **Frequency:** annual. **Type:** recognition. **Recipient:** for military residents for best poster presentation. **Formerly:** (1952) Society of Military Otolaryngologists. **Conventions/Meetings:** annual meeting and luncheon, in conjunction with American Academy of Otolaryngology - Head and Neck Surgery.

14949 ■ Uniformed Services Academy of Family Physicians (USAFP)
2301 N Parham Rd., Ste.4
Richmond, VA 23229
Ph: (804)968-4436
Fax: (804)968-4418
E-mail: tschulte@vafp.org
URL: http://www.usafp.org
Contact: Terrence J. Schulte, Exec. Dir.
Founded: 1972. **Members:** 2,000. **Staff:** 6. **Description:** Family physicians, teachers of family medicine, medical students, and residents in the armed services, public health service, or Indian health service. Sponsors continuing education program. Sponsors educational programs. **Awards:** Family Physician of the Year. **Frequency:** annual. **Type:** recognition. **Recipient:** for exemplifying the tradition of family doctor. **Affiliated With:** American Academy of Family Physicians. **Publications:** The Uniformed Family Physician. Journal. Alternate Formats: online. **Conventions/Meetings:** annual meeting (exhibits).

Minerals

14950 ■ International Bioliron Society (IBIS)
1111 N Plaza Dr., Ste.550
Schaumburg, IL 60173
Ph: (847)517-7225
Fax: (847)517-7229
E-mail: info@bioiron.org
URL: http://www.bioiron.org
Contact: Pierre Brissot MD, Pres.-Elect
Membership Dues: regular, $50 (annual) ● training, $20 (annual). **Multinational. Description:** Seeks to advance biological and medical roles of iron, as well as disorders due to iron deprivation or excess. **Awards:** IBIS Marcel Simon Award. **Frequency:** biennial. **Type:** recognition. **Committees:** Founding; Nomenclature. **Conventions/Meetings:** annual meeting.

Mining

14951 ■ International Society of Mine Safety Professionals (ISMSP)
PO Box 772
Jasper, GA 30143
Ph: (706)253-3675
Fax: (706)253-2678
E-mail: info@ismsp.com
URL: http://www.ismsp.com
Contact: Chris Bise, Contact
Founded: 1991. **Membership Dues:** regular, $150 (annual). **Multinational. Description:** Represents individuals working in the field of mine safety. Promotes the development of health and safety professionals throughout the international mining community. Seeks to save lives and reduce injuries through better leadership, planning, and practice. Offers networking opportunities among members. **Awards: Frequency:** annual. **Type:** recognition. **Recipient:** for outstanding accomplishments in mine health and safety. **Telecommunication Services:** electronic mail, cxb7@psu.edu. **Publications:** The Society Review, quarterly. Newsletter. Contains up-to-date information on the latest regulatory developments. Alternate Formats: online.

Multiple Birth

14952 ■ Center for the Study of Multiple Birth (CSMB)
333 E Superior St., Ste.464
Chicago, IL 60611
Ph: (312)695-1677
Fax: (312)908-8777
E-mail: lgk395@northwestern.edu
URL: http://www.multiplebirth.com
Contact: Dr. Louis G. Keith, Pres.
Founded: 1977. **Staff:** 3. **Description:** Medical research foundation concerned with the study of multiple birth and the care of multiple birth children. Disseminates information on the medical risks of multiple birth. Encourages funding for the support of medical and social research. Serves as resource center for the media and the public through informative website. **Computer Services:** Information services, articles. **Formerly:** (1981) Center for Study of Multiple Gestation.

Musculoskeletal Disorders

14953 ■ Council of Musculoskeletal Specialty Societies (COMSS)
6300 N River Rd., Ste.727
Rosemont, IL 60018-4226
Ph: (847)384-4330
Fax: (847)823-0536
E-mail: schneider@aaos.org
Contact: Andrew N. Pollak MD, Chm.
Description: Advocates the interests of its orthopedic specialty societies while promoting and encouraging orthopedic unity among the specialty societies and the American Academy of Orthopedic Surgeons and the American Association of Orthopedic Surgeons.

14954 ■ Musculoskeletal Tumor Society (MSTS)
c/o Marla Holderby
Vanderbilt Orthopaedic Inst.
Medical Center East, South Tower, Ste.4200
1215 21st Ave. S
Nashville, TN 37232-8774
Ph: (615)343-4400
Fax: (615)343-1028
E-mail: msts@vanderbilt.edu
URL: http://msts.org
Contact: Marla Holderby, Contact
Founded: 1977. **Members:** 164. **Staff:** 1. **Description:** Seeks to advance the science of orthopaedic oncology and promote high standards of patient care. **Committees:** Education; Research.

Mycology

14955 ■ Medical Mycological Society of the Americas (MMSA)
c/o Dr. James Harris
2501 Timberline Dr.
Austin, TX 78746
Ph: (512)458-7566
Fax: (512)458-7697
E-mail: jim.harris@tdh.state.tx.us
URL: http://www.mycologicalsociety.org
Contact: Ms. Annette W. Fothergill MA, Sec.-Treas.
Founded: 1966. **Members:** 300. **Membership Dues:** $20 (annual). **Description:** Medical professionals interested in fungi and fungal diseases. Seeks to exchange professional information; promotes continuing education in medical mycology in association with American Society for Microbiology. **Awards: Type:** recognition. **Affiliated With:** American Society for Microbiology. **Publications:** Bulletin, quarterly ● Directory, periodic. **Conventions/Meetings:** annual meeting, held in conjunction with ASM.

Naprapathy

14956 ■ American Naprapathic Association (ANA)
164 Div. St., Ste.714
Elgin, IL 60120
Ph: (847)214-8642
Fax: (847)214-8645
E-mail: anafordns@aol.com
URL: http://www.naprapathy.org
Contact: Dr. George G. Stretch DN, Pres.
Founded: 1909. **Members:** 300. **Description:** Composed of naprapathic physicians. (Naprapathy is the science and system of therapeutic manipulation of tissue structures that have become damaged due to stress and strain.) Promotes and publishes the principles of natural healing; seeks to further legislation and recognition of the system of treatment based on the belief that many functional disorders are caused by abnormal connective tissue and ligamentous changes and can be corrected by manipulation. Sponsors Naprapathic Education and Research Foundation. Conducts seminars and educational programs. Maintains speakers' bureau. **Libraries: Type:** not open to the public. **Subjects:** medical, alternative health. **Awards: Type:** recognition. **Publications:** *Back Pain* ● *Headache: A Warning* ● *Naprapathy: A Scientific Approach to Natural Healing* ● *The Three Facets of Naprapathy* ● *Voice of Naprapathy.* Booklet. Includes articles on nutrition and health topics. **Price:** free. **Circulation:** 5,000 ● *Why Manipulation?* ● Directory, periodic. **Conventions/Meetings:** annual Educational Conference (exhibits) - always June ● annual meeting (exhibits) - always January.

Natural Hygiene

14957 ■ International Association of Hygienic Physicians (IAHP)
4620 Euclid Blvd.
Youngstown, OH 44512
Ph: (330)788-0526
Fax: (330)788-0093
E-mail: mhuberman@zoominternet.net
URL: http://www.iahp.net
Contact: Atty. Mark A. Huberman, Sec.-Treas.
Founded: 1978. **Members:** 45. **Membership Dues:** graduate student, $10 (annual) ● regular, $50 (annual) ● fasting institute supplement, $200 (annual). **Staff:** 1. **Description:** Doctors of medicine, osteopathy, chiropractic, and naturopathy who specialize in the supervision of therapeutic fasting as part of a natural hygiene regimen. Promotes clinical advancement and ethical responsibility. Works for the health freedom of members. Provides certification for professionals and accreditation for schools and training programs; offers internship programs. Funds research. **Formerly:** (1995) International Association of Professional Natural Hygienists. **Publications:** *IAHP Newsletter*, quarterly. Includes association news, bibliography, book reviews, case studies, medical journal reviews, and reports from foreign countries. **Price:** included in membership dues. **Circulation:** 100. **Conventions/Meetings:** annual conference and convention.

14958 ■ National Health Association (NHA)
PO Box 30630
Tampa, FL 33630
Ph: (813)855-6607
Fax: (813)855-8052
E-mail: info@healthscience.org
URL: http://www.healthscience.org
Contact: Lynn Grudnik, Exec. Dir.
Founded: 1948. **Members:** 4,000. **Membership Dues:** regular, in U.S. and Canada, $35 (annual) ● regular, outside U.S. and Canada, $55 (annual) ● century club, $100 (annual). **Staff:** 2. **Budget:** $500,000. **Multinational. Description:** Public health education organization dedicated to teaching and preserving a tradition of health freedom and independence. Promotes health maintenance through natural

means such as natural foods, fresh air, pure water, sunshine, fasting, exercise, and rest. Emphasizes a lifestyle that encourages people to maximize their health by living in harmony with their physiological needs. Operates Natural Hygiene Press; maintains Herbert Shelton Library on fasting, natural hygiene, and related subjects. **Committees:** Education; Permanent Home Site. **Affiliated With:** International Association of Hygienic Physicians. **Formerly:** American Physiological and Natural Hygiene Society; (2003) American Natural Hygiene Society. **Publications:** *Health Science*, quarterly. Magazine. **Price:** included in membership dues. ISSN: 0883-8216. **Circulation:** 7,000. Alternate Formats: online. Also Cited As: *Vegetarian Health Science* ● Also publishes and distributes books and tapes. **Conventions/Meetings:** annual conference.

Naturopathy

14959 ■ American Association of Naturopathic Physicians (AANP)
4435 Wisconsin Ave. NW, Ste.403
Washington, DC 20016
Ph: (202)237-8150
Free: (866)538-2267
Fax: (202)237-8152
E-mail: member.services@naturopathic.org
URL: http://www.naturopathic.org
Contact: Karen E. Howard, Exec. Dir.
Founded: 1985. **Members:** 2,000. **Membership Dues:** regular, graduate, $400 (annual) ● international, retired/inactive, associate, supporting, $265 (annual) ● student, $60 (annual) ● leader, $545 (annual). **Staff:** 7. **Budget:** $700,000. **State Groups:** 36. **Description:** Naturopathic physicians. Unites naturopathic physicians and represents their legislative interests; promotes high educational standards and uniform criteria for licensing; increases public awareness of naturopathic medicine. **Computer Services:** Mailing lists, $1,000 for ND. **Telecommunication Services:** phone referral service, $50 charge for National Referral Directory and information brochures. **Publications:** *Journal of Naturopathic Medicine* ● Newsletter, quarterly. **Price:** included in membership dues. **Circulation:** 1,500. **Advertising:** accepted. **Conventions/Meetings:** annual conference (exhibits) ● annual convention, with continuing professional education program (exhibits).

14960 ■ American Naturopathic Medical Association (ANMA)
PO Box 96273
Las Vegas, NV 89193
Ph: (702)897-7053
Fax: (702)897-7140
E-mail: webmaster@anma.com
URL: http://www.anma.com
Contact: Julie Morgan, Contact
Founded: 1981. **Members:** 4,000. **Membership Dues:** professional/associate, $350 (annual) ● student/supporting, retired, $295 (annual). **Multinational. Description:** Strives to explore new frontiers of mind, body, medicine and health. **Publications:** *ANMA Monitor Online*, quarterly. Magazine. **Price:** free for members. **Circulation:** 10,000. **Advertising:** accepted. Alternate Formats: online. **Conventions/Meetings:** annual convention and seminar (exhibits).

14961 ■ Association of Natural Medicine Pharmacists (ANMP)
PO Box 150727
San Rafael, CA 94915-0727
Ph: (415)479-1512
Fax: (415)472-2559
E-mail: anmpnet@aol.com
URL: http://www.anmp.org
Contact: Constance Grauds RPh, Pres.
Founded: 1994. **Membership Dues:** individual, $35 (annual) ● student, $20 (annual) ● foreign, $45 (annual) ● sponsor, $500 (annual) ● corporate, $1,000 (annual). **Description:** Represents the interests of pharmacists and individuals in the field of natural medicine. Provides continuing education programs

for the advancement of natural medicine and pharmacy. **Computer Services:** Information services, natural medicine and healing related literature. **Boards:** Advisory. **Publications:** *The Source*, bimonthly. Newsletter. Alternate Formats: online.

Nephrology

14962 ■ American Association of Kidney Patients (AAKP)
3505 E Frontage Rd., Ste.315
Tampa, FL 33607
Ph: (813)636-8100
Free: (800)749-2257
Fax: (813)636-8122
E-mail: info@aakp.org
URL: http://www.aakp.org
Contact: Kris Robinson, Exec. Dir./CEO
Founded: 1969. **Members:** 12,000. **Membership Dues:** patient, family, $25 (annual) ● professional, $45 (annual) ● sustaining, physician, $100 (annual) ● institutional, dialysis unit, transplant center, $200 (annual) ● life, $1,000. **Staff:** 8. **Budget:** $1,500,000. **Regional Groups:** 16. **State Groups:** 16. **Local Groups:** 16. **National Groups:** 16. **Languages:** English, Spanish. **Description:** Works to improve the lives of fellow kidney patients and their families by helping them deal with the physical, emotional and social impact of kidney disease; provides educational and supportive programs and reading materials. **Awards:** Medal of Excellence. **Frequency:** annual. **Type:** medal. **Recipient:** to renal physician. **Formerly:** National Association of Patients on Hemodialysis; National Association of Patients on Hemodialysis and Transplantation. **Publications:** *AAKP Public Policy Briefing*, monthly. Newsletter. Alternate Formats: online ● *AAKP Renal Flash*, monthly. Newsletter. Provides information about living with kidney disease, current news and AAKP activities. Alternate Formats: online ● *AAKPRENALIFE*, bimonthly. Magazine. Provides articles, news and healthcare information of interest to kidney patients. **Price:** included in membership dues. **Circulation:** 20,000. **Advertising:** accepted. Alternate Formats: online ● *Americans with Disabilities Act of 1990.* Brochure. Explains the Americans with Disabilities Act. ● *Blood Chemistry Levels.* Brochure ● *Dietary Counters.* Brochure ● *Kidney Beginnings*, quarterly. Magazine. Features information on the kidneys and common questions about chronic kidney disease. **Price:** included in membership dues. **Circulation:** 40,000. Alternate Formats: online ● *Kidney Beginnings: The Electronic Newsletter*, monthly. Alternate Formats: online ● *Kidney Transplant Today*, monthly. Newsletter. Alternate Formats: online ● Also publishes other informational materials including care of the kidneys, treatment options and conditions that may affect the kidneys. **Conventions/Meetings:** annual convention and conference, covers advancements in kidney disease and allows individuals to exchange ideas and share experiences (exhibits) - August/September.

14963 ■ American Kidney Fund (AKF)
6110 Executive Blvd., Ste.1010
Rockville, MD 20852
Ph: (301)881-3052
Free: (800)638-8299
Fax: (301)881-0898
E-mail: helpline@kidneyfund.org
URL: http://www.kidneyfund.org
Contact: Karen M. Sendelback CFRE, Exec. Dir.
Founded: 1971. **Staff:** 30. **Budget:** $5,400,000. **Regional Groups:** 1. **Languages:** English, German, Spanish. **Description:** Works to alleviate the financial burdens caused by kidney disease; improves the quality of life for kidney patients; promotes kidney health care nationwide. Provides direct financial assistance to needy kidney disease victims with costs specific to their treatment. Raises funds through direct mail from the public. Supports dialysis center emergency funds. Presents programs include: American Kidney Fund Clinical Scientist in Nephrology program, which provides assistance to nephrology

students pursuing scholarship in the provision of clinical care; patient and community services; public and professional education; kidney donor development; and clinical research. **Awards:** Clinical Scientist in Nephrology Fellowships. **Frequency:** annual. **Type:** fellowship. **Recipient:** for U.S. citizens who have completed their residency in Internal Medicine or Pediatric Medicine. **Telecommunication Services:** additional toll-free number, (866)300-2900. **Divisions:** Community Services; Kidney Donor Development; Patient Services Program; Planned Giving; Public Education; Research. **Programs:** Minority Intervention and Kidney Education; Summer Enrichment. **Publications:** *American Kidney Fund—Annual Report.* Price: free. Alternate Formats: online ● *Clinical Strategies Newsletter for Health Professionals,* semiannual. Price: free. Circulation: 4,500 ● *Professional Advocate.* Newsletter. Highlights the spectrum of American Kidney Fund programs and activities. Price: free. Alternate Formats: online ● Brochures. **Conventions/Meetings:** semiannual Board of Trustees Meeting - seminar - usually May and November ● quadrennial regional meeting, address issues of quality of care and life for renal patients ● annual Torchbearer Award - dinner, held in conjunction with the annual Peritoneal Dialysis Conference.

14964 ■ American Lithotripsy Society (ALS)
305 Second Ave., Ste.200
Waltham, MA 02451-1122
Ph: (781)895-9098
Fax: (781)895-9088
E-mail: info@lithotripsy.org
URL: http://www.lithotripsy.org
Contact: Wesley E. Harrington, Exec.Dir.
Founded: 1987. **Members:** 1,207. **Membership Dues:** physician, $195 (annual) ● allied health professional, $65 (annual) ● corporate, $1,500 (annual). **Staff:** 5. **Budget:** $800,000. **Description:** Promotes trade and public awareness of Lithotripsy. (Lithotripsy is a non-invasive procedure to treat kidney stones and gall stones.) Disseminates information; conducts educational programs, quality improvement and certification programs. **Awards:** Distinguished Guest Lecturer. **Frequency:** annual. **Type:** monetary. **Publications:** *ALS Quarterly.* Newsletter. **Conventions/Meetings:** annual convention (exhibits).

14965 ■ American Nephrology Nurses' Association (ANNA)
Box 56, E Holly Ave.
Pitman, NJ 08071
Ph: (856)256-2320
Free: (888)600-2662
Fax: (856)589-7463
E-mail: anna@ajj.com
URL: http://www.annanurse.org
Contact: Mike Cunningham, Exec. Dir.
Founded: 1969. **Members:** 11,905. **Membership Dues:** active, $60 (annual) ● associate, $50 (annual) ● international, $75 (annual) ● student, $30 (annual). **Staff:** 60. **Budget:** $3,000,000. **Regional Groups:** 4. **Local Groups:** 106. **Description:** Registered nurses; physicians, dietitians, social workers, and technicians. Promotes continuing education of members at national, regional, and local levels. **Awards:** Outstanding Contribution to ANNA. **Frequency:** annual. **Type:** recognition. **Recipient:** for a nurse who has made outstanding contributions to the goals of ANNA ● Rod Brady Memorial Award for Excellence in Volunteer Leadership. **Frequency:** annual. **Type:** recognition. **Recipient:** for an individual who has demonstrated outstanding leadership ● Spirit of Nephrology Nursing Award. **Frequency:** annual. **Type:** recognition. **Recipient:** for a nurse who demonstrates outstanding performance as a mentor. **Computer Services:** database ● mailing lists ● online services. **Committees:** Awards and Scholarship; Conferences; Distance Learning; Ethics; Health Policy; Leadership Development; Professional Practice; Research. **Formerly:** (1984) American Association of Nephrology Nurses and Technicians. **Publications:** *ANNA RenalWEB E-News,* biweekly. Bulletin. Alternate Formats: online ● *ANNA Update,* bimonthly. Newsletter ● *Building Your Career in Dialysis.* Video.

Price: $29.00 ● *Contemporary Nephrology Nursing Textbook.* **Price:** $88.00 for members; $103.00 for nonmembers ● *Core Curriculum for Nephrology Nursing.* **Price:** $70.00 for members; $90.00 for nonmembers ● *Nephrology Nursing: A Guide to Professional Development.* **Price:** $35.00 for members; $50.00 for nonmembers ● *Nephrology Nursing Certification Review Guide.* **Price:** $20.00 for members; $30.00 for nonmembers ● *Nephrology Nursing Journal,* bimonthly. **Price:** $36.00 /year for individuals; $54.00 /year for individuals outside U.S.; $50.00 /year for institutions; $68.00 /year for institutions outside U.S. **Circulation:** 14,000. **Advertising:** accepted ● *RPA Shared Decision-Making in the Appropriate Initiation of and Withdrawal from Dialysis.* **Price:** $10.00 for members ● *Standardized Training Program for the Patient Care Technician in Hemodialysis - Instructor's Guide.* **Price:** $18.00 ● *Standardized Training Program for the Patient Care Technician in Hemodialysis - Learner's Guide.* **Price:** $28.00 ● *Standards and Guidelines of Clinical Practice for Nephrology Nursing.* **Price:** $35.00 for members; $50.00 for nonmembers ● *Standards of Clinical Practice for Continuous Renal Replacement Therapy.* This publication is included in Standards of Clinical Practice for Nephrology Nursing. **Price:** $10.00 for members; $15.00 for nonmembers. **Conventions/Meetings:** annual symposium (exhibits) - always spring. 2008 Apr. 27-30, Philadelphia, PA.

14966 ■ American Society of Diagnostic and Interventional Nephrology (ASDIN)
c/o Dianna Garvey
131 Continental Dr., Ste.405
Newark, DE 19713
Ph: (302)658-7596
Fax: (302)658-9669
E-mail: asdin@medsocdel.org
URL: http://www.asdin.org
Contact: Arif Asif MD, Pres.
Founded: 2000. **Membership Dues:** regular, $200 (annual) ● associate/fellow, $100 (annual). **Description:** Improves the quality of patient care. Promotes the proper application of new and existing procedures in the practice of nephrology. Conducts training programs and courses. **Publications:** *Seminars in Dialysis,* bimonthly. Journal. Focuses on cutting-edge clinical aspects of dialysis therapy. **Conventions/Meetings:** annual meeting.

14967 ■ American Society of Nephrology (ASN)
1725 I St. NW, Ste.510
Washington, DC 20006
Ph: (202)659-0599
Fax: (202)659-0709
E-mail: email@asn-online.org
URL: http://www.asn-online.org
Contact: Karen L. Campbell PhD, Exec. Dir.
Founded: 1967. **Members:** 7,500. **Membership Dues:** active in North America and Central America, $250 (annual) ● affiliate/corresponding outside North America and Central America, $275 (annual) ● emeritus, $97 (annual). **Staff:** 18. **Budget:** $75,000,000. **Description:** Nephrologists united for the exchange of scientific information. Seeks to contribute to the education of members and to improve the quality of patient care. Conducts educational courses. Maintains placement service. **Libraries:** Type: by appointment only. Holdings: 250; periodicals. **Awards:** ASN Career Enhancement Grant. **Frequency:** annual. **Type:** fellowship ● ASN/NKF Fellowships. **Frequency:** annual. **Type:** fellowship ● ASN Research Scholar Award. **Frequency:** annual. **Type:** fellowship ● Belding H. Scribner Award. **Frequency:** annual. **Type:** recognition. **Recipient:** for individuals who have made outstanding contributions that had a direct impact on the care of patients ● Homer H. Smith Award. **Frequency:** annual. **Type:** recognition. **Recipient:** for an individual who has made outstanding contribution that fundamentally affect the science of nephrology ● John P. Peters Award. **Frequency:** annual. **Type:** recognition. **Recipient:** for individuals who have made substantial research contributions to the discipline of nephrology ● Young Investigator Award. **Frequency:**

annual. **Type:** recognition. **Recipient:** for an individual with an outstanding record of achievement and creativity in basic or patient-oriented research. **Computer Services:** Mailing lists, of members. **Committees:** Awards; Basic Science; Clinical Science; Education; Grants Review; Nominating; Policy and Public Affairs; Postgraduate Education. **Publications:** *Abstracts Issue,* annual. Journal. Contains programs and abstracts for annual scientific meeting. **Price:** $50.00. **Circulation:** 10,000. **Advertising:** accepted. Also Cited As: *The Journal of the American Society of Nephrology* ● *ASN Highlights,* annual. Newsletter ● *ASN's Renal Express,* monthly. Newsletter. Alternate Formats: online ● *ASN's Renal Policy Express,* monthly. Newsletter. Alternate Formats: online ● *Clinical Journal of the American Society of Nephrology.* Alternate Formats: online ● *Journal of the American Society of Nephrology,* monthly. **Advertising:** accepted. Alternate Formats: online ● *NephSAP Nephrology Self-Assessment Program* ● Membership Directory. Alternate Formats: online. **Conventions/Meetings:** annual Board Review Course - meeting ● annual Meeting and Scientific Exposition (exhibits).

14968 ■ American Society of Pediatric Nephrology (ASPN)
3400 Res. Forest Dr., Ste.B
The Woodlands, TX 77381
Ph: (281)419-0052
Fax: (281)419-0052
E-mail: info@aspneph.com
URL: http://www.aspneph.com
Founded: 1969. **Members:** 550. **Staff:** 1. **Description:** Committed to optimal care for children with renal disease and to disseminate advances in the clinical practice and basic science of pediatric nephrology. **Awards:** Founders Award. **Frequency:** annual. **Type:** recognition. **Recipient:** for active or honorary member of ASPN, greater than 55 years, having made significant clinical, scientific and/or leadership contributions to the field of pediatric nephrology. **Publications:** *KIDney Notes,* bimonthly. Newsletter. Alternate Formats: online. **Conventions/Meetings:** annual meeting.

14969 ■ Board of Nephrology Examiners Nursing and Technology (BONENT)
1901 Pennsylvania Ave. NW, Ste.607
Washington, DC 20006
Ph: (202)462-1252
Fax: (202)463-1257
E-mail: president@bonent.org
URL: http://www.bonent.org
Contact: R.J. Picciano BA, Pres.
Founded: 1974. **Members:** 1,900. **Staff:** 4. **Description:** Registered nurses, licensed practical nurses, licensed vocational nurses, and dialysis technicians. Provides nephrology nursing and technology certification examinations. Through certification, seeks to ensure: safe, competent practitioners in nephrology nursing and technology; excellence in the quality of care of the nephrology patient; the continued study and advance of the science of nursing and technological fields in nephrology. Compiles statistics. **Computer Services:** Mailing lists. **Committees:** Bylaws; Credentials; Examination; Fundraising/Marketing; Host Review; Legislative; Membership; Policies and Procedures; Publications; Regional Representative. **Formerly:** (2002) Board of Nephrology Examiners - Nursing and Technology. **Publications:** *Bonent Update,* quarterly. Newsletter. Price: included in membership dues. Circulation: 4,000. Advertising: accepted. **Conventions/Meetings:** biennial meeting.

14970 ■ DaVita Patient Citizens (DPC)
1155 15th St. NW, Ste.1100
Washington, DC 20005
Free: (866)877-4242
Fax: (202)457-0452
E-mail: dpc@dialysispatients.org
URL: http://www.dialysispatients.org
Contact: Chad Lennox, Exec. Dir.
Founded: 2004. **Members:** 19,000. **Description:** Works to improve the quality of life for all dialysis patients through advocacy, education and motivation. Raises awareness of dialysis issues. Fosters and

strengthens partnerships among patients and caregivers. **Publications:** Newsletter, quarterly. Alternate Formats: online.

14971 ■ International Pediatric Nephrology Association (IPNA)

c/o Isidro B. Salusky, MD, Treas.
David Geffen School of Medicine at UCLA
10833 Le Conte Ave.
CHS 27-066, MC 169717
Los Angeles, CA 90095
Ph: (310)694-8250
Fax: (310)206-9440
E-mail: isalusky@mednet.ucla.edu
URL: http://www.ipna-online.org
Contact: Isidro B. Salusky MD, Treas.

Founded: 1973. **Members:** 1,432. **Membership Dues:** individual, $175 (annual) ● emeritus individual, $88 (annual). **Staff:** 2. **Budget:** $500,000. **Regional Groups:** 7. **Multinational. Description:** Specialists in children's kidney disease. Promotes communication and disseminates information among pediatric nephrologists. Maintains training facilities. **Libraries: Type:** not open to the public. **Awards:** Ira Greifer Award and Medal. **Type:** recognition. **Committees:** Continuing Medical Education; National and International Disaster. **Councils:** International. **Publications:** *Pediatric Nephrology*, monthly. Journal. Peer review journal, peer reviewed original research, clinical data. **Price:** included in membership dues. ISSN: 0931-041X. **Circulation:** 2,214. **Advertising:** accepted. Alternate Formats: online ● Proceedings, triennial. **Conventions/Meetings:** triennial congress and symposium (exhibits).

14972 ■ National Association of Nephrology Technicians/Technologists (NANT)

PO Box 2307
Dayton, OH 45401-2307
Ph: (937)586-3705
Free: (877)607-6268
Fax: (937)586-3699
E-mail: nant@meinet.com
URL: http://www.nant.biz
Contact: Francine W. Rickenbach, Exec. Dir.

Founded: 1983. **Members:** 1,200. **Membership Dues:** full/associate, $50 (annual) ● student, $35 (annual). **Staff:** 3. **Budget:** $250,000. **State Groups:** 22. **Description:** Nephrology technicians and technologists. Promotes the recognition, job security, and employment opportunities of nephrology technicians and technologists. Sets forth standards for the dialysis industry; educates dialysis practitioners; promotes research; disseminates new ideas; addresses technician and technologist practice issues. **Awards:** James Boag Lifetime Contribution Award. **Frequency:** annual. **Type:** recognition. **Recipient:** to an individual who has made an ongoing contribution to the field of nephrology technology ● The President's Award. **Frequency:** annual. **Type:** recognition. **Computer Services:** Mailing lists. **Formerly:** (1994) National Association of Nephrology Technologists. **Publications:** *A Manual on Water Treatment for Hemodialysis*. Book. Discusses each component of a hemodialysis water treatment system. **Price:** $20.00 for members; $40.00 for nonmembers ● *Dialysis Technology, Third Edition*. Book. Contains information on dialysis technology, used in training programs and for preparing for certification exams. **Price:** $45.00 for members; $60.00 for nonmembers ● *NANT News*, bimonthly. Newsletter. **Advertising:** accepted ● *Study Guide for Technologists, Third Edition*. Book. **Price:** $20.00 for members; $30.00 for nonmembers. **Conventions/Meetings:** annual convention, dialysis technology education (exhibits).

14973 ■ National Kidney Foundation (NKF)

30 E 33rd St.
New York, NY 10016
Ph: (212)889-2210
Free: (800)622-9010
Fax: (212)689-9261

E-mail: info@kidney.org
URL: http://www.kidney.org
Contact: John Davis, CEO

Founded: 1950. **Staff:** 101. **Budget:** $60,000,000. **Local Groups:** 200. **Languages:** English, Spanish. **Description:** Supports research, patient services, professional and public education, organ and tissue donor program, and community service. Affiliates conduct community and patient services including: drug banks; transportation; early screening; patient seminars. Sponsors symposium in health care professionals. Maintains speakers' bureau and biographical archives; compiles statistics. **Awards: Type:** recognition. **Committees:** Affiliate Relations; Bylaws and Policies; Communications; Continuing Medical Education; Emeritus; Executive; Finance; Fund Raising; Leadership; Minority Outreach; Nominating; Patient Services; Personnel; Planned Giving; Public Education; Public Policy; Research Endowment Board; Volunteer Development. **Councils:** Diabetic Kidney Disease; Dialysis; Glomerulonephritis; Hypertension; National Donor Family; Nephrology Nurses and Technicians; Nephrology Social Workers; Patient and Family; Pediatric Nephrology and Urology; Polycystic Kidney Disease; Renal Nutrition; TransAction; Transplantation. **Absorbed:** (2003) National Enuresis Society. **Formerly:** (1958) National Nephrosis Foundation; (1964) National Kidney Disease Foundation. **Publications:** *Advances in Renal Replacement Therapy*, quarterly. Journal ● *American Journal of Kidney Diseases*, monthly. Covers research in kidney and urinary tract diseases. Includes annual index and conference reports. **Price:** included in membership dues. ISSN: 0272-6386. **Advertising:** accepted ● *CNNT Newsletter*, quarterly. Contains employment opportunity listings and regional news. **Price:** included in membership dues ● *CNSW Newsletter*, quarterly. Includes calendar of events, information on current literature, employment opportunities, and legislative and regional reports. **Price:** included in membership dues ● *CRN News and Briefs*, quarterly. Newsletter. Contains employment opportunity listings, legislative news, and research reports. **Price:** included in membership dues. **Circulation:** 1,200 ● *Journal of Nephrology Social Work*, annual ● *Journal of Renal Nutrition*, quarterly ● *National Kidney Foundation—Clinical Nephrology Meetings Proceedings Book*. **Conventions/Meetings:** annual Clinical Nephrology Meeting - conference (exhibits).

14974 ■ North American Society for Dialysis and Transplantation (NASDAT)

c/o Laura Brazil-Nichols, Exec. Dir.
4010 Bentley Dr.
Pearland, TX 77584
Ph: (281)997-1944
E-mail: lbrazil@nasdat.org
URL: http://www.nasdat.org
Contact: Laura Brazil-Nichols, Exec. Dir.

Founded: 1981. **Members:** 200. **Description:** Represents professionals active in the area of teaching, manufacturing, and administration in the fields of nephrology and transplantation including nephrologists, transplant surgeons and physicians, registered nurses, dialysis nurses, and transplant coordinators. Promotes education and research and disseminates current knowledge and technology in the field of kidney dialysis and transplantation. **Publications:** none. **Conventions/Meetings:** annual meeting.

14975 ■ Oxalosis and Hyperoxaluria Foundation (OHF)

201 E 19th St., Ste.12E
New York, NY 10003
Ph: (212)777-0470
Free: (888)OHF-8699
Fax: (212)777-0471
E-mail: kimh@ohf.org
URL: http://www.ohf.org
Contact: Brett Rosen, Pres.

Founded: 1989. **Members:** 900. **Membership Dues:** individual, $25 (annual) ● professional, $50 (annual) ● small business, $100 (annual) ● corporate, $500 (annual). **Staff:** 1. **Description:** Individuals affected by oxalosis and hyperoxaluria; health care professionals. Hyperoxaluria is a metabolic disease affecting the kidneys. Oxalosis occurs when calcium crystals have deposited elsewhere in the body, often the eyes, bones, and joints. Provides support services and information regarding the conditions and their affects. Encourages research. Operates referral service. **Awards: Frequency:** annual. **Type:** grant. **Recipient:** for hyperoxaluria and oxalosis researchers. **Computer Services:** database, patient registry. **Telecommunication Services:** electronic mail, ohf@ohf.ultranet.com. **Affiliated With:** Genetic Alliance; National Organization for Rare Disorders. **Publications:** *In Touch*, semiannual. Newsletter. Contains issues that concern patients, families, medical professionals affected by Oxalosis and PH. **Price:** included in membership dues. Alternate Formats: online ● *Understanding Hyperoxaluria and Oxalosis*. Brochure. **Conventions/Meetings:** annual conference, held in conjunction with the American Society of Nephrology (exhibits).

14976 ■ Rainbow Celebration of Hope Network (RCHN)

PO Box 20621
Houston, TX 77225-0621
Free: (866)849-3853
E-mail: sheliabailey@rainc-hope.org
Contact: Shelia Robey-Bailey, Dir./Founder

Founded: 1999. **Members:** 10. **Membership Dues:** regular, $20 (annual). **Budget:** $10,000. **Languages:** English, Spanish. **Description:** Provides spiritual and educational resources for individuals on dialysis; also provides means of support. **Awards:** Rainbow Celebration of Hope Network Achievement Award. **Type:** recognition. **Subgroups:** Rainbow Pals. **Publications:** Newsletter, annual. Covers past and future events and organizations. **Conventions/Meetings:** monthly meeting - every 3rd Thursday in Houston, TX.

14977 ■ Renal Physicians Association (RPA)

1700 Rockville Pike, Ste.220
Rockville, MD 20852
Ph: (301)468-3515
Fax: (301)468-3511
E-mail: rpa@renalmd.org
URL: http://www.renalmd.org
Contact: Dale Singer MHA, Exec. Dir.

Founded: 1973. **Members:** 3,100. **Membership Dues:** physician, $375 (annual) ● practice manager, physician assistant, advanced practice nurse, $275 (annual) ● retired, $100 (annual). **Staff:** 9. **Budget:** $2,000,000. **Description:** Physicians specializing in the treatment of renal (kidney) diseases. Promotes optimal care and high standards of treatment for patients. Serves as a national representative for physicians engaged in the study and management of patients with kidney and related disorders; specifically, expresses the concerns and needs of renal physicians to congressional and governmental agencies legislating, executing, and regulating the federal End Stage Renal Disease Program. Provides resources for the development of national policies concerning kidney disease such as ESRD legislative and network activities, federal funding for related research, and studies relative to treatment procedures and clinical practices. Conducts educational programs. Membership is open to practice managers who are responsible for billing and coding in nephrologists' offices. **Committees:** Clinical Practice; Government Affairs; Health Care Payment; Nominating; Practice Managers; Program; Quality, Safety and Accountability. **Publications:** *Collaborative Leadership for ESRD Patient Safety*. Report. Alternate Formats: online ● *RPA News*, bimonthly. Newsletter. **Price:** included in membership dues. **Circulation:** 3,100. **Advertising:** accepted ● Papers. Alternate Formats: online. **Conventions/Meetings:** annual assembly and symposium (exhibits).

14978 ■ Renal Support Network (RSN)

1311 N Maryland Ave.
Glendale, CA 91207
Ph: (818)543-0896
Fax: (818)244-9540

E-mail: info@rsnhope.org
URL: http://www.rsnhope.org
Contact: Lori Hartwell, Exec. Dir./Pres./Founder
Founded: 1993. **Description:** Provides non-medical services to those affected by chronic kidney disease (CKD). Strives to help patients develop their personal coping skills, special talents and employability through education, advocacy and employment resources. Provides lawmakers and policymakers with the patients' perspective on the needs and capabilities of people with CKD. Helps patients find resources to manage their disease. Offers patients and family education on life enhancement and illness-related issues. **Publications:** *Live & Give Newsletter*, quarterly. **Price:** free. Alternate Formats: online ● Brochure. Alternate Formats: online.

Neuro-Ophthalmology

14979 ■ Neuro-Optometric Rehabilitation Association, International (NORA)
PO Box 14934
Irvine, CA 92623-4934
Free: (866)222-3887
E-mail: wpadula@padulainstitute.com
URL: http://www.nora.cc
Contact: Don P. Fong OD, Pres.
Membership Dues: level 1, $500 ● level 2, $170 ● level 3, $130 ● level 4, $50. **Multinational. Description:** Advances the art and science of habilitation/rehabilitation of the neurologically and cognitively injured. Emphasizes treatment designed to optimize visual-motor abilities, visual perception and visual information-processing in the neurologically affected person. Recognizes the crucial role of vision in human performance. **Awards:** Advancement of Neuro-Optometric Rehabilitation Award. **Frequency:** annual. **Type:** recognition. **Recipient:** for contributions in the advancement of the art and science of neuro-optometric rehabilitation ● Advancement of Sciences Award. **Frequency:** annual. **Type:** recognition. **Recipient:** for unique and valuable contribution to the science of neuro-optometric rehabilitation. **Publications:** Newsletter, quarterly. Contains news about the activities and achievements of the organization. **Price:** free. Alternate Formats: online.

Neurological Disorders

14980 ■ Accelerated Cure Project for Multiple Sclerosis
300 Fifth Ave.
Waltham, MA 02451
Ph: (781)487-0008
Fax: (781)487-0009
E-mail: info-web0107@acceleratedcure.org
URL: http://www.acceleratedcure.org
Contact: Art Mellor, Pres./CEO/Co-Founder/Dir.
Founded: 2001. **Description:** Represents individuals dedicated to curing Multiple Sclerosis (MS) by determining the cause of MS. Stimulates, supports, and coordinates research into the cause, treatment, and cure of Multiple Sclerosis. Works to stop the progress of MS and repair the damage already caused in patients with MS. **Telecommunication Services:** electronic mail, art@bostoncure.org. **Publications:** *Multiple Sclerosis Update*, quarterly. Newsletter. Alternate Formats: online ● Annual Report, annual. Alternate Formats: online ● Articles. Alternate Formats: online.

14981 ■ American Academy of Health Care Providers in the Addictive Disorders
314 W Superior St., Ste.508
Duluth, MN 55802
Ph: (218)727-3940
Free: (888)429-3701
Fax: (218)722-0346
E-mail: info@americanacademy.org
URL: http://www.americanacademy.org
Contact: Lorraine D. Grymala, Exec. Dir.
Founded: 1989. **Description:** Nurses, doctors, psychiatrists, social workers, and

counselors. Established and maintains Certified Addiction Specialist (CAS) credentials. Strives to create a national unity of standards. **Boards:** International Advisory; Trustees. **Formerly:** (2003) American Academy of Health Care Providers. **Publications:** *Academy News*, semiannual. Newsletter. Includes information on contemporary research findings and treatment techniques. **Price:** free for members. **Advertising:** accepted. Alternate Formats: online ● *E-News*, bimonthly. Newsletter. **Price:** free. Alternate Formats: online ● Handbooks ● Books.

14982 ■ American Association of Neuromuscular and Electrodiagnostic Medicine (AANEM)
2621 Superiod Dr. NW
Rochester, MN 55901
Ph: (507)288-0100
Fax: (507)288-1225
E-mail: aanem@aanem.org
URL: http://www.aanem.net
Contact: Shirlyn A. Adkins JD, Exec. Dir.
Founded: 1953. **Members:** 5,000. **Membership Dues:** fellow, associate, active, $270 (annual) ● junior, $75 (annual) ● fellow, active, associate outside U.S., $140 (annual). **Staff:** 13. **Budget:** $1,500,000. **Description:** M.D.'s and D.O.'s or equivalent foreign degrees who practice or are interested in electrodiagnostic medicine. Increases and extends knowledge of electromyography and electrodiagnostic medicine, and to improve patient care. **Libraries: Type:** reference. **Holdings:** 23; audiovisuals. **Subjects:** electrodiagnostic medicine. **Awards:** Advocacy Award. **Frequency:** annual. **Type:** recognition. **Recipient:** for members or non-members who have made significant advocacy contributions for physicians specializing in neuromuscular medicine ● Distinguished Physician Award. **Frequency:** annual. **Type:** recognition. **Recipient:** for members and/or educators who have provided distinguished service for a number of years ● Distinguished Researcher Award. **Frequency:** annual. **Type:** recognition. **Recipient:** for members who have made continuous significant contributions to clinical neurophysiology research ● Golseth Young Investigator Award. **Frequency:** annual. **Type:** recognition. **Recipient:** for original research in clinical neurophysiology; based on scientific merit and methodology ● Lifetime Achievement Award. **Frequency:** annual. **Type:** recognition. **Recipient:** to individuals recognized as major contributors to the field by virtue of teaching, research, and scholarly publications. **Computer Services:** Mailing lists, of members ● online services, career service. **Subgroups:** Communications Services; Education Services; Meeting Operations Manager; Member and Diplomate Services; Policy/Legislative. **Formerly:** (1990) American Association of Electromyography and Electrodiagnosis. **Publications:** *AAEM Case Reports*, periodic. Monograph. **Price:** $8.00 for members; $10.00 for nonmembers ● *AAEM Minimonographs*, 2-3/year. **Price:** $10.00 for members; $15.00 for nonmembers ● *American Association of Electrodiagnostic Medicine—Membership Directory*, annual. **Price:** included in membership dues; $50.00 for nonmembers ● *Guidelines*, periodic. **Price:** $75.00 for members; $150.00 for nonmembers; $10.00 each, for individual chapters to members; $20.00 each, for individual chapters to nonmembers ● *Muscle and Nerve*, monthly. **Price:** included in fellow/associate membership. ISSN: 6148-639X ● Also publishes course syllabi. **Conventions/Meetings:** annual Scientific Meeting - seminar and workshop (exhibits) - usually September or October.

14983 ■ American Parkinson Disease Association (APDA)
135 Parkinson Ave.
Staten Island, NY 10305
Ph: (718)981-8001
Free: (800)223-2732
Fax: (718)981-4399
E-mail: apda@apdaparkinson.org
URL: http://www.apdaparkinson.org
Contact: Vincent N. Gattullo, Pres.
Founded: 1961. **Members:** 2,000. **Staff:** 17. **Regional Groups:** 90. **Local Groups:** 400. **Descrip-**

tion: Works to find the cure for Parkinson's disease and to alleviate the suffering of its victims by subsidizing information and referral centers and providing funds for research. Offers counseling services to patients and their families. Maintains 57 information and referral centers and 250 support groups. Conducts symposia. **Libraries: Type:** not open to the public. **Subjects:** Parkinson's disease. **Awards:** Fred Springer Award. **Frequency:** annual. **Type:** recognition. **Recipient:** for a scientist who made an outstanding contribution to the study of the disease ● Salvatore J. Esposito Coordinators Award. **Frequency:** annual. **Type:** recognition. **Recipient:** for an Information and Referral Center coordinator who contributed to create a better quality of life for people with Parkinson's Disease ● Salvatore J. Esposito Volunteers Award. **Frequency:** annual. **Type:** recognition. **Recipient:** for a volunteer who contributed to create a better quality of life for people with Parkinson's Disease. **Boards:** Scientific Advisory. **Publications:** *Aquatic Exercise for Parkinson's Disease* (in English). Booklet ● *Be Active! A Suggested Exercise Program for People with Parkinson's Disease*. Booklet ● *Be Independent! To Help the Patient with Parkinson's Disease in the Activities of Daily Living*. Booklet ● *Good Nutrition* (in English). Booklet ● *Parkinson's Disease Handbook*. Booklet ● *Speaking Effectively - Speech Problems and Swallowing Problems in Parkinson's Disease*. Booklet ● Newsletter, quarterly. Includes association and research news, and calendar of events. **Price:** free. **Circulation:** 250,000. Alternate Formats: online ● Annual Report, annual ● Also publishes educational supplements. **Conventions/Meetings:** biennial Coordinators' and Chapter Presidents' Conference (exhibits) - always August ● periodic regional meeting.

14984 ■ American Syringomyelia Alliance Project (ASAP)
PO Box 1586
Longview, TX 75606-1586
Ph: (903)236-7079
Free: (800)ASAP-282
Fax: (903)757-7456
E-mail: info@asap.org
URL: http://www.asap.org
Contact: Patricia Maxwell, Operations Admin.
Founded: 1988. **Members:** 4,000. **Membership Dues:** friend, $30 ● supporter, $60 ● sponsor, $100 ● patron, $250 ● benefactor, $500 ● Bobby Jones Society, $1,000. **Staff:** 4. **Description:** Seeks to increase awareness of and promote research on syringomyelia, a rare spinal disorder. Conducts fundraising activities and children's services. **Libraries: Type:** reference. **Holdings:** articles, video recordings. **Subjects:** syringomyelia chiari malformation. **Awards:** Volunteer of the Year Award. **Frequency:** annual. **Type:** recognition. **Recipient:** for outstanding service. **Computer Services:** database ● mailing lists, of members ● online services, message board. **Committees:** Fundraising; Medical Advisory. **Publications:** *ASAP Connections*, bimonthly. Newsletter. **Circulation:** 4,200 ● *What Is Syringomyelia*. Brochure ● Videos. **Price:** $15.00. **Conventions/Meetings:** annual Syringomyelia Conference - convention.

14985 ■ Amyotrophic Lateral Sclerosis Association (ALSA)
27001 Agoura Rd., Ste.150
Calabasas Hills, CA 91301-5104
Ph: (818)880-9007
Free: (800)782-4747
Fax: (818)880-9006
E-mail: alsinfo@alsa-national.org
URL: http://www.alsa.org
Contact: Gary A. Leo, Pres./CEO
Founded: 1985. **Members:** 250,000. **Staff:** 36. **Budget:** $10,300,000. **Regional Groups:** 135. **Languages:** English, Spanish. **Description:** Patients; relatives and friends of patients; doctors, neurologists, physical therapists, nurses, and professional organizations dedicated to finding the cause, prevention, and cure for Amyotrophic Lateral Sclerosis (ALS). Offers help and information to ALS patients and their families. Funds ALS-specific research at major medical institutions. Works with other agen-

cies, including the government, to increase their involvement on a priority basis in ALS research. Conducts patient meetings. **Libraries: Type:** reference. **Awards: Frequency:** annual. **Type:** grant. **Recipient:** for ALS research. **Computer Services:** Electronic publishing, ALSAexchange ● online services, Patient Services Resource Directory. **Committees:** Medical Advisory; Scientific Review. **Also Known As:** ALS Association. **Formed by Merger of:** National ALS Foundation; Amyotrophic Lateral Sclerosis Society of America. **Publications:** *A Reason for Hope,* semiannual. Magazine. Alternate Formats: online ● Newspaper, quarterly. Includes book reviews and research and chapter news. **Price:** free. **Circulation:** 75,000. **Advertising:** accepted ● Also publishes fact sheets and pamphlets on ALS and patient care. **Conventions/Meetings:** annual conference, leadership development (exhibits) ● biennial conference.

14986 ■ Angioma Alliance
107 Quaker Meeting House Rd.
Williamsburg, VA 23188
Ph: (757)258-3355
Free: (866)432-5226
E-mail: info@angiomaalliance.org
URL: http://www.angiomaalliance.org
Contact: Connie Lee, Pres.
Languages: English, Portuguese, Spanish. **Multinational. Description:** Improves the quality of life of individuals with cavernous angiomas through education, support and promotion of research. Raises public awareness and understanding of cavernous angioma. **Computer Services:** Information services, cavernous angioma facts and resources ● mailing lists ● online services, chat ● online services, community forum. **Publications:** Newsletter ● Annual Report.

14987 ■ Attention Deficit Information Network (AD-IN)
58 Prince St.
Needham, MA 02492
Ph: (781)455-9895 (781)449-3018
E-mail: adin@gis.net
Contact: Libby Ostrofsky, Pres.
Founded: 1988. **Membership Dues:** initial support group fee, $50 ● renewal, $35 (annual). **Regional Groups:** 41. **State Groups:** 20. **Description:** People with Attention Deficit Disorders (ADD), their families, and other individuals with an interest in ADD. Promotes improved quality of life for people with ADD. Works to expand home, school, and work-based strategies for aiding people with ADD; advocates for improved responsiveness to the needs of people with ADD by schools, businesses, and organizations. Provides support and information to families of people with ADD; conducts educational programs; maintains speakers' bureau. **Awards:** AD-IN Scholarship. **Frequency:** annual. **Type:** scholarship. **Computer Services:** Mailing lists. **Publications:** Brochure. Alternate Formats: online. **Conventions/Meetings:** periodic board meeting ● periodic conference.

14988 ■ Avenues, National Support Group for Arthrogryposis Multiplex Congenita
c/o Lynn Staheli, MD, Dir. of Orthopedics
Children's Orthopedic Hosp. and Medical Center
4800 Sand Point Way NE
Seattle, WA 98105
E-mail: info@avenuesforamc.com
URL: http://www.avenuesforamc.com/index.htm
Contact: Jim Schmidt, Contact
Founded: 1980. **Members:** 1,200. **Description:** Individuals with arthrogryposis multiplex congenita (AMC), their families and friends, and interested professionals. (AMC, a birth defect, is a muscle and/or nerve syndrome affecting some or all of the body's limbs.) Shares positive attitudes and self-help ideas for the handicapped and for all who deal with them. **Libraries: Type:** reference. **Holdings:** clippings. **Subjects:** medical information on AMC. **Publications:** *Avenues,* semiannual. Newsletter. Lists doctors and families interested in corresponding with others about arthrogryposis. **Price:** included in membership dues; $10.00 annual donation requested for members in U.S.; $15.00 annual donation re-

quested for members outside U.S. **Circulation:** 1,200 ● Audiotapes ● Bibliography ● Pamphlet. **Price:** $1.00/copy ● Also a $3.00 Resource Packet for Doctors, Therapists, Pen Pals Families, Clinics, Support Groups. **Conventions/Meetings:** annual seminar.

14989 ■ Batten Disease Support and Research Association (BDSRA)
166 Humphries Dr.
Reynoldsburg, OH 43068
Ph: (740)927-4298
Free: (800)448-4570
Fax: (740)927-7683
E-mail: bdsra1@bdsra.org
URL: http://www.bdsra.org
Contact: Lance W. Johnston, Exec. Dir.
Founded: 1986. **Members:** 1,000. **Membership Dues:** family, professional, $20 (annual). **Staff:** 2. **Budget:** $350,000. **State Groups:** 18. **Languages:** English, Spanish. **Description:** Represents the interests of individuals with Batten Disease, and their families. (Batten Disease is a degenerative neurological disease affecting children, causing seizures, dementia, loss of motor skills, and blindness.) Seeks to educate the public and professional community concerning the needs of Batten Disease patients. Provides information and referral services. Conducts support group activities. Maintains registry. **Libraries: Type:** reference. **Holdings:** articles, audiovisuals. **Subjects:** Batten's disease. **Awards:** Batten Disease Research. **Frequency:** annual. **Type:** grant. **Recipient:** for pertinent research. **Computer Services:** database. **Committees:** Chapter Development; Education; Family and Sibling Outreach; Medical Liaison. **Publications:** *Batten Disease: An Easy to Understand Guide.* Book ● *Family Directory,* annual. **Price:** free; available to member families only. **Circulation:** 350 ● *Illuminator,* quarterly. Newsletter. Alternate Formats: online ● *The Lighthouse,* quarterly. Newsletter. Bereavement newsletter. Alternate Formats: online ● *Teach and Be Taught: A Guide for Teachers Having a Student with Batten Disease.* Book. **Conventions/Meetings:** annual Family Conference (exhibits).

14990 ■ Benign Essential Blepharospasm Research Foundation (BEBRF)
PO Box 12468
Beaumont, TX 77726-2468
Ph: (409)832-0788
Fax: (409)832-0890
E-mail: bebrf@blepharospasm.org
URL: http://www.blepharospasm.org
Contact: Mary Lou Thompson, Pres.
Founded: 1981. **Members:** 8,900. **Staff:** 2. **Budget:** $300,000. **Regional Groups:** 4. **State Groups:** 50. **Local Groups:** 170. **Description:** Victims of Benign Essential Blepharospasm (BEB), a rare disorder of unknown cause characterized by an involuntary forcible closure of the eyelids. Undertakes, promotes, and develops research into the cause and cure of BEB and related disorders and infirmities of the facial musculature, such as Meige's Syndrome (involving muscle spasms of the eyes, lower face, mouth, tongue, throat, and respiratory system) and hemifacial spasm (one side of the face only). Seeks to foster public awareness of the disorder in order to guarantee detection at the onset of symptoms. Encourages continuity and cooperation among neurologists, neuro-ophthalmologists, ophthalmologists, plastic surgeons, psychologists, psychiatrists, and other medical professionals in rendering correct diagnoses, implementing effective treatment, improving surgical procedure, and discovering a cure. Organizes seminars, clinical studies, and other programs in continuing education; sponsors fundraising activities. Endeavors to locate sufferers of the disorder and to compile data in order to determine the incidence of BEB and to advise on available treatment. Carries out research activities in areas such as brain tissue collection and experimental treatments. **Libraries: Type:** reference. **Holdings:** articles, books, periodicals. **Subjects:** blepharospasm, meige, hemifacial spasm, dry eye, blepharitis, apraxia of eyelid opening. **Awards:** Fellowship. **Frequency:** annual. **Type:** grant. **Recipient:** for research ● Research Grants.

Frequency: annual. **Type:** grant. **Computer Services:** Mailing lists. **Telecommunication Services:** electronic bulletin board, where patients can communicate with one another. **Affiliated With:** American Academy of Neurology; American Academy of Ophthalmology; National Organization for Rare Disorders. **Publications:** *Benign Essential Blepharospasm, Meige and Other Related Disorders.* Brochure. **Price:** $10.00/copy ● *Eye Opening Recipes.* Book. Includes 495 favorite recipes of patients. **Price:** $10.00/copy ● *Physician Reprint Articles* ● Newsletter, bimonthly. Includes research reports and statistics, medical articles, and patient stories. **Price:** $15.00/year in U.S.; $20.00/year in Canada and Mexico; $25.00/year elsewhere. **Circulation:** 6,800 ● Pamphlets. **Conventions/Meetings:** annual conference, scientific meeting for doctors and patients.

14991 ■ Care4Dystonia (C4D)
c/o Beka Serdans, RN, Founder/Acting Exec. Dir.
440 E 78th St.
New York, NY 10021
Free: (800)984-0433
E-mail: infoc4d@aol.com
URL: http://www.care4dystonia.org
Contact: Beka Serdans RN, Founder/Acting Exec. Dir.
Founded: 2000. **Description:** Seeks to improve the quality of direct clinical patient care. Raises awareness and understanding of dystonia. Empowers patients to ask questions, seek care, and educate themselves and their families about dystonia. Creates a forum to entice scientists and researchers into the area of dystonia research and invoke the need for multidisciplinary care. Facilitates communication and cooperation among organizations, business ventures and companies providing specific services to movement disorders. **Libraries: Type:** reference. **Holdings:** books, video recordings. **Subjects:** dystonia. **Publications:** *In Motion,* monthly. Newsletter. Alternate Formats: online.

14992 ■ Charcot-Marie-Tooth Association (CMTA)
2700 Chestnut St.
Chester, PA 19013-4867
Ph: (610)499-9264
Free: (800)606-CMTA
Fax: (610)499-9267
E-mail: info@charcot-marie-tooth.org
URL: http://www.charcot-marie-tooth.org
Contact: Patrick Torchia, Chm.
Founded: 1983. **Members:** 15,000. **Membership Dues:** individual, $40 (annual). **Staff:** 3. **Budget:** $500,000. **Regional Groups:** 25. **Languages:** English, Spanish. **Description:** Charcot-Marie-Tooth patients and their families, medical professionals treating the disorder, and interested individuals. (Charcot-Marie-Tooth Disease, also known as peroneal muscular atrophy or hereditary motor sensory neuropathy, is a progressive neurological disorder beginning in childhood or adult life with weakness and muscle wasting in feet, legs, hands, and arms.) Works to inform and educate patients and their families, the medical community, and the public about medical treatment for CMT. Offers support groups for patients and their families; disseminates educational materials; encourages and funds research; sponsors lay and professional symposia. **Libraries: Type:** reference. **Holdings:** archival material. **Computer Services:** database, for researchers on CMT. **Boards:** Medical Advisory. **Formerly:** (1990) National Foundation for Peroneal Muscular Atrophy. **Publications:** *Charcot-Marie-Tooth Disorders.* Pamphlets ● *Charcot-Marie-Tooth Disorders: A Handbook for Primary Care Physicians.* **Price:** $20.00 for nonmembers; $15.00 for members ● *CMT Brochure.* Includes information on CMT. **Price:** free ● *CMT Facts I,* periodic. Booklets. **Price:** $3.00 for members; $5.00 for nonmembers ● *CMT Facts II,* periodic. Booklets. **Price:** $5.00 for members; $7.00 for nonmembers ● *CMT Facts III,* periodic. Booklets. Contains articles on CMT topics, research news, patient profiles, and meeting and program announcements. **Price:** $5.00 for members; $7.00 for nonmembers. ISSN: 1067-0181. **Circulation:** 10,000 ● *CMT Facts IV,* periodic.

Booklets. **Price:** $8.00 for members; $10.00 for nonmembers ● *CMT Facts V*, periodic. Booklets. **Price:** $12.00 for members; $15.00 for nonmembers ● *CMTA Report*, bimonthly. Newsletter. Contains articles on CMT topics, research news, patient profiles, and meeting and program announcements. **Price:** included in membership dues. ISSN: 1067-0181. **Circulation:** 10,000. **Conventions/Meetings:** periodic conference (exhibits) - 4-6/year.

14993 ■ Children and Adults With Attention Deficit/Hyperactivity Disorder (CHADD)
8181 Professional Pl., Ste.150
Landover, MD 20785
Ph: (301)306-7070
Free: (800)233-4050
Fax: (301)306-7090
E-mail: national@chadd.org
URL: http://www.chadd.org
Contact: E. Clarke Ross DPA, CEO
Founded: 1987. **Members:** 20,000. **Membership Dues:** individual/family/educator in U.S., $45 (annual) ● individual/family/educator outside U.S., professional in U.S., $100 (annual) ● professional outside U.S., $190 (annual) ● student, $35 (annual) ● student outside U.S., $75 (annual) ● organization, $275 (annual) ● organization outside U.S. and Canada, $425 (annual). **Staff:** 20. **Budget:** $3,900,000. **Local Groups:** 250. **Languages:** English, Spanish. **Description:** Works to improve the lives of people affected by AD/HD through collaborative leadership, advocacy, research, education and support. Provides support network for parents and caregivers, a forum for continuing education; works to be a community resource, disseminates accurate evidence-based information about AD/HD to parents, educators, adults, professionals and the media; promotes ongoing research; advocated on behalf of AD/HD community. **Awards: Type:** recognition. **Departments:** Development. **Programs:** Medical Benefits; Vehicle Donation. **Formerly:** (1993) Children with Attention-Deficit Disorders; (2001) Children and Adults With Attention Deficit Disorder. **Publications:** *ATTENTION*, bimonthly. Magazine. **Price:** included in membership dues. **Circulation:** 86,000. **Advertising:** accepted. Alternate Formats: online ● Booklets ● Brochures ● Annual Report, annual. Alternate Formats: online ● Also publishes fact sheets. **Conventions/Meetings:** annual conference (exhibits) - always October/November. 2007 Nov. 7-10, Washington, DC; 2008 Nov. 13-15, Anaheim, CA; 2010 Nov. 11-14, Atlanta, GA.

14994 ■ Children's Tumor Foundation (CTF)
95 Pine St., 16th Fl.
New York, NY 10005
Ph: (212)344-6633
Free: (800)323-7938
Fax: (212)747-0004
E-mail: info@ctf.org
Contact: John W. Risner, Pres.
Founded: 1978. **Members:** 1,700. **Staff:** 25. **Budget:** $3,500,000. **State Groups:** 37. **Description:** The leading resource on neurofibromatosis, a genetic disorder that causes tumors to grow along nerves throughout the body. Provides direct services to children and adults with NF, as well as information and resources to the public and medical professionals via a toll-free number and a website. **Libraries: Type:** reference; open to the public. **Holdings:** books. **Subjects:** neurofibromatosis. **Awards:** Basic Grant. **Frequency:** annual. **Type:** grant. **Recipient:** for research in neurofibromatosis ● Young Investigator Grant. **Frequency:** annual. **Type:** grant. **Recipient:** for research in neurofibromatosis. **Computer Services:** database. **Formerly:** (2005) National Neurofibromatosis Foundation. **Publications:** *Neurofibromatosis News*, quarterly. Newsletter. **Price:** free for members. **Conventions/Meetings:** annual meeting, for members.

14995 ■ Communication Independence for the Neurologically Impaired (CINI)
c/o Kornreich Technology Center
201 I.U. Willets Rd.
Albertson, NY 11507

Ph: (516)465-1629
Fax: (516)465-3744
E-mail: cini@cini.org
URL: http://www.cini.org
Contact: Peter Strugatz, Pres.
Description: Works to improve the quality of life for those with ALS/MND (Lou Gehrig's Disease). **Telecommunication Services:** electronic mail, peter@cini.org. **Publications:** *Communication and Swallowing Solutions for the ALS/MND Community.* Manual. **Price:** $11.50.

14996 ■ Dysautonomia Foundation
315 W 39th St., Ste.701
New York, NY 10018
Ph: (212)279-1066
Fax: (212)279-2066
E-mail: info@familialdysautonomia.org
URL: http://www.familialdysautonomia.org
Contact: Lenore F. Roseman, Exec. Dir.
Founded: 1954. **Members:** 14,000. **Staff:** 3. **Budget:** $1,000,000. **Description:** Parents, relatives, friends, and benefactors of children afflicted with Familial dysautonomia, a Jewish genetic disease of the autonomic nervous system. **Awards:** Research Grants. **Frequency:** annual. **Type:** monetary. **Recipient:** for postdoctoral research into FD. **Publications:** *DYS/COURSE*, semiannual. Newsletter. Includes research updates. **Price:** free. **Circulation:** 11,000 ● *Dysautonomia Foundation—Journal*, annual. **Price:** free upon ad of $300 or more. **Circulation:** 500. **Advertising:** accepted. **Conventions/Meetings:** annual International FD Day - meeting, for parents and patients to gather for a yearly progress report of the illness and treatment updates - always second Sunday in June.

14997 ■ Dysautonomia Youth Network of America (DYNA)
c/o Debra L. Dominelli, Pres./Exec. Dir.
1301 Greengate Ct.
Waldorf, MD 20601
Ph: (301)705-6995
Fax: (301)638-DYNA
E-mail: info@dynakids.org
URL: http://www.dynakids.org
Contact: Debra L. Dominelli, Pres./Exec. Dir.
Description: Works to help young people who are diagnosed with various dysautonomia conditions. Provides positive support to young people who have dysautonomia. Raises awareness of dysautonomia conditions and treatments. Promotes compassion, support and understanding of the various challenges that youth with dysautonomia face within educational facilities. **Publications:** *The Young and the Dizzy.* Newsletter. Features news and articles about medical issues pertaining to Dysautonomia. Alternate Formats: online ● Brochure. **Price:** free. Alternate Formats: online.

14998 ■ Dystonia Medical Research Foundation
1 E Wacker Dr., Ste.2430
Chicago, IL 60601-1905
Ph: (312)755-0198
Free: (800)377-DYST
Fax: (312)803-0138
E-mail: dystonia@dystonia-foundation.org
URL: http://www.dystonia-foundation.org
Contact: Janet Hieshetter, Exec. Dir.
Founded: 1977. **Members:** 25,000. **Membership Dues:** voluntary, $30 (annual). **Staff:** 7. **Budget:** $1,600,000. **Regional Groups:** 8. **State Groups:** 100. **Local Groups:** 2. **National Groups:** 5. **Description:** Dystonia patients and their families; medical personnel; health agencies; interested individuals. Promotes and funds research and encourages increased public awareness of dystonia, a neurologic muscular disorder causing muscles to jerk and contract into abnormal positions. Disseminates information concerning dystonia. Sponsors patient and family support groups. **Libraries: Type:** open to the public. **Holdings:** books. **Subjects:** dystonia treatment and diagnosis. **Awards:** Research Grant. **Frequency:** annual. **Type:** grant. **Recipient:** for Dystonia research. **Computer Services:** Mailing lists, of members. **Boards:** Junior Advisory; Scientific Advi-

sory. **Councils:** Parents. **Publications:** *Dystonia Dialogue*, 3/year. Magazine. Includes foundation and chapter news and research updates. **Price:** free. **Circulation:** 12,000 ● Brochures. **Conventions/Meetings:** periodic International Symposium on Dystonia ● biennial symposium.

14999 ■ Facioscapulohumeral (FSH) Society
3 Westwood Rd.
Lexington, MA 02420
Ph: (781)860-0501
Fax: (781)860-0599
E-mail: carol.perez@fshsociety.org
URL: http://www.fshsociety.org
Contact: Carol A. Perez, Exec.Dir.
Founded: 1992. **Members:** 1,000. **Membership Dues:** regular, $35 (annual) ● sustaining, $70 (annual) ● professional, professional individual, $100 (annual) ● professional sustaining, $200 (annual) ● sponsor, $250 (annual) ● corporate, benefactor, professional fellow, $1,000 (annual) ● donor, professional associate, $500 (annual). **Staff:** 1. **Budget:** $400,000. **Regional Groups:** 6. **Description:** Individuals, families, and medical and business professionals interested in Facioscapulohumeral Muscular Dystrophy. (FSHD is an inheritable disease that causes a progressive loss of skeletal muscle with weakness of facial, scapular, and upper arm muscles.) Promotes research, solicits contributions and grants, and disperses information on FSHD. Offers support groups, acts as clearinghouse for researchers, clinicians and patients to facilitate participation in FSHD studies. Funds Research on FSHD. **Libraries: Type:** not open to the public. **Awards:** Marjorie Bronfman Grant. **Frequency:** semiannual. **Type:** grant. **Recipient:** for FSHD research ● 1 Delta Railroad Construction Fellowship. **Frequency:** annual. **Type:** fellowship. **Recipient:** for FSHD research. **Boards:** Scientific Advisory. **Publications:** *FSH WATCH*, quarterly. Newsletter. Contains updates on FSHD Internationally and cites current research articles. **Circulation:** 4,000. **Advertising:** accepted. Alternate Formats: online ● Also publishes a patient brochure in English and Spanish. **Conventions/Meetings:** annual conference (exhibits).

15000 ■ Families of S.M.A. (FSMA)
PO Box 196
Libertyville, IL 60048-0196
Ph: (847)367-7620
Free: (800)886-1762
Fax: (847)367-7623
E-mail: sma@fsma.org
URL: http://www.fsma.org
Contact: Kenneth Hobby, Exec. Dir.
Founded: 1984. **Members:** 3,500. **Membership Dues:** family/friend, $30 (annual) ● professional, $35 (annual) ● international, $40 (annual). **Regional Groups:** 1. **State Groups:** 21. **Local Groups:** 22. **Languages:** Chinese, English, French, German, Greek, Hebrew, Italian, Polish, Portuguese, Russian, Spanish, Yiddish. **Description:** Individuals with Spinal Muscular Atrophy; their families; medical professionals; and interested others. Major funder of SMA research. Promotes public awareness. SMA diseases include: Infantile Progressive SMA (Werdnig-Hoffman Disease), Juvenile Progressive SMA (Kugelberg-Welander Disease) and Adult Progressive SMA (Aran-Duchenne Type). Offers support to families. **Libraries: Type:** reference. **Holdings:** photographs, reports. **Computer Services:** Mailing lists. **Additional Websites:** http://curesma.com. **Telecommunication Services:** electronic mail, audrey@fsma.org. **Projects:** Cure SMA. **Publications:** *Direction*, quarterly. Newsletter. Includes research updates and information network. **Price:** $25.00/year for families in U.S.; $35.00/year for professionals in U.S.; $40.00/year outside U.S. **Circulation:** 3,000. **Advertising:** accepted ● *Living with SMA.* Video ● *Understanding Muscular Atrophy* (in English, French, and Spanish). **Conventions/Meetings:** annual conference and workshop (exhibits).

15001 ■ Fibromuscular Dysplasia Society of America (FMDSA)
PO Box 999
Hudson, OH 44236

Ph: (330)653-8416
E-mail: admin@fmdsa.org
URL: http://www.fmdsa.org
Contact: Pamela Mace, Chair
Founded: 2003. **Description:** Educates the public and medical communities about Fibromuscular Dysplasia. Provides research grants. **Publications:** Newsletter, quarterly.

15002 ■ Forbes Norris MDA/ALS Research Center

2324 Sacramento St., Ste.150
San Francisco, CA 94115
Ph: (415)600-3604
Fax: (415)673-5184
URL: http://www.cpmc.org/services/als
Contact: Robert G. Miller MD, Dir.
Founded: 1981. **Staff:** 17. **Budget:** $300,000. **Local Groups:** 3. **Description:** Serves as a clearinghouse for laboratory and clinical research into neuromuscular diseases, primarily Amyotrophic Lateral Sclerosis (Lou Gehrig's Disease). ALS is a paralytic and usually fatal disease of the motor neurons, nerves which innervate the muscles to allow movement. Although patients maintain their full intellectual capacities, they gradually lose their ability to move, talk, and breathe. Sponsors the ALS Research Center at the California Pacific Medical Center in San Francisco, CA and maintains an extensive bank of ALS patient information. Offers educational programs and a speakers' bureau. **Convention/Meeting:** none. **Libraries: Type:** reference. **Holdings:** video recordings. **Subjects:** patient care. **Formerly:** (1994) ALS and Neuromuscular Research Foundation; (1999) ALS Forbes Norris Research Center. **Publications:** *Forbes Norris Research Center — Support Group Newsletter*, monthly. **Price:** free ● Newsletter, semiannual.

15003 ■ Global Neuro Rescue (GNR)

5539 Riverton Ave.
North Hollywood, CA 91601
Ph: (818)516-6346
Fax: (818)557-7311
URL: http://www.globalneurorescue.com
Contact: Dr. Jorge A. Lazareff MD, CEO/Founder
Founded: 2002. **Multinational. Description:** Seeks to improve the livelihood of children and adults suffering from neurological diseases in developing nations throughout the world. Performs medical procedures on infants and children for the treatment of hydrocephalus, myelomeningocele and intra-cranial pathology. Coordinates treatment and disease prevention campaigns through a worldwide voluntary relief effort.

15004 ■ Global and Regional Asperger Syndrome Partnership (GRASP)

135 E 15th St.
New York, NY 10003
Ph: (646)242-4003
Fax: (212)529-9996
E-mail: info@grasp.org
URL: http://www.grasp.org
Contact: Michael John Carley, Exec. Dir.
Founded: 2003. **Multinational. Description:** Seeks to improve the quality of life of people with Asperger Syndrome. Increases public awareness of Asperger Syndrome and high-functioning Autism. Serves as a support network for people with Asperger Syndrome and their families. **Publications:** Brochure. Alternate Formats: online ● Articles. Alternate Formats: online.

15005 ■ Guardians of Hydrocephalus Research Foundation (GHRF)

2618 Ave. Z
Brooklyn, NY 11235-2037
Ph: (718)743-4473
Fax: (718)743-1171
E-mail: ghrf2618@aol.com
URL: http://ghrf.homestead.com/ghrf.html
Contact: Mrs. Marie Fischetti, Co-Founder
Founded: 1977. **Members:** 5,000. **Membership Dues:** individual, $25 (annual) ● parent, $30 (annual). **Staff:** 2. **State Groups:** 11. **Local Groups:** 2. **Description:** Hydrocephalics and their families, health care professionals, and other concerned

individuals. Seeks to find the cause and cure of hydrocephalus. (Hydrocephalus is the buildup of cerebrospinal fluid in the brain cavity, which can cause brain damage or death if untreated.) Disseminates information on hydrocephalus; conducts public awareness and fundraising projects. Plans to conduct research and educational programs, and to operate computerized services. **Additional Websites:** http://ghrforg.org. **Committees:** Fund Raising; Public Awareness. **Publications:** *An Introduction to Hydrocephalus*. Book ● *Journal Ad Book*, annual ● Newsletter, quarterly. Includes news briefs and fundraising and project information. **Price:** included in membership dues ● Makes available documentary film.

15006 ■ Guillain-Barre Syndrome Foundation International (GBSFI)

PO Box 262
Wynnewood, PA 19096
Ph: (610)667-0131
Fax: (610)667-7036
E-mail: info@gbsfi.com
URL: http://www.guillain-barre.com
Contact: Estelle L. Benson, Exec.Dir.
Founded: 1980. **Members:** 20,000. **Staff:** 2. **National Groups:** 148. **Languages:** English, French, German, Spanish. **Multinational. Description:** Individuals concerned with Guillain-Barre syndrome (Acute Idiopathic Polyneuritis), a rare, paralyzing, potentially catastrophic disorder of the peripheral nerves. Aims to: educate the public and medical community about the availability of support groups and maintain their awareness of the disorder; foster research on cause, prevention, and treatment; encourage financial support for research; develop nationwide support groups. Arranges for recovered or recovering patients to visit patients in acute care and rehabilitation hospitals; assists patients in dealing with disabilities should complete recovery not occur. Maintains steering committee of physicians, some of who have had the disorder. **Computer Services:** Online services, chat room ● online services, discussion forum ● online services, web store. **Formerly:** (1988) Guillain-Barre Syndrome Support Group; (1990) Guillian-Barre Syndrome Support Group International. **Publications:** *Communicator*, quarterly. Newsletter ● *Guide for Caregivers*. Handbook ● *Guillain-Barre Syndrome, an Overview for the Layperson*. Booklet. **Conventions/Meetings:** periodic Support Meetings - regional meeting ● biennial symposium ● symposium.

15007 ■ Hereditary Disease Foundation (HDF)

3960 Broadway, 6th Fl.
New York, NY 10032
Ph: (212)928-2121
Fax: (212)928-2172
E-mail: cures@hdfoundation.org
URL: http://www.hdfoundation.org
Contact: Nancy S. Wexler PhD, Pres.
Founded: 1968. **Staff:** 5. **Description:** Aims to fund basic biomedical research on the causes, prevention, diagnosis, treatment, and cure of genetic disorders and in particular Huntington's Disease, an inherited neurological disorder. Maintains grant programs to support scientific projects in major medical and basic science laboratories throughout the U.S. Offers grants and postdoctoral fellowships. Sponsors a series of interdisciplinary workshops to stimulate new ideas and approaches to understanding hereditary problems. Helps maintain two tissue banks for research purposes. Disseminates information to organizations and individuals. **Awards:** John J. Wasmuth Award. **Type:** scholarship. **Recipient:** for postdoctoral fellowships ● Lieberman Award. **Frequency:** annual. **Type:** grant. **Recipient:** for innovative research for treatment or cure of Huntington's disease ● Milton Wexler Award. **Type:** scholarship. **Recipient:** for postdoctoral fellowships. **Computer Services:** Mailing lists, of members. **Committees:** Scientific Advisory Board. **Publications:** Newsletter, quarterly. **Price:** free. **Circulation:** 70. **Conventions/Meetings:** bimonthly workshop, science workshop.

15008 ■ Huntington's Disease Society of America (HDSA)

505 8th Ave., Ste.902
New York, NY 10018
Ph: (212)242-1968
Free: (800)345-4372
Fax: (212)239-3430
E-mail: hdsainfo@hdsa.org
URL: http://www.hdsa.org
Contact: Barbara T. Boyle, Exec. Dir./CEO
Founded: 1986. **Members:** 50,000. **Staff:** 25. **Budget:** $10,000,000. **Regional Groups:** 34. **Local Groups:** 3,331. **Languages:** English, Spanish. **Description:** Individuals and groups of volunteers concerned with Huntington's disease, an inherited and terminal neurological condition causing progressive brain and nerve deterioration. Identifies HD families. Educates the public and professionals, with emphasis on increasing consumer awareness of HD. Promotes and supports basic and clinical research into the causes and cure of HD. Maintains patient services program, coordinated with various community services, to assist families in meeting the social, economic, and emotional problems resulting from HD. Works to change the attitude of the working community toward the HD patient, enhance the HD patient's lifestyle, and promote better health care and treatment, both in the community and in facilities. **Libraries: Type:** reference. **Holdings:** audio recordings. **Awards: Frequency:** periodic. **Type:** grant. **Recipient:** for researchers investigating a treatment or cure for Huntington's Disease. **Computer Services:** Mailing lists, of members. **Telecommunication Services:** electronic mail, barbaraboyle@hdsa.org. **Councils:** National Science. **Affiliated With:** Community Health Charities; National Health Council. **Formed by Merger of:** Huntington Disease Foundation of America; National Huntington's Disease Association. **Publications:** *Huntington's Disease Society of America - The Marker*, semiannual. Magazine. **Price:** free. **Circulation:** 45,000 ● *Toward A Cure*, semiannual. Newsletter ● Booklets ● Pamphlets ● Videos. **Conventions/Meetings:** annual convention (exhibits).

15009 ■ Hydrocephalus Association (HA)

870 Market St., Ste.705
San Francisco, CA 94102
Ph: (415)732-7040
Free: (888)598-3789
Fax: (415)732-7044
E-mail: info@hydroassoc.org
URL: http://www.hydroassoc.org
Contact: Ms. Dory Kranz, Exec. Dir.
Founded: 1983. **Members:** 2,000. **Membership Dues:** individual/family, $30-$250 (annual) ● professional/organization, $50-$500 (annual). **Staff:** 4. **Description:** People with hydrocephalus and their families, health care professionals with an interest in hydrocephalus, and interested businesses and foundations. Works to improve the quality of life of people with hydrocephalus through education. Conducts training for families of people with hydrocephalus; sponsors social gatherings; facilitates networking among families of people with hydrocephalus and between organizations representing people with hydrocephalus. **Libraries: Type:** open to the public. **Awards:** Anthony Abbene Scholarship. **Type:** scholarship. **Recipient:** for young adults with hydrocephalus ● Gerard Swartz Fudge Scholarship. **Frequency:** 3/year. **Type:** scholarship. **Recipient:** for persons age 18 to 30 with hydrocephalus ● Morris L. Ziskind Memorial Scholarship. **Type:** scholarship. **Recipient:** for young adults with hydrocephalus. **Programs:** Link; Outreach. **Publications:** *About Hydrocephalus - A Book for Families* (in English and Spanish). Booklet. Provides information on hydrocephalus diagnosed in childhood. ● *About Normal Pressure Hydrocephalus-A Book for Adults and Their Families*. Booklet. Discusses the diagnosis and treatment of adult-onset normal pressure hydrocephalus. ● *Directory of Hydrocephalus Support Groups*, periodic ● *Directory of Neurosurgeons for Adult Hydrocephalus*. Contains names and addresses of neurosurgeons who treat adult-onset normal pressure hydrocephalus. ● *Directory of Pediatric Neurosurgeons*. Lists

130 neurosurgeons geographically and alphabetically. ● *Fact Sheet 12 Different Topics.* Pamphlet ● *Hydrocephalus Diagnosed in Young and Middle-Aged Adults.* Booklet. Discusses the diagnosis and treatment of hydrocephalus that occurs in young and middle-aged adults. ● *Prenatal Hydrocephalus - A Book for Parents.* Booklet. Provides information about the diagnosis of prenatal-onset hydrocephalus. ● *Resource Guide.* Bibliography. Includes over 600 published articles regarding hydrocephalus. ● *Teachers Guide to Hydrocephalus.* Book. Discusses education needs of children with hydrocephalus. ● Newsletter, quarterly. **Price:** included in membership dues. Alternate Formats: online. **Conventions/Meetings:** semiannual conference, for people, families and professionals working with hydrocephalus (exhibits).

15010 ■ International Essential Tremor Foundation (IETF)
PO Box 14005
Lenexa, KS 66285-4005
Ph: (913)341-3880
Free: (888)387-3667
Fax: (913)341-1296
E-mail: staff@essentialtremor.org
URL: http://www.essentialtremor.org
Contact: Catherine S. Rice, Exec. Dir.
Founded: 1988. **Members:** 44,000. **Membership Dues:** individual, $30 (annual). **Staff:** 4. **Budget:** $500,000. **State Groups:** 92. **Description:** Provides services, support, research, funds, and education to families, friends, and individuals suffering from Benign Essential Tremor. Current treatment includes drug therapy and surgical intervention. Provides patient information and referrals to physicians who specialize in Essential Tremor. **Libraries: Type:** reference. **Holdings:** 80; articles, books, papers, periodicals. **Subjects:** essential tremor. **Awards:** IETF Research Grant Award. **Frequency:** annual. **Type:** grant. **Recipient:** for research in essential tremor. **Doing business as:** (2002) IETF. **Formerly:** (2003) International Tremor Foundation. **Publications:** Newsletter, quarterly. Includes research reports and networking information. **Price:** included in membership dues. **Circulation:** 25,000. **Conventions/Meetings:** symposium - 2-5/year.

15011 ■ International Organization of Glutaric Acidemia (IOGA)
RD No. 4, Box 299-A
Blairsville, PA 15717
Ph: (724)459-0179
E-mail: mmetil@helicon.net
URL: http://www.glutaricacidemia.org
Contact: Mike Metil, Dir.
Founded: 1995. **Members:** 100. **Multinational. Description:** Enhances early detection and prevention of neurological damage. Assists in the treatment and rehabilitation of people affected by Glutaric Aciduria. Provides support, advocacy, networking services and medical referrals. **Computer Services:** Online services, message board. **Publications:** *The IOGA Community.* Newsletter.

15012 ■ International Research Council of Neuromuscular Disorders (IRCND)
Address Unknown since 2006
Founded: 1982. **Members:** 82. **Budget:** $150,000. **Description:** Health professionals interested in neuromuscular diseases of the human body. Purpose is to advance and disseminate information on the causes, effects, occurrence, cure, and prevention of neuromuscular disorders and associated topics related to the human spine. Coordinates and encourages basic research and the exchange of ideas and related materials between professionals in the field. Prepares teaching and educational materials. Compiles statistics for distribution; sponsors seminars and speakers' bureau. Is currently developing a library. **Publications:** *Information/Newsletter,* annual. **Conventions/Meetings:** annual conference.

15013 ■ International Rett Syndrome Association (IRSA)
9121 Piscataway Rd., No. 2B
Clinton, MD 20735
Ph: (301)856-3334
Free: (800)818-RETT

Fax: (301)856-3336
E-mail: admin@rettsyndrome.org
URL: http://www.rettsyndrome.org
Contact: Kathy Hunter, Pres./Founder
Founded: 1985. **Members:** 3,500. **Membership Dues:** individual outside U.S., $40 (annual) ● family, $35 (annual) ● individual in U.S., $30 (annual) ● life, $500. **Staff:** 7. **Budget:** $1,500,000. **State Groups:** 20. **Description:** Parents of children with Rett Syndrome; interested professionals and supporters. (A child afflicted with Rett Syndrome, which strikes predominately in females, seems normal until 7 to 18 months of age, when a regression leads to loss of psychomotor and communication skills. Autistic-like withdrawal often sets in; though this symptom eases in time, higher brain functions are compromised. The child also loses purposeful use of her hands, wringing them in a constant "hand-washing" movement in front of the face or chest. The syndrome is named for Dr. Andreas Rett, of Vienna, Austria, who described it in 1966. The cause of Rett Syndrome has been traced to a defective gene, called the MeCP2 on the X chromosome.) Provides support to parents; encourages research; collects and disseminates information. Assists in identifying patients; conducts activities aimed at the prevention, treatment, and eventual eradication of Rett Syndrome. **Libraries: Type:** open to the public. **Subjects:** Rett Syndrome. **Awards:** Research Grant. **Frequency:** annual. **Type:** grant. **Recipient:** for individuals approved by a Professional Advisory Board. **Computer Services:** database ● mailing lists. **Telecommunication Services:** electronic mail, khunter@rettsyndrome.org. **Boards:** Professional Advisory. **Committees:** Family Support; Fundraising; Public Awareness; Strategic Plan. **Funds:** Angel. **Formerly:** (1985) International Rett's Syndrome Association. **Publications:** *International Rett Syndrome Association—Newsletter Rett Gazette,* quarterly. **Price:** included in membership dues. **Circulation:** 3,500 ● *IRSAlert.* Newsletter. Alternate Formats: online ● *Rett Gazette,* quarterly. Newsletter. Alternate Formats: online ● *Rett Syndrome: A Closer Look.* Video. **Price:** $20.00 for members; $25.00 for nonmembers ● *Rett Syndrome: A Conversation with Families.* Video. **Price:** $20.00 for members; $25.00 for nonmembers ● *Rett Syndrome: A Physician's Approach.* Video. **Price:** $20.00 for members; $25.00 for nonmembers ● *Rett Syndrome: A Therapeutic Approach.* Video. **Price:** $20.00 for members; $25.00 for nonmembers ● *The Rett Syndrome Handbook* (in English and Spanish). **Price:** $15.00 each ● *Silent Angels: The Rett Syndrome Story.* Video. **Price:** $19.95 ● Bibliography. Contains scientific articles from medical periodicals. Alternate Formats: online. **Conventions/Meetings:** annual conference, program includes distinguished faculty members, parent led sessions, medical research updates (exhibits).

15014 ■ Lewy Body Dementia Association (LBDA)
PO Box 451429
Atlanta, GA 31145-9429
Ph: (404)935-6444
Free: (800)539-9767
Fax: (480)422-5434
E-mail: lbda@ldba.org
URL: http://www.lewybodydementia.org
Contact: Robert DeBusk, CEO
Multinational. Description: Promotes scientific advances in medical research on Lewy body dementia. Provides assistance to patients, their families, and caregivers by organizing support groups. Raises public awareness on Lewy body dementia through education and outreach services. **Awards:** Volunteer of the Year. **Frequency:** annual. **Type:** recognition. **Recipient:** to an individual who has demonstrated exemplary service and commitment to voluntary work. **Publications:** *The Thistle,* quarterly. Newsletter. Alternate Formats: online ● Pamphlet. Alternate Formats: online ● Annual Report, annual. Alternate Formats: online.

15015 ■ Lissencephaly Network
c/o Dianna Fitzgerald, Pres.
10408 Bitterroot Ct.
Fort Wayne, IN 46804

Ph: (260)432-4310
Fax: (260)432-4310
E-mail: lissnet@lissencephaly.org
URL: http://www.lissencephaly.org/network/index.htm
Contact: Dianna Fitzgerald, Pres.
Membership Dues: family (initial one time fee), $20 ● family (maintenance fee), $10 (annual). **Multinational. Description:** Works to serve children with lissencephaly, or other neuronal migration disorders, and their families. **Libraries: Type:** lending. **Subjects:** toys. **Programs:** Sibling Pen Pal. **Publications:** *Directory of Families,* updated 3/year ● Newsletter, 3/year. **Conventions/Meetings:** periodic conference ● semiannual Lissencephaly Network Get Together - convention.

15016 ■ MAAP Services for Autism and Asperger Syndrome
c/o Susan J. Moreno, Pres./Founder/Ed.
PO Box 524
Crown Point, IN 46308
Ph: (219)662-1311
Fax: (219)662-0638
E-mail: info@maapservices.org
URL: http://maapservices.org
Contact: Susan J. Moreno, Pres./Founder/Ed.
Founded: 1984. **Membership Dues:** individual (diagnosed with Asperger's Syndrome or related condition), $15 (annual) ● individual or family, $35 (annual) ● professional, $55 (annual). **Description:** Individuals, families, professionals such as doctors, psychologists, educators, therapists. Promotes understanding of Asperger Syndrome and related conditions, including pervasive developmental disorder, not otherwise specified; high functioning autism; nonverbal learning disability; semantic-pragmatic disorder, hyperlexia. Seeks to develop a nationwide support group assistance program, provide leadership training, and produce products, services and educational materials. **Formerly:** Asperger Syndrome Coalition of the United States. **Publications:** *Asperger Info Packet.* Papers. **Price:** $15.00 in U.S.; $18.00 outside U.S. ● *High-Functioning Individuals with Autism* (in English and Spanish). Booklet. **Price:** $6.00 in U.S.; $8.00 outside U.S. ● *The MAAP,* quarterly. Newsletter. **Price:** $22.00/year. Alternate Formats: online. **Conventions/Meetings:** annual conference, with presentations by various presenters (exhibits).

15017 ■ Multiple Sclerosis Foundation (MSF)
6350 N Andrews Ave.
Fort Lauderdale, FL 33309-2130
Ph: (954)776-6805
Free: (800)225-6495
Fax: (954)938-8708
E-mail: director@msfocus.org
URL: http://www.msfocus.org
Contact: Jules Kuperberg, Exec. Dir.
Founded: 1986. **Staff:** 100. **Budget:** $4,900,000. **Description:** Helps to create "A Brighter Tomorrow" for those with MS. Offers a wide array of free services, including: information and referral, subsidized home care and outreach, educational programs, free publications, a quarterly news magazine, and more to improve the quality of life for those affected by MS. **Libraries: Type:** reference. **Holdings:** 500; audiovisuals, books, clippings, periodicals. **Subjects:** MS, health, complementary and alternative medicine. **Computer Services:** Online services, provides a forum for the MS community to ask the advice of a medical professional. **Publications:** *MS Fact Sheets.* Booklets. **Price:** free ● *MSFocus Magazine,* quarterly. **Circulation:** 20,000. **Advertising:** accepted ● *MS-FYi,* monthly. Newsletter. Internet newsletter. Alternate Formats: online ● *Multiple Sclerosis: Helpful Information for Patients and Families.* Booklet.

15018 ■ Muscular Dystrophy Association (MDA)
3300 E Sunrise Dr.
Tucson, AZ 85718
Ph: (520)529-2000
Free: (800)344-4863
Fax: (520)529-5300

E-mail: mda@mdausa.org
URL: http://www.mda.org
Contact: Mr. Jerry Weinberg, Pres./CEO
Founded: 1950. **Staff:** 1,000. **Local Groups:** 157. **Description:** Serves as national voluntary health agency fostering research into the cause and cure of neuromuscular diseases in the following 8 categories. Supports international programs of some 350 research awards, major university-based neuromuscular disease research/clinical centers, and 230 outpatient clinics in hospitals in the U.S. and Puerto Rico. Renders services to patients locally through its chapters, including: diagnostic examinations; follow-up medical evaluations; wheelchairs; leg braces; physical therapy; flu shots; summer camps. Maintains 28 centers across the nation offering research and care for persons affected by Lou Gehrig's disease. **Awards:** Neuromuscular Disease Research Grants. **Frequency:** semiannual. **Type:** grant. **Recipient:** to individual scientific investigators; must meet eligibility requirements set by MDA. **Computer Services:** Online services, chat ● online services, employment. **Committees:** Medical Advisory; Scientific Advisory. **Programs:** Patient and Community Services; Public Health Education. **Task Forces:** Genetics. **Publications:** *MDA/ALS News-Magazine*, bimonthly ● *Quest*, bimonthly. Magazine. Contains stories, research updates, etc. of concern to those with neuromuscular diseases. **Price:** free to individuals served by MDA. **Advertising:** accepted ● Annual Report, annual ● Booklets. Covers each disease in MDA's program. ● Also publishes general and technical literature on muscular dystrophy and other neuromuscular diseases.

15019 ■ Myasthenia Gravis Foundation of America (MGFA)

1821 Univ. Ave. W, Ste.S256
St. Paul, MN 55104
Ph: (651)917-6256
Free: (800)541-5454
Fax: (651)917-1835
E-mail: mgfa@myasthenia.org
URL: http://www.myasthenia.org
Contact: Ms. Janet Golden, Chief Exec.
Founded: 1952. **Members:** 20,000. **Staff:** 3. **Budget:** $750,000. **State Groups:** 31. **Description:** Facilitates the timely diagnosis and optimal care of individuals affected by myasthenia gravis and closely related disorders. Improves their lives through programs of patient services, public information, medical research, professional education, advocacy and patient care. **Libraries: Type:** not open to the public. **Subjects:** myasthenia gravis. **Awards:** Henry R. Viets Students Medical Students Fellowships. **Frequency:** annual. **Type:** fellowship. **Recipient:** for pre-med students ● Kermit E. Osserman/Hilbert Sosin/Blance McClure Post-Doctoral Fellowship. **Frequency:** annual. **Type:** fellowship. **Recipient:** for clinical or basic research pertinent to myasthenia gravis or related neuromuscular disorders. **Committees:** Education; Public Education; Public Relations; Resource Development; Services. **Formerly:** (1998) Myasthenia Gravis Foundation. **Publications:** Brochures, annual. Alternate Formats: online ● Handbooks. For patients. ● Manuals. For physicians and nurses. ● Pamphlets. **Conventions/Meetings:** annual meeting (exhibits) ● annual Scientific Session - meeting, held in conjunction with the American Neurological Association - usually December.

15020 ■ The Myositis Association (TMA)

1233 20th St. NW, Ste.402
Washington, DC 20036
Ph: (202)887-0088
Free: (800)821-7356
Fax: (202)466-8940
E-mail: tma@myositis.org
URL: http://www.myositis.org
Contact: Bob Goldberg, Exec.Dir.
Founded: 1993. **Members:** 2,000. **Membership Dues:** $35 (annual). **Staff:** 5. **Budget:** $500,000. **Regional Groups:** 65. **Description:** Seeks to educate members in ways to avoid future degeneration process of myositis, give emotional support, investigate the different causes of the disease, act as a

clearinghouse to physicians and scientists, and disseminate information to patients to inform on some of the known causes, pursue additional funding for research, investigate the most effective medical treatments available that have the least side effects and, most important, research a cure into these debilitating diseases. **Formerly:** (2002) Myositis Association of America. **Publications:** *JM Companion*, quarterly. Magazine ● *Myositis Monitor*, bimonthly. Newsletter. Alternate Formats: online ● *Myositis Update*, 4-6/ year. Newsletter ● *OutLook Extra*, semiannual. Magazine ● *Outlook for the Inflammatory Myopathies*, quarterly. Magazine. **Advertising:** accepted. **Conventions/Meetings:** conference, with medical panels and speakers ● annual meeting.

15021 ■ National Ataxia Foundation (NAF)

2600 Fernbrook Ln. N, No. 119
Minneapolis, MN 55447
Ph: (763)553-0020
Fax: (763)553-0167
E-mail: naf@ataxia.org
URL: http://www.ataxia.org
Contact: Michael Parent, Exec. Dir.
Founded: 1957. **Members:** 3,000. **Membership Dues:** individual in U.S., $25 (annual) ● medical professional, $45 (annual) ● individual outside U.S., $40 (annual). **Staff:** 7. **Budget:** $850,000. **Local Groups:** 61. **National Groups:** 6. **Description:** Membership is open to any individual who wishes to contribute to the eradication of ataxia (a genetic disease characterized by the degeneration of the nerves of the spinal cord and the cerebellum, causing a loss of coordination and disturbance in gait and related conditions such as peroneal muscular atrophy, hereditary spastic paraplegia, and hereditary tremor. Ataxia may be inherited as a recessive or dominant trait and may strike persons from a very early age up to and even beyond 50 years of age. Ataxia is very similar to multiple sclerosis; however, multiple sclerosis is not inherited and has a different origin.) Aims to: make an early diagnosis of ataxia by locating all potential victims and encouraging them to have an examination; educate the public and the helping professions about ataxia; initiate basic research and coordinate efforts of worldwide research centers. Focuses on locating and understanding the genes responsible. Provides services and information to ataxia victims and their families. **Awards:** Ataxia Research Grant. **Frequency:** annual. **Type:** grant. **Computer Services:** Information services, sign up for membership, donations, request information, grant applications and current research. **Boards:** Medical and Research Advisory. **Publications:** *Generations*, quarterly. Newsletter. Includes foundation news, calendar of events, and research updates. **Price:** free for members and those who suffer from ataxia. **Circulation:** 12,000 ● *Together There is Hope*. Video ● *Together There is Understanding*. Video ● Brochures ● Also publishes Together. (video) and brochures. **Conventions/Meetings:** annual meeting (exhibits).

15022 ■ National Attention Deficit Disorder Association (National ADDA)

15000 Commerce Pkwy., Ste.C
Mount Laurel, NJ 08054
Ph: (856)439-9099
Fax: (856)439-0525
E-mail: mail@add.org
URL: http://www.add.org
Contact: Linda S. Anderson MCC, Pres.
Founded: 1989. **Membership Dues:** individual, $45 (annual) ● family, $55 (annual) ● professional, $150 (annual). **Description:** Seeks to: promote a greater public awareness of the multiple needs of individuals with ADD and their families; address their educational, psychological, and social needs; encourage more responsiveness with regard to ADD in the academic and health care communities. **Computer Services:** database, of support groups throughout the country. **Formerly:** (1992) Attention-Deficit Disorder Association. **Publications:** *Addalog*. Catalog. Lists books, brochures, monographs, and other materials available for purchasing. ● *Focus*, quarterly. Newsletter. **Price:** included in membership dues ● Monographs

● Pamphlets. **Conventions/Meetings:** annual Adult ADD Conference - conference and workshop (exhibits).

15023 ■ National Brain Tumor Foundation (NBTF)

22 Battery St., Ste.612
San Francisco, CA 94111-5520
Ph: (415)834-9970
Free: (800)934-CURE
Fax: (415)834-9980
E-mail: nbtf@braintumor.org
URL: http://www.braintumor.org
Contact: Rob Tufel, Exec. Dir.
Founded: 1981. **Staff:** 10. **Budget:** $1,600,000. **Languages:** English, Spanish. **Description:** Comprises of medical researchers, doctors, brain tumor patients, and relatives working together to improve the quality of life for brain tumor patients and their families and find a cure through research. Raises funds for brain tumor research; offers patient services such as educational materials, a toll-free brain tumor information line, a quarterly newsletter, information about support groups and patient networks, caregiver trainings, free publications, a medical information nurse and national and regional conferences. **Awards:** Research Grants. **Frequency:** annual. **Type:** grant. **Recipient:** for research. **Doing business as:** Brain Tumor Foundation of America. **Formerly:** (1989) Friends of Brain Tumor Research. **Publications:** *Brain Tumors: A Guide* (in English and Spanish). Booklet. Contains information on brain tumors. **Price:** 1st copy is free; $6.00 each (additional copy) ● *Coping With Your Loved One's Brain Tumor*. Brochure ● *Glioblastoma Multiforme*. Brochure ● *Returning to Work*. Brochure ● *Search*, quarterly. Newsletter. Informs readers of advances in treatment and psychosocial support. **Circulation:** 15,000. Alternate Formats: online ● *Understanding Brain Metastases*. Brochure ● Pamphlets. **Conventions/Meetings:** meeting.

15024 ■ National CFIDS Foundation (NCF)

103 Aletha Rd.
Needham, MA 02492
Ph: (781)449-3535
Fax: (781)449-8606
E-mail: info@ncf-net.org
URL: http://www.ncf-net.org
Contact: Gail R. Kansky, Pres.
Founded: 1997. **Members:** 4,000. **Membership Dues:** individual in U.S., $30 (annual) ● individual in Canada, C$45 (annual) ● supporter, individual outside U.S. and Canada, $50 (annual) ● sponsor, $100 (annual) ● patron, $500 (annual) ● benefactor, $1,000 (annual). **Description:** Provides education, advocacy and fundraising for research. **Awards:** B&D. **Type:** grant. **Recipient:** for research into causal matters. **Publications:** *The National Forum*, quarterly. Newsletter. **Price:** included in membership dues.

15025 ■ National Coalition for Research in Neurological Disorders (NCR)

Address Unknown since 2007
Founded: 1952. **Members:** 57. **Staff:** 3. **Budget:** $65,000. **Description:** Represents voluntary health agencies and professional societies concerned with obtaining funds for neurological research. Seeks to stimulate public information regarding the field of neurological disorders. Lobbies for increased funding for training and research in neurological disorders. **Committees:** Citizens Budget; Government Liaison; Public and Governmental Information; Review. **Formerly:** National Committee for Research in Neurological Disorders; (1988) National Committee for Research in Nerualogical and Communicative Disorders; (1989) National Coalition for Research in Neurological and Communicative Disorders. **Publications:** *NCR News*, quarterly. **Conventions/Meetings:** annual meeting and symposium.

15026 ■ National Fibromyalgia Research Association (NFRA)

PO Box 500
Salem, OR 97308
Ph: (503)315-7257

Fax: (503)315-7205
E-mail: nfra@firstpac.com
URL: http://www.nfra.net
Founded: 1992. **Description:** Focuses on education, treatment and finding a cure for fibromyalgia. Produces a Fibromyalgia Awareness Pin to raise public awareness and research dollars. **Computer Services:** Information services, fibromyalgia resources.

15027 ■ National Institute of Neurological Disorders and Stroke (NINDS)

PO Box 5801
Bethesda, MD 20824
Ph: (301)496-5751 (301)468-5981
Free: (800)352-9424
E-mail: brainfo@ninds.nih.gov
URL: http://www.ninds.nih.gov
Contact: Story C. Landis PhD, Dir.
Founded: 1950. **Description:** Works to identify the causes and ways to prevent, diagnose and treat neurological disorders and stroke. **Awards: Type:** fellowship ● Grants-in-aid. **Type:** grant. **Recipient:** to public and private institutions. **Boards:** Scientific Counselors. **Committees:** Muscular Dystrophy Coordinating. **Subgroups:** Brain Tumor Progress Review; The Stroke Progress Review. **Conventions/Meetings:** periodic Regular Study Section Meetings ● periodic Special Emphasis Panel Meetings.

15028 ■ National Multiple Sclerosis Society (NMSS)

733 3rd Ave.
New York, NY 10017
Ph: (212)986-3240
Free: (800)344-4897
Fax: (212)986-7981
E-mail: info@nmss.org
URL: http://www.nationalmssociety.org
Contact: Joyce M. Nelson, Pres./CEO
Founded: 1946. **Members:** 470,000. **Membership Dues:** regular, $25 (annual). **Staff:** 120. **Budget:** $58,000,000. **State Groups:** 93. **Description:** Stimulates, supports, and coordinates research into the cause, treatment, and cure of multiple sclerosis; provides services for persons with MS and related diseases and their families; aids in establishing MS clinics and therapy centers. Conducts Creative Will, biennial competition for artists with MS. Maintains numerous committees including international and research and medical programs, and services. Maintains speakers' bureau; compiles statistics. **Libraries: Type:** reference; open to the public. **Holdings:** 1,000. **Subjects:** multiples sclerosis and related topics. **Awards:** John Dystel Prize. **Frequency:** annual. **Type:** recognition. **Recipient:** for outstanding contributions to MS research ● Mother/Father of the Year. **Frequency:** annual. **Type:** recognition ● Public Education Award. **Frequency:** annual. **Type:** recognition. **Recipient:** for magazine writing and radio or television reporting. **Computer Services:** Electronic publishing, Teen InsideMS ● information services, press room ● online services, chat ● online services, message boards ● online services, searching of biomedical databases. **Affiliated With:** Multiple Sclerosis International Federation. **Formerly:** (1947) Association for Advancement of Research on Multiple Sclerosis. **Publications:** *Inside MS,* quarterly. Magazine. Contains book reviews, research updates, legislative updates, and annual report. **Price:** included in membership dues. ISSN: 0739-9774. **Circulation:** 400,000. **Advertising:** accepted. **Conventions/Meetings:** annual National Leadership Conference (exhibits).

15029 ■ National Organization for Disorders of the Corpus Callosum (NODCC)

PMB 363
18032-C Lemon Dr.
Yorba Linda, CA 92886
Ph: (714)747-0063
Fax: (714)693-0808

E-mail: info@nodcc.org
URL: http://www.nodcc.org
Contact: Lynn K. Paul PhD, Pres.
Founded: 2002. **Members:** 2,000. **Membership Dues:** individual, $25 (annual) ● family, $50 (annual). **Description:** Enhances the quality of life of individuals with Agenesis of the Corpus Callosum (ACC) and other disorders of the corpus callosum. Gathers and distributes information regarding ACC. Works in collaboration with The ACC Network and several neuropsychological research programs. Sponsors conferences for families and professionals.

15030 ■ National Parkinson Foundation (NPF)

1501 NW 9th Ave.
Miami, FL 33136-1494
Ph: (305)243-6666
Free: (800)327-4545
Fax: (305)243-5595
E-mail: contact@parkinson.org
URL: http://www.parkinson.org
Contact: Daniel Arty, Pres.
Founded: 1957. **Staff:** 50. **Budget:** $6,000,000. **Languages:** English, French, Spanish. **Description:** Doctors, nurses, scientists, pharmacologists, and therapists who research, diagnose, and treat Parkinsonism. Supports basic and clinical research for Parkinsonism and related neurological disorders and provides physical, speech, and occupational therapy. NPF is associated with the University of Miami School of Medicine, and supports the National Parkinson Institute, which provides diagnosis, treatment, care, and rehabilitation. Conducts educational programs. Distributes literature to medical libraries, nurses training schools, health clinics, physicians, and patients. Sponsors regional patient self-support groups where problems are discussed and experiences are exchanged under guidance of physicians, social workers, and psychologists. **Awards:** Research Grants. **Frequency:** annual. **Type:** grant. **Publications:** *How to Start and Run a Support Group* ● *Membership List,* periodic ● *The Parkinson Handbook* ● *Parkinson Report,* quarterly. Newsletter. Contains research reports. **Price:** included in membership dues; available free of charge to others upon request. **Circulation:** 115,000 ● Also publishes other books and brochures. **Conventions/Meetings:** annual Fundraising Dinner - meeting ● semiannual International Symposium - meeting ● annual symposium.

15031 ■ National Spasmodic Dysphonia Association (NSDA)

300 Park Blvd., Ste.415
Itasca, IL 60143
Free: (800)795-6732
Fax: (630)250-4505
E-mail: nsda@dysphonia.org
URL: http://www.dysphonia.org
Contact: Ms. Kimberly Kuman, Exec. Dir.
Founded: 1989. **Members:** 8,200. **Membership Dues:** voluntary, $35 (annual). **Staff:** 7. **National Groups:** 45. **Description:** Works to advance medical research into the causes of and treatments for Spasmodic Dysphonia (SD), promotes physician and public awareness of the disorder, and sponsors support groups for patients and their families. Represents people with SD, healthcare professionals, dedicated volunteers, friends and families. Helps to improve the lives of people dealing with SD, and works to support research in order to bring understanding to this disorder. (Spasmodic Dysphonia is an unusual neurological voice disorder that most people have never heard of, yet it affects over 50,000 people in North America and probably many more since it is often undiagnosed or misdiagnosed as chronic laryngitis, allergies, acid reflux or even stress. Living with Spasmodic Dysphonia leaves many people feeling alone and isolated because the ability to communicate is impaired.). **Libraries: Type:** reference. **Holdings:** 6; books, video recordings. **Subjects:** Spasmodic Dysphonia. **Publications:** *NSDA Newsletter,* biennial. **Price:** free for members; $35.00 for nonmembers. **Circulation:** 8,200. **Conventions/Meetings:** annual symposium and regional meeting.

15032 ■ National Spasmodic Torticollis Association (NSTA)

9920 Talbert Ave.
Fountain Valley, CA 92708
Ph: (714)378-7837
Free: (800)487-8385
Fax: (714)378-7830
E-mail: nstamail@aol.com
URL: http://www.torticollis.org
Contact: Ms. Vi Tran, Office Mgr.
Founded: 1980. **Members:** 3,400. **Membership Dues:** individual, $30 (annual) ● donor, $50 (annual) ● patron, $100 (annual). **Staff:** 30. **Budget:** $150,000. **Regional Groups:** 85. **Local Groups:** 48. **Description:** Persons afflicted with spasmodic torticollis or ST, (a syndrome in which the muscles on one side of the neck contract and pull the head to the side, sometimes pushing the chin up or down. ST usually occurs in adults and can sometimes be treated successfully with medication and physical therapy. Educates the public on ST so that persons with early symptoms know to seek proper medical help from a neurologist or neurosurgeon.) Provides forum for discussion among ST sufferers and their families in order to share information and experiences, and diminish feelings of alienation and self-consciousness. **Libraries: Type:** not open to the public. **Holdings:** articles, books, periodicals. **Subjects:** treatments, symptoms, diagnosis. **Absorbed:** (1993) American Spasmodic Torticollis Association. **Formerly:** Project S.T. **Publications:** *NSTA News Magazine,* quarterly. Includes medical advisor's column. **Price:** included in membership dues. **Circulation:** 3,500 ● *P.T. In-Home Videotape.* **Price:** $24.00 for members ● *Physicians Referral Directory,* annual. Lists neurologists who treat spasmodic torticollis. **Price:** free ● *Series of - Helpful Hints Letters* ● *What is NSTA?* ● Also publishes fact sheet. **Conventions/Meetings:** annual symposium - for three days.

15033 ■ National Tay-Sachs and Allied Diseases Association (NTSAD)

2001 Beacon St., Ste.204
Boston, MA 02135
Ph: (617)277-4463
Free: (800)906-8723
Fax: (617)277-0134
E-mail: info@ntsad.org
URL: http://www.ntsad.org
Contact: Diana Pangonis, Interim Exec. Dir.
Founded: 1956. **Members:** 400. **Membership Dues:** individual, $50 (annual). **Staff:** 3. **Budget:** $500,000. **Regional Groups:** 4. **Languages:** English, Russian, Spanish. **Multinational. Description:** Supports educational, prevention, family service, and research programs concerning Tay-Sachs and allied degenerative lysosomal and leukodystrophy and neurological diseases occurring in infants, children, and adults. Provides educational literature on Tay-Sachs and allied diseases; serves as a referral agency for the layperson and professional on all aspects of Tay-Sachs and related diseases; promotes mass screening programs and appropriate legislation locally and nationally. Sponsors International Laboratory Quality Control and Reference Sample Center for TSD laboratories. Offers support groups and services for parents of children with Tay-Sachs and related diseases, grandparents and extended family members. Compiles statistics; operates Speaker's Bureau. **Libraries: Type:** reference; lending. **Holdings:** 150; books, periodicals. **Subjects:** bereavement, living. **Awards:** Research Initiative. **Frequency:** annual. **Type:** grant. **Committees:** Education; Family Services; Fundraising; Research Initiative; Scientific Advisory. **Affiliated With:** Genetic Alliance; National Organization for Rare Disorders. **Formerly:** (1966) National Tay-Sachs Association. **Publications:** *Breakthrough,* semiannual. Newsletter. **Circulation:** 10,000. **Advertising:** accepted ● *Home Care Manual.* **Price:** $5.00 includes shipping and handling ● *Lay-Onset Tay-Sachs.* Contains information sheet. **Price:** free ● *Lifeline,* quarterly. Newsletter. Distributed to affected families only. ● *National Tay-Sachs and Allied Diseases Association—Breakthrough,* semiannual. Newsletter ● *What Every Family Should*

Know, annual. Manual. **Price:** $5.00 ● *What Is Canavan Disease?* ● *What Is Tay-Sachs Disease?* ● . **Price:** Also makes available brochures and educational materials. **Conventions/Meetings:** annual conference, for family and care providers, professional clinicians and researchers (exhibits) - usually April/May ● symposium, on basic research conducted on TSD and allied diseases ● symposium, on carrier detection and psychosocial implications.

15034 ■ NBIA Disorders Association
2082 Monaco Ct.
El Cajon, CA 92019-4235
Ph: (619)588-2315
Fax: (619)588-4093
E-mail: info@nbiadisorders.org
URL: http://www.nbiadisorders.org
Contact: Patricia V. Wood, Pres.
Founded: 1991. **Description:** Educates the public about the Neurodegeneration with Brain Iron Accumulation (NBIA) disease. Provides emotional support to families affected by NBIA. Monitors and supports NBIA research. **Formerly:** (2003) Hallervorden-Spatz Syndrome Association.

15035 ■ Neurobehavioral Teratology Society (NBTS)
c/o Susan M. Melnick, PhD, Sec.
SK Bio-Pharmaceuticals
22-10 State Rte. 208 S
Fair Lawn, NJ 07410
E-mail: melnicks@skbp.com
URL: http://www.nbts.org
Contact: Susan M. Melnick PhD, Sec.
Membership Dues: full, $75 (annual) ● associate (includes journal subscription), $55 (annual). **Description:** Promotes study of functional brain deficits (like learning disorders) resulting from abnormal neurological development. **Awards:** Conference Award. **Frequency:** 5/year. **Type:** grant. **Recipient:** for students or postdoctoral students who attended the conference and presented a deserving abstract ● New Investigator. **Frequency:** annual. **Type:** grant. **Recipient:** for a PhD within 5 years of graduation who published a paper in the last calendar year, which is relevant to NBTS. **Committees:** Constitution and Bylaws; Nominations; Public Affairs; Publications. **Conventions/Meetings:** annual meeting.

15036 ■ Neuroleptic Malignant Syndrome Information Service (NMSIS)
PO Box 1069
Sherburne, NY 13460-1069
Ph: (607)674-7920 (607)674-7901
Fax: (607)674-7910
E-mail: info@nmsis.org
URL: http://www.nmsis.org
Contact: Dianne Daugherty, Exec. Dir.
Founded: 1997. **Membership Dues:** basic, $35. **Multinational. Description:** Serves as an international resource center for educational and research initiatives to promote awareness, improve patient safety and reduce morbidity and mortality in relation to heat-related disorders. Disorders covered include Neuroleptic Malignant Syndrome, Serotonin Syndrome, Malignant Catatonia, Heatstroke and Hyperthermia associated with drugs of abuse. **Computer Services:** database, research on neuroleptic malignant syndrome and related conditions. **Telecommunication Services:** hotline, (888)667-8367. **Affiliated With:** Malignant Hyperthermia Association of the United States. **Publications:** *A typical Antipsychotics and Neuroleptic Malignant Syndrome.* **Price:** free ● *Catatonia, Lethal Catatonia, and Neuroleptic Malignant Syndrome.* **Price:** free ● *Central Dopamine Hypoactivity and the Pathogenesis of Neuroleptic Malignant Syndrome.* **Price:** free ● *Frequently Asked Questions about NMS.* Brochure ● *NMS Packet for Medical Professionals.* **Price:** $15.00/copy ● *NMS Packet for Patients.* **Price:** $10.00/copy ● *NMS Recognition, Diagnosis and Treatment.* Brochure ● *NMSIS News*, biennial. Newsletter ● *Role of Calcium Peripheral Catecholamines in the Pathophysiology of Neuroleptic Malignant Syndrome.* **Price:** free ● *The Serotonin Syndrome.* **Price:** free ● *Treatment of Neuroleptic Malignant Syndrome.* **Price:** free ● Brochure.

15037 ■ Parents of Infants and Children with Kernicterus (PICK)
One W. Superior St., Ste.2410
Chicago, IL 60610
Ph: (312)274-9695
E-mail: info@pickonline.org
URL: http://www.pickonline.org
Contact: Karen E. Dixon PhD, Co-Founder/Pres.
Founded: 2000. **Description:** Aims to prevent all new cases of kernicterus through a system-wide change in jaundice management. Develops a parent/ healthcare partnership model for addressing preventable disabilities in newborns. Prevents kernicterus through a program of education, objective screening, follow up, diagnosis and treatment. Provides information and support to families. Identifies effective therapies and treatment that could improve the quality of life for children and adults with kernicterus. **Telecommunication Services:** electronic mail, karendixon@pickonline.org. **Publications:** *PICK Educational Video.* Alternate Formats: online ● Newsletter. Alternate Formats: online ● Report. Alternate Formats: online ● Brochure. Alternate Formats: online.

15038 ■ Parkinson Alliance
PO Box 308
Kingston, NJ 08528-0308
Ph: (609)688-0870
Free: (800)579-8440
Fax: (609)688-0875
URL: http://www.parkinsonalliance.net
Contact: Carol J. Walton, Exec. Dir.
Founded: 1999. **Description:** Fosters philanthropic activities to raise funds for promising medical research in finding a cure for Parkinson's disease. Creates public awareness and support for research on Parkinson's disease. Seeks to improve the quality of life in the DBS (deep brain stimulation) community. Organizes special fundraising and charitable events. **Awards:** Research Grant. **Frequency:** annual. **Type:** grant. **Recipient:** for promising and scientifically validated Parkinson's disease research programs. **Publications:** *The Catalyst*, semiannual. Newsletter. **Price:** $25.00. Alternate Formats: online.

15039 ■ Parkinson's Disease Foundation (PDF)
1359 Broadway, Ste.1509
New York, NY 10018
Ph: (212)923-4700
Free: (800)457-6676
Fax: (212)923-4778
E-mail: info@pdf.org
URL: http://www.pdf.org
Contact: Robin Anthony Elliott, Exec. Dir.
Founded: 1957. **Staff:** 18. **Nonmembership. Description:** Raises funds for support of scientific research into causes, prevention, and cure of Parkinson's disease. Supports its own laboratories for research in Parkinsonism. Prepares and distributes information on patient care and rehabilitation including list of clinics where treatment is available, and a list of patient self-help groups. Supports a brain bank to permit anatomical and chemical studies. Sponsors scientific symposia. Offers patient and family counseling and advocacy services. Maintains research advisory board. Sponsors summer fellowship program for medical students and undergraduate. **Awards:** Center Grants. **Frequency:** 3/year. **Type:** grant. **Recipient:** to major Parkinson's research centers ● H. Houston Merritt Fellowship. **Type:** fellowship. **Recipient:** for postdoctoral students at Columbia University's College of Physicians and Surgeons and other institutions ● International Research Grants. **Frequency:** annual. **Type:** grant. **Recipient:** to investigators to pursue Parkinson's science ● Postdoctoral Program and Named Postdoctoral Fellowship. **Type:** fellowship. **Formerly:** (1999) United Parkinson Foundation. **Publications:** *Information Packet.* Booklets. **Price:** free ● *PDF Newsletter*, 3-4/year. Covers developments in Parkinson's disease research, hints for daily living, and advice to health care professionals. Includes case studies. **Price:** free. **Circulation:** 98,000 ● Brochures.

15040 ■ Pediatric Neurotransmitter Disease Association
c/o Nancy Speller, Pres.
6 Nathan Dr.
Plainview, NY 11803
Ph: (516)937-0049
Fax: (516)937-0049
E-mail: pnd@pndassoc.org
URL: http://www.pndassoc.org
Contact: Nancy Speller, Pres.
Founded: 1998. **Description:** Provides information and support to patients and families affected by pediatric neurotransmitter diseases. Increases public awareness of pediatric neurotransmitter diseases. Acts as a source of information for health care professionals. Establishes and coordinates a network among affected families, health care professionals and the research community. Promotes public and private support and funding for pediatric neurotransmitter disease research. **Awards:** PND Research Grant Award. **Frequency:** periodic. **Type:** grant. **Recipient:** for research related to the detection, diagnosis and treatment of diseases of neurotransmitter metabolism ● Young Investigator Award. **Frequency:** periodic. **Type:** monetary. **Recipient:** for outstanding researchers on pediatric neurotransmitter diseases. **Telecommunication Services:** electronic mail, nancyjka@optonline.net.

15041 ■ Polio Society (PS)
PMB 106-273
4200 Wisconsin Ave. NW
Washington, DC 20016
Ph: (301)897-8180 (202)897-8180
Fax: (202)994-3153
E-mail: poliosociety@yahoo.com
URL: http://www.poliosociety.org
Founded: 1984. **Members:** 3,500. **Membership Dues:** institutional, $50 (annual) ● individual, $25 (annual). **Staff:** 1. **Budget:** $10,000. **Local Groups:** 3. **Description:** Polio survivors and health care professionals interested in the long-term health of patients who have had the disease. Gathers and disseminates information on post-polio syndrome. (PPS is a condition in which polio survivors suffer unaccustomed fatigue, joint and muscle pain, weakening or loss of muscle function, and respiratory problems.) Acts as liaison between members and medical facilities; maintains outreach program and referral service; sponsors support groups. Advocates on issues of disability and benefits. **Libraries:** Type: reference. **Holdings:** archival material. **Formerly:** Post-Polio League for Information and Outreach. **Publications:** *Options*, quarterly. Newsletter ● Brochures. Contains informational brochures. ● Also publishes information packets. **Conventions/Meetings:** bimonthly meeting ● monthly support group meeting.

15042 ■ Reflex Sympathetic Dystrophy Syndrome Association of America (RSDSA)
PO Box 502
Milford, CT 06460
Ph: (203)877-3790
Free: (877)662-7737
Fax: (203)882-8362
E-mail: info@rsds.org
URL: http://www.rsds.org
Contact: James W. Broatch MSW, Exec. Dir.
Founded: 1984. **Members:** 6,579. **Membership Dues:** regular, in U.S., $15 (annual) ● regular, outside U.S., $25 (annual). **Staff:** 3. **Budget:** $500,000. **Local Groups:** 100. **Languages:** English, French, Spanish. **Description:** People with Reflex Sympathetic Dystrophy Syndrome, also known as Complex Regional Pain Syndrome Type I and Type II; health care professionals treating RSDS patients. (RSDS is a disorder of the autonomic nervous system whose onset is usually preceded by a minor trauma such as a muscle sprain; surgery; symptoms of RSDS include severe pain, loss of muscle motion and use, swelling, skin and nail changes, and softening of the bones in affected areas.) Promotes increased awareness of RSDS among health care professionals and the public; conducts media campaigns; maintains national network of physicians involved in RSDS treatment and research. Encour-

ages and supports RSDS research; has a national data bank for the coordination of RSDS research and treatment information. Aids in the formation of support groups for people with RSDS; develops inservice programs and seminars for use at hospitals and educational institutions. Makes available referral services. Conducts educational programs; maintains speakers' bureau; compiles statistics, funds research, has published clinical practice guidelines for diagnosis, treatment, and management of RSDS/CRPS. **Libraries:** Type: reference. **Holdings:** periodicals. **Awards:** Rachel Tobias Young Investigator Award. **Frequency:** annual. **Type:** fellowship. **Recipient:** for research in basic or clinical science related to CRPS ● RSDSA Fellowship Grant. **Frequency:** annual. **Type:** grant. **Recipient:** for research. **Computer Services:** Online services, electronic alerts. **Formerly:** (1998) Reflex Sympathetic Dystrophy Association. **Publications:** *Clinical Practice Guidelines for Diagnosis, Treatment, and Management of RSD/CRPS* ● *Do You Have Reflex Sympathetic Dystrophy/Complex Regional Pain Syndrome?*, quarterly. Newsletter. **Price:** included in membership dues. **Circulation:** 4,500. **Advertising:** accepted ● *Helping Children/Youth with RSD/CRPS Succeed in School* ● *In Pain and Agonizing Over the BillsResources for People with CRPS*, annual. Booklet. Alternate Formats: online ● *RSDSA Review*, quarterly. Newsletter. **Price:** included in membership dues. **Circulation:** 4,500. **Advertising:** accepted ● *Telltale Signs of RSD/CRPS Type I* ● *Treating Complex Regional Pain Syndrome/Reflex Sympathetic Dystrophy Syndrome: A Guide for Therapy* ● Also publishes fact sheets. **Conventions/Meetings:** meeting - 3/year.

15043 ■ Sturge-Weber Foundation (SWF)

PO Box 418
Mount Freedom, NJ 07970-0418
Ph: (973)895-4445
Free: (800)627-5482
Fax: (973)895-4846
E-mail: swf@sturge-weber.com
URL: http://www.sturge-weber.com
Contact: Karen Ball, Pres./CEO
Founded: 1986. **Members:** 4,500. **Staff:** 5. **Budget:** $300,000. **Regional Groups:** 21. **Description:** Persons with Sturge-Weber syndrome and their families; concerned professionals and supporters. Serves as an information clearinghouse on Sturge-Weber syndrome, port-wine stains, and Klippel-Trenaunay Weber syndrome. Sturge-Weber syndrome is a congenital neurological disorder characterized by facial port-wine stains, seizures, glaucoma, and loss of motor control, accompanied in rare cases by internal organ irregularities. Disseminates information; offers support to afflicted persons; maintains speakers' bureau and compiles statistics. Funds research. **Libraries:** Type: reference. **Holdings:** audiovisuals, books, clippings. **Subjects:** epilepsy, lectures. **Awards:** Frequency: annual. **Type:** grant. **Recipient:** for research into port wine stains, glaucoma, and Sturge-Weber. **Computer Services:** database. **Committees:** Education. **Publications:** *Branching Out Newsletter*, quarterly. **Advertising:** accepted ● *Sturge-Weber Syndrome*. Book ● *Sturge-Weber Syndrome Resource Guide for a Reason, a Season, a Lifetime*. Book ● Brochures. **Conventions/Meetings:** biennial conference, for members; with speakers, workshops and support for new families (exhibits).

15044 ■ Take Charge! Cure Parkinson's (TCCP)

1489 W Palmetto Park Rd., Ste.442
Boca Raton, FL 33486
Ph: (561)620-1970
Fax: (561)488-5726
E-mail: cureparkinsons@aol.com
URL: http://www.cureparkinsons.org
Contact: Fran Landes, Co-Founder
Founded: 1999. **Description:** Seeks to improve the quality of life for people with Parkinson's disease. Empowers people with Parkinson's and their care partners. Increases awareness and understanding of Parkinson's disease through education and advocacy.

Supports research efforts to find a cure for Parkinson's disease.

15045 ■ Tourette Syndrome Association (TSA)

42-40 Bell Blvd.
Bayside, NY 11361-2820
Ph: (718)224-2999
Free: (888)4TOURET
Fax: (718)224-9596
E-mail: ts@tsa-usa.com
URL: http://www.tsa-usa.org
Contact: Monte N. Redman, Chm.
Founded: 1972. **Members:** 40,000. **Membership Dues:** individual, $45 (annual) ● physician, $100 (annual) ● allied professional, family, $60 (annual) ● individual (plus support for a scholarship member), $90 (annual) ● contributing, $125 (annual) ● corporate, sustaining, $250 (annual) ● patron, $500 (annual) ● benefactor, $1,000 (annual) ● life, $5,000. **Staff:** 20. **Budget:** $1,800,000. **Regional Groups:** 5. **State Groups:** 50. **Local Groups:** 300. **Description:** People with Tourette Syndrome (TS) and their families and friends; physicians, nurses, teachers, psychologists, social workers, and other professionals; organizations such as mental health agencies. (TS is characterized by involuntary muscular movements and utterances of sounds or words, and is often undiagnosed or misdiagnosed.) Develops and disseminates educational materials to families, professionals, and agencies involved in health care, education, and governments. Schedules meetings and seminars for professionals and families to explore the latest information on TS. Stimulates support for research into the nature and causes of the disorder. Apprises members of rights, services, and benefits provided by the government and other organizations. **Libraries:** Type: reference. **Holdings:** articles. **Subjects:** scientific. **Awards:** Permanent Research Fund Award. **Frequency:** annual. **Type:** grant. **Recipient:** for research. **Affiliated With:** National Association of Councils on Developmental Disabilities; National Coalition for Research in Neurological Disorders; National Health Council; National Organization for Rare Disorders. **Formerly:** Gilles de la Tourette Syndrome Association. **Publications:** *Leadership Bulletins*, quarterly. **Price:** free. **Circulation:** 50 ● *Medical Letter: Summary of the Recent Literature*, annual ● *Tourette Syndrome Association Newsletter*, quarterly. Includes book reviews. **Price:** included in membership dues. **Conventions/Meetings:** biennial meeting (exhibits).

15046 ■ Transverse Myelitis Association (TMA)

c/o Sanford J. Siegel, Pres./Newsletter Ed.
1787 Sutter Pkwy.
Powell, OH 43065-8806
Ph: (614)766-1806
E-mail: ssiegel@myelitis.org
URL: http://www.myelitis.org
Contact: Sanford J. Siegel, Pres./Newsletter Ed.
Founded: 1944. **Languages:** Chinese, Dutch, English, French, German, Italian, Polish, Portuguese, Romanian, Spanish. **Multinational. Description:** Advocates for individuals who have rare neuroimmunologic diseases of the central nervous system, including Transverse Myelitis (TM), Acute Disseminated Encephalomyelitis (ADEM), Optic Neuritis, and Neuromyelitis Optica (Devic's disease). Facilitates support and networking opportunities among TM families. Supports research and innovative treatment of TM. **Computer Services:** Information services, ADEM resources ● information services, Devic's disease resources ● information services, TM resources ● online services, chat room ● online services, message forum. **Programs:** Equipment Exchange. **Publications:** Newsletter, semiannual. Contains articles by physicians, patients, and healthcare providers. Alternate Formats: online ● Membership Directory, annual.

15047 ■ Tremor Action Network (TAN)

PO Box 5013
Pleasanton, CA 94566
Ph: (925)462-0111 (510)681-6565

Fax: (925)369-0485
E-mail: tremor@tremoraction.org
URL: http://www.tremoraction.org
Contact: Janice Bolick, Dir.
Multinational. Description: Aims to spread awareness of essential tremor, focal dystonia, and tremor related movement disorders by advocating for a cure through research. Educates the public about the millions of children and adults worldwide afflicted with essential tremor, focal dystonia, and tremor related movement disorders. Connects a community of persons with common interest to inform government agencies and the health care industry on the universal necessity for diagnosis, contemporary diagnostic tests, treatments, and options. Ameliorates the quality of life physical, emotional, financial, and educational challenges people face after the diagnosis of a movement disorder. **Publications:** *Spikes & Spasms*, quarterly. Newsletter. Provides informative articles for a better understanding of living with related movement disorders. Alternate Formats: online ● Videos. Alternate Formats: online.

15048 ■ Trigeminal Neuralgia Association (TNA)

925 NW 56th Terr., Ste.C
Gainesville, FL 32605-6402
Ph: (352)331-7009
Free: (800)923-3608
Fax: (352)331-7078
E-mail: tnanational@tna-support.org
URL: http://www.tna-support.org
Contact: Michael G. Pasternak PhD, Pres.
Founded: 1990. **Members:** 20,000. **Staff:** 9. **Budget:** $75,000. **Local Groups:** 67. **National Groups:** 18. **Description:** Individuals with trigeminal neuralgia, a neurological disorder characterized by sudden attacks of pain along the distribution of one or more branches of the trigeminal nerve in the face and head, and related facial pain conditions. Works to increase public and professional awareness and understanding of the disorder. Provides a forum for discussion among individuals with trigeminal neuralgia in order to share information and experiences and offer support to patients and their families. Offers physician referrals. Conducts educational programs. **Additional Websites:** http://www.endthepain.org. **Boards:** Directors; Medical Advisory. **Affiliated With:** National Organization for Rare Disorders. **Publications:** *Striking Back*. Book. Presents a comprehensive guide for the layperson about TN. **Price:** $14.00 plus shipping and handling ● *TNAlert*, 3/year. Newsletter. Contains the most up-to-date news and information on advancements in the care and management of TN and related facial pain conditions. **Price:** free. **Circulation:** 14,000. Alternate Formats: online ● *Trigeminal Neuralgia - An Overview for Patients and Their Families* ● *Trigeminal Neuralgia and Face Pain*. Handbook. Describes all aspects of TN and provides information and resources for patients, family, and medical professionals. **Price:** $24.95/copy. **Conventions/Meetings:** annual conference (exhibits) ● periodic support group meeting (exhibits).

15049 ■ Tuberous Sclerosis Alliance (TS Alliance)

801 Roeder Rd., Ste.750
Silver Spring, MD 20910
Ph: (301)562-9890
Free: (800)225-6872
Fax: (301)562-9870
E-mail: info@tsalliance.org
URL: http://www.tsalliance.org
Contact: Nancy L. Taylor, CEO
Founded: 1974. **Members:** 8,000. **Membership Dues:** regular, in U.S., $50 (annual) ● regular, outside U.S., $75 (annual). **Staff:** 12. **Budget:** $1,700,000. **Languages:** English, Spanish. **Description:** Encourages and provides grants for research into the diagnosis, cause, management, and cure of tuberous sclerosis. (Tuberous sclerosis is a genetic disease characterized by one or more of the following: epileptic seizures, mental retardation, behavioral problems, non-malignant tumors, or skin lesions). Provides support to families affected by the disease

through a nationwide network of volunteer area representatives and the distribution of informational packets. Conducts educational programs for medical and allied professionals. **Libraries: Type:** reference. **Holdings:** periodicals. **Subjects:** tuberous sclerosis. **Awards:** Gomez Award. **Type:** grant. **Recipient:** for research ● Rothberg Courage Award. **Type:** grant. **Recipient:** for research ● TS Champion Award. **Type:** recognition. **Boards:** Professional Advisory. **Subgroups:** Community Alliances; Support Network. **Formerly:** (2001) National Tuberous Sclerosis Association. **Publications:** *Perspective*, quarterly. Newsletter. Contains research articles, resources for patients and parents, and legislative news. **Price:** available to members only. **Circulation:** 15,000. Alternate Formats: online ● Also publishes brochures, fact sheets, patient journal, Life Stages Guide. **Conventions/ Meetings:** annual Medical Education Conference Series - conference and board meeting ● National Family Conference.

15050 ■ United Leukodystrophy Foundation (ULF)

2304 Highland Dr.
Sycamore, IL 60178
Ph: (815)895-3211
Free: (800)728-5483
Fax: (815)895-2432
E-mail: office@ulf.org
URL: http://www.ulf.org
Contact: Ron Brazeal, Exec. Dir.
Founded: 1982. **Members:** 12,000. **Membership Dues:** family, $25 (annual) ● professional, $50 (annual) ● organization, $50 (annual). **Staff:** 3. **Budget:** $340,000. **Multinational. Description:** Leukodystrophy patients, their families, and medical care professionals. (Leukodystrophy refers to a group of disorders, which affect the brain, spinal cord, and peripheral nerves by damaging the insulating sheath around nerve strands, interfering with the flow of electrical impulses.) Provides information on leukodystrophy to patients, their families, and the general public; assists in identifying sources of medical care, social services, and counseling; coordinates a communication network among affected families. Promotes and supports research into the causes, treatment, and prevention of white matter disorders. Coordinates cooperation between donor and government agencies, scientific programs, and the private sector. Conducts educational and research programs. Offers second opinion program for those with undiagnosed white matter disorders. **Libraries: Type:** lending; reference; open to the public. **Holdings:** 1,000; audiovisuals. **Subjects:** homecare, issues related to leukodystrophy, psycho-social. **Awards:** Mark Giese Humanitarian Award. **Frequency:** annual. **Type:** recognition. **Recipient:** for extraordinary efforts on behalf of ULF or leukodystrophy families. **Publications:** *The Facts About Leukodystrophy*. Brochures ● *ULF News*, quarterly. Newsletter. **Price:** included in membership dues. **Circulation:** 3,000. **Advertising:** accepted ● *What to Expect When the Diagnosis is a Neurodegenerative Disease*. Booklet. **Conventions/ Meetings:** annual Love & Science - conference - in July.

15051 ■ World Federation of Neurology Research Group on Motor Neuron Diseases

c/o Robert G. Miller, MD, Chm.
Dept. of Neurology
2324 Sacramento St., No. 150
San Francisco, CA 94115
Ph: (415)563-4321
Fax: (415)673-5184
E-mail: rmiller@cooper.cpmc.org
URL: http://www.wfnals.org/membership/index.html
Contact: Robert G. Miller MD, Chm.
Founded: 1998. **Membership Dues:** regular, $89 (annual). **Multinational. Description:** Advances knowledge concerning Amyotrophic Lateral Sclerosis (ALS). Fosters research and the education and training of clinicians and scientists concerning the problem of ALS and other motor neuron diseases throughout the world. Facilitates properly designed clinical trials of putative therapeutic agents in ALS. Involves appropriate Centers and Consortia of investigators in

ALS clinical trials. Facilitates collaboration in all aspects of research, including the design, execution and analysis of clinical trials. **Affiliated With:** World Federation of Neurology. **Publications:** *Amyotrophic Lateral Sclerosis and Other Motor Neuron Disorders*, quarterly. Journal. Covers all aspects of the diagnosis and management of ALS. **Price:** included in membership dues. ISSN: 1466-0822. Alternate Formats: online.

15052 ■ Young Onset Parkinson's Association (YOPA)

22136 Westheimer Pkwy., No. 343
Katy, TX 77450-8296
Free: (888)937-9672
E-mail: directors@yopa.org
URL: http://www.yopa.org
Contact: Mark Davis, Treas.
Description: Strives to help all young-onset Parkinson's patients, particularly the recently diagnosed. Provides a forum for patients to form affiliations with fellow sufferers. Supports and raises funds for research leading to a cure for Parkinson's. Collaborates with other Parkinson's organizations and corporations. **Telecommunication Services:** electronic mail, mark@yopa.org. **Publications:** *YOPA News*, semiannual. Newsletter. Alternate Formats: online.

Neurology

15053 ■ American Academy of Clinical Neurophysiology (AACN)

c/o Dr. Keith H. Chiappa, Ed.
Massachusetts Gen. Hosp.
Boston, MA 02114
Ph: (617)726-8737
Fax: (617)726-2019
E-mail: chiappa@helix.mgh.harvard.edu
URL: http://mitpress.mit.edu/e-journals/JCN
Contact: Dr. Keith H. Chiappa, Ed.
Founded: 1985. **Members:** 700. **Membership Dues:** student, $30 (annual) ● associate, $40 (annual) ● active, $150 (annual) ● corporate/laboratory, $225 (annual). **Staff:** 5. **Description:** Clinical neurophysiologists. Fosters an understanding of the function of the nervous system among health professionals, scientists, and the public by serving as a forum for interaction and the communication of new developments. Offers educational programs. **Publications:** *Neurology and Clinical Neurophysiology*. Journal. **Price:** $75.00 individuals; $200.00 institutions. Alternate Formats: online. Also Cited As: *NCN*. **Conventions/Meetings:** annual meeting (exhibits).

15054 ■ American Academy of Neurology (AAN)

1080 Montreal Ave.
St. Paul, MN 55116
Ph: (651)695-2717
Free: (800)879-1960
Fax: (651)695-2791
E-mail: memberservices@aan.com
URL: http://www.aan.com
Contact: Catherine M. Rydell, Exec. Dir.
Founded: 1948. **Members:** 18,000. **Membership Dues:** junior, $130 (annual) ● affiliate, $205 (annual) ● associate in U.S. and Canada, active, $395 (annual) ● associate international, corresponding active, $325 (annual). **Staff:** 92. **Budget:** $20,000,000. **Description:** Professional society of medical doctors specializing in brain and nervous system diseases. Maintains placement service. Sponsors research and educational programs. Compiles statistics. Publishes scientific journal. **Libraries: Type:** reference. **Holdings:** books, periodicals. **Subjects:** neurology. **Awards:** Bruce S. Schoenberg International Award and Lecture in Neuroepidemiology. **Frequency:** annual. **Type:** scholarship. **Recipient:** for a young investigator from a developing country who has completed neuroepidemiological study ● Extended Neuroscience Award. **Frequency:** annual. **Type:** monetary. **Recipient:** for research by a medical student for over one year ● Founders Award. **Fre-**

quency: annual. **Type:** monetary. **Recipient:** for clinical research by a physician in a training program ● G. Milton Shy Award in Clinical Neurology. **Frequency:** annual. **Type:** monetary. **Recipient:** for research by a medical student in clinical aspects for less than one year ● John Jay Dystel Prize. **Frequency:** annual. **Type:** monetary. **Recipient:** for multiple sclerosis and related diseases research ● Lawrence C. McHenry Award. **Frequency:** annual. **Type:** recognition. **Recipient:** for excellence in research in the history of neurology ● Potamkin Prize. **Frequency:** annual. **Type:** monetary. **Recipient:** for research in Pick's, Alzheimer's, and related diseases ● Roland P. McKay Award in Historical Aspects. **Frequency:** annual. **Type:** monetary. **Recipient:** for research by a medical student in historical aspects for less than one year ● S. Weir Mitchell Award. **Frequency:** annual. **Type:** monetary. **Recipient:** for basic research by a physician in a training program ● Saul R. Korey Award in Experimental Neurology. **Frequency:** annual. **Type:** monetary. **Recipient:** for research by a medical student in experimental aspects for less than one year. **Computer Services:** Mailing lists, upon request (fee applies). **Committees:** Ad Hoc; Standing; Task Force. **Subcommittees:** Annual Meeting Management; Archives; Bylaws; Neuromuscular Pathology; Sections. **Publications:** *AAN Governmental Report*, bimonthly. Newsletter. Includes news on legislative affairs. ● *AANnews*, monthly. Newsletter. Contains general information and placement publication. ● *American Academy of Neurology Membership Directory*, annual ● *ICD-9-CM for Neurologists*. Booklet. Aids users of ICD-9 diagnostic codes. ● *Medical Specialty of Neurology*. Brochure. Discusses neurology as a career. ● *Neurologist*. Brochure. For patients. ● *Neurology*, monthly. Journal. Includes research reports. ● *Patient Information Guide for Neurology*. Handbook. Helps patients find educational information about disorders. **Conventions/Meetings:** annual meeting (exhibits) - 2008 Apr. 5-12, Chicago, IL.

15055 ■ American College of Osteopathic Neurologists and Psychiatrists (ACONP)

28595 Orchard Lake Rd., Ste.200
Farmington Hills, MI 48334
Ph: (248)553-0010
Fax: (248)553-0818
E-mail: acn-aconp@msn.com
Contact: Louis Rentz DO, Exec. Dir.
Founded: 1937. **Description:** Osteopathic neurologists and psychiatrists. Promotes adherence to high standards of training, ethics, and practice within the fields of osteopathic neurology and psychiatry. Conducts examinations and confers certification upon qualified osteopathic neurologists and psychiatrists; sponsors continuing professional development courses. **Conventions/Meetings:** annual conference.

15056 ■ American Neurological Association (ANA)

5841 Cedar Lake Rd. S, Ste.204
Minneapolis, MN 55416
Ph: (952)545-6284
Fax: (952)545-6073
E-mail: ana@llmsi.com
URL: http://www.aneuroa.org
Contact: Timothy A. Pedley, Pres.
Founded: 1875. **Members:** 960. **Staff:** 2. **Budget:** $400,000. **Description:** Physicians and scientists interested in the form, functioning, and disorders of the nervous system. Conducts research programs. **Awards:** Distinguished Neurology Teacher Award. **Frequency:** annual. **Type:** recognition. **Recipient:** for contributions by gifted and talented teachers of neurology ● F.E. Bennett Memorial Lecture. **Frequency:** annual. **Type:** grant. **Recipient:** for research and education in neurology and psychiatry ● Young Neurological Scholar Award. **Frequency:** annual. **Type:** recognition. **Recipient:** to a young member who has achieved a significant stature in neurological research. **Committees:** Annals of Neurology Oversight; Career Development; Education; Ethical Affairs; History; Local Arrangements; Long Range Planning; Nominating. **Publications:** *Annals of Neurol-*

ogy, monthly. Journal. Includes book reviews. **Price:** included in membership dues; $68.00 /year for nonmembers; $84.00 /year for institutions; $52.50/ year for students. **Advertising:** accepted. **Conventions/Meetings:** annual meeting (exhibits) - 2007 Oct. 7-10, Washington, DC.

15057 ■ American Society for Experimental Neuro Therapeutics (ASENT)
342 N Main St., Ste.301
West Hartford, CT 06117-2507
Ph: (860)586-7570
Fax: (860)586-7550
E-mail: info@asent.org
URL: http://www.asent.org
Contact: Ms. M. Suzanne C. Berry, Exec. Dir.
Founded: 1997. **Members:** 300. **Membership Dues:** ordinary, $250 (annual) ● trainee, $100 (annual) ● government, $50 (annual) ● advocacy, $125 (annual). **Staff:** 3. **Budget:** $350,000. **Description:** Neurologists and other medical professionals with an interest in experimental neuro therapeutics. Seeks to advance the development of improved therapies for diseases and disorders of the nervous system and promotes professional advancement of members. Serves as a forum for the exchange of information among those concerned with the development of neuro therapeutics; works to maintain friendly and cooperative relationships between members and government agencies and industries with an interest in neurology; assists in the formulation of public policies affecting experimental neuro therapeutics; and provides support to health care professionals and research scientists pursuing careers in neuro therapeutics. **Publications:** *ASENT Membership Directory*, annual ● *NeuroRx*, quarterly. Journal. Features reviews focused on a single topic relating to the treatment of neurological disorders. Alternate Formats: online. **Conventions/Meetings:** annual meeting (exhibits).

15058 ■ American Society for Neural Transplantation and Repair (ASNTR)
c/o Donna C. Morrison, Conference Coor./Office Mgr.
Dept. of Neurosurgery, MDC-78
Center for Aging and Brain Repair
Univ. of South Florida COM
12901 Bruce B. Downs Blvd.
Tampa, FL 33612-4799
Ph: (813)974-3154
Fax: (813)974-3078
E-mail: dmorriso@hsc.usf.edu
URL: http://www.asntr.org
Contact: Donna C. Morrison, Conference Coor./Office Mgr.
Founded: 1994. **Members:** 250. **Description:** Basic and clinical neuroscientists who utilize transplantation and related technologies to better understand the way the nervous system functions. Provides an interactive forum for scientists to discuss their data and important issues in the areas of neural transplantation, nervous system regeneration, and plasticity. Also provides leadership in the area of education with the emphasis on the training and education of young investigators. **Computer Services:** Information services. **Formerly:** (2003) American Society for Neural Transplantation. **Conventions/Meetings:** annual conference.

15059 ■ American Society of Neurophysiological Monitoring (ASNM)
333 E Lancaster Ave., No. 327
Wynnewood, PA 19096
Free: (800)479-7979
Fax: (800)479-7989
E-mail: info@asnm.org
URL: http://www.asnm.org
Contact: Mark Stecker MD, Pres.
Founded: 1990. **Membership Dues:** full, $100 (annual). **Description:** Promotes the interests of the individuals involved in neurophysiological monitoring. Fosters the growth and stature of neurophysiological monitoring as a profession. Provides a forum for education and dissemination of knowledge in the field of neurophysiological monitoring. **Committees:** Credential and Competency; Cross-Education; Educa-

tion; Ethics; Government Relations; Patient Safety; Practice Management. **Subcommittees:** Fellow Selection. **Publications:** *The ASNM Monitor*, monthly. Newsletter. Alternate Formats: online.

15060 ■ American Society of Neurorehabilitation (ASNR)
5841 Cedar Lake Rd., Ste.204
Minneapolis, MN 55416
Ph: (952)545-6324
Fax: (952)545-6073
E-mail: asnr@llmsi.com
URL: http://www.asnr.org
Contact: David C. Good MD, Pres.
Founded: 1990. **Members:** 500. **Membership Dues:** active non-physician, $175 (annual) ● active physician, $250 (annual) ● physician-in-training, $150 (annual). **Staff:** 2. **Description:** Neurologists, neurosurgeons, psychiatrists, pediatricians, and other medical professionals interested in disorders of the nervous system. Rehabilitates and monitors patients with neurological disabilities. Acts as an advocate for patients; liaises with other neurological organizations. Conducts research. **Libraries: Type:** not open to the public. **Awards:** Presidential Award. **Frequency:** annual. **Type:** recognition. **Recipient:** for best poster presentation based on abstract. **Committees:** Certification and Re-certification; Communications; Fellowship; Meetings Program; Practice; Web Site. **Publications:** *Neurorehabilitation and Neural Repair*, quarterly. Journal. Includes articles on clinical practice, research, brief communications, case reports, reviews, and media reviews. **Price:** $188.00 /year for individuals; $588.00 /year for institutions; included in membership dues. ISSN: 1545-9683. **Circulation:** 600. **Advertising:** accepted ● Newsletter, semiannual. **Conventions/Meetings:** annual conference (exhibits) ● annual workshop.

15061 ■ Association for Comprehensive NeuroTherapy (ACN)
PO Box 1967
Tarpon Springs, FL 34688-1967
Ph: (561)798-0472
Fax: (561)798-9820
E-mail: acn@latitudes.org
URL: http://www.latitudes.org
Contact: Sheila Rogers, Dir.
Description: Practitioners and lay persons. Dedicated to exploring advanced and complementary treatments for neurological conditions, focusing on autism, Tourette syndrome, attention deficit disorder/ hyperactivity, obsessive compulsive disorder, and learning disabilities. Articles, editorials, and letters, as well as a survey on Tourette Syndrome, are available through their website. **Publications:** *ACN Today*. Newsletter. **Price:** free for members. Alternate Formats: online ● *Latitudes*, quarterly. Magazine. Contains articles, research updates, and clinical findings about autism, Tourette syndrome, attention disorders and learning problems. **Price:** $40.00/year; $65.00 for two years. **Circulation:** 6,000. **Advertising:** accepted.

15062 ■ Association of Neuroscience Departments and Programs (ANDP)
41218 Roundup Rd.
Magnolia, TX 77354
Ph: (281)259-6737
Fax: (281)356-2837
E-mail: andp@andp.org
URL: http://www.andp.org
Contact: Alison K. Hall, Pres.
Membership Dues: graduate, postdoctoral, $265 (annual) ● undergraduate, $100 (annual) ● international affiliate, $50 (annual). **Description:** Works to advance education and research in neuroscience. **Awards:** Award for Education in Neuroscience. **Frequency:** annual. **Type:** recognition. **Recipient:** for outstanding contributions in the field of neuroscience ● Distinguished Service Award. **Frequency:** annual. **Type:** recognition. **Recipient:** for individuals who have developed a policies related to neuroscience training. **Publications:** *Survey Report*. Alternate Formats: online ● Reports. Alternate Formats: online.

15063 ■ Cajal Club (CC)
c/o Dr. Charles E. Ribak, Sec.-Treas.
Dept. of Anatomy and Neurobiology
Univ. of California at Irvine
School of Medicine
Irvine, CA 92697-1275
E-mail: ribak@uci.edu
URL: http://www.cajalclub.org
Contact: Dr. Charles E. Ribak, Sec.-Treas.
Founded: 1947. **Members:** 450. **Membership Dues:** active, $30 (annual) ● student/postdoc, $10 (annual). **Description:** Consists of neuroanatomists who meet for discussion and the presentation of papers on prospective research, technique, and history of neurology. (Club is named after Sr. Don Santiago Ramon y Cajal, a founder of and Nobel laureate for the science of neuroanatomy.) **Awards:** Cajal Medal. **Frequency:** annual. **Type:** recognition. **Recipient:** for outstanding research on the cerebral cortex ● Certificate of Recognition. **Frequency:** annual. **Type:** recognition. **Recipient:** for outstanding research on the cerebral cortex ● Krieg Cortical Kudos. **Frequency:** annual. **Type:** recognition. **Publications:** *History of Cajal Club*, quinquennial ● Proceedings, periodic. **Conventions/Meetings:** annual meeting, held in conjunction with the American Association of Anatomists at Federated Societies for Experimental Biology.

15064 ■ Child Neurology Society (CNS)
1000 W County Rd. E, Ste.290
St. Paul, MN 55126
Ph: (651)486-9447
Fax: (651)486-9436
E-mail: nationaloffice@childneurologysociety.org
URL: http://www.childneurologysociety.org
Contact: Mary Currey, Exec. Dir.
Founded: 1972. **Members:** 1,300. **Membership Dues:** junior, $30 (annual) ● active, $225 (annual). **Staff:** 2. **Budget:** $200,000. **Description:** Neurologists certified by the American Board of Psychiatry and Neurology (see separate entry) and specializing in child neurology; individuals eligible for the certifying examination and those who have made significant contributions to the field of child neurology; individuals enrolled in approved child neurology training programs. Advances child neurology by establishing a scientific forum for professionals in the field; Defines areas of pediatric neurological practices and to make known these procedures among professionals and medical students. Promotes interest in the field of child neurology among medical students. Advertises positions available in pediatric neurology. **Awards:** Dreifuss-Penry Epilepsy Award. **Frequency:** annual. **Type:** recognition. **Recipient:** for physicians who, in the early stages of their careers, have made an independent contribution to epilepsy research. **Committees:** Archives; Awards; Bylaws; Electronic Communications; Ethics; International Affairs; Legislative Affairs; Nominating. **Publications:** *Annals of Neurology*, monthly. Journal ● Booklets. **Conventions/Meetings:** annual conference (exhibits).

15065 ■ Dana Alliance for Brain Initiatives
745 Fifth Ave., Ste.900
New York, NY 10151
Ph: (212)223-4040
Fax: (212)317-8721
E-mail: dabiinfo@dana.org
URL: http://www.dana.org/about/dabi
Contact: William Safire, Chm.
Founded: 1992. **Members:** 250. **Description:** Provides information about the personal and public benefits of brain research. Works to find the genes that increase risk for schizophrenia and manic-depressive illness. Understands, prevents and treats Alzheimer's, Parkinson's, and other major neurodegenerative disorders. Improves the treatment of strokes and spinal cord injuries. Develops new approaches to the management of pain. Applies noninvasive methods to the diagnosis of many neurological and psychiatric disorders. **Publications:** *Brain Connections: Your Source Guide to Information on Brain Diseases and Disorders*. Booklet. Lists more than 240 organizations likely to help people with a

brain-related disorder. **Price:** free. Alternate Formats: online ● Report. Alternate Formats: online.

15066 ■ International Academy for Child Brain Development (IACBD)
c/o Institutes for the Achievement of Human Potential
8801 Stenton Ave.
Wyndmoor, PA 19038
Ph: (215)233-2050
Fax: (215)233-9312
E-mail: institutes@iahp.org
URL: http://www.iahp.org
Contact: Janet Doman, Dir.
Founded: 1984. **Languages:** English, French, German, Italian, Japanese, Spanish. **Description:** Professionals from a variety of disciplines including physicians, psychologists, and anthropologists, who are interested in the physical and psychological processes involved in child brain development. Seeks to gain recognition for the study of child brain development as a discipline in itself and establish criteria for the certification of child brain developmentalists. Provides a forum for presentation of scholarly works in the field; offers courses in child-brain development; conducts field research and prepares reports of results. **Awards:** Statuette With Pedestal. **Type:** recognition. **Recipient:** for significant contributions to the field of child brain development. **Affiliated With:** Institutes for the Achievement of Human Potential; World Organization for Human Potential. **Publications:** *The In-Report*, quarterly. Journal. Includes list of victories of brain-injured children. **Price:** $25.00 in U.S.; $28.00 in Canada and Mexico; $30.00 outside U.S. **Conventions/Meetings:** annual meeting - always the last week of November in Philadelphia, PA.

15067 ■ International Functional Electrical Stimulation Society (IFESS)
c/o Paul Meadows, MS, Pres.
1854 Los Encinos Ave.
Glendale, CA 91208-2240
Ph: (661)362-1755
Fax: (818)956-2181
E-mail: paul.meadows@bionics.com
URL: http://www.ifess.org
Contact: Paul Meadows MS, Pres.
Founded: 1995. **Membership Dues:** student, $20 (annual) ● general, user/consumer individual, user/consumer group, $30 (annual) ● corporate, $250 (annual) ● life, $300. **Multinational. Description:** Represents academic leaders in the field of biomedical engineering, physical therapists, medical doctors, members of the electrical stimulation manufacturing community, and students and users of functional electrical stimulation (FES) technology. Promotes the research, application, and understanding of electrical stimulation as it is utilized in the field of medicine. Facilitates cooperation and fellowship among members. **Awards:** Vodovnik Award. **Frequency:** annual. **Type:** recognition. **Recipient:** to the best three papers submitted and presented at IFESS conferences by students. **Publications:** *IFESS Annual Conference DVDROM.* Video. Contains proceedings of the International Functional Electrical Stimulation Society's annual conferences. **Price:** $40.00 ● *Neuromodulation*, quarterly. Journal. Disseminates scientific and clinical information relevant to the field of neuromodulation. **Price:** $100.00. Alternate Formats: online.

15068 ■ International Neural Network Society (INNS)
2810 Crossroads Dr., Ste.3800
Madison, WI 53718
Ph: (608)443-2461
Fax: (608)443-2478
E-mail: inns@reesgroupinc.com
URL: http://www.inns.org
Contact: Fredric M. Ham, Pres.
Founded: 1987. **Members:** 2,000. **Membership Dues:** regular, $85 (annual) ● student, $25 (annual) ● individual (without journal), $30 (annual). **Staff:** 3. **Multinational. Description:** Individuals interested in theoretical and computational understanding of the

brain. Provides forum for neurocomputing and theoretical approaches to neuroscience. Promotes research into behavioral processes and models of the brain. Encourages development of computing applications that use neural modeling concepts. **Awards:** Gabor Award. **Frequency:** annual. **Type:** recognition. **Recipient:** for outstanding achievement in engineering ● Hebb Award. **Frequency:** annual. **Type:** recognition. **Recipient:** for outstanding achievement in biological learning ● Helmholtz Award. **Frequency:** annual. **Type:** recognition. **Recipient:** for outstanding achievement in sensation/perception ● Leadership Awards. **Frequency:** annual. **Type:** recognition ● Young Investigator. **Frequency:** annual. **Type:** recognition. **Recipient:** for outstanding research. **Computer Services:** Mailing lists. **Subgroups:** Biomedical Applications; Business/Economics; Control, Automation, and Robotics; Electronics/VLSI; Expert Networks; Higher Level Cognitive Processes; Mathematics and Theory; Mental Function and Dysfunction; Neuroscience; Optics; Philosophy and Evolution; Power Engineering; Pulsed Networks. **Publications:** *INNS Newsletter*, 9/year. Includes calendar of events and special interest group information. ● *Neural Networks*, 10/year. Journal. **Price:** included in membership dues ● Membership Directory. Alternate Formats: online. **Conventions/Meetings:** biennial International Joint Conference on Neural Networks.

15069 ■ International Neuromodulation Society (INS)
2000 Van Ness Ave., Ste.402
San Francisco, CA 94109
Ph: (415)567-1219
Fax: (415)567-2534
E-mail: ins@neuromodulation.com
URL: http://www.neuromodulation.com
Contact: Tia Sofatzis, Exec. Dir.
Founded: 1989. **Members:** 400. **Membership Dues:** regular, $125 (annual). **Staff:** 1. **Regional Groups:** 5. **Multinational. Description:** Individuals with an interest in implantable technologies that impact on the nervous system. Promotes advancement of neuromodulation technologies and techniques; encourages continuing professional development of members. Serves as a forum for the exchange of scientific information on neuromodulation; conducts research and educational programs. **Computer Services:** database. **Affiliated With:** North American Neuromodulation Society. **Publications:** *Neuromodulation*, quarterly. Journal. **Price:** included in membership dues. ISSN: 1094-7159. **Advertising:** accepted. Alternate Formats: online. **Conventions/Meetings:** biennial congress.

15070 ■ International Neuropsychological Society (INS)
700 Ackerman Rd., Ste.625
Columbus, OH 43202
Ph: (614)263-4200
Fax: (614)263-4366
E-mail: ins@osu.edu
URL: http://www.the-ins.org
Contact: Robert A. Bornstein PhD, Exec. Sec.
Founded: 1967. **Members:** 4,500. **Membership Dues:** regular, $120 (annual) ● associate, $60 (annual). **Staff:** 2. **Multinational. Description:** Works to promote research, service and education in neuropsychology and to enhance communication among the scientific disciplines that contribute to the understanding of brain-behavior relationships. **Telecommunication Services:** electronic mail, bornstein.1@osu.edu. **Publications:** *Journal of the International Neuropsychological Society*, bimonthly. **Price:** included in membership dues. Alternate Formats: online. Also Cited As: *JINS*. **Conventions/Meetings:** annual meeting (exhibits) - 2008 Feb. 6-9, Waikoloa, HI; 2009 Feb. 11-14, Atlanta, GA.

15071 ■ International Society for Neuroimmunomodulation (ISNIM)
c/o Jeannine A. Majde-Cottrell, PhD, Exec. Dir.
PO Box 41269
Arlington, VA 22204-8269
Fax: (703)521-3462

E-mail: isnim@aol.com
URL: http://www.isnim.org
Contact: Jeannine A. Majde-Cottrell PhD, Exec. Dir.
Founded: 1986. **Members:** 150. **Membership Dues:** regular, $125 (annual) ● student, $40 (annual) ● retired, $35 (annual) ● regular, $350 (triennial). **Staff:** 2. **Budget:** $15,000. **Multinational. Description:** Professional society for scientists involved in interdisciplinary research in the molecular and cellular aspects of neurobiology, neuroendocrinology, immunology, and the behavioral sciences. Focuses on discerning the integrative elements underlying communication and modulation between the central nervous, endocrine, and immune systems, and upon related disease states. **Awards:** Novera Herbert Spector Lectureship. **Frequency:** triennial. **Type:** monetary. **Committees:** International; Program Planning; Publications. **Publications:** *NeuroImmunoModulation*, bimonthly. Journal. **Conventions/Meetings:** triennial International Congress ● periodic meeting.

15072 ■ International Society for Neuronal Regulation (ISNR)
3620 W 10th St., Unit B
PMB 128
Greeley, CO 80634-1821
Free: (800)488-3867
Fax: (775)305-9379
E-mail: office@isnr.org
URL: http://www.isnr.org
Contact: Darlene Nelson, Exec. Dir.
Founded: 1995. **Members:** 500. **Membership Dues:** individual, $160 (annual) ● individual, $290 (biennial) ● corporate, $350 (annual) ● for two, $280 (annual) ● retired, $120 (annual) ● student, $60 (annual) ● intern, $90 (annual). **Staff:** 2. **Multinational. Description:** Promotes professionals in the fields of neurotherapy, neurofeedback, training and research. **Formerly:** (1999) Society for the Study of Neuronal Regulation; (2003) Society for Neuronal Regulation. **Publications:** *Journal of Neurotherapy*, quarterly. **Price:** included in membership dues. ISSN: 1087-4208. **Advertising:** accepted. Alternate Formats: online. **Conventions/Meetings:** annual conference and workshop.

15073 ■ International Society of NeuroVirology (ISNV)
c/o Kamel Khalili, PhD, Treas./Ed.-in-Chief
Temple Univ.
Bio-Life Sciences Bldg.
1900 N 12th St., Rm. 203-N
Philadelphia, PA 19122
Ph: (215)204-0680
Fax: (215)204-0681
E-mail: mail@isnv.org
URL: http://www.isnv.org
Contact: Kamel Khalili PhD, Treas./Ed.-in-Chief
Founded: 1998. **Members:** 245. **Membership Dues:** faculty/research scientist (with journal subscription), $240 (annual) ● faculty/research scientist (without journal subscription), $100 (annual) ● student/postdoctoral (without journal subscription), $40 (annual). **Staff:** 1. **Multinational. Description:** Advances collaboration among scientists in all aspects of neurovirology and related disciplines to further the knowledge in the area. Promotes the clinical application of this knowledge. Aims to prevent and treat neurodegenerative and neoplastic disease in the nervous system. **Awards:** Pioneer in NeuroVirology Award. **Frequency:** annual. **Type:** monetary. **Recipient:** for outstanding contribution to the field of neurovirology. **Publications:** *Journal of NeuroVirology*, bimonthly. Features articles on basic and clinical research in neurovirology. **Price:** included in membership dues. ISSN: 1355-0284. **Circulation:** 300. **Advertising:** accepted. Alternate Formats: online. Also Cited As: *j neurovirol* ● Newsletter, periodic. **Price:** free for members. Alternate Formats: online. **Conventions/Meetings:** annual International Symposium on Neurovirology - conference, scientific conference on neurovirology.

15074 ■ National Foundation for Brain Research (NFBR)
c/o BrainNet.org
PO Box 390
Solomons, MD 20688
Ph: (202)250-3845
URL: http://www.brainnet.org
Contact: Lawrence S. Hoffheimer Esq., Exec. Dir.
Founded: 1989. **Description:** Promotes the prevention and cure of disorders and diseases of the brain. Supports brain research. Collects, organizes, and disseminates information relating to the Decade of the Brain (the years 1990-2000, which were so designated by United States Congress and President George Bush to acknowledge the importance of neurological and mental research). Maintains the Decade of the Brain Coalition which strives to achieve by the end of the decade a large increase in federal funding for research on the brain. Seeks to increase public awareness of the importance of brain research through sponsoring educational symposia, the distribution of reports and pamphlets, and the organization of traveling museum exhibits. Provides educational programs for professionals. **Awards:** Silvio O. Conte Decade of the Brain Award. **Frequency:** annual. **Type:** recognition. **Recipient:** for outstanding achievements in neuroscience research. **Publications:** *Decade of the Brain News*, quarterly. Newsletter. Alternate Formats: online. **Conventions/Meetings:** annual Decade of the Brain Symposium (exhibits) - always in Washington, DC.

15075 ■ National Neurotrauma Society
c/o Linda Garcia
PO Box 143060
Gainesville, FL 32614
Ph: (352)271-1169
Fax: (305)704-3814
E-mail: garcialinda@cox.net
URL: http://www.neurotrauma.org
Contact: Linda Garcia, Contact
Members: 500. **Membership Dues:** individual (with journal subscription), $245 (annual) ● individual (without journal subscription), $100 (annual) ● student (with journal subscription), $195 (annual) ● student (without journal subscription), $50 (annual). **Description:** Conducts scientific research in neurotrauma field. Promotes neurotrauma research by enhancing communications, providing a forum, and increasing support on the national and international level. **Awards:** Student Travel Award. **Frequency:** annual. **Type:** monetary. **Publications:** *Journal of Neurotrauma*, monthly. **Price:** $626.00 /year for individuals; $1,169.00 /year for institutions. **Advertising:** accepted. Alternate Formats: online. **Conventions/Meetings:** annual meeting.

15076 ■ Neuro-Developmental Treatment Association (NDTA)
1540 S Coast Hwy., Ste.203
Laguna Beach, CA 92651
Free: (800)869-9295
Fax: (949)376-3456
E-mail: info@ndta.org
URL: http://www.ndta.org
Contact: Paul Myers, Assoc. Exec. Dir.
Founded: 1967. **Members:** 2,500. **Membership Dues:** NDT trained individual, $95 (annual) ● retired or student, $55 (annual) ● family, $45 (annual) ● agency, $250 (annual). **Staff:** 4. **Budget:** $325,000. **Regional Groups:** 14. **Description:** Physical and occupational therapists, speech pathologists, special educators, physicians, parents, and others interested in neurodevelopmental treatment. (NDT is a form of therapy for individuals who suffer from central nervous system disorders resulting in abnormal movement. Treatment attempts to initiate or refine normal stages and processes in the development of movement.) Informs members of new developments in the field and with ideas that will eventually improve fundamental independence. Locates articles related to NDT. **Awards:** Award of Excellence. **Frequency:** annual. **Type:** recognition ● Certificate of Appreciation. **Type:** recognition ● Research Grant Award. **Frequency:** annual. **Type:** grant. **Committees:** Finance; Membership; Public Relations; Publications;

Research. **Subgroups:** Instructors; Region Chairs. **Task Forces:** Curriculum; Theoretical Base. **Formerly:** International Bobath Alumni Association. **Publications:** *NDTA Network*, bimonthly. Newsletter. **Advertising:** accepted ● *Neuro-Developmental Treatment Approach: Theoretical Foundations and Principles of Clinical Practice*, bimonthly. Newsletter. **Advertising:** accepted. **Conventions/Meetings:** annual Plasticity and Recovery Across the Lifespan - conference (exhibits).

15077 ■ The Neuropathy Association (TNA)
60 E 42 St., Ste.942
New York, NY 10165
Ph: (212)692-0662
Free: (800)247-6968
Fax: (212)692-0668
E-mail: info@neuropathy.org
URL: http://www.neuropathy.org
Contact: Catherine Law, Chief Financial Off.
Founded: 1995. **Members:** 100,000. **Membership Dues:** benefactor, $1,000 (annual) ● sponsoring, $100-$750 (annual) ● contributing, $50-$75 (annual) ● basic, $35 (annual). **Staff:** 4. **Local Groups:** 200. **Languages:** English, Spanish. **Description:** Offers support to persons suffering from disorders affecting the peripheral nerves; provides patient support and education, advocates for patients' interests, promotes research into the causes and cure for peripheral neuropathies. **Awards:** **Frequency:** periodic. **Type:** grant. **Committees:** Medical Advisory; Research Advisory. **Councils:** National Advisory. **Publications:** *A Guide to the Peripheral Neuropathies*. Booklet. **Price:** included in membership dues; $10.00 for nonmembers ● *Exercising with Neuropathy*. Booklet. **Price:** included in membership dues; $10.00 for nonmembers ● *Explaining Peripheral Neuropathy*. Booklet. **Price:** included in membership dues; $10.00 for nonmembers ● *Neuropathy News*. Newsletter. **Price:** included in membership dues. Alternate Formats: online ● Survey. Alternate Formats: online.

15078 ■ North American Skull Base Society (NASBS)
12100 Sunset Hills Rd., Ste.130
Reston, VA 20190
Ph: (703)437-4377
Fax: (703)435-4390
E-mail: info@nasbs.org
URL: http://www.nasbs.org
Contact: Kathy Hoskins, Exec. Dir.
Founded: 1989. **Members:** 500. **Membership Dues:** active, affiliate, international, candidate, $100 (annual). **Staff:** 2. **Budget:** $250,000. **Description:** Neurosurgeons, otolaryngologists, and others with an interest in diseases associated with the skull base. Promotes advancement of medical practice relating to diseases of the skull base. Conducts continuing professional education programs. **Publications:** *Skull Base*, quarterly. Journal. **Advertising:** accepted. **Conventions/Meetings:** annual meeting (exhibits) - 2008 Sept. 11-14, Vancouver, BC, Canada.

15079 ■ North American Spine Society (NASS)
7075 Veterans Blvd.
Burr Ridge, IL 60527
Ph: (630)230-3600
Free: (877)774-6337
Fax: (630)230-3700
E-mail: info@spine.org
URL: http://www.spine.org
Contact: Eric J. Muehlbauer CAE, Exec. Dir.
Founded: 1985. **Members:** 3,400. **Membership Dues:** professional, associate, $525 (annual) ● affiliate, $225-$275 (annual) ● corresponding, $125-$225 (annual) ● in training, $100 (annual). **Staff:** 30. **Budget:** $6,100,000. **Multinational. Description:** Organization of physicians, osteopaths, orthopedists, neurosurgeons, physiatrists, radiologists, and other professionals that advances quality spine care through education, research and advocacy. Works to improve the quality of scientific practice in spinal disorders; exchange ideas and disseminate scientific information about clinical techniques; investigate and propagate methods by which malfunction of the spine

can be corrected. Makes inquiries into practice characteristics, language usage and terminology, and treatment methods. **Awards:** Research Grant. **Frequency:** annual. **Type:** monetary. **Recipient:** for quality research on spinal care. **Computer Services:** Mailing lists, rental. **Committees:** Awards and Grants; Clinical Guidelines; Continuing Medical Education; Core Curriculum; Outcomes. **Formed by Merger of:** (1987) American College of Spine Surgeons; (1987) North American Lumbar Spine Association. **Publications:** *Common Coding Scenarios for Comprehensive Spine Care*, annual. Book. **Price:** $70.00 for members; $85.00 for nonmembers ● *Contemporary Concepts in Spine Care*, bimonthly. Paper. **Price:** $10.00/copy for members; $15.00/copy for nonmembers; $150.00/set for members; $225.00/set for nonmembers ● *Phase III Clinical Guidelines on Herniated Discs and Unremitting Low Back Pain*. Book ● *The Spine Journal*, bimonthly. Contains news on association activities, peer-reviewed research topics. **Price:** included in membership dues; $106.00 /year for nonmembers; $237.00 /year for institutions. **Circulation:** 4,000. **Advertising:** accepted. Alternate Formats: online. Also Cited As: *TSJ* ● *SpineLine*, bimonthly. Magazine. Contains news on association activities and peer-reviewed research topics. **Price:** included in membership dues; $100.00 /year for nonmembers. **Circulation:** 4,000. **Advertising:** accepted. Alternate Formats: online. **Conventions/Meetings:** annual meeting, educational conference (exhibits).

15080 ■ World Spine Society (WSS)
22 Calendar Ct., 2nd Fl.
La Grange, IL 60525
E-mail: wade@worldspine.org
URL: http://www.worldspine.org
Contact: Laura Scott Wade, Managing Dir.
Founded: 2003. **Membership Dues:** regular, $50 (annual) ● in-training, $10 (annual) ● corporate, $1,000 (annual). **Multinational. Description:** Aims to improve the quality of scientific knowledge and pursuit of excellence in patient care among professionals in the field of spinal disorders. Seeks to improve communication with and support for scientists and clinicians in honing their diagnostic and clinical skills. Strives to investigate and promulgate concepts and methods by which spine pathology may be detected and treated. **Telecommunication Services:** electronic mail, membership@worldspine.org. **Publications:** *World Spine Journal*. Alternate Formats: online. Also Cited As: *WSJ*. **Conventions/Meetings:** periodic congress.

Neuroscience

15081 ■ American Autonomic Society (AAS)
c/o Ms. Anita Zeller, Exec. Sec.
18915 Inca Ave.
Lakeville, MN 55044
Ph: (952)469-5837
Fax: (952)469-8424
E-mail: zeller.anita@mayo.edu
URL: http://www.americanautonomicsociety.org
Contact: Ms. Anita Zeller, Exec. Sec.
Membership Dues: regular, $200 (annual) ● trainee, $100 (annual). **Description:** Seeks to bring together individuals from diverse disciplines who share an interest in the structure and function of the autonomic nervous system and in the pathology, treatment, and prevention of its disorders. Aims to provide advice and support in identifying and obtaining research support for members. Facilitates communication and cooperation among the many interested clinical and basic scientists. **Publications:** *Clinical Autonomic Research*. Journal. Contains information for individuals working in areas involving the autonomic nervous system. **Price:** included in membership dues. ISSN: 0959-9851. Alternate Formats: online. Also Cited As: *CAR*.

15082 ■ Cognitive Neuroscience Society (CNS)
c/o Center for Mind and Brain
Univ. of California, Davis
One Shields Ave.
Davis, CA 95616

Ph: (805)705-9014
Fax: (530)792-1489
E-mail: cnsinfo@cogneurosociety.org
URL: http://www.cogneurosociety.org
Contact: Cathy Harding, Exec. Dir.
Founded: 1994. **Members:** 2,000. **Membership Dues:** student, $25 (annual) ● post-doctoral, $50 (annual) ● faculty, $65 (annual). **Multinational. Description:** Aims to advance mind and brain research with focus on the psychological, computational and neuroscientific bases of cognition. Facilitates public, professional and scientific discourse through research and dialogues. Fosters cooperation among its members through a formation of a network of scientists and scholars who are engaged in the interface of mind, brain and behavior research. **Awards:** George A. Miller Prize in Cognitive Neuroscience. **Frequency:** annual. **Type:** recognition. **Recipient:** to individual whose career is characterized by distinguished and sustained scholarship and research at the cutting-edge of cognitive neuroscience ● Graduate Students Presents Award. **Frequency:** annual. **Type:** recognition. **Recipient:** for the best research abstract ● Young Investigator Awards. **Frequency:** annual. **Type:** recognition. **Recipient:** for outstanding contributions by scientists early in their careers. **Publications:** *Journal of Cognitive Science*, monthly. Investigates brain-behavior interaction and promotes lively interchange among the mind sciences. ISSN: 0898-929X. **Advertising:** accepted ● Newsletter, monthly. Contains news and articles pertaining to Cognitive Neuroscience. **Advertising:** accepted. Alternate Formats: online. **Conventions/Meetings:** annual meeting.

15083 ■ International Behavioral Neuroscience Society (IBNS)
c/o Marianne Van Wagner, Exec. Coor.
8181 Tezel Rd., No. 10269
San Antonio, TX 78250
Ph: (830)796-9393
Free: (866)377-4416
Fax: (830)796-9394
E-mail: ibns@ibnshomepage.org
URL: http://www.ibnshomepage.org
Contact: Marianne Van Wagner, Exec. Coor.
Founded: 1992. **Members:** 587. **Membership Dues:** regular, affiliate, $60 (annual) ● student, $25 (annual). **Multinational. Description:** Represents clinicians, teachers, scientists and therapists with background and interest in the field of behavioral neuroscience. Promotes and encourages education and research in the field of behavioral neuroscience. Collaborates with public and private organizations and assists in the coordination of efforts or formulation of research and clinical programs. **Publications:** *IBNS News*, semiannual. Newsletter. Alternate Formats: online.

Neurosurgery

15084 ■ American Academy of Neurological and Orthopaedic Surgeons (AANOS)
10 Cascade Creek Ln.
Las Vegas, NV 89113
Ph: (702)388-7390
Fax: (702)871-4728
E-mail: aanos@aanos.org
URL: http://www.aanos.org
Contact: Prof. Kazem Fathie MD, Chm.
Founded: 1974. **Members:** 240. **Membership Dues:** regular, $600 (annual). **Description:** Neurological and orthopaedic surgeons, neurologists, physiatrists, and professionals in allied medical or surgical specialties. Provides and encourages information about and understanding of neurological and orthopaedic medicine and surgery, a branch of medicine that deals with diseases and injuries to the human neuromusculo-skeletal system; seeks to improve patient care. Maintains American Board of Neurological and Orthopaedic Medicine and Surgery and American Board of Spinal Surgery. Sponsors charitable program. Maintains a complete collection of recordings of scientific meetings since 1977. Oper-

ates 40 colleges of experts in individual disciplines related to neurological and orthopaedic medicine and surgery. **Libraries: Type:** reference. **Holdings:** 400; archival material, articles, biographical archives. **Subjects:** neurological surgery, orthopaedic surgery, spinal surgery. **Awards:** AANOS Scholarship Fund. **Frequency:** annual. **Type:** recognition. **Recipient:** for abstract submission and presentation. **Subcommittees:** American Board of Medical Accreditation; Annual Meeting; Credentials; Education; Ethics and Grievances; Examinations; Fund Raising; Journal. **Publications:** *Journal of Neurological and Orthopaedic Medicine and Surgery (JONOMS)*. Alternate Formats: online. **Conventions/Meetings:** annual Scientific Meeting - general assembly, with presentations from neurological, orthopaedic specialists and surgeons (exhibits) ● seminar.

15085 ■ American Association of Neurological Surgeons (AANS)
5550 Meadowbrook Dr.
Rolling Meadows, IL 60008
Ph: (847)378-0500
Free: (888)566-2267
Fax: (847)378-0600
E-mail: info@aans.org
URL: http://www.aans.org
Contact: Ms. Susan Funk, Governance Admin.
Founded: 1931. **Members:** 6,000. **Staff:** 45. **Budget:** $5,700,000. **Regional Groups:** 4. **Multinational. Description:** Neurological surgeons united to promote excellence in neurological surgery and its related sciences. Provides funding to foster research in the neurosciences. Conducts specialized education, provides products and publications. **Libraries: Type:** reference. **Holdings:** 300; archival material. **Awards:** Van Wagenen Fellowship. **Frequency:** annual. **Type:** recognition. **Computer Services:** Mailing lists, of members. **Committees:** Annual Meeting; Bylaws; Development; Digital and Technology; Education and Practice Management; Ethics; Finance; International Outreach; Long-Range Planning; Maintenance of Certification; Membership; Professional Conduct; Professional Liability; Public Relations; Publications; Scientific Program; Young Neurosurgeons. **Projects:** Devices and Drugs; Member Benefits; Military Neurosurgeons; Neurosurgical Research and Education Foundation. **Sections:** Cerebrovascular Surgery; Disorders of the Spine and Peripheral Nerves; Functional and Stereotactic Surgery; History of Neurological Surgery; Neurotrauma and Critical Care; Pain; Pediatric Neurological Surgery; Tumors. **Affiliated With:** World Federation of Neurosurgical Societies. **Formerly:** (1966) Harvey Cushing Society. **Publications:** *AANS Membership Directory of Neurological Surgery*, annual. Includes an electronic directory on CD-ROM. **Price:** $50.00 for members. **Circulation:** 5,000. **Advertising:** accepted. Alternate Formats: CD-ROM ● *American Association of Neurological Surgeons Bulletin*, quarterly. Magazine. **Price:** included in membership dues. **Circulation:** 4,976. **Advertising:** accepted ● *Journal of Neurosurgery*, monthly. **Price:** $100.00 /year for members; $110.00 /year for nonmembers; $60.00/year for residents. **Circulation:** 12,000. **Advertising:** accepted ● *Journal of Neurosurgery: Pediatrics*, monthly ● *Journal of Neurosurgery: Spine*, bimonthly ● *Neurosurgical Focus*, bimonthly. Journal. Alternate Formats: online ● *Neurosurgical Operative Atlas*. Booklets. **Conventions/Meetings:** semiannual Master Series - meeting, advanced neurosurgical and clinical courses ● annual meeting, neurosurgeons, residents, nurses and P.A.'s (exhibits) ● periodic seminar, various Practice Management, Oral Board Review, Socioeconomic, and Clinical courses.

15086 ■ American Board of Neurological Surgery (ABNS)
6550 Fannin St., Ste.2139
Houston, TX 77030
Ph: (713)441-6015
Fax: (713)794-0207
E-mail: abns@tmh.tmc.edu
URL: http://www.abns.org
Contact: Mary Louise Sanderson, Admin.
Founded: 1940. **Membership Dues:** actively practicing diplomate, diplomate certified in 1999 and after,

$275 (annual). **Staff:** 2. **Description:** Works to stimulate development of adequate training facilities and aids in evaluating residencies under consideration by the Residency Review Committee for Neurological Surgery of the Accreditation Council on Graduate Medical Education. **Committees:** Credentials; Educational Requirements and Subspecialization; Maintenance of Certification; Oral Examination; Professional Practice Data; Written Examination. **Publications:** *Newsletter to Diplomates*, annual. **Price:** free. **Conventions/Meetings:** semiannual meeting - always May and November. 2007 Nov. 6-9, Houston, TX - **Avg. Attendance:** 36.

15087 ■ American Society for Stereotactic and Functional Neurosurgery (ASSFN)
Dept. of Neurosurgery
New Jersey Medical Scholarship
90 Bergen St., Ste.8100
Newark, NJ 07103-2499
Ph: (973)972-2907
Fax: (973)972-2333
E-mail: schulder@umdnj.edu
URL: http://www.assfn.org
Contact: Dr. Michael Schulder, Pres.
Founded: 1968. **Members:** 300. **Membership Dues:** associate, $50 (annual) ● resident, fellow, $25 (annual) ● active, $325 (annual). **Staff:** 2. **Description:** Aims to foster the use of stereotactic and functional neurological methods for the treatment of diseases of the nervous system. Seeks to advance stereotactic and functional neurosurgery and related sciences, to improve patient care, to support meaningful basic and clinical research, to provide leadership in undergraduate and graduate education and continuing education, and to provide administrative facilities necessary to meet these goals. Provides a forum for the review of the basic form and function of the human nervous system in order to improve stereotactic and/or functional neurosurgical procedures that alleviate human disease and suffering through diagnosis or treatment of the function of the nervous system. **Libraries: Type:** reference. **Holdings:** archival material. **Awards:** Resident's Award. **Frequency:** annual. **Type:** recognition. **Recipient:** abstract. **Computer Services:** Mailing lists. **Affiliated With:** American Association of Neurological Surgeons; Congress of Neurological Surgeons; World Society for Stereotactic and Functional Neurosurgery. **Formerly:** (1972) International Society for Research in Stereoencephalotomy, American Branch. **Publications:** *Stereotactic and Functional Neurosurgery*, bimonthly. Journal. **Advertising:** accepted. **Conventions/Meetings:** quadrennial congress (exhibits) ● biennial Scientific Meeting.

15088 ■ Congress of Neurological Surgeons (CNS)
10 N Martingale Rd., Ste.190
Schaumburg, IL 60173
Ph: (847)240-2500
Free: (877)517-1267
Fax: (847)240-0804
E-mail: info@1cns.org
URL: http://www.neurosurgeon.org
Contact: P. David Adelson MD, Sec.
Founded: 1951. **Members:** 5,300. **Staff:** 11. **Multinational. Description:** Professional society of neurological surgeons in the United States and 55 other countries who meet annually to express their views on various aspects of the principles and practice of neurological surgery; to exchange technical information and experience; to join study of the developments in scientific fields allied to neurological surgery. Promotes interest of neurological surgeons in their practice; provides placement service; honors a living leader in the field of neurological surgery annually. **Computer Services:** Mailing lists, of members. **Committees:** Drugs and Devices; Education; International; Placement; Resident; Socio-Economic; Spinal Disorders; Trauma; Tumor. **Publications:** *Clinical Neurosurgery*, annual ● *Neurosurgery*, monthly. Journal ● *Neurosurgery News*, quarterly. Newsletter. Provides update on practice management, socioeconomic and policy issues facing neurosurgeons today. ● *U.S. and Canada Directory*, annual ● *World Directory*, bien-

nial. **Conventions/Meetings:** annual meeting (exhibits) - 2007 Sept. 15-20, San Diego, CA; 2008 Sept. 20-25, Orlando, FL.

15089 ■ Neurosurgeons to Preserve Health Care Access (NPHCA)

5550 Meadowbrook Dr.
Rolling Meadows, IL 60008
Ph: (202)628-2883
E-mail: korrico@neurosurgery.org
Contact: Katie Orrico, Contact
Description: Promotes sound public policies that preserve patient access to healthcare. Seeks to identify and remove barriers that hinder patients' access to quality neurosurgical health care. Educates the public on ways in which they can assist in improving patients' access quality neurosurgical health care. Cooperates with other organizations and individuals in preserving and improving patients' access to health care. **Telecommunication Services:** electronic mail, bpeck@neurosurgery.org. **Publications:** Brochure. Alternate Formats: online.

15090 ■ Neurosurgery International

c/o Seattle Neuroscience Institute
1600 E Jefferson, Ste.200
Seattle, WA 98122
Ph: (206)320-2028
E-mail: gfoltz@nsinternational.org
URL: http://www.nsinternational.org
Contact: Dr. Greg Foltz, Contact
Founded: 2000. **Multinational. Description:** Improves neurosurgical surgery and related health care in developing countries. Promotes international neurosurgery education and training for physicians and other health care professionals. Provides medical relief missions and physician exchange programs. Facilitates internet-based doctor-to-doctor consultation network. **Computer Services:** Online services, discussion board. **Programs:** Doctor to Doctor. **Projects:** Medical Assistance; Physician Exchange.

15091 ■ Society of Neurological Surgeons (SNS)

c/o Robert J. Dempsey, MD, Sec.
Univ. of Wisconsin - Madison
600 Highland Ave.
Madison, WI 53792
Ph: (608)263-9585
Fax: (608)263-1728
E-mail: dempsey@neurosurg.wisc.edu
URL: http://www.societyns.org
Contact: Robert J. Dempsey MD, Sec.
Founded: 1920. **Members:** 350. **Membership Dues:** active, $250 (annual). **Description:** Neurological surgeons interested in and contributing to education. **Committees:** Accreditation of Subspecialty Training; Grass Foundation; Program; Tellers. **Conventions/ Meetings:** annual meeting (exhibits) - 2008 May 18-20, Madison, WI.

15092 ■ Society of Neurosurgical Anesthesia and Critical Care (SNACC)

520 N Northwest Hwy.
Park Ridge, IL 60068-2573
Ph: (847)825-5586
Fax: (847)825-5658
E-mail: snacc@asahq.org
URL: http://www.snacc.org
Contact: Cornelis J. Kalkman MD, Pres.
Founded: 1973. **Members:** 500. **Membership Dues:** active, $275 (annual) ● international (with journal), $285 (annual) ● resident/emeritus (with journal), $175 (annual) ● active and international (without journal), $125 (annual) ● resident/emeritus (without journal), $25 (annual). **Staff:** 8. **Description:** Neurosurgeons and anesthesiologists interested in the care of patients with neurological disorders. Sponsors continuing medical education and research concerning the care of neurosurgical patients. **Awards:** Frequency: annual. **Type:** recognition. **Recipient:** to a resident physician for research essay ● Teacher of the Year Award. **Frequency:** annual. **Type:** recognition. **Recipient:** for outstanding teacher of healthcare professionals in the areas of neuroscience, neurosurgical anesthesiology and neurocritical care. **Commit-**

tees: Education. **Publications:** *Annual Summary of Society Meeting Proceedings*, annual ● *Society Membership*, annual. Membership Directory ● Newsletter, 3-4/year ● Journal, quarterly. ISSN: 0898-4921. Alternate Formats: online. **Conventions/Meetings:** annual meeting, held in conjunction with American Society of Anesthesiologists (exhibits) - 2007 Oct. 12, San Francisco, CA.

15093 ■ World Federation of Neurosurgical Societies (WFNS)

c/o Edward R. Laws
Stanford Univ. Medical Center
Advanced Medicine Ctr.
875 Blake Wilbur Dr.
Stanford, CA 94305-5821
Ph: (650)725-0701
E-mail: erlaws@stanford.edu
URL: http://www.wfns.org
Contact: Edward R. Laws, Contact
Founded: 1957. **Members:** 64. **Membership Dues:** individual, $5 (annual). **Staff:** 1. **Budget:** $65,000. **Regional Groups:** 5. **Multinational. Description:** National neurosurgical societies representing approximately 17,400 neurosurgeons. Works for the advancement of neurological surgery. **Awards:** Gold Medal of Honor. **Frequency:** quadrennial. **Type:** monetary. **Recipient:** for excellence in neurosurgery ● Scoville Award. **Frequency:** quadrennial. **Type:** monetary. **Recipient:** for excellence in neurosurgery ● Young Neurosurgeons Award. **Frequency:** quadrennial. **Type:** monetary. **Recipient:** for excellence in neurosurgery. **Committees:** Ethics and Medical Legal Affairs; Liaison and Public Relations; Materials and Devices; Neurooncology; Neurosurgical Education; Neurotraumatology; Pediatric Neurosurgery; Sterotactical and Functional Neurosurgery. **Publications:** *Critical Reviews in Neurosurgery*. Journal ● *Federation News*, quarterly. Newsletter. **Price:** $75.00. **Circulation:** 19,000. **Advertising:** accepted ● *Journal on Neurology and Neurosurgery*. Alternate Formats: online ● *Journal on Neurosurgical and Allied Disciplines*. Alternate Formats: online ● *Proceedings of International Congress*, quadrennial ● *World Directory*, periodic. **Conventions/Meetings:** quadrennial World Congress of Neurological Surgery (exhibits) - 2009 Aug. 23-28, Boston, MA - **Avg. Attendance:** 3001.

15094 ■ World Society for Stereotactic and Functional Neurosurgery (WSSFN)

c/o Michael Schulder, MD, Asst. Sec.-Treas.
UMDNJ-New Jersey Medical School
90 Bergen St., Ste.8100
Newark, NJ 07103
Ph: (973)972-2907
Fax: (973)972-2333
E-mail: schulder@umndj.edu
URL: http://www.wssfn.org
Contact: Andres M. Lozano PhD, Pres.
Founded: 1963. **Members:** 600. **Membership Dues:** full, $325 (annual). **Staff:** 2. **Regional Groups:** 4. **National Groups:** 3. **Multinational. Description:** Neurosurgeons and professors dedicated to the advancement of stereotactic studies and procedures. Original manuscripts submitted at meetings are published and used as reference books throughout the world. **Libraries: Type:** reference. **Holdings:** archival material. **Awards:** Spiegel-Wycis Medal. **Frequency:** quadrennial. **Type:** medal. **Recipient:** to senior neurosurgeons who have contributed to the advancement of the field of Stereotactic and Functional Neurosurgery ● Young Investigator Award. **Frequency:** annual. **Type:** recognition. **Recipient:** to neurosurgeons with the best presentations, poster or oral at the quadrennial WSSFN meeting. **Also Known As:** World Stereotactic Society; WSSFN. **Formerly:** (1973) International Society for Research in Stereoencephalotomy. **Publications:** *Stereotactic and Functional Neurosurgery*, quarterly. Journal. **Circulation:** 2,000. **Advertising:** accepted ● *Studies in Stereoencephalotomy*, quadrennial. **Conventions/ Meetings:** quadrennial congress and symposium (exhibits).

Nuclear Medicine

15095 ■ American Board of Nuclear Medicine (ABNM)

4555 Forest Park Blvd., Ste.119
St. Louis, MO 63108
Ph: (314)367-2225
Fax: (314)362-2806
E-mail: abnm@abnm.org
URL: http://www.abnm.org
Contact: Henry D. Royal MD, Exec. Dir.
Founded: 1971. **Members:** 12. **Staff:** 4. **Description:** A primary medical specialty board and member of the American Board of Medical Specialties. Provides educational standards and evaluates the competence of physicians in nuclear medicine; establishes requirements for certification. Conducts examinations and issues certification. Maintains registry of certificate holders. Aids in the assessment and accreditation of nuclear medicine programs in hospitals and institutions offering graduate training. **Publications:** *American Board of Nuclear Medicine Information, Policies and Procedures*, annual. Brochure. Provides information on the annual certifying examination. **Price:** free. **Conventions/Meetings:** semiannual conference.

15096 ■ American Board of Science in Nuclear Medicine (ABSNM)

1850 Samuel Morse Dr.
Reston, VA 20190
Ph: (703)708-9000
Fax: (703)708-9013
E-mail: absnm@snm.org
URL: http://www.snm.org/absnm
Contact: Subhash M. Danak MS, Pres.
Founded: 1976. **Staff:** 2. **Nonmembership. Description:** Certifies scientists in nuclear medicine; promotes nuclear medicine science, including nuclear medicine physics and instrumentation, nuclear pharmaceutical science, radiochemistry, and radiation protection. **Publications:** *Nuclear Medicine Science Syllabus, 4th Edition*.

15097 ■ American College of Nuclear Medicine (ACNM)

c/o Robert P. Powell, Exec. Dir.
101 W Broad St., Ste.614
Hazleton, PA 18201
Ph: (570)501-9661
Fax: (570)450-0863
E-mail: rpowell@ptd.net
URL: http://www.acnucmed.com
Contact: Harry J. Lessig MD, Chm.
Founded: 1972. **Members:** 500. **Description:** Physicians and medical scientists in nuclear medicine united to: advance the science of nuclear medicine; improve its benefits to patients; study the socioeconomic aspects of the practice of nuclear medicine; encourage improved and continuing education for practitioners in this and allied fields. **Libraries: Type:** reference. **Holdings:** articles. **Subjects:** nuclear medicine from 1941 to present. **Awards:** Gold Medal Award. **Type:** recognition. **Recipient:** for outstanding service and accomplishment. **Committees:** Board of Representatives. **Publications:** *ACNM Directory*, biennial ● *ACNM Report*, bimonthly. Newsletter. **Conventions/Meetings:** annual conference ● annual Scientific Program - meeting.

15098 ■ American College of Nuclear Physicians (ACNP)

1850 Samuel Morse Dr.
Reston, VA 20190-5316
Ph: (703)326-1190
Fax: (703)708-9015
E-mail: vpappas@snm.org
URL: http://www.acnponline.org
Contact: Virginia Pappas, CEO
Founded: 1974. **Members:** 1,600. **Membership Dues:** full, $175 (annual) ● associate, affiliate (industry employee), $150 (annual) ● corresponding (international), $250 (annual). **Staff:** 1. **Budget:** $800,000. **Description:** Nuclear medicine physicians, scientists, and corporations. Fosters the highest

standards of nuclear medicine service and consultation to the public, hospitals, and referring physicians. Advances the science of nuclear medicine and improve nuclear medicine consultation and service through study, education, and improvement of the socioeconomic aspects of the practice of nuclear medicine. Promotes the continuing competence of practitioners of nuclear medicine. Conducts educational seminars and continuing education program. Maintains speakers' bureau. **Libraries: Type:** reference. **Holdings:** biographical archives, books. **Awards: Type:** fellowship ● **Type:** recognition. **Committees:** Corporate; Credentials; Equipment Service and Performance; Ethics; Governmental Affairs; Nuclear Medicine Science; Practice Management and Economics; Professional and Public Information Program; Quality Assurance and Practice Audit Certification; Radiopharmaceutical; Standardization of Nuclear Medicine Instrumentation; Technologists Affairs. **Programs:** Proficiency Testing. **Publications:** *Scanner*, 10/year. Newsletter. Alternate Formats: online ● Directory, annual. **Conventions/Meetings:** annual meeting, scientific session.

15099 ■ Nuclear Medicine Technology Certification Board (NMTCB)
3558 Habersham at Northlake, Bldg. I
Tucker, GA 30084
Ph: (404)315-1739
Fax: (404)315-6502
E-mail: board@nmtcb.org
URL: http://www.nmtcb.org
Contact: Bhaskar R. Dawadi PhD, Exec. Dir.
Founded: 1977. **Members:** 21,000. **Membership Dues:** certified, $35 (annual). **Staff:** 5. **Budget:** $1,500,000. **Description:** Aims to provide for the certification of nuclear medical technologists and to develop, assess, and administer basic and specialty examinations relevant to nuclear medicine technology. **Convention/Meeting:** none. **Committees:** Bylaws; Credentials; Disciplinary; Examination; Executive; Finance; Long Range Planning; Publications; Specialty Examination; Task Analysis. **Affiliated With:** American Association of Physicists in Medicine; Society of Nuclear Medicine; Society of Nuclear Medicine Technologist Section. **Publications:** *NMTCB Examination Report*, annual. **Price:** free ● *NMTCB News*, semiannual. **Price:** free for members. **Circulation:** 13,500 ● Brochures.

15100 ■ Society of Nuclear Medicine (SNM)
1850 Samuel Morse Dr.
Reston, VA 20190-5316
Ph: (703)708-9000
Fax: (703)708-9015
E-mail: vpappas@snm.org
URL: http://www.snm.org
Contact: Virginia M. Pappas, CEO
Founded: 1954. **Members:** 16,000. **Membership Dues:** associate (plus local chapter fees), $170 (annual) ● full (plus local chapter fees), $260 (annual) ● associate technologist (plus local chapter fees), $112 (annual) ● affiliate (plus local chapter fees), $195 (annual) ● regular technologist (plus local chapter fees), $97 (annual). **Staff:** 45. **Budget:** $5,000,000. **Regional Groups:** 15. **Description:** Professional society of physicians, physicists, chemists, radiopharmacists, nuclear medicine technologists, and others interested in nuclear medicine, nuclear magnetic resonance, and the use of radioactive isotopes in clinical practice, research, and teaching. Disseminates information concerning the utilization of nuclear phenomena in the diagnosis and treatment of disease. Oversees the Technologist Section of the Society of Nuclear Medicine. **Awards:** Outstanding Educator Award. **Frequency:** annual. **Type:** recognition. **Recipient:** for members who have significantly contributed to providing knowledge which advances and promotes the field of medicine technology through outstanding work in education ● Outstanding Technologist Award. **Frequency:** annual. **Type:** recognition. **Recipient:** for outstanding service and dedication to the field of nuclear medicine technology ● Pilot Research Grant. **Frequency:** annual. **Type:** grant. **Recipient:** for innovative ideas in clinical or basic research ● Student Fellowship Award. **Fre-**

quency: annual. **Type:** fellowship. **Recipient:** for students enrolled in medical school, or graduate school and undergraduates demonstrating outstanding competence in nuclear research. **Computer Services:** Mailing lists. **Committees:** Awards; Commercial Exhibits; Competence and Certification; Government Relations; Public Relations; Socio-Economics. **Councils:** Academic; Brain Imaging; Cardiovascular; Computer and Instrumentation; Correlative Imaging; Nuclear Oncology Diagnosis and Therapy; Pediatric Imaging; Radiopharmaceutical. **Affiliated With:** American Board of Science in Nuclear Medicine; American College of Nuclear Physicians. **Publications:** *The Journal of Nuclear Medicine*, monthly. Includes advertisers' index, case reports, technical notes, book reviews, calendar of events and information on new products. **Price:** included in membership dues; $120.00 /year for nonmembers; $130.00 /year for nonmembers in Canada and Mexico; $160.00 /year for nonmembers outside North America. ISSN: 0161-5505. **Circulation:** 16,000. **Advertising:** accepted. Alternate Formats: microform; online ● *Journal of Nuclear Medicine Technology*, quarterly. Includes teaching editorials, commentaries, continuing education, and technologist news. Contains advertisers' index and calendar of events. **Price:** included in membership dues; $70.00 /year for nonmembers; $75.00 /year for nonmembers in Canada and Mexico; $80.00 /year for nonmembers outside North America. ISSN: 0091-4916. **Circulation:** 8,000. **Advertising:** accepted ● *Society of Nuclear Medicine Membership Directory*, semiannual. Lists members arranged geographically and alphabetically. **Price:** included in membership dues; $100.00/issue, for nonmembers. **Circulation:** 15,000 ● Also publishes other books and patient pamphlets; produces audiovisual materials. **Conventions/Meetings:** annual meeting (exhibits) - always June. 2008 June 14-18, New Orleans, LA; 2009 June 13-17, Toronto, ON, Canada.

15101 ■ Society of Nuclear Medicine Technologist Section (SNMTS)
1850 Samuel Morse Dr.
Reston, VA 20190
Ph: (703)708-9000
Fax: (703)708-9020
E-mail: vpappas@snm.org
URL: http://interactive.snm.org/index.
cfm?PageID=936&RPID=10
Contact: Virginia M. Pappas CAE, CEO
Founded: 1970. **Members:** 7,000. **Membership Dues:** technologist (plus chapter dues), $97 (annual). **Staff:** 45. **Budget:** $1,100,000. **Regional Groups:** 15. **Description:** Members of the Society of Nuclear Medicine who have received formal training in nuclear medicine technology. Purposes are to: promote the continued development and improvement of nuclear medicine technology; enhance the development of nuclear medicine technologists; stimulate continuing education; develop a forum for the exchange of ideas and information. Serves as the central source of information for those interested and involved in the field of nuclear medicine technology. Represents the field in areas of licensure, accreditation, and certification. Sponsors training sessions. Conducts surveys; compiles statistics. **Awards: Type:** recognition. **Computer Services:** database, membership list ● mailing lists. **Committees:** Academic Affairs; Advocacy; Continuing Education; Entry Level Education; Government Relations; Nominating; Scholarships, Grants, and Awards; Socio-Economic Affairs. **Affiliated With:** Society of Nuclear Medicine. **Formerly:** (2003) Technologist Section of the Society of Nuclear Medicine. **Publications:** *Journal of Nuclear Medicine Technology*, quarterly. **Price:** included in membership dues. ISSN: 0091-4910. **Advertising:** accepted ● Books ● Membership Directory, biennial ● Videos. **Conventions/Meetings:** annual conference, held in conjunction with SNM (exhibits) ● workshop.

Nursing

15102 ■ Academy of Medical Surgical Nurses (AMSN)
PO Box 56
Pitman, NJ 08071-0056
Free: (866)877-AMSN

E-mail: amsn@ajj.com
URL: http://www.medsurgnurse.org/cgi-bin/WebObjects/AMSNMain.woa
Contact: Cecelia Gatson Grindel PhD, Pres.
Membership Dues: full, $84 (annual) ● senior-full, senior associate, $75 (annual) ● new graduate-full, new graduate associate, $70 (annual) ● student, $50 (annual) ● NSNA student, $45 (annual). **Description:** Adult/health, medical-surgical nurses. Promotes standards of nursing. Collaborates with other nursing organizations to provide educational programs, practice guidelines and new ideas for its members. **Awards:** Academy of Medical-Surgical Nurses Competence in Aging Award. **Frequency:** annual. **Type:** recognition. **Recipient:** to a member who has displayed excellence in providing care to older adults and serves as a role model and mentor to other healthcare providers ● Academy of Medical-Surgical Nurses Convention Grant. **Frequency:** annual. **Type:** grant. **Recipient:** for members ● Academy of Medical-Surgical Nurses Research Grant. **Frequency:** annual. **Type:** grant. **Recipient:** for members ● Career Mobility Scholarship Award. **Frequency:** annual. **Type:** scholarship. **Recipient:** for members ● Medical-Surgical Nursing Certification Grant. **Frequency:** annual. **Type:** grant. **Recipient:** for members. **Committees:** Chapter Development; Clinical Practice; End-of-Life; Legislative Policies and Issues; Program Planning; Research. **Special Interest Groups:** Geriatric; Military. **Publications:** *Certification Review Course Manual*. Provides continuing nursing education. ● *Certification Review Questions*. Book ● *MedSurg Matters*, quarterly. Newsletter ● *MEDSURG Nursing*. Journal. Features comprehensive description and discussion of today's clinical issues in adult health nursing. **Price:** included in membership dues ● Membership Directory. Alternate Formats: online ● Brochure. Alternate Formats: online. **Conventions/Meetings:** annual Medical-Surgical Nursing: Creating the Future of Adult Care - convention - 2007 Oct. 24-29, Las Vegas, NV.

15103 ■ Air and Surface Transport Nurses Association (ASTNA)
7995 E Prentice Ave., Ste.100
Greenwood Village, CO 80111
Ph: (720)488-0492
Free: (800)897-6362
Fax: (303)770-1614
E-mail: astna@gwami.com
URL: http://www.astna.org
Contact: Karen Wojdyla, Exec. Dir.
Founded: 1981. **Members:** 1,700. **Membership Dues:** active, $90 (annual) ● affiliate or inactive, $85 (annual) ● student, military, $75 (annual) ● international military, $95 (annual) ● international, $115 (annual). **Budget:** $230,000. **Regional Groups:** 10. **Description:** Transport nurses. Seeks to promote the quality of transport nursing by developing standards for the profession and exploring educational opportunities. Seeks optimum working conditions for members. Provides assistance to hospitals for developing air medical services programs. Maintains Speaker's Bureau. **Libraries: Type:** reference. **Awards: Type:** recognition. **Computer Services:** Mailing lists, of members. **Committees:** Certification; Education; Liaison; Research; Special Interest Groups; Standards; Transport Nurse Advance Trauma Course. **Also Known As:** (1999) National Flight Nurses Association. **Publications:** *Air Medical Journal*, bimonthly ● *Wings, Wheels & Rotors*, quarterly. Newsletter ● Also produces educational learning module. **Conventions/Meetings:** annual conference, held in conjunction with Association of Air Medical Services, National Flight Paramedics Association, and National EMS Pilots Association (exhibits) - usually October ● annual conference - always mid-year ● annual seminar.

15104 ■ American Academy of Ambulatory Care Nursing (AAACN)
E Holly Ave.
Box 56
Pitman, NJ 08071-0056
Ph: (856)256-2350
Free: (800)262-6877

Fax: (856)589-7463
E-mail: aaacn@ajj.com
URL: http://www.aaacn.org
Contact: Cynthia R. Nowicki Hnatiuk EdD, Exec. Dir.
Founded: 1978. **Members:** 1,900. **Membership Dues:** active, $130 (annual) ● LPN/LVN, affiliate, $105 (annual) ● senior, student, $70 (annual) ● corporate affiliate, $250 (annual) ● corporate, $1,500 (annual). **Budget:** $500,000. **Local Groups:** 17. **Description:** Advances the art and science of ambulatory care nursing. Serves as the voice of ambulatory care nursing; promotes professional practices; and stimulates innovative thinking. Builds collaborating relationships and strengthens the Academy's resource base. **Awards:** Excellence Award. **Frequency:** annual. **Type:** recognition ● Research Grant. **Frequency:** annual. **Type:** grant ● Research Scholarship. **Frequency:** annual. **Type:** scholarship. **Formerly:** American Academy of Ambulatory Nursing Administration. **Publications:** *Ambulatory Care Nursing Administration and Practice Standards*, periodic. Manual. Serves as a reference manual. **Price:** $15.00 for members; $25.00 for nonmembers ● *Dermatology Nursing*. Journal ● *MedSurg Nursing*. Journal ● *Nursing Economics*, bimonthly. Journal ● *Pediatric Nursing*. Journal ● *Viewpoint*, bimonthly. Newsletter. Includes legislative updates and synopses of articles in current journals. **Price:** included in membership dues; $80.00 institutional. **Advertising:** accepted. **Conventions/Meetings:** annual conference, includes wide array of education for nurses in ambulatory settings (exhibits).

15105 ■ American Academy of Nurse Practitioners (AANP)

PO Box 12846
Austin, TX 78711
Ph: (512)442-4262
Fax: (512)442-6469
E-mail: admin@aanp.org
URL: http://www.aanp.org
Contact: Dr. Judith Dempster, Exec. Dir.
Founded: 1985. **Members:** 19,600. **Membership Dues:** regular, associate, $99 (annual) ● student, retired, $49 (annual). **Staff:** 30. **Description:** Represents the interests of approximately 85,000 nurse practitioners around the country; continually advocates for the active role of nurse practitioners as providers of high-quality, cost-effective healthcare. **Awards:** Fellows of the American Academy of Nurse Practitioners. **Frequency:** annual. **Type:** fellowship. **Recipient:** for nurse practitioner leaders who have made outstanding contributions to health care ● **Frequency:** annual. **Type:** grant. **Recipient:** for members ● **Frequency:** annual. **Type:** scholarship. **Recipient:** for members. **Computer Services:** Online services, personal and professional information. **Publications:** *AANP Monitor*, quarterly. Newsletter ● *AANP SmartBrief*, Monday-Friday. Newsletter. Alternate Formats: online ● *Journal of the American Academy of Nurse Practitioners*, monthly. Focuses on clinical practice, management, and education. **Price:** included in membership dues. **Advertising:** accepted. Alternate Formats: online. Also Cited As: *JAANP ● Your Partner in Health—The Nurse Practitioner* (in English and Spanish). Brochure. Available upon request. **Price:** $8.00 for members; $12.00 for nonmembers ● Papers. Alternate Formats: online ● Annual Report, annual. Alternate Formats: online. **Conventions/Meetings:** annual conference and trade show.

15106 ■ American Academy of Nursing (AAN)

555 E Wells St., Ste.1100
Milwaukee, WI 53202
Ph: (414)287-0289
Fax: (414)276-3349
E-mail: info@aannet.org
URL: http://www.aannet.org
Contact: Ms. Annette Hess, Dir. of Admin. and Operations
Founded: 1973. **Members:** 800. **Membership Dues:** active fellow, $365 (annual) ● emeritus fellow, $75 (annual). **Staff:** 3. **Budget:** $400,000. **Description:** Aims to advance new concepts in nursing and health

care. Identifies and explores issues in health, the professions, and society that concern nursing. Examines interrelationships among the segments within nursing and the interaction among nurses as these affect the development of the nursing profession. Identifies and proposes resolutions to issues and problems confronting nursing and health, including alternative plans for implementation. Sponsors symposia. **Awards:** Media Award. **Frequency:** annual. **Type:** recognition. **Recipient:** for accurate representation of the nursing profession. **Computer Services:** Mailing lists. **Affiliated With:** American Nurses Association. **Publications:** *American Academy of Nursing Directory*, annual. **Price:** included in membership dues ● *Nursing Outlook*, bimonthly. Journal. Includes calendar of events, obituaries, and research reports. **Price:** included in membership dues; $25.00 /year for nonmembers. **Advertising:** accepted. **Conventions/Meetings:** annual meeting (exhibits).

15107 ■ American Assembly for Men in Nursing (AAMN)

c/o Byron McCain
PO Box 130220
Birmingham, AL 35213
Ph: (205)802-7551 (205)322-6400
Fax: (205)802-7553
E-mail: aamn@aamn.org
URL: http://aamn.org
Contact: Demetrius Porche DNS, Pres.
Founded: 1971. **Members:** 2,300. **Membership Dues:** full, $80 (annual) ● associate, $25-$40 (annual) ● international (based on the standard national income), $10-$30 (annual). **Staff:** 1. **Regional Groups:** 5. **State Groups:** 4. **Description:** Registered nurses. Works to: help eliminate prejudice in nursing; interest men in the nursing profession; provide opportunities for the discussion of common problems; encourage education and promote further professional growth; advise and assist in areas of professional inequity; help develop sensitivities to various social needs; promote the principles and practices of positive health care. Acts as a clearinghouse for information on men in nursing. Conducts educational programs. Promotes education and research about men's health issues. **Awards:** Best Nursing School/College for Men in Nursing. **Frequency:** annual. **Type:** recognition. **Recipient:** for a nursing school or college that provided significant efforts in recruiting and retaining men in nursing ● Best Workplace for the Men in Nursing. **Frequency:** annual. **Type:** recognition. **Recipient:** for employers who have implemented significant efforts in recruiting and retaining men in nursing workplace culture supportive of men in nursing ● Lee Cohen Award. **Frequency:** annual. **Type:** recognition. **Recipient:** to an individual who fulfills the purposes and meets the criteria of the award ● Luther Christman Award. **Frequency:** annual. **Type:** recognition. **Recipient:** for outstanding contributions to nursing that also reflect highly on men in nursing or significantly contribute to the purposes of the organization. **Committees:** By-laws; Chapters; Education; Nominations. **Formerly:** (1982) National Male Nurse Association. **Publications:** *Interaction*, quarterly. Newsletter. Contains statement of objectives and information on officers, events, and activities. **Price:** included in membership dues. **Advertising:** accepted. **Conventions/Meetings:** annual Breaking Barriers to Men's Health - conference (exhibits).

15108 ■ American Association of Critical-Care Nurses (AACN)

101 Columbia
Aliso Viejo, CA 92656-4109
Ph: (949)362-2000
Free: (800)899-2226
Fax: (949)362-2020
E-mail: info@aacn.org
URL: http://www.aacn.org
Contact: Mary Fran Tracy RN, Pres.
Founded: 1969. **Members:** 65,000. **Membership Dues:** active/affiliate, $78 (annual) ● active/affiliate, $148 (biennial) ● active/affiliate, $211 (triennial) ● student/emeritus/retired/disabled, $52 (annual) ●

emeritus, $99 (biennial). **Staff:** 96. **Local Groups:** 275. **Description:** Represents the interests of professional critical care nurses. Aims to provide continuing education programs for nurses specializing in critical care and to develop standards of nursing care of critically ill patients. Conducts educational programs. Offers certification program for critical care nurses through Certification Corporation. Seeks liaison with other professional nursing organizations and related health agencies. **Awards:** Community Service Award. **Frequency:** annual. **Type:** recognition. **Recipient:** for critical care nurses (individuals or groups) who make a difference in their community ● Critical Care Mentoring Award. **Frequency:** annual. **Type:** recognition. **Recipient:** for individuals or groups who develop and enhance another's intellectual and technical skills, acculturating them to the professional community and modeling a way of life and professional achievement ● Educational Advancement Scholarships. **Frequency:** annual. **Type:** scholarship. **Recipient:** to members who are registered nurses completing a baccalaureate or graduate degree program in nursing ● Excellence in Caring Practices. **Frequency:** annual. **Type:** recognition. **Recipient:** for critical care nurses whose caring practices are paramount in making possible the empowerment of patients and/or their families ● Excellence in Critical Care Clinical Practice. **Frequency:** annual. **Type:** recognition. **Recipient:** for critical care nurses who embody and exemplify the principles of critical care nursing practice ● Excellence in Critical Care Education. **Frequency:** annual. **Type:** recognition. **Recipient:** for critical care nurse educators who facilitate the acquisition and advancement of the knowledge and skills required for competent practice and positive patient outcomes ● Excellence in Critical Care Management. **Frequency:** annual. **Type:** recognition. **Recipient:** for critical care managers who demonstrate excellence in coordination of available resources to efficiently and effectively care for critically ill patients ● Innovision Award. **Frequency:** annual. **Type:** recognition. **Recipient:** for initiatives and programs that innovatively and collaboratively meet the needs of families of the acute and critically ill ● Media Awards. **Frequency:** annual. **Type:** recognition. **Recipient:** for print and broadcast media excellence in the portrayal of healthcare providers, especially critical care nurses, contributing to a healthcare system driven by the needs of patients and families ● Multidisciplinary Team Award. **Frequency:** annual. **Type:** recognition. **Recipient:** for multidisciplinary team that clearly practices key principles of collaboration and multidisciplinary practice ● Outstanding Clinical Nurse Specialist. **Frequency:** annual. **Type:** recognition. **Recipient:** for critical care clinical nurse specialists who function as expert practitioners ● Special Contributor Award. **Frequency:** annual. **Type:** recognition. **Recipient:** for significant contributions that affect the profession of critical care nursing. **Computer Services:** Mailing lists. **Telecommunication Services:** electronic mail, aacnnews@aacn.org. **Formerly:** (1970) American Association of Cardiovascular Nurses. **Publications:** *AACN Clinical Issues*, quarterly. Journal. Contains peer-reviewed articles on clinically relevant topics. **Price:** $49.30 /year for members; $58.00 /year for nonmembers; $90.00 /year for institutions. ISSN: 1046-7467. **Circulation:** 4,000 ● *AACN News*, monthly. Newsletter. **Advertising:** accepted. Alternate Formats: online ● *American Journal of Critical Care*, bimonthly. Covers original research in critical care. Contains directory of educational programs. **Price:** included in membership dues; $45.00 /year for nonmembers; $110.00 /year for institutions. ISSN: 1062-3264. **Circulation:** 80,000. **Advertising:** accepted. Also Cited As: *AJCC ● Core Curriculum for Critical-Care Nursing ● Critical Care Newsline*, weekly. Newsletter. Contains news and information important to critical care nurses. Alternate Formats: online ● *Critical Care Nurse*, bimonthly. Journal. Focuses on critical care clinical practice. Contains listing of educational programs. **Price:** included in membership dues; $27.00 /year for nonmembers; $45.00 /year for institutions. ISSN: 0279-5442. **Circulation:** 100,000. **Advertising:** accepted. Also Cited As: *CCN*. **Conventions/Meetings:** annual National Teaching Institute and Critical Care Exposition - convention (exhibits).

15109 ■ American Association of Managed Care Nurses (AAMCN)
4435 Waterfront Dr., Ste.101
Glen Allen, VA 23060
Ph: (804)747-9698
Fax: (804)747-5316
E-mail: lgivens@aamcn.org
URL: http://www.aamcn.org
Contact: Laura Givens, Exec. Admin.
Founded: 1994. **Members:** 2,500. **Membership Dues:** individual, $70-$85 (annual) ● student, $15 (annual) ● professional, $125 (annual) ● group of five, $300 (annual) ● group of ten, $600 (annual) ● sustaining, $2,000 ● participating, $1,500 ● contributing, $1,000. **Staff:** 12. **Budget:** $300,000. **Description:** Managed health care professionals, including registered nurses, licensed practical nurses, and nurse practitioners. Seeks to enhance the abilities of members to meet the future needs of the managed health care profession through education. Provides a home study program as a pre-requisite for the Certified Managed Care Nurse (CMCN) exam. **Committees:** Education; Informatics; Managed Care Nursing Practice Standards; Membership; Publications. **Publications:** *Nurses' Notes*, quarterly. **Price:** included in membership dues. **Advertising:** accepted. Alternate Formats: online. **Conventions/ Meetings:** annual Managed Care Nursing: Tomorrow's Healthcare Today - conference, educational (exhibits) ● meeting, all aspects of managed care nursing, including UM, QM, risk management, and medical informatics (exhibits) - 3/year.

15110 ■ American Association of Neuroscience Nurses (AANN)
4700 W Lake Ave.
Glenview, IL 60025
Ph: (847)375-4733
Free: (888)557-2266
Fax: (877)734-8677
E-mail: info@aann.org
URL: http://www.aann.org
Contact: Stacy Sochacki, Exec. Dir.
Founded: 1968. **Members:** 4,000. **Membership Dues:** individual, $98 (annual) ● associate, $73 (annual) ● student, $49 (annual). **Staff:** 5. **Budget:** $750,000. **State Groups:** 50. **Description:** Registered nurses engaged in or primarily interested in neurosurgical or neurological nursing. Fosters interest, education, and high standards of practice in the field of neuroscience nursing. Encourages continuing growth in the field. Provides a medium for communication among neuroscience nurses in the U.S. and Canada. Has developed core curriculum for neuroscience nursing practice. **Awards:** Excellence in Advanced Practice Nursing Award. **Frequency:** annual. **Type:** recognition. **Recipient:** for a nurse who demonstrates excellence in nursing care and advances neuroscience nursing as a specialty through the development and support of nurses ● Excellence in Clinical Practice. **Frequency:** annual. **Type:** recognition. **Recipient:** for excellence in clinical practice of an experienced neuroscience nurse ● Excellence in Neuroscience Education Awards. **Frequency:** annual. **Type:** recognition. **Recipient:** for excellence in neuroscience nursing through contributions that inspire, develop, and support nurses in the provision of care to neuroscience patients ● Outstanding Chapter of the Year Award. **Frequency:** annual. **Type:** recognition. **Recipient:** for an outstanding chapter that supports and advances the mission and vision of AANN ● Rising Star in Clinical Practice Award. **Frequency:** annual. **Type:** recognition. **Recipient:** for a neuroscience nurse with 1-3 years of neuroscience nursing experience. **Affiliated With:** American Board of Neuroscience Nursing. **Publications:** *Core Curriculum for Neuroscience Nursing* ● *Journal of Neuroscience Nursing*, bimonthly. Includes book reviews, pharmacology update, and research reports. **Price:** included in membership dues; $137.00 /year for individuals; $168.00 /year for institutions. ISSN: 0888-0395. **Circulation:** 6,000. **Advertising:** accepted ● *Synapse*, bimonthly. Newsletter. Includes calendar of events, continuing education course listings, employment listings, and information on new members and publications. **Price:** included in mem-

bership dues. **Circulation:** 4,000. **Advertising:** accepted. **Conventions/Meetings:** annual conference (exhibits) ● annual meeting.

15111 ■ American Association of Nurse Anesthetists (AANA)
222 S Prospect Ave.
Park Ridge, IL 60068
Ph: (847)692-7050
Fax: (847)692-6968
E-mail: info@aana.com
URL: http://www.aana.com
Contact: Jeffery M. Beutler, Exec. Dir.
Founded: 1931. **Members:** 34,208. **Membership Dues:** full, $495 (annual). **Staff:** 95. **State Groups:** 52. **Description:** Represents active registered, professional, advanced-practice nurses who have successfully completed an accredited program in nurse anesthesia and passed a national certification examination. Advances the art and science of anesthesia; promotes research in anesthesia; develops educational standards and techniques for the administration of anesthesia. Sponsors continuing education; promotes biennial recertification. **Libraries:** **Type:** open to the public. **Holdings:** 3,000; books. **Subjects:** anesthesia and nursing. **Awards:** Agatha Hodgins Award for Outstanding Accomplishment. **Frequency:** annual. **Type:** recognition. **Recipient:** for individuals with foremost dedication to excellence that has furthered the art and science of nurse anesthesia ● Helen Lamb Outstanding Educator Award. **Frequency:** annual. **Type:** recognition. **Recipient:** to a Certified Registered Nurse Anesthetist (CRNA) who has made a significant contribution to the education of nurse anesthetists. **Computer Services:** Mailing lists. **Additional Websites:** http://www.anesthesiapatientsafety.com. **Councils:** Accreditation; Certification; Public Interest; Recertification. **Publications:** *AANA News Bulletin*, monthly. Contains legislative news, president's message, calendar of events, and employment listings. **Price:** included in membership dues. ISSN: 0199-2554. **Circulation:** 26,908. **Advertising:** accepted ● *American Association of Nurse Anesthetists List of Recognized Educational Programs*, semiannual ● Journal, bimonthly. Contains clinical, practical, theoretical, and research articles. Includes advertisers' index, and alphabetical index by organization. **Price:** included in membership dues; $24.00 /year for nonmembers. ISSN: 0094-6354. **Circulation:** 26,408. **Advertising:** accepted. Alternate Formats: microform. **Conventions/Meetings:** annual convention and meeting, with medical equipment and supplies, including pharmaceutical products, recruiters, and publications (exhibits).

15112 ■ American Association of Nurse Life Care Planners (AANLCP)
3267 E 3300 S, No. 309
Salt Lake City, UT 84109
Ph: (801)274-1184
Free: (888)575-4047
Fax: (801)274-1535
E-mail: hmcdaniel@aanlcp.org
URL: http://www.aanlcp.org
Contact: Helen McDaniel RN, Pres.
Membership Dues: regular, $96 (annual). **Description:** Represents professional registered nurses concerned with nurse life care planning. Promotes the professional practice that registered nurses deliver to the life care planning process. Fosters education, collegiality, collaboration, research and standards on nurse life care planning. **Publications:** *The Journal of Nurse Life Care Planning*, quarterly. Contains news updates and related information on life care planning. **Price:** included in membership dues.

15113 ■ American Association of Occupational Health Nurses (AAOHN)
2920 Brandywine Rd., Ste.100
Atlanta, GA 30341
Ph: (770)455-7757
Fax: (770)455-7271

E-mail: ann@aaohn.org
URL: http://www.aaohn.org
Contact: Ann Cox, Exec. Dir.
Founded: 1942. **Members:** 9,000. **Membership Dues:** active, $185 (annual). **Staff:** 20. **Budget:** $3,000,000. **Regional Groups:** 1. **State Groups:** 33. **Local Groups:** 106. **Description:** Represents registered professional nurses employed by business and industrial firms; nurse educators, nurse editors, nurse writers, and others interested in occupational health nursing. Promotes and sets standards for the profession. Provides and approves continuing education; maintains governmental affairs program; offers placement service. **Awards:** AAOHN Fellowship. **Frequency:** annual. **Type:** fellowship. **Recipient:** for significant contributions to the field of occupational and environmental health nursing ● Business Recognition Awards. **Frequency:** annual. **Type:** recognition. **Recipient:** for small and large businesses that support and promote the occupational and environmental health nursing profession ● Innovations in Occupational Health Award. **Frequency:** annual. **Type:** recognition. **Recipient:** for individual occupational health nurses or nurse teams with innovative ideas to improve the delivery of occupational health care services ● Mary Louise Brown Research Recognition. **Frequency:** annual. **Type:** recognition. **Recipient:** for occupational and environmental health nurses who have contributed to the advancement of occupational and environmental health field through research ● Nurse in Washington Internship Grants. **Frequency:** annual. **Type:** grant. **Recipient:** for members. **Computer Services:** database ● mailing lists. **Formerly:** (1977) American Association of Industrial Nurses. **Publications:** *AAOHN Core Curriculum Study Guide*. Includes guidelines for Occupational Health and Safety Services. ● *AAOHN News*, monthly. Newsletter ● *Foundation Blocks*. Booklet ● *Official Journal of the American Association of Occupational Health Nurses*, monthly. **Circulation:** 15,000. **Advertising:** accepted ● *Success Tools: Strategies for Thriving and Surviving in Business*. Includes guidelines for Occupational Health and Safety Services. **Conventions/Meetings:** annual conference, premier educational, informational and networking event for occupational and environmental health professionals (exhibits).

15114 ■ American Association of Office Nurses (AAON)
52 Park Ave., Ste.B-4
Park Ridge, NJ 07656
Ph: (201)391-2600
Free: (800)457-7504
Fax: (201)573-8543
E-mail: aaonmail@aaon.org
Contact: Michelle Aronowitz, Dir.
Founded: 1988. **Members:** 2,000. **Membership Dues:** individual, $99 (annual). **Staff:** 3. **Budget:** $350,000. **Regional Groups:** 21. **Description:** Nurses working primarily in physicians' offices. Promotes improvement of the image of the office nurse. Encourages professional growth and development; facilitates exchange of information among members. Provides continuing education opportunities. Issues publications. **Awards:** Office Nurse Patient Educator of the Year Award. **Frequency:** annual. **Type:** monetary. **Recipient:** acknowledges and applauds the role of the office nurse in all aspects of ambulatory nursing care. **Publications:** *Medical Office Nurse*, monthly. Booklets. **Price:** $39.00; included in membership dues ● *NEON*, quarterly. Newsletter. **Price:** included in membership dues. **Conventions/ Meetings:** annual meeting and convention (exhibits).

15115 ■ American Association of Spinal Cord Injury Nurses (AASCIN)
75-20 Astoria Blvd.
East Elmhurst, NY 11370
Ph: (718)803-3782
Fax: (718)803-0414
E-mail: aascin@unitedspinal.org
URL: http://www.aascin.org
Contact: Sara Lerman MPH, Program Mgr.
Founded: 1983. **Members:** 1,200. **Membership Dues:** individual, $115 (annual). **Staff:** 5. **Descrip-**

tion: Nurses who care for patients with spinal cord impairment; nurses interested in the field of spinal cord impairment; persons who have provided extraordinary service to improve the quality of life for spinal cord impairment patients. Purposes are to: promote and improve nursing care of spinal cord impairment patients; develop and advance related education and research; recognize nurses whose careers are devoted to the problems of spinal cord impairment; keep medical personnel informed of state-of-the-art techniques. Focuses on topics such as sexuality and spinal cord impairment, care of respiratory dependent spinal cord impairment patients, alcohol and drug dependent spinal cord impairment patients, and planning for care in the community. Monitors and participates in legislative and regulatory activities affecting spinal cord impairment and professional nursing practice. Conducts research and educational programs. **Libraries: Type:** reference. **Awards:** Expanded Pole Award for Excellence in SCI Nursing. **Frequency:** annual. **Type:** recognition. **Recipient:** for an active member who is a role model ● James J. Peters Award for Distinguished Service. **Frequency:** annual. **Type:** recognition. **Recipient:** for outstanding contributions on spinal cord injury nursing ● Staff Nurse Award for Excellence in SCI Nursing. **Frequency:** annual. **Type:** recognition. **Recipient:** for a staff nurse who is a role model in providing competent and passionate care to individuals with SCI. **Computer Services:** Mailing lists, Medline. **Committees:** Clinical Practice; Editorial Board; Education; Membership; Nominating; Professional Issues; Program; Research. **Publications:** *Clinical Practice Guideline: Autonomic Dysreflexia.* Pamphlet. **Price:** $10.00 ● *SCI Nursing*, quarterly. Journal. Contains articles on all facets of spinal cord injury patient care and association news. **Price:** included in membership dues; $65.00 /year for individuals in U.S. and Canada; $75.00 /year for institutions in U.S. and Canada; $105.00 /year for individuals outside U.S. and Canada. **Circulation:** 2,500 ● *Standards of Spinal Cord Injury Nursing Practice.* Pamphlet. **Price:** $6.00. **Conventions/Meetings:** annual Going Platinum: Distinctions & Achievements - conference (exhibits) - in September.

15116 ■ American Board of Managed Care Nursing (ABMCN)
4435 Waterfront Dr., Ste.101
Glen Allen, VA 23060
Ph: (804)527-1905
Fax: (804)747-5316
E-mail: keads@abmcn.org
URL: http://www.abmcn.org
Contact: Katie Eads, Contact
Founded: 1998. **Staff:** 2. **Description:** Seeks to advance the study, teaching, and practice of managed care nursing. Conducts examinations and bestows certification upon qualified nurses.

15117 ■ American Board of Neuroscience Nursing (ABNN)
4700 W Lake Ave.
Glenview, IL 60025
Ph: (847)375-4733
Free: (888)557-2266
Fax: (877)734-8677
E-mail: info@aann.org
URL: http://www.aann.org
Contact: Louise Miller, Exec. Dir.
Founded: 1978. **Members:** 1,500. **Staff:** 3. **Description:** Certifying body for registered nurses who have passed a written examination demonstrating achievement in neuroscience nursing. Promotes excellence in the field by encouraging professional growth and individual study. Grants neuroscience nursing certification, measures knowledge and level of theory required for certification, and establishes certification standards. Administers certifying examination. **Publications:** none. **Affiliated With:** American Association of Neuroscience Nurses. **Formerly:** (1984) Neurosurgical Nurses. **Conventions/Meetings:** annual board meeting.

15118 ■ American Board of Nursing Specialties (ABNS)
610 Thornhill Ln.
Aurora, OH 44202

Ph: (330)995-9172
Fax: (330)995-9743
E-mail: abnsceo@aol.com
URL: http://www.nursingcertification.org
Contact: Dottie Roberts MSN, Pres.-Elect
Founded: 1991. **Members:** 25. **Membership Dues:** regular, $250-$1,000 (annual) ● associate, $125-$500 (annual) ● affiliate, $375-$1,500 (annual). **Staff:** 1. **Budget:** $93,000. **Description:** National nursing certification boards and nursing organizations concerned with nursing credential issues. National peer review program for specialty nursing certification bodies. **Libraries: Type:** reference. **Holdings:** articles, monographs. **Subjects:** nursing certification. **Conventions/Meetings:** semiannual assembly and meeting.

15119 ■ American Board for Occupational Health Nurses (ABOHN)
201 E Ogden Ave., Ste.114
Hinsdale, IL 60521-3652
Ph: (630)789-5799
Free: (888)842-2646
Fax: (630)789-8901
E-mail: info@abohn.org
URL: http://www.abohn.org
Contact: Ms. Georgia M. Knuth RN, Exec. Dir.
Founded: 1972. **Members:** 6,772. **Staff:** 5. **Budget:** $700,000. **Description:** Occupational health nurses. Establishes standards and confers initial and ongoing certification in occupational health nursing. Conducts semiannual certification examination. **Convention/Meeting:** none. **Awards:** ABOHN Employer Award. **Frequency:** annual. **Type:** recognition. **Recipient:** for firms that promote certification of occupational health nurses ● ABOHN Research Award. **Frequency:** annual. **Type:** monetary. **Recipient:** for a research related to occupational health ● Marguerite Ahern Graff Excellence Award. **Frequency:** annual. **Type:** recognition. **Recipient:** for an occupational health nurse who received the highest score on the previous year's COHN certification exam ● Mayrose Snyder Excellence Award. **Frequency:** annual. **Type:** recognition. **Recipient:** for an occupational health nurse who received the highest score on the previous year's COHN-S certification exam. **Computer Services:** database. **Publications:** *The ABOHN Report*, semiannual. Newsletter ● *Directory of Certified Occupational Health Nurses*, annual. Contains contact information for certified occupational health nurses. ● *Reference Guide for Examination Preparation* ● Also publishes position papers on occupational health nursing issues.

15120 ■ American Board of Perianesthesia Nursing Certification (ABPANC)
475 Riverside Dr., 6th Fl.
New York, NY 10115-0089
Free: (800)622-7262
Fax: (212)367-4256
E-mail: abpanc@proexam.org
URL: http://www.cpancapa.org
Contact: Bonnie Niebuhr MS, CEO
Founded: 1985. **Staff:** 2. **Description:** Administers examination to individuals wishing to attain perianesthesia nursing certification. **Libraries: Type:** reference. **Holdings:** 72; books. **Subjects:** nursing. **Publications:** *Certification Newsletter.* **Price:** free for members. **Circulation:** 5,500. **Conventions/Meetings:** annual conference (exhibits).

15121 ■ American College of Nurse-Midwives (ACNM)
8403 Colesville Rd., Ste.1550
Silver Spring, MD 20910
Ph: (240)485-1800
Fax: (240)485-1818
E-mail: info@acnm.org
URL: http://www.midwife.org
Contact: Kathleen Przybylski, Assoc. Dir.
Founded: 1955. **Members:** 6,200. **Membership Dues:** friend, $120 (annual) ● student, associate, $130 (annual) ● retired/disabled/active-first year, $205 (annual) ● active, $335 (annual) ● life, $5,025. **Staff:** 38. **Budget:** $2,200,000. **Regional Groups:** 6. **Local Groups:** 53. **Description:** Seeks to develop

and support the profession of certified nurse-midwives in order to promote the health and well-being of women and infants within their families and communities. Represents licensed health care practitioner educated in the two disciplines of nursing and midwifery. Provides gynecological services and care of mothers and babies throughout the maternity cycle. Cooperates with allied groups to enable nurse-midwives to concentrate their efforts in the improvement of services for mothers and newborn babies. Studies and evaluates activities of nurse-midwives in order to establish qualifications. Conducts research and continuing education workshops. sponsors research. Compiles statistics. Maintains speakers' bureau and archives; offers placement service. **Awards: Type:** recognition. **Computer Services:** Mailing lists, of members. **Committees:** Clinical Practice; International Health; Minority Affairs; Pre-Certification; Publicity and Public Relations. **Divisions:** Accreditation; Competency Assessment; Education; Research; Standards and Practice; Women's Health Policy and Leadership. **Absorbed:** (1968) American Association of Nurse-Midwives. **Formerly:** (1969) American College of Nurse-Midwifery. **Publications:** *American College of Nurse-Midwives Membership Directory Supplement*, annual. **Price:** included in membership dues ● *Directory of Nurse-Midwifery Practices*, annual. Contains computer listing of certified nurse-midwives by state. **Price:** included in membership dues; $10.00 /year for nonmembers ● *Journal of Midwifery and Women's Health*, bimonthly. Covers topics relevant to maternal and newborn health, obstetrics, well-woman gynecology, family planning, and midwifery education. **Price:** included in membership dues; $48.00 /year for nonmembers; $69.00 /year for institutions. ISSN: 0091-2182. **Circulation:** 4,300. **Advertising:** accepted. Alternate Formats: microform; online ● *Quickening*, bimonthly. Newsletter. Includes activities, calendar of events, employment listings, and legislative updates. **Price:** included in membership dues. ISSN: 0196-3805. **Advertising:** accepted ● Also publishes pamphlets and brochures. **Conventions/Meetings:** annual conference (exhibits).

15122 ■ American College of Nurse Practitioners (ACNP)
1501 Wilson Blvd., Ste.509
Arlington, VA 22209
Ph: (703)740-2529
Fax: (703)740-2533
E-mail: acnp@acnpweb.org
URL: http://www.acnpweb.org
Contact: Carolyn Hutcherson, CEO
Founded: 1993. **Members:** 2,800. **Membership Dues:** individual/associate, $110 (annual) ● individual with affiliate discount, $95 (annual) ● student, $55 (annual). **Staff:** 3. **Budget:** $500,000. **Description:** Licensed and student nurse practitioners; state and national associations representing nurse practitioners. Seeks to strengthen the voice of nurse practitioners within the medical profession; promotes advancement in the study, teaching, and practice of nursing. Aims to unite and represent nurse practitioners on policy and professional issues, in order to ensure an appropriate, prevention-based health care system that meets the needs of individuals, families and communities. Provides advocacy on federal policy issues, publishes continuing education materials, and provides a range of professional networking opportunities. **Awards:** ACNP Nurse Practitioner Student Scholarship. **Frequency:** annual. **Type:** scholarship. **Recipient:** for education of student nurse practitioners ● Margie Koehler Legislative Advocacy Award. **Frequency:** annual. **Type:** recognition. **Recipient:** to an individual NP or lay person who has demonstrated a commitment to ACNP's legislative priorities and has shown outstanding political and legislative leadership ● Sharp Cutting Edge Award. **Frequency:** annual. **Type:** recognition. **Recipient:** for a nurse or lay person who has demonstrated extraordinary belief in NPs and has shown efforts to improve the image and visibility of NPs. **Publications:** *Forum*, quarterly. Newsletter ● *Journal for Nurse Practitioners*, 10/year. **Advertising:** accepted. Alternate Formats: online. Also Cited As: *JNP* ● *Nurse Practitioner World News*,

periodic. Newsletter ● *Washington Word*, monthly. Newsletter. Contains updates on legislation of interest to Nurse Practitioners, membership information, affiliate updates, and meeting information. **Conventions/Meetings:** annual National Clinical Conference - held in October. 2007 Oct. 24-28, San Antonio, TX ● annual National Nurse Practitioner Summit - symposium - held in February.

15123 ■ American Forensic Nurses (AFN)
255 N El Cielo, Ste.195
Palm Springs, CA 92262
Ph: (760)322-9925
Fax: (760)322-9914
E-mail: info@amrn.com
URL: http://www.amrn.com
Contact: Faye Battiste, Pres.
Founded: 1983. **Description:** Promotes and assists forensic nurses to meet the needs of law enforcement agencies in the collection of forensic evidence. **Libraries: Type:** reference. **Holdings:** articles, books, periodicals. **Subjects:** forensic sciences.

15124 ■ American Licensed Practical Nurses Association (ALPNA)
Address Unknown since 2007
Founded: 1984. **Members:** 6,200. **Budget:** $150,000. **Description:** Licensed practical nurses. Promotes the practical nursing profession; lobbies and maintains relations with the government on issues and legislation that may have an impact on LPNs. Conducts continuing education classes. Facilitates discussion of issues affecting the nursing and health professions. **Publications:** Pamphlets. Contain information on legislation and nursing standards. ● Papers. **Conventions/Meetings:** annual conference (exhibits) - always August.

15125 ■ American Nurses Association (ANA)
8515 Georgia Ave., Ste.400
Silver Spring, MD 20910
Ph: (301)628-5000
Free: (800)274-4262
Fax: (301)628-5001
E-mail: memberinfo@ana.org
URL: http://www.nursingworld.org
Contact: Rebecca M. Patton MS, Pres.
Founded: 1896. **Members:** 150,000. **Membership Dues:** direct individual, $171 (annual). **Staff:** 168. **State Groups:** 54. **Local Groups:** 860. **National Groups:** 11. **Description:** Membership association representing registered nurses. **Libraries: Type:** reference; not open to the public. **Holdings:** monographs, periodicals. **Subjects:** nursing. **Awards:** Hall of Fame. **Frequency:** biennial. **Type:** recognition. **Recipient:** for lifelong contributions in nursing ● Honorary Awards. **Frequency:** biennial. **Type:** recognition. **Recipient:** for significant contributions and accomplishments. **Subgroups:** American Academy of Nursing; American Nurses Association - Political Action Committee; American Nurses Credentialing Center; American Nurses Foundation; Congress on Nursing Practice and Economics; Constituent Assembly; International Nursing Center. **Affiliated With:** International Council of Nurses. **Formerly:** (1911) Nurses Associated Alumnae of United States and Canada. **Publications:** *The American Nurse*, monthly. Newspaper. Includes employment listings. **Price:** included in membership dues; $20.00 /year for nonmembers; $10.00/year for full-time nursing students. ISSN: 0098-1486. **Circulation:** 160,000. **Advertising:** accepted. Alternate Formats: microform ● *Proceedings of the House of Delegates*, periodic ● Catalog, annual ● Also publishes nursing standards and professional literature. **Conventions/Meetings:** biennial convention (exhibits) ● annual House of Delegates - meeting.

15126 ■ American Nurses Foundation (ANF)
8515 Georgia Ave., Ste.400 W
Silver Spring, MD 20910
Ph: (301)628-5227
Free: (800)274-4ANA
Fax: (301)628-5357

E-mail: anf@ana.org
URL: http://www.nursingworld.org/anf
Contact: Leo Schargorodski, Exec. Dir.
Founded: 1955. **Staff:** 18. **Budget:** $2,380,000. **Description:** Research, education, and charitable arm of the American Nurses' Association (see separate entry). Promotes nursing and consumers wherever nurses practice. Mission accomplished through four major functions: fundraising, Nursing Research Grants, grant development and management, and American Nurses Publishing. **Awards:** Distinguished Contribution to Nursing Science Award. **Frequency:** semiannual. **Type:** recognition ● **Type:** grant. **Recipient:** for nurse researchers. **Additional Websites:** http://www.anfonline.org. **Telecommunication Services:** hotline, Nursing Research Grants Program, (202)651-7298 - do not use for general information. **Committees:** Research Review. **Councils:** Corporate Advisory. **Affiliated With:** American Nurses Association. **Publications:** Books. **Conventions/Meetings:** board meeting - 3/year.

15127 ■ American Nursing Informatics Association (ANIA)
1908 S El Camino Real, Ste.H
San Clemente, CA 92672
E-mail: mbrs@ania.org
URL: http://www.ania.org
Contact: Jim Cato RN, Pres.
Founded: 1992. **Members:** 350. **Membership Dues:** associate/full (licensed nurse), $50 (annual) ● student, $35 (annual). **Description:** Licensed nurses, nursing students, and individuals involved with clinical, administrative and educational aspects of healthcare information systems. Provides networking, education, and information resources to members; serves as a forum for the advancement of nursing and nursing professionals in informatics. Makes available discounts on professional program attendance and conference tuition to members. **Publications:** *Input-Output*, quarterly. Newsletter. Features the latest happening in the field of nursing informatics. **Price:** free for members. **Advertising:** accepted. Alternate Formats: online. **Conventions/Meetings:** annual conference - usually April or May.

15128 ■ American Organization of Nurse Executives (AONE)
c/o Liberty Place
325 Seventh St. NW
Washington, DC 20004
Ph: (202)626-2240
Fax: (202)638-5499
E-mail: aone@aha.org
URL: http://www.aone.org
Contact: Pamela A. Thompson RN, CEO
Founded: 1967. **Members:** 4,000. **Membership Dues:** full/affiliate, $200 (annual) ● retired, $150 (annual) ● associate/student, $75 (annual). **Staff:** 10. **Budget:** $2,700,000. **State Groups:** 69. **Description:** Provides leadership, professional development, advocacy, and research to advance nursing practice and patient care, promote nursing leadership and excellence, and shape healthcare public policy. Supports and enhances the management, leadership, educational, and professional development of nursing leaders. Offers placement service through Career Development and Referral Center. **Awards:** Research Award. **Frequency:** annual. **Type:** recognition ● **Type:** scholarship. **Computer Services:** database, membership ● mailing lists, of members. **Committees:** Bylaws; Education and Research; Institute Operations; Membership Services; Nominations; Political Action; Publications; Strategic Planning. **Task Forces:** Patient Care Delivery System; Regulatory Monitoring; Rural Care Delivery. **Affiliated With:** American Hospital Association. **Formerly:** (1977) American Society for Hospital Nursing Service Administrators; (1984) American Society for Nursing Service Administrators. **Publications:** *AONE eNews Update*, weekly. Newsletter. Contains bulleted update of information related to nursing administration. **Price:** included in membership dues. **Advertising:** accepted ● *Nurse Leader*, bimonthly. Journal. Contains discussions on how to make the transition from management to leadership. **Price:** $22.00/year for students

and residents; $53.00 /year for individuals; $115.00 /year for institutions. **Circulation:** 4,638. Alternate Formats: online ● *Voice of Nursing Leadership*, bimonthly. Newsletter. Features communicating news on nursing leadership profession. **Price:** included in membership dues. **Advertising:** accepted ● Books ● Membership Directory, annual. **Price:** included in membership dues ● Monographs ● Videos. **Conventions/Meetings:** annual meeting (exhibits).

15129 ■ American Pediatric Surgical Nurses Association (APSNA)
PO Box 1605
Lansdale, PA 19446
Ph: (614)722-3900
E-mail: webadmin@apsna.org
URL: http://www.apsna.org
Contact: Ana Haga, Pres.
Founded: 1992. **Members:** 240. **Membership Dues:** individual, $80 (annual). **Description:** Supports the practice of pediatric surgical nurses through continuing education, networking and mentoring. **Awards:** Founders Award. **Frequency:** annual. **Type:** recognition ● Research and Scholarship Gift Fund. **Type:** scholarship. **Publications:** *Sutureline*, quarterly. Newsletter. **Price:** included in membership dues. **Circulation:** 240. **Advertising:** accepted. Alternate Formats: online. **Conventions/Meetings:** annual meeting, with awards.

15130 ■ American Psychiatric Nurses Association (APNA)
1555 Wilson Blvd., Ste.602
Arlington, VA 22209
Ph: (703)243-2443
Free: (866)243-2443
Fax: (703)243-3390
E-mail: inform@apna.org
URL: http://www.apna.org
Contact: Nick Croce Jr., Exec. Dir.
Founded: 1987. **Members:** 3,900. **Membership Dues:** regular, affiliate, $120 (annual) ● student, retired, $66 (annual) ● international, $126 (annual). **Staff:** 2. **Budget:** $800,000. **State Groups:** 28. **Description:** Provides leadership to advance psychiatric mental health nursing practice, improve mental health care for culturally diverse families, individuals, groups and communities, and shape health policy for the delivery of mental health services. **Computer Services:** Mailing lists, rental. **Publications:** *APNA News*, bimonthly. Newsletter. **Advertising:** accepted ● *Journal of the American Psychiatric Nurses Association*, bimonthly. Journal. **Price:** included in membership dues. **Advertising:** accepted. Alternate Formats: online. **Conventions/Meetings:** annual conference (exhibits) - always October. 2007 Oct. 3-7, Orlando, FL; 2008 Oct. 15-18, Minneapolis, MN.

15131 ■ American Radiological Nurses Association (ARNA)
7794 Grow Dr.
Pensacola, FL 32514
Ph: (850)474-7292
Free: (866)486-2762
Fax: (850)484-8762
E-mail: arna@puetzamc.com
URL: http://www.arna.net
Contact: Ms. Harriet McClung, Account Exec.
Founded: 1981. **Members:** 1,950. **Membership Dues:** active, associate, $95 (annual) ● international, $110 (annual). **National Groups:** 24. **Description:** Represents nurses practicing diagnostic and therapeutic imaging environments. Maintains continuity of quality patient care in imaging environments such as general diagnostic, neurointerventional/cardiovascular, interventional ultrasonography, computerized tomography, nuclear medicine, magnetic resonance, breast health and radiation oncology. **Awards:** Dorothy Budnek Scholarship. **Frequency:** annual. **Type:** scholarship. **Publications:** *Images*, quarterly. Journal. Conveys news related to developments in practice, technology, and research. **Price:** free for members; $15.00/copy for nonmembers; $50.00 /year for nonmembers. ISSN: 1055-1476. **Circulation:** 2,000. **Advertising:** accepted ● *Vision*, quarterly. Newsletter. Conveys news of the association. **Price:**

free for members. **Conventions/Meetings:** annual convention, education and business.

15132 ■ American Society of Ophthalmic Registered Nurses (ASORN)

PO Box 193030
San Francisco, CA 94119-3030
Ph: (415)561-8513
Fax: (415)561-8531
E-mail: asorn@aao.org
URL: http://www.asorn.org
Contact: Lisa Brown, Meeting Mgr.
Founded: 1976. **Members:** 1,100. **Membership Dues:** regular, $85 (annual) ● individual affiliate, $65 (annual) ● retired RN, $50 (annual). **Staff:** 6. **Local Groups:** 27. **Description:** Registered nurses and other ophthalmic medical personnel specializing in the field of ophthalmology. Promotes excellence in ophthalmic nursing for the best and safest care of patients with eye disorders or injuries. Facilitates continuing education through the study, discussion, and exchange of knowledge, experience, and ideas in the field. Represents members' interests before governmental agencies, hospitals, industries, research organizations, technical societies, universities, and other professional associations. Conducts educational programs. **Awards:** ASORN Honor Award. **Frequency:** annual. **Type:** recognition. **Recipient:** for members who have made significant contributions to the society ● ASORN Local Chapter Honor Award. **Frequency:** annual. **Type:** recognition. **Recipient:** for a local chapter that has made significant contributions or service ● Edna Ashy Award. **Frequency:** annual. **Type:** recognition. **Recipient:** for outstanding research in the field by a member of the association ● Manuscript Award. **Frequency:** annual. **Type:** recognition. **Recipient:** for best manuscripts submitted by ASORN members ● Paul C. Haffey/Advanced Educational Scholarships. **Frequency:** annual. **Type:** recognition. **Recipient:** for a member of the association who is currently working on his/her degree ● Research Grant. **Frequency:** annual. **Type:** grant. **Recipient:** for authors of ophthalmic nursing proposal. **Computer Services:** database, mailing labels ● mailing lists, of members. **Additional Websites:** http://webeye.ophth.uiowa.edu/asorn. **Committees:** Education; Nursing Practice; Research. **Publications:** *Insight: The Journal of the American Society of Ophthalmic Registered Nurses,* quarterly. Covers trends in ophthalmology, standards of care, and legislative issues. Includes society news, calendar of events, and chapter news. **Price:** included in membership dues; $26.00/year for students and residents; $53.00 /year for individuals; $93.00 /year for institutions. ISSN: 1060-135X. **Circulation:** 1,800. **Advertising:** accepted ● Ophthalmic Procedures, A Nursing Perspective - Office & Clinic; Ophthalmic Procedures, A Nursing Perspective - Operating Room. Core curriculum for Ophthalmic Nursing; Care & Handling of Ophthalmic Microsurgical Instruments; Standards of Ophthalmic Clinical Nursing Practice. Recommended Practices in Laser Refractive Surgery. **Conventions/Meetings:** annual conference (exhibits) - 2007 Nov. 9-12, New Orleans, LA; 2008 Nov. 7-10, Atlanta, GA.

15133 ■ American Society for Pain Management Nursing (ASPMN)

PO Box 15473
Lenexa, KS 66285-5473
Ph: (913)752-4975
Free: (888)34A-SPMN
Fax: (913)599-5340
E-mail: aspmn@goamp.com
URL: http://www.aspmn.org
Contact: Annabel Edwards APRN, Pres.
Founded: 1990. **Members:** 1,600. **Membership Dues:** active, $95 (annual) ● international, $105 (annual) ● student, $40 (annual) ● corporate, $1,000 (annual) ● associate, $80 (annual). **National Groups:** 26. **Description:** Professional nurses. Dedicated to promoting and providing optimal care to patients with pain. **Awards:** ASPMN Chapter Award. **Frequency:** annual. **Type:** recognition. **Recipient:** to a chapter, in recognition of development and activity for support of pain management nursing ● ASPMN

Nurse Exemplar Award. **Frequency:** annual. **Type:** recognition. **Recipient:** to a nurse with outstanding contribution to the field of pain management nursing ● ASPMN Nurses Distinguished Service Award. **Frequency:** annual. **Type:** recognition. **Recipient:** to a member with outstanding leadership and contribution to the society ● **Frequency:** annual. **Type:** grant. **Recipient:** for research in pain management. **Committees:** Achievement and Recognition; Chapter Development; Clinical Practice; Government Relations; Nominating; Program Planning; Research. **Publications:** *Pain Management Nursing,* quarterly. Journal. Contains original and reviewed articles in pain management. ● *Pathways,* 3/year. Newsletter. Includes news, clinical topics, job opportunities and literature reviews. **Conventions/Meetings:** annual conference (exhibits).

15134 ■ American Society of PeriAnesthesia Nurses (ASPAN)

10 Melrose Ave., Ste.110
Cherry Hill, NJ 08003-3696
Ph: (856)616-9600
Free: (877)737-9696
Fax: (856)616-9601
E-mail: aspan@aspan.org
URL: http://www.aspan.org
Contact: Kevin Dill, CEO
Founded: 1980. **Members:** 10,000. **Membership Dues:** active, $70 (annual) ● retiree, student, $55 (annual) ● international/affiliate, $100 (annual). **Staff:** 9. **Budget:** $1,800,000. **Regional Groups:** 40. **Local Groups:** 100. **National Groups:** 3. **Multinational. Description:** Nurses practicing in all phases of ambulatory surgery, pre-anesthesia and post anesthesia care. Promotes quality and cost-effective care for patients, their families, and the community through public and professional education, research and standards of practice. Offers continuing education programs. **Awards:** Gold Leaf Component of the Year Award. **Frequency:** annual. **Type:** recognition. **Recipient:** for excellence in component leadership ● Star Recognition Award. **Frequency:** annual. **Type:** recognition. **Recipient:** for members who made significant, positive contribution to the association. **Formerly:** (2001) American Society of Post Anesthesia Nurses. **Publications:** *Breathline,* bimonthly. Newsletter. **Advertising:** accepted ● *The Journal of PeriAnesthesia Nursing,* bimonthly ● Also publishes a manual of forms and the Core Curriculum for Post Anesthesia Nursing Practice. **Conventions/Meetings:** annual conference (exhibits) - 2008 May 4-8, Dallas, TX; 2009 Apr. 19-23, Washington, DC.

15135 ■ American Society of Plastic Surgical Nurses (ASPSN)

7794 Grow Dr.
Pensacola, FL 32514
Ph: (850)473-2443
Free: (800)272-0136
Fax: (850)484-8762
E-mail: aspsn@puetzamc.com
URL: http://www.aspsn.org
Contact: Ms. Patricia Barlow, Account Exec.
Founded: 1975. **Members:** 1,700. **Membership Dues:** regular, $125 (annual) ● associate, $80 (annual) ● student, $50 (annual). **Regional Groups:** 5. **State Groups:** 30. **Multinational. Description:** Registered nurses, licensed practical nurses, and licensed vocational nurses working with plastic surgeons or interested in plastic and reconstructive nursing. Objectives are: to enhance leadership qualities of nurses in the field of plastic surgery; to increase the skills, knowledge, and understanding of personnel in plastic surgery nursing through continuing education; to study existing practices and new developments in the field; to encourage participation and interest in professional organizations; to cooperate with others in the profession. **Awards: Frequency:** annual. **Type:** grant. **Affiliated With:** American Society of Plastic Surgeons and Plastic Surgery Education Foundation. **Formerly:** (2001) American Society of Plastic and Reconstructive Surgical Nurses. **Publications:** *ASPS News,* quarterly. Newsletter. **Price:** available to members only. **Advertising:** accepted ● *Core Curriculum for Plastic Surgical Nursing.* Book ● *Plastic*

Surgical Nursing, quarterly. Journal. **Conventions/Meetings:** annual conference (exhibits) - 2007 Oct. 27-31, Baltimore, MD; 2008 Oct. 25-29, Honolulu, HI.

15136 ■ Anthroposophical Nurses Association of America (ANAA)

5909 SE Div. St.
Portland, OR 97206
Ph: (503)235-9067
Fax: (503)234-2367
E-mail: artemisia@anthroposophy.org
URL: http://www.artemisia.net/anaa
Contact: Rise Smythe-Freed, Pres.
Founded: 1985. **Members:** 90. **Membership Dues:** senior, $70 (annual) ● affiliate, associate, $85 (annual) ● general, $100 (annual). **Description:** Seeks to further the practice of anthroposophical nursing in the U.S. (Anthroposophy is a 20th century body of knowledge centering on human development.) Encourages nurses to apply their knowledge of humankind to nursing practices. Promotes members' continued education. **Committees:** Education. **Publications:** Newsletter, annual. **Price:** $12.00. **Circulation:** 400. Alternate Formats: online. **Conventions/Meetings:** annual conference.

15137 ■ Asian American/Pacific Islander Nurses Association (AAPINA)

c/o SeonAe Yeo, PhD, Pres.
Univ. of Michigan
School of Nursing
Div. of Hea. Promotion and Risk Reduction
400 N Ingalls St., Ste.3160
Ann Arbor, MI 48109-0482
E-mail: info@aapina.org
URL: http://www.aapina.org
Contact: SeonAe Yeo PhD, Pres.
Founded: 1991. **Membership Dues:** full, $50 ● student, $25. **Multinational. Description:** Seeks to identify and support the health care needs of Asian Pacific Islanders (API) in the United States and globally. Implements strategies to act on issues, registration and public policies affecting the health of APIs. Collaborates with other interdisciplinary health and professional organizations. **Telecommunication Services:** electronic mail, syeo@aapina.org. **Publications:** Newsletter, 3/year. **Price:** included in membership dues.

15138 ■ Association of Camp Nurses (ACN)

8630 Thorsonveien NE
Bemidji, MN 56601
Ph: (218)586-2633
E-mail: acn@campnurse.org
URL: http://www.campnurse.org
Contact: Linda Ebner Erceg RN, Exec. Dir.
Founded: 1990. **Members:** 500. **Membership Dues:** regular, $50 (annual). **Staff:** 1. **Budget:** $30,000. **Regional Groups:** 9. **National Groups:** 2. **Multinational. Description:** Works to promote and develop the nursing practice in the camp community. Maintains resource center; provides consulting services; supports camp nursing research; conducts educational programs. **Libraries: Type:** reference; not open to the public. **Holdings:** archival material, audiovisuals, books, business records, clippings, periodicals. **Subjects:** camp nursing. **Awards:** Jean Otto Award. **Frequency:** periodic. **Type:** recognition. **Recipient:** for extraordinary contribution to camp nursing practice. **Computer Services:** database ● mailing lists. **Additional Websites:** http://www.acn.org. **Publications:** *Compass Point,* quarterly. Newsletter. **Price:** included in membership dues; $50.00 for nonmembers. **Circulation:** 500. **Conventions/Meetings:** annual Camp Nurse Symposium (exhibits) ● annual conference.

15139 ■ Association of Child Neurology Nurses (ACNN)

c/o Rita Brockway
Arkansas Children's Hosp.
Div. of Neurology
800 Marshall St.
Little Rock, AR 72202-3591

E-mail: cathy5114@aol.com
URL: http://www.acnn.org
Contact: Cathy Asher, Contact
Membership Dues: general, $75 (annual). **Multinational. Description:** Represents nurses and allied health personnel caring for children with neurological conditions. Improves the quality of life of children with neurological problems and their families. Promotes nursing research, education and professional growth of members.

15140 ■ Association of Community Health Nursing Educators (ACHNE)
10200 W 44th Ave., No. 304
Wheat Ridge, CO 80033
Ph: (303)422-0769
Fax: (303)422-8894
E-mail: achne@resourcecenter.com
URL: http://www.achne.org
Contact: Derryl Block MPH, Pres.
Founded: 1978. **Members:** 350. **Membership Dues:** active, contributing, $90 ● student, full-time, $45 ● student, part-time, $65 ● affiliate, $450 ● retired, $25. **Staff:** 90. **Regional Groups:** 5. **Description:** Nurses and graduate students. Committed to "excellence in community and public health nursing education, research, and practice". **Publications:** ACHNE Accents, quarterly. Newsletter. **Price:** included in membership dues. Alternate Formats: online. **Conventions/Meetings:** annual Spring Institute and Research - conference (exhibits).

15141 ■ Association of Pediatric Hematology/Oncology Nurses (APHON)
4700 W Lake Ave.
Glenview, IL 60025
Ph: (847)375-4724
Fax: (877)734-8755
E-mail: info@aphon.org
URL: http://www.aphon.org
Contact: Ms. Louise Miller, Exec. Dir.
Founded: 1973. **Members:** 2,500. **Membership Dues:** active outside U.S., $118 (annual) ● graduate nursing student in U.S., $78 (annual) ● active in U.S., graduate nursing student outside U.S., $98 (annual) ● associate in U.S., $88 (annual) ● associate outside U.S., $108 (annual) ● nursing student (NSNA members only), $25 (annual). **Regional Groups:** 42. **Description:** Represents pediatric hematology/oncology nurses and other pediatric hematology/oncology healthcare professionals. Provides expert practice in pediatric hematology/oncology nursing to its members and the public at large. Promotes optimal nursing care for children, adolescents, and young adults with cancer and blood disorders, and their families. Provides leadership and expertise to pediatric hematology/oncology nurses by defining and promoting the highest standards of practice and care to the pediatric, adolescent, and young adult communities. **Awards:** APHON Distinguished Researcher Award. **Frequency:** annual. **Type:** recognition. **Recipient:** for member investigators who have built a strong record of independent initiated research ● APHON Local Chapter Community Service Award. **Frequency:** annual. **Type:** recognition. **Recipient:** for a local chapter that has made a significant contribution to the community ● APHON Local Chapter Excellence Award. **Frequency:** annual. **Type:** recognition. **Recipient:** for a local chapter that has excelled in promoting the mission, vision and goals of APHON ● APHON Novice Researcher Award. **Frequency:** annual. **Type:** recognition ● Casey Hooke Distinguished Service Award. **Frequency:** annual. **Type:** monetary. **Recipient:** for a member who has demonstrated excellence in service to and leadership of APHON ● Dr. Patricia Greene Leadership Award. **Frequency:** annual. **Type:** monetary. **Recipient:** for a registered professional nurse who has demonstrated exemplary service through leadership to the APHON in a particular year ● Jean Fergusson Excellence in Pediatric Hematology/Oncology Nursing Education Award. **Frequency:** annual. **Type:** monetary. **Recipient:** to a registered professional nurse (must be an APHON member) ● Jean Fergusson Excellence in Pediatric Hematology/Oncology Nursing Practice Award. **Frequency:** annual. **Type:** monetary. **Recipi-**

ent: to a registered professional nurse (must be an APHON member) ● Patient/Family Education Materials Award. **Frequency:** annual. **Type:** monetary. **Recipient:** to a registered professional nurse (must be an APHON member). **Computer Services:** Mailing lists, of members (not for rent). **Committees:** Conference; Education Provider; Journal; Local Chapter; Newsletter; Nominations; Program; Steering. **Formerly:** (2006) Association of Pediatric Oncology Nurses. **Publications:** APHON Counts, quarterly. Newsletter. **Price:** included in membership dues. **Advertising:** accepted ● Journal of Pediatric Oncology Nursing, bimonthly. **Price:** included in membership dues. **Advertising:** accepted. Also Cited As: JOPON. **Conventions/Meetings:** annual conference (exhibits).

15142 ■ Association of PeriOperative Registered Nurses (AORN)
2170 S Parker Rd., Ste.300
Denver, CO 80231-5711
Ph: (303)755-6304
Free: (800)755-2676
Fax: (303)755-4511
E-mail: custsvc@aorn.org
URL: http://www.aorn.org
Contact: Mary Jo W. Steiert RN, Pres.
Founded: 1949. **Members:** 41,000. **Membership Dues:** standard, associate (non-RN), $100 (annual) ● student, $20 (annual) ● retired, $40 (annual). **Staff:** 100. **Budget:** $10,000,000. **Local Groups:** 350. **Multinational. Description:** Professional perioperative (operating room) nurses. Provides education, representation, and standards for quality patient care. **Libraries: Type:** reference. **Holdings:** articles, books, periodicals. **Subjects:** OR nursing, surgery, nursing management. **Awards:** Award for Excellence in Perioperative Nursing. **Frequency:** annual. **Type:** recognition. **Recipient:** for a current member whose work and accomplishment must have had global implications on perioperative nursing ● Next Generation Achievement Award. **Frequency:** annual. **Type:** recognition. **Recipient:** for a current member who has demonstrated outstanding contributions to perioperative nursing that will have impact on the future of AORN ● Outstanding Achievement in Mentorship. **Frequency:** annual. **Type:** recognition. **Recipient:** for a current member who has demonstrated outstanding achievement in mentorship ● Outstanding Achievement in Perioperative Clinical Nursing Education Award. **Frequency:** annual. **Type:** recognition. **Recipient:** for a current member who has demonstrated outstanding achievement in perioperative academic nursing education ● Outstanding Achievement in Perioperative Clinical Nursing Practice. **Frequency:** annual. **Type:** recognition. **Recipient:** for a current member who has demonstrated outstanding achievement in perioperative clinical nursing practice ● Outstanding Achievement in Perioperative Nursing Management Award. **Frequency:** annual. **Type:** recognition. **Recipient:** for a current member who has demonstrated outstanding achievement in perioperative nursing management ● Outstanding Achievement in Perioperative Nursing Research Award. **Frequency:** annual. **Type:** recognition. **Recipient:** for a current member who has demonstrated outstanding achievement in perioperative nursing research ● Outstanding Achievement in Perioperative Patient Education. **Frequency:** annual. **Type:** recognition. **Recipient:** for a current member who has demonstrated outstanding achievement in perioperative patient education. **Computer Services:** Mailing lists, of members. **Boards:** Editorial; Scholarship. **Commissions:** Patient Safety. **Committees:** Awards; Continuing Education Approval; Legislation; Nursing Practices; Professional Standards; Recommended Practices; Research. **Sections:** Advanced Technology: Lasers and MIS; Ambulatory Surgery; Business, Industry, Consulting; Cardiothoracic; Informatics; Management Leadership; Nurse Educator/Clinical Nurse Specialist; Orthopedic; Pediatric; RN First Assistant; Rural/Small Hospital. **Subgroups:** Neurosurgery. **Formerly:** (1999) Association of Operating Room Nurses. **Publications:** AORN Journal, monthly. Includes film and book reviews, educational opportunities, employment listings, and legislation.

Price: included in membership dues; $95.00 /year for nonmembers in U.S. ISSN: 0001-2092. **Circulation:** 46,000. **Advertising:** accepted. Alternate Formats: microform ● Surgical Services Management, bimonthly. Contains information about trends in management and the surgical environment, changing policies and regulations, clinical practice, and other issues. ISSN: 1079-8269. **Advertising:** accepted. **Conventions/Meetings:** annual congress and conference (exhibits).

15143 ■ Association of Rehabilitation Nurses (ARN)
4700 W Lake Ave.
Glenview, IL 60025-1485
Ph: (847)375-4710
Free: (800)229-7530
Fax: (877)734-9384
E-mail: info@rehabnurse.org
URL: http://www.rehabnurse.org
Contact: Terrie Sue Patterson MSN, Pres.
Founded: 1974. **Members:** 5,600. **Membership Dues:** voting and non-voting, $110 (annual) ● corporate and facility, $2,000 (annual). **Staff:** 9. **Budget:** $2,500,000. **Local Groups:** 63. **Description:** Registered nurses concerned with or actively engaged in the practice of rehabilitation nursing; others interested in rehabilitation. Works to advance the quality of rehabilitation nursing practice through educational opportunities and to facilitate the exchange of ideas. Committees involve members in issues of organizational, local, and national importance and provide an avenue to effect change. Has formed the Rehabilitation Nursing Foundation to promote, develop, and engage in scientific research in the rehabilitation field. **Awards:** Mary Ann Mikulic Scholarship. **Frequency:** annual. **Type:** scholarship. **Recipient:** for currently practicing registered nurses ● RNF Research Grant. **Frequency:** annual. **Type:** grant. **Recipient:** for nurses. **Computer Services:** database, mailing labels ● mailing lists, of members. **Committees:** Awards; Health Policy; Research. **Programs:** Certified Rehabilitation Registered Nurse; Continuing Education Approval and Provider. **Affiliated With:** American Nurses Association; Continuing Care Accreditation Commission. **Publications:** ARN Network, bimonthly. Newsletter. Informs members on the latest professional and organizational news. **Advertising:** accepted ● Make a Difference. Brochure. Contains information on the practice of rehabilitation nursing. **Price:** $10.00/packet of 25 ● Rehabilitation Nursing, bimonthly. Journal. Provides up-to-date information on nursing topics. **Price:** free for members; $105.00 /year for individuals; $160.00 /year for institutions. ISSN: 0278-4807. **Circulation:** 10,300. **Advertising:** accepted. Alternate Formats: microform. **Conventions/Meetings:** annual Succeeding in the Complex World of Rehab - conference (exhibits).

15144 ■ Association of Women's Health, Obstetric and Neonatal Nurses (AWHONN)
2000 L St. NW, Ste.740
Washington, DC 20036
Ph: (202)261-2400
Free: (800)673-8499
Fax: (202)728-0575
E-mail: customerservice@awhonn.org
URL: http://www.awhonn.org
Contact: Karen Tucker Thomas CAE, Exec. Dir.
Founded: 1969. **Members:** 22,000. **Membership Dues:** full, $149 (annual) ● student, retired, disabled, $75 (annual) ● associate, $132 (annual) ● international, $173 (annual). **Staff:** 48. **Budget:** $8,000,000. **State Groups:** 52. **Local Groups:** 165. **Languages:** English, French. **Multinational. Description:** Members are registered nurses and other health care providers who specialize in obstetric, women's health, and neonatal nursing. Promotes and establishes the highest standards of women's health, obstetric and neonatal nursing practice, education, and research; advocates for nursing, women's needs and newborn health issues at federal and state levels; sponsors educational meetings, audiovisual programs, and continuing education courses; publishes journals, magazines, books, and other nursing and consumer-related publications. **Libraries: Type:** by appoint-

ment only; lending; reference. **Holdings:** 2,000. **Subjects:** women's health, perinatal nursing, newborn nursing, pregnancy and health. **Computer Services:** Mailing lists, available for rental ● online services, information on education and clinical practice; membership and industry programs. **Formerly:** (1993) Nurses Association of the American College of Obstetricians and Gynecologists. **Publications:** *AWHONN Lifelines*, bimonthly. Magazine. Includes reports on health care trends, current practice issues, annual index, calendar of events, employment listings, and legislation. **Price:** included in membership dues; $85.00 /year for individuals (the Americas); EUR 71.00 /year for individuals (Europe); 47.00 /year for individuals (rest of the world). ISSN: 1091-5923. **Circulation:** 24,000. **Advertising:** accepted ● *Every Woman*, annual. Magazine. Contains current health information for women of all ages and ethnic origin. **Price:** free to site distributors (min. 500 copies). **Circulation:** 1,000,000. **Advertising:** accepted ● *Journal of Obstetric, Gynecologic, and Neonatal Nursing*, bimonthly. Contains research and evidence-based articles. **Price:** $92.00 /year for individuals (the Americas); EUR 77.00 /year for individuals (Europe); 51.00 /year for individuals (rest of the world). ISSN: 0884-2175. **Circulation:** 30,000. **Advertising:** accepted. Alternate Formats: online. Also Cited As: *JOGNN* ● Also publishes evidence-based clinical practice guidelines, practice standards, monographs and other educational resources.

15145 ■ Baromedical Nurses Association (BNA)
PO Box 531190
San Diego, CA 92153
Ph: (303)918-9686
Fax: (619)651-7543
E-mail: kathyfurnas611@msn.com
URL: http://www.hyperbaricnurses.org
Contact: Justin Everts, Pres.

Founded: 1985. **Members:** 160. **Membership Dues:** full, $50 (annual) ● affiliate, $25 (annual). **Staff:** 1. **Regional Groups:** 6. **Description:** Registered nurses practicing baromedicine (hyperbaric medicine), involved in research related to baromedical nursing, completing basic orientation in baromedicine, or contributing to literature on baromedicine or baromedical nursing. Defines, develops, and promotes the status and standards of baromedical nursing. Facilitates professional activities and continuing education programs. Provides a forum for the exchange of ideas, information, and support; maintains speakers' bureau. **Libraries: Type:** not open to the public. **Subjects:** hyperbaric medicine, hyperbaric nursing. **Awards:** Diane Norkool Award. **Frequency:** annual. **Type:** recognition. **Recipient:** for excellence in baromedical nursing. **Computer Services:** Mailing lists. **Publications:** *BNA Update*, quarterly. Newsletter. Includes research findings, safety and educational information, and upcoming events. **Price:** free, for members only. **Circulation:** 200. **Advertising:** accepted ● Membership Directory, periodic. **Conventions/Meetings:** annual conference (exhibits).

15146 ■ Certifying Board of Gastroenterology Nurses and Associates (CBGNA)
401 N Michigan Ave.
Chicago, IL 60611-4267
Free: (800)245-SGNA
Fax: (312)673-6723
E-mail: info@cbgna.org
URL: http://www.cbgna.org
Contact: Nancy Eisemon RN, Pres.

Founded: 1986. **Description:** Maintains and improves the knowledge, understanding and skill of nurses in the fields of gastroenterology and gastroenterology endoscopy; administers certification program. **Awards:** Certification Scholarship. **Frequency:** annual. **Type:** scholarship. **Recipient:** to an individual who is currently employed in gastroenterology ● Recertification Scholarship. **Frequency:** annual. **Type:** scholarship. **Recipient:** to an individual who is currently employed in gastroenterology. **Committees:** Awards/Scholarship; Education; Grievance; Item Writers; Market and Communications; Nominations;

Recertification and GI Specific CEU. **Publications:** *Certification Handbook*. Alternate Formats: online ● *Recertification Handbook*. Alternate Formats: online.

15147 ■ Commission on Graduates of Foreign Nursing Schools (CGFNS)
3600 Market St., Ste.400
Philadelphia, PA 19104
Ph: (215)222-8454
Fax: (215)662-0425
E-mail: bnichols@cgfns.org
URL: http://www.cgfns.org
Contact: Barbara L. Nichols RN, CEO

Founded: 1977. **Staff:** 101. **Description:** Established to help ensure safe nursing and other health care for the American public while assisting health care professionals educated outside the United States in assessing their ability to become licensed, as well as to practice, in the U.S. Offers a certification program with credentials review and exam of nursing knowledge and English-language proficiency for foreign-educated registered nurses. Administers the Visascreen: Visa credentials assessment through its division, the International Commission on Healthcare Professions, which meets federal requirements for a screening and assessment service for foreign-born healthcare professionals seeking certain occupational visas in the U.S. Provides the CGFNS Credentials Evaluation Service which can evaluate any health care professional's academic records and registration/licensure in terms of U.S. comparability. Conducts studies and surveys; participates in policy discussions concerning international nursing education, licensure, and practice. **Libraries: Type:** reference; not open to the public. **Holdings:** 1,200; archival material, articles, books, periodicals. **Subjects:** international nursing education and licensure, secondary education. **Subgroups:** LPN Standards; Medical Technologists Standards; Occupational Therapists Standards; Physical Therapists Standards; Research and Evaluation; Speech Language Standards; Strategic Planning. **Affiliated With:** American Nurses Association; National League for Nursing. **Publications:** *An Assessment of North American Nursing* (in English, French, and Spanish). Book ● *Characteristics of Foreign Nurse Graduates in the U.S. Workforce 2000-2001*. **Price:** $20.00 ● *How to Study: Preparing for the CGFNS Qualifying Exam and the NCLEX-RN Examination*. Book. **Price:** $12.00 ● *How To Take Tests: Strategies for the CGFNS Qualifying Exam and The NCLEX-RN Examination*. Book. **Price:** $20.00 ● *Official Study Guide for the CGFNS Qualifying Exam, 5th Edition*. Book. **Price:** $45.00 ● *Practice English Audio Tape and Booklet - Series 1*. Includes audiotape. **Price:** $16.00 ● *Practice English Audio Tape and Booklet - Series 2*. Includes audiotape. **Price:** $16.00 ● *Western Regional Directory of U.S. Hospitals, Nursing Licensure Agencies and INS Offices*. Book. **Price:** $13.00.

15148 ■ Consortium of Behavioral Health Nurses and Associates (CBHNA)
PMB 1214
1733 H St., Ste.330
Blaine, WA 98230
Ph: (360)332-9105
Free: (800)876-2236
Fax: (360)332-2280
E-mail: cbhna@aol.com
Contact: Randy Bryson, Exec. Dir.

Founded: 1987. **Members:** 1,000. **Membership Dues:** individual, $75 (annual). **Regional Groups:** 21. **State Groups:** 21. **Description:** Professional nurses specializing in behavioral health with focus on chemical dependency. Aims are: to increase the effectiveness of nursing services for behavioral health; to establish a professional standard in chemical dependency nursing through a system of competency-based testing and programs of professional development and certification. Seeks to increase public awareness of the need for chemical dependency treatment and nurses specializing in this field. Encourages the growth of knowledge, skills, and competency in chemical dependency nursing. Offers certification exam for nurses with 4000 hours experience in the previous 5 years and 30 hours of

chemical dependency coursework; conducts educational programs. Maintains Speaker's Bureau. **Computer Services:** Mailing lists. **Formerly:** (2003) National Consortium of Chemical Dependency Nurses. **Publications:** *CD Nurse Briefing*, quarterly. Newsletter. Covers issues of interest of NCCDN membership. **Price:** available to members only. **Circulation:** 2,000. **Advertising:** accepted ● Pamphlets. **Conventions/Meetings:** annual CD Nurse Conference - meeting (exhibits).

15149 ■ Council on Certification of Nurse Anesthetists (CCNA)
222 S Prospect Ave.
Park Ridge, IL 60068
Ph: (847)692-7050
Fax: (847)692-7082
E-mail: certification@aana.com
URL: http://www.aana.com
Contact: Linda Vitek, Dir., Certification

Founded: 1975. **Members:** 11. **Staff:** 3. **Description:** Sets certification standards and policies; confers certification upon entry-level nurse anesthetists. Conducts research. Works within the framework of the American Association of Nurse Anesthetists. **Affiliated With:** American Association of Nurse Anesthetists. **Supersedes:** Exam Committee, American Association of Nurse Anesthetists. **Conventions/Meetings:** semiannual meeting.

15150 ■ Dermatology Nurses' Association (DNA)
E Holly Ave.
PO Box 56
Pitman, NJ 08071-0056
Ph: (856)256-2330
Free: (800)454-4362
Fax: (856)589-7463
E-mail: dna@ajj.com
URL: http://www.dnanurse.org
Contact: Cynthia Hnatiuk, Exec. Dir.

Founded: 1982. **Members:** 3,100. **Membership Dues:** nurse, $60 (annual) ● associate, $50 (annual). **Staff:** 4. **Description:** Addresses professional issues involving dermatology nurses; develops high standards of dermatological nursing care; facilitates communication and interdisciplinary cooperation among members. Conducts educational meetings. **Commissions:** Web Site. **Committees:** Annual Program; Awards; Bylaws and Policies; Education; Legislative; Nominating; Public Relations; Resource Center. **Publications:** *Dermatology Nursing Journal*, bimonthly. Features state-of-the-art, peer-reviewed articles on all aspects of skin and wound care. **Price:** $38.00 /year for individuals in U.S.; $52.00 /year for institutions in U.S.; $56.00 /year for individuals outside U.S.; $70.00 /year for institutions outside U.S. ● Newsletter, bimonthly. **Conventions/Meetings:** annual convention (exhibits).

15151 ■ Developmental Disabilities Nurses Association (DDNA)
PMB 1214
1733 H St., Ste.330
Blaine, WA 98230-5107
Free: (800)888-6733
Fax: (360)332-2280
E-mail: ddnahq@aol.com
URL: http://www.ddna.org
Contact: Randy Bryson RN, Exec. Dir.

Founded: 1992. **Members:** 1,100. **Membership Dues:** active, $65 (annual). **Staff:** 2. **Regional Groups:** 35. **State Groups:** 35. **Description:** Works to serve individuals with developmental disabilities, as well as having a certification program for RN's, and a developing program for LPN/LVN's. **Awards:** Mary Gage Award. **Frequency:** annual. **Type:** recognition. **Publications:** *DDNA News Network*, quarterly. Newsletter. Contains information on the activities of the association and its members. Includes report from the president and news from regional networks. **Conventions/Meetings:** annual conference.

15152 ■ Federation for Accessible Nursing Education and Licensure (FANEL)

PO Box 1418
Lewisburg, WV 24901
Ph: (304)645-4357
Fax: (304)645-4357
E-mail: nurse@fanel.org
URL: http://www.fanel.org
Contact: Twyla Wallace, Pres.
Founded: 1983. **Membership Dues:** individual associate, $15 (annual) ● individual regular, $25 (annual) ● individual sustaining, $50 (annual) ● organizational associate, $175 (annual) ● organizational regular, $400 (annual). **Description:** Registered nurses, licensed practical nurses, educators, health organizations, schools, and hospital administrators seeking to maintain licensure through current educational programs for RNs and LPNs. **Publications:** Brochures ● Newsletter, biennial. **Conventions/Meetings:** semiannual board meeting - always February and October.

15153 ■ Frontier Nursing Service (FNS)

132 FNS Dr.
Wendover, KY 41775
Ph: (606)672-2317
Fax: (606)672-3022
E-mail: fnstour@yahoo.com
URL: http://www.frontiernursing.org
Contact: Jane Leigh Powell, Chair
Founded: 1925. **Members:** 15. **Staff:** 350. **Description:** Provides health care to persons in approximately 1,000 square miles of eastern Kentucky using a 40-bed hospital, two primary care centers, three rural health clinics, and a home health agency. Operates Frontier School of Midwifery and Family Nursing. Provides social and ancillary services; conducts research on health services; compiles statistics; offers educational programs. Maintains a hall of fame and museum. **Libraries: Type:** reference. **Holdings:** 2,000; periodicals. **Subjects:** FNS general information. **Awards: Type:** scholarship. **Recipient:** for nurses in higher education. **Publications:** *Quarterly Bulletin.* **Price:** $5.00 for individuals; $10.00 for institutions. **Circulation:** 8,500 ● Brochure, annual. For Christmas appeal. **Circulation:** 10,000. **Conventions/Meetings:** quarterly Board of Governors Meeting - general assembly.

15154 ■ Helene Fuld Health Trust

HSBC Bank USA
452 Fifth Ave., 17th Fl.
New York, NY 10018-2706
Ph: (212)525-2418
Fax: (212)525-2395
E-mail: marianne.caskran@hsbcpb.com
URL: http://www.fuld.org
Contact: Ms. Marianne Caskran, Grants Admin.
Founded: 1965. **Description:** Strives to support the improvement of the health, welfare, and education of student nurses. **Awards: Type:** grant.

15155 ■ Home Healthcare Nurses Association (HHNA)

PO Box 91486
Washington, DC 20090
Ph: (202)547-7424
Free: (800)558-4462
Fax: (202)547-3660
E-mail: hhna_info@nahc.org
URL: http://www.hhna.org
Contact: Margaret J. Cushan, Exec. Dir.
Founded: 1999. **Members:** 800. **Membership Dues:** individual, $100 (annual) ● student, $45 (annual). **Staff:** 1. **Local Groups:** 10. **Description:** Works to develop and promote the specialty of home healthcare nursing. Provides a forum for members to exchange information; influences public policy affecting the practice; fosters excellence in practice. **Computer Services:** database ● mailing lists. **Telecommunication Services:** electronic bulletin board. **Special Interest Groups:** Cardiac; Diabetes; Education; Psychiatric-Mental Health; Telehealth. **Affiliated With:** National Association for Home Care and Hospice. **Publications:** *Home Healthcare Nurse*, 10/year. Journal. Contains clinical, operational and educational home care nursing issues. **Price:** included in membership dues; $45.00 /year for nonmembers. **Circulation:** 13,000. **Advertising:** accepted. **Conventions/Meetings:** semiannual convention (exhibits) ● annual Psych-Mental Health Conference (exhibits).

15156 ■ Hospice and Palliative Nurses Association (HPNA)

One Penn Ctr. W, Ste.229
Pittsburgh, PA 15276
Ph: (412)787-9301
Fax: (412)787-9305
E-mail: hpna@hpna.org
URL: http://www.hpna.org
Contact: Judy Lentz, CEO
Founded: 1987. **Members:** 5,000. **Membership Dues:** associate, $85 (annual) ● LP/VN, $70 (annual) ● nursing student, senior, $45 (annual) ● RN, $85 (annual) ● nursing assistant, $35 (annual). **Staff:** 8. **Budget:** $600,000. **Regional Groups:** 10. **Description:** Registered nurses engaged in end of life care in all settings. Promotes excellence in the specialties of hospice and palliative nursing. Conducts education and research programs. Has the only certification boards in hospice and palliative nursing. **Awards:** CHPN of the Year. **Frequency:** annual. **Type:** recognition ● Yearly Innovation in End-of-Life Care. **Frequency:** annual. **Type:** recognition. **Computer Services:** Mailing lists ● online services, membership directory. **Formerly:** (1998) Hospice Nurses Association. **Publications:** *Core Curriculum for the Hospice and Palliative Nursing Assistant.* **Price:** $35.00 for members; $45.00 for nonmembers ● *Journal of Hospice and Palliative Nursing*, quarterly. **Price:** $50.00. **Circulation:** 5,000. **Advertising:** accepted. **Alternate Formats:** online. Also Cited As: *JHPN* ● *Study Guide for the Generalist Hospice & Palliative Nurse.* **Price:** $35.00 for members; $55.00 for nonmembers ● Newsletter. **Price:** included in membership dues. Alternate Formats: online. **Conventions/Meetings:** annual assembly.

15157 ■ International Association of Forensic Nurses (IAFN)

1517 Ritchie Hwy., Ste.208
Arnold, MD 21012
Ph: (410)626-7805
Fax: (410)626-7804
E-mail: info@iafn.org
URL: http://www.iafn.org
Contact: Ms. Carey Goryl, Exec.Dir.
Founded: 1992. **Members:** 2,500. **Membership Dues:** student, $65 (annual) ● individual, $115 (annual) ● associate, $95 (annual) ● life, $1,400. **Staff:** 7. **Budget:** $125,000. **State Groups:** 15. **Description:** Represents registered nurses working in the medico-legal arena. Aims to develop, promote, and disseminate information about the science of forensic nursing internationally. Works with other nursing organizations to set standards of practice and strives to foster growth and development of forensic nursing as an emerging area of nursing expertise. Promotes the exchange of ideas and the transmission of developing knowledge among its members and with other interested professionals. **Awards: Frequency:** annual. **Type:** recognition. **Computer Services:** database ● mailing lists. **Councils:** Clinical Forensic Specialists; Death Investigation; Forensic Psychiatric/Correctional Nurses; Interpersonal Violence Specialists; Legal Nurse Consultants; Research; Sexual Assaults Nurse Examiners. **Publications:** *Journal of Forensic Nursing*, quarterly. **Price:** included in membership dues ● *On the Edge*, quarterly. Newsletter. **Price:** included in membership dues. **Advertising:** accepted. **Conventions/Meetings:** annual Scientific Assembly - conference (exhibits).

15158 ■ International Nurses Society on Addictions (IntNSA)

2170 S Parker Rd., Ste.229
Denver, CO 80231
Ph: (484)318-6739
E-mail: info@intnsa.org
URL: http://www.intnsa.org
Contact: Jim Scarborough, Exec. Dir.
Founded: 1975. **Members:** 600. **Membership Dues:** regular, $120 (annual) ● student, $75 (annual) ● international full, $140 (annual) ● retired, $90 (annual) ● associate, individual, $100 (annual) ● corporate, $1,000 (annual). **Staff:** 4. **Regional Groups:** 10. **Multinational. Description:** Promotes quality-nursing care for persons addicted to alcohol and other drugs, and their families. Fosters continuing education and development of skills among nurses involved in the field; works to enhance the professional image of addictions nurses. Participates in public policy and social issues related to alcohol or chemical abuse. Serves as liaison between members and professional groups with common goals. Represents members' interests before national organizations. Regional groups sponsor workshops. Provides certification program. **Awards: Frequency:** periodic. **Type:** grant. **Committees:** Education; International; Legislative; Marketing; Peer Assistance. **Programs:** Mentor. **Absorbed:** (1999) Consolidated Association of Nurses in Substance Abuse International. **Formerly:** (1983) National Nurses Society on Alcoholism; (2001) National Nurses Society on Addictions. **Publications:** *The Care of Clients with Addictions: Dimensions of Nursing Practice and Standards of Addictions.* Book ● *CARN Study Guide.* Book ● *The Core Curriculum of Addictions Nursing.* Book ● *IntNSA Position Papers* ● *Journal of Addiction Nursing*, quarterly ● *NNSA Today*, quarterly. Newsletter. Includes articles on clinical and research areas of addictions field. **Price:** available to members only. **Circulation:** 1,200. **Advertising:** accepted ● *Nursing Care Planning with the Addicted Client.* Book ● *Nursing Practice with Selected Diagnoses and Criteria.* Book ● Monographs. **Conventions/Meetings:** annual Educational Conference (exhibits).

15159 ■ International Nursing Association for Clinical Simulation and Learning (INACSL)

c/o Dr. Christine Hooper, VP of Finance
San Jose State Univ. - School of Nursing
One Washington Sq.
San Jose, CA 95192-0057
E-mail: spunt@son.umaryland.edu
URL: http://www.inacsl.org
Contact: Debbie Spunt, Co-Founding Pres.
Membership Dues: individual, $75 (annual) ● international, $80 (annual) ● life, $750. **Multinational. Description:** Promotes the development and advancement of clinical simulation and learning resource centers. **Committees:** Communications. **Task Forces:** On-Line Journal. **Publications:** Journal. Alternate Formats: online.

15160 ■ International Organization of Multiple Sclerosis Nurses (IOMSN)

PO Box 450
Teaneck, NJ 07666
Ph: (201)837-0727
Fax: (201)837-9414
E-mail: info@iomsn.org
URL: http://www.iomsn.org
Contact: June Halper MSN, Exec. Dir.
Membership Dues: active, junior, affiliate, $35 (annual). **Languages:** English, French, Italian, Spanish. **Multinational. Description:** Seeks to improve the lives of people diagnosed with multiple sclerosis through the provision of appropriate healthcare services. Facilitates the development of a specialized branch of nursing in multiple sclerosis. Aims to establish standards of nursing care in multiple sclerosis. Supports research on multiple sclerosis nursing. Raises awareness of the disease by educating the healthcare community and the general public. **Awards:** June Halper Award for Excellence in Nursing. **Frequency:** annual. **Type:** recognition. **Recipient:** for leadership and creativity in the care of people with multiple sclerosis and their families. **Publications:** *IOMSN Update*, quarterly. Journal. Alternate Formats: online ● Membership Directory. **Price:** included in membership dues. Alternate Formats: online ● Monographs. Alternate Formats: online.

15161 ■ International Society of Psychiatric-Mental Health Nurses (ISPN)

2810 Crossroads Dr., Ste.3800
Madison, WI 53718
Ph: (608)443-2463
Free: (866)330-7227

Fax: (608)443-2474
E-mail: info@ispn-psych.org
URL: http://www.ispn-psych.org
Contact: Geraldine S. Pearson PhD, Pres.-Elect
Founded: 1999. **Members:** 900. **Membership Dues:**
full (primary division), $143 (annual) ● student, retired
(primary division), $75 (annual) ● full (secondary divi-
sion), $68 (annual) ● student, retired (secondary divi-
sion), $37 (annual). **Staff:** 6. **Local Groups:** 25.
Multinational. Description: Psychiatric and mental
health nurses. Seeks to advance the study, teaching,
and practice of psychiatric and mental health nursing.
Represents members' professional and economic
interests. **Awards:** Robert O. Gilbert Foundation
Research Award. **Frequency:** annual. **Type:** monetary. **Computer Services:** Mailing lists. **Telecommunication Services:** electronic mail, pearsong@
psychiatry.uchc.edu. **Councils:** Education; Legislative; Practice; Research. **Divisions:** Adult and
Geropsychiatric-Mental Health Nurses; Association of
Child and Adolescent Psychiatric Nurses; International Society of Psychiatric Consultation Liaison
Nurses; Society of Education and Research in
Psychiatric-Mental Health Nursing. **Formerly:** (1992)
Advocates for Child Psychiatric Nursing; (1999) Association of Child and Adolescent Psychiatric Nurses.
Publications: *Archives of Psychiatric Nursing*,
quarterly. Journal. **Price:** $43.00 /year for nonmem-
bers; included in membership dues. **Advertising:** accepted ● *ISPN Connections*, 3/year. Newsletter.
Price: included in membership dues; $20.00 for
nonmembers. **Circulation:** 900. **Advertising:** accepted. Alternate Formats: online ● *Journal of Child
and Adolescent Psychiatric Nursing*, quarterly. **Price:**
included in membership dues; $43.00 for nonmem-
bers. **Advertising:** accepted. Alternate Formats:
microform ● *Perspectives in Psychiatric Care*. Journal
● Membership Directory. **Conventions/Meetings:**
annual conference (exhibits) - usually April.

**15162 ■ International Transplant Nurses
Society (ITNS)**
PO Box 351
1739 E Carson St.
Pittsburgh, PA 15203-0351
Ph: (412)343-4867
Fax: (412)343-3959
E-mail: itns@msn.com
URL: http://www.itns.org
Contact: Beth Kassalen MBA, Exec. Dir.
Founded: 1992. **Members:** 950. **Membership Dues:**
active, $75 (annual) ● associate, $50 (annual). **Staff:**
2. **Budget:** $150,000. **Regional Groups:** 16. **Local
Groups:** 17. **Description:** Nurses, LVNs, LPNs, and
others involved in patient care for organ transplanta-
tion. Works to encourage cooperation among all
medical disciplines involved in transplantation, dis-
seminate information, and establish certification for
this nursing specialty. **Awards:** Nursing Research
Grants. **Frequency:** annual. **Type:** grant. **Recipient:**
for grant proposal. **Computer Services:** Mailing lists,
website, job postings - transplant ● online services.
Committees: Nominating; Symposium. **Programs:**
Transplant Nurse Mentoring. **Special Interest
Groups:** Abstract Reviewer; Certification; Research.
Publications: *Heart Transplant Patient Education
Booklet*. Alternate Formats: online ● *ITNS Newslet-
ter*, quarterly. Contains clinical transplant articles,
society updates. **Price:** included in membership dues.
Circulation: 1,000. **Advertising:** accepted. Alternate
Formats: online ● *Kidney/Pancreas Transplant
Patient Education Booklet* (in English and Spanish).
Alternate Formats: online ● *Progress in Transplanta-
tion*, quarterly. Journal. **Price:** $55.00 for nonmem-
bers; included in membership dues. ISSN: 1526-
9248. **Circulation:** 3,000 ● Membership Directory.
Alternate Formats: online ● Brochure. Alternate
Formats: online. **Conventions/Meetings:** annual
symposium (exhibits) - 2007 Oct. 4-6, Denver, CO.

15163 ■ NANDA International
100 N 20th St., 4th Fl.
Philadelphia, PA 19103
Ph: (215)545-8105
Free: (800)647-9002
Fax: (215)545-8107

E-mail: info@nanda.org
URL: http://www.nanda.org
Contact: T. Heather Herdman PhD, Pres.
Founded: 1973. **Members:** 400. **Membership Dues:**
regular/associate, $100 (annual) ● student, $29 (annual) ● retired, $65 (annual). **Staff:** 8. **Languages:**
Chinese, English, French, German, Icelandic, Italian,
Japanese, Portuguese, Russian, Spanish. **Multinational. Description:** Registered nurses; individuals
interested in nursing language and informatics.
Develops, refines, and promotes a taxonomy of nursing terminology for use by professional nurses. **Libraries: Type:** reference. **Holdings:** 6; archival
material, artwork, books, business records, monographs, periodicals. **Subjects:** nursing diagnosis,
language development. **Awards:** Unique Contribution Award. **Frequency:** biennial. **Type:** recognition.
Computer Services: Mailing lists. **Committees:** Diagnosis Review; Informatics; Nursing Diagnosis
Development; Taxonomy. **Affiliated With:** American
Nurses Association; American Nursing Informatics
Association. **Also Known As:** North American Nursing Diagnosis Association. **Publications:** *Critical
Thinking and Nursing Diagnoses: Case Studies and
Analyses*. Book. **Price:** $24.95 plus shipping and
handling ● *NANDA Nursing Diagnoses: Definitions
and Classification 2001-2002* (in Chinese, English,
French, German, Icelandic, Italian, Japanese, Portu-
guese, and Spanish), biennial. Book. Includes 167
NANDA International-approved nursing diagnoses.
Price: $19.95 plus shipping and handling; $15.95 for
members. **Circulation:** 10,000 ● *Nursing Diagnosis
Journal*, quarterly. **Price:** $42.00 /year for nonmem-
bers; $54.00 /year for members outside U.S. ISSN:
0890-7188. **Advertising:** accepted. **Conventions/
Meetings:** biennial Nursing Language and Informatics - conference, developing, linking and integrating
nursing language and informatics (exhibits).

**15164 ■ National Alliance of Nurse
Practitioners (NANP)**
Address Unknown since 2006
Founded: 1985. **Members:** 25,000. **National
Groups:** 6. **Description:** Nurse practitioners. Seeks
to emphasize the role of Nurse Practitioners in ef-
ficient and cost-effective health care services.
Promotes continuing education for all health care
professionals. Promotes and supports legislation &
health policy for NPs. **Committees:** Political Action.
Conventions/Meetings: semiannual meeting.

**15165 ■ National American Arab Nurses
Association (NAANA)**
PO Box 43
Dearborn Heights, MI 48127
Ph: (313)680-5049 (313)982-4070
Fax: (313)996-3185
E-mail: info@n-aana.org
URL: http://www.n-aana.org
Contact: Rose Khalifa RN, Dir./Pres.
Founded: 2003. **Membership Dues:** active, $50 (an-
nual) ● associate, $130 (annual) ● member-at-large,
$50 (annual) ● student, $10 (annual) ● retired nurse,
$60 (annual) ● retired nurse (life), $500 ● corporate/
business/professional organization, $1,000-$3,000
(annual). **Description:** Serves as a voice, a network
and a resource for men and women in their pursuit of
employment and advancement within the nursing
profession. Fosters knowledge of cultural diversity
and sensitivity between members and the community
in the area of transcultural health care. Encourages
and supports the recruitment of student nurses.
Promotes the image of American-Arab nurses in the
profession and to patients. Works to advance the
knowledge and career status of nurses. Educates
healthcare providers about cultural practices that
impact the healthcare of the Arab-American community. **Awards:** NAANA Scholarship. **Frequency:**
annual. **Type:** scholarship. **Recipient:** for deserving
Arab-American nursing students. **Publications:**
Brochure. Alternate Formats: online. **Conventions/
Meetings:** annual conference, for nurses and other
allied health practitioners - 2008 Oct. 8-10, Detroit,
MI.

**15166 ■ National Association of Catholic
Nurses - USA (NACN-USA)**
PO Box 3016
Lisle, IL 60532-3016
E-mail: info@nacn-usa.org
URL: http://www.nacn-usa.org
Contact: Sookie Escandon-Dominguez RN, Pres.
Membership Dues: full (nurse), $35 (annual) ● as-
sociate (non-nurse), $30 (annual) ● student nurse,
$20 (annual) ● retiree, $30 (annual). **Description:**
Promotes Catholic/Christian beliefs through nursing
education, practice, research and health policy. Sup-
ports opportunities for nurses to explain spirituality in
all aspects of professional lives. Allows nurses of different backgrounds but with the same Roman Catholic values to work together.

**15167 ■ National Association of Clinical
Nurse Specialists (NACNS)**
2090 Linglestown Rd., Ste.107
Harrisburg, PA 17110
Ph: (717)234-6799
Fax: (717)234-6798
E-mail: nacnsorg@nacns.org
URL: http://www.nacns.org
Contact: Kelly A. Goudreau RN, Pres.
Founded: 1995. **Members:** 1,200. **Membership
Dues:** student, $65 (annual) ● regular, $110 (annual).
Staff: 3. **Regional Groups:** 11. **Description:** Repre-
sents clinical nurse specialists. Works to promote
and advance the practice of nursing. **Awards:** CNS
of the Year. **Frequency:** annual. **Type:** recognition.
Recipient: for clinical nurse specialists ● Graduate
Student Scholarship. **Frequency:** annual. **Type:**
scholarship. **Recipient:** for graduate students. **Computer Services:** Mailing lists, job postings. **Committees:** Affiliate Advisory; Communications and Marketing; Education; Legislative/Regulatory; Nominating;
Practice; Publications; Research. **Publications:** *Clinical Nurse Specialist*, bimonthly. Journal. Features
information on current trends and methodologies.
Price: included in membership dues; $91.95 for
nonmembers in U.S.; $201.95 /year for institutions.
ISSN: 0887-6274. Alternate Formats: online ● *Statement on Clinical Nurse Specialist Practice and Education*. Handbook. **Price:** $15.00 for members; $25.00
for nonmembers ● Newsletter. **Price:** included in
membership dues ● Membership Directory, annual.
Price: included in membership dues ● Papers.
Alternate Formats: online ● Proceedings, annual.
Alternate Formats: online. **Conventions/Meetings:**
annual CNS Vision - meeting (exhibits) ● annual
conference.

**15168 ■ National Association of Directors of
Nursing Administration in Long Term Care
(NADONA/LTC)**
10101 Alliance Rd., No. 140
Cincinnati, OH 45242
Ph: (513)791-3679
Free: (800)222-0539
Fax: (513)791-3699
E-mail: info@nadona.org
URL: http://www.nadona.org
Contact: Charlotte Eliopoulos, Interim Exec. Dir.
Founded: 1986. **Members:** 5,000. **Membership
Dues:** national, $85 (annual) ● individual, $105-$125
(annual). **Staff:** 4. **Budget:** $500,000. **Regional
Groups:** 5. **State Groups:** 40. **Description:** Directors, assistant directors, and former directors of nursing in long term care. Aims are: to create and
establish an acceptable ethical standard for practices
in long term care nursing administration and to
promote and encourage research in the profession;
to develop and provide a consistent program of
education and certification for the positions of director, associate director, and assistant director; to
promote a positive image of the long-term health care
industry. Encourages members to share concerns
and experiences; sponsors research programs.
Advocates legislation pertaining to the practice of
professional nursing. Maintains speakers' bureau.
Libraries: Type: reference. **Holdings:** 1,150. **Subjects:** long term care, clinical nursing. **Awards:**
Above and Beyond. **Frequency:** annual. **Type:**
scholarship. **Recipient:** upon request ● Caring. **Fre-**

quency: annual. **Type:** scholarship ● Nursing Administrator of the Year. **Frequency:** annual. **Type:** recognition. **Recipient:** for outstanding contributions to the field of long term nursing care ● Upward Bound. **Frequency:** annual. **Type:** scholarship. **Computer Services:** database ● mailing lists ● online services, DON Certification ● online services, forum. **Telecommunication Services:** electronic mail, gary@nadona.org. **Committees:** Audit; By Laws; Education/Scholarship; Ethics; Legislation; Nomination; Program; Publicity. **Publications:** *The Director*, quarterly. Journal. Includes research, clinical papers and news items. **Price:** included in membership dues. **Circulation:** 22,000. **Advertising:** accepted. **Conventions/Meetings:** annual conference (exhibits) ● seminar and symposium ● workshop.

15169 ■ National Association of Hispanic Nurses (NAHN)

1501 Sixteenth St. NW
Washington, DC 20036
Ph: (202)387-2477
Fax: (202)483-7183
E-mail: info@thehispanicnurses.org
URL: http://www.thehispanicnurses.org
Contact: Maria T. Villot BSN, Pres.

Founded: 1976. **Members:** 1,000. **Membership Dues:** full, $75 (annual) ● associate, affiliate, international, $60 (annual) ● retired, $50 (annual) ● student, $25 (annual) ● corporate, $5,000 (annual). **Staff:** 1. **State Groups:** 10. **Local Groups:** 24. **Languages:** English, Spanish. **Description:** Nurses on all educational levels, from all Hispanic sub-groups; non-Hispanic nurses concerned about the health delivery needs of the Hispanic community; nursing students. Serves the nursing and health care delivery needs of the Hispanic community and the professional needs of Hispanic nurses. Provides a forum in which Hispanic nurses can analyze, research, and evaluate the health care needs of the Hispanic community. Disseminates findings of that research to local, state, and federal agencies so as to affect policy-making and resource allocation. Aims to ensure that Hispanic nurses have equal access to educational, professional, and economic opportunities. **Libraries: Type:** reference. **Holdings:** archival material. **Awards:** Henrietta Villaescusa Award. **Frequency:** annual. **Type:** recognition. **Recipient:** for members who have contributed to the improvement of health in the Hispanic community ● Ildaura Murillo-Rhode Awards. **Frequency:** annual. **Type:** recognition. **Recipient:** for members who have distinguished themselves in scholarship and nursing education ● Janie Menchaca Wilson Leadership Award. **Type:** recognition. **Recipient:** to a member in nursing leadership roles ● Juanita Robles-Lopez/Pampers Parenting Institute & Proctor & Gamble Scholarship. **Frequency:** annual. **Type:** scholarship. **Recipient:** for a member pursuing master's degree in maternal-child nursing program ● National Association of Hispanic Nurses Scholarship Awards. **Frequency:** annual. **Type:** scholarship. **Recipient:** for members enrolled in associate, diploma, baccalaureate, graduate, or practical/vocational nursing program ● Sarah Gomez Erlach Humanitarian. **Frequency:** annual. **Type:** recognition. **Recipient:** for an individual, group or organization that has taken an active role in promoting the welfare, growth or social reform of the society. **Computer Services:** Mailing lists, of members. **Formerly:** (1979) National Association of Spanish Speaking-Spanish Surnamed Nurses. **Publications:** *Hispanic Health Care International*, quarterly. Journal. **Price:** $58.00 /year for individuals in U.S.; $68.00 /year for individuals outside U.S.; $128.00 /year for institutions in U.S.; $148.00 /year for institutions outside U.S. **Conventions/Meetings:** annual conference (exhibits).

15170 ■ National Association of Neonatal Nurses (NANN)

4700 W Lake Ave.
Glenview, IL 60025-1485
Ph: (847)375-3660
Free: (800)451-3795
Fax: (888)477-6266

E-mail: info@nann.org
URL: http://www.nann.org
Contact: Peggy Gordin MS, Pres.

Founded: 1984. **Members:** 5,600. **Membership Dues:** regular, in U.S. and Canada, $95 (annual) ● regular, outside U.S. and Canada, $131 (annual) ● student, $85 (annual). **Staff:** 10. **Budget:** $1,600,000. **Regional Groups:** 60. **Description:** Represents neonatal nurses providing evidence-based care to high-risk neonatal patients; acts as the recognized voice that influences standards of practice through advocacy, collaboration, and leadership. **Awards:** Distinguished Neonatal Nursing Leader. **Frequency:** periodic. **Type:** recognition. **Recipient:** for contribution to neonatal nursing profession ● Robyn Main. **Frequency:** annual. **Type:** recognition. **Recipient:** for excellence in practice ● SIG Leadership. **Frequency:** annual. **Type:** recognition. **Recipient:** for excellence in a leadership role. **Publications:** *Advances in Neonatal Care*, bimonthly. Journal ● *Central Lines*, bimonthly. Newsletter. Contains organizational news, product updates and neonatal practices. **Circulation:** 12,000. **Advertising:** accepted ● *Practice Guidelines* ● *Technical Bulletins*. **Conventions/Meetings:** annual conference, educational for neonatal nursing (exhibits).

15171 ■ National Association of Nurse Massage Therapists (NANMT)

6749 Willow Creek Dr.
PO Box 24004
Huber Heights, OH 45424
Ph: (937)235-0872
Free: (800)262-4017
Fax: (800)262-4017
E-mail: nanmtadmin@nanmt.org
URL: http://www.nanmt.org
Contact: Arlene Frederick, Pres.

Founded: 1987. **Members:** 200. **Membership Dues:** active, $85 (annual) ● student/senior, $50 (annual) ● corporate supporting, $150 (annual) ● individual supporting, $75 (annual). **Staff:** 5. **Description:** Nurses and other healthcare professionals who practice massage therapy. Promotes the integration of massage and other therapeutic forms of body work into existing healthcare practice. Promotes Nurse Massage Therapists as specialists within the nursing profession. Establishes standards of professional practice and criteria for national certification of Nurse Massage Therapists. Educates the medical community and the general public about bodywork therapies. Monitors legislation. **Computer Services:** database ● mailing lists. **Committees:** Education; Legislative. **Publications:** *NANMT Membership Directory*, annual. **Price:** included in membership dues. Alternate Formats: online ● *NANMT News*, quarterly. Newsletter ● Brochure. Alternate Formats: online. **Conventions/Meetings:** Nurse Massage Therapy for the Aging Population - conference (exhibits).

15172 ■ National Association of Nurse Practitioners in Women's Health (NPWH)

505 C St. NE
Washington, DC 20002
Ph: (202)543-9693
Fax: (202)543-9858
E-mail: info@npwh.org
URL: http://www.npwh.org
Contact: Susan Wysocki RNC, Pres./CEO

Founded: 1980. **Members:** 3,500. **Membership Dues:** student, retired, $35 (annual) ● active, associate, $75 (annual) ● supporting, $150 (annual). **Staff:** 5. **Description:** Nurse practitioners involved in women's healthcare. Advocates quality healthcare to be inclusive of an individual's physical, emotional, and spiritual needs. Promotes women as decision-makers for their own healthcare. Encourages nurses to participate in continuing education programs. Disseminates information. **Awards:** Pharmacia/NPWH Nurse Practitioner of the Year. **Frequency:** annual. **Type:** recognition. **Formerly:** (2001) National Association of Nurse Practitioners in Reproductive Health. **Publications:** *The Monthly Cycle*. Newsletter. **Price:** available to members only. **Circulation:** 2,000. **Conventions/Meetings:** annual Women's

Health Care in the New Millennium - conference, clinical national meeting (exhibits).

15173 ■ National Association of Orthopaedic Nurses (NAON)

401 N Michigan Ave., Ste.2200
Chicago, IL 60611
Free: (800)289-6266
Fax: (312)527-6658
E-mail: noan@smithbucklin.com
URL: http://www.orthonurse.org
Contact: Kaye Englebrecht, Exec. Dir.

Founded: 1980. **Members:** 8,300. **Membership Dues:** general, $85 (annual) ● associate, $75 (annual) ● student, $35-$45 (annual). **Budget:** $2,000,000. **Local Groups:** 154. **Description:** Registered, licensed practical, or licensed vocational nurses involved or knowledgeable in orthopedic nursing. Enhances the personal and professional growth of orthopedic nurses through continuing education programs. Promotes research development and advances in orthopedic nursing; promotes an awareness of patients' rights. Stresses the concept of man's physical, psychological, social, emotional, and spiritual needs in the development of patient care plans. Maintains liaison with and serves as resource to hospitals, universities, industries, and government agencies. Operates special interest groups. Sponsors workshops; maintains speakers' bureau; offers research grants. Makes available audiovisual presentation. **Computer Services:** Mailing lists, of members. **Telecommunication Services:** electronic mail, kenglebrecht@smithbucklin.com. **Committees:** Education; Political Action; Research. **Publications:** *News*, bimonthly ● *Orthopaedic Nursing*, bimonthly. Journal. Provides continuing education for orthopaedic nurses and focuses on a wide variety of settings. **Price:** $49.00 /year for individuals in U.S.; $139.00 /year for institutions in U.S.; $89.00 /year for individuals outside U.S.; $189.00 /year for institutions outside U.S. ISSN: 0744-6020. Alternate Formats: online ● Bibliographies ● Monographs ● Proceedings. **Conventions/Meetings:** annual congress and convention (exhibits) - usually May. 2008 May 17-21, San Jose, CA.

15174 ■ National Association of Pediatric Nurse Practitioners (NAPNAP)

20 Brace Rd., Ste.200
Cherry Hill, NJ 08034-2634
Ph: (856)857-9700
Fax: (856)857-1600
E-mail: info@napnap.org
URL: http://www.napnap.org
Contact: Karen Kelly Thomas, Exec. Dir./CEO

Founded: 1973. **Members:** 7,000. **Membership Dues:** student, retired, $65 (annual) ● individual, $130 (annual). **Staff:** 13. **State Groups:** 49. **Description:** Pediatric, school, and family nurse practitioners and interested persons. Seeks to improve the quality of infant, child, and adolescent health care by making health care services accessible and providing a forum for continuing education of members. Facilitates and supports legislation designed to promote the role of pediatric nurse practitioners; promotes salary ranges commensurate with practitioners' responsibilities; facilitates exchange of information between prospective employers and job seekers in the field. Supports research programs; compiles statistics. **Libraries: Type:** not open to the public. **Awards:** NAPNAP/McNeil Scholarship. **Frequency:** semiannual. **Type:** scholarship. **Recipient:** for students entering pediatric nurse practitioner programs ● **Type:** recognition. **Computer Services:** database, on pediatric nurse practitioner members ● mailing lists. **Publications:** *Journal of Pediatric Health Care*, bimonthly. Includes annual index, book reviews, legislative news, literature abstracts, multi-media reviews, and product news. **Price:** $55.00 /year for individuals; $104.00 /year for institutions; $28.00/year for students. ISSN: 0891-5245. **Advertising:** accepted. Alternate Formats: microform ● *Pediatric Nurse Practitioner*, bimonthly. Newsletter. Contains calendar of events and legislative news. **Price:** free for members. ISSN: 0097-9805. **Circulation:** 5,800. **Advertising:** accepted ● Brochures. **Conventions/Meetings:** annual Nursing Conference on Pediatric Primary Care (exhibits).

15175 ■ National Association of Physician Nurses (NAPN)
900 S Washington St., No. G-13
Falls Church, VA 22046
Ph: (703)237-8616
Fax: (703)533-1153
Contact: Susan Young, Dir.
Founded: 1973. **Members:** 2,000. **Membership Dues:** individual, $30 (annual). **Staff:** 4. **Budget:** $50,000. **Description:** Physicians' nurses united to bring added stature and purpose to their profession and to create for themselves the benefits normally limited to members of specialized professional and fraternal groups. **Awards: Type:** scholarship. **Publications:** *The Nightingale*, monthly. Newsletter. **Price:** included in membership dues; $15.00 /year for nonmembers. ISSN: 0894-5780. **Circulation:** 2,000. **Advertising:** accepted ● *Salary Survey Report* ● Also publishes special reports.

15176 ■ National Association of School Nurses (NASN)
8484 Georgia Ave., Ste.420
Silver Spring, MD 20910
Ph: (240)821-1130
Free: (866)627-6767
Fax: (301)585-1791
E-mail: nasn@nasn.org
URL: http://www.nasn.org
Contact: Amy Garcia RN, Exec. Dir.
Founded: 1969. **Members:** 12,000. **Membership Dues:** active/associate, $90 (annual) ● corporate/business/professional organization, $130 (annual) ● student, $44 (annual) ● retired, $50 (annual). **Staff:** 18. **Budget:** $3,000,000. **State Groups:** 47. **Description:** Improves health and educational success of children and youth by developing and providing leadership to advance school nursing practice. **Libraries: Type:** not open to the public. **Awards:** School Nurse of the Year. **Frequency:** annual. **Type:** recognition. **Computer Services:** Mailing lists, labels. **Committees:** Annual Conference; Finance; Policy; Professional Development; Research; Standards. **Formerly:** (1977) Department of School Nurses/NEA. **Publications:** *Journal of School Nursing*, bimonthly. Magazine. Includes book reviews, resources, education topics and legislative updates. **Price:** included in membership dues; $70.00 /year for nonmembers. ISSN: 0048-945X. **Advertising:** accepted ● *NAS-Newsletter*, bimonthly. **Price:** included in membership dues. **Advertising:** accepted. Alternate Formats: online ● *Postural Screening*. **Price:** $7.00 for members; $11.00 for nonmembers ● *Scope and Standards of Professional School Nursing Practice*. **Price:** $10.00 for members; $15.00 for nonmembers ● *Vision Screening Guidelines for School Nurses*. **Price:** $7.00 for members; $11.00 for nonmembers ● Offers various guides, brochures, manuals, and other publications. **Conventions/Meetings:** annual conference (exhibits) - usually last weekend in June.

15177 ■ National Association of State School Nurse Consultants (NASSNC)
PO Box 708
Kent, OH 44240-0013
Ph: (608)266-8857
Fax: (608)267-3746
E-mail: linda.caldart-olson@dpi.state.wi.us
URL: http://www.tjcats.net/nassnc
Description: Registered nurses employed by state departments of education or health. Promotes development of standards of practice among school nurse consultants; facilitates continuing professional advancement of members. Serves as a forum for the exchange of information among members and between members and related professionals; promotes and supports research activities; formulates nursing standards; sponsors educational programs. **Publications:** Papers. **Conventions/Meetings:** semiannual meeting - always spring and fall.

15178 ■ National Association of Traveling Nurses (NATN)
PO Box 35215
Chicago, IL 60707-0215
Ph: (708)453-0080
Fax: (708)453-0083
E-mail: natn@rentamark.com
URL: http://www.travelingnurse.org
Contact: L. David Stoller, Chm.
Founded: 1990. **Members:** 78,951. **Membership Dues:** individual and company, $25 (annual). **Staff:** 10. **Description:** Members of the medical profession. Provides travel information. Provides information to nurses, health care professionals on traveling assignments and job placement opportunities. Offers substantial discounts for members at major hotels, resorts, and car rental agencies. Provides members with complete list of approved travel industry suppliers, including travel agents, vendors, airlines, cruise ship companies, and hotels. **Libraries: Type:** reference; not open to the public. **Holdings:** 1,000. **Subjects:** travel, medicine. **Awards:** Nurse of the Year Award. **Frequency:** annual. **Type:** recognition ● Travel Industry Award. **Type:** recognition ● Traveling Nurse of the Year Award. **Frequency:** annual. **Type:** recognition. **Computer Services:** Mailing lists ● online services, product endorsements to support member benefits. **Additional Websites:** http://www.medicalassociation.net. **Publications:** *Journal of Traveling Nurses*, quarterly. Online journal. **Price:** for members. **Circulation:** 100,000. **Advertising:** accepted. Alternate Formats: online ● *National Online.* Newsletter. National invites authors to submit articles in "WORD" format via email for publication in the national online journal. **Conventions/Meetings:** annual conference and convention.

15179 ■ National Association of Vietnamese Nurses (NAVN)
PO Box 9692
Fountain Valley, CA 92728-9692
Ph: (714)330-1243
Fax: (206)888-2684
E-mail: diepnp@netscape.net
URL: http://www.navn.us
Contact: Diep Pham MBA, Pres./Founder
Founded: 2002. **Membership Dues:** active, $75 (annual) ● associate, $40 (annual) ● student, retired, $20 (annual) ● corporate, $500 (annual). **Description:** Promotes the interests of Vietnamese nurses. Improves the quality of health of Vietnamese communities. Provides a forum for networking and professional development of Vietnamese nurses. Offers education, leadership and mentorship programs. **Publications:** Newsletter, quarterly. **Price:** included in membership dues.

15180 ■ National Black Nurses Association (NBNA)
8630 Fenton St., Ste.330
Silver Spring, MD 20910-3803
Ph: (301)589-3200
Free: (800)575-6298
Fax: (301)589-3223
E-mail: nbna@erols.com
URL: http://www.nbna.org
Contact: Millicent Gorham, Exec. Dir.
Founded: 1971. **Members:** 3,000. **Membership Dues:** student, $35 (annual) ● retired/first year graduate, $75 (annual) ● regular, $150 (annual) ● life, $2,000. **Staff:** 4. **National Groups:** 76. **Description:** Registered nurses, licensed practical nurses, licensed vocational nurses, and student nurses. Functions as a professional support group and as an advocacy group for the black community and their health care. Recruits and assists blacks interested in pursuing nursing as a career. Compiles statistics; maintains biographical archives. **Awards:** NBNA Scholarship Program. **Frequency:** annual. **Type:** scholarship. **Recipient:** for students. **Committees:** Editorial; History; Policy; Publicity and Public Relations; Scholarship and Awards. **Publications:** *Journal of Black Nurses Association*, semiannual. **Price:** included in membership dues; $35.00 /year for nonmembers ● *National Black Nurses Association—Book of Reports*, annual ● *National Black Nurses Association—Proceedings*,

periodic ● *NBNA Newsletter*, quarterly. Includes calendar of events, research updates, scholarships, grants, and fellowships. **Price:** included in membership dues; $25.00 /year for nonmembers. **Circulation:** 3,000. Alternate Formats: online ● Annual Report. **Conventions/Meetings:** annual conference, includes institute (exhibits) ● regional meeting.

15181 ■ National Certification Corporation for the Obstetric, Gynecologic and Neonatal Nursing Specialties (NCC)
PO Box 11082
Chicago, IL 60611-0082
Ph: (312)951-0207
Free: (800)367-5613
Fax: (312)951-9475
E-mail: bburns@nccnet.org
URL: http://www.nccnet.org
Contact: Betty Burns CAE, Exec. Dir.
Founded: 1975. **Members:** 55,000. **Staff:** 5. **Budget:** $2,500,000. **Description:** Promotes quality nursing care by encouraging nurses to demonstrate special knowledge by participating in a voluntary national certification program for obstetric/gynecologic nurse practitioners, in-patient obstetric nurses, neonatal intensive care nurses, neonatal nurse practitioners, low-risk neonatal nurses, telephone nurses, electronic fetal monitoring, menopause, and maternal newborn nurses. **Formerly:** (1991) NAACOG Certification Corporation. **Publications:** *NCC News*, periodic. Newsletter. **Advertising:** accepted ● *Self Assessment Program*. Brochure. **Conventions/Meetings:** annual meeting.

15182 ■ National Coalition of Ethnic Minority Nurse Associations (NCEMNA)
c/o Dr. Betty Smith Williams, RN, Pres.
6101 W Centinela Ave., Ste.378
Culver City, CA 90230
Ph: (310)258-9515
Fax: (310)258-9513
E-mail: bwilliams@ncemna.org
URL: http://www.ncemna.org
Contact: Dr. Betty Smith Williams RN, Pres.
Founded: 1998. **Description:** Advocates for equity and justice in nursing and health care for ethnic minority populations. Promotes the professional and educational advancement of ethnic nurses. Fosters education of consumers, health care professionals and policy makers on the health issues of ethnic minority populations. Develops ethnic minority nurse leaders in the areas of health policy, practice, education and research. **Conventions/Meetings:** annual Creating Research Careers: Your Pathways to Success - conference.

15183 ■ National Council of State Boards of Nursing (NCSBN)
111 E Wacker Dr., Ste.2900
Chicago, IL 60601
Ph: (312)525-3600
Free: (866)293-9600
Fax: (312)279-1032
E-mail: info@ncsbn.org
URL: http://www.ncsbn.org
Contact: Kathy Apple, Exec. Dir.
Founded: 1978. **Members:** 61. **Staff:** 60. **Description:** State boards of nursing. Assists member boards in administering the National Council Licensure Examinations for Registered Nurses and Practical Nurses and works to insure relevancy of the exams to current nursing practice. Aids boards in the collection and analysis of information pertaining to the licensure and discipline of nurses. Provides consultative services, conducts research, develops model nursing legislation and administrative regulations, and sponsors educational programs. **Computer Services:** Information services, membership. **Publications:** *Council Connector*, bimonthly. Newsletter. Contains news about committee activities and updates from NCSBN departments. Alternate Formats: online ● *NCLEX Exam Test Plans*, annual. Booklets. Contains educational information. ● Also publishes research results and monographs. **Conventions/Meetings:** annual meeting - mid-year. 2008 Mar. 3-5, Chicago, IL ● annual meeting and as-

sembly, includes delegate assembly - 2008 Aug. 5-8, Nashville, TN.

15184 ■ National Federation of Licensed Practical Nurses (NFLPN)
605 Poole Dr.
Garner, NC 27529
Ph: (919)779-0046
Fax: (919)779-5642
E-mail: cbarbour@mgmt4u.com
URL: http://www.nflpn.org
Contact: Charlene Barbour, Exec. Dir.
Founded: 1949. **Members:** 5,000. **Membership Dues:** active, $100 (annual) ● retired, $65 (annual) ● student, $25 (annual) ● military, international, individual, $70 (annual) ● affiliate, $60 (annual). **Staff:** 3. **Budget:** $200,000. **State Groups:** 22. **Description:** Federation of state associations of licensed practical and vocational nurses. Aims to: preserve and foster the ideal of comprehensive nursing care for the ill and aged; improve standards of practice; secure recognition and effective utilization of LPNs; further continued improvement in the education of LPNs. Acts as clearinghouse for information on practical nursing and cooperates with other groups concerned with better patient care. Maintains loan program. **Computer Services:** database, continuing education. **Committees:** Ethics; Leadership Training; Legislation; Members State Boards of Nursing; Nursing Practice; Personnel Review; State Presidents. **Programs:** Continuing Education; Lobbying. **Publications:** *Licensed Practical Nurse*, quarterly. Journal. Includes state and legislative news and list of new members. **Price:** included in membership dues. **Circulation:** 10,000. **Advertising:** accepted ● *LPN*, quarterly. Magazine. **Conventions/Meetings:** annual convention (exhibits).

15185 ■ National League for Nursing (NLN)
61 Broadway, 33rd Fl.
New York, NY 10006
Ph: (212)363-5555
Free: (800)669-1656
Fax: (212)812-0391
E-mail: generalinfo@nln.org
URL: http://www.nln.org
Contact: Ms. Karen Klestzick, Communications Dir.
Founded: 1893. **Members:** 14,000. **Membership Dues:** individual, $90 (annual) ● agency, (based on number of graduations), $935-$1,375 (annual) ● graduate student, retired, $75 (annual). **Staff:** 30. **Budget:** $9,500,000. **State Groups:** 20. **Languages:** English, Spanish. **Description:** Champions the pursuit of quality nursing education. A professional association of nursing faculty, education agencies, health care agencies, allied/public agencies, and public members whose mission is to advance quality nursing education that prepares the nursing workforce to meet the needs of diverse populations in an ever-changing health care environment. Serves as the primary source of information about every type of nursing education program, from the LVN and LPN to the EdD and PhD. There are 20 affiliated constituent leagues that provide a local forum for members. The National League for Nursing Accrediting Commission is an independent corporate affiliate of the NLN, responsible for providing accreditation services to all levels of nursing education. **Awards:** Award for Outstanding Leadership in Workforce Development. **Frequency:** annual. **Type:** recognition. **Recipient:** to individual or organization ● NLN Award for Excellence in Nursing Education Research. **Frequency:** annual. **Type:** recognition. **Recipient:** to nurse scholar ● NLN Award for Excellence in Teaching. **Frequency:** annual. **Type:** recognition. **Recipient:** to nurse educator ● NLN Award for Outstanding Leadership in Nursing Education. **Frequency:** annual. **Type:** recognition. **Recipient:** to nurse educator ● NLN Award for Public Service. **Frequency:** annual. **Type:** recognition. **Recipient:** to lay person of national stature. **Divisions:** Assessment and Evaluation; Finance; Office of CEO; Office of COO; Research and Professional Development. **Formed by Merger of:** Association of Collegiate Schools of Nursing; Joint Committee on Careers in Nursing; National Committee for the Improvement of Nursing Services; National

League of Nursing Education; National Nursing Accrediting Service; National Organization for Public Health Nursing. **Publications:** *Nursing Data Review*, annual. Book. Contains tables and graphs of data. ● *Nursing Education Perspectives*, bimonthly. Journal. Contains news, legislative updates, education, service analyses, and editorials. **Circulation:** 18,000. **Advertising:** accepted ● *State Approved Schools of Nursing - LPN*, annual ● *State Approved Schools of Nursing - RN*, annual. Books. Covers education, leadership, nursing history, culture and diversity, theory development, and professional issues. ● *Undergraduate & Graduate Nursing Programs, 2nd Ed.*. Book. Comprehensive guide to U.S. nursing programs. ● Books. Covers education, leadership, nursing history, culture and diversity, theory development, and professional issues. **Conventions/Meetings:** annual Education Summit - conference, with keynote speakers and multiple concurrent sessions (exhibits) - 2007 Sept. 26-29, Phoenix, AZ ● annual Faculty Development Institute - conference ● annual Nursing Education Research Conference ● annual Nursing Education Research Institute - conference.

15186 ■ National Nursing Staff Development Organization (NNSDO)
7794 Grow Dr.
Pensacola, FL 32514
Ph: (850)474-0995
Free: (800)489-1995
Fax: (850)484-8762
E-mail: nnsdo@puetzamc.com
URL: http://www.nnsdo.org
Contact: Kari Schmidt MS, Pres.
Founded: 1989. **Members:** 1,995. **Membership Dues:** regular or foreign, $95 (annual) ● contributing, $100 (annual) ● executive, $250 (annual) ● retired, $80 (annual). **National Groups:** 38. **Description:** Advances the specialty practice of staff development for the enhancement of quality healthcare outcomes. Provides a forum for networking among staff development educators. **Awards:** Affiliate Excellence in Quality Programs Awards. **Frequency:** annual. **Type:** recognition ● Belinda E. Puetz Award. **Frequency:** annual. **Type:** recognition ● Excellence Awards. **Frequency:** quarterly. **Type:** recognition ● **Frequency:** annual. **Type:** grant. **Publications:** *Journal for Nurses in Staff Development*, bimonthly ● *Trendlines*, bimonthly. Newsletter. **Conventions/Meetings:** annual convention (exhibits).

15187 ■ National Organization for Associate Degree Nursing (N-OADN)
7794 Grow Dr.
Pensacola, FL 32514
Ph: (850)484-6948
Free: (877)966-6236
Fax: (850)484-8762
E-mail: noadn@puetzamc.com
URL: http://www.noadn.org
Contact: Belinda Puetz, Exec. Dir.
Founded: 1984. **Members:** 750. **Membership Dues:** individual, $115-$140 (annual) ● associate, $90-$110 (annual) ● agency, $400-$500 (annual). **Staff:** 8. **Budget:** $500,000. **State Groups:** 10. **Description:** Individuals interested in retaining current competency level examinations and endorsement of RN licensure from state to state for associate degree nursing graduates. Represents and advances the status of associate degree nursing education and practice. Provides networking among members to facilitate the exchange of legislative information and support. Offers clearinghouse for interpretation of legal issues and liability insurance. **Awards:** Naomi Brack. **Frequency:** annual. **Type:** scholarship. **Recipient:** for students. **Formerly:** (1986) National Organization for Advancement of Associate Degree Nursing. **Publications:** *First Tuesday*, monthly. Newsletter. Contains updates from the Board of Directors. Alternate Formats: online ● *N-OADN Newsletter*, quarterly. **Advertising:** accepted. Alternate Formats: online ● *Teacher and Learning in Nursing*. Journal ● Newsletter, quarterly. Includes national and state association news, activities, and information. ● Also issues position papers. **Conventions/Meetings:** annual convention (exhibits) ● seminar ● workshop.

15188 ■ National Organization of Nurse Practitioners Faculties (NONPF)
1522 K St. NW, Ste.702
Washington, DC 20005
Ph: (202)289-8044
Fax: (202)289-8046
E-mail: nonpf@nonpf.org
URL: http://www.nonpf.com
Contact: Joanne Pohl PhD, Pres.
Founded: 1981. **Members:** 1,000. **Membership Dues:** individual, $125 (annual) ● group, $500 (annual) ● associate, $100 (annual) ● retired, $50 (annual) ● student, $75 (annual). **Staff:** 2. **Budget:** $250,000. **Description:** Works to promote public health by developing and implementing nurse practitioner education. Disseminates research related to nurse practitioner education; provides a forum for the exchange of information; works to influence policy affecting nurse practitioners; and develops national guidelines and criteria for nurse practitioner educational programs. **Awards:** Achievement in Research Award. **Frequency:** annual. **Type:** recognition ● Outstanding Group Faculty Practice Award. **Frequency:** annual. **Type:** recognition ● Outstanding Nurse Practitioner Educator Award. **Frequency:** annual. **Type:** recognition ● Small Grant Research Award. **Frequency:** annual. **Type:** grant. **Publications:** *The Mentor*, quarterly. Newsletter. Alternate Formats: online ● *National Directory of NP Programs*, biennial ● Brochure. **Conventions/Meetings:** annual conference and board meeting (exhibits) - always April ● annual meeting - 2008 Apr. 10-13, Louisville, KY.

15189 ■ National Organization of Nurses with Disabilities (NOND)
1640 W Roosevelt Rd., Rm. 736
Chicago, IL 60608
E-mail: info@nond.org
URL: http://www.nond.org
Contact: Karen McCulloh, Pres.
Founded: 2003. **Membership Dues:** standard, $25 ● silver, $250 ● gold, $500 ● platinum, $800 ● titanium, $1,000. **Description:** Promotes the full inclusion and acceptance of people with disabilities and chronic health conditions into nursing careers. Educates and advocates for the full participation of nurses with disabilities in all aspects of nursing practice. Promotes the development of curricula in graduate schools of nursing that focus on masters and doctoral degrees in "Disability and Nursing". Advocates for students with disabilities to gain equal access to nursing educational programs. **Telecommunication Services:** electronic mail, bmarks1@uic.edu.

15190 ■ Nurse Practitioner Associates for Continuing Education (NPACE)
209 W Central St., Ste.228
Natick, MA 01760
Ph: (508)907-6424
Fax: (508)907-6425
E-mail: npace@npace.org
URL: http://www.npace.org
Contact: Maureen Fischer, Exec. Dir.
Founded: 1980. **Description:** Represents and promotes nurse practitioners and other nurses in advanced practice to improve healthcare in the U.S. **Computer Services:** database, nurse practitioners, demographic data, salary surveys, practice information ● mailing lists. **Telecommunication Services:** electronic mail, mfischer@npace.org. **Publications:** *Clinical Excellence for Nurse Practitioners*, quarterly. Journal. **Price:** $62.00 /year for individuals in U.S.; $72.00 /year for individuals outside U.S.; $134.00 /year for institutions in U.S.; $154.00 /year for institutions outside U.S. **Advertising:** accepted. Alternate Formats: online. **Conventions/Meetings:** periodic National Primary Care Conference and Acute Care Specialty Track (exhibits) - 2007 Sept. 19-21, St. Louis, MO; 2007 Oct. 21-24, NEW YORK, NY.

15191 ■ Nurses Educational Funds (NEF)
304 Park Ave. S, 11th Fl.
New York, NY 10010
Ph: (212)590-2443

Fax: (212)590-2446
E-mail: info@n-e-f.org
URL: http://www.n-e-f.org
Contact: Kathleen M. Dirschel PhD, Pres.
Founded: 1954. **Members:** 30. **Staff:** 1. **Budget:** $120,000. **Description:** Seeks to establish, maintain, and administer funds to provide financial assistance to registered nurses studying for advanced degrees; masters/doctoral level only formulate policies for the administration of such funds; collect and manage all funds contributed to it. Masters study must be full-time only GRE/or MAT scores are required. **Awards: Frequency:** annual. **Type:** scholarship. **Recipient:** for RN, member of professional nursing, full-time student at Master's Level, full or part-time at doctoral level, U.S. Citizen, enrolled in or applying to NLNAC or CCNE accredited nursing masters program or at doctoral level; for academic and service leader. **Formerly:** (1954) Isabel Hampton Robb Memorial Fund. **Publications:** Annual Report, annual. Includes NEF activity highlights and financial summary for the fiscal year. **Price:** available to members and donors only. **Conventions/Meetings:** National Nursing Convention (exhibits).

15192 ■ Nurses' House
Veronica M. Driscoll Center for Nursing
2113 Western Ave., Ste.2
Guilderland, NY 12084-9559
Ph: (518)456-7858
Fax: (518)452-3760
E-mail: mail@nurseshouse.org
URL: http://www.nurseshouse.org
Contact: Susan Fraley, Exec. Dir.
Founded: 1925. **Members:** 1,100. **Staff:** 2. **Budget:** $163,500. **Regional Groups:** 6. **Description:** Registered nurses and interested individuals united to assist registered nurses in financial and other crises. Provides short-term financial aid for shelter, food, and utilities until nurses obtain entitlements or jobs. Offers counseling and referrals. Encourages homebound or retired nurses through a volunteer corps. **Awards:** Distinguished Service Award. **Type:** recognition. **Affiliated With:** American Nurses Association; National League for Nursing. **Publications:** Appeal, annual. Newsletter ● The Dolphin, semiannual. Newsletter ● Also publishes promotional flyer.

15193 ■ Nurses Organization of Veterans Affairs (NOVA)
1726 M St. NW, Ste.1101
Washington, DC 20036
Ph: (202)296-0888
Fax: (202)833-1577
E-mail: nova@vanurse.org
URL: http://www.vanurse.org
Contact: Deborah Beck, Exec. Dir.
Founded: 1980. **Members:** 3,200. **Membership Dues:** active, $90 (annual) ● associate, $50 (annual) ● legacy, $200 (quinquennial). **Staff:** 3. **Budget:** $300. **Regional Groups:** 99. **Description:** Provides VA nurses with the opportunity to preserve and improve quality care and professionalism through legislative influence. Conducts seminars, and educational programs. **Libraries: Type:** open to the public. **Subjects:** membership yearbook. **Awards:** Distinguished Member Award. **Frequency:** annual. **Type:** recognition. **Recipient:** to an individual or group for distinguished service to the nursing profession of the Veteran's Health Care System ● Veterans Award. **Frequency:** annual. **Type:** recognition. **Recipient:** to an individual veteran or group of veterans in recognition of dedication, accomplishment, and sacrifice to the country. **Computer Services:** Mailing lists. **Formerly:** (1989) Nurses Organization of the Veterans Administration. **Publications:** News From NOVA, quarterly. Newsletter. **Price:** $40.00 /year for nonmembers. **Advertising:** accepted. Alternate Formats: online ● Also publishes Legislatively Speakings. **Conventions/Meetings:** annual meeting (exhibits).

15194 ■ Oncology Nursing Certification Corporation (ONCC)
125 Enterprise Dr.
Pittsburgh, PA 15275-1214
Ph: (412)859-6104
Free: (877)769-ONCC

Fax: (412)859-6168
E-mail: oncc@ons.org
URL: http://www.oncc.org
Contact: Patricia D. Baldwin RN, Pres.
Founded: 1984. **Description:** Provides oncology nursing certification to improve patient care and professional practice. **Awards:** Advanced Oncology Certified Nurse of the Year Award. **Frequency:** annual. **Type:** recognition. **Recipient:** for outstanding individuals who have supported and promoted Oncology Nursing Certification ● CPON of the Year. **Frequency:** annual. **Type:** recognition. **Recipient:** for outstanding individuals in the field of Pediatric Oncology Nursing and Oncology Nursing Service ● Employer Recognition Award. **Frequency:** annual. **Type:** recognition. **Recipient:** to an organization that supports Oncology Nursing Certification ● OCN of the Year. **Frequency:** annual. **Type:** recognition. **Recipient:** for outstanding individuals in the field of Oncology Nursing and Oncology Nursing Service ● Roberta Scofield Memorial Certification Award. **Frequency:** annual. **Type:** recognition. **Recipient:** for nurses who are committed to Oncology Nursing. **Affiliated With:** Oncology Nursing Society. **Publications:** ONCC News. Newsletter. Alternate Formats: online ● Oncology Nursing Certification Bulletin.

15195 ■ Oncology Nursing Society (ONS)
125 Enterprise Dr.
Pittsburgh, PA 15275
Ph: (412)859-6100
Free: (877)369-5497
Fax: (412)859-6162
E-mail: customer.service@ons.org
URL: http://www.ons.org
Contact: Georgia M. Decker RN, Pres.
Founded: 1975. **Members:** 35,000. **Membership Dues:** active/associate, $93 (annual) ● student/senior/physically challenged, $46 (annual). **Staff:** 115. **Budget:** $20,000,000. **Local Groups:** 215. **Description:** Registered nurses and other health care professionals with an interest in oncology. Seeks to: promote high professional standards in oncology nursing; provide a network for the exchange of information, resources, and peer support; encourage nurses to specialize in oncology; promote and develop educational programs in oncology nursing extending through the graduate level; identify, encourage, and foster nursing research in improving the quality of patient care. Conducts instructional and abstract sessions. Compiles statistics. **Libraries: Type:** not open to the public. **Holdings:** audio recordings, books, periodicals, video recordings. **Subjects:** oncology nursing, association management, oncology. **Awards:** Excellence Awards. **Frequency:** annual. **Type:** recognition. **Recipient:** for research, clinical practice, education, administration. **Computer Services:** Online services, publication. **Telecommunication Services:** additional toll-free number, (866)257-4ONS. **Committees:** Nominating. **Councils:** Publishing; Steering. **Projects:** Awards; Congress; Institutes of Learning; Others on an ad hoc basis. **Publications:** Clinical Journal of Oncology Nursing, bimonthly. **Price:** $130.00 for institutions in U.S.; $145.00 for institutions outside U.S. ISSN: 1538-067X. **Circulation:** 33,000. **Advertising:** accepted. Alternate Formats: online. Also Cited As: CJON ● Oncology Nursing Forum, bimonthly. Journal. Contains advertisers' index, calendar of events, information on new products, employment opportunity listings, chapter directory, and promotion news. **Price:** $130.00 for institutions in U.S.; $145.00 for institutions outside U.S. ISSN: 1538-0688. **Circulation:** 34,500. **Advertising:** accepted. Alternate Formats: online. Also Cited As: ONF ● ONS News, monthly. Newsletter. Contains Washington, DC, news, calendar of events, employment opportunity listings, member news, and chapter news. **Price:** included in membership dues; $260.00 /year for nonmembers. **Circulation:** 30,000. **Advertising:** accepted. Alternate Formats: online. **Conventions/Meetings:** annual congress, includes roundtables, instructional session, abstracts, posters, discussion sessions (exhibits) ● annual Institute of Learning - symposium, educational session (exhibits).

15196 ■ Pediatric Nursing Certification Board (PNCB)
800 S Frederick Ave., Ste.204
Gaithersburg, MD 20877-4152
Ph: (301)330-2921
Free: (888)641-2767
Fax: (301)330-1504
E-mail: pncb@pncb.org
URL: http://www.pncb.org/ptistore/control/index
Contact: Janet S. Wyatt PhD, CEO
Founded: 1976. **Members:** 15,000. **Staff:** 10. **Budget:** $1,500,000. **Description:** Provides national and international pediatric nursing certification, exams, and continuing education programs. Credentials offered in Certified Pediatric Nurse Practitioner (CPNP) and Certified Pediatric Nurse (CPN). **Libraries: Type:** reference. **Committees:** CPNP Certification and Self-Assessment Exercise. **Affiliated With:** American Academy of Pediatrics; National Association of Pediatric Nurse Practitioners; Society of Pediatric Nurses. **Formerly:** (1989) National Board of Pediatric Nurse Practitioners and Associates; (2004) National Certification Board of Pediatric Nurse Practitioners and Nurses. **Conventions/Meetings:** semiannual board meeting.

15197 ■ Preventive Cardiovascular Nurses Association (PCNA)
613 Williamson St., Ste.205
Madison, WI 53703
Ph: (608)250-2440
Fax: (608)250-2410
E-mail: info@pcna.net
URL: http://www.pcna.net
Contact: Sue Koob MPA, Exec. Dir.
Founded: 1992. **Members:** 1,800. **Membership Dues:** student, $50 (annual) ● regular, $75 (annual). **Staff:** 5. **Regional Groups:** 16. **Description:** Works to prevent cardiovascular disease through assessing risk, facilitating lifestyle changes, and guiding individuals to achieve treatment goals. **Awards: Type:** grant. **Computer Services:** Mailing lists. **Telecommunication Services:** electronic mail, skoob@pcna.net. **Subgroups:** Marketing; Protocols; Publishing; Reimbursement. **Formerly:** (2001) Lipid Nurse Task Force. **Publications:** A Guide to Developing a Cardiovascular Risk Reduction Program. Manual. **Price:** $40.00 for nonmembers; $25.00 for members ● Diabetes - CVD Tool Kit. Alternate Formats: CD-ROM ● Get Tough on Angina Patient Handbook and Resource Tool Kit ● Journal of Cardiovascular Nursing, bimonthly. Also Cited As: JCN ● PCNA Forms: A Companion to the Pocket Guide-Practical Information for Your Cardiovascular Risk Reduction. Manual. **Price:** $25.00 for members; $40.00 for nonmembers. Alternate Formats: online ● Reducing Cardiovascular Risk in the Insulin Resistant Patient. Book. **Price:** $25.00 for members; $40.00 for nonmembers. **Conventions/Meetings:** annual symposium (exhibits).

15198 ■ Respiratory Nursing Society (RNS)
c/o Casey Norris, Pres.-Elect
708 Gladstone CR
Maryville, TN 37804
E-mail: cnorris@etch.com
URL: http://www.respiratorynursingsociety.org
Contact: Casey Norris, Pres.-Elect
Founded: 1990. **Members:** 400. **Membership Dues:** voting/associate, $75 (annual) ● student/retired, $50 (annual) ● corporate, $1,500 (annual). **Local Groups:** 2. **Description:** Nurses who care for clients with pulmonary dysfunction, and who are interested in the promotion of pulmonary health. Fosters the personal and professional development of respiratory nurses, and quality care of their clients. Provides educational opportunities and promotes research in the field. **Computer Services:** Mailing lists, rental. **Telecommunication Services:** electronic mail, joann_frey@trihealth.com. **Publications:** Perspectives in Respiratory Nursing, 4 to 6/year. Newsletter. Contains clinically based articles and news. Alternate Formats: online ● Respiratory Exchange, quarterly. Newsletter. **Advertising:** accepted. **Conventions/Meetings:** annual conference (exhibits).

15199 ■ School Nurse Achievement Program (SNAP)

c/o University of Colorado Health Sciences Center
PO Box 6508, Mail Stop F-541
Aurora, CO 80045-0508
Ph: (303)724-0644
Free: (866)724-0645
Fax: (303)724-0905
E-mail: osh.librarian@uchsc.edu
URL: http://www.uchsc.edu/schoolhealth/ed_pages/ed_index.htm
Founded: 1980. **Membership Dues:** student, $275 ● undergraduate, $453 ● graduate, $604. **Description:** Network of registered nurses who conduct courses in the treatment of handicapped children in a school setting. Trains and certifies state course coordinators. Maintains library of materials pertaining to treatment of handicapped children in a school setting. **Convention/Meeting:** none.

15200 ■ Society of Otorhinolaryngology and Head/Neck Nurses (SOHN)

202 Julia St., Ste.A
New Smyrna Beach, FL 32168
Ph: (386)428-1695
Fax: (386)423-7566
E-mail: info@sohnnurse.com
URL: http://www.sohnnurse.com
Contact: Sandra L. Schwartz RN, Exec. Dir.
Founded: 1976. **Members:** 1,200. **Membership Dues:** full, associate, $85 (annual). **Staff:** 2. **Local Groups:** 20. **Description:** Registered nurses specializing in otorhinolaryngology and head and neck nursing. Seeks to: promote awareness of professional techniques and new developments in the field; enhance professional standards; create a channel for the exchange of ideas, concerns, and information; develop interaction with similar groups. Offers programs and seminars that have been approved for continuing education credits by the American Nurses' Association (see separate entry). **Awards:** Excellence in ORL Nursing Award. **Frequency:** annual. **Type:** recognition. **Recipient:** for individual members who have constantly demonstrated excellence in the delivery of skilled and compassionate care to the ORL-Head and Neck Patient. **Telecommunication Services:** electronic mail, sohnnet@aol.com. **Publications:** ORL-Head and Neck Nursing, quarterly. Journal. Includes book reviews and current trends in nursing. **Price:** included in membership dues; $40.00 /year for nonmembers in U.S.; $45.00 /year for nonmembers outside U.S. **Circulation:** 1,500. **Advertising:** accepted ● Update, bimonthly. Newsletter. Includes employment opportunity listings. **Price:** included in membership dues. **Advertising:** accepted. **Conventions/Meetings:** annual Congress and Nursing Symposium (exhibits) - 2007 Sept. 14-18, Washington, DC; 2008 Sept. 19-23, Chicago, IL; 2009 Sept. 11-15, San Diego, CA.

15201 ■ Society of Pediatric Nurses (SPN)

7794 Grow Dr.
Pensacola, FL 32514
Ph: (850)494-9467
Free: (800)723-2902
Fax: (850)484-8762
E-mail: spn@puetzamc.com
URL: http://www.pedsnurses.org
Contact: Dr. Sandra R. Mott RN, Pres.
Founded: 1990. **Members:** 2,225. **Membership Dues:** associate/student, $60 (annual) ● regular, $105 (annual). **Staff:** 7. **National Groups:** 30. **Description:** Promotes excellence in nursing care of children and their families through support of members' clinical practice, education, research and advocacy. Advocates for accessible, affordable, comprehensive healthcare services for children and their families; advancing the art and science of pediatric nursing through interactive efforts among all nurses in clinical practice, research, education and administration; establishing position statements and standards of practice; and collaborating with other healthcare professionals with similar purposes, child health advocates, and organizations. **Libraries:** Type: reference; not open to the public. **Holdings:** articles, books, periodicals. **Subjects:** pediatric nurs-

ing. **Awards:** Barbara A. Larson Humanitarian Award. **Frequency:** periodic. **Type:** recognition ● Corinne J. Barnes Research Grant. **Frequency:** annual. **Type:** grant ● Educational Scholarship Award. **Frequency:** annual. **Type:** scholarship ● Excellence in Advanced Practice Award. **Frequency:** annual. **Type:** recognition ● Excellence in Clinical Practice Award. **Frequency:** annual. **Type:** recognition ● Excellence in Education Award. **Frequency:** annual. **Type:** recognition ● Excellence in Research Award. **Frequency:** annual. **Type:** recognition ● Margaret Miles Distinguished Service Award. **Frequency:** periodic. **Type:** recognition. **Computer Services:** database. **Committees:** Chapter Development; Clinical Practice; Education; Nominating; Professional Development and Program; Program; Public Policy; Public Policy and Research; Research. **Task Forces:** Advanced Practice; Corporate Membership; Nurse Competency in Aging. **Publications:** Journal of Pediatric Nursing, bimonthly. **Advertising:** accepted ● SPN News, bimonthly. Newsletter. **Advertising:** accepted. **Conventions/Meetings:** annual Pediatric Nursing: Expanding Our Boundaries - conference (exhibits).

15202 ■ Society of Trauma Nurses (STN)

1926 Waukegan Rd., Ste.1
Glenview, IL 60025
Ph: (847)657-6745
Fax: (847)657-6819
E-mail: info@traumanursesoc.org
URL: http://www.traumanurses.org
Contact: Ms. Joyce Paschall, Exec. Dir.
Founded: 1989. **Members:** 1,100. **Membership Dues:** individual in U.S., $100 (annual) ● individual outside U.S., $115 (annual). **Budget:** $450,000. **Description:** Nurses involved in all facets of trauma care. Seeks to communicate trauma nursing information and recognize excellence and innovation in trauma nursing. Addresses legislative issues; assists in the development of standards. Facilitates research. **Awards:** STN Service Award. **Frequency:** annual. **Type:** recognition. **Recipient:** for commitment and dedication to ideals and goals of STN ● Trauma Leadership Award. **Frequency:** annual. **Type:** recognition. **Recipient:** for outstanding leadership in trauma and trauma issues of a medical or nonmedical individual ● Trauma Nursing Lifetime Achievement Award. **Frequency:** annual. **Type:** recognition. **Recipient:** to a nurse with service of more than 10 years in trauma nursing ● Trauma Nursing Service Award. **Frequency:** annual. **Type:** recognition. **Recipient:** for outstanding leadership of an STN nurse/management. **Computer Services:** Mailing lists, membership list - mailing addresses only, no email or phone provided. **Telecommunication Services:** electronic mail, joycep@tcag.com. **Boards:** Directors; Editorial. **Special Interest Groups:** Advanced Practice Trauma Nursing; Injury Prevention; Neurotrauma; Pediatric Trauma; Rural Trauma. **Publications:** Journal of Trauma Nursing, quarterly. **Price:** included in membership dues; $70.00 /year for nonmembers in U.S.; $85.00 /year for nonmembers outside U.S.; $110.00 /year for libraries in U.S. **Advertising:** accepted ● Papers. Alternate Formats: online. **Conventions/Meetings:** annual conference - 2008 Apr. 9-11, New Orleans, LA.

15203 ■ Society of Urologic Nurses and Associates (SUNA)

c/o Anthony J. Jannetti
E Holly Ave., Box 56
Pitman, NJ 08071-0056
Ph: (856)256-2335
Free: (888)827-7862
Fax: (856)589-7463
E-mail: suna@ajj.com
URL: http://www.suna.org
Contact: Anthony J. Jannetti, Contact
Founded: 1972. **Members:** 3,000. **Membership Dues:** senior, $30 (annual) ● active, $60 (annual) ● sustaining, $100 (annual). **Staff:** 6. **Regional Groups:** 4. **Local Groups:** 30. **Description:** Nurses and other health care providers working in the field of urology. Promotes excellence in urological education; establishes standards of care for urology patients. Conducts educational programs; holds examinations

and bestows professional certification; facilitates communication among members. **Libraries:** Type: reference. **Holdings:** books, periodicals. **Subjects:** urology, nursing. **Awards:** Literary Excellence Award. **Frequency:** annual. **Type:** recognition. **Recipient:** for writer of the best manuscript appearing in Urologic Nursing Journal ● MacFarlane Award. **Frequency:** annual. **Type:** recognition. **Recipient:** for the highest scorer on CBUNA certification examination ● Presidents Trophies. **Frequency:** annual. **Type:** recognition. **Recipient:** for two outstanding contributors to the practice of urologic nursing. **Publications:** Uro-Gram, bimonthly. Newsletter ● Urologic Nursing, bimonthly. Journal. **Advertising:** accepted. **Conventions/Meetings:** annual conference, with speakers (exhibits).

15204 ■ Society for Vascular Nursing (SVN)

203 Washington St.
Salem, MA 01970
Ph: (978)744-5005
Fax: (978)744-5029
E-mail: svn@administrare.com
URL: http://www.svnnet.org
Contact: Diane Treat-Johnson PhD, Pres.
Founded: 1982. **Members:** 700. **Membership Dues:** active/associate in U.S. and Canada, $110 (annual) ● active/associate outside U.S. and Canada, $125 (annual) ● student/graduate (1 year) nurse, $55 (annual). **Budget:** $250,000. **Local Groups:** 16. **Description:** Nurses and other health care professionals interested in providing comprehensive care for persons with vascular disease. Seeks to educate public about prevention of PVD. Provides educational programs; conducts research. **Awards:** Distinguished Service Award. **Frequency:** annual. **Type:** recognition ● **Frequency:** annual. **Type:** scholarship. **Computer Services:** database, membership ● mailing lists. **Committees:** Professional Education and Practice; Research. **Formerly:** (1992) Society for Peripheral Vascular Nursing. **Publications:** Journal of Vascular Nursing, quarterly. **Price:** included in membership dues. ISSN: 1062-0303. **Circulation:** 1,100. **Advertising:** accepted ● SVN.prn. Newsletter ● Also publishes patient educational materials. **Conventions/Meetings:** annual convention (exhibits).

15205 ■ Transcultural Nursing Society (TCNS)

Madonna Univ.
Coll. of Nursing and Hea.
36600 Schoolcraft Rd.
Livonia, MI 48150
Free: (888)432-5470
Fax: (734)432-5463
E-mail: staff@tcns.org
URL: http://www.tcns.org
Contact: Beverly Horn PhD, Exec. Dir.
Founded: 1974. **Members:** 400. **Membership Dues:** regular, $100 (annual) ● retired or full-time student, $50 (annual). **Staff:** 1. **Regional Groups:** 6. **Multinational. Description:** Nurses interested in advancing transcultural nursing in education and practice. Seeks to discuss health care of diverse cultures, disseminate transcultural nursing knowledge, improve and maintain quality healthcare, and promote transcultural nursing policies, practices, and leadership skills. Supports and conducts research; provides consultation services. **Awards:** Research Award. **Frequency:** annual. **Type:** monetary. **Recipient:** for research whose primary focus involves transcultural nursing. **Publications:** Journal of Transcultural Nursing, quarterly. **Price:** included in membership dues. **Advertising:** accepted. **Conventions/Meetings:** annual conference (exhibits).

15206 ■ Visiting Nurse Associations of America (VNAA)

99 Summer St., Ste.1700
Boston, MA 02110
Ph: (617)737-3200
Free: (800)426-2547
Fax: (617)737-1144

E-mail: vnaa@vnaa.org
URL: http://www.vnaa.org
Contact: Ms. Carrie Gardner, Exec. Asst.
Founded: 1982. **Members:** 210. **Staff:** 9. **Budget:** $1,300,000. **Description:** Home health care agencies. Develops competitive strength among community-based nonprofit visiting nurse organizations; works to strengthen business resources and economic programs through contracting, marketing, governmental affairs and publications. **Libraries: Type:** not open to the public. **Awards:** Clinician of the Year. **Frequency:** annual. **Type:** recognition ● Mentor of the Year. **Frequency:** annual. **Type:** recognition ● Program Manager of the Year. **Frequency:** annual. **Type:** recognition ● Volunteer of the Year - Agency Board Member. **Frequency:** annual. **Type:** recognition ● Volunteer of the Year - Individual Care Provider. **Frequency:** annual. **Type:** recognition. **Computer Services:** Information services, referrals to local visiting nurse associations ● mailing lists, community-based, nonprofit visiting nurse organizations. **Telecommunication Services:** additional toll-free number, (888)866-8773. **Committees:** Agency Board Member; Education; Forum of Coalitions; Government Affairs; Membership. **Formerly:** (1985) American Affiliation of Visiting Nurses Associations and Services. **Publications:** *Nursing Procedure Manual*, monthly. **Price:** free for members and CEOs. **Circulation:** 25. **Advertising:** accepted. **Conventions/Meetings:** annual meeting (exhibits).

15207 ■ Wound, Ostomy and Continence Nurses Society: An Association of E.T. Nurses (WOCN)
15000 Commerce Pkwy., Ste.C
Mount Laurel, NJ 08054
Free: (888)224-9626
Fax: (856)439-0525
E-mail: wocn_info@wocn.org
URL: http://www.wocn.org
Contact: Nicolette Zuecca, Exec. Dir.
Founded: 1969. **Members:** 4,000. **Membership Dues:** active, $110 (annual) ● associate, $105 (annual) ● retired-active, retired-associate, student, $65 (annual). **Staff:** 8. **Budget:** $2,000,000. **Regional Groups:** 11. **Local Groups:** 20. **Description:** Enterostomal therapy (ET) nurses, wound, ostomy and continence care nurses in 10 countries trained in WOCN accredited schools; individuals interested in objectives of the association who hold a valid license in medicine or nursing; health-related firms. Seeks to support ET, wound, ostomy, and continence nurses by promoting educational, clinical, and research opportunities and to guide the delivery of expert health care to individuals with wounds, ostomies, and incontinence. **Awards:** ET/WOC Nursing Education Programs and Advanced Degree Scholarships. **Frequency:** quarterly. **Type:** scholarship. **Committees:** Accreditation; Clinical Practice; Communications; Continuing Education; Guideline/Pathways; Legislative Response; National Conference Planning; Nominations; Professional Practice; Publications; Regulatory/Reimbursement; Scholarship; Web Team. **Formerly:** Wound, Ostomy and Continence Nurses Society, An Association of E.T. Nurses; (1993) International Association for Enterostomal Therapy. **Publications:** *Guideline for Management of Wounds in Patients with Lower-Extremity Arterial Disease*. **Price:** $10.00 for members; $15.00 for nonmembers ● *Journal of Wound, Ostomy and Continence Nursing*, bimonthly. Provides continuing education for the entire scope of WOCN nursing practice. **Price:** $72.49 /year for individuals in U.S.; $235.49 /year for institutions in U.S.; $97.49 /year for individuals in U.S.; $256.49 /year for institutions outside U.S. ISSN: 1071-5754. **Circulation:** 5,000. **Advertising:** accepted. Alternate Formats: online. Also Cited As: *JWOCN* ● *Management of Urinary Incontinence*. Slides and handout. **Price:** $50.00 for members; $85.00 for nonmembers ● *Patient Information Data System*. **Price:** $95.00 for members; $125.00 for nonmembers ● *Professional Practice Manual*. **Price:** $85.00 for members; $125.00 for nonmembers ● *Standards of Care Guidelines for Management*. Booklets ● *WOCN News*, quarterly. Newsletter. **Price:** included in membership dues ●

Membership Directory, annual. **Price:** $35.00 for members; $50.00 for nonmembers ● Fact Sheets and Position Statements N/C. **Conventions/Meetings:** annual Wound, Ostomy and Continence Conference (exhibits) - always June.

15208 ■ Wound, Ostomy and Continence Nursing Certification Board (WOCNCB)
555 E Wells St., Ste.1100
Milwaukee, WI 53202-3823
Ph: (414)289-8721
Free: (888)496-2622
Fax: (414)276-2146
E-mail: info@wocncb.org
URL: http://www.wocncb.org
Contact: Kathy Wright RN, Pres.
Description: Works to promote consumer safety and protection; provides credentialing in wound, ostomy, and continence care nursing. **Publications:** *The Board's BULLETIN*, semiannual. Newsletter.

Nursing Homes

15209 ■ American College of Health Care Administrators (ACHCA)
300 N Lee St., Ste.301
Alexandria, VA 22314
Ph: (703)739-7900
Free: (888)88-ACHCA
Fax: (703)739-7901
E-mail: mgrachek@achca.org
URL: http://www.achca.org
Contact: Marianna Kern Grachek, Pres./CEO
Founded: 1962. **Members:** 6,360. **Membership Dues:** full, fellow, $273 (annual) ● affiliate, $355 (annual) ● senior, $150 (annual) ● student, $50 (annual). **Staff:** 16. **Budget:** $2,500,000. **Regional Groups:** 11. **State Groups:** 48. **Description:** Persons actively engaged in the administration of long-term care facilities, such as nursing homes, retirement communities, assisted living facilities, and sub-acute care programs. Administers professional certification programs for assisted living, sub-acute and nursing home administrators. Works to elevate the standards in the field and to develop and promote a code of ethics and standards of education and training. Seeks to inform allied professions and the public that good administration of long-term care facilities calls for special formal academic training and experience. Encourages research in all aspects of geriatrics, the chronically ill, and administration. Maintains placement service. Holds special education programs; facilitates networking among administrators. **Libraries: Type:** reference. **Holdings:** 500; books, papers, periodicals. **Subjects:** long-term care administration, geriatrics, gerontology. **Awards: Type:** recognition. **Computer Services:** Online services. **Committees:** Advancement; Advocacy; Awards; Bylaws; Development; Education and Research; Ethics and Standards; Nominating; Professional Certification. **Task Forces:** Assisted Living; Cultural Diversity. **Formerly:** American College of Nursing Home Administrators. **Publications:** *ACHCA Update*, 10/year. Newsletter. News and articles of interest to the Profession. **Price:** included in membership dues. **Advertising:** accepted ● *Monday Morning Memo*, biweekly. Newsletter. Contains information on initiatives and industry updates. **Price:** included in membership dues. **Advertising:** accepted. Alternate Formats: online. Also Cited As: *MMM* ● Also publishes educational materials. **Conventions/Meetings:** annual convention (exhibits) - always spring ● annual Winter Marketplace - meeting (exhibits) - December.

15210 ■ American Medical Directors Association (AMDA)
10480 Little Patuxent Pkwy., Ste.760
Columbia, MD 21044
Ph: (410)740-9743 (410)992-3126
Free: (800)876-2632
Fax: (410)740-4572

E-mail: info@amda.com
URL: http://www.amda.com
Contact: Lorraine Tarnove, Exec. Dir.
Founded: 1975. **Members:** 8,000. **Membership Dues:** physician, $198 (annual) ● retiree, $35 (annual) ● interdisciplinary team, $99 (annual) ● physician in training, $75 (annual). **Staff:** 24. **Budget:** $4,000,000. **State Groups:** 39. **Description:** Physicians providing care in long-term facilities including nursing homes. Sponsors continuing medical education in geriatrics and medical administration. Promotes improved long-term care. **Libraries: Type:** reference. **Holdings:** archival material, audiovisuals, books, clippings, periodicals. **Subjects:** long-term care and geriatrics, medical administration. **Awards: Type:** recognition. **Computer Services:** Mailing lists. **Publications:** *AMDA Reports*, quarterly. Newsletter. Includes calendar of events, reviews of articles, publications, and other resources. **Price:** available to members only. **Circulation:** 8,000 ● *Caring for the Ages*, monthly. Newspaper. Features information related to medical direction. **Price:** included in membership dues; $137.00 /year for individuals in U.S.; $220.00 /year for institutions in U.S.; $197.00 /year for individuals outside U.S. ISSN: 1526-4114. **Circulation:** 47,000. **Advertising:** accepted ● *JAMDA*, 9/year. Journal. **Price:** included in membership dues; $138.00 for 42 copies. ISSN: 1525-8610. **Circulation:** 8,000. **Advertising:** accepted. **Conventions/Meetings:** annual conference and symposium (exhibits).

15211 ■ Lemko Housing Organization (LHO)
Address Unknown since 2007
Description: Individuals and organizations. Promotes availability of housing and living assistance for elderly people or people with disabilities of Slavic descent. Purchases property and constructs housing and assisted care facilities; provides programs and services to people with disabilities and the elderly.

15212 ■ National Association of Boards of Examiners of Long Term Care Administrators (NAB)
1444 I St. NW, No. 700
Washington, DC 20005-6542
Ph: (202)712-9040
Fax: (202)216-9646
E-mail: nab@bostrom.com
URL: http://www.nabweb.org
Contact: Randy Lindner, Exec. Dir.
Founded: 1972. **Members:** 550. **Membership Dues:** state licensing board, $1,200 (annual) ● associate, subscribing, $70 (annual). **Staff:** 4. **Budget:** $1,600,000. **Description:** State boards responsible for licensing nursing homes administrators. Produces exam to test the competence of nursing home administrators; operates continuing education review service; disseminates information and educational materials on nursing home administration. **Computer Services:** database, disciplinary. **Formerly:** National Association of Boards of Examiners of Nursing Home Administrators. **Publications:** *NAB/AIT Preceptor's Domains of Practice Internship Manual*. Book. Offers a detailed set of AIT activities based on the five major practice areas. **Price:** $55.00 ● *NAB Study Guide: How To Prepare For the Nursing Home Administrators Examination*. Book. **Price:** $130.00 ● *RC/AL AIT Preceptor's Domains of Practice Internship Manual*. Book. **Price:** $55.00 ● *RC/AL Study Guide: How to Prepare for the Residential Care/Assisted Living Administrators Examination*. Book. **Price:** $130.00. Alternate Formats: CD-ROM. **Conventions/Meetings:** annual conference ● annual Mid-Year Meeting.

15213 ■ National Association of Professional Geriatric Care Managers (GCM)
1604 N Country Club Rd.
Tucson, AZ 85716
Ph: (520)881-8008
Fax: (520)325-7925
E-mail: vtobin@kellencompany.com
URL: http://www.caremanager.org
Contact: Victoria Tobin, Exec. Dir.
Founded: 1986. **Members:** 1,700. **Membership Dues:** care manager/affiliate, $245 (annual). **Staff:**

18. **Budget:** $500,000. **Regional Groups:** 1. **State Groups:** 11. **Description:** Promotes quality services and care for elderly citizens. Provides referral service and distributes information to individuals interested in geriatric care management. Maintains referral network. **Awards:** Adell Elkind Award. **Frequency:** annual. **Type:** recognition. **Recipient:** for contribution to care management. **Formerly:** National Association of Private Geriatric Care Managers. **Publications:** *GCM Journal*, quarterly. **Price:** $95.00/year. **Circulation:** 1,700 ● *Inside GCM*, quarterly. Newsletter. **Advertising:** accepted ● Membership Directory, annual. **Conventions/Meetings:** annual conference (exhibits).

Nutrition

15214 ■ American Association of Nutritional Consultants (AANC)
401 Kings Hwy.
Winona Lake, IN 46590
Ph: (574)267-6165
Free: (888)828-2262
Fax: (574)268-2120
E-mail: registrar@aanc.net
URL: http://www.aanc.net
Contact: Adrienne Naibauer, Admin.

Founded: 1980. **Members:** 5,000. **Membership Dues:** diplomate/professional/association, $60 (annual) ● corporate, $500 (annual). **Staff:** 5. **Description:** Professional nutritional consultants. Seeks to create a forum for exchange of nutritional information. Offers benefits such as car rental and laboratory discounts. **Absorbed:** (1984) International Academy of Nutritional Consultants. **Publications:** *Health-Keepers*, quarterly. Magazine. Focuses on innovation in the field of professional nutritional counseling, and vitamin, mineral, and food therapies. Includes nutrition digest. **Price:** available to members only. ISSN: 8750-2370. **Circulation:** 4,000. **Advertising:** accepted ● Membership Directory. **Conventions/Meetings:** annual convention (exhibits).

15215 ■ American Board of Nutrition (ABN)
Address Unknown since 2007
URL: http://main.uab.edu/ipnc/show.asp-?durki=38578

Founded: 1948. **Members:** 524. **Staff:** 1. **Budget:** $27,000. **Description:** Currently inactive. Physicians qualified to treat nutritional and metabolic disorders; doctoral recipients working on problems of human nutrition and nutrient requirements. Establishes standards for qualification of persons as specialists in the field of clinical human nutrition; holds examinations and certifies those who meet its qualifications. **Publications:** *Directory of Diplomates in Human Nutrition and Clinical Nutrition*, biennial. **Price:** free. **Advertising:** not accepted. **Conventions/Meetings:** annual Certification Exam - meeting - in the fall.

15216 ■ American Board of Physician Nutrition Specialists (ABPNS)
c/o University of Alabama at Birmingham
439 Susan Mott Webb Nutrition Sciences Bldg.
1675 Univ. Blvd.
Birmingham, AL 35294-3360
Ph: (205)996-2513
Fax: (205)934-7050
E-mail: shreid@uab.edu
URL: http://main.uab.edu/ipnc/show.asp-?durki=37725
Contact: Caroline M. Apovian MD, Pres.

Founded: 2001. **Description:** Provides a credential that recognizes physician expertise in clinical nutrition. **Publications:** *Handbook and Application for Candidates* ● *Progress Report*. Annual Report.

15217 ■ American Celiac Society/Dietary Support Coalition (ACS/DSC)
PO Box 23455
New Orleans, LA 70183-0455
Ph: (504)737-3293

E-mail: amerceliacsoc@onebox.com
URL: http://www.americanceliacsociety.org
Contact: Annette Bentley, Pres.

Founded: 1970. **Members:** 7,000. **Membership Dues:** individual - suggested contribution, $25 (annual) ● individual outside U.S., $45 (annual). **Staff:** 7. **Regional Groups:** 76. **Local Groups:** 57. **National Groups:** 4. **Languages:** English, Italian, Spanish. **Description:** Individuals interested in a gluten-free diet; physicians who diagnose and care for individuals with gluten-sensitive intestinal disease, dietitians, nutritionists, and agencies that serve or have an interest in individuals with gluten-sensitive enteropathy, also known as celiac sprue. Provides information on how to follow a gluten-free diet; assists members in locating specialty foods that are gluten-free; encourages retailers to make gluten-free products available. Coordinates activities with other international celiac societies. Maintains speakers' bureau for patients and health care professionals. **Computer Services:** database ● mailing lists. **Telecommunication Services:** electronic mail, info@americanceliacsociety.org. **Affiliated With:** Digestive Disease National Coalition; National Digestive Diseases Information Clearinghouse. **Absorbed:** (1989) Whoo Who Sprue. **Formerly:** (1990) America Celiac Society. **Publications:** *Whoo's Report*, 3/year. Newsletter. **Circulation:** 6,000. **Advertising:** accepted. **Conventions/Meetings:** annual conference (exhibits).

15218 ■ American College of Nutrition (ACN)
300 S Duncan Ave., Ste.225
Clearwater, FL 33755
Ph: (727)446-6086
Fax: (727)446-6202
E-mail: office@amcollnutr.org
URL: http://www.amcollnutr.org
Contact: Dr. Geltrude Mingrone, Exec. Dir.

Founded: 1959. **Members:** 1,170. **Membership Dues:** fellow/regular, $150 (annual) ● student/trainee, $60 (annual). **Staff:** 5. **Budget:** $350,000. **Regional Groups:** 1. **Multinational. Description:** Physicians, research scientists, nutritionists, dietitians, allied health personnel, and postbaccalaureate students and trainees in these fields. Provides education on clinical, scientific, and experimental developments in the field of nutrition. Stimulates the exchange of information between nutrition scientists and physicians interested in applying research findings to the care of patients; encourages nutrition education in medical schools; provides for continuing education of physicians and other scientists on nutritional subjects. Sponsors a postgraduate course on nutritional problems. Advises physicians on nutrition developments of clinical importance. Certifies credentials of professional nutritionists, including by formal examination. **Awards:** ACN Award Lecture. **Frequency:** annual. **Type:** recognition ● ACN Humanitarian Award. **Frequency:** annual. **Type:** recognition ● Best International Presentation Award. **Frequency:** annual. **Type:** recognition ● Best Poster Awards. **Frequency:** annual. **Type:** recognition ● Best Review Paper in JACN Award. **Frequency:** annual. **Type:** recognition ● Charles E. Rogus Award for Best Scientific Paper in JACN. **Frequency:** annual. **Type:** recognition ● Grace A. Goldsmith Award Lecture. **Frequency:** annual. **Type:** recognition. **Recipient:** for a scientist under the age of 50 ● Mark Bieber Awards. **Frequency:** annual. **Type:** recognition ● New Investigator Award. **Frequency:** annual. **Type:** recognition ● Seelig Magnesium Award. **Frequency:** annual. **Type:** recognition. **Recipient:** for an individual with outstanding contribution defining the role of magnesium in nutrition. **Computer Services:** Mailing lists. **Councils:** Bone Health; Cardiovascular Diseases; Endocrinology; Enteral and Parenteral Tube Feeding; Gastroenterology; Gerontology; Laboratory Diagnosis of Nutritional Status; Magnesium, Trace Minerals, and Vitamins; Nephrology; Neurosciences; Obesity and Eating Disorders; Oncology and Hematology; Pediatrics and Perinatology; Surgery. **Publications:** *ACN Newsletter*, quarterly. Contains member news, calendar of events, and nutritional articles. **Price:** free ● *Journal of the American College of Nutrition*, bimonthly. Contains

peer-reviewed articles. **Price:** included in membership dues; $90.00 /year for nonmembers in U.S.; $235.00 /year for institutions in U.S.; $130.00 /year for nonmembers outside U.S. ISSN: 0731-5724. **Circulation:** 1,300. **Advertising:** accepted. Alternate Formats: online. **Conventions/Meetings:** annual meeting - 2007 Sept. 19-23, Orlando, FL ● annual Symposium on Advances in Clinical Nutrition - conference and symposium (exhibits).

15219 ■ American Council of Applied Clinical Nutrition (ACACN)
PO Box 509
Florissant, MO 63032
Ph: (314)921-3997
Free: (800)826-5366
Fax: (314)921-8485
Contact: Dr. Clarence T. Smith PhD, Pres.

Founded: 1974. **Members:** 500. **Staff:** 6. **Description:** Clinical nutrition specialists. Offers structured academic course and certification; conducts research.

15220 ■ American Dietetic Association (ADA)
120 S Riverside Plz., Ste.2000
Chicago, IL 60606-6995
Ph: (312)899-0040
Free: (800)877-1600
Fax: (312)899-1979
E-mail: rmoen@eatright.org
URL: http://www.eatright.org
Contact: Ronald S. Moen, CEO

Founded: 1917. **Members:** 67,000. **Membership Dues:** active, $200 (annual) ● retired, $100 (annual) ● student, $43 (annual) ● international, $170 (annual). **Staff:** 150. **Budget:** $33,000,000. **State Groups:** 52. **Multinational. Description:** Represents food and nutrition professionals. Promotes nutrition, health and well-being. **Libraries: Type:** not open to the public. **Holdings:** 3,000; audiovisuals, books, periodicals. **Subjects:** foods, nutrition, dietetics practice. **Awards: Type:** recognition ● **Type:** scholarship. **Divisions:** Education and Research; Management Practices. **Publications:** *Dieting for Dummies, 2nd Ed.*. Book. **Price:** $21.99 ● *The Healthy Beef Cookbook*. Books ● *Journal of the American Dietetic Association*, monthly. Contains research and practice articles, association news, literature abstracts, and a list of new publications. **Price:** included in membership dues; $98.00 /year for nonmembers; $315.00 /year for institutions. ISSN: 0002-8223. **Circulation:** 65,000. **Advertising:** accepted. Alternate Formats: microform; online ● *365 Days of Healthy Eating from the American Dietetic*. Book. Contains practical hints, tips, and strategies for healthy diet. **Price:** $14.95. **Conventions/Meetings:** annual Food & Nutrition Conference and Expo (exhibits) - 2007 Sept. 29-Oct. 2, Philadelphia, PA.

15221 ■ American Society for Clinical Nutrition (ASCN)
9650 Rockville Pike
Bethesda, MD 20814-3998
Ph: (301)634-7110
Fax: (301)634-7892
E-mail: schlicker@verizon.net
URL: http://www.nutrition.org
Contact: Sandra A. Schlicker PhD, Exec. Dir.

Founded: 1959. **Members:** 1,565. **Membership Dues:** associate, emeritus, regular, or student, $235 (annual). **Staff:** 10. **For-Profit. Description:** Physicians and scientists actively engaged in clinical nutrition research. Promotes teaching, research, and reporting of progress in clinical nutrition. Offers annual postgraduate course. **Computer Services:** Mailing lists. **Committees:** Clinical Practice Issues in Health and Disease; Continuing Medical Education; Food and Nutrition Science; Professional Nutrition Education; Public Affairs; Public Information. **Affiliated With:** American Society for Nutrition. **Formerly:** (1997) American Institute of Nutrition. **Publications:** *The American Journal of Clinical Nutrition*, monthly. Contains original research findings. Includes book reviews, commentaries, letters to the editor, and editorials. **Price:** $60.00 /year for members; $120.00 /year for nonmembers in U.S.; $140.00 /year for nonmembers outside U.S.; $50.00/year for students.

ISSN: 0002-9165. **Circulation:** 7,600. **Advertising:** accepted. Alternate Formats: microform ● Publishes 6-8 supplements per year. **Conventions/Meetings:** annual Experimental Biology - meeting (exhibits) ● annual meeting.

15222 ■ American Society for Nutrition (ASN)

9650 Rockville Pike, Ste.4500
Bethesda, MD 20814-3998
Ph: (301)634-7050
Fax: (301)634-7892
E-mail: sec@asnutrition.org
URL: http://www.asnutrition.org
Contact: John Courtney, Exec. Off.

Founded: 1928. **Members:** 3,500. **Membership Dues:** regular/associate, $150 (annual) ● postdoctoral, $50 (annual) ● student, $30 (annual) ● emeritus, $25 (annual). **Staff:** 6. **Budget:** $1,000,000. **Description:** Serves as professional society of nutrition research scientists from universities, government, and industry. **Libraries: Type:** reference. **Holdings:** archival material. **Awards:** Bio-Serv Award in Experimental Animal Nutrition. **Frequency:** annual. **Type:** recognition. **Recipient:** for an individual with meritorious research in nutrition ● Centrum Center for Nutrition Science Award. **Frequency:** annual. **Type:** recognition. **Recipient:** for an individual with significance to the understanding of human nutrition ● Conrad A. Elvehjem Award. **Frequency:** annual. **Type:** recognition. **Recipient:** for an individual with distinguished service to the public through the science of nutrition ● Dannon Institute Mentorship Award. **Frequency:** annual. **Type:** recognition. **Recipient:** for an individual with outstanding mentorship in success of nutritional research ● ELR Stokstad Award. **Frequency:** annual. **Type:** recognition. **Recipient:** for a scientist with outstanding fundamental research in nutrition ● **Frequency:** annual. **Type:** fellowship. **Recipient:** to pre-doctoral students ● Mead Johnson Award. **Frequency:** annual. **Type:** recognition. **Recipient:** for an investigator with single outstanding piece of nutrition research ● Nutrition Science Journalism Award. **Frequency:** annual. **Type:** recognition. **Recipient:** for individuals with exceptional achievements in nutrition science journalism ● Osborne and Mendel Award. **Frequency:** annual. **Type:** recognition. **Recipient:** for an individual with outstanding basic research in nutrition ● Peter Reeds Memorial Young Investigator Award. **Frequency:** annual. **Type:** recognition. **Recipient:** for an individual with outstanding research in macronutrient metabolism. **Committees:** Graduate Nutrition Education; History of Nutrition; Industry Liaison; Predoctoral Fellowship; Public Information; Public Policy. **Affiliated With:** American Society for Clinical Nutrition. **Formerly:** (1997) American Institute of Nutrition; (2006) American Society for Nutritional Sciences. **Publications:** *Journal of Nutrition*, monthly. Covers all aspects of experimental nutrition, critical reviews, biographies, and commentaries on controversial issues. **Price:** included in membership dues; $150.00 /year for nonmembers in U.S.; $250.00 /year for nonmembers outside U.S.; $585.00 /year for institutions. ISSN: 0022-3166. **Circulation:** 4,000. Alternate Formats: online ● *Nutrition Notes*, quarterly. Newsletter. Provides information about the Institute's activities as well as topical national and international issues in nutrition. **Price:** included in membership dues; $30.00 /year for nonmembers. **Circulation:** 3,300. Alternate Formats: online. **Conventions/Meetings:** annual meeting, held in conjunction with Experimental Biology.

15223 ■ American Society for Parenteral and Enteral Nutrition (ASPEN)

8630 Fenton St., Ste.412
Silver Spring, MD 20910-3805
Ph: (301)587-6315
Free: (800)727-4567
Fax: (301)587-2365
E-mail: aspen@nutr.org
URL: http://www.nutritioncare.org
Contact: Marion Winkler, Pres.

Founded: 1975. **Members:** 6,000. **Membership Dues:** active, in U.S., $120-$185 (annual) ● student in U.S., $65 (annual) ● chapter, $5-$20 (annual) ●

active, outside U.S., $140-$205 (annual) ● student outside U.S., $85 (annual). **Staff:** 20. **Budget:** $2,500,000. **State Groups:** 49. **Description:** Physicians, dietitians, nurses, pharmacists, and members of the industry. Works to promote quality patient care, education, and research in the field of nutrition and metabolic support in all health care settings. Educates health care professionals. Conducts postgraduate courses and research programs; compiles statistics. **Awards:** Discipline Research Awards. **Frequency:** annual. **Type:** monetary. **Recipient:** for a research done by a nurse, dietitian, and pharmacist members of ASPEN ● Dudrick Research Scholar Award. **Frequency:** annual. **Type:** monetary. **Recipient:** for past research accomplishments of a young investigator in the field of nutrition support ● RHOADS Foundation Research Award. **Frequency:** annual. **Type:** monetary. **Recipient:** for nutrition researchers in the early stages of their careers, to encourage research in the fields of nutrition and metabolic support and related areas of clinical nutrition ● Vars Award. **Frequency:** annual. **Type:** monetary. **Recipient:** for best research by a young investigator at each Clinical Congress. **Computer Services:** Mailing lists. **Committees:** Education and Professional Development; Industry Liaison; Public Policy; Research and Data; Standards. **Councils:** Advisory Board. **Publications:** *Advances in Nutrition Support: An Anthology.* Book. Contains review articles from Nutrition in Clinical Practice and the Journal of Parental and Enteral Nutrition. **Price:** $40.00 for members; $60.00 for nonmembers ● *ASPEN's Guidelines (2002) and Standards.* Book. Contains guidelines for the use of parental and enteral nutrition in adult and pediatric patients. **Price:** $70.00 for members; $140.00 for nonmembers ● *Clinical Guidelines Pocket Guide 2002.* Handbook. **Price:** $20.00 for members; $30.00 for nonmembers ● *Journal of Parenteral and Enteral Nutrition,* bimonthly. Includes current research, book reviews, case reports, and citations from world literature. **Price:** included in membership dues; $45.00/year for students; $165.00 /year for institutions; $90.00 /year for individuals. ISSN: 0148-6071. **Circulation:** 10,500. **Advertising:** accepted. Also Cited As: *JPEN* ● *Nutrition in Clinical Practice,* bimonthly. Journal. Contains abstracts of literature in the field from other publications, ASPEN news, case reports, legislative news, and a list of new products. **Price:** included in membership dues; $45.00/year for students; $115.00 /year for institutions; $65.00 /year for individuals. ISSN: 0884-5336. **Circulation:** 9,000. **Advertising:** accepted ● *Nutrition Support Core Curriculum, 3rd Edition.* Manual. Includes general and disease-specific nutrition concepts, self-assessment Q&A, summary tables, and extensive index. **Price:** $40.00 for members; $70.00 for nonmembers ● *Nutrition Support Practice Manual.* Covers product resources. **Price:** $50.00 ● Monographs ● Also publishes course syllabi on a variety of clinical nutrition topics, self-assessment programs, and reference anthologies. **Conventions/Meetings:** annual Clinical Congress - conference (exhibits) - always January or February.

15224 ■ Commission on Dietetic Registration (CDR)

120 S Riverside Plz., Ste.2000
Chicago, IL 60606-6995
Ph: (312)899-0040
Fax: (312)899-4772
E-mail: cdr@eatright.org
URL: http://www.cdrnet.org
Contact: Chris Reidy, Dir.

Members: 11. **Multinational. Description:** Credentialing agency for the American Dietetic Association. Exists to serve the public by establishing and enforcing standards for certification, recertification, and the code of ethics, and by issuing credentials to individuals who meet these standards; has sole and independent authority in all matters pertaining to certification including, but not limited to standard setting, establishment of fees, finances and administration. Awards five separate and distinct credentials: Registered Dietitian; Dietetic Technician, Registered; Board Certified Specialist in Renal Nutrition; Board Certified Specialist in Pediatric Nutrition; and Fellow of the

American Dietetic Association. **Affiliated With:** National Organization for Competency Assurance.

15225 ■ Community Nutrition Institute (CNI)

419 W Broad St., Ste.204
Falls Church, VA 22046
Ph: (703)532-0030
Fax: (703)532-5780
E-mail: rl@communitynutrition.org
URL: http://www.communitynutrition.org
Contact: Rodney E. Leonard, Exec.Dir.

Founded: 1970. **Staff:** 5. **Description:** Citizen advocates specializing in food and nutrition issues including hunger, food quality and safety, nutrition research, food programs, education, and food labeling and marketing. Aims to secure a food system that provides access to a diet that sustains cultural and social values and maintains human health. Offers advocacy-training courses for federal, state, and community impact. Supports litigation on food policy issues. Assists federal agencies in analyzing and implementing food programs and research. Develops standards for food products and lobbies for USDA and FDA ratification. **Libraries: Type:** open to the public. **Holdings:** 30. **Subjects:** nutrition policy, food safety. **Publications:** *CFNP Report,* biweekly. Newsletter. Contains news about CFNP and related issues affecting low-income people. Alternate Formats: online ● *Nutrition Week,* weekly. Newsletter. Includes association news, employment listings, research notes, and statistics. **Price:** $85.00/year. ISSN: 0736-0096. **Circulation:** 2,000 ● Booklets. **Circulation:** 2,000 ● Also publishes training materials. **Conventions/Meetings:** seminar ● workshop.

15226 ■ Community Systems Foundation (CSF)

219 S Main St., Ste.206
Ann Arbor, MI 48104
Ph: (734)761-1357
Fax: (734)761-1356
E-mail: sswestrin@communitysystemsfoundation.org
URL: http://www.umich.edu/~csfound
Contact: Kris S. Oswalt MBA, Pres.

Founded: 1963. **Members:** 10. **Staff:** 25. **Budget:** $1,000,000. **Description:** Commits in improving the quality of life through applied research and direct assistance to communities, governmental agencies, and service-oriented entities in the private sector. Focuses on community learning and encourages citizen involvement. Works to develop systems for evaluating, monitoring, and implementing programs of nutrition and family planning such as UNICEF's ChildInfo System. **Libraries: Type:** reference. **Holdings:** 2,500. **Computer Services:** database, research ● information services, management and geographic. **Publications:** *Research Reports.*

15227 ■ Comparative Nutrition Society (CNS)

c/o Wendy R. Hood, Sec./Webmaster
PO Box 261954
Conway, SC 29528
E-mail: wrhood@coastal.edu
URL: http://www.cnsweb.org
Contact: Wendy R. Hood, Sec./Webmaster

Founded: 1996. **Membership Dues:** full, associate, $50 (annual) ● student, $20 (annual). **Description:** Aims to promote and establish a professional concept of comparative nutrition. Facilitates communication among laboratory and field scientists from various disciplines with interests in comparative nutrition. Encourages education and professional development in the field of comparative nutrition. **Publications:** *The CNS News.* Newsletter. Alternate Formats: online ● Proceedings.

15228 ■ Consultant Dietitians in Health Care Facilities (CDHCF)

2219 Cardinal Dr.
Waterloo, IA 50701
Ph: (319)235-0991
Free: (800)877-1600
Fax: (319)235-7224

E-mail: fewalker@stellarnet.com

URL: http://www.cdhcf.org

Contact: Jojo Dantone-DeBarbieris MS, Chair

Founded: 1975. **Members:** 6,100. **Membership Dues:** individual, $30 (annual). **Staff:** 1. **Budget:** $250,000. **Regional Groups:** 7. **State Groups:** 50. **Description:** A special interest group of the American Dietetic Association. Dietitians employed in extended care facilities, nursing homes, homecare, and a variety of food service operations. Disseminates information; assists in solving their problems in the field. Conducts workshops; offers networking opportunities for professionals. **Awards:** Best Practice Award. **Frequency:** quarterly. **Type:** recognition. **Recipient:** for innovations in practice ● CDHCF Circle Award. **Frequency:** annual. **Type:** recognition. **Recipient:** for outstanding support for the Consultant Dietitian ● CDHCF Distinguished Member Award. **Frequency:** annual. **Type:** recognition. **Recipient:** for significant contributions by a member ● CDHCF Horizon Award. **Frequency:** annual. **Type:** scholarship ● CDHCF Scholarship Award. **Frequency:** annual. **Type:** scholarship ● Gaynold Jenson Educational Stipend. **Frequency:** annual. **Type:** scholarship. **Recipient:** for educational programs ● Ross Leadership Award. **Frequency:** annual. **Type:** recognition. **Recipient:** for outstanding leadership. **Computer Services:** database ● mailing lists. **Telecommunication Services:** electronic mail, jojodantone@aol.com. **Committees:** Allied Organizations; Legislative; Marketing; Public Relations; Quality Assurance. **Formerly:** Consultant Dieticians Special Interest Group. **Publications:** The Consultant Dietitian, quarterly. Newsletter. **Price:** $25.00/year. **Circulation:** 6,100 ● Dining Skills ● Inservice Manual ● Pocket Resource for Nutrition Assessment. **Price:** $10.50 ● Tool Box (Adults with Developmental Disabilities) ● Video Tapes on Dining Skills. Videos. **Conventions/Meetings:** annual meeting and seminar, held in conjunction with ADA (exhibits).

15229 ■ Dietary Managers Association (DMA)

406 Surrey Woods Dr.

St. Charles, IL 60174

Ph: (630)587-6336

Free: (800)323-1908

Fax: (630)587-6308

E-mail: info@dmaonline.org

URL: http://www.dmaonline.org/index.html

Contact: Erma L. O'Neil CDM, Chair

Founded: 1960. **Members:** 14,000. **Membership Dues:** active/associate, $97 (annual) ● student, $35 (annual). **Staff:** 14. **Budget:** $1,800,000. **State Groups:** 50. **Description:** Dietary managers united to maintain a high level of competency and quality in dietary departments through continuing education. Provides educational programs and placement service. **Libraries:** **Type:** not open to the public. **Holdings:** 74; books. **Subjects:** food, nutrition management, food services, recipe, health, associations. **Awards:** State Achievement Award. **Frequency:** annual. **Type:** recognition. **Recipient:** for states that fulfill requirements. **Computer Services:** Mailing lists, of members. **Committees:** Political Action. **Formerly:** Hospital, Institution and Educational Food Service Society. **Publications:** Accounting and Finance Fundamentals. Book. **Price:** $50.00 for members; $60.00 for nonmembers. Alternate Formats: online ● Alzheimer's Disease. Book. Provides strategies to assist patients/residents at each stage of the disease. **Price:** $20.00 for members; $30.00 for nonmembers ● Diet Therapy for the Dietary Manager. Book. **Price:** $47.50 for nonmembers ● Dietary Manager, bimonthly. Magazine. **Price:** $40.00/year. **Circulation:** 17,000. **Advertising:** accepted. Alternate Formats: online ● DMA Master Track Human Resource. Booklet. **Price:** $60.00 for members; $90.00 for nonmembers ● DMA Master Track Operations Management. Booklet. **Price:** $100.00 for members; $150.00 for nonmembers ● Managing Foodservice Operations. Book ● Professional Procurement Practices. Book. **Conventions/Meetings:** annual conference and meeting, with expo (exhibits) - 2008 July 27-31, Philadelphia, PA; 2009 Aug. 9-13, Atlanta, GA.

15230 ■ Egg Nutrition Center (ENC)

1900 L St. NW, Ste.725

Washington, DC 20036

Ph: (202)833-8850

Fax: (202)463-0102

E-mail: enc@enc-online.org

URL: http://www.enc-online.org

Contact: Donald J. McNamara PhD, Exec. Dir.

Founded: 1984. **Description:** Commercial egg producers and processors, health promotion agencies, and consumers. Provides scientifically accurate information on egg nutrition and the role of eggs in health and nutrition. Monitors nutrition research reports and nutrition policy development. **Publications:** Healthy Habits for the Best of Your Life. Brochure. Alternate Formats: online ● Nutrition Close-Up, quarterly. Newsletter. Reviews and summarizes recent research reports. Alternate Formats: online ● Nutrition Realities. Newsletter. Alternate Formats: online.

15231 ■ Feingold Association of the United States (FAUS)

554 E Main St., No. 301

Riverhead, NY 11901

Ph: (631)369-9340

Free: (800)321-3287

Fax: (631)369-2988

E-mail: help@feingold.org

URL: http://www.feingold.org

Contact: Jane Hersey, Natl. Dir.

Founded: 1976. **Members:** 30,000. **Membership Dues:** first year, $69. **Staff:** 8. **Budget:** $360,000. **Regional Groups:** 8. **Description:** Works to help people determine if certain foods or synthetic food additives are triggering various learning, health, or behavior problems; program eliminates synthetic dye, artificial flavor, and three preservatives. Provides comprehensive materials to assist people in finding suitable brand-name products. Disseminates information, including medical studies that link diet to behavior and health problems. **Committees:** Adults on the Diet; Educational Aides; Product Information Research; School Foods; Scientific Advisory. **Publications:** Healthier Food for Busy People: 20 little rules to help you navigate the supermarket. Book ● Pure Facts, 10/year. Newsletter. **Price:** included in membership dues; $38.00 /year for nonmembers. **Circulation:** 10,000 ● School Year Calendar, annual ● What are all those funny things in food? . and should I eat them?. Audiotape ● Why Can't My Child Behave?. Book. Provides guidance to parents through process of using diet to help children. **Price:** $38.00. **Conventions/Meetings:** annual conference.

15232 ■ Food and Nutrition Board (FNB)

c/o Institute of Medicine

500 5th St. NW

Washington, DC 20001

Ph: (202)334-2352

Fax: (202)334-1412

E-mail: fnb@nas.edu

URL: http://www.iom.edu/?id=3788&redirect=0

Contact: Linda D. Meyers PhD, Dir.

Founded: 1940. **Members:** 13. **Staff:** 25. **Budget:** $2,000,000. **Description:** Evaluates and offers advice to the federal government concerning the relationship between food consumption, nutritional status, and public health. **Committees:** Dietary Reference Intakes; Food Chemicals Codex; Food Forum; International Nutrition; Military Nutrition Research; Nutrient Requirement of Military Women; WIC Program Evaluation. **Affiliated With:** Institute of Medicine; National Academy of Sciences. **Publications:** Booklets ● Monographs. Covers nutrition, public health and food safety. ● Report. **Conventions/Meetings:** annual symposium.

15233 ■ Gluten Intolerance Group (GIG)

31214 14th Ave. SE

Auburn, WA 98092-3667

Ph: (206)246-6652

Fax: (206)246-6531

E-mail: info@gluten.net

URL: http://www.gluten.net

Contact: Cynthia Kupper RD, Exec. Dir.

Founded: 1974. **Members:** 3,000. **Membership Dues:** individual in U.S., $35 (annual) ● individual in Canada and Mexico, $45 (annual) ● individual (international), $50 (annual). **Staff:** 2. **Budget:** $200,000. **Local Groups:** 2. **Languages:** English, Spanish. **Description:** Persons with gluten-sensitive enteropathy (celiac sprue) or dermatitis herpetiformis, family members, physicians, dietitians, and celiac sprue societies. (Gluten is a protein found in wheat, rye, and barley. Gluten-sensitive enteropathy is an inherited disorder characterized by gluten-related destruction of the small intestine. Symptoms include diarrhea, weight loss, fatigue, and anemia.) Works to educate patients, health care personnel, and the public; to offer psychological support to celiac sprue patients and their families in dealing with the adjustment and nutritional limitations of the disease; to conduct research into the causes. Promotes practical application in specific food research, such as recipe development and information on gluten content of products. Offers children's services and group and individual counseling. **Libraries:** **Type:** reference. **Holdings:** 26; books, video recordings. **Subjects:** celiac disease, dermatitis herpetiformis, associated autoimmune disorders, diet and nutrition, medications, cooking gluten-free. **Awards:** Campership. **Frequency:** annual. **Type:** scholarship ● Membership. **Frequency:** annual. **Type:** scholarship. **Formerly:** (1985) Gluten Intolerance Group; (2003) Gluten Intolerance Group of North America. **Publications:** GIG Newsletter, quarterly. Provides book reviews, product information, recipes, and research reports to help in monitoring diets for persons with celiac sprue and dermatitis. **Price:** $30.00/year in U.S. ISSN: 0890-507X. **Advertising:** accepted ● Gluten-Free Diet-A Comprehensive Resource Guide. Book. **Price:** $17.95 ● Kids with Celiac Disease-A Family Guide to Raising Happy, Healthy, Gluten-Free Children. Book. **Price:** $15.95 ● Living Well with Celiac Disease Abundance beyond Wheat and Gluten. Book. **Price:** $15.95 ● Wheat-Free Worry-Free The Art of Happy, Healthy, Gluten-Free Living. Book. **Price:** $13.00 ● Videos ● Also publishes cookbook and fact sheets. **Conventions/Meetings:** annual Education Conference - meeting, regarding food products (exhibits) - usually June ● monthly meeting.

15234 ■ International and American Association of Clinical Nutritionists (IAACN)

15280 Addison Rd., Ste.130

Addison, TX 75001

Ph: (972)407-9089

Fax: (972)250-0233

E-mail: ddc@clinicalnutrition.com

URL: http://www.iaacn.org

Contact: Kevin P. Henry, Exec. Dir.

Founded: 1971. **Membership Dues:** student, $45 (annual) ● corporate, $900 (annual) ● professional, $395 (annual) ● professional associate, $360 (annual) ● associate, $300 (annual). **Staff:** 4. **State Groups:** 7. **Description:** Physicians (medical, osteopathic, chiropractic), dentists, veterinarians, clinical nutritionists, pharmacists, nurses and scientists; practitioners hold accredited undergraduate, graduate or professional degrees in science and/or nutrition, or in fields related to nutrition with the addition of required core courses. Sponsors the Certified Clinical Nutritionist (CCN) credential under the responsibility of the Clinical Nutrition Certification Board (CNCB). Members work in the U.S. and other countries to stimulate and encourage research in the nutritional aspects of disease, promote the science and study of nutrition and complementary therapies in medical and dental schools, hospitals, colleges and research institutions. Provides a referral service for people seeking nutrition/preventive health care providers. Holds an annual scientific symposium with world-class faculty. **Libraries:** **Type:** reference. **Subjects:** all aspects of nutrition. **Formed by Merger of:** International College of Applied Nutrition; International Academy of Preventive Medicine. **Formerly:** (1998) International Academy of Nutrition and Preventative Medicine. **Publications:** The IAACN Insight, bimonthly. **Newsletter.** Provides latest news and information. ● *Journal of Applied Nutrition*, quarterly. **Price:** $67.00 /year for members; $90.00 /year for nonmembers and institutions; $40.00/year for student; $110.00/year outside U.S. **ISSN:** 0021-8960. **Circulation:** 750. **Advertising:** accepted. **Alternate Formats:** microform; CD-ROM ● *Your Health*, bimonthly. Newsletter. Includes information on nutrition and preventative medicine applied to a variety of health issues. **Price:** included in membership dues. **Circulation:** 750. **Advertising:** accepted. **Conventions/ Meetings:** annual Nutritional Advancements in Pediatric and Adolescent Care - symposium.

15235 ■ International Life Sciences Institute - North America (ILSINA)
1 Thomas Cir. NW, 9th Fl.
Washington, DC 20005
Ph: (202)659-0074
Fax: (202)659-3859
E-mail: rfisher@ilsi.org
URL: http://www.ilsina.org
Contact: Robert Fisher PhD, Exec. Dir.
Founded: 1985. **Members:** 44. **Staff:** 11. **Budget:** $4,000,000. **Multinational. Description:** Advances the understanding of scientific issues related to the nutritional quality and safety of the food supply, as well as health issues related to consumer self-care products. Sponsors relevant research programs, professional education programs and workshops, seminars, and publications, as well as providing a neutral forum for government, academic, and industry scientists to discuss and resolve scientific issues of common concern for the well-being of the general public. Fosters career development of outstanding new scientists. Programs are supported primarily by its industry membership. **Awards:** Future Leader Awards. **Frequency:** annual. **Type:** grant. **Recipient:** to a resident of North America with a doctoral degree within the past 7 years. **Committees:** Caffeine; Carbohydrates; Energy; Flavonoids; Food Components for Health Promotion; Food Microbiology; Food Nutrition and Safety; Food Toxicology and Safety Assessment; Hydration; Lifestyle and Weight Management; Lipids; Science, Self-care and Health; Sodium; Tolerable Upper Levels. **Affiliated With:** International Life Sciences Institute, European Branch. **Formed by Merger of:** (1985) Nutrition Foundation; (1985) North American Branch of International Life Sciences Institute. **Formerly:** (1991) International Life Sciences Institute - Nutrition Foundation. **Publications:** Newsletter. Contains information on programs and people in the news. Alternate Formats: online ● Also publishes monographs, reprints, scientific reports, and educational materials. **Conventions/Meetings:** periodic symposium, with seminars and workshops.

15236 ■ International Society of Sports Nutrition (ISSN)
c/o Maelu Fleck, Exec. Dir.
600 Pembrook Dr.
Woodland Park, CO 80863
Free: (866)472-4650
Fax: (719)687-5184
E-mail: issn@sportsnutritionsociety.org
URL: http://www.sportsnutritionsociety.org
Contact: Dr. Jose Antonio PhD, CEO/Co-Founder
Membership Dues: professional, fellow, $150 (annual) ● affiliate, $125 (annual) ● student, $75 (annual) ● professional, fellow, $270 (biennial) ● affiliate, $225 (biennial) ● student, $135 (biennial) ● professional, fellow, $349 (triennial) ● affiliate, $299 (triennial) ● student, $179 (triennial). **Multinational. Description:** Represents scientists, sports nutritionists, personal trainers, industry professionals and other individuals with interests in the field of sports nutrition. Promotes and supports the science and application of sports nutrition. Facilitates communication and cooperation among members. **Telecommunication Services:** electronic mail, drjoseantonio@aol. com. **Publications:** *Journal of the International Society of Sports Nutrition*. Covers aspects of sports nutrition, supplementation, exercise metabolism, and scientific policies related to sports nutrition. **Price:** included in membership dues. **ISSN:** 1550-2783. Alternate Formats: online. Also Cited As: *JISSN* ●

Newsletter, bimonthly. Contains latest news in sports nutrition. **Price:** included in membership dues. Alternate Formats: online ● Books ● Videos.

15237 ■ International Union of Nutritional Sciences (IUNS)
c/o Dr. Osman M. Galal, Sec.Gen.
UCLA School of Public Hea.
Dept. of Community Hea. Sciences
PO Box 951772
Los Angeles, CA 90095-1772
Ph: (310)206-9639
Fax: (310)794-1805
E-mail: info@iuns.org
URL: http://www.iuns.org
Contact: Dr. Osman M. Galal, Sec.Gen.
Founded: 1946. **Members:** 80. **Multinational. Description:** National nutritional societies. Promotes international cooperation in the scientific study of nutrition and its applications. Encourages research and the exchange of scientific information. Cooperates with the Food and Agriculture Organization of the United Nations, the United Nations Educational, Scientific and Cultural Organization, and the World Health Organization. Maintains 9 task forces. **Awards:** IUNS Award. **Frequency:** quadrennial. **Type:** monetary ● IUNS Fellow. **Frequency:** quadrennial. **Type:** recognition. **Conventions/Meetings:** quadrennial International Congress of Nutrition (exhibits) - 2009 Oct. 4-9, Bangkok, Thailand - **Avg. Attendance:** 4000.

15238 ■ International Vitamin A Consultative Group (IVACG)
c/o ILSI Human Nutrition Institute
One Thomas Cir. NW
Washington, DC 20005-5802
Ph: (202)659-9024
Fax: (202)659-3617
E-mail: hni@ilsi.org
URL: http://ivacg.ilsi.org/index.cfm?pubentityid=16
Founded: 1975. **Staff:** 4. **Description:** Offers consultation and guidance to operating and donor agencies that are seeking to reduce vitamin A deficiencies. Prepares guidelines and recommendations for assessing the regional distribution and magnitude of vitamin A deficiency, developing intervention methods and strategies against the deficiency, evaluating the effectiveness of implemented programs, and conducting research needed to support the assessment of intervention. Conducts task forces globally. **Affiliated With:** International Life Sciences Institute - North America. **Publications:** *A Brief Guide to Current Methods of Assessing Vitamin A Status*. **Price:** $3.50 ● *The Bioavailability of Dietary Carotenoids: Current Concepts*. **Price:** $3.50. Alternate Formats: online ● *Biochemical Methodology for the Assessment of Vitamin A Status, and Reprints of Selected Methods for the Analysis of Vitamin A and Carotenoids*. Book. **Price:** $18.00/set of 2 books ● *Combining Vitamin A Distribution with EPI Contacts*. **Price:** $3.50. Alternate Formats: online ● *Delivery of Vitamin A Supplements with DPT/Polio and Measles Immunization*. **Price:** $3.50. Alternate Formats: online ● *IVACG Meeting Reports*. **Price:** free ● *IVACG Policy Statement on Vitamin A, Diarrhea and Measles*. **Price:** $3.50. Alternate Formats: online ● *IVACG Policy Statement on Vitamin A Status and Childhood Mortality*. **Price:** $3.50. Alternate Formats: online ● *IVACG Statement on Clustering of Xerophthalmia and Vitamin A Deficiency Within Communities and Families*. **Price:** $3.50. Alternate Formats: online ● *IVACG Statement on Maternal Night Blindness: Extent and Associated Risk Factors*. **Price:** $3.50. Alternate Formats: online ● *IVACG Statement on Safe Doses of Vitamin A During Pregnancy and Lactation*. **Price:** $3.50. Alternate Formats: online ● *IVACG Statement on Vitamin A and Iron Interactions*. **Price:** $3.50. Alternate Formats: online ● *Nutrition Communications in Vitamin A Programs: A Resource Book*. **Price:** $3.50 ● *The Safe Use of Vitamin A*. **Price:** $3.50 ● *The Safe Uses of Vitamin A by Women During the Reproductive Years*. **Price:** $3.50 ● *Status of the Studies on Vitamin A and Human Immunodeficiency Virus Infection*. **Price:** $3.50. Alternate Formats: online ● *Strategic Placement of IVACG in the Evolving Micronutrient*

Field. **Price:** $3.50. Alternate Formats: online ● *Vitamin A Conversions to SI*. **Price:** free. Alternate Formats: online ● *Vitamin A Supplements: A Guide to their Use in the Treatment and Prevention of Vitamin A Deficiency and Xerophthalmia*. **Price:** $3.50 ● Also publishes monographs, guidelines, and books. **Conventions/Meetings:** conference (exhibits) - every 18 months.

15239 ■ Intersociety Professional Nutrition Education Consortium (IPNEC)
c/o University of Alabama at Birmingham
439 Susan Mott Webb Nutrition Sciences Bldg.
1675 Univ. Blvd.
Birmingham, AL 35294-3360
Ph: (205)996-2513
Fax: (205)934-7050
E-mail: shreid@uab.edu
URL: http://main.uab.edu/ipnec/show.asp-
?durki=35204
Contact: Douglas C. Heimburger MD, Sec.-Treas.
Multinational. Description: Works to achieve national consensus on the identity, training, and certification of physician nutrition specialists.

15240 ■ National Association of Nutrition and Aging Services Programs (NANASP)
1612 K St. NW, Ste.400
Washington, DC 20006
Ph: (202)682-6899
Fax: (202)223-2099
E-mail: eross@matzblancato.com
URL: http://www.nanasp.org
Contact: Sharon TerHaar, Pres.
Membership Dues: non-profit, $150 (annual) ● corporate/for-profit, $300 (annual) ● retiree, $75 (annual). **Description:** Dedicated to supporting a broad, comprehensive range of nutrition and other support services for the aging living in community dwellings; helps shape national policy; provides training for service providers; advocates on behalf of senior citizens. **Awards:** Star Awards. **Frequency:** annual. **Type:** recognition. **Conventions/Meetings:** annual conference, training conference, with awards (exhibits) ● annual meeting.

15241 ■ Nutrition for Optimal Health Association (NOHA)
PO Box 380
Winnetka, IL 60093
Ph: (847)604-3258
E-mail: nohareplies@yahoo.com
URL: http://www.nutrition4health.org
Contact: Neil E. Levin, Pres.
Founded: 1972. **Members:** 230. **Membership Dues:** individual, $60 (annual) ● couple, $75 (annual) ● senior individual, $50 (annual) ● business, $100 (annual). **Budget:** $30,000. **Description:** Consists of individuals interested in making informed health decisions through better nutrition. Promotes good nutrition as a means of achieving and maintaining optimal health. Advances and disseminates scientifically based information on the practical application of sound nutritional principles to daily living. Offers nutrition education programs and seminars. Maintains tape list. **Libraries: Type:** reference. **Holdings:** 200. **Publications:** *NOHA News*, quarterly. Newsletter. Includes association news, book reviews and articles by members of NOHA's Professional Advisory Board. **Price:** included in membership dues; $8.00 /year for nonmembers. **Circulation:** 700. Alternate Formats: online. **Conventions/Meetings:** monthly board meeting ● monthly lecture - usually September-May.

15242 ■ Price-Pottenger Nutrition Foundation (PPNF)
7890 Broadway
Lemon Grove, CA 91945
Ph: (619)462-7600
Free: (800)366-3748
Fax: (619)433-3136
E-mail: info@price-pottenger.org
URL: http://www.ppnf.org
Contact: Joan Grinzi RN, Exec. Dir.
Founded: 1952. **Members:** 2,000. **Membership Dues:** individual, $40 (annual) ● student, senior, $30

(annual) ● professional, $100 (annual) ● international (individual), $55 (annual) ● international (senior and student), $45 (annual) ● international (professional), $115 (annual) ● domestic/international friend, $1,000 (annual). **Staff:** 4. **Budget:** $200,000. **Multinational. Description:** Seeks to increase awareness of natural health, organic gardening, nutrition and ecology. Disseminates information to the medical and dental professions, as well as to the public, through publications, seminars, classes, study groups, and scientific exhibits. Stresses the benefits of chemically-untreated "whole" foods. Named in honor of Weston A. Price, DDS and Francis M. Pottenger, Jr., MD, known for their work in nutrition research. **Libraries: Type:** not open to the public; reference. **Holdings:** 10,000; articles, audio recordings, books, films, periodicals, video recordings. **Subjects:** nutrition, natural health, organic gardening, ecology. **Awards:** Greater San Diego Science and Engineering Fair Awards. **Frequency:** annual. **Type:** recognition. **Computer Services:** database, library and archival records. **Telecommunication Services:** information service, about health and nutrition, natural environmental care, farming and gardening, pet care. **Formerly:** (1954) Santa Barbara Medical Research Foundation; (1965) Weston A. Price Memorial Foundation; (1973) Price-Pottenger Foundation. **Publications:** *Nutrition and Physical Degeneration*, biennial. Book ● *Pottenger's Cats: A Study in Nutrition*, periodic. Book ● *PPNF Health Journal: Health and Healing Wisdom*, quarterly. Contains articles on health, book reviews, recipes, and a calendar. **Price:** $35.00/year; $100.00/year for professionals. **Circulation:** 2,000. **Advertising:** accepted ● *Root Canal Cover Up*, biennial. Book. **Price:** $19.95. **Conventions/Meetings:** periodic seminar (exhibits).

15243 ■ Seventh-Day Adventist Dietetic Association (SDADA)
PO Box 400
6100 Leoni Rd.
Grizzly Flats, CA 95636-0400
Ph: (407)897-6701
E-mail: veggie@sdada.org
URL: http://www.sdada.org
Contact: Sherri Flynt RD, VP
Founded: 1956. **Members:** 505. **Membership Dues:** regular/associate, $25 (annual) ● life, $500 ● retired, $10 (annual) ● student, $5 (annual). **Description:** Seventh-Day Adventist registered dietitians; dietitians working in Seventh-Day Adventist institutions. Strives to motivate members to attain high professional standards and to actively promote Seventh-Day Adventist health principles. Provides resources and guidance concerning vegetarian lifestyles to dietitians. Disseminates nutrition information. **Awards:** Dietetic Student Scholarship Awards. **Frequency:** annual. **Type:** scholarship. **Recipient:** for Seventh-Day Adventist dietetic students. **Computer Services:** Mailing lists. **Telecommunication Services:** electronic mail, cherylflynt@flhosp.org. **Committees:** Awards; Diet Manual; Editorial Review. **Affiliated With:** American Dietetic Association. **Publications:** *Health Gems*. Brochures. Alternate Formats: online ● *Manual de Dietas y Nutricion, 2nd Edition* (in English and Spanish). **Price:** $30.00 plus shipping and handling ($3) ● *SDADA News*, quarterly. Newsletter. **Price:** free; available to members only. Alternate Formats: online ● *Vegetarian Resource, 4th Edition*. Includes vegetarian options. **Price:** $40.00 plus shipping and handling ($3). Alternate Formats: CD-ROM. **Conventions/Meetings:** annual convention - always October ● periodic seminar.

15244 ■ Society for Nutrition Education (SNE)
7150 Winton Dr., Ste.300
Indianapolis, IN 46268
Ph: (317)328-4627
Free: (800)235-6690
Fax: (317)280-8527
E-mail: info@sne.org
URL: http://www.sne.org
Contact: Mary Ann Passi CAE, Exec. Dir.
Founded: 1967. **Members:** 1,000. **Membership Dues:** individual, professional, $170 (annual) ●

retired, $94 (annual) ● international, $85 (annual) ● student, $69 (annual) ● organizational, $3,500 (annual) ● organizational (non-profit), $1,000 (annual). **Staff:** 5. **Budget:** $600,000. **Regional Groups:** 15. **Description:** Represents nutrition educators from the fields of dietetics, public health, home economics, medicine, industry and education (elementary, secondary, college, university and consumer affairs). Works toward the fulfillment of its vision of having healthy people in healthy communities. **Computer Services:** Mailing lists. **Committees:** Advisory; Nominating. **Divisions:** Communications; Food and Nutrition Extension Education; Higher Education; International Nutrition Education; Nutrition Education for Children. **Programs:** Public Policy. **Publications:** *Journal of Nutrition Education*, bimonthly. For educators, practitioners and researchers on nutrition education. Includes book reviews and employment opportunity listings. **Price:** included in membership dues; $119.00 /year for individuals; $170.00 /year for institutions; $60.00 /year for individuals in-training. **Circulation:** 4,500. **Advertising:** accepted ● Also publishes journal supplements. **Conventions/Meetings:** annual conference, nutrition-related, for educating the public and educators (exhibits).

15245 ■ Vitamin Angel Alliance
1450 Orange Grove Ave.
Santa Barbara, CA 93105
Ph: (805)565-9919
Fax: (805)565-9916
E-mail: info@vitaminangel.org
URL: http://www.vitaminangelalliance.com
Contact: Howard Schiffer, Pres./Founder
Founded: 1994. **Multinational. Description:** Strives to fight malnutrition and childhood blindness around the world. Provides health education and nutritional supplements to individuals, families, and communities that are medically underserved or at risk of a specific condition or illness. Supports grassroots community programs to promote and strengthen self sufficiency. Develops collaborative initiatives with other organizations to provide more comprehensive programs. **Publications:** Newsletter. Alternate Formats: online.

15246 ■ Weston A. Price Foundation (WAPF)
PMB 106-380
4200 Wisconsin Ave. NW
Washington, DC 20016
Ph: (202)363-4394
Fax: (202)363-4396
E-mail: info@westonaprice.org
URL: http://www.westonaprice.org
Contact: Sally Fallon, Pres.
Founded: 1999. **Members:** 9,000. **Membership Dues:** regular, $40 (annual) ● foreign, $50 (annual) ● student, senior, $25 (annual) ● special, $100 (annual) ● sponsor, $250 (annual) ● patron, $500 (annual). **Staff:** 4. **Budget:** $300,000. **Local Groups:** 300. **Languages:** English, Spanish. **Description:** Seeks to disseminate the research of Dr. Weston Price and restore nutrient-dense foods to the human diet through education, research, and activism. **Programs:** A Campaign for Real Milk. **Publications:** *Wise Traditions in Food, Farming, and the Healing Arts*, quarterly. Journal. Contains information on worldwide dietary, agricultural, and medical traditions. **Price:** included in membership dues. **Circulation:** 2,600. **Advertising:** accepted. **Conventions/Meetings:** annual Wise Traditions - conference.

Obesity

15247 ■ American Board of Bariatric Medicine (ABBM)
700 N Colorado Blvd., No. 348
Denver, CO 80206
Ph: (303)779-0279
Fax: (303)779-0965
E-mail: info@abbmcertification.org
URL: http://www.abbmcertification.org
Contact: Kelly Dycus, Exec. Dir.
Founded: 1997. **Membership Dues:** ASBP, $100 (annual) ● non-ASBP, $200 (annual). **Description:**

Works to certify physicians in the field of bariatric medicine through comprehensive testing and review process.

15248 ■ American Obesity Association (AOA)
1250 24th St. NW, Ste.300
Washington, DC 20037
Ph: (202)776-7711
Fax: (202)776-7712
E-mail: executive@obesity.org
URL: http://www.obesity.org
Contact: Morgan Downey, Exec. Dir.
Founded: 1995. **Members:** 450. **Membership Dues:** individual, $15 (annual) ● professional provider, $90 (annual) ● obesity special clinic, $500 (annual) ● center of excellence, $1,000 (annual) ● corporation, $5,000 (annual) ● non-profit/government/small business, $200 (annual). **Staff:** 3. **Budget:** $500,000. **Description:** Health professionals. Supports research and education about obesity including the discrimination against the obese. Actively seeks government funding and advocates for insurance coverage for the obese. **Computer Services:** database, provider directory. **Projects:** OPERATE. **Publications:** *AOA Report*, quarterly. Newsletter. Alternate Formats: online.

15249 ■ American Society of Bariatric Physicians (ASBP)
2821 S Parker Rd., Ste.625
Aurora, CO 80014
Ph: (303)770-2526
Free: (877)266-6834
Fax: (303)779-4834
E-mail: info@asbp.org
URL: http://www.asbp.org
Contact: Judith Robinson PhD, Interim Exec. Dir.
Founded: 1950. **Members:** 1,000. **Membership Dues:** physician, $450 (annual) ● physician-in-training, $100 (annual) ● student, $50 (annual) ● associate, $195 (annual) ● affiliate, $125 (annual). **Staff:** 4. **Budget:** $900,000. **State Groups:** 2. **Description:** Physicians with a special interest in the study and treatment of obesity and associated conditions. Encourages excellence in the practice of bariatric medicine through exchange of information, research, and continuing education. Sponsors regional courses and clinical research programs. Offers a physician referral service. **Libraries: Type:** reference. **Holdings:** audio recordings, books, clippings. **Awards:** Bariatrician of the Year Award. **Frequency:** annual. **Type:** recognition. **Recipient:** for a nominated physician ● Dr. Raymond E. Dietz Meritorious Service Award. **Frequency:** annual. **Type:** recognition. **Recipient:** for a physician member who made continuing contributions to the Society ● Fellow. **Frequency:** annual. **Type:** recognition. **Recipient:** for outstanding, long-term member of the society. **Computer Services:** Information services, physician referral lists. **Committees:** Ethics; Honors and Awards; Membership; Program; Public Relations; Research. **Publications:** *The Bariatrician*, quarterly. Journal. Includes articles on health, fitness, nutrition, and current treatments for obesity. **Price:** $48.00/year in U.S.; $72.00/year outside U.S. **Circulation:** 1,800. **Advertising:** accepted. Also Cited As: *American Journal of Bariatric Medicine* ● *News from ASBP*, bimonthly. Newsletter. **Price:** available to members only. **Circulation:** 1,500. **Advertising:** accepted ● Membership Directory, annual. **Advertising:** accepted ● Manuals ● Pamphlets. **Conventions/Meetings:** annual Obesity & Associated Conditions Symposium, 50 booth displays of related products, services for bariatric physician (exhibits) - in October ● annual Regional Obesity Course - meeting - May.

15250 ■ North American Association for the Study of Obesity (NAASO)
c/o Ann Kenworthy, Interim Exec. Dir.
8630 Fenton St., Ste.918
Silver Spring, MD 20910
Ph: (301)563-6526
Fax: (301)563-6595

E-mail: annk@naaso.org
URL: http://www.naaso.org
Contact: Thomas A. Wadden PhD, Pres. **Founded:** 1982. **Members:** 2,000. **Membership Dues:** regular, $200 (annual) ● overseas, $210 (annual) ● student, $10 (annual). **Multinational. Description:** Promotes research, education and advocacy to better understand, prevent and treat obesity and improve the lives of those affected. Assists in the development of programs designed to prevent obesity. Ensures patients have access to quality medical care for obesity treatment. **Computer Services:** Mailing lists, of members ● online services, member forums. **Publications:** *Obesity*, monthly. Journal. Contains original scientific articles, commentaries and medical news. **Price:** $225.00 for members; $325.00 for institutions; $235.00 for members overseas. **Advertising:** accepted. Alternate Formats: online ● *The Obesity Society*, monthly. Newsletter. Contains information about awards, meetings, education programs and case studies. Alternate Formats: online ● *The Practical Guide: Identification, Evaluation and Treatment of Overweight and Obesity in Adults*. Handbook. Provides tools needed for overweight and obese adult patient management. Alternate Formats: online. **Conventions/Meetings:** annual meeting, scientific meeting.

15251 ■ Obesity Action Coalition (OAC)
4511 N Himes Ave., Ste.250
Tampa, FL 33614
Ph: (813)872-7835
Free: (800)717-3117
Fax: (813)873-7838
E-mail: info@obesityaction.org
URL: http://www.obesityaction.org
Contact: Joseph Nadglowski Jr., Pres./CEO
Membership Dues: patient/family, $20 (annual) ● allied health professional, $50 (annual) ● physician, $100 (annual) ● surgeon, $150 (annual) ● institutional, $500 (annual) ● chairman's council, $1,000 (annual). **Description:** Educates patients, family members and the public on obesity and morbid obesity. Works to improve access to medical treatments for obese patients. Advocates for safe and effective treatments. Strives to eliminate the negative stigma associated with all types of obesity. **Publications:** *OAC News*, quarterly. Newsletter. Features different articles and stories on obesity-related topics, geared towards patients. **Price:** included in membership dues. Alternate Formats: online ● *Obesity Action Alert*, monthly. Newsletter. Contains articles and research on obesity and its effects. **Price:** included in membership dues. Alternate Formats: online ● Brochure. Alternate Formats: online.

15252 ■ Weight-Control Information Network (WIN)
1 WIN Way
Bethesda, MD 20892-3665
Ph: (202)828-1025
Free: (877)946-4627
Fax: (202)828-1028
E-mail: win@info.niddk.nih.gov
URL: http://win.niddk.nih.gov/index.htm
Founded: 1994. **Description:** Provides health professionals and consumer with science-based information on obesity, weight control, and nutrition. **Programs:** Sisters Together: Move More, Eat Better. **Publications:** *Clinical Weight Loss and Control Lecture Series*. Videos ● *Conference Proceedings* ● *Fact Sheets* ● *WIN Notes*, quarterly. Newsletter. Features latest information on obesity, weight control, and weight-related nutritional disorders. ● *Workshop Proceedings* ● Reports ● Articles ● Brochures.

Obstetrics and Gynecology

15253 ■ American Academy of Husband-Coached Childbirth (AAHCC)
PO Box 5224
Sherman Oaks, CA 91413-5224
Ph: (818)788-6662
Free: (800)4-A-BIRTH

Fax: (818)788-1580
URL: http://www.bradleybirth.com
Contact: Marjie Hathaway, Exec. Dir. **Founded:** 1970. **Members:** 1,200. **For-Profit. Description:** Trains instructors in the Bradley method of natural childbirth. Provides referrals to Bradley teachers. **Publications:** *Directory of Instructors*, 2-3/year. **Price:** free ● *Fetal Advocate*, periodic.

15254 ■ American Association of Birth Centers (AABC)
3123 Gottschall Rd.
Perkiomenville, PA 18074
Ph: (215)234-8068
Fax: (215)234-8829
E-mail: aabc@birthcenters.org
URL: http://www.birthcenters.org
Contact: Kate E. Bauer MBA, Exec. Dir.

Founded: 1983. **Members:** 400. **Membership Dues:** established birth center (with gross receipts of less than $100,000), developing birth center (renewal), $400 (annual) ● established birth center (with gross receipts of less than $500,000), $600 (annual) ● established birth center (with gross receipts of more than $500,000), $1,200 (annual) ● developing birth center (first year), $800 (annual) ● institutional, $450 (annual) ● individual, $85 (annual) ● associate, $40 (annual) ● life, $2,025. **Staff:** 4. **Budget:** $250,000. **Regional Groups:** 6. **State Groups:** 2. **Description:** Works on public and policy levels in government, industry and the health professions. Commits in developing quality, holistic services for childbearing families that promote self-reliance and confidence in birth and parenting. Collects and disseminates information on birth centers. Sets national standards for birth center operation, promotes state regulation for licensure, and national accreditation by the Commission for the Accreditation of Birth Centers. Provides a Parent Information Service for consumers looking for birth centers. Provides information on birth center. **Libraries:** Type: reference. **Holdings:** articles. **Awards:** NACC Achievement Award. **Frequency:** annual. **Type:** recognition. **Recipient:** for outstanding achievement in four categories: professional, public advocate, media, and community activist. **Computer Services:** Mailing lists, of members. **Committees:** Bylaws; International; Legislative; Nominating; Program; Research; Standards. **Formerly:** (2006) National Association of Childbearing Centers. **Supersedes:** Cooperative Birth Center Network. **Publications:** *The Birth Center Brochure*. Contains information describing freestanding birth centers; designed for public education and promotion of the concept of birth centers. **Price:** $49.00/100 brochures ● *Birth Center Information Packet*. Articles. Covers growth and development, regulation, costs, reimbursement, research, and selected issues of NACC News. **Price:** $30.00 ● *The Birth Center Video*. Increases public awareness of the presence of birth centers. **Price:** $39.95 ● *Continuous Quality Improvement Manual*. Contains forms and instructions for implementing a continuous quality improvement/risk management program in birth centers. **Price:** $99.95 for members; $149.95 for nonmembers ● *How to Review a Managed Care Contract*. Video. **Price:** $49.95 for members; $59.95 for nonmembers ● *How to Start a Birth Center*. Manual. **Price:** $499.95 for members; $549.95 for nonmembers ● *Marketing the Birth Center- A Complete Presentation*. **Price:** $199.95 for members; $299.95 for nonmembers ● *NACC Membership Directory*, annual. **Price:** included in membership dues ● *NACC News*, 3/year. Newsletter. **Advertising:** accepted ● *NACC Uniform Data Set*. **Price:** $299.00 for members; $599.00 for nonmembers ● *National Birth Center Study*. Reprint. **Price:** $1.00 ● *Sample Birth Center Policy and Procedure Manual*. Contains sample policies and procedures of an accredited birth center. Includes diskettes for customization. **Price:** $200.00 for members; $300.00 for nonmembers ● *Standards for Birth Centers*, annual. **Price:** $14.95 for members; $29.95 for nonmembers ● *Survey Report of Birth Center Experience*. **Price:** $10.00 for members; $20.00 for nonmembers ● Audiotapes. **Conventions/Meetings:** annual convention and meeting, clinical

and administrative issues (exhibits) ● quarterly How to Start a Birth Center - workshop.

15255 ■ American Association of Gynecologic Laparoscopists (AAGL)
6757 Katella Ave.
Cypress, CA 90630-5105
Ph: (714)503-6200
Free: (800)554-2245
Fax: (714)503-6201
E-mail: generalmail@aagl.com
URL: http://www.aagl.org
Contact: Linda Michels, Exec. Dir.
Founded: 1971. **Members:** 6,000. **Membership Dues:** first-time, $145 (annual) ● practicing physician, $250 (annual) ● resident/fellow-in-training, $110 (annual). **Staff:** 14. **Description:** Physicians who specialize in obstetrics and gynecology and who are interested in gynecological endoscopic procedures. Purposes are to: teach; demonstrate; exchange ideas; distribute literature; stimulate interest in gynecological laparoscopy; maintain and improve medical standards in medical schools and hospitals regarding gynecological laparoscopy; maintain and improve the ethics, practice, and efficiency of the medical practice pertaining to obstetrics and laparoscopy. Conducts seminars and workshops. **Awards:** Best Scientific Poster Award. **Frequency:** annual. **Type:** recognition ● Carol Romanini Award for Best Paper on Endoscopy. **Frequency:** annual. **Type:** recognition ● Circon ACMI Golden Hysteroscope Award. **Frequency:** annual. **Type:** recognition. **Recipient:** to the best submitted paper on hysteroscopy by a physician ● Daniel F. Kott Award for Best New Instrumentation. **Frequency:** annual. **Type:** recognition ● Kurt Semm Award. **Frequency:** annual. **Type:** recognition ● Olympus Golden Laparoscope Award. **Frequency:** annual. **Type:** recognition. **Recipient:** to the best submitted surgical video/film on gynecologic endoscopy by a physician ● Postgraduate Prize Paper. **Frequency:** annual. **Type:** monetary. **Recipient:** to the best submitted paper on gynecologic endoscopy by a resident or fellow physician ● Computer **Services:** Mailing lists, list rental. **Committees:** Advisory; Bylaws; CME; Editorial; Ethics; Long-Range Planning; Membership; Nominating; Research-Survey; Residents and Fellows; Technical Bulletin. **Formerly:** (2003) American Association of Gynecological Laparoscopists. **Publications:** *Annual Meeting Videos*. **Price:** $35.00 for members; $50.00 for nonmembers ● *Hysteroscopy: Principles and Practice*. Book. Covers many aspects of hysteroscopy. **Price:** $45.00 ● *Journal of Minimally Invasive Gynecology*, quarterly, February, May, August, November. Covers endoscopic procedures. **Price:** $140.00. ISSN: 1074-3804. **Circulation:** 4,500. **Advertising:** accepted. Alternate Formats: online ● *News Scope*. Newsletter. Contains multitude topics in ob-gyn field. Alternate Formats: online ● *Primer-Gynecologic Endoscopy*. Book. **Price:** $90.00. **Conventions/Meetings:** periodic Endoscopic Skills Development - workshop (exhibits) ● annual Global Congress on Gynecologic Endoscopy - 2008 Oct. 29-Nov. 1, Las Vegas, NV ● annual World Congress of Gynecologic Endoscopy - convention (exhibits).

15256 ■ American Board of Obstetrics and Gynecology (ABOG)
2915 Vine St.
Dallas, TX 75204
Ph: (214)871-1619
Fax: (214)871-1943
E-mail: info@abog.org
URL: http://www.abog.org
Contact: Norman F. Gant MD, Exec. Dir.
Founded: 1930. **Members:** 35,277. **Description:** Certification board to establish qualifications, conduct examinations, and certify as diplomates those doctors whom the board finds qualified to specialize in obstetrics and gynecology. **Committees:** Female Pelvic Medicine and Reconstructive Surgery; Residency Review. **Divisions:** Gynecologic Oncology; Maternal Fetal Medicine; Reproductive Endocrinology and Infertility. **Publications:** Bulletin, annual. Contains the latest news and upcoming events.

Alternate Formats: online. **Conventions/Meetings:** annual Directors' Meeting.

15257 ■ American College of Domiciliary Midwives (ACDM)

3889 Middlefield Rd.
Palo Alto, CA 94303-4718
Ph: (650)328-8491
E-mail: info@collegeofmidwives.org
URL: http://www.collegeofmidwives.org/acdm01/college.htm
Contact: Faith Gibson LM, Exec. Dir.
Founded: 1993. **Members:** 75. **Membership Dues:** physician, midwife, birth educator, $45 (annual) ● parent, consumer, $25 (annual). **Staff:** 5. **Budget:** $10,000. **State Groups:** 2. **Description:** Strives to preserve lawful access to home-based maternity care as provided by community midwives and family-practice physicians. **Libraries: Type:** reference. **Holdings:** 120; books, periodicals. **Subjects:** history and politics of midwifery, childbirth, midwifery practice. **Computer Services:** database. **Telecommunication Services:** electronic mail, goodnews@best.com. **Committees:** Characteristics of Clinical Competencies. **Publications:** *International Journal of Domiciliary Midwifery*, quarterly. Includes historical and contemporary articles on the history, politics, and practice of independent midwifery. **Price:** free. Alternate Formats: CD-ROM; online. **Conventions/Meetings:** periodic workshop.

15258 ■ American College of Obstetricians and Gynecologists (ACOG)

PO Box 96920
Washington, DC 20090-6920
Ph: (202)638-5577
Fax: (202)484-8107
E-mail: resources@acog.org
URL: http://www.acog.org
Contact: Ralph Hale MD, Exec. VP
Founded: 1951. **Members:** 41,000. **Staff:** 200. **Budget:** $40,000,000. **Regional Groups:** 10. **State Groups:** 50. **Description:** Physicians specializing in childbirth and the diseases of women. Sponsors continuing professional development program. **Libraries: Type:** reference; not open to the public. **Holdings:** 12,000; archival material, audio recordings, books, periodicals, video recordings. **Awards: Frequency:** annual. **Type:** recognition. **Formerly:** (1956) American Academy of Obstetrics and Gynecology. **Publications:** *ACOG Today*, monthly. Newsletter ● *Committee Opinions, Practice Bulletins, and Technology Assessments*, periodic. Includes technical information. ● *Obstetrics and Gynecology*, monthly. Journal. **Price:** $70.00 medical students/ residents; $160.00 personal; $255.00 libraries. ISSN: 0029-7844. **Circulation:** 40,000. **Advertising:** accepted ● Manuals. **Conventions/Meetings:** annual convention (exhibits).

15259 ■ American College of Osteopathic Obstetricians and Gynecologists (ACOOG)

2615 Merrick St.
Fort Worth, TX 76107
Ph: (817)377-0421
Free: (800)875-6360
Fax: (817)377-0439
E-mail: info@acoog.org
URL: http://www.acoog.org
Contact: Laura S. Dalton, Pres.
Founded: 1934. **Members:** 1,100. **Membership Dues:** regular, $200 (annual) ● associate, $50 (annual). **Staff:** 4. **Budget:** $500,000. **Description:** Osteopathic physicians and surgeons specializing in obstetrics and gynecology. Conducts educational programs, and reviews osteopathic obstetric and gynecologic residency training programs. Holds annual postgraduate course and annual convention. **Awards:** Annual ORTHO-ACOOG Resident Thesis Competition. **Frequency:** annual. **Type:** monetary. **Recipient:** for research papers. **Computer Services:** database. **Telecommunication Services:** electronic mail, rec@acoog.org ● electronic mail, membership@acoog.org ● electronic mail, cme@acoog.org ● electronic mail, newsletter@acoog.org. **Committees:** Bylaws; Continuing Medical Education; Edito-

rial, Research and Awards; Ethical and Professional Standards; Finance; Medical Education Foundation; Membership and Promotional; Nominating; Residency Evaluation; Strategic Planning. **Affiliated With:** American Osteopathic Association. **Publications:** *ACOOG Newsletter*, quarterly. Includes legislative news, calendar of events, employment listings, and lists of residents completing training and newly certified physicians. **Price:** free. **Circulation:** 12,000. **Advertising:** accepted. Alternate Formats: online ● *American College of Osteopathic Obstetricians and Gynecologists Membership Directory*, annual. **Price:** included in membership dues. **Circulation:** 1,200 ● Also publishes medical education brochures. **Conventions/Meetings:** annual convention, with awards and ceremonials (exhibits) - usually March ● annual Ortho Resident Thesis Competition - meeting.

15260 ■ American Foundation for Maternal and Child Health (AFMCH)

Address Unknown since 2007
Founded: 1972. **Staff:** 1. **Description:** Serves as a clearinghouse for interdisciplinary research on maternal and child health; focuses on the perinatal or birth period and its effect on infant development. Sponsors medical research designed to improve application of technology in maternal and child health; conducts educational programs; compiles statistics. Operates extensive reference library. **Affiliated With:** National Women's Health Network.

15261 ■ American Gynecological and Obstetrical Society (AGOS)

c/o Cassandra Larkins, Admin. Dir.
409 12th St. SW
Washington, DC 20024-2125
Ph: (202)863-1648
Fax: (202)554-0453
E-mail: clarkins@acog.org
URL: http://www.agosonline.org
Contact: James E. Ferguson II, Sec.
Founded: 1981. **Members:** 243. **Staff:** 1. **Description:** Works to cultivate and promote knowledge concerning obstetrics and gynecology. **Awards:** Association Foundation Prize. **Type:** recognition. **Recipient:** for the gathering, promotion, and dissemination of theoretical and practical knowledge on subjects relating to obstetrics and gynecology ● Charles A. Hunter, Jr. Prize Thesis Award. **Frequency:** annual. **Type:** recognition. **Formed by Merger of:** American Gynecological Society; American Association of Obstetricians and Gynecologists. **Publications:** *Transactions*, annual ● Newsletter. Alternate Formats: online. **Conventions/Meetings:** annual meeting - 2007 Sept. 26-29, Chicago, IL; 2008 Sept. 10-13, Carlsbad, CA.

15262 ■ American Pregnancy Association (APA)

1425 Greenway Dr., Ste.440
Irving, TX 75038
Ph: (972)550-0140
Free: (800)672-2296
Fax: (972)550-0800
E-mail: info@americanpregnancy.org
URL: http://www.americanpregnancy.org
Contact: Brad Imler PhD, Pres.
Founded: 1995. **Description:** Promotes reproductive and pregnancy wellness through education, research, advocacy and community awareness. Aims to support women and families by lobbying the legislature, businesses and insurance providers to promote pregnancy and family health issues. Increases public awareness of the reproductive and pregnancy needs, concerns and resources necessary to address these needs. **Telecommunication Services:** electronic mail, questions@americanpregnancy.org. **Publications:** Newsletter, weekly. **Price:** free. Alternate Formats: online.

15263 ■ American Society of Childbirth Educators (ASCE)

PO Box 2282
Sedona, AZ 86339
Ph: (928)284-9897
Fax: (928)284-9897

E-mail: jsasmor@sedona.net
Contact: Dr. James C. Sasmor, Corporate Sec.
Founded: 1972. **Description:** Seeks to provide a medium for the exchange and dissemination of information relating to prepared childbirth as a shared family experience and disseminate information to qualified professionals regarding standards, techniques, and skills relevant to the concept of prepared birth.

15264 ■ American Society for Colposcopy and Cervical Pathology (ASCCP)

20 W Washington St., Ste.1
Hagerstown, MD 21740
Ph: (301)733-3640
Free: (800)787-7227
Fax: (301)733-5775
E-mail: kpoole@asccp.org
URL: http://www.asccp.org
Contact: Kathleen G. Poole, Exec. Dir.
Founded: 1964. **Members:** 3,500. **Membership Dues:** individual, active, $140 (annual) ● individual, active with HSC Slides, $165 (annual). **Staff:** 6. **Budget:** $1,700,000. **Description:** Gynecologists, family physicians, pathologists, nurses, and other individuals interested in promoting the accurate and ethical application of colposcopy (the examination of the lower genital tract by means of a colposcope), and the diagnosis and treatment of lower genital tract disease. Organizes and approves training programs and audio visual materials in the diagnosis and management of lower genital tract disease and in regards to HPV and the HPV vaccines. Conducts accredited postgraduate courses. **Libraries: Type:** reference. **Holdings:** 27; periodicals. **Subjects:** colposcopy, cervical screening, pathology of the lower genital tract, cancer of the cervix, vagina, vulva, HPV. **Awards:** Colposcopy Mentorship Program Certificate. **Frequency:** quarterly. **Type:** recognition. **Recipient:** for completion of a 3-tiered beginning colposcopy training program ● Colposcopy Recognition Award. **Frequency:** annual. **Type:** recognition. **Recipient:** to members who have successfully passed a written and slide examination ● Distinguished Scientific Achievement Award. **Frequency:** biennial. **Type:** recognition ● G. Trombetta Teaching Award. **Frequency:** biennial. **Type:** recognition. **Recipient:** for best resident paper. **Computer Services:** database, membership list ● online services, forums. **Committees:** Ad-Hoc Assessment; APC Task Force; Editorial; Education; Mentorship; Nominating; Pathology; Practice; Program. **Formerly:** American Society for Colposcopy and Colpomicroscopy. **Publications:** *A Classical Approach to Vulvar Disease.* **Price:** $150.00 for members; $180.00 for nonmembers. Alternate Formats: CD-ROM ● *Advanced Colposcopy CD-ROM 2002.* **Price:** $175.00 for members; $195.00 for nonmembers. Alternate Formats: CD-ROM ● *ASCCP Algorithms from the Consensus Guidelines for the Management of Women with Cervical Cytological Abnormalities.* Booklet. **Price:** $3.45/booklet (non-government); $1.45/booklet (government) ● *ASCCP Patient Education*, quarterly. Pamphlets. Includes topics like Cervical Cryotherapy, Genital Warts, HIV-AIDS, Human Papillomavirus, Pap Smear, Sexuality and Pain: A Real Challenge, etc. **Price:** $20.00/pack (50 pamphlets/pack) ● *ASCCP Videoguide to Colposcopy.* Features a 30-minute video on colposcopy, LGSIL, HGSIL, and cancer. **Price:** $40.00 in U.S. ● *Clinical Uses of Human Papillomavirus (HPV) DNA Testing Self-Assessment Booklet.* **Price:** $2.50. **Advertising:** accepted ● *Colposcopy Image Library CD-ROM 2003.* **Price:** $170.00 for members; $190.00 for nonmembers. Alternate Formats: CD-ROM ● *Home Study Course*, quarterly. **Price:** $25.00 /year for members; $35.00 /year for nonmembers. Alternate Formats: CD-ROM ● *Journal of Lower Genital Tract Disease*, quarterly. **Advertising:** accepted ● *Modern Colposcopy Textbook & Atlas, 2nd Ed..* **Price:** $295.00 for members; $350.00 for nonmembers. Alternate Formats: CD-ROM. **Conventions/Meetings:** annual Advanced Colposcopy and Lower Genital Tract Dermatology - meeting (exhibits) ● quarterly Comprehensive Colposcopy - regional meeting (exhibits) ● biennial meeting ● annual Postgraduate Courses - meeting.

15265 ■ Association for Childbirth at Home, International (ACHI)
c/o The Natural Birth and Women's Center
14140 Magnolia Blvd.
Sherman Oaks, CA 91423
Ph: (818)386-1082
Fax: (818)386-9374
E-mail: naturalbirthcntr@aol.com
URL: http://gr8birth.com
Contact: Tonya Brooks, Founder/Pres.
Founded: 1972. **Members:** 30,000. **Staff:** 8. **Budget:** $150,000. **Regional Groups:** 9. **State Groups:** 40. **Local Groups:** 120. **Description:** Parents, midwives, doctors, childbirth educators, other professionals, and interested individuals, all of whom support childbirth at home. Seeks to: bring accurate information and competent support to parents seeking home birth and safe hospital birth; identify and implement correct obstetrical and pediatric practice. Offers parent education classes, leader training programs, international resource and referral service, and professional education seminars and programs; instructs parents, childbirth educators, midwives, doulas, midwifery assistants, and physicians in safe home birth and noninterventive alternative techniques. Conducts research; compiles statistics. Maintains speakers' bureau. **Libraries: Type:** reference. **Holdings:** 500. **Awards:** Great Humanitarian Award. **Type:** recognition ● Outstanding Teacher Award. **Type:** recognition ● Outstanding Trainee Award. **Type:** recognition. **Committees:** Research. **Formerly:** Association for Childbirth at Home. **Publications:** *Birth Notes*, quarterly. Newsletter. **Price:** $25.00/year. **Circulation:** 10,000. **Advertising:** accepted ● *Founder's Letter*, 6/year ● *Giving Birth at Home*. Handbook ● Brochures. **Conventions/Meetings:** annual meeting - always October.

15266 ■ Association of Professors of Gynecology and Obstetrics (APGO)
2130 Priest Bridge Dr., Ste.7
Crofton, MD 21114
Ph: (410)451-9560
Fax: (410)451-9568
E-mail: apgoadmin@apgo.org
URL: http://www.apgo.org
Contact: Donna Wachter, Exec. Dir.
Founded: 1962. **Members:** 1,500. **Membership Dues:** individual/fellow, $185 (annual) ● university department, $1,250 (annual) ● institutional department, $1,000 (annual) ● international, $270 (annual). **Staff:** 6. **Budget:** $600,000. **Description:** Departments of obstetrics and gynecology in approved medical schools in the U.S. and Canada, and in non-university teaching hospitals with active educational program for undergraduate medical students in OB/GYN. Works to consider problems relating to the departments of obstetrics and gynecology; to advance and improve the study of gynecology and obstetrics; to provide a means of exchanging information relating to the programs of study, teaching methods, and research activities of such departments. Compiles statistics. **Awards:** APGO Web Site Award of Excellence. **Frequency:** annual. **Type:** recognition. **Recipient:** for programs whose sites provide outstanding and innovative content for use by medical students in the context of their clerkships, and by student interest groups, as well as other relevant curricula ● Excellence in Teaching Award. **Frequency:** annual. **Type:** recognition. **Recipient:** to an outstanding teacher in ob-gyn medical education ● Medical Education. **Frequency:** annual. **Type:** recognition. **Committees:** Undergraduate Medical Education. **Publications:** *Academic Position Report*, 3/year. Includes information on job openings in the academic OB/GYN community. **Price:** $5.00 ● *APGO Membership Directory*, annual. **Price:** $20.00 for members; $30.00 for nonmembers ● *The APGO Reporter*, 3/year. Newsletter ● *Basic Laparoscopy*. Video. **Price:** $30.00 for members; $40.00 for nonmembers ● *The Challenge of Pelvic Adhesions: Strategies for the Prevention and Management*. Monograph. **Price:** $5.00 for members; $7.00 for nonmembers ● *Medical Student Educational Objectives*. **Price:** $20.00 for members; $30.00 for nonmembers ● *Radical Hysterectomy*. Video. **Price:** $30.00 for members; $40.00

for nonmembers ● *Strategies for the Management of Headache*. Monograph. **Price:** $5.00 for members; $7.00 for nonmembers ● *Women's Health: A Teaching Guide to Psychosocial Issues*. **Price:** $35.00 for members; $45.00 for nonmembers. **Conventions/Meetings:** annual meeting, educational ob/gyn (exhibits) - always February or March. 2008 Mar. 5-8, Lake Buena Vista, FL.

15267 ■ C/SEC
13 Alfred Rd.
Framingham, MA 01701
Ph: (508)877-8266
Contact: Norma Shulman, Dir.
Founded: 1972. **Members:** 2,000. **Description:** Childbirth groups, doctors, laypersons, and nurses. Established out of concern for the lack of resources available to couples who anticipate or have had a cesarean delivery. Goals are to: improve the cesarean childbirth experience and make the cesarean delivery a good and meaningful childbirth experience for each couple; provide information and promote education on cesarean prevention and vaginal birth after cesarean; change attitudes and policies that affect the cesarean childbirth experience. Offers support for cesarean couples through informal discussion meetings, telephone contact, and personal reply to letters. Provides information on many aspects of cesarean childbirth in order to make couples aware of exactly what the procedure entails and what options are available. Works with doctors, hospitals, childbirth educators, and others in the medical community to effect policy changes and to promote family-centered maternity care for cesarean couples. Conducts inservice programs for hospital staffs and has spoken at conventions and workshops on childbirth. Acronym C/SEC stands for Cesareans/Support, Education and Concern. **Committees:** Correspondence and Counseling; Parent Education; Research; Support Groups. **Formerly:** (1976) C/SEC (Cesarean Sections: Education and Concern). **Publications:** *Frankly Speaking*. Book. Contains discussion of cesarean birth. **Price:** $4.00 ● *Preventing Unnecessary Cesareans: A Guide to Labor Management and Detailed Bibliography*. Pamphlet. Outlines avoidable factors that may lead to preventable cesareans. **Price:** $2.00.

15268 ■ Center for Humane Options in Childbirth Experiences (CHOICE)
3474 N High St.
Columbus, OH 43214
Ph: (614)263-2229
E-mail: shortstork@aol.com
URL: http://choicemidwives.org
Contact: Abby J. Kinne CPM, Exec. Dir.
Founded: 1977. **Members:** 1,200. **Local Groups:** 1. **Description:** Medical professionals, paraprofessionals, and interested individuals. Teaches and encourages parents, parents-to-be, groups, and interested individuals working in family-oriented childbirth in hospital birth centers and out-of-hospital situations. Trains and certifies attendants to attend or coach births. Acts as consumer advocate for hospital births. Services include medical referrals, childbirth education classes, and supplementary prenatal care. Sponsors community educational programs; operates speakers' bureau; compiles statistics. **Convention/Meeting:** none. **Libraries: Type:** reference. **Affiliated With:** International Association of Parents and Professionals for Safe Alternatives in Childbirth.

15269 ■ Childbirth Connection
281 Park Ave. S, 5th Fl.
New York, NY 10010
Ph: (212)777-5000
Fax: (212)777-9320
E-mail: info@maternitywise.org
URL: http://www.childbirthconnection.org
Contact: Maureen P. Corry MPH, Exec. Dir.
Founded: 1918. **Staff:** 6. **Budget:** $1,000,000. **Description:** Provides national leadership in identifying and demonstrating innovative and effective ways to improve maternity care and the birth experience for mothers and their babies. These innovations, which include prenatal care, nurse-midwifery education, prenatal, childbirth and parenting education, and care

in out-of-hospital birth centers, have resulted in significant, positive change. Works to promote safe, effective and satisfying maternity care for all women and their families through research, education and advocacy. **Libraries: Type:** reference. **Holdings:** 2,500; archival material, audiovisuals, books, clippings, monographs, periodicals. **Subjects:** maternal and child health care, midwifery. **Awards:** Hazel Corbin/Maternity Center Association Grant for Evidence-Based Midwifery Care. **Frequency:** annual. **Type:** grant. **Recipient:** for individuals who are enrolled in ACNM accredited certification programs. **Programs:** Maternity Wise. **Affiliated With:** American Association of Birth Centers. **Formerly:** (2005) Maternity Center Association. **Publications:** *Birth Atlas*. Book. Contains instructional aide. **Price:** $70.00 plus shipping and handling. **Advertising:** accepted ● *Growing Uterus Seven Chart Set and Guide*. **Price:** $56.00/set. **Advertising:** accepted ● *Journey to Parenthood: Your Guide Through Pregnancy, Birth & Beyond*. Booklet. **Price:** $6.00/copy (1-50 copies); $5.50/copy (51-100 copies); $5.00/copy (101 copies or more) ● *The Nature and Management of Labor Pain*. Papers. **Price:** $12.00/copy, plus shipping and handling ● *The Rights of Childbearing Women*. Brochure ● *Statements of Rights of Childbearing Women* ● *What Every Pregnant Woman Needs to Know About Cesarean Section*. Booklet. **Price:** $4.00/copy (1-50 copies); $3.80/copy (51-100 copies); $3.60/copy (101-200 copies); $3.20/copy (201-200 copies) ● *Women Supporting Women During Childbirth*. Booklet. **Price:** $2.25/copy, plus shipping and handling ● *Your Guide to Safe and Effective Care During Labor and Birth*. Booklet. **Price:** $2.25/booklet, plus shipping and handling ● Also publishes teaching aids for health professionals, charts, and slides. **Conventions/Meetings:** annual board meeting - December.

15270 ■ Coalition for Improving Maternity Services (CIMS)
PO Box 2346
Ponte Vedra Beach, FL 32004
Ph: (904)285-1613
Free: (888)282-CIMS
Fax: (904)285-2120
E-mail: info@motherfriendly.org
URL: http://www.motherfriendly.org
Founded: 1996. **Description:** Promotes a wellness model of maternity care that improves birth outcomes and reduces costs. **Publications:** *CIMS Mother-Friendly Childbirth Initiative Slide Show*. Film. Presents the creation and mission, the development of MFCI, and the philosophy behind its 10 Steps. **Price:** $125.00/set ● *Having A Baby? Ten Questions To Ask* (in Czech, English, French, and Portuguese). Article. Contains ten questions for prospective mothers to ask of their chosen birth center, hospital, or home birth service. **Price:** free online; $2.00 in U.S. (printed copy); $3.00 in Canada and Mexico (printed copy); $5.00 international (printed copy). Alternate Formats: online ● *MFCI Video*. Contains a series of photographs depicting the elements of Mother-Friendly care. **Price:** $25.00 in VHS format; $35.00 in CD format; $45.00 in DVD format ● *The Mother-Friendly Childbirth Initiative* (in Czech, English, French, and Portuguese). Paper. Contains definition of Mother-Friendly care. Alternate Formats: online.

15271 ■ Council on Resident Education in Obstetrics and Gynecology (CREOG)
c/o American College of Obstetricians and Gynecologists
PO Box 96920
Washington, DC 20090-6920
Ph: (202)863-2554
Fax: (202)863-4994
E-mail: creog@acog.org
URL: http://www.acog.org/departments/dept_web.cfm?recno=1
Contact: DeAnne Nehra, Assoc. Dir.
Founded: 1967. **Members:** 450. **Staff:** 3. **Description:** A semiautonomous nonregulatory organization founded by the American College of Obstetricians and Gynecologists (see separate entry) and comprised of national specialty organizations. Works to

promote and maintain high standards of resident training in obstetrics and gynecology. **Services** include: consultative site visits to residency programs; clearinghouse for residency positions; conferences; a resident data bank; national in-training examination. **Committees:** Education; In-Training Examination; Program Directors Services. **Publications:** *A Design for Resident Education in Obstetrics and Gynecology* ● *Basic Science Monographs in Obstetrics and Gynecology*, periodic. Covers metabolism, genetics, maternal physiology, pharmacology, microbiology, and other aspects of reproductive health. **Price:** $10.00 for members; $15.00 for nonmembers ● *Council on Resident Education in Obstetrics and Gynecology—Council News*, 3/year. Newsletter. Contains membership activities and *CREOG Directory of Obstetric and Gynecologic Residency Programs* update. Alternate Formats: online ● *CREOG Directory of Obstetric and Gynecologic Residency Programs and Directors*, annual. Lists accredited residency programs in the U.S. and Canada. **Price:** $10.00 ● *Educational Objectives for Residents in Obstetrics and Gynecology.* **Conventions/Meetings:** annual conference ● annual retreat, for directors.

15272 ■ DONA International (DONA)
PO Box 626
Jasper, IN 47547-0626
Free: (888)788-DONA
Fax: (812)634-1491
E-mail: info@dona.org
URL: http://www.dona.org
Contact: Susan Martensen, Pres.
Founded: 1992. **Members:** 5,842. **Membership Dues:** individual in U.S., $45 (annual) ● individual in U.S., $80 (biennial) ● individual in Canada, $36 (annual) ● individual in Mexico, $56 (biennial) ● individual in Canada, $65 (biennial) ● individual in Mexico, $29 (annual). **Staff:** 4. **Regional Groups:** 9. **State Groups:** 50. **Languages:** English, Spanish. **Multinational. Description:** Seeks to help Doulas provide quality labor support to birthing women. Offers certification program for Doulas; provides continuing education opportunities; establishes standards of practice and code of ethics; compiles statistics. **Awards:** Annie Kennedy Award. **Type:** recognition. **Recipient:** for an outstanding Doula group ● John Kennel & Marshall Klaus Award. **Type:** recognition. **Recipient:** for an individual who has shown good understanding about Doula care ● Penny Simkin Award. **Type:** recognition. **Recipient:** for outstanding Doulas ● Phyllis Klaus Award. **Type:** recognition. **Recipient:** for outstanding Doulas. **Telecommunication Services:** information service, Doula referrals, information, education. **Committees:** Education. **Formerly:** (2006) Doulas of North America. **Publications:** *DONA Referral Directory* ● *eDoula* (in English and Spanish), monthly. Newsletters. **Price:** free for members. Alternate Formats: online ● *The International Doula*, quarterly. Magazine. **Advertising:** accepted ● *The International Doula Trainer*, quarterly. Newsletter. Alternate Formats: online ● *Introducing the Doula.* Video. **Price:** $15.00 for members; $20.00 for nonmembers. **Conventions/Meetings:** annual conference and board meeting (exhibits) ● annual international conference ● workshop.

15273 ■ Endometriosis Association (EA)
8585 N 76th Pl.
Milwaukee, WI 53223
Ph: (414)355-2200
Free: (800)992-3636
Fax: (414)355-6065
E-mail: endo@endometriosisassn.org
URL: http://www.endometriosisassn.org
Contact: Mary Lou Ballweg, Pres./CEO
Founded: 1980. **Members:** 6,000. **Membership Dues:** individual (diagnosed with endometriosis), $35 (annual) ● associate (others interested), $40 (annual) ● family (teens and their parents), $50 (annual). **Staff:** 10. **Regional Groups:** 200. **Multinational. Description:** Provides help and support to those affected by endometriosis; educates public and medical community about the disease. Promotes and funds research. **Libraries:** Type: reference. **Hold-**

ings: audiovisuals, books, clippings, periodicals. **Subjects:** endometriosis, women's health, nutrition, healthcare. **Awards:** Media Excellence Awards. **Frequency:** annual. **Type:** recognition. **Recipient:** for accuracy and style/accessibility of Endo coverage. **Computer Services:** Mailing lists ● online services. **Additional Websites:** http://www.endo-online.org. **Committees:** Community Education; Correspondence; Crisis Call; Data Bank; Library; Scientific. **Councils:** Advisors; Hispanic; Nurses. **Publications:** *Are You a Teenager?*, bimonthly. Brochure. Available in 2 languages. **Price:** included in membership dues. ISSN: 0897-1870 ● *Endometriosis Association Newsletter*, 4-6/year. Includes news, tips, reviews, and research reports; also covers association and chapter news and activities. **Price:** included in membership dues. ISSN: 0897-1870 ● *Endometriosis: Libro de Consulta* (in Spanish). Book. **Price:** $27.95 each ● *The Endometriosis Sourcebook.* **Price:** $15.95 each ● *Endometriosis: The Complete Reference for Taking Charge of Your Health.* Book. **Price:** $17.95 each ● *Overcoming Endometriosis*, quarterly. Book. Includes information for teen/family members. **Price:** $14.95 each ● *Teens Speak Out on Endometriosis.* Video. Available in 28 languages. **Price:** $14.95 each ● *Teensource*, quarterly. Newsletter. Includes information for teen/family members. **Price:** $2.00/issue ● *What is Endometriosis?.* Brochure. Contains information about endometriosis and available in 28 languages. **Price:** free. **Conventions/Meetings:** quadrennial conference (exhibits).

15274 ■ Gynecologic Surgery Society (GSS)
2440 M St. NW, Ste.801
Washington, DC 20037-1474
Ph: (202)293-5205
Fax: (202)778-6195
E-mail: gsswebmaster@fertilitynet.net
URL: http://www.gynecologicsurgerysociety.org
Contact: Rafael Valle MD, Pres.
Founded: 1979. **Members:** 700. **Membership Dues:** active, $95 (annual). **Staff:** 2. **Budget:** $200,000. **Description:** Individuals interested in gynecologic surgery. Facilitates communication among members. Conducts educational programs and demonstrations of new surgical techniques. **Computer Services:** Mailing lists. **Publications:** *Journal of Gynecologic Surgery*, quarterly. **Price:** $908.00 /year for institutions in U.S.; $1,104.00 /year for institutions outside U.S. ISSN: 1042-4067. **Advertising:** accepted ● Newsletter, periodic. **Conventions/Meetings:** annual conference and board meeting ● periodic seminar.

15275 ■ Hysterectomy Educational Resources and Services Foundation (HERS)
422 Bryn Mawr Ave.
Bala Cynwyd, PA 19004
Ph: (610)667-7757
Free: (888)750-HERS
Fax: (610)667-8096
E-mail: hersfdn@earthlink.net
URL: http://www.uterinearteryembolization.com
Contact: Nora W. Coffey, Pres.
Founded: 1982. **Staff:** 8. **Budget:** $125,000. **Languages:** English, French, German, Spanish. **Multinational. Description:** Helps women make informed decisions regarding hysterectomy and alternatives to surgery. Provides medical journal articles and other educational materials concerning hysterectomy and alternative procedures, networking with other women on a one-to-one basis, referral to physicians and telephone counseling by appointment. **Libraries:** Type: reference. **Holdings:** 4,000; audio recordings, video recordings. **Subjects:** women's health, physical, social and political issues. **Additional Websites:** http://www.hersfoundation.com. **Also Known As:** HERS Foundation. **Publications:** *HERS Annual Hysterectomy Conference Proceedings.* **Price:** $70.00/set. Alternate Formats: diskette ● *HERS Newsletter*, quarterly. Contains book reviews, medical and scientific literature reviews, writer's chronicle of journal, and letters from readers. **Price:** $20.00/year; $6.00/copy. ISSN: 0892-628X. **Circulation:** 5,000 ● *Hysterectomy and Castration.* Pamphlet. Includes comprehensive information. **Price:** $6.00/copy ● Reprints ● Also makes available reading list and cop-

ies of medical journal articles; distributes audio cassettes and other related materials. **Conventions/Meetings:** semiannual Hysterectomy Conference.

15276 ■ Informed Homebirth/Informed Birth and Parenting (IH/IBP)
Address Unknown since 2007
URL: http://www.informedfamilylife.org
Founded: 1977. **Staff:** 2. **Description:** Expectant and new parents, childbirth educators, midwives, nurses, preschool and elementary school teachers, and others interested in safe childbirth alternatives. Seeks to provide information on alternatives in childbirth methods, parenting, and developmental education. Childbirth Educator Training Program leading to certification as Childbirth Educator; Childbirth Assistant Training emphasizing practical skills to help the birthing woman and the primary caregiver. **Libraries:** Type: reference. **Holdings:** audiovisuals, books, periodicals. **Subjects:** birth, pregnancy, parenting. **Divisions:** Book Service; Educational. **Also Known As:** Informed Family Life. **Formerly:** (1981) Informed Homebirth. **Conventions/Meetings:** annual Early Childhood: The Magical Years - conference - always April.

15277 ■ International Association of Parents and Professionals for Safe Alternatives in Childbirth (NAPSAC)
Rte. 4, Box 646
Marble Hill, MO 63764
Ph: (573)238-2010
Fax: (573)238-2010
E-mail: napsac@clas.net
Contact: David Stewart PhD, Exec. Dir.
Founded: 1975. **Members:** 1,000. **Membership Dues:** individual in U.S., $20 (annual) ● individual outside U.S., $22 (annual) ● professional in U.S., $50 (annual) ● professional outside U.S., $52 (annual). **Staff:** 2. **Budget:** $50,000. **Local Groups:** 20. **National Groups:** 20. **Description:** Parents, midwives, physicians, nurses, health officials, social workers, and childbirth educators in 10 countries who are "dedicated to exploring, examining, implementing, and establishing family-centered childbirth programs which meet the needs of families as well as provide the safe aspects of medical science." Promotes education concerning the principles of natural childbirth; facilitates communication and cooperation among parents, medical professionals, and childbirth educators; assists in the establishment of maternity and childbearing centers. Provides educational opportunities to parents and parents-to-be, enabling them to assume more personal responsibility for pregnancy, childbirth, infant care, and child rearing. **Libraries:** Type: not open to the public. **Holdings:** 21; articles, books, periodicals. **Subjects:** pregnancy, childbirth, parenting, health, midwifery. **Computer Services:** database ● mailing lists. **Formerly:** (1979) National Association of Parents and Professionals for Safe Alternatives in Childbirth. **Publications:** *Childbirth Activists Handbook.* **Price:** $15.95. **Circulation:** 1,500 ● *Emergency Childbirth.* **Price:** $18.95 ● *Five Standards for Safe Childbearing.* **Price:** $19.95 ● *NAPSAC Directory of Alternative Birth Services and Consumer Guide*, annual. **Price:** $7.95 for nonmembers, plus shipping and handling; $6.95 for members ● *NAPSAC News*, quarterly. Newsletter. Includes association news, book reviews, and calendar of events. **Price:** included in membership dues. ISSN: 0192-1223. **Circulation:** 2,000. **Advertising:** accepted ● *Safe Alternatives in Childbirth.* **Price:** $12.95 ● *Transitions.* **Price:** $10.95 ● *21st Century Obstetrics Now.* **Price:** $14.95/2 volumes. **Conventions/Meetings:** quadrennial conference (exhibits).

15278 ■ International Cesarean Awareness Network (ICAN)
1304 Kingsdale Ave.
Redondo Beach, CA 90278
Ph: (310)542-6400
Free: (800)686-ICAN
Fax: (310)697-3056

E-mail: info@ican-online.org
URL: http://www.ican-online.org
Contact: Tonya Jamois, Pres.
Founded: 1982. **Members:** 600. **Membership Dues:** in U.S., $30 (annual) ● outside U.S., $40 (annual) ● life, $500 ● professional, $80 (annual) ● supporter, $31-$499 (annual). **Staff:** 11. **Local Groups:** 50. **Languages:** English, Spanish. **Description:** Men and women and birth professionals concerned with the increasing rate of cesarean births. Aims to oppose and lower through education the high cesarean rate currently prevalent and to offer encouragement, information and support to those women who wish to have a vaginal birth after previous cesarean(s) or VBAC. Endeavors to share information about the prevention of unnecessary cesareans and to encourage vaginal birth; to encourage positive birthing assistance that is non-interventive in nature; to refer mothers desiring a VBAC to birth attendants who will assist them; to inform the public as to VBAC option; and to offer direct encouragement, counseling and support to women pursuing a VBAC. Assists and encourages the establishment of local associations, committees, and support groups to further the purposes outlined above. Promotes the safety of vaginal birth vs. cesarean section through printed and other media nationwide. Provides information on cesarean and VBAC issues via website and through printed media. **Libraries: Type:** reference. **Holdings:** 300; books, clippings, periodicals. **Subjects:** cesareans, VBAC. **Computer Services:** Mailing lists. **Formerly:** (1992) Cesarean Prevention Movement. **Publications:** *The Clarion*, quarterly. Newsletter. Includes research and informational articles, book reviews and chapter news. **Price:** included in membership dues; one free copy for nonmembers; $30.00 for basic subscriber in U.S.; $40.00 for basic subscriber outside U.S. **Circulation:** 2,000. **Advertising:** accepted ● *ICAN E-news Line*, semimonthly. Newsletter. **Price:** free. Alternate Formats: online ● Papers. Alternate Formats: online. **Conventions/Meetings:** biennial Reclaiming Our Choices in Childbirth - conference.

15279 ■ International Childbirth Education Association (ICEA)
PO Box 20048
Minneapolis, MN 55420
Ph: (952)854-8660
Fax: (952)854-8772
E-mail: info@icea.org
URL: http://www.icea.org
Contact: Jane Hanrahan MEd, Pres.
Founded: 1960. **Members:** 12,000. **Membership Dues:** individual, $50 (annual) ● individual, $140 (triennial) ● supporting, $100 (annual) ● supporting, $290 (triennial). **Staff:** 8. **Budget:** $500,000. **Local Groups:** 275. **Description:** Furthers the educational, physical, and emotional preparation of expectant parents for childbearing and breastfeeding; increases public awareness on current issues related to childbearing; cooperates with physicians, nurses, physical therapists, hospitals, health, education, and welfare agencies, and other individuals and groups interested in furthering parental participation and minimal obstetric intervention in uncomplicated labors; promotes development of safe, low-cost alternatives in childbirth that recognize the rights and responsibilities of those involved. Develops, publishes, and distributes literature pertaining to family-centered maternity care. Offers a teacher certification program for childbirth educators. Conducts workshops. Operates mail order book store in Minneapolis, MN which makes available literature on all aspects of childbirth education and family-centered maternity care. **Awards:** ICEA Virginia Larson Research Award. **Type:** recognition. **Committees:** Breastfeeding; Cesarean Options; Community Outreach. **Programs:** Certification. **Publications:** *ICEA Bookmarks*, quarterly. Catalog ● *International Journal of Childbirth Education*, quarterly. **Price:** included in membership dues. **Advertising:** accepted. Alternate Formats: online ● Membership Directory, annual ● Also publishes pamphlets. **Conventions/Meetings:** annual meeting (exhibits).

15280 ■ Lamaze Birth Without Pain Education Association
20134 Snowden
Detroit, MI 48235
Ph: (313)341-3816 (313)345-9850
Fax: (313)341-3816
E-mail: cat-flora@juno.com
Contact: Flora Hommel, Exec.Dir./Founder
Founded: 1958. **Members:** 2,000. **Membership Dues:** regular, $20 (annual) ● nurse, $35 (annual) ● physician, $50 (annual). **Staff:** 5. **Budget:** $30,000. **Regional Groups:** 3. **State Groups:** 3. **Local Groups:** 1. **National Groups:** 8. **Languages:** English, French. **Description:** Former and current students of the Lamaze method of painless childbirth; physicians, nurses, midwives, students, former students and interested individuals. Sponsors classes and films for women with or without partners, nurses, midwives and medical and lay groups about the method, which is based on conditioned reflexes to help prevent or reduce pain, thus allowing for normal, usually drug- and intervention free childbirth. Works to provide a method-trained person (monitrice) in attendance at the birth where possible. Collects data for further development of the method; surveys maternity services. Sponsors childbirth teacher and monitrice training and certification nationally with workshops. Provides teen pregnancy programs. Offers some referral service. **Libraries: Type:** reference. **Holdings:** 100; articles, books, periodicals. **Subjects:** methods of childbirth preparation, psychoprophylatic and family-centered maternity care, birth centers, case reports. **Awards:** Volunteer of the Year Award. **Frequency:** annual. **Type:** recognition. **Computer Services:** Information services, referral and consulting services. **Committees:** Film; Speakers' Bureau. **Divisions:** Certification; Consultant; Education and Workshops; Research. **Also Known As:** Childbirth Without Pain Education Association. **Publications:** *Childbirth Without Pain Education Association Memo*, bimonthly. Newsletter. Includes association news and book reviews, and current practices and research, also available on video. **Price:** included in membership dues; $50.00/year for physicians; $35.00 /year for nonmembers and nurses; $16.00/year for alumni. **Circulation:** 1,000. **Advertising:** accepted. **Conventions/Meetings:** biennial lecture and workshop (exhibits). - always in Detroit, MI ● annual meeting and general assembly (exhibits) - always June.

15281 ■ Lamaze International
2025 M St. NW, Ste.800
Washington, DC 20036-3309
Ph: (202)367-1128
Free: (800)368-4404
Fax: (202)367-2128
E-mail: info@lamaze.org
URL: http://www.lamaze.org
Contact: Linda L. Harmon MPH, Exec. Dir.
Founded: 1960. **Members:** 5,000. **Membership Dues:** in U.S., $95 (annual) ● in Mexico, $75 (annual) ● in Canada, $85 (annual). **Staff:** 7. **Budget:** $1,800,000. **Local Groups:** 25. **Languages:** English, Spanish. **Description:** Physicians, nurses, nurse-midwives, certified teachers of psychoprophylatic (Lamaze) method of childbirth, other professionals, parents, and others interested in Lamaze childbirth preparation and family-centered maternity care. Disseminates information about the theory and practical application of psychoprophylaxis in obstetrics; administers teacher training courses and certifies qualified Lamaze teachers; provides educational lectures, public forums, films, and written materials; maintains national teacher referral service. Presents materials to prospective parents concerning the demands of childrearing. Serves as information office clearinghouse. **Libraries: Type:** reference. **Awards:** Lamaze Childbirth Educator Program Scholarship. **Frequency:** annual. **Type:** scholarship. **Recipient:** for members enrolled in Lamaze Childbirth Educator Program who demonstrate financial need ● Marjorie Karmel Award. **Frequency:** annual. **Type:** recognition ● President's Award. **Frequency:** annual. **Type:** recognition. **Computer Services:** Mailing lists, educational programs. **Committees:** Appeals and

Mediation; Certification; Chapter Formation and Development; Education and Public Information. **Task Forces:** Outreach. **Formerly:** (1998) American Society for Psychoprophylaxis in Obstetrics. **Publications:** *Genesis*, quarterly. Newsletter. Contains book and film reviews and calendar of events. **Price:** included in membership dues. **Circulation:** 5,000. **Advertising:** accepted. Alternate Formats: online ● *Journal of Perinatal Education*, quarterly. Includes issues, clinical practice, perinatal education and clinical research. **Price:** free for members; $180.00 /year for institutions; $60.00 /year for nonmembers. ISSN: 1058-1243. **Circulation:** 5,000. **Advertising:** accepted. **Conventions/Meetings:** annual conference (exhibits) - always September. 2007 Sept. 7-9, Phoenix, AZ.

15282 ■ Midwest Parentcraft Center (MPC)
Address Unknown since 2007
Founded: 1950. **Staff:** 2. **Description:** Prenatal instructors, parents, and professionals involved in parenting and pregnancy. To instruct and educate expectant mothers and others in the Gamper Method of childbirth. (The Gamper Method, based on the teachings of several 19th century physicians and developed by Margaret Gamper in 1946, is designed to prepare the prospective mother for childbirth by instilling self-determination and confidence in her ability to work with the physiological changes of her body during pregnancy, labor, and delivery.) Conducts prenatal and grandparenting classes and workshops; operates in-service programs for hospitals and clinics; sponsors programs on topics such as grieving and history of birth procedures. Disseminates teaching aids including slides, films, records, and tapes. Grants childbirth educator certificates to qualified applicants who have taught Gamper Method classes under the supervision of an instructor. Operates charitable program and speakers' bureau; maintains library of 6000 volumes on childbirth, midwifery, marriage, sex, and childcare. The center's activities are currently concentrated in Ohio, Illinois, Indiana, Wisconsin, and Michigan. **Affiliated With:** International Childbirth Education Association. **Publications:** *Heir Raising News*, quarterly ● *Preparation for the Heir Minded*. **Conventions/Meetings:** annual conference.

15283 ■ Midwives Alliance of North America (MANA)
375 Rockbridge Rd., Ste.172-313
Lilburn, GA 30047
Free: (888)923-6262
Fax: (417)777-6181
E-mail: info@mana.org
URL: http://www.mana.org
Contact: Diane Holzer, Pres.
Founded: 1982. **Members:** 1,000. **Membership Dues:** midwife (based on family income), $60-$125 (annual) ● student/apprentice (based on family income), $40-$55 (annual) ● supporting, $40 (annual). **Budget:** $55,000. **Regional Groups:** 10. **Description:** Midwives, student/apprentice midwives, and persons supportive of midwifery. Seeks to expand communication and support among midwives. Works to promote basic competency in midwives; develops and encourages guidelines for their education. Offers legal, legislative, and political information and resource referrals; conducts networking on local, state, and regional bases; compiles statistics. **Awards: Type:** recognition. **Committees:** Affirmative Action; Education; Insurance; Legislative; Media Response Team; Public Education; Public Relations. **Sections:** CPM; Midwives of Color. **Affiliated With:** International Confederation of Midwives. **Publications:** *MANA Committee Reports*. Alternate Formats: online ● *MANA News*, quarterly. Newsletter. **Price:** included in membership dues. Alternate Formats: online ● Brochures ● Also publishes information packets. **Conventions/Meetings:** annual conference (exhibits) ● periodic regional meeting.

15284 ■ Museum of Menstruation and Women's Health (MUM)
PO Box 2398
Landover Hills Br.
Hyattsville, MD 20784-0398

Ph: (301)459-4450
E-mail: hfinley@mum.org
URL: http://www.mum.org
Contact: Barbara Czerwinski PhD, Dir.
Founded: 1994. **Members:** 310. **Membership Dues:** individual, $20 (annual). **Staff:** 2. **Budget:** $10,000. **Languages:** English, German. **For-Profit. Description:** Seeks to educate the public on the cultural history of menstruation. Conducts research and statistical studies. Offers assistance to individuals conducting patent and advertising research, and scholarly work, museum displays of advertising history and menstrual devices. **Convention/Meeting:** none. **Libraries: Type:** reference; open to the public; by appointment only. **Holdings:** 4,000; archival material, artwork, books, business records, clippings, monographs. **Subjects:** menstruation, menstrual hygiene, advertising, history, menstrual devices, underwear, kitsch, tampons, pads. **Boards:** Museum of Menstruation. **Publications:** Booklets. Alternate Formats: online ● Directories. Contains list of essays, myths, poetry, and zines. Alternate Formats: online.

15285 ■ National Healthy Mothers, Healthy Babies Coalition
2000 N Beauregard St., 6th Fl.
Alexandria, VA 22311
Ph: (703)837-4792
Fax: (703)684-5968
E-mail: info@hmhb.org
URL: http://www.hmhb.org
Contact: Ms. Judy Meehan, Exec. Dir.
Founded: 1981. **Members:** 110. **Membership Dues:** volunteer organization, $50 (annual) ● individual associate, $30 (annual) ● based on annual budget/revenues, $75-$500 (annual). **Staff:** 11. **Budget:** $1,000,000. **State Groups:** 21. **Local Groups:** 30. **National Groups:** 110. **Description:** Coalition of national and state organizations concerned with maternal and child health. Serves as a network through which members share ideas and information regarding issues such as prenatal care, nutrition for pregnant women, and infant mortality. **Awards:** National Achievement Awards. **Frequency:** annual. **Type:** recognition. **Recipient:** for local health education programs. **Computer Services:** Mailing lists. **Committees:** Adolescent Health and Pregnancy Prevention; Breastfeeding Promotion; Community Perinatal Outreach Workers; Fathers/Male Involvement; Immunization Education and Action; Injury and Violence Prevention; Substance Use and Pregnancy. **Formerly:** (1999) Healthy Mothers, Healthy Babies. **Publications:** Community Health Workers' Views on Technology and the Promotion of Breastfeeding: Findings from Focus Groups in Three Cities. Report ● Healthy Mothers, Healthy Babies Newsletter, quarterly. **Price:** free. **Circulation:** 6,000 ● IEAC News, quarterly. Newsletter. **Price:** free. **Circulation:** 6,000 ● Power News, quarterly. **Price:** free. **Circulation:** 6,000. **Conventions/Meetings:** biennial conference and workshop (exhibits) - always summer or fall.

15286 ■ National Healthy Start Association (NHSA)
PO Box 25227
Baltimore, MD 21229-0327
Ph: (410)525-1600
Fax: (410)525-1601
E-mail: natlhealthystart@mindspring.com
URL: http://www.healthystartassoc.org
Contact: Bea Haskins, Operations Mgr.
Founded: 1998. **Membership Dues:** individual, $25 (annual) ● community-based organization, local business or corporation, $50 (annual) ● state or regional organization, business or corporation, $100 (annual) ● national organization, business or corporation, $200 (annual). **Description:** Promotes the development of community-based maternal and child health programs, with emphasis on issues of infant mortality, low birthweight and racial disparities in perinatal outcomes. Increases public awareness of the needs of pregnant women, infants, children and families. Develops strategies to sustain the Healthy Start program and other community-based maternal and child health programs. **Publications:** Getting Off to a

Healthy Start, quarterly. Newsletter. Contains information on maternal and child health issues. Alternate Formats: online ● Report. Alternate Formats: online ● Proceedings. Alternate Formats: online.

15287 ■ North American Menopause Society (NAMS)
PO Box 94527
Cleveland, OH 44101
Ph: (440)442-7550
Fax: (440)442-2660
E-mail: info@menopause.org
URL: http://www.menopause.org
Contact: Wulf H. Utian PhD, Exec. Dir.
Founded: 1989. **Members:** 2,500. **Membership Dues:** regular, in North America, $215 (annual) ● regular, outside North America, $235 (annual). **Staff:** 9. **Description:** Physicians, scientists, research and clinical personnel, and other health care professionals are active members; student or physicians serving residencies or fellowships are associate members. Promotes understanding of menopause in women. Advances the exchange of research plans and experience between members. Offers educational programs. **Awards: Frequency:** annual. **Type:** grant. **Computer Services:** database. **Publications:** Flashes, 3/year. Newsletter. **Price:** included in membership dues ● Menopause Management, bimonthly. Serves as a review publication. **Price:** included in membership dues. **Circulation:** 35,000. **Advertising:** accepted ● Menopause: The Journal of the North American Menopause Society, bimonthly. **Price:** included in membership dues. **Circulation:** 3,500. **Advertising:** accepted. **Conventions/Meetings:** annual conference (exhibits).

15288 ■ Polycystic Ovarian Syndrome Association
PO Box 3403
Englewood, CO 80111
E-mail: info@pcosupport.org
URL: http://www.pcosupport.org
Contact: Ms. Christine Dezarn, Founder/CEO
Founded: 1997. **Members:** 2,500. **Membership Dues:** general, associate, $40 (annual) ● professional individual, $175 (annual) ● regular, $25 (annual). **Staff:** 16. **Budget:** $250,000. **Local Groups:** 12. **Languages:** English, Spanish. **Multinational. Description:** Provides support, education and advocacy for women suffering from Polycystic Ovary Syndrome (PCOS). Hosts educational events combining lectures with support sessions. Advocates for women with PCOS in the media and medical community. **Libraries: Type:** not open to the public. **Holdings:** articles, audiovisuals, books, monographs, periodicals. **Subjects:** Polycystic Ovary Syndrome, infertility, drug treatments, hirsutism, diabetes, Syndrome X, obesity, diet, nutrition. **Awards:** Chair's Award. **Frequency:** annual. **Type:** recognition. **Recipient:** for outstanding service of an individual volunteer ● Director's Award. **Frequency:** annual. **Type:** recognition. **Recipient:** for outstanding service of an individual volunteer ● Founder's Award. **Frequency:** annual. **Type:** recognition. **Recipient:** for outstanding service of an individual volunteer ● **Frequency:** periodic. **Type:** scholarship. **Recipient:** to those who indicate need. **Computer Services:** Mailing lists, of members. **Conventions/Meetings:** annual PCOSupport Conference - lecture, 2-3 days, includes support sessions (exhibits).

15289 ■ Sidelines National High-Risk Pregnancy Support Network
PO Box 1808
Laguna Beach, CA 92652
Ph: (949)497-2265
Free: (888)447-4754
Fax: (949)497-5598
E-mail: sidelines@sidelines.org
URL: http://www.sidelines.org
Contact: Candace Hurley, Exec. Dir./Founder
Founded: 1991. **Members:** 20,000. **Staff:** 35. **Regional Groups:** 32. **Languages:** Chinese, English, Japanese, Spanish. **Description:** Former high-risk mothers dedicated to supporting women and their families experiencing a complicated or high-risk

pregnancy. (A pregnancy is termed "complicated" when the life or health of the mother and/or baby may be at risk.) Works to help women overcome the risks of preterm birth, low birth weight, and other serious consequences of high risk pregnancies. Operates the One-On-One program where a mother and her family are paired with a trained "Phone Friend" who has previously been through a complicated pregnancy. Offers prenatal care information and grief and loss counseling. Provides the families with resources and referrals to local businesses, agencies, and services that can assist them. **Convention/Meeting:** none. **Libraries: Type:** lending. **Holdings:** articles, books, video recordings. **Subjects:** prenatal care, pregnancy, high-risk pregnancy, pregnancy loss. **Computer Services:** Online services, chat. **Formerly:** (2002) Sidelines National Support Network. **Publications:** Left Side Lines, annual. Magazine. Contains articles, tips and insights related to the challenges of coping with a high-risk pregnancy. **Price:** $5.00 plus shipping and handling ● Sidelines Parent Pack. Book. **Price:** $15.00 ● That's What Friends Are For. Includes a guide for helping the bedresting Mom and her family. ● When Pregnancy Isn't Perfect. **Price:** $12.00.

15290 ■ Society for Gynecologic Investigation (SGI)
409 12th St. SW
Washington, DC 20024-2125
Ph: (202)863-2544 (202)863-2407
Fax: (202)863-0739
E-mail: sgiava@aol.com
URL: http://sgionline.org
Contact: Charles J. Lockwood, Pres.
Founded: 1953. **Members:** 963. **Membership Dues:** regular, $262 (annual) ● in-training, $50. **Staff:** 4. **Description:** Present and former faculty members of institutions interested or engaged in fundamental gynecologic research. Aims to stimulate, encourage, assist, and conduct gynecologic research. **Awards:** Solvay/Joseph Mortoln Research Grant. **Frequency:** annual. **Type:** grant. **Computer Services:** database ● mailing lists. **Boards:** Executive. **Publications:** Journal of the Society for Gynecologic Investigation, bimonthly. **Advertising:** accepted. **Conventions/Meetings:** annual meeting - always March. 2008 Mar. 26-29, San Diego, CA.

15291 ■ Society for Menstrual Cycle Research (SMCR)
c/o Mary Anna Friederich, MD, Sec.-Treas.
10559 N 104th Pl.
Scottsdale, AZ 85258
Ph: (480)451-9731
Fax: (480)451-9731
E-mail: maryannafriederich@msn.com
URL: http://menstruationresearch.org
Contact: Mary Anna Friederich MD, Sec.-Treas.
Founded: 1977. **Members:** 100. **Membership Dues:** individual in U.S. and Canada, $50 (annual) ● individual outside U.S. and Canada, $65 (annual) ● individual in U.S. and Canada, $125 (triennial) ● student, $20 (annual). **Description:** Physicians, nurses, endocrinologists, geneticists, physiologists, psychologists, sociologists, researchers, educators, students, and others interested in the health needs of women as related to the menstrual cycle. Aims to identify research priorities, recommend research strategies, and promote interdisciplinary research on the menstrual cycle. Establishes a communication network for facilitating interdisciplinary dialogue on menstrual cycle events. Disseminates information and promote discussion of issues among public groups. **Awards:** Linda McKeever Student Prize. **Frequency:** biennial. **Type:** scholarship. **Recipient:** for a student who presents paper at meeting. **Publications:** Changing Perspectives on Menopause. Book ● Culture, Society and Menstruation. Book ● Membership Roster, annual. Membership Directory ● Menarche: The Transition from Girl to Woman. Book ● The Menstrual Cycle, Volume 1: A Synthesis of Interdisciplinary Research ● The Menstrual Cycle, Volume 2: Research and Implications for Women's Health ● Menstrual Health in Women's Lives ● Menstruation, Health, and Illness ● Mind-Body Rhythmic-

ity, A Menstrual Cycle Prospective. Book ● Proceedings 8th Conference Society for Menstrual Cycle Research ● Newsletter, quarterly. **Conventions/Meetings:** biennial Research Conference (exhibits).

15292 ■ Vulvar Pain Foundation (VPF)
203 1/2 N Main St., Ste.203
Graham, NC 27253
Ph: (336)226-0704
Fax: (336)226-8518
URL: http://www.vulvarpainfoundation.org
Contact: Joanne Yount, Exec. Dir.
Founded: 1992. **Members:** 7,741. **Membership Dues:** network/friend in U.S., $45 (annual) ● network/friend in Canada and Mexico, $55 (annual) ● network/friend outside U.S. and Canada, professional in U.S., $60 (annual) ● professional in Canada and Mexico, $70 (annual) ● professional outside U.S. and Canada, $75 (annual). **Staff:** 6. **Budget:** $225,000. **Regional Groups:** 17. **Multinational. Description:** Represents women who have vulvar pain and related disorders (fibromyalgia, interstitial cystitis, irritable bowel), family members, and interested health care professionals. Educates patients, physicians, and the public about successful treatment and current research. Identifies interested health care professionals, promotes scientific research, coordinates support networks and groups. **Libraries: Type:** reference; not open to the public. **Holdings:** 500; articles, books, clippings, periodicals, video recordings. **Subjects:** vulvar pain and related disorders. **Committees:** Scientific Research. **Also Known As:** The VP Foundation. **Publications:** The Low Oxalate Cookbook. Contains dietary guidelines, recipes, and other related information. **Price:** $32.00 for nonmembers; $23.00 for members. **Circulation:** 4,000 ● The VP Foundation Newsletter. **Price:** $2.00 for members; $10.00 for nonmembers. **Circulation:** 2,300 ● Brochure. Describes the purposes, activities, and membership benefits of the foundation. **Price:** free. **Conventions/Meetings:** periodic Regional Seminars, presentations on research and effective treatment; offers support and networking opportunities.

Occupational Medicine

15293 ■ Academy of Organizational and Occupational Psychiatry (AOOP)
PO Box 343
Ridgefield Park, NJ 07660
Free: (877)789-2667
Fax: (877)789-6050
E-mail: staff@aoop.org
URL: http://www.aoop.org
Contact: Steven Pflanz MD, Pres.
Founded: 1990. **Members:** 160. **Membership Dues:** general, associate, $725 (annual). **Multinational. Description:** Strives to provide a forum for exchanging ideas between psychiatry and the world of work. Dedicated to the advancement of psychiatric solutions to the problems of organizations, workers, and leaders. **Publications:** The Bulletin of Organizational and Occupational Psychiatry, quarterly. Contains scholarly articles regarding occupational and organizational psychiatry for publication. **Price:** included in membership dues. **Circulation:** 160. Alternate Formats: online ● Membership Directory. Alternate Formats: online. **Conventions/Meetings:** annual meeting.

15294 ■ American Academy of Physician Assistants in Occupational Medicine (AAPA-OM)
950 N Washington St.
Alexandria, VA 22314-1552
Free: (800)596-4398
Fax: (703)684-1924
E-mail: aapaom@aapa.org
URL: http://www.aapa.org/paom.html
Contact: Thomas Powell PA, Pres.
Founded: 1981. **Members:** 200. **Membership Dues:** fellow, $75 (annual) ● affiliate, $50 (annual) ● student, $10 (annual). **Staff:** 1. **Description:** Physicians, physician assistants, students and graduates

of PA programs. Designed for an exchange of information and ideas within occupational health field. Endorses the code of ethical conduct established by the American College of Occupational Medicine. **Publications:** AAPA-OM Newsletter, quarterly. **Price:** included in membership dues. Alternate Formats: online ● Membership Directory. **Price:** included in membership dues. Alternate Formats: online.

15295 ■ American Board of Industrial Hygiene (ABIH)
6015 W St. Joseph, Ste.102
Lansing, MI 48917
Ph: (517)321-2638
Fax: (517)321-4624
E-mail: abih@abih.org
URL: http://www.abih.org
Contact: Lynn C. O'Donnell CIH, Exec. Dir.
Founded: 1960. **Members:** 12. **Membership Dues:** renewal, $75 (annual). **Staff:** 5. **Budget:** $800,000. **Description:** Certifies industrial hygienists and promotes high standards within the profession. Maintains a record of holders of certificates. **Publications:** ABIH Candidate Handbook. Contains all the background information, instructions, equations sheets, and plates. **Conventions/Meetings:** triennial board meeting.

15296 ■ American College of Occupational and Environmental Medicine (ACOEM)
25 NW Point Blvd., Ste.700
Elk Grove Village, IL 60007-1030
Ph: (847)818-1800
Fax: (847)818-9266
E-mail: acoeminfo@acoem.org
URL: http://www.acoem.org
Contact: Barry S. Eisenberg CAE, Exec. Dir.
Founded: 1916. **Members:** 6,000. **Membership Dues:** regular active, $365 (annual) ● associate, affiliate, $225 (annual) ● student, resident, $35 (annual). **Staff:** 24. **Regional Groups:** 31. **Description:** Physicians specializing in occupational and environmental medicine. Promotes maintenance and improvement of the health of workers; works to increase awareness of occupational medicine as a medical specialty. Sponsors educational programs; maintains placement service. **Awards:** Corporate Health Achievement Award. **Frequency:** annual. **Type:** recognition. **Recipient:** for an organization ● Kammer Merit in Authorship Award. **Frequency:** annual. **Type:** recognition ● Kehoe Award of Merit. **Frequency:** annual. **Type:** recognition ● Knudsen Award. **Frequency:** annual. **Type:** recognition. **Computer Services:** database ● mailing lists. **Formed by Merger of:** American Occupational Medical Association; American Academy of Occupational Medicine. **Formerly:** (1992) American College of Occupational Medicine. **Publications:** ACOEM Report, 10/year. Newsletter. Covers Occupational Safety and Health Administration rulings. **Price:** included in membership dues. **Circulation:** 6,000 ● Journal of Occupational and Environmental Medicine, monthly. Contains book reviews, calendar of events, and employment listings. ISSN: 1076-2752. **Circulation:** 7,000. **Advertising:** accepted ● MRO Update, 10/year. Newsletter. Designed for medical review officers and provides latest information on alcohol and drug testing. **Price:** $210.00 for members; $235.00 for nonmembers. ISSN: 1079-3291. **Circulation:** 600 ● Membership Directory, annual. Arranged alphabetically and geographically. **Price:** included in membership dues; $195.00 for nonmembers. **Circulation:** 6,000. **Advertising:** accepted. **Conventions/Meetings:** annual American Occupational Health Conference (exhibits) ● annual State of the Art Conference - in fall.

15297 ■ American Conference of Governmental Industrial Hygienists (ACGIH)
1330 Kemper Meadow Dr.
Cincinnati, OH 45240
Ph: (513)742-2020 (513)742-6163
Fax: (513)742-3355

E-mail: mail@acgih.org
URL: http://www.acgih.org
Contact: A. Anthony Rizzuto CAE, Exec. Dir.
Founded: 1938. **Members:** 4,000. **Membership Dues:** regular, associate, $175 (annual) ● student, $20 (annual) ● retired, $30 (annual) ● organization, $600 (annual). **Staff:** 17. **Budget:** $3,200,000. **Description:** Professional society of occupational and environmental safety and health professionals. Devoted to the development of administrative and technical aspects of worker health protection. Functions mainly as a medium for the exchange of ideas and the recommendation of exposure guidelines in industrial hygiene and occupational safety and health. **Libraries: Type:** reference. **Holdings:** 2,000. **Subjects:** industrial hygiene, occupational and environmental health and safety. **Awards:** Herbert E. Stokinger Award. **Frequency:** annual. **Type:** recognition. **Recipient:** for individuals who have made significant contributions to the profession through their leadership and dedication ● Meritorious Achievement Award. **Frequency:** annual. **Type:** recognition. **Recipient:** for members who have made an outstanding, long-term contribution to the progress of occupational and environmental hygiene ● William Steiger Memorial Award. **Frequency:** annual. **Type:** recognition. **Recipient:** for individuals from the social/political sphere whose efforts have contributed to advancements in occupational health and safety. **Formerly:** (1945) National Conference of Governmental Industrial Hygienists. **Publications:** Air Sampling Instruments ● Applied Occupational and Environmental Hygiene, monthly. Journal. Includes book reviews, peer-reviewed scientific/technical articles and columns, employment listings and information on new products and literature. **Price:** included in membership dues; $118.00 /year for nonmembers; $204.00 for institutions. ISSN: 0882-8032. **Circulation:** 6,100. **Advertising:** accepted ● Bioaerosols: Assessment and Control ● Documentation of the Threshold Limit Values with Other Worldwide Occupational Exposure Values CD-ROM. Audiotape. Alternate Formats: CD-ROM ● Guide to Occupational Exposure Values. Handbook ● Industrial Ventilation—A Manual of Recommended Practice ● Threshold Limit Values and Biological Exposure Indices ● Ventilation System Testing ● Also publishes other manuals, guides, and studies.

15298 ■ American Industrial Health Council (AIHC)
Address Unknown since 2007
Founded: 1977. **Members:** 38. **Staff:** 10. **Budget:** $1,400,000. **Description:** Advocates the importance of sound science in regulatory decision-making on chronic human health hazards. Promotes the sound use of scientific principles and procedures in the assessment and regulation of risks of chronic human health effects and ecological health effects. Does not act as an advocate for any product or substance. **Libraries: Type:** not open to the public. **Publications:** AIHC Bulletin, weekly. **Price:** included in membership dues. **Circulation:** 200. **Advertising:** not accepted ● AIHC Newsletter, monthly. **Price:** included in membership dues. **Circulation:** 550. **Advertising:** not accepted ● Committe brochures and white papers; exposure factors scourcebook; FOB manual. **Conventions/Meetings:** annual conference - Washington, DC - **Avg. Attendance:** 200.

15299 ■ American Industrial Hygiene Association (AIHA)
2700 Prosperity Ave., Ste.250
Fairfax, VA 22031
Ph: (703)849-8888
Fax: (703)207-3561
E-mail: infonet@aiha.org
URL: http://www.aiha.org
Contact: Steven H. Davis CAE, Exec. Dir.
Founded: 1939. **Members:** 11,600. **Membership Dues:** full, associate, affiliate, $166 (annual). **Staff:** 58. **Budget:** $13,000,000. **Regional Groups:** 76. **Local Groups:** 70. **Languages:** English, Spanish. **Description:** Professional society of industrial hygienists. Promotes the study and control of environmental factors affecting the health and well-being of

workers. Sponsors continuing education courses in industrial hygiene, government affairs program, and public relations. Accredits laboratories. Maintains 40 technical committees and a foundation. Operates placement service. Conducts educational and research programs. **Awards:** Alice Hamilton Award. **Frequency:** annual. **Type:** recognition. **Recipient:** to an outstanding woman who has shown a definitive and lasting achievement in the field of occupational and environmental hygiene through public and community service ● Cummings Memorial Award. **Frequency:** annual. **Type:** recognition. **Recipient:** for outstanding contributions to the knowledge and practice of the industrial hygiene profession ● Distinguished Service Award. **Frequency:** annual. **Type:** recognition. **Recipient:** for distinguished service in the advancement of industrial hygiene and technical contributions to the goals of AIHA ● Edward J. Baier Technical Achievement Award. **Frequency:** annual. **Type:** recognition. **Recipient:** for the most significant contribution to industrial hygiene in recent years ● Kusnetz Award. **Frequency:** annual. **Type:** recognition. **Recipient:** to a certified hygienist. **Computer Services:** Mailing lists. **Absorbed:** (1999) Academy of Industrial Hygiene. **Publications:** *The AIHA Journal*, bimonthly. Includes peer-reviewed technical and scientific articles. ISSN: 0002-8894. **Circulation:** 15,000. **Advertising:** accepted. Alternate Formats: online ● *The Synergist*, monthly. Magazine. Includes news magazine covering occupational and environmental health and safety issues. **Price:** $65.00/year in U.S.; $90.00/year international. **Circulation:** 13,000. **Advertising:** accepted. Alternate Formats: online ● *Who's Who in Industrial Hygiene*, annual. Directory ● Books ● Manuals ● Videos. **Conventions/Meetings:** annual American Industrial Hygiene Conference and Exposition (exhibits) - usually in May.

15300 ■ American Occupational Therapy Foundation (AOTF)

4720 Montgomery Ln.
PO Box 31220
Bethesda, MD 20824-1220
Ph: (301)652-6611
Free: (800)729-2682
Fax: (301)656-3620
E-mail: aotf@aotf.org
URL: http://www.aotf.org
Contact: Martha Kirkland, Exec. Dir.

Founded: 1965. **Staff:** 12. **Budget:** $1,300,000. **Nonmembership. Description:** Encourages practice, research and scholarship in occupation and occupational therapy. Educates the public and professionals about occupation and occupational therapy. **Libraries: Type:** not open to the public. **Holdings:** 4,000; archival material, books, periodicals. **Subjects:** occupational therapy, rehabilitation. **Awards:** A. Jean Ayres Award. **Frequency:** annual. **Type:** recognition. **Recipient:** for occupational therapy clinicians, educators and researchers ● Leadership Service Commendation. **Frequency:** annual. **Type:** recognition. **Recipient:** for retiring members of the foundation ● Meritorious Service Award. **Frequency:** annual. **Type:** recognition. **Recipient:** for members who have made sustained and exemplary contributions in support of the foundation's mission ● Student Scholarships. **Frequency:** annual. **Type:** scholarship. **Recipient:** for full-time student in accredited OT program ● Virginia Scardina Award of Excellence. **Frequency:** annual. **Type:** recognition. **Recipient:** for clinical therapy technician who has demonstrated sustained commitment, excellence and/or innovation in sensory integration and brain behavior relationships in the practice of occupational therapy. **Computer Services:** database ● mailing lists. **Programs:** Center for Outcomes Research and Education; OJTR: Occupation, Participation and Health; Scholarships; Student Research Grants; Wilma L. West Library. **Task Forces:** Occupation in Societal Crises. **Affiliated With:** American Occupational Therapy Association. **Publications:** *Connection*. Newsletter. Alternate Formats: online ● *Occupation, Participation and Health*. Journal ● *The Occupational Therapy Journal of Research*, quarterly ● Annual Report, an-

nual. Alternate Formats: online. **Conventions/Meetings:** annual conference (exhibits).

15301 ■ Association of Occupational and Environmental Clinics (AOEC)

1010 Vermont Ave. NW, Ste.513
Washington, DC 20005
Ph: (202)347-4976
Free: (888)347-AOEC
Fax: (202)347-4950
E-mail: aoec@aoec.org
URL: http://www.aoec.org
Contact: Katherine H. Kirkland MPH, Exec. Dir.

Founded: 1987. **Members:** 324. **Membership Dues:** individual, $40 (annual) ● clinic, $250 (annual) ● associate, $200 (annual). **Staff:** 4. **Budget:** $2,000,000. **Description:** Seeks to enhance the practice of occupational and environmental medicine. Shares information. Provides educational and research programs. **Libraries: Type:** lending; not open to the public. **Subjects:** environmental and occupational medicine. **Awards: Type:** grant. **Computer Services:** database. **Publications:** *AOEC News*, quarterly. Newsletter. **Advertising:** accepted. Alternate Formats: online. **Conventions/Meetings:** board meeting ● conference ● regional meeting.

15302 ■ Association of Occupational Health Professionals in Healthcare (AOHP)

109 VIP Dr., Ste.220
Wexford, PA 15090
Free: (800)362-4347
Fax: (724)935-1560
E-mail: info@aohp.org
URL: http://www.aohp.org
Contact: Denise Strode RN, Exec. Pres.

Founded: 1981. **Members:** 1,000. **Membership Dues:** active, $125 (annual) ● student, $50 (annual) ● retired, $25 (annual). **Staff:** 3. **Regional Groups:** 5. **Description:** Occupational health professionals. Promotes the health and safety of workers in healthcare. Provides occupational health education and networking opportunities. **Awards:** Continuing Education Scholarship. **Frequency:** annual. **Type:** scholarship. **Recipient:** for members ● Editor's Fund Scholarship. **Frequency:** annual. **Type:** scholarship. **Recipient:** for members ● Julie Schmid Original Research Scholarship. **Frequency:** annual. **Type:** scholarship. **Recipient:** for members. **Computer Services:** Mailing lists. **Committees:** Continuing Education; Governmental Affairs; National Conference; Nominations; Planning. **Publications:** *Getting Started Manual*. **Price:** included in membership dues ● *Journal of the Association of Occupational Health Professionals in Healthcare*, bimonthly. **Price:** included in membership dues. **Advertising:** accepted ● Membership Directory. **Price:** included in membership dues. Alternate Formats: online ● Report. Alternate Formats: online ● Brochure. Alternate Formats: online. **Conventions/Meetings:** annual conference - 2007 Sept. 26-29, Savannah, GA.

15303 ■ Association for Repetitive Motion Syndromes (ARMS)

PO Box 471973
Aurora, CO 80047-1973
Ph: (303)369-0803
E-mail: arms@lightspeed.net
URL: http://www.certifiedpst.com/arms/index.html
Contact: Stephanie S. Barnes MA, Exec. Dir./ Founder

Founded: 1990. **Membership Dues:** individual, $20 (annual) ● professional, $75 (annual) ● corporate, $150 (annual). **Staff:** 1. **Budget:** $10,000. **Regional Groups:** 1. **State Groups:** 1. **Description:** Individuals suffering from repetitive motion injuries; other interested individuals and organizations. Promotes the welfare of persons at risk of developing repetitive motion injuries. Works to increase public awareness of repetitive motion injuries and prevention and treatment. Develops and implements occupational safety standards and educational programs. Compiles, analyzes, and disseminates data; conducts research programs; and clearinghouse. **Absorbed:** (1993) American Carpal Tunnel Syndrome Association. **Publications:** *ARMS News*, quarterly. Newsletter. **Price:**

$20.00 for individuals; $75.00 for professionals; $150.00 for organizations. **Advertising:** accepted. **Conventions/Meetings:** monthly support group meeting.

15304 ■ Council for Accreditation in Occupational Hearing Conservation (CAOHC)

555 E Wells St., Ste.1100
Milwaukee, WI 53202-3823
Ph: (414)266-5338
Fax: (414)276-2146
E-mail: info@caohc.org
URL: http://www.caohc.org
Contact: Ms. Barbara Lechner, Exec. Dir.

Founded: 1973. **Members:** 22,000. **Staff:** 2. **Budget:** $350,000. **Description:** Establishes and maintains standards for the training and certification of audiometric technicians (persons certified to conduct pure tone air conduction hearing tests and related duties as part of an occupational hearing conservation program). Trains and certifies instructors for those courses known as Course Directors. Trains and certifies audiologists and physicians as the Professional Supervisor of the Audiometric Component of Hearing Conservation Programs. Council members represent professional associations in the hearing conservation field. **Affiliated With:** American Academy of Otolaryngology - Head and Neck Surgery; American Association of Occupational Health Nurses; American College of Occupational and Environmental Medicine; American Industrial Hygiene Association; American Society of Safety Engineers; American Speech Language Hearing Association; Institute of Noise Control Engineering. **Publications:** *Occupational Hearing Conservation Manual, 4th Edition*. Contains information on the hearing conservationist's mission, training, and role; and federal and state regulations. **Price:** $75.00. **Circulation:** 10,000 ● *The Update*, 3/year. Newsletter. **Price:** $20.00/year. **Circulation:** 22,000. **Advertising:** accepted. Alternate Formats: online. **Conventions/Meetings:** semiannual Course Director Workshop, certification requirement for certifying course directors - spring and fall.

15305 ■ Society for Occupational and Environmental Health (SOEH)

6728 Old McLean Village Dr.
McLean, VA 22101
Ph: (703)556-9222
Fax: (703)556-8729
E-mail: soeh@degnon.org
URL: http://www.soeh.org
Contact: George K. Degnon CAE, Exec. Dir.

Founded: 1972. **Members:** 350. **Membership Dues:** regular, $90 (annual) ● student and emeritus, $30 (annual). **Staff:** 2. **Budget:** $50,000. **Description:** Scientists, academicians, and industry and labor representatives. Seeks to improve the quality of both working and living places by operating as a neutral forum for conferences involving all aspects of occupational health. Focuses public attention on scientific, social, and regulatory problems; studies specific categories of hazards, methods for assessment of health effects, and diseases associated with particular jobs. Identifies hazards in the occupational and general environment and proposes actions to reduce their danger. **Computer Services:** Mailing lists. **Publications:** *Health Impacts of Global Climate Change*. Video. **Price:** $23.00 each, in U.S.; $35.00 each, outside U.S. ● *Society for Occupational and Environmental Health—Bulletin*, quarterly. Newsletter. **Price:** included in membership dues. **Circulation:** 350. Also Cited As: *SOEH Bulletin*. **Conventions/Meetings:** annual conference.

Occupational Safety and Health

15306 ■ Voluntary Protection Programs Participants' Association (VPPPA)

7600-E Leesburg Pike, Ste.440
Falls Church, VA 22043-2004
Ph: (703)761-1146
Fax: (703)761-1148

E-mail: administration@vpppa.org
URL: http://www.vpppa.org
Contact: R. Davis Layne, Exec. Dir.

Members: 1,200. **Membership Dues:** full (based on site employee count), $90-$2,500 (annual) ● corporate, $250 (annual) ● agency, $360-$4,500 (annual) ● non-profit, $360 (annual) ● union, $100 (annual). **Staff:** 10. **Description:** Companies participating in Voluntary Protection Programs and other workplace environmental protection, health, and safety programs. Promotes cooperation between labor, management, and government agencies to insure safe and environmentally sustainable workplaces. Works closely with federal environmental and safety agencies to develop and implement cooperative programs; provides information on environmental health and workplace safety to congressional committees considering legislation. **Awards:** Safety and Health Achievement Award. **Frequency:** annual. **Type:** recognition. **Recipient:** for non-safety and health professionals in recognition of their contributions in the field of safety, health and environmental program management ● Safety and Health Outreach Award. **Frequency:** annual. **Type:** recognition. **Recipient:** for an individual, company, or worksite that has achieved an outstanding level of outreach in the safety and health arena ● VPP Innovation Award. **Frequency:** annual. **Type:** recognition. **Recipient:** for a site or company that has developed and successfully implemented an innovation ● VPP Outreach Award. **Frequency:** annual. **Type:** recognition. **Recipient:** for VPP ambassadors who achieved an outstanding level of outreach activity and results ● VPPPA June Brothers Scholarship. **Frequency:** annual. **Type:** scholarship. **Recipient:** for students pursuing either an undergraduate or graduate degree in the safety/health/environmental field ● VPPPA Stephen Brown Scholarship. **Frequency:** annual. **Type:** scholarship. **Recipient:** for students pursuing a degree in the trades. **Programs:** Mediation; Mentoring. **Publications:** *The Leader*, quarterly. Magazine. **Price:** $25.00 for nonmembers; included in membership dues. ISSN: 1081-261X. **Circulation:** 8,000. **Advertising:** accepted ● *On the Wire*, bimonthly. Newsletter. Informs members of Association activities. **Price:** free for members. Alternate Formats: online ● *Safety News Network*, biweekly. Newsletter. Alternate Formats: online ● *Washington Update*, monthly. Newsletter. Keeps members abreast of groundbreaking news on regulations, policy developments and legislative news. Alternate Formats: online. **Conventions/Meetings:** annual conference (exhibits) - 2008 Aug. 24-28, Anaheim, CA; 2009 Aug. 23-27, San Antonio, TX.

Oncology

15307 ■ American Association for Cancer Research (AACR)
615 Chestnut St., 17th Fl.
Philadelphia, PA 19106-4406
Ph: (215)440-9300
Free: (866)423-3965
Fax: (215)440-7228
E-mail: aacr@aacr.org
URL: http://www.aacr.org
Contact: Margaret Foti PhD, CEO

Founded: 1907. **Members:** 19,000. **Membership Dues:** active, $245 (annual) ● associate, $70 (annual) ● affiliate, $115 (annual) ● student, $10 (annual) ● emeritus, $35 (annual). **Staff:** 100. **Budget:** $3,000,000. **Local Groups:** 3. **Multinational. Description:** Works to facilitate communication and dissemination of information among scientists and others dedicated to cancer research; seeks to advance understanding of cancer etiology, prevention, diagnosis and treatment throughout the world. Fosters research on cancer, public and science education and training. **Awards:** American Cancer Society Award for Research Excellence in Cancer Epidemiology and Prevention. **Frequency:** annual. **Type:** recognition. **Recipient:** for outstanding research accomplishments in cancer epidemiology, biomarkers, and prevention ● Award for Outstanding Achieve-

ment in Cancer Research. **Frequency:** annual. **Type:** recognition. **Recipient:** to a young investigator on the basis of meritorious achievement in cancer research ● Bruce F. Cain Memorial Award. **Frequency:** annual. **Type:** recognition. **Recipient:** for outstanding preclinical research in the fields of medicinal chemistry, biochemistry, or tumor biology as related to drug discovery ● DeWitt S. Goodman Memorial Lectureship. **Frequency:** annual. **Type:** recognition. **Recipient:** to individuals with significant contributions to the field of nutrition and cancer and cancer prevention ● G.H.A. Clowes Memorial Award. **Frequency:** annual. **Type:** recognition. **Recipient:** for outstanding recent accomplishments in basic cancer research ● Gertrude Elion Cancer Research Award. **Frequency:** annual. **Type:** recognition ● Joseph H. Burchenal Clinical Research Award. **Frequency:** annual. **Type:** monetary ● Landon-AACR Prize in Translational Cancer Research. **Frequency:** annual. **Type:** recognition. **Recipient:** to an individual who has made significant fundamental contributions to cancer research, either through a single scientific discovery or a body of work ● Landon-AACR Prizes for Basic and Translational Cancer Research. **Frequency:** annual. **Type:** monetary. **Recipient:** for medical or graduate students ● Pezcoller Foundation-AACR International Award for Cancer Research. **Frequency:** annual. **Type:** recognition. **Recipient:** for a major scientific discovery in basic cancer research or significant contributions to translational cancer research ● Richard and Hinda Rosenthal Foundation Award. **Frequency:** annual. **Type:** recognition. **Recipient:** for investigators ● Scholar-in-Training Awards. **Frequency:** annual. **Type:** grant. **Recipient:** for graduate students, medical students and residents, clinical fellows or equivalent, and postdoctoral fellows who have highly rated proffered papers ● Travel Award-Scientific Meetings. **Frequency:** annual. **Type:** monetary. **Recipient:** for medical or graduate students ● Women in Cancer Research-Charlotte Friend Memorial Lectureship. **Frequency:** annual. **Type:** recognition. **Recipient:** for an outstanding scientist who has made meritorious contributions to the field of cancer research. **Computer Services:** database, membership ● mailing lists. **Committees:** Clinical Cancer Research; International Affairs; Nominating; Publications; Science Education; Science Policy and Legislative Affairs; Special Conferences; Tellers. **Publications:** *Cancer Epidemiology, Biomarkers and Prevention*, monthly. Journal. Contains original research on causes and prevention of cancer. **Price:** $165.00 /year for nonmembers; included in membership dues. ISSN: 1044-9523. **Circulation:** 2,700. **Advertising:** accepted. Alternate Formats: online ● *Cancer Research*, semimonthly. Journal. Contains reports in subfields of cancer research: biochemistry, biophysics, carcinogenesis, endocrinology, immunology, and molecular biology. **Price:** included in membership dues; $640.00 /year for nonmembers. ISSN: 0008-5472. **Circulation:** 9,600. **Advertising:** accepted. Alternate Formats: microform; online ● *Clinical Cancer Research*, monthly. Journal. Features articles on clinical and translational cancer research. **Price:** $225.00 /year for nonmembers; included in membership dues. ISSN: 1078-0432. **Circulation:** 5,000. **Advertising:** accepted. Alternate Formats: online ● *Molecular Cancer Research*, monthly. Journal. Includes peer-reviewed research on the molecular and cellular biology of cancer. **Price:** $145.00 /year for nonmembers; included in membership dues. ISSN: 1541-7786. **Circulation:** 2,200. **Advertising:** accepted. Alternate Formats: online. Also Cited As: *Cell Growth and Differentiation* ● *Molecular Cancer Therapeutics*, monthly. Journal. Contains research on emerging disciplines with implications for cancer therapeutics. **Price:** $100.00 /year for nonmembers; included in membership dues. ISSN: 1535-7163. **Circulation:** 3,159. **Advertising:** accepted. Alternate Formats: online ● *Supplement to Journal*, periodic ● *Directory*, annual ● *Proceedings*, annual. **Conventions/Meetings:** annual convention (exhibits) - 2008 Apr. 12-16, San Diego, CA; 2009 Apr. 18-22, Denver, CO; 2010 Apr. 17-21, Washington, DC.

15308 ■ American College of Mohs Micrographic Surgery and Cutaneous Oncology (ACMMSCO)
555 E Wells St., Ste.1100
Milwaukee, WI 53202-3823

Ph: (414)347-1103
Free: (800)500-7224
Fax: (414)276-2146
E-mail: info@mohscollege.org
URL: http://www.mohscollege.org
Contact: Georganne Dixon, Exec. Dir.

Founded: 1967. **Members:** 800. **Membership Dues:** physician in U.S., $450 (annual) ● physician outside U.S., $275 (annual). **Description:** Physicians, dermatologists, surgeons, plastic surgeons, and other specialists who have had a minimum of one year of training in Mohs surgery at an approved institution. (Mohs surgery is used for the microscopically controlled excision of skin cancer.) Provides a means for recognition of physicians who have become proficient in the method; facilitates education and the exchange of ideas. **Formerly:** (1987) American College of Chemosurgery. **Publications:** *Mohs Micrographic Surgery Pamphlet* (in English and Spanish). Demonstrates the procedure using text and step-by-step diagrams. **Price:** $27.00/package for members; $49.00/package for nonmembers. **Conventions/Meetings:** annual meeting, combined ASDS/ACMMSCO meeting (exhibits).

15309 ■ American Joint Committee on Cancer (AJCC)
633 N St. Clair St.
Chicago, IL 60611
Ph: (312)202-5313
Fax: (312)202-5009
E-mail: kpollitt@facs.org
URL: http://www.cancerstaging.org
Contact: Karen Pollitt, Admin.

Founded: 1959. **Members:** 40. **Staff:** 2. **Budget:** $250,000. **Description:** Surgeons, physicians, radiologists, pathologists, American Cancer Society (see separate entry) representatives, and National Cancer Institute representatives. Formulates and publishes systems of classification for cancer staging and end results reporting for the purpose of selecting the most effective treatment, determining prognosis, and continuing evaluation of cancer control measures. Promotes the use of developed systems of classification of cancer and evaluates systems of recording and reporting data. **Committees:** Editorial and Publications; Education and Promotions; Executive. **Task Forces:** Bone; Breast; Central Nervous System; Foregut; Genitourinary; Gynecologic; Head and Neck; Hepatobiliary; Hindgut; Lung and Esophagus; Lymphoma; Melanoma and Non-Skin Melanoma; Ophthalmic; Soft Tissue Sarcoma; Statistical. **Affiliated With:** American Cancer Society; American College of Physicians-American Society of Internal Medicine; American College of Radiology; American College of Surgeons; College of American Pathologists; National Cancer Center. **Formerly:** (1981) American Joint Committee for Cancer Staging and End Results Reporting. **Publications:** *AJCC Cancer Staging Atlas*, published as necessary. Book. Includes more than 400 black and white illustrations for the AJCC Cancer Staging Atlas to depict the anatomic extent of disease for T, N and M. **Price:** $59.95 ● *AJCC Cancer Staging Handbook, 6th Edition*. **Price:** $39.95. Alternate Formats: CD-ROM ● *AJCC Manual for Staging of Cancer, 6th Edition*, quadrennial. Includes classification for cancer staging and end results reporting for selecting treatment, determining prognosis and evaluating cancer. **Price:** $59.95. Alternate Formats: CD-ROM; online ● *Cancer Staging - What You Need to Know* (in English and Spanish). Brochure. Presents the concept of cancer staging for patients and families. **Conventions/Meetings:** annual meeting, for full, executive and nominating committees only - always September.

15310 ■ American Psychosocial Oncology Society (APOS)
2365 Hunters Way
Charlottesville, VA 22911
Ph: (434)293-5350
Fax: (434)977-1856
E-mail: info@apos-society.org
URL: http://www.apos-society.org
Contact: Ms. Elliott Graham, Exec. Dir.

Membership Dues: full, associate, $175 (annual) ● member-in-training, $125 (annual). **Description:**

Seeks to advance the science and practice of psychosocial care for people with cancer. Raises the level of awareness of health professionals and the public about psychological, social, behavioral, and spiritual domains of care for patients with cancer. Promotes education and training of health professionals in the psychological, social, behavioral, and spiritual domains of cancer. Provides a forum for professionals and individuals interested in the areas of psychological, social, behavioral, spiritual and physical aspects of cancer and allied diseases. **Awards:** Distinguished Public Service Award. **Frequency:** annual. **Type:** recognition. **Recipient:** for a leader with outstanding contributions to the field of psychosocial oncology ● Holland Distinguished Leadership Award. **Frequency:** annual. **Type:** recognition. **Recipient:** for APOS or community member who has made an outstanding contribution to the field of psychosocial oncology ● New Investigator Award. **Frequency:** annual. **Type:** recognition. **Recipient:** for outstanding research contributions to the field of psychosocial oncology ● Outstanding Clinical Care Award. **Frequency:** annual. **Type:** recognition. **Recipient:** for outstanding clinical contributions to the field of psychosocial oncology. **Telecommunication Services:** electronic mail, egraham@apos-society.org. **Publications:** *Psycho-Oncology*, monthly. Journal. Contains research articles on psychosocial oncology. **Price:** included in membership dues. **Conventions/Meetings:** annual conference, for supporters, contributors and individuals; with leisure opportunities (exhibits) - 2008 Feb. 28-Mar. 8, Irvine, CA.

15311 ■ American Radium Society (ARS)
11300 W Olympic Blvd., Ste.600
Los Angeles, CA 90064
Ph: (310)437-0581
Fax: (310)437-0585
E-mail: info@americanradiumsociety.org
URL: http://www.americanradiumsociety.org
Contact: Ms. Jaclyn Weinstein, Exec. Dir.

Founded: 1916. **Members:** 500. **Membership Dues:** active, $275 (annual). **Description:** Represents radiation oncologists, surgical oncologists, gynecological oncologists and medical oncologists. Promotes the study of cancer in all of its aspects, encourages liaison among the various medical specialists and allied scientists concerned with the treatment of cancer, and continues scientific study of the treatment of the cancer patient through its annual meeting and educational publications. **Awards:** Janeway Lecture Award. **Frequency:** annual. **Type:** recognition. **Recipient:** to a leader in oncology ● Young Oncologist Awards. **Frequency:** annual. **Type:** grant. **Recipient:** to residents and fellows. **Computer Services:** Online services, abstracts. **Committees:** Constitution and Bylaws; Educational Resources; Executive; Industry Relations/Development; Janeway Lecture; Membership and Credentials; Nominating; Resident and Attending Educational; Scientific Program; Website and Public Relations. **Publications:** *American Radium Society—Membership Directory*, annual. **Price:** included in membership dues. **Circulation:** 10,000. Alternate Formats: online ● *Oncology*, annual. Journal. **Conventions/Meetings:** annual meeting, with half day scientific sessions and half day exploration of location (exhibits) - 2008 May 2-7, Laguna Niguel, CA - **Avg. Attendance:** 300.

15312 ■ American Society of Clinical Oncology (ASCO)
1900 Duke St., Ste.200
Alexandria, VA 22314
Ph: (703)299-0150
Fax: (703)299-1044
E-mail: asco@asco.org
URL: http://www.asco.org
Contact: Gabriel N. Hortobagyi, Pres.

Founded: 1964. **Members:** 25,000. **Membership Dues:** active, $495 (annual) ● active-junior, $295 (annual) ● active-allied, $125 (annual) ● active-allied (with JCO), $415 (annual) ● affiliate, $100 (annual) ● affiliate (with JCO), $390 (annual) ● international corresponding, associate (with JCO), $50 (annual). **Staff:** 85. **Budget:** $16,000,000. **Description:** Physi-

cians who treat people with cancer. Sets the standard for patient care worldwide, and leads the fight for more effective cancer treatments, increased funding for clinical and translational research. **Awards:** Karnofsky Memorial Lecture Awards. **Frequency:** annual. **Type:** recognition. **Recipient:** for individuals who have changed the way oncologists think about the general practice of oncology. **Committees:** Bylaws; Cancer Communications; Cancer Education; Cancer Prevention; Cancer Research; Career Development; Clinical Practice; Ethics. **Publications:** *ASCO Daily News*, annual. Newspaper. Alternate Formats: online ● *ASCO News*, quarterly. Magazine. **Price:** included in membership dues. Alternate Formats: online ● *Educational Book*. **Price:** $60.00 for members; $75.00 for nonmembers ● *Journal of Clinical Oncology*, monthly. **Price:** included in membership dues; $487.00 for nonmembers, in U.S.; $678.00 for nonmembers, international; $35.00/single copy, for nonmembers in U.S. ISSN: 0732-183X. Alternate Formats: online. Also Cited As: *JCO* ● *JCO Policy Watch Weekly*. Newsletter. **Price:** included in membership dues. Alternate Formats: online ● Directory, annual ● Proceedings, annual. **Price:** $60.00 for members; $75.00 for nonmembers ● Membership Directory. **Price:** included in membership dues. **Conventions/Meetings:** annual meeting (exhibits).

15313 ■ American Society for Mohs Surgery (ASMS)
Private Mail Box 391
5901 Warner Ave.
Huntington Beach, CA 92649-4659
Ph: (714)379-6262
Free: (800)616-ASMS
Fax: (714)379-6272
E-mail: info@mohssurgery.org
URL: http://www.mohssurgery.org
Contact: Novella Rodgers, Exec. Dir.

Founded: 1990. **Members:** 850. **Membership Dues:** fellow, $250 (annual) ● affiliate, associate, international, $200 (annual) ● mohs technician-related professional, $50 (annual). **Multinational. Description:** Provides advocacy for Mohs surgeons from a variety of Mohs training backgrounds. Supports members in the area of practice resources. Offers educational programs in Mohs surgery to the dermatologic community. **Awards:** Corporate Exhibitor/Educational Grant. **Frequency:** annual. **Type:** grant. **Recipient:** for corporate exhibitors of the annual Clinical Symposium. **Publications:** *Mohs Surgery: Fundamentals and Techniques*. Book. **Price:** $165.00 each ● *Patient Information Brochure*. **Price:** $38.00 minimum package for members; $72.00 minimum package for nonmembers.

15314 ■ American Society of Preventive Oncology (ASPO)
c/o Heidi Sahel, Exec. Dir.
330 WARF Bldg.
610 Walnut St.
Madison, WI 53726
Ph: (608)263-9515
Fax: (608)263-4497
E-mail: hasahel@facstaff.wisc.edu
URL: http://www.aspo.org
Contact: Heidi Sahel, Exec. Dir.

Founded: 1976. **Members:** 420. **Membership Dues:** individual, $200 (annual) ● student/postdoc trainee, $35 (annual) ● emeritus, $85 (annual). **Staff:** 2. **Budget:** $200,000. **Description:** Professionals in clinical, educational, or research disciplines concerned with the field of cancer prevention. Promotes the exchange of information and ideas relating to cancer prevention and the causes of human cancer, including environmental exposures and lifestyles; encourages research. Works to implement programs for the prevention and early detection of cancer. Evaluates programs intended to reduce cancer incidence, mortality, and morbidity. Encourages professional and public education regarding cancer prevention. Maintains communication and liaison with other oncological societies. Provides expert advice to scientific, public health, and governmental organizations and agencies. **Awards:** Distinguished Achievement Award. **Frequency:** annual. **Type:** recognition. **Re-**

cipient: for contribution in area of cancer prevention. **Computer Services:** Mailing lists. **Subgroups:** Behavioral Oncology; Chemoprevention; Diet and Nutrition; Molecular Epidemiology; Screening Molecular Epidemiology; Tobacco. **Publications:** *Cancer Epidemiology, Biomarkers, and Prevention*, monthly. Journal. Contains original, peer-reviewed research on cancer causation, mechanisms of carcinogenesis, prevention, and survivorship. **Price:** included in membership dues. **Conventions/Meetings:** annual conference and workshop.

15315 ■ Association of Residents in Radiation Oncology (ARRO)
c/o Steven Smith, Liaison
12500 Fair Lakes Cir., Ste.375
Fairfax, VA 22033
Ph: (703)839-7326
Fax: (703)502-7852
E-mail: stevens@astro.org
URL: http://www.arro.org
Contact: Joshua Petit MD, Chm.

Founded: 1983. **Members:** 550. **Membership Dues:** corporate, allied, $20 ● associate, corresponding, international, $10. **Description:** Medical residents in the field of radiation oncology. Seeks to "formalize resident input into professional organizations affecting radiation oncology residents". Serves as a clearinghouse on radiation oncology; fosters communication and cooperation among members. **Awards:** ASTRO Gold Medal Award. **Frequency:** annual. **Type:** medal. **Recipient:** to members with outstanding contributions to oncology ● ASTRO Honorary Membership. **Frequency:** annual. **Type:** recognition. **Recipient:** to cancer researchers. **Publications:** *ARROgram*, periodic. Newsletter. Alternate Formats: online. **Conventions/Meetings:** annual meeting, in conjunction with the American Society for Therapeutic Radiation and Oncology.

15316 ■ Chemotherapy Foundation (CF)
183 Madison Ave., Rm. 403
New York, NY 10016
Ph: (212)213-9292
Fax: (212)213-3831
E-mail: scox@chemotherapyfoundation.org
URL: http://www.chemotherapyfoundation.org
Contact: Shirley Cox, Exec. Dir.

Founded: 1968. **Members:** 2,500. **Staff:** 3. **Budget:** $900,000. **Description:** Supports laboratory and clinical research for the control, cure, and prevention of cancer through innovative medical therapies; conducts professional symposia to enable oncologists to incorporate advances in cancer treatment into the care of their patients; distributes free educational literature. Grant allocations currently include five major metropolitan medical centers. **Boards:** Associate Medical Directors; Honorary Board of Trustees; Trustees. **Councils:** Scientific Advisory. **Publications:** *Anniversary Journal*, annual ● *Chemotherapy Today: New Drugs, New Approaches, and New Strategies*. Booklet ● *Major Research Achievements of The Chemotherapy Foundation Grant Programs 1968-2005*. Booklet ● *Meet Our Research Grant Recipients*, annual. Booklet ● *Prostate Cancer: A Chronic Disease With Multiple Treatment Options*. Booklet ● *Symposium Abstracts*, annual. Booklet. For medical oncologists. **Price:** $15.00/copy ● *What Every Woman and Her Doctor Should Discuss About Ovarian Cancer*. Booklet. Contains educational material for patients and the public. **Price:** free ● Newsletter, semiannual. **Conventions/Meetings:** annual Innovative Cancer Therapy for Tomorrow - symposium.

15317 ■ Connective Tissue Oncology Society (CTOS)
c/o Barbara Rapp, Exec. Dir.
PO Box 19611
Alexandria, VA 22320-0611
Ph: (301)502-7371
Fax: (703)548-4882
E-mail: ctos@ctos.org
URL: http://www.ctos.org
Contact: Barbara Rapp, Exec. Dir.

Founded: 1995. **Members:** 400. **Membership Dues:** regular, $100 (annual) ● allied healthcare professional, $50 (annual) ● resident, fellow, $25 (annual). **Multinational. Description:** Represents physicians and scientists with primary interest in the tumors of connective tissues. Advances the care of patients with connective tissue tumors. Increases knowledge of all aspects of the biology of connective tissue tumors.

15318 ■ Gynecologic Oncology Group (GOG)

4 Penn Ctr.
1600 JFK Blvd., Ste.1020
Philadelphia, PA 19103
Ph: (215)854-0770
Free: (800)225-3053
Fax: (215)854-0716
E-mail: cgaloppo@gog.org
URL: http://www.gog.org
Contact: Philip J. Disaia, Chm.

Founded: 1970. **Members:** 65. **Staff:** 10. **Budget:** $800,000. **Description:** Institutions and teaching hospitals conducting research in gynecological oncology. Sponsored by the American College of Obstetricians and Gynecologists. **Affiliated With:** American College of Obstetricians and Gynecologists. **Publications:** Newsletter, semiannual. **Conventions/Meetings:** semiannual meeting (exhibits).

15319 ■ International Association for Comparative Research on Leukemia and Related Diseases (IACRLRD)

c/o The de Burlo Group
50 Fed. St.
Boston, MA 02110
Fax: (617)338-6077
E-mail: deburlo@erols.com
Contact: C. Russell de Burlo DBA, Treas.

Founded: 1963. **Members:** 500. **Membership Dues:** scientific, $45 (annual) ● scientific, $80 (biennial). **Budget:** $700,000. **Description:** Promotes cooperation and coordination of basic and clinical research on leukemia and related diseases. Emphasizes comparative aspects of different disciplines in order to develop new hypotheses and introduce comparable working methods. Sponsors educational programs. **Awards:** NIH/NCI: Leukemia Society of America Awards. **Type:** recognition. **Computer Services:** Mailing lists. **Committees:** World (Advisory and Policy). **Publications:** *Symposium Proceedings*, biennial. **Price:** free for members; $35.00/issue for nonmembers. **Conventions/Meetings:** biennial symposium (exhibits).

15320 ■ International Society for Preventive Oncology (ISPO)

c/o Herbert E. Nieburgs, Sec. Gen./Ed.
Cancer Detection and Prevention
Univ. of Massachusetts Medical School
365 Plantation St., Ste.175
Worcester, MA 01605-2398
Ph: (508)856-1822
Fax: (508)856-1824
E-mail: journal@cancerprev.org
URL: http://www.cancerprev.org/ISPO
Contact: Herbert E. Nieburgs, Sec. Gen./Ed.

Founded: 1980. **Members:** 400. **Staff:** 2. **Budget:** $150,000. **Description:** Physicians and other professionals at the doctoral level; individuals with professional equivalence that are actively engaged in preventive oncology. Promotes the prevention of cancer through the identification and control of cancer causing factors; fosters secondary prevention through detection and treatment of cancer in its earliest, most curable stages. Sponsors basic research on cancer prevention and early detection and provides a forum for information exchange between scientists engaged in research and those working on preventive and clinical oncology. Conducts workshops. **Awards:** Tumor Markers in Cancer Control Award. **Type:** recognition. **Telecommunication Services:** electronic mail, accounting@cancerprev.org ● electronic mail, webmaster@cancerprev.org. **Publications:** *Cancer Detection and Prevention*, bimonthly. Journal. **Price:** free for members ● *Proceedings of International Symposium on Immunobiology of Cancer and Allied Immune Dysfunctions*, biennial ● *Proceedings of the International Conference on Human Tumor Markers*,

biennial ● *Proceedings of the International Symposium on Prevention and Detection of Cancer*, biennial. **Conventions/Meetings:** regional meeting ● semiannual symposium.

15321 ■ National Association for Proton Therapy

1301 Highland Dr.
Silver Spring, MD 20910
Ph: (301)587-6100
Fax: (301)587-6100
E-mail: lenarzt@proton-therapy.org
URL: http://www.proton-therapy.org
Contact: Leonard Arzt, Contact

Founded: 1989. **Members:** 5. **Staff:** 1. **Budget:** $100,000. **Description:** Oncologists and other health care professionals with an interest in the treatment of cancer. Promotes use of proton therapy to treat cancer patients. Conducts research and educational programs; gathers and disseminates information. **Publications:** *Proton News*, periodic. Newsletter.

15322 ■ National Cancer Center (NCC)

88 Sunnyside Blvd., Ste.307
Plainview, NY 11803-1507
Ph: (516)349-0610
Fax: (516)349-1755
E-mail: info@nationalcancercenter.org
URL: http://www.nationalcancercenter.org
Contact: Jack Sherman, Pres.

Founded: 1953. **Staff:** 4. **Description:** Supports cancer research and educational programs. Concentrates on cytology, immunology, detection, and prevention of cancer, and on invention and perfection of new methods and instruments for early diagnosis of cancer. **Awards:** **Frequency:** annual. **Type:** recognition. **Committees:** Scientific Advisory. **Formerly:** (1954) Eugene L. Garey Cancer Foundation; (1965) Cancer Cytology Foundation of America; (1986) National Cancer Cytology Center. **Publications:** Brochures. Alternate Formats: online.

15323 ■ National Cancer Registrars Association (NCRA)

1340 Braddock Pl., Ste.203
Alexandria, VA 22314
Ph: (703)299-6640
Fax: (703)299-6620
E-mail: info@ncra-usa.org
URL: http://www.ncra-usa.org
Contact: Lori Swain BA, Exec. Dir.

Founded: 1974. **Members:** 4,000. **Membership Dues:** active, $80 (annual) ● inactive, $50 (annual) ● associate, $65 (annual) ● sustaining, $150 (annual) ● student, $15 (annual) ● international, $40 (annual). **Staff:** 5. **Budget:** $1,000,000. **Description:** Represents cancer registry professionals and Certified Tumor Registrars. Cancer Registrars capture a complete summary of patient history, diagnosis, treatment, and status for every cancer patient in the U.S. Cancer Registrars work for better treatments, and ultimately, a cure. Promotes education, credentialing, and advocacy for cancer registry professionals; serves professionals providing data that makes a difference in the war on cancer. Participate in programs to improve and standardize the compiling of tumor-related information; interact with professional and governmental organizations that use data derived from tumor registries. Conducts national educational programs including: coding and tumor registry workshops; symposia on head and neck tumors, lymphatic and hematopoietic neoplasms, and non-Hodgkin's lymphoma; tumor registry training program and seminars. Sponsors registry management training program at the University of Pittsburgh School of Health Related Professions to instruct tumor registrars. Offers certification examinations for tumor registrars; provides continuing education. **Libraries:** **Type:** reference. **Holdings:** archival material, audio recordings. **Awards:** Conference Scholarship. **Frequency:** annual. **Type:** scholarship. **Recipient:** to an active NCRA member ● Distinguished Member Award. **Frequency:** annual. **Type:** recognition. **Recipient:** to a member of NCRA for outstanding contributions to the profession ● Educational Achievement Award. **Frequency:** annual. **Type:** recognition.

Recipient: to members for significant contributions to cancer registry education ● Literary Award. **Frequency:** annual. **Type:** recognition. **Recipient:** to members for preparation of important published materials related to the cancer registry ● Outstanding New Professional. **Frequency:** annual. **Type:** recognition. **Recipient:** to a new member for significant involvement to the profession. **Additional Websites:** http://www.creducationcenter.org. **Committees:** Alternative Methods; Bylaws; Credentials; Education; Ethics; Finance; Legislative/Grants; Membership; Program Recognition; Public Relations/Communications; Web Site. **Task Forces:** AHIMA Collaboration; Informatics; Nominations Process; Recruitment and Retention; Workload. **Formerly:** National Tumor Registrars Association. **Publications:** *Connection*, quarterly. Newsletter. Contains articles on NCRA topics. **Price:** included in membership dues. **Circulation:** 2,500. **Advertising:** accepted ● *Journal of Registry Management*, quarterly. Includes book reviews, peer reviewed scientific articles and lists of employment opportunities. **Price:** included in membership dues; $40.00 /year for nonmembers in U.S.; $55.00 /year for nonmembers outside U.S. **Circulation:** 2,500. **Advertising:** accepted ● *National Cancer Registrars Association—Membership Roster*, annual. Membership Directory. **Price:** included in membership dues. **Circulation:** 2,500 ● *National Cancer Registrars Association—Proceedings/Annual Report*. **Price:** included in membership dues ● Surveys. Contains information on compensation. **Circulation:** 2,500. **Advertising:** accepted ● Also publishes educational materials. **Conventions/Meetings:** annual Education Conference (exhibits) ● periodic regional meeting.

15324 ■ National Foundation for Cancer Research (NFCR)

4600 E West Hwy., Ste.525
Bethesda, MD 20814
Ph: (301)654-1250
Free: (800)321-2873
Fax: (301)654-5824
E-mail: info@nfcr.org
URL: http://www.nfcr.org
Contact: Franklin C. Salisbury Jr., Pres.

Founded: 1974. **Staff:** 11. **Budget:** $13,000,000. **Description:** Conducts basic cancer research and provides prevention education focusing on understanding how and why cells become cancerous. **Libraries:** **Type:** reference. **Holdings:** articles, films, papers. **Awards:** Scientific Grants. **Frequency:** biennial. **Type:** grant. **Recipient:** for research and discovery that will lead to the cure for cancer. **Formerly:** (1975) Bethesda National Foundation of Massachusetts. **Publications:** *E-Newsletter Series*, monthly. **Price:** $1.00. **Circulation:** 55,000. **Advertising:** accepted. Alternate Formats: online ● *Research for a Cure*, quarterly. Newsletters. Contains updates on cancer research projects. **Price:** $1.00. **Circulation:** 120,000. **Advertising:** accepted. Alternate Formats: online ● Annual Report, annual. **Price:** $1.00. **Circulation:** 12,000. Alternate Formats: online ● Also publishes booklets and papers.

15325 ■ Radiation Therapy Oncology Group (RTOG)

1818 Market St., Ste.1600
Philadelphia, PA 19103
Ph: (215)574-3189
Free: (800)277-5463
Fax: (215)928-0153
E-mail: info@rtog.org
URL: http://www.rtog.org
Contact: Thomas J. Wudarski, Admin.

Founded: 1968. **Members:** 290. **Staff:** 110. **Description:** Clinical radiation therapy investigative centers united to conduct cooperative clinical trials and studies to improve the care of patients with cancer. Maintains 50 committees. **Committees:** Data Monitoring; Medical Oncology; Medical Physics; Membership Evaluation; New Investigators; Nominating; Outcomes and Health Services Research; Pathology. **Publications:** *RA Reporter*. Newsletter. Alternate Formats: online ● *RTOG Report*. Reprint. **Conven-**

tions/Meetings: semiannual meeting - 2008 Jan. 17-20, San Diego, CA; 2008 June 19-22, Philadelphia, PA.

15326 ■ Society of Gynecologic Oncologists (SGO)
230 W Monroe St., Ste.710
Chicago, IL 60606
Ph: (312)235-4060
Fax: (312)235-4059
E-mail: sgo@sgo.org
URL: http://www.sgo.org
Contact: Mary C. Eiken, Exec. Dir.
Founded: 1969. **Members:** 1,100. **Membership Dues:** full, associate, candidate, $480 (annual). **Staff:** 9. **Description:** Aims to improve the care of patients with gynecological cancer; encourage research in gynecologic oncology; advance knowledge in the field; and upgrade standards of practice. Evaluates and seeks to address the trends in gynecologic oncology and assesses the future of the field. **Publications:** *SGO Issues*, 3/year. Newsletter. Contains information about the society and its activities. ● *State of the State of Gynecologic Cancers*, annual. Annual Report. Contains reports on scientific and medical knowledge about the most common gynecologic cancers that affect most women. Alternate Formats: online. **Conventions/Meetings:** annual meeting (exhibits) ● seminar.

15327 ■ Society of Surgical Oncology (SSO)
85 W Algonquin Rd., Ste.550
Arlington Heights, IL 60005
Ph: (847)427-1400
Fax: (847)427-9656
E-mail: webmaster@surgonc.org
URL: http://www.surgonc.org
Contact: Nicholas J. Petrelli MD, Pres.
Founded: 1940. **Members:** 2,000. **Membership Dues:** regular, $150 (annual). **Staff:** 6. **Budget:** $1,200,000. **Description:** Represents physicians and scientists working in the field of cancer. **Awards: Type:** monetary. **Recipient:** for outstanding basic cancer scientist ● **Type:** monetary. **Recipient:** for outstanding clinical scientist ● **Type:** monetary. **Recipient:** for outstanding clinical layman ● **Frequency:** annual. **Type:** recognition. **Recipient:** for a medical resident who is performing an original research project. **Committees:** Clinical Affairs; Constitution and Bylaws; Continuing Medical Education; Corporate Relations; Fellowship and Research Grant; Issues and Government Affairs; Local Arrangements; Nominating. **Formerly:** (1974) James Ewing Society. **Publications:** *Annals of Surgical Oncology*, 10/year. Journal. Includes proceedings of the society's annual scientific sessions. ISSN: 1068-9265. **Circulation:** 1,700. **Advertising:** accepted. Alternate Formats: online ● *SSO News*. Newsletter. Alternate Formats: online ● *Surgical Oncology: Yesterday, Today and Tomorrow*. Bibliography. **Conventions/Meetings:** annual Scientific Session - meeting (exhibits) - always March. 2008 Mar. 13-16, Chicago, IL.

Ophthalmology

15328 ■ American Academy of Ophthalmology (AAO)
PO Box 7424
San Francisco, CA 94120-7424
Ph: (415)561-8500
Fax: (415)561-8533
E-mail: customer_service@aao.org
URL: http://www.aao.org
Contact: H. Dunbar Hoskins Jr., Exec. VP
Founded: 1896. **Members:** 27,000. **Membership Dues:** active fellow, osteopathic fellow, professional, $825 (annual) ● second year in practice, $600 (annual) ● first year in practice, $400 (annual). **Staff:** 190. **Description:** Works to achieve accessible, appropriate and affordable eye care for the public by serving the educational and professional needs of the ophthalmologist. Provides clinical education, ophthalmic practice, federal and state advocacy, patient information, and other services to its members.

Provides accurate, appropriate and timely information to the public through its media and public information programs. Current activities of EyeCare America include multiple eye care programs for which individuals may qualify: Glaucoma EyeCare, Diabetes EyeCare, AMD Eyecare, Seniors EyeCare and Children's EyeCare. **Libraries: Type:** reference. **Holdings:** 100. **Subjects:** ophthalmology, general medicine. **Awards:** Achievement Award. **Frequency:** annual. **Type:** recognition. **Recipient:** for an individual ● International Blindness Prevention. **Frequency:** annual. **Type:** recognition. **Recipient:** for significant contribution to the prevention of blindness or restoration of sight ● Life Achievement Honor Award. **Frequency:** annual. **Type:** recognition. **Recipient:** for an individual ● Outstanding Humanitarian Service Award. **Frequency:** annual. **Type:** recognition. **Recipient:** for participation in charitable activities, indigent care, community service, or other humanitarian activity ● Senior Achievement Award. **Frequency:** annual. **Type:** recognition. **Recipient:** for an individual ● Special Recognition Award. **Frequency:** annual. **Type:** recognition. **Recipient:** to an individual or organization for outstanding service in a specific effort or cause that improves the quality of eye care. **Departments:** Communications; Controller's Office; Education; Foundation of the AAO; Governmental Relations; Meetings; Ophthalmic Practice; Personnel. **Absorbed:** (1981) American Association of Ophthalmology. **Publications:** *Basic and Clinical Science Course*, annual. **Price:** $895.00 ● *Eye Net*, monthly. Magazine. **Price:** included in membership dues; $128.00 /year for members in U.S.; $180.00 /year for nonmembers in U.S.; $20.00 for inactive members. **Circulation:** 17,404. **Advertising:** accepted. Alternate Formats: online ● *Ophthalmology*, monthly. Journal ● Directory, biennial ● Manuals ● Videos ● Also publishes slide script packages and study guides, special interest newsletters, modules, procedures assessments, issue briefs, brochures. **Conventions/Meetings:** annual meeting (exhibits).

15329 ■ American Association of Certified Orthoptists (AACO)
c/o Camille Phillips
63 Old Greenfield Rd.
Peterborough, NH 03458
Ph: (603)924-0284
E-mail: ron.biernacki@vanderbilt.edu
URL: http://www.orthoptics.org
Contact: Ronald Biernacki CO, Pres.
Founded: 1940. **Members:** 250. **Membership Dues:** certified orthoptist, $150 (annual). **Regional Groups:** 4. **Description:** Orthoptists certified by the American Orthoptic Council (see separate entry), after completing a minimum of 24 months' special training, to treat defects in binocular function. Assists in postgraduate instruction courses; conducts programs and courses at international, national, and regional meetings; helps individual orthoptists with special or unusual problem cases; trains new orthoptists. Operates a placement listing. **Libraries: Type:** reference. **Holdings:** audiovisuals, books, clippings, periodicals. **Subjects:** motility, neuro-anatomy, neuro physiology, binocular vision, ophthalmic pharmacology, eye photography. **Awards:** Lancaster Award. **Frequency:** annual. **Type:** recognition. **Recipient:** for meritorious contributions. **Formerly:** (1963) American Association of Orthopic Technicians. **Publications:** *American Association of Certified Orthoptists—Directory*, annual. **Price:** included in membership dues. **Circulation:** 400 ● *American Orthoptic Journal*, annual. Presents new material in the fields of amblyopia and strabismus. Includes book reviews and abstracts of current English and French literature. **Price:** $25.00/copy for individuals; $56.00/copy for institutions. ISSN: 0065-955X. **Circulation:** 1,300. **Advertising:** accepted ● *The Prism*, quadrennial. Newsletter. **Advertising:** accepted. **Conventions/Meetings:** annual convention, held in conjunction with the American Academy of Ophthalmology (exhibits).

15330 ■ American Association of Dispensing Ophthalmologists (AADO)
PO Box 655
Jarrettsville, MD 21084
Free: (800)705-2236

Fax: (410)692-0334
E-mail: contact@aado.net
URL: http://www.aado.net
Contact: Pamela B. Fritz, Exec. Dir.
Founded: 2000. **Membership Dues:** ophthalmology practice, $250 (annual) ● ophthalmology practice, $400 (biennial) ● ophthalmology practice, $500 (triennial). **Description:** Brings together ophthalmologists and management staff for the purpose of education in the area of optical dispensing. Provides an opportunity for ophthalmologists who wish to pursue optical dispensing in their practices. Presents programs that support the development, training and expansion of optical dispensing in an ophthalmology practice. **Publications:** *MD Dispensing News*, monthly. Newsletter. **Price:** free for members. Alternate Formats: online ● *Pure Optics*. Book. Contains information for mastering the skills in opticianry. **Price:** $125.00 for nonmembers; $99.00 for members; free with 2-3 year membership.

15331 ■ American Association for Ophthalmic Standardized Echography (AAOSE)
c/o Karl C. Ossoinig, MD, Pres.
1345 Cedar St.
Iowa City, IA 52245
Ph: (319)337-4066
Fax: (319)338-0377
E-mail: kcossoinig@mchsi.com
URL: http://www.echography.com
Contact: Karl C. Ossoinig MD, Pres.
Description: Promotes the practice of Ophthalmic Standardized Echography. Coordinates with other ophthalmology organizations for information exchange. Facilitates communication among members. Provides updates on the state of Ophthalmic Standardized Echography in the country and other related issues.

15332 ■ American Association for Pediatric Ophthalmology and Strabismus (AAPOS)
PO Box 193832
San Francisco, CA 94119-3832
Ph: (415)561-8505
Fax: (415)561-8531
E-mail: aapos@aao.org
URL: http://www.aapos.org
Contact: Christie L. Morse MD, Pres.
Founded: 1974. **Members:** 844. **Budget:** $140,000. **Description:** Ophthalmologists who limit their practice largely to children. Encourages quality eye care for children by establishing high ethical standards of practice, supporting educational training programs for pediatric ophthalmologists, and promoting basic research in children's eye diseases. Conducts research programs. **Computer Services:** Mailing lists, labels. **Formerly:** (1978) American Association of Pediatric Ophthalmology. **Publications:** *Journal of AAPOS*, bimonthly. Contains information on children's eye diseases and on strabismus as it impacts all age groups. **Price:** $156.00 individual in U.S.; $79.00 student in U.S.; $194.00 individual outside U.S.; $97.00 student outside U.S. ISSN: 1091-8531 ● Membership Directory, annual. **Conventions/Meetings:** annual Scientific Sessions - meeting (exhibits).

15333 ■ American Board of Ophthalmology (ABO)
111 Presidential Blvd., Ste.241
Bala Cynwyd, PA 19004-1075
Ph: (610)664-1175
Fax: (610)664-6503
E-mail: info@abop.org
URL: http://www.abop.org
Contact: John G. Clarkson MD, Exec. Dir.
Founded: 1916. **Members:** 17. **Staff:** 6. **Description:** Medical specialty board to determine the adequacy of training, the professional preparation, and ophthalmic knowledge of ophthalmologists who wish to be certified. Works to improve the standards of graduate medical education and the facilities for special ophthalmic training. **Formerly:** (1933) American Board for Ophthalmic Examinations. **Publications:** *ABO News*, annual. Newsletter. Details current events, new policies, and board news. Alternate

Formats: online ● *Certification Brochure*, annual. Details the Board's certification and recertification procedures, policies, fees, and dates and deadlines for that year's examinations. Alternate Formats: online. **Conventions/Meetings:** semiannual Oral Examination - meeting.

15334 ■ American Ophthalmological Society (AOS)
PO Box 193940
San Francisco, CA 94119-3940
Ph: (415)561-8578
Fax: (415)561-8531
E-mail: admin@aosonline.org
URL: http://www.aosonline.org
Contact: Lisa Brown, Contact

Founded: 1864. **Members:** 325. **Staff:** 3. **Description:** Professional honorary society of physicians specializing in the functions and treatment of the eye. **Awards:** Howe Medal. **Frequency:** annual. **Type:** medal. **Recipient:** for a member's outstanding achievement in ophthalmology. **Publications:** *Transactions of the American Ophthalmological Society*, annual. Journal. Contains papers presented at annual meeting and accepted theses. **Price:** $55.00. **Circulation:** 500. Alternate Formats: online. **Conventions/Meetings:** annual meeting, scientific and business meeting.

15335 ■ American Orthoptic Council (AOC)
c/o Ms. Leslie France, CO, Admin.
3914 Nakoma Rd.
Madison, WI 53711
Ph: (608)233-5383
Fax: (608)263-4247
E-mail: lwfranceco@att.net
URL: http://www.orthoptics.org
Contact: Ms. Leslie France CO, Admin.

Founded: 1935. **Members:** 20. **Staff:** 1. **Description:** Ophthalmologists and orthoptists. Directs practice of orthoptics; determines qualifications of candidates; regulates training and certification of orthoptists; supervises the practice of orthoptists after certification. Regulates standards for training programs. Recertifies orthoptists annually. Organizes scientific symposia. **Affiliated With:** American Academy of Ophthalmology; American Association of Certified Orthoptists; American Association for Pediatric Ophthalmology and Strabismus; American Ophthalmological Society. **Publications:** *A Career in Orthoptics*, annual. Pamphlet. Contains list of current programs and general description of profession. **Price:** free ● *American Orthoptic Journal*, annual. Covers ocular motility and visual physiology. Contains abstracts of ophthalmic literature. **Price:** included in membership dues; $37.00 /year for individuals; $102.00 /year for libraries and institutions. ISSN: 0065-955X. **Circulation:** 1,000. **Advertising:** accepted. Alternate Formats: online. Also Cited As: *AOJ* ● *Orthoptic Training Centers*, annual. Pamphlet ● *Syllabus of Orthoptic Instruction*, annual. Monograph. Contains outline of instruction. **Price:** $50.00. **Conventions/Meetings:** annual meeting, in conjunction with the Academy of Ophthalmology - usually October ● quarterly regional meeting.

15336 ■ American Osteopathic Colleges of Ophthalmology and Otolaryngology-Head and Neck Surgery (AOCOO-HNS)
4764 Fishburg Rd., Ste.F
Huber Heights, OH 45424
Ph: (937)233-5653
Free: (800)455-9404
Fax: (937)233-5673
E-mail: info@aocoohns.org
URL: http://www.aocoohns.org
Contact: Dr. Alvin D. Dubin DO, Exec. VP

Founded: 1916. **Members:** 670. **Membership Dues:** osteopathic, $475 (annual). **Staff:** 2. **Budget:** $250,000. **Description:** Osteopathic physicians who have completed formal specialty training or are acquiring such training in ophthalmology, otorhinolaryngology, and facial plastic surgery, and those who are certified specialists in one or more of the above named areas. Develops application of osteopathic concepts in this specialty; determines minimum

standards of education at undergraduate and postgraduate levels. Sponsors research programs. **Awards: Type:** recognition. **Committees:** Audit; Awards; Editorial; Ethics; Medical Education; Quality Improvement; Strategic Planning Adhoc. **Formerly:** Osteopathic College of Ophthalmology and Otorhinolaryngology. **Publications:** *Quarterly Report*. Newsletter. **Price:** included in membership dues. **Circulation:** 580. Alternate Formats: online ● Journal, annual ● Directory, periodic ● Also publishes collected papers. **Conventions/Meetings:** annual seminar and assembly, includes clinical assembly (exhibits).

15337 ■ American Society of Cataract and Refractive Surgery (ASCRS)
4000 Legato Rd., Ste.700
Fairfax, VA 22033
Ph: (703)591-2220
Fax: (703)591-0614
E-mail: ascrs@ascrs.org
URL: http://www.ascrs.org
Contact: Richard L. Lindstrom MD, Pres.

Founded: 1974. **Members:** 8,000. **Membership Dues:** in U.S., $465 (annual) ● international physician or resident, military in U.S., $230 (annual). **Staff:** 31. **Budget:** $9,000,000. **Description:** Ophthalmologists interested in anterior segment surgery and refractive corneal surgery. Offers continuing medical education to ophthalmologists on cataract and refractive surgery techniques, intraocular lens designs, and related research areas; assists allied health care professionals in ophthalmology on medical and surgical care of pseudophakic (lens implant) patients. Works to improve public education in the field of eye care. Conducts research in ocular pathology in cataract and refractive surgery. Compiles statistics. **Awards:** Binkhorst Medal. **Frequency:** annual. **Type:** medal. **Recipient:** for an individual ● Charles D. Kelman Innovator's Lecture. **Frequency:** annual. **Type:** recognition. **Recipient:** for an individual ● Honored Guest. **Frequency:** annual. **Type:** recognition. **Recipient:** for a guest at the annual symposium ● Ophthalmology Hall of Fame. **Frequency:** annual. **Type:** recognition. **Recipient:** for an individual. **Computer Services:** Mailing lists. **Telecommunication Services:** hotline, emergency consultation hotline, (800)451-1339. **Committees:** Cataract; Continuing Education; Cornea; Pediatric; Practice Management; Refractive; Young Physicians and Residents. **Subcommittees:** Glaucoma Programming. **Affiliated With:** American Medical Association; American Society of Ophthalmic Administrators. **Formerly:** (1986) American Intra-Ocular Implant Society. **Publications:** *Administrative Eyecare*, quarterly. Contains current information about ophthalmic office administration. **Price:** included in membership dues; $60.00 /year for nonmembers. **Advertising:** accepted ● *ASCRS Roster*, biennial. Membership Directory. **Price:** free for members ● *ASCRS Washington Watch*, weekly. Newsletter. Provides the latest information on congressional and regulatory issues affecting the practice of cataract and refractive surgery. **Price:** included in membership dues ● *Journal of Cataract and Refractive Surgery*, monthly. Addresses cataract surgery techniques and technology and advances in refractive surgery. **Price:** included in membership dues; $149.00 /year for nonmembers. **Advertising:** accepted ● Newsletter, monthly. **Conventions/Meetings:** annual meeting and symposium, topics include cataract surgery, intraocular lens technology, laser procedures (exhibits) - always spring. 2008 Apr. 12-16, Chicago, IL; 2009 Apr. 4-8, San Francisco, CA; 2010 Apr. 10-14, Washington, DC.

15338 ■ American Society of Contemporary Medicine, Surgery, and Ophthalmology
7250 N Cicero Ave., Lower Level 6
Lincolnwood, IL 60712
Ph: (312)440-0699
Free: (800)621-4002
Fax: (312)677-9094
E-mail: iaos@aol.com
Contact: Randall T. Bellows MD, Dir.

Founded: 1966. **Members:** 500. **Membership Dues:** professional/ophthalmologist, $275 (annual). **Staff:** 2. **Description:** Ophthalmologists interested in promot-

ing clinical investigative advances in ophthalmology. Offers continuing medical education courses approved by the American Council for Continuing Medical Education (ACCME) on new ophthalmic developments in medical, therapeutic, diagnostic, and surgical procedures. **Awards:** Certificate of Advanced Studies in Ophthalmology. **Type:** recognition. **Recipient:** for ophthalmologists who earn 150 credits in continuing medical education in a three-year period ● Charles Schepens Award. **Type:** recognition. **Recipient:** for outstanding achievement in retina studies ● Distinguished Service Award in Ophthalmology. **Type:** recognition. **Recipient:** for meritorious experimental or clinical work ● Sir Stewart Duke-Elder Glaucoma Award. **Type:** recognition. **Affiliated With:** International Association of Ocular Surgeons. **Formerly:** (1970) Society for Cryo-Ophthalmology; (2006) American Society of Contemporary Ophthalmology. **Publications:** *Annals of Ophthalmology*, 3/year. Journal. Includes book reviews and information on educational activities and new products. A continuing medical education publication for ophthalmologist. **Price:** $160.00. ISSN: 1079-4794. **Circulation:** 600. **Advertising:** accepted.

15339 ■ American Society for Ophthalmic Ultrasonography (ASOU)
c/o Suzanne W. Daly, BSN, Sec.-Treas.
Weill Cornell Medical Coll.
Dept. of Ophthalmology
1300 York Ave., Box 112
New York, NY 10021
Ph: (212)746-2504
E-mail: sdaly@med.cornell.edu
URL: http://www.asou.us
Contact: Suzanne W. Daly BSN, Sec.-Treas.

Description: Represents physicians, scientists, engineers, technicians, nurses, and sonographers who are involved or concerned with ultrasonography of the eye. Serves as a central source of information regarding issues affecting the practice of ophthalmic ultrasonography. Provides a forum for exchange of ideas and experience, scientific communication, and discussion of the clinical practice of ophthalmic ultrasonography. **Publications:** Papers, annual.

15340 ■ American Uveitis Society
c/o Rudolph M. Franklin, MD, Exec. Sec.
3535 Bienville Ave., Ste.W380
New Orleans, LA 70119
URL: http://www.uveitissociety.org
Contact: Rudolph M. Franklin MD, Exec. Sec.

Founded: 1990. **Membership Dues:** full, associate, $100 (annual). **Description:** Serves as a resource for individuals with an interest in inflammatory eye diseases, including patients, families, researchers, ophthalmologists and other healthcare providers. Promotes and disseminates knowledge of the treatment of uveitis to the public. Encourages and develops uveitis investigation and research. **Computer Services:** Information services, resources for patients ● mailing lists, for members ● online services, patients discussion group.

15341 ■ Association for Macular Diseases (AMD)
210 E 64th St., 8th Fl.
New York, NY 10021
Ph: (212)605-3719
Fax: (212)605-3795
E-mail: association@retinal-research.org
URL: http://www.macula.org
Contact: Nikolai Stevenson, Pres.

Founded: 1978. **Members:** 8,000. **Membership Dues:** regular, $20 (annual). **Description:** Individuals afflicted with macular diseases, and their families. (The macula of the eye is the posterior middle portion of the retina responsible for central vision. Disorders involving the macula include inflammations, tumors, retinal growths, and degenerative problems.) Disseminates information on available resources such as recorded material and low vision aids. Promotes public awareness of macular diseases. Encourages growth of research into the causes, treatment, and possible prevention of macular diseases. Informs the public of the need for postmortem donation of eyes having a history of macular disease and advises on procedures for making such a donation. Provides counseling programs and group sharing for afflicted persons and their families. **Formerly:** Association for Mascular Degeneration. **Publications:** *Eyes Only*, quarterly. Newsletter. Updates members on medical advances in the field of macular diseases. **Price:** included in membership dues. **Circulation:** 10,000. **Conventions/Meetings:** monthly meeting.

15342 ■ Association of Nurses Endorsing Transplantation (ANET)

Address Unknown since 2007
Founded: 1983. **Members:** 75. **Membership Dues:** active, $45 (annual) ● nonprofit organization, $250 (annual) ● corporate, $350 (annual). **Staff:** 2. **Description:** Registered nurses, LVNs, LPNs, student nurses, chaplains, social workers, hospitals, health care facilities and individuals interested in the promotion of organ and tissue donation for transplantation and research. **Libraries: Type:** reference. **Holdings:** audio recordings, papers, video recordings. **Subjects:** transplantation. **Awards:** Chapter of the Year. **Frequency:** annual. **Type:** recognition ● Nurse of the Year. **Frequency:** annual. **Type:** recognition. **Computer Services:** Mailing lists. **Committees:** Membership and Public Relations. **Formerly:** (1983) Consortium of Registered Nurses for Eye Acquisition. **Publications:** *ANET Newsletter*, quarterly. **Advertising:** not accepted ● *Handbook*, annual. **Conventions/Meetings:** annual conference, with seminars (exhibits) - always September ● Life - Keep It Going.

15343 ■ Association for Ocular Pharmacology and Therapeutics (AOPT)

c/o Dr. Achim H. Krauss, PhD, Treas.
Pfizer Inc.
10724 Sci. Center Dr.
San Diego, CA 92121
Ph: (858)638-3748
E-mail: achim.krauss@pfizer.com
URL: http://www.aopt.org
Contact: Dr. Achim H. Krauss PhD, Treas.
Membership Dues: regular, $340 (annual) ● associate, $30 (annual) ● contributing, $2,000 (annual). **Multinational. Description:** Serves as a global forum for the exchange of information about ocular pharmacology. Seeks to meet the needs of vision scientists and eye care professionals for the advancement of vision research and the treatment of ophthalmic disorders worldwide. Develops program to support recruitment, retention, and education of young scientists to ocular pharmacology. **Publications:** *Journal of Ocular Pharmacology and Therapeutics*, bimonthly. Covers basic and clinical research about ocular pharmacology and therapeutics. **Price:** included in membership dues.

15344 ■ Association for Research in Vision and Ophthalmology (ARVO)

12300 Twinbrook Pkwy., Ste.250
Rockville, MD 20852-1606
Ph: (240)221-2900
Fax: (240)221-0370
E-mail: arvo@arvo.org
URL: http://www.arvo.org
Contact: Ms. Joanne G. Angle, Exec. Dir.
Founded: 1928. **Members:** 10,500. **Membership Dues:** in-training predoctoral, $85 (annual) ● in-training postdoctoral, $90 (annual) ● family, $300 (annual) ● contributing, sustaining, $255 (annual) ● life, $4,000 ● regular, $200 (annual) ● life (family), $6,000. **Staff:** 18. **Budget:** $4,500,000. **Multinational. Description:** Professional society of researchers in vision and ophthalmology. Encourages ophthalmic research in the field of blinding eye disease. Operates placement service. Maintains 13 scientific sections. **Awards:** ARVO/Pfizer Ophthalmic Translational Research. **Frequency:** annual. **Type:** recognition. **Recipient:** for excellence in research and fundamental scientific discoveries, concepts, and novel technologies ● Cogan Award. **Frequency:** annual. **Type:** recognition. **Recipient:** for significant contributions to research in ophthalmology or visual science ● Kupfer Award. **Frequency:** annual. **Type:** recognition. **Recipient:** for distinguished public

service on behalf of eye and vision research ● Mildred Weisenfeld Award for Excellence in Ophthalmology. **Frequency:** annual. **Type:** recognition. **Recipient:** for scholarly contributions to the clinical practice of ophthalmology ● Proctor Medal and Friedenwald Award. **Frequency:** annual. **Type:** recognition. **Recipient:** for outstanding research of senior scientists in the basic or clinical sciences as applied to ophthalmology ● Special Recognition Award. **Frequency:** periodic. **Type:** recognition. **Recipient:** for outstanding service to the association or the vision research community. **Computer Services:** Mailing lists. **Committees:** Animals in Research; Awards; Ethics and Regulation; Members-in-Training; University. **Programs:** Commercial Relations. **Sections:** Anatomy and Pathology; Biochemistry and Molecular Biology; Clinical and Epidemiologic Research; Cornea; Eye Movements, Strabismus, Amblyopia and Neuro-ophthalmology; Glaucoma; Immunology and Microbiology; Lens; Physiology and Pharmacology; Retina; Retinal Cell Biology; Visual Neurophysiology, Visual Psychophysics and Physiological Optics. **Affiliated With:** American Academy of Ophthalmology; Federation of American Societies for Experimental Biology; Society for Neuroscience. **Formerly:** (1970) Association for Research in Ophthalmology. **Publications:** *Investigative Ophthalmology and Visual Science*, monthly. Journal. Includes announcements and information for authors. **Price:** included in membership dues; $710.00 /year for institutions in U.S.; $865.00 /year for institutions outside U.S.; $485.00 /year for individuals in U.S. ISSN: 0146-0404. **Advertising:** accepted. Alternate Formats: online ● Also publishes membership brochure; makes available posters. **Conventions/Meetings:** annual meeting (exhibits) - usually in May. 2008 Apr. 27-May 1, Fort Lauderdale, FL.

15345 ■ Association for Retinopathy of Prematurity and Related Diseases (ROPARD)

PO Box 250425
Franklin, MI 48025
Free: (800)788-2020
E-mail: ropard@yahoo.com
URL: http://www.ropard.org
Contact: Susan Campbell, Admin. Dir.
Founded: 1990. **Membership Dues:** general, $20 (annual) ● sponsor, $50 (annual) ● patron, $100 (annual) ● benefactor, $600 (annual). **Description:** Works to eliminate the problems of low vision and blindness in children caused by premature birth and other pediatric retinal diseases. Funds clinical research to eliminate retinopathy of prematurity and associated retinal diseases. **Libraries: Type:** by appointment only. **Holdings:** books, video recordings. **Subjects:** low vision aids and devices, child development. **Computer Services:** Information services, retinopathy of prematurity related resources ● online services, bulletin board. **Publications:** Newsletter. Alternate Formats: online.

15346 ■ Association of Technical Personnel in Ophthalmology (ATPO)

2025 Woodlane Dr.
St. Paul, MN 55125-2998
Ph: (651)731-7239 (651)731-2944
Free: (800)482-4858
Fax: (651)731-0410
E-mail: atpomembership@jcahpo.org
URL: http://www.atpo.org
Contact: Deborah McDonald COT, Pres.
Founded: 1969. **Members:** 1,200. **Membership Dues:** student, $20 (annual) ● regular, $65 (annual) ● regular, $250 (triennial) ● student, $175 (triennial). **Staff:** 2. **Budget:** $150,000. **State Groups:** 4. **Description:** Ophthalmic assistants, technicians, technologists, surgical and keratorefractive techs, photographers, nurses, and orthoptists. Promotes high standards and professional ethics dedicated to quality ophthalmic medical care under the direction of an ophthalmologist. Recognizes the utilization of ophthalmic medical personnel to perform certain non-medical procedures or tests as a means of enhancing the productivity of ophthalmologists and thereby increasing the availability of ophthalmologists to provide the highest level of medical service and

comprehensive vision care to their patients. **Libraries: Type:** reference. **Holdings:** archival material. **Awards:** Fellow. **Frequency:** annual. **Type:** recognition. **Recipient:** for an individual. **Computer Services:** Mailing lists. **Committees:** Continuing Education; Representatives to CoA-OMPElections. **Affiliated With:** Joint Commission on Allied Health Personnel in Ophthalmology. **Formerly:** (1989) American Association of Certified Allied Health Personnel in Ophthalmology. **Publications:** *Viewpoints*, quarterly. Newsletter. **Price:** free for members. **Advertising:** accepted. Alternate Formats: online. **Conventions/Meetings:** annual Scientific Sessions and Tech Bowl - convention and meeting, includes educational program for ophthalmic medical personnel (exhibits) - 2007 Nov. 10-13, New Orleans, LA; 2008 Nov. 8-11, Atlanta, GA.

15347 ■ Association of University Professors of Ophthalmology (AUPO)

PO Box 420369
San Francisco, CA 94142-0369
Ph: (415)561-8548
Fax: (415)561-8531
E-mail: aupo@aao.org
URL: http://www.aupo.org
Contact: Bartly J. Mondino MD, Exec. VP
Founded: 1966. **Members:** 246. **Staff:** 3. **Description:** Heads of departments or divisions of ophthalmology in accredited medical schools throughout the U.S. and Canada; directors of ophthalmology residency programs in institutions not connected to medical schools. Promotes medical education, research, and patient care relating to ophthalmology. Operates Ophthalmology Matching Program and faculty placement service, which aids ophthalmologists interested in being associated with university ophthalmology programs to locate such programs. **Awards:** Straatsma Award for Excellence in Resident Education. **Frequency:** annual. **Type:** recognition. **Recipient:** for an outstanding program director in ophthalmology. **Committees:** Department Management, Education Patient Care, and Research. **Subcommittees:** Fellowship Education; Medical Student Education; Residency Education. **Publications:** *News & Views*, quarterly. Newsletter. Alternate Formats: online ● Membership Directory, annual. **Conventions/Meetings:** annual meeting.

15348 ■ Association of Veterans Affairs Ophthalmologists (AVAO)

PO Box 193940
San Francisco, CA 94119-3940
Ph: (415)561-8523
Fax: (415)561-8531
E-mail: avao@aao.org
URL: http://www.avao.org
Contact: Francisco Garcia-Ferrer MD, Sec.-Treas./ Ed.
Membership Dues: active/associate, $35 (annual). **Multinational. Description:** Seeks to improve patient care, medical education and research in eye disorders in the Veterans Administration medical system. Brings together ophthalmologists from the U.S. and Puerto Rico in an effort to improve eye care delivery. **Publications:** Newsletter.

15349 ■ Association of Vision Educators

c/o Kate Keilman
111 Hekili St., Ste.A, No. 206
Kailua, HI 96734
E-mail: info@visioneducators.org
URL: http://www.visioneducators.org
Contact: Kate Keilman, Contact
Founded: 1999. **Membership Dues:** general, $60 (annual). **Multinational. Description:** Seeks to increase public awareness of natural and integrated vision care. Encourages education, communication, and research in the field of natural and integrated vision. **Computer Services:** database, practitioners and teachers ● information services, case histories ● information services, natural vision improvement resources. **Telecommunication Services:** electronic mail, updates@visioneducators.org.

15350 ■ Better Vision Institute (BVI)
1700 Diagonal Rd., Ste.500
Alexandria, VA 22314
Ph: (703)548-4560
Fax: (703)548-4580
E-mail: vca@visionsite.org
URL: http://www.visionsite.org
Contact: Joseph LaMountain, VP of Strategic Communications
Founded: 1929. **Members:** 10. **Description:** Advisory council of the Vision Council of America. Carried out in consultation with a board of eye care professionals who inform the public of the need for more adequate vision care. **Boards:** Directors. **Committees:** Exhibitors Advisory; Public Relations; Show; Speakers' Bureau. **Publications:** *Perspective.* Article ● Pamphlets ● Also publishes charts, posters, and press releases; produces school kits and counter displays for vision care practitioners, schools, and the public.

15351 ■ Children's Eye Foundation (CEF)
1527 W State Hwy. 114, Ste.500, No. 216
Grapevine, TX 76051
Ph: (817)891-1144
Fax: (817)329-5532
E-mail: admin@childrenseyefoundation.org
URL: http://www.childrenseyefoundation.org
Contact: Dr. John D. Baker MD, Pres.
Founded: 1970. **Staff:** 3. **Budget:** $350,000. **Non-membership. Description:** Seeks to optimize the quality of life of infants, children, and families by fostering normal development and protection of vision through promoting programs of prevention, detection, treatment, research and education. **Awards:** Fellowship Loans. **Frequency:** annual. **Type:** fellowship. **Recipient:** to fund fellowships in pediatric ophthalmology ● Research Grant. **Frequency:** annual. **Type:** grant. **Recipient:** for research in children's eye disorders and diseases. **Boards:** Directors. **Committees:** Medical Advisory. **Projects:** Magnetoencephalography (MEG) and Amblyopia Treatment. **Affiliated With:** American Academy of Ophthalmology; American Academy of Pediatrics; American Association for Pediatric Ophthalmology and Strabismus. **Formerly:** (1982) Children's Eye Care Foundation; (2004) National Children's Eye Care Foundation. **Publications:** Annual Report, annual ● Brochures. **Conventions/Meetings:** annual board meeting ● periodic symposium.

15352 ■ Contact Lens Association of Ophthalmologists (CLAO)
c/o John S. Massare, PhD, Exec. Dir.
2025 Woodland Dr.
St. Paul, MN 55125
Ph: (651)731-2944
Free: (877)501-3937
Fax: (651)731-0410
E-mail: eyes@clao.org
URL: http://www.clao.org
Contact: John S. Massare PhD, Exec. Dir.
Founded: 1963. **Members:** 1,500. **Membership Dues:** regular (more than 3 years in practice)/regular international, $295 (annual) ● allied health, $95 (annual) ● associate, $275 (annual) ● affiliate, $245 (annual) ● group, $959 (annual) ● regular (1st year in practice), $60 (annual) ● regular (2nd year in practice), $160 (annual). **Staff:** 3. **Budget:** $500,000. **Description:** Advances the quality medical eyecare for the public by providing comprehensive ophthalmologists and other eye care professionals with education and training in contact lenses, and related eyecare science. **Awards:** Travel Grant. **Type:** grant. **Recipient:** for young investigators. **Additional Websites:** http://www.ContactLensDocs.com. **Affiliated With:** American Academy of Ophthalmology; American Medical Association; American National Standards Institute. **Publications:** *CLAOgram*, monthly. Bulletin. Alternate Formats: online ● *Eye and Contact Lens: Science and Clinical Practice*, bimonthly. Journal. **Price:** included in membership dues; $145.00 /year for institutions in U.S.; $159.00 /year for nonmembers outside U.S.; $139.00 /year for nonmembers in U.S. ISSN: 1542-2321. **Circulation:** 2,500. **Advertising:** accepted. Alternate Formats: on-

line ● Report ● Also publishes Contact Lenses: The CLAO Guide to Basic Science and Clinical practice Third Edition, and The CLAO Pocket Guide to Contact Lens Fitting and patient information pamphlets. **Conventions/Meetings:** annual conference and meeting (exhibits) - in January.

15353 ■ Focus
c/o Marilyn T. Miller
1855 W Taylor St.
Chicago, IL 60612
Ph: (312)996-7445
E-mail: marimill@uic.edu
Contact: Dr. Marilyn Miller, Pres.
Founded: 1961. **Members:** 100. **Description:** Volunteer eye surgeons. Allows American ophthalmologists the opportunity to represent their profession and country by working overseas in an area of desperate need. Doctors pay their own transportation and expenses, and contribute two working weeks of their vacation time to treating patients in Nigeria, where eye care would otherwise not be available. Medical equipment and drugs have been donated by U.S. drug and medical supply firms to the clinics operated by Focus in these countries. Group is unrelated to association of same name. **Publications:** Newsletter, 4-6/month.

15354 ■ The Glaucoma Foundation (TGF)
80 Maiden Ln., Ste.1206
New York, NY 10038
Ph: (212)285-0080 (212)651-1900
Fax: (212)651-1888
E-mail: info@glaucomafoundation.org
URL: http://www.glaucomafoundation.org
Contact: Scott R. Christensen, Pres./CEO
Founded: 1984. **Staff:** 6. **Budget:** $2,100,000. **Description:** Individuals who have been affected by glaucoma and interested others. Works to increase public awareness and to provide research funding. Provides information about glaucoma to the medical and lay communities. Targets and funds the following areas for research: optic nerve regeneration; molecular genetics. Sponsors scientific research. **Awards:** Award of Merit. **Type:** recognition ● **Type:** grant. **Computer Services:** Mailing lists. **Programs:** Glaucoma Screening. **Formed by Merger of:** (1994) National Glaucoma Trust and The Glaucoma Foundation. **Publications:** *Doctor, I Have a Question.* Booklet. Answers the basic questions about glaucoma and treatments. **Circulation:** 25,000. Alternate Formats: online ● *Eye to Eye*, quarterly. Newsletter. Provides up-to-date information on advances in research and development. **Circulation:** 52,000. Alternate Formats: online ● Annual Report, annual. Alternate Formats: online. **Conventions/Meetings:** annual Scientific Think Tank - conference, by invitation only.

15355 ■ Glaucoma Research Foundation
251 Post St., Ste.600
San Francisco, CA 94108
Free: (800)826-6693
Fax: (415)986-3763
E-mail: info@glaucoma.org
URL: http://www.glaucoma.org
Contact: Ms. Jennifer Rulon, Research and Education Specialist
Founded: 1978. **Staff:** 7. **Budget:** $3,000,000. **Languages:** English, Spanish. **Description:** Aims to protect the sight and independence of individuals with glaucoma through research and education, with the ultimate goal of finding a cure. Funds pilot project grants. **Libraries: Type:** reference. **Awards:** Pilot Project. **Frequency:** annual. **Type:** grant. **Recipient:** for research. **Formerly:** (1993) Foundation for Glaucoma Research. **Publications:** *Childhood Glaucoma.* Provides information for people with glaucoma and their families regarding glaucoma in children. **Price:** free ● *Gleams*, 3/year. Newsletter. Includes research updates, foundation news, and medical column. **Price:** free. ISSN: 1072-7906. **Circulation:** 45,000. Alternate Formats: online ● *Understanding and Living With Glaucoma.* Serves as a reference guide for people with glaucoma.

15356 ■ International Association of Ocular Surgeons (IAOS)
Address Unknown since 2007
Founded: 1981. **Members:** 100. **Membership Dues:** ophthalmologist, optometrist, $275 (annual). **Staff:** 2. **Description:** A division of the American Society of Contemporary Ophthalmology. Seeks to develop a global community of ophthalmic surgeons who examine and deliberate on all aspects of ocular surgery; encourage information exchange among members; and disseminate information about contemporary diagnostic and surgical procedures. **Libraries: Type:** reference. **Holdings:** 100. **Computer Services:** database. **Publications:** *Annals of Ophthalmology*, 3/year. Journal. Features topics for continuing medical education for ophthalmologists. **Price:** $160.00. ISSN: 1530-4086. **Circulation:** 600. **Advertising:** accepted. **Conventions/Meetings:** seminar ● workshop.

15357 ■ International Eye Foundation (IEF)
10801 Connecticut Ave.
Kensington, MD 20895-2134
Ph: (240)290-0263
Fax: (240)290-0269
E-mail: ief@iefusa.org
URL: http://www.iefusa.org
Contact: Victoria M. Sheffield, Exec. Dir.
Founded: 1961. **Staff:** 21. **Budget:** $2,500,000. **Description:** Works to restore sight and prevent blindness in poor countries around the world. Focuses on making eye clinics financially self-sufficient. Develops eye health services. Trains ophthalmologists and para-medicals, and fights vitamin A deficiency, trachoma and river blindness. Strives to help clinics become less dependent on outside donors and government funds. **Publications:** *International Eye Foundation—Eye to Eye*, semiannual. Newsletter. Involves with the prevention of blindness in the developing countries; includes information on foundation programs. **Price:** free. **Circulation:** 2,000 ● Annual Report, annual. **Circulation:** 1,500 ● Also publishes fact sheets and Primary Eye Care Manual: Eye Care in Developing Nations.

15358 ■ International Federation of Ophthalmological Societies (IFOS)
c/o Bruce E. Spivey, MD, Pres.
945 Green St.
San Francisco, CA 94133
Ph: (415)409-8410
Fax: (415)409-8403
E-mail: info@icoph.org
URL: http://www.icoph.org
Contact: Bruce E. Spivey MD, Pres.
Founded: 1857. **Members:** 120. **Staff:** 2. **Budget:** $160,000. **Regional Groups:** 5. **National Groups:** 125. **Description:** Represents ophthalmologic organizations throughout the world. Aims to create an international exchange in ophthalmology. Encourages the study and improvement of ophthalmologic education; formulates international standards. Advocates the prevention and treatment of preventable blindness in developing nations, particularly Africa. Supports the International Agency for the Prevention of Blindness. **Libraries: Type:** not open to the public. **Holdings:** archival material. **Subjects:** history of the organization. **Awards:** Gonin Medal. **Frequency:** quadrennial. **Type:** medal. **Recipient:** for special contributions to ophthalmology ● Internation Duke Elder Medal. **Frequency:** quadrennial. **Type:** medal. **Recipient:** for special contributions to ophthalmology ● Jules Francois Golden Medal. **Frequency:** quadrennial. **Type:** medal. **Committees:** Advisory; Advocacy; Education; Standards; Supranational. **Conventions/Meetings:** biennial International Congress of Ophthalmology - conference, with scientific program and technical exhibits - 2008 June 28-July 2, Hong Kong, People's Republic of China; 2010 June 6-10, Berlin, Germany; 2012 Nov. 10-13, Chicago, IL.

15359 ■ International Iridology Practitioners Association (IIPA)
PO Box 339
Pinehurst, TX 77362
Free: (888)682-2208

Fax: (888)682-2208
E-mail: iipacentraloffice@iridologyassn.org
URL: http://www.iridologyassn.org
Contact: Dave Carpenter ND, Pres.
Founded: 1982. **Members:** 300. **Membership Dues:** professional, $165 (annual). **Staff:** 1. **Languages:** English, French, Spanish. **Multinational. Description:** Studies the eye for indications of body stresses that may influence health. Offers members educational classes and information, conventions, research and certification. **Libraries: Type:** reference. **Holdings:** 30; periodicals. **Computer Services:** database, supplies names of certified Iridologists around the world ● information services, Iridology resources. **Telecommunication Services:** electronic mail, jhwnur@earthlink.net. **Formerly:** (1999) National Iridology Research Association; (2002) International Iridology Research Association. **Publications:** *IIPA Insights*, quarterly. Newsletter. Contains news in the field of Iridology. **Price:** included in membership dues ● *The Iridology Review*, quarterly. Article. Presents research in Iridology. **Circulation:** 300. **Conventions/Meetings:** semiannual conference and board meeting - February/August.

15360 ■ International Perimetric Society (IPS)
c/o Dr. Richard P. Mills, MD
Glaucoma Consultants Northwest
1221 Madison St., Ste.1124
Seattle, WA 98104
Ph: (206)682-3447
Fax: (206)682-8219
E-mail: rmillswa@msn.com
URL: http://www.perimetry.org
Contact: Dr. Richard P. Mills MD, Contact
Founded: 1974. **Members:** 200. **Membership Dues:** individual, $65 (annual). **Staff:** 5. **Budget:** $30,000. **Description:** Ophthalmologists, scientists, and technicians in 20 countries working in the field of perimetry (visual field testing) and related areas. Promotes the study of normal and abnormal visual function and encourages worldwide cooperation and friendship among those working in the field. **Libraries: Type:** not open to the public. **Holdings:** 13. **Publications:** *Perimetry Update*, biennial. Proceedings. **Circulation:** 300. **Conventions/Meetings:** biennial symposium, posters and manufacturers (exhibits).

15361 ■ International Refractive Surgery Club (IRSC)
c/o Marcie B. Stein
4000 Legato Rd., No. 850
Fairfax, VA 22033
Ph: (703)591-2220
Fax: (703)591-0614
E-mail: mstein@ascrs.org
URL: http://www.refractive.org
Contact: Richard L. Lindstom MD, Pres.
Multinational. Description: Represents Ophthalmic Surgeons who have proficient skill in the methods of surgical correction for myopia (near sightedness), hyperopia (far sightedness), and astigmatism. Creates and promotes awareness of advanced knowledge in the correction of myopia, hyperopia, astigmatism and presbyopia. Provides avenues for the fraternal and cooperative exchange of ideas.

15362 ■ International Society for Imaging in the Eye (ISIE)
6900 Grove Rd., Bldg. 100
Thorofare, NJ 08086-0308
Ph: (856)994-9400
Free: (888)960-0256
Fax: (856)348-6680
E-mail: smonteith@vindicomeded.com
URL: http://www.isie.net
Contact: David Greenfield MD, Sec.-Treas.
Membership Dues: regular, $150 (annual). **Multinational. Description:** Strives to advance the field of ophthalmic imaging. Provides information and education related to imaging in the eye. Acts as a forum for the presentation of current clinical and basic science advances in glaucoma, retina, cornea, anterior segment, orbit and neuro imaging in ophthalmology. **Pub-**

lications: *Ophthalmic Surgery, Lasers & Imaging.* Journal. **Price:** included in membership dues.

15363 ■ International Society on Metabolic Eye Disease (ISMED)
1125 Park Ave.
New York, NY 10128
Ph: (212)427-1246
Fax: (212)360-7009
E-mail: optoedcorp@aol.com
URL: http://www.ismed.info
Contact: Dr. Heskel M. Haddad MD, Sec.-Treas.
Founded: 1971. **Members:** 600. **Membership Dues:** individual, $20 (annual). **Description:** Ophthalmologists, pediatricians, endocrinologists, internists, and paramedical personnel in 20 countries. Promotes the study of metabolic eye problems and biochemical and genetic aspects of such problems. **Libraries: Type:** reference. **Holdings:** books, periodicals. **Subjects:** ophthalmology, metabolic eye disease. **Publications:** *Metabolic, Pediatric, and Systemic Ophthalmology*, quarterly. Journal. **Price:** $160.00/year ● Book. **Conventions/Meetings:** biennial meeting and symposium (exhibits).

15364 ■ Joint Commission on Allied Health Personnel in Ophthalmology (JCAHPO)
2025 Woodlane Dr.
St. Paul, MN 55125-2998
Ph: (651)731-2944
Free: (800)284-3937
Fax: (651)731-0410
E-mail: jcahpo@jcahpo.org
URL: http://www.jcahpo.org/newsite/index.htm
Contact: Lynn D. Anderson PhD, Exec. Dir./Sec.
Founded: 1969. **Staff:** 26. **Description:** Serves as a certifying agency for allied health personnel. Aims to encourage the establishment of medically oriented programs for training allied health personnel in ophthalmology; to develop standards of education and training in the field; to examine, certify, and recertify ophthalmic medical personnel, and encourage their continued occupational development. Conducts national certifying examinations. **Departments:** Accounting; Administrative Services; Certification; Communications/Marketing; Education. **Publications:** *Booklet and Application for Recertification.* **Price:** free. Alternate Formats: online ● *Career of Ophthalmic Medical Assisting* ● *Certification - Why & How* ● *Educational Programs for Ophthalmic Medical Personnel* ● *JCAHPO Criteria for Certification and Recertification.* Book. Provides information on the eligibility, application and preparation for the COA, COT, COMT & Ophthalmic Surgical Assisting examinations. **Price:** free ● *Open Your Eyes to a Bright Future!*. Brochure. **Price:** free ● *The President's Report*, annual. Annual Report. **Price:** free. **Circulation:** 6,000 ● *Viewpoints*, quarterly. Newsletter. **Price:** free to certified ophthalmic medical personnel; $20.00/year. **Circulation:** 17,500. Alternate Formats: online. **Conventions/Meetings:** annual Continuing Education Program for Ophthalmic Medical Personnel - meeting and lecture, held in conjunction with American Academy of Ophthalmology (exhibits).

15365 ■ National Association of Vision Professionals (NAVP)
1775 Church St. NW
Washington, DC 20036
Ph: (202)234-1010
Fax: (202)234-1020
E-mail: contact@visionpros.org
URL: http://members.tripod.com/charlie216
Contact: Michele D. Hartlove, VP
Founded: 1976. **Members:** 200. **Membership Dues:** individual, $35 (annual). **Staff:** 1. **Budget:** $25,000. **Description:** Individuals responsible for or connected with vision conservation and eye health programs in public or private agencies and institutions. Serves as a forum for ideas and programs, cooperates with other agencies, and promotes professional standards. Certifies vision screening personnel. **Additional Websites:** http://visionpros.com. **Committees:** Certification; Editorial Review. **Formerly:** (1986) National Association of Vision Program Consultants. **Publications:** *National Association of Vision Professionals—*

Newsletter, quarterly. **Price:** included in membership dues. Alternate Formats: online. **Conventions/Meetings:** annual conference (exhibits).

15366 ■ National Examining Board of Ocularists (NEBO)
c/o David M. Bulgarelli, Exec. Dir.
625 1st Ave., Ste.220
Coralville, IA 52241-2101
Ph: (319)339-1125
Fax: (319)354-3465
E-mail: nebo@neboboard.org
URL: http://www.neboboard.org
Contact: David M. Bulgarelli, Exec. Dir.
Founded: 1980. **Description:** Promotes uniform standards in field of ophthalmic prosthetics (artificial eyes). **Affiliated With:** American Academy of Ophthalmology; American Society of Ocularists; National Organization for Competency Assurance.

15367 ■ North American Neuro-Ophthalmology Society (NANOS)
5841 Cedar Lake Rd., Ste.204
Minneapolis, MN 55416
Ph: (952)646-2037
Fax: (952)545-6073
E-mail: info@nanosweb.org
URL: http://www.nanosweb.org
Contact: Lori J. Anderson, Exec. Dir.
Founded: 1975. **Members:** 400. **Membership Dues:** general, $325 (annual). **Staff:** 2. **Budget:** $400,000. **Multinational. Description:** Ophthalmologists and neurologists. Seeks to promote the field of neuro-ophthalmology. Supports education; encourages research; promotes clinical expertise. **Awards:** Best Abstract Award. **Frequency:** annual. **Type:** recognition. **Recipient:** for best poster or platform presentation by a resident or fellow ● Thomas and Susan Carlow Young Investigator Award. **Frequency:** annual. **Type:** recognition. **Recipient:** for young researchers. **Publications:** *Journal of Neuro-Ophthalmology*, quarterly. **Advertising:** accepted. Alternate Formats: online. **Conventions/Meetings:** annual meeting (exhibits).

15368 ■ Ophthalmic Photographers' Society (OPS)
c/o Barbara S. McCalley, Exec. Dir.
1869 W Ranch Rd.
Nixa, MO 65714-8262
Ph: (417)725-0181
Free: (800)403-1677
Fax: (417)724-8450
E-mail: ops@opsweb.org
URL: http://www.opsweb.org
Contact: Barbara S. McCalley, Exec. Dir.
Founded: 1969. **Members:** 1,200. **Membership Dues:** regular, $80 (annual). **Staff:** 1. **Budget:** $250,000. **Regional Groups:** 3. **Description:** Represents ophthalmologists, pathologists, medical and ophthalmic photographers, nurses, ophthalmic assistants, technicians, technologists, researchers, and engineers; organizations and individuals who are actively involved with ophthalmology or ophthalmic photography. Encourages the highest quality of ophthalmic photography and to promote development of new and improved techniques and equipment. (Ophthalmic photography involves photography of the eye for documentation and diagnostic purposes.) Provides continuing education and technical information. Serves as a forum for the discussion of ophthalmic photography. Provides testing, and subsequent certification as Certified Retinal Angiographer in performance of ophthalmic photography. **Awards:** **Type:** recognition. **Recipient:** for performance and contributions to ophthalmic photography. **Computer Services:** Mailing lists. **Publications:** *Journal of Ophthalmic Photography*, semiannual. **Price:** $26.00 for nonmembers in U.S.; $31.00 for nonmembers outside U.S.; included in membership dues. **Circulation:** 1,400. **Advertising:** accepted ● *OPS Directory*, annual ● *OPS Newsletter*, bimonthly. **Conventions/Meetings:** semiannual Education Program - meeting, educational lectures and workshops - 2007 Nov. 9-13, New Orleans, LA - **Avg. Attendance:** 500.

15369 ■ ORBIS International

520 8th Ave., 11th Fl.
New York, NY 10018
Ph: (646)674-5500
Free: (800)ORBIS-US
Fax: (646)674-5599
E-mail: info@orbis.org
URL: http://www.orbis.org
Contact: Geoffrey Holland, Exec. Dir.
Founded: 1973. **Staff:** 160. **Budget:** $27,000,000.
Languages: Amharic, Bengali, Cantonese, English,
French, Hindi, Mandarin Dialects, Vietnamese. **Multinational. Description:** Dedicated to saving sight and
eliminating avoidable blindness worldwide. Responds
to the needs of developing nations, where ninety
percent of blind people live, with hands-on training
for eye care professionals, public education about
blindness, and technical assistance to improve access to quality ophthalmic services. Has the world's
only flying eye hospital, a DC-10 that has been
converted into a state-of-the-art medical facility, and
flies to developing countries to provide intensive,
comprehensive eye care training. Has long-term
country programs in Bangladesh, China, Ethiopia,
India and Vietnam. **Libraries: Type:** reference; not
open to the public. **Holdings:** 500; articles, books,
periodicals. **Subjects:** ophthalmology, nursing,
anesthesia, biomedical engineering, community
health. **Formerly:** Project Orbis. **Publications:** *ORBIS Observer*, quarterly. Newsletter. **Price:** free. **Circulation:** 20,000. Alternate Formats: online ● *ORBIS
Observer - Hong Kong.* Newsletter ● *ORBIS Observer - U.K..* Newsletter ● Brochures. Alternate
Formats: online. **Conventions/Meetings:** annual
meeting, in conjunction with AAO (exhibits).

15370 ■ Outpatient Ophthalmic Surgery Society (OOSS)

c/o Ms. Claudia A. McDougal, Exec. Dir.
6564 Umbers Cir.
Arvada, CO 80007
Free: (866)892-1001
Fax: (303)940-7780
E-mail: claudiamcdougal@ooss.org
URL: http://www.ooss.org
Contact: Ms. Claudia A. McDougal, Exec. Dir.
Founded: 1981. **Members:** 700. **Membership Dues:**
facility (fewer than 1000 procedures per year),
president's council (per person), $1,500 (annual) ●
facility (more than 1000 procedures per year), $2,500
(annual). **Description:** Represents ophthalmic
surgeons. Gathers and share information about
outpatient eye surgery in order to promote high-quality, low-cost patient care. **Affiliated With:** Accreditation Association for Ambulatory Health Care.
Publications: *Outlook Magazine Online*, quarterly.
Newsletter. Details about society activities and
articles. **Price:** included in membership dues. Alternate Formats: online ● *Washington Update Online*,
Published as necessary. Bulletins. Contains current
upcoming legislative issues. ● Also publishes books;
produces videotapes. **Conventions/Meetings:** annual meeting ● annual symposium, for new technologies, efficiencies, networking, marketing, coding,
operating room expansion formulas, new facility
advice - 2007 Oct. 5-6, Atlanta, GA.

15371 ■ Pan-American Association of Ophthalmology (PAAO)

1301 S Bowen Rd., Ste.365
Arlington, TX 76013
Ph: (817)275-7553
Fax: (817)275-3961
E-mail: info@paao.org
URL: http://www.paao.org
Contact: Teresa J. Bradshaw, Exec. Dir.
Founded: 1939. **Members:** 14,000. **Membership
Dues:** ophthalmologist, $150 (annual) ● resident/
fellow, $50 (annual). **Staff:** 2. **Budget:** $200,000.
Languages: English, Portuguese, Spanish. **Description:** Represents ophthalmologists throughout the
Western Hemisphere. Seeks to improve the treatment of eye diseases and prevention of blindness in
the Americas through the exchange of ideas and
treatments. **Awards:** Benjamin F. Boyd Humanitarian
Award. **Frequency:** biennial. **Type:** recognition. **Re-**

cipient: for ophthalmological service and blindness
prevention activities ● **Type:** fellowship ● Gillingham
- Pan American Fellowship. **Frequency:** annual.
Type: grant. **Recipient:** for education. **Committees:**
Congresses; Educational Programs; Eye Banking;
Fellowships; Independent Review Financial; Institutional Courses; Visiting Professors. **Affiliated With:**
American Academy of Ophthalmology. **Publications:**
Vision Pan-America, quarterly. **Conventions/Meetings:** biennial Pan-American Congress of Ophthalmology - meeting (exhibits).

15372 ■ Pediatric Keratoplasty Association (PKA)

c/o Dr. Gerald W. Zaidman, MD, Assoc. Dir.
Westchester Medical Ctr.
Dept. of Ophthalmology
Valhalla, NY 10595
Ph: (914)493-1599
Fax: (914)493-7445
E-mail: pedkera@aol.com
URL: http://www.pedkera.org
Contact: Dr. Gerald W. Zaidman MD, Assoc. Dir.
Description: Assists pediatric ophthalmologists,
corneal surgeons, and others in the diagnosis and
management of pediatric corneal cases through the
exchange of ideas and information. Facilitates data
collection on the success rate associated with various types of surgical procedures. Addresses non-ophthalmic issues that arise in the care of the
children. **Publications:** Newsletter. Alternate Formats: online.

15373 ■ Seniors EyeCare Program (SEP)

c/o Eye Care America
PO Box 429098
San Francisco, CA 94142
Free: (877)887-6327
Fax: (415)561-8567
E-mail: pubserv@aao.org
URL: http://www.eyecareamerica.org/eyecare/care/
senior-eyecare.cfm
Contact: Richard P. Mills MD, Chm.
Founded: 1986. **Staff:** 8. **Description:** Ophthalmologists dedicated to ensuring eye care for the elderly,
particularly those who are economically disadvantaged. Provides medical and surgical eye care to
individuals 65 and over who normally would not have
access or the means to consult an ophthalmologist.
Disseminates information on participating physicians
and eye diseases. Offers referral services; a project
of the Foundation of the American Academy of
Ophthalmology. **Telecommunication Services:** 24-hour hotline, helpline, (800)222-3937. **Formerly:**
(2004) National Eye Care Project. **Publications:**
Publishes a fact sheet and information packet.

15374 ■ Society for Excellence in Eyecare (SEE)

PO Box 6139
Palm Harbor, FL 34684-0739
Ph: (630)699-1929
Fax: (727)786-6622
E-mail: info@excellenteyesurgery.com
URL: http://www.excellenteyesurgery.com
Contact: Trent Roark, Exec. Dir.
Founded: 1989. **Members:** 80. **Membership Dues:**
ophthalmologist, $1,000 (annual) ● optometrist, $750
(annual). **Staff:** 2. **Description:** Seeks excellence in
eye surgery and peri-operative care and is committed
that patients with ocular problems are afforded safe,
high quality and cost-effective care of the eye.
Endeavors to seek education, training and advocacy,
those policies, procedures and technologies that
promote patient access to vision restoring treatment.
Awards: Frequency: annual. **Type:** fellowship. **Recipient:** to members who attain certain standards
and/or criteria related to patient advocacy. **Conventions/Meetings:** annual CME Credit Seminar (exhibits).

15375 ■ Society of Eye Surgeons (SES)

c/o International Eye Foundation
10801 Connecticut Ave.
Kensington, MD 20895
Ph: (240)290-0263

Fax: (240)290-0269
E-mail: ief@iefusa.org
URL: http://www.iefusa.org
Contact: R.D. Thulasiraj, Exec. Dir.
Founded: 1968. **Members:** 1,000. **Membership
Dues:** regular, in U.S., $100 (annual) ● regular,
outside U.S., $50 (annual). **Description:** Ophthalmologist promoting the science of ophthalmic surgery
worldwide. Supports the blindness prevention efforts
of the International Eye Foundation. Provides educational, training, and eye care services by sponsoring
teaching teams and professors to visit countries
worldwide; fosters social exchange among physicians
and scientists in the field of ophthalmology. **Awards:**
Derrick Vail Medal. **Type:** recognition. **Recipient:** for
outstanding ophthalmic achievement. **Publications:**
Eye to Eye, semiannual. Newsletter. Provides program news. **Conventions/Meetings:** periodic congress ● periodic meeting.

Opticianry

15376 ■ American Board of Opticianry (ABO)

6506 Loisdale Rd., Ste.209
Springfield, VA 22150-1815
Ph: (703)719-5800
Free: (800)296-1379
Fax: (703)719-9144
E-mail: mail@abo-ncle.org
URL: http://www.abo.org
Contact: Michael H. Robey, Exec. Mgr.
Founded: 1979. **Members:** 38,000. **Staff:** 8. **Budget:**
$1,300,000. **Multinational. Description:** Provides
uniform standards for dispensing opticians by administering the National Opticianry Competency Examination and by issuing the Certified Optician Certificate
to those passing the exam. Administers the Master in
Ophthalmic Optics Examination and issues certificates to opticians at the advanced level passing the
exam. Maintains records of persons certified for
competency in eyeglass dispensing. Adopts and
enforces continuing education requirements; assists
and encourages state licensing boards in the use of
the National Opticianry Competency Examination for
licensure purposes. **Affiliated With:** Contact Lens
Society of America; National Academy of Opticianry;
Opticians Association of America. **Publications:** *Professional Dispensing*. Newsletter. Alternate Formats:
online. **Conventions/Meetings:** periodic board meeting.

15377 ■ BiOptic Driving Network - USA

c/o Susan Baillely
7775 Ivygate Ln.
Cincinnati, OH 45242
Ph: (513)745-9677
Fax: (413)638-6941
URL: http://www.biopticdriving.org
Contact: Susan Baillely, Contact
Founded: 2001. **Membership Dues:** general, 100
(annual). **Description:** Promotes the use of BiOptics
for driving. Seeks to provide assistance, technical
and experiential information, guidance and counseling to people with professional or personal interests.
Raises awareness of BiOptic driving for people with
stable low vision. **Telecommunication Services:** hotline, members only telephone helpline, (413)306-4263.

15378 ■ Commission on Opticianry Accreditation (COA)

c/o Ellen Stoner, Dir. of Accreditation
PO Box 4342
Chapel Hill, NC 27515
Ph: (703)468-0566
E-mail: info@coaccreditation.com
URL: http://www.coaccreditation.com
Contact: Ellen Stoner, Dir. of Accreditation
Founded: 1979. **Members:** 26. **Membership Dues:**
accredited program, $950 (annual). **Staff:** 1. **Budget:**
$90,000. **Description:** Accrediting agency for ophthalmic dispensing and ophthalmic laboratory technology programs in postsecondary institutions. Conducts
an evaluator's workshop to train on-site evaluators.

Telecommunication Services: electronic mail, coa@coaccreditation.com. **Publications:** *Accreditation Guide for Laboratory Technician Programs.* Manual. **Price:** $10.00 ● *Accreditation Guide for Ophthalmic Dispensing Programs.* Manual. **Price:** $10.00 ● *Essentials of an Accredited Educational Program for Ophthalmic Laboratory Technician Programs.* Handbook ● *Essentials of an Accredited Educational Program for Opticianry Programs.* Handbook ● *Evaluator's Checklist for Ophthalmic Dispensing Programs.* Manual ● *Evaluator's Checklist for Ophthalmic Laboratory Technology Programs.* Manual ● *Evaluator's Handbook for Ophthalmic Dispensing Programs* ● *Evaluator's Handbook for Ophthalmic Laboratory Technology Programs* ● *Self-Study Report Format for Ophthalmic Dispensing Programs.* Manual ● *Self-Study Report Format for Ophthalmic Laboratory Technology Program.* Manual. **Conventions/Meetings:** semiannual executive committee meeting.

15379 ■ National Academy of Opticianry (NAO)
8401 Corporate Dr., Ste.605
Landover, MD 20785
Ph: (301)577-4828
Free: (800)229-4828
Fax: (301)577-3880
E-mail: info@nao.org
URL: http://www.nao.org
Contact: Jim Iciek Jr., Exec. Dir.
Founded: 1963. **Members:** 5,000. **Membership Dues:** fellow and associate, $75 (annual). **Staff:** 7. **Budget:** $600,000. **Description:** Offers review courses for national certification and state licensure examinations to members. Maintains speakers' bureau and Career Progression Program. **Awards:** Beverly Myers Achievement Award. **Frequency:** annual. **Type:** recognition ● Hall of Fame. **Frequency:** annual. **Type:** recognition. **Formed by Merger of:** American Board of Opticianry; International Academy of Opticianry. **Publications:** *Academy Newsletter,* quarterly. **Circulation:** 6,000 ● *Exam Review for Ophthalmic Dispensing* ● *Ophthalmic Dispensing Review Book* ● *Optical Math Review* ● Brochure ● Videos. **Conventions/Meetings:** competition ● seminar.

15380 ■ National Federation of Opticianry Schools (NFOS)
c/o Randall L. Smith, Exec. Mgr.
1238 Robinson Point Rd.
Mountain Home, AR 72653
Ph: (870)492-6623
Fax: (870)492-6623
E-mail: rsmith@asumh.edu
URL: http://www.nfos.org
Contact: Randall L. Smith, Exec. Mgr.
Description: Promotes formal opticianry education offered by accredited educational institutions. Strives to develop formal education programs in identified areas of need; upgrade standards of opticianry education; facilitate exchange of teaching methods; achieve uniformity of formal education in opticianry; and assist national opticianry organizations.

15381 ■ Opticians Association of America (OAA)
441 Carlisle Dr.
Herndon, VA 20170
Ph: (703)437-8780
Free: (800)433-8997
Fax: (703)437-0727
E-mail: oaa@oaa.org
URL: http://www.oaa.org
Contact: Ms. Catherine Langley, Exec. Dir.
Founded: 1926. **Members:** 10,000. **Membership Dues:** individual, $65 (annual) ● honored fellow, $75 (annual) ● student, $10 (annual) ● associate, $500 (annual) ● firm, $400 (annual). **Staff:** 4. **Budget:** $500,000. **State Groups:** 22. **Description:** Retail dispensing opticians who fill prescriptions for glasses or contact lenses written by a vision care specialist. Works to advance the science of ophthalmic optics. Conducts research and educational programs. Maintains museum and speakers' bureau. Compiles statistics. **Libraries: Type:** reference. **Holdings:**

1,000. **Subjects:** opticianry. **Awards:** Russell Fritz Memorial Scholarship. **Frequency:** annual. **Type:** scholarship. **Recipient:** for a first year student in an opticianry program accredited by the Commission on Opticianry Accreditation. **Committees:** Political Action. **Formerly:** (1972) Guild of Prescription Opticians of America. **Publications:** *American Optician,* quarterly. Magazine. Contains calendar of events and research reports. **Price:** included in membership dues. **Circulation:** 10,000. **Advertising:** accepted. **Conventions/Meetings:** annual National Opticians Convention (exhibits).

Optometry

15382 ■ Accreditation Council on Optometric Education (ACOE)
243 N Lindbergh Blvd., 1st Fl.
St. Louis, MO 63141-7881
Ph: (314)991-4100
Fax: (314)991-4101
E-mail: acoe@aoa.org
URL: http://www.theacoe.org
Contact: Joyce L. Urbeck, Admin. Dir.
Founded: 1934. **Members:** 11. **Staff:** 3. **Description:** Accrediting body for professional Optometric Degree (O.D.) programs (examination, diagnosis, and treatment and management of diseases and disorders of the vision system, the eyes and associated structures as well as diagnosis of related systemic conditions), paraoptometric educational programs, and optometric residency programs. Members are appointed by the president of the American Optometric Association (see separate entry). Works to ensure the quality of optometric education by establishing and applying valid educational standards and announces list of accredited programs. **Affiliated With:** American Optometric Association. **Formerly:** (2002) Council on Optometric Education. **Conventions/Meetings:** annual meeting, held in conjunction with AOA - always June ● annual meeting - always October or November ● annual meeting - always February.

15383 ■ American Academy of Optometry (AAO)
6110 Executive Blvd., Ste.506
Rockville, MD 20852
Ph: (301)984-1441
Fax: (301)984-4737
E-mail: aaoptom@aaoptom.org
URL: http://www.aaopt.org
Contact: Dr. Richard E. Weisbarth, Pres.
Founded: 1922. **Members:** 5,000. **Membership Dues:** fellow, $325 (annual) ● emeritus fellow, $80 (annual) ● student, $30 (annual) ● senior fellow, $225 (annual). **Staff:** 11. **Budget:** $3,600,000. **Local Groups:** 26. **Multinational. Description:** Optometrists, educators, and scientists interested in optometric education, and standards of care in visual problems. Conducts continuing education for optometrists and visual scientists. Sponsors 4-day annual meeting. **Awards:** Carol C. Koch Award. **Frequency:** annual. **Type:** recognition. **Recipient:** for outstanding service in interprofessional relations ● Charles F. Prentice Medal. **Frequency:** annual. **Type:** recognition. **Recipient:** for outstanding research in vision ● Founder's Award. **Frequency:** annual. **Type:** recognition. **Recipient:** for outstanding contribution to clinical aspects of contact lens fitting ● Garland W. Clay Award. **Frequency:** annual. **Type:** recognition. **Recipient:** for best published paper on clinical optometry ● Glenn A. Fry Award. **Frequency:** annual. **Type:** recognition. **Recipient:** for invited recognized scientist ● Julius Neumueller Award. **Frequency:** annual. **Type:** recognition. **Recipient:** for best paper on optics by a professional student ● William Feinbloom Award. **Frequency:** annual. **Type:** recognition. **Recipient:** for outstanding contributions to clinical optometry. **Computer Services:** Mailing lists, of members. **Boards:** Editorial. **Committees:** Admittance; Awards; Communication; Exhibits; Lectures and Workshops; Research; Scientific Program. **Sections:** Binocular Vision, Perception, and Pediatric

Optometry; Cornea and Contact Lenses; Disease; Low Vision; Optometric Education; Primary Care; Public Health and Environmental Optometry; Vision Science. **Affiliated With:** American Optometric Foundation. **Publications:** *Eye Mail Monthly.* Newsletter ● *Optometry and Vision Science,* monthly. Journal. Includes academy news, book reviews, and periodic index. **Price:** included in membership dues; $305.00 /year for nonmembers in U.S.; $396.00 /year for institutions in U.S.; $35.00/year for students. ISSN: 1040-5488. **Circulation:** 5,500. **Advertising:** accepted. **Conventions/Meetings:** annual conference, latest research and patient treatments (exhibits) - 2007 Oct. 24-27, Tampa, FL; 2008 Oct. 22-25, Anaheim, CA.

15384 ■ American Optometric Association (AOA)
243 N Lindbergh Blvd., 1st Fl.
St. Louis, MO 63141-7881
Ph: (314)991-4100
Free: (800)365-2219
Fax: (314)991-4101
E-mail: lmbaumstark@aoa.org
URL: http://www.aoa.org
Founded: 1898. **Members:** 34,500. **Membership Dues:** regular, $611 (annual). **Staff:** 97. **Budget:** $19,600,000. **State Groups:** 53. **Local Groups:** 500. **Description:** Professional association of optometrists, students of optometry, and paraoptometric assistants and technicians. Purposes are: to improve the quality, availability, and accessibility of eye and vision care; to represent the optometric profession; to help members conduct their practices; to promote the highest standards of patient care. Monitors and promotes legislation concerning the scope of optometric practice, alternate health care delivery systems, health care cost containment, Medicare, and other issues relevant to eye/vision care. Supports the International Library, Archives and Museum of Optometry which includes references on ophthalmic and related sciences with emphasis on the history and socioeconomic aspects of optometry. Operates Vision U.S.A. program, which provides free eye care to the working poor, and the InfantSEE program, which provides free vision assessments for infants between six and twelve months of age. Conducts specialized education programs; operates placement service; compiles statistics. Maintains museum. Conducts Seal of Acceptance Program. **Libraries: Type:** reference; open to the public; lending. **Holdings:** 8,500; archival material, audiovisuals, books, clippings, periodicals. **Subjects:** vision, eye care, optometry. **Awards:** Apollo Award. **Frequency:** annual. **Type:** recognition. **Recipient:** for individuals, organizations, educational institutions or programs outside optometry which have made a significant contribution to the visual welfare of Americans ● Distinguished Service Award. **Frequency:** annual. **Type:** recognition. **Recipient:** to an optometrist for unusually significant contributions and outstanding achievements contributing to the advancement of the profession of optometry ● National Optometrist of the Year Award. **Frequency:** annual. **Type:** recognition. **Recipient:** for an optometrist for outstanding service on behalf of the profession and to the visual welfare of the public ● Paraoptometric of the Year Award. **Frequency:** annual. **Type:** recognition. **Recipient:** for the optometric assistant or technician who has made the most outstanding and worthwhile contributions to the profession of optometry, paraoptometry, and the general public ● Young Optometrist of the Year Award. **Frequency:** annual. **Type:** recognition. **Recipient:** for optometrists who have been in practice for less than 10 years, and show remarkable leadership skills when serving their patients, their profession and their community. **Computer Services:** Mailing lists, of members. **Commissions:** Ophthalmic Standards; Quality Assessment and Improvement. **Committees:** Clinical Guidelines Coordinating; Clinical Programs; Congress and Conferences; Environmental/Occupational Vision; Ethics and Values; Federal Relations; Health Care Legislation; Industry Relations; Insurance; International Affairs; Licensure and Regulation; Professional Relations; Public Health and Disease Prevention; State Statutory Scope; Vi-

sion USA. **Councils:** Judicial; Optometric Education; Research. **Sections:** Contact Lens; Low Vision; Paraoptometric; Sports Vision. **Subgroups:** Clinical Care; Communications; Eye Care Benefits; Federal Government Relations; Member Services; State Government Relations. **Formerly:** (1903) American Optical Association. **Publications:** *American Optometric Association—News*, semimonthly. Magazine. Includes employment listings, classified ads, promotional news, and obituaries. **Price:** $80.00 /year for nonmembers; $95.00/year in U.S. and Canada; $103.00/year outside U.S. and Canada. ISSN: 0094-9620. **Circulation:** 30,000. **Advertising:** accepted ● *Optometry: Journal of the American Optometric Association*, monthly. Includes research articles, book reviews, calendar of events, legislative news, new products information, and advertisers' index. **Price:** $95.00/year in U.S.; $130.00/year in Canada; $145.00/year outside U.S. and Canada. ISSN: 0003-0244. **Circulation:** 30,000. **Advertising:** accepted. Alternate Formats: microform. **Conventions/Meetings:** annual congress (exhibits).

15385 ■ American Optometric Foundation (AOF)
c/o American Academy of Optometry
6110 Executive Blvd., Ste.506
Rockville, MD 20852
Ph: (301)984-4734
Free: (800)368-6AOF
Fax: (301)984-4737
E-mail: bullimore.1@osu.edu
URL: http://www.aaopt.org/aof/about/index.asp
Contact: Mark Bullimore, Pres.
Founded: 1947. **Staff:** 1. **Budget:** $300,000. **Description:** Optometrists, optometric organizations, corporations, and the public. Promotes research, education, literature, and professional advancement in the visual sciences. Supports fellowships in graduate research. **Awards:** Antoinette Molinari Memorial. **Frequency:** annual. **Type:** scholarship. **Recipient:** for student pursuing a doctorate of optometry ● Vincent Salierno Memorial Scholarship. **Frequency:** annual. **Type:** scholarship. **Recipient:** for colleges and institutions ● Vistakon Research. **Frequency:** annual. **Type:** grant. **Recipient:** for optometric research in soft disposable contact lenses ● William Ezell Fellowship. **Frequency:** annual. **Type:** grant. **Recipient:** for post graduate research. **Committees:** Communications; Fundraising; Membership. **Affiliated With:** American Academy of Optometry. **Publications:** *The Torch*, quarterly. Newsletter. Updates on foundation's activities. **Price:** free. **Circulation:** 4,000. Alternate Formats: online. **Conventions/Meetings:** annual American Academy of Optometry Meeting - conference (exhibits) - always December.

15386 ■ American Optometric Student Association (AOSA)
c/o American Optometric Association
243 N Lindbergh
St. Louis, MO 63141
Free: (800)365-2291
Fax: (314)991-4101
E-mail: cmfrei@aol.com
URL: http://www.theaosa.org
Contact: Carol Freihaut, Exec. Dir.
Founded: 1972. **Members:** 5,600. **Membership Dues:** non-profit, $25 (annual). **Staff:** 2. **Local Groups:** 19. **Languages:** English, French, Spanish. **Description:** Optometric students, state optometric associations, and family members of optometric students. Collects updated information on progress in the optometry field. Provides members with opportunities to work in areas of health care need such as local community health projects, school curriculum changes, and health manpower legislation. Works to improve optometric education and health care for the general population. Maintains active liaison with other optometric associations. Conducts communications program. **Awards:** Raymond I. Myers Award. **Frequency:** annual. **Type:** recognition. **Recipient:** for the person who contributes most to the organization's efforts to benefit students and the profession ● Student Award in Clinical Ethics. **Frequency:** annual. **Type:** recognition. **Recipient:** for optometry student.

Committees: Benefits; Conference Attendance; Foresight; Membership Development; Speaker Selection. **Publications:** *AOSA Foresight: Optometry Looking Forward*, semiannual. Newsletter. Reports information concerning scholarships, grants, internships, and other educational issues related to the study of optometry. **Price:** included in membership dues. **Circulation:** 7,000. **Advertising:** accepted ● *Communicator*, 9/year. Newsletter. **Conventions/Meetings:** annual Optometry's Meeting - congress and conference, with ophthalmic equipment and services (exhibits).

15387 ■ Asia-Pacific Council of Optometry (APCO)
c/o Dr. Willard B. Bleything, Sec.Gen.
2043 Coll. Way
Forest Grove, OR 97116
Ph: (503)352-2170
Free: (877)722-8648
Fax: (503)352-2929
E-mail: bleythiw@pacificu.edu
URL: http://www.asiapacificoptometry.org
Contact: Dr. Willard B. Bleything, Sec.Gen.
Founded: 1978. **Members:** 26. **Description:** National associations of optometrists in 20 countries. Improves the delivery of eye care and standards of visual welfare to people in the the Asian-Pacific region. **Committees:** Education; Legislation. **Formerly:** International Federation of Asian and Pacific Associations of Optometrists. **Conventions/Meetings:** biennial Asian Pacific Optometric Congress (exhibits).

15388 ■ Association of Regulatory Boards of Optometry (ARBO)
1750 S Brentwood Blvd., Ste.503
St. Louis, MO 63144
Ph: (314)785-6000
Fax: (314)785-6002
E-mail: arbo@arbo.org
URL: http://www.arbo.org
Contact: Ms. Jennifer Parker, Exec. Dir.
Founded: 1919. **Members:** 56. **Staff:** 6. **Budget:** $630,000. **State Groups:** 56. **Multinational. Description:** Represents the North American regulatory boards of optometry. Works to assist member licensing agencies in regulating the practice of optometry for the public welfare. **Councils:** Endorsed Licensure Mobility for Optometrists; Optometric Practitioner Education. **Programs:** Tracker (Optometric Education Tracker). **Affiliated With:** National Board of Examiners in Optometry. **Formerly:** (1999) International Association of Boards of Examiners in Optometry. **Publications:** *ARBO Greensheet*, 3/year. Newsletter ● *Directory of Boards of Optometry*, annual. Lists members of state boards with addresses and phone/fax. **Circulation:** 600. Alternate Formats: online. **Conventions/Meetings:** annual meeting ● regional meeting, held in conjunction with other regional optometric associations - 3/year.

15389 ■ Association of Schools and Colleges of Optometry (ASCO)
6110 Executive Blvd., Ste.510
Rockville, MD 20852
Ph: (301)231-5944
Fax: (301)770-1828
E-mail: porourke@opted.org
URL: http://www.opted.org
Contact: Martin A. Wall CAE, Exec. Dir.
Founded: 1941. **Members:** 19. **Membership Dues:** active (institutional member), $25,000 (annual). **Staff:** 6. **Budget:** $810,000. **Description:** Works to achieve excellence in optometric education and to helping its member schools/colleges prepare well-qualified graduates for entrance into the profession of optometry. Aims to serve the American public through the continued advancement and promotion of all aspects of academic optometry. **Committees:** Academic Affairs; Clinical Affairs; Financial Affairs; Government Affairs; Residency Affairs; Student Affairs. **Publications:** *Faculty Directory*. Online directory. Alternate Formats: online ● *Faculty Survey Report*, annual. Contains survey report. **Price:** $25.00/copy in U.S.; $31.00/copy outside U.S. ● *Optometric Education*,

quarterly. Journal. **Price:** included in membership dues; $30.00 for nonmembers in U.S.; $40.00 for nonmembers outside U.S. ● *Residency Online Directory*. Alternate Formats: online ● *Student Survey Report*, annual. **Price:** $100.00/copy in U.S.; $110.00/copy outside U.S. **Conventions/Meetings:** semiannual board meeting - 3rd weekend of October, 3rd weekend of March ● annual meeting, educational - always June ● annual Special Interest Groups Workshop/Business Meetings - workshop and meeting, educational - usually December.

15390 ■ College of Optometrists in Vision Development (COVD)
215 W Garfield Rd., Ste.210
Aurora, OH 44202
Ph: (330)995-0718
Free: (888)268-3770
Fax: (330)995-0719
E-mail: info@covd.org
URL: http://www.covd.org
Contact: Ms. Pamela R. Happ CAE, Exec. Dir.
Founded: 1970. **Members:** 2,800. **Membership Dues:** fellow/associate, $320 (annual) ● affiliate/therapist, $85 (annual). **Staff:** 3. **Budget:** $600,000. **Regional Groups:** 3. **State Groups:** 50. **Multinational. Description:** Optometrists involved in developmental vision care and vision therapy with emphasis on visual information processing in visually related learning problems. Seeks to establish a body of practitioners who are knowledgeable in functional and developmental concepts of vision, to insure that the public will receive continually improving vision care; to enable members to maintain the highest standards of professional knowledge and competency; to educate and encourage optometrists to qualify for membership and fellowship in the college; to certify optometrists skilled in this specialty. Conducts national educational programs and public information programs. **Awards:** A.M. Skeffington Award. **Frequency:** annual. **Type:** recognition. **Recipient:** for excellence in optometric writing ● G.N. Getman Award. **Frequency:** annual. **Type:** recognition. **Recipient:** for outstanding contributions in developmental vision care ● Presidents Award. **Frequency:** annual. **Type:** recognition. **Recipient:** for contributions to the organization. **Boards:** International Examination and Certification. **Committees:** Education; Insurance; Membership; Peer Review; Public Information; Research. **Affiliated With:** Optometric Extension Program Foundation. **Formed by Merger:** of (1970) National Optometric Society for Developmental Vision Care; (1970) National Society for Vision and Perception Training; (1970) Southwest Developmental Vision Society. **Publications:** *College of Optometrists in Vision Development—Membership Directory*, annual. Presents a listing of associate and fellow members. **Price:** included in membership dues; $3.50/copy, for nonmembers. **Advertising:** accepted ● *Optometry and Vision Development Journal*, quarterly. **Price:** $65.00/year. **Circulation:** 1,800. **Advertising:** accepted ● *Visions Newsletter*, bimonthly. **Price:** included in membership dues ● Brochures ● Monographs ● Also publishes research reviews. **Conventions/Meetings:** annual meeting (exhibits).

15391 ■ Intercontinental Federation of Behavioral Optometry (IFBO)
c/o Robert Williams, Exec. Dir.
1921 E Carnegie Ave., Ste.3L
Santa Ana, CA 92705
E-mail: oep@oep.org
URL: http://www.ifbo.net
Contact: Robert Williams, Exec. Dir.
Founded: 1996. **Membership Dues:** regular, $200 (annual). **Multinational. Description:** Promotes the worldwide development of behavioral vision care. Fosters communication and cooperation between various organizations that are committed to the study and application of behavioral vision care. Facilitates information sharing among members.

15392 ■ International Association of Optometric Executives (IAOE)
1454 30th St., Ste.204
West Des Moines, IA 50266

Ph: (515)222-5679
Fax: (515)222-9073
Contact: Gary Ellis, Exec.Dir.
Members: 75. **Staff:** 1. **Description:** Executives of optometric associations in 10 countries. Promotes continuing education in optometric association management. **Libraries: Type:** reference. **Subjects:** management. **Affiliated With:** American Optometric Association; American Society of Association Executives. **Formerly:** Society of Association Optometric Executives. **Conventions/Meetings:** annual congress, held in conjunction with American Optometric Association - always June ● meeting - held in fall.

15393 ■ National Association of Optometrists and Opticians (NAOO)
PO Box 459
Marblehead, OH 43440
Ph: (419)798-2031
Fax: (419)798-8548
E-mail: fdrozak@cros.net
Contact: Franklin D. Rozak, Sec.-Treas.
Founded: 1960. **Members:** 13,225. **Description:** Licensed optometrists, opticians, and corporations. Conducts public affairs programs of mutual importance to members; serves as an organizational center for special purpose programs; acts as a clearinghouse for information affecting the retail optical industry. **Formerly:** National Optical Association. **Conventions/Meetings:** semiannual meeting.

15394 ■ National Board of Examiners in Optometry (NBEO)
200 S Coll. St., No. 1920
Charlotte, NC 28202
Ph: (704)332-9565
Free: (800)969-EXAM
Fax: (704)332-9568
E-mail: nbeo@optometry.org
URL: http://www.optometry.org
Contact: Jack Terry PhD, Exec. Dir.
Founded: 1951. **Staff:** 10. **Budget:** $2,500,000. **Description:** Administers entry-level criterion-referenced credentialing examinations to students and graduates of accredited schools and colleges of optometry for use by individual state licensing boards. Provides other evaluation, assessment, and survey services to the profession. **Committees:** Examination Operations; Examination Policy; External Relations. **Publications:** *Candidates Guide*, annual ● *Test Points*, 3/year. Newsletter ● Annual Report, annual ● Manuals. **Conventions/Meetings:** annual meeting - always June.

15395 ■ National Contact Lens Examiners (NCLE)
6506 Loisdale Rd., Ste.209
Springfield, VA 22150-1815
Ph: (703)719-5800
Free: (800)296-1379
Fax: (703)719-9144
E-mail: mail@abo-ncle.org
URL: http://www.abo.org
Contact: Lawrence Tom Graves, Chm.
Founded: 1979. **Members:** 9,000. **Membership Dues:** certification, $85 (triennial). **Staff:** 8. **Budget:** $350,000. **Description:** Serves as National certifying agency promoting continued development of opticians and technicians as contact lens fitters by formulating standards and procedures for determination of entry-level competency. Assists in the continuation, development, administration, and monitoring of a national Contact Lens Registry Examination (CLRE), which verifies entry-level competency of contact lens fitters. Issues certificates. Activities include: maintaining records of those certified in contact lens fitting; encouraging state occupational licensing and credentialing agencies to use the CLRE for licensure purposes; identifying contact lens dispensing education needs as a result of findings of examination programs; disseminating information to sponsors of contact lens continuing education programs. **Affiliated With:** American Board of Opticianry. **Publications:** *Professional Dispensing*. Newsletter. Alternate Formats: online. **Conventions/Meetings:** periodic board meeting.

15396 ■ National Eye Research Foundation (NERF)
Address Unknown since 2007
URL: http://www.nerf.org
Founded: 1955. **Members:** 300. **Membership Dues:** $400 (annual). **Staff:** 10. **Budget:** $400,000. **Description:** Persons with graduate degrees in the eye professions; persons without graduate degrees but employed in the field of eye care; others participating in the work of the foundation for charitable or public welfare purposes. Works to sponsor research and education relating to the eye and contact lenses and to promote interprofessional relations for better eye care. Serves as public information center for questions on eye care. Supports Vision Foundation for Blind Youth. Conducts research and certification program. **Libraries: Type:** reference. **Holdings:** 40; articles. **Subjects:** optometry. **Awards:** Leo Award. **Frequency:** annual. **Type:** recognition. **Recipient:** for significant impact in vision and health. **Computer Services:** database, optometrist. **Divisions:** International Orthokeratology. **Publications:** *Contacto*, quarterly. Journal. **Price:** included in membership dues; $85.00/year for nonmembers. **Advertising:** accepted ● *The Pinnacle*, monthly. Newsletter. **Conventions/Meetings:** annual Post-Graduate Congress, post graduate education for optometrist (exhibits) ● quarterly regional meeting.

15397 ■ National Optometric Association (NOA)
c/o Dr. Charles Comer, Mgr.
3723 Main St.
PO Box F
East Chicago, IN 46312
Ph: (219)398-4483
Free: (877)394-2020
Fax: (219)398-1077
E-mail: ddodpc@verizon.net
URL: http://www.natoptassoc.org
Contact: Dr. Daniel Desrivieres, Pres.
Founded: 1969. **Members:** 450. **Membership Dues:** optometrist (based on year graduated), $100-$175 (annual). **Staff:** 1. **Budget:** $50,000. **Regional Groups:** 5. **Description:** Represents optometrists dedicated to increasing awareness of the status of eye/vision health in the minority community and the national community at-large. Strives to make known the impact of the eye/vision dysfunction on the effectiveness and productivity of citizens and the academic proficiency of students. Conducts national minority recruiting programs, job placement, assistance programs for graduates, practitioners, and optometric organizations, and the promotion of delivery of care. Maintains speakers' bureau. Offers specialized education program. **Awards:** Cave Award. **Frequency:** annual. **Type:** recognition ● Founder's Award. **Frequency:** annual. **Type:** recognition ● Optometrist of the Year. **Frequency:** annual. **Type:** recognition. **Computer Services:** Mailing lists. **Affiliated With:** American Optometric Association; National Health Council. **Publications:** Newsletter, semiannual. **Price:** free. **Circulation:** 500. **Advertising:** accepted. Alternate Formats: online. **Conventions/Meetings:** annual convention (exhibits) - usually July.

15398 ■ National Optometry Association (NOA)
PO Box 35215
Chicago, IL 60707-0215
Ph: (708)453-0080
Fax: (708)453-0083
E-mail: noa@rentamark.com
Founded: 1975. **Members:** 68,786. **Membership Dues:** individual, $25 (annual) ● business, $100 (annual) ● corporate sponsor, $250 (annual). **Staff:** 10. **Description:** Optometrists. Seeks to increase members' public visibility and professional influence. Provides members with further education and recommends books to help the profession. Provides benefits. **Libraries: Type:** not open to the public. **Holdings:** 10,000. **Subjects:** optometry. **Computer Services:** Mailing lists. **Publications:** *NOA-E Journal*, monthly. Alternate Formats: online.

15399 ■ Optometric Extension Program Foundation (OEPF)
1921 E Carnegie Ave., Ste.3L
Santa Ana, CA 92705-5510
Ph: (949)250-8070
Fax: (949)250-8157
E-mail: smc.oep@worldnet.att.net
URL: http://www.healthy.net/oep
Contact: Beverly A. Roberts, Pres.
Founded: 1928. **Members:** 4,000. **Membership Dues:** individual, $275 (annual). **Staff:** 12. **Description:** Represents registered optometrists and optometric assistants enrolled for continuing education courses. Maintains speakers' bureau. Sponsors educational programs. **Libraries: Type:** reference. **Holdings:** 2,000; archival material, audiovisuals, books, monographs, periodicals. **Subjects:** behavioral optometry. **Awards: Type:** recognition. **Additional Websites:** http://www.oep.org. **Telecommunication Services:** electronic mail, beverleyroberts@oep.org. **Departments:** Continuing Education; Optometry Student Services; Paraoptometrics; Public Education; Research. **Publications:** *Journal of Behavioral Optometry*, bimonthly. Includes professional articles, calendar of events, and current affairs. **Price:** $65.00/year. ISSN: 1045-8395. **Circulation:** 4,000. **Advertising:** accepted ● *Optometric Extension Program Foundation—Curriculum II*, annual. Covers text of 6-8 courses on various optometry subjects. Includes literature and research reviews and annual index. **Price:** $350.00. **Circulation:** 2,000 ● *Reference Directory*, biennial ● Pamphlets ● Booklets ● Videos. **Conventions/Meetings:** Graduate Clinical Seminar ● biennial Leadership Conference ● regional meeting and congress ● seminar, provides visual training.

15400 ■ Optometric Historical Society (OHS)
243 N Lindbergh Blvd.
St. Louis, MO 63141
Free: (800)365-2219
Fax: (314)991-4101
E-mail: ilovesylvan@bellsouth.net
URL: http://www.opt.indiana.edu/ohs/optohiso.html
Contact: Melvin Wolfberg, Pres.
Founded: 1969. **Membership Dues:** regular, $25 (annual) ● patron, $50 (annual). **Description:** Represents optometrists and other individuals or groups interested in optometry, optics, and related disciplines. Encourages the collection and preservation of materials relating to the history of optometry. Assists in the care of archives of optometric interest. **Awards: Type:** recognition. **Publications:** *Hindsight*, quarterly. Newsletter. **Conventions/Meetings:** annual meeting - always December.

15401 ■ Tear Film and Ocular Surface Society (TFOS)
PO Box 130146
Boston, MA 02113
E-mail: amy@tearfilm.org
URL: http://www.tearfilm.org
Contact: Amy G. Sullivan, Exec. Dir.
Founded: 2000. **Members:** 500. **Membership Dues:** full, $120 (annual) ● student, fellow, $30 (annual). **Multinational. Description:** Advances the research, literacy and educational aspects of the scientific field of tear film and ocular surface. Promotes a better understanding of the study of the tear film and ocular surface. Stimulates interaction among members and seeks to attract possible memberships from other professionals with diverse interests and expertise. **Awards:** TFOS Travel Award. **Frequency:** annual. **Type:** monetary. **Recipient:** to a postdoctoral fellow, graduate student or young investigator whose abstract demonstrates significant scientific achievement ● TFOS Travel Fellowship. **Frequency:** annual. **Type:** monetary. **Recipient:** to a graduate student or a postdoctoral fellow involved in a primary research activity related to tear film and ocular surface. **Publications:** *The Ocular Surface*, quarterly. Journal. Contains major reviews of important work in Laboratory Science, Clinical Science and Clinical Practice. **Price:** $149.00 individual in U.S. and Canada; $229.00 institution in U.S. and Canada; $185.00 individual outside U.S. and Canada; $269.00 institu-

tion outside U.S. and Canada. **Advertising:** accepted. Alternate Formats: online. **Conventions/ Meetings:** triennial international conference - 2007 Sept. 5-8, Sicily, Italy.

15402 ■ Vision USA
243 N Lindbergh Blvd.
St. Louis, MO 63141-7881
Free: (800)766-4466
Fax: (314)991-4101
E-mail: visionusa@aoa.org
URL: http://www.aoa.org/x5607.xml
Contact: Gen. Colin L. Powell, Founding Chm.
Founded: 1991. **Description:** Commits to help low-income, uninsured working Americans and their families who have no other means of obtaining care, by providing basic eye health and vision care services free of charge. Services are given to individuals who have a job or live in a household where there is one member working at least part-time, have no insurance that covers eye exams, not have had an eye exam within the past 24 months, and have income below an established level based on household size. **Affiliated With:** American Optometric Association; Connecticut Association of Optometrists.

15403 ■ World Council of Optometry (WCO)
8360 Old York Rd., 4th Fl. W
Elkins Park, PA 19027
Ph: (215)780-1320
Fax: (215)780-1325
E-mail: wco@pco.edu
URL: http://www.worldoptometry.org
Contact: Ms. Melissa Padilla, Exec. Dir.
Founded: 1927. **Members:** 84. **Staff:** 3. **Regional Groups:** 3. **National Groups:** 54. **Description:** National optical and optometric organizations in 60 countries. Promotes optometry and vision care worldwide. Works to develop optometry through education, legal and legislative advice, discussion with authorities, and support of similar associations. Is concerned with protecting optometry from what the league sees as proposed restrictive legislation, and apathy toward the profession. Establishes educational standards; offers evaluation program for schools and colleges of optometry; provides consulting services. **Awards:** International Optometrist of the Year Award. **Frequency:** annual. **Type:** recognition ● IOOL Medal. **Frequency:** annual. **Type:** medal. **Committees:** Education; Future Planning; International Contact Lens Body; Legal and Legislative; Optometric Development; Publicity. **Affiliated With:** American Optometric Association. **Publications:** *International Country Contact Register*, periodic. Directory ● *Interoptics*, quarterly. Newsletter ● *Members' Journals*, periodic ● *Optometric Mailing Directory*, periodic. Lists information on optometric organizations. ● *Publications List*, periodic ● *Register of Schools and Colleges of Optometry*, periodic. Directory ● Brochure, periodic. **Conventions/Meetings:** annual General Delegates Meeting - conference and symposium - always spring ● annual seminar.

Oral and Maxillofacial Surgery

15404 ■ American Association of Oral and Maxillofacial Surgeons (AAOMS)
9700 W Bryn Mawr Ave.
Rosemont, IL 60018-5701
Ph: (847)678-6200
Free: (800)822-6637
Fax: (847)678-6286
E-mail: inquiries@aaoms.org
URL: http://www.aaoms.org
Contact: Dr. Robert Rinaldi, Sec.
Founded: 1918. **Members:** 8,000. **Staff:** 50. **Budget:** $9,000,000. **Regional Groups:** 9. **State Groups:** 51. **Description:** Oral surgeons and dentists specializing in disease diagnosis and surgical, adjunctive and esthetic treatment of diseases, injuries, and defects of the oral and maxillofacial region (jaw deformities, dental implants, infections and oral cancer). **Awards:** Committeeman of the Year. **Frequency:** annual. **Type:** recognition ● Distinguished Service Award.

Type: recognition ● **Frequency:** annual. **Type:** fellowship. **Recipient:** for research ● **Type:** fellowship. **Recipient:** for clinical surgery ● **Type:** Foundation Fellowship. **Type:** fellowship ● **Frequency:** annual. **Type:** grant. **Recipient:** for two qualified individual ● **Frequency:** annual. **Type:** monetary. **Recipient:** for five outstanding research ($1000 each) ● **Frequency:** annual. **Type:** recognition. **Recipient:** for research. **Computer Services:** Mailing lists, oral surgery continuing education. **Committees:** Anesthesia; Coding and Nomenclature; Governmental Affairs; Health Care Programs; Hospital Affairs; Political Action; Practice Management; Professional Conduct; Public Information; Research; Residency Education and Training; Scientific Sessions. **Divisions:** Communication; Development; Education; Government Relations; Health Care Delivery. **Formerly:** (1944) American Society of Exodontists; (1977) American Society of Oral Surgeons. **Publications:** *AAOMS Forum*, quarterly ● *AAOMS Today*, bimonthly. Newsletter. Contains association news and events. **Circulation:** 8,000. **Advertising:** accepted. Alternate Formats: online ● *Journal of Oral Maxillofacial Surgery*, monthly ● *Office Anesthesia Evaluation Manual* ● *Report of Annual Meeting* ● *Surgical Update*, 3/year ● Directory, annual ● Annual Report. **Conventions/Meetings:** annual conference (exhibits) - midwinter ● annual Scientific Session - conference (exhibits).

15405 ■ American Board of Oral and Maxillofacial Surgery (ABOMS)
625 N Michigan Ave., Ste.1820
Chicago, IL 60611
Ph: (312)642-0070
Fax: (312)642-8584
E-mail: aenriquez@aboms.org
URL: http://www.aboms.org
Contact: Mr. Alex Enriquez, Admin. Asst.
Founded: 1946. **Members:** 3,580. **Membership Dues:** regular, $100 (annual). **Staff:** 3. **Description:** Establishes qualifications, conducts examinations, and certifies surgeons whom the board finds qualified to practice oral and maxillofacial surgery, including diagnostic, surgical, and adjunctive treatment of the diseases, injuries, and defects of the oral and maxillofacial regions. **Affiliated With:** American Association of Oral and Maxillofacial Surgeons; American Dental Association. **Formerly:** (1978) American Board of Oral Surgery. **Conventions/Meetings:** annual meeting.

15406 ■ American College of Oral and Maxillofacial Surgeons (ACOMS)
2025 M St., NW
Washington, DC 20036
Ph: (202)367-1182
Free: (800)522-6676
Fax: (202)367-2182
E-mail: acoms@smithbucklin.com
URL: http://www.acoms.org
Contact: Brian Lagana, Exec. Dir.
Founded: 1975. **Members:** 2,500. **Membership Dues:** individual, $295 (annual). **Staff:** 2. **Budget:** $500,000. **Multinational. Description:** Diplomates of the American Board of Oral and Maxillofacial Surgery who practice oral and maxillofacial surgery. Aims to advance the integrity of the profession through continuing education, exchange of ideas, certification procedures, and cooperation with allied groups. **Libraries: Type:** reference. **Holdings:** archival material, periodicals. **Awards:** Humanitarian Award. **Frequency:** annual. **Type:** recognition. **Recipient:** for individual accomplishments ● W. Harry Archer Award. **Frequency:** annual. **Type:** recognition. **Recipient:** for individual accomplishments. **Committees:** Bylaws; Communications; Continuing Education; Nominating; Research, Education and Humanitarian Foundation. **Affiliated With:** American Board of Oral and Maxillofacial Surgery. **Formerly:** (1975) Association of Diplomates of the American Board of Oral Surgery. **Publications:** *The Archives of Oral and Maxillofacial Surgery*, quarterly. Journal. Alternate Formats: online; CD-ROM. **Conventions/Meetings:** annual Cosmetic Surgery - symposium ● annual Scientific Meeting - conference (exhibits).

15407 ■ American Society of Maxillofacial Surgeons (ASMS)
444 E Algonquin Rd.
Arlington Heights, IL 60005
Ph: (847)228-3338
Free: (800)849-4682
Fax: (847)849-4682
E-mail: admin@maxface.org
URL: http://www.maxface.org
Contact: Peggy O'Carroll, Admin. Mgr.
Founded: 1947. **Members:** 475. **Membership Dues:** active, senior, international, honorary and associate, $350 (annual). **Staff:** 1. **Description:** Professional society of doctors of medicine and doctors of dental surgery who have at least five years of recognized graduate training and experience in maxillofacial surgery. Seeks to stimulate and advance knowledge of the science and art of maxillofacial surgery and improve and elevate the standard of practice. **Awards:** Research Grant Awards. **Frequency:** annual. **Type:** monetary. **Telecommunication Services:** electronic mail, po@plasticsurgery.org. **Publications:** *Maxillofacial News*, quarterly. Newsletter. **Circulation:** 500. **Advertising:** accepted. **Conventions/Meetings:** annual conference and meeting (exhibits) - always in September or October.

15408 ■ International Association of Oral and Maxillofacial Surgeons (IAOMS)
17 W 220 22nd St., Ste.420
Oakbrook Terrace, IL 60181
Ph: (630)833-0945
Fax: (630)833-1382
E-mail: info@iaoms.org
URL: http://www.iaoms.org
Contact: Dr. John F. Helfrick, Exec. Dir.
Founded: 1965. **Members:** 4,000. **Membership Dues:** trainee, $75 (annual) ● fellow, $150 (annual) ● associate, $150 (annual). **Staff:** 1. **National Groups:** 63. **Description:** Seeks to improve the quality of healthcare worldwide through the advancement of patient care, education, and research in oral and maxillofacial surgery. **Computer Services:** Mailing lists, of members. **Foreign language name:** Association Internationale de Chirurgie Buccale et Maxillo-Faciale. **Publications:** *International Journal of Oral and Maxillofacial Surgery*, bimonthly. **Advertising:** accepted ● *Registry of Fellows* ● *Rules and Regulations of the IAOMS* ● Newsletter, semiannual. **Conventions/Meetings:** biennial International Conference of Oral and Maxillofacial Surgeons (exhibits).

15409 ■ Uplift Internationale
PO Box 582
Wheat Ridge, CO 80034
Ph: (303)707-1361
E-mail: info@upliftinternationale.org
URL: http://www.upliftinternationale.org
Contact: Jaime Yrastorza DMD, Pres.
Founded: 1989. **Multinational. Description:** Aims to give a life-changing gift to children with facial deformities by mending faces. Recruits healthcare and support personnel who are willing to share their expertise and provide care to indigent children in rural Philippines. **Projects:** Operation Taghoy. **Publications:** Newsletter. Alternate Formats: online.

Orgonomy

15410 ■ American College of Orgonomy (ACO)
PO Box 490
Princeton, NJ 08542
Ph: (732)821-1144
Fax: (732)821-0174
E-mail: aco@orgonomy.org
URL: http://www.orgonomy.org
Contact: Dr. Gary A. Karpf MD, Pres.
Founded: 1968. **Members:** 12. **Staff:** 2. **Description:** Represents physicians and social scientists seeking to promote and advance the science of orgonomy. (Orgonomy is derived from the theory formulated by Wilhelm Reich, M.D. "that all space is filled with a specific form of energy called orgone

energy which accounts for life and living functions.") Provides training in medical orgonomy and character analysis for physicians. Sponsors training and research for physicians and scientists in orgone physics, orgone biology, and weather control. Holds laboratory workshops for physicians and scientists. Offers referral service. Conducts specialized education. **Libraries: Type:** reference. **Holdings:** 1,000. **Subjects:** medical and social orgonomy, education, psychiatry. **Awards: Type:** recognition. **Computer Services:** Mailing lists ● online services. **Committees:** Ethics and Credentials; Executive; Public Education; Publications; Referral Service; Research; Training and Education; Weather Control. **Publications:** *Journal of Orgonomy,* semiannual. Contains articles on scientific topics related to Orgonomy, socio-political and case studies. **Price:** $40.00/year, in U.S.; $45.00/year, outside U.S., surface rate; $55.00/year, outside U.S. and Canada, airmail. **Circulation:** 500 ● *Man in the Trap.* Book. **Price:** $24.95 paperback ● *Orgonomic Medicine* ● Booklets. **Conventions/Meetings:** annual conference and seminar, presentations and panel discussions on recent work in orgonomy - usually first Sunday in October or last weekend in September.

Oriental Healing

15411 ■ Accreditation Commission for Acupuncture and Oriental Medicine (ACAOM)
7501 Greenway Ctr. Dr., Ste.820
Greenbelt, MD 20770
Ph: (301)313-0855
Fax: (301)313-0912
E-mail: dort.bigg@acaom.org
URL: http://www.acaom.org
Contact: Dort S. Bigg JD, Exec. Dir.
Founded: 1982. **Members:** 51. **Staff:** 6. **Budget:** $450,000. **Description:** Acts as an independent body to evaluate first professional master's degree and first professional master's level certificate and diploma programs in acupuncture and in Oriental medicine with concentrations in both acupuncture and herbal therapy for a level of performance, integrity and quality that entitles them to the confidence of the educational community and the public they serve. Evaluates doctoral programs in oriental medicine. Establishes accreditation criteria, arranges site visits, evaluates those programs that desire accredited status and publicly designates those programs that meet the criteria. **Formerly:** (1998) National Accreditation Commission for Schools and Colleges of Acupuncture and Oriental Medicine. **Publications:** *Accreditation Handbook.* **Price:** $40.00 ● *Acupuncture and Oriental Medicine Accreditation,* semiannual. Newsletter. Contains flow of information, policies and procedures among educators, practitioners and state legislatures. **Price:** free. **Circulation:** 1,100. Alternate Formats: online ● Brochure ● Manuals. **Conventions/Meetings:** semiannual meeting - usually May and November.

15412 ■ American Academy of Medical Acupuncture (AAMA)
4929 Wilshire Blvd., Ste.428
Los Angeles, CA 90010
Ph: (323)937-5514
Fax: (323)937-0959
E-mail: jdowden@prodigy.net
URL: http://www.medicalacupuncture.org
Contact: C. James Dowden, Exec. Administrator
Founded: 1987. **Members:** 1,830. **Membership Dues:** student, $75 (annual) ● affiliate, international affiliate, $125 (annual) ● full, associate, $300 (annual). **Staff:** 4. **Budget:** $1,000,000. **State Groups:** 8. **Description:** Professional society of physicians and osteopaths who utilize acupuncture in their practices. Provides ongoing training and information related to the Chinese practice of puncturing the body at specific points to cure disease or relieve pain. Offers educational and research programs. **Committees:** ABMA Examination; Budget; Continuing Education; Investment; Medical Acupuncture Advisory; Review Course; Volunteer and Activism. **Publica-**

tions: *Medical Acupuncture,* 3/year. Journal. ISSN: 1050-5695. **Circulation:** 4,000. **Advertising:** accepted ● Newsletter, bimonthly. Provides news and information regarding legislative, regulatory and practice developments in acupuncture. Alternate Formats: online. **Conventions/Meetings:** annual symposium and trade show (exhibits).

15413 ■ American Acupuncture Association (AAA)
4262 Kissena Blvd.
Flushing, NY 11355
Ph: (718)886-4431 (212)752-9227
Fax: (718)463-0808
Contact: Dr. David P.J. Hung, Chm.
Founded: 1972. **Members:** 400. **Description:** Physicians, nurses, acupuncturists, physical therapists, and herbologists. Promotes acceptance of acupuncture as a viable medical method. Works to legalize acupuncture on the state level. Offers continuing education course. Maintains speakers' bureau. Conducts lectures to educate public on acupuncture. **Publications:** *Journal of Chinese Acupuncture,* annual. **Conventions/Meetings:** annual meeting - always December, New York City ● monthly symposium.

15414 ■ American Association of Oriental Medicine (AAOM)
PO Box 162340
Sacramento, CA 95816
Ph: (916)443-4770
Free: (866)455-7999
Fax: (916)443-4766
E-mail: info@aaom.org
URL: http://www.aaom.org
Contact: Leslie McGee RN, Pres.
Founded: 1981. **Members:** 2,600. **Membership Dues:** joint professional, $200 (annual) ● student, friend of OM, $50 (annual) ● practitioner, $100-$250 (annual) ● professional practitioner, allied professional and organization, $250 (annual) ● professional partnership, $225 (annual) ● school of OM, general business, $450 (annual). **Staff:** 6. **Budget:** $1,500,000. **Regional Groups:** 32. **State Groups:** 32. **Languages:** Chinese, English. **Multinational. Description:** Professional acupuncturists and Oriental Medicine Practitioners. Seeks to: elevate the standards of education and practice of acupuncture and oriental medicine; establish laws governing acupuncture; provide a forum to share information on acupuncture techniques; increase public awareness of acupuncture; support research in the field. Conducts educational programs; compiles statistics. Operates speakers' bureau. **Libraries: Type:** open to the public. **Subjects:** acupuncture, oriental medicine or complimentary medicine. **Awards:** Acupuncture Patient of the Year. **Frequency:** annual. **Type:** recognition ● Acupuncturist of the Year. **Frequency:** annual. **Type:** recognition ● Legislator of the Year. **Frequency:** annual. **Type:** recognition. **Computer Services:** Mailing lists. **Committees:** Ethics; Fundraising; Herbal Medicine; Insurance; Policies and Procedures; Public Health; Research/IRB; State Association. **Formerly:** (1996) American Association for Acupuncture and Oriental Medicine. **Publications:** *American Acupuncturist Newsletter,* semiannual. Contains political and educational news and information. **Circulation:** 1,600. **Advertising:** accepted ● *American Acupuncturist Update,* quarterly. Newsletter. Contains political and educational news and info. **Circulation:** 1,200. **Advertising:** accepted. Alternate Formats: online ● Membership Directory, annual. Contains listing of U.S. acupuncture and oriental medicine practitioners. **Price:** $12.00/copy. **Circulation:** 1,600. **Advertising:** accepted. Alternate Formats: online; CD-ROM. **Conventions/Meetings:** semiannual board meeting, with concurrent education meetings (exhibits) ● annual conference, membership convention, meetings, training (exhibits).

15415 ■ Council of Colleges of Acupuncture and Oriental Medicine (CCAOM)
3909 Natl. Dr., Ste.125
Burtonsville, MD 20866
Ph: (301)476-7790

Fax: (301)476-7792
E-mail: ccaomcnt@verizon.net
URL: http://www.ccaom.org
Contact: David M. Sale JD, Exec. Dir.
Founded: 1982. **Members:** 51. **Staff:** 2. **Description:** Represents acupuncture and oriental medicine colleges. Aims to advance the status of acupuncture and oriental medicine through educational programs. Works to provide high-quality classroom and clinical instruction. Promotes the improvement of research and teaching methods. **Formerly:** (1992) National Council of Acupuncture Schools and Colleges. **Publications:** Newsletter, annual. Alternate Formats: online. **Conventions/Meetings:** semiannual meeting.

15416 ■ East West Academy of Healing Arts (EWAHA)
117 Topaz Way
San Francisco, CA 94131
Ph: (415)285-9400
Fax: (415)647-5745
E-mail: eastwestqi@aol.com
URL: http://www.eastwestqi.com
Contact: Dr. Effie Chow, Founder
Founded: 1973. **Staff:** 3. **Description:** Promotes holistic health, Qigong, and Oriental medicine. Sponsors educational and research programs; provides clinical services.

15417 ■ G-Jo Institute
PO Box 1460
Columbus, NC 28722-1460
Ph: (828)863-4660
Free: (800)747-0306
Fax: (828)863-4575
E-mail: office@g-jo.com
URL: http://www.g-jo.com
Contact: Michael Blate, Exec. Dir.
Founded: 1976. **Members:** 3,000. **Description:** People interested in "self-health" techniques that are natural, require no drugs or medications, and are based on traditional Oriental healing philosophies, especially acupuncture and acupressure. Aims to promote the use of self-health techniques. Makes available charts and teaching guides. Provides classes in self-health methods and natural (vegetarian) cooking. Conducts radio program and research on natural health and healing. Sponsors Vegetarian Gourmet Society; Institute derives name from G-Jo, the easiest form of acupressure. **Libraries: Type:** reference. **Holdings:** 5,000. **Publications:** *Advanced G-Jo Training.* Manual. Contains the unique, virtually unknown method for balancing the inner organs and glands. ● *Basic G-Jo Training.* Video. Contains step-by-step through finding and triggering some of the most powerful and broad-acting Basic G-Jo Points. ● Newsletter, periodic. Explains how and when to use a specific G-Jo acupressure point. Alternate Formats: online ● Publishes self-health reports. **Conventions/Meetings:** seminar ● workshop.

15418 ■ Jin Shin Do Foundation for Bodymind Acupressure (JSDF)
PO Box 416
Idyllwild, CA 92549
Ph: (951)659-5707
Fax: (951)659-5707
E-mail: teegers@earthlink.net
URL: http://www.jinshindo.org
Contact: Iona Marsaa Teeguarden MA, Exec. Dir.
Founded: 1982. **Members:** 2,000. **Membership Dues:** teacher, $100 (annual) ● practitioner, $50 (annual) ● student, $7 (annual). **Staff:** 2. **Languages:** English, French, German, Italian. **Multinational. Description:** A referral and educational organization of teachers and practitioners of the Jin Shin Do acupressure method. (Jin Shin Do acupressure integrates a traditional Japanese acupressure technique with classical Chinese acu-theory, Taoist philosophy and Qigong breathing exercises, and Western psychology.) Outlines tension points associated with common physical problems and distressing feelings, and teaches points and exercises that help release physical and emotional tensions. Conducts continuing education classes, practicums, and workshops for students. **Computer Services:** database. **Affiliated**

With: American Organization for Bodywork Therapies of Asia. **Publications:** *A Complete Guide to Acupressure.* Book. **Price:** $29.00 ● *Acupressure News* (in English, French, German, and Italian), annual. Newsletter. Contains general association information; claps catalog; product catalog. **Price:** $2.50. **Circulation:** 5,000. Alternate Formats: online ● *The Acupressure Way of Health: Jin Shin Do.* Book. **Price:** $17.00 ● *Directory of Registered Practitioners and Authorized Teachers*, annual. Includes listing of authorized basic, intermediate, and advanced teachers. **Price:** $1.00 ● *Fundamentals of Self-Acupressure.* Booklet. **Price:** $6.00 ● *Joy of Feeling: Bodymind Acupressure.* Book. **Price:** $26.00 ● *JSD Strange Flows Wall Chart.* **Price:** $10.00. **Conventions/ Meetings:** periodic meeting.

15419 ■ National Certification Commission for Acupuncture and Oriental Medicine (NCCAOM)
76 S Laura St., Ste.1290
Jacksonville, FL 32202
Ph: (904)598-1005
Fax: (904)598-5001
E-mail: info@nccaom.org
URL: http://www.nccaom.org
Contact: Dr. Kory Ward-Cook, CEO
Founded: 1982. **Members:** 13,000. **Staff:** 18. **Budget:** $2,500,000. **Description:** Serves as national certification agency for practitioners of acupuncture, Chinese herbology, and Asian bodywork therapy in the United States. Establishes and maintains standards of competence for the safe and effective practice of Oriental medicine; to evaluate an applicant's qualifications in relation to these established standards through the administration of national board examinations; to certify practitioners who meet these standards. Acts as a consultant to state agencies in regulation, certification, and licensing of the practice of acupuncture and Oriental medicine. **Computer Services:** Online services, publication. **Formerly:** (1997) National Commission for the Certification of Acupuncturists. **Publications:** *The Diplomate*, semiannual. Newsletter. **Advertising:** accepted. Alternate Formats: online ● *NCCAOM Directory of Diplomates*, annual. Alternate Formats: online. **Conventions/Meetings:** Examinations - meeting - 3/year.

15420 ■ Ohashi Institute (OI)
147 W 25th St., 6th Fl.
New York, NY 10001
Ph: (646)486-1187
Free: (800)810-4190
Fax: (646)486-1409
E-mail: info@ohashiatsu.org
URL: http://www.ohashiatsu.org
Contact: Wataru Ohashi, Dir.
Founded: 1974. **Staff:** 64. **State Groups:** 4. **National Groups:** 30. **Languages:** English, Japanese. **For-Profit. Description:** Dedicated to the promotion and teaching of the Oriental healing arts, specifically Ohashiatsu - a method of bodywork that elevates traditional Japanese shiatsu to a more complete experience of self-development and healing to promote health of body, mind and spirit. Program focuses on expanding awareness of self and others through the use of exercise, meditation and touch techniques based on Oriental healing philosophies. Courses for both laypeople and professionals in beginning, intermediate, advanced and post-graduate Ohashiatsu are offered. Instructor certification program available. Operates programs in the United States, South America and Europe. **Formerly:** (1983) Shiatsu Education Center of America. **Publications:** *The Art of Ohashi Series.* Video. Sold only as a set of 4: Front & Back, Side Position, Seated Position, The Neck. ● *Beyond Shiatsu: Ohashi's Bodywork Method.* Book. **Price:** $19.95 ● *Do-It-Yourself Shiatsu, How to Perform the Ancient Japanese Art of Acupressure.* Book. **Price:** $18.00 ● *Facelift & Vital Eyes.* Video. For skincare professionals. **Price:** $39.95 ● *Healthy Hair.* Video. For hairstylists. **Price:** $39.95 ● *Natural Childbirth, the Eastern Way, A Healthy Pregnancy and Delivery Through Shiatsu.* Book. Contains fully illustrated step-by-step exercises to use alone or in conjunction with Lamaze and other

Western childbirth methods. **Price:** $15.00 ● *Ohashiatsu.* Video. For pregnant women. **Price:** $39.00 ● *Ohashiatsu News.* Newsletter ● *Reading the Body: Ohashi's Book of Oriental Diagnosis.* **Price:** $21.00 ● *Touch For Love: Shiatsu For Your Baby.* Book. Features step-by-step guides through the world of touch. **Price:** $15.00 ● *Ultimate Relaxation.* Video. For spa professionals. **Price:** $39.95 ● *Zen Shiatsu, How to Harmonize Yin and Yang for Better Health.* Book.

Orthopedics

15421 ■ AAMED - The American Association of Multiple Enchondroma Diseases
357 Redwood Rd.
Venice, FL 34293
Ph: (941)492-5117
E-mail: aameddirector@aol.com
URL: http://www.aamed.net
Contact: Susan Challen, CEO/Natl. Dir. of Research
Founded: 1998. **Members:** 500. **Membership Dues:** donation, $25 (annual). **Staff:** 25. **State Groups:** 1. **Local Groups:** 1. **Languages:** English, German. **Multinational. Description:** Assists persons afflicted with Multiple Enchondroma Disease - Ollier's Disease, Maffucci's Syndrome. Provides news and information, research participation, a message board, and other services. Disseminates information on conditions and/or diseases associated with multiple enchondromatosis including chondrosarcoma. **Libraries: Type:** reference. **Holdings:** articles, video recordings. **Subjects:** Olliers disease, Maffucci Syndrome. **Formerly:** (1998) Ollier's Disease Self-Help Group; (2004) Ollier's/Maffucci Self-Help Group. **Publications:** *The ABC's of Multiple Enchondromatosis.* Booklets. **Price:** $3.00 ● *Baby in a Frame (Ilizarov Fixation).* Videos. **Price:** $5.00.

15422 ■ Academic Orthopaedic Society (AOS)
6300 N River Rd., Ste.505
Rosemont, IL 60018-4262
Ph: (847)823-7186
Fax: (847)823-8125
E-mail: hackett@aaos.org
URL: http://www.aaos.org
Contact: Karen L. Hackett, CEO
Founded: 1971. **Description:** Chairpersons and faculty members of orthopedic departments and divisions of medical schools; directors of orthopedic residency programs; fellowship directors. Provides forum for discussion of administrative and departmental problems concerning undergraduate and graduate orthopedics education in medical schools. Coordinates and plans activities requiring cooperation between orthopedic departments and residencies. Acts as liaison between orthopedic organizations and organizations interested in medical education. **Formerly:** (1989) Association of Orthopaedic Chairmen; (1991) American Orthopaedic Society. **Publications:** *Presidential Newsletter*, semiannual ● *Directory*, annual. **Conventions/Meetings:** annual conference, held in conjunction with the Association of American Medical Colleges.

15423 ■ American Academy of Craniofacial Pain (AACP)
516 W Pipeline Rd.
Hurst, TX 76053
Ph: (817)282-1501
Free: (800)322-8651
Fax: (817)282-8012
E-mail: central@aacfp.org
URL: http://www.aacfp.org
Contact: Cordelia Mason, Exec. Dir.
Founded: 1985. **Members:** 525. **Membership Dues:** regular, $300 (annual). **Staff:** 2. **Description:** Health Care Practitioners who treat head, facial, and neck pain. Functions as a referral service for patients suffering from head, facial, and neck pain worldwide. Plans to establish computerized medical procedures and insurance database. **Formerly:** (2005) American Academy of Head, Neck and Facial Pain. **Publica-

tions:** *CRANIO: The Journal of Temporomandibular Practice.* **Price:** free, for members only ● *TMDiary*, semiannual. Journal. **Price:** free, for members only. Alternate Formats: online ● *Membership Directory*, periodic. **Circulation:** 6,000. **Advertising:** accepted. **Conventions/Meetings:** annual lecture (exhibits).

15424 ■ American Academy of Orthopaedic Surgeons (AAOS)
6300 N River Rd.
Rosemont, IL 60018-4262
Ph: (847)823-7186
Free: (800)346-AAOS
Fax: (847)823-8125
E-mail: custserv@aaos.org
URL: http://www.aaos.org
Contact: James H. Beaty MD, Pres.
Founded: 1933. **Members:** 26,000. **Membership Dues:** fellow, $750 (annual) ● candidate, international affiliate, $350 (annual). **Staff:** 234. **Budget:** $41,000,000. **Multinational. Description:** Promotes the highest quality musculoskeletal health, the interests of all patients, the profession of orthopedics, and unity and collaboration among all orthopedic organizations through education, health services research, advocacy, support of academic orthopedics and communication. Promotes physician education and skills enhancement by offering textbooks, clinical videotapes, courses and self-assessment exams. **Libraries: Type:** reference. **Holdings:** 500; periodicals. **Awards:** Diversity Award. **Frequency:** annual. **Type:** monetary. **Recipient:** for significant contributions to advancing diversity in orthopedics through recruiting, mentoring, leadership and the treatment of diverse populations ● Humanitarian Award. **Frequency:** annual. **Type:** monetary. **Recipient:** for achievements in public service related to orthopaedic health care ● Kappa Delta. **Frequency:** annual. **Type:** monetary. **Recipient:** for achievements in orthopaedic research. **Additional Websites:** http://orthoinfo.aaos.org. **Telecommunication Services:** information service, fax on demand ● information service, listservs. **Councils:** Academic Affairs; Communications; Education; Health, Policy and Practice; Research and Scientific Affairs. **Absorbed:** (1993) Advisory Council for Orthopedic Resident Education. **Publications:** *AAOS Report*, monthly. Newsletter ● *Academy News*, annual. Newspaper. Released during annual meeting. **Advertising:** accepted ● *Arthroscopic Meniscal Repair Monograph.* Contains proper preparation, technique and new suturing tools for procedure. **Price:** $50.00 for nonmembers, resident; $40.00 for members, resident ● *Arthroscopy Brochures* (in English and Spanish). Features techniques and details the advantage of this popular surgical procedure. **Price:** $43.00 ● *Bulletin*, bimonthly. Magazine. **Advertising:** accepted ● *Journal of the American Academy of Orthopaedic Surgeons: A Comprehensive Review* (in English, Italian, Spanish, and Turkish), monthly. Contains peer-reviewed articles focused on clinical diagnosis and management. **Price:** included in membership dues; $185.00 /year for individuals in U.S.; $310.00 /year for institutions in U.S.; $90.00/year for residents. ISSN: 1067-151X. **Circulation:** 29,000. **Advertising:** accepted. Alternate Formats: online; CD-ROM ● *Knee Arthroscopy Patient Education.* Booklet. Contains treatment-specific information. **Price:** $2.50 ● *Orthopaedic Medical Legal Advisor*, quarterly. Newsletter ● *Patient Safety Update*, quarterly. Newsletter. Electronic. **Conventions/Meetings:** annual meeting, business meeting, affiliate meetings, scientific paper/poster presentations, scientific and technical exhibits (exhibits) - 2008 Mar. 5-9, San Francisco, CA; 2009 Feb. 25-Mar. 1, Las Vegas, NV.

15425 ■ American Association of Orthopedic Medicine (AAOM)
600 Pembrook Dr.
Woodland Park, CO 80863
Free: (800)992-2063
Fax: (719)687-5184
E-mail: aaom@aaomed.org
URL: http://www.aaomed.org
Contact: Maelu Fleck, Exec. Dir.
Founded: 1982. **Members:** 450. **Membership Dues:** active, $275 (annual) ● allied, $185 (annual) ● intern/

resident, $15 (annual) ● student, $75 (annual). **Budget:** $180,000. **Description:** Represents physicians and allied health professionals interested in the advancement of knowledge, diagnosis, and nonsurgical treatment of musculoskeletal and related disorders. Seeks to: advance the standards of practice and quality of service in the field of orthopedic medicine; unite the common interests and skills of medicine and osteopathy; serve as a forum of learning for all of the specialties that deal with pain and dysfunction in the neural, muscular, skeletal, and vascular systems. Encourages research and the dissemination of results. Provides training and continuing medical education in orthopedic medicine; conducts regional seminars every two to three months. **Awards:** AAOM Lifetime Achievement Award. **Frequency:** annual. **Type:** recognition. **Recipient:** for a member having lifetime work contribution to the AAOM and to Orthopaedic Medicine. **Committees:** Clinical and Educational Research; Liaison; Medical Practice; Public Relations. **Supersedes:** Prolotherapy Association. **Publications:** *AAOM Membership Directory*, annual ● *AAOM News*, quarterly. Newsletter ● *The Journal of Orthopaedic Medicine*, 3/year. Contains scientific papers and articles, editorials, and book reviews. **Price:** included in membership dues. **Advertising:** accepted. **Conventions/Meetings:** annual meeting and seminar (exhibits).

15426 ■ American Back Society (ABS)
2647 Intl. Blvd., Ste.401
Oakland, CA 94601
Ph: (510)536-9929
Fax: (510)536-1812
E-mail: info@americanbacksoc.org
URL: http://www.americanbacksoc.org
Contact: Scott Haldeman MD, Pres.
Founded: 1982. **Membership Dues:** licensed health care professional, $225 ● non-licensed health care professional, attorney, health organization, $125 ● student, $25. **Description:** Orthopedic and neurological surgeons, physical therapists, chiropractors, and other health care professionals with an interest in back and spinal health. Promotes continuing professional development of members; seeks to advance the prevention, diagnosis, and treatment of back and spinal disorders. Serves as a clearinghouse on spinal health; sponsors research and educational programs; facilitates exchange of information among members.

15427 ■ American Board of Orthopaedic Surgery (ABOS)
400 Silver Cedar Ct.
Chapel Hill, NC 27514
Ph: (919)929-7103
Fax: (919)942-8988
URL: http://www.abos.org
Contact: Dr. G. Paul DeRosa MD, Exec. Dir.
Founded: 1934. **Members:** 12. **Description:** Works to establish qualifications, conduct annual examinations, and certify as diplomates those whom the board finds qualified to practice orthopaedic surgery. **Committees:** Certificate Renewal; Credentials; Examinations; Graduate Education. **Affiliated With:** American Academy of Orthopaedic Surgeons; American Medical Association; American Orthopaedic Association. **Publications:** *The ABOS Diplomate*. Newsletter. Alternate Formats: online ● *Directory of Diplomates*, annual. Alternate Formats: online.

15428 ■ American Fracture Association (AFA)
Address Unknown since 2007
Founded: 1938. **Members:** 500. **Description:** Orthopedic, general, industrial, plastic, traumatic, and dental surgeons and physicians interested in the care and treatment of fractures. Seeks to further and create interest in the study of the various accepted types of bone fracture therapy. **Formerly:** American Ambulatory Fracture Association. **Publications:** *Orthopedic Transactions*, annual ● Directory, periodic. **Conventions/Meetings:** annual Henry W. Meyerding Essay Contest - competition, for essays on fractures or injuries to the soft tissues ● annual meeting, scientific (exhibits) - usually spring.

15429 ■ American Orthopaedic Association (AOA)
6300 N River Rd., Ste.505
Rosemont, IL 60018
Ph: (847)318-7330
Fax: (847)318-7339
E-mail: info@aoassn.org
URL: http://www.aoassn.org
Contact: Kristin Olds Glavin JD, Exec. Dir.
Founded: 1887. **Members:** 10,000. **Membership Dues:** senior, $500 (annual) ● corresponding, $100 (annual). **Staff:** 7. **Budget:** $1,500,000. **Description:** Serves as professional society of bone and joint surgeons. Seeks to further knowledge in the diagnosis and treatment of crippling diseases. **Awards:** Alfred R. Shands Award. **Frequency:** annual. **Type:** recognition. **Recipient:** for a United States or Canadian citizen who has made significant contributions to orthopedics ● Smith & Nephew Endoscopy Distinguished Clinician Educator Award. **Frequency:** annual. **Type:** recognition. **Recipient:** for an individual who has personal achievement and broad contribution to orthopedics ● Zimmer Award. **Frequency:** annual. **Type:** recognition. **Recipient:** for an individual who has outstanding leadership in the advancement of the art and science of orthopaedics. **Publications:** *American Orthopedic Association—Newsletter*, 3/year. Journal. Also Cited As: *AOA News* ● *Journal on Bone and Joint Surgery*, 8/year. **Conventions/Meetings:** annual meeting - 2008 June 4-7, Quebec, QC, Canada; 2009 June 10-13, Bonita Springs, FL.

15430 ■ American Orthopaedic Foot and Ankle Society (AOFAS)
6300 N River Rd., Ste.510
Rosemont, IL 60018
Ph: (847)698-4654
Free: (800)235-4855
Fax: (847)692-3315
E-mail: aofasinfo@aofas.org
URL: http://www.aofas.org
Contact: Ms. Lousanne Lofgren CAE, Exec. Dir.
Founded: 1969. **Members:** 1,800. **Membership Dues:** active, $475 (annual) ● resident, fellow, $75 (annual) ● international, active military, candidate military, $250 (annual) ● candidate, $425 (annual). **Staff:** 14. **Budget:** $1,500,000. **Description:** Represents medical doctors who specialize in orthopaedic foot and ankle surgery. Promotes quality, ethical and cost-effective patient care through education, research and training of orthopaedic surgeons and other health care providers. Creates public awareness for the prevention and treatment of foot and ankle disorders. Provides leadership and serves as a resource for government and industry and the national and international health care communities. Sponsors several educational programs, research grants, an overseas outreach project, and a traveling fellowship awards program. **Libraries:** Type: reference. **Subjects:** foot and ankle disorders and treatment. **Awards:** Leonard Goldner Award. **Frequency:** annual. **Type:** monetary. **Recipient:** for outstanding basic science paper submitted for the AOFAS Annual Summer Meeting ● Research Grants. **Frequency:** 5/year. **Type:** grant. **Recipient:** for research on foot and ankle conditions and treatment ● Roger A. Mann Award. **Frequency:** annual. **Type:** monetary. **Recipient:** for outstanding clinical paper submitted for the AOFAS Summer Meeting ● Traveling Fellowship Awards Program. **Frequency:** annual. **Type:** fellowship. **Recipient:** three-week fellowship award for travel and visit to foot and ankle research and education centers. **Computer Services:** Mailing lists, for rent. **Affiliated With:** American Academy of Orthopaedic Surgeons. **Formerly:** (1983) American Orthopaedic Foot Society. **Publications:** *The Adult Foot*. Pamphlet ● *The Diabetic Foot*. Pamphlet ● *Foot and Ankle International*, monthly. Journal. **Price:** included in membership dues; $149.00 /year for nonmembers; $180.00 /year for institutions; $11.00/copy for nonmembers. **Circulation:** 5,500. **Advertising:** accepted ● *Ten Points of Proper Shoe Fit*. Pamphlet ● *Workers Compensation Manual*. Features anatomy, basic science, diagnosis, management, and prognosis of simple and complex injuries of the foot and ankle.

Price: $39.95 for members; $49.95 for nonmembers. **Conventions/Meetings:** annual meeting (exhibits) - always summer.

15431 ■ American Osteopathic Academy of Orthopedics (AOAO)
PO Box 291690
Davie, FL 33329-1690
Ph: (954)262-1700
Free: (800)741-2626
Fax: (954)262-1748
E-mail: exec@aoao.org
URL: http://www.aoao.org
Contact: Morton Morris DO, Exec. Dir.
Founded: 1941. **Members:** 851. **Membership Dues:** active, $350 (annual) ● physician assistant, $175 (annual). **Staff:** 5. **Description:** Serves as professional society of osteopathic orthopedic surgeons. **Awards:** Fellow of the AOAO. **Type:** fellowship. **Committees:** Documents and Ceremonial Procedures; Female Orthopedics; Grants in Aid; Historical; Physician Assistant; Publications; Research; Strategic Planning. **Affiliated With:** American Osteopathic Association. **Publications:** *American Osteopathic Academy of Orthopedics—Membership Roster*, annual. Membership Directory. Arranged alphabetically and geographically; also lists resident candidates and AOAO-approved residency programs. **Price:** free ● *AOAO Newsletter*, 3/year. **Price:** included in membership dues. **Advertising:** accepted. Alternate Formats: online ● *Orthopod*, semiannual. **Price:** included in membership dues. **Advertising:** accepted. **Conventions/Meetings:** annual Clinical Assembly of Osteopathic Specialists - conference (exhibits) - 2007 Oct. 18-21, San Francisco, CA; 2008 Sept. 11-14, Boca Raton, FL ● annual Post Graduate Seminar - usually May. 2008 Apr. 4-6, Chicago, IL.

15432 ■ American Society of Orthopaedic Physician's Assistants (ASOPA)
8365 Keystone Crossing, Ste.107
Indianapolis, IN 46240
Free: (800)280-2390
Fax: (317)205-9481
E-mail: asopa@hp-assoc.com
URL: http://www.asopa.org
Contact: Hal Blank, Pres.
Founded: 1976. **Membership Dues:** fellow, affiliate, $200 (annual). **Description:** Physician's assistants who specialize in orthopaedic board-certified surgery. Aims to enhance the quality of medical treatment of orthopaedic patients. Provides information on advances in the field through continuing education, certification, publications, and meetings. **Publications:** *The Update*, quarterly. Newsletter. Alternate Formats: online.

15433 ■ American Society of Orthopedic Professionals (ASOP)
PO Box 7440
Seminole, FL 33775
Ph: (727)394-1700
E-mail: cbarocas@asop.org
URL: http://www.asop.org
Contact: Charles Barocas, Contact
Founded: 1999. **Members:** 1,846. **Membership Dues:** individual, $150 (biennial). **Staff:** 3. **Description:** Promotes continuing education for members and raises awareness of the orthopedic allied professional. **Awards:** Orthopedic Allied Professional of the Year. **Frequency:** annual. **Type:** recognition. **Recipient:** for lifetime achievement. **Publications:** Newsletter, bimonthly. **Conventions/Meetings:** meeting ● workshop.

15434 ■ Arthroscopy Association of North America (AANA)
6300 N River Rd., Ste.104
Rosemont, IL 60018
Ph: (847)292-2262
Fax: (847)292-2268
E-mail: info@aana.org
URL: http://www.aana.org
Contact: Edward A. Goss, Exec. Dir.
Founded: 1981. **Members:** 1,500. **Membership Dues:** individual, $450 (annual). **Staff:** 8. **Budget:**

$700,000. **Description:** Orthopedic surgeons. Advances arthroscopy, a diagnostic or surgical procedure in which an arthroscope, is inserted into a joint; the surgeon can either look directly into the arthroscope or observe on a screen the view projected by the arthroscope. In this way the surgeon can diagnose a condition using only a small incision for insertion of the arthroscope. The arthroscope also allows certain surgical procedures to be performed within viewing range of the scope. Sponsors research and continuing education programs. **Awards:** Richard O'Connor. **Frequency:** annual. **Type:** recognition. **Recipient:** for the best paper presented during the AANA annual meeting. **Computer Services:** database ● mailing lists. **Committees:** Archives; Bylaws; Communications; Data Retrieval; Education; Ethics and Standards; Fellowship; Health Policy and Practice; Learning Center; Research. **Publications:** AANA Membership Directory, annual. Contains alphabetical and geographical membership listings. **Price:** included in membership dues. **Circulation:** 1,500 ● Arthroscopy: The Journal of Arthroscopic and Related Surgery, quarterly. Enables its readers put into perspective the usefulness of the various emerging arthroscopic techniques. **Price:** $170.00 /year for individuals in U.S.; $220.00 /year for institutions; $497.00 /year for individuals outside U.S.; $353.00/year for students outside U.S. ISSN: 0749-8063. **Circulation:** 5,500. **Advertising:** accepted ● Inside AANA, quarterly. Newsletter. **Circulation:** 1,500 ● Patient Education. Brochure. Contains description of arthroscopy, possible problems, treatments, and recovery. **Price:** $37.50 for members; $43.75 for nonmembers. **Conventions/Meetings:** annual meeting (exhibits) - usually April or May. 2008 Apr. 24-27, Washington, DC; 2009 Apr. 30-3, San Diego, CA ● annual Fall Course - meeting (exhibits) - usually November. 2007 Nov. 1-3, Orlando, FL; 2008 Nov. 13-16, Phoenix, AZ; 2009 Nov. 12-15, Palm Desert, CA.

15435 ■ Association of Bone and Joint Surgeons (ABJS)
6300 N River Rd., Ste.727
Rosemont, IL 60018-4226
Ph: (847)698-1636
Fax: (847)823-4921
E-mail: abjs@aaos.org
URL: http://www.abjs.org
Contact: Colette Iocca Hohimer, Exec. Dir.
Founded: 1947. **Members:** 265. **Staff:** 2. **Description:** Orthopedic surgeons interested in clinical aspects of orthopedics and in training of leaders in the specialty. **Libraries: Type:** open to the public. **Subjects:** orthopedic surgery. **Awards:** Marshall R. Urist Young Investigator Award. **Frequency:** annual. **Type:** recognition. **Recipient:** for paper that deals with clinically relevant laboratory ● Nicolas Andry Award. **Frequency:** annual. **Type:** monetary. **Recipient:** for patient oriented research. **Telecommunication Services:** electronic mail, hohimer@aaos.org. **Committees:** Awards; Program. **Formerly:** ABJS. **Publications:** Clinical Orthopaedics and Related Research, monthly. Journal. Contains the latest and most important research, discoveries and informed opinions that shape today's orthopedic practice. **Price:** $331.00 /year for individuals in U.S.; $712.00 /year for institutions in U.S.; $535.00 /year for individuals outside U.S.; $826.00 /year for institutions outside U.S. ISSN: 0009-921. **Advertising:** accepted. Alternate Formats: online. **Conventions/Meetings:** annual meeting - 2008 June 13-17, Jackson, WY.

15436 ■ Bones Society
6300 N River Rd., Ste.727
Rosemont, IL 60018-4226
Free: (800)247-9699
Fax: (847)823-4921
E-mail: bones@bonessociety.org
URL: http://www.bonessociety.org
Contact: Thomas Potts, Pres.
Founded: 1969. **Members:** 1,400. **Membership Dues:** individual, $200 (annual). **Description:** Solo practitioners, private group practices and university-affiliated groups of all sizes. Dedicated to the professional development of the orthopedic practice admin-

istrator through educational and research programs and peer interaction. **Publications:** BONEFIDE News. Newsletter. Features orthopedic practice management related issues, society activities, and industry news. **Price:** included in membership dues. **Conventions/Meetings:** annual conference (exhibits) - 2008 Apr. 13-16, Charlotte, NC; 2009 May 3-6, Austin, TX.

15437 ■ Christian Orthopaedic Partners (COP)
PO Box 4712
Crofton, MD 21114
Ph: (301)261-3211
Fax: (410)721-4647
E-mail: copcmm@olg.com
URL: http://www.christianorthopartners.com
Contact: David S. Hungerford MD, Chm./Co-Founder
Multinational. Description: Serves as fellowship of healthcare providers promoting orthopaedic services to the poor and indigent worldwide. **Affiliated With:** Children's Medical Ministries. **Publications:** Manuals.

15438 ■ Clinical Orthopaedic Society (COS)
2209 Dickens Rd.
Richmond, VA 23230-2005
Ph: (804)565-6366
Fax: (804)282-0090
E-mail: cos@societyhq.com
URL: http://www.cosociety.org
Contact: Kenneth L. Moore MD, Pres.
Founded: 1912. **Members:** 700. **Description:** Orthopedic surgeons practicing in cities of the Midwest. **Awards:** Travelling Fellowship. **Frequency:** annual. **Type:** fellowship. **Recipient:** for physicians up to the age of 45. **Committees:** Ad Hoc Committee on Emeritus Member; Ad Hoc Grants and Funding; Continuing Medical Education; Nominating; Publication; Residents Paper; Travelling Fellowship; Visiting Professor. **Publications:** Directory, annual. **Conventions/Meetings:** annual meeting (exhibits) - usually during the fall. 2007 Sept. 27-29, Memphis, TN.

15439 ■ Conservative Orthopedics International Association (COIA)
Address Unknown since 2007
Founded: 1982. **Members:** 4,417. **Staff:** 5. **Budget:** $6,000,000. **For-Profit. Description:** Medical doctors, osteopaths, chiropractors, orthopedists, psychiatrists, and physical therapists. Promotes continuing education, research, and practice of conservative orthopedics. (Conservative orthopedics concentrates on nonoperative, nonradical, preventive and rehabilitative treatment of musculoskeletal disorders.) Seeks to advance the science and art of conservative orthopedics as they relate to the whole person. Operates charitable program; compiles statistics. Maintains speakers' bureau; offers educational and research programs. Sponsors hall of fame. **Libraries: Type:** reference. **Awards: Type:** recognition. **Publications:** Conservative Orthopedics International Bulletin, annual ● Updates, periodic ● Membership Directory, periodic ● Newsletter, quarterly. **Conventions/Meetings:** convention - 6-15/year ● lecture ● seminar ● workshop.

15440 ■ Council on Chiropractic Orthopedics (CCO)
c/o Gary L. Carver, Treas.
4409 Sterling Ave.
Kansas City, MO 64133-1854
Ph: (816)358-5100
Fax: (816)358-6565
E-mail: gcdc7@earthlink.net
URL: http://www.ccodc.org
Contact: Gary L. Carver, Treas.
Founded: 1967. **Members:** 750. **Membership Dues:** certified/supporting, $100 (annual) ● faculty/associate, $50 (annual) ● retired, $25-$35 (annual). **Budget:** $50,000. **Description:** Licensed doctors of chiropractic who have completed 360 hours of postgraduate courses in orthopedics; chiropractic physicians with an interest in orthopedics. Objectives are: to assist in the advancement of chiropractic as a science and healing art; to protect the welfare and

interests of members; to encourage and maintain the highest standards of moral and ethical conduct; to promote research; to encourage the standardization of terminology; to disseminate information; to encourage the teaching of chiropractic orthopedics at all levels. Reviews and revises postgraduate courses in chiropractic. Fosters seminars and courses in personal, athletic, and industrial injuries; provides consulting. **Committees:** Credentials; Ethics; Insurance; Public Relations; Publications; Research. **Affiliated With:** American Chiropractic Association. **Publications:** Orthopedic Briefs, bimonthly ● Brochure ● Directory, annual. **Conventions/Meetings:** annual meeting ● annual symposium.

15441 ■ Hip Society
c/o Karen V. Andersen, Exec. Dir.
951 Old County Rd., No. 182
Belmont, CA 94002
Ph: (650)596-6190
Fax: (650)508-2040
URL: http://www.hipsoc.org
Contact: Karen V. Andersen, Exec. Dir.
Founded: 1968. **Description:** Dedicated to the advancement of knowledge relating to the hip joint. **Awards:** Frank Stinchfield Award. **Frequency:** annual. **Type:** monetary. **Recipient:** to a resident or fellow for outstanding contribution to hip problems ● John Charnley Award. **Frequency:** annual. **Type:** monetary. **Recipient:** for innovative research on hip disorders management ● Otto Aufranc Award. **Frequency:** annual. **Type:** monetary. **Recipient:** for innovative research on hip disorders management. **Conventions/Meetings:** annual meeting - every summer. 2007 Sept. 20-22, Pasadena, CA ● annual Open Scientific Meeting, with award paper sessions; in conjunction with AAHKS - 2008 Mar. 8, San Francisco, CA.

15442 ■ International College of Cranio-Mandibular Orthopedics (ICCMO)
c/o Hallie Truswell, Exec. Dir.
619 N 35th St., Ste.307
Seattle, WA 98103
Ph: (206)633-4355
Free: (800)446-1763
Fax: (206)633-4352
E-mail: hallietruswell@tmj-iccmo.org
URL: http://tmj-iccmo.org
Contact: Hallie Truswell, Exec. Dir.
Founded: 1979. **Members:** 550. **Membership Dues:** individual, $350 (annual). **Description:** Craniomandibular orthopedists. Seeks to advance the study and practice of cranio-mandibular orthopedics. Conducts continuing professional development courses for members. **Awards: Frequency:** annual. **Type:** fellowship. **Recipient:** for an individual with the highest level of achievement in diagnosis and treatment of TMD ● Mastership. **Frequency:** annual. **Type:** recognition. **Publications:** Journal of Craniomandibular Orthopedics, 3/year. **Circulation:** 1,000. **Advertising:** accepted ● Newsletter, 3/year. **Circulation:** 1,000. **Advertising:** accepted. Alternate Formats: online. **Conventions/Meetings:** annual Bernard Jankelson Memorial Lecture Forum - board meeting, scientific congress ● annual conference.

15443 ■ International Society of Arthroscopy, Knee Surgery and Orthopaedic Sports Medicine (ISAKOS)
2678 Bishop Dr., Ste.250
San Ramon, CA 94583-2338
Ph: (925)807-1197
Fax: (925)807-1199
E-mail: isakos@isakos.com
URL: http://www.isakos.com
Contact: John A. Bergfeld, Pres.
Founded: 1978. **Members:** 1,700. **Membership Dues:** associate, active, $240 (annual). **Staff:** 4. **Budget:** $150,000. **Multinational. Description:** Orthopaedic surgeons specializing in problems of the knee, arthroscopy, and orthopaedic sports medicine. **Awards:** Achilles Orthopaedic Sports Medicine Research. **Frequency:** biennial. **Type:** recognition. **Recipient:** for a researcher who has done outstanding laboratory research in the field of sport medicine

● Albert Trillat Young Investigator's Award. **Frequency:** biennial. **Type:** monetary. **Recipient:** for a young researcher who has done outstanding clinical research about knee injuries prevention ● John J. Joyce Award. **Frequency:** biennial. **Type:** monetary. **Recipient:** for the best paper presented during the ISAKOS congress. **Computer Services:** Electronic publishing, contains biannual newsletter, hosts a "Current Concepts" section, provides a link to the official journal ● online services, membership services. **Committees:** Arthroscopy; Education; Knee; Program; Scientific; Site Selection; Sports Medicine; Strategic Planning. **Formerly:** International Arthroscopy Association; (1995) International Society of the Knee. **Publications:** *Arthroscopy: The Journal of Arthroscopic and Related Surgery.* Enables its readers to put into perspective the usefulness of the various emerging arthroscopic techniques. **Price:** $386.00 /year for individuals in U.S.; $517.00 /year for individuals outside U.S.; $367.00/year for students outside U.S. ISSN: 0749-8063. **Advertising:** accepted ● Newsletter, semiannual. Features meeting information, committee updates and timely articles on ISAKOS events and happenings. **Price:** included in membership dues. Alternate Formats: online. **Conventions/Meetings:** biennial congress and convention, held in conjunction with the International Arthroscopy Association (exhibits).

15444 ■ International Society for Computer Assisted Orthopaedic Surgery (CAOS-International)
Inst. for Cmpt. Assisted Orthopaedic Surgery
The Western Pennsylvania Hosp.
Mellon Pavillon, Ste.242
4815 Liberty Ave.
Pittsburgh, PA 15224
Ph: (412)578-2267
Free: (866)883-2267
Fax: (412)605-6376
E-mail: tony@pfcusa.org
URL: http://www.caos-international.org
Contact: Stephen Murphy MD, 2nd VP
Founded: 2000. **Membership Dues:** active, $150 (annual) ● student, $75 (annual) ● active plus CAOS-France, $160 (annual) ● student plus CAOS-France, $80 (annual) ● active plus ISCAS, $180 (annual). **Multinational. Description:** Seeks to bring together individuals interested in Computer Assisted Orthopaedic Surgery (CAOS) throughout the world. Serves as a forum for the exchange of information of both an investigative and clinical nature by means of computer assistance. Promotes partnerships between orthopaedic surgeons and technologists. Stimulates basic and clinical research, and organizes postgraduate teaching programs. **Awards:** Best Paper Awards. **Frequency:** annual. **Type:** recognition. **Recipient:** for the best podium presentations at the annual CAOS-International meeting ● Best Poster Awards. **Frequency:** annual. **Type:** recognition. **Recipient:** for the best poster presentations at the annual CAOS-International meeting ● Maurice E. Muller Award for Excellence in Computer Assisted Surgery. **Frequency:** annual. **Type:** recognition. **Recipient:** for individuals whose contribution fostered excellence in Computer Assisted Surgery to the present. **Telecommunication Services:** electronic mail, caos@caos-international.org. **Publications:** *Computer Aided Surgery.* Journal. **Price:** included in membership dues ● Yearbook, annual. **Price:** included in membership dues. Alternate Formats: online.

15445 ■ Jaw Joints and Allied Musculo-Skeletal Disorders Foundation (JJAMD)
c/o The Forsyth Institute
140 Fenway
Boston, MA 02115-3782
Ph: (617)266-2550 (617)262-5200
Fax: (617)267-9020
E-mail: tmjoints@aol.com
URL: http://www.tmjoints.org
Contact: Renee Glass, Co-Founder/Pres.
Founded: 1982. **Description:** Promotes public awareness of TemporoMandibular Joint disorder (TMJ) and related musculoskeletal disorders. Pro-

vides information on prevention, treatment, and responsible diagnosis. Conducts research and educational programs; monitors legislative activities. Provides advocacy, networking, patients, professionals, governmental agencies, healthcare, academic, research communities, insurance providers, and support group activities. **Libraries:** Type: reference. **Holdings:** articles, reports. **Computer Services:** database. **Publications:** *JJAMD TMJ Update.* Newsletter. Alternate Formats: online ● *Plain Talk Guide to TMJ; with Self-Help Tips to Keep Your Jaw Joints Healthy.* Pamphlet ● Articles. Alternate Formats: online. **Conventions/Meetings:** periodic TMJ - Implications for Health Care Costs - conference.

15446 ■ National Board for Certification of Orthopaedic Technologists (NBCOT)
4736 Onondaga Blvd., No. 166
Syracuse, NY 13219
Free: (866)466-2268
Fax: (315)476-8840
E-mail: gonbcot@aol.com
URL: http://www.nbcot.net
Contact: Mr. Jeffery Virgo, Chm.
Founded: 1982. **Members:** 5,500. **Staff:** 2. **Description:** Offers National Certification in Orthopaedic Technology to those Orthopaedic Technologists that have met the standards set forth by the NBCOT; allows re-certification by retesting or by obtaining Continuing Education Units. **Affiliated With:** National Association of Orthopaedic Technologists. **Publications:** *NBCOT Study Guide,* 5/year. Handbooks. Contains 150 question sample examination with references. **Price:** $30.00 ● *Role Delineation.* Serves as a study guide for the Orthopaedic Technologist exam and the Orthopaedic Technologist-Surgery Certified exam.

15447 ■ National Osteoporosis Foundation (NOF)
1232 22nd St. NW
Washington, DC 20037-1202
Ph: (202)223-2226
E-mail: communications@nof.org
URL: http://www.nof.org
Contact: Judith Cranford, Exec. Dir.
Founded: 1984. **Members:** 300,000. **Membership Dues:** individual, $20 (annual) ● individual outside North America, $35 (annual) ● healthcare professional, $49 (annual) ● health service, $125 (annual) ● Professional Partners Network, $550 (annual). **Staff:** 25. **Budget:** $7,000,000. **Description:** A national voluntary health organization dedicated to reducing the widespread prevalence of osteoporosis. (Osteoporosis is an excessive loss of bone tissue which often results in fractures of the hip, spine, and wrist.) Seeks to: increase public awareness and knowledge about osteoporosis; provide information about osteoporosis to sufferers and their families; educate physicians and allied health professionals; advocate for increased governmental support for research on osteoporosis; and support basic biomedical, epidemiological, clinical, behavioral, and social research and research training. Sponsors Research Grant Award program; conducts public and professional education programs. **Awards:** Research Grant Awards. **Frequency:** annual. **Type:** grant. **Formerly:** (1985) The Osteoporosis Foundation. **Publications:** *Boning Up on Osteoporosis.* Handbook. **Price:** $5.00/copy, for nonmembers; included in membership dues ● *Falls and Related Fractures ● How Strong Are Your Bones,* periodic ● *Living with Osteoporosis ● Medications and Bone Loss ● Osteoporosis Education Kit ● Osteoporosis Report,* quarterly. Newsletter. Includes current medical journal references and listing of consumer publications and recent articles related to the subject of osteoporosis. **Price:** included in membership dues ● *Stand Up to Osteoporosis.* **Conventions/Meetings:** annual Osteoporosis: Translating Research into Clinical Practice - symposium, pharmaceutical companies, medical testing equipment, publishers.

15448 ■ Orthopaedic Research Society (ORS)
6300 N River Rd., Ste.727
Rosemont, IL 60018-4226
Ph: (847)698-1625

Fax: (847)823-4921
E-mail: ors@ors.org
URL: http://www.ors.org
Contact: Brenda Frederick, Exec. Dir.
Founded: 1954. **Members:** 1,870. **Membership Dues:** active, $245 (annual) ● associate, $75 (annual). **Staff:** 3. **Budget:** $450,000. **Description:** Orthopedic surgeons and other investigators who are elected as active members on the basis of previous scientific activity, continued participation in the field of research, and accomplishments in orthopedic surgery. Promotes orthopedic research and provides a meeting place for presentation and discussion of orthopedic research activities. **Libraries:** Type: reference. **Awards:** Marshall Urist Award. **Frequency:** annual. **Type:** recognition. **Recipient:** for an investigator who has established himself as a cutting edge researcher in tissue generation ● New Investigator Recognition Awards. **Frequency:** annual. **Type:** recognition. **Recipient:** for outstanding work in orthopedics ● The Shands. **Frequency:** annual. **Type:** recognition. **Recipient:** for a U.S. or Canadian citizen who has made significant contributions to orthopaedics ● The Steindler. **Frequency:** biennial. **Type:** recognition. **Recipient:** for a senior scientist, clinician and educator ● William Harris Award. **Frequency:** annual. **Type:** recognition. **Recipient:** for the best paper submitted to a review committee of ORS members. **Computer Services:** database. **Telecommunication Services:** electronic mail, frederick@aaos.org. **Boards:** Directors. **Committees:** Education and Special Projects; Mentoring; Professional Liaison. **Publications:** *Journal of Orthopedic Research,* quarterly. Published for Musculoskeletal investigators. **Price:** $164.00 in U.S.; $190.00 outside U.S. **Advertising:** accepted ● *Transactions of Annual Meeting.* Proceedings. **Price:** $45.00 ● Newsletters, semiannual. **Price:** included in membership dues. Alternate Formats: online. **Conventions/Meetings:** annual workshop and meeting (exhibits) - 2008 Mar. 2-5, San Francisco, CA.

15449 ■ Orthopaedic Trauma Association (OTA)
6300 N River Rd., Ste.727
Rosemont, IL 60018-4226
Ph: (847)698-1631
Free: (800)346-2267
Fax: (847)823-0536
E-mail: franzon@aaos.org
URL: http://www.ota.org
Contact: Nancy E. Franzon, Exec.Dir.
Founded: 1983. **Members:** 620. **Membership Dues:** active/research, $600 ● associate/community, $500 ● international, $100 ● allied health, $130 ● resident, $50. **Staff:** 4. **Description:** Physicians and other health care professionals with an interest in orthopedic trauma. Seeks to advance research and education in the practice of orthopedics; promotes development of improved orthopedic trauma treatment techniques; and works to educate the public regarding safety issues in motor vehicle accidents. Serves as a clearinghouse on orthopedic trauma; and conducts continuing professional development courses. **Awards:** Edwin G. Bovill, Jr., MD Award. **Frequency:** annual. **Type:** recognition. **Recipient:** to the author of the most outstanding OTA Annual Meeting scientific paper ● Orthopaedic Trauma Fellowship. **Frequency:** periodic. **Type:** fellowship. **Computer Services:** database, membership directory. **Telecommunication Services:** electronic mail, ota@aaos.org. **Programs:** Research Mentor. **Publications:** *Fracture Lines,* quarterly. Newsletter. **Price:** free, for members only. Alternate Formats: online ● *Journal of Orthopaedic Trauma,* periodic ● Abstracts of lectures given at annual meeting in JBJS and online. **Conventions/Meetings:** annual meeting (exhibits) ● annual Residence Advanced Trauma Techniques Course - conference (exhibits) ● annual Residents Comprehensive Fracture Course - meeting and lecture, with lectures, skills labs, small group discussions.

15450 ■ Orthopaedics Overseas (OO)
1900 L St. NW, Ste.310
Washington, DC 20036
Ph: (202)296-0928

Fax: (202)296-8018
E-mail: info@hvousa.org
URL: http://www.hvousa.org
Contact: Nancy Kelly, Exec. Dir.
Founded: 1959. **Members:** 775. **Membership Dues:** individual, $100 (annual). **Staff:** 12. **Budget:** $5,000,000. **Description:** Orthopedic surgeons interested in volunteering as consultants in developing countries. Trains physicians in developing countries in diagnostic, conservative, and operative management techniques. Addresses chronic and acute orthopedic problems and crippling diseases such as polio and arthritis. Operates programs in Cambodia, Bhutan, Nepal, Malawi, Kenya, St. Lucia, South Africa, Uganda, Vietnam, and Ethiopia. Formerly a project of CARE, the group is a division of Health Volunteers Overseas. HVO also sponsors Anesthesia Overseas, Dentistry Overseas, Nursing Overseas, Oral and Maxillofacial Surgery Overseas, and Pediatrics Overseas, Internal Medicine Overseas, Nurse Anesthesia Overseas, and Physical Therapy Overseas. **Conventions/Meetings:** annual conference.

15451 ■ Osteogenesis Imperfecta Foundation (OIF)
804 W Diamond Ave., Ste.210
Gaithersburg, MD 20878
Ph: (301)947-0083
Free: (800)981-2663
Fax: (301)947-0456
E-mail: bonelink@oif.org
URL: http://www.oif.org
Contact: Ms. Mary Beth Huber, Information and Resource Dir.
Founded: 1970. **Members:** 4,500. **Membership Dues:** individual, $30 (annual). **Staff:** 9. **Budget:** $800,000. **State Groups:** 35. **Description:** Helps people cope with Osteogenesis Imperfecta. Aims to improve the quality of life for individuals affected by OI through education, awareness, mutual support and research into the treatment and potential cure of the disorder. Provides information to individuals who have OI and their families, medical professionals and other members of the community. Resources and programs include a quarterly newsletter, a physician information service, written literature, informative videos, national conferences and local support groups. Compiles statistics. **Awards:** Michael Geisman Memorial Fellowship and Seed Awards. **Frequency:** annual. **Type:** grant. **Recipient:** for research contribution ● **Type:** monetary. **Recipient:** for OI research projects. **Committees:** Medical Advisory Board; Scientific Review. **Affiliated With:** Genetic Alliance; National Organization for Rare Disorders. **Publications:** *Breakthrough*, quarterly. Newsletter. Contains medical reports, foundation news, and activities. **Price:** free for members; $12.00 /year for nonmembers. **Circulation:** 3,500 ● *Caring for Infants and Children with Osteogenesis Imperfecta*. Brochure ● *Children with Osteogenesis Imperfecta: Strategies to Enhance Performance*. Book ● *Going Places*. Video ● *Growing Up With OI: A Guide for Children*. Book ● *Growing Up With OI: A Guide for Families & Caregivers*. Book ● *Jason's First Day!*. Book ● *Managing Osteogenesis Imperfecta: A Medical Manual*. Book. **Price:** $28.50 ● *Osteogenesis Imperfecta: A Guide for Medical Professionals, Individuals, Families Affected by OI*. Brochure ● *Osteogenesis Imperfecta: A Guide for Nurses*. Book ● *Plan for Success: An Education's Guide to Students with Osteogenesis Imperfecta*. Brochure ● *Therapeutic Strategies for OI: A Guide for Physical Therapists and Occupational Therapists*. Brochure ● Also publishes other medical and general literature. **Conventions/Meetings:** biennial conference, features 45 workshops (exhibits).

15452 ■ Pediatric Orthopedic Society of North America (POSNA)
6300 N River Rd., Ste.727
Rosemont, IL 60018-4226
Ph: (847)698-1692
Fax: (847)823-0536
E-mail: goldberg@aaos.org
URL: http://www.posna.org
Contact: Sharon Goldberg, Exec. Dir.
Founded: 1983. **Members:** 800. **Membership Dues:** active, associate, corresponding, candidate, senior,

$300 (annual). **Staff:** 3. **For-Profit. Description:** Pediatric orthopedic surgeons. Aims to provide continuing education to members. Conducts tutorial programs. **Awards:** Huene Award. **Frequency:** annual. **Type:** monetary. **Recipient:** for past and future research in pediatric orthopedics. **Computer Services:** database. **Publications:** Bulletin, quarterly. **Price:** available to members only ● Membership Directory, annual. **Conventions/Meetings:** annual meeting and seminar ● One-Day Course - workshop ● Specialty Day - specialty show.

15453 ■ Ruth Jackson Orthopaedic Society (RJOS)
c/o Teri Stech, Mgr.
6300 N River Rd., Ste.727
Rosemont, IL 60018-4226
Ph: (847)698-1626
Fax: (847)823-4921
E-mail: rjos@aaos.org
URL: http://www.rjos.org
Contact: Teri Stech, Mgr.
Founded: 1983. **Members:** 469. **Membership Dues:** active, associate/affiliate, $250 (annual) ● resident/fellowship, $50 (annual) ● student, $25 (annual). **Staff:** 2. **Description:** Women orthopaedic surgeons, residents, fellows, and medical students. Seeks to advance the science of orthopaedic surgery and to provide support for women orthopaedic surgeons. Named for practicing orthopaedic surgeon Dr. Ruth Jackson (1902-94), the first woman certified by the American Board of Orthopaedic Surgery and the first female member of the American Academy of Orthopaedic Surgeons. Conducts educational programs; operates placement service and speakers' bureau, holds biennial meeting, sponsors mentoring program, offers traveling fellowship and resident research award. **Libraries:** Type: reference. **Holdings:** articles, biographical archives. **Subjects:** orthopaedic surgery. **Awards:** Jacquelin Perry, MD Resident Research Award. **Frequency:** annual. **Type:** monetary. **Recipient:** for a female resident in accredited orthopaedic surgical residency programs ● RJOS Traveling Fellowship. **Frequency:** annual. **Type:** monetary. **Recipient:** for interest in promoting the general cause of women in orthopaedics. **Computer Services:** database. **Committees:** Communications; Mentoring; Nominating; Scientific. **Publications:** *Membership List*, periodic. Newsletter. **Price:** $150.00. **Circulation:** 469 ● *Ruth Jackson Society Newsletter*, semiannual. Includes articles on international members and careers and personal life; also contains calendar of events, upcoming meetings and courses. **Price:** free for members only. **Circulation:** 507. **Conventions/Meetings:** annual luncheon, in conjunction with AAOS annual meeting - always March ● annual meeting.

Orthotics and Prosthetics

15454 ■ American Academy of Orthotists and Prosthetists (AAOP)
526 King St., Ste.201
Alexandria, VA 22314
Ph: (703)836-0788
Fax: (703)836-0737
E-mail: prosenstein@oandp.org
URL: http://www.oandp.org
Contact: Peter D. Rosenstein CAE, Exec. Dir.
Founded: 1970. **Members:** 2,400. **Membership Dues:** active/associate, $300 (annual) ● affiliate/professional, $175 (annual) ● candidate/resident/student, $36 (annual). **Staff:** 8. **Budget:** $1,800,000. **State Groups:** 15. **Description:** Professional practitioners certified by the American Board for Certification in Orthotics and Prosthetics. Works to advance the profession and improve patient care. Provides continuing education designed to increase professional competence of the individual practitioner. **Libraries:** Type: not open to the public. **Awards:** Distinguished Practitioner. **Frequency:** annual. **Type:** recognition. **Recipient:** for professional excellence ● Titus-Ferguson Award. **Frequency:** annual. **Type:** recognition. **Computer Services:** Online services.

Committees: AOPA Government Relations; Chapter Presidents; Interprofessional Relations; Legislative Advocacy. **Councils:** Education Development; Member Services; Professional Issues. **Task Forces:** O&P Awareness. **Publications:** *Academician Xpress*, monthly. Newsletter. **Price:** included in membership dues. Alternate Formats: online ● *Journal of Prosthetics and Orthotics*, quarterly. Contains scientific and research articles on latest products, fitting techniques and patient care regimens. ● *JPO Selected Readings* ● Handbooks ● Manuals ● Also publishes home study videos. **Conventions/Meetings:** annual conference and symposium (exhibits).

15455 ■ American Board for Certification in Orthotics, Prosthetics and Pedorthics (ABC)
330 John Carlyle St., Ste.210
Alexandria, VA 22314
Ph: (703)836-7114
Fax: (703)836-0838
E-mail: info@abcop.org
URL: http://www.abcop.org
Contact: Catherine Carter, Exec. Dir.
Founded: 1958. **Members:** 1,400. **Staff:** 5. **Budget:** $385,000. **Description:** Certified Pedorthists. (Pedorthists fit and provide prescription footwear, footwear modifications and foot orthoses to clients referred by physicians.) Sponsors certification program; sets standards of practice in pedorthics and requires continuing education of certificants to maintain certification. **Libraries:** Type: not open to the public. **Computer Services:** database, candidate handbook. **Formed by Merger of:** (2007) Board for Certification in Pedorthics and American Board for Certification in Orthotics, Prosthetics and Pedorthics. **Publications:** *Pedorthic Candidate's Handbook*, annual. Alternate Formats: online ● *Study Guide for Pedorthic Skills Examination*. **Conventions/Meetings:** semiannual board meeting - April and November.

15456 ■ Association of Children's Prosthetic-Orthotic Clinics (ACPOC)
6300 N River Rd., Ste.727
Rosemont, IL 60018-4226
Ph: (847)698-1637 (847)384-4235
Fax: (847)823-0536
E-mail: raymond@aaos.org
URL: http://www.acpoc.org
Contact: Melody Raymond, Coor.
Founded: 1980. **Members:** 450. **Membership Dues:** physician, $150 (annual) ● non-physician, $75 (annual) ● corresponding outside U.S. and Canada, $50 (annual). **Staff:** 2. **Description:** Prosthetic-orthotic clinics for children. Promotes the exchange of information concerning children's prosthetic-orthotic devices. Fosters cooperative research development and evaluative efforts among member clinics. Seeks to improve care in member clinics. **Computer Services:** Mailing lists. **Publications:** Newsletter, quarterly. **Advertising:** accepted. **Conventions/Meetings:** annual meeting (exhibits).

15457 ■ Board for Orthotist/Prosthetist Certification (BOC)
7150 Columbia Gateway Dr., Ste.G
Columbia, MD 21046-1151
Ph: (443)539-3810
Free: (877)776-2200
Fax: (410)872-9298
E-mail: info@bocusa.org
URL: http://www.bocusa.org
Contact: Kay Zehms BOCO, Chair
Founded: 1984. **Staff:** 7. **Budget:** $700,000. **Description:** Certifies orthotists and prosthetists based on comprehensive performance and examinations. Accredits orthotic and prosthetic facilities and maintains a registry of Orthotic Fitters and Mastectomy Fitters. **Computer Services:** database, IMIS Millennium. **Programs:** Approved Continuing Professional Education; Certification; Family Accreditation. **Publications:** *The BOC Advantage*, quarterly. Newsletter. **Advertising:** accepted. Alternate Formats: online ● *Candidate Handbook*, annual. **Conventions/Meetings:** semiannual board meeting.

15458 ■ National Association for the Advancement of Orthotics and Prosthetics (NAAOP)
1875 Eye St. NW, 12th Fl.
Washington, DC 20006-5409
Ph: (202)624-0064
Free: (800)622-6740
Fax: (202)785-1756
E-mail: naaop@oandp.com
URL: http://www.oandp.com/resources/organizations/ naaop
Contact: Peter W. Thomas, Gen. Counsel
Founded: 1987. **Membership Dues:** individual, $250 (annual) ● independent, $1,000 (annual) ● supplier or manufacturer, $500 (annual). **Description:** Advocates for the advancement of orthotics and prosthetics. Educates and informs the Orthotics and Prosthetics field of relevant legislative and regulatory issues. Creates a federal research and development program in orthotics and prosthetics.

Osteology

15459 ■ American Society for Bone and Mineral Research (ASBMR)
2025 M St. NW, Ste.800
Washington, DC 20036-3309
Ph: (202)367-1161
Fax: (202)367-2161
E-mail: asbmr@asbmr.org
URL: http://www.asbmr.org
Contact: Steven R. Goldring MD, Pres.
Founded: 1977. **Members:** 3,100. **Membership Dues:** full, $215 (annual) ● trainee, $80 (annual). **Staff:** 4. **Description:** Represents physicians, dentists, veterinarians, clinical investigators, and researchers interested in bone and mineral metabolism. Provides placement service. **Awards:** Frederic C. Bartter Award. **Frequency:** annual. **Type:** recognition. **Recipient:** for outstanding clinical investigation in disorders of mineral and bone metabolism ● Fuller Albright Award. **Frequency:** annual. **Type:** recognition. **Recipient:** for meritorious scientific accomplishment in the bone and mineral field ● Gideon A. Rodan Excellence in Mentorship Award. **Frequency:** annual. **Type:** recognition. **Recipient:** for outstanding support provided by a senior scientist ● Louis V. Avioli Founders Award. **Frequency:** annual. **Type:** recognition. **Recipient:** for fundamental contributions to bone and mineral basic research ● President's Book Award. **Frequency:** annual. **Type:** recognition. **Recipient:** for highest ranking abstract submitted by a student ● Shirley Hohl Service Award. **Frequency:** annual. **Type:** recognition. **Recipient:** for significant contributions to the mission of the ASBMR ● William F. Neuman Award. **Frequency:** annual. **Type:** recognition. **Recipient:** for outstanding and major scientific contributions in the area of bone and mineral research ● Young Investigators Award. **Frequency:** annual. **Type:** recognition. **Recipient:** for young investigators. **Computer Services:** Mailing lists. **Committees:** Awards; Development; Education; Public Affairs; Publications. **Publications:** *ASBMRNews*, quarterly. Newsletter ● *Journal of Bone and Mineral Research* (in English and Japanese), monthly. **Price:** $495.00 /year for individuals, in U.S.; $590.00 /year for institutions, in U.S.; $570.00 /year for individuals, outside U.S.; $635.00 /year for institutions, outside U.S. ISSN: 0884-0431. **Advertising:** accepted. Alternate Formats: CD-ROM. Also Cited As: *JMBR* ● *Primer on the Metabolic Bone Diseases and Disorders of Mineral Metabolism.* Book. **Price:** $49.95 for members. Alternate Formats: online ● Membership Directory, annual. **Conventions/Meetings:** annual congress (exhibits).

15460 ■ International Society for Clinical Densitometry (ISCD)
342 N Main St.
West Hartford, CT 06117-2507
Ph: (860)586-7563
Fax: (860)586-7550
E-mail: iscd@iscd.org
URL: http://www.iscd.org
Contact: M. Suzanne C. Berry MBA, Exec. Dir.
Founded: 1993. **Members:** 6,000. **Membership Dues:** clinician, scientist, researcher, industry - full, $195 (annual) ● technologist, associate, retired - regular, $50 (annual) ● technologist, associate, retired - upgraded, $70 (annual) ● technologist, associate, retired - full, $110 (annual). **Multinational. Description:** Raises awareness and understanding of the clinical application of bone mass measurement technology. Seeks to adopt an industry and technology neutral approach towards advances in the field. Encourages improvements in patient care through appropriate utilization of densitometry. Fosters continuing professional education and certification for clinicians and technologists. **Awards:** Dr. John P. Bilezikian ISCD Global Leadership Award. **Frequency:** annual. **Type:** recognition. **Recipient:** to a member for his/her distinguished service and leadership in the global promotion of the bone densitometry field and the society ● Dr. Oscar S. Gluck ISCD Humanitarian Award. **Frequency:** annual. **Type:** recognition. **Recipient:** to a member with a history of contributing to the alleviation of human suffering, protection of life, outstanding service to the community, or the promotion of health in underserved populations ● Dr. Paul D. Miller ISCD Service Award. **Frequency:** annual. **Type:** recognition. **Recipient:** to a member for his/her distinguished service and dedication to the society ● ISCD Clinician of the Year Award. **Frequency:** annual. **Type:** recognition. **Recipient:** to an outstanding ISCD clinician for his/her distinguished service to the field of densitometry in the areas of publication, education, or leadership ● ISCD Super Tech Award. **Frequency:** annual. **Type:** recognition. **Recipient:** to the best ISCD technologists for their contributions to the practice of densitometry ● ISCD Technologist of the Year Award. **Frequency:** annual. **Type:** recognition. **Recipient:** to an outstanding ISCD technologist for his/her distinguished service to the field of densitometry in the areas of publication, education, or leadership. **Telecommunication Services:** electronic mail, sberry@ iscd.org. **Publications:** *Journal of Clinical Densitometry.* Contains clinical research articles on the uses of bone mass and density measurements in medical practice. **Price:** included in membership dues. Alternate Formats: online. Also Cited As: *JCD* ● *SCAN*, quarterly. Newsletter. Covers society news and information on bone mass measurement, bone mass imaging technologies, and bone mass health/ economics. **Price:** included in membership dues. Alternate Formats: online ● Audiotape. Contains audio recordings of past ISCD annual meetings. **Price:** $9.00 per copy; $329.00 per set. Alternate Formats: CD-ROM ● Membership Directory. Alternate Formats: online. **Conventions/Meetings:** annual meeting - 2008 Mar. 12-15, San Francisco, CA; 2009 Mar. 11-14, Orlando, FL.

Osteopathic Medicine

15461 ■ Advocates for the American Osteopathic Association (AAOA)
142 E Ontario St.
Chicago, IL 60611-2864
Ph: (312)202-8190
Free: (800)621-1773
Fax: (312)202-8218
E-mail: info@aaoa4u.org
URL: http://www.aaoa4u.org
Contact: Bridget L. Price, Interim Exec. Dir.
Founded: 1940. **Members:** 5,000. **Membership Dues:** student, $5 (annual) ● widow retired, $10 (annual) ● regular, $50 (annual). **Staff:** 3. **Description:** Immediate family members of osteopathic physicians; spouses of students of osteopathic medicine. Promotes public health education; provides funds for scholarships for the training of osteopathic physicians and surgeons, and for research and other activities at osteopathic colleges; encourages establishment and continuation of volunteer service organizations in nonprofit osteopathic hospitals; participates in national and community health programs. Sponsors summer seminars. **Awards:** Osteopathic Medical Explorers Scholarships. **Type:** scholarship. **Recipient:** for life career education program for young men and women. **Programs:** Osteoporosis Prevention; Voter Registration; Women and Heart Disease; Red Dress; Yellow Ribbon Teen Suicide Prevention. **Affiliated With:** American Osteopathic Association; American Osteopathic College of Anesthesiologists. **Formerly:** (2006) Auxiliary to the American Osteopathic Association. **Publications:** *AAOA Accent*, quarterly. Newsletter. Covers osteopathic medicine and related subjects such as safety projects, public health information, and osteopathic college scholarship awards. **Price:** included in membership dues. **Circulation:** 7,000. Also Cited As: *AAOA Record* ● *Newsbriefs*, bimonthly. Newsletter ● *Roster of Affiliates*, annual ● Annual Report ● Also publishes handbooks. **Conventions/Meetings:** annual meeting.

15462 ■ American Academy of Osteopathy (AAO)
3500 DePauw Blvd., Ste.1080
Indianapolis, IN 46268
Ph: (317)879-1881
Fax: (317)879-0563
E-mail: snoone@academyofosteopathy.org
URL: http://www.academyofosteopathy.org
Contact: Stephen J. Noone CAE, Exec. Dir.
Founded: 1937. **Members:** 7,000. **Membership Dues:** US-trained osteopathic physician, $225 (annual). **Staff:** 6. **Budget:** $1,300,000. **Regional Groups:** 14. **Multinational. Description:** Represents doctors of osteopathy. Seeks to develop and teach the science and art of osteopathic manipulative treatment and encourage greater proficiency in the use of osteopathic structural diagnostic and therapeutic procedures. Conducts graduate courses and seminars; offers structural consultation and treatment service at meetings. Conducts research. **Libraries:** Type: reference. **Awards:** A. T. Still Medallion of Honor. **Frequency:** annual. **Type:** medal. **Recipient:** for outstanding contributions in the field. **Computer Services:** Mailing lists, membership labels. **Committees:** Education; Louisa Burns Osteopathic Research; OPTI Liaison; Postdoctoral Standards and Evaluation; Structural Consultation and Treatment Service; Undergraduate Academies. **Formerly:** (1944) Osteopathic Manipulative Therapeutic and Clinical Research Association; (1970) Academy of Applied Osteopathy. **Publications:** *American Academy of Osteopathy—Quarterly Journal.* **Price:** $60.00/year. **Circulation:** 4,100. **Advertising:** accepted. Alternate Formats: online ● *Contributions to Osteopathic Literature - Myron C. Beal, DO, FAAO,* periodic. Yearbook. **Price:** $25.00 ● Yearbooks. Contains collection of 52 yearbooks on one CD-ROM, over 9,000 pages of osteopathic literature. Alternate Formats: CD-ROM ● Membership Directory, annual. **Conventions/Meetings:** annual Neuromusculoskeletal Medicine: An Osteopathic Evolution - convention (exhibits).

15463 ■ American Association of Colleges of Osteopathic Medicine (AACOM)
5550 Friendship Blvd., Ste.310
Chevy Chase, MD 20815-7231
Ph: (301)968-4100
Fax: (301)968-4101
E-mail: president@aacom.org
URL: http://www.aacom.org
Contact: Stephen C. Shannon DO, Pres./CEO
Founded: 1898. **Members:** 23. **Staff:** 21. **Budget:** $4,325,385. **Description:** Represents osteopathic medical colleges. Operates centralized application service; monitors and works with Congress and other government agencies in the planning of health care programs. Gathers statistics on osteopathic medical students, on innovations in medical education, and faculty. **Awards:** Sherry R. Arnstein Minority Student Scholarship. **Frequency:** annual. **Type:** scholarship. **Recipient:** for qualifying current and incoming minority student at a U.S. college of osteopathic medicine. **Boards:** Deans. **Committees:** AACOMAS Advisory. **Councils:** Development and Alumni Relations Profes-

sionals; Educational Council on Osteopathic Principles; Fiscal Officers; Marketing and Communications Advisory; Osteopathic Medical Student Services; Osteopathic Student Government Presidents; Society of Osteopathic Medical Educators. **Sections:** Chairmen of Departments of Family Medicine; Student Affairs Officers. **Affiliated With:** American Osteopathic Association. **Formerly:** (1970) American Association of Osteopathic Colleges. **Publications:** *American Association of Colleges of Osteopathic Medicine—Annual Statistical Report.* Covers activities of the colleges of osteopathic medicine. Provides information on enrollment, student costs, scholarships and loans. **Price:** $18.00/copy. **Circulation:** 1,500. Alternate Formats: online ● *Clinical Osteopathically Integrated Learning Scenarios.* Book. Provides an overview of how osteopathic principles and manipulative medicine are integrated into care for patients with specific conditions. **Price:** $30.00/copy ● *College Information,* annual. Book. Contains description of each of the 20 osteopathic medical colleges, admissions criteria, class enrollment, application and tuition. Alternate Formats: online ● *Debts and Career Plans of Osteopathic Medical Students,* annual. Book. Reports describing financial debt and career plans of freshmen and seniors in osteopathic colleges. Contains statistics on debts. **Price:** $18.00/copy. **Circulation:** 1,500.

15464 ■ American Association of Physician Specialists (AAPS)

2296 Henderson Mill Rd., Ste.206
Atlanta, GA 30345
Ph: (770)939-8555
Fax: (770)939-8559
E-mail: wcarbone@aapsga.org
URL: http://www.aapsga.org
Contact: William J. Carbone, CEO
Founded: 1950. **Members:** 2,900. **Membership Dues:** resident/retired, $100 (annual) ● regular/diplomat, $595 (annual) ● military regular, $225 (annual) ● military diplomat, $250 (annual). **Staff:** 14. **Budget:** $3,000,000. **Description:** Represents twelve major specialties and twelve sub-specialties of medicine. Accepts qualified physicians into membership with either an allopathic (MD) or osteopathic (DO) degree. Serves as the official headquarters for 15 academies of medicine and boards of certification in the following specialties: anesthesiology, dermatology, disaster medicine, emergency medicine, family practice, internal medicine, geriatric medicine, neurology/psychiatry, obstetrics/gynecology, orthopedic surgery, plastic/reconstructive surgery, radiology, surgery. **Awards:** Degree of Fellow Recipients. **Frequency:** annual. **Type:** fellowship. **Recipient:** for physicians ● E.O. Martin. **Frequency:** annual. **Type:** recognition. **Recipient:** for an individual who has made significant contributions to the AAPS ● Physician of the Year. **Frequency:** annual. **Type:** recognition. **Recipient:** for an individual who has contributed to the growth, recognition and leadership of the academy. **Boards:** Anesthesiology; Critical Care; Dermatology; Emergency Medicine; Family Practice; Geriatric Medicine; Internal Medicine; Neurology and Psychiatry; Obstetrics/Gynecology; Orthopedic Surgery; Plastic and Reconstructive Surgery; Radiology; Surgery. **Committees:** Basic Documents; Continuing Medical Education; Executive; External Relations; Finance; Governmental Affairs; Membership; PAC; Personnel; Program and Meetings; Strategic Planning. **Formerly:** American Association of Osteopathic Specialists; (1984) American Academy of Osteopathic Surgeons. **Publications:** *AAPS Directory,* annual. Provides alphabetical and geographical list of members. **Price:** included in membership dues. **Circulation:** 2,500. **Advertising:** accepted ● *The American Journal of Clinical Medicine (AJCM),* quarterly. Contains detail on how to improve the practice of clinical medicine by providing up to date education for today's practitioners. **Advertising:** accepted. Alternate Formats: online ● *E-Member Notes,* quarterly. Newsletter. **Advertising:** accepted. **Conventions/Meetings:** annual convention and meeting (exhibits).

15465 ■ American College of Osteopathic Family Physicians (ACOFP)

330 E Algonquin Rd., Ste.1
Arlington Heights, IL 60005
Free: (800)323-0794

Fax: (847)228-9755
E-mail: membership@acofp.org
URL: http://www.acofp.org
Contact: Peter L. Schmelzer CAE, Exec. Dir.
Founded: 1950. **Members:** 20,000. **Membership Dues:** active, $125-$250 (annual) ● associate, $150 (annual) ● retired, military, $50 (annual). **Staff:** 16. **Budget:** $4,300,000. **State Groups:** 35. **Description:** Provides information, education and advocacy for osteopathic physicians practicing family medicine. **Awards:** Fellow. **Frequency:** annual. **Type:** recognition. **Recipient:** for outstanding contributions in education to the college. **Telecommunication Services:** electronic mail, peters@acofp.org. **Committees:** Reference. **Formerly:** (1993) American College of General Practitioners in Osteopathic Medicine and Surgery. **Publications:** *Osteopathic Family Physician News,* monthly. Journal. Includes calendar of events and member news. **Price:** free for members. **Circulation:** 15,000. **Advertising:** accepted. Alternate Formats: online. **Conventions/Meetings:** annual convention, pharmaceutical, medical equipment, supplies for physician offices (exhibits) - usually March.

15466 ■ American College of Osteopathic Internists (ACOI)

3 Bethesda Metro Ctr., Ste.508
Bethesda, MD 20814
Ph: (301)656-8877
Free: (800)327-5183
Fax: (301)656-7133
E-mail: bjd@acoi.org
URL: http://www.acoi.org
Contact: Brian J. Donadio, Exec. Dir.
Founded: 1943. **Members:** 1,300. **Membership Dues:** associate, retired, $200 (annual) ● subspecialty section, $50 (annual) ● regular, $400 (annual). **Staff:** 5. **Description:** Osteopathic doctors who limit their practice to internal medicine and various subspecialties and who intend, through postdoctoral education, to qualify as certified specialists in the field. Aims to provide educational programs and to improve educational standards in the field of osteopathic internal medicine. Sponsors competitions. Compiles statistics; offers placement service. **Awards:** Humanism and Excellence in Teaching Award. **Frequency:** annual. **Type:** recognition. **Recipient:** for residents who have demonstrated excellence in clinical teaching ● Teacher, Internist and Researcher of the Year Awards. **Frequency:** annual. **Type:** recognition. **Recipient:** for members with outstanding achievement. **Committees:** Advisory Council on Clinical Investigation; Clinical Practice; Communications; Constitution and Bylaws; Council on Education and Evaluation; Credentials; Editorial; Ethics and Grievances; Exhibits; Government Relations; Honors and Awards; Hospital; Program; Research; Young Internists. **Publications:** *ACOInformation,* monthly. Newsletter. Provides information on CME. **Price:** included in membership dues. **Advertising:** accepted ● *Resident News,* quarterly. Newsletter. **Price:** included in membership dues ● Directory, annual. **Conventions/Meetings:** annual convention (exhibits) - 2007 Oct. 10-14, Boston, MA; 2008 Oct. 8-12, Marco Island, FL.

15467 ■ American College of Osteopathic Pediatricians (ACOP)

2209 Dickens Rd.
Richmond, VA 23230-2005
Free: (877)231-ACOP
Fax: (804)282-0090
E-mail: acop@acopeds.org
URL: http://www.acopeds.org
Contact: Lee J. Herskowitz MBA, Pres.
Founded: 1940. **Members:** 365. **Membership Dues:** intern, $20 (annual) ● resident, $30 (annual) ● general/fellow/associate, $300 (annual). **Description:** Osteopathic physicians who have received or are receiving advanced training in pediatrics and who are specializing in pediatric practice. **Publications:** *ACOP Pulse,* quarterly. Newsletter. Reports on new regulations and sources of information in the field of osteopathic pediatrics. **Price:** included in membership dues. **Circulation:** 375. **Advertising:** accepted ● Membership Directory, annual. **Conventions/**

Meetings: semiannual Scientific Meeting - meeting and seminar - always spring and fall.

15468 ■ American College of Osteopathic Sclerotherapeutic Pain Management (ACOSPM)

303 S Ingram Ct.
Middletown, DE 19709
Ph: (302)376-8080
Free: (800)471-6114
Fax: (302)376-8081
E-mail: admin@acopms.com
URL: http://acopms.com
Contact: Linda J. Pavina, Exec. Sec.
Founded: 1938. **Membership Dues:** general, $200. **Description:** Osteopathic medical therapists. Seeks to improve the practice of and disseminate knowledge about sclerotherapy. Supports research and education. **Awards:** **Frequency:** annual. **Type:** scholarship. **Recipient:** for the osteopathic medical student submitting the best paper on sclerotherapy. **Formerly:** (2005) American College of Osteopathic Pain Management and Sclerotherapy. **Conventions/Meetings:** semiannual seminar and convention.

15469 ■ American College of Osteopathic Surgeons (ACOS)

123 N Henry St.
Alexandria, VA 22314-2903
Ph: (703)684-0416
Free: (800)888-1312
Fax: (703)684-3280
E-mail: info@facos.org
URL: http://www.facos.org
Contact: Guy D. Beaumont Jr., Exec. Dir.
Founded: 1927. **Members:** 1,950. **Membership Dues:** active, $535 (annual) ● dual, $270 (annual) ● U.S. military/public health service, $322 (annual) ● life (full-time practice), $402 ● life (not in practice), $115 ● life (part-time), $201 ● associate/inactive/retired, $60 (annual) ● resident, $110 (annual) ● student, $20. **Staff:** 8. **Budget:** $1,700,000. **Description:** Professional society of osteopathic physicians specializing in surgery and surgical specialties. Maintains placement service; conducts seminars in continuing surgical education. **Awards:** Resident's Awards. **Frequency:** annual. **Type:** recognition. **Computer Services:** Mailing lists, of members. **Committees:** Awards; Ethics; Government Affairs; Grants and Commercial Exhibits; Scientific Exhibits and Posters; Training Standards and Evaluation. **Sections:** Cardiothoracic and Vascular Surgery; General Surgery; Neurological Surgery; Plastic and Reconstructive Surgery; Urology. **Affiliated With:** American Osteopathic Association. **Publications:** *ACOS News,* monthly. Newsletter. Covers association activities and legislative and regulatory issues affecting osteopathic surgeons. Includes calendar of events. **Price:** included in membership dues. **Advertising:** accepted. **Conventions/Meetings:** Annual Clinical Assembly - assembly and seminar, with surgical education seminars and commercial and scientific exhibits (exhibits) - 2007 Oct. 18-21, San Francisco, CA; 2008 Sept. 11-14, Boca Raton, FL ● annual Indepth Review Seminar (exhibits) - usually January.

15470 ■ American Osteopathic Association (AOA)

142 E Ontario St.
Chicago, IL 60611
Ph: (312)202-8000
Free: (800)621-1773
Fax: (312)202-8200
E-mail: info@osteotech.org
URL: http://www.osteopathic.org
Contact: John B. Crosby JD, Exec. Dir.
Founded: 1897. **Members:** 32,300. **Membership Dues:** regular, $590 (annual) ● allied/international physician, $400 (annual) ● retired/associate, $90 (annual) ● postdoctoral training, $60 (annual). **Budget:** $8,000,000. **Regional Groups:** 4. **State Groups:** 50. **Description:** Osteopathic physicians, surgeons, and graduates of approved colleges of osteopathic medicine. Associate members include teaching, research, administrative, and executive employees of approved colleges, hospitals, divisional societies, and

affiliated organizations. Forms (with its affiliates) an officially recognized structure of the osteopathic profession. Promotes the public health to encourage scientific research, and to maintain and improve high standards of medical education in osteopathic colleges. Inspects and accredits colleges and hospitals; conducts a specialty certification program; sponsors a national examining board satisfactory to state licensing agencies; maintains mandatory program of continuing medical education for members. **Awards:** Research Awards. **Frequency:** annual. **Type:** recognition. **Recipient:** for essential contribution of research ● **Type:** scholarship. **Committees:** Colleges; Continuing Medical Education; Hospital Accreditation; Organizational Structure; Osteopathic Progress Fund; Osteopathic Specialties; Political Action; Postdoctoral Training. **Councils:** Federal Health Programs. **Publications:** *AOA Yearbook and Directory of Osteopathic Physicians.* Alternate Formats: online ● *The D.O.,* monthly. Magazine. Contains news about the profession and its members. **Price:** $75.00 /year for nonmembers in U.S.; $130.00 /year for nonmembers outside U.S. Alternate Formats: online ● *Journal of AOA,* monthly. Contains documentation and articles on clinical teaching. **Price:** $75.00 /year for nonmembers in U.S.; $130.00 /year for nonmembers outside U.S. Alternate Formats: online ● *What is a DO?.* Brochures. Explains osteopathic medicine from historical perspective. **Price:** $20.00 for nonmembers. Alternate Formats: online. **Conventions/Meetings:** annual meeting and seminar (exhibits).

15471 ■ American Osteopathic Board of Family Physicians (AOBFP)
330 E Algonquin Rd., Ste.6
Arlington Heights, IL 60005
Ph: (847)640-8477
Free: (800)390-5801
E-mail: aobfp@aobfp.org
URL: http://www.aobfp.org
Contact: Carol A. Thoma MBA, Exec. Dir.
Founded: 1972. **Staff:** 2. **Description:** Certifying board for osteopathic physicians. Prepares and administers semiannual certification examination and annual recertification exam. **Affiliated With:** American College of Osteopathic Family Physicians; American Osteopathic Association. **Formerly:** (1993) American Osteopathic Board of General Practice. **Conventions/Meetings:** annual meeting.

15472 ■ American Osteopathic Board of Pediatrics (AOBP)
142 E Ontario St.
Chicago, IL 60611
Ph: (312)202-8267
Free: (800)621-1773
E-mail: aobp@osteopathic.org
URL: http://www.aobp.org
Contact: Jay D. Johnson DO, Sec.-Treas.
Founded: 1940. **Description:** Certification board for osteopathic pediatricians. Standards are formulated by the American Osteopathic Association. Certification is conducted by annual examination. **Conventions/Meetings:** annual conference.

15473 ■ American Osteopathic Board of Preventive Medicine (AOBPM)
142 E Ontario St., 4th Fl.
Chicago, IL 60611-2864
Free: (800)621-1773
Fax: (602)268-3042
E-mail: aobmp@osteopathic.org
URL: http://www.aobpm.org
Contact: James L. Fleming DO, Sec.
Description: Evaluates and recommends osteopathic board certification in the specialty areas of preventive medicine/aerospace medicine, preventive medicine/occupational-environmental medicine, and preventive medicine/public health-community medicine.

15474 ■ American Osteopathic College of Occupational and Preventive Medicine (AOCOPM)
c/o Mr. Jeffrey J. LeBoeuf, Pres.
Associates Innovators, LCC
5620 Cedar Park Dr., Ste.1-B
Jackson, MS 39206
Free: (800)558-8686

Fax: (601)366-2868
E-mail: jeffrey@moma-net.org
URL: http://www.aocopm.org
Contact: Mr. Jeffrey J. LeBoeuf, Pres.
Founded: 1982. **Members:** 250. **Staff:** 3. **Budget:** $200,000. **Description:** Osteopathic doctors. Prepares and educates doctors of osteopathy who wish to specialize in aerospace medicine, occupational/environmental medicine, or public health preventive medicine. Seeks to foster an understanding of these fields of study among osteopathic doctors and the public. Provides consultant services to other physicians. Maintains speakers' bureau. Conducts studies. **Awards:** Frank Lovejoy Memorial Lecture. **Type:** recognition ● Kenneth Riland Memorial Lecture. **Type:** recognition. **Recipient:** for individuals who have exhibited outstanding performance in his or her specialization ● Loren Hatch Memorial Lecture. **Type:** recognition ● Murray Goldstein Memorial Lecture. **Type:** recognition. **Computer Services:** database ● mailing lists ● online services, e-mail broadcast. **Telecommunication Services:** electronic mail, srees@reesgroupinc.com. **Divisions:** Aerospace Medicine; Disability and Impairment Evaluation Medicine; Occupational and Environmental Medicine; Public Health/General Preventive Medicine. **Affiliated With:** American Osteopathic Association. **Formed by Merger of:** American Osteopathic Academy of Public Health and Preventive Medicine; American Osteopathic Occupational Medical Association. **Formerly:** (2003) American Osteopathic College of Preventive Medicine. **Publications:** *AOCOPM News,* semiannual. Newsletter. Alternate Formats: online ● Membership Directory, annual. **Price:** free for members. **Advertising:** accepted. Alternate Formats: online; CD-ROM. **Conventions/Meetings:** semiannual conference ● annual symposium.

15475 ■ American Osteopathic College of Ophthalmology and the American Osteopathic College of Otolaryngology-Head and Neck Surgery (AOCOO-HNS)
4764 Fishburg Rd., Ste.F
Huber Heights, OH 45424
Ph: (937)233-5653
Free: (800)455-9404
Fax: (937)233-5673
E-mail: info@aocoohns.org
URL: http://www.aocoohns.org
Contact: Debra L. Bailey, Admin. Dir.
Founded: 1918. **Members:** 670. **Membership Dues:** physician, $475 (annual). **Staff:** 2. **Budget:** $250,000. **Description:** Osteopathic ophthalmologists and osteopathic otolaryngologists/facial plastic surgeons. Created to improve quality of training, education and practice of osteopathic ophthalmologists and facial plastic surgeons. Provides "members only" access to areas of professional interest, including basic documents and committee matters. **Awards:** Patrick Murray Award. **Frequency:** annual. **Type:** monetary. **Recipient:** to the highest scoring resident in the annual OKAP examination. **Computer Services:** Online services. **Committees:** Adhoc; Audit; Editorial; Ethics; Medical Education; Nominating; Quality Improvement; Strategic Planning Adhoc. **Publications:** *Quarterly Report.* Newsletter. Alternate Formats: online. **Conventions/Meetings:** annual assembly.

15476 ■ American Osteopathic College of Pathologists (AOCP)
142 E Ontario St.
Chicago, IL 60611-8224
Ph: (312)202-8197
Fax: (312)202-8224
URL: http://www.aocp-net.org
Contact: Jason Friske, Interim Exec. Dir.
Founded: 1954. **Members:** 180. **Membership Dues:** active, $300 ● 1st year in practice, $150 ● retired, $100 ● candidate (resident), $10. **Description:** Osteopathic physicians who have completed residency training programs in pathology and clinical pathology; candidate members are in residency training in pathology. Establishes guidelines for training programs in pathology and clinical pathology for osteopathic physicians; maintains standards in residency training programs. Offers placement service and mid-

year tutorial program. Maintains collection of slide study sets. **Libraries: Type:** open to the public. **Holdings:** reports. **Subjects:** pathology. **Awards:** Distinguished Service Award. **Frequency:** annual. **Type:** recognition. **Recipient:** for pathologist of the year ● Founders Memorial Lecture. **Frequency:** annual. **Type:** recognition. **Recipient:** for a resident with an outstanding paper. **Committees:** Editorial; Evaluating; Graduate Education; Membership and Public Relations; National Laboratory Standards and Inspections; Program; Resolutions; Rules and Regulations. **Publications:** *American Osteopathic College of Pathologists Directory,* annual ● *Nova,* monthly. Newsletter. Includes reports on employment opportunities and topics of interest. **Price:** included in membership dues. **Conventions/Meetings:** annual convention and meeting (exhibits).

15477 ■ American Osteopathic College of Physical Medicine and Rehabilitation (AOCPMR)
PO Box 732
Dover, NH 03821-0732
Ph: (603)343-1937
Fax: (603)343-1938
E-mail: executive.director@aocpmr.org
URL: http://www.aocpmr.org
Contact: Brenda L. Woods DO, Pres.
Founded: 1954. **Members:** 225. **Membership Dues:** active/associate, $295 (annual). **Description:** Osteopathic physicians with a strong interest in physical and rehabilitation medicine as a specialty. Active members are those certified in the specialty by the American Osteopathic Board of Rehabilitation Medicine of Physical Medicine & Rehabilitation, an affiliate of the American Osteopathic Association (see separate entry). Stimulates study, extends knowledge, and improves practice in rehabilitation medicine. Co-sponsors training programs; sponsors competitive writing for pre-doctoral osteopathic medical students, interns, and residents. **Committees:** Coding and Reimbursement; Constitution and By-laws; Education; Evaluating; Nominating; Publication; Special Awards. **Formerly:** (1955) American Osteopathic Academy of Physical Medicine and Rehabilitation; (1970) American Osteopathic College of Physical Medicine and Rehabilitation; (2001) American Osteopathic College of Rehabilitation Medicine. **Publications:** Directory, annual ● Newsletter, periodic. **Conventions/Meetings:** annual meeting, in conjunction with AOA.

15478 ■ American Osteopathic Foundation (AOF)
142 E Ontario St., Ste.502
Chicago, IL 60611
Ph: (312)202-8234
Free: (800)621-1773
Fax: (312)202-8216
E-mail: info@aof-foundation.org
URL: http://www.aof-foundation.org
Contact: Stephen S. Downey, Exec. Dir.
Founded: 1949. **Members:** 9,300. **Membership Dues:** individual, $35 (annual) ● century, $100 (annual) ● gentry, $250 (annual) ● patron, $500 (annual) ● benefactor, $1,000 (annual) ● Andrew T. Still Society, grand patron (corporate), $15,000 (annual) ● sponsor (corporate), $2,500 (annual) ● sustaining (corporate), $5,000 (annual) ● patron (corporate), $10,000 (annual). **Staff:** 5. **Budget:** $350,000. **Description:** Osteopathic physicians and laypersons interested in raising and administering funds for osteopathic medical education, research, colleges, and hospitals. Functions as philanthropic affiliate of the American Osteopathic Association (see separate entry); seeks to foster understanding of osteopathic principles and practice. **Awards:** Bristol-Myers Squibb Outstanding Resident Award. **Frequency:** annual. **Type:** grant. **Recipient:** for a 2nd or 3rd year osteopathic medical resident in Family Practice, Internal Medicine, or Pediatrics ● Donna Jones Moritsugu Memorial Award. **Frequency:** annual. **Type:** recognition. **Recipient:** for a spouse of a graduating osteopathic medical student ● Russell C. McCaughan Education Scholarship. **Frequency:** annual. **Type:** scholarship. **Recipient:** for an osteopathic medical

student ● Zeneca Pharmaceuticals Underserved Healthcare Grant. **Frequency:** annual. **Type:** scholarship. **Recipient:** for one or two students in the colleges of osteopathic medicine, demonstrating commitment to practice in underserved or minority populations. **Telecommunication Services:** electronic mail, sdowney@aof-foundation.org. **Boards:** Directors; Foundation Advisory. **Committees:** Development; Educational Grants; Fundraising; Program Administration; Student Loan Fund. **Affiliated With:** American Osteopathic Association. **Formerly:** (1960) Osteopathic Foundation; (1998) National Osteopathic Foundation. **Publications:** *AOF In Touch*, triennial. Newsletter. **Price:** free, for members only. **Conventions/Meetings:** board meeting - 3/year ● executive committee meeting - 3/year.

15479 ■ Association of Military Osteopathic Physicians and Surgeons (AMOPS)
1796 Seven Hills Ln.
Severn, MD 21144-1061
Ph: (410)519-8217
Fax: (410)519-7657
E-mail: jyonts@amops.org
URL: http://www.amops.org
Contact: Jim Yonts, Exec. Dir.
Founded: 1977. **Membership Dues:** active, $90 (annual) ● intern, resident, $20 (annual) ● student, $5 (annual) ● associate, $40 (annual). **Description:** Represents the interests of osteopathic physicians in the uniformed services. Promotes the advancement of osteopathic principles in military and federal institutions. **Publications:** Newsletter, quarterly. Alternate Formats: online.

15480 ■ Association of Osteopathic Directors and Medical Educators (AODME)
142 E Ontario St.
Chicago, IL 60611
Ph: (312)202-8211
Fax: (312)202-8224
E-mail: gmoorma1@hfhs.org
URL: http://www.aodme.org
Contact: James W. Cole DO, Pres.
Members: 250. **Membership Dues:** active, $300 (annual) ● associate, $100 (annual). **Staff:** 5. **Regional Groups:** 8. **Description:** Provides leadership for the development, improvement, and evaluation of education and training of osteopathic physicians at all levels in order to further the quality of the osteopathic profession. Offers educational programs. **Awards:** Collegium of Fellows. **Frequency:** annual. **Type:** recognition. **Recipient:** for contributions to the association and to the profession of osteopathic medical education. **Boards:** Trustees. **Committees:** Education; Internship Evaluation; Membership; Program/Education. **Publications:** *Osteopathic Progress*. Newsletter. **Conventions/Meetings:** annual Osteopathic Partners in Progress Convention - convention and board meeting.

15481 ■ Association of Osteopathic State Executive Directors (AOSED)
2007 Apalache Pkwy.
Tallahassee, FL 32301-4867
Ph: (850)878-7364
Fax: (850)942-7538
E-mail: admin@foma.org
URL: http://www.osteopathic.org/index.
  cfm?PageID=lcl_affil
Contact: Michelle Winn, Contact
Founded: 1919. **Members:** 75. **Staff:** 1. **Budget:** $30,000. **Description:** Divisional and affiliated societies of the American Osteopathic Association (see separate entry). Seeks to promote and improve associations and procedures among members; to examine and develop procedures and policies that will bring about an efficient unit of operation within the divisional societies; to disseminate information on the activities of members and foster and participate in the objectives of the AOA. **Additional Websites:** http://www.do-online.osteotech.org/index. cfm?PageID=lcl_aosedmain. **Publications:** *Directory of Osteopathic Publications*, biennial ● Newsletter. **Conventions/Meetings:** semiannual conference and seminar.

15482 ■ Bureau of Professional Education of the American Osteopathic Association (BPEAOA)
Amer. Osteopathic Assn.
142 E Ontario St.
Chicago, IL 60611
Ph: (312)202-8000
Free: (800)621-1773
Fax: (312)202-8200
E-mail: info@osteotech.org
URL: http://www.osteopathic.org
Members: 13. **Description:** Membership comprises of American Osteopathic Associations representatives from other AOA affiliates, and public representatives. Approves policy regarding new and/or different intern and residency training programs in approved osteopathic hospitals. Serves as accrediting agency for colleges of osteopathic medicine. Oversees osteopathic continuing medical education activities. **Publications:** *Accreditation of Colleges of Osteopathic Medicine*. Handbook. Contains accreditation standards, policies and procedures. **Conventions/Meetings:** meeting - 3/year, January, June, October.

15483 ■ Cranial Academy (CA)
8202 Clearvista Pkwy., No. 9-D
Indianapolis, IN 46256
Ph: (317)594-0411
Fax: (317)594-9299
E-mail: info@cranialacademy.org
URL: http://www.cranialacademy.com
Contact: Sidney N. Dunn, Exec. Dir.
Founded: 1947. **Members:** 1,200. **Membership Dues:** regular, $155 (annual) ● associate, $120 (annual) ● affiliate, $130 (annual) ● intern, resident, $40 (annual) ● student, $25 (annual) ● life, $2,325. **Staff:** 2. **Budget:** $350,000. **Description:** A component society of the American Academy of Osteopathy. Osteopathic physicians interested in the study and development of osteopathic cranial concepts and techniques of diagnosis and treatment in structural manipulation of the body; members have taken a Cranial Academy approved basic course in Osteopathy in the cranial field. Promotes research programs. **Awards: Type:** recognition. **Committees:** Bylaws; Communications; Credentials; Editorial Board; Education; Publications; Research. **Task Forces:** Critical Issues. **Formerly:** (1960) Osteopathic Cranial Association. **Publications:** *Clinical Cranial Osteopathy*. Book. Contains articles in the cranial field. **Price:** $45.00 for members; $50.00 for nonmembers ● *The Cranial Bowl*. Book. **Price:** $15.00 for members; $17.00 for nonmembers ● *The Cranial Bowl*. Brochure. Contains extracts from lectures relative to the cranial concept. **Price:** $1.00 for nonmembers ● *The Cranial Concept*. Brochure. **Price:** $27.00/100 copies for members; $30.00/100 copies for nonmembers ● *The Cranial Letter*, quarterly. Newsletter. Contains articles related to new developments in cranial osteopathy. **Price:** $60.00 /year for individuals. **Circulation:** 1,250. **Advertising:** accepted ● *Journal of OCA 1948, 49, 54, 57, & 58*. **Price:** $18.00 for members; $20.00 for nonmembers ● *Manual of Cranial Technique*. Book. Contains medical reference for health care professionals. **Price:** $22.50 for members; $25.00 for nonmembers ● *Member Information Directory*, annual. **Price:** included in membership dues. **Conventions/Meetings:** annual Cranial in Special Needs Populations - conference (exhibits) - always third weekend in June.

15484 ■ National Board of Osteopathic Medical Examiners (NBOME)
8765 W Higgins Rd., Ste.200
Chicago, IL 60631-4174
Ph: (773)714-0622
Fax: (773)714-0631
E-mail: candidateservice@nbome.org
URL: http://www.nbome.org
Contact: Frederick G. Meoli DO, Pres.
Founded: 1935. **Members:** 12. **Description:** Examining and evaluating board that investigate the qualifications of, and administer examinations and grant diplomate status to osteopathic physicians. **Formerly:** (1986) National Board of Examiners for Osteopathic Physicians and Surgeons. **Publications:**

Bulletin of Information, annual. Alternate Formats: online. **Conventions/Meetings:** annual meeting - always May, in Des Plaines, IL.

15485 ■ Pain Management and Sclerotherapy
303 S Ingram Ct.
Middletown, DE 19709-7935
Ph: (302)376-8080
Free: (800)471-6114
Contact: Linda Pavina, Exec. Sec.
Founded: 1938. **Members:** 145. **Description:** Dedicated to improving the practice of and disseminating knowledge about sclerotherapy. (The academy defines sclerotherapy as the stimulation of the formation of fibrous-connective tissues by the body, in a specific location, by the specific application of a sclerosing modality.) The most frequently used modality is the injection of certain medications, known as sclerosants. Primary studies involve the treatment of: unstable joints, venous abnormalities, and tendeno-osseous points of hyper-irritability. Supports research program; maintains speakers' bureau. **Awards: Frequency:** annual. **Type:** scholarship. **Recipient:** to an osteopathic medical student submitting the best paper on sclerotherapy; students are invited to present paper at academy convention. **Formed by Merger of:** American Osteopathic Society of Herniologists; Central States Osteopathic Herniologists. **Formerly:** (1956) American Osteopathic Academy of Sclerotherapy; (1959) American Academy of Sclerotherapy. **Publications:** *Get the Point*, semiannual. Newsletter. Reports on the results of studies; evaluates differing sclerotherapeutic treatments. **Price:** included in membership dues. **Circulation:** 145 ● Directory, periodic. **Conventions/Meetings:** semiannual seminar (exhibits).

15486 ■ Student Osteopathic Medical Association (SOMA)
142 E Ontario St.
Chicago, IL 60611
Ph: (312)202-8193
Free: (800)621-1773
Fax: (312)202-8200
E-mail: somanat@studentdo.com
URL: http://www.studentdo.com
Contact: Elizabeth Hodor, Natl. Admin.
Founded: 1970. **Members:** 6,000. **Membership Dues:** regular (medical student), $60 (annual). **Description:** Seeks to improve the quality of healthcare delivery; contributes to the education of osteopathic medical students, aims to improve awareness of osteopathic medicine, and establishes communication between healthcare professionals. **Awards:** SOMA Spirit Award. **Frequency:** annual. **Type:** monetary. **Recipient:** for the best, most spirited and creative NOM week activities. **Programs:** AT Still Memorial Scholarship; Doctors' Debt Management Loan Consolidation; International Health; Medically Underserved; Osteopathic Principles and Practices; Political Development; Pre-SOMA; Preventive Medicine. **Publications:** *Student Doctor*. Magazine. **Price:** included in membership dues. Alternate Formats: online ● Newsletter. Alternate Formats: online.

Otorhinolaryngology

15487 ■ Acoustic Neuroma Association (ANA)
600 Peachtree Pkwy., Ste.108
Cumming, GA 30041-6899
Ph: (770)205-8211
Free: (877)200-8211
Fax: (770)205-0239
E-mail: info@anausa.com
URL: http://www.anausa.org
Contact: Agnes Garino, Pres.
Founded: 1981. **Members:** 5,000. **Membership Dues:** basic, $35 (annual) ● basic (international), $50 (annual) ● medical professional, $100 (annual). **Staff:** 2. **Budget:** $190,000. **Local Groups:** 43. **Description:** Provides information and support to patients who have been diagnosed with or experienced an acoustic neuroma or other benign problem

affecting the cranial nerves. The association also furnishes information on patient rehabilitation to physicians and health care personnel, promotes research on acoustic neuroma, thus promoting early diagnosis and successful treatment. **Computer Services:** database. **Publications:** *A Glimpse of the Brain.* Booklet ● *Acoustic Neuroma, Basic Overview.* Booklet ● *The Acoustic Neuroma Experience 1988/ Member Survey.* Booklet ● *ANA Notes,* quarterly. Newsletter ● *Diagnosis Acoustic Neuroma: What Next?.* Booklet ● *Eye Care after Acoustic Neuroma Surgery.* Booklet ● *Facial Nerve and Acoustic Neuroma: Possible Damage and Rehabilitation.* Booklet ● *Headache Following Acoustic Neuroma.* Booklet ● *Improving Balance Following Treatment for AN.* Booklet ● Newsletter, quarterly. Covers advances in the treatment of acoustic neuroma, patient letters and support group information. **Price:** included in membership dues. **Circulation:** 4,800 ● Booklets. **Price:** included in membership dues. **Conventions/ Meetings:** biennial symposium (exhibits).

15488 ■ American Academy of Otolaryngology - Head and Neck Surgery (AAO-HNS)
1 Prince St.
Alexandria, VA 22314-3354
Ph: (703)836-4444
Fax: (703)299-1124
E-mail: webmaster@entnet.org
URL: http://www.entnet.org
Contact: Richard T. Miyamoto MD, Pres.

Founded: 1896. **Members:** 11,000. **Membership Dues:** fellow, $75-$525 (annual) ● associate, $425 (annual) ● affiliate, $100 (annual). **Staff:** 75. **Budget:** $15,000,000. **Description:** Professional society of medical doctors specializing in otolaryngology (diseases of the ear, nose, and throat) and head and neck surgery. Represents otolaryngology in governmental and socioeconomic areas and provides high-quality medical education for otolaryngologists. Coordinates Combined Otolaryngological Spring Meetings for ten national otolaryngological societies. Operates job information exchange service and museum. **Libraries: Type:** reference. **Holdings:** archival material, books, monographs, periodicals. **Subjects:** otolaryngology - head and neck surgery. **Awards: Type:** grant. **Recipient:** for research ● Honor Award. **Frequency:** annual. **Type:** recognition ● Humanitarian Efforts Award. **Frequency:** annual. **Type:** recognition ● Presidential Award. **Frequency:** annual. **Type:** recognition. **Computer Services:** On-line services, Physician Directory. **Telecommunication Services:** teletype, (703)519-1585. **Committees:** Allergy and Immunology; Computer; Environment; Ethics; Facial Nerve Disorders; Geriatric Otolaryngology; Head and Neck Surgery and Oncology; Health Policy; Hearing and Equilibrium; Humanitarian Efforts; Infectious Disease; Interprofessional Relations; Laser Surgery; Latin American Medicine; Long Range Planning; Manpower; Medical Devices and Drugs; Otolaryngic Pathology; Pediatric Otolaryngology; Plastic and Reconstructive Surgery; Practice Management; Professional Liability; Professional Relations and Public Education; Quality Assurance; Reimbursement Programs; Relative Values; Research in Otolaryngology; Rhinology and Paranasal Sinus Disease; Skull Base Surgery; Sleep Disorders; Speech, Voice and Swallowing Disorders. **Programs:** Annual Otolaryngology Exam; Audiocassette; Continuing Education With Television; Home Study Courses; Patient of the Month; Self-Instructional Package. **Publications:** *American Academy of Otolaryngology-Head and Neck Surgery—Bulletin,* monthly. Magazine. Includes academy news, calendar of events, employment opportunity listings, legislative news, and research updates. **Price:** included in membership dues; $55.00 /year for nonmembers. ISSN: 0731-8359. **Circulation:** 11,000. **Advertising:** accepted ● *Conjoint Directory of the American Academy of Otolaryngology - Head and Neck Surgery,* semiannual ● *Otolaryngology - Head and Neck Surgery,* monthly. Journal. **Price:** included in membership dues; $205.00 /year for nonmembers in U.S.; $365.00 /year for institutions in U.S. ●

Monographs ● Videos. **Conventions/Meetings:** annual OTO Expo - conference (exhibits).

15489 ■ American Board of Otolaryngology (ABOto)
5615 Kirby Dr., Ste.600
Houston, TX 77005
Ph: (713)850-0399
Fax: (713)850-1104
E-mail: czw@aboto.org
URL: http://www.aboto.org
Contact: Robert H. Miller MD, Exec. Dir.

Founded: 1924. **Staff:** 8. **Description:** Aims to elevate standards of practice in otolaryngology (the medical specialty dealing with ear, nose, throat, head, and neck surgery); holds examinations and certify qualified otolaryngologists; advances the cause of the field. Conducts annual in-training, written and oral examinations. **Telecommunication Services:** electronic mail, vam@aboto.org. **Publications:** Newsletter, semiannual.

15490 ■ American Head and Neck Society (AHNS)
11300 W Olympic Blvd., Ste.600
Los Angeles, CA 90064
Ph: (310)437-0559
Fax: (310)437-0585
E-mail: admin@ahns.info
URL: http://www.headandneckcancer.org
Contact: Gregory T. Wolf MD, Pres.

Founded: 1959. **Members:** 1,635. **Membership Dues:** active, $300 (annual) ● corresponding, associate, $75 (annual) ● candidate, $25 (annual). **Staff:** 1. **Budget:** $100,000. **Description:** Otolaryngologists and other physicians with board certification whose primary interest is head and neck oncology. Associate membership is for other practitioners who treat head and neck cancer. Seeks to advance knowledge relevant to treatment of diseases of the head and neck, including reconstruction and rehabilitation. Promotes development of programs of training in head and neck oncology. **Libraries: Type:** reference. **Holdings:** archival material, reports. **Awards:** Alando J. Ballantyne Award. **Type:** monetary. **Recipient:** for the best grant application by a resident ● Research Award. **Frequency:** annual. **Type:** grant. **Recipient:** for best head and neck cancer research ● Resident Awards. **Type:** recognition ● Robert Maxwell Byers Award. **Type:** monetary. **Recipient:** for the best clinical paper. **Computer Services:** Mailing lists. **Councils:** Advanced Training; Executive. **Formerly:** (1998) Society of Head and Neck Surgeons; (1999) American Society for Head and Neck Surgery; (2000) American Society of Head and Neck Surgeons. **Publications:** *Head and Neck Cancer Practice Guidelines.* Contains practice Guidelines for Head and Neck Oncology. **Price:** $5.00 for members; $10.00 for nonmembers. **Conventions/Meetings:** quadrennial Conference on Head and Neck Cancer (exhibits) - 2008 July 19-23, San Francisco, CA ● annual meeting, held in conjunction with Society of Surgical Oncology.

15491 ■ American Laryngological Association (ALA)
c/o Ms. Maxine Cunningham, Admin.
Dept. of Otolaryngology
Vanderbilt Univ. Medical Ctr.
1215 21st Ave. S
7302 Medical Center E
Nashville, TN 37232-8783
Ph: (615)322-6326 (615)812-6170
Fax: (615)322-9102
E-mail: maxine@alahns.org
URL: http://www.alahns.org
Contact: Ms. Maxine Cunningham, Admin.

Founded: 1879. **Members:** 232. **Membership Dues:** corresponding fellowship, $150 (annual) ● active fellowship, $300 (annual). **Multinational. Description:** Serves as professional medical society of otorhinolaryngologists (specialists in ear, nose, and throat diseases). Works to advance research in medicine and surgery, with emphasis on the upper aerodigestive tract. **Libraries: Type:** reference. **Holdings:** archival material. **Awards:** Casselberry Award. **Fre-**

quency: annual. **Type:** monetary. **Recipient:** for outstanding manuscripts or accomplishments in Laryngology and Rhinology ● Seymour R. Cohen Award. **Frequency:** annual. **Type:** monetary. **Recipient:** for basic science research in pediatric laryngology/neurolaryngology. **Committees:** Casselberry Fund; DeRoaldes Fund; Newcomb Award. **Publications:** *Transactions,* annual. **Conventions/Meetings:** annual competition, in conjunction with other societies - always May ● annual meeting (exhibits).

15492 ■ American Laryngological, Rhinological and Otological Society (ALROS)
555 N 30th St.
Omaha, NE 68131
Ph: (402)346-5500
Fax: (402)346-5300
E-mail: info@triological.org
URL: http://www.triological.org
Contact: David F. Wilson MD, Pres.

Founded: 1895. **Members:** 1,300. **Membership Dues:** resident in U.S. and Canada, $55 (annual) ● active fellow, $50 (annual) ● post-graduate, $85 (annual). **Staff:** 4. **Regional Groups:** 4. **Description:** Serves as professional society of medical specialists dealing with the ear, nose, and throat. **Also Known As:** Triological Society. **Publications:** *The Laryngoscope,* monthly. Journal. Covers annual meeting; includes membership list. **Price:** included in membership dues; $252.00 for nonmembers in U.S. (individual); $469.00 for nonmembers in U.S. (institutional); $103.00 for nonmembers in U.S. (in-training). ISSN: 0023-852X. **Advertising:** accepted. Alternate Formats: online ● *Triologistics.* Newsletter. Alternate Formats: online. **Conventions/Meetings:** annual Scientific Session - meeting (exhibits) - 2008 May 1-4, Orlando, FL.

15493 ■ American Otological Society (AOS)
c/o Ms. Shirley Gossard, Admin.
3096 Riverdale Rd.
The Villages, FL 32162
Ph: (352)751-0932
Fax: (352)751-0696
E-mail: segossard@aol.com
URL: http://www.americanotologicalsociety.org
Contact: Antonio De La Cruz MD, Pres.

Founded: 1868. **Members:** 294. **Membership Dues:** associate, $100 (annual) ● corresponding, $200 (annual). **Budget:** $35,000. **Description:** Otologists and contributors to the advancement of otology. Encourages study and research in otology (the science of the ear and its diseases). Aims to advance and promote medical and surgical otology, including the rehabilitation of the hearing impaired, and to encourage and promote research in otology and related disciplines. Maintains research fund for advanced studies of otosclerosis. **Libraries: Type:** reference. **Subjects:** otology. **Awards:** Award of Merit. **Frequency:** annual. **Type:** recognition. **Recipient:** for individual ● Clinician-Scientist. **Frequency:** annual. **Type:** scholarship. **Recipient:** for clinician scientist ● Guest of Honor. **Frequency:** annual. **Type:** recognition. **Recipient:** for individual ● Research Training. **Frequency:** annual. **Type:** fellowship. **Recipient:** for physician only. **Publications:** *Otology & Neurotology,* 8/year. Journal. **Price:** $410.00/year subscription for active member; $420.00/year subscription for international active member. ISSN: 1531-7129 ● Newsletter. Alternate Formats: online. **Conventions/Meetings:** annual meeting - spring.

15494 ■ American Rhinologic Society (ARS)
c/o Wendi Perez, Admin.
9 Sunset Terr.
Warwick, NY 10990
Ph: (845)988-1631
Fax: (845)986-1527
E-mail: arsinfo@american-rhinologic.org
URL: http://www.american-rhinologic.org
Contact: Wendi Perez, Admin.

Founded: 1954. **Members:** 1,087. **Membership Dues:** fellow/regular, $240 (annual) ● associate, $100 (annual) ● international, $140 (annual). **Staff:** 1. **Description:** Physicians who are diplomates of the American Board of Otolaryngology, the American

Board of Plastic Surgery (see separate entries), and other boards and who have had additional training and interest in the study of medical and surgical rhinology. Works to advance knowledge of rhinology (branch of medicine that relates to the nose and its diseases) internationally through short, frequent teaching courses at universities in conjunction with their faculties. Conducts research in nasal physiology, rhinomanometry, and anatomy. **Libraries: Type:** reference. **Holdings:** 20,000; audio recordings, audiovisuals. **Subjects:** rhinology. **Awards:** Dr. Maurice H. Cottle Honor Award. **Frequency:** annual. **Type:** recognition. **Recipient:** for original clinical and laboratory research in rhinology. **Computer Services:** database ● mailing lists ● online services. **Committees:** Audit; Awards; By-Laws; Credentials; Education; Friendship; Information Technology; Nominating; Patient Advocacy; Public Relations; Research; Rhinomanometry Standardization. **Publications:** *American Journal of Rhinology*, bimonthly. **Price:** $177.00/year. **Advertising:** accepted ● Membership Directory, biennial ● Newsletter, 4-5/year. **Conventions/Meetings:** semiannual COSM - meeting (exhibits).

15495 ■ Association for Research in Otolaryngology (ARO)
19 Mantua Rd.
Mount Royal, NJ 08061
Ph: (856)423-0041
Fax: (856)423-3420
E-mail: headquarters@aro.org
URL: http://www.aro.org
Contact: Robert V. Shannon PhD, Pres.
Founded: 1973. **Members:** 2,100. **Membership Dues:** associate, $50 (annual) ● regular, $120 (annual). **Description:** Medical professionals, scientists, and researchers with an interest in otolaryngology. Promotes increased understanding of basic science and clinical practice associated with hearing, speech, balance, the senses of taste and smell, and diseases of the head and neck. Conducts educational programs; facilitates exchange of information among members. **Awards:** Midwinter Meeting Travel Award. **Frequency:** annual. **Type:** grant. **Computer Services:** Mailing lists, sale of member list. **Committees:** Animal Research; Diversity and Minority Affairs; Education; Government Relations; Long Range Planning; Nominating; Physician Research Training; Publications. **Publications:** *ARO News*, annual. Newsletter. Features articles on current issues, upcoming meetings, and member recognition. Alternate Formats: online ● *Journal of the Association for Research in Otolaryngology (JARO)*, quarterly. ISSN: 1525-3961. **Advertising:** accepted. Alternate Formats: online ● Membership Directory, annual. Contains membership information. **Conventions/Meetings:** periodic board meeting ● annual Mid Winter Research Meeting (exhibits) ● annual Research Forum - seminar ● annual trade show.

15496 ■ Ear Foundation (EF)
PO Box 330867
Nashville, TN 37203
Ph: (615)627-2724
Free: (800)545-HEAR
Fax: (615)627-2728
E-mail: info@earfoundation.org
URL: http://www.earfoundation.org
Contact: Suzanne Wyatt, Exec. Dir.
Founded: 1971. **Staff:** 2. **Description:** Benefactors dedicated to advance medical knowledge concerning ear diseases and to encourage public understanding of such disorders. Offers professional and public education programs; research directed towards Eustachian tube disorders, ear diseases, and related disorders such as hearing loss, tinnitus, and vertigo. **Awards:** Minnie Pearl Scholarship. **Type:** scholarship. **Recipient:** for hearing impaired students. **Publications:** *Steady*, periodic. Newsletter. Contains helpful tips on coping with Meniere's Disease. ● Brochures ● Monographs.

15497 ■ Meniere's Network (MN)
c/o The Ear Foundation
PO Box 330867
Nashville, TN 37203

Ph: (615)627-2724
Free: (800)545-HEAR
Fax: (615)627-2728
E-mail: info@earfoundation.org
URL: http://www.earfoundation.org
Contact: Suzanne Wyatt, Exec. Dir.
Founded: 1987. **Members:** 1,500. **Membership Dues:** regular, $25 (annual). **Staff:** 3. **Description:** Persons suffering from Meniere's disease, an inner ear disorder of unknown cause that results in vertigo, tinnitus, and hearing fluctuation or loss. Seeks to develop a network of peer support groups to help integrate hearing- and balance-impaired people into mainstream society. Operates pen pals and phone buddies services; offers educational programs and materials. **Publications:** *A Dietary Guidebook for Meniere's Disease; An Introduction to Meniere's Disease; Meniere's Disease-Coping Skills.* Booklet. **Price:** $1.35 pack of 3 ● *Steady*, quarterly. Newsletter. Provides medical information and lists self-help support groups, pen pals, "phone buddies" and "email buddies". **Price:** $40.00. **Circulation:** 1,500. **Conventions/Meetings:** monthly support group meeting.

15498 ■ Society for Ear, Nose, and Throat Advances in Children (SENTAC)
c/o Anthony E. Magit, MD, Sec.
Children's Hosp. of San Diego
3030 Children's Way, Ste.402
San Diego, CA 92123
Ph: (858)576-4085
E-mail: amagit@chsd.org
URL: http://www.sentac.org
Contact: Anthony E. Magit MD, Sec.
Founded: 1973. **Members:** 350. **Membership Dues:** fellow, associate, $100 (annual). **Description:** Otolaryngologists, pediatricians, audiologists, speech pathologists, and related professionals. Works to evaluate the science and practice of medicine, surgery, and rehabilitation as related to diseases and disorders of the ear, nose, and throat in infants and children; to improve quality of care; to promote and coordinate research; to foster scientific exchange and coordination among professionals from related disciplines. Sponsors lectures and symposia. Provides forum for interchange of information on practice and research. **Publications:** *Directory and Meeting Abstracts*, annual ● Brochure. **Conventions/Meetings:** annual meeting - usually December.

15499 ■ Society of University Otolaryngologists - Head and Neck Surgeons (SUO-HNS)
c/o Donna Hoffman, MA, Exec. Admin.
USC School of Medicine
Dept. of Otolaryngology
1200 N State St.
Box 795
Los Angeles, CA 90033
Ph: (323)226-7315
Fax: (323)226-2780
E-mail: dhquilt@earthlink.net
URL: http://www.suo-aado.org/SUO/index.html
Contact: Donna Hoffman MA, Exec. Admin.
Founded: 1964. **Members:** 500. **Membership Dues:** active, $80 (annual). **Staff:** 1. **Budget:** $60,000. **Description:** Otolaryngologists affiliated with universities through an approved residency training program, faculty appointment, or teaching or research position. Promotes the advancement of the art and science of otolaryngology by the development and improvement of undergraduate and graduate teaching programs. Encourages basic research and clinical investigation as an integral part of university training programs. Sponsors annual course; maintains society records. **Telecommunication Services:** electronic mail, rweber@mdanderson.org. **Committees:** Continuing Education; Research; Resident Education; Undergraduate Education. **Affiliated With:** Association of American Medical Colleges. **Formerly:** (1983) Society of University Olodaryngologists. **Publications:** Directory, annual. **Conventions/Meetings:** annual meeting.

15500 ■ Vestibular Disorders Association (VEDA)
PO Box 13305
Portland, OR 97213
Ph: (503)229-7705
Free: (800)837-8428
Fax: (503)229-8064
E-mail: veda@vestibular.org
URL: http://www.vestibular.org
Contact: Lisa Haven, Exec. Dir.
Founded: 1983. **Members:** 4,000. **Membership Dues:** basic-new, in U.S., $30 (annual) ● basic-new, outside U.S., $40 (annual) ● basic-renewing, in U.S., $25 (annual) ● basic-renewing, outside U.S., $35 (annual) ● professional-new, $100 (annual) ● professional-renewing, $95 (annual) ● basic-renewing, $60 (triennial) ● professional-new, $255 (triennial) ● professional-renewing, $250 (triennial). **Staff:** 3. **Budget:** $170,000. **Local Groups:** 115. **Languages:** English, Spanish. **Multinational. Description:** Individuals suffering from vestibular disorders, their families and friends, and health care professionals. (Vestibular disorders are characterized by persistent dizziness or vertigo which often indicates a problem in the inner ear.) Provides support services including information and referrals; encourages public education about vestibular disorders and their effects. **Libraries: Type:** reference. **Holdings:** books, papers, periodicals, video recordings. **Subjects:** vestibular disorders, Meniere's disease, vestibular neuronitis, labyrinthitis, BPPU, ototoxicity, perilymph fistula. **Awards:** Communicator Award. **Frequency:** semiannual. **Type:** recognition. **Affiliated With:** Acoustic Neuroma Association; American Tinnitus Association; Brain Injury Association of America; CFIDS Association of America; Ear Foundation; National Stroke Association. **Formerly:** (1989) Dizziness and Balance Disorders Association. **Publications:** *Balancing Act, 2nd Edition.* Book. **Price:** $17.95 ● *BPPV: What You Need to Know.* Book. **Price:** $24.95 softbound; $29.95 hardbound ● *Getting Better: Diagnosis and Treatment; Managing Your Symptoms; Psychological/Cognitive Impacts - Helping the Family Understand.* Video. Includes a closed caption VHS tape or DVD. **Price:** $34.95 ● *Meniere's Disease: What You Need to Know.* Book. **Price:** $24.95 softbound; $34.95 hardbound ● *On the Level*, quarterly. Newsletter. Includes coping tips, health-related items, reviews, and association news. **Price:** included in membership dues. **Circulation:** 5,000 ● *Stories and Strategies: Coping with Vestibular Disorders.* Booklet ● Audiotapes ● Bibliographies ● Pamphlets ● Reports.

Pain

15501 ■ Alliance of State Pain Initiatives (ASPI)
1300 Univ. Ave., Rm. 4720
Madison, WI 53706
Ph: (608)265-4013
Fax: (608)265-4014
E-mail: aspi@mailplus.wisc.edu
URL: http://aspi.wisc.edu
Contact: Debora Treu, Dir.
Description: Supports the efforts of State Cancer Pain initiatives. Works to remove the barriers that impede pain relief through education, advocacy and institutional improvement. Provides education and advocacy to healthcare providers, cancer patients and their families. **Telecommunication Services:** electronic mail, dltreu@wisc.edu. **Formerly:** (2006) American Alliance of Cancer Pain Initiatives. **Conventions/Meetings:** annual meeting.

15502 ■ American Academy of Pain Management
13947 Mono Way, Ste.A
Sonora, CA 95370
Ph: (209)533-9744
Fax: (209)533-9750
E-mail: aapm@aapainmanage.org
URL: http://www.aapainmanage.org
Contact: Kathryn A. Padgett PhD, Exec. Dir.
Founded: 1988. **Members:** 6,000. **Membership Dues:** general, $195 (annual) ● student, $50 (an-

nual) ● health care facility, $500 (annual) ● corporate, $5,000 (annual). **Staff:** 12. **Budget:** $2,000,000. **Description:** Establishes the core body of knowledge necessary to become a pain management professional. Provides educational and research programs and speakers' bureau. **Awards:** Janet Travell Pain Management Award. **Frequency:** annual. **Type:** recognition ● John C. Liebeskind Pain Research Award. **Frequency:** annual. **Type:** recognition. **Computer Services:** database ● information services, pain management resources. **Publications:** *American Journal of Pain Management*, quarterly. Contains pain management-related reviews, original contributions, editorial commentaries, updates and descriptions of new technologies. **Price:** included in membership dues; $65.00 /year for nonmembers in U.S.; $75.00 /year for nonmembers outside U.S. ● *The Pain Practitioner*, quarterly. Magazine. **Price:** $35.00/year ● *Weiner's Pain Management: A Practical Guide for Clinicians*. Book. Includes contributions from over 100 pain management experts. **Price:** $289.95. **Conventions/Meetings:** annual Clinicians United to Manage Pain - conference and board meeting (exhibits).

15503 ■ American Academy of Pain Medicine (AAPM)
4700 W Lake Ave.
Glenview, IL 60025
Ph: (847)375-4731
Fax: (877)734-8750
E-mail: info@painmed.org
URL: http://www.painmed.org
Contact: B. Todd Sitzman, MD, Pres.
Founded: 1983. **Members:** 1,200. **Membership Dues:** regular, $325 (annual) ● corporate, $5,000 (annual). **Staff:** 3. **Budget:** $1,000,000. **Description:** Anesthesiologists, internists, neurologists, neurosurgeons, orthopedic surgeons, physiatrists, and psychiatrists. Promotes a socioeconomic and political climate conducive to the effective and efficient practice of pain medicine. Ensures quality medical care by physicians specializing in pain medicine. Participates in networking and liaison activities with other organizations dealing in pain medicine. Conducts educational programs. Holds a seat in the American Medical Association House of Delegates. **Awards:** **Frequency:** annual. **Type:** recognition. **Recipient:** for a professional in the field of pain medicine. **Computer Services:** database ● mailing lists ● online services. **Affiliated With:** American Academy of Neurology; American Academy of Physical Medicine and Rehabilitation; American Headache Society; American Medical Association; American Pain Society; American Psychiatric Association; American Society of Anesthesiologists; Continuing Care Accreditation Commission. **Formerly:** American Academy of Algology. **Publications:** *A Guide to Pain Medicine*. Brochure ● *AAPM Membership Directory*, annual. Lists primary care and specialty physicians with an interest in pain medicine. **Circulation:** 1,200. **Advertising:** accepted. Alternate Formats: magnetic tape ● *Pain Medicine*, bimonthly. Journal. Contains clinical articles, research information, articles concerning socioeconomic issues, and news. **Price:** included in membership dues; $45.00/issue; for nonmembers; $90.00/issue; for institutions. ISSN: 1526-2375. **Circulation:** 3,000. **Advertising:** accepted ● *Pain Medicine Network*, quarterly. Newsletter. Covers news about the academy and its members. **Advertising:** accepted. Alternate Formats: online. **Conventions/Meetings:** annual conference, focuses on socioeconomic and governmental issues and chronic pain issues; with review course (exhibits) ● annual meeting, with networking opportunities and presentations by recognized faculty leaders in the field - 2008 Feb. 13-16, Orlando, FL ● periodic Review Course in Pain Medicine - seminar, program providing information on current concepts and practices in pain control, held in conjunction with annual conference.

15504 ■ American Board of Pain Medicine (ABPM)
4700 W Lake Ave.
Glenview, IL 60025-1468
Ph: (847)375-4726

Fax: (877)734-8751
E-mail: info@abpm.org
URL: http://www.abpm.org
Contact: Kenneth Follett PhD, Pres.
Founded: 1991. **Members:** 1,335. **Description:** Develops and administers practice-related examinations in the field of pain medicine. Awards certification to physicians successfully completing the examination and credentialing process. **Publications:** none. **Convention/Meeting:** none. **Formerly:** American College of Pain Medicine.

15505 ■ American Chronic Pain Association (ACPA)
PO Box 850
Rocklin, CA 95677
Ph: (916)632-0922
Free: (800)533-3231
Fax: (916)632-3208
E-mail: acpa@pacbell.net
URL: http://www.theacpa.org
Contact: Penney Cowan, Founder
Founded: 1980. **Membership Dues:** regular, $30 (annual). **Staff:** 4. **Budget:** $50,000. **National Groups:** 235. **Languages:** English, Russian, Spanish. **Description:** Works to facilitate peer support and education for individuals with chronic pain and their families so that these individuals may live more fully in spite of pain; aims to raise awareness among the health care community, policy makers, and the public at large about issues of living with chronic pain. **Publications:** *ACPA Chronicle*, quarterly. Newsletter ● *ACPA Facilitation Guide*, periodic. Directory. Features how-to's for ACPA group development and ongoing resources. ● *Family Manual* ● *From Patient to Person: First Steps*, periodic. Helps anyone who has a chronic pain problem gain an understanding of how to cope with the problems that their pain creates. **Price:** $25.00/copy ● *Reflections of You*. Journal. Contains daily meditation. ● *Staying Well: Advanced Pain Management for Members Workbook*. Handbook. Provides additional skills necessary to continue to move forward in the journey to wellness. **Price:** $20.00. **Conventions/Meetings:** annual workshop and conference, for all ACPA members.

15506 ■ American Pain Foundation (APF)
201 N Charles St., Ste.710
Baltimore, MD 21201-4111
Free: (888)615-7246
Fax: (410)385-1832
E-mail: info@painfoundation.org
URL: http://www.painfoundation.org
Contact: Will Rowe, Exec. Dir.
Founded: 1997. **Nonmembership. Description:** Aims to improve the quality of life for all people affected by pain. Publishes and distributes practical information, sponsors initiatives to reduce regulatory and other barriers to effective pain management. **Telecommunication Services:** electronic bulletin board, PainAid online support community ● information service, toll-free information and order line. **Committees:** Pain Community Advisory; Scientific Advisory. **Publications:** *Pain Action Guide*. Brochure. Provides information about finding good pain care and taking control of pain. Alternate Formats: online ● *Pain Bulletin: Project Update*, monthly. Newsletter. Alternate Formats: online ● *Pain Community News*, quarterly. Newsletter. Alternate Formats: online ● *Pain Monitor*, monthly. Newsletter. Alternate Formats: online.

15507 ■ American Pain Society (APS)
4700 W Lake Ave.
Glenview, IL 60025
Ph: (847)375-4715
Free: (877)734-8758
Fax: (877)734-8758
E-mail: info@ampainsoc.org
URL: http://www.ampainsoc.org
Contact: Judith A. Paice PhD, Pres.
Founded: 1977. **Members:** 3,500. **Membership Dues:** regular, $120-$275 (annual) ● individual affiliate, $150 (annual) ● student/trainee, $50 (annual). **Staff:** 6. **Budget:** $1,200,000. **Regional Groups:** 6. **Description:** Physicians, dentists, psychologists,

nurses, and other health professionals interested in the study and treatment of pain. Purposes are to: promote control, management, and understanding of pain through scientific meetings and research activities; develop standards for training and ethical management of pain patients. Conducts scientific conferences. **Awards:** Distinguished Service Award. **Frequency:** annual. **Type:** recognition. **Recipient:** for individuals or groups who advance the mission of the society in a significant and lasting way ● F.W.L. Kerr Basic Science Research Award. **Frequency:** annual. **Type:** recognition. **Recipient:** to a pain professional, for individual excellence and achievements in pain research ● John and Emma Bonica Public Service Award. **Frequency:** annual. **Type:** recognition. **Recipient:** for individuals or organization that has an outstanding achievement through direct public service, dissemination of information and public education, or activities that enhanced the field of pain management ● John C. Liebeskind Early Career Scholar Award. **Frequency:** annual. **Type:** recognition. **Recipient:** for individuals who have achieved or shown a promise of significant scholarly distinction ● Wilbert E. Fordyce Clinical Investigator Award. **Frequency:** annual. **Type:** recognition. **Recipient:** for an individual who has made outstanding contributions to the field of clinical pain research. **Telecommunication Services:** electronic mail, j-paice@northwestern.edu. **Affiliated With:** International Association for the Study of Pain. **Publications:** *APS Bulletin*, bimonthly. Newsletter. **Advertising:** accepted ● *Guideline for the Management of Acute and Chronic Pain in Sickle Cell Disease*. Provides comprehensive evidence-based guideline to address treatment of the pain of sickle-cell disease. **Price:** $7.50 for members; $9.00 for nonmembers ● *Guideline for the Management of Cancer Pain in Adults and Children (2003)*. **Price:** $15.00 for members; $20.00 for nonmembers ● *Guideline for the Management of Pain in Osteoarthritis, Rheumatoid Arthritis, and Juvenile Chronic Arthritis (2nd Edition)*. **Price:** $15.00 for members; $20.00 for nonmembers ● *The Journal of Pain*, monthly. Contains original articles related to all aspects of pain, including clinical and basic research, patient care, education, and health policy. **Price:** included in membership dues. **Advertising:** accepted ● *Pain Facilities Directory* ● *Principles of Analgesic Use in the Treatment of Acute Pain and Cancer Pain (5th Edition)*, periodic. Includes information on appropriate drug selection, dosing variation among patient populations, and side effect minimization. **Price:** $5.00 for members; $8.00 for nonmembers. **Conventions/Meetings:** annual meeting, scientific meeting (exhibits) - 2008 May 7-10, Tampa, FL; 2009 May 6-9, San Diego, CA.

15508 ■ American Society of Interventional Pain Physicians (ASIPP)
81 Lakeview Dr.
Paducah, KY 42001
Ph: (270)554-9412
Fax: (270)554-5394
E-mail: asipp@asipp.org
URL: http://www.asipp.org
Contact: Melinda Martin, Dir. of Operations
Founded: 1998. **Members:** 3,692. **Membership Dues:** life (active), $5,000 ● life (associate), $2,500 ● active, $300 (annual) ● military physician, $150 (annual) ● fellow/resident/associate, $100 (annual) ● medical student, $25 (annual) ● corporate sponsorship, $50,000 (annual). **Description:** Improves the delivery of interventional pain management services. Promotes the development and practice of safe, high quality and cost-effective interventional pain management techniques for the diagnosis and treatment of pain and other related disorders. Advances patient safety, cost effectiveness and accountability. **Publications:** *Pain Physician*, quarterly. Journal. Addresses the science and practice of interventional pain management. **Advertising:** accepted ● *Pain Physician News*, quarterly. Magazine. Covers news from the interventional pain management field. **Advertising:** accepted. Alternate Formats: online. **Conventions/Meetings:** periodic Comprehensive Interventional Cadaver Workshop and FIPP Review Course and Examination ● periodic Interventional Techniques

Review Course and Comprehensive Interventional Cadaver Workshop - 2007 Oct. 5-7, Memphis, TN; 2007 Nov. 30-Dec. 2, Memphis, TN ● annual meeting.

15509 ■ American Society of Pain Educators (ASPE)

PO Box 1548
Montclair, NJ 07042
Ph: (973)233-5570
Free: (877)733-9797
Fax: (973)453-8246
E-mail: df@paineducators.org
URL: http://www.paineducators.org
Contact: Darryl Fossa, Exec. Dir.

Membership Dues: individual, $175 (annual) ● student, resident, $75 (annual) ● group (10 members, based on the amount of savings), $750-$1,450 (annual). **Description:** Seeks to improve the standards of clinical pain practice. Strives to improve the quality of life of those suffering from pain, as well as serve as an in-house resource for their healthcare professional peers. Provides pain-related educational programs that specifically focus on the transfer of knowledge from professional to patient and peer to peer. Creates and administers credentialing examinations. **Publications:** *PainView*, quarterly. Newsletter. **Price:** included in membership dues.

15510 ■ Chronic Pain Support Group (CPSG)

c/o Andrea R. Kramer, Facilitator
Shady Grove Hosp., Maple Rm.
9901 Medical Center Dr.
Rockville, MD 20850
Ph: (301)670-0134
Fax: (301)947-8555
E-mail: andreakram@outofpain.com
URL: http://www.chronicpainsupport.org
Contact: Andrea R. Kramer, Facilitator

Founded: 1985. **Description:** Individuals suffering from chronic pain, their families and friends. Provides a forum for pain sufferers to help themselves through communication with other members. Promotes public awareness of chronic pain and its victims; encourages medical research on causes and treatments. Operates Speaker's Bureau; conducts educational programs. **Convention/Meeting:** none. **Additional Websites:** http://www.outofpain.com. **Telecommunication Services:** electronic mail, andreakram@aol.com. **Publications:** *Stop Pain*, monthly. Newsletter. Covers coping skills. **Price:** $25.00/year. **Advertising:** accepted. Alternate Formats: online.

15511 ■ International Adhesions Society (IAS)

c/o Dr. David Wiseman, PhD, Founder
Synechion, Inc.
6757 Arapaho Rd., Ste.711, No. 238
Dallas, TX 75248
Ph: (972)931-5596
Fax: (972)931-5476
E-mail: david.wiseman@adhesions.org
URL: http://www.adhesions.org
Contact: Dr. David Wiseman PhD, Founder

Founded: 1996. **Multinational. Description:** Promotes treatment for adhesions and chronic pelvic pain. Adhesions are scars that form an abnormal connection between two parts of the body, including non-surgical insults such as endometriosis, infection, chemotherapy, radiation and cancer, or from surgical procedures. Assists formation of support groups. **Publications:** *Connections*. Newsletter. Alternate Formats: online ● Audiotapes. Features a set of lecture tapes from the March 12, 2001 IAS conference held in Detroit, Michigan. **Price:** included with $50 member donation.

15512 ■ International Association for the Study of Pain (IASP)

111 Queen Anne Ave. N, Ste.501
Seattle, WA 98109-4955
Ph: (206)547-6409
Fax: (206)283-9403

E-mail: iaspdesk@iasp-pain.org
URL: http://www.iasp-pain.org
Contact: Katherine Kreiter, Exec. Dir.

Founded: 1973. **Members:** 7,000. **Membership Dues:** individual, $175 (annual) ● trainee, $40 (annual). **Staff:** 12. **Budget:** $2,000,000. **National Groups:** 67. **Multinational. Description:** Represents scientists, physicians, and other health professionals interested in pain research and therapy. Encourages research on pain mechanisms and syndromes; seeks to improve management of patients with acute and chronic pain. Promotes education and training in the field of pain; informs the public of results of current research. Fosters development of an international data bank, adoption of a uniform classification and definition regarding pain and pain syndromes, and creation of a uniform records system on information relating to pain mechanisms, syndromes, and management. Promotes the formation of national associations for the study and treatment of pain. **Awards:** IASP Award for Excellence in Pain Research and Management. **Frequency:** triennial. **Type:** grant. **Recipient:** for excellence in pain research and management of an individual or a team ● IASP Collaborative Research Grants. **Frequency:** annual. **Type:** grant. **Recipient:** for collaborative research between two or more research groups located in different countries ● IASP Developing Countries Education Programs Grant. **Frequency:** annual. **Type:** grant. **Recipient:** for pain education programs in developing countries ● IASP Research Symposium. **Frequency:** annual. **Type:** grant. **Recipient:** for a symposium about pain research and management ● John J. Bonica Distinguished Lecture Award. **Frequency:** triennial. **Type:** recognition ● John J. Bonica Trainee Fellowship. **Frequency:** annual. **Type:** fellowship. **Recipient:** to support training in clinical and basic science research in the field of pain ● Patrick D. Wall Young Investigator Award for Clinical Science. **Frequency:** triennial. **Type:** grant. **Recipient:** for an individual who has achieved a level of independence as a scholar in the field of pain in clinical science ● Ronald Dubner Research Prize. **Frequency:** triennial. **Type:** grant. **Recipient:** for trainees in the field of pain ● Ulf Lindblom Young Investigator Award for Basic Science. **Frequency:** triennial. **Type:** grant. **Recipient:** for an individual who has achieved a level of independence as a scholar in the field of pain in basic science. **Additional Websites:** http://www.painbooks.org. **Committees:** Education; History; Local Arrangements; Public Information; Research and Ethical Issues; Scientific Program. **Special Interest Groups:** Acute Pain; Clinical/Legal Issues in Pain; Neuropathic Pain; Orofacial Pain; Pain and Movement; Pain and the Sympathetic Nervous System; Pain in Childhood; Pain in Non-Human Species; Pain in Older Persons; Pain of Urogenital Origin; Pain Related to Torture, Organized Violence, and War; Placebo; Sex, Gender, and Pain; Systematic Reviews in Pain. **Task Forces:** Taxonomy. **Publications:** *Acute and Procedure Pain in Infants and Children*. Book ● *The Child With Headache: Diagnosis and Treatment*. Book ● *Chronic and Recurrent Pain in Children and Adolescents*. Book ● *Complex Regional Pain Syndrome*. Book ● *Epidemiology of Pain*. Book ● *Genetics of Pain*. Book. **Price:** $78.00 for nonmembers; $59.00 for members ● *Hyperalgesia: Molecular Mechanisms and Clinical Implications*. Book. **Price:** $71.00 for members; $89.00 for nonmembers ● *Manual de Farmacoes Utilizados en el Tratamiento del Dolor Cronico*. Book ● *Measurement of Pain in Infants and Children*. Book ● *Molecular Neurobiology of Pain*. Book ● *Neuropathic Pain: Pathophysiology and Treatment*. Book ● *Opiod Sensitivity of Chronic Noncancer Pain*. Book ● *Opioids and Pain Relief: A Historical Perspective*. Book. **Price:** $51.00 for members; $68.00 for nonmembers ● *Pain*, 15/year. Journal ● *Pain and Suffering*. Book ● *Pain: Clinical Updates*. Newsletter ● *Pain System in Normal and Pathological States: A Primer for Clinicians*. Book. **Price:** $57.00 for members; $71.00 for nonmembers ● *Pediatric Pain: Biological and Social Context*. Book. **Price:** $57.00 for members; $76.00 for nonmembers ● *Psychological Methods of Pain Control: Basic Science and Clinical Perspectives*. Book. **Price:** $51.00 for members; $63.00 for nonmembers ● *Psychoso-*

cial Aspects of Pain: A Handbook for Health Care Providers. **Price:** $69.00 for members; $89.00 for nonmembers. **Conventions/Meetings:** triennial World Congress on Pain (exhibits).

15513 ■ International MYOPAIN Society (IMS)

c/o Barbara Runnels, MEd, Admin. Off.
PO Box 690402
San Antonio, TX 78269
Ph: (210)567-4661
Fax: (210)567-6669
E-mail: russell@uthscsa.edu
URL: http://www.myopain.org
Contact: Barbara Runnels MEd, Admin. Off.

Founded: 1997. **Members:** 600. **Membership Dues:** regular, $100 (annual) ● sponsor, $500-$10,000 ● associate, $70 (annual). **Multinational. Description:** Research scientists, physicians, other health care professionals, individuals in training toward a health-related career, institutions, foundations, and commercial companies. Promotes information exchange, research, and education about soft tissue pain syndrome such as myofascial pain syndrome and fibromyalgia syndrome. **Publications:** *Journal of Musculoskeletal Pain*, quarterly. Covers topic of soft tissue pain. **Price:** $75.00 for individual in U.S.; $375.00 for institution, agency/library in U.S.; $101.00 for individual in U.S. and Canada; $544.00 for institution, agency/library in U.S. and Canada. **Conventions/Meetings:** triennial conference.

15514 ■ International Pelvic Pain Society (IPPS)

c/o C. Paul Perry, MD, Board Chm.
C. Paul Perry Pelvic Pain Center
2006 Brookwood Medical Center Drive, Ste.402
Women's Medical Plz.
Birmingham, AL 35209
Ph: (205)877-2950 (847)517-8712
Free: (800)624-9676
Fax: (205)877-2973
E-mail: pelvicpain@aol.com
URL: http://www.pelvicpain.org
Contact: C. Paul Perry MD, Board Chm.

Founded: 1996. **Membership Dues:** professional (with less than $50000 annual income), $50 (annual) ● professional (with an annual income of $50000-$100000), $100 (annual) ● professional (with an annual income of over $100000), $200 (annual) ● patient, $35 (annual). **Multinational. Description:** Educates health care professionals on how to diagnose and manage chronic pelvic pain. Supports women who suffer from chronic pelvic pain by raising public awareness and impacting individual lives. **Computer Services:** Information services, health resources ● online services. **Publications:** *Chronic Pelvic Pain* (in English and Spanish). Booklet. Contains basic information about chronic pelvic pain. Alternate Formats: online ● *Vision*. Newsletter. Features articles relevant to pelvic pain and pelvic pain research and findings. Alternate Formats: online.

15515 ■ National Chronic Pain Outreach Association (NCPOA)

PO Box 274
Millboro, VA 24460
Ph: (540)862-9437
Fax: (540)862-9485
URL: http://www.chronicpain.org
Contact: Mike Troyer, Pres.

Founded: 1980. **Members:** 1,000. **Membership Dues:** individual, $25 (annual) ● friend and professional, $50 (annual) ● medical facility and patron, $100 (annual) ● benefactor, $250 (annual) ● angel, $500 (annual) ● corporate, $1,000 (annual). **Staff:** 3. **Budget:** $75,000. **Description:** Disseminates information about chronic pain and its management in an effort to lessen the suffering caused by chronic pain. Operates information clearinghouse for pain sufferers, family members, and health care professionals. Provides a Support Group Starter Kit to encourage the formation of local chronic pain support groups. Provides referrals to member health care providers and facilities. **Computer Services:** database, physician and pain clinic referral. **Publications:** *Chronic*

Pain and the Family. Article. Contains an overview of the impact of chronic pain on the family system as a whole. ● *Lifeline*, quarterly. Newsletter. Includes pain management information and book reviews. **Price:** available to members only. ISSN: 1043-0776. **Circulation:** 5,000. **Advertising:** accepted ● *Making Breaking Commitments - A Personal Reflection*. Article ● *The Stigma of Chronic Pain*. Article. Alternate Formats: online ● Audiotapes ● Booklets ● Brochures ● Pamphlets. **Conventions/Meetings:** periodic conference.

15516 ■ National Chronic Pain Society (NCPS)
10700 Fuqua St., No. 194
Houston, TX 77082
Ph: (281)357-4673
Fax: (281)357-4514
E-mail: ncps@houston.rr.com
URL: http://www.ncps-cpr.org/index.php
Contact: Helen Dearman, Exec. Dir.
Membership Dues: general, $25 (annual). **Description:** Provides peer support groups for people with chronic pain and their families. Educates the public about chronic pain. Encourages members to become proactive in their health care by becoming informed, equipped and empowered to fight chronic pain. **Publications:** *Chronic Pain Report*. Newsletter. **Price:** included in membership dues.

15517 ■ National Pain Education Council (NPEC)
c/o CME Scholar
1010 Washington Blvd., 7th Fl.
Stamford, CT 06901
Free: (888)536-7545
E-mail: support@npecweb.org
URL: http://www.npecweb.org
Contact: Richard Payne MD, Co-Chm.
Description: Aims to advance the clinical management of pain through education and communication. Fosters professional development by helping primary care physicians and other healthcare professionals to improve their skills and enhance their knowledge of analgesic pharmacotherapy. Provides pain specialists with materials to assist them in educating nonspecialists. **Publications:** *JournalToGo*. Covers the latest medical literature and news about pain management. **Price:** free. Alternate Formats: online ● Monographs. Alternate Formats: online.

15518 ■ North American Neuromodulation Society (NANS)
4700 W Lake Ave.
Glenview, IL 60025
Ph: (847)375-4714
Fax: (877)594-6704
E-mail: vmobley@connect2amc.com
URL: http://www.neuromodulation.org
Contact: Claudio Feler, Pres.
Founded: 1994. **Membership Dues:** active, $260 (annual). **Description:** Aims to advance the field of neuromodulation therapies through clinical research, education and print material within the U.S; aims to increase avenues of development for members through professional networking systems, ongoing communication and other opportunities. **Formerly:** (1994) American Neuromodulation Society. **Publications:** *Economic Newsletter*. Contains topics such as coding, reimbursement rates (RVU), payor coverage, and hospital topics. ● *Neuromodulation*, quarterly. Journal. Contains scientific and clinical information relevant to the field of neuromodulation. ISSN: 1094-7159. **Advertising:** accepted.

15519 ■ RSDHope Group (RSDS)
PO Box 875
Harrison, ME 04040
Ph: (207)583-4589
Fax: (207)583-4978
E-mail: stonehed@megalink.net
URL: http://www.rsdhope.org
Contact: Keith Orsini, Exec. Dir.
Founded: 1995. **Membership Dues:** angel, $25 (annual) ● guardian angel, $50 (annual) ● archangel, $100 (annual). **Languages:** English, French, Ger-

man, Spanish. **Multinational. Description:** Patients suffering from Reflex Sympathetic Dystrophy Syndrome, Chronic Pain, their parents and friends. Dedicated to increasing the awareness of Reflex Sympathetic Dystrophy Syndrome (RSDS), chronic pain. **Publications:** Newsletter. Alternate Formats: online. **Conventions/Meetings:** periodic reunion and lecture ● annual seminar and workshop.

15520 ■ Society of Chest Pain Centers and Providers
3000 W Broad St., Box 9
Columbus, OH 43204
Ph: (614)274-9710
Fax: (614)274-9716
E-mail: info@scpcp.org
URL: http://www.scpcp.org
Contact: Robert Weisenburger Lipetz MBA, Exec. Dir.
Founded: 1998. **Membership Dues:** physician, $200 (annual) ● associate, non-physician, $100 (annual) ● facility, $500 (annual) ● nonmedical, $150 (annual). **Description:** Promotes development, coordination, and comprehensiveness of chest pain centers; promotes guidelines for quality chest pain center care. **Libraries: Type:** reference. **Holdings:** articles, papers. **Subjects:** chest pain, acute coronary syndromes, heart failure. **Telecommunication Services:** electronic mail, director@scpcp.org. **Publications:** *Critical Pathways in Cardiology*, quarterly. Journal. Alternate Formats: online. **Conventions/Meetings:** biennial congress.

15521 ■ TMJ Association (TMJA)
PO Box 26770
Milwaukee, WI 53226-0770
Ph: (262)432-0350
Fax: (262)432-0375
E-mail: info@tmj.org
URL: http://www.tmj.org
Contact: Terrie Cowley, Pres.
Founded: 1986. **Staff:** 1. **Budget:** $100,000. **Non-membership. Multinational. Description:** Provides updated information on temporomandibular problems; serves as a support network to patients; educated health care professionals, policymakers, research investigators and the general public about TMJ diseases and disorders; advocated in the public and private sectors for quality research that will yield evidence-based treatments and prevention of TMJ diseases and disorders; communicates with members of Congress, government agencies, and others in position to set agendas to ensure ongoing research on TMJ diseases and disorders. **Publications:** *Temporomandibular Joint Diseases and Disorders*, annual. Brochure. Contains overview of TMJDs, causes and treatments. ● *TMJ Communique*, quarterly. Newsletter. Provides news and updates. Alternate Formats: online ● *TMJ Science*, biennial. Journal. Contains meeting summary and recommendations. Alternate Formats: online ● Annual Report, annual. Alternate Formats: online.

Pancreatic Diseases

15522 ■ Pancreatic Cancer Action Network (PanCAN)
2141 Rosecrans Ave., Ste.7000
El Segundo, CA 90245
Ph: (310)725-0025
Free: (877)272-6226
Fax: (310)725-0029
E-mail: info@pancan.org
URL: http://www.pancan.org
Contact: Julie Fleshman, Pres./CEO
Founded: 1999. **Description:** Works to focus national attention on the need to find a cure for pancreatic cancer. Promotes treatments, prevention programs, research and early detection of pancreatic cancer through support, services and advocacy. **Computer Services:** Information services, pancreatic cancer facts and services ● mailing lists.

Pathology

15523 ■ American Academy of Oral and Maxillofacial Pathology (AAOMP)
214 N Hale St.
Wheaton, IL 60187
Ph: (630)579-3252
Free: (888)552-2667
Fax: (630)510-4501
E-mail: aaomp@b-online.com
URL: http://www.aaomp.org
Contact: Ms. Liz Lenard, Co-Exec. Dir.
Founded: 1946. **Members:** 700. **Membership Dues:** regular, $120 (annual) ● fellow, $300 (annual). **Staff:** 3. **Budget:** $110,000. **Description:** Professional society of oral pathologists. **Awards:** Dental Student Award. **Frequency:** annual. **Type:** recognition. **Recipient:** for student determined by dental school ● Gorlin Award. **Frequency:** annual. **Type:** monetary. **Recipient:** for residents who are primary researcher on the AAOMP essay/abstract ● Shafter Award. **Frequency:** annual. **Type:** monetary. **Recipient:** to the highest scorer on AAOMP fellowship exam ● Student Travel Award. **Frequency:** annual. **Type:** monetary. **Recipient:** for undergraduates who are not in an oral pathology program and are interested in the field. **Computer Services:** database ● mailing lists ● online services. **Affiliated With:** American Board of Oral and Maxillofacial Pathology. **Formerly:** (1994) American Academy Oral Pathology. **Publications:** *Oral Surgery, Oral Medicine, Oral Pathology*, monthly. **Conventions/Meetings:** annual meeting, with continuing education program (exhibits) - 2008 June 22-26, San Francisco, CA - **Avg. Attendance:** 400; 2009 May 16-20, Montreal, QC, Canada - **Avg. Attendance:** 220.

15524 ■ American Association of Neuropathologists (AANP)
c/o Dr. George Perry, Sec.-Treas.
Dept. of Pathology
Case Western Reserve Univ.
2103 Cornell Rd., WRB 5101
Cleveland, OH 44106
Ph: (216)368-3671
Fax: (216)368-8964
E-mail: aanp@case.edu
URL: http://www.neuropath.org
Contact: Dr. George Perry, Sec.-Treas.
Founded: 1959. **Members:** 800. **Membership Dues:** associate, $155 (annual) ● affiliate, $140 (annual) ● active, $165 (annual). **Budget:** $110,000. **Description:** Promotes neuropathology, especially the study of diverse aspects of diseases of the nervous system including changes at tissue, cellular, subcellular, and molecular levels with consideration of etiology and pathophysiology, genetics, epidemiology and clinical manifestations of such diseases. **Awards:** Moore Award. **Frequency:** annual. **Type:** recognition. **Recipient:** for the best paper on Clinicopathologic Correlation ● Rubinstein Award. **Frequency:** annual. **Type:** recognition. **Recipient:** for the best paper on Neuro-Oncology ● Weil Award. **Frequency:** annual. **Type:** recognition. **Recipient:** for the best paper on Experimental Neuropathology. **Formerly:** (1932) Club of Neuropathologists. **Publications:** *Journal of Neuropathology and Experimental Neurology*, monthly ● Membership Directory, annual. Alternate Formats: online. **Conventions/Meetings:** annual congress and symposium, with scientific sessions, special course, Korey lecture, diagnostic slide session, Moore lecture (exhibits) - always June.

15525 ■ American Association of Pathologists' Assistants (AAPA)
Rosewood Off. Plz.
1711 W County Rd. B, Ste.300 N
Roseville, MN 55113-4036
Ph: (651)697-9264
Free: (800)532-AAPA
E-mail: oei@assocmgmt.org
URL: http://www.pathologistsassistants.org
Contact: Larry Marquis, Pres.
Founded: 1972. **Members:** 1,000. **Membership Dues:** affiliate, $150 (annual) ● fellow, $100 (annual)

● student of NAACLS accredited training program (one time fee), $45 ● sustaining, $400 (annual) ● institutional, $300 (annual). **Description:** Pathologists' assistants and individuals qualified by academic and practical training to provide service in anatomic pathology under the direction of a qualified pathologist who is responsible for the performance of the assistant. Promotes the mutual association of trained pathologists' assistants and informs the public and the medical profession concerning the goals of this profession. Compiles statistics on salaries, geographic distribution, and duties of pathologists' assistants. Sponsors a continuing medical education program; offers a job hotline for members only. **Telecommunication Services:** electronic mail, msok@assocmgmt.org. **Publications:** *AAPA Newsletter*, quarterly. **Price:** included in membership dues. **Circulation:** 1,000. **Conventions/Meetings:** annual Continuing Education and Business Conference (exhibits) - 2008 Sept. 13-19, Long Beach, CA.

15526 ■ American Board of Oral and Maxillofacial Pathology (ABOMP)
PO Box 25915
Tampa, FL 33622-5915
Ph: (813)286-2444
Fax: (813)289-5279
URL: http://www.abomp.org
Contact: Mrs. Clarita Scioscia, Exec. Sec.
Founded: 1948. **Members:** 260. **Description:** Works to encourage, promote, and improve the study and practice of oral pathology; seeks to arrange, conduct, and control examinations to determine the competence of applicants; provides grant and issues certificates. **Affiliated With:** American Academy of Oral and Maxillofacial Pathology. **Formerly:** American Board of Oral Pathology. **Conventions/Meetings:** annual meeting, with examination - 2007 Oct. 4-5, Tampa, FL.

15527 ■ American Board of Pathology (ABP)
PO Box 25915
Tampa, FL 33622-5915
Ph: (813)286-2444
Fax: (813)289-5279
E-mail: bdbennett@abpath.org
URL: http://www.abpath.org
Contact: Betsy D. Bennett MD, Exec. VP
Founded: 1936. **Members:** 12. **Staff:** 12. **Description:** Seeks to encourage study of pathology; maintain professional standards and advance practice in the field; maintain registry of certified pathologists; participate in the evaluation and review of graduate medical education programs in pathology. Examines doctors of medicine or osteopathy who have had three to four years postgraduate training in laboratory medicine and pathology. Certifies qualified and successful applicants as specialists in pathology. **Telecommunication Services:** electronic mail, questions@abpath.org. **Publications:** *Information Booklet*, annual ● Newsletter, 2-3/year. **Conventions/Meetings:** semiannual meeting.

15528 ■ American Pathology Foundation (APF)
1540 S Coast Hwy., No. 203
Laguna Beach, CA 92651
Ph: (949)464-9810 (949)376-3456
Free: (877)993-9935
E-mail: brad@isaminc.com
URL: http://www.apfconnect.org
Contact: Edward J. Stygar Jr., Exec. Dir.
Founded: 1959. **Members:** 750. **Membership Dues:** active/associate, affiliate, $250 (annual) ● patron (minimum), $350 (annual) ● special status, $200 (annual) ● junior, $50 (annual). **Staff:** 3. **Description:** Board-certified pathologists. Objectives are: to promote the practice of pathology in private laboratories; to provide for exchange of information that will improve anatomic and clinical pathology; to cooperate in the development of the art and sciences of medicine and pathology. Compiles statistics. **Awards:** **Type:** recognition. **Formerly:** Private Practitioners of Pathology Foundation. **Publications:** *American Pathology Review*, quarterly. Newsletter. ISSN: 1066-9906 ● Directory, annual. **Conventions/Meetings:**

annual convention and meeting, educational ● semiannual seminar, provides information on direct billing and management.

15529 ■ American Registry of Pathology (ARP)
c/o Armed Forces Institute of Pathology
14th St. and Alaska Ave. NW, Bldg. 54
Washington, DC 20306-6000
Free: (800)898-1870
Fax: (800)899-8569
E-mail: aasinfo@afip.osd.mil
URL: http://www.afip.org/ARP/index.html
Contact: Dr. William Gardner, Exec. Dir.
Founded: 1976. **Staff:** 8. **Budget:** $3,100,000. **Description:** Engages in cooperative enterprises in medical research and education with the Armed Forces Institute of Pathology. Functions as a fiscal agent in the management of research grants and monies derived from tuition fees, publications, and contributions. Serves as a link between, and encourages cooperation among, the military and civilian medical, dental, and veterinary communities for the mutual benefit of military and civilian medicine. Provides personnel and other services in support of research. Offers 38 continuing medical education courses annually. **Awards:** John Hill Brinton Award. **Frequency:** annual. **Type:** recognition. **Recipient:** for an outstanding young researcher ● John Shaw Billings Lifetime Achievement Award. **Frequency:** annual. **Type:** recognition. **Recipient:** for a senior AFIP staff member. **Conventions/Meetings:** annual meeting.

15530 ■ American Society for Clinical Pathology (ASCP)
33 W Monroe, Ste.1600
Chicago, IL 60603
Ph: (312)541-4999
Free: (800)267-2727
Fax: (312)541-4998
E-mail: info@ascp.org
URL: http://www.ascp.org
Contact: Dr. John R. Ball, Exec. VP
Founded: 1922. **Members:** 150,000. **Membership Dues:** medical affiliate, $176 (annual) ● international BOR certified, PhD, $65 (annual) ● BOR certified, PhD, $79 (annual) ● fellow, $329 (annual) ● international - fellow, $100 (annual). **Staff:** 135. **Description:** Works to promote public health and safety by the appropriate application of pathology and laboratory medicine. Provides educational programs for pathologists and laboratory professionals throughout the year, certification for laboratory professionals, and publishes scientific journals and reference textbooks. **Awards:** **Type:** recognition. **Telecommunication Services:** electronic mail, membership@ascp.org. **Formerly:** (2002) American Society of Clinical Pathologists. **Publications:** *American Journal of Clinical Pathology*, monthly ● *ASCP Member News*, monthly. Newsletter ● *Laboratory Medicine*, monthly. Journal ● *Pathology Patterns*, semiannual ● *Pathology Today*, bimonthly. Magazine. Contains important news and information on professional, economic and regulatory issues, along with the latest news about ASCP activities. ● Membership Directory, triennial. **Conventions/Meetings:** annual meeting and conference (exhibits) - April-June ● annual meeting and conference (exhibits) - September/October. 2007 Oct. 18-21, New Orleans, LA.

15531 ■ American Society for Investigative Pathology (ASIP)
9650 Rockville Pike
Bethesda, MD 20814-3993
Ph: (301)634-7130
Fax: (301)634-7990
E-mail: asip@asip.org
URL: http://www.asip.org
Contact: Mark E. Sobel PhD, Exec. Off.
Founded: 1900. **Members:** 2,000. **Membership Dues:** regular, in U.S. (with print/online of AJP/JMD), $195 (annual) ● regular, in Canada and Mexico (with print/online of AJP/JMD), $270 (annual) ● regular, in other country (with print/online of AJP/JMD), $290 (annual) ● regular, in U.S. and international (online

AJP/JMD only), $160 (annual) ● associate (with print/online of AJP/JMD), $125 (annual) ● associate (online AJP/JMD only), $85 (annual) ● trainee (with print/online of AJP/JMD), $95 (annual) ● trainee (online AJP/JMD only), $50 (annual). **Staff:** 17. **Budget:** $500,000. **Description:** Experimental research pathologists who have made significant contributions to the knowledge of disease. **Awards:** Amgen Outstanding Investigator Award. **Frequency:** annual. **Type:** monetary. **Recipient:** for an ASIP member under age 43 at time of meeting for meritorious research in experimental pathology ● Experimental Pathologist-in-Training Award. **Type:** recognition. **Recipient:** for individuals who have excelled in their investigative efforts as trainees in studying mechanisms of disease ● Gold Headed Cane Award. **Frequency:** annual. **Type:** recognition. **Recipient:** for recognition of long-term contributions to pathology, including meritorious research, outstanding teacher and general excellence ● Minority Trainee Travel Awards. **Type:** recognition. **Recipient:** for underrepresented minority scientists and minority-serving institutions into the mainstream of the basic science community ● Rous-Whipple Award. **Type:** monetary. **Recipient:** for a pathologist age 50 years or older with a distinguished career in research and continued productivity at the time of the award ● Trainee Travel Awards. **Frequency:** annual. **Type:** recognition. **Recipient:** for young scientists into the mainstream of the basic science community ● Young Pathologist Fellowship. **Type:** fellowship. **Recipient:** offers 12 graduate students in pathology an opportunity to attend symposia, lectures and poster sessions, network with career pathologists and explore career pathways at the Experimental Biology Meeting. **Telecommunication Services:** electronic mail, mesobel@asip.org. **Affiliated With:** Federation of American Societies for Experimental Biology. **Formed by Merger of:** (1992) American Association of Pathologists and Bacteriologists; American Society for Experimental Pathology. **Formerly:** (1992) American Association of Pathologists. **Publications:** *The American Journal of Pathology*, monthly. Research papers in experimental pathology. Covers cell injury and death, inflammatory reactions, disturbances in circulation, and neoplastic growth. **Price:** included in membership dues; $195.00 /year for nonmembers; $350.00 /year for institutions. ISSN: 0002-9440. **Circulation:** 550. **Advertising:** accepted. Alternate Formats: microform; online. Also Cited As: *AJP* ● *ASIP Bulletin*, semiannual. Newsletter. Contains articles on public policy issues and research opportunities. Includes new members and personnel promotions and appointments. **Price:** included in membership dues. **Circulation:** 2,300. Alternate Formats: online ● *FASEB Directory*, annual ● *The Journal of Molecular Diagnostics*, quarterly. Research papers in experimental pathology. Covers cell injury and death, inflammatory reactions, disturbances in circulation, and neoplastic growth. **Price:** included in membership dues; $195.00 /year for nonmembers; $350.00 /year for institutions. ISSN: 0002-9440. **Circulation:** 550. **Advertising:** accepted. Alternate Formats: microform; online. Also Cited As: *JMD*. **Conventions/Meetings:** annual Experimental Biology - meeting (exhibits) - 2008 Apr. 5-9, San Diego, CA; 2009 Apr. 18-22, New Orleans, LA; 2010 Apr. 24-28, Anaheim, CA.

15532 ■ Association of Indian Pathologists in North America (AIPNA)
c/o Rajal Shah, MD, Treas.
2G332UH, 1500 E Medical Center Dr.
Dept. of Pathology
Ann Arbor, MI 48109-0054
E-mail: info@aipna.org
URL: http://www.aipna.org
Contact: Megha Joshi MD, Pres.

Membership Dues: regular, $50 (annual) ● life, $500 ● resident, $25 (annual). **Description:** Works to advance the profession of pathology. Transfers knowledge of pathology and laboratory medicine to Indian hospitals and laboratories. **Publications:** Newsletter. Alternate Formats: online. **Conventions/Meetings:** annual meeting.

15533 ■ Association for Molecular Pathology (AMP)
9650 Rockville Pike
Bethesda, MD 20814-3993
Ph: (301)634-7939 (301)634-7130
Fax: (301)634-7990
E-mail: amp@asip.org
URL: http://www.amp.org
Contact: Mark E. Sobel MD, Exec. Off.
Founded: 1995. **Members:** 1,400. **Membership Dues:** associate, $75 (annual) ● regular, for profit company, $175 (annual) ● non-profit institution, $100 (annual). **Description:** Individuals interested in, or engaged in the practice of, molecular pathology. Promotes clinical practice, basic research, and education in the field. Represents members' interests within the health care industry. Develops and maintains liaison with other organizations and agencies concerned with molecular pathology; serves as a forum for the exchange of ideas and information among members. Participates in the development of regulatory and credentialing policies applied to molecular pathology; promulgates guidelines for molecular pathology training programs. Conducts educational programs to increase public awareness of molecular pathology. **Awards:** AMP Leadership Award. **Frequency:** annual. **Type:** recognition. **Recipient:** for an AMP member who has demonstrated exceptional leadership in the accomplishment of the mission and goals of AMP ● Award for Excellence in Molecular Diagnostics. **Frequency:** annual. **Type:** recognition. **Recipient:** for professionals in the fields of molecular biology, molecular pathology, pathology, genetics, microbiology and basic medical sciences ● Technologist Award. **Frequency:** annual. **Type:** recognition. **Recipient:** for the best abstracts submitted by AMP members who are non-doctoral technologists or medical technologists ● Young Investigator Awards. **Frequency:** annual. **Type:** recognition. **Recipient:** for trainees who are AMP members, presents an outstanding basic or applied research in poster format. **Computer Services:** Online services. **Committees:** Meetings and Membership Services; Professional Relations; Publications; Scientific Programs; Strategic Planning; Training and Education. **Special Interest Groups:** Education; Genetics; Hematology; Infectious Diseases; Solid Tumors; Technical Topics. **Publications:** AMP Membership Directory, annual. **Circulation:** 870 ● Newsletter, periodic. **Conventions/Meetings:** annual Scientific/Business Meeting (exhibits) - 2007 Nov. 7-10, Los Angeles, CA - **Avg. Attendance:** 850.

15534 ■ Association of Pathology Chairs (APC)
9650 Rockville Pike
Bethesda, MD 20814-3993
Ph: (301)634-7880
Fax: (301)634-7990
E-mail: apc@asip.org
URL: http://www.apcprods.org
Contact: James M. Crawford MD, Pres.
Founded: 1967. **Members:** 144. **Staff:** 2. **Regional Groups:** 4. **Description:** Chairs of medical school departments of pathology. Acts as a communications center for exchange of information and for workshops on innovations for teaching and resident training, department administration, and relationships with governmental and other non-university agencies. Compiles statistics. **Awards:** Distinguished Service Award. **Frequency:** annual. **Type:** recognition. **Recipient:** for individual. **Telecommunication Services:** electronic mail, pmarkwood@asip.org. **Committees:** Graduate Medical Education; Practice and Management; Research. **Sections:** Program Directors. **Formerly:** (1970) American Association of Chairmen of Medical School Departments of Pathology; (1993) Association of Pathology Chairmen. **Publications:** Newsletter, semiannual. **Price:** available to members only. **Circulation:** 350. Alternate Formats: online. **Conventions/Meetings:** annual meeting - 2008 July 16-19, Colorado Springs, CO.

15535 ■ Association for Pathology Informatics (API)
9650 Rockville Pike
Bethesda, MD 20814-3993
Ph: (301)634-7820
Fax: (301)634-7990
E-mail: api@asip.org
URL: http://www.pathologyinformatics.org
Contact: Ulysses J. Balis, Pres.
Membership Dues: sponsoring, $225 (annual) ● regular, $115 (annual) ● associate, $50 (annual) ● for-profit organization, $1,500 (annual) ● non-profit organization, $500 (annual). **Description:** Promotes the field of pathology informatics as an academic and clinical subspecialty of pathology. Strives to support advances in the field of pathology informatics. Seeks to develop standards for reporting, transferring, storing, and merging confidential and other pathology-related information. **Awards:** API Honorary Informatics Fellow Award. **Frequency:** annual. **Type:** recognition. **Recipient:** to individuals who have made significant contributions to the development of pathology informatics as a clinical and academic subspecialty of pathology ● Peter J. Becich Educational Grant. **Frequency:** annual. **Type:** grant. **Recipient:** for a full membership rebate to associate members. **Telecommunication Services:** electronic mail, ulysses@umich.edu. **Affiliated With:** American Society for Investigative Pathology.

15536 ■ Clinical Cytometry Society (CCS)
10517 Ocean Hwy., Unit 4, Ste.306
Pawleys Island, SC 29585
Ph: (312)238-9068
Free: (866)235-1018
Fax: (312)896-5614
E-mail: admin@cytometry.org
URL: http://www.cytometry.org
Contact: J. Philip McCoy Jr., Pres.
Membership Dues: regular, $75 (annual). **Description:** Fosters the development and implementation of cytometry in relation to human pathology. **Publications:** Clinical Cytometry, bimonthly. Journal ● Newsletter. **Conventions/Meetings:** annual meeting.

15537 ■ College of American Pathologists (CAP)
325 Waukegan Rd.
Northfield, IL 60093-2750
Ph: (847)832-7000
Free: (800)323-4040
Fax: (847)832-8000
URL: http://www.cap.org
Contact: Nicki M. Norris, Exec. VP
Founded: 1947. **Members:** 15,467. **Membership Dues:** fellow, $270 (annual) ● life fellow, $4,000 ● affiliate, $100 (annual). **Staff:** 453. **Budget:** $100,000,000. **Description:** Physicians practicing the specialty of pathology (diagnosis, treatment, observation, and understanding of the progress of disease or medical condition) obtained by morphologic, microscopic, chemical, microbiologic, serologic, or any other type of laboratory examination made on the patient. Fosters improvement of education, research, and medical laboratory service to physicians, hospitals, and the public. Provides job placement information for members. Conducts laboratory accreditation program and laboratory proficiency testing surveys. Maintains spokespersons network; provides free health information to the public; compiles statistics; sponsors educational programs. **Divisions:** Communications Services; Education; Finance and Administrative Services; Human Resources; Information Services; Laboratory Improvement; Membership and Advocacy; SNOMED International. **Publications:** Archives of Pathology and Laboratory Medicine, monthly. Journal. **Price:** included in membership dues; $225.00/year in U.S. and Canada; $340.00/year outside U.S. and Canada. ISSN: 0003-9985. **Circulation:** 15,000. **Advertising:** accepted ● CAP TODAY, monthly. Magazine. Includes scientific abstracts. **Price:** included in membership dues; $75.00/year in U.S.; $95.00/year in Canada; $165.00/year outside U.S. and Canada. **Circulation:** 50,000. **Advertising:** accepted ● College of American Pathologists—Directory, annual. **Price:** included in membership dues ● College of American Pathologists-Positions Listing Service. Provides job listings. **Price:** included in membership dues. Alternate Formats: online ● Also publishes other materials of interest to pathologists and the public. **Conventions/Meetings:** annual meeting - 2007 Sept. 30-Oct. 3, Chicago, IL; 2008 Sept. 25-28, San Diego, CA.

15538 ■ Department of Environmental and Toxicologic Pathology
c/o Armed Forces Institute of Pathology
6825 16th St. NW
Washington, DC 20306-6000
Ph: (202)782-2125
E-mail: mullick@afip.osd.mil
URL: http://www.afip.org/Departments/environmental
Contact: Florabel G. Mullick MD, Principal Deputy Dir.
Founded: 1966. **Staff:** 13. **Multinational**. **Description:** Evaluates biopsy and autopsy material on adverse drug-reaction cases and environment-related diseases; has collected over 18,000 such cases. Functions in areas of consultation, investigation, and education. **Computer Services:** database, INTOX Data Center. **Telecommunication Services:** electronic mail, draleyd@afip.osd.mil. **Departments:** Biophysics; Dermatopathology; Endocrine and Otorhino; Environmental and Tox; Genitourinary; Gyn and Breast; Hematopathology; Hepatic and Gastrointestinal; Infectious and Parasitic; Legal Medicine. **Affiliated With:** Armed Forces Institute of Pathology. **Formerly:** (1979) Registry of Tissue Reactions to Drugs; (1990) Department of Environmental and Drug-Induced Pathology. **Publications:** Reprints. **Conventions/Meetings:** semiannual seminar.

15539 ■ International Academy of Pathology (IAP)
c/o Dr. Florabel G. Mullick, Sec.
WRAMC, Bldg. 54, Rm. N1610
14th St. and Alaska Ave. NW
Washington, DC 20306-6000
Fax: (202)782-7166
E-mail: mullick@afip.osd.mil
URL: http://iaphomepage.org
Contact: Dr. Florabel G. Mullick, Sec.
Founded: 1906. **Members:** 8,300. **Regional Groups:** 32. **Multinational**. **Description:** Professional society of pathologists and medical scientists. Aims to improve methods of teaching pathology. Coordinates anatomical pathology, pathologic physiology, and comparative pathology; promotes research in pathology in medical schools, laboratories, hospitals, and medical museums. **Formerly:** (1954) International Association of Medical Museums. **Publications:** International Pathology, quarterly. Newsletter. **Price:** included in membership dues. ISSN: 0020-8205. **Conventions/Meetings:** biennial congress (exhibits).

15540 ■ International Society for Plastination (ISP)
c/o Robert W. Henry, PhD, Treas.
Univ. of Tennessee
Dept. of Animal Sciences, Rm. A-130
2407 River Dr.
Knoxville, TN 37996
Ph: (423)974-5822
Fax: (423)974-2215
E-mail: rhenry@utk.edu
URL: http://anatomie.meduni-graz.at/plast
Contact: Robert W. Henry PhD, Treas.
Founded: 1984. **Members:** 200. **Membership Dues:** full, library, institution, $75 (biennial). **Description:** Anatomists, pathologists, and technologists. Seeks to share information about plastination, a means of infiltrating biological specimens with curable polymers. **Telecommunication Services:** electronic mail, david.hostler.1@ohio.edu. **Publications:** Journal of the International Society for Plastination, annual. **Price:** $40.00/year. ISSN: 1090-2171. **Circulation:** 200. **Advertising:** accepted. **Conventions/Meetings:** biennial international conference, posters/exhibits of specimens (exhibits).

15541 ■ Intersociety Council for Pathology Information (ICPI)
9650 Rockville Pike
Bethesda, MD 20814-3993
Ph: (301)634-7200

Fax: (301)634-7990
E-mail: icpi@asip.org
URL: http://www.pathologytraining.org
Contact: Donna Stivers, Admin./Managing Ed.
Founded: 1957. **Members:** 5. **Staff:** 2. **Description:** One representative from each sponsoring society: American Society for Investigative Pathology; American Society for Clinical Pathology; Association of Pathology Chairs; College of American Pathologists; U.S. and Canadian Academy of Pathology. Disseminates information about the medical practice and research achievements of pathology. Produces career information, especially training of residents and postdoctoral fellows in pathology. **Telecommunication Services:** electronic mail, dstivers@asip.org. **Affiliated With:** American Society for Clinical Pathology; American Society for Investigative Pathology; Association of Pathology Chairs; College of American Pathologists; United States and Canadian Academy of Pathology. **Formerly:** (2004) Intersociety Committee on Pathology Information. **Publications:** *Directory of Pathology Training Programs: Residencies and Fellowships in US and Canada,* annual. **Price:** $25.00 others, in U.S. and Canada; $5.00 for medical students/residents; free for medical schools/medical libraries. **Circulation:** 2,500 ● *Pathology as a Career in Medicine.* Brochure.

15542 ■ Renal Pathology Society (RPS)

c/o Dr. Helen Liapis, Sec.-Treas.
Dept. of Pathology and Immunology
Washington Univ. School of Medicine
660 S Euclid Ave.
St. Louis, MO 63110
Fax: (314)747-2040
E-mail: sum2013@med.cornell.edu
URL: http://www.renalpathsoc.org
Contact: Dr. Helen Liapis, Sec.-Treas.
Founded: 1993. **Members:** 236. **Membership Dues:** regular member, $75 (annual). **Multinational.** **Description:** Works to spread and increase knowledge of pathology of the kidney and seeks to develop renal pathology as a subspecialty. Conducts research and educational programs. **Awards:** Jacob Churg Award. **Frequency:** annual. **Type:** recognition ● Young Investigator Award. **Frequency:** biennial. **Type:** monetary. **Computer Services:** database ● mailing lists ● online services. **Committees:** Auditing; Communication and Publications; Education and Scientific; Nominating and Awards; Program; Research; Training Programs. **Publications:** Directory. Alternate Formats: online ● Bulletin. Alternate Formats: online. **Conventions/Meetings:** semiannual conference and board meeting.

15543 ■ Society for Applied Immunohistochemistry

c/o Richard W. Cartun, PhD, Sec.-Treas.
Dept. of Pathology
Hartford Hosp.
80 Seymour St.
Hartford, CT 06102
Ph: (860)545-1596
Fax: (860)545-0174
E-mail: rcartun@harthosp.org
URL: http://www.appliedimmuno.org
Contact: Richard W. Cartun PhD, Sec.-Treas.
Founded: 1991. **Membership Dues:** general, $40 (annual). **Description:** Gathers data and disseminates information on immunohistochemistry. Provides an online forum for its members. Offers courses on immunohistochemistry.

15544 ■ Society for Hematopathology (SH)

3643 Walton Way Extension
Augusta, GA 30909
Ph: (706)733-7570
Fax: (706)733-8033
E-mail: sh@uscap.org
URL: http://socforheme.org
Contact: Roger A. Warnke MD, Pres.
Founded: 1981. **Members:** 500. **Staff:** 1. **Description:** Physicians; doctors of science, osteopathy, veterinary medicine, and dental surgery. Promotes exchange of information and encourages clinical, morphological, and functional investigation of the he-

matopoietic (pertaining to the formation of blood cells) and lymphoreticular (regarding reticuloendothelial cells of the lymph glands) systems. **Awards:** Pathologist-in-Training Award. **Frequency:** annual. **Type:** recognition. **Telecommunication Services:** electronic mail, rwarnke@stanford.edu. **Publications:** Newsletter. **Conventions/Meetings:** annual meeting and symposium.

15545 ■ Society for Pediatric Pathology (SPP)

c/o United States and Canada Academy of Pathology (USCAP)
3643 Walton Way Extension
Augusta, GA 30909
Ph: (706)364-3375
Fax: (706)733-8033
E-mail: spp@uscap.org
URL: http://www.spponline.org
Contact: Deborah Perry, Pres.
Founded: 1965. **Members:** 520. **Membership Dues:** regular, $200 (annual) ● affiliate, $120 (annual) ● junior, $100 (annual). **Staff:** 1. **Description:** Pediatric pathologists. Seeks to advance the science and practice of pediatric pathology. Facilitates the integration of scientific developments in the field; conducts continuing medical education programs. **Awards:** A. James McAdams Short-Term Study Stipend. **Frequency:** annual. **Type:** monetary. **Recipient:** to a pediatric pathologist or pathology trainee ● Gordon L. Vawter Pathologist-in-Training Award. **Frequency:** annual. **Type:** recognition. **Recipient:** for the best platform or poster presentation by a pathologist in training ● Harry B. Neustein Memorial Award. **Frequency:** annual. **Type:** recognition. **Recipient:** for meritorious work involving electron microscopy in the study of children's disorders ● Lotte Strauss Prize. **Frequency:** annual. **Type:** monetary. **Recipient:** for meritorious work by an individual 40 years of age or younger in a subject germane to pediatric pathology ● Resident's Case Presentation Award. **Frequency:** annual. **Type:** recognition. **Recipient:** for residents interested in pediatric pathology ● Young Investigator Research Grant. **Frequency:** annual. **Type:** grant. **Recipient:** for young investigators in the field of pediatric pathology. **Publications:** *Pediatric and Developmental Pathology,* bimonthly. Journal. Features pathology of disease from conception through adolescence. Alternate Formats: online ● *Perspectives in Pediatric and Developmental Pathology,* annual. Book. Covers comprehensive treatment of specific topics germane to pediatric pathology. Alternate Formats: online ● Newsletter, semiannual. Features updates on Society news and pertinent national and international information. Alternate Formats: online. **Conventions/Meetings:** annual meeting.

15546 ■ Society of Toxicologic Pathology (STP)

1821 Michael Faraday Dr., Ste.300
Reston, VA 20190
Ph: (703)438-7508
Fax: (703)438-3113
E-mail: stp@toxpath.org
URL: http://www.toxpath.org
Contact: Sue Pitsch, Exec. Dir.
Founded: 1971. **Members:** 980. **Membership Dues:** student, $50-$150 (annual) ● full, associate (in U.S., Canada, Mexico, Central and South America), $205 (annual). **Staff:** 3. **Regional Groups:** 5. **National Groups:** 800. **Description:** Promotes the advancement of the individuals interested in toxicology and toxicologic pathology from industry, academic institutions, and government. **Awards:** Achievement Award. **Frequency:** annual. **Type:** monetary ● Student Investigator Awards. **Frequency:** annual. **Type:** monetary. **Computer Services:** Mailing lists. **Committees:** Continuing Education Course; Education Fund; Education Symposium; External Affairs; Internet; Journal; Membership; Newsletter; Regulatory Affairs; Scientific and Regulatory Affairs; Strategic Planning. **Formerly:** (2003) Society of Toxicologic Pathologists. **Publications:** *Communique,* quarterly. Newsletter. **Price:** available to members only. **Circulation:** 700. **Advertising:** accepted. Alternate For-

mats: online ● *Toxicologic Pathology,* bimonthly. Journal. **Price:** $240.00 /year for individuals in U.S.; $360.00 /year for individuals outside U.S. ISSN: 0192-6233. **Circulation:** 1,000. **Advertising:** accepted. **Conventions/Meetings:** annual symposium (exhibits) - always May/June.

15547 ■ Society for Ultrastructural Pathology

c/o Dr. John Shelburne, Sec.-Treas.
Box 3712
Dept. of Pathology
Duke Univ. Medical Center
Durham, NC 27710-3712
Ph: (919)286-6907
Fax: (919)416-5950
E-mail: john.shelburne@med.va.gov
URL: http://sup.ultrakohl.com
Contact: Dr. John Shelburne, Sec.-Treas.
Founded: 1986. **Members:** 185. **Membership Dues:** technologist, pathologist in training, $20 (annual) ● PhD, research associate, pathologist, $30 (annual). **Description:** Promotes the art and science of diagnostic electron microscopy. Fosters the application of electron microscopy in the diagnosis and research of human diseases. Provides an opportunity for the exchange of information, particularly ultrastructural and immunohistochemical, relevant to diagnostic pathology. Focuses on the relevance of molecular pathology techniques to tumor pathology. **Awards:** Pathologist in Training Award. **Frequency:** annual. **Type:** monetary. **Recipient:** for best poster with ultrastructural study. **Publications:** *Organelles in Tumor Diagnosis: An Ultrastructural Atlas.* Book. Features an Atlas designed to identify diagnostic cell structures and tumors through the use of electron microscopy. **Price:** $39.50/copy ● *Ultrastructural Pathology with Related Surgical and Molecular Pathology,* bimonthly. Journal. **Price:** $292.00/copy. **Advertising:** accepted. **Conventions/Meetings:** annual meeting (exhibits) ● biennial UltraPath - conference (exhibits).

15548 ■ United States and Canadian Academy of Pathology

3643 Walton Way Extension
Augusta, GA 30909
Ph: (706)733-7550
Fax: (706)733-8033
E-mail: iap@uscap.org
URL: http://www.uscap.org
Contact: Fred Silva MD, Sec.-Treas./Exec. Dir.
Founded: 1906. **Members:** 8,200. **Membership Dues:** regular, $150 (annual) ● junior, $25 (annual). **Staff:** 5. **Budget:** $1,500,000. **Description:** Works for the advancement of pathology teaching, practice, and research. Disseminates information to members. Sponsors educational programs to serve the needs of pathologists of various levels of experience. Presents Maude Abbott Lectureship to a recognized and respected person in contemporary pathology. **Awards:** Benjamin Castleman Award. **Frequency:** annual. **Type:** monetary. **Recipient:** for a pathologist or pathologist-in-training under 40 years old who has written an outstanding paper on human pathology in English ● Council's Distinguished Pathologist Award. **Frequency:** annual. **Type:** recognition. **Recipient:** for an individual who has made a major contribution to pathology over the years ● F. K. Mostofi Distinguished Service Award. **Frequency:** annual. **Type:** recognition. **Recipient:** for a member who has rendered outstanding service to the Academy and the International Academy of Pathology ● President's Award. **Frequency:** annual. **Type:** recognition. **Recipient:** for outstanding service to the field of pathology ● Stowell-Orbison Awards for Pathologists-in-Training. **Type:** monetary. **Recipient:** for authors of outstanding papers ● Young Investigator Award. **Frequency:** annual. **Type:** recognition. **Recipient:** for a body of work that has contributed to the diagnosis of human disease. **Committees:** Castleman Award; Education; Nominating; Publications; Vogel Award; Young Investigator Award. **Affiliated With:** International Academy of Pathology. **Publications:** *Laboratory Investigation,* monthly. Journal. Focuses on significant advances in research dealing with human and experimental diseases. **Price:** free for members

● *Modern Pathology*, bimonthly. Journal. Concentrates on the practice of diagnostic human pathology. **Price:** free for members ● Membership Directory. Alternate Formats: online ● Books. Alternate Formats: online. **Conventions/Meetings:** annual meeting and conference, includes courses (exhibits) - always late winter or early spring.

Pediatrics

15549 ■ Ambulatory Pediatric Association (APA)

6728 Old McLean Village Dr.
McLean, VA 22101
Ph: (703)556-9222
Fax: (703)556-8729
E-mail: info@ambpeds.org
URL: http://www.ambpeds.org
Contact: Marge Degnon, Exec. Dir.

Founded: 1960. **Members:** 2,000. **Membership Dues:** physician, $200 (annual) ● non-physician, $100 (annual) ● in training, $50 (annual). **Staff:** 3. **Budget:** $300,000. **Regional Groups:** 10. **Description:** Health care providers interested in the care of children in ambulatory care facilities, particularly directors of outpatient departments in private, university, and other teaching hospitals and those engaged in public health work or private practice. Aims to improve methods of care of children. Studies methods of research and the teaching of outpatient care. Conducts collaborative research; compiles statistics; presents annual scientific program. **Awards:** Health Care Delivery Award. **Frequency:** annual. **Type:** recognition. **Recipient:** to residents or medical students for innovative and effective program that provides health care in the context of a teaching setting ● Public Policy Award. **Frequency:** annual. **Type:** recognition. **Recipient:** for individual, pediatric department or program whose public policy advocacy efforts at the state, regional, national, or international level have improved the health and well-being of infants, children and adolescents ● Research Award. **Frequency:** annual. **Type:** recognition. **Recipient:** for individuals who advanced their pediatrics knowledge through excellence in research ● Teaching Award. **Frequency:** annual. **Type:** recognition. **Recipient:** for individuals who excel in educational teaching methods. **Committees:** Chronic Illness and Research; Education; Fellowship; Graduate Education; Health Care Delivery; International Health; Manpower; Research; Social/Political Action; Undergraduate Education. **Formerly:** (1967) Association for Ambulatory Pediatric Services. **Publications:** *Ambulatory Pediatric Association—Membership Directory*, biennial. **Price:** included in membership dues ● *Ambulatory Pediatric Association—Newsletter*, 3/year. Includes book reviews, calendar of events, listing of employment opportunities, research reports, and statistics. **Price:** included in membership dues. **Circulation:** 2,000 ● *Ambulatory Pediatrics*, bimonthly. Journal ● Also publishes abstracts of scientific papers. **Conventions/Meetings:** annual meeting and workshop, scientific research presentations, interest groups (exhibits).

15550 ■ American Academy of Pediatrics (AAP)

141 NW Point Blvd.
Elk Grove Village, IL 60007-1098
Ph: (847)434-4000
Fax: (847)434-8000
E-mail: kidsdocs@aap.org
URL: http://www.aap.org
Contact: Jay Berkelhamer MD, Pres.

Founded: 1930. **Members:** 55,000. **Membership Dues:** fellow/specialty fellow (from 1st to 2nd year), $297-$526 (annual) ● married fellow/specialty fellow, $229 (annual) ● candidate (from 1st year to 7th year), $233-$398 (annual) ● associate, $294 (annual) ● corresponding fellow, $323 (annual) ● retired fellow, $176 (annual) ● emeritus fellow, $63 (annual) ● international, $391 (annual) ● medical student, $16 (annual) ● section affiliate, $60 (annual) ● ACP-ASIM (dual fellow), $480 (annual) ● Canadian Paediatric

Society (dual fellow), $412 (annual) ● resident/post-residency training, $88 (annual). **Staff:** 250. **State Groups:** 66. **Description:** Professional medical society of pediatricians and pediatric subspecialists. Maintains 42 committees, councils, and tasks forces including: Accident and Poison Prevention; Early Childhood, Adoption and Dependent Care; Infectious Diseases. Operates 47 sections. Sponsors Pediatrics Review and Education Program (PREP), a self-assessment, continuing education program for practicing pediatricians. **Libraries:** Type: reference. **Holdings:** books, periodicals. **Subjects:** pediatric medicine, office practice, child health care policy. **Awards:** AAP Education Award. **Frequency:** annual. **Type:** recognition. **Recipient:** to a member whose educational activities have made a broad and positive impact on the health and well-being of children and adolescents ● Andrew Margileth Award. **Frequency:** annual. **Type:** recognition. **Recipient:** to a uniformed services pediatrician who has the best research paper ● Anne Dyson Child Advocacy Award. **Frequency:** annual. **Type:** recognition. **Recipient:** to physicians-in-training who had outstanding efforts as they work through their residency training program ● Arnold J. Capute Award. **Frequency:** annual. **Type:** recognition. **Recipient:** to a pediatrician who makes a notable contribution to the health and well-being of children with disabilities ● Award for Outstanding Service to Maltreated Children. **Frequency:** annual. **Type:** recognition. **Recipient:** to a pediatrician or pediatric subspecialist who has demonstrated outstanding clinical care of and service to abused and neglected children and their families ● Awards of Chapter Excellence. **Frequency:** annual. **Type:** recognition. **Recipient:** for individuals or chapters who have excellent programs that promote the health and welfare of children. **Publications:** *AAP News*, monthly. Newspaper. Covers the social, economic, and professional aspects of pediatric care. Includes association news and chapter news. **Price:** included in membership dues; $40.00 for nonmembers. **Circulation:** 55,000. **Advertising:** accepted ● *Fellowship List*, annual. Directory ● *Pediatrics* (in English, Italian, Polish, Portuguese, and Spanish), monthly. Journal. Includes employment listings. **Price:** $167.00 for nonmembers in U.S.; $202.00 for nonmembers outside U.S.; $119.00 in training/allied health professional in U.S.; $154.00 in training/allied health professional outside U.S. ISSN: 0031-4005. **Circulation:** 63,000. **Advertising:** accepted. Alternate Formats: microform; online ● *Pediatrics in Review*, monthly. Journal. Contains review articles and abstracts. Subscribers are eligible for Category/Continuing Medical Education credit. **Price:** $149.00 for members; $189.00 for nonmembers; $139.00 for candidate fellow; $139.00 for allied health professional/in training. ISSN: 0191-9601. **Circulation:** 28,000. Alternate Formats: online ● Also publishes professional manuals and patient education materials. **Conventions/Meetings:** annual meeting (exhibits).

15551 ■ American Board of Pediatrics (ABP)

111 Silver Cedar Ct.
Chapel Hill, NC 27514
Ph: (919)929-0461
Fax: (919)929-9255
E-mail: abpeds@abpeds.org
URL: http://www.abp.org
Contact: James A. Stockman MD, Pres.

Founded: 1933. **Members:** 250. **Staff:** 60. **Description:** Certification board to establish qualifications, conduct examinations, and certify as diplomates those whom the board finds qualified as specialists in pediatrics. **Affiliated With:** American Board of Medical Specialties. **Publications:** *American Board of Pediatrics—Booklet of Information*, annual. Outlines requirements for admission to certifying examinations; includes details of examinations. **Price:** free ● *American Board of Pediatrics—Informal Newsletter to Members*, periodic. Alternate Formats: CD-ROM ● *American Board of Pediatrics—Newsletter for Diplomates*, annual. **Price:** free. Alternate Formats: online ● *Newsletter to Pediatric Training Program Directors*. **Price:** free. **Conventions/Meetings:** quarterly meeting, for board of directors and various committees.

15552 ■ American Pediatric Society (APS)

3400 Res. Forest Dr., Ste.B-7
The Woodlands, TX 77381
Ph: (281)419-0052
Fax: (281)419-0082
E-mail: info@aps-spr.org
URL: http://www.aps-spr.org
Contact: Kathy A. Cannon, Assoc. Exec. Dir.

Founded: 1888. **Members:** 1,700. **Membership Dues:** $255 (annual). **Staff:** 9. **Budget:** $300,000. **Description:** Professional academic society of MD educators and researchers interested in the study of children and their diseases, prevention of illness, and promotion of health in childhood. Maintains archives. **Awards:** John Howland Award. **Frequency:** annual. **Type:** medal. **Recipient:** for individuals who contributed to the advancement in pediatrics health care. **Telecommunication Services:** electronic mail, kathyc@aps-spr.org. **Publications:** *Pediatric Research*, monthly. Journal. **Advertising:** accepted ● *Program and Abstracts of Annual Meeting*, annual. Annual Report. **Conventions/Meetings:** annual meeting (exhibits) - 2008 May 2-6, Honolulu, HI; 2009 May 2-5, Baltimore, MD; 2010 May 5-8, Vancouver, BC, Canada; 2011 Apr. 30-May 3, Denver, CO.

15553 ■ American Pediatric Surgical Association (APSA)

60 Revere Dr., Ste.500
Northbrook, IL 60062
Ph: (847)480-9576
Fax: (847)480-9282
E-mail: eapsa@eapsa.org
URL: http://www.eapsa.org
Contact: Melanie Stanton, Exec. Dir.

Founded: 1970. **Members:** 863. **Membership Dues:** regular, associate, international, $525 (annual) ● candidate, $75 (annual). **Description:** Pediatric surgeons who are certified by the American Board of Surgery for competence in dealing with surgical problems of infancy and childhood. Seeks to provide competent medical care for children. Serves as a forum for discussion of ethics involving childcare. Presents new concepts and advances in surgical care of infants and children. **Computer Services:** Mailing lists. **Committees:** Cancer; Critical Care; Education; Endoscopic Surgery; Ethics and Advocacy; Fetal Therapy; Informatics and Telemedicine; International Relations; Membership and Credentials; Nominating; Outcomes and Clinical Trials; Practice; Program; Publications; Transplant; Trauma. **Task Forces:** Special Task Force on Manpower (Workforce). **Publications:** *Annual Program Booklet*, annual ● *Business Meeting Minutes*, annual ● *Cancer Newsletter*, annual ● *Journal of Pediatric Surgery*, monthly ● Membership Directory, annual ● Newsletter, semiannual. **Conventions/Meetings:** annual meeting (exhibits) - always May. 2008 May 29-June 1, Phoenix, AZ.

15554 ■ Association of Medical School Pediatric Department Chairs (AMSPDC)

c/o Jean Bartholomew, Coor.
Amer. Bd. of Pediatrics
111 Silver Cedar Ct.
Chapel Hill, NC 27514-1651
Ph: (919)942-1993
Fax: (919)929-9255
E-mail: jbartholomew@abpeds.org
URL: http://www.amspdc.org
Contact: Aaron Friedman MD, Sec.-Treas.

Founded: 1961. **Members:** 148. **Membership Dues:** regular, $495 (annual). **Description:** Chairmen of the department of pediatrics of each accredited medical school in the United States and Canada. Fosters education and research in the field of child health and human development. Cooperates with other national pediatric groups to consider problems of pediatric education, research, and care. **Awards:** Pediatric Scientist Award. **Type:** recognition. **Telecommunication Services:** electronic mail, afriedman@lifespan.org. **Publications:** Membership Directory, annual. **Conventions/Meetings:** annual meeting - always March. 2008 Mar. 6-10, Santa Fe, NM - **Avg. Attendance:** 275; 2009 Mar. 4-10, Savannah, GA.

15555 ■ Association of Pediatric Oncology Social Workers (APOSW)
c/o Dr. Barbara Jones, Pres.
Univ. of Texas
Austin School of Social Work
1 Univ. St., D3500
Austin, TX 78712
Ph: (512)475-9367
Fax: (512)471-9600
E-mail: barbarajones@mail.utexas.edu
URL: http://www.aposw.org
Contact: Dr. Barbara Jones, Pres.
Founded: 1977. **Members:** 360. **Membership Dues:** full, $60 (annual) ● associate, $50 (annual). **Description:** Social workers involved with pediatric cancer patients in health care and community based settings nationwide. Aims to: advance the practice, enhance knowledge, and develop policy and programs of pediatric oncology social work; foster quality and effectiveness of the social work practice of pediatric oncology; promote solidarity among social workers; provide community and professional education; formulate and record local and federal legislation related to pediatric oncology. **Publications:** Brochure ● Newsletter, quarterly. Alternate Formats: online. **Conventions/Meetings:** annual conference.

15556 ■ Council of Pediatric Subspecialties (CoPS)
6728 Old McLean Village Dr.
McLean, VA 22101
Ph: (703)556-9222
Fax: (703)556-8729
E-mail: info@pedsubs.org
URL: http://www.pedsubs.org
Contact: Vicky Norwood, Chair
Description: Strives to ensure excellence in pediatric subspecialty medicine. Integrates approaches to subspecialty education, research, and patient care. Serves as the common voice for pediatric subspecialties. **Telecommunication Services:** electronic mail, vfn6t@hscmail.mcc.virginia.edu.

15557 ■ Federation of Pediatric Organizations (FOPO)
3723 Haven Rd., MS 3705-190
Menlo Park, CA 94025
Ph: (650)839-1933
Fax: (650)839-1933
E-mail: karen@fopo.org
URL: http://www.fopo.org
Contact: Karen Kowaki, Sec.
Description: Promotes high standards of health care for infants, children, adolescents and young adults. Fosters high quality education and training of pediatricians both in residency and throughout their careers. Advances research and development of new knowledge for the improvement of children's health and well being. Promotes education of the public, the government and other organizations regarding the development and maintenance of high standards of care. **Publications:** Newsletter. Alternate Formats: online.

15558 ■ International Association of Pediatric Laboratory Medicine (IAPLM)
6728 Old McLean Village Dr.
McLean, VA 22101
E-mail: klausp.kohse@t-online.de
URL: http://www.uni-oldenburg.de/ec4/iaplm.htm
Contact: Jocelyn Hicks PhD, Pres.
Founded: 1994. **Membership Dues:** full, $115 (annual) ● non-journal, $80 (annual). **Multinational. Description:** Aims to enhance the science and practice of pediatric laboratory medicine. Encourages the development of scientific knowledge and use of improved methods, practices, and techniques applied to pediatric laboratory medicine. Seeks to advance the interests of pediatric clinical pathologists and scientists through continuing education. Fosters camaraderie and networking among international leaders in laboratory medicine. **Telecommunication Services:** electronic mail, jhicks@cnmc.org. **Publications:** *Pediatric and Developmental Pathology*, bimonthly. Journal. **Price:** included in membership

dues (full membership only) ● Newsletter. **Price:** included in membership dues.

15559 ■ International Pediatric Endosurgery Group (IPEG)
11300 W Olympic Blvd., No. 600
Los Angeles, CA 90064
Ph: (310)437-0553
Fax: (310)437-0585
E-mail: admin@ipeg.org
URL: http://www.ipeg.org
Contact: Atsuyuki Yamataka MD, Pres.
Multinational. Description: Doctors, surgeons, pediatricians, and those in the medical field. Presents materials and articles keeping up to date on pediatric endosurgery and endoscopy, offer open forum for discussions and ideas, and extend support.

15560 ■ National Pediatrics AIDS Network
c/o Gary Gale, Dir.
PO Box 1032
Boulder, CO 80306
Free: (800)646-1001
E-mail: gary@npan.org
URL: http://www.npan.org
Contact: Gary Gale, Dir.
Description: Works as a resource for children and adolescents with HIV/AIDS around the world.

15561 ■ North American Society for Pediatric Medicine (NASPEM)
c/o Pat Nixon, PhD, Pres.
Exercise Sci. Dept.
Syracuse Univ.
Women's Bldg., Rm. 201
820 Comstock Ave.
Syracuse, NY 13244-5040
Ph: (336)758-4642
Fax: (336)758-4680
E-mail: nixonpa@wfu.edu
URL: http://www.naspem.org
Contact: Pat Nixon PhD, Pres.
Founded: 1985. **Description:** Promotes exercise science, physical activity, and fitness in the health and medical care of children and adolescents. **Computer Services:** database, training programs. **Programs:** Student Research Grant; Training. **Publications:** Newsletter. Alternate Formats: online.

15562 ■ Pediatric Cardiac Intensive Care Society (PCICS)
c/o Anthony C. Chang, MD, Pres.
CHOC Heart Indus.
455 S Main St., LLW-108
Orange, CA 92868
Ph: (714)532-7576
Fax: (714)289-4962
URL: http://www.pcics.com
Contact: Anthony C. Chang MD, Pres.
Members: 250. **Membership Dues:** regular, $100 (annual) ● associate, $50 (annual). **National Groups:** 12. **Multinational. Description:** Promotes excellence in pediatric cardiac critical care medicine. Encourages collegial relationships among pediatric specialists. Improves the level of care of pediatric and adult patients with congenital heart disease, pediatric patients with acquired cardiovascular disease and pediatric patients after cardiac surgery. Promotes basic and clinical research related to pediatric patients in the peri-operative period. Provides related educational material through established and developing communication technologies. **Conventions/Meetings:** annual symposium - 2008 Dec. 2-7, Miami Beach, FL.

15563 ■ Pediatric Digestion and Motility Disorders Society (PEDS)
PO Box 1360
Buffalo, NY 14205
URL: http://www.pedsgi.org
Description: Volunteers. Works towards finding cures. Hosts events to fund research. Promotes public awareness.

15564 ■ Pediatric Endocrinology Nursing Society (PENS)
7794 Grow Dr.
Pensacola, FL 32514
Ph: (850)484-5223
Free: (877)936-7367
Fax: (850)484-8762
E-mail: pens@puetzamc.com
URL: http://www.pens.org
Contact: Helen Grosskreuz, Pres.
Founded: 1986. **Members:** 375. **Staff:** 1. **Description:** Pediatric endocrine nurses. Promotes professional responsibility, accountability, ethics and respect; dedicated to the advancement of the art and science of pediatric endocrine nursing; establishes and maintains standards of practice; enhances nursing research, clinical expertise and recognition of excellence in nursing. **Awards:** Academic Education Scholarships. **Type:** scholarship. **Recipient:** for nursing academic programs (BSN, MSN, PhD) ● Continuing Education Scholarships. **Type:** scholarship. **Recipient:** to assist members attending PENS annual conference ● Manual Chapter Author Grant. **Type:** monetary. **Recipient:** provides financial support to active members authoring an original or revised chapter for the manual ● Poster Presentation Grant. **Type:** monetary. **Recipient:** for materials necessary to create a poster presentation for the PENS annual conference ● Research Grants. **Type:** monetary. **Recipient:** to support pediatric endocrinology nursing research projects. **Telecommunication Services:** electronic bulletin board. **Committees:** Communications; Conference Planning; Education; Membership/ Bylaws; Nominations; Research and Special Projects. **Councils:** Advisory. **Publications:** *PENS Manual*. Contains individual chapters authored by nurses in the field of pediatric endocrinology. ● *PENS Reporter*, quarterly. Newsletter. Includes society news, committee reports, deadlines, articles with focus on endocrine disorders and nursing research, lay organization information. **Price:** included in membership dues. **Conventions/Meetings:** annual conference, educational.

15565 ■ Pediatric Network for Chronic Fatigue Syndrome, Fibromyalgia, and Orthostatic Intolerance
c/o Mary Robinson, Co-Founder
507 Park Ave.
Medina, NY 14103-1519
E-mail: founders@pediatricnetwork.org
URL: http://www.pediatricnetwork.org
Contact: Mary Robinson, Co-Founder
Founded: 2002. **Members:** 250. **Description:** Supports parents, youth, professionals concerned with chronic fatigue syndrome, fibromyalgia, and orthostatic intolerance. **Computer Services:** Information services, Lyndonville News archive of articles ● mailing lists ● online services, monthly chats ● online services, newsletter listserv. **Publications:** *Pediatric Network News*, monthly. Newsletter. Alternate Formats: online ● Brochure.

15566 ■ Pediatric Pharmacy Advocacy Group (PPAG)
7975 Stage Hills Blvd., Ste.No. 6
Memphis, TN 38133
Ph: (901)380-3617
Fax: (901)266-4751
E-mail: matthew.helms@ppag.org
URL: http://www.ppag.org
Contact: Matthew Helms, Exec.Dir.
Members: 600. **Membership Dues:** individual/associate, $150 (annual) ● resident/fellow, $55 (annual) ● pharmacy technician/student, $35 (annual). **Staff:** 1. **Description:** Dedicated to safe and effective medication use in children. **Publications:** *Journal of Pediatric Pharmacology and Therapeutics*, quarterly. **Circulation:** 900. **Advertising:** accepted. Also Cited As: *JPPT*. **Conventions/Meetings:** annual meeting (exhibits) - October and April.

15567 ■ Puerto Rico Association of Pediatric Surgeons
PO Box 10426
Caparra Heights Sta.
San Juan, PR 00922-0426

Ph: (787)777-3535
Fax: (787)720-6103
E-mail: titolugo@coqui.net
URL: http://home.coqui.net/titolugo/praps.htm
Contact: Humberto Lugo-Vicente MD, Ed.
Founded: 1997. **Description:** General pediatric surgeons. Strives to improve the care of newborns, infants, children, adolescent and young adults with surgically related diseases. Provides educational forum, research and teaching of surgery, consults and recommends programs and policy statements. **Computer Services:** database, pediatric surgery update.

15568 ■ Society for Developmental and Behavioral Pediatrics (SDBP)
6728 Old McLean Village Dr.
McLean, VA 22101
Ph: (703)556-9222
Fax: (703)556-8729
E-mail: info@sdbp.org
URL: http://www.sdbp.org
Contact: Laura Degnon CAE, Exec. Dir.
Founded: 1982. **Members:** 750. **Membership Dues:** trainee, non-doctorate, or developing nation, $105 (annual) ● regular, $190 (annual). **Staff:** 2. **Budget:** $250,000. **Regional Groups:** 2. **State Groups:** 2. **Description:** Pediatricians, child psychologists, and other allied health care professionals. Seeks to improve the health care of infants, children, and adolescents by promoting research, teaching, and clinical care in the area of developmental-behavioral pediatrics. **Awards:** SDBP Lectureship Award. **Frequency:** annual. **Type:** recognition. **Recipient:** for significant contributions to the field of developmental-behavioral pediatrics, either academically or in a leadership role. **Telecommunication Services:** electronic mail, sdbp@ahint.com. **Committees:** Advocacy; Communications; Education; Funding; Practice Issues; Program; Research. **Formerly:** Society for Behavioral Pediatrics. **Publications:** *Behavioral Developments*, semiannual. Newsletter. Alternate Formats: online ● *Journal of Developmental and Behavioral Pediatrics*, bimonthly. Includes original scientific articles, book and journal article reviews, commentaries, and letters to the editor. **Price:** included in membership dues; $277.00 /year for individuals in U.S.; $337.00 /year for individuals outside U.S. ISSN: 0196-206X. **Circulation:** 1,440. **Advertising:** accepted. **Conventions/Meetings:** annual meeting and workshop, limited to publishers of books in developmental-behavioral pediatrics and psychological testing instruments (exhibits).

15569 ■ Society for Pediatric Research (SPR)
3400 Res. Forest Dr., Ste.B-7
The Woodlands, TX 77381
Ph: (281)419-0052
Fax: (281)419-0082
E-mail: info@aps-spr.org
URL: http://www.aps-spr.org
Contact: Debbie Anagnostelis, Exec. Dir.
Founded: 1929. **Members:** 3,200. **Membership Dues:** active, $180 (annual) ● senior, $95 (annual) ● affiliate, $35 (annual). **Staff:** 9. **Budget:** $300,000. **Description:** Physicians and scientists under age 50 who are engaged in research in diseases of infancy and childhood; those over age 50 are senior members. **Awards:** David G. Nathan Award in Hematology/Oncology. **Frequency:** annual. **Type:** monetary. **Recipient:** for an individual who served as mentor to young physicians ● Douglas K. Richardson Award for Perinatal and Pediatric Health Care Research. **Frequency:** annual. **Type:** recognition. **Recipient:** for an investigator who has made a substantive contribution ● E. Mead Johnson Award. **Frequency:** annual. **Type:** monetary. **Recipient:** for outstanding achievement for research accomplishments in pediatrics ● Fellow House Officer Student Research Awards. **Frequency:** annual. **Type:** monetary. **Recipient:** for students, house officers and fellows engaged in pediatric research ● Maureen Andrew Mentorship Award. **Frequency:** annual. **Type:** monetary. **Recipient:** for an individual who served as an exemplary mentor for trainees and junior faculty ● Medical Student Award. **Frequency:** annual. **Type:** recogni-

tion ● Richard D. Rowe Award in Perinatal Cardiology. **Frequency:** annual. **Type:** monetary. **Recipient:** for an individual who earned MD, PhD, or equivalent degree ● Young Investigator Research Awards. **Frequency:** annual. **Type:** monetary. **Recipient:** for an individual who has an excellent contribution dedicated to unraveling the mysteries of childhood development or disease. **Computer Services:** Mailing lists ● online services, membership database. **Councils:** Public Policy. **Publications:** *Pediatric Research*, monthly. Journal. Includes calendar of events, and abstracts. **Price:** $110.00/year. **Advertising:** accepted. **Conventions/Meetings:** annual Pediatric Academic Societies - convention, to current and future research related to the health and well being of children (exhibits) - 2008 May 3-6, Honolulu, HI; 2009 May 2-5, Baltimore, MD.

Perinatology

15570 ■ National Perinatal Association (NPA)
2090 Linglestown Rd., Ste.107
Harrisburg, PA 17110
Free: (888)971-3295
Fax: (717)920-1390
E-mail: npa@nationalperinatal.org
URL: http://www.nationalperinatal.org
Contact: Shelia S. Sorkin, Exec. Dir.
Founded: 1976. **Members:** 1,500. **Membership Dues:** individual, $75 (annual) ● nonprofit, $200 ● corporate, $5,000. **Staff:** 3. **Budget:** $250,000. **Regional Groups:** 1. **State Groups:** 27. **National Groups:** 20. **Description:** Organizations and individuals interested in perinatal health care. Seeks to promote improved patient care, education, research, advocacy and delivery systems for perinatal health. **Libraries:** **Type:** reference. **Awards:** National Perinatal Association Award. **Frequency:** annual. **Type:** recognition. **Recipient:** for contribution to maternal/child health ● Stanley N. Graven Leadership Award. **Frequency:** annual. **Type:** recognition ● State Initiative. **Frequency:** annual. **Type:** monetary. **Computer Services:** database ● mailing lists. **Committees:** Awards; By Laws; Education; Finance; Legislative; Marketing; Membership; Nominations; Personnel; Program; Research; State Forum; Strategic Planning. **Publications:** *Journal of Perinatology*, bimonthly. Examines all facets of perinatology/neonatology from a variety of perspectives. **Price:** included in membership dues; $40.00 /year for nonmembers. ISSN: 0743-8346. **Circulation:** 2,400. **Advertising:** accepted ● Newsletter, quarterly. Includes article reviews and legislative news. **Price:** included in membership dues. **Circulation:** 1,400. **Advertising:** accepted ● Proceedings. **Conventions/Meetings:** Clinical Conference, focuses on the needs and interests of health care professionals who are committed to perinatal health issues (exhibits) - always fall ● annual meeting.

15571 ■ National Perinatal Information Center (NPIC)
225 Chapman St., Ste.200
Providence, RI 02905
Ph: (401)274-0650
Fax: (401)455-0377
E-mail: npic@npic.org
URL: http://www.npic.org
Contact: David E. Gagnon MPH, Pres.
Founded: 1985. **Members:** 2,000. **Membership Dues:** hospital, $5,750 (annual) ● individual, $60 (annual). **Staff:** 12. **Budget:** $1,000,000. **Description:** Gathers extensive patient data on hospital stays. Serves as perinatal research center for Maternal and Child Health Clearinghouse. Provides educational and research programs. Maintains speakers' bureau. Performs children's services. **Libraries:** **Type:** reference; by appointment only. **Holdings:** clippings. **Subjects:** perinatal, maternal health, children's health. **Computer Services:** database ● mailing lists. **Councils:** Women and Infants Specialty Hospital. **Programs:** SStar; SStarbirth; Vulnerable Infants. **Projects:** Family Strengthening; Link. **Publications:** *NPIC Newsletter*, quarterly. Contains articles on NPIC

research. **Price:** included in membership dues. **Circulation:** 1,000. Alternate Formats: online ● Brochure, annual ● Directory ● Reports, quarterly. Contains comparative data on topic relevant to the perinatal community. **Conventions/Meetings:** annual conference and board meeting.

15572 ■ Society for Maternal-Fetal Medicine (SMFM)
409 12th St. SW
Washington, DC 20024-2125
Ph: (202)863-2476 (202)863-2480
Fax: (202)554-1132
E-mail: smfm@smfm.org
URL: http://www.smfm.org
Contact: Patricia D. Stahr, Exec. Dir.
Founded: 1977. **Members:** 2,000. **Membership Dues:** individual, $425 (annual) ● coding, $100 (annual) ● associate, affiliate, $375 (annual) ● associate fellow-in-training, resident, $50 (annual). **Staff:** 3. **Description:** Obstetricians specializing in maternal-fetal medicine. Works to improve perinatal care through promotion and expansion of education in obstetrical perinatology. Provides forum for exchange between members. **Awards:** Achievement Award. **Frequency:** annual. **Type:** recognition. **Recipient:** for an outstanding member ● Award for Research. **Frequency:** annual. **Type:** recognition. **Recipient:** for the best paper presented ● Honorary Membership. **Frequency:** annual. **Type:** recognition. **Recipient:** for an outstanding member ● SMFM/AAOGF Scholar Award. **Frequency:** annual. **Type:** scholarship. **Recipient:** for research. **Formerly:** (1999) Society of Perinatal Obstetricians. **Publications:** *American Journal of Obstetrics and Gynecology*, periodic. **Conventions/Meetings:** annual Clinical Meeting (exhibits) - 2008 Jan. 28-Feb. 2, Dallas, TX.

15573 ■ Society for Obstetric Anesthesia and Perinatology (SOAP)
2 Summit Park Dr., No. 140
Cleveland, OH 44131-2571
Ph: (216)447-7863
Fax: (216)447-8970
E-mail: soaphq@soap.org
URL: http://www.soap.org
Contact: Gurinder M.S. Vasdev MD, Pres.
Founded: 1968. **Members:** 1,000. **Membership Dues:** active, associate, $125 (annual) ● resident, retired, $40 (annual). **Staff:** 14. **Budget:** $500,000. **Description:** Physicians and scientists interested in perinatal health care. Purpose is to improve the health care of pregnant women and their unborn children. Conducts specialized education programs; compiles statistics. **Awards:** OAPEF/SOAP Research Starter Grant. **Type:** grant. **Recipient:** for young members who wish to launch an academic career in obstetric anesthesia. **Publications:** *Society for Obstetric Anesthesia and Perinatology Newsletter*, quarterly. **Price:** included in membership dues. **Circulation:** 1,500. Alternate Formats: online. **Conventions/Meetings:** annual meeting (exhibits) - 2008 Apr. 30-May 4, Chicago, IL.

Personal Development

15574 ■ International Enneagram Association (IEA)
4100 Executive Park Dr., Ste.16
Cincinnati, OH 45241
Ph: (513)232-5054
Fax: (513)563-9734
E-mail: theiea@aol.com
URL: http://www.internationalenneagram.org
Contact: Sandy Perry Hatmaker, Admin.
Membership Dues: participating, $70 (annual) ● professional, $130 (annual) ● corporate, $300 (annual). **Description:** Works to promote the highest human values through the insights of the Enneagram. Sponsors open and constructive interactions among various schools of Enneagram thought; encourages innovative application of the Enneagram and builds community through grass roots regional participation.

Publications: *Nine Points Bulletin*, quarterly. Newsletter. **Price:** free for members. Alternate Formats: online.

Pharmacy

15575 ■ Academy of Managed Care Pharmacy (AMCP)
100 N Pitt St., Ste.400
Alexandria, VA 22314
Ph: (703)683-8416
Free: (800)827-2627
Fax: (703)683-8417
E-mail: amcp@amcp.org
URL: http://www.amcp.org
Contact: Judith A. Cahill, Exec. Dir.
Founded: 1989. **Members:** 4,800. **Membership Dues:** student, $35 (annual) ● health care practitioner/pharmacist, $240 (annual) ● associate, $440 (annual) ● resident/fellow/graduate, $85 (annual). **Staff:** 27. **Budget:** $7,000,000. **Description:** Dedicated to the concept and practice of pharmaceutical care in managed health care environments. Promotes the development and application of pharmaceutical care in order to ensure appropriate health care outcomes for all individuals. Represents the views and interest of managed care pharmacy. **Awards:** Foundation Award. **Frequency:** annual. **Type:** recognition. **Publications:** *AMCP News*, monthly. Newsletter. **Circulation:** 4,800. **Advertising:** accepted ● *Concept Series in Managed Care Pharmacy*, periodic. Paper ● *Journal of Managed Care Pharmacy*, 9/year. **Price:** $10.00 each; $60.00 /year for individuals and institutions in U.S.; $80.00 /year for individuals and institutions outside U.S. ● *Who's Who*, annual. Directory. **Conventions/Meetings:** annual Educational Conference - 2007 Oct. 24-27, Boston, MA ● annual meeting (exhibits) - always spring.

15576 ■ Academy of Pharmaceutical Research and Science (APRS)
c/o American Pharmacists Association
1100 15th St. NW, Ste.400
Washington, DC 20005-1707
Ph: (202)628-4410
Free: (800)237-2742
Fax: (202)783-2351
E-mail: apha-aprs@aphanet.org
URL: http://www.aphanet.org
Contact: Gary Smith, Pres.
Founded: 1965. **Members:** 3,000. **Membership Dues:** regular, $185 (annual). **Staff:** 3. **Description:** A part of American Pharmaceutical Association (see separate entry). Pharmaceutical scientists from industry and academia. Serves the profession of pharmacy by developing knowledge and integrating the process of science into the profession. Sponsors national meetings to provide a forum for presentation and discussion of original research, controversial topics, and continuing communication. Provides consultation and advice to pharmacists on scientific matters as they relate to policy; congressional committees on bills of interest to pharmaceutical scientists and governmental agencies. **Awards:** Ebert Prize. **Frequency:** annual. **Type:** medal. **Recipient:** for the best essay or written communication containing investigation of a medical substance ● Kilmer Prize. **Frequency:** annual. **Type:** recognition. **Recipient:** for both undergraduate and graduate students in schools or colleges of pharmacy ● Postgraduate Best Paper Awards. **Frequency:** annual. **Type:** monetary. **Recipient:** for the author of the best contributed paper presented at each APhA Annual Meeting ● Research Achievement Award. **Frequency:** annual. **Type:** monetary. **Recipient:** for an APhA member ● Takeru Higuchi Research Prize. **Frequency:** triennial. **Type:** monetary. **Recipient:** for scientists who have demonstrated effective and persistent efforts in pioneering a new concept applicable to pharmaceutical sciences ● Wiederholt Prize-Best Published Paper in the Economic, Social, and Administrative Sciences. **Frequency:** annual. **Type:** recognition. **Recipient:** for an APhA member. **Telecommunication Services:** electronic mail, gsmith@rx.umary-

land.edu. **Sections:** Basic Pharmaceutical Sciences; Clinical Sciences; Economic, Social, and Administrative Sciences. **Formerly:** (1987) Academy of Pharmaceutical Sciences. **Publications:** *Abstracts of Papers*, annual. Article. Published in Journal of the American Pharmaceutical Association. **Circulation:** 45,000. **Advertising:** accepted ● *APhA DrugInfoLine*, monthly. Newsletter. Contains information designed to keep frontline pharmacists up-to-date on the latest trends in the biomedical literature. **Price:** included in membership dues ● *Journal of Pharmaceutical Sciences*, monthly. **Price:** included in membership dues; $325.00 for nonmembers in U.S.; $385.00 for nonmembers outside U.S. **Circulation:** 6,000. **Advertising:** accepted. Alternate Formats: online ● *Journal of the American Pharmacists Association*, monthly. Provides information on pharmaceutical care, drug therapy, diseases and other health issues, trends in pharmacy practice and therapeutics. Alternate Formats: online ● *Pharmacy Student*, bimonthly. Journal. Provides news and information that affects reader's daily lives. **Price:** included in membership dues. **Advertising:** accepted ● *Pharmacy Today*, monthly. Magazine. Features extensive coverage of advances in medications, therapies, and patient care. **Price:** $200.00 /year for members. **Advertising:** accepted ● Manuals ● Monographs. **Conventions/Meetings:** annual meeting, held in conjunction with APhA (exhibits).

15577 ■ Accreditation Council for Pharmacy Education (ACPE)
20 N Clark St., Ste.2500
Chicago, IL 60602-5109
Ph: (312)664-3575
Fax: (312)664-4652
E-mail: info@acpe-accredit.org
URL: http://www.acpe-accredit.org
Contact: Peter H. Vlasses PharmD, Exec. Dir.
Founded: 1932. **Staff:** 10. **Description:** National agency for accreditation of professional degree programs in pharmacy and providers of continuing pharmaceutical education, including certificate programs in pharmacy. **Telecommunication Services:** electronic mail, pvlasses@acpe-accredit.org. **Committees:** Curriculum; Executive; Self-Study. **Formerly:** (2004) American Council on Pharmaceutical Education. **Publications:** *Accredited Professional Programs of Colleges and Schools of Pharmacy*, annual. Directory ● *Accredited Providers of Continuing Pharmacy Education*, annual. Directory. **Conventions/Meetings:** semiannual board meeting - January and June ● biennial Conference on Continuing Pharmacy Education.

15578 ■ Alliance for the Prudent Use of Antibiotics (APUA)
75 Kneeland St.
Boston, MA 02111-1901
Ph: (617)636-0966
Fax: (617)636-3999
E-mail: apua@tufts.edu
URL: http://www.tufts.edu/med/apua
Contact: Ms. Kathleen T. Young, Exec. Dir.
Founded: 1981. **Members:** 1,000. **Membership Dues:** student, $20 (annual) ● individual, $45 (annual) ● individual, $70 (biennial) ● supporting, $55 (annual) ● supporting, $95 (biennial) ● library/nonprofit organization, $100 (annual) ● friend, $250 (annual). **Staff:** 9. **National Groups:** 24. **Languages:** Chinese, English, Italian, Korean, Russian, Spanish. **Multinational. Description:** International membership of physicians, scientists, and medical and public health personnel; other individuals supporting prudent use of antibiotics. (Believes that abuse of antibiotics leads to development of resistant strains of pathogenic and common, nonpathogenic bacteria with resistance traits transferable from one bacterium to others. These resistant strains are no longer susceptible to antibiotics and therefore can undermine treatment of infectious bacterial diseases.) Advocates and defines "good usage" of antibiotics; informs and educates the public about the dangers of misusing and overusing antibiotics and other antimicrobial agents; provides data to individuals and organizations interested in preventing antibiotic misuse and

overuse. Informs and educates medical and paramedical personnel worldwide about the defined and specific action of antibiotics and the necessity of controlling their dispensation and prescription. Supports research projects. Maintains Speaker's Bureau. **Publications:** *APUA Newsletter*, quarterly. Includes pharmacology reviews. **Price:** included in membership dues. **Circulation:** 7,000. **Conventions/Meetings:** symposium and seminar.

15579 ■ American Association of Colleges of Pharmacy (AACP)
1426 Prince St.
Alexandria, VA 22314
Ph: (703)739-2330
Fax: (703)836-8982
E-mail: mail@aacp.org
URL: http://www.aacp.org
Contact: Amy B. Connelly, Dir., Development
Founded: 1900. **Members:** 3,000. **Membership Dues:** affiliate, $100 (annual). **Staff:** 15. **Budget:** $3,200,000. **Description:** College of pharmacy programs accredited by American Council on Pharmaceutical Education; corporations and individuals. Compiles statistics. **Awards:** Paul Dawson Biotechnology Award. **Frequency:** annual. **Type:** monetary. **Recipient:** to an individual member of AACP for contributions to contemporary teaching and scholarship in biotechnology and its related science ● Robert L. Chalmers Distinguished Pharmacy Educator Award. **Frequency:** annual. **Type:** monetary. **Recipient:** to an individual member of AACP holding a full-time faculty appointment in a U.S. member college or school of pharmacy with excellence in pharmacy education ● The Volwiler Research Achievement Award. **Frequency:** annual. **Type:** medal. **Recipient:** to individual members of AACP with a demonstrated commitment to the mission and objectives of pharmacy education. **Telecommunication Services:** electronic mail, aconnelly@aacp.org. **Committees:** Academic Affairs; Professional Affairs; Program, Research and Graduate Affairs. **Councils:** Deans; Faculties. **Sections:** Biological Sciences; Chemistry; Continuing Professional Education; Librarians/Education Resources; Pharmaceutics; Pharmacy Practice; Social and Administrative Sciences. **Special Interest Groups:** Curriculum; Development Directors; Electronic-Based Instructional Resources; Geriatric Pharmacy; Laboratory Instructors; Liberal Education; Pharmacy Ethics; Substance Abuse Education and Assistance. **Affiliated With:** Accreditation Council for Pharmacy Education. **Formerly:** (1925) American Conference of Pharmaceutical Faculties. **Publications:** *AACP News*, monthly. Newsletter. Includes information on association activities, employment opportunities, and new members. **Price:** included in membership dues; $100.00 /year for nonmembers. **Circulation:** 6,000 ● *American Association of Colleges of Pharmacy—Graduate Programs in the Pharmaceutical Sciences*, annual. Directory. Lists graduate programs in pharmacy; provides comparative analysis of pharmacy schools and admissions criteria for graduate programs. **Price:** $25.00/copy ● *American Journal of Pharmaceutical Education*, quarterly. Includes book reviews, listing of recent publications, and statistics. **Price:** included in membership dues; $40.00 /year for nonmembers in U.S. and Canada; $65.00 /year for nonmembers outside U.S. and Canada; $100.00 /year for libraries. ISSN: 0002-9459. **Circulation:** 2,500. **Advertising:** accepted. Alternate Formats: microform; online ● *Pharmacy School Admission Requirements*, annual. Directory. Lists pharmacy schools arranged by state; provides comparative analysis of pharmacy schools and admissions criteria for professional programs. **Price:** $25.00/copy. ISSN: 0149-1113 ● *Prescription for a Rewarding Career*, periodic. Booklet. Provides prospective students with an overview of pharmacy career options and the vital role that pharmacists play in the health care delivery system. **Price:** $75.00/copy ● *Roster of Faculty and Professional Staff*, annual. Directory. Contains more than 5,000 full and part-time pharmacy faculty members and valuable information about AACP. **Price:** $10.00 for members; $100.00 for nonmembers ● *Roster of Teaching Personnel in Colleges of Pharmacy*, annual. Direc-

tory. Includes calendar of events. **Price:** included in membership dues; $100.00/copy for nonmembers. **Conventions/Meetings:** competition ● annual meeting (exhibits) - 2008 July 19-23, Chicago, IL; 2009 July 18-22, Boston, MA; 2010 July 10-14, Seattle, WA ● annual board meeting - 2008 July 17-18, Chicago, IL; 2009 July 16-17, Boston, MA; 2010 July 8-9, Seattle, WA.

15580 ■ American Association of Pharmacy Technicians (AAPT)
PO Box 1447
Greensboro, NC 27402
Ph: (336)333-9356
Free: (877)368-4771
Fax: (336)333-9068
E-mail: aapt@pharmacytechnician.com
URL: http://www.pharmacytechnician.com
Contact: Sandra Covington CPhT, Pres.
Membership Dues: active, $50 (annual) ● active-joint, $75 (annual) ● associate, $65 (annual) ● technician student, $25 (annual) ● retired, $16 (annual). **Description:** Pharmacy technicians. Promotes professional advancement of members. Represents members before health care and public organizations; conducts continuing professional development courses; publicizes the role of the pharmacy technician as an "integral part of the patient care team". **Conventions/Meetings:** annual convention.

15581 ■ American Chinese Pharmaceutical Association (ACPA)
PO Box 2623
Cherry Hill, NJ 08034
Ph: (609)394-6121
E-mail: clau@chsnj.org
URL: http://www.acpa-rx.org
Contact: Yih-Chain Huang PhD, Pres.
Membership Dues: regular, associate, international associate, $40 (annual) ● student, $10 (annual). **Description:** Pharmacists and pharmaceutical scientists. Seeks to advance the professional well being of pharmacists and pharmaceutical scientists of Chinese heritage; encourages exchange of ideas; provides educational opportunities; promotes health-related issues to the Chinese community. Encourages development of pharmacy practice in China, Taiwan, and Hong Kong. **Programs:** Scholarship. **Publications:** Newsletter, quarterly. Contains organization's events, activities, and membership news. Alternate Formats: online ● Membership Directory. Alternate Formats: online.

15582 ■ American College of Apothecaries (ACA)
2830 Summer Oaks Dr.
Bartlett, TN 38134-3811
Ph: (901)383-8119
Free: (800)828-5933
Fax: (901)383-8882
E-mail: aca@acainfo.org
URL: http://www.acainfo.org
Contact: Mr. D.C. Huffman Jr., Exec. VP
Founded: 1940. **Members:** 1,000. **Staff:** 7. **Budget:** $250,000. **Regional Groups:** 13. **State Groups:** 24. **Description:** Professional society of pharmacists owning and operating ethical prescription pharmacies, including hospital pharmacists, pharmacy students, and faculty of colleges of pharmacy. Translates, transforms, and disseminates knowledge, research data, and recent developments in the pharmaceutical industry and public health. Offers continuing education courses and certificate program. Conducts research programs; sponsors charitable program; compiles statistics; operates speakers' bureau. **Awards:** Type: recognition. **Committees:** Community Pharmacy Services; Contractual Pharmacy Services; Professional Pharmacy Services. **Publications:** *American College of Apothecaries—Directory*, annual. **Price:** included in membership dues. **Circulation:** 1,000 ● *American College of Apothecaries Newsletter*, monthly. Covers membership activities and developments affecting the profession. **Price:** included in membership dues. **Circulation:** 1,000 ● *American College of Apothecaries—Patron's Newsletter*, monthly. Provides tips on health

and medications for patrons of member pharmacists. **Price:** included in membership dues. **Circulation:** 500 ● *American College of Apothecaries—Physician's Newsletter*, monthly. Provides health tips on the use of drugs and medications. **Price:** included in membership dues. **Circulation:** 500 ● *Voice of the Pharmacist*, quarterly. Newsletter. Provides information on issues affecting pharmacy practice, including legislative developments. **Price:** included in membership dues; $40.00 /year for nonmembers. **Circulation:** 1,000 ● Books ● Handbooks ● Also publishes bylaws. **Conventions/Meetings:** semiannual conference.

15583 ■ American College of Clinical Pharmacology (ACCP)
3 Ellinwood Ct.
New Hartford, NY 13413-1115
Ph: (315)768-6117
Fax: (315)768-6119
E-mail: accp1ssu@aol.com
URL: http://www.accp1.org
Contact: Susan S. Ulrich, Exec. Dir.
Founded: 1969. **Members:** 1,000. **Membership Dues:** associate, $150 (annual) ● member, $175 (annual) ● fellow, $250 (annual). **Staff:** 4. **Budget:** $1,000,000. **Local Groups:** 2. **Description:** Strives to be the premier professional society with the size, influence, and diversity of membership consistent with the breadth of the discipline of clinical pharmacology. Provides educational programs and forum for membership, health professionals, students, and the public. Assists in the development and dissemination of basic and clinical knowledge to improve rational drug use and patient outcomes. Serves as a forum for active public debate to influence scientific, regulatory, and public health policy issues. Provides opportunities to influence future directions of the college. Supports and encourages the discovery and development efforts designed to provide improved therapeutic modalities. **Awards:** Bristol-Myers Squibb Mentorship in Clinical Pharmacology Award. **Frequency:** biennial. **Type:** recognition. **Recipient:** for individuals who have provided guidance to those studying clinical pharmacology ● Distinguished Investigator Award. **Frequency:** annual. **Type:** recognition. **Recipient:** for superior scientific expertise and accomplishments by a senior investigator, usually involving a distinct area of research in basic or clinical pharmacology for which the individual is internationally known ● Distinguished Service Award. **Frequency:** annual. **Type:** recognition. **Recipient:** for outstanding service to the college, or the discipline of clinical pharmacology ● Honorary Fellowship Award. **Frequency:** annual. **Type:** recognition. **Recipient:** for overall contributions to the field of clinical pharmacology by a senior investigator ● McKeen Cattell Memorial Award. **Frequency:** annual. **Type:** recognition. **Recipient:** for best paper published in the journal of clinical pharmacology during the prior year ● Tanabe Young Investigator Award. **Frequency:** biennial. **Type:** recognition. **Recipient:** for scientific contributions of a young investigator. **Computer Services:** Mailing lists. **Committees:** Credentials; Education; Finance; Program; Publications. **Publications:** *American College of Clinical Pharmacology—Directory*, annual. Membership Directory. **Price:** included in membership dues ● *Journal of Clinical Pharmacology*, monthly. **Price:** included in membership dues; $295.00 for nonmembers in U.S.; $365.00 for nonmembers outside U.S. ISSN: 0091-2700. **Circulation:** 1,900. **Advertising:** accepted ● Newsletter, 3/year. **Price:** included in membership dues. **Circulation:** 1,000. **Conventions/Meetings:** annual conference (exhibits) - 2007 Sept. 9-11, San Francisco, CA - **Avg. Attendance:** 300.

15584 ■ American College of Clinical Pharmacy (ACCP)
13000 W 87th St. Pkwy.
Lenexa, KS 66215-4530
Ph: (913)492-3311
Fax: (913)492-0088
E-mail: accp@accp.com
URL: http://www.accp.com
Contact: Robert M. Elenbaas PhD, Exec. Dir.
Founded: 1979. **Members:** 6,900. **Membership Dues:** full, associate out of training, affiliate, $200

(annual) ● associate fellow, associate resident, $70 (annual) ● associate student, $35 (annual). **Staff:** 28. **Budget:** $5,000,000. **Regional Groups:** 16. **Description:** Clinical pharmacists dedicated to: promoting rational use of drugs in society; advancing the practice of clinical pharmacy and interdisciplinary health care; assuring high quality clinical pharmacy by establishing and maintaining standards in education and training at advanced levels. Encourages research and recognizes excellence in clinical pharmacy. Offers educational programs, symposia, research forums, fellowship training, and college-funded grants through competitions. Maintains placement service. **Awards:** Education Award. **Frequency:** annual. **Type:** recognition. **Recipient:** for an ACCP member who has shown excellence in the classroom or clinical training site ● Paul F. Parker Medal for Distinguished Service to the Profession of Pharmacy. **Type:** medal ● Practice Award. **Frequency:** annual. **Type:** recognition. **Recipient:** for an ACCP member who has developed an innovative clinical pharmacy service ● Russell R. Miller Award. **Frequency:** annual. **Type:** recognition. **Recipient:** for an ACCP member who has made substantial contributions to the literature of clinical pharmacy ● Service Award. **Frequency:** annual. **Type:** recognition. **Recipient:** for an ACCP member who has outstanding contributions to the vitality of ACCP or to the advancement of its goals that are well above the usual devotion of time, energy or material goods ● Therapeutic Frontiers Lecture Award. **Frequency:** annual. **Type:** recognition. **Recipient:** for a scientist whose research is actively advancing the frontiers of pharmacotherapy ● Young Investigator Award. **Frequency:** annual. **Type:** recognition. **Recipient:** for an ACCP member who has made a major impact in an aspect of clinical pharmaceutical science. **Computer Services:** Mailing lists, of members. **Publications:** *ACCP Report*, monthly. Newsletter. **Price:** free ● *Pharmacotherapy Self-Assessment Program: Fourth Edition*, annual. Booklets. **Price:** $135.00 for members; $160.00 for nonmembers ● *Pharmacotherapy: The Journal of Human Pharmacology and Drug Therapy*, monthly. **Price:** included in membership dues. ISSN: 0277-0008. **Circulation:** 8,000. **Advertising:** accepted ● *Residency and Fellowship Programs Offered by ACCP Members*, annual. Directory. Contains training programs in clinical pharmacy. **Price:** free. **Conventions/Meetings:** annual meeting, for pharmaceutical companies and pharmacy services (exhibits).

15585 ■ American College of Neuropsychopharmacology (ACNP)
545 Mainstream Dr., Ste.110
Nashville, TN 37228
Ph: (615)324-2360
Fax: (615)324-2361
E-mail: acnp@acnp.org
URL: http://www.acnp.org
Contact: Ronnie Wilkins EdD, Exec. Dir.
Founded: 1961. **Members:** 735. **Staff:** 8. **Description:** Experienced investigators whose work is related to neuropsychopharmacology. Promotes and encourages the scientific study and application of neuropsychopharmacology. Conducts study groups and plenary sessions. **Awards:** Daniel Efron Award. **Frequency:** annual. **Type:** recognition. **Recipient:** for outstanding research in the field ● Joel Elkes Award. **Frequency:** annual. **Type:** recognition. **Recipient:** for outstanding research in the field. **Publications:** *Mailings*, monthly. Journal ● *Neuropsychopharmacology*, monthly. Journal. Focuses on clinical and basic science contributions to neuropharmacology. **Price:** included in membership dues. **Advertising:** accepted ● Directory, annual. **Conventions/Meetings:** annual Invitational Meeting - always December. 2007 Dec. 9-13, Boca Raton, FL; 2008 Dec. 7-11, Scottsdale, AZ.

15586 ■ American Foundation for Pharmaceutical Education (AFPE)
1 Church St., Ste.202
Rockville, MD 20850-4184
Ph: (301)738-2160
Fax: (301)738-2161

E-mail: info@afpenet.org
URL: http://www.afpenet.org
Contact: Robert M. Bachman CAE, Pres.
Founded: 1942. **Members:** 40. **Staff:** 2. **Budget:** $1,200,000. **Description:** Established by pharmaceutical and drug trade associations to improve pharmaceutical education, colleges of pharmacy, and pharmacy student performance. Accepts and administers gifts, legacies, bequests, and funds and makes disbursements for fellowships and the promotion of pharmaceutical education. **Boards:** Grants. **Committees:** Century Club; Education; Patrons; Planning. **Publications:** *Annual Progress Report*, annual. Contains reports on contributions and programs. **Price:** free. **Circulation:** 5,000. **Conventions/Meetings:** annual board meeting ● annual executive committee meeting.

15587 ■ American Institute of the History of Pharmacy (AIHP)
777 Highland Ave.
Madison, WI 53705-2222
Ph: (608)262-5378
E-mail: aihp@aihp.org
URL: http://www.pharmacy.wisc.edu/aihp
Contact: Dr. Gregory J. Higby, Exec. Dir.
Founded: 1941. **Members:** 1,000. **Membership Dues:** individual in U.S., $50 (annual) ● individual outside U.S., $60 (annual). **Staff:** 4. **Budget:** $200,000. **Description:** Pharmacists, firms, and organizations interested in historical and social aspects of the pharmaceutical field. Maintains pharmaceutical Americana collection; conducts research programs. **Libraries: Type:** reference. **Holdings:** biographical archives. **Awards:** AIHP Student Certificate Program. **Frequency:** annual. **Type:** recognition. **Recipient:** for schools and colleges of pharmacy ● Fischelis Grants. **Frequency:** annual. **Type:** grant. **Recipient:** for established scholars ● Grant-in-Aid Toward Thesis Expenses Related to the History of Pharmacy. **Frequency:** annual. **Type:** grant. **Recipient:** for graduate students with good standing at an institution. **Committees:** Historical Markers; Popular History; Teaching the History of Pharmacy. **Sections:** Contributed Papers. **Publications:** *AIHP Notes*, quarterly. Newsletter. **Price:** included in membership dues ● *Pharmacy in History*, quarterly. Journal. Contains writings on the history of pharmaceutical practice, including drugs and therapeutics and related facets of the medical sciences. **Price:** included in membership dues. ISSN: 0031-7047. **Circulation:** 1,000. **Advertising:** accepted. Alternate Formats: microform ● Booklets. **Conventions/Meetings:** annual meeting, held in conjunction with the American Pharmaceutical Association.

15588 ■ American Pharmacists Association - Academy of Pharmacy Practice and Management (APhA-APPM)
c/o APhA
1100 15th St. NW, Ste.400
Washington, DC 20005-1707
Ph: (202)628-4410
Free: (800)237-APHA
Fax: (202)783-2351
E-mail: apha-appm@aphanet.org
URL: http://www.aphanet.org
Contact: Jean-Venable R. Goode, Pres.
Founded: 1965. **Members:** 26,000. **Staff:** 2. **Description:** Pharmacists concerned with rendering professional services directly to the public, without regard for status of employment or environment of practice. Aims to provide a forum and mechanism whereby pharmacists may meet to discuss and implement programs and activities relevant and helpful to the practitioner of pharmacy; to recommend programs and courses of action which should be undertaken or implemented by the profession; to coordinate academy efforts so as to be an asset to the progress of the profession. Provides and co-sponsors continuing education meetings, seminars, and workshops; produces audiovisual materials. **Awards:** APHA-APPM Merit Award. **Frequency:** annual. **Type:** recognition. **Recipient:** for contributions to pharmacy practice ● Daniel B. Smith Practice Excellence

Award. **Frequency:** annual. **Type:** recognition. **Recipient:** for outstanding professional performance by a pharmacist in any practice setting ● Distinguished Achievement Award: Administrative Practice. **Frequency:** annual. **Type:** recognition. **Recipient:** for outstanding professional contributions by a pharmacist ● Distinguished Achievement Award: Clinical/Pharmacotherapeutic Practice. **Frequency:** annual. **Type:** recognition. **Recipient:** for outstanding professional contributions by a pharmacist ● Distinguished Achievement Award: Community/Ambulatory Practice. **Frequency:** annual. **Type:** recognition. **Recipient:** for outstanding professional contributions by a pharmacist ● Distinguished Achievement Award: Hospital/Institution. **Frequency:** annual. **Type:** recognition. **Recipient:** for outstanding contributions. **Additional Websites:** http://www.pharmacist.com. **Telecommunication Services:** electronic mail, jrgoode@vcu.edu. **Sections:** Administrative Practice; Clinical/Pharmacotherapeutic Practice; Community and Ambulatory Practice; Hospital and Institutional Practice; Nuclear Pharmacy Practice; Specialized Pharmaceutical Services. **Formerly:** (1966) General Practice Section of APhA; (1975) Academy of General Practice of Pharmacy; (1987) Academy of Pharmacy Practice; (1995) Academy of Pharmacy Practice and Management; (2003) American Pharmaceutical Association - Academy of Pharmacy Practice and Management. **Publications:** *APhA DrugInfoLine*, monthly. Newsletter. Contains information designed to keep frontline pharmacists up-to-date on the latest trends in the biomedical literature. **Price:** included in membership dues ● *Journal of Pharmaceutical Sciences*, monthly. Contains articles, communications, notes, reviews, minireviews, and commentaries. **Price:** included in membership dues; $325.00 for nonmembers; $385.00 for nonmembers outside North America. **Advertising:** accepted ● *Journal of the American Pharmacists Association*, monthly. Provides information on pharmaceutical care, drug therapy, diseases and other health issues. Alternate Formats: online ● *Pharmacy Student*, bimonthly. Journal. Provides news and information that affects reader's daily lives. **Price:** included in membership dues. **Advertising:** accepted ● *Pharmacy Today*, monthly. Magazine. Features extensive coverage of advances in medications, therapies, and patient care. **Price:** $200.00 /year for members. **Advertising:** accepted. **Conventions/Meetings:** annual meeting (exhibits) - 2008 Mar. 14-17, San Diego, CA.

15589 ■ American Pharmacists Association Academy of Student Pharmacists (APhA-ASP)
1100 15th St. NW, Ste.400
Washington, DC 20005-1707
Ph: (202)628-4410
Free: (800)237-2742
Fax: (202)783-2351
E-mail: apha-asp@aphanet.org
URL: http://www.aphanet.org
Contact: Daniel A. Zlott, Pres.
Founded: 1954. **Members:** 18,000. **Staff:** 3. **Regional Groups:** 8. **Local Groups:** 79. **Description:** A division of the American Pharmaceutical Association, the national professional society of pharmacy students. Keeps members informed of the affairs of the association and the profession. Provides a forum for the expression of student opinion on activities and policies. Seeks to strengthen the program whereby student members, upon graduation, become active members of the association. Encourages participation by pharmacy students in interdisciplinary projects that attempt to find solutions to social problems; works in community-oriented drug education programs; supports interdisciplinary clinical training for pharmacists. **Awards:** Chapter Achievement. **Frequency:** annual. **Type:** recognition. **Recipient:** for outstanding achievements, activities and programs of APhA-ASP Chapters ● Linwood F. Tice Friend. **Frequency:** annual. **Type:** recognition. **Recipient:** for individual whose long-term service has benefited APhA-ASP and student pharmacists nationwide ● Outstanding Chapter Advisor. **Frequency:** annual. **Type:** recognition. **Recipient:** for outstanding chapters, faculty advisors, and friends of ASP ● Outstand-

ing Dean. **Frequency:** annual. **Type:** recognition. **Recipient:** for school or college pharmacy dean ● Student Leadership. **Frequency:** annual. **Type:** recognition. **Recipient:** for outstanding achievement and leadership ability in APhA-ASP member at the local, regional and national levels. **Committees:** Awards; Communications; Education; Policy. **Formerly:** (1969) American Pharmaceutical Association Student Section; (1988) Student American Pharmaceutical Association; (2003) Academy of Students of Pharmacy; (2003) American Pharmaceutical Association Academy of Students of Pharmacy. **Publications:** *APhA DrugInfoLine*, monthly. Newsletter. Keeps frontline pharmacists up-to-date on the latest trends in the biomedical literature. **Price:** included in membership dues ● *Student Pharmacist Magazine*, bimonthly. **Price:** included in membership dues; $25.00 /year for nonmembers. **Advertising:** accepted. **Conventions/Meetings:** annual meeting (exhibits) - always March ● annual National Patient Counseling Competition - always March ● annual regional meeting - always October or November.

15590 ■ American Society for Clinical Pharmacology and Therapeutics (ASCPT)
528 N Washington St.
Alexandria, VA 22314-2314
Ph: (703)836-6981 (703)836-6982
Fax: (703)836-5223
E-mail: info@ascpt.org
URL: http://www.ascpt.org
Contact: Sharon J. Swan CAE, Exec. Dir.
Founded: 1900. **Members:** 2,150. **Membership Dues:** full/associate (not in training) in U.S., $330 (annual) ● associate (in training) in U.S., $125 (annual) ● student in U.S., $50 (annual) ● full/associate (not in training) outside U.S., $363 (annual) ● associate (in training) outside U.S., $158 (annual) ● student outside U.S., $83 (annual). **Staff:** 5. **Budget:** $2,000,000. **Multinational. Description:** Advances the discipline and practice of clinical pharmacology for the benefit of patients and society. **Awards:** Gary Neil Prize for Innovation in Drug Development. **Frequency:** annual. **Type:** recognition. **Recipient:** for outstanding individuals or teams who have been leaders in the application of innovative science to clinical drug development ● Henry W. Elliott Distinguished Service Award. **Frequency:** annual. **Type:** recognition. **Recipient:** for an individual who has an excellent record of service to the society ● Leon I. Goldberg Young Investigator Award. **Frequency:** annual. **Type:** recognition. **Recipient:** for young scientists who are active in the field in which they have earned their doctoral degrees ● Oscar B. Hunter Memorial Award in Therapeutics. **Frequency:** annual. **Type:** recognition. **Recipient:** for outstanding contributions to clinical pharmacology and therapeutics throughout his/her professional career ● Rawls-Palmer Progress in Medicine Award. **Frequency:** annual. **Type:** recognition. **Recipient:** for significant contributions to drug investigation that incorporate the efforts of modern drug research in the care of patients ● William B. Abrams Award in Geriatric Clinical Pharmacology. **Frequency:** annual. **Type:** recognition. **Recipient:** for a young clinical pharmacologist in the field of geriatric clinical pharmacology. **Computer Services:** Mailing lists, of members ● online services, Career Center. **Sections:** Analgesiology and Inflammation; Cardiovascular and Pulmonary; Dermatologic and Allergic Diseases; Drug Development and Regulatory Science; Gastrointestinal, Endocrine and Metabolic Diseases; Geriatric Clinical Pharmacology; Hematologic and Neoplastic Diseases; Infectious Diseases and Antimicrobial Agents; Nephrology and Hypertension; Neuropsycholpharmacological Agents; Pediatric and Maternal Pharmacology; Pharmacoepidemiology, Drug Safety and Outcomes Research; Pharmacogenetics and Molecular Therapeutics; Pharmacokinetics and Drug Metabolism; Pharmacometrics and Biostatistics; Therapeutic Drug and Toxicology Monitoring. **Formed by Merger of:** (1993) American Therapeutic Society; American Society of Clinical Pharmacology and Chemotherapy. **Publications:** *Clinical Pharmacology and Therapeutics*, monthly. Journal. Features clinical articles and case reports. **Price:** included in membership dues. ISSN: 0009-9236. **Advertising:**

accepted. Alternate Formats: online. **Conventions/ Meetings:** annual meeting and symposium (exhibits).

15591 ■ American Society of Clinical Psychopharmacology (ASCP)

PO Box 40395
Glen Oaks, NY 11004
Ph: (718)470-4007
Fax: (718)343-7739
E-mail: jrusso@lij.edu
URL: http://www.ascpp.org
Contact: Dr. John M. Kane, Pres.

Founded: 1992. **Members:** 900. **Membership Dues:** professional, $100 (annual). **Staff:** 2. **Description:** Works to encourage clinical research in psychopharmacology and provide continuing education for members. Sponsors research; facilitates exchange of information; conducts professional educational programs; provides educational programs on the treatment of psychiatric disorders for patients and families; develops relationships with mental health advocacy groups; advocates public policies which promote research and the delivery of high quality care. **Awards:** Residency Travel Award. **Frequency:** annual. **Type:** monetary. **Recipient:** to 4 outstanding psychiatry residents. **Publications:** *ASCP Update*, quarterly. Newsletter. **Price:** free for members. **Circulation:** 1,200. **Conventions/Meetings:** annual Psychopharmacology: State of the Art - meeting, lectures given for continuing medical education credit (exhibits) - usually February or November.

15592 ■ American Society of Consultant Pharmacists (ASCP)

1321 Duke St.
Alexandria, VA 22314-3563
Ph: (703)739-1300
Free: (800)355-2727
Fax: (703)739-1321
E-mail: info@ascp.com
URL: http://www.ascp.com
Contact: John Feather, Exec. Dir./CEO

Founded: 1969. **Members:** 7,000. **Membership Dues:** active (retired), $44 (annual) ● pledge, $87 (annual) ● associate, $108 (annual) ● active, $210 (annual) ● active (spouse), $100 (annual). **Staff:** 45. **Budget:** $9,000,000. **State Groups:** 20. **Description:** Provides leadership, education, advocacy, and resources to advance the practice of senior care pharmacy. Conducts surveys of long-term care pharmacy operations. Sponsors educational and research programs. Maintains information center, hall of fame, and speakers' bureau; operates placement service; compiles statistics. **Awards:** George F. Archambault Award. **Frequency:** annual. **Type:** recognition. **Recipient:** for outstanding contributions to consultant pharmacy ● Leadership in Education Award. **Frequency:** annual. **Type:** recognition. **Recipient:** for members with unique and innovative educational endeavors ● Richard S. Berman Service Award. **Frequency:** annual. **Type:** recognition. **Recipient:** for outstanding contributions to the society. **Computer Services:** database, member demographics ● mailing lists. **Committees:** Education Advisory; Government Affairs. **Councils:** Organizational Affairs; Professional Affairs; Public Affairs. **Publications:** *UPDATE*, bimonthly. Newsletter. **Price:** included in membership dues ● Also publishes books and manuals. **Conventions/Meetings:** annual Legislative and Regulatory Conference, pharmaceutical manufacturers, computer vendors, drug packaging vendors, and other representatives of related industries (exhibits) - in March ● annual Midyear - meeting (exhibits) ● annual Senior Care Pharmacy - conference and trade show - in November. 2007 Nov. 14-17, Philadelphia, PA; 2008 Nov. 9-12, New Orleans, LA; 2009 Nov. 17-20, Anaheim, CA; 2010 Nov. 10-13, Orlando, FL.

15593 ■ American Society of Health System Pharmacists (ASHP)

7272 Wisconsin Ave.
Bethesda, MD 20814
Ph: (301)657-3000
Free: (866)279-0681
Fax: (301)664-8867

E-mail: membership@ashp.org
URL: http://www.ashp.org
Contact: Henri R. Manasse Jr., Exec. VP/CEO

Founded: 1942. **Members:** 30,000. **Membership Dues:** active (full), international associate, $230 (annual) ● new practitioner (1st year to 5th year), $78-$230 (annual) ● joint, $120 (annual) ● retired, $75 (annual) ● student, $35 (annual) ● technician (without journal), $68 (annual) ● technician (with journal), $178 (annual). **Staff:** 200. **Budget:** $30,000,000. **State Groups:** 50. **Description:** Professional society of pharmacists employed by hospitals, HMOs, clinics, and other health systems. Provides personnel placement service for members; sponsors professional and personal liability program. Conducts educational and exhibit programs. Has 30 practice interest areas, special sections for home care practitioners and clinical specialists, and research and education foundation. **Libraries: Type:** reference. **Holdings:** 3,200; books, periodicals. **Subjects:** medicine, pharmacy. **Awards:** Award for Distinguished Leadership of Health-System Pharmacy Practice. **Frequency:** annual. **Type:** recognition. **Recipient:** for excellence in practice leadership ● Board of Director's Award of Honor. **Frequency:** annual. **Type:** recognition. **Recipient:** for significant contributions to the health field ● Donald E. Francke Medal. **Frequency:** annual. **Type:** medal. **Recipient:** for significant international contributions to health system pharmacy ● Harvey A.K. Whitney Lecture Award. **Frequency:** annual. **Type:** recognition. **Recipient:** for outstanding contributions to health system pharmacy. **Computer Services:** database, consumer drug information full text ● database, drug information full text ● database, drug product information file ● database, international pharmaceutical abstracts information system. **Telecommunication Services:** electronic mail, custserv@ashp.org. **Boards:** Canvassers. **Committees:** Delegates to APhA House of Delegates; Goals; Harvey A.K. Witney Selection; Nominations; Publications. **Councils:** Administrative Affairs; Educational Affairs; Legal and Public Affairs; Organizational Affairs; Professional Affairs. **Affiliated With:** American Hospital Association; American Nurses Association. **Publications:** *AHFS Drug Handbook*, annual. Contains the most accurate recommendations on drug therapy. **Price:** $163.00 /year for individuals. ISSN: 8756-6028. Alternate Formats: CD-ROM; online ● *American Journal of Health System Pharmacy*, semimonthly. **Price:** included in membership dues ● $137.00 /year for nonmembers in U.S. ISSN: 0002-9289. **Advertising:** accepted ● *ASHP Newsletter*, monthly. Covers developments in pharmacy and health care. Includes information on legislation and regulations and association news. **Price:** included in membership dues. **Circulation:** 30,000 ● *Handbook on Injectable Drugs*, biennial. **Price:** $158.00. Alternate Formats: CD-ROM ● *International Pharmaceutical Abstracts*, semimonthly. **Price:** $100.00 /year for members; $425.00 /year for nonmembers in U.S.; $450.00 /year for nonmembers outside U.S.; $20.00/copy ● Books ● Videos ● Also publishes user manuals and aids, and produces software, CD-ROMS, and training programs. **Conventions/Meetings:** annual meeting (exhibits) - always June ● annual Midyear Clinical Meeting, offers continuing education programs (exhibits).

15594 ■ American Society of Pharmacognosy (ASP)

c/o David J. Slatkin, Treas.
853 Sanders Rd., No. 260
Northbrook, IL 60062
Ph: (773)995-3748
Fax: (847)656-2800
E-mail: okuda@sjsu.edu
URL: http://www.phcog.org
Contact: Roy K. Okuda, Pres.

Founded: 1959. **Members:** 1,200. **Membership Dues:** active, $75 (annual) ● associate (student), $25 (annual) ● emeritus, $10 (annual). **Staff:** 2. **Budget:** $300,000. **Multinational. Description:** Serves as a professional society of pharmacognosists (persons engaged in the study of drugs from a natural origin) and others interested in the biological sciences

and secondary metabolites. **Awards:** Matt Suffness Award. **Frequency:** annual. **Type:** recognition. **Recipient:** for up to 2 young researchers (less than 12 years post PhD) who have done significant work travel and registration expenses for AGM ● Norman R Farnsworth Research Achievement Award. **Frequency:** annual. **Type:** recognition. **Recipient:** for major scientific contribution to the field ● Travel Awards. **Type:** recognition. **Recipient:** for undergraduate students, graduate students, and postdoctoral investigators involved in research. **Telecommunication Services:** electronic mail, asphcog@aol.com. **Supersedes:** Plant Science Seminar. **Publications:** *ASP Newsletter*, quarterly ● *Journal of Natural Products*, monthly. **Conventions/Meetings:** annual meeting, with major exchange of professional and scientific information (exhibits) - 2008 Aug. 3-8, Athens, Greece; 2009 June 27-July 1, Honolulu, HI.

15595 ■ American Society for Pharmacology and Experimental Therapeutics (ASPET)

9650 Rockville Pike
Bethesda, MD 20814-3995
Ph: (301)634-7060
Fax: (301)634-7061
E-mail: info@aspet.org
URL: http://www.aspet.org
Contact: Christine K. Carrico PhD, Exec. Off.

Founded: 1908. **Members:** 4,500. **Membership Dues:** student, $30 (annual) ● affiliate, $105 (annual) ● regular, $140 (annual). **Staff:** 16. **Description:** Scientific society of investigators in pharmacology and toxicology interested in research and promotion of pharmacological knowledge and its use among scientists and the public. **Awards:** ASPET-Astellas Awards in Translational Pharmacology. **Frequency:** annual. **Type:** monetary ● Benedict R. Lucchesi Distinguished Lectureship in Cardiac Pharmacology. **Frequency:** biennial. **Type:** monetary ● Bernard B. Brodie Award. **Frequency:** biennial. **Type:** recognition. **Recipient:** for outstanding original research contribution ● Drug Metabolism Early Career Achievement Award. **Frequency:** biennial. **Type:** monetary ● Epilepsy Research Award. **Frequency:** biennial. **Type:** monetary. **Recipient:** for active participation and accomplishment in research ● Goodman & Gilman Award. **Frequency:** biennial. **Type:** recognition. **Recipient:** for research contributions ● John J. Abel Award. **Frequency:** annual. **Type:** monetary. **Recipient:** for original research in the field of pharmacology ● Julius Axelrod Award. **Frequency:** annual. **Type:** monetary ● P.B. Dews Award for Research in Behavioral Pharmacology. **Frequency:** biennial. **Type:** monetary. **Recipient:** for lifetime achievements in research, teaching and professional service ● Paul M. Vanhoutte Distinguished Lectureship in Vascular Pharmacology. **Frequency:** biennial. **Type:** monetary ● Pharmacia-ASPET Award. **Frequency:** annual. **Type:** medal. **Recipient:** for outstanding research in pharmacology and experimental therapeutics ● Torald Sollmann Award. **Frequency:** biennial. **Type:** monetary. **Recipient:** for significant contributions. **Computer Services:** Mailing lists. **Committees:** Diversity; Graduate Recruitment and Education; Public Affairs; Women in Pharmacology. **Divisions:** Behavioral Pharmacology; Cardiovascular Pharmacology; Clinical Pharmacology, Pharmacogenomics and Translational Medicine; Drug Discovery, Development and Regulatory Affairs; Drug Metabolism; Molecular Pharmacology; Neuropharmacology; Pharmacology Education; Systems and Integrative Pharmacology; Toxicology. **Affiliated With:** Federation of American Societies for Experimental Biology. **Publications:** *Drug Metabolism and Disposition*, monthly. Journal. Presents original research that contributes significant and novel information on xenobiotic metabolism, transport, and disposition. **Price:** $96.00 /year for members (print only); $184.00 /year for nonmembers in U.S. (print and online); $254.00 /year for nonmembers outside U.S. (print and online); $353.00 /year for institutions in U.S. (print and online) ● *Journal of Pharmacology and Experimental Therapeutics*, monthly. Presents original research dealing with the interactions of chemicals with biological systems. **Price:** $999.00 /year for institutions outside U.S.

(print and online); $765.00 /year for institutions (online only); $333.00 /year for nonmembers (online only); $182.00 /year for members (print). ISSN: 0090-9556. **Circulation:** 650. **Advertising:** accepted. Alternate Formats: online ● *Molecular Interventions*, bimonthly. Journal. Highlights cutting-edge research from all avenues of pharmacology. **Price:** $284.00 /year for institutions (print and online); $236.00 /year for institutions (online only); $77.00 /year for nonmembers (online only); $85.00 /year for nonmembers (print and online). ISSN: 0022-3565. **Circulation:** 1,300. **Advertising:** accepted. Alternate Formats: online ● *Molecular Pharmacology*, monthly. Journal. Presents original applications. **Price:** $699.00 /year for institutions (print and online); $554.00 /year for institutions (online only); $226.00 /year for nonmembers (online only); $131.00 /year for members (print). ISSN: 1534-0384. **Advertising:** accepted. Alternate Formats: online ● *Pharmacological Reviews*, quarterly. Journal. Showcases important review articles on topics of high current interest. **Price:** $287.00 /year for institutions outside U.S. (print and online); $124.00 /year for nonmembers (online only); $220.00 /year for institutions (online only); $77.00 /year for members (print). ISSN: 0026-6895. **Advertising:** accepted. Alternate Formats: online ● *The Pharmacologist*, quarterly. Newsletters. **Price:** $65.00 /year for nonmembers and institutions outside U.S.; $45.00 /year for nonmembers and institutions in U.S.; $20.00 /year for members (print). ISSN: 0031-6997. **Circulation:** 4,500. **Advertising:** accepted. Alternate Formats: online ● Brochures. **Price:** $40.00 /year for nonmembers and institutions in U.S. (print only); $60.00 /year for nonmembers and institutions outside U.S. (print only); $20.00 /year for members (print only). ISSN: 0031-7004. Alternate Formats: online ● Also distributes listings of schools of medicine and pharmacy. **Conventions/Meetings:** annual Experimental Biology - meeting (exhibits) - 2008 Apr. 5-9, San Diego, CA; 2009 Apr. 18-22, New Orleans, LA.

15596 ■ ASHP Foundation
7272 Wisconsin Ave.
Bethesda, MD 20814
Ph: (301)664-8612
Fax: (301)634-5712
E-mail: foundation@ashp.org
URL: http://www.ashpfoundation.org
Contact: Stephen J. Allen MS, Sec.
Founded: 1968. **Description:** Established for pharmaceutical care and research purposes. Offers anticoagulation, asthma, stem cell transplantation, diabetes, pain management, oncology, and traineeships. **Awards: Type:** fellowship. **Recipient:** for the study of practice areas such as oncology drug therapy, psychiatric drug therapy, clinical pharmacokinetics, cardiovascular drug therapy, critical care, drug information, and pharmacy nutritional support ● Literature Awards. **Frequency:** annual. **Type:** recognition. **Recipient:** for the most significant contribution to literature in the areas of research and practice ● Student Leadership Award. **Frequency:** annual. **Type:** monetary. **Recipient:** for interest in pharmacy practice in health systems practice ● Student Research Award. **Frequency:** annual. **Type:** grant. **Recipient:** for research and special projects. **Also Known As:** American Society of Hospital Pharmacists Research and Education Foundation; ASHP Research and Education Foundation. **Publications:** *Resource Book on Progressive Pharmaceutical Services.*

15597 ■ Association of Clinical Research Professionals (ACRP)
500 Montgomery St., Ste.800
Alexandria, VA 22314
Ph: (703)254-8100
Fax: (703)254-8101
E-mail: office@acrpnet.org
URL: http://www.acrpnet.org
Contact: Thomas L. Adams CAE, Pres./CEO
Founded: 1976. **Members:** 20,001. **Membership Dues:** individual, $120 (annual). **Staff:** 29. **Budget:** $8,200,000. **Local Groups:** 54. **National Groups:** 7. **Multinational. Description:** Individuals engaged in clinical pharmacology and other related research

professions, including clinical monitors and research associates, nurses, pharmacists, pharmacologists, physicians, and regulatory professionals. Promotes professional growth in the field through the dissemination of information, the exchange of ideas, and the development of educational programs. Provides continuing education credits to pharmacy and nursing professionals through the American Council on Pharmaceutical Education and the American Nurses Association. **Computer Services:** Online services, member services: forum discussion groups, directory, cancer center. **Committees:** Continuing Education; Financial; Nominations; Program. **Formerly:** (1997) Associates of Clinical Pharmacology. **Publications:** *ACRP Membership Directory.* **Price:** free, for members only. Alternate Formats: online ● *ACRP White Paper*, annual. Papers. **Price:** $20.00 single copy ● *ACRP Wire*, monthly. Newsletter. Alternate Formats: online ● *The Monitor*, bimonthly. Magazine. Includes activities information and committee reports, industry news, calendar of events, and clinical research articles. **Price:** free, for members only. **Advertising:** accepted. **Conventions/Meetings:** annual conference (exhibits) - every spring. 2008 Apr. 25-29, Boston, MA; 2009 Apr. 24-28, Denver, CO ● annual European Meeting - convention (exhibits) - in the fall.

15598 ■ Christian Pharmacists Fellowship International (CPFI)
PO Box 24708
West Palm Beach, FL 33416-4708
Free: (888)253-6885
E-mail: info@cpfi.org
URL: http://www.cpfi.org
Contact: Fred Eckel, Exec. Dir.
Founded: 1984. **Members:** 1,200. **Membership Dues:** student, $20 (annual) ● supporting, $250 (annual) ● regular, $70 (annual) ● contributing, $125 (annual) ● sustaining, $500 (annual). **Staff:** 2. **Budget:** $90,500. **Regional Groups:** 3. **State Groups:** 3. **Local Groups:** 7. **Description:** Promotes and maintains fellowship among Christian pharmacists. Establishes clubs and chapters at universities, colleges, schools, hospitals, and in communities; sponsors activities and retreats for Christian pharmacists and their families. Encourages active Christian witness and evangelism; teaches pharmacists how to share and present the Gospel of Jesus Christ in their practice; disseminates information among Christian pharmacists; identifies areas of service for pharmacists in missions worldwide and sponsors missionaries in the field. Provides and promotes Christian pharmacist-speakers. **Awards:** Scholarship Award. **Frequency:** annual. **Type:** scholarship. **Computer Services:** Mailing lists. **Telecommunication Services:** electronic mail, fred@ncpharmacists.org ● electronic mail, jennifer_hudson@pba.edu. **Committees:** Missions. **Publications:** *Christian Pharmacists Fellowship International—Newsletter*, bimonthly. Reports on the activities of members and the fellowship, as well as Christian events in pharmacy. Includes book reviews and directory. **Price:** free. **Circulation:** 2,000 ● *Christianity and Pharmacy*. Journal. Alternate Formats: online ● *The Faith Script*, quarterly. Newsletter. Alternate Formats: online ● Membership Directory, biennial. **Conventions/Meetings:** annual meeting and seminar.

15599 ■ Collegium Internationale Neuro-Psychopharmacologicum (CINP)
c/o Oakley Ray, PhD, Exec.Sec.
1608 17th Ave. S
Nashville, TN 37203
Ph: (615)297-3144
Fax: (615)385-3174
E-mail: cinp@cinp.org
URL: http://www.cinp.org
Contact: Oakley Ray PhD, Exec.Sec.
Founded: 1957. **Members:** 1,000. **Description:** Individuals engaged in experimental and clinical neuropsychopharmacological research and teachers in this field. Purposes are to advance the experimental and clinical aspects of the neuropsychopharmacological sciences; facilitate international relations between branches of the neuropsychopharmacological disci-

plines; further the international exchange of information and promote personal relations; consider the medico-social problems of psychopharmacology. **Awards:** The Dr. Paul Janssen Schizophrenia Research Award. **Frequency:** biennial. **Type:** recognition. **Recipient:** to a young investigator who has performed outstanding research in the field of Basic or Clinical Neuroscience of Schizophrenia at a University, Institute, or any other acknowledged scientific institution ● Pioneers in Psychopharmacology Award. **Frequency:** biennial. **Type:** grant. **Recipient:** for those who have made major contributions to the field as it has developed. **Telecommunication Services:** electronic mail, oray@cinp.org. **Committees:** Constitution and Bylaws; Corresponding Organizations; Credentials; Education; Fellowship and Awards; History; International Scientific Program; National Organizing. **Publications:** *Mailings*, periodic. Journal ● Proceedings. Covers symposia and congresses. ● Reports ● Also publishes abstracts. **Conventions/Meetings:** biennial conference (exhibits) ● symposium.

15600 ■ Commission for Certification in Geriatric Pharmacy (CCGP)
1321 Duke St.
Alexandria, VA 22314-3507
Ph: (703)535-3038
Fax: (703)739-1500
E-mail: info@ccgp.org
URL: http://www.ccgp.org
Contact: Lance O. Hoxie, Exec. Dir.
Founded: 1997. **Description:** Works to promote excellence in Geriatric Health Care through education and certification.

15601 ■ Drug Information Association (DIA)
800 Enterprise Rd., Ste.200
Horsham, PA 19044-3595
Ph: (215)442-6100
Fax: (215)442-6199
E-mail: dia@diahome.org
URL: http://www.diahome.org
Contact: William Brassington, Acting Exec. Dir.
Founded: 1964. **Members:** 27,000. **Membership Dues:** individual, $130 (annual) ● individual, EUR 130 (annual) ● individual, 14,700 (annual). **Staff:** 70. **Multinational. Description:** Provides neutral, global forum promoting exchange of information critical to professional performance and achievement in the discovery, development, regulation, surveillance, or marketing of pharmaceuticals or related products. **Awards:** Distinguished Career Award. **Frequency:** annual. **Type:** recognition. **Recipient:** for individuals who have established an extensive record for excellence in drug information science research ● Research Award Grant. **Frequency:** annual. **Type:** grant ● Special Recognition Award. **Frequency:** periodic. **Type:** recognition. **Recipient:** for members who have sustained a level of outstanding service over a long period of time. **Committees:** Audit; Compensation; Continuing Education; Governance; Nomination. **Special Interest Groups:** Biotechnology Special Interest Area Community. **Publications:** *DIA Forum*, quarterly. Magazine. Career development resource. **Price:** included in membership dues. **Advertising:** accepted. Alternate Formats: online ● *DIA Today*, quarterly. Newsletter. **Price:** included in membership dues. **Advertising:** accepted. Alternate Formats: online ● *Drug Information Association-CSO Directory*, annual. **Price:** included in membership dues; $125.00/copy for nonmembers. Alternate Formats: online ● *Drug Information Journal*, quarterly. **Price:** included in membership dues. **Advertising:** accepted. Alternate Formats: online ● Annual Report, annual. **Conventions/Meetings:** annual EuroMeeting (exhibits) - March ● annual meeting (exhibits) - June.

15602 ■ Ethiopian Pharmacists Association in North America (EPANA)
13208 Bellevue St.
Silver Spring, MD 20904
Ph: (202)806-4214

E-mail: bhailemeskel@howard.edu
URL: http://www.ethioworld.com/epana.htm
Contact: Bisrat Hailemeskel PhD, Pres.
Founded: 1999. **Multinational. Description:** Serves Ethiopians who reside in the U.S. and practice in the pharmaceutical field to network with each other to achieve their professional career endeavors. Joins with pharmacy professionals in Ethiopia to contribute to the pharmaceutical needs of Ethiopians. Participates in the pharmaceutical education of pharmacy professionals in Ethiopia and in the United States.

15603 ■ Foreign Pharmacy Graduate Examination Committee (FPGEC)

c/o Carmen A. Catizone, MS, Exec. Dir./Sec.
Natl. Assn. of Boards of Pharmacy
1600 Feehanville Dr.
Mount Prospect, IL 60056
Ph: (847)391-4406
Fax: (847)391-4502
E-mail: custserv@nabp.net
URL: http://www.nabp.net
Contact: Carmen A. Catizone MS, Exec. Dir./Sec.
Founded: 1982. **Staff:** 6. **Description:** A committee of the National Association of Boards of Pharmacy. Provides information to foreign pharmacy graduates regarding entry into the U.S. pharmacy profession and health care systems. Evaluates qualifications of foreign pharmacy graduates. Gathers and disseminates data on foreign graduates; maintains information on foreign pharmacy schools in order to produce an examination that measures academic competence with regard to U.S. pharmacy school standards. **Affiliated With:** National Association of Boards of Pharmacy. **Formerly:** (1988) Foreign Pharmacy Graduate Examination Commission. **Conventions/Meetings:** biennial Foreign Pharmacy Graduate Equivalency Examination Administration - meeting - usually December and June.

15604 ■ HealthCare Compliance Packaging Council (HCPC)

131 E Broad St., Ste.206
Falls Church, VA 22046
Ph: (703)538-4030
Fax: (703)538-6305
E-mail: pgmayberry@aol.com
URL: http://www.unitdose.org
Contact: Peter G. Mayberry, Exec. Dir.
Founded: 1990. **Members:** 80. **Membership Dues:** individual, $195 (annual) ● full, $6,000 (annual) ● associate, nonvoting corporate, $3,000 (annual) ● educational institution, consultant, $500 (annual) ● trade association, testing company, $1,000 (annual). **Staff:** 3. **Budget:** $300,000. **Description:** Promotes the benefits of "unit-dose blister and strip packaging" for pharmaceutical as a means of insuring better patient compliance with drug regimens. Sponsors research and provide educational programs. **Awards:** Compliance Package of the Year Award. **Frequency:** annual. **Type:** recognition. **Publications:** Unit Dose Alert, quarterly. Magazine. **Circulation:** 3,000. **Conventions/Meetings:** annual National Symposium on Patient Compliance (exhibits).

15605 ■ International Academy of Compounding Pharmacists (IACP)

PO Box 1365
Sugar Land, TX 77487
Ph: (281)933-8400
Free: (800)927-4227
Fax: (281)495-0602
E-mail: iacpinfo@iacprx.org
URL: http://www.iacprx.org
Contact: L.D. King, Exec. Dir.
Founded: 1991. **Members:** 1,800. **Membership Dues:** pharmacist in U.S., $500 (annual) ● pharmacist outside U.S., $300 (annual) ● technician/professor/retired pharmacist/physician, $65 (annual) ● student/patient, $25 (annual). **Staff:** 6. **Multinational. Description:** Pharmacists who compound custom medications to meet unique patient needs. Seeks to "enhance credibility and respect of the compounding pharmacy practice to the health care community and its patients"; promotes empowerment of compounding pharmacists. Develops and enforces codes of

ethics and practice for members; facilitates cooperation and exchange of information among members; sponsors research and educational programs. **Programs:** Fellowship. **Publications:** The eLink, weekly. Newsletter. Alternate Formats: online ● The Pharmacists' Link, quarterly. Newsletter. **Conventions/Meetings:** annual Compounders on Capital Hill - meeting.

15606 ■ International Biopharmaceutical Association (IBPA)

PMB 143
11521 N FM 620, No. 250
Austin, TX 78726
Ph: (914)206-4640
Fax: (914)206-4640
E-mail: info@ibpassociation.org
URL: http://www.ibpassociation.org
Contact: Ms. Kristin Hudasek, Coor.
Members: 7,000. **Membership Dues:** junior, $45 (annual) ● full, $90 (annual). **Multinational. Description:** Brings together biopharmaceutical and clinical research institutions and organizations from different countries. Provides assistance for professionals seeking to join the industry. Acts as a channel between professionals and institutions within the biopharmaceutical industry. Provides access to networking resources. **Awards:** IBPA Scholarship. **Frequency:** annual. **Type:** scholarship. **Recipient:** to IBPA member who has the right educational background to take part in a professional development program. **Publications:** BioAuditor, quarterly. Journal. Alternate Formats: online ● Careers in Clinical Research and the Biopharmaceutical Industry. Brochure. Alternate Formats: online ● Careers in the Biopharmaceutical Industry, monthly. Newsletter. Contains information on upcoming events in the biopharmaceutical industry around the world. **Price:** included in membership dues. **Advertising:** accepted. Alternate Formats: online ● The Proceedings of the International Biopharmaceutical Association, quarterly. Journal. Alternate Formats: online.

15607 ■ International Society for Pharmacoeconomics and Outcomes Research (ISPOR)

3100 Princeton Pike, Bldg. 3, Ste.E
Lawrenceville, NJ 08648
Ph: (609)219-0773
Fax: (609)219-0774
E-mail: info@ispor.org
URL: http://www.ispor.org
Contact: Marilyn Dix Smith RPh, Founding Exec. Dir.
Founded: 1995. **Members:** 2,200. **Membership Dues:** active, $175 (annual) ● student, $70 (annual) ● university/organization, $1,000 (annual) ● institution, $5,000 (annual). **Staff:** 12. **Budget:** $1,000,000. **Regional Groups:** 3. **National Groups:** 13. **Multinational. Description:** Researchers who study the cost effectiveness of treatments. Researchers and users of cost-effectiveness information; and health care decision makers. **Awards:** Global Outcomes Leadership Award. **Frequency:** annual. **Type:** recognition. **Recipient:** for an individual, nationally or internationally, who has made major advances in or contributions to the field of health outcomes ● ISPOR Aredis Donabedian Outcomes Research Lifetime Achievement Award. **Frequency:** annual. **Type:** recognition. **Recipient:** for an individual's outstanding achievement in the area of improving health outcomes ● ISPOR Bernie J. O'Brien New Investigator Award. **Frequency:** annual. **Type:** grant. **Recipient:** for an individual who honors the long-standing commitment of Bernie J. O'Brien, PhD, to training and mentoring new scientists in the fields of outcomes research and pharmacoeconomics ● ISPOR Best Contributed Poster Presentation Award. **Frequency:** annual. **Type:** recognition. **Recipient:** for scientific merit exhibited on the poster ● Research Excellence Award. **Frequency:** annual. **Type:** recognition. **Recipient:** for recent publications on pharmacoeconomics and outcomes research. **Computer Services:** Online services, publication. **Special Interest Groups:** Health Technology Assessment; Medication Compliance and Persistence; Patient Registry; Patient Reported Outcomes; Retrospective Database; Risk Management; Translating Research to Clinical

Practice; Value-Based Reimbursement. **Publications:** Health Care Cost, Quality, and Outcomes: ISPOR Book of Terms. **Price:** $60.00 for nonmembers; $36.00 for members; $33.00 for student, library, and academic ● ISPOR Connections, bimonthly. Newsletter. Contains news on pharmacoeconomics. **Price:** included in membership dues. **Advertising:** accepted. Alternate Formats: online ● ISPOR eBulletin, monthly. Features updates of recent ISPOR activities and events. **Price:** included in membership dues. **Advertising:** accepted. Alternate Formats: online ● Value in Health, bimonthly. Journal. Provides information on pharmacoeconomics and outcomes research; and health policy development. **Price:** $165.00 for nonmembers in U.S. and Canada; included in membership dues. **ISSN:** 1098-3015. **Circulation:** 2,000. **Advertising:** accepted. Alternate Formats: online. Also Cited As: The Journal of the International Society for Pharmacoeconomics and Outcomes Research. **Conventions/Meetings:** annual congress, with European scientific contributions, health policy development, health decision sessions ● annual international conference, with scientific presentations, health policy development and health decision sessions (exhibits).

15608 ■ Medical Letter (ML)

1000 Main St.
New Rochelle, NY 10801
Ph: (914)235-0500
Free: (800)211-2769
Fax: (914)632-1733
E-mail: custserv@medicalletter.org
URL: http://www.medletter.com
Contact: Joanne Valentino, Dir. of Marketing and Communications
Founded: 1959. **Languages:** English, French. **Description:** Gathers and publishes information on the therapeutic and side effects of drugs for the benefit of physicians and other members of the health professions. Emphasizes on new drugs. **Libraries:** **Type:** reference. **Holdings:** 150; periodicals. **Subjects:** pharmacology and therapeutics. **Telecommunication Services:** electronic mail, joanne@medicalletter.org. **Formerly:** Drug and Therapeutic Information. **Publications:** Advice for Travelers, semiannual. Provides quick access to information about specific countries, diseases and travel-related risks. **Price:** $139.00 ● Handbook of Antimicrobial Therapy, biennial. Contains information on the treatment of infectious diseases. **Price:** $25.00/issue ● Medical Letter: A Searchable Collection on CD-ROM, annual. Permits users to quickly access, search and print articles. **Price:** $65.00. Alternate Formats: CD-ROM ● Medical Letter Handbook of Adverse Drug Interactions. **Price:** $22.00 for nonmembers; $12.00 for members. Alternate Formats: diskette ● Medical Letter on Drugs and Therapeutics, biweekly. Newsletter. Evaluates drugs for physicians. **Price:** $76.00 /year for individuals. **Circulation:** 150,000.

15609 ■ Medication Compliance Institute (MCI)

PO Box 437
Lakeside, CA 92040
Ph: (619)443-0531
Fax: (619)443-1023
E-mail: asme.1@juno.com
Contact: Daryl L. Bell-Greenstreet, Exec. Dir.
Founded: 2001. **Members:** 7. **Membership Dues:** for profit organization, $1,000 (annual). **Staff:** 3. **Budget:** $500,000. **Languages:** English, Spanish. **Multinational. Description:** Works for the discovery and identification of factors driving non-professional medication errors, research and development strategies, systems, and processes for ameliorating or eliminating causes of such errors, education of public and healthcare community on all matters relating to self-administration of medications to outpatients. **Libraries:** **Type:** reference. **Holdings:** archival material. **Subjects:** medication error-related information. **Subgroups:** Education; Research.

15610 ■ Multidisciplinary Association for Psychedelic Studies (MAPS)

10424 Love Creek Rd.
Ben Lomond, CA 95005

Ph: (831)336-4325
Fax: (831)336-3665
E-mail: askmaps@maps.org
URL: http://www.maps.org
Contact: Dr. Rick Doblin PhD, Pres.
Founded: 1986. **Members:** 1,800. **Membership Dues:** student/low income, $20-$34 (annual) ● basic, $35-$49 (annual) ● integral, $50-$99 (annual) ● supporting, $100-$249 (annual) ● patron, $250 (annual). **Staff:** 3. **Budget:** $250,000. **Description:** Promotes the development of beneficial, socially sanctioned uses of psychedelic drugs and marijuana. Helps researchers design, obtain government approval for, fund, conduct and report on psychedelic research in human volunteers; funds MDMA psychotherapy studies; facilitates research and FDA approval for marijuana to be prescribed for medical uses. **Libraries: Type:** reference; not open to the public. **Awards: Type:** grant. **Computer Services:** database, bibliography of psychedelic research. **Publications:** *Maps Bulletin*, quarterly. Magazine. Contains reports on MAPS activities, current research and feature articles. **Price:** $10.00/issue. ISSN: 1080-8981. **Circulation:** 4,000. Alternate Formats: online ● The Secret Chief: Conversations with a Pioneer of the Underground Psychedelic Therapy Movement. **Conventions/Meetings:** periodic conference.

15611 ■ National Alliance of State Pharmacy Associations (NASPA)
5501 Patterson Ave., Ste.202
Richmond, VA 23226
Ph: (804)285-4431
Fax: (804)285-4227
E-mail: becky@naspa.us
URL: http://www.ncspae.org
Contact: Rebecca P. Snead, Exec. VP/CEO
Founded: 1927. **Members:** 52. **Membership Dues:** individual, $300 (annual) ● associate, $750 (annual). **Staff:** 1. **Budget:** $150,000. **State Groups:** 52. **Description:** Professional society of the executive officers of state pharmacy associations. **Awards:** Merck Grant. **Frequency:** annual. **Type:** grant. **Recipient:** for state pharmacy association. **Formerly:** (1964) National Conference of State Pharmaceutical Association Secretaries; (1992) National Council of State Pharmaceutical Association; (2006) National Council of State Pharmacy Association Executives. **Conventions/Meetings:** semiannual meeting, held in conjunction with American Pharmaceutical Association and NCPA annual meetings.

15612 ■ National Association of Boards of Pharmacy (NABP)
1600 Feehanville Dr.
Mount Prospect, IL 60056
Ph: (847)391-4406
Fax: (847)391-4502
E-mail: custserv@nabp.net
URL: http://www.nabp.net
Contact: Carmen A. Catizone MS, Exec. Dir./Sec.
Founded: 1904. **Members:** 68. **Membership Dues:** active or associate, $250 (annual). **Staff:** 50. **Budget:** $8,000,000. **Description:** Pharmacy boards of several states, District of Columbia, Puerto Rico, Virgin Islands, several Canadian provinces, the states of Victoria, Australia, and New South Wales, the Pharmaceutical Society of New Zealand, and the South African Pharmacy Council. Provides for interstate reciprocity in pharmaceutic licensure based upon a uniform minimum standard of pharmaceutic education and uniform legislation; improves the standards of pharmaceutical education licensure and practice. Provides legislative information; sponsors uniform licensure examination; also provides information on accredited school and college requirements. Maintains pharmacy and drug law statistics. **Awards:** Fred T. Mahaffey Award. **Frequency:** annual. **Type:** recognition. **Recipient:** to an individual state board of pharmacy ● Henry Cade Award. **Frequency:** annual. **Type:** recognition. **Recipient:** for individuals who have supported the association ● Honorary President. **Frequency:** annual. **Type:** recognition. **Recipient:** for lifetime achievements ● Lester E. Hosto Distinguished Service Award. **Frequency:** annual. **Type:** recognition. **Recipient:** for significant contribu-

tions to the association ● President's Award. **Frequency:** annual. **Type:** recognition. **Recipient:** for active participation and dedication in pharmacy practice. **Computer Services:** database, state laws pertaining to pharmacy. **Committees:** Advisory; Constitution and Bylaws; Examinations; Law Enforcement and Legislation; Resolutions. **Task Forces:** Pharmacy Technicians. **Publications:** *Annual Meeting Proceedings*, annual ● *Pre-NAPLEX*, annual. Contains practice examination. **Price:** $50.00 each. Alternate Formats: online ● *State Newsletters Program*, quarterly. Covers 34 states. **Price:** $100.00 /year for individuals ● *Survey of Pharmacy Law*, annual. Provides summary data about topical issues in pharmacy. **Price:** $20.00/issue ● Newsletter, 10/year. Reports on regulation and licensure in the pharmacy profession. Contains information on NABP competency assessment programs. **Price:** $35.00 /year for individuals. **Circulation:** 1,500 ● Surveys ● Also publishes periodically updated guides and examination manuals. **Conventions/Meetings:** Fall Legislative Conference ● annual meeting, with pharmacy software (exhibits) - every spring, generally in May. 2008 May 17-20, Baltimore, MD ● seminar ● workshop.

15613 ■ National Catholic Pharmacists Guild of the United States (NCPG)
1012 Surrey Hills Dr.
St. Louis, MO 63117-1438
Ph: (314)645-0085
Contact: John Paul Winkelmann, Exec.Dir./Co-Pres.
Founded: 1962. **Members:** 400. **Membership Dues:** individual, $20 (annual) ● life, $150. **Staff:** 1. **National Groups:** 1. **Description:** Catholic pharmacists, pharmacy graduates, students, and pharmacy technicians. Upholds the principles of the Catholic faith and all laws of church and country, especially those pertaining to the practice of pharmacy; assists ecclesiastical authorities in the diffusion of Catholic pharmacy ethics; promotes donations of funds and supplies to the needy; opposes the sale of pornographic literature, especially that which is being sold in pharmacies; fosters solidarity and goodwill among all pharmacists. Provides pharmaceuticals and funds for people worldwide. **Libraries: Type:** reference. **Holdings:** biographical archives. **Awards:** Award of Merit Certificate. **Type:** recognition ● Catholic Pharmacist of the Year. **Type:** recognition ● Church and Profession Award. **Type:** recognition. **Recipient:** for distinguished and outstanding service ● Honorary President of the Year. **Frequency:** annual. **Type:** recognition. **Committees:** Charitable Appeals; Pro-Life. **Publications:** *The Catholic Pharmacist*, quarterly. Journal. Includes obituaries, membership and professional news, new member listings, and book reports as well as other reports and issues. **Price:** included in membership dues; $20.00/year for members only. **Circulation:** 400. **Advertising:** accepted.

15614 ■ National Council on Patient Information and Education (NCPIE)
4915 St. Elmo Ave., Ste.505
Bethesda, MD 20814-6082
Ph: (301)656-8565
Fax: (301)656-4464
E-mail: ncpie@ncpie.info
URL: http://www.talkaboutrx.org
Contact: Phillip Schneider MA, Chm.
Founded: 1982. **Members:** 160. **Membership Dues:** for-profit company, $7,500 (annual) ● non-profit health professional organization, $750 (annual) ● public sector/consumer or patient advocacy group/university/non-profit organization, $150 (annual). **Staff:** 4. **Budget:** $600,000. **Languages:** English, Spanish. **Description:** Health care professional organizations, pharmaceutical manufacturing organizations, federal agencies, voluntary health agencies, and consumer groups. Increases the availability of information and improves the dialogue between consumers and health care providers about prescription medicines; increases professional awareness of the need to give adequate information on prescription therapy; expands consumers' participation with health professionals on matters of drug therapy. Com-

municates with health care providers on the importance of giving consumers oral and written information on prescription medicines and encourages consumers to ask questions about medicines and explain factors that may affect their ability to follow prescriptions. **Awards:** Paul G. Rogers Medication Communicators Award. **Frequency:** semiannual. **Type:** recognition. **Additional Websites:** http://www. bemedwise.org. **Committees:** Conference; Fund Development; Public Relations. **Councils:** Business; Consumer Advisory; Healthcare Professional Advisory. **Publications:** *Alcohol and Medicine: Ask Before You Mix*. Brochure. Features an easy-to-read chart listing common interactions of both prescription and over-the-counter medicines with alcohol. **Price:** $10. 00/pack of 100. Alternate Formats: online ● *Be Med-Wise: Use Over-the-Counter Medicines Wisely* (in English and Spanish). Brochure. Contains expert tips on how to take OTC medicines correctly by learning how to read the product label. **Price:** $20.00/pack of 100. Alternate Formats: online ● *Get the Answers Wallet Card* (in English and Spanish). Records all prescription and non-prescription medicines, allergies, emergency contact names. **Price:** $15.00/pack of 100 ● *Get the Most From Your Medicines: Managing Side Effects*. Pamphlet. **Price:** $15.00/pack of 100. Alternate Formats: online ● *Medicine: Before You Take It, Talk About It*. Brochure. Features 10 simple questions to help patients use their medicines safely. **Price:** $10.00/pack of 100. Alternate Formats: online ● *NCPIE E-News*, bimonthly. Newsletter. Alternate Formats: online ● *Talk About Prescriptions: Month Planning Kit*, annual. Articles. Includes ideas for practical TAP activities, reproducible articles on dietary supplements. **Price:** $15.00 ● *Your Medicine: Play It Safe*. Brochure. Contains guides on how to take medicine safely. **Price:** $15.00/pack of 80. Alternate Formats: online. **Conventions/Meetings:** biennial conference (exhibits) - odd numbered years.

15615 ■ National Pharmaceutical Association (NPhA)
107 Kilmayne Dr., Ste.C
Cary, NC 27511
Free: (800)944-NPHA
Fax: (919)469-5870
E-mail: npha@npha.net
URL: http://www.npha.net
Contact: JoAnn Spearmon, Pres.
Founded: 1947. **Members:** 2,235. **Membership Dues:** active/associate, $125 (annual) ● retired/auxiliary, $25 (annual) ● life, $2,500 ● affiliate, $250 (annual). **Description:** State and local associations of professional minority pharmacists. Provides a means whereby members may "contribute to their common improvement, share their experiences, and contribute to the public good". **Telecommunication Services:** electronic mail, president@npha.net. **Publications:** *Inside NPhA*, periodic. Newsletter. Alternate Formats: online ● *Journal of the NPhA*, quarterly. **Price:** $20.00 /year for individuals in U.S.; $35.00 /year for institutions in U.S.; $30.00 /year for individuals outside U.S.; $45.00 /year for institutions outside U.S. ISSN: 0027-9897. **Conventions/Meetings:** annual convention (exhibits).

15616 ■ Pharmacy Benefit Management Institute (PBMI)
8679 E San Alberto Dr., Ste.101
Scottsdale, AZ 85258-4368
Ph: (480)730-0814
Fax: (480)222-4229
E-mail: pbmi@pbmi.com
URL: http://www.pbmi.com
Contact: Dana Hoernig Felthouse, Pres.
Membership Dues: individual plan sponsor, $100 (annual) ● Pharmacy Benefit Manager, industry partner, $2,500 (annual). **Description:** Represents and supports the pharmacy benefit management industry. **Publications:** *Customer Satisfaction Survey*, annual. Report. Examines the quality of services provided by PBMs. **Price:** $150.00/copy ● *eBulletin*, monthly. Alternate Formats: online ● *PBMinews*, quarterly. Newsletter. Contains tips and information on how to manage prescription drug benefit plans. **Price:** free ● *Prescription Drug Benefit Plan Cost*

and Plan Design Report. Documents the decisions organizations make about drug exclusions and utilization management. **Price:** free ● *Rx Reimbursement Brief,* monthly. Newsletter. Alternate Formats: online. **Conventions/Meetings:** annual Prescription Drug Utilization Management - conference.

15617 ■ Public Hospital Pharmacy Coalition (PHPC)
1875 Eye St. NW, 12th Fl.
Washington, DC 20006
Ph: (202)466-6550
Fax: (202)785-1756
E-mail: ted.slafsky@phpcrx.org
URL: http://www.phpcrx.org
Contact: Ted Slafsky, Exec. Dir.
Membership Dues: hospital (with 100 beds or more), $1,250-$5,000 (annual) ● hospital (with 51-99 beds), $625-$2,500 (annual) ● hospital (with 50 beds or less), $375-$1,500 (annual). **Description:** Represents public and private non-profit hospitals and health systems that participate in the public health service 340B drug discount program. Aims to increase the affordability and accessibility of pharmaceutical care for the poor and underserved population. Monitors, educates and serves as an advocate on federal legislative and regulatory issues pertaining to drug pricing and other pharmacy matters. **Publications:** *The Federal Drug Discount and Compliance Monitor,* monthly. Newsletter. **Price:** included in membership dues; $400.00 for-profit organization (online access); $200.00 non-profit organization/government (online); $100.00 printed copy. **Advertising:** accepted. Alternate Formats: online.

15618 ■ Safety Pharmacology Society (SPS)
PO Box 7033
Audubon, PA 19407
Ph: (610)630-0991
Fax: (610)630-1544
E-mail: execdir@safetypharmacology.org
URL: http://www.safetypharmacology.org
Contact: R. Sarazan, Pres.
Membership Dues: general, $50 (annual). **Description:** Promotes knowledge, development, application and training in safety pharmacology. Furthers the discovery, development and safe use of biologically active chemical entities. Supports the human safety of drugs and biologicals by fostering scientific research, education and dissemination of scientific information. **Awards:** Distinguished Service Award. **Frequency:** annual. **Type:** recognition. **Recipient:** to an individual who has substantially contributed to the field of safety pharmacology ● Junior Investigator Travel Award. **Frequency:** annual. **Type:** recognition. **Recipient:** to a junior investigator engaged in safety pharmacology who will be attending the SPS annual meeting ● Student Travel Award. **Frequency:** annual. **Type:** recognition. **Recipient:** to a student who will be attending the SPS annual meeting.

15619 ■ Society of Infectious Diseases Pharmacists (SIDP)
823 Cong. Ave., Ste.230
Austin, TX 78701
Ph: (512)479-0425
Fax: (512)495-9031
E-mail: sidp@eami.com
URL: http://www.sidp.org
Contact: Michael Klepser, Pres.
Founded: 1990. **Membership Dues:** trainee, $25 (annual) ● active/associate, $35 (annual). **Description:** Pharmacists with a primary interest and practice in infectious diseases pharmacotherapy, and who have spent at least two years performing pharmacotherapeutic researches are active members; pharmacists and other individuals not meeting the requirements for active membership, but who share an interest in infectious diseases pharmacotherapy, are associate members. Seeks to advance the study and practice of infectious diseases pharmacotherapy, and to enhance the professional status of members. Serves as a forum for discussion and exchange of information among members. Encourages pharmacotherapeutic research. **Awards:** SIDP/Abbott Award for Outcomes Research. **Frequency:** annual. **Type:**

monetary. **Recipient:** for an established researcher making a significant contribution to the field of infectious diseases pharmacotherapy ● SIDP/Ortho McNeil Scientist Preceptorship Award. **Frequency:** annual. **Type:** monetary. **Recipient:** for research groups wishing to visit their collaborators ● SIDP Young Investigator's Award. **Frequency:** annual. **Type:** recognition. **Recipient:** for outstanding young pharmacotherapeutic researcher. **Publications:** *News Update,* monthly. Newsletter ● Newsletter, 3/year. **Conventions/Meetings:** annual meeting.

15620 ■ United States Pharmacopeia (USP)
12601 Twinbrook Pkwy.
Rockville, MD 20852-1790
Ph: (301)881-0666
Free: (800)822-8772
E-mail: webmaster@usp.org
URL: http://www.usp.org
Contact: Roger L. Williams MD, Exec. VP/CEO
Founded: 1820. **Members:** 500. **Staff:** 385. **Budget:** $53,000,000. **Languages:** Chinese, English, French, German, Spanish. **Multinational. Description:** Promotes the public health by establishing and disseminating officially recognized standards of quality and authoritative information for the use of medicines and other health care technologies by health professionals, patients and consumers. Helps to monitor quality and prevent medication errors through national reporting programs. Achieves its goals through the contributions of volunteers representing pharmacy, medicine, and other health care professions, as well as science, academia, the U.S. government, the pharmaceutical industry, and consumer organizations. **Libraries: Type:** reference. **Holdings:** books, periodicals. **Subjects:** drug standards and information. **Awards: Type:** fellowship. **Recipient:** for students of drug standards and information. **Committees:** Information Expert; Revision; Standard and Cross-Cutting Expert. **Departments:** Business; Corporate Service Officers; Science. **Programs:** Dietary Supplement Verification; Drug Information; Patient Safety; Professional and Public Affairs; Reference Standards and Publications. **Formerly:** U.S. Pharmacopeial Convention. **Publications:** *Pharmacopeial Forum,* bimonthly. Journal. Features in process revisions, pharmacopeial reviews and policies and announcements of USP. ● *Proceedings of Quinquennial Meetings* ● *The United States Pharmacopeia and the National Formulary,* annual. Includes semiannual supplement. ● *USAN and USP Dictionary of Drug Names,* annual. Book. Provides important drug information, reference for drug names and chemical structure. **Price:** $299.00/copy ● *USP-National Formulary* (in English and Spanish), annual. Book. Contains standards for medicines, dosage forms, drugs substances, medical devices and dietary supplements. **Price:** $665.00/copy ● *USP Press,* quarterly. Newsletter ● Annual Report, annual. **Conventions/Meetings:** quinquennial convention.

Philanthropy

15621 ■ Grantmakers in Health (GIH)
1100 Connecticut Ave. NW, Ste.1200
Washington, DC 20036
Ph: (202)452-8331
Fax: (202)452-8340
E-mail: lleroy@gih.org
URL: http://www.gih.org
Contact: Lauren LeRoy PhD, Pres./CEO
Founded: 1982. **Description:** Dedicated to helping foundations and corporate giving programs to improve the nation's health. **Awards:** Terrance Keenan Leadership Award. **Frequency:** annual. **Type:** recognition. **Recipient:** to a grantmaker whose leadership and thoughtful application of philanthropic dollars has forged permanent improvements in health through creativity, risk taking, and boldness **Computer Services:** database. **Publications:** *GIH Bulletin,* biweekly. Newsletter. Contains news and information on the field including new grants, people, surveys and studies. Alternate Formats: online ● *Issue Dialogue Briefs.* Reports. Provides a synthesis of

available data and evaluation results, private and public sector activities, and opportunities for grantmakers. Alternate Formats: online ● *Perspectives on Philanthropy.* Reports. Covers topics pertaining to the practice of health philanthropy. Alternate Formats: online ● Annual Reports, annual. Alternate Formats: online ● Brochure. Alternate Formats: online. **Conventions/Meetings:** annual meeting ● periodic workshop.

Philosophy

15622 ■ Opening Mind Academy (OMA)
PO Box 444
Huntington Beach, CA 92648
Ph: (714)379-4911
E-mail: mind@openingmind.com
URL: http://www.openingmind.com
Contact: Pierre Grimes PhD, Founder/Pres.
Founded: 1983. **Membership Dues:** website, $50 (annual) ● general, $50 (monthly) ● student, $35 (monthly) ● sustaining, $100 (monthly) ● friend of the Academy, $2,500 (annual). **Description:** Promotes the philosophical midwifery movement, the exploration and study of dreams, and problems experienced by students during meditation. **Awards:** Work Scholarships. **Type:** scholarship. **Divisions:** Academic Forum. **Programs:** Artemis. **Publications:** Videos ● Books ● Pamphlets.

Physical Fitness

15623 ■ Aerobics and Fitness Association of America (AFAA)
15250 Ventura Blvd., Ste.200
Sherman Oaks, CA 91403-3297
Free: (877)968-7263
Fax: (818)990-5468
E-mail: contactafaa@afaa.com
URL: http://www.afaa.com
Contact: Linda D. Pfeffer RN, Pres.
Founded: 1983. **Members:** 155,000. **Membership Dues:** individual, $68 (annual). **Staff:** 60. **Languages:** English, French, German, Greek, Italian, Japanese, Korean, Spanish, Swedish. **For-Profit. Multinational. Description:** Promotes safety and excellence in exercise instruction. Offers certifications in Primary Group Exercise, Personal Trainer, Advanced Personal Trainer, Yoga, Step, KickBoxing, Emergency Response, Fitness Practitioner, and the New Wave Workout. **Telecommunication Services:** hotline, (800)YOUR-BODY. **Publications:** *American Fitness,* bimonthly. Magazine. Features exercise trends, research, interviews, products, health, and nutrition. **Price:** included in membership dues; $27.00 /year for nonmembers. ISSN: 0893-5238. **Circulation:** 42,000. **Advertising:** accepted. Alternate Formats: online ● *Fitness Theory and Practice.* Book. Contains expert advice on anatomy, kinesiology and sports medicine. **Price:** $44.00 ● Brochures. Alternate Formats: online ● Manuals. **Conventions/Meetings:** monthly meeting and workshop.

15624 ■ African-American Association of Fitness Professionals (AAAFP)
1507 E 53rd St. No. 495
Chicago, IL 60615
Ph: (630)268-7332
Fax: (312)755-0376
E-mail: aaafp93@hotmail.com
Contact: Darmea S. McCoy, Pres.
Membership Dues: fitness professional, $45 (annual) ● fitness associate, $35 (annual) ● friend of AAAFP, $20 (annual). **Description:** Provides fitness education, motivation and training to all people. Increases the number of African-Americans who start and stay physically active. **Computer Services:** database, referral lists ● information services, fitness tips and recipes. **Publications:** Newsletter. Alternate Formats: online.

15625 ■ American Council on Exercise (ACE)
4851 Paramount Dr.
San Diego, CA 92123
Ph: (858)279-8227
Free: (888)825-3636
Fax: (858)279-8064
E-mail: pr@acefitness.org
URL: http://www.acefitness.org
Contact: Scott Goudeseune, Pres.

Founded: 1985. **Members:** 45,000. **Staff:** 50. **Description:** Promotes the benefits of physical activity and protects consumers against unsafe and ineffective fitness products, and instruction. Sponsors university-based exercise science research and testing that targets fitness products and trends. Sets standards for fitness professionals. **Libraries:** Type: reference. **Holdings:** 500; audiovisuals, books, clippings, periodicals. **Subjects:** exercise, fitness, sports medicine, nutrition. **Awards:** Joe Q. Bryant American Council on Exercise Educational Scholarship. **Frequency:** annual. **Type:** scholarship. **Recipient:** for Pennsylvania State students ● William J. Merriman American Council on Exercise Educational Scholarship. **Frequency:** annual. **Type:** scholarship. **Recipient:** for Manhattan College students ● William Shannon American Council on Exercise Educational Scholarship. **Frequency:** annual. **Type:** scholarship. **Recipient:** for Duke University students. **Departments:** Academy; Certifications; Customer Service; GymJob.com; Professional Services; Resource Center. **Programs:** Academy; Operation Fit Kids. **Publications:** *ACE Certified News*, bimonthly. Magazine. Provides information for ACE-certified fitness professional. **Circulation:** 37,000. **Advertising:** accepted ● *ACE Faculty Network* ● *ACE Fitness Matters*, bimonthly. Magazine. **Price:** $25.00/year; $60.00/3 years; $33.00/year in North America; $49.00/year outside North America. **ISSN:** 1082-0361. **Circulation:** 39,000 ● *Certification and Education Programs*. Brochure. Alternate Formats: online ● *Fall 2004 ACE Product Catalog* ● *Newsletters*. Alternate Formats: online.

15626 ■ American Council for Fitness and Nutrition (ACFN)
PO Box 33396
Washington, DC 20033-3396
Free: (800)953-1700
E-mail: info@acfn.org
URL: http://www.acfn.org
Contact: Dr. Susan Finn, Chair

Founded: 2003. **Members:** 93. **Description:** Aims to find a comprehensive and achievable solutions to obesity. Provides parents, teachers and children with information and resources on making the best lifestyle choices regarding physical activities and nutrition. **Programs:** All Communities Exercise Day; Cristo Rey School-Based Nutrition; Eat Healthy, Stay Fit; Fun, Food and Fitness; Illinois Achievement Awards for Workplace Wellness; Texas on the Move; Texas Trails Registry; Virginia on the Move.

15627 ■ American Senior Fitness Association (SFA)
PO Box 2575
New Smyrna Beach, FL 32170
Ph: (386)423-6634
Free: (800)243-1478
Fax: (386)427-0613
E-mail: sfa@ucnsb.net
URL: http://www.seniorfitness.net
Contact: Janie Clark MA, Pres.

Founded: 1992. **Description:** Promotes excellence in older adult fitness. Provides comprehensive training, recognized certification, professional resources and member support for fitness professionals who serve older adults. Offers senior fitness specialist courses for colleges and universities. **Telecommunication Services:** electronic mail, sfa@seniorfitness.net. **Publications:** *Experience!*, semimonthly. Newsletter. **Price:** free for members. Alternate Formats: online ● *Mature Fitness*, quarterly. Magazine.

15628 ■ Cooper Institute
12330 Preston Rd.
Dallas, TX 75230
Ph: (972)341-3200
Free: (800)635-7050
Fax: (972)341-3227
E-mail: courses@cooperinst.org
Contact: Kenneth H. Cooper MD, Chm.

Founded: 1970. **Staff:** 70. **Budget:** $12,000,000. **Local Groups:** 2. **Multinational. Description:** Promotes understanding of the relationship between living habits and health. Provides leadership in enhancing the physical and emotional well-being of individuals. Promotes participation in aerobics. Seeks to increase the quality and quantity of fitness programs within major institutions. Conducts innovative studies on health and living habits and methods of facilitating changes in living habits; promotes the awareness and skills needed to develop a positive life-style. Sponsors workshops and seminars; conducts weekly training course and certification testing of fitness leaders in education, government, human services and corporate sectors. **Divisions:** Behavioral Sciences; Continuing Education-Consultation/Certification; Epidemiology; Exercise-Physiology; Research Dissemination. **Projects:** Hypertension; Nutrition; Stress Management; Women's Health Studies; Youth Fitness and Health. **Affiliated With:** American College of Sports Medicine. **Formerly:** (2000) Institute for Aerobics Research; (2004) Cooper Institute for Aerobics Research. **Publications:** *Fitness After 50*. Book. Offers a practical approach for everyone over 50 who want to be fit. **Price:** $20.00/copy ● *Providing Dietary Guidance Course*. Manual. Covers fundamental aspects of nutrition and practical applications that provide information to assess clients' general dietary practices. **Price:** $35.00/copy ● *Steps to Better Health*. Booklet. Contains information on how to support and enhance the use of step counters among adults and children. **Price:** $6.95/copy ● *The Walking Handbook*. Includes treadmill and elliptical trainer workouts, walking to control blood pressure, weight, stress and diabetes. **Price:** $10.00/copy; $15.00.

15629 ■ Exercise Safety Association (ESA)
PO Box 547916
Orlando, FL 32854-7916
Ph: (407)246-5090
Fax: (407)246-5090
E-mail: askesa@aol.com
URL: http://www.exercisesafety.com
Contact: Sharon Foy, Dir. of Education and Training

Founded: 1978. **Members:** 20,000. **Membership Dues:** certified, associate, business, professional, $25 (annual). **Staff:** 5. **Local Groups:** 150. **Description:** Fitness instructors, personal trainers, health spas, YMCAs, community recreation departments, and hospital wellness programs. Purposes are: to improve the qualifications of exercise instructors; to train instructors to develop safe exercise programs that will help people avoid injury while exercising; to prepare instructors for national certification. Offers training in aerobics and exercise and on the physiological aspects of exercise. Conducts exercise safety and research programs. Sponsors charitable program; maintains speakers' bureau. Offers instructor placement services. **Libraries:** Type: reference. **Awards:** Type: recognition. **Computer Services:** Mailing lists, of members. **Formerly:** Exer-Safety Association; (1985) International Exer-Safety Association. **Publications:** *ESA Member Directory*, annual. Membership Directory ● *Exercise Safety Association Newsletter*, bimonthly. Provides exercise information based on current scientific research. Includes schedule of upcoming programs. **Price:** included in membership dues. **Circulation:** 10,000. **Advertising:** accepted. **Conventions/Meetings:** annual Moving With Power Conference ● annual Music and Movements Conference - convention (exhibits).

15630 ■ Fitness for Life (FFL)
Address Unknown since 2007
Founded: 1984. **Staff:** 4. **Budget:** $250,000. **For-Profit. Local. Description:** Personal fitness training massages. **Computer Services:** Mailing lists. **Publications:** *On Purpose*, quarterly. Newsletter ● *On*

Purpose Manual. **Conventions/Meetings:** monthly board meeting.

15631 ■ IDEA Health and Fitness Association
10455 Pacific Center Ct.
San Diego, CA 92121-3773
Ph: (858)535-8979
Free: (800)999-IDEA
Fax: (858)535-8234
E-mail: contact@ideafit.com
URL: http://www.ideafit.com
Contact: Kathie Davis, Exec. Dir.

Founded: 1982. **Members:** 23,000. **Membership Dues:** personal trainer, $99 (annual) ● business, $185 (annual) ● student, $59 (annual) ● mind-body, $99 (annual) ● associate, $75 (annual) ● group fitness, $79 (annual) ● program director, $160 (annual). **Staff:** 50. **Languages:** English, Filipino, French, Italian, Japanese, Spanish. **For-Profit. Description:** Provides continuing education for fitness professionals including; fitness instructors, personal trainers, program directors, and club/studio owners. Offers workshops for continuing education credits. **Libraries:** Type: by appointment only; not open to the public; reference. **Holdings:** articles, artwork, clippings, photographs, reports, software. **Awards:** IDEA Fitness Instructor of the Year. **Frequency:** annual. **Type:** recognition. **Recipient:** for member who demonstrates strong leadership skills through community and industry involvement and has superior instructional abilities ● IDEA Personal Trainer of the Year Award. **Frequency:** annual. **Type:** recognition ● IDEA Program Director of the Year. **Frequency:** annual. **Type:** recognition. **Affiliated With:** American Heart Association. **Formerly:** (1982) IDEA: International Dance Exercise Association; (1989) IDEA: The Association for Fitness Professionals; (1997) Idea, The Health & Fitness Source; (2004) IDEA, The Health and Fitness Source. **Publications:** *IDEA Fitness Manager*, 5/year. Newsletter ● *IDEA Health & Fitness Source*, 10/year. Magazine. Includes articles on exercise science, teaching techniques, and business management. Also includes annual index to articles and calendar of events. **Price:** included in membership dues. **Circulation:** 23,000. **Advertising:** accepted ● *IDEA Personal Trainer*, 10/year. Magazine. Includes marketing client relationship and business information. **Circulation:** 7,000. **Advertising:** accepted ● Brochures ● Pamphlets ● Videos. **Conventions/Meetings:** annual IDEA Fitness Fusion - international conference, for group fitness instructors and personal trainers (exhibits) ● annual IDEA Personal Trainer - international conference, training for serious trainers (exhibits) - 2007 Oct. 12-14, Orlando, FL ● annual international conference, for fitness professionals around the globe (exhibits).

15632 ■ Medical Fitness Association
PO Box 73103
Richmond, VA 23235-8026
Ph: (804)327-0330
Fax: (804)327-1630
E-mail: info@medicalfitness.org
URL: http://www.medicalfitness.org
Contact: Cary Wing EdD, Exec.Dir.

Founded: 1991. **Members:** 450. **Membership Dues:** regular, $195 (annual) ● regular facility, $500 (annual) ● student, $75 (annual) ● advisory, $2,500 (annual) ● corporate/vendor, $800 (annual) ● corporate/vendor advisory, $6,000 (annual). **Staff:** 3. **Budget:** $500,000. **Description:** Hospitals, organizations, and medically based fitness and wellness center professionals. Seeks to reduce community health care costs through preventive care. Promotes strengthened operations and standards in fitness centers maintained by hospitals and organizations; works to improve the financial viability of fitness facilities. Serves as a network linking fitness professionals and facilities. Conducts research and educational programs; compiles statistics. **Awards:** Distinguished Achievement. **Frequency:** annual. **Type:** recognition. **Recipient:** for exemplary medical fitness centers and directors. **Computer Services:** Mailing lists. **Telecommunication Services:** electronic mail, avoigt@medicalfitness.org. **Formerly:** (1998) Association of Hospital Health and Fitness. **Publications:** *Medical*

Fitness Centers, 4th Edition, biennial. Directory. Comprehensive listing/profile of medical fitness centers in North America. **Price:** $295.00. **Advertising:** accepted ● *Re: Source, Journal of the Medical Fitness Association*, quarterly. Contains industry news, center profiles, and programming ideas. **Circulation:** 3,000. **Advertising:** accepted. Also Cited As: *Hospital Fitness News.* **Conventions/Meetings:** annual Strategies for Today's Healthcare Leaders - conference, on medical fitness (exhibits) - fall.

15633 ■ National Association for Health and Fitness (NAHF)
c/o Be Active New York State
65 Niagara Sq., Rm. 607
Buffalo, NY 14202
Ph: (716)583-0521
Free: (800)227-3988
Fax: (716)851-4309
E-mail: phaberstro@city-buffalo.org
URL: http://www.physicalfitness.org
Contact: Philip Haberstro, Exec. Dir.
Founded: 1977. **Members:** 100. **Membership Dues:** state council/coalition, $160 (annual) ● corporate, $125 (annual) ● community organization and public sector, $90 (annual) ● individual, $45 (annual). **Staff:** 2. **Budget:** $100,000. **Regional Groups:** 4. **State Groups:** 40. **Description:** State governor's fitness councils, corporations/nonprofit and public sector organizations, and individuals. Works with states to establish and maintain governor's councils and or state coalitions on physical fitness and health. Seeks to promote the quality of life for individuals in the U.S. through physical fitness, sports, and healthy lifestyles. Conducts Annual National conference; regional meetings; National EMPLOYEE Health and Fitness day (celebrated third Wednesday of May each year), trainings/technical assistance, networking, national newsletters, resources and members benefits program, and Annual Gold Star Awards program. **Awards:** Dorothy Harris Endowed Scholarship. **Frequency:** annual. **Type:** scholarship. **Recipient:** to female graduate students in Physical Education, Sports Management, Sports Psychology or Sports Sociology ● RYKA Women's Fitness Grant. **Frequency:** annual. **Type:** grant. **Recipient:** to organizations and programs that enhance women's lives through health and fitness. **Computer Services:** Online services, links to resources. **Subgroups:** Planning Groups for National Meeting and Employee Fitness Day; Regional Meetings for Northeast, Southeast, Central and Western states. **Formerly:** (2000) National Association of Governor's Councils on Physical Fitness and Sport. **Conventions/Meetings:** annual National Employee Health and Fitness Day - rally, for employers from all sectors - always 3rd Wednesday of May.

15634 ■ National Fitness Therapy Association (NFTA)
PO Box 522
Winter Park, CO 80482
Ph: (970)726-0697
E-mail: fitnesstherapy@nfta.org
URL: http://www.nfta.org
Contact: Patrick Pine, Founder/Pres.
Membership Dues: accredited facility, associate, $300 (annual) ● accredited fitness professional, $50 (annual). **Description:** Aims to improve the quality, standards and outcomes of preventive health care services. Seeks to educate and inform the public on health, fitness and wellness issues. Provides accreditation for medical fitness professionals and facilities offering post-rehabilitation exercise therapy services, preventive health care services and exercise programs for referrals with clinically diagnosed conditions.

15635 ■ Shape Up America (SUA)
PO Box 149
Clyde Park, MT 59018
E-mail: info@shapeup.org
URL: http://www.shapeup.org
Contact: Barbara J. Moore PhD, Pres./CEO
Staff: 6. **Description:** Educates the public on the importance of the achievement and maintenance of a

healthy body weight. Encourages sensible eating and increased physical activities of individuals. **Computer Services:** database, fitness and weight management directory ● information services, breakfast benefits ● information services, childhood obesity ● information services, Diabesity ● online services, body fat lab. **Telecommunication Services:** electronic mail, member-info@shapeup.org ● electronic mail, customer-care@shapeup.org. **Committees:** Scientific Advisory. **Programs:** Eating Out Quiz; Fitness Focus Quiz; Portion Control Quiz; Shape Up and Drop 10; 10,000 Steps.

15636 ■ Truth in Fitness
204 E 204th St.
Costa Mesa, CA 92627
E-mail: chazz@truthinfitness.org
Contact: Chazz Weaver, Contact
Founded: 2004. **Description:** Conducts academic and scientific research on the relationships between exercise, diet and nutrition. Educates the general public on health and fitness. **Computer Services:** Online services, discussion forum ● online services, survey. **Projects:** Before and After; The McDonald's Diet; Starting Over at 54. **Publications:** Newsletter.

Physical Therapy

15637 ■ American Academy of Orthopaedic Manual Physical Therapists (AAOMPT)
2104 Delta Way, Ste.7
Tallahassee, FL 32303
Ph: (850)222-0397
Fax: (850)222-0342
E-mail: aaompt@lewisweb.net
URL: http://www.aaompt.org
Contact: Craig Crosby, Exec. Dir.
Founded: 1992. **Membership Dues:** regular, $95 (annual) ● institutional, $160 (annual) ● student (without journal), $15 (annual) ● student (with journal), $60 (annual) ● regular, in North America, $105 (annual) ● overseas, $115 (annual). **Description:** Promotes excellence in orthopaedic manual physical therapy practice, education and research, and collaborates with national and international associations. Promotes research in orthopaedic manual physical therapy and fosters the principles of evidence-based practice within the membership. Develops and updates professional and post-professional education guidelines and continuing education programming relevant to the practice of orthopaedic manual physical therapy. **Telecommunication Services:** electronic mail, ccrosby@fpta.org. **Publications:** *Articulations.* Newsletter ● *Journal of Manual and Manipulative Therapy.*

Physician Assistants

15638 ■ Accreditation Review Commission on Education for the Physician Assistant (ARC-PA)
12000 Findley Rd., Ste.240
Duluth, GA 30097
Ph: (770)476-1224
Fax: (770)476-1738
E-mail: johnmccarty@arc-pa.org
URL: http://www.arc-pa.org
Contact: John E. McCarty, Exec. Dir.
Founded: 1971. **Members:** 16. **Budget:** $125,000. **Description:** Serves as an accrediting body for physician assistant education nationwide. **Libraries:** Type: reference. **Holdings:** archival material. **Affiliated With:** Commission on Accreditation of Allied Health Education Programs. **Formerly:** (1972) Joint Review Committee on Educational Programs for Physician's Assistants; (1987) Joint Review Committee on Educational Programs for Physician Assistants; (1989) Accreditation Committee on Education for Physicians Assistants; (2000) Accreditation Review Committee on Education for Physician Assistants. **Conventions/Meetings:** semiannual meeting.

15639 ■ American Academy of Physician Assistants (AAPA)
950 N Washington St.
Alexandria, VA 22314-1552
Ph: (703)836-2272
Fax: (703)684-1924
E-mail: aapa@aapa.org
URL: http://www.aapa.org
Contact: Steve Crane, Exec. VP/CEO
Founded: 1968. **Members:** 37,000. **Membership Dues:** fellow, $215 (annual) ● associate, $200 (annual) ● sustaining/physician/affiliate/student, $75 (annual). **Staff:** 87. **Budget:** $9,000,000. **Regional Groups:** 5. **State Groups:** 57. **Local Groups:** 59. **Description:** Physician assistants and other interested parties. Seeks to promote quality, cost-effective, and accessible healthcare, and the professional and personal development of PAs. Provides services for members. Organizes annual National PA Day. Develops research and education programs; compiles statistics. **Libraries:** Type: reference. **Awards:** Type: scholarship. **Telecommunication Services:** electronic mail, steve@aapa.org. **Committees:** Political Action. **Affiliated With:** Physician Assistant Education Association. **Publications:** *AAPA News*, biweekly. Newsletter. News on physician assistant programs, AAPA's activities, and employment information and opportunities. **Price:** included in membership dues. ISSN: 0894-0509. **Circulation:** 27,000. **Advertising:** accepted ● *Journal of the American Academy of Physician Assistants*, monthly. Covers clinical and scholarly research. Includes book reviews. **Price:** included in membership dues; $50.00 /year for nonmembers; $75.00 /year for institutions. **Circulation:** 27,000. **Advertising:** accepted ● *Legislative Watch*, monthly ● Membership Directory, annual. **Conventions/Meetings:** annual conference (exhibits) - 2008 May 24-29, San Antonio, TX; 2009 May 23-28, San Diego, CA; 2010 May 29-June 3, Atlanta, GA; 2011 May 26-31, Las Vegas, NV.

15640 ■ Association of Neurosurgical Physician Assistants (ANSPA)
4267 NW Fed. Hwy.
PMB 202
Jensen Beach, FL 34957
Free: (888)94A-NSPA
Fax: (772)388-3457
E-mail: theanspa@aol.com
URL: http://www.anspa.org
Contact: Linda Kotrba, Exec. Dir.
Founded: 1990. **Members:** 250. **Membership Dues:** student, $20 (annual) ● fellow, $100 (annual). **Staff:** 2. **Description:** Physician assistants active in the field of neurosurgery; students enrolled in accredited physician assistant education programs. Promotes professional advancement of members. Represents members before medical organizations; conducts continuing professional development and educational and training programs. **Publications:** *Brainwaves*, quarterly. Newsletter. **Conventions/Meetings:** annual board meeting.

15641 ■ National Commission on Certification of Physician Assistants (NCCPA)
12000 Findley Rd., Ste.200
Duluth, GA 30097
Ph: (678)417-8100
Fax: (678)417-8135
E-mail: nccpa@nccpa.net
URL: http://www.nccpa.net
Contact: Janet Lathrop MBA, Pres.
Founded: 1975. **Staff:** 9. **Description:** Certifies physician assistants at the entry level and for continued competence; has certified 22,750 physician assistants. **Telecommunication Services:** electronic mail, janetl@nccpa.net. **Formerly:** (1987) National Commission on Certification of Physician's Assistants. **Publications:** *Directory of Physician Assistants - Certified*, annual ● Newsletter, quarterly. **Conventions/Meetings:** annual meeting.

15642 ■ Physician Assistant Education Association (PAEA)
300 N Washington St., Ste.505
Alexandria, VA 22314-2544
Ph: (703)548-5538

Fax: (703)548-5539
E-mail: info@paeaonline.org
URL: http://www.paeaonline.org
Contact: Jonna Holden, Admin. Asst.
Founded: 1972. **Members:** 135. **Membership Dues:** institutional, $1,500 (annual) ● individual, $75 (annual) ● international colleague, $150 (annual) ● program, $2,875 (annual). **Staff:** 7. **Budget:** $1,300,000. **Regional Groups:** 6. **Description:** Represents physician assistant (PA) educational programs in the United States. Assists PA educational programs-institutions with training programs for physician assistants to primary care and surgical physicians. Assists in the development and organization of educational curricula for PA programs to assure the public of competent PA's. Contributes to defining the roles of PA's in the field of medicine to maximize their benefit to the public; serves as a public information center on the profession; coordinates program logistics such as admissions and career placements; and is currently initiating a centralized application service for PA applicants. Sponsors the Annual Survey of Physician Assistant Educational Programs in the United States. Conducts and sponsors research projects; compiles statistics; offers ongoing training for PA leadership and faculty. **Telecommunication Services:** electronic mail, jholden@paeaonline.org. **Affiliated With:** American Academy of Physician Assistants. **Formerly:** (2006) Association of Physician Assistant Programs. **Publications:** *Annual Report on Physician Assistant Education in the U.S.*, annual. Provides data on physician assistant education, employment, and trends affecting the profession. Includes statistics. **Price:** $50.00/copy; free for members. ISSN: 0883-0703. **Circulation:** 300 ● *Journal of Physician Assistant Education*, quarterly. **Price:** $75.00 /year for nonmembers in U.S.; $95.00 /year for nonmembers outside U.S.; free for members. Also Cited As: *JPAE* ● *PAEA Networker*, monthly. Newsletter. Contains information for physician assistant program faculty. **Price:** included in membership dues. Alternate Formats: online. **Conventions/Meetings:** annual meeting, exhibits include computer software, medical devices, publishers and APAP products and services (exhibits).

15643 ■ Society of Army Physician Assistants (SAPA)
PO Box 07490
Fort Myers, FL 33919
Ph: (239)482-2162
Fax: (239)482-2162
E-mail: hal.slusher@juno.com
URL: http://www.sapa.org
Contact: Harold E. Slusher PAC, Exec. Dir.
Founded: 1976. **Members:** 1,000. **Membership Dues:** fellow, associate, affiliate, $25 (annual) ● student, $5 (annual). **Multinational. Description:** Represents and supports the U.S. Army Physician Assistant, including, former, active, retired, reserve and National Guard PA's. Aims to provide a forum for discussion, representation with the AAPA; provides low cost continuing medical education (CME) to members and the PA profession. **Programs:** Corporate Associate. **Affiliated With:** American Academy of Physician Assistants. **Publications:** Newsletter, bimonthly. **Price:** included in membership dues ● Membership Directory. **Price:** included in membership dues. **Conventions/Meetings:** annual PA Refresher Course - conference, pharmaceutical, medical, medical equipment, recruitment, military (exhibits).

15644 ■ Society of Dermatology Physician Assistants (SDPA)
PO Box 701461
San Antonio, TX 78270
Free: (800)380-3992
Fax: (830)438-5425
E-mail: sdpa@dermpa.org
URL: http://www.dermpa.org
Contact: Daniel B. Hickey, Pres.
Founded: 1994. **Members:** 1,100. **Membership Dues:** fellow, associate, affiliate, $100 (annual) ● student, $75 (annual). **Budget:** $15,000. **Description:** Physician assistants who are employed in or

have an interest in the practice of dermatology. Seeks to advance the practice of dermatology physician assistants supervised by dermatologists; promotes continuing professional development of members. Acts as liaison between members and the American Academy of Dermatology; educates physicians and the public regarding the role of members in the practice of dermatology; assists in the training of dermatology physician assistants and students. Maintains writers' bureau. **Telecommunication Services:** electronic mail, dhickey@dermpa.org. **Affiliated With:** American Academy of Physician Assistants. **Also Known As:** (1995) Physician Assistants in Dermatology. **Publications:** Newsletter, periodic. **Price:** free, for members only ● Brochure. Alternate Formats: online. **Conventions/Meetings:** annual conference, includes dermatology CME, held in conjunction with Academy of Dermatology - 2007 Oct. 31-Nov. 3, Nashville, TN; 2008 Nov. 4-8, Tampa, FL.

15645 ■ Society of Emergency Medicine Physician Assistants (SEMPA)
222 S Westmonte Dr., No. 101
Altamonte Springs, FL 32714
Ph: (407)774-7880
Fax: (407)774-6440
E-mail: info@sempa.org
URL: http://www.sempa.org
Contact: Barbara FitzGerald Beatty, Exec. Dir.
Founded: 1990. **Members:** 700. **Membership Dues:** fellow, $75 (annual) ● associate, affiliate, $100 (annual) ● student, $25 (annual). **Staff:** 1. **Regional Groups:** 6. **Description:** Works to collect demographic data to share with the PA profession and other agencies; strives to devise a more standardized approach to credentialing the development and granting of clinical privileges. Seeks to enhance the EM PA's ability to provide the best quality patient care. **Publications:** *SEMPA News*, quarterly. Newsletter. **Conventions/Meetings:** annual conference.

15646 ■ Society for Physician Assistants in Pediatrics (SPAP)
950 N Washington St.
Alexandria, VA 22314-1552
E-mail: spap@aapa.org
URL: http://www.aapa.org/spec/SPAP
Contact: Daniel Wood, Pres.
Founded: 1994. **Members:** 250. **Membership Dues:** fellow, $35 (annual) ● associate, affiliate, $50 (annual) ● student, $10 (annual). **Staff:** 1. **Description:** Gathers and disseminates information affecting the practice of pediatric physician assistants. Collects demographic data to share within the profession or with other organizations. Assists in developing guidelines for physician assistant utilization in clinical settings, and enhances the relationship with the American Academy of Pediatrics. **Awards:** Frequency: annual. Type: scholarship. Recipient: for PA student with documented interest in pediatric practice. **Publications:** *Physician Assistants in Pediatrics*, quarterly. Newsletter. **Price:** included in membership dues.

Physicians

15647 ■ Academy of Clinical Laboratory Physicians and Scientists (ACLPS)
c/o Elizabeth Frank, PhD, Sec.-Treas.
500 Chipeta Way
Salt Lake City, UT 84108
Ph: (801)583-2787
Fax: (801)584-5207
E-mail: e.frank@aruplab.com
URL: http://www.aclps.org
Contact: Elizabeth Frank PhD, Sec.-Treas.
Founded: 1966. **Members:** 500. **Membership Dues:** regular, $100 (annual). **Multinational. Description:** Represents physicians, scientists, and educators. Encourages and promotes the highest standards of education, service and research in clinical pathology at universities and medical schools. Sponsors journal. **Awards:** Cotlove Lectureship. Frequency: annual.

Type: recognition. **Recipient:** to a scientist for outstanding contributions to the science of laboratory medicine ● Ellis Benson Award. **Frequency:** annual. **Type:** recognition ● Gerald T. Evans Award. **Frequency:** annual. **Type:** recognition. **Recipient:** to a member for outstanding leadership and/or service to the society ● Paul E. Strandjord Young Investigator Award. **Frequency:** annual. **Type:** recognition. **Recipient:** for young investigators. **Publications:** *The American Journal of Clinical Pathology*. Alternate Formats: online ● Newsletter, periodic. **Price:** included in membership dues. Alternate Formats: online. **Conventions/Meetings:** annual Continuing Medical Education Seminar ● annual meeting.

15648 ■ Aesculapian Club (AC)
25 Shattuck St., Bldg. A Rm. 206
Harvard Medical School
Boston, MA 02115
Ph: (617)432-1000
URL: http://www.hms.harvard.edu
Founded: 1902. **Description:** Social organization of graduates of Harvard Medical School or physicians who have held teaching appointments there for three years.

15649 ■ Air Medical Physician Association (AMPA)
c/o Pat Petersen, Exec. Dir.
951 E Montana Vista Ln.
Salt Lake City, UT 84124
Ph: (801)263-2672
Fax: (801)434-0434
E-mail: patp@ampa.org
URL: http://www.ampa.org
Contact: Pat Petersen, Exec. Dir.
Founded: 1992. **Members:** 400. **Membership Dues:** academic, $300 (annual) ● physician, voting, active, $200 (annual) ● non-physician, non-voting, affiliate, $75 (annual) ● individual, medical student, resident, non-voting, $50 (annual). **Staff:** 1. **Description:** Physicians and professionals involved in medical transport. Promotes safe and effective patient transportation through medical direction, research, education, leadership, and collaboration. **Awards:** AMPA Distinguished Physician. **Frequency:** annual. **Type:** recognition. **Recipient:** for physicians of AMPA ● Medical Director of the Year. **Frequency:** annual. **Type:** recognition. **Recipient:** for outstanding physician. **Task Forces:** AirMed and Air Medical Journal; Budget/Financial Projection; Position Papers; Promotion; Website. **Affiliated With:** Air and Surface Transport Nurses Association; National Flight Paramedics Association. **Publications:** *Air Medical Journal*, quarterly. Peer-reviewed journal. ● *Air Medical Physician Handbook*. **Price:** included in membership dues; $65.00 for nonmembers; $50.00 additional copy for members ● Newsletter. Alternate Formats: online. **Conventions/Meetings:** annual Critical Care Transport Medicine Conference (exhibits) ● annual meeting - held at the end of October.

15650 ■ American Academy on Communication in Healthcare (AACH)
16020 Swingley Ridge Rd., Ste.300
Chesterfield, MO 63017
Ph: (636)449-5080
Fax: (636)449-5051
E-mail: chris@aachonline.org
URL: http://www.aachonline.org
Contact: Chris Pallozola, Exec. Dir.
Founded: 1978. **Description:** Fosters best patient care by advocating a relationship-centered approach to healthcare communication, education and research. Focuses on strengths, resources and needs of patients, physicians and other professionals. Develops skills that integrate biological, psychosocial and social domains. Applies existing scholarship from multiple disciplines and develops new knowledge through research. Promotes collaborative relationships between doctors and patients, teachers and learners, and other involved professionals. Incorporates core values of respect, empathy and genuineness in human relationships and the importance of self-awareness in all activities. **Awards:** Type: grant ● Type: scholarship. **Formerly:** (2006) American

Academy on Physician and Patients. **Publications:** *Medical Encounter*, quarterly. **Price:** included in membership dues ● *Patient Education and Counseling*. Journal. Contains information on educational, counseling and communication models in health care. **Price:** $98.00 for members; $168.00 for nonmembers. **Conventions/Meetings:** biennial international conference (exhibits) - 2007 Oct. 9-12, Charleston, SC.

15651 ■ American Academy of Hospice and Palliative Medicine (AAHPM)
4700 W Lake Ave.
Glenview, IL 60025
Ph: (847)375-4712
Free: (877)734-8671
Fax: (877)734-8671
E-mail: info@aahpm.org
URL: http://www.aahpm.org
Contact: Ronald S. Schonwetter MD, Pres.

Founded: 1988. **Membership Dues:** physician, $325 (annual) ● affiliate, $160 (annual) ● fellow, $100 (annual). **Description:** Works to further and foster the practice of hospice/palliative care for the terminally ill and their families. **Publications:** *AAHPM Bulletin*, quarterly. Newsletter. **Price:** included in membership dues ● *Journal of Palliative Medicine*, bimonthly. **Price:** included in membership dues. **Conventions/Meetings:** Congress of the European Association for Palliative Care.

15652 ■ American Association of Clinical Directors (AACD)
520 N Northwest Hwy.
Park Ridge, IL 60068-2573
Ph: (847)825-5586
Fax: (847)825-5658
E-mail: aacd@asahq.org
URL: http://www.aacdhq.org
Contact: Sean K. Kennedy MD, Pres.

Founded: 1988. **Membership Dues:** physician, associate, international (with subscription to the journal), $150 (annual) ● active, associate (with subscription to the journal), $225 (annual) ● international, $50 (annual). **Description:** Improves the quality of anesthesia care in the US and other nations where anesthesia directors may be associated with. Provides a forum for anesthesiologists whose primary responsibility is operating room management. Offers physicians with an interest in the business aspect of operating room management as an opportunity to share ideas with colleagues who have more experience in the field and share in a common forum for the discussion of problems and issues. **Computer Services:** database, member directory ● information services, procedural glossary ● mailing lists, of members ● online services, discussion forum. **Publications:** *Journal of Clinical Anesthesia*. **Price:** included in membership dues ● Newsletter. Alternate Formats: online.

15653 ■ American Association of Physicians of Indian Origin (AAPI)
600 Enterprise Dr., Ste.108
Oak Brook, IL 60523
Ph: (630)530-2277
Fax: (630)990-2281
E-mail: info@aapiusa.net
URL: http://www.aapiusa.net
Contact: Hemantkumar Patel MD, Pres.

Founded: 1984. **Members:** 100. **Membership Dues:** regular, $100 (annual) ● young physician, $50 (annual) ● life - patron, $750 ● life - joint patron, $1,000 ● joint, $150 (annual) ● life - patron (if spouse is already a patron member), $250. **Description:** Serves as a forum to facilitate and enable Indian American physicians to excel in patient care, teaching, and research. **Committees:** Academic Affairs; Charitable Foundation; Women Physicians. **Programs:** Clerkship. **Publications:** Journal, bimonthly. Contains articles on medical and social matters related to Indian physicians and public health. **Conventions/Meetings:** annual convention.

15654 ■ American Association of Professional Ringside Physicians (AAPRP)
40 Heights Rd., Ste.201
Darien, CT 06820
Ph: (203)662-8900
Fax: (203)662-8906
E-mail: ringsidemd@aol.com
URL: http://www.aaprp.org
Contact: Dr. Michael B. Schwartz, Pres./Chm.

Founded: 1997. **Membership Dues:** individual, $125 (annual). **Description:** Physicians who provide ringside services during boxing matches. Seeks to create and develop protocols and guidelines for ringside physicians; works to ensure the safety and protection of professional boxers. Facilitates communication and cooperation among members; develops standards of practice for ringside physicians; serves as a clearinghouse on the medical aspects of boxing. **Publications:** *Ring Sports Magazine*.

15655 ■ Association of American Indian Physicians (AAIP)
1225 Sovereign Row, Ste.103
Oklahoma City, OK 73108
Ph: (405)946-7072
Fax: (405)946-7651
E-mail: aaip@aaip.com
URL: http://www.aaip.com
Contact: Margaret Knight, Exec. Dir.

Founded: 1971. **Members:** 270. **Membership Dues:** individual, $100 (annual). **Staff:** 5. **Budget:** $700,000. **Description:** Physicians (MD or DO) of American Indian descent. Encourages American Indians to enter the health professions. Provides a forum for the interchange of ideas and information of mutual interest to physicians of Indian descent. Establishes contracts with government agencies to provide consultation and other expert opinion regarding health care of American Indians and Alaskan Natives; receives contracts and grant monies and other forms of assistance from these sources. Supports and encourages all other agencies and organizations, Indian and non-Indian, working to improve health conditions of American Indians and Alaskan Natives. Locates scholarship funds for Indian professional students; provides counseling assistance; preserves American Indian culture. Conducts seminars for students interested in health careers and for counselors in government and other schools where American Indian children are taught. **Committees:** Internet. **Programs:** Health Careers Opportunity; HIV/AIDS; National Institutes of Health Information Dissemination; National Native American Youth Initiative; Native Research Network; Tobacco Prevention and Control. **Publications:** Newsletter, quarterly. **Circulation:** 5,500. **Advertising:** accepted. **Conventions/Meetings:** annual National Indian Health Conference (exhibits).

15656 ■ Association of American Physicians and Surgeons (AAPS)
1601 N Tucson Blvd., Ste.9
Tucson, AZ 85716
Free: (800)635-1196
Fax: (520)326-3529
E-mail: aaps@aapsonline.org
URL: http://www.aapsonline.org
Contact: Jane M. Orient MD, Exec. Dir.

Founded: 1943. **Members:** 4,500. **Membership Dues:** regular, $325 (annual) ● builder, $390 (annual) ● sustainer, $550 (annual) ● life, $2,000 ● house officer, $30 (annual) ● professional associate, $150 (annual) ● associate, $95 (annual). **Staff:** 3. **Description:** Physicians dedicated to preserving and promoting quality medical care. Represents physicians in the socioeconomic and legal aspects of medical practice such as medical economics, public relations, and legislation. Makes available legal consultation services. **Committees:** PAC; Program. **Publications:** *AAPS News*, monthly. Newsletter. Covers developments affecting health care and the profession. Includes legislative news, calendar of events, and health law commentary. **Price:** included in membership dues; $35.00 /year for nonmembers. ISSN: 8750-9687 ● *AAPS 2004 Annual Meeting*. Audiotapes. Contains the events happened in the an-

nual meeting of the association. **Price:** $15.00 for audio CD copy; $30.00 for audio DVD copy. Alternate Formats: CD-ROM ● *Journal of American Physicians and Surgeons*, quarterly. Takes on controversial issues. **Price:** free for members. **Conventions/Meetings:** annual meeting.

15657 ■ Association of Chinese American Physicians (ACAP)
c/o Ms. Randi Lee
PO Box 1565
New York, NY 10159-1565
Ph: (212)684-9038
Fax: (212)937-3158
E-mail: rlee@medicalit.net
URL: http://www.acaponline.org
Contact: Ms. Randi Lee, Contact

Membership Dues: life, $500 ● full, $50 (annual) ● associate, $30 (annual) ● student, $10 (annual). **Description:** Fosters programs that enable physicians to form a professional community in the practice of medicine. Provides opportunities for physicians to participate in the governance and decision-making of health care policies that affect the communities that they serve. Promotes and develops a cooperative working relationship among physicians. **Publications:** *ACAP Newsletter* (in Chinese and English). Alternate Formats: online ● *ACAP Quarterly*. Journal.

15658 ■ Association of Nigerian Physicians in the Americas (ANPA)
7221 Pineville Matthews Rd., Ste.200
Charlotte, NC 28226
Ph: (330)677-0400
Fax: (330)677-0400
E-mail: anpa@sbcglobal.net
URL: http://www.anpa.org
Contact: Akinyele Aluko MD, Pres.

Founded: 1995. **Membership Dues:** licensed medical doctor, osteopathic doctor, dentist and podiatrist of Nigerian descent, $365 (annual). **Description:** Physicians and surgeons of Nigerian descent practicing in the United States and Canada. Promotes professional advancement of members; seeks to stimulate interest in matters affecting the health of people of Nigerian descent; encourages adherence to high standards of professional ethics and practice by members. Serves as a clearinghouse on professional opportunities available to physicians of Nigerian descent in North America; conducts charitable, social, educational, and scientific activities. **Publications:** *Directory of Nigerian Physicians in the United States and Canada*, annual. Alternate Formats: online ● *Quarterly News Bulletin*. Newsletter ● Articles. Alternate Formats: online. **Conventions/Meetings:** annual convention.

15659 ■ Association of Pakistani Physicians of North America (APPNA)
6414 S Cass Ave.
Westmont, IL 60559
Ph: (630)968-8585 (630)968-8606
Fax: (630)968-8677
E-mail: info@appna.org
URL: http://www.appna.org
Contact: Dr. Nadeem A. Kazi, Pres.

Founded: 1976. **Members:** 1,200. **Membership Dues:** current, $125 (annual) ● affiliate, $62 (annual) ● life, $1,875. **Staff:** 2. **Budget:** $150,000. **Languages:** Baluchi, English, Panjabi, Pashto, Sindhi. **Description:** Physicians and dentists who are native to Pakistan but now live and practice in North America. Supports medical education and research and advances the interests of medicine and medical organizations. Fosters scientific development and education in order to improve the quality of medicine and health care. Facilitates better relations among Pakistani physicians and between them and the people of North America. Assists Pakistani physicians newly arrived in North America in orientation and adjustment. Arranges for donation of medical literature and medical supplies to Pakistan, and for lecture tours, medical conferences, and seminars to be held there. Participates in medical relief and charitable activities in Pakistan and North America. **Telecommunication Services:** electronic mail, president@appna.org. **Committees:** Communication; Ethics and Grievance; Gold Medal Task Force and Awards; Hotel Selection and Negotiation; Nominations and Election; Office Management; Project Evaluation; Publication; Research, Education and Scientific Affairs; Resource Development; Social Welfare and Disaster; Women's Auxiliary. **Formerly:** (2003) Association of Pakistani Physicians. **Publications:** Bulletin, monthly ● Newsletter, quarterly. **Conventions/Meetings:** annual International Conference on Health - always December, in Pakistan ● annual meeting - always summer.

15660 ■ Association of Philippine Physicians in America (APPA)
PO Box 452164
Los Angeles, CA 90045
Fax: (310)889-7131
E-mail: masmd@aboutappa.org
Contact: Dr. Rodolfo V. Punzalan MD, Special Presidential Asst.
Founded: 1972. **Members:** 3,000. **Staff:** 3. **Budget:** $130,000. **State Groups:** 27. **National Groups:** 27. **Description:** Individuals from the Philippines who are licensed to practice medicine in the U.S. Seeks to: render free medical care to indigent persons; establish a continuing medical education program for physicians; provide aid for education of physicians; support medical research. Sends medical missions to the Philippines. Provides medical residency program placement service. Maintains speakers' bureau; compiles statistics. **Libraries: Type:** not open to the public. **Subjects:** educational, charitable products, social. **Awards:** APPA Physician of the Year. **Frequency:** annual. **Type:** recognition. **Recipient:** for individual ● **Frequency:** annual. **Type:** recognition. **Computer Services:** database ● electronic publishing ● mailing lists. **Committees:** Awards; Continuing Medical Education; Foreign Medical Graduates; Medico-Legal Aid; Philippine Medical Aid Program; Political Action; Public Relations; Unification. **Councils:** Legislation. **Formerly:** (1986) Association of Philippine Practicing Physicians in America. **Publications:** Directory of Physicians, biennial ● Leadership Roster of Officers, annual ● Philippine Physician, periodic. Newsletter. Association and professional newsletter. **Price:** free. **Advertising:** accepted ● Also publishes CME abstracts; plans to publish journal of medicine. **Conventions/Meetings:** annual meeting and seminar, pharmaceutical, home health products (exhibits).

15661 ■ Association of Staff Physician Recruiters (ASPR)
1711 W County Rd. B, Ste.300N
Roseville, MN 55113
Free: (800)830-2777
Fax: (651)635-0307
E-mail: admin@aspr.org
URL: http://www.aspr.org
Contact: David Nyman, Pres.
Founded: 1990. **Members:** 500. **Membership Dues:** active/associate, $200 (annual) ● interim, $75 (annual). **Regional Groups:** 19. **Multinational. Description:** Recruits physicians and other healthcare providers to staff hospitals, clinics and managed care organizations where the members are employed. Sponsors educational programs and meetings on various recruitment issues. **Publications:** Membership Directory, annual ● Newsletter, quarterly. **Price:** for members. **Conventions/Meetings:** annual meeting.

15662 ■ Catholic Medical Association (CMA)
333 E Lancaster Ave., No. 348
Wynnewood, PA 19096-1929
Ph: (215)877-9099
Fax: (215)701-6577
E-mail: info@cathmed.org
URL: http://www.cathmed.org
Contact: Robert J. Saxer MD, Pres.
Founded: 1932. **Members:** 3,500. **Membership Dues:** associate (friend, individual), $100 (annual) ● active (practicing physician/dentist), $300 (annual) ● active (retired physician/dentist), $150 (annual) ● active (physician in training), associate (allied health professional, organization, clergy, religious, deacon, graduate student), $100 (annual) ● associate (medical student, nursing student, seminarian, undergraduate), $35 (annual). **Staff:** 2. **Budget:** $200,000. **Local Groups:** 90. **Description:** Catholic physicians and dentists dedicated to upholding the principles of the Catholic faith in the practice of medicine. **Committees:** Medical Mission. **Formerly:** (1998) National Federation of Catholic Physicians Guilds. **Publications:** Homosexuality and Hope Booklet. **Price:** $5.00 for members ● Homosexuality and Hope Pamphlet. **Price:** $1.50 for members ● The Linacre Quarterly. Journal. Contains information about bioethics. **Price:** $60.00/year in U.S.; $70.00 /year for institutions; $75.00/year outside U.S. ● Newsletter. **Price:** included in membership dues. Alternate Formats: online. **Conventions/Meetings:** annual conference.

15663 ■ Educational Commission for Foreign Medical Graduates (ECFMG)
3624 Market St.
Philadelphia, PA 19104-2685
Ph: (215)386-5900
Fax: (215)386-9196
E-mail: info@ecfmg.org
URL: http://www.ecfmg.org
Contact: Nancy E. Gary MD, Pres./CEO
Founded: 1956. **Members:** 20. **Staff:** 80. **Description:** Sponsoring organizations are American Board of Medical Specialties; American Medical Association; Association of American Medical Colleges; Association for Hospital Medical Education; the Federation of State Medical Boards of the U.S; National Medical Association. Aims to provide information to graduates of foreign medical schools regarding entry into graduate medical education and the U.S. health care system; evaluate the qualifications of graduates of foreign medical schools; identify the cultural and professional needs of graduates of foreign medical schools and assist in the establishment of educational policies and programs; provides international access to testing and evaluation programs to meet theses needs. Sponsors exchange visitor program to enable physicians from other countries to participate in graduate medical education or training. Gathers and disseminates data about graduates of foreign medical schools. **Convention/Meeting:** none. **Libraries: Type:** open to the public. **Holdings:** photographs. **Sections:** Certification; Credential Evaluation; English Testing; Examination; Information. **Formerly:** (1974) Educational Council for Foreign Medical Graduates. **Publications:** Educational Commission for Foreign Medical Graduates—Annual Report. Details organizations history and programs. **Price:** free. **Circulation:** 8,000 ● Educational Commission for Foreign Medical Graduates—Information Booklet, annual. Provides procedures for fulfilling ECFMG examination and certification requirements. **Price:** free. **Circulation:** 320,000.

15664 ■ Federal Physicians Association (FPA)
12427 Hedges Run Dr., Ste.104
Lake Ridge, VA 22192
Ph: (703)323-9888
Free: (800)403-3374
Fax: (800)528-3492
E-mail: info@fedphy.org
URL: http://www.fedphy.org
Contact: Dennis W. Boyd, Exec. Dir.
Founded: 1979. **Members:** 500. **Membership Dues:** individual, $100 (annual) ● retired, $25 (annual). **Staff:** 1. **Budget:** $40,000. **Regional Groups:** 1. **State Groups:** 1. **Description:** Physicians employed by or retired from the federal government. Objectives are: to improve the health care of patients served by federal physicians; to advance the practice of medicine within the federal government; to improve the working conditions and benefits of federal physicians. Conducts specialized education programs. **Awards:** Federal Health Care Award. **Frequency:** periodic. **Type:** recognition. **Recipient:** for materially improved federal health care programs. **Formerly:** (1982) American Academy of Federal Civil Service Physicians. **Publications:** The Federal Physician, bimonthly. Newsletter. **Price:** $37.50/year. ISSN:

1070-9029. **Circulation:** 500. **Advertising:** accepted. **Conventions/Meetings:** annual conference (exhibits).

15665 ■ Federation of State Physician Health Programs (FSPHP)
c/o Vickie Grosso
Amer. Medical Assn.
515 N State St.
Chicago, IL 60610
Ph: (312)464-4574
E-mail: vickie.grosso@ama-assn.org
URL: http://www.fsphp.org
Contact: Luis T. Sanchez, Pres.
Founded: 1990. **Description:** Provides a forum for education and exchange of information among state programs. Enhances awareness of issues related to physician health and impairment. Advocates for physicians and their health issues at local, state and national levels. Assists state programs in their quest to protect the public. **Publications:** Newsletter.

15666 ■ Interamerican College of Physicians and Surgeons (ICPS)
233 Broadway, Ste.771
New York, NY 10279
Ph: (212)777-3642
Fax: (212)267-5394
E-mail: info@icps.org
URL: http://www.icps.org
Contact: Dr. Rene F. Rodriguez MD, Pres.
Founded: 1979. **Members:** 4,000. **Membership Dues:** licensed physician under the age of 62, $60 (annual) ● physician 62 years old and above, $40 (annual) ● resident and medical school student, $25 (annual) ● adjunct, $50 (annual) ● life (under 62 years old), $300 ● life (age 62 and older), $175 ● corporate gold, $10,000 (annual) ● corporate silver, $15,000 (annual) ● corporate platinum, $25,000 (annual). **Staff:** 10. **Languages:** English, Spanish. **Description:** Physicians in countries of the Americas. Encourages understanding and communication among members concerning all aspects of medical practice. Promotes health education in Hispanic communities in the Western Hemisphere. **Computer Services:** database ● mailing lists. **Publications:** Interamerican Medical Directory, biennial ● Medico Interamericano (in English and Spanish), monthly. Journal. **Circulation:** 40,000. **Advertising:** accepted. Alternate Formats: online. **Conventions/Meetings:** annual conference (exhibits).

15667 ■ International Association of Physicians in AIDS Care (IAPAC)
33 N LaSalle St., Ste.1700
Chicago, IL 60602-2601
Ph: (312)795-4930
Fax: (312)795-4938
E-mail: iapac@iapac.org
URL: http://www.iapac.org
Contact: Jose M. Zuniga, Pres./CEO
Founded: 1995. **Members:** 12,000. **Membership Dues:** contributing, $190 (annual) ● regular, $150 (annual) ● AIDS service organization, $50 (annual) ● affiliate, student, $30 (annual) ● associate, $110 (annual). **Staff:** 2. **Regional Groups:** 22. **Languages:** English, Spanish. **Multinational. Description:** Provides educational programs to caregivers, physicians and patients. Promotes public policy reform and research. **Awards:** Dag Hammarksjold Award. **Frequency:** periodic. **Type:** recognition. **Recipient:** to world leaders instituting bold approaches to various aspects of the AIDS pandemic ● IAPAC Hero in Medicine. **Frequency:** periodic. **Type:** recognition ● Jonathan Mann Health & Human Rights Award. **Frequency:** periodic. **Type:** recognition. **Computer Services:** database, confidential. **Departments:** Publications. **Divisions:** African Regional Office; European Regional Office. **Programs:** Diflucan Partnership; Health and Human Rights; HIV Care Provider Advocacy; Physicians Sponsorship. **Absorbed:** (1995) Physicians Assoc. for AIDS Care. **Publications:** JIAPAC, quarterly. Journal. Contains clinical and social articles. **Price:** included in membership dues. ISSN: 1081-454X. **Circulation:** 9,000. **Advertising:** accepted. Alternate Formats: online ● Also

publishes IAPAC monthly AIDS public policy and medical conference coverage. **Conventions/Meetings:** annual Healthcare Resource Allocation for HIV/AIDS - international conference, promoting economic and ethical considerations in AIDS policy ● annual HIV Treatment Adherence - international conference.

15668 ■ International Association of Physicians and Health Care Professionals
PO Box 13089
Tallahassee, FL 32317
Ph: (850)878-3134
Fax: (850)878-1291
Contact: R.S. Rhinehart, Pres./CEO
Founded: 1996. **Members:** 85. **Membership Dues:** regular, $45 (annual). **Staff:** 2. **Budget:** $40,000. **Multinational. Description:** Serves as an organization for physicians and allied health care workers.

15669 ■ Islamic Medical Association of North America (IMANA)
101 W 22nd St., Ste.106
Lombard, IL 60148
Ph: (630)932-0000
Fax: (630)932-0005
E-mail: hq@imana.org
URL: http://www.imana.org
Contact: Sheik N. Hassan MD, Pres.
Founded: 1967. **Members:** 6,000. **Membership Dues:** resident, $30 (annual) ● life, $2,000 ● practicing physician, $200 (annual) ● nurse, allied health professional, $50 (annual) ● joint (husband and wife physicians), $300 (annual) ● joint life, $3,000. **Staff:** 5. **Budget:** $125,000. **Languages:** Arabic, Bengali, English. **Description:** Muslim physicians and allied health professionals. Unites Muslim physicians and allied health professionals in the U.S. and Canada for the improvement of professional and social contact; provides assistance to Muslim communities worldwide. Charitable programs include: donation of books, journals, and educational and research materials to medical institutions; donation of medical supplies and equipment to charity medical institutions in Muslim countries. Maintains speakers' bureau to present Islamic viewpoints on medical topics; sponsors placement service; offers assistance in orientation. **Awards: Type:** scholarship. **Computer Services:** database, Muslim physicians by special interest ● mailing lists ● online services. **Committees:** CME; Education; Ethics; Internship and Resident; Publications; Red Crescent; Scientific. **Formerly:** (2001) Islamic Medical Association. **Publications:** *IMANA News.* Newsletter. Alternate Formats: online ● *The Journal of IMA*, quarterly. **Price:** free for members; $50.00 /year for nonmembers in U.S. and Canada; $60.00 /year for nonmembers outside U.S. and Canada. **Circulation:** 2,500. **Advertising:** accepted. Alternate Formats: online. Also Cited As: *JIMA.* **Conventions/Meetings:** annual convention, accredited CME meeting (exhibits) ● Islamic Medicine - seminar - always April ● periodic meeting ● workshop.

15670 ■ National Association of Locum Tenens Organization (NALTO)
222 S Westmonte Dr., Ste.101
Altamonte Springs, FL 32714
Ph: (407)774-7880
Fax: (407)774-6440
E-mail: info@nalto.org
URL: http://www.nalto.org
Contact: David Baldridge, Pres.
Membership Dues: general, $475 (annual). **Description:** Promotes the interests of locum tenens physician industry. Educates the healthcare industry about the benefits of locum tenens staffing. Provides a forum for companies offering locum tenens services. **Publications:** Brochure. **Price:** $478.00 500 copies, plus shipping and handling; $544.00 1000 copies, plus shipping and handling.

15671 ■ National Association of Managed Care Physicians (NAMCP)
4435 Waterfront Dr., Ste.101
PO Box 4765
Glen Allen, VA 23058
Ph: (804)527-1905
Free: (800)722-0376
Fax: (804)747-5316
E-mail: info@namcp.com
URL: http://www.namcp.com
Contact: W.C. Williams III, Exec. VP
Founded: 1991. **Members:** 8,000. **Membership Dues:** associate, $300 (annual) ● physician, $195 (annual) ● student, $25 (annual) ● nurse, $50 (annual). **Staff:** 16. **Budget:** $750,000. **Description:** Licensed physicians and allied health professionals working in managed health care programs; medical residents and students interested in managed health care; corporations or agencies providing services or goods to the industry; interested others. Enhances the ability of practicing physicians to proactively participate within the managed health care arena through research, communication, and education. Provides a forum for members to communicate their concerns about the changing health care environment, integrate into managed health care delivery systems, and assure continuous improvement in the quality of health care services provided. Develops practice criteria, quality assurance measures, and appropriate utilization management criteria. Offers educational programs; maintains speakers' bureau and placement services; conducts research programs; develops informational clearinghouse. **Computer Services:** Online services, e-mail discussion groups. **Committees:** Education; Informatics; Medical Directors; Membership; Publications. **Publications:** *Managed Care Medicine*, bimonthly. Journal. **Price:** $95.00/year. **Circulation:** 30,000. **Advertising:** accepted. Alternate Formats: online ● *NAMCP Guide to Managed Care.* Monograph ● *Profiles*, quarterly. Newsletter. **Conventions/Meetings:** annual The Three P's Leadership Forum - conference (exhibits).

15672 ■ National Association of Physician Recruiters (NAPR)
222 S Westmonte Dr., Ste.101
Altamonte Springs, FL 32714
Ph: (407)774-7880
Free: (800)726-5613
Fax: (407)774-6440
E-mail: napr@napr.org
URL: http://www.napr.org
Contact: Bill Kautter CAE, Exec. VP
Founded: 1983. **Members:** 300. **Membership Dues:** active, $395-$1,595 (annual) ● institutional, $237 (annual) ● vendor, $465 (annual). **Staff:** 5. **Budget:** $280,000. **Description:** Physician search firms (companies that recruit resident physicians or practicing physicians to fill positions nationwide). Promotes a positive public image of physician recruiting services. Seeks to establish accreditation standards for the field. Provides marketing services to the physician recruiting industry. Maintains speakers' bureau. Sponsors educational programs and seminars. Compiles statistics. **Libraries: Type:** not open to the public. **Holdings:** articles. **Subjects:** physician recruiting. **Awards:** President's Award. **Frequency:** annual. **Type:** recognition. **Recipient:** for outstanding committee chairman. **Computer Services:** database, membership list. **Publications:** *NAPA Business Report (Newsletter)*, annual. Brochures. **Advertising:** accepted ● *NAPR Business Report*, quarterly. Newsletter. **Advertising:** accepted ● *NAPR Pulse.* Newsletter ● *Recruiter News.* Newsletter. Alternate Formats: online. **Conventions/Meetings:** annual conference (exhibits) ● annual convention ● annual Fly-In - conference and workshop.

15673 ■ National Association of VA Physicians and Dentists (NAVAPD)
PO Box 15458
Arlington, VA 22215-0458
Ph: (703)418-0723
Fax: (703)418-0724
E-mail: service@navapd.org
URL: http://www.navapd.org
Contact: Samuel V. Spagnolo MD, Pres.
Founded: 1975. **Members:** 2,000. **Membership Dues:** individual, $170 (annual). **Description:** Physicians and dentists at Department of Veterans Affairs Medical Centers. Strengthens and improves the quality of care and conditions at VA health care facilities. Works to assure that veterans receive quality care. **Publications:** *NAVAPD News*, bimonthly. Newsletter. Brings in-depth coverage of what is going on throughout the VA health care system as well as on Capitol Hill. **Price:** included in membership dues. **Circulation:** 2,000. **Advertising:** accepted ● *NAVAPD Notes*, bimonthly. **Conventions/Meetings:** annual meeting - always May.

15674 ■ National Commission on Human Life, Reproduction and Rhythm (NCHLRR)
PO Box 101501
Pittsburgh, PA 15237
Ph: (724)444-8045
Contact: Dr. Brian W. Donnelly MD, Sec.-Treas.
Founded: 1967. **Members:** 25. **Staff:** 3. **Budget:** $60,000. **Description:** Physicians united to strengthen the family unit and support traditional concepts of marriage, sex, and life. Encourages physicians to place more emphasis on personal attention to patients and less emphasis on the prescribing of medication; promotes pro-life values. Conducts scientific meetings dealing with subjects including: the role of the mother, particularly during her child's first three years; sex education; natural family planning; obstetric delivery; breastfeeding; abortion. Sponsors public meetings. **Libraries: Type:** not open to the public. **Publications:** *Child and Family*, quarterly. Journal. Contains scientific and philosophical articles in support of the traditional family. Consists primarily of reprinted material. **Price:** $12.00/year in U.S.; $16.00/year outside U.S. ISSN: 0009-3882. **Circulation:** 1,000 ● Also publishes reprint booklets. **Conventions/Meetings:** periodic meeting.

15675 ■ National Physicians Alliance (NPA)
1902 Assn. Dr., Ste.200
Reston, VA 20191
Ph: (703)254-8972
Fax: (703)620-5873
E-mail: npa@npalliance.org
URL: http://npalliance.org
Contact: David Evans MD, Contact
Membership Dues: resident/fellow, $60 (annual) ● physician, $120 (annual). **Description:** Advances the core values of the medical profession (service, integrity and advocacy). Works to improve health and well being, and to ensure equitable, affordable, high quality health care for all people. Seeks collaborative and creative solutions with other health professionals to protect and improve public health. **Publications:** *NPA News.* Newsletter. Contains up-to-date news on the organization's work. **Price:** included in membership dues. Alternate Formats: online ● Brochure.

15676 ■ National Physician's Association (NPA)
PO Box 35215
Chicago, IL 60707-0215
Ph: (708)453-0080
Fax: (708)453-0083
E-mail: npa@rentamark.com
Founded: 1975. **Members:** 89,741. **Membership Dues:** individual, $25 (annual) ● business, $100 (annual) ● corporate sponsor, $250 (annual). **Staff:** 10. **Description:** Physicians. Seeks to increase members' public visibility and professional influence. Provides trademark licensing and product and service endorsement services to support members' activities. Serves as a platform for doctors to find new patients and receive information about the latest healthcare "breakthroughs", and receive advice on healthcare matters. **Libraries: Type:** not open to the public. **Holdings:** 10,500. **Subjects:** medicine. **Awards:** Physician of the Year. **Frequency:** annual. **Type:** recognition. **Computer Services:** Mailing lists ● online services, product endorsements to support member benefits. **Publications:** *National Physicians Journal*, quarterly. Contains articles submitted by authors via email. **Price:** included in membership dues. **Circulation:** 100,000. **Advertising:** accepted. Alternate Formats: online. **Conventions/Meetings:** convention.

15677 ■ Society of Correctional Physicians (SCP)
1145 W Diversey Pkwy.
Chicago, IL 60614
Free: (800)229-7380
Fax: (773)880-2424
E-mail: scp@corrdocs.org
URL: http://www.corrdocs.org
Contact: Lynn F. Sander MD, Pres.
Founded: 1993. **Membership Dues:** regular, $100 (annual). **Description:** Provides a forum for the support, education, and professional development of physicians delivering healthcare in a correctional setting. Enrolls qualified correctional physicians in a national educational and scientific society. Encourages research in correctional health care issues. Reviews, promotes and establishes ethical ideals and service standards in correctional medicine. Supports, encourages and develops more humane and effective correctional environments and health services. **Awards:** Armond Start Award of Excellence. **Frequency:** annual. **Type:** recognition. **Recipient:** for members who have represented the highest of ideals in correctional medicine. **Publications:** *CorrDocs*, quarterly. Newsletter. Provides current information on Society activities and correctional medicine. **Price:** included in membership dues. Alternate Formats: online.

15678 ■ Thai Physicians Association of America
1350 Covington Ct.
Crown Point, IN 46307
Ph: (219)757-6077 (219)663-6330
Fax: (219)757-6261
E-mail: tvachir@yahoo.com
URL: http://www.tpaa.us
Contact: Thongchai Vachirasomboon MD, Pres.
Membership Dues: general, $50 (annual) ● life (age 50 or over), $250 ● life, $500. **Regional Groups:** 4. **Description:** Fosters measures for sustenance and advancement of health care delivery and education in the Thai community. Conducts medical missions in Thailand and other countries. **Committees:** Communication; Medical Education; Medical Mission. **Councils:** Educational.

15679 ■ World Federation of Doctors Who Respect Human Life (United States Section) (WFDRHL)
PO Box 101501
Pittsburgh, PA 15237
Ph: (724)444-8045
Contact: Dr. Brian W. Donnelly, Sec.-Treas.
Founded: 1976. **Members:** 1,400. **Description:** Physicians united to restore the "traditional Hippocratic medical position" through firm opposition to abortion, suicide, and direct euthanasia. Sponsors educational programs and seminars. **Affiliated With:** National Commission on Human Life, Reproduction and Rhythm. **Publications:** *Primum Non Nocere*, quarterly. Newsletter. **Conventions/Meetings:** periodic meeting.

Physics

15680 ■ American Association of Physicists in Medicine (AAPM)
One Physics Ellipse
College Park, MD 20740
Ph: (301)209-3350
Fax: (301)209-0862
E-mail: 2007.aapm@aapm.org
URL: http://www.aapm.org
Contact: Angela R. Keyser, Exec. Dir.
Founded: 1958. **Members:** 5,000. **Membership Dues:** full, associate, $285 (annual) ● junior, $200 (annual) ● student, $29 (annual) ● emeritus, $40 (annual). **Staff:** 20. **Budget:** $5,000,000. **Regional Groups:** 20. **Multinational. Description:** Persons professionally engaged in application of physics to medicine and biology in medical research and educational institutions; encourages interest and training in medical physics and related fields; pro-

motes high professional standards; disseminates technical information. Maintains placement service. Conducts research programs. Member society of American Institute of Physics (see separate entry). **Libraries: Type:** not open to the public. **Holdings:** 100; books, monographs, periodicals, reports. **Subjects:** medical physics: from acceptance testing to x-ray imaging. **Awards:** Farrington Daniels Award. **Frequency:** annual. **Type:** recognition. **Recipient:** for best article on Radiation Dosimetry published in *Medical Physics Journal* for the calendar year ● John R. Cameron Award. **Type:** recognition. **Recipient:** for best presentation by a Young Investigator for the calendar year ● Sylvia Sorkin Greenfield Award. **Frequency:** annual. **Type:** recognition. **Recipient:** for best paper published in *Medical Physics* Journal for the calendar year ● William D. Coolidge Award. **Frequency:** annual. **Type:** recognition. **Recipient:** for distinguished contributions to medical physics professions. **Computer Services:** Information services, homepage on the Net, medical physics info and organization info ● online services, membership application ● online services, membership directory ● online services, placement service. **Councils:** Education; Professional; Science. **Affiliated With:** American Institute of Physics; International Organization for Medical Physics. **Publications:** *Medical Physics*, monthly. Journal. Contains articles broadly concerned with the relationship of human biology and medicine. **Price:** included in membership dues; $300.00 for nonmembers in U.S.; $350.00 for nonmembers in Canada, Mexico, Central and South America. ISSN: 0094-2405. **Circulation:** 5,500. **Advertising:** accepted ● Membership Directory, annual. **Price:** free, for members only. **Advertising:** accepted. Alternate Formats: online. **Conventions/Meetings:** annual meeting, technical exhibition and scientific presentation (exhibits) - always summer. 2008 July 27-31, Houston, TX; 2009 July 26-30, Anaheim, CA; 2010 July 18-22, Philadelphia, PA.

15681 ■ American Board of Health Physics (ABHP)
1313 Dolley Madison Blvd., Ste.402
McLean, VA 22101
Ph: (703)790-1745
Fax: (703)790-2672
E-mail: njohnson@burkinc.com
URL: http://www.hps1.org/aahp/abhp/abhp.htm
Contact: Nancy J. Johnson, Exec. Sec.
Founded: 1960. **Members:** 8. **Description:** Certifying body. Promotes the health physics profession by establishing standards and procedures for certification and conducting certification examinations. Issues written proof of certification. **Conventions/Meetings:** annual conference.

15682 ■ American College of Medical Physics (ACMP)
12100 Sunset Hills Rd., Ste.130
Reston, VA 20190-5202
Ph: (703)481-5001
Fax: (703)435-4390
E-mail: acmp@acmp.org
URL: http://www.acmp.org
Contact: Laureen Rowland, Exec. Dir.
Founded: 1982. **Members:** 450. **Membership Dues:** provisional, $125 (annual) ● full, $250 (annual) ● trainee, $25 (annual). **Staff:** 2. **Regional Groups:** 9. **Description:** Focuses on socio-economic aspects of practice, management issues, reimbursement, licensure, and practice standards. **Awards:** ACMP Graduate Scholarship Award. **Frequency:** annual. **Type:** scholarship ● Marvin M.D. Williams Professional Achievement Award. **Frequency:** annual. **Type:** recognition. **Recipient:** to a member of the college who has made a significant contribution to the field of medical physics during his/her career. **Telecommunication Services:** electronic mail, lrowland@drohanmgmt.com. **Committees:** Continuing Education; Ethics; History; Journal Business Management; Meeting; Organizational Liaison; Reimbursement; Rules. **Publications:** *Diagnostic Radiology*. Report. **Price:** $25.00 for nonmembers ● *Magnetic Resonance Imaging*. Report. **Price:** $25.00 for nonmembers ● *Mammography*. Report. **Price:** $25.00 for

nonmembers ● *Medical Laser Systems*. Report. **Price:** $25.00 for nonmembers ● *Nuclear Medicine*. Report. **Price:** $25.00 for nonmembers ● *Radiation Oncology*. Report. **Price:** $25.00 for nonmembers ● Newsletter, 3-4/year ● Brochure. **Conventions/Meetings:** annual symposium and meeting (exhibits).

15683 ■ Health Physics Society (HPS)
1313 Dolley Madison Blvd., Ste.402
McLean, VA 22101
Ph: (703)790-1745
Fax: (703)790-2672
E-mail: hps@burkinc.com
URL: http://www.hps.org
Contact: Richard J. Burk Jr., Exec. Sec.
Founded: 1956. **Members:** 6,890. **Membership Dues:** fellow/plenary/associate, $105 (annual) ● emeritus/fellow, $30 (annual) ● affiliate, $500-$3,800 (annual) ● student, $10 (annual). **Staff:** 10. **Local Groups:** 41. **Description:** Persons engaged in some form of activity in the field of health physics (the profession devoted to radiation protection). Strives to improve public understanding of the problems and needs in radiation protection. Promotes health physics as a profession. Maintains Elda E. Anderson Memorial Fund to be used for teachers, researchers, and others. Provides placement service at annual meeting. Co-sponsors American Board of Health Physics (see separate entry) for certification of health physicists. **Committees:** Awards; Homeland Security; Nominating; Placement; Public Information; Rules; Standards; State and Federal Legislation. **Affiliated With:** National Academy of Sciences. **Publications:** *Health Physics Journal*, monthly. Contains refereed technical publications in the general field of radiation protection. Alternate Formats: online ● *Health Physics News*, monthly. Newsletter. **Price:** included in membership dues. **Advertising:** accepted ● *Membership Handbook*, annual. **Conventions/Meetings:** annual conference (exhibits) - always June or July. 2008 July.13-17, Pittsburgh, PA; 2009 July 12-16, Minneapolis, MN ● annual Midyear Topical - meeting (exhibits) - always January. 2008 Jan. 27-30, Oakland, CA ● annual symposium.

15684 ■ International Organization for Medical Physics (IOMP)
c/o Saiyid M. Shah, PhD, Corporate Liaison Off.
Evansville Cancer Center
706 N Burkhardt Rd.
Evansville, IN 47715-2740
Ph: (812)474-1110
Fax: (812)476-2917
E-mail: smshah@evcancntr.net
URL: http://www.iomp.org
Contact: Prof. Barry Allen PhD, Pres.
Founded: 1963. **Members:** 16,000. **Staff:** 5. **Budget:** $180,000. **Regional Groups:** 3. **State Groups:** 73. **Multinational. Description:** A member of the International Union of Physical and Engineering Sciences in Medicine (see separate entry). International organizations of medical physics representing 16,000 individuals. Fosters international cooperation in medical physics; promotes communication between various branches of medical physics and allied subjects. Conducts training programs. Has established 43 libraries in developing countries. **Awards:** Marie Sklodowska-Curie Award. **Frequency:** triennial. **Type:** recognition. **Committees:** Awards and Honors; Education and Training; Nominating; Professional Relations; Publications; Rules; Science. **Affiliated With:** American Association of Physicists in Medicine; International Council for Science; International Union of Pure and Applied Physics - USA. **Publications:** *Clinical Physics and Physiological Measurement*, semiannual. Newsletter. **Circulation:** 16,000. **Advertising:** accepted. Alternate Formats: online ● *Medical Physics World*, semiannual ● *Physics in Medicine and Biology*, monthly. **Conventions/Meetings:** congress, in developing countries ● international conference.

Physiology

15685 ■ American Society of Exercise Physiologists (ASEP)
c/o The College of St. Scholastica
1200 Kenwood Ave.
Duluth, MN 55811

Ph: (218)723-6297
E-mail: contact@asep.org
URL: http://www.asep.org
Contact: Tommy Boone PhD, Co-Founder/Board Member
Founded: 1997. **Membership Dues:** professional, $80 (annual) ● certified professional, fellow, $70 (annual) ● affiliate, international, $100 (annual) ● student, $40 (annual). **Regional Groups:** 4. **State Groups:** 9. **Description:** Works for the advancement of exercise physiologists. Promotes the exchange of scientific information between organizations interested in health promotion, disease prevention, rehabilitation, sports fitness and athlete training. **Computer Services:** Information services, exercise physiology resources ● online services, public forum. **Boards:** Accreditation. **Committees:** Licensure; Public Education; Research. **Publications:** Newsletter, quarterly ● Journal, monthly. Alternate Formats: online ● Membership Directory.

Pituitary

15686 ■ Human Growth Foundation (HGF)
997 Glen Cove Ave., Ste.5
Glen Head, NY 11545-1584
Free: (800)451-6434
Fax: (516)671-4055
E-mail: hgf1@hgfound.org
URL: http://www.hgfound.org
Contact: Patricia D. Costa, Exec. Dir.
Founded: 1965. **Members:** 1,000. **Membership Dues:** family, $35 (annual) ● supporting, $50 (annual) ● patron/institutional, $200 (annual) ● century club (personal), $1,000 (annual) ● century club (corporate), $1,500 (annual). **Staff:** 3. **National Groups:** 30. **Languages:** English, Spanish. **Description:** Families of children with physical growth problems, adults with growth hormone deficiency, and interested persons united to help medical science better understand the process of growth. Distributes money for basic and clinical growth research. Disseminates informative literature and presents educational programs to families and physicians. **Formerly:** (1971) Human Growth. **Publications:** Fourth Friday, quarterly. Newsletter. **Price:** included in membership dues ● Growing UP. Book. Features topics about kid's growth and other related concerns. **Price:** $4.50 each. **Conventions/Meetings:** annual conference.

15687 ■ National Hormone and Pituitary Program (NHPP)
Harbor - UCLA Medical Ctr.
1000 W Carson St.
Torrance, CA 90509
Ph: (310)222-3537
Fax: (310)222-3432
E-mail: parlow@humc.edu
URL: http://www.humc.edu/hormones
Contact: Dr. A.F. Parlow, Scientific Dir.
Founded: 1963. **Staff:** 4. **Description:** Collects human pituitary glands obtained through autopsies and extracts from the human Growth Hormone (hGH), human Follicle Stimulating Hormone (hFSH), human Luteinizing Hormone (hLH), human Adrenocorticotrophic Hormone (ACTH), human Thyroid Stimulating Hormone (hTSH), human prolactin, and beta-lipotropin. These and similar hormones of rat, ovine, bovine, porcine, and monkey origin are distributed to doctors in research centers for research in endocrinology. Promotes basic studies with all pituitary hormones and seeks to make these available to investigators. **Formerly:** (1983) National Pituitary Agency. **Conventions/Meetings:** annual meeting, with advisory board meeting.

15688 ■ Pituitary Network Association (PNA)
PO Box 1958
Thousand Oaks, CA 91358
Ph: (805)499-9973
Fax: (805)480-0633

E-mail: pna@pituitary.org
URL: http://www.pituitary.org
Contact: Robert Knutzen, Chm./CEO
Founded: 1992. **Members:** 5,000. **Membership Dues:** regular, $45 (annual) ● sponsor, $200 (annual) ● physician, psychiatry, $295 (annual) ● life, $500 ● patron, $100 (annual) ● mental health professional, $150 (annual). **Staff:** 4. **Budget:** $300,000. **Regional Groups:** 8. **State Groups:** 4. **National Groups:** 4. **Languages:** English, Norwegian, Spanish. **Description:** Patients supplying information to other patients, families and health care professionals. Publishes books and news magazines on pituitary issues. **Libraries: Type:** not open to the public. **Holdings:** 150. **Subjects:** pituitary and hormones. **Awards:** Gentle Giant Award. **Frequency:** annual. **Type:** recognition. **Recipient:** to an individual or entity for distinguished contribution in field of pituitary/endocrine medicine. **Computer Services:** Information services, Referral Program. **Formerly:** (1993) PTNA; (2002) Pituitary Tumor Network Association. **Publications:** Handbook of Acromegaly ● NETWORK Magazine, quarterly ● Pituitary Patient Resource Guide, biennial. Book. Contains information for pituitary patients, families, physicians, and all health care providers. **Price:** $39.95 for members; $49.95 for nonmembers. **Circulation:** 10,000. **Advertising:** accepted ● PNA Newsletter, monthly. **Conventions/Meetings:** Awareness Days - conference and convention - 4-6/year ● annual Gentle Giant Award Dinner.

Podiatry

15689 ■ Academy of Ambulatory Foot and Ankle Surgery (AAFS)
1601 Walnut, Ste.1005
Philadelphia, PA 19102
Ph: (215)569-3303
Free: (800)433-4892
Fax: (215)569-3310
E-mail: jasp@arnet.com.ar
URL: http://www.academy-afs.org
Contact: Dr. Borys Markewych, Pres.
Founded: 1972. **Members:** 1,500. **Membership Dues:** full/associate, $395 (annual) ● international, $245 (annual) ● fellow, $395 (annual). **Description:** Physicians who advocate performing foot and ankle surgery in their offices or on an outpatient basis, thereby keeping patients ambulatory and able to function normally, and lowering the patients' medical costs. Promotes the advancement of foot and ankle surgical procedures that can eliminate the necessity of hospital admission. Sponsors national and regional continuing medical education seminars and semiannual research program. Compiles statistics. **Awards: Type:** recognition. **Committees:** Convention; Faculty; International; International Scientific; Internet; Office Accreditation; Peer Review; Scientific & Exhibitor. **Publications:** Ask the Doc. Newsletter ● Journal of the Academy of Ambulatory Foot Surgery, periodic ● Directory, periodic. **Conventions/Meetings:** annual meeting (exhibits).

15690 ■ American Academy of Podiatric Practice Management (AAPPM)
10 Maple St., Ste.301
Middleton, MA 01949
Ph: (978)646-9091
Fax: (978)646-9092
E-mail: office@aappm.org
URL: http://www.aappm.com
Contact: Gary W. Adams, Exec. Dir.
Founded: 1961. **Members:** 750. **Membership Dues:** active, $269 (annual) ● associate, $169 (annual) ● assistant, $139 (annual) ● resident, $89 (annual). **Staff:** 3. **Description:** Doctors of podiatric medicine interested in practice administration. Works to standardize office management procedures to create more efficient podiatry practices; develops formalized procedures for obtaining and training podiatry office assistants. Disseminates pedal information and material on practice management. Investigates methods of delivering improved podiatric care to an increasing

number of patients; seeks effective participation in the public health team. Sponsors seminars and workshops. **Affiliated With:** American Podiatric Medical Association. **Formerly:** (1969) American Academy of Practice Management in Podiatry; (1970) American Academy of Podiatric Management; (1993) American Academy Podiatric Administration. **Publications:** AAPPM News, quarterly. Newsletter. **Conventions/Meetings:** quarterly convention (exhibits).

15691 ■ American Association of Colleges of Podiatric Medicine (AACPM)
15850 Crabbs Br. Way, Ste.320
Rockville, MD 20855
Ph: (301)948-9760
Free: (800)922-9266
Fax: (301)948-1928
E-mail: info@aacpm.org
URL: http://www.aacpm.org
Contact: Moraith G. North, Exec. Dir.
Founded: 1932. **Members:** 8. **Staff:** 8. **Budget:** $700,000. **Description:** Represents U.S. colleges of podiatric medicine and institutions that sponsor graduate podiatric medical training programs. Provides vocational guidance material for secondary schools and colleges. Conducts public affairs activities and legislative advocacy. **Programs:** Central Application Service for Podiatric Residencies; Enrollment Management Services. **Affiliated With:** American Podiatric Medical Association. **Formerly:** American Association of Colleges of Chiropody; (1970) American Association of Colleges of Podiatry. **Conventions/Meetings:** periodic meeting, meetings of the board and "fly-in" meetings.

15692 ■ American Association of Hospital Podiatrists (AAHP)
c/o Frank Rinaldi, Exec. Dir.
8508 18th Ave.
Brooklyn, NY 11214
Ph: (718)259-1822
Fax: (718)259-4002
E-mail: info@hospitalpodiatrists.org
URL: http://www.hospitalpodiatrists.org
Contact: Frank Rinaldi, Exec. Dir.
Founded: 1950. **Members:** 800. **Membership Dues:** general, $50 (annual) ● student, $15 (annual). **Description:** A general specialty group of the American Podiatric Medical Association (see separate entry). Podiatrists (trained and certified persons dealing in the care and diseases of the foot) who are affiliated with hospitals. Seeks to: elevate the standards of podiatry practices in hospitals and health institutions; standardize hospital podiatry procedures, charting, recording forms, and methods; promote understanding among personnel in podiatry, medicine, and allied health professions; aid podiatrists in attaining institutional affiliations; assist in the educational and teaching programs of health institutions and hospitals; foster the development of podiatric internships and residencies in hospitals and institutions. Compiles statistics. **Committees:** Charts and Records; Grievance and Ethics; Hospital Protocol; Internship and Residencies. **Publications:** The Hospital Podiatrist, annual ● Newsletter, annual. **Conventions/Meetings:** annual meeting, in conjunction with APMA.

15693 ■ American Association for Women Podiatrists (AAWP)
c/o Kathleen Satterfield, DPM, Pres.
138 Dresden Wood
Boerne, TX 78006
Ph: (830)229-5444
E-mail: vksatterfielddpm@aol.com
URL: http://www.aawpinc.org
Contact: Kathleen Satterfield DPM, Pres.
Founded: 1965. **Members:** 997. **Membership Dues:** active, $80 (annual) ● associate, $30 (annual) ● friend, $175 (annual) ● life, $750. **Staff:** 1. **Budget:** $50,000. **Regional Groups:** 14. **Description:** Promotes the advancement of the educational, political, financial and social well-being of members. Provides networking opportunities, consulting and financial assistance to student members. Maintains Speaker's Bureau. **Libraries: Type:** reference. **Holdings:** archival material, articles, audiovisuals, business

records, clippings. **Subjects:** women, business, podiatry. **Awards:** Founders Scholarship. **Frequency:** annual. **Type:** scholarship. **Recipient:** for female student member of AAWP. **Computer Services:** Mailing lists. **Boards:** Executive. **Committees:** Membership; Publicity. **Publications:** *AAWP Newsletter*, quarterly. **Price:** included in membership dues; free to students. **Circulation:** 1,850. **Advertising:** accepted. **Conventions/Meetings:** biennial Educational Seminar - board meeting, with spa (exhibits) ● annual meeting.

15694 ■ American Board of Lower Extremities Surgery

6421 Inkster Rd., Ste.102
Bloomfield Hills, MI 48301
Ph: (248)855-7740
Fax: (248)855-7743
E-mail: accpps1@juno.com
Contact: Howard L. Lazar DPM, Exec. Dir.

Founded: 1982. **Members:** 650. **Staff:** 7. **Description:** Promotes the profession of podiatric medicine and surgery. Gains equal acceptance for all podiatrists by hospitals and managed care organizations. **Libraries: Type:** not open to the public. **Holdings:** 350. **Subjects:** Federal and Michigan podiatry and law. **Computer Services:** database ● mailing lists. **Formerly:** (2006) American Council of Certified Podiatric Physicians and Surgeons. **Conventions/Meetings:** semiannual meeting (exhibits) - always spring and fall ● annual seminar (exhibits) - April or May.

15695 ■ American Board of Multiple Specialties in Podiatry

1350 Broadway, Ste.1705
New York, NY 10018
Ph: (212)356-0690
Free: (888)852-1442
Fax: (212)356-0678
E-mail: msp@ptcny.com
URL: http://www.abmsp.org
Contact: Leonard Feigenblatt, Admin.

Founded: 1986. **Members:** 700. **Staff:** 2. **Budget:** $235,500. **Description:** Seeks to insure high standards of training, ethics, and practice in the field of podiatric medicine, podiatric surgery and the prevention and treatment of diabetic foot wounds. Facilitates professional advancement of members. **Computer Services:** database, membership ● mailing lists, membership. **Formerly:** (2000) American Podiatric Multiple Specialties Board; (2004) American Board of Medical Specialties in Podiatry. **Publications:** Newsletter, periodic ● Directory, annual ● Brochure, periodic. **Conventions/Meetings:** board meeting - 2-3/year.

15696 ■ American Board of Podiatric Orthopedics and Primary Podiatric Medicine (ABPOPPM)

3812 Sepulvada Blvd., Ste.530
Torrance, CA 90505
Ph: (310)375-0700
Fax: (310)375-1386
E-mail: admin@abpoppm.org
URL: http://www.abpoppm.org
Contact: Marc A. Benard DPM, Exec. Dir.

Founded: 1975. **Members:** 3,000. **Membership Dues:** board qualified, $175 (annual) ● board certified, $250 (annual). **Staff:** 3. **Budget:** $750,000. **Description:** Podiatrists who have taken a competency exam prepared by the board. Offers certifying examinations in podiatric orthopedics and primary podiatric medicine aims at improving public health by encouraging and elevating standards for practicing podiatrics. **Committees:** Credentials; Examinations. **Affiliated With:** American Podiatric Medical Association. **Formerly:** American Board of Podiatric Orthopedics; (2003) American Board of Podiatric Orthopedics and Primary Medicine. **Publications:** *Directory of Diplomates*, annual. Membership Directory. Includes alphabetical and geographical listing of members. **Price:** free ● Newsletter, semiannual. **Price:** included in membership dues. **Conventions/Meetings:** annual meeting, held in conjunction with the American Podiatric Medical Association - usually in August.

15697 ■ American Board of Podiatric Surgery (ABPS)

c/o James A. Lamb, Exec. Dir.
445 Fillmore St.
San Francisco, CA 94117-3404
Ph: (415)553-7800
Fax: (415)553-7801
E-mail: info@abps.org
URL: http://www.abps.org
Contact: James A. Lamb, Exec. Dir.

Founded: 1975. **Members:** 5,800. **Membership Dues:** diplomate, $280 (annual) ● board qualified, $125 (annual). **Staff:** 10. **Budget:** $2,860,000. **Description:** Podiatrists certified as diplomates. Protects and improves public health by advancing the science of foot surgery and by encouraging the study and evaluation of standards of foot surgery. Acts upon application for certification of legally licensed podiatrists to ascertain their competency in foot surgery. Grants certificates to candidates who have met all qualifications. **Computer Services:** Online services, applications, verifications, member services. **Affiliated With:** American Podiatric Medical Association. **Publications:** Membership Directory. **Price:** $150.00/item. Alternate Formats: CD-ROM. **Conventions/Meetings:** annual meeting - always February.

15698 ■ American College of Foot and Ankle Orthopedics and Medicine (ACFAOM)

5272 River Rd., Ste.630
Bethesda, MD 20816
Ph: (301)718-6505
Free: (800)265-8263
Fax: (301)656-0989
E-mail: info@acfaom.org
URL: http://www.acfaom.org
Contact: Norman Wallis PhD, Exec. Dir.

Founded: 1949. **Members:** 1,300. **Membership Dues:** student, $15 (annual) ● resident, $50 (annual) ● associate/fellow, $350 (annual). **Staff:** 3. **Budget:** $350,000. **Description:** Professional society of podiatrists sanctioned as specialists to practice foot orthopedics (deformities and diseases of bones, joints, and muscles of the foot) and primary podiatric medicine. **Awards:** Timothy Holbrook Awards. **Frequency:** annual. **Type:** recognition. **Recipient:** for clinical and academic excellence. **Committees:** Education and Scientific Affairs; Executive; Membership Services; Nominating; Publicity and Government/Political Affairs; Student Liaison. **Affiliated With:** American Podiatric Medical Association. **Formerly:** (1993) American CLG of Foot Orthopedists. **Publications:** *ACFAOM News*, quarterly. Newsletter. **Price:** included in membership dues; $5.00 for nonmembers. **Circulation:** 1,300 ● *Review Text in Podiatric Orthopedics and Primary Podiatric Medicine*. Book. **Price:** $149.00 each; $99.00 each, for students. **Conventions/Meetings:** annual conference (exhibits) - always August ● annual seminar.

15699 ■ American College of Foot and Ankle Pediatrics (ACFAP)

Address Unknown since 2007

Founded: 1977. **Members:** 200. **Membership Dues:** individual, $50 (annual) ● $15 (annual). **Staff:** 1. **Description:** Podiatric physicians and surgeons, general physicians and surgeons, psychologists, and physical therapists. Seeks to bring together all professionals interested in children's foot health. Goals are to: disseminate information; consider all forms of therapy of value in foot and ankle pediatrics; bring to all those interested the most advanced and valuable forms of therapy through publications, seminars, and research sessions; establish teaching courses on foot and ankle pediatrics so that more podiatric students will consider specializing in the field. Encourages individual research projects; maintains speakers' bureau. **Awards: Type:** recognition. **Recipient:** for outstanding practitioner. **Affiliated With:** American Podiatric Medical Association. **Formerly:** (1993) American College of Podopediatrics. **Publications:** *ACP Abstracts*, bimonthly. Newsletter ● Newsletter, annual. **Conventions/Meetings:** annual Pediatric Foot and Ankle Disorders - seminar.

15700 ■ American College of Foot and Ankle Surgeons (ACFAS)

8725 W Higgins Rd., Ste.555
Chicago, IL 60631-2724
Ph: (773)693-9300
Free: (800)421-2237
Fax: (773)693-9304
E-mail: info@acfas.org
URL: http://www.acfas.org
Contact: J.C. Mahaffey CAE, Exec. Dir.

Founded: 1942. **Members:** 5,600. **Membership Dues:** resident, $105 (annual) ● fellow/associate, $490 (annual). **Staff:** 15. **Budget:** $4,200,000. **Regional Groups:** 14. **Description:** Promotes and disseminates information on podiatric surgery among the public, podiatric surgeons, and other health professionals; encourage and publish research findings and related literature; provide intensive programs for clinical and experimental research to improve podiatric surgery and to promote its members' professional and socioeconomic activities. **Awards:** Abstract Award. **Frequency:** annual. **Type:** monetary ● Journal Article Award. **Frequency:** annual. **Type:** monetary ● Research Award. **Frequency:** annual. **Type:** monetary. **Affiliated With:** American Podiatric Medical Association. **Formerly:** (1993) American College of Foot Surgeons. **Publications:** *Current Trends in the Management of Foot and Ankle Infections*. Monographs. Features collections of reference tools about foot and ankle infections. ● *Journal of Foot and Ankle Surgery*, bimonthly. Includes book reviews and journal abstracts. **Price:** included in membership dues; $130.00 /year for nonmembers in U.S.; $171.00 /year for nonmembers outside U.S. ISSN: 0449-2544. Alternate Formats: microform ● *Membership Roster*, annual. Membership Directory ● *Update*, bimonthly. Newsletter. **Price:** included in membership dues. **Advertising:** accepted. Alternate Formats: online. **Conventions/Meetings:** annual meeting and convention, includes scientific seminar and expo (exhibits).

15701 ■ American College of Podiatric Medical Review (ACPMR)

c/o Dr. Craig Gastwirth, DPM, Sec.-Treas.
3800 Woodward Ave., Ste.318
Detroit, MI 48201-2066
Ph: (313)833-3091
E-mail: cmgfootdr@pol.net
URL: http://www.acpmr.org
Contact: Dr. Craig Gastwirth DPM, Sec.-Treas.

Members: 60. **Membership Dues:** individual, $165 (annual). **Budget:** $5,000. **Description:** Licensed podiatric professionals. Works to elevate standards, improve education, standardize guidelines, and develop universal methods for peer and claims review. Acts as clearinghouse and liaison for the podiatric medical profession, the public and government agencies.

15702 ■ American Podiatric Circulatory Society (APCS)

c/o Dr. Stanley Goldstein, Pres.
5704 18th Ave.
Brooklyn, NY 11204
Ph: (718)236-7952
Fax: (718)236-7953
E-mail: goldsteinopm@att.net
Contact: Dr. Stanley Goldstein, Pres.

Founded: 1979. **Members:** 900. **Membership Dues:** individual, $35 (annual). **Description:** Podiatrists. Disseminates information on the Suffuse Osmotic Chemisorb Asphyxiation (SOCA) therapy, now known as the Tereno Method, devised by Dr. Isaac Tereno for treatment of geriatric patients suffering from arterial blockage in their limbs. (The Tereno Method uses vitamins to enrich the blood and enlarge subcutaneous capillaries and lymph vessels, thus creating an alternate circulatory network, which bypasses blocked arteries. It is an alternative to major surgery and/or amputation in geriatric patients with poor circulation in their limbs.) Conducts research; maintains speakers' bureau. **Awards: Type:** recognition. **Publications:** *American Podiatric Circulatory Society Bulletin*, quarterly. Contains case studies of patients treated using the Tereno Method. **Circulation:** 1,000.

Advertising: accepted. Conventions/Meetings: annual Wound Care - conference (exhibits).

15703 ■ American Podiatric Medical Association (APMA)
9312 Old Georgetown Rd.
Bethesda, MD 20814-1621
Ph: (301)571-9200
Free: (800)FOOTCARE
Fax: (301)530-2752
E-mail: gbgastwirth@apma.org
URL: http://www.apma.org
Contact: Glenn B. Gastwirth DPM, Exec. Dir.
Founded: 1912. Members: 11,500. Staff: 53. Budget: $6,770,000. State Groups: 53. Description: Serves as professional society of doctors of podiatric medicine. Awards: Journalism Award. Frequency: annual. Type: recognition. Committees: Appeals and Control; Governmental/Federal Health Policy; Graduate Educational Assistance; International Relations; Liaison on Podiatric Medical Education and Practice; Membership and Student Liaison; National Data Base; Physicians' Recovery Network; Podiatric Seals; Podiatry Political Action; Public Affairs and Professional Information; Public Health and Preventive Podiatric Medicine. Councils: Podiatric Medical Education. Formerly: (1958) National Association of Chiropodists; (1984) American Podiatry Association. Publications: APMA News, monthly. Magazine. Includes calendar of events, research updates, and statistics. Price: included in membership dues; $50.00 /year for nonmembers. ISSN: 8750-2585. Circulation: 12,500. Advertising: accepted ● Desk Reference of the APMA, annual ● Journal of the American Podiatric Medical Association, monthly. Price: included in membership dues; $90.00 for nonmembers. ISSN: 0003-0538. Circulation: 14,500. Advertising: accepted ● Brochures. Price: free for members ● Also publishes foot health literature. Conventions/Meetings: annual Scientific Seminar (exhibits).

15704 ■ American Podiatric Medical Students' Association (APMSA)
9312 Old Georgetown Rd.
Bethesda, MD 20814
Ph: (301)493-9667
E-mail: apmsadcm@apma.org
URL: http://www.apmsa.org
Contact: Dorothy Cahill McDonald, Exec. Dir.
Founded: 1954. Members: 2,000. Staff: 1. Description: Podiatric medical students enrolled at seven podiatric schools in the U.S. Works to represent the interests of podiatric medical students in legislative, professional, and educational programs. Cosponsors seminars and writing contests. Compiles statistics. Formerly: American Podiatric Students Association. Publications: First Step, quarterly. Newsletter ● Graduation Handbook, annual. Serves as a reference guide. Conventions/Meetings: semiannual conference, held in conjunction with American Podiatric Medical Association - always summer and winter. 2009 Aug., Washington, DC ● annual Midwest Podiatry Conference - 2008 Mar. 27-30, Chicago, IL; 2009 Apr. 2-5, Chicago, IL.

15705 ■ American Podiatric Medical Writers Association (APMWA)
PO Box 750129
Forest Hills, NY 11375
Ph: (718)897-9700
Fax: (718)896-5747
E-mail: bblock@prodigy.net
Contact: Dr. Barry H. Block, Exec. Dir.
Founded: 1985. Members: 100. Membership Dues: podiatrist, $50 ● non-podiatrist, $25. Staff: 2. Budget: $26,000. Description: Podiatric medical writers. Promotes the improvement of writing on podiatric topics. Awards: Golden Quill Award. Frequency: annual. Type: recognition ● Type: recognition ● Student Writing Award. Frequency: annual. Type: monetary. Publications: American Podiatric Medical Writers Association—Membership Directory, annual. Price: free. Circulation: 100. Advertising: accepted ● American Podiatric Medical Writers Association—Newsletter, quarterly. Lists new members. Price:

free; provide self-addressed stamped envelope. Circulation: 100. Advertising: accepted. Conventions/Meetings: semiannual conference (exhibits) - always February and August ● seminar, on writing.

15706 ■ American Society of Podiatric Medical Assistants (ASPMA)
2124 S Austin Blvd.
Cicero, IL 60804
Ph: (708)863-6303
Free: (888)88ASPMA
E-mail: aspmaex@aol.com
URL: http://www.aspma.org
Contact: Sandra Lohrentz PMAC, Exec. Dir.
Founded: 1964. Members: 1,350. Membership Dues: individual, $69 (annual). Staff: 12. Budget: $30,000. Regional Groups: 14. State Groups: 12. Description: Represents podiatric assistants. Holds educational seminars and administers certification examinations. Libraries: Type: reference. Holdings: archival material. Awards: Type: scholarship ● Zelda W. Vicha Memorial Scholarship Fund. Type: scholarship. Recipient: for academic standing based on financial need. Computer Services: Mailing lists. Committees: Focus Forward; Qualifying and Examining. Affiliated With: American Podiatric Medical Association. Publications: Journal of the American Society of Podiatric Medical Assistants, quarterly. Price: free for members. Circulation: 1,350. Advertising: accepted. Conventions/Meetings: annual meeting, education sessions - always August ● annual seminar.

15707 ■ American Society of Podiatrists and Chiropractors (ASPC)
PO Box 35215
Chicago, IL 60707-0215
Ph: (708)453-0080
Fax: (708)453-0083
E-mail: aspc@rentamark.com
URL: http://www.rentamark.com/aspc
Contact: L. Stroller, Contact
Founded: 1975. Members: 58,989. Membership Dues: individual, $25 (annual) ● business, $100 (annual) ● corporate sponsor, $250 (annual). Staff: 10. Description: Podiatrists and chiropractors. Seeks to increase members' public visibility and professional influence. Provides trademark licensing and product and service endorsement services to support members' activities. Serves as a platform to network Podiatrists and Chiropractors with patients on the net. Libraries: Type: not open to the public. Holdings: 10,601. Subjects: podiatry and chiropractory. Awards: Doctor of the Year. Frequency: annual. Type: recognition. Computer Services: Mailing lists, Ad banner (468X60 pixel), product endorsements to support member benefits. Publications: Journal. Contains information on the association. Price: included in membership dues. Circulation: 100,000. Advertising: accepted. Alternate Formats: online. Conventions/Meetings: annual convention (exhibits).

15708 ■ Council on Podiatric Medical Education (CPME)
9312 Old Georgetown Rd.
Bethesda, MD 20814-1621
Ph: (301)581-9200
Fax: (301)571-4903
E-mail: sbsaylor@apma.org
URL: http://www.cpme.org
Contact: Alan R. Tinkleman MPA, Dir.
Founded: 1918. Members: 11. Staff: 7. Budget: $670,000. Description: Accrediting agency for colleges of podiatric medicine, podiatric residency programs and continuing education programs in podiatry. Conducts in-service training programs for members engaged in accrediting activities. Committees: Accreditation; Continuing Education; Joint Residency Review; Specialty Boards. Affiliated With: American Podiatric Medical Association. Formerly: (1984) Council on Podiatry Education. Publications: Council on Podiatric Medical Education—Annual Report ● Standards and Requirements for Accreditation ● Also publishes lists of accredited institutions and approved programs.

15709 ■ Federation of Podiatric Medical Boards (FPMB)
6551 Malta Dr.
Boynton Beach, FL 33437
Ph: (561)752-3735
E-mail: fpmb@fpmb.org
URL: http://www.fpmb.org
Contact: Larry I. Shane, Exec. Dir.
Founded: 1936. Members: 45. State Groups: 52. Description: State boards of podiatry examiners. Goals are to: serve as a repository for information relating to common problems among boards of podiatry examiners; promote competency examinations with national standards to be utilized by examining boards; monitor and catalog legislation pertaining to podiatry. Conducts business sessions and educational programs on topics concerning the licensure and regulation of health professions. Compiles statistics. Computer Services: database, disciplinary data file ● online services, score reports for state podiatric medical licensing examinations. Formerly: (1985) Federation of Podiatry Boards; (1986) Federation of Podiatry Medical Boards. Publications: Disciplinary Data Reports, semiannual. Conventions/Meetings: annual meeting.

15710 ■ Fund for Podiatric Medical Education (FPME)
c/o American Podiatric Medical Association
9312 Old Georgetown Rd.
Bethesda, MD 20814
Ph: (301)581-9200
Fax: (301)530-2752
E-mail: askapma@apma.org
URL: http://www.apma.org
Founded: 1959. Nonmembership. Description: Open to all People who wish to join. Offers financial support to third and fourth year podiatric medical students. Awards scholarships. Awards: Frequency: annual. Type: scholarship. Recipient: to third and fourth year podiatric medical students with highest financial and academic qualifications.

15711 ■ International Federation of Foot and Ankle Societies (IFFAS)
6300 N River Rd., Ste.510
Rosemont, IL 60018
Ph: (847)698-4654
Fax: (847)692-3315
E-mail: iffas@globalfoot.org
URL: http://www.globalfoot.org
Contact: Lousanne Lofgren CAE, Exec. Dir.
Founded: 1999. Multinational. Description: Seeks to bring together all foot and ankle organizations around the world. Promotes the development of foot and ankle surgery. Initiates, promotes and develops international scientific relations between students of the foot. Develops and spreads knowledge about all aspects of anatomy, physiology and pathology of the foot. Aims to advance education, study and research in the foot and ankle surgery specialty. Telecommunication Services: electronic mail, zlofgren@globalfoot.org. Publications: Brochure. Alternate Formats: online. Conventions/Meetings: triennial meeting - 2008 Sept. 18-20, Salvador, BH, Brazil.

15712 ■ National Board of Podiatric Medical Examiners (NBPME)
PO Box 510
Bellefonte, PA 16823
Ph: (814)357-0487
Fax: (814)357-0581
E-mail: nbpmeofc@aol.com
URL: http://www.nbpme.com
Contact: Robert A. Christman MEd, Pres.
Founded: 1956. Members: 12. Staff: 2. Description: Professional podiatrists. Prepares and administers examinations for podiatry students seeking state licensure. Monitors test validity and reliability. Committees: Testing. Affiliated With: American Association of Colleges of Podiatric Medicine; American Podiatric Medical Association. Formerly: (1985) National Board of Podiatry Examiners. Publications: Annual Report, annual ● Bulletin, annual ● Membership Directory, annual. Conventions/Meetings: semiannual board meeting.

15713 ■ National Podiatric Medical Association (NPMA)
1706 E 87th St.
Chicago, IL 60617
Ph: (773)374-5300
Fax: (773)374-5860
E-mail: npmadebby@sbcglobal.net
URL: http://www.npmaonline.org
Contact: Debby Burton, Exec. Dir.

Founded: 1971. **Members:** 200. **Membership Dues:** individual, $300 (annual) ● retired practitioner, $50 (annual) ● guild, $100 (annual) ● life, $1,500. **Staff:** 3. **Description:** Minority podiatrists, predominantly black. Promotes the science and art of podiatry. Seeks to: improve public health; raise the standards of the podiatric profession and education; stimulate a favorable relationship between all podiatrists; nurture growth and diffusion of podiatric information; stimulate public education concerning public health and features of podiatric medicine. Sponsors proposal of podiatric laws; works to eliminate religious and racial discrimination and segregation in American medical institutions. **Formerly:** (1987) National Podiatry Association. **Publications:** *Annual Seminar Ad Book*, annual ● *National Podiatric Medical Association— Newsletter*, annual. Includes calendar of events and news from student-affiliated associations. **Price:** included in membership dues. **Circulation:** 450. **Advertising:** accepted. **Conventions/Meetings:** annual conference - usually March or April.

Polio

15714 ■ International Post Polio Support Organization (IPPSO)
6901 Old Stage Rd., No. 3
Central Point, OR 97502
Ph: (541)664-4348
Fax: (541)664-4348
E-mail: president@ippso-world.org
URL: http://www.ippso-world.org
Contact: Harald Hasle, Pres./Co-Founder

Founded: 2001. **Membership Dues:** regular, $15 (annual). **Multinational. Description:** Provides assistance to persons suffering from post polio syndrome, their families and friends. Guides patients in the purchase and/or acquisition of physical support devices, medical treatment for post polio syndrome, and assistance in their application for disability. Educates the public and the medical community about the effects, symptoms, possible treatment and places to obtain treatment for post polio syndrome. **Publications:** *IPPSO Online Magazine*. Alternate Formats: online.

Preventive Medicine

15715 ■ American Association for Health Freedom
PO Box 458
Great Falls, VA 22066
Ph: (703)294-6244
Free: (800)230-2762
Fax: (703)294-6380
E-mail: healthfreedom2000@yahoo.com
URL: http://www.healthfreedom.net
Contact: Brenna Hill, Exec. Dir.

Founded: 1992. **Members:** 500. **Membership Dues:** consumer, $20 (annual) ● healthcare professional, $350 (annual) ● corporate sponsor, $6,000 (annual). **Staff:** 4. **Budget:** $450,000. **Description:** Strives to promote health care freedom. Protects practitioners through complementary and alternative therapies. **Awards:** Benjamin Rush Award. **Frequency:** annual. **Type:** recognition. **Recipient:** for an individual who has shown true dedication in achieving health care freedom. **Computer Services:** Mailing lists. **Formerly:** (2002) American Preventive Medical Association. **Publications:** *Eye on Health Freedom*, monthly. Newsletter.

15716 ■ American Board of Preventive Medicine (ABPM)
330 S Wells St., Ste.1018
Chicago, IL 60606-7106
Ph: (312)939-2276
Fax: (312)939-2218
E-mail: abpm@abprevmed.org
URL: http://www.abprevmed.org
Contact: James M. Vanderploeg MD, Exec. Dir.

Founded: 1948. **Members:** 11. **Staff:** 3. **Description:** Determines requirements, administers examinations, and certifies qualified physicians in the specialty areas of public health and general preventive medicine, aerospace medicine, occupational medicine and in the subspecialty areas of medical toxicology and undersea and hyperbaric medicine. **Telecommunication Services:** electronic mail, execdir@abprevmed. org. **Formerly:** (1952) American Board of Preventive Medicine and Public Health. **Publications:** *ABPM Booklet of Information*, annual. Covers board requirements. **Price:** free ● *Study Guide*. Includes outlines of examinations. **Conventions/Meetings:** semiannual board meeting - always January and August ● annual Certification Exam - meeting - always November, in Chicago, IL.

15717 ■ American College for Advancement in Medicine (ACAM)
24411 Ridge Rte., No. 115
Laguna Hills, CA 92653
Ph: (949)309-3520
Free: (800)532-3688
Fax: (949)309-3539
E-mail: info@acam.org
URL: http://www.acam.org
Contact: Sharon Urch, Exec. Dir.

Founded: 1973. **Members:** 1,000. **Membership Dues:** active physician in U.S., $430 (annual) ● active physician outside U.S., $330 (annual) ● affiliate in U.S., $345 (annual) ● affiliate outside U.S., $255 (annual) ● adjunct in U.S., $215 (annual) ● adjunct outside U.S., $160 (annual) ● associate in U.S., $250 (annual) ● associate outside U.S., $225 (annual). **Staff:** 5. **Budget:** $1,000,000. **Multinational. Description:** Physicians organized for the promotion of preventive medicine throughout the world. Conducts research and educational programs in the fields of chelation therapy, nutritional medicine, and other preventive modalities. Maintains physician referrals. Offers specialized education program. **Libraries: Type:** reference. **Awards: Type:** recognition. **Committees:** Education; Scientific. **Formerly:** (1987) American Academy of Medical Preventics. **Publications:** *ACAM Update*, monthly. Newsletter. Contains abstracts on issues and developments in preventive medicine. **Price:** included in membership dues. **Circulation:** 2,500. **Advertising:** accepted ● *Membership Directory*, annual. **Conventions/Meetings:** semiannual conference and workshop (exhibits) - usually May and November.

15718 ■ American College of Preventive Medicine (ACPM)
1307 New York Ave. NW, No. 200
Washington, DC 20005
Ph: (202)466-2044
Fax: (202)466-2662
E-mail: info@acpm.org
URL: http://www.acpm.org
Contact: Mike Barry, Exec. Dir.

Founded: 1954. **Members:** 2,200. **Membership Dues:** resident, $65 (annual) ● affiliate, $130 (annual) ● ordinary, associate, fellow, $285 (annual) ● emeritus, $15 (annual) ● student, $25 (annual) ● associate, $85 (annual). **Staff:** 6. **Budget:** $1,000,000. **Description:** Professional society of medical doctors specializing in preventive medicine, public health, aerospace medicine, and occupational medicine. Sponsors educational programs. **Awards:** Distinguished Service Award. **Frequency:** annual. **Type:** recognition. **Recipient:** for outstanding service to ACPM ● Resident Award. **Frequency:** annual. **Type:** recognition. **Recipient:** for outstanding achievement in community service, scholarship, research, teaching and overall leadership ● Rising Star. **Frequency:** annual. **Type:** recognition. **Recipient:** to a member

of ACPM who is within seven years of completion of residency training and who is certified by the American Board of Preventive Medicine ● Special Recognition Award. **Frequency:** annual. **Type:** recognition. **Recipient:** for outstanding achievement in or contribution to the field of preventive medicine. **Computer Services:** Mailing lists. **Telecommunication Services:** electronic mail, mbarry@acpm.org. **Committees:** Adolescent Health; Association of Preventive Medicine Residents; Awards; Corporate Council; Development; Education; External Relations; International Health; Practice Guidelines; Prevention Policy; Science. **Publications:** *ACPM News*, quarterly. Newsletter. Reports on continuing medical education, legislative activities, and programs of the college. Includes calendar of events and research updates. **Price:** included in membership dues; $25.00 /year for nonmembers. ISSN: 1044-4211. **Circulation:** 2,200. **Advertising:** accepted ● *American Journal of Preventive Medicine*, 8/year. **Price:** $295.00 for members; $340.00 for nonmembers ● *Careers in Preventive Medicine* ● *Directory of Residency Programs*, periodic. **Conventions/Meetings:** annual Preventive Medicine - conference (exhibits).

15719 ■ American Institute for Preventive Medicine (AIPM)
30445 Northwestern Hwy., Ste.350
Farmington Hills, MI 48334
Ph: (248)539-1800
Free: (800)345-2476
Fax: (248)539-1808
E-mail: aipm@healthylife.com
URL: http://www.healthylife.com
Contact: Don R. Powell PhD, Pres./CEO

Founded: 1983. **Staff:** 26. **Description:** Promotes positive health behaviors by developing and distributing effective health promotion programs, publications, and products. Trains and certifies health care organizations and corporations to offer its services or deliver its programs through a nationwide network of health care affiliates. Conducts educational programs. Maintains speakers' bureau. **Publications:** *A Year of Health Hints - 365 Practical Ways to Feel Better and Live Longer* (in Chinese, English, and Spanish). Book. **Price:** $19.95 ● *Being a Wise Healthcare Consumer* ● *Guide to Mental Fitness* ● *Guide to Self Care* ● *Health at Home: Your Complete Guide to Symptoms, Solutions, and Self-Care* (in English and Spanish). Book. **Price:** $17.95 for English edition; $19.95 for Spanish edition ● *Healthy Self: The Guide to Self Care and Wise Consumers*. Book. **Price:** $7.95 ● *Hotlines to Health Directory*, annual. **Price:** $2.95. **Circulation:** 200,000 ● *Self Care: Your Family Guide to Symptoms and How to Treat Them*. Book. **Price:** $14.95 ● *Seniors Health at Home*. Book. **Price:** $19.95 ● Catalog.

15720 ■ Association for Prevention Teaching and Research (APTR)
1001 Connecticut Ave. NW, Ste.610
Washington, DC 20036
Ph: (202)463-0550
Free: (866)520-APTR
Fax: (202)463-0555
E-mail: info@aptrweb.org
URL: http://www.atpm.org
Contact: David R. Garr MD, Pres.

Founded: 1942. **Members:** 900. **Membership Dues:** individual, $175 (annual) ● academic unit/practice institution/health agency, $700 (annual) ● student, $65 (annual) ● retired, $90 (annual). **Staff:** 16. **Budget:** $500,000. **Description:** Advances individual and community health promotion and disease prevention in the education of physicians and other health professionals. Individual members are teachers, researchers, practitioners, administrators, residents and students. Institutional members include preventive medicine and related departments in medical schools, schools and graduate programs in public health and preventive medicine, other health professions schools and various health agencies. **Awards:** Duncan Clark Award. **Frequency:** annual. **Type:** recognition. **Recipient:** for a distinguished record of achievement in the areas of teaching, research and/or advocacy ● F. Marian Bishop Educator of the

Year Award. **Frequency:** annual. **Type:** recognition. **Recipient:** for teachers who have contributed to the instruction of students or residents in the field of public health and preventive medicine ● Outstanding Educational Program of the Year Award. **Frequency:** annual. **Type:** recognition. **Recipient:** for an innovative program, department or academic institution's involvement in advancing undergraduate education in prevention and public health. **Computer Services:** Mailing lists. **Committees:** Awards; Education; Research; Special Populations. **Councils:** Departments of Preventive Medicine Chairs; Graduate Programs of Preventive Medicine; Residency Programs. **Formerly:** (1955) Conference of Professors of Preventive Medicine; (2006) Association of Teachers of Preventive Medicine. **Publications:** *American Journal of Preventive Medicine*, 8/year. Publishes articles in the areas of prevention research, teaching, practice and policy. ● *APTR News Now!*, weekly. Newsletter. Alternate Formats: online ● *APTR Quarterly*. Newsletter. Provides members with information on APTR members, projects, programs and activities. ● *Directory and Profile of Academic Units in Preventive Medicine*, periodic. **Conventions/Meetings:** annual Teaching Prevention: Linking the Prevention Education Community - conference, on prevention.

15721 ■ Center for Sports and Osteopathic Medicine (CDM)

c/o Dr. Richard M. Bachrach, DO, Pres.
317 Madison Ave.
New York, NY 10017
Ph: (212)685-8113
Fax: (212)697-4541
E-mail: bonesdoctor@bonesdoctor.com
URL: http://www.bonesdoctor.com
Contact: Dr. Richard M. Bachrach DO, Pres.
Founded: 1978. **Description:** Educates dancers about their bodies and preventive medicine in order to help them avoid injuries. Activities are currently concentrated in New York City area. **Formerly:** (1997) CTR for Dance Medicine. **Conventions/Meetings:** seminar and workshop.

15722 ■ Hearing Education and Awareness for Rockers (HEAR)

1405 Lyon St.
San Francisco, CA 94115
Ph: (415)409-3277
Fax: (415)409-5683
E-mail: hear@hearnet.com
URL: http://www.hearnet.com
Contact: Kathy Peck, Co-Founder/Exec. Dir.
Founded: 1988. **Staff:** 3. **Budget:** $100,000. **Description:** Musicians, music industry professionals, and music lovers. Seeks to prevent hearing loss and Tinnitus by promoting public awareness regarding the dangers of over amplified music and noise. Promotes the use of hearing protection and enhancement devices, especially among young people. Produces public service announcements recording artists, school programs, distributes ear protection and information at music events, conducts free hearing screening programs and provides hearing information and resources and affiliate referrals. **Computer Services:** Mailing lists. **Telecommunication Services:** 24-hour hotline, (415)773-9590. **Publications:** *Can't Hear You Knocking*. Video. **Price:** $39.95. **Advertising:** accepted ● *HEAR Information Packet*. **Price:** $10.00.

15723 ■ National Wellness Institute (NWI)

PO Box 827
Stevens Point, WI 54481-0827
Ph: (715)342-2969
Fax: (715)342-2979
E-mail: nwi@nationalwellness.org
URL: http://www.nationalwellness.org
Contact: Bill Hettler MD, Pres.
Founded: 1977. **Members:** 1,800. **Membership Dues:** core individual, $94 (annual) ● student, $59 (annual) ● core organization, $214 (annual) ● core plus individual, $184 (annual) ● core plus organization, $349 (annual). **Staff:** 8. **Multinational. Description:** Aims to provide national leadership in the wellness movement; to assist professionals working in

health and wellness promotion in all types of settings, and organizations with planning, development, implementation, and evaluation of wellness programs; and to assist in the development of high quality wellness products and services. Acts as clearinghouse on wellness information. Provides consultations; offers professional development conferences. Sponsors National Wellness Association. **Libraries: Type:** reference. **Holdings:** audio recordings, books, clippings, periodicals, video recordings. **Subjects:** health and wellness promotion. **Awards:** National Wellness Institute Research Merit Award. **Frequency:** annual. **Type:** scholarship. **Recipient:** for original research in health and wellness that is not yet published. **Computer Services:** Mailing lists. **Telecommunication Services:** electronic mail, members@nationalwellness.org. **Publications:** *American Journal of Health Promotion*, bimonthly ● *Health Issues Update/Resource News*, bimonthly. Newsletter. **Price:** included in membership dues. ISSN: 1073-6794. **Circulation:** 1,800. Alternate Formats: online ● *Health Promotion Practitioner*, bimonthly. Newsletter. Alternate Formats: online ● *Testwell Assessment Series* ● *Wellness Management*, quarterly. Newsletter. **Price:** included in membership dues. ISSN: 1062-1156. **Circulation:** 2,500. Alternate Formats: online ● *Wellness Resource Directory*. **Advertising:** accepted. Alternate Formats: online ● Brochures. **Conventions/Meetings:** annual National Wellness Conference, professional development for health and wellness promotion professionals (exhibits) - always third week in July, Stevens Point, WI.

15724 ■ Wellness Associates

PO Box 8422
Asheville, NC 28814
Ph: (206)984-0948
Fax: (206)984-0948
E-mail: info@thewellspring.com
URL: http://www.thewellspring.com
Contact: John W. Travis MD, Founder
Founded: 1975. **Staff:** 3. **Budget:** $20,000. **Non-membership. Description:** Provides high quality resource materials for lifestyle improvement integrating the major components of wellness: self-responsibility, stress management, nutrition, and physical awareness. Expands wellness education into the fields of emotional and psychological health. Recognizes spiritual growth and the search for meaning to be essential elements in the experience of wellness. Offers wellness publications and resources for helping professionals to assist them in realizing the principles of wellness in their own lives and to help their clients experience their own capacity for good health and well-being. Provides consultation for wellness centers, individuals, universities, agencies, hospitals, and government groups. **Computer Services:** Online services, wellness inventory. **Formerly:** (1979) Wellness Resource Center. **Publications:** *A Change of Heart: The Global Wellness Inventory*. Book. **Price:** $8.00 ● *Simply Well: Choices for a Healthy Life*. Book. **Price:** $9.95 ● *Wellness for Helping Professionals*. Book. **Price:** $39.00 ● *Wellness Index*. Booklet. **Price:** $4.95 ● *Wellness Inventory*. Booklet. **Price:** $2.95 ● *Wellness Workbook*. **Price:** $19.95.

Proctology

15725 ■ American Board of Colon and Rectal Surgery (ABCRS)

20600 Eureka Rd., Ste.600
Taylor, MI 48180
Ph: (734)282-9400
Fax: (734)282-9402
E-mail: admin@abcrs.org
URL: http://www.abcrs.org
Contact: Irene Babcock, Exec. Asst.
Founded: 1934. **Staff:** 3. **Description:** Certification board established to investigate qualifications, administer examinations, and provide certification as diplomats for medical doctors specializing in colon and rectal surgery. **Formerly:** American Board of Proctology. **Publications:** *American Board of Colon*

and Rectal Surgery—Newsletter to Diplomates, annual. Includes research updates. **Price:** included in membership dues. **Conventions/Meetings:** annual meeting - always fall ● annual meeting - always spring.

15726 ■ American Society of Colon and Rectal Surgeons (ASCRS)

85 W Algonquin Rd., Ste.550
Arlington Heights, IL 60005
Ph: (847)290-9184
Fax: (847)290-9203
E-mail: ascrs@fascrs.org
URL: http://www.fascrs.org
Contact: Lester Rosen MD, Pres.
Founded: 1899. **Members:** 2,600. **Membership Dues:** regular, $400 (annual). **Staff:** 5. **Regional Groups:** 20. **Description:** Professional society of surgeons specializing in the diagnosis and treatment of diseases of the colon, rectum, and anus. Offers placement service; conducts research programs. **Awards:** Career Development. **Frequency:** annual. **Type:** grant. **Recipient:** for young staff's academic career development in the field of diseases of the colon, rectum and anus ● International Research. **Frequency:** annual. **Type:** grant. **Recipient:** for residents and clinical investigators in U.S. or Canada ● Limited Project Grant. **Frequency:** semiannual. **Type:** grant ● **Type:** recognition ● RFP for Clinical Studies on Benign Colorectal Disorders. **Frequency:** annual. **Type:** grant. **Recipient:** for outstanding research in specific areas of colorectal diseases or disorders. **Publications:** *ASCRS News*, semiannual. Newsletter. Alternate Formats: online ● *Diseases of the Colon and Rectum*, monthly. Journal. **Price:** free for members. **Advertising:** accepted. **Conventions/Meetings:** annual convention, scientific (exhibits) - 2008 June 7-12, Boston, MA - **Avg. Attendance:** 2000.

15727 ■ International Association of Colon Therapy (I-ACT)

c/o A.R. Hoenninger, III, Exec. Dir.
PO Box 461285
San Antonio, TX 78246-1285
Ph: (210)366-2888
Fax: (210)366-2999
E-mail: homeoffice@i-act.org
URL: http://www.iact.org
Contact: A.R. Hoenninger III, Exec. Dir.
Founded: 1988. **Members:** 2,500. **Membership Dues:** full, $150 (annual). **Budget:** $250,000. **Regional Groups:** 15. **Description:** Professional colon hydrotherapists and other health care practitioners. Works to unite the community of colon hydrotherapy professionals and increase visibility and recognition in the health care industry. Promotes the establishment of uniform guidelines and standards of practice and the establishment of accredited colon hydrotherapy schools. Conducts research and educational programs; plans to operate referral service. Maintains library. **Committees:** Accreditation; Certification; Conference Planning; Education; Fundraising. **Formerly:** (1993) American Colon Therapy Association. **Publications:** *I-ACT Newsletter*, quarterly. Provides organization updates, convention schedule, and continuing education course schedule. **Price:** included in membership dues. **Circulation:** 2,500. **Advertising:** accepted. **Conventions/Meetings:** annual conference and convention (exhibits).

Psychiatry

15728 ■ American Academy of Addiction Psychiatry (AAAP)

345 Blackstone Blvd., 2nd Fl. - RCH
Providence, RI 02906
Ph: (401)524-3076
Fax: (401)272-0922
URL: http://www.aaap.org
Contact: Becky Stein, Exec. Dir.
Founded: 1985. **Members:** 1,000. **Membership Dues:** medical student, $50 (annual) ● resident, $60 (annual) ● regular, affiliate, $215 (annual) ● interna-

tional, $205 (annual) ● retired, $123 (annual). **Regional Groups:** 9. **Description:** Psychiatrists and other health care and mental health professionals treating people with addictive behaviors. Promotes accessibility to highest quality treatment for all who need it; promotes excellence in clinical practice in addiction psychiatry; educates the public to influence public policy regarding addictive illness; provides continuing education for addiction professionals; disseminates new information in the field of addiction psychiatry; and encourages research on the etiology, prevention, identification, and treatment of the addictions. **Awards:** Founders Award. **Frequency:** annual. **Type:** recognition ● Medical Student Scholarships. **Frequency:** annual. **Type:** scholarship. **Recipient:** for medical students ● **Frequency:** annual. **Type:** monetary ● Resident Scholarships. **Frequency:** annual. **Type:** scholarship. **Recipient:** for resident members. **Computer Services:** Mailing lists, of members. **Publications:** *AAAP News*, 3/year. Newsletter. Contains information on the organization's activities and membership. **Advertising:** accepted ● *American Journal on Addictions*, 5/year. Contains latest research findings. **Circulation:** 1,500. **Advertising:** accepted. Alternate Formats: online ● Membership Directory. **Conventions/Meetings:** annual meeting and symposium (exhibits) ● biennial Review Course on Addiction Psychiatry - workshop.

15729 ■ American Academy of Child and Adolescent Psychiatry (AACAP)
3615 Wisconsin Ave. NW
Washington, DC 20016-3007
Ph: (202)966-7300
Free: (800)333-7636
Fax: (202)966-2891
E-mail: executive@aacap.org
URL: http://www.aacap.org
Contact: Dr. Thomas Anders MD, Pres.
Founded: 1953. **Members:** 8,000. **Membership Dues:** active, $350 (annual) ● affiliate, $295 (annual) ● corresponding, $215 (annual) ● resident, $60 (annual). **Staff:** 32. **Budget:** $6,000,000. **Regional Groups:** 60. **Description:** Serves as professional society of degreed physicians who have completed an additional five years of residency in child and adolescent psychiatry. Seeks to stimulate and advance medical contributions to the knowledge and treatment of psychiatric illnesses of children and adolescents. **Awards:** AACAP George Tarjan Award for Contributions in Mental Retardation. **Frequency:** annual. **Type:** recognition. **Recipient:** for the understanding or care of those with mental retardation and developmental disabilities ● AACAP Irving Philips Award for Prevention. **Frequency:** annual. **Type:** recognition. **Recipient:** to a child and adolescent psychiatrist and Academy member who has made significant contributions in a lifetime career or single seminal work for the prevention of mental illness in children and adolescents ● AACAP Rieger Service Program Award for Excellence. **Frequency:** annual. **Type:** recognition. **Recipient:** for innovative programs that address prevention, diagnosis or treatment of mental illnesses in children and adolescents, and serve as model programs to the community ● AACAP Sidney Berman Award for the Study and Treatment of Learning Disabilities. **Frequency:** annual. **Type:** recognition. **Recipient:** to a child and adolescent psychiatrist and AACAP member who has shown outstanding leadership in the public education and treatment of learning disabilities ● Elaine Schlosser Lewis Award for Research on Attention-Deficit Disorder. **Frequency:** annual. **Type:** monetary. **Recipient:** for the best paper published in the journal on attention-deficit disorder written by a child and adolescent psychiatrist ● Klingestein Third Generation Foundation Award for Research in Depression or Suicide. **Frequency:** annual. **Type:** monetary. **Recipient:** for the best paper on suicide and/or depression published in the journal during the past year ● Norbert and Charlotte Rieger Award for Scientific Achievement. **Frequency:** annual. **Type:** monetary. **Recipient:** for the most significant paper by a child and adolescent psychiatrist published in the journal during the past year ● Robert Cancro Academic Leadership Award. **Frequency:** annual. **Type:** recognition.

Recipient: to a currently serving General Psychiatry Training Director, Medical School Dean, CEO of a Training Institution or Chair of a Department of Pediatrics for his or her contributions to the promotion of child and adolescent psychiatry. **Computer Services:** Mailing lists ● online services. **Formerly:** (1986) American Academy of Child Psychiatry. **Publications:** *AACAP News*, bimonthly. Newsletter. Includes listing of employment opportunities, research updates, and statistics. **Price:** included in membership dues. **Circulation:** 6,000. **Advertising:** accepted ● *Journal of the AACAP*, monthly. **Price:** included in membership dues. **Circulation:** 9,245. **Advertising:** accepted ● Bulletin, periodic ● Catalog ● Manuals ● Membership Directory, periodic. **Conventions/Meetings:** annual meeting (exhibits) - 2007 Oct. 23-28, Boston, MA; 2008 Oct. 28-Nov. 2, Chicago, IL; 2009 Oct. 27-Nov. 1, Honolulu, HI.

15730 ■ American Academy of Clinical Psychiatrists (AACP)
PO Box 458
Glastonbury, CT 06033
Ph: (860)635-5533 (314)747-2013
Fax: (860)613-1650
E-mail: aacp@cox.net
URL: http://www.aacp.com
Contact: Carol S. North MD, Pres.
Founded: 1975. **Members:** 600. **Membership Dues:** active, $175 (annual) ● affiliate, $90 (annual) ● early career, $50 (annual). **Staff:** 1. **Budget:** $125,000. **Description:** Practicing board-eligible or board-certified psychiatrists. Promotes the scientific practice of psychiatric medicine. Conducts educational and teaching research. **Libraries: Type:** not open to the public. **Holdings:** 6. **Awards:** Clinical Research Award. **Frequency:** annual. **Type:** recognition. **Computer Services:** database ● mailing lists. **Telecommunication Services:** electronic mail, aacpoffice@aol.com. **Publications:** *Annals of Clinical Psychiatry*, quarterly. Journal. **Price:** included in membership dues. **Circulation:** 600. **Advertising:** accepted. **Conventions/Meetings:** annual conference (exhibits) - always fall ● annual The Last Straw: Suicide - competition.

15731 ■ American Association of Chairs of Departments of Psychiatry (AACDP)
c/o Lucille F. Meinsler, Exec. Sec.
1594 Cumberland St.
Lebanon, PA 17042
Ph: (717)270-1673
Fax: (717)270-1673
E-mail: aacdp@verizon.net
URL: http://www.aacdp.org
Contact: Lucille F. Meinsler, Exec. Sec.
Founded: 1967. **Members:** 136. **Membership Dues:** institutional, $525 (annual). **Staff:** 1. **Budget:** $40,000. **Description:** Chairmen of departments of psychiatry in colleges of medicine. Purposes are: to promote medical education, research, and patient care, particularly as these concern psychiatry; to promote the growth and continuing development of psychiatry; to provide a forum for discussion and exchange of ideas among the chairmen of departments of psychiatry in medical schools; to provide appropriate liaison between chairmen and individuals and organizations whose activities bear on the objectives of the association. **Publications:** Membership list. **Conventions/Meetings:** semiannual meeting, for membership - always fall and spring.

15732 ■ American Association of Community Psychiatrists (AACP)
c/o Frances M. Roton
PO Box 570218
Dallas, TX 75228-0218
Ph: (972)613-0985
Fax: (972)613-5532
E-mail: frda1@airmail.net
URL: http://www.wpic.pitt.edu/aacp
Contact: Wesley Sowers MD, Pres.
Founded: 1984. **Members:** 350. **Membership Dues:** general, $150 (annual) ● international, $150 (annual) ● group (per person), $75 (annual) ● liaison (non-psychiatrist), $100 (annual). **Regional Groups:** 7.

Description: Psychiatrists and psychiatry residents practicing in community mental health centers (CMHCs) or similar programs that provide care to populations of the mentally ill regardless of their ability to pay. Works to address issues faced by psychiatrists who practice within CMHCs, with the goal of ensuring quality patient care. Clarifies and solves mutual problems regarding community mental health psychiatric practice. Informs and educates the public about the community psychiatrist's role in treating the mentally ill. Encourages research and training in psychiatry in the community mental health setting. Establishes liaison with similar professional associations and foster local and regional groups interested in public community psychiatry. **Publications:** *Community Psychiatrist*, quarterly. Newsletter ● Membership Directory, annual. **Conventions/Meetings:** annual meeting, held in conjunction with the Institute on Hospital and Community - always fall.

15733 ■ American Association of Directors of Psychiatric Residency Training (AADPRT)
c/o Lucille F. Meinsler, Admin. Mgr.
Executive Off.
1594 Cumberland St.
Lebanon, PA 17042
Ph: (717)270-1673
E-mail: aadprt@verizon.net
URL: http://www.aadprt.org
Contact: Lucille F. Meinsler, Admin. Mgr.
Founded: 1973. **Members:** 525. **Membership Dues:** institutional, $300 (annual) ● individual, $100 (annual) ● affiliate, $250 (annual). **Staff:** 1. **Description:** Creates, reviews and maintains standards for Psychiatric residency training programs. **Awards:** AADPRT IMG Mentorships. **Frequency:** annual. **Type:** recognition. **Recipient:** for psychiatry residents ● Fromm-Reichmann Fellowship Award. **Type:** fellowship. **Recipient:** for AADPRT residents ● Ginsberg/AADPRT Fellowship. **Frequency:** annual. **Type:** fellowship. **Recipient:** for AADPRT residents ● Henderson Memorial Award. **Frequency:** annual. **Type:** recognition. **Recipient:** for AADPRT residents. **Computer Services:** Mailing lists. **Publications:** *Academic Psychiatry*, quarterly. Journal. Also Cited As: *Journal of Psychiatric Education* ● Newsletter, quarterly ● Membership Directory. **Conventions/Meetings:** annual conference - always March.

15734 ■ American Association for Geriatric Psychiatry (AAGP)
7910 Woodmont Ave., Ste.1050
Bethesda, MD 20814-3069
Ph: (301)654-7850
Fax: (301)654-4137
E-mail: main@aagponline.org
URL: http://www.aagpgpa.org
Contact: Christine deVries MD, CEO
Founded: 1978. **Members:** 1,468. **Membership Dues:** full, in U.S. and Canada, $220 (annual) ● full, outside U.S. and Canada, $325 (annual) ● retired, $110 (annual) ● in-training, $75 (annual) ● regular student, $45 (annual) ● student (without access to AJGP), $10 (annual) ● affiliate, $170 (annual). **Staff:** 13. **Budget:** $2,500,000. **Description:** Psychiatrists interested in promoting better mental health care for the elderly. Maintains placement service and speakers' bureau. **Committees:** Clinical Practice; Diversity; Education; Nominations; Public Policy and Communications; Research; Teaching and Training. **Publications:** *AAGP Membership Directory*, annual ● *American Journal of Geriatric Psychiatry*, monthly. **Price:** free for members. Alternate Formats: online ● *Geriatric Psychiatry News*, bimonthly. Newsletter. Provides brief articles on psychiatric topics and case reports pertaining to elderly patients; includes association news, and employment listings. **Price:** free for members ● *Growing Older and Wiser*. Covers consumer and general public information. **Price:** $14.00. **Conventions/Meetings:** annual meeting (exhibits) - always February/March.

15735 ■ American Association of Psychiatric Technicians (AAPT)
1220 S St., Ste.100
Sacramento, CA 95814-7138

Ph: (916)443-1701
Free: (800)391-7589
Fax: (916)329-9145
E-mail: loger@psychtechs.net
URL: http://www.psychtechs.org
Contact: Ms. Debi Loger, Exec. Dir.
Founded: 1991. **Members:** 2,500. **Membership Dues:** individual, $45 (annual). **Staff:** 1. **Description:** Administers the Nationally Certified Psychiatric Technician examination to non-licensed direct-care workers in the fields of mental illness, developmental disabilities and substance abuse. **Libraries: Type:** reference.

15736 ■ American Association for Technology in Psychiatry (AATP)
PO Box 11
Bronx, NY 10464-0011
Ph: (718)502-9469
E-mail: aatp@techpsych.org
URL: http://www.techpsych.org
Contact: Naakesh A. Dewan MD, Pres.
Founded: 1995. **Membership Dues:** professional, $75 (annual) ● trainee, $20 (annual). **Description:** Promotes the understanding and use of informatics and information technology in psychiatry. Fosters technology in psychiatry and mental health as a recognized body of knowledge. Promotes the development and dissemination of standards and best practices for use of technology in psychiatry and mental health. Informs and influences public policy in the use of technology in psychiatry and mental health. **Publications:** *Tech Psych Review.* Journal. Alternate Formats: online.

15737 ■ American Board of Psychiatry and Neurology (ABPN)
500 Lake Cook Rd., Ste.335
Deerfield, IL 60015-5635
Ph: (847)945-7900
Fax: (847)945-1146
E-mail: questions@abpn.com
URL: http://www.abpn.com
Contact: Larry R. Faulkner MD, Exec. VP
Founded: 1934. **Nonmembership. Description:** Determines training and admission requirements of applicants for certification and maintenance of certification examinations, administers examinations, and certifies physicians with specialized training in psychiatry, neurology, child neurology, addiction psychiatry, child and adolescent psychiatry, clinical neurophysiology, forensic psychiatry, geriatric psychiatry, hospice and palliative medicine, neuromuscular medicine, neurodevelopmental disabilities, pain medicine, psychosomatic medicine, sleep medicine, and vascular neurology. Member of the American Board of Medical Specialties. **Convention/Meeting:** none. **Publications:** *ABPN Update.* Newsletter. Alternate Formats: online ● *eDiplomate.* Newsletter. Alternate Formats: online.

15738 ■ American College of Neuropsychiatrists (ACN)
28595 Orchard Lake Rd., Ste.200
Farmington Hills, MI 48334
Ph: (248)553-0010
Fax: (248)553-0818
E-mail: acn-aconp@msn.com
Contact: Louis E. Rentz, Exec. Dir.
Founded: 1937. **Members:** 420. **Staff:** 2. **Description:** Psychiatrists, neurologists, physicians in training, and persons in interrelated professions. Promotes study and research in neurology and psychiatry in the osteopathic profession. Maintains specialized education programs. **Committees:** Colleges; Public and Professional Relations; Training Institutions. **Divisions:** Educational Evaluation. **Publications:** *Journal of the American College of Neuropsychiatrists,* semiannual. Reports information on medical developments, case studies, and analysis of political actions. Includes calendar of events and research updates. **Price:** included in membership dues. **Circulation:** 500 ● Directory, annual. **Conventions/Meetings:** competition, for residents writing ● annual conference, held in conjunction with American Osteopathic Association.

15739 ■ The American College of Psychiatrists (TACP)
122 S Michigan Ave., Ste.No. 1360
Chicago, IL 60603
Ph: (312)662-1020
Fax: (312)662-1025
E-mail: angel@acpsych.org
URL: http://www.acpsych.org
Contact: Fawzy I. Fawzy, Pres.
Founded: 1963. **Members:** 1,000. **Membership Dues:** $350 (annual). **Staff:** 6. **Budget:** $2,000,000. **Description:** Established to honor men and women who have made a significant contribution to psychiatry. Members, in turn, invite into membership younger psychiatrists whose scholarly work and demonstrated clinical excellence indicate that they show promise of becoming leaders in the field. **Awards:** Honorary Fellows. **Frequency:** annual. **Type:** recognition. **Recipient:** for distinguished physicians and scientists whose outstanding scientific and clinical contributions are significant to the field of psychiatry ● Laughlin Fellowship. **Frequency:** annual. **Type:** recognition. **Recipient:** for ten residents from the U.S. and Canada to attend two annual programs ● PRITE Fellowship. **Frequency:** annual. **Type:** recognition. **Recipient:** for two residents, one PRITESM (Psychiatry Resident In-Training Examination) and one CHILD PRITESM Fellow from the U.S. and Canada ● Research in Geriatric Psychiatry. **Frequency:** annual. **Type:** monetary. **Recipient:** for an individual or group who made major contributions to research in geriatric psychiatry. **Committees:** Awards; Continuing Medical Education; Contributions; Dean Award; Education; Education Award; Ethics; Honorary Fellowship; Long-Range Planning and Policy; Membership Development; Psychiatrists in Practice Examinations; Scientific Programs. **Publications:** *ACP News,* quarterly. Newsletter ● Handbook ● Membership Directory, annual. **Conventions/Meetings:** annual meeting - always February. 2008 Feb. 27-Mar. 2, Koloa, HI; 2009 Feb. 25-Mar. 1, Tucson, AZ ● annual seminar, graduate education.

15740 ■ American Neuropsychiatric Association (ANPA)
700 Ackerman Rd., Ste.625
Columbus, OH 43202
Ph: (614)447-2077
Fax: (614)263-4366
E-mail: anpa@osu.edu
URL: http://www.anpaonline.org
Contact: Fred Ovsiew MD, Pres.
Founded: 1988. **Members:** 750. **Membership Dues:** regular, $175 (annual). **Staff:** 1. **Budget:** $40,000. **Description:** Aims to work together in a collegial fashion to advance knowledge of brain-behavior relations. Provides a forum for learning, promote excellent, scientific and compassionate care. **Awards:** Career Development Award. **Frequency:** annual. **Type:** monetary. **Recipient:** for advanced trainees in psychiatry, neurology, or neuropsychology whose accomplishments during training offer promise of a successful career in neuropsychiatry and the clinical neurosciences ● Young Investigator Awards. **Frequency:** annual. **Type:** monetary. **Recipient:** for the best abstract submissions to the annual meeting by trainees. **Publications:** *Journal of Neuropsychiatry and Clinical Neurosciences.* **Circulation:** 5,000. **Conventions/Meetings:** annual meeting - 2008 Mar. 1-4, Savannah, GA.

15741 ■ American Orthopsychiatric Association (ORTHO)
PO Box 1104
Tempe, AZ 85280-1104
Ph: (480)727-7518
Fax: (480)965-8544
E-mail: americanortho@gmail.com
URL: http://www.amerortho.org
Contact: Nancy Felipe Russo PhD, Exec. Off./Ed.
Founded: 1924. **Members:** 4,500. **Membership Dues:** regular, $105 (annual) ● fellow, $115 (annual) ● student, $25 (annual). **Budget:** $600,000. **Description:** Represents psychiatrists, psychologists, social workers, educators, psychiatric nurses and lawyers, and others in related fields, including anthropology,

sociology, and economics. Seeks to unite and provide a common meeting ground for those engaged in the study and treatment of problems of human behavior. Fosters research and disseminates information concerning scientific work in the field of mental health. **Awards:** Blanche F. Ittleson. **Frequency:** annual. **Type:** recognition. **Recipient:** for outstanding contributions to understanding the growth and psychology of women ● Marion F. Langer. **Frequency:** annual. **Type:** recognition. **Recipient:** for outstanding achievement in the areas of social advocacy and philanthropy ● Max Hayman Award. **Frequency:** annual. **Type:** recognition. **Recipient:** for persons who have furthered the understanding of genocide and the Holocaust ● Vera S. Paster Award. **Frequency:** annual. **Type:** recognition. **Recipient:** for an outstanding professional who has contributed to the mental well-being of minorities. **Computer Services:** Mailing lists. **Study Groups:** Adolescence; Adoption and Foster Care; Alternative Therapies; Asian-American/Pacific Rim; Disability; Divorce and Family Mediation; Education; Family Therapy; Gay and Lesbian Issues; International Human Rights; Latino Affairs; Prevention and Early Intervention; Professional Training Issues; Racism; Women's Issues. **Publications:** *American Journal of Orthopsychiatry,* quarterly. Covers therapeutic work with children and adults, community mental health, studies in interpersonal relations, and other related topics. **Price:** included in membership dues; $94.00 /year for nonmembers; $180.00 /year for institutions. ISSN: 0002-9432. **Circulation:** 10,000. **Advertising:** accepted. Alternate Formats: microform. **Conventions/Meetings:** annual conference (exhibits).

15742 ■ American Psychiatric Association (APA)
1000 Wilson Blvd., Ste.1825
Arlington, VA 22209-3901
Ph: (703)907-7300
Free: (888)357-7924
Fax: (703)907-1085
E-mail: apa@psych.org
URL: http://www.psych.org
Contact: Alan F. Schatzberg MD, Pres./Chm.
Founded: 1844. **Members:** 40,000. **Membership Dues:** international (based on country of residence income group category), $50-$180 (annual). **Staff:** 237. **Budget:** $25,000,000. **Regional Groups:** 74. **State Groups:** 2. **Multinational. Description:** Psychiatrists. Seeks to further the study of the nature, treatment, and prevention of mental disorders. Assists in formulating programs to meet mental health needs; compiles and disseminates facts and figures about psychiatry; furthers psychiatric education and research. **Libraries: Type:** by appointment only. **Holdings:** 11,000. **Subjects:** psychiatry, mental illness, history of psychiatry. **Commissions:** Addiction Psychiatry; AIDS; Government Relations; Judicial Action; Public Affairs. **Councils:** Aging; Children, Adolescents, and Their Families; Economic Affairs; Internal Organization; International Affairs; Medical Education and Career Development; Mental Health Services; National Affairs; Psychiatric Services; Psychiatry and Law; Research. **Formerly:** (1892) Association of Medical Superintendents of American Institutions for Insane; (1921) American Medico Psychological Association. **Publications:** *American Journal of Psychiatry,* monthly. Includes book reviews. **Price:** free for members in U.S.; $193.00 /year for nonmembers in U.S., /year for members outside U.S.; $290.00 /year for nonmembers outside U.S. ISSN: 0002-953X. **Circulation:** 45,413. **Advertising:** accepted. Alternate Formats: microform. Also Cited As: *American Journal of Insanity* ● *Let's Talk Facts.* Pamphlets ● *Psychiatric News,* semimonthly. Newsletter. **Price:** free for members in U.S.; $88.00 /year for nonmembers in U.S.; $87.00 /year for members outside U.S.; $158.00 /year for nonmembers outside U.S. ● *Psychiatric Services,* monthly. Journal. Covers the delivery of mental health services in organized settings. Includes book reviews and research reports. **Price:** free for members in U.S.; $91.00 /year for nonmembers in U.S.; $73.00 /year for members outside U.S.; $184.00 /year for nonmembers outside U.S. ISSN: 1075-2730. **Circulation:** 22,900. **Adver-**

tising: accepted. **Alternate Formats:** microform ● Books ● Membership Directory, biennial. **Conventions/Meetings:** annual meeting (exhibits) - always May. 2008 May 3-8, Washington, DC; 2009 May 16-21, San Francisco, CA.

15743 ■ American Psychiatric Association Alliance (APAA)

c/o Angela Poblocki, Exec. Dir.
PO Box 285
North Boston, NY 14110
E-mail: ang3689@aol.com
URL: http://www.apaalliance.org
Contact: Angela Poblocki, Exec. Dir.
Membership Dues: general, $45 (annual) ● sustaining, $100 ● life, $500. **Description:** Advocates for people with mental illness. Supports and assists members of the American Psychiatric Association. Fosters collaboration among people concerned with the medical, psychological and legal aspects of mental illness. Educates the public on the medical training of psychiatrists. **Awards:** Elsa Barton Educational Scholarship Fund. **Frequency:** annual. **Type:** scholarship. **Recipient:** for the post secondary educational needs of a spouse/partner or dependent of a disabled or deceased physician who is unable to provide family income. **Projects:** When Not to Keep a Secret. **Publications:** Newsletter, quarterly. **Price:** included in membership dues.

15744 ■ American Society for Adolescent Psychiatry (ASAP)

PO Box 570218
Dallas, TX 75357-0218
Ph: (972)686-6166 (972)613-0985
Fax: (972)613-5532
E-mail: info@adolpsych.org
URL: http://www.adolpsych.org
Contact: Frances M. Bell, Exec. Dir.
Founded: 1967. **Members:** 800. **Membership Dues:** regular, $245 (annual) ● society, $15 (annual) ● in-training, $105 (annual). **Regional Groups:** 20. **Multinational. Description:** Qualified psychiatrists concerned with the behavior of adolescents. Provides for the exchange of psychiatric knowledge; encourages the development of adequate standards and training facilities; stimulates research in the psychopathology and treatment of adolescents. Consults with national organizations interested in the welfare of youth and adolescence. **Awards:** Distinguished Service Award. **Frequency:** annual. **Type:** recognition ● Gralnick Research Award. **Frequency:** annual. **Type:** recognition ● William A. Schonfeld Award. **Frequency:** annual. **Type:** recognition. **Recipient:** to individuals with outstanding contributions to the field of adolescent psychiatry. **Computer Services:** Mailing lists. **Committees:** Educational and Scientific Affairs; Fellowships in Adolescent Psychiatry; Topical Studies. **Publications:** Adolescent Psychiatry, annual. Book. Contains articles and case studies on adolescent psychiatry. **Price:** included in membership dues. **Circulation:** 1,200. **Advertising:** accepted. Also Cited As: The Annals of Adolescent Psychiatry ● ASAP Membership Directory, biennial ● Handbook of Adolescent Health Risk Behavior. Includes chapters on theories of adolescent risk-taking behavior, tobacco, alcohol and drug use, and suicide and unintentional injury. **Price:** $75.00/copy ● Journal of Youth and Adolescence, bimonthly ● Treating Abused Adolescents. Book. Includes brief overviews of the developmental psychopathology of abuse. **Price:** $42.00 for hardcover; $18.95 for softcover ● Newsletter, quarterly. Includes society news, calendar of events, and research updates. **Price:** included in membership dues; $10.00 /year for nonmembers in U.S. and Canada; $15.00 /year for nonmembers outside U.S. and Canada. **Circulation:** 2,500. **Conventions/Meetings:** annual Clinical Review and Update on Adolescent Psychiatry - conference (exhibits) ● annual meeting ● symposium, on topics relating to adolescent psychiatry.

15745 ■ Antipsychiatry Coalition

c/o Carrie L. Drake
2040 Polk St.
Box 234
San Francisco, CA 94109
E-mail: openedbook@earthlink.net
URL: http://www.antipsychiatry.org
Contact: Carrie L. Drake, Contact
Languages: Dutch, English, French, Greek, Italian, Japanese, Polish, Portuguese, Romany, Russian, Spanish. **Multinational. Description:** Advocates against psychiatric treatment; promotes mental health reform. **Telecommunication Services:** electronic mail, antipsychiatrycoalition@usa.net.

15746 ■ Association for Ambulatory Behavioral Healthcare (AABH)

247 Douglas Ave.
Portsmouth, VA 23707
Ph: (757)673-3741
Fax: (757)966-7734
E-mail: info@aabh.org
URL: http://www.aabh.org
Contact: Mickey Wright, Exec. Dir.
Founded: 1965. **Members:** 350. **Membership Dues:** individual, $295 (annual) ● program, $495 (annual) ● system, $695 (annual). **Staff:** 3. **Budget:** $200,000. **Regional Groups:** 20. **Description:** Individuals interested in the development and improvement of the continuum of psychiatric treatment. Supports, encourages, and stimulates the expansion of ambulatory behavioral health services. Sponsors educational discussions on partial hospitalization, intensive outpatient and rehabilitative services including clinical research and administrative issues. Provides consultation services to stimulate and support the study, evaluation, and implementation of ambulatory behavioral health services. Collaborates with other groups in establishing standards of operation and performance in the field. Monitors local and national legislative activity directly related to behavioral healthcare. **Computer Services:** Mailing lists. **Committees:** Legislative/Advocacy; Training & Research. **Formerly:** (1975) Partial Hospitalization Study Group; (1979) Federation of Partial Hospitalization Study Groups; (1996) American Association for Partial Hospitalization. **Publications:** Insurance and Partial Hospitalization ● Milieu, bimonthly. Newsletter ● Standards and Guidelines for Child and Adolescent Partial Hospitalization ● Standards and Guidelines for Partial Hospitalization. **Conventions/Meetings:** annual seminar (exhibits) - usually August.

15747 ■ Association of Medicine and Psychiatry (AMP)

c/o Michael R. Hanlon, Exec. Dir.
3815 Kanawha Ave. SE
Charleston, WV 25304-1543
Ph: (304)925-9366
E-mail: medpsych@charter.net
URL: http://www.amedpsych.com
Contact: Michael R. Hanlon, Exec. Dir.
Founded: 1991. **Membership Dues:** regular, $150 (annual) ● associate, $125 (annual). **Description:** Represents primary care physicians and psychiatrists interested in improving the health of patients with concurrent physical and psychiatric issues. Promotes high quality patient care for those with concurrent physical and psychiatric difficulties. Develops guidelines for services and training experiences specifically designed to address the problems of these patients. Fosters basic and applied research at the interface of medicine and psychiatry. **Awards:** Martin Fenton Award. **Frequency:** annual. **Type:** recognition. **Recipient:** to an outstanding resident in a combined internal medicine/psychiatry or family medicine/psychiatry residency. **Publications:** Primary Care Companion to the Journal of Clinical Psychiatry. Contains articles that address neuropsychiatric problems. **Price:** $89.00 regular in U.S.; $64.00 student/in-training in U.S.; $133.00 regular outside U.S. Also Cited As: PCC ● Newsletter. Provides news and information about health and psychiatry. **Alternate Formats:** online.

15748 ■ Association for Research in Nervous and Mental Disease (ARNMD)

c/o Weill Medical College of Cornell University
Dept. of Psychiatry
1300 York Ave., Box 171, Rm. F-1231
New York, NY 10021
Ph: (570)839-0296
Fax: (570)839-0297
E-mail: amgooder@med.cornell.edu
URL: http://www.arnmd.org/arnmd
Contact: Dr. Annlouise R. Goodermuth, Exec. Dir.
Founded: 1920. **Members:** 950. **Membership Dues:** regular, $150 (annual) ● associate, senior, $75 (annual). **Budget:** $25,000. **Description:** Individuals engaged in the practice or research of neurology, neurosurgery, or psychiatry who are members of neurologic or psychiatric societies. **Formerly:** (1922) Neuropsychiatric Research Society. **Publications:** Clinical Neuroscience Research. Journal. Includes articles on the cellular, neuropsychological, and molecular functioning of the nervous system. **Price:** included in membership dues. ISSN: 1566-2772. **Conventions/Meetings:** annual symposium - always first weekend of December, New York City.

15749 ■ Disaster Psychiatry Outreach (DPO)

50 Broad St., No. 1714
New York, NY 10004
Ph: (212)598-9995
Fax: (212)785-2141
E-mail: info@disasterpsych.org
Contact: Anastasia Holmes, Exec. Dir.
Founded: 1998. **Members:** 1,100. **Staff:** 5. **Budget:** $1,100,000. **Description:** Works to provide high quality disaster mental health services. **Computer Services:** Mailing lists. **Telecommunication Services:** electronic mail, holmes@disasterpsych.org. **Committees:** Child/Adolescent; Clinical; Educational; International. **Task Forces:** Crisis Team; Curriculum; Speakers' Bureau. **Conventions/Meetings:** annual International Congress on Disaster Psychiatry - international conference and congress.

15750 ■ Group for the Advancement of Psychiatry (GAP)

PO Box 570218
Dallas, TX 75357-0218
Ph: (972)613-3044
Fax: (972)613-5532
E-mail: frda1@airmail.net
URL: http://www.groupadpsych.org
Contact: Paul Jay Fink MD, Pres.
Founded: 1946. **Members:** 300. **Membership Dues:** regular, $810 (biennial). **Staff:** 2. **Budget:** $750,000. **Description:** Independent group of psychiatrists organized in working committees interested in applying the principles of psychiatry toward the study of human relations. Works closely with specialists in many other disciplines. Investigates such subjects as school desegregation, use of nuclear energy, religion, psychiatry in the armed forces, mental retardation, cross-cultural communication, medical uses of hypnosis, and the college experience. Maintains 25 committees. **Libraries: Type:** reference. **Holdings:** books, monographs. **Subjects:** psychiatry. **Publications:** Reports. **Conventions/Meetings:** semiannual conference - always April and November, White Plains, NY.

15751 ■ Institute on Psychiatric Services/American Psychiatric Association

1000 Wilson Blvd., Ste.1825
Arlington, VA 22209-3901
Ph: (703)907-7300
Free: (888)357-7924
Fax: (703)907-1085
E-mail: apa@psych.org
URL: http://www.psych.org
Contact: Jill L. Gruber CMP, Assoc. Dir.
Founded: 1949. **Staff:** 13. **Description:** Annual meeting sponsored by the American Psychiatric Association. Open to Physicians and all mental health professionals of all psychiatric and related health and educational facilities. Includes lectures by experts in the field and workshops and accredited courses on problems, programs, and trends. Offers on-site Job Bank, which lists opportunities for mental health professionals. Organized scientific exhibits. **Awards: Type:** recognition. **Recipient:** for outstanding programs in the mental health field. **Affiliated With:** American Psychiatric Association. **Formerly:** (1995) Institute on Hospital and Community Psychiatry. **Pub-

lications: *Psychiatric Services*, monthly. Journal. **Price:** $45.00 for individuals; $75.00 for institutions; $22.50 for students. **ISSN:** 1075-2730. **Circulation:** 20,000. **Advertising:** accepted. Alternate Formats: CD-ROM; microform. **Conventions/Meetings:** annual conference (exhibits) - always October. 2007 Oct. 11-14, New Orleans, LA - **Avg. Attendance:** 2000.

15752 ■ International Center for the Study of Psychiatry and Psychology (ICSPP)
c/o Dr. Robert Sliclen
450 Washington Ave.
Township of Washington, NJ 07676-4031
Ph: (212)861-7400 (212)664-2566
E-mail: djriccio@aol.com
URL: http://www.icspp.org
Contact: Dominick Riccio PhD, Exec. Dir.
Founded: 1971. **Membership Dues:** general, $100 (annual) ● international, $110 (annual). **Description:** Concentrates on the critical study of the mental health movement and theories on public policy and the effects of therapeutic practices upon individual well-being, personal freedom, and community and family values. Members include psychiatrists, psychologists, social workers, philosophers, counselors, therapists and psychiatric victims and survivors worldwide, and include journalists, editors, academics, practitioners and interested lay people. **Libraries: Type:** not open to the public. **Holdings:** archival material, clippings, papers, periodicals. **Programs:** Children First!. **Formerly:** (1995) Center for the Study of Psychiatry; (2003) Center for the Study of Psychiatry and Psychology. **Publications:** *Ethical Human Psychology and Psychiatry*, 3/year. Journal. Features scientific research, literature reviews, clinical reports, and book reviews that draw on ethical and scientific perspectives. **Price:** $60.00 /year for individuals; $125.00 /year for institutions ● *Ethical Human Sciences and Services*, quarterly. Journal. Also Cited As: *EHSS*.

15753 ■ International Society for Adolescent Psychiatry and Psychology (ISAPP)
c/o Rosalie J. Landy, Admin. Dir. for USA-Asia-SA
223 Sunset Blvd.
Bronx, NY 10473
Ph: (718)892-4868
E-mail: isapp.newyork@isapp.org
URL: http://www.isapp.org
Contact: Rosalie J. Landy, Admin. Dir. for USA-Asia-SA
Founded: 1984. **Members:** 500. **Membership Dues:** in U.S., Canada, Europe, Asia and some other country, EUR 100 (annual) ● in Eastern Europe, South America, and Africa, EUR 20 (annual). **Staff:** 1. **Languages:** English, French. **Multinational. Description:** Psychiatrists, psychologists, psychoanalysts, social workers, sociologists, pediatricians, educators, and health care professionals involved in the treatment of adolescents. Seeks to advance treatment of psychiatric illnesses of adolescents. Maintains research and educational programs. **Publications:** *International Annals of Adolescent Psychiatry*, triennial. Monograph. **Price:** included in membership dues ● Newsletter, 3/year. **Price:** included in membership dues. Alternate Formats: online. **Conventions/Meetings:** triennial congress ● periodic international conference.

15754 ■ International Society for Research on Impulsivity (ISRI)
c/o Christina Oyervides, Managing Sec.
Univ. of Texas at Houston
1300 Moursund Ave., Ste.206
Houston, TX 77030
Ph: (713)500-2550
Fax: (713)500-2553
E-mail: secretary@impulsivity.org
URL: http://www.impulsivity.org
Contact: Christina Oyervides, Managing Sec.
Multinational. Description: Promotes research collaboration on impulsivity and impulse control disorders by scientists around the world. Fosters international research collaboration on impulsivity and its psychiatric and social consequences. Establishes

guidelines for measurement of impulsivity that would make comparisons across research projects more meaningful. Disseminates clinical and pre-clinical impulsivity research to other researchers and clinicians. **Publications:** Newsletter. Alternate Formats: online.

15755 ■ International Transactional Analysis Association (ITAA)
2186 Rheem Dr., No. B-1
Pleasanton, CA 94588
Ph: (925)600-8110
Fax: (925)600-8112
E-mail: ken@itaa-net.org
URL: http://www.itaa-net.org
Contact: Ken Foselman, Contact
Founded: 1958. **Members:** 1,600. **Membership Dues:** regular, $115 (annual) ● associate, student, $69 (annual). **Staff:** 2. **Budget:** $258,000. **Description:** Educational corporation of persons in medical and behavioral sciences, including psychiatrists, psychologists, social workers, nurses, educators, marriage and family counselors, clergy, and organizational consultants. Maintains standards of practice and teaching of transactional analysis, which involves group therapy, social dynamics, and personality theory based on analysis of the "transactions" or interactions between persons. **Libraries: Type:** reference. **Holdings:** 1,500. **Subjects:** transactional analysis, psychiatry. **Awards:** Eric Berne Memorial Award. **Frequency:** annual. **Type:** recognition. **Recipient:** for scientific research in transactional analysis ● Eric Berne Research Grant. **Type:** grant. **Computer Services:** Mailing lists, available professional transactional analysis therapists. **Telecommunication Services:** electronic mail, info@itaa-net. org. **Formerly:** (1961) San Francisco Social Psychiatry Seminar. **Publications:** *Script*, 9/year. Newsletter. **Advertising:** accepted ● *Transactional Analysis Journal*, quarterly. **Conventions/Meetings:** annual International Transactional Analysis Conference - conference and workshop.

15756 ■ National Association for Children's Behavioral Health (NACBH)
1025 Connecticut Ave. NW, Ste.1012
Washington, DC 20036-3536
Ph: (202)857-9735
Fax: (202)362-5145
E-mail: nacbh@verizon.net
URL: http://www.nacbh.org
Contact: Joy Midman, Exec. Dir.
Founded: 1983. **Members:** 80. **Membership Dues:** board eligible, association, $4,950-$10,890 (annual) ● multi facility system, $13,800 (annual) ● additional facility or program, $2,000 (annual). **Staff:** 2. **Budget:** $350,000. **Description:** Treatment centers and programs for children and adolescents with or at risk of serious emotional or behavioral disorders, providing a full array of mental health and related services including residential treatment, partial hospitalization, outpatient treatment, therapeutic foster care, group homes, independent living programs, in-home treatment, intensive case management, and accredited education, special education, and alternative education programs. **Formerly:** (2005) National Association of Psychiatric Treatment Centers for Children. **Publications:** *Friday Facts*, weekly ● *Member Facilities*, annual. Directory ● Brochures. Contains informational material. **Conventions/Meetings:** annual conference - always March or April or May ● annual Mid-Year Technical Meeting - always fall.

15757 ■ National Association of Psychiatric Health Systems (NAPHS)
701 13th St. NW, Ste.950
Washington, DC 20005-3995
Ph: (202)393-6700
Fax: (202)783-6041
E-mail: naphs@naphs.org
URL: http://www.naphs.org
Contact: Edward Irby, Pres.
Founded: 1933. **Members:** 292. **Staff:** 7. **Budget:** $2,000,000. **Description:** Advocates for behavioral health. Represents provider systems that are committed to the delivery of responsive, accountable, and

clinically effective preventing treatment, and care for children, adolescents, and adults with mental and substance use disorders. **Awards: Type:** recognition. **Computer Services:** Mailing lists. **Committees:** Political Action. **Formerly:** (1993) National Association of Private Psychiatric Hospitals. **Conventions/Meetings:** annual conference (exhibits).

15758 ■ Radical Caucus in Psychiatry (RCP)
Address Unknown since 2007
Founded: 1969. **Members:** 75. **Membership Dues:** $10 (annual). **Staff:** 2. **Description:** Members of the American Psychiatric Association (see separate entry) and individuals interested in mental health issues who take a politically progressive stand in psychiatry. Objective is to examine the socioeconomic and sociopolitical aspects of mental health issues from a left-oriented perspective. Areas of study have included a critical analysis of biological psychiatry, patient rights, and psychiatric treatment of mental patients in Latin America. Presents research findings to professionals and laypersons. Maintains speakers' bureau. **Affiliated With:** American Psychiatric Association. **Publications:** Newsletter, annual. **Conventions/Meetings:** annual conference and symposium ● seminar.

15759 ■ Section for Psychiatric and Substance Abuse Services (SPSPAS)
c/o American Hospital Association
One N Franklin
Chicago, IL 60606-3421
Ph: (312)422-3300
Fax: (312)422-4590
E-mail: rchickey@aha.org
URL: http://www.aha.org/aha/member-center/ constituency-sections/Psychiatric/index.html
Contact: Rebecca Chickey, Contact
Founded: 1969. **Members:** 1,400. **Description:** Institutional members, both general hospitals and freestanding specialty hospitals, of the American Hospital Association (see separate entry) who provide psychiatric, substance abuse, clinical psychology, and other behavioral health services. Assists the AHA in development and implementation of policies and programs to promote improvement of and advocacy for the nation's behavioral health care providers. Works on formulating and commenting on federal legislation and regulations relating to psychiatric and substance abuse services. Develops and maintains liaison relationships with key organizations important to behavioral health providers. **Awards:** AHA-McKesson Quest for Quality Prize. **Type:** monetary. **Recipient:** for best in hospital leadership and innovation in quality, safety and commitment to patient care ● Caroline Boone Lewis Living the Vision Award. **Type:** recognition. **Recipient:** to the organization and individuals living AHA's vision "a society of healthy communities where all individuals reach their highest potential for health" ● Hospitals Awards for Volunteer Excellence. **Type:** recognition. **Recipient:** for outstanding contributions of organized programs of volunteer service ● Shirley Ann Munroe Leadership Development Award. **Type:** recognition. **Recipient:** for small or rural hospital chief executives and administrators who have achieved improvements in local health delivery and health status through their leadership and direction. **Affiliated With:** American Hospital Association. **Formerly:** (1972) Psychiatric Hospital Section; (1984) Psychiatric Services Section; (1991) Special Constituency Section for Mental Health and Psychiatric Services; (1997) Special Constituency Section for Psychiatric and Substance Abuse Services.

15760 ■ Social Psychiatry Research Institute (SPRI)
150 E 69th St., Ste.2H
New York, NY 10021
Ph: (212)628-4800
Free: (888)345-7774
Fax: (212)249-8546
E-mail: akiev@spristudy.com
Contact: Ari Kiev MD, Pres.
Founded: 1970. **Description:** Promotes, supports, and conducts research in the fields of mental health

and psychiatry in and outside the U.S; assembles data and findings for mental health and psychiatry. Currently conducts Phase I through Phase IV inpatient and outpatient research medication studies for depression, anxiety, bipolar disorder, schizophrenia, schizoaffective disorder and Alzheimer's disease. Has supported several suicide prevention and drug abuse projects. Has developed a 15-week home-study program on panic and agoraphobia.

15761 ■ Society of Biological Psychiatry (SBP)

c/o Mayo Clinic of Jacksonville
Research-Birdsall 310
4500 San Pablo Rd.
Jacksonville, FL 32224
Ph: (904)953-2842
Fax: (904)953-7117
E-mail: maggie@mayo.edu
URL: http://www.sobp.org
Contact: Maggie Peterson MBA, Exec. Dir.
Founded: 1945. **Members:** 950. **Membership Dues:** active, $150 (annual). **Staff:** 1. **Budget:** $275,000. **Description:** International professional society of psychiatrists, neurologists, neurosurgeons, pharmacologists, neuropharmacologists, physiologists, psychologists, and physicians in related biological studies. Studies the neuronal basis of human behavior and the biological basis of psychiatry. Compiles statistics. **Libraries:** Type: reference. **Holdings:** archival material, business records. **Awards:** A.E. Bennett Award. **Frequency:** annual. **Type:** recognition ● George N. Thompson Distinguished Service Award. **Frequency:** annual. **Type:** recognition ● Gold Medal Award. **Frequency:** annual. **Type:** recognition ● Lilly Fellowship. **Frequency:** annual. **Type:** fellowship ● Ziskind-Somerfeld Award. **Frequency:** annual. **Type:** recognition. **Committees:** Public Relations; Research Awards; Scientific Informational Opportunities. **Publications:** *Biological Psychiatry*, bimonthly. Journal. Alternate Formats: CD-ROM ● *Membership Roster*, annual. Membership Directory. **Conventions/Meetings:** annual convention (exhibits) - 2008 May 1-3, Washington, DC; 2009 May 14-16, San Francisco, CA.

15762 ■ Society of Professors of Child and Adolescent Psychiatry (SPCAP)

3615 Wisconsin Ave. NW
Washington, DC 20016
Ph: (202)333-7636
Fax: (202)464-0131
E-mail: rlhendren@ucdavis.edu
URL: http://www.spcap.org
Contact: Mr. Earl Magee, Admin.
Founded: 1969. **Members:** 150. **Membership Dues:** individual, $150 (annual). **Staff:** 1. **Budget:** $20,000. **Description:** Division directors from university psychiatric departments who meet annually to discuss issues in child and adolescent psychiatry. **Awards:** Type: recognition. **Computer Services:** Mailing lists, adhesive, electronic. **Formerly:** (1987) Society of Professors of Child Psychiatry. **Publications:** *SPCAP Membership Directory*, annual. **Circulation:** 150. **Conventions/Meetings:** annual meeting and conference, scientific meeting.

15763 ■ World Association of Cultural Psychiatry (WACP)

c/o Wen-Shing Tseng, MD, Pres.
1356 Lusitana St.
Honolulu, HI 96813-2421
E-mail: president@waculturalpsy.org
URL: http://www.waculturalpsychiatry.org
Contact: Wen-Shing Tseng MD, Pres.
Founded: 2004. **Membership Dues:** group A (high income), $60 (annual) ● group A (high income), $100 (biennial) ● group B (upper-middle income), $40 (annual) ● group B (upper-middle income), $70 (biennial) ● group C (lower-middle income), $30 (annual) ● group C (lower-middle income), $50 (biennial). **Multinational. Description:** Promotes the exchange of scientific knowledge, research initiatives and clinical experiences in the field of cultural psychiatry worldwide. Encourages the development of cultural psychiatric activities and organizations within nations

and larger regions throughout the world. Assists the coordination of working relations between national, regional and international organizations in the field of cultural psychiatry. **Publications:** *WACP Newsletter*. **Price:** included in membership dues. Alternate Formats: online ● *World Cultural Psychiatry Research Review*, quarterly. Journal. Reviews published and unpublished scientific articles relating to cultural psychiatry. **Price:** included in membership dues. ISSN: 1932-6270. Also Cited As: *WCPRR*.

15764 ■ World Association for Infant Mental Health (WAIMH)

Univ. Outreach and Engagement
Kellogg Ctr., Garden Level, No. 24
Michigan State Univ.
East Lansing, MI 48824
Ph: (517)432-3793
Fax: (517)432-3694
E-mail: waimh@msu.edu
URL: http://www.msu.edu/user/waimh
Contact: Hiram E. Fitzgerald, Exec. Dir.
Founded: 1992. **Members:** 850. **Membership Dues:** professional in U.S., $115 (annual) ● professional in Canada, $118 (annual) ● professional outside U.S. and Canada, $127 (annual) ● student in U.S., $85 (annual) ● student in Canada, $88 (annual) ● student outside U.S. and Canada, $97 (annual). **Staff:** 1. **Regional Groups:** 19. **Languages:** English, French. **Description:** Child development specialists, child psychiatrists, child psychoanalysts, infant care workers, linguists, nurses, obstetricians, pediatricians, psychologists, and social workers. Works to further research and understanding of mental development and disorders in children from conception through age 3. Promotes studies on the conditions affecting the mental health of infants, their parents, and other caregivers; explores mental development during infancy and its subsequent effects on psychopathological development. Advocates international multidisciplinary discussions of research and intervention in infant psychiatry within the framework of the total life cycle. Facilitates communication and exchange of information and theories; fosters discussion of questions, problems, and issues in infant mental health. **Awards:** New Investigator Award. **Frequency:** periodic. **Type:** recognition. **Recipient:** for promising new investigators in infant mental health ● Serge Lebovici Award. **Frequency:** periodic. **Type:** recognition. **Recipient:** for significant contributions to the international development of infant mental health ● Sonya Bemporad Award. **Frequency:** periodic. **Type:** recognition. **Recipient:** for significant contributions to the advancement of social and public policies ● WAIMH Award. **Frequency:** periodic. **Type:** recognition. **Recipient:** for significant contribution to the association. **Formed by Merger of:** World Association for Allied Disciplines and Infant Psychiatry; International Association for Infant Mental Health. **Publications:** *Infant Mental Health Journal*, bimonthly. **Price:** $45.00 for members in U.S.; $58.00 for members outside U.S.; $75.00 for nonmembers in U.S. ISSN: 0163-9641. **Circulation:** 1,000 ● *The Signal*, quarterly. Newsletter. **Price:** $99.00 for nonmembers outside U.S. ISSN: 0163-9641. **Circulation:** 1,000. **Conventions/Meetings:** biennial congress (exhibits) ● biennial World Congress - meeting.

15765 ■ World Association for Social Psychiatry (WASP)

656 Romero Canyon Rd.
Santa Barbara, CA 93108
Ph: (805)969-1376
Fax: (805)969-1376
E-mail: jlcmd@cox.net
Contact: John L. Carleton MD, Honorary Pres.
Founded: 1964. **Members:** 3,000. **Membership Dues:** individual, $15 (annual). **Staff:** 1. **Regional Groups:** 26. **Languages:** English, French, German, Spanish. **Multinational. Description:** Professionals, contributors, and interested individuals active in allied fields of social psychiatry including anthropology, social work, nursing, or occupational therapy. Aims to: study the nature of man and his surrounding culture; research methods to prevent and treat internal changes and behavioral disorders; advance

the physical, social, and philosophic well-being of mankind. Fosters collaboration among members and distributes theoretical and practical information. Conducts workshops and demonstrations of rehabilitation centers. **Formerly:** (1978) International Association for Social Psychiatry. **Publications:** *French Journal of Social Psychiatry* (in English and French), quarterly. **Advertising:** accepted ● *International Journal of Social Psychiatry*, quarterly ● *World Journal of Social Psychiatry* (in English and French), quarterly. **Advertising:** accepted. **Conventions/Meetings:** biennial congress (exhibits).

15766 ■ World Psychiatric Association (WPA)

c/o Prof. Juan E. Mezzich, Jr., Pres.
Intl. Center for Mental Hea.
Mt. Sinai School of Medicine of New York Univ.
Fifth Ave. & 100th St.
Box 1093
New York, NY 10029-6574
Ph: (718)334-5094
Fax: (718)334-5096
E-mail: wpasecretariat@wpanet.org
URL: http://www.wpanet.org
Contact: Prof. Juan E. Mezzich Jr., Pres.
Founded: 1950. **Members:** 116. **Regional Groups:** 18. **National Groups:** 114. **Languages:** English, French, German, Spanish. **Description:** Psychiatric societies and individuals in 90 countries. Aims are: to promote international cooperation in the field of psychiatry; to advance inquiry into the etiology, pathology, and treatment of mental illness; to strengthen relations among psychiatrists working in various fields. Encourages the exchange of information concerning the medical problems of mental diseases; sponsors educational and research programs. Comprises 40 sections representing different specialties in psychiatry. **Publications:** *WPA News*, quarterly. Newsletter. **Circulation:** 800. **Conventions/Meetings:** Thematic Conference - 3-4/year. 2008 June 19-21, Granada, Spain ● triennial World Congress of Psychiatry - convention, educational activities and exchange of information (exhibits) - 2008 Sept. 19-25, Prague, Czech Republic.

Psychoanalysis

15767 ■ American Academy of Psychoanalysis and Dynamic Psychiatry (AAPDP)

PO Box 30
1 Regency Dr.
Bloomfield, CT 06002
Ph: (860)243-3977
Free: (888)691-8281
Fax: (860)286-0787
E-mail: aap@ssmgt.com
URL: http://aapdp.org
Contact: Jacquelyn T. Coleman CAE, Exec. Dir.
Founded: 1956. **Members:** 600. **Membership Dues:** regular, $475 (annual). **Staff:** 3. **Budget:** $275,000. **Description:** Psychoanalysts are fellows of the academy; psychiatric members are psychiatrists who meet specific requirements; associates are psychiatrists, scientists, or educators; candidates. Seeks to develop communication among psychoanalysts and persons in other disciplines in science and the humanities; provides a forum for inquiry into the phenomena of individual motivation and social behavior; encourages and supports research in psychoanalysis; fosters acceptance of psychoanalysis. Sponsors seminars and symposia. **Computer Services:** Mailing lists. **Committees:** Children and Adolescents; History; Human Rights and Social Issues; Psychoanalysis and Religion; Psychoanalysis and Women; Psychoanalytic Education; Research; Transcultural Psychiatry. **Formerly:** (1966) Academy of Psychoanalysis; (2001) American Foundation for Psychoanalysis and Psychoanalysis in Groups; (2003) American Academy of Psychoanalysis. **Publications:** *Academy Forum*, biennial. Magazine. Contains articles on psychoanalysis and related topics and book reviews. **Price:** $20.00. **Advertising:** accepted ● *Academy News*. Newsletter. Alternate

Formats: online ● *Journal of the American Academy of Psychoanalysis and Dynamic Psychiatry*, quarterly. **Price:** $70.00 /year for individuals; $250.00 /year for institutions. **Conventions/Meetings:** semiannual conference (exhibits).

15768 ■ American Psychoanalytic Association (APSAA)
309 E 49th St.
New York, NY 10017-1601
Ph: (212)752-0450
Fax: (212)593-0571
E-mail: info@apsa.org
URL: http://www.apsa.org
Contact: Dottie Jeffries, Dir. of Public Affairs
Founded: 1911. **Members:** 3,500. **Staff:** 14. **Budget:** $2,300,000. **Local Groups:** 43. **Description:** Psychoanalysts who have graduated from or are currently attending an accredited institute. Seeks to establish and maintain standards for the training of psychoanalysts and for the practice of psychoanalysis; fosters the integration of psychoanalysis with other branches of medicine; encourages research. Conducts educational programs. **Computer Services:** Mailing lists. **Affiliated With:** International Psychoanalytical Association. **Publications:** *The American Psychoanalyst*, quarterly. Newsletter. **Price:** free for members. **Circulation:** 3,500. **Advertising:** accepted. Alternate Formats: online ● *Journal of the American Psychoanalytic Association*, quarterly. ISSN: 0003-0651 ● *Roster*, biennial. Membership Directory ● *Title Key Word and Author Index to Psychoanalytic Journals* ● Also publishes material on psychoanalytic education and research. **Conventions/Meetings:** semiannual conference (exhibits).

15769 ■ American Psychoanalytic Foundation (APF)
c/o American Psychoanalytic Association
309 E 49th St.
New York, NY 10017
Ph: (212)752-0450
Fax: (212)593-0571
E-mail: info@apsa.org
URL: http://www.apsa.org
Contact: Dean K. Stein, Exec. Dir.
Description: Dedicated to the advancement of psychoanalysis through community outreach, education, research, clinical programs. **Funds:** Psychoanalytic Assistance. **Absorbed:** (2004) Psychoanalytic Assistance Fund. **Conventions/Meetings:** annual meeting, benefit.

15770 ■ American Society of Psychoanalytic Physicians (ASPP)
13528 Wisteria Dr.
Germantown, MD 20874
Ph: (301)540-3197
Fax: (301)540-3511
E-mail: cfcotter@aspp.net
URL: http://www.aspp.net
Contact: Christine Cotter, Exec. Dir.
Founded: 1985. **Members:** 275. **Membership Dues:** individual, $250 (annual). **Staff:** 1. **Description:** Physicians, psychiatrists, and psychoanalysts united to: foster a wider understanding and utilization of psychoanalytic concepts; provide an opportunity to study psychoanalytic theory from all schools of thought; encourage clinical and didactic research; promote social and professional fraternalism among members in the field and maintain good relationships with other professional groups. Offers lectures on therapy that combines psychoanalytic orientation with other disciplines. **Awards:** Dr. Henry P. and Page Laughlin Award. **Frequency:** annual. **Type:** recognition. **Recipient:** for achievement in the teaching and practice of psychoanalysis and research ● Sigmund Freud Award. **Frequency:** annual. **Type:** recognition. **Recipient:** for achievement in the teaching and practice of psychoanalysis and research. **Formed by Merger of:** American Association of Psychoanalytic Physicians; American Society of Physician Analysts. **Publications:** *The Bulletin*, semiannual. **Price:** included in membership dues. ISSN: 1055-4572. **Conventions/Meetings:** annual conference - always May.

15771 ■ Association for Advancement of Psychoanalysis (of the Karen Horney Psychoanalytic Institute and Center) (AAP)
329 E 62nd St.
New York, NY 10021
Ph: (212)838-4333
E-mail: theclinic@karenhorneyclinic.org
URL: http://karenhorneyclinic.org
Contact: Jacqueline Simon, Dir. of Internship Training
Founded: 1941. **Members:** 80. **Membership Dues:** full, $100 (annual) ● associate, $50 (annual). **Staff:** 2. **Description:** Certified psychoanalysts interested in encouraging training in psychoanalysis and disseminating psychoanalytic principles to the medical-psychiatric profession and the general community. Conducts scientific meetings. Maintains a consultation and referral service, placement service, and speakers' bureau. Supports research programs; sponsors public educational lectures; maintains library of 4000 volumes. **Libraries: Type:** not open to the public. **Holdings:** 4,000. **Subjects:** psychoanalysis. **Committees:** Bookshop; Journal; Karen Horney Lecture; Library; Public Education; Public Relations; Referral; Scientific Lectures. **Affiliated With:** Karen Horney Clinic. **Publications:** *The American Journal of Psychoanalysis*, quarterly. Includes book reviews. **Price:** $59.00 for individuals (print only); $360.00 for libraries and institutions. ISSN: 0002-9548. Alternate Formats: microform ● Newsletter, semiannual. **Conventions/Meetings:** annual Karen Horney Lecture - meeting - always in New York City.

15772 ■ Association for Child Psychoanalysis (ACP)
7820 Enchanted Hills Blvd., No. A-233
Rio Rancho, NM 87144
Ph: (505)771-0372
Fax: (866)534-7555
E-mail: childanalysis@comcast.net
URL: http://www.childanalysis.org
Contact: Ms. Tricia Hall, Admin.
Founded: 1965. **Members:** 650. **Membership Dues:** full, $150 (annual) ● candidate, $50 (annual). **Staff:** 1. **Description:** Child psychoanalysts united to provide a forum for discussion and dissemination of information in their field. Conducts national and international scientific meetings. **Awards:** Award of Excellence. **Frequency:** annual. **Type:** recognition. **Recipient:** for outstanding work in promoting child analysis. **Computer Services:** database ● mailing lists. **Committees:** Arrangements; Awards; Continued Education; Eastern European; Extension; Grants; Liaison; Membership; Newsletter; Program; Study Groups. **Formerly:** (1971) American Association for Child Psychoanalysis. **Publications:** *Abstracts*, triennial ● *Association for Child Psychoanalysis— Newsletter*, semiannual. Covers child analysis methods, child psychoanalysis training, and the treatment and education of children throughout the world. **Price:** included in membership dues ● *Membership Roster*. Membership Directory. Alternate Formats: online. **Conventions/Meetings:** annual Scientific Meeting, with workshops, lectures, plenary sessions with group discussion.

15773 ■ Association for Psychoanalytic Medicine (APM)
c/o Dr. Lila J. Kalinich, MD, Pres.
333 Central Park W
New York, NY 10025
Ph: (718)548-6088
Fax: (718)548-8302
E-mail: gsagi@mac.com
URL: http://theapm.org
Contact: Dr. Lila J. Kalinich MD, Pres.
Founded: 1945. **Members:** 241. **Membership Dues:** active, $300 (annual) ● candidate, $50 (annual). **Description:** Represents physicians who are psychoanalysts. Provides forum on psychoanalytic developments for membership and community. Conducts postgraduate seminars. Sponsors speakers for community or medical groups. Conducts research on psychoanalytic involvement in social issues. **Awards:** George E. Daniels Merit Award. **Frequency:** annual. **Type:** recognition. **Recipient:** for outstanding contri-

butions to psychoanalysis through research or teaching ● Lionel Ovesey Award. **Frequency:** annual. **Type:** monetary. **Recipient:** for a candidate who has been significantly involved in original research, contributed to the psychoanalytic literature, or has developed an innovative teaching. **Committees:** Arrangements; Awards; Ethics; Lectureship; Legislation and Professional Practice; RAPS and Continuing Education. **Affiliated With:** American Psychoanalytic Association. **Formerly:** (1946) Association for Psychoanalytic and Psychosomatic Medicine. **Publications:** *Between Analyst and Patient.* Book ● *The Bulletin*, semiannual. Alternate Formats: online ● *The Psychology of Men.* Book ● *Roster*, biennial. Membership Directory. **Conventions/Meetings:** monthly Scientific Meeting - October through June at New York Academy of Medicine ● annual symposium.

15774 ■ International Association for Relational Psychoanalysis and Psychotherapy (IARRP)
22 Cortlandt St., 20th Fl.
New York, NY 10007
Ph: (212)669-6123
E-mail: info@iarpp.org
URL: http://www.iarpp.org
Contact: Hazel Ipp PhD, Pres.
Founded: 2001. **Membership Dues:** standard in U.S., $135 (annual) ● non-practicing, academic, candidate in U.S., $85 (annual) ● graduate student in U.S., $45 (annual) ● standard (in Canada, Western Europe, Japan, Australia & New Zealand), $90 (annual) ● non-practicing, academic, candidate (in Canada, Western Europe, Japan, Australia & New Zealand), $57 (annual) ● graduate student (in Canada, Western Europe, Japan, Australia & New Zealand), $30 (annual) ● standard (Israel, Latin America, Eastern Europe, Asia & Africa), $67 (annual) ● non-practicing, academic, candidate (Israel, Latin America, Eastern Europe, Asia & Africa), $42 (annual) ● graduate student (Israel, Latin America, Eastern Europe, Asia & Africa), $22 (annual). **Multinational. Description:** Promotes the development of relational psychoanalysis. Develops relational perspectives and explores similarities and differences with other approaches to analysis and psychotherapy. Encourages the formation of a space in which an open and democratic community of creative thinkers and practitioners can flourish. **Telecommunication Services:** electronic mail, office@iarpp.org. **Publications:** *IARPP eNews*, quarterly. Newsletter. **Price:** included in membership dues. Alternate Formats: online. **Conventions/Meetings:** annual conference.

15775 ■ Karen Horney Clinic (KHC)
329 E 62nd St.
New York, NY 10021
Ph: (212)838-4333
E-mail: theclinic@karenhorneyclinic.org
URL: http://www.karenhorneyclinic.org
Contact: Henry Paul MD, Exec. Dir.
Founded: 1955. **Staff:** 60. **Budget:** $1,600,000. **Description:** Promotes psychoanalytic and psychotherapeutic treatment of individuals and groups focusing on the special problems of children, adolescents, victims of violent crimes, adult survivors of childhood sexual abuse, and persons with psychoneurotic and emotional problems. Named for Karen Horney (1885-1952), German/American psychoanalyst and author of several books on neurosis, psychoanalysis, and related topics. Conducts children's services. **Libraries: Type:** reference. **Holdings:** 4,000. **Subjects:** psychoanalytic and mental health. **Additional Websites:** http://www.nycagainstrape.org/resource_23.html. **Affiliated With:** Association for Advancement of Psychoanalysis (of the Karen Horney Psychoanalytic Institute and Center). **Formerly:** (1979) Karen Horney Psychoanalytic Clinic. **Publications:** *American Journal of Psychoanalysis*, quarterly. **Advertising:** accepted ● *Association for the Advancement of Psychoanalysis*, periodic.

15776 ■ National Association for the Advancement of Psychoanalysis (NAAP)
80 8th Ave., Ste.1501
New York, NY 10011-7158
Ph: (212)741-0515

Fax: (212)366-4347
E-mail: info@naap.org
URL: http://www.naap.org
Contact: Margery Quackenbush, Exec. Dir.
Founded: 1972. **Members:** 1,700. **Membership Dues:** psychoanalyst or psychoanalytic psychotherapist, $175 (annual) ● candidate-in-training, $100 (annual). **Staff:** 5. **Budget:** $240,000. **Multinational. Description:** Psychoanalytic organizations and individual psychoanalysts from a variety of schools of psychoanalytic thought united for the advancement of psychoanalysis as a profession. Establishes standards for psychoanalytic training and works to improve its quality. Sets standards for certification of individual psychoanalysts; registers those who have met its training standards. **Libraries: Type:** open to the public. **Subjects:** psychoanalysis. **Awards:** Gradiva Award. **Frequency:** annual. **Type:** recognition. **Recipient:** for publications, movies, and plays ● Vision Award. **Frequency:** annual. **Type:** recognition. **Recipient:** for advancing psychoanalysis. **Computer Services:** Mailing lists ● online services. **Committees:** Analyst-in-Training; Conference; Continuing Education; Cultural Affairs; Educational Outreach; Ethics; Gradiva Awards; Membership Registration. **Formerly:** (2000) National Association for the Advancement of Psychoanalysis and the American Board for Accreditation in Psychoanalysis. **Publications:** *NAAP News*, quarterly. Newsletter. Covers institute, committee, and membership activities. Includes legislative news, calendar of events, and obituaries. **Price:** included in membership dues; $12.00 /year for nonmembers. **Advertising:** accepted ● *Registry of Psychoanalysts*, annual. Directory. Lists qualified psychoanalysts and candidates-in-training. Includes list of member organizations and geographic index. **Price:** $15.00/copy. **Advertising:** accepted. **Conventions/Meetings:** annual conference, book and institute exhibits (exhibits).

15777 ■ National Psychological Association for Psychoanalysis (NPAP)
150 W 13th St.
New York, NY 10011-7891
Ph: (212)924-7440
Fax: (212)989-7543
E-mail: info@npap.org
URL: http://www.npap.org
Contact: Paul Kaiser, Pres.
Founded: 1948. **Members:** 365. **Staff:** 2. **Languages:** English, French, German. **Description:** Professional society for practicing psychoanalysts. Conducts training program leading to certification in psychoanalysis. Offers information and private referral service for the public. Operates speakers' bureau. **Libraries: Type:** reference. **Holdings:** periodicals. **Subjects:** psychoanalysis. **Computer Services:** Mailing lists, for a fee. **Publications:** *National Psychological Association for Psychoanalysis—Bulletin*, biennial. **Price:** free ● *National Psychological Association for Psychoanalysis—News and Reviews*, semiannual. **Price:** included in membership dues. **Advertising:** accepted ● *Psychoanalytic Review*, bimonthly. Journal. Includes book reviews. ISSN: 0033-2836. **Advertising:** accepted ● *What is Psychoanalysis?*. Brochure. Alternate Formats: online ● Membership Directory. Alternate Formats: online.

15778 ■ Psychoanalytic Research Society
c/o Pamela A. Foelsch, Pres.
550 Mamaroneck Ave., Ste.102
Harrison, NY 10528
Ph: (914)533-0302
Fax: (914)381-6971
E-mail: pfoelsch@mail.med.cornell.edu
URL: http://www.division39section6.org
Contact: Pamela A. Foelsch, Pres.
Membership Dues: individual, $20 (annual) ● student, $10 (annual). **Description:** Promotes psychoanalytic research of an empirical, theoretical and clinical nature, including the planning and conducting of psychoanalytic research and dissemination of findings. **Committees:** Archivist; Education and Training; International Liaison; Professional Liaison; Program; Psychoanalytic Research

Fund Advisory; Public Policy; Publication. **Publications:** Bulletin.

15779 ■ Psychohistory Forum (PF)
627 Dakota Trail
Franklin Lakes, NJ 07417
Ph: (201)891-7486
E-mail: pelovitz@aol.com
Contact: Paul H. Elovitz PhD, Dir.
Founded: 1983. **Members:** 100. **Membership Dues:** patron, $250 (annual) ● sustaining, $150 (annual) ● supporting, $100 (annual) ● contributing, $50 (annual) ● contributing outside U.S., $53 (annual) ● full time student, $25 (annual) ● benefactor, $500 (biennial). **Staff:** 2. **Budget:** $25,000. **Description:** Psychologists, psychiatrists, Psychotherapists, social workers, historians, psychohistorians, and laypeople having a scholarly interest in the integration of depth psychology and history. (Psychohistory is the study of psychobiography, group process, the mechanisms of defense, the history of childhood, creativity, dreams, and the difference between stated intention and actual behavior). Seeks to further psychohistory through the exchange of information. Conducts bimonthly workshops on topics related to psychohistory and training seminars on dream analysis, innovation, teaching, and methodology. Aids individuals in psychohistorical research. Holds lecture series. lecture series. lecture series. **Libraries: Type:** reference. **Holdings:** 4,500. **Awards:** Halpern Award for the Best Psychohistorical Idea. **Frequency:** annual. **Type:** recognition ● Halpern Graduate Student Award. **Frequency:** annual. **Type:** monetary. **Recipient:** for the best psychohistorical idea ● Student Award. **Type:** recognition. **Recipient:** year's membership. **Projects:** Childhood, Personality and Psychology of Presidents; Columbian Cocaine (in Columbia); Dreamwork; Empathy; The Makers of Psychohistory; Teaching Psychohistory and Psychohistorically; War, Peace and Conflict Resolution. **Publications:** *Clio's Psyche: Understanding the Why of Culture Current Events, History and Society*, quarterly. Journal. **Price:** included in membership dues; $25.00 for nonmembers in U.S.; $35.00 for nonmembers outside U.S.; $48.00 for nonmembers in U.S. for 2 years. ISSN: 1080-2622. **Circulation:** 300 ● *Immigrant Experience: Personal Narrative and Psychological Analysis*. Monograph. **Price:** $58.00 for nonmembers outside U.S. for 2 years. ISSN: 1080-2622. **Circulation:** 300. **Conventions/Meetings:** meeting - 5-6/year.

15780 ■ Sandtray Network
1946 Clemens Rd.
Oakland, CA 94602
Ph: (510)530-1383
E-mail: sandtray@rcn.com
URL: http://www.sandtray.org
Membership Dues: individual, $30 (annual) ● couple, $45 (annual). **Multinational. Description:** Promotes learning, healing and creativity through the use of the sandtray. Disseminates information about the different sandtray methods. Explores the use of the sandtray as an interpersonal communication tool to bridge ethnic and cross-cultural barriers. **Computer Services:** Information services, sandplay facts. **Telecommunication Services:** electronic mail, sandworldplay@rcn.com. **Publications:** Journal. Contains articles about all aspects of sandtray use.

15781 ■ Sigmund Freud Archives (SFA)
c/o Manuscript Division of the Library Congress
101 Independence Ave. SE
Washington, DC 20540-4680
Ph: (516)621-6850
E-mail: haroldpblum@cs.com
URL: http://www.freudarchives.org
Contact: Dr. Harold P. Blum, Exec. Sec.
Founded: 1951. **Members:** 18. **Staff:** 1. **Description:** Psychoanalysts interested in the preservation and collection of scientific and personal writings of Sigmund Freud (1856-1939), Austrian neurologist and founder of psychoanalysis. Assists in research on Freud's life and work and the evolution of psychoanalytic thought; collects and classifies all documents, papers, publications, personal correspondence, and historical data written by, to, and on

Freud. **Libraries: Type:** open to the public. **Subjects:** Freud and psychoanalysis. **Conventions/Meetings:** annual meeting - usually October or November, New York City.

15782 ■ World Organization and Public Education Corporation of the National Association for the Advancement of Psychoanalysis (WOPAC NAAP)
80 8th Ave., Ste.1501
New York, NY 10011-5126
Ph: (212)741-0515 (212)741-0516
Fax: (212)366-4347
E-mail: info@naap.org
URL: http://www.naap.org
Contact: Margery Quackenbush, Exec. Dir.
Founded: 1995. **Staff:** 6. **Budget:** $25,000. **Multinational. Description:** Works for public education for the National Association for the Advancement of Psychoanalysis. **Awards:** Gradiva Awards. **Frequency:** annual. **Type:** recognition. **Recipient:** for work that advances psychoanalysis ● Vision Awards. **Frequency:** annual. **Type:** scholarship. **Recipient:** for work that advances psychoanalysis. **Formerly:** (2000) Public Education Corp. of the National Association for the Advancement of Psychoanalysis. **Publications:** Brochure. **Conventions/Meetings:** monthly seminar ● annual Trauma and Change: Psychoanalysis In a Time of Crisis - conference, with books and training information (exhibits).

Psychology

15783 ■ Alfred Adler Institute (AAI)
594 Broadway, Ste.1213
New York, NY 10012
Ph: (212)254-1048
Fax: (212)254-8271
E-mail: alfredadler@ny.com
URL: http://www.alfredadler-ny.org
Contact: Guilford Bartlett EdD, Exec. Dir.
Founded: 1948. **Members:** 220. **Staff:** 46. **Budget:** $80,000. **Description:** Offers training in psychotherapy, analytic psychotherapy and analysis to psychiatrists, psychologists, social workers, teachers, clergymen, lawyers, counselors and other related professional persons. Conducts part-time, evening three-year-plus programs to provide an understanding of the dynamics of personality and interpersonal relationships and to teach therapeutic methods and techniques. Presents the theory of Individual Psychology as formulated by the Austrian psychiatrist Alfred Adler (1870-1937). Maintains the Alfred Adler Consultation Center. **Libraries: Type:** reference. **Holdings:** 2,000. **Subjects:** psychotherapy, psychology, psychiatry, counseling. **Committees:** Arrangement; Students. **Affiliated With:** North American Society of Adlerian Psychology. **Formerly:** Alfred Adler Institute for Individual Psychology. **Publications:** *Journal of Individual Psychology*, quarterly ● Bulletin, annual ● Newsletter, quarterly. **Conventions/Meetings:** annual meeting ● semiannual seminar.

15784 ■ American Academy of Counseling Psychology (AACoP)
c/o Steve K.D. Eichel, PhD, Pres.
409 Nottingham Rd.
Newark, DE 19711
Ph: (302)598-1330
Free: (866)538-9048
Fax: (215)698-7873
E-mail: steve@dreichel.com
URL: http://www.aacop.net
Contact: Steve K.D. Eichel PhD, Pres.
Founded: 1992. **Description:** Consists of counseling psychologists who are Board Certified Diplomates of the American Board of Professional Psychology (ABPP). Promotes standards of professional practice and conduct within the specialization of Counseling Psychology; seeks to protect the well-being of the public, the profession, and the Academy. Provides education and training. **Formerly:** (2005) Academy of Counseling Psychology. **Publications:** *Bulletin of the American Academy of Counseling Psychology*,

annual. Alternate Formats: online. **Conventions/ Meetings:** biennial meeting.

15785 ■ American Association of Applied and Preventive Psychology (AAAPP)

PO Box 3822
Tucson, AZ 85722
Ph: (520)621-9182
Fax: (520)621-9306
E-mail: aaapp@u.arizona.edu
Contact: Lee Sechrest, Pres.
Members: 500. **Multinational. Description:** Protects the interests of clinical and preventive psychology in science, professional application and other means of improving human welfare. Promotes clinical and preventive research. **Computer Services:** Online services, discussion group. **Committees:** Psychology Medicalization. **Publications:** *Applied and Preventive Psychology.* Journal ● *The Scientist Practitioner.* Newsletter.

15786 ■ American Board of Professional Neuropsychology (ABPN)

c/o Michael J. Raymond, PhD, Exec. Dir.
John Heinz Rehabilitation Inst.
150 Mundy St.
Wilkes-Barre, PA 18702
Ph: (570)826-3771 (732)741-2552
E-mail: mjrphd@epix.net
URL: http://abpn.net
Contact: Michael J. Raymond PhD, Exec. Dir.
Founded: 1982. **Description:** Represents professional neuropsychologists. **Awards:** Distinguished Neuropsychologist Award. **Frequency:** annual. **Type:** recognition. **Recipient:** for outstanding neuropsychologist. **Committees:** Awards; Continuing Education; Examination; Long Term Planning; Training Site. **Publications:** *The Professional Neuropsychologist.* Newsletter. Alternate Formats: online ● Directory. Contains detailed listing of diplomates' services, subspecialties, ages served, and geographic locations. ● Membership Directory. Alternate Formats: online.

15787 ■ American Board of Professional Psychology (ABPP)

300 Drayton St., 3rd Fl.
Savannah, GA 31401
Ph: (912)234-5477
Free: (800)255-7792
Fax: (912)234-5120
E-mail: office@abpp.org
URL: http://www.abpp.org
Contact: Dr. David R. Cox, Exec. Off.
Founded: 1947. **Members:** 3,950. **Membership Dues:** regular, $165 (annual). **Staff:** 4. **Budget:** $350,000. **National Groups:** 13. **Description:** Conducts oral examinations and awards diplomas to advanced specialists in 11 professional specialties: psychoanalysis, rehabilitation psychology, behavioral psychology, clinical psychology, industrial and organizational psychology, forensic psychology, counseling psychology, clinical neuropsychology, family psychology, health psychology and school psychology. Candidates must have three years of qualifying experience in psychological practice. **Awards:** Distinguished Professional Achievement Award. **Frequency:** annual. **Type:** recognition. **Recipient:** for meritorious contributions to the psychology profession. **Affiliated With:** Association of State and Provincial Psychology Boards. **Absorbed:** American Board of Clinical Neuropsychology; American Board of Forensic Psychology; American Board of Family Psychology; American Board of Cognitive and Behavioral Psychology; American Board of Clinical Psychology; American Board of Counseling Psychology; American Board of School Psychology; American Board of Clinical Health Psychology; American Board of Organizational and Business Consulting; American Board of Rehabilitation Psychology; American Board of Psychoanalysis in Psychology; American Board of Examiners in Professional Psychology; American Board of Clinical Child and Adolescent Psychology; American Board of Group Psychology. **Formed by Merger of:** (1968) American Board of Examiners in Professional Psychology. **Publications:** *Policies and Procedures,* annual ● *The Specialist,* semiannual.

Newsletter. **Price:** included in membership dues. **Circulation:** 3,750. **Advertising:** accepted. Alternate Formats: online. **Conventions/Meetings:** annual board meeting, for Board of Trustees.

15788 ■ American Psychological Association (APA)

750 First St. NE
Washington, DC 20002-4242
Ph: (202)336-5500
Free: (800)374-2721
Fax: (202)336-6069
E-mail: president@apa.org
URL: http://www.apa.org
Contact: Sharon Stephens PhD, Pres.
Founded: 1892. **Members:** 150,000. **Membership Dues:** subsequent (member), $216 (annual) ● graduate student affiliate, $35 (annual) ● undergraduate student affiliate, $27 (annual) ● subsequent associate, $155 (annual) ● international affiliate, $27 (annual) ● high school teacher affiliate, $32 (annual). **Staff:** 540. **Budget:** $91,000,000. **Regional Groups:** 7. **State Groups:** 58. **Description:** Scientific and professional society of psychologists; students participate as affiliates. Advances psychology as a science, a profession, and as a means of promoting health, education and the human welfare. **Libraries:** Type: lending; open to the public; by appointment only. **Holdings:** 2,500; archival material, audiovisuals, books, periodicals. **Subjects:** psychology, mental health. **Computer Services:** database, PsycLit, PsycInfo. **Divisions:** Addictions; Adult Development and Aging; American Psychology-Law Society; Applied Experimental and Engineering Psychologists; Child, Youth, and Family Services; Clinical Neuropsychology; Clinical Psychology; Consulting Psychology; Counseling Psychology; Developmental Psychology; Educational Psychology; Evaluation, Measurement, and Statistics; Exercise and Sport Psychology; Experimental Analysis of Behavior; Experimental Psychology; Family Psychology; General Psychology; Group Psychology and Group Psychotherapy; Health Psychology; History of Psychology; Humanistic Psychology; Media Psychology; Mental Retardation and Developmental Disabilities; Military Psychology; Peace Psychology; Physiological and Comparative Psychology; Population and Environmental Psychology; Psychoanalysis; Psychological Hypnosis; Psychologists in Independent Practice; Psychologists in Public Service; Psychology and the Arts; Psychology of Religion; Psychology of Women; Psychopharmacology and Substance Abuse; Psychotherapy; Rehabilitation Psychology; School Psychology; Society for Community Research and Action; Society for Consumer Psychology; Society for Industrial and Organizational Psychology; Society for the Psychological Study of Ethnic Minority Issues; Society for the Psychological Study of Lesbian and Gay Issues; Society for the Psychological Study of Men and Masculinity; Society for the Psychological Study of Social Issues; Society of Personality and Social Psychology; State Psychological Association Affairs; Teaching of Psychology; Theoretical and Philosophical Psychology. **Affiliated With:** Psi Chi, the National Honor Society in Psychology. **Absorbed:** Psychologists Interested in the Advancement of Psychotherapy. **Publications:** *American Psychologist,* monthly. Journal. Publishes articles on current issues in psychology as well as empirical, theoretical, and practical articles on broad aspects of psychology. **Price:** included in membership dues; $180.00 /year for nonmembers in U.S.; $220.00 /year for nonmembers outside U.S.; $332.00 /year for institutions in U.S. ISSN: 0003-066X. **Circulation:** 103,000. **Advertising:** accepted ● *APA Monitor,* monthly. Newspaper. Reports on the science, profession, and social responsibility of psychology, plus legislative developments affecting mental health and education. **Price:** included in membership dues; $30.00 /year for nonmembers in U.S.; $48.00 /year for institutions in U.S.; $35.00 /year for nonmembers outside U.S. ISSN: 0001-2114. **Circulation:** 103,000. **Advertising:** accepted ● *Behavioral Neuroscience,* bimonthly. Journal. Publishes original research papers in the broad field of the biological bases of behavior. Includes reviews and theoretical articles. **Price:**

$83.00 /year for members; $166.00 /year for non-members in U.S.; $186.00 /year for nonmembers outside U.S.; $332.00 /year for institutions in U.S. ISSN: 0735-7044. **Circulation:** 1,300. **Advertising:** accepted ● *Clinician's Research Digest,* monthly. Newsletter. Contains selections and summaries of articles from clinical research journals. **Price:** $46.00 /year for members in U.S.; $83.00 /year for nonmembers in U.S.; $123.00 /year for nonmembers outside U.S.; $110.00 /year for institutions in U.S. ISSN: 8756-3207. **Circulation:** 6,000 ● *Contemporary Psychology,* monthly. Journal. Contains critical reviews of books, films, tapes, and other media relevant to psychology. **Price:** $73.00 /year for members; $145.00 /year for nonmembers in U.S.; $185.00 /year for nonmembers outside U.S.; $291.00 /year for institutions in U.S. ISSN: 0010-7549. **Circulation:** 3,000. **Advertising:** accepted ● *Developmental Psychology,* bimonthly. Journal. Publishes articles that advance knowledge and theory about human development across the life span. **Price:** $72.00 /year for members; $144.00 /year for nonmembers in U.S.; $164.00 /year for nonmembers outside U.S.; $284.00 /year for institutions in U.S. ISSN: 0012-1649. **Circulation:** 5,500. **Advertising:** accepted ● *Directory of the American Psychological Association,* quinquennial. Membership Directory. Lists names, addresses, telephone numbers, and divisional affiliations of members. **Price:** $50.00 for members and affiliates. **Circulation:** 3,000 ● *Health Psychology,* bimonthly. Journal. Covers research on the relationships between behavioral principles and physical health and illness. **Price:** $37.00 /year for members in U.S.; $73.00 /year for nonmembers in U.S.; $93.00 /year for nonmembers outside U.S.; $180.00 /year for institutions in U.S. ISSN: 0278-6133. **Circulation:** 9,500. **Advertising:** accepted ● *Journal of Abnormal Psychology,* quarterly. Publishes articles on basic research and theory in the broad field of abnormal behavior and its determinants and correlates. **Price:** $45.00 /year for members; $90.00 /year for nonmembers in U.S.; $105.00 /year for nonmembers outside U.S.; $180.00 /year for institutions in U.S. ISSN: 0021-843X. **Circulation:** 6,000. **Advertising:** accepted ● *Journal of Applied Psychology,* bimonthly. Includes original quantitative investigations that contribute new knowledge and understanding to fields of applied psychology. **Price:** $69.00 /year for members; $138.00 /year for nonmembers in U.S.; $158.00 /year for nonmembers outside U.S.; $277.00 /year for institutions in U.S. ISSN: 0021-9010. **Circulation:** 6,000. **Advertising:** accepted ● *Journal of Consulting and Clinical Psychology,* bimonthly. Presents original research on techniques of diagnosis and treatment in disordered behavior and studies of populations of clinical interest. **Price:** $83.00 /year for members; $166.00 /year for nonmembers in U.S.; $186.00 /year for nonmembers outside U.S.; $327.00 /year for institutions in U.S. ISSN: 0022-006X. **Circulation:** 8,000. **Advertising:** accepted ● *Journal of Counseling Psychology,* quarterly. Contains empirical studies about counseling processes and interventions, theoretical articles in counseling, and studies of counseling programs. **Price:** $38.00 /year for members; $76.00 /year for nonmembers in U.S.; $91.00 /year for nonmembers outside U.S.; $152.00 /year for institutions in U.S. ISSN: 0022-0167. **Circulation:** 9,000. **Advertising:** accepted ● *Journal of Educational Psychology,* quarterly. Publishes original investigations dealing with learning and cognition, social and emotional processes, and human development. **Price:** $48.00 /year for members; $97.00 /year for nonmembers in U.S.; $112.00 /year for nonmembers outside U.S.; $194.00 /year for institutions in U.S. ISSN: 0022-0663. **Circulation:** 5,500. **Advertising:** accepted ● *Journal of Experimental Psychology: Human Perception and Performance,* bimonthly. Publishes studies on perception, formulation and control of action and related cognitive processes. **Price:** $104.00 /year for members; $185.00 /year for nonmembers in U.S.; $205.00 /year for nonmembers outside U.S.; $358.00 /year for institutions in U.S. ISSN: 0096-1523. **Circulation:** 1,800. **Advertising:** accepted ● *Journal of Experimental Psychology: Learning, Memory, and Cognition,* bimonthly. Publishes original experimental studies or non-empirical reports on cognition, learning, memory, imagery, concept formation, and related subjects. **Price:** $104.00 /year for members; $185.00 /year for non-members in U.S.; $205.00 /year for nonmembers outside U.S.; $358.00 /year for institutions in U.S. ISSN: 0278-7393. **Circulation:** 3,600. **Advertising:** accepted ● *Journal of Family Psychology*, quarterly. Includes articles on the study of family systems. Includes reviews, reports, and theoretical articles. **Price:** $42.00 /year for members in U.S.; $70.00 /year for nonmembers in U.S.; $85.00 /year for nonmembers outside U.S.; $103.00 /year for institutions in U.S. ISSN: 0893-3200. **Circulation:** 4,000. **Advertising:** accepted ● *Journal of Personality and Social Psychology*, monthly. Contains research results on attitudes and social cognition, interpersonal relations, group and individual processes and individual differences. **Price:** $140.00 /year for members; $290.00 /year for nonmembers in U.S.; $330.00 /year for nonmembers outside U.S.; $622.00 /year for institutions in U.S. ISSN: 0022-3514. **Circulation:** 5,800. **Advertising:** accepted ● *Psychological Assessment*, quarterly. Journal. Contains empirical articles on clinical assessment and evaluation. **Price:** $42.00 /year for members; $83.00 /year for nonmembers in U.S.; $98.00 /year for nonmembers outside U.S.; $166.00 /year for institutions in U.S. ISSN: 1040-3590. **Circulation:** 6,700. **Advertising:** accepted ● *Psychological Bulletin*, bimonthly. Journal. Provides evaluative and integrative reviews and interpretations of critical substantive and methodological issues in scientific psychology. **Price:** $73.00 /year for members; $145.00 /year for nonmembers in U.S.; $165.00 /year for nonmembers outside U.S.; $274.00 /year for institutions in U.S. ISSN: 0033-2909. **Circulation:** 7,700. **Advertising:** accepted ● *Psychological Methods*, quarterly. Journal. Includes development and dissemination of methods for collecting, understanding, and interpreting psychological data. **Price:** $55.00 /year for nonmembers in U.S.; $70.00 /year for nonmembers outside U.S.; $110.00 /year for institutions in U.S.; $28.00 /year for members. ISSN: 1082-989X. **Advertising:** accepted. **Conventions/Meetings:** annual convention (exhibits).

15789 ■ American Psychological Association - Division of of Family Psychology
c/o American Psychological Association
750 First St. NE
Washington, DC 20002-4242
Ph: (202)336-6013
Fax: (202)218-3599
E-mail: cindy.carlson@mail.utexas.edu
URL: http://www.apa.org/divisions/div43
Contact: William H. Watson PhD, Pres.
Founded: 1984. **Members:** 2,000. **Membership Dues:** full, $31 (annual) ● student, $15 (annual) ● affiliate, $50 (annual). **Description:** A division of the American Psychological Association (see separate entry). Psychologists interested in research, teaching, prevention, treatment, evaluation and public interest initiatives in family psychology. Seeks to promote human welfare through the development, dissemination and application of knowledge about the dynamics, structure and functioning of the family. Conducts research and specialized education programs. Maintains speakers' bureau. **Awards: Frequency:** annual. **Type:** recognition. **Committees:** Addictive Behaviors; Aging; AIDS; At-Risk Children; Awards; Chronic Illness/Disability; Continuing Education; Critical Issues in Families; Education and Training; Ethical Concerns; Families and Healthcare Concerns; Families and Schools; Families and Workplace; Family Violence; Fellows; Gender Concerns; Lesbian and Gay Family Issues; Mental Illness; Minority and Ethnocultural Concerns; Research; Rural Family Psychology; Sexuality and Families; Student Development; Trauma. **Task Forces:** Diagnosis and Classification; Investment in Diversity in Family Psychology; Specialty Guidelines in Family Psychology. **Affiliated With:** American Psychological Association. **Supersedes:** Academy of Family Psychology. **Publications:** *The Family Psychologist*, quarterly. Bulletin. **Circulation:** 4,000. **Advertising:** accepted. **Conventions/Meetings:** annual convention, in conjunction with American Psychology Association (exhibits) ● annual meeting, in conjunction

with APA Divisions of Psychotherapy and Independent Practice - always mid-winter.

15790 ■ American Psychological Association Division of Independent Practice (APADIP)
c/o Jeannie Beeaff
Div. 42, Central Off.
919 W Marshall Ave.
Phoenix, AZ 85013
Ph: (602)246-6768
Fax: (602)246-6577
E-mail: div42apa@cox.net
URL: http://www.apa.org/about/division/div42.html
Contact: Laura H. Barbanel EdD, Pres.
Founded: 1982. **Members:** 8,600. **Membership Dues:** fellow, $42 (annual). **Description:** Members of the American Psychological Association (APA) engaged in independent practice. Works to insure that the needs and concerns of independent psychology practitioners are considered by the APA. Gathers and disseminates information on legislation affecting the practice of psychology, managed care and other developments in the health care industries, office management, malpractice risk and insurance, hospital management. Offers continuing professional education programs. **Awards:** Distinguished Psychologists of the Year. **Frequency:** annual. **Type:** recognition. **Recipient:** for a psychologist with distinguished and sustained service to the practice of psychology ● Rosalee G. Weiss Award. **Frequency:** annual. **Type:** recognition. **Recipient:** for outstanding leader in the arts or sciences who has contributed to psychology. **Additional Websites:** http://www.division42.org. **Publications:** *Independent Practitioner*, quarterly. Newsletter. **Advertising:** accepted. **Conventions/Meetings:** semiannual board meeting and convention - always March and the second week of August.

15791 ■ American Psychological Association of Graduate Students (APAGS)
750 1st St. NE
Washington, DC 20002-4242
Ph: (202)336-6014
E-mail: apags@apa.org
URL: http://www.apa.org/apags
Contact: Kristi Sands Van Sickle, Chair
Founded: 1988. **Membership Dues:** graduate, $43 (annual) ● undergraduate, $41 (annual). **Description:** Establishes and maintains channels of communication between APAGS and the psychological community. Promotes the highest standards in the research, teaching and practice of psychology for further education and development of all psychology students. Promotes graduate student leadership development in order to communicate and advocate the concerns of psychology students. **Awards:** APA/APAGS Award for Distinguished Graduate Student in Professional Psychology. **Frequency:** annual. **Type:** monetary. **Recipient:** to a graduate student for outstanding practice and application of psychology ● APAGS Award for Outstanding State, Provincial or Territorial Psychological Association of the Year. **Frequency:** annual. **Type:** monetary. **Recipient:** for superior performance in promoting graduate student development, involvement, and joint APAGS/SPTA membership ● APAGS Scholarships. **Frequency:** annual. **Type:** scholarship. **Recipient:** to graduate student members in good standing ● Department of the Year Award. **Frequency:** annual. **Type:** monetary. **Recipient:** to a graduate psychology department that has exemplified an outstanding level of commitment towards graduate students and graduate student life. **Telecommunication Services:** electronic mail, kristivansickle@msn.com. **Publications:** *APAGS Campus Representative Bulletin*, quarterly. Alternate Formats: online ● *gradPSYCH*, quarterly. Magazine. Provides information on innovative psychology careers. **Price:** included in membership dues.

15792 ■ American Psychology-Law Society (AP-LS)
c/o Ms. Lynn Peterson, Admin. Asst.
PO Box 638
Niwot, CO 80544
Ph: (303)652-9154
Fax: (303)652-2723

E-mail: div41apa@comcast.net
URL: http://www.ap-ls.org
Contact: Ms. Lynn Peterson, Admin. Asst.
Founded: 1968. **Members:** 2,000. **Membership Dues:** general, $60 (annual) ● student, $30 (annual). **Staff:** 1. **Budget:** $200,000. **Multinational. Description:** Works as a division of American Psychological Association. Aims to: promote exchanges between the disciplines of psychology and law in regard to teaching, research, administration of justice, jurisprudence, and other matters at the psychology-law interface; foster research relevant to legal problems using psychological knowledge and methods and advance psychological research using the legal setting and related legal research techniques; promote education of lawyers at all levels regarding psychology, and of psychologists at all levels regarding the law; encourage legislation and social policies consistent with current states of psychological knowledge; promote the effective use of psychologists in the legal processes. **Awards:** American Psychology-Law Society Book Award. **Frequency:** biennial. **Type:** trophy. **Recipient:** for the best book on a psychology law topic published within the last two years ● Dissertation Award. **Frequency:** annual. **Type:** monetary. **Recipient:** for the best dissertation on a psychology and law topic ● Outstanding Teaching and Mentoring Award. **Frequency:** annual. **Type:** monetary. **Recipient:** for outstanding teacher and mentor in the field of psychology and law (in even years); for a professor at a teaching-oriented institution (in odd years) ● Saleem Shah Early Career Award. **Frequency:** annual. **Type:** monetary. **Recipient:** for outstanding early career contributions to the field of psychology and law within the first six years. **Committees:** Grants-in-Aid; Mentorship. **Affiliated With:** American Psychological Association. **Publications:** *Law and Human Behavior*, bimonthly. Journal. Contains scholarly research on psychology-law topics including jury decision-making, eyewitness identification, expert witnesses and mental health. **Price:** included in membership dues. **Advertising:** accepted ● *Monograph Series*, periodic. Monographs ● Newsletter, quarterly. Covers association activities; lists opportunities in psychology and law. **Price:** included in membership dues. **Advertising:** accepted. **Conventions/Meetings:** annual conference, held in conjunction with APA (exhibits).

15793 ■ Association for the Advancement of Gestalt Therapy (AAGT)
c/o Sylvie Falschlunger, Admin. Asst.
60 Waller Ave.
White Plains, NY 10605
Ph: (914)686-3477
E-mail: info@aagt.org
URL: http://www.aagt.org
Contact: Peter Philippson, Pres.
Membership Dues: full-time professional, $100 (annual) ● part-time, new professional, $50 (annual) ● retiree, student, $25 (annual) ● supporting, $150 (annual). **Multinational. Description:** Represents psychiatrists, psychologists, social workers, teachers, academics, writers, artists, performers, organizational consultants and political and social analysts, activists, and students. Seeks to advance theory, philosophy, practice and research in Gestalt Therapy and its various applications, including but not limited to, personal growth, mental health, education, organization and systems development, political and social development and change, and the fine and performing arts. **Telecommunication Services:** electronic mail, peterphilippson@gmail.com. **Committees:** Gestalt Applications to Diverse and Special Populations; Gestalt Community Development, Networking and Support; Gestalt Theory Development and Philosophy; Gestalt Therapy and Social Change; Gestalt Therapy in Academia and Higher Education; Gestalt Therapy with Children; Gestalt Training Institutes Liaison; Gestalt Training Materials Development. **Publications:** *AAGT Newsletter*. **Advertising:** accepted. Alternate Formats: online. **Conventions/Meetings:** international conference and workshop ● annual meeting - usually held during conferences.

15794 ■ Association for the Advancement of Psychology (AAP)
PO Box 38129
Colorado Springs, CO 80937-8129
Free: (800)869-6595

Fax: (719)520-0375
E-mail: smpfeiffer@aapnet.org
URL: http://www.aapnet.org
Contact: Stephen M. Pfeiffer PhD, Exec. Dir.
Founded: 1974. **Members:** 6,000. **Membership Dues:** individual, $95 (annual) ● sponsoring organization, $150 (annual) ● student, $10 (annual). **Description:** Members of the American Psychological Association (see separate entry) or other national psychological associations, students of psychology, and organizations with a primarily psychological focus. Aims to advance psychology and represent the interests of all psychologists (professional, social, and scientific) in the public policy arena. Maintains Psychologists For Legislative Action Now, a political action and education committee. **Absorbed:** (1975) Council for the Advancement of Psychological Professions and Sciences. **Publications:** *AAP Advance*, quarterly. Newsletter. Includes calendar of events and research updates. **Price:** included in membership dues. **Circulation:** 6,000. Alternate Formats: online.

15795 ■ Association for Birth Psychology (ABP)
444 E 82nd St.
New York, NY 10028
Ph: (212)988-6617
E-mail: birthpsychology@aol.com
URL: http://birthpsychology.org
Contact: Leslie Feher PhD, Exec. Dir.
Founded: 1978. **Members:** 352. **Membership Dues:** individual, $50 (annual). **Description:** Obstetricians, pediatricians, midwives, nurses, psychotherapists, psychologists, counselors, social workers, sociologists, and others interested in birth psychology, a developing discipline concerned with the experience of birth and the correlation between the birth process and personality development. Seeks to promote communication among professionals in the field; encourage commentary, research, and theory from different points of view; establish birth psychology as an autonomous science of human behavior; develop guidelines and give direction to the field. **Libraries: Type:** reference. **Subjects:** birth. **Publications:** *Birth Psychology Bulletin*, semiannual. Journal. Covers conception to the first year of life. Includes book reviews, research reports, calendar of events, and case reports. **Price:** included in membership dues; $20.00 /year for nonmembers. ISSN: 0734-3124. **Circulation:** 1,000 ● Books. **Conventions/Meetings:** annual conference ● regional meeting ● workshop.

15796 ■ Association of Black Psychologists (ABPsi)
PO Box 55999
Washington, DC 20040-5999
Ph: (202)722-0808
Fax: (202)722-5941
E-mail: abpsi_office@abpsi.org
URL: http://www.abpsi.org
Contact: Robert Atwell, Pres.
Founded: 1968. **Members:** 1,400. **Membership Dues:** life, $2,500 ● supporting, $250 (annual) ● professional/associate/adjunct, $150 (annual) ● affiliate, $160 (annual) ● graduate student, $50 (annual) ● undergraduate student, $30 (annual) ● institutional, $300 (annual). **Staff:** 4. **Budget:** $500,000. **Regional Groups:** 4. **State Groups:** 29. **Local Groups:** 35. **Description:** Professional psychologists and others in associated disciplines. Aims to: enhance the psychological well being of black people in America; define mental health in consonance with newly established psychological concepts and standards; develop policies for local, state and national decision-making that have impact on the mental health of the black community; support established black sister organizations and aid in the development of new, independent black institutions to enhance the psychological, educational, cultural and economic situation. Offers training and information on AIDS. Conducts seminars, workshops and research. **Committees:** AIDS; Black Family; Black Mental Health Month; Communications; Ethics; Research and Development; Social Action; Social Work Liaison; Student Affairs; Testing. **Publications:** *Association of Black*

Psychologists Publications Manual ● *Journal of Black Psychology*, quarterly. Provides research results. Includes book reviews. **Price:** $30.00 /year for individuals; $50.00 /year for institutions. ISSN: 0095-7984. **Circulation:** 2,500. **Advertising:** accepted ● *Monographs From the Journal of Black Psychology*, biennial ● *Proceedings of Annual Convention* ● *Psych Discourse*, monthly. Journal. Includes calendar of events and research updates. **Price:** included in membership dues; $95.00 /year for nonmembers. **Circulation:** 2,500 ● *Resource Manual for Black Psychology Students* ● *Sourcebook on the Teaching of Black Psychology* ● Also publishes brochures, bulletins and research projects; distributes videotapes on issues in black psychology. **Conventions/Meetings:** periodic conference (exhibits) ● annual convention (exhibits) - always August.

15797 ■ Association for Clinical Psychosocial Research (ACPR)
c/o Lisa Dixon, MD, Membership Chair
Dept. of Psychology
Univ. of Maryland
685 W Baltimore St.
Baltimore, MD 21201-1549
Ph: (215)842-4550
Fax: (215)843-3441
E-mail: ldixon@umaryland.edu
URL: http://www.wpic.pitt.edu/acpr
Contact: Katherine Shear MD, Pres.
Description: Professionals active in psychosocial research who show promise as independent investigators. Seeks to improve research and enhance prevention, treatment and rehabilitation. Conducts annual meetings and seminars.

15798 ■ Association for Humanistic Psychology (AHP)
1516 Oak St., No. 320A
Alameda, CA 94501-2958
Ph: (510)769-6495
Fax: (510)769-6433
E-mail: ahpoffice@aol.com
URL: http://www.ahpweb.org
Contact: Mr. Garroy U. Ferguson, Pres.
Founded: 1962. **Members:** 2,000. **Membership Dues:** introductory, limited income, $49 (annual) ● regular, $69 (annual) ● humanistic professional, $110 (annual) ● organization, $149 (annual) ● couple, $89 (annual). **Staff:** 4. **Budget:** $350,000. **State Groups:** 1. **Local Groups:** 2. **National Groups:** 2. **Description:** Psychologists, social workers, clergy, educators, psychiatrists, and others engaged in humanistic practice. Functions as an international community of people who are dedicated to the exploration, healing, and expansion of the human mind, body and soul, and to building a society that advances humans' ability to choose, to grow, and to create. Aims to realize a vision of the possible for humanity. **Awards:** Pathfinder Award. **Frequency:** periodic. **Type:** recognition. **Recipient:** for a person who has contributed to forwarding humanistic principles. **Computer Services:** Mailing lists, for rental or promotion of sponsored events. **Committees:** The Oregon Community; Somatics and Wellness Community. **Formerly:** American Association for Humanistic Psychology. **Publications:** *AHP Perspective*, bimonthly. Magazine. Covers growth therapies, holistic education, interdisciplinary humanistic practices, and social concerns. Includes calendar of events. **Price:** included in membership dues. **Circulation:** 5,000. **Advertising:** accepted ● *Journal of Humanistic Psychology*, quarterly. **Conventions/Meetings:** annual Winter Professional Training - workshop, 1 or 2-day training seminar on specified topic - always in Cancun, Mexico.

15799 ■ Association for Psychoanalytic Self Psychology (APSP)
c/o Helena Johansson, Membership Mgr.
7916 Convoy Ct.
San Diego, CA 92111-1212
Ph: (858)565-9921
Fax: (858)565-9954

E-mail: iapsp@pcmisandiego.com
URL: http://www.psychologyoftheself.com
Contact: James L. Fosshage PhD, Founding Pres.
Founded: 1987. **Membership Dues:** regular (prorated over the year), $80-$200 (annual) ● student/candidate (prorated over the year), $40-$100 (annual). **Multinational. Description:** Provides a forum for discussion and study of self psychology. Sponsors theoretical and clinical presentations on self psychology.

15800 ■ Association for Psychological Science (APS)
1010 Vermont Ave. NW, 11th Fl.
Washington, DC 20005-4918
Ph: (202)783-2077
Fax: (202)783-2083
E-mail: aps@psychologicalscience.org
URL: http://www.psychologicalscience.org
Contact: Alan G. Kraut, Exec. Dir.
Founded: 1988. **Members:** 15,000. **Membership Dues:** individual, $150 (annual) ● graduate student affiliate, $58 (annual) ● post-doctoral, retired, $89 (annual) ● spouse, $72 (annual) ● life, $3,000 ● undergraduate student affiliate, $35 (annual). **Staff:** 15. **Budget:** $2,000,000. **Description:** Aims for the advancement of scientific psychology and its representation at the national level. Seeks to promote, protect, and advance the interests of scientifically oriented psychology in research, application, teaching, and the improvement of human welfare. **Awards:** James McKeen Cattell Fellow Award. **Frequency:** annual. **Type:** scholarship. **Recipient:** for outstanding contributions to the area of applied psychological research ● William James Fellow Award. **Frequency:** annual. **Type:** scholarship. **Recipient:** for significant intellectual contributions to the basic science of psychology. **Computer Services:** Mailing lists, of members ● online services, job listings. **Formerly:** (2006) American Psychological Society. **Publications:** *APS Observer*, monthly. Magazine. Educates and informs the association on matters affecting the research, academic, and applied disciplines of psychology. **Price:** free for members; $75.00 for nonmembers. ISSN: 1050-4672. **Circulation:** 14,400. **Advertising:** accepted. Alternate Formats: online ● *Current Directions in Psychological Science*, bimonthly. Journal. Contains concise reviews spanning all of scientific psychology and its applications. ISSN: 0963-7214. **Circulation:** 15,000. **Advertising:** accepted. Alternate Formats: online ● *Psychological Science*, monthly. Journal. Publishes authoritative articles of interest across all of scientific psychology's subdisciplines. ISSN: 0956-7976. **Circulation:** 15,000. **Advertising:** accepted. Alternate Formats: online ● *Psychological Science in the Public Interest*, 3/year. Monographs. Alternate Formats: online. **Conventions/Meetings:** annual convention and symposium, offers variety of programs that span across all disciplines of scientific psychology (exhibits) - 2008 May 21-24, Chicago, IL - **Avg. Attendance:** 3500.

15801 ■ Association for Psychological Type International (APTi)
9650 Rockville Pike
Bethesda, MD 20814-3998
Ph: (301)634-7450
Free: (800)847-9943
Fax: (301)634-7455
E-mail: info@aptinternational.org
URL: http://www.aptinternational.org
Contact: John Lord, Exec. Dir.
Founded: 1979. **Members:** 5,000. **Membership Dues:** regular, in U.S. and Canada, $95 (annual) ● regular, outside North America, $105 (annual) ● shared publication fee, $75 (annual) ● full-time student, $45 (annual) ● retiree, $65 (annual). **Staff:** 7. **Budget:** $1,300,000. **Regional Groups:** 7. **Local Groups:** 60. **Description:** Individuals involved in organizational development, religion, management, education, and counseling, and who are interested in psychological type, the Myers-Briggs Type Indicator, and the works of Carl G. Jung (1875-1961). Aims to bring together and share ideas related to the uses of MBTI and the application of psychological type theory in any area; promotes research, development, and

education in the field. Sponsors seminars conferences and training sessions on the use of psychological type. **Divisions:** Careers and Occupations; Counseling and Psychotherapy; Education; Management and Organizational Development; Multi-Cultural; Psychological Theory; Religious and Spiritual; Research. **Publications:** *Bulletin of Psychological Type*, quarterly. Covers interest area issues, upcoming events, and book reviews. **Price:** included in membership dues. **Advertising:** accepted ● *Journal of Psychological Type*, semiannual. Discusses type theory and research. **Price:** included in membership dues. **Advertising:** accepted. **Conventions/Meetings:** biennial conference (exhibits).

15802 ■ Association of State and Provincial Psychology Boards (ASPPB)

PO Box 241245
Montgomery, AL 36124-1245
Ph: (334)832-4580
Fax: (334)269-6379
E-mail: asppb@asppb.org
URL: http://www.asppb.org
Contact: Kenneth G. Roy, Pres.

Founded: 1961. **Members:** 62. **Membership Dues:** individual, $35 (annual). **Staff:** 12. **Budget:** $2,000,000. **Description:** State boards of psychology from across the U.S. and Canada. Promotes the development and administration of the national EPPP examination for certification for the practice of psychology. Provides legal counsel to the member boards as well as keeping them abreast of changes in the field of psychology. Provides Certificate of Professional Qualification in Psychology (CPQ) to qualified psychologists for licensure in multiple jurisdictions. **Libraries: Type:** reference. **Holdings:** 500. **Subjects:** licensure, certification, credentialing of psychologists. **Awards:** Ming Fisher Award. **Frequency:** annual. **Type:** recognition. **Recipient:** for significant contributions as administrator or other employee of a psychology Board ● Norma P. Simon Award. **Frequency:** annual. **Type:** recognition. **Recipient:** for significant contributions to psychology credentialing on the national or international level ● Roger C. Smith Award. **Frequency:** annual. **Type:** recognition. **Recipient:** for significant contributions to psychology licensing and/or certification efforts at the state or provincial level. **Computer Services:** database, disciplinary actions against psychologists, Examination for Professional Practice in Psychology (EPPP) scores, roster of CPQ holders. **Formerly:** American Association of State Psychology Boards. **Publications:** *Avoiding Liability in Mental Health Practice.* **Price:** $45.00/copy ● *Ethical Dilemmas Facing Psychologists.* Video. **Price:** $125.00/copy ● *Items from Previous Examinations.* Contains 250 retired questions from previous version of the Examination for Professional Practice of Psychology (EPPP). **Price:** $75.00/copy ● *Research Digest.* **Price:** $25.00/copy ● Newsletter, quarterly. **Price:** $8.00/year. **Conventions/Meetings:** annual meeting - every October ● annual Midwinter Delegates Meeting - midwinter in February.

15803 ■ Association for Women in Psychology (AWP)

c/o Prof. Suzanna Rose, PhD, Dir. of Women's Studies
Florida Intl. Univ.
Women's Stud. Center
DM 212, Univ. Park
Miami, FL 33199
Ph: (305)348-2408
Fax: (305)348-3143
E-mail: srose@fiu.edu
URL: http://www.awpsych.org
Contact: Prof. Suzanna Rose PhD, Dir. of Women's Studies

Founded: 1969. **Members:** 2,400. **Membership Dues:** student in North America, $15 (annual) ● institution in North America, $30 (annual) ● individual in North America, $85 (annual) ● student outside North America, $25 (annual) ● institution outside North America, $40 (annual) ● individual outside North America, $95 (annual). **Budget:** $67,000. **Description:** Seeks to: end the role that the association

feels psychology has had in perpetuating unscientific and unquestioned assumptions about the "natures" of women and men; encourage unbiased psychological research on sex and gender in order to establish facts and expose myths; encourage research and theory directed toward alternative sex-role socialization, child rearing practices, life-styles, and language use; educate and sensitize the science and psychology professions as well as the public to the psychological, social, political, and economic rights of women; combat the oppression of women of color; encourage research on issues of concern to women of color; achieve equality of opportunity for women and men within the profession and science of psychology. Conducts business and professional sessions at meetings of regional psychology associations. Maintains Hall of Fame and speakers' bureau. Monitors sexism in the American Psychological Association. **Libraries: Type:** reference. **Holdings:** archival material. **Subjects:** history of organization. **Awards:** Distinguished Publication Award. **Frequency:** annual. **Type:** recognition. **Recipient:** selection by committee ● Jewish Women's Caucus Award for Scholarship. **Frequency:** annual. **Type:** scholarship. **Recipient:** for projects and papers published, also unpublished documents ● Lesbian Psychologies Unpublished Manuscript Award. **Frequency:** annual. **Type:** recognition ● Student Research Prize. **Frequency:** annual. **Type:** recognition. **Recipient:** for research on women and gender ● Women of Color Psychologies Award. **Frequency:** annual. **Type:** recognition. **Computer Services:** Mailing lists, POWR-L. **Caucuses:** Bisexual and Sexual Diversity; Experimental Psychology; Jewish Women's; Mothering Issues; Older Women's; Student; Women of Color. **Formerly:** (1970) Association for Women Psychologists. **Publications:** *AWP Membership Directory*, annual. **Price:** free for members. **Circulation:** 2,400. **Advertising:** accepted ● *AWP Newsletter*, quarterly. Provides news about the association's activities and with information and scholarly material consonant with association's goals. **Advertising:** accepted. **Conventions/Meetings:** annual Feminist Psychology Conference, with books, crafts, feminist-made products (exhibits) - always March.

15804 ■ C. G. Jung Foundation for Analytical Psychology

28 E 39th St.
New York, NY 10016-2587
Ph: (212)697-6430
Fax: (212)953-3989
E-mail: cgjungny@aol.com
URL: http://www.cgjungny.org
Contact: Janet M. Careswell, Exec. Dir.

Founded: 1963. **Members:** 1,000. **Membership Dues:** individual, $75 (annual). **Staff:** 5. **Budget:** $350,000. **Description:** Analysts who follow the precepts of Carl G. Jung (1875-1961), Swiss psychologist; persons interested in analytical psychology. Provides information on analytical psychology. Sponsors public lectures, films, continuing education courses and professional seminars. Operates book service, which provides publications on analytical psychology and related topics, and lectures on audiocassettes. **Libraries: Type:** reference. **Holdings:** archival material. **Subjects:** archetypal symbolism. **Publications:** *Quadrant*, semiannual. Journal. **Circulation:** 1,000. **Advertising:** accepted ● Annual Report. **Conventions/Meetings:** lecture ● seminar ● symposium ● workshop.

15805 ■ Center for Applications of Psychological Type (CAPT)

2815 NW 13th St., Ste.401
Gainesville, FL 32609-2865
Ph: (352)375-0160
Free: (800)777-2278
Fax: (352)378-0503
E-mail: info@capt.org
URL: http://www.capt.org
Contact: Mr. Robert McPeek PhD, Dir. of Marketing

Founded: 1975. **Staff:** 25. **Budget:** $2,600,000. **Nonmembership. Multinational. Description:** Represents counselors and consultants; educators, researchers, and psychologists; business and reli-

gious leaders; and self-directed individuals. Provides products and services like training materials. Publishes and distributes books, exercises, and training materials, used by counselors, consultants, and psychologists: to invigorate training courses; to aid in career development, relationship enhancement, self-actualization, and other self-improvement initiatives; and to help individuals, teams, and organizations understand their strengths and challenges and reach new levels of success and satisfaction. Offers variety of workshops and training courses for use and application of various assessment tools. **Libraries: Type:** by appointment only; reference. **Holdings:** 4,000; archival material. **Subjects:** personality theory, personality research, dissertations, theses, assessment instruments, leadership, team performance, personality development, biographies. **Computer Services:** Bibliographic search ● database, MBTI computer scoring. **Telecommunication Services:** information service, consultation regarding research past, present, and future regarding personality assessment and development. **Divisions:** Library and Research Services; Marketing and Customer Service. **Publications:** *Atlas of Type Tables* ● *Bibliography of the MBTI*, semiannual ● *Journal of Psychological Type*, monthly. Contains research on applications and use of psychological type as defined by Carl Jung and Isabel Myers. **Price:** $36.00 /year for individuals. ISSN: 0895-8750 ● Books ● Reports ● Also publishes papers, training exercises, and other materials.

15806 ■ Christian Association for Psychological Studies (CAPS)

c/o Paul Regan, EdD, Exec. Dir.
PO Box 365
Batavia, IL 60510-0365
Ph: (630)639-9478
Fax: (630)454-3799
E-mail: info@caps.net
URL: http://www.caps.net
Contact: Paul Regan EdD, Exec. Dir.

Founded: 1956. **Members:** 2,100. **Membership Dues:** regular, $110 (annual) ● associate, spousal, $60 (annual) ● student, $50 (annual) ● life, $1,100. **Staff:** 8. **Budget:** $167,000. **Regional Groups:** 7. **Local Groups:** 65. **Description:** Psychologists, marriage and family therapists, social workers, educators, physicians, nurses, ministers, researchers, pastoral counselors, and rehabilitation workers and others professionally engaged in the fields of psychology, counseling, psychiatry, pastoring, and related areas. Association is based upon a genuine commitment to superior clinical, pastoral, and scientific enterprise in the theoretical and applied social sciences and theology, assuming persons in helping professions will be guided to professional and personal growth and a greater contribution to others in this way. Aims to help members cooperatively as Christians to explore the fields of psychology, pastoring, and psychotherapy for a better insight into personality and interpersonal relations and to articulate and promote the lordship of Christ in these scientific disciplines. **Awards:** Distinguished Member Award. **Frequency:** annual. **Type:** recognition. **Recipient:** for research, graduate student achievement, and distinguished member. **Committees:** Continuing Education; Endowment; Pastoral Care and Ethics. **Publications:** *CAPS Report*, quarterly. Newsletter. Includes information on membership activities and schedule of events. **Price:** included in membership dues ● *Christian Monograph Series*, periodic ● *International Directory of the Christian Association for Psychological Studies*, annual. Membership Directory. Contains separate listings for libraries. **Price:** $12.00. **Circulation:** 2,500 ● *Journal of Psychology and Christianity*, quarterly. Contains articles on clinical and theoretical topics. Includes book reviews and professional employment opportunities. **Price:** included in membership dues; $50.00 /year for nonmembers; $65.00 /year for libraries. ISSN: 0733-4273. **Circulation:** 2,500. **Advertising:** accepted. **Conventions/Meetings:** annual conference (exhibits) ● regional meeting - 5/year ● workshop.

15807 ■ Council for the National Register of Health Service Providers in Psychology (NRHSPP)

c/o National Register
1120 G St. NW, Ste.330
Washington, DC 20005

Ph: (202)786-7663
Fax: (202)347-0550
E-mail: jacquie@nationalregister.org
URL: http://www.e-psychologist.org
Contact: Judy E. Hall PhD, Exec. Off.
Founded: 1974. **Members:** 13,000. **Membership Dues:** credentialing organization, $145 (annual). **Staff:** 14. **Budget:** $1,900,000. **Description:** Psychologists who are licensed or certified by a state/provincial/territorial board of examiners of psychology and who have met council criteria as health service providers in psychology. Advances psychology as a profession and improve the delivery of high quality health services to the public. Disseminates standards for evaluating the education and training of licensed psychologists. Evaluates programs that enhance the education, training, and delivery of services by psychologists. Reviews the practices and ethics of psychologists to ensure integrity in the profession and quality of patient care. Provides information on psychologists to the health care community and to the general public. **Awards:** Alfred M. Wellner Award. **Frequency:** annual. **Type:** recognition. **Recipient:** for outstanding contributions by a registrant with more than 10 years of postdoctoral experience ● Judy E. Hall PhD Early Career Psychologist Award. **Frequency:** annual. **Type:** recognition. **Recipient:** for outstanding contribution by a registrant with less than 10 years of postdoctoral experience ● The National Psychologist Trainee Register Credentialing Scholarships. **Frequency:** semiannual. **Type:** monetary. **Recipient:** for doctoral students interested in becoming credentialed by the national register through the National Psychologist Trainee Register (NPTR) ● The National Register Early Career Psychologist Credentialing Scholarships. **Frequency:** semiannual. **Type:** monetary. **Recipient:** for the national register of health service providers in psychology. **Computer Services:** database, of 13,000 credentialed psychologists. **Additional Websites:** http://www.nationalregister.org, http://www.findapsychologist.org. **Publications:** *Designated Doctoral Programs in Psychology*, periodic. Directory. Lists doctoral programs in psychology that have been approved by the ASPPB/National Register Designation Project. Alternate Formats: online. Also Cited As: *Designation List* ● *National Register of Health Service Providers in Psychology*, periodic. Membership Directory. **Price:** $599.00 for organizations; free to registrants and the public. **Advertising:** accepted. Also Cited As: *The National Register* ● *Psychologist's Legal Updates*, periodic. Articles ● *The Register Report*, semiannual. Magazine. Includes current issues in practice. **Conventions/Meetings:** semiannual board meeting - always May and November.

15808 ■ False Memory Syndrome Foundation (FMSF)
1955 Locust St.
Philadelphia, PA 19103-5766
Ph: (215)940-1040
Fax: (215)940-1042
E-mail: mail@fmsfonline.org
URL: http://www.fmsfonline.org
Contact: Pamela Freyd PhD, Exec. Dir.
Founded: 1992. **Staff:** 3. **Budget:** $275,000. **Description:** Explores the scientific, political, legal therapeutic, and economic issues that arise when adults claim to have recovered long-repressed memories of childhood abuse. (False Memory Syndrome is based on the notion that memory is "a creative process that often involves reinterpretation and reconstruction of events, therefore our experiences are often recalled inaccurately.") Researches the question: "what is the evidence that would be accepted that a person accused of abuse was not guilty?". **Committees:** Program. **Publications:** *The False Memory Syndrome Phenomenon*. Booklet. Contains articles exploring some of the questions that arise when adults claim to have recovered long-repressed memories of childhood abuse. **Price:** $3.00 ● *Frequently Asked Questions*. **Price:** $1.50 ● Newsletter, bimonthly. **Price:** $30.00. Alternate Formats: online.

15809 ■ International Association of Pastoral Psychologists (IAPP)
981 S Third St.
Louisville, KY 40203

E-mail: docestill@docestill.com
Contact: Dr. Estill Maddox, Pres.
Founded: 1959. **Multinational. Description:** Represents individuals in the area of medicine, mental health, education and faith based service. Fosters, educates and promotes Pastoral Psychology. Promotes safe care in the practice of religious philosophy.

15810 ■ International Society for Comparative Psychology (ISCP)
c/o Dr. Ty Partridge, Treas.
Dept. of Psychology
Wayne State Univ.
71 W Waren
Detroit, MI 48202
Ph: (313)577-2813
Fax: (313)577-7636
E-mail: tpartrid@sun.science.wayne.edu
URL: http://www.comparativepsychology.org
Contact: Dr. Ty Partridge, Treas.
Founded: 1980. **Members:** 80. **Membership Dues:** entry level, $30 (annual) ● renewal, $50. **Description:** Psychologists, biologists, anthropologists, and neuroscientists who work in or are interested in comparative psychology. Aims to promote the international development of comparative psychology; establish worldwide communication among comparative psychologists; encourage the study of the development and evolution of behavior. **Publications:** *Advances in Comparative Psychology*, semiannual. **Price:** $35.00. **Circulation:** 200 ● *International Journal of Comparative Psychology*, quarterly. **Price:** free for members; $95.00 for nonmembers. ISSN: 0889-3667. **Circulation:** 100. **Advertising:** accepted. Alternate Formats: online. **Conventions/Meetings:** biennial meeting, held in conjunction with International Union of Psychological Sciences (exhibits) - always even-numbered years.

15811 ■ International Society for Developmental Psychobiology (ISDP)
8181 Tezel Rd., No. 10269
San Antonio, TX 78250
Free: (866)377-4416
E-mail: isdp@isdpcentraloffice.org
URL: http://www.isdp.org
Contact: Marianne Van Wagner, Contact
Founded: 1967. **Members:** 335. **Membership Dues:** student associate, $78 (annual) ● postdoctoral, $100 (annual) ● regular, $140 (annual) ● retired, spouse of regular, $38 (annual). **Multinational. Description:** Research scientists in the field of developmental psychobiology; biology and psychology students. Promotes research in the field of developmental psychobiology, the study of the brain and behavior throughout the life span and in relation to other biological processes. Stimulates communication and interaction among scientists in the field. Provides the editorship for the journal, *Development Psychobiology*. Compiles statistics. **Computer Services:** Mailing lists. **Affiliated With:** Federation of Behavioral, Psychological, and Cognitive Sciences. **Publications:** *Developmental Psychobiology*, bimonthly. Journal. Features the anatomical, physiological, biochemical, hormonal, pharmacological, genetic, and evolutionary aspects of behavioral development. **Price:** included in membership dues; $2,155.00 /year for nonmembers in U.S.; $2,251.00 /year for nonmembers in Canada and Mexico; $2,307.00 /year for nonmembers outside U.S., Canada and Mexico. ISSN: 0012-1630 ● Membership Directory, every 1-2 years ● Newsletter, 2-3/year. **Conventions/Meetings:** annual conference - always November.

15812 ■ International Society of Political Psychology (ISPP)
ISPP Central Off.
Moynihan Inst. of Global Affairs
346 Eggers Hall
Syracuse Univ.
Syracuse, NY 13244
Ph: (315)443-4470
Fax: (315)443-9085

E-mail: ispp@maxwell.syr.edu
URL: http://ispp.org
Contact: Bruce Dayton, Exec. Dir.
Founded: 1978. **Members:** 1,400. **Membership Dues:** student, $30 (annual) ● retired, $40 (annual) ● regular (based on income), $70-$100 (annual) ● contributing, $150 (annual) ● sponsor, $200 (annual) ● life, $1,700. **Staff:** 1. **Budget:** $70,000. **Multinational. Description:** Psychologists, psychiatrists, psychoanalysts, political scientists, historians, sociologists, economists, anthropologists, media representatives, and government officials. Promotes understanding and scientific interest in the relationship between psychological, political, social, and economic processes. Seeks to facilitate communication among members and to increase the quality and application of work in political psychology. Examines relationships between psychological and political events. Areas of interest include: political violence and terrorism; socialization and the media; human rights conflict resolution; bureaucracy negotiation and mediation; totalitarianism. Sponsors the Summer Institute in Political Psychology in conjunction with Ohio State University. Conducts panel discussions. **Awards:** Alexander George Award. **Frequency:** annual. **Type:** recognition ● Alfred M. Freedman Award. **Frequency:** annual. **Type:** recognition. **Recipient:** for best paper presented at the annual meeting ● Erik H. Erikson Award. **Frequency:** annual. **Type:** recognition. **Recipient:** for early career achievements in political psychology ● Harold D. Lasswell Award. **Frequency:** annual. **Type:** recognition. **Recipient:** for distinguished scientific contribution to political psychology ● Jeanne N. Knutson Award. **Type:** recognition. **Recipient:** for distinguished service ● Nevitt Sanford Award. **Frequency:** annual. **Type:** recognition. **Recipient:** for distinguished professional contribution to the field. **Computer Services:** Online services, list service discussion. **Committees:** Junior Scholars. **Study Groups:** Ethical and Social Responsibilities of Political Psychologists; Legal Rights and Responsibilities in Social Research; Training in Political Psychology. **Publications:** *ISPPNews*, semiannual. Newsletter. Contains information on activities and news of the organization; includes availability of fellowships, grants, and visiting scholar programs. **Price:** free for members. **Circulation:** 1,400. **Advertising:** accepted. Alternate Formats: online ● *Political Psychology*, bimonthly. Journal. Covers classics in political psychology, interdisciplinary foundations of political psychology, and issues in professional development. ● Membership Directory. Alternate Formats: online. **Conventions/Meetings:** annual Scientific Meeting (exhibits) ● workshop.

15813 ■ International Society of Sports Psychology (ISSP)
c/o Judy Van Raalte, VP
Psychology Dept.
263 Alden St.
Springfield, MA 01109
Ph: (413)748-3388
Fax: (413)748-3854
E-mail: jvanraal@spfldcol.edu
URL: http://www.issponline.org
Contact: Judy Van Raalte, VP
Founded: 1965. **Members:** 1,000. **Membership Dues:** individual, $10-$40 (annual) ● group, $40-$100 (annual) ● organizational affiliate, $40 (annual). **Staff:** 16. **Budget:** $35,000. **State Groups:** 5. **National Groups:** 10. **Multinational. Description:** Professionally qualified individuals in 47 countries interested in sports psychology. Supports and promotes scientific research and professional relations between scholars in the field; participates in information and documentation services in sports psychology; advises and facilitates the establishment of other continental, regional, and national societies of sport psychology. Provides the International Olympic Committee and United States Olympic Committee with information on sport psychology services. Maintains speakers' bureau. **Awards:** ISSP Developing Scholar. **Frequency:** quadrennial. **Type:** recognition. **Recipient:** for developing sports psychologist ● ISSP Distinguished International Sport Psychologist Award. **Frequency:** quadrennial. **Type:** recognition. **Recipi-**

ent: for original contributions to the advancement of sport psychology ● ISSP Honor Award. **Frequency:** quadrennial. **Type:** recognition. **Recipient:** for significant contributions to national and international sports psychology ● Young Scholar Award. **Frequency:** quadrennial. **Type:** recognition. **Publications:** *International Journal of Sport and Exercise Psychology*, quarterly. Reports scientific and applied issues in sport and exercise psychology. **Price:** $90.00/year. **Advertising:** accepted ● Newsletter, semi-annual. Covers professional issues in sports psychology; includes conference reports, employment opportunities, and membership list. **Price:** included in membership dues. **Circulation:** 900. **Advertising:** accepted. Alternate Formats: online ● Also publishes proceedings. **Conventions/Meetings:** quadrennial World Sport Psychology Congress (exhibits).

15814 ■ Jean Piaget Society: Society for the Study of Knowledge and Development (JPSSSKD)

c/o Nancy Budwig, Pres.
Dept. of Psychology
Clark Univ.
950 Main St.
Worcester, MA 01610-1477
Ph: (508)793-7250
Fax: (508)793-7265
E-mail: nbudwig@clarku.edu
URL: http://www.piaget.org
Contact: Nancy Budwig, Pres.
Founded: 1970. **Members:** 500. **Membership Dues:** student (without journal), $50 (annual) ● individual (includes Journal Cognitive Development and annual book), $115 (annual) ● student (with journal), $85 (annual). **Description:** Scholars, teachers, and researchers interested in exploring the nature of the developmental construction of human knowledge. Furthers research on knowledge and development, especially in relation to the work of Jean Piaget (1896-1980), a Swiss developmentalist noted for his work in child psychology, the study of human development, and the origin and growth of human knowledge. Conducts small meetings and programs. **Formerly:** (1989) Jean Piaget Society. **Publications:** *Cognitive Development*, quarterly. Journal. **Price:** included in membership dues; $80.00 for nonmembers ● *Jean Piaget Symposium Series*, annual. **Price:** included in membership dues; $80.00 for nonmembers ● *Newsletter of the JPS*, annual. Covers the nature of human knowledge. **Price:** included in membership dues. ISSN: 0740-9583. **Circulation:** 500. **Advertising:** accepted. **Conventions/Meetings:** annual meeting (exhibits).

15815 ■ Midwestern Psychological Association (MPA)

Dept. of Psychology
Indiana University-Purdue Univ. Ft. Wayne
2101 E Coliseum Blvd.
Fort Wayne, IN 46815
Ph: (260)481-6400
Fax: (260)481-6972
E-mail: mpa@ipfw.edu
URL: http://www.midwesternpsych.org
Contact: Elaine Blakemore, Sec.-Treas.
Members: 3,000. **Membership Dues:** regular, $45 (annual) ● regular, $120 (triennial) ● graduate, $20 (annual). **Description:** Psychological association, with interests in the physiology of vision to social stereotyping, from political psychology to medical psychology, from organizational behavior to children's language development, from memory to depression, from sex roles to drug addiction. **Conventions/Meetings:** annual meeting, promotes current developments in psychological research, theory, and practice (exhibits).

15816 ■ National Academy of Neuropsychology (NAN)

2121 S Oneida St., Ste.550
Denver, CO 80224-2594
Ph: (303)691-3694
Fax: (303)691-5983

E-mail: office@nanonline.org
URL: http://www.nanonline.org
Contact: Ms. Dorothy Shadrick MBA, Exec. Dir.
Founded: 1975. **Members:** 3,024. **Membership Dues:** fellow, professional, associate, affiliate, $125 (annual) ● student, special, $50 (annual) ● postdoctoral fellows, $75 (annual). **Description:** Clinical neuropsychologists and others interested in brain-behavior relationships. Works to preserve and advance knowledge regarding the assessment and remediation of neuropsychological disorders. Promotes the development of neuropsychology as a science and profession; develops standards of practice and training guidelines for the field; fosters communication between members; represents the professional interests of members; serves as an information resource; facilitates the exchange of information among related organizations. Offers continuing education programs; conducts research. **Libraries: Type:** not open to the public. **Awards:** Distinguished Clinical Neuropsychologist Award. **Frequency:** annual. **Type:** recognition ● Early Career Achievement Award. **Type:** recognition. **Computer Services:** Mailing lists. **Publications:** *Archives of Clinical Neuropsychology*, bimonthly. Journal. **Price:** included in membership dues; $185.00/year for nonmember institutions. ISSN: 0887-6177. **Circulation:** 3,064. **Advertising:** accepted. Alternate Formats: microform ● *Bulletin of the National Academy of Neuropsychologists*, quarterly. **Price:** included in membership dues. **Circulation:** 3,064. **Advertising:** accepted. **Conventions/Meetings:** annual workshop and symposium, includes paper sessions (exhibits).

15817 ■ National Association of Psychometrists (NAP)

c/o April German, Membership Chair
Cincinnati Children's Hosp. Medical Center
Dept. of Behavioral Medicine and Clinical Psychology
MLC 3015
3333 Burnet Ave.
Cincinnati, OH 45229
Ph: (513)636-2092
Fax: (513)636-7756
E-mail: vicki.gedert@cchmc.org
URL: http://www.napnet.org
Contact: Vicki Gedert CSP, Pres.
Founded: 1995. **Membership Dues:** general, $30 (annual). **Description:** Promotes the education and training of individuals who are employed to administer neuropsychological, psychological and educational tests under the supervision of neuropsychologists, psychologists and other authorized users. Advocates for the careful application of standardized procedures for administration and scoring as set forth by the test developer. Collaborates with other professional groups and test developers in the review of the testing process involving the standard administration and scoring of tests. **Publications:** *The Network*. Newsletter.

15818 ■ National Association of School Psychologists (NASP)

4340 E West Hwy., Ste.402
Bethesda, MD 20814
Ph: (301)657-0270
Free: (866)331-NASP
Fax: (301)657-0275
E-mail: membership@naspweb.org
URL: http://www.nasponline.org
Contact: Susan Gorin, Exec. Dir.
Founded: 1969. **Members:** 23,000. **Membership Dues:** student, $50 (annual) ● regular, associate in Canada, $160 (annual) ● international, $170 (annual) ● student transition, $105 (annual) ● retired, $60 (annual) ● common address, $125 (annual). **Staff:** 17. **Budget:** $2,700,000. **Regional Groups:** 5. **State Groups:** 51. **Description:** School psychologists. Serves the mental health and educational needs of all children and youth. Encourages and provides opportunities for professional growth of individual members. Informs the public on the services and practice of school psychology, and advances the standards of the profession. Operates national school psychologist certification system. Sponsors children's

services. **Awards:** School Psychologist of the Year. **Frequency:** annual. **Type:** recognition. **Computer Services:** Mailing lists, of members. **Telecommunication Services:** TDD, (301)657-4155. **Committees:** Political Action. **Publications:** *Communique Newspaper*, 8/year. **Advertising:** accepted ● *School Psychology Review*, quarterly. Journal. **Advertising:** accepted ● Catalog. Lists publications. ● Monographs ● Reports. **Conventions/Meetings:** symposium ● workshop ● annual convention (exhibits) - 2008 Feb. 5-9, New Orleans, LA; 2009 Feb. 24-28, Boston, MA; 2010 Mar. 2-6, Chicago, IL.

15819 ■ National Register of Health Service Providers in Psychology

1120 G St. NW, Ste.330
Washington, DC 20005
Ph: (202)783-7663
Fax: (202)347-0550
E-mail: support@nationalregister.org
URL: http://www.nationalregister.org
Contact: Morgan T. Sammons PhD, Pres./Chm.
Founded: 1974. **Members:** 14,000. **Membership Dues:** credentialing organization, $115 (annual). **Staff:** 14. **Budget:** $1,800,000. **Description:** Licensed psychologists. Aims to contribute to the continuous improvement of health services to the public by developing, reviewing and disseminating standards for evaluating credentials, disseminating information, conducting ethics programs, and evaluating education programs. Developed the subsidiary, HSP verified, to develop electronic solutions for providing credentialing services. **Publications:** *The Register Report*, 3/year. Magazine. Alternate Formats: online. **Conventions/Meetings:** semiannual board meeting.

15820 ■ North American Society of Adlerian Psychology (NASAP)

614 Old W Chocolate Ave.
Hershey, PA 17033
Ph: (717)579-8795
Fax: (717)533-8616
E-mail: info@alfredadler.org
URL: http://www.alfredadler.org
Contact: Becky LaFountain, Exec. Dir.
Founded: 1951. **Members:** 750. **Membership Dues:** individual/affiliate, $125 (annual) ● retired, family, student (with journal), $45 (annual) ● associate, student (without journal), $25 (annual). **Staff:** 2. **Budget:** $85,000. **Local Groups:** 20. **Description:** Psychiatrists, psychologists, educators, social workers, clergy, and others interested in promoting the knowledge, training, and teaching of individual psychology, developed by the Austrian psychiatrist Alfred Adler (1870-1937). Encourages development of professional workers and groups in individual psychology; establishes standards for professional activities of members. Conducts research in child behavior and psychology, counseling, psychotherapy, group therapy, and treatment of the mentally ill. Sponsors training institutes and summer school program. Promotes the establishment of family education associations and parent study groups. **Computer Services:** Mailing lists, of members. **Boards:** Directors. **Councils:** Representatives. **Affiliated With:** International Association of Individual Psychology. **Formerly:** (1977) American Society of Alderian Psychology. **Publications:** *Alfred Adler: As We Remember Him*. Book ● *An Adlerian Resource Book* ● *Journal of Individual Psychology*, quarterly. ISSN: 0277-7010 ● *Membership List*, biennial. Membership Directory ● *North American Society of Adlerian Psychology—Newsletter*, bimonthly. Includes calendar of events. **Price:** included in membership dues; $20.00 /year for nonmembers. ISSN: 0889-9428. **Circulation:** 1,000. **Conventions/Meetings:** annual meeting and workshop (exhibits).

15821 ■ Orthodox Christian Association of Medicine, Psychology and Religion (OCAMPR)

50 Goddard Ave.
Brookline, MA 02445
Ph: (904)396-5383

E-mail: frniko@aol.com
URL: http://ocampr.org
Contact: Very Rev. Nicholas T. Graff, Pres.
Founded: 1986. **Members:** 200. **Membership Dues:** full, $100 (annual) ● associate, $50 (annual) ● student, $25 (annual). **Staff:** 1. **Budget:** $30,000. **Regional Groups:** 5. **Languages:** English, Greek. **Description:** Represents professionals in medicine, psychology, and religion. Facilitates interdisciplinary programs and community understanding of Orthodox Christianity concerning interdisciplinary studies. Encourages Christian fellowship among professionals. Sponsors charitable activities. Operates research center. **Libraries: Type:** open to the public. **Holdings:** 60; articles, books. **Subjects:** integration of medicine, psychology and religion from an Orthodox Christian perspective. **Awards:** S.S. Kosmos and Damian Award. **Frequency:** annual. **Type:** recognition. **Recipient:** for contributions to the development of the integration of medicine, psychology and religion from an Orthodox Christian perspective. **Committees:** Ethics. **Publications:** Conference Proceedings, annual. Contains formal papers and reports of ethical, medical, and religious issues. ● Synergia, quarterly. Magazine ● Membership Directory, periodic. Contains listing of Orthodox Health Professionals. **Price:** $2.50. **Advertising:** accepted. **Conventions/Meetings:** annual Cancer: The Power of Faith and Prayer - conference (exhibits).

15822 ■ Psychology of Religion
c/o America Psychological Association
Div. Services Off.
750 1st St. NE
Washington, DC 20002-4242
Ph: (202)218-3599
Fax: (202)336-6013
E-mail: mark.mcminn@wheaton.edu
URL: http://www.apa.org/divisions/div36/homepage. html
Contact: Mark McMinn, Pres.
Founded: 1948. **Members:** 1,350. **Membership Dues:** general, $17 (annual). **Description:** A division of the American Psychological Association (see separate entry). Seeks to encourage and accelerate research, theory, and practice in the psychology of religion and related areas. Facilitates the dissemination of data on religious and allied issues and on the integration of these data with current psychological research, theory, and practice. **Formerly:** (1971) American Catholic Psychological Association; (1993) Psychologists Interested in Religious Issues. **Publications:** Psychology of Religion—Newsletter, quarterly. Contains articles, interviews, book reviews, and announcements focusing on psychology and religion. **Price:** included in membership dues; $5.00 /year for nonmembers. **Circulation:** 1,400. **Conventions/Meetings:** annual meeting, held in conjunction with APA.

15823 ■ Psychology Society (PS)
100 Beekman St.
New York, NY 10038-1810
Ph: (212)285-1872
Fax: (212)285-1872
Contact: Dr. Pierre C. Haber, Exec. Dir.
Founded: 1960. **Members:** 4,600. **Membership Dues:** full, $175 (annual) ● associate, $125 (annual). **Staff:** 5. **Budget:** $750,000. **Regional Groups:** 5. **Local Groups:** 4. **Languages:** English, French, German, Spanish. **Description:** Professional membership is limited to psychologists who have a doctorate and are certified/licensed as such in the state where they practice. Associate membership is intended for teachers and researchers as well as persons who will attain professional status shortly. Seeks to further the use of psychology in therapy, family and social problems, behavior modification, and treatment of drug abusers and prisoners. Encourages the use of psychology in the solution of social and political conflicts. Operates an information bureau to answer inquiries of authors and media. Sponsors biennial overseas trip to enable members and their spouses to observe other programs and institutions. Collaborates with other associations. Evaluates programs in the use of psychology. Recommends

legislation; appears in court cases where issues of mental health occur as expert and impartial witness. **Libraries: Type:** not open to the public. **Holdings:** 2,500; books. **Subjects:** psychology, human applications. **Publications:** PS Newsletter, monthly. Includes book reviews, calendar of events, and research updates. **Price:** included in membership dues. **Circulation:** 5,100 ● PS Quarterly. Journal. **Price:** included in membership dues. **Circulation:** 5,100 ● Psychology Society-Summary of Research in Psychology, biennial. Membership Directory. **Conventions/Meetings:** annual congress, for members - always October/November for national meeting, April/May for the four regional meetings.

15824 ■ Psychometric Society (PS)
c/o Carol Earey, Office Mgr.
Center for Educational Res. & Evaluation
210 Curry Bldg.
Univ. of North Carolina
PO Box 26171
Greensboro, NC 27402-6171
Fax: (336)256-0405
E-mail: ccearey@uncg.edu
URL: http://www.psychometricsociety.org
Contact: Carol Earey, Office Mgr.
Founded: 1935. **Members:** 2,200. **Membership Dues:** student, $25 (annual) ● regular, $90 (annual) ● family, $110 (annual). **Staff:** 5. **Budget:** $130,000. **Description:** Persons interested in development of quantitative models for psychological phenomena and quantitative methodology in the social and behavioral sciences. **Awards:** Psychometric Society Dissertation Award. **Frequency:** annual. **Type:** monetary. **Recipient:** for a dissertation reviewed by a committee of three past presidents. **Publications:** Psychometrika, quarterly. Journal. Covers statistical models of psychological phenomena. Includes book and software reviews. **Price:** included in membership dues; $100.00 for organizations and nonmembers. ISSN: 0033-3123. **Circulation:** 2,100. **Conventions/Meetings:** annual conference (exhibits) ● periodic meeting.

15825 ■ Psychonomic Society (PS)
1710 Fortview Rd.
Austin, TX 78704
Ph: (512)462-2442
Fax: (512)462-1101
E-mail: rlorch@uky.edu
URL: http://www.psychonomic.org
Contact: Robert F. Lorch Jr., Sec.-Treas.
Founded: 1959. **Members:** 2,500. **Membership Dues:** full, $91 (annual) ● associate, $50 (annual). **Staff:** 18. **Budget:** $1,000,000. **Description:** Persons qualified to conduct and supervise scientific research in psychology or allied sciences; members must hold a Ph.D. degree or its equivalent and must have published significant research other than the doctoral dissertation. Promotes the communication of scientific research in psychology and allied sciences. **Computer Services:** Mailing lists, of members. **Publications:** Behavior Research Methods, quarterly. Journal. Contains articles in the areas of methods, techniques, and instrumentation of research in experimental psychology. **Price:** $224.00 /year for institutions; $90.00 /year for individuals; $45.00/year for students; $212.80/year for agency. ISSN: 0743-3808. **Circulation:** 900. **Advertising:** accepted. Alternate Formats: microform; online ● Cognitive, Affective, and Behavioral Neuroscience, quarterly. Journal. **Price:** $224.00 /year for institutions; $90.00 /year for individuals; $45.00/year for students; $212.80/year for agency. ISSN: 1530-7026. **Circulation:** 700. **Advertising:** accepted. Alternate Formats: microform; online ● Learning and Behavior, quarterly. Journal. Covers animal learning, motivation, emotion, and behavior, including classical and operant conditioning, sensory effects, and imprinting. **Price:** $178.00 /year for institutions; $75.00 /year for individuals; $38.00/year for students; $169.10/year for agency. ISSN: 0090-4996. **Circulation:** 1,300. **Advertising:** accepted. Alternate Formats: microform; online ● Memory and Cognition, 8/year. Journal. Covers human memory and learning, conceptual processes, thinking, decision making, and skilled perfor-

mance. **Price:** $270.00 /year for institutions; $115.00 /year for individuals; $60.00/year for students; $256. 50/year for agency. ISSN: 0090-502X. **Circulation:** 1,800. **Advertising:** accepted. Alternate Formats: microform; online ● Perception and Psychophysics, 8/year. Journal. Provides articles on sensory processes, perception, and psychophysics, including reports of experimental investigations. **Price:** $125.00 /year for institutions; $314.00 /year for individuals; $65.00/year for students; $298.30/year for agency. ISSN: 0031-5117. **Circulation:** 1,700. **Advertising:** accepted. Alternate Formats: microform; online ● Program of the Annual Meeting of the Psychonomic Society. Contains schedule and abstracts. **Circulation:** 2,400. **Advertising:** accepted ● Psychonomic Bulletin and Review, bimonthly. Journal. Contains short reports and full length review articles covering all areas of experimental psychology. **Price:** $80.00 /year for individuals; $200.00 /year for institutions; $42.00/year for students; $190.00/year for agency. ISSN: 0090-5054. **Circulation:** 1,300. **Advertising:** accepted. Alternate Formats: microform. **Conventions/Meetings:** annual conference ● annual meeting - 2007 Nov. 15-18, Long Beach, CA; 2008 Nov. 20-24, Chicago, IL.

15826 ■ Psychosynthesis International
PO Box 4237
Oceanside, CA 92052
Fax: (562)696-7484
E-mail: psyninter@yahoo.com
URL: http://www.healthy.net/psi
Contact: Robert A. Anderson MD, Pres.
Founded: 1984. **Multinational. Description:** Seeks to increase awareness, facilitate personal healing, and educate on mental, emotional, physical, and spiritual levels through pyschosynthesis, the psychology of the soul that deals with the whole person-physical, emotional, mental, and spiritual.

15827 ■ Radical Psychology Network (RadPsyNet)
c/o Dennis Fox, Co-Founder/Archivist
PO Box 470783
Brookline Village, MA 02447-0783
Ph: (650)493-5000
E-mail: info@radpsynet.org
URL: http://www.radpsynet.org
Contact: Dennis Fox, Co-Founder/Archivist
Founded: 1993. **Members:** 322. **National Groups:** 34. **Multinational. Description:** International network of psychologists and others who seek to bring about social justice and create a society better able to meet human needs. **Committees:** Coordinating. **Publications:** Radical Psychology, semiannual. Journal. Peer-reviewed online academic journal on radical/critical psychology. Alternate Formats: online.

15828 ■ Society for Applied Psychological Research in the Performing Arts (SAPRPA)
3 E Wilson St.
Batavia, IL 60510
Free: (877)761-8230
Fax: (630)406-0313
E-mail: markzinn@saprpa.org
URL: http://www.saprpa.org
Contact: Dr. Marcie Zinn PhD, Pres.
Membership Dues: professional, $135 (annual) ● affiliate, $75 (annual) ● graduate/trainee, $35 (annual) ● student, $15 (annual). **Description:** Represents individuals committed to finding research-based solutions for those in performing arts. Advances research, education, treatment and professional practice of Applied Psychological Research in the Performing Arts. Facilitates and integrates research into common practice within the performing arts community. **Publications:** Journal of Applied Psychological Research in the Performing Arts, quarterly. Contains scholarly articles and current issues with commentaries on controversial subjects. **Price:** included in membership dues ● Performing Arts Psychology Connections, quarterly. Newsletter. Includes information on recent trends in the discipline, notice of other related events and other information. **Price:** included in membership dues. Alternate Formats: online ● SAPRPA Mentoring Handbook.

Contains information for mentors. ● Membership Directory, annual. Features complete listings of all SAPRPA members alphabetically, geographically and by specialty. Alternate Formats: online.

15829 ■ Society of Clinical Child and Adolescent Psychology (SCCAP)

c/o Richard Abidin, EdD, Treas.
PO Box 170231
Atlanta, GA 30317
Fax: (404)373-8251
E-mail: rra@virginia.edu
URL: http://www.clinicalchildpsychology.org
Contact: Richard Abidin EdD, Treas.
Membership Dues: full, associate, $40 (annual) ● foreign affiliate (except Canada), $45 (annual) ● student, $20 (annual). **Description:** Aims to serve children, adolescents, and families with the best possible clinical care based on psychological science. Focuses on issues of cultural and ethnic diversity among its membership and within the science and practice of clinical child and adolescent psychology. Initiates programs designed to increase the attention of clinical child and adolescent psychologists on issues of diversity. Increases diversity among the next generation of clinical child and adolescent psychologists. **Awards:** Student Research Award. **Frequency:** annual. **Type:** recognition. **Recipient:** for science-oriented doctoral students in clinical child and adolescent psychology. **Publications:** *InBalance*, 3/year. Newsletter. **Price:** included in membership dues. Alternate Formats: online ● *Journal of Clinical Child and Adolescent Psychology*, quarterly. **Price:** included in membership dues. Alternate Formats: online. Also Cited As: *JCCAP*.

15830 ■ Society for Industrial and Organizational Psychology (SIOP)

PO Box 87
Bowling Green, OH 43402-0087
Ph: (419)353-0032
Fax: (419)352-2645
E-mail: siop@siop.org
URL: http://www.siop.org
Contact: Mr. David Nershi CAE, Exec. Dir.
Founded: 1982. **Members:** 6,600. **Membership Dues:** professional, associate or international affiliate, $55 (annual) ● student affiliate or student international affiliate, $25 (annual). **Staff:** 7. **Budget:** $1,000,000. **Multinational. Description:** Promotes human welfare through various applications of psychology to all types of organizations providing goods and services. **Awards: Frequency:** annual. **Type:** recognition. **Computer Services:** Online services, consultant locator, media resources, pub-hub (book sales). **Affiliated With:** American Psychological Association; Association for Psychological Science. **Publications:** *The Industrial-Organizational Psychologist*, quarterly. Newsletter. Contains information about Society activities and articles of interest to those in the field. **Price:** included in membership dues, or for a small charge to others. ISSN: 0739-1110. **Circulation:** 6,200. **Advertising:** accepted. Alternate Formats: online. **Conventions/Meetings:** annual conference and convention, offers papers, special addresses, and other programs (exhibits).

15831 ■ Society of Multivariate Experimental Psychology (SMEP)

c/o Prof. Patrick Shrout, Sec.-Treas.
New York Univ.
Dept. of Psychology
6 Washington Pl.
New York, NY 10003
Ph: (212)998-7895
E-mail: pat.shrout@nyu.edu
URL: http://www.smep.org
Contact: Prof. Patrick Shrout, Sec.-Treas.
Founded: 1960. **Members:** 65. **Description:** Aims to advance experimental and quasi-experimental psychology by developing multivariate designs and analysis. Promotes substantive research and scientific discovery through mathematical/statistical models that are designed to enrich psychological theory. Facilitates meaningful interactions during meetings. **Awards:** Cattell Award for Distinguished Multivariate

Research. **Type:** recognition. **Affiliated With:** Federation of Behavioral, Psychological, and Cognitive Sciences. **Publications:** *Multivariate Behavioral Research*, quarterly. **Conventions/Meetings:** annual conference.

15832 ■ Society for Pediatric Psychology (SPP)

PO Box 170231
Atlanta, GA 30317
Ph: (404)373-1099
Fax: (404)373-8251
E-mail: pedpsychol@aol.com
URL: http://www.apa.org/divisions/div54
Contact: Alan Delamater PhD, Pres.
Founded: 1968. **Members:** 1,500. **Membership Dues:** psychologist/physician/allied professional, $45 (annual) ● active psychology student, $20 (annual) ● retired, $30 (annual). **Staff:** 1. **Budget:** $125,000. **Multinational. Description:** A section of the American Psychological Association. Psychologists working in children's hospitals, developmental clinics, and pediatric and medical group practices. Fosters the development of theory, research, training, and professional practice in pediatric psychology and the application of psychology to medical and psychological problems of children, youths, and their families. Supports legislation benefiting children's health and welfare. Sponsors colloquia and symposia; provides speakers. **Libraries: Type:** not open to the public. **Holdings:** periodicals. **Awards:** Distinguished Professional Contribution Award. **Frequency:** annual. **Type:** recognition. **Recipient:** for major contribution to the field ● Research Contribution Award. **Frequency:** annual. **Type:** recognition ● Routh Student Research. **Frequency:** annual. **Type:** grant. **Recipient:** for student members of the society ● Student Research Award. **Frequency:** annual. **Type:** recognition. **Computer Services:** Mailing lists, student listserve. **Affiliated With:** American Psychological Association. **Formerly:** (1999) Division 54, APA. **Publications:** *Handbook of Pediatric Psychology*. Provides a state-of-the-art science review of research and practice at the interface of psychology and pediatric medicine. **Price:** $45.00 ● *Journal of Pediatric Psychology*, quarterly. Includes research reports, literature and book reviews, case studies, graphs, tables, charts, and society meeting minutes. **Price:** included in membership dues; $170.00 /year for nonmembers; $678.00 /year for institutions; $75.00/year for non-member students. ISSN: 0146-8693. **Circulation:** 1,700. **Advertising:** accepted. Alternate Formats: online ● *Progress Notes, Newsletter of the Society for Pediatric Psychology*, 3/year. Contains research articles on pediatric psychology. Includes abstracts of published research, society news, and lists of employment opportunities. **Price:** included in membership dues. **Circulation:** 1,500. Alternate Formats: online. **Conventions/Meetings:** biennial National Conference on Child Health Psychology (exhibits).

15833 ■ Society for Personality Assessment (SPA)

6109 H Arlington Blvd.
Falls Church, VA 22044
Ph: (703)534-4772
Fax: (703)534-6905
E-mail: manager@spaonline.org
URL: http://www.personality.org
Contact: Dr. Paula Garber, Admin. Dir.
Founded: 1938. **Members:** 2,200. **Membership Dues:** individual, associate, $98 (annual) ● student, $25 (annual). **Staff:** 2. **Multinational. Description:** Psychologists, behavioral scientists, anthropologists, and psychiatrists. Promotes the study, research, development, and application of personality assessment. **Libraries: Type:** reference. **Awards:** Beck and Klopfer Award. **Frequency:** annual. **Type:** recognition ● Margarete Hertz Lecture. **Frequency:** annual. **Type:** recognition ● Mary Cerney Award. **Frequency:** annual. **Type:** recognition. **Computer Services:** Online services, dues payment, annual meeting registration, nominations and ballots. **Formerly:** (1938) Rorschach Research Exchange; (1958) Society for Projective Techniques and Rorschach Institute;

(1970) Society for Projective Techniques and Personality Assessment. **Publications:** *Journal of Personality Assessment*, bimonthly. Includes book reviews, case reports, and annual directory. **Price:** included in membership dues; $70.00 /year for nonmembers; $270.00 /year for institutions. ISSN: 0022-3891 ● *SPA Exhange*, semiannual. Newsletter. **Conventions/Meetings:** annual conference and meeting, book exhibits from publishers (exhibits) - always around March ● symposium ● workshop.

15834 ■ Society for Police and Criminal Psychology (SPCP)

c/o Gary S. Aumiller, PhD, Exec. Dir.
750 Veterans Memorial Hwy.
Hauppauge, NY 11788
Ph: (631)724-5522
Fax: (631)858-1600
E-mail: sineater@msn.com
URL: http://psychweb.cisat.jmu.edu/spcp
Contact: JoAnne Brewster PhD, Sec.
Founded: 1973. **Membership Dues:** individual, $50 (annual) ● student, $35 (annual) ● institutional, $100 (annual). **Languages:** English, Italian. **Multinational. Description:** Promotes the scientific study of the criminal justice system, focusing on law enforcement, the judicial, and the corrections elements in criminal justice. Research includes the full range of human behaviors, motivations, and actions within the criminal justice system, along with causation of crime, victimization, and organizational influences. **Awards:** The Michael F. Serafino Award. **Frequency:** annual. **Type:** recognition. **Recipient:** to the best student paper. **Publications:** *Journal of Police and Criminal Psychology*, semiannual, spring and fall. Contains information on issues relevant to practitioners and academicians in the field of criminal justice. **Price:** included in membership dues; $100.00 institution. **Conventions/Meetings:** annual conference.

15835 ■ Society for the Psychological Study of Lesbian, Gay and Bisexual Issues (SPSLGBI)

c/o American Psychological Association
750 First St. NE
Washington, DC 20002
E-mail: c.martell@comcast.net
URL: http://www.apadivision44.org
Contact: Christopher Martell, Pres.
Founded: 1985. **Members:** 1,600. **Membership Dues:** member, associate, affiliate, $30 (annual) ● student, $10 (annual). **Multinational. Description:** Psychologists, graduate students in psychology, and others interested in the psychological study of lesbian, gay, and bisexual issues and the delivery of affirmative mental health services to gay, lesbian, and bisexual individuals. Promotes scholarship in the study of psychology as it relates to bisexual, gay, and lesbian issues; provides training for psychologists in the field. Cooperates with other groups sharing similar goals, including other divisions of the American Psychological Association. Conducts scholarly programs. **Awards:** Distinguished Contributions Awards. **Frequency:** annual. **Type:** recognition. **Recipient:** for contributions to the interest and goals of Division 44 ● Malyon-Smith Scholarship Award. **Frequency:** annual. **Type:** scholarship. **Recipient:** for graduate student research. **Computer Services:** Mailing lists. **Committees:** Bisexuality; Education Training; Public Policy; Racial/Ethnic Diversity; Science; Youth and Family. **Affiliated With:** American Psychological Association. **Formerly:** (1998) Society for the Psychological Study of Lesbian and Gay Issues. **Publications:** *Division 44 Newsletter*, 3/year. **Price:** included in membership dues. **Circulation:** 2,200. **Advertising:** accepted. Alternate Formats: online ● *Psychological Book Series on Lesbian and Gay Issues*, periodic. **Conventions/Meetings:** annual meeting, held in conjunction with APA (exhibits).

15836 ■ Society for the Psychological Study of Men and Masculinity (SPSMM)

c/o Mark Stevens, Pres.
Univ. Counseling Services
CSUN 18111 Nordhoff St.
Northridge, CA 91330-8217

Ph: (818)677-2364
Fax: (818)677-2371
E-mail: mark.stevens@csun.edu
URL: http://www.apa.org/divisions/div51
Contact: Mark Stevens, Pres.
Founded: 1995. **Members:** 1,000. **Membership Dues:** regular, associate, affiliate, $25 (annual) ● student affiliate, $5 (annual). **Description:** Advances knowledge in the psychology of men. Fosters research, education, training, public policy and improved clinical practice of psychology of men and masculinity. Promotes the critical study of how gender shapes and constricts men's lives. Enhances men's capacity to experience their full human potential. Endeavors to erode constraining definitions of masculinity. **Publications:** *Psychology of Men & Masculinity*, quarterly. Journal. Contains research, theory, and clinical scholarship that advances the discipline of the psychology of men and masculinity. **Price:** included in membership dues. ISSN: 1524-9220. Alternate Formats: online ● Newsletter. Alternate Formats: online.

15837 ■ Society for the Psychological Study of Social Issues (SPSSI)
208 I St. NE
Washington, DC 20002-4340
Ph: (202)675-6956
Fax: (202)675-6902
E-mail: spssi@spssi.org
URL: http://www.spssi.org
Contact: Shari Miles PhD, Exec. Dir.
Founded: 1936. **Members:** 3,000. **Membership Dues:** full (introductory rate), $30 (annual) ● graduate student, retired, $25 (annual) ● affiliate, $50 (annual) ● life, $1,500 ● gift, $10 (annual). **Staff:** 3. **Description:** Psychologists, sociologists, anthropologists, psychiatrists, political scientists, and social workers. Works to: obtain and disseminate to the public scientific knowledge about social change and other social processes; promote psychological research on significant theoretical and practical questions of social issues; encourage application of findings to problems of society. **Libraries:** Type: not open to the public. **Holdings:** 100; books. **Subjects:** social issues. **Awards:** Applied Social Issues Internship Program. **Frequency:** annual. **Type:** monetary ● Clara Mayo Grants Program. **Type:** monetary ● Dalmas A. Taylor Summer Minority Fellow. **Frequency:** annual. **Type:** fellowship ● Gordon Allport Intergroup Relations Prize. **Frequency:** annual. **Type:** monetary ● Grants-In-Aid Program. **Frequency:** annual. **Type:** monetary ● James Marshall Public Policy Scholar. **Frequency:** biennial. **Type:** fellowship ● Kurt Lewin Memorial Award. **Type:** recognition ● Louise Kidder Early Career Award. **Type:** monetary ● Otto Klineberg Intercultural and International Relations Award. **Frequency:** annual. **Type:** monetary ● SAGES Grant Program. **Type:** monetary ● Social Issues Dissertation Award. **Type:** monetary. **Computer Services:** Mailing lists, listserv. **Committees:** Awards; Publications; Student. **Councils:** Governing. **Publications:** *Analyses of Social Issues and Public Policy (ASAP)*, quarterly. Journal. **Price:** included in membership dues; $74.00 for nonmembers. Alternate Formats: online ● *Journal of Social Issues*, quarterly. **Price:** included in membership dues; $74.00 for nonmembers. Also Cited As: *JSI* ● *Social Psychological Applications to Social Issues*, 3/year. Books ● *SPSSI Newsletter*, 3/year. **Conventions/Meetings:** biennial convention (exhibits).

15838 ■ Society for Psychophysiological Research (SPR)
2810 Crossroads Dr., Ste.3800
Madison, WI 53718
Ph: (608)443-2472
Fax: (608)443-2474
E-mail: spr@reesgroupinc.com
URL: http://www.sprweb.org
Contact: Susan Rees, Dir.
Founded: 1960. **Members:** 1,020. **Membership Dues:** full, $82 (annual) ● student, $41 (annual) ● early career, $63 (annual). **Budget:** $30,000. **Multinational. Description:** Research group comprising

representatives from psychology, psychiatry, physiology, medicine, and biomedical engineering concerned with the interrelationship between behavioral and biological processes. Conducts research including the evaluation of biofeedback in the treatment of disease states. Maintains historical archives. Conducts workshops. **Awards:** Early Career Award. **Frequency:** annual. **Type:** recognition. **Committees:** Archives; Bylaws; Convention Sites; Early Career Award; Education Training; Ethical Standards. **Publications:** *Psychophysiology*, bimonthly. Journal. **Conventions/Meetings:** annual meeting - always October.

15839 ■ Society for a Science of Clinical Psychology (SSCP)
c/o Denise M. Sloan, PhD, Sec.-Treas.
Dept. of Psychology
Weiss Hall
Temple Univ.
Philadelphia, PA 19122
E-mail: dsloan@temple.edu
URL: http://www.bsos.umd.edu/sscp
Contact: Denise M. Sloan PhD, Sec.-Treas.
Founded: 1966. **Members:** 350. **Membership Dues:** division (Division 12 of APA), full, associate, $35 (annual) ● student, $10 (annual). **Description:** Promotes the integration of the scientist and the practitioner in training, research, and applied undertakings in the field of clinical psychology. **Awards:** Dissertation Grant Awards. **Frequency:** annual. **Type:** grant ● Distinguished Scientist Award. **Frequency:** annual. **Type:** recognition. **Recipient:** to an individual who has made contributions to the science of clinical psychology. **Affiliated With:** American Psychological Association. **Publications:** *Clinical Science*. Newsletter. Alternate Formats: online.

15840 ■ Sufi Psychology Association (SPA)
PO Box 2221
Davis, CA 95617-2221
E-mail: sufipsy@comcast.net
URL: http://www.sufipsychology.org
Contact: Cheryl Crumpler PhD, Contact
Founded: 1997. **Membership Dues:** supporter, $100 (annual) ● professional, $50 (annual) ● student, $15 (annual) ● regular, $35 (annual). **Description:** Psychologists, psychotherapists, psychiatrists and researchers. Promotes Sufi Psychology. **Computer Services:** Mailing lists. **Publications:** *The Science of the Soul*, semiannual. Journal. **Price:** included in membership dues; $5.95 each, for nonmembers in U.S. (plus $2.95 postage & handling); $12.00 /year for nonmembers outside U.S. Alternate Formats: online. **Conventions/Meetings:** meeting and conference.

15841 ■ United States Association for Body Psychotherapy (USABP)
PMB 294
7831 Woodmont Ave.
Bethesda, MD 20814
Ph: (202)466-1619
E-mail: usabp@usabp.org
URL: http://www.usabp.org
Contact: Elliot Greene MA, Pres.
Founded: 1996. **Membership Dues:** clinical, $150 (annual) ● associate, $125 (annual) ● student, $50 (annual) ● affiliate, $75 (annual) ● institutional, $250 (annual). **Description:** Aims to develop and advance the art, science, and practice of body therapy. **Awards:** Lifetime Achievement Award. **Frequency:** periodic. **Type:** recognition. **Recipient:** for individual with outstanding contribution in the field of body psychotherapy ● Outstanding Research in the field of Body Psychotherapy. **Frequency:** periodic. **Type:** recognition. **Recipient:** for the best research in the field of body psychotherapy ● **Type:** recognition. **Committees:** Conference; Ethics; Strategic Planning. **Publications:** *USA Body Psychotherapy Journal*, semiannual. **Advertising:** accepted ● Newsletter.

15842 ■ Workplace Bullying Institute
PO Box 29915
Bellingham, WA 98228
Ph: (360)656-6630 (360)656-6603

E-mail: admin@bullyinginstitute.org
URL: http://bullyinginstitute.org
Contact: Gary Namie PhD, Dir.
Description: Seeks to raise awareness of health-impairing workplace psychological violence prevalence; conducts research; disseminates self-help strategies for involved individuals; serves as a liaison with media; provides technical assistance to public policy makers regarding workplace bullying. **Formerly:** (2006) Workplace Bullying and Trauma Institute. **Publications:** *The Bully At Work*. Book ● *2003 Comprehensive Research Report on Abusive Workplaces*. Alternate Formats: online ● Brochure. **Conventions/Meetings:** conference ● Freedom from Bullies Week - meeting - 3rd week of October.

Psychopathology

15843 ■ American Psychopathological Association (APPA)
c/o Linda B. Cottler, PhD, Treas.
Dept. of Psychiatry
Washington Univ. School of Medicine
40 N Kings Hwy., Ste.4
St. Louis, MO 63108
Fax: (314)286-2265
E-mail: cottler@epi.wustl.edu
URL: http://www.appassn.org
Contact: Linda B. Cottler PhD, Treas.
Founded: 1910. **Members:** 500. **Membership Dues:** individual/fellow/corresponding, $100 (annual) ● student, $50 (annual) ● life, $50. **Staff:** 7. **Budget:** $40,000. **Description:** Physicians and scientists interested in the field of psychopathology. Investigates scientific problems of abnormal psychology including: study of phenomena arising from abnormal mental processes; study of organic pathological conditions directly connected with abnormal mental processes; study of means which may remove or modify social or individual factors operating in the production of mental disease; study of relationship between psychopathological and social or cultural problems. **Awards:** Paul Moch Award. **Frequency:** annual. **Type:** monetary. **Recipient:** for academy distinction ● Samuel Hamilton Award. **Frequency:** annual. **Type:** recognition ● Zubin Award. **Frequency:** annual. **Type:** monetary. **Recipient:** for an individual who has been a seminal figure in psychopathology research. **Publications:** *Comprehensive Psychiatry*, quarterly. Journal. Provides a forum for clinicians and investigators of markedly divergent concepts, methods and orientations. **Advertising:** accepted. Alternate Formats: online ● *Proceedings of Annual Meeting*. **Conventions/Meetings:** annual conference, with books - always March. 2008 Mar. 6-8, New York, NY.

15844 ■ American Society of Psychopathology of Expression (ASPE)
c/o Dr. Irene Jakab, Pres.
74 Lawton St.
Brookline, MA 02446
Ph: (617)738-9821
Fax: (617)975-0411
Contact: Dr. Irene Jakab, Pres.
Founded: 1964. **Members:** 137. **Membership Dues:** individual, $25 (annual) ● fellow, $25 (annual) ● distinguished fellow, $25 (annual). **Budget:** $10,000. **Description:** Psychiatrists, psychologists, art therapists, sociologists, art critics, artists, social workers, linguists, educators, criminologists, writers, and historians. At least two-thirds of the members must be physicians. Fosters collaboration among specialists in the United States who are interested in the problems of expression and in the artistic activities connected with psychiatric, sociological, and psychological research. Disseminates information about research and clinical applications in the field of psychopathology of expression. Sponsors consultations, seminars, and lectures on art therapy. **Libraries:** Type: reference. **Holdings:** business records. **Awards:** Ernst Kris Award. **Frequency:** biennial. **Type:** recognition. **Recipient:** for professional excellence. **Sections:** Children's Drawing; Documentation; Dramatic and Films; Expressions of Criminals and

Delinquents; Language; Musical; Plastic. **Publications:** *American Society of Psychopathology of Expression—Newsletter*, 3/year. Includes obituaries and book reviews. **Price:** included in membership dues. **Circulation:** 100 ● *Art Media as a Vehicle of Communication.* **Price:** $33.00 ● *The Personality of the Therapist* ● *The Role of the Imagination in the Healing Process* ● *Stress Management Through Art.* **Price:** $18.00 ● Proceedings, semiannual. **Conventions/Meetings:** biennial International Congress - conference, with exhibits of patient's art products and books (exhibits).

15845 ■ Association for Comprehensive Energy Psychology (ACEP)
PO Box 910244
San Diego, CA 92191-0244
Ph: (619)861-2237 (858)487-7759
Fax: (760)804-3704
E-mail: member_admin@energypsych.org
URL: http://www.energypsych.org
Contact: Larry Stoler PhD, Pres.
Founded: 1999. **Members:** 800. **Membership Dues:** standard, $85 (annual) ● patron, $150 (annual) ● student (grad student in health field), $45 (annual) ● grand patron, $250 (annual) ● angel, $1,000 (annual). **Staff:** 1. **Budget:** $250,000. **Regional Groups:** 11. **Multinational. Description:** Professionals in psychotherapeutic practice, allied health professionals, researchers, organizations, students, and interested laypersons. Promotes understanding of energy psychology in order to establish the field's credibility among health professionals, particularly psychotherapists; creates collegial atmosphere for collaboration in order to produce treatments for the public. **Computer Services:** Mailing lists, of members. **Telecommunication Services:** electronic mail, dorotheah@aol.com ● electronic mail, glotao@cox.net. **Publications:** *The Energy Field*, quarterly. Newsletter. **Price:** included in membership dues. **Advertising:** accepted. Alternate Formats: online. **Conventions/Meetings:** annual Energy Psychology Conference - International (EPC-I) (exhibits).

15846 ■ National Association of Cognitive-Behavioral Therapists (NACBT)
PO Box 2195
Weirton, WV 26062
Ph: (304)723-3982
Free: (800)853-1135
Fax: (304)723-3982
E-mail: nacbt@nacbt.org
URL: http://www.nacbt.org
Contact: Aldo R. Pucci MA/LPC, Pres.
Founded: 1995. **Membership Dues:** professional in U.S., graduate student outside U.S., $25 (annual) ● graduate student in U.S., $10 (annual) ● professional outside U.S., $50 (annual). **Description:** Promotes and supports the teaching and practice of cognitive-behavior psychotherapy and to support those professionals and students seeking to practice it; sets standards for credentialing. **Computer Services:** database, referral service. **Conventions/Meetings:** workshop.

15847 ■ Society for Psychotherapy Research (SPR)
c/o Jacques P. Barber, PhD, Pres.-Elect
Center for Psychotherapy Res.
Dept. of Psychiatry
Univ. of Pennsylvania School of Medicine
3535 Market St., Rm. 648
Philadelphia, PA 19104-3309
E-mail: barberj@mail.med.upenn.edu
URL: http://www.psychotherapyresearch.org
Contact: Jacques P. Barber PhD, Pres.-Elect
Members: 1,000. **Membership Dues:** regular, $95 (annual) ● regular (in Latin America), $85 (annual) ● student, $40 (annual) ● retired, $45 (annual). **Regional Groups:** 4. **Multinational. Description:** Works for the scientific study of psychotherapy. **Awards:** Distinguished Career (Senior) Award. **Frequency:** annual. **Type:** recognition. **Recipient:** for a lifetime of scientific work that constitutes a major and significant contribution to psychotherapy research ● Early Career Contribution Award. **Frequency:** an-

nual. **Type:** recognition. **Computer Services:** database, membership ● mailing lists. **Publications:** *Psychotherapy Research.* Journal. **Price:** included in membership dues. Alternate Formats: online ● Newsletter. Alternate Formats: online. **Conventions/Meetings:** annual meeting, international - 2008 June 18-22, Barcelona, Spain.

Psychosomatic Medicine

15848 ■ Academy of Psychosomatic Medicine (APM)
5272 River Rd., Ste.630
Bethesda, MD 20816-1453
Ph: (301)718-6520
Fax: (301)656-0989
E-mail: apm@apm.org
URL: http://www.apm.org
Contact: Norman Wallis PhD, Exec. Dir.
Founded: 1954. **Members:** 1,000. **Membership Dues:** full, $175 (annual) ● associate, $125 (annual) ● postgraduate fellow/resident/intern/student, $55 (annual). **Staff:** 1. **Budget:** $300,000. **Description:** Interdisciplinary organization of health care professionals dedicated to the concept of total health care of the physical and emotional needs of the patient. Objectives are: to advance scientific knowledge and the practice of medicine relating to the interaction of mind, body, and environment through study and research; to cooperate with other workers in these and related disciplines; to provide a forum for the presentation and discussion of these problems; to publish the results of research; to facilitate total and comprehensive care. **Awards:** Academy Fellowship. **Frequency:** annual. **Type:** fellowship. **Recipient:** for academy members with active participation as educators, researchers, or administrators in psychiatry and psychosomatic medicine ● Award of Special Recognition. **Frequency:** annual. **Type:** recognition. **Recipient:** to individuals for outstanding service to the field on a local or national level ● Distinguished Service Award. **Frequency:** annual. **Type:** recognition. **Recipient:** for academy members with invaluable assistance to the organization ● Dorfman Journal Paper Award. **Frequency:** annual. **Type:** recognition. **Recipient:** for best articles published in Psychosomatics Journal.● Research Award. **Frequency:** annual. **Type:** recognition. **Recipient:** for an active researcher in the field of psychopathology in the medically ill ● Thomas P. Hackett Award. **Frequency:** annual. **Type:** recognition. **Recipient:** for an individual with outstanding achievement in psychosomatic medicine. **Committees:** Credentials; Education and Scientific; Professional Liaison; Public Relations. **Publications:** *Academy of Psychosomatic Medicine—Directory,* annual. **Circulation:** 1,000 ● *Psychosomatics,* bimonthly. Journal. Includes book reviews and calendar of events. **Price:** included in membership dues; $164.00 /year for nonmembers in U.S.; $195.00 /year for nonmembers outside U.S.; $121.00/year for students. ISSN: 0033-3182. Alternate Formats: microform; online ● Newsletter, semiannual. Alternate Formats: online. **Conventions/Meetings:** annual meeting.

15849 ■ American Psychosomatic Society (APS)
6728 Old McLean Village Dr.
McLean, VA 22101
Ph: (703)556-9222
Fax: (703)556-8729
E-mail: info@psychosomatic.org
URL: http://www.psychosomatic.org
Contact: Laura E. Degnon CAE, Assoc. Exec. Dir.
Founded: 1943. **Members:** 900. **Membership Dues:** associate, $50 (annual) ● regular, $125 (annual). **Staff:** 2. **Description:** Promotes scientific understanding of interrelationships among biological, psychological, social and behavioral factors in human health and disease, and the integration of the fields of science that separately examine them, fosters this understanding in education and improved health care. **Awards:** Type: recognition. **Computer Services:** Mailing lists, of members. **Formerly:** (1948) American

Society for Research in Psychosomatic Problems. **Publications:** *APS Newsletter,* semiannual ● *Psychosomatic Medicine,* bimonthly. Journal. **Price:** $339.00 /year for individuals; $658.00 /year for institutions.

Psychotherapy

15850 ■ Albert Ellis Institute (AEI)
45 E 65th St.
New York, NY 10021
Ph: (212)535-0822
Free: (800)323-4738
Fax: (212)249-3582
E-mail: info@albertellis.org
URL: http://www.rebt.org
Contact: Kristene A. Doyle PhD, Assoc. Exec. Dir.
Founded: 1968. **Staff:** 15. **Budget:** $1,253,000. **Description:** Provides professional training; moderate-cost treatment services, including individual and group psychotherapy, marriage and family counseling, and crisis intervention; consultative services for mental health professionals, corporations, and community agencies; research programs in applied psychology. Operates speakers' bureau. Rational emotive behavior therapy, the institute's chief treatment approach, is a psychological theory and technique devised in 1955 based on the assumption that human beings become disturbed through acquiring irrational thoughts, beliefs, philosophies, or attitudes. Asserts that people can be taught to change their negative and disturbed feelings and behaviors by consciously correcting the false beliefs and inaccurate perceptions that underlie and accompany these feelings. **Absorbed:** (1982) Institute for Rational Living. **Formerly:** (1978) Institute for Advanced Study in Rational Psychotherapy; (1996) Institute for Rational-Emotive Therapy. **Publications:** *A Guide to Personal Happiness.* Book. **Price:** $10.00 ● *A Guide to Successful Marriage.* Book. **Price:** $7.00 ● *Journal of Rational Emotive and Cognitive-Behavior Therapy,* quarterly. **Price:** $70.00 individual in U.S.; $80.00 individual outside U.S.; $110.00/year for friend ● Newsletter. Alternate Formats: online. **Conventions/Meetings:** quinquennial conference ● periodic workshop, for the public in problems of everyday living.

15851 ■ American Academy of Psychotherapists (AAP)
605 Poole Dr.
Garner, NC 27529
Ph: (919)779-5051
Fax: (919)779-5642
E-mail: aap@mgmt4u.com
URL: http://www.coe.iup.edu/aap
Contact: Debora Steenson, Exec. Dir.
Founded: 1955. **Members:** 725. **Staff:** 1. **Regional Groups:** 4. **Description:** Professional society of psychologists, psychiatrists, clergy, and social workers engaged in the practice of psychotherapy. Provides meeting ground for psychotherapists of differing backgrounds and orientations. Facilitates cross-discipline thinking, planning, and research in psychotherapy. **Computer Services:** Mailing lists, open to members of the academy. **Committees:** Continuing Education; Ethics; Research. **Publications:** *AAP Newsletter,* quarterly ● *Voices,* 3/year. Journal. Focuses on the personal struggles and growth of therapists and the influences of therapists on the process of psychotherapy. **Price:** $50.00/year in U.S.; $75.00/year outside U.S. and Canada; $25.00 back issue; $65.00/year in Canada ● Directory, biennial. **Conventions/Meetings:** annual Psychotherapy's Challenge: Courage in the Face of Adversity - conference ● annual workshop.

15852 ■ American Art Therapy Association (AATA)
5999 Stevenson Ave.
Alexandria, VA 22304
Ph: (703)212-2238
Free: (888)290-0878

E-mail: info@arttherapy.org
URL: http://www.arttherapy.org
Contact: Paula Howie, Pres.
Founded: 1969. **Members:** 4,300. **Budget:** $775,000. **Local Groups:** 30. **Description:** Art therapists, students, and individuals in related fields. Supports the progressive development of therapeutic uses of art, the advancement of research, and improvements in the standards of practice. Has established specific professional criteria for training art therapists. Facilitates the exchange of information and experience. Compiles statistics. **Awards:** Cay Drachnik Minorities Fund. **Frequency:** annual. **Type:** monetary. **Recipient:** to members of a minority group who are enrolled in an AATA approved program and who can demonstrate financial need ● Distinguished Service Awards. **Frequency:** annual. **Type:** recognition ● Gladys Agell Award for Excellence in Research. **Frequency:** annual. **Type:** recognition. **Recipient:** to the most outstanding project, completed within the past year, by an art therapist using a statistical measure in the area of applied art therapy ● Myra Levick Scholarship Fund. **Frequency:** annual. **Type:** scholarship. **Recipient:** to students who demonstrate financial need, acceptance into an AATA approved graduate art therapy program, and an undergraduate GPA of at least 3.0 ● Rawley Silver Scholarship Fund. **Frequency:** annual. **Type:** scholarship. **Recipient:** to persons whose academic record or prior experience is deemed excellent and who are enrolled in an AATA approved art therapy program. **Computer Services:** database. **Publications:** *American Art Therapy Association—Newsletter*, quarterly. Provides information on related organizations and available resources; includes calendar of events, legislative news, and member news. **Price:** included in membership dues; $16.00 /year for nonmembers. ISSN: 1066-4076. **Circulation:** 3,800. **Advertising:** accepted ● *Art Therapy*, quarterly. Journal. Includes referred articles and illustrations, news and summaries of national conferences, books reviews, media, and commentaries. **Price:** included in membership dues; $40.00 /year for nonmembers in U.S.; $57.00 /year for institutions; $64.00 /year for nonmembers outside U.S. ISSN: 0742-1656. **Circulation:** 4,200. **Advertising:** accepted ● *Proceedings of Annual Conference*. **Conventions/Meetings:** competition ● annual Education Conference (exhibits) ● seminar.

15853 ■ American Association for Marriage and Family Therapy (AAMFT)
112 S Alfred St.
Alexandria, VA 22314-3061
Ph: (703)838-9808
Fax: (703)838-9805
E-mail: central@aamft.org
URL: http://www.aamft.org
Contact: Scott Johnson PhD, Pres.
Founded: 1942. **Members:** 23,000. **Membership Dues:** student, $50 (annual) ● associate, $133 (annual) ● affiliate, $147 (annual) ● clinical, $183 (annual) ● clinical outside U.S., $117 (annual). **Staff:** 32. **Budget:** $4,500,000. **Regional Groups:** 53. **Description:** Professional society of marriage and family therapists. Assumes a major role in developing and maintaining the highest standards of excellence in this field. Conducts 76 accredited training programs throughout the U.S. Sponsors educational and research programs. **Libraries:** Type: reference. **Awards:** Cumulative Contribution to Family Therapy Research Award. **Frequency:** annual. **Type:** recognition ● Distinguished Leadership Award. **Frequency:** annual. **Type:** recognition ● Distinguished Professional Contribution to Family Therapy Award. **Frequency:** annual. **Type:** recognition ● Divisional Contribution Award. **Frequency:** annual. **Type:** recognition ● Ethnic Minority Fellowships Awards. **Type:** monetary ● Ethnic Minority Honorable Mention Awards. **Type:** monetary ● Graduate Student Research Grant Award. **Frequency:** annual. **Type:** recognition ● Organizational Contribution Award. **Frequency:** annual. **Type:** recognition ● Outstanding Scholarly Publication in Family Therapy Research Award. **Frequency:** annual. **Type:** recognition ● Significant Contribution to the Field of Marriage and

Family Therapy Award. **Frequency:** annual. **Type:** recognition. **Computer Services:** database ● mailing lists, of members. **Commissions:** Accreditation. **Committees:** Ethics; Judicial; Political Action; Standards. **Councils:** Divisional Affairs. **Formerly:** (1970) American Association of Marriage Counselors; (1978) American Association of Marriage and Family Counselors. **Publications:** *A Career for the Future: Marriage and Family Therapy*. Brochures. **Price:** $8.75 for members; $11.25 for nonmembers ● *AAMFT's Guide to Ethical and Legal Practices*. Booklet. Contains common legal and ethical issues that arise in marriage and family therapy practices. **Price:** $29.95 for nonmembers; $19.95 for members ● *Effectiveness Research in MFT*. Book. **Price:** $49.95 for nonmembers; $39.95 for members ● *Family Therapy Glossary*. Book. Includes an overview of family therapy terms aimed at new MFTs. **Price:** $15.95 for nonmembers; $12.95 for members ● *Family Therapy Magazine*, bimonthly. Provides report on current events and clinical developments in the MFT profession and in the mental health community. **Price:** included in membership dues; $10.00 for nonmembers ● *Family Therapy News*, bimonthly. Newsletter. Includes research news, interviews, reports on legislative, organization activities, and activities calendar, **Price:** included in membership dues; $25.00 /year for nonmembers ● $40.00 /year for institutions. **Circulation:** 25,000. **Advertising:** accepted ● *Journal of Marital and Family Therapy*, quarterly. Includes articles on clinical practice, research, theory, training and book reviews. **Price:** included in membership dues; $70.00 /year for nonmembers; $110.00 /year for institutions. ISSN: 0194-472X. **Circulation:** 22,000. **Advertising:** accepted. Also Cited As: *Journal of Marriage and Family Counseling* ● Also publishes other brochures and books; produces series of professional training videos. **Conventions/Meetings:** annual conference, professional development conference for MFTs (exhibits) - usually fall.

15854 ■ American Board of Examiners of Psychodrama, Sociometry, and Group Psychotherapy (ABEPSGP)
c/o American Board of Examiners
PO Box 15572
Washington, DC 20003-0572
Ph: (202)483-0514
E-mail: drjglass@pacbell.net
URL: http://perso.wanadoo.fr/a.ancelin.schutzenberger/usboardex.htm
Contact: Dale Richard Buchanan PhD, Exec.Dir.
Founded: 1975. **Members:** 389. **Staff:** 1. **Budget:** $42,000. **Description:** Certifying body for professionals in the fields of group psychotherapy, psychodrama, and sociometry. (Psychodrama was developed by Dr. Jacob L. Moreno, 1889-1974, and is used to afford catharsis and social relearning. Sociometry studies interpersonal relationships in groups of people.) Works to establish and maintain national professional standards. Administers annual exam which includes on-site observation. Compiles statistics. **Libraries:** Type: reference. **Holdings:** biographical archives. **Affiliated With:** American Society of Group Psychotherapy and Psychodrama. **Publications:** *Board News*, semiannual. Newsletter. **Price:** available to members only. **Circulation:** 400 ● Directory, annual. **Price:** free ● Also publishes standards for psychodramatists. **Conventions/Meetings:** semiannual executive committee meeting.

15855 ■ American Board of Medical Psychotherapists and Psychodiagnosticians (ABMPP)
345 24th Ave. N, Ste.200
Park Plaza Medical Bldg.
Nashville, TN 37203-1520
Ph: (615)327-2984
Fax: (615)327-9235
E-mail: americanbd@aol.com
Contact: Alex Horowitz MD, Exec. Off.
Founded: 1982. **Members:** 2,900. **Membership Dues:** fellow and diplomate, $400 (annual) ● renewal, $100 (annual). **Staff:** 4. **Description:** Psychiatrists, psychologists, social workers, and psychiatric nurses

working in public or private facilities. Promotes high standards of professional practice of medical psychotherapy. (Medical psychotherapy is the treatment of psychiatric and/or medical disorders from a mental health perspective.) Offers certification review and continuing education programs. Compiles statistics. **Libraries:** Type: reference. **Holdings:** 10; archival material. **Subjects:** mental health. **Awards:** Career Achievement Award. **Frequency:** annual. **Type:** recognition. **Recipient:** for research productivity and clinical excellence. **Publications:** *Advances in Medical Psychotherapy and Psychodiagnosis Volume 10*, annual. Journal. Scholarly articles of interest to mental health practitioners. **Price:** $48.00/volume. **Circulation:** 4,000. **Advertising:** accepted ● *Medical Psychotherapist*, semiannual. Newsletter. Includes listing of board certification recipients; activities and announcements of general interest for members. **Price:** $20.00/year ● *National Directory of Medical Psychotherapists*, annual. Includes geographic index. **Price:** $32.00/copy. **Advertising:** accepted. **Conventions/Meetings:** annual conference (exhibits).

15856 ■ American Dance Therapy Association (ADTA)
2000 Century Plz., Ste.108
10632 Little Patuxent Pkwy.
Columbia, MD 21044
Ph: (410)997-4040
Fax: (410)997-4048
E-mail: info@adta.org
URL: http://www.adta.org
Contact: Robyn Flaum Cruz PhD, Pres.
Founded: 1966. **Members:** 1,200. **Membership Dues:** professional, $160 (annual) ● associate, $130 (annual) ● contributing, $200 (annual) ● student, $100 (annual) ● retired, $78 (annual) ● chapter, $20 (annual). **Description:** Individuals professionally practicing dance therapy, students interested in becoming dance therapists, university departments with dance therapy programs, and individuals in related therapeutic fields. Establishes and maintains high standards of professional education and competence in dance therapy. Acts as information center; develops guidelines for educational programs and for approval of programs; maintains registry of qualified dance therapists. Maintains Marian Chace Memorial Fund to be used for educational, literary, or scientific projects related to dance in the field of mental health. **Computer Services:** Mailing lists, of members. **Committees:** Approval (of Graduate Training Programs); Communications; Credentials; Education; Government Affairs; Standards and Ethics. **Publications:** *American Journal of Dance Therapy*, semiannual ● *Capturing the Essence of Chase: A Teacher's Journey Schmais*. Book. Details the specifics of teaching some of the basic concepts of dance therapy. **Price:** $15.00 ● *Conference Proceedings*. **Price:** $25.00 for members; $30.00 for nonmembers ● *Dance Therapy Bibliography* ● *Dance Therapy Notebook*. Contains the clinical practice of an experienced dance therapist working in long-term, interpersonal treatment. **Price:** $12.00 for members; $15.00 for nonmembers ● *Metamorphosis in Movement: Mart Stark Whitehouse - a Video Retrospective*. Includes Whitehouse teaching a class and interviews with Jane Manning Cathy McFann and Neala Haze. **Price:** $25.00 ● Membership Directory, annual. Alternate Formats: online ● Monographs ● Newsletter, quarterly. **Conventions/Meetings:** annual conference - 2007 Sept. 27-30, New York, NY.

15857 ■ American Group Psychotherapy Association (AGPA)
25 E 21st St., 6th Fl.
New York, NY 10010
Ph: (212)477-2677
Free: (877)668-2472
Fax: (212)979-6627
E-mail: info@agpa.org
URL: http://www.agpa.org
Contact: Marsha S. Block CAE, CEO
Founded: 1942. **Members:** 4,500. **Membership Dues:** associate/adjunct/academic/research, $130 (annual) ● professional/student, $65 (annual). **Staff:** 4. **Budget:** $1,000,000. **Regional Groups:** 40. **De-**

scription: Psychiatrists, psychologists, social workers, psychiatric nurses, and other mental health professionals who meet specific educational and professional requirements. Sponsors educational and research programs. **Awards: Type:** recognition. **Programs:** Group Psychotherapy Foundation. **Publications:** *The Group Circle*, quarterly. Newsletter. **Advertising:** accepted. Alternate Formats: online ● *Group Works!*, quarterly. Brochure. Contains information about group psychotherapy. **Price:** included in membership dues. **Circulation:** 4,500. **Advertising:** accepted ● *Guidelines for Training of Group Psychotherapists*, quarterly. Journal. Includes calendar of events and research updates. **Price:** included in membership dues. **Circulation:** 4,500. **Advertising:** accepted ● *International Journal of Group Psychotherapy*, quarterly. **Price:** included in membership dues; $90.00 /year for nonmembers; $375.00 /year for institutions. ISSN: 0020-7284. **Advertising:** accepted ● Membership Directory, biennial. **Conventions/Meetings:** annual meeting (exhibits) - 2008 Feb. 18-23, Washington, DC.

15858 ■ American Music Therapy Association (AMTA)
8455 Colesville Rd., Ste.1000
Silver Spring, MD 20910
Ph: (301)589-3300
Fax: (301)589-5175
E-mail: info@musictherapy.org
URL: http://www.musictherapy.org
Contact: Dr. Andrea Farbman, Exec. Dir.
Founded: 1950. **Members:** 4,000. **Membership Dues:** professional/associate, $200 (annual) ● undergraduate/graduate student, $75 (annual) ● retired, $125 (annual) ● crescendo patron, $1,200 (annual) ● educational affiliate, affiliate, $300 (annual) ● patron, $600 (annual) ● virtuoso patron, $2,500 (annual). **Staff:** 10. **Budget:** $900,000. **Regional Groups:** 8. **Description:** Supports the therapeutic use of music in hospital, rehabilitation, educational and community settings. Monitors the clinical practice of music therapy to insure the services provided to persons with disabilities are the highest quality possible. Serves as the national voice advocating for the development and expansion of music therapy services and programs. **Councils:** Association Services; Education and Clinical Training; Professional Practices. **Formerly:** (1998) National Association for Music Therapy; (2001) American Association for Music Therapy. **Publications:** *AMTA Membership Sourcebook*, annual. Membership Directory. Contains statistical information and association documents. **Price:** included in membership dues; $50.00 /year for nonmembers. **Advertising:** accepted ● *Journal of Music Therapy*, quarterly. **Price:** included in membership dues; $40.00 for nonmembers. ISSN: 0022-2917. **Circulation:** 5,000 ● *Music Therapy and Medicine: A Satellite Broadcast Video*. **Price:** $50.00 for nonmembers; $35.00 for members ● *Music Therapy as a Career*. Brochures. Contains a listing of AMTA-approved schools offering degree programs in music therapy. **Price:** $10.00 for nonmembers; $5.00 for members ● *Music Therapy Clinical Training Facilities Handbook*. Lists approved facilities and programs offering music therapy internships, available on website. Alternate Formats: online ● *Music Therapy Matters*, quarterly. Newsletter. **Price:** included in membership dues. **Circulation:** 3,500. **Advertising:** accepted. Alternate Formats: online ● *Music Therapy Perspectives*, semiannual. **Price:** included in membership dues. ISSN: 0734-6875. **Circulation:** 3,500. **Advertising:** accepted ● *Music Therapy Public Education*. Brochures. Contains in-depth overview of the benefits and uses of music therapy. **Price:** $10.00 for nonmembers; $5.00 for members ● *Music Therapy Responding to Crisis and Trauma Resource Kit*. Video. Includes case study, fact sheet on trauma, caring for yourself as you care for others, and Post Traumatic Stress Disorder resources. **Price:** $45.00 for nonmembers; $30.00 for members. **Conventions/Meetings:** annual conference (exhibits) - always October or November.

15859 ■ American Psychological Association - Division of Psychotherapy
c/o Tracey Martin
Div. 29 Central Off.
6557 E Riverdale St.
Mesa, AZ 85215-0722

Ph: (602)363-9211
Fax: (480)854-8966
E-mail: leon.vandecreek@wright.edu
URL: http://www.divisionofpsychotherapy.org
Contact: Leon VandeCreek PhD, Pres.
Founded: 1964. **Members:** 6,500. **Membership Dues:** regular, $40 (annual) ● student, $29 (annual). **Staff:** 1. **Budget:** $300,000. **Description:** A division of the American Psychological Association. Psychologists and psychotherapists interested in exchanging scientific and technical information about psychotherapy. Conducts continuing education workshops. **Awards:** Rosalee G. Weiss Lecture. **Frequency:** annual. **Type:** recognition. **Computer Services:** Mailing lists. **Additional Websites:** http://www.apa.org/about/division/div29.html?CFID=2214516&CFTOKEN=97970692. **Committees:** Midwinter Planning. **Task Forces:** Families With Parents In Prison. **Publications:** *The Anatomy of Psychotherapy: Viewer's Guide to the APA Psychotherapy Videotape Series*. Book. **Price:** $11.95 for members. **Advertising:** accepted ● *History of Psychotherapy: A Century of Change*. Book. **Price:** $29.95 for members. **Advertising:** accepted ● *Psychotherapy Bulletin*. Alternate Formats: online ● Brochures. **Conventions/Meetings:** annual meeting (exhibits).

15860 ■ American Psychotherapy Association (APA)
2750 E Sunshine St.
Springfield, MO 65804
Ph: (417)823-0173
Free: (800)205-9165
Fax: (417)823-9959
URL: http://www.americanpsychotherapy.com
Contact: Daniel J. Reidenberg PsyD, Chm.
Founded: 1997. **Members:** 5,000. **Membership Dues:** associate, $130 (annual). **Staff:** 5. **Description:** Counselors, social workers, marriage and family therapists, psychologists, psychiatrists, psychoanalysts, pastoral counselors and nurse psychotherapists. Seeks to enhance public perception of psychotherapy. Serves as a forum for the discussion, development, and dissemination of ethical and professional standards for psychotherapists. Works to establish guidelines, promotes education and training confirm the professional identity of members, educate the public about benefits of psychotherapy; provides networking and resource development. Operates library and biographical archives. Compiles statistics; sponsors competitions. Maintains Board of Examiners in Psychotherapy to evaluate training, experience, and professional excellence of individuals. **Publications:** *The Annals of the American Psychotherapy Association*, quarterly. Journal. Peer-reviewed journal. ISSN: 1535-4075. **Advertising:** accepted.

15861 ■ American Society of Group Psychotherapy and Psychodrama (ASGPP)
301 N Harrison St., Ste.508
Princeton, NJ 08540
Ph: (609)452-1339
Fax: (732)605-7033
E-mail: asgpp@asgpp.org
URL: http://www.asgpp.org
Contact: Eduardo Garcia, Exec. Dir.
Founded: 1942. **Members:** 650. **Membership Dues:** regular, $100 (annual) ● student, $50 (annual). **Staff:** 2. **Budget:** $180,000. **State Groups:** 8. **Local Groups:** 6. **National Groups:** 4. **Description:** Social workers, psychologists, psychiatrists, clergy members, nurses, and others interested in group psychotherapy, psychodrama, and sociometry. Conducts educational programs; compiles statistics. **Awards:** J.L. Moreno Award. **Frequency:** annual. **Type:** recognition. **Recipient:** for sustained contribution to psychodrama. **Publications:** *The International Journal of Action Methods, Psychodrama Skill Training and Role Playing*, quarterly. Discusses the application of action methods to the fields of psychotherapy, counseling, education and organizational development. ISSN: 1096-7680 ● *Psychodrama*

Network News, quarterly. Newsletter. **Advertising:** accepted. **Conventions/Meetings:** annual meeting (exhibits).

15862 ■ American Society for Philosophy Counseling and Psychotherapy (ASPCP)
c/o Dr. Kenneth F.T. Cust, RPN, Co-Exec. Dir.
Dept. of English and Philosophy
Central Missouri State Univ.
Warrensburg, MO 64093
Ph: (660)543-4268
Fax: (660)543-8544
E-mail: kencust@philosophical-services.com
URL: http://www.aspcp.org
Contact: Dr. Kenneth F.T. Cust RPN, Co-Exec. Dir.
Founded: 1992. **Membership Dues:** general, $35 (annual). **Description:** Promotes both the professional and academic sides of philosophical counseling and philosophy as a private practice profession. **Publications:** Newsletter. **Price:** included in membership dues.

15863 ■ Association for the Advancement of Psychotherapy (AAP)
c/o T. Byram Karasu, MD, Ed.-in-Chief
Belfer Educ. Ctr., Rm. 405
1300 Morris Park Ave.
Bronx, NY 10461
Ph: (718)430-3503
Fax: (718)430-8907
E-mail: info@ajp.org
URL: http://www.ajp.org
Contact: T. Byram Karasu MD, Ed.-in-Chief
Founded: 1939. **Staff:** 5. **Description:** Works to create a forum where all concepts of psychotherapeutic thought can be aired for the advancement of psychotherapy in practice, research, and training. **Libraries: Type:** reference. **Holdings:** books, monographs, periodicals. **Subjects:** psychotherapy. **Publications:** *American Journal of Psychotherapy*, quarterly. Includes book reviews and software reviews. **Price:** $78.00 /year for individuals in U.S.; $110.00 /year for institutions in U.S.; $86.00 /year for individuals in Canada; $119.00 /year for institutions in Canada. ISSN: 0002-9564. **Advertising:** accepted. Alternate Formats: online; microform. **Conventions/Meetings:** periodic conference.

15864 ■ Association for Applied Poetry (AAP)
81 Shadymere Ln.
Columbus, OH 43213
Ph: (614)986-1881
E-mail: info@puddinghouse.com
URL: http://www.puddinghouse.com
Contact: Jennifer Bosveld, Pres.
Founded: 1984. **Membership Dues:** regular in U.S., $19 (annual). **Staff:** 8. **Description:** Poets, teachers, therapists, social workers, creative artists, librarians, and interested individuals. Promotes the application of poetry and creative writing to human services, healing, and self-awareness and self-actualization. Conducts support groups and tutorials. Operates Pudding House Bed and Breakfast retreat at Puddings House Writers Resource Center. Maintains speakers' bureau. Conducts educational programs. **Libraries: Type:** reference. **Holdings:** 3,000; archival material, books. **Subjects:** poetry therapy, poetry in schools, poetry affecting career, relationships, education. **Awards: Type:** recognition. **Publications:** *Pudding Magazine: The International Journal of Applied Poetry*, periodic. Contains poetry essays and reviews applicable to education and human services and art. **Price:** included in membership dues. **Circulation:** 2,000 ● *Topics for Getting in Touch: A Poetry Therapy Sourcebook* ● Also publishes articles, chapbooks, and educational materials. **Conventions/Meetings:** periodic workshop and meeting, frequently on writing and/or publishing poetry and on poetry therapy.

15865 ■ Association of Mormon Counselors and Psychotherapists (AMCAP)
2540 E 1700 S
Salt Lake City, UT 84108
Ph: (801)583-6227

E-mail: mail@amcap.net
URL: http://www.amcap.net
Contact: O. Kent Berg, Founder
Membership Dues: professional and associate, $60 (annual) ● student, retired, and international, $30 (annual) ● life, $750. **Multinational. Description:** Represents and supports counselors, psychotherapists and others in helping professions to adhere to the principles and standards of the Church of Jesus Christ of Latter-day Saints. **Awards:** Distinguished Service to AMCAP Award. **Frequency:** annual. **Type:** recognition. **Recipient:** for members who have served on the leadership council ● Distinguished Service to Humanity Award. **Frequency:** annual. **Type:** recognition. **Recipient:** for outstanding service to the community or church ● Professional Liaison. **Frequency:** periodic. **Type:** recognition. **Additional Websites:** http://www.ldscounselors.net. **Publications:** *AMCAP Networker* ● Journal. Alternate Formats: online. **Conventions/Meetings:** semiannual convention.

15866 ■ Certification Board for Music Therapists (CBMT)
506 E Lancaster Ave., Ste.102
Downingtown, PA 19335
Ph: (610)269-8900
Free: (800)765-CBMT
E-mail: info@cbmt.com
URL: http://www.cbmt.org
Contact: Joy S. Schneck, Exec. Dir.
Founded: 1982. **Members:** 3,330. **Staff:** 2. **Budget:** $200,000. **Description:** Board-certified professional music therapists. Certifies and recertifies (every 5 years) professional music therapists through examination and continuing professional education. Monitors competence and professional growth of certificants. **Convention/Meeting:** none. **Computer Services:** database, listings of CBMT Approved Providers ● database, listings of clinical settings and populations served by music therapists ● information services, Music Therapy resources. **Committees:** Continuing Education; Examination; Legislative/Regulatory Affairs; Practice Analysis. **Publications:** *BC-Status,* semiannual. Newsletter. Includes a list of new members and updates on recertification process. **Price:** free for members. **Circulation:** 3,000. **Advertising:** accepted ● *Candidate Handbook* ● *Recertification Manual* ● *Recertification, Self-Growth, and You.*

15867 ■ Community Guidance Service (CGS)
155 W 68th St., Ste.1618
New York, NY 10023
Ph: (212)724-1091
Fax: (212)724-1091
E-mail: rcatcc@aol.com
Contact: Alphrodite Clamar PhD, Dir.
Founded: 1953. **Staff:** 30. **Languages:** English, Greek, Spanish, Yiddish. **Description:** Service agency providing low-cost psychotherapy services at private offices throughout the New York City area. Staff includes psychologists, and social workers. **Formerly:** Group for Community Guidance Centers. **Conventions/Meetings:** periodic meeting.

15868 ■ EMDR International Association (EMDRIA)
5806 Mesa Dr., Ste.360
Austin, TX 78731
Ph: (512)451-5200
Free: (866)451-5200
Fax: (512)451-5256
E-mail: info@emdria.org
URL: http://www.emdria.org
Contact: Scott Blech CAE, Exec. Dir.
Founded: 1995. **Members:** 4,000. **Membership Dues:** full, $120 (annual) ● associate, $95 (annual) ● student/intern, $70 (annual). **Multinational. Description:** Represents mental health professionals dedicated to the highest standards of excellence and integrity in EMDR (Eye Movement Desensitization and Reprocessing). Establishes and upholds standards of practice, training, certification and research. Provides information, education and advocacy. Assists practitioners in fulfilling their responsibilities to

the public. Advocates for EMDR's broader inclusion in the mental health field. Seeks to encourage and cultivate leadership skills among members. **Publications:** *EMDR for Professionals.* Brochure ● *EMDRIA E-News,* monthly. Newsletter. Alternate Formats: online ● *What is EMDR?* (in English and Spanish). Brochure ● Newsletter, quarterly. **Price:** included in membership dues. **Advertising:** accepted. Alternate Formats: online. **Conventions/Meetings:** annual conference - 2007 Sept. 28-30, Dallas, TX - **Avg. Attendance:** 1000.

15869 ■ Equine Assisted Growth and Learning Association (EAGALA)
PO Box 993
Santaquin, UT 84655
Ph: (801)754-0400
Free: (877)858-4600
Fax: (801)754-0401
E-mail: equine@eagala.org
URL: http://www.eagala.org
Contact: David Currie LMFT, Chm.
Founded: 1999. **Membership Dues:** individual, $45 (annual) ● organization, $135 (annual) ● individual, $80 (biennial) ● organization, $255 (biennial) ● life, $500. **Multinational. Description:** Promotes, educates and provides standards of practice, ethics and safety in the field of Equine Assisted Psychotherapy (EAP). Addresses the need for resources, education and professionalism in the field of EAP. Strives to provide public understanding and awareness of the EAP profession. **Computer Services:** Information services, EAP resources ● online services, forum. **Telecommunication Services:** electronic mail, information@eagala.org. **Publications:** *EAGALA News,* quarterly. Newsletter. Contains the latest information in the field of Equine Assisted Psychotherapy.

15870 ■ Institute for Expressive Analysis (IEA)
50 W 97th St., No. 1H
New York, NY 10025
Ph: (212)362-2167 (212)980-4664
URL: http://www.ieany.com
Contact: Claudia Bader MPS, Exec. Dir.
Founded: 1976. **Members:** 64. **Membership Dues:** regular, $50. **Staff:** 20. **Budget:** $15,000. **Local Groups:** 1. **Description:** Practicing art, dance, and music therapists, social workers, art teachers, and psychotherapists trained in expressive analysis (a psychotherapy that strives to develop the left and right brain activities to achieve body-mind integration and the mobilization of creative energies). Sponsors lectures and workshops for the public and professionals. Provides advanced courses leading to certification as associate, fellow, or full member of the institute. Maintains educational and counseling center. **Libraries: Type:** not open to the public. **Holdings:** 400. **Subjects:** psychoanalysis, expressive analysis. **Committees:** Educational Evaluation; Public Relations. **Formerly:** Center for Expressive Analysis; Center for Expressive Psychotherapy. **Publications:** Journal, annual. **Conventions/Meetings:** board meeting - every 6-8 weeks ● annual meeting.

15871 ■ International Association for Cognitive Psychotherapy (IACP)
c/o Lata K. McGinn, PhD, Sec.-Treas./Membership Coor.
Amer. Inst. for Cognitive Therapy
136 E 57th St., Ste.1101
New York, NY 10022
Ph: (718)430-3965
Fax: (212)308-3099
E-mail: iacpmembership@yahoo.com
URL: http://www.cognitivetherapyassociation.org
Contact: Lata K. McGinn PhD, Sec.-Treas./Membership Coor.
Founded: 1990. **Membership Dues:** individual, $65 (annual) ● individual, $120 (biennial) ● individual, $180 (triennial) ● student, $50 (annual). **Multinational. Description:** Facilitates the utilization and growth of cognitive psychotherapy as a professional activity and scientific discipline. Advances the theory and practice of Cognitive Psychotherapy. Encour-

ages the development of the conceptual and scientific basis of cognitive psychotherapy as an empirical approach to applied problems. Serves as a resource and information center for matters related to cognitive psychotherapy. **Telecommunication Services:** electronic mail, lmcginn@aecom.yu.edu. **Publications:** *Cognitive Therapy,* quarterly. Newsletter. **Price:** included in membership dues ● *Journal of Cognitive Psychotherapy: An International Quarterly.* **Price:** included in membership dues. Alternate Formats: online. Also Cited As: *JCP.*

15872 ■ International Neuro-Linguistic Programming Association (INLPA)
42 Spruce Ridge, Rte. 9P
Saratoga Springs, NY 12866
Ph: (518)587-3478
E-mail: barb@inlpa.org
URL: http://www.inlpa.org
Contact: Barbara Faraone, Exec. Dir.
Founded: 1983. **Members:** 1,300. **Membership Dues:** individual, associate, $100 (annual) ● institute, $250 (annual). **Budget:** $125,000. **Regional Groups:** 9. **Multinational. Description:** Certified neuro-linguistic programming practitioners and programmers (355); certified master programmers (393); certified NLP trainers (152); individuals with some training in NLP (400). (NLP is a discipline that examines the structure of human thought and response and is used in counseling, psychotherapy, and business applications.) Provides an international network for the exchange of ideas, materials, and services. Sets standards for the ethical use of NLP and for NLP training and certification. Encourages and supports research and development; fosters utilization of new technologies in NLP; seeks to integrate the skills and ideas of other disciplines with those of NLP. Promotes greater public understanding of NLP and its objectives. Sponsors NLP workshops. Cooperates with other professional organizations. **Formerly:** (1991) International Association for Neuro-Linguistic Programming; (1993) International Association of Neuro-Linguistic Programming; (1995) North American Association of Neuro-Linguistic Programming; (2003) International Association of Neuro-Linguistic Programming. **Publications:** Membership Directory, annual ● Newsletter, bimonthly. **Conventions/Meetings:** annual meeting (exhibits).

15873 ■ International REST Investigators Society (IRIS)
Address Unknown since 2007
Founded: 1983. **Description:** Scientists and individuals interested in exploring the psychophysiological effects of floating. Serves as an information exchange for researchers, therapists, and individuals interested in restricted environmental stimulation techniques (REST). (Restricted environmental stimulation techniques include methods of producing a relaxed environment to create changes in consciousness and behavior such as floatation or isolation tanks.) Clinically, REST is being used in conjunction with relaxation training, biofeedback, psychotherapy, and a variety of stress-related disorders. Organizes meetings where members and other interested individuals can communicate current interests, exchange ideas and suggestions, and form collaborative research groups. **Publications:** *REST and Self-Regulation Conference Proceedings,* periodic ● Bulletin, 3/year ● Also publishes bibliography. **Conventions/Meetings:** biennial conference (exhibits).

15874 ■ Milton H. Erickson Foundation (MHEF)
3606 N 24th St.
Phoenix, AZ 85016
Ph: (602)956-6196
Fax: (602)956-0519
E-mail: jeff@erickson-foundation.org
URL: http://www.erickson-foundation.org
Contact: Jeffrey K. Zeig PhD, Dir.
Founded: 1979. **Staff:** 10. **Budget:** $250,000. **Languages:** English, Spanish. **Description:** Seeks to promote and advance the contributions made to health sciences by Milton H. Erickson, M.D. (1901-1980), regarded as an authority on hypnotherapy and

brief strategic therapy; dedicated to the training of health and restricted to mental health professionals. **Libraries: Type:** reference. **Holdings:** archival material, audiovisuals, books, clippings, periodicals, photographs. **Subjects:** Milton H. Erickson, other mental health professionals. **Awards:** Lifetime Achievement Award. **Frequency:** periodic. **Type:** recognition ● **Frequency:** periodic. **Type:** scholarship. **Computer Services:** Mailing lists, of members. **Publications:** *A Teaching Seminar with Milton H. Erickson, M.D.*. Book. Contains transcript with commentary of a one-week teaching seminar. ● *Ericksonian Methods: The Essence of the Story*. Book ● *Ericksonian Monographs*, 3/year. Contains selected articles on Ericksonian hypnosis and psychotherapy, including technique, theory, and research topics. ● *M.H. Erickson Foundation Newsletter*, 3/year. Contains articles and notices relating to Ericksonian approaches to psychotherapy and hypnosis. ● *The Process of Hypnotic Induction: A Training Videotape Featuring Inductions Conducted by Milton H. Erickson in 1964*. Discusses the process and describes the microdynamics of Erickson's techniques. ● *Symbolic Hypnotherapy*. Video. Presents information regarding the use of symbols in psychotherapy and hypnosis. ● *What Is Psychotherapy?: Contemporary Perspectives*. Book. Contains edited commentaries of eminent clinicians. **Conventions/Meetings:** quinquennial Evolution of Psychotherapy - conference ● biennial International Congress on Ericksonian Approaches to Hypnosis and Psychotherapy (exhibits) - always Western United States. 2007 Dec. 6-9, Phoenix, AZ.

15875 ■ National Association for Drama Therapy (NADT)
15 Post Side Ln.
Pittsford, NY 14534
Ph: (585)381-5618
Fax: (585)383-1474
E-mail: nadt.office@nadt.org
URL: http://www.nadt.org
Contact: Barbara McKechnie, Pres.

Founded: 1979. **Members:** 550. **Membership Dues:** registered drama therapist, $95 (annual) ● registered drama therapist (Board Certified Trainer), $115 (annual) ● student, alternative training student, $35 (annual) ● allied professional, $55 (annual) ● senior (65 years old and above), $45 (annual) ● organization, school, $100 (annual) ● individual, $55 (annual). **Staff:** 1. **Regional Groups:** 3. **Multinational. Description:** Represents drama therapists (those trained in the therapeutic applications of creative drama and theatre) and others interested in the field of drama therapy, including those in the psychotherapy, rehabilitation, and education professions. (The association defines drama therapy as the intentional use of drama and theatrical processes to achieve the therapeutic goals of symptom relief, emotional and physical integration, and personal growth. It is used with individuals, groups, and families to maintain health and to treat emotional disorders, learning difficulties, geriatric problems, and social maladjustments.) Purposes are to: develop criteria and standards of training for drama therapists; maintain a system of registration and peer review; encourage research and development of professional training opportunities in drama therapy; represent the interests of members to legislative and regulatory agencies regarding the inclusion of drama therapy in mental health and education bills, state job lines, and insurance policies. Sponsors educational events; maintains speakers' bureau. **Awards:** Gertrude Shattner Award. **Frequency:** periodic. **Type:** recognition. **Recipient:** for distinguished contribution to the field of drama therapy in education, publication, practice, and service ● NADT Research Award. **Frequency:** annual. **Type:** recognition. **Recipient:** for significant contributions to the field through research demonstrating the efficacy of drama therapy ● NADT Service Award. **Frequency:** annual. **Type:** recognition. **Recipient:** to a member who has volunteered substantial time and effort serving the association on committees, subcommittees, or regional chapters on a specific project or series of projects ● NADT Student Service Award. **Frequency:** annual. **Type:**

recognition. **Recipient:** to a student member who has volunteered substantial time and effort serving the association, the student members of NADT, and/or students of drama therapy at-large on a project or series of projects in the past year ● The Raymond Jacobs Memorial Diversity Award. **Frequency:** periodic. **Type:** recognition. **Recipient:** for outstanding dedication to diversity in the field of drama therapy, through advocacy, championing a diverse membership, or working to increase skill, awareness and cultural competence. **Committees:** Communications; Education; Public and Government Affairs; Registry; Standards and Ethics; Trainer Review. **Publications:** *Dramascope*, 3/year. Newsletter. Includes book reviews, calendar of events, employment listings, descriptions of treatment programs and methods, and commentaries and reports. **Price:** included in membership dues; $20.00/year. **Circulation:** 500 ● *Membership List/Registry*, annual. Membership Directory ● *Proceedings of Annual Conference*, annual ● Bibliography ● Monographs ● Survey ● Also publishes information on workshops and courses in drama therapy. **Conventions/Meetings:** annual conference (exhibits) - always November.

15876 ■ National Association for Poetry Therapy (NAPT)
c/o Lauren Keller, Admin. Asst.
777 E Atlantic Ave., No. 243
Delray Beach, FL 33483
Free: (866)844-NAPT
E-mail: info@poetrytherapy.org
URL: http://www.poetrytherapy.org
Contact: Lauren Keller, Admin. Asst.

Founded: 1981. **Members:** 380. **Membership Dues:** regular, $115 (annual) ● student, retired/disabled, $80 (annual) ● institutional, $250 (annual). **Staff:** 1. **Regional Groups:** 16. **Description:** Psychiatrists, psychologists, social workers, teachers, nurses, librarians, occupational therapists, paraprofessionals, ministers, counselors, recreation and rehabilitation specialists, and poets and professors of English and psychology. Promulgates the principles and techniques of poetry therapy for healing and personal growth. (Poetry therapy is used with patients in a variety of mental states ranging from "normal neurosis" to acute psychosis, as well as the physically handicapped and the learning disabled. Methods of using poetry for therapy vary and include reading poems and encouraging clients to write their own poetry. Leads the person into talking or writing about himself or herself and bringing out emotions not previously shown or discussed.) Sponsors two degrees in the field of poetry therapy: Certified Poetry Therapist (CPT) and Registered Poetry Therapist (RPT). **Computer Services:** Mailing lists, of members. **Boards:** Praise of Muses Advisory. **Committees:** Conference; Credentials; Diversity; Education; Ethics; Government Affairs; Institutional Outreach; Research. **Affiliated With:** National Coalition of Creative Arts Therapy Associations. **Formerly:** World Poetry Therapy Association; (1981) Association for Poetry Therapy. **Publications:** *Giving Sorrow Words*. Book. **Price:** $4.00 for nonmembers, plus shipping and handling; $3.00 for members, plus shipping and handling ● *Journal of Poetry Therapy*, quarterly. **Price:** included in membership dues; $77.00 /year for nonmembers; $540.00 /year for institutions. ISSN: 0889-3675. Alternate Formats: online ● *NAPT Museletter*, 3/year. Newsletter. Includes training and conference information. **Price:** included in membership dues; $25.00 /year for nonmembers in U.S.; $35.00 /year for nonmembers outside U.S. **Circulation:** 500 ● *The National Federation for Biblio/Poetry Therapy Guide to Training Requirements*. Book. **Price:** $30.00. Also Cited As: *CPT/RPT Guidebook* ● *Trainee's and Trainer's Guide*. **Price:** $20.00. **Conventions/Meetings:** annual Words for Life - conference and workshop (exhibits) - 2008 Apr. 2-7, Minneapolis, MN.

15877 ■ National Coalition of Creative Arts Therapy Associations (NCCATA)
c/o AMTA
8455 Colesville Rd., Ste.1000
Silver Spring, MD 20910

Ph: (703)250-3414
Fax: (703)250-3414
E-mail: dianne.dulicai@cox.net
URL: http://www.nccata.org
Contact: Diane Dulicai PhD, Co-Chair

Founded: 1979. **Members:** 8,000. **Budget:** $200,000. **National Groups:** 6. **Description:** Creative arts therapists. Promotes therapeutic and rehabilitative uses of the arts in medicine, mental health, special education, and forensic and social services; coordinates member associations' activities and efforts in meeting common objectives while supporting and advancing each group's discipline. Works to: represent members' interests in legislative activities; define joint positions on public policy issues; facilitate communication among members; initiate educational and research programs. Compiles statistics. **Libraries: Type:** reference. **Holdings:** 200. **Subjects:** art therapies in a broad range of settings. **Committees:** Database; Joint Commission on Accreditation of Health Care Organizations; Legislative; Licensing. **Affiliated With:** American Art Therapy Association; American Dance Therapy Association; American Music Therapy Association; American Society of Group Psychotherapy and Psychodrama; National Association for Drama Therapy; National Association for Poetry Therapy. **Formerly:** (2002) National Coalition of Arts Therapy Associations. **Conventions/Meetings:** quinquennial conference (exhibits) ● seminar.

15878 ■ National Federation for Biblio/Poetry Therapy (NFBPT)
c/o Linda Hendrick, Admin.
7857 S Univ. Way
Centennial, CO 80122
Ph: (720)200-1015
E-mail: admin@nfbpt.com
URL: http://www.nfbpt.com
Contact: Linda Hendrick, Admin.

Founded: 1983. **Nonmembership. Description:** Establishes standards for individuals, organizations, and institutions engaged in the training of biblio/poetry therapists or the practice of biblio/poetry therapy as a profession. (Biblio/poetry therapy uses literature or poetry to help patients "respond to an emotional impact which can then be integrated in self-awareness and self-understanding".) A credentialing committee grants certification and the most advanced level, registration as a poetry therapist. **Affiliated With:** National Association for Poetry Therapy. **Conventions/Meetings:** annual conference.

15879 ■ National Remotivation Therapy Organization (NRTO)
PO Box 440
York Harbor, ME 03911
Ph: (207)363-7577
E-mail: jmeixsell@theraskills.com
URL: http://www.remotivation.fws1.com
Contact: Michael Stotts, Exec. Dir.

Founded: 1971. **Members:** 412. **Membership Dues:** individual, $25 (annual) ● retired, $15 (annual) ● supporting institution, $30 (annual). **State Groups:** 5. **Description:** Certified remotivation therapists organized to provide a forum for the discussion of ideas and information related to the field. Remotivation therapy involves the use of small group sessions to stimulate and revitalize individuals who have experienced a decline in interest in their surroundings, themselves, and other people. Conducts discussions of methods that allow patients an opportunity for verbal expression, renewal of listening skills, and resocialization. **Libraries: Type:** open to the public. **Holdings:** articles. **Subjects:** remotivation therapy. **Awards:** Remotivator of the Year. **Frequency:** annual. **Type:** recognition. **Affiliated With:** American Psychiatric Association. **Also Known As:** National Remotivation Technique Organization. **Publications:** *Remotivation Therapy Information*. Brochure ● *Remotivator*, quarterly. Newsletter. **Advertising:** accepted ● Newsletter, quarterly. **Price:** $20.00/year. **Advertising:** accepted. **Conventions/Meetings:** annual National Remotivation Institute - meeting and workshop (exhibits).

15880 ■ Postgraduate Center for Mental Health (PCMH)
c/o Vocational Services Department
344 W 36th St.
New York, NY 10018-1843
Ph: (212)560-6720
Fax: (212)563-1291
E-mail: crichards@pqcmh.org
URL: http://www.webstrats.com/pcmhvoc.htm
Contact: Dr. Jacob Barak, Pres./CEO
Founded: 1945. **Staff:** 540. **Budget:** $14,000,000. **For-Profit. Description:** Provides therapy for individuals, groups, couples, and families; training; psychiatric day and evening care program; community services and public educational programs. Conducts research. Maintains social rehabilitation clinic; child/adolescent and family clinic; adult clinic; employee support service; group residence for the mentally ill preparing for independent living. Gives training opportunities include Adult Fellowship, Advanced Training for Social Workers, Child and Adolescent Counseling, Family Therapy, Group Therapy, Pastoral Counseling, Psychology Internship, and Social Work Internship. Offers mental health and organizational consultation to industry and government agencies. Maintains six residential facilities (supported housing) for homeless mentally ill. Oversees distribution of funds for programs providing housing and supportive services to people with HIV/AIDS. **Libraries: Type:** reference. **Holdings:** 11,000; books, monographs, periodicals. **Subjects:** psychiatry, clinical psychology, psychotherapy, psychoanalysis. **Awards: Type:** recognition. **Additional Websites:** http://www.pgcmh.org. **Formerly:** Institute for Research in Psychotherapy; (1962) Postgraduate Center for Psychotherapy. **Publications:** *Psychoanalysis and Psychotherapy*, semiannual. Journal. Includes professional book reviews and author and title indexes. **Price:** $37.50/year. ISSN: 9736-508X. **Conventions/Meetings:** annual Group Therapy Workshops, three-day weekend, intensive group experience for mental health professionals.

15881 ■ Psychotherapy Network
5135 MacArthur Blvd. NW
Washington, DC 20016
Ph: (202)537-8950
Free: (888)408-2452
Fax: (202)537-6869
E-mail: info@psychnetworker.org
Contact: Richard Simon, Ed.
Founded: 1976. **Members:** 65,000. **Staff:** 6. **Description:** Promotes the exchange of ideas and information among psychotherapists. **Formerly:** (2003) Family Therapy Network. **Publications:** *Psychotherapy Networker*, bimonthly. Magazine. Contains case studies, calendar of events, listing of employment opportunities, and book and movie reviews. **Price:** $18.00 /year for individuals in U.S.; $24.00 /year for individuals outside U.S. ISSN: 1535-573X. **Circulation:** 65,000. **Advertising:** accepted. **Conventions/Meetings:** annual Networker Symposium, includes workshops relating to theory, techniques, business and tapping one's creative resources (exhibits) - always March.

15882 ■ Rabbinic Center for Research and Counseling (RCRC)
c/o Rabbinic Center Synagogue
128 E Dudley Ave.
Westfield, NJ 07090
Ph: (908)233-0419
Fax: (908)233-6459
E-mail: ihf@rcrconline.org
URL: http://www.rcrconline.org
Contact: Rabbi Irwin H. Fishbein, Dir.
Founded: 1970. **Staff:** 3. **Description:** Operates outpatient facility for treatment of emotional and mental disabilities by the application of psychotherapeutic knowledge and religious guidance. Provides psychotherapy for the general public, particularly for individuals and couples involved in interfaith marriages. Specializes in helping interfaith couples cope with issues relating to diverse ethnic and religious backgrounds. Offers courses, workshops and counseling for interfaith couples. Conducts research on

interfaith marriage with particular emphasis on the impact of intermarriage on the marital relationship and upbringing of children. Conducts quadrennial surveys to determine rabbinic views on interfaith marriage. Provides list of nearly 350 rabbis who officiate at intermarriages and offer counsel and support to intermarrying couples. **Publications:** *Central Conference of American Rabbis Report of Committee on Mixed Marriage*. Article. Alternate Formats: online ● *Intermarriage and Outreach: Facing Contemporary Challenges*. Article. Alternate Formats: online. **Conventions/Meetings:** semiannual meeting - always June and December ● seminar.

15883 ■ Recovery, Inc.
802 N Dearborn St.
Chicago, IL 60610
Ph: (312)337-5661
Fax: (312)337-5756
E-mail: inquiries@recovery-inc.org
URL: http://www.recovery-inc.org
Contact: Kathleen Garcia, Exec. Dir.
Founded: 1937. **Members:** 3,500. **Membership Dues:** regular, $20 (annual) ● contributing, $40 (annual) ● supporting, $80 (annual) ● sustaining, $160 (annual) ● life, $1,000. **Staff:** 6. **Budget:** $600,000. **Local Groups:** 650. **Languages:** English, Spanish. **Multinational. Description:** Community mental health organization offering a self-help method developed by the neuropsychiatrist Dr. Abraham A. Low; the Recovery method is a system of techniques for controlling temperamental behavior and changing attitudes toward nervous symptoms and fears. **Libraries: Type:** reference. **Holdings:** archival material, books, clippings, periodicals. **Computer Services:** Mailing lists, of members. **Also Known As:** Recovery, Inc., The Association of Nervous and Former Mental Patients. **Publications:** *Manage Your Fears Manage Your Anger: A Psychiatrist Speaks*. Book. **Price:** $20.00 ● *Mental Health Through Will Training* (in English, French, and Spanish). Book. Contains the main techniques of the Recovery method. **Price:** $20.00 ● *Mental Illness, Stigma, and Self Help: The Founding Recovery, Inc.*. Book. **Price:** $20.00 ● *Recovery Reporter*, bimonthly. Magazine. **Price:** included in membership dues. **Circulation:** 3,500. **Advertising:** accepted ● *Recovery, Inc. Reports*. Newsletter. Contains information for professionals. Alternate Formats: online ● *Selections from Works*. Book. **Price:** $20.00. **Conventions/Meetings:** annual meeting.

15884 ■ Social/Vocational Rehabilitation Clinic (SVRC)
Address Unknown since 2007
Founded: 1959. **Description:** Clinic employing a comprehensive therapeutic clinical program for psychiatric outpatients. Aims at reducing hospital admissions and creating a therapeutic and social experience resulting in independent living, improved interpersonal relationships, and productivity in the work field. Offers a program of "therapeutic groups of creative, recreational, experiential, and work activities." Provides individual counseling, activity and therapy, and medication therapy; offers placement service; operates case management services. Sponsors vocational activities, family therapy, internship program, and community outreach activities. Functions as a psychotherapeutic service of the Postgraduate Center for Mental Health (see separate entry). **Formerly:** The Living Room; (1975) Social Rehabilitation Clinic; (1977) Psychiatric Day and Evening Clinic; (1988) Social Rehabilitation Clinic.

15885 ■ Society for the Exploration of Psychotherapy Integration (SEPI)
3100 N Leisure World Blvd., No. 1021
Silver Spring, MD 20906
Ph: (301)598-0969
Fax: (301)598-2436
E-mail: geostricker@comcast.net
URL: http://cyberpsych.org/sepi
Contact: Dr. George Stricker, Treas.
Founded: 1984. **Members:** 750. **Membership Dues:** student, $29 (annual) ● individual, $59 (annual). **Staff:** 1. **Regional Groups:** 15. **Multinational. De-**

scription: Mental health professionals interested in the integration of theories and methods of psychotherapy. Encourages communication among members. Promotes collaborative work among psychotherapists who adhere to different theories and methods. **Awards:** Student Presentation Award. **Frequency:** annual. **Type:** monetary. **Recipient:** to student members presenting at annual meeting to help with conference expense. **Computer Services:** Mailing lists. **Publications:** *Journal of Psychotherapy Integration*, quarterly. Contains professional articles and book reviews. **Circulation:** 1,000. **Advertising:** accepted. **Conventions/Meetings:** annual conference (exhibits).

15886 ■ William Glasser Institute
22024 Lassen St., Ste.118
Chatsworth, CA 91311
Ph: (818)700-8000
Free: (800)899-0688
Fax: (818)700-0555
E-mail: wginst@wglasser.com
URL: http://www.wglasser.com
Contact: Linda S. Harshman MSW, Exec. Dir.
Founded: 1967. **Staff:** 7. **Regional Groups:** 9. **Description:** Teaches Reality Therapy, Choice Theory, and Lead Management concepts to those who wish to use the knowledge in various working environments. **Formerly:** Institute for Reality Therapy; (1998) Institute for Control Therapy, Reality Therapy, and Quality Management. **Publications:** *Every Student Can Succeed*. Booklet. **Price:** $14.00 ● *Fibromyalgia: Hope from a Completely New Perspective*. Booklet. **Price:** $12.00 ● *For Parents and Teenagers-Dissolving the Barrier Between You and Your Teen*. Booklet. **Price:** $15.00 ● *International Journal of Reality Therapy*, semiannual. Contains contributions from individual/s around the world. **Price:** included in membership dues; $14.00 for nonmembers ● *Warning: Psychiatry Can Be Hazardous To Your Health*. Booklet. **Price:** $15.00 ● Newsletter, 3/year. **Conventions/Meetings:** annual international conference.

Public Health

15887 ■ American Association for Health Education (AAHE)
1900 Assn. Dr.
Reston, VA 20191-1599
Ph: (703)476-3437
Free: (800)213-7193
Fax: (703)476-6638
E-mail: aahe@aahperd.org
URL: http://www.aahperd.org/aahe
Contact: Dr. Becky J. Smith PhD, Exec. Dir.
Founded: 1937. **Members:** 6,000. **Membership Dues:** health educator, $125 (annual). **Staff:** 4. **Description:** Professionals who have responsibility for health education in schools, colleges, communities, hospitals and clinics, and industries. Purposes are advancement of health education through program activities and federal legislation; encouragement of close working relationships between all health education and health service organizations; achievement of good health and well-being for all Americans automatically, without conscious thought and endeavor. Member of the American Alliance for Health, Physical Education, Recreation and Dance. **Awards:** AAHE Scholar Award. **Frequency:** annual. **Type:** recognition. **Recipient:** for outstanding research in health education and promotion ● Barbara Cooley Scholarship. **Frequency:** annual. **Type:** scholarship. **Recipient:** to an outstanding masters degree candidate in health education ● Bill Kane Scholarship. **Frequency:** annual. **Type:** scholarship. **Recipient:** to an outstanding undergraduate major in health education ● Delbert Oberteuffer Scholarship. **Frequency:** annual. **Type:** scholarship. **Recipient:** to an outstanding doctoral candidate in health education ● Distinguished Service to Health Education Award. **Frequency:** annual. **Type:** recognition. **Recipient:** for outstanding service to the association ● Health Education Professionals of the Year Award. **Frequency:** annual. **Type:** recognition. **Recipient:** to

individuals in six different venues where health educators are employed ● Horizon Award. **Frequency:** annual. **Type:** recognition. **Recipient:** for outstanding new professional ● Marion Pollock Fellowship. **Frequency:** annual. **Type:** fellowship. **Recipient:** to an outstanding masters degree student in school health education ● Outstanding Undergraduate Health Education Majors. **Frequency:** annual. **Type:** recognition. **Recipient:** to undergraduate students in each health education/promotion majors program at US colleges/universities preparing health education/promotion majors ● Professional Service to Health Education Award. **Frequency:** annual. **Type:** recognition ● Will Rogers Institute Fellowship. **Frequency:** annual. **Type:** fellowship. **Recipient:** to an outstanding doctoral candidate in health education who has a research interest or experience in lung related health education and promotion. **Computer Services:** database, job bank. **Additional Websites:** http://heawards.org. **Formerly:** (1974) School Health Division of American Association for Health, Physical Education and Recreation; (1997) Association for the Advancement of Health Education. **Publications:** *American Journal of Health Education,* bimonthly. **Price:** $120.00. **Circulation:** 10,000 ● *Directory of Institutions Offering Undergraduate and Graduate Degree Programs in Health Education,* biennial. Features appearance in the Journal of Health Education. ● *HExtra,* quarterly. Reports on health education programs across the nation. Includes association news and research updates. **Price:** included in membership dues. **Circulation:** 6,000. **Advertising:** accepted. Alternate Formats: online ● *International Electronic Journal of Health Education* (in Chinese, English, French, and Spanish). ISSN: 1529-1944. **Circulation:** 10,000. Alternate Formats: online ● Also publishes books, reports, proceedings, CD-Roms. **Conventions/Meetings:** annual convention (exhibits) - always April.

15888 ■ American Association of Public Health Physicians (AAPHP)
3433 Kirchoff Rd.
Rolling Meadows, IL 60008-1842
Ph: (847)371-1502
Fax: (847)255-0559
E-mail: aaphp@reachone.com
URL: http://www.aaphp.org
Contact: Alfio Rausa MD, Pres.
Founded: 1954. **Members:** 200. **Membership Dues:** life, $950 ● active, $95 (annual) ● retiree, $40 (annual). **Staff:** 1. **Budget:** $10,000. **Description:** Physicians actively engaged in public health. Promotes leadership in the field of public health; speaks for its membership on proposed health legislation at various levels; supports coordination of public health responsibilities in a variety of agencies. Conducts or co-sponsors educational seminars. **Awards:** **Frequency:** periodic. **Type:** recognition. **Recipient:** for distinguished service. **Publications:** *American Association of Public Health Physicians—Bulletin,* quarterly. Newsletter. **Price:** included in membership dues. **Circulation:** 200. **Conventions/Meetings:** semiannual conference, held in conjunction with American Public Health Association.

15889 ■ American Public Health Association (APHA)
800 I St. NW
Washington, DC 20001
Ph: (202)777-2742
Fax: (202)777-2534
E-mail: comments@apha.org
URL: http://www.apha.org
Contact: Allen Baker, Chief of Staff
Founded: 1872. **Members:** 32,000. **Membership Dues:** individual regular, $160 (annual) ● individual student, $50 (annual) ● contributing, $210 (annual) ● special health worker, retired, consumer, $65 (annual). **Staff:** 65. **Budget:** $13,400,000. **Description:** Professional organization of physicians, nurses, educators, academicians, environmentalists, epidemiologists, new professionals, social workers, health administrators, optometrists, podiatrists, pharmacists, dentists, nutritionists, health planners, other community and mental health specialists, and interested

consumers. Seeks to protect and promote personal, mental, and environmental health. Services include: promulgation of standards; establishment of uniform practices and procedures; development of the etiology of communicable diseases; research in public health; exploration of medical care programs and their relationships to public health. Sponsors job placement service. **Libraries:** **Type:** not open to the public. **Awards:** Award for Excellence. **Frequency:** annual. **Type:** recognition. **Recipient:** to individuals for outstanding contributions to the improvement of public health ● David P. Rall Award. **Frequency:** annual. **Type:** recognition. **Recipient:** for outstanding contributions to public health through science-based advocacy ● Distinguished Public Health Legislator of the Year Award. **Frequency:** annual. **Type:** recognition. **Recipient:** for individuals at the federal, state or local levels who supports public health issues and have taken action in the name of public health ● Drotman Award. **Frequency:** annual. **Type:** recognition. **Recipient:** for a young health professional who demonstrates potential in the health field ● Martha May Eliot Award. **Frequency:** annual. **Type:** recognition. **Recipient:** for exceptional achievements in the field of maternal and child health ● Sedgwick Memorial Medal. **Frequency:** annual. **Type:** medal. **Recipient:** for those who have advanced public health knowledge and practices. **Telecommunication Services:** teletype, (202)777-2500. **Boards:** Action; Program Development. **Caucuses:** Academic Public Health; American Indian, Alaska Native & Native Hawaiian; Asian Pacific Islander; Black Caucus of Health Workers. **Special Interest Groups:** Community Health Workers; Veterinary Public Health. **Publications:** *American Journal of Public Health,* monthly. Includes news briefs and annual leadership directory. **Price:** included in membership dues; $185.00 /year for nonmembers. ISSN: 0090-0036. **Circulation:** 37,000. **Advertising:** accepted. Alternate Formats: microform; online ● *The Nation's Health,* monthly. Newspaper. Reports on current and proposed legislation, regulations, and policy issues affecting public health; includes reports on current health issues. **Price:** included in membership dues; $45.00 /year for nonmembers. ISSN: 0028-0496. **Circulation:** 33,000. **Advertising:** accepted. Alternate Formats: online ● Also publishes books, manuals, and pamphlets; maintains publications service. **Conventions/Meetings:** annual meeting (exhibits) - fall. 2007 Nov. 3-7, Washington, DC; 2008 Oct. 25-29, San Diego, CA; 2009 Nov. 7-11, Philadelphia, PA.

15890 ■ Asia Pacific Public Health Nutrition Association (APPHNA)
Address Unknown since 2007
Description: Public health practitioners and nutritionists. Promotes nutrition as a vital component of good health. Develops and implements national and international public health nutrition strategies; sponsors research and educational programs.

15891 ■ Association for Community Health Improvement (ACHI)
180 Montgomery St., Ste.1520
San Francisco, CA 94104
Ph: (415)248-8408 (415)248-8411
Fax: (415)296-0519
E-mail: communityhlth@aha.org
URL: http://www.communityhlth.org/communityhlth_app/index.jsp
Contact: Michael Bilton, Exec. Dir.
Founded: 2002. **Members:** 430. **Membership Dues:** individual (based on employer's budget), $110-$210 (annual) ● organizational (based on number of people), $550-$1,000 (annual) ● student/retired, $70 (annual). **Multinational.** **Description:** Aims to strengthen community health through education, peer networking and dissemination of practical tools. Strives to ensure that underserved populations gain access to primary and specialty health care. Convenes and supports leaders from the health care, public health, community, and philanthropic sectors to identify and achieve shared community health goals. **Telecommunication Services:** electronic mail, mbilton@aha.org. **Publications:** *ACHI Members' Bulletin.* Features exclusive and advance notice

of member benefits and events, premium news and funding announcements. **Price:** for members only. Alternate Formats: online ● *Community Benefit Bulletin,* 1-3 times/month. Contains news and reports on charity care, non-profit tax-exempt status, and hospital community benefit programs. ● *Community Health News,* weekly. Newsletter. Covers health trends and statistics, prevention programs, policy initiatives, funding opportunities, tools and best practices. **Price:** free. **Circulation:** 2,300. Alternate Formats: online.

15892 ■ Association of Public Health Laboratories (APHL)
8515 Georgia Ave., Ste.700
Silver Spring, MD 20910
Ph: (240)485-2745
Fax: (240)485-2700
E-mail: info@aphl.org
URL: http://www.aphl.org
Contact: Scott J. Becker MS, Exec. Dir.
Founded: 1951. **Members:** 460. **Membership Dues:** public health institutional, associate institutional, $500-$4,000 (annual) ● individual, $85 (annual) ● student, $50 (annual). **Staff:** 60. **Languages:** English, French, Hindi, Portuguese, Spanish. **Description:** Represents national, state, and local public health laboratories. Collaborates with partners in private and public sectors in advocating sound public health and environmental health policies, and providing technical assistance and training. **Computer Services:** database ● mailing lists ● online services. **Publications:** *The APHL Minute.* Newsletter. **Price:** free for members ● *APHL Washington Bulletin,* monthly. Features legislation update. **Conventions/Meetings:** annual conference.

15893 ■ Association of Schools of Public Health (ASPH)
1101 15th St. NW, Ste.910
Washington, DC 20005
Ph: (202)296-1099
Fax: (202)296-1252
E-mail: info@asph.org
URL: http://www.asph.org
Contact: Harrison C. Spencer MD, Pres./CEO
Founded: 1941. **Members:** 28. **Membership Dues:** institution, $14,000 (annual). **Staff:** 13. **Budget:** $350,000. **Description:** Accredited graduate schools of public health. Provides focus for the enhancement of academic public health programs. Serves as an information center for governmental and private groups, and individuals whose concerns overlap those of higher education for public health. **Libraries:** **Type:** reference. **Holdings:** books. **Subjects:** school catalogs, environmental brochures, minority recruitment. **Telecommunication Services:** electronic mail, hspencer@asph.org. **Committees:** CEPH Liaison; Continuing Education; Data; Education; International Health; Legislation; Marketing/Recruiting. **Publications:** *Gerontology Programs and Curricula in U.S. Schools of Public Health* ● *Public Health Career Information* ● *Reach.* Brochure. Outlines potential careers and job opportunities in public health. **Price:** $1.75 plus shipping and handling. **Conventions/Meetings:** annual Deans' Meeting - conference - always fall.

15894 ■ Commonwealth Fund
1 E 75th St.
New York, NY 10021
Ph: (212)606-3800
Fax: (212)606-3500
E-mail: info@cmwf.org
URL: http://www.cmwf.org
Contact: Karen Davis, Pres.
Founded: 1918. **Members:** 12. **Staff:** 50. **Description:** Aims to promote a high performing health care system that achieves better access, improved quality, and greater efficiency, particularly for society's most vulnerable, including low-income people, the uninsured, minority Americans, young children, and elderly adults. Carries out this mandate by supporting independent research on health care issues and making grants to improve health care practice and policy. Serves an international program in health policy that

is designed to stimulate innovative policies and practices in the United States and other industrialized countries.

15895 ■ Council on Education for Public Health (CEPH)
800 Eye St. NW, Ste.202
Washington, DC 20001-3710
Ph: (202)789-1050
Fax: (202)789-1895
E-mail: lking@ceph.org
URL: http://www.ceph.org
Contact: Laura Rasar King MPH, Exec. Dir.

Founded: 1974. **Members:** 2. **Staff:** 3. **Budget:** $400,000. **Description:** Participants are professional associations representing public health practice (American Public Health Association) and public health education (Association of Schools of Public Health) (see separate entries). Seeks to strengthen educational programs in schools of public health and graduate public health programs through accreditation, consultation, research, and other appropriate services; and to encourage the development of experimental and innovative programs that will ensure educational quality. **Affiliated With:** American Public Health Association; Association of Schools of Public Health. **Publications:** *Manuals for Accreditation of Graduate Schools of Public Health and Graduate Public Health Programs.* **Conventions/Meetings:** semiannual board meeting.

15896 ■ Health Education Foundation (HEF)
2600 Virginia Ave. NW, Ste.502
Washington, DC 20037
Ph: (202)338-3501
Fax: (202)965-6520
E-mail: hefmona@erols.com
Contact: Morris E. Chafetz MD, Pres.

Founded: 1975. **Staff:** 3. **Description:** Seeks to develop cost-effective health promotion programs for government, industry, and the business community; helps people make informed decisions about their physical and mental health; participates in research for analysis and development of standards and programs to meet public health needs. **Convention/Meeting:** none. **Publications:** *Conference Proceedings,* periodic ● *Health Fact Tips,* semiannual ● *HEF News: Perspectives on Health, Behavior, and Lifestyle,* quarterly. Newsletter. **Price:** $15.00/year. **Circulation:** 1,000 ● Monograph ● Pamphlets.

15897 ■ National Association of Local Boards of Health (NALBOH)
1840 E Gypsy Lane Rd.
Bowling Green, OH 43402
Ph: (419)353-7714
Fax: (419)352-6278
E-mail: nalboh@nalboh.org
URL: http://www.nalboh.org
Contact: Marie M. Fallon MHSA, Exec. Dir.

Founded: 1992. **Members:** 800. **Membership Dues:** institutional, $95-$120 (annual) ● affiliate, sponsor (for profit), $300 (annual) ● associate, sponsor (nonprofit), $60 (annual) ● retired, $12 (annual) ● student, $20 (annual). **Staff:** 7. **Budget:** $500,000. **Regional Groups:** 7. **State Groups:** 11. **Local Groups:** 3,200. **Description:** Represents the interests of local boards of health throughout the United States and relates their concerns to individuals responsible for developing public health policy at the national level. Offers training, technical assistance and advocacy. **Awards:** Everett I. Hageman Award. **Frequency:** annual. **Type:** recognition. **Recipient:** to a member of a local Board of Health ● Presidential. **Type:** recognition. **Computer Services:** database, 3172 local Boards of Health. **Telecommunication Services:** electronic mail, marie@nalboh.org. **Publications:** *NewsBrief,* quarterly. Newsletter. **Circulation:** 8,000. **Advertising:** accepted. Alternate Formats: online. **Conventions/Meetings:** annual Boards of Health: The Stewards of Local Public Health - conference (exhibits) - 2007 Sept. 19-21, Anchorage, AK.

15898 ■ National Association of Rural Health Clinics (NARHC)
2 E Main St.
Fremont, MI 49412
Free: (866)306-1961
Fax: (231)924-4882
E-mail: info@narhc.org
URL: http://www.narhc.org
Contact: John Gill, Pres.

Membership Dues: independent/provider-based RHC, government institution, $400 (annual) ● corporate, consultant, $550 (annual). **Description:** Represents groups of rural hospitals, community health centers and individual practitioners dedicated to improving the delivery of quality, cost-effective health care in rural underserved areas through Rural Health Clinics (RHC) programs. Promotes and protects the interests of rural clinics. **Publications:** *NARHC News,* quarterly. Newsletter.

15899 ■ National Conference of Local Environmental Health Administrators (NCLEHA)
c/o University of Washington
Dept. of Environmental Hea.
PO Box 357234
Seattle, WA 98195-7234
Ph: (206)616-2097
Fax: (206)543-8123
E-mail: ctreser@u.washington.edu
URL: http://www.ncleha.org
Contact: Dave Riggs, Sec.

Founded: 1939. **Members:** 220. **Membership Dues:** regular, $25 (annual). **Description:** Professional environmental health personnel engaged in or officially concerned with municipal (city, county, or district) environmental health administration or teaching of environmental health. Promotes improvement and greater use of science and practice of environmental health in community life. **Committees:** Accident Prevention; Administration of Air Pollution Control Programs; Environmental Health Planning; Hospital and Institutional Sanitation; Housing and Urban Renewal; Swimming Pools and Bathing Places; Water Supply. **Affiliated With:** National Environmental Health Association. **Formerly:** (1969) Conference of Municipal Public Health Engineers; (1981) Conference of Local Environmental Health Administrators. **Publications:** Newsletter, quarterly. **Conventions/Meetings:** annual meeting, held in conjunction with NEHA (exhibits) - always June.

15900 ■ National Pediculosis Association (NPA)
50 Kearney Rd.
Needham, MA 02494
Ph: (781)449-6487
Fax: (781)449-8129
E-mail: npa@headlice.org
URL: http://www.headlice.org
Contact: Deborah Z. Altschuler, Pres.

Founded: 1983. **Staff:** 5. **Languages:** English, Spanish. **Description:** Parents, physicians, school nurses, and individuals representing hospitals and county health departments. Works to eliminate the incidence, particularly among children, of pediculosis (head lice). Conducts public education campaign to make pediculosis control a public health priority; acts as consumer advocate to ensure the quality and safety of products for treating pediculosis and scabies; encourages scientific research to discover methods of treatment that minimize the use of pesticides, which may harm pregnant and nursing women as well as infants and children. Disseminates information on identifying, treating, and preventing pediculosis, with emphasis on finding and removing nits (louse eggs) in the hair. Provides consultations to schools, camps, and other organizations. **Affiliated With:** American Camp Association; National Association of Chain Drug Stores; National Association of School Nurses. **Publications:** *Keep Your Wits Not Your Nits* ● *Latest Greatest Coloring Book About Lice.* **Conventions/Meetings:** annual meeting.

15901 ■ National Rural Health Association (NRHA)
521 E 63rd St.
Kansas City, MO 64110-3329
Ph: (816)756-3140
Fax: (816)756-3144
E-mail: mail@nrharural.org
URL: http://www.nrharural.org
Contact: Alan Morgan, CEO

Founded: 1978. **Members:** 2,000. **Membership Dues:** advocate, student, $35 (annual) ● individual, $200 (annual) ● supporting, $3,500 (annual). **Staff:** 13. **Description:** Administrators, physicians, nurses, physician assistants, health planners, academicians, and others interested or involved in rural health care. Creates a better understanding of health care problems unique to rural areas; utilizes a collective approach in finding positive solutions; articulates and represents the health care needs of rural America; supplies current information to rural health care providers; serves as a liaison between rural health care programs throughout the country. Offers continuing education credits for medical, dental, nursing, and management courses. **Libraries:** Type: not open to the public. **Holdings:** articles, books, periodicals. **Subjects:** rural health. **Awards:** Frequency: annual. **Type:** recognition. **Recipient:** for persons involved in rural health. **Telecommunication Services:** electronic mail, morgan@nrharural.org. **Absorbed:** American Small and Rural Hospital Association. **Formed by Merger of:** American Rural Health Association; National Rural Health Care Association. **Publications:** *Journal of Rural Health,* quarterly. Includes rural health research, book reviews, abstracts of published research, and research reviews. **Price:** included in membership dues; $55.00 /year for nonmembers; $160.00 /year for institutions. ISSN: 0890-765X. **Circulation:** 2,500. **Advertising:** accepted. Alternate Formats: online ● *Rural Clinical Quarterly.* Newsletter ● *Rural Roads.* Magazine. **Price:** $20.00/year ● Also publishes many other resources. **Conventions/Meetings:** annual Minority and Multicultural Conference (exhibits) ● annual Rural Health - conference (exhibits) ● annual Rural Health Policy Institute - conference - 2008 Jan. 28-30, Washington, DC.

15902 ■ NSF International
789 N Dixboro Rd.
PO Box 130140
Ann Arbor, MI 48113-0140
Ph: (734)769-8010
Free: (800)NSF-MARK
Fax: (734)769-0109
E-mail: info@nsf.org
URL: http://www.nsf.org
Contact: Nancy Quay, Exec. Dir.

Founded: 1944. **Staff:** 230. **Nonmembership. Description:** Specializes in the areas of public health and environmental quality focusing on water quality, food safety, indoor air health and the environment. Develops standards, operates product certification and listings programs for products that meet or exceed public health safety standards. Maintains a worldwide network of auditors who conduct unannounced inspections of manufacturer facilities to ensure compliance and to protect the integrity of the NSF Certification Mark. Provides special research and testing services to industry, government, and foundations. **Awards:** Walter F. Snyder. **Frequency:** annual. **Type:** recognition. **Recipient:** for excellence in public health and environmental safety. **Computer Services:** database, on official product listings: individual models or product types by plant, company, and standard. **Telecommunication Services:** electronic mail, nquay@nsf.org. **Committees:** Council of Public Health Consultants; Joint Industry User and Public Health. **Programs:** Packaged Ice. **Formerly:** (1993) National Sanitation Foundation. **Publications:** *Bottled Water and Packaged Ice,* periodic ● *Class II Biohazard Cabinetry,* periodic. Book. Alternate Formats: online ● *Drinking Water Additives-Health Effects,* periodic ● *Drinking Water Treatment Units and Related Products, Components, and Materials,* periodic ● *Environmental Management Systems Standards and Guidance Documents* ● *Food Equip-*

ment and Related Products, Components, and Materials, periodic ● Plastics Piping Components and Related Materials, periodic ● Swimming Pools, Spas, and Hot Tubs, periodic ● Wastewater Treatment Units and Related Products and Components, periodic ● Also publishes educational material.

15903 ■ Public Citizen Health Research Group (PCHRG)
1600 20th St. NW
Washington, DC 20009
Ph: (202)588-1000 (202)588-7735
Fax: (202)588-7796
E-mail: hrg1@citizen.org
URL: http://www.citizen.org/hrg
Contact: Sidney M. Wolfe MD, Dir.

Founded: 1971. **Membership Dues:** friend, $10-$50 (annual) ● regular, $20-$100 (annual) ● partner, $500-$5,000 (annual). **Staff:** 10. **Description:** Works on issues of health care delivery, workplace safety and health, drug regulation, food additives, medical device safety, and environmental influences on health. Petitions or sues federal agencies on consumers' behalf, testifies before Congress on health matters, and monitors the enforcement of health and safety legislation. Publicizes important health findings; makes available to the public a broad spectrum of research and consumer action materials in the form of books and reports. **Publications:** Health Letter, monthly. Newsletter. Contains reports on health and health policy issues. **Price:** $18.00/year. ISSN: 0882-598X. **Circulation:** 40,000 ● Worst Pills, Best Pills News, monthly. Newsletter. Contains reports on drug safety issues. **Price:** $20.00/year. ISSN: 1080-2479. Alternate Formats: online ● Directory, annual. Includes list of association publications.

15904 ■ Public Health Foundation (PHF)
1300 L St. NW, Ste.800
Washington, DC 20005
Ph: (202)218-4400
Fax: (202)218-4409
E-mail: info@phf.org
URL: http://www.phf.org
Contact: Ronald Bialek MPP, Pres.

Founded: 1970. **Staff:** 15. **Nonmembership. Description:** Strives to achieve healthy communities through research, training, and technical assistance. **Telecommunication Services:** electronic mail, rbialek@phf.org. **Publications:** PHF E-News. Newsletter. Promotes projects, products and plans. **Price:** free for members. **Circulation:** 60,000. Alternate Formats: online.

15905 ■ Public Health Leadership Society (PHLS)
1515 Poydras St., Ste.1200
New Orleans, LA 70112
Ph: (504)301-9821
Fax: (504)301-9820
E-mail: awilliams@lphi.org
URL: http://www.phls.org
Contact: Ms. An Nguyen, Coor.

Membership Dues: regular, $125 (annual) ● retired alumnus/alumna, $75 (annual). **Description:** Comprised of alumni from leadership programs for senior public health professionals. Provides opportunities for alumni to continue their learning experiences and leadership development, maintain and develop professional and personal relations, and contribute to innovative thinking about public health issues. **Committees:** Annual Program; Book Club; Educational Services; Public Health Code of Ethics. **Publications:** Newsletter.

15906 ■ Society for the Analysis of African-American Public Health Issues (SAAPHI)
PO Box 360350
Decatur, GA 30036
E-mail: jvr4@cdc.gov
URL: http://www.saaphi.org
Contact: Jessie Richardson Hood, Pres.

Membership Dues: general, $20 (annual). **Description:** Promotes the health of African-American individuals and communities through scientifically-

based interventions, intervention-guided research and health policy advocacy. Increases public awareness of and solutions to health problems of African-American communities through education and information dissemination. **Computer Services:** Mailing lists.

15907 ■ Society for Public Health Education (SOPHE)
750 First St. NE, Ste.910
Washington, DC 20002-4241
Ph: (202)408-9804
Fax: (202)408-9815
E-mail: info@sophe.org
URL: http://www.sophe.org
Contact: Libby Howze ScD, Pres.

Founded: 1950. **Members:** 2,200. **Membership Dues:** active, $130 (annual) ● emeritus, $75 (annual) ● student, $60 (annual). **Staff:** 7. **Budget:** $1,000,000. **Local Groups:** 24. **National Groups:** 9. **Multinational. Description:** Researchers and practitioners in health education/health promotion concerned with individual and population health problems. Seeks to promote, encourage, and contribute to the advancement of health of all people by encouraging research, improving health practices, elevating standards of achievement in public health education, and advocating for public health policies. **Awards:** Chapter Innovation. **Frequency:** annual. **Type:** monetary. **Recipient:** for chapters that recognize replicable methods implemented by the society and deliver one or more core member services ● Distinguished Fellow. **Frequency:** annual. **Type:** recognition. **Recipient:** for individuals who have made significant and lasting contribution to the society and professional health education ● Health Education Mentor Award. **Frequency:** annual. **Type:** recognition. **Recipient:** for individuals who have provided excellence in mentorship in health educators in their preparation, performance and practice ● Honorary Fellow. **Frequency:** annual. **Type:** recognition. **Recipient:** for an individual who made an exemplary and lasting contribution in the field of health education and public health ● Program Excellence Award. **Frequency:** annual. **Type:** recognition. **Recipient:** for outstanding health education programs in existence for at least three years ● Student Research Paper. **Frequency:** annual. **Type:** recognition. **Recipient:** for outstanding graduate students who excel in creative and innovative research ● Vivian Drenckhahn Scholarship Award. **Frequency:** annual. **Type:** recognition. **Recipient:** for both graduate and undergraduate level student who pursued educational and professional development in health education. **Computer Services:** Mailing lists, rental. **Subgroups:** Anthropology; Children and Adolescent School Health; Community Health; Health Communications; International Health; Medical Care; Social Marketing; Students/New Proposals; University Faculty; Worksite Health. **Formerly:** Society of Public Health Educators. **Publications:** Health Education and Behavior, bimonthly. Journal. Contains topics on critical health issues for a broad range of professionals interested in understanding factors associated with health behavior. **Price:** included in membership dues. **Advertising:** accepted. Also Cited As: formerly Health Education Quarterly ● Health Promotion Practice, quarterly. Journal. Contains information on health promotion/health education policy, applications, practice. **Price:** included in membership dues. **Advertising:** accepted ● News and Views, bimonthly. Newsletter. Features latest trends, public policies, meetings and resources. **Conventions/Meetings:** semiannual conference (exhibits) ● annual meeting, in conjunction with American Public Health Association - 2007 Nov. 1-3, Washington, DC.

15908 ■ U.S.-Mexico Border Health Association (USMBHA)
5400 Suncrest Dr., Ste.C-5
El Paso, TX 79912-5615
Ph: (915)833-6450
Fax: (915)833-7840
E-mail: mail@usmbha.org
URL: http://www.usmbha.org
Contact: Dr. Manuel Robles Linares, Exec. Dir.

Founded: 1943. **Members:** 500. **Membership Dues:** individual (based on annual income), $25-$75 (an-

nual) ● student/community health worker, $15 (annual). **Languages:** English, Spanish. **Description:** Physicians, public health administrators, nurses, sanitary engineers, veterinarians, scientists, laboratory workers, and other health officers from the 4 American and 6 Mexican states bordering the two countries. Seeks to make easier and more efficient the improvement of public health along both sides of the border; provides for exchange of experiences, discussion of mutual problems in human and animal diseases, and development of personal and professional contacts necessary for carrying out health projects. Sponsors seminars and workshops covering topics such as: food handling; rabies; tuberculosis; epidemiological principles; sexually transmitted diseases. Compiles statistics. **Libraries: Type:** reference. **Holdings:** biographical archives. **Subjects:** US-Mexico border. **Awards:** Honorary Member. **Frequency:** annual. **Type:** recognition ● Outstanding Health Worker. **Frequency:** annual. **Type:** recognition. **Computer Services:** Mailing lists, of members. **Committees:** Awards; Education and Training. **Councils:** Binational Health. **Sections:** Disease Control; Environmental Health; Family Health; Geriatrics; Health Administration; Mental Health; Nursing; Oral Health. **Formerly:** (1975) United States-Mexico Border Health Association. **Publications:** Journal of Border Health (in English and Spanish), quarterly. Contains articles on U.S.-Mexico border health issues. **Price:** $5.00/issue. **Circulation:** 800. **Advertising:** accepted ● Report of Activities, annual ● U.S.-Mexico Border Health Association—News/Noticias, quarterly. Newsletter. Informs the members on activities carried out by members and issues relevant to the border. **Conventions/Meetings:** annual conference (exhibits) - always June ● quarterly meeting.

15909 ■ Women's International Public Health Network (WIPHN)
7100 Oak Forest Ln.
Bethesda, MD 20817
Ph: (301)469-9210
Fax: (301)469-8423
E-mail: wiphn@erols.com
Contact: Dr. Naomi Baumslag, Pres.

Founded: 1987. **Members:** 12,500. **Membership Dues:** individual, $25 (annual) ● organization, $50 (annual). **Staff:** 2. **Budget:** $25,000. **Description:** Individuals and organizations with an interest in women's health issues. Promotes adoption of public health policies and programs providing greater access to health care for women. Conducts educational programs. **Libraries: Type:** open to the public. **Holdings:** 25. **Subjects:** health, nutrition, public health, women's health issues. **Computer Services:** database. **Telecommunication Services:** electronic bulletin board. **Publications:** WIPHN News, 3/year. Newsletter. **Price:** $35.00 /year for individuals; $50.00/year for organizations. **Circulation:** 12,000. **Advertising:** accepted.

15910 ■ World Federation of Public Health Associations (WFPHA)
c/o American Public Health Association
800 I St. NW
Washington, DC 20001-3710
Ph: (202)777-2490 (202)777-2487
Fax: (202)777-2533
E-mail: bhatcher@wfpha.org
URL: http://www.wfpha.org
Contact: Barbara J. Hatcher PhD, Sec. Gen.

Founded: 1967. **Members:** 70. **Membership Dues:** sustaining, $1,000 (annual) ● regular, $300-$3,000 (annual). **Staff:** 2. **Regional Groups:** 5. **National Groups:** 64. **Multinational. Description:** Represents national public health associations, regional public health associations, and regional associations of schools of public health united "to strengthen the public health profession and to improve community health throughout the world." Encourages formation of national public health associations. Organizes projects; conducts special studies; offers lectures; compiles reports; sponsors triennial world congress. **Awards:** The Leavell Lectureship. **Frequency:** triennial. **Type:** recognition. **Recipient:** for leadership in public health at the national or international level.

Projects: Global Tobacco Control; Handwashing; Human Resources for Health; Persistent Organic Pollutants. **Affiliated With:** U.S. Fund for UNICEF. **Publications:** *Reports of Triennial International Congresses* ● *WFPHA Report*, quarterly. Newsletter. Provides information on the activities of the Federation, its member associations, and international organizations. Alternate Formats: online. **Conventions/Meetings:** annual meeting - always May in Geneva, Switzerland ● triennial World Congress on Public Health.

Publishing

15911 ■ International Society for Medical Publication Professionals (ISMPP)
PO Box 2523
Briarcliff Manor, NY 10510
Ph: (914)945-0507
Fax: (914)945-0307
E-mail: kgoldin@ismpp.org
URL: http://www.ismpp.org
Contact: Kimberly Goldin, Exec. Dir.
Founded: 2005. **Membership Dues:** regular, $150 (annual). **Multinational. Description:** Promotes excellence in medical publishing. Supports publication professionals through education in fields associated with publication development and planning. Facilitates and encourages communication among publication professionals within the pharmaceutical industry, medical publishers, medical communications companies and other research, regulatory and educational groups. Fosters a consensus for policies related to publication planning and medical publishing. **Conventions/Meetings:** annual meeting - 2008 Apr. 28-30, Philadelphia, PA.

Quality Assurance

15912 ■ American Board of Quality Assurance and Utilization Review Physicians (ABQAURP)
6640 Cong. St.
New Port Richey, FL 34653
Ph: (727)569-0190
Free: (800)998-6030
Fax: (727)569-0195
E-mail: info@abqaurp.org
URL: http://www.abqaurp.org
Contact: Arthur I. Border MD, Chm.
Founded: 1977. **Members:** 6,351. **Membership Dues:** diamond (corporate), $15,000 (annual) ● platinum (corporate), $10,000 (annual) ● gold (corporate), $5,000 (corporate), ● silver (corporate), $2,500 (annual). **Staff:** 7. **Budget:** $1,250,000. **Description:** Seeks to maintain and improve the process of health care quality and management through development, administration, and supervision of a certification program in the field. Provides continuing education for physicians, RNs and other health care professionals and makes available study material. **Computer Services:** database, diplomates. **Divisions:** The American Institute for Healthcare Quality. **Publications:** *The PSQH*, bimonthly. Journal. **Price:** $49.00/year. ISSN: 1553-6637 ● Books. **Conventions/Meetings:** quarterly Continuing Education Seminar (exhibits).

15913 ■ American College of Medical Quality (ACMQ)
4334 Montgomery Ave., Ste.B
Bethesda, MD 20814
Ph: (301)913-9149
Free: (800)924-2149
Fax: (301)913-9142
E-mail: acmq@acmq.org
URL: http://www.acmq.org
Contact: Bridget Brodie, Exec. VP
Founded: 1973. **Members:** 900. **Membership Dues:** physician, $285 (annual) ● affiliate, $115 (annual) ● corporate/institutional, $1,200 (annual). **Staff:** 4. **Budget:** $500,000. **Regional Groups:** 4. **Description:** Physicians, affiliates, and institutions. Seeks to

educate and set standards of competence in the field of quality improvement and management. Offers a core curriculum in quality. Maintains Speaker's Bureau. **Libraries: Type:** reference. **Awards:** Founders Award. **Frequency:** annual. **Type:** recognition ● Institutional Leadership in Quality Award. **Frequency:** annual. **Type:** recognition ● Service Award. **Frequency:** annual. **Type:** recognition. **Computer Services:** database ● mailing lists. **Committees:** Bylaws; Continuing Medical Education; Education; Ethics and Professional Policy; Grants and Sponsorships; Membership. **Special Interest Groups:** Health Information Technology; Healthcare Quality in Diverse and Underserved Communities; Quality in Managed Care. **Formerly:** (1988) ACURP. **Publications:** *American College of Medical Quality Newsletter - Focus*, bimonthly. Includes topical articles and college and chapter news. **Price:** included in membership dues. **Circulation:** 1,000. **Advertising:** accepted ● *American Journal of Medical Quality*, bimonthly. Covers topics concerning evaluation of quality in health care, DRGs, Medicare and Medicaid, risk management, and other areas of interest. **Price:** included in membership dues; $423.00 /year for institutions; $189.00 /year for nonmembers. ISSN: 0885-713X. **Advertising:** accepted. **Conventions/Meetings:** annual Medical Quality - conference (exhibits).

15914 ■ American Health Quality Association (AHQA)
1155 21st St. NW
Washington, DC 20036
Ph: (202)331-5790
Fax: (202)331-9334
E-mail: info@ahqa.org
URL: http://www.ahqa.org
Contact: Arja P. Adair Jr., Pres.
Founded: 1973. **Members:** 1,400. **Membership Dues:** individual, $125 (annual) ● associate, $5,000 (annual). **Staff:** 11. **Budget:** $1,900,000. **State Groups:** 53. **Local Groups:** 11. **Description:** Institutions and individuals. Develops communication programs for physicians, institutions, and others interested in peer review organizations (PROs). Provides a national forum for the interchange of ideas, techniques, and information relating to medical quality assessment. Conducts courses and on-site educational programs to increase physicians' involvement and leadership in PROs, improve practice patterns through review, understand and use PRO data to improve service delivery, pre-admission review, profile analysis, retrospective review, and organizational development. Sponsors placement service; maintains a speakers' bureau and a library. **Committees:** Ambulatory Review; Confidentiality and Information Disclosure; Continuing Care; Continuing Medical Education; Credentials; Legislative Affairs; Quality Improvement. **Formerly:** (1982) American Association of Professional Standards Review Organizations; (1997) American Medical Peer Review Association. **Publications:** *AHQA Bulletin*, periodic. Covers medical regulatory and legislative developments. **Price:** included in membership dues. **Circulation:** 75 ● *Legislative Monitor*, periodic. **Price:** free for members ● *Physician Advisor Manual* ● *Quality Advocate*, quarterly. Newsletter. Includes Policy Outlook, Innovation, Washington Update, Legislative Update, Calendar of Events columns and job announcements. **Price:** included in membership dues; $75.00 /year for nonmembers. **Circulation:** 1,400. **Advertising:** accepted ● *Resource Document and Private Review Manual* ● *Tapes of Conference Programs*. Audiotape ● Membership Directory, annual. **Conventions/Meetings:** annual Data Finance and Medical Review Conference and Health Policy Symposium - conference and symposium (exhibits) ● annual meeting (exhibits) - 2008 Feb. 25-29, San Francisco, CA; 2009 Feb. 23-27, Tampa, FL.

15915 ■ Institute for Medical Quality (IMQ)
221 Main St., Ste.210
San Francisco, CA 94105
Ph: (415)882-5151 (415)882-5169
Fax: (415)882-5149

E-mail: jsilverman@imq.org
URL: http://www.imq.org
Contact: Jill K. Silverman MSPH, Pres./CEO
Description: Works to improve the quality of care to patients across the continuum of health care. **Programs:** Ambulatory; Consolidated Accreditation and Licensure Survey; Continuing Medical Education Accreditation; Continuing Medical Education Certification; Continuing Medical Education Consultation; Corrections and Detentions Survey; Medical Staff Consultation and Quality Education; Peer Review Consultation.

15916 ■ National Association for Healthcare Quality (NAHQ)
4700 W Lake Ave.
Glenview, IL 60025
Ph: (847)375-4720
Free: (800)966-9392
Fax: (877)218-7939
E-mail: heidi_benson@northcrest.com
URL: http://www.nahq.org
Contact: Heide Benson, Pres.
Founded: 1976. **Members:** 5,200. **Membership Dues:** individual, $115 (annual) ● institution, $450 (annual). **Staff:** 7. **Budget:** $1,000,000. **State Groups:** 47. **Description:** Healthcare professionals in quality assessment and improvement, utilization and risk management, case management, infection control, managed care, nursing, and medical records. Objectives are: to encourage, develop, and provide continuing education for all persons involved in health care quality; to give the patient primary consideration in all actions affecting his or her health and welfare; to promote the sharing of knowledge and encourage a high degree of professional ethics in health care quality. Offers accredited certification in the field of healthcare quality, utilization, and risk management. Facilitates communication and cooperation among members, medical staff, and health care government agencies. Conducts educational seminars and conferences. **Awards:** Award for Association Excellence. **Frequency:** annual. **Type:** recognition. **Recipient:** to the state healthcare quality association that provides exceptional membership services and benefits ● Clare Glover Award. **Frequency:** annual. **Type:** recognition. **Recipient:** to a dynamic and passionate member who has demonstrated enthusiasm for the association ● Distinguished Member Award. **Frequency:** annual. **Type:** recognition. **Recipient:** to an outstanding member who has made significant contributions to the healthcare quality profession ● HQF Career Development Grant. **Frequency:** annual. **Type:** grant. **Recipient:** for a member who has been in the healthcare quality field at least 5 years and is a Certified Professional in Healthcare Quality ● HQF New Quality Professional Grant. **Frequency:** annual. **Type:** grant. **Recipient:** for a member who has been in the healthcare quality field less than 2 years and is not yet a Certified Professional in Healthcare Quality ● JHQ Golden Pen Award. **Frequency:** annual. **Type:** recognition. **Recipient:** for members who have demonstrated excellence in writing for the Journal for Healthcare Quality ● Stumph Award for Excellence in Publication. **Frequency:** annual. **Type:** monetary. **Computer Services:** Mailing lists, of members. **Boards:** Editorial Review; Fellowship Review; Healthcare Quality Certification; Healthcare Quality Foundation. **Committees:** Awards; Conference Planning; Nominating. **Formerly:** (1979) National Association of Utilization Review Coordinators; (1991) National Association of Quality Assurance Professionals. **Publications:** *Journal for Healthcare Quality*, bimonthly. **Price:** $115.00 /year for individuals in U.S.; $170.00 /year for institutions in U.S.; $190.00 /year for individuals and institutions outside U.S. ISSN: 1062-2551. **Circulation:** 8,000. **Advertising:** accepted ● *NAHQ Guide to Quality Management* ● *NAHQ News*, quarterly. Newsletter. **Conventions/Meetings:** annual Educational Conference (exhibits).

15917 ■ National Committee for Quality Assurance (NCQA)
2000 L St. NW, Ste.500
Washington, DC 20036

Ph: (202)955-3500
Free: (888)275-7585
Fax: (202)955-3599
E-mail: customersupport@ncqa.org
URL: http://www.ncqa.org
Contact: Margaret E. O'Kane, Pres.

Founded: 1979. **Nonmembership. Description:** Represents employers, consumer and labor representatives, health plans, quality experts, regulators and representatives from organized medicine. Aims to improve the quality of health care delivered everywhere. Accredits quality assurance programs in prepaid managed health care organizations. Develops and coordinates programs for assessing the quality of care and service in the managed health care industry. Conducts research; holds training and educational seminars; operates speakers' bureau. **Programs:** Accreditation; Certification; HEDIS; Physician Recognition; Quality Plus. **Publications:** Health Plan Employer Data and Information Set, annual. Handbook. Also Cited As: HEDIS ● Quality Matters, 3/year. Newsletter. Discusses quality-related activities in the managed care industry and at NCQA. **Price:** $90.00/year. Alternate Formats: online ● 2006-2007 Publications and Products, annual. Catalog. Alternate Formats: online ● Annual Report, annual. Alternate Formats: online ● Brochures ● Reports. Alternate Formats: online. **Conventions/Meetings:** conference.

15918 ■ PSRC of America

200 Madison Ave., Ste.2108
New York, NY 10016
Ph: (646)419-4020
Fax: (212)779-9307
E-mail: info@psrc-of-america.org
URL: http://www.psrc-of-america.org
Contact: Carol A. Wielk, Exec. Dir.

Founded: 1977. **Description:** Physicians, nurses, health care administrators, and consumers. Monitors the quality, appropriateness, and cost of health care given to patients in hospitals, ambulatory clinics, nursing facilities, and physicians' offices. Carries out work on behalf of managed care companies, health care institutions and facilities, insurance carriers and governmental entities. **Divisions:** Administrative Support. **Formerly:** (1999) Professional Standards Review Council of America. **Publications:** Informational Health Care Bulletin, periodic. **Conventions/Meetings:** biweekly Training Session - seminar.

Radiation

15919 ■ American College of Radiation Oncology (ACRO)

5272 River Rd.
Bethesda, MD 20816
Ph: (301)718-6515
Fax: (301)656-0989
E-mail: nwallis@paimgmt.com
URL: http://www.acro.org
Contact: Norman Wallis PhD, Exec. Sec.

Founded: 1989. **Members:** 1,500. **Membership Dues:** active, $350 (annual) ● associate, $230 (annual) ● corporate, $2,000 (annual). **Staff:** 5. **Budget:** $500,000. **Description:** Radiation oncologists, physicists, and administrators. Seeks to ensure that regulatory legislation is fair to radiation oncologists and their patients. Lobbies on behalf of radiation oncology physicians and their patients. Represents physicians in fee disputes with Medicare. Offers educational opportunities to assist radiation oncologists stay current. **Awards:** Howard Wong Scholarships. **Frequency:** annual. **Type:** scholarship. **Recipient:** for residents who wish to do a rotation at another facility during their residency training. **Computer Services:** Online services. **Publications:** ACRO Bulletin, quarterly. Newsletter. **Price:** included in membership dues. **Circulation:** 1,500. **Advertising:** accepted. **Conventions/Meetings:** annual meeting (exhibits) - in May.

15920 ■ Association of Freestanding Radiation Oncology Centers (AFROC)

1501 M St. NW, 7th Fl.
Washington, DC 20005
Ph: (202)872-6767
Free: (888)334-4542
Fax: (202)785-0564
E-mail: sgell@ppsv.com
URL: http://www.afroc.org
Contact: Sheila Gell MA, Exec. Dir.

Founded: 1987. **Members:** 300. **Membership Dues:** gold (less than 10 physicians), $5,000 (annual) ● individual, $500 (annual) ● gold (more than 10 physicians), $10,000 (annual). **Staff:** 2. **Budget:** $250,000. **Description:** Freestanding radiation oncology center employees; radiologists; oncologists; physicists; radiation therapists; laboratory clinicians. Promotes the interests of freestanding radiation oncology centers to insure high quality care for patients. Upgrades management services offered. Represents members in legal matters and to other associations. **Computer Services:** Mailing lists, available for purchase. **Committees:** Ethics; Publications; Quality Assurance; Standards. **Affiliated With:** American College of Radiology; American Society for Therapeutic Radiology and Oncology. **Publications:** The Source, bimonthly. Newsletter ● Directory, annual. **Conventions/Meetings:** annual meeting and conference (exhibits) - spring ● annual Reception and Roundtable Discussion - meeting.

15921 ■ International RadioSurgery Association (IRSA)

3005 Hoffman St.
Harrisburg, PA 17110
Ph: (717)260-9808
Fax: (717)260-9809
E-mail: office@irsa.org
URL: http://www.irsa.org
Contact: Douglas Kondziolka, Contact

Multinational. Description: Works to provide educational information on stereotactic radiosurgery to governments, regulatory agencies, insurers and referring physicians. Provides emotional support, education, and referrals for treatment to patients worldwide. **Publications:** Brain Talk. Newsletter. Alternate Formats: online.

15922 ■ Radiation and Public Health Project (RPHP)

PO Box 60
Unionville, NY 10988
Free: (800)582-3716
E-mail: bill@radiation.org
URL: http://www.radiation.org
Contact: Joseph Mangano, Natl. Coor.

Founded: 1994. **Description:** Represents scientists and physicians dedicated to understanding the relationships between low-level, nuclear radiation and public health. Promotes public awareness and responsible public policy related to radiation and public health. Publishes the results of research dealing with the impact of low-level radiation on public health and disseminates this information to the public, media, policy makers and the scientific community. **Publications:** Nuclink: Journal of Current Radiation and Public Health Issues. Alternate Formats: online ● Books.

Radiology

15923 ■ American Association for Women Radiologists (AAWR)

4550 Post Oak Pl., Ste.342
Houston, TX 77027
Ph: (713)965-0566
Fax: (713)960-0488
E-mail: admin@aawr.org
URL: http://www.aawr.org
Contact: Judith Amorosa MD, Pres.

Founded: 1981. **Members:** 1,400. **Membership Dues:** active, associate, $125 (annual) ● emeritus, $25 (annual) ● corresponding, $15 (annual). **Staff:** 2. **Local Groups:** 3. **Description:** Physicians involved in diagnostic or therapeutic radiology, nuclear medicine, or radiologic physics. Facilitates exchange of knowledge and information as it relates to women in radiology; encourages publication of materials on radiology and medicine by members; supports women who are training in the field and encourages women at all levels to participate in radiological societies. **Awards:** Alice Ettinger Distinguished Achievement Award. **Frequency:** annual. **Type:** recognition. **Recipient:** to a radiologist, radiation oncologist, or other person who has made long term contributions to radiology ● Eleanor Montague Distinguished Resident Award in Radiation Oncology. **Frequency:** annual. **Type:** recognition. **Recipient:** to residents who are in training in an accredited radiology department ● Lucy Frank Squire Distinguished Resident Award in Diagnostic Radiology. **Frequency:** annual. **Type:** recognition. **Recipient:** to residents who are in training in an accredited radiology department ● Marie Sklodowska-Curie Award. **Frequency:** annual. **Type:** recognition. **Recipient:** to a radiologist, radiation oncologist, or other person who has been a mentor, role model, or leader in radiology. **Computer Services:** Online services. **Subgroups:** AAWR Research and Education Foundation. **Formerly:** (1991) American Association of Women Radiologists. **Publications:** AAWR Focus, quarterly. Newsletter. Price: included in membership dues. **Circulation:** 1,400 ● AAWR Membership Directory, biennial. Price: included in membership dues. **Circulation:** 1,400 ● Journal of Women's Imaging, quarterly. Price: $60.00 for members; $113.00 for non-members ● Survival Guide for Women Radiologists: The AAWR Pocket Mentor. Handbook. Contains guidance and advice on many work-related and personal matters. Price: included in membership dues. **Conventions/Meetings:** annual meeting and lecture, business meeting, awards presentation ● annual seminar, refresher courses held in conjunction with Radiological Society of North America.

15924 ■ American Board of Radiology (ABR)

5441 E Williams Blvd., Ste.200
Tucson, AZ 85711
Ph: (520)790-2900
Fax: (520)790-3200
E-mail: information@theabr.org
URL: http://www.theabr.org
Contact: Dr. Robert R. Hattery, Exec. Dir.

Founded: 1934. **Members:** 23. **Description:** Certification board to establish qualifications, conduct examinations, and certify physicians in the specialty of radiation oncology, diagnostic radiology and radiological physics (science dealing with X-rays or rays from radioactive substances for medical use). **Publications:** Booklets. Contains topics on examinations in diagnostic radiology, radiological physics, radiation oncology and special competence in nuclear radiology. **Conventions/Meetings:** annual meeting, with examination.

15925 ■ American Chiropractic Registry of Radiologic Technologists (ACRRT)

52 W Colfax St.
Palatine, IL 60067
Ph: (847)705-1178
Fax: (847)705-1178
URL: http://www.acrrt.com
Contact: Dr. Edward Maurer, Exec. VP

Founded: 1982. **Members:** 2,000. **Staff:** 2. **Description:** Chiropractic assistants and radiologic technologists employed in chiropractic offices. Educates the general public concerning the importance of having highly skilled radiologic technologists (those who administer X-rays) in chiropractic offices. Serves as a national certifying agency for individuals in the field; maintains registry of certified chiropractic radiologic technologists. **Publications:** Self-Instructed Readings, annual. Articles. Contains information relating to the practice of radiologic technology. ● Wavelengths, periodic. Newsletter. Contains information on members, events, programs, and articles on radiologic technology. **Conventions/Meetings:** semiannual board meeting.

15926 ■ American College of Radiology (ACR)
1891 Preston White Dr.
Reston, VA 20191
Ph: (703)648-8900
Free: (800)227-5463
Fax: (703)264-2093
E-mail: info@acr.org
URL: http://www.acr.org
Contact: Harvey L. Neiman MD, Exec. Dir.

Founded: 1923. **Members:** 32,000. **Membership Dues:** active/associate, $60 (annual) ● international, $175 (annual) ● physicist, $200 (annual). **Staff:** 300. **Budget:** $38,700,000. **State Groups:** 53. **Description:** Principal organization serving radiologists with programs that focus on the practice of radiology and the delivery of comprehensive radiological health services. These programs in medical sciences, education, and in practice management, serve the public interest and the interests of the medical community in which radiologists serve in both diagnostic and therapeutic roles. Seeks to "advance the science of radiology, improve radiologic service to the patient, study the economic aspects of the practice of radiology, and encourage improved and continuing education for radiologists and allied professional fields". **Libraries: Type:** reference. **Holdings:** 2,000. **Awards:** Gold Medal. **Frequency:** annual. **Type:** fellowship. **Committees:** Cancer; Diagnostic Radiology; Equipment; Human Resources; Magnetic Resonance; Marketing; Nuclear Medicine Accreditation; Radiation Therapy; Radiologic Practice; Ultrasound Accreditation. **Affiliated With:** International Society of Radiology. **Publications:** Booklets ● Books ● Bulletin, monthly ● Directory, annual ● Pamphlets ● Also publishes textbooks, reprints, kits, and slides. **Conventions/Meetings:** annual meeting - always in Washington, DC. 2008 May 17-22, Washington, DC; 2009 May 2-7, Washington, DC.

15927 ■ American Healthcare Radiology Administrators (AHRA)
490B Boston Post Rd., No. 101
Sudbury, MA 01776
Ph: (978)443-7591
Free: (800)334-2472
Fax: (978)443-8046
E-mail: info@ahraonline.org
URL: http://www.ahraonline.org
Contact: Edward J. Cronin Jr., Exec. Dir.

Founded: 1973. **Members:** 4,000. **Membership Dues:** individual, $180 (annual). **Staff:** 10. **Budget:** $2,600,000. **Description:** Promotes leaders in radiology and imaging sciences, including administrators and managers of imaging services in hospitals, imaging centers, and physician practices. Publishes benchmarking research studies that include compensation and benefits, utilization of imaging staff, image management, and patient care quality. **Awards:** Award for Excellence. **Frequency:** annual. **Type:** recognition. **Recipient:** for radiology administrators for excellence and leadership. **Telecommunication Services:** electronic mail, ecronin@ahraonline.org. **Committees:** Annual Meeting; Editorial Review Board; Member Recognition; Nominations. **Formerly:** (1986) American Hospital Radiology Administrators. **Publications:** Link, monthly. Newsletter. **Price:** included in membership dues. **Circulation:** 4,000. **Advertising:** accepted. Also Cited As: AHRA Link ● Radiology Management, bimonthly. Journal. **Price:** $65.00 in U.S.; $80.00 in Canada; $100.00 other foreign countries. **Advertising:** accepted ● Radiology Policy & Procedure. Manual. **Price:** $265.00 for members; $365.00 for nonmembers. Alternate Formats: CD-ROM ● Membership Directory, annual, updated weekly. Alternate Formats: online. **Conventions/Meetings:** annual convention (exhibits).

15928 ■ American Osteopathic College of Radiology (AOCR)
119 E 2nd St.
Milan, MO 63556-1331
Ph: (660)265-4011
Free: (800)258-AOCR
Fax: (660)265-3494

E-mail: donna@aocr.org
URL: http://www.aocr.org
Contact: Bruno F. Borin DO, Pres.

Founded: 1941. **Members:** 730. **Membership Dues:** active, $495 (annual) ● associate, $250 (annual) ● affiliate, $55 (annual) ● active-military, $220 (annual) ● active-subspecialty training, retired, candidate, $110 (annual). **Staff:** 5. **Budget:** $400,000. **Description:** Certified radiologists, residents-in-training, and others active in the field of radiology. **Publications:** Viewbox, quarterly. Newsletter ● Membership Directory, annual. **Conventions/Meetings:** annual convention (exhibits) - 2007 Sept. 24-28, Boca Raton, FL.

15929 ■ American Roentgen Ray Society (ARRS)
44211 Slatestone Ct.
Leesburg, VA 20176-5109
Ph: (703)729-3353
Free: (800)438-2777
Fax: (703)729-4839
E-mail: info@arrs.org
URL: http://www.arrs.org
Contact: Anton N. Hasso MD, Pres.

Founded: 1900. **Members:** 14,000. **Membership Dues:** active, associate, allied science, physics, $250 (annual) ● training, $85 (annual) ● international, $320 (annual). **Staff:** 28. **Multinational. Description:** Trade association for radiologists worldwide. Offers many educational programs. **Libraries: Type:** reference. **Holdings:** books, periodicals. **Subjects:** radiology, history of society. **Awards:** ARRS Gold Medal. **Frequency:** annual. **Type:** recognition. **Recipient:** for distinguished service in radiology field ● ARRS Scholar. **Frequency:** annual. **Type:** scholarship. **Recipient:** for a practicing radiologist. **Formerly:** (1906) Roentgen Society of the U.S. **Publications:** American Journal of Roentgenology, monthly. Contains clinically useful information designed for radiologist. **Price:** $289.00 /year for individuals in U.S.; $379.23 /year for individuals in Canada; $363.00 /year for individuals, international. ISSN: 0361-803X. **Circulation:** 26,000. **Advertising:** accepted ● ARRS Memo, quarterly. Newsletter ● Categorical Course Syllabi. **Conventions/Meetings:** annual Scientific Meeting - meeting and symposium (exhibits) - 2008 Apr. 13-18, Washington, DC - **Avg. Attendance:** 3000; 2009 Apr. 26-May 1, Boston, MA; 2010 Apr. 28-May 3, San Diego, CA.

15930 ■ American Society of Emergency Radiology (ASER)
4550 Post Oak Pl., Ste.342
Houston, TX 77027
Ph: (713)965-0566
Fax: (713)960-0488
E-mail: aser@meetingmanagers.com
URL: http://www.erad.org
Contact: Carlos J. Sivit MD, Pres.

Founded: 1988. **Membership Dues:** active and associate, $250 (annual) ● training, $55. **Staff:** 3. **Description:** Works to advance the quality of diagnosis and treatment of ill or injured patients through medical imaging. **Telecommunication Services:** electronic bulletin board, Job Board. **Committees:** Annual Meeting; Audit; Community Radiology; Editorial; Education; Fellowship; Nominating; Sponsor Support. **Publications:** Newsletter. Alternate Formats: online ● Membership Directory. Alternate Formats: online ● Journal. Alternate Formats: online. **Conventions/Meetings:** Scientific Meetings.

15931 ■ American Society of Head and Neck Radiology (ASHNR)
2210 Midwest Rd., Ste.207
Oak Brook, IL 60523-8205
Ph: (630)574-0220
Fax: (630)574-0661
E-mail: kcammarata@asnr.org
URL: http://www.ashnr.org
Contact: Kenneth F. Cammarata, Business Mgr.

Founded: 1976. **Members:** 400. **Membership Dues:** active, associate, $175 (annual). **Budget:** $400,000. **Description:** Promotes education in the field of radiation research. **Awards:** Radiologist in Training. **Frequency:** annual. **Type:** monetary. **Telecommunica-**

tion Services: electronic mail, bmack@asnr.org. **Committees:** Ad Hoc Program; American College of Radiology Representatives; Education; International Relations; Nominating; Publications; Rules; Scientific. **Publications:** American Journal of Neuroradiology, 10/year. **Price:** included in membership dues; $235.00 for nonmembers in U.S.; $295.00 for nonmembers outside U.S.; $115.00 fellow-in-training. Alternate Formats: online ● ASHNR News, 3/year. Newsletters. Provides news and information about the society and the field of head and neck radiology. **Price:** free for members. Alternate Formats: online ● Membership Directory. **Price:** included in membership dues. **Conventions/Meetings:** annual meeting (exhibits) - 2007 Sept. 26-30, Seattle, WA; 2008 Sept. 10-14, Toronto, ON, Canada; 2009 Sept. 9-13, New Orleans, LA.

15932 ■ American Society of Interventional and Therapeutic Neuroradiology (ASITN)
3975 Fair Ridge Dr., Ste.400 N
Fairfax, VA 22033
Ph: (703)691-2272
Fax: (703)691-1855
E-mail: info@asitn.org
URL: http://www.asitn.org
Contact: Ms. Marie Williams, Exec. Dir.

Founded: 1992. **Membership Dues:** senior/active, $300 (annual) ● corresponding, $150 (annual) ● associate, $100 (annual) ● junior/clinical associate, $50 (annual). **Description:** Represents physicians and scientists interested in interventional and therapeutic neuroradiology. Develops and supports standards of post-graduate training and practice in interventional and therapeutic neuroradiology. Advances the development of interventional and therapeutic neuroradiology through education and scientific research. **Publications:** American Journal of Neuroradiology ● The Embolus, quarterly. Newsletter.

15933 ■ American Society of Neuroimaging (ASN)
5841 Cedar Lake Rd., Ste.204
Minneapolis, MN 55416
Ph: (952)545-6291
Fax: (952)545-6073
E-mail: asn@llmsi.com
URL: http://www.asnweb.org
Contact: Camilo R. Gomez MD, Pres.

Founded: 1977. **Members:** 800. **Membership Dues:** active, associate, $300 (annual) ● sustaining, $525 (annual) ● junior, $100 (annual) ● technologist, $105 (annual) ● corresponding, $140 (annual). **Staff:** 3. **Budget:** $500,000. **Description:** Neurologists, neurosurgeons, neuroradiologists, and scientists. Promotes the development of Computerized Tomography (CT scanning), Magnetic Resonance Imaging (MRI), neurosonology, and other neurodiagnostic techniques for clinical service, teaching, and research. Encourages the collaboration of members to improve techniques through educational programs and scientific research. Holds annual certification exam in MRI and neurosonology. **Awards:** William H. Oldendorf, M.D. Award. **Frequency:** annual. **Type:** recognition. **Recipient:** for outstanding research in MRI/CT/PET/SPECT ● William McKinney, M.D. Award. **Type:** recognition. **Recipient:** for outstanding research work in neurosonology. **Formerly:** (1980) Society for Computerized Tomography and Neuroimaging. **Publications:** Journal of Neuroimaging, quarterly. **Circulation:** 1,000. **Advertising:** accepted ● Newsletter, semiannual. Alternate Formats: online. **Conventions/Meetings:** annual meeting - 2008 Jan. 17-20, Tucson, AZ.

15934 ■ American Society of Neuroradiology (ASNR)
2210 Midwest Rd., Ste.207
Oak Brook, IL 60523
Ph: (630)574-0220
Fax: (630)574-0661
E-mail: jgantenberg@asnr.org
URL: http://www.asnr.org
Contact: James B. Gantenberg, Exec. Dir./CEO

Founded: 1962. **Members:** 3,258. **Membership Dues:** regular, $425 (annual) ● senior (for first year),

$475 (annual) ● regular (interim), $25 ● senior (interim), $100. **Staff:** 18. **Description:** Neuroradiologists who spend at least half of their time practicing neuroradiology. Fosters education, basic science research, and communication in neuroradiology. **Awards:** Berlex/NER Foundation Fellowship in Basic Science Fellowship. **Frequency:** periodic. **Type:** fellowship. **Recipient:** for basic science research ● Cornelius G. Dyke Memorial Award. **Frequency:** annual. **Type:** recognition. **Recipient:** for best paper discussing original work by fellow or junior staff member ● NERF/Boston Scientific-Target Fellowship in Cerebrovascular Disease Research. **Frequency:** annual. **Type:** fellowship. **Recipient:** for best paper discussing original work by fellow or junior staff member ● Neuroradiology Education and Research Foundation Scholar Award in Neuroradiology Research. **Frequency:** annual. **Type:** fellowship. **Recipient:** for science research. **Publications:** *American Journal of Neuroradiology*, 10/year. **Price:** included in membership dues; $235.00 print and online (add $60 if outside U.S.); $270.00 /year for nonmembers outside U.S.; $115.00 fellow, in-training. ISSN: 0195-6108. **Circulation:** 6,500. **Advertising:** accepted. Alternate Formats: online ● *Membership Roll*, annual. Membership Directory. **Conventions/Meetings:** annual meeting, with scientific courses (exhibits) - 2008 May 31-June 6, New Orleans, LA; 2009 May 16-22, Vancouver, BC, Canada.

15935 ■ American Society of Pediatric Neuroradiology (ASPNR)

2210 Midwest Rd., Ste.207
Oak Brook, IL 60523-8205
Ph: (630)574-0220
Fax: (630)574-0661
E-mail: bmack@asnr.org
URL: http://www.aspnr.org
Contact: Jill V. Hunter MD, Pres.-Elect
Founded: 1993. **Members:** 346. **Budget:** $150,000. **Description:** Promotes the profession of pediatric neuroradiology. **Publications:** *American Journal of Neuroradiology* ● *Gyrations*, periodic. Newsletters. Provides news and information about the society and field of pediatric neuroradiology. Alternate Formats: online.

15936 ■ American Society of Spine Radiology (ASSR)

2210 Midwest Rd., Ste.207
Oak Brook, IL 60523-8205
Ph: (630)574-0220
Fax: (630)574-0661
E-mail: kcammarata@asnr.org
URL: http://www.asnr.org
Contact: Ken Cammarata, Business Mgr.
Founded: 1993. **Members:** 600. **Membership Dues:** radiologist, $75 (annual) ● active, $25 (annual). **Budget:** $200,000. **Description:** Radiologists. Provides support and exchange ideas and information concerning spine radiology. Holds meetings, lectures, and discussions. **Libraries:** Type: reference. **Holdings:** papers, video recordings. **Additional Websites:** http://www.theassr.org. **Committees:** Ad Hoc Awards; Ad Hoc Corporate Support; Ad Hoc Informatics; Ad Hoc Interventional Spine Program; Ad Hoc Mentor; Ad Hoc Research; Meeting Planning; Program. **Publications:** *The Myelon*, quarterly. Newsletter. Alternate Formats: online. **Conventions/Meetings:** annual symposium - February.

15937 ■ American Society for Therapeutic Radiology and Oncology (ASTRO)

8280 Willow Oaks Corporate Dr., Ste.500
Fairfax, VA 22031
Ph: (703)502-1550
Free: (800)962-7876
Fax: (703)502-7852
E-mail: bethb@astro.org
URL: http://www.astro.org
Contact: Ms. Laura Thevenot, CEO
Founded: 1958. **Members:** 8,500. **Membership Dues:** active, allied, affiliate, $375 (annual) ● associate, corresponding, $40 (annual) ● international, $270 (annual). **Staff:** 36. **Budget:** $8,200,000. **Description:** Physicians who limit their practice to radia-

tion therapy; associate members are scientists and health care personnel who have a major interest "in furthering the aims of the society"; junior members are residents who have completed one year of training in radiation therapy. Aims to extend the benefits of radiation therapy to patients with cancer or other disorders, to advance its scientific basis, and to provide for the education and professional fellowship of its members. **Awards:** Gold Medal. **Frequency:** annual. **Type:** recognition. **Recipient:** for lifetime achievement in radiation oncology. **Computer Services:** Mailing lists. **Affiliated With:** Association of Residents in Radiation Oncology. **Formerly:** (1983) American Society of Therapeutic Radiologists. **Publications:** *ASTRO News*, quarterly. Magazine. **Price:** included in membership dues. **Circulation:** 7,200. **Advertising:** accepted ● *The International Journal of Radiation Oncology, Biology and Physics*, 15/year. **Advertising:** accepted. **Conventions/Meetings:** annual conference and meeting, education and exhibits for radiation oncologists, biologists, physicists, radiation therapists and radiation oncology nurses (exhibits).

15938 ■ Association of University Radiologists (AUR)

820 Jorie Blvd.
Oak Brook, IL 60523
Ph: (630)368-3730
Fax: (630)571-7837
E-mail: aur@rsna.org
URL: http://www.aur.org
Contact: Lise Steg Thorsby, Exec. Dir.
Founded: 1953. **Members:** 4,000. **Membership Dues:** full, $220 (annual) ● associate, $200 (annual) ● junior, $60 (annual). **Staff:** 6. **Description:** Physician and non-physician scientists who have been appointed to a university faculty. Seeks to encourage excellence in laboratory and clinical investigation, teaching, and clinical practice; stimulates interest in academic radiology as a medical career; advances radiology as a medical science; provides a forum for university based radiologists to present and discuss results of research, teaching, and administrative issues. **Awards:** Memorial Award. **Frequency:** annual. **Type:** recognition. **Recipient:** to a resident in radiology for best research paper ● Stauffer Awards. **Frequency:** annual. **Type:** recognition. **Recipient:** to the author of the most outstanding work ● Whitley Award. **Frequency:** annual. **Type:** recognition. **Recipient:** for the best education-based paper. **Committees:** Awards; Bylaws; Corporate Support; Education; Membership; Nominating; Program; Symposium. **Divisions:** Alliance of Medical Student Educators in Radiology; American Alliance of Academic Chief Residents in Radiology; Radiology Alliance for Health Services Research; Radiology Research Alliance. **Affiliated With:** Association of Program Directors in Radiology; Society of Chairmen of Academic Radiology Departments. **Publications:** *Academic Radiology*, monthly. Journal. **Circulation:** 5,000. **Advertising:** accepted. Alternate Formats: online ● Also publishes award and scientific papers. **Conventions/Meetings:** annual conference - always spring ● annual meeting (exhibits).

15939 ■ Computerized Medical Imaging Society (CMIS)

Address Unknown since 2007
Founded: 1976. **Members:** 350. **Staff:** 2. **Description:** Physicians and other medical personnel concerned with computerized tomography (a diagnostic technique using X-ray photographs in which the shadows of structures before and behind the section under scrutiny do not show), and other radiological diagnostic procedures. Provides a forum for the exchange of information concerning the medical use of computerized tomography in radiological diagnosis. **Formerly:** (1983) Computerized Tomography Society; (1988) Computerized Radiology Society. **Publications:** *Computerized Medical Imaging and Graphics*, bimonthly.

15940 ■ Council on Diagnostic Imaging (CDI)

PO Box 190
Cheney, KS 67025
Ph: (316)542-3400

E-mail: drgould@chc.kscoxmail.com
URL: http://www.dacbr.com/cdi_homepage.htm
Contact: Dr. Glynna Rangel DC, Pres.
Founded: 1936. **Members:** 2,000. **Membership Dues:** general, $60 (annual) ● student, $15 (annual). **Staff:** 1. **Budget:** $100,000. **Description:** Professional society of chiropractic roentgenologists, educators, students, and chiropractors interested in roentgenology. **Formerly:** (1963) National Council of Chiropractic Roentgenologists; (1968) American Council on Chiropractic Roentgenology; (1970) American Chiropractic Council on Roentgenology; (1983) Council on Roentgenology to the American Chiropractic Association. **Publications:** *Topics in Diagnostic Radiology and Advanced Imaging*, quarterly. Journal. Covers diagnostic radiology, advanced imaging, thermology, and case studies. **Circulation:** 2,000. **Advertising:** accepted. **Conventions/Meetings:** annual regional meeting and symposium (exhibits) - always May.

15941 ■ International Skeletal Society (ISS)

c/o Lynne S. Steinbach
Univ. of California San Francisco
Dept. of Radiology
San Francisco, CA 94143-0628
Fax: (415)353-2643
E-mail: wendy.turner@roh.nhs.uk
URL: http://www.internationalskeletalsociety.com
Contact: Jeremy Kaye MD, Pres.
Founded: 1973. **Members:** 500. **Description:** Physicians and scientists interested in skeletal muscle disease. Seeks to advance the science of skeletal radiology; brings together radiologists and individuals in related disciplines; provides continuing education courses. **Committees:** Auditing; Awards; Closed Program; Convention Planning; Editorial; Evaluation of Research Grants; Nominating; Rules. **Publications:** *Skeletal Radiology*, monthly. Journal. Contains scientific articles and case reports. **Price:** included in membership dues. ISSN: 0364-2348. **Circulation:** 1,200. **Advertising:** accepted ● Membership Directory, annual ● Newsletter, semiannual. **Conventions/Meetings:** annual meeting (exhibits).

15942 ■ International Society for Magnetic Resonance in Medicine (ISMRM)

2118 Milvia St., Ste.201
Berkeley, CA 94704
Ph: (510)841-1899
Fax: (510)841-2340
E-mail: info@ismrm.org
URL: http://www.ismrm.org
Contact: Roberta A. Kravitz, Exec. Dir.
Founded: 1994. **Members:** 5,000. **Membership Dues:** full, $350 (annual) ● student, $240 (annual) ● associate, $30 (annual). **Staff:** 12. **Regional Groups:** 2. **Multinational. Description:** Aims to further the development and application of MRI and its techniques in medicine and biology. Sponsors educational and research programs. **Libraries:** Type: reference; open to the public. **Holdings:** books. **Subjects:** MRI, spectroscopy. **Awards:** Young Investigator's Award/Student Stipends. **Frequency:** annual. **Type:** monetary. **Computer Services:** Mailing lists. **Telecommunication Services:** electronic mail, roberta@ismrm.org. **Study Groups:** Brain Function; Cardiac MR; Diffusion and Perfusion; Dynamic NMR Spectroscopy; High Field Systems and Applications; Hyperpolarized Noble Gas MR; Interventional MR; Molecular and Cellular Imaging; MR Engineering; MR Flow and Motion Quantitation; MR in Drug Research; MR of Cancer; Musculoskeletal; Psychiatric MR Spectroscopy and Imaging; White Matter Diseases. **Formerly:** (1995) Society for Magnetic Resonance. **Publications:** *Journal of Magnetic Resonance Imaging*, monthly. **Price:** included in membership dues. Alternate Formats: online ● *Magnetic Resonance in Medicine*, monthly. Journal. **Price:** included in membership dues. Alternate Formats: online ● *MR-Pulse*, 3/year. Newsletter ● Brochure ● Directory. **Conventions/Meetings:** annual meeting and workshop (exhibits) - 2008 May 3-9, Toronto, ON, Canada; 2009 Apr. 18-24, Honolulu, HI.

15943 ■ International Society of Radiology (ISR)

7910 Woodmont Ave., Ste.800
Bethesda, MD 20814
Ph: (301)657-2652
Fax: (301)907-8768
E-mail: otha.linton@isradiology.org
URL: http://www.isradiology.org
Contact: Otha W. Linton MSJ, Exec. Dir.

Founded: 1953. **Members:** 84. **Staff:** 1. **Regional Groups:** 4. **National Groups:** 84. **Languages:** English, French, German. **Multinational. Description:** Seeks to promote medical radiology worldwide through the work of its sections and international commissions. Undertakes business referred by member societies. Provides financial support for the work of its commissions. **Commissions:** Radiation Units and Measurements; Radiological Education; Radiological Protection. **Publications:** *Congress Programs*, biennial ● *Reports of Commissions of ISR*, periodic ● Newsletter, semiannual. Alternate Formats: online. **Conventions/Meetings:** biennial International Congress of Radiology - meeting, scientific radiology related topics (exhibits) - 2008 Oct. 19-24, Buenos Aires, Argentina.

15944 ■ Magnetic Resonance Managers Society (MRMS)

1533 Spruce Ct.
Lombard, IL 60148
Ph: (801)262-3441
Fax: (801)265-8968
E-mail: info@mrms.org
URL: http://www.mrms.org
Contact: Linda Monty, Pres.

Founded: 1988. **Members:** 110. **Membership Dues:** single, $125 (annual) ● single, $225 (biennial). **Description:** Strives to advance the profession of magnetic resonance management. **Telecommunication Services:** electronic mail, tlcmonty4@msn.com. **Publications:** Newsletter, quarterly. **Price:** included in membership dues ● Membership Directory. **Price:** included in membership dues. **Conventions/Meetings:** annual conference, educational (exhibits).

15945 ■ Radiological Society of North America (RSNA)

820 Jorie Blvd.
Oak Brook, IL 60523
Ph: (630)571-2670 (630)571-7866
Free: (800)381-6660
Fax: (630)571-7837
E-mail: membership@rsna.org
URL: http://www.rsna.org
Contact: R. Gilbert Jost MD, Pres.

Founded: 1915. **Members:** 35,000. **Membership Dues:** active/associate, $355 (annual) ● corresponding, $445 (annual) ● radiologist assistant, $177 (annual). **Staff:** 125. **Budget:** $30,000,000. **Description:** Radiologists and scientists in fields closely related to radiology. Promotes study and practical application of radiology, radium, electricity, and other branches of physics related to medical science. **Libraries: Type:** not open to the public. **Awards:** Research and Education Fund. **Frequency:** annual. **Type:** fellowship. **Recipient:** for physicians nearing the end of their radiologic training ● RSN Gold Medal. **Frequency:** annual. **Type:** recognition. **Recipient:** for outstanding contribution in radiology field. **Committees:** Refresher Course; Scientific Exhibits; Scientific Program; Technical Exhibits. **Councils:** Education. **Formerly:** (1918) Western Roentgen Society. **Publications:** *Radiographics*, bimonthly. Journal. Features pictorial presentations of selected scientific exhibits from the society's annual meeting. Includes case studies. ISSN: 0271-5333. **Circulation:** 26,000. **Advertising:** accepted. Alternate Formats: online ● *Radiology*, monthly. Journal. Covers diagnostic radiology, neuroradiology, nuclear medicine, pediatric radiology, therapeutic radiology, cardiovascular radiology, and ultrasound. ISSN: 0033-8419. **Circulation:** 36,000. **Advertising:** accepted ● *RSNA Educational Materials*, annual. Catalog. Lists video/slide set series for CME credits. ● *RSNA News*, monthly. Magazine. Alternate Formats: online ●. Membership Directory, annual. **Con-**

ventions/Meetings: annual Scientific Assembly - assembly and meeting (exhibits) - always in Chicago, IL. 2007 Nov. 25-30, Chicago, IL; 2008 Nov. 30-Dec. 5, Chicago, IL; 2009 Nov. 29-Dec. 4, Chicago, IL; 2010 Nov. 28-Dec. 3, Chicago, IL.

15946 ■ Society for the Advancement of Women's Imaging (SAWI)

PO Box 885
Schererville, IN 46375
Ph: (219)864-3065
Fax: (219)864-3067
E-mail: ahealy@sawi.org
URL: http://www.sawi.org
Contact: Teresita L. Angtuaco MD, Pres.

Founded: 1993. **Membership Dues:** practicing radiologist, $100 (annual). **Description:** Promotes a sub-specialty within diagnostic radiology devoted to the diagnostics and treatment of diseases and conditions unique to women. Supports residency and fellowship training in the sub-specialty of women's imaging. Encourages research pertaining to all aspects of women's imaging. **Telecommunication Services:** electronic mail, angtuacoteresital@uams.edu.

15947 ■ Society of Breast Imaging (SBI)

1891 Preston White Dr.
Reston, VA 20191-4397
Ph: (703)715-4390
Fax: (703)716-1283
E-mail: sbi@acr.org
URL: http://www.sbi-online.org
Contact: R. James Brenner MD, Pres.

Founded: 1985. **Membership Dues:** regular, $125 (annual) ● physicist, $75 (annual) ● affiliate, $50 (annual). **Description:** Promotes the field of breast imaging. **Awards:** Gold Medal. **Frequency:** biennial. **Type:** medal. **Committees:** Breast Imaging Practice Evaluation; Bylaws; Fellows Program; Nominating; Representatives. **Publications:** Newsletter, quarterly. **Price:** free for members. Alternate Formats: online. **Conventions/Meetings:** biennial Postgraduate Course - meeting (exhibits).

15948 ■ Society of Chairmen of Academic Radiology Departments (SCARD)

c/o Lise Steg Thorsby, Account Exec.
820 Jorie Blvd.
Oak Brook, IL 60523
Ph: (630)368-3731
Fax: (630)571-7837
E-mail: scard@comresource.net
Contact: Lise Steg Thorsby, Account Exec.

Founded: 1966. **Members:** 141. **Membership Dues:** active, $1,000 (annual) ● Canadian, $150 (annual). **Description:** Radiology department chairpersons. Works to advance the art and science of radiology; promotes medical education, research and patient care, the development of methods of teaching in radiology; provides a forum for problem solving and mutual interests. **Telecommunication Services:** electronic mail, lthorsby@rsna.org.

15949 ■ Society of Computed Body Tomography and Magnetic Resonance (SCBT/MR)

1891 Preston White Dr.
Reston, VA 20191
Ph: (703)476-1117
E-mail: info@scbtmr.org
URL: http://www.scbtmr.org
Contact: Jeffrey C. Weinreb MD, Pres.

Founded: 1977. **Members:** 100. **Membership Dues:** active, $250 (annual) ● active, $475 (biennial) ● active, $675 (triennial). **Staff:** 4. **Description:** Radiologists. Provides continuing medical educational courses on computed tomography and magnetic resonance imaging of the body. **Awards:** Scientific Research Awards. **Frequency:** annual. **Type:** recognition. **Formerly:** (1991) Society of Computed Body Tomography. **Publications:** Course syllabus. **Conventions/Meetings:** annual meeting, educational course (exhibits) - 2008 Mar. 31-Apr. 4, Charleston, SC ● annual Summer Practicum - meeting - 2008 Aug. 10-14, Napa, CA ● symposium - fall.

15950 ■ Society of Gastrointestinal Radiologists (SGR)

c/o International Meeting Managers, Inc.
4550 Post Oak Pl., Ste.342
Houston, TX 77027
Ph: (713)965-0566
Fax: (713)960-0488
E-mail: imm@meetingmanagers.com
URL: http://www.sgr.org
Contact: Michael P. Federle MD, Pres.

Founded: 1971. **Description:** Strives to furnish leadership and fosters advances in diagnostic, interventional, gastrointestinal and abdominal radiology; works to exchange knowledge pertaining to research practice and education in gastrointestinal and abdominal radiology. Conducts annual lecture in memory of Walter B. Cannon, the pioneer physiologist who initiated gastrointestinal radiology and an annual postgraduate course in gastrointestinal radiology. **Conventions/Meetings:** annual Abdominal Radiology Course - meeting.

15951 ■ Society for Imaging Informatics in Medicine (SIIM)

19440 Golf Vista Plz., Ste.330
Leesburg, VA 20176
Ph: (703)723-0432
Fax: (703)723-0145
E-mail: info@siimweb.org
URL: http://www.siimweb.org
Contact: Anna Marie Mason, Exec. Dir.

Founded: 1980. **Members:** 2,000. **Membership Dues:** student, resident in U.S. and Canada, $100 (annual) ● regular in U.S. and Canada, $150 (annual) ● regular outside U.S. and Canada, $200 (annual) ● corporate sponsor, $2,000 (annual) ● institution in U.S., $600 (annual) ● institution outside U.S., $800 (annual) ● institutional level II, $1,050 (annual) ● institutional multi-facility, $3,000 (annual). **Staff:** 6. **Description:** Represents individuals, corporations, and health care facilities devoted to advanced computer applications and information technology in medical imaging through education and research. **Awards:** Fellow. **Frequency:** annual. **Type:** recognition. **Telecommunication Services:** electronic mail, amason@siimweb.org. **Special Interest Groups:** APUG; FUSUN; IRISS. **Absorbed:** (1998) Radiology Information System Consortium. **Formerly:** (2006) Society for Computer Applications in Radiology. **Publications:** *Journal of Digital Imaging*, quarterly. ISSN: 0897-1889. **Advertising:** accepted. Alternate Formats: online ● *SCAR University Primer 5: Security Issues in the Digital Medical Enterprise, 2nd Edition*. Book. **Price:** $34.95 for members; $39.95 for nonmembers ● *SCAR University Primer 4: Electronic Reporting in the Digital Medical Enterprise*. Book. **Price:** $34.95 for members; $39.95 for nonmembers ● *SCAR University Primer 3: QA: Meeting the Challenge of the Digital Medical Enterprise*. Book. **Price:** $34.95 for members; $39.95 for nonmembers ● *SCAR University Primer 2: Archiving Issues in the Digital Medical Enterprise*. Book. **Price:** $34.95 for members; $39.95 for nonmembers ● *SIIM News*, quarterly. Newsletter. Alternate Formats: online ● *Understanding Image Compression*. Handbook. **Price:** $8.00/copy ● *Understanding Teleradiology*. Handbook. **Price:** $8.00/copy. **Conventions/Meetings:** annual meeting (exhibits).

15952 ■ Society of Interventional Radiology (SIR)

3975 Fair Ridge Dr., Ste.400 N
Fairfax, VA 22033
Ph: (703)691-1805
Free: (800)488-7284
Fax: (703)691-1855
E-mail: info@sirweb.org
URL: http://www.sirweb.org
Contact: Peter B. Lauer CAE, Exec. Dir.

Founded: 1973. **Members:** 4,000. **Membership Dues:** active, $560 (annual) ● associate, $450 (annual) ● clinical associate, $290 (annual) ● corresponding, $280 (annual) ● medical student, $25 (annual) ● member-in-training, $50 (annual) ● military, public health, $410 (annual). **Staff:** 27. **Description:** Physicians who are leaders in the field of interventional radiology. Facilitates exchange of new ideas and techniques and provides educational courses for all physicians working in the field. Conducts annual postgraduate course. Conducts Interventional Radiology Political Action. **Libraries: Type:** reference. **Holdings:** audio recordings, photographs, reports, video recordings. **Awards:** Young Investigator Award. **Frequency:** annual. **Type:** monetary. **Telecommunication Services:** electronic bulletin board. **Formerly:** (2003) Society of Cardiovascular and Interventional Radiology. **Publications:** *Directory of Angiography and Interventional Radiology Fellowship Programs* ● *Journal of Vascular and Interventional Radiology*, bimonthly. **Advertising:** accepted ● *SIR Membership Directory*, annual ● *SIR Newsletter*, bimonthly. **Conventions/Meetings:** annual convention (exhibits) - usually March.

15953 ■ Society for Pediatric Radiology (SPR)
1891 Preston White Dr.
Reston, VA 20191
Ph: (703)648-0680
E-mail: spr@acr.org
URL: http://www.pedrad.org
Contact: Jennifer K. Boylan, Exec. Dir.
Founded: 1958. **Members:** 800. **Membership Dues:** active, associate, $400 (annual) ● corresponding, $25 (annual). **Budget:** $160,000. **Description:** Physicians working in the field of pediatric radiology. Seeks to advance knowledge in pediatric imaging and improve medical care of infants and children. **Awards:** Heidi Patriquin International Fellowship for Education. **Frequency:** annual. **Type:** fellowship. **Recipient:** for a pediatric radiologist who resides and practices outside North America ● Jack O. Haller Award for Excellence in Teaching. **Frequency:** annual. **Type:** recognition. **Recipient:** for an individual who has demonstrated evidence of outstanding ability to educate trainees ● N. Thorne Griscom Award for Education in Pediatric Radiology. **Frequency:** biennial. **Type:** monetary. **Recipient:** for investigators involved in pediatric radiology education ● Research Fellow. **Frequency:** annual. **Type:** grant. **Recipient:** for young investigators in radiologic sciences ● Seed Grant. **Frequency:** annual. **Type:** grant. **Recipient:** for investigators ● Walter Berdon Award. **Frequency:** annual. **Type:** recognition. **Recipient:** for the best clinical and science papers submitted to the Journal of Pediatric Radiology. **Telecommunication Services:** electronic mail, jboylan@acr.org. **Publications:** *RadioGraphics*, bimonthly. Journal. Contains medical education in radiology. **Price:** $135.00 for nonmembers in North America; $170.00 for nonmembers outside North America. **Advertising:** accepted. Alternate Formats: online ● *Radiology*, monthly. Journal. Contains original research, authoritative reviews, well-balanced commentary on significant articles, and expert opinion on new technologies. **Price:** $25.00/copy; $250.00 /year for nonmembers in North America; $325.00 /year for nonmembers outside North America. Alternate Formats: online ● Membership Directory, annual. **Conventions/Meetings:** annual meeting - always spring. 2008 May 6-10, Scottsdale, AZ; 2009 Apr. 21-25, Carlsbad, CA.

15954 ■ Society for Radiation Oncology Administrators (SROA)
5272 River Rd., Ste.630
Bethesda, MD 20816
Ph: (301)718-6510 (913)541-4623
Free: (866)458-7762
Fax: (301)656-0989
E-mail: sroa@paimgmt.com
URL: http://www.sroa.org
Contact: Darrin L. Kistler, Pres.
Founded: 1984. **Members:** 500. **Membership Dues:** contributing, $250 (annual) ● active, $175 (annual). **Staff:** 11. **Budget:** $125,000. **For-Profit. Description:** Individuals with managerial responsibilities in radiation oncology at the executive, divisional, or departmental level, and whose functions include personnel, budget, and development of operational procedures and guidelines for therapeutic radiology departments. Strives to improve the administration of

the business and nonmedical management aspects of therapeutic radiology, to promote the field of therapeutic radiology administration, to provide a forum for communication among members, and to disseminate information among members. Maintains speakers' bureau; offers placement service. **Committees:** Ballot Validating; Constitution and Bylaws; Education; Long Range Planning; Manpower and Recruitment; Membership; Program; Publications; Reimbursement and Economics. **Formerly:** (1985) Radiation Oncology Administrators. **Publications:** *SROA Membership Directory*, annual. **Price:** included in membership dues. **Circulation:** 500. **Advertising:** accepted ● *SROA Newsletter*, quarterly. Includes calendar of events and employment listings. **Price:** included in membership dues; $50.00 for nonmembers in U.S.; $60.00 for nonmembers outside U.S. **Circulation:** 520. **Advertising:** accepted. **Conventions/Meetings:** annual meeting - 2008 Sept. 21-24, Cambridge, MA; 2009 Nov. 1-4, San Antonio, TX; 2010 Oct. 31-Nov. 3, San Diego, CA.

15955 ■ Society of Radiologists in Ultrasound (SRU)
44211 Slatestone Ct.
Leesburg, VA 20176-5109
Ph: (703)858-9210
Fax: (703)729-4839
E-mail: srumembership@acr.org
URL: http://www.sru.org
Contact: Beverly G. Coleman MD, Pres.
Founded: 1975. **Membership Dues:** general, $200 (annual) ● transitional, $100 (annual). **Description:** Board certified and Board eligible radiologists interested in ultrasound imaging. Promotes the interests of radiologists in ultrasound. Funds research; educates non-physician health care professionals. **Awards: Frequency:** annual. **Type:** grant. **Recipient:** for clinical ultrasound research. **Telecommunication Services:** electronic mail, beverly.coleman@uphs.upenn.edu. **Publications:** *Managing Ultrasound Benefits*. Newsletter. Contains the latest ultrasound techniques and examinations. **Circulation:** 10,000 ● Newsletter, 3/year. Alternate Formats: online. **Conventions/Meetings:** annual Advances in Sonography - meeting and seminar - always October.

15956 ■ Society of Skeletal Radiology (SSR)
1111 N Plaza Dr., Ste.550
Schaumburg, IL 60173
Ph: (847)517-3302
Fax: (847)517-7229
E-mail: admin@skeletalrad.org
URL: http://www.skeletalrad.org
Contact: Dr. Cheryl A. Petersilge MD, Pres.
Founded: 1978. **Members:** 340. **Membership Dues:** full, international, $200 (annual). **Description:** Practicing radiologists. Represents the subspecialty of musculoskeletal radiology. **Conventions/Meetings:** annual meeting.

15957 ■ Society of Thoracic Radiology (STR)
PO Box 7169
Rochester, MN 55903-7169
Ph: (507)288-5620
Fax: (507)288-0014
E-mail: str@thoracicrad.org
URL: http://www.thoracicrad.org
Contact: Jud Gurney, Pres.
Founded: 1982. **Members:** 500. **Membership Dues:** senior/associate in U.S., $290 (annual) ● senior/associate in Canada, C$295 (annual) ● senior/associate (other country), $294 (annual) ● training, $185 (annual) ● training in Canada, C$190 (annual) ● training (other country), $189 (annual). **Description:** Represents radiologists interested in and dedicated to cardiopulmonary radiology. Provides for continuing medical education. **Committees:** Education; Electronic Media; Research; Scientific Session. **Conventions/Meetings:** annual World Congress of Thoracic Imaging - seminar and workshop.

15958 ■ World Federation of Neuroradiological Societies (WFNRS)
2210 Midwest Rd., Ste.207
Oak Brook, IL 60523-8205
Ph: (630)574-0220

Fax: (630)574-0661
E-mail: jgantenberg@asnr.org
URL: http://www.wfnrs.org
Contact: James Gantenberg, Exec. Dir.
Founded: 1993. **Multinational. Description:** Fosters international scientific and educational programs in neuroradiology. Advances neuroradiology in all its aspects. Establishes and maintains cooperation between neuroradiological organizations worldwide. Facilitates the exchange and dissemination of knowledge and ideas in the field of Neuroradiology. **Publications:** *Handbook of Worldwide Neuroradiologic Manpower and Resources*.

Rehabilitation

15959 ■ American Academy of Physical Medicine and Rehabilitation (AAPM&R)
330 N Wabash Ave., Ste.2500
Chicago, IL 60611-7617
Ph: (312)464-9700
Fax: (312)464-0227
E-mail: info@aapmr.org
URL: http://www.aapmr.org
Contact: Joel M. Press MD, Pres.
Founded: 1938. **Members:** 6,700. **Membership Dues:** student, $55 (annual) ● affiliate, $70 (annual) ● corresponding, $215 (annual) ● academic, researcher, $240 (annual) ● fellow, $175 (annual) ● associate, $100 (annual). **Staff:** 30. **Budget:** $5,200,000. **Description:** National medical specialty society of physical medicine and rehabilitation physicians whose patients include people with physical disabilities and chronic, disabling illnesses. Mission is to maximize quality of life, minimize the incidence and prevalence of impairments, disability, and handicaps, promote societal health, and enhance the understanding and development of psychiatry. Offers educational opportunities and advocacy support to members and provides information, referrals, and patient education materials. **Libraries: Type:** reference. **Holdings:** archival material. **Awards:** Distinguished Member Award. **Frequency:** annual. **Type:** recognition. **Recipient:** for AAPM&R members who provided invaluable service to the specialty ● The Frank H. Krusen Award. **Frequency:** annual. **Type:** medal. **Recipient:** for outstanding and unique contributions to the specialty ● Recognition Award for Distinguished Clinicians. **Frequency:** annual. **Type:** recognition. **Recipient:** for physiatrists who achieved distinction on the basis of their scholarly level of teaching and outstanding performance in patient care activities ● Recognition Award for Distinguished Public Service. **Frequency:** annual. **Type:** recognition. **Recipient:** for individuals who, in the course of their public service activities, have made significant contributions to the development of educational, research, and service activities ● The Richard and Hinda Rosenthal Foundation Lecture. **Frequency:** annual. **Type:** recognition. **Recipient:** to a physiatrist under the age of 45 whose endeavors have constituted a noteworthy advancement in the non-surgical clinical care of low back pain ● The Walter J. Zeiter Lecture. **Frequency:** annual. **Type:** recognition. **Recipient:** for physiatrists who have made consistent contributions to the specialty and have earned the respect and admiration of their peers for outstanding accomplishments in the field of PM&R. **Committees:** Health Policy and Legislation; Medical Education; Research. **Formerly:** (1956) American Society of Physical Medicine and Rehabilitation. **Publications:** *AAPM&R Membership Directory*, annual. Arranged alphabetically, geographically, and by special interest group. **Price:** included in membership dues. **Circulation:** 6,200. **Advertising:** accepted ● *Archives of Physical Medicine and Rehabilitation*, monthly. Journal. Provides original research and clinical reports to health professionals who work with the disabled, elderly, and handicapped. **Price:** included in membership dues; $159.00 /year for nonmembers; $200.00 /year for institutions; $72.00/year for students. ISSN: 0003-9993. **Circulation:** 10,000. **Advertising:** accepted. Alternate Formats: microform ● *The Physiatrist*, 10/year. Newsletter. Provides information

on organizational activities, legislative and practice issues. Includes research updates, calendar, and quarterly inserts. **Price:** included in membership dues. **Circulation:** 6,200. **Advertising:** accepted ● *Study Guide.* Manual. Published part of Self-Directed Medical Knowledge Program. **Conventions/Meetings:** annual assembly (exhibits) - 2007 Sept. 27-30, Boston, MA; 2008 Nov. 20-23, San Diego, CA; 2009 Oct. 22-25, Austin, TX.

15960 ■ American Board of Disability Analysts (ABDA)

345 24th Ave. N, Ste.200
Park Plaza Medical Bldg.
Nashville, TN 37203
Ph: (615)327-2984
Fax: (615)327-9235
E-mail: americanbd@aol.com
URL: http://www.americandisability.org
Contact: Alexander E. Horwitz MD, Exec. Off. Emeritus
Founded: 1989. **Members:** 7,600. **Membership Dues:** regular, $80 (annual) ● life, $950. **Description:** Physicians, nurses, speech therapists, psychologists, physical therapists, osteopaths, occupational therapists, chiropractors, case managers, rehabilitation counselors, professional counselors, dentists, insurance claims adjusters, educators, economists, attorneys, engineers, and correctional specialists. Serves as a multidisciplinary credentialing association for all disciplines dealing with the physically and/or mentally disabled. Provides continuing education programs. **Awards:** Career Achievement Award-Scholar in Residence. **Frequency:** annual. **Type:** recognition. **Recipient:** for professional excellence. **Publications:** *The Catastrophic Injury Handbook (2003).* **Price:** $140.00 includes shipping and handling ● *Disability Analysis Handbook: Tools for Independent Practice (1996).* **Price:** $125.00 includes shipping and handling. **Advertising:** accepted ● *Disability Analysis in Practice: Framework for an Interdisciplinary.* Book. **Price:** $75.00 includes shipping and handling ● *The Disability Analyst,* 3/year. Newsletter. **Price:** $18.00. **Circulation:** 8,000. **Advertising:** accepted. Alternate Formats: online ● *International Directory of Disability Analysts.* **Price:** $150.00 includes shipping and handling. **Advertising:** accepted. **Conventions/Meetings:** semiannual meeting, for training of disability analysts.

15961 ■ American Board of Physical Medicine and Rehabilitation (ABPMR)

3015 Allegro Park Ln. SW
Rochester, MN 55902-4139
Ph: (507)282-1776
Fax: (507)282-9242
E-mail: info@abpmr.org
URL: http://www.abpmr.org
Contact: Anthony M. Tarvestad JD, Exec. Dir.
Founded: 1947. **Members:** 6,515. **Staff:** 10. **Description:** Certification board to establish qualifications, conduct examinations, and certify physicians who have completed the requirements in physical medicine and rehabilitation. **Committees:** Credentials; Examination. **Affiliated With:** American Board of Medical Specialties. **Publications:** *Certification,* annual. Booklet. Contains information concerning Board requirements, policies and procedures. **Price:** free for members. Alternate Formats: online ● *Diplomate News,* semiannual. Newsletter. Alternate Formats: online ● *Residency Program Director Newsletter,* annual. Contains the annual survey of residency programs. **Conventions/Meetings:** annual meeting.

15962 ■ American Congress of Rehabilitation Medicine (ACRM)

6801 Lake Plaza Dr., Ste.B-205
Indianapolis, IN 46220
Ph: (317)915-2250
Fax: (317)915-2245
E-mail: acrm@acrm.org
URL: http://www.acrm.org
Contact: Dr. Gerben DeJong, Pres.
Founded: 1923. **Members:** 1,100. **Membership Dues:** active, $240 (annual) ● corresponding, associate, consumer, $215 (annual) ● emeritus, resident, student, $75 (annual) ● Brain Injury Interdisciplinary Special Interest Group, $30 (annual). **Staff:** 4. **Budget:** $450,000. **Description:** Represents physicians, nurses, physical therapists, psychologists, occupational therapists, social workers, speech/language pathologists, and other allied health specialists active in and contributing to advancement in the field of medical rehabilitation. **Awards:** Annual Professional in Rehabilitation Essay Award. **Frequency:** annual. **Type:** recognition. **Recipient:** for professionals in rehabilitation ● The Conrad Jobst Foundation Prize. **Frequency:** annual. **Type:** monetary. **Recipient:** to physicians and members of the allied health professions for the best unpublished scientific paper pertaining to peripheral vascular disease or circulation in the extremities ● The Distinguished Member Award. **Frequency:** annual. **Type:** recognition. **Recipient:** to ACRM members who significantly contributed to the development and functioning of ACRM, demonstrating leadership skills, organizational abilities, and public service ● The Edward Lowman Award. **Frequency:** annual. **Type:** recognition. **Recipient:** to an ACRM member whose career reflects an energetic promotion of the spirit of interdisciplinary rehabilitation ● Gold Key Award. **Frequency:** annual. **Type:** recognition. **Recipient:** for members of the medical and allied professions who have rendered extraordinary service to the cause of rehabilitation ● John Stanley Coulter Lecture. **Frequency:** annual. **Type:** recognition. **Recipient:** for an individual who has professional achievement that contributed significantly to the field of rehabilitation. **Computer Services:** Mailing lists. **Committees:** Dissemination; Education and Training; Policy and Legislation. **Special Interest Groups:** Brain Injury; Measurement and Evaluation; Neuroscience; Spinal Cord Injury. **Formerly:** American Congress of Physical Medicine; American Congress of Physical Medicine and Rehabilitation. **Publications:** *ACRM Membership Directory,* annual. **Advertising:** accepted ● *Archives of Physical Medicine and Rehabilitation,* monthly. Journal. ISSN: 0003-9993. **Circulation:** 10,000. **Advertising:** accepted ● *Rehabilitation Outlook,* quarterly. Newsletter. **Advertising:** accepted. **Conventions/Meetings:** annual conference (exhibits) - 2007 Oct. 3-7, Washington, DC ● annual Technology and Inventor: Advancing Rehabilitation Research and Practice - meeting (exhibits).

15963 ■ American Kinesiotherapy Association (AKTA)

118 Coll. Dr., No. 5142
Hattiesburg, MS 39406
Free: (800)296-AKTA
E-mail: helen.fuller@usm.edu
URL: http://www.akta.org
Contact: Jon VonderHaar, Pres.
Founded: 1946. **Members:** 600. **Membership Dues:** active, $175 (annual) ● associate, $45 (annual) ● emeritus, $11 (annual) ● student, $15 (annual). **Staff:** 1. **Regional Groups:** 7. **State Groups:** 1. **Description:** Professional society of kinesiotherapists, associate and student members with interest in therapeutic exercise and education. Kinesiotherapy is the application of scientifically-based exercise principles adapted to enhance the strength, endurance and mobility of individuals with functional limitations of those requiring extended physical reconditioning. Seeks to serve the interest of members and represent the profession to the public through the promotion of continuing competency and continuing educational opportunities. **Awards: Frequency:** annual. **Type:** recognition ● **Type:** recognition. **Committees:** Awards; By Laws; Governmental Affairs; Nominations; Professional Standards; Public Relations; Research; Scholarship. **Divisions:** Council on Professional Standards. **Affiliated With:** American Alliance for Health, Physical Education, Recreation and Dance; American College of Sports Medicine; American Hospital Association; American Therapeutic Recreation Association; Aquatic Exercise Association; Association of Schools of Allied Health Professions; Medical Fitness Association; National Athletic Trainers' Association; National Council on the Aging; National Strength and Conditioning Association. **Formerly:** (1968) Association for Physical and Mental Rehabilitation; (1987) American Corrective Therapy Association. **Publications:** *Clinical Kinesiology,* quarterly. Journal. Online manuscripts of professional and scientific nature in disciplines relates to kinesiotherapy. **Price:** $25.00 /year for individuals; $45.00 /year for libraries or institutions. ISSN: 0896-9620. **Advertising:** accepted. Alternate Formats: online ● *Kinesiotherapy: An Overview.* Brochure ● *Mobility,* quarterly. Newsletter. **Conventions/Meetings:** annual conference (exhibits) - October. 2007 Oct. 2-6, Richmond, VA - **Avg. Attendance:** 250.

15964 ■ American Medical Rehabilitation Providers Association (AMRPA)

1710 North St. NW
Washington, DC 20036
Ph: (202)223-1920
Free: (888)346-4624
Fax: (202)223-1925
E-mail: czollar@13x.com
URL: http://www.amrpa.org
Contact: Carolyn C. Zollar, VP
Founded: 1997. **Members:** 450. **Staff:** 4. **Budget:** $2,000,000. **State Groups:** 29. **Description:** Rehabilitation facilities in the U.S. and Canada; agencies operating established medical, residential and vocational rehabilitation facilities. Promotes expansion and improvement of rehabilitation services to disabled persons as provided in rehabilitation facilities. Represents the concerns of rehabilitation providers before Congress and government agencies. Is concerned with quality operation of rehabilitation centers and facilities. Conducts research and development programs in national rehabilitation policy. Sponsors seminars and provides specialized education programs. **Libraries: Type:** reference. **Holdings:** books, periodicals. **Subjects:** rehabilitation center services. **Awards: Type:** recognition. **Computer Services:** Information services, AMRPA News Bureau. **Divisions:** Medical; Residential; State Chapters; State Use; Vocational. **Formed by Merger of:** National Association of Sheltered Workshops and Homebound Programs; Association of Rehabilitation Centers. **Formerly:** (1975) International Association of Rehabilitation Facilities; (1980) Association of Rehabilitation Facilities; (1994) National Association of Rehabilitation Facilities; (1998) American Rehabilitation Association. **Publications:** *AMRPA Magazine,* monthly. Analyzes insurance issues relevant to rehabilitation services. **Price:** included in membership dues. **Advertising:** accepted. Alternate Formats: online ● *Rehabilitation Review,* weekly. Newsletter. Monitors developments in the rehabilitation industry. Includes research updates and a calendar of events. **Price:** included in membership dues; $125.00 /year for nonmembers. **Circulation:** 1,500 ● Books ● Monographs ● Videos. **Conventions/Meetings:** conference (exhibits) - 3/year ● annual meeting - fall/spring ● annual Mid-Winter Issues Forum - meeting.

15965 ■ American Rehabilitation Counseling Association (ARCA)

c/o Irmo Marini, PhD, Pres.
Univ. of Texas
Pan Amer. Dept. of Rehabilitation
Coll. of Hea. Sciences and Human Services
1201 W Univ. Dr.
Edinburg, TX 78539-2999
Ph: (956)316-7035 (956)316-7036
Free: (800)347-6647
Fax: (956)380-6499
E-mail: imarini@panam.edu
URL: http://www.arcaweb.org
Contact: Irmo Marini PhD, Pres.
Founded: 1958. **Members:** 2,329. **Membership Dues:** professional, regular, $70 (annual) ● student, $15 (annual). **Description:** A division of the American Counseling Association (see separate entry). Rehabilitation counselors and interested professionals and students. Aims to improve the rehabilitation counseling profession and its services to individuals with disabilities. Promotes high standards in rehabilitation counseling, practice, research, and education. Encourages the exchange of information between rehabilitation professionals and consumer groups.

Serves as liaison among members and public and private rehabilitation counselors across the country. Sponsors educational and training programs. **Affiliated With:** American Counseling Association. **Publications:** *ARCA News*, quarterly. Newsletter. Provides information on the procedures and problems involved in rehabilitation counseling and special education for the disabled and the aged. **Price:** included in membership dues. **Circulation:** 3,500. Alternate Formats: online ● *Rehabilitation Counseling Bulletin*, quarterly. Journal. **Price:** included in membership dues; $18.00/year for nonmembers. **ISSN:** 0034-3552. **Circulation:** 3,456. **Advertising:** accepted. **Conventions/Meetings:** annual meeting, held in conjunction with ACA (exhibits).

15966 ■ American Rehabilitation Economics Association (AREA)
127 N Westwind Dr.
El Cajon, CA 92020-2955
Free: (800)317-AREA
Fax: (619)593-9989
E-mail: areaorg@cox.net
URL: http://www.a-r-e-a.org
Contact: Margy Ashby, Sec.-Treas.
Founded: 1989. **Members:** 97. **Membership Dues:** professional/associate, $110 (annual) ● registered, $275 (annual) ● certified, $475 (annual) ● student, $55 (annual). **Staff:** 1. **Description:** Forensic specialists with expertise in evaluating the medical, vocational, and economic aspects of injury. Strives to bring recognition to the combined use of vocational rehabilitation and earnings loss assessment as a distinct discipline. Provides a peer-exchange forum for vocational, economic, and legal experts who practice in this field. **Computer Services:** Information services ● mailing lists ● online services, listserv. **Publications:** *AREA News*. Newsletter ● *The Earnings Analyst*, annual, every October. Journal. Contains research and practice issues in the areas of forensic vocational and economic evaluation and testimony. **Price:** $25.00 for members. **ISSN:** 1547-240X. **Conventions/Meetings:** annual conference - spring.

15967 ■ American Therapeutic Recreation Association (ATRA)
1414 Prince St., Ste.204
Alexandria, VA 22314
Ph: (703)683-9420
Fax: (703)683-9431
E-mail: national@atra-tr.org
URL: http://www.atra-tr.org/atra.htm
Contact: Ann D. Huston, Exec. Dir.
Founded: 1984. **Members:** 2,800. **Membership Dues:** professional, $115 (annual). **Staff:** 8. **Budget:** $869,000. **Regional Groups:** 32. **Description:** Therapeutic recreation professionals and students; interested others. (Therapeutic recreation is often referred to as recreational therapy and uses treatment modalities to improve the physical, mental, and emotional functions of persons with illnesses or disabling conditions.) Promotes the use of therapeutic recreation in hospitals, mental rehabilitation centers, physical rehabilitation centers, senior citizen treatment centers, and other public health facilities. Conducts discussions on certification, legislative and regulatory concerns that affect the industry. Sponsors seminars and workshops; conducts research. **Libraries: Type:** reference. **Subjects:** therapeutic recreation practice. **Awards:** Fellow Professional Member of the Year. **Frequency:** annual. **Type:** recognition. **Computer Services:** database ● mailing lists. **Committees:** Education and Professional Development; Protocol; Quality Assurance; Standards of Practice. **Publications:** *Annual in Therapeutic Recreation*, annual. Journal. Published in conjunction with American Association for Leisure and Recreation. **Price:** included in membership dues. **Circulation:** 3,750 ● *ATRA Newsletter*, bimonthly. **Price:** included in membership dues. **Circulation:** 4,200. **Advertising:** accepted ● *Employment Update*, monthly. Features employment and internship opportunities for therapeutic recreation professionals. **Price:** included in membership dues. **Circulation:** 4,200. **Advertising:** accepted ● *Evaluation of Therapeutic Recreation through Quality Assurance* ● *Risk Management in*

Therapeutic Recreation. **Conventions/Meetings:** periodic Academics - workshop - throughout the year ● annual conference (exhibits) - always September or October and March ● annual conference - always spring.

15968 ■ Association of Academic Physiatrists (AAP)
1106 N Charles St., Ste.201
Baltimore, MD 21201
Ph: (410)637-8300
Fax: (410)637-8399
E-mail: aap@physiatry.org
URL: http://www.physiatry.org
Contact: Carolyn L. Braddom-Ritzler EdD, Exec. Dir.
Founded: 1967. **Members:** 1,400. **Membership Dues:** diplomate, associate, $385 (annual) ● academic affiliate, administrative affiliate, $315 (annual) ● emeritus, $145 (annual) ● in-training, medical student, fellow, $95 (annual) ● international, $300 (annual). **Staff:** 8. **Budget:** $800,000. **Description:** Academic physicians practicing physical medicine and rehabilitation and certified by the American Board of Physical Medicine and Rehabilitation. Aims are: to advance teaching and research in physical medicine and rehabilitation within the area of academic medicine; to promote the dissemination of information to future physicians planning to work in this field; to become involved in the exchange of information from other areas of medicine both in basic sciences and in the clinical areas of teaching and research. **Libraries: Type:** reference. **Holdings:** articles, biographical archives, papers, reports. **Computer Services:** Mailing lists. **Committees:** Academic Affairs; Education; Public Affairs; Research. **Affiliated With:** Association of American Medical Colleges. **Publications:** *AAP Newsletter*, quarterly. Contains information regarding the availability of clinical and research fellowships and research grants and contracts for projects. **Advertising:** accepted ● *American Journal of Physical Medicine and Rehabilitation*, biennial. **Price:** included in membership dues; $254.00/year for nonmembers in U.S. - individual; $395.00/year for nonmembers in U.S. - institutional; $154.00/year for nonmembers in U.S. - in-training. **ISSN:** 0894-9115. **Advertising:** accepted. Alternate Formats: online ● *Residency Program Directory*, annual. Alternate Formats: online ● Membership Directory, annual ● Brochures, periodic. Features information directly or indirectly related to the field of PM&R. **Conventions/Meetings:** annual meeting and conference (exhibits) - 2008 Feb. 19-24, Anaheim, CA; 2009 Feb. 24-28, Colorado Springs, CO.

15969 ■ Brain Injury Resource Center
PO Box 84151
Seattle, WA 98124-5451
Ph: (206)621-8558
Fax: (206)329-0912
E-mail: brain@headinjury.com
URL: http://www.headinjury.com
Contact: Constance Miller MA, Contact
Founded: 1985. **Staff:** 5. **Description:** Founded and operated by head injury activists. Serves as a place where visitors can get information, join a discussion group, build advocacy skills, and self-care skills. Integrates resources from diverse organizations including support groups, rehabilitation, and research sites, as well as lay and professional journals and more. Maintains speaker's bureau. **Libraries: Type:** reference. **Formerly:** (1993) Phoenix Project; (2004) Head Injury Hotline. **Publications:** *From the Ashes: A Head Injury Self-Advocacy Guide*, periodic. Contains worksheets to assist in locating and assessing doctors and therapists; self-assessment inventories; glossary of commonly-used phrases. **Price:** $20.00/copy (plus $5 shipping and handling). **Conventions/Meetings:** annual meeting - always May, Seattle, WA.

15970 ■ Continuing Care Accreditation Commission (CCAC)
4891 E Grant Rd.
Tucson, AZ 85712
Ph: (520)325-1044
Free: (888)281-6531

Fax: (520)318-1129
E-mail: education@carf.org
URL: http://www.carf.org
Contact: Brian J. Boon PhD, Pres./CEO
Founded: 2003. **Description:** Sponsored by rehabilitation, employment, and aging services organizations. The commission is the standard setting and accrediting authority for organizations providing rehabilitation services. Encourages development and improvement of uniformly high standards of performance for all organizations serving individuals with developmental, physical, or emotional disabilities. Surveys and accredits rehabilitation organizations; conducts research and educational activities related to standards for organizations offering programs in comprehensive inpatient rehabilitation, spinal cord injury, chronic pain management, brain injury, outpatient medical rehabilitation, work hardening, infant and early childhood development, vocational evaluation, work adjustment, occupational skill training, job placement, work services, supported employment, industry-based programs, community living, psychosocial programs, respite programs, alcoholism and other drug abuse rehabilitation programs, community mental health programs and aging services. Has accreditation program that is administered by a 53-member appointed board of trustees. **Computer Services:** Mailing lists. **Status Note:** (2003) CARF, Commission on Accreditation of Rehabilitation Facilities. **Publications:** *CARF Connection*, bimonthly. Newsletter. Covers commission activities. **Price:** free. Alternate Formats: online ● *CCAC Today*. Newsletter. Alternate Formats: online ● *Standards Manual for Employment Community Services*, annual. Describes accreditation standards for programs providing services; includes glossary. **Price:** $90.00/year. **Conventions/Meetings:** annual seminar - always in Tucson, AZ.

15971 ■ Council on Rehabilitation Education (CORE)
300 N Martingale Rd., Ste.460
Schaumburg, IL 60173
Ph: (847)944-1345
Fax: (847)944-1324
E-mail: mkuehn@emporia.edu
URL: http://www.core-rehab.org
Contact: Marv Kuehn PhD, Exec. Dir.
Founded: 1972. **Members:** 97. **Staff:** 2. **Budget:** $75,000. **Description:** Sponsored by the American Rehabilitation Counseling Association, Council of State Administrators of Vocational Rehabilitation, American Rehabilitation Counseling Association, National Council on Rehabilitation Education, and the National Rehabilitation Counseling Association. Promotes effective delivery of rehabilitation services to people with disabilities. Surveys, critiques, and works to improve rehabilitation educational programs at the postgraduate level. **Commissions:** Standards and Accreditation. **Affiliated With:** American Medical Rehabilitation Providers Association; American Rehabilitation Counseling Association; Commission on Rehabilitation Counselor Certification; Council of State Administrators of Vocational Rehabilitation; National Council on Rehabilitation Education; National Rehabilitation Counseling Association; Vocational Evaluation and Career Assessment Professionals. **Publications:** *CORE News*, annual. Newsletter. Lists recognized rehabilitation counselor education programs. Alternate Formats: online. **Conventions/Meetings:** annual meeting.

15972 ■ Council of State Administrators of Vocational Rehabilitation (CSAVR)
4733 Bethesda Ave., Ste.330
Bethesda, MD 20814
Ph: (301)654-8414
Fax: (301)654-5542
E-mail: carlsuter@rehabnetwork.org
URL: http://www.rehabnetwork.org
Contact: Carl Suter, Exec. Dir.
Founded: 1940. **Members:** 81. **Staff:** 4. **Budget:** $900,000. **Regional Groups:** 10. **State Groups:** 81. **Description:** Administrators of state vocational rehabilitation agencies. Serves as an advisory body to federal agencies and the public in the develop-

ment of policies affecting rehabilitation of handicapped persons; acts as a forum for discussion on the provision of quality rehabilitation services. Compiles statistics. **Libraries: Type:** reference. **Holdings:** papers. **Committees:** Deaf & Hard of Hearing; Direct Client Services; Employment; Human Resources Development; Legislative; Management Services; Rehabilitation Research; Social Security Relationships. **Publications:** *CSAVR Memorandum*, semimonthly ● *Proceedings of Conferences*, semiannual ● *State Rehabilitation Directors*, periodic. Directory ● Manuals ● Reports. **Conventions/Meetings:** semiannual conference - held in fall and spring ● annual seminar, provides information for new state rehabilitation directors and professional training sessions (exhibits).

15973 ■ Hospitalized Veterans Writing Project (HVWP)

5920 Nall, Rm. 105
Mission, KS 66202-3456
Ph: (913)432-1214
URL: http://www.veteransvoices.org
Contact: Priscilla Chansky, Admin. Mgr.

Founded: 1946. **Membership Dues:** general, $20 (annual) ● family, $30 (annual) ● associate, $50 (annual) ● sponsor, $100 (annual). **Staff:** 1. **Budget:** $40,000. **Description:** Individuals and organizations united to encourage hospitalized U.S. veterans to write for pleasure and rehabilitation during their hospital stay. Maintains speakers' bureau and slide program with commentary. Conducts writing sessions in hospitals. **Awards: Frequency:** 3/year. **Type:** monetary. **Recipient:** for prose, poetry, cartoon, drawing, and photographs. **Publications:** *Veterans' Voices*, 3/year. Magazine. Contains prose, poetry, artwork, and cartoons submitted by hospitalized veterans. **Price:** $10.00/year for hospitalized veterans and outpatients; $20.00/year for others. ISSN: 0504-0779. **Circulation:** 7,000.

15974 ■ International Association of Rehabilitation Professionals (IARP)

1926 Waukegan Rd., Ste.1
Glenview, IL 60025
Ph: (847)657-6964
Fax: (847)657-6963
E-mail: debbiew@tcag.com
URL: http://www.rehabpro.org
Contact: Debbie Witt, Exec. Dir.

Founded: 1981. **Members:** 3,300. **Membership Dues:** individual professional, $127 (annual) ● associate, $85 (annual) ● student, $40 (annual). **Staff:** 3. **Budget:** $800,000. **State Groups:** 36. **Description:** Private rehabilitation companies, insurance companies, rehabilitation nurses, and rehabilitation professionals in the private sector. Seeks to promote the field of private rehabilitation and to provide for information exchange on rehabilitation issues and techniques. **Formerly:** (2000) National Association of Rehabilitation Professionals in the Private Sector. **Publications:** *IARP Journal*, quarterly. Includes book reviews and case studies. **Price:** included in membership dues; $60.00 /year for nonmembers; $35.00 /year for libraries and schools. **Circulation:** 3,300. **Advertising:** accepted ● *NARPPS National Directory*, annual. Contains membership listings by state; includes member name and advertisers indexes. **Price:** included in membership dues; $50.00/copy for nonmembers. **Circulation:** 3,500. **Advertising:** accepted ● *Rehabilitation Professional*, bimonthly. Newsletter. **Circulation:** 3,500. **Advertising:** accepted. **Conventions/Meetings:** annual conference (exhibits).

15975 ■ National Association of Multicultural Rehabilitation Concerns (NAMRC)

c/o Paul Leung, PhD, Pres.
PO Box 311456
Denton, TX 76203-1456
Ph: (940)369-7939
Fax: (940)565-3960
E-mail: pleung@unt.edu
URL: http://www.namrc.org
Contact: Paul Leung PhD, Pres.

Founded: 1969. **Membership Dues:** regular, $20 (annual) ● affiliate/student, $10 (annual). **Descrip-**

tion: Rehabilitation professionals, human services providers, educators, researchers, students, and other individuals with an interest in rehabilitation and people with disabilities. Promotes increased awareness of the barriers created by cultural insensitivity; seeks to ensure availability and quality of rehabilitation services to people of all cultural and ethnic backgrounds. Conducts continuing education courses and certification programs for rehabilitation professionals; supports legislation that encourages multiculturalism in American society and benefits people with disabilities. **Awards:** Bobbie Atkins Research Award. **Frequency:** annual. **Type:** recognition. **Recipient:** for producing significant volume of exemplary research and associated publications ● Joyce Keener Meritorious Service Award. **Frequency:** annual. **Type:** recognition. **Recipient:** for continuous and loyal service and leadership to the association ● Sylvia Walker Education Award. **Frequency:** annual. **Type:** recognition. **Recipient:** for excellence in rehabilitation education at the graduate or undergraduate level ● T.K. Bridges Practitioner Award. **Frequency:** annual. **Type:** recognition. **Recipient:** for providing extended, dedicated and exemplary service to persons with disabilities from culturally diverse backgrounds. **Publications:** *Cultural Network Newsletter*, quarterly. **Alternate Formats:** online.

15976 ■ National Association of Rehabilitation Instructors (NARI)

c/o Nancy Pendegraph
3000 Johnson Rd. SW
Huntsville, AL 35805-5844
Free: (800)671-6840
Fax: (256)650-8250
Contact: Julie Brock, Contact

Members: 87. **State Groups:** 50. **Description:** Promotes rehabilitation of all persons with disabilities. Acts as a medium through which rehabilitation instructors can coordinate their efforts with other instructors, facilities, workshops, individuals, and organizations serving persons with disabilities. Conducts training workshops at the state level. **Publications:** *NARI Newsletter*, 3/year. Bulletin. **Conventions/Meetings:** annual conference and workshop, in conjunction with National Rehabilitation Association.

15977 ■ National Association for Rehabilitation Leadership (NARL)

c/o National Rehabilitation Association
633 S Washington St.
Alexandria, VA 22314
Ph: (703)836-0850
Fax: (703)836-0848
E-mail: email@narl.us
URL: http://www.homestead.com/prosites-nraa
Contact: Ray Feroz, Pres.

Membership Dues: professional, $30 (annual) ● student, $15 (annual). **Description:** Represents nonprofit rehabilitation instructors, state agency vocational rehabilitation instructors, and private instructors. Promotes continuing professional development of members. Conducts professional training sessions. **Awards: Frequency:** periodic. **Type:** grant. **Recipient:** for professionals in the fields of rehabilitation administration and supervision ● Guy Hubbard Award. **Frequency:** annual. **Type:** recognition. **Recipient:** for excellent supervision and administration ● Mary Switzer Award. **Frequency:** annual. **Type:** recognition. **Recipient:** for leadership ● NARL President's Award. **Frequency:** annual. **Type:** recognition. **Recipient:** for contribution to the association. **Formerly:** (2004) National Rehabilitation Administration Association. **Publications:** *Journal of Rehabilitation Administration*, periodic ● *NARL Newsletter*, periodic. **Alternate Formats:** online.

15978 ■ National Association of Rehabilitation Providers and Agencies (NARA)

PO Box 1440
Oldsmar, FL 34677-1440
Ph: (813)855-9168
Fax: (813)855-6449

E-mail: nara@naranet.org
URL: http://www.naranet.org
Contact: Gregg Altobella, Pres.

Founded: 1978. **Members:** 100. **Membership Dues:** active, $750-$1,250 (annual) ● associate, $500 (annual). **Staff:** 2. **Budget:** $250,000. **Description:** Members are rehabilitation companies servicing patients (including Medicare recipients) with physical therapy, occupational therapy and speech pathology services in outpatient and long-term care settings. Associate members are rehabilitation vendors. **Awards:** NARA Award of Merit. **Type:** recognition ● NARA Service Award. **Type:** recognition. **Committees:** Political Action. **Publications:** *NARA News*, quarterly. Newsletter. Provides legislative news for rehabilitation companies; contains articles on Medicare, business management, etc. **Price:** included in membership dues. **Advertising:** accepted. **Alternate Formats:** online. **Conventions/Meetings:** annual conference (exhibits).

15979 ■ National Association of Rehabilitation Support Staff (NARSS)

c/o National Rehabilitation Association
633 S Washington St.
Alexandria, VA 22314
Ph: (703)836-0850 (703)836-0849
Fax: (703)836-0848
E-mail: info@nationalrehab.org
URL: http://www.nationalrehab.org/website/divs/narss.html

Membership Dues: professional, $20 (annual). **Description:** Office support staff in a rehabilitation setting. Promotes professional advancement of members; seeks to insure more effective rehabilitation services for people with disabilities. Conducts advocacy activities on behalf of people with disabilities; sponsors training courses for rehabilitation support staff; provides support and services to organizations representing people with disabilities. **Awards:** Secretary Service Award. **Frequency:** annual. **Type:** recognition. **Publications:** *NARSS Newsletter*, periodic.

15980 ■ National Association of Service Providers in Private Rehabilitation (NASPPR)

c/o National Rehabilitation Association
633 S Washington St.
Alexandria, VA 22314
Ph: (703)836-0850
Fax: (703)836-0848
E-mail: info@nationalrehab.org
URL: http://www.nationalrehab.org/website/divs/nasppr.html

Membership Dues: professional/affiliate, $30 (annual) ● student, $5 (annual). **Description:** Rehabilitation nurses and counselors, physical therapists, job placement professionals, and other individuals with an interest in the rehabilitation and employment of people with disabilities. Seeks to improve practice and outcomes in both the medical and placement phases of the rehabilitation process. Serves as a forum for the exchange of information among rehabilitation professionals; facilitates cooperation among members; sponsors educational and training programs. **Telecommunication Services:** TDD, (703)-836-0849.

15981 ■ National Council on Rehabilitation Education (NCRE)

c/o Sharon Benshoff, Admin. Sec.
2012 W Norwood Dr.
Carbondale, IL 62901
Ph: (618)549-3267
Fax: (618)457-3632
E-mail: sbenshoff@ncre-admin.org
URL: http://www.rehabeducators.org
Contact: Jorge Garcia, Pres.

Founded: 1961. **Members:** 600. **Membership Dues:** student, $30 (annual) ● individual, $50 (annual) ● associate individual, $75 (annual) ● associate institution, $250 (annual) ● institution, $450 (annual). **Staff:** 2. **Budget:** $136,000. **Regional Groups:** 10. **Description:** Represents academic institutions and organizations, professional educators, researchers, and students. Goals are to: assist in the documentation of the effect of education in improving services to persons with disability; determine the skills and training necessary for effective rehabilitation services; develop models, standards, and uniform licensure and certification requirements for rehabilitation personnel; interact with consumers and public and private sector policy makers. Disseminates information and provides forum for discussion. Sponsors specialized education and placement service. Compiles statistics. Works closely with agencies and associations serving persons with disabilities. **Libraries: Type:** open to the public. **Holdings:** reports. **Computer Services:** database ● mailing lists. **Formerly:** (1976) Council of Rehabilitation Counselor Educators. **Publications:** *Rehabilitation Education*, quarterly. Journal. Features original contributions. **Price:** included in membership dues. **Circulation:** 400. **Advertising:** accepted ● Newsletter, quarterly. Features member news. **Circulation:** 600. Alternate Formats: online ● Membership Directory, annual. **Price:** $25.00 ● Monographs ● Report, quarterly. **Conventions/Meetings:** annual conference - every October in Washington, DC ● annual conference - every February in Tucson, AZ ● annual Rehabilitation Educators' Conference.

15982 ■ National Rehabilitation Association (NRA)

633 S Washington St.
Alexandria, VA 22314
Ph: (703)836-0850
Fax: (703)836-0848
E-mail: info@nationalrehab.org
URL: http://www.nationalrehab.org/website/index. html
Contact: Daniel C. Lustig, Ed.
Founded: 1925. **Members:** 9,000. **Membership Dues:** professional, $126 (annual) ● organizational, $500 (annual) ● student, $35 (annual) ● friend, family/consumer, retiree, $75 (annual). **Staff:** 8. **Regional Groups:** 7. **State Groups:** 52. **National Groups:** 9. **Description:** Provides opportunities through knowledge and diversity for professionals in the fields of rehabilitation of people with disabilities. **Awards:** E.B. Whitten Silver Medallion Award. **Frequency:** annual. **Type:** medal. **Recipient:** for notable leadership ● Max T. Prince Meritorious Service Award. **Frequency:** annual. **Type:** recognition. **Recipient:** for faithful service and leadership ● NRA Chapter of the Year Award. **Frequency:** annual. **Type:** recognition. **Recipient:** for outstanding achievement ● Organizational Award. **Frequency:** annual. **Type:** recognition. **Recipient:** for outstanding record of service to individuals with disabilities. **Computer Services:** Mailing lists, sales. **Telecommunication Services:** TDD, (703)836-0849. **Committees:** Executive; Switzer Planning. **Divisions:** Job Placement and Development; Multi-Cultural Rehabilitation Concerns; National Association for Independent Living; National Association of Rehabilitation Instructors; National Association of Rehabilitation Support Staff; Rehabilitation Administration; Rehabilitation Counseling; Service Providers in Private Rehabilitation; Vocational Evaluation and Work Adjustment Association (see separate entries). **Publications:** *Contemporary Rehab*, bimonthly. Newsletter. Includes calendar of events, listing of employment opportunities, chapter news, human interest stories, and practice information. **Price:** included in membership dues. ISSN: 0279-5507. **Circulation:** 11,000. **Advertising:** accepted ● *Journal of Rehabilitation*, quarterly. Includes articles on rehabilitation research and new technology. Also includes book reviews and annual index. **Price:** included in membership dues; $65.00 /year for nonmembers in U.S.; $75.00 /year for individuals in Canada; $90.00 /year for individuals outside U.S. and Canada. ISSN: 0022-4154. **Circulation:** 16,000. **Advertising:** accepted. Alternate Formats: online ● *Switzer Monographs*. Reports the writings, discussions and recommendations. **Price:** $15.00 each for members; $20.00 each for nonmembers. **Conventions/Meetings:** annual Governmental Affairs - seminar - spring ● annual Training Conference and Showcase (exhibits) - fall.

15983 ■ National Rehabilitation Counseling Association (NRCA)

PO Box 4480
Manassas, VA 20108

Ph: (703)361-2077
Fax: (703)361-2489
E-mail: nrcaoffice@aol.com
URL: http://nrca-net.org
Contact: Jeanne B. Patterson EdD, Pres.
Founded: 1958. **Members:** 1,650. **Membership Dues:** professional, $70 (annual) ● student, $20 (annual) ● affiliate, $40 (annual). **Staff:** 2. **Regional Groups:** 7. **Description:** An independent Association of Professional and student rehabilitation counselors. Works to expand the role of counselors in the rehabilitation process and seeks to advance members' professional development. Supports legislation favoring the profession. **Publications:** *Journal of Applied Rehabilitation Counseling*, quarterly. Includes research information, literature and book reviews. **Price:** included in membership dues; $15.00 for nonmembers; $30.00 for institutions. ISSN: 0047-2220. **Circulation:** 4,800. **Advertising:** accepted. Alternate Formats: microform. **Conventions/Meetings:** annual conference, held in conjunction with NRA (exhibits) ● annual Professional Development Symposium, with concurrent training sessions.

15984 ■ National Rehabilitation Information Center (NARIC)

4200 Forbes Blvd., Ste.202
Lanham, MD 20706
Ph: (301)459-5900
Free: (800)346-2742
Fax: (301)459-4263
E-mail: naricinfo@heitechservices.com
URL: http://www.naric.com
Contact: Mark X. Odum, Dir.
Founded: 1977. **Staff:** 9. **Languages:** English, Spanish. **Description:** Aims to improve delivery of information to the rehabilitation community. Disseminates the findings of programs funded by the National Institute on Disability and Rehabilitation Research; prepares custom bibliographies; helps locate answers to reference questions; searches for relevant materials in other commercially available databases. **Libraries: Type:** open to the public. **Holdings:** 60,000; audiovisuals, books, reports. **Subjects:** disability, rehabilitation. **Computer Services:** database, abstracts collection, info on current research, disability organizations ● online services, virtual reference through php-live chat. **Telecommunication Services:** TDD, (301)459-5984. **Publications:** *NIDRR Program Directory*, annual. **Price:** $5.00 each. Alternate Formats: online ● *REHABDATA Thesaurus*. Annual Reports. **Price:** $25.00 each. Alternate Formats: online ● Directory, annual. Available online only. Alternate Formats: online.

15985 ■ Rehabilitation International (RI)

25 E 21st St., 4th Fl.
New York, NY 10010
Ph: (212)420-1500
Fax: (212)505-0871
E-mail: ri@riglobal.org
URL: http://www.rehab-international.org
Contact: Mr. Thomas Lagerwall, Sec. Gen.
Founded: 1922. **Members:** 150. **Description:** Distributes information to 150 countries conducting programs for the rehabilitation of people with physical and mental disabilities. Disseminates information on every phase of disability prevention and rehabilitation. Assists experts in planning work or study programs outside their own countries; aids in practical development of national rehabilitation programs. Participates in the International Disability Alliance and the International Working Group on Disability and Development. **Awards:** Certificate of Gratitude. **Type:** recognition. **Recipient:** to express RI's gratitude for services provided by individuals or organizations ● The Fenmore R. Seton Distinguished Volunteer Award. **Frequency:** quadrennial. **Type:** recognition. **Recipient:** for a volunteer who made the most special and meaningful contribution nationally and/or internationally to the improvement of the quality of life for persons with disabilities ● Henry H. Kessler Awards. **Frequency:** quadrennial. **Type:** recognition. **Recipient:** for three individuals or organizations whose achievements in a specified area of activity have contributed significantly to mankind's ability to

overcome the occurrence and the disadvantages of physical, mental and/or sensory disability ● President's Citation. **Type:** recognition. **Recipient:** for distinguished accomplishments by individuals or organizations that are in support of RI's purpose ● Rehabilitation International Presidential Award. **Type:** recognition. **Recipient:** for an individual or organization whose work and accomplishments over an extended period of time have contributed significantly to the progress of international efforts to prevent or overcome physical, mental and/or sensory disability. **Commissions:** Education; Health and Functioning; Policy and Services; Social; Sports, Leisure and Recreation; Technical Aids, Building, and Transportation; Vocational; Work and Employment. **Affiliated With:** Council of Europe; Organization of American States; United Nations; United Nations Economic and Social Commission for Asia and the Pacific; World Health Organization. **Formerly:** (1939) International Society for Crippled Children; (1960) International Society for the Welfare of Cripples; (1976) International Society for Rehabilitation of the Disabled. **Publications:** *International Journal of Rehabilitation Research*, quarterly ● *International Rehabilitation Review*, triennial. Newsletter. Provides coverage of United Nations agencies, discusses the elimination of architectural and environmental barriers for the disabled. **Price:** $45.00 /year for individuals. **Circulation:** 10,000 ● *One-In-Ten* (in Arabic, English, French, and Spanish), semiannual. Newsletter. Features programs to improve the situation of children with disabilities. ● *Proceedings of World Congress*, quadrennial ● *Rehabilitation* (in English and Spanish), semiannual ● Directory, annual ● Also publishes booklets and papers. **Conventions/Meetings:** annual Regional Conference - meeting - 2007 Oct. 20-26, Djerba, Tunisia ● quadrennial World Congress (exhibits).

15986 ■ Rehabilitation Technology Association

Address Unknown since 2007
Founded: 1982. **Members:** 1,000. **Description:** Individuals involved in the rehabilitation field. Uses technology to enhance performance in their jobs. **Telecommunication Services:** Telnet: enable.WVnet.edu ● electronic bulletin board, Project Enable BBS (304)766-2690. **Publications:** *RTA Online Newsletter*, quarterly. Contains articles on rehabilitation and information technologies. **Price:** free. **Circulation:** 5,000. **Advertising:** accepted. Alternate Formats: online. **Conventions/Meetings:** annual symposium (exhibits); **Avg. Attendance:** 150.

15987 ■ Sister Kenny Rehabilitation Institute

800 E 28th St.
Minneapolis, MN 55407
Ph: (612)863-4466
E-mail: sisterkenny@allina.com
URL: http://www.allina.com/ahs/ski.nsf
Contact: Dick Pettingill, Exec. Dir.
Founded: 1942. **Staff:** 287. **Description:** Investigates, evaluates, promotes, and supports projects in rehabilitation and provide rehabilitative patient care. (Named for Elizabeth Kenny, 1886-1952, an Australian nurse who developed a method for treating poliomyelitis with thermal compresses and physical therapy.) Compiles statistics on research activities and patient care activities. Specializes in the treatment of acutely and chronically disabled patients. A large number of patients are stroke victims, spinal cord-injured, or brain-damaged. Rehabilitation services are also used by patients with arthritis, cerebral palsy, Parkinson's disease, polio residuals, or other neuromuscular disorders or muskuloskeletal injuries. Offers professional education programs to instruct medical and allied health professionals in the most recent and most relevant rehabilitation practices. Teaches rehabilitation personnel nursing skills needed to fill the special requirements of chronically ill and physically disabled people. **Departments:** Development. **Formerly:** (1965) Sister Kenny Foundation; (1976) American Rehabilitation Foundation; (2002) Sister Kenny Institute. **Publications:** *Clinical Rehab Perspectives*, quarterly. Newsletter. Highlights recent research, clinical practices and advances in

rehabilitation. Alternate Formats: online ● *Kenny Independent*, quarterly. Newsletter. Highlights the institute's programs, staff and patient stories. Alternate Formats: online.

15988 ■ United States Psychiatric Rehabilitation Association (USPRA)
601 Global Way, Ste.106
Linthicum, MD 21090
Ph: (410)789-7054
Fax: (410)789-7675
E-mail: info@uspra.org
URL: http://www.uspra.org
Contact: Marcie Granahan CAE, CEO
Founded: 1976. **Members:** 1,900. **Membership Dues:** individual, $90 (annual) ● organization, $170-$4,000 (annual) ● associate individual, $30 (annual) ● associate organization, $565 (annual). **Staff:** 8. **Budget:** $1,000,000. **Regional Groups:** 2. **State Groups:** 32. **Local Groups:** 32. **National Groups:** 2. **Description:** Individuals and organizations serving adults with a psychiatric disability. Promotes the advancement of the role, scope, and quality of service designed to facilitate the readjustment into the community of the adults with psychiatric disabilities. Provides a forum for the exchange of ideas, experiences, and contributions to the field. Offers technical assistance to organizational members; sponsors regional training conferences. **Awards:** Armin Loeb Award. **Frequency:** annual. **Type:** recognition ● Consumer Advocate Award. **Frequency:** annual. **Type:** recognition ● Irv Rutman Award. **Frequency:** annual. **Type:** recognition ● Research Award. **Frequency:** annual. **Type:** recognition. **Committees:** Awards; Consumer; Cultural Diversity; Governance; Managed Care; Membership; Nominations; Public Policy; Publications; Research; Training/Certification; U.S. Public Policy. **Formerly:** (2004) International Association of Psychosocial Rehabilitation Services. **Publications:** *An Introduction to Psychiatric Rehabilitation.* Book. **Price:** $35.00 for members; $50.00 for nonmembers ● *Best Practices in Psychosocial Rehabilitation.* Book. **Price:** $45.00 for members; $60.00 for nonmembers ● *Consumers as Providers in Psychiatric Rehabilitation.* Book. **Price:** $35.00 for members; $50.00 for nonmembers ● *PSR Connection*, quarterly. Newsletter. **Price:** included in membership dues. **Circulation:** 1,500. **Advertising:** accepted. Alternate Formats: online ● *Psychosocial Rehabilitation Journal*, quarterly. Includes calendar of events and research reports. **Price:** included in membership dues; $115.00 /year for institutions; $55.00 /year for nonmembers. ISSN: 0147-5622. **Circulation:** 3,000. **Advertising:** accepted ● Also publishes legislative bulletins, documents, and professional information. **Conventions/Meetings:** annual conference (exhibits) - always spring.

15989 ■ Vocational Evaluation and Career Assessment Professionals (VECAP)
PO Box 2958
Salina, KS 67402-2958
Ph: (785)404-2105
Fax: (785)404-2105
E-mail: office@vecap.org
URL: http://www.vecap.org
Contact: Wesley Greenwood MA, Pres.
Founded: 1967. **Members:** 100. **Membership Dues:** professional, associate, $70 (annual) ● student, $10 (annual). **Regional Groups:** 7. **National Groups:** 2. **Multinational. Description:** Specialists in vocational evaluation and work adjustment whose goals are to improve and advance the field and to promote high ethical practices through training and research. Conducts educational programs at state, regional, and national levels. Works with other organizations to develop a certification program for vocational evaluators and work adjustment personnel. Keeps legislators informed of the needs of persons with disabilities; promotes adequate funding of state and federal programs benefiting persons with disabilities. Disseminates employment information to members. **Libraries: Type:** reference. **Holdings:** video recordings. **Awards: Type:** grant. **Recipient:** to members for small research projects ● Paul R. Hoffman

Service Award. **Type:** recognition. **Committees:** Certification; Standards; Student Affairs. **Formerly:** (2003) Vocational Evaluation and Work Adjustment Association. **Publications:** *VECAP Newsletter*, quarterly. Alternate Formats: online ● Bulletin, quarterly ● National Directory of Vocational Evaluation and Assessment Professionals. **Conventions/Meetings:** annual conference, held in conjunction with NRA (exhibits).

15990 ■ World Association for Psychosocial Rehabilitation - U.S. Branch (WAPR)
c/o AAPR
19 E 93rd St.
New York, NY 10128
E-mail: office@wapr.net
Contact: Dr. Zebulon Taintor, Pres.
Founded: 1987. **Members:** 500. **Membership Dues:** regular, $50 (annual) ● sponsoring, $1,000 (annual) ● student, consumer, family, $25. **Description:** Professionals in the mental health field concerned with research, study, and training in psychosocial rehabilitation. (Psychosocial rehabilitation assists individuals whose primary problems or pathologies are related to psychiatric dysfunctions that limit their social, personal, or occupational functioning.) Conducts research and educational programs; maintains speakers' bureau and placement services. **Libraries: Type:** reference. **Holdings:** archival material. **Awards: Type:** recognition. **Computer Services:** database ● mailing lists. **Committees:** Advanced Institute; Advocacy and Policy; Aging; Cognitive Rehabilitation; Culture; Developing Countries; Editorial; Education; Epidemiology. **Publications:** *Bulletin WAPR* (in English, French, and Spanish), periodic. **Price:** free, for members only. **Circulation:** 2,000 ● *International Journal of Mental Health*, quarterly. **Price:** $50.00 to members. **Circulation:** 1,200 ● Newsletter, periodic. **Conventions/Meetings:** biennial international conference ● annual UN Awards Luncheon - meeting and luncheon.

Religion

15991 ■ Health Ministries Association (HMA)
295 W Crossville Rd., Ste.130
Roswell, GA 30075
Ph: (770)640-9955
Free: (800)280-9919
Fax: (770)640-1095
E-mail: info@hmassoc.org
URL: http://www.hmassoc.org
Contact: Dr. Peggy Matteson PhD, Pres.
Founded: 1989. **Members:** 1,000. **Membership Dues:** student, retiree, $80 (annual) ● standard, $120 (annual). **Staff:** 4. **Regional Groups:** 22. **Description:** Serves as the professional organization for Faith Community Nurses (formerly called parish nurses), Clergy, Academic faculty, Health Educators, Lay Health Ministers, and Program Coordinators assisting faith communities to attain and maintain spiritual, mental, and physical health. Provides a forum for sharing of ideas and programming. **Awards:** Wilkerson-Droege Award. **Frequency:** periodic. **Type:** recognition. **Recipient:** to an individual who has made a difference in peoples' lives through health ministry beyond the local faith community. **Computer Services:** Information services, for members only section that provides discussion groups, articles describing programs, e-announcements, and quarterly newsletters. **Special Interest Groups:** Clergy; Faculty; Faith Community Nurses; Health Educators; Lay Health Ministers; Program Coordinators. **Publications:** *A Guide to Developing a Health Ministry*, semiannual. Book. Provides information on how to start and/or maintain a health ministry. **Price:** $54.95 for members. Alternate Formats: CD-ROM ● *Faith Community Nursing: Scope and Standards of Practice*, as needed. Book. Describes the scope and minimum standards of practice of this specialty in professional nursing. **Price:** $12.00 for members; $15.00 for nonmembers ● *Healing and Wholeness: The Church's Role in Health*. Book. Defines health and wholeness within the context of the Congrega-

tion and Theology. **Price:** $5.00 for members; $7.00 for nonmembers ● *Healing and Wholeness: The Role of the Congregation in Health*. Video. Demonstrates the importance of the church's involvement in health. **Price:** $34.95 for members; $44.95 for nonmembers ● *The Healing Team*. Video. Covers the church's role in developing a health ministry. **Price:** $16.00 for members; $18.00 for nonmembers. Alternate Formats: CD-ROM ● *Health Ministry Journal*, quarterly. **Price:** $35.00 for members; $55.00 for nonmembers; $95.00 for institutions. ISSN: 1550-3992. **Circulation:** 300. **Advertising:** accepted. **Conventions/Meetings:** annual conference, with key note speakers, and workshops (exhibits).

Religious Administration

15992 ■ HealthCare Chaplaincy (HCC)
315 E 62nd St., 4th Fl.
New York, NY 10021-7767
Ph: (212)644-1111
Fax: (212)758-9959
E-mail: wsmith@healthcarechaplaincy.org
URL: http://www.healthcarechaplaincy.org
Contact: Rev. Dr. Walter J. Smith, Pres./CEO
Founded: 1961. **Staff:** 65. **Description:** Seeks to advance pastoral care, education and research; dedicated to spiritual care of all individuals. **Libraries: Type:** reference. **Holdings:** articles, books, periodicals. **Subjects:** healthcare chaplaincy. **Awards:** Wholeness of Life Award. **Frequency:** annual. **Type:** recognition. **Recipient:** for individuals who embody the spirit of the organization's mission. **Publications:** *The Beacon*. Newsletter. Alternate Formats: online ● *Community Outreach Programs* ● *JIPC News & Notes* ● *Partners in Caring* ● *Plain-Views*. Newsletter. Alternate Formats: online ● *Professional Chaplaincy: Its Role & Importance in Healthcare*. Paper. Alternate Formats: online ● Annual Report, annual. Alternate Formats: online.

Reproductive Health

15993 ■ Maternal Life International (MLI)
326 S Jackson St.
Butte, MT 59701
Ph: (406)782-1719
Fax: (406)782-1719
E-mail: usacares@in-tch.com
URL: http://www.mlionline.org
Founded: 1996. **Multinational. Description:** Provides safe, practical, life-affirming and innovative programs in maternal health care, AIDS prevention, and fertility awareness.

15994 ■ North American Society for the Study of Hypertension in Pregnancy (NASSHP)
c/o Chaur-Dong Hsu, MD
New York Medical Coll. - Westchester Medical Ctr.
19 Bradhurst Ave., Ste.2700
Hawthorne, NY 10532
Ph: (914)593-8950
Fax: (914)593-8960
E-mail: hsuc@wcmc.com
URL: http://www.nasshp.org
Contact: Chaur-Dong Hsu, Contact
Membership Dues: general, $50 (annual). **Description:** Promotes knowledge, research and education on all aspects of hypertensive complications of pregnancy. Promotes the exchange of professional information related to maternal-fetal medicine.

15995 ■ Society for Male Reproduction and Urology (SMRU)
1209 Montgomery Hwy.
Birmingham, AL 35216-2809
Ph: (205)978-5000
Fax: (205)978-5005

E-mail: asrm@asrm.org
URL: http://www.smru.org
Contact: Craig S. Niederberger MD, Pres.
Founded: 1995. **Membership Dues:** active, $75 (annual) ● associate, $35 (annual). **Description:** Promotes the advancement of male reproductive physiology and management of male infertility. Provides a forum for the dissemination of both basic and clinical research information of male reproductive physiology. Supports educational programs for male reproduction. **Computer Services:** database, member directory. **Affiliated With:** American Society for Reproductive Medicine. **Publications:** Newsletter. Alternate Formats: online.

15996 ■ Society for the Study of Male Reproduction (SSMR)

1111 N Plaza Dr., Ste.550
Schaumburg, IL 60173
Ph: (847)517-7225
Fax: (847)517-7229
E-mail: info@ssmr.org
URL: http://www.ssmr.org
Contact: Wendy J. Weiser, Exec. Dir.
Membership Dues: active, $100 (annual). **Description:** Aims to improve the quality of care of the subfertile male. Promotes the role of urology in the evaluation and treatment of the infertile male. Seeks to develop standards and guidelines for male reproduction research and practices. Produces educational programs related to clinical practice and government and reimbursement issues. **Publications:** *SSMR News*, semiannual. Newsletter. **Price:** included in membership dues. Alternate Formats: online.

Reproductive Medicine

15997 ■ Institute for Female Alternative Medicine

1500 S Central Ave., Ste.214
Glendale, CA 91204
Ph: (818)956-3391
Free: (800)505-IFAM
URL: http://www.alternativesurgery.com
Contact: Dr. Tirso del Junco Jr., Founder
Staff: 10. **Description:** Focuses on alternative surgical procedures for the treatment of benign female pathologies (i.e: fibroids, ovarian cystic disease, endometriosis); philosophy is "reconstructive" with extensive use of lasers, not removal of pelvic organs. **Formerly:** (1998) Institute for Reproductive Health. **Publications:** *Women's Health Quarterly*. **Conventions/Meetings:** periodic meeting.

15998 ■ Society for Assisted Reproductive Technology (SART)

c/o American Society for Reproductive Medicine
1209 Montgomery Hwy.
Birmingham, AL 35216-2809
Ph: (205)978-5000
Fax: (205)978-5015
E-mail: jzeitz@asrm.org
URL: http://www.sart.org
Contact: Joyce Zeitz, Exec. Admin.
Founded: 1987. **Members:** 390. **Membership Dues:** practice, $300 (annual). **Staff:** 1. **Description:** Institutions conducting assisted reproductive procedures. Works to extend knowledge of human in vitro fertilization techniques. Conducts educational programs; gathers and disseminates information and outcome statistics on art. **Conventions/Meetings:** annual meeting, held in conjunction with American Society for Reproductive Medicine (exhibits) ● annual meeting - always midyear.

15999 ■ Society for Prevention of Human Infertility (SPHI)

877 Park Ave.
New York, NY 10021
Ph: (212)744-5500
Fax: (212)744-6536

E-mail: info@frfbaby.com
URL: http://www.frfbaby.com
Contact: Dr. Masood A. Khatamee, Exec. Dir.
Founded: 1990. **Members:** 500. **Membership Dues:** regular, $50 (annual) ● sponsor, $100 (annual) ● benefactor, $1,000 (annual) ● scholarship fund, $10,000. **Regional Groups:** 100. **Languages:** English, Farsi, Spanish, Urdu. **Description:** Physicians specializing in obstetrics and gynecology; scientists representing public and private teaching hospitals, medical school faculties, and university research departments; practitioners who work with infertile men and women. Works to: study Sexually Transmitted Infectious Diseases (STDs) and their effects on human fertility; and reduce the incidence of infection and the possibility of resulting infertility. Coordinates and encourages research that can lead to successful forms of treatment and control of STDs, thus enhancing the opportunities for childless couples to achieve intrauterine pregnancies and bear healthy children. Encourages the exchange of information among those involved in research on and treatment of STDs. Designs educational and informational strategies intended for the prevention of infertility. **Formerly:** (1991) International Society of Infectious Diseases and Human Infertility. **Conventions/Meetings:** annual international conference, held in conjunction with American Medical Association and American Fertility Society (exhibits) ● lecture ● seminar ● symposium.

16000 ■ Society for Reproductive Endocrinology and Infertility (SREI)

c/o American Society for Reproductive Medicine
1209 Montgomery Hwy.
Birmingham, AL 35216-2809
Ph: (205)978-5000
Fax: (205)978-5005
E-mail: asrm@asrm.org
URL: http://www.socrei.org
Contact: Marc A. Fritz MD, Pres.
Founded: 1984. **Members:** 810. **Membership Dues:** active, $90 (annual) ● associate, $25 (annual). **Staff:** 2. **Description:** Medical doctors with American Board of Obstetrics and Gynecology subspecialty certification as reproductive endocrinologists. Works to extend knowledge of human reproduction and endocrinology; makes available to members continuing education programs. Conducts seminars. **Publications:** *SREI Feedback*, quarterly. Newsletter. Includes information for members on SREI activities. **Price:** included in membership dues. **Conventions/Meetings:** annual convention and meeting, held in conjunction with American Society for Reproductive Medicine ● annual meeting - always fall.

16001 ■ Society of Reproductive Surgeons (SRS)

1209 Montgomery Hwy.
Birmingham, AL 35216-2809
Ph: (205)978-5000
Fax: (205)978-5005
E-mail: asrm@asrm.org
URL: http://www.reprodsurgery.org
Contact: Ricardo Azziz MD, Pres.
Founded: 1984. **Members:** 450. **Membership Dues:** active, $75 (annual) ● associate, $25 (annual). **Description:** Reproductive surgeons. Gathers and disseminates information on reproductive surgery; conducts continuing education programs for members. Makes available referrals list. **Awards:** SRS Prize Paper. **Frequency:** annual. **Type:** monetary. **Recipient:** for the best paper based on peer review. **Committees:** Associate Member Development; Industry Relations; International Relations; MIS/AAGL/SRS Fellowship; Postgraduate; Practice; Residency Directors Coordination; Website. **Publications:** Newsletter, semiannual. **Conventions/Meetings:** annual meeting, held in conjunction with American Society for Reproductive Medicine ● annual meeting - fall.

16002 ■ Society for the Study of Reproduction (SSR)

1619 Monroe St.
Madison, WI 53711-2063
Ph: (608)256-2777

Fax: (608)256-4610
E-mail: ssr@ssr.org
URL: http://www.ssr.org
Contact: Mitch Eddy, Pres.
Founded: 1967. **Members:** 2,500. **Membership Dues:** regular in U.S., associate in U.S., $170 (annual) ● regular outside U.S., associate outside U.S., $190 (annual) ● postdoctoral fellow, $45 (annual) ● graduate student, $30 (annual) ● emeritus, $85 (annual). **Staff:** 1. **Budget:** $1,500,000. **Description:** Researchers in obstetrics and gynecology, urology, zoology, animal husbandry, and physiology; clinicians in human and veterinary medicine. Promotes the study of reproduction by fostering interdisciplinary communication within the science. **Awards:** Carl G. Hartman Award. **Frequency:** annual. **Type:** recognition. **Recipient:** for research and activities in the field of reproductive biology ● Merit Awards for Travel. **Frequency:** annual. **Type:** grant. **Recipient:** for trainee members active in research ● SSR Distinguished Service Award. **Frequency:** annual. **Type:** recognition. **Recipient:** for unselfish service and leadership ● SSR New Investigator Award. **Frequency:** annual. **Type:** recognition. **Recipient:** for research published within ten years ● SSR Research Award. **Frequency:** annual. **Type:** recognition. **Recipient:** for outstanding research published during the previous six years ● Trainee Research Award. **Frequency:** annual. **Type:** recognition. **Recipient:** for best paper research. **Computer Services:** Mailing lists, available for rental. **Committees:** Animal Care and Use; Awards; Bylaws; Development; Education; Minority Affairs; Program; Public Affairs. **Publications:** *Biology of Reproduction*, monthly, plus one supplement per year. Journal. Includes peer-reviewed scientific research in the field of reproductive biology. **Price:** included in membership dues; $575.00 for nonmembers outside U.S. ISSN: 0006-3363. **Circulation:** 3,700. **Advertising:** accepted. Alternate Formats: online. Also Cited As: *Biol Reprod* ● *Biology of Reproduction Monograph Series 1: Equine Reproduction VI* ● Newsletter, 3/year, always February, June and October. **Price:** included in membership dues. **Conventions/Meetings:** annual conference and meeting (exhibits).

Research

16003 ■ International Society for Interferon and Cytokine Research (ISICR)

c/o Federation of American Societies for
   Experimental Biology
9650 Rockville Pike
Bethesda, MD 20814-3998
Ph: (301)634-7250
Fax: (301)634-7420
E-mail: isicr@faseb.org
URL: http://www.isicr.org
Contact: Otto Haller, Pres.
Members: 650. **Membership Dues:** regular, $50 (annual) ● postdoctoral fellow, student, $10 (annual) ● life, $500 ● emeritus, $25 (annual). **Multinational**. **Description:** Conducts research in the fields of interferon, cytokine, and chemokine cell biology, molecular biology, biochemistry, and the clinical use of these biological response modifiers. **Awards:** Christina Fleischmann Memorial Award. **Frequency:** annual. **Type:** monetary. **Recipient:** for women members who have made notable contributions to either basic or clinical research within 10 years after receiving their PhD or MD ● Milstein Award. **Frequency:** annual. **Type:** recognition. **Recipient:** for individuals who have made exceptional contributions to research related to interferons and cytokines either in basic or clinical field ● Milstein Young Investigator Awards. **Frequency:** annual. **Type:** monetary. **Recipient:** for members who have made notable contributions to either basic or clinical research within 8 years after receiving their PhD or MD ● Travel Awards. **Frequency:** annual. **Type:** monetary. **Recipient:** for members who intend to attend the annual meeting of ISICR. **Computer Services:** Information services, resources and catalogs ● online services, cytokine-interferon forum. **Telecommunica-**

tion Services: electronic mail, otto.haller@uniklinik-freiburg.de. Boards: Advisory. Committees: Archives; Meetings; Nomenclature; Publications; Standards. Publications: *Journal of Interferon and Cytokine Research*, monthly. Covers all aspects of interferons and cytokines from basic science to clinical applications. ISSN: 1079-9907. Advertising: accepted ● Newsletter, 3/year. Alternate Formats: online. Conventions/Meetings: annual meeting, with speakers and scientific program.

Respiratory Diseases

16004 ■ Allergy and Asthma Network Mothers of Asthmatics (AANMA)
2751 Prosperity Ave., Ste.150
Fairfax, VA 22031
Free: (800)878-4403
Fax: (703)573-7794
E-mail: aanma@aol.com
URL: http://www.aanma.org
Contact: Nancy Sander, Pres./Founder
Founded: 1985. Members: 6,000. Membership Dues: individual/family, $35 (annual) ● medical professional, $100 (annual) ● gift, $25 (annual). Staff: 15. Budget: $1,000,000. Description: Represents individuals, parents, physicians, patients, educators and professional associations. Works to the education and support of people with allergies and asthma. Formerly: (1991) Mothers of Asthmatics; (1993) National Allergy and Asthma Network. Publications: *Allergy and Asthma Today* (in English and Spanish), quarterly. Magazine. Provides in-depth coverage of allergy and asthma issues from leading medical and consumer experts. Includes a mini-magazine for kids. Price: free for members; $4.95 each (back issues) ● *Breathing Easy with Day Care*. Booklet ● *Consumer Update on Asthma*. Report ● *How Asthma Makes Me Feel*, periodic. Book. Includes pictures, essays and artwork about living with asthma. Price: $9.00/copy for members; $10.00/copy for nonmembers ● *I'm a Meter Reader*. Video ● *MA Report*, monthly. Newsletter. Provides patients and families of children with asthma and allergies with coping strategies, medical information, product reviews & how to articles. Price: $25.00/year ● *So You Have Asthma Too!* (in English and Spanish). Book. Conventions/Meetings: Asthma Awareness Day on Capitol Hill - meeting.

16005 ■ Alpha-1 Association
2937 SW 27th Ave., Ste.106
Miami, FL 33133
Ph: (305)648-0088
Free: (800)521-3025
Fax: (305)648-0089
E-mail: info@alpha1.org
URL: http://www.alpha1.org
Contact: Miriam O'Day, Sr. Dir. for Public Policy
Founded: 1989. Members: 700. Membership Dues: patient, $25 (annual) ● family, $40 (annual) ● professional, non-patient, $50 (annual) ● life, $500. Staff: 6. State Groups: 35. Local Groups: 2. National Groups: 81. Languages: English, German, Spanish. Description: Seeks to identify those affected by Alpha-1 Antitrypsin Deficiency and to improve the quality of their lives through support, education, advocacy, and research. Formerly: (1991) Alpha 1 Antitrypsin Support Group. Publications: *Alpha 1 News*, quarterly. Newsletter. Price: free for members. Circulation: 3,300. Conventions/Meetings: annual National Educational Conference (exhibits).

16006 ■ American Lung Association (ALA)
61 Broadway, 6th Fl.
New York, NY 10006
Ph: (212)315-8700
E-mail: info@lungusa.org
URL: http://www.lungusa.org
Contact: John L. Kirkwood, Pres./CEO
Founded: 1904. Staff: 100. Local Groups: 78. Description: Commits in fighting Big Tobacco, Bad Air and the Asthma Epidemic through research and education. Advocates in an effort to prevent lung disease and promotes lung health. Awards: Biomedi-

cal Research Grant. Frequency: annual. Type: monetary. Recipient: for investigators researching the mechanisms of lung disease ● Career Investigator. Frequency: annual. Type: monetary. Recipient: for national leadership role in investigative work related lung disease ● Lung Health Dissertation Grant. Frequency: annual. Type: monetary. Recipient: for students with academic focus or nurses pursuing a doctoral degree ● Senior Research Training Fellowship. Frequency: annual. Type: monetary. Recipient: for professionals with further academic training. Committees: Awards; Cultural Diversity; Fields Operations; Lung Disease Action; Nominating; Planning. Task Forces: Policies and Guidelines; Stakeholder Learning. Formerly: (1918) National Association for the Study and Prevention of Tuberculosis; (1968) National Tuberculosis Association; (1973) National Tuberculosis and Respiratory Disease Association. Publications: *LUNGhealth*, quarterly. Magazine ● *Lungs @ Work*, quarterly. Newsletter. Features the latest lung health news and information. Alternate Formats: online.

16007 ■ Association of Asthma Educators (AAE)
1215 Anthony Ave.
Columbia, SC 29201-1701
Free: (888)988-7747
Fax: (803)254-3773
E-mail: franciscob@health.missouri.edu
URL: http://www.asthmaeducators.org
Contact: Benjamin Francisco RN, Pres.
Founded: 1998. Members: 460. Membership Dues: individual, $50 (annual) ● group (6 or more persons), $45 (annual). Description: Promotes asthma education as an integral component of a comprehensive asthma program. Aims to raise the competence of health care professionals who educate individuals and families affected by asthma. Seeks to raise the standard of asthma care for patients. Publications: *Talking About Asthma*, quarterly. Newsletter. Features articles on asthma education, care and management. Price: included in membership dues ● Annual Report, annual. Alternate Formats: online.

16008 ■ Coalition for Pulmonary Fibrosis (CPF)
1659 Branham Ln., Ste.F, No. 227
San Jose, CA 95118
Free: (888)222-8541
Fax: (866)683-9458
E-mail: info@coalitionforpf.org
URL: http://www.coalitionforpf.org
Contact: Mr. Mark A. Shreve, CEO
Founded: 2001. Multinational. Description: Seeks to advance education, patient support, and research for pulmonary fibrosis, specifically idiopathic pulmonary fibrosis (IPF). Affiliated With: Caring Voice Coalition; Second Wind Lung Transplant Association. Publications: *Action Alert*. Newsletter. Alternate Formats: online ● *Let's Talk About IPF*, annual. Brochure. Alternate Formats: online ● *Lung Transplantation: What Every Patient with IPF Should Know*, annual. Brochure. Alternate Formats: online ● *Pulmonary Rehabilitation and Oxygen Management for the IPF Patient*, annual. Brochure. Alternate Formats: online. Conventions/Meetings: seminar.

16009 ■ Congress of Lung Association Staff (CLAS)
1150 18th St. NW
Washington, DC 20036-3816
Ph: (202)785-3355
Fax: (202)452-1805
E-mail: jwidmer@lungusadc.org
URL: http://www.thoracic.org
Contact: Janet Widmer, Exec. Dir.
Founded: 1912. Members: 800. Membership Dues: individual, $25 (annual). Staff: 2. Budget: $200,000. Description: Professional society of executives and staff members of the American Lung Association. Sponsors network opportunities and staff development and training programs. Awards: Type: recognition. Computer Services: database, membership. Affiliated With: American Lung Association. Formerly: National Conference of Tuberculosis Secretar-

ies; (1968) National Conference of Tuberculosis Workers; (1973) National Respiratory Disease Conference. Publications: *CLAS Action Report*, quarterly ● Booklets ● Membership Directory, annual. Conventions/Meetings: annual meeting (exhibits) - usually May.

16010 ■ Cystic Fibrosis Foundation (CFF)
6931 Arlington Rd.
Bethesda, MD 20814
Ph: (301)951-4422
Free: (800)344-4823
Fax: (301)951-6378
E-mail: info@cff.org
URL: http://www.cff.org
Contact: Robert J. Beall PhD, Pres./CEO
Founded: 1955. Local Groups: 85. Nonmembership. Description: Supports medical research, professional education, and care centers to benefit patients with Cystic Fibrosis (CF), an inherited fatal disease among children and adults. (With this disease a thick mucus clogs the lungs, creating breathing difficulties and high susceptibility to infection; the digestive system and other organs are also affected.) Has more than 113 care centers affiliated with the foundation provide patient services. Conducts medical programs that provides support for a national network of multidisciplinary basic and clinical research grants. Awards: Clinical Research Grants. Frequency: annual. Type: grant. Recipient: for the study and treatment of CF ● Research Fellowship. Frequency: annual. Type: fellowship. Recipient: for clinical or research training, professional education, accreditation, and development of treatment centers. Computer Services: Mailing lists. Committees: Campaign Executive; CF Center; Medical Advisory Council; Patient Registry; Professional Education/Clinical Training; Research; Research Training. Councils: Research Development. Supersedes: Children's Exocrine Foundation; (1975) National Cystic Fibrosis Research Foundation. Publications: *Commitment*, quarterly. Newsletter. Features updates on research news and fund-raising news. Price: free. Circulation: 80,000. Alternate Formats: online ● Annual Report, annual ● Also publishes consumer fact sheets. Conventions/Meetings: annual North American Cystic Fibrosis Conference (exhibits) ● symposium, medical and scientific.

16011 ■ Cystic Fibrosis Worldwide (CFW)
c/o Ms. Christine Noke, Program Dir.
210 Park Ave., No. 267
Worcester, MA 01609
Ph: (508)733-6120
E-mail: info@cfww.org
URL: http://www.cfww.org
Contact: Ms. Christine Noke, Program Dir.
Founded: 2003. Languages: English, French, German, Italian, Spanish. Multinational. Description: Works to promote access to appropriate care and education for those people living with Cystic Fibrosis (CF) in developing countries. Improves the knowledge of CF among medical professionals and governments worldwide. Acts as an international platform for the exchange of information. Supports the search for a cure to Cystic Fibrosis. Promotes linkage between countries in order to share experiences, research and education. Awards: Research Project Grants. Frequency: annual. Type: grant. Recipient: for internationally relevant projects of a globally applicable nature ● Frequency: annual. Type: scholarship. Recipient: for individuals working in the field of clinical CF care wishing to improve their knowledge in a recognized CF center worldwide ● Training Courses for Allied Health Professionals. Frequency: annual. Type: grant. Recipient: for courses both in the applicant's country or abroad ● Visiting Expert. Frequency: annual. Type: grant. Recipient: for highly qualified CF experts. Telecommunication Services: electronic mail, cnoke@cfww.org. Publications: Newsletter. Alternate Formats: online ● Annual Report, annual. Alternate Formats: online.

16012 ■ Fundacion Alfa-1 de Puerto Rico
PO Box 6729
Bayamon, PR 00960-9007
Ph: (787)743-0268

Fax: (787)743-0268
E-mail: fundacion.alfa1@alfa1.org
URL: http://www.alfa1.org
Contact: Elaine Alfonzo, Pres.
Founded: 1996. **Staff:** 5. **Languages:** English, Portuguese, Spanish. **Nonmembership. Multinational. Description:** Offers support and education for the Spanish-speaking Alpha 1-Antitrypsin Deficiency patients and their families. Distributes Spanish educational materials. Works to increase awareness about Alpha 1-Antitrypsin Deficiency and the importance of early detection and treatment. **Computer Services:** Mailing lists. **Telecommunication Services:** electronic mail, ealfonzo@alfa1.org. **Affiliated With:** Alpha-1 Association. **Formerly:** (1999) Puerto Rico Alpha 1 Support Group. **Publications:** Brochures. Alternate Formats: online. **Conventions/Meetings:** annual symposium.

16013 ■ National Jewish Medical and Research Center (NJMRC)
1400 Jackson St.
Denver, CO 80206
Ph: (303)388-4461
Free: (800)222-5864
E-mail: lungline@njc.org
URL: http://www.nationaljewish.org
Contact: Michael Salem MD, Pres./CEO
Founded: 1899. **Staff:** 1,000. **Budget:** $85,000,000. **Description:** Focuses on treatment, research, and education in chronic respiratory diseases and immunological disorders such as asthma, tuberculosis, cystic fibrosis, chronic bronchitis, emphysema, interstitial lung disease, and systemic lupus erythematosus. Accepts non-sectarian patients of all ages. Disseminates information to the public. **Libraries: Type:** reference. **Holdings:** 15,000. **Awards: Frequency:** annual. **Type:** recognition. **Recipient:** for outstanding civic and community service. **Formed by Merger of:** National Jewish Hospital and Research Center; National Asthma Center. **Formerly:** (1978) National Jewish Hospital/National Asthma Center; (1998) National Jewish Center for Immunology and Respiratory Medicine. **Publications:** Lung Line Letter, quarterly. Newsletter. **Price:** free for members ● National Jewish Medical and Research Center—Annual Report. **Price:** free for members ● National Jewish Medical and Research Center—Medical Scientific Update, monthly. Newsletter. **Price:** free for members ● New Directions, quarterly. Newsletter. Updates the center's research programs. **Price:** free for members. **Conventions/Meetings:** annual board meeting - usually September.

16014 ■ Second Wind Lung Transplant Association
c/o Mary Hardy, Treas.
23609 Talbot St.
St. Clair Shores, MI 48082
Ph: (586)294-3162
Free: (888)855-9463
E-mail: secondwind@netzero.net
URL: http://www.2ndwind.org
Contact: Mary Hardy, Treas.
Founded: 1995. **Members:** 800. **Membership Dues:** patient/family, $25 (annual) ● professional, $50 (annual) ● corporate, $100 (annual) ● associate, $35 (annual). **Staff:** 3. **Description:** People who have received a lung transplant, or who are considering undergoing the procedure, and their families; health care professionals; corporations supplying medication, supplies, or services to people with respiratory diseases. Promotes improved quality of life for people with respiratory diseases. Serves as a forum for exchange of information among members. Sponsors establishment of lung transplant housing near transplantation centers for use by candidate and recipient transplant patients and their families. **Formerly:** (2003) Second Wind Organization. **Publications:** Air-Ways, bimonthly. Newsletter. Alternate Formats: online ● The Lung Transplantation Handbook. **Price:** $29.98. Also Cited As: Things You Should Know About Lung Transplantation: Before, During and After. **Conventions/Meetings:** annual Education Conference.

16015 ■ United Mitochondrial Disease Foundation (UMDF)
8085 Saltsburg Rd., Ste.201
Pittsburgh, PA 15239
Ph: (412)793-8077
Fax: (412)793-6477
E-mail: info@umdf.org
URL: http://www.umdf.org
Contact: Charles A. Mohan Jr., CEO/Exec. Dir.
Founded: 1995. **Members:** 3,000. **Membership Dues:** regular, outside U.S. and Canada, $60 (annual) ● regular, in U.S. and Canada, $50 (annual). **Staff:** 13. **Regional Groups:** 20. **State Groups:** 1. **Local Groups:** 1. **Description:** Promotes research and education for the diagnosis, treatment and cure of mitochondrial disorders; provides support to affected individuals and families. Patients, parents or guardians, friends, relatives, medical professionals, hospitals, and other organizations are welcome to contact the foundation for information. **Libraries: Type:** reference. **Holdings:** articles. **Subjects:** mitochondrial disease. **Awards:** Research grants. **Frequency:** annual. **Type:** grant. **Recipient:** for researchers conducting research about the diagnosis, treatments, and cures for mitochondrial disease. **Computer Services:** database, patient registry. **Boards:** Scientific Advisory; Trustees. **Programs:** Physician Education. **Publications:** Mitochondrial News, quarterly. Newsletter. Alternate Formats: online. **Conventions/Meetings:** annual Streams of Energy - symposium, both family and scientific tracks.

16016 ■ United States Adult Cystic Fibrosis Association (USACFA)
PO Box 1618
Gresham, OR 97030-0519
Ph: (503)669-3561
Fax: (503)669-3561
E-mail: cfroundtable@usacfa.org
URL: http://www.usacfa.org
Contact: Paul Feld, Pres.
Founded: 1990. **Description:** Provides a source of information for Cystic Fibrosis (CF) adults regarding the basis, nature and progression of the disease. Assists in the psycho-social aspects of coping with CF on a day-to-day basis. Provides a network and a forum for communication among adults who have CF, their families, and medical professionals. **Telecommunication Services:** electronic mail, pfeld@usacfa.org. **Publications:** CF Roundtable, quarterly. Newsletter. **Price:** $10.00 /year for individuals; $15.00 outside U.S.; $25.00 /year for institutions.

Reticuloendothelial System

16017 ■ Society for Leukocyte Biology (SLB)
9650 Rockville Pike
Bethesda, MD 20814
Ph: (301)634-7810
Fax: (301)634-7813
E-mail: slb@faseb.org
URL: http://www.leukocytebiology.org
Contact: Debbie Weinstein PhD, Exec. Dir.
Founded: 1954. **Members:** 1,000. **Membership Dues:** regular in U.S., $50 (annual). **Multinational. Description:** Persons holding MD and/or PhD degrees who conduct research with universities; private, industrial, and government institutes; hospital clinics; members of the pharmaceutical industry. Facilitates the association of persons studying the reticuloendothelial system; fosters research in the field. (The reticuloendothelial system comprises all the cells of the blood and body tissues, including macrophages, lymphocytes, and granulocytes. It is involved in the immune response and in inflammation and functions in host defense against such problems as malignancies, infection, and environmental pathogens.) Sponsors workshop on macrophage methodology. **Awards:** G. Jeanette Thorbecke Award. **Frequency:** annual. **Type:** recognition ● Marie T. Bonazinga Awards. **Type:** recognition. **Recipient:** for excellence in research relating to the biology of the macrophage ● Presidential Awards. **Type:** recognition. **Recipient:** for the best papers presented by

students in training ● Young Investigator Award. **Type:** recognition. **Recipient:** for the best paper by an investigator under the age of 36. **Computer Services:** Mailing lists. **Formerly:** (1988) Reticuloendothelial Society. **Publications:** Directory and Constitution, annual ● Journal of Leukocyte Biology, monthly ● SLB Newsletter, semiannual ● Books. **Conventions/Meetings:** periodic international conference ● annual meeting (exhibits) - usually October. 2007 Oct. 11-13, Cambridge, MA.

Reye's Syndrome

16018 ■ National Reye's Syndrome Foundation (NRSF)
426 N Lewis
PO Box 829
Bryan, OH 43506
Ph: (419)636-2679
Fax: (419)636-9897
E-mail: nrsf@reyessyndrome.org
URL: http://www.reyessyndrome.org
Contact: Ms. Kathleen Rohrbaugh, Office Mgr.
Founded: 1974. **Members:** 5,000. **Membership Dues:** regular, $25 (annual). **Staff:** 2. **Budget:** $90,000. **Regional Groups:** 6. **State Groups:** 47. **Local Groups:** 148. **Description:** Families of children who have had Reye's Syndrome; doctors, scientists, nurses, and other health professionals and concerned individuals. (Reye's Syndrome is a disease affecting the liver and brain. Cause and cure unknown, its mortality rate is over 57 percent. Death may occur within a few hours after onset.) Aims to disseminate information to the public and the medical community and to raise and provide funds for research into the cause, treatment, cure, and prevention of the disease through research grants to individual scientists. Gives support and guidance to families experiencing Reye's Syndrome; assists federal and state agencies in obtaining data on Reye's cases; encourages governmental funding of research. Promotes service through a resource clearinghouse, support groups, and referral services. Promotes awareness via lay-oriented literature, information services, professional training, lay/professional slide presentations, and emergency room posters. Sponsors National Reye's Syndrome Month in September. Compiles statistics; maintains speakers' bureau. **Libraries: Type:** reference. **Awards: Frequency:** annual. **Type:** grant. **Recipient:** based on merit of study as determined by scientific advisory board; must be related to the study of Reye's Syndrome. **Telecommunication Services:** additional toll-free number, (800)233-7393, information and counseling hotline. **Committees:** Aspirin. **Programs:** Trick-Or-Treat Information Packets. **Projects:** Awareness Campaigns, Research Campaigns. **Working Groups:** School Superintendent Mailing. **Absorbed:** (1985) Reye's Syndrome Society; (1990) American Reye's Syndrome Society. **Publications:** National Reye's Syndrome Foundation—In the News, biennial. Newsletter. **Price:** included in membership dues. **Circulation:** 5,000. **Conventions/Meetings:** annual meeting - usually June.

Rheumatic Diseases

16019 ■ American College of Rheumatology (ACR)
1800 Century Pl., Ste.250
Atlanta, GA 30345-4300
Ph: (404)633-3777
Fax: (404)633-1870
E-mail: acr@rheumatology.org
URL: http://www.rheumatology.org
Contact: Neil S. Birbaum MD, Pres.
Founded: 1934. **Members:** 8,200. **Membership Dues:** fellow (in U.S., Canada and Mexico), clinical (international), $355 (annual) ● researcher, $242 (annual) ● trainee, $100 (annual) ● emeritus, $50 (annual). **Staff:** 48. **Budget:** $11,500,000. **Multinational. Description:** Rheumatologists and rheumatology health professionals. Provides unified leadership in

research, education, and the care of people with rheumatic diseases. **Awards:** ACR Research and Education Foundation Awards. **Frequency:** annual. **Type:** monetary. **Recipient:** for students, health professionals, researchers and institutions. **Committees:** Education; Executive; Government Affairs; Journal Publications; Research; Rheumatologic Care. **Sections:** Pediatric Rheumatology; Rehabilitative Rheumatology. **Affiliated With:** Association of Rheumatology Health Professionals. **Formerly:** (1989) American Rheumatism Association. **Publications:** *ACR Membership Directory*, annual. Alternate Formats: online ● *ACR Scientific Program*, annual ● *Arthritis and Rheumatism*, monthly. Journal. Covers research and trends in the treatment and investigation in the field. Includes book reviews, calendar of events, and employment opportunities. **Price:** included in membership dues; $325.00 /year for nonmembers - individual; $699.00 /year for nonmembers - institution. ISSN: 0004-3591. **Circulation:** 9,000. **Advertising:** accepted. Alternate Formats: microform; online ● *Arthritis Care and Research*, quarterly. Journal. For health professionals interested in the rheumatic diseases. **Price:** $145.00 institution in U.S.; $82.00 individual in U.S.; $174.00 institution in Canada and Mexico; $109.00 individual in Canada and Mexico. ISSN: 0893-7524. **Circulation:** 1,500. **Advertising:** accepted. Alternate Formats: microform; online. **Conventions/Meetings:** annual meeting (exhibits).

16020 ■ American Juvenile Arthritis Organization (AJAO)
1330 W Peachtree St., Ste.100
Atlanta, GA 30309
Ph: (404)965-7538
Free: (800)283-7800
Fax: (404)872-9559
URL: http://www.arthritis.org/communities/juvenile_arthritis/about_ajao.asp
Contact: Renee Thomas, Chair
Founded: 1980. **Members:** 3,000. **Membership Dues:** regular, $20 (annual). **Staff:** 1. **State Groups:** 58. **Description:** Parents, health care professionals, and others interested in the problems of juvenile arthritis. Serves as advocate for the needs of those affected by juvenile arthritis. A council of the Arthritis Foundation. **Libraries: Type:** reference. **Awards: Type:** recognition. **Recipient:** for parents, young people and health professionals who have shown exceptional strength and leadership in dealing with juvenile arthritis. **Publications:** *Alternative Therapies for Arthritis: An A to Z Guide*. Book. **Price:** $13.95 ● *Arthritis in Children*. Brochure. **Price:** $22.00 ● *Arthritis Today*. Magazine. Brings latest news about arthritis care, treatment and research. ● *Kids Get Arthritis, Too*, bimonthly. Newsletter. Covers activities, current research, legislative topics, and medical and scientific updates. **Price:** $20.00 for nonmembers; included in membership dues ● *When Your Student Has Arthritis*. Brochure. Contains an overview of arthritis. Includes a checklist for student activities, education rights and how teachers can help. **Price:** $22.00. **Conventions/Meetings:** annual conference and regional meeting, national - always summer.

16021 ■ Arthritis Foundation (AF)
PO Box 7669
Atlanta, GA 30357-0669
Ph: (404)872-7100 (404)965-7888
Free: (800)568-4045
Fax: (404)872-0457
E-mail: contactus@arthritis.org
URL: http://www.arthritis.org
Contact: Dr. John H. Klippel MD, CEO/Pres.
Founded: 1948. **Members:** 700,000. **Staff:** 750. **Local Groups:** 71. **Description:** Seeks to: discover the cause and improve the methods for the treatment and prevention of arthritis and other rheumatic diseases; increase the number of scientists investigating rheumatic diseases; provide training in rheumatic diseases for more doctors; extend knowledge of arthritis and other rheumatic diseases to the lay public, emphasizing the socioeconomic as well as medical aspects of these diseases. **Awards: Frequency:** annual. **Type:** recognition. **Recipient:** for

writing. **Sections:** American Juvenile Arthritis Organization. **Formerly:** Arthritis and Rheumatism Foundation. **Publications:** *All You Need to Know About Back Pain*. Book. Contains information on how to manage your back problems. **Price:** $19.95 ● *Arthritis Today*, bimonthly. Magazine. Includes research reports and self-help tips from readers. **Price:** included in membership dues. ISSN: 0890-1120. **Circulation:** 700,000. **Advertising:** accepted ● *Bulletin on the Rheumatic Diseases*, bimonthly. Contains articles on developments in research and management of rheumatic diseases; geared for the nonrheumatologist. **Price:** free. ISSN: 0007-5248. **Circulation:** 12,000. Alternate Formats: online ● *Index of Rheumatology*, annual ● *Kids Get Arthritis Too*, bimonthly. Newsletter. Contains information on the family needs to live successfully with arthritis. **Price:** free for members. **Conventions/Meetings:** annual meeting.

16022 ■ Association of Rheumatology Health Professionals (ARHP)
c/o American Colorado of Rheumatology
1800 Century Pl., Ste.250
Atlanta, GA 30345-4300
Ph: (404)633-3777
Fax: (404)633-1870
E-mail: arhp@rheumatology.org
URL: http://www.rheumatology.org/arhp/index.asp
Contact: David Haag, Exec. Dir.
Founded: 1965. **Members:** 1,000. **Membership Dues:** student, associate, $75 (annual) ● emeritus, $25 (annual) ● individual, international, $125 (annual). **Staff:** 5. **Budget:** $700,000. **Description:** Advanced practice nurses, physician assistants, nurses, occupational and physical therapists, social workers, psychologists, vocational counselors, pharmacists, and other health professionals concerned with the practice, education, and research of rheumatic diseases. Seeks to establish a scientific base of knowledge to improve the quality and provision of health services to individuals with rheumatic diseases. Disseminates information regarding the study and treatment of rheumatic diseases. Develops and implements medical and scientific programs in the field of rheumatology. A division of the American College of Rheumatology. **Libraries: Type:** reference. **Holdings:** papers, reports. **Awards:** Addie Thomas Service Award. **Frequency:** annual. **Type:** recognition. **Recipient:** for individuals who have been active volunteers ● Distinguished Scholar Award. **Frequency:** annual. **Type:** recognition. **Recipient:** for exceptional achievements in scholarly activities in rheumatic diseases ● Membership Recruitment Award. **Frequency:** annual. **Type:** recognition. **Recipient:** for members who recruit the most number of new members in the present year ● President's Award. **Frequency:** annual. **Type:** recognition. **Recipient:** for outstanding service within the present year. **Computer Services:** Mailing lists. **Committees:** Education; Educational Products; Nominations; Practice; Research. **Subcommittees:** Program. **Task Forces:** Clinical Focus Course; Web Enhancement. **Formerly:** (1993) Arthritis Health Professions Association. **Publications:** *ARHP News*, quarterly. Newsletter. **Price:** included in membership dues ● *Arthritis Care and Research*, quarterly. Journal. **Price:** $145.00 institution in U.S.; $82.00 individual in U.S.; $174.00 institution in Canada and Mexico; $109.00 individual in Canada and Mexico. **Circulation:** 7,000. **Advertising:** accepted. Alternate Formats: online ● *Book for Clinicians*, periodic. Includes research updates. **Price:** included in membership dues. **Circulation:** 2,000. **Advertising:** accepted ● *Clinical Care in the Rheumatic Diseases*, periodic. Book. **Price:** $10.00 for members; $15.00 for nonmembers. **Conventions/Meetings:** annual Scientific Meeting, in conjunction with the American College of Rheumatology.

16023 ■ National Institute of Arthritis and Musculoskeletal and Skin Diseases Information Clearinghouse (NIAMS)
c/o National Institutes of Health
1 AMS Cir.
Bethesda, MD 20892-3675

Ph: (301)495-4484 (301)565-2966
Free: (877)22-NIAMS
Fax: (301)718-6366
E-mail: niamsinfo@mail.nih.gov
URL: http://www.niams.nih.gov
Contact: Dr. Stephen I. Katz, Dir.
Languages: English, Spanish. **Description:** Collects, publishes, and disseminates professional and public educational materials for persons concerned with Arthritis and musculoskeletal and skin diseases. **Formerly:** (1999) National Arthritis and Musculoskeletal and Skin Diseases Information Clearinghouse (NAMSIC). **Publications:** Reports.

16024 ■ National Sjogren's Syndrome Association (NSSA)
PO Box 22066
Beachwood, OH 44122
Ph: (216)292-3866
Free: (800)395-6772
Fax: (216)292-4955
E-mail: nickofohio@aol.com
URL: http://www.sjogrenssyndrome.org
Contact: Barbara Henry, Exec. Dir.
Founded: 1990. **Members:** 4,500. **Membership Dues:** family, individual, $25 (annual) ● regular, outside U.S., $35 (annual) ● friend, $50 (annual) ● investor, $100 (annual) ● life, $250 ● grantor, $500 (annual) ● humanitarian, $1,000 (annual). **Staff:** 6. **Budget:** $120,000. **Description:** Promotes public awareness of Sjogren's Syndrome; encourages research into the cause and cure of the disorder. Sponsors chapters and offers information to the medical community. Conducts educational and research programs; maintains speakers' bureau. **Libraries: Type:** open to the public. **Holdings:** 7; articles, books, periodicals, video recordings. **Subjects:** educating Sjogren's Syndrome. **Awards:** Fellow in Rheumatology. **Frequency:** annual. **Type:** scholarship ● Student of Ophthalmology. **Frequency:** annual. **Type:** scholarship. **Affiliated With:** National Organization for Rare Disorders. **Publications:** *Learning to Live with Sjogren's Syndrome*. Video. **Price:** $25.00 ● *Patient Education Series*, quarterly. **Advertising:** accepted ● *Sjogren's Digest*, quarterly. Newsletter. **Price:** included in membership dues. **Advertising:** accepted. **Conventions/Meetings:** annual conference (exhibits).

16025 ■ OsteoArthritis Research Society International (OARSI)
15000 Commerce Pkwy., Ste.C
Mount Laurel, NJ 08054
Ph: (856)439-1385
Fax: (856)439-0525
E-mail: oarsi@orsi.org
URL: http://www.oarsi.org
Contact: Martin Lotz MD, Pres.
Founded: 1990. **Membership Dues:** associate, $125 (annual) ● regular, $195 (annual) ● industry partner, $6,000 (annual) ● allied health professional, $125 (annual) ● student, $50 (annual). **Description:** Researchers and health care professionals with an interest in osteoarthritis. Seeks to promote and encourage fundamental and applied research on osteoarthritis and its treatment. Gathers and disseminates information on osteoarthritis and related research; sponsors educational programs. **Awards:** OARSI Basic Science Research Award. **Frequency:** annual. **Type:** monetary. **Recipient:** for basic research in the field of osteoarthritis ● OARSI Clinical Research Award. **Frequency:** annual. **Type:** monetary. **Recipient:** for excellence in clinical research related to osteoarthritis ● Student Scholarship. **Frequency:** periodic. **Type:** scholarship. **Recipient:** for students. **Committees:** Corporate Development; Publications; Scientific Advisory; Website. **Publications:** *OA Today*, quarterly. Newsletter ● *Osteoarthritis and Cartilage*, monthly. Journal. Includes information on osteoarthritis. **Price:** $257.00 /year for individuals; $695.00 /year for institutions. ISSN: 1063-4584. **Advertising:** accepted ● Membership Directory, annual. **Conventions/Meetings:** annual World Congress on Osteoarthritis - 2007 Dec. 6-9, Miami Beach, FL; 2008 Sept. 18-21, Rome, Italy.

16026 ■ Roger Wyburn-Mason and Jack M. Blount Foundation for the Eradication of Rheumatoid Disease (RDF)
7376 Walker Rd.
Fairview, TN 37062-8141
Ph: (615)799-1002
Fax: (615)799-1002
E-mail: admin@arthritistrust.org
URL: http://www.arthritistrust.org
Contact: Perry A. Chapdelaine, Exec. Dir./Sec.
Founded: 1982. **Members:** 60,000. **Membership Dues:** supporting, $15 (annual). **Staff:** 1. **Budget:** $1,570,000. **Multinational. Description:** Seeks to eradicate rheumatoid disease and related arthritis. Where funds are available, performs or supports research. Provides physician list recommends publications primarily to show various causes of arthritis and treatments that must be explored to achieve wellness. Does not seek to over-emphasize a particular treatment program, but encourages removing burdens that stress the immune system, thus permitting the body to recover. These burdens may include, but may not be limited to, proper nutrition, candidiasis, food allergies, microorganism infections, foci of infection from root canals or extracted teeth, intestinal tract, or mercury poisoning from amalgams or other forms of dental metals, plus storage of herbicides and pesticides in fatty (lipids) parts of cells. **Boards:** Controlling. **Committees:** Audit; Physician and Scientist Advisory. **Also Known As:** Rheumatoid Disease Foundation; The Arthritis Trust of America. **Publications:** *The Arthritis Trust Newsletter*, quarterly. Contains interesting articles related to arthritis such as causations of arthritis. **Price:** $15.00/year. **Circulation:** 3,000. Alternate Formats: online ● Also publishes several papers and articles on topics related to arthritis.

16027 ■ Sjogren's Syndrome Foundation (SSF)
6707 Democracy Blvd., Ste.325
Bethesda, MD 20817
Ph: (301)530-4420
Free: (800)475-6473
Fax: (301)530-4415
E-mail: staylor@sjogrens.org
URL: http://www.sjogrens.org
Contact: Steven Taylor, CEO
Founded: 1983. **Members:** 8,700. **Membership Dues:** in U.S., $32 (annual) ● in Canada, $38 (annual) ● overseas resident, $45 (annual) ● healthcare professional, $50 (annual). **Staff:** 4. **Budget:** $750,000. **Local Groups:** 80. **Multinational. Description:** Individuals who have Sjogren's Syndrome, xerostomia (dry mouth), or keratoconjunctivitis sicca (dry eyes); Specialists, Internists, Immunologists, Rheumatologists, Otolaryngologists, Ophthalmologists, Gynecologists, Gastroenterologists, Pulmonologists, Dermatologists, Neurologists, Urologists, pharmaceutical companies, and dentists. (Sjogren's Syndrome is a disorder marked by dryness of all mucous membranes, resulting from deficient secretion of the glands, particularly the lacrimal and salivary glands, those of the upper respiratory tract, the sweat glands, and the vaginal area. Approximately 50&percent; of Sjogren's Syndrome patients also have rheumatoid arthritis, lupus, or scleroderma.) Seeks to increase public awareness and medical knowledge about Sjogren's Syndrome, educate patients and their families, and allow patients to share information on coping with the syndrome. Supports research. Sponsors support groups with meetings in which doctors speak on aspects of the syndrome. Compiles statistics. **Libraries: Type:** reference. **Holdings:** audiovisuals. **Awards:** Outstanding Abstract Award. **Frequency:** annual. **Type:** recognition. **Recipient:** for distinguished research in the field ● Research Grant. **Frequency:** periodic. **Type:** grant. **Recipient:** for a team with innovative researched proposal regarding the field ● Student Fellowship. **Frequency:** annual. **Type:** monetary. **Recipient:** for medical or dental students working in the field. **Computer Services:** Mailing lists. **Formerly:** (1985) Moisture Seekers. **Publications:** *Moisture Seekers Newsletter*, monthly. Covers information on new products, treatments, and developments, status of

research, and discussion by specialists. **Price:** included in membership dues; $25.00 for nonmembers. **Circulation:** 11,000. **Advertising:** accepted ● *The New Sjogren's Syndrome Handbook*. **Price:** $24.00 for members; $28.00 for nonmembers ● Articles ● Brochure. **Conventions/Meetings:** periodic regional meeting ● semiannual symposium (exhibits).

16028 ■ Spondylitis Association of America (SAA)
PO Box 5872
Sherman Oaks, CA 91413
Ph: (818)981-1616
Free: (800)777-8189
E-mail: info@spondylitis.org
URL: http://www.spondylitis.org
Contact: Katherine Culpepper, Exec. Dir.
Founded: 1983. **Members:** 4,000. **Membership Dues:** regular, $25 (annual) ● in Canada/Mexico, $30 (annual) ● other foreign, $35 (annual) ● supporting, $50 (annual) ● sustaining, $100 (annual) ● sponsor, $250 (annual) ● patron, $500 (annual) ● President's Circle, $1,000 (annual). **Staff:** 9. **Description:** Individuals affected by Ankylosing Spondylitis, psoriatic spondylitis, spondylitis associated with inflammatory bowel/Crohn's disease, undifferentiated spondyloarthropathy, and Reiter's Syndrome; and their families and friends; health care professionals; scientific researchers. (Ankylosing Spondylitis is a chronic condition most often affecting those between 17-40 years of age and characterized by pain or stiffness in the back. Although the cause and cure are not known, the condition may be managed through a program of medicines, posture awareness, and regular, therapeutic exercise; it is believed to be a hereditary condition.) Disseminates information; promotes public awareness and research; conducts educational programs; sponsors national support groups. **Libraries: Type:** reference. **Formerly:** (1993) Ankylosing Spondylitis Association. **Publications:** *A Family of Related Diseases*. Booklet ● *Back in Action*. Videos. **Price:** $15.00 ● *Guidebook for Patients* ● *Juvenile AS*. Booklet ● *Physical Therapy Exercises*. Audiotapes ● *Spondylitis Plus*, bimonthly. Newsletter. Includes information on treatment, research, and coping with the condition. **Price:** included in membership dues. **Circulation:** 10,000. **Advertising:** accepted ● *Straight Talk on Spondylitis*. Book. **Price:** $14.00 ● *The Water Workout*. Video. **Price:** $15.00. **Conventions/Meetings:** periodic StoPain - symposium ● annual symposium (exhibits).

Russian

16029 ■ Russian American Medical Association (R-AMA)
36100 Euclid Ave., Ste.330-B
Willoughby, OH 44094
Ph: (440)953-8055
Fax: (440)953-0242
E-mail: info@russiandoctors.org
URL: http://www.russiandoctors.org
Contact: Boris Vinogradsky MD, Chm.
Founded: 2002. **Membership Dues:** practicing physician, $100 (annual) ● full-time researcher, $30 (annual) ● resident, student, $15 (annual). **Multinational. Description:** Serves as a forum to facilitate and enable Russian American medical professionals to excel in patient care, teaching and research. Advances the professional and educational qualifications of medical professionals and students in the United States. Provides medical support and assistance to medically indigent residents. **Computer Services:** Online services, discussion forum. **Telecommunication Services:** electronic mail, boris@russiandoctors.org. **Programs:** Charitable Foundation; Heart Health Awareness; Medical Missions; Observanship; Partnership; Research Collaboration; Scholarship. **Publications:** *R-AMA Journal*. Alternate Formats: online.

Safety

16030 ■ International Healthcare Safety Professional Certification Board (IHSPCB)
11900 Parklawn Dr., Ste.451
Rockville, MD 20852

Ph: (301)770-2540
Fax: (301)770-2183
E-mail: info@chcm-chsp.org
URL: http://www.chcm-chsp.org
Contact: Harold M. Gordon, Exec.Dir.
Founded: 1976. **Description:** Individuals working or consulting in hospitals or healthcare facilities who are responsible for the handling and control of hazardous materials. Areas of concern include: emergency and disaster planning; biological, chemical, and physical hazards; ventilation; fire prevention and protection; maintenance and engineering; personal protective equipment; sanitation; life safety code. Grants affiliate, associate, and executive level distinctions for the title of Certified Healthcare Safety Professional. Encourages exchange of ideas and information to improve performance. Sponsors HSP Academy, which conducts professional development activities. **Publications:** *A Management Approach to Hazard Control*. Book. Provides presentation of the management principles, concepts and techniques that should be employed to achieve an effective Hazard Control Program. **Price:** $8.95/copy, plus $1.75 for postage; $7.25 for diplomates, $1.75 for postage ● *Directory of Certified Healthcare Safety Professionals*, annual ● *Healthcare Hazard Control and Safety Management*. Book. Provides candidates with focus and direction regarding the CHSP certification examination. ● Brochure.

16031 ■ International Sharps Injury Prevention Society (ISIPS)
10046 Prestwick Cir.
South Jordan, UT 84095
Ph: (801)280-8797
Fax: (801)280-8798
E-mail: info@yisips.org
URL: http://www.isips.org
Contact: Ron Stoker, Exec. Dir.
Membership Dues: profitable company, $4,000 (annual) ● not-currently-profitable company, $1,500 (annual) ● gold, $10,000 (annual) ● platinum charter, $15,000 (annual). **Multinational. Description:** Aims to reduce the number of accidental sharps injury cases by promoting the use of safety-engineered products and services. Provides information on needlestick and sharps injuries, and related healthcare issues. Maintains the "Sharps Injury Prevention Center", an online information resource that features educational presentations on various sharps safety and blood exposure prevention products, and safety practices that help reduce needlestick and blood exposure. **Awards:** Sharps Injury Prevention Award. **Frequency:** annual. **Type:** recognition. **Recipient:** for outstanding achievement in needlestick reduction. **Telecommunication Services:** electronic mail, ron@isips.org. **Publications:** *ISIPS Newsletter*, weekly. Contains the latest information on sharps injury prevention, needlesticks, and other infection control issues. Alternate Formats: online.

16032 ■ National Alliance for the Primary Prevention of Sharps Injuries (NAPPSI)
126 Main St.
PO Box 10
Milner, GA 30257
Ph: (770)358-7860
Fax: (770)358-6793
E-mail: info@nappsi.org
URL: http://www.nappsi.org
Contact: Ms. Lynn Hadaway, Exec. Dir.
Description: Strives to promote techniques, technologies, and practices that must be employed for primary prevention of sharps injuries. Primary prevention is the total removal of sharp devices from the healthcare workplace while secondary prevention is the re-engineering of sharp devices to render them safer. Primary and secondary prevention must both be employed to reach the safest healthcare environment. Provides resources, education and solutions to minimize sharps exposure. **Awards:** Sharps Safety Award. **Frequency:** annual. **Type:** recognition. **Recipient:** for healthcare facilities that have instituted primary prevention methods to create a safer environment for their workers. **Computer Services:** database, lists of safety devices ● information services,

featured technologies ● information services, primary prevention resources. **Publications:** Newsletter.

16033 ■ National Organization of Alternative Programs (NOAP)
PO Box 10703
Austin, TX 78766
Ph: (512)467-7027
E-mail: administration@alternativeprograms.org
URL: http://www.alternativeprograms.org
Contact: Laura Clarkson RN, Pres.

Founded: 1999. **Membership Dues:** full, $200 (annual) ● associate, $150 (annual) ● organizational, $400 (annual). **Description:** Promotes public safety through the development and maintenance of programs that serve as alternatives to licensure discipline. Fosters safe practice and retention of health care professionals through monitoring, rehabilitation, and recovery in alternative programs. Encourages research, education, ethical practices and standardization of alternative programs. **Publications:** Newsletter, quarterly. **Price:** included in membership dues, for members only ● Membership Directory, annual. **Price:** included in membership dues ● Brochure. Alternate Formats: online.

Sanitarians

16034 ■ American Academy of Sanitarians (AAS)
c/o Gary Noonan, Exec. Sec.-Treas.
1568 LeGrand Cir.
Lawrenceville, GA 30043-8191
Ph: (678)407-1051
Fax: (678)407-1051
E-mail: gnoonan@charter.net
URL: http://sanitarians.org
Contact: Gary Noonan, Exec. Sec.-Treas.

Founded: 1966. **Members:** 250. **Membership Dues:** diplomate, $50 (annual). **Description:** Legally registered sanitarians who possess at least a master's degree in public health, environmental health sciences, or environmental management. Aims to improve the environmental health status of humanity through certification of those sanitarians who have helped or who are helping to achieve this long-range goal. **Awards:** Davis Calvin Wagner Sanitarian Award. **Frequency:** annual. **Type:** recognition. **Recipient:** for excellence in the practice of environmental public health. **Formerly:** American Intersociety Academy for Certification of Sanitarians. **Publications:** Register of Professional Sanitarians, quinquennial ● Roster of Diplomates, annual ● Newsletter, semiannual. **Conventions/Meetings:** annual meeting, held in conjunction with National Environmental Health Association (exhibits) - always June.

16035 ■ American Association of Medical Milk Commissions (AAMMC)
c/o Dr. Paul Fleiss, MD, Pres.
1824 N Hillhurst Ave.
Los Angeles, CA 90027
Ph: (323)664-1977
Fax: (323)664-0870
E-mail: fleiss@usc.edu
Contact: Dr. Paul Fleiss MD, Pres.

Founded: 1907. **Members:** 5. **Description:** Professional society of physician members of local Medical Milk Commissions, including veterinarians, sanitarians, and bacteriologists who supervise production of certified milk (milk from dairies conforming to official standards of sanitation). **Libraries: Type:** open to the public. **Committees:** Methods and Standards; Research. **Publications:** Methods and Standards for the Production of Certified Milk, annual. **Conventions/Meetings:** meeting - in June.

16036 ■ National Restaurant Association Quality Assurance Study Group
c/o National Restaurant Association
1200 17th St. NW
Washington, DC 20036
Ph: (202)331-5900 (202)973-3678
Free: (800)424-5156

Fax: (202)331-2429
E-mail: jcolindres@dineout.org
URL: http://www.restaurant.org/studygroups/qa/index.cfm
Contact: Steven C. Anderson CAE, Pres./CEO

Members: 208. **Description:** Professional quality assurance and quality control personnel sanitarians from the National Restaurant Association working in foodservice facilities. Provides members with the opportunity to share common goals, concerns, ideas, and problems. Conducts research and educational programs and semiannual study group meeting. **Computer Services:** Mailing lists.

Scalp

16037 ■ National Alopecia Areata Foundation (NAAF)
PO Box 150760
San Rafael, CA 94915-0760
Ph: (415)472-3780
Fax: (415)472-5343
E-mail: info@naaf.org
URL: http://www.naaf.org
Contact: Vicki Kalabokes, CEO

Founded: 1981. **Members:** 56,000. **Staff:** 8. **Budget:** $1,000,002. **Regional Groups:** 4. **State Groups:** 6. **Local Groups:** 2. **National Groups:** 65. **Description:** Individuals concerned about alopecia areata, a disease causing partial scalp hair loss, total scalp hair loss (alopecia totalis), or total loss of body hair (alopecia universalis); cause and cure are unknown and the course of the disease is unpredictable. Objectives are to: develop public awareness of the disease; provide a support network; raise funds for research; keep patients medically informed with explanations about AA and the latest treatments. Maintains medical advisory board; operates information booth at meetings of the American Academy of Dermatology. **Libraries: Type:** not open to the public. **Holdings:** 250; books, periodicals. **Subjects:** dermatology, immunology research, hair biology, alopecia areata. **Awards:** National Alopecia Areata Foundation Research Grants. **Frequency:** annual. **Type:** grant. **Recipient:** for research on Alopecia Areata. **Committees:** Government Relations; Mental Health. **Affiliated With:** National Health Council; National Organization for Rare Disorders. **Publications:** National Alopecia Areata Foundation Newsletter, quarterly. Covers treatment, research, and developments. Includes wig and cosmetic tips. **Price:** included with donation of $35 or more. **Circulation:** 1,000. **Advertising:** accepted ● Also publishes medical description of AA and assorted brochures. **Conventions/Meetings:** annual International Patients Conference (exhibits) - in summer.

Scleroderma

16038 ■ International Scleroderma Network (ISN)
7455 France Ave. S, No. 266
Edina, MN 55435
Ph: (952)831-3091
Free: (800)564-7099
E-mail: isn@sclero.org
URL: http://www.sclero.org
Contact: Shelley Ensz, Founder/Pres.

Founded: 2002. **Membership Dues:** email, $25 (annual) ● postal, $35 (annual). **Languages:** English, French, German, Greek, Hebrew, Hungarian, Italian, Japanese, Korean, Portuguese, Russian, Spanish. **Multinational. Description:** Provides medical and support information about scleroderma in several languages. Raises awareness on scleroderma and other related illnesses. Supports international research in collaboration with the Scleroderma Clinical Trials Consortium. Maintains an online support community. **Telecommunication Services:** electronic mail, shelley-ensz@sclero.org. **Publications:** ISN Insider, quarterly. Newsletter. Includes an "Ask the Doctor" column by leading world experts in scleroderma. **Price:** included in membership dues ● Voices

of Scleroderma. Book. Contains medical and support information for scleroderma patients and caregivers. **Price:** $25.00/copy, plus shipping and handling ● Brochure (in English, Japanese, and Spanish). Alternate Formats: online.

16039 ■ Juvenile Scleroderma Network (JSDN)
1204 W 13th St.
San Pedro, CA 90731
Ph: (310)519-9511
Free: (866)338-5892
E-mail: jsdinfo@jsdn.org
URL: http://www.jsdn.org
Contact: Kathy Gaither, Pres./Founder

Founded: 1999. **Membership Dues:** regular, in U.S., $20 (annual) ● regular, outside U.S., $25 (annual). **Description:** Children afflicted with scleroderma, parents and families, and doctors. Provides online support, pen-pal programs, information, facts, and literature. **Programs:** Family Outreach. **Publications:** For Kids' Sake. Newsletter. Alternate Formats: online.

16040 ■ Scleroderma Foundation (SF)
300 Rosewood Dr., Ste.105
Danvers, MA 01923
Ph: (978)463-5843
Free: (800)722-4673
E-mail: sfinfo@scleroderma.org
URL: http://www.scleroderma.org
Contact: Mr. Joseph Camerino, Chm.

Founded: 1983. **Members:** 16,000. **Membership Dues:** individual in U.S., $25 (annual) ● individual outside U.S., $35 (annual). **Staff:** 7. **Budget:** $1,300,000. **Regional Groups:** 75. **Description:** Scleroderma organizations. Promotes medical research to find a cure for scleroderma, a chronic systemic disease affecting all organs resulting from uncontrolled growth of connective tissue. Seeks to foster an understanding of the disease through media and outreach programs; raises funds. Provides patients with educational materials and referrals to local organizations and medical specialists. Offers encouragement and consultation services towards the formation and development of local support groups. Acts as a clearinghouse for information about scleroderma research, drugs, and therapies. Conducts accredited programs for professionals. Maintains speakers' bureau; compiles statistics. Funds one million dollars a year in new research. **Libraries: Type:** reference. **Awards:** Research Grant. **Frequency:** annual. **Type:** grant. **Recipient:** for medical research. **Computer Services:** Mailing lists. **Boards:** Medical Advisory. **Committees:** Advocacy; Awareness; Publications; Technology. **Absorbed:** (1992) Scleroderma Association of New England. **Formerly:** (1984) International Scleroderma Federation; (1998) Scleroderma Federation. **Publications:** About Scleroderma. Brochure ● Helpful Hints for Living with Scleroderma ● Newsline, quarterly. **Price:** included in membership dues ● Scleroderma Voice, quarterly. Magazine. Features latest research and treatments, articles and practical tips. **Price:** included in membership dues ● Understanding and Managing Scleroderma. Booklet. **Conventions/Meetings:** annual conference, for patient and physician education (exhibits).

16041 ■ Scleroderma Research Foundation (SRF)
220 Montgomery St., Ste.1411
San Francisco, CA 94104
Ph: (415)834-9444
Free: (800)441-CURE
Fax: (415)834-9177
E-mail: info@sclerodermaresearch.org
URL: http://www.srfcure.org
Contact: Luke Evnin PhD, Chm.

Founded: 1978. **Staff:** 6. **Regional Groups:** 1. **Languages:** English, Greek. **Description:** Seeks to find a cure for scleroderma, a life-threatening and degenerative illness. Funds and facilitates research and public awareness. **Libraries: Type:** not open to the public. **Holdings:** 200; articles. **Subjects:** Scleroderma. **Awards:** SRF Postdoctoral Fellowship

Awards. **Frequency:** annual. **Type:** fellowship. **Recipient:** for outstanding postdoctoral fellows with strong records of accomplishment ● Thomas Jefferson University Grant. **Type:** grant. **Recipient:** for research projects. **Computer Services:** Mailing lists. **Boards:** Scientific Advisory. **Programs:** Cure Advocate; Government Affairs. **Affiliated With:** Scleroderma Foundation. **Publications:** *Scleroderma Handbook & Resource Guide* ● *Scleroderma Research Foundation Newsletter*, semiannual. **Price:** included in membership dues. **Circulation:** 1,500. **Advertising:** accepted. Alternate Formats: online.

16042 ■ Scleroderma Support Group (SSG)
18 Talbot Manor
Cranston, RI 02905
Ph: (401)781-5013
E-mail: scleroderma@hotmail.com
URL: http://ri.sclerodermasupportgroup.net
Contact: Carole Cowell, Pres.
Founded: 1989. **Members:** 1,000. **Membership Dues:** regular, $20 (annual). **State Groups:** 2. **Languages:** English, German, Spanish. **Description:** Scleroderma patients and interested individuals. Serves as a support group for patients. Provides information; raises funds for research; holds medical meetings and rap sessions. **Conventions/Meetings:** bimonthly meeting.

Scoliosis

16043 ■ Adolescent Scoliosis Society of North America
PO Box 1178
Rocky Mount, NC 27802-1178
Fax: (252)754-8268
E-mail: jmoste84@aol.com
URL: http://www.teenscolinet.org
Contact: Justin Oswalt, Pres.
Members: 100. **Description:** Aims to help scoliosis patients and their families deal with the diagnosis and treatment of scoliosis. Seeks to obtain support and participation from scoliosis physicians and their staff to help the patient, parent, and family. Provides physical scoliosis treatment, support and information. **Publications:** *Scoliocity*, periodic. Newsletter.

16044 ■ National Scoliosis Foundation (NSF)
5 Cabot Pl.
Stoughton, MA 02072-4624
Free: (800)673-6922
Fax: (781)341-8333
E-mail: nsf@scoliosis.org
URL: http://www.scoliosis.org
Contact: Joseph P. O'Brien, Pres./CEO
Founded: 1976. **Members:** 25,000. **Budget:** $140,000. **State Groups:** 3. **Description:** Supporters are businesses, organizations, and individuals concerned with the early detection and prevention of progressing scoliosis, kyphosis, and structural lordosis. Purposes are to promote programs and activities leading to the elimination of the crippling effects of scoliosis and to educate the public about all abnormal spinal curvatures. Assists local groups in identifying available medical resources and personnel to help conduct volunteer screening programs; encourages legislation requiring scoliosis screening for each student in the 5th through 10th grades throughout the US. Maintains resource center for individuals or schools seeking information on abnormal spinal curvatures. **Committees:** Benefit; Development; Education; Legal; Public Relations; Volunteer Services. **Publications:** *Spinal Connection*, biennial. Newsletter. Contains information about the different activities for members. **Price:** free. **Circulation:** 25,000 ● Booklets ● Brochures ● Manuals ● Also publishes resource lists and produces school audiovisual materials. **Conventions/Meetings:** annual meeting.

16045 ■ Scoliosis Association, Inc. (SAI)
PO Box 811705
Boca Raton, FL 33481-1705
Ph: (561)994-4435
Free: (800)800-0669

Fax: (561)994-2455
E-mail: normlipin@aol.com
URL: http://www.scoliosis-assoc.org
Contact: Stanley Sacks, CEO
Founded: 1976. **Members:** 5,000. **Membership Dues:** individual, in U.S., $20 (annual) ● professional, in U.S., $50 (annual) ● individual, foreign, $30 (annual) ● professional, foreign, $60 (annual) ● general public, $20 (annual). **Local Groups:** 52. **Description:** Individuals or families involved or interested in scoliosis (lateral or sidewards curvature of the spine). Educates the public about scoliosis and other spinal deviations. Encourages and supports spinal screening programs in schools throughout the U.S. and Canada. Sponsors the formation of scoliosis chapters throughout the country which serve as support groups for the scoliosis patient and his or her family. Aids the patient in attaining a positive social and emotional adjustment during treatment of scoliosis. Plans to compile statistics; works with researchers in scoliosis. Raises funds for scoliosis research. Has sponsored scoliosis spinal conferences with several hospitals and leading spinal orthopaedists. **Libraries: Type:** reference. **Holdings:** articles, audiovisuals, books, papers, periodicals, video recordings. **Publications:** *Backtalk*, periodic. Newsletter. Contains research and chapter news, article reprints, book reviews, and listings of publications. **Price:** $30.00 for individuals outside U.S.; $40.00 for institutions. **Circulation:** 5,000. **Advertising:** accepted ● *Scoliosis, An Adult Perspective*. Video. **Price:** $19.95 ● Bibliography. Lists books, articles, pamphlets, and papers on scoliosis. **Price:** $6.00 for part one; $3.00 for part two; $8.00 for parts one and two ● Brochure ● Also issues posters. **Conventions/Meetings:** biennial board meeting.

16046 ■ Scoliosis Research Society (SRS)
555 E Wells St., Ste.1100
Milwaukee, WI 53202-3823
Ph: (414)289-9107
Fax: (414)276-3349
E-mail: info@srs.org
URL: http://www.srs.org
Contact: Tressa Goulding CAE, Exec. Dir.
Founded: 1966. **Members:** 870. **Staff:** 3. **Multinational. Description:** Orthopedic surgeons and physicians. Furthers research and education in spinal deformities, particularly scoliosis, a twisting of the spine to one side. Most cases are of unknown cause, though scoliosis can result from a birth defect, polio, or spinal injury and usually develops in children during the growth spurt between ages ten to fifteen. Early detection followed with use of a brace and exercise can halt the curvature and prevent deformity. **Awards: Frequency:** periodic. **Type:** grant. **Committees:** Adult Deformity; Aging Spine; Etiology; Global Outreach; Historical; Instrumentation; International Affairs; Morbidity and Mortality. **Publications:** *SRS Textbook - Spinal Deformities the Comprehensive Text*. Contains all the facts and information necessary to successfully manage spinal deformities. **Price:** $259.95/copy. **Conventions/Meetings:** annual conference and meeting, scientific - mid September. 2007 Sept. 4-8, Edinburgh, United Kingdom; 2008 Sept. 9-13, Salt Lake City, UT.

Semantics

16047 ■ International Society of Neuro-Semantics (ISNS)
c/o L. Michael Hall, PhD, Co-Founder
PO Box 8
Clifton, CO 81520
Ph: (970)523-7877
Fax: (970)523-5790
E-mail: meta@onlinecol.com
URL: http://www.neurosemantics.com
Contact: L. Michael Hall PhD, Co-Founder
Founded: 1996. **Membership Dues:** regular, $25 (annual). **Multinational. Description:** Works to model the structure of excellence, expertise, and mastery of Neuro-Semantics. Aims to eliminate the knowing-doing gap that prevents the full experiencing

of the great ideas and principles. Applies Meta-States to new areas and develops new models and patterns that affect health and fitness, leadership, cultural change, and political change. **Publications:** Brochures. Alternate Formats: online.

Sexual Health

16048 ■ Abstinence Clearinghouse
801 E 41st St.
Sioux Falls, SD 57105
Ph: (605)335-3643
Free: (888)577-2966
E-mail: info@abstinence.net
URL: http://www.abstinence.net
Contact: Leslee J. Unruh, Pres./Founder
Founded: 1997. **Members:** 1,800. **Membership Dues:** friend, $25 (semiannual) ● hand-holder, $50 (annual) ● embracer, $180 (annual) ● engager, $480 (annual) ● diamond, $1,500 (biennial). **Staff:** 25. **Regional Groups:** 1. **State Groups:** 1. **Local Groups:** 1. **Description:** Promotes the practice of sexual abstinence through age-appropriate, factual and medically-accurate materials. **Libraries: Type:** open to the public. **Holdings:** 1,600; books, periodicals, video recordings. **Subjects:** marriage, family, abstinence, dating, sex. **Computer Services:** Mailing lists ● online services, technical assistance to SPRANS and Title V grantees. **Councils:** International Abstinence; Medical Abstinence; National Advisory. **Publications:** *Abstinence Clearinghouse Directory of Abstinence Resources*, semiannual. Contains abstinence-until-marriage resources. **Price:** $20.00. **Advertising:** accepted ● *The Abstinence Network*, quarterly. Newsletter. Assists those working with young people to abstain from premarital sexual intercourse. **Conventions/Meetings:** annual International Abstinence Leadership Conference (exhibits).

16049 ■ American Association of Sexuality Educators, Counselors and Therapists (AASECT)
PO Box 1960
Ashland, VA 23005-4960
Ph: (804)752-0026
Fax: (804)752-0056
E-mail: aasect@aasect.org
URL: http://www.aasect.org
Contact: Stephen Conley PhD, Exec. Dir.
Founded: 1967. **Members:** 1,700. **Membership Dues:** student, $90 (annual) ● retired, $110 (annual) ● individual, $195 (annual) ● institutional, $475 (annual) ● certified individual, $225 (annual). **Staff:** 4. **Budget:** $350,000. **Regional Groups:** 4. **Multinational. Description:** Represents professionals concerned with sex education, counseling, and therapy; and students pursuing degrees in the field. Certifies sex educators, counselors, and therapists. Provides educational services. Acts as a referral service for the general public. **Libraries: Type:** not open to the public. **Telecommunication Services:** electronic mail, drsconley@aasect.org. **Committees:** Certification; Continuing Education; Ethics; Public Relations. **Formerly:** (1976) American Association of Sex Educators and Counselors. **Publications:** *Contemporary Sexuality*, monthly. Newsletter. **Price:** $42.00. **Conventions/Meetings:** annual conference (exhibits) ● annual The Tapestry of Sexuality: Focus on Legal and Ethical Issues - conference.

16050 ■ American Board of Sexology (ABS)
PO Box 1166
Winter Park, FL 32790-1166
Ph: (407)645-1641 (407)574-5708
Free: (800)533-3521
Fax: (407)574-8943
E-mail: billeast@cfl.rr.com
URL: http://www.sexologist.org
Contact: William B. Easterling PhD, Pres.
Founded: 1986. **Membership Dues:** general, $200 (triennial). **Description:** Aims to take certification out of area of subjectivity to a process based on academic achievement in the field of clinical sexology.

16051 ■ Council for Sex Information and Education (CSIE)
2272 Colorado Blvd., No. 1228
Los Angeles, CA 90041
Fax: (323)344-8594
Contact: Joel Adams, Dir.
Founded: 1977. **Description:** A national clearinghouse for information on sexuality and related topics. Premise is that adequate knowledge and understanding of sexuality contributes not only to sexual well-being but to physical and emotional well-being and that helpful information should be readily available. **Formerly:** Sex Information Council of America.

16052 ■ Exodus Trust (ET)
1523 Franklin St.
San Francisco, CA 94109
Ph: (415)928-1133
Fax: (415)928-8061
Contact: Ted McIlvenna, Pres.
Founded: 1968. **Staff:** 9. **Description:** Established to: educate and train professionals interested in sex counseling, therapy, education, or research; provide sex education, counseling, and therapy for adults; research human sexuality; produce films, slides, and literature for use in sex counseling, therapy, and education. Conducts continuing education programs for physicians and nurses, and workshops and counseling programs for professional and laypeople in San Francisco, CA and other cities. **Convention/Meeting:** none. **Formerly:** (1989) National Sex Forum.

16053 ■ Family Care International (FCI)
588 Broadway, Ste.503
New York, NY 10012
Ph: (212)941-5300
Fax: (212)941-5563
E-mail: info@familycareintl.org
URL: http://familycareintl.org
Contact: James Sligar Esq., Sec.
Founded: 1986. **National Groups:** 170. **Multinational. Description:** Works to improve women's sexual and reproductive health and rights in developing countries, especially safer pregnancy and childbirth.

16054 ■ International Professional Surrogates Association (IPSA)
3428 Motor Ave.
Los Angeles, CA 90034
Ph: (310)836-1662
E-mail: info@surrogatetherapy.org
URL: http://www.ipsa.us
Contact: Vena Blanchard DHS, Pres.
Founded: 1973. **Members:** 40. **Membership Dues:** certified surrogate partner, $50 (annual) ● therapist, $25 (annual) ● associate, $25 (annual). **Staff:** 1. **Multinational. Description:** Aims to provide information, training, and referrals. Offers therapists referrals to certified professional surrogate partners and client referrals to sex therapists and surrogate-and-therapist teams, who have expertise in Surrogate Partner Therapy. Sponsors initial training for surrogate partners, and provides continuing education to sex therapists, psychotherapists, and surrogate partners. Sponsors personal enrichment courses for individuals and couples. The Code of Ethics established by the association helps maintain the highest professional standards within the field of Surrogate Partner Therapy. **Libraries: Type:** by appointment only. **Holdings:** archival material, articles, books, clippings, films, papers. **Subjects:** surrogate partner therapy, surrogate-assisted therapy, sex therapy, sex surrogates. **Computer Services:** Information services, providing information and referrals. **Additional Websites:** http://www.surrogatepartners.org, http://www.surrogatetherapy.org. **Committees:** Ethics; Training. **Affiliated With:** American Association of Sexuality Educators, Counselors and Therapists; Society for the Scientific Study of Sexuality; Society for the Scientific Study of Sexuality, Western Region. **Publications:** *Code of Ethics.* Brochure. Alternate Formats: online ● *Intensive Therapy.* Brochure. Alternate Formats: online ● *IPSA Training.* Brochure. Alternate Formats: online ● *Membership Newsletter* ● *Sur-*

rogate Partner Therapy. Brochure. Alternate Formats: online. **Conventions/Meetings:** periodic conference, continuing education for surrogate partners and therapists.

16055 ■ International Society for the Study of Women's Sexual Health (ISSWSH)
1111 N Plaza Dr., Ste.550
Schaumburg, IL 60173
Ph: (847)517-7225
Fax: (847)517-7229
E-mail: info@isswsh.org
URL: http://www.isswsh.org
Contact: Wendy J. Weiser, Exec. Dir.
Membership Dues: active, affiliate, $95 (annual). **Multinational. Description:** Provides opportunities for communication among scholars, researchers, and practitioners about women's sexual function and experience. Supports high standards of ethics and professionalism in research, education, and clinical practice of women's sexuality. Seeks to provide the public with accurate information about women's sexuality and sexual health. **Publications:** *Journal of Sex and Marital Therapy.* Also Cited As: *JSMT* ● Books. Contains information from past meetings of the association. **Price:** $30.00 for members; $75.00 for nonmembers.

16056 ■ Sexual Medicine Society of North America (SMS)
1111 N Plaza Dr., Ste.550
Schaumburg, IL 60173
Ph: (847)517-7225
Fax: (847)517-7229
E-mail: sms@wjweiser.com
URL: http://www.smsna.org
Contact: Wendy J. Weiser, Exec. Dir.
Founded: 1994. **Membership Dues:** active, corresponding, industry, $100 (annual). **Description:** Aims to further the understanding of the science of human sexual function and dysfunction. Promotes, encourages and supports high standards of practice, research, education, and ethics in the study of the anatomy, physiology, pathology, diagnosis, and treatment of human sexual function and dysfunction. Provides a forum for the exchange and discussion of ideas, thoughts and concepts in the field of sexual medicine. **Awards:** Fellowship Award. **Frequency:** annual. **Type:** fellowship. **Recipient:** for research relating to erectile dysfunction. **Telecommunication Services:** electronic mail, sueo@wjweiser.com. **Affiliated With:** American Urological Association; International Society for Sexual Medicine. **Publications:** Reports. Alternate Formats: online. **Conventions/Meetings:** annual meeting - 2007 Dec. 6-9, Chicago, IL.

16057 ■ Sexuality Information and Education Council of the U.S. (SIECUS)
130 W 42nd St., Ste.350
New York, NY 10036-7802
Ph: (212)819-9770
Fax: (212)819-9776
E-mail: siecus@siecus.org
URL: http://www.siecus.org
Contact: Joseph DiNorcia Jr., Pres./CEO
Founded: 1964. **Staff:** 21. **Budget:** $1,378,972. **Languages:** English, Spanish. **Description:** Promotes education about sexuality. Advocates "the right of individuals to make responsible sexual choices". Disseminates information. **Libraries: Type:** by appointment only; reference; open to the public. **Holdings:** 7,000; archival material, books, clippings, periodicals. **Subjects:** sexuality education, human sexuality. **Computer Services:** Mailing lists, of members. **Divisions:** Education Programs and Computer Services; Information and Library Services; Management; Public Relations. **Sections:** Educational Services; Public Information. **Formerly:** (1998) Sex Information and Education Council of the U.S. **Publications:** *Fact Sheets* ● *SIECUS Report.* Journal ● Manuals ● Pamphlets ● Booklets ● Bibliographies ● Also publishes guidelines for comprehensive sexuality education and position statement. Publications catalog available on request.

16058 ■ Society for the Scientific Study of Sexuality (SSSS)
c/o David L. Fleming, Exec. Dir.
PO Box 416
Allentown, PA 18105-0416
Ph: (610)530-2483
Fax: (610)530-2485
E-mail: thesociety@sexscience.org
URL: http://www.sexscience.org
Contact: David L. Fleming, Exec. Dir.
Founded: 1957. **Members:** 1,200. **Membership Dues:** associate, $185 (annual) ● couple, $230 (annual) ● retired, $120 (annual) ● graduate/undergraduate student, $95 (annual) ● $185 (annual). **Staff:** 2. **Budget:** $320,000. **Regional Groups:** 3. **State Groups:** 4. **Multinational. Description:** Aims to advance the knowledge of sexuality. Supports research and interdisciplinary network of collaborating scholars. **Libraries: Type:** reference. **Holdings:** archival material. **Subjects:** sex research. **Awards:** Student Research Grant. **Frequency:** semiannual. **Type:** monetary. **Recipient:** to student members who are doing sexuality research; must be enrolled in a degree granting institution. **Committees:** Accreditation; Awards; Elections; Ethics; Fellows; Historical; Scientific and Professional Affairs. **Formerly:** (1998) Society for the Scientific Study of Sex. **Publications:** *Annual Review of Sex Research,* annual. Contains review articles on selected topics in the field of sexology. **Price:** $83.00/volume for agencies; $56.00/volume for individuals ● *Journal of Sex Research,* quarterly. Contains book reviews and case studies. **Price:** included in membership dues; $110.00/year for nonmembers; $160.00/year for libraries. ISSN: 0022-4499. **Circulation:** 1,900. **Advertising:** accepted. Alternate Formats: microform; CD-ROM ● *Society for the Scientific Study of Sex—Membership Handbook/Directory.* Membership Directory. **Price:** available to members only ● *Society for the Scientific Study of Sex—Newsletter,* quarterly. Includes calendar of events. **Price:** included in membership dues; $20.00/year for nonmembers. **Circulation:** 1,200. **Advertising:** accepted ● Also publishes research and clinical material. **Conventions/Meetings:** annual conference (exhibits) - always November ● annual meeting (exhibits) ● meeting, for presentation of research papers ● regional meeting - 3/year ● seminar ● symposium ● workshop.

16059 ■ Society for Sex Therapy and Research (SSTAR)
PO Box 96920
Washington, DC 20090-6920
Ph: (202)863-1644
E-mail: maurice@interchange.ubc.ca
URL: http://www.sstarnet.org
Contact: Bonnie R. Saks MD, Pres.
Founded: 1975. **Members:** 200. **Membership Dues:** student, $30 (annual) ● individual in U.S., $125 (annual) ● individual outside U.S., $90 (annual). **Budget:** $50,000. **Description:** Professionals in social work, nursing, physiology, gynecology, urology, internal medicine, primate research, psychiatry, and psychology who have clinical or research interests in human sexual concerns. Seeks to facilitate communications among clinicians who treat problems of sexual identity, sexual function, and reproductive life. Provides a forum for exchange of ideas between researchers and patient care providers. **Awards:** Masters and Johnson Award. **Frequency:** annual. **Type:** recognition. **Recipient:** for exceptional contributions in the field ● Student Research Award. **Type:** recognition. **Recipient:** to scholarly work of students who are developing a career in the field of sexual disorders. **Computer Services:** Mailing lists. **Telecommunication Services:** electronic mail, ycousins@acog.com. **Committees:** Ad Hoc Recommendations; Membership. **Formerly:** (1979) Eastern Academy of Sexual Therapy. **Publications:** *Journal of Sex and Marital Therapy,* 5/year. **Price:** $240.00/year for institutions; $106.00/year for individuals. Alternate Formats: online ● *Sexual and Relationship,* quarterly. Journal. **Price:** $676.00/year for institutions; $225.00/year for individuals. **Conventions/Meetings:** annual meeting - 2008 Mar. 13-16, Chicago, IL.

Sexually Transmitted Diseases

16060 ■ American Foundation for the Prevention of Venereal Disease (AFPVD)
Address Unknown since 2007
Founded: 1967. **Description:** Provides educational material to the public on the prevention of sexually transmitted diseases. Encourages every individual to assume responsibility for his or her own health; stresses the importance of proper personal hygiene. Seeks to eliminate the feelings of guilt and shame that are associated with sexually transmitted diseases. **Formerly:** (1967) New York Alliance for the Eradication of Venereal Disease, Inc. **Publications:** *Sexually Transmitted Disease Prevention for Everyone*, periodic. Brochure. **Advertising:** not accepted.

16061 ■ American Social Health Association (ASHA)
PO Box 13827
Research Triangle Park, NC 27709
Ph: (919)361-8400
Fax: (919)361-8425
E-mail: info@ashastd.org
URL: http://www.ashastd.org
Contact: Lynn Barclay MD, Pres./CEO
Founded: 1914. **Staff:** 250. **Budget:** $9,100,000. **Description:** A national voluntary health agency dedicated to stopping sexually transmitted diseases and their harmful consequences to individuals, families and communities. Works to expand biomedical research, provide information and education programs, upgrade clinical care, and improve public policy. Provides leadership in public policy issues. Supplies public health agencies with patient education materials. Engages directly in biomedical research through its ASHA Research Fund. Operates Herpes Resource Center, a national program for those infected with the genital herpes virus, and HPV Support Program, a national program for those infected with the human papilloma virus. **Telecommunication Services:** hotline, Herpes Resource Center Hotline, (919)361-8488 ● hotline, National AIDS Hotline, (800)342-2437 ● hotline, National AIDS Hotline in Spanish, (800)344-7432 ● hotline, National STD Hotline, (800)227-8922 ● teletype, service for the Deaf, (800)243-7889. **Formerly:** (1959) American Social Hygiene Association. **Publications:** *Helper*, quarterly. Newsletter. Reports on the latest research on the herpes simplex virus; includes information on strategies for coping with the virus and on treatments. **Price:** $25.00/year. **Circulation:** 10,000 ● *HPV News*, quarterly. Newsletter. Includes latest research on HPV/genital warts and information on coping strategies. **Price:** $25.00/year. **Circulation:** 3,000 ● *Managing Herpes*. Book. **Price:** $19.75 plus shipping and handling ● Brochures ● Pamphlets. **Conventions/Meetings:** semiannual board meeting - usually May and November.

16062 ■ Citizens Alliance for VD Awareness (CAVDA)
800 W Central Rd., Ste.128
Mount Prospect, IL 60056
Ph: (847)398-3378
Fax: (847)398-7309
E-mail: cavdarx@earthlink.net
Contact: Howard A. Mirsky, Pres.
Founded: 1972. **Members:** 125. **Staff:** 2. **Description:** Businessmen, corporations, social service agencies, public health agencies, physicians, nurses, and pharmacists. Provides information to the public, especially to high incidence groups, about symptoms, treatment, and prevention of sexually transmitted diseases, including AIDS (Acquired Immune Deficiency Syndrome). Seeks to increase commitment of health professionals and the public to venereal disease and AIDS control. Conducts demonstrations, public service messages, and surveys. **Committees:** Editorial; Media; Public Relations. **Projects:** Citizens AIDS. **Formed by Merger of:** (1974) Chicago VD Alliance Committee; Chicago Alliance for VD Awareness. **Publications:** *STD Spotlight: Dedicated to Thought and Activity in STD Information-Education Programs*, quarterly. Newsletter. **Price:** $24.00/year.

Circulation: 350. Also Cited As: *VD Spotlight* ● Pamphlets ● Also publishes fact sheets. **Conventions/Meetings:** annual conference ● workshop and seminar.

16063 ■ Herpes Resource Center - American Social Health Association (HRC)
PO Box 13827
Research Triangle Park, NC 27709
Ph: (919)361-8400
Free: (800)227-8922
Fax: (919)361-8425
E-mail: hsvnet@ashastd.org
URL: http://www.ashastd.org/hrc
Contact: Anna Wald MD, Medical Advisor/Chair
Founded: 1979. **Local Groups:** 98. **Description:** Individuals with recurrent genital herpes infections; individuals interested in the dissemination of information about genital herpes. (Herpes is a sexually transmitted disease which is as yet incurable.) Works to give emotional support to individuals, and to provide current information about herpes. Offers referrals to local support groups (HELP) throughout the U.S. and Canada for people living with herpes; HELP groups provide a safe, confidential environment in which to obtain accurate information about HPV and share experiences with other people concerned about herpes. Compiles statistics. **Libraries: Type:** reference. **Awards: Type:** fellowship ● **Type:** grant. **Affiliated With:** American Social Health Association. **Publications:** *The Helper*, quarterly. Newsletter. Contains information about all issues surrounding herpes including, leading research, treatment and testing options, and partner communication. **Price:** $25.00/year ● *Herpes: Questions & Answers* (in English and Spanish). Pamphlet. **Price:** free for members ● *HPV E-News*, bimonthly. Newsletter. Provides information on genital warts, cervical cancer prevention, the latest scientific discoveries and the newest treatment information. **Price:** $25.00/year. Alternate Formats: online ● *HPV in Perspective: A Patient Guide*. Booklet. Contains information about HPV and genital warts using clear, easy-to-understand language. **Price:** $7.00 plus shipping and handling ● *Managing Herpes: How to Live and Love with a Chronic STD*. Handbook. Features reassuring patient-oriented approach to the impact of herpes, the basic facts, and the latest science. **Price:** $26.95 plus shipping and handling ● *Understanding Herpes*. Booklet. Explains how herpes is transmitted, the symptoms, treatment issues, and how to deal with the social and psychological pressures. **Price:** $7.00 each.

16064 ■ HPV Support Program - American Social Health Association
PO Box 13827
Research Triangle Park, NC 27709
Ph: (919)361-8400
Free: (800)783-9877
Fax: (919)361-8425
E-mail: info@ashastd.org
URL: http://www.ashastd.org
Contact: James R. Allen MD, Pres./CEO
Founded: 1991. **Local Groups:** 15. **Description:** Disseminates information and educational materials about Human Papilloma Virus (HPV). Offers assistance to local support groups and/or people living with HPV. **Libraries: Type:** reference. **Affiliated With:** American Social Health Association. **Publications:** *HPV in Perspective: A Patient Guide*. Brochure. Summarizes the latest information about HPV and genital warts using clear and easy-to-understand language. **Price:** $5.00 each ● *HPV News*, quarterly. Journal. Covers medical and psychosocial information about HPV and genital warts. **Price:** $25.00/year ● *HPV Questions and Answers* (in English and Spanish). Pamphlet.

16065 ■ International Union Against Sexually Transmitted Infections, Regional Office for North America
c/o Dr. Jonathan M. Zenilman, MD, Regional Dir.
Johns Hopkins Bayview Medical Ctr.
4940 Eastern Ave.
Baltimore, MD 21224

Ph: (410)550-0501
Fax: (410)550-1169
E-mail: jzenilma@jhmi.edu
URL: http://www.iusti.org
Contact: Dr. Jonathan M. Zenilman MD, Regional Dir.
Founded: 1923. **Description:** Represents governmental and nongovernmental agencies and individuals working in the field of venereal disease control. Encourages campaigns, both medical and social, against venereal diseases and treponematoses. **Telecommunication Services:** electronic mail, bmcgroga@jhmi.edu. **Formerly:** (1998) International Union Against the Venereal Diseases and the Treponematoses, Regional Office for North America. **Publications:** Proceedings, biennial. **Conventions/Meetings:** biennial World General Assembly - meeting.

Sickle Cell Anemia

16066 ■ American Sickle Cell Anemia Association (ASCAA)
10300 Carnegie Ave.
Cleveland Clinic/East Off. Bldg. (EEb18)
Cleveland, OH 44106
Ph: (216)229-8600
Fax: (216)229-4500
E-mail: irabragg@ascaa.org
URL: http://ascaa.org
Contact: Ira Bragg-Grant, Exec. Dir.
Founded: 1971. **Staff:** 8. **Budget:** $450,000. **Description:** Ensures the availability and accessibility of quality, comprehensive sickle cell services. Provides quality and quantity counseling, education, testing services, and promotes public professional awareness about sickle cell anemia and its hemoglobin diseases and trait variants. **Formerly:** (2001) American Sickle Cell Society; (2002) American Sickle Cell Anemia Society.

Sikh

16067 ■ North American Sikh Medical and Dental Association (NASMDA)
c/o Dr. Baljit Singh Sidhu, MD, Sec.
13801 Allied Rd.
Chester, VA 23836
Ph: (804)691-1906
E-mail: gurmitchilana@yahoo.com
URL: http://sikhdocs.org
Contact: Gurmit Singh Chilana MD, Pres.
Founded: 1992. **Membership Dues:** active, $100 (annual) ● active associate (resident), $25 (annual) ● life, $1,000 ● patron, $10,000 (annual). **Multinational. Description:** Promotes the interests of Sikh physicians and dentists in the United States, Canada and elsewhere. Supports Sikh physicians, dentists and other Sikh professionals pursuing their careers in those fields or any other fields. Assists Sikh medical and dental graduates to establish practices and help them obtain adequate post-graduate training. Seeks to improve the medical education and delivery of medical care in the parent homeland. Compiles a comprehensive directory of Sikh physicians and dentists residing in North America.

Sleep

16068 ■ Academy of Dental Sleep Medicine (ADSM)
One Westbrook Corporate Center, Ste.920
Westchester, IL 60154
Ph: (708)273-9366
Fax: (708)492-0943
E-mail: info@dentalsleepmed.org
URL: http://www.dentalsleepmed.org
Founded: 1991. **Members:** 650. **Membership Dues:** regular, $295 (annual). **Staff:** 1. **Description:** Dentists, physicians, and PhDs active in sleep disorder medicine. Seeks to improve the treatment of patients

with sleep disorders through the involvement of dental practitioners and use of oral appliances in overall therapy and to enhance the lives of people suffering form sleep disorders. Supports research in application of dental appliances in the treatment of sleep disorders, such as snoring and sleep apnea; conducts educational and certification programs; establishes dental treatment protocol; disseminates information on sleep disorder treatment; facilitates the exchange of information; operates the SDDS Resource Center. **Awards:** Best Abstract in Dental Sleep Medicine. **Frequency:** annual. **Type:** recognition. **Recipient:** for the most significant abstract in dental sleep medicine presented at the APSS annual meeting ● Distinguished Service Award. **Frequency:** annual. **Type:** recognition. **Recipient:** for individuals who have exhibited exceptional initiative, leadership and service in the field of dental sleep medicine ● Pierre Robin Academic Award. **Frequency:** annual. **Type:** recognition. **Recipient:** for individuals who have exhibited exceptional initiative and progress in the areas of education and academic research in the field of dental sleep medicine. **Committees:** Awards; Education and Curriculum; Professional Relations; Program; Reimbursement. **Publications:** *ADSM Dialogue*, quarterly. Newsletter. Contains articles about dental sleep medicine, dental and medical issues, media reviews, government issues and calendar of upcoming events. **Circulation:** 650. Alternate Formats: online ● *Sleep and Breathing*. Journal. Alternate Formats: online. **Conventions/Meetings:** annual meeting (exhibits).

16069 ■ American Academy of Sleep Medicine (AASM)

One Westbrook Corporate Ctr., Ste.920
Westchester, IL 60154
Ph: (708)492-0930
Fax: (708)492-0943
E-mail: info@aasmnet.org
URL: http://www.aasmnet.org
Contact: Jerome Barrett, Exec. Dir.

Founded: 1975. **Members:** 4,700. **Membership Dues:** regular, fellowship, nurse/technician, $100 (annual) ● student (with journal), $60 (annual) ● student (without journal), $30 (annual) ● industry, $200 (annual). **Staff:** 30. **Budget:** $1,300,000. **Description:** Sleep disorders centers and individuals united to provide full diagnostic and treatment services and to improve the quality of care for patients with all types of sleep disorders. Fosters educational activities at medical schools and in continuing medical education programs; conducts site visits to assure minimum standards at member centers; trains and evaluates the competence of individuals who care for patients with sleep disorders. Conducts research programs, including a cooperative case study series on all patients seen by sleep disorders centers throughout the country. **Libraries: Type:** reference. **Holdings:** books, monographs, periodicals. **Awards:** Mark O. Hatfield Public Policy Award. **Frequency:** annual. **Type:** recognition. **Recipient:** for an individual who has made an outstanding contribution to public policy affecting the healthy sleep of all Americans ● Nathaniel Kleitman Distinguished Service Award. **Frequency:** annual. **Type:** recognition. **Recipient:** for service to the field of sleep research and sleep disorders medicine ● William C. Dement Academic Achievement Award. **Frequency:** annual. **Type:** recognition. **Recipient:** for individuals who have made unique and monumental contributions in the areas of sleep education and academic research. **Committees:** Accreditation; Behavioral Sleep Medicine; Clinical Practice Review; Continuing Medical Education; Education; Fellowship Training; Government Affairs; Health Policy; Nosology; Polysomnographic Technologist Issues; Reimbursement; Research; Standards of Practice. **Sections:** Dreams; Pediatrics. **Affiliated With:** Associated Professional Sleep Societies. **Formerly:** American Association of Sleep Disorders Centers; (1987) Association of Sleep Disorders Centers; (2000) American Association of Sleep Disorders. **Publications:** *Bulletin*, quarterly. Newsletter. Informs members on the latest news and important happenings. **Advertising:** accepted ● *Journal of Clinical Sleep Medicine*. Includes some original

manuscripts such as clinical trials as well as clinical reviews, clinical commentary and debate. **Price:** included in membership dues; $60.00 /year for individuals in U.S. - nonmember; $90.00 /year for individuals outside U.S. - nonmember; $120.00 /year for institutions outside U.S. **Advertising:** accepted ● *SLEEP*, 9/year. Journal. Contains original findings pertaining to sleep and circadian rhythms. **Price:** included in membership dues; $195.00 /year for individuals in U.S. - nonmember; $260.00 /year for individuals outside U.S. - nonmember; $290.00 /year for institutions in U.S. ISSN: 0161-8105. **Circulation:** 5,000. **Advertising:** accepted ● Also publishes a roster of centers. **Conventions/Meetings:** annual Scientific Meeting (exhibits) - usually June.

16070 ■ American Academy of Somnology (AAS)

PO Box 27077
Las Vegas, NV 89126-1077
Ph: (702)371-0947 (702)437-1113
Fax: (702)438-1118
E-mail: somnology@aol.com
URL: http://www.hopperinstitute.com/aas_intro.html
Contact: Dr. David L. Hopper PhD, Founder/Pres.

Founded: 1986. **Members:** 75. **Staff:** 6. **Description:** Clinicians, researchers, and students in the field of somnology; interested individuals. Promotes advancement of somnology as a health care specialty. (Somnology is the study of sleep and sleep disorders.) Advocates standardization of university programs in somnology and a multidisciplinary approach to the study and treatment of sleep disorders; conducts continuing education program. Sponsors American Board of Somnology to evaluate qualifications of applicants, administer examinations, and confer diplomate status on qualified individuals. Provides a forum for somnology clinicians and researchers to present findings and exchange ideas. Maintains speakers' bureau. **Awards:** Fellow of the American Academy of Somnology. **Frequency:** annual. **Type:** recognition. **Recipient:** for diplomates who demonstrate outstanding achievements. **Committees:** Education; Legislative. **Publications:** *AAS Membership Directory*, annual ● *Certification Handbook*, periodic ● *Journal of Somnology*, annual ● *The Somnologist*, quarterly ● Also publishes constitution, ethical standards, and bylaws.

16071 ■ American Board of Sleep Medicine (ABSM)

One Westbrook Corporate Ctr., Ste.920
Westchester, IL 60154
Ph: (708)492-1290
Fax: (708)492-0943
E-mail: absm@absm.org
URL: http://www.absm.org
Contact: Becky Nowlin, Examination Coor.

Founded: 1991. **Description:** Works to encourage the study and elevate the standards of sleep medicine. Offers certification in sleep medicine to licensed physicians and individuals with PhDs in health related fields. **Publications:** Brochure. Contains information for applicants. **Conventions/Meetings:** annual board meeting.

16072 ■ American Sleep Apnea Association (ASAA)

1424 K St. NW, Ste.302
Washington, DC 20005
Ph: (202)293-3650
Fax: (202)293-3656
E-mail: asaa@sleepapnea.org
URL: http://www.sleepapnea.org
Contact: Edward Grandi, Exec. Dir.

Founded: 1990. **Members:** 5,000. **Membership Dues:** individual, $25 (annual) ● supporter, $100 ● investor, $250 ● patron, $500 ● sponsor, $1,000 ● friend/foreign, $50. **Staff:** 2. **Budget:** $250,000. **Local Groups:** 225. **Description:** Individuals affected by sleep apnea; health care professionals. Promotes public awareness of sleep apnea; encourages research on the causes and treatments of breathing abnormalities during sleep. Sponsors educational programs and support groups through the A.W.A.K.E. Network. Serves as an advocate for people with sleep

apnea. **Libraries: Type:** reference. **Holdings:** audiovisuals, books, clippings, periodicals. **Subjects:** sleep disorders, obstructive sleep apnea for adults and children, central sleep apnea. **Additional Websites:** http://www.apneasupport.org. **Committees:** A.W.A.K.E. Network; Program. **Publications:** *Get the Facts about Sleep Apnea*. Brochure ● *Wake Up Call The Wellness Letter for Snoring and Apnea*, quarterly. Newsletter. Includes articles of interest to people affected by sleep apnea. **Price:** included in membership dues. **Circulation:** 5,000 ● Choosing a CPAP, Choosing a Mask and Headgear, Sleep and the Internet, Sleep Apnea and Driving, Reprints of newsletter articles.

16073 ■ Associated Professional Sleep Societies (APSS)

1 Westbrook Corporate Ctr., Ste.920
Westchester, IL 60154
Ph: (708)492-0930
Fax: (708)273-9354
E-mail: info@aasmnet.org
URL: http://www.apss.org
Contact: Jerome A. Barrett, Exec. Dir.

Founded: 1985. **Staff:** 30. **Budget:** $1,000,000. **Nonmembership. Description:** Members are the Sleep Research Society and American Academy of Sleep Medicine (see separate entries). Works to facilitate sleep research and development of sleep disorder medicine by encouraging cooperation and exchange of information among members. **Awards:** Dement/Kleitman/Hatfield. **Frequency:** annual. **Type:** monetary. **Recipient:** for academic achievement/ distinguished service/public policy. **Affiliated With:** American Academy of Sleep Medicine; Sleep Research Society. **Formerly:** Association of Professional Sleep Societies. **Publications:** *SLEEP*, 8/year. Journal. **Price:** $129.00 /year for individuals; $185.00 /year for institutions; $159.00/year for foreign individuals; $220.00/year for foreign institutions. ISSN: 0161-8105. **Circulation:** 6,500. **Advertising:** accepted. **Conventions/Meetings:** annual meeting, scientific meeting (exhibits).

16074 ■ Association of Polysomnographic Technologists (APT)

1 Westbrook Corporate Ctr., Ste.920
Westchester, IL 60154
Ph: (708)492-0796
Fax: (708)273-9344
E-mail: cwaring@aptweb.org
URL: http://www.aptweb.org
Contact: Cynthia Mattice, Pres.

Founded: 1978. **Members:** 2,600. **Membership Dues:** active, $100 (annual). **Description:** Individuals who practice polysomnography in research or clinical settings. (Polysomnographic technology deals with the measurement and recording of multiple physiological activity, such as eye movement and heart rate, during sleep.) Seeks to establish standards for polysomnographic technology and provide education and training for people entering in the field. Acts as a forum for communication among members. **Awards:** Carskadon Research. **Frequency:** annual. **Type:** monetary. **Computer Services:** database ● mailing lists. **Telecommunication Services:** electronic mail, apt@aptweb.org. **Boards:** Registered Polysomnographic Technologists. **Committees:** Communications; Education; Legislative Action; Regional Activities; Standards and Guidelines. **Affiliated With:** Associated Professional Sleep Societies. **Publications:** *A2Zzz Newsletter*, quarterly. **Advertising:** accepted. Alternate Formats: online. **Conventions/Meetings:** annual conference and workshop (exhibits) - always June.

16075 ■ Better Sleep Council (BSC)

501 Wythe St.
Alexandria, VA 22314-1917
Ph: (703)683-8371
Fax: (703)683-4503
E-mail: nshark@sleepproducts.org
URL: http://www.bettersleep.org
Contact: Mrs. Nancy Shark, VP for Communications

Founded: 1978. **Description:** Represents mattress manufacturers and suppliers. Increases public awareness of the importance of sleep to good health, quality of life, and the role of the sleep system in pursuit of a good night's sleep. **Formerly:** (1987) Better Sleep Council (of the National Association of Bedding Manufacturers); (1993) Better Sleep Council (of the International Sleep Products Association). **Publications:** *Better Sleep Guide.* Brochure. A consumer guide to sleep and mattresses. ● Also publishes press kits.

16076 ■ Community Dreamsharing Network (CDN)
Address Unknown since 2007
Founded: 1982. **Members:** 600. **Membership Dues:** individual, $15 (annual). **Staff:** 4. **Budget:** $43,000. **Regional Groups:** 7. **State Groups:** 5. **Local Groups:** 10. **National Groups:** 150. **Description:** Social groups of individuals interested in discussing and understanding their dreams. Works to organize local dreamsharing groups which meet weekly and encourages networking between these groups. Refers qualified dreamsharing activity helpers to schools and groups. Trains elementary and high school teachers in using the dreams of students. Sponsors training sessions in dream understanding methods; conducts research. Maintains speakers' bureau and placement service. Maintains a database of dreamsharing groups. **Libraries: Type:** reference. **Holdings:** reports. **Subjects:** dreamsharing, understanding dreams. **Computer Services:** database ● online services. **Affiliated With:** National Self-Help Clearinghouse. **Formerly:** (1970) Center for Dream Drama; (1982) New York/New Jersey DreamSharing Network; (1988) Dreamsharing Grassroots Network. **Publications:** *Dream Switchboard,* quarterly. Newsletter. Includes networking notices. **Price:** $15.00 /year for individuals. **Circulation:** 2,000. **Advertising:** not accepted. Alternate Formats: online. **Conventions/Meetings:** periodic Regional Weekend Workshop - conference and workshop, to share ideas, acquire referrals, promote social relationships; **Avg. Attendance:** 100.

16077 ■ International Association for the Study of Dreams (IASD)
1672 Univ. Ave.
Berkeley, CA 94703
Ph: (209)724-0889
Fax: (209)724-0889
E-mail: jccampb@aol.com
URL: http://www.asdreams.org
Contact: Jean Campbell MA, Pres.
Founded: 1984. **Members:** 900. **Membership Dues:** student, $65 (annual) ● individual, business, $100 (annual) ● couple, patron, $150 (annual). **Staff:** 1. **Budget:** $250,000. **Multinational. Description:** Medical professionals, sociologists, counselors, educators, researchers, students, and others whose disciplines are involved in the study of dreams and dreaming. Provides an international interdisciplinary forum for the promotion and public dissemination of information regarding research into the physiological and therapeutic aspects of dreams and their interpretation. **Formerly:** (2005) Association for the Study of Dreams. **Publications:** *Dream Time,* quarterly. Magazine. Contains research reports, clinical reports, interviews, case studies, and book reviews. **Price:** included in membership dues. **Circulation:** 900. **Advertising:** accepted ● *Dreaming,* quarterly. Journal. Contains scholarly articles on every aspect of dreams and dreaming. Includes book reviews. **Price:** included in membership dues ● Audiotapes. Contains conference lectures. **Conventions/Meetings:** annual Dreams Building Bridges - conference and workshop ● regional meeting.

16078 ■ Narcolepsy Network
PO Box 294
Pleasantville, NY 10570
Ph: (401)667-2523
Free: (888)292-6522
Fax: (401)633-6567
E-mail: narnet@narcolepsynetwork.org
URL: http://www.narcolepsynetwork.org
Contact: Dr. Eveline Honig, Exec. Dir.
Founded: 1986. **Membership Dues:** individual, $35 (annual) ● sleep professional, $75 (annual) ● sleep

center, $150 (annual). **Staff:** 3. **Local Groups:** 60. **Description:** Individuals with narcolepsy, their friends and families, sleep professionals, and interested others. Seeks to improve the quality of life of individuals who have narcolepsy. Works to educate members and the general public about narcolepsy. Fosters communication among members. Offers referral service. Supports research; disseminates information. **Awards: Frequency:** periodic. **Type:** grant. **Recipient:** for research. **Publications:** *Narcolepsy: A Guide to Understanding* ● *The Network,* quarterly. Newsletter. Contains news, articles, and regular columns. **Conventions/Meetings:** annual conference ● periodic support group meeting.

16079 ■ National Sleep Foundation (NSF)
1522 K St. NW, Ste.500
Washington, DC 20005
Ph: (202)347-3471
Fax: (202)347-3472
E-mail: nsf@sleepfoundation.org
URL: http://www.sleepfoundation.org
Contact: Barbara A. Phillips MD, Chair
Founded: 1990. **Membership Dues:** individual, $15 (annual) ● professional, $49 (annual) ● CSAP network, $295 (annual) ● life, $1,500 ● sustaining, $500 (annual) ● supporting, $250 (annual) ● contributing, $100 (annual) ● Chairman's Circle, $1,000 (annual). **Staff:** 13. **Budget:** $20,000. **Languages:** English, Spanish. **Description:** Works to improve the quality of life of people suffering from sleep disorders and to prevent accidents related to sleep disorders. (Sleep disorders include: insomnia, narcolepsy, sleep apnea syndrome, sudden infant death syndrome, stroke, epilepsy, and other disorders of sleep and daytime alertness.) Educates health care professionals and the public about the existence and treatment of sleep disorders. Promotes the development of patient services, community resources, and support groups for individuals affected by sleep disorders. Sponsors educational and research programs. **Awards:** Pickwick Club and Narcolepsy Fellowships. **Frequency:** annual. **Type:** grant ● **Type:** scholarship. **Publications:** *Sleepmatters,* quarterly. Magazine. Alternate Formats: online ● Brochures. **Conventions/Meetings:** annual International Forum on Sleeplessness and Crashes - meeting and conference, drowsy driving conference.

16080 ■ Sleep Research Society (SRS)
c/o John Slater, Coor.
1 Westbrook Corporate Center, Ste.920
Westchester, IL 60154
Ph: (708)492-1093
Fax: (708)492-0943
E-mail: jslater@srsnet.org
URL: http://www.sleepresearchsociety.org
Contact: Mark R. Opp PhD, Pres.
Founded: 1961. **Members:** 850. **Membership Dues:** full, $180 (annual) ● dual, $150 (annual) ● associate, postdoctoral fellow, $90 (annual) ● predoctoral student, $45 (annual). **Staff:** 2. **Description:** Physiologists, psychologists, and physicians with research interests in the study of sleep. Disseminates scientific papers on the physiological and psychological aspects of sleep. Facilitates communication among research workers in this field, but do not sponsor research investigations on its own. **Awards:** Distinguished Scientist Award. **Frequency:** annual. **Type:** recognition. **Recipient:** for scientific advances in the field of sleep research ● Young Investigator Award. **Frequency:** annual. **Type:** recognition. **Recipient:** to an outstanding research effort by a new investigator in the field of sleep research. **Committees:** Awards; Communications; Educational Program; Research; Trainee and Education Advisory. **Formerly:** (1983) Association for the Psychophysiological Study of Sleep. **Publications:** *Sleep,* monthly. Journal. Includes book reviews and bibliography of recent literature. **Price:** included in membership dues; $195.00 /year for nonmembers in U.S.; $290.00 /year for institutions in U.S.; $260.00 /year for nonmembers outside U.S. ISSN: 0161-8105. **Advertising:** accepted. Alternate Formats: online ● *Sleep Research Society—Sleep Research,* annual. Monograph. Contains author and keyword-in-context index. **Price:**

$220.00 /year for institutions outside U.S.; included in membership dues. ISSN: 0161-8105. **Circulation:** 5,000. **Advertising:** accepted. **Conventions/Meetings:** annual meeting, courses, symposia, lecture, discussion groups on sleep, sleep disorders and related topics (exhibits).

16081 ■ World Association of Sleep Medicine (WASM)
c/o Sudhansu Chokroverty, Pres.-Elect
JFK New Jersey Neuroscience Inst.
65 James St.
Edison, NJ 08818
E-mail: schok@worldnet.att.net
URL: http://www.wasmonline.org
Contact: Sudhansu Chokroverty, Pres.-Elect
Founded: 2003. **Membership Dues:** full, EUR 80 (annual) ● without journal, EUR 40 (annual). **Multinational. Description:** Works to advance sleep health. Promotes and encourages education, research and patient care throughout the world. Acts as a bridge between different sleep societies and cultures. Supports and encourages worldwide exchange of clinical information and scientific studies related to sleep medicine. Seeks to encourage development and exchange of information for worldwide and regional standards of practice for sleep medicine. **Telecommunication Services:** electronic mail, schok@att.net ● electronic mail, secretary@wasmonline.org. **Publications:** *Sleep Medicine.* Journal. **Price:** included in membership dues ● *Sleep Medicine Worldwide.* Newsletter. Alternate Formats: online.

Smoking

16082 ■ Action on Smoking and Health (ASH)
2013 H St. NW
Washington, DC 20006
Ph: (202)659-4310
Fax: (202)833-3921
E-mail: webmaster@ash.org
URL: http://www.ash.org
Contact: John F. Banzhaf III, Exec. Dir.
Founded: 1967. **Membership Dues:** individual, $25 (annual). **Staff:** 10. **Languages:** Dutch, English, French, Italian, Spanish. **Description:** Works for the rights of nonsmokers against the problems of smoking. Provides scientific, educational, legal, and advocacy services. Includes accomplishments such as: ban of tobacco ads from radio and television; establishment of no-smoking sections on airplanes, trains, and interstate buses; persuading the National Association of Insurance Commissioners to adopt a resolution urging insurance companies to force smokers to pay their fair share of health insurance costs by charging them higher rates than non smokers; sued the Occupational Safety and Health Administration (OSHA) to ban smoking in all workplaces. **Libraries: Type:** reference. **Computer Services:** Mailing lists. **Publications:** *ASH Smoking and Health Review,* bimonthly. Newsletter. Covers medical, legal, regulatory, commercial, institutional, and humorous news related to smoking. **Price:** $25.00/year. **Circulation:** 30,000 ● Also publishes informational handouts on addiction to nicotine, effects of passive smoking, workplace smoking costs, workplace nonsmokers' rights, filing for workers' compensation, and other materials. **Conventions/Meetings:** quarterly meeting.

16083 ■ Americans for Nonsmokers' Rights American Nonsmokers' Rights Foundation (ANR)
2530 San Pablo Ave., Ste.J
Berkeley, CA 94702
Ph: (510)841-3032
Fax: (510)841-3071
E-mail: anr@no-smoke.org
URL: http://www.no-smoke.org
Contact: Cynthia Hallett, Exec. Dir.
Founded: 1976. **Members:** 15,000. **Membership Dues:** basic, $40 (annual) ● contributor, $50 (annual) ● major donor, $100 (annual) ● supporter, $250 (an-

nual) ● sponsor, $500 (annual) ● advocate, $1,000 (annual) ● defender, $5,000 (annual) ● champion, $10,000 (annual). **Staff:** 19. **Description:** Seeks to protect the rights of nonsmokers in the workplace and other public settings. Maintains American Non-smokers' Rights Foundation, which promotes smoking prevention, educational programs, and public education about secondhand smoke issues. **Libraries: Type:** not open to the public. **Formerly:** (1976) California Group Against Smoking Pollution; (1986) Californians for Nonsmokers' Rights; (2001) Americans for Nonsmokers' Rights. **Publications:** *ANR Materials.* Alternate Formats: diskette; CD-ROM ● *ANR Update,* quarterly. Newsletter. Provides information on issues important to nonsmokers. **Price:** included in membership dues. **Circulation:** 10,000 ● *Clearing the Air.* Book ● *Secondhand Smoke.* Manual ● *Teens Take Action Guidebook: How to Butt In Tobacco Smoke and the Non-Smoker.* Brochure.

16084 ■ National Center for Tobacco-Free Kids

1400 Eye St. NW, Ste.1200
Washington, DC 20005
Ph: (202)296-5469
Fax: (202)296-5427
E-mail: info@tobaccofreekids.org
URL: http://www.tobaccofreekids.org
Contact: Matthew L. Myers, Pres.
Founded: 1995. **Description:** People interested in helping kids keep tobacco-free. Fights to protect America's kids from tobacco. Increases the number of organizations and individuals fighting against tobacco. Sponsors federal initiatives. **Also Known As:** (2005) Campaign for Tobacco-Free Kids.

16085 ■ SmokeFree Educational Services

c/o Michael Tacelosky
Smokescreen
1502 21st St. NW
Washington, DC 20036
Ph: (202)955-9099
E-mail: tac@smokescreen.org
URL: http://www.tobacco.org
Contact: Michael Tacelosky, Contact
Founded: 1987. **Members:** 100,000. **Budget:** $250,000. **Languages:** English, French. **Description:** Mission statement is "to win the right to live and work in a smoke free environment, and to educate people about the unhealthy and socially undesirable consequences of tobacco addiction". Works for: more education for people on the consequences of tobacco addiction; tobacco-free schools; larger health warnings on cigarette ads and cigarette packs; health warnings on cigarettes sold to less developed countries; ending tobacco sponsorship of youth oriented events; eliminating cigarette vending machines; and 100&percent; smoke free public places. **Convention/Meeting:** none. **Awards: Type:** recognition. **Computer Services:** Mailing lists, of members. **Telecommunication Services:** electronic mail, tac@smokefree.net. **Also Known As:** Smokefree America. **Publications:** *SmokeFree Air,* quarterly. Newsletter. **Circulation:** 110,000.

16086 ■ Smokenders

PO Box 316
Kensington, MD 20895
Free: (800)828-HELP
E-mail: info@smokenders.com
URL: http://www.smokenders.com
Contact: Kay Willcuts, VP
For-Profit. Description: Teaches smokers to quit smoking through seminars or self-help kits.

Sonography

16087 ■ American Institute of Ultrasound in Medicine (AIUM)

14750 Sweitzer Ln., Ste.100
Laurel, MD 20707-5906
Ph: (301)498-4100
Free: (800)638-5352
Fax: (301)498-4450

E-mail: admin@aium.org
URL: http://www.aium.org
Contact: Carmine M. Valente PhD, CEO
Founded: 1952. **Members:** 8,000. **Membership Dues:** non-physician, $140 (annual) ● physician, $250 (annual). **Staff:** 30. **Budget:** $4,500,000. **Description:** A multidisciplinary organization dedicated to advancing the art and science of ultrasound in medicine through its educational, scientific, literary and professional activities. Membership comprises professionals from many medical specialties, as well as basic scientists, engineers, manufacturers, nurses, physicists, radiologic technologists, sonographers and veterinarians involved with diagnostic medical ultrasound. **Libraries: Type:** reference. **Holdings:** archival material. **Awards:** Joseph Holmes Pioneer. **Frequency:** annual. **Type:** recognition ● Memorial Hall of Fame. **Frequency:** annual. **Type:** recognition ● Research Grants. **Frequency:** annual. **Type:** grant ● Sonographer. **Frequency:** annual. **Type:** recognition ● William Fry. **Frequency:** annual. **Type:** recognition. **Committees:** Annual Convention; Bioeffects; CME; Education and Research Fund; Educational Resource; Ethics and Professional Standards; Finance; International Relations; Patient Resource; Technical Standards. **Sections:** Basic Sciences and Instrumentation; Cardio/Vascular Ultrasound; General and Abdominal Ultrasound; Interventional-Intraoperative; Musculoskeletal Ultrasound; Neurosonology; OB/GYN Ultrasound; Ophthalmologic Ultrasound; Pediatric Ultrasound; Sonography. **Publications:** *Acoustic Output Labeling Standard for Diagnostic Ultrasound Equipment,* monthly. Book. Covers institute activities and developments in diagnostic ultrasound. Includes listing of continuing education courses and employment opportunities. **Price:** $15.00 for members; $30.00 for nonmembers. **Advertising:** accepted ● *Acoustic Output Measurement Standard for Diagnostic Ultrasound Equipment,* monthly. Book. Contains research papers and case reports covering all aspects of diagnostic ultrasound, advances in instrumentation, and biological effects. **Price:** $22.00 for members; $44.00 for nonmembers; $190.00 /year for institutions. ISSN: 0278-4297. **Circulation:** 13,000. **Advertising:** accepted. Alternate Formats: microform ● *AIUM Sound Waves,* 10/year. Newsletter. Covers institute activities and developments in diagnostic ultrasound. **Price:** included in membership dues. **Circulation:** 9,000. **Advertising:** accepted. Alternate Formats: online ● *Bioeffects and Safety of Diagnostic Ultrasound.* Book. **Price:** $17.00 for members; $34.00 for nonmembers ● *Evaluation of Research Reports: Bioeffects Literature Reviews 1985-1991.* Book. **Price:** $16.00 for members; $30.00 for nonmembers ● *Evaluation of Research Reports: Bioeffects Literature Reviews 1962-1982.* Book. **Price:** $9.00 for members; $16.00 for nonmembers ● *Journal of Ultrasound in Medicine,* monthly. Contains research papers and case reports covering all aspects of diagnostic ultrasound, advances in instrumentation, and biological effects. **Price:** included in membership dues; $265.00 /year for nonmembers; $295.00 /year for institutions. ISSN: 0278-4297. **Circulation:** 10,000. **Advertising:** accepted. Alternate Formats: microform; online ● *Mechanical Bioeffects from Diagnostic Ultrasound: AIUM Consensus Statements.* **Price:** $25.00 ● *Medical Ultrasound Safety.* **Price:** $10.00 for members; $19.00 for nonmembers ● *Obstetrical Measurements Used in A Routine Examination.* **Price:** $20.00 for members; $40.00 for nonmembers ● *Perf. Criteria and Measurements for Doppler U/S Devices: Tech. Discussions-2nd Ed..* **Price:** $18.00 for members; $36.00 for nonmembers ● Videos. Alternate Formats: CD-ROM ● *AIUM Annual Convention Proceedings,* annual. **Price:** $12.00/copy for members; $22.00/copy for nonmembers. Also Cited As: *American Institute of Ultrasound in Medicine—Official Book of Abstracts and Supplement to Journal of Ultrasound in Medicine* ● *Is Sonography the Career for You?.* **Price:** $55.00 for members, bulk; $120.00 for nonmembers, bulk. **Advertising:** accepted. Also Cited As: *American Institute of Ultrasound in Medicine—Official Book of Abstracts and Supplement to Journal of Ultrasound in Medicine.* **Conventions/Meetings:** annual convention (exhibits) - usually June.

16088 ■ American Registry of Diagnostic Medical Sonographers (ARDMS)

51 Monroe St.
Plz. East One
Rockville, MD 20850-2400
Ph: (301)738-8401
Free: (800)541-9754
Fax: (301)738-0312
E-mail: admin@ardms.org
URL: http://www.ardms.org
Contact: Diane Kawamura PhD, Chair
Founded: 1975. **Members:** 42,000. **Membership Dues:** certification, $45 (annual). **Staff:** 28. **Budget:** $5,100,000. **Description:** Administers examinations in the field of diagnostic medical sonography and vascular technology throughout the U.S. and Canada and registers candidates passing those exams in the specialties of their expertise. Maintains central office for administering examination plans and schedules and assisting registered candidates and those interested in becoming registered. **Convention/Meeting:** none. **Computer Services:** Mailing lists. **Committees:** Certification. **Task Forces:** Examination Development. **Publications:** *American Registry of Diagnostic Medical Sonographers Directory,* annual. **Price:** free ● *Continuing Competency Requirements.* Brochure ● *Information and Examination Application Booklet.* Alternate Formats: online ● *Informational Brochure,* annual ● *Mailing List Brochure.*

16089 ■ Society of Diagnostic Medical Sonography (SDMS)

2745 N Dallas Pkwy., Ste.350
Plano, TX 75093-8730
Ph: (214)473-8057
Free: (800)229-9506
Fax: (214)473-8563
E-mail: dsanchez@sdms.org
URL: http://www.sdms.org
Contact: Dawn Sanchez, Membership Marketing and Services Dir.
Founded: 1972. **Members:** 15,500. **Membership Dues:** student (in U.S., Canada and Mexico), $40 (annual) ● student (international), $50 (annual) ● active/associate/supporting (in Canada and Mexico), $105 (annual) ● active/associate/supporting (in U.S.), $119 (annual) ● active/associate/supporting (international), $134 (annual) ● corporate/business/institution, $495 (annual). **Staff:** 6. **Budget:** $2,500,000. **Regional Groups:** 7. **Description:** Works to enhance the art and science of medicine by advancing medical sonography. **Awards:** Distinguished Educator Award. **Frequency:** annual. **Type:** recognition. **Recipient:** for outstanding educators in the field of diagnostic medical sonography ● Joan Baker Award. **Type:** recognition ● Scientific Award. **Type:** recognition ● W. Frederick Sample Award. **Type:** recognition. **Computer Services:** Mailing lists. **Committees:** Awards; Bylaws; Conference Management; Continuing Education; Educators; Finance; Government Relations; Membership; Nominating. **Formerly:** (1980) American Society of Ultrasound Technical Specialists. **Publications:** *Coding Reference Guides.* Book. **Price:** $81.00/issue for members; $90.00/issue for nonmembers; $112.00/CD for members; $125.00/CD for nonmembers. Alternate Formats: CD-ROM ● *Journal of Diagnostic Medical Sonography,* bimonthly. **Price:** free for members ● *National Certification Examination Review.* Manuals. Contains CME post-tests presented in an easy-to-use outline format. Offers an excellent review of each specialty area covered. **Price:** $420.00 for members (all 10 specialty areas); $660.00 for nonmembers (all 10 specialty areas) ● *News Wave,* bimonthly. Newsletter ● *SDMS Annual Conference Videotapes & DVDs.* Videos ● *Sonography Benchmark Survey Annual Income* ● *Sound News,* monthly. Newsletter. Contains late-breaking news and special announcements. Alternate Formats: online ● Books. **Conventions/Meetings:** annual conference (exhibits) - 2007 Oct. 11-14, Las Vegas, NV.

Speech and Hearing

16090 ■ American Academy of Audiology (AAA)

11730 Plaza Am. Dr., Ste.300
Reston, VA 20190

Ph: (703)790-8466
Free: (800)AAA-2336
Fax: (703)790-8631
E-mail: info@audiology.org
URL: http://www.audiology.org
Contact: Laura Fleming Doyle CAE, Exec. Dir.
Founded: 1988. **Members:** 10,000. **Membership Dues:** individual, $155 (annual). **Staff:** 26. **Budget:** $4,800,000. **Description:** Professionals in the field of audiology. Seeks to "enhance the ability of members to achieve career and practice objectives through professional development." Conducts research and educational programs; sponsors public education campaigns to raise awareness of hearing disorders and audiological services. **Publications:** *Audiology Today*, bimonthly. Magazine. **Price:** $40.00 /year for individuals; $85.00 /year for libraries and institutions. ISSN: 1535-2609. **Circulation:** 11,000. **Advertising:** accepted ● *Journal of the American Academy of Audiology*, 10/year. **Advertising:** accepted. **Conventions/Meetings:** annual meeting, largest gathering of audiologists in the world (exhibits).

16091 ■ American Institute for Stuttering Treatment and Professional Training (AIS)

27 W 20th St., Ste.1203
New York, NY 10011-3707
Ph: (212)633-6400
Free: (877)378-8883
Fax: (212)220-3922
E-mail: ais@stutteringtreatment.org
URL: http://www.stutteringtreatment.org
Contact: Catherine Otto Montgomery MS, Exec. Dir.
Founded: 1995. **Staff:** 4. **Languages:** English, Spanish. **Description:** Provides both intensive and non-intensive treatment options for people of all ages who stutter, while also providing clinical training to both new and established speech-language pathologists. **Affiliated With:** Friends: The National Association of Young People Who Stutter; National Stuttering Association; Stuttering Foundation of America. **Formerly:** (1998) Total Immersion Fluency Training.

16092 ■ American Neurotology Society (ANS)

c/o Shirley Gossard, Admin.
3096 Riverdale Rd.
The Villages, FL 32162
Ph: (352)751-0932
Fax: (352)751-0696
E-mail: segossard@aol.com
URL: http://www.americanneurotologysociety.com
Contact: Shirley Gossard, Admin.
Founded: 1965. **Members:** 500. **Membership Dues:** associate, fellow, senior, honorary, $150 (annual). **Description:** Physicians and audiologists interested in the diagnosis and treatment of hearing and balance disorders. Promotes education and research in the field of neurotology. **Awards:** Neurotology Fellows Award. **Frequency:** annual. **Type:** monetary. **Recipient:** for scientific excellence ● Nicholas Torok Vestibular Award. **Frequency:** annual. **Type:** monetary. **Recipient:** for an innovative observation, experience or technique in the field of vestibular basic science or clinical science ● Trainee Award. **Frequency:** annual. **Type:** monetary. **Recipient:** for the best clinical or basic science paper in neurotology submitted by a resident or fellow in training in the field of Otolaryngology-Head and Neck Surgery. **Computer Services:** Mailing lists. **Committees:** Audiology; Vestibulology. **Formerly:** (1965) ENG Study Group. **Publications:** Directory, annual. Published in conjunction with American Academy of Otolaryngology - Head and Neck Surgery. **Conventions/Meetings:** semiannual conference - May and September.

16093 ■ American Speech Language Hearing Association (ASHA)

10801 Rockville Pike
Rockville, MD 20852
Free: (800)638-8255
Fax: (301)897-7355
E-mail: actioncenter@asha.org
URL: http://www.asha.org
Contact: Alex F. Johnson, Pres.
Founded: 1925. **Members:** 123,000. **Staff:** 220. **Description:** Consumers of speech, language, and hearing services and their families. Provides educational and referral information on speech, language, and hearing disabilities. **Awards:** Media Award. **Frequency:** annual. **Type:** recognition. **Telecommunication Services:** teletype, (301)897-5700. **Divisions:** Consumer Affairs. **Programs:** Academic; Doctoral; Graduate. **Formerly:** (1922) American Association for the Hard of Hearing; (1935) American Federation of Organizations for the Hard of Hearing; (1946) American Society for the Hard of Hearing; (1966) American Hearing Society; (1974) National Association of Hearing and Speech Agencies; (1999) National Association for Hearing and Speech Action. **Publications:** Pamphlets. Covers a wide range of communication disorders and development of speech, language, and hearing in children. ● Newsletter, bimonthly. **Alternate Formats:** online. **Conventions/Meetings:** annual convention (exhibits).

16094 ■ American Tinnitus Association (ATA)

PO Box 5
Portland, OR 97207-0005
Ph: (503)248-9985
Free: (800)634-8978
Fax: (503)248-0024
E-mail: tinnitus@ata.org
URL: http://www.ata.org
Contact: Mr. David Fagerlie, CEO
Founded: 1971. **Members:** 18,000. **Membership Dues:** regular, $35-$99 (annual) ● supporting, $100-$249 (annual) ● contributing, $250-$499 (annual) ● sustaining, $500-$999 (annual) ● champion, $1,000 (annual). **Staff:** 10. **Budget:** $1,000,000. **State Groups:** 42. **Description:** Commits in tinnitus research and educates patients, and professionals through conferences, books, brochures, videos and journal. Supports tinnitus awareness, prevention and treatment under its guiding principles Education, Advocacy, Research and Support. Offers prevention programs in schools, urges governmental and private organizations to support hearing conservation, funds the nation's brightest researchers and facilitates self-help groups around the country. **Awards:** ATA Research Grants. **Frequency:** semiannual. **Type:** monetary. **Recipient:** for research. **Computer Services:** Mailing lists. **Committees:** Medical Advisory. **Programs:** Advocacy; Education; Research. **Publications:** *Coping With the Stress of Tinnitus* (in English and Spanish). Brochure ● *If You Have Tinnitus - The First Steps To Take.* Brochure ● *Information About Tinnitus.* Brochure ● *Noise - Its Effects on Hearing and Tinnitus.* Brochure ● *Tinnitus Bibliography* ● *Tinnitus Today*, quarterly, March, July, September, December. Journal. Includes book reviews, calendar of events, research updates, and statistics. **Price:** $2.50/issue for members; $5.00/issue for nonmembers. ISSN: 0897-6368. **Circulation:** 80,000. **Advertising:** accepted ● *Tinnitus Treatments - What's New, What Works.* Brochure ● *Understanding Tinnitus - Advice for Family and Friends.* Brochure. **Conventions/Meetings:** annual conference and regional meeting.

16095 ■ Childhood Apraxia of Speech Association (CASANA)

1151 Freeport Rd., No. 243
Pittsburgh, PA 15238
Ph: (412)767-6589
Fax: (412)767-0534
URL: http://www.apraxia-kids.org
Contact: Kathleen H. Bauer, Sec.
Founded: 2000. **Description:** Represents children with apraxia (verbal dyspraxia) and their families, professionals caring for them, and researchers. **Libraries:** Type: reference. Holdings: articles. **Subjects:** apraxia. **Computer Services:** Mailing lists, of members. **Boards:** Professional Advisory. **Publications:** *Apraxia-KIDS*, monthly. Newsletter. Includes articles about apraxia of speech. **Price:** free. **Alternate Formats:** online ● *Hope Speaks: An Introduction to Childhood Apraxia of Speech.* Video. **Price:** $29.99.

16096 ■ Friends: The National Association of Young People Who Stutter

c/o Lee Caggiano
38 S Oyster Bay Rd.
Syosset, NY 11791
Free: (866)866-8335
E-mail: lcaggiano@aol.com
URL: http://www.friendswhostutter.org
Contact: Lee Caggiano, Contact
Founded: 1998. **Membership Dues:** individual, $20 (annual). **Staff:** 2. **Budget:** $20,000. **Description:** Children and teenagers who stutter; family members of young people who stutter; professionals working with people who stutter. Seeks to create a network of love and support for members; promotes increased self-esteem among young people who stutter. Facilitates communication among members. **Publications:** *Reaching Out*, 9/year. Journal. **Circulation:** 1,500. **Conventions/Meetings:** annual convention.

16097 ■ House Ear Institute (HEI)

2100 W 3rd St.
Los Angeles, CA 90057
Ph: (213)483-4431
Free: (800)388-8612
Fax: (213)483-8789
E-mail: info@hei.org
URL: http://www.hei.org
Contact: Karen Hall, Exec. Asst.
Founded: 1946. **Staff:** 184. **Description:** Develops conceptual and technically feasible approaches to resolving hearing and balance disorders through applied research. Conducts research on subjects including hearing aids, auditory implants, aging ear, brain mapping, neuroanatomy, infant hearing diagnosis, and acoustic tumor. Offers seminars and classes for senior residents and practicing physicians. Operates children's center to serve profoundly deaf children and their families. Maintains library of 2800 volumes and 180 journal titles on otology. Sponsors videotape seminars and conducts courses on the use of hearing devices and how to evaluate hearing disorders. Provides support for parents raising a deaf or hard of hearing child. Compiles statistics; offers children's services; maintains speakers' bureau. **Libraries:** Type: open to the public. Holdings: 2,800; articles, books, video recordings. **Subjects:** otology, otolaryngology, audiology, psychoacoustics, cell and molecular biology. **Awards:** Type: recognition. **Telecommunication Services:** TDD, (213)484-2642. **Committees:** Research. **Formerly:** (1972) Los Angeles Foundation of Otology; (1981) Ear Research Institute. **Publications:** *House Calls*, semiannual. Magazine. Contains scientific studies and ongoing achievements in hearing research. ● Annual Report, annual ● Manuals ● Monographs ● Papers ● Brochures. **Conventions/Meetings:** periodic workshop.

16098 ■ International Foundation for Stutterers (IFS)

304 Hampshire Dr.
Plainsboro, NJ 08536
Ph: (609)275-3806
E-mail: elliotdennis@yahoo.com
Contact: Elliot Dennis, Contact
Founded: 1980. **Members:** 1,100. **Description:** Individuals who stutter, their families, speech therapists, and other interested persons. Aims to provide for the treatment and cure of stuttering through speech therapy in conjunction with self-help groups. Believes it is imperative for stutterers to reinforce techniques learned through speech therapy in an atmosphere outside of clinics and with the support of other stutterers. Establishes, maintains, and encourages formation of regional self-help groups for individuals undergoing therapy. Aims to make the public aware of the availability of professional treatment for stutterers. Conducts research to examine the causes and treatments of stuttering and to provide findings to the public. Sponsors seminars for speech therapists. Maintains speakers' bureau. **Publications:** *Look Who's Talking*, quarterly. Newsletter. **Price:** $18.00/year. **Conventions/Meetings:** annual meeting.

16099 ■ National Black Association for Speech-Language and Hearing (NBASLH)

800 Perry Hwy., Ste.3
Pittsburgh, PA 15229
Ph: (412)366-1177
Fax: (412)366-8804

E-mail: nbaslh@nbaslh.org
URL: http://www.nbaslh.org
Contact: Ronald Jones PhD, Chm.
Founded: 1978. **Members:** 500. **Membership Dues:** student, $25 (annual) ● associate, $50 (annual) ● professional, $75 (annual). **Description:** Professionals and other individuals concerned with communicatively handicapped blacks. Strongly encourages the recruitment and training of black professionals to work with individuals suffering from speech, language, and hearing problems; maintains that conditions such as race, socioeconomic class, and cultural differences must be taken into account in order to understand and sensitively study the communicative process, and to treat communicative disorders. Supports related research; solicits, and provides, financial support for the training of black students in speech-language pathology and audiology. Disseminates information. **Awards:** Competition Research Scholarship Award. **Frequency:** annual. **Type:** recognition. **Recipient:** for any African-American student who is enrolled at least part time in a Masters Degree program in speech-language pathology, audiology or the speech and hearing sciences. **Publications:** *Echo*, quarterly. Journal. **Price:** $7.00. **Circulation:** 500. **Advertising:** accepted. Alternate Formats: online. **Conventions/Meetings:** annual meeting (exhibits).

16100 ■ National Center for Neurogenic Communication Disorders (NCNCD)
Univ. of Arizona
PO Box 210071
Tucson, AZ 85721-0071
Ph: (520)621-1472
E-mail: bayles@u.arizona.edu
URL: http://cnet.shs.arizona.edu
Contact: Kathryn A. Bayles PhD, Assoc. Dir.
Description: Promotes research into speech and language disorders caused by diseases of the nervous system, with special interest in American Indian and Hispanic cultures.

16101 ■ National Center for Stuttering (NCS)
200 E 33rd St.
New York, NY 10016
Ph: (212)532-1460
Free: (800)221-2483
E-mail: executivedirector@stuttering.com
URL: http://www.stuttering.com
Contact: Dr. Martin F. Schwartz, Exec. Dir.
Founded: 1974. **Staff:** 10. **Budget:** $100,000. **Languages:** English, French, Spanish, Yiddish. **For-Profit. Description:** Furnishes information to parents of children who stutter. Provides treatment for children and adults who stutter and training on the latest practices and theories for speech pathologists. **Libraries: Type:** not open to the public. **Holdings:** articles, books. **Subjects:** stuttering. **Formerly:** Center for Speech Pathology. **Publications:** *Annual Review of Published Literature*, annual ● *Stutter No More*. Book ● Newsletter, quarterly.

16102 ■ National Center for Voice and Speech (NCVS)
c/o The Denver Center for the Performing Arts
1101 13th St.
Denver, CO 80204-5319
Ph: (303)446-4834
Fax: (303)893-6487
E-mail: ititze@dcpa.org
URL: http://www.ncvs.org
Contact: Ingo R. Titze PhD, Exec. Dir.
Founded: 1990. **Description:** Works to prevent, diagnose, treat voice and speech disorders through understanding underlying processes, including molecular, neurophysiologic, biomechanic, aerodynamic, acoustic. **Libraries: Type:** reference. **Holdings:** books. **Subjects:** private collections, scientific journals. **Publications:** *Vocal Vibrations*, biennial. Magazine. **Circulation:** 5,500. **Conventions/Meetings:** conference ● meeting ● seminar ● workshop.

16103 ■ National Cued Speech Association/Deaf Children's Literacy Project (NCSA)
c/o Sarina Roffe, Pres.
23970 Hermitage Rd.
Cleveland, OH 44122-4008
Fax: (718)421-5596
E-mail: info@cuedspeech.org
URL: http://www.cuedspeech.org
Contact: Sarina Roffe, Pres.
Founded: 1982. **Members:** 500. **Membership Dues:** individual, family, $35 (annual) ● association, business, $45 (annual) ● individual outside U.S., $40 (annual). **Staff:** 3. **Budget:** $100,000. **Regional Groups:** 2. **State Groups:** 8. **Description:** Promotes and supports the effective use of Cued Speech for communication, language acquisition, and literacy. Provides information, referral and support for persons with language, hearing, speech, and learning needs. Sponsors instructional programs, exhibits, and family learning vacations. **Awards:** Best of the Combined Federal Campaign. **Frequency:** annual. **Type:** monetary. **Recipient:** to the organizations with fiscal integrity. **Telecommunication Services:** TDD, (800)-459-3529. **Doing business as:** (2002) Deaf Children's Literacy Project. **Publications:** *Cued Speech Journal*, periodic. Covers various aspects of Cued Speech. **Price:** included in membership dues; $10.00 /year for nonmembers. Alternate Formats: online ● *On Cue*, quarterly. Newsletter. Contains calendar of events and regional reports. **Price:** included in membership dues; $25.00 /year for nonmembers. **Conventions/Meetings:** annual Cue Camps - conference, all ages learning vacations for families and professionals - always held in May through September; in various places in the United States and Europe.

16104 ■ National Student Speech Language Hearing Association (NSSLHA)
c/o Dawn D. Dickerson, Dir. of Operations
10801 Rockville Pike
Rockville, MD 20852
Free: (800)498-2071
Fax: (301)571-0481
E-mail: nsslha@asha.org
URL: http://www.nsslha.org
Contact: Dawn D. Dickerson, Dir. of Operations
Founded: 1972. **Members:** 12,000. **Membership Dues:** individual, $60 (annual). **Staff:** 2. **Budget:** $724,300. **Local Groups:** 300. **Description:** Serves as preprofessional organization for undergraduate and graduate students in speech-language pathology, speech and hearing sciences, and audiology. **Awards:** Honors of NSSLHA, CICSD Editors' Award. **Frequency:** annual. **Type:** recognition. **Recipient:** for outstanding students, faculty, chapters and individuals who have made significant contributions to both associations on a national and local level. **Formed by Merger of:** (1980) Student Journal Group of the American Speech and Hearing Association; Sigma Alpha Eta. **Formerly:** National Student Speech and Hearing Association. **Publications:** *Contemporary Issues in Communication Science and Disorders*, semiannual. Journal. **Price:** included in membership dues; $20.00 for nonmembers. ISSN: 0736-0312. **Circulation:** 16,000. **Advertising:** accepted ● *NSSLHA Now!*. Newsletter. **Conventions/Meetings:** annual meeting, held in conjunction with American Speech, Language, and Hearing Association (exhibits) - always November.

16105 ■ National Stuttering Association (NSA)
119 W 40th St., 14th Fl.
New York, NY 10018
Ph: (212)944-4050
Free: (800)937-8888
Fax: (212)944-8244
E-mail: info@westutter.org
URL: http://www.WeStutter.org
Contact: Ms. Elaine Saitta, Exec. Dir.
Founded: 1977. **Members:** 4,000. **Membership Dues:** regular, $35 (annual) ● student/low income, $20 (annual). **Staff:** 1. **Budget:** $180,000. **Local Groups:** 79. **Languages:** English, Spanish. **Descrip-**

tion: Serves as self-help organization of people who stutter, parents of children who stutter, and speech pathologists. Seeks to provide a safe, supportive environment for stutterers and their families through chapter meetings, special programs, workshops, tape series, and self-help groups. Concentrates on issues such as improving self-image and assuming personal responsibility rather than focusing on speech fluency. Educates the public about stuttering and functions as a referral service for those seeking professional help. (Does not provide speech therapy or trained therapists.) Offers consulting in program development and technical assistance to school districts, speech clinics, hospitals, rehabilitation centers, and other agencies involved in speech services. Advises members on how to be wise consumers of speech and related therapies. Maintains speakers' bureau. **Libraries: Type:** open to the public. **Subjects:** stuttering. **Publications:** *Letting Go, Care, Stutter Buddies*, bimonthly. Newsletter. Benefits parents, children and adults. **Price:** $35.00 ● *Letting Go, Stutter Buddies*. Audiotapes. Publication for children. ● Audiotapes ● Brochures ● Pamphlets. **Conventions/Meetings:** annual conference (exhibits).

16106 ■ Speak Easy International Foundation (SEIF)
233 Concord Dr.
Paramus, NJ 07652
Ph: (201)262-0895 (201)848-0455
Fax: (201)262-0895
E-mail: speakezusa@juno.com
Contact: Robert Gathman, Pres.
Founded: 1977. **Membership Dues:** regular, associate, member-at-large, $80 (annual). **Staff:** 7. **State Groups:** 8. **Local Groups:** 1. **Languages:** English, German. **Description:** Support group and information source for individuals with a speech dysfluency (stuttering). Seeks to instill confidence in stutterers and reinforce fluency in their speech. Educates public, families, and friends on the problems of speech diffluent individuals. **Libraries: Type:** reference. **Holdings:** books, clippings. **Subjects:** stuttering. **Awards: Frequency:** periodic. **Type:** scholarship. **Publications:** *Speak Easy Newsletter* (in English and German), quarterly. Contains activities of self-help groups, research reports on stuttering; convention schedules. **Price:** $40.00/year; $60.00/ two years. **Circulation:** 400 ● *Why Can't We Talk*. Video. Contains theatre-piece on stuttering. **Price:** $129.95 for institutions; $25.00 for individuals. **Conventions/Meetings:** annual meeting and retreat - in fall ● annual symposium and workshop, includes keynote speakers - during the summer.

16107 ■ Stuttering Foundation of America (SFA)
3100 Walnut Grove Rd., Ste.603
PO Box 11749
Memphis, TN 38111-0749
Ph: (901)452-7343
Free: (800)992-9392
Fax: (901)452-3931
E-mail: info@stutteringhelp.org
URL: http://www.stutteringhelp.org
Contact: Jane H. Fraser, Pres.
Founded: 1947. **Membership Dues:** nonprofit organization, $5 (annual). **Staff:** 7. **Budget:** $1,000,000. **Languages:** English, French, Spanish. **Description:** Provides comprehensive materials, including videotapes, books and brochures, on stuttering to both the public and professionals. Seeks to bring together speech pathologists concerned with the prevention and treatment of stuttering. Provides referrals to speech-language pathologists specializing in stuttering. Provides support for research into the causes of stuttering. **Libraries: Type:** open to the public. **Holdings:** 50; articles, books, periodicals. **Subjects:** stuttering. **Awards:** SFA Award for Excellence in Reporting. **Frequency:** annual. **Type:** monetary. **Computer Services:** Mailing lists. **Telecommunication Services:** electronic mail, webmaster@stutteringhelp.org ● additional toll-free number, (800)967-7700. **Formerly:** (1991) Speech Foundation of America. **Publications:** *Advice to Those Who Stutter* (in English and Spanish). Book. **Price:** $2.00

● *The Child Who Stutters: To the Health Care Provider*. Book. **Price:** $2.00 ● *The Child Who Stutters: To the Pediatrician, 2nd Edition*. Book ● *Do You Stutter: A Guide for Teens, 3rd Edition*. Book ● *If Your Child Stutters: A Guide for Parents, 5th Edition*. Book ● *The School-Age Child Who Stutters: Working Effectively with Attitudes and Emotions*. **Price:** $15.00 ● *Self Therapy for the Stutterer, 10th Edition*. Book. **Price:** $3.00 ● *Sometimes I Just Stutter*. Book. **Price:** $2.00 ● *Stuttering and Your Child: Help for Families*. Video. **Price:** $10.00 ● *Stuttering and Your Child: Questions and Answers, 3rd Edition*. Book. **Price:** $2.00 ● Newsletter, quarterly. Contains SFA activities and information on stuttering. **Price:** free. Alternate Formats: online ● Brochures. Alternate Formats: online. **Conventions/Meetings:** annual Practical Ideas for the School Clinician - workshop, focuses on ways to work with school-age children who stutter (exhibits) - 2nd week of June ● annual Practical Ideas for Working With School Age Children Who Stutter - workshop - usually in Seattle, Washington; Boston, Massachusetts; Tallahassee, Florida, in June ● annual Stuttering Therapy: Workshop for Specialists, cosponsored with Iowa University - usually 2nd or 3rd week in July.

16108 ■ Voice Foundation (VF)

1721 Pine St.
Philadelphia, PA 19103
Ph: (215)735-7999
Fax: (215)735-9293
E-mail: office@voicefoundation.org
URL: http://www.voicefoundation.org
Contact: Robert Thayer Sataloff MD, Chm.
Founded: 1969. **Members:** 350. **Membership Dues:** domestic professional, $250 (annual) ● domestic associate, $50 (annual) ● foreign associate, $75 (annual) ● sustaining, $125 (annual) ● foreign professional, $275 (annual) ● institutional, $500 (annual) ● corporate, $2,500 (annual) ● life, $5,000 ● foreign sustaining, $150 (annual). **Staff:** 2. **Description:** Sponsors research and education on the causes, prevention, and treatment of voice disorders. Sponsors educational programs. Holds fundraising events. **Libraries: Type:** reference. **Holdings:** audiovisuals, papers. **Subjects:** vocal care. **Awards: Type:** recognition ● **Type:** scholarship ● Voice Education Research Awareness Award. **Frequency:** annual. **Type:** grant. **Recipient:** to individuals with unusual interest and contribution in voice communication. **Computer Services:** Mailing lists, of members. **Publications:** *Journal of Voice*, quarterly. **Price:** $131.00 /year for individuals in U.S.; $151.00 /year for individuals outside U.S.; $281.00 /year for libraries and institutions in U.S.; $301.00 /year for libraries and institutions outside U.S. ISSN: 0892-1997. **Circulation:** 1,000. Alternate Formats: online ● *Voice Foundation Newsletter*, 3-4/year. **Price:** included in membership dues ● Videos. **Conventions/Meetings:** annual symposium (exhibits) - always May/June, Philadelphia, PA.

Spina Bifida

16109 ■ Spina Bifida Association of America (SBAA)

4590 MacArthur Blvd. NW, Ste.250
Washington, DC 20007-4226
Ph: (202)944-3285
Free: (800)621-3141
Fax: (202)944-3295
E-mail: sbaa@sbaa.org
URL: http://www.sbaa.org
Contact: Ms. Cindy Brownstein, CEO
Founded: 1973. **Members:** 6,000. **Membership Dues:** student, $20 (annual) ● family, individual, $25 (annual) ● professional/agency/school, $40 (annual) ● international, $50 (annual). **Staff:** 8. **Budget:** $400,000. **State Groups:** 60. **Local Groups:** 60. **Description:** Individuals with spina bifida; their parents, relatives, and friends; concerned professionals. (Spina bifida, or "open spine," is the second most common disabling birth defect and results in muscle weakness or paralysis and incontinence. Its cause is

unknown and there is no complete cure.) Aims are to: develop an information service of materials relating to spina bifida; conduct research into the causes of the birth defect; improve vocational training of individuals with spina bifida; monitor development of legislation applying to disabled persons. Promotes public awareness and action through national media; provides referral services; participates in appropriate legislative activities; holds seminars on scientific, social, medical, and educational programs. Provides training of competent personnel to aid in the treatment, care, education, adjustment, and rehabilitation of individuals with spina bifida. **Awards: Frequency:** annual. **Type:** scholarship. **Committees:** Adoption Information; Adult Network; Chapter Development; Education; Government Affairs; Professional Advisory; Public Affairs; Publication Review; Research. **Publications:** *Insights* (in English and Spanish), bimonthly. Newsletter. **Price:** included in membership dues. **Advertising:** accepted ● *Spina Bifida Insights*, bimonthly. Newsletter. Reports on the developments in medicine, education, and legislation affecting the problems and needs of persons with spina bifida. **Price:** included in membership dues; $25.00 /year for nonmembers in U.S.; $40.00/year for professionals; $50.00 /year for nonmembers outside U.S. **Advertising:** accepted ● Pamphlets ● Reports. **Conventions/Meetings:** annual conference (exhibits) - always June.

Spinal Injury

16110 ■ American Association of Spinal Cord Injury Psychologists and Social Workers (AASCIPSW)

75-20 Astoria Blvd.
Jackson Heights, NY 11372
Ph: (718)803-3782
Fax: (718)803-0414
E-mail: aascipsw@unitedspinal.org
URL: http://www.aascipsw.org
Contact: Dr. Vivian Beyda, Assoc. Exec. Dir.
Founded: 1986. **Members:** 430. **Membership Dues:** active, associate, $125 (annual). **Staff:** 5. **Budget:** $450,000. **Description:** Psychologists, social workers, and counselors (CRC and LPC) who treat patients with spinal cord impairment; others interested in the spinal injury field. Promotes improved psychosocial care of spinal cord injury patients; develops and enhances related education and research programs. Focuses on topics such as sexuality and spinal cord injury, alcohol and drug dependent spinal cord injury patients, adjusting to spinal cord injuries, and planning for care in the community. **Awards:** Clinical Performance Award. **Frequency:** annual. **Type:** recognition ● Essie Morgan Excellence Award. **Frequency:** annual. **Type:** recognition ● James J. Peters Distinguished Service Award. **Frequency:** annual. **Type:** recognition ● Organizational Award. **Frequency:** annual. **Type:** recognition. **Publications:** *SCI Psychosocial Process*, quarterly. Journal. **Price:** included in membership dues. **Circulation:** 2,500. **Advertising:** accepted ● Also publishes Suggested Reading List, Standards for SCI Psychosocial Rehabilitation and practice guidelines. **Conventions/Meetings:** annual conference (exhibits) - Labor Day week.

16111 ■ American Paraplegia Society (APS)

75-20 Astoria Blvd.
Jackson Heights, NY 11372
Ph: (718)803-3782
Fax: (718)803-0414
E-mail: aps@unitedspinal.org
URL: http://www.apssci.org
Contact: Vivian Beyda PhD, Assoc. Exec. Dir.
Founded: 1954. **Members:** 500. **Membership Dues:** individual (active, associate), $200 (annual). **Staff:** 5. **Budget:** $625,000. **Description:** Represents physicians and researchers in the spinal cord injury field. Aims to advance and foster improved health care of spinal cord injury patients, and develop and promote education and research in the neuroscience fields. Sponsors seminars; maintains library. Conducts annual educational program. **Libraries: Type:** refer-

ence. **Subjects:** spinal cord injury, disease health issues, legal architecture. **Awards:** Ernest Bors Award. **Frequency:** annual. **Type:** recognition. **Recipient:** for clinical skills and accomplishment in the field of spinal cord impairment ● Estin Comarr Memorial Award. **Frequency:** annual. **Type:** recognition. **Recipient:** for clinical service ● Excellence Award. **Frequency:** annual. **Type:** recognition. **Recipient:** for outstanding leadership. **Publications:** *Journal of Spinal Cord Medicine*, quarterly. **Circulation:** 3,000. **Conventions/Meetings:** annual conference (exhibits) - Labor Day week.

16112 ■ American Spinal Injury Association (ASIA)

2020 Peachtree Rd. NW
Atlanta, GA 30309-1402
Ph: (404)355-9772
Fax: (404)355-1826
E-mail: asiaoffice@shepherd.org
URL: http://www.asia-spinalinjury.org
Contact: Marcalee Sipski Alexander MD, Pres./Dir.
Founded: 1973. **Members:** 450. **Membership Dues:** full, MD, $350 (annual) ● corresponding, associate, non-MD, $125 (annual) ● doctoral level, $225 (annual). **Staff:** 3. **Budget:** $350,000. **Description:** Medical doctors and Allied Health Care professionals who have been trained in the care of spinal injury patients and who are either actively engaged in the field and acknowledged to be competent by their peers or who have made a significant contribution to the advancement of the basic sciences or one of the clinical fields of practice as they are applicable to the treatment of spinal cord injury. Aims are to: develop knowledge and investigation of the causes, cure, and prevention of spinal injury and related trauma; pursue excellence in spinal injury patient care; promote and exchange ideas between professionals in the field; standardize medical terminology in spinal cord injury; foster and encourage basic research in the field; develop teaching and educational material; foster education of the medical profession and laity in the prevention and proper management of spinal injury, including the necessity for specialized regional spinal injury centers, provision for educational and vocational training, removal of architectural barriers, and promotion of a society more sensitive to individuals with a physical disability, including adequate housing and transportation; establish criteria for centers and/or systems of total spinal injury management so as to provide optimal care of a person with spinal injury. Conducts annual scientific sessions. Sponsors G. Heiner Sell Distinguished Lectureship. **Awards:** Best Journal Article by a Member Award. **Type:** recognition ● Best Paper Awards. **Type:** recognition ● Erica Nader Award. **Frequency:** annual. **Type:** recognition ● Lifetime Achievement Award. **Frequency:** annual. **Type:** grant ● Synthes Award. **Type:** recognition. **Computer Services:** Mailing lists. **Committees:** Awards; Education; International Relations; Legislative Issues; Membership; Prevention; Research; Spine; Standards; Urology. **Publications:** *International Standards of Neurological Classification of Spinal Injuries*. Article. Includes videos and manuals. **Conventions/Meetings:** annual Scientific Sessions - meeting.

16113 ■ Cervical Spine Research Society (CSRS)

6300 N River Rd., Ste.727
Rosemont, IL 60018-4226
Ph: (847)698-1628
Fax: (847)823-0536
E-mail: wlezien@aaos.org
URL: http://www.csrs.org
Contact: Peggy Wlezien, Dir.
Founded: 1973. **Members:** 310. **Membership Dues:** active, corresponding, $200 (annual). **Staff:** 3. **Multinational. Description:** Promotes the exchange and development of ideas and philosophy regarding the diagnosis and treatment of cervical spine injury and disease. **Computer Services:** Online services, directory. **Committees:** Archives; Clinical Outcomes; Communications; Continuing Education; Development and Industry Relations; Editorial; Exhibits; Instructional Course Planning. **Publications:** News-

letter. **Alternate Formats:** online. **Conventions/Meetings:** annual meeting, with instructional course - 2007 Nov. 29-Dec. 1, San Francisco, CA - **Avg. Attendance:** 400; 2008 Dec. 5-6, New Orleans, LA; 2009 Dec. 3-5, Salt Lake City, UT.

16114 ■ Christopher Reeve Foundation (CRF)
636 Morris Tpke., Ste.3A
Short Hills, NJ 07078
Ph: (973)379-2690
Free: (800)225-0292
Fax: (973)912-9433
E-mail: info@christopherreeve.org
URL: http://www.christopherreeve.org
Contact: Joel M. Faden, Exec. Committee Chm.
Founded: 1982. **Staff:** 15. **Regional Groups:** 1. **Description:** Seeks to encourage and support research to find a cure for paralysis caused by spinal cord injury and other central nervous system disorders. Offers the Christopher and Dana Reeve Paralysis Resource Center to assist people with paralysis with their questions. Provides a free lending library and free book "Paralysis Resource Guide" in English and Spanish. **Libraries: Type:** open to the public. **Holdings:** 3,500; audio recordings, audiovisuals, books, periodicals, video recordings. **Subjects:** paralysis. **Awards: Type:** grant. **Recipient:** to research laboratories and individuals for postgraduate study ● **Type:** grant. **Recipient:** to physicians and scientists conducting research on the spinal cord and central nervous system. **Additional Websites:** http://www.paralysis.org. **Councils:** Science Advisory. **Divisions:** Research. **Absorbed:** Paralysis Cure Research Foundation. **Formerly:** (1981) Kent Waldrep International Spinal Cord Research Foundation; (2002) American Paralysis Association; (2006) Christopher Reeve Paralysis Foundation. **Publications:** *American Paralysis Association Progress in Research*, semiannual. Newsletter ● *Annual Review*, annual ● *Paralysis Resource Guide*. Book. Contains free 310-page book in English or Spanish. **Conventions/Meetings:** periodic conference.

16115 ■ International Intradiscal Therapy Society (IITS)
810 North St.
Belgium, WI 53004-9531
Ph: (262)285-4487
Fax: (262)285-4231
E-mail: ellen.yolich@iits.org
URL: http://www.iits.org
Contact: Ellen M. Yolich, Exec. Sec.
Founded: 1987. **Members:** 268. **Membership Dues:** active, $200 (annual) ● associate, $100 (annual). **Multinational. Description:** Provides information on the most effective techniques to treat intradiscal spinal disorders. **Awards:** Golf Awards. **Frequency:** annual. **Type:** recognition ● Lyman Smith Award. **Frequency:** periodic. **Type:** recognition. **Recipient:** for best paper ● Meeting Awards. **Frequency:** annual. **Type:** monetary. **Publications:** Newsletter. **Conventions/Meetings:** annual meeting (exhibits) ● workshop.

16116 ■ International Spinal Development and Research Foundation
600 S Rancho Dr., Ste.101
Las Vegas, NV 89108
E-mail: spine@spine-research.org
URL: http://www.spine-research.org
Contact: John S. Thalgott MD, Clinical Dir.
Founded: 1994. **Multinational. Description:** Promotes development of new techniques, approaches, instruments, and implants for spinal surgery; disseminates research. Does not perform spinal cord injury research or act as a watchdog. Oversees education of U.S. and foreign born spinal surgeons.

16117 ■ International Spine Intervention Society (ISIS)
c/o Jordon Moncrief, Chief Operating Off.
5 Ash Ave.
Kentfield, CA 94904-1504
Ph: (415)457-4747
Free: (888)255-0005
Fax: (415)457-3495

E-mail: isisfiles@msn.com
URL: http://www.spinalinjection.com
Contact: Jordon Moncrief, Chief Operating Off.
Founded: 1989. **Membership Dues:** general, $300. **Multinational. Description:** Physicians interested in the development, implementation, and standardization of percutaneous techniques for the precision diagnosis of spinal pain. **Formerly:** (2005) International Spinal Injection Society. **Publications:** *ISIS Scientific Newsletter.* Alternate Formats: online ● *Practice Guidelines: Spinal Diagnostic and Treatment Procedures.* Book. **Price:** $75.00 for members; $225.00 for nonmembers, institutions. **Conventions/Meetings:** lecture ● annual meeting.

16118 ■ Kent Waldrep National Paralysis Foundation
Address Unknown since 2007
Founded: 1985. **Description:** Works for increased rate of recovery for newly injured victims through drug therapies and treatments, and a cure for those afflicted with chronic or long-term paralysis. **Publications:** *One Step*, quarterly. Newsletter. Alternate Formats: online.

16119 ■ National Spinal Cord Injury Association (NSCIA)
6701 Democracy Blvd., Ste.300-9
Bethesda, MD 20817
Free: (800)962-9629
Fax: (301)990-0445
E-mail: info@spinalcord.org
URL: http://www.spinalcord.org
Contact: Marcie Roth, Exec. Dir.
Founded: 1948. **Members:** 11,000. **Staff:** 6. **Budget:** $500,000. **Local Groups:** 50. **Description:** Seeks to inform and educate the medical and allied professions, persons with spinal cord injury or disease, their families, and the public on spinal cord injury. Provides information, referral and resource services to individuals with spinal cord injuries and diseases and their families to maximize quality of life. Offers activities in public and professional prevention and education programs and services. Conducts recreation, advocacy, support group, and peer counseling programs through national network of chapters and support groups. **Libraries: Type:** reference. **Awards: Type:** recognition. **Telecommunication Services:** electronic mail, resource@spinalcord.org. **Committees:** Prevention; Scientific Advisory; Services. **Affiliated With:** Paralyzed Veterans of America. **Formerly:** National Spinal Cord Injury Foundation; (1979) National Paraplegia Foundation. **Publications:** *Spinal Cord Injury Life*, quarterly. Journal. Provides news and articles concerning persons with spinal cord injuries caused by trauma or disease. Includes book reviews. **Price:** included in membership dues; $40.00/year. **Circulation:** 12,000. **Advertising:** accepted. Also Cited As: *SCI Life* ● Also publishes fact sheets on research, sexuality and other topics. **Conventions/Meetings:** biennial Educational Conference (exhibits).

16120 ■ Spinal Cord Society (SCS)
19051 County Hwy. 1
Fergus Falls, MN 56537-7609
Ph: (218)739-5252 (218)739-5261
Fax: (218)739-5262
URL: http://members.aol.com/scsweb
Contact: Dr. Chas E. Carson PhD, Pres.
Founded: 1978. **Members:** 9,000. **Membership Dues:** individual in U.S., $30 (annual) ● individual outside U.S., $45 (annual). **Staff:** 4. **Local Groups:** 170. **Description:** Spinal cord injury victims and their friends and families; physicians, nurses, physical and rehabilitation therapists, and other medical professionals. Aims to promote research and increase public awareness concerning the potential for a cure of paralysis due to spinal cord injury. Focuses on the cure rather than rehabilitation for paralysis due to spinal injury. Promotes funding of reversal-oriented pure and applied medical research; encourages establishment of spinal injury centers in conjunction with existing hospitals and medical centers; maintains data bank of chronic spinal cord injury case histories, continuously monitored and upgraded for improving

treatment, guiding research, and screening patients for referral to other physicians or to a spinal injury center. Through concentration on research, data, and treatment, seeks to provide a base of information, statistical analysis, and experience, with accelerated progress and minimal duplication of effort. Maintains medical center in Minneapolis, MN that applies state-of-art treatment to paralysis victims. **Publications:** *Spinal Cord Society Newsletter*, monthly. Includes convention news, letters, and information on services. **Price:** $30.00/year. **Circulation:** 4,000. **Conventions/Meetings:** annual conference.

16121 ■ Think First National Injury Prevention Foundation
26 S La Grange Rd., Ste.103
La Grange, IL 60525
Ph: (708)588-2000
Free: (800)844-6556
Fax: (708)588-2002
E-mail: thinkfirst@thinkfirst.org
URL: http://www.thinkfirst.org
Contact: David A. Cavanaugh MD, Chm.
Founded: 1986. **Staff:** 4. **Budget:** $750,000. **State Groups:** 20. **Local Groups:** 200. **Description:** Works to educate young people about personal vulnerability and the consequences of risk taking behavior. Aims to prevent permanent brain, spinal cord, and other traumatic injuries. Conducts school-based educational programs, reinforcement activities, general public education and public policy initiatives. **Libraries: Type:** reference. **Holdings:** articles, audiovisuals. **Subjects:** brain and spinal cord injury prevention. **Formerly:** (2000) Think First Foundation: National Injury Prevention Programs. **Publications:** *Prevention Pages*, quarterly. Newsletter ● *Think First for Kids Curriculum Packet.* Contains instructional materials for children in grades 1-3. **Price:** $249.00. **Conventions/Meetings:** semiannual conference and board meeting - spring and fall.

Sports Medicine

16122 ■ American Academy of Podiatric Sports Medicine (AAPSM)
109 Greenwich Dr.
Walkersville, MD 21793
Ph: (301)845-9887
Free: (888)854-FEET
Fax: (301)845-9888
E-mail: info@aapsm.org
URL: http://www.aapsm.org
Contact: Rita J. Yates, Exec. Dir.
Founded: 1970. **Members:** 600. **Membership Dues:** general, $200 (annual). **Staff:** 2. **Description:** Represents podiatrists, medical doctors, and athletic trainers interested in promoting professional participation and research in sports medicine. Directs 12 committees that deal with individual sports. Compiles statistics. **Awards:** Golden Foot Award. **Frequency:** annual. **Type:** recognition ● Robert Barnes Distinguished Service Award. **Frequency:** annual. **Type:** recognition. **Affiliated With:** American Podiatric Medical Association. **Publications:** *AAPSM Newsletter*, quarterly. Features articles on the treatment of sports injuries in the field of podiatry. Includes calendar of events and research updates. **Price:** included in membership dues. **Circulation:** 1,300. **Advertising:** accepted. **Conventions/Meetings:** annual meeting (exhibits).

16123 ■ American Academy of Sports Physicians (AASP)
17445 Oak Creek Ct.
Encino, CA 91316
Ph: (818)501-8855
Fax: (818)501-8855
E-mail: aasp-@mindspring.com
Contact: Janie Zimmer, Coor.
Founded: 1979. **Members:** 150. **Membership Dues:** regular, $150 (annual) ● associate - nurse practitioner/physician assistant, $100 (annual) ● associate - fellow/resident, $75 (annual). **Description:** Clinical physicians engaged in the practice of sports medicine

who have made contributions in research, academics, or related fields. Objectives are to educate and inform physicians whose practices comprise mainly sports medicine and to register and recognize physicians who have expertise in sports medicine. Sponsors seminars. **Awards: Type:** recognition. **Publications:** Newsletter, quarterly. **Conventions/Meetings:** annual meeting.

16124 ■ American College of Sports Medicine (ACSM)
401 W Michigan St.
Indianapolis, IN 46202-3233
Ph: (317)637-9200
Fax: (317)634-7817
E-mail: publicinfo@acsm.org
URL: http://www.acsm.org
Contact: James R. Whitehead, Exec. VP
Founded: 1954. **Members:** 20,000. **Membership Dues:** professional, $195 (annual) ● professional-in-training, $145 (annual) ● associate, $135 (annual) ● graduate/undergraduate student, $80 (annual). **Staff:** 35. **Budget:** $6,000,000. **Regional Groups:** 12. **Description:** Promotes and integrates scientific research, education, and practical applications of sports medicine and exercise science to maintain and enhance physical performance, fitness, health, and quality of life. Certifies fitness leaders, fitness instructors, exercise test technologists, exercise specialists, health/fitness program directors, and U.S. military fitness personnel. Grants Continuing Medical Education (CME) and Continuing Education Credits (CEC). Operates more than 50 committees. **Libraries: Type:** reference. **Subjects:** exercise science, sports medicine. **Awards:** Honor Award. **Frequency:** annual. **Type:** recognition. **Recipient:** for outstanding contribution to sports medicine. **Computer Services:** Mailing lists, of members. **Absorbed:** (2004) Association for Worksite Health Promotion. **Publications:** *ACSM Fitness Book.* Gives guidelines on daily fitness programs and training regimens. **Price:** $15.00. ISSN: 8801-1783 ● *ACSM's Guidelines for Exercise Testing and Prescription, 6th Ed.* ● *ACSM's Health/ Fitness Facility Standards and Guidelines* ● *ACSM's Resource Manual for Guidelines for Exercise Testing and Prescription* ● *American College of Sports Medicine Directory of Graduate Programs in Sports Medicine and Exercise Science,* annual. Lists graduate programs in fields related to exercise science and sports medicine at North American institutions. **Price:** $20.00. **Circulation:** 1,000 ● *American College of Sports Medicine Guidelines for the Team Physician* ● *Exercise and Sport Sciences Reviews,* annual. Monographs. **Price:** included in membership dues; $88.00 /year for nonmembers. **Circulation:** 20,000 ● *Medicine and Science in Sports and Exercise,* monthly. Journal. **Price:** included in membership dues; $303.00 /year for nonmembers ● *Medicine and Science in Sports and Exercise Cumulative Index* ● *Sports Medicine Bulletin,* bimonthly. Magazine. Covers association activities and professional topics. Includes book reviews, calendar of events, and information on membership and fellowship. **Price:** included in membership dues. **Circulation:** 20,000. Alternate Formats: online ● Also publishes position stands, current comments and health and fitness brochures. **Conventions/Meetings:** annual conference, for health, fitness, or nutrition professionals (exhibits) ● annual meeting, medical and scientific (exhibits) ● seminar ● workshop.

16125 ■ American Medical Equestrian Association/Safe Riders Foundation (AMEA/SRF)
PO Box 91883
Albuquerque, NM 87199
Free: (866)441-2632
E-mail: ameasrf@equestriansafety.com
URL: http://www.ameaonline.org
Contact: Ms. Wanda Franks, Admin. Off.
Founded: 1990. **Members:** 175. **Membership Dues:** individual, $50 (annual) ● organization, $100 (annual) ● organization (over 200 members), $250 (annual). **Staff:** 1. **Budget:** $15,000. **Description:** Physicians, health personnel, and individuals interested in equestrian safety. Seeks to decrease accidents

related to horseback riding through education and awareness programs. Advocates use of headgear for riders. Offers recommendations, consultations, and leadership to equestrian organizations. Conducts studies and surveys. Compiles statistics. **Libraries: Type:** reference. **Holdings:** 100; periodicals. **Subjects:** horse-related accidents, injuries of rider/caregiver. **Awards:** Ayer-Hammett. **Frequency:** annual. **Type:** recognition. **Recipient:** for safety leadership. **Computer Services:** Mailing lists, available to members. **Formerly:** (2003) American Medical Equestrian Association. **Publications:** *AMEA News,* quarterly. Newsletter. Includes articles and statistics on horse-related human injuries. **Price:** included in membership dues. **Circulation:** 400 ● *Planning Event Coverage.* Booklet ● *When Can My Child Ride a Horse.* Brochure. **Conventions/Meetings:** annual conference (exhibits) - fall.

16126 ■ American Medical Society for Sports Medicine (AMSSM)
11639 Earnshaw
Overland Park, KS 66210
Ph: (913)327-1415
Fax: (913)327-1491
E-mail: office@amssm.org
URL: http://www.amssm.org
Contact: Paul Stricker MD, Pres.
Founded: 1991. **Membership Dues:** associate, affiliate, $300 (annual) ● provisional, $225 (annual) ● resident, $150 (annual). **Description:** Sports medicine specialists. Provides a forum specific for primary care non-surgical sports medicine physicians. **Awards: Frequency:** annual. **Type:** scholarship. **Recipient:** for an individual who is planning a career in Sports Medicine. **Computer Services:** Mailing lists. **Publications:** *AMSSM Newsletter* ● *Clinical Journal of Sports Medicine* ● Directory. Alternate Formats: online. **Conventions/Meetings:** annual conference.

16127 ■ American Orthopaedic Society for Sports Medicine (AOSSM)
6300 N River Rd., Ste.500
Rosemont, IL 60018
Ph: (847)292-4900
Free: (877)321-3500
Fax: (847)292-4905
E-mail: aossm@aossm.org
URL: http://www.sportsmed.org
Contact: Irvin E. Bomberger, Exec. Dir.
Founded: 1972. **Members:** 2,000. **Membership Dues:** associate, active, affiliate, $450 (annual). **Staff:** 11. **Budget:** $3,000,000. **Description:** Promotes sports medicine education, research, communication and fellowship; disseminates information to orthopaedic surgeons working in sports medicine. **Awards:** Excellence in Research. **Frequency:** annual. **Type:** monetary. **Computer Services:** Mailing lists. **Publications:** *American Journal of Sports Medicine,* bimonthly. Reports on the diagnosis, treatment, prevention, and rehabilitation of sports-related injury and disease; also includes society news and book reviews. **Price:** $80.00 /year for individuals; $100.00 /year for institutions; $30.00/year for students. ISSN: 0363-5465. **Circulation:** 11,000. **Advertising:** accepted. Alternate Formats: microform. **Conventions/Meetings:** annual meeting, instructional and fraternal (exhibits) - usually June or July.

16128 ■ American Osteopathic Academy of Sports Medicine (AOASM)
2810 Crossroads Dr., Ste.3800
Madison, WI 53718
Ph: (608)443-2477
Fax: (608)443-2474
E-mail: info@aoasm.org
URL: http://www.aoasm.org
Contact: Susan M. Rees, Exec. Dir.
Founded: 1975. **Members:** 500. **Membership Dues:** physician, affiliate, $325 (annual) ● resident, intern, fellow, associate, $230 (annual) ● student, $130 (annual). **Description:** Members of the American Osteopathic Association and students enrolled in approved colleges of osteopathic medicine. Promotes education, development of high ethical standards, communication, and research in the field of sports

medicine. Conducts study programs, lectures, forums, and seminars. Encourages publication of articles and dissertations in scientific and professional journals. Sponsors student academy organizations at osteopathic education institutions. Maintains speakers' bureau. **Awards:** Fellow, American Osteopathic Academy of Sports Medicine. **Frequency:** annual. **Type:** fellowship. **Recipient:** for applicants who have completed residency in the following specialties: family practice, emergency medicine, internal medicine, pediatrics, physical medicine, rehabilitation and manipulative medicine. **Computer Services:** Mailing lists. **Telecommunication Services:** electronic mail, srees@reesgroupinc.com. **Committees:** Certification; Continuing Medical Education; Editorial Board. **Publications:** *Clinical Journal of Sports Medicine,* bimonthly. Reviews research and educational programs in sports medicine. Contains calendar of events. **Price:** included in membership dues. ISSN: 1050-642X. **Circulation:** 3,000. **Advertising:** accepted ● Membership Directory, annual. **Conventions/Meetings:** annual Clinical Conference (exhibits).

16129 ■ American Sports Medicine Institute (ASMI)
2660 10th Ave. S, Ste.505
Birmingham, AL 35205
Ph: (205)918-0000 (205)918-2127
Fax: (205)918-0800
E-mail: ljohnson@asmi.org
URL: http://www.asmi.org
Contact: Lanier Johnson, Exec. Dir.
Description: Aims to improve the understanding, prevention, and treatment of sports-related injuries through research and education. **Libraries: Type:** reference. **Holdings:** books. **Subjects:** orthopaedics, sports medicine. **Awards:** James R. Andrews Award for Excellence in Baseball Sports Medicine. **Frequency:** annual. **Type:** recognition. **Recipient:** to an individual or group that made significant contribution to baseball sports medicine. **Publications:** *American Journal of Sports Medicine* ● *Conditioning Program for Baseball Pitchers.* Booklet. **Price:** $10.00 plus shipping and handling ● *Sports Engineering.* **Conventions/Meetings:** annual Injuries in Baseball Course - seminar.

16130 ■ Association for the Advancement of Applied Sport Psychology (AAASP)
2810 Crossroads Dr., Ste.3800
Madison, WI 53718
Ph: (608)443-2475
Fax: (608)443-2474
E-mail: president-elect@aaasponline.org
URL: http://www.aaasponline.org
Contact: Vikki Krane, Pres.
Founded: 1986. **Members:** 1,300. **Membership Dues:** professional, affiliate, $135 (annual) ● student, $75 (annual). **Multinational. Description:** Promotes the development of research, theory, and intervention strategies in sport psychology. Deals with ethical and professional issues related to the development of sport psychology and to the provision of psychological services in sport and exercise settings. Sponsors research and educational programs. **Awards:** Dissertation Award. **Frequency:** annual. **Type:** recognition. **Recipient:** for excellence in doctoral dissertations conducted on a topic involving exercise or sport psychology ● Distinguished International Scholar. **Frequency:** periodic. **Type:** recognition. **Recipient:** for an international scholar recognized for his/her research in applied sport psychology ● Distinguished Professional Practice Award. **Frequency:** periodic. **Type:** recognition. **Recipient:** for contribution to the development of the practice of sport psychology ● Dorothy V. Harris Memorial Award. **Frequency:** periodic. **Type:** recognition. **Recipient:** for AAASP scholar/practitioner in the early stage of his/her scientific and/or professional career ● Thesis Award. **Frequency:** annual. **Type:** recognition. **Recipient:** for excellence in thesis research. **Publications:** *Directory of Graduate Programs in Applied Sport Psychology.* Alternate Formats: online ● *Journal of Applied Sport Psychology,* quarterly. ISSN: 1041-3200 ● Newsletter, 3/year. Contains professional articles,

organization information, and book reviews. **Circulation:** 1,300. **Advertising:** accepted ● Membership Directory. Alternate Formats: online. **Conventions/Meetings:** annual conference (exhibits).

16131 ■ Big Picture Alliance (BPA)
1315 Walnut St., Ste.1616
Philadelphia, PA 19107
Ph: (215)735-5750
Fax: (215)735-9291
E-mail: info@bigpicturealliance.org
URL: http://www.bigpicturealliance.org
Contact: Jeffrey A. Seder, Exec. Dir./Co-Founder
Founded: 1976. **Members:** 50. **Staff:** 9. **Budget:** $600,000. **Description:** Seeks to educate and support the efforts of disadvantaged and underserved youth to develop self-expression, life skills, and job skills by engaging students in the inspiring and collaborative process of creating communications projects and media arts. Partners with schools, community centers and arts organizations with programs that support students in accessing advanced technologies, including digital media, computer arts and the Internet; uses intensive, hands-on training to engage young people's interest in media and media making and thereby developing language and communication skills, critical thinking, teamwork and self-esteem. **Libraries: Type:** reference. **Holdings:** 1,000; video recordings. **Subjects:** sports medicine, violence. **Awards: Type:** recognition. **Telecommunication Services:** electronic mail, staff@bigpicturealliance.org. **Divisions:** Equine; Human. **Also Known As:** (1995) Association for The Advancement of Social Potential. **Formerly:** (1997) Association for the Advancement of Sports Potential. **Publications:** Newsletter, quarterly. **Conventions/Meetings:** annual Children's Film Festival - meeting.

16132 ■ International Academy for Sports Dentistry (IASD)
c/o Shelly Lott, Exec. Sec.
118 Faye St.
Farmersville, IL 62533
Ph: (217)227-3431
Free: (800)273-1788
Fax: (217)227-3438
E-mail: sportsdentistry@consolidated.net
URL: http://www.sportsdentistry-asd.org
Contact: Shelly Lott, Exec. Sec.
Founded: 1983. **Members:** 750. **Membership Dues:** dentist, $150 (annual) ● student, $120 (annual) ● corporate, $185 (annual). **Staff:** 1. **Description:** Dentists, dental students, physicians, athletic trainers, and others interested in the study and prevention of dental injuries incurred during sports participation. Fosters research, development, and education in all sciences related to sports dentistry and its relationship to the body as a whole. Encourages utilization of this knowledge in promoting better approaches to the prevention and treatment of athletic injuries and oral disease. Facilitates the exchange of ideas and experience among members. **Libraries: Type:** open to the public. **Subjects:** mouth guards, sports trauma. **Computer Services:** Mailing lists. **Formerly:** (2002) Academy for Sports Dentistry. **Publications:** ASD Newsletter, 2-3/year. Provides information on the use of craniofacial protection such as helmets, mouthguards, and faceguards. **Price:** included in membership dues. **Circulation:** 1,000 ● Membership Directory, annual. **Conventions/Meetings:** annual symposium (exhibits).

16133 ■ International Sports Massage Federation (ISMF)
Address Unknown since 2007
Founded: 1989. **Members:** 43. **Membership Dues:** $25 (annual). **Description:** National sports massage federations. Facilitates exchange of techniques and ideas among members; emphasizes improving relations between Socialist and non-Socialist countries. Conducts international exchange programs. Plans to publish newsletter and hold annual meeting. **Libraries: Type:** not open to the public. **Holdings:** 1,000; artwork, audio recordings, books, periodicals, video recordings. **Subjects:** sports massage. **Awards:** Art of Caring. **Frequency:** annual. **Type:** recognition.

Publications: Sports Massage Journal, quarterly. **Price:** $35.00/year. **Advertising:** accepted. **Conventions/Meetings:** annual International Sports Massage Congress - congress and workshop (exhibits).

16134 ■ Joint Commission on Sports Medicine and Science (JCSMS)
c/o Eve Becker-Doyle, CAE, Exec. Dir.
Natl. Athletic Trainers' Assn.
2952 Stemmons Fwy. 200
Dallas, TX 75247
Ph: (214)637-6282
Free: (214)879-6282
Fax: (214)637-2206
E-mail: kimmelcw@apsu.org
URL: http://www.nata.org
Contact: Charles Kimmel Jr., Pres.
Founded: 1966. **Description:** Provides a forum and acts as a catalyst for the promotion of increased communication among the various organizations interested in the health and safety of sports participants and to help them convey to the public necessary information on that subject. Seeks to stimulate various organizations for continuous research on pertinent questions and problems in the field of sports injury prevention and care and for the acquisition of valid statistics on the incidence and epidemiology of injuries in sports activities. Plays a role in helping corporations contact those sports organizations so that they can be of mutual benefit to each other. **Formerly:** (1988) Joint Commission on Competitive Safeguards and the Medical Aspects of Sports. **Conventions/Meetings:** annual meeting, features major organizations involved in the sports medicine field - 2008 June 17-21, St. Louis, MO; 2009 June 17-21, San Antonio, TX.

16135 ■ National Youth Sports Safety Foundation (NYSSF)
1 Beacon St., Ste.3333
Boston, MA 02108
Ph: (617)367-6677
Fax: (617)722-9999
E-mail: nyssf@aol.com
URL: http://www.nyssf.org
Contact: Michelle Klein, Exec. Dir.
Founded: 1989. **Membership Dues:** student, $15 (annual) ● individual, $35 (annual) ● professional, $75 (annual) ● contributing, $100 (annual). **Description:** Works to promote the safety and well-being of children and adolescents participating in sports. Strives to reduce the number and severity of injuries youth sustain in sports and fitness activities. Sponsors educational programs. Maintains speakers' bureau. **Libraries: Type:** by appointment only. **Holdings:** articles, audiovisuals, books, clippings, periodicals. **Subjects:** sports injury prevention, sports injuries, exercise science, sports, coaching education psychology, nutrition, steroids. **Formerly:** National Youth Sports Foundation for the Prevention of Athletic Injuries. **Publications:** Sidelines, quarterly. Newsletter. **Price:** included in membership dues; $9.50 /year for nonmembers. **Circulation:** 10,000 ● Yearbook of Youth Sports Safety. **Conventions/Meetings:** quarterly board meeting ● conference (exhibits).

16136 ■ United States Sports Massage Federation (USMF)
3556 Kenwood Dr.
Spring Valley, CA 91977-2021
Ph: (619)464-0999
E-mail: drmyk_smti@netzero.com
Contact: Dr. M.K. Hungerford PhD, Pres.
Founded: 1989. **Members:** 17. **Description:** Sports massage therapists. Facilitates exchange of techniques and ideas among members. Promotes more widespread use of massage therapy by U.S. professional sports teams. **Libraries: Type:** reference. **Holdings:** books. **Conventions/Meetings:** annual International Sports Massage Congress - conference (exhibits).

16137 ■ World Sports Medicine Association of Registered Therapists (WORLD SMART)
206 Marine Ave.
PO Box 5642
Newport Beach, CA 92662

Ph: (626)445-1978
E-mail: americansportsmedicine@hotmail.com
Contact: Joe Borland, Contact
Founded: 1993. **Members:** 4,000. **Membership Dues:** certified trainer, $60 (annual) ● registered personal fitness trainer, $60 ● athletic registered trainer, $75 ● registered sports medicine therapist/trainer/technician, $100 (annual). **Staff:** 3. **Languages:** English, Spanish. **Description:** Sports medicine therapist, trainer, technician, and individuals involved in sports medicine and certified by any nationally recognized athletic trainers association. Establishes standards of competency for trainers, therapists, and sports medicine care providers that are recognized worldwide. **Libraries: Type:** not open to the public; reference. **Awards: Frequency:** annual. **Type:** recognition. **Recipient:** for a registered professor, trainer, instructor and therapist. **Computer Services:** database. **Also Known As:** World Smart. **Publications:** World Smart News. Newsletter ● Brochure. **Price:** free. **Advertising:** accepted. Alternate Formats: CD-ROM; diskette ● Bulletin, periodic ● Newsletter, quarterly. **Price:** included in membership dues. **Advertising:** accepted. **Conventions/Meetings:** annual conference.

Stress

16138 ■ American Institute of Stress (AIS)
124 Park Ave.
Yonkers, NY 10703
Ph: (914)963-1200
Fax: (914)965-6267
E-mail: stress125@optonline.net
URL: http://www.stress.org
Contact: Paul J. Rosch MD, Pres./Chm.
Founded: 1979. **Members:** 600. **Membership Dues:** lay, $75 (annual) ● professional (domestic), $90 (annual) ● sustaining, professional (foreign), $100 (annual) ● sponsoring/organizational, $1,000 (annual). **Staff:** 2. **Budget:** $80,000. **Description:** Physicians, health professionals, scholars, and others from varied disciplines constitute board of trustees. Explores the personal and social consequences of stress. Compiles research data on topics such as: relationships between emotional factors and cardiovascular disease; stress and the immune system with specific emphasis on cancer; stress reduction programs for industry; occupational stress (for example, that of law enforcement officers or air traffic controllers); executive stress ("burn out"); and pharmacological and holistic methods of stress reduction. Seeks a definition of health that recognizes the need for harmony between the individual and the physical and social environments as well as the effects of positive emotions such as creativity, faith, and humor on health. Evaluates ongoing research efforts and stress management programs in the U.S. and abroad. Disseminates information to individuals, institutions, and organizations. Serves as a network for rapid communication among individuals in different disciplines. Sponsors consulting services. **Libraries: Type:** by appointment only. **Holdings:** 4,000. **Subjects:** stress. **Awards:** Hans Selye Award. **Frequency:** annual. **Type:** recognition. **Recipient:** for past achievements in stress research. **Computer Services:** database ● mailing lists ● online services. **Publications:** Health and Stress: The Newsletter of the American Institute of Stress, monthly. **Price:** $35.00 in U.S.; $45.00 outside U.S. **Circulation:** 3,000 ● Readings in Oncology. Book ● Also publishes papers and speeches and issues reprints on stress. **Conventions/Meetings:** annual International Montreux Congress on Stress (exhibits) ● seminar ● symposium ● workshop.

16139 ■ Cell Stress Society International (CSSI)
c/o MCB Dept.
The Univ. of Connecticut
91 N Eagleville Rd.
Storrs Mansfield, CT 06269-3125
Fax: (860)486-5709

E-mail: helen.neumann@uconn.edu
URL: http://web.uconn.edu/cssi
Contact: Helen Neumann, Contact
Membership Dues: regular, $225 (annual) ● student/post doctoral, individual from a developing country, $45 (annual) ● life, $1,000. **Multinational. Description:** Promotes the clinical and industrial applications of basic research in cellular stress. Informs the public of the goal and major advances in stress response research. **Computer Services:** Online services, cellular stress response forum. **Publications:** *Cell Stress and Chaperones*, quarterly. Journal. Alternate Formats: online. **Conventions/Meetings:** annual workshop.

16140 ■ International Society for Traumatic Stress Studies (ISTSS)
60 Revere Dr., Ste.500
Northbrook, IL 60062
Ph: (847)480-9028
Fax: (847)480-9282
E-mail: istss@istss.org
URL: http://www.istss.org
Contact: Rick Koepke, Exec. Dir.
Founded: 1985. **Members:** 2,500. **Membership Dues:** student, $65-$85 (annual) ● regular, $135-$155 (annual). **Staff:** 8. **Budget:** $650,000. **Multinational. Description:** Professionals who treat individuals suffering from traumatic stress. (Traumatic stress is a medical term applied to persons who experience severe mental or emotional reactions to extraordinary stressful situations such as war, crime, natural disasters, and high-stress occupations.) Conducts research in the treatment of these cases; disseminates information. **Awards:** Chaim Danieli Award. **Frequency:** annual. **Type:** recognition. **Recipient:** for an individual who has completed his or her training within five years ● Lifetime Achievement Award. **Frequency:** annual. **Type:** recognition. **Recipient:** for an individual who has made great lifetime contributions to the field of PTSD ● Robert S. Laufer Award. **Frequency:** annual. **Type:** recognition. **Recipient:** for an individual or group who has made an outstanding contribution to research in the PTSD field ● Sarah Haley Award. **Frequency:** annual. **Type:** recognition. **Recipient:** for a clinician or a group of clinicians in direct service to traumatized individuals. **Computer Services:** Mailing lists. **Committees:** Board of Directors. **Formerly:** Society for Traumatic Stress Studies. **Publications:** *Journal of Traumatic Stress*, bimonthly. Reports on the latest findings and innovations in the study and treatment of those affected by traumatic stress. ISSN: 0894-9867. **Advertising:** accepted. Alternate Formats: online ● *Membership List*, periodic. Directory. **Price:** $500.00 flat fee ● *Traumatic Stress Points* (in English and Spanish), quarterly. Newsletter. Contains book reviews, topical articles, and association news. **Price:** included in membership dues. **Circulation:** 2,750. **Advertising:** accepted. Alternate Formats: online. **Conventions/Meetings:** annual conference and meeting (exhibits) - always fall.

16141 ■ National Center for Post Traumatic Stress Disorder (NCPTSD)
VA Medical Center 116D
215 N Main St.
White River Junction, VT 05009
Ph: (802)296-5132 (802)296-6300
Fax: (802)296-5135
E-mail: ncptsd@ncptsd.org
URL: http://www.ncptsd.va.gov
Contact: Matthew J. Friedman PhD, Exec. Dir.
Founded: 1989. **Description:** Promotes studies on the effects of psychological trauma. **Publications:** *NCP Clinical Quarterly*. Provides an overview of the major clinical, theoretical and programmatic developments in the field of PTSD. ● *PTSD Research Quarterly*. Contains review articles written by guest-experts on specific topics related to PTSD. **Price:** free. Alternate Formats: online ● Videos.

Stress Management

16142 ■ International Critical Incident Stress Foundation (ICISF)
3290 Pine Orchard Ln., Ste.106
Ellicott City, MD 21042

Ph: (410)750-9600 (410)313-2473
Fax: (410)750-9601
E-mail: info@icisf.org
URL: http://www.icisf.org
Contact: Mark J. Maggio PhD, Chm.
Membership Dues: level one in U.S., $40 (annual) ● level one outside U.S., $45 (annual) ● level two in U.S., $88 (annual) ● level two outside U.S., $103 (annual). **Multinational. Description:** Promotes prevention and mitigation of disabling stress through education, training, and support services for all emergency services professions. Offers continuing education and training in Emergency Mental Health Services for psychologists, psychiatrists, social workers, and licensed professional counselors. Holds consultations on the establishment of Crisis and Disaster Response Programs for varied organizations and communities worldwide.

Stroke

16143 ■ American Stroke Association (ASA)
Natl. Center
7272 Greenville Ave.
Dallas, TX 75231
Ph: (214)706-1890
Free: (888)478-7653
E-mail: strokeinfo@heart.org
URL: http://www.strokeassociation.org
Contact: Ellen Magnis, Contact
Founded: 1998. **Members:** 23,000. **Membership Dues:** premium professional, $150 (annual) ● early career, $55 (annual) ● student/trainee, $40 (annual) ● general professional, $35 (annual). **Description:** Strives to reduce disability and death from stroke through research, education, fundraising, and advocacy. **Publications:** *Stroke Connection*, bimonthly. Magazine. **Price:** included in membership dues. **Advertising:** accepted ● *Stroke Information Alliance*, monthly. Newsletter. Alternate Formats: online ● *Stroke: Journal of the American Heart Association*, monthly. **Circulation:** 15,300. Alternate Formats: online. **Conventions/Meetings:** American Stroke Challenge - meeting, with golf tournament, co-sponsored with Bayer Aspirin ● annual international conference.

16144 ■ Children's Hemiplegia and Stroke Association (CHASA)
4101 W Green Oaks Blvd., Ste.305, No. 149
Arlington, TX 76016
Ph: (817)492-4325
E-mail: info437@chasa.org
URL: http://www.chasa.org
Contact: Nancy Atwood, Pres./Founder
Founded: 1999. **Description:** Provides support and information to families of children who have hemiplegia, hemiparesis or childhood stroke. Raises funds to help children who have hemiplegia, hemiparesis or childhood stroke. Provides a network for stroke survivors and concerned persons. Furthers the study of all aspects of stroke. **Awards: Frequency:** annual. **Type:** scholarship. **Recipient:** for young adults who have hemiplegia or are pediatric stroke survivors. **Telecommunication Services:** electronic mail, list@hemikids.org ● electronic mail, lg@chasa.org. **Publications:** *Helping Hands*. Newsletter. Alternate Formats: online ● Brochures.

16145 ■ National Stroke Association (NSA)
9707 E Easter Ln., Bldg. B
Centennial, CO 80112
Ph: (303)649-9299
Free: (800)STROKES
Fax: (303)649-1328
E-mail: info@stroke.org
URL: http://www.stroke.org
Contact: Lindsey Larson, Dir. of Communications
Founded: 1984. **Members:** 7,500. **Membership Dues:** individual, $20 (annual) ● professional, $50 (annual) ● hospital/organization, $200 (annual). **Staff:** 40. **Budget:** $4,850,000. **State Groups:** 16. **Local Groups:** 1,200. **Description:** Stroke survivors and their families; health care professionals and institutions; lay com-

munity. Seeks to reduce the incidence and impact of stroke by promoting research, educating the public, and providing a network for stroke survivors and concerned persons. Serves as an information referral clearinghouse on stroke; makes available educational materials on stroke prevention, treatment, rehabilitation, resocialization, and research. Offers guidance in the development of stroke support groups, and clubs. Maintains speakers' bureau and Stroke Information and Referral Center; compiles statistics. Conducts educational symposiums/meetings. **Libraries: Type:** reference. **Holdings:** 100; books, clippings, periodicals. **Subjects:** cerebrovascular disorders. **Awards:** Community Education Award. **Frequency:** annual. **Type:** grant. **Recipient:** for medical facilities and community organization ● Research Fellowship Award in Cerebrovascular Disease. **Frequency:** annual. **Type:** fellowship. **Recipient:** for doctors dedicated to the field of stroke as a career. **Committees:** Scientific Advisory. **Publications:** *Hope: The Stroke Recovery Guide*. Book. Alternate Formats: online ● *Journal of Stroke and Cerebrovascular Diseases*, bimonthly. **Price:** $129.00 /year for individuals in U.S.; $204.00 /year for institutions; $161.00 individual outside U.S. ISSN: 1052-3057. **Advertising:** accepted ● *State Listing of Stroke Clubs*, periodic. Directory ● *Stroke: Clinical Updates*, bimonthly. Newsletter. **Price:** included in membership dues. **Circulation:** 10,000 ● *Stroke Smart*, bimonthly. Magazine. **Price:** free. **Circulation:** 80,000. **Conventions/Meetings:** annual North American Stroke Meeting (exhibits).

16146 ■ Stroke Awareness for Everyone (SAFE)
c/o Bernadette Manion, Treas.
PO Box 36186
Los Angeles, CA 90036
E-mail: aboutsafe@strokesafe.org
URL: http://www.strokesafe.org
Contact: Bernadette Manion, Treas.
Founded: 1995. **Multinational. Description:** Represents stroke survivors and their families. Addresses the need for support and recognition of stroke-affected individuals from all over the world. Provides support to stroke survivors in need regardless of age, background, creed or disability. Serves as the voice on issues pertaining to stroke, what it means to live with stroke, and how to prevent stroke from happening to others. **Telecommunication Services:** electronic mail, safeboard@strokesafe.org ● electronic mail, webmaster@strokesafe.org. **Publications:** *Stroke Caregivers Handbook*. Contains information about stroke. Alternate Formats: online.

16147 ■ Stroke Clubs, International (SCI)
Address Unknown since 2007
Founded: 1968. **Members:** 12,000. **Staff:** 2. **Description:** Active members are stroke victims; associate members are individuals interested in the problems of stroke victims. To unite stroke victims for the purpose of aiding each other; to instruct them and their families regarding the nature of stroke and the means for overcoming the resulting handicaps; to aid them in finding employment; and to give the stroke victim hope and encouragement. At monthly meetings, qualified speakers discuss the medical aspects of strokes and member stroke victims discuss their progress and problems. Maintains list of over 1,000 clubs throughout the U.S. **Libraries: Type:** open to the public. **Holdings:** archival material. **Formerly:** (1973) The Stroke Club; (1978) Stroke Club of America. **Publications:** *Stroke Club International Bulletin*, annual. Includes book and cassette recommendations. **Conventions/Meetings:** annual meeting.

16148 ■ Stroke Network
PO Box 492
Abingdon, MD 21009
URL: http://www.strokenetwork.org
Contact: Steve Mallory, CEO
Founded: 1996. **Multinational. Description:** Stroke survivors and caregivers. Promotes stroke awareness, provides support to stroke survivors, offers information for those suffering physical problems

such as Central Pain and emotional scars. Offers Web Casts, private chat rooms, and bookstore. **Libraries: Type:** reference. **Holdings:** articles, video recordings. **Computer Services:** Mailing lists, of members. **Publications:** Newsletter, monthly.

Stuttering

16149 ■ International Stuttering Association (ISA)
c/o Judith Eckardt, Sec.
65208 E Desert Sands Ct.
Tucson, AZ 85739
Ph: (520)825-9875
E-mail: info@stutterisa.org
URL: http://www.stutterisa.org
Contact: Judith Eckardt, Sec.
Founded: 1995. **Membership Dues:** association (based on annual budget), EUR 60-EUR 180 (annual). **Languages:** Arabic, Chinese, Dutch, English, French, German, Japanese, Russian, Spanish. **Multinational. Description:** Seeks to provide a means whereby the voices of people who stutter can be heard at the international level. Improves the conditions of all individuals whose lives are affected by stuttering. Facilitates interaction and communication among people who stutter, parents of children who stutter and therapists and researchers from all disciplines. Educates the general public about stuttering and the needs and capabilities of persons who stutter. **Telecommunication Services:** electronic mail, jjjudithe@msn.com. **Publications:** One Voice. Newsletter. **Price:** included in membership dues. Alternate Formats: online.

Substance Abuse

16150 ■ American Association for the Treatment of Opioid Dependence (AATOD)
217 Broadway, Ste.304
New York, NY 10007
Ph: (212)566-5555
Fax: (212)349-2944
E-mail: info@aatod.org
URL: http://www.aatod.org
Contact: Mark W. Parrino MPA, Pres.
Founded: 1984. **Membership Dues:** individual, $125 (annual) ● program, $250 (annual). **Description:** Enhances the quality of patient care in treatment programs. Promotes the growth and development of methadone treatment services. Educates providers and communities on opioid treatment. **Computer Services:** Information services, methadone and opioid treatment resources. **Projects:** Hepatitis Education for Opioid Treatment Providers; Prevalence of Prescription Opioid Abuse. **Publications:** The Media. Video. Contains fundamental elements of effective media communication. **Conventions/Meetings:** annual conference - 2007 Oct. 20-24, San Diego, CA.

16151 ■ American Osteopathic Academy of Addiction Medicine (AOAAM)
142 E Ontario St.
Chicago, IL 60611
Free: (800)621-1773
Fax: (312)202-8224
E-mail: info@aoaam.org
URL: http://www.aoaam.org
Contact: Jason Friske, Exec. Dir.
Founded: 1986. **Members:** 100. **Membership Dues:** active (osteopathic physician), $150 (annual) ● associate, $75 (annual) ● resident/fellow, $50 (annual) ● intern, student, $25 (annual). **Staff:** 3. **Description:** Conducts research into the diagnosis, intervention, and treatment of substance abuse problems. Seeks to educate society, and to influence the passage of legislation regarding drug abuse. Provides seminars and lectures to students, physicians, medical and dental societies, civic groups, religious organizations, bar associations, and law enforcement bodies. **Awards:** Fellow in AOAAM. **Frequency:** annual. **Type:** recognition. **Recipient:** for service to the

association and to the field of addiction medicine. **Affiliated With:** American Osteopathic Association. **Formerly:** (1996) American Osteopathic Academy Addictionology. **Publications:** AOAAM News, quarterly. Newsletter. Alternate Formats: online. **Conventions/Meetings:** annual meeting (exhibits).

16152 ■ American Society of Addiction Medicine (ASAM)
4601 N Park Ave., Upper Arcade No. 101
Chevy Chase, MD 20815
Ph: (301)656-3920
Fax: (301)656-3815
E-mail: email@asam.org
URL: http://www.asam.org
Contact: Eileen McGrath JD, Exec. VP/CEO
Founded: 1954. **Members:** 3,000. **Membership Dues:** regular, $150 (annual) ● international, $225 (annual) ● retired, $125 (annual) ● resident, $35 (annual). **Staff:** 12. **Budget:** $2,000,000. **State Groups:** 28. **Description:** Physicians with special interest and experience in the field of alcoholism and other drug dependencies and who wish to share this experience with other professionals in order to extend their knowledge of addictive diseases; promote dissemination of that knowledge; enlighten the public regarding these problems; advance education and research in the field of addiction. Holds annual Ruth Fox Course for Physicians, annual Medical-Scientific Conference and five other conferences/courses. **Awards:** ASAM Annual Awards. **Frequency:** annual. **Type:** recognition. **Recipient:** for contributions to the field ● John P. McGovern Award and Lecture. **Frequency:** annual. **Type:** recognition. **Recipient:** to an individual who has made meritorious contributions to public policy, research, or prevention which has increased understanding of the relationship of addiction and society ● R. Brinkley Smithers Distinguished Scientist Lecture. **Frequency:** annual. **Type:** recognition. **Recipient:** for contributions to study/treatment of alcoholism. **Computer Services:** Mailing lists, certification verification ● online services, membership directory. **Committees:** Advocacy; Certification; Chapters; Constitution and Bylaw; Medical Education; Medical Societies; Nominations and Awards; Organizational Relations. **Formerly:** (1967) New York City Medical Society on Alcoholism; (1989) American Medical Society on Alcoholism and Other Drug Dependencies. **Publications:** ASAM News, bimonthly. Newsletter. **Price:** $25.00. **Circulation:** 3,200. **Advertising:** accepted. Alternate Formats: online ● Guidelines for Facilities Treating Chemically Dependent Patients at Risk for AIDS ● Journal of Addictive Diseases, quarterly. **Advertising:** accepted. Alternate Formats: online ● Patient Placement Criteria ● Principles of Addiction Medicine. Book. **Price:** $175.00 for members; $199.00 for nonmembers ● Membership Directory. Contains contact information of American Society of Addiction Medicine members. Alternate Formats: online. **Conventions/Meetings:** annual conference, addiction-related (exhibits) - 2008 Apr. 10-13, Toronto, ON, Canada.

16153 ■ Center for Substance Abuse Prevention (CSAP)
c/o SAMHSA
1 Choke Cherry Rd.
Rockville, MD 20857
Ph: (240)276-2420 (240)276-2401
Free: (800)773-8546
E-mail: info@samhsa.gov
URL: http://www.prevention.samhsa.gov
Contact: Dennis O. Romero, Acting Dir.
Founded: 1992. **Description:** Works to disseminate information, increase dialog, and promote community empowerment to combat alcohol and other drug problems. Maintains Speakers' bureau.

16154 ■ Drug Strategies
1616 P St. NW, Ste.220
Washington, DC 20036
Ph: (202)289-9070
Fax: (202)414-6199

E-mail: dspolicy@aol.com
URL: http://www.drugstrategies.org
Contact: Dr. Robert B. Millman, Chm.
Founded: 1993. **Description:** Works towards more effective approaches to the nation's drug problems. Supports private and public efforts to reduce demand for drugs. **Awards:** Nancy Dickerson Whitehead Awards. **Frequency:** annual. **Type:** recognition. **Recipient:** to journalists who have demonstrated the highest standards of reporting on drug issues. **Publications:** Keeping Score, annual. Report ● Revised Making the Grade: A Guide to School Drug Prevention Programs. Book. **Price:** $16.95 each (1-4 copies), plus shipping and handling; $14.95 each (5 or more copies), plus shipping and handling ● Safe Schools, Safe Students: A Guide to Violence Prevention Strategies. Book. **Price:** $16.95 each (1-4 copies), plus shipping and handling; $14.95 each (5 or more copies), plus shipping and handling ● Reports.

16155 ■ International Council on Alcohol, Drugs and Traffic Safety (ICADTS)
c/o Barry M. Sweedler
3798 Mosswood Dr.
Lafayette, CA 94549
Ph: (925)962-1810
Fax: (925)962-1810
E-mail: sweedlb@hotmail.com
URL: http://www.icadts.org
Contact: Ralph Hingson, Pres.
Founded: 1950. **Members:** 150. **Membership Dues:** full, affiliate, $60 (annual). **Description:** Works to reduce mortality and morbidity brought about by misuse of alcohol and drugs by operators of vehicles in all modes of transportation. Sponsors international and regional conferences to collect, disseminate and share essential information among professionals in the fields of law, medicine, public health, economics, law enforcement, public information and education, human factors and public policy. **Publications:** ICADTS Reporter, quarterly. Newsletter ● Journal of Traffic Medicine, quarterly. **Price:** included in membership dues. **Conventions/Meetings:** conference - every 2-3 years.

16156 ■ International Nurses Anonymous (INA)
c/o Kathy Kavanaugh, RN, Sec.-Treas.
14542 Greenpoint Ln.
Huntersville, NC 28078
Ph: (704)992-0678
E-mail: wkavanaugh@aol.com
URL: http://members.aol.com/IntNursesAnon
Contact: Kathy Kavanaugh RN, Sec.-Treas.
Founded: 1988. **Members:** 500. **Description:** Nurses, nursing students, and former nurses who are involved in a 12-step recovery program. Provides mutual support and networking; serves as a resource for newly recovering nurses. **Computer Services:** database, membership list ● mailing lists. **Publications:** Newsletter, semiannual. **Price:** free for members. **Conventions/Meetings:** annual meeting and retreat.

16157 ■ International Society for Biomedical Research on Alcoholism (ISBRA)
PO Box 202332
Denver, CO 80220-8332
Ph: (303)355-6420
Fax: (303)355-1207
E-mail: isbra@isbra.com
URL: http://www.isbra.com
Contact: R. Adron Harris, Pres.
Founded: 1980. **Members:** 730. **Membership Dues:** regular (ESBRA, RSA or JMSAS member), $35 (annual) ● regular (not a member of ESBRA, RSA or JMSAS), $60 (annual). **Regional Groups:** 3. **Multinational. Description:** Physicians, psychologists, biologists, and other scientists in over 20 countries who conduct research on biological factors in the etiology and treatment of alcoholism and its medical complications. Official collaborating agency of the World Health Organization. Conducts international collaborative research projects and training courses. **Publications:** Advances in Biomedical Alcohol Research, biennial. Book. Contains proceedings of the

biennial congresses. ● *Alcoholism: Clinical and Experimental Research*, bimonthly. Journal. **Price:** $55.00 for members; $110.00 for nonmembers. ISSN: 0145-6008. **Advertising:** accepted. **Conventions/Meetings:** biennial congress (exhibits).

16158 ■ Moderation Management (MM)
22 W 27th St., 5th Fl.
New York, NY 10001
Ph: (212)871-0974
Fax: (212)213-6582
E-mail: mm@moderation.org
URL: http://www.moderation.org
Contact: Ana Kosok, Exec. Dir.
Membership Dues: basic, $100 (annual) ● silver, $250 (annual) ● gold, $500 (annual) ● platinum, small business, $1,000 (annual) ● life, $5,000 ● medium business, $2,500 (annual) ● foundation or large business, $10,000 (annual). **Staff:** 1. **Description:** People concerned about their drinking. Behavioral change program and national support group to aid people to reduce drinking and make positive lifestyle changes; empowers individuals to accept responsibility for their actions, whether its moderation or abstinence; promotes early self-recognition of risky drinking behavior.

16159 ■ Mothers Against Misuse and Abuse (MAMA)
5217 SE 28th Ave.
Portland, OR 97202
Ph: (503)233-4202
Fax: (541)298-2842
E-mail: mama@mamas.org
URL: http://www.mamas.org
Contact: Sandee Burbank, Dir.
Founded: 1982. **Membership Dues:** basic, $25 ● supporting, $50 ● sustaining, $125 ● benefactor, $500. **Description:** Promotes personal responsibility and informed decision making on issues of substance use, abuse, and misuse. **Publications:** *Drug Consumer Safety*. Handbook. Explains the guidelines on how to reduce the harm from side effects and adverse reactions. ● *Using Alcohol Responsibly*. Booklet. Tells about the risks of using alcohol in a variety of circumstances.

16160 ■ NAADAC The Association for Addiction Professionals (NAADAC)
901 N Washington St., Ste.600
Alexandria, VA 22314
Ph: (703)741-7686
Free: (800)548-0497
Fax: (703)741-7698
E-mail: naadac@naadac.org
URL: http://www.naadac.org
Contact: Cynthia Moreno Touhy, Exec. Dir.
Founded: 1972. **Members:** 14,000. **Membership Dues:** individual full, $85-$210 (annual) ● individual student, $40-$67 (annual) ● organization, $500-$2,000 (annual). **Staff:** 10. **Budget:** $2,500,000. **Regional Groups:** 8. **State Groups:** 47. **Description:** Promotes excellence in care by promoting the highest quality and most up-to-date, science-based services to clients, families and communities. Provides education, clinical training and certification. Among the organization's national certification programs are the National Certified Addiction Counselor, Tobacco Addiction Credential and the Masters Addiction Counselor designations. **Awards:** Lora Roe Memorial Alcoholism and Drug Abuse Counselor of the Year. **Frequency:** annual. **Type:** recognition. **Recipient:** to a counselor who has made an outstanding contribution to the profession of addiction counseling ● Mel Schulstad Professional of the Year. **Frequency:** annual. **Type:** recognition. **Recipient:** for outstanding and sustained contributions to the advancement of the addiction counseling profession ● NAADAC Organizational Achievement Award. **Frequency:** annual. **Type:** recognition. **Recipient:** to organizations that have demonstrated a strong commitment to the addiction profession ● William F. "Bill" Callahan Award. **Frequency:** annual. **Type:** recognition. **Recipient:** for sustained and meritorious service at the national level. **Computer Services:** Mailing lists. **Commissions:** NAADAC Certification. **Com-**

mittees: Clinical Issues; Conference Review; Editorial Review; Ethics; Political Action; Public Policy. **Formerly:** (2001) National Association of Alcoholism and Drug Abuse Counselors. **Publications:** *Addiction Professional*, bimonthly. Magazine. Includes book, pamphlet, and film list. Contains notices of employment and educational opportunities. **Price:** included in membership dues. **Circulation:** 19,000. **Advertising:** accepted. Alternate Formats: online ● *The Basics of Addiction Counseling: A Desk Reference and Study Guide*, periodic. Handbook. Caters to the unique learning styles of each counselor, incorporating charts, graphics, and diagrams to illustrate important points. **Price:** $120.00 ● *Basics Of Addiction Counseling Independent Study Course*, periodic. Handbook. Includes the Basics of Addiction Counseling: Desk Reference and Study Guide and an examination. **Price:** $155.00 ● *NAADAC News*, bimonthly. Newsletter. Covers events, education and stories that impact on addiction professionals. **Price:** included in membership dues. **Circulation:** 14,000. **Advertising:** accepted. Alternate Formats: online ● Also publishes annual conference papers. **Conventions/Meetings:** annual conference (exhibits) ● periodic workshop and seminar.

16161 ■ National Acupuncture Detoxification Association (NADA)
PO Box 1927
Vancouver, WA 98668-1927
Ph: (360)254-0186
Free: (888)765-NADA
Fax: (360)260-8620
E-mail: nadaoffice@acudetox.com
URL: http://www.acudetox.com
Contact: Kenny O. Carter MPH, Pres.
Founded: 1985. **Members:** 1,200. **Membership Dues:** regular, $65 (annual). **Staff:** 4. **Budget:** $100,000. **State Groups:** 2. **Multinational. Description:** Works to promote the use of acupuncture in the treatment of addictions. Provides training and educational materials. **Libraries: Type:** reference. **Holdings:** articles, audiovisuals, clippings. **Publications:** *Guidepoints: News from NADA*, bimonthly. Newsletter. **Price:** $185.00/year. ISSN: 1070-8200. **Conventions/Meetings:** annual conference (exhibits).

16162 ■ National Alliance of Advocates for Buprenorphine Treatment (NAABT)
PO Box 333
Farmington, CT 06034
Ph: (860)269-4391 (860)810-0768
Fax: (860)269-4391
E-mail: makecontact@naabt.org
URL: http://www.naabt.org
Contact: Nancy Jean Barmashi, Contact
Founded: 2005. **Description:** Educates the public about the disease of opioid addiction and the buprenorphine treatment option. Helps to reduce the stigma and discrimination associated with patients with addiction disorders. Serves as a conduit connecting patients in need of treatment to qualified treatment providers. **Telecommunication Services:** electronic mail, nbarmashi@naabt.org. **Publications:** *Keeping You Informed*. Newsletter. Contains the latest information about NAABT and its website, treatment studies, and law changes. Alternate Formats: online.

16163 ■ National Association on Alcohol, Drugs and Disability (NAADD)
2165 Bunker Hill Dr.
San Mateo, CA 94402-3801
Ph: (650)578-8047
Fax: (650)286-9205
E-mail: solanda@sbcglobal.net
Contact: John de Miranda, Exec. Dir.
Description: Promotes awareness and education about substance abuse among people with co-existing disabilities; aims to create public awareness of issues related to alcoholism, drug addiction, and substance abuse faced by persons with co-existing disabilities; provides a peer approach to enhance access to services, information, education and prevention through collaborative efforts of individuals and organizations. Sponsors the California Technology

Assistance and Training Project. **Publications:** *The NAADD Report: The Newsletter on Alcohol, Drugs and Disability*, annual. Alternate Formats: online.

16164 ■ National Clearinghouse for Alcohol and Drug Information (NCADI)
PO Box 2345
Rockville, MD 20847-2345
Ph: (301)468-2600
Free: (800)729-6686
Fax: (301)468-6433
E-mail: info@health.org
URL: http://ncadi.samhsa.gov
Multinational. Description: Provides current information and materials concerning substance abuse. **Libraries: Type:** open to the public. **Holdings:** 85,000. **Subjects:** alcohol, tobacco, drugs, social science. **Computer Services:** database, information on drugs and alcohol ● database, prevention materials ● database, treatment resources. **Telecommunication Services:** TDD, (800)487-4889 ● additional toll-free number, Hablamos Espanol, (877)767-8432. **Publications:** *Fact Sheets* ● Brochures.

16165 ■ National Inhalant Prevention Coalition (NIPC)
322-A Thompson St.
Chattanooga, TN 37405
Ph: (423)265-4662
Free: (800)269-4237
Fax: (423)265-4889
E-mail: nipc@io.com
URL: http://www.inhalants.org
Contact: Harvey Weiss, Exec. Dir.
Founded: 1992. **Languages:** English, Spanish. **Description:** Promotes awareness and prevention of the use of inhalants as dangerous drugs. **Publications:** *ViewPoint*, quarterly. Newsletter. Contains the latest research findings.

16166 ■ National Organization on Fetal Alcohol Syndrome (NOFAS)
900 17th St. NW, Ste.910
Washington, DC 20006
Ph: (202)785-4585
Free: (800)66-NOFAS
Fax: (202)466-6456
E-mail: varillas@nofas.org
URL: http://www.nofas.org
Contact: Tom Donaldson, Pres.
Founded: 1990. **Description:** Works to eliminate birth defects caused by alcohol consumption during pregnancy. **Awards:** FASD Hall of Fame. **Frequency:** periodic. **Type:** recognition. **Recipient:** to an advocate, family or researcher who has dedicated his/her time and effort to working on fetal alcohol spectrum disorders issues ● Mike Synar Memorial Award. **Frequency:** annual. **Type:** monetary. **Recipient:** to American Indian medical school students from Oklahoma. **Computer Services:** Information services, FASD resources. **Programs:** Affiliate. **Projects:** Low-Literacy FAS. **Task Forces:** National. **Publications:** *State-by-State Resource Directory* ● Newsletter, monthly. **Price:** free. **Conventions/Meetings:** workshop.

16167 ■ Rational Recovery Systems (RRS)
PO Box 800
Lotus, CA 95651
Ph: (530)621-2667 (530)621-4374
Free: (800)303-CURE
Fax: (530)622-4296
E-mail: info@rational.org
URL: http://www.rational.org
Contact: Jack Trimpey, Pres.
Founded: 1986. **Staff:** 6. **For-Profit. Description:** Focuses on rational recovery (self-recovery from substance addiction through planned abstinence). Advocates for complete abstinence from substance abuse using Addictive Voice Recognition Technique (AVRT). **Libraries: Type:** open to the public. **Holdings:** 10, archival material. **Subjects:** alcohol, drugs, eating disorders, sexual abuse. **Computer Services:** Online services. **Subgroups:** AVRT Courses. **Publications:** *Addictive Voice Recognition Technique Live*. Videos. Includes complete 12-video VHS set. **Price:**

$449.00 ● *Exploring AVRT.* Audiotapes. **Price:** $39.95 ● *Greater Expectations.* Video. **Price:** $39.95 ● *Journal of Rational Recovery,* quarterly. Contains articles by recovered addicts of alcohol, drugs, and eating disorders and others. **Price:** $40.00/year, plus shipping and handling. ISSN: 1065-2019. **Circulation:** 6,000. **Advertising:** accepted ● *Rational Recovery/The New Cure for Substance Addiction.* **Price:** $15.95 ● *The Small Book: A Revolutionary Alternative for Overcoming Alcohol and Drug Dependence.* **Price:** $15.95 ● *Taming the Feast Beast.* **Price:** $14.95 ● *There's Nothing Wrong With You.* Video. **Price:** $89.95. **Advertising:** accepted. **Conventions/Meetings:** bimonthly workshop, four days each.

16168 ■ Research Society on Alcoholism (RSA)

7801 N Lamar Blvd., Ste.D-89
Austin, TX 78752-1038
Ph: (512)454-0022
Fax: (512)454-0812
E-mail: debbyrsa@sbcglobal.net
URL: http://www.RSOA.org
Contact: Debra Sharp, Dir.

Founded: 1976. **Members:** 1,400. **Membership Dues:** associate, student, $20 (annual) ● regular/postdoctoral, $150 (annual) ● regular/postdoctoral outside North America, $195 (annual). **Staff:** 3. **Description:** Scientists who hold an MD or PhD degree and others actively engaged in research on alcoholism and alcohol-related problems; doctoral students; professionals in related fields who are interested in supporting alcohol research. Purposes are to: serve as a forum for researchers working in the field; aid and further the application of research to problems related to alcoholism; disseminate scientific information; protect the rights of researchers and human research subjects; assess research priorities; enlighten the public about problems of alcoholism. Provides opportunities for communication and discussion among scientists, clinicians, and lay workers in alcoholism research, diagnosis, and treatment. Conducts lectures. **Awards:** Distinguished Researcher Award. **Frequency:** annual. **Type:** recognition. **Recipient:** for research accomplishments ● Seixas Award. **Frequency:** annual. **Type:** recognition. **Recipient:** for an extraordinary contribution to the advancement of alcohol research ● Young Investigator Award. **Frequency:** annual. **Type:** recognition. **Recipient:** for research accomplishments. **Computer Services:** Mailing lists. **Committees:** Awards; National Advocacy. **Publications:** *Alcoholism: Clinical and Experimental Research,* monthly. Journal. Includes book reviews and research reports. **Price:** $395.00 in the Americas; EUR 384.00 in Europe; 256.00 rest of the world. ISSN: 0145-6008. Alternate Formats: microform ● *Recent Developments in Alcoholism,* annual. Monograph. **Price:** $382.00 in Canada and Mexico; $406.00 for nonmembers, foreign. ISSN: 0145-6008. Alternate Formats: microform ● *RSA Directory,* periodic. **Price:** available to members only. ISSN: 0738-422X. **Conventions/Meetings:** annual meeting - 2008 June 28-July 3, Washington, DC; 2009 June 20-25, San Diego, CA ● annual Scientific Conference (exhibits).

16169 ■ Road Recovery Foundation

PO Box 1680
Radio City Sta.
New York, NY 10101-1680
Ph: (212)489-2425
Fax: (212)333-7226
E-mail: contact@roadrecovery.com
URL: http://www.roadrecovery.com
Contact: Gene Bowen, Founder

Founded: 1998. **Description:** Promotes a substance-free existence to young people, concertgoers and local communities. **Computer Services:** database, Road Crew Personnel Databank. **Publications:** Newsletter ● Annual Report, annual. **Conventions/Meetings:** Performance Programs - meeting.

16170 ■ SMART Recovery

7537 Mentor Ave., Ste.306
Mentor, OH 44060

Ph: (440)951-5357
Free: (866)951-5357
Fax: (440)951-5358
E-mail: info@smartrecovery.org
URL: http://www.smartrecovery.org
Contact: Shari Allwood, Contact

Description: Brings together recovered, recovering and never addicted individuals committed to abstinence from addictive behavior, including alcohol, other substances, and activities. **Programs:** SMART Recovery Training Programs. **Conventions/Meetings:** meeting, discussion sessions.

16171 ■ Society for Prevention Research (SPR)

11240 Waples Mill Rd., Ste.200
Fairfax, VA 22030
Ph: (703)934-4850
Fax: (703)359-7562
E-mail: info@preventionresearch.org
URL: http://www.preventionresearch.org
Contact: Anthony Biglan PhD, Pres.

Founded: 1992. **Members:** 650. **Membership Dues:** regular, $145 (annual) ● student, $70 (annual). **Staff:** 2. **Multinational. Description:** Scientists, practitioners, advocates, administrators, and policy makers concerned with the prevention of social, physical and mental health problems and the promotion of health, safety and well-being. Promotes the advancement of science-based prevention programs and policies through empirical research. Facilitates communication and cooperation among prevention interventionist working in fields that include etiology, epidemiology, and the social sciences. **Awards:** Community, Culture, and Prevention Science Award. **Frequency:** annual. **Type:** recognition. **Recipient:** for contributions to the field of prevention science in the area of community and culture ● Early Career Award. **Frequency:** annual. **Type:** recognition. **Recipient:** for an individual who has shown commitment to prevention science through research, policy or practice ● Federal Achievement Award. **Type:** recognition ● Friend of ECPN Award. **Frequency:** annual. **Type:** recognition. **Recipient:** to a mid-career or senior preventionist ● International Collaborative Prevention Research Award. **Frequency:** annual. **Type:** recognition. **Recipient:** for contributions to the field of prevention science in the area of international collaboration ● Lifetime Achievement Award. **Type:** recognition ● Nan Tobler Award for Review of the Prevention Science Literature. **Frequency:** annual. **Type:** recognition. **Recipient:** for contributions to the summarization or articulation of the empirical evidence relevant to prevention science ● Presidential Award. **Frequency:** annual. **Type:** recognition. **Recipient:** for individuals who have made a specific contribution to prevention science research ● Prevention Science Award. **Frequency:** annual. **Type:** recognition. **Recipient:** for individuals who have made a significant body of research that has applied scientific methods to test one or more preventive interventions or policies ● Public Service Award. **Frequency:** annual. **Type:** recognition. **Recipient:** for individuals who have made an extensive and effective advocacy for prevention science and science/research-based programs ● Science to Practice Award. **Frequency:** annual. **Type:** recognition. **Recipient:** for continued support to the implementation of research based prevention practices ● Service to SPR Award. **Frequency:** annual. **Type:** recognition. **Recipient:** for outstanding service to the organization ● Society for Prevention Research Award. **Type:** recognition ● State Achievement Award. **Type:** recognition ● Travel scholarships. **Frequency:** annual. **Type:** scholarship. **Committees:** Conference Planning; Partner Organization; Prevention Science Advocacy; Recognition and Honors; Training. **Task Forces:** International; Minority Scholarship; Standards of Evidence. **Publications:** *Prevention Science,* quarterly. Journal. **Circulation:** 600. **Conventions/Meetings:** annual meeting, bridging disciplines, building paradigms, and crossing borders in prevention science (exhibits).

16172 ■ Substance Abuse Program Administrators Association (SAPAA)

12 Cottage Field Ct.
Germantown, MD 20874

Ph: (301)540-2783
Fax: (301)540-1756
E-mail: exdir@sapaa.com
URL: http://www.sapaa.com
Contact: Dennis Kerns, Pres.

Members: 300. **Membership Dues:** regular, classification A, $550 (annual) ● regular, classification B, $175 (annual). **Multinational. Description:** Represents substance abuse program administrators. **Publications:** *Substance Abuse Professional Guidelines Handbook,* periodic ● Catalogs, periodic ● Brochure. Alternate Formats: online. **Conventions/Meetings:** annual conference.

Sudden Infant Death Syndrome

16173 ■ American Guild for Infant Survival (AGIS)

301 Eastwood Cir.
Virginia Beach, VA 23454-4014
Ph: (757)463-3845
E-mail: agis@mail.arczip.com
URL: http://www.sids-supportguild.org
Contact: Scott Hessek, Pres.

Founded: 1972. **Members:** 170. **Staff:** 4. **Regional Groups:** 1. **Local Groups:** 2. **Description:** Works to reduce infant mortality, especially Sudden Infant Death Syndrome. Develops low-tech innovations to reduce infant mortality, such as the AFGIS test, which scores risk categories of infants and fetuses. Promotes the home monitoring program. Conducts educational and research programs. Compiles statistics. Maintains speakers' bureau. Offers children's services. **Libraries:** Type: reference; by appointment only. **Holdings:** archival material, articles, audiovisuals, books, clippings, periodicals. **Subjects:** SIDS, research, public policy, public education. **Awards:** **Frequency:** annual. **Type:** grant. **Recipient:** for research. **Computer Services:** Mailing lists, of members. **Also Known As:** American Forces Guild for Infant Survival; Tidewater Guild for Infant Survival, Inc. **Publications:** *The Baby and Family Newspaper,* semiannual. **Circulation:** 10,000. **Advertising:** accepted ● Brochures ● Directory. **Conventions/Meetings:** annual Baby Fest - trade show (exhibits) - mid-August ● annual board meeting - always October ● monthly regional meeting.

16174 ■ American Sudden Infant Death Syndrome Institute (ASIDSI)

509 Augusta Dr.
Marietta, GA 30067
Ph: (770)426-8746
Free: (800)232-SIDS
Fax: (770)426-1369
E-mail: prevent@sids.org
URL: http://www.sids.org
Contact: Marc Peterzell, Chm.

Founded: 1983. **Staff:** 4. **Regional Groups:** 1. **Description:** Participants include health care professionals, researchers, and laypeople concerned about sudden infant death syndrome (SIDS); families who have lost babies to SIDS. Works to identify the cause and cure of SIDS. Promotes infant health through research, education, and support for SIDS families. Conducts research on siblings of SIDS babies; sponsors research programs seeking the cause and cure of SIDS. Conducts seminars for health care professionals and laypeople; maintains speakers' bureau. **Libraries:** Type: reference. **Holdings:** articles, reports. **Also Known As:** American SIDS Institute. **Publications:** Brochures ● Also publishes research results. **Conventions/Meetings:** quarterly board meeting ● annual Physician Symposium.

16175 ■ Association of SIDS and Infant Mortality Programs (ASIP)

8280 Greensboro Dr., Ste.300
McLean, VA 22102-3807
Free: (800)930-7437
Fax: (703)902-1320

E-mail: asip@asip1.org
URL: http://www.asip1.org
Contact: Mary Adkins, Pres.
Founded: 1987. **Members:** 110. **Membership Dues:** full, $65 (annual) ● associate, $40 (annual). **Description:** Health and human services professionals who provide support services to those affected by Sudden Infant Death Syndrome (SIDS). Represents SIDS information and counseling services at the national, state, and international levels. Acts as an advocate for continued developmental and expansion of SIDS and bereavement services. Organizes activities which promote professional growth, develops practice standards and links together practitioners working with SIDS families. Supports research. **Committees:** Legislative; Research; Service Delivery. **Formerly:** (1998) Association for SIDS Program Professionals. **Publications:** *SIDs and Sleeping Position: Counseling Implications*, annual. Newsletter. **Circulation:** 500 ● *Standards of Service* ● Papers. Alternate Formats: online ● Brochure. **Conventions/Meetings:** annual Infant Mortality and Sudden Infant Death Syndrome: Meeting the Challenge of National Priorities - conference (exhibits).

16176 ■ First Candle/SIDS Alliance (SIDSA)
1314 Bedford Ave., Ste.210
Baltimore, MD 21208
Ph: (410)653-8226
Free: (800)221-SIDS
Fax: (410)653-8709
E-mail: info@firstcandle.org
URL: http://www.sidsalliance.org
Contact: Ms. Deborah Boyd, Exec. Dir.
Founded: 1991. **Local Groups:** 50. **Description:** Unites concerned citizens, health professionals, and parents who have lost a child to Sudden Infant Death Syndrome (SIDS), a condition commonly known as "crib death" that accounts for about 6000 infant deaths annually in the United States. (Deaths of this type usually occur at night and during the cold weather months among apparently healthy infants generally under 6 months of age.) Although the common causes and methods of prevention have yet to be determined, recent research findings suggest an increased risk of SIDS for infants sleeping on the stomach, sleeping on soft bedding, exposed to smoke, or overheated. Serves as a central source of medical and scientific information about SIDS. Works to eliminate SIDS through research; Assists bereaved parents who have lost a child to SIDS; seeks to make the public aware of SIDS and related issues. **Libraries: Type:** reference. **Holdings:** articles, books, papers. **Subjects:** reducing the risks for SIDS, bereavement, SIDS research, specialized info for mothers, fathers, grandparents, siblings, day care providers, medical professionals. **Awards:** Medical Research Grants Program. **Frequency:** annual. **Type:** recognition. **Committees:** Finance and Administration; Marketing; Public Education. **Councils:** Family Services Advisory; Medical and Scientific Advisory. **Formed by Merger of:** National Sudden Infant Death Syndrome Foundation; Sudden Infant Death Syndrome Alliance. **Formerly:** (2004) Sudden Infant Death Syndrome (SIDS) Alliance. **Publications:** *Synopsis*, periodic. Newsletter. **Advertising:** accepted. **Conventions/Meetings:** annual Alliance National Conference (exhibits).

16177 ■ National SIDS/Infant Death Resource Center (NSIDRC)
8280 Greensboro Dr., Ste.300
McLean, VA 22102
Ph: (703)821-8955
Free: (866)866-7437
Fax: (703)821-2098
E-mail: sids@circlesolutions.com
URL: http://www.sidscenter.org
Contact: Carol Kennedy, Proj. Dir.
Founded: 1980. **Staff:** 4. **Description:** Funded by Maternal and Child Health Bureau, Health Resources and Services Administration, U.S. Department of Health and Human Services, National SIDS/Infant Death Resource Center. Provides resources, referrals, and technical assistance to SIDS families, public health and other professionals, and the general

public. **Libraries: Type:** reference. **Subjects:** SIDS, related topics, bereavement, effects on family members and siblings, epidemiology, etiology, pathologic findings, theories of causation. **Computer Services:** database, research and public awareness materials on SIDS. **Formerly:** (1991) National Sudden Infant Death Syndrome Clearinghouse. **Publications:** *Fact Sheets ● Information Exchange*, semiannual. Newsletter. Includes list of resources, calendar of events, and national, state and legislative news. Alternate Formats: online ● *Table of SIDS Deaths and Mortality Rates*, annual ● Bibliographies, annual. Contains research bibliographies. ● Also publishes fact sheets and educational publications.

16178 ■ StopSIDS.org
1673 Rte. 9, Ste.2
Clifton Park, NY 12065
Free: (888)521-9499
E-mail: info@stopsids.org
URL: http://www.stopsids.org
Contact: Dr. Craig Wehrenberg, Exec. Dir.
Founded: 2000. **Description:** Focuses on research and education in order to end Sudden Infant Death Syndrome (SIDS) and other infant deaths; promotes health in babies and children through chiropractic-atlas correction and other healthy lifestyle choices. **Publications:** *The Best-Kept Secret to Raising a Healthy Child.and the Possible Prevention of Sudden Infant Death Syndrome (SIDS)*. Book. **Price:** $14.95 plus shipping and handling.

Support Groups

16179 ■ Angelman Syndrome Foundation (ASF)
3015 E New York St., Ste.A2265
Aurora, IL 60504
Ph: (630)978-4245
Free: (800)432-6435
Fax: (630)978-7408
E-mail: info@angelman.org
URL: http://www.angelman.org
Contact: Eileen Braun, Exec. Dir.
Founded: 1992. **Members:** 750. **Membership Dues:** family, $50 (annual). **Staff:** 3. **Regional Groups:** 3. **Description:** Works to advance the awareness and treatment of Angelman Syndrome through education and information, research, and support for individuals with Angelman Syndrome, their families, and other concerned parties. **Telecommunication Services:** electronic bulletin board ● information service. **Publications:** *Voices of Angels*, quarterly. Newsletter. **Conventions/Meetings:** biennial conference (exhibits).

16180 ■ Biliary Atresia and Liver Transplant Network (BALT)
3835 Richmond Ave.
Box 190
Staten Island, NY 10312
Ph: (718)987-6200
Fax: (718)987-6200
E-mail: organtrans@msn.com
URL: http://www.transweb.org/people/recips/resources/support/oldbilitree.html
Contact: Lisa Carroccio, CEO
Founded: 1994. **Members:** 2,000. **Description:** Offers support for families of children born with biliary atresia (both pre-liver and post-liver transplant). **Libraries: Type:** reference. **Subjects:** biliary atresia, liver transplantation, other issues. **Committees:** Support Team. **Divisions:** Spanish. **Programs:** Parent Matching; Twin Registry. **Sections:** Angels Above Us; Baby Formula Network; Tree House Club.

16181 ■ CDG Family Network Foundation
c/o Cynthia Wren-Gray, Pres.
PO Box 860847
Plano, TX 75074
Free: (800)250-5273

E-mail: cdgaware@aol.com
URL: http://www.cdgs.com
Contact: Cynthia Wren-Gray, Pres.
Founded: 1996. **Description:** Promotes awareness of Carbohydrate-deficient Glycoprotein Syndrome, also known as Congenital Disorders of Glycosylation. **Awards:** Research Grants. **Type:** grant. **Computer Services:** Information services, email listserv. **Affiliated With:** National Organization for Rare Disorders. **Publications:** *CDG: The Long Road To Diagnosis*. Video ● Newsletter, semiannual, every spring and summer, or fall and winter ● Brochure. **Conventions/Meetings:** annual Family Conferences.

16182 ■ Families of Adults Afflicted with Asperger's Syndrome (FAAAS)
PO Box 514
Centerville, MA 02632
Ph: (508)790-1930
E-mail: faaas@faaas.org
URL: http://www.faaas.org
Contact: Karen E. Rodman, Pres./Founder
Founded: 1997. **Membership Dues:** regular, $9 (annual). **Multinational. Description:** Provides support to family members of adult individuals afflicted with the neurological disorder, Asperger's Syndrome. Promotes public awareness to families and medical communities. **Computer Services:** Mailing lists. **Publications:** *The Book of FAAAS*. Contains essays and poems written by spouses/partners and parents of adults afflicted with the neurological disorder, Asperger's Syndrome. ● Audiotapes ● Brochure. Alternate Formats: online. **Conventions/Meetings:** annual conference and lecture.

16183 ■ Fatty Oxidation Disorders (FOD) Family Support Group
c/o Deb Lee Gould, MEd, Dir.
2041 Tomahawk
Okemos, MI 48864
Ph: (517)381-1940
E-mail: deb@fodsupport.org
URL: http://www.fodsupport.org
Contact: Deb Lee Gould MEd, Dir.
Founded: 1991. **Description:** Offers support to families of children born with the metabolic disorder, fatty oxidation disorder (FOD). **Computer Services:** Mailing lists. **Publications:** *FOD Family Support Group*. Brochure. Alternate Formats: online ● *FOD Support*, semiannual. Newsletter ● Surveys.

16184 ■ FG Syndrome Family Alliance (FGSFA)
946 NW Circle Blvd., No. 290
Corvallis, OR 97330
Ph: (617)577-9050
E-mail: info@fg-syndrome.org
URL: http://www.fg-syndrome.org
Contact: Jackie Morford, Pres.
Founded: 1996. **Members:** 150. **Multinational. Description:** Offers support and advocacy to families impacted by FG Syndrome. **Computer Services:** Online services. **Publications:** *Family Album ● FlaGstone*, bimonthly. Newsletter. Contains scientific feedback, family support, parent education and humor. **Price:** $15.00/year ● Brochure.

16185 ■ Five P Minus Society
PO Box 268
Lakewood, CA 90714
Ph: (562)804-4506
Free: (888)970-0777
Fax: (562)920-5240
E-mail: director@fivepminus.org
URL: http://www.criduchat.org
Contact: Greg Abbruzzese, Pres.
Founded: 1986. **Members:** 300. **Membership Dues:** individual and family, $25 (annual). **Staff:** 1. **Description:** Seeks to encourage and facilitate communication among families with a member who has 5P-Syndrome also known as Cri du Chat Syndrome. Promotes awareness of 5P- Syndrome. **Libraries: Type:** reference. **Holdings:** 2; archival material, articles, video recordings. **Subjects:** 5-P Syndrome also known as Cri du Chat Syndrome. **Awards:** Family Assistance Program. **Frequency:** annual. **Type:**

scholarship. **Recipient:** to five (5) families who will attend annual conference. **Additional Websites:** http://www.fivepminus.org. **Telecommunication Services:** information service. **Councils:** Professional Advisory Board. **Also Known As:** (2005) Cri du Chat Syndrome Society; (2005) 5P- Society. **Publications:** *5p- News*, quarterly. Newsletter. **Price:** $2.50. Alternate Formats: online. **Conventions/Meetings:** annual meeting.

16186 ■ FRAXA Research Foundation
45 Pleasant St.
Newburyport, MA 01950
Ph: (978)462-1866
Fax: (978)463-9985
E-mail: info@fraxa.org
URL: http://www.fraxa.org
Contact: Katherine Clapp, Pres./Co-Founder
Membership Dues: regular, $25 (annual). **Description:** Supports research aimed at treatment for Fragile X syndrome. **Also Known As:** (2004) FRAXA, the Fragile X Research Foundation. **Publications:** *Educating Boys with Fragile X Syndrome*. Book. **Price:** $10.00 ● *Fragile X - A to Z: A Guide for Families*. Book. **Price:** $15.00 ● *Fragile X Information Cards*. **Price:** $5.00/75 cards ● *FRAXA*. Newsletter. **Price:** included in membership dues; $5.00 on CD-Rom. Alternate Formats: CD-ROM ● *Me and the X-Man*. Journal. Alternate Formats: online ● *Medication Guide for Fragile X Syndrome*. Book. **Price:** $20.00 ● *My Brother has Fragile X*. Book.

16187 ■ Genetic Alliance (GA)
4301 Connecticut Ave. NW, Ste.404
Washington, DC 20008
Ph: (202)966-5557
Free: (800)336-4363
Fax: (202)966-8553
E-mail: info@geneticalliance.org
URL: http://www.geneticalliance.org
Contact: Sharon Terry, Pres./CEO
Founded: 1986. **Staff:** 12. **Languages:** English, Spanish. **Description:** Works to increase the capacity of advocacy organizations to achieve their mission and leverages the voices of millions of individuals and families living with genetic conditions. Builds communication and mentoring networks, designs and sponsors rigorous training courses, and provides infrastructure that strengthens and empowers its 600 member organizations. The technical assistance provided to advocacy organizations results in measurable growth: increased funding for research, access to services and support for emerging technologies. **Awards:** Art of Advocacy. **Frequency:** annual. **Type:** recognition ● Art of Industry Partnership. **Frequency:** annual. **Type:** recognition ● Art of Listening Award. **Frequency:** annual. **Type:** recognition ● Art of Reporting Award. **Frequency:** annual. **Type:** recognition. **Computer Services:** database, membership. **Committees:** Education; Family Service; Public Policy. **Formerly:** (2001) Alliance of Genetic Support Groups. **Publications:** *G.ADVOCACY*, quarterly. Newsletter. Includes announcements, calendar of events, and membership information. **Price:** free, for members only. Alternate Formats: online. **Conventions/Meetings:** annual conference.

16188 ■ International Center for Fabry Disease (ICFD)
Dept. of Human Genetics
Mt. Sinai School of Medicine, Box 1498
5th Ave. at 100th St.
New York, NY 10029
Free: (866)322-7963
E-mail: fabry.disease@mssm.edu
URL: http://www.mssm.edu/genetics/fabry/index.shtml
Contact: Charlene Pearlman, Contact
Description: Offers diagnosis and treatment to Fabry patients and their families.

16189 ■ Klinefelter Syndrome and Associates (KSA)
11 Keats Ct.
Coto de Caza, CA 92679
Ph: (949)858-9428
Free: (888)999-9428

Fax: (949)858-3443
E-mail: khenry@genetic.org
URL: http://www.genetic.org
Contact: Melissa Aylstock, Founding Dir.
Founded: 1989. **Members:** 2,000. **Membership Dues:** regular, $25 (annual). **Staff:** 2. **Regional Groups:** 3. **Languages:** English, Spanish. **Description:** Individuals affected by Klinefelter Syndrome and their families. (Klinefelter syndrome is a genetic alteration, occurring only in males, identified by the presence of an extra "X" chromosome on the chromosome chain that determines gender.) Provides support services; facilitates networking and exchange of information. Conducts educational programs. **Computer Services:** database, telephone numbers and addresses ● mailing lists. **Also Known As:** KS and Associates. **Publications:** *The Even Exchange*, periodic. Newsletter. **Price:** $25.00/year in U.S.; $28.00/year in Canada and Mexico; $30.00/year outside U.S., Canada and Mexico ● Brochure. Contains information about Klinefelter Syndrome. **Conventions/Meetings:** annual conference (exhibits).

16190 ■ LMBS Network
c/o Foundation Fighting Blindness
11435 Cronhill Dr.
Owings Mills, MD 21117-2220
Ph: (410)568-0150
Free: (888)394-3937
E-mail: info@blindness.org
URL: http://www.blindness.org
Founded: 1980. **Members:** 50. **Staff:** 2. **Description:** Individuals with LMBS and family members. Offers support to individuals and family members. **Libraries:** **Type:** open to the public. **Subjects:** yearly newsletters. **Subgroups:** Foundation Fighting Blindness. **Affiliated With:** Foundation Fighting Blindness. **Publications:** *Network*, semiannual. Newsletter. Contains profiles and informations. **Price:** free. **Circulation:** 100 ● Brochure, annual. Contains general information on disease, profile of cases, addresses of contacts. **Circulation:** 100. **Conventions/Meetings:** biennial Visions (Rare Syndrome Group) - conference, with low visual aids (exhibits).

16191 ■ Miscarriage Infant Death and Stillbirth Support Group (MIDS)
PO Box 6345
Parsippany, NJ 07054
Ph: (973)884-1016
E-mail: mids1982@yahoo.com
URL: http://www.midsinc.org
Contact: Janet Tischler, Founder/Pres.
Founded: 1982. **Members:** 900. **Staff:** 10. **Budget:** $8,000. **State Groups:** 2. **Local Groups:** 4. **Description:** Offers friendship and support to parents who have experienced miscarriage, infant death, or stillbirth. Provides monthly meetings, friendships, in-hospital visits, workshops, and speakers. **Libraries:** **Type:** lending. **Holdings:** articles, books, clippings. **Subjects:** perinatal loss, miscarriage, infant death, stillbirth. **Awards:** **Type:** recognition. **Publications:** Brochure. **Conventions/Meetings:** board meeting.

16192 ■ MUMS National Parent-to-Parent Network (MUMS)
c/o Julie Gordon, Pres.
150 Custer Ct.
Green Bay, WI 54301-1243
Ph: (920)336-5333
Free: (877)336-5333
Fax: (920)339-0995
E-mail: mums@netnet.net
URL: http://www.netnet.net/mums
Contact: Julie Gordon, Pres.
Founded: 1979. **Members:** 20,500. **Membership Dues:** professional, $25 (quarterly) ● parent, $15 (quarterly) ● matching fee, $5 (quarterly). **Staff:** 2. **Budget:** $25,000. **Regional Groups:** 61. **State Groups:** 32. **Local Groups:** 28. **Languages:** Arabic, English, French, German, Italian, Norwegian, Polish, Russian, Spanish. **Description:** Parents or care providers of a child with any disability, rare disorder, chromosomal abnormality or health condition. Seeks to provide support to parents in the form of a networking system that matches parents with other parents

whose children have the same or similar condition, including rare disorders. Informs and updates families and professionals about services available. Refers parents to support groups and assists in forming new groups. **Computer Services:** database, over 18000 families covering over 3200 disorders in 54 countries. **Formerly:** Mothers United for Moral Support. **Publications:** *MUMS National Parent to Parent Network Matchmaker*, quarterly. Newsletter. **Price:** included in membership dues; $15.00/year. **Circulation:** 9,000. **Advertising:** accepted. Alternate Formats: online.

16193 ■ Myotubular Myopathy Resource Group
2602 Quaker Dr.
Texas City, TX 77590
Ph: (409)945-8569
Fax: (409)945-2162
E-mail: gscoggin@mtmrg.org
URL: http://www.mtmrg.org
Description: Offers advice, support, and advocacy to parents of children diagnosed with myotubular myopathy. **Publications:** Newsletter, periodic. Alternate Formats: online.

16194 ■ National Necrotizing Fasciitis Foundation (NNFF)
c/o Donna Batdorff, Co-Founder
2731 Porter SW
Grand Rapids, MI 49509
Ph: (616)261-2538
E-mail: nnfffeb@aol.com
URL: http://www.nnff.org
Contact: Donna Batdorff, Co-Founder
Founded: 1997. **Description:** Strives to educate and offer support to those affected by necrotizing fasciitis (flesh-eating bacteria). **Publications:** *Surviving the "Flesh-Eating Bacteria": Understanding, Preventing, Treating and Living with the Effects of Necrotizing Fasciitis*. Book. **Price:** $15.95/copy.

16195 ■ National Potter Syndrome Support Group
c/o Delores Schlegel
8221 Township Rd. 323
Holmesville, OH 44633
Ph: (330)279-4374
E-mail: potterssyndrome@hotmail.com
URL: http://www.potterssyndrome.org
Contact: Delores Schlegel, Contact
Founded: 1995. **Members:** 105. **Description:** Supports and disseminates information to families affected with Potter Syndrome. **Libraries:** **Type:** reference. **Holdings:** articles. **Subjects:** Potter Syndrome, renal abnormalities. **Computer Services:** Mailing lists, Parent Match Program. **Publications:** *National Potter Syndrome Support Group Newsletter*, biennial. Alternate Formats: online.

16196 ■ Nevus Network
c/o The Congenital Nevus Support Group
PO Box 305
West Salem, OH 44287
Ph: (419)853-4525 (405)377-3403
E-mail: info@nevusnetwork.org
URL: http://www.nevusnetwork.org
Contact: BJ Bett, Co-Founder
Founded: 1983. **Members:** 1,200. **Regional Groups:** 6. **Languages:** English, French, German, Spanish. **Multinational. Description:** Supports people with a large congenital nevus (large brown birth marks) or a related condition called neurocutaneous melanosis. Offers pen pals and information. **Libraries:** **Type:** lending; not open to the public; by appointment only. **Holdings:** articles, clippings, photographs. **Subjects:** giant congenital nevus, neurocutaneous melanosis, large congenital melanocytic nevi. **Computer Services:** database ● online services. **Publications:** *Nevus Network News*, periodic. Newsletter. **Price:** free. **Circulation:** 1,200. **Advertising:** accepted ● Brochure. **Conventions/Meetings:** regional meeting.

16197 ■ Parents Network for the Post Institutionalized Child (PNPIC)
PO Box 613
Meadow Lands, PA 15347
Ph: (724)222-1766
E-mail: thais1@earthlink.net
URL: http://www.pnpic.org
Contact: Thais Pepper, Co-Founder
Founded: 1993. **Description:** Devoted to understanding the medical, developmental, emotional and educational needs of children adopted from hospitals, orphanages and institutions worldwide. **Telecommunication Services:** electronic mail, pnpic@aol.com. **Projects:** Child Emotion Research Laboratory. **Study Groups:** Language Research on Children Adopted from Eastern European Orphanages. **Publications:** *International Adoptions: Challenges and Opportunities.* Book. **Price:** $33.00 in U.S., plus shipping and handling; $35.00 in Canada, plus shipping and handling ● *The POST.* Newsletter. **Price:** $5.00 single copy. Alternate Formats: online.

16198 ■ Progeria Research Foundation (PRF)
PO Box 3453
Peabody, MA 01961-3453
Ph: (978)535-2594
Fax: (978)535-5849
E-mail: info@progeriaresearch.org
URL: http://www.progeriaresearch.org
Contact: Audrey Gordon Esq., Pres./Exec. Dir.
Multinational. Description: Provides information and support to individuals and families affected by Progeria; promotes research; seeks to find a cure for children living with this disorder.

16199 ■ Reach Out for Youth with Ileitis and Colitis
84 Northgate Cir.
Melville, NY 11747
Ph: (631)293-3102
E-mail: info@reachoutforyouth.org
URL: http://www.reachoutforyouth.org
Contact: Susan Spellman, Exec. Dir./Founder
Founded: 1979. **Membership Dues:** general, $30 (annual). **Description:** Works to provide support groups for families whose children have Inflammatory Bowel Disease (IBD). Provides educational and emotional support to patients and families; conducts fund-raising events; and promotes research into the cause and treatment of IBD. **Awards:** College Scholarship Award. **Frequency:** annual. **Type:** scholarship. **Recipient:** for graduating high school students. **Publications:** *The Inner Circle,* quarterly. Newsletter. Keeps members in touch with the activities and news about association. **Price:** free for members ● *The Inside Story.* Brochure.

16200 ■ Restless Legs Syndrome Foundation (RLS)
819 2nd St. SW
Rochester, MN 55902-2985
Ph: (507)287-6465
Free: (877)463-6757
Fax: (507)287-6312
E-mail: rlsfoundation@rls.org
URL: http://www.rls.org
Contact: Georgianna Bell, Exec. Dir.
Founded: 1990. **Members:** 12,000. **Membership Dues:** regular, in U.S., $25 (annual) ● regular, in Canada, $30 (annual) ● international, $40 (annual). **Staff:** 10. **Budget:** $1,000,000. **Description:** Sufferers of restless leg syndrome and other interested people. Supports research of effective treatments and a cure. Acts as and develops support groups for sufferers and their friends and families. Educates physicians, patients and the public to increase awareness. **Awards:** Research Grants. **Frequency:** annual. **Type:** grant. **Recipient:** for promising scientists whose works address the goals of the foundation. **Computer Services:** database ● online services. **Boards:** Medical Advisory; Scientific Advisory. **Programs:** Impact Giving; Physician Referral. **Publications:** *Healthcare Provider Directory.* Alternate Formats: online ● *Night Walkers,* quarterly. Newsletter. Includes information on research, support groups, and news. **Price:** $25.00 /year for members. **Circula-**

tion: 15,000. Alternate Formats: online ● *Understanding and Diagnosing RLS.* Video ● Annual Report, annual. Alternate Formats: online ● Bulletin. Alternate Formats: online ● Brochures. Alternate Formats: online.

16201 ■ Ryan's Reach
2953 Edinger Ave.
Tustin, CA 92780
Ph: (949)733-0046
URL: http://www.ryansreach.com
Contact: Lindy Michaelis, Contact
Description: Works to meet the demanding and complex needs of brain injury victims and their families. **Programs:** High Hopes Neurological Recovery Group.

16202 ■ Shwachman-Diamond Syndrome Foundation (SDSF)
710 Brassie Dr.
Grand Junction, CO 81506
Ph: (614)939-2324
Free: (877)737-4685
Fax: (970)255-8293
E-mail: 4sskids@shwachman-diamond.org
URL: http://www.shwachman-diamond.org
Contact: Debbie Kadel, Pres.
Founded: 1994. **Description:** Provides emotional support to patients and their families; educates the medical community and general public about Schwachman-Diamond Syndrome; encourages training of and research by medical professionals; advocates support of research; links families through exchange of experience and ideas; disseminates current medical information; supports an International Patient Registry/Database. **Formerly:** (2004) Shwachman-Diamond Syndrome International. **Publications:** Newsletter, quarterly. Alternate Formats: online. **Conventions/Meetings:** conference.

16203 ■ Vasculitis Foundation (VF)
PO Box 28660
Kansas City, MO 64188-8660
Ph: (816)436-8211
Free: (800)277-9474
Fax: (816)436-8211
E-mail: vf@vasculitisfoundation.org
URL: http://www.vasculitisfoundation.org
Contact: Joyce Kullman, Exec. Dir.
Founded: 1986. **Members:** 5,000. **Membership Dues:** regular, $25 (annual) ● regular, outside U.S., $35 (annual). **Staff:** 2. **Budget:** $150,000. **Regional Groups:** 127. **State Groups:** 58. **Local Groups:** 4. **National Groups:** 12. **Description:** Seeks to raise public awareness of Wegener's Granulomatosis. Alleviates the isolation of having the disease. Wegener's Granulomatosis is an uncommon life threatening disease, a form of vasculitis and an autoimmune disease. Disseminates information. **Computer Services:** database ● information services ● mailing lists. **Formerly:** (1999) Wegener's Granulomatosis Support Group; (2003) Wegener's Granulomatosis Support Group International; (2006) Wegener's Granulomatosis Association. **Publications:** *Wegener's Granulomatosis Support Group, Inc. International,* bimonthly. Pamphlet. **Circulation:** 6,700. **Advertising:** accepted. Alternate Formats: online ● *Wegener's Symposium,* biennial. Videos ● Brochures. Contains basic information on Wegener's Granulomatosis. Alternate Formats: online. **Conventions/Meetings:** biennial Wegener's Granulomatosis International Symposium, noted medical experts speaking on WG and its treatment patients and families meeting, learning, asking questions, sharing experiences (exhibits).

16204 ■ Well Spouse Association (WSA)
63 W Main St., Ste.H
Freehold, NJ 07728
Ph: (732)577-8899
Free: (800)838-0879
Fax: (732)577-8644

E-mail: info@wellspouse.org
URL: http://www.wellspouse.org
Contact: Mr. Richard Anderson, Pres.
Founded: 1988. **Members:** 1,700. **Membership Dues:** individual, supporting, $25 (annual) ● individual outside U.S., $30 (annual) ● organization, $50 (annual). **Staff:** 2. **Budget:** $60,000. **Local Groups:** 60. **Description:** Husbands, wives, and partners of chronically ill patients. Supports network functioning to raise public consciousness about and advocate for the spouses of the chronically ill and/or disabled. Establishes local support groups, publishes a quarterly newsletter, conducts respite weekends, coordinates mentorship and letter writing programs. Compiles statistics; conducts educational programs. **Awards:** Well Spouse of the Year. **Frequency:** annual. **Type:** recognition. **Computer Services:** database ● mailing lists. **Committees:** Advocacy. **Formerly:** National Well Spouse Foundation; (2005) Well Spouse Foundation. **Publications:** *Mainstay,* quarterly. Newsletter. Contains membership news and information, advocacy issues, and helpful hints. **Price:** included in membership dues. **Circulation:** 3,000. **Conventions/Meetings:** annual conference and workshop, provides workshops on various spousal caregiving topics such as relationships, finances, coping, and intimacy.

16205 ■ Wide Smiles
PO Box 5153
Stockton, CA 95205-0153
Ph: (209)942-2812
Fax: (209)464-1497
E-mail: josmiles@yahoo.com
URL: http://www.widesmiles.org
Contact: Joanne Green, Dir.
Founded: 1991. **Description:** Offers support to families of children born with cleft lip and palate.

16206 ■ Woman to Woman Support Network
1341 W Main Rd., Airport Plz., Unit 5
Middletown, RI 02842
Ph: (401)841-9211
E-mail: newportoceanside@hotmail.com
URL: http://www.thombs.com/woman2woman
Description: Provides free support and referrals to women experiencing a problem on pregnancy. **Telecommunication Services:** electronic mail, jmartellino@home.com.

16207 ■ World Arnold Chiari Malformation Association (WACMA)
c/o Bernie Meyer
31 Newtown Woods Rd.
Newtown Square, PA 19073
Ph: (610)353-4737
E-mail: internautbhm2@comcast.net
URL: http://www.pressenter.com/~wacma
Contact: Bernie Meyer, Contact
Multinational. Description: Offers support, current information, and understanding to those affected by the Arnold Chiari malformation and syringomyelia. **Computer Services:** Mailing lists.

Surgery

16208 ■ American Association for Accreditation of Ambulatory Surgery Facilities (AAAASF)
5101 Washington St., Ste.2F
Gurnee, IL 60031
Ph: (847)775-1970
Free: (888)545-5222
Fax: (847)775-1985
E-mail: info@aaaasf.org
URL: http://www.aaaasf.org
Contact: Jeff Pearcy, Exec. Dir.
Founded: 1981. **Members:** 1,200. **Staff:** 5. **Description:** Board-certified surgeon-operated ambulatory surgical facilities. Maintains high standards through adherence to a voluntary program of inspection, evaluation and accreditation of ambulatory surgery facilities and ASC's. **Telecommunication Services:** electronic mail, jeff@aaaasf.org. **Committees:** Inves-

tigative. **Affiliated With:** American Society for Aesthetic Plastic Surgery; American Society of Plastic Surgeons and Plastic Surgery Education Foundation. **Formerly:** (1994) American Association for Accreditation of Ambulatory Plastic Surgery Facilities. **Publications:** *ASF Source: Ambulatory Surgery Facilities*, 3/year. Newsletter. **Advertising:** accepted. Alternate Formats: online. **Conventions/Meetings:** semiannual board meeting (exhibits).

16209 ■ American Association of Ambulatory Surgery Centers (AAASC)
PO Box 5271
Johnson City, TN 37602-5271
Ph: (423)915-1001
Fax: (423)282-9712
E-mail: info@aaasc.org
URL: http://www.aaasc.org
Contact: John J. Duggan MD, Pres.
Founded: 1978. **Members:** 500. **Membership Dues:** facility, $250-$1,750 (annual) ● state association, $500 (annual) ● professional/consultant, $550 (annual) ● corporate (bronze business partner), $2,800 (annual) ● corporate (silver business partner), $4,300 (annual) ● corporate (gold business partner), $6,300 (annual). **Staff:** 4. **Description:** Assists physicians, corporations, healthcare administrators to provide excellence in ambulatory care; provides information to build free-standing surgery center by addressing legal, accreditation and leadership issues. **Telecommunication Services:** electronic mail, aaasc@mtgsunlimited.com. **Boards:** Advisory. **Formerly:** (1986) Society for Office-Based Surgery; (1996) American Society of Outpatient Surgeons. **Publications:** *Monitor*, quarterly. Newsletter. **Advertising:** accepted ● Membership Directory, annual. **Price:** free for members. **Advertising:** accepted. **Conventions/Meetings:** annual symposium and meeting (exhibits).

16210 ■ American Association of Hip and Knee Surgeons (AAHKS)
6300 N River Rd., Ste.615
Rosemont, IL 60018
Ph: (847)698-1200
Fax: (847)698-0704
E-mail: helpdesk@aahks.org
URL: http://www.aahks.org
Contact: Daniel J. Berry MD, Pres.
Founded: 1991. **Members:** 814. **Membership Dues:** regular, $600 (annual). **Staff:** 1. **Budget:** $500,000. **Description:** Provides current educational, research and communication opportunities and promotes quality management of arthritic disorders of the hip and knee. **Awards:** Research Grant. **Frequency:** annual. **Type:** grant. **Funds:** OREF Endowment. **Publications:** Newsletter, quarterly. Contains association information for members. **Price:** included in membership dues. Alternate Formats: online. **Conventions/Meetings:** annual Combined Specialty Day - meeting ● annual meeting (exhibits) - always November in Dallas, TX.

16211 ■ American Association of Surgical Physician Assistants (AASPA)
4267 NW Fed. Hwy.
PMB 201
Jensen Beach, FL 34957
Free: (888)882-2772
Fax: (772)388-3457
E-mail: aaspa@aaspa.com
URL: http://www.aaspa.com
Contact: Linda Kotrba, Exec. Dir.
Founded: 1973. **Members:** 1,000. **Membership Dues:** fellow, $125 (annual) ● student, $75 (annual). **Staff:** 2. **Budget:** $40,000. **Description:** Surgical physician assistants and students in accredited physician assistant programs. Purposes are to promote academic and clinical excellence among members, to respond to the needs of surgical physician assistants, and to educate the medical community and the public about the role of surgical physician assistants in health care. **Awards:** John W. Kirklin MD Award. **Frequency:** periodic. **Type:** recognition. **Recipient:** for professional excellence. **Formerly:** (1996) American Association of Surgeon Assistants. **Publications:** *Surgical Physician Assistant*, monthly.

Journal. ISSN: 1080-6393. **Circulation:** 15,000. **Advertising:** accepted ● *Sutureline*, quarterly. Journal. **Price:** included in membership dues. **Circulation:** 650. **Advertising:** accepted. **Conventions/Meetings:** annual Reception and Membership Meeting, held in conjunction with American College of Surgeons.

16212 ■ American Board of Abdominal Surgery (ABAS)
1 E Emerson St.
Melrose, MA 02176
Ph: (781)665-6102
Fax: (781)665-4127
E-mail: office@abdominalsurg.org
URL: http://www.abdominalsurg.org/board.html
Contact: Louis F. Alfano MD, Exec. Sec.
Founded: 1957. **Members:** 800. **Staff:** 4. **Description:** Specialists in abdominal surgery. Improves the quality of graduate education for abdominal surgery. Establishes minimum educational and training standards for the specialty. Determines whether candidates have received adequate preparation as defined by the board. Provides comprehensive examinations to determine the ability and fitness of candidates. Certifies surgeons who have satisfied the requirements of the board as a protection to the public and the profession. Gives oral and written examinations in abdominal surgery. **Libraries: Type:** reference. **Holdings:** 825. **Awards:** Distinguished Service Award. **Frequency:** annual. **Type:** recognition ● Residency Award. **Frequency:** annual. **Type:** recognition. **Publications:** *ASAS Journal*, annual. **Price:** free for members. **Circulation:** 1,865 ● *Surgeon*, semiannual. **Price:** free for members. **Circulation:** 1,865. **Conventions/Meetings:** annual congress.

16213 ■ American Board of Facial Plastic and Reconstructive Surgery (ABFPRS)
115C S St. Asaph St.
Alexandria, VA 22314
Ph: (703)549-3223
Fax: (703)549-3357
E-mail: tshill@abfprs.org
URL: http://www.abfprs.org
Contact: T. Susan Hill, Exec. Dir.
Founded: 1986. **Description:** Works to improve the quality of facial plastic surgery available to the public. **Awards:** Anderson Prize for Scholastic Excellence. **Type:** recognition ● Larry D. Schoenrock Distinguished Service Award. **Type:** recognition.

16214 ■ American Board of Surgery (ABS)
1617 John F. Kennedy Blvd., Ste.860
Philadelphia, PA 19103
Ph: (215)568-4000
Fax: (215)563-5718
E-mail: flewis@absurgery.org
URL: http://www.absurgery.org
Contact: Frank R. Lewis MD, Exec. Dir.
Founded: 1937. **Members:** 29. **Description:** Examining and certifying board in general surgery; also certifies in Pediatric Surgery, Vascular Surgery, Surgical Critical Care, and Hand Surgery. Membership is drawn from 23 national and regional surgical and specialty societies and organizations. Offers Recertification in General Surgery, Pediatric Surgery, Vascular Surgery, and Surgical Critical Care. **Committees:** Credentials; Examination; Issues; Plans. **Publications:** *ABMS Directories of Certified Specialists* ● *Directory of Medical Specialists* ● *Service Booklets of Information*, annual. **Conventions/Meetings:** semiannual conference - always January and June ● annual meeting - always April/May.

16215 ■ American College of Eye Surgeons (ACES)
334 E Lake Rd., No. 135
Palm Harbor, FL 34685-2427
Ph: (727)366-1487
Fax: (727)836-9783
E-mail: quality@aces-abes.org
URL: http://www.aces-abes.org
Contact: Brenda S. Sheets, Exec. Dir.
Founded: 1986. **Members:** 700. **Membership Dues:** Founder's Circle, $2,000 (annual) ● academic, $100

(annual) ● regular/physician, $750 (annual). **Description:** Ophthalmic surgeons. Promotes and seeks to "sustain excellence in eye surgery while supporting self-direction and self-regulation" in the field of ophthalmic surgery. Works to ensure the quality and availability of ophthalmic health and surgical services. Conducts examinations and certifies qualified surgeons in ophthalmic surgical subspecialties; conducts continuing professional education courses for members; serves as a clearinghouse on emerging ophthalmic surgical techniques and technologies. **Awards:** Resident Award. **Frequency:** annual. **Type:** recognition. **Affiliated With:** American Numismatic Association. **Publications:** *American Board of Eye Surgery Directory*, annual. **Price:** $2.00 ● *Synergism*, periodic. Newsletter. **Conventions/Meetings:** annual Quality Surgery Meeting - symposium (exhibits).

16216 ■ American College of Surgeons (ACS)
633 N Saint Clair St.
Chicago, IL 60611-3211
Ph: (312)202-5000
Free: (800)621-4111
Fax: (312)202-5001
E-mail: ms@facs.org
URL: http://www.facs.org
Contact: Thomas R. Russell MD, Exec. Dir.
Founded: 1913. **Members:** 70,000. **Staff:** 210. **Budget:** $38,000,000. **Local Groups:** 67. **Description:** Serves as professional association of surgeons worldwide organized primarily to improve the quality of care for surgical patients by elevating the standards of surgical education and practice. Conducts nationwide programs to improve emergency medical services and hospital cancer programs. Sponsors continuing education and self-assessment courses for surgeons in practice. **Libraries: Type:** by appointment only; reference. **Holdings:** books, periodicals. **Subjects:** surgery. **Awards:** Australia/New Zealand Traveling Fellowship. **Frequency:** periodic. **Type:** fellowship ● Distinguished Service Award. **Frequency:** annual. **Type:** recognition ● International Guest Scholarship. **Frequency:** periodic. **Type:** scholarship. **Recipient:** for surgeons from overseas ● Research Scholarship. **Frequency:** periodic. **Type:** scholarship. **Computer Services:** database, National Cancer; cancer registry ● database, National TRACS Program; trauma registry. **Commissions:** Cancer. **Committees:** Allied Health Personnel; Coding and Reimbursement; Continuing Education; Development; Emerging Surgical Technology and Education; Ethics; Forum on Fundamental Surgical Problems; Graduate Medical Education; Informatics; International Relations; Medical Motion Pictures; Operating Room Environment; Pre- and Postoperative Care; Professional Liability; Scholarships; Surgical Education in Medical Schools; Surgical Research and Education; Trauma; Young Surgeons. **Publications:** *ACS Publications and Services Catalog*, annual. Lists publications. **Price:** free. Alternate Formats: online ● *Bulletin of the American College of Surgeons*, monthly. Includes ACS and Washington news. **Price:** included in membership dues. ISSN: 0002-8045. **Circulation:** 67,779 ● *Journal of the American College of Surgeons*, monthly. Includes The Surgeon at Work Section, collective literature reviews, and book reviews. ISSN: 1072-7515. **Advertising:** accepted ● *NewsScope*, weekly. Newsletter. Alternate Formats: online ● *Resources for Optimal Care of the Injured Patient*. **Price:** $15.00 ● *Surgery News*. Newspaper. **Conventions/Meetings:** annual Clinical Congress (exhibits) - always fall ● annual meeting (exhibits) - always spring.

16217 ■ American Hernia Society (AHS)
PO Box 4834
Englewood, CO 80155
Ph: (303)567-7899
Fax: (303)771-2550
E-mail: contact@americanherniasociety.org
URL: http://www.americanherniasociety.org
Contact: Shelburn M. Wilkes, Exec. Dir.
Founded: 1997. **Members:** 600. **Membership Dues:** individual, $160 (annual). **Staff:** 2. **Budget:** $100,000. **Multinational. Description:** Surgeons interested in

the management of hernias. Seeks to advance the diagnosis and treatment of hernias; promotes continuing professional development of members. Serves as a forum for the exchange of information among members; gathers and disseminates information on emerging methods of hernia surgery and management. **Publications:** *Hernia,* quarterly. Journal. **Price:** $60.00/copy. **Circulation:** 1,000. **Advertising:** accepted. **Conventions/Meetings:** Hernia Repair - convention, includes vendors with medical supply equipment (exhibits).

16218 ■ American Shoulder and Elbow Surgeons (ASES)
6300 N River Rd., Ste.727
Rosemont, IL 60018-4226
Ph: (847)698-1629
Fax: (847)823-0536
E-mail: jones@aaos.org
URL: http://www.ases-assn.org
Contact: Dr. W.Z. Burkhead Jr., Pres.
Founded: 1982. **Members:** 206. **Description:** Orthopedic surgeons. Works to promote the exchange and dissemination of information on shoulder and elbow surgery and treatment. Sponsors educational courses. **Awards:** Neer Award. **Frequency:** annual. **Type:** recognition. **Recipient:** for the most outstanding research paper. **Committees:** Education. **Publications:** *ASES News.* Newsletter. Alternate Formats: online. **Conventions/Meetings:** annual meeting.

16219 ■ American Society of Abdominal Surgeons (ASAS)
1 E Emerson St.
Melrose, MA 02176
Ph: (781)665-6102
Fax: (781)665-4127
E-mail: office@abdominalsurg.org
URL: http://www.abdominalsurg.org
Contact: Louis F. Alfano MD, Exec. Sec.
Founded: 1959. **Members:** 2,400. **Staff:** 4. **Description:** Medical doctors specializing in abdominal surgery. Sponsors extensive program of surgical education including study courses, postgraduate programs, lectures, and demonstrations. **Libraries:** **Type:** reference. **Holdings:** 825; articles, books, periodicals. **Subjects:** medicine, surgery. **Awards:** Distinguished Service Award. **Frequency:** periodic. **Type:** recognition ● Dr. Blaise F. Alfano Award in Colorectal Surgery. **Frequency:** annual. **Type:** recognition. **Recipient:** for clinical investigations and laboratory experimentation. **Councils:** Advisory on Surgical Education. **Publications:** *The Surgeon,* semiannual. Newsletter. Includes calendar of events. **Price:** available to members only. **Circulation:** 3,900 ● Journal, annual. **Price:** available to members only. **Circulation:** 3,900. **Advertising:** accepted ● Books. **Conventions/Meetings:** annual Clinical Congress of Abdominal Surgeons and Hepato-Biliary Symposium - congress and symposium (exhibits).

16220 ■ American Society for Bariatric Surgery (ASBS)
100 SW 75th St., Ste.201
Gainesville, FL 32607
Ph: (352)331-4900
Fax: (352)331-4975
E-mail: info@asbs.org
URL: http://www.asbs.org
Contact: Georgeann Mallory RD, Exec. Dir.
Founded: 1983. **Members:** 2,000. **Membership Dues:** regular, $305 (annual) ● affiliate, $260 (annual) ● associate, $195 (annual). **Staff:** 8. **Description:** Works to advance the art and science of bariatric surgery. Supports clinical and laboratory investigations; promotes guidelines for ethical patient care; conducts educational programs for physicians, paramedicals and lay people; provides a forum for the exchange of ideas. **Awards:** Resident/Trainee Award. **Frequency:** annual. **Type:** monetary. **Recipient:** for a resident or trainee in the field of bariatric surgery. **Publications:** *ASBS Newsletter,* periodic ● *Surgery for Obesity and Related Diseases,* bimonthly. Journal. Serves as an interdisciplinary forum for communicating latest research and surgical techniques. **Price:** $350.00 /year for institutions; $180.00 /year for

individuals. ISSN: 0960-8923. **Advertising:** accepted. **Conventions/Meetings:** annual conference (exhibits) - always June. 2008 June 15-20, Washington, DC; 2009 June 21-26, Grapevine, TX.

16221 ■ American Society of Breast Surgeons
5950 Symphony Woods Rd., Ste.212
Columbia, MD 21044
Ph: (410)992-5470
Free: (877)992-5470
Fax: (410)992-5472
E-mail: contact@breastsurgeons.org
URL: http://www.breastsurgeons.org
Contact: Jane Schuster, Exec. Dir.
Founded: 1995. **Members:** 1,900. **Membership Dues:** active, associate, affiliate, $295 (annual) ● candidate, $50 (annual). **Description:** Encourages the study of breast surgery. Promotes research and development of advanced surgery techniques. Improves the standards of practice for breast surgery in the United States. **Publications:** *The American Journal of Surgery.* Provides the latest news and technologies for medical specialists concerned with breast diseases. **Price:** included in membership dues ● Newsletter, quarterly. Reports on the latest procedures, education programs, clinical trials and activities of the society. **Price:** free for members. **Conventions/Meetings:** annual meeting.

16222 ■ American Society of General Surgeons (ASGS)
PO Box 4834
Englewood, CO 80155
Ph: (303)771-5948
Free: (800)998-8322
Fax: (303)771-2550
E-mail: asgs-info@theasgs.org
URL: http://www.theasgs.org
Contact: J. Barry McKernan MD, Pres.
Founded: 1993. **Members:** 3,600. **Membership Dues:** active, associate, $125 (annual) ● candidate, corresponding, $50 (annual) ● resident, $25 (annual) ● senior, $100 (annual). **Budget:** $500,000. **Description:** Board certified general surgeons who perform procedures within the scope of general surgery. **Programs:** Expert Witness Certification; Fellowship; Laparoscopic Certification; Reimbursement and Coding. **Publications:** *Issues and Insights.* Newsletter, Alternate Formats: online ● *Surgfax,* monthly. Features timely updates on current issues. Alternate Formats: online ● Membership Directory. Alternate Formats: online ● Brochure. **Conventions/Meetings:** annual meeting, with scientific program (exhibits).

16223 ■ American Society of Lipo-Suction Surgery (ASLSS)
c/o American Academy of Cosmetic Surgery
737 N Michigan Ave., Ste.2100
Chicago, IL 60611-5405
Ph: (312)981-6760
Fax: (312)981-6787
E-mail: info@cosmeticsurgery.org
URL: http://www.cosmeticsurgery.org
Contact: Craig M. Sondalle, Exec. Dir.
Founded: 1982. **Members:** 400. **Staff:** 8. **Budget:** $2,000,000. **Description:** Surgeons specializing in dermatology, general surgery, gynecology, otolaryngology, plastic and reconstructive surgery, and cosmetic surgery. Trains surgeons in the art and methods of lipo-suction surgery. Conducts workshops and seminars. **Computer Services:** Mailing lists. **Councils:** Advisory. **Publications:** *American Journal of Cosmetic Surgery,* quarterly. Features occasional special issues that address numerous state-of-the-art cosmetic surgery procedures, topics and breakthroughs. **Price:** $128.00 in U.S.; $154.00 outside U.S. ISSN: 0748-8068 ● *Membership Roster,* annual. Membership Directory ● *Newsline,* bimonthly. Newsletter. **Conventions/Meetings:** annual meeting, held in conjunction with American Academy of Cosmetic Surgery (exhibits) - 2007 Oct. 29-31, Dubai, United Arab Emirates.

16224 ■ American Society for Reconstructive Microsurgery (ASRM)
20 N Michigan Ave., Ste.700
Chicago, IL 60602
Ph: (312)456-9579
Fax: (312)782-0553
E-mail: contact@microsurg.org
URL: http://www.microsurg.org
Contact: Krista A. Greco, Exec. Dir.
Founded: 1984. **Members:** 500. **Multinational. Description:** Aims to encourage, foster, and advance the art and science of reconstructive microneurovascular surgery and to establish a forum for teaching, research, and free discussion of reconstructive microsurgical methods and principles among members. **Publications:** Newsletter, semiannual. **Advertising:** accepted. **Conventions/Meetings:** annual meeting - 2008 Jan. 12-15, Beverly Hills, CA; 2009 Jan. 10-13, Wailea, HI.

16225 ■ American Society for Reconstructive Surgery (ASRM)
20 N Michigan Ave., Ste.700
Chicago, IL 60602
Ph: (312)456-9579
Fax: (312)782-0553
E-mail: contact@microsurg.org
URL: http://www.microsurg.org
Contact: Krista A. Greco, Exec. Dir.
Description: Healthcare professionals. Strives to facilitate information flow for reconstructive microsurgery professionals. **Computer Services:** database. **Publications:** *Reconstructive Microsurgery,* semiannual. Newsletter. Alternate Formats: online ● Membership Directory. **Conventions/Meetings:** annual meeting (exhibits) - 2008 Jan. 12-15, Los Angeles, CA; 2009 Jan. 10-13, Maui, HI; 2010 Jan. 9-12, Boca Raton, FL.

16226 ■ American Surgical Association (ASA)
900 Cummings Ctr., Ste.221-U
Beverly, MA 01915
Ph: (978)927-8330
Fax: (978)524-8890
E-mail: asa@prri.com
URL: http://www.americansurgical.info
Contact: Courtney M. Townsend Jr., Pres.
Founded: 1880. **Members:** 949. **Staff:** 1. **Description:** Represents surgeons organized to promote the science and art of surgery. **Awards:** American Surgical Association Foundation Fellowship. **Frequency:** annual. **Type:** grant. **Recipient:** for a US citizen or permanent resident with an MD or equivalent medical degree who has completed an ACGME approved residency and hold a faculty appointment in an accredited medical school or similar medical institution ● ASA Medallion for Scientific Achievement. **Frequency:** annual. **Type:** recognition. **Recipient:** for scientific achievement. **Publications:** *Annals of Surgery,* monthly ● *Transactions,* annual. **Conventions/Meetings:** annual meeting.

16227 ■ Association for Academic Surgery (AAS)
11300 W Olympic Blvd., Ste.600
Los Angeles, CA 90064
Ph: (310)437-1606
Fax: (310)437-0585
E-mail: aaron@aasurg.org
URL: http://www.aasurg.org
Contact: Christina Kaserndof, Exec. Dir.
Founded: 1967. **Members:** 2,736. **Membership Dues:** active, $180 (annual) ● candidate, $15 (annual) ● senior, $80 (annual). **Staff:** 10. **Description:** Active and senior surgeons with backgrounds in all surgical specialties in academic surgical centers at chief resident level or above. Encourages young surgeons to pursue careers in academic surgery; supports them in establishing themselves as investigators and educators by providing a forum in which senior surgical residents and junior faculty members may present papers on subjects of clinical or laboratory investigations; promotes interchange of ideas between senior surgical residents, junior faculty, and established academic surgeons; facilitates com-

munication among academic surgeons in all surgical fields. Maintains placement service. **Awards:** Astra-Zeneca Resident Research Fellowship Award. **Frequency:** biennial. **Type:** recognition. **Recipient:** to residents and fellows completing at least 2 years of postgraduate training, and planning to spend 2 years in full-time research with active AAS member ● Joel J. Roslyn, MD Faculty Award. **Frequency:** biennial. **Type:** recognition. **Recipient:** to full-time faculty ● Research Fellowship Award. **Frequency:** biennial. **Type:** recognition. **Recipient:** to residents and fellows completing at least 2 years of postgraduate training, and planning to spend 2 years in full-time research with active AAS member ● Student Research Award. **Frequency:** annual. **Type:** recognition. **Recipient:** to senior medical students planning academic surgical career. **Telecommunication Services:** electronic mail, christina@aasurg.org. **Committees:** Education; Informatics and Technology; Issues; Membership; Nominating; Program. **Publications:** *Journal of Surgical Research*, monthly. **Price:** included in membership dues; $65.00 for nonmembers ● Newsletter, semiannual. **Conventions/Meetings:** annual meeting (exhibits).

16228 ■ Association of Program Directors in Surgery (APDS)
PO Box 342260
Bethesda, MD 20827-2260
Ph: (301)320-1200
Fax: (301)263-9025
E-mail: cd005258@mindspring.com
URL: http://www.apds.org
Contact: R. James Valentine MD, Pres.
Founded: 1978. **Members:** 507. **Membership Dues:** associate, $125 ● regular, $170. **Staff:** 5. **Description:** Represents program directors in surgery. Conducts educational programs and scientific meetings. **Computer Services:** Mailing lists, of surgery program directors and surgery residency coordinators ● online services, library. **Publications:** *Current Surgery*, 9/year. **Price:** $40.00 for members. **Advertising:** accepted. **Conventions/Meetings:** annual meeting (exhibits).

16229 ■ Association of Program Directors in Vascular Surgery (APDVS)
c/o Dr. Bauer E. Sumpio, MD, Sec.-Treas.
Yale Univ. School of Medicine
333 Cedar St., Surgery, FMB 137
New Haven, CT 06510
E-mail: bauer.sumpio@yale.edu
URL: http://apdvs.vascularweb.org
Contact: Dr. Bauer E. Sumpio MD, Sec.-Treas.
Description: Represents directors of all vascular surgery residency programs in the United States. Addresses the educational, regulatory, and financial issues which impact on the education of future vascular surgeons. Fosters the professional development of vascular surgery residents. **Telecommunication Services:** electronic mail, pburton@vascularsociety.org.

16230 ■ Association of Women Surgeons (AWS)
5204 Fairmont Ave., Ste.208
Downers Grove, IL 60515
Ph: (630)655-0392
Fax: (630)493-0798
E-mail: info@womensurgeons.org
URL: http://www.womensurgeons.org
Contact: Judith Keel, Exec. Dir.
Founded: 1981. **Members:** 1,700. **Membership Dues:** life, $3,000 ● new surgeon, $125 (annual) ● resident, $25 (annual) ● student, $15 (annual) ● associate, $150 (annual) ● regular, $200 (annual) ● institutional, $500 (annual). **Description:** Women surgeons, interns, and residents; retired women surgeons; women in medical school interested in a career in surgery; interested individuals. Promotes the professional and personal goals of women surgeons and women involved and interested in the medical profession. Encourages interaction between women surgeons internationally. Serves as a network for the exchange of ideas and information. **Libraries: Type:** open to the public. **Awards:** Distinguished

Member Award. **Frequency:** annual. **Type:** recognition. **Recipient:** to a member surgeon who exemplifies the ideals and mission of the association ● Honorary Member Award. **Frequency:** annual. **Type:** recognition. **Recipient:** to individuals supportive of the goals of the association ● Nina Starr Braunwald Award. **Frequency:** annual. **Type:** recognition. **Recipient:** for exceptional service to women in surgery ● Outstanding Woman Resident Award. **Frequency:** annual. **Type:** recognition. **Recipient:** to a woman who demonstrates great potential as a future leader in surgery ● Pat Numann, MD, Award. **Frequency:** annual. **Type:** recognition. **Recipient:** for female medical students. **Computer Services:** database ● mailing lists ● online services. **Committees:** Academic Practice; Chapter Development and Liaison; Fundraising; Grants/Awards; Honors; Information Technology; Liaison/Networking; Marketing. **Publications:** *AWS Connections*, quarterly. Newsletter. Includes notice of meetings, lists employment opportunities, and profiles of outstanding women surgeons. **Price:** included in membership dues. **Advertising:** accepted. Alternate Formats: online ● *Pocket Mentor*. Handbook. Features information for residents and interns. **Price:** included in membership dues ● *Sexual Harassment Resource Manual*, biennial. Serves as a networking device among members. **Conventions/Meetings:** annual Fall Conference, held in conjunction with American College of Surgeons Clinical Congress - always fall.

16231 ■ Children's Corrective Surgery Society (CCSS)
338 W 3rd Ave.
Escondido, CA 92025
Ph: (760)735-9065
Fax: (760)735-2977
E-mail: ccss@coad.org
URL: http://www.coad.org
Contact: John M. Martin, Pres.
Founded: 1972. **Multinational. Description:** Provides free plastic surgery to disfigured children in countries where medical assistance of this kind is limited. Participates in disaster relief and provides medicine to needy parts of the world.

16232 ■ CyberKnife Society (CKS)
c/o Dianna Brogden
1310 Chesapeake Terr.
Sunnyvale, CA 94089
Ph: (408)716-4663
Free: (888)522-3740
Fax: (408)716-4620
E-mail: admin@cksociety.org
URL: http://www.cksociety.org
Contact: Dianna Brogden, Contact
Founded: 2002. **Membership Dues:** physician, $200 (annual) ● non-physician, $100 (annual). **Multinational. Description:** Fosters scholarly exchange of clinical information pertaining to CyberKnife radiosurgical ablation. Seeks to improve results achieved in the field of radiosurgery. Encourages and enhances Cyberknife adoption and radiosurgical techniques in the worldwide medical community and among healthcare providers and patients. **Publications:** *CyberKnife Stereotactic Radiosurgery System Peer Reviewed Bibliography*. Alternate Formats: online.

16233 ■ Federated Ambulatory Surgery Association (FASA)
1012 Cameron St.
Alexandria, VA 22314
Ph: (703)836-8808
Fax: (703)549-0976
E-mail: fasa@fasa.org
URL: http://www.fasa.org
Contact: Kathy Bryant, Pres.
Founded: 1974. **Members:** 1,425. **Membership Dues:** facility, $500-$2,000 (annual) ● supporter, $500 (annual). **Staff:** 12. **Budget:** $2,500,000. **Description:** Physicians, nurses, health administrators, and other individuals representing more than 1,400 ambulatory surgery centers. Promotes the concept of ambulatory (outpatient) surgical care. Facilitates exchange of knowledge and ideas regarding the care of ambulatory surgical patients. Represents members'

interests at national level. Provides information to members, other organizations, and the public regarding government activities, legislation, statistical studies, group purchase programs, and the availability of malpractice insurance. Sponsors seminars, educational programs, and panel discussions; conducts studies and surveys in the field. **Libraries: Type:** open to the public. **Holdings:** books, periodicals. **Computer Services:** database ● mailing lists, of members. **Committees:** Nurses. **Formerly:** Society for the Advancement of Freestanding Ambulatory Surgical Care; (1986) Freestanding Ambulatory Surgery Association. **Publications:** *FASA Update*, bimonthly. Newsletter. **Price:** $125.00 /year for nonmembers; included in membership dues. **Advertising:** accepted ● *Protecting your ASC: A Legal Handbook*. **Price:** $59.95 for members; $79.95 for nonmembers ● Membership Directory, annual. **Conventions/Meetings:** annual conference (exhibits) - 2008 May 14-17, San Antonio, TX.

16234 ■ International College of Surgeons (ICS)
1516 N Lake Shore Dr.
Chicago, IL 60610
Ph: (312)642-3555
Fax: (312)787-1624
E-mail: info@icsglobal.org
URL: http://www.icsglobal.org
Contact: Max C. Downham, Exec. Dir.
Founded: 1935. **Members:** 8,000. **Staff:** 6. **Budget:** $1,000,000. **Regional Groups:** 6. **National Groups:** 70. **Multinational. Description:** General surgeons and surgical specialists in 110 countries maintaining official relations with the World Health Organization. Promotes the universal teaching and advancement of surgery and its allied sciences. Maintains International Museum of Surgical Science containing specialty rooms showing the growth and perfection of many surgical specialties. Maintains library open to researchers, individuals working in the profession, and the public. Organizes postgraduate clinics around the world; conducts lecture series and periodic congresses; offers grants, scholarships, and loans for residencies, research, and advanced study in surgery. Sends surgical teaching teams to developing countries. Bestows honorary fellowships. **Libraries: Type:** not open to the public. **Holdings:** 5,000; books. **Subjects:** general surgery, surgical specialties. **Awards:** International Master Surgeon. **Frequency:** annual. **Type:** recognition. **Recipient:** by recommendation of International Honors Committee. **Publications:** *International College of Surgeons Newsletter*, quarterly. Covers college news and business. **Circulation:** 10,000. **Advertising:** accepted ● *International Surgery*, quarterly. Journal. Presents papers on clinical, experimental, cultural, and historical topics pertinent to surgery and related fields. Contains book reviews. **Price:** $25.00 /year for members; $50.00 /year for nonmembers. ISSN: 0020-8868. **Circulation:** 10,000. **Advertising:** accepted. **Conventions/Meetings:** biennial conference (exhibits).

16235 ■ International Society for Vascular Surgery (ISVS)
11 Scott Dr.
Smithtown, NY 11787
Ph: (631)979-3780
Fax: (631)360-7263
E-mail: info@isvs.com
URL: http://www.isvs.com
Contact: Pauline T. Mayer, Exec. Dir.
Founded: 2003. **Membership Dues:** full, $250 (annual) ● in training, $175 (annual) ● developing country, $75 (annual) ● senior/retired, $125 (annual) ● non-physician, $150 (annual). **Multinational. Description:** Enhances and promotes the recognition of vascular surgery as an independent and distinct specialty throughout the world. Encourages the dissemination of knowledge regarding vascular disease and vascular surgery to the public and to the profession. Develops international standards of practice and training in vascular surgery. Encourages international exchange for training in vascular surgery. **Telecommunication Services:** electronic mail, isvs@isvs.com. **Publications:** *VASCULAR*, bimonthly.

Journal. Publishes opinion pieces and other non-scientific articles dealing with issues important to vascular surgery. **Price:** included in membership dues. **Advertising:** accepted ● Newsletter. **Price:** included in membership dues.

16236 ■ National Surgical Assistant Association (NSAA)

2615 Amesbury Rd.
Winston-Salem, NC 27103
Ph: (336)768-4443
Free: (888)633-0479
Fax: (336)768-4445
E-mail: nsaa@namgmt.com
URL: http://www.nsaa.net
Contact: Ms. Ruth Helein, Exec. Dir.
Founded: 1983. **Members:** 907. **Staff:** 1. **State Groups:** 5. **Description:** Professional surgical assistants throughout the United States. Provides standard guidelines and regulations. Establishes rules for those who practice and function as surgical assistants. Examines, reviews, and certifies the training, duration, experience, skills, and knowledge of its members. **Publications:** CSA Node, quarterly. Newsletter. Provides articles on latest surgical techniques and trends in the operating room. Alternate Formats: online ● Membership Directory. **Conventions/Meetings:** annual conference ● seminar ● annual show, exhibits at the American College of Surgeons Clinical Congress (exhibits).

16237 ■ Prosthetics Outreach Foundation (POF)

400 E Pine St., Ste.225
Seattle, WA 98122
Ph: (206)726-1636
Fax: (206)726-1637
E-mail: info@pofsea.org
URL: http://www.pofsea.org
Contact: Winfried Danke, Exec. Dir.
Founded: 1989. **Staff:** 4. **Budget:** $500,000. **Description:** Strives to restore mobility and independence to disadvantaged amputees worldwide through sharing of clinical and technical experience and expertise from working more than one decade in prosthetics. Seeks to help the Developing World walks again through local manufacturing of prosthetic and orthotic components (feet, knee joints, etc.), local fabrication and fitting of comfortable, custom-made prostheses, and orthopedic surgical assistance. **Projects:** Vietnam Knee. **Formerly:** (1993) Prosthetics Research Foundation. **Publications:** Newsletter, semiannual. **Price:** free for members. Alternate Formats: online.

16238 ■ Society of Air Force Clinical Surgeons

5350 Dunlay Dr., Unit 214
Sacramento, CA 95835-1563
Ph: (916)924-0352
Fax: (916)923-5987
E-mail: rose@safcs.org
URL: http://www.safcs.org
Contact: Rose Thomas, Exec. Dir.
Founded: 1949. **Members:** 640. **Membership Dues:** resident, $25 (annual) ● active, $75 (annual) ● senior, associate, $110 (annual). **Staff:** 1. **Budget:** $60,000. **Description:** Air Force Clinical Surgeons. Promotes excellence in surgery within the Air Force, serves as a forum for the presentation of scientific papers, fosters esprit de corps, and promulgates military surgical objectives. **Awards:** Clinical Surgeons Award. **Frequency:** annual. **Type:** monetary. **Recipient:** for the best original paper written and presented by a resident or fellow at the annual meeting ● Excaliber Award. **Type:** recognition. **Recipient:** for outstanding Active Duty member who has made significant contributions to academic or clinical Air Force surgery and exemplifies the highest dedication, process, competence, character and vision of a career Air Force Officer ● Paul W. Myers Award for Excellence in Resident Research. **Type:** recognition ● Trauma/Critical Care Award. **Frequency:** annual. **Type:** monetary. **Recipient:** for the best scientific and best clinical paper presented. **Conventions/Meetings:** annual symposium - held every other odd

year in San Antonio and is rotated among Centers during the even years.

16239 ■ Society of Interventional Pain Management Surgery Centers (SIPMS)

81 Lakeview Dr.
Paducah, KY 42001
Ph: (270)554-9412 (270)554-8373
Fax: (270)554-5394
E-mail: drm@asipp.org
URL: http://www.asipp.org/sipms.html
Contact: Laxmaiah Manchikanti MD, Pres.
Membership Dues: individual (physician, administrator, coordinator, nurse), $500 (annual) ● surgery center (based on qualifications), $2,000-$25,000 (annual). **Description:** Aims to limit or eliminate impending dramatic cuts in Medicare payment for ambulatory surgery centers' (ASC) services. Addresses the issues of providing interventional pain management procedures in the ASC setting. Seeks to improve the current situation of ambulatory surgery centers involved in interventional pain management.

16240 ■ Society of Laparoendoscopic Surgeons (SLS)

7330 SW 62nd Pl., Ste.410
Miami, FL 33143-4825
Ph: (305)665-9959
Free: (800)446-2659
Fax: (305)667-4123
E-mail: info@sls.org
URL: http://www.sls.org
Contact: Paul Alan Wetter MD, Chm.
Founded: 1990. **Members:** 6,700. **Membership Dues:** physician, $250 (annual) ● resident-in-training, nurse, technician, fellow-in-training, retired physician, $75 (annual). **Staff:** 8. **Description:** Works to ensure standards for the practice of laparoscopic, endoscopic, and minimally invasive surgery. Serves physicians from various specialties and other health professionals who are interested in advancing expertise in the diagnostic and therapeutic uses of laparoendoscopic techniques. Accredited by the Accreditation Council for Continuing Medical Education to provide continuing medical education for physicians. **Libraries:** Type: not open to the public. **Holdings:** 100; video recordings. **Subjects:** laparoscopy, endoscopy. **Awards:** Excel Award. **Frequency:** annual. **Type:** recognition. **Recipient:** for outstanding contribution to the practice and education of laparoscopy and/or endoscopy ● SLS Innovation Award. **Frequency:** periodic. **Type:** recognition. **Recipient:** for innovative work in the fields of laparoscopy, endoscopy or minimally invasive surgery. **Computer Services:** Mailing lists, available for purchase. **Publications:** Journal of the Society of Laparoendoscopic Surgeons, quarterly. Contains original articles on basic science and technical topics pertaining to laparoscopy, endoscopy and minimally invasive surgery. **Price:** $250.00 for nonmembers in U.S.; included in membership dues. ISSN: 1086-8089. **Circulation:** 8,000. **Advertising:** accepted. Also Cited As: JSLS ● Laparoscopy and SLS Report, semiannual. Newsletter. Serves as a resource of information for SLS members. **Price:** $85.00. ISSN: 1060-8458. **Circulation:** 80,000. **Advertising:** accepted. **Conventions/Meetings:** biennial Asian American MultiSpecialty Congress of Laparoscopy & Minimally Invasive Surgery ● biennial Euro American MultiSpecialty Congress of Laparoscopy & Minimally Invasive Surgery - regional meeting ● annual International Congress and Endo Expo - meeting (exhibits) - 2007 Sept. 5-8, San Francisco, CA ● periodic regional meeting.

16241 ■ Society for Surgery of the Alimentary Tract (SSAT)

900 Cummings Ctr., Ste.221-U
Beverly, MA 01915
Ph: (978)927-8330
Fax: (978)524-8890
E-mail: ssat@prri.com
URL: http://www.ssat.com
Contact: Mr. Robert P. Jones Jr., Exec. Dir.
Founded: 1960. **Members:** 2,600. **Membership Dues:** active, $155 (annual) ● resident in a surgical

training program or GI Fellowship (restricted to US/Canadian residents), $20 (annual) ● candidate not more than 4 years out of residency (includes all non-North American residents), $80 (annual). **Multinational. Description:** Licensed physicians with an interest in surgical aspects of digestive diseases. Seeks to advance the study, teaching, and practice of surgery of the alimentary tract; promotes continuing professional development of members. Serves as a forum for the discussion of new alimentary surgical techniques; encourages training opportunities and funding for alimentary surgical research. **Awards:** Career Development Award. **Frequency:** annual. **Type:** monetary. **Recipient:** for young faculty members ● Traveling Fellowship for Surgeons in Academic Practice. **Frequency:** annual. **Type:** monetary. **Recipient:** for junior academic surgeons in the SSAT with surgical units overseas ● Traveling Fellowship for Surgeons within the U.S. or Canada. **Frequency:** annual. **Type:** monetary. **Recipient:** for U.S./Canadian SSAT members and affiliated U.S./Canadian universities. **Computer Services:** database ● mailing lists. **Publications:** Journal of Gastrointestinal Surgery, monthly. **Advertising:** accepted. Alternate Formats: online ● Patient Care Guidelines. Alternate Formats: online. **Conventions/Meetings:** annual meeting, digestive disease week (exhibits) - always May. 2008 May 17-21, San Diego, CA.

16242 ■ Society of University Surgeons (SUS)

341 N Maitland Ave., Ste.130
Maitland, FL 32751
Ph: (407)647-7714
Fax: (407)629-2502
E-mail: info@susweb.org
URL: http://www.susweb.org
Contact: Michael T. Longaker, Pres.
Founded: 1938. **Members:** 1,280. **Membership Dues:** active, $150 (annual) ● senior, $180 (annual). **Staff:** 1. **Budget:** $50,000. **Description:** Professional society of surgeons connected with university teaching. Works to advance the art and science of surgery by encouraging original investigations both in the clinic and in the laboratory and by developing methods of graduate teaching of surgery with particular reference to the resident system. **Awards:** SUS Foundation. **Frequency:** annual. **Type:** fellowship. **Recipient:** for members who have completed two years of training, and agree to spend one or two years in full-time research in the laboratory. **Committees:** Social and Legislative Issues; Surgical Education. **Publications:** Surgery, monthly. Journal. **Conventions/Meetings:** annual congress.

16243 ■ Western Surgical Association (WSA)

c/o Gregory J. Jurkovich, MD, Sec.
UW Harborview Medical Center
325 Ninth Ave.
Seattle, WA 98104-2420
Ph: (206)731-8485
Free: (800)354-9527
Fax: (206)731-3656
E-mail: jerryj@u.washington.edu
URL: http://www.westernsurg.org
Contact: Gregory J. Jurkovich MD, Sec.
Founded: 1891. **Members:** 700. **Membership Dues:** regular, $150 (annual). **Staff:** 1. **Description:** Surgeons who have contributed to surgical education and advancement. Objectives are: to cultivate, promote, and diffuse knowledge of the art and science of surgery; to sponsor and maintain the highest standards of practice; to deliver the best possible care to all people. **Awards:** J. Bradley Aust Award. **Frequency:** annual. **Type:** monetary. **Recipient:** for best paper presented by a new member. **Committees:** Executive; Membership. **Publications:** Western Surgical Association Newsletter, quarterly. Includes information on new members and information on upcoming meetings. **Price:** free ● Western Surgical Association Program, annual. Book. Contains abstracts of papers to be presented at annual meeting, also includes transactions. **Conventions/Meetings:** annual meeting - 2007 Nov. 4-7, Colorado Springs, CO; 2008 Nov. 9-12, Santa Fe, NM.

T'ai Chi

16244 ■ American Tai Chi Association (ATCA)
13130 Thornapple Pl.
Herndon, VA 20171
Ph: (703)477-8878
E-mail: contact@americantaichi.net
URL: http://www.americantaichi.org
Contact: Dr. Li-Chuan Chen, Board Member
Founded: 2001. **Membership Dues:** premium professional, $75 (annual) ● regular professional, $50 (annual) ● associate, $35 (annual). **Description:** Promotes Tai Chi as a complementary and alternative medicine and as a physical activity for fitness and wellness. Educates the public on the role and benefits of Tai Chi. Represents Tai Chi coaches nationwide. **Libraries: Type:** reference. **Holdings:** archival material, articles, audio recordings, audiovisuals, video recordings. **Subjects:** Tai Chi. **Boards:** Advisory. **Publications:** Newsletter, monthly. Contains health association and industry news, advice, useful tips and feature articles. **Price:** free.

Technology

16245 ■ Section for Magnetic Resonance Technologists (SMRT)
2118 Milvia St., Ste.201
Berkeley, CA 94704
Ph: (510)841-1899
Fax: (510)841-2340
E-mail: smrt@ismrm.org
URL: http://www.ismrm.org/smrt
Contact: Roberta A. Kravitz, Exec. Dir.
Membership Dues: basic, $75 (annual) ● technologist (with 1 journal), $180 (annual) ● technologist (with 2 journals), $285 (annual) ● student, $25 (annual) ● student (with 1 journal), $130 (annual) ● student (with 2 journals), $235 (annual). **Multinational. Description:** Seeks to advance education and training for Magnetic Resonance Imaging and Science technologists globally. **Awards: Type:** recognition. **Boards:** Policy. **Committees:** Awards; Bylaws; Education; External Relations; Local Chapter; Membership; Nominating; Program; Publications; Regionals. **Publications:** *Magnetic Resonance Imaging*. Journal. **Price:** included in membership dues ● *Magnetic Resonance in Medicine*. Journal. **Price:** included in membership dues ● *Signals*, quarterly. Newsletter ● *SMRT Continuing Education Credit Activity Report* ● Membership Directory. **Conventions/Meetings:** annual meeting (exhibits) ● seminar.

Telecommunications

16246 ■ American Telemedicine Association (ATA)
1100 Connecticut Ave. NW, Ste.540
Washington, DC 20036
Ph: (202)223-3333
Fax: (202)223-2787
E-mail: info@americantelemed.org
URL: http://www.americantelemed.org
Contact: Jonathan D. Linkous, Exec. Dir.
Founded: 1993. **Members:** 2,000. **Membership Dues:** individual, $225 (annual) ● student, resident, $100 (annual) ● institution, $1,400 (annual) ● President's Circle, $5,750 (annual) ● corporate, regular, $1,725 (annual) ● sustaining, $1,000 (annual). **Staff:** 7. **Description:** Works to promote improvement in health care delivery by applying telecommunications technology. Supports telemedical research and education; develops policy and standards; educates government leaders, public and professional organizations; serves as a clearinghouse for telemedical information and services. **Awards:** President's Award. **Frequency:** annual. **Type:** monetary. **Recipient:** to a project, program, institution or individual who made a substantial contribution to telemedicine. **Special Interest Groups:** Emergency Preparedness and Response; Home Telehealth; Hu-

man Factors; Ocular Telehealth; Technology; Teledermatology; Telenursing; Telepathology. **Publications:** *Journal of Telemedicine and Telecare*, 6-8/year. **Price:** $109.00 for members; $380.00 for nonmembers ● *Member Update*, bimonthly. Newsletter. Contains news briefs about the latest events affecting telemedicine. Alternate Formats: online ● *Professional Journal*, quarterly ● *Telemedicine and e-Health Journal*, quarterly. Includes all aspects of clinical telemedicine practice. **Price:** included in membership dues. **Conventions/Meetings:** annual convention (exhibits).

16247 ■ Council for Responsible Telemedicine (CRT)
Address Unknown since 2007
Description: Seeks to improve quality and effective access to telemedicine and health care in general.

Therapy

16248 ■ Adventures in Movement for the Handicapped (AIM)
945 Danbury Rd.
Dayton, OH 45420
Ph: (937)294-4611
Free: (800)332-8210
Fax: (937)294-3783
E-mail: aimforthehandicapped@aimforthehandicapped.org
URL: http://www.aimforthehandicapped.org
Contact: Dr. Jo A. Geiger, Natl. Exec. Dir.
Founded: 1958. **Members:** 4,000. **Staff:** 6. **Budget:** $450,000. **Description:** Organizes activities for people with physical and mental challenges. **Libraries: Type:** open to the public. **Subjects:** the AIM method, adventures in movement. **Awards:** Certificate of Recognition. **Frequency:** annual. **Type:** recognition. **Recipient:** to a volunteer for 1 year. **Formerly:** (1969) DANCE, Inc. **Publications:** *Adventures in Movement*. Book ● Brochure. **Conventions/Meetings:** periodic Adventures in Movement - meeting, training in AIM method for teachers and volunteers (exhibits).

16249 ■ American Academy of Health Physics (AAHP)
1313 Dolley Madison Blvd., Ste.402
McLean, VA 22101
Ph: (703)790-1745
Fax: (703)790-2672
E-mail: aahp@burkinc.com
URL: http://www.hps1.org/aahp
Contact: James S. Bogard, Pres.
Description: Certified Health Physicists. Works to promote the profession. Actively participates in the certification program. **Awards:** William A. McAdams Outstanding Service Award. **Frequency:** annual. **Type:** recognition. **Recipient:** to a CHP who has made a significant contribution to the advancement of professionalism in health physics and to the certification process. **Computer Services:** Mailing lists. **Telecommunication Services:** electronic bulletin board. **Committees:** Appeals; Continuing; Development; Education; Examination Site; Nominating; Professional; Selection. **Publications:** *CHP Corner*. Newsletter. Alternate Formats: online.

16250 ■ American Association for Respiratory Care (AARC)
9425 N MacArthur Blvd., Ste.100
Irving, TX 75063-4706
Ph: (972)243-2272
Fax: (972)484-2720
E-mail: info@aarc.org
URL: http://www.aarc.org
Contact: Sam Giordano, Exec. Dir.
Founded: 1947. **Members:** 35,000. **Membership Dues:** active/special/associate in U.S., $102 (annual) ● associate outside U.S., $117 (annual) ● student, $50 (annual). **Staff:** 40. **Budget:** $8,000,000. **State Groups:** 50. **National Groups:** 4. **Languages:** English, Spanish. **Description:** Allied health society of respiratory therapists and other respiratory car-

egivers employed by hospitals, skilled nursing facilities, home care companies, group practices, educational institutions, and municipal organizations. Encourages, develops, and provides educational programs for persons interested in the profession of respiratory care; and advances the science of respiratory care. **Sections:** Adult Acute Care; Continuing Care-Rehabilitation; Diagnostics; Education; Home Care; Long-Term Care; Management; Neonatal-Pediatrics; Sleep; Surface and Air Transport. **Formerly:** (1954) Inhalation Therapy Association; (1967) American Association of Inhalation Therapists; (1973) American Association for Inhalation Therapy; (1986) American Association for Respiratory Therapy. **Publications:** *AARC Times: The Magazine for the Respiratory Care Professional*, monthly. Includes advertisers' index, calendar of events, employment opportunities, and legislative update. **Price:** included in membership dues; $75.00 /year for nonmembers in U.S.; $90.00 /year for nonmembers outside U.S. ISSN: 0893-8520. **Circulation:** 37,000. **Advertising:** accepted ● *Respiratory Care* (in English, French, Italian, and Japanese), monthly. Journal. Provides original studies, case reports, and method/device evaluations in cardiopulmonary clinical medicine. **Price:** included in membership dues; $89.75 /year for nonmembers in U.S. ISSN: 0020-1324. **Circulation:** 40,000. **Advertising:** accepted. Alternate Formats: microform. **Conventions/Meetings:** annual International Respiratory Congress - convention (exhibits).

16251 ■ American Hippotherapy Association (AHA)
136 Bush Rd.
Damascus, PA 18415
Free: (888)851-4592
Fax: (570)224-4462
E-mail: info@americanhippotherapyassociation.org
URL: http://www.americanhippotherapyassociation.org
Contact: Karen McPhail MOT, Pres.
Membership Dues: standard, $40 (annual) ● professional, $65 (annual) ● premium, international, $100 (annual) ● legacy, $50 (monthly) ● life, $1,000. **Multinational. Description:** Represents medical professionals and individuals who are interested in the use of equine movement as a treatment strategy. Promotes the use of the movement of the horse as a treatment strategy in physical, occupational and speech therapy sessions for people with disabilities. Raises awareness of the contributions of Hippotherapy. **Computer Services:** Information services, Hippotherapy resources ● online services, message board. **Committees:** Education and Workshops; Outreach; Research; Standards and Practice. **Affiliated With:** North American Riding for the Handicapped Association. **Publications:** Newsletter. Alternate Formats: online.

16252 ■ American Horticultural Therapy Association (AHTA)
3570 E 12th Ave., Ste.206
Denver, CO 80206
Ph: (303)322-2482
Free: (800)634-1603
Fax: (303)322-2485
E-mail: info@ahta.org
URL: http://www.ahta.org
Contact: Ms. Joy Harrison, Exec. Dir.
Founded: 1973. **Members:** 800. **Membership Dues:** student in U.S., $55 (annual) ● student outside U.S. and Canada, $95 (annual) ● student in Canada, $80 (annual) ● professional in U.S., $145 (annual) ● professional outside U.S. and Canada, $185 (annual) ● professional in Canada, $170 (annual) ● institutional in U.S., $300 (annual) ● institutional in Canada, $350 (annual) ● institutional outside U.S. and Canada, $400 (annual) ● individual in U.S., $95 (annual) ● individual outside U.S. and Canada, $135 (annual) ● individual in Canada, $120 (annual). **Staff:** 2. **Budget:** $115,000. **Regional Groups:** 12. **Description:** Represents professional horticultural therapists and rehabilitation specialists, horticultural therapy students, institutions and commercial organizations. Promotes and encourages the development of horticulture and related activities as a therapeutic

and rehabilitative medium. Coordinates efforts of professional and educational organizations and conducts regional workshops and seminars. Provides resource information; offers papers at various conferences. Registers professional horticultural therapists. **Awards:** Alice Burlingame Humanitarian Service Award. **Frequency:** annual. **Type:** recognition. **Recipient:** for an individual or group with remarkable contributions in horticultural therapy ● Ann Lane Mavromatis Scholarship. **Frequency:** annual. **Type:** scholarship. **Recipient:** for deserving students in the field of horticultural therapy ● John Walker Community Service Award. **Frequency:** annual. **Type:** recognition. **Recipient:** for excellent propagation of horticultural therapy in the community ● Rhea McCandliss Professional Service Award. **Frequency:** annual. **Type:** recognition. **Recipient:** for a member with significant contribution in the organization ● Therapeutic Garden Design Awards. **Frequency:** annual. **Type:** recognition. **Recipient:** for an individual or group with excellent design in therapeutic garden. **Publications:** *AHTA Annual Membership Directory*, annual. **Price:** free for members; $35.00 for nonmembers. **Advertising:** accepted ● *Journal of Therapeutic Horticulture Volumes I-XV*, annual. Journals. Contains research and programmatic articles. **Price:** $13.00 for members; $16.00 for nonmembers. **Circulation:** 1,000 ● *Newsletter American Horticulture Therapy Association*, biennial. Includes association news, program features, horticultural therapy activities, and member profiles. **Price:** $35.00/year; $3.00/issue. **Circulation:** 1,000. Also Cited As: *National Council for Therapy and Rehabilitation Through Horticulture—Newsletter* ● Books. Contains information about gardening and horticultural therapy. **Conventions/Meetings:** annual conference (exhibits).

16253 ■ American Occupational Therapy Association (AOTA)
4720 Montgomery Ln.
PO Box 31220
Bethesda, MD 20824-1220
Ph: (301)652-2682
Free: (800)377-8555
Fax: (301)652-7711
E-mail: execdept@aota.org
URL: http://www.aota.org
Contact: Frederick P. Somers, Exec. Dir.
Founded: 1917. **Members:** 36,000. **Membership Dues:** professional, $187 (annual). **Staff:** 95. **Budget:** $15,000,000. **State Groups:** 52. **Description:** Occupational therapists and occupational therapy assistants. Provides services to people whose lives have been disrupted by physical injury or illness, developmental problems, the aging process, or social or psychological difficulties. Occupational therapy focuses on the active involvement of the patient in specially designed therapeutic tasks and activities to improve function, performance capacity, and the ability to cope with demands of daily living. **Libraries:** **Type:** reference. **Holdings:** 4,100; books, video recordings. **Subjects:** occupational therapy and rehabilitation. **Awards:** **Frequency:** annual. **Type:** scholarship. **Recipient:** for students accepted in an occupational therapy education program. **Computer Services:** Information services, library catalog and bibliography ● mailing lists, rental. **Commissions:** Education; Practice; Standards and Ethics. **Committees:** Accreditation; Credentials Review and Accountability; Political Action; Standards Review. **Sections:** Administration and Management; Developmental Disabilities; Education; Gerontology; Home and Community Health; Mental Health; Physical Disabilities; School Systems; Sensory Integration; Technology; Work Programs. **Affiliated With:** American Occupational Therapy Association. **Formerly:** National Society for the Promotion of Occupational Therapy. **Publications:** *American Journal of Occupational Therapy*, bimonthly. ISSN: 0272-9490. **Circulation:** 59,000. **Advertising:** accepted ● *OT Practice*, biweekly. **Advertising:** accepted ● *Publications Catalog* ● Also publishes more than 100 single titles. **Conventions/Meetings:** annual conference, with expo (exhibits).

16254 ■ American Physical Therapy Association (APTA)
1111 N Fairfax St.
Alexandria, VA 22314-1488

Ph: (703)684-2782
Free: (800)999-2782
Fax: (703)684-7343
E-mail: frankmallon@apta.org
URL: http://www.apta.org
Contact: Mr. Frank Mallon Esq., CEO
Founded: 1921. **Members:** 67,000. **Membership Dues:** individual physical therapist, $265 (annual) ● individual physical therapist assistant, $180 (annual). **Staff:** 165. **Budget:** $29,000,000. **Regional Groups:** 52. **State Groups:** 52. **National Groups:** 18. **Description:** Professional organization of physical therapists and physical therapist assistants and students. Fosters the development and improvement of physical therapy service, education, and research; evaluates the organization and administration of curricula; directs the maintenance of standards and promotes scientific research. Acts as an accrediting body for educational programs in physical therapy. Establishes standards. Offers advisory and consultation services to schools of physical therapy and facilities offering physical therapy services; provides placement services at conference. **Libraries:** **Type:** reference. **Holdings:** archival material, books, periodicals. **Subjects:** physical therapy, rehabilitation. **Awards:** **Frequency:** annual. **Type:** recognition ● **Type:** recognition. **Computer Services:** Online services, catalog, membership. **Telecommunication Services:** TDD, (703)683-6748. **Boards:** American Board of Physical Therapy Specialties; Clinical Instructor Education; Directors. **Commissions:** Accreditation in Physical Therapy Education; Foundation for Physical Therapy. **Committees:** Annual Conference Program; Awards; Catherine Worthingham Fellows; Chapters and Sections; Clinical Residency and Fellowship Program Credentialing; Cultural Competence; Ethics and Judicial; Physical Therapist Assistant Recognition; Reference; Risk Management and Member Benefits; Screening Proposals/ Abstracts; Trustees of the American Physical Therapy Congressional Action. **Councils:** Advisory Panel on Education; Advisory Panel on Member Recruitment and Retention; Advisory Panel on Physical Therapist Assistants; Advisory Panel on Practice; Advisory Panel on Public Relations; Advisory Panel on Reimbursement Policy and Planning; Advisory Panel on Research. **Divisions:** Administration and Communications; Education; Governance, Components, Meetings; Practice and Research. **Formerly:** (1921) American Women's Physical Therapeutic Association; (1947) American Physiotherapy Association. **Publications:** *Physical Therapy*, monthly. Journal. Features peer-reviewed scientific and professional articles, continuing education course listings, abstracts of current literature, and book reviews. **Price:** included in membership dues; $80.00 /year for nonmembers; $10.00/single issue. ISSN: 0031-9023. **Circulation:** 72,000. **Advertising:** accepted. Alternate Formats: microform; online ● *PT Bulletin Online*, weekly. Newsletter. Includes public affairs and member news, plus information on upcoming seminars. **Price:** included in membership dues. ISSN: 0888-1618. **Circulation:** 105,000 ● *PT Magazine*, monthly. Journal. Features columns on risk management and reimbursement strategies. Contains advertisers' index and information on new products and literature. **Price:** included in membership dues; $70.00 /year for nonmembers; $10.00/copy. ISSN: 0276-8038. **Circulation:** 72,000. **Advertising:** accepted. Alternate Formats: microform; online ● Brochures ● Monographs ● Also issues bulletins to chapters and publishes anthologies, handbooks, and educational resource guides. **Conventions/Meetings:** annual Combined Sections Meeting - conference (exhibits) - in February ● annual conference, educational programming, social events, networking opportunities (exhibits).

16255 ■ Animal Assisted Therapy Foundation
15632 Hwy. 110 S, Ste.7
Whitehouse, TX 75791
E-mail: mail@therapet.com
URL: http://www.therapet.com
Contact: Shari Bernard-Curran OTR, Exec. Dir.
Description: Facilitates the use of animals in healing and rehabilitation of acute and chronically ill individu-

als. **Publications:** *A Comprehensive Look at Animal Assisted Therapy*. Brochure.

16256 ■ Association for Applied and Therapeutic Humor (AATH)
Historic Mill Hill District
247 E Front St.
Trenton, NJ 08611
Ph: (609)392-0200
Fax: (609)392-0244
E-mail: staff@aath.org
URL: http://www.aath.org
Contact: Lenny Dave, Pres.
Founded: 1987. **Members:** 550. **Membership Dues:** regular, $97 (annual) ● gold, $147 (annual) ● student, $37 (annual) ● senior, $67 (annual) ● international, $25 (annual). **Staff:** 3. **Budget:** $112,000. **Description:** Health care providers, clergy, and educators; other interested individuals. Promotes the use of humor as a therapeutic technique; disseminates public information about laughter and humor; offers networking service to further understanding of therapeutic humor; conducts research programs that incorporate therapeutic uses of humor. Maintains speakers' bureau. **Libraries:** **Type:** reference. **Holdings:** archival material. **Awards:** Book Award. **Frequency:** annual. **Type:** monetary. **Recipient:** for the author of a book which best furthers the organization's mission ● Doug Fletcher Lifetime Achievement Award. **Frequency:** annual. **Type:** recognition. **Recipient:** for dedication and service to the association and for significant contribution to the understanding and application of humor and/or laughter over an entire career with a definable body of work ● Ed Dunkelblau Scholarship. **Frequency:** annual. **Type:** scholarship. **Recipient:** to a practitioner of color interested in the cultural applications of therapeutic humor ● Patty Wooten Scholarship. **Frequency:** annual. **Type:** recognition. **Recipient:** to a nurse who is involved in creating humor interventions that are being used in a therapeutic manner for patients, family or staff. **Formerly:** American Association for Therapeutic Humor. **Publications:** *Humor Connection*, quarterly. Newsletter. Contains articles, interviews and book reviews about issues important to the advancement of humor and laughter. **Advertising:** accepted. Alternate Formats: online ● *Laugh It Up*, quarterly. Newsletter ● *Laugh It Update*, bimonthly. Monograph ● Bibliographies ● Also makes available tapes. **Conventions/Meetings:** annual conference.

16257 ■ Association of Pediatric Therapists (APT)
PO Box 194191
San Francisco, CA 94119
E-mail: info@bayareaapt.org
URL: http://www.aptbayarea.org
Contact: Karen Cowell, Co-Chair
Membership Dues: student, $20 (annual) ● therapist, $35 (annual). **Description:** Occupational, physical, and speech therapists, certified assistants, and students. Promotes continuing professional development of members. Works as a communication network-linking members. Cooperates with other organizations representing professionals in related fields. Conducts continuing professional education programs. **Libraries:** **Type:** reference. **Holdings:** audio recordings, books, software, video recordings. **Subjects:** pediatric therapy. **Publications:** *Resource Directory*, annual ● Newsletter, 10/year. Alternate Formats: online. **Conventions/Meetings:** monthly meeting and board meeting, with educational event.

16258 ■ Association for Play Therapy (APT)
2060 N Winery Ave., No. 102
Fresno, CA 93703
Ph: (559)252-2278
Fax: (559)252-2297
E-mail: info@a4pt.org
URL: http://www.a4pt.org
Contact: William M. Burns CAE, Exec. Dir.
Founded: 1982. **Members:** 5,000. **Membership Dues:** professional, $80 (annual) ● international, $70 (annual) ● affiliate, $45 (annual). **Staff:** 4. **Budget:** $750,000. **Description:** Promotes play therapy; addresses the professional needs of members. **Librar-**

ies: **Type:** open to the public. **Holdings:** 7. **Subjects:** play therapy. **Awards:** Service Award. **Type:** recognition. **Recipient:** for outstanding services and contributions for play therapy ● Student Research Award. **Frequency:** annual. **Type:** recognition. **Recipient:** for graduate students who have completed research on play therapy while enrolled in an accredited program. **Computer Services:** Mailing lists, of members. **Publications:** *Association for Play Therapy Newsletter*, quarterly. **Price:** included in membership dues. **Circulation:** 4,400. **Advertising:** accepted ● *International Journal of Play Therapy*, semiannual. **Price:** included in membership dues. **Circulation:** 4,400. **Advertising:** accepted. **Conventions/Meetings:** annual conference (exhibits) - always October. 2007 Oct. 9-14, Hollywood, CA; 2008 Oct. 14-19, Dallas, TX; 2009 Oct. 6-11, Atlanta, GA.

16259 ■ Association for Therapeutic Eurythmy in North America (ATHENA)
c/o Susanne Zipperlen
2110 W Arthur Ave., Apt. 2
Chicago, IL 60645
Ph: (773)761-0833
E-mail: zippster@earthlink.net
URL: http://www.artemisia.net/athena
Contact: Susanne Zipperlen, Contact
Multinational. Description: Promotes the development and practice of therapeutic eurythmy in North America. Fulfills and supports the needs, endeavors, initiatives and achievements of therapeutic eurythmists. Provides education, mentoring, certification and research.

16260 ■ Biomagnetic Therapy Association (BTA)
PO Box 394
Lyons, CO 80540
Ph: (303)823-0307
E-mail: info@biomagnetic.org
URL: http://www.biomagnetic.org
Contact: Suzy Balliett, Founder
Founded: 1995. **Members:** 150. **Membership Dues:** general/certified, $45 (annual). **Staff:** 3. **Description:** Represents health care professionals and other individuals with an interest in biomagnetic therapy. Biomagnetic therapy is the art and science of applying and removing magnetic fields for health benefits. Seeks to advance the study and practice of biomagnetic therapy; and promotes increased use of biomagnetic therapy in the treatment of a wide variety of disorders. Serves as a clearinghouse on biomagnetic and related therapies; conducts continuing professional education programs; and sponsors research. **Awards:** William Philpott, MD Scholarship. **Frequency:** annual. **Type:** scholarship. **Recipient:** for members. **Publications:** *Biomagnetic Therapy Association Newsletter*, quarterly. **Price:** $45.00/year. **Conventions/Meetings:** annual meeting - always summer.

16261 ■ Committee on Accreditation for Respiratory Care (COARC)
1248 Harwood Rd.
Bedford, TX 76021-4244
Ph: (817)283-2835
Free: (800)874-5615
Fax: (817)354-8519
E-mail: richwalker@coarc.com
URL: http://www.coarc.com
Contact: William W. Goding, Interim Exec. Dir.
Founded: 1963. **Members:** 13. **Staff:** 3. **Description:** Physicians (6); respiratory therapists (6); public representative (1). Purposes are to develop standards and requirements for accredited educational programs of respiratory therapy for recommendation to the American Medical Association; to conduct evaluations of educational programs that have applied for accreditation of the AMA and to make recommendations to the AMA's Committee on Allied Health Education and Accreditation; to maintain a working liaison with other organizations interested in respiratory therapy education and evaluation. **Affiliated With:** American Medical Association; Commission on Accreditation of Allied Health Education Programs. **For-**

merly: (1970) Board of Schools of Inhalation Therapy; (1998) Joint Review Committee for Respiratory Therapy Education. **Publications:** Publishes lists of programs. **Conventions/Meetings:** annual meeting - always November ● workshop.

16262 ■ Delta Society (DS)
875 124th Ave. NE, Ste.101
Bellevue, WA 98005
Ph: (425)679-5500
Fax: (425)679-5539
E-mail: info@deltasociety.org
Contact: Lawrence J. Norvell, Pres.
Founded: 1977. **Members:** 10,000. **Membership Dues:** general public, $50 (annual). **Staff:** 10. **Budget:** $2,479,000. **Description:** Doctors, nurses, veterinarians, therapists, nursing home personnel, animal trainers and breeders, pet owners, academicians, and students of gerontology, psychology, therapeutic recreation, and other health fields. Improves human health through service and therapy animals, trains and registers volunteers to provide animal assisted activities/therapy in their communities worldwide through a therapy animal program called Pet Partners. Provides training to for persons seeking to establish and maintain programs that involve animals in animal-assisted activities/therapy. Operates National Service Dog Center serving people with disabilities via a website. **Libraries: Type:** open to the public. **Holdings:** 1,500. **Subjects:** service dogs, animal-assisted therapy, therapeutic riding pet loss, human animal interactions, health benefits of animals, companion animals. **Boards:** Honorary. **Affiliated With:** International Association of Human-Animal Interaction Organizations. **Publications:** *InterActions*, biennial. Magazine. ISSN: 8755-5875 ● Journal.

16263 ■ Family Therapy Section of the National Council on Family Relations (FTSNCFR)
3989 Central Ave. NE, No. 550
Minneapolis, MN 55421
Ph: (248)370-3069 (763)781-9331
Free: (888)781-9331
Fax: (763)781-9348
E-mail: info@ncfr.com
URL: http://www.oakland.edu/~blume/ncfr
Contact: Thomas W. Blume PhD, Ed.
Founded: 1955. **Members:** 400. **Description:** A section of the National Council on Family Relations. Practicing family therapists and family therapy supervisors, educators, and researchers. Seeks to improve the practice of family therapy through the development of theory, research, and training. Promotes communication between family therapy researchers and clinicians; functions as a network for family therapy research projects; conducts educational programs. **Awards:** Family Therapy Section Awards. **Frequency:** annual. **Type:** monetary. **Recipient:** to student members. **Affiliated With:** National Council on Family Relations. **Formerly:** (1991) National Council on Family Relations Family Therapy Section. **Conventions/Meetings:** annual conference (exhibits).

16264 ■ Foundation for Physical Therapy (FPT)
c/o American Physical Therapy Association
1111 N Fairfax St.
Alexandria, VA 22314-1488
Free: (800)875-1378
Fax: (703)706-8536
E-mail: foundation@apta.org
URL: http://www.apta.org/Foundation
Contact: Christine A. Williams, COO
Founded: 1979. **Staff:** 6. **Budget:** $1,300,000. **Nonmembership. Description:** Supports the physical therapy profession's research needs by funding scientific and clinically-relevant physical therapy research. **Awards:** Mary McMillan Doctoral Scholarship. **Frequency:** annual. **Type:** scholarship. **Recipient:** for physical therapists who have completed one full year of doctoral coursework ● Research Grants. **Type:** grant. **Recipient:** for individuals and groups of researchers to pursue scientifically based and clini-

cally related physical therapy research. **Telecommunication Services:** TDD, (703)683-6748. **Committees:** Scientific Review. **Affiliated With:** American Physical Therapy Association. **Publications:** Annual Report, annual. Alternate Formats: online.

16265 ■ Infusion Nurses Society (INS)
315 Norwood Park S
Norwood, MA 02062
Ph: (781)440-9408
Free: (800)694-0298
Fax: (781)440-9409
E-mail: bill.talbot@ins1.org
URL: http://www.ins1.org
Contact: Mary Alexander, CEO
Founded: 1973. **Members:** 5,300. **Membership Dues:** general, $90 (annual). **Staff:** 18. **Budget:** $2,600,000. **Regional Groups:** 62. **Local Groups:** 62. **Description:** Registered nurses involved in infusion therapy; licensed practical nurses and pharmacists. Works to promote the education of individuals practicing infusion therapy. Conducts certification program for nurses and advanced studies program in infusion nursing. Maintains speakers' bureau; compiles statistics. **Awards:** Gardner Foundation Scholarship. **Frequency:** annual. **Type:** scholarship. **Recipient:** for INS members who wish to pursue careers in infusion therapy. **Computer Services:** database ● mailing lists. **Telecommunication Services:** electronic mail, phyllis.gerome@ins1.org. **Committees:** Alternate Site; Certification; National Council on Education; Research; Standards. **Departments:** Education; Marketing; Meetings; Memberships and Finance; Publications. **Programs:** Annual Meeting; National Academy of Intravenous Therapy. **Formerly:** (2002) Intravenous Nurses Society. **Publications:** *Infusion Nursing Standards of Practice*, periodic. **Price:** $15.00 for members; $45.00 for nonmembers. ISSN: 15331458 ● *Journal of Infusion Nursing*, bimonthly. Includes information on meetings, clinical manuscripts, products, and certification and recertification exams. **Price:** included in membership dues; $102.00 /year for nonmembers; $256.00 /year for institutions; $42.00/year for nonmember students. ISSN: 15331458. **Advertising:** accepted ● *Newsline*, bimonthly. Newsletter. Includes convention news, legislative network information, chapter agendas, and calendar of events. **Advertising:** accepted ● *Policies and Procedures for Infusion Nursing*, periodic ● Also publishes news releases and nursing standards. **Conventions/Meetings:** annual meeting, meeting and industrial exhibition providing continuing education (exhibits) ● annual National Academy of Infusion Nursing - seminar, continuing education.

16266 ■ International Association of Human-Animal Interaction Organizations (IAHAIO)
c/o Delta Society
875 124th Ave. NE, Ste.101
Bellevue, WA 98005-2531
Ph: (425)226-7357
Fax: (425)235-1076
E-mail: info@iahaio.org
URL: http://www.iahaio.org
Contact: Larry Norvell, Contact
Founded: 1990. **Members:** 22. **Budget:** $16,000. **National Groups:** 22. **Languages:** English, French, German, Japanese. **Description:** Provides a forum for exchange of ideas and information among organizations concerned with the study of the mutual welfare of people and animals. Encourages research and promotes educational and practical developments in the field of human-animal interactions. Hosts an international conference every three years. **Affiliated With:** Delta Society. **Formerly:** (1990) International Society for the Study of the Human-Companion Animal Bond. **Publications:** *Proceedings of International Conference*, triennial. Includes papers presented at international conference. ● Also contributes to and distributes *Anthrozoos: Journal of the Delta Society*. **Conventions/Meetings:** International Conference on Human-Animal Interactions (exhibits).

16267 ■ International Association for Oxygen Therapy (IAOT)
PO Box 502
Nordman, ID 83848

Ph: (208)443-4319 (208)443-6633
Fax: (775)227-9353
E-mail: oxytherapies@yahoo.com
Contact: Nicole S. Sacks, Contact
Founded: 1898. **Members:** 4,500. **Membership Dues:** individual, $100 (annual). **Staff:** 5. **Budget:** $250,000. **Regional Groups:** 12. **State Groups:** 30. **Local Groups:** 50. **Languages:** English, French, Spanish. **Description:** Oxidation therapists. Promotes the use of oxidation enhancing therapies to physicians and the general public. Compiles statistics. Conducts research, educational, and charitable programs. Maintains museum and speakers' bureau. **Libraries: Type:** lending; not open to the public. **Holdings:** 25,000; audiovisuals, books, business records, clippings, monographs, periodicals. **Subjects:** oxidation, scientific and medical information. **Awards:** Blass Oxidation Therapy Award. **Frequency:** annual. **Type:** recognition. **Recipient:** for outstanding oxidation therapists. **Computer Services:** database ● electronic publishing, on net ● mailing lists ● online services. **Divisions:** World Missionary Association. **Publications:** *IAOT Newsletter (Oxidation News)*, quarterly. Features international journal of WNHO. **Price:** free sample; included in membership dues. **Circulation:** 5,000. Alternate Formats: online. Also Cited As: *WNHO Journal*. **Conventions/Meetings:** annual convention (exhibits).

16268 ■ International Association for Regression Research and Therapies (IARRT)
PO Box 20151
Riverside, CA 92516
Ph: (951)784-1570
Fax: (951)784-8440
E-mail: info@iarrt.org
URL: http://www.iarrt.org
Contact: Connie Brooks, Exec. Dir.
Founded: 1980. **Members:** 800. **Membership Dues:** certified in U.S., $135 (annual) ● certified outside U.S., $135 (annual) ● non-certified in U.S., $110 (annual) ● non-certified outside U.S., $110 (annual) ● supporting in U.S., $70 (annual) ● supporting outside U.S., $70 (annual). **Staff:** 1. **State Groups:** 20. **Description:** Represents psychiatrists, psychologists, counselors, and students; organizations and individuals interested in past-life regression therapy. Promotes past-life therapy as a means of helping individuals realize their capacity to change and improve their lives. Works for progressive application of the therapy and the establishment of clinical standards for training therapists. Acts as a communications network for the exchange of information and experiences. Disseminates information to the public about benefits of the therapy. Registers therapists. Promotes research in the field. **Libraries: Type:** reference. **Awards:** Life Time Membership Award. **Type:** recognition. **Computer Services:** Mailing lists. **Formerly:** Association for Past Life Research and Therapies; (1991) Association for Past-Life Research and Therapy; (2002) Association for Past-Life Research and Therapies. **Publications:** *Journal of Regression Therapy*, annual. **Price:** $26.00/volume for nonmembers; included in membership dues; $3.00/issue for nonmembers. ISSN: 1054-0830. **Circulation:** 800. Alternate Formats: online ● *Past Life Research and Therapies*, quarterly. Newsletter. Contains editorials, Open Forum, reviews, and calendar of events. **Price:** $10.00 /year for nonmembers; included in membership dues. ISSN: 1054-0792. **Circulation:** 900. **Advertising:** accepted. Alternate Formats: online ● Audiotapes. Audios of all conference lectures, workshops and pre/post conference institutes by top individuals in the field. ● Directory, periodic. Alternate Formats: online ● Videos. **Conventions/Meetings:** semiannual conference - always spring and fall.

16269 ■ International Board for Regression Therapy (IBRT)
3702 Mt. Diablo Blvd.
Lafayette, CA 94549
Ph: (925)283-3941
E-mail: freedman@dreamscape.com
URL: http://www.ibrt.org
Contact: Janet Cunningham PhD, Pres.
Founded: 1998. **Multinational. Description:** Therapists, researchers, training programs. Provides

documentation, training, and certification. Promotes public awareness of regression therapy. **Publications:** Books.

16270 ■ International EECP Therapists Association (IETA)
PO Box 650005
Vero Beach, FL 32965-0005
Ph: (772)794-0861
Free: (800)376-3321
Fax: (772)299-6219
E-mail: secretary@ietaonline.com
URL: http://www.ietaonline.com
Contact: Joanne Giordano, Sec.-Treas.
Membership Dues: individual, $45 (annual) ● business, $200 (annual). **Multinational. Description:** Seeks to advance the profession of Enhanced External Counterpulsation (EECP) therapy. Aims to set and support standards of excellence in the delivery of EECP. Offers CET credentialing examinations to members and non-members. **Publications:** Newsletter, quarterly. **Price:** included in membership dues.

16271 ■ International Institute of Reflexology
PO Box 12642
St. Petersburg, FL 33733-2642
Ph: (727)343-4811 (727)343-1722
Fax: (727)381-2807
E-mail: iir@tampabay.rr.com
URL: http://www.reflexology-usa.net
Contact: Mr. Dwight Byers, Pres.
Founded: 1972. **Members:** 25,000. **Multinational. Description:** Promotes the ancient art of reflexology, scientifically based on the premise that there are zones and reflex areas in the feet and hands which correspond to all glands, organs, parts and systems of the body. **Conventions/Meetings:** workshop.

16272 ■ International Palmtherapy Association (IPTA)
PO Box 7453
Van Nuys, CA 91409-7453
Ph: (661)944-4909
E-mail: info@palmtherapy.com
URL: http://www.palmtherapy.com
Founded: 1995. **Membership Dues:** certified palmtherapist, $100 (biennial). **Multinational. Description:** Dedicated to the research of the "hand/mind connection". Palm therapy is the art and practice of "enhancing optimum potential, self-growth, fulfillment and success in all aspects of life through the massage stimulation of specific lines and areas of the hand". Offers seminars. **Programs:** Palmtherapy Certification. **Conventions/Meetings:** periodic Palmtherapy Seminar for Healthcare Providers.

16273 ■ Laughter Therapy (LT)
PO Box 827
Monterey, CA 93942
URL: http://www.candidcamera.com/cc7/cc7.html
Contact: Mr. Allen A. Funt, Pres.
Founded: 1981. **Staff:** 3. **Description:** Provides tapes of Candid Camera to patients, nursing homes, doctors, hospices, and clinics. (Candid Camera was a regular weekly comedy series on CBS that ran from 1960-67 and was produced by Allen Funt. The program displayed people from all walks of life and their reactions to strange or unexpected occurrences or situations.) Because studies and experiences have shown that humor is one of the most useful forms of therapy, the tapes are being used in a variety of cases where terminal illness, depression, or other ailments are evident. Maintains library of 6 one-hour tapes.

16274 ■ Love on a Leash - The Foundation for Pet Provided Therapy
PO Box 4115
Oceanside, CA 92052-4115
Ph: (760)740-2326

E-mail: info@loveonaleash.org
URL: http://www.loveonaleash.org
Contact: Liz Palika, Founder
Founded: 1984. **Members:** 600. **Membership Dues:** individual, associate, $20 (annual) ● individual (under 18), $10 (annual). **Description:** Promotes positive interaction between pets and people.

16275 ■ National Association of Myofascial Trigger Point Therapists (NAMTPT)
PO Box 42446
Pittsburgh, PA 15223
Ph: (412)303-5889
E-mail: namtpt@hotmail.com
URL: http://www.myofascialtherapy.org
Contact: Heather Wimbish, Sec.
Membership Dues: professional, associate professional, $130 (annual) ● student, supporting, $55 (annual). **Description:** Seeks to establish and promote professional standards of myofascial trigger point therapy. Aims to advance continuing education for those who are interested in the study of myofascial pain and dysfunction. Provides resources and support to all members. **Telecommunication Services:** electronic mail, hwimbish@myofascialtherapy.org. **Publications:** Newsletter. **Price:** included in membership dues. Alternate Formats: online ● Membership Directory. **Price:** included in membership dues. **Conventions/Meetings:** annual convention.

16276 ■ National Board for Certification in Occupational Therapy (NBCOT)
The Eugene B. Casey Bldg.
800 S Frederick Ave., Ste.200
Gaithersburg, MD 20877-4150
Ph: (301)990-7979
Fax: (301)869-8492
E-mail: webmaster@nbcot.org
URL: http://www.nbcot.org
Contact: Linda Florey PhD, Chair
Founded: 1986. **Staff:** 22. **Description:** Participants are occupational therapists and occupational therapy assistants. Administers certification program and maintains certification records of certificants; operates disciplinary mechanisms. **Committees:** Certification Examination Development; Disciplinary Action; Program Directors Advisory; Research Advisory; State Association Presidents Advisory; State Regulatory Advisory. **Formerly:** (1996) AOTCB; (1998) American Occupational Therapy Certification Board. **Publications:** *Report to the Profession*, semiannual. Newsletters ● Brochures ● Reports ● Annual Report, annual. **Conventions/Meetings:** board meeting - 3/year ● periodic executive committee meeting.

16277 ■ National Board for Respiratory Care (NBRC)
8310 Nieman Rd.
Lenexa, KS 66214-1510
Ph: (913)599-4200
Fax: (913)541-0156
E-mail: nbrc-info@nbrc.org
URL: http://www.nbrc.org
Contact: Ms. Lauren Vorbeck, Admin. Coor.
Founded: 1960. **Members:** 16,000. **Membership Dues:** individual, $20 (annual). **Description:** Offers credentialing examinations for respiratory therapists, respiratory therapy technicians, pulmonary technologists, and perinatal/pediatric respiratory care specialists. **Affiliated With:** American Association for Respiratory Care; American College of Chest Physicians; American Society of Anesthesiologists; American Thoracic Society. **Formerly:** (1974) American Registry of Inhalation Therapists; (1982) National Board for Respiratory Therapy. **Publications:** *NBRC Horizons*, bimonthly. Newsletter. Alternate Formats: online. **Conventions/Meetings:** semiannual board meeting.

16278 ■ National Council for Therapeutic Recreation Certification (NCTRC)
7 Elmwood Dr.
New City, NY 10956
Ph: (845)639-1439
Fax: (845)639-1471

E-mail: nctrc@nctrc.org
URL: http://www.nctrc.org
Contact: James J. Shea, Treas.
Founded: 1981. **Members:** 17,170. **Membership Dues:** professional certification, $65 (annual). **Staff:** 15. **Budget:** $1,500,000. **Description:** Objectives are to: establish standards for certification and recertification of individuals who work in the therapeutic recreation field; grant recognition to individuals who voluntarily apply and meet established standards; monitor adherence to standards by certified personnel. **Boards:** Hearing Committee; Standards Review. **Affiliated With:** American Therapeutic Recreation Association; National Therapeutic Recreation Society. **Publications:** *National Council for Therapeutic Recreation Certification: Certification Standards*. Book ● *NCTRC Newsletter*, semiannual. Alternate Formats: magnetic tape.

16279 ■ National Therapeutic Recreation Society (NTRS)

22377 Belmont Ridge Rd.
Ashburn, VA 20148-4501
Ph: (703)858-0784
Free: (800)626-6772
Fax: (703)858-0794
E-mail: ntrsnrpa@nrpa.org
URL: http://www.nrpa.org/content/default.aspx?documentId=530
Contact: Dr. Terry Robertson, Pres.
Founded: 1966. **Members:** 2,000. **Membership Dues:** professional, $100 (annual). **Staff:** 2. **Description:** Serves as a branch of the National Recreation and Park Association. Professionals, educators, and students involved in the provision of therapeutic recreation services for persons with disabilities in clinical and residential facilities and in the community. Offers technical assistance services to agencies, institutions, and individuals. **Libraries:** Type: open to the public. **Holdings:** 10,000; archival material. **Subjects:** recreation, programming. **Awards:** NTRS Annual Awards Program. **Frequency:** annual. **Type:** recognition. **Computer Services:** Online services, technical, listserv, bookstore, registration for education, CELL's. **Councils:** State and Regional Advisory. **Affiliated With:** National Recreation and Park Association. **Formed by Merger of:** (1966) National Association of Recreation Therapists; Hospital Section of the American Recreation Society. **Publications:** *Parks and Recreation*, monthly. Magazine. **Price:** included in membership dues ● *Philosophy of Therapeutic Recreation: Ideas and Issues* ● *Preparing for a Career in Therapeutic Recreation* ● *Therapeutic Recreation Journal*, quarterly. **Price:** $28.00 for members in U.S.; $34.00 for members outside U.S.; $66.00 for nonmembers in U.S.; $72.00 for nonmembers outside U.S. ISSN: 0040-5914. **Circulation:** 2,800. Also Cited As: *TRJ*. **Conventions/Meetings:** annual conference and workshop (exhibits).

16280 ■ Option Institute International Learning and Training Center

2080 S Undermountain Rd.
Sheffield, MA 01257-9643
Ph: (413)229-2100 (413)229-8063
Free: (800)714-2779
Fax: (413)229-5030
E-mail: participantsupport@option.org
URL: http://www.option.org
Contact: Barry Neil Kaufman, Founder
Founded: 1983. **Staff:** 60. **Multinational. Description:** Provides individuals, couples, families, businesses and groups empowering personal growth programs and seminars using life changing, experiential learning techniques that can greatly improve relationships, career, health and quality of life. Process counseling sessions with Certified Option Process Mentors/Counselors are offered. **Computer Services:** Mailing lists ● online services, message board. **Programs:** Autism Treatment Center of America; Son-Rise. **Formerly:** (2004) Option Institute and Fellowship. **Publications:** *A Miracle to Believe In*. Book ● *A Sacred Dying*. Book ● *Giant Steps*. Book ● *Happiness Is a Choice*. Book ● *Out-Smarting Your Karma*. Book ● *Personal Growth Program Catalog*. **Price:** free ● *Power Dialogues*. Book ● *Son-*

Rise: The Miracle Continues. Book ● *To Love Is To Be Happy With*. Book. **Conventions/Meetings:** workshop.

16281 ■ Orthopaedic Section, American Physical Therapy Association

2920 East Ave. S, Ste.200
La Crosse, WI 54601
Ph: (608)788-3982
Free: (800)444-3982
Fax: (608)788-3965
E-mail: tdeflorian@orthopt.org
URL: http://www.orthopt.org
Contact: Terri DeFlorian, Exec. Dir.
Founded: 1974. **Members:** 15,500. **Membership Dues:** orthopaedic physical therapist, $50 (annual) ● physical therapist assistant, $30 (annual) ● student, $15 (annual). **Staff:** 5. **Budget:** $1,300,000. **Description:** Orthopaedic physical therapists and physical therapist assistants who belong to the American Physical Therapy Association; physical therapy educators and students. Supports the continued growth of the physical therapy profession through education and research; promotes development of a standard certification procedure for the field. Seeks to assure the quality of physical therapy curricula at both the undergraduate and postgraduate levels. Facilitates communication among orthopedic physical therapists and other health care professionals. Gathers and disseminates information on the care of musculoskeletal disorders. Provides access to a network of orthopaedic study groups. **Computer Services:** Online services, membership list. **Committees:** Awards; Practice; Public Relations; Research; Specialization. **Programs:** Education. **Special Interest Groups:** Animal Physical Therapy; Foot and Ankle; Occupational Health; Pain Management; Performing Arts. **Publications:** *Journal of Orthopaedic and Sports Physical Therapy*, monthly. **Price:** $253.00 /year for institutions in U.S.; $152.00 /year for individuals in U.S.; $85.00/year for students in U.S.; $209.00 /year for individuals outside U.S. **Circulation:** 17,000. **Advertising:** accepted. Alternate Formats: online ● *Orthopaedic Physical Therapy Practice*, quarterly. Magazine. **Advertising:** accepted.

16282 ■ Outpatient Intravenous Infusion Therapy Association (OPIVITA)

Address Unknown since 2007
Description: Strives to educate physicians and their team members in the provision of safe and effective outpatient parenteral infusion therapy (OPAT).

16283 ■ People-Animals-Love (PAL)

4900 Massachusetts Ave. NW, Ste.330
Washington, DC 20016
Ph: (202)966-2171
E-mail: palinfo@peopleanimalslove.com
URL: http://www.peopleanimalslove.com
Contact: Mr. Joe Cavarretta, Exec. Dir.
Founded: 1981. **Staff:** 4. **Budget:** $350,000. **Description:** Brings people and animals together, brightening the lives of the lonely, easing the pain of the sick, and enriching the world of at-risk children. Its volunteer corps is made up of caring adults, children, and eager animals committed to bringing people and animals together in meaningful, mutually life-affirming ways. This is accomplished through programs that fall into two broad areas: pet visiting and at-risk youth education. **Affiliated With:** Delta Society. **Publications:** *PAL Companion*, quarterly. Newsletter. **Conventions/Meetings:** monthly board meeting ● seminar, for volunteer training.

16284 ■ Private Practice Section/American Physical Therapy Association (PPS)

1055 N Fairfax St., Ste.100
Alexandria, VA 22314
Ph: (703)299-2410
Free: (800)517-1167
Fax: (703)299-2411

E-mail: privatepracticesection@apta.org
URL: http://www.ppsapta.org
Contact: Stephen E. Anderson, Pres.
Founded: 1956. **Members:** 3,750. **Membership Dues:** active, $175 (annual) ● affiliate, $105 (annual) ● student, $50 (annual) ● post professional student, $150 (annual) ● retired, $120 (annual) ● life, $60. **Staff:** 6. **Budget:** $1,500,000. **Description:** Physical therapists who are members of the American Physical Therapy Association (see separate entry) and who are in private practice. Purposes are: to provide physical therapists with information on establishing and managing a private practice; to promote high standards of private practice physical therapy; to represent private practitioners before governmental and professional agencies; to disseminate information relating to private practice. Monitors federal and state legislation. Holds forums and seminars. **Awards:** Friends of Private Practice Award. **Type:** recognition. **Recipient:** for a non-member who has promoted the goals of the section and enhanced benefits to section member ● Practice Award. **Type:** recognition. **Recipient:** for an individual member who has made outstanding and enduring contributions to the practice of physical therapy ● Robert G. Dicus Award. **Type:** recognition. **Recipient:** for a single member whose contributions to the section has been of exceptional value ● Section Achievement Award. **Type:** recognition. **Recipient:** for an individual who has performed exceptional service. **Computer Services:** Mailing lists, of members. **Committees:** Governmental Affairs. **Publications:** *The Acquisition or Sale of a Physical Therapy Practice*. Book. **Price:** $45.00 PPS member; $50.00 APTA member; $70.00 non-APTA member ● *An Employer's Guide to Obtaining Physical Therapy Services* ● *Hire for Fit*. Pamphlet. **Price:** $25.00 PPS member; $35.00 APTA member; $40.00 non-APTA member ● *How to Start a PT Private Practice* ● *IMPACT*, monthly. Magazine. Covers practice management, marketing, clinical developments, legislative and regulatory news, and research and professional issues. **Circulation:** 4,000 ● *Private Practice Physical Therapy: The How-To Manual*. Book. **Price:** $89.00 PPS member; $125.00 APTA member; $145.00 non-APTA member ● *Private Practice Section Membership Directory*. Arranged alphabetically and geographically. **Price:** included in membership dues. Alternate Formats: online ● *Private Practice Valuation Primer - How to Value a Practice for Sale or Purchase* ● *Private Practices: Strategies for Everyday Management*, monthly. Magazine. Covers practice management, marketing, clinical developments, legislative and regulatory news, and research and professional issues. **Price:** $45.00 PPS member; $65.00 APTA member; $90.00 non-APTA member. **Circulation:** 8,000 ● *Safeguarding Your Practice: The Corporate Compliance Manual*, annual. Membership Directory. Arranged alphabetically and geographically. Includes meeting schedule. **Price:** $125.00 PPS member; $175.00 non-PPS member. **Circulation:** 5,000. **Advertising:** accepted ● *Twenty Questions About Private Practice*. Pamphlet ● *Understanding Computers in Healthcare: A Guidebook for Rehabilitation Professionals*. **Price:** $25.00 PPS member; $35.00 APTA member; $40.00 non-APTA member ● *The Valuation of a Physical Therapy Practice*. Book. **Price:** $55.00 PPS member; $77.00 APTA member; $88.00 non-APTA member. **Conventions/Meetings:** annual conference (exhibits) - usually October/November. 2007 Nov. 6-10, San Diego, CA.

16285 ■ Project Magic (PM)

c/o Stormont-Vail West
3707 SW 6th Ave.
Topeka, KS 66606
Ph: (785)270-4610
Free: (888)221-8199
Fax: (785)232-8545
URL: http://www.dcopperfield.com
Contact: David Copperfield, Contact
Founded: 1982. **Staff:** 1. **Description:** Provides information and facilitates communication between magicians, occupational therapists, and patients with physical, psychosocial, and developmental disabilities. Created by television magician David Cop-

perfield, the project works to rehabilitate patients by teaching them magic tricks instead of, or in addition to, traditional therapy techniques. Seeks to motivate patients to develop new skills and improve their self-image by demonstrating magical tricks. Tricks such as sleight-of-hand teach physical dexterity and mental puzzles help people to improve memory, concentration, and the ability to think sequentially. Provides interested magicians and occupational therapists with information and written material on the therapeutic value of magic for disabled persons. Sponsors educational seminars and workshops for rehabilitation facilities and health professionals. **Libraries: Type:** open to the public. **Publications:** *David Copperfield's Project Magic Booklet*, periodic.

16286 ■ Sandplay Therapists of America (STA)
PO Box 4847
Walnut Creek, CA 94596
Ph: (925)825-9277
Fax: (925)687-9985
E-mail: sta@sandplay.org
URL: http://www.sandplay.org
Contact: Daniel Nelson PhD, Chm.
Membership Dues: general, $75 (annual). **Description:** Advances the profession and practice of sandplay therapy. Promotes education, training, and research in sandplay therapy. **Computer Services:** Mailing lists. **Publications:** *Journal of Sandplay Therapy*, semiannual. **Price:** $46.00 for nonmembers; free for members.

16287 ■ Society for Light Treatment and Biological Rhythms (SLTBR)
4648 Main St.
Chincoteague Island, VA 23336
Fax: (757)336-5777
E-mail: sltbrinfo@aol.com
URL: http://www.sltbr.org
Contact: Kathleen Matikonis, Exec. Dir.
Founded: 1988. **Members:** 400. **Membership Dues:** regular, associate, $85 (annual) ● student, $15 (annual) ● corporate, $600 (annual). **Staff:** 1. **Budget:** $75,000. **Multinational. Description:** Fosters research, professional development, and clinical applications in the fields of light therapy and biological rhythms. **Awards:** Young Investigator Award. **Frequency:** annual. **Type:** recognition. **Recipient:** for research done in clinical aspect of biological rhythms. **Publications:** *Chronobiology International*. Journal ● *Journal of Biological Rhythms*. **Conventions/Meetings:** annual meeting (exhibits).

16288 ■ Soul Friends
401 Center St.
Wallingford, CT 06492
Ph: (203)679-0849
Fax: (203)670-0348
E-mail: info@soul-friends.org
URL: http://www.soul-friends.org
Contact: Kate Nicoll MSW, Pres./Dir. of Clinical Services
Description: Promotes the benefits of the human-animal bond for children through clinical and educational programs. Studies the human-animal bond, and its impact on the physical and emotional health of children, adolescents and adults. Offers holistic animal assisted therapy programs. Addresses the emotional, therapeutic and educational needs of children and adolescents. Promotes the benefits of incorporating a therapeutic animal as part of a treatment plan or educational program under the close supervision of a licensed professional. **Telecommunication Services:** electronic mail, kate@soul-friends.org ● electronic mail, customersupport@soul-friends.org.

16289 ■ Therapy Dogs International (TDI)
88 Bartley Rd.
Flanders, NJ 07836
Ph: (973)252-9800
Fax: (973)252-7171

E-mail: tdi@gti.net
URL: http://www.tdi-dog.org
Contact: Ursula A. Kempe, Pres./CEO
Founded: 1976. **Members:** 10,000. **Membership Dues:** initial, $35 ● regular, $30 (annual). **Regional Groups:** 32. **Description:** Works for the regulation, testing, selection, and registration of qualified dogs and handlers for the purpose of visitations to hospitals, nursing homes, and other institutions where therapy dogs are needed. **Libraries: Type:** not open to the public. **Holdings:** articles, books, periodicals. **Awards:** ID Active Volunteer. **Frequency:** periodic. **Type:** recognition. **Recipient:** for outstanding volunteer, if member achieved 50 visits. **Publications:** Newsletter, 3/year. **Price:** included in membership dues ● Brochures. Alternate Formats: online.

Thermal Analysis

16290 ■ Society for Thermal Medicine (STM)
10105 Cottesmore Ct.
Great Falls, VA 22066-3540
Ph: (703)757-0044
Fax: (703)757-0454
E-mail: info@thermalmedicine.org
URL: http://www.thermaltherapy.org
Contact: Ellen L. Jones PhD, Pres.
Founded: 1986. **Members:** 200. **Membership Dues:** active, associate, $200 (annual) ● student, $25 (annual). **Multinational. Description:** Promotes researchers in the field of thermal therapy; seeks to advance communication between theoreticians, experimentalists, and clinical practitioners; aims to increase understanding and use of hyperthermia; disseminates research findings. **Formerly:** (2005) North American Hyperthermia Society. **Publications:** *International Journal of Hyperthermia*, 8/year. Features research and clinical studies and trials on hyperthermia. **Price:** included in membership dues; $1,923.00 /year for nonmembers.

Thoracic Medicine

16291 ■ American Association for Thoracic Surgery (AATS)
900 Cummings Ctr., Ste.221U
Beverly, MA 01915-6183
Ph: (978)927-8330
Fax: (978)524-8890
E-mail: aats@prri.com
URL: http://www.aats.org
Contact: Tirone E. David MD, Pres.
Founded: 1917. **Members:** 1,200. **Staff:** 12. **Description:** Represents specialists in surgery of the chest region, including cardiovascular surgeons. Encourages investigation and study of intrathoracic physiology, pathology, and therapy. **Awards:** Evarts A. Graham Memorial Traveling Fellowship. **Frequency:** annual. **Type:** fellowship. **Recipient:** for an outstanding non-North American in the final year of residency ● **Type:** scholarship. **Computer Services:** database ● mailing lists, available to CME accredited programs only- $250. **Committees:** Education; Ethics; Historian; Local Arrangements; Nominating; Program; Scientific and Government Relations; Seminars in Thoracic and Cardiovascular Surgery. **Publications:** *Journal of Thoracic and Cardiovascular Surgery*, monthly. **Price:** included in membership dues ● *Operative Techniques in Thoracic and Cardiovascular Surgery*, quarterly. Journal ● *Seminars in Thoracic and Cardiovascular Surgery*, quarterly. Journal ● Membership Directory, annual. **Conventions/Meetings:** annual meeting (exhibits) - always April or May.

16292 ■ American Board of Thoracic Surgery (ABTS)
633 N St. Clair St., Ste.2320
Chicago, IL 60611
Ph: (312)202-5900
Fax: (312)202-5960

E-mail: info@abts.org
URL: http://www.abts.org
Contact: William A. Gay Jr., Exec. Dir.
Founded: 1948. **Description:** Serves as medical certification board that certifies surgeons specializing in thoracic surgery. **Formerly:** Board of Thoracic Surgery.

16293 ■ American Thoracic Society (ATS)
61 Broadway
New York, NY 10006
Ph: (212)315-8600
Fax: (212)315-6498
E-mail: atsinfo@thoracic.org
URL: http://www.thoracic.org
Contact: Carl Booberg, Exec. Dir.
Founded: 1905. **Members:** 13,300. **Membership Dues:** full (doctoral), $350 (annual) ● full (non-doctoral), $250 (annual) ● in training, $75 (annual) ● in-transition, $200 (annual) ● senior, $100 (annual) ● affiliate, $130 (annual). **Staff:** 53. **Budget:** $18,500,000. **State Groups:** 43. **Multinational. Description:** International Educational and scientific Society for respiratory and critical care medicine. Seeks to prevent and fight respiratory diseases through research, education and patient advocacy. **Committees:** Allergy, Immunology, Inflammation; Behavioral Science; Clinical Problems; Critical Care; Environmental and Occupational Health; Microbiology, Tuberculosis and Pulmonary Infections; Nursing; Pediatrics; Pulmonary Circulation; Respiratory Cell and Molecular Biology; Respiratory Neurobiology and Sleep; Respiratory Structure and Function. **Affiliated With:** American Lung Association. **Formerly:** (1939) American Sanatorium Association; (1960) American Trudeau Society. **Publications:** *American Journal of Respiratory and Critical Care Medicine*, semimonthly. Includes society news, book reviews, and case reports. **Price:** included in membership dues. ISSN: 0003-0805. **Advertising:** accepted ● *American Journal of Respiratory Cell and Molecular Biology*, monthly. **Price:** included in membership dues. ISSN: 1044-1549. **Circulation:** 10,000 ● *ATS News*, monthly. Newsletter. Includes summary of health legislation and annual index. **Price:** included in membership dues. **Circulation:** 13,300 ● Membership Directory, biennial. **Conventions/Meetings:** annual conference, held in conjunction with ALA (exhibits).

16294 ■ Society of Thoracic Surgeons (STS)
633 N St. Clair St., No. 2320
Chicago, IL 60611
Ph: (312)202-5800
Fax: (312)202-5801
E-mail: sts@sts.org
URL: http://www.sts.org
Contact: Robert A. Wynbrandt, Exec. Dir.
Founded: 1964. **Members:** 5,000. **Membership Dues:** active, individual, $750 (annual). **Staff:** 10. **Budget:** $1,500,000. **Description:** Surgeons who confine their practice to the field of thoracic-cardiovascular surgery. Objectives are: to improve the quality and practice of thoracic and cardiovascular surgery as a specialty; to strengthen and establish basic standards in training programs; to encourage clinical and basic research; to promote the professional development of those surgeons specializing in the field; to represent and sponsor those surgeons who have recently entered the field. Conducts annual postgraduate program and three-day scientific session. **Publications:** *Annals of Thoracic Surgery*, monthly ● *STS News*, quarterly. Newsletter ● *Thoracic & Cardiac surgery SourceBook*. **Price:** $569.00/ year. **Conventions/Meetings:** annual meeting (exhibits).

Thyroid

16295 ■ American Thyroid Association (ATA)
6066 Leesburg Pike, Ste.550
Falls Church, VA 22041
Ph: (703)998-8890
Free: (800)THYROID

Fax: (703)998-8893
E-mail: thyroid@thyroid.org
URL: http://www.thyroid.org
Contact: Barbara R. Smith, Exec. Dir.
Founded: 1923. **Members:** 650. **Membership Dues:** active (with subscription), $260 (annual) ● corresponding international (with subscription), $240 (annual) ● senior (with subscription), $190 (annual) ● associate, $50 (annual). **Staff:** 4. **Description:** Represents endocrinologists, surgeons, pathologists, radiologists, and research scientists interested in the thyroid gland and its disorders. **Awards:** Distinguished Service Award. **Frequency:** annual. **Type:** recognition. **Recipient:** for members with remarkable contributions to the association ● Paul Starr Clinical Day Lectureship Prize. **Frequency:** annual. **Type:** recognition ● Sidney H. Ingbar Prize Lectureship Award. **Frequency:** annual. **Type:** recognition ● Van Meter Award. **Frequency:** annual. **Type:** recognition. **Recipient:** for excellence in thyroidology research. **Committees:** Awards; Bylaws; Clinical Affairs; Development; Education; History and Archives; Nominating; Research. **Formerly:** (1948) American Association for the Study of Goiter; (1961) American Goiter Association. **Publications:** *Clinical Thyroidology*, 3/year. **Price:** free. Alternate Formats: online ● *Signal*, 3/year. Newsletter. Contains news and other thyroid-related issues. **Price:** included in membership dues. Alternate Formats: online ● *Thyroid*, monthly. Journal. **Price:** included in membership dues ● Membership Directory, annual. **Conventions/Meetings:** annual workshop (exhibits) ● annual meeting (exhibits) - 2007 Oct. 4-7, New York, NY; 2008 Oct. 2-5, Chicago, IL; 2009 Sept. 24-27, Palm Beach, FL.

16296 ■ National Graves' Disease Foundation (NGDF)
PO Box 1969
Brevard, NC 28712
Ph: (828)877-5251
Free: (877)NGDF123
E-mail: admin@ngdf.org
URL: http://www.ngdf.org
Contact: Nancy H. Patterson PhD, Exec. Dir./ Founder
Founded: 1990. **Members:** 900. **Membership Dues:** individual, $30 (annual) ● physician, professional, $125 (annual) ● benefactor, $100 (annual). **Staff:** 1. **Budget:** $60,000. **State Groups:** 19. **Local Groups:** 25. **Languages:** English, Spanish. **Description:** People with Graves' disease; families of those affected; physicians and other professionals. Facilitates establishments of support groups for members in all states. Fosters public awareness and education on the causes, effects, and treatment of Graves' disease, a result of hyperthyroidism (the excess production by the body of thyroxine and triiodothyronine) in which the thyroid gland may be slightly enlarged, and symptoms such as a rapid heartbeat, eye problems, weight loss, or fatigue may occur. Participates in research on Graves' disease. **Libraries: Type:** open to the public. **Holdings:** 53. **Subjects:** Graves' disease. **Computer Services:** database ● information services, Graves' disease resources ● mailing lists, for research only ● online services, bulletin board. **Telecommunication Services:** electronic mail, nancy@ngdf.org. **Boards:** Medical Advisory. **Also Known As:** Graves' Disease Foundation. **Publications:** Bulletin, periodic. Features information regarding specific Graves' Disease topics. ● Newsletter, quarterly. **Conventions/Meetings:** annual A Bridge to Wellness - conference, for patients, family and caregivers (exhibits).

16297 ■ Thyroid Cancer Survivors' Association (ThyCa)
PO Box 1545
New York, NY 10159-1545
Free: (877)588-7904
Fax: (630)604-6078
E-mail: thyca@thyca.org
URL: http://www.thyca.org
Contact: Gary Bloom, Chm.
Founded: 1995. **Membership Dues:** general, $25 (annual) ● life, $225. **Description:** Provides a network of communication for thyroid cancer survi-

vors, family members and health care professionals. Increases awareness of thyroid cancer diseases. Supports research to prevent thyroid cancer. **Computer Services:** Information services, thyroid cancer resources. **Publications:** *Membership Messenger*. Newsletter. **Price:** free for members ● *ThyCa Journeys*. Newsletter. **Price:** free for members. Alternate Formats: online. **Conventions/Meetings:** annual conference, with workshops.

16298 ■ Thyroid Foundation of America (TFA)
One Longfellow Pl., Ste.1518
Boston, MA 02114
Ph: (617)534-1500
Free: (800)832-8321
Fax: (617)534-1515
E-mail: info@allthyroid.org
URL: http://www.allthyroid.org
Contact: Dr. Lawrence C. Wood, Pres.
Founded: 1985. **Members:** 4,500. **Membership Dues:** regular, $45 (annual) ● senior citizen, $25 (annual). **Staff:** 5. **Regional Groups:** 1. **State Groups:** 2. **Local Groups:** 1. **Description:** Individuals with thyroid conditions; health professionals. Provides education and support for thyroid patients and health professionals; promotes public awareness of thyroid problems. Conducts educational programs. Operates referral service. **Libraries: Type:** open to the public. **Holdings:** 100; articles, books, periodicals. **Subjects:** thyroid disease. **Affiliated With:** American Thyroid Association; Community Health Charities. **Publications:** *The Bridge*, quarterly. Newsletter. Reports on current research, articles of interest to individuals with thyroid disorders. **Price:** included in membership dues. **Circulation:** 4,000 ● Brochures. **Conventions/Meetings:** annual Pat Bradley Pro-AM Golf Classic - competition, fundraising, golf tournament.

16299 ■ Thyroid Society for Education and Research
Address Unknown since 2007
Staff: 3. **Description:** Promotes public awareness about thyroid disease. Provides patient education materials. **Publications:** *Could It Be My Thyroid?*. Book. Contains reference information for thyroid patients. **Price:** $22.00.

Tissue

16300 ■ Ehlers Danlos National Foundation (EDNF)
3200 Wilshire Blvd., Ste.1601
South Tower
Los Angeles, CA 90010
Ph: (213)368-3800
Fax: (213)427-0057
E-mail: staff@ednf.org
URL: http://www.ednf.org
Contact: Cindy Lauren, Pres./CEO
Founded: 1985. **Members:** 2,000. **Membership Dues:** access, $15 (annual) ● standard, $25 (annual) ● supporting, $50 (annual) ● international, $40 (annual). **Staff:** 3. **Budget:** $160,000. **Local Groups:** 25. **Description:** Individuals who are affected with Ehlers Danlos Syndrome (EDS); medical professionals involved in the treatment of EDS. (Ehlers Danlos Syndrome, which is named after dermatologists Edward L. Ehlers (1863-1937) and Henri A. Danlos (1844-1912), is an inheritable connective tissue disorder characterized by fragile skin, hypermobile joints, and poor wound healing.) Provides networking among members for communication and support. Local branches and support groups throughout the U.S. provide support, educational materials and public awareness to people affected by EDS, their families and health care professionals. **Computer Services:** database ● online services, free email services, message boards, chat and online contact databases. **Boards:** Medical Advisory. **Publications:** *Emergency Room Physician's Guide to EDS Vascular Type*. Newsletter. Alternate Formats: CD-ROM; online ● *The Facts about Ehlers Danlos Syndrome*. Brochures.

Includes the types of Ehlers Danlos Syndrome and genetic inheritance pattern to Ehlers Danlos Syndrome. ● *Loose Connections*, quarterly. Newsletter. Includes medical updates on EDS, personal interest stories, local branch information. **Price:** included in membership dues. **Circulation:** 2,000. **Advertising:** accepted. Alternate Formats: online ● *The Types of Ehlers Danlos Syndrome*. Pamphlets. **Conventions/Meetings:** annual convention and workshop (exhibits) - usually July.

16301 ■ National Marfan Foundation (NMF)
22 Manhasset Ave.
Port Washington, NY 11050-2023
Ph: (516)883-8712
Free: (800)862-7326
Fax: (516)883-8040
E-mail: staff@marfan.org
URL: http://www.marfan.org
Contact: Carolyn Levering, Pres./CEO
Founded: 1981. **Members:** 25,000. **Membership Dues:** basic, $35 (annual). **Staff:** 15. **Budget:** $1,400,000. **State Groups:** 15. **Local Groups:** 60. **Description:** Serves persons affected with the Marfan syndrome and related connective tissue disorders; families of affected persons; genetic counselors; cardiologists, ophthalmologists, orthopedists, and other medical professionals. (Marfan syndrome is a heritable disorder of the connective tissue affecting the skeleton, lungs, eyes, heart, and blood vessels.) Objectives are to: disseminate accurate and timely information on Marfan syndrome; act as support network and provide a means for patients and relatives to share experiences; improve medical care. Supports and fosters research. **Libraries: Type:** reference. **Holdings:** articles, books, periodicals, video recordings. **Subjects:** Marfan Syndrome and related connective tissue disorders including all body systems affected by MFS. **Awards:** NMF Research Grant. **Frequency:** annual. **Type:** grant. **Recipient:** for basic and clinical research on Marfan Syndrome and related connective tissue disorders. **Affiliated With:** America's Charities; Genetic Alliance; National Health Council; National Organization for Rare Disorders. **Publications:** *Connective Issues*, quarterly. Newsletter. Includes research reports, chapter news, and legislative reports. **Price:** included in membership dues. ISSN: 8756-9086. **Circulation:** 25,000 ● *How Do Your Genes Fit? Marfan Syndrome: The Heart of the Matter*. Video. Explains about genetic disorders, especially, Marfan Syndrome. Contains information for middle school students, families and support groups. ● *The Marfan Syndrome*. Booklet ● *The Marfan Syndrome: A Booklet for Teachers* ● *Marfan Syndrome: Emergency Diagnosis and Treatment of Aortic Dissection*. Booklet ● Brochures. Features overview of related disorders and physical activity guidelines. **Conventions/Meetings:** annual conference, with symposia (exhibits) - always summer.

Tobacco

16302 ■ Association for the Treatment of Tobacco Use and Dependence (ATTUD)
c/o Ken Wassum, Pres.
Free & Clear, Inc.
999 3rd Ave., Ste.2100
Seattle, WA 98104
Ph: (206)876-2198
E-mail: ken.wassum@freeclear.com
URL: http://www.attud.org
Contact: Ken Wassum, Pres.
Membership Dues: full, $75 (annual) ● student, $35 (annual). **Description:** Promotes the implementation and increased access to evidence-based tobacco treatment. Seeks to establish standards for core competencies, training, and credentialing of tobacco treatment providers. Acts as an advocate for tobacco users to promote awareness and availability of effective tobacco treatments. Serves as a reliable resource of tobacco use and dependence treatment for the health care community, regulatory agencies, private

foundations, and tobacco users. **Publications:** *AT-TUD Newsletter.* Alternate Formats: online.

Touch-Healing

16303 ■ International Foundation of Bio-Magnetics (IFBM)
5634 E Pima St.
Tucson, AZ 85712
Ph: (520)323-7951
Free: (888)GREET-12
Fax: (520)760-1536
E-mail: arizona@justtouch.com
URL: http://www.justtouch.com
Membership Dues: supporting, $10 (annual). **Multinational. Description:** Promotes bio-magnetic touch healing. **Computer Services:** Online services. **Programs:** Bio-House; Certified Practitioner; Instructor; Practitioner Training. **Publications:** *Awakening Athena.* Book. **Price:** $25.00/copy ● *Just Touch News,* quarterly. Newsletter. **Price:** included in membership dues ● *Quick Reference Pocket Manual.* **Price:** $2.00/copy.

Toxic Exposure

16304 ■ Asbestos Disease Awareness Organization (ADAO)
1525 Aviation Blvd., Ste.318
Redondo Beach, CA 90278
E-mail: info@asbestosdiseaseawareness.org
URL: http://www.asbestosdiseaseawareness.org
Contact: Linda Reinstein, Exec. Dir./Co-Founder
Multinational. Description: Seeks to give asbestos victims and concerned citizens a united voice to help ensure that their rights are fairly represented and protected. Raises public awareness of the dangers of asbestos exposure and often deadly asbestos-related diseases. **Computer Services:** Information services, asbestos disease facts and resources ● online services, bulletin board. **Telecommunication Services:** electronic mail, linda@asbestosdiseaseawareness.org. **Publications:** Newsletter. Alternate Formats: online.

16305 ■ Chemical Injury Information Network (CIIN)
PO Box 301
White Sulphur Springs, MT 59645
Ph: (406)547-2255
Fax: (406)547-2455
E-mail: chemicalinjury@ciin.org
URL: http://ciin.org
Contact: Cynthia Wilson, Exec. Dir.
Founded: 1990. **Members:** 5,000. **Membership Dues:** fixed income, $15 (annual) ● employed individual, $30 (annual) ● professional, $50 (annual). **Multinational. Description:** Fosters education and supports research on multiple chemical sensitivities (MCS). Raises funds to support research on MCS. Serves as a clearinghouse of information on the adverse health effects of chemical exposures. Creates awareness on multiple chemical sensitivities as a global health problem and the need to address health related issues that are associated with the disease. **Publications:** *Our Toxic Times,* monthly. Magazine. **Price:** included in membership dues. **Advertising:** accepted.

Toxicology

16306 ■ America Board of Clinical Metal Toxicology (ABCMT)
c/o James E. Smith, DO
4889 Smith Rd.
West Chester, OH 45069
Ph: (513)863-6277
Free: (800)356-2228
Fax: (513)942-3934

E-mail: treasurer@abcmt.org
URL: http://www.abcmt.com
Contact: Jack Hank, Exec. Dir.
Founded: 1982. **Members:** 220. **Staff:** 1. **Description:** Works to define and establish qualifications required of licensed physicians and surgeons for certification in the field of chelation therapy. Stresses that proper use of chelation therapy requires knowledge of nutrition and exercise and expertise in assisting patients in implementing lifestyle changes. Refers candidate physicians to sponsor in organizations for teaching workshops, audio and video learning aids, and reading and study materials. Has created series of testing procedures designed to be comprehensive and unbiased. Administers oral and written examinations and conducts reviews of candidates' background experience and patient records. Maintains standards through process of recertification and reexamination. **Committees:** Credentials; Examination; Review. **Affiliated With:** American College for Advancement in Medicine; American Holistic Medical Association. **Formerly:** (2005) American Board of Chelation Therapy. **Publications:** Newsletter. Contains relevant information from the media. **Conventions/Meetings:** semiannual meeting ● meeting, held in conjunction with ICIM.

16307 ■ American Academy of Clinical Toxicology (AACT)
777 E Park Dr.
PO Box 8820
Harrisburg, PA 17105-8820
Ph: (717)558-7847
Free: (888)633-5784
Fax: (717)558-7841
E-mail: swilson@pamedsoc.org
URL: http://www.clintox.org
Contact: Susie Wilson, Exec. Dir.
Founded: 1968. **Members:** 600. **Membership Dues:** full, $165 (annual) ● student, $100 (annual). **Staff:** 2. **Budget:** $150,000. **Description:** Physicians, veterinarians, pharmacists, nurses research scientists, and analytical chemists. Objectives are to: unite medical scientists and facilitate the exchange of information; encourage the development of therapeutic methods and technology; Conducts professional training in poison information and emergency service personnel. **Awards:** AACT/Texaco Fellowship. **Frequency:** annual. **Type:** recognition. **Recipient:** for financial support of training in clinical toxicology ● AACT/Texaco Research Award. **Frequency:** annual. **Type:** recognition. **Recipient:** for financial support of a research project ● Clinton H. Thienes Memorial Lecture Award. **Frequency:** biennial. **Type:** recognition ● Donald Kunke-Kenneth Lampe Award. **Frequency:** biennial. **Type:** recognition. **Computer Services:** Mailing lists, of members. **Telecommunication Services:** electronic mail, aact@pamedsoc.org. **Committees:** Bylaws; Communications and Technology; Education; Fellowship; Long Range Planning; Multicenter Research; Pediatric Toxicology; Research Awards. **Publications:** *AACTion.* Newsletter. **Price:** included in membership dues ● *Journal of Toxicology-Clinical Toxicology,* 7/year. Contains current research and review articles relevant to the clinical toxicologist. **Price:** included in membership dues. ISSN: 0731-3810. **Advertising:** accepted ● Current Awareness-Publication of Contemporary References in clinical toxicology and AACTion-organization newsletter. **Conventions/Meetings:** annual North American Congress of Clinical Toxicology - meeting (exhibits).

16308 ■ American Association of Poison Control Centers (AAPCC)
3201 New Mexico Ave., Ste.330
Washington, DC 20016
Ph: (202)362-7217
Fax: (202)362-3240
E-mail: info@aapcc.org
URL: http://www.aapcc.org
Contact: Stuart E. Heard, Pres.-Elect
Founded: 1958. **Members:** 1,400. **Membership Dues:** individual, $200 (annual) ● sustaining, $7,500 (annual) ● company (for profit), $2,000 (annual) ● animal poison center, $1,000 (annual) ● associate,

poison prevention education center, $500 (annual) ● U.S. Poison Center, $2,500 (annual). **Staff:** 8. **Regional Groups:** 70. **Description:** Individuals and organizations engaged in operation of poison control centers and/or interested in poison prevention. Has established standards for poison information, control centers and specialists in poison information. Compiles statistics about poison exposures in the United States. Coordinates nationwide toll-free poison emergency hotline. **Awards:** AAPCC Recognition Award. **Frequency:** annual. **Type:** recognition. **Recipient:** for significant contributions to AAPCC's work ● **Frequency:** annual. **Type:** fellowship. **Computer Services:** database, national poisoning. **Telecommunication Services:** hotline, (800)222-1222. **Committees:** Data Collection; Epidemiology/Data Collection; Managers; Poison Control Center Personnel Proficiency; Public Education; Regional Center Certification; Research Fellowship; Scientific Review. **Publications:** *Annual Report of the American Association of Poison Control Centers Toxic Exposure Surveillance System,* annual. Features articles in the American Journal of Emergency Medicine. **Price:** included in membership dues ● *The Poison Line,* bimonthly. Newsletter. **Price:** included in membership dues. **Conventions/Meetings:** annual North American Congress of Clinical Toxicology, research about epidemiology and treatment of poison exposures (exhibits) - always September or October.

16309 ■ American College of Medical Toxicology (ACMT)
1901 N Roeselle Rd., Ste.920
Schaumburg, IL 60195
Ph: (847)885-0674
Fax: (847)885-8393
E-mail: info@acmt.net
URL: http://www.acmt.net
Contact: Keith K. Burkhart MD, Pres.
Founded: 1993. **Members:** 400. **Staff:** 4. **Description:** Seeks to advance the science, study and practice of medical toxicology by fostering the development of medical toxicology in its provision of emergency, consultation, forensic, legal, community and industrial services; and by otherwise striving to advance and elevate the science, study and practice of medical toxicology. **Libraries:** Type: open to the public. **Holdings:** 3; books. **Subjects:** medical toxicology. **Awards:** ACMT Research Award. **Frequency:** annual. **Type:** monetary. **Computer Services:** database, membership. **Committees:** Award; Bylaws; Education; Fellowship; Grants and External Contracts; Liaison; Nominating; Research. **Formerly:** American Board of Medical Toxicology. **Publications:** *ACMT Newsletter,* quarterly. Alternate Formats: online ● *Internet Journal of Medical Toxicology,* quarterly. ISSN: 1523-5130. **Advertising:** accepted. Alternate Formats: online. **Conventions/Meetings:** annual North American Congress of Clinical Toxicology - conference, in conjunction with AACT.

16310 ■ Behavioral Toxicology Society (BTS)
Wayne State Univ.
71 W Warren Ave.
Detroit, MI 48201
Ph: (313)577-9546
E-mail: scott.bowen@wayne.edu
URL: http://www.behavioraltoxicology.org
Contact: Scott E. Bowen PhD, Treas.
Founded: 1982. **Membership Dues:** regular, $77 (annual) ● student, post-doc, $10 (annual) ● student, post-doc (journal subscription included), $67 (annual). **Description:** Promotes scientific research into the effects of toxic agents on behavior and the nervous system; provides a forum for presentation and discussion of research. Stimulates new growth and interest in behavioral toxicology in scientists engaged in the broader areas of behavioral sciences, neuroscience, toxicology, pharmacology, and risk assessment. **Publications:** *Neurotoxicology and Teratology.* Journal. A joint publication of BTS and the Neurobehavioral Teratology Society. **Conventions/Meetings:** annual meeting.

16311 ■ National Eosinophilia-Myalgia Syndrome Network (NEMSN)
c/o Jann Heston, Pres.
155 Delaware Ave.
Lexington, OH 44904-1212

E-mail: nemsn2005@aol.com
URL: http://www.nemsn.org
Contact: Jann Heston, Pres.
Description: Provides emotional and peer support to Eosinophilia-Myalgia Syndrome (EMS) survivors and their families. Encourages research to improve treatment for L-tryptophan induced EMS. Increases awareness of the cause and effects of the disease and other similar auto-immune disorders. **Publications:** *National EMS Network Newsletter*, quarterly. Alternate Formats: online.

Transplantation

16312 ■ American Association of Tissue Banks (AATB)
1320 Old Chain Bridge Rd., Ste.450
McLean, VA 22101
Ph: (703)827-9582
Fax: (703)356-2198
E-mail: aatb@aatb.org
URL: http://www.aatb.org
Contact: James Forsell PhD, Pres.
Founded: 1976. **Members:** 1,200. **Membership Dues:** individual, $185 (annual). **Staff:** 7. **Description:** Aims to encourage the development of regional tissue banks and the establishment of guidelines and standards for the retrieval, preservation, storage, and distribution of tissues for transplantation. **Committees:** Accreditation; Bylaws; Ethics; Medical Advisory. **Councils:** Musculoskeletal; Reproductive; Skin; Tissue Bank. **Publications:** *AATB Newsletter*, quarterly. **Price:** available to members only ● *American Association of Tissue Banks—Technical Manual*, periodic ● *Standards for Tissue Banking*, periodic. **Conventions/Meetings:** annual meeting (exhibits) - every spring ● annual meeting - 2007 Sept. 15-18, Boston, MA ● periodic workshop - 2007 Nov. 15-17, Lake Buena Vista, FL.

16313 ■ American Organ Transplant Association (AOTA)
21175 Tomball Pkwy. No. 194
Houston, TX 77070
Ph: (713)344-2402
Fax: (713)344-9420
URL: http://aota.schipul.net
Contact: Pamela H. Terry, Pres.
Founded: 1986. **Description:** Helps patients obtain and sustain transplantation. Provides fundraising assistance for patients needing a life-saving transplant and aftercare. Provides patients free transportation to and from the transplant center for evaluation, surgery and aftercare. Promotes organ, marrow and tissue donation. **Publications:** Newsletter. Alternate Formats: online.

16314 ■ American Society for Blood and Marrow Transplantation (ASBMT)
85 W Algonquin Rd., Ste.550
Arlington Heights, IL 60005
Ph: (847)427-0224 (201)336-8664
Fax: (847)427-9656
E-mail: mail@asbmt.org
URL: http://www.asbmt.org
Contact: Robert Soiffer MD, Pres.
Founded: 1993. **Members:** 1,400. **Membership Dues:** regular, associate, $175 (annual) ● affiliate, $125 (annual) ● in-training, $75 (annual). **Staff:** 3. **Budget:** $2,000,000. **Description:** Individuals, organizations, and corporations with an interest in stem cell therapy and blood and marrow transplantation. Seeks to advance blood and marrow transplantation techniques; and promotes professional advancement of physicians and support personnel engaged in blood and marrow transplantation. Facilitates exchange of information among members; serves as a clearinghouse on blood and marrow transplantation; and sponsors educational programs. **Telecommunication Services:** electronic mail, rsoiffer@partners.org. **Publications:** *ASBMT eNEWS*, monthly. Newsletter. Alternate Formats: online ● *Biology Blood and Marrow Transplantation*, monthly. Journal. Contains original research reports,

reviews, editorials and commentaries. **Price:** $260.00 /year for individuals; $375.00 /year for institutions; $130.00 for student; $36.00/issue. **Advertising:** accepted. Alternate Formats: online ● *Blood and Marrow Transplantation Reviews*, quarterly. Bulletin. Alternate Formats: online ● Audiotapes. **Price:** $13.00. Alternate Formats: CD-ROM. **Conventions/Meetings:** annual BMT Tandem Meetings, joint meeting with the International Bone Marrow Transplant Registry (exhibits).

16315 ■ American Society of Multicultural Health and Transplant Professionals (ASMHTP)
700 N 4th St.
Richmond, VA 23219
Free: (866)276-4871
Fax: (804)782-4816
E-mail: info@asmhtp.org
URL: http://www.asmhtp.org
Contact: Tina Evans Caines, Pres.
Founded: 1992. **Membership Dues:** active, individual, $125 (annual) ● corporate associate, $200 (annual) ● friend, $60 (annual) ● corporate sponsor, $1,000 (annual). **Description:** Promotes organ and tissue donation and transplantation among minorities. **Formerly:** (2003) American Society of Minority Health and Transplant Professionals.

16316 ■ American Society of Transplant Surgeons (ASTS)
2461 S Clark St., Ste.640
Arlington, VA 22202
Ph: (703)414-7870
Fax: (703)414-7874
E-mail: matas001@tc.umn.edu
URL: http://www.asts.org
Contact: Arthur J. Matas MD, Pres.
Founded: 1975. **Members:** 1,000. **Staff:** 3. **Description:** Surgeons specializing in transplantation. Promotes and encourages education and research, especially in transplantation surgery; collaborates with public and private organizations; participates and assists in developing programs and coordinates efforts on projects that will benefit organ recipients. **Awards:** Type: recognition ● Type: scholarship. **Committees:** Advisory Committee on Issues; Bylaws; Education; Heart Transplantation; Issues and Ethics Advisory; Local Arrangements; Medical Data Review; Nominations; Organ Procurement Standards; Postgraduate Course and Government Relations; Scientific Studies; Thoracic Organ Transplantation. **Programs:** Certification of Postdoctoral Fellowship Training; Sandoz Fellowship. **Publications:** *American Journal of Transplantation*, monthly. **Price:** included in membership dues ● *Chimera*, quarterly. Newsletter. **Conventions/Meetings:** annual Scientific Meeting (exhibits) - always May/June.

16317 ■ American Society of Transplantation (AST)
15000 Commerce Pkwy., Ste.C
Mount Laurel, NJ 08054
Ph: (856)439-9986
Fax: (856)439-9982
E-mail: ast@ahint.com
URL: http://www.a-s-t.org
Contact: Susan J. Nelson CAE, Exec. VP
Founded: 1982. **Members:** 1,300. **Membership Dues:** regular, $420 (annual) ● international, $300 (annual) ● trainee, $90 (annual) ● associate, $110 (annual). **Staff:** 9. **Budget:** $2,000,000. **Description:** Promotes and encourages education and research with respect to transplantation medicine and immunology; provides a forum for exchange of scientific information related to transplantation across solid organ specialties. **Awards:** AST Fujisawa Fellowship in Transplantation. **Frequency:** annual. **Type:** grant ● AST President's Award. **Frequency:** annual. **Type:** grant ● AST Sandoz Fellowship in Transplantation. **Frequency:** biennial. **Type:** grant ● Faculty Development. **Frequency:** annual. **Type:** grant ● Novartis Fellowship in Transplantation. **Frequency:** annual. **Type:** grant ● Roche New Investigator Award. **Frequency:** annual. **Type:** grant ● Upjohn Young Investigators Award. **Type:** recognition. **Computer**

Services: Mailing lists, for members. **Committees:** Awards; Development; Education; Intrathoracic Organs; Kidney-Pancreas; Liver and Intra-Abdominal Organs and Advisory; Membership; Patient and Education; Pediatric; Program; Public Policy; Scientific Studies; Training and Manpower. **Publications:** *AST Newsletter*, quarterly. **Price:** included in membership dues. **Circulation:** 1,000 ● *AST Primer on Transplantation* ● *AST Washington Round-Up*, monthly. **Conventions/Meetings:** annual meeting (exhibits).

16318 ■ American Transplant Association (ATA)
47 W Polk St., Ste.100-133
Chicago, IL 60605
Free: (800)494-4527
Fax: (847)494-4527
E-mail: ata@americantransplant.org
URL: http://www.americantransplant.org
Contact: Mr. John Butorac, Exec.Dir.
Founded: 1995. **Members:** 1,200. **Membership Dues:** individual, family, $12 (annual). **Staff:** 1. **Budget:** $100,000. **Description:** Provides patient-oriented education, services and support to transplant patients and their families and friends. **Publications:** *A Patient's Guide to Transplantation*. Book. **Price:** included in membership dues; $10.00 for nonmembers. **Circulation:** 5,000 ● *reOrganized!*, monthly. Newsletter. **Price:** included in membership dues. **Circulation:** 1,500 ● *Transcend*, 3/year. Newsletter. For contributors and supporters. **Circulation:** 500.

16319 ■ Center for Organ Recovery and Education (CORE)
204 Sigma Dr.
RIDC Park
Pittsburgh, PA 15238
Free: (800)366-6777
Fax: (412)963-3563
E-mail: ccain@core.org
URL: http://www.core.org
Contact: Susan A. Stuart, Pres.
Founded: 1977. **Staff:** 70. **Description:** Manages organ, tissue and eye donation activities. Offers families the opportunity to donate; coordinates the surgical recovery of the organs, tissue and eyes, and facilitates the computerized matching of donating organs and placement of corneas. Maintains permanent tribute to donors. Delivers continuing education programs for health professionals in regional hospitals and associations. Provides speakers for presentation to civic organizations and schools or corporations. **Libraries:** Type: reference. **Subjects:** medical. **Computer Services:** database. **Telecommunication Services:** electronic mail, sstuart@core.org. **Affiliated With:** American Association of Tissue Banks; Eye Bank Association of America; North American Transplant Coordinators Organization. **Formerly:** (1984) Transplant Organ Procurement Organization; (1992) Pittsburgh Transplant Foundation. **Publications:** *The COREnection*, quarterly. Newsletter ● Pamphlets ● Also publishes protocols.

16320 ■ International Liver Transplantation Society (ILTS)
15000 Commerce Pkwy., Ste.C
Mount Laurel, NJ 08054
Ph: (856)439-0500
Fax: (856)439-0525
E-mail: ilts@ahint.com
URL: http://www.ilts.org
Contact: Diann Stern MS, Exec. Dir.
Founded: 1992. **Members:** 700. **Membership Dues:** active, $190 (annual) ● non-physician, $90 (annual) ● trainee, $75 (annual). **Multinational. Description:** Individuals interested in liver transplantation. Seeks to educate members on liver transplantation. Offers post graduate courses and mini-symposia. **Committees:** Development; Newsletter; Publications; Scope. **Publications:** *Liver Transplantation*, monthly. Journal. Includes articles on surgical techniques, clinical investigations and drug research. **Circulation:** 1,500. **Advertising:** accepted ● Newsletter, quarterly. **Conventions/Meetings:** annual conference and congress ● periodic symposium.

16321 ■ International Pediatric Transplant Association (IPTA)
15000 Commerce Pkwy., Ste.C
Mount Laurel, NJ 08054
Ph: (856)439-0500
Fax: (856)439-0525
E-mail: ipta@ahint.com
URL: http://www.iptaonline.org
Contact: Elizabeth McDannell, Exec. Dir.
Membership Dues: regular, $195 (annual) ● regular, allied professional, trainee (developing country), $50 (annual) ● allied professional, trainee, $100 (annual) ● regular, $350 (biennial) ● regular, allied professional, trainee (developing country), $90 (biennial) ● allied professional, trainee, $180 (annual). **Multinational. Description:** Promotes the advancement of the science and practice of transplantation in children worldwide. Fosters technical and scientific advances in pediatric transplantation. Serves as a unified voice for the special needs of pediatric transplant recipients. Provides a forum that highlights the recent advances in clinical and basic sciences related to pediatric transplantation. Develops educational programs for pediatric transplant professionals in underserved regions of the world. **Awards:** Travel Grant. **Frequency:** periodic. **Type:** grant. **Recipient:** for the best abstract submitter. **Telecommunication Services:** electronic mail, emcdannell@ahint.com. **Publications:** *Pediatric Solid Organ Transplantation.* Book. **Price:** $165.00 per copy ● *Pediatric Transplantation,* 8/year. Journal. Covers all areas of solid organ transplantation, stem cell transplantation, immunobiology, and infectious diseases. **Price:** included in membership dues. ISSN: 1397-3142. **Advertising:** accepted.

16322 ■ International Society for Heart and Lung Transplantation (ISHLT)
14673 Midway Rd., Ste.200
Addison, TX 75001
Ph: (972)490-9495
Fax: (972)490-9499
E-mail: ishlt@ishlt.org
URL: http://www.ishlt.org
Contact: Amanda W. Rowe, Exec. Dir.
Founded: 1981. **Members:** 2,250. **Membership Dues:** resident/student, $105 (annual) ● regular, $260 (annual). **Staff:** 4. **Budget:** $2,000,000. **Multinational. Description:** Medical doctors, PhD's, nurses, researchers, and others interested in artificial hearts and in heart and heart-lung failure and transplantation. Provides a center for discussion, exchange of information, and activities that promote the interests of heart and lung transplantation. Seeks to heighten awareness of public and governmental agencies regarding developments in the field. Maintains the International Heart and Lung Transplantation Registry. **Awards:** Caves Award. **Frequency:** annual. **Type:** monetary. **Recipient:** for best abstract by student/resident ● Nursing and Social Sciences Excellence in Research Award. **Frequency:** annual. **Type:** recognition. **Recipient:** for outstanding nursing and social science research ● Nursing Research Grant. **Frequency:** annual. **Type:** grant. **Recipient:** for deserving members of the organization ● Ortho Biotech/ISHLT Research Fellowship Award. **Frequency:** annual. **Type:** monetary. **Recipient:** for young researchers ● Roche/ISHLT Research Fellowship Award. **Frequency:** annual. **Type:** monetary. **Recipient:** for young researchers. **Computer Services:** database, membership ● mailing lists, transplant registry, slides, statistical reports. **Formerly:** (1991) International Society for Heart Transplantation. **Publications:** *ISHLT Society News,* semiannual. Newsletter ● *The Journal of Heart and Lung Transplantation,* monthly. **Price:** included in membership dues. **Circulation:** 3,600. **Advertising:** accepted. Also Cited As: *The Journal of Heart Transplantation.* **Conventions/Meetings:** annual meeting, with scientific sessions (exhibits) - 2008 Apr. 9-12, Boston, MA.

16323 ■ Kidney Transplant/Dialysis Association (KT/DA)
PO Box 51362 GMF
Boston, MA 02205-1362
Ph: (781)641-4000
E-mail: ktda1@rcn.com
URL: http://users.rcn.com/ktda1
Contact: Dr. Richard Faber, Past Pres.
Founded: 1964. **Members:** 2,200. **Membership Dues:** individual, $15 (annual) ● family, $20 (annual) ● health professional, $35 (annual) ● corporate/facility, $150 (annual) ● regular, outside U.S. and Canada, $25 (annual). **Description:** Provides support to artificial kidney and kidney transplant patients, families, friends, and health professionals. **Awards: Type:** recognition ● **Type:** scholarship. **Recipient:** to kidney patients or members of their immediate families. **Committees:** Patient Assistance. **Publications:** *KT/DA Patient Handbook, 4th Edition* (in English and Spanish). Alternate Formats: online ● *RenalGram,* quarterly. Newsletter. Informs members about recent medical advances, treatment, events, legislation. **Price:** included in membership dues. Alternate Formats: online. **Conventions/Meetings:** meeting, with health professional speakers - every two months, except during summer.

16324 ■ National Bone Marrow Transplant Link (NBMTL)
20411 W 12 Mile Rd., Ste.108
Southfield, MI 48076
Ph: (248)358-1886
Free: (800)546-5268
E-mail: info@nbmtlink.org
URL: http://www.nbmtlink.org
Contact: Myra Jacobs MA, Exec. Dir./Founder
Founded: 1992. **Description:** Assists patients, caregivers, families and health care communities in facing the challenges of bone marrow transplant by providing vital information and support services. **Libraries: Type:** reference. **Holdings:** articles, books. **Subjects:** bone marrow, stem cell transplant patients. **Computer Services:** Information services, resource referrals, health resources. **Publications:** *Caregiver's Guide for Bone Marrow/Stem Cell Transplant.* Book. Offers practical suggestions for getting through the difficult days dealing with bone marrow transplant. **Price:** $12.00/copy (1-10 copies); $10.00/copy (for 11 copies or more). Alternate Formats: online ● *The New Normal.* Video. Features bone marrow transplant experiences. **Price:** free of charge for a single copy; $20.00 for additional copy ● *Resource Guide for Bone Marrow/Stem Cell Transplant.* Booklet. Provides an overview of the transplant process. **Price:** $5.00/copy (1-10 copies); $3.00/copy (for 11 copies or more). Alternate Formats: online ● *Stem Cell Transplant.* Booklet. Provides information for women undergoing a stem cell transplant for breast cancer. **Price:** $2.00 ● Newsletter. Alternate Formats: online.

16325 ■ National Council on Minority Education in Transplantation (COMET)
c/o Diana Carter, Pres./Founder
PO Box 7401
Freeport, NY 11520
Fax: (516)546-4253
E-mail: physicals1@aol.com
URL: http://www.transweb.org/comet
Contact: Diana Carter, Pres./Founder
Membership Dues: individual, $50 (annual) ● chapter/organizational, $150 (annual) ● corporate sponsorship, $500 (annual). **Description:** Seeks to increase organ and tissue awareness and donation, with emphasis on minority involvement. Addresses issues that may have an impact on the transplant community at large. Provides information and education about organ and tissue donation to the public.

16326 ■ National Foundation for Transplants (NFT)
1102 Brookfield, Ste.200
Memphis, TN 38119
Ph: (901)684-1697
Free: (800)489-3863
Fax: (901)684-1128
E-mail: info@transplants.org
URL: http://www.transplants.org
Contact: Janice Hill, Communications Mgr.
Founded: 1983. **Staff:** 11. **Nonmembership. Description:** Provides financial assistance, advocacy and support to organ and tissue transplant candidates and recipients nationwide. **Libraries: Type:** lending; reference; open to the public. **Holdings:** books, business records, clippings, video recordings. **Subjects:** transplantation. **Formerly:** National Organ Transplant Fund. **Publications:** *NFT Newsletter,* quarterly ● *Raising Money, Raising Hope.* Brochure. Describes the services of NFT. ● Annual Report, annual.

16327 ■ National Institute of Transplantation (NIT)
2200 W 3rd St., Ste.100
Los Angeles, CA 90057
Ph: (213)413-2779
Fax: (213)484-6652
E-mail: nit@transplantation.com
URL: http://www.transplantation.com
Contact: Justin Dooley, CEO
Description: Works to advance the science and art of organ transplantation. **Awards:** Transplant Surgery Fellowship Program. **Type:** fellowship ● Visiting Clinical Fellowship Program. **Type:** fellowship. **Publications:** *NIT Newsletter,* semiannual. Alternate Formats: online.

16328 ■ National Transplant Society (NTS)
3149 Dundee Rd., Ste.314
Northbrook, IL 60062
Ph: (847)962-3441
Fax: (847)792-4108
E-mail: info@organdonor.org
URL: http://www.organdonor.org
Contact: Michael R. Reed, Pres./Founder
Membership Dues: individual, $20 (annual). **Description:** Advocates for issues relating to organ and tissue donation and transplantation. Seeks to enhance the availability of organs and human tissue for medical transplants. Maintains registry of donors; supports research. **Telecommunication Services:** electronic mail, feedback@organdonor.org. **Publications:** *Life Notes.* Newsletter.

16329 ■ North American Transplant Coordinators Organization (NATCO)
PO Box 15384
Lenexa, KS 66285-5384
Ph: (913)492-3600
Fax: (913)599-5340
E-mail: natco-info@goamp.com
URL: http://www.natco1.org
Contact: Marian A. O'Rourke RN, Pres.
Founded: 1979. **Members:** 1,800. **Membership Dues:** practitioner, colleague, $150 (annual) ● elite, $50,000 (annual) ● patron, $10,000 (annual) ● benefactor, $25,000 (annual). **Staff:** 5. **Budget:** $700,000. **Description:** Nurses and allied health professionals working with organ recipients and those working to obtain and distribute human organs and tissues to waiting victims of end-stage organ failure. Seeks to influence increased procurement and use of transplantable organs and tissues under the direction of individuals and institutions responsible for the employment of members. Disseminates information to members, medical personnel, technicians, and the public regarding the benefits of organ transplantation, new techniques in organ procurement, advancements in immunology and preservation, transplant surgery, and other aspects of organ transplantation. Promotes and supports training and development programs for new transplant coordinators. Sponsors seminars, workshops, and annual training course on procurement for transplant coordinators. Offers job referral information. **Computer Services:** database ● mailing lists. **Committees:** Communications; Education; Ethics/Public Policy; National Affairs; Operations; Professional Practice; Research; Strategic Plan. **Publications:** *InTouch,* bimonthly. Newsletter. Includes calendar of events, employment opportunity listings, legislative updates, and conference reports. **Price:** included in membership dues ● *North American Transplant Coordinators Organization—Membership Directory,* annual. **Price:** included in membership dues. **Advertising:** accepted ● *Progress in Transplantation,* quarterly. Journal. Includes clinical articles addressing transplantation issues. **Price:** included in membership dues; $65.00 /year for nonmembers in U.S.; $99.00 /year for nonmembers outside U.S. **Ad-**

vertising: accepted. **Conventions/Meetings:** annual meeting (exhibits) - 2008 Aug. 11-14, Boston, MA.

16330 ■ Transplant Recipients International Organization (TRIO)

2100 M St. NW, No. 170-353
Washington, DC 20037-1233
Ph: (202)293-0980
Free: (800)TRIO-386
E-mail: info@trioweb.org
URL: http://www.trioweb.org
Contact: J.T. Rhodes, Pres., Board of Dir.
Founded: 1987. **Members:** 3,500. **Membership Dues:** individual, $20 (annual). **Staff:** 5. **Budget:** $500,000. **Regional Groups:** 6. **Languages:** English, Italian, Japanese, Spanish. **Description:** Transplant candidates, recipients, family members, donor families, and medical personnel. Provides support and medical information to patients and their families. Conducts educational programs. **Libraries: Type:** open to the public. **Holdings:** 100. **Subjects:** transplantation. **Awards: Frequency:** annual. **Type:** scholarship. **Recipient:** for transplant recipients, donors and their family members. **Computer Services:** Online services. **Publications:** *TRIO Lifelines*, bimonthly. Newsletter. Includes chapter activities and current transplantation news. **Price:** included in membership dues. **Circulation:** 4,000. **Conventions/Meetings:** annual conference (exhibits) - October/November ● monthly regional meeting.

16331 ■ Transplant Speakers International (TSI)

PO Box 6395
Freehold, NJ 07728-6395
Free: (877)609-4615
E-mail: fbodino@transplant-speakers.org
URL: http://www.transplant-speakers.org
Contact: Frank X. Bodino, Pres.
Multinational. Description: Seeks to improve or save lives through public education given via a donor-recipient perspective. Raises public awareness of organ donors and transplants. Provides educational programs with the goal of making organ and tissue donation the norm in the United States and beyond.

16332 ■ United Network for Organ Sharing (UNOS)

PO Box 2484
Richmond, VA 23218-2484
Ph: (804)782-4800
Free: (888)894-6361
Fax: (804)782-4817
E-mail: editor@unos.org
URL: http://www.unos.org
Contact: Walter K. Graham MD, Exec. Dir.
Founded: 1984. **Members:** 412. **Staff:** 197. **Budget:** $12,000,000. **Regional Groups:** 11. **Description:** Transplant and organ procurement centers, tissue-typing labs, and health care professionals engaged in organ transplant operations. Administers the National Organ Procurement and Transplantation Network and the U.S. Scientific Registry for Organ Transplantation, as mandated by law under contract with the U.S. Department of Health and Human Services. Maintains national waiting list for transplant candidates. Operates the Organ Center, which matches patients in need of transplants with donated organs. Formulates and implements national policies on equitable access and organ allocation and organ procurement standards. Conducts professional education courses for transplant personnel. Maintains and publicizes national statistics on organ donation and transplantation. **Libraries: Type:** reference. **Holdings:** 400; audiovisuals, books, clippings, monographs, periodicals. **Subjects:** organ transplantation, donation. **Computer Services:** database, case histories of transplanted organ recipients in the U.S. ● information services, registry of patients awaiting donated organs in the U.S. **Committees:** Ad Hoc on Public Solicitation of Organs; Histo; Kidney/Pancreas Transplantation; Liver/Intestine Transplantation; Living Donor; Minority Affairs; Organ Availability; Patient Affairs. **Also Known As:** UNOS. **Publications:** *UNOS Update*, bimonthly. Newsletter. **Price:** free for domestic subscribers; $100.00/year overseas. Circu-

lation: 15,000. **Advertising:** accepted. Alternate Formats: online. **Conventions/Meetings:** annual Members Forum - meeting (exhibits).

Trauma

16333 ■ American Academy of Experts in Traumatic Stress (AAETS)

368 Veterans Memorial Hwy.
Commack, NY 11725
Ph: (631)543-2217
Fax: (631)543-6977
E-mail: info@aaets.org
URL: http://www.aaets.org
Contact: Mark D. Lerner PhD, Pres.
Members: 200. **Membership Dues:** full, $125 (annual) ● associate, $80 (annual). **National Groups:** 41. **Description:** Committed to the advancement of intervention for survivors of trauma. **Computer Services:** Online services, discussion forum. **Programs:** Board Certification. **Publications:** *The Academy Update* ● *Trauma Response*. Newsletter. Alternate Formats: online.

16334 ■ American Academy of Wound Management (AAWM)

1155 15th St. NW, Ste.500
Washington, DC 20005
Ph: (202)457-8408
Fax: (202)530-0659
E-mail: cmurphy@aawm.org
URL: http://www.aawm.org
Contact: Christopher M. Murphy, Exec. Dir.
Founded: 1995. **Members:** 2,000. **Membership Dues:** diplomate, $150 (annual). **Staff:** 2. **Budget:** $400,000. **Description:** Medical practitioners representing numerous professional specialties with an interest in wound management. Seeks to advance the study and practice of wound treatment. Formulates standards of wound management practice; sponsors examinations and confers certification. Conducts continuing professional education programs. **Telecommunication Services:** electronic mail, jmargeson@aawm.org. **Publications:** *AAWM Quarterly News Briefing*. Journal. **Circulation:** 5,000 ● *National Registry of Board Certified Wound Specialists*, annual. **Circulation:** 5,000. **Advertising:** accepted ● Brochure.

16335 ■ American Association for the Surgery of Trauma (AAST)

633 N St. Clair, No. 2400
Chicago, IL 60611
Ph: (312)202-5252
Free: (800)789-4006
Fax: (312)202-5013
E-mail: sgautschy@aast.org
URL: http://www.aast.org
Contact: Ms. Sharon Gautschy, Exec. Dir.
Founded: 1938. **Members:** 1,100. **Membership Dues:** $400 (annual). **Budget:** $1,000,000. **Description:** Comprises of surgeons interested in the cultivation and improvement of the science and art of the surgery of trauma and allied sciences. Offers opportunities for medical students and residents to participate at a reduced rate and supports a minimum of two scholarships a year. **Awards:** Research and Education Scholarship. **Frequency:** annual. **Type:** scholarship. **Committees:** Acute Care Surgery; Critical Care; Honors; Injury Assessment and Outcome; Nominating; Prevention; Program; Publication; Scholarship. **Publications:** *Journal of Trauma*, monthly. **Conventions/Meetings:** annual conference, three days of scientific sessions, with dinner/dance (exhibits) - every September. 2007 Sept. 27-29, Las Vegas, NV - **Avg. Attendance:** 700.

16336 ■ American Professional Wound Care Association (APWCA)

853 Second St. Pike, Ste.A1
Richboro, PA 18954
Ph: (215)364-4100
Fax: (215)364-1146

E-mail: wounds@apwca.org
URL: http://www.apwca.org
Contact: Steven R. Kravitz DPM, Exec. Dir./Founder
Membership Dues: physician, $175 (annual) ● nurse, $125 (annual) ● student, resident, $65 (annual). **Description:** Incorporates all of the various medical specialties involved in treating complex wounds. Aims to decrease the rate of lower limb amputation and other chronic wounds such as sacral decubiti. Provides quality interactive and interdisciplinary medical education. Serves as an informational resource for the at-risk patient as well as the public. **Computer Services:** Information services, wound and wound-related resources. **Boards:** Medical Advisory. **Committees:** Authors; Conference Scientific; Insurance. **Programs:** Insurance Initiative. **Affiliated With:** American Board of Podiatric Orthopedics and Primary Podiatric Medicine; American College of Foot and Ankle Orthopedics and Medicine; American College of Foot and Ankle Surgeons; American Diabetes Association; American Podiatric Medical Association; Amputee Coalition of America. **Publications:** *Advances in Skin and Wound Care*, 9/year. Journal. **Price:** $66.91 /year for individuals in U.S.; $222.96 /year for institutions in U.S.; $122.94 /year for individuals outside U.S.; $255.94 /year for institutions outside U.S. ISSN: 1527-7941. **Advertising:** accepted. Alternate Formats: online ● *Puncture Wounds and Lacerations from Hurricane Damage*. Article. Alternate Formats: online ● *Synergy*, semiannual. Newsletter. Contains articles, news, activities and information about the organization. Alternate Formats: online. **Conventions/Meetings:** annual conference, with lectures (exhibits).

16337 ■ American Trauma Society (ATS)

8903 Presidential Pkwy., Ste.512
Upper Marlboro, MD 20772
Ph: (301)420-4189
Free: (800)556-7890
Fax: (301)420-0617
E-mail: info@amtrauma.org
URL: http://www.amtrauma.org
Contact: Harry Teter, Exec. Dir.
Founded: 1968. **Members:** 3,000. **Membership Dues:** resident, $30 (annual) ● general/nurse/social worker/trauma coordinator/trauma registrar/EMS personnel, $50 (annual) ● EMS squad, $100 (annual) ● physician, $145 (annual) ● corporate/institutional, $1,500 (annual). **Staff:** 5. **Budget:** $1,000,000. **State Groups:** 22. **Description:** Represents physicians, nurses, EMT personnel, other healthcare professionals, institutions, corporations, and interested individuals. Seeks to prevent trauma situations; improves trauma care through professional and paraprofessional education; educates the public through campaigns and dissemination of information. **Awards:** Shari Zougras Scholarship. **Frequency:** annual. **Type:** recognition. **Recipient:** for an active trauma registrar. **Councils:** Hospital; Trauma Registrars. **Subcommittees:** Data. **Publications:** *Promotional Media Resource Catalog* ● *Trauma Watch*, biweekly. Newsletter. Provides summaries of the nation's trauma related news. **Price:** included in membership dues ● *Traumagram Newsletter*, quarterly. Includes prevention activities, news on the annual meeting, and legislative and research updates. **Price:** included in membership dues. **Circulation:** 5,000 ● *TraumaView Newsletter*. **Price:** included in membership dues. **Conventions/Meetings:** annual conference and symposium (exhibits).

16338 ■ Harvard Injury Control Research Center (HICRC)

Harvard School of Public Hea.
677 Huntington Ave., 3rd Fl.
Boston, MA 02115
Ph: (617)432-3420
Fax: (617)432-3699
E-mail: hemenway@hsph.harvard.edu
URL: http://www.hsph.harvard.edu/hicrc
Contact: Dr. David Hemenway PhD, Dir.
Founded: 1998. **Staff:** 16. **Budget:** EUR 3,500,000. **Nonmembership. Description:** Serves as a comprehensive CDC-funded Center. Works for the interdisciplinary study of the causes and etiology of injury

among vulnerable populations and applications for primary prevention and intervention strategies and policy. Focuses on violence primarily youth and family violence and cross-cutting issues including alcohol and drug use, firearm use and treatment setting. Offers graduate courses, internships, conferences, trainings, grand rounds, and a Seminar Series, and provides technical assistance to State Health Departments and Regional Networks. **Libraries: Type:** reference. **Subjects:** faculty and staff publications. **Formerly:** (1998) Injury Control Center; (2001) Injury Control Research Center.

16339 ■ Trauma Foundation at San Francisco General Hospital
San Francisco Gen. Hosp., Bldg. 1, Rm. 300
San Francisco, CA 94110
Ph: (415)821-8209
Fax: (415)821-8202
E-mail: tf@traumaf.org
URL: http://www.traumaf.org
Contact: Andrew McGuire, Exec. Dir.
Founded: 1981. **Description:** Works to improve the lives of survivors of traumatic injuries and provides injury prevention issues and policies, including fire safe cigarettes, automobile safety, gun control, and alcohol policy. **Libraries: Type:** reference. **Holdings:** articles, books, reports. **Subjects:** violence, injury prevention. **Publications:** Videos.

Tropical Medicine

16340 ■ American Academy of Tropical Medicine (AATM)
Address Unknown since 2007
Founded: 1984. **Members:** 2,600. **Staff:** 12. **Regional Groups:** 10. **National Groups:** 10. **Multinational. Description:** Physicians and allied health professionals interested in tropical medicine. Provides postgraduate continuing medical education; confers certificates and diplomas. Maintains speakers' bureau; provides placement service. Conducts research and compiles statistics. Conducts educational programs; offers children's services. **Libraries: Type:** reference. **Holdings:** 2,800; archival material. **Subjects:** scientific, medical. **Awards:** Membership and Fellowship. **Frequency:** annual. **Type:** fellowship. **Recipient:** for physicians and allied health professionals. **Computer Services:** database ● mailing lists ● online services. **Affiliated With:** American Board of Alternative Medicine. **Publications:** Journal of the American Academy of Tropical Medicine, semiannual. Includes book reviews, employment opportunities, and information on new diagnostic equipment. **Price:** $125.00/year. **ISSN:** 0891-544X. **Circulation:** 4,500. **Advertising:** accepted. Alternate Formats: online ● Monographs ● Newsletter, periodic ● Also publishes case studies and plans to publish directory of physicians and hospitals in tropical countries. **Conventions/Meetings:** competition (exhibits) ● annual Themes in Tropical Medicine and Diseases - meeting (exhibits) - always July 15-18.

16341 ■ American Society of Tropical Medicine and Hygiene (ASTMH)
60 Revere Dr., Ste.500
Northbrook, IL 60062
Ph: (847)480-9592
Fax: (847)480-9282
E-mail: info@astmh.org
URL: http://www.astmh.org
Contact: Sally Finney, Exec. Dir.
Founded: 1951. **Members:** 3,000. **Membership Dues:** individual, $195 (annual) ● pre-doctoral student, $65 (annual) ● post-doctoral student, $95 (annual) ● life, $3,900 ● patron, $5,000 (annual) ● donor, $1,000-$4,999 (annual) ● contributor, $500-$999 (annual). **Staff:** 4. **Budget:** $1,000,000. **For-Profit. Description:** Professional society of physicians and scientists interested in tropical medicine and hygiene, including the areas of arbovirology, entomology, medicine, nursing, parasitology, immunology, infectious disease, and travelers' health. **Awards:** Ashford Medal. **Frequency:** triennial. **Type:**

medal ● Ben Kean Medal. **Frequency:** triennial. **Type:** recognition ● LePrince Medal. **Frequency:** triennial. **Type:** medal ● Mackay Medal. **Frequency:** triennial. **Type:** medal ● Walter Reed Medal. **Frequency:** triennial. **Type:** medal ● Young Investigator Award. **Frequency:** annual. **Type:** recognition. **Computer Services:** database ● mailing lists. **Committees:** Arbovirology; Clinical Tropical Medicine and Travelers' Health; Medical Entomology; Molecular, Cellular and Immunoparasitology. **Formed by Merger of:** (1951) National Malaria Society; American Society of Tropical Medicine. **Publications:** American Journal of Tropical Medicine and Hygiene, monthly. **Price:** included in membership dues; $520.00 /year for nonmembers. **Circulation:** 4,200. **Advertising:** accepted ● Health Hints for the Tropics. Book. **Price:** $10.00/copy ● Tropical Medicine and Hygiene News, quarterly. Alternate Formats: online. **Conventions/Meetings:** annual convention (exhibits) ● annual meeting - 2007 Nov. 4-8, Philadelphia, PA; 2008 Dec. 7-11, New Orleans, LA; 2009 Nov. 18-22, Washington, DC; 2010 Nov. 3-7, Atlanta, GA.

16342 ■ Royal College of Physicians and Surgeons of the United States of America (RCPSUS)
PO Box 24224
485 Allard Rd.
Detroit, MI 48224-0224
Ph: (313)882-0641
Fax: (313)882-0979
E-mail: info@rcpsus.com
URL: http://www.rcpsus.com
Contact: Martin H. Savitz MD, Vice Chancellor
Founded: 1984. **Members:** 12,500. **Staff:** 15. **Budget:** $500,000. **Regional Groups:** 30. **State Groups:** 4. **Local Groups:** 28. **National Groups:** 32. **Languages:** Arabic, Chinese, English. **Multinational. Description:** Physicians and allied health professionals interested in advancement of medical science and research. Provides postgraduate continuing medical education; confers certificates, fellowship, and diplomas. Maintains speakers' bureau and hall of fame and provides placement service. Conducts research and educational programs; compiles statistics. **Libraries: Type:** reference. **Holdings:** 26,000; archival material. **Subjects:** scientific, medicine, pharmacology, surgery, laboratory medicine. **Awards:** FRCP. **Frequency:** quarterly. **Type:** fellowship. **Recipient:** for physicians ● FRCS. **Frequency:** quarterly. **Type:** fellowship. **Recipient:** for physicians ● FROG. **Frequency:** quarterly. **Type:** fellowship. **Recipient:** for physicians ● MRCP. **Frequency:** quarterly. **Type:** fellowship. **Recipient:** for physicians ● MRCS. **Frequency:** quarterly. **Type:** fellowship. **Recipient:** for physicians. **Computer Services:** database, research and information services ● mailing lists, for members only ● online services, CME; education and networking. **Subgroups:** Research. **Publications:** Bare Facts for Practicing Doctors, semiannual. Magazine. Provides clinical information to doctors in developing countries. **Circulation:** 2,400. **Advertising:** accepted ● Journal of the Royal College of Physicians and Surgeons, semiannual. Focuses on continuing medical education and certificate/diploma award. **Price:** $50.00 for members; $75.00 for nonmembers; $110.00 for institutions. **Circulation:** 4,500. **Advertising:** accepted. Alternate Formats: online ● Proceedings of the Royal College of Physicians and Surgeons, semiannual. **Price:** $100.00. **ISSN:** 0895-544X. **Advertising:** accepted. **Conventions/Meetings:** annual Clinical and Research Basics for AIDS Virus/Spines and Spinal Cord/Specialized Medicine - convention, medical and medical educator and equipment, books, instruments, labwork, financial planning (exhibits) - always July 15-18 ● competition.

Twins

16343 ■ Conjoined Twins International (CTI)
PO Box 10895
Prescott, AZ 86304-0895
Ph: (928)445-2777

E-mail: dwdegeraty@myexcel.com
Contact: Will L. Degeraty, Founder/Dir.
Founded: 1996. **Multinational. Description:** Fosters support for families of conjoined twins, both medical and non-medical. **Libraries: Type:** lending. **Holdings:** video recordings. **Subjects:** conjoined twins. **Computer Services:** Information services, conjoined twins resources.

Ultrasound

16344 ■ Musculoskeletal Ultrasound Society (MUSOC)
3588 Plymouth Rd., No. 249
Ann Arbor, MI 48105
Ph: (734)973-7462
Free: (866)768-7253
E-mail: holsbeeck@musoc.com
URL: http://www.musoc.com
Contact: Marnix van Holsbeeck MD, Co-Dir.
Multinational. Description: Promotes Musculoskeletal Ultrasound. Focuses on the ideals of Ultrasound application to the musculoskeletal system. Teaches the anatomy, techniques and interventions applicable to the musculoskeletal system using Ultrasound. **Conventions/Meetings:** annual meeting.

Undersea Medicine

16345 ■ Undersea and Hyperbaric Medical Society (UHMS)
PO Box 1020
Dunkirk, MD 20754
Ph: (410)257-6606
Fax: (410)257-6617
E-mail: uhms@uhms.org
URL: http://www.uhms.org
Contact: Donald R. Chandler, Exec. Dir.
Founded: 1967. **Members:** 2,500. **Membership Dues:** regular, $225 (annual) ● regular (international), $175 (annual) ● government employee/academic employee, $125 (annual) ● physician in training, $85 (annual) ● associate, $40 (annual) ● student, $30 (annual). **Staff:** 5. **Budget:** $600,000. **Regional Groups:** 4. **Description:** Diving physiologists, physicians, biologists, and bioengineers with subsea or hyperbaric interests. Seeks to develop and advance undersea and hyperbaric medicine and its supporting sciences; provides channels of scientific communication among researchers dedicated to the safe penetration of the oceans by man; disseminates information on diving problems. Conducts courses on diving medicine for physicians. **Libraries: Type:** not open to the public. **Holdings:** articles, books, periodicals. **Subjects:** diving physiology, clinical hyperbarics. **Awards:** **Frequency:** annual. **Type:** recognition. **Recipient:** for outstanding contributors to the field. **Computer Services:** Mailing lists ● record retrieval services, scientific literature retrieval service (abstracts). **Committees:** Awards; Budget; Bylaws; Diving; Education; Hyperbaric Chamber Fire Safety; Hyperbaric Oxygen; International Affairs; One Atmospheric Vehicles and Submarine Medicine; Research; Scientific Program. **Task Forces:** Federal and Regulatory Affairs. **Formerly:** (1986) Undersea Medical Society. **Publications:** Case Histories of Diving and Hyperbaric Accidents. Book. **Price:** $30.00/issue ● Directory of Hyperbaric Chambers ● Diving Accident Management. Report. **Price:** $35.00/issue ● Diving Physiology in Plain English. Book. **Price:** $30.00/issue ● Fitness to Dive. Report. **Price:** $20.00/issue ● Flying After Diving. Report. **Price:** $20.00/issue ● Handbook and Membership Directory, biennial ● Hyperbaric Oxygen Therapy: A Committee Report. **Price:** $40.00/issue ● Key Documents of the Biomedical Aspects of Deep Diving. **Price:** $100.00/CD ● Near Drowning. Report. **Price:** $20.00/issue ● Pressure, bimonthly. Newsletter. Includes book reviews and obituaries. **Price:** $30.00 /year for individuals. **ISSN:** 0889-0242. **Circulation:** 3,000. **Advertising:** accepted. Alternate Formats: CD-ROM ● Treatment of Decompression Illness. Report. **Price:** $45.00/issue ● Undersea & Hyperbaric Medicine,

bimonthly. **Journal. Price:** $200.00 /year for individuals. ISSN: 1066-2936. **Circulation:** 2,000 ● *Underwater and Hyperbaric Medicine: Abstracts from the Literature*, bimonthly ● *Women in Diving*. Report. **Price:** $15.00/issue ● Are Asthmatics Fit to Dive. **Conventions/Meetings:** annual meeting (exhibits).

Urology

16346 ■ American Association of Clinical Urologists (AACU)
2 Woodfield Lake
1100 E Woodfield Rd., Ste.520
Schaumburg, IL 60173
Ph: (847)517-7225
Fax: (847)517-7229
E-mail: info@aacuweb.org
URL: http://aacuweb.org
Contact: Gary Michael Kirsh MD, Pres.
Founded: 1970. **Members:** 5,600. **Membership Dues:** active/affiliate, $175 (annual). **Staff:** 8. **Budget:** $400,000. **Description:** Represents clinical urologists who are members of the American Urological Association or its sections and the American Medical Association (see separate entries). Stimulates interest in the science and practice of urology. Promotes understanding of socioeconomic and political affairs affecting medical practice. **Computer Services:** database. **Committees:** Political Action. **Affiliated With:** American Medical Association. **Publications:** *AACU Fax*, 3-4/year. Newsletter. **Price:** included in membership dues ● *AACU News*. Newsletter. Provides information on socioeconomics surrounding urology. **Price:** included in membership dues ● Membership Directory, annual ● Journal, bimonthly. **Conventions/Meetings:** annual meeting - always March in Washington, DC.

16347 ■ American Association of Genito-Urinary Surgeons (AAGUS)
41 Mall Rd.
Burlington, MA 01803-4136
Ph: (781)744-5796
Fax: (781)744-5767
E-mail: barbara.t.lamont@lahey.org
URL: http://www.aagus.org
Contact: David Barrett MD, Sec.-Treas.
Founded: 1886. **Members:** 180. **Membership Dues:** active (less than 65 years of age), $250 (annual) ● fellow (at least age 65), international, $140 (annual). **Staff:** 1. **Description:** Serves as a professional society of physicians specializing in genito-urinary surgery. Bestows Keyes and Barringer medals; membership by invitation only. **Awards:** The Barringer Medal. **Type:** medal. **Recipient:** for a member who has achieved fame and distinguished accomplishments ● The Keyes Medal. **Type:** medal. **Recipient:** for an individual with outstanding contributions in the advancement of Urology ● The Spence Medal. **Type:** medal. **Recipient:** for outstanding achievements in Urology. **Conventions/Meetings:** annual conference.

16348 ■ American Board of Urology (ABU)
2216 Ivy Rd., Ste.210
Charlottesville, VA 22903
Ph: (434)979-0059
Fax: (434)979-0266
E-mail: staff@abu.org
URL: http://www.abu.org
Contact: Stuart S. Howards MD, Exec. Sec.
Founded: 1935. **Members:** 12. **Staff:** 8. **Description:** Conducts examinations and certifies physicians in the specialty of urology (branch of medicine that is concerned with the genito-urinary tract). **Publications:** *Information for Applicants and Candidates*, annual. Handbook. Includes certification details and schedule of exams. **Price:** free.

16349 ■ American Prostate Society
PO Box 870
Hanover, MD 21076
Ph: (410)859-3735
Fax: (410)850-0818

E-mail: ameripros@mindspring.com
URL: http://www.americanprostatesociety.com
Contact: Claude Gerard, Chm.
Founded: 1991. **Members:** 51,000. **Staff:** 4. **Local Groups:** 1. **Description:** Works to increase the public's awareness of prostate disease. Encourages men to get annual exams. Aids hospitals and other health care facilities that are dedicated exclusively to detection and treatment of prostate disease. Sponsors Prostate Awareness Week. Conducts speakers' bureau. Sponsors educational programs. **Convention/Meeting:** none. **Publications:** *Update*, quarterly. Newsletter. Contains review and special reports on developments in prostate disease. **Price:** free. **Circulation:** 55,000 ● Brochures, annual.

16350 ■ American Society of Andrology (ASA)
1100 E Woodfield Rd., Ste.No. 520
Schaumburg, IL 60173
Ph: (847)619-4909
Fax: (847)517-7229
E-mail: info@andrologysociety.com
URL: http://www.andrologysociety.com
Contact: Wendy J. Weiser, Exec. Dir.
Founded: 1975. **Members:** 800. **Membership Dues:** active in U.S., $180 (annual) ● active outside U.S., $190 (annual) ● trainee, $40 (annual) ● life, $3,000. **Description:** Individuals interested in andrology, the science and medicine of the male reproductive system. Promotes advancement of knowledge of the male reproductive system and its diseases. Fosters interdisciplinary communication within the field of andrology; cooperates with other organizations holding similar interests. Conducts educational programs. **Awards:** Distinguished Andrologist Award. **Frequency:** annual. **Type:** recognition. **Recipient:** to individual who made an outstanding contribution to progress of Andrology ● Research Excellence Award. **Frequency:** annual. **Type:** recognition. **Recipient:** for female qualified to be trainee member who has presented a meritorious original laboratory or clinical research report ● Thomas S.K. Chang Trainee Travel Award. **Frequency:** annual. **Type:** recognition. **Recipient:** for trainee members of ASA ● Young Andrologists Award. **Frequency:** annual. **Type:** recognition. **Recipient:** to active member of the American Society of Andrology who made significant contributions in the field of Andrology. **Committees:** Archives and History; Development; Diversity; International Liaison; Local Arrangements; Nominating; Public Affairs and Policy; Publications. **Publications:** *Handbook of Andrology*, periodic ● *Journal of Andrology*, bimonthly. **Price:** included in membership dues; $370.00 for institutions in U.S.; $400.00 for institutions outside U.S. **Circulation:** 1,120. **Advertising:** accepted. Alternate Formats: online. **Conventions/Meetings:** periodic international conference ● annual meeting and symposium ● periodic workshop.

16351 ■ American Urogynecologic Society (AUGS)
2025 M St. NW, Ste.800
Washington, DC 20036-3309
Ph: (202)367-1167
Fax: (202)367-2167
E-mail: info@augs.org
URL: http://www.augs.org
Contact: Ingrid Nygaard MD, Pres.
Founded: 1979. **Members:** 1,000. **Membership Dues:** medical student, physician in training, $150 (annual) ● allied health professional, researcher, pharmacist, $200 (annual). **Staff:** 5. **Budget:** $750,000. **Description:** Physicians and health professionals actively engaged in providing quality urogynecologic care to women. Conducts research and education in urogynecology and works to improved care for women with lower urinary tract disorders. **Libraries: Type:** open to the public. **Subjects:** pelvic floor. **Awards:** Health Science Award. **Frequency:** annual. **Type:** monetary. **Computer Services:** Mailing lists. **Committees:** Coding and Nomenclature; Education; Government Relations; Public Relations; Research. **Publications:** *Quarterly Report*. Newsletter. Contains case reports and articles. **Price:** $30.00/year. **Circulation:** 785. **Con-**

ventions/Meetings: Postgraduate Courses - meeting - 3/year ● semiannual retreat, for research ● annual meeting, scientific issues (exhibits) - 2007 Sept. 27-29, Hollywood, FL; 2008 Sept. 4-6, Chicago, IL; 2009 Sept. 24-26, Hollywood, FL.

16352 ■ American Urological Association (AUA)
1000 Corporate Blvd.
Linthicum, MD 21090
Ph: (410)689-3700
Free: (866)746-4282
Fax: (410)689-3800
E-mail: aua@auanet.org
URL: http://www.auanet.org
Contact: Mr. Michael T. Sheppard CPA, Exec. Dir.
Founded: 1902. **Members:** 15,000. **Membership Dues:** active/associate, $425 (annual) ● associate fast-track, $130 (annual) ● candidate, $115 (annual) ● corresponding, $275 (annual) ● affiliate, $150 (annual). **Staff:** 100. **Budget:** $20,000,000. **Regional Groups:** 8. **Description:** Serves as professional society of physicians specializing in urology. Provides education and formulation of health care policy for urologists. **Libraries: Type:** reference. **Holdings:** reports. **Committees:** Education; Electronic Media; Health Policy; Research. **Publications:** *AUA News*, monthly. Magazine. **Circulation:** 13,000. **Advertising:** accepted ● *Health Policy Brief*, monthly. Newsletter ● *Journal of Urology*, monthly. **Price:** included in membership dues; $190.00/year for affiliate, honorary and senior members; $585.00 /year for nonmembers in U.S.; $784.00 /year for nonmembers outside U.S. **Advertising:** accepted ● *Membership Roster*, biennial. Membership Directory. **Conventions/Meetings:** annual Scientific Meeting (exhibits).

16353 ■ American Urological Association Foundation (AUAF)
1000 Corporate Blvd.
Linthicum, MD 21090
Ph: (410)689-3700
Free: (866)746-4282
Fax: (410)689-3800
E-mail: auafoundation@auafoundation.org
URL: http://www.auafoundation.org
Contact: Lawrence S. Ross MD, Pres.
Founded: 1987. **Membership Dues:** chairman, $1,000 ● president, $500 ● benefactor, $250 ● patron, $125 ● advocate, $75 ● supporter, $50 ● individual, $35. **Staff:** 9. **Description:** Medical research and education organization working to broaden the base of urological research and enhance public and health care providers awareness of urologic disease in the U.S. Conducts public educational programs on topics including childhood urological problems, prostate disease, and bladder disorders. Encourages advocacy among urologic disease and cancer survivors. Makes available research fellowships and grants. **Libraries: Type:** reference. **Holdings:** reports. **Awards:** AUA Foundation/Astellas Rising Star in Urology Research Award. **Frequency:** annual. **Type:** grant. **Recipient:** for board-certified or eligible urologists with externally funded, peer-reviewed career development awards for salary supplementation ● AUA Foundation Bridge Awards. **Frequency:** annual. **Type:** grant. **Recipient:** to AUA members for research efforts ● AUA Foundation/NIDDK Surgeon-Scientist Award. **Frequency:** annual. **Type:** grant. **Recipient:** for board-certified or eligible urologists with NIDDK or NCI career development funding ● AUA Foundation Research Scholars Program. **Frequency:** annual. **Type:** fellowship. **Recipient:** for MD and PhD researchers ($30,000 award requires institutional match) ● Pfizer/AUA Fellowship in Urology. **Frequency:** annual. **Type:** fellowship. **Recipient:** for board-certified or eligible urologists. **Additional Websites:** http://www.urologyhealth.org. **Programs:** Prostate Cancer Support Network; Research Scholar. **Affiliated With:** American Urological Association. **Formerly:** (2005) American Foundation for Urologic Diseases. **Conventions/Meetings:** annual meeting (exhibits) - 2008 May 17-22, Orlando, FL.

16354 ■ Certification Board for Urologic Nurses and Associates (CBUNA)
Box 56
East Holly Ave.
Pitman, NJ 08071-0056
Ph: (856)256-2351
Free: (888)827-7862
Fax: (856)589-7463
E-mail: cbuna@ajj.com
URL: http://www.suna.org
Contact: Tina Yancey CURN, Pres.
Founded: 1972. **Members:** 500. **Staff:** 1. **Description:** Conducts certification exam for urological professionals. **Libraries: Type:** reference. **Subjects:** urologic nursing. **Awards:** Macfarlane Award. **Frequency:** annual. **Type:** recognition. **Recipient:** for highest score on certification examination. **Formerly:** American Board of Urologic Allied Health Professionals. **Conventions/Meetings:** annual board meeting.

16355 ■ Continence Restored, Inc. (CRI)
407 Strawberry Hill Ave.
Stamford, CT 06902
Ph: (203)348-0601
E-mail: annejyoung@aol.com
Contact: Anne Smith-Young, Pres.
Founded: 1985. **State Groups:** 2. **Nonmembership. For-Profit. Description:** Participants are people with bladder control problems and interested individuals. Organizes support groups. Provides information on incontinence devices and treatment; offers referrals. Compiles statistics. **Conventions/Meetings:** seminar - every 1-3 months, always New York City.

16356 ■ Interstitial Cystitis Association (ICA)
110 N Washington St., Ste.340
Rockville, MD 20850
Ph: (301)610-5300
Free: (800)HELPICA
Fax: (301)610-5308
E-mail: icamail@ichelp.org
URL: http://www.ichelp.org
Contact: Vicki Ratner MD, Pres.
Founded: 1984. **Membership Dues:** in U.S., $45 (annual) ● outside U.S., $60 (annual). **Staff:** 17. **Budget:** $1,200,000. **Description:** Supports network for patients suffering or suspected of suffering from interstitial cystitis, an inflammation of the bladder wall that primarily affects women; its cause and cure are unknown. Works to inform the public and especially the medical profession about the seriousness of IC. Raises funds for research into treatments and cures; maintains a medical advisory board. Is establishing a national registry to record facts about IC. **Awards:** Pilot Award. **Type:** grant. **Recipient:** for worthy research connected. **Publications:** ICA Update, quarterly. Newsletter. Covers IC research and political and educational activities of the ICA. **Price:** $45.00/year ● Annual Report, annual. Alternate Formats: online. **Conventions/Meetings:** annual meeting.

16357 ■ National Association for Continence (NAFC)
PO Box 1019
Charleston, SC 29402-1019
Ph: (843)377-0900
Free: (800)252-3337
Fax: (843)377-0905
E-mail: memberservices@nafc.org
URL: http://www.nafc.org
Contact: Nancy Muller, Exec. Dir.
Founded: 1982. **Members:** 140,000. **Membership Dues:** consumer in U.S. and Canada, $25 (annual) ● non-physician in U.S. and Canada, $75 (annual) ● physician in U.S. and Canada, non-physician outside U.S. and Canada, $125 (annual) ● consumer outside U.S. and Canada, $50 (annual) ● physician outside U.S. and Canada, $175 (annual). **Staff:** 6. **Budget:** $965,000. **Languages:** English, Spanish. **Multinational. Description:** Works to help individuals who have bladder control problems. Acts as a clearinghouse of information involving incontinence and assistive devices for consumers and their families as well as medical, nursing, and social service organizations. **Libraries: Type:** reference. **Holdings:** articles, audiovisuals, books. **Subjects:** incontinence.

Awards: Continence Care Champion. **Frequency:** periodic. **Type:** grant. **Computer Services:** database, continence referral service. **Formerly:** Help for Incontinent People. **Publications:** Quality Care, quarterly. Newsletter. **Price:** $25.00/year for consumer; $100.00/year for professional; $250.00/year for group professional. **Circulation:** 90,000. **Advertising:** accepted ● Resource Guide: Products and Services for Incontinence. Directory. **Price:** $16.00 for nonmembers; included in membership dues.

16358 ■ National Kidney and Urologic Diseases Information Clearinghouse (NKUDIC)
3 Info. Way
Bethesda, MD 20892-3580
Free: (800)891-5390
Fax: (703)738-4929
E-mail: nkudic@info.niddk.nih.gov
URL: http://www.kidney.niddk.nih.gov/index.htm
Contact: Kathy Kranzfelder, Dir.
Founded: 1987. **Languages:** English, Spanish. **Description:** An information and referral service of the National Institute of Diabetes and Digestive Kidney Diseases. Responds to written inquiries, develops and distributes publications about kidney and urologic diseases, and provides referrals to kidney and urologic organizations, including support groups. Maintains a database of patient and professional educational materials and performs searches. Provides bulk orders of publications to health and information professionals planning patient health education programs. Established by the National Institutes of Health. **Computer Services:** database, combined health information. **Publications:** KU Notes. Newsletter. Features news about kidney and urologic diseases research, special events, professional and patient organizations. ● Research Updates in Kidney and Urologic Health, semiannual. Newsletter. Alternate Formats: online ● Booklets ● Directories ● Also publishes a variety of patient education materials including fact sheets and literature searches from the Combined Health Information Database (CHID).

16359 ■ Simon Foundation for Continence (SFC)
PO Box 815
Wilmette, IL 60091
Ph: (847)864-3913
Free: (800)237-4666
Fax: (847)864-9758
E-mail: cbgartley@simonfoundation.org
URL: http://www.simonfoundation.org
Contact: Ms. Jasmine Schmidt, Dir. of Education
Founded: 1983. **Members:** 140,000. **Staff:** 6. **Description:** Represents persons with urinary and bowel incontinence; family members, doctors, medical personnel, and others concerned with the condition. Seeks to educate the public on urinary and bowel problems, to provide information to persons with incontinence, and to remove the stigma attached to the condition. Acts as support group. Organizes "I Will Manage" self help groups. Conducts research on the number of people who have the problems, and the types and causes of incontinence; compiles statistics. Maintains speakers' bureau. **Awards:** Defeating Stigma in Healthcare Award. **Frequency:** annual. **Type:** recognition. **Recipient:** to individuals, organizations, and companies who strive to defeat stigma in healthcare ● John J. Humpal Award. **Frequency:** annual. **Type:** recognition. **Recipient:** for outstanding dedication in finding incontinence solutions ● Mimi Van Slyke Award. **Frequency:** annual. **Type:** recognition. **Recipient:** for excellence in incontinence not-for-profit management. **Absorbed:** (1984) Step-Up Foundation. **Formerly:** Simon Foundation. **Publications:** A Time for Action. Video ● The Choice Is Yours. Video ● The Informer: Helping People with Incontinence, quarterly. Newsletter. **Price:** included in membership dues. **Circulation:** 150,000. **Advertising:** accepted ● Managing Incontinence: A Guide to Living with the Loss of Bladder Control. Book ● The Solution Starts with You. Video. **Conventions/Meetings:** periodic meeting.

16360 ■ Society for Basic Urologic Research (SBUR)
1111 N Plaza Dr., Ste.550
Schaumburg, IL 60173
Ph: (847)517-7225
Fax: (847)517-7229
E-mail: info@sbur.org
URL: http://www.sbur.org
Contact: Wendy J. Weiser, Exec. Dir.
Membership Dues: active, $75 (annual) ● trainee, $50 (annual) ● life, $1,000. **Description:** Molecular biologists, immunologists, epidemiologists, biochemists and clinical urologic scientists. Provides a forum for the presentation and discussion of urology; promotes collaborative investigations among member scientists; serves as a liaison between member scientists and funding agencies, industry representatives and academic institutions. **Committees:** Academic Operations; Advocacy; Bylaws; Development, Finance and Fundraising; Executive; Industry Operations; Membership; NIH Operations; Nominating; SBUR/Merck Awards. **Publications:** Newsletter. **Conventions/Meetings:** annual meeting.

16361 ■ Society for Fetal Urology (SFU)
c/o Ms. Kris Greiner, Admin. Coor.
Dept. of Urology
Univ. of Iowa
200 Hawkins Dr., 3 RCP
Iowa City, IA 52242-1089
Ph: (319)353-7871
Fax: (319)356-3900
E-mail: kristina-greiner@uiowa.edu
URL: http://www.fetalurology.org
Contact: Ms. Kris Greiner, Admin. Coor.
Founded: 1984. **Members:** 267. **Membership Dues:** regular, $75 (annual). **Multinational. Description:** Physicians committed to fetal and perinatal care. Seeks to improve the care of patients with fetal or perinatal urologic problems, especially hydronephrosis. Promotes communication between specialists; supports research; provides consultation. **Affiliated With:** American Urological Association. **Publications:** Newsletter, semiannual. **Price:** included in membership dues. Alternate Formats: online. **Conventions/Meetings:** semiannual meeting.

16362 ■ Society of Government Service Urologists (SGSU)
PO Box 681965
San Antonio, TX 78268-7202
Ph: (210)681-5800
Fax: (210)680-7725
E-mail: sgsu@satx.rr.com
URL: http://www.sgsu.org
Contact: Ltc. Douglas W. Soderdahl MD, Pres./Co-Course Dir.
Founded: 1952. **Members:** 731. **Membership Dues:** urologist, $50 (annual). **Staff:** 2. **Budget:** $200,000. **Description:** Urologists. Promotes exchange of information on advancements in urological research. **Libraries: Type:** reference. **Holdings:** business records. **Awards:** Kimbrough Seminar Award. **Frequency:** annual. **Type:** recognition. **Recipient:** for writer of clinical paper on urology. **Computer Services:** Mailing lists. **Publications:** Newsletter, quarterly. **Price:** free. **Circulation:** 700. **Conventions/Meetings:** annual Kimbrough Urological Seminar (exhibits) - always January. 2008 Jan. 20-25, San Diego, CA.

16363 ■ Society for Pediatric Urology (SPU)
900 Cummings Ctr., Ste.221-U
Beverly, MA 01915
Ph: (978)927-8330
Fax: (978)524-8890
E-mail: spu@prri.com
URL: http://www.spuonline.org
Contact: Aurelie M. Alger JD, Exec. Dir.
Founded: 1941. **Members:** 300. **Membership Dues:** elected, $60 (annual). **Budget:** $80,000. **Local Groups:** 45. **Description:** Represents medical doctors who are specialists in urology (relating to the genito-urinary tract in health and disease) and who have a special interest in the field of childhood urological problems. Seeks to encourage the study,

improve the practice, elevate the standards, and further the advancement of pediatric urology. Conducts educational programs. **Awards:** John W. Duckett, Jr. AFUD Pediatric Research Scholarship. **Frequency:** annual. **Type:** scholarship. **Recipient:** for outstanding scientific contributions. **Publications:** *Dialogues in Pediatric Urology*, bimonthly. Journal. **Price:** $75.00 /year for nonmembers in U.S.; $100.00 /year for nonmembers outside U.S.; included in membership dues ● *Pediatric Urology*, monthly. Newsletter. **Price:** included in membership dues ● Audiotapes ● Books ● Pamphlets ● Videos. **Conventions/Meetings:** annual meeting.

16364 ■ Society of University Urologists (SUU)

1111 N Plaza Dr., Ste.550
Schaumburg, IL 60173
Ph: (847)517-7225
Fax: (847)517-7229
E-mail: info@suunet.org
URL: http://www.suunet.org
Contact: Robert Roy Bahnson MD, Pres.
Founded: 1967. **Members:** 460. **Membership Dues:** regular, $70 (annual). **Staff:** 1. **Description:** Represents urologists holding faculty or teaching positions in residency training programs. Seeks to promote high standards in the field by: acting as a forum for the interchange of ideas and materials relative to university urology educational programs. Fosters balance of all phases of academic work in urology. **Committees:** Research; Residency Standards. **Publications:** *Objectives for Urology Residency Education*. **Conventions/Meetings:** annual conference, in conjunction with American Urology Association Annual Meeting.

16365 ■ Society of Uroradiology (SUR)

4550 Post Oak Pl., Ste.342
Houston, TX 77027
Ph: (713)965-0566
Fax: (713)960-0488
E-mail: info@uroradiology.org
URL: http://www.uroradiology.org
Contact: Richard H. Cohan, Pres.
Founded: 1966. **Members:** 281. **Description:** Works to advance urinary tract and gynecological imaging, with emphasis on the integration of conventional radiography, sonography, computer tomography, magnetic resonance imaging, nuclear medicine and interventional procedures. **Awards:** Gold Medal. **Type:** recognition ● Research Award. **Frequency:** annual. **Type:** monetary. **Recipient:** to research projects. **Committees:** Ethics; Gold Medal; Membership; Nominating; Research; Rules and Bylaws. **Conventions/Meetings:** annual Abdominal Radiology Course - meeting.

16366 ■ Society of Women in Urology (SWIU)

1111 N Plaza Dr., Ste.550
Schaumburg, IL 60173-4946
Ph: (847)517-7225
Fax: (847)517-7229
E-mail: info@swiu.org
URL: http://www.swiu.org
Contact: Wendy J. Weiser, Exec. Dir.
Founded: 1992. **Members:** 260. **Membership Dues:** active, affiliate, $100 (annual). **Description:** Represents women working in the field of urology. **Awards:** Christina Manthos Mentoring Award. **Frequency:** annual. **Type:** recognition. **Recipient:** for mentors of female urologists ● Elisabeth Pickett Research Award. **Frequency:** annual. **Type:** grant. **Recipient:** for basic science or clinical urologic research. **Publications:** *SWIU News*. Newsletter. **Conventions/Meetings:** annual meeting and breakfast.

Vascular System

16367 ■ American College of Angiology (ACA)

Address Unknown since 2007
Founded: 1959. **Members:** 1,700. **Membership Dues:** fellowship, $410 (annual). **Multinational.** **De-**

scription: Scientists from 27 countries interested in the field of vascular medicine and surgery and dedicated to scientific advancement and continued education in angiology (the study of the circulatory, or vascular system). Seeks to: define, represent, and foster the growth and development of the specialty practice of angiology; improve patient care by advising physicians on recent developments in the field; provide a common forum for the exchange of ideas, technical research, and clinical experiences. Conducts continuing medical education programs. Disseminates original research findings related to cerebrovascular, cardiovascular, and peripheral vascular diseases, diagnostic methods, therapeutic procedures, clinical and laboratory research, and case reports. Holds clinical, diagnostic, and therapeutic symposia and seminars. **Awards:** Young Investigators Award. **Frequency:** annual. **Type:** monetary. **Computer Services:** database ● mailing lists. **Committees:** Continuing Medical Education; Scientific. **Publications:** *The Journal of the American College of Angiology*, bimonthly. **Advertising:** accepted. **Conventions/Meetings:** annual World Congress (exhibits).

16368 ■ American College of Phlebology (ACP)

100 Webster St., Ste.101
Oakland, CA 94607-3724
Ph: (510)834-6500
Fax: (510)832-7300
E-mail: acp@amsinc.org
URL: http://www.phlebology.org
Contact: Mr. Bruce Sanders CAE, Exec. Dir.
Founded: 1985. **Members:** 1,500. **Membership Dues:** active physician, $350 (annual) ● physician, nonphysician, $150 (annual) ● member-in-training, $50 (annual). **Staff:** 6. **Budget:** $1,000,000. **Description:** Physicians and Allied Health Professionals with an interest in the evaluation and management of patients with varicose veins, thrombophlebitis, thrombosis, and venous leg ulcers. Seeks to advance the study, teaching, and practice of phlebology; promotes continuing professional development of members. Serves as a network facilitating cooperation and exchange of information among medical professionals with an interest in phlebology; conducts educational programs; functions as a clearinghouse on medical techniques and technologies applicable to the practice of phlebology. **Awards:** BSN-JOBST Research Grant. **Frequency:** annual. **Type:** grant ● Walter DeGroot Fellowship Award. **Frequency:** annual. **Type:** fellowship. **Sections:** Ambulatory Phlebectomy. **Formerly:** (1997) North American Society of Phlebology. **Publications:** *Journal of Dermatologic Surgery*, monthly. **Circulation:** 18,000. **Advertising:** accepted ● *Phlebology*, quarterly. Journals ● *Vein Line*, quarterly. Newsletter ● *Venous Digest*, quarterly. Newsletter. **Conventions/Meetings:** annual congress (exhibits) ● semiannual regional meeting and symposium ● annual workshop and international conference.

16369 ■ American Venous Forum (AVF)

203 Washington St.
PMB 311
Salem, MA 01970
Ph: (978)744-5005
Fax: (978)744-5029
E-mail: venous-info@administrare.com
URL: http://www.venous-info.com
Contact: Michael C. Dalsing MD, Pres.
Founded: 1988. **Members:** 225. **Membership Dues:** associate, $100 (annual) ● candidate, $25 (annual) ● active, international, $150 (annual). **Description:** Board-certified vascular surgeons. Provides a forum intent on improving the quality care to patients suffering venous and lymphatic disorders. Assists in research and offers guidelines for clinical trials. **Awards:** BSN-Jobst, Inc. Research Fellowship. **Frequency:** annual. **Type:** grant. **Recipient:** to a research fellow/resident chosen through competitive peer review selection process ● Sigvaris Traveling Fellowship. **Frequency:** annual. **Type:** grant. **Recipient:** to medical students, residents or fellows ● Venous Research Award. **Frequency:** annual. **Type:**

recognition. **Recipient:** for the best abstract on clinical or experimental work on venous diseases. **Computer Services:** database. **Committees:** Arrangements of the Annual Meeting; Honorary Membership; International Relations; Issues; Nominating; Program; Research. **Publications:** *A New Perspective on DVT*. Article. Alternate Formats: online ● *AVForum*, periodic. Newsletter. Alternate Formats: online ● *Getting a Leg Up on Varicose Vein Treatment Choices*. Article. Alternate Formats: online ● *Handbook of Venous Disorders*. Provides guidelines in the evaluation and management of patients with venous and lymphatic disorders. **Price:** 115.00/copy. Alternate Formats: online. **Conventions/Meetings:** annual meeting (exhibits).

16370 ■ Association for Vascular Access (AVA)

134 Fairmont St., Ste.B
Clinton, MS 39056
Ph: (601)924-2233
Free: (877)924-AVA1
Fax: (601)924-0720
E-mail: info@avainfo.org
URL: http://www.avainfo.org
Contact: Mary Lea Nations, Exec. Dir.
Founded: 1988. **Members:** 1,300. **Membership Dues:** individual, $95 (annual) ● bronze, $2,500 (annual) ● silver, $5,000 (annual) ● gold, $10,000 (annual) ● platinum, $15,000 (annual). **Staff:** 2. **Local Groups:** 10. **Description:** Physicians, pharmacists, nurses, and manufacturers involved in the care and management of patients with vascular access devices. Seeks to advance the effectiveness of vascular access devices; promotes professional development of members. Serves as a network linking members; conducts educational programs. **Awards:** AVA/Suzanne LaVere Herbst Award. **Frequency:** annual. **Type:** monetary. **Formerly:** (2003) National Association of Vascular Access Networks. **Publications:** *JVAD*, quarterly. Journal. **Price:** included in membership dues; $9.95/issue for nonmembers; $100.00 /year for individuals; $200.00 /year for institutions. **Advertising:** accepted. **Conventions/Meetings:** annual conference (exhibits) - always September.

16371 ■ Association of Vascular and Interventional Radiographers (AVIR)

12100 Sunset Hills Rd., Ste.130
Reston, VA 20190
Ph: (703)234-4055
Fax: (703)435-4390
E-mail: info@avir.org
URL: http://www.avir.org
Contact: Greg Philips RT, Pres.
Founded: 1988. **Members:** 1,100. **Membership Dues:** active, $60 (annual) ● associate, $50 (annual) ● student, $30 (annual) ● international, $85 (annual). **Staff:** 2. **Description:** Cardiovascular and interventional radiographers and allied health care professionals. **Publications:** *AVIR Interventional Informer*, quarterly. Newsletter. **Price:** included in membership dues; $35.00 for nonmembers ● Membership Directory. **Price:** included in membership dues. **Conventions/Meetings:** annual Educational Meeting - 2008 Mar. 15-20, Washington, DC; 2009 Mar. 7-12, San Diego, CA.

16372 ■ International College of Angiology (ICA)

5 Daremy Ct.
Nesconset, NY 11767-1547
Ph: (631)366-1429
Fax: (631)366-3609
E-mail: denisemrossignol@cs.com
URL: http://www.intlcollegeofangiology.org
Contact: Denise M. Rossignol, Exec. Dir.
Founded: 1958. **Members:** 600. **Membership Dues:** fellow, $400 (annual) ● associate fellow, $225 (annual) ● regular, $175 (annual). **Staff:** 1. **Budget:** $250,000. **Multinational.** **Description:** Dedicated to advancement and education in angiology, the study of the circulatory and vascular system. **Awards:** Dr. John B. Chang Research Achievement Award. **Frequency:** annual. **Type:** recognition. **Recipient:** to a fellow of the International College of Angiology in

recognition of knowledge in the field of cardiovascular medicine or surgery ● Young Investigator Award Scholarship. **Frequency:** annual. **Type:** scholarship. **Recipient:** for promising young investigators in the field of cardiovascular disciplines. **Subgroups:** Venous Society of America. **Publications:** *International Journal of Angiology*, quarterly. Promotes multidisciplinary approaches to all aspects of vascular disease. **Price:** included in membership dues. **Advertising:** accepted. Alternate Formats: online. **Conventions/Meetings:** annual congress and workshop, to bring together basic and clinical scientists to share universally current knowledge and techniques in angiology to update the pathophysiology of disease, clinical diagnostic methods and treatment for improved healthcare (exhibits).

16373 ■ International Society of Endovascular Specialists (ISES)
1928 E Highland Ave., Ste.F104-605
Phoenix, AZ 85016
Ph: (602)650-1334
Fax: (602)266-6018
E-mail: admin@isesonline.org
URL: http://www.isesonline.org
Founded: 1992. **Members:** 2,300. **Membership Dues:** regular, $295 (annual) ● physician in training, $150 (annual). **Multinational. Description:** Endovascular surgeons promoting the development of endovascular technologies and therapies. **Computer Services:** Online services. **Publications:** *Journal of Endovascular Therapy*, bimonthly. **Price:** included in membership dues. ISSN: 1526-6028. **Advertising:** accepted. **Conventions/Meetings:** annual meeting and luncheon.

16374 ■ Intersocietal Commission for the Accreditation of Vascular Laboratories (ICAVL)
8830 Stanford Blvd., Ste.306
Columbia, MD 21045-5442
Ph: (410)872-0100
Free: (800)838-2110
Fax: (410)872-0030
E-mail: katanick@intersocietal.org
URL: http://www.icavl.org
Contact: Sandra Katanick CAE, Exec. Dir.
Founded: 1990. **Description:** Establishes industry standards. **Computer Services:** Mailing lists. **Additional Websites:** http://www.icael.org, http://www.icamrl.org. **Formerly:** (2000) Intersocietal Commission for the Accreditation of Vascular Laboratories. **Publications:** Newsletter. Alternate Formats: online.

16375 ■ Microcirculatory Society (MCS)
c/o Dr. Cynthia Meininger, Pres.
Dept. of Systems Biology and Translational Medicine
Coll. of Medicine
Texas A&M Hea. Sci. Center
College Station, TX 77843-1114
Ph: (254)742-7037
Fax: (254)742-7145
E-mail: cjm@tamu.edu
URL: http://microcirc.org
Contact: Dr. Cynthia Meininger, Pres.
Founded: 1954. **Members:** 450. **Membership Dues:** regular, associate, $105 (annual) ● student (without journal subscription), $10 (annual) ● student (with journal subscription), $70 (annual). **Budget:** $30,000. **Description:** Encourages the exchange and dissemination of information on microcirculation. **Libraries: Type:** by appointment only. **Holdings:** 1; archival material, audiovisuals, biographical archives, monographs, papers, video recordings. **Awards:** August Krogh Young Investigator Award. **Frequency:** annual. **Type:** monetary. **Recipient:** to a graduate student, PhD, or MD in the early stages of a research career in order to encourage excellence in microcirculatory research ● Benjamin W. Zweifach Award. **Frequency:** periodic. **Type:** medal. **Recipient:** for achievements of internationally renowned individuals whose careers have been noteworthy and who have made outstanding contributions to the knowledge of the microcirculation ● Eugene M. Landis Research Award. **Frequency:** annual. **Type:** monetary. **Recipient:** for an outstanding investigator in the field of mi-

crocirculation ● Microcirculatory Society Award for Excellence in Lymphatic Research. **Frequency:** annual. **Type:** monetary. **Recipient:** for meritorious research of the lymph, lymphatics, or interstitium by a young investigator ● Microcirculatory Society Travel Award for Outstanding Young Investigators. **Frequency:** annual. **Type:** monetary. **Recipient:** for outstanding young investigators to reward meritorious research in the field of microcirculation by supporting the recipients' visits to laboratories abroad ● Zweifach Student/Postdoc Award. **Frequency:** annual. **Type:** monetary. **Recipient:** to encourage meeting participation by young scientists in training in the field of microcirculation. **Committees:** Awards; Communications; Development; Historical; Liaison; Nominating; Publications. **Publications:** *Microcirculatory Society Directory*, annual. Membership Directory ● *Microcirculatory Society Newsletter*, 3/year. **Conventions/Meetings:** annual conference (exhibits).

16376 ■ North American Vascular Biology Organization (NAVBO)
18501 Kingshill Rd.
Germantown, MD 20874-2211
Ph: (301)760-7745
Fax: (301)540-6903
E-mail: bernadette@navbo.org
URL: http://www.navbo.org
Contact: Bernadette Englert, Admin.
Founded: 1994. **Members:** 600. **Membership Dues:** regular, $100 (annual) ● trainee, $40 (annual). **Description:** Brings together vascular biologists from diverse disciplines and promotes the interchange of knowledge and ideas among these scientists. **Awards:** Earl P. Benditt Award. **Frequency:** annual. **Type:** recognition. **Recipient:** for outstanding discovery in understanding vascular biology or pathology. **Computer Services:** Mailing lists. **Committees:** Development; Meritorious Awards; Program. **Publications:** Newsletter. **Conventions/Meetings:** annual conference, part of experimental biology (exhibits) ● biennial Vascular Matrix Biology and Bioengineering - workshop, focuses on extracellular matrix, vascular calcification, tissue engineering, and bioengineering - 2008 Jan. 30-Feb. 3, Monterey, CA.

16377 ■ Society for Vascular Medicine and Biology (SVMB)
2400 N St. NW
Washington, DC 20037-1153
Ph: (202)375-6189
Fax: (202)375-6839
URL: http://www.svmb.org
Contact: John P. Cooke MD, Pres.
Founded: 1989. **Members:** 270. **Membership Dues:** fellow/regular, $160 (annual). **Staff:** 5. **Description:** Represents individuals with professional interest in vascular medicine, surgery, or nursing, involved in training programs and those who have demonstrated leadership in vascular medicine teaching, practice, or research. Promotes advancement in the disciplines of vascular medicine and vascular biology. Provides consultation and advice to educational institutions, government agencies, and health care policy makers. Facilitates formation of vascular medicine training programs; promotes establishment of Centers of Excellence for the diagnosis and treatment of vascular diseases. Promulgates standards for postgraduate continuing medical education curricula. **Computer Services:** Mailing lists, of accredited programs. **Publications:** *Vascular Medicine*, quarterly. Journal. **Price:** included in membership dues. Alternate Formats: online ● *Vascular Medicine Directory*, periodic ● Newsletter. Alternate Formats: online. **Conventions/Meetings:** annual meeting (exhibits) ● annual Scientific Meeting.

16378 ■ Society for Vascular Surgery (SVS)
633 N St. Clair, 24th Fl.
Chicago, IL 60611
Ph: (312)202-5600
Free: (800)258-7188
Fax: (312)202-5610

E-mail: vascular@vascularsociety.org
URL: http://www.vascularweb.org
Contact: K. Craig Kent MD, Pres.
Founded: 1947. **Members:** 2,300. **Membership Dues:** active/affiliate, $450 (annual) ● corresponding (depends upon country of practice), $150-$450 (annual) ● candidate, $50 (annual). **Description:** Represents surgeons dedicated to advancing excellence and innovation in vascular health. Provides continuing medical education for vascular surgeons, and advocates on behalf of vascular patients and surgeons in Washington, DC. Promotes public awareness about vascular disease and supports career development for young vascular researchers. **Publications:** *Journal of Vascular Surgery*, monthly. Provides vascular, cardiothoracic, and general surgeons with the most recent information in vascular surgery. Alternate Formats: online ● *Vascular Specialist*, bimonthly. Newspaper. Features clinical news, meeting coverage, expert commentary, results of clinical trials and updates on news devices. **Price:** included in membership dues. **Conventions/Meetings:** annual meeting (exhibits).

16379 ■ Society for Vascular Ultrasound (SVU)
4601 Presidents Dr., Ste.260
Lanham, MD 20706-4831
Ph: (301)459-7550
Free: (800)788-8346
Fax: (301)459-5651
E-mail: svuinfo@svunet.org
URL: http://www.svunet.org
Contact: Melissa A. Vickery, Pres.
Founded: 1977. **Members:** 3,800. **Membership Dues:** regular in U.S. and Canada, $110 (annual) ● regular outside U.S. and Canada, $135 (annual) ● student, $60 (annual) ● retired, $45 (annual). **Staff:** 5. **Budget:** $1,000,000. **Regional Groups:** 20. **State Groups:** 5. **Local Groups:** 25. **Description:** Represents vascular technologists and others in the field of noninvasive vascular technology. Seeks to establish an information clearinghouse providing reference and assistance in matters relating to noninvasive vascular technology. Facilitates cooperation among noninvasive vascular facilities and other health professions. Provides continuing education for individuals in the field. Represents members on various regulatory issues. **Libraries: Type:** reference. **Holdings:** periodicals. **Subjects:** vascular technology. **Awards:** D.E. Strandness, MD, Scientific Award for Excellence in Research. **Frequency:** annual. **Type:** monetary. **Recipient:** to a member who is the primary author and presenter of a scientific paper selected for presentation at the annual conference ● Distinguished Service Award. **Frequency:** annual. **Type:** recognition. **Recipient:** to a member for outstanding service ● Leadership Award. **Frequency:** annual. **Type:** recognition. **Recipient:** to members who have made outstanding contributions ● Pioneer Award. **Frequency:** annual. **Type:** monetary. **Recipient:** to individual for contribution in the scientific field of noninvasive vascular diagnosis. **Computer Services:** database, membership ● mailing lists, of members. **Committees:** Abstracts; Academics; Annual Conference; Awards; Certification; Chapters; Continuing Education; Ethics; Finance; Government Relations; Meetings; Membership; Nominations; Products; Screening. **Formerly:** (1988) Society of Non-Invasive Vascular Technology; (2002) Society of Vascular Technology. **Publications:** *e-Spectrum*, monthly. Newsletter. **Price:** included in membership dues; $50.00 /year for nonmembers in U.S. and Canada; $55.00 /year for nonmembers outside U.S. and Canada. **Circulation:** 6,000. **Advertising:** accepted. Alternate Formats: online ● *Glossary of Terms*. Handbook. Contains terms used in the vascular ultrasound profession. **Price:** $10.00 for members; $20.00 for nonmembers ● *Journal for Vascular Ultrasound*, quarterly. Contains original scientific and educational articles, case studies, book reviews, viewpoints, letters to the editor, and CME tests. **Price:** included in membership dues; $105.00 /year for nonmembers in U.S. and Canada; $140.00 /year for nonmembers outside U.S. and Canada; $205.00 /year for institutions in U.S. and Canada. ISSN: 1044-4122. **Circula-**

tion: 10,000. **Advertising:** accepted. Alternate Formats: online. Also Cited As: *Bruit* ● *Medicare Compliance Manual*. Contains policies and procedures designed to identify and correct regulatory and legal issues. **Price:** $250.00 for members; $350.00 for nonmembers ● *Patient Education Guides*. Booklets. Covers peripheral arterial, venous, and cerebrovascular diseases. ● *Referenced Study Outline*. Booklet. **Price:** $10.00 for members; $15.00 for nonmembers ● *Vascular Registry Review*. Booklet. Contains two-volume (three-ring binder) set. **Price:** $75.00 for members; $100.00 for nonmembers ● Brochures ● Videos ● Also publishes information kits. **Conventions/Meetings:** annual conference, discussion of the scientific, clinical management, and regulatory developments affecting vascular laboratories (exhibits) ● annual Current Issues - conference - November. 2007 Nov. 2-3, Arlington, VA ● bimonthly Vascular Laboratory Interpretation Courses - seminar.

16380 ■ Venous Society of America (VSA)
c/o Denise M. Rossignol, Exec. Dir.
5 Daremy Ct.
Nesconset, NY 11767-1547
Ph: (631)366-1429
Fax: (631)366-3609
E-mail: denisemrossignol@cs.com
Contact: Dr. John B. Chang, Chm.
Founded: 1962. **Members:** 300. **Membership Dues:** associate or full, $300 (annual). **Staff:** 1. **Description:** Physicians and scientists with an interest in phlebitis and other diseases of the vascular system. Seeks to advance the diagnosis and treatment of peripheral vascular disease. Serves as a certifying board for professional phlebologists; functions as a clearinghouse on phlebology; facilitates exchange of information among members. Conducts educational programs. **Awards:** Young Investigator Award. **Frequency:** annual. **Type:** monetary. **Recipient:** for presentation and originality of research. **Computer Services:** Mailing lists. **Affiliated With:** International College of Angiology. **Formerly:** (2004) Phlebology Society of America. **Publications:** *International Journal of Angiology*, quarterly. Peer-reviewed journal. ISSN: 1061-1711. **Circulation:** 2,000. **Advertising:** accepted. Alternate Formats: CD-ROM. Also Cited As: *IJA*. **Conventions/Meetings:** annual conference (exhibits) ● annual Scientific Meeting ● periodic seminar.

Veterinary Medicine

16381 ■ Academy of Veterinary Allergy and Clinical Immunology (AVACI)
c/o Dr. Frederick Feibel, DVM, Membership Chm.
328 W Main St.
Avon, CT 06001
Ph: (203)678-1122
Fax: (203)677-0086
E-mail: richlge@aol.com
URL: http://www.avaci.org
Contact: Dr. Frederick Feibel DVM, Membership Chm.
Founded: 1960. **Members:** 300. **Description:** Represents veterinarians, research MD's, and allergy extract firms. Promotes education and research in veterinary and comparative allergy and immunology. **Awards: Frequency:** annual. **Type:** recognition. **Publications:** *Membership List*, periodic. Membership Directory ● *Veterinary Allergist*, quarterly. Journal ● Journal, quarterly. Contains articles and studies. **Price:** $75.00/year in U.S.; $80.25/year in Canada; $89.00/year, international. **Conventions/Meetings:** annual conference, in conjunction with the American Animal Hospital Association.

16382 ■ Academy of Veterinary Emergency and Critical Care Technicians (AVECCT)
c/o Veterinary Emergency and Critical Care Society
6335 Camp Bullis Rd., Ste.14
San Antonio, TX 78257
Ph: (210)698-5575
Fax: (210)698-7138

E-mail: info@avecct.org
URL: http://www.veccs.org
Contact: Leslie Carter RVT, Pres.
Description: Promotes veterinary emergency and critical care technicians; provides certification. **Additional Websites:** http://www.avecct.org. **Publications:** *International Veterinary Emergency and Critical Care Symposium*. Proceedings. Alternate Formats: CD-ROM ● *Journal of Veterinary Emergency and Critical Care or Veterinary Technician*. Contains applied and clinical research articles. ISSN: 1479-3261. Alternate Formats: online. **Conventions/Meetings:** symposium.

16383 ■ Academy of Veterinary Homeopathy (AVH)
PO Box 9280
Wilmington, DE 19809
Free: (866)652-1590
Fax: (866)652-1590
E-mail: office@theavh.org
URL: http://www.theavh.org
Contact: Karen Komisar DVM, Chair
Founded: 1996. **Membership Dues:** individual, $125 (annual) ● student, $25 (annual). **Description:** Works to promote education and research in veterinary homeopathy. Offers an accreditation training program for veterinarians; provides referrals to the public; sponsors continuing education conferences; supports practical and clinical research. **Conventions/Meetings:** bimonthly seminar ● periodic Veterinary Homeopathic Case Conference.

16384 ■ American Academy of Veterinary and Comparative Toxicology (AAVCT)
c/o Dr. Ramesh Gupta, Pres.
Murray State Univ. in Kentucky
Breathitt Veterinary Center
715 North Dr.
PO Box 2000
Hopkinsville, KY 42240
Ph: (270)886-3959
Fax: (270)886-4295
E-mail: ramesh.gupta@murraystate.edu
URL: http://Breathitt.murraystate.edu
Contact: Dr. Ramesh Gupta, Pres.
Founded: 1957. **Members:** 82. **Membership Dues:** fellow, associate fellow, student, charter, $60 (annual). **Staff:** 7. **Budget:** $20,000. **Description:** Veterinarians specializing in toxicology and others interested in veterinary comparative toxicology. Sponsors and encourages scientific and technical meetings and promotes discussion and interchange of information in the following fields of veterinary comparative toxicology: teaching, research and development, diagnosis, nomenclature, public health, and other problems of common interest. Reviews manuscripts and literature pertaining to toxicology and keeps a file of such literature for use by its members. Encourages the use of uniform toxicologic nomenclature. Facilitates and implements the exchange of proven methods among veterinary comparative toxicologists. **Formerly:** American College of Veterinary Toxicologists. **Publications:** *Veterinary and Human Toxicology*, quarterly. Journal. Contains annual directory. **Conventions/Meetings:** annual meeting and symposium, held in conjunction with American Association of Veterinary Laboratory Diagnosticians.

16385 ■ American Academy of Veterinary Nutrition (AAVN)
c/o Wilbur B. Amand, VMD, Exec. Dir.
6 N Pennel Rd.
Media, PA 19063-5520
Ph: (610)892-4812
Fax: (610)892-4813
E-mail: wbamand@aol.com
URL: http://www.aavn.org
Contact: Wilbur B. Amand VMD, Exec. Dir.
Founded: 1956. **Members:** 200. **Membership Dues:** regular, $40 (annual) ● international, $50 (annual). **Budget:** $25,000. **Multinational. Description:** Veterinarians and nutritional scientists interested in animal nutrition and health. Works to promote research and discussion in fields where health of animals may be influenced by nutrition. Sponsors

programs on animal nutrition. Maintains speakers' bureau. **Committees:** Nominating; Program; Public Relations. **Formerly:** (1978) American Association of Veterinary Nutritionists. **Publications:** *Proceedings of the American Academy of Veterinary Nutrition (AAVN) Clinical Nutrition and Research Symposium*, annual. Contains the abstracts of papers/posters presented at the annual meeting of the AAVN. **Conventions/Meetings:** annual symposium.

16386 ■ American Academy of Veterinary Pharmacology and Therapeutics (AAVPT)
c/o Dr. Joe S. Gloyd, Sec.-Treas.
Gloyd Gp.
3 Penny Lane Ct.
Wilmington, DE 19803-4023
Ph: (302)761-9690
Fax: (302)761-9680
E-mail: aavptsec@aol.com
URL: http://www.aavpt.org
Contact: Dr. Joe S. Gloyd, Sec.-Treas.
Founded: 1977. **Members:** 187. **Membership Dues:** fellow, $60 (annual) ● regular, $45 (annual) ● student, $10 (annual). **Description:** Veterinary pharmacologists and clinicians interested in clinical therapeutics; representatives of academia, industry, and government; private practitioners. Supports and promotes education and research in comparative pharmacology, clinical veterinary pharmacology, and other aspects of pharmacology of interest to the veterinary profession; aims to enhance the exchange of educational materials and ideas among veterinary pharmacologists. Organizes committees of experts to research and make recommendations to the profession on current problems in veterinary therapeutics. Sponsors and conducts workshops and other scientific and educational meetings. **Awards:** Lloyd E. Davis Award. **Frequency:** biennial. **Type:** recognition. **Recipient:** for significant contributions over an entire career to the advancement and extension of knowledge in the fields of veterinary or comparative pharmacology ● Research Award. **Frequency:** biennial. **Type:** recognition. **Recipient:** for significant research contributions to the fields of veterinary or comparative pharmacology or therapeutics ● Service Award. **Frequency:** biennial. **Type:** recognition. **Recipient:** for significant service to the fields of veterinary or comparative pharmacology or therapeutics ● Teaching Award. **Frequency:** biennial. **Type:** recognition. **Recipient:** for significant teaching activities in the fields of veterinary or comparative pharmacology or therapeutics. **Publications:** *Journal of Veterinary Pharmacology and Therapeutics*, bimonthly ● Directory, periodic ● Newsletter, quarterly. **Conventions/Meetings:** annual meeting, in conjunction with American Veterinary Medical Association ● biennial Scientific Symposium ● periodic symposium, on contemporary issues.

16387 ■ American Animal Hospital Association (AAHA)
12575 W Bayaud Ave.
Lakewood, CO 80228
Ph: (303)986-2800
Free: (800)252-2242
Fax: (303)986-1700
E-mail: info@aahanet.org
URL: http://www.aahanet.org
Contact: Mr. Derek Woodbury, Public Relations Mgr.
Founded: 1933. **Members:** 36,000. **Staff:** 60. **Description:** Represents veterinary care providers who treat companion animals. Accredits veterinary hospitals throughout the U.S. and Canada. Conducts stringent accreditation process that covers patient care, client service and medical protocols. **Awards:** AAHA Award. **Type:** recognition ● Practitioner-of-the-Year Award. **Frequency:** annual. **Type:** recognition. **Computer Services:** database ● mailing lists. **Publications:** *American Animal Hospital Association Scientific Proceedings*, annual. Includes manuscripts of papers delivered at AAHA meeting. Contains authors index. **Price:** included in membership dues; $55.00 for nonmembers, plus shipping and handling. **Circulation:** 5,000. **Advertising:** accepted ● *Journal of the American Animal Hospital Association*, bimonthly. Includes advertisers' index. **Price:** included

in membership dues; $107.00 /year for nonmembers in U.S. and Canada; $127.00 /year for nonmembers outside U.S. and Canada. ISSN: 0587-2871. **Circulation:** 13,200. **Advertising:** accepted. Alternate Formats: microform ● *NEWStat*, biweekly. Newsletter. Contains latest veterinary news and information. **Price:** included in membership dues ● *TRENDS Magazine*, bimonthly. Covers management trends, social issues, paraprofessional topics in veterinary medicine; includes association news, and CE calendar. **Price:** included in membership dues; $60.00 /year for nonmembers in U.S. and Canada; $70.00 /year for nonmembers outside U.S. and Canada; $20.00/copy for nonmembers. ISSN: 0883-1696. **Circulation:** 13,000. **Advertising:** accepted ● Membership Directory, annual. **Circulation:** 13,000. **Advertising:** accepted ● Has also published atlases for ophthalmology, behavior, oncology, dermatology, cytology, and cardiology and a manual of standards. **Conventions/Meetings:** annual lecture, with veterinary industry exhibits (exhibits) ● seminar ● workshop.

16388 ■ American Association of Avian Pathologists (AAAP)
953 Coll. Sta. Rd.
Athens, GA 30602-4875
Ph: (706)542-5645
Fax: (706)542-0249
E-mail: aaap@uga.edu
URL: http://www.aaap.info
Contact: Charles Hofacre, Sec.-Treas.
Founded: 1957. **Members:** 1,100. **Membership Dues:** full/associate in U.S., $130 (annual) ● full/associate outside U.S., $195 (annual) ● student, $60 (annual). **Description:** Represents graduates of recognized veterinary colleges and individuals that are engaged in some form of avian medicine. Maintains 29 committees. **Awards:** Bayer-Snoeyenbos New Investigator Award. **Frequency:** annual. **Type:** monetary. **Recipient:** to a member or associate member of AAAP whose career as an independent investigator in poultry medicine began less than seven years ago ● Bruce W. Calnek Applied Poultry Research Achievement Award. **Frequency:** annual. **Type:** monetary. **Recipient:** to a member who has made outstanding research contributions resulting directly or indirectly in a measurable, practical impact on the control of one or more important diseases of poultry ● C.A. Bottorf Award. **Frequency:** annual. **Type:** monetary. **Recipient:** to an avian diagnostician/technical service veterinarian who has contributed significantly to the poultry health program in North America in the past 10 years ● L. Dwight Schwartz Travel Scholarship. **Frequency:** annual. **Type:** scholarship. **Recipient:** to an outstanding student ● P.P. Levine Award. **Frequency:** annual. **Type:** recognition ● Reed Rumsey Student Award. **Frequency:** annual. **Type:** recognition. **Recipient:** to an outstanding student ● Special Service Award. **Frequency:** annual. **Type:** recognition. **Recipient:** to a person who has made outstanding contributions within the field of avian medicine. **Publications:** *Avian Diseases*, quarterly. Journal. Contains case reports. **Price:** included in membership dues; $160.00 /year for nonmembers in U.S.; $195.00 /year for nonmembers outside U.S. ISSN: 0005-2086. **Circulation:** 1,800. **Advertising:** accepted ● Manuals ● Videos. **Conventions/Meetings:** annual meeting, scientific ● symposium.

16389 ■ American Association of Bovine Practitioners (AABP)
PO Box 3610
Auburn, AL 36831-3610
Ph: (334)821-0442
Fax: (334)821-9532
E-mail: aabphq@aabp.org
URL: http://www.aabp.org
Contact: Dr. M. Gatz Riddell, Exec. VP
Founded: 1965. **Members:** 5,800. **Membership Dues:** active, $125 (annual) ● student, $20 (annual). **Staff:** 3. **Budget:** $900,000. **Description:** Represents veterinarians who practice bovine medicine. Aims to elevate standards in the field; cooperates with veterinary and agricultural organizations and regulatory agencies. **Awards:** Amstutz Scholarship. **Fre-**

quency: annual. **Type:** scholarship. **Recipient:** to students enrolled in colleges of veterinary medicine in Canada and the United States ● Bovine Veterinary Student Recognition Award. **Frequency:** annual. **Type:** monetary. **Recipient:** to student members ● Externship Grant. **Frequency:** annual. **Type:** grant. **Recipient:** to student members ● Research Assistantship. **Frequency:** annual. **Type:** monetary. **Recipient:** to member and graduate veterinarian. **Computer Services:** Mailing lists. **Affiliated With:** World Association for Buiatrics. **Publications:** *AABP Newsletter*, monthly. Contains meetings calendar. **Price:** included in membership dues. **Circulation:** 5,000. **Advertising:** accepted ● *American Association of Bovine Practitioners Directory*, annual. Includes annual supplements. **Price:** included in membership dues; $25.00/copy for nonmembers. **Circulation:** 5,000 ● *American Association of Bovine Practitioners Proceedings of Annual Meeting*. **Price:** included in membership dues; $40.00/copy for nonmembers. **Advertising:** accepted ● *Bovine Practitioner*, annual. Journal. Covers new developments in bovine practice. **Price:** included in membership dues; $20.00 /year for nonmembers. **Advertising:** accepted. **Conventions/Meetings:** annual conference and convention, with scientific programs for veterinarians (exhibits) - 2007 Sept. 20-22, Vancouver, BC, Canada; 2008 Sept. 25-27, Charlotte, NC; 2009 Sept. 10-12, Omaha, NE; 2010 Sept. 16-18, Albuquerque, NM.

16390 ■ American Association of Equine Practitioners (AAEP)
4075 Iron Works Pkwy.
Lexington, KY 40511
Ph: (859)233-0147
Free: (800)443-0177
Fax: (859)233-1968
E-mail: aaepoffice@aaep.org
URL: http://www.aaep.org
Contact: Sally J. Baker, Dir. of Public Relations
Founded: 1954. **Members:** 6,500. **Membership Dues:** individual, $210 (annual). **Staff:** 13. **Budget:** $2,800,000. **Description:** Veterinarians who specialize in equine medicine and surgery. Disseminates the latest scientific information relative to the practice of equine medicine; promotes research on horses. Maintains 10 professional committees. **Awards:** AAEP/American Live Stock Insurance Co. **Frequency:** annual. **Type:** scholarship ● AAEP Research Program. **Frequency:** annual. **Type:** grant. **Computer Services:** database ● mailing lists. **Publications:** *AAEP Guardian*, monthly. Newsletter ● *Annual Convention Proceedings*, annual. **Price:** $37.00 for members; $74.00 for nonmembers. **Circulation:** 6,000 ● Directory, annual. **Conventions/Meetings:** annual conference (exhibits) - 2007 Dec. 1-5, Orlando, FL; 2008 Dec. 6-10, San Diego, CA; 2009 Dec. 4-9, Las Vegas, NV.

16391 ■ American Association of Equine Veterinary Technicians (AAEVT)
2604 Lake Cove
Highland Village, TX 75077
Ph: (972)966-3440
Fax: (972)966-3605
E-mail: dreeder@cox.net
URL: http://www.aaevt.org
Contact: Deborah Reeder RVT, Pres./Exec. Dir.
Membership Dues: regular, $50 (annual) ● international, $60 (annual) ● student, $25 (annual). **Multinational. Description:** Promotes the health and welfare of horses through the education and professional enrichment of equine veterinary technicians. Provides continuing educational opportunities that are relevant and accessible to equine technicians and assistants. Encourages and improves communications between equine technicians and assistants. **Publications:** Newsletter.

16392 ■ American Association of Feline Practitioners (AAFP)
203 Towne Centre Dr.
Hillsborough, NJ 08844-4693
Ph: (908)359-9351
Free: (800)874-0498
Fax: (908)359-7619

E-mail: info@aafponline.org
URL: http://www.aafponline.org
Contact: Rick Alampi, Exec. Dir.
Founded: 1970. **Members:** 1,800. **Membership Dues:** general, $165 (annual) ● fellow, $215 (annual) ● student, $80 (annual). **Staff:** 1. **Description:** Doctors of veterinary medicine who specialize or have a general interest in the field of feline medicine and surgery. Works to promote the interests and improve the public stature of feline practice and to increase the knowledge of veterinarians in the field. Cooperates with other veterinary and cat fancier organizations. **Awards:** **Type:** recognition. **Recipient:** for student achievement ● Research Grant. **Frequency:** annual. **Type:** grant. **Recipient:** for feline research. **Computer Services:** Mailing lists, of members. **Publications:** *Journal of Feline Medicine and Surgery*, bimonthly. Includes original research, review articles and case reports relevant to your own work within this specialized field. ● Newsletter, 3/year. Includes information such as meeting abstracts, pharmacology information, practice tips and capsule reports. **Advertising:** accepted ● Membership Directory, annual. Contains listing of over 1,500 feline practitioners world wide, and with multiple cross-referenced sections. **Conventions/Meetings:** semiannual conference (exhibits).

16393 ■ American Association of Food Hygiene Veterinarians (AAFHV)
c/o Linda Tollefson, Immediate Past Pres.
U.S. Food and Drug Admin.
5600 Fishers Ln., Rm. 14C06 HF33
Rockville, MD 20857
Ph: (301)827-3040 (301)527-1950
Fax: (301)827-3042
E-mail: linda.tollefson@fda.hhs.gov
URL: http://www.avma.org/aafhv
Contact: Linda Tollefson, Immediate Past Pres.
Membership Dues: regular (US, Canada, Mexico), $35 (annual) ● other international, $45 (annual). **Description:** Increases the knowledge of veterinarians engaged in food animal practice, education, and/or the practice of food inspection, hygiene and safety. Promotes the interests and professional expertise of food hygiene veterinarians. **Computer Services:** Information services, food safety resources. **Subgroups:** Food Animal Advisory Panel. **Publications:** Newsletter, periodic. Includes articles of interest to food hygiene veterinarians.

16394 ■ American Association of Housecall Veterinarians (AAHV)
c/o Shannon Stanek, DVM
1694 Swamp Pike
Gilbertsville, PA 19525
E-mail: stanekvet@comcast.net
URL: http://www.athomevet.org
Contact: Shannon Stanek DVM, Contact
Description: Assists pets in getting quality veterinary care. Promotes the services of housecall veterinarians for better pet care. Promotes safety, public awareness, health and the highest quality of veterinary care possible for pets.

16395 ■ American Association of Public Health Veterinarians (AAPHV)
c/o Dr. Joe Horman, Treas.
5649 Horman Ln.
Frederick, MD 21701
Fax: (410)333-6333
E-mail: jthdvmmph@aol.com
Contact: Dr. Joe Horman, Treas.
Founded: 1953. **Members:** 100. **Membership Dues:** active, $5,000 (annual) ● individual, $20 (annual). **Description:** Executive veterinary public health administrators in each state. Works to guide and develop veterinary public health programs in the states and on the national level. **Formerly:** (1968) Association of State Public Health Veterinarians; (1979) Association of State and Territorial Public Health Veterinarians; (1984) National Association of State and Territorial Public Health Veterinarians; (2002) National Association of State Public Health Veterinarians. **Publications:** *Annual National Com-*

pendium of Animal Rabies Control, annual. **Conventions/Meetings:** annual conference.

16396 ■ American Association of Retired Veterinarians
Address Unknown since 2007
Founded: 1986. **Members:** 425. **Membership Dues:** onetime, $20 (annual) ● life membership, $200 (annual). **Description:** Individuals with a degree in veterinary medicine who are retired or considering retiring, and their spouses. Seeks to advance the science and art of veterinary medicine. Encourages friendship among those in the profession. Promotes social and professional lives of retired veterinarians. Attempts to assist future retirees in achievement of their goals in retirement life. Organizes group trips and cruises. **Publications:** *AARV Newsletter* ● Membership Directory, periodic. **Conventions/Meetings:** annual meeting, in conjunction with the American Veterinary Medical Association.

16397 ■ American Association of Small Ruminant Practitioners (AASRP)
2413 Nashville Rd., Ste.112 MS-C13
Bowling Green, KY 42101
Ph: (270)793-0781
Fax: (502)413-6625
E-mail: aasrp@aasrp.org
URL: http://www.aasrp.org
Contact: Peggy Logsdon, Admin.
Founded: 1968. **Members:** 1,250. **Membership Dues:** veterinarian/non-veterinarian associate in U.S. and Canada, $75 (annual) ● student in U.S. and Canada, $15 (annual) ● student outside U.S. and Canada, $20 (annual) ● veterinarian/non-veterinarian associate outside U.S. and Canada, $100 (annual). **Staff:** 2. **Languages:** English, Spanish. **Description:** Represents practicing veterinarians and veterinary students, producers, feeders, hobbyists, and others interested in sheep, goats, llamas, deer, and exotic small ruminants. Aims are to: elevate standards of practice in the field; further research programs that will assist in solving small ruminant health problems; foster communication between veterinarians, owners, and researchers in order to improve small ruminant health management programs. Sponsors specialized education programs. Conducts educational programs. Maintains speakers' bureau. **Libraries: Type:** reference. **Holdings:** archival material. **Awards:** George McConnell Award and Practitioner of the Year. **Frequency:** annual. **Type:** recognition. **Recipient:** for professional service ● Sam Guss Student Grant Fund. **Type:** grant. **Recipient:** for student research and extern purposes. **Computer Services:** database ● mailing lists ● online services. **Committees:** Program and Continuing Education for Veterinarians; Students Educational Opportunities. **Formerly:** (1988) American Association of Sheep and Goat Practitioners. **Publications:** *The Health and Disease of Small Ruminants*, annual. Brochure. Contains annual summary of papers from nationwide educational programs. ● *Wool & Wattles*, quarterly. Newsletter. Offers reviews, association reports, practical exchange of techniques, association reports, technology and regulatory news, and grant opportunities. **Price:** included in membership dues. **Circulation:** 1,300 ● Membership Directory, annual. Provides a list of members who can be a source for referrals, consultation and collaboration. ● Also publishes fact sheets and abstracts. **Conventions/Meetings:** annual meeting and convention, held in conjunction with American Veterinary Medical Association.

16398 ■ American Association of Swine Veterinarians (AASV)
902 1st Ave.
Perry, IA 50220-1703
Ph: (515)465-5255
Fax: (515)465-3832
E-mail: aasv@aasv.org
URL: http://www.aasv.org
Contact: Dr. Tom Burkgren, Exec. Dir.
Founded: 1969. **Members:** 1,500. **Membership Dues:** active/associate, $160 (annual) ● full-time graduate student, $80 (annual) ● student, $15 (annual). **Staff:** 3. **Budget:** $800,000. **Multinational.**

Description: Represents veterinarians concerned with swine health and nutrition. Improves public stature and increase the knowledge of veterinarians in the field of swine practice. **Awards:** AASV Meritorious Service Award. **Frequency:** annual. **Type:** recognition ● Howard Dunne Memorial Award. **Frequency:** annual. **Type:** recognition ● Swine Practitioner of the Year. **Frequency:** annual. **Type:** recognition. **Formerly:** (2000) American Association of Swine Practitioners. **Publications:** *Journal of Swine Health and Production*, bimonthly. Includes reports of swine-related research. **Price:** $102.50/year in North America; $117.50/year outside North America. ISSN: 1536-209X ● *Proceedings of the AASV Annual Meeting*, annual. Includes papers of the AASV annual meeting. **Price:** $70.00 plus shipping and handling; $35.00 CD-Rom, plus shipping and handling. Alternate Formats: CD-ROM ● *Swine Disease Manual*, periodic. Provides a current and concise overview of swine diseases encountered in production systems. **Price:** $25.00/copy. **Conventions/Meetings:** annual meeting, continuing education (exhibits) - 2008 Mar. 8-11, Columbus, OH; 2009 Feb. 28-Mar. 3, Charlotte, NC.

16399 ■ American Association of Veterinary Clinicians (AAVC)
37 W Broad St., Ste.480
Columbus, OH 43215-4132
Ph: (614)358-0417
Fax: (614)241-2215
E-mail: tking@craiggroup.com
URL: http://www.craiggroup.com/AAVC.htm
Contact: Molly K. McKee, Exec. Dir.
Founded: 1958. **Description:** Veterinary clinicians engaged in teaching and/or research at the professional, graduate or postgraduate level. Strives to enhance the quality of teaching, service and research, provides a forum for exploration and creative resolution of clinical issues. Hosts educational programs and sponsors achievement awards. **Awards:** Faculty Achievement Award. **Frequency:** annual. **Type:** recognition. **Recipient:** to a member who has achieved national recognition through his/her efforts on behalf of veterinary medicine ● Residents Award. **Frequency:** annual. **Type:** recognition. **Recipient:** for two individuals who have achieved a high degree of excellence in their chosen specialty. **Conventions/Meetings:** annual meeting.

16400 ■ American Association of Veterinary Immunologists (AAVI)
c/o Eileen L. Thacker, PhD, Sec.-Treas.
2118 Vet Med Bldg.
Veterinary Microbiology and Preventive Medicine
Iowa State Univ.
Ames, IA 50011
Ph: (515)294-5097
Fax: (515)294-8500
E-mail: ethacker@iastate.edu
URL: http://www.theaavi.org
Contact: Eileen L. Thacker PhD, Sec.-Treas.
Founded: 1979. **Members:** 260. **Membership Dues:** regular, $50 (annual). **Description:** Holders of BS or DVM degrees with an interest in veterinary immunology. Promotes development and dissemination of knowledge in the field of veterinary immunology. Conducts research and educational programs. **Awards:** Student Awards. **Frequency:** annual. **Type:** recognition. **Recipient:** for oral and poster presentation competition. **Publications:** *AAVI Newsletter*, periodic. Alternate Formats: online. **Conventions/Meetings:** annual Business and Scientific Meeting - always November ● annual symposium.

16401 ■ American Association of Veterinary Laboratory Diagnosticians (AAVLD)
PO Box 1770
Davis, CA 95617
Ph: (530)754-9719
Fax: (530)752-5680
E-mail: areitz@cahfs.ucdavis.edu
URL: http://www.aavld.org
Contact: Allison Reitz, Sec.
Founded: 1957. **Members:** 1,200. **Membership Dues:** full, $75 (annual) ● resident, associate, retired,

graduate student, $25 (annual). **Staff:** 3. **Budget:** $100,000. **Multinational. Description:** Represents each state official delegate and individuals active in veterinary laboratory diagnostic medicine. Disseminates information on diagnosis of animal disease; coordinates diagnostic activities of regulatory, research, and service laboratories; establishes uniform diagnostic techniques; seeks to improve existing diagnostic techniques and facilitate the development of new ones; establishes guides for personnel qualifications and facilities; acts as consultant to the U.S. Animal Health Association on uniform diagnostic criteria. **Affiliated With:** United States Animal Health Association. **Publications:** *Journal of Veterinary Diagnostic Investigation*, bimonthly. **Price:** included in membership dues. **Circulation:** 1,500. Also Cited As: *JVDI* ● Newsletter, 3/year. Contains association news and information on employment opportunities. **Price:** included in membership dues. **Circulation:** 1,500. **Advertising:** accepted.

16402 ■ American Association of Veterinary Parasitologists (AAVP)
c/o Dr. Alan A. Marchiondo, Sec.-Treas.
IVX Animal Hea., Inc.
3915 S 48th St. Terr.
St. Joseph, MO 64503-4711
Ph: (816)676-6171
Fax: (816)676-6874
E-mail: alan_marchiondo@ivax.com
URL: http://www.aavp.org
Contact: Dr. Alan A. Marchiondo, Sec.-Treas.
Founded: 1956. **Members:** 450. **Description:** Persons actively engaged in teaching and researching parasitology. Encourages education and research in the field; provides for exchange of information. Compiles summaries of papers presented at annual scientific meeting. **Publications:** *Annual Meeting Proceedings*, annual ● Directory, biennial ● Newsletter, quarterly. **Conventions/Meetings:** annual assembly, in conjunction with American Veterinary Medical Association.

16403 ■ American Association of Veterinary State Boards (AAVSB)
4106 Central St.
Kansas City, MO 64111
Ph: (816)931-1504
Free: (877)698-8482
Fax: (816)931-1604
E-mail: aavsb@aavsb.org
URL: http://www.aavsb.org
Contact: Robyn Kendrick, Exec. Dir.
Founded: 1957. **Members:** 56. **Membership Dues:** state board, $500 (annual). **Staff:** 4. **Description:** Represents state boards of examiners in veterinary medicine. Aids state boards of veterinary medicine in the protection of the public health and welfare. Acts as a clearing house for research, collects and disseminates information about legal regulation of the veterinary profession. Works to simplify and standardize licensing and certification processes for veterinarians and veterinary technicians. Assists member boards in fulfilling statutory, public, and ethical obligations in legal regulation and enforcement. Cooperates with the National Board Examination Committee in the design and use of entry level, relicensure and disciplinary examinations. Collects and disseminates information regarding disciplinary actions taken by member boards. Provides veterinary medical educational programs. **Computer Services:** database, services-members only. **Committees:** Grievance; Reciprocity/Endorsement. **Formerly:** (1968) Association of American Board of Examiners in Veterinary Medicine; (1974) American Association State Boards, Veterinary. **Publications:** *State Board Directory*. Includes contact information for all State Veterinary Boards. ● *Veterinary Regulation News*, quarterly. Newsletter. Includes current issues. Alternate Formats: online. **Conventions/Meetings:** annual conference and meeting, in conjunction with American Veterinary Medical Association - always July.

16404 ■ American Association of Wildlife Veterinarians (AAWV)
c/o Dr. Mark Cunningham, Sec.
Florida Fish and Wildlife Conservation Commission
4005 S Main St.
Gainesville, FL 32601

E-mail: mark.cunningham@fwc.state.fl.us
URL: http://www.aawv.net
Contact: Dr. Mark Cunningham, Sec.
Founded: 1979. **Members:** 350. **Membership Dues:** veterinarian/active, subscriber, $40 (annual) ● veterinary student, $20 (annual). **Budget:** $10,000. **Description:** Veterinarians in state and federal wildlife resource agencies, universities, private practice, public health service agencies, agricultural agencies, and diagnostic laboratories; veterinary students; and interested individuals. Deals with problems confronting veterinarians who work with free-ranging wildlife. Encourages colleges of veterinary medicine to increase emphasis on management of and preventive medicine for free-ranging species; educates governmental agencies and wildlife resource interest groups; promotes utilization of veterinarians in the field of wildlife resource management and research; encourages cooperation among resource management professionals and wildlife veterinarians; promotes continuing education programs for wildlife veterinarians; emphasizes interrelationships of man, domestic animals, and wildlife with disease; encourages recognition of disease syndromes as potentially influenced by habitat succession, alteration, and pollution. **Affiliated With:** American Veterinary Medical Association; Wildlife Disease Association. **Publications:** *AAWV Newsletter*, quarterly ● Membership Directory, periodic. **Conventions/Meetings:** annual conference - always August.

16405 ■ American Association of Zoo Veterinarians (AAZV)
c/o Dr. Robert Hilsenroth, Exec. Dir.
581705 White Oak Rd.
Yulee, FL 32097
Ph: (904)225-3275
Fax: (904)225-3289
E-mail: rhilsenrothaazv@aol.com
URL: http://www.aazv.org
Contact: Dr. Robert Hilsenroth, Exec. Dir.
Founded: 1960. **Members:** 1,200. **Membership Dues:** active, $205 (annual) ● associate, $195 (annual) ● student, $90 (annual). **Staff:** 3. **Budget:** $325,000. **Multinational. Description:** Veterinarians actively engaged in the practice of zoo and wildlife medicine for at least four years; veterinarians who do not qualify for active membership; persons interested in diseases of wildlife; students of veterinary medicine in any accredited veterinary school. Purposes are to: advance programs for preventive medicine, husbandry, and scientific research dealing with captive and free-ranging wild animals; provide a forum for the presentation and discussion of problems related to the field; enhance and uphold the professional ethics of veterinary medicine. **Awards:** Dolensek Award. **Frequency:** periodic. **Type:** recognition ● Ullrey Award. **Frequency:** periodic. **Type:** recognition. **Recipient:** for research and support of the AAZV. **Committees:** Animal Welfare; Editorial; Education; Ethics; Infectious Disease; ISIS/Computer Data; Legislative; Programs; Public Relations. **Publications:** *Conference Proceedings*, annual. Contains papers presented at the annual conference. **Price:** $55.00/year. Alternate Formats: CD-ROM ● *Journal of Zoo and Wildlife Medicine*, quarterly. Contains original manuscripts, book and paper reviews and research notes/case reports. **Price:** included in membership dues; $115.00 /year for nonmembers in U.S.; $130.00 /year for nonmembers outside U.S.; $245.00 /year for institutions and libraries. ISSN: 1042-7260. **Advertising:** accepted. Also Cited As: *Journal of Zoo Animal Medicine*. **Conventions/Meetings:** annual conference (exhibits) - 2007 Oct. 20-26, Knoxville, TN - **Avg. Attendance:** 650.

16406 ■ American Board of Veterinary Practitioners (ABVP)
c/o Jeff Allen, Exec. Dir.
618 Church St., Ste.220
Nashville, TN 37219
Ph: (615)250-7794 (615)254-3687
Free: (800)697-3583
Fax: (615)254-7047

E-mail: abvp@xmi-amc.com
URL: http://www.abvp.com
Contact: Jeff Allen, Exec. Dir.
Founded: 1978. **Members:** 750. **Membership Dues:** individual, $250 (annual). **Staff:** 2. **Budget:** $200,000. **Description:** Veterinarians. Seeks to recognize excellence in clinical, species-oriented specialty practice. Works to insure delivery of superior, comprehensive, multidisciplinary veterinary services. Confers certification; conducts educational programs. **Computer Services:** database ● mailing lists ● online services. **Committees:** Credentials. **Publications:** *ABVP News*, quarterly. Newsletter. Includes directory. **Circulation:** 700. **Advertising:** accepted. Alternate Formats: online ● Proceedings. Alternate Formats: online. **Conventions/Meetings:** annual Practitioner's Symposium - conference, continuing education.

16407 ■ American Board of Veterinary Specialties (ABVS)
c/o American Veterinary Medical Association
1931 N Meacham Rd., Ste.100
Schaumburg, IL 60173
Ph: (847)925-8070
Free: (800)248-2862
Fax: (847)925-1329
E-mail: jgranstrom@avma.org
URL: http://www.avma.org
Contact: Julie Granstrom, Admin. Asst.
Founded: 1959. **Members:** 22. **Staff:** 1. **Budget:** $22,000. **Description:** Serves as board of the American Veterinary Medical Association. Represents veterinarians with advanced training in one or more specialty areas of veterinary practice, research, or study whose purpose is to recognize and supervise organizations that provide certification to qualified specialists. **Formerly:** Advisory Board on Veterinary Specialties. **Publications:** *Policies and Procedures Manual*, periodic. **Price:** first copy free; $1.00/additional copy. **Conventions/Meetings:** annual board meeting.

16408 ■ American Board of Veterinary Toxicology (ABVT)
c/o Dr. Randall A. Lovell, Candidate Coor.
FDA/Center for Veterinary Medicine
Division of Animal Feeds, HFV-222
7519 Standish Pl., Rm. 226
Rockville, MD 20855
Ph: (240)453-6857
Fax: (240)453-6882
E-mail: randall.lovell@fda.org
URL: http://www.abvt.org
Contact: Dr. Randall A. Lovell, Candidate Coor.
Founded: 1967. **Members:** 100. **Description:** Seeks to further education and scientific progress in veterinary toxicology. Encourages research and training. Establishes and maintains the highest possible standards of training and experience for qualification in toxicology. Recognizes qualified specialists through certification. Conducts annual examination. **Awards:** ASPCA-APCC Intervet Student Paper Award. **Frequency:** annual. **Type:** monetary. **Recipient:** for best paper relating to veterinary toxicology. **Affiliated With:** American Veterinary Medical Association. **Publications:** *American Board of Veterinary Toxicology—Directory of Diplomates*, annual. Lists diplomates certified as veterinary toxicologists by the board. **Conventions/Meetings:** annual Business Meeting.

16409 ■ American Canine Sports Medicine Association (ACSMA)
PO Box 07412
Fort Myers, FL 33919
E-mail: postmaster@acsma.org
URL: http://www.acsma.org
Contact: Edward S. Aycock DVM, Contact
Founded: 1991. **Members:** 200. **Membership Dues:** in U.S., $35 (annual) ● in Canada and other address outside U.S., $45 (annual) ● professional student, intern, resident, graduate student in U.S., $10 (annual) ● graduate student outside U.S., $15 (annual). **Description:** Promotes interests of members. Conducts research and educational programs. **Publications:** Newsletter, quarterly. **Price:** included in

membership dues. **Conventions/Meetings:** annual symposium (exhibits).

16410 ■ American College of Laboratory Animal Medicine (ACLAM)
c/o Dr. Melvin W. Balk, Exec. Dir.
96 Chester St.
Chester, NH 03036
Ph: (603)887-2467
Fax: (603)887-0096
E-mail: mwbaclam@gsinet.net
URL: http://www.aclam.org
Contact: Dr. Melvin W. Balk, Exec. Dir.
Founded: 1957. **Members:** 706. **Description:** Represents veterinarians specializing in laboratory animal medicine. Establishes standards of training and experience for qualification of specialists in the field, administers examinations, and certifies eligible specialists. Encourages education, training, and research in laboratory animal medicine. Sponsors symposia on infectious and metabolic diseases of laboratory animals. Conducts continuing education forums for diplomates on topics including quality assurance, biohazards, and animal production. **Committees:** Continuing Education; Credentials; Examination; Nominating. **Formerly:** American Board of Laboratory Animal Medicine. **Publications:** *The Biology of the Laboratory Rabbit*. Book ● Membership Directory, annual ● Newsletter, quarterly. Alternate Formats: online. **Conventions/Meetings:** annual meeting, held in conjunction with American Veterinary Medical Association - always July. 2008 July 19-23, New Orleans, LA; 2009 July 11-15, Seattle, WA; 2010 July 31-Aug. 4, Atlanta, GA.

16411 ■ American College of Theriogenologists (ACT)
PO Box 3065
Montgomery, AL 36109
Ph: (334)395-4666
Fax: (334)270-3399
E-mail: charles@franzmgt.com
URL: http://www.theriogenology.org
Contact: Charles F. Franz DVM, Exec. Dir.
Founded: 1970. **Members:** 350. **Description:** Represents veterinarians specializing in animal reproduction. Advances knowledge, education, and services in theriogenology. Acts as certifying agency for theriogenologists. Sponsors scientific programs. Conducts educational programs. **Awards:** Theriogenologist of the Year. **Frequency:** annual. **Type:** recognition. **Programs:** Mentorship. **Affiliated With:** Society for Theriogenology. **Publications:** *Newsletter of ACT*, bimonthly. **Price:** free. **Circulation:** 350 ● Directory, annual. **Conventions/Meetings:** annual conference, held in conjunction with the Society for Theriogenology (exhibits) ● periodic symposium, held in conjunction with annual conference some years.

16412 ■ American College of Veterinary Anesthesiologists (ACVA)
c/o Dr. Lydia Donaldson, Exec. Sec.
PO Box 1100
Middleburg, VA 20118
E-mail: ldonldsn@earthlink.net
URL: http://www.acva.org
Contact: Dr. Lydia Donaldson, Exec. Sec.
Founded: 1975. **Description:** Veterinary anesthesiologists and other individuals with an interest in the field. Promotes high standards of practice in veterinary anesthesiology; facilitates continuing professional development of members. Establishes practice guidelines and certification criteria; conducts examinations; bestows certification. Advises the American Veterinary Medical Association regarding accreditation of veterinary anesthesiology training programs. **Telecommunication Services:** electronic mail, execdir@acva.org. **Publications:** *Veterinary Anaesthesia and Analgesia*, bimonthly. Journal. **Price:** $178.00 /year for individuals (the Americas); EUR 146.00 /year for individuals (Europe - Euro zone); 97.00 /year for individuals (Europe - non Euro zone); 106.00 /year for individuals (rest of the world). ISSN: 1467-2987. **Advertising:** accepted.

16413 ■ American College of Veterinary Dermatology (ACVD)
c/o Kim Boyanowski, DVM
1411 El Camino Real
Redwood City, CA 94063
Ph: (650)365-6826
Fax: (650)365-6858
E-mail: kboyanowski@yahoo.com
URL: http://www.acvd.org
Contact: Kim Boyanowski DVM, Contact
Founded: 1982. **Members:** 133. **Membership Dues:** full, $150 (annual). **Staff:** 1. **Description:** Specialists in veterinary dermatology who have satisfied examination requirements; individuals with national reputation and standing are charter diplomates. Promotes veterinary dermatology and enhances the competency of professionals in the field. Seeks to develop guidelines for postdoctoral education and to establish experience prerequisites for certification in veterinary dermatology. Administers examinations and certifies veterinarians as veterinary dermatology specialists. Encourages research and other contributions in areas of pathogenesis, diagnosis, therapy, prevention, and control of diseases affecting the skin of animals. Authorizes training programs in the field. **Awards:** ACVD Award of Excellence. **Frequency:** annual. **Type:** monetary. **Recipient:** for excellence in research, teaching, and service in the field of veterinary dermatology. **Committees:** Credentials; Education; Examination. **Affiliated With:** American Veterinary Medical Association. **Conventions/Meetings:** annual conference (exhibits).

16414 ■ American College of Veterinary Emergency and Critical Care (ACVECC)
c/o Dr. Armelle de Laforcade, DVM, Exec. Sec.
Tufts Cummings School of Veterinary Medicine
200 Westboro Rd.
North Grafton, MA 01536
Ph: (508)839-5395 (508)887-4415
E-mail: armelle.delaforcade@tufts.edu
URL: http://www.acvecc.org
Contact: Dr. Armelle de Laforcade DVM, Exec. Sec.
Founded: 1989. **Members:** 179. **Membership Dues:** individual, $350 (annual). **Staff:** 2. **Budget:** $75,000. **Description:** Aims to promote advancement of practice in the field of veterinary emergency and critical care medicine; establish requirements and foster development of residency and alternative training programs for post-doctoral education and experience prerequisite to certification in the specialty of Veterinary Emergency and Critical Care Medicine; to examine and certify veterinarians as specialists in Veterinary Emergency and Critical Care Medicine; to encourage research and other contributions to knowledge relating to diagnosis, therapy, prevention and control of animal disease requiring emergency or critical care management; to promote communication and dissemination of knowledge relating to veterinary emergency and critical care medicine and to recognize individuals for outstanding contributions to the specialty. **Awards:** ACVECC Scientific Achievement Award. **Frequency:** annual. **Type:** recognition. **Recipient:** for outstanding scientific contributions to some aspect of veterinary emergency and critical care ● Research Grant. **Frequency:** annual. **Type:** grant. **Recipient:** for research in veterinary emergency and critical care. **Publications:** Journal of Veterinary Emergency and Critical Care, quarterly. Reviews articles of interest in the field. **Advertising:** accepted. Alternate Formats: CD-ROM; online. Also Cited As: JVECC. **Conventions/Meetings:** annual International Veterinary Emergency and Critical Care Symposium - international conference (exhibits) - September.

16415 ■ American College of Veterinary Internal Medicine (ACVIM)
1997 Wadsworth Blvd., Ste.A
Lakewood, CO 80214-5293
Ph: (303)231-9933
Free: (800)245-9081
Fax: (303)231-0880

E-mail: acvim@acvim.org
URL: http://www.acvim.org
Contact: Ms. June Pooley, Exec. Dir.
Founded: 1972. **Members:** 1,434. **Staff:** 6. **Budget:** $1,500,000. **Description:** Veterinarians certified in internal medicine and related specialties such as cardiology, neurology, and oncology. Works to advance the scope and ideals of veterinary internal medicine and to increase the competence of those practicing in the field. Issues certifying diplomas. **Committees:** Appeals; Credentials; Examination; Forum; Residency Training. **Affiliated With:** American Veterinary Medical Association. **Publications:** ACVIM Proceedings, annual. Contains papers submitted by speakers at annual conference. **Price:** $49.00 in U.S.; $49.00 outside U.S. Alternate Formats: CD-ROM ● Journal of Veterinary Internal Medicine, bimonthly. **Price:** $60.00 /year for individuals in U.S.; $80.00 /year for individuals outside U.S.; $500.00 /year for institutions in U.S.; $525.00 /year for institutions outside U.S. **Conventions/Meetings:** annual meeting (exhibits) - 2008 June 4-7, San Antonio, TX; 2009 June 3-6, Montreal, QC, Canada; 2010 June 9-12, Anaheim, CA.

16416 ■ American College of Veterinary Ophthalmologists (ACVO)
PO Box 1311
Meridian, ID 83680
Ph: (208)466-7624
Fax: (208)466-7693
E-mail: office06@acvo.org
URL: http://www.acvo.com
Contact: Stacee Daniel, Exec. Dir.
Founded: 1969. **Members:** 245. **Membership Dues:** individual, $10 (annual). **Staff:** 2. **Description:** Represents veterinarians certified by examination in veterinary ophthalmology. Works to continue education, research, and practice in veterinary ophthalmology; establishment of standards of training and experience; recognition of individuals who have fulfilled such standards; certification of qualified veterinarians. **Publications:** Directory of Diplomates, annual. **Price:** included in membership dues. **Circulation:** 245. **Advertising:** accepted. Alternate Formats: online ● Veterinary Ophthalmology, bimonthly. Journal. Contains articles written by academic researchers, specialists and general practitioners with a strong ophthalmology interest. **Price:** $97.00 /year for members in U.S.; $146.00 /year for nonmembers in U.S.; $65.00 /year for institutions. ISSN: 1463-5216. **Conventions/Meetings:** annual meeting and seminar ● annual conference (exhibits) - 2007 Oct. 21-28, Waikoloa, HI; 2008 Oct. 15-18, Boston, MA; 2009 Nov. 4-7, Chicago, IL.

16417 ■ American College of Veterinary Pathologists (ACVP)
2810 Crossroads Dr., Ste.3800
Madison, WI 53718-7961
Ph: (608)443-2466
Fax: (608)443-2474
E-mail: info@acvp.org
URL: http://www.acvp.org
Contact: Wendy Coe, Exec. Dir.
Founded: 1949. **Members:** 1,450. **Membership Dues:** regular, $200 (annual) ● emeritus, $55 (annual). **Staff:** 6. **Budget:** $500,000. **Description:** Comprised of specialists in veterinary pathology (origin, nature, and course of diseases in animals). Aims to further scientific progress in the specialty of veterinary pathology; to establish standards of training and experience for qualification of specialists in veterinary pathology; to further the recognition of such qualified specialists by suitable certification and other means. Recognized as the certifying agency for the specialty of veterinary pathology in the U.S. and Canada. Conducts specialized education programs and certifying exams. **Committees:** Editorial; Examination. **Publications:** American College of Veterinary Pathologists—Newsletter, quarterly. Covers developments in veterinary pathology; also includes association news, calendar of events, obituaries, and listing of employment opportunities. **Price:** included in membership dues. **Circulation:** 1,450. Alternate Formats: online ● Membership List, annual. Member-

ship Directory ● Veterinary Pathology: An International Journal of Natural and Experimental Disease in Animals, bimonthly. Includes book reviews and periodic special supplements on a scientific topic. **Price:** $75.00/year. ISSN: 0300-9858. **Circulation:** 1,700. **Advertising:** accepted ● Proceedings, annual. **Conventions/Meetings:** annual meeting (exhibits).

16418 ■ American College of Veterinary Radiology (ACVR)
PO Box 8820
Harrisburg, PA 17105-8820
Ph: (717)558-7865
Fax: (717)558-7841
E-mail: administration@acvr.org
URL: http://www.acvr.org
Contact: Dr. Robert D. Pechman Jr., Exec. Dir.
Founded: 1964. **Members:** 215. **Membership Dues:** diplomate, $150 (annual). **Staff:** 2. **Budget:** $40,000. **Description:** Diplomate members (215) are veterinarians certified by the college in veterinary radiology; individuals distinguished in radiological science but who are not certified veterinary radiologists. Works to advance the art and science of radiology. Certifies candidates who have demonstrated proficiency in veterinary radiology. Encourages the development of teaching personnel and training facilities in veterinary radiology. Aids in the evaluation of residencies and fellowships in veterinary radiology under consideration by the Council on Education of the American Veterinary Medical Association. Advises veterinarians who desire certification in veterinary radiology. Conducts continuing education seminars in conjunction with other veterinary organizations. **Libraries:** Type: reference. **Holdings:** archival material, business records. **Awards:** Research Grant. **Frequency:** annual. **Type:** grant ● Resident Authored Paper. **Frequency:** annual. **Type:** recognition. **Recipient:** for best resident-authored paper. **Special Interest Groups:** Nuclear Medicine; Radiation Oncology; Veterinary Ultrasound. **Formerly:** (1969) American Board of Veterinary Radiology. **Publications:** Veterinary Radiology and Ultrasound, bimonthly. Journal. Covers diagnostic and therapeutic radiology, ultrasound, MR, CT, and scintigraphy. **Price:** included in membership dues; $78.00 /year for institutions. ISSN: 0196-3627. **Advertising:** accepted ● Brochure. **Conventions/Meetings:** annual conference, held in conjunction with the Radiology Society of North America (exhibits).

16419 ■ American College of Veterinary Surgeons (ACVS)
11 N Washington St., Ste.720
Rockville, MD 20850
Ph: (301)610-2000
Fax: (301)610-0371
E-mail: acvs@acvs.org
URL: http://www.acvs.org
Contact: Ann T. Loew EdM, Exec. Dir.
Founded: 1965. **Members:** 1,150. **Membership Dues:** certified veterinary surgeon, $400 (annual). **Staff:** 6. **Budget:** $1,250,000. **Description:** Acts as certification board for veterinary surgeons. **Publications:** ACVS Newsletter, 3/year. **Price:** included in membership dues. **Circulation:** 1,700. **Advertising:** accepted ● American College of Veterinary Surgeons—Directory of Diplomates, biennial. Membership Directory. Includes photographic and biographical information on each member; includes alphabetical name and geographic region indexes. **Price:** included in membership dues. **Advertising:** accepted ● Veterinary Surgery, bimonthly. Journal. Presents clinical and research papers on veterinary surgery; topics include surgical techniques and management of the surgical patient. **Price:** $156.00 /year for individuals; $256.00 /year for institutions. **Advertising:** accepted. Alternate Formats: online ● Who is the ACVS?, annual. Brochure. **Conventions/Meetings:** annual ACVS Veterinary Symposium - meeting, veterinary surgery continuing education (exhibits).

16420 ■ American Heartworm Society (AHS)
PO Box 667
Batavia, IL 60510
Ph: (630)262-1997

Fax: (630)208-8398
E-mail: info@heartwormsociety.org
URL: http://www.heartwormsociety.org
Contact: Eve C. Larocca, Exec. Dir.
Founded: 1974. **Members:** 1,200. **Membership Dues:** individual, $35 (annual) ● individual, $70 (biennial) ● individual, $105 (triennial). **Staff:** 2. **Description:** Veterinarians, physicians, parasitologists, and other scientists. Promotes scientific programs for the study of heartworm disease, caused by the filarial parasite, dilofilaria immitis. Encourages standardization of procedures for diagnosis, treatment, and prevention of heartworm disease. Keeps members abreast of current research and recent developments concerning the disease. **Publications:** *Heartworm Disease in Dogs.* Brochure. **Price:** $20.00 for members (100 copies); $25.00 for nonmembers (500 copies) ● *Recent Advances in Heartworm Disease; Symposium '98.* Proceedings ● Bulletin, quarterly. Contains topical commentary, synopsis of clinical and scientific literature and society news. **Price:** included in membership dues; $38.00 /year for nonmembers. **Circulation:** 1,200. **Advertising:** accepted. Alternate Formats: online. **Conventions/Meetings:** triennial symposium and meeting, lectures, abstracts and panel discussions (exhibits).

16421 ■ American Holistic Veterinary Medical Association (AHVMA)

2218 Old Emmorton Rd.
Bel Air, MD 21015
Ph: (410)569-0795
Fax: (410)569-2346
E-mail: office@ahvma.org
URL: http://www.ahvma.org
Contact: Dr. Carvel G. Tiekert, Exec. Dir.
Founded: 1982. **Members:** 1,000. **Membership Dues:** graduate veterinarian in U.S., $135 (annual) ● graduate veterinarian in Canada, $150 (annual) ● graduate veterinarian outside U.S. and Canada, $165 (annual) ● retired in U.S., $67 (annual) ● retired in Canada, $82 (annual) ● retired outside U.S. and Canada, $97 (annual) ● subscriber in U.S., $95 (annual) ● subscriber in Canada, $110 (annual) ● subscriber outside U.S. and Canada, $125 (annual) ● student in U.S., $20 (annual) ● student in Canada, $35 (annual) ● student outside U.S. and Canada, $50 (annual) ● 2nd-year graduate veterinarian in U.S., $67 (annual) ● 2nd-year graduate veterinarian in Canada, $82 (annual) ● 2nd-year graduate veterinarian outside U.S. and Canada, $97 (annual). **Staff:** 4. **Budget:** $125,000. **Description:** Veterinarians and others interested in exploring alternative approaches in veterinary medicine, including clinical nutrition, homeopathy, and herbal medicine. **Formerly:** (1985) American Veterinary Holistic Medical Association. **Publications:** *Journal of the AHVMA,* quarterly. Includes association news and book reviews. **Price:** included in membership dues. **Circulation:** 1,000. **Advertising:** accepted. Also Cited As: *American Holistic Veterinary Medical Association—Newsletter.* **Conventions/Meetings:** annual conference (exhibits).

16422 ■ American Pre-Veterinary Medical Association (APVMA)

c/o Arvind Badrinarayanan, Sec.
303 W Green St.
Champaign, IL 61820
E-mail: vet.arvind@gmail.com
URL: http://www.apvma.us
Contact: Arvind Badrinarayanan, Sec.
Membership Dues: club with 20 members or less, $20 (annual) ● club with greater than 20 members ($1 per member), $1 (annual) ● non-club affiliated ($10 per individual), $10 (annual). **Description:** Brings together pre-veterinary students from all across America. Promotes and stimulates interest in the field of veterinary medicine. Provides its member clubs with sources of information regarding sister clubs and the field of veterinary medicine. **Awards:** Outstanding Club Project Award. **Frequency:** annual. **Type:** recognition. **Recipient:** for the best club project ● Outstanding Community Service Award. **Frequency:** annual. **Type:** recognition. **Recipient:** for innovative and effective community service project ●

Outstanding Senior Award. **Frequency:** annual. **Type:** recognition. **Recipient:** for students belonging to APVMA member pre-veterinary clubs, who have senior status within their institution ● **Frequency:** annual. **Type:** scholarship. **Recipient:** for students belonging to APVMA member pre-veterinary clubs. **Publications:** Newsletter. Alternate Formats: online.

16423 ■ American Society of Veterinary Ophthalmology (ASVO)

1416 W Liberty Ave.
Stillwater, OK 74075
E-mail: membership@asvo.org
URL: http://www.asvo.org
Contact: Dr. Virginia Schultz DVM, Sec.
Founded: 1957. **Members:** 250. **Membership Dues:** veterinarian, $40 (annual) ● student, $25 (annual). **Description:** Veterinarians with a special interest in ophthalmology (the science of the eye and its diseases). Sponsors research proposal competition. **Computer Services:** Mailing lists. **Publications:** Directory, annual ● Newsletter, periodic ● Proceedings, annual. **Conventions/Meetings:** annual meeting, in conjunction with American Animal Hospital Association (exhibits).

16424 ■ American Veterinarian Service Association (AVSA)

7115 W North Ave., Ste.272
Oak Park, IL 60302
Ph: (708)453-0080
Contact: Richard Johnson, VP
Founded: 1985. **Members:** 79,009. **Membership Dues:** professional, $95 (annual). **Staff:** 10. **Description:** Veterinarians ad animal care professionals. Seeks to increase members' public visibility and professional influence. Provides trademark licensing and product and service endorsement services to support members' activities. A platform for veterinarians and animal care professionals to learn about new medicines and receive the latest animal health care advice. **Libraries: Type:** not open to the public. **Holdings:** 10,000. **Subjects:** veterinarian. **Awards:** Vet of the Year. **Frequency:** annual. **Type:** recognition. **Computer Services:** Mailing lists, ad banner advertising opportunities on (468X60 pixel) AUSA "website". Also Known As: (2000) Veterinarian Association. **Publications:** *AUSA Journal,* quarterly. **Price:** included in membership dues. **Circulation:** 70,000. **Advertising:** accepted. Alternate Formats: online. **Conventions/Meetings:** annual convention (exhibits).

16425 ■ American Veterinary Chiropractic Association (AVCA)

442154 E 140 Rd.
Bluejacket, OK 74333
Ph: (918)784-2231
Fax: (918)784-2675
E-mail: avcainfo@junct.com
URL: http://www.animalchiropractic.org
Contact: Paul D. Rowan DVM, Chm.
Founded: 1989. **Members:** 550. **Membership Dues:** doctor associate, $300 (annual) ● non-doctor associate, $100 (annual) ● life (AVCA certified professional), $1,500 ● life (associate professional), $2,000 ● life (non-doctor associate), $1,500 ● professional certified, $200 (annual). **Description:** Serves as a professional association that sets animal chiropractic education standards, board examinations and legislative issues. **Libraries: Type:** reference.

16426 ■ American Veterinary Dental Society (AVDS)

PO Box 803
Fayetteville, TN 37334
Ph: (931)438-0238
Free: (800)332-AVDS
Fax: (931)433-8289
E-mail: avds@avds-online.org
URL: http://www.avds-online.org
Contact: Dee Ann Walker CAE, Exec. Sec.
Founded: 1976. **Members:** 1,000. **Membership Dues:** in U.S., $85 (annual) ● in Canada, $95 (annual) ● outside North America, $100 (annual). **Regional Groups:** 1. **Description:** Dentists, veterinar-

ians, and others dedicated to the scientific advancement of dentistry for animals. Conducts continuing education seminars on veterinary dentistry; serves as a forum for exchange of experience and ideas. **Computer Services:** database. **Publications:** *Journal of Veterinary Dentistry,* quarterly. Includes association news and clinical reports. **Price:** included in membership dues; $195.00 /year for nonmembers in U.S.; $235.00 /year for nonmembers outside U.S. **Circulation:** 750. **Advertising:** accepted ● Membership Directory, periodic ● Membership Directory ● Proceedings. **Price:** $45.00. **Conventions/Meetings:** annual conference and seminar.

16427 ■ American Veterinary Medical Association (AVMA)

1931 N Meacham Rd., Ste.100
Schaumburg, IL 60173
Ph: (847)925-8070
Free: (800)248-2862
Fax: (847)925-1329
E-mail: avmainfo@avma.org
URL: http://www.avma.org
Contact: Diane A. Fagen, Librarian
Founded: 1863. **Members:** 74,000. **Membership Dues:** active, $250 (annual) ● associate/affiliate, $225 (annual). **Staff:** 100. **Budget:** $14,000,000. **State Groups:** 52. **Local Groups:** 433. **Description:** Professional society of veterinarians. Conducts educational and research programs. Provides placement service. Sponsors American Veterinary Medical Association Foundation (also known as AVMF Foundation) and Educational Commission for Foreign Veterinary Graduates. Compiles statistics. Accredits veterinary medical education programs and veterinary technician education programs. **Libraries: Type:** reference. **Computer Services:** database, Noah ● mailing lists. **Boards:** American Board of Veterinary Specialties. **Committees:** Animal Agriculture Liaison; Animal Welfare; Aquatic Veterinary Medicine; Clinical Practitioners Advisory; Disaster and Emergency Issues; Educational Commission for Foreign Veterinary Graduates; Environmental Issues; Food Safety Advisory; Human-Animal Bond; Political Action; Veterinary Technician Education and Activities. **Councils:** Biologic and Therapeutic Agents; Education; Judicial; Public Health and Regulatory Medicine; Research; Veterinary Service. **Divisions:** Governmental Relations. **Sections:** Laboratory Animal Medicine; Large Animal; Poultry; Public Health; Regulatory Veterinary Medicine; Research; Small Animal. **Formerly:** (1988) United States Veterinary Medical Association. **Publications:** *American Journal of Veterinary Research,* monthly. **Price:** $205.00 /year for individuals in U.S.; $215.00 /year for individuals outside U.S.; $25.00/copy in U.S.; $30.00/ copy outside U.S. **Advertising:** accepted. Also Cited As: *AJVR* ● *AVMA Convention Notes,* annual ● *AVMA Disaster Preparedness & Response Guide.* Handbook ● *AVMA Membership Directory and Resource Manual,* annual. Contains list of members, governance documents, related professional organizations, related industry organizations, related governmental units. **Price:** $150.00. ISSN: 0898-6657. **Circulation:** 73,000 ● *Economic Report on Veterinarians and Veterinary Practices,* semiannual ● *Journal of the American Veterinary Medical Association,* semimonthly. **Price:** $165.00 /year for nonmembers in U.S.; $185.00 /year for nonmembers outside U.S.; $15.00/copy for members in U.S.; $20.00/copy for members outside U.S. **Advertising:** accepted. Also Cited As: *JAVMA* ● *US Pet Ownership and Demographic Sourcebook,* semiannual. **Conventions/Meetings:** annual meeting, with scientific program (exhibits).

16428 ■ American Veterinary Society of Animal Behavior (AVSAB)

c/o Lisa Radosta, DVM, Sec.-Treas.
PO Box 210636
Royal Palm Beach, FL 33421-0636
Fax: (561)795-8537
E-mail: avsabe@yahoo.com
URL: http://www.avsabonline.org
Contact: Lisa Radosta DVM, Sec.-Treas.
Founded: 1975. **Members:** 440. **Membership Dues:** regular, affiliate - with PhD in animal behavior or

closely related field, $40 (annual) ● student, $7 (annual). **Description:** Veterinarians and veterinary students. Promotes inquiry and research into animal behavior. Seeks to advance ethological knowledge regarding the care and utilization of captive, domesticated, and free-living animals. Promotes and facilitates the exchange of information among those concerned with animal behavior and well-being; encourages discussion on veterinary aspects of animal behavior and the publication of materials in the field. **Awards:** Student Excellence in Applied Animal Research. **Frequency:** annual. **Type:** monetary. **Committees:** Education; Future Directions; Human/Animal Bond; Laboratory Animal; Large Animal; Small Animal. **Formerly:** (1984) American Society of Veterinary Ethology. **Publications:** Newsletter, quarterly. **Price:** included in membership dues; $30.00 /year for nonmembers. **Circulation:** 500. **Conventions/Meetings:** annual conference, in conjunction with the American Veterinary Medical Association.

16429 ■ Animal Health Foundation (AHF)
3615 Bassett Rd.
Pacific, MO 63069
E-mail: info@ahf-laminitis.org
URL: http://www.animalhealthfoundation.com
Contact: Donald Walsh, Contact
Founded: 1984. **Members:** 1,000. **Membership Dues:** donation, $10. **Description:** Represents individuals interested in finding the causes, treatments, and cure for the crippling equine disease laminitis/founder syndrome. (Laminitis is an inflammation of the laminae, the semi-rigid internal supporting structures of the horse's foot; founder is the crippling result of laminitis in which the coffin bone in the horse's foot puts pressure on the sole of the foot, and sometimes actually penetrates the sole.) These ailments affect horses of any age or breed, and are counted as the second ranking disease leading to the need to euthanize horses. Supports extensive research and collects range of related data. **Libraries: Type:** reference. **Holdings:** reports. **Awards: Type:** grant. **Publications:** AHF Newsletter, periodic. **Circulation:** 2,000 ● Brochure.

16430 ■ Association of Avian Veterinarians - USA (AAV)
PO Box 811720
Boca Raton, FL 33481
Ph: (561)393-8901
Fax: (561)393-8902
E-mail: aavctrlofc@aav.org
URL: http://www.aav.org
Contact: Adina Rae Freedman CAE, Exec. Dir.
Founded: 1980. **Members:** 3,300. **Membership Dues:** active, $140-$155 (annual) ● veterinary technician, $85-$100 (annual) ● student, $45-$60 (annual). **Staff:** 5. **Budget:** $450,000. **Multinational. Description:** Veterinarians; veterinary students; breeders and importers of captive birds. Works to further knowledge in the field of avian medicine; conducts educational programs. Organizes student chapters. Operates speakers' bureau. **Publications:** AAV Membership Directory, annual ● Journal of the Avian Medicine Surgery, quarterly. Includes referred articles and practice tips. **Price:** included in membership dues; $70.00 /year for nonmembers. **Advertising:** accepted ● Proceedings of Annual Seminars ● Technical Proceedings, annual ● Also publishes information packets. **Conventions/Meetings:** annual conference (exhibits) - always August or September.

16431 ■ Association of Exotic Mammal Veterinarians (AEMV)
PO Box 396
Weare, NH 03281-0396
Fax: (603)529-4980
E-mail: info@aemv.org
URL: http://aemv.org
Contact: Angela M. Lennox DVM, Pres.
Founded: 2000. **Membership Dues:** veterinarian, $95 (annual) ● veterinary resident, intern, technician, $70 (annual) ● veterinary student, $50 (annual). **Description:** Represents veterinarians interested in advancing the veterinary care of ferrets, guinea pigs,

rodents and other small exotic mammals. Advocates for the advancement of veterinary education. Assists veterinarians interested in avian and zoo animal medicine. **Telecommunication Services:** electronic mail, birddr@aol.com. **Publications:** Journal of Exotic Mammal Medicine and Surgery. **Price:** included in membership dues. Also Cited As: JEMMS ● Seminar in Exotic Pet Medicine, quarterly. Newsletter. **Price:** included in membership dues. **Conventions/Meetings:** annual conference, with business meeting (exhibits).

16432 ■ Association of Reptilian and Amphibian Veterinarians (ARAV)
c/o Wilbur B. Amand, VMD, Exec. Dir.
PO Box 605
Chester Heights, PA 19017
Ph: (610)892-4812
Fax: (610)892-4813
E-mail: aravets@aol.com
URL: http://www.arav.org
Contact: Wilbur B. Amand VMD, Exec. Dir.
Founded: 1991. **Members:** 1,250. **Membership Dues:** veterinary technician, $75 (annual) ● regular in North America, $115 (annual) ● veterinary student, $75 (annual) ● library/institution in North America, $145 (annual) ● veterinary technician outside North America, $90 (annual) ● regular outside North America, $130 (annual) ● veterinary student outside North America, $90 (annual) ● library/institution outside North America, $160 (annual). **Staff:** 1. **Budget:** $165,000. **Multinational. Description:** Veterinarians specializing in the treatment of reptiles and amphibians. Seeks to advance the study and practice of reptilian and amphibian veterinary medicine; and promotes ongoing professional development of members. Serves as a clearinghouse on reptilian and amphibian veterinary medicine; sponsors educational programs; and facilitates communication and cooperation among members. **Awards:** Lifetime Achievement Award. **Frequency:** periodic. **Type:** recognition. **Committees:** Research and Conservation. **Publications:** Journal of Herpetological Medicine and Surgery, quarterly. **Price:** included in membership dues. ISSN: 1529-9651. **Circulation:** 1,200. **Advertising:** accepted. Alternate Formats: online. Also Cited As: ARAV Bulletin ● Membership Directory. **Price:** included in membership dues. Alternate Formats: online. **Conventions/Meetings:** annual conference (exhibits).

16433 ■ Association of Shelter Veterinarians (ASV)
c/o Julie D. Dinnage, DVM
MSPCA
350 S Huntington Ave.
Boston, MA 02130
E-mail: jdddvm@sheltervet.org
URL: http://www.sheltervet.org
Contact: Julie D. Dinnage DVM, Contact
Members: 300. **Membership Dues:** active, student chapter, $25 (annual) ● student, $5 (annual) ● affiliate, $15 (annual). **Multinational. Description:** Serves as an advocate for the profession of shelter veterinary medicine. Aims to advance the practice of shelter medicine. Seeks to further veterinary education and research, with focus on animals' health in a shelter environment. **Publications:** Shelter Veterinarian. Newsletter. **Price:** included in membership dues. Alternate Formats: online ● Membership Directory. **Price:** for members only.

16434 ■ Association of Veterinary Hematology and Transfusion Medicine (AVHTM)
c/o Dr. Larry DeLuca, Exec. Dir.
2509 N Campbell Ave., No. 304
Tucson, AZ 85719-3304
E-mail: larry@sunstates.org
URL: http://www.vetmed.wsu.edu/org-AVHTM/index.asp
Contact: Dr. Larry DeLuca, Exec. Dir.
Membership Dues: individual, $35 (annual) ● institutional, $75 (annual). **Description:** Aims to advance the scientific study of veterinary hematology and transfusion medicine. Promotes and supports

education and research in veterinary transfusion medicine and hematology. Facilitates exchange of information among its members and other health professionals who have a special interest in veterinary hematology and transfusion medicine.

16435 ■ Association for Women Veterinarians (AWV)
c/o Magnolia Association Management Affiliates
310 N Indian Hill Blvd.
Box 337
Claremont, CA 91711-4611
E-mail: mama.la@verizon.net
URL: http://www.vet.ksu.edu/AWV/index.htm
Contact: Heidi Hulon, Sec.
Founded: 1947. **Members:** 400. **Membership Dues:** full, $50 (annual) ● veterinary student/retiree, $5 (annual) ● new graduate/associate, $10 (annual). **Description:** Works to support veterinary medicine by providing leadership in women's issues. **Awards:** AWV Service Award. **Frequency:** annual. **Type:** recognition. **Recipient:** to individual contributing to the advancement of women in veterinary medicine ● Outstanding Woman Veterinarian. **Frequency:** annual. **Type:** recognition. **Recipient:** for contributions to veterinary medicine ● Student Scholarship. **Frequency:** annual. **Type:** scholarship. **Recipient:** for second or third year veterinary students. **Committees:** Archives; Historical; Outstanding Woman Veterinarian; Publicity; Scholarship; Survey. **Formerly:** (1981) Women's Veterinary Medical Association. **Publications:** AWV Bulletin, quarterly. **Price:** included in membership dues; $10.00 /year for nonmembers. **Advertising:** accepted ● Roster of Women Veterinarians, periodic. Directory. **Conventions/Meetings:** annual convention, held in conjunction with American Veterinary Medical Association (exhibits).

16436 ■ Association of Zoo Veterinary Technicians (AZVT)
c/o Mr. Joel Pond, CVT, Exec.Dir.
Lincoln Park Zoo
2001 N Clark St.
Chicago, IL 60614-6064
Ph: (312)742-7211
Fax: (312)742-7823
E-mail: jpond@lpzoo.org
URL: http://www.AZVT.org
Contact: Mr. Joel Pond CVT, Exec.Dir.
Founded: 1981. **Members:** 350. **Membership Dues:** active, associate, $35 (annual) ● subscribing, $17 (annual) ● institutional, $60 (annual). **Description:** Represents zoo veterinary technicians. **Libraries: Type:** not open to the public. **Holdings:** 22. **Subjects:** veterinary medicine. **Awards:** Laurie Page-Peck Scholarship. **Frequency:** annual. **Type:** scholarship. **Recipient:** for veterinary technician students with interest in zoo medicine; must write a paper for presentation at annual conference. **Computer Services:** database. **Publications:** AZVT News, quarterly. Newsletter. **Price:** included in membership dues. **Circulation:** 400. **Advertising:** accepted. Alternate Formats: online. **Conventions/Meetings:** annual conference (exhibits) - in fall.

16437 ■ Canine Cancer Awareness (CCA)
340 Oak Hill Rd.
Litchfield, ME 04350
E-mail: ccancerawareness@aol.com
URL: http://www.caninecancerawareness.org
Contact: Linda Desrosier, Pres./Treas.
Membership Dues: associate, $15 (annual) ● junior, $10 (annual). **Description:** Alerts and educates the general public about the prevalence of canine cancer, its effects and available treatment options. Increases public awareness through the distribution of printed educational materials. Promotes the Canine Cancer Awareness program and assists in fundraising efforts.

16438 ■ Center for Veterinary Medicine (CVM)
c/o Food and Drug Administration
Communications Staff
7519 Standish Pl., HFV-12
Rockville, MD 20855

Ph: (240)276-9300 (240)276-9000
Fax: (240)276-9115
E-mail: cvmhomep@cvm.fda.gov
URL: http://www.fda.gov/cvm/default.html
Contact: Dr. Stephen F. Sundlof, Dir.
Description: Regulates manufacture and distribution of food additives and drugs given to animals, including animals used for human foods, food additives, and drugs for pets. **Computer Services:** Information services, Veterinary Master Files. **Publications:** *FDA Veterinarian*, bimonthly. Newsletter. **Price:** $17.00/ year domestic; $23.80/year foreign. Alternate Formats: online ● *The Green Book*, annual. **Price:** $100.00 first copy; $75.00 additional copies to same name and address; $120.00 first copy, in Canada and other countries. Alternate Formats: online.

16439 ■ Conference of Research Workers in Animal Diseases (CRWAD)
c/o Dr. Robert P. Ellis, Exec. Dir.
Colorado State Univ.
Dept. of Microbiology, Immunology and Pathology
Microbiology Bldg., Rm. A 102
Fort Collins, CO 80523-1682
Ph: (970)491-5740
Fax: (970)491-1815
E-mail: robert.ellis@colostate.edu
URL: http://www.cvmbs.colostate.edu/microbiology/crwad/index.htm
Contact: Dr. Robert P. Ellis, Exec. Dir.
Founded: 1920. **Members:** 550. **Membership Dues:** regular, $70 (annual). **Staff:** 2. **Multinational. Description:** Represents research workers in animal diseases. **Awards:** Annual Meeting Dedicatee. **Frequency:** annual. **Type:** recognition. **Recipient:** for life members with significant contributions to CRWAD. **Computer Services:** Mailing lists. **Publications:** *Proceedings of the Annual Meeting—CRWAD*, annual. Journal. Contains abstracts presented at annual meeting. **Price:** $15.00/year. **Circulation:** 800. **Conventions/Meetings:** annual conference - always November.

16440 ■ Cornell Feline Health Center
Coll. of Veterinary Medicine
Cornell Univ., Box 13
Ithaca, NY 14853-6401
Ph: (607)253-3414
Free: (800)548-8937
Fax: (607)253-3419
URL: http://www.vet.cornell.edu/fhc
Contact: Dr. James R. Richards DVM, Dir.
Founded: 1975. **Members:** 6,000. **Membership Dues:** supporting, $40 (annual) ● international, $45 (annual) ● standard, $15 (annual). **Staff:** 6. **Description:** Professionals devoted to cats. Seeks to unravel the mysteries of feline health, nutrition, and behavior. Works to educate veterinarians and cat owners, and to aid veterinarians when new or unknown diseases occur. Provides educational programs. **Publications:** *CatWatch*, monthly. Newsletter. Informs cat fanciers of news on cat diseases and activities at the center. **Price:** free for members; $20.00 for nonmembers in U.S.; $26.00 for nonmembers in Canada; $42.00 for nonmembers overseas ● *The Cornell Book of Cats, Second Edition*. **Price:** $35.00 each ● *Cornell Veterinary Magazine* ● *Dog Watch*. Newsletter. **Price:** $39.00 /year for individuals ● *Feline Health Topics*, monthly ● *Pre-Veterinary*, bimonthly. Newsletters ● Annual Report, annual. Alternate Formats: online ● Brochures. **Conventions/Meetings:** seminar.

16441 ■ International Association for Aquatic Animal Medicine (IAAAM)
c/o Judy St. Leger, DVM, Membership Chair
500 Sea World Dr.
San Diego, CA 92109-7904
Ph: (619)225-4259
Fax: (619)226-3951
E-mail: membership@iaaam.org
URL: http://iaaam.org
Contact: Judy St. Leger DVM, Membership Chair
Founded: 1969. **Members:** 450. **Membership Dues:** full, $40 (annual) ● student, $25 (annual) ● institution/library, $60 (annual) ● sustaining, $250 (annual). **Multinational. Description:** Veterinarians, PhD's,

and marine biologists involved in aquatic animal medicine and husbandry. Works to advance the art of aquatic animal medicine; to promote the free exchange of knowledge in the interest of improving the health care and husbandry of domestic aquatic animals and the proper management of aquatic animal resources in the wild; to provide an organization in which interested and professionally qualified individuals can work together to achieve these objectives; to provide a setting in which the development of the practice of aquatic animal medicine may be facilitated and enhanced; to promote the application of veterinary medical principles to aquatic animal disease problems. **Committees:** Conservation; Interorganizational Liaison; Student Liaison. **Publications:** *Diagnostic Techniques in Aquatic Animal Medicine*. Booklet. Provides a review of the basic principles of traditional and novel techniques used by clinical and anatomic pathologists. ● *IAAAM Conference Proceedings*, annual. Contains annual conference abstracts. **Price:** included in membership dues; $40.00 for nonmembers. **Circulation:** 600. Alternate Formats: CD-ROM ● *IAAAM News*, 3/year. Newsletter. Includes association news, book reviews, calendar of events, and research updates. **Price:** included in membership dues ● Membership Directory, annual. Included in proceedings book. **Price:** free for members. **Conventions/Meetings:** annual conference (exhibits) - usually May.

16442 ■ International Embryo Transfer Society (IETS)
1111 N Dunlap Ave.
Savoy, IL 61874
Ph: (217)356-3182 (217)398-4697
Fax: (217)398-4119
E-mail: iets@assochq.org
URL: http://www.iets.org
Contact: Naida M. Loskutoff PhD, Pres.
Founded: 1974. **Members:** 1,100. **Membership Dues:** full/associate, $150 (annual) ● student, $70 (annual). **Staff:** 1. **Budget:** $180,000. **Description:** Veterinarians; researchers in reproductive physiology, animal science, genetics, endocrinology, and immunology; representatives of regulatory agencies such as government agencies and breed associations; sales representatives of drugs or equipment; students. Works to disseminate scientific and educational information; to promote more effective research; to foster and maintain high standards of education and ethics. Conducts Code Numbers to Identify Units Freezing Embryos Program, through which containers of frozen embryos are labeled with a permanent, recognized identification number. Sponsors exhibits of drugs and equipment used in embryo transfer. Conducts student competition to promote excellence in research. Maintains speakers' bureau. **Awards:** Pioneer Award. **Frequency:** annual. **Type:** recognition. **Recipient:** for early research in the field of embryo transfer. **Committees:** Companion Animal, Non-Domestic and Endangered Species (CANDES); Heath And Safety Advisory. **Affiliated With:** American Embryo Transfer Association. **Publications:** *IETS Manual* (in English, French, and Spanish). Manuals. Covers information on minimum sanitary standards for embryo transfer procedures. **Price:** $25.00/piece ● *IETS Newsletter*, quarterly ● *Proceedings of Annual Symposium and Conference*. **Conventions/Meetings:** annual conference and symposium (exhibits) - 2008 Jan. 5-9, Denver, CO; 2009 Jan. 3-6, New Orleans, LA.

16443 ■ International Society of Veterinary Dermatopathology (ISVD)
c/o Emily J. Walder, VMD, Treas.
626 Venice Blvd.
Venice, CA 90291
Fax: (310)574-3330
E-mail: ejwalder@gte.net
URL: http://www.isvd.org
Contact: Emily J. Walder VMD, Treas.
Membership Dues: regular, $50 (annual). **Multinational. Description:** Aims to advance the study of veterinary and comparative dermatopathology. Assists and coordinates the adaptation and implementation of emerging technologies for the diagnosis of

skin diseases in animals. Promotes training of pathology and dermatology residents in dermatopathology. Provides opportunities for graduate veterinarians to learn advanced techniques and new concepts in veterinary dermatopathology. **Awards:** ISVD Research Grants. **Frequency:** annual. **Type:** grant. **Recipient:** for research projects on veterinary dermatopathology. **Telecommunication Services:** electronic mail, vets@vetcutis.co.uk.

16444 ■ International Veterinary Acupuncture Society (IVAS)
PO Box 271395
Fort Collins, CO 80527-1395
Ph: (970)266-0666
Fax: (970)266-0777
E-mail: office@ivas.org
URL: http://www.ivas.org
Contact: Vikki Weber MBA, Exec. Dir.
Founded: 1974. **Membership Dues:** certified/associate, $140 (annual) ● affiliate, $85 (annual) ● student/retired, $40 (annual). **Staff:** 4. **Budget:** $750,000. **National Groups:** 6. **Multinational. Description:** Veterinarians and veterinary students. Encourages knowledge and research of the philosophy, technique, and practice of veterinary acupuncture. Fosters high standards in the field; promotes scientific investigation. Accumulates resources for scientific research and education; collects data concerning clinical and research cases where animals have been treated with acupuncture; disseminates information to veterinary students, practitioners, other scientific groups, and the public. Offers 120-contact hour basic veterinary acupuncture course; administers certification examination; also offers advanced traditional Chinese herbal veterinary medicine. **Libraries:** Type: not open to the public. **Holdings:** video recordings. **Subjects:** scientific, TCM veterinary acupuncture, herbal medicine. **Awards:** Research Grant. **Frequency:** annual. **Type:** grant. **Computer Services:** database, membership directory ● mailing lists. **Committees:** Education; Examination. **Also Known As:** IVAS. **Conventions/Meetings:** annual International Congress on Veterinary Acupuncture - conference, three-day professional meeting (exhibits).

16445 ■ International Veterinary Ultrasound Society (IVUSS)
PO Box 46391
Madison, WI 53744
Ph: (608)827-7239
Fax: (608)836-1745
E-mail: wallerk@svm.vetmed.wisc.edu
URL: http://www.ivuss.org
Contact: Kenneth R. Waller III, Treas./Webmaster
Founded: 2001. **Membership Dues:** general, $25 (annual). **Multinational. Description:** Represents private veterinary practitioners, academic veterinarians, diagnostic medical sonographers, and researchers interested in veterinary diagnostic ultrasound or echocardiography of domestic and zoological species. Promotes and encourages ultrasound research and education within the veterinary community. **Publications:** Proceedings.

16446 ■ Mid-Atlantic States Association of Avian Veterinarians (MASAAV)
610 N Main St.
Memorial Bldg., Ste.291
Blacksburg, VA 24060-3311
Ph: (540)951-2559
Fax: (540)953-0230
E-mail: office@masaav.org
URL: http://www.masaav.org
Contact: Dr. Keath L. Marx, Conference Co-Chair
Founded: 1979. **Members:** 125. **Membership Dues:** veterinarian, intern, resident, and associate (technician, nurse), $45 (annual) ● veterinary and veterinary technician student, $20 (annual). **Staff:** 1. **Regional Groups:** 1. **State Groups:** 9. **Multinational. Description:** Represents veterinary medicine, surgery or research professional and related student. Works to address the needs of the veterinarians and technicians interested in avian medicine. Discusses avian veterinary medicine and surgery to improve the health and longevity of avian patients. Provides conference

proceedings to libraries in third world countries. Conducts avian medicine and surgery educational conference. Makes donations for avian research. Keeps members informed regarding legislation of interest to the profession. **Libraries: Type:** not open to the public. **Holdings:** 25; articles, business records, monographs, papers, periodicals, reports. **Subjects:** annual avian medicine and surgery conference proceedings, association history, newsletters. **Awards:** E.L. Stubbs Research Grant. **Frequency:** periodic. **Type:** grant. **Recipient:** for researchers in avian medicine and surgery ● Pamela Slack Award for Excellence. **Frequency:** annual. **Type:** scholarship. **Recipient:** for a veterinary college junior. **Computer Services:** Online services, locator service for member veterinarians ● online services, resources from past Avian Medicine and Surgery conferences. **Committees:** Legislative; Newsletter. **Affiliated With:** American Veterinary Medical Association. **Publications:** *Conference Proceedings Book*, annual. Contains the annual conference on avian medicine and surgery proceedings. **Price:** $56.00 overseas air; $45.00 in North America. **Circulation:** 200. **Advertising:** accepted. Alternate Formats: online; CD-ROM. Also Cited As: *Proceedings MASAAV Annual Conference on Avian Medicine and Surgery* ● *MASAAView*, 3/year. Newsletter. **Circulation:** 200. **Advertising:** accepted. **Conventions/Meetings:** annual Avian Medicine and Surgery - conference, with continuing education for veterinary profession related personnel (exhibits) - every April for 2 1/2 days, Sunday through Tuesday. 2008 Apr. 28-30, Williamsburg, VA.

16447 ■ National Association of Federal Veterinarians (NAFV)
1910 Sunderland Pl. NW
Washington, DC 20036-1608
Ph: (202)223-4878
Fax: (202)223-4877
E-mail: vragan@nafv.org
URL: http://users.erols.com/nafv
Contact: Dr. Douglas L. Fulnechek, Pres.
Founded: 1918. **Members:** 1,600. **Membership Dues:** active, $260 (annual) ● affiliate (non-federal veterinarian), restricted, $45 (annual) ● affiliate (student), $20 (annual). **Staff:** 4. **Budget:** $200,000. **State Groups:** 30. **Description:** Professional society of veterinarians employed by the U.S. Government. Maintains speakers' bureau. **Awards:** Dr. Daniel E. Salmon Award. **Frequency:** annual. **Type:** monetary. **Recipient:** for federally employed veterinarians with not more than 10 years service. **Affiliated With:** American Veterinary Medical Association. **Formerly:** Bureau of Animal Industry Veterinarians; (1943) National Association of Bureau of Animal Industry Veterinarians. **Publications:** *Federal Veterinarian*, monthly. Newsletter. Includes abstracts, obituaries, federal regulatory and legislative news, and association news. **Price:** included in membership dues; $45.00 /year for nonmembers, in U.S.; $60.00 /year for nonmembers, outside U.S. ISSN: 0164-6257. **Circulation:** 1,500. **Advertising:** accepted ● *National Association of Federal Veterinarians—Directory*, annual. **Price:** $4.00 for members only. **Conventions/Meetings:** semiannual meeting, held in conjunction with AVMA in summer and held in conjunction with United States Animal Health Association in fall.

16448 ■ National Association of Veterinary Technicians in America (NAVTA)
PO Box 224
Battle Ground, IN 47920
Ph: (765)742-2216
Fax: (765)742-2216
E-mail: navta@navta.net
URL: http://www.navta.net
Contact: A. Patrick Navarre BS, Exec. Dir.
Membership Dues: active/associate, $50 (annual) ● student, $25 (annual). **Description:** Focuses on career growth and the advancement of the veterinary technology profession. **Publications:** *The NAVTA Journal*, quarterly. **Price:** included in membership dues. ISSN: 1552-4663. **Advertising:** accepted. Alternate Formats: online. **Conventions/Meetings:** Leadership Conference.

16449 ■ National Veterinarian Service Association (NVSA)
PO Box 35215
Chicago, IL 60707-0215
Ph: (708)453-0080
Fax: (708)453-0083
E-mail: nvsa@rentamark.com
Contact: Boyd J. Landry, Exec.Dir.
Membership Dues: individual, $25 (annual) ● business, $100 (annual) ● corporate sponsor, $250 (annual). **Description:** Promotes health care and grooming of animals. Disseminates information on products and services related to animal health care. Provides national certification, accreditation and recognition to members. **Computer Services:** database, member directory.

16450 ■ NMC
421 S Nine Mound Rd.
Verona, WI 53593
Ph: (608)848-4615
Fax: (608)848-4671
E-mail: anne@nmconline.org
URL: http://www.nmconline.org
Contact: Ms. Anne Saeman, Exec. Dir.
Founded: 1961. **Members:** 2,000. **Membership Dues:** individual, $90 (annual) ● student, $25 (annual). **Description:** Seeks to resolve the problem of bovine mastitis (inflammation of the udder) by developing and distributing factual information on mastitis control and encouraging mastitis research. Conducts research and education programs. Helps organize and coordinate the activities of state councils. **Committees:** Education; Research; Technical Advisory. **Formerly:** (2006) National Mastitis Council. **Publications:** *National Mastitis Council— Annual Meeting Proceedings*. Contains papers on topics related to the production of high quality milk and the prevention of mastitis. **Price:** included in membership dues; $15.00 for nonmembers. **Circulation:** 2,000 ● *Udder Topics*, bimonthly. Newsletter. Covers topics related to the production of high quality milk. **Price:** included in membership dues. **Circulation:** 2,000 ● Also publishes books, brochures, flyers, and monographs. **Conventions/Meetings:** annual meeting - 2008 Jan. 20, New Orleans, LA.

16451 ■ Options for Animals International (OFA)
4267 Virginia Rd.
Wellsville, KS 66092
Ph: (309)658-2920
Fax: (785)883-4710
URL: http://www.animalchiro.com
Contact: Dr. Dennis Eschbach, Owner/Chiropractor
Founded: 1988. **Members:** 120. **Multinational. Description:** Promotes chiropractic healthcare for animals and encourages interaction and communication with healthcare professionals and pet owners regarding current developments in non-invasive animal healthcare. Disseminates information; conducts and promotes research. Operates speakers' bureau. **Formerly:** (1998) Options for Animals Foundation; (2005) Options for Animals. **Publications:** *Options Newsletter*, bimonthly. Provides regular updates on future classes as well as schedules and OFA news. Alternate Formats: online.

16452 ■ Orthopedic Foundation for Animals (OFA)
2300 E Nifong Blvd.
Columbia, MO 65201-3806
Ph: (573)442-0418
Fax: (573)875-5073
E-mail: ofa@offa.org
URL: http://www.offa.org
Contact: Dr. G.G. Keller, Proj. Dir.
Founded: 1967. **Description:** National and local dog clubs and individual breeders. Acts as a clearinghouse for information on orthopedic diseases of animals, particularly hip dysplasia in dogs (a hereditary condition resulting in abnormal development of the hip joints). Develops a national control program through monitoring animals and conducting selective breeding and research. Conducts educational seminars; compiles statistics; sponsors a national referral

service for animal breeders. Maintains library of all breed canine pelvic radiographs. **Awards: Type:** grant. **Recipient:** for research. **Publications:** *The Advocate*, quarterly. Newsletter. Alternate Formats: online ● *Proceedings of Canine Hip Dysplasia Symposium and Workshop*.

16453 ■ Society for Theriogenology (SFT)
PO Box 3007
Montgomery, AL 36109
Ph: (334)395-4666
Fax: (334)270-3399
E-mail: charles@franzmgt.com
URL: http://www.therio.org
Contact: Charles Franz DVM, Exec. Dir.
Founded: 1954. **Members:** 2,508. **Membership Dues:** active, $110 (annual) ● student, $10 (annual). **Staff:** 4. **Budget:** $300,000. **Description:** Represents veterinarians. Promote the practice of qualified veterinarians examining animals for breeding soundness; facilitates these procedures by standardization of the criteria used by veterinarians; assembles and evaluates the measurements of breeding soundness from literature and from unbiased records accumulated from all sources and distribute this information to all members. (Theriogenology is a branch of veterinary medicine that deals with reproduction, veterinary obstetrics, gynecology, and seminology.) Distributes morphology stain for use in making breeding soundness evaluations and standard forms for use in recording such evaluations. Maintains speakers' bureau. **Awards:** Bartlett Award. **Frequency:** annual. **Type:** recognition. **Recipient:** for distinguished theriogenologist. **Telecommunication Services:** electronic mail, tammy@therio.org. **Formerly:** (1975) American Veterinary Society for the Study of Breeding Soundness. **Publications:** *Proceedings of Annual Meeting*, annual. **Price:** $50.00 ● *SFT News*, quarterly. Newsletter. Alternate Formats: online. **Conventions/Meetings:** annual meeting ● seminar.

16454 ■ Society for Tropical Veterinary Medicine (STVM)
c/o Dr. Thomas E. Walton, Sec.-Treas.
555 S Howes
Fort Collins, CO 80521
Ph: (970)490-8100
Fax: (970)490-8099
E-mail: stvmwalton@comcast.net
URL: http://www.soctropvetmed.org
Contact: Dr. Thomas E. Walton, Sec.-Treas.
Founded: 1978. **Membership Dues:** professional, $40 (annual) ● student, $20 (annual). **Multinational. Description:** Promotes the advancement of tropical veterinary medicine and related disciplines. Focuses on strategies to deal with established and changing patterns of diseases affecting animals in the tropics. Develops better diagnosis, treatment and control methods for tropical diseases of livestock species. **Awards:** Career Development Award. **Frequency:** biennial. **Type:** monetary. **Recipient:** for participating in a workshop in an area of tropical veterinary medicine ● Norval-Young Award. **Frequency:** biennial. **Type:** monetary. **Recipient:** for contribution to the understanding of tickborne diseases in the tropics. **Publications:** Newsletter, monthly. Alternate Formats: online ● Proceedings, biennial. Alternate Formats: online ● Membership Directory.

16455 ■ Society for Veterinary Medical Ethics (SVME)
c/o John S. Wright, DVM, Treas.
Coll. of Veterinary Medicine, Univ. of Minnesota
Dept. of Small Animal Clinical Sciences
C339 Veterinary Teaching Hosp.
1352 Boyd Ave.
St. Paul, MN 55108
Ph: (509)335-2956
Fax: (509)335-6725
E-mail: wrigh008@umn.edu
URL: http://www.vetmed.wsu.edu/org_SVME
Contact: John S. Wright DVM, Treas.
Founded: 1994. **Members:** 160. **Membership Dues:** regular, $25 (annual) ● student, $5 (annual). **Description:** Promotes teaching of ethical and value issues at colleges of veterinary medicine. Encourages ethi-

cal practices and appropriate professional conduct of veterinarians in all aspects of the profession. Maintains archives of pertinent documents and materials related to veterinary medicine. **Awards:** Dr. Robert Shomer Award. **Frequency:** annual. **Type:** recognition. **Recipient:** to an individual who has made a significant contribution to the field of veterinary medical ethics ● Society for Veterinary Medical Ethics Student Essay Award. **Frequency:** annual. **Type:** recognition. **Recipient:** for the best written essay dealing with specific veterinary issues. **Publications:** Newsletter, periodic. Alternate Formats: online.

16456 ■ Student American Veterinary Medical Association (SAVMA)
c/o AVMA
1931 N Meacham Rd., Ste.100
Schaumburg, IL 60173
Ph: (847)925-8070
Free: (800)248-2862
Fax: (847)925-1329
E-mail: savma@cvm.tamu.edu
URL: http://www.avma.org/savma/default.asp
Contact: Justin Sobota, Pres.
Founded: 1969. **Members:** 8,000. **Regional Groups:** 28. **Multinational. Description:** Seeks to advance science and art of veterinary medicine, including its relationship to agriculture and public health. **Awards:** AVMA Student Chapter Certificates. **Frequency:** annual. **Type:** recognition. **Recipient:** for SAVMA member graduates from the AVMA. **Committees:** Animal Welfare; Education and Licensure; Emerging Issues; Government Affairs; International Veterinary Student Relations; Multicultural Student Affairs; Native American Project; Public Relations; Symposium. **Publications:** *INTERVET*, quarterly. Journal. Alternate Formats: online ● Brochure. Alternate Formats: online. **Conventions/Meetings:** semiannual board meeting, for House of Delegates ● annual Educational Symposium - held in spring.

16457 ■ Student Veterinary Emergency and Critical Care Society (SVECCS)
c/o Desiree Broach, Externship Coor.
14 Chrisaren Ln.
Athens, GA 30601
E-mail: desib11@yahoo.com
URL: http://www.sveccs.org
Contact: Desiree Broach, Externship Coor.
Multinational. Description: Promotes the education and involvement of veterinary students in all aspects of emergency and critical care medicine. Fosters the advancement of knowledge to students of veterinary medicine and veterinary technician training. Raises public awareness and understanding of emergency medicine and critical care. Encourages the inclusion of emergency medicine and critical care topics in the curriculum for those colleges of veterinary medicine having student chapters. **Telecommunication Services:** electronic mail, dbroach@uga.edu ● electronic mail, mchickey@wisc.edu. **Publications:** *Vital Signs*. Newsletter. Alternate Formats: online.

16458 ■ United States Animal Health Association (USAHA)
PO Box K227
8100 Three Chopt Rd., Ste.203
Richmond, VA 23288
Ph: (804)285-3210
Fax: (804)285-3367
E-mail: usaha@usaha.org
URL: http://www.usaha.org
Contact: Linda B. Ragland, Contact
Founded: 1897. **Members:** 1,400. **Membership Dues:** official, allied organization, $600 (annual) ● individual, $120 (annual). **Staff:** 2. **Budget:** $150,000. **Regional Groups:** 4. **Description:** Veterinarians, livestock producers, and transportation and livestock companies concerned with the improvement of the health of livestock and poultry through disease control and eradication. Develop solutions for animal health issues. **Computer Services:** Mailing lists, of members. **Committees:** Animal Disease Surveillance; Animal Welfare; Environmental Residue; Epizootic Attack Plans; Food Safety; Foreign Animal Diseases; Infectious Diseases of Cattle; Infectious Diseases of

Horses; Livestock Identification; Parasitic Diseases; Pharmaceutical and Toxicology; Public Health and Environmental Quality; Transmissible Diseases of Poultry; Transmissible Diseases of Swine; Wild and Marine Life Diseases; Zoological Animals. **Absorbed:** National Assembly of Chief Livestock Health Officials. **Formerly:** Association of State Sanitary Boards; United States Livestock Sanitary Association. **Publications:** *Foreign Animal Diseases Diagnosis and Control*, quarterly. Newsletter ● Proceedings, annual. **Price:** $30.00. **Conventions/Meetings:** annual conference, veterinary medical supplies (exhibits) ● annual meeting.

16459 ■ Veterinary Botanical Medicine Association (VBMA)
c/o Jasmine C. Lyon, Exec. Dir.
1785 Poplar Dr.
Kennesaw, GA 30144
E-mail: office@vbma.org
URL: http://www.vbma.org
Contact: Jasmine C. Lyon, Exec. Dir.
Membership Dues: regular, associate, primary multiple (first member), $75 (annual) ● affiliate, $175 (annual) ● veterinary student, $10 (annual) ● multiple (for each additional member), $40 (annual) ● developing country, $25 (annual). **Description:** Promotes responsible herbal practice. Seeks to increase the professional acceptance of herbal medicine for animals. Encourages ethical clinical research in herbal veterinary medicine. Offers certification to both veterinary and non-veterinary herbalists. **Libraries: Type:** reference. **Holdings:** biographical archives, books, papers, periodicals. **Subjects:** herbal medicine in animals, general herbal medicine. **Publications:** *Journal of Veterinary Botanical Medicine*, quarterly. Contains articles about veterinary medical herbalism. Alternate Formats: online. Also Cited As: *JVBM* ● Membership Directory. Alternate Formats: online ● Newsletter. **Price:** included in membership dues. **Conventions/Meetings:** annual meeting - 2007 Oct. 6-7, Tulsa, OK.

16460 ■ Veterinary Cancer Society (VCS)
PO Box 1763
Spring Valley, CA 91979-1763
Ph: (619)474-8929
Fax: (619)474-8947
E-mail: vcs@cox.net
URL: http://www.vetcancersociety.org
Contact: Dr. Barbara J. McGehee, Exec. Dir.
Founded: 1974. **Members:** 800. **Membership Dues:** veterinarian, $100 (annual) ● intern, resident, student, technician, $25 (annual). **Staff:** 1. **Budget:** $100,000. **Description:** Veterinarians and others who have an interest in cancer in animals. Goals are to: achieve and maintain high standards of diagnosis, treatment, and prevention of animal cancers; advance interdisciplinary research in neoplastic diseases of animals; collect and disseminate information about animal tumors; conduct and evaluate studies, including cooperative clinical trials, of animal neoplasms. **Publications:** *VCS Newsletter*, quarterly. **Circulation:** 1,000. **Advertising:** accepted ● Directory, periodic. **Conventions/Meetings:** semiannual meeting and conference, on scientific information (exhibits) ● seminar.

16461 ■ Veterinary Hospital Managers Association (VHMA)
PO Box 2280
Alachua, FL 32616-2280
Ph: (518)433-8911
Free: (877)599-2707
Fax: (518)320-8575
E-mail: admin@vhma.org
URL: http://www.vhma.org
Contact: Christine Shupe, Exec. Dir.
Founded: 1981. **Membership Dues:** individual, consultant, $160 (annual) ● hospital, $260 (annual) ● student, $90 (annual). **Description:** Individuals involved in veterinary practice management. Seeks to advance the study, teaching, and practice of veterinary practice management. Serves as a forum for the exchange of information among members; sponsors continuing professional development

courses; formulates standards of ethics and practice for veterinary medical managers. **Programs:** Mentor. **Publications:** Newsletter, monthly. Features management articles. ● Membership Directory, biennial. **Conventions/Meetings:** annual conference and meeting ● annual meeting ● annual retreat.

16462 ■ Veterinary Institute of Integrative Medicine (VIIM)
c/o Julie Andrus, Educational Consultant
PO Box 740053
Arvada, CO 80006
Ph: (303)277-8227
E-mail: julieandrus@viim.org
URL: http://www.viim.org
Contact: Julie Andrus, Educational Consultant
Founded: 1998. **Description:** Seeks to advance the benefits of an integrative approach to animal healthcare. **Computer Services:** Online services, location of Holistic Vet. **Publications:** *Dictionary*. Contains terms used in holistic practices. Alternate Formats: online ● *Veterinary Desk Reference*. Manual. Contains a comprehensive manual for veterinarians using nutritional supplementation. **Price:** free for members. Alternate Formats: online ● Monographs. Alternate Formats: online.

16463 ■ Veterinary Orthopedic Society (VOS)
PO Box 705
Okemos, MI 48805-0705
Ph: (517)381-2468
Fax: (517)381-2468
E-mail: vosdvmsecretary@sbcglobal.net
URL: http://www.vosdvm.org
Contact: Maralyn R. Probst, Exec. Sec.
Founded: 1972. **Members:** 600. **Membership Dues:** international, $100 (annual) ● intern/resident, $25 (annual). **Staff:** 1. **Multinational. Description:** Veterinarians interested in orthopedic surgery. Promotes education and research in veterinary orthopedic surgery. Provides a forum for the exchange of ideas among veterinarians in academia, research, and practice. **Awards:** Hohn-Johnson Research Awards. **Frequency:** annual. **Type:** monetary. **Recipient:** for research ● Mark S. Bloomberg Memorial Resident Research Award. **Frequency:** annual. **Type:** grant. **Recipient:** for outstanding resident abstract submitted to the VOS scientific program. **Publications:** *Membership List*, periodic. Membership Directory ● *Veterinary and Comparative Orthopaedics and Traumatology*, quarterly. Journal. **Price:** $66.00 /year for members. Also Cited As: *VCOT* ● *VOS Newsletter*, annual. **Price:** included in membership dues ● Brochure, annual. Includes information of annual events. **Conventions/Meetings:** annual meeting and conference (exhibits) - 2008 Mar. 8-15, Big Sky, MT.

16464 ■ Western Veterinary Conference (WVC)
2425 E Oquendo Rd.
Las Vegas, NV 89120
Ph: (702)739-6698
Fax: (702)739-6420
E-mail: carolyn@wvc.org
URL: http://www.wvc.org
Contact: Dr. Stephen Crane, Exec. Dir.
Founded: 1928. **Members:** 13,500. **Staff:** 6. **Budget:** $4,000,000. **Description:** Provides practical continuing education for veterinarians, veterinary technicians, and animal hospital administrators. Topics of study at conference include small and large animal medicine and surgery, general medicine, emergency clinic operation, radiographic and clinical pathologic methods, and cutting edge clinical updates in the medical sciences. Autotutorial programs are available. **Libraries: Type:** not open to the public. **Holdings:** 400. **Subjects:** veterinary medicine, clinical procedures. **Awards: Frequency:** annual. **Type:** scholarship. **Recipient:** for third year veterinary students. **Formerly:** (1986) Intermountain Veterinary Medical Association. **Publications:** *Clinical Notes*, annual. **Price:** $45.00/year. **Circulation:** 400. Alternate Formats: CD-ROM; online. **Conventions/Meetings:** annual conference (exhibits) - always Las Vegas, NV.

16465 ■ World Association for the Advancement of Veterinary Parasitology (WAAVP)
PO Box 8
North Aurora, IL 60542
Ph: (970)494-2342
Fax: (970)482-6184
E-mail: info@waavp.org
URL: http://www.waavp.org
Contact: Dr. Ann R. Donoghue DVM, Sec.-Treas.
Founded: 1963. **Members:** 560. **Membership Dues:** regular, associate, $15 (annual) ● corporate, $1,000 (annual). **Staff:** 1. **Budget:** $10,000. **Languages:** English, French, German, Spanish. **Description:** Represents veterinarians and other scientists in 60 countries interested in veterinary parasitology. Aims to encourage research in veterinary parasitology, to promote the exchange of information and material between organizations and individuals, and to organize meetings for the study of parasites of veterinary importance. Maintains scientific committees. **Awards:** Excellence in Teaching Veterinary Parasitology. **Frequency:** biennial. **Type:** recognition. **Recipient:** for research, publications, service ● Outstanding Contributions to Research in Veterinary Parasitology. **Frequency:** biennial. **Type:** recognition. **Recipient:** for research, publications, service ● Peter Nancen Award for Young Scientists. **Frequency:** biennial. **Type:** recognition. **Recipient:** for research, publications, service ● **Type:** recognition. **Recipient:** for outstanding contributions to Research in Veterinary Parasitology; for excellence in teaching veterinary parasitology. **Affiliated With:** World Veterinary Association. **Also Known As:** Association Mondiale pour l'Advancement de Parasitologie Veterinaire. **Publications:** *Proceedings of Scientific Conferences*, biennial. ISSN: 0304-4017. Also Cited As: *Veterinary Parasitology* ● *Statutes - List of Members*, biennial. Membership Directory ● Newsletter, 3/year ● Membership Directory, annual. **Conventions/Meetings:** biennial conference (exhibits).

16466 ■ World Association of Veterinary Laboratory Diagnosticians (WAVLD)
c/o Dr. Craig N. Carter, Sec.-Treas.
PO Box 14125
Lexington, KY 40512-4125
Ph: (859)253-0571
Fax: (859)255-1624
E-mail: craig.carter@uky.edu
URL: http://www.wavld.org
Contact: Dr. Craig N. Carter, Sec.-Treas.
Founded: 1977. **Members:** 650. **National Groups:** 5. **Languages:** English, French, Spanish. **Description:** Individuals in 30 countries engaged in laboratory diagnosis of animal diseases. Coordinates activities of regulatory, research, and service laboratories. Maintains guidelines for personnel qualifications and facility standards. Establishes uniform laboratory methods and seeks to improve and develop existing diagnostic techniques. Disseminates information; maintains speakers' bureau. **Committees:** Awards and Honors; Membership Services. **Affiliated With:** American Association of Veterinary Laboratory Diagnosticians; Food and Agriculture Organization of the United Nations - Regional Office for Europe. **Publications:** *Symposium Proceedings*, triennial. **Circulation:** 400. **Conventions/Meetings:** biennial symposium (exhibits).

Visually Impaired

16467 ■ Achromatopsia Network
PO Box 214
Berkeley, CA 94701-0214
Ph: (510)540-4700
Fax: (510)540-4767
E-mail: editor@achromat.org
URL: http://www.achromat.org
Contact: Frances Futterman, Ed.
Founded: 1994. **Description:** Provides information and support for individuals and families concerned with the vision disorder achromatopsia, including both rod monochromacy and blue cone monochromacy.

Publications: *Living with Achromatopsia*. Book. Consists entirely of comments from persons who know firsthand about living with achromatopsia. Alternate Formats: online ● *Understanding and Coping with Achromatopsia*. Book. Presents a substantial amount of helpful and interesting information pertaining to achromatopsia. Alternate Formats: online.

16468 ■ American Action Fund for Blind Children and Adults (AAFBCA)
1800 Johnson St., Ste.100
Baltimore, MD 21230
Ph: (410)659-9315
Fax: (410)685-5653
E-mail: actionfund@actionfund.org
URL: http://www.actionfund.org
Founded: 1919. **Nonmembership. Description:** Works to assist blind persons in securing reading material, to educate the public about blindness, to give aid to the deaf-blind and to improve the quality of life for blind persons. Provides information and referral services on Social Security Disability Insurance, employment, civil rights, products and aids, education of blind children and public rehabilitation agencies; disseminates information on Braille and sign language; distributes publications free of charge to libraries and schools. **Libraries: Type:** lending. **Holdings:** books. **Subjects:** Braille. **Awards:** Kenneth Jernigan Scholarship. **Frequency:** annual. **Type:** scholarship. **Recipient:** to an individual who has changed the perceptions regarding the capabilities of the blind. **Formerly:** (1990) American Brotherhood for the Blind. **Publications:** *Action Line*, monthly. Newsletter. Alternate Formats: online ● *Great Documents Series*. Books. Features Braille copies of Great American documents. ● *Oh! Say Can You See*. Book. Alternate Formats: online ● *Twin Vision*. Books. Contains side-by-side Braille print for children. ● Also publishes Braille calendars. **Conventions/Meetings:** board meeting.

16469 ■ American Council of the Blind (ACB)
1155 15th St. NW, Ste.1004
Washington, DC 20005
Ph: (202)467-5081
Free: (800)424-8666
Fax: (202)467-5085
E-mail: info@acb.org
URL: http://www.acb.org
Contact: Melanie Brunson, Exec. Dir.
Founded: 1961. **Members:** 20,000. **Membership Dues:** member-at-large, $5 (annual). **Staff:** 7. **State Groups:** 51. **National Groups:** 19. **Description:** Blind and visually impaired persons. Provides information about social security and supplemental security income programs, radio reading services, special library services, state rehabilitation services, and low vision technology. Offers professional assistance in public interest, class action litigation, and public education about blindness and the abilities of visually impaired people. **Awards:** Floyd Qualls Memorial Scholarships. **Frequency:** annual. **Type:** scholarship. **Recipient:** for blind postsecondary students ● **Type:** scholarship. **Affiliated With:** ACB Radio Amateurs; American Association of Visually Impaired Attorneys; American Council of the Blind Lions; Blind Information Technology Specialists; Braille Revival League; Council of Citizens With Low Vision International; Council of Families with Visual Impairment; Friends-in-Art of American Council of the Blind; Guide Dog Users, Inc.; Independent Visually Impaired Enterprisers; Library Users of America; National Alliance of Blind Students; National Association of Blind Teachers; Randolph-Sheppard Vendors of America; Visually Impaired Veterans of America. **Publications:** *Braille Forum*, 10/year. Magazine. Concerned with legislative developments, new products and services, medical and technological advances, and human interest stories for the blind. **Price:** $25.00/year for companies or agencies. **Circulation:** 25,000. Alternate Formats: online; diskette. **Conventions/Meetings:** annual convention (exhibits).

16470 ■ American Council of the Blind Enterprises and Services (ACBES)
120 S 6th St., Ste.1005
Minneapolis, MN 55402

Ph: (612)332-3242
Free: (800)866-3242
Fax: (612)332-7850
E-mail: acbesall@ix.netcom.com
URL: http://www.acb.org
Founded: 1978. **Members:** 16. **Staff:** 4. **Budget:** $5,400,000. **Description:** Board of directors of the American Council of the Blind (see separate entry). Owns and operates 8 ACB thrift stores which help finance ACB and its programs and aid the blind and visually impaired in leading productive and independent lives. **Awards: Frequency:** annual. **Type:** scholarship. **Publications:** *The Braille Forum*, monthly. Magazine. Contains information of interest both to ACB members and the general public. Alternate Formats: magnetic tape; online. **Conventions/Meetings:** quarterly board meeting ● annual convention.

16471 ■ American Council of Blind Government Employees (ACBGE)
c/o Billie Jean Keith, Pres.
737 N Buchanan St.
Arlington, VA 22203
E-mail: billiejean@2keiths.com
URL: http://www.acb.org/affiliates
Contact: Billie Jean Keith, Pres.
Founded: 1978. **Members:** 50. **Description:** Government employees, retirees from government employment who are blind or visually handicapped, and other interested persons. Strives to improve opportunities in government employment for the blind and visually impaired; provides career development material; works with personnel policymakers. Members participate as speakers and panelists in workshops and other meetings. Offers technical assistance through specialized education program. **Affiliated With:** American Council of the Blind. **Formerly:** (1991) American Council of Blind Federal Employees. **Publications:** Newsletter, periodic. **Conventions/Meetings:** annual meeting (exhibits) - usually July.

16472 ■ American Council of the Blind Lions (ACBL)
c/o Alan Beatty, Pres.
PO Box 2312
Fort Collins, CO 80522
Ph: (970)484-2598
URL: http://www.acb.org/acbl
Contact: Alan Beatty, Pres.
Founded: 1970. **Members:** 141. **Membership Dues:** regular, $5 (annual). **Description:** Legally blind members of Lions Clubs International (see separate entry). Informs the public of the needs and capabilities of blind persons; exchanges information on club activities benefiting work for the blind; encourages blind people to join Lions Clubs and other civic organizations. Supports speakers' bureau. **Computer Services:** Mailing lists. **Affiliated With:** American Council of the Blind; Lions Clubs International. **Formerly:** (1985) World Council of Blind Lions; (1986) Council of Blind Lions. **Publications:** Newsletter, quarterly. **Conventions/Meetings:** annual conference (exhibits).

16473 ■ American Foundation for the Blind (AFB)
11 Penn Plz., Ste.300
New York, NY 10001
Ph: (212)502-7600
Free: (800)232-5463
Fax: (212)502-7777
E-mail: afbinfo@afb.net
URL: http://www.afb.org
Contact: Ms. Caitlin McFeely, Communications Coor.
Founded: 1921. **Staff:** 125. **Description:** Aims to expand possibilities for people with vision loss. Seeks to broaden access to technology; elevate the quality of information and tools for the professionals who serve people with vision loss; and promote independent and healthy living for people with vision loss by providing them and their families with relevant and timely resources. Provides members with vision loss information and services. **Libraries: Type:** reference. **Holdings:** 125,000; archival material. **Subjects:**

blindness. **Awards:** Delta Gamma Foundation Memorial Scholarship. **Frequency:** annual. **Type:** scholarship. **Recipient:** to undergraduate juniors, seniors, or graduate students who are legally blind, of good character, have exhibited academic excellence, and are studying in the field of rehabilitation and/or education of persons who are visually impaired or blind ● Ferdinand Torres AFB Scholarship. **Frequency:** annual. **Type:** scholarship. **Recipient:** to a full-time post-secondary student who is legally blind and who presents evidence of economic need ● Frederick A. Downes Scholarship. **Type:** scholarship. **Recipient:** to persons who are 22 years of age or younger, legally blind, and enrolled in a course of study leading to credentials in a profession or vocation ● Gladys C. Anderson Memorial Scholarship. **Type:** scholarship. **Recipient:** to a woman who is legally blind, studying religious or classical music at the college level ● Rudolph Dillman Memorial Scholarship. **Frequency:** annual. **Type:** scholarship. **Recipient:** to graduate and undergraduate students who are legally blind and studying in the field of rehabilitation and/or education of persons who are visually impaired or blind ● Telesensory Scholarship. **Type:** scholarship. **Recipient:** to a full-time undergraduate student who is legally blind and does not meet criteria for other AFB scholarships. **Telecommunication Services:** TDD, (212)502-7662. **Publications:** *AFB Directory of Services for Blind and Visually Impaired Persons in the U.S. and Canada.* Lists over 3000 local, state, regional, and national services, including educational, informational, rehabilitative, low-vision, and aging services. **Price:** $70.00/copy. Alternate Formats: CD-ROM ● *AFB eNews*, monthly. Newsletter. Highlights events, programs, recent awards/grants, new publications, timely policy work, and/or activities directly related to AFB. **Price:** free. Alternate Formats: online ● *Journal of Visual Impairment and Blindness*, monthly. Contains articles on research and practice in the areas of rehabilitation, psychology, education, legislation, medicine, and sensory devices. **Price:** $130.00 /year for individuals in U.S. and Canada; $160.00 /year for individuals outside U.S. and Canada; $180.00 /year for institutions in U.S. and Canada; $210.00 /year for institutions outside U.S. and Canada. ISSN: 0145-482X. **Circulation:** 3,000. **Advertising:** accepted ● Also publishes textbooks, training manuals, and resource guides, videos, and educational materials for teachers. **Conventions/Meetings:** annual Josephine L. Taylor Leadership Institute - meeting.

16474 ■ American Israeli Lighthouse (AIL)
20 E 46th St., Rm. 1401
New York, NY 10017-9244
Ph: (212)838-5322
Contact: Mrs. Leonard F. Dank, Pres.
Founded: 1927. **Members:** 1,500. **Staff:** 2. **State Groups:** 8. **Local Groups:** 7. **Description:** Works to raise funds for the maintenance of a rehabilitation center in Kiriat Haim, Israel for adult blind and physically handicapped persons. Promotes research in the development of techniques in education, vocational training, and rehabilitation. **Publications:** *The Tower*, annual. **Conventions/Meetings:** biennial meeting.

16475 ■ American Nystagmus Network (ANN)
303-D Beltline Pl., No. 321
Decatur, AL 35603
E-mail: jlowry@nystagmus.org
URL: http://www.nystagmus.org
Contact: Jeff Lowry, Pres.
Founded: 1999. **Members:** 600. **Membership Dues:** regular, $25 (annual) ● family, $45 (annual) ● life, $250. **Description:** Serves the needs and interests of people affected by nystagmus. Seeks to provide technical and experiential information about nystagmus and its manifestations. Provides help in coping with nystagmus through the exchange of information and ideas, guidance and counseling. **Computer Services:** Information services, website and e-mail listserv. **Publications:** *ANNagram*, semiannual. Newsletters. Contains articles on the social and daily living aspects of nystagmus. **Price:** free for members; $25.00 /year for nonmembers.

16476 ■ American Printing House for the Blind (APH)
PO Box 6085
1839 Frankfort Ave.
Louisville, KY 40206-0085
Ph: (502)895-2405
Free: (800)223-1839
Fax: (502)899-2274
E-mail: info@aph.org
URL: http://www.aph.org
Contact: Dr. Tuck Tinsley III, Pres.
Founded: 1858. **Staff:** 320. **Budget:** $14,000,000. **Description:** Produces literature in all media (Braille, large type, recorded, computer disc) for the blind. Manufactures special products for use by visually impaired students and adults, such as preschool and vocational materials and talking software. Conducts ongoing educational research program. Conducts art contest, tours of the plant and of the APH Museum of artifacts from the education of the blind field. **Libraries: Type:** reference. **Holdings:** 3,500; articles, books, periodicals. **Subjects:** blindness, handicapped persons. **Awards:** Wings of Freedom Award. **Frequency:** periodic. **Type:** recognition. **Recipient:** for individuals demonstrating exemplary leadership in the areas of education or rehabilitation of visually impaired persons. **Computer Services:** database, Louis. **Telecommunication Services:** electronic mail, ttinsley@aph.org. **Committees:** Compensation; Educational Research and Development; Finance and Audit; Publications. **Absorbed:** (1983) Instructional Materials Reference Center. **Publications:** *APH News*, monthly. Newsletter. Contains information on the products, services and training opportunities of the organization. Alternate Formats: online ● *APH Slate*, quarterly. Newsletter. Provides information on new products for the visually impaired; includes organization news and activities. **Price:** free. ISSN: 1081-5198. **Circulation:** 8,890. Alternate Formats: online; diskette ● *APH Technology Update: Technology for People Who Are Visually Impaired*, annual. Newsletter. Covers computer and other high-tech products designed for blind persons. **Price:** free. ISSN: 1081-518X. **Circulation:** 2,500. Alternate Formats: diskette; online ● Annual Report ● Makes available Newsweek, Readers Digest, and Weekly Reader in Braille, tape, or large type. **Conventions/Meetings:** Meeting of Ex Officio Trustees - assembly, for extended Board of Directors - always 2nd or 3rd week in October, in Louisville, KY.

16477 ■ Associated Blind
315 5th Ave., Ste.807
New York, NY 10016
Ph: (212)683-4950
Fax: (212)683-4975
E-mail: memberservices@esight.org
URL: http://www.tabinc.org
Contact: Nancy O'Connell, Exec. Dir.
Founded: 1938. **Staff:** 2. **Budget:** $245,000. **Regional Groups:** 1. **Local Groups:** 1. **Description:** Provides employment and career management services for blind or visually impaired individuals through direct service programs and online. Assists corporations and other organizations with all accessibility consulting services, including web accessibility and disability awareness and sensitivity training, and emergency preparedness. Conducts internship programs that enable blind and visually impaired college students to participate in national internships along with sighted peers. **Libraries: Type:** lending; reference; not open to the public. **Holdings:** audio recordings. **Subjects:** music, culture, education, entertainment, radio stations, computer training, adaptive equipment. **Additional Websites:** http://www.esight.org. **Committees:** Accessibility Resources Exchange; Adaptive Computer Education; Adaptive Solutions Institute; Information Access Center; Library; Social Services; Volunteers. **Programs:** Professional Development. **Publications:** *eSight Careers Network.* Provides information for job seekers and prospective employers about what works best for a range of disability employment issues. **Circulation:** 800. Alternate Formats: online ● *eSight NetWork News*, weekly. Newsletter. Alternate Formats: online. **Conventions/Meetings:** annual Adap-

tive Solutions - meeting, tech expo with adaptive computer equipment.

16478 ■ Associated Services for the Blind (ASB)
919 Walnut St.
Philadelphia, PA 19107
Ph: (215)627-0600
Fax: (215)922-0692
E-mail: asbinfo@asb.org
URL: http://www.asb.org
Contact: Patricia C. Johnson, CEO/Pres.
Founded: 1983. **Staff:** 75. **Budget:** $2,900,000. **Languages:** English, Spanish. **Description:** Serves as multiservice agency that provides services to blind and visually impaired people. Aims to help the blind and visually impaired people to live independently. Operates a braille printing house that transcribes print materials into braille; radio reading service that reads newspapers and magazines over closed-circuit radio. Offers rehabilitation program, social services, and recorded periodicals. **Formed by Merger of:** Volunteer Services for the Blind; Nevil Institute for Rehabilitation and Service; Radio Information Center for the Blind. **Publications:** *ASB Visions*, quarterly. Newsletter. Alternate Formats: online ● Annual Report, annual. Reports on services, board, and finances. ● Brochure.

16479 ■ Association for the Advancement of Blind and Retarded (AABR)
PO Box 560247
College Point, NY 11356
Ph: (718)321-3800
Fax: (718)321-8688
E-mail: email@aabr.org
URL: http://aabr.org
Contact: Audrey Sachs Jr., Pres.
Founded: 1956. **Staff:** 560. **Budget:** $21,000. **Nonmembership. Description:** Community groups and individuals interested in multi-handicapped blind and severely retarded adults. Operates 19 group residences providing intermediate care and individual residential alternative facilities for blind and retarded adults; two treatment centers for blind, multi-handicapped, and severely retarded adults; NYS approved special education program for autistic children from pre-school to school age. Provides information and referral services. **Programs:** Adult Day Treatment; Day Habilitation; Recreation. **Formerly:** (1974) Association for Advancement of Blind Children. **Publications:** *AABR Newsletter*, 3/year. Contains donor update letter. **Price:** free.

16480 ■ Association for Education and Rehabilitation of the Blind and Visually Impaired (AERBVI)
1703 N Beauregard St., Ste.440
Alexandria, VA 22311
Ph: (703)671-4500
Free: (877)492-2708
Fax: (703)671-6391
E-mail: jgandorf@aerbvi.org
URL: http://www.aerbvi.org
Contact: Jim Gandorf CAE, Exec. Dir.
Founded: 1984. **Members:** 4,000. **Membership Dues:** regular, international, $130 (annual) ● household, transition, $100 (annual) ● retired, support/clerical, student, $55 (annual). **Staff:** 4. **Budget:** $950,000. **State Groups:** 44. **Description:** Provides support and assistance to professionals "who work in all phases of education and rehabilitation of blind and visually impaired persons of all ages". **Awards:** William and Dorothy Ferrell Scholarship. **Frequency:** biennial. **Type:** scholarship. **Recipient:** to two selected applicants who are legally blind and are studying for a career in the field of services to persons who are blind or visually impaired. **Formed by Merger of:** (1993) American Association of Workers for the Blind; Association for Education of the Visually Handicapped. **Publications:** *AER Report*, quarterly, plus annual year end edition. Magazine. Contains information about blind and visually impaired persons. Includes legislative and membership news. **Price:** included in membership dues. **Circulation:** 5,000. **Advertising:** accepted ● *Association for*

Education and Rehabilitation of the Blind and Visually Impaired—Job Exchange, monthly. Bulletin. Lists job openings in the field of services to blind and visually impaired children and adults. **Price:** free for members (online). **Circulation:** 300. Alternate Formats: online ● *Re:View*, quarterly. Journal. **Conventions/Meetings:** annual AER-Lift Leadership Conference (exhibits) ● biennial international conference - even numbered years.

16481 ■ Blind Children's Fund (BCF)

311 W Broadway St., Ste.1
Mount Pleasant, MI 48858
Ph: (989)779-9966
Fax: (989)779-0015
E-mail: bcf@blindchildrensfund.org
URL: http://www.blindchildrensfund.org
Contact: Karla B. Storrer, Exec. Dir./CEO
Founded: 1978. **Members:** 1,300. **Staff:** 2. **Regional Groups:** 1. **Multinational. Description:** Aims to encourage the development, education and welfare of children with visual and/or multiple impairments. Seeks to increase global awareness regarding the need for early and continuing intervention services, and to provide children, parents and professionals with information and resources for promoting the independence and dignity of children with disabilities. **Libraries: Type:** reference. **Holdings:** 1,800; audiovisuals, books, periodicals. **Subjects:** preschool, blindness, early childhood. **Formerly:** (1987) International Institute for the Visually Impaired. **Publications:** *Get A Wiggle On.* Booklet. For parents of blind or visually impaired infants with suggestions for assisting development form birth to the walking stage. **Price:** $5.00 ● *Get Ready.Get Set.Go!*. Teaches techniques for the parent or educator of the blind child, focusing on self-help skills. **Price:** $7.00 ● *Learning to Look.* Book. Contains specific suggestions on how to help your child use what vision she/he has or may have; for parents of severely visually impaired children. **Price:** $9.00 ● *Move It.* Booklet. Contains suggestions for the development of a preschool blind or visually impaired child from walking to school entrance age. **Price:** $5.00 ● *Movement Education.* Serves as a movement curriculum for preschoolers. **Price:** $13.00 ● *Our Kids Are Great!.* Booklet. Contains short stories parents of visually impaired children about what their children can do because of their help, love, and attention. **Price:** $3.00 ● *Parent & Teacher Packet No. 1.* Booklet. Includes activities to teach skills at home, toys to make, how to stimulate language, and readings on blindness for parents and children. **Price:** $7.00 ● *VIP Newsletter*, quarterly. Contains information and articles for parents of blind or visually impaired children. **Price:** $10.00/year in U.S.; $15.00/year outside U.S. ISSN: 0738-7091 ● *Watch Me Grow* (in English and Spanish). Book. Contains month by month suggestions for assisting the development of a blind or visually impaired infant from birth to age three. **Price:** $12.00.

16482 ■ Blind Information Technology Specialists (BITS)

c/o Robert R. Rogers, Treas.
1121 Morado Dr.
Cincinnati, OH 45238-4436
Ph: (513)921-3186
E-mail: rrrogers@nuvox.net
URL: http://www.acb.org/bits
Contact: Robert R. Rogers, Treas.
Founded: 1969. **Members:** 75. **Membership Dues:** corporate/organization, $25 (annual) ● full, $20 (annual) ● student, $10 (annual) ● ACB, life, $15. **Budget:** $500. **Description:** Visually impaired electronic data processing employees; those seeking employment; employers, instructors, manufacturers, and students in the electronic data processing field. Advocates high standards in training visually impaired students. Seeks to increase employment opportunities; encourages the exchange of work technique ideas and the development of new equipment. Works with agencies to increase the availability of braille and recorded materials. Supports a speakers' bureau. **Awards:** Kelly Cannon Memorial Scholarship. **Frequency:** annual. **Type:** scholarship. **Recipient:** to a

person pursuing post secondary or graduate studies in computer technology. **Computer Services:** Mailing lists ● online services. **Committees:** Constitution and Bylaws; Convention Program; John R. Mattioli Jr. Technical Inventor Award; Projects. **Affiliated With:** American Council of the Blind. **Formerly:** (2003) Visually Impaired Data Processors International. **Publications:** *Bytes from BITS*, quarterly. Newsletter. **Conventions/Meetings:** annual convention (exhibits).

16483 ■ Blind Service Association (BSA)

17 N State St., Ste.1050
Chicago, IL 60602-3510
Ph: (312)236-0808
Fax: (312)236-8679
E-mail: blindsrvc@aol.com
Contact: Debbie Grossman, Exec. Dir.
Founded: 1924. **Members:** 550. **Staff:** 6. **Budget:** $495,000. **Description:** Organization that has supported the independence of blind and partially blind Chicago residents since 1924. The association maintains reading rooms for daily oral readings of textbooks and work-related material primarily to blind students, senior citizens, and business and professional people; records textbooks on cassette tapes for blind people's home, study, work and leisure needs; supplies visual aids, field trips, and other assistance to blind and visually handicapped children in Chicago, IL schools; operates senior program and a consortium of blind computer users. **Awards: Type:** grant. **Recipient:** for blind college students ● Harry G. Hershenson Memorial Award. **Type:** recognition. **Recipient:** for outstanding contribution to blind people ● **Frequency:** annual. **Type:** scholarship. **Committees:** Associates. **Conventions/Meetings:** annual meeting - always May.

16484 ■ Blinded Veterans Association (BVA)

477 H St. NW
Washington, DC 20001
Ph: (202)371-8880
Free: (800)669-7079
Fax: (202)371-8258
E-mail: bva@bva.org
URL: http://www.bva.org
Contact: Mr. Thomas H. Miller, Exec. Dir.
Founded: 1945. **Members:** 10,500. **Membership Dues:** individual, $8 (annual) ● life, $80. **Staff:** 22. **Budget:** $4,000,000. **Regional Groups:** 54. **Description:** Veterans who lost their sight as a result of military service in the armed forces of the U.S; associate members are veterans whose loss of sight was not connected with military service. Assists blinded veterans in attaining benefits and employment and with reestablishing themselves as adjusted, active, and productive citizens in their communities. Offers placement service; supports research programs; compiles statistics. Constructs initiatives designed to improve blind rehabilitation programs for veterans. **Awards:** David Schnair Award. **Frequency:** annual. **Type:** recognition. **Recipient:** for excellence in the giving of voluntary service ● Irving Diener Award. **Type:** recognition. **Recipient:** for the service of regional groups ● Kathern F. Gruber Scholarship. **Frequency:** annual. **Type:** scholarship. **Recipient:** for spouses and dependent children of blinded veterans ● Major General Melvin T. Maas Achievement Award. **Frequency:** annual. **Type:** recognition. **Recipient:** for service connected blinded veteran. **Computer Services:** Mailing lists, of members. **Programs:** Field Service. **Publications:** *BVA Bulletin*, quarterly. Newsletter. Reports on legislation, benefits, and Department of Veterans Affairs programs affecting blind veterans. ISSN: 0005-3430. **Circulation:** 13,000. **Conventions/Meetings:** annual meeting (exhibits) - always August ● annual seminar.

16485 ■ Braille Authority of North America (BANA)

c/o Braille & Talking Book Library
Perkins School for the Blind
175 N Beacon St.
Watertown, MA 02472
Ph: (617)972-7249 (617)972-7240
Free: (888)965-8965

Fax: (617)972-7363
E-mail: kim.charlson@perkins.org
URL: http://www.brailleauthority.org
Contact: Ms. Kim Charlson, Chair
Founded: 1976. **Members:** 12. **Membership Dues:** organization, $500 (annual) ● full, $675 (annual). **Description:** Braille publishers, producers, and transcribers; representatives of consumer groups; educators of the visually handicapped; professional organizations. Aims to promote and facilitate the use, teaching, and production of Braille texts and other Braille items. Promulgates rules, makes interpretations, and renders opinions concerning literary and technical Braille codes and related forms and formats of embossed materials for the blind. **Committees:** Braille Research; Computer Notations; Linear; Literary; Mathematics; Music; Textbook. **Publications:** *Braille Textbook Code Formats and Techniques* ● *English Braille, American Edition* ● *Learning the Nemeth Code* ● *Nemeth Code of Braille Mathematics and Scientific Notation* ● Directory, annual. **Conventions/Meetings:** semiannual meeting - always fall and spring.

16486 ■ Braille Revival League (BRL)

57 Grandview Ave.
Watertown, MA 02472
Ph: (617)926-9198
Free: (800)424-8666
Fax: (617)923-0004
E-mail: kimcharlson@earthlink.net
Contact: Kim Charlson, Contact
Founded: 1981. **Members:** 1,000. **Membership Dues:** $15 (annual). **State Groups:** 6. **Description:** Blind and visually impaired persons; professionals interested in promoting the use, production, and teaching of Braille. Encourages blind people to read and write in Braille; advocates the mandatory use of Braille instruction in educational facilities for the blind; promotes use of Braille material available through libraries and printing houses. Lends support to the Braille Authority of North America. Conducts research into Braille efficiency. **Committees:** Braille Literacy Project; Braille Writing Contest. **Affiliated With:** American Council of the Blind; Braille Authority of North America. **Publications:** *BRL Memorandum*, quarterly. Newsletter. Volumes are in Braille, large print, and computer diskette. **Conventions/Meetings:** annual conference (exhibits) - always July.

16487 ■ Carroll Center for the Blind (CCB)

770 Centre St.
Newton, MA 02458
Ph: (617)969-6200
Free: (800)852-3131
Fax: (617)969-6204
E-mail: dina.rosenbaum@carroll.org
URL: http://www.carroll.org
Contact: Rachel Ethier Rosenbaum, Pres.
Founded: 1936. **Staff:** 62. **Budget:** $3,800,000. **Description:** Serves persons of all ages who are blind or visually impaired. Provides individualized short-term programs that teach adaptive methods for living independently, using technology, seeking employment, performing successfully in school, and living a full and productive life; also manages the statewide materials center of books in Braille and large print books for all ages, kindergarten through 12th grade. **Libraries: Type:** reference. **Holdings:** 1,000. **Awards:** Father Carroll Award. **Frequency:** annual. **Type:** recognition. **Recipient:** to an outstanding employee who is blind, in Massachusetts ● **Type:** recognition. **Telecommunication Services:** electronic mail, mccleary@aol.com. **Departments:** Community Rehabilitation Services; Computer Training; Low Vision for Employment; Public Education; Residential Rehabilitation; Volunteer Services. **Formerly:** (1972) Catholic Guild for All the Blind; (1974) Carroll Rehabilitation Center for the Visually Impaired. **Publications:** *Blindness: What It Is, What It Does, and How to Live With It.* **Price:** $15.00 ● *Carroll Center for the Blind—Focus*, semiannual. Newsletter. Covers membership activities. Includes information for donors and new program information. **Price:** free ● *Computer Access, Resource Manual.* **Price:** $20.00 ● *Educational Software, Compiled Listing.*

Price: $5.00 ● *Facing the Wind.* Price: $25.00 ● *Mapping.* Price: $15.00 ● *Medical Transcription Training Manual.* Price: $125.00 ● *Resource Manual for Teaching Blind Persons to Use Computers,* annual. Price: $20.00/year; $10.00 for tape ● *Selected Exercises in Sensory Training.* Price: $15.00 ● *Sensory Training.* Price: $15.00 ● *Videation and Spatial Orientation, Vols. I and II.* Price: $50.00. **Conventions/Meetings:** semiannual meeting (exhibits) - always spring and fall, Newton, MA.

16488 ■ Christian Blind Mission International (CBMI)
450 E Park Ave.
Greenville, SC 29601
Ph: (864)239-0065
Free: (800)YES-CBMI
Fax: (864)239-0069
E-mail: info@cbmiusa.org
URL: http://www.cbmiusa.org
Contact: Ms. Larae Harvey, Dir., Marketing and Communications
Founded: 1908. **Members:** 7. **Staff:** 9. **National Groups:** 10. **Multinational. Description:** Interdenominational Christian organization dedicated to service of the blind, visually impaired, and physically handicapped in more than 113 countries. Supports national activities of missions, churches, and voluntary organizations in developing countries with financial aid to cover operational expenses and the provision of equipment, drugs, medicines, and instruments. Fosters prevention of visually disabling ailments such as glaucoma, trachoma, and blinding cataracts. Assists in education and rehabilitation of all disabled individuals through establishment of vocational training centers and a corps of community volunteers to coordinate and stimulate project participation. Contributes to international efforts in the battle against blindness; conducts research on onchocerciasis, xerophthalmia, and glaucoma. Sponsors rural education programs on personal and environmental hygiene and nutrition. **Affiliated With:** International Agency for the Prevention of Blindness. **Publications:** *Case for Support: Portraits.* Brochure ● *CBMI Report,* annual ● *Human Interest Stories,* monthly. **Circulation:** 10,000 ● *Light,* quarterly. Newsletter. **Circulation:** 15,000. **Conventions/Meetings:** annual board meeting ● workshop.

16489 ■ Christian Record Services (CRS)
PO Box 6097
Lincoln, NE 68506-0097
Ph: (402)488-0981
Fax: (402)488-7582
E-mail: info@christianrecord.org
URL: http://www.christianrecord.org
Contact: Larry Pitcher, Pres.
Founded: 1899. **Staff:** 165. **Languages:** English, Spanish. **Description:** Provides free Christian publications and programs for persons with visual impairments. Produces six magazines in Braille, large print, and on cassette tape. Hosts Bible correspondence school, National Camps for Blind Children and Adults. **Libraries: Type:** reference; lending. **Holdings:** 2,000; audio recordings, books. **Subjects:** general information, religion, inspirational materials. **Awards:** CRS College Scholarships. **Frequency:** annual. **Type:** scholarship. **Recipient:** to legally blind young people striving to obtain a college education. **Affiliated With:** American Camp Association; Association for Education and Rehabilitation of the Blind and Visually Impaired; Christian Camping International/U.S.A. **Formerly:** Christian Record Benevolent Association; (1989) Christian Record Braille Foundation. **Publications:** *Christian Record,* quarterly. Magazine. Contains contemporary interest stories presented from a Christian viewpoint. ● *Christian Record Talking Magazine,* quarterly. Contains inspirational stories, articles and interviews of contemporary interest presented from a Christian viewpoint. Alternate Formats: online ● *Encounter,* bimonthly. Magazine. Features a regular sermon-of-the-month, Bible-oriented discussions, questions and answers from the Bible and in-depth studies of Bible prophecy. ● *Lifeglow,* quarterly. Magazine. Contains articles and stories from a Christian perspective. ● *The Student,*

monthly. Magazine. Focuses on a particular book of the Bible. Alternate Formats: online ● Also publishes Braille cards. **Conventions/Meetings:** annual conference ● Winter Camps - meeting.

16490 ■ Christian Services for the Blind
1124 Fair Oaks Ave.
PO Box 26
South Pasadena, CA 91031-0026
Ph: (626)799-3935
Free: (888)511-3935
Fax: (626)403-9460
E-mail: frank@csbonline.org
URL: http://www.csbonline.org
Contact: Dr. Franklin D. Tucker, Exec.Dir.
Founded: 1949. **Staff:** 5. **Local Groups:** 1. **Description:** Makes available books on cassette for blind and Braille books for deaf-blind individuals. **Libraries: Type:** reference. **Holdings:** 310; books. **Subjects:** Christian books in Braille and on tape. **Formerly:** Christian Fellowship for the Blind. **Publications:** *Bartimaeus Review,* 3/year. Newsletter. **Price:** free. **Circulation:** 3,500. **Conventions/Meetings:** annual Bible Camp - meeting.

16491 ■ Council of Families with Visual Impairment (CFVI)
c/o Cindy Van Winkle, Pres.
6686 Capricorn Ln. NE
Bremerton, WA 98311
E-mail: wcbprez@msn.com
URL: http://www.acb.org/affiliates
Contact: Cindy Van Winkle, Pres.
Founded: 1979. **Members:** 100. **Description:** Sighted parents of blind and visually impaired children; blind and visually impaired parents, professionals, and interested individuals. Offers forum for support and outreach, sharing of experiences in parent-child relationships, and educational and cultural information about child development. Monitors developments in technical and legislative arenas. **Affiliated With:** American Council of the Blind. **Formerly:** (1990) American Council of the Blind Parents. **Publications:** *Reflections,* 3/year. Newsletter. Published in large print. **Price:** $6.00/copy; $8.00 for tape. **Conventions/Meetings:** annual conference, in conjunction with the ACB.

16492 ■ DB-Link: The National Information Clearinghouse On Children Who Are Deaf-Blind
345 N Monmouth Ave.
Monmouth, OR 97361
Free: (800)438-9376
Fax: (503)838-8150
E-mail: dblink@tr.wou.edu
URL: http://www.dblink.org
Contact: Dr. John Reiman, Dir.
Founded: 1992. **Languages:** English, Spanish. **Description:** Parents, service providers, administrators, and others interested in services. Identifies, coordinates, and disseminates information related to children and youth who are deaf-blind. Collaborative effort of the Helen Keller National Center, Perkins School for the Blind, and Teaching Research of Western Oregon University. **Libraries: Type:** reference. **Holdings:** audiovisuals, books, clippings, periodicals. **Subjects:** deaf-blindness. **Computer Services:** database. **Telecommunication Services:** TDD, (800)854-7013. **Programs:** Hilton/Perkins. **Affiliated With:** American Association of the Deaf-Blind; Helen Keller National Center for Deaf-Blind Youths and Adults. **Formerly:** (2004) DB-Link. **Publications:** *Deaf-Blind Perspectives,* 3/year. Newsletter. Available in standard print, Braille, large print and ASCII. **Price:** free to subscribers ● Also publishes 10 fact sheets related to deaf-blindness. (7 of which are also in Spanish) Available full text also on web site.

16493 ■ Fidelco Guide Dog Foundation
103 Old Iron Ore Rd.
Bloomfield, CT 06002
Ph: (860)243-5200
Fax: (860)243-7215

E-mail: jackhayward@fidelco.org
URL: http://www.fidelco.org
Contact: George Salpietro, Exec. Dir.
Founded: 1960. **Members:** 25,000. **Staff:** 17. **Description:** Works to breed, train, and place Fidelco German shepherd guide dogs with persons who are blind (the Fidelco shepherd is a special breed ideally suited for guide work because of its intelligence, strength, health, and stability). Utilizes genetic processes and clinical methods to improve and refine the breed and maintain an ongoing program for development and improvement of training methods. Conducts on-going performance reviews of the guide dog team to see that the dog and recipients are working together as required. **Committees:** Selection. **Formerly:** Fidelco Foundation; (1981) Fidelco Breeder's Foundation. **Publications:** *Fidelco Annual Report,* annual ● *Fidelco News,* quarterly. Newsletter ● *On-command,* quarterly. Newsletters. Alternate Formats: online. **Conventions/Meetings:** board meeting - 3/year.

16494 ■ Foundation Fighting Blindness (FFB)
11435 Cronhill Dr.
Owings Mills, MD 21117-2220
Ph: (410)568-0150
Free: (800)683-5555
Fax: (410)363-2393
E-mail: info@blindness.org
URL: http://www.fightblindness.org
Contact: Ms. Mitsy Palmer, Constituent Services Coor.
Founded: 1971. **Members:** 65,000. **Staff:** 69. **Local Groups:** 35. **Description:** Drives the research that will provide preventions, treatments, and cures for people affected by retinitis pigmentosa, macular degeneration, Usher syndrome and the entire spectrum of retinal degenerative diseases. Offers information and referral services for affected individuals and their families as well as for doctors and eye care professionals. Provides comprehensive information kits on retinitis pigmentosa, muscular degeneration, and usher syndrome. **Telecommunication Services:** TDD, (410)363-7139 ● TDD, (800)683-5551. **Formerly:** RP Foundation Fighting Blindness. **Publications:** *InFocus,* 3/year. Newsletter ● Information kits or retinitis pigmentosa (RP), macular degeneration and Usher Syndrome. **Conventions/Meetings:** biennial VISIONS - conference (exhibits).

16495 ■ Gospel Association for the Blind (GAB)
1450 SW 10th Ave., Bldg. B-2
Delray Beach, FL 33444-1299
Ph: (386)586-5885
E-mail: care@careministries.org
URL: http://www.careministries.org/resourcelist.html
Contact: George Montanus, Pres.
Founded: 1947. **Staff:** 10. **Description:** Religious corporation supported by contributions "to evangelize the physically blind by presenting the Gospel of the Lord Jesus Christ." Provides counseling and summer camp. **Convention/Meeting:** none. **Libraries: Type:** reference. **Holdings:** 10,000; audio recordings, books. **Subjects:** religion, devotion, fiction, Christian life topics in Braille. **Publications:** *The Gospel Messenger,* monthly. Newsletter. Carries the message of the Gospel to the blind. Contains religious stories, poems, and articles; available on cassette. **Price:** free for blinds. **Circulation:** 650 ● *Jottings,* monthly. Newsletter. Christian-oriented; includes profiles of blind people. **Price:** free. **Circulation:** 5,000.

16496 ■ Guide Dog Foundation for the Blind (GDFB)
371 E Jericho Tpke.
Smithtown, NY 11787-2976
Ph: (631)930-9000 (631)930-9010
Free: (800)548-4337
Fax: (631)930-9009
E-mail: info@guidedog.org
URL: http://www.guidedog.org
Contact: Wells B. Jones CAE, CEO
Founded: 1946. **Members:** 180,000. **Staff:** 80. **Budget:** $5,000,000. **Description:** Works to provide independence and mobility for qualified blind ap-

plicants free of charge. Dogs are raised in volunteer homes for the first year, then trained for an additional four to six months with qualified instructor. Conducts 25-day residential training program for blind persons and guide dogs at Smithtown, NY. **Awards: Type:** recognition. **Telecommunication Services:** electronic mail, wells@guidedog.org. **Departments:** Breeding; Consumer Services; Development/Fund-Raising; Human Resources; Public Relations; Puppy. **Programs:** Volunteer. **Also Known As:** GDF; Second Sight; Guide Dog Foundation. **Publications:** *Digital Guide*, monthly. Newsletter. Contains the latest news and happenings in the Foundation. **Price:** free. Alternate Formats: online ● *Guideway*, quarterly. Newsletter. Updates the foundation's activities. **Price:** free. **Circulation:** 10,000. Alternate Formats: online ● Annual Report, annual. Alternate Formats: online.

16497 ■ Guide Dog Users, Inc. (GDUI)
14311 Astrodome Dr.
Silver Spring, MD 20906
Ph: (301)598-5771
Free: (888)858-1008
Fax: (301)871-7591
E-mail: info@gdw.org
URL: http://www.gdui.org
Contact: Jane Sheehan, Office Mgr./Treas.
Founded: 1969. **Members:** 1,000. **Membership Dues:** general, $15 (annual) ● life, $250. **State Groups:** 20. **Multinational. Description:** Persons who are visually handicapped or blind and who use guide dogs; other interested individuals. Conducts seminars, workshops, and public relations programs. Encourages promotion of aids for mobility skills and employment of the blind; promotes self-help concept for blind persons. Operates speakers' bureau. **Telecommunication Services:** electronic mail, treasurer@gdui.org ● hotline, for guide dog handlers, (800)858-9600 ● additional toll-free number, advocacy services, (888)858-2481 ● additional toll-free number, empathizer services, (888)858-2227. **Committees:** Advocacy; Fund Raising; Legislative Affairs; Products; Public Relations. **Affiliated With:** American Council of the Blind. **Formed by Merger of:** Coordinating Committee of Guide Dog Users; National Society of Guide Dog Users. **Publications:** *Pawtracks*, quarterly. Newsletter. Provides medical, legal, and financial information on canine maintenance. Gives specific emphasis on needs of guide dogs. **Price:** included in membership dues; $25.00 /year for nonmembers. **Circulation:** 1,000. Alternate Formats: CD-ROM ● Brochures. **Conventions/Meetings:** annual conference - usually early July.

16498 ■ Guide Dogs of America (GDA)
13445 Glenoaks Blvd.
Sylmar, CA 91342
Ph: (818)362-5834
Fax: (818)362-6870
E-mail: mail@guidedogsofamerica.org
URL: http://www.guidedogsofamerica.org
Contact: Jay A. Bormann, Pres./Dir.
Founded: 1948. **Staff:** 39. **Budget:** $1,250,000. **Languages:** English, French, Spanish. **Description:** Breeds, raises and trains guide dogs for legally blind men and women throughout the U.S. and Canada and provides instruction in the use of these "special" dogs for safe mobility. All GDA services that include guide dog, specially designed harness, individualized 28 day in-residence training, and life-time follow up is free of charge. Supported by donations from individuals, companies, foundations, organizations, and service clubs. Maintains speakers' bureau. Tours available by appointment. **Awards:** Gift of Sight Award. **Frequency:** annual. **Type:** recognition. **Recipient:** for outstanding support of GDA. **Programs:** Breeding; Guide Dog; Puppy Raising. **Formerly:** (1993) International Guiding Eyes. **Publications:** *Partners*, quarterly. Newsletter. **Conventions/Meetings:** annual board meeting and show, union industry show, open house (exhibits).

16499 ■ Guide Dogs for the Blind (GDB)
PO Box 151200
San Rafael, CA 94915-1200
Ph: (415)499-4000
Free: (800)295-4050

Fax: (415)499-4035
E-mail: information@guidedogs.com
URL: http://www.guidedogs.com
Contact: Robert L. Phillips, Pres./CEO
Founded: 1942. **Staff:** 269. **Budget:** $27,858. **Multinational. Description:** Provides guide dogs and training on their use to visually impaired people throughout the U.S. and Canada; services are free to those served through the generosity of donors and support volunteers. **Departments:** Development; Kennel; Veterinary. **Programs:** Breeding.

16500 ■ Guiding Eyes for the Blind (GEB)
611 Granite Springs Rd.
Yorktown Heights, NY 10598
Ph: (914)245-4024
Free: (800)942-0149
Fax: (914)962-1403
E-mail: info@guidingeyes.org
URL: http://guidingeyes.org
Contact: Ms. Bev Klayman, Admissions Mgr.
Founded: 1954. **Staff:** 100. **Budget:** $8,600,000. **Multinational. Description:** Breeds and provides fully trained guide dogs and instruction in their use to visually impaired and blind individuals including special needs students with additional challenges. Conducts 3-year course for instructors and 4-week training programs for blind persons in proper use and care of guide dogs at Yorktown Heights, NY. Provides in-service education for staff and seminars for orientation and mobility instructors and other rehabilitation professionals. Maintains speakers' bureau of program graduates; provides home training. **Telecommunication Services:** additional toll-free number, (800)421-1220. **Publications:** *Guide Lines*, quarterly. Newsletter.

16501 ■ Helen Keller International (HKI)
352 Park Ave. S, 12th Fl.
New York, NY 10010
Ph: (212)532-0544
Free: (877)535-5374
Fax: (212)532-6014
E-mail: info@hki.org
URL: http://www.hki.org
Contact: Ms. Kathy Spahn, Pres./CEO
Founded: 1915. **Staff:** 50. **Budget:** $26,184,389. **Multinational. Description:** Assists governments and voluntary agencies throughout Asia, Africa, and the Americas (including the United States) to establish and integrate, into their national health and welfare systems, services to prevent or cure malnutrition and eye diseases and blindness and to rehabilitate and educate visually disabled persons. Focuses on programs in the prevention and treatment of blindness caused by malnutrition, trachoma, onchocerciasis and cataracts. Trains health workers at all levels in the use of specially developed materials to diagnose and treat eye problems and to refer patients to hospitals. Compiles statistics. Provides free prescription eyeglasses to junior high school students in the U.S. and a growing number of countries overseas through the Childsight Program. **Libraries: Type:** not open to the public. **Holdings:** 3,000; articles, audio recordings, audiovisuals, books, video recordings. **Subjects:** public health. **Awards:** Helen Keller Global Legacy Award. **Type:** recognition. **Recipient:** for display of humanitarian qualities ● Spirit of Helen Keller Award. **Type:** recognition. **Recipient:** for display of humanitarian qualities. **Committees:** Sponsors. **Programs:** Eye Health; Health and Nutrition; Poverty Reduction. **Affiliated With:** 20/20 Vision National Project; Global Health Council; Interaction/American Council for Voluntary International Action. **Absorbed:** (1952) Association for the Chinese Blind. **Formerly:** (1925) Permanent Blind Relief War Fund; (1946) American Braille Press for War and Civilian Blind; (1977) American Foundation for Overseas Blind; (1999) Helen Keller International; (2000) Helen Keller Worldwide. **Publications:** *Insight*, quarterly. Newsletter. **Price:** free. **Circulation:** 1,000 ● Annual Report, annual. Highlights previous year and forecasts coming year. **Price:** free. Alternate Formats: online ● Also publishes fact sheets, technical reports, training materials on detection and treatment of infectious diseases and nutritional blindness,

and educational materials. **Conventions/Meetings:** semiannual board meeting.

16502 ■ Independent Visually Impaired Enterprisers (IVIE)
c/o Ardis Bazyn, Pres.
500 S 3rd St., Apt. H
Burbank, CA 91502
Ph: (818)238-9321
E-mail: abazyn@bazyncommunications.com
URL: http://www.acb.org/affiliates
Contact: Ardis Bazyn, Pres.
Founded: 1980. **Members:** 50. **Membership Dues:** general, $15 (annual). **Description:** Blind and visually impaired people who own or operate small businesses. Seeks to: broaden vocational opportunities in business for the blind and visually impaired; improve rehabilitational facilities for all types of business enterprises; publicize capabilities of the blind and visually impaired. Maintains speakers' bureau. **Affiliated With:** American Council of the Blind. **Publications:** *IVIE Motivator*, quarterly. Newsletter. **Price:** $15.00 for nonmembers. **Circulation:** 75. **Conventions/Meetings:** annual meeting, held in conjunction with the ACB National Convention.

16503 ■ International Association of Audio Information Services (IAAIS)
c/o Rob Munro, Treas.
65 Forest Oaks Dr.
Durham, NC 27705
Ph: (540)989-8900
Free: (800)280-5325
Fax: (540)776-2727
E-mail: hlusignan@nbrscanada.com
URL: http://www.iaais.org
Contact: Heather Lusignan, Pres.
Founded: 1977. **Members:** 140. **Membership Dues:** associate, $100 (annual) ● full voting, $200 (annual) ● satellite, $50 (annual). **Staff:** 1. **Budget:** $17,860. **Multinational. Description:** Helps members to provide access to current printed information not available to print disabled people. Represents volunteers broadcast daily newspapers, community news updates, grocery ads, and death notices. Advocates access to printed material as a key issue under the Americans with Disabilities Act and that the Internet needs to be accessible to people with disabilities. Compiles statistics; holds competitions; maintains speakers' bureau. **Libraries: Type:** reference; not open to the public. **Holdings:** archival material, articles, audiovisuals, books, periodicals. **Subjects:** radio, disabilities, legislation, regulation. **Awards:** C. Stanley Potter Lifetime Achievement. **Frequency:** annual. **Type:** recognition ● PR/Awareness. **Frequency:** annual. **Type:** recognition ● Program of the Year. **Frequency:** annual. **Type:** recognition. **Computer Services:** database ● mailing lists, of members ● online services, referral and webcasting. **Telecommunication Services:** electronic bulletin board, radio-reading and audio information. **Committees:** External Affairs; Future Priorities and Goals; Internal Affairs. **Formerly:** National Association of Radio Reading Services. **Publications:** *Directory of Radio Reading Services*, annual. **Price:** $150.00. **Circulation:** 200. **Advertising:** accepted ● *HEARSSAY*, quarterly. Newsletter ● *IAAIS Newsletter*, quarterly. Contains audio information industry news. **Price:** free. **Circulation:** 1,000. **Advertising:** accepted. Alternate Formats: magnetic tape; diskette ● Membership Directory, annual. **Conventions/Meetings:** annual conference and meeting (exhibits).

16504 ■ International Children's Anophthalmia Network (ICAN)
c/o Center for Developmental Medicine and Genetics
5501 Old York Rd.
Genetics, Levy 2 W
Philadelphia, PA 19141
Free: (800)580-4226
E-mail: ican@anophthalmia.org
URL: http://www.anophthalmia.org
Contact: Sherry Salatto, Pres.
Founded: 1993. **Membership Dues:** individual/family, $25 (annual) ● professional, $50 (annual). **Multinational. Description:** Provides support for individu-

als with anophthalmia, micropthalmia, coloboma, and their families. Provides a forum for parents with affected children to share personal experiences, information and support. Provides referrals to genetic counseling, support groups and other services. Promotes professional and patient education. **Telecommunication Services:** electronic mail, aemcgenetics2@hotmail.com. **Publications:** *The Conformer*, semiannual. Newsletter. Contains stories, event information and research advancements. **Price:** included in membership dues. Alternate Formats: online.

16505 ■ International Trachoma Initiative (ITI)
441 Lexington Ave., Ste.1101
New York, NY 10017-3910
Ph: (212)490-6460
Fax: (212)490-6461
E-mail: info@trachoma.org
URL: http://www.trachoma.org
Contact: Dr. Jacob Kumaresan, Pres.

Founded: 1998. **Multinational. Description:** Seeks to eliminate the cause of preventable blindness. Promotes "SAFE: surgery, antibiotics, face washing and environmental change" as a strategy to eliminate blinding trachoma. **Computer Services:** Information services, trachoma resources ● mailing lists. **Committees:** Trachoma Expert. **Programs:** Applied Research; Communications and Advocacy. **Publications:** Newsletter, periodic. Alternate Formats: online.

16506 ■ Interprofessional Fostering of Ophthalmic Care for Underserved Sectors (InFOCUS)
19728 Saums Rd.
PMB No. 136
Houston, TX 77084
Ph: (281)398-7525
Free: (866)398-7525
Fax: (281)398-7428
E-mail: info@infocusonline.org
URL: http://www.infocusonline.org
Contact: Dr. Ian B. Berger MD, Dir.

Founded: 1987. **Staff:** 4. **Description:** Works in cooperation with eye care specialists, public health care professionals, health care providers and humanitarian organizations to develop sustainable eye care practices in areas with underserved populations; encourages community self-reliance. Conducts educational and charitable programs; sponsors research on appropriate technology for primary eye care. **Libraries: Type:** reference. **Holdings:** artwork, audio recordings, books, clippings, periodicals, video recordings. **Subjects:** vision science, ophthalmology, public health.

16507 ■ InTouch Networks (ITN)
c/o Jewish Guild for the Blind
15 W 65th St.
New York, NY 10023
Ph: (212)769-6270
E-mail: intouchinfo@jgb.org
URL: http://www.jgb.org/InTouch/default.asp

Founded: 1974. **Members:** 1,000,000. **Staff:** 5. **Budget:** $325,000. **Description:** Volunteer service that allows blind or physically impaired people to listen to readings of articles from more than 100 newspapers and magazines via closed-circuit radio. Broadcasts nationally accessible on Galaxy 4 satellite. **Awards:** International Association of Audio Information Services Best Program of the Year. **Frequency:** annual. **Type:** recognition. **Recipient:** to radio reading stations nationwide. **Computer Services:** database ● mailing lists. **Publications:** *Program Guide*, annual. Alternate Formats: magnetic tape.

16508 ■ JBI International - Jewish Braille Institute of America (JBI)
110 E 30th St.
New York, NY 10016
Ph: (212)889-2525
Free: (800)433-1531
Fax: (212)689-3692

E-mail: admin@jbilibrary.org
URL: http://www.jbilibrary.org
Contact: Dr. Ellen Isler, Pres./CEO

Founded: 1931. **Staff:** 29. **Budget:** $3,000,000. **Languages:** English, Hebrew, Hungarian, Polish, Russian, Yiddish. **Multinational. Description:** Serves the cultural, religious, educational and communal needs of the visually impaired and blind in over 50 countries, including the U.S., Israel and the former Soviet Union and in six languages (English, Russian, Hebrew, Hungarian, Yiddish, Polish). Distributes materials free on audiocassette, in large print and in Braille. Maintains a collection of 10,000 titles covering fiction and non-fiction, liturgical materials, and 7 monthly magazines. **Libraries: Type:** reference; lending. **Holdings:** 168,000; audio recordings, books, periodicals. **Subjects:** fiction, non-fiction, liturgical materials, Braille volumes in Hebrew, Yiddish and English. **Computer Services:** Online services, catalogs to subscribers in subject/interest areas. **Programs:** International; Outreach. **Formerly:** (2003) Jewish Braille Institute of America. **Publications:** *Hebrew Braille Bible* ● *Hebrew Self-Taught* (in Hebrew). Serves as a Braille primer. ● *JBI Voice*, 10/year. Magazine. Includes articles on Jewish-related topics, politics, stories, and poetry. Available in cassette format. **Price:** free to blind and visually impaired persons. **Circulation:** 2,000 ● *Jewish Reference Calendar*, annual. Comes in large print, 18-month with secular holidays and candle lighting times. ● *Passover Haggadah*. Available in large print edition. ● Also publishes prayer books and religious texts in Hebrew.

16509 ■ Jewish Guild for the Blind (JGB)
15 W 65th St.
New York, NY 10023
Ph: (212)769-6200
Free: (800)284-4422
Fax: (212)769-6266
E-mail: info@jgb.org
URL: http://www.jgb.org
Contact: Alan R. Morse, Pres./CEO

Founded: 1914. **Staff:** 700. **Languages:** Chinese, English, French, Hebrew, Russian, Spanish. **Non-membership. Description:** Medical and vision services for blind, visually impaired, and multihandicapped people of all ages, races, and creeds. Provides social work, counseling, and AIDS case management; job development, placement, and training; support group services; rehabilitation, including vocational, high school equivalency training, orientation and mobility, activities of daily living, and computer training; adapted physical education; communication skills; adult day health care program, GuildCare in New York City, Yonkers, Bronx, Buffalo, Niagara Falls, Albany, New York, and at Greater Boston Guild for the Blind, The Guild's Boston subsidiary. Operates Early Intervention Program for infants and preschoolers (up to age 5); school for multihandicapped children; state licensed psychiatric clinic for emotionally disturbed blind persons and their families; day treatment programs for multihandicapped blind adults; Low Vision Services; Comprehensive Outpatient Rehabilitation Facility (C.O.R.F.) and a Center for Diabetes Care. J.G.B. Health Facilities Corporation, the residential health care subsidiary, operates the Home for Aged Blind (a nursing home), and the Newman Center for Alzheimer's Care in Yonkers, NY. Co-sponsors health fairs/vision screenings for the community; operates GuildNet, a long-term managed health care program; SightCare, an education program for caregivers, and InTouch Networks, a national radio reading service. **Awards:** The Alfred W. Bressler Prize in Vision Science. **Frequency:** annual. **Type:** monetary. **Recipient:** to a professional who has published research or clinical work that has contributed to the advancement of vision care, the treatment of eye disease or the rehabilitation of people with vision impairment ● The GuildScholar Program. **Frequency:** annual. **Type:** scholarship. **Recipient:** for college-bound high school students who are legally blind. **Formerly:** (1960) New York Guild for the Jewish Blind. **Publications:** *The Guild*, quarterly. Newsletter. Contains guild programs and events involving professional and volunteer sup-

porters of Guild services. **Price:** free. **Circulation:** 25,000. **Conventions/Meetings:** annual board meeting.

16510 ■ Keren Or
350 7th Ave., Ste.701
New York, NY 10001
Ph: (212)279-4070
Fax: (212)279-4043
E-mail: info@keren-or.org
URL: http://www.keren-or.org
Contact: Albert Hornblass MD, Pres.

Founded: 1956. **Staff:** 4. **Budget:** $1,800,000. **Languages:** English, Hebrew. **Description:** Maintains the Keren-Or Center for Multi-Handicapped Blind Children in Jerusalem which houses, rehabilitates, and trains over 70 severely disabled blind children and young adults. Funds acquired through public contributions and Israeli government funding. **Libraries: Type:** not open to the public. **Holdings:** 300. **Awards:** Ray of Light. **Frequency:** annual. **Type:** recognition. **Computer Services:** database ● mailing lists ● online services. **Divisions:** Women's; Young Leadership. **Formerly:** (1987) Jerusalem Institutions for the Blind. **Publications:** *InSights*, semiannual. Newsletter. Gives updates on all the activities at Keren-Or. Alternate Formats: online. **Conventions/Meetings:** quarterly board meeting.

16511 ■ Leader Dogs for the Blind (LDB)
1039 S Rochester Rd.
Rochester, MI 48307
Ph: (248)651-9011
Free: (888)777-5332
Fax: (248)651-5812
E-mail: leaderdog@leaderdog.org
URL: http://www.leaderdog.org
Contact: William C. Hansen, Pres./CEO

Founded: 1939. **Staff:** 105. **Budget:** $8,910,000. **Multinational. Description:** Trains dogs to serve as guides for blind persons and conducts a supervised course of training to coordinate blind persons and their Leader Dogs as operating teams; there is no charge for the service. Conducts research to determine the most satisfactory breed of dog for Leader Dog purposes. Places puppies into volunteer homes in preparation for formal adult dog training; facilities include a kennel, veterinary hospital, residence facility and training center. **Telecommunication Services:** TDD, (248)651-3715 ● teletype, (248)651-3713. **Programs:** Accelerated Mobility; Universities. **Affiliated With:** Association for Education and Rehabilitation of the Blind and Visually Impaired. **Formerly:** Path-Finder Guide Dogs; (1952) Leader Dog League for the Blind. **Publications:** *Leader Dog Overview and Tour*. Videos. **Price:** free ● *Leader Dog Update*, quarterly. Newsletter. Available in large print, Braille, and tape. **Price:** free. **Circulation:** 18,000 ● *Orientation of Dog Guide Users to New Environments* ● Also produces taped cassettes of all written materials available to the visually impaired. **Conventions/Meetings:** annual board meeting.

16512 ■ Lighthouse International
111 E 59th St.
New York, NY 10022-1202
Ph: (212)821-9200 (212)821-9713
Free: (800)829-0500
Fax: (212)821-9707
E-mail: info@lighthouse.org
URL: http://www.lighthouse.org
Contact: Tara A. Cortes PhD, Pres./CEO

Founded: 1906. **Multinational. Description:** Provides free literature and information on blindness, low vision, vision rehabilitation, eye conditions and diseases, assistive computer technology, financial aid, magnifiers and other products, etc. Also provides nationwide and international listings of low vision doctors, agencies, and support groups. **Awards:** Career Awards Program. **Frequency:** annual. **Type:** recognition. **Recipient:** for students who are blind or partially sighted ● College-bound Award. **Frequency:** annual. **Type:** scholarship. **Recipient:** for high seniors or recent high school graduates ● Graduate Award. **Frequency:** annual. **Type:** scholarship. **Recipient:** for college graduates or college seniors planning to pursue a graduate level program ● Undergraduate Award I. **Frequency:** annual. **Type:** scholarship. **Recipient:** for college students ● Undergraduate Award II. **Frequency:** annual. **Type:** scholarship. **Recipient:** for college students pursuing an undergraduate degree. **Programs:** Arlene R. Gordon Research Institute; Career Services; Independent Living Skills; Lighthouse Child Development Center; Lighthouse Continuing Education; Lighthouse Music School; Low Vision Services. **Publications:** *Aging & Vision News.* Newsletter. Alternate Formats: online ● *EnVision.* Newsletter. Contains issues of visually impaired children. Alternate Formats: online ● *Sharing Solutions,* 3/year. Newsletter. **Price:** free for members. Alternate Formats: online ● *Visionary Philanthropy.* Newsletter. Alternate Formats: online ● Annual Report; "Aging & Vision News"; literature on eye conditions and other aspects of vision loss.

16513 ■ Lutheran Braille Evangelism Association (LBEA)
1740 Eugene St.
White Bear Lake, MN 55110-3312
Ph: (651)426-0469
E-mail: lbea@qwest.net
URL: http://www.users.qwest.net/~lbea/index.htm
Contact: Rev. Roger Schwartz, Pres.
Founded: 1952. **Members:** 2,000. **Membership Dues:** sponsor, $150 (annual). **Staff:** 2. **Budget:** $45,000. **Multinational. Description:** Fosters provision of religious material to the visually impaired in Braille, audio cassette, extra large print and digital formats. Supported by contributions of members. **Additional Websites:** http://www.lbea.org. **Publications:** *Braille Evangelism Bulletin,* quarterly. Newsletter. Contains membership activities, and services and materials available. **Price:** free. **Circulation:** 1,100 ● *Christian Magnifier,* 11/year. Magazine. Contains large-print Christian inspirational readings. **Price:** $7.00/year ● *Tract Messenger,* 11/year. Magazine. Contains information about Christian devotional readings and LBEA news. **Price:** free for the blind ● Also provides religious material in Braille, large print and audio cassette, such as the Holy Bible. **Conventions/Meetings:** annual meeting and banquet - always May.

16514 ■ Lutheran Braille Workers (LBW)
PO Box 5000
Yucaipa, CA 92399
Ph: (909)795-8977
Fax: (909)795-8970
E-mail: lbw@lbwinc.org
URL: http://www.lbwinc.org
Founded: 1943. **Members:** 7,000. **Staff:** 18. **Budget:** $1,750,000. **National Groups:** 206. **Description:** Volunteers staffing 206 work centers worldwide, through which they seek to bring the Bible to the blind and visually impaired. Assists sighted volunteers to transcribe printed material into Braille and large print. Produces and distributes free biblical and devotional material in Braille and large print in over 40 languages. Works to constantly upgrade the systems necessary for the production of Braille materials. **Departments:** Braille; Large Print. **Affiliated With:** World Blind Union. **Publications:** *Lutheran Braille Workers—Newsletter,* quarterly. Covers association activities. **Price:** free ● *Work Center Directory,* annual ● *Work Center Memo,* monthly. Newsletter. Provides information to LBW work centers. **Conventions/Meetings:** triennial meeting.

16515 ■ MAB Community Services (MAB)
313 Pleasant St.
Watertown, MA 02472-2821
Ph: (617)926-4232
Free: (800)852-3029
Fax: (617)926-1412
E-mail: fweisse@mabcommunity.org
URL: http://www.mabcommunity.org
Contact: Fran Weisse, Asst. Regional Dir.
Founded: 1903. **Staff:** 50. **Budget:** $2,000,000. **State Groups:** 3. **Languages:** English, Spanish. **Nonmembership. Description:** Serves individuals who are newly blind or partially sighted, and those with progressive eye disease, as well as individuals

who are blind. Provides information and referral, self-help support groups, special services for elders, community volunteer services, recording studio, Braille program, brain injury program and DD community services program (Developmental Disabilities). **Libraries: Type:** reference. **Awards:** Uncommon Vision Award. **Frequency:** annual. **Type:** recognition. **Computer Services:** database, information in print, large print, and speech. **Formed by Merger of:** (1998) Massachusetts Association for the Blind and Vision Foundation. **Formerly:** (2001) Vision Community Services; (2004) Vision Community Services - A Division of the Massachusetts Association for the Blind. **Publications:** *MABCS Resource Update,* quarterly. Newsletter. **Conventions/Meetings:** annual board meeting - usually October.

16516 ■ Macular Degeneration Foundation (MDF)
PO Box 531313
Henderson, NV 89053
Free: (888)633-3937
Fax: (702)450-3396
E-mail: ed@eyesight.org
URL: http://www.eyesight.org
Contact: Dr. Edmund J. Aleksandrovich, Founder/Chm./Pres./CEO
Founded: 1992. **Staff:** 3. **Budget:** $59,000. **Nonmembership. Description:** Encourages medical research and education into the vision disease macular degeneration. **Publications:** *The Magnifier.* Newsletter. Features breaking news regarding clinical trials, reports, and resources. **Price:** free. **Circulation:** 16,000. Alternate Formats: online.

16517 ■ National Accreditation Council for Agencies Serving the Blind and Visually Impaired (NAC)
21475 Lorain Rd.
Cleveland, OH 44126
Ph: (440)409-0340
Fax: (440)409-0173
E-mail: steve@nacasb.org
URL: http://www.nacasb.org
Contact: Steven K. Hegedeos, Exec. Dir.
Founded: 1966. **Members:** 48. **Membership Dues:** regular, $300-$3,000 (annual). **Staff:** 2. **Budget:** $160,000. **Description:** Accredits schools, agencies and programs serving people who are blind or visually impaired. Constitutes with the broad-based support of national organizations in the field of blindness, many state and local organizations, and the U.S. Department of Health, Education and Welfare. Influences special schools and agencies that serve people who are blind or visually impaired to meet established standards that promote effective, sound, and publicly accountable education and rehabilitation programs. **Formerly:** (2003) National Accreditation Council for Agencies Serving the Blind and Visually Handicapped. **Publications:** *NAC News.* Newsletter. Alternate Formats: online ● *The Standard-Bearer,* annual. Annual Report. Alternate Formats: online ● Also publishes self-study and evaluation guides, incorporating standards for management and services of agencies and schools for people who are blind and visually handicapped; publications are available in print, Braille, and recorded editions. **Conventions/Meetings:** annual meeting.

16518 ■ National Alliance of Blind Students (NABS)
c/o American Council of the Blind
1155 15th St. NW, Ste.1004
Washington, DC 20005
Ph: (202)467-5081
Free: (800)424-8666
Fax: (202)467-5085
E-mail: rj.hodson@verizon.net
Contact: Rebecca Hodson, Pres.
Founded: 1974. **Members:** 150. **Membership Dues:** general student, $15 (annual) ● junior (under 18), $8 (annual). **State Groups:** 8. **Description:** Postsecondary students in academic, vocational, trade, and professional programs as well as disabled student service personnel. Aims to educate agencies, governments, institutions, and the public dealing with blind

students as to their needs and educational pursuits in accredited postsecondary educational programs. Acts to protect rights and interests of blind students. Participates in annual National Student Seminar at the national convention of the American Council of the Blind. **Computer Services:** Mailing lists. **Publications:** *Student Advocate,* quarterly. Newsletter. **Price:** free for members. Alternate Formats: online. **Conventions/Meetings:** annual conference (exhibits) - July.

16519 ■ National Alliance for Eye and Vision Research (NAEVR)
12300 Twinbrook Pkwy., Ste.250
Rockville, MD 20852
Ph: (240)221-2905
Fax: (240)221-0370
E-mail: jamesj@eyeresearch.org
URL: http://www.eyeresearch.org
Contact: Stephen J. Ryan MD, Pres.
Founded: 1997. **Description:** Represents the interests of professionals, consumers and industry organizations involved in eye and vision research. Educates the Congress and the public about the value of eye and vision research. Works to contain health costs and improve the quality of life for millions of Americans. **Telecommunication Services:** electronic mail, sryan@doheny.org. **Publications:** *Contributor Report,* quarterly. Newsletter. Highlights activity in support of eye and vision research community. Alternate Formats: online.

16520 ■ National Association for Parents of Children With Visual Impairments (NAPVI)
PO Box 317
Watertown, MA 02471
Ph: (617)972-7441
Free: (800)562-6265
Fax: (617)972-7444
E-mail: napvi@perkins.org
URL: http://www.spedex.com/napvi
Contact: Susan LaVenture, Exec. Dir.
Founded: 1980. **Members:** 2,000. **Membership Dues:** parent/guardian, associate, $25 (annual) ● professional, $40 (annual) ● agency/community group, $250 (annual) ● supporting, $50-$200 (annual) ● sponsoring, $200-$1,000 (annual) ● patron, $1,000 (annual). **Regional Groups:** 7. **State Groups:** 16. **Languages:** English, Spanish. **Description:** Parents and families of visually impaired children; community groups and agencies; interested individuals. Provides support for members and promotes public understanding of the needs and rights of the visually impaired child. Seeks to address parental needs for: emotional support; information about care, education, and treatment for their children; aid in establishing local, state, and regional groups; quality services for blind and impaired children; communication of their expertise and expectations with other parents and federal, state, and local service agencies; assurance that their children are accepted by society. Conducts workshops for parents and research programs. **Computer Services:** Bibliographic search ● information services, camps and agencies serving blind and visually impaired children. **Affiliated With:** American Foundation for the Blind; American Printing House for the Blind; Association for Education and Rehabilitation of the Blind and Visually Impaired; National Accreditation Council for Agencies Serving the Blind and Visually Impaired. **Formerly:** (2003) National Association for Parents of the Visually Impaired. **Publications:** *Awareness,* quarterly. Newsletter. **Price:** included in membership dues. **Circulation:** 2,000. **Advertising:** accepted ● *How to Pack 'Em In: A Guide to Planning Workshops* ● *Mainstreaming Your Visually Impaired Child: Legislative Handbook for Parents.* **Price:** $5.50 for nonmembers; $5.00 for members ● *Parents to the Rescue.* Book ● *Preschool Learning Activities for the Visually Impaired Child: A Guide for Parents.* Book. **Price:** $9.50 for nonmembers; $8.00 for members ● *Take Charge!: A Resource Guide for Parents of the Visually Impaired* ● *Your Child's Information Journal* ● Audiotapes ● Brochures ● Reprints ● Videos. **Conventions/Meetings:** annual board meeting ● annual Families Connecting with Families Conference.

16521 ■ National Association for Visually Handicapped (NAVH)
22 W 21st St., 6th Fl.
New York, NY 10010
Ph: (212)889-3141 (212)255-2804
Free: (888)205-5951
Fax: (212)727-2931
E-mail: navh@navh.org
URL: http://www.navh.org
Contact: Dr. Lorraine H. Marchi, Founder/CEO
Founded: 1954. **Members:** 7,530. **Membership Dues:** individual (full), $50 (annual). **Staff:** 15. **Regional Groups:** 2. **Languages:** English, Italian, Mandarin Dialects, Russian, Spanish, Yiddish. **Description:** Individuals, clubs, organizations, and foundations support NAVH's work in publishing and distributing large-print informational literature for the partially seeing. Acts as information clearinghouse regarding all public and private services available to the partially seeing. Offers guidance and counseling to parents of partially seeing children and to partially seeing adults. Educates the public and the professional community about the needs of the partially seeing. **Libraries: Type:** reference; lending. **Holdings:** 8,500; books. **Subjects:** classical and contemporary large-print reading material. **Telecommunication Services:** electronic mail, staffca@navh.org. **Formerly:** (1972) National Aid to Visually Handicapped. **Publications:** *About Children's Eyes.* Large print only. **Price:** free ● *It's All Right to Be Angry* ● *Knitting Instructions* ● *Large Print Loan Library Catalog,* biennial. Lists books in large print commercial publishers available from NAVH. ● *National Association for Visually Handicapped—Bulletin: Annual Program Report,* annual. Newsletter. Reports on association activities and programs. Includes obituaries. ● *NAVH Update,* quarterly. Newsletter. Provides updates on issues and devices for the visually handicapped. ● *Visual Aids and Information Materials.* Catalog. Features visual aids available from NAVH. ● Also publishes (in English, Russian, Spanish, and some Chinese) pamphlets, guides, booklets, and manuals on eye diseases and services for visually impaired; also books on tape. **Conventions/Meetings:** bimonthly Senior Discussion Group - support group meeting, support group for visually impaired seniors - every 1st and 3rd Wednesday ● annual Showcase and Counseling Center in NYC - meeting, open to the public (exhibits) - always spring.

16522 ■ National Braille Association (NBA)
3 Townline Cir.
Rochester, NY 14623-2513
Ph: (585)427-8260
Fax: (585)427-0263
E-mail: nbaoffice@nationalbraille.org
URL: http://nationalbraille.org
Contact: Mr. David Shaffer, Exec. Dir.
Founded: 1945. **Members:** 1,500. **Membership Dues:** regular in U.S., $40 (annual) ● regular outside U.S., $45 (annual) ● sustaining, $60 (annual) ● patron, $150 (annual) ● life, $500. **Staff:** 5. **Budget:** $360,800. **Description:** Provides continuing education to those who prepare braille, and provides braille materials to persons who are visually impaired. Cooperates with other organizations in developing and expanding use of advanced braille codes; offers training workshops for transcribers and tactile illustrators. NBA Braille Book Bank maintains over 2000 titles and 500 standard technical tables in braille for immediate duplication; offers a transcribing service for braille readers. **Libraries: Type:** not open to the public. **Holdings:** 12,665; books. **Subjects:** math, science, music, foreign languages, general interest - all in braille. **Awards:** Merit Awards. **Frequency:** annual. **Type:** recognition. **Recipient:** for volunteer service. **Subgroups:** Board of Directors; Skills Committees. **Affiliated With:** Braille Authority of North America. **Formerly:** (1964) National Braille Club. **Publications:** *Braille Technical Table Catalog,* periodic. Contains technical tables in the NBA collection. Covers the fields of mathematics, statistics, chemistry, physics, computer science, and business. **Price:** free ● *National Braille Association—Bulletin,* quarterly. Newsletter. Features articles of interest to members and persons working in the field of services

to the visually impaired. Contains calendar of events. **Price:** included in membership dues; $40.00 /year for nonmembers in U.S.; $50.00 /year for nonmembers outside U.S. ISSN: 0550-5666. **Circulation:** 2,500. Alternate Formats: CD-ROM ● *National Braille Association—General Interest Catalog,* periodic. Topics include work, recreation, and daily living. Directory of titles available in braille from NBA collection. Available in print and braille. **Price:** free ● *National Braille Association—Music Catalog,* periodic. Directory of music titles available in braille from NBA collection. Available in print and braille. **Price:** free ● *National Braille Association—Textbook Catalog,* periodic. Includes titles of braille books from NBA collection of college-level and technical materials. Available in print and braille. **Price:** free ● *NBA Publications.* Manuals. Covers tape recording, tactile graphics, mathematics and science braille, textbook format braille, computer-assisted transcription, and large type. **Conventions/Meetings:** biennial Professional Development Conference - conference and workshop, includes workshops for preparers of reading matter for the blind (exhibits) ● semiannual regional meeting - spring and fall.

16523 ■ National Braille Press (NBP)
88 St. Stephen St.
Boston, MA 02115-4302
Ph: (617)266-6160
Free: (888)965-8965
Fax: (617)437-0456
E-mail: orders@nbp.org
URL: http://www.nbp.org
Contact: Bill Raeder, Pres.
Founded: 1927. **Staff:** 31. **Budget:** $3,200,000. **Description:** Publishes books and magazines in Braille, including booklets on computers, self-help, and children's books (also in print). Supported by private gifts and legacies. Sponsors Children's Braille Book Club, offering monthly selections of print-braille books. **Telecommunication Services:** additional toll-free number, for ordering, (800)548-7323. **Programs:** ReadBooks!. **Publications:** *National Braille Press Release,* 3/year. Newsletter. Alternate Formats: online ● *Our Special,* bimonthly ● *Syndicated Columnists Weekly* ● *Annual Report,* annual. Alternate Formats: online. **Conventions/Meetings:** annual Corporate Meeting.

16524 ■ National Federation of the Blind (NFB)
1800 Johnson St.
Baltimore, MD 21230
Ph: (410)659-9314
Fax: (410)685-5653
E-mail: nfb@nfb.org
URL: http://www.nfb.org
Contact: Marc Maurer, Pres.
Founded: 1940. **Members:** 50,000. **Staff:** 100. **State Groups:** 52. **Local Groups:** 700. **Description:** Federation of states (50 plus Washington, DC and Puerto Rico) and local (700) organizations representing over 50,000 blind people. Seeks the complete equality and integration of the blind into society. Monitors all legislation affecting the blind; evaluates present programs for the blind; stimulates and assists in promoting needed services. Supports and conducts scholarly research and publication of results. Works to improve policies toward the blind in such places as the U.S. Office of Personnel Management. Sponsors National White Cane Week annually for fundraising and educational purposes. Distributes information. Maintains National Blindness Information Center. **Awards:** Hermione Grant Calhoun Scholarship. **Frequency:** annual. **Type:** scholarship. **Recipient:** for blind women students ● Howard Brown Rickard Scholarship. **Type:** scholarship. **Recipient:** for blind students of the professions ● **Type:** recognition. **Recipient:** for greatest contribution to the welfare of the blind ● **Type:** scholarship. **Recipient:** for blind postsecondary students ● **Type:** scholarship. **Recipient:** for blind students. **Divisions:** Blind Merchants; Computer Users; Human Services Workers; Lawyers; Parents of Blind Children; Public Employees; Secretaries and Transcribers; Students; Teachers; Workshop Employees. **Programs:** Braille is Beautiful; Job

Referral; Leadership Training for Blind Leaders; Online Education; Senior Blind; Web Certification. **Publications:** *Braille Monitor,* monthly. Magazine. Reports on action by the NFB on current legislative issues, legal cases, and social concerns affecting the blind; gives news of aids and appliances. **Price:** included in membership dues; available to nonmembers by donation. **Circulation:** 30,000. Alternate Formats: online ● *Future Reflections,* quarterly. Magazine. Offers guidance in the day-to-day aspects of raising a blind child. Includes literature reviews, calendar of events, and new product list. **Price:** included in membership dues; $15.00 /year for nonmembers. ISSN: 0883-3419. **Circulation:** 10,000. Alternate Formats: online ● *If Blindness Comes.* Book. Serves as a general information book with answers to common questions about blindness. ● *The Kernel Books.* Features a series of books written by the blind. ● *Voice of the Diabetic,* quarterly. Newspaper. Contains personal stories and practical guidance from blind diabetics and medical professionals, medical news, resource column and recipe corner. **Price:** included in membership dues. **Circulation:** 60,000. Alternate Formats: online ● Brochures ● Pamphlets. **Conventions/Meetings:** annual conference (exhibits) - always late June to early July ● seminar.

16525 ■ National Industries for the Blind (NIB)
1310 Braddock Pl.
Alexandria, VA 22314-1691
Ph: (703)310-0500
E-mail: info@nib.org
URL: http://www.nib.org
Contact: Jim Gibbons, Pres./CEO
Founded: 1938. **Members:** 87. **Staff:** 120. **Description:** Association of agencies employing blind persons who undertake the production of certain goods and services for the federal government under the Javits-Wagner-O'Day Act. Offers gainful employment in these industries, located in 38 states, Puerto Rico, and the District of Columbia for those blind or multi-disabled blind persons who are able and willing to work. Researches and recommends new products, prices, and price revisions to the Committee for Purchase From People Who Are Blind or Severely Disabled; allocates federal work orders among these agencies. Devises quality control systems; provides management and engineering services to increase plant efficiency and broaden opportunities for blind persons; assists the industries in procurement of raw materials. **Awards:** Blind Employee of the Year. **Frequency:** annual. **Type:** recognition. **Publications:** *Opportunity,* quarterly. Magazine. Covers news and feature articles on agencies for the blind; describes industries, agencies, and projects that employ blind workers. ● *60 Years of Success,* annual. Annual Report ● Report. Alternate Formats: diskette; magnetic tape. **Conventions/Meetings:** semiannual conference - always spring and fall.

16526 ■ National Organization of Parents of Blind Children (NOPBC)
1800 Johnson St.
Baltimore, MD 21230-4998
Ph: (410)659-9314
Fax: (410)685-5653
E-mail: bcheadle@nfb.org
URL: http://www.nfb.org/nfb/Parents_and_Teachers.
asp?SnID=2114452487
Contact: Barbara Cheadle, Pres.
Membership Dues: general, $8 (annual). **State Groups:** 30. **Description:** Provides information and support to parents of blind children. Develops and expands resources available to parents and their children. Aims to eliminate discrimination and prejudice against the blind. **Committees:** Adoption and Blindness Network; Blind Multiple Disabled; Parents in Partnership for Deaf-Blind Children. **Affiliated With:** National Federation of the Blind. **Publications:** *Future Reflections,* quarterly. Magazine. **Price:** free for members. Alternate Formats: online.

16527 ■ Parents Active for Vision Education (PAVE)
4135 54th Pl.
San Diego, CA 92105-2303

Ph: (619)287-0081
Free: (800)PAVE-988
Fax: (619)287-0084
E-mail: info@pavevision.org
URL: http://www.pavevision.org
Contact: Marjie Thompson, Pres.
Founded: 1988. **Membership Dues:** family, individual, $20 (annual) ● supporting, $40-$99 (annual) ● century, $100-$499 (annual) ● benefactor, $500-$999 (annual) ● angel funder, $1,000,000. **Staff:** 1. **Budget:** $55,000. **Local Groups:** 1. **Description:** Parents and teachers with children in their homes and classrooms who suffer or have suffered from the effects of undiagnosed vision problems. Works to raise public awareness of learning related vision problems. Supports the development of comprehensive learning related vision screenings, vision education, and vision hygiene programs in schools and communities. Maintains speakers' bureau. **Libraries: Type:** reference. **Holdings:** audio recordings, books, periodicals, video recordings. **Subjects:** efficient vision. **Boards:** Directors. **Publications:** *The Hidden Disability* (in English and Spanish). Pamphlet. **Price:** $26.00 100 copies, includes shipping and handling ● *The Hidden Disability: Undetected Vision Problems.* Video. **Price:** $65.00/copy, plus shipping and handling ● *Pavestones*, semiannual. Newsletter. **Price:** free. **Circulation:** 2,900 ● *Some Heroes Are Small* (in English and Spanish). Book. **Price:** $7.70/copy, plus shipping and handling. **Conventions/Meetings:** bimonthly seminar (exhibits) - always in San Diego, CA.

16528 ■ Pilot Dogs (PD)
625 W Town St.
Columbus, OH 43215
Ph: (614)221-6367
Fax: (614)221-1577
URL: http://www.pilotdogs.org
Contact: Steven Kahn, Pres.
Founded: 1950. **Members:** 20,841. **Membership Dues:** active, $10 (annual) ● sustaining, $50 (annual) ● life, $100 ● perpetual, $500 (annual). **Staff:** 30. **Budget:** $1,200,000. **Description:** Provides guide dogs and training for the blind. **Publications:** *Pilot Light*, quarterly. Newsletter. **Conventions/Meetings:** annual convention - always July.

16529 ■ Prevent Blindness America
211 W Wacker Dr., Ste.1700
Chicago, IL 60606
Free: (800)331-2020
E-mail: info@preventblindness.org
URL: http://www.preventblindness.org
Contact: Hugh R. Parry, Pres./CEO
Founded: 1908. **Members:** 40,000. **Staff:** 125. **State Groups:** 22. **Local Groups:** 22. **Description:** Charitable organization committed to preventing blindness and preserving sight through nationwide comprehensive programs of public and professional education, research, industrial, and community services. Services include promotion and support of local glaucoma screening programs, pre-school vision testing, industrial eye safety, and collection of statistical and other data on nature and extent of causes of blindness and impaired vision. Operates a toll-free information center dealing with eye health and safety topics. Through PBA Investigator Awards, the organization awards postdoctoral awards and grants in aid for medical research. Sponsors Wise Owl Program to promote widespread use of safety eyewear for various activities and occupations. Compiles statistics. **Libraries: Type:** reference. **Holdings:** 3,000. **Subjects:** ophthalmology, optometry, vision care, eye safety, health. **Awards:** Grant-In-Aid. **Frequency:** annual. **Type:** grant. **Recipient:** for funding of research in vision and ophthalmology ● Postdoctoral Fellowship. **Frequency:** annual. **Type:** fellowship. **Recipient:** for basic or clinical research in vision and ophthalmology. **Computer Services:** database ● mailing lists ● online services, library catalog. **Committees:** Community Programs; Development; Expansion; Eye Safety Advisory; Field Relations; Glaucoma Advisory; Government Relations; Marketing; Pediatric Advisory; Retina Advisory; Scientific Advisory; Strategic Planning. **Absorbed:** (1961)

Ophthalmological Foundation. **Formed by Merger of:** (1913) American Medical Association for the Conservation of Vision; New York State Committee for the Prevention of Blindness. **Formerly:** (1915) National Committee for the Prevention of Blindness; (1928) National Society for the Prevention of Blindness; (1978) National Society to Prevent Blindness. **Publications:** *Prevent Blindness America—Annual Report.* Covers highlights and accomplishments of the previous fiscal year. Includes financial statements. **Price:** free. **Circulation:** 10,000. Alternate Formats: online ● *Prevent Blindness America News*, 3/year. Newsletter. Contains information on eye health and safety. **Price:** $12.00/year. **Circulation:** 40,000. Alternate Formats: online. **Conventions/Meetings:** annual general assembly and meeting (exhibits) - always November.

16530 ■ Prevent Blindness in Premature Babies
Address Unknown since 2007
Description: Provides support and information to individuals and parents of children who have retinopathy of prematurity, a retinal disease that prevents the eye from developing properly.

16531 ■ Protestant Guild for Human Services (PGHS)
411 Waverley Oaks Rd., Ste.104
Waltham, MA 02452
Ph: (781)893-6000
Fax: (781)893-1171
E-mail: admin@protestantguild.org
URL: http://www.protestantguild.org
Contact: Edmund T. Hagerty, Exec. Dir.
Founded: 1946. **Staff:** 165. **Budget:** $8,000,000. **Local Groups:** 2. **Nonmembership. Description:** Non-sectarian organization with a volunteer board and highly-trained professional staff dedicated to serving individuals with special needs. Provides a wide spectrum of services to children, adolescents and young adults with a variety of developmental disabilities. **Programs:** Car Donation; Church Liaison. **Formerly:** Protestant Guild for the Blind. **Publications:** *PGHS News*, semiannual. Newsletter. **Circulation:** 4,000 ● Annual Report, annual. **Conventions/Meetings:** annual meeting.

16532 ■ Recording for the Blind and Dyslexic (RFB&D)
20 Roszel Rd.
Princeton, NJ 08540
Free: (800)803-7201
Fax: (609)987-8116
E-mail: custserv@rfbd.org
URL: http://www.rfbd.org
Contact: Mark Zustovich, Contact
Founded: 1948. **Members:** 40,000. **Membership Dues:** individual, $35 (annual) ● institutional (depends on the level), $350-$950 (annual). **Staff:** 105. **Budget:** $10,000,000. **Regional Groups:** 31. **Description:** Provides library services, computerized books, books on audiotape, and other educational materials free of charge to individuals who are unable to read standard print because of a visual, physical, or perceptual disability. Materials are produced by 4800 volunteers at 31 recording studios throughout the U.S. Titles recorded supplement, but do not duplicate, those of the Library of Congress Talking Book program. **Libraries: Type:** reference. **Holdings:** 90,000; books. **Subjects:** educational. **Awards:** Marion Huber Learning Through Listening Award. **Frequency:** annual. **Type:** recognition. **Recipient:** to outstanding learning disabled high school seniors ● Mary P. Oenslager Scholastic Achievement Award. **Frequency:** annual. **Type:** recognition. **Recipient:** to outstanding blind college seniors. **Computer Services:** Online services, subject reference system. **Absorbed:** (1991) Computerized Books for the Blind. **Formerly:** (1951) National Committee for Recording for the Blind; (2000) Recording for the Blind. **Publications:** *Disk Catalog*, quarterly. **Price:** $16.00/year. **Circulation:** 800. Alternate Formats: diskette ● *Recorded Catalog*, quarterly. **Price:** $16.00/year. **Circulation:** 1,000 ● *Recording for the Blind—Catalog Supplement*, periodic ● *RFB and D Impact*, quarterly.

Newsletter. Provides news for donors, agencies, and schools serving the blind and print-disabled. **Price:** free. **Circulation:** 25,000 ● Annual Report, annual. Includes financial statements for the fiscal year as well as highlights from the previous year. **Price:** free. **Circulation:** 12,000. **Conventions/Meetings:** annual meeting, of volunteer unit chairmen ● annual meeting, of studio directors.

16533 ■ Research to Prevent Blindness (RPB)
645 Madison Ave., 21st Fl.
New York, NY 10022-1010
Ph: (212)752-4333
Free: (800)621-0026
Fax: (212)688-6231
E-mail: inforequest@rpbusa.org
URL: http://www.rpbusa.org
Contact: Diane S. Swift, Pres.
Founded: 1960. **Membership Dues:** eye care specialist, $150 (annual). **Staff:** 9. **Budget:** $15,971,000. **Description:** National voluntary health foundation supported by foundations, corporations, and voluntary gifts and bequests from individuals. Works to stimulate basic and applied research into the causes, prevention, and treatment of blinding eye diseases. Grants funds for equipment, eye research professorships with up to 7 year salary support, assistance in financing construction campaigns for eye research laboratory facilities, and travel expenses for international scholars for short-term collaborative research in the U.S. through seminars and other means, encourages communication among scientists, practicing ophthalmologists, and the public. Maintains scientific advisory panel. **Awards:** Career Development Award. **Type:** grant. **Recipient:** to young physicians and scientists who wish to conduct eye research ● **Frequency:** annual. **Type:** grant. **Recipient:** for eye research to departments of ophthalmology at university medical schools ● Jules and Doris Stein Professorship. **Type:** grant. **Recipient:** for outstanding basic scientists from other disciplines who conduct relevant clinical research in ophthalmology ● Lew R. Wasserman Merit Award. **Type:** recognition. **Recipient:** for mid-career scientists who hold primary positions within departments of ophthalmology and who are actively engaged in eye research ● Physician-Scientist Award. **Type:** recognition. **Recipient:** for nationally recognized and established MDs engaged in clinical eye research ● Senior Scientific Investigator Award. **Type:** grant. **Recipient:** for investigators who have deeply influenced the course of eye research ● Special Research Scholars Award. **Type:** recognition. **Recipient:** for outstanding young scientists conducting research of exceptional merit and promise. **Committees:** Ad Hoc Advisory; Scientific Advisory Panel. **Publications:** *Eye Research News*, annual. Newsletter. Contains reports on latest developments in eye research. **Price:** free ● *Eye Research Seminar Papers*, annual ● *Research to Prevent Blindness—Annual Report*. Contains information on RPB's activities in support of scientific research into the causes, treatment, and prevention of blindness. **Price:** free. **Circulation:** 56,000.

16534 ■ Retinitis Pigmentosa International (RPI)
PO Box 900
Woodland Hills, CA 91365
Ph: (818)992-0500
Free: (800)FIGHT-RP
Fax: (818)992-3265
E-mail: info@rpinternational.org
URL: http://www.rpinternational.org
Contact: Helen Harris, Pres./Founder
Founded: 1972. **Members:** 30,000. **Staff:** 8. **Budget:** $350,000. **State Groups:** 4. **Local Groups:** 1. **Description:** Seeks to raise funds to support research and provide human service programs to assist the visually impaired. Offers charitable services. Maintains research programs. Also describes motion picture and television programs for the blind. Produces annual television special "The Eyes of Christmas" with celebrity memories and a motion picture described for the blind and vision impaired. **Awards:** Vision Awards. **Frequency:** annual. **Type:** recogni-

tion. **Computer Services:** database. **Additional Websites:** http://www.theatrevision.org. **Publications:** *Nightlighter, Sound Bites,* annual. Newsletter. **Conventions/Meetings:** board meeting.

16535 ■ Seeing Eye
PO Box 375
Morristown, NJ 07963-0375
Ph: (973)539-4425
Fax: (973)539-0922
E-mail: info@seeingeye.org
URL: http://www.seeingeye.org
Contact: Dr. James A. Kutsch Jr., Pres.
Founded: 1929. **Staff:** 170. **Budget:** $17,000,000. **Languages:** English, Spanish. **Multinational. Description:** Seeks to enhance the independence, dignity, and self-confidence of blind and visually impaired persons; provides assistance to graduates and their seeing-eyed dogs; educates the public in consideration of public policy. **Libraries: Type:** by appointment only; reference. **Holdings:** archival material, books, papers, reports. **Subjects:** guide dog management. **Awards:** Veterinary Recognition Awards. **Frequency:** annual. **Type:** recognition. **Recipient:** for veterinarians. **Computer Services:** Online services, technology center with speech access software. **Programs:** Breeding; Dog Adoption; Puppy Raising. **Subgroups:** Half Century Club. **Publications:** *Every Step Forward.* Book. Contains inspiring biographical accounts of accomplished Seeing Eye graduates. **Price:** $20.00 ● *Puppy Raising Manual* ● *The Seeing Eye Guide,* quarterly. Annual Report ● Book. Features complete history of The Seeing Eye. **Price:** $10.00 ● Magazine, 3/year ● Also distributes holiday cards.

16536 ■ Surgical Eye Expeditions International (SEE)
7200 Hollister Ave., Unit A
Goleta, CA 93117-2807
Ph: (805)963-3303
Free: (800)20-TO-SEE
Fax: (805)965-3564
E-mail: seeintl@seeintl.org
URL: http://www.seeintl.org
Contact: George Primbs MD, Co-Founder/Pres./CEO
Founded: 1974. **Members:** 756. **Membership Dues:** affiliate in U.S. and Canada, Australia, Western Europe, New Zealand, $108 (annual) ● affiliate in U.S. and Canada, Australia, Western Europe, New Zealand, $216 (biennial) ● affiliate in U.S. and Canada, Australia, Western Europe, New Zealand, $324 (triennial) ● other country, $10 (annual) ● nurse, tech, resident, medical student, $50 (annual). **Staff:** 12. **Budget:** $1,200,000. **Languages:** English, Spanish. **Multinational. Description:** Humanitarian organization providing medical, surgical and educational services by volunteer ophthalmic surgeons with the primary objective of restoring sight to disadvantaged blind individuals worldwide. **Awards:** Spirit of Sight Award. **Frequency:** annual. **Type:** recognition. **Boards:** Geriatric; Pediatric. **Publications:** *SEE Vision,* quarterly. Newsletter. Provides recap of programs for professional members. **Circulation:** 1,000 ● Annual Report. **Conventions/Meetings:** annual meeting, held during AAO and ASCRS conventions (exhibits) ● annual meeting, in conjunction with the American Academy of Ophthalmology and ASCRS.

16537 ■ Vision World Wide
5707 Brockton Dr., Ste.302
Indianapolis, IN 46220-5481
Ph: (317)254-1332
Free: (800)431-1739
Fax: (317)251-6588
E-mail: info@visionww.org
URL: http://www.visionww.org
Contact: Patricia Price, Founder/Pres./Managing Ed.
Founded: 1995. **Multinational. Description:** Aims to improve the lives of the visually impaired and their families by providing medical information and assistance. Seeks to enlighten the general public about issues concerning people with impaired vision. Serves as a consumer protection organization against unscrupulous predators who victimize or take advantage of unsuspecting victims of vision loss and impair-

ment. **Publications:** *Vision Enhancement,* quarterly. Journal. Features the latest medical and scientific developments in the field of ophthalmology and optometry. **Price:** $7.50. ISSN: 1094-8635. Alternate Formats: online.

16538 ■ Visually Impaired Veterans of America (VIVA)
c/o American Council of the Blind
1155 15th St. NW, Ste.1004
Washington, DC 20005
Ph: (202)467-5081 (909)825-3067
Free: (800)424-8666
Fax: (202)467-5085
E-mail: viva_info@worldnet.att.net
URL: http://www.acb.org/viva
Contact: John A. Fleming, Pres.
Founded: 1975. **Members:** 117. **Membership Dues:** regular, $15 (annual). **Description:** Veterans of the armed forces of the U.S. who have blindness or visual impairment. Maintains and fosters the well-being and rehabilitation of all visually impaired veterans; preserves the legal rights of all visually impaired veterans on the local, state, and national levels; maintains, promotes, and fosters the social, economic, and cultural level of these veterans and to promote opportunities to increase their knowledge of educational, professional, and rehabilitation standards and methods. Seeks to acquire, preserve, and disseminate information relative to the functions and accomplishments of visually impaired veterans. Encourages research and development of new products for the blind. Maintains speakers' bureau; offers specialized education program. **Awards: Type:** recognition. **Recipient:** for service and achievement. **Telecommunication Services:** electronic mail, bj2kiowa@worldnet.att.net. **Affiliated With:** American Council of the Blind. **Publications:** *VIVA Viewpoints,* quarterly. Newsletter. For blind veterans. **Price:** included in membership dues. **Circulation:** 200 ● Membership Directory, annual. Includes newsletter. **Conventions/Meetings:** annual conference (exhibits).

16539 ■ Xavier Society for the Blind (XSB)
154 E 23rd St.
New York, NY 10010
Ph: (212)473-7800
Contact: Rev. Alfred Caruana S.J., Dir.
Founded: 1900. **Members:** 11,000. **Staff:** 14. **Budget:** $1,200,000. **Description:** A center for publications, primarily Catholic, for the blind and visually handicapped, supported by charitable contributions. Transcribes numerous titles, including religious textbooks. Maintains a circulating library of books and other materials in Braille, large type, and on tape. Items are loaned by mail from catalogs of titles in each of 3 formats. Tapes are also circulated to the physically handicapped. **Convention/Meeting:** none. **Libraries: Type:** not open to the public. **Holdings:** 1,525; audio recordings, books. **Subjects:** religion, inspirational. **Publications:** *Catholic Review,* bimonthly. Magazine. Available in Braille, large print and on tape.

Women

16540 ■ AACR-Women in Cancer Research (WICR)
615 Chestnut St., 17th Fl.
Philadelphia, PA 19106-4404
Ph: (215)440-9300
Fax: (215)440-9412
E-mail: wicr@aacr.org
URL: http://www.aacr.org/default.aspx?p=5510
Contact: Anne W. Hamburger PhD, Chair
Members: 1,700. **Description:** Promotes professional development and achievements of women in the field of cancer research. **Awards:** Charlotte Friend Memorial Lectureship. **Frequency:** annual. **Type:** recognition. **Recipient:** to a scientist who has made outstanding contribution in cancer research ● WICR-Brigid G. Leventhal Scholar Awards. **Frequency:** annual. **Type:** scholarship. **Recipient:** to scientists-in-training members. **Committees:** Brigid

D. Leventhal Scholar Awards; Charlotte Friend Memorial Lecture; Communications; Nominating; Professional Advancement. **Programs:** Mentorship. **Subcommittees:** Leadership; Networking Roundtable. **Affiliated With:** American Association for Cancer Research. **Formerly:** (2004) Women in Cancer Research. **Conventions/Meetings:** annual Charlotte Friend Memorial Lecture.

16541 ■ American Menopause Foundation (AMF)
350 5th Ave., Ste.2822
New York, NY 10118
Ph: (212)714-2398
Fax: (212)714-1252
E-mail: menopause@earthlink.net
URL: http://www.americanmenopause.org
Contact: Marie Lugano, Pres./Founder
Founded: 1993. **Description:** Provides support and assistance on all issues related to menopause. **Publications:** *A Review of Progesterone,* semiannual. Article ● *Bone Health During Menopause.* Article ● *The Challenge of Menopause: Denial vs. Constructive Coping.* Article ● *Highlights from Our Third Annual Menopause Symposium.* Article ● *Hormone Replacement Therapy: What's Science and What's Speculation? What More Do We Need to Know?.* Article ● *Managing Anxiety During Menopause.* Article ● *New Research on Diet and Uterine Myomas.* Article ● *Nonhormonal Management of Menopause for Women: Phytoestrogens.* Article ● *Premature Ovarian Failure is not an Early Menopause.* Article ● *Preventing Coronary Artery Disease in Women.* Article ● Newsletter. **Conventions/Meetings:** annual Menopause Symposium - September, New York City.

16542 ■ Black Women's Health Imperative
1420 K St. NW, 10th Fl., Ste.1000
Washington, DC 20005
Ph: (202)548-4000
Fax: (202)543-9743
E-mail: nbwhp@nbwhp.org
URL: http://www.blackwomenshealth.org
Contact: Eleanor Hinton Hoytt PhD, Pres./CEO
Founded: 1983. **Membership Dues:** sister's circle, $25 (annual) ● leader's circle, $50 (annual) ● president's circle, $100 (annual) ● chair's circle, $500 (annual) ● founder's circle, $1,000 (annual). **Staff:** 12. **Budget:** $3,000,000. **Regional Groups:** 5. **State Groups:** 26. **Local Groups:** 150. **Description:** Provides education, advocacy, research and leadership development focusing on health issues that disproportionately affect black women across lifespan, devoted solely to the health of black women groups. Also notes that black infant mortality is twice that of whites and that black women are often victims of family violence. Offers seminars outlining demographic information, chronic conditions, the need for health information and access to services, and possible methods of improving the health status of black women. Sponsors Center for Black Women's Wellness. Maintains library, database, and speakers' bureau. Conducts gender and race specific health research programs. Plans to: establish black women's wellness centers; develop Empowerment Through Wellness curriculum. **Computer Services:** Mailing lists. **Formerly:** (1984) Black Women's Health Project; (2004) National Black Women's Health Project. **Publications:** *Body and Soul: A Black Women's Guide to Health and Well-Being.* Book ● *It's Ok to Peek.* Video ● *It's Up to Us.* Video ● *Let Me Know What's Going On? My Body, My Self, My Life.* Video ● *On Becoming a Woman: Mothers and Daughters Talking Together.* Video ● *Our Bodies, Our Voices, Our Choices: A Black Women's Primer on Reproductive Health and Rights.* Book ● Also publishes conference reports, brochures, and health fact sheets. Makes available educational films. **Conventions/Meetings:** annual convention - spring/summer.

16543 ■ Command Trust Network (CTN)
11301 W Olympic Blvd., Ste.332
Los Angeles, CA 90064

E-mail: info@commandtrust.org
URL: http://www.commandtrust.org
Contact: Sybil Niden Goldrich, Co-Founder
Founded: 1988. **Description:** Individuals concerned with the effects of silicone breast implants. Seeks to inform the public and motivate women with implants to consider all possible options. Disseminates information on medical studies, legal referrals, research, choosing a doctor, implant removal procedures, and other related topics. Maintains speakers' bureau for consumer, medical, or legal meetings on breast implants. **Computer Services:** Online services. **Publications:** Newsletter, quarterly.

16544 ■ Global Alliance for Women's Health (GAWH)

823 UN Plz., Ste.712
New York, NY 10017
Ph: (212)286-0424
Fax: (212)286-9561
E-mail: contactus@gawh.org
URL: http://www.gawh.org
Contact: Elaine M. Wolfson PhD, Pres.
Founded: 1994. **Description:** Individuals and organizations working to improve the quality of women's health worldwide. Gathers and disseminates information on topics including primary health care, education of healthcare providers, cultural practices affecting the health of women and girls, occupational health and safety, sexually transmitted diseases, domestic violence, and mental health. Develops model health programs addressing women's needs. Conducts research; compiles statistics. **Publications:** *Women's Health Compendium.* Book.

16545 ■ International Dalkon Shield Victims Education Association (IDEA)

PO Box 84151
Seattle, WA 98124
Ph: (206)329-1371
Fax: (206)329-0912
Contact: Constance Miller, Treas.
Founded: 1986. **Members:** 2,000. **Membership Dues:** $25 (annual). **Staff:** 1. **State Groups:** 2. **Description:** Women who have contracted illnesses and/or been disabled through use of the Dalkon Shield intrauterine contraceptive device; their supporters. Promotes public education about the dangers of using the Dalkon Shield. Disseminates information regarding Dalkon Shield injuries, claim resolution, and related topics. Offers seminars. Maintains speakers' bureau. **Libraries: Type:** reference. **Conventions/Meetings:** annual meeting - always June, Seattle, WA.

16546 ■ International Women's Health Coalition (IWHC)

333 7th Ave., 6th Fl.
New York, NY 10001
Ph: (212)979-8500
Fax: (212)979-9009
E-mail: info@iwhc.org
URL: http://www.iwhc.org
Contact: Adrienne Germain, Pres.
Founded: 1984. **Staff:** 24. **Budget:** $5,500,000. **Languages:** English, French, Portuguese, Spanish. **Multinational. Description:** Guided by the principle that global well-being and social and economic justice can only be achieved by ensuring women's rights. Committed to three main goals: comprehensive sexuality education and services for adolescents, worldwide access to safe abortion, and expansion of sexual rights for women and girls. Provides technical and financial support to local organizations and networks in Africa, Asia, Latin America, and Eastern Europe working to promote these rights. Advocates directly for women's health and rights on an international level: informs public debate at home and abroad through its multilingual publications, media involvement, and web site; collaborates with UN agencies, donor governments, and private foundations on health sector reform and global health initiatives; participates in major UN conferences on health, population, women and children. **Formerly:** (1980) National Women's Health Coalition. **Publications:** *Expanding Access to Safe Abortion: Strategies for Action.* Report ● *Sexuality and Human Rights.* Bibliography ● *Taking Steps of Courage: Teaching Adolescents About Sexuality and Gender in Nigeria and Cameroon.* Report. Explores the importance of the study of sexuality and gender-based power relations to reproductive health policies and programs.

16547 ■ Melpomene Institute

550 Rice St., Ste.104
St. Paul, MN 55103
Ph: (651)789-0140
Fax: (651)292-9417
E-mail: shawne@melpomene.org
URL: http://www.melpomene.org
Contact: Rachel Seidman, Dir.
Founded: 1982. **Members:** 1,350. **Membership Dues:** individual, $40 (annual) ● student, $25 (annual) ● life, $500. **Staff:** 8. **Budget:** $363,000. **Description:** Individuals professionally trained in healthcare, physical activity, and sports for girls and women. Conducts research and disseminates information on issues such as body image, osteoporosis, athletic amenorrhea, exercise and pregnancy, and aging. Offers undergraduate and graduate internships, and volunteer programs. Provides consulting services for program evaluations. Operates speakers' bureau. **Libraries: Type:** reference. **Holdings:** 5,500. **Subjects:** women's and girls' health issues, physical activity. **Awards:** Melpomene Outstanding Achievement Award. **Frequency:** periodic. **Type:** recognition. **Recipient:** for outstanding contributions to women's cause. **Computer Services:** Mailing lists. **Formerly:** (2002) Melpomene Institute for Women's Health Research. **Publications:** *The Bodywise Woman.* Book. Provides information for women on physical activity and health. **Price:** $16.95/copy ● *Breast Cancer: A Handbook* (in English and Spanish) ● *Heroes: Growing Up Female and Strong.* Video. Concerns self-esteem in adolescent girls. **Price:** $19. 95/copy; $29.95 for curriculum ● *HRT: Is It For Me?.* Booklet. Helps individuals make a more informed decision about Hormone Replacement Therapy. **Price:** $2.50 ● *Let's Get Moving.* Booklet. Contains information about physical activity for women over 50. **Price:** $4.50 ● *Melpomene Journal,* 3/year. Examines the relationship between physical activity and lifestyles. Features research reports, scientific bibliographies, and personal profiles. **Price:** included in membership dues; $5.00/issue for nonmembers. ISSN: 1043-8734. **Circulation:** 2,500. Alternate Formats: online. Also Cited As: *Melpomene Report ● Of Heroes, Hopes and Level Playing Fields.* Book. **Price:** $10.00/copy.

16548 ■ National Asian Women's Health Organization (NAWHO)

1 Embarcadero Ctr., Ste.500
San Francisco, CA 94111
Ph: (415)773-2838
Fax: (415)773-2872
E-mail: info@nawho.org
URL: http://www.nawho.org
Contact: Afton Kobayashi, CEO
Founded: 1993. **Description:** Asian American women. Promotes increased awareness of the unique health needs of Asian American women among health care professionals and the public. Serves as a clearinghouse on Asian American women's health issues; conducts advocacy campaigns; compiles statistics. **Projects:** Empowering Avenues for Community Action in Mental Health; National Asian American Reproductive Health and Rights; Promoting Prevention for Healthy Communities; Transforming Information into Action. **Publications:** *A Profile on Cervical Cancer And Asian American Women.* Report. Provides recommendations for educational programs. Alternate Formats: online ● *Community Solutions: Meeting the Challenge of STDs in Asian Americans and Pacific Islanders.* Report. Features strategies in bringing reproductive and sexual health education to under-served Asian American and Pacific Islander women. Alternate Formats: online ● *Making a Difference: Highlights From A National Symposia Series On Asian Americans and Diabetes.* Proceedings. Provides a comprehensive look at key issues for Asian Americans in the prevention and management of diabetes. ● *NAWHO Diabetes Questionnaire.* Report. Provides findings on the attitude of adults about obesity and type II diabetes among American children. Alternate Formats: online.

16549 ■ National Association of Postpartum Care Services (NAPCS)

800 Detroit St.
Denver, CO 80206
Ph: (303)321-3287
Free: (800)453-6852
Fax: (303)321-4058
E-mail: doulacare@napcs.org
Contact: Lois Ecker, Treas.
Founded: 1988. **Membership Dues:** general, $55 (annual) ● general, $90 (biennial). **Description:** Provides care services for women suffering from postpartum depression. **Publications:** *Fourth Trimester News.* Newsletter.

16550 ■ National Association for Women's Health (NAWH)

300 W Adams St., Ste.328
Chicago, IL 60606-5101
Ph: (312)786-1468
Fax: (312)786-0376
URL: http://nawh.org
Founded: 1987. **Description:** Health care professionals from a broad range of disciplines with a common interest in improving health outcomes for women. Seeks to "promote excellence and provide leadership, resources, and collegial support to all professionals who influence, develop, and champion quality health care programs for women". Works with community organizations to increase awareness of health care issues among women; sponsors continuing professional development courses for members; designs and implements community education programs. **Formerly:** (2003) National Association of Professionals in Women's Health. **Publications:** *Focus,* quarterly. Newsletter. Features women's health issues. **Advertising:** accepted ● Membership Directory, annual. Contains information about member expertise and specialized programs in women's health. **Advertising:** accepted ● Handbook ● Audiotape.

16551 ■ National Council on Women's Health (NCWH)

1300 York Ave.
New York, NY 10021
Ph: (212)746-6967
E-mail: info@ncwh.org
URL: http://www.ncwh.org
Contact: Gayatri Devi MD, Pres.
Founded: 1979. **Members:** 500. **Membership Dues:** individual, $40 (annual) ● corporate, $500 (annual) ● board, $75 (annual). **Description:** Works in partnership of health professionals and consumers whose mission is to educate the public and policy-makers on women's health issues and empower women to make informed healthcare choices. Open to everyone concerned with furthering the goals of the Council, fostering better quality health care, increased availability of information to patients, and improving doctor-patient relationship; the goals of the organization are accomplished through a variety of educational efforts including forums and conferences for the general public, publications for professionals and the public, and networking with a wide range of organizations concerned with women's health. **Publications:** Newsletter, quarterly. **Conventions/Meetings:** periodic conference (exhibits).

16552 ■ National Vulvodynia Association (NVA)

PO Box 4491
Silver Spring, MD 20914-4491
Ph: (301)299-0775
Fax: (301)299-3999
E-mail: mate@nva.org
URL: http://www.nva.org
Contact: Phyllis Mate, Exec. Dir.
Founded: 1994. **Members:** 2,500. **Membership Dues:** individual in U.S., $45 (annual) ● individual outside U.S., $50 (annual). **Staff:** 3. **Budget:**

$60,000. **National Groups:** 80. **Description:** Strives to improve the lives of individuals affected by Vulvodynia, a spectrum of chronic vulvar pain disorders. **Publications:** *NVA News*, 3/year. Newsletter. **Price:** included in membership dues. **Circulation:** 3,300.

16553 ■ National Women's Health Network (NWHN)
514 10th St. NW, Ste.400
Washington, DC 20004
Ph: (202)347-1140 (202)628-7814
Fax: (202)347-1168
E-mail: nwhn@nwhn.org
URL: http://www.nwhn.org
Contact: Cynthia Pearson, Exec. Dir.
Founded: 1975. **Members:** 8,000. **Membership Dues:** individual, $25 (annual) ● organizational, $50. **Staff:** 7. **Budget:** $1,000,000. **Description:** Serves as an advocacy organization giving women a greater voice in the health care system in the United States. Provides women with unbiased health information through its clearinghouse. Monitors federal legislation to ensure that women's needs are not overlooked. **Libraries: Type:** by appointment only. **Publications:** *Women's Health Activist*, bimonthly. Newsletter. Keeps readers informed about the important developments in women's health, provides ways to improve one's health, recommends books. **Price:** included in membership dues. ISSN: 8755-867X. **Circulation:** 10,000. Alternate Formats: online ● Also publishes health information packets, booklets, and brochures.

16554 ■ National Women's Health Resource Center (NWHRC)
157 Broad St., Ste.315
Red Bank, NJ 07701
Ph: (732)530-3425
Free: (877)986-9472
Fax: (732)530-3347
E-mail: info@healthywomen.org
URL: http://www.healthywomen.org
Contact: Audrey Sheppard, Pres./CEO
Founded: 1988. **Staff:** 7. **Nonmembership. Description:** Disseminates information about women's health. Serves as the national clearinghouse for women's health information. Provides comprehensive, unbiased health information. **Libraries: Type:** not open to the public. **Holdings:** articles, books. **Subjects:** all women's health topics. **Computer Services:** database, health information ● database, national resource ● mailing lists. **Boards:** Director's; Medical Advisory. **Publications:** *National Women's Health Report*, bimonthly. Newsletter. Contains information on current women's health issues. **Price:** $35.00 /year for individuals; $85.00/year for organizations. ISSN: 0741-9147. **Circulation:** 15,000. Alternate Formats: online. Also Cited As: *NWHR*.

16555 ■ Native American Women's Health Education Resource Center
PO Box 572
Lake Andes, SD 57356-0572
Ph: (605)487-7072
Fax: (605)487-7964
E-mail: nativewoman@igc.apc.org
URL: http://www.nativeshop.org/nawherc.html
Multinational. Description: Individuals and organizations interested in the health status of Native American women. Promotes improved health and access to health services for Native American women. Works to redress Eurocentrism in American society. Gathers and disseminates information on women's health and related topics. Conducts educational programs. **Publications:** *Wicozanni Wowapi*, quarterly. Newsletter.

16556 ■ Our Bodies, Ourselves (OBOS)
34 Plympton St.
Boston, MA 02118
Ph: (617)451-3666
Fax: (617)451-3664
E-mail: office@bwhbc.org
URL: http://www.ourbodiesourselves.org
Contact: Judy Norsigian, Exec. Dir.
Founded: 1969. **Staff:** 4. **Languages:** English, Spanish. **Description:** Promotes increased awareness of women's health issues among health care professionals and the public. Gathers and disseminates information on health topics of concern to women. Maintains speakers' bureau. **Also Known As:** (2003) Boston Women's Health Book Collective. **Formerly:** BWHBC. **Publications:** *Nuestros Cuerpos, Nuestras Vidas* (in Spanish). Book. Contains information pertaining to health and other issues affecting Latin American women. **Price:** $24.00/copy ● *Our Bodies, Ourselves for the New Century*. Book. Contains comprehensive information regarding women's health. **Price:** $24.00/copy.

16557 ■ Society for Women's Health Research (SWHR)
1025 Connecticut Ave. NW, Ste.701
Washington, DC 20036
Ph: (202)223-8224
Fax: (202)833-3472
E-mail: info@womenshealthresearch.org
URL: http://www.womenshealthresearch.org
Contact: Phyllis Greenberger MSW, Pres./CEO
Founded: 1990. **Membership Dues:** patron, $500 (annual) ● friend, $35 (annual) ● friend, $25 (annual) ● contributor, $50 (annual) ● supporter, $100 (annual) ● sponsor, $250 (annual). **Staff:** 18. **Budget:** $3,500,000. **Description:** Seeks to improve the health of women by promoting equity in research. Advocates policies which promotes the inclusion of women in clinical trials; informs government agencies and private industry of issues affecting women's health and sex-based biology; educates women consumers on conditions that affect women; promotes funding for women's health research. **Awards:** Excellence in Media. **Frequency:** annual. **Type:** monetary. **Recipient:** for excellence in reporting research on women's health. **Formerly:** (2001) Society for the Advancement of Women's Health Research. **Publications:** *Journal of Women's Health*, 10/year ● *Sexx Matters*, quarterly. Newsletter. Covers recent activities of the Society and research news related to women's health. **Price:** included in membership dues. **Conventions/Meetings:** annual Scientific Advisory Meeting, with updates in the scientific and health care communities on recent research on sex differences in biology ● annual Scientific Advisory Meeting: Update on Women's Health - conference.

Abortion

16558 ■ Elliot Institute
PO Box 7348
Springfield, IL 62791-7348
Ph: (217)525-8202
Fax: (217)525-8212
E-mail: elliotinst@afterabortion.org
URL: http://www.afterabortion.org
Contact: David C. Reardon PhD, Dir.
Founded: 1988. **Staff:** 3. **Description:** Seeks to promote post abortion healing and reconciliation through research and education on the after affects of abortion on women, men, children and society. Conducts educational and research programs; compiles statistics; maintains Speaker's Bureau. **Also Known As:** (1999) Elliot Institute for Social Sciences Research. **Publications:** *Ending Abortion With Compassion.* Brochure ● *The Post-Abortion Review,* quarterly. Newsletter. Contains original articles reporting on post-abortion research of trends in post-abortion healing and advocacy. **Price:** $20.00/year. ISSN: 1083-9496. **Circulation:** 1,200.

16559 ■ Legal Action for Women (LAW)
PO Box 11061
Pensacola, FL 32524
Ph: (334)962-3554
Free: (888)9-WOMENS
E-mail: law@gulftel.com
URL: http://www.legalactionforwomen.org
Contact: Vicky Conroy, Contact
Founded: 1985. **Staff:** 1. **Budget:** $12,000. **Description:** Provides legal referral for women injured by abortions. Conducts research on medical malpractice; promotes action on abortion safety. **Telecommunication Services:** additional toll-free number, (800)822-6783.

16560 ■ National Abortion Rights Action League (NARAL)
1156 15th St. NW, Ste.700
Washington, DC 20005
Ph: (202)973-3000 (202)973-3018
Fax: (202)973-3096
E-mail: can@prochoiceamerica.org
URL: http://www.naral.org
Contact: Nancy Keenan, Pres.
Description: Politically involved in the pro-choice movement. Outspoken advocate of reproductive freedom and choice. Protects and preserves the right to choose. Promotes policies and programs to improve women's health. Seeks to make abortion less necessary.

16561 ■ National Network of Abortion Funds (NNAF)
42 Seaverns Ave.
Boston, MA 02130-2865
Ph: (617)524-6040
Free: (800)772-9100
Fax: (617)524-6042
E-mail: info@nnaf.org
URL: http://www.nnaf.org
Contact: M.J. Maccardini, Admin. Dir.
Founded: 1993. **Members:** 98. **Membership Dues:** regular (based on the size of individual's fund), $25-$100 (annual). **Staff:** 3. **Budget:** $500,000. **Local Groups:** 96. **Description:** Local abortion funds. Promotes increased access to abortion services; seeks to insure freedom of reproductive choice among women in the United States. Facilitates networking and mutual support among members; conducts outreach activities and encourages formation of new local abortion funds. **Publications:** *Abortion Funding: Matter of Justice.* Report. Alternate Formats: online ● *Building an Abortion Fund: An Organizing Guide.* Handbook. **Price:** free ● *Legal But Out of Reach.* Video. **Price:** $25.00 for allied organizations; $50.00 for institutions. **Conventions/Meetings:** periodic board meeting ● annual conference ● periodic regional meeting.

Accounting

16562 ■ International Budget Project of the Center on Budget and Policy Priorities (IBP)
820 1st St. NE, Ste.510
Washington, DC 20002
Ph: (202)408-1080
Fax: (202)408-8173
E-mail: info@internationalbudget.org
URL: http://www.internationalbudget.org
Contact: Warren Krafchik, Proj. Dir.
Founded: 1997. **Staff:** 4. **National Groups:** 55. **Languages:** English, French, German, Italian, Portuguese, Spanish. **Multinational. Description:** Works to assist civil society organizations globally to improve budget policies and decision-making processes. **Libraries: Type:** open to the public. **Holdings:** 240; articles, books, periodicals. **Subjects:** budget analysis, budget training, budget process transition, economies, budget transparency, development economics, fiscal decentralization, taxation and revenue issues, public expenditure management. **Computer Services:** Mailing lists, listserv. **Publications:** *A Guide to Budget Work for NGOs* (in English, Russian, and Spanish). Handbook. Serves as a guide for applied budget analysis training. **Price:** free. **Advertising:** accepted. Alternate Formats: online ● *A Taste of Success: Examples of the Budget Work of NGOs* ● *Can Civil Society Add Value to Budget Decision-Making?* (in English and Spanish). Alternate Formats: online ● *IBP Newsletter* (in English and Spanish), bimonthly. **Advertising:** accepted. Alternate Formats: online ● *Reports on Budget Transparency* ● Reports. Focuses on wide range of policies at national and state levels. ● Papers. Alternate Formats: online. **Conventions/Meetings:** biennial International Budget Conference.

Accreditation

16563 ■ National Committee for Certifying Agencies (NCCA)
2025 M St. NW, Ste.800
Washington, DC 20036-3309
Ph: (202)367-1165
Fax: (202)367-2165
E-mail: info@noca.org
URL: http://www.noca.org/ncca/ncca.htm
Contact: Ashley K. Robinson, Coor.
Description: Works to ensure health, welfare, and safety of public through accreditation of certification programs/organizations, exceeding requirements set forth by the American Psychological Association and U.S. Equal Employment Commission.

Afghanistan

16564 ■ Afghanistan Peace Association (APA)
41-36 Coll. Point Blvd., Ste.2A
Flushing, NY 11355
Ph: (718)461-6799
Fax: (718)886-8616
E-mail: info@afghanistanpeace.com
URL: http://www.arianainteractive.com/apa
Contact: Dr. Ahmad Dawer Nadi, Pres.
Founded: 1989. **Languages:** Dari, English, Pashto. **Description:** Promotes peace in Afghanistan. **Libraries: Type:** reference. **Holdings:** books. **Committees:** Administrative Affairs; External Affairs; Inter-Afghan Relations; Internal Affairs; Press and Culture; Social Services; Youth Affairs. **Councils:** Fundamental.

Africa

16565 ■ Africa Action
1634 Eye St. NW, No. 810
Washington, DC 20006
Ph: (202)546-7961
Fax: (202)546-1545
E-mail: africaaction@igc.org
URL: http://www.africaaction.org
Contact: Nii Akuetteh, Exec. Dir.
Founded: 1953. **Staff:** 5. **Budget:** $1,000,000. **Non-membership. Description:** Works for political, economic and social justice in Africa. **Computer Services:** Mailing lists. **Absorbed:** (2002) The Africa Fund. **Formerly:** (2002) American Committee on Africa. **Publications:** *Action Alerts* ● *Fact Sheets,* periodic ● Pamphlets. **Conventions/Meetings:** periodic conference.

16566 ■ Africa-America Institute (AAI)
Graybar Bldg.
420 Lexington Ave., Ste.1706
New York, NY 10170
Ph: (212)949-5666
Fax: (212)682-6174
E-mail: aainy@aaionline.org
URL: http://www.aaionline.org
Contact: Mora McLean, Pres./CEO
Founded: 1953. **Staff:** 64. **Budget:** $15,600,000. **Languages:** English, French. **Multinational. Description:** Works to further development in Africa, improve African-American understanding, and inform

Americans about Africa. Engages in training, development assistance, and informational activities. Sponsors African-American conferences, media and congressional workshops, and regional seminars. Maintains training and visitor program offices in Washington, DC and representatives in 21 African countries. **Committees:** AFGRAD Executive Committee of Graduate Deans. **Councils:** International Advisory. **Formerly:** (1999) African-American Institute. **Publications:** Annual Report, annual. Provides historical overview of the work of AAI. ● Bulletin, periodic. **Conventions/Meetings:** annual dinner.

16567 ■ Africa Faith and Justice Network (AFJN)
3035 4th St. NE
Washington, DC 20017
Ph: (202)884-9780
Fax: (202)884-9774
E-mail: afjn@afjn.org
URL: http://www.afjn.org
Contact: Rev. Rocco Puopolo, Exec. Dir.
Founded: 1983. **Members:** 950. **Membership Dues:** $50 (annual). **Staff:** 3. **Multinational. Description:** Catholic network of individual and group members focused on Africa and the experience of its people. Committed in faith to collaborate in the task of transforming United States' mentality and policy on Africa through research analysis, education, and advocacy. **Awards:** AFJN Award. **Frequency:** annual. **Type:** recognition. **Recipient:** for commitment to social justice in Africa. **Publications:** AFJN Newsletter, monthly. **Price:** included in membership dues. **Circulation:** 600 ● Around Africa, 8/year. Newsletter. Alternate Formats: online ● Documentation Pamphlets, quarterly. **Conventions/Meetings:** annual Looking Back, Moving Forward - meeting.

16568 ■ Africa News Service (AFRICA NEWS)
920 M St. SE
Washington, DC 20003
Ph: (202)546-0777
Fax: (202)546-0676
E-mail: newsdesk@africanews.org
URL: http://allafrica.com
Contact: J. Reed Kramer, CEO
Founded: 1973. **Staff:** 13. **Description:** News agency whose purpose is to supply material on Africa for broadcast and print media. Covers African politics, economy and culture, and U.S. policy and international issues affecting Africa. Obtains news by monitoring African radio stations on short-wave equipment, by subscribing to African publications, and through a network of reporters based in Africa. Also produces investigative stories on U.S. policy and its implications. Provides audio news and programming for radio, articles and graphics for newspapers and magazines, and prints for libraries and institutions. Carries out research for feature articles, news programs, and individuals. Maintains 5000 volume library along with 90 file cabinets of clippings and documents related to Africa. **Computer Services:** Information services, material from Africa News available through Newsnet, Human Rights Internet, Nexis and University Microfilms. **Publications:** Africa News, biweekly. Newsletter. Covers current events in Africa; includes annual index. **Price:** $30.00 /year for individuals; $48.00 /year for institutions; $95.00/year for first class postal service. ISSN: 0191-6521. **Circulation:** 3,500. Alternate Formats: online ● The Africa News Cookbook: African Cooking for Western Kitchens. **Price:** $16.95 ● Index, annual.

16569 ■ AFRICALINK
c/o USAID
1325 G St. NW, Ste.400
Washington, DC 20005
Ph: (202)712-4810 (202)712-0000
Fax: (202)216-3524
E-mail: africalink@usaid.gov
URL: http://www.usaid.gov/regions/afr/alnk
Contact: Jeffrey Cochrane, Contact
Description: Individuals and organizations with an interest in the economic and community development of Africa. Promotes sustainable development suitable to local needs and capacities. Identifies and distrib-

utes appropriate technologies; facilitates establishment of improved communications networks; sponsors research and educational programs.

16570 ■ African Development Institute (ADI)
PO Box 1644
New York, NY 10185
Free: (888)619-7535
Fax: (908)850-3016
E-mail: ca498@bfn.org
URL: http://www.africainstitute.com
Contact: Dr. Kwame Akonor, Dir.
Founded: 1995. **Members:** 20. **Membership Dues:** individual, $50 (annual). **Staff:** 5. **Multinational. Description:** Seeks to find practical solutions to Africa's developmental crisis through non-partisan policy research. Conducts study and discussion forums, special events and educational outreach programs. Compiles statistics; maintains Speaker's Bureau. **Publications:** Sankofa: African Visions, quarterly. Newsletter. Contains solution oriented articles focusing on African development. Alternate Formats: online. **Conventions/Meetings:** annual board meeting (exhibits) - always June.

16571 ■ Africare
440 R St. NW
Washington, DC 20001
Ph: (202)462-3614
Fax: (202)387-1034
E-mail: development@africare.org
URL: http://www.africare.org
Contact: Julius E. Coles, Pres.
Founded: 1970. **Members:** 372. **Membership Dues:** life, $1,500. **Staff:** 98. **Budget:** $35,600,000. **Languages:** Arabic, English, French, Portuguese. **Multinational. Description:** Commits in African aid. Works to improve the quality of life in Africa; addresses needs in the principal areas of food security and agriculture as well as health and HIV/AIDS. Supports water resource development, environmental management, basic education, microenterprise development, governance initiatives, and emergency humanitarian aid. **Libraries: Type:** reference. **Holdings:** 3,300. **Subjects:** African development. **Awards:** Bishop John T. Walker Humanitarian Award. **Frequency:** annual. **Type:** recognition. **Recipient:** selected by Africare Board of Directors. **Computer Services:** database, internal use only ● mailing lists, internal use only. **Programs:** Civil-Society Development and Governance; Emergency Humanitarian Response; Food Security and Agriculture; Health and HIV/AIDS. **Publications:** Habari, semiannual. Newsletter. Alternate Formats: online ● Annual Report, annual. Alternate Formats: online.

16572 ■ All-African People's Revolutionary Party (AAPRP)
PO Box 863
New York, NY 10116
E-mail: culturevue@aol.com
URL: http://members.aol.com/aaprp
Contact: Mark Kornbluh, Exec. Dir.
Founded: 1971. **Members:** 783. **Staff:** 1. **Regional Groups:** 5. **State Groups:** 34. **Description:** Africans and persons of African descent who support Pan-Africanism, "the total liberation and unification of Africa under an all-African socialist government". Conducts seminars, conferences and symposia; compiles statistics. Maintains speakers' bureau. **Libraries: Type:** reference. **Subjects:** African history and politics, politics of the Western Left, revolutionary forces. **Additional Websites:** http://www.freewebs.com/aaprp_atlanta. **Committees:** Political Education; Program. **Publications:** Brochures. **Conventions/Meetings:** annual African Liberation Day - meeting (exhibits) - always in Washington, DC.

16573 ■ Association of Concerned African Scholars (ACAS)
c/o Meredeth Turshen, Co-Chair
School of Planning and Public Policy
Rutgers Univ.
New Brunswick, NJ 08903

E-mail: turshen@rci.rutgers.edu
URL: http://www.prairienet.org/acas
Contact: Meredeth Turshen, Co-Chair
Founded: 1977. **Members:** 275. **Membership Dues:** individual (based on income), $35-$70 (annual) ● sustainer, $105 (annual) ● institution, $60 (annual). **Description:** Individuals and institutions. Facilitates scholarly analysis and opinion in order to impact U.S. policy toward Africa; formulates alternative government policy toward Africa and disseminates it to the public; works to develop a communication and action network among African scholars. Mobilizes support on current issues; participates in local public education programs; stimulates research on policy-oriented issues and disseminates findings; informs and updates members on international policy developments. **Committees:** Political Action; Research. **Publications:** ACAS Bulletin, quarterly. **Price:** included in membership dues. ISSN: 1051-0842. Alternate Formats: online. **Conventions/Meetings:** annual meeting, held in conjunction with African Studies Association.

16574 ■ Constituency for Africa (CFA)
316 F St. NE, Ste.100
Washington, DC 20002
Ph: (202)371-0588
Fax: (202)371-9017
URL: http://www.constituencyforafrica.org
Contact: Melvin P. Foote, Exec. Dir.
Description: Committed to the progress and empowerment of Africa and African peoples.

16575 ■ Debts AIDS Trade Africa (DATA)
1400 Eye St. NW, Ste.1125
Washington, DC 20005
Ph: (202)639-8010
E-mail: data@data.org
URL: http://www.data.org
Contact: Bobby S. Shriver, Chm.
Founded: 2002. **Multinational. Description:** Works to raise awareness of the crises facing Africa - unpayable debts, uncontrolled spread of AIDS, and unfair trade rules that keep Africans poor. Calls on the governments of wealthy nations to put more resources towards Africa, and to adopt a policy that helps rather than hinders Africa in achieving long-term prosperity. **Computer Services:** Information services, Africa resources. **Telecommunication Services:** electronic mail, media@data.org.

16576 ■ Global Alliance for Africa
703 W Monroe
Chicago, IL 60661
Ph: (312)382-0607
Fax: (312)382-8850
E-mail: director@globalallianceafrica.org
URL: http://www.globalallianceafrica.org
Contact: Thomas Derdak PhD, Exec. Dir./Founder
Membership Dues: student, $15 (annual) ● individual, $40 (annual). **Staff:** 2. **Budget:** $400,000. **Description:** Promotes community-based health care development programs for impoverished people living in remote rural areas and urban slums throughout Africa. **Publications:** Newsletter.

16577 ■ Global Coalition for Africa (GCA)
1818 H St., Rm. H2-200
Washington, DC 20433
Ph: (202)458-4338 (202)458-4272
Fax: (202)522-3259
URL: http://www.gcacma.org
Contact: Mr. Hage G. Geingob, Exec. Sec.
Founded: 1990. **Languages:** English, French. **Description:** Intergovernmental policy forum. Other participants include international development and finance organizations. Seeks to "forge policy consensus on development priorities among African governments and their northern partners". Serves as a catalyst for development action; works to improve cooperation between African and overseas development programs and agencies; assists African governments in the formulation of public development programs and policies. Conducts outreach activities. **Also Known As:** Coalition Mondiale Pour L'Afrique. **Publications:** African Social and Economic Trends

(in English and French), annual. Annual Report. Features IT reviews and economic trends in Africa supported by relevant Sub-Saharan development indicators. Alternate Formats: online. **Conventions/ Meetings:** annual Policy Forum - meeting.

16578 ■ Guinea Development Foundation

140 W End Ave., Ste.17G
New York, NY 10023
Ph: (212)874-2911
Fax: (212)496-9549
E-mail: gdf@guineadev.org
URL: http://www.guineadev.org
Contact: Dr. Sekou M. Sylla, Pres.
Founded: 1988. **Members:** 96. **Staff:** 25. **Budget:** $75,000. **Regional Groups:** 7. **State Groups:** 34. **Local Groups:** 27. **National Groups:** 19. **Languages:** English, French. **Description:** Promotes health care delivery system and children's services, HIV/AIDS prevention and education, culture, community development in the rural area of the Republic of Guinea, West Africa. **Libraries: Type:** reference. **Holdings:** business records. **Subjects:** health, education, social culture, community development. **Awards: Frequency:** annual. **Type:** monetary. **Computer Services:** Mailing lists, of members. **Boards:** Advisory. **Publications:** *Health for All* (in English and French), annual. Report. **Price:** free for members ● Pamphlets. Contains information about community development. **Conventions/Meetings:** periodic Health Issues in Rural Areas of Guinea - seminar.

16579 ■ Information Project for Africa (IPFA)

Address Unknown since 2006
Founded: 1990. **Staff:** 3. **Budget:** $60,000. **Languages:** Arabic, English, French, Portuguese, Spanish. **Description:** Print and broadcast journalists. Conducts research on foreign affairs, development programs, lending conditions, strategic considerations, demographic and political implications, and related issues. Examines international trends from an African perspective. Operates a news service (Baobab Press), which is available to journalists in the southern hemisphere. Maintains a speaker's bureau and offers research and educational programs. **Convention/Meeting:** none. **Libraries: Type:** reference. **Holdings:** archival material, books, clippings, monographs, periodicals. **Subjects:** international relations, covert activities in the southern hemisphere, population control, military issues. **Formerly:** International Project for Africa. **Publications:** *Critical Mass.* Booklet ● *Excessive Force.* Book. **Price:** $13.00 ● *Genocide,* semimonthly. Booklet. Contains briefings for journalists, editors, news organizations overseas. **Circulation:** 1,000. **Advertising:** not accepted.

16580 ■ Operation Crossroads Africa (OCA)

PO Box 5570
New York, NY 10027
Ph: (212)289-1949
Fax: (212)289-2526
E-mail: oca@igc.org
URL: http://operationcrossroadsafrica.org
Contact: Willis Logan, Pres.
Founded: 1957. **Members:** 7,800. **Staff:** 2. **Budget:** $3,500,000. **Description:** Students and professionals, mostly from the U.S., who live and work with African counterparts during July and August on self-help community development projects in Africa and Brazil. Provides opportunities for interaction with village elders, educators, and political and other community leaders. Emphasizes community growth from within a "Third World" structure. Before departure, participants make an intensive study of Africa; after their return, they give speeches about their experiences. Participants pay the cost of the project. **Programs:** African and Diaspora Overseas. **Publications:** *Crossroads,* annual ● Annual Report ● Also publishes brochure. **Conventions/Meetings:** annual board meeting.

16581 ■ Saharan People's Support Committee (SPSC)

217 E Lehr Ave.
Ada, OH 45810
Ph: (419)634-3666
Contact: Anne Lippert, Chair
Founded: 1977. **Description:** Persons concerned with the right of Sahrawi people of Western Sahara to self-determination. Provides information to the U.S. government and the public on the decolonization and status of Western Sahara. Makes available lectures and slides. Maintains relations with organizations concerned with human rights in Africa. Compiles statistics. **Publications:** *SPSC Letter,* quarterly. Newsletter. Reports on the war in Western Sahara. Includes information on refugees. **Price:** $5.00. ISSN: 0891-608X. **Circulation:** 800 ● Also publishes bibliographies and occasional papers.

16582 ■ TransAfrica Forum (TAF)

1629 K St. NW, Ste.1100
Washington, DC 20006
Ph: (202)223-1960
Fax: (202)223-1966
E-mail: info@transafricaforum.org
URL: http://www.transafricaforum.org
Contact: Harry Belafonte, Pres.
Founded: 1977. **Members:** 18,000. **Membership Dues:** student, $20 (annual) ● associate, $25 (annual) ● supporter, $75 (annual) ● sustainer, $125 (annual) ● advocate, $500 (annual) ● champion, $1,000 (annual). **Staff:** 5. **Budget:** $300,000. **Description:** Concerned with the political and human rights of people in Africa and the Caribbean, and those of African descent throughout the world. Attempts to influence U.S. foreign policy in these areas by informing the public of violations of social, political, and civil rights, and by advocating a more progressive attitude in the U.S. policy stance. Supports the work of the United Nations in Africa. Sponsors TransAfrica Action Alert to mobilize black opinion nationally on foreign policy issues by contacting influential policymakers. **Libraries: Type:** reference. **Holdings:** 10,000; audiovisuals, books, clippings, maps, periodicals, photographs. **Subjects:** African and Caribbean issues. **Formerly:** (2004) TransAfrica. **Publications:** *Globalization Monitor,* periodic. Journal. Focuses on how African world is affected by globalization. Alternate Formats: online ● *Public Policy Report* ● *TransAfrica Forum Newsletter.* Alternate Formats: online. **Conventions/Meetings:** annual banquet - always June in Washington, DC.

16583 ■ Washington Office on Africa (WOA)

212 E Capitol St.
Washington, DC 20003
Ph: (202)547-7503
Fax: (202)547-7505
E-mail: woa@igc.org
URL: http://www.woaafrica.org
Contact: Mhizha Edmund Chifamba, Exec. Dir.
Founded: 1972. **Membership Dues:** individual, $30 (annual). **Staff:** 2. **Budget:** $100,000. **Description:** Monitors and analyzes developments in U.S. policy toward Africa. Promotes "a just American policy toward Africa." Mobilizes grassroots pressure on Congress to support sustainable development and peace-keeping efforts in Africa. **Computer Services:** Mailing lists. **Publications:** *Action Alerts,* periodic ● *Legislative Bulletin,* periodic ● *Washington Notes on Africa,* 3/year. **Price:** $3.00. Alternate Formats: online.

African-American

16584 ■ The Black Agenda

PO Box 9726
Columbus, OH 43209
Ph: (614)338-8383
Fax: (614)231-9592
E-mail: info@blackagenda.com
URL: http://www.BlackAgenda.com
Contact: F. Leon Wilson PhD, Natl. Dir.
Founded: 1985. **Members:** 950,000. **Membership Dues:** scholastic, $25 (annual) ● college student, $50 (annual) ● general, $125 (annual) ● life, $12,000 ● corporate, $225,000 (3/year) ● family, $175 (annual). **Staff:** 126. **Budget:** $5,500,000. **Regional**
Groups: 8. **State Groups:** 52. **Local Groups:** 26. **Description:** Dedicated to enhancing the political, economic, social, and cultural status of African-Americans. Fosters communication among members. Conducts educational programs. **Libraries: Type:** by appointment only; not open to the public; reference. **Holdings:** 500,000; archival material, articles, audio recordings, books, clippings, papers. **Awards:** Black Agenda's Scientific and Technology Scholarships. **Frequency:** annual. **Type:** scholarship. **Recipient:** for individuals who have shown commitment in developing solutions that enhance the quality of life for people of color ● Black Agenda's Writers Scholarships. **Frequency:** annual. **Type:** scholarship. **Recipient:** for individuals writing about all aspects pertaining to the lives, treatment, philosophy, influences and time for people of color during the 1950 through 2006 ● Neely Fuller Junior Scholarship. **Frequency:** annual. **Type:** scholarship. **Recipient:** for college student researching white supremacy. **Computer Services:** database ● electronic publishing, all materials of interest to people of color ● information services, nationwide information and research network ● mailing lists, for rental. **Caucuses:** Black. **Publications:** *The Black Agenda Resource Guide* (in English, French, and Spanish), annual. Directory. Contains information about people of colour. **Price:** $250.00. **Advertising:** accepted. Alternate Formats: CD-ROM; online ● *State of Black America,* semiannual. Book ● Journal, quarterly. **Conventions/Meetings:** annual international conference (exhibits).

16585 ■ Black Holocaust Society (BHS)

6622 N Bourbon St., Rm. 16
Milwaukee, WI 53224
Ph: (414)446-4377
E-mail: pclaser@mailexcite.com
URL: http://www.blackwallstreet.freeservers.com
Contact: Dr. Gregory E. Brown, Dir.
Description: Promotes dispute resolution using truth, religion, history, law, education, reason and common sense; fights racism. **Awards:** Black Holocaust Society Leadership Award. **Type:** recognition. **Publications:** *A Black Holocaust in America: The East St. Louis Massacre.* Book. **Price:** $19.95 plus shipping and handling ($5) ● *Tulsa Riot Final Report.* Book. **Price:** $19.95 plus shipping and handling ($5); $9.95 for printable MS Word version.

16586 ■ Congress of Racial Equality (CORE)

817 Broadway, 3rd Fl.
New York, NY 10003
Ph: (212)598-4000
Fax: (212)598-4141
E-mail: core@core-online.org
URL: http://www.core-online.org
Contact: Roy Innis, Natl. Chm./CEO
Founded: 1942. **Membership Dues:** general, $50 (annual) ● active, $25 (annual) ● professional, patron, $100 (annual) ● corporate, $500 (annual) ● student, $15 (annual). **Staff:** 60. **Budget:** $2,000,000. **Regional Groups:** 5. **State Groups:** 39. **Local Groups:** 141. **Description:** Civil rights organization; seeks the right of black people to govern themselves in those areas which are demographically and geographically defined as theirs. Compiles statistics; engages in research. Maintains placement service, charitable program, and speakers' bureau. Sponsors Project Independence, a job training program; offers immigration and legal services. **Awards:** Harmony Awards. **Frequency:** annual. **Type:** recognition ● Martin Luther King Jr. Holiday Award. **Frequency:** annual. **Type:** recognition. **Programs:** Community Outreach & Crisis Intervention; Crime Victims/Witness Assistance; Education, Image & Values Enhancement; Equal Opportunity Affairs; Ex-offender Stabilization & Rehabilitation; Immigration Crisis & Counseling Center; Independence; Legal Services & Complaints Center. **Publications:** *CORE Magazine,* quarterly. **Advertising:** accepted ● *The Corelator,* quarterly. Newsletter ● *Equal Opportunity Employment Journal,* quarterly ● *Population Studies* ● *Profiles in Black.* **Conventions/Meetings:** annual Health Care Awareness Festival - conference, street fair (exhibits).

16587 ■ Lincoln Institute for Research and Education (LIRE)
PO Box 254
Great Falls, VA 22066
Ph: (703)759-4278
E-mail: contactus@lincolnreview.com
URL: http://www.lincolnreview.com
Contact: Jay A. Parker, Pres.
Founded: 1978. **Staff:** 6. **Description:** Studies public policy issues affecting middle-class black Americans and disseminates research findings to elected officials and the public. Re-evaluates theories and programs that it feels are harmful to the long-range interests of blacks. Transmits pro-private enterprise views to public policymakers at local, state, and federal levels. Emphasizes the common national destiny of black and white Americans; supports a strong, steadily growing economy and a strong national defense. Sponsors and cosponsors conferences, seminars, and symposia on current issues. Maintains a comprehensive research and education program. **Publications:** Lincoln Review, quarterly. Journal. Contains public policy articles, essays, and reviews on issues affecting middle-class black Americans. **Price:** $12.00/year. **Advertising:** accepted. Alternate Formats: online.

16588 ■ National Association of African Americans for Positive Imagery (NAAAPI)
1231 N Broad St.
Philadelphia, PA 19122
Ph: (215)235-6488
Fax: (215)235-6491
E-mail: naaapi@msn.com
URL: http://www.naaapi.org
Contact: Rev. Jesse W. Brown Jr., Exec. Dir.
Founded: 1991. **Membership Dues:** regular, $25 (annual). **Description:** Dedicated to ending excessive marketing of alcohol, tobacco, and other harmful products in communities of color. **Programs:** Environmental Tobacco Smoke. **Publications:** Breathe Free!. Booklet. Provides information on indoor air quality around cultural issues that are part of the African American experience. ● Words to the Wise, bimonthly. Newsletter. **Price:** included in membership dues. Alternate Formats: online.

16589 ■ National Association of Black Citizens Action (NABCA)
PO Box 182
St. Martinville, LA 70582-0182
E-mail: nabca@blackaction.net
URL: http://www.blackaction.net/nabca.htm
Description: Works for the development of African-American and poor people through education, political and social change. Establishes realistic and progressive media networks within the greater Black community. Promotes and supports Black media outlets that seek progressive change.

16590 ■ National Black United Federation of Charities (NBUFC)
40 Clinton St., 5th Fl.
Newark, NJ 07102
Ph: (973)648-3767
Fax: (973)643-8350
E-mail: info@nbufcharities.org
URL: http://www.nbufcharities.org
Contact: Charlene Taylor, Exec. Dir.
Description: Black charities. Works to help national and local organizations gain resources in order to provide for the needs of Black communities. Conducts fundraisers.

16591 ■ National Coalition of Blacks for Reparations in America (N'COBRA)
PO Box 90604
Washington, DC 20090
Ph: (202)291-8400
Fax: (202)291-4600
E-mail: nationalncobra@aol.com
URL: http://www.ncobra.org
Contact: H. Khalif Khalitah, Contact
Founded: 1989. **Members:** 5,000. **Membership Dues:** individual, $10 (annual) ● local organization,

$25 (annual) ● national organization, $50 (annual) ● life, $500. **Budget:** $20,000. **Regional Groups:** 5. **State Groups:** 24. **Local Groups:** 40. **National Groups:** 20. **Description:** Seeks to obtain reparations from the United States government, other governments, and corporations that profited from the labor of African people who were treated as slaves and for the vestiges of enslavement. Compiles statistics; offers educational and research programs; maintains a speakers' bureau. **Libraries: Type:** reference. **Holdings:** 7; archival material, clippings. **Subjects:** legal, social, religious, discussion on reparations. **Awards: Frequency:** annual. **Type:** recognition. **Commissions:** Economic Development; Human Resources; Information and Education; International; Legal Strategies and Litigation; Legislative; Membership and Organizational Development; Youth. **Publications:** ENCOBRA, semiannual. Magazine. **Price:** $4.00. **Advertising:** accepted ● Reparation/N'COBRA NEWS, quarterly. Newsletter. **Conventions/Meetings:** annual board meeting - always June.

16592 ■ National Juneteenth Observance Foundation (NJOF)
1100-15th St. NW, Ste.No. 300
Washington, DC 20005
Ph: (202)331-8864
Fax: (202)331-8876
E-mail: myersfound@aol.com
URL: http://www.juneteenth.us
Contact: Rev. Ronald V. Myers MD, Chm./Founder
Membership Dues: regular, $60 (annual) ● affiliate, $120 (annual). **Description:** Aims to unite Americans in celebration of the common bond of freedom through the historic preservation of Juneteenth in America (June 19, 1865 is considered the date of freeing the last remaining slaves in America). **Additional Websites:** http://www.njof.org, http://www.19thofJune.com. **Commissions:** National Juneteenth Art; National Juneteenth Choir; National Juneteenth Economic Development; National Juneteenth Education; National Juneteenth Farming and World Trade; National Juneteenth Film; National Juneteenth Food; National Juneteenth Historical; National Juneteenth Jazz; National Juneteenth Labor; National Juneteenth Legal; National Juneteenth Medical; National Juneteenth Orchestra; National Juneteenth Pain Patients; National Juneteenth Poetry; National Juneteenth Tourism; National Juneteenth Youth.

16593 ■ National Trust for the Development of African American Men (NTDAAM)
1608 Nordic Hill Cir.
Silver Spring, MD 20906
Ph: (301)933-6151
Fax: (301)887-0405
Contact: Dr. Garry A. Mendez Jr., Exec. Dir.
Founded: 1989. **Description:** Individuals interested in improving the self-esteem of African-American men. Promotes increased understanding of and appreciation for traditional African value systems; works to "create and diffuse a new consciousness in the African rooted people in America." Conducts research and educational programs, with emphasis on issues facing incarcerated men and their families. **Awards:** Trust Awards. **Frequency:** annual. **Type:** recognition. **Computer Services:** Online services, TrustNet Information Service. **Formerly:** The Trust. **Publications:** Annual Report. **Price:** free ● Brochures ● Pamphlets. **Conventions/Meetings:** annual Planning - meeting.

16594 ■ United Black Church Appeal (UBCA)
c/o Christ Church
860 Forest Ave.
Bronx, NY 10456
Ph: (718)665-6688
Founded: 1980. **Members:** 500. **Description:** Black clergy and laity. Objective is to awaken the power of the black clergy and the black church to provide leadership for the liberation of the black community. Is concerned with black economic development and political power, and the strengthening of black families and churches. Believes pastors in black churches should reestablish legitimate leadership

roles within the black community. Works with troubled black youths in the community; rallies against drugs in urban areas. Supports community betterment projects including surplus food programs and distribution of food to needy families. Raises funds to alleviate hunger in Puerto Rico, Mexico, Colombia, and Africa. Plans to establish Black Church Center to house a hall of fame, museum, and library dedicated to preserving the history and restoring the importance of the black church. **Conventions/Meetings:** annual Black Empowerment and Leadership Conference.

Agriculture

16595 ■ American Agri-Women (AAW)
11425 Pedee Creek Rd.
Monmouth, OR 97361
Ph: (503)581-6610
Fax: (503)362-2253
E-mail: info@americanagriwomen.org
URL: http://www.americanagriwomen.org
Contact: Yvonne Erickson, Pres.
Founded: 1974. **Members:** 42. **Membership Dues:** single, $20 (annual) ● collegiate, $10 (annual) ● life, $500. **Budget:** $60,000. **State Groups:** 20. **Description:** Farm and ranch women's organizations representing 35,000 interested persons. Promotes agriculture; seeks to present the real identity of American farmers to the rest of the population and to develop an appreciation of "the interdependence of the components of the agricultural system". Supports a marketing system that makes quality food and fiber available to all on a reasonable cost basis and at a fair profit to the farmer. Believes that the family farm system is the bulwark of the private enterprise system, and as such must be preserved. Works in areas of legislation, regulations, consumer relations, and education. Maintains resource center and speakers' bureau. Establishes an oral history project of America's farm and ranch women entitled From Mules to Microwaves; conducts research programs. **Awards:** Leaven Award. **Type:** recognition. **Recipient:** for outstanding achievement within AWW's guidelines. **Committees:** Agriculture Chemical; Agriculture Labor/Management; Animal Welfare; Dairy; Energy; Food Safety; Fruit and Vegetables; Grain; Land Use; Legislation; Livestock; Religion; Rural Economic Development; Trade and Marketing; Water Resources. **Publications:** American Agri-Women—Directory, annual. Contains listing of officers of affiliate organizations of farm and ranch women. **Price:** available to members and sponsors only ● Voice of the American Agri-Woman, bimonthly. Newsletter. Concerns farm and ranch women. **Price:** $10.00 for members and sponsors only. **Circulation:** 5,000. Alternate Formats: online. **Conventions/Meetings:** annual meeting (exhibits) - always November.

16596 ■ American Agri-Women Resource Center (AAWRC)
c/o Eleanor Kiner, Dir.
27703 Kiner Rd. N
Almira, WA 99103
E-mail: aawrc@americanagriwomen.org
URL: http://www.americanagriwomen.org
Contact: Mary Ann Graff, Pres.
Founded: 1977. **Members:** 45,000. **Membership Dues:** individual, $20 (annual) ● collegiate, $10 (annual) ● life, $500. **Budget:** $62,000. **Regional Groups:** 27. **State Groups:** 22. **National Groups:** 6. **Description:** Represents farm women concerned with the advancement of agricultural production within the free enterprise system. Aims to formulate and disseminate educational materials that accurately represent agripolitan America for use by teachers and the public. Initiates and promotes educational program to advance the interests and welfare of agriculture. Provides training for women in leadership, public relations, and communications. Conducts workshops, seminars, symposia which illustrate, explain, and inform in various subject areas from kindergarten to adult levels. **Awards:** Daughters of American Agriculture Scholarship. **Frequency:** annual. **Type:** monetary ● Helen Whitmore Scholar-

ship. **Frequency:** annual. **Type:** monetary. **Recipient:** for interest in Ag leadership, 21-35 to attend 1st AAW Convention sponsored by AAW affiliates. **Publications:** *The Voice*, bimonthly. Newsletter. **Advertising:** accepted. **Conventions/Meetings:** annual meeting and workshop (exhibits) ● annual meeting, committee and policy development - mid-year ● annual meeting, legislative tour and reception.

16597 ■ American Agriculture Movement (AAM)
c/o Larry Matlack, Pres.
13118 E Stroud Rd.
Burrton, KS 67020
Ph: (620)463-3513
E-mail: larry@stingerltd.com
URL: http://www.aaminc.org
Contact: Larry Matlack, Pres.
Founded: 1977. **Membership Dues:** regular, $100 (annual). **Staff:** 4. **Budget:** $200,000. **State Groups:** 35. **Description:** Family farmers and ranchers concerned with governmental agricultural policy. Seeks to: establish a mechanism through which farmers can initiate and approve changes in federal agricultural policies; ensure that foreign and domestically produced agricultural products sell for the same price in the U.S. Promotes: political candidates favoring higher prices for agricultural products; borrower's rights as defined in recent farm credit legislation; cooperation among farmers' organizations and between farm and urban interests; worldwide agricultural supply management and higher prices for agricultural products in international markets. Opposes federal subsidies, excise tax increases, and the patenting of genetically-engineered animals. Achievements include: organization of a grassroots lobbying campaign; bringing the views of U.S. farmers to the attention of international agricultural bodies; changes in elevator bankruptcy laws and FmHa foreclosure procedures. Drafts opinions and supplies information to media on federal and international farm policy issues. **Formerly:** (1977) American Agricultural Movement. **Publications:** *American Agriculture*. Brochure ● *American Agriculture Movement Reporter*, monthly. **Price:** $15.00 /year for members; $20.00 /year for nonmembers ● *The Impact of Excise Taxes on Rural Americans*. Brochure ● *Where Do Higher Excise Taxes Hit a Farmer?*. Brochure ● Newsletter. Alternate Formats: online. **Conventions/Meetings:** annual conference (exhibits).

16598 ■ American Farmland Trust (AFT)
1200 18th St. NW, Ste.800
Washington, DC 20036
Ph: (202)331-7300
Free: (800)431-1499
Fax: (202)659-8339
E-mail: info@farmland.org
URL: http://www.farmland.org
Contact: Ralph Grossi, Pres.
Founded: 1980. **Members:** 33,000. **Membership Dues:** basic, $20 (annual) ● corporate affiliate, $500 (annual) ● corporate associate, Barnraisers Society, $1,000 (annual). **Staff:** 60. **Budget:** $8,000,000. **Regional Groups:** 3. **State Groups:** 5. **Description:** Works to stop the loss of productive farmland and promote farming practices that lead to a healthy environment. Disseminates information on safeguarding farmlands, through conservation easements and other voluntary conservation programs. Encourages and assists policy makers to revise federal, state, and local policies on farmland preservation. Conducts policy development assistance, public education, and land project programs. Aids landowners in private conservancy transactions. **Convention/Meeting:** none. **Publications:** *American Farmland*, quarterly. Magazine. Discusses major challenges confronting farmland today and offers the latest information on tools and techniques being used. **Price:** included in membership dues ● Annual Report, annual. Alternate Formats: online.

16599 ■ Center for Rural Affairs (CFRA)
PO Box 136
Lyons, NE 68038-0136
Ph: (402)687-2100

Fax: (402)687-2200
E-mail: info@cfra.org
URL: http://www.cfra.org
Contact: Chuck Hassebrook, Exec. Dir.
Founded: 1973. **Staff:** 30. **Budget:** $2,100,000. **Nonmembership. Description:** Works to strengthen small businesses, family farms and ranches, and rural communities through action oriented programs addressing social, economic and environmental issues. **Programs:** Rural Enterprise Assistance; Rural Opportunities and Stewardship; Rural Policy; Rural Research and Analysis. **Projects:** Conservation and Environment; Farm Opportunity; Rural Development; Sustainable Agriculture. **Publications:** *Center for Rural Affairs Newsletter*, monthly. Contains survey of events affecting rural America. ISSN: 1085-4975. **Circulation:** 7,000. Alternate Formats: online. **Conventions/Meetings:** annual general assembly (exhibits) - usually winter.

16600 ■ Farm Aid
11 Ward St., Ste.200
Somerville, MA 02143
Ph: (617)354-2922
Free: (800)FARM-AID
Fax: (617)354-6992
E-mail: info@farmaid.org
URL: http://www.farmaid.org
Contact: Carolyn Mugar, Exec. Dir.
Founded: 1985. **Staff:** 8. **Budget:** $850,000. **Description:** Works to raise public awareness of the plight of the American family farmer and to provide aid to families dependent on agriculture. Provides funds to organizations aiding farmers, and to programs focusing on long-term solutions to problems faced by farmers. **Publications:** *Farm Aid Update*, quarterly. Newsletter. Covers family farm organizations and issues. **Price:** $35.00/year. **Advertising:** accepted. **Conventions/Meetings:** annual show - fall.

16601 ■ Groundswell Inc. of Minnesota (MG)
PO Box 338
Wanda, MN 56294
Ph: (507)342-5797
Fax: (507)342-5797
Contact: Diane Irlbeck, Office Mgr.
Founded: 1974. **Members:** 2,500. **Budget:** $160,000. **State Groups:** 48. **Description:** Farmers and other individuals who seek to preserve the existence of the family farm and to aid the rural economy in Minnesota and the U.S. as a whole. Educates farmers on their legal rights and the availability of assistance programs. Collects and distributes clothing, and other necessities to needy farmers. Supports legal, peaceful actions to improve the rural economy. Informs members of legislative activity and secures media attention for farmers and the rural economy in general. Maintains speakers' bureau. **Formerly:** (1992) Minnesota Groundswell. **Publications:** *Groundswell Newsletter*, monthly. **Conventions/Meetings:** annual board meeting.

16602 ■ Institute for Agriculture and Trade Policy
2105 1st Ave. S
Minneapolis, MN 55404
Ph: (612)870-0453
Fax: (612)870-4846
E-mail: iatp@iatp.org
URL: http://www.iatp.org
Contact: Dr. Jim Harkness, Pres.
Founded: 1983. **Staff:** 33. **Budget:** $3,000,000. **Languages:** English, French, German, Spanish. **Description:** Individuals concerned with the current plight of the small farm in the U.S. Seeks to educate voters about federal farm legislation. Conducts research and disseminates information on government farm policies. Provides funds for lobbying farm issues. Promotes adoption of U.S. farm policies that will benefit the international farming community as well as domestic farmers. Maintains speakers' bureau. **Libraries: Type:** reference. **Holdings:** archival material, audiovisuals, books, clippings, periodicals. **Subjects:** trade, agriculture, global institutions, North-South relations, intellectual prop-

erty rights. **Computer Services:** Online services, trade and development information, sustainable development, multilateralism information. **Projects:** Eat Well Guide; Environment and Agriculture; Fish and Marine Conservation; Food and Agriculture; Food and Health; Food and Society Policy Fellows; Forestry; Trade and Global Governance. **Formerly:** (2001) League of Rural Voters Education Project. **Publications:** *Food Safety and Health*, monthly. Bulletin. Follows issues relating to pesticides, chlorine, dioxin and food safety. ● *Global Food Watch*, bi-weekly. Bulletin. Surveys food security issues globally. ● *IATP News*, triennial. Bulletin. Highlights IATP current activities. ● *Intellectual Property and Biodiversity News* (in English and Spanish), weekly. Bulletin. Surveys intellectual property and biodiversity issues around the world. ● Also maintains numerous listserves on agriculture, trade, and environment. **Conventions/Meetings:** periodic meeting.

16603 ■ National Family Farm Coalition (NFFC)
110 Maryland Ave. NE, Ste.307
Washington, DC 20002
Ph: (202)543-5675
Free: (800)639-3276
Fax: (202)543-0978
E-mail: kozer@nffc.net
URL: http://www.nffc.net
Contact: Katherine Ozer, Exec. Dir.
Founded: 1986. **Members:** 39. **Membership Dues:** organizational, $250-$1,000 (annual). **Staff:** 3. **Description:** Small farm and rural organizations including the Federation of Southern Cooperatives and Land Assistance Fund, Groundswell Inc. of Minnesota, North American Farm Alliance, and the RAFI-USA. Seeks to assure U.S. consumers of ample quantities of domestically produced food that is affordably priced and of high quality, and to reestablish a stable rural society by preserving economically viable family-owned and operated farms. Strives to increase the political participation and awareness of rural Americans, and works to develop an alliance with supportive urban Americans. Supports sustainable agriculture, the restoration of federal farm price supports and effective supply management, debt restructuring programs, and emergency aid to farm families in need of food, shelter, and health care. Coalition is distinct from group of same name listed in index as defunct. **Affiliated With:** American Agriculture Movement; Federation of Southern Cooperatives Land Assistance Fund; Groundswell Inc. of Minnesota; Institute for Agriculture and Trade Policy; Rural Advancement Foundation International - USA. **Formerly:** (1988) National Save the Family Farm Coalition. **Publications:** *Family Farm Agenda*, quarterly. Newsletter. **Conventions/Meetings:** annual conference.

16604 ■ National Organization for Raw Materials (NORM)
680 E 5 Point Hwy.
Charlotte, MI 48813
Ph: (517)543-0111
E-mail: rccook@voyager.net
URL: http://www.normeconomics.com
Contact: Randy C. Cook, Pres.
Founded: 1971. **Members:** 100. **Membership Dues:** $100 (annual). **Staff:** 1. **State Groups:** 48. **Multinational. Description:** Studies the U.S. and world economies, emphasizing the interaction between agricultural parity prices and general prosperity. Supports the enactment of a National Economic Stability Act which would establish a pricing structure for specific agricultural commodities thereby stabilizing monetary purchasing power and generating sufficient national income to achieve solvency. Conducts seminars; compiles statistics. **Libraries: Type:** reference; not open to the public. **Holdings:** 350; archival material, audio recordings, books, monographs, reports, video recordings. **Subjects:** business cycles, economics, US history, monetary history, legislative history, agricultural history, statistical records. **Publications:** *Economic Report of the Producers*, annual. Features statistical analysis of the economic position of the productive segments of the national economy.

Price: $10.00 ● *National Organization for Raw Materials—Newsletter*, quarterly. Features topics on agricultural raw materials economics, equity in international trade, and the growing U.S. public and private debt. **Price:** included in membership dues; $2.00/copy for nonmembers. Also Cited As: *NORM Newsletter*. **Conventions/Meetings:** annual general assembly, held in conjunction with AcresUSA December conference.

16605 ■ U.S. Farmers Association (USFA)
c/o William Gudex
W 2561 Sunset Dr.
Campbellsport, WI 53010
Ph: (920)533-8020 (712)263-2679
Contact: William Gudex, Editor
Founded: 1952. **Members:** 500. **Membership Dues:** $15 (annual). **Staff:** 2. **Budget:** $10,000. **Description:** Progressive organizations across the U.S. and Canada interested in parity for farmers, civil rights, and peace. **Awards: Type:** recognition. **Publications:** *Parity, A Program That Works* ● *Peace and Parity* ● *Truth About Farm Betrayal* ● *U.S. Farm News*, quarterly. Newspaper. **Price:** $5.00/year. ISSN: 0041-7637. **Circulation:** 1,000. **Conventions/Meetings:** annual board meeting - always late October or early November. Mason City, IA - **Avg. Attendance:** 6.

16606 ■ Winrock International (WI)
2101 Riverfront Dr.
Little Rock, AR 72202
Ph: (501)280-3000
Fax: (501)280-3090
E-mail: information@winrock.org
URL: http://www.winrock.org
Contact: Dr. Frank Tugwell, Pres./CEO
Founded: 1985. **Staff:** 700. **Nonmembership. Multinational. Description:** Works with people in the United States and around the world to increase economic opportunity, sustain natural resources, and protect the environment. Matches innovative approaches in agriculture, natural resources management, clean energy, and leadership development with the unique needs of its partners. By linking local individuals and communities with new ideas and technology, it increases long-term productivity, equity, and responsible resource management to benefit the poor and disadvantaged of the world. **Libraries: Type:** reference. **Holdings:** 7,000; audiovisuals, books, maps, periodicals. **Subjects:** agriculture, sustainable agriculture, environment, economic development. **Awards: Frequency:** periodic. **Type:** scholarship. **Recipient:** for women in developing countries who are studying agriculture or environmental sciences. **Formed by Merger of:** (1985) International Agriculture Development Service; (1985) Winrock International Livestock Research and Training Center; Agricultural Development Council. **Formerly:** (2004) Winrock International Institute for Agricultural Development. **Publications:** Annual Report, annual. ISSN: 1049-6165 ● Also publishes research and study reports. **Conventions/Meetings:** periodic conference.

16607 ■ Women Involved in Farm Economics (WIFE)
c/o Doris Ourecky, Membership Chair
1635 County Rd. 1950
Wilber, NE 68465-2592
Ph: (402)821-2574
Fax: (402)821-3554
E-mail: dorisourecky@diodecom.net
URL: http://www.wifeline.com
Contact: Doris Ourecky, Membership Chair
Founded: 1976. **Members:** 2,000. **Membership Dues:** regular, $30 (annual). **State Groups:** 17. **Local Groups:** 190. **For-Profit. Description:** Works to improve profitability in production agriculture through educational, legislative, and cooperative programs. Promotes public and governmental awareness of the importance of agriculture in the American economy; maintains that agriculture is the most vital renewable industry and that economic prosperity in the United States is dependent upon economic prosperity in agriculture. Upholds the "family farm" concept for the

production of food and fiber in the U.S. Works with governmental agencies and Congress to promote stability in the agricultural industry. Encourages communication regarding agricultural issues. Cooperates with other agricultural organizations and commodity groups in an effort to provide a unified voice for the industry. Conducts educational activities. Sponsors National Ag Day promotions. **Libraries: Type:** reference. **Holdings:** archival material. **Subjects:** WIFE history and proceedings. **Committees:** Commodity; Education; Energy; Farm Credit; Labor; Membership; Natural Resources; Public Relations; Resolutions; Safety; Taxation; Trade; Transportation. **Programs:** Ag in the Classroom. **Publications:** *Directory and Policy Summaries*, annual. **Price:** available to members only ● *WIFEline*, monthly. Newspaper. Includes editorials and reports on commodities. **Price:** $10.00. **Circulation:** 4,000 ● Brochure. **Conventions/Meetings:** annual conference and seminar, government affairs ● annual convention - always November ● seminar.

AIDS

16608 ■ ACT UP
332 Bleecker St., Ste.G5
New York, NY 10014
Ph: (212)642-5499
Fax: (212)966-4873
E-mail: actupny@panix.com
URL: http://www.actupny.org
Contact: Maxine Wolfe, Contact
Founded: 1987. **Description:** Represents individuals "united in anger and committed to direct action to end the AIDS crisis." Seeks to increase public awareness and government involvement in the fight against AIDS. Conducts rallies and demonstrations aimed at public figures or institutions that the group feels should be doing more to combat AIDS. Lobbies for quicker availability of experimental AIDS drugs. **Libraries: Type:** reference. **Holdings:** archival material. **Subjects:** AIDS, drugs, alternative medicine. **Caucuses:** Lesbian. **Committees:** Act Up Americans; Alternative and Holistic; Prison Committee: No Time To Lose; Youth Education Life-Line. **Working Groups:** AIDS Cure; Giuliani; Global AIDS. **Also Known As:** AIDS Coalition to Unleash Power. **Publications:** *Act Up Americans*. Catalog ● *AIDS, Act Up and Activism*. Handbook ● *Merchandise Catalog*. **Price:** free upon request. Alternate Formats: online ● *Time to Become an AIDS Activist*. Manual. Alternate Formats: online ● *Women and AIDS Handbook*. **Conventions/Meetings:** weekly meeting - every Monday night.

16609 ■ Children's AIDS Fund
PO Box 16433
Washington, DC 20041
Ph: (703)433-1560
Free: (866)829-1560
Fax: (703)433-1561
E-mail: info@childrensaidsfund.org
URL: http://www.childrensaidsfund.org
Contact: Anita M. Smith, Pres.
Founded: 1987. **Staff:** 17. **Nonmembership. Multinational. Description:** Serves children and families who are HIV impacted through direct assistance referrals, counseling, and resource materials. Advisory board of doctors, public health professionals, legislators, educators, and clergy assisting in the formulation of a sound public policy on HIV/AIDS that will be understood and promoted by the public. Encourages the public to react compassionately toward persons affected, infected, or ill with HIV or AIDS. Advocates early diagnosis; promotes reducing transmission of the epidemic through public health intervention strategies such as confidential and voluntary partner notification. Supports development of treatments, diagnostics, vaccines, and an eventual cure for the disease. Promotes health care access for individuals infected with HIV and AIDS. Testifies before national, state, and local government agencies. Operates Speaker's Bureau. **Libraries: Type:** reference. **Subjects:** medical, social, legislative,

religious issues with regard to HIV and AIDS. **Awards:** Thomas Parran Award. **Frequency:** annual. **Type:** recognition. **Recipient:** for significant contributions to limiting the spread of HIV/AIDS. **Formerly:** (1993) Americans for a Sound AIDS Policy; (1998) Americans for a Sound AIDS/HIV Policy. **Publications:** *AIDS/HIV News*, bimonthly. **Price:** $25.00/ year. ISSN: 1056-0890. **Circulation:** 7,500 ● *Christians in the Age of AIDS: How We Can be Good Samaritans Responding to the AIDS Crisis*. Book ● *The Church's Response to the Challenge of AIDS/ HIV*. Compiled in conjunction with MAP International. ● *Guide to Federal Funding of HIV Disease*, periodic ● Audiotapes ● Brochures ● Videos ● Also issues literature, conference transcripts, and testimonies. **Conventions/Meetings:** periodic conference.

16610 ■ Elton John AIDS Foundation (EJAIDSF)
PO Box 17139
Beverly Hills, CA 90209-3139
E-mail: eric.washer@ejaf.org
URL: http://www.ejaf.org
Contact: John Scott, Contact
Founded: 1992. **Staff:** 4. **Budget:** $2,500,000. **Description:** Individuals and organizations. Promotes increased access to, and improved quality of, patient care services for people with AIDS. Provides financial assistance to AIDS care programs and prevention projects; conducts fundraising activities. **Awards:** Service and Prevention Grants. **Frequency:** quarterly. **Type:** grant.

16611 ■ HIV/AIDS Prevention Grants Program
c/o United States Conference of Mayors
1620 I St. NW
Washington, DC 20006
Ph: (202)293-7330
Fax: (202)293-2352
E-mail: info@usmayors.org
URL: http://www.usmayors.org
Contact: J. Thomas Cochran, Exec. Dir.
Founded: 1983. **Description:** AIDS prevention program of the United States Conference of Mayors. Acts as a forum for information exchange among members; provides policy information to the media. Operates speakers' bureau and conducts educational programs. **Convention/Meeting:** none. **Formerly:** (2003) HIV/AIDS Program. **Publications:** *AIDS Information Exchange*, bimonthly. Newsletter ● *Local AIDS Policy* ● *Local AIDS Services: A National Directory*, periodic.

16612 ■ Infoshare International (II)
584 Castro St., Ste.671
San Francisco, CA 94114
Ph: (415)437-1873
Fax: (415)843-4066
E-mail: infoshare1@aol.com
URL: http://www.spiral.com/infoshare/welcome.html
Contact: Julie Stachowiak, Exec. Dir.
Founded: 1993. **Staff:** 3. **Budget:** $230,000. **Languages:** English, Russian. **Description:** AIDS organizations in Russia and the United States. Promotes increased public awareness of AIDS and HIV and their prevention and treatment. Serves as a clearinghouse on AIDS and HIV; provides clothing, food, and support services to people with HIV and their families; makes available technical and administrative assistance to grass roots AIDS organizations; conducts educational programs. **Libraries: Type:** reference. **Holdings:** articles, books, periodicals. **Subjects:** AIDS, HIV. **Computer Services:** database, AIDS and HIV, social services for people with AIDS.

16613 ■ Mobilization Against AIDS (MAA)
c/o Health Gap
429 W 127th St., 2nd Fl.
New York, NY 10027
Ph: (212)537-0575
E-mail: info@healthgap.org
URL: http://www.healthgap.org
Contact: Phillip Machingura, Program Asst.
Founded: 1984. **Members:** 1,000. **Membership Dues:** individual, $35 (annual). **Staff:** 3. **Budget:** $250,000. **Local Groups:** 1. **Languages:** English,

Spanish. **Description:** Individuals supporting increased government expenditure on AIDS research, treatment, and social services. Purposes are to: lobby Congress, the Food and Drug Administration, and the National Institutes of Health to provide support and funding to AIDS organizations; mobilize people into public expressions of support for persons with AIDS; oppose civil rights attacks on persons with AIDS. Organizes annual International AIDS candlelight vigil, marches, and the Just Sign IT postcard campaign. Provides speakers on the civil rights ramifications of the AIDS crisis. **Formerly:** (1987) Mobilization Against AIDS; (1992) National Mobilization Against AIDS. **Publications:** *Action Alert*, quarterly. Newsletter. **Price:** included in membership dues ● *International AIDS Candlelight Memorial and Mobilization*. Booklet.

16614 ■ National Alliance of State and Territorial AIDS Directors (NASTAD)
444 N Capitol St. NW, Ste.339
Washington, DC 20001
Ph: (202)434-8090
Fax: (202)434-8092
E-mail: nastad@nastad.org
URL: http://www.nastad.org
Contact: Julie M. Scofield, Exec. Dir.
Founded: 1992. **Members:** 59. **Staff:** 30. **Budget:** $5,000,000. **State Groups:** 59. **Description:** State and territorial directors of public state health HIV/AIDS programs and services. Aims to reduce the incidence of HIV infection in the U.S. and territories, providing comprehensive, compassionate, and quality care to all persons living with HIV/AIDS, and the development of responsible and compassionate public policies. **Programs:** Global Aids; HIV Care and Treatment; HIV Prevention; Viral Hepatitis. **Publications:** *HIV Prevention Bulletin*, monthly. **Circulation:** 1,000 ● Annual Report, annual. Alternate Formats: online. **Conventions/Meetings:** annual meeting - always in spring.

16615 ■ National Native American AIDS Prevention Center (NNAAPC)
436-14th St., Ste.1020
Oakland, CA 94612
Ph: (510)444-2051
Fax: (510)444-1593
E-mail: information@nnaapc.org
URL: http://www.nnaapc.org
Contact: Yvonne M. Davis, Pres./Interim Exec. Dir.
Founded: 1987. **Staff:** 11. **For-Profit. Description:** Network of concerned Native people. Works to stop the spread of HIV and related diseases, including sexually transmitted disease and tuberculosis, among American Indians, Alaska Natives, and Native Hawaiians by improving their health status through empowerment and self determination. Serves as a resource to Native communities and to support community efforts by providing education and information services, thereby enhancing the physical, spiritual, and economic health of Native people. Sponsors educational programs. Maintains speakers' bureau. Compiles statistics. **Libraries: Type:** reference; not open to the public. **Holdings:** articles, books, periodicals. **Subjects:** AIDS prevention. **Telecommunication Services:** information service, Fax-On-Demand, (800)-283-6880. **Formerly:** (1998) National Indian AIDS Hotline. **Publications:** *Season*, annual. Journal. **Conventions/Meetings:** periodic board meeting ● periodic conference.

16616 ■ Solidarity and Action Against the HIV Infection in India (SAATHI)
PO Box 14635
Chicago, IL 60614
Ph: (312)423-7899
E-mail: saathiiusa@yahoo.com
URL: http://www.saathi.org
Contact: Prasanthi Gandhi, Dir.
Founded: 2000. **Multinational. Description:** Seeks to strengthen and expand HIV/AIDS prevention and treatment services throughout India. Mobilizes increased attention and political commitment to HIV/AIDS. **Computer Services:** Information services,

HIV/AIDS resources ● mailing lists ● online services, forum. **Publications:** Newsletter.

Albanian

16617 ■ Albanian American Civic League (AACL)
PO Box 70
Ossining, NY 10562
Ph: (914)762-5530
Fax: (914)762-5102
E-mail: jjd@aacl.com
URL: http://aacl.com
Contact: Joseph DioGuardi, Founder
Founded: 1989. **Membership Dues:** regular, individual, $100 (annual) ● family, $250 (annual) ● student, $25 (annual). **Multinational. Description:** Represents the concerns and interests of the Albanian people. Works to end the repression and oppression of Albanians living under hostile Slavic Communist regimes in the Balkans. Preserves the culture, identity and human rights of Albanians. **Computer Services:** Information services, Albania resources ● mailing lists. **Publications:** Newsletter.

Alcoholic Beverages

16618 ■ Free the Grapes!
2700 Napa Valley Corporate Dr., Ste.H
Napa, CA 94558
Ph: (707)254-1107
Fax: (707)254-0433
E-mail: fedup@freethegrapes.org
URL: http://www.freethegrapes.org
Contact: Jeremy Benson, Exec. Dir.
Founded: 1998. **Description:** Represents the interests of consumers and wineries who seek to remove restrictions in 22 states that prohibit consumers from purchasing wines directly from out-of-state wineries. Seeks a workable solution that efficiently serves the needs of adult wine lovers and state regulators in a dynamic marketplace. **Publications:** Newsletter. Alternate Formats: online.

American

16619 ■ Common Dreams
PO Box 443
Portland, ME 04112-0443
Ph: (207)775-0488
Fax: (207)775-0489
E-mail: editor@commondreams.org
URL: http://www.commondreams.org
Contact: Craig Brown, Exec. Dir./Ed.
Founded: 1997. **Description:** Works to bring Americans together and to promote visions for America's future; committed to the use of the Internet as a political organizing tool, and creating new models for Internet activism. **Publications:** *Daily Clips*. Alternate Formats: online.

American Indian

16620 ■ American Indian Law Alliance (AILA)
611 Broadway, Ste.632
New York, NY 10012
Ph: (212)477-9100
Fax: (212)477-0004
E-mail: aila@ailanyc.org
URL: http://www.ailanyc.org/staffandboard.htm
Contact: Kent Lebsock, Exec. Dir.
Founded: 1989. **Multinational. Description:** Works with indigenous nations, communities and organizations for the promotion of human rights, sovereignty and social justice for American Indians. Protects indigenous cultures, environments, and lands through representation in international forums. **Computer Services:** Information services, documents and reports. **Projects:** Legal Service. **Publications:** *Border Crossing Rights*. Handbook. Alternate Formats:

online ● *Our Own Voices*. Booklet. Contains the words of Amerindian leaders and elders throughout the years of struggle for voice and freedom. Alternate Formats: online.

Americas

16621 ■ Americas Society (AS)
680 Park Ave.
New York, NY 10021
Ph: (212)249-8950
Fax: (212)249-1880
E-mail: inforequest@as-coa.org
URL: http://www.americas-society.org
Contact: Susan L. Segal, Pres./CEO
Founded: 1965. **Members:** 800. **Membership Dues:** individual, $85 (annual) ● senior/student, $35 (annual) ● dual/family, $150 (annual) ● contributing, $250 (annual) ● sustaining, $500 (annual) ● president's circle, $1,000 (annual) ● sponsor, $3,000 (annual) ● patron, $5,000 (annual). **Staff:** 50. **Budget:** $3,000,000. **Languages:** English, Portuguese, Spanish. **Description:** Works to educate U.S. citizens about the other nations of the Americas. Fosters mutual understanding of the economic, political, and cultural issues facing Latin America, the Caribbean, and Canada today. Promotes appreciation of the cultures of the Western Hemisphere. **Libraries: Type:** open to the public. **Holdings:** 3,000; books, periodicals. **Subjects:** Spanish literature, poetry. **Councils:** Chairman's International Advisory. **Divisions:** Cultural Affairs; Public Policy Programs. **Affiliated With:** Council of the Americas. **Publications:** *Review: Latin American Literature and Arts*, biennial. Magazine. Focuses on Latin American literature and arts. **Circulation:** 5,000. **Advertising:** accepted ● Books ● Brochure ● Catalogs. **Conventions/Meetings:** weekly conference and seminar, business and cultural (exhibits).

16622 ■ Council on Hemispheric Affairs (COHA)
1250 Connecticut Ave. NW, Ste.1C
Washington, DC 20036
Ph: (202)223-4975
Fax: (202)223-4979
E-mail: coha@coha.org
URL: http://www.coha.org
Contact: Larry Birns, Dir.
Founded: 1975. **Membership Dues:** associate, $150 (annual). **Staff:** 30. **Budget:** $165,000. **Languages:** English, Portuguese, Spanish. **Description:** Leaders of national trade union, professional, religious, academic, Hispanic, and civic groups and members of Congress. Nonpartisan education and research organization that seeks to monitor the full spectrum of U.S.-Canadian, U.S.-Latin American, and Canadian-Latin American relations and to raise public and governmental understanding and concern with respect to current diplomatic, economic, social, and political realities in Latin America. Brings together volunteer undergraduate and graduate interns, retired professionals, and academic specialists to engage in objective and knowledgeable analyses of policies concerning inter-American relations. Trains volunteer interns. **Libraries: Type:** reference. **Holdings:** 2,500; archival material, books, clippings. **Subjects:** U.S. and Canadian relations with Latin America. **Computer Services:** database, Internet, Latin American. **Publications:** *Survey of Press Freedom in Latin America*, annual. Booklet. Contains country-by-country analyses of government treatment of print and electronic media. Cites acts of censorship and press intimidation. **Price:** $8.95/year, plus shipping. **Circulation:** 2,500 ● *Washington Report on the Hemisphere*, biweekly. Newsletter. Covers U.S. relations with Latin America from a Washington perspective, including political, economic, and diplomatic issues. **Price:** $285.00 /year for individuals; $465.00 /year for institutions. ISSN: 1275-5599. **Circulation:** 1,000. **Conventions/Meetings:** annual banquet ● annual symposium - always in New York City.

16623 ■ International Relations Center (IRC)

PO Box 2178
Silver City, NM 88062
Ph: (505)388-0208
Fax: (505)388-0619
E-mail: irc@irc-online.org
URL: http://www.irc-online.org
Contact: Debra Preusch, Exec. Dir.
Founded: 1979. **Membership Dues:** basic, $35 (annual) ● amiga/amigo, $50 (annual) ● campanera/companero, $100 (annual) ● comadre/compadre, $250 (annual) ● sustainer, $1,000 (annual). **Staff:** 11. **Budget:** $700,000. **Multinational. Description:** Policy studies center that works to make the USA a more responsible member of the global community by promoting progressive strategic dialogue that leads to new citizen-based agendas. **Libraries: Type:** reference. **Holdings:** books, clippings, periodicals. **Subjects:** Central America, Mexico, labor, human rights, economics, U.S. foreign policy. **Computer Services:** database, names, addresses, and descriptions of individuals and organizations involved in U.S./Mexico relations. **Formerly:** New Mexico People and Energy; Inter-Hemispheric Education Resource Center; (2005) Interhemispheric Resource Center. **Publications:** *Boletin Americas* (in English and Spanish), biweekly. Magazine ● *Crossborder Updater* (in English and Spanish), weekly. Magazine. Alternate Formats: online ● *Foreign Policy In Focus*, monthly. Newsletter. **Price:** $30.00/20 issues; $60.00/50 issues ● *Global Good Neighbor News*, biweekly. Magazine ● *Rightweb News*, weekly. Magazine. Alternate Formats: online ● *World Beat*, weekly. Magazine. Alternate Formats: online.

16624 ■ North American Congress on Latin America (NACLA)

38 Greene St., 4th Fl.
New York, NY 10013
Ph: (646)613-1440
Fax: (646)613-1443
E-mail: nacweb@nacla.org
URL: http://www.nacla.org
Contact: Marshall Beck, Ed.
Founded: 1966. **Staff:** 4. **Budget:** $350,000. **Description:** Independent research organization founded to analyze and report on Latin American and U.S. foreign policy. **Libraries: Type:** reference. **Holdings:** 8,600; books, periodicals. **Publications:** *NACLA Report on the Americas*, bimonthly. Magazine. Covers political, economic and social trends in Latin America and U.S. Policy in the region. **Price:** $36.00 /year for individuals in U.S.; $60.00 /year for institutions in U.S.; $46.00 /year for individuals outside U.S.; $70.00 /year for institutions outside U.S. ISSN: 1071-4839. **Circulation:** 9,000. **Advertising:** accepted.

16625 ■ Organization of American States (OAS)

17th St. and Constitution Ave. NW
Washington, DC 20006
Ph: (202)458-3000 (202)458-6046
Fax: (202)458-6319
E-mail: oasweb@oas.org
URL: http://www.oas.org
Contact: Jose Miguel Insulza, Sec. Gen.
Founded: 1890. **Members:** 35. **Staff:** 688. **Budget:** $83,752,028. **Languages:** English, French, Portuguese, Spanish. **Description:** Works to strengthen the peace and security of the continent; promotes and consolidates representative democracy, with due respect for the principle of non-intervention; aims to prevent possible causes of difficulties and to ensure the peaceful settlement of disputes that may arise among the member states; provides for a common action in the event of aggression; seeks the solution of political, juridical and economic problems that may arise among them; promotes, by cooperative action, their economic, social and cultural development; works to achieve an effective limitation of conventional weapons; and devotes the largest amount of resources to the economic and social development of member states. **Libraries: Type:** reference. **Holdings:** 300,819; archival material, monographs, papers, periodicals. **Subjects:** inter-American system, human rights, democracy, Latin America and Caribbean drugs, trade, sustainable development, women in the Americas. **Awards:** Andres Bello Award. **Frequency:** annual. **Type:** recognition. **Recipient:** for education ● Bernardo A. Houssay Award. **Frequency:** annual. **Type:** recognition. **Recipient:** for science ● Gabriela Mistral Award. **Frequency:** annual. **Type:** recognition. **Recipient:** for culture ● Manuel Noriega Morales Award. **Frequency:** annual. **Type:** recognition. **Recipient:** for science and technology. **Computer Services:** Mailing lists. **Commissions:** Inter-American Drug Abuse Control Commission; Inter-American Juridical; Inter-American Telecommunication. **Committees:** General; Hemispheric Security; Inter-American Summits Management and Civil Society Participation; Judicial and Political Affairs. **Subgroups:** Working. **Affiliated With:** Inter-American Children's Institute; Inter-American Commission of Women; Pan American Health Organization. **Formerly:** (1948) Pan American Union. **Publications:** *Americas* (in English and Spanish), bimonthly. Magazine. Discusses culture, economy, history, and lifestyles of the Americas. **Price:** $18.00 /year for individuals in U.S.; $24.00 /year for individuals in Canada and Mexico; $31.00 /year for individuals in Europe and South America. ISSN: 0397-0940. **Circulation:** 60,000 ● *Secretary General Annual Report*. **Conventions/Meetings:** annual general assembly.

16626 ■ Pan American Development Foundation (PADF)

1889 F St. NW
Washington, DC 20006
Ph: (202)458-3969
Fax: (202)458-6316
E-mail: padf-dc@padf.org
URL: http://www.padf.org
Contact: David J. S. Winfield, Exec. Dir.
Founded: 1962. **Staff:** 25. **Budget:** $23,000,000. **Languages:** English, Portuguese, Spanish. **Description:** Utilizes grants from the public and private sectors to improve the quality of life in Latin America and the Caribbean. Fulfills its mission through municipal training and democracy strengthening environmental preservation, microenterprise development, and in-kind medical and vocational tools donations. **Awards:** Leadership Award. **Frequency:** annual. **Type:** recognition. **Recipient:** for heads of state of OAS member nations. **Boards:** Advisory. **Affiliated With:** Organization of American States. **Publications:** *Pan American Development Foundation—Newsletter*, semiannual. Covers foundation activities and programs. **Price:** free for members ● Annual Report (in English and Spanish), annual. **Price:** free for members. **Circulation:** 8,000. **Conventions/Meetings:** biennial Contact Series - conference.

16627 ■ Partners of the Americas

1424 K St. NW, Ste.700
Washington, DC 20005
Ph: (202)628-3300
Fax: (202)628-3306
E-mail: info@partners.net
URL: http://www.partners.net
Contact: Malcolm Butler, Pres./CEO
Founded: 1964. **Members:** 20,000. **Staff:** 31. **Budget:** $8,400,000. **Languages:** English, Portuguese, Spanish. **Description:** Volunteer private citizens organized in 60 partnerships linking U.S. states with Latin American and Caribbean countries. Goals are to encourage innovative, community-based projects and joint planning among local partnerships; to provide a stimulus to local partnerships in generating additional resources for their technical and cultural exchange projects; to assist in the implementation of effective and ongoing development projects in the Latin American, Mexican, and Caribbean partner areas. Partnerships form the basis for exchange projects in agriculture, public health, culture, rehabilitation, community education, sports, and other areas of hemispheric development. **Awards:** Foundation Grants. **Frequency:** annual. **Type:** grant. **Recipient:** for partnership projects ● **Type:** recognition ● Volunteer Travel Grant. **Frequency:** annual. **Type:** monetary. **Recipient:** for travel for selected volunteer technicians. **Programs:** Awards; Conservation Corps. **Formerly:** (1971) National Association of the Partners of the Alliance. **Publications:** *A Good Idea That Works*. Video ● *Partners*, quarterly. Newsletter. Reports on technical assistance projects and exchanges between the United States and Latin America. **Price:** $25.00 /year for individuals ● Annual Report ● Booklets ● Brochures. **Conventions/Meetings:** annual convention.

Anarchism

16628 ■ Voluntary Cooperation Movement (VCM)

c/o Ed Stamm
PO Box 1402
Lawrence, KS 66044-8402
E-mail: ed.stamm@excite.com
URL: http://www.geocities.com/voluntary_cooperation_movement/start.html
Contact: Ed Stamm, Contact
Founded: 1991. **Members:** 35. **Staff:** 1. **Multinational. Description:** An address exchange network linking individuals who favor education and self-organization as the preferred method of achieving a voluntary, egalitarian and cooperative society. **Convention/Meeting:** none. **Formerly:** Affinity Group of Evolutionary Anarchists. **Publications:** *Any Time Now*, quarterly. Newsletter. **Price:** $1.00. Alternate Formats: online ● *Consent or Coercion*. Booklet. An Anarchist case for social transformation. **Price:** $1.50 includes postage. Alternate Formats: online ● *Studies in Mutualist Political Economy*. Book. **Price:** $20.00 each.

16629 ■ Workers Solidarity Alliance (WSA)

339 Lafayette St., Rm. 202
New York, NY 10012
Ph: (212)979-8353
Fax: (973)773-9337
E-mail: wsany@hotmail.com
URL: http://www.workersolidarity.org
Founded: 1984. **Membership Dues:** individual (making between $8-$12 per hour), $15 (quarterly) ● individual (making more than $12 per hour), $20 (quarterly) ● individual (making between $5-$8 per hour), $10 (quarterly) ● student, retired, unemployed, employed person (making less than $5 per hour), $6 (quarterly). **Regional Groups:** 4. **Local Groups:** 16. **Description:** Wage working, unemployed, and working class people. Seeks to "emancipate society from capitalism" and create a new society based on collective workers' control of the economy. Advocates direct democracy, with basic decisions made in assemblies, not imposed by leaders. Encourages the formation of action committees in workplaces as well as networks of anti-authoritarian workers in industries or companies. Conducts educational programs; maintains speakers' bureau. **Conventions/Meetings:** convention.

Animal Welfare

16630 ■ Equus Sanctuary

PO Box 9
Ravendale, CA 96123
Ph: (530)931-0108
E-mail: mustangsb@hughes.net
URL: http://www.equus.org
Contact: Barbara Clarke, Contact
Description: Domestic no-kill horse preserve for horses pulled from slaughter and healthy young horses too small or wild to be placed in homes; advocates against any inhumane treatments of animals or horses used for human consumption, does not seek modifications in slaughter procedures. **Telecommunication Services:** electronic mail, designteam@aviddstudio.com.

16631 ■ Return to Freedom (RTF)

PO Box 926
Lompoc, CA 93438
Ph: (805)737-9246

Fax: (805)800-0868
E-mail: admin@returntofreedom.org
URL: http://www.returntofreedom.org
Contact: William S. DeMayo, Dir./Sec.-Treas.
Founded: 1997. **Membership Dues:** family, $45 ●
student, youth (12 and under), $10 ● senior, $15 ●
adult, $25. **Description:** Aims to protect and save
the American wild horse, ensuring its freedom and
diversity. **Telecommunication Services:** electronic
mail, programs@returntofreedom.org. **Publications:**
Return to Freedom Newsletter, quarterly. Alternate
Formats: online. **Conventions/Meetings:** monthly
Sanctuary Tour - first and third Saturday of April
through October.

**16632 ■ Thoroughbred Retirement
Foundation (TRF)**
PMB 351
450 Shrewsbury Plz.
Shrewsbury, NJ 07702-4332
Ph: (732)957-0182
Fax: (732)671-7538
E-mail: diana@trfinc.org
URL: http://www.trfinc.org
Contact: Diana Pikulski, Exec. Dir.
Founded: 1982. **Staff:** 3. **Description:** Provides
lifetime haven for retired racehorses. **Publications:**
Renews, quarterly. Newsletter. Alternate Formats: on-
line.

Anti-Communism

**16633 ■ American Security Council
Foundation (ASCF)**
1239 Pennsylvania Ave. SE
Washington, DC 20003
Ph: (202)546-5200
Fax: (202)546-2100
E-mail: info@ascfusa.org
URL: http://www.ascfusa.org
Contact: Dr. Henry A. Fischer, Pres.
Founded: 1958. **Description:** Educational institution
created by several national organizations and private
institutions to further public understanding of the
"basic foundations of American strength and freedom,
the Communist challenge to American freedom and
how a free society can meet the Communist challenge." Serves as educational secretariat of the
Congressional Caucus on National Security. Sponsors U.S. Congressional Advisory Board which disseminates information to members of Congress.
Conducts concentrated training programs for free
world leaders in both public and private sectors;
maintains the National Security Speakers' Bureau.
Formerly: (1977) Institute for American Strategy;
(1980) American Security Council Education Foundation. **Publications:** *A Strategy for Peace Through
Strength* ● Also publishes monographs, handbooks,
and studies; has produced documentary films for
television. **Conventions/Meetings:** annual meeting.

16634 ■ Anti-Communist International (ACI)
PO Box 1095, Grand Central Sta.
New York, NY 10163-1095
E-mail: kshedaker5154@monroecollege.edu
Contact: Kathleen Shedaker, CEO
Founded: 1959. **Members:** 12. **Staff:** 2. **Budget:**
$100,000. **National Groups:** 23. **Multinational. De-
scription:** Ethnic and religious organizations. Coordi-
nates activities among members and others oppos-
ing communist ideology. Conducts research; compiles
statistics. Organizes seminars; bestows awards.
Awards: ACI Gold & Silver Cold War Victory Medals.
Frequency: annual. **Type:** medal. **Recipient:** for
contribution to anti-Communism. **Publications:** *ACI
Reports*. Country reports. **Price:** $100.00/report.
Alternate Formats: CD-ROM; diskette; online. **Con-
ventions/Meetings:** biennial international conference
● periodic seminar.

16635 ■ Captive Nations Committee (CNC)
PO Box 540
Gracie Sta.
New York, NY 10028-0005

E-mail: captivenationscommitteeinc2@yahoo.com
URL: http://www.captivenationscommitteeinc2.org/
preview
Contact: Horst Adolf Uhlich, Pres.
Founded: 1959. **Members:** 20,000. **Description:**
Represents ethnic groups and concerned individuals
organized to carry out activities that support their
anti-communist beliefs. Supports freedom for all the
captive nations; promotes boycott of merchandise
from communist nations. Sponsors annual parade
and seven-day educational program in New York City
during Captive Nations Week. Conducts demonstrations, commemorations, and lectures; attends and
supports anti-communist activities sponsored by other
organizations. **Awards: Type:** recognition. **Committees:** Folklore; Parade; Park; Public Relations; St.
Patrick's Cathedral; Security; Signs. **Formerly:** Captive Nations Committee New York. **Conventions/
Meetings:** annual meeting - always late April, in New
York City.

**16636 ■ Cardinal Mindszenty Foundation
(CMF)**
PO Box 11321
St. Louis, MO 63105
Ph: (314)727-6279
Fax: (314)727-5897
E-mail: info@mindszenty.org
URL: http://www.mindszenty.org
Contact: Eleanor Schlafly, Pres.
Founded: 1958. **Members:** 10,000. **Membership
Dues:** individual, $20 (annual). **Staff:** 6. **State
Groups:** 4. **Description:** Conducts educational and
research activities concerning Communists objec-
tives, tactics, and propaganda through study groups,
lectures, radio programs, and conferences. Maintains
research files. **Libraries: Type:** open to the public;
by appointment only. **Holdings:** 1,000; books,
periodicals. **Awards:** Freedom Award. **Frequency:**
annual. **Type:** recognition. **Computer Services:** Mailing lists. **Publications:** *Mindszenty Report*, monthly.
Newsletter. Contains current concerns on faith, family
and freedom. **Price:** $20.00 /year for individuals in
U.S.; $36.00 for 2 years; $28.00 /year for individuals
outside U.S. **Circulation:** 9,000. Alternate Formats:
online ● Videos. **Conventions/Meetings:** annual
conference, with religion, educational materials
(exhibits) - held for one day in Chicago, IL, Dallas,
TX, Louisville, KY and Anaheim, CA.

16637 ■ CAUSA International
401 5th Ave.
New York, NY 10016
E-mail: info@causainternational.org
URL: http://familyfed.org/causa
Contact: Dr. Thomas Ward, Contact
Founded: 1980. **Members:** 21. **Multinational. Description:** A worldwide network of nonsectarian
educational and social organizations founded by Rev.
Sun Myung Moon (who also founded the Unification
Church). Objectives are: to promote a viable God-
centered alternative to the Marxist worldview of the
society of the future; to alert and inform the public
regarding rising threats to democracy throughout the
world. Advocates a new ideological perspective on
world democracy. Based upon religious principles,
CAUSA holds that positive social change can be effected only through the unity of "God-accepting,
conscientious" people bound by a common goal;
strives to propagate this worldview as the means to
fight communist ideologies. **Conventions/Meetings:**
periodic meeting ● seminar.

**16638 ■ Christian Anti-Communism Crusade
(CACC)**
PO Box 129
Manitou Springs, CO 80829
Ph: (719)685-9043
URL: http://www.schwarzreport.org
Contact: Dr. David Noebel, Pres.
Founded: 1953. **Staff:** 4. **Budget:** $300,000. **Multi-
national. Description:** Aims to inform Christians and
others of the philosophy, morality, organization,
strategy, and tactics of Communism and allied forces.
Holds rallies, organizes lectures, debates, and forums
at universities. Sponsors anti-subversive seminars in

various cities, with the aid of local citizens' committees; has supported anti-communist projects in 21
countries including India, Australia, Brazil, the Philippines, and Kenya. **Publications:** *Beating the Unbeat-
able Foe*. Book. **Price:** $34.95 ● *The Three Faces of
Revolution* ● *What Is Communism?* ● *Why Communism Kills* ● *Why I Am Against Communism*.
Booklet ● *You Can Trust the Communists (to be
Communists)*. Book. **Price:** $5.00 ● Newsletter,
monthly. ISSN: 0195-9387.

16639 ■ Selous Foundation (SF)
325 Pennsylvania Ave. SE, 2nd Fl.
Washington, DC 20003
Ph: (202)547-6963
Contact: Morgan Norval, Exec.Dir.
Founded: 1985. **Members:** 50,000. **Staff:** 3. **Budget:**
$750,000. **Description:** Dedicated to the study of
conflict and providing for a strong national defense.
Libraries: Type: not open to the public. **Holdings:**
350. **Subjects:** terrorism, revolutionary, warfare. **Pub-
lications:** Book ● Booklets.

Appropriate Technology

16640 ■ Aprovecho Research Center
80574 Hazelton Rd.
Cottage Grove, OR 97424
Ph: (541)942-8198
E-mail: apro@efn.org
URL: http://www.aprovecho.net
Founded: 1981. **Members:** 150. **Membership Dues:**
regular, $30 (annual). **Staff:** 12. **Budget:** $60,000.
Regional Groups: 1. **Description:** Provides a basis
for scientific research on appropriate technologies
and techniques for simple and cooperative living, and
to serve an educational role in disseminating information on such technologies and techniques. Offers a
10-week internship program. Trains Peace Corps
volunteers and development workers worldwide.
(Aprovecho is a Spanish word which means "I make
the best use of."). **Libraries: Type:** reference. **Committees:** Buildings; Permaculture. **Departments:** Appropriate Technology; Environmental Education; Fuel
Conserving Stoves; Organic Gardening; Public
Information; Sustainable Forestry; Sustainable Land
Use. **Formerly:** (1997) Aprovecho Institute. **Publications:** *Capturing Heat*. Manual ● *Capturing Heat II*.
Manual ● *News From Aprovecho*, quarterly. Newsletter. Provides information on permaculture, stoves,
nonconsumptive lifestyles, and notices of upcoming
events. **Price:** $30.00/year (suggested donation). **Cir-
culation:** 2,500. **Advertising:** accepted ● Also
publishes technical guide. **Conventions/Meetings:**
meeting, ten-week internship - 3/year.

16641 ■ Domestic Technologies (DTI)
PO Box 44
Evergreen, CO 80437-2043
Ph: (303)674-7700
Fax: (303)674-7772
E-mail: dti@domtech.com
Contact: Malcolm Lillywhite, Pres.
Founded: 1977. **Staff:** 6. **Budget:** $3,000,000. **Na-
tional Groups:** 6. **Languages:** English, French,
Portuguese, Spanish. **For-Profit. Multinational. Description:** Develops and promotes business/
economic developing using conservation and renewable technologies and hybrid power systems for eco-
tourism, community electrification, natural resource
management, and related programs throughout the
world. Defines domestic technology as a systematic
way of applying technology to solve community,
economic, food and energy problems while developing the local economy. Conducts natural resource
management, research, training, and community
development programs. Programs emphasize
hands-on training and range from constructing and
operating simple solar systems to designing and
building integrated ethanol fuel processing systems.
Offers design and engineering consulting, survey and
assessment, and speaker services. Has designed
and managed renewable energy program for the
governments, villagers, and refugee camps of Sudan

Somalia, Kenya, Botswana, Lesotho, Swaziland, Zimbabwe, Belize, Indonesia, Tibet, Madagascar, Brazil, the Caribbean, and Morocco. Has also developed a site-built solar water treatment system; implemented a Low Impact Tourism as a Strategy for Sustaining Natural Resource and Cultural Conservation Project in Tibet, China, Botswana, Madagascar, the Caribbean, Brazil, Indonesia, Central America, and with Native Americans in the USA. **Libraries: Type:** reference. **Holdings:** 200,000; audiovisuals, books, clippings, periodicals. **Subjects:** renewable energy, natural resource management, tourism. **Computer Services:** database, Energy Consumption Tourism Market Trends ● mailing lists, Computer Design Solar House Construction Plans ● online services, hard copy catalogue or electronic available. **Formerly:** (2003) Domestic Technology Institute. **Publications:** Reports ● Also publishes solar house and greenhouse plans and ethanol fuel plant plans. **Conventions/Meetings:** workshop, on organic gardening, passive solar food drying and dehydration, site-built collectors, greenhouses, eco-tourism, and renewable energy for tourism industry and renewable energy hybrid power systems for remote locations.

16642 ■ E. F. Schumacher Society (EFSS)
140 Jug End Rd.
Great Barrington, MA 01230
Ph: (413)528-1737
Fax: (413)528-4472
E-mail: efssociety@smallisbeautiful.org
URL: http://www.smallisbeautiful.org
Contact: Susan Witt, Exec. Dir.
Founded: 1980. **Members:** 500. **Membership Dues:** individual, $50 (annual) ● student, senior, $15 (annual). **Staff:** 2. **Budget:** $150,000. **Description:** Works for the promotion of the economic philosophy of British economist Ernst Friedrich Schumacher (1911-77), author of *Small is Beautiful: Economics As If People Mattered*. Schumacher advocated small-scale, environmentally-conscious economic development that fosters decentralization, bioregional awareness (a bioregion is a soft-boundary geographic zone based on ecological and cultural criteria), local community awareness (a sense of place), and production "from local resources, for local needs." Believes that ecological laws must form the basis of long-term social systems: agricultural, economic, political, and technological. Designs and implements programs to strengthen the regional economy, including local currencies, community micro-lending, and community land trusts. **Libraries: Type:** reference. **Holdings:** 9,000; archival material, articles, audio recordings, books, periodicals, video recordings. **Subjects:** community building, economic development, organic farming, rural and environmental issues, sustainability, decentralism, personal library and archives of Fritz Schumacher. **Computer Services:** Online services. **Publications:** *A New Lease on Farmland*. Pamphlet. **Price:** $5.00 postage included ● *Community Land Trust: Handbook of Legal Documents*. Handbooks ● *Lecture Reprints*, annual ● *Local Currencies*. Pamphlets. **Price:** $5.00 postage included ● *People, Land and Community: Collected E.F. Schumacher Society Lectures*. Book. **Price:** $21.00 paperback ● *Small is Beautiful*. Book. **Price:** $23.00 paperback ● Monographs ● Pamphlets. **Price:** $5.00 postage included ● Papers ● Reports ● Also publishes lectures, information packets, and other materials. **Conventions/Meetings:** annual E. F. Schumacher Lectures - conference - every 4th Saturday in October.

16643 ■ EnterpriseWorks/VITA
1825 Connecticut Ave. NW, Ste.630
Washington, DC 20009
Ph: (202)293-4600
Fax: (202)293-4598
E-mail: info@enterpriseworks.org
URL: http://www.enterpriseworks.org
Contact: Don Feil, Pres./CEO
Founded: 1978. **Staff:** 25. **Languages:** English, French. **Multinational. Description:** Works to create profitable, environmentally responsible businesses in the developing world. Enables small-scale farmers and microentrepreneurs in Africa, Asia, and Latin America to increase incomes, expand operations and markets, and forge new regional and international business links. **Libraries: Type:** reference. **Subjects:** international socio-economic literature on appropriate technology. **Formed by Merger of:** (2005) EnterpriseWorks Worldwide and Volunteers in Technical Assistance. **Formerly:** (1999) Appropriate Technology International. **Publications:** *Occasional Working Papers*, 4-6/year ● *WhatWorks*, monthly. Newsletter. Showcases successful approaches to small business development and poverty reduction programs. Alternate Formats: online ● Annual Report.

16644 ■ Intermediate Technology Development Group of North America (ITDG/NA)
777 UN Plz., Ste.3C
New York, NY 10017
Ph: (212)972-9877 (914)271-6500
Free: (800)316-2739
Fax: (212)972-9878
E-mail: cipany@igc.apc.org
Contact: Ward Morehouse, Chm.
Founded: 1979. **Staff:** 2. **Budget:** $50,000. **Description:** Community groups, educational institutions, and other individuals and organizations interested in intermediate technology. (Intermediate technology refers to techniques and institutions providing goods and services that are environmentally sustainable and operate on a local level, representing an alternative to prevailing, conventional, large-scale technologies.) Objectives are to create jobs at the local level through the use of intermediate technology and thus effect community revitalization, and to create an atmosphere where workers enjoy, take pride in, and exercise greater control over the work they do. Encourages greater economic decentralization and community self-reliance; promotes employment systems that are more labor-intensive and less capital-intensive; fosters international cooperation in development of intermediate technology. Disseminates information on new approaches to economic issues, emphasizing human values and environmental sustainability; applications of intermediate technology to housing problems, especially those of low-income people; decentralization of energy production in harmony with the environment and responsive to community concerns; diversification of food production; conservation and reuse of agricultural land; reduction of costs of transportation and packaging. **Programs:** Bootstrap Press. **Publications:** *A World that Works*. Book ● *Building Sustainable Communities*. Book ● *Future Wealth*. Book ● *Greening Cities*. Book ● *Humanistic Economics*. Book ● Also distributes publications on intermediate technology and social economics as they apply to agriculture, building and housing, cooperatives, energy, health, industry and business management, and rural development.

16645 ■ National Center for Appropriate Technology (NCAT)
PO Box 3838
Butte, MT 59702
Ph: (406)494-4572
Free: (800)ASK-NCAT
Fax: (406)494-2905
E-mail: information@ncat.org
URL: http://www.ncat.org
Contact: Kathleen Hadley, Exec. Dir.
Founded: 1976. **Staff:** 80. **Budget:** $3,000,000. **Description:** Seeks to develop, apply, research, and transfer applications of appropriate technologies that meet long-term human needs for energy, shelter, environment, and sustainable agriculture, particularly the needs of low-income individuals. Provides information in the areas of renewable energy sources, resource conservation, and low-input sustainable agriculture. Conducts research and analysis on demand side management. **Libraries: Type:** reference. **Holdings:** 6,600; books, periodicals. **Subjects:** energy, sustainable agriculture, shelter, and environment. **Awards:** Distinguished Appropriate Technology Award. **Frequency:** annual. **Type:** recognition. **Computer Services:** Online services, Appropriate Technology Management Information system, accessible through DIALOG. **Programs:** Sustainable Agriculture and Rural Development; Sustainable Communities; Sustainable Energy. **Projects:** Center for Resourceful Building Technology; Low-Income Home Energy Assistance Program Clearinghouse; Million Solar Roofs; National Energy Assistance Referral; Residential Solar Electric Demonstration; Wind Energy. **Publications:** Bibliographies ● Booklet. Includes consumer materials. ● Report. Includes research materials. ● Annual Report, annual. Alternate Formats: online.

16646 ■ Planet Drum Foundation (PDF)
PO Box 31251
Shasta Bioregion, USA
San Francisco, CA 94131
Ph: (415)285-6556
Fax: (415)285-6563
E-mail: planetdrum@igc.org
URL: http://www.planetdrum.org
Contact: Peter Berg, Dir.
Founded: 1973. **Members:** 500. **Membership Dues:** regular, in North America, $25 (annual) ● regular, outside North America, $30 (annual). **Staff:** 8. **Budget:** $50,000. **Regional Groups:** 300. **Local Groups:** 425. **Description:** Aids social change organizations, libraries, and individuals interested in bioregionalism. Defines a bioregion as a "whole life-place, a distinct area with coherent and interconnected plant and animal communities, often defined by a watershed. Bioregionalism provides an effective grass roots approach to ecology that emphasizes sustainability, community self-determination and regional self-reliance". Encourages people to become aware of the environment and adapt to its existing natural systems: inhabiting or reinhabiting life-places. Conducts bioregional research and publishes information on the relationship between human culture and natural processes of the planetary biosphere. Promotes the concept of bioregionalism, through workshops and lectures. Networks nationally and internationally for bioregional movement. Maintains speakers' bureau. Publishes online calendar of various ecological events in the Bay area. Also publishes an all-bioregional calendar online. **Libraries: Type:** open to the public. **Holdings:** articles, books, periodicals. **Subjects:** bioregionalism, ecology, environmentalism. **Telecommunication Services:** electronic mail, mail@planetdrum.org. **Committees:** Benefit. **Programs:** Green City. **Projects:** Eco Ecuador; Olympic Actions. **Publications:** *A Green City Program for the San Francisco Bay Area and Beyond*. Book. Describes how to make cities more sustainable. **Price:** $10.00 plus shipping and handling ● *Backbone-The Rockies*. Book. **Price:** $10.00 plus shipping and handling ● *Directory of North American Bioregional Groups*, periodic ● *Discovering Your Life-Place: A First Bioregional Workbook*. **Price:** $10.00 plus shipping and handling ● *Eco-Decentralist Design*. Book ● *Planet Drum Bundles*, periodic ● *Planet Drum Pulse*. Newsletter. **Price:** included in membership dues ● *Raise the Stakes*, semiannual ● *Reinhabiting a Separate Country: A Bioregional Anthology of Northern California*. Book. **Price:** $7.00 plus shipping and handling. **Conventions/Meetings:** periodic conference.

16647 ■ Program for Appropriate Technology in Health (PATH)
1455 NW Leary Way
Seattle, WA 98107-5136
Ph: (206)285-3500
Fax: (206)285-6619
E-mail: info@path.org
URL: http://www.path.org
Contact: Mahmoud Fahmy Fathalla, Chm.
Founded: 1977. **Staff:** 260. **Budget:** $37,307,000. **Description:** Works to improve reproductive and child health, immunization programs, and diagnostic technologies in developing countries. Focuses on the effectiveness, availability, safety, and appropriateness of technologies for health and family planning. Conducts research and development, field assessment, communications, and technology transfer programs. Offers loans to assist developing countries

in producing the essential health products. **Libraries: Type:** reference; lending; not open to the public. **Holdings:** archival material, artwork, audiovisuals, books, clippings, periodicals. **Subjects:** health, family planning. **Councils:** Leadership. **Absorbed:** Program for the Introduction and Adaptation of Contraceptive Technology. **Supersedes:** Health Division of Program for the Introduction and Adaptation of Contraceptive Technology. **Publications:** *Lending for Health*, semiannual ● *Outlook*, quarterly. Features news on reproductive health issues. **Price:** $40.00 /year for individuals. ISSN: 0737-3732 ● Annual Report, annual. Focuses on the organization's progress and milestones. **Conventions/Meetings:** annual board meeting.

16648 ■ Servants in Faith and Technology (SIFAT)
2944 County Rd. 113
Lineville, AL 36266
Ph: (256)396-2017 (256)396-2015
Fax: (256)396-2501
E-mail: corsont@sifat.org
URL: http://www.sifat.org
Contact: Tom Corson, Exec. Dir.
Founded: 1979. **Staff:** 20. **Budget:** $750,000. **Languages:** English, Spanish. **Multinational. Description:** Churches, church groups, and Christian individuals concerned with development through the use of appropriate technology. Purposes are: to provide education and training in practical technology; to conduct research and development on appropriate technology; to act as a clearinghouse of appropriate technology information. Aims to enable people to meet their own basic needs. Gives seminars and training courses; offers consulting service. **Libraries: Type:** open to the public. **Holdings:** 2,250. **Subjects:** appropriate technology, agriculture, conservation, development, energy, transportation, sanitation, water, geographical regions, church, missions, ethics, philosophy, world religions, sociology, psychology, cross cultural communication, village industries, health, medicine, housing, communication. **Divisions:** Alternative Energies; Cross-Cultural Communication; Health; Livestock for Self-Sufficiency; Poverty-Related Issues; Small-Scale Food Production and Preservation; Village Industries and Skills; Water. **Also Known As:** Southern Institute for Appropriate Technology. **Publications:** *SIFAT Journal*, monthly. Reports happenings at SIFAT, news about staff, students, learn and serve teams, and information about appropriate technologies. **Price:** free for contributors ● Also publishes brochures, technical papers, bibliographies, and course guidelines. **Conventions/Meetings:** semiannual Summer Training Practicum - board meeting.

16649 ■ TRANET
4457 Bethany Rd., Bldg. F
Mason, OH 45040
Ph: (513)459-8700
Fax: (513)459-8515
E-mail: info@tranet.com
URL: http://tranet.com
Contact: Tim Rudy, Pres.
Founded: 1976. **Members:** 1,000. **Staff:** 5. **Description:** Individuals and groups participating in appropriate/alternative technologies (the development and application of technologies geared to needs and conditions of specific areas). Works to serve appropriate/alternative technologies around the world by helping to develop bilateral exchanges and by promoting communication on appropriate technology concepts. Establishes Third World appropriate technology libraries. Conducts educational programs. **Libraries: Type:** reference. **Holdings:** 5,000; archival material. **Subjects:** the alternative movements. **Computer Services:** database, appropriate technology organizations and publications. **Telecommunication Services:** electronic bulletin board, information on networkers ● electronic mail, timrudy@tranet.com. **Also Known As:** Trans-National Network of Appropriate/Alternative Technology. **Publications:** Newsletter, bimonthly. Includes calendar of events and directory of services. **Price:** included in membership dues. ISSN: 0739-0971. **Circulation:** 3,000.

Arab

16650 ■ Arab American Leadership Council (ALC)
1600 K St. NW, Ste.601
Washington, DC 20006
Ph: (202)429-9210
Fax: (202)429-9214
E-mail: jzogby@aaiusa.org
URL: http://www.aaiusa.org
Contact: Dr. James Zogby, Pres./CEO
Founded: 1989. **Members:** 250. **Budget:** $40,000. **Description:** Network of elected, appointed, and party officials of Arab descent. Provides information, technical assistance, and campaign support to Arab American candidates; supports public service appointments sought by its members. **Libraries: Type:** reference. **Holdings:** archival material. **Committees:** Arab American Democrats; Arab American Republicans; Democratic and Republican Caucuses. **Absorbed:** Arab American Republican Federation; (1989) Arab American Democratic Federation. **Publications:** *Roster of Arab Americans in Political Life*, biennial. Directory. Listing of Arab Americans who hold elected, appointed office or party committee position. **Conventions/Meetings:** annual meeting.

Artists

16651 ■ Pollock-Krasner Foundation (PKF)
863 Park Ave.
New York, NY 10021
Ph: (212)517-5400
Fax: (212)288-2836
E-mail: grants@pkf.org
URL: http://www.pkf.org
Contact: Eugene Victor Thaw, Pres. Emeritus
Founded: 1985. **Multinational. Description:** Provides financial assistance to individual working artists of established ability through the generosity of the late Lee Krasner, one of the leading abstract expressionist painters and the widow of Jackson Pollock. **Awards:** The Grant. **Type:** grant. **Recipient:** for visual artists who are painters, sculptors, and artists who work on paper, including printmakers.

Asia

16652 ■ The Asia Foundation (TAF)
PO Box 193223
San Francisco, CA 94119-3223
Ph: (415)982-4640
Fax: (415)392-8863
E-mail: info@asiafound.org
URL: http://www.asiafoundation.org
Contact: Doug Bereuter, Pres.
Founded: 1954. **Members:** 300. **Staff:** 300. **Multinational. Description:** Supported by U.S. government grants and private contributions. Works to strengthen government and institutions in Asia and the Pacific Islands; promotes Asian-Pacific cooperation; and develops closer Asian-American relations. Supports projects that: strengthen representative government, build effective legal systems, foster market economies, increase accountability in the public and private sectors, develop independent and responsible media, and encourage the development of human resources. Maintains Books for Asia program which distributes over one million books and journals each year to Asian schools, universities, libraries, and research centers; and Asian-American Exchange program which offers in-country opportunities to Asians and Pacific Islanders to share professional training and academic study with Americans. **Programs:** Books for Asia. **Publications:** *The Asia Foundation Bulletin*, quarterly. Newsletter. Alternate Formats: online ● *Program Profiles*. Report ● Annual Report, annual. Includes yearly activities and financial report. ● Working Paper Series; Asian Perspectives Series; Projects List; Occasional Reports. **Conventions/Meetings:** quarterly board meeting.

16653 ■ Committee Against Anti-Asian Violence (CAAAV)
2473 Valentine Ave.
Bronx, NY 10458
Ph: (718)220-7391
Fax: (718)220-7398
E-mail: justice@caaav.org
URL: http://www.caaav.org
Contact: Jane S. Bai, Exec. Dir.
Founded: 1986. **Members:** 300. **Staff:** 8. **Languages:** Cantonese, English, Korean, Mandarin, Mandarin Dialects, Urdu, Vietnamese. **Description:** Community-based organization committed to building the capacity of poor and low-income Asian immigrant communities to contribute to the struggles for racial, economic, women's, and environmental justice. Addresses police brutality, housing, welfare, immigration, labor, public education, and other issues related to anti-Asian violence. **Projects:** Chinatown Justice; Women Workers; Youth Leadership. **Also Known As:** (2000) CAAAV: Organizing Asian Communities. **Publications:** *CAAAV Voice*, annual. Newsletter. Describes organizational work and analysis and updates of other justice struggles. **Price:** $25.00/year. **Circulation:** 2,500.

16654 ■ Free Burma Coalition (FBC)
PO Box 9573
Berkeley, CA 94709
Ph: (510)685-4170
Fax: (510)559-0003
E-mail: mandalay1886@yahoo.com
URL: http://www.freeburmacoalition.org
Contact: Mr. Christopher Tun, Technical Advisor
Founded: 1995. **Languages:** Burmese, English. **Description:** Aims to support Burmese people's aspirations and struggle for democracy and human rights through boycotts, pro-sanctions advocacy and Burma awareness promotion. Organizes anti-apartheid-style pro-sanctions campaigns. Supports efforts to interact and engage with the country. Encourages travel and tourism, educational exchange, policies aimed to support people's livelihoods, institutional and capacity building, and humanitarian assistance. **Telecommunication Services:** information service, majordomo@igc.apc.org. **Publications:** *Free Burma Online*, biweekly. Alternate Formats: online. **Conventions/Meetings:** annual international conference.

16655 ■ National Advisory Council for South Asian Affairs (NACSAA)
3105 Beaverwood Ln.
Silver Spring, MD 20906
Ph: (301)460-7090
Contact: Dr. Vasant G. Telang, Exec. Dir.
Founded: 1979. **Members:** 40. **Membership Dues:** regular, $200 (annual). **Languages:** Bengali, English, Hindi, Urdu. **For-Profit. Description:** Represents Americans who immigrated to the United States from South Asian countries. Monitors and shapes United States foreign policy issues, particularly those regarding South Asia. Holds discussions and dialogues. **Computer Services:** Mailing lists. **Publications:** Newsletter, semiannual. **Conventions/Meetings:** semiannual conference ● seminar.

16656 ■ U.S.-Asia Institute (USAI)
232 E Capitol St. NE
Washington, DC 20003
Ph: (202)544-3181
Fax: (202)543-1748
E-mail: usasiainstitute@verizon.net
URL: http://www.usasiainstitute.org
Contact: Esther G. Kee, Pres.
Founded: 1979. **Members:** 25. **Staff:** 6. **Budget:** $325,000. **Description:** Americans of Asian descent, individuals with an interest in U.S.-Asia relations, U.S. institutions and companies doing business with Asia, and Asian institutions and companies doing business with the U.S. Aims to strengthen ties between the East and the West and foster cooperation, communication, and cultural exchange between the U.S. and Asia. Places special emphasis on the "unique capabilities" of Asian Americans to assist in this process, and on the contribution of Asian Americans to the cultural, social, and economic

mainstream of American life. Promotes a firm under-standing in Asia of the issues important to the development of American domestic and foreign poli-cies through research, symposia, and special pro-grams. Sponsors American Perspective Series of educational seminars for Asian leaders and groups on issues concerning U.S.-Asia Relations and U.S. congressional aides planning visits to Indonesia, Japan, Malaysia, and the People's Republic of China. **Awards:** Kay Sugahara Award. **Frequency:** annual. **Type:** recognition. **Recipient:** for the contributions of young American Asians ● USAI Achievement Award. **Frequency:** annual. **Type:** recognition. **Recipient:** for Asian-Americans who have made outstanding contributions to America in their individual fields. **Councils:** U.S.-Asia Foreign Policy. **Publications:** *An Asian/Pacific American Perspective: Future Direc-tions of U.S.* ● *The Communications Revolution: Key to U.S.-Asia Relations* ● *U.S.-Asia Economic Rela-tions: Policies and Prospects* ● *US-Asia Institute—Policy Forum,* quarterly. Newsletter. Covers eco-nomic, political, and strategic relations between the United States and Asia; also covers institute activities and programs. **Price:** included in membership dues. **Circulation:** 1,500 ● *US-Asia National Leadership Conference Proceedings,* annual. **Price:** free to conference attendees; $25.00/copy for non-attendees ● *US-Asia Update,* semiannual. Newsletter. Alternate Formats: online. **Conventions/Meetings:** annual National Leadership Conference - meeting.

16657 ■ U.S.-Vietnam Trade Council (USVTC)
731 8th St. SE
Washington, DC 20003
Ph: (202)547-3800
Fax: (202)546-5248
E-mail: virginia.foote@usvtc.org
URL: http://www.usvtc.org
Contact: Virginia B. Foote, Pres./Co-Founder
Founded: 1989. **Members:** 120. **Multinational. De-scription:** Serves as a focal point for American private sector leadership aimed at achieving normal-ized diplomatic and economic relations. Valuable information source and key player in the strengthen-ing of U.S.-Vietnam relations. Hosts senior Vietnam-ese officials in Washington for high level meetings and conferences; organizes delegations to Vietnam for Cabinet officials and members of Congress. **For-merly:** (1998) Commission on U.S.-Asian Relations. **Publications:** *Update,* periodic. Newsletter. Alternate Formats: online ● Report, periodic. **Conventions/Meetings:** periodic meeting - usually in Washington, DC area.

16658 ■ Vets With a Mission (VWAM)
PO Box 202
Newberry, SC 29108
Ph: (803)405-9926 (803)351-9953
Fax: (803)405-9926
E-mail: vetswithamission@backroads.net
URL: http://www.vwam.com
Contact: Chuck Ward, Exec. Dir.
Founded: 1989. **Staff:** 2. **Budget:** $174,000. **Non-membership. Multinational. Description:** Imple-ments various humanitarian programs and carries out a number of projects in that part of the country formerly known as the Republic of South Vietnam. Focuses on services of humanitarian medical teams, the construction of rural health care communes or small medical clinics in the city, and other specialized projects. Is involved in ministry to the Vietnamese Church and support of Vietnamese Christians. Works to "heal the deep wounds and devastating effects that war has inflicted on South East Asia on both sides" and to express the purpose and love of Christ according to II Corinthians 5:18. **Libraries: Type:** not open to the public; by appointment only; reference. **Holdings:** 100; articles, audiovisuals, books, films, periodicals, photographs. **Subjects:** Vietnam War. **Telecommunication Services:** electronic mail, thewards@backroads.net. **Boards:** Directors. **Publi-cations:** *VWAMessenger,* annual. Newsletter. **Price:** free.

Atlantic

16659 ■ Atlantic Council of the United States (ACUS)
1101 15th St. NW, 11th Fl.
Washington, DC 20005

Ph: (202)463-7226 (202)778-4957
Fax: (202)463-7241
E-mail: info@acus.org
URL: http://www.acus.org
Contact: Jam M. Lodal, Pres.
Founded: 1961. **Members:** 700. **Membership Dues:** counselor, $250 (annual) ● associate counselor, $100 (annual) ● senior counselor, $500 (annual) ● patron counselor, $1,000 (annual) ● chairman's associate, $10,000 (annual). **Staff:** 20. **Budget:** $3,000,000. **Regional Groups:** 1. **Languages:** English, French. **Description:** Conducts programs to: promote better understanding of major international security, politi-cal, and economic problems; foster informed public debate on these issues; make substantive policy recommendations to both the Executive and Legisla-tive branches of the U.S. government, as well as to appropriate international organizations. Sponsors young leaders seminars; offers counselors program for high-level senior advisers. **Programs:** Asia; British-North American Committee; Economics, Energy and Environment; International Security; Of-fice of Education and the Successor Generations; Transatlantic Relations. **Affiliated With:** Atlantic Treaty Association. **Publications:** *Atlantic Council News,* biennial. Newsletter. **Price:** free for members. **Circulation:** 2,000. Alternate Formats: online ● *Bul-letins,* periodic. Monographs ● *Occasional Papers,* periodic ● *Policy Papers,* periodic ● *Program Sum-mary,* annual. **Conventions/Meetings:** annual Award Dinner - meeting and dinner, with reception and speaker on major foreign affairs topic.

Automobile

16660 ■ Coalition for Vehicle Choice (CVC)
c/o E. Bruce Harrison & Co.
1440 New York Ave. NW
Washington, DC 20005
Free: (800)288-6411
Contact: Diane Steed, Pres.
Members: 40,000. **Description:** Automotive, con-sumer, farm, insurance, law enforcement, recreation and safety groups. Works to preserve the freedom of Americans to choose motor vehicles that meet their needs and their freedom to travel.

16661 ■ Seat Belt Choice Coalition (SBCC)
c/o Nedd Kareiva, Dir.
6000 S Central, No. 8
Chicago, IL 60638
E-mail: nedd_@seatbeltchoice.com
URL: http://www.seatbeltchoice.com
Contact: Nedd Kareiva, Dir.
Description: Committed to repealing mandatory seat belt laws. **Publications:** *Buckled Down or Knuckled Under.* **Price:** $5.00.

Awards

16662 ■ Francena Purchase Applied Honors Society
PO Box 7421
Grand Rapids, MI 49510
Contact: Francena Purchase, Pres.
Founded: 1999. **Multinational. Description:** Profes-sional society of students and others who have displayed outstanding contributions and understand-ing of various learning environments that have impacted communities. **Libraries: Type:** not open to the public; reference; by appointment only. **Holdings:** articles, artwork, books. **Awards:** International Who's Who of Information Technology. **Frequency:** periodic. **Type:** recognition ● International Who's Who of Professionals. **Frequency:** periodic. **Type:** recogni-tion.

Baltic

16663 ■ Baltic American Freedom League (BAFL)
PO Box 65056
Los Angeles, CA 90065-0056

Ph: (949)837-7135 (310)231-0018
Fax: (530)481-5514
E-mail: asinlab@cox.net
URL: http://www.bafl.com
Contact: Alnis Briedis, Co-Pres.
Founded: 1981. **Members:** 16,000. **Membership Dues:** life, $100. **Staff:** 1. **Budget:** $30,000. **Lan-guages:** English, Estonian, Latvian, Lithuanian. **Mul-tinational. Description:** Americans of Baltic ances-try; human rights activists in the Baltic nations of Estonia, Latvia, and Lithuania. Disseminates informa-tion on Baltic history, culture, and current events. Provides interviews to television, radio, and com-munity programs. Maintains speakers' bureau. **Awards:** Baltic Freedom Award. **Frequency:** annual. **Type:** recognition. **Recipient:** for people who make important contributions to the development of democ-racy and security of the Baltic countries ● President's Award. **Frequency:** annual. **Type:** recognition. **Publi-cations:** *Baltic Bulletin,* quarterly. **Price:** $30.00 ● *Baltic Caucus Update,* periodic, monthly when Congress is in session. Newsletter. **Price:** free. **Con-ventions/Meetings:** annual Awards Banquet - usu-ally March or April ● annual Foreign Policy and Defense Issues (USA) - conference (exhibits) - usu-ally March or April.

16664 ■ Joint Baltic American National Committee (JBANC)
400 Hurley Ave.
Rockville, MD 20850-3121
Ph: (301)340-1954
Fax: (301)309-1406
E-mail: jbanc@jbanc.org
URL: http://www.jbanc.org
Contact: Karl Altau, Managing Dir.
Founded: 1961. **Members:** 9. **Staff:** 5. **Description:** Representatives of the American Latvian Association in the U.S., the Lithuanian American Council, and the Estonian American National Council. Coordinates the presentation of issues relating to the Baltic states of Estonia, Latvia, and Lithuania to the U.S. govern-ment and public. Works for the preservation of Baltic culture for the Baltic peoples. Conducts summer internship program for interested students of U.S.-Baltic affairs. **Affiliated With:** American Latvian As-sociation; Estonian American National Council; Lithuanian American Council. **Formerly:** (1977) Joint Baltic American Committee. **Publications:** *JBANC Annual Report,* annual. Includes coverage of Baltic Freedom Day, activist projects, and current Baltic legislation updates. **Price:** free. **Circulation:** 500. **Advertising:** accepted. Alternate Formats: online ● *JBANC Chronicle,* quarterly. Newsletter. Covers events of Baltic interest with a Washington perspec-tive. **Price:** $20.00 /year for individuals. Alternate Formats: online ● *Legislative Updates,* periodic. Contains information on issues affecting Baltic Americans as they are debated in Congress. **Con-ventions/Meetings:** biennial Baltic Security Confer-ence.

Banking

16665 ■ Single Global Currency Association (SGCA)
PO Box 390
Newcastle, ME 04553
Ph: (207)586-6078
E-mail: morrison@singleglobalcurrency.org
URL: http://www.singleglobalcurrency.org
Contact: Morrison Bonpasse, Contact
Founded: 2003. **Membership Dues:** supporter, $20 (annual) ● contributor, $200 (annual) ● sustainer, $2,006 (annual) ● benefactor, $20,006 (annual). **Mul-tinational. Description:** Promotes the implementa-tion of single global currency. Increases awareness of the benefits of single global currency in the economic development. **Publications:** *The Single Global Currency - Common Cents for the World.* Book. Explains the multicurrency foreign exchange system. **Price:** EUR 22.00. Alternate Formats: online ● *Single Global Currency Journal.* Presents articles, news and comments about the single global currency

and related matters. Alternate Formats: online. Also Cited As: *SGCJ*. Conventions/Meetings: annual conference.

Bicycle

16666 ■ America Bikes
1612 K St. NW, Ste.800
Washington, DC 20006
Ph: (202)833-8080
Fax: (202)822-1334
E-mail: info@americabikes.org
URL: http://www.americabikes.org
Contact: Matt Winfield, Campaign Mgr.
Description: Promotes bicycling for transportation. Advocates for positive outcomes for bicycling in the federal transportation funding bill. Believes that bicycling can improve the economic prosperity of communities throughout the United States.

Biological Weapons

16667 ■ Chemical and Biological Arms Control Institute (CBACI)
1747 Pennsylvania Ave. NW, 7th Fl.
Washington, DC 20006
Ph: (202)296-3550
Fax: (202)296-3574
E-mail: cbaci@cbaci.org
Contact: Michael Moodie, Pres.
Membership Dues: $3,500 (annual). **Description:** Promotes the goals of arms control, non-proliferation, and threat reduction, focusing on elimination of chemical and biological weapons. **Projects:** Beyond Proliferation - The Challenge of Technology Diffusion; CBRN Terrorism Campaigns: Response Requirements & Capabilities; Countering Biological Threats: Engaging the Biotechnology Industry; Developing a Strategic Concept for Communications Information & Dissemination as part of a CBRN Terrorism Response Architecture; The New Global Security Environment; Promoting International Cooperation in the Fight Against CBRN Terrorism; Vaccines & National Security: Issues, Concerns, & "Lessons Learned". **Publications:** *Appeasing Wilson's Ghost: The Expanded Role of New Vaccines in International Diplomacy.* Paper ● *The Arena*, 10/year. Paper. Issue paper series focusing on security agenda. ● *CBACI Report: Bioterrorism in the United States: Threat, Preparedness, and Response* ● *Critical Information Flows in the Alfred P. Murrah Building Bombing: A Case Study.* Report ● *Health, Security, & U.S. Global Leadership.* Report ● *Industry Insights*, 10/year. Newsletter. Contains analyses of issues of specific concern to industry. ● *Reducing the Chemical & Biological Weapons Threat: What Contribution from Arms Control?.* Report. **Conventions/Meetings:** annual conference and seminar ● Seminar Series: Responding to the BW Challenge, with speakers - meets every 6-8 weeks.

Bisexual

16668 ■ Bi Without Borders (BWB)
PO Box 581037
Minneapolis, MN 55458
E-mail: biwithoutborders@coolmail.com
URL: http://www.bisexual.org/g/biwithoutborders
Membership Dues: regular, $20 (annual) ● family, $50 (annual). **Description:** Works to serve bisexuals and their friends and families. Advocates for the well being of bisexuals.

Broadcasting

16669 ■ Citizens for Independent Public Broadcasting (CIPB)
901 Old Hickory Rd.
Pittsburgh, PA 15243
Ph: (412)341-1967

Fax: (412)341-6533
E-mail: jmstarr@adelphia.net
URL: http://www.cipbonline.org
Contact: Jerold M. Starr, Exec. Dir.
Membership Dues: includes training manual, $15 (annual) ● includes training manual and book, $30 (annual) ● includes training manual, book and video, $40 (annual). **Description:** Promotes public broadcasting; supports local initiatives to democratize programming on local public broadcasting stations. Acts as a national clearinghouse. **Telecommunication Services:** electronic mail, cipb@cipbonline.org. **Committees:** National Advisory. **Publications:** *Air Wars: The Fight to Reclaim Public Broadcasting.* Book. **Price:** $10.00 plus shipping and handling ● *How to Make Public Broadcasting Accountable to Your Community: A Manual for Activists.*

16670 ■ National Association of Public Affairs Networks (NAPAN)
21 Oak St., Ste.605
Hartford, CT 06106
Ph: (860)246-1553
Fax: (860)246-1547
E-mail: paul.giguere@napan.net
URL: http://napan.net
Contact: Paul Giguere, Pres.
Membership Dues: regular, $250 (annual) ● associate (individual), $50 (annual) ● associate (new start), $100 (annual) ● associate (affinity organization), $250 (annual). **Description:** Supports the establishment and expansion of non-commercial networks devoted to providing citizens with access to unbiased information about state government deliberations and public policy events. Advances public understanding and participation in political processes and the development of public policy.

Bulgaria

16671 ■ Bulgarian National Front (BNF)
PO Box 46250
Chicago, IL 60646
Ph: (847)692-5460
Fax: (847)692-5460
E-mail: alexd906@aol.com
Contact: Alex Darvodelsky, Pres.
Founded: 1948. **Members:** 960. **Membership Dues:** $20 (annual). **State Groups:** 5. **Local Groups:** 12. **Description:** Americans of Bulgarian origin; American friends of Bulgaria. Works to promote and defend "the democratization of Bulgaria and the return to free market economy and Western values; and to make known in America the culture and history of Bulgaria for establishing friendly relations between the U.S. and Bulgaria." Compiles statistics; is preparing to open a museum. **Libraries: Type:** reference. **Holdings:** 6,000; archival material. **Awards:** Fight for Liberation of Bulgaria Medal. **Frequency:** periodic. **Type:** recognition. **Committees:** Placement; Welfare. **Publications:** *Borba* (in Bulgarian and English), bimonthly. Magazine. **Circulation:** 5,000. **Advertising:** accepted ● Pamphlets. **Conventions/Meetings:** annual conference ● biennial congress ● seminar.

Capital Punishment

16672 ■ Campaign to End the Death Penalty (CEDP)
PO Box 25730
Chicago, IL 60625
Ph: (773)955-4841
Fax: (773)955-4842
E-mail: cedp@nodeathpenalty.org
URL: http://www.nodeathpenalty.org
Contact: Julien Ball, Admin. Coor.
Description: Works to abolish the death penalty. **Publications:** *New Abolitionist*, bimonthly. Newsletter. **Price:** $12.00/year. Alternate Formats: online. **Conventions/Meetings:** meeting ● rally.

16673 ■ Capital Punishment Project (CPP)
c/o John Holdridge, Dir.
201 W Main St., Ste.402
Durham, NC 27701
Ph: (919)682-5659
URL: http://www.aclu.org/capital/general/
10521res20040409.html
Contact: John Holdridge, Dir.
Founded: 1976. **Staff:** 2. **Description:** A project of the American Civil Liberties Union (see separate entry). Seeks to abolish the death penalty and prevent execution in the U.S. Serves as a source of data on capital punishment; acts as a public policy advocate. Compiles statistics; operates speakers' bureau. **Libraries: Type:** reference. **Holdings:** 100.

16674 ■ Death Penalty Information Center (DPIC)
1101 Vermont Ave. NW, Ste.701
Washington, DC 20005
Ph: (202)289-2275
Fax: (202)289-7336
E-mail: rdieter@deathpenaltyinfo.org
URL: http://www.deathpenaltyinfo.org
Contact: Richard Dieter, Exec. Dir.
Founded: 1990. **Staff:** 4. **Description:** Works to educate the public about the death penalty in America, primarily through the media. Examines problems that affect the death penalty including: poverty and mental deficiency of defendants; racism; ineffective legal representation. **Awards:** Thurgood Marshall Journalism Award. **Frequency:** annual. **Type:** monetary. **Recipient:** for the best print or electronic media stories about capital punishment. **Publications:** *Chattahoochee Judicial District: The Buckle of the Death Belt*, annual. Reports. Reports on the death penalty. **Price:** $5.00. Alternate Formats: online ● *The Death Penalty in Black & White: Who Lives, Who Decides (1998).* Report ● *The Future of the Death Penalty in the U.S.: A Texas-Sized Crisis.* Report ● *Innocence and the Death Penalty: Assessing the Danger of Mistaken Executions.* Report ● *International Perspectives on the Death Penalty: A Costly Isolation for the U.S. (1999).* Report ● *Justice on the Cheap: The Philadelphia Story.* Report ● *Killing for Votes: The Dangers of Politicizing the Death Penalty Process.* Report ● *Killing Justice: Government Misconduct and the Death Penalty.* Report ● *Millions Misspent: What Politicians Don't Say About the High Costs of the Death Penalty.* Report. Contains national opinion survey. ● *On the Front Line: Law Enforcement Views on the Death Penalty 1995.* Report. Contains national opinion survey. ● *Racial Disparities in Federal Death Penalty Prosecutions: 1988-1994.* Report ● *Representation and The Death Penalty in 1995: Year End Report* ● *Sentencing for Life: Americans Embrace Alternative to the Death Penalty.* Report ● *Twenty Years of Capital Punishment: A Re-evaluation.* Report ● *With Justice for Few: The Growing Crisis in Death Penalty.* Report.

16675 ■ Lamp of Hope Project (LHP)
PO Box 305
League City, TX 77574-0305
E-mail: ksebung@lampofhope.org
URL: http://www.lampofhope.org
Contact: Karen Sebung, Exec. Dir.
Founded: 1991. **Membership Dues:** regular, $20 (annual) ● contributing, $50 (annual) ● sustaining, $100 (annual). **Staff:** 16. **State Groups:** 1. **Description:** Death row prisoners, their families, and other interested individuals. Works to address victim's rights concerns and legal issues; the effects of poverty on crime; and the concerns of children and other family members of incarcerated individuals, especially those on Death Row. Strives for the enhancement of public understanding of the death penalty; seeks the protection of Death Row prisoners' interests and civil rights by addressing such issues as unwarranted oppressive prison conditions. **Publications:** *Death Row Journal*, bimonthly. **Price:** included in membership dues. **Conventions/Meetings:** annual conference.

16676 ■ Murder Victims' Families for Reconciliation (MVFR)
PO Box 202875
Austin, TX 78720-2875
Ph: (512)782-9895
E-mail: info@mvfr.org
URL: http://www.mvfr.org
Contact: Pat Clark, Chair
Founded: 1976. **Description:** Represents murder victims' families seeking to abolish the death penalty. **Programs:** Speakers Bureau. **Formerly:** Murder Victims' Families Against the Death Penalty. **Publications:** Not in Our Name: Murder Victims' Families Speak Out Against the Death Penalty. Booklet ● The Voice, semiannual. Newsletter. Alternate Formats: online.

16677 ■ National Coalition to Abolish the Death Penalty (NCADP)
1717 K St. NW, Ste.510
Washington, DC 20036
Ph: (202)331-4090
Fax: (202)331-4099
E-mail: info@ncadp.org
URL: http://www.ncadp.org
Contact: Diann Rust-Tierney, Exec. Dir.
Founded: 1976. **Members:** 3,000. **Membership Dues:** new, $25 (annual) ● student, restricted income, $10 (annual) ● sustaining, $35 (annual) ● abolitionist, $1,000 (annual) ● champion, $500 (annual) ● patron, $250 (annual) ● supporter, $100 (annual) ● friend, $50 (annual). **Staff:** 6. **State Groups:** 80. **National Groups:** 40. **Description:** National and regional religious, community, human and civil rights, public-interest law, minority, political, and professional organizations. Works to abolish the death penalty in the U.S. and to avert all executions. Believes the death penalty to be ineffective as a deterrent to crime. Provides a national podium and works with related groups on regional, state, and local levels. Compiles statistics on the number of juveniles on death row and race classifications of the condemned and their victims. **Libraries:** Type: reference. **Computer Services:** Information services, execution alerts accessible through website. **Committees:** Litigation; National Execution Alert Network (see separate entry); Outreach; Religious. **Formerly:** (1987) National Coalition Against the Death Penalty; (1997) National Execution Alert Network. **Publications:** The Abolitionist's Directory, annual. Lists organizations working to end capital punishment. **Price:** $3.00/copy ● Legislative Action to Abolish the Death Penalty ● Lifelines/Execution Alert, monthly. Bulletin. Provides information on the activities and resources available for citizens seeking alternatives to the death penalty. **Price:** $15.00/year. **Circulation:** 9,000 ● Also distributes pamphlets, reprints, and other research and advocacy materials. **Conventions/Meetings:** annual conference ● regional meeting - 3/year.

16678 ■ People of Faith Against the Death Penalty (PFADP)
110 W Main St., Ste.2-G
Carrboro, NC 27510
Ph: (919)933-7567
Fax: (919)933-5611
E-mail: info@pfadp.org
URL: http://www.pfadp.org
Contact: Stephen Dear, Exec. Dir.
Founded: 1994. **Membership Dues:** congregation/organization, $100 (annual) ● individual, $25 (annual) ● household, $40 (annual). **Description:** Seeks to educate and mobilize faith communities to act to abolish the death penalty in the United States. Reaches out to all citizens regardless of faith, race or ethnic group, income, political affiliation, age and ability. Encourages members to urge their pastors, rabbis or leaders to preach against the death penalty. **Publications:** Newsletter, monthly. Alternate Formats: online ● Brochure. Alternate Formats: online.

16679 ■ Project Hope to Abolish the Death Penalty (PHADP)
PO Box 1362
Lanett, AL 36863
Ph: (334)499-0003

E-mail: beesther@earthlink.net
URL: http://www.phadp.org
Contact: Esther Brown, Contact
Multinational. Description: Represents inmates and individuals committed to abolish the death penalty worldwide. **Publications:** On Wings of Hope, quarterly. **Price:** free.

16680 ■ Southern Center for Human Rights (SCHR)
83 Poplar St. NW
Atlanta, GA 30303-2122
Ph: (404)688-1202
Fax: (404)688-9440
E-mail: sbright@schr.org
URL: http://www.schr.org
Contact: Stephen B. Bright, Pres./Sr. Counsel
Founded: 1976. **Description:** Aims to protect civil and human rights of individuals facing the death penalty in prisons and jails of the South. **Programs:** Human Rights Internship. **Publications:** Capital Punishment and the Criminal Justice System: Courts of Vengeance or Courts of Justice?. Alternate Formats: online ● Death in Texas. Article ● The Death Penalty: Casualties and Costs of the War on Crime. Alternate Formats: online ● Drum Majors for Justice. Alternate Formats: online ● Electric Chair and the Chain Gang: Choices and Challenges for America's Future. Alternate Formats: online ● Is Fairness Irrelevant? The Evisceration of Federal Habeas Corpus Review and Limits on the Ability of State Courts to Protect Fundamental Rights. Alternate Formats: online ● Keep the Dream of Equal Justice Alive. Alternate Formats: online ● Politics of Crime and the Death Penalty: Not 'Soft on Crime', But Hard on the Bill of Rights. Alternate Formats: online ● Right to Counsel, Indigent Defense. Article ● Will the Death Penalty Remain Alive in the Twenty-First Century?. Alternate Formats: online.

Censorship

16681 ■ Adult Video Association (AVA)
8033 Sunset Blvd., No. 851
West Hollywood, CA 90046
Ph: (323)436-0060
Fax: (323)876-6642
E-mail: bmargold@aol.com
Contact: William Margold, Creative Consultant
Founded: 1987. **Members:** 400. **Description:** Trade organization that believes adults should be able to watch what they choose in the privacy of their own homes. Challenges the constitutionality of laws affecting adult videos; provides legal information and referrals. Lobbies government agencies; produces publicity campaigns. Supports other anti-censorship organizations. Maintains speakers' bureau; conducts educational programs. **Awards:** Lifetime Achievement Awards. **Type:** recognition. **Publications:** Newsletter, periodic. **Conventions/Meetings:** monthly board meeting ● annual meeting.

16682 ■ Anti-Censorship and Deception Union
PO Box 400297
Cambridge, MA 02140
Ph: (617)491-0433
E-mail: rbercaw@alumni-mail.gs.columbia.edu
Contact: Roy Bercaw, Pres.
Founded: 1990. **Description:** Opposes censorship and deception by government and corporations by press release, letters, essays, articles, videos and newsletter. Petitions local, state, and federal governments, journalists. **Libraries:** Type: reference. **Subjects:** political, government, media, historical deception. **Awards:** Deceiver Achiever Award. **Type:** recognition. **Publications:** Enough Room, periodic. Articles.

16683 ■ Families Against Internet Censorship (FAIC)
2135 Wickes Rd.
Colorado Springs, CO 80919
Ph: (719)548-4989

E-mail: faic@netfamilies.org
URL: http://www.netfamilies.org
Contact: Barry S. Fagin PhD, Co-Founder
Founded: 1995. **Members:** 500. **Description:** Families committed to opposing censorship on the Internet. Provides a resource for anti-censorship families; disseminates information on commercial products for filtering objectional material on the net; opposes government regulation of Internet content. **Computer Services:** database, families willing to speak out against Internet censorship.

16684 ■ Freedom to Read Foundation (FTRF)
50 E Huron St.
Chicago, IL 60611
Ph: (312)280-4226
Free: (800)545-2433
Fax: (312)280-4227
E-mail: ftrf@ala.org
URL: http://www.ala.org/ala/ourassociation/other-groups/ftrf/freedomreadfoundation.htm
Contact: Judith F. Krug, Sec./Exec. Dir.
Founded: 1969. **Members:** 2,000. **Membership Dues:** regular, $35 (annual) ● student, $10 (annual) ● contributing, $50 (annual) ● sponsor, $100 (annual) ● patron, $500 (annual) ● benefactor, $1,000 (annual). **Staff:** 3. **Description:** Individuals, associations, corporations, and other organizations concerned with protecting and defending freedom of speech and freedom of the press, particularly as these relate to librarians and libraries. Promotes the recognition and acceptance of libraries as repositories of knowledge and protects the public right of access to them; supports the right of librarians to make available to the public any creative work legally acquired. Supplies legal counsel and other support to librarians and libraries suffering from legal injustices by reason of their defense of freedom of speech and freedom of press. **Awards:** Roll of Honor. **Frequency:** annual. **Type:** recognition. **Recipient:** to a member or participant in FTRF litigation. **Programs:** Lawyers for Libraries. **Affiliated With:** American Library Association; Media Coalition. **Absorbed:** National Freedom Fund for Librarians. **Publications:** News, quarterly. Newsletter. **Price:** included in membership dues. **Circulation:** 2,000. **Conventions/Meetings:** annual meeting, in conjunction with American Library Association - midwinter.

16685 ■ International Freedom to Publish Committee (IFTPC)
c/o Association of American Publishers
71 5th Ave., 2nd Fl.
New York, NY 10003
Ph: (212)255-0200
Fax: (212)255-7007
E-mail: lclark@publishers.org
URL: http://www.iftpc.org
Contact: Lily Clark, Membership Dir.
Founded: 1975. **Members:** 28. **Description:** Committee of the Association of American Publishers. Protects and promotes the rights of publishers and authors throughout the world, especially where they are threatened by oppressive and tyrannical governments. Monitors relations between writers and publishers and their governments, and takes action to remove barriers to the freedom to publish raised by governments. Works closely with publishers' and authors' groups worldwide. Discusses the issue of freedom to publish with the U.S. government, other governments, and international organizations having responsibilities for protecting writers. Makes recommendations to these organizations and issues public statements. **Awards:** Jeri Laber International Freedom to Publish Award. **Frequency:** annual. **Type:** recognition. **Recipient:** for a publisher who demonstrated courage in defending freedom of expression. **Additional Websites:** http://www.publishers.org. **Affiliated With:** Association of American Publishers. **Formerly:** (2002) Committee on International Freedom to Publish.

16686 ■ National Coalition Against Censorship (NCAC)
275 7th Ave., No. 1504
New York, NY 10001
Ph: (212)807-6222

Fax: (212)807-6245
E-mail: ncac@ncac.org
URL: http://www.ncac.org
Contact: Joan E. Bertin, Exec. Dir.
Founded: 1974. **Members:** 29,000. **Membership Dues:** regular, $30 (annual). **Staff:** 7. **Budget:** $900,000. **Description:** Participants are 50 national nonprofit organizations united to preserve and advance freedom of thought, inquiry, and expression. Holds that "freedom of communication is the indispensable condition of a healthy democracy," and that "censorship constitutes an unacceptable dictatorship over our minds, and a dangerous opening to religious, political, artistic, and intellectual repression." Helps participating organizations to educate their own members about the dangers of censorship and how to oppose it. Helps organize state and local anti-censorship groups. Works with individuals on front lines in local community controversies. Sponsors public meetings on First Amendment issues; carries out educational work through the media and the public. **Committees:** Sex and Censorship. **Programs:** Countering Censorship in Schools and Libraries; Resisting Homophobic Attacks on Education and the Arts. **Projects:** Arts Advocacy; Free Expression Policy. **Publications:** *Censorship News*, quarterly. Newsletter. **Price:** $30.00 /year for nonmembers; included in membership dues. ISSN: 0749-6001. **Circulation:** 30,000. Alternate Formats: online ● *Conference Report* ● *Meese Commission Exposed*. Proceedings. **Price:** $6.00 plus shipping and handling ● *Public Education, Democracy, Free Speech: The Ideas That Define and Unite Us.* Booklet. **Price:** $2.50 plus shipping and handling ● *The Sex Panic: Women, Censorship, and Pornography.* Report. Contains a report of the conference of NCAC's Working Group on Women, Censorship, and Pornography. **Price:** $5.00 plus shipping and handling ● *25 Years: Defending Freedom of Thought, Inquiry and Expression.* Brochure. **Price:** $2.50 plus shipping and handling ● Also distributes reprints and videos. **Conventions/Meetings:** semiannual luncheon and meeting.

16687 ■ Project Censored (PC)
Sonoma State Univ.
1801 E Cotati Ave.
Rohnert Park, CA 94928
Ph: (707)664-2500
Fax: (707)664-2108
E-mail: censored@sonoma.edu
URL: http://www.projectcensored.org
Contact: Peter Phillips PhD, Dir.
Founded: 1976. **Members:** 200. **Staff:** 4. **Budget:** $150,000. **Description:** Seeks to explore and publicize the extent of censorship by locating stories on significant issues of which the public is unaware. Recognizes and promotes good investigative journalism and encourages the public to demand coverage of controversial issues or to seek information from other sources. **Awards:** Most Censored News Stories. **Frequency:** annual. **Type:** recognition. **Recipient:** for best censored stories of the year, submitted by individuals who feel that an issue of national social significance should have received more coverage by the mass media. **Computer Services:** Mailing lists ● online services. **Publications:** *Censored 2003: The News That Didn't Make The News.* Pamphlet. **Price:** $16.95.

16688 ■ Rock Out Censorship (ROC)
PO Box 147
Jewett, OH 43986
E-mail: roc@theroc.org
URL: http://www.theroc.org
Founded: 1989. **Membership Dues:** full, in U.S., $15 (annual) ● full, outside U.S., $27 (annual). **Description:** Works as a voice of opposition to censorship of popular music. **Computer Services:** database, Know Your Friends ● database, Music Link ● mailing lists, of members. **Publications:** *ROC News.* Bulletin. Alternate Formats: online ● *The ROC - The Voice of Rock Out Censorship.* Newspaper. **Price:** included in membership dues; $2.00/copy for nonmembers. **Advertising:** accepted. Alternate Formats: online.

16689 ■ Rock the Vote (RTV)
409 N Pacific Coast Hwy., No. 589
Redondo Beach, CA 90277
Ph: (310)234-0665 (202)478-2858
URL: http://www.rockthevote.org
Contact: Jehmu S. Greene, Pres.
Founded: 1990. **Staff:** 11. **Budget:** $1,500,000. **Local Groups:** 50. **Description:** Works to protect freedom of expression and empower young people to change the world. **Subgroups:** Community Street Teams.

Central America

16690 ■ Hermandad
430 Shore Rd., Apt. 6D
Long Beach, NY 11561
Ph: (516)431-6602
Fax: (516)897-2981
E-mail: hermandadi@aol.com
URL: http://www.hermandad.org
Contact: George R. Gerardi, Exec. Dir.
Founded: 1975. **Languages:** English, Spanish. **Description:** Works to help the rural poor in Latin America and the Caribbean. Conducts self-help projects at the community level, including irrigation, potable water, reforestation, technical assistance in agriculture, improving nutrition, and conserving soil and natural resources. Works in the Dominican Republic, past projects are in Honduras and Guatemala. **Libraries: Type:** reference. **Holdings:** audio recordings, business records, periodicals, video recordings. **Conventions/Meetings:** annual meeting.

16691 ■ Institute for Regional and International Studies (IRIS)
5735 Arapahoe Ave., No. A-5
Boulder, CO 80303
E-mail: giesen@csupomona.edu
URL: http://www.csupomona.edu/~ige/www_iris/iris. htm
Contact: Dr. George Eisen, Dir.
Founded: 1983. **Staff:** 2. **Description:** Nonpolitical organization of individuals who seek to aid small and poor countries (particularly Central American nations) in dealing with what the institute believes is externally supported internal violence and terrorism. Recruits and supports public safety instructors to assist defense and public safety institutions in El Salvador. Conducts research on the nature and causes of terrorism and political violence in Central America. **Additional Websites:** http://www.iris-bg.org.

16692 ■ Katalysis Partnership
c/o Christina Jennings, Exec. Dir.
Katalysis Bootstrap Fund
3601 Pacific Ave.
Stockton, CA 95211
Ph: (209)644-6245
Fax: (866)403-6571
E-mail: information@katalysis.org
URL: http://www.katalysis.org
Contact: Christina Jennings, Exec. Dir.
Founded: 1984. **Staff:** 23. **Budget:** $2,328,200. **Regional Groups:** 7. **Languages:** English, Spanish. **Description:** Fights poverty through the "Bootstrap Banking" model of economic development. Provides small loans and basic business training to low-income micro-entrepreneurs through local partner organizations in Nicaragua, Honduras, Guatemala, and El Salvador, thereby giving enterprising women the resources they need to "pull themselves up by their own bootstraps." Current outstanding portfolio is $6.4 million, reaching more than 27,000 Central American entrepreneurs, 97&percent; or whom repay their loans on time with interest. **Awards:** Robert E. Graham Development Entrepreneur of the Year Award. **Frequency:** annual. **Type:** recognition. **Recipient:** for individuals who have demonstrated significant dedication to the mission of the Partnership. **Programs:** Institutional Strengthening; Micro-Enterprise Development; Women's Community Banking. **Formerly:** Katalysis Foundation; (2000) Katalysis North/South Development Partnership.

Publications: *Beyond the Annual Campaign: A Handbook for Sustainable Fundraising* ● *Bootstrap Bank Accounts*, semiannual. Newsletter ● *Choosing Partnership: The Evolution of the Katalysis Model.* Booklet. **Price:** $5.00 ● *Katalysis.* Video. **Price:** $20.00 ● *Perfecting the Alliance: Viable Fundraising for International Partnerships.* Booklet.

16693 ■ National Labor Committee for Worker and Human Rights (NLC)
540 W 48th St., 3rd Fl.
New York, NY 10036
Ph: (212)242-3002
Fax: (212)242-3821
E-mail: nlc@nlcnet.org
URL: http://www.nlcnet.org
Contact: Charles Kernaghan, Exec. Dir.
Founded: 1981. **Description:** Promotes and defends the rights of workers. Educates and actively involves the public in actions aimed at ending labor abuses, improving living conditions for workers and their families and promoting the concept of a living wage and true independent monitoring. **Formerly:** (1998) National Labor Committee in Support of Democracy and Human Rights in El Salvador; (2004) National Labor Committee in Support of Worker and Human Rights in Central America. **Publications:** *Worker Rights and the New World Order/El Salvador, Honduras, Guatemala.*

16694 ■ Neighbor to Neighbor (N2N)
1550 Blue Spruce Dr.
Fort Collins, CO 80524
Ph: (970)488-2369
Fax: (970)407-7045
E-mail: wrobinson@n2n.org
URL: http://www.n2n.org
Contact: Wendie Robinson, Exec. Dir.
Founded: 1985. **Members:** 52,000. **Staff:** 15. **Budget:** $1,500,000. **Regional Groups:** 1. **State Groups:** 3. **Languages:** English, Spanish. **Description:** Began as a project of the Institute for Food and Development Policy. Publicized, organized, and lobbied to change U.S. policy in Central America. Now works for comprehensive, secure healthcare in the U.S. (single payer health care) as a social justice issue. Seeks to refocus U.S. military aid to reconstruction aid. Maintains 3 funds: Action Fund for lobbying and legislative activities; Education Fund for public education through grass roots organization and the media. Encourages participation in grass roots organizing to affect legislation. Distributes information packets. Conducts public opinion polls. **Committees:** Neighbor to Neighbor Political Action Committee. **Departments:** Fundraising; Media; Membership; Organizing; Political. **Publications:** *Grounds for Action*, quarterly. Newsletter. **Price:** included in membership dues. **Circulation:** 45,000 ● Brochures. **Conventions/Meetings:** annual meeting.

16695 ■ Office of the Americas (OOA)
8124 W 3rd St., Ste.202
Los Angeles, CA 90048
Ph: (323)852-9808
Fax: (323)852-0655
E-mail: ooa@igc.org
URL: http://www.officeoftheamericas.org
Contact: Theresa Bonpane, Exec. Dir.
Founded: 1983. **Members:** 3,000. **Staff:** 2. **Description:** Professionals, technicians, and other individuals dedicated to furthering justice and peace in the Western Hemisphere through educational programs and media. Seeks to provide "reliable facts and humane perspectives about Latin American issues" so that U.S. citizens can make educated decisions about U.S. foreign policy. Works to generate increased support for the principles of self-determination for Latin American countries and nonintervention by the U.S. Activities include sending delegations to areas of conflict, assisting in visits of Central American political and cultural leaders to the U.S., organizing demonstrations, providing information about legislative issues, and working with and providing services to other peace organizations. Maintains speakers' bureau. **Convention/Meeting:** none. **Libraries: Type:** reference. **Subjects:** justice

and peace issues in the Western Hemisphere. **Awards:** Office of the Americas Peace and Justice Award. **Frequency:** annual. **Type:** recognition. **Recipient:** for dedication to peace and justice in the Americas. **Computer Services:** Online services, Peace Net. **Committees:** Special Events. **Publications:** *Focus*, 3/year. Newsletter. Alternate Formats: online ● *News Analysis of Americas*, periodic. **Price:** $25.00/year.

16696 ■ Religious Task Force on Central America and Mexico (RTFCAM)
3053 4th St. NE
Washington, DC 20017-1102
Ph: (202)529-0441
E-mail: general@rtfcam.org
URL: http://www.rtfcam.org
Contact: Scott Wright, Dir.
Founded: 1980. **Staff:** 2. **Description:** Organizations, priests, nuns, and other individuals interested in social justice and contemporary church involvement with the disadvantaged in Central America. Strives to stop U.S. intervention in and military aid to Central American countries and to educates people about circumstances there with hopes that they will take action. Serves as resource center for people seeking accurate information about human rights economics and U.S. involvement in Central America. Provides national coordination of religious-based Central American campaigns. **Libraries: Type:** open to the public. **Holdings:** 23. **Subjects:** human rights, US policy, global economics, peace and justice. **Formerly:** (1982) Religious Task Force on El Salvador; (1996) Religious Task Force on Central America. **Publications:** *Central America/Mexico Report*, bimonthly. Newsletter. Contains regional news, analysis, reflection and current policy. **Price:** $25.00 /year for individuals in U.S.; $35.00 /year for institutions. **Circulation:** 2,500 ● *Like Grains of Wheat: A Spirituality of Solidarity*. Book. **Price:** $18.00/issue ● *Resource Packets*, annual ● *Oscar Romero: Prophet to the Americas*.

Chemicals

16697 ■ Citizens Against Chemtrails U.S. (CACTUS)
c/o Clifford E. Carnicom
PO Box 4653
Santa Fe, NM 87502
E-mail: cactusmailbox@yahoo.com
URL: http://www.geocities.com/cactusmailbox/ CACTUS.html
Contact: Clifford E. Carnicom, Contact
Description: Promotes grassroots group dedicated to halting the aerial spraying of America that is believed to have caused increased epidemics of death due to disease pathogens.

Child Health

16698 ■ Generation Green
PO Box 7027
Evanston, IL 60201
Free: (800)652-0827
E-mail: info@generationgreen.org
URL: http://www.generationgreen.org
Contact: Rochelle Davis, Founder/Exec. Dir.
Founded: 1998. **Membership Dues:** basic, $25 (annual) ● supporter, $50 (annual) ● benefactor, $250 (annual). **Description:** Aims to reduce toxins and pesticide exposure through food for the health of the next generation. Gives parents an effective voice in advocating for an environmental policy that protects children. Encourages members and the public to be environmentally conscious consumers. Educates parents and other concerned citizens about children's environmental health issues. **Publications:** *The Green Report*. Newsletter. **Price:** included in membership dues. Alternate Formats: online ● Annual Report, annual. Alternate Formats: online.

16699 ■ Locks of Love
2925 10th Ave. N, Ste.102
Lake Worth, FL 33461
Ph: (561)963-1677
Free: (888)896-1588
Fax: (561)963-9914
E-mail: info@locksoflove.org
URL: http://www.locksoflove.org
Contact: Madonna W. Coffman, Pres.
Founded: 1997. **Staff:** 4. **Description:** Provides hairpieces to financially disadvantaged children, under the age of 18, across the U.S., suffering from long-term medical hair loss.

Child Welfare

16700 ■ American Association for Home-Based Early Interventionists (AAHBEI)
Utah State Univ.
6500 Old Main Hill
Logan, UT 84322-6500
Free: (800)396-6144
Fax: (435)797-5580
E-mail: fpayne@cc.usu.edu
URL: http://www.aahbei.org
Contact: Kathy de la Pena, Pres.
Founded: 1992. **Members:** 850. **Membership Dues:** life, $250 ● professional/specialist, $35 (annual) ● professional/specialist, $65 (biennial) ● parent, $20 (annual) ● parent, $35 (biennial) ● student currently enrolled in preschool program, $20 (annual). **Regional Groups:** 5. **Description:** Represents childhood special education teachers and other specialists, including parents and families, early interventionists, teachers, students, administrators, and physicians. Works to provide services and support for children with special needs; parent support and networking; professional development and networking; local, regional and national representation, and provides knowledge, linkage, leadership and resources to members. **Publications:** *AAHBEI News Exchange*, quarterly. Newsletter. Contains practical information on innovative techniques and technologies, publications, products, and resources. **Price:** included in membership dues. **Advertising:** accepted. Alternate Formats: online. **Conventions/Meetings:** regional meeting.

16701 ■ Fight Crime: Invest in Kids
1212 New York Ave. NW, Ste.300
Washington, DC 20005
Ph: (202)776-0027
E-mail: snewman@fightcrime.org
URL: http://www.fightcrime.org
Contact: Sanford A. Newman J.D., Pres.
Founded: 1996. **Members:** 2,000. **Description:** Represents experts in criminology, child development and law enforcement working to keep kids from becoming criminals.

16702 ■ Grandparents United for Children's Rights (GUCR)
c/o Ethel Dunn, Exec. Dir.
137 Larkin St.
Madison, WI 53705-5115
Ph: (608)238-8751 (608)236-0480
Fax: (608)238-8751
E-mail: sedun@inexpress.net
URL: http://www.geocities.com/Heartland/Prairie/ 6866
Contact: Ethel Dunn, Exec. Dir.
Description: Provides support to grandparents and other kin in issue resolution support services, and information referral and retrieval nationwide. **Publications:** Newsletter, quarterly.

16703 ■ Mothers and Fathers Aligned Saving Kids (MASK)
2566 Nostrand Ave.
Brooklyn, NY 11210
Ph: (718)758-0400
Fax: (718)758-9515

E-mail: maskparents@aol.com
URL: http://www.maskparents.org
Contact: Ruchama Bistritzky-Clapman, Founder/Dir.
Languages: Hebrew, Yiddish. **Description:** Volunteers. Provides support groups, educational forums and financial guidance for parents of teens with problems. Referral to organizations and private counselors. **Libraries: Type:** lending. **Holdings:** audio recordings, books, video recordings. **Subjects:** self-help, parental advice. **Telecommunication Services:** hotline, (718)758-0400, 10 a.m.-10 p.m. **Programs:** Starr.

China

16704 ■ Free the Fathers (FF)
1120 Applewood Cir.
Signal Mountain, TN 37377
Ph: (423)634-0644
E-mail: president@ftf.org
URL: http://www.ftf.org
Contact: John Davies, Pres.
Founded: 1983. **Members:** 25,000. **Budget:** $300,000. **Description:** Concerned individuals who work to secure freedom for imprisoned Catholic priests, nuns, and laity in communist and other totalitarian countries, particularly the People's Republic of China. According to the organization, Catholic priests are being tortured and imprisoned in China because they are "devout Christians in a nation where atheism still rules with an iron hand". Conducts news media interviews to alert people to the issue. Sponsors letter-writing campaigns to foreign officials; contacts U.S. leaders on behalf of the persecuted. Maintains speakers' bureau. **Computer Services:** Mailing lists, of members. **Publications:** Newsletter, periodic.

16705 ■ Friends of Falun Gong
24 W Railroad Ave., PMB No. 124
Tenafly, NJ 07670
Free: (866)343-7436
URL: http://www.fofg.org
Contact: Alan Adler, Exec. Dir.
Founded: 2000. **Description:** Supports and advocates for freedom of belief and other human rights, particularly to free Falun Gong prisoners of conscience in the People's Republic of China and end persecution there. **Publications:** Newsletter. Includes news about upcoming events, updates on developments in China, special features on prisoners of conscience.

16706 ■ Independent Federation of Chinese Students and Scholars (IFCSS)
733 15th St. NW, Ste.700
Washington, DC 20005
Ph: (202)347-0017
Fax: (202)737-0024
E-mail: webmaster@ifcss.net
URL: http://www.ifcss.net
Contact: Liu Yong-chuan, Pres.
Founded: 1989. **Members:** 50,000. **Staff:** 4. **Budget:** $350,000. **Local Groups:** 150. **Languages:** Chinese, English. **Description:** Organizations representing the interests of over 50,000 Chinese students and scholars in the U.S.A. Promotes democracy and human rights in China. Seeks to educate Americans about the suppression of the democratic movement in China by the Chinese government. Researches and analyzes developments and explores possibilities for a peaceful transition to democracy and political pluralism. Facilitates communication between activists in China and supporters in the U.S; provides the Chinese people with "accurate information, unavailable from the Chinese media". Offers assistance regarding financial aid, employment, housing, and immigration to Chinese students in the U.S. Maintains collection of historical documents on the "89 Democracy Movement". Conducts research and educational programs; offers placement service. **Awards:** Human Rights Award. **Frequency:** annual. **Type:** recognition. **Computer Services:** database, Chinese society and culture ● mailing lists, China-

Net ● online services. **Committees:** China's Economic Development; Chinese Professional Club; Community Information Center; Fund-raising; Human Rights; Humanitarian Assistance; Political Action; Public Relations and Government Affairs; Scientific, Cultural, and Educational Exchange; Student Affairs; Student Service; Theoretic Research. **Absorbed:** (1991) June 4th Foundation. **Publications:** *IFCSS Newsletter*, monthly. **Circulation:** 3,000. **Advertising:** accepted. Alternate Formats: online ● *Press Freedom Herald*, weekly. **Advertising:** accepted ● Also publishes flyers. **Conventions/Meetings:** annual congress.

16707 ■ June 4th Foundation
733 15th St. NW, Ste.700
Washington, DC 20005
Ph: (202)347-0017
Fax: (202)737-0024
E-mail: hq@ifcss.org
URL: http://www.ifcss.org
Contact: Danxuan Yi, Pres.
Founded: 1989. **Staff:** 6. **Description:** A division of the Independent Federation of Chinese Students and Scholars. Chinese students studying at more than 40 U.S. universities and colleges. Goal is to bear witness to and preserve the historic record of the June 4, 1989 assault by soldiers on students demonstrating for democracy in Tiananmen Square, Beijing, People's Republic of China. Seeks to preserve "the terrible truth" of what occurred in Tiananmen Square before "the Chinese government's systematic campaign of intimidation and distortion succeeds in erasing forever the memories of what was done to Chinese men and women." Works to: document a complete list of the names of the dead, injured, and missing Chinese in the aftermath of the Tiananmen Square assault through eyewitness accounts; transmit radio broadcasts into China from Hong Kong, using technology that would make such broadcasts difficult to jam by the Chinese government; maintain the flow of information into China through fax machines, telephones, telecommunication scramblers for the preservation of security, and computers; create a permanent archive of film, videotape, still photograph, and radio records of the events in Tiananmen Square. Works to secure haven in the West for students and reformers fleeing China. Plans to erect a memorial statue in Washington, DC to honor the students who died and hopes to raise a similar, larger memorial in Tiananmen Square "when Democracy comes to China.". **Publications:** Newsletter, periodic ● Also publishes press releases and monographs. **Conventions/Meetings:** annual congress.

16708 ■ National Committee on United States-China Relations (NCUSCR)
71 W 23rd St., Ste.1901
New York, NY 10010-4102
Ph: (212)645-9677
Fax: (212)645-1695
E-mail: info@ncuscr.org
URL: http://www.ncuscr.org
Contact: Stephen A. Orlins, Pres.
Founded: 1966. **Members:** 700. **Staff:** 12. **Budget:** $1,500,000. **Languages:** Chinese, English. **Description:** Nonpartisan educational organization that encourages understanding of the People's Republic of China and the United States among citizens of both countries. Membership includes Americans who share the belief that increased public knowledge of China and of the relations between the U.S. and China enhances international understanding, contributes to the effective conduct of foreign policy, and strengthens the U.S.-China relationship. Focuses on exchanges, educational programs, and policy activities in the fields of international relations, economic management and development, legal affairs and governance, administration, mass communications, environmental and global issues, and education. Offers consultation and referrals to corporations, foundations, institutions, and individuals traveling to or otherwise concerned with China, Taiwan, and Hong Kong. **Computer Services:** database, Rule of Law; academic programs and non-governmental organizations. **Programs:** Exchanges; Public Educa-

tion; Public Intellectuals; U.S.-China Student Leaders Exchange; United States-China Student Teachers Exchange; Young Leaders Forum. **Publications:** *National Committee China Policy Series*, periodic. Reports on policy issues in U.S.-China relations. **Price:** $3.00. **Circulation:** 5,000 ● *Notes From the National Committee*, semiannual. Newsletter. **Price:** free for members and libraries; $5.00 /year for nonmembers ● Brochure, annual ● Annual Report, annual. Alternate Formats: online ● Newsletter, 3/year. Alternate Formats: online. **Conventions/Meetings:** annual meeting - always in New York City.

16709 ■ Organization of Chinese Americans (OCA)
1001 Connecticut Ave. NW, No. 601
Washington, DC 20036
Ph: (202)223-5500
Fax: (202)296-0540
E-mail: oca@ocanatl.org
URL: http://www.ocanatl.org
Contact: Dorothy Wong, Exec. Dir.
Founded: 1973. **Members:** 10,000. **Staff:** 5. **Budget:** $800,000. **Local Groups:** 44. **Description:** U.S. citizens and permanent residents over the age of 18, most of whom are Chinese-Americans. Strives to advance the cause and foster public awareness of the needs and concerns of Chinese-Americans in the U.S., to promote participation through advancement of equal rights, responsibilities, and opportunities, to promote cultural awareness, to unite Chinese-Americans, and to uphold the U.S. Constitution. Provides activities such as eradicating negative stereotypes. Conducts organizational, cultural, educational, and political seminars and charitable programs. **Libraries: Type:** reference. **Holdings:** archival material. **Awards:** Community Service Award. **Frequency:** annual. **Type:** recognition. **Recipient:** for a committed and exemplary corporate employee ● Corporate Partner Award. **Frequency:** annual. **Type:** recognition. **Recipient:** for an active member company ● OCA-Verizon Scholarship Program. **Type:** scholarship. **Recipient:** for financially disadvantaged APA high school seniors ● **Type:** recognition. **Recipient:** for distinguished Chinese Americans. **Programs:** College Affiliates. **Projects:** Allstate Hate Crimes. **Publications:** *A Place Called Chinese America* ● Convention Program, annual ● *IMAGE*, quarterly. Newsletter ● *National Directory of Asian Pacific American Organizations*, biennial ● Also publishes chapter newsletters, advocacy alerts, and textbook on the Chinese in America. **Conventions/Meetings:** competition ● annual convention (exhibits).

16710 ■ U.S.-China Peoples Friendship Association (USCPFA)
c/o Robert Sanborn, Pres.
402 E 43rd St.
Indianapolis, IN 46205
Ph: (317)283-7735
E-mail: info@uscpfa.org
URL: http://www.uscpfa.org
Contact: Robert Sanborn, Pres.
Founded: 1974. **Members:** 2,500. **Membership Dues:** individual, $20 (annual). **Staff:** 4. **Budget:** $80,000. **Regional Groups:** 4. **Local Groups:** 62. **Description:** Individuals and groups united to build active and lasting friendship based on mutual understanding between the people of the U.S. and the People's Republic of China. Works to develop cultural, academic, and people-to-people relations between the two countries. Assists other organizations in developing ties with China. Arranges study tours to China and hosts visiting Chinese delegations. Promotes the short- and long-term exchange of visitors. Operates Center for Teaching About China (see separate entry). Maintains speakers' bureau; conducts charitable programs. **Awards:** Koji Aryoshi Award. **Frequency:** biennial. **Type:** recognition. **Telecommunication Services:** electronic mail, robert@uscpfa.org ● electronic mail, membership@uscpfa.org. **Committees:** Center for Teaching about China Program; Tours. **Affiliated With:** Center for Teaching About China. **Publications:** *U.S.-China Review*, quarterly. Magazine. **Price:** $22.00/year regular;

$25.00 /year for institutions; $30.00/year overseas. ISSN: 0164-3886. **Circulation:** 3,000 ● Catalogs ● Pamphlets ● Also publishes and distributes films, photo exhibits, and curriculum material for American schools. **Conventions/Meetings:** biennial convention ● biennial seminar, on U.S.-China relations - always held in Washington, DC.

Christianity

16711 ■ Center for Reclaiming America
PO Box 632
Fort Lauderdale, FL 33302
Free: (877)725-8872
E-mail: cfra@coralridge.org
URL: http://www.reclaimamerica.org
Contact: Dr. D. James Kennedy, Founder
Founded: 1996. **Description:** Provides non-partisan, non-denominational information, training, and support to all those interested in positively affecting the culture and renewing the vision of the Founding Fathers. **Projects:** ACLU Expose; Judge Moore Defense; Operation Outcry; Shake the Nation Back to Life. **Publications:** Books ● Videos ● Audiotapes.

Citizenship

16712 ■ American Citizenship Center (ACC)
2501 E Memorial Rd.
Box 11000
Oklahoma City, OK 73136-1100
Ph: (405)425-5032
Fax: (405)425-5108
E-mail: pen.woods@oc.edu
Contact: Pendleton Woods, Dir.
Founded: 1957. **Staff:** 1. **Description:** Seeks to create an appreciation and understanding of the American way of life. Develops an employee education program in free enterprise and personal development. Conducts Freedom Forums, Youth Citizen Leadership, Building Your Own Business, and graduate seminars for students. Sponsors competitions. **Libraries: Type:** reference. **Holdings:** books, films, video recordings. **Subjects:** American heritage, governmental and economic systems. **Awards: Type:** recognition. **Publications:** *Libertas*, quarterly. Magazine. **Circulation:** 2,000. Also Cited As: *National Program Letter* ● Books. Publishes in conjunction with National Education Program. ● Pamphlets. **Conventions/Meetings:** meeting and seminar, one day forums and four day seminars for young people.

16713 ■ American Legion Auxiliary Girls Nation (GN)
Natl. 4-H Conf. Center
7100 Connecticut Ave.
Chevy Chase, MD 20815
Ph: (317)955-3845
Fax: (317)955-3884
E-mail: alahq@legion-aux.org
URL: http://www.legion-aux.org
Contact: Kris Nelson, Dir.
Founded: 1947. **Members:** 96. **Staff:** 35. **State Groups:** 49. **Description:** Serves as youth citizenship training program conducted annually by the American Legion Auxiliary national organization (see separate entry) to give high school juniors practical experience in the processes of federal government and a clear understanding of their approaching citizenship responsibilities. Conducts Girls State sessions, which are sponsored by 50 states of the ALA, and held each June or July in state capitals or on centrally located campuses. Elects two senators from each Girls State, to represent their constituents at Girls Nation in July in Washington, DC. Teaches local, county, and state level government; at Girls Nation the emphasis is on national government. Has representatives that organize political parties, hold conventions, run campaigns, elect officers, enact legislation, and visit government agencies. (LA does not participate in Girls Nation, but has a Girls State program). **Libraries: Type:** reference. **Holdings:** archival material, audiovisuals, clippings. **Subjects:**

government. **Awards: Frequency:** annual. **Type:** scholarship. **Recipient:** to GN president, vice-president, and outstanding senator. **Additional Websites:** http://girlsnation-auxiliary.com. **Committees:** National Girls State. **Affiliated With:** American Legion Auxiliary. **Publications:** *American Legion Auxiliary Girls State.* Brochure. **Price:** free. **Conventions/Meetings:** annual Girls Nation - congress, with citizenship training and model senate sessions.

16714 ■ Center for the Study of the Presidency (CSP)
1020 19th St. NW, Ste.250
Washington, DC 20036
Ph: (202)872-9800
Fax: (202)872-9811
E-mail: center@thepresidency.org
URL: http://www.thepresidency.org
Contact: Dr. David M. Abshire, Pres./CEO
Founded: 1965. **Members:** 600. **Membership Dues:** student, retired professor, $50 (annual) ● professional, faculty, public policy, $80 (annual) ● contributing, $150 (annual) ● life, $2,000. **Staff:** 10. **Budget:** $1,700,000. **Description:** College and university faculty and students; business and professional leaders; governmental leaders; corporations; colleges and universities; foundations. Counsels the White House and Executive Branch on policy issues critical to strengthening Presidential leadership and improving Executive-Congressional relations. Promotes citizenship education, especially of youth, and a better understanding of the U.S. political and economic systems. Conducts roundtables and special studies. Maintains research clearinghouse on the presidency. **Libraries: Type:** reference. **Holdings:** 2,000; archival material. **Subjects:** American presidency. **Awards:** Center Fellow. **Frequency:** annual. **Type:** fellowship. **Recipient:** for 80 graduate and undergraduate students from top academic institutions ● Donald B. Marron and James R. Moffet. **Frequency:** annual. **Type:** recognition. **Recipient:** for best two Center fellow papers ● Publius Award. **Frequency:** annual. **Type:** recognition. **Recipient:** for distinguished public service. **Programs:** Communicating America; Global Economic Vulnerabilities; Homeland Security; Marshalling the Nation's Science and Technology Resources. **Formerly:** (1970) Library of Presidential Papers. **Publications:** *Presidential Studies Quarterly.* Journal. Examines public policy issues with special reference to the American presidency and its relationships with Congress and the courts. **Price:** included in membership dues. ISSN: 0360-4918. **Circulation:** 2,000. **Advertising:** accepted. Alternate Formats: microform; online ● *Triumphs and Tragedies: Seventy-Six Case Studies in Presidential Leadership,* annual. Annual Report. Describes programs, publications, services, and contributions. **Price:** included in membership dues ● Reports. **Conventions/Meetings:** semiannual Center Fellows Leadership Conference - conference and symposium - April and November.

16715 ■ Claremont Institute
937 W Foothill Blvd., Ste.E
Claremont, CA 91711
Ph: (909)621-6825
Fax: (909)626-8724
E-mail: info@claremont.org
URL: http://www.claremont.org
Contact: Brian T. Kennedy, Pres.
Founded: 1979. **Membership Dues:** general, $25-$99 ● Patriot's Club, $100-$499 ● Churchill Club, $500-$999 ● President's Club, $1,000-$4,999 ● Madison Club, $5,000 ● Founder's Circle (minimum), $50,000. **Description:** Works to restore the principles of the American founding to their rightful, preeminent authority in national life. Engages Americans in an informed discussion of the principles and policies necessary to rebuild civic institutions. **Programs:** American Family; Investment Security; Publius Fellowship. **Projects:** Ballistic Missile Defense. **Sections:** Center for Constitutional Jurisprudence; Center for Local Government. **Publications:** *Claremont Review of Books,* quarterly. **Price:** $19.50/year ● *Local Liberty,* quarterly. Newsletter. Alternate Formats: online ● *The Proposition,* monthly. Newslet-

ter. Includes excerpts of essays and speeches by Claremont Institute scholars. **Price:** free ● *The Public View,* quarterly. Newsletter.

16716 ■ Close Up Foundation
44 Canal Center Plz.
Alexandria, VA 22314-1592
Ph: (703)706-3300
Free: (800)256-7387
Fax: (703)706-0000
E-mail: webmaster@closeup.org
URL: http://www.closeup.org
Contact: Timothy S. Davis, Pres./CEO
Founded: 1970. **Staff:** 190. **Budget:** $34,000,000. **Description:** Encourages responsible participation in the democratic process by citizens of all ages and backgrounds; promotes increased civic awareness, involvement, and achievement through non-partisan educational programs in government and citizenship. Operates Close Up Washington, a government studies program for middle school and high school students and teachers from the U.S. and other countries, including hearing and visually impaired students. Other programs include the Civil Rights Trail, Pacific Basin (Honolulu); Program for New Americans (recently immigrated students). Broadcasts public affairs programs over the Cable Satellite Public Affairs Network; produces award-winning publications, simulations, and videos for the classroom. **Councils:** Executive. **Publications:** *The American Economy.* Book. **Price:** $14.00/issue ● *The Bill of Rights: A User's Guide.* Book. **Price:** $20.00/issue ● *Bill of Rights Series,* annual. Videos ● *Current Issues,* annual. Book. **Price:** $15.00/issue ● *Democracy and Rights.* Video ● *Destination America: Perspectives on U.S. Immigration Policy.* Video ● *Exploring Race and Affirmation Action.* Video ● *Fight for Freedom: The Inspiring Story of African American Civil War Soldiers.* Video ● *International Relations.* Book. **Price:** $16.00/issue ● *Ordinary Americans: U.S. History Through the Eyes of Everyday People, 2nd Edition.* Book. **Price:** $23.00/issue ● *Perspectives.* Video ● *Public Policy and the Information Superhighway.* Video ● *The Source Book* ● *Talking Peace with Jimmy Carter.* Video ● *The Washington Notebook.* **Conventions/Meetings:** weekly Close Up Washington - meeting and workshop, with tours.

16717 ■ Ethics Resource Center (ERC)
1747 Pennsylvania Ave. NW, Ste.400
Washington, DC 20006
Ph: (202)737-2258
Free: (800)777-1285
Fax: (202)737-2227
E-mail: ethics@ethics.org
URL: http://www.ethics.org
Contact: Patricia J. Harned PhD, Pres.
Founded: 1977. **Staff:** 15. **Budget:** $1,700,000. **Description:** Seeks to serve as a catalyst to improve the ethical practices of individuals and organizations from the classroom to the boardroom. Fulfills its mission through three distinct areas of expertise: as a leader in the fields of organizational/business ethics consulting; as a provider and facilitator of character education programs; and as an ethics information clearinghouse. **Libraries: Type:** reference. **Subjects:** ethics. **Awards:** Stanley C. Pace Distinguished Lecture Award on Leadership in Ethics. **Frequency:** annual. **Type:** recognition. **Recipient:** for contribution to ethical business conduct. **Computer Services:** database, ethics-related literature. **Absorbed:** (1942) Citizenship Educational Service. **Formerly:** (1942) American Viewpoint Society; (1980) American Viewpoint. **Publications:** *Charter Education.* Video ● *Common Sense and Everyday Ethics* ● *Creating a Workable Company Code of Ethics.* **Price:** $25.00. Alternate Formats: online ● *Ethical Basis of Economic Freedom* ● *Ethics at Work.* Video ● *Ethics Education in American Business Schools* ● *Ethics Policies and Programs in American Business* ● *Ethics Today,* monthly. Newsletter. Covers ethics and character education in business, education, and government. **Price:** free. ISSN: 1060-0698. **Circulation:** 19,000. Alternate Formats: online.

16718 ■ National Conference on Citizenship (NCoC)
PO Box 15129
Chevy Chase, MD 20825
Ph: (202)467-8833
Fax: (202)467-8900
E-mail: info@ncoc.net
URL: http://www.ncoc.net
Contact: A.G. Newmyer III, Mgr.
Founded: 1946. **Staff:** 2. **Description:** Promotes citizenship activities and spirit of cooperation on part of all citizens. Leads annual Citizenship Day on September 17 to recognize youth reaching voting age and salutes foreign-born receiving citizenship through naturalization. **Awards:** Citizen of the Year. **Frequency:** annual. **Type:** recognition. **Recipient:** for exemplary service to the country. **Conventions/Meetings:** annual conference - always September, in National Capital area.

Civics

16719 ■ Association of Americans for Civic Responsibility (AACR)
13316 Foxhall Dr.
Silver Spring, MD 20906
Ph: (301)933-1494
E-mail: aacri@aacri.org
URL: http://www.aacri.org
Contact: Dr. Joy Cherian, Chair/Pres./CEO
Description: Seeks to educate and encourage individuals, institutions, organizations and businesses to advance the commonweal (the public good) through acts of civic responsibility. Organizes educational programs, seminars and conferences on personal civic responsibility for youth leaders across the United States. Develops and distributes educational materials. Promotes corporate social responsibilities including customer relations, consumer service and ethical behavior. **Publications:** Articles. Alternate Formats: online.

16720 ■ Innovations in Civic Participation (ICP)
1776 Massachusetts Ave. NW, Ste.201
Washington, DC 20036
Ph: (202)775-0290
Fax: (202)833-8581
E-mail: info@icicp.org
URL: http://www.icicp.org
Contact: Susan E. Stroud, Founder/Exec. Dir.
Founded: 2001. **Multinational. Description:** Promotes civic participation as a strategy to address important issues around the world. Supports the development of service as an emerging social institution. Provides technical assistance to organizations and governments for service policy and program development. Stimulates new thinking in the field of national and community service in the United States and around the world. Encourages dialogue between disciplines in order to illustrate the potential of service in addressing critical social issues. **Telecommunication Services:** electronic mail, stroud@icicp.org. **Publications:** Newsletter, monthly.

16721 ■ National Voice
2105 First Ave. S
Minneapolis, MN 55404
Ph: (612)879-7500
Free: (866)428-7228
Fax: (612)870-4846
E-mail: info@nationalvoice.org
URL: http://www.nationalvoice.org
Description: Works to maximize public participation in the nation's democratic process. Helps local groups incorporate voter education and registration activities into their work. **Computer Services:** Mailing lists ● online services, library.

Civil Defense

16722 ■ Minuteman Civil Defense Corps
6501 Greenway Pkwy., Ste.103-640
Scottsdale, AZ 85254
Ph: (520)829-3112

E-mail: info@minutemanhq.com
URL: http://www.minutemanhq.com/hq
Membership Dues: registration fee, $50. **Description:** Seeks to assist the U.S. Border Patrol in turning back the tidal wave of people entering the United States illegally. Reports and directs the Border Patrol to suspected illegal aliens or illegal activities. Encourages volunteers to use restraint and stay within the boundaries of the law. **Computer Services:** Information services, The Minuteman Pledge ● information services, Standard Operating Procedure for Minuteman Project ● mailing lists. **Projects:** The Minuteman. **Publications:** Manual. Alternate Formats: online.

Civil Rights and Liberties

16723 ■ A. Philip Randolph Educational Fund (APREF)
c/o Clayola Brown
815 16th St. NW, 5th Fl.
Washington, DC 20006
Ph: (202)508-3710
Fax: (202)508-3711
Contact: Clayola Brown, Pres.
Founded: 1964. **Staff:** 10. **Description:** Seeks to: eliminate prejudice and discrimination from all areas of life; educate individuals and groups on their rights and responsibilities; defend human and civil rights; assist in the employment and education of the underprivileged; combat community deterioration, delinquency, and crime.

16724 ■ Afghans for Civil Society (ACS)
806 N Charles St.
Baltimore, MD 21201
Ph: (410)385-1445
Fax: (410)385-1475
E-mail: baltimore@afghansforcivilsociety.org
URL: http://www.afghansforcivilsociety.org
Contact: Qayum Karzai, Founder/Chm.
Founded: 1998. **Multinational. Description:** Promotes a democratic alternative for Afghanistan that opposes violence and extremism and encourages the rebirth of civil society in the country. Envisions a society based on the rule of law, where participation by ordinary citizens, including women, can have an effect. **Computer Services:** Online services, photo gallery. **Programs:** Focus Groups; Rebuilding Bomb-Damaged Houses; Research and Policy Studies; Restoration of Historical Monuments; Sister School; Vocational Training Center; Women's Forum; Women's Income Generation Project. **Affiliated With:** Women for Afghan Women. **Publications:** *Geopolitics of an Afghan Settlement.* Report. Alternate Formats: online ● *Letters From The South, Policy Statements.* Paper. Alternate Formats: online ● *Loya Jirga Focus Group Report.* Alternate Formats: online ● *Shamalan Canal Socio-Economic Study.* Report. Alternate Formats: online ● *Violations of Human Rights in Afghanistan from the Soviets' Withdrawal to the Rise of the Taliban.* Report. Alternate Formats: online.

16725 ■ All One Heart
12190 Perris Blvd., Ste.F-141
Moreno Valley, CA 92557
Fax: (909)924-1882
E-mail: michele@alloneheart.com
URL: http://www.alloneheart.com
Contact: Michele Orgell, Pres./Exec. Dir./Founder
Description: Promotes harmony among people of different cultures, races, religions, age groups, sexual gender and orientation, and physical and mental abilities. Encourages tolerance through raised consciousness, education and experience. Teaches how to love, respect and build self esteem and individuality. **Publications:** *e-HeartBeat.* Newsletter. **Advertising:** accepted. Alternate Formats: online.

16726 ■ American-Arab Anti-Discrimination Committee (ADC)
1732 Wisconsin Ave. NW
Washington, DC 20007
Ph: (202)244-2990
Free: (800)654-2200
Fax: (202)244-7968
E-mail: adc@adc.org
URL: http://www.adc.org
Contact: Mary Rose Oakar MD, Pres.
Founded: 1980. **Membership Dues:** student, $5 (annual) ● basic, $10 (annual) ● sustaining, $75 (annual) ● contributing, $100-$499 (annual) ● sponsoring, $500-$999 (annual) ● President's Club, $1,000-$4,999 (annual) ● Chair's Council, $5,000-$9,999 (annual) ● Benefactor's Circle, $10,000 (annual). **Staff:** 25. **Description:** Serves as grassroots organization representing Arab-Americans. Seeks to protect the rights of people of Arab descent. Promotes and defends the Arab-American heritage. Serves the needs of the Arab-American community. Works through its Action Network and Media Monitoring Groups to end the stereotyping of Arabs in the media and discrimination against Arab-Americans in employment, education, and politics. Operates ADC Research Institute and conducts internship program for college students. Organizes protests against racist advertisements and other media. Maintains speakers' bureau. Conducts charitable program. Provides resources and information for teachers. **Libraries: Type:** not open to the public. **Holdings:** 300. **Awards: Frequency:** annual. **Type:** recognition. **Recipient:** to Arab-Americans for notable achievements. **Computer Services:** database, membership. **Divisions:** Legal; Organizing; Outreach and Education; Press; Publications. **Publications:** *ADC Times,* semimonthly. Magazine. Includes reports on U.S. Middle East policy and Arab American issues. **Price:** included in membership dues. ISSN: 0749-2642. **Circulation:** 25,000. **Advertising:** accepted ● *Issue Papers,* periodic. Monographs. ISSN: 1041-8911 ● *Special Reports,* periodic ● *Taking Root* ● Also publishes guides. **Conventions/Meetings:** annual Arab-Americans: A Pro-Active Agenda - conference (exhibits).

16727 ■ American Citizens for Justice (ACJ)
PO Box 2735
Southfield, MI 48037
E-mail: rededication20@yahoo.com
URL: http://www.americancitizensforjustice.org
Contact: Roland Hwang, Pres.
Founded: 1983. **Members:** 600. **Membership Dues:** student, senior, low-income, $10 (annual) ● individual, $20 (annual) ● family, $30 (annual) ● sponsor, $50 (annual) ● bronze, $100 (annual) ● silver, $250 (annual) ● gold, $500 (annual) ● platinum, $1,000 (annual). **Staff:** 1. **Budget:** $40,000. **Languages:** Chinese, English, Filipino, Hindi, Japanese, Korean, Vietnamese. **Description:** Asian Pacific Americans and other individuals concerned with discrimination against ethnic groups. Works to combat and prevent racial intolerance. Operates the Asian American Center for Justice. Monitors legislation and law enforcement. Community education of Asian Pacific American history and culture. **Awards:** Leadership Recognition. **Frequency:** annual. **Type:** recognition ● Legal Scholarship. **Frequency:** annual. **Type:** scholarship. **Publications:** *Justice Update,* quarterly. Newsletter. **Circulation:** 850. **Advertising:** accepted. **Conventions/Meetings:** annual dinner (exhibits).

16728 ■ American Civil Liberties Union (ACLU)
125 Broad St., 18th Fl.
New York, NY 10004
Ph: (212)549-2500
Free: (888)567-ACLU
Fax: (212)549-2646
E-mail: membership@aclu.org
URL: http://www.aclu.org
Contact: Anthony D. Romero, Exec. Dir.
Founded: 1920. **Members:** 275,000. **Membership Dues:** individual, $20 (annual) ● joint, $30 (annual). **Staff:** 125. **Budget:** $20,000,000. **State Groups:** 53. **Local Groups:** 200. **Description:** Champions the rights set forth in the Bill of Rights of the U.S. Constitution: freedom of speech, press, assembly, and religion; due process of law and fair trial; equality before the law regardless of race, color, sexual orientation, national origin, political opinion, or religious belief. Conducts activities including litigation, advocacy, and public education. Sponsors litigation projects on topics such as women's rights, gay and lesbian rights, and children's rights. **Awards:** Medal of Liberty. **Frequency:** biennial. **Type:** monetary. **Recipient:** for lifetime contribution to civil liberties in U.S. **Telecommunication Services:** electronic mail, media@aclu.org. **Publications:** Also publishes policy statements, handbooks, reprints, and pamphlets. **Conventions/Meetings:** biennial conference.

16729 ■ American Civil Liberties Union Foundation (ACLUF)
125 Broad St., 18th Fl.
New York, NY 10004
Ph: (212)549-2500
Free: (800)775-2258
Fax: (212)549-2654
E-mail: media@aclu.org
URL: http://www.aclu.org
Contact: Nadine Strossen, Pres.
Founded: 1966. **Staff:** 81. **Regional Groups:** 2. **Description:** Established as the tax-exempt arm of the American Civil Liberties Union (see separate entry). Conducts legal defense, research, and public education on behalf of civil liberties including freedom of speech, press, and other First Amendment rights; has litigation projects on topics such as capital punishment, censorship, women's rights, immigration, prisoners' rights, voting rights, and lesbian and gay rights. Provides research and public education projects to enable citizens to know and assert their rights. Seeks funds to protect liberty guaranteed by the Bill of Rights and the Constitution. **Formerly:** (1969) Roger Baldwin Foundation of ACLU. **Publications:** *Civil Liberties,* semiannual. Newsletter. Covers the legal defense, research, and public education projects of the foundation. Includes legislative news. **Price:** included in membership dues ● Annual Report, annual.

16730 ■ American Civil Rights Institute
PO Box 188350
Sacramento, CA 95818-8350
Ph: (916)444-2278
Fax: (916)444-2279
E-mail: todd@bollenbach.com
URL: http://www.acri.org
Contact: Ward Connerly, Chm.
Founded: 1997. **Description:** Educates the public about racial and gender preferences. **Publications:** *The Egalitarian,* quarterly. Newsletter. **Price:** free. Alternate Formats: online.

16731 ■ American Sons of Liberty (ASL)
1142 S Diamond Bar Blvd., Ste.305
Diamond Bar, CA 91765
E-mail: americansonsofliberty@americansonsofliberty.com
URL: http://www.americansonsofliberty.com
Contact: Gene S. Whitehead, Pres./Founder
Founded: 1998. **Members:** 300. **Membership Dues:** single, $35 (annual) ● senior, veteran, active military, college student, $30 (annual) ● junior, $22 (annual) ● life, $320-$475 ● family, $120 (annual). **Staff:** 5. **Description:** Represents politically conservative individuals seeking to defend the U.S. Constitution. Concentrates efforts on the right to keep and bear arms; opposes gun control, including restrictions on semiautomatic weapons. "Maintains that mandatory gun registration precedes confiscation, which infringes upon individual freedom. Claims that less than one percent of registered guns are used for illegal purposes, therefore gun control would constitute harassment of 99&percent; of gun owners." Provides information on the right to bear arms. Compiles statistics; operates speakers' bureau. **Libraries: Type:** reference. **Holdings:** 95; archival material. **Subjects:** firearms. **Computer Services:** Information services. **Telecommunication Services:** electronic mail, gene@americansonsofliberty.com. **Publications:** *Liberty Report,* quarterly. Newsletter ● Journal, periodic. **Conventions/Meetings:** annual meeting.

16732 ■ **American Spanish Committee (ASC)**
PO Box 42
Leonia, NJ 07605-0042
Ph: (201)567-7417
Fax: (201)816-9797
E-mail: americanspanishcommittee@yahoo.com
Contact: Mr. Anthony F. Gonzalez LLb, Chm./CEO
Founded: 1962. **Languages:** English, Spanish. **Description:** Represents Spanish-surnamed white citizens. Protects the civil and religious rights of Spanish-surnamed White American citizens in the U.S. and abroad. Monitors activities of international human rights groups. Sponsors charitable programs. Maintains speakers' bureau, and compiles statistics. **Libraries: Type:** reference. **Holdings:** 2,000; archival material. **Awards: Type:** recognition. **Subcommittees:** Research and Development. **Affiliated With:** World Spanish Congress. **Publications:** *New World* ● Newsletter, bimonthly. Covers committee activities. **Price:** free. **Conventions/Meetings:** periodic conference.

16733 ■ **Americans to Ban Cloning (ABC)**
1100 H St. NW, Ste.700
Washington, DC 20005
Ph: (202)347-6840
Fax: (202)347-6849
E-mail: media@cloninginformation.org
URL: http://cloninginformation.org
Contact: Gene Tarne, Contact
Description: Promotes a global and comprehensive ban on human cloning. **Computer Services:** database, cloning commentaries ● database, cloning new archive ● database, radio ads ● information services, cloning resources. **Telecommunication Services:** electronic mail, jpcarter@cbhd.org.

16734 ■ **Americans for Religious Liberty (ARL)**
PO Box 6656
Silver Spring, MD 20916
Ph: (301)260-2988
Fax: (301)260-2989
E-mail: info@arlinc.org
URL: http://www.arlinc.org
Contact: Edd Doerr, Pres.
Founded: 1981. **Members:** 9,000. **Membership Dues:** student, limited income, $10 (annual) ● individual, $25 (annual) ● family, $30 (annual) ● sustaining, $50 (annual) ● supporting, $100 (annual) ● sponsoring, $500 (annual) ● patron, $1,000 (annual). **Staff:** 3. **Budget:** $200,000. **Description:** Individuals dedicated to preserving religious, intellectual, and personal freedom, the constitutional principle of separation of church and state, democratic secular public education, reproductive rights, and the Jeffersonian-Madisonian ideal of a pluralistic secular democracy. Counter attacks on church-state separation by sectarian special interests. Maintains speakers' bureau; conducts research programs; engages in litigation. **Libraries: Type:** not open to the public. **Holdings:** 1,000. **Absorbed:** (1982) Center for Moral Democracy. **Formerly:** (1983) Voice of Reason. **Publications:** *The Case Against School Vouchers.* Book. Includes member and research news. **Price:** included in membership dues; $15.95 for nonmembers. **Circulation:** 9,000 ● *Catholic Schools: The Facts.* Book. **Price:** $10.00 ● *Church Schools and Public Money - the Politics of Parochiaid.* Book. **Price:** $14.95 ● *The December Wars.* Book. **Price:** $18.95 ● *The Great Quotations on Religious Freedom.* Book. **Price:** $18.00 ● *Maryland's 1992 Abortion Rights Referendum.* Book ● *Religion and Public Education - Common Sense and the Law.* Book. **Price:** $5.00 ● *Religious Liberty and State Constitutions.* Book. **Price:** $14.95 ● *Religious Liberty in Crisis.* Book ● *Visions of Reality: What Fundamentalist Schools Teach.* Book. **Price:** $14.95 ● *Voice of Reason,* quarterly. Newsletter. **Price:** $20.00 /year for nonmembers; included in membership dues. **Circulation:** 9,000. Alternate Formats: online.

16735 ■ **Anti-Defamation League (ADL)**
823 UN Plz.
New York, NY 10017
Ph: (212)885-7700
Fax: (212)867-9406
E-mail: webmaster@adl.org
URL: http://www.adl.org
Contact: Abraham H. Foxman, Natl. Dir.
Founded: 1913. **Staff:** 400. **Budget:** $45,000,000. **Regional Groups:** 28. **Description:** Seeks to stop the defamation of the Jewish people and to secure justice and fair treatment to all citizens alike. Educates Americans about Israel; promotes all citizens alike. Fights bigotry of all kinds; exposes extremist individuals and organizations; builds bridges to better interfaith and intergroup relations; works against anti-Semitism; of understanding between racial, religious, and ethnic groups; educates about Israel; trains educators on counteracts anti-democratic extremism and diversity; champions separation of church and state. **Libraries: Type:** reference. **Holdings:** articles, books, periodicals. **Subjects:** anti-Semitism, holocaust denial, first amendment, racism, extremism, hate groups, American democracy and pluralism. **Awards:** America's Democratic Legacy Award. **Type:** recognition ● The Courage to Care Award. **Type:** recognition ● Dore Schary Student Achievement Award. **Frequency:** annual. **Type:** recognition. **Recipient:** for student of film and video productions ● Hubert H. Humphrey First Amendment Freedoms Prize. **Type:** recognition ● Joseph Prize for Human Rights. **Type:** recognition ● Special Jury Award. **Frequency:** annual. **Type:** recognition. **Recipient:** for amateur and professional filmmakers. **Divisions:** Civil Rights; Community Service; Development; Intergroup Relations; International Affairs; Leadership; Marketing and Communications. **Absorbed:** (1965) Institute for Democratic Education. **Also Known As:** Anti Defamation League of B'nai B'rith. **Publications:** *ADL on the Frontline,* bimonthly. Newsletter. **Price:** $12.00 /year for individuals. ISSN: 1061-5202. **Circulation:** 80,000. Alternate Formats: online ● *Dimensions,* semiannual. Journal ● *Law Enforcement Bulletin,* semiannual. **Price:** free for members ● *Middle East Insight,* quarterly ● *PLO Watch,* periodic ● *Terrorism Update* ● Also publishes monographs, articles, and teaching materials. **Conventions/Meetings:** annual National Commission - meeting (exhibits) - always fall.

16736 ■ **Anti-Racist Action-Los Angeles/People Against Racist Terror (ARA-LA/PART)**
PO Box 1055
Culver City, CA 90232-1055
Ph: (310)495-0299
E-mail: antiracistaction_la@yahoo.com
URL: http://www.geocities.com/ara_losangeles
Contact: Michael Novick, Exec. Off.
Founded: 1987. **Members:** 500. **Membership Dues:** individual, $16 (annual) ● organizational/institutional/international, $26 (annual) ● supporting (sustaining), $50 (annual). **Staff:** 1. **Budget:** $4,800. **Regional Groups:** 6. **Languages:** English, French, Spanish. **Multinational. Description:** Engages in anti-racist and anti-colonial activities. Promotes freedom, equality, self-determination, and respect for all; opposes white and male supremacy and racist and sexist discrimination in any form. **Libraries: Type:** reference. **Holdings:** 75; audiovisuals, books, clippings, periodicals. **Subjects:** racism and sexism. **Additional Websites:** http://www.antiracistaction.ca, http://www.antiracistaction.us. **Committees:** Political Action. **Formerly:** (1987) People Against Racist Terror; (2005) Anti-Racist Action/People Against Racist Terror. **Publications:** *Turning the Tide: Journal of Anti-Racist Action, Research and Education* (in English and Spanish), bimonthly. Magazine. Covers youth-oriented, anti-racist activities. **Price:** $16.00 /year for members; $26.00 /year for institutions; $2.00/issue. ISSN: 1082-6491. **Circulation:** 8,000. **Advertising:** accepted ● All reports have been incorporated into: "White Lies, White Power: The Fight Against White Supremacy and Reactionary Violence," by Michael Novick, published by Common Courage Press, Monroe, ME. **Conventions/Meetings:** monthly meeting, educational forum, speaker or film plus discussion - always third Saturday ● semiannual regional meeting - usually April and October.

16737 ■ **Anti-Repression Resource Team (ARRT)**
PO Box 210
Bellefonte, PA 16823-0210
E-mail: writerkl@aol.com
Contact: Ken Lawrence, Dir.
Founded: 1979. **Description:** Combats all forms of political repression including: police violence and misconduct; Ku Klux Klan and Nazi terrorism; spying and covert action by secret police and intelligence agencies. Focuses on research, writing, lecturing, organizing, and publishing. Conducts training workshops for church, labor, and community organizations. Maintains speakers' bureau. **Libraries: Type:** reference. **Subjects:** spying, repression, covert action, terrorism, civil liberties. **Supersedes:** Mississippi Surveillance Project of the American Friends Service Committee.

16738 ■ **Asian American Center for Justice of the American Citizens for Justice**
Address Unknown since 2007
Founded: 1983. **Members:** 600. **Membership Dues:** student/senior citizen, $10 (annual) ● adults, $20 (annual) ● family, $30 (annual). **Staff:** 1. **Budget:** $40,000. **Languages:** Chinese, Filipino, Hindi, Japanese, Korean, Thai, Vietnamese. **Description:** Works to eradicate racism and violence against Asian Americans. Offers legal consultation and education. Monitors violence against Asians. Conducts civil rights education project. Maintains speakers' bureau. Improves understanding of APA history, contributions, problems and cultures. **Libraries: Type:** reference. **Holdings:** archival material, audio recordings, clippings, video recordings. **Awards:** Vincent Chin Justice Scholarship. **Frequency:** annual. **Type:** scholarship. **Recipient:** bestowed to Asian Pacific American in law school. **Publications:** *Justice Update,* monthly. **Advertising:** not accepted. **Conventions/Meetings:** annual dinner (exhibits).

16739 ■ **Asian American Legal Defense and Education Fund (AALDEF)**
99 Hudson St., 12th Fl.
New York, NY 10013
Ph: (212)966-5932
Free: (800)966-5946
Fax: (212)966-4303
E-mail: info@aaldef.org
URL: http://www.aaldef.org
Contact: Margaret Fung, Exec. Dir.
Founded: 1974. **Membership Dues:** basic, $50 (annual) ● joint, $75 (annual) ● associate, $100 (annual) ● contributing, $250 (annual) ● sustaining, $500 (annual) ● patron, $1,000 (annual). **Staff:** 17. **Budget:** $1,400,000. **Languages:** Bengali, Chinese, English, Korean, Tagalog. **Description:** Attorneys, legal workers, and members of the community who seek to employ legal, advocacy, and educational methods to address civil rights issues in Asian American communities. Provides bilingual legal counseling and representation for people who cannot obtain access to legal assistance; areas of concern include immigration, employment, voting rights, racially-motivated violence against Asian Americans, affirmative action and language rights. Litigates cases that have the potential of improving the quality of life in the Asian American community. Monitors and reports on incidents of racial discrimination against Asian Americans. Sponsors training sessions to inform community workers and residents of their rights and benefits before legal problems arise. Conducts student intern program to provide law and undergraduate students with legal experience in a community setting; is supported by foundation and corporate grants, special events, and individuals. **Awards:** Justice in Action. **Frequency:** annual. **Type:** recognition. **Projects:** Affirmative Action; Economic Justice for Workers; Elimination of Anti-Asian Violence, Police Misconduct and Human Trafficking; Immigration and Immigrants' Rights; Language Access to Services; Voting Rights; Youth Rights and Equity. **Publications:** *The Asian American Vote 2004: A Report on the Multilingual Exit Poll in the 2004 Presidential Election.* Alternate Formats: online ● *Outlook,* semiannual. Newsletter. **Price:** free for

members ● *Righting Wrongs*, monthly. Newsletter ● Pamphlet (in Chinese, English, Japanese, and Korean). **Conventions/Meetings:** seminar ● workshop.

16740 ■ Center for the Community Interest (CCI)

Lincoln Bldg.
60 E 42nd St., Ste.2112
New York, NY 10165
Ph: (212)909-2620
Fax: (212)909-2620
E-mail: mail@communityinterest.org
URL: http://www.communityinterest.org
Contact: David Castro, Exec. Dir.
Founded: 1989. **Members:** 4,000. **Membership Dues:** regular, $20 (annual). **Staff:** 4. **Budget:** $500,000. **Regional Groups:** 1. **Description:** Dedicated to restoring the link between rights and responsibilities in public policy debates, court decisions, and the daily life of individual Americans. Raises awareness of the decline in civic responsibility in the U.S; identifies local solutions to community problems; promotes citizenship through community service; provides information to grassroots activists and local governments; recruits law firms to provide pro bono legal services to community groups; maintains information clearinghouse on rights and responsibility issues; conducts policy research; maintains Speaker's Bureau. **Formerly:** (1998) American Alliance for Rights and Responsibilities. **Publications:** *Rights and Responsibilities*. Newsletter ● *The Winnable War: A Community Guide to Eradicating Street Drug Markets*. Manual. **Price:** $12.50 plus shipping and handling. **Conventions/Meetings:** board meeting.

16741 ■ Center for Constitutional Rights (CCR)

666 Broadway, 7th Fl.
New York, NY 10012
Ph: (212)614-6464
Fax: (212)614-6499
E-mail: info@ccr-ny.org
URL: http://www.ccr-ny.org
Contact: E. Vincent Warren, Exec. Dir.
Founded: 1966. **Staff:** 22. **Budget:** $2,000,000. **Description:** Represents legal and educational organization dedicated to advancing and protecting "the rights guaranteed by the United States Constitution and the Universal Declaration of Human Rights." Advocates the "creative use of law" as a positive force for social change. Sponsors the Ella Baker Student Program. **Computer Services:** Mailing lists. **Absorbed:** (1997) National Emergency Civil Liberties Committee. **Formerly:** (1967) Civil Rights Legal Defense Fund; (1970) Law Center for Constitutional Rights. **Publications:** *CCR News*, semiannual. Newsletter. Alternate Formats: online ● *Jailhouse Lawyer's Handbook*. Alternate Formats: online ● Annual Report, annual. Includes listing of litigation and educational programs of the center. ● Also publishes pamphlets on international and domestic human rights.

16742 ■ Center for Democratic Renewal (CDR)

PO Box 50469
Atlanta, GA 30303
Ph: (404)221-0025
Fax: (404)221-0045
E-mail: info@thecdr.org
URL: http://www.thecdr.org
Contact: Beni Ivey, Exec. Dir.
Founded: 1979. **Membership Dues:** regular, $35 (annual). **Staff:** 9. **Budget:** $600,000. **Description:** Advocates federal prosecution of the Ku Klux Klan and any groups or individuals involved in racist violence. Seeks to build public opposition to racist groups and their activities, and assist victims of bigoted violence. Works with trade unions, public officials, and religious, women's, civil rights, and grass roots organizations. Programs include education, research, victims' assistance, community organizing, leadership training, and public advocacy. Acts as a national clearinghouse for community-based re-

sponse to hate group activities. Maintains network of lawyers and archive on far-right activities, individuals, and organizations; conducts seminars, specialized education programs, and research on trends in the far right; compiles data; maintains speakers' bureau. **Libraries: Type:** reference. **Holdings:** audiovisuals, books, monographs. **Subjects:** right-wing groups, hate violence. **Divisions:** Research Unit. **Subgroups:** African Americans; Educators; Labor; Media; Minorities; Religious; Women; Youth. **Formerly:** (1985) National Anti-Klan Network. **Publications:** *Bitter Harvest: Gordon Kahl and the Posse Comitatus: Murder in the Heartland.* **Price:** $12.00 ● *Blood in the Face: The KKK, Aryan Nations, Nazi Skinheads and the Rise of a New White Culture.* **Price:** $18.95 ● *Christian Identity Movement* ● *Chronology of Violence, 1980-1986* ● *Epidemic Hangman's Noose in the Workplace: The Economic and Social Cost of Noose Harassment.* Report ● *The Monitor*, 3/year. Reports on white supremacist efforts and activities. **Price:** $35.00. **Circulation:** 11,000 ● *National Alliance: A House Divided.* Report ● *Near the Cross: A Ten-Year Chronology.* Report ● *Quarantines and Death: The Far Right's Homophobic Agenda.* **Price:** $5.00 ● *Solidarity and Division* ● *Special Report: Lost in the U.S.A.: INS Special Registration* ● *When Hate Groups Come to Town.* Manual. **Price:** $18.95. **Conventions/Meetings:** semiannual meeting.

16743 ■ Center for Third World Organizing (CTWO)

1218 E 21st St.
Oakland, CA 94606
Ph: (510)533-7583
Fax: (510)533-0923
E-mail: ctwo@ctwo.org
URL: http://www.ctwo.org
Contact: Danielle Mahones, Exec. Dir.
Founded: 1980. **Staff:** 17. **Budget:** $1,000,000. **Local Groups:** 200. **Description:** Provides training and resources to sustain direct action organizing in communities of color in the United States. Provides issue analysis research and leads a national campaign for welfare rights. **Awards:** George Wiley Award. **Frequency:** annual. **Type:** recognition. **Publications:** *CTWO Times*, bimonthly. Newsletter. Alternate Formats: online ● *Directory of Church Funding Sources*, periodic ● *Images of Color: A Guide to Media from and for Asian, Black, Latino, and Native American Communities* ● *Issue Pac*, quarterly ● *Surviving America: What You're Entitled to and How to Get it* ● *Third Force*, bimonthly. **Price:** $22.00 /year for individuals. ISSN: 1067-3237. **Circulation:** 6,000. **Advertising:** accepted ● Manuals. **Conventions/Meetings:** seminar, on issues affecting minorities.

16744 ■ Children's Rights

330 7th Ave., 4th Fl.
New York, NY 10001
Ph: (212)683-2210
Fax: (212)683-4015
E-mail: info@childrensrights.org
URL: http://www.childrensrights.org
Contact: Marcia Robinson Lowry Esq., Founder/Exec. Dir.
Founded: 1995. **Staff:** 30. **Budget:** $3,200,000. **Description:** Fights for the rights of poor children who are dependent on government systems. **Libraries: Type:** not open to the public. **Formerly:** Children's Rights Project - ACLU. **Publications:** *Continuing Danger: A Study of Child Fatalities in NYC.* Report ● *Impact*, quarterly. Newsletter. Alternate Formats: online ● *Time Running Out! Teens in Foster Care.* Report ● Annual Report, annual. Alternate Formats: online.

16745 ■ Chinese for Affirmative Action (CAA)

17 Walter U. Lum Pl.
San Francisco, CA 94108
Ph: (415)274-6750
Fax: (415)397-8770
E-mail: info@caasf.org
URL: http://www.caasf.org
Contact: Vincent Pan, Exec. Dir.
Founded: 1969. **Membership Dues:** regular, $40 (annual). **Staff:** 10. **Languages:** Chinese, English,

Mandarin Dialects. **Description:** Works towards equal rights and justice for Asian Americans, women and other people of color. Conducts policy advocacy in the areas of education, employment, hate crimes and affirmative action. Provides direct services for people interested in non-traditional blue collar work where women and people of color have been historically underrepresented. **Publications:** *Chinese for Affirmative Action—Newsletter*, quarterly. Informs readers of career counseling services and employment and apprenticeship opportunities. Announces organization events. **Price:** included in membership dues. **Circulation:** 2,000 ● Annual Report, annual. **Conventions/Meetings:** annual meeting.

16746 ■ Christian Anti-Defamation League (CADL)

PO Box 4
Palm Harbor, FL 34683-2141
Ph: (727)771-0635
E-mail: cadlinc@earthlink.net
URL: http://www.christian-adl-inc.org
Contact: William S. Hollis PhD, Pres.
Founded: 1996. **Nonmembership. Multinational. Description:** Provides and facilitates Christian anti-defamation legal services, including litigation and supporting services in defense of the rights and interests of Christians under the US Bill of Rights with particular emphasis on the freedom of religion clause of the First Amendment. Advocates for the elimination of defamation of Christians and other religious and ethnic groups, as well as advance proper understanding among all peoples in order to preserve and translate into greater effectiveness the principles of freedom, equality and democracy.

16747 ■ Citizens for a Better America (CFABA)

PO Box 7647
Van Nuys, CA 91409-7647
Ph: (818)757-1776
E-mail: hq@cfaba.org
URL: http://www.cfaba.org
Contact: Robert Colaco, Volunteer Natl. Chm./Founder
Founded: 1992. **Membership Dues:** individual, $60 (annual) ● individual, $5 (monthly). **Description:** Focuses on electing morality and values-based candidates from the very lowest to the very highest political positions all over the United States of America, who are pro-America first, pro-traditional family, pro-life, pro-Second Amendment, pro-USA sovereignty, pro-constitutional candidates. **Awards:** Good Guys List. **Type:** recognition. **Additional Websites:** http://www.haveyoubeenliedto.org, http://www.goodguys-list.org, http://www.stateprops.com. **Affiliated With:** Witness for Peace. **Publications:** *Commentary and News Release List (TM).* Newsletter ● *The Good News Report (TM)*, monthly. Newsletter. **Price:** free for members ● *Have you Been Lied To? (TM).* Article. Alternate Formats: online ● *110-Year Report.*

16748 ■ Citizens' Commission on Civil Rights (CCCR)

2000 M St. NW, Ste.400
Washington, DC 20036
Ph: (202)659-5565
Free: (800)552-6843
Fax: (202)223-5302
E-mail: citizen@cccr.org
URL: http://www.cccr.org
Contact: Dianne M. Piche, Exec. Dir.
Founded: 1982. **Members:** 16. **Description:** Bipartisan organization of former federal cabinet officials concerned with achieving the goal equality of opportunity. Aims to: monitor the federal government's enforcement of laws barring discrimination on the basis of race, sex, religion, ethnic background, age, or handicap; foster public understanding of civil rights issues; formulate constructive policy recommendations. **Telecommunication Services:** electronic mail, dpiche@cccr.org. **Programs:** Civil Rights Monitoring; Education Reform and Advocacy; Pursuing Justice. **Publications:** *Barriers to Registration and Voting: An Agenda for Reform* ● *Choosing Better Schools: A report on student transfers under the No Child Left*

Behind Act. Alternate Formats: online ● *Lost Opportunities: The Civil Rights Record of the Bush Administration at MidTerm* ● *New Opportunities: Civil Rights at a Crossroads.* Report ● *One Nation Indivisible: The Civil Rights Challenge for the 1990s* ● *Rights At Risk: Equality in an Age of Terrorism.* Report. Alternate Formats: online ● *Title I in California: Will the State Pass the Test?.* Reports. Covers broad range of civil rights issues including housing education, voting, employment, judicial nominations and hate crimes. ● Reports. Covers broad range of civil rights issues including housing education, voting, employment, judicial nominations and hate crimes. Alternate Formats: online ● Also provides press releases.

16749 ■ Citizens Committee for the Right to Keep and Bear Arms (CCRKBA)
Liberty Park
12500 NE 10th Pl.
Bellevue, WA 98005
Ph: (425)454-4911
Free: (800)486-6963
Fax: (425)451-3959
E-mail: informationrequest@ccrkba.org
URL: http://www.ccrkba.org
Contact: Joe Waldron, Exec. Dir.
Founded: 1971. **Members:** 650,000. **Membership Dues:** regular, $15 (annual) ● regular, $50 (quinquennial) ● life, $150 ● patron, $1,000 (annual). **Staff:** 40. **Budget:** $3,600,000. **State Groups:** 50. **Local Groups:** 140. **Description:** Citizens interested in defending the Second Amendment; more than 150 members of Congress serve on the advisory board. Conducts educational and political activities, in-depth studies on gun legislation and lobbying activities. Sponsors speakers' bureau; compiles statistics. **Awards: Type:** recognition. **Telecommunication Services:** electronic mail, adminforweb@ccrkba.org. **Committees:** Right to Bear Arms Political Victory Fund Political Action. **Absorbed:** Firearms Lobby of America. **Formerly:** (1973) National Citizens Committee for the Right to Keep and Bear Arms; (1989) National Association of Gun and Knife Shows. **Publications:** *Gottlieb-Tartaro Report,* monthly. Newsletter. Features what's happening in the gun rights movement. **Price:** $30.00/year ● *Gun Rights Fact Book - An Individual Right.* Contains report of the subcommittee on the Constitution Judiciary Committee of the 97th Congress. ● *Point Blank,* monthly. Newsletter. Fosters public awareness on the right of citizens to bear arms. Reports on gun control legislation, pro-gun candidates, and committee activities. **Price:** included in membership dues; $15.00 /year for nonmembers. **Circulation:** 100,000. **Advertising:** accepted ● *Politically Correct Guns.* Book. Lists some of America's most "outrageous" gun laws. **Price:** $14.95 ● *Politically Correct Hunting.* Book. Contains hunting humor; discusses the moral and ethical aspects of hunting. **Price:** $14.95 ● *The Rights of Gun Owners.* **Conventions/Meetings:** annual Gun Rights Policy Conference, for gun rights activists, constitutional scholars, and organization leaders (exhibits) ● seminar.

16750 ■ Citizens for Sensible Safeguards (CSS)
c/o OMB Watch
1742 Connecticut Ave. NW
Washington, DC 20009
Ph: (202)234-8494
Fax: (202)234-8584
E-mail: rushingr@ombwatch.org
URL: http://www.ombwatch.org/article/articleview/208/1/69
Contact: Robert Shull, Contact
Founded: 1995. **Members:** 300. **Description:** Coalition of over 300 organizations concerned with environmental, educational, civil rights, disability, health, and social services issues. Works to improve laws and safeguards that protect citizens and believes the federal government plays an important role in protecting the public interest. Opposes actions taken by Congress to dismantle federal laws and safeguards. Operates an information clearing house; coordinates lobbying and media efforts of member

organizations. **Additional Websites:** http://www.sensiblesafeguards.org. **Committees:** Grassroots Strategy; Media/Message; National Strategy; Steering. **Publications:** Papers. Alternate Formats: online ● Reports. Alternate Formats: online ● Publishes position papers and action alerts on relevant issues, especially regulatory reform.

16751 ■ Commission for Social Justice (CSJ)
219 E St. NE
Washington, DC 20002
Ph: (202)547-2900
Free: (800)552-OSIA
Fax: (202)547-0121
E-mail: csj@osia.org
URL: http://www.osia.org/public/commission/commission.asp
Contact: Philip R. Piccigallo PhD, Natl. Exec. Dir.
Founded: 1979. **Membership Dues:** individual, $25 (annual). **Staff:** 8. **State Groups:** 25. **Description:** Serves as the anti-defamation arm of the Order Sons of Italy in America (see separate entry). Monitors businesses, schools, and the media to combat negative portrayals of Italian-Americans. Seeks to gain positive recognition for the contributions of Italians and Americans of Italian descent. Conducts surveys and evaluations regarding the image of Italian-Americans throughout the country; compiles statistics. **Affiliated With:** Order Sons of Italy in America. **Formerly:** (1981) Institute for Liberty and Justice. **Publications:** *Italian-American Characters in TV Entertainment.* Report ● *Survey of Italian-American Representation in the Top 800 Companies in the U.S..* **Conventions/Meetings:** periodic conference ● symposium.

16752 ■ Death with Dignity National Center (DDNC)
520 SW 6th Ave., Ste.1030
Portland, OR 97204
Ph: (503)228-4415
Fax: (503)228-7454
E-mail: info@deathwithdignity.org
URL: http://www.deathwithdignity.org
Contact: Eli D. Stutsman JD, Dir.
Founded: 1994. **Members:** 20. **Membership Dues:** helper, $25 (annual) ● caregiver, $50 ● patron, $100. **Staff:** 4. **Budget:** $350,000. **Description:** Diverse group of people who believe in an inherent right to make their own choices regarding their health care and end-of-life decisions. Informs and educates the public about physician aid-in-dying so that they can make informed decisions regarding issues related to end-of-life choices. Provides forums for public and professional education. Disperses information in non-technical language. Places physician aid-in-dying in the context of recent social policy such as Living Wills, the Durable Power of Attorney and the Federal Patient Self Determination Act. Works with professional organizations to expand the scope of care and support available to terminally ill patients. **Libraries: Type:** not open to the public. **Doing business as:** (2002) Death With Dignity National Center. **Formerly:** Death With Dignity Education Fund; (1998) Death With Dignity Education Center. **Publications:** *Network,* semiannual. Newsletter. **Price:** free. **Conventions/Meetings:** Leaders' Forum - symposium - 3/year.

16753 ■ Department of Civil, Human and Women's Rights, AFL-CIO
815 16th St. NW
Washington, DC 20006
Ph: (202)637-5000
Fax: (202)637-5058
E-mail: feedback@aflcio.org
URL: http://www.aflcio.org
Contact: Linda Chavez-Thompson, Exec. VP
Founded: 1955. **Description:** Staff arm AFL-CIO Civil Rights Committee. Serves as official liaison with women's and civil rights organizations and government agencies working in the field of equal opportunity; helps to implement state and federal laws and AFL-CIO civil rights policies; aids affiliates in the development of affirmative programs to expand opportunities for minorities and women; prepares and

disseminates special materials on civil rights; speaks at union and civil rights institutes, conferences, and conventions; helps affiliates resolve complaints involving unions under Title VII of the 1964 Civil Rights Act and Executive Order 11246. **Affiliated With:** AFL-CIO. **Formerly:** (2004) Department of Civil Rights, AFL-CIO. **Publications:** *America @Work,* monthly. Magazine. **Conventions/Meetings:** biennial convention.

16754 ■ Discussion Club
Address Unknown since 2007
Founded: 1955. **Members:** 300. **Membership Dues:** individual, $30 (annual) ● family, $45 (annual) ● corporate, $180 (annual). **Description:** Individuals with an interest in individual freedom and the expansion of government activities in the 20th century. Promotes increased understanding of the impact of "government expansion into almost all walks of life" on civil rights. Serves as a clearinghouse on the rights of the individual; sponsors research and educational programs. **Awards: Frequency:** periodic. **Type:** recognition. **Publications:** *The Discussion Club 1955-1995.* Booklet ● Brochure. **Conventions/Meetings:** monthly dinner ● monthly lecture.

16755 ■ Drug Policy Alliance (DPA)
925 15th St. NW, 2nd Fl.
Washington, DC 20005
Ph: (202)216-0035
Fax: (202)216-0803
E-mail: dc@drugpolicy.org
URL: http://www.drugpolicy.org
Contact: Ethan Nadelmann, Exec. Dir.
Founded: 1986. **Members:** 15,500. **Membership Dues:** individual in U.S., $35 (annual) ● individual outside U.S., $50 (annual). **Staff:** 42. **State Groups:** 1. **National Groups:** 7. **Description:** Promotes alternative methods such as legalization, decriminalization, and medicalization of currently illegal substances including marijuana and heroin, to curb drug abuse while protecting the rights of the individual. Believes that legal drugs, clean needles, and effective drug treatment would vastly improve the health of addicts, slow the spread of AIDS, and decrease crime. Opposes the use of urine tests in employment. Sponsors debates and seminars on drug policy issues. Conducts research. **Libraries: Type:** reference; open to the public. **Holdings:** 11,000; articles, books, periodicals, reports. **Subjects:** drugs, treatment, drug policy, education. **Additional Websites:** http://www.dpf.org. **Projects:** California Proposition 36; Drug Testing Fails Our Youth; ProtectLiveMusic; Real Reform; Safety First. **Formerly:** Drug Policy Foundation; (2000) Lindesmith Center. **Publications:** *About Methadone,* periodic. Booklet ● *The Ally,* semiannual. Newsletter ● *The Marijuana Conviction.* Book ● *Marijuana Myths, Marijuana Facts.* Book. Provides reliable information about marijuana's effects on people. ● *Psychedelic Drugs Reconsidered.* Book ● *Safety First,* periodic. Booklet. **Conventions/Meetings:** biennial conference (exhibits).

16756 ■ European/American Issues Forum (E/AIF)
c/o Lou Calabro, Pres.
PMB 253, 1212H El Camino Real
San Bruno, CA 94066
Ph: (650)312-8284
Fax: (650)869-7215
E-mail: eaifpres@aol.com
URL: http://www.eaif.org
Contact: Lou Calabro, Pres.
Founded: 1997. **Members:** 300. **Membership Dues:** student, retiree, $15 (annual) ● family, individual, $25 (annual) ● organizational, $100 (annual) ● patron, $250 (annual) ● benefactor, $500 (annual). **Staff:** 1. **Budget:** $8,500. **Regional Groups:** 1. **Local Groups:** 1. **Description:** Individuals of European descent living in the United States. Functions as an advocate for the civil rights of Americans of European descent; encourages cultural and ethnic diversity in American life. Works to change the prevailing social perception of European Americans as culturally bland and politically and socially oppressive. "Rejects use of the term 'white', which the group believes ignores

European ethnic and cultural diversity. Opposes affirmative action, which the group believes to be the use of racial preference in educational admissions and hiring." Conducts cultural and educational programs. **Awards: Frequency:** annual. **Type:** recognition. **Recipient:** for an individual contributing to European American movement. **Computer Services:** database ● mailing lists. **Publications:** *Voices*, monthly. Newsletter. **Price:** included in membership dues. **Advertising:** accepted.

16757 ■ European-American Unity and Rights Organization (EURO)
c/o David Duke, PhD, Pres.
PO Box 188
Mandeville, LA 70470
Ph: (985)626-7714
Fax: (985)624-3351
E-mail: info44@davidduke.com
URL: http://www.whitecivilrights.com
Contact: David Duke PhD, Pres.
Founded: 2000. **Membership Dues:** associate, $25 (annual) ● principal, $100 (annual). **Description:** Works to defend the rights and interests of European-Americans. Increases public awareness and understanding of issues vital to the rights and well being of European-Americans. **Computer Services:** Online services, update list. **Publications:** Report.

16758 ■ First Amendment Foundation
3321 12th St. NE
Washington, DC 20017
Ph: (202)529-4225
Fax: (202)526-4611
E-mail: info@firstamend.org
URL: http://www.firstamend.org
Contact: Kit Gage, Exec. Dir.
Founded: 1985. **Staff:** 1. **Budget:** $50,000. **Description:** Seeks to protect the rights of free expression for individuals and organizations. Disseminates educational information on the first amendment. Conducts research. **Libraries: Type:** reference. **Holdings:** archival material, books. **Awards:** Thomas I. Emerson First Amendment Protector Tribute Award. **Frequency:** periodic. **Type:** recognition. **Recipient:** for active protection of First Amendment rights. **Publications:** *At War With Peace: U.S. Covert Operations.* Monograph. Summarizes the history and covert operations by the CIA, 1947-1990. ● *The FBI vs. Black Voting Rights.* Pamphlet ● *The FBI vs. the First Amendment.* Book ● *Political Smears - A Technique for Suppression.* Pamphlet ● *Terrorism and the Constitution.* Book ● *Uncertain Future: Thought Control and Repression During the Reagan-Bush Era.* Book ● *The Vigil: Remembering Lovejoy.* Film. **Conventions/Meetings:** annual board meeting ● periodic conference ● seminar.

16759 ■ Freedom of Expression Foundation (FOEF)
UTC 106
California State Univ.
Long Beach, CA 90840-2801
Ph: (562)985-4313 (562)434-2284
Fax: (562)985-4259
E-mail: crsmith@csulb.edu
URL: http://www.csulb.edu/~crsmith/1amendment.html
Contact: Dr. Craig R. Smith, Pres.
Founded: 1983. **Members:** 300. **Membership Dues:** corporation, $2,500 (annual). **Staff:** 5. **Budget:** $125,000. **Description:** Corporations, foundations, broadcasters, producers, academics, publishers, and other individuals interested in First Amendment rights. Seeks to provide information to Congress and the public concerning freedom of speech as guaranteed by the First Amendment. Maintains Education and Research Fund which informs the public of issues. Funds the Center for First Amendment Studies on the campus of California Statue University, Long Beach. **Publications:** *Filings with FCC*, periodic ● *The First Amendment in the Information Age* ● *First Amendment Rights of Advertisers*, annual. Book. Includes commercial and advertising. **Price:** $30.00. Alternate Formats: online ● *Freedom of Expression Foundation—Newsletter*, quarterly. **Price:** included in

membership dues. **Circulation:** 500 ● *The Quest for Charisma (Praeger, 2000)* ● *Silencing the Opposition: Government Strategies of Suppression (State University of NY Press, 1996)* ● *To Form a More Perfect Union (U. Press of America, 1993)* ● Videos.

16760 ■ Freedom Forum
1101 Wilson Blvd.
Arlington, VA 22209
Ph: (703)528-0800
Fax: (703)284-3770
E-mail: news@freedomforum.org
URL: http://www.freedomforum.org
Contact: Peter S. Prichard, Pres.
Founded: 1991. **Multinational. Description:** Works for free press, free speech, and free spirit for all people. **Awards:** Al Neuharth Free Spirit of the Year Award. **Frequency:** annual. **Type:** monetary. **Recipient:** to an individual who has demonstrated exceptional free spirit. **Divisions:** First Amendment Freedoms; Newseum; Newsroom Diversity; World Press Freedom. **Publications:** *The Freedom Forum Annual Report*, annual. Alternate Formats: online.

16761 ■ Gay and Lesbian Advocates and Defenders (GLAD)
30 Winter St., Ste.800
Boston, MA 02108
Ph: (617)426-1350
Free: (800)455-GLAD
Fax: (617)426-3594
E-mail: gladlaw@glad.org
URL: http://www.glad.org
Contact: Lee Swislow, Exec. Dir.
Founded: 1978. **Staff:** 16. **Budget:** $525,000. **Languages:** English, Spanish. **Description:** Attorneys working to defend the civil rights of lesbians, gay men, transgendered individuals, and people with HIV. Operates AIDS Law Project. Conducts educational programs, impact litigation, advocacy, and a lawyer and referral service within New England. **Publications:** *GLAD Briefs*, periodic. Newsletter. Includes information on recent cases, legislation affecting civil rights issues, and organization activities. ● Annual Report, annual.

16762 ■ The Generation After (TGA)
Box 14, Homecrest Sta.
Brooklyn, NY 11229
Ph: (718)743-6640
Contact: John Ranz, Exec.Dir.
Founded: 1979. **Members:** 3,000. **Membership Dues:** universal, $20 (annual). **Staff:** 2. **State Groups:** 1. **Local Groups:** 1. **Description:** Individuals working to eradicate anti-Semitism and racism, ethnic prejudice and human injustices by exhorting human rights and social justice. Seeks to: accumulate and store data of neo-Nazi groups, their leaders' names and addresses; share such information with local authorities to prevent violence that might be caused by such groups; monitor neo-Nazi newspapers in the United States. Conducts educational outreach at schools and colleges offering a strong humanistic view of life and warning against the evils of Nazism and racism. Has organized demonstrations at deportation hearings for Nazi war criminals, against apartheid and the South African government, and against former president Ronald Reagan's visit to Bitburg, Germany. Sends speakers to colleges, high schools, synagogues, churches, and senior centers. Maintains museum; operates speakers' bureau; conducts educational, charitable, and research programs. **Libraries: Type:** reference. **Holdings:** books, clippings, periodicals. **Absorbed:** Holocaust Survivors Association, U.S.A. **Publications:** *The Generation After*, quarterly. Newsletter. Contains information relevant to the struggle for a better world. **Price:** included in membership dues. **Circulation:** 4,000. **Conventions/Meetings:** annual congress (exhibits) ● monthly Forum - meeting (exhibits).

16763 ■ Independence Institute (II)
13952 Denver W Pkwy., Ste.400
Golden, CO 80401
Ph: (303)279-6536
Fax: (303)279-4176

E-mail: jess@i2i.org
URL: http://i2i.org
Contact: Jon Caldara, Pres.
Founded: 1985. **Description:** Resolves important issues facing communities, including education, healthcare costs, economic freedom, violent crime. Emphasizes private-sector and community-based solutions. **Publications:** *Independent Inking*, bimonthly. Newsletter ● *Independent Voices*. Audiotape ● *Issue Backgrounders*. Articles. Provides a short but in-depth investigation of timely policy issues. Alternate Formats: online ● Papers. **Conventions/Meetings:** conference ● monthly meeting, with issue speakers.

16764 ■ Intelligence Project
400 Washington Ave.
Montgomery, AL 36104
Ph: (334)956-8200
URL: http://www.splcenter.org/intel
Contact: Joe Roy, Dir.
Founded: 1981. **Budget:** $230,000. **Description:** Gathers and disseminates information about the Ku Klux Klan and creates a body of law to protect the rights of those the Klan is attacking. Collects information from 13,000 U.S. publications and other sources concerning the Klan. Conducts educational programs and distributes films for school children. Compiles statistics. **Convention/Meeting:** none. **Libraries: Type:** reference. **Holdings:** books, periodicals. **Subjects:** white supremacy. **Affiliated With:** Southern Poverty Law Center. **Formerly:** (1998) Klanwatch. **Publications:** *Free at Last* ● *Hate, Violence, and White Supremacy - A Decade Review 1980-1990.* Report ● *Hatewatch*, monthly. Newsletter. Alternate Formats: online ● *Intelligence Report*, quarterly. Magazine. Updates law enforcement, the media, and the public on the activity it investigates. ● *Klanwatch Intelligence Report*, bimonthly. Contains updates on white supremacy activities throughout the United States. **Price:** free. **Circulation:** 6,000 ● *Klanwatch Law Report*, quarterly. Contains updates on the activities of Klanwatch and the Southern Poverty Law Center. **Price:** free. **Circulation:** 120,000 ● *The Ku Klux Klan: A History of Racism and Violence* ● *Terror in Our Neighborhoods: Report on Housing Violence*.

16765 ■ Jews for the Preservation of Firearms Ownership (JPFO)
PO Box 270143
Hartford, WI 53027
Ph: (262)673-9745
Free: (800)869-1884
Fax: (262)673-9746
E-mail: jpfo@jpfo.org
URL: http://www.jpfo.org
Contact: Aaron Zelman, Founder/Exec. Dir.
Founded: 1989. **Members:** 7,000. **Membership Dues:** individual in U.S., $25 (annual) ● life, $500 ● individual outside U.S., $35 (annual). **Staff:** 3. **Budget:** $175,000. **State Groups:** 1. **Description:** Individuals dedicated to advancing the civil right of law abiding persons to be armed. Works toward "destroying the concept that gun control is a beneficial policy". Conducts research programs. Promotes public education regarding citizens' right to bear arms, and maintains that it is dangerous to individuals' safety and rights for the government to have guns while the public is disarmed. **Libraries: Type:** not open to the public. **Holdings:** 500. **Subjects:** Holocaust, world genocides, government, history, Bill of Rights. **Computer Services:** Mailing lists, of members. **Publications:** *Bill of Rights Sentinel*, periodic. Magazine. **Price:** $5.00/copy. **Circulation:** 7,000. Alternate Formats: online ● *Death by Gun Control: The Human Cost of Victim Disarmament.* Booklet ● *Dial 911 and Die.* Contains opinions about the truth of police protection myth. ● *Gun Control: Gateway to Tyranny.* Book. Compares the texts of the U.S. Gun Control Act of 1968 and the Nazi Weapons Law of 1938. **Price:** $22.90 ● *Hope: A Novel About A New President Who Practices Strict Bill of Rights Enforcement.* Booklet ● *I Will Live Free.* Includes musical CD-Rom. Alternate Formats: CD-ROM ● *The State vs. the People: Re-Rise of the American Police State.* Booklet. Alternate Formats: online ● *Television*

Documentary: Innocents Betrayed. Booklet ● *The Warsaw Ghetto Uprising.*

16766 ■ Judge David L. Bazelon Center for Mental Health Law

1101 15th St. NW, Ste.1212
Washington, DC 20005
Ph: (202)467-5730
Fax: (202)223-0409
E-mail: info@bazelon.org
URL: http://www.bazelon.org
Contact: Robert Bernstein PhD, Exec. Dir.

Founded: 1972. **Staff:** 27. **Budget:** $2,600,000. **Description:** Aims to clarify, establish, and advance the legal rights of people with mental and developmental disabilities. Provides technical assistance and training to lawyers, consumer groups, providers of mental health and supported housing services, and policymakers at federal, state, and local levels. Has staff attorneys that have represented individual plaintiffs and leading national consumer and professional associations in landmark lawsuits that have established many rights of people with mental and developmental disabilities including the rights to: appropriate education, compensation for institution-maintaining labor, and fair consideration for access to federal assistance. Works to expand community-living opportunities for adults and children with disabilities and to protect their civil rights under the American With Disabilities Act and Fair Housing Act. **Libraries: Type:** reference. **Holdings:** 1,500. **Subjects:** mental disability, law. **Telecommunication Services:** TDD, (202)467-4232. **Committees:** Leadership 21. **Formerly:** (1993) Mental Health Law Project. **Publications:** *A Family Advocate's Guide: Managed Behavioral Health Care for Children and Youth.* Handbook ● *Arrested? What Happens to Your Benefits If You Go to Jail or Prison?.* Booklet. **Price:** $2.50. Alternate Formats: online ● *At Home: Strategies for Serving Older People with Mental Disabilities in the Community.* Report. **Price:** $11.50 ● *Digest of Cases and other Resources on Fair Housing for People with Disabilities* ● *Elders Assert Their Rights.* Booklet. Guides residents, family members and advocates to the legal rights of elderly people with mental disabilities in nursing homes. **Price:** $6.95 each (for 1-4 copies); $6.00 each (for 5-14 copies); $5.35 each (for 15-49 copies); $4.50 each (for 50 or more copies) ● *Finding the Key to Successful Transition from Jail to Community.* Booklet. **Price:** $3.00 ● *In Brief,* quarterly. Newsletter. **Price:** free. Alternate Formats: online ● *Integration of Primary Care and Behavioral Health.* Report. **Price:** $4.00. Alternate Formats: online ● *Making Child Welfare Work.* Booklet. Describes Alabama's unique system reform. **Price:** $12.40 ● *Making Sense of Medicaid for Children with Serious Emotional Disturbance.* Report. **Price:** $18.90 ● *Minority Advocacy Notebook.* Handbook. **Price:** $11.00 ● *Outreach and Advocacy for Black and Hispanic People with Mental Disabilities.* Manual. Contains information for cross-cultural training of advocates. Includes research articles. **Price:** $63.00 ● *Relinquishing Custody: The Tragic Results of Failing to Meet Children's Mental Health Needs.* Reprint. Covers why parents in at least half the states are having to give up custody to access mental health services for their child. **Price:** $10.00 ● *What "Fair Housing" Means for People with Disabilities.* Handbook ● *Where to Turn: Confusion in Medicaid Policies on Screening Children for Mental Health Needs.* Report. **Price:** $12.90 ● *Your Family and Managed Care.* Booklet ● Annual Report, annual. Alternate Formats: online.

16767 ■ Leadership Conference on Civil Rights (LCCR)

1629 K St. NW, 10th Fl.
Washington, DC 20006
Ph: (202)466-3311
Fax: (202)466-3435
E-mail: grassroots@civilrights.org
URL: http://www.civilrights.org
Contact: Wade Henderson Esq., Pres./CEO

Founded: 1950. **Members:** 185. **Description:** Coalition of national organizations working to promote passage of civil rights, social and economic legislation, and enforcement of laws already on the books; has released studies examining former President Ronald Reagan's tax and budget programs in areas including housing, elementary and secondary education, social welfare, and Indian affairs, and tax cuts. Evaluates the enforcement of activities in civil rights by the U.S. Department of Justice; has also reviewed civil rights activities of the U.S. Department of Education. **Awards:** Hubert H. Humphrey Civil Rights Award. **Frequency:** annual. **Type:** recognition. **Recipient:** for individuals or organizations that best exemplify Vice President Humphrey's legacy of selfless and devoted service in the cause of equality. **Committees:** Compliance and Enforcement; Education; Employment; Federal Regulatory Agencies; Health and Welfare; Housing; Legislative; Veteran's Affairs; Women's Rights. **Formerly:** Civil Rights Mobilization. **Publications:** *LCCR Memo* ● Reports. Alternate Formats: online. **Conventions/Meetings:** annual conference.

16768 ■ League of the South (LS)

PO Box 760
Killen, AL 35645
Ph: (256)757-6789
Free: (800)888-3163
Fax: (256)757-6768
E-mail: 76071.326@compuserve.com
URL: http://www.dixienet.org
Contact: Dr. Michael Hill, Pres.

Founded: 1994. **State Groups:** 18. **Description:** Advances the cultural, social, economic and political well-being and independence of the Southern people. **Computer Services:** Mailing lists, of members. **Publications:** *Dixienet Gazette.* Paper. Contains a collection of essays about Confederate issues and freedom. Alternate Formats: online ● *Southern Patriot,* bimonthly. Journal. Alternate Formats: online.

16769 ■ Media Coalition

275 Seventh Ave., Ste.1504
New York, NY 10003
Ph: (212)587-4025
Fax: (212)587-2436
E-mail: info@mediacoalition.org
URL: http://www.mediacoalition.org
Contact: David Horowitz, Exec. Dir.

Founded: 1973. **Members:** 12. **Staff:** 2. **Budget:** $350,000. **Description:** Trade associations united to defend the First Amendment right to produce and distribute books, magazines, recordings, videogames and videotapes. Monitors censorship legislation at the federal and state level; files legal challenges to unconstitutional laws and amicus curial briefs in cases involving First Amendment rights of producers and distributors of constitutionally protected works. Gathers and disseminates material, including public opinion polls and reports, on censorship and First Amendment issues. **Libraries: Type:** reference. **Holdings:** books, reports. **Subjects:** violence, censorship, hate speech, religious right, legal history, sexually explicit materials, biography, women's studies, general selections, television, film, youth violence, video games, pornography, internet, zoning effects, legislation, First Amendment, Catherine MacKinnon. **Formed by Merger of:** Media Coalition and Americans for Constitutional Freedom. **Formerly:** (2003) Media Coalition/Americans for Constitutional Freedom. **Publications:** *Catharine A. MacKinnon: The Rise of a Feminist Censor, 1983-1993.* Report. Alternate Formats: online ● *The Rev. Donald Wildmon's Crusade for Censorship, 1977-1992.* Report. Alternate Formats: online ● *Sense and Censorship: The Vanity of Bonfires.* Report ● *Shooting the Messenger: Why Censorship Won't Stop Violence.* Report. Alternate Formats: online.

16770 ■ National Alliance Against Racist and Political Repression (NAARPR)

1325 S Wabash Ave., Ste.105
Chicago, IL 60605
Ph: (312)939-2750
Fax: (773)929-2613
URL: http://www.naarpr.org/chicago/home/index.php
Contact: Clarice Durham, Co-Chair

Founded: 1970. **Members:** 38. **Membership Dues:** individual, $15 (annual). **State Groups:** 5. **Local Groups:** 5. **Description:** Aims to give justice to those who are condemned by the criminal justice system. Campaigns against official and unofficial police crimes, and works to abolish the death penalty. Works to defend and extend affirmative action programs. **Awards:** Human Rights Award. **Frequency:** annual. **Type:** recognition. **Recipient:** for outstanding contributions in human rights. **Formerly:** (1995) Alliance to End Repression. **Publications:** *The Illinois Organizer,* quarterly. Newsletter.

16771 ■ National Association for the Advancement of Colored People (NAACP)

4805 Mt. Hope Dr.
Baltimore, MD 21215
Ph: (410)580-5777
Free: (877)NAACP-98
Fax: (410)358-3818
E-mail: info@naacp.org
URL: http://www.naacp.org
Contact: Bruce S. Gordon, Pres./CEO

Founded: 1909. **Members:** 400,000. **Membership Dues:** youth age 17 and under (without magazine subscription), $10 (annual) ● youth age 18-20 (with magazine subscription), $15 (annual) ● regular adult (age 21 and older), $30 (annual) ● corporate, $5,000 (annual) ● junior life, $100 ● bronze life, $400 ● silver life, $750 ● gold life, $1,500 ● diamond life, $2,500. **Staff:** 132. **Local Groups:** 1,802. **Description:** Persons "of all races and religions" who believe in the objectives and methods of the NAACP. Works to achieve equal rights through the democratic process and eliminate racial prejudice by removing racial discrimination in housing, employment, voting, schools, the courts, transportation, recreation, prisons, and business enterprises. Offers referral services, tutorials, job referrals, and day care. Sponsors seminars; maintains law library. Sponsors the NAACP National Housing Corporation to assist in the development of low and moderate income housing for families. Compiles statistics. **Awards:** Spingarn Medal. **Frequency:** annual. **Type:** medal. **Recipient:** to a black American for his/her distinguished achievement. **Committees:** Health; International Affairs; Legal; Spingarn Medal; Walter White Award. **Departments:** Economic Development; Voter Education and Registration; Washington Bureau. **Programs:** Prison; Youth. **Publications:** *Crisis,* 10/year. Magazine. **Advertising:** accepted. Alternate Formats: online ● Annual Report, annual. **Conventions/Meetings:** annual meeting - usually June/July.

16772 ■ National Association for the Advancement of Colored People Legal Defense and Educational Fund (LDF)

99 Hudson St., Ste.1600
New York, NY 10013
Ph: (212)965-2200
Free: (800)221-7822
Fax: (212)226-7592
E-mail: gworley@naacpldf.org
URL: http://www.naacpldf.org
Contact: Theodore M. Shaw, Pres./Dir.-Counsel

Founded: 1940. **Staff:** 68. **Budget:** $8,900,000. **Description:** Legal arm of the civil rights movement, functioning independently from and no longer part of the National Association for the Advancement of Colored People (see separate entry) since the mid-1950s. Works to provide and support litigation in behalf of blacks, other racial minorities, and women defending their legal and constitutional rights against discrimination in employment, education, housing, and other areas. Represents civil rights groups as well as individual citizens who have bonafide civil rights claims. Contributed funds are used to finance court actions for equality in schools, jobs, voting, housing, municipal services, land use, and delivery of health care services. Has organized litigation campaign for prison reform and the abolition of capital punishment. Maintains Herbert Lehman Education Fund, through which scholarships are awarded to black students attending state universities; sponsors Earl Warren Legal Training Program (see separate entry), which provides scholarships to black law students. Compiles statistics on capital punishment. Committee of 100, a voluntary cooperative group of individuals, has sponsored the appeal of the fund since 1943. **Libraries: Type:** not open to the public. **Holdings:** 15,000. **Subjects:** law. **Absorbed:** (1974) National Office for the Rights of the Indigent. **Publications:** *Equal Justice*, quarterly. Newsletter. Alternate Formats: online ● Annual Report, annual. Alternate Formats: online ● Also publishes legal materials, brochures, press releases, and occasional watchdog reports.

16773 ■ National Association of Korean Americans (NAKA)

3883 Plaza Dr.
Fairfax, VA 22030
Ph: (703)267-2388
Fax: (703)267-2396
E-mail: nakausa@naka.org
URL: http://www.naka.org
Contact: William T. Cho, Pres.

Founded: 1994. **Members:** 900. **Membership Dues:** associate, student, limited income, $10 (annual) ● life, $1,000 ● regular, $30 (annual). **Staff:** 4. **Regional Groups:** 3. **Description:** Individuals of Korean descent living in the United States. Seeks to safeguard the human and civil rights of Korean Americans; promotes friendly relations between Korean-Americans and other racial and ethnic groups. Conducts educational programs. **Awards:** NAKA Award. **Frequency:** annual. **Type:** recognition. **Publications:** *Korean American Voice*, quarterly. Newsletter ● Brochure ● Papers. Alternate Formats: online. **Conventions/Meetings:** annual board meeting and luncheon, with panel discussions, workshops, and cultural performances (exhibits) ● annual convention.

16774 ■ National Association for Rights Protection and Advocacy (NARPA)

PO Box 40585
Tuscaloosa, AL 35404
Ph: (205)464-0101
E-mail: narpa@aol.com
URL: http://www.narpa.org
Contact: Jim Gottstein, Pres.

Founded: 1980. **Membership Dues:** basic, $35 (annual) ● sponsor, $50 (annual) ● organization, $100 (annual) ● subsidized, $25 (annual). **Description:** Represents individuals working or interested in rights protection and advocacy for recipients of mental health services. Aims to work for better rights protection and advocacy services and to provide a means of sharing information and support among those working in the field. Maintains speakers' bureau. **Publications:** *Membership Roster*, annual. Membership Directory ● *The Rights Tenet*, quarterly. Newsletter. Alternate Formats: online ● Proceedings, annual. **Conventions/Meetings:** annual conference (exhibits).

16775 ■ National Catholic Conference for Interracial Justice (NCCIJ)

c/o The White House
1600 Pennsylvania Ave. NW
Washington, DC 20500
Ph: (202)456-1414 (202)529-6480
Fax: (202)456-2461
URL: http://clinton4.nara.gov/Initiatives/OneAmerica/
   Practices/pp_19980803.17202.html
Contact: Rev. Joseph M. Conrad Jr., Exec. Dir.

Founded: 1960. **Members:** 6,000. **Membership Dues:** individual, $35 (annual) ● organization, $200 (annual) ● parish, $100 (annual). **Staff:** 4. **Description:** Represents Catholic organization working for interracial justice and social concerns in America. Initiates programs within and outside the Catholic Church to end discrimination in community development, education, and employment. **Publications:** *Commitment*, quarterly. Newsletter. **Advertising:** accepted ● *LASER: Creating Unity in Diversity* ● *Martin Luther King Jr. Holiday Celebration Packet* ● *Pentecost: A Feast for all Peoples* ● *Workshops on Racism* ● Pamphlets. **Conventions/Meetings:** annual meeting.

16776 ■ National Committee Against Repressive Legislation (NCARL)

3321 12th St. NE
Washington, DC 20017
Ph: (202)529-4225
Fax: (202)526-4611
E-mail: info@ncarl.org
URL: http://ncarl.org
Contact: Kit Gage, Dir.

Founded: 1960. **Staff:** 1. **Budget:** $25,000. **Description:** Promotes First Amendment Rights as they oppose repressive laws and inquisitorial activities of government. Focuses special concern on reform of federal criminal laws and control of federal intelligence gathering agencies; seeks to ban covert operations by the CIA and what the group feels is political spying and harassment by the FBI. Maintains speakers' bureau, prepares and distributes literature, and carries out other educational and political action programs. Conducts research. **Libraries: Type:** reference. **Holdings:** books. **Subjects:** civil liberties. **Awards:** Lillian Hellman-Dashiell Hammett Award. **Frequency:** periodic. **Type:** recognition. **Committees:** Coordinating. **Formerly:** (1960) National Committee to Abolish HUAC; (1970) Committee to Abolish HUAC/HISC. **Publications:** *At War with Peace: U.S. Covert Operations* ● *NCARL Letter*, monthly. Newsletter. Alternate Formats: online. **Conventions/Meetings:** annual meeting.

16777 ■ National Committee to Reopen the Rosenberg Case (NCRRC)

c/o Richard Corey, Co-Dir.
PO Box 1100
New York, NY 10113-1100
Ph: (718)667-4740
E-mail: mail@rosenbergtrial.org
URL: http://www.rosenbergtrial.org
Contact: Richard Corey, Co-Dir.

Founded: 1960. **Members:** 9,000. **Description:** Aims to reopen the Rosenberg-Sobell case legally, legislatively, and politically, and to establish the innocence of Ethel and Julius Rosenberg and Morton Sobell. (The Rosenbergs were convicted at the height of McCarthyism in 1951 and electrocuted June 19, 1953, for conspiring to commit espionage. Sobell received a 30-year prison sentence.) Campaigns to open all Rosenberg files under the Freedom of Information Act as amended in 1974, and for appointment of a congressional or government commission of inquiry. Rosenberg sons, Robert and Michael Meeropol, instituted a lawsuit against a number of government agencies due to inadequate response to requests for information, with partial success. Urges proclamation for full pardon for Julius and Ethel Rosenberg and Morton Sobell. Maintains speakers' bureau; sponsors research and educational programs. **Libraries: Type:** reference. **Holdings:** archival material, artwork, books, clippings, periodicals. **Subjects:** Rosenberg case. **Publications:** *The Kaufman Papers* ● *National Committee to Reopen the Rosenberg Case—Newsletter*, periodic. Includes book reviews and newly discovered evidence. **Price:** free ● *Poems and Songs for Ethel and Julius Rosenberg* ● Film, semiannual. **Price:** free ● Also publishes press releases and fact sheets. **Conventions/Meetings:** annual Memorial for Julius and Ethel Rosenberg - conference (exhibits) - held around June 19th ● periodic seminar.

16778 ■ National Drug Strategy Network (NDSN)

c/o Criminal Justice Policy Foundation
8730 Georgia Ave., Ste.400
Silver Spring, MD 20910
Ph: (301)589-6020
Fax: (301)589-5056
E-mail: ndsn@ndsn.org
URL: http://www.ndsn.org
Contact: Eric E. Sterling, Coor.

Founded: 1989. **Description:** Government officials, business leaders, scholars, religious leaders, attorneys, civil libertarians, health care professionals, criminal justice officials, and community activists sharing information on the "War on Drugs". Sponsors training seminars; maintains speakers' bureau. Li-

braries: **Type:** not open to the public. **Holdings:** 1,000. **Subjects:** drugs, crime, politics, law. **Computer Services:** Online services, publication. **Publications:** *News Briefs*. Newsletter. Provides complete citations to news stories, journal articles, research, legislation and regulations. Alternate Formats: online.

16779 ■ National Organization for the Reform of Marijuana Laws (NORML)

1600 K St. NW, Ste.501
Washington, DC 20006-2832
Ph: (202)483-5500
Fax: (202)483-0057
E-mail: norml@norml.org
URL: http://www.norml.org
Contact: Stephen W. Dillon Esq., Chm.

Founded: 1970. **Members:** 80,000. **Membership Dues:** $25-$250 (annual) ● life, $2,500. **Staff:** 5. **Budget:** $400,000. **State Groups:** 80. **Languages:** English, Spanish. **Description:** Serves as a public education organization working for change in U.S. policy regarding marijuana. Seeks a more reasonable treatment of marijuana consumers in federal, state, and local laws and policies. Provides speakers for interested groups; collects and disseminates educational materials; provides testimony for legislative committees; coordinates chapters around the country. Provides information on urinalysis testing. **Libraries: Type:** reference. **Holdings:** 10,000; articles, books, clippings. **Subjects:** marijuana, marijuana prohibition, medicinal marijuana, hemp. **Computer Services:** Online services. **Committees:** Emergency Coalition for Medical Cannabis; Legal. **Councils:** Marijuana and Health. **Publications:** *Citizen's Guide to Marijuana Laws*, annual. State-by-state breakdown of penalties and regulations for marijuana offenses. ● *The Leaflet*, quarterly. Newsletter. Provides the facts, analysis, and activist tips needed to reform marijuana laws. Contains updates on current legislation and research. **Price:** included in membership dues. **Circulation:** 10,000. **Advertising:** accepted. Alternate Formats: online ● *Legislative Bulletin*, quarterly. Newsletter. **Price:** included in membership dues. Alternate Formats: online ● *Ongoing Briefing*, monthly. Provides detailed background information on policy, legislation, judicial action, and marijuana related research. ● *Potpourri*, monthly. Reviews important marijuana related developments in the news. ● Reports, periodic. Features an in-depth analysis of issues such as military involvement in the Drug War, marijuana potency, and myths about marijuana. ● Pamphlets. Covers health, economics, justice, medicinal marijuana, children, and urinalysis. **Conventions/Meetings:** annual conference (exhibits) ● annual seminar.

16780 ■ National Urban League (NUL)

120 Wall St., 8th Fl.
New York, NY 10005
Ph: (212)558-5300
Fax: (212)344-5332
E-mail: info@nul.org
URL: http://www.nul.org
Contact: Marc H. Morial, Pres./CEO

Founded: 1910. **Members:** 50,000. **Staff:** 100. **Budget:** $18,900,000. **Local Groups:** 114. **Description:** Voluntary nonpartisan community service agency of civic, professional, business, labor, and religious leaders with a staff of trained social workers and other professionals. Aims to eliminate racial segregation and discrimination in the United States and to achieve parity for blacks and other minorities in every phase of American life. Works to eliminate institutional racism and to provide direct service to minorities in the areas of employment, housing, education, social welfare, health, family planning, mental retardation, law and consumer affairs, youth and student affairs, labor affairs, veterans' affairs, and community and minority business development. Maintains research department in Washington, DC. **Programs:** Black Executive Exchange; National Urban League Incentives To Excel and Succeed; Social Welfare; Summer Internship. **Projects:** Seniors in Community Service; Teenage Pregnancy. **Publications:** *BEEP Newsletter*, quarterly. Describes BEEP courses. Includes member news and listing of publications. ● *Com-*

munity Surveys and Reports, periodic ● *Opportunity Journal*, periodic. Magazine. Contains in-depth and scholarly analysis of issues. **Price:** $4.95 plus shipping and handling ● *The State of Black America*, annual. Journal. Addresses the issues central to black America. **Price:** $29.95 plus shipping and handling ● *The Urban League News*, quarterly. Newsletter. Features information on league program and activities. **Price:** included in membership dues. **Circulation:** 50,000. **Conventions/Meetings:** annual meeting (exhibits).

16781 ■ New Age Citizen (NAC)

PO Box 419
Dearborn Heights, MI 48127
Ph: (313)704-0021
E-mail: newagecitizenx@comcast.net
URL: http://www.newagecitizen.com
Contact: Bruce W. Cain, Ed.
Founded: 1989. **Members:** 1,200. **Staff:** 4. **State Groups:** 3. **Description:** Drug, environmental, and social policy reform activists. Works to legalize marijuana and other psychotropic drugs. Promotes public awareness of what the group believes to be the benefits of ending drug prohibition and the negative constitutional, social, and economic consequences of continuing with current drug policy. Sponsors International Drug Policy Day. Maintains Speaker's Bureau. **Libraries:** Type: reference. **Holdings:** 8. **Subjects:** drug policy and legalization. **Formerly:** (2001) New Age Patriot. **Publications:** *Regulated Drug Legalization, Education, and Rehabilitation: A Framework for Safely Legalizing All Drugs* ● Magazine, quarterly. **Price:** $15.00/year. **Circulation:** 8,000. **Advertising:** accepted. Alternate Formats: CD-ROM.

16782 ■ Omega First Amendment Legal Fund (OFALF)

c/o Mark H. Carson and Associates, P.C.
1790 30th St., Ste.418
Boulder, CO 80301
Ph: (303)449-3060
Fax: (303)449-2747
E-mail: mark@bouldercpas.com
URL: http://www.bouldercpas.com
Contact: Mark H. Carson JD, Contact
Founded: 1988. **Description:** Raises funds to appeal a court judgment against Omega Group Ltd., publisher of *Soldier of Fortune* magazine. (Omega Group was ordered to pay $9.4 million in damages to the family of a woman whose killer was hired through a *Soldier of Fortune* classified advertisement. Omega Group maintains that the magazine was exercising its First Amendment rights by publishing the advertisement and that the ruling is an infringement of those rights).

16783 ■ Online Privacy Alliance (OPA)

c/o Christine Varney, Pres.
Hogan and Hartson
555 13th St. NW
Washington, DC 20004
Ph: (202)637-5600
E-mail: webmaster@privacyalliance.org
URL: http://www.privacyalliance.org
Contact: Christine Varney, Pres.
Members: 90. **Description:** Represents companies and associations. Works to promote privacy online and privacy practices.

16784 ■ Partnership for Civil Justice Legal Defense and Education Fund (PCJ LDEF)

c/o Partnership for Civil Justice
10 G St. NE, Ste.650
Washington, DC 20002
Ph: (202)789-4330
Fax: (202)789-4333
E-mail: demo_support@justiceonline.org
URL: http://www.justiceonline.org
Contact: Atty. Carl Messineo, Co-Founder
Description: Founded by civil rights attorneys in Washington, DC. Provides and supports exclusively charitable and educational activities that secure and advance civil rights under the law, and that work towards the elimination of discrimination and preju-

dice. **Projects:** Emergency Campaign to Defend Dissent and Advance Civil Rights.

16785 ■ People for the American Way (PFAW)

2000 M St. NW, Ste.400
Washington, DC 20036
Ph: (202)467-4999
Free: (800)326-7329
Fax: (202)293-2672
E-mail: pfaw@pfaw.org
URL: http://www.pfaw.org
Contact: Ralph G. Neas, Pres.
Founded: 1980. **Members:** 600,000. **Membership Dues:** individual, $35 (annual). **Staff:** 90. **Budget:** $4,200,000. **State Groups:** 6. **Description:** Nonpartisan constitutional liberties organization. Religious, business, media, and labor figures committed to reaffirming the traditional American values of pluralism, diversity, and freedom of expression and religion. Believes that the individual still matters in the society. Improves the quality of life by strengthening the things that unite citizens. Engages in a mass media campaign to create a positive climate of tolerance and respect for diverse peoples, religions, and values. Maintains speakers' bureau; conducts research programs; compiles statistics. Operates National Resource Center, a collection of printed and visual materials. **Libraries:** Type: open to the public. **Holdings:** 1,000; articles, books, periodicals, video recordings. **Subjects:** first amendment, political right. **Awards:** Spirit of Liberty. **Frequency:** annual. **Type:** recognition. **Recipient:** for extraordinary contributions. **Subgroups:** Administration; Center for Values in American Life; Communications; Development; Public Policy; Research; Strategic Planning; Young People For Project. **Absorbed:** (1982) Moral Alternatives; (1985) Citizens for Constitutional Concerns. **Publications:** Also publishes issue papers, reports, and books. **Conventions/Meetings:** semiannual board meeting.

16786 ■ People's Rights Fund

39 W 14th St., No. 206
New York, NY 10011
Ph: (212)633-6646
Fax: (212)633-2889
E-mail: donations@peoplesrightsfund.org
URL: http://www.peoplesrightsfund.org
Founded: 1986. **Description:** Provides an alternative to mainstream charities. Provides funding for educational programs on peace, civil rights, civil liberties, economic inequality, anti-repression and social justice issues. Allocates grants which fund conferences, meetings, seminars, classes, national speaking tours and other activities around the country which fulfill its goal of educating the public about important international and local issues. Seeks to provide funding for the dissemination of information not found in the daily print or electronic media; donates funds to organizations for the purposes of publishing books, pamphlets, fact sheets and other literature and for producing videos which educate the public about the above issues. **Awards:** Type: grant. **Projects:** Colombia; People's Video Network.

16787 ■ Peoples Rights Organization (PRO)

4444 Indianola Ave.
Columbus, OH 43214-2226
Ph: (614)268-0122
Fax: (614)268-0122
E-mail: terenceregan@peoplesrights.org
URL: http://www.peoplesrights.org
Contact: Terence Regan, Chm.
Founded: 1989. **Membership Dues:** individual, $30 (annual) ● life, $360. **Description:** Protects human rights set forth in the U.S. Constitution, especially in regards to the Second Amendment. **Publications:** *PROponent*. Newsletter. **Price:** included in membership dues.

16788 ■ Prejudice Institute/Center for the Applied Study of Ethnoviolence

2743 Maryland Ave.
Baltimore, MD 21218
Ph: (410)366-9654 (410)243-6987
Fax: (410)366-9656

E-mail: prejinst@aol.com
URL: http://www.prejudiceinstitute.org
Contact: Howard J. Ehrlich PhD, Exec. Dir.
Founded: 1985. **Staff:** 3. **Description:** Works to study and respond to the problems of prejudice, discrimination, conflict, and violence. Collects, analyzes, produces, and disseminates information and materials on programs of prevention and response. Conducts research on the causes and prevalence of prejudice and violence and their effects on victims and society; provides technical assistance to public agencies, voluntary organizations, schools, and communities in conflict; analyzes and drafts model legislation; conducts educational and training programs. **Libraries:** Type: reference. **Formerly:** Center for the Applied Study of Prejudice and Ethnoviolence; (1986) Institute for Prevention and Control of Violence and Extremism; (1993) National Institute Against Prejudice and Violence. **Publications:** *Ethnoviolence in the Workplace: Summary of Major Findings*. Report. **Price:** $10.00/copy ● *Perspectives: The Newsletter on Prejudice, Ethnoviolence and Social Policy*, bimonthly. **Price:** $50.00 subscription. ISSN: 1097-5955. **Circulation:** 1,000. Alternate Formats: online. **Conventions/Meetings:** periodic conference ● periodic convention and symposium, encourages information exchange among experts ● periodic regional meeting.

16789 ■ Private Citizen, Inc. (PCI)

PO Box 233
Naperville, IL 60566
Ph: (630)393-1555
Free: (800)CUT-JUNK
E-mail: pci@private-citizen.com
URL: http://www.privatecitizen.com
Contact: Robert Bulmash, Pres.
Founded: 1988. **Members:** 4,000. **Membership Dues:** business and personal, $20 (annual). **Staff:** 2. **State Groups:** 5. **For-Profit. Description:** Works to allow individuals to preserve their privacy and regulate the intrusion of junk phone calls and junk mail. Subscribers authorize PCI to notify telemarketers not to solicit them; if telemarketers persist in such solicitation, they are levied with a $500 charge for the subscriber's time. Conducts lobbying for the regulation of telemarketing. Operates speakers' bureau and compiles statistics. **Convention/Meeting:** none. **Libraries:** Type: reference. **Holdings:** 2,000; books, clippings, monographs, periodicals. **Subjects:** direct and database marketing. **Computer Services:** database, names and addresses of telemarketing firms, marketing list sellers and compilers. **Publications:** *Private Citizen Directory*, semiannual. Lists subscribers. **Price:** free. **Circulation:** 1,700. Alternate Formats: diskette; online ● *The Private Citizen News*, annual. Newsletter. **Price:** included in membership dues. **Circulation:** 7,000 ● *So.You want to Sue a Telemarketer*. Book. **Price:** $10.00 for nonmembers; $5.00 for members ● Also publishes list of telemarketers receiving the *Private Citizen Directory*.

16790 ■ Project Equality (PE)

7132 Main St.
Kansas City, MO 64114-1406
Ph: (816)361-9222
Fax: (816)361-8997
E-mail: ces@projectequality.org
URL: http://www.projectequality.org
Contact: Mr. Carlos E. Salazar, Exec. Dir.
Founded: 1965. **Members:** 150. **Membership Dues:** individual, $35-$500 (annual) ● congregational, $50-$500 (annual) ● institutional, $50-$1,000 (annual) ● business, $100-$1,000 (annual) ● corporate, $1,500-$10,000 (annual). **Staff:** 4. **Budget:** $285,000. **State Groups:** 1. **Local Groups:** 2. **Description:** Provides a nationwide interfaith program enabling religious organizations, institutions, and others to support equal opportunity employers with their purchasing power. Includes services such as: validation of hotels for conventions and meetings of organizations, validations of suppliers to member organizations and institutions, and consultant and educational services to assist employers in affirmative action and equal employment opportunity programs. **Computer Services:** Mailing lists, of members, prospective mem-

bers, and participating members. **Publications:** *PE Update, Action, EEO News,* quarterly. Newsletter. Provides information about project advocacy, action focus, and program work with employers and members, equal employment opportunities. **Price:** included in membership dues. **Circulation:** 2,000 ● *Project Equality—Buyer's Guide,* annual. Directory. Lists employers that have provided current equal employment opportunity data and have been validated by the project. **Price:** included in membership dues; $25.00/copy for nonmembers. **Conventions/ Meetings:** annual meeting and seminar (exhibits).

16791 ■ Puerto Rican Legal Defense and Education Fund (PRLDEF)
99 Hudson St., 14th Fl.
New York, NY 10013-2815
Ph: (212)219-3360
Free: (800)328-2322
Fax: (212)431-4276
E-mail: info@prldef.org
URL: http://www.prldef.org
Contact: Cesar A. Perales, Pres./Gen. Counsel

Founded: 1972. **Staff:** 21. **Languages:** English, Spanish. **Description:** Seeks to secure, promote and protect the civil and human rights of the Puerto Rican and wider Latino community. (Three divisions, Legal, Policy and Education, carry out the core program areas - Civil and Human Rights, Civic Engagement and Empowerment, Civil Society and Culture and Equitable Educational Opportunities -the pursuit of a legal career for Puerto Ricans and other minorities via its LSAT prep course, Law Day and other programs.). **Awards:** Law School Scholarship. **Frequency:** annual. **Type:** scholarship. **Recipient:** for Latino law students in the United States. **Telecommunication Services:** electronic mail, cesar_perales@prldef.org. **Divisions:** Development; Education; Legal; Policy. **Programs:** Pro Bono Cooperating Counsel. **Projects:** Lawbound. **Publications:** *Justicia,* quarterly. Newsletter. **Price:** free ● *Politica Social.* Newsletter. Alternate Formats: online ● *PRLDEF In The News.* **Conventions/Meetings:** annual banquet, with awards ● quarterly board meeting ● workshop.

16792 ■ Resisting Defamation
440 El Camino Real
Sunnyvale, CA 94087
E-mail: bosears@resistingdefamation.org
URL: http://www.resistingdefamation.org
Contact: Mr. Bo Sears, Co-Pres.

Founded: 1992. **Members:** 86. **Membership Dues:** family, $20 (annual). **Description:** Works to identify and eliminate ethnic slurs and negative stereotypes, especially those expressed against Americans of European origins. **Libraries: Type:** not open to the public. **Holdings:** 267; books. **Subjects:** English literature, contemporary works on defamation and political correctness, analyses of epistemology and psychology. **Computer Services:** Electronic publishing, online syllabus. **Publications:** *Sensitivity toward European Americans: Diversity within Diversity,* annual. Booklet. Contains a syllabus for free, one-hour seminars. **Price:** $3.00. **Conventions/Meetings:** annual conference.

16793 ■ Rigoberta Menchu Tum Foundation (RMTF)
8 W 40th St., Ste.1610
New York, NY 10017
Ph: (718)836-0424
Fax: (718)836-0424
E-mail: frmtny2002@hotmail.com
URL: http://www.frmt.org

Founded: 1992. **Languages:** English, Spanish. **Multinational. Description:** Works to defend and promote human rights, particularly the rights of indigenous peoples. Conducts educational and health care programs in Guatemala; develops projects relating to housing, urban planning and farming; works to strengthen unity between different groups of indigenous peoples. Maintains Speaker's Bureau. **Publications:** Brochure ● Newsletter.

16794 ■ Second Amendment Foundation (SAF)
12500 NE 10th Pl.
James Madison Bldg.
Bellevue, WA 98005
Ph: (425)454-7012
Free: (800)426-4302
Fax: (425)451-3959
E-mail: adminforweb@saf.org
URL: http://www.saf.org
Contact: Alan Gottlieb, Founder

Founded: 1974. **Members:** 550,000. **Membership Dues:** individual, $15 (annual). **Staff:** 16. **Budget:** $4,400,000. **Description:** Individuals dedicated to promoting a better understanding of "your constitutional right to privately own and possess firearms." Compiles statistics. Operates Speaker's Bureau, and legal referral service. **Libraries: Type:** reference. **Holdings:** 80; archival material. **Subjects:** right to keep and bear arms. **Awards:** James Madison Award. **Frequency:** quarterly. **Type:** recognition. **Recipient:** to pro-gun rights columnists and editorialists in remembrance of Madison's contribution toward protecting the individual right to keep and bear arms. **Publications:** *The Gottlieb-Tartaro Report,* monthly. Features insiders' news for Gun Rights. **Price:** $30.00. **Circulation:** 5,000 ● *Gun News Digest,* quarterly ● *Gun Week Newspaper,* periodic ● *Publications Catalog* ● *Second Amendment Reporter,* quarterly ● *Women and Guns,* bimonthly. Magazine ● Videos. Analyzes the gun control debate. **Conventions/ Meetings:** annual Gun Rights Policy Conference - meeting (exhibits).

16795 ■ Section of Individual Rights and Responsibilities (SIRR)
c/o American Bar Association
740 15th St. NW
Washington, DC 20005-1009
Ph: (202)662-1030
Free: (800)285-2221
Fax: (202)662-1032
E-mail: irr@abanet.org
URL: http://www.abanet.org/irr
Contact: Robert E. Stein, Chm.

Founded: 1966. **Members:** 3,000. **Membership Dues:** lawyer, $45 (annual) ● law student, $10 (annual). **Staff:** 5. **Description:** A section of the American Bar Association. Represents lawyers, law students, and other individuals. Concentrates on law and public policy as they relate to civil and constitutional rights, civil liberties, and human rights in the United States and internationally. Projects include legal issues in AIDS/HIV and death penalty moratorium. **Awards:** Thurgood Marshall Award. **Frequency:** annual. **Type:** recognition. **Recipient:** for long-term contributions to the furtherance of civil rights, civil liberties, or human rights in the U.S. **Affiliated With:** American Bar Association. **Publications:** *Human Rights Magazine,* quarterly. **Price:** included in membership dues. **Circulation:** 3,500 ● *IRR E-Newsletter,* quarterly. Alternate Formats: online. **Conventions/Meetings:** quarterly Council Meetings.

16796 ■ Southern Christian Leadership Conference (SCLC)
PO Box 89128
Atlanta, GA 30312
Ph: (404)522-1420
Fax: (404)527-4333
E-mail: president@sclcnational.org
URL: http://www.sclcnational.org
Contact: Mr. Charles Steele Jr., Pres./CEO

Founded: 1957. **Membership Dues:** youth, senior, $10 (annual) ● student, $15 (annual) ● general, $25 (annual) ● Faithful Servant, $50 (annual) ● Freedom Fighter, $100 (annual) ● life, $1,000. **Staff:** 12. **Description:** Nonsectarian coordinating and service agency for local organizations seeking full citizenship rights, equality, and the integration of African-Americans in all aspects of life in the U.S. and subscribing to the Ghandian philosophy of nonviolence. Works primarily in 16 southern and border states to improve civic, religious, economic, and cultural conditions. Fosters nonviolent resistance to

all forms of racial injustice, including state and local laws and practices. Conducts leadership training program embracing such subjects as registration and voting, social protest, use of the boycott, picketing, nature of prejudice, and understanding politics. Sponsors citizenship education schools to teach reading and writing, help persons pass literacy tests for voting, and provide information about income tax forms, tax-supported resources, aid to handicapped children, public health facilities, how government is run, and social security. Conducts Crusade for the Ballot, which aims to double the black vote in the South through increased voter registrations. Sponsors lectures; disseminates literature. **Publications:** Newsletter, monthly. **Price:** included in membership dues ● Magazine, 5/year. Serves as a vital educational and informational link between SCLC's national headquarters and constituency throughout the country. **Circulation:** 400,000. **Conventions/Meetings:** annual convention.

16797 ■ Southern Poverty Law Center (SPLC)
400 Washington Ave.
Montgomery, AL 36104
Ph: (334)956-8200 (334)956-8483
Free: (888)414-7752
Fax: (334)264-0629
URL: http://www.splcenter.org
Contact: J. Richard Cohen, Pres./CEO

Founded: 1971. **Staff:** 113. **Budget:** $25,000,000. **Multinational. Description:** Works to combat hate, intolerance and discrimination through education and litigation. **Publications:** *Intelligence Report,* quarterly. **Price:** free ● *SPLC Report,* quarterly. Newspaper ● *Teaching Tolerance,* semiannual. Magazine.

16798 ■ Southern Regional Council (SRC)
1201 W Peachtree St. NE, Ste.2000
Atlanta, GA 30309
Ph: (404)522-8764
Fax: (404)522-8791
E-mail: info@southerncouncil.org
URL: http://www.southerncouncil.org
Contact: Toni Fannin, Interim Exec. Dir.

Founded: 1919. **Members:** 123. **Membership Dues:** individual, $50 (annual) ● institution, $100 (annual). **Staff:** 15. **Budget:** $1,000,000. **Description:** Promotes racial justice, protects democratic rights, and broadens civic participation in the southern United States. **Libraries: Type:** reference. **Holdings:** audio recordings, books, films, periodicals, video recordings. **Subjects:** civil rights, civil liberties, politics, suffrage, labor, American South, history. **Awards:** Lillian Smith Book Award. **Frequency:** annual. **Type:** recognition. **Recipient:** for fiction and nonfiction books that deal honestly with the condition of racial and social inequity in the South and propose a vision of justice. **Computer Services:** Mailing lists, services ● online services, training. **Telecommunication Services:** electronic mail, tfannin@southerncouncil.org. **Boards:** Executive; Focus Group. **Committees:** Youth Empowerment Project Advisory Group. **Programs:** Fair Representation. **Supersedes:** (1919) Commission on Interracial Cooperation. **Publications:** *Remedies to Racial Inequality-Seeking an America as Good as its Promise: The Public's Views.* Reports. Focuses on gaining a better understanding of the attitudes of white Americans. ● *Southern Actions.* Newsletter ● *Southern Changes,* quarterly. Journal. Covers the politics, history, literature, and racial, social, and economic conditions of the South. Includes book reviews. **Price:** included in membership dues; $75.00 /year for institutions; $30.00 /year for individuals. ISSN: 0193-2446. **Advertising:** accepted. Alternate Formats: microform ● *Voting Rights Review,* annual. Newsletter. Provides information and analysis about trends in voting rights at national and local levels. Includes listings of current voting rights action. **Price:** included in membership dues. **Advertising:** accepted ● *Will the Circle Be Unbroken?.* Audiotape. **Price:** $145.00 cassette tape set; $160.00 CD set ● Reports, biennial. Covers organizational programs, work, and budget. **Price:** free to associate members. **Conventions/Meetings:** annual conference, with Lillian Smith Book Awards announcement and forum to discuss relevant issues.

16799 ■ Special Committee on the Situation with Regard to the Implementation of the Declaration on the Granting of Independence to Colonial Countries and Peoples
UN HQ, Rm. S-2977
First Ave. at 46th St.
New York, NY 10017
Ph: (212)963-3051
Fax: (212)963-9223
E-mail: cherniavsky@un.org
URL: http://www.un.org
Contact: Mr. Julian R. Hunte, Chm.
Founded: 1961. **Members:** 27. **Staff:** 4. **Languages:** Arabic, Chinese, English, French, Russian, Spanish. **Multinational. Description:** United Nations committee comprising representatives of 27 nations concerned with the progress of people under colonial rule toward self-determination and independence. Considers situations in 16 territories based on information received from administering powers or local governments, non-governmental organizations, published sources, and observations of the committee's visiting missions. Reviews activities of foreign economic interests in colonial territories; enlists support of United Nations specialized agencies and international institutions to assist decolonization efforts, especially through aid to colonial people; seeks to mobilize public opinion in support of decolonization by disseminating information. **Also Known As:** Special Committee on Decolonization; Special Committee of 24. **Conventions/Meetings:** annual meeting.

16800 ■ Trade Union Leadership Council (TULC)
8670 Grand River Ave.
Detroit, MI 48204
Ph: (313)894-0303
Fax: (313)894-0311
Contact: Larry K. Lewis, Pres.
Founded: 1957. **Members:** 2,500. **Description:** Primarily black trade unionists in Michigan, but membership is open to anyone. Seeks to eradicate injustices perpetrated upon people because of race, religion, sex, or national origin. Seeks increased leadership and job opportunities for blacks. Maintains Nelson Jack Edwards Educational Centre. **Committees:** Civil Rights; Inter-Cultural Relations; Inter-Organizational; Political Action; Public Relations; Religious Affairs; Sick. **Programs:** HUD Housing; Training for Building Trades. **Sections:** Women's Auxiliary; Youth Council. **Publications:** *Vanguard,* quarterly.

16801 ■ Workers' Defense League (WDL)
275 7th Ave.
New York, NY 10001
Ph: (212)627-1931
Fax: (212)627-4628
Contact: Jon Bloom, Exec.Dir.
Founded: 1936. **Members:** 500. **Description:** Labor-oriented human rights organization. Provides counseling to workers on employment-related problems via telephone. Conducts educational campaigns to defend and advance workers' rights. Maintains speakers' bureau. Offers referral service regarding unemployment insurance claims. **Awards:** David Clendenin Award. **Frequency:** annual. **Type:** recognition. **Recipient:** for distinguished service to labor rights. **Absorbed:** (1981) Fund for Human Rights. **Publications:** *Know Your Rights* ● *WDL News,* quarterly ● Also publishes reports leaflet series on benefits, discrimination, health, job security, occupational safety, and unemployment insurance in English, Spanish, Creole, and Chinese.

Communications

16802 ■ Accuracy in Media (AIM)
4455 Connecticut Ave. NW, Ste.330
Washington, DC 20008
Ph: (202)364-4401
Free: (800)787-4567

Fax: (202)364-4098
E-mail: info@aim.org
URL: http://www.aim.org
Contact: Don Irvine, Chm.
Founded: 1969. **Members:** 3,500. **Membership Dues:** regular, $40 (annual). **Staff:** 8. **Budget:** $1,000,000. **Description:** Nonpartisan, news media watchdog organization. Receives complaints from the public on factual errors made by the news media. Researches specific complaints; if they are justified, asks that errors be corrected publicly; publicizes failure of news media to do so. Hosts a daily three-minute radio program, Media Monitor, which is aired on approximately 200 stations around the country. **Awards: Type:** recognition. **Recipient:** for outstanding achievement in the field of fair and accurate journalism. **Additional Websites:** http://www.conservativemall.com. **Affiliated With:** Accuracy in Academia. **Publications:** *AIM Report,* semimonthly. Newsletter. Covers inaccurate and biased reporting. **Price:** $40.00. **Circulation:** 3,500. Alternate Formats: CD-ROM ● *The Clinton Legacy.* Video ● *How to Write Letters To The Media,* semiannual. Booklet. Alternate Formats: CD-ROM ● *Index of AIM Reports,* semiannual. Alternate Formats: CD-ROM ● *TWA800 - The Search for Truth.* Video ● Also publishes weekly column in approximately 100 newspapers. **Conventions/Meetings:** conference, with speakers (exhibits) - 3-4/year ● annual conference.

16803 ■ Alliance for Community Media (ACM)
666 11th St. NW, Ste.740
Washington, DC 20001
Ph: (202)393-2650
Fax: (202)393-2653
E-mail: acm@alliancecm.org
URL: http://www.alliancecm.org
Contact: Anthony Riddle, Exec. Dir.
Founded: 1976. **Members:** 900. **Membership Dues:** individual, $60 (annual) ● organization, $305 (annual). **Staff:** 3. **Budget:** $400,000. **Regional Groups:** 7. **State Groups:** 9. **Local Groups:** 20. **Description:** Individual access producers, community producers, public access organizations, public access professionals, cable television firms, cable regulators, and other interested organizations and individuals. Seeks to make cable programming more responsive to the needs of individuals, local groups, and communities by providing assistance in local access efforts and by serving as an advocate at the federal level. Maintains information referral services. **Libraries: Type:** reference. **Holdings:** books, video recordings. **Subjects:** media. **Awards:** Hometown U.S.A. Awards. **Frequency:** annual. **Type:** recognition. **Recipient:** for best community generated videotapes. **Computer Services:** database ● mailing lists. **Committees:** Equal Opportunity; Information Services; International; Organizational Development; Public Policy. **Formerly:** (1976) National Federation of Local Cable Programmers. **Publications:** *Community Media Review,* quarterly. Journal. **Price:** $2.00 /year for members; $4.00 /year for nonmembers. Alternate Formats: online ● Books ● Journals ● Also publishes educational packet series concerning public educational and government access, cable television, lease access, local origination, and the franchising process. **Conventions/Meetings:** periodic international conference (exhibits) ● periodic regional meeting.

16804 ■ American Family Association (AFA)
PO Drawer 2440
Tupelo, MS 38803
Ph: (662)844-5036
Fax: (662)842-7798
E-mail: afa@afa.net
URL: http://www.afa.net
Contact: Donald E. Wildmon, Founder/Chm.
Founded: 1977. **Staff:** 25. **Local Groups:** 560. **Description:** Fosters "the biblical ethic of decency in American society with a primary emphasis on television and other media." Urges viewers to write letters to networks and sponsors, protesting shows that promote "violence, immorality, profanity and vulgarity" and encouraging the airing of programs that are "clean, constructive, wholesome and family oriented." Compiles statistics on television broadcasts of scenes

involving sex, profanity, and violence. Maintains Speaker's Bureau. **Projects:** Glossy Garbage; In God We Trust; Meet at City Hall; Movie Gallery. **Formerly:** (1988) National Federation for Decency. **Publications:** *AFA Journal,* monthly. **Advertising:** accepted. Alternate Formats: online.

16805 ■ Association for Progressive Communications (APC)
c/o International Global Communications
PO Box 29047
San Francisco, CA 94129-0047
E-mail: webeditor@apc.org
URL: http://www.apc.org
Contact: Anriette Esterhuysen, Exec. Dir.
Membership Dues: very small organization from developing countries, $300 (annual) ● very small to small organization, $500 (annual) ● small to medium organization, $1,000 (annual) ● medium organization, $2,000 (annual) ● large organization and small for-profit, $5,000 (annual) ● for-profit, $5,001 (annual). **Languages:** English, Spanish. **Multinational. Description:** Aims to provide low cost computer communication services to individuals and organizations working for environmental sustainability, human rights, and social and economic justice. Seeks to empower local, indigenous organizations by encouraging expertise in computer networking.

16806 ■ Black Awareness in Television (BAIT)
30 Josephine St., 3rd Fl.
Detroit, MI 48202-1810
Ph: (313)871-3333
E-mail: davidrambeau@hotmail.com
URL: http://www.projectbait.blakgold.net
Contact: David Rambeau, Dir.
Founded: 1970. **Members:** 100. **Staff:** 10. **Local Groups:** 3. **Languages:** English, French. **Description:** Produces black media programs for television, video, radio, film, and theatre. Trains individuals in the media and conducts research projects including surveys. Produces public affairs, cultural arts, soap opera, and exercise programs. Sponsors theatre companies. Seeks television exposure for black-produced products and black performing artists; promotes September as Black Reading Month program, the Afrikan World Language and Culture Fair, and the Black Arts Festival. **Publications:** *The Afrikan World Journal of Language and Culture* ● *Project Bait Business Magazine.* **Conventions/Meetings:** triennial meeting.

16807 ■ Caucus for Television Producers, Writers, and Directors (CPWD)
PO Box 11236
Burbank, CA 91510-1236
Ph: (818)843-7572
Fax: (818)846-2159
E-mail: caucuspwd@aol.com
URL: http://caucus.org
Contact: Vin Di Bona, Chm.
Founded: 1973. **Members:** 150. **Budget:** $80,000. **Description:** Represents producers, writers, and directors in the television industry. Seeks to improve prime time television quality by lessening network control over production, thereby increasing artistic integrity and creative control. Acts as a liaison between the creative community and public groups. **Libraries: Type:** reference. **Holdings:** archival material. **Awards:** Distinguished Service Award. **Frequency:** annual. **Type:** recognition ● Executive of the Year Award. **Frequency:** annual. **Type:** recognition ● Member of the Year Award. **Frequency:** annual. **Type:** recognition. **Computer Services:** Mailing lists. **Telecommunication Services:** electronic bulletin board, for members only ● electronic mail, info@caucus.org. **Committees:** Bill of Rights; Industry Issues; Inter-Guild; Membership; Special Events; Website. **Formerly:** (1974) Hyphenate Lobby. **Publications:** *The Caucus Journal,* quarterly. Contains information on creative rights, censorship, and other issues of importance to members. **Price:** $5.00. **Circulation:** 2,000. **Conventions/Meetings:** quarterly meeting - always in Beverly Hills, CA.

16808 ■ Center for Asian American Media
145 9th St., Ste.350
San Francisco, CA 94103
Ph: (415)863-0814
Fax: (415)863-7428
E-mail: info@asianamericanmedia.org
URL: http://www.asianamericanmedia.org
Contact: Stephen Gong, Exec. Dir.
Founded: 1980. **Members:** 300. **Membership Dues:** senior, student, $35 (annual) ● friend, $50 (annual) ● supporter, $100 (annual) ● patron, $250 (annual) ● Director's Circle, $500 (annual) ● benefactor, $1,000 (annual) ● advocate, $2,500 (annual) ● visionary, $5,000 (annual). **Staff:** 25. **Description:** Provides stories that convey the richness and diversity of Asian-American experiences to the broadest audience possible. Does funding, producing, distributing and exhibiting works in film, television, and digital media. **Awards:** James T. Yee Fellowship Program. **Frequency:** annual. **Type:** fellowship. **Recipient:** for Asian Pacific American producers ● Open Door Completion Fund. **Frequency:** semiannual. **Type:** monetary. **Recipient:** for applicants with projects in the final post-production phase. **Formerly:** (2006) National Asian American Telecommunications Association. **Publications:** CAAM Connect, biweekly. Newsletters. Contains electronic newsletter with the latest in Asian American film and media. Alternate Formats: online ● Distribution Catalog, biennial. Alternate Formats: online ● San Francisco International Asian American Film Festival Program Guide, annual. Catalog. Lists all the films playing at the annual San Francisco International Asian American Film Festival. Alternate Formats: online ● Year in Review, annual. Annual Report. **Conventions/Meetings:** annual Film Festival - conference and festival - every March.

16809 ■ Center For Democracy and Technology (CDT)
1634 Eye St. NW, Ste.1100
Washington, DC 20006
Ph: (202)637-9800
Fax: (202)637-0968
E-mail: feedback@cdt.org
URL: http://www.cdt.org
Contact: Jerry Berman, Pres.
Founded: 1994. **Staff:** 10. **Budget:** $1,500,000. **Nonmembership. Description:** Works to promote democratic values and constitutional liberties in the digital age. Seeks practical solutions to enhance free expression and privacy in global communications technologies. Dedicates to building consensus among all parties interested in the future of the Internet and other new communications media. Champions the right of individuals to communicate, publish and obtain an unprecedented array of information the Internet, challenges invasive government policies, and educates the public about current policy issues. Develops user empowerment solutions. Coordinates a series of working groups in areas of online privacy, digital security, and free expression. **Computer Services:** Mailing lists, of members. **Committees:** Advisory. **Publications:** Privacy Journal, monthly ● PrivacyTimes, biweekly. Newsletter. Includes summaries of court decisions on the Freedom of Information Act and other relevant statutes.

16810 ■ Center for Investigative Reporting (CIR)
2927 Newbury St., Ste.A
Berkeley, CA 94703-2565
Ph: (510)809-3160
Fax: (510)849-1813
E-mail: center@cironline.org
URL: http://www.muckraker.org
Contact: Erica Baker, Operations Mgr.
Founded: 1977. **Staff:** 8. **Budget:** $1,500,000. **Description:** Investigative journalists engaged in the indepth reporting of economic, environmental, energy, social justice, public policy, and constitutional government issues. Produces investigative television documentaries, newspaper and magazine articles, books, and reports; provides investigative and editorial consulting services to television news, publications, and nonprofit organizations. Conducts intern-

ship program, and classes for journalism students and others on techniques of investigative reporting; the center's articles have helped spark congressional hearings and legislation, public-interest lawsuits, and United Nations resolutions. **Libraries: Type:** reference. **Holdings:** 1,000. **Publications:** Circle of Poison. Book. Includes reports on pesticides-too dangerous for unrestricted use in the US-that are being shipped to underdeveloped countries. **Price:** $5.95 ● The Electronic Sweatshop. Booklet. Includes list of resources for high-tech workers at risk, health professionals and other interested readers. **Price:** $4.50 ● Global Dumping Ground. Video. Features the investigation of Correspondent Bill Moyers on the international export of toxic waste. **Price:** $19.98 ● Nuclear California. Book. Details the secret story behind nuclear California: the accidents, cover-ups, scandals, terrorist threats and more. **Price:** $5.95 ● Paper Trails ● Paper Trails: A Guide to Public Records in California. Includes information on how to access records online. **Price:** $18.95 ● Raising Hell: A Citizens Guide to the Fine Art of Investigation ● Raising Hell: How the Center for Investigative Reporting Gets the Story ● Troubled Water ● Yakuza: The Explosive Account of Japan's Criminal Underworld. Book. Explores the culture and history of the Japanese organized crime world. **Price:** $18.95. **Conventions/Meetings:** seminar ● workshop.

16811 ■ Center for Media and Public Affairs (CMPA)
2100 L St. NW, Ste.300
Washington, DC 20037
Ph: (202)223-2942
Fax: (202)872-4014
E-mail: mail@cmpa.com
URL: http://www.cmpa.com
Contact: Dr. S. Robert Lichter, Pres.
Founded: 1986. **Staff:** 14. **Description:** Analyzes scientifically how the media treat social and political issues. Conducts surveys to determine media impact on public opinion. Performs rapid response media analyses, enabling the impact of media coverage to be determined as it occurs. **Publications:** Media Monitor, bimonthly. Newsletter. Contains reports on press behavior. **Price:** $50.00/year ● When Should the Watchdogs Bark? Media Coverage of Clinton Scandals. Book. **Price:** $12.95 plus shipping ● Monographs. **Price:** $15.00.

16812 ■ Center for War, Peace, and the News Media (CWPNM)
418 Lafayette St., Ste.518
New York, NY 10003
Ph: (212)998-7960
Fax: (212)995-4143
E-mail: war.peace.news@nyu.edu
URL: http://www.bu.edu/globalbeat
Contact: Robert Manoff, Dir.
Founded: 1985. **Staff:** 10. **Multinational. Description:** Supports journalists and news organizations in their efforts to sustain an informed and engaged global citizenry. Current activities are concentrated in several areas: assisting journalists in the U.S. and abroad in their coverage of international issues relating to security, interdependence and globalization; working with leading journalists in Russia, Asia and the U.S. to improve coverage of nuclear questions; developing and implementing programs dedicated to transforming ethno national, religious and racial conflict with and through the media worldwide; enhancing the potential of new media technologies to assist journalism organizations operating in politically or economically difficult circumstances. Funding for Center programs comes primarily from private U.S. and European foundations, with additional support from several governmental and international agencies. **Computer Services:** database, archive of press clippings and videotapes of television news broadcasts. **Programs:** Media and Conflict. **Projects:** Global Reporting Network; Mid-East/American Media. **Publications:** Global Beat, weekly. Contains research and commentary on international security issues. **Price:** free for members and working journalists ● Occasional Papers, triennial. **Conventions/Meetings:** periodic conference.

16813 ■ Citizens Communications Center Project of the Institute for Public Representation (CCCPIPR)
c/o Georgetown University Law Center
600 New Jersey Ave. NW
Washington, DC 20001
Ph: (202)662-9535 (202)662-9000
Fax: (202)662-9634
E-mail: gulcipr@law.georgetown.edu
URL: http://www.law.georgetown.edu/clinics/ipr/telecom.html
Contact: Angela J. Campbell, Dir.
Founded: 1971. **Staff:** 3. **Description:** Project of the Institute for Public Representation of the Georgetown University Law Center. Represents non-profit organization before the FCC and courts. Seeks to open the regulatory process to participation by citizens. Aids citizens and groups without resources or technical skills in participating the regulatory and decision-making process relating to communications policy. **Telecommunication Services:** TDD, (202)662-9538. **Formerly:** For Responsive Media: Citizens Communication Center; (1989) Citizens Communication Center of the Institute for Public Representation.

16814 ■ Committee to Protect Journalists (CPJ)
330 7th Ave., 11th Fl.
New York, NY 10001
Ph: (212)465-1004 (212)465-9344
Fax: (212)465-9568
E-mail: info@cpj.org
URL: http://www.cpj.org
Contact: Joel Simon, Exec. Dir.
Founded: 1981. **Members:** 468. **Membership Dues:** general/participant, $45 (annual) ● student, $20 (annual) ● contributor, $100 (annual) ● supporter, $500 (annual) ● benefactor, $1,000 (annual) ● friend, $5,000 (annual). **Staff:** 25. **Budget:** $1,800,000. **Languages:** Arabic, English, French, German, Hebrew, Russian, Spanish. **Description:** Media organizations, human rights groups, and journalists. Supports journalists around the world who have been subjected to human rights and press freedom violations; is concerned about efforts by governments to limit the ability of foreign correspondents and local journalists to practice their profession. Keeps U.S. and foreign journalists informed about such practices and organizes protests on behalf of those whose rights have been violated. Compiles and publicizes human rights abuses. Brings exiled journalists to the U.S. for interviews and press conferences; sends delegations of journalists to areas of the world where there are especially serious and continuous problems. Maintains liaison with press groups worldwide to exchange information and launch campaigns on urgent human rights abuse cases. Maintains information files and speakers' bureau; compiles statistics. Conducts research programs. **Libraries: Type:** reference. **Holdings:** books, periodicals. **Subjects:** journalism, law, human rights. **Awards:** International Press Freedom Awards. **Frequency:** annual. **Type:** recognition. **Computer Services:** database, press freedom information. **Publications:** Attacks on the Press, annual. Book. Documents incidents of abuse worldwide. **Price:** $15.00 for members; $30.00 for nonmembers. Alternate Formats: online ● Bouch Pe: The Crackdown on Haiti's Media Since the Overthrow of Aristide ● Dangerous Assignments, semiannual. Newsletter. Covers recent cases of press abuse. **Price:** included in membership dues; $45.00 /year for nonmembers ● Don't Force Us to Lie (The Struggle of Chinese Journalists in the Reform Era) ● Journalism Under Occupation ● Journalists Advisory on Yugoslavia. **Conventions/Meetings:** luncheon and seminar.

16815 ■ Committee on Public Doublespeak (CPD)
c/o National Council of Teachers of English
1111 W Kenyon Rd.
Urbana, IL 61801-1096
Ph: (217)328-3870
Free: (877)369-6283
Fax: (217)328-0977

E-mail: public_info@ncte.org
URL: http://www.ncte.org/about/awards/council/jrnl/
106868.htm
Contact: Margaret Chambers, Contact
Founded: 1972. **Members:** 22. **Description:** A committee of the National Council of Teachers of English, comprising NCTE members who are concerned with and interested in the study of public doublespeak and who are willing to speak or write on this subject. Works to study dishonest and inhumane uses of language, especially as transmitted through the mass media. Brings these misuses to public attention. Proposes classroom techniques for the study of public language. **Awards:** Doublespeak Award. **Frequency:** annual. **Type:** recognition. **Recipient:** to a glaring example of deceptive language by a public spokesperson ● George Orwell Award. **Frequency:** annual. **Type:** recognition. **Recipient:** for outstanding contributions to the study of public language. **Computer Services:** Online services, discussion group. **Affiliated With:** National Council of Teachers of English. **Conventions/Meetings:** annual meeting, held in conjunction with NCTE (exhibits) - always November.

16816 ■ Empowerment Project (EP)
8218 Farrington Mill Rd.
Chapel Hill, NC 27517
Ph: (919)928-0382
E-mail: info@empowermentproject.org
URL: http://www.empowermentproject.org
Founded: 1984. **Staff:** 4. **Nonmembership. Description:** Progressive video and filmmakers; activists. Produces documentary videos and films; works to democratize access to the media and expand the distribution of progressive films and videos; acts as a support group for individuals involved in such activity. Provides video production and editing services and facilities to individuals and organizations working to further important social, political and artistic purposes; also offers pre-production, production, and post-production consulting and assistance. Presents films and delivers keynote addresses at college, universities, and organizations nationwide. **Publications:** *Coverup: Behind the Iran Contra Affair.* Video ● *Destination Nicaragua.* Video ● *Gatewood: Facing the White Canvas.* Video ● *Is War the Answer?.* Video ● *The Panama Deception.* Video. **Price:** $24.95 for individuals and non-profits; $75.00 for institutional viewing ● *Soldiers Speak Out.* Video ● *Taking it to the Theaters.* Booklet ● *Waging Peace.* Video.

16817 ■ Essential Information (EI)
PO Box 19405
Washington, DC 20036
Ph: (202)387-8030
Fax: (202)234-5176
E-mail: info@essential.org
URL: http://www.essential.org
Contact: John Richard, Contact
Founded: 1982. **Description:** Promotes investigative journalism and public education regarding social, environmental, corporate, political, and global affairs. Offers young people resources and training designed to help them provide information to the public on topics that have been neglected by the mass media, policy-makers and academics. Provides training to allow students to pursue investigative projects for school newspapers and in professional positions. Offers grants to journalists investigating social, political, and global topics such as defense spending, U.S. activities in Central America, nuclear power safety violations, and environmental hazards. **Publications:** *Multinational Monitor,* bimonthly. Magazine.

16818 ■ Fairness and Accuracy in Reporting (FAIR)
112 W 27th St.
New York, NY 10001
Ph: (212)633-6700
Free: (800)847-3993
Fax: (212)727-7668
E-mail: fair@fair.org
URL: http://www.fair.org
Contact: Hilary Goldstein, Development Dir.
Founded: 1986. **Members:** 15,000. **Staff:** 10. **Description:** Promotes the rights of U.S. citizens to a

free press and free speech; encourages pluralism in media. Brings public attention to the performance of the media in specific areas; suggests ways in which U.S. media can improve the quality of coverage and performance. Participates in public forums on topics pertaining to the U.S. media. Maintains speakers' bureau; compiles statistics. **Convention/Meeting:** none. **Publications:** *Extra!,* bimonthly. Journal. **Price:** $19.00. **Circulation:** 20,000.

16819 ■ Foundation for American Communications (FACS)
85 S Grand Ave.
Pasadena, CA 91105
Ph: (626)584-0010
Fax: (626)584-0627
URL: http://www.facsnet.org
Contact: Robert E. Wood, Pres./CEO
Founded: 1976. **Members:** 19. **Staff:** 7. **Budget:** $1,400,000. **Description:** Seeks to improve mutual understanding between major American institutions and the news media. Works with individuals, associations, organizations, corporations, and institutions at every point in the communication process. Sponsors short-term professional education programs for the working journalist (from both broadcast and print media) who wants to improve his or her understanding of important issues including economics, business, energy, technology, the environment, ethics, law, corporate and governmental practices, and foreign affairs. Conducts Business/News Media Conferences involving business executives and journalists in an effort to improve the participants' understanding of the news media and its relationship to corporate credibility. Organizes communications programs for individual corporations. Sponsors communications programs for non-profit organizations. **Publications:** *Communications Conference Workbook* ● *Human Heart Replacement.* Book. **Price:** $5.00 ● *Journalism Ethics.* Book. **Price:** $10.00 ● *Knowledge, Resources and Perspectives.* Video. **Price:** $10.00 ● *Media Resource Guide.* **Price:** $5.00 ● *Reporting on Risk: A Journalist's Handbook on Environmental Risk Assessment.* **Price:** $10.00 ● Report ● Books.

16820 ■ Fund for Investigative Journalism (FIJ)
PO Box 60184
Washington, DC 20039-0184
Ph: (202)362-0260
Fax: (301)576-0804
E-mail: johnchyde@yahoo.com
URL: http://www.fij.org
Contact: John Hyde, Exec. Dir.
Founded: 1969. **Staff:** 1. **Budget:** $225,000. **Description:** Makes grants to enable writers to probe abuses of authority or the malfunctioning of institutions and systems that harm the public. Writers must have publication commitment from editor or producer. These factual reports are broadcast or published as books or articles. Has awarded over 900 grants; two grantees have won Pulitzer Prizes. More than 50 investigative books have been written with fund support. Administers program for media criticism. Subjects investigated by fund grantees include environmental hazards, political corruption, invasion of privacy, organized crime, threats to civil rights, defense and foreign policy, and abuses of corporate and union authority. **Conventions/Meetings:** board meeting - always Washington, DC; March, July, November.

16821 ■ Fund for Objective News Reporting (FONR)
1 Massachusetts Ave. NW, Ste.600
Washington, DC 20001
Ph: (202)216-0600
Free: (800)787-7557
Fax: (202)216-0611
E-mail: customerservice@humaneventsonline.com
URL: http://www.humanevents online.com
Contact: Thomas Winter, Exec. Off.
Founded: 1974. **Staff:** 1. **Description:** Nonpartisan organization working to correct bias in the major news media. Provides grants to journalists conducting

media research. Plans to sponsor seminars on the media and fair reporting.

16822 ■ Hispanic Public Relations Association (HPRA)
PO Box 86760
Los Angeles, CA 90086-0760
Ph: (310)473-2031 (213)239-6555
Fax: (213)239-6550
E-mail: romina.bongiovanni@edelman.com
URL: http://www.hpra-usa.org
Contact: Romina Bongiovanni, Pres.
Founded: 1984. **Members:** 150. **Membership Dues:** professional (with 2 years or less professional experience), $75 (annual) ● professional (with 3 or more years professional experience), $100 (annual) ● student, $30 (annual). **Budget:** $50,000. **Regional Groups:** 1. **Description:** Hispanic professionals in public relations. Promotes a positive image of Hispanics in the media. **Libraries: Type:** reference. **Awards:** PREMIO HPRA. **Frequency:** annual. **Type:** recognition. **Recipient:** for outstanding communicators ● **Frequency:** annual. **Type:** scholarship. **Recipient:** to Hispanic students majoring in communications. **Computer Services:** Mailing lists. **Councils:** Advisory. **Publications:** *The Buzz,* quarterly. Newsletter. Features industry news. **Price:** included in membership dues. **Circulation:** 250. **Advertising:** accepted. **Conventions/Meetings:** monthly meeting.

16823 ■ Inter American Press Association (IAPA)
1801 SW 3rd Ave.
Jules Dubois Bldg.
Miami, FL 33129
Ph: (305)634-2465
Free: (877)747-4272
Fax: (305)635-2272
E-mail: info@sipiapa.org
URL: http://www.sipiapa.com
Contact: Julio E. Munoz, Exec. Dir.
Founded: 1942. **Members:** 1,383. **Membership Dues:** active (based on circulation), $145-$1,435 (annual) ● corporate, $2,100-$5,250 (annual) ● news agency (based on feature services), $1,435-$2,975 (annual) ● associate individual, $1,100 (annual) ● associate corporate, $3,300 (annual) ● teacher of journalism, $70 (annual) ● syndicated columnist, $110 (annual) ● cybernetic newspaper, $525 (annual). **Staff:** 10. **Budget:** $900,000. **Languages:** English, Portuguese, Spanish. **Description:** Newspapers, magazines, educators, and other individuals in allied fields. Promotes and protects freedom of the press in the Americas. **Libraries: Type:** open to the public. **Holdings:** books, papers, periodicals, reports. **Subjects:** journalism, mass media, media law, human rights, press freedom. **Awards:** Cartoon Award. **Frequency:** annual. **Type:** monetary. **Recipient:** for cartoons with news and/or news humor content ● Features Award. **Frequency:** annual. **Type:** monetary. **Recipient:** for special reports (well-written, accurate articles with impact) produced not under deadline pressure ● Grand Prize for Press Freedom. **Frequency:** annual. **Type:** monetary. **Recipient:** for outstanding work by one or more persons in the Americas ● Human Rights and Service to the Community Award. **Frequency:** annual. **Type:** monetary. **Recipient:** for news reports or series designed to highlight cases or situations that affect or lessen respect for human rights in the Americas ● IAPA Scholarships. **Frequency:** annual. **Type:** scholarship. **Recipient:** for journalists or journalism school seniors or graduates ● In-Depth Reporting Award. **Frequency:** annual. **Type:** monetary. **Recipient:** for major investigative reporting or campaigns that required extensive investigative work ● Infographics Award. **Frequency:** annual. **Type:** monetary. **Recipient:** for the most creative infographics, reflecting the capabilities of this specialty ● News Coverage Award. **Frequency:** annual. **Type:** monetary. **Recipient:** for any kind of news reporting ● Newspaper in Education Award. **Frequency:** annual. **Type:** monetary. **Recipient:** for NIE program with best content and educational value ● Opinion Award. **Frequency:** annual. **Type:** monetary. **Recipient:** for reasoned opinion pieces (not series) including, where possible,

recommendations ● Pedro Joaquin Chamorro Inter-American Relations Award. **Frequency:** annual. **Type:** monetary. **Recipient:** for news reports or series designed to highlight, improve or resolve issues or problems in relations among the countries of the Americas ● Photography Award. **Frequency:** annual. **Type:** monetary. **Recipient:** for one or more news photos. **Committees:** Awards; Freedom of the Press; International Affairs; Legal. **Publications:** *Hora de Cierre* (in English and Spanish), quarterly. Magazine ● *IAPA News*, bimonthly. Newspaper ● *Manual de Estilo* (in English and Spanish), periodic. Includes rules on grammar, consultation manual, and orientation on the work of journalists and ordinary writers. ● *Manual de Periodistas* (in English and Spanish), periodic. Contains guide for the professional exercise; also, detailed and exact advice of Malcolm F. Mallete. ● *Manual Diario En La Educacion* (in English and Spanish), periodic. Features project that ties a social segment with the newspaper. ● *Noticiero SIP* (in English and Spanish), bimonthly. Book ● *Periodismo Sobre Catastrofes* (in English and Spanish), periodic. Manual. Features information on how to be prepared for catastrophes, whether by natural or human causes. **Price:** $20.00/copy. **Conventions/Meetings:** annual general assembly - October ● semiannual meeting (exhibits) - March.

16824 ■ Media Access Project (MAP)
1625 K St. NW, Ste.1000
Washington, DC 20006
Ph: (202)232-4300
Fax: (202)466-7656
E-mail: info@mediaaccess.org
URL: http://www.mediaaccess.org
Contact: Andrew Jay Schwartzman, Pres./CEO
Founded: 1972. **Staff:** 6. **Description:** Serves as public interest law firm that works to assure that the print and electronic media inform the public fully and fairly on important issues involving the environment, consumerism, civil rights, the economy, and the political process. Participates in conferences and seminars designed to maximize citizen group ability to gain access to radio and television audiences. Advises local and national organizations seeking to make broadcast stations more responsive in the areas of programming and employment. Represents these groups in their efforts to obtain access to the broadcast and print media. Has successfully used the Freedom of Information Act to obtain access to government information for clients. Grants law students internships. **Publications:** Annual Report, annual. Alternate Formats: online ● Brochure. Alternate Formats: online.

16825 ■ Media Alliance (MA)
1904 Franklin St., Ste.500
Oakland, CA 94612
Ph: (510)832-9000
Fax: (510)238-8557
E-mail: information@media-alliance.org
URL: http://www.media-alliance.org
Contact: Jeff Pearlstein, Exec. Dir.
Founded: 1975. **Members:** 3,800. **Membership Dues:** contributing, $25 (annual) ● standard, $65 (annual) ● professional, $95 (annual). **Staff:** 3. **Budget:** $550,000. **Languages:** English, Spanish. **Description:** Writers, photographers, editors, broadcast workers, public relations practitioners, videographers, filmmakers, commercial artists and other media workers and aspiring media workers. Supports free press and independent, alternative journalism that services progressive politics and social justice. **Libraries:** **Type:** reference. **Holdings:** 200; periodicals. **Subjects:** media. **Awards:** Mitford Memorial Scholarship. **Frequency:** annual. **Type:** scholarship. **Recipient:** for an outstanding youth journalist. **Computer Services:** Mailing lists ● online services, publication. **Publications:** *Freelance Markets*, periodic, every 3-4 years. Serves as a guide to Bay Area periodicals. ● *MediaFile*, semiannual. Newsletter. **Price:** free. **Circulation:** 8,000 ● *People Behind the News*, semiannual. Book. Includes the Bay Area Media Press list. **Price:** $35.00. **Circulation:** 1,200. Alternate Formats: online.

16826 ■ The Media Institute (TMI)
2300 Clarendon Blvd., Ste.503
Arlington, VA 22201
Ph: (703)243-5700
Fax: (703)243-8808
E-mail: info@mediainstitute.org
URL: http://www.mediainstitute.org
Contact: Patrick D. Maines, Pres.
Founded: 1979. **Staff:** 7. **Budget:** $750,000. **Description:** Serves as research foundation specializing in media and communication's policy issues. Seeks to foster freedom of speech, a competitive communications industry, and excellence in journalism through publications, studies, and filing court briefs and regulatory comments. **Awards:** American Horizon Award. **Frequency:** annual. **Type:** recognition ● Freedom of Speech Award. **Frequency:** annual. **Type:** recognition. **Recipient:** to an individual who has made important contributions to the advancement and protection of free speech. **Councils:** Board of Trustees; Communications Policy; First Amendment Advisory; Public Interest. **Publications:** *Commercial Speech Digest*, quarterly. Contains news and analysis of legal and regulatory development affecting advertising rights. Alternate Formats: online ● *The First Amendment and the Media - 2000*, annual. Book. Includes analysis of government actions affecting First Amendment rights of media speakers. **Price:** $14.95. Alternate Formats: online ● *Protecting Kids Online*, annual. Book. Contains detailed information on what 46 corporate and non-profit groups are doing to protect kids from pornography and violence on the internet. **Price:** $10.95. ISSN: 9377-9049. Alternate Formats: online ● *Rationales and Rationalizations: Regulating the Electronic Media*. Book. Contains seven essays exploring why none of the government's rationales for continued media regulation can be justified. **Price:** $15.95 ● Papers. Alternate Formats: online. **Conventions/Meetings:** periodic conference.

16827 ■ Media Watch (MW)
PO Box 618
Santa Cruz, CA 95061-0618
Ph: (831)423-6355
Free: (800)631-6355
E-mail: info@mediawatch.com
URL: http://www.mediawatch.com
Contact: Ann Simonton, Founder/Dir.
Founded: 1984. **Members:** 1,500. **Staff:** 2. **Budget:** $10,000. **Local Groups:** 3. **National Groups:** 3. **Multinational. Description:** Dedicated to challenging the biases found in commercial media. Exposes the dangerous consequences of living amid "discriminatory, violent and corporate controlled media." Does not believe in any form of censorship. Stages public protests, boycotts, letter writing campaigns, and fundraising events. Maintains speakers' bureau and biographical archives; conducts children's programs and educational workshops and seminars. Compiles statistics. Creates educational videos and DVDs. **Libraries:** **Type:** reference. **Holdings:** 1,050; articles, books, periodicals, video recordings. **Subjects:** feminism, media portrayal, pornography, commercialism. **Awards:** Silver Apple Award. **Type:** recognition. **Recipient:** for national educational video and film festival. **Affiliated With:** Fairness and Accuracy in Reporting. **Publications:** *The Media May Be Hazardous to Your Health*. Video ● Report. Challenges sexism and violence in the media through education and action; includes announcements of current boycott campaigns. **Circulation:** 3,000. Alternate Formats: online. **Conventions/Meetings:** bimonthly board meeting.

16828 ■ National Council for Families and Television (NCFT)
c/o Leo Burnett Advertising
6500 Wilshire Blvd., Ste.1950
Los Angeles, CA 90048
Ph: (323)866-6020
Fax: (310)208-5984
E-mail: ncft@yahoo.com
Contact: Tricia McLeod Robin, Pres.
Founded: 1977. **Budget:** $350,000. **Description:** Advisory board comprises television producers, writ-

ers, and programming executives; advertisers; educators. Aims to enhance the quality of life for families and children by positively affecting the creation and uses of primetime television entertainment. Conducts seminars, symposia, and invitational weekends where television creators meet with experts to discuss issues that are important to the American family. **Formerly:** (1984) National Council for Children and Television. **Publications:** *Television & Families*. Magazine. **Conventions/Meetings:** annual meeting.

16829 ■ National Hispanic Media Coalition (NHMC)
1201 W 5th St., Ste.T-205
Los Angeles, CA 90017-2019
Ph: (213)534-3026
Fax: (213)534-3027
E-mail: info@nhmc.org
URL: http://www.nhmc.org
Contact: Alex Nogales, Pres./CEO
Founded: 1986. **Members:** 55,000. **Staff:** 2. **Budget:** $75,000. **Regional Groups:** 5. **National Groups:** 12. **Description:** Promotes the employment and image of Hispanic Americans in radio, television, and film. **Convention/Meeting:** none. **Awards:** Impact Awards. **Frequency:** annual. **Type:** recognition. **Recipient:** for excellence in industry. **Publications:** *Positive Images*, annual. Newsletter. **Price:** free. **Circulation:** 7,000.

16830 ■ Progress and Freedom Foundation (PFF)
1444 Eye St. NW, Ste.500
Washington, DC 20005
Ph: (202)289-8928
Fax: (202)289-6079
E-mail: mail@pff.org
URL: http://www.pff.org
Contact: Daniel W. Caprio Jr., Pres.
Founded: 1993. **Description:** Seeks to study the digital revolution and its implications for public policy. Presents monographs to educate policy leaders. **Publications:** *Competition, Innovation and the Microsoft Monopoly: Antitrust in the Digital Marketplace* ● *The Digital Economy Factbook*. Presents comprehensive information regarding the impact of the digital economy. **Conventions/Meetings:** annual Aspen Summit - conference, focuses on "the big picture" regarding digital technologies, attracting leading commentators, policy experts and policymakers.

16831 ■ Public Conversations Project (PCP)
46 Kondazian St.
Watertown, MA 02472-2832
Ph: (617)923-1216
Fax: (617)923-2757
E-mail: info@publicconversations.org
URL: http://www.publicconversations.org
Contact: Laura Chasin MA, Founder/Board Chair
Founded: 1989. **Description:** Promotes constructive conversations and relationships among those who have differing values, world views and positions about divisive public issues. Helps people with fundamental disagreements over divisive issues develop the mutual understanding and trust essential for strong communities and positive action. Seeks to avoid repeating unproductive debates and to develop new modes of communicating that lead to mutual understanding, respect and trust. **Telecommunication Services:** electronic mail, lchasin@publicconversations.org. **Publications:** Newsletter, monthly. Alternate Formats: online.

16832 ■ Public Media Center (PMC)
466 Green St., Ste.300
San Francisco, CA 94133
Ph: (415)434-1403
Fax: (415)986-6779
E-mail: info@publicmediacenter.org
URL: http://www.publicmediacenter.org
Contact: Herbert Chao Gunther, Exec. Dir./Creative Dir.
Founded: 1974. **Staff:** 20. **Description:** Serves as public interest advertising agency that helps produce information campaigns for non-profit organizations working for social change. Seeks to educate people

about the uses and possibilities of media and tries to organize access to media. Believes that every segment of society should have access to the mass media and to mass communication skills. Executes local, regional, national, and international campaigns on topics ranging from reproductive rights to nuclear power. Distributes campaigns on current issues to broadcasters and community groups. **Formerly:** (1974) Public Interest Communications. **Publications:** *The Hazard Connection* ● *Index to Progressive Funders* ● *Looking Out for Number 1* ● *Talking Back: Citizen's Guide to the Fairness Doctrine* ● *Worker's Rights Handbook* ● Directory. Alternate Formats: online.

16833 ■ Radio Free Europe/Radio Liberty (RFE/RL)
1201 Connecticut Ave. NW
Washington, DC 20036
Ph: (202)457-6947 (202)457-6900
Fax: (202)457-6992
E-mail: jensend@rferl.org
URL: http://www.rferl.org
Contact: Don Jensen, Dir. of Communications
Founded: 1976. **Staff:** 593. **Budget:** $79,127,000. **Description:** Private, international communications service to Eastern and Southeastern Europe, Russia, the Caucasus, Central Asia, the Middle East, and Southwest Asia, funded by the U.S. Congress through the Broadcasting Board of Governors. "Listeners in 25 countries stretching from Belarus to Bosnia and from the Arctic Sea to the Persian Gulf, rely on RFE/RL's daily news, analysis and current affairs programming in 34 languages (none in English) to provide a coherent, objective account of events in their region and the world." Provides publications that are available at website, via email and fax subscription. Maintains pre-1995 archives that are held at Hoover Institution (Stanford University, CA) and Open Society Archives (Central European University, Budapest). **Formed by Merger of:** Free Europe; Radio Liberty Committee. **Publications:** *RFE/RL Afghanistan Report*, weekly. Newsletter ● *RFE/RL Balkan Report*, weekly. Newsletter ● *RFE/RL Baltic States Report*, weekly. Newsletter ● *RFE/RL Caucasus Report*, weekly. Newsletter ● *RFE/RL Central Asia Report*, weekly. Newsletter ● *RFE/RL East European Perspectives*, biweekly. Newsletter ● *RFE/RL Iran Report*, weekly. Newsletter ● *RFE/RL Iraq Report*, weekly. Newsletter ● *RFE/RL Media Matters*, weekly. Newsletter ● *RFE/RL Newsline*, daily. Newsletter. Alternate Formats: online ● *RFE/RL Organized Crime and Terrorism Watch*, weekly. Newsletter ● *RFE/RL Poland, Belarus, and Ukraine Report*, weekly. Newsletter ● *RFE/RL Russian Political Weekly*. Newsletter ● *RFE/RL South Slavic Report*, weekly. Newsletter ● *RFE/RL (Un)Civil Societies*, weekly. Newsletter ● Also publishes indexes. **Conventions/Meetings:** periodic Briefings - meeting, held at Washington office and at Prague Broadcasting Center; presentations by prominent opinion leaders from broadcast regions and persons of interest to broadcast audience; opening presentations followed by Q&A.

16834 ■ Reporters Committee for Freedom of the Press (RCFP)
1101 Wilson Blvd., Ste.1100
Arlington, VA 22209
Ph: (703)807-2100
Free: (800)336-4243
Fax: (703)807-2109
E-mail: rcfp@rcfp.org
URL: http://www.rcfp.org
Contact: Lucy Dalglish, Exec. Dir.
Founded: 1970. **Members:** 2,000. **Membership Dues:** individual, $30 (annual). **Staff:** 11. **Budget:** $426,000. **Description:** Upholds the First Amendment to the U.S. Constitution and protecting the freedom of information rights of the working press of all media. Conducts studies on the impact of subpoenaing reporters' notes or journalists' testimonies upon their ability to gather news from confidential sources; examines efforts to close criminal justice proceedings to the public and press; has acted as plaintiff or friend-of-court in most major lawsuits affecting the

First Amendment rights of working news reporters and editors since 1972. Provides free legal advice to reporters whose First Amendment Rights are infringed upon by subpoenas or other legal pressures. Sponsors in-house legal fellowships and semester internships for journalism students. Maintains a 200 volume library on media law and the Freedom of Information Service Center to aid journalists in obtaining government information. **Computer Services:** Mailing lists ● online services. **Publications:** *News Media and the Law*, quarterly. Magazine. **Price:** $7.50/issue. ISSN: 0149-0737. **Circulation:** 2,000 ● *News Media Update*, biweekly.

16835 ■ Society for the Eradication of Television (SET)
Box 10491
Oakland, CA 94610-0491
E-mail: set2@eyeopeners.info
URL: http://www.webwm.com/set
Contact: Steve Wagner, Dir.
Founded: 1980. **Members:** 700. **Regional Groups:** 8. **State Groups:** 6. **Local Groups:** 23. **Description:** Households that do not have a working television. Encourages others to remove televisions from their homes. Believes television retards the inner life of human beings, destroys human interaction, squanders time, and draws viewers into abject addiction. Maintains speakers' bureau for radio programs, schools, churches, and civic groups. **Libraries: Type:** reference. **Holdings:** archival material, artwork, books, clippings, periodicals. **Subjects:** television, communications, propaganda. **Publications:** *Propaganda War Comix*, periodic. **Circulation:** 20,000 ● *S.E.T. Free: The Newsletter Against Television*, quarterly. Contains original articles, reprints, and resources. Concerned with the effects of television viewing. **Circulation:** 1,200 ● *Talking Back to Television*. Pamphlet. **Conventions/Meetings:** annual conference - always September 21, in Berkeley, CA.

16836 ■ Student Press Law Center (SPLC)
1101 Wilson Blvd., Ste.1100
Arlington, VA 22209
Ph: (703)807-1904
Fax: (703)807-2109
E-mail: splc@splc.org
URL: http://www.splc.org
Contact: Mark Goodman, Exec. Dir.
Founded: 1974. **Staff:** 4. **Description:** Supporters are high school and college student journalists and journalism educators. Aims to protect the First Amendment rights of high school and college journalists. Provides information clearinghouse for student editors and others interested in preserving press freedom at student level. Offers legal aid and advice to students and teachers experiencing censorship; acts as amicus curiae in major censorship cases. Monitors important litigation. Maintains speakers' bureau. **Convention/Meeting:** none. **Awards:** Scholastic Press Freedom Award. **Frequency:** annual. **Type:** recognition. **Recipient:** for high school or college student journalists or publications. **Publications:** *Law of The Student Press*. Book. Covers press law for student journalists. **Price:** $18.00. ISSN: 0964-3574 ● *Rights, Restrictions and Responsibilities*. Booklet ● *Student Press Law Center—Report*, 3/year. Newsletter. Provides news, information, and advice on such topics as libel, censorship, and freedom of information. **Price:** $15.00/year; $28.00/2 years. ISSN: 0160-3825. **Circulation:** 5,300. Alternate Formats: online ● *Student Press Legal Center Legal Alert*, September through May. Newsletter. Alternate Formats: online.

16837 ■ Telecommunications Research and Action Center (TRAC)
PO Box 27279
Washington, DC 20005
E-mail: trac@trac.org
URL: http://www.trac.org
Contact: Samuel A. Simon, Chm.
Founded: 1967. **Members:** 32. **Membership Dues:** individual, $25 (annual) ● business, $50 (annual) ● student, $10 (annual) ● sustaining, $250 (annual). **Staff:** 1. **Description:** Offers computerized long

distance telephone analysis for cost comparison for long distance companies. **Publications:** *Teletips*, semiannual.

16838 ■ Union for Democratic Communications (UDC)
c/o Jennifer Proffitt
Dept. of Commun.
Florida State Univ.
Univ. Ctr., Bldg. C, Ste.3100
Tallahassee, FL 32306-2664
Ph: (850)644-8748
E-mail: jennifer.proffitt@comm.fsu.edu
URL: http://www.udc.org
Contact: James R. Compton, Coor.
Founded: 1981. **Members:** 300. **Membership Dues:** regular, $50 (annual) ● student/low-income, $25 (annual). **Budget:** $9,200. **Local Groups:** 8. **Multinational. Description:** Researchers, teachers, media producers, and community activists committed to more democratic, participatory communications. Fosters critical perspectives in communication theory and media production; unites media producers, communications researchers, and grass roots communications workers; facilitates media productions. **Awards:** Dallas Smythe Award. **Type:** recognition. **Publications:** *Democratic Communique*, quarterly. Newsletter. Reports on and analyzes issues relating to democratic communications; reprints pertinent conference statement and other documents; reviews resources. **Price:** $30.00 /year for individuals; $65.00 /year for institutions; $55.00/2 years for individuals; $120.00/2 years for institutions. **Circulation:** 450. **Advertising:** accepted. Alternate Formats: online. **Conventions/Meetings:** biennial conference (exhibits) ● periodic regional meeting.

16839 ■ Unison Institute
1742 Connecticut Ave. NW
Washington, DC 20009
Ph: (202)797-7200
Fax: (202)234-8584
E-mail: unison@unison.org
URL: http://chelen.net
Founded: 1989. **Staff:** 5. **Description:** Works to provide a center for computer systems and software technology in the public interest in cooperation with other groups, including OMB Watch, to monitor the Environmental Protection Agency's responsibilities toward the Toxic Release Inventory. Operates the Right-to-Know Network (RTK NET), a computer online system which provides community groups and activists with government information. Conducts research for community groups, provides training around the country on the use of computer technology, and provides technical assistance to groups trying to tap into the system. **Computer Services:** database, environmental, housing, demographic and geographic, and campaign finance. **Publications:** Newsletter, quarterly. Alternate Formats: online.

16840 ■ Willow Mixed Media (WMM)
PO Box 194
Glenford, NY 12433
Ph: (845)657-2914
Free: (888)731-4237
E-mail: video@hvc.rr.com
URL: http://www.hvw.com/willow
Contact: Tobe Carey, Exec. Off.
Founded: 1979. **Description:** Seeks to develop and produce projects for videotape, cable television, and art shows for educational purposes. **Publications:** *The Bomb Shelter*. Video. **Price:** $14.95 each ● *Cancer: Just a Word.Not a Sentence*. Video. **Price:** $29.95 for home use; $69.95 for public performance ● *Deep Water: Building the Catskill Water System*. Video. **Price:** $19.95 each ● *Flags: Post 9/11*. Video ● *Giving Birth*. Video. **Price:** $29.95 each ● *The Hudson River PCB Story: A Toxic Heritage*. Video. **Price:** $14.95 each ● *The Infertility Tape: A Couple's Guide*. Video. **Price:** $29.95 for home use ● *Living With Tomorrow*. Video. **Price:** $14.95 each ● *The March for Disarmament*. Video. **Price:** $19.95 each ● *Radiation Workers: Reprocessing*. Video. **Price:** $19.95 each ● *Stream a Meditation*. Video ● *The Touch: Preventing Sexual Misconduct in Law Enforcement*.

Video. **Price:** $195.00 for public performance ● *Will Our Children Thank Us.* Video. **Price:** $29.95 each ● *Woodstock Summer of '94: Not the Music.Just the Scene.* Video. **Price:** $19.95 each.

16841 ■ Women's Institute for Freedom of the Press (WIFP)
1940 Calvert St. NW
Washington, DC 20009-1502
Ph: (202)265-6707
E-mail: mediademocracy@wifp.org
URL: http://www.wifp.org
Contact: Martha Leslie Allen PhD, Dir./Pres.

Founded: 1972. **Members:** 500. **Description:** Seeks to publish works both theoretical and practical on media democracy issues. Encourages discussion and ideas on the restructuring of the world's communications systems so that freedom of the press can be for individuals, not big corporations. Works toward a system where people can speak for themselves, not just have others portraying them. **Libraries: Type:** not open to the public. **Subjects:** media democracy, women and media. **Publications:** *A National Citizens' Network of Radio and Television.* Booklet ● *Directory of Women's Media,* annual. Book. Spiral-bound. ● *Media Democracy: Past, Present, and Future.* Booklet ● *The Media Liberation Movement.* Booklet ● *The Media Technology Road to Democracy and Equality.* Booklet ● *Media Without Democracy and What to Do About It.* Booklet ● *Source of Power for Women: A Strategy to Equalize Media Outreach.* Booklet ● *What's Wrong With Mass Media for Women.*

16842 ■ World Press Freedom Committee (WPFC)
11690-C Sunrise Valley Dr.
Reston, VA 20191
Ph: (703)715-9811
Fax: (703)620-6790
E-mail: freepress@wpfc.org
URL: http://www.wpfc.org
Contact: Richard N. Winfield, Chm.

Founded: 1976. **Staff:** 4. **Description:** Journalistic organizations united to support freedom of the press, especially in Third World and Eastern European countries. Speaks out against "those who seek to deny truth in news and those who abuse newsmen." Encourages high professional standards and performance of the news media. Offers professional and technical print and broadcast assistance to Third World journalists; conducts seminars; has sponsored over 150 projects in Africa, Asia, Latin America, Eastern Europe, and the Caribbean including organization of training programs and preparation of manuals for practitioners. **Publications:** Newsletter, 4-8/year ● Also publishes papers, manuals, declarations, and reports. **Conventions/Meetings:** biennial meeting.

16843 ■ World Press Institute (WPI)
Macalester Coll.
1576 Summit Ave.
St. Paul, MN 55105
Ph: (651)696-6360
Fax: (651)696-6306
E-mail: wpi@macalester.edu
URL: http://www.worldpressinstitute.org
Contact: John H. Ullmann, Exec. Dir.

Founded: 1961. **Members:** 506. **Staff:** 4. **Budget:** $600,000. **Description:** Organizes a four-month work, study, and travel program in the U.S. for 10 experienced professional journalists from foreign countries. Aims to provide a personal, informal perspective about U.S. business, politics, social issues, communication, science and technology, and culture and to focus on the workings of a free press in a democracy. Program includes: seminars; interviews with government officials, business leaders, academics, editors, and ordinary citizens. **Awards:** World Press Institute Fellowship. **Frequency:** annual. **Type:** fellowship. **Recipient:** for professional non-U.S. citizen journalists with at least 5 years experience. **Conventions/Meetings:** board meeting - always March, July and October; 3/year.

Community Action

16844 ■ Join Hands Day
1315 W 22nd St., Ste.400
Oak Brook, IL 60523
Ph: (630)522-6322
Fax: (630)522-6327
E-mail: actioncenter@joinhandsday.org
URL: http://www.joinhandsday.org
Contact: Frederick H. Grubbe, Pres.

Founded: 1999. **Description:** Targets and develops relationships between young persons and adults through neighborhood volunteering. **Awards:** Excellence Awards. **Frequency:** annual. **Type:** recognition. **Recipient:** for outstanding youth/adult partnerships that take place across America. **Publications:** *Join Hands Day Action Guide.* Manuals ● *Join Hands Day Report of the Day.* Alternate Formats: online ● Brochure.

16845 ■ Praxis Project
1750 Columbia Rd. NW, 2nd Fl.
Washington, DC 20009
Ph: (202)234-5921
Fax: (202)234-2689
E-mail: info@thepraxisproject.org
URL: http://www.thepraxisproject.org
Contact: Makani Themba-Nixon, Exec. Dir.

Description: Builds partnerships with local groups to influence policymaking to address the underlying systemic causes of community problems. Trains partner organizations and provides research, technical assistance and financial support. Designs community-based plans and develops media strategies and policy initiatives to achieve sustainable results. **Telecommunication Services:** electronic mail, mthemba@thepraxisproject.org. **Publications:** *Praxis News and Notes.* Newsletter. Alternate Formats: online.

Community Development

16846 ■ ACCION International (ACCION)
56 Roland St., Ste.300
Boston, MA 02129
Ph: (617)625-7080
Free: (866)245-0783
Fax: (617)625-7020
E-mail: info@accionusa.org
URL: http://www.accion.org
Contact: Maria Otero, Pres./CEO

Founded: 1961. **Staff:** 125. **Budget:** $13,100,000. **Regional Groups:** 27. **State Groups:** 8. **Languages:** English, French, Portuguese, Spanish. **Multinational.** **Description:** Provides financial services to poor and low-income people in 15 countries in Latin America and the Caribbean, 5 in Africa and in over 30 U.S. cities and towns. Works to reduce poverty and unemployment by providing loans and business support to microentrepreneurs in low-income communities through a network of affiliated institutions. **Libraries: Type:** reference. **Subjects:** microfinance. **Additional Websites:** http://www.accionusa.org. **Councils:** President's. **Publications:** *ACCION International Publications,* annual. Annual Report ● *The Business of Fighting Poverty,* annual. Annual Report ● *Ventures,* biennial. Newsletter ● Books ● Brochures ● Catalog. Alternate Formats: online ● Monographs ● Papers. **Conventions/Meetings:** annual conference.

16847 ■ American Congress of Community Supports and Employment Services (ACCSES)
1875 Eye St. NW, 12th Fl.
Washington, DC 20006-5409
Ph: (202)466-3355
Fax: (202)466-7571
E-mail: mkilmer@accses.org
URL: http://www.accses.org
Contact: Brenda Maxey, Pres./CEO/Chair

Founded: 1998. **Members:** 45. **Membership Dues:** general, $3,000-$5,000 (annual). **Staff:** 1. **Budget:** $250,000. **Languages:** English, Spanish. **Description:** Community members and service organizations. Aims to maximize employment opportunities and independent living for individuals with mental and physical disabilities. Sponsors annual meetings and conventions, publishes newsletters and weekly fact sheets, and networking of the various committees. **Publications:** *ACCSES Update,* monthly. Newsletter ● *Fact Sheet,* weekly ● *News From the Capital,* monthly. Newsletter. **Price:** free, for members only. **Conventions/Meetings:** annual Legislative Fly-In Conference, with legislative updates ● annual seminar.

16848 ■ Association of Metropolitan Planning Organizations (AMPO)
1029 Vermont Ave. NW, Ste.710
Washington, DC 20005
Ph: (202)296-7051
Fax: (202)296-7054
E-mail: staff@ampo.org
URL: http://www.ampo.org
Contact: DeLania Hardy, Exec. Dir.

Founded: 1994. **Membership Dues:** associate, $500-$2,500 (annual) ● individual associate, $75 (annual) ● student/intern, $25 (annual). **Description:** Enhances the Metropolitan Planning Organizations' (MPOs) abilities to improve metropolitan transportation systems. Serves the needs and interests of MPOs nationwide. Promotes planning, programming and coordination of federal highway and transit investments. Provides training, forum, conferences and workshops for transportation policy development. **Awards:** Honorable Mention National Award for Outstanding Achievement in Metropolitan Transportation Planning - MPOs Over 200000. **Frequency:** annual. **Type:** recognition. **Recipient:** for outstanding achievement in Metropolitan Transportation Planning for an MPO over 200,000 ● National Award for Outstanding Achievement in Metropolitan Transportation Planning - MPOs Over 200000. **Frequency:** annual. **Type:** recognition. **Recipient:** for outstanding achievement in Metropolitan Transportation Planning for an MPO over 200,000 ● National Award for Outstanding Technical Merit in Metropolitan Transportation Planning - MPOs Over 200000. **Frequency:** annual. **Type:** recognition. **Recipient:** for outstanding technical achievement in Metropolitan Transportation Planning for an MPO over 200,000 ● National Award for Outstanding Technical Merit in Metropolitan Transportation Planning - MPOs Under 200000. **Frequency:** annual. **Type:** recognition. **Recipient:** for outstanding achievement in Metropolitan Transportation Planning for small MPOs ● Outstanding Achievement in Metropolitan Transportation Planning as an Elected Official. **Frequency:** annual. **Type:** recognition. **Recipient:** for outstanding elected official leadership ● Outstanding Professional Achievement in Metropolitan Transportation Planning. **Frequency:** annual. **Type:** recognition. **Recipient:** for outstanding individual leadership in metropolitan transportation planning ● Senator Daniel Patrick Moynihan Award. **Frequency:** annual. **Type:** recognition. **Recipient:** for outstanding individual in the field of urban affairs and transportation. **Task Forces:** Transit Development. **Working Groups:** Air Quality; Travel Modeling. **Publications:** *aMPO eMAIL,* biweekly. Newsletter. Alternate Formats: online ● *ITS,* quarterly. Newsletter ● *Metros,* quarterly. Newsletter.

16849 ■ Center for Neighborhood Technology (CNT)
2125 W North Ave.
Chicago, IL 60647
Ph: (773)278-4800
Fax: (773)278-3840
E-mail: info@cnt.org
URL: http://www.cnt.org
Contact: Scott Bernstein, Pres.

Founded: 1978. **Members:** 31. **Staff:** 26. **Budget:** $18,000,000. **Description:** Formulates public policy recommendations on community development and the environment and carries out demonstration projects that foster sustainable communities. **Computer Services:** Mailing lists ● online services, housing abandonment early warning system. **Depart-**

ments: Energy Service; Housing; Industrial Development; Public Issues. **Projects:** Chicagoland Transportation and Air Quality Commission; Clean Air Counts; Community Energy Cooperative; Community Information Technology and Neighborhood Early Warning System; Connections for Community Ownership; Green Infrastructure Regional Mapping; I-GO Car Sharing; LEGInfo.org. **Publications:** *The Neighborhood Works.* Magazine. **Price:** $30.00/year. **Circulation:** 2,000 ● *Place Matters,* 3/year. Newsletter. **Circulation:** 6,000 ● Annual Report, annual. **Circulation:** 1,000 ● Report, biennial. Alternate Formats: online.

16850 ■ Center for New Community (CNC)
PO Box 479327
Chicago, IL 60647
Ph: (312)266-0319
Fax: (312)266-0278
URL: http://www.newcomm.org
Description: Works to revitalize congregations and communities for social, economic and political democracy. **Projects:** Building Democracy Initiative. **Conventions/Meetings:** conference.

16851 ■ Center for Reflective Community Practice (CRCP)
Massachusetts Inst. of Tech.
Dept. of Urban Stud. and Planning, Rm. 7-307
77 Massachusetts Ave.
Cambridge, MA 02139
Ph: (617)253-3216
Fax: (617)258-6515
E-mail: crcp@mit.edu
URL: http://crcp.mit.edu
Contact: Dr. Ceasar McDowell, Dir.
Founded: 1970. **Staff:** 3. **Description:** Provides opportunity for minority community activists and local governmental officials (10 to 12 per year) to spend a year of reflection, study, and research at the Massachusetts Institute of Technology. The Program is being redesigned to capture the potential of new information technologies for poor communities and communities of color. **Programs:** Community Fellows; MLK Fellowship. **Projects:** Boston Community Learning. **Special Interest Groups:** Design Studio for Social Intervention. **Study Groups:** Springfield Practicum (Fall 06). **Formerly:** Community Fellows Program.

16852 ■ Community Associations Institute (CAI)
225 Reinekers Ln., Ste.300
Alexandria, VA 22314
Ph: (703)548-8600
Free: (888)CAI-4321
Fax: (703)684-1581
E-mail: caidirect@caionline.org
URL: http://www.caionline.org
Contact: Thomas M. Skiba, CEO
Founded: 1973. **Members:** 16,000. **Membership Dues:** national corporate, $7,500 (annual) ● community management company, $350 (annual) ● volunteer leader, $85 (annual) ● community manager, $95 (annual) ● business partner, $495 (annual). **Staff:** 50. **Budget:** $7,000,000. **State Groups:** 55. **Description:** Condominium and homeowner associations, cooperatives, and association-governed planned communities of all sizes and architectural types; community or property managers and management firms; individual homeowners; community association managers and management firms; public officials; and lawyers, accountants, engineers, reserve specialists, builder/developers and other providers of professional services and products for CAs. Seeks to educate and represent America's 250,000 residential condominium, cooperative and homeowner associations and related professionals and service providers. Aims to foster vibrant, responsive, competent community associations that promote harmony, community and responsible leadership. **Libraries: Type:** not open to the public. **Holdings:** 3,000; articles. **Awards:** National Community Association of the Year. **Frequency:** annual. **Type:** recognition. **Recipient:** for effective management and operation of a community association. **Computer**

Services: database, Credentialed Professionals. **Programs:** Accredited Association Management Company Accreditation; Association Management Specialist Designation; Professional Community Associations Manager Designation; Professional Management Development; Reserve Specialist Designation. **Publications:** *CEO Insights.* Newsletter. Contains easy to read information about professional trends and strategies. Alternate Formats: online ● *Common Ground,* bimonthly. Magazine. Covers the community association industry. Includes book reviews and research reports. **Price:** $65.00 /year for nonmembers; $39.00 /year for members. ISSN: 0885-6133. **Circulation:** 30,000. **Advertising:** accepted ● *Community Association Law Reporter,* monthly. Newsletter. Reports on court cases, legal trends, and legislative developments concerning community associations. **Price:** $125.00 /year for members; $208.00 /year for nonmembers. ISSN: 0190-1192. **Circulation:** 3,000 ● *Community Management,* bimonthly. Newsletter. **Price:** $35.00 for members; $59.00 for nonmembers. **Circulation:** 4,000 ● *Fast Tracks,* monthly. Newsletter. Consists of articles focusing on industry trends and issues. Alternate Formats: online ● *Ledger Quarterly.* Newsletter. Covers financial issues of concern to community associations. **Price:** $40.00 for members; $67.00 /year for nonmembers. **Circulation:** 3,000 ● *Product and Service Providers.* Directory. Alternate Formats: online. **Conventions/Meetings:** semiannual conference (exhibits) - May and October ● annual Law Seminar - January or February ● workshop.

16853 ■ Community Development Society (CDS)
17 S High St., Ste.200
Columbus, OH 43215
Ph: (614)221-1900
Fax: (614)221-1989
E-mail: cds@assnoffices.com
URL: http://www.comm-dev.org
Contact: Randy Adams, Pres.
Founded: 1969. **Members:** 1,100. **Membership Dues:** student, $35 (annual) ● retiree, $60 (annual) ● regular, $85 (annual) ● family, $130 (annual). **Budget:** $75,000. **State Groups:** 21. **Description:** Professionals and practitioners in community development; international, national, state, and local groups interested in community development efforts. Provides a forum for exchange of ideas and experiences; disseminates information to the public; advocates excellence in community programs, scholarship, and research; promotes citizen participation as essential to effective community development. Sponsors educational programs. **Awards:** CD Achievement Award. **Frequency:** annual. **Type:** recognition. **Recipient:** for outstanding contribution to community development ● Duane L. Gibson Distinguished Service Award. **Frequency:** annual. **Type:** recognition. **Recipient:** for superior and long standing service ● Innovative Program. **Frequency:** annual. **Type:** recognition. **Recipient:** for superior innovative program using the principles of good practice ● New Professional Award. **Frequency:** annual. **Type:** recognition. **Recipient:** for contribution to the field of community development ● Outstanding Program. **Frequency:** annual. **Type:** recognition. **Recipient:** for outstanding program utilizing the principles of good practice ● Student Achievement, Research. **Frequency:** annual. **Type:** recognition. **Recipient:** for contribution to the community through an article, project or internship. **Telecommunication Services:** electronic mail, adamsrmk@aol.com. **Committees:** Local Arrangements. **Publications:** *CDS Membership Directory,* annual ● *Journal of the Community Development Society,* semiannual. **Price:** $12.00/ issue; $65.00/year outside U.S. ISSN: 0010-3829. Alternate Formats: microform ● *Vanguard,* quarterly. Newsletter. Contains current activities, topical issues and ideas. Alternate Formats: online ● Books ● Brochures ● Community Development Practice (quarterly - 608 pages). **Conventions/Meetings:** annual conference (exhibits).

16854 ■ Community Service (CS)
PO Box 243
Yellow Springs, OH 45387

Ph: (937)767-2161
E-mail: info@communitysolution.org
URL: http://www.smallcommunity.org
Contact: Faith Morgan, Board Pres.
Founded: 1940. **Members:** 400. **Membership Dues:** regular, $25 (annual). **Staff:** 2. **Budget:** $80,000. **Description:** Individuals concerned with various aspects of small local community development including economic, educational, cultural, and spiritual. Promotes understanding of the nature and possibilities of the small local community as essential to a wholesome society. Provides information and counseling on intentional communities and land trusts. **Libraries: Type:** reference. **Holdings:** 1,500; books, periodicals. **Subjects:** small local community, sociology, rural life, correspondence of the commune movement since the 1940s, economics, sustainability. **Committees:** Community Journal; Earth Institute; Land Trust; Small Community Course on Website. **Also Known As:** SmallCommunity.org. **Publications:** *Annual Booklist,* annual. Bibliography. **Price:** free. ISSN: 0277-6189 ● *Community Journal,* quarterly. Magazine. Contains book reviews and articles about small community and economic issues, land trusts, education, and community improvement. **Price:** $25.00/year; included in membership dues. **Circulation:** 400 ● *The Great Community.* Pamphlet ● *The Small Community.* Book ● Membership Directory, annual. **Conventions/Meetings:** annual conference and workshop (exhibits) - in October, Yellow Springs, OH.

16855 ■ Do Something
24-32 Union Sq. E, 4th Fl.
New York, NY 10003
Fax: (212)254-2391
E-mail: help@dosomething.org
URL: http://www.dosomething.org
Contact: Michelle Bellinger, Office Mgr.
Founded: 1993. **Description:** Educators helping young people who are committed to community improvement. **Programs:** Kindness and Justice Challenge. **Publications:** *Do Something E-Newsletter.* Alternate Formats: online ● Annual Report. Alternate Formats: online.

16856 ■ Fellowship for Intentional Community (FIC)
RR 1 Box 156-W
Rutledge, MO 63563-9720
Ph: (660)883-5545
Free: (800)995-8342
Fax: (660)883-5545
E-mail: fic@ic.org
URL: http://www.ic.org
Contact: Laird Schaub, Exec. Sec.
Founded: 1948. **Members:** 265. **Membership Dues:** individual, $30 (annual) ● individual with low income, $15 (annual) ● community, $40-$100 (annual) ● organization, $50 (annual) ● supporting, $100 (annual) ● sustaining, $250 (annual) ● sponsoring, $500 (annual). **Staff:** 10. **Budget:** $175,000. **Regional Groups:** 6. **State Groups:** 1. **Description:** Promotes the establishment of communal, cooperative living groups; encourages increased public awareness, understanding, and acceptance of "intentional communities." Demonstrates and facilitates application of communal experiences to the larger society; cites intentional communities as models of ecological options, opportunities for personal and community development, and methods for nurturing peaceful social transformation. Facilitates exchange of information, skills, and economic support among existing and newly formed intentional communities; encourages wider social interaction among communities. Operates speaker's bureau, revolving loan fund, and referral service; conducts research and educational programs; compiles statistics. **Computer Services:** Mailing lists, communities and resource groups. **Additional Websites:** http://fic.ic.org. **Affiliated With:** Community Service; Federation of Egalitarian Communities. **Formerly:** (1986) Fellowship of International Communities. **Publications:** *Communities Directory,* quadrennial. Includes maps, charts, and articles. **Price:** $24.00 plus shipping and handling. ISSN: 0960-2714. **Circulation:** 18,000. **Advertising:**

accepted ● *Communities: Journal of Cooperative Living,* quarterly. **Price:** $20.00/year; $6.00/issue. **ISSN:** 0199-9346. **Circulation:** 5,000. **Advertising:** accepted ● *FIC Newsletter* ● *Visions of Utopia: Experiment in Sustainable Culture.* Video. **Price:** $33.00. **Conventions/Meetings:** semiannual Art of Community - conference and workshop, weekend event social opportunities (exhibits) - always spring and fall.

16857 ■ Foundation for International Community Assistance (FINCA)
1101 14th St. NW, Ste.1100
Washington, DC 20005
Ph: (202)682-1510
Fax: (202)682-1535
E-mail: info@villagebanking.org
URL: http://www.villagebanking.org
Contact: Rupert Scofield, Exec. Dir.
Founded: 1984. **Staff:** 30. **Languages:** English, Spanish. **Multinational. Description:** Provides financial services to the world's poorest families so they can create their own jobs, raise household incomes and improve standard of living. Aims to deliver these services through a global network of locally managed, self-supporting institutions. **Awards:** Village Banking Award. **Type:** recognition. **Publications:** *The Case for Village Banking* ● *Village Banknotes,* quarterly. Newsletter. Contains Success Story of the Month and news from field offices. ● Annual Report.

16858 ■ HOUR Money Network
Box 365
Ithaca, NY 14851
Ph: (607)272-4330
E-mail: paglo@lightlink.com
URL: http://www.ithacahours.com
Contact: Paul Glover, Founder
Founded: 1991. **Members:** 5,000. **Membership Dues:** individual, $25 (annual). **Staff:** 1. **Local Groups:** 65. **Languages:** Spanish. **Description:** Anyone who agrees to accept HOURS, local currency, backed by local goods and services. Seeks to reduce dependency on multinational corporations and bankers by promoting local paper money called HOURS. (HOURS have been valued at $10 because $10 per hour is the average County wage.) Finds that the benefits of connecting the HOUR systems nationwide are: adding to reliable local money supply; raising minimum wage to $10 per hour; benefiting businesses by adding to local spending power, reinforcing trade among local businesses and individuals; providing grants of HOURS to local organizations; making business loans without charging interest; and expanding a mutual enterprise system which allows more people to meet and help one another. **Libraries: Type:** reference. **Holdings:** archival material. **Subjects:** local currency. **Awards:** Hour Grants. **Frequency:** monthly. **Type:** grant. **Recipient:** to local organizations. **Publications:** *Hometown Money Starter Kit.* Book. **Price:** $27.00 ● *Hour Town,* bimonthly. Newsletter ● *Ithaca Hour Video.* **Price:** $15.00. **Conventions/Meetings:** quarterly Barter Potlucks - general assembly.

16859 ■ Independence Plan for Neighborhood Councils (IPNC)
201 W Maple
Independence, MO 64050
Ph: (816)833-4225
Fax: (816)833-4251
E-mail: pauljr@ipnc.net
URL: http://www.ipnc.net
Contact: Paul Erickson Jr., Contact
Founded: 1971. **Members:** 23,000. **Staff:** 4. **Budget:** $500,000. **Local Groups:** 42. **Description:** Aims to act as a model group for communities worldwide and to promote community leadership by pooling human resources for neighborhood and community development. Maintains 20 committees on subjects such as health, fire, family life, energy and environment, and social services. Establishes community programs including Indevestors, Community Foundation for Independence, Independence Think Tank, and Blue Ribbon Jury. Holds monthly neighborhood and citywide meetings. Sponsors events such as Citywide

Police Recognition Program, Family Fun Festival, Children's Christmas Party, Community Messiah Sing, and Good Neighbor Recognition Program. Sponsors neighborhood competitions; offers Community Leaders Training Course. **Libraries: Type:** open to the public. **Holdings:** 15,000; articles, books, periodicals. **Awards:** Lifetime Achievement Award. **Frequency:** annual. **Type:** recognition. **Computer Services:** database ● mailing lists ● online services. **Publications:** *Biennial Report.* Magazine. **Price:** $10.00 donation ● *Leadership Digest,* semiannual. Pamphlets. **Conventions/Meetings:** annual Fall Leadership Rendezvous - conference and workshop - always held weekend after Thanksgiving.

16860 ■ Industrial Areas Foundation (IAF)
220 W Kinzie St., 5th Fl.
Chicago, IL 60610
Ph: (312)245-9211
Fax: (312)245-9744
E-mail: iaf@industrialareasfoundation.org
URL: http://www.industrialareasfoundation.org
Contact: Edward T. Chambers, Exec. Dir.
Founded: 1940. **Staff:** 12. **Multinational. Description:** Supplies techniques and personnel to help people in poor, working, and middle class communities, especially within larger municipalities, to organize themselves on a democratic basis so that they have power in matters that affect their own interests. Works against established authority in dealing with problems of slum dwellings, housing, urban renewal, racial discrimination, unresponsive politicians, and overcrowded schools. Maintains a training institute to develop citizens into politically literate, competent organizers and leaders. **Telecommunication Services:** electronic mail, iaf@iafil.org. **Publications:** *Going Public.* Book. **Price:** $15.75 ● *Roots for Radicals: Organizing for Power, Action and Justice.* Book. **Price:** $12.89 ● *Rules for Radicals.* Book. **Price:** $9.00.

16861 ■ Institute for Community Economics (ICE)
57 School St.
Springfield, MA 01105-1331
Ph: (413)746-8660
Fax: (413)746-8862
E-mail: info@iceclt.org
URL: http://www.iceclt.org
Contact: Yesenia Perez, Exec. Asst.
Founded: 1967. **Membership Dues:** affiliate, $100 (annual) ● associate, $1,500 (annual). **Staff:** 14. **Budget:** $2,370,000. **Description:** Provides technical and organizational assistance and low cost financing to community-based groups such as Community Land Trusts (CLTs), Community Loan Funds (CLFs), and limited-equity housing cooperatives; these groups in turn help rural and urban low-income communities gain access to land, housing, and capital and other resources. Operates Revolving Loan Fund to aid community-based non-profit organizations such as CLTs and other non-profit housing organizations. **Telecommunication Services:** electronic mail, yesenia@iceclt.org. **Funds:** Revolving Loan. **Programs:** Financial Services; Technical Assistance. **Absorbed:** (1978) National Community Land Trust Center. **Formerly:** (1978) International Independence Institute. **Publications:** *CLT Handbook, Revised 2002* ● *Community Land Trusts Legal Manual.* Provides information about legal issues regarding organizational structure, separate ownership of land and buildings, and ground leases. **Price:** $100.00 each; $50.00 for CLT Network members ● *Homes and Hands: Community Land Trusts in Action* (in English and Spanish). Video. **Price:** $100.00 for institutions; $60.00 for community organizations; $20.00 for developing CLTs ● *ICE Update,* semiannual. Newsletter ● *Introducing Community Land Trusts.* Brochure. **Price:** $25.00 for 100 copies ● *Managing the Money Side: Financial Management for Community-Based Housing Organizations.* Handbook. **Price:** $25.00 ● Annual Report, annual ● Also publishes educational and technical materials on community land trusts and property reform solutions to the affordable housing crises. **Conventions/Meetings:** annual Community Land

Trust Conference and Affiliate Meeting (exhibits) ● semiannual seminar.

16862 ■ International Coalition for Sustainable Production and Consumption (ICSPAC)
c/o Integrative Strategies Forum
11426 Rockville Pike, No. 306
Rockville, MD 20852
Ph: (301)770-6375
E-mail: info@icspac.net
URL: http://www.icspac.net
Contact: Jeffrey Barber, Contact
Founded: 1999. **Multinational. Description:** Aims to provide information exchange and a networking vehicle for NGOs and citizen organizations promoting Sustainable Production and Consumption (SPAC) policies and practices. Raises public awareness and engagement on SPAC issues, trends and policies. Encourages governments to implement their commitments to eliminate unsustainable production and consumption patterns.

16863 ■ Leadership Development Network (LDN)
PO Box 70
Silver Point, TN 38582
Ph: (931)858-6399
Fax: (603)372-1271
E-mail: info@leadershipdevelopmentnetwork.com
URL: http://www.leadershipdevelopmentnetwork.com
Contact: Tommy Roberts, Pres.
Description: Association of individuals working in community economic development who are dedicated to moving the field toward practices which dismantle racism, empower community residents, build locally controlled institutions, nurture and develop the capacity of individuals, families, organizations and communities to realize hope, recognize and construct options, and to take positive action towards creating healthy communities.

16864 ■ Local Initiatives Support Corporation (LISC)
501 7th Ave.
New York, NY 10018
Ph: (212)455-9800
Fax: (212)682-5929
E-mail: info@lisc.org
URL: http://www.lisc.org
Contact: Michael Rubinger, Pres./CEO
Founded: 1979. **Description:** Seeks to help independent community-based organizations in deteriorated areas to improve local, physical, and economic conditions while strengthening their own management and financial capabilities. Matches funds contributed by local corporations and foundations with those provided by national donors and investors; offers loans and grants to local organizations and projects. Administers national community development loan programs in cooperation with major financial institutions. **Convention/Meeting:** none. **Publications:** *LISC eNewsletter,* 3/year. Alternate Formats: online ● Annual Report, annual.

16865 ■ National Association for County Community and Economic Development (NACCED)
2025 M St. NW, Ste.800
Washington, DC 20036-3309
Ph: (202)367-1149
Fax: (202)367-2149
E-mail: snusser@smithbucklin.com
URL: http://www.nacced.org
Contact: John C. Murphy, Exec. Dir.
Founded: 1978. **Members:** 130. **Membership Dues:** large non-entitlement county, $725 (annual) ● medium county, $450 (annual) ● small county, $225 (annual) ● associate, $400 (annual). **Staff:** 3. **Description:** Community development directors and principal community and economic development staff members from counties that are members of the National Association of Counties (see separate entry). Aims to stimulate and contribute to the implementation of community and economic development and

housing programs within counties; and to act as a liaison between the counties and the Department of Housing and Urban Development; has established a peer-to-peer matching network for directors needing assistance on specific issues. Sponsors workshops and seminars on community development and housing issues. **Awards:** Awards of Excellence. **Frequency:** annual. **Type:** recognition. **Recipient:** for counties in America with effective, innovative and exemplary activities ● John C. Murphy Scholarship. **Frequency:** annual. **Type:** scholarship. **Recipient:** to an undergraduate and graduate student currently attending a college or university with a chosen field of study in the areas of affordable housing. **Committees:** Community Development; Economic Development; Housing; Program Support. **Programs:** HOME Technical Assistance. **Formerly:** (1987) National Association of County Community Development Directors. **Publications:** *NACCED Alerts*, periodic. Contains analyses on federal legislation and regulations and reports on current developments in the field. **Price:** included in membership dues ● *NACCED Insights*, bimonthly. Newsletter. Includes reviews of award-winning programs and county case studies. **Price:** included in membership dues ● *National Association for County Community and Economic Development—Directory*, annual ● Annual Report, annual. Alternate Formats: online. **Conventions/Meetings:** annual conference - always fall.

16866 ■ National Association of Development Organizations Research Foundation (NADO)
400 N Capitol St. NW, Ste.390
Washington, DC 20001
Ph: (202)624-7806
Fax: (202)624-8813
E-mail: info@nado.org
URL: http://www.nado.org
Contact: Laurie Thompson, Deputy Exec. Dir.
Founded: 1988. **Budget:** $1,500,000. **Regional Groups:** 250. **Description:** Identifies, studies and promotes regional solutions and approaches to improving local prosperity and services through the nationwide network of regional development organizations. Shares best practices and offer professional development training, analyzes the impact of federal policies and programs on regional development organizations, and examines the latest developments and trends in small metro and rural America. Provides federal advocacy, informative research, special reports and training to the nation's rural regional development organizations. **Awards:** Congressional Partnership Award. **Frequency:** biennial. **Type:** recognition ● Innovations Award. **Frequency:** annual. **Type:** recognition. **Recipient:** for members. **Computer Services:** database, 1000 records on innovative economic development projects. **Affiliated With:** National Association of Development Organizations. **Conventions/Meetings:** annual Training Conference (exhibits).

16867 ■ National Center for Neighborhood Enterprise (NCNE)
1625 K St. NW, Ste.1200
Washington, DC 20006
Ph: (202)518-6500
Fax: (202)588-0314
E-mail: info@cneonline.org
URL: http://www.cneonline.org
Contact: Robert L. Woodson Sr., Pres./Founder
Founded: 1981. **Staff:** 14. **Budget:** $2,000,000. **Description:** Empowers neighborhood leaders to promote solutions that reduce crime and violence, restore families, revitalize low-income communities and create economic enterprise. Provides training, technical assistance, public policy initiatives, and linkages to sources of support. **Awards:** Achievement Against the Odds. **Frequency:** annual. **Type:** recognition. **Recipient:** for low income individuals who have overcome significant adversity and helped others. **Funds:** Compassion Capital. **Programs:** Alabama Rural Initiative; Neighborhood Leadership Development Institute; Violence Free Zone; Weed and Seed. **Projects:** Financial Literacy. **Publications:** *A Companion Manual to the HUD Comprehensive Improvement and Assistance Program Handbook*

- Guide to Understanding CIAP. **Price:** $9.95 ● *On the Road to Economic Freedom: An Agenda for Black Progress* ● *The Reverse Commute Training Manual: Guide to Developing a Reverse Commute Transportation Business.* **Price:** $9.95 ● *The Triumphs of Joseph.* Book ● Newsletter. Alternate Formats: online ● Videos ● Brochure. Alternate Formats: online.

16868 ■ National Coalition Building Institute (NCBI)
1120 Connecticut Ave. NW, Ste.450
Washington, DC 20036
Ph: (202)785-9400
Fax: (202)785-3385
E-mail: ncbiinc@aol.com
URL: http://www.ncbi.org
Contact: Cherie R. Brown, Exec. Dir.
Founded: 1984. **Multinational. Description:** Strives to eliminate prejudice and intergroup conflict in communities worldwide. **Programs:** Leadership Training. **Conventions/Meetings:** workshop.

16869 ■ National Community Development Association (NCDA)
522 21st St. NW, No. 120
Washington, DC 20006
Ph: (202)293-7587
Fax: (202)887-5546
E-mail: ncda@ncdaonline.org
URL: http://www.ncdaonline.org
Contact: Nancy Haney, Pres.
Founded: 1973. **Members:** 500. **Membership Dues:** affiliate, $2,500 (annual) ● subscriber, non-entitlement, $375 (annual) ● alumni, $450 (annual) ● entitlement (based on population), $550-$3,365 (annual). **Staff:** 4. **Regional Groups:** 10. **Description:** Represents community development program directors. Supports the interests of Community Development Block Grant Programs as well as other community and economic development issues; disseminates information; operates workshops on various aspects of housing, economic, and community development. **Computer Services:** database, peer assistance line ● online services, yellow pages. **Committees:** Community Development Funding; Legislative; Organizational Structure. **Affiliated With:** National League of Cities; United States Conference of Mayors. **Formerly:** (1973) National Model Cities Directors Association; (1977) National Model Cities Community Development Directors Association. **Publications:** *Washington Report*. Newsletter. Alternate Formats: online. **Conventions/Meetings:** annual conference - always spring in Washington, DC.

16870 ■ National Community Reinvestment Coalition (NCRC)
727 15th St. NW, Ste.900
Washington, DC 20005
Ph: (202)628-8866
Fax: (202)628-9800
E-mail: jtaylor@ncrc.org
URL: http://www.ncrc.org
Contact: John Taylor, Pres./CEO
Founded: 1990. **Members:** 500. **Membership Dues:** local non-profit (with operating budget of less than $500,000; with voting privileges), $150 (annual) ● local non-profit (with operating budget of over $500,000; with voting privileges), $250 (annual) ● individual, $500 (annual) ● community-based non-profit (with budget of over $1,000,000), $400 (annual) ● public sector/government agency, $1,000 (annual) ● educational institution or local government agency, $500 (annual) ● national non-profit, $600 (annual) ● sustaining national non-profit, $6,000 (annual) ● student, $35 (annual) ● TA provider-for-profit, $250 (annual). **Staff:** 7. **Budget:** $600,000. **Description:** Works with national and local nonprofit organizations and banks to increase the level of money going into low income, minority, and disadvantaged communities through the Community Reinvestment Act (CRA). Monitors legislation related to the CRA. Provides information to organizations seeking to establish CRA agreements with local lending institutions. Disseminates legislative and regulatory updates. Offers many member services. **Libraries: Type:** reference. **Holdings:** books, clippings, periodicals. **Subjects:**

Community Reinvestment Act, legislation, CRA ratings and agreements. **Councils:** Banker/Community Collaborative. **Publications:** *Compendium* ● *Reinvest Works*, quarterly. Newsletter. Includes articles by NCRC members. Alternate Formats: online ● Brochures. Alternate Formats: online. **Conventions/Meetings:** annual meeting (exhibits) - usually March.

16871 ■ National Neighborhood Coalition (NNC)
1221 Connecticut Ave. NW, 2nd Fl.
Washington, DC 20036
Ph: (202)429-0790
Fax: (202)429-0795
E-mail: info@neighborhoodcoalition.org
URL: http://www.neighborhoodcoalition.org
Contact: Anne Pasmanick, Exec. Dir.
Founded: 1979. **Members:** 125. **Membership Dues:** profit, government agency, $1,000 (annual) ● individual, $50 (annual) ● regular, $3,000 (annual). **Staff:** 3. **Budget:** $300,000. **Description:** National membership organization that works with inner-city neighborhood groups. Serves as information and educational clearinghouse on national policies and federal programs that affect low and moderate-income neighborhoods. Sponsors regular 2-hour information forums on issues such as housing, community reinvestment banking, and community-based development. **Awards:** Making a Difference. **Frequency:** annual. **Type:** recognition. **Programs:** The Forum; Neighborhood Voices. **Affiliated With:** National Council of La Raza. **Formerly:** (1983) Neighborhood Coalition. **Publications:** *Connectivity*, quarterly. Magazine ● *The Voice*, quarterly. Newsletter. Contains updates on legislation, appropriations, and issues on inner city neighborhoods. **Price:** $50.00 for organizations; $25.00 for individuals ● Reports. Alternate Formats: online ● Articles. Alternate Formats: online ● Videos. Alternate Formats: online ● Audiotapes. Alternate Formats: online.

16872 ■ National Trust Main Street Center
1785 Massachusetts Ave. NW
Washington, DC 20036
Ph: (202)588-6219
Fax: (202)588-6050
E-mail: mainstreet@nthp.org
URL: http://www.mainst.org
Contact: Doug Loescher, Dir.
Founded: 1980. **Members:** 1,700. **Membership Dues:** allied network, $495 (annual). **Staff:** 20. **State Groups:** 40. **Description:** Commercial district revitalization, using historic preservation, grassroots economic development. **Libraries: Type:** reference. **Holdings:** articles, books, periodicals. **Subjects:** volunteer recruitment, business retention, insurances, conferences. **Awards:** Main Street GAMSA Awards. **Frequency:** annual. **Type:** recognition ● Main Street Leadership Awards. **Frequency:** annual. **Type:** recognition. **Computer Services:** Mailing lists, for members only. **Additional Websites:** http://www.mainstreet.org. **Affiliated With:** National Trust for Historic Preservation. **Publications:** *Main Street News*, monthly. Journal. **Price:** included in membership dues. Alternate Formats: online. **Conventions/Meetings:** annual conference (exhibits) - early May.

16873 ■ New York New Visions (NYNV)
c/o Center for Architecture
536 LaGuardia Pl.
New York, NY 10012
Ph: (212)683-0023
E-mail: info@aiany.org
Contact: Ms. Annie Kurtin, Programs Coor.
Description: Committed to rebuilding and revitalizing Lower Manhattan, New York. **Publications:** Reports. Alternate Formats: online.

16874 ■ Opportunity Finance Network
Public Ledger Bldg.
620 Chestnut St., Ste.572
Philadelphia, PA 19106
Ph: (215)923-4754
Fax: (215)923-4755

E-mail: info@opportunityfinance.net
URL: http://www.opportunityfinance.net
Contact: Mark Pinsky, Pres./CEO
Founded: 1986. **Members:** 154. **Membership Dues:** with less than $2 million in assets, $250 (annual) ● with $2 million to $4,999,999 in assets, $500 (annual) ● with $5 million to $14,999,999 in assets, $1,000 (annual). **Staff:** 22. **Budget:** $729,000. **Regional Groups:** 22. **State Groups:** 9. **Local Groups:** 13. **Description:** Promotes community investment and facilitates cooperation among Community Development Loan Funds (CDLFs). Seeks to assist those who need capital by providing capital, credit, and technical assistance to promote economic and community development and economic democracy. Engages those who have capital by providing opportunities for socially responsible community investment and stimulating a dialogue on the social and ethical responsibilities of wealth. Encourages and challenges those who manage capital by providing information, overcoming prejudice, and broadening institutional commitments. **Libraries: Type:** reference. **Holdings:** papers. **Subjects:** development and management of a CDFI. **Committees:** Financial Services; Member Services; Public Policy. **Formerly:** (1998) National Association of Community Development Loan Funds; (2006) National Community Capital Association. **Publications:** *Community Investment Monitor*, quarterly. Newsletter ● *National Directory of Community Development Finance Institutions*, periodic ● *Operations Guide for Community Development Finance Institutions*. **Conventions/ Meetings:** annual conference and seminar.

Community Improvement

16875 ■ Alliance for a Paving Moratorium (APM)
c/o Culture Change
PO Box 4347
Arcata, CA 95518
Ph: (215)243-3144
Fax: (215)243-3144
E-mail: info@culturechange.org
URL: http://www.culturechange.org/apm_page.htm
Contact: Jan Lundberg, Contact
Founded: 1990. **Members:** 400. **Membership Dues:** regular, $30 (annual) ● life, $100. **Staff:** 3. **Budget:** $80,000. **Local Groups:** 10. **National Groups:** 115. **Description:** Groups, businesses, and individuals opposed to the construction of new roads and parking lots. Works to stop any construction of new roads or parking lots anywhere in the world. Advocates economic and transportation alternatives. Alliance coordinated by Fossil Fuels Policy Action Institute. **Convention/Meeting:** none. **Publications:** *Paving Moratorium Update/Auto-Free Times*, quarterly. Magazine. **Price:** included in membership dues; $2.00 for nonmembers. **Circulation:** 10,000. **Advertising:** accepted ● *Road-Fighters' Alert*.

16876 ■ Architectural League of New York (AL)
The Urban Center
457 Madison Ave.
New York, NY 10022
Ph: (212)753-1722
Fax: (212)486-9173
E-mail: info@archleague.org
URL: http://www.archleague.org
Contact: Rosalie Genevro, Exec. Dir.
Founded: 1881. **Members:** 1,200. **Membership Dues:** active (over 35 years of age), $85 (annual) ● active (under 35 years of age), $50 (annual) ● student, senior, $25 (annual) ● non-resident, $40 (annual) ● dual, $125 (annual) ● contributing, $250 (annual) ● supporting, $500 (annual) ● sustaining, $1,000 (annual) ● league circle, $2,500 (annual) ● corporate council patron, $5,000 (annual) ● corporate council benefactor, $10,000 (annual). **Staff:** 6. **Budget:** $600,000. **Description:** Represents persons in the field of architecture or (as related to architecture) city planning, painting, sculpture, landscape and site planning, engineering, education, crafts, decoration,

interior design, and photography. Promotes art and architecture; serves as a forum for new and experimental ideas in the arts. Sponsors exhibitions. **Awards:** Deborah J. Norden Fund Grant. **Frequency:** annual. **Type:** monetary. **Recipient:** for recent graduates ● Young Architects Forum Competition. **Frequency:** annual. **Type:** monetary. **Recipient:** for juried portfolio competition. **Telecommunication Services:** electronic mail, genevro@archleague.org. **Publications:** *Charlotte Perriand: An Art of Living*. Book ● *The League*, weekly. Newsletter. Contains information about the League programs and events. **Price:** included in membership dues. Alternate Formats: online ● *Ten Shades of Green*. Brochure. **Price:** $5.00 ● *Urban Life: Housing in the Contemporary City*. Catalog. **Price:** $10.00. **Conventions/ Meetings:** periodic competition ● lecture.

16877 ■ Experimental Cities, Inc. (ECI)
PO Box 731
Pacific Palisades, CA 90272-0731
Ph: (323)935-4585 (323)428-8580
E-mail: drmarcus@pacbell.net
Contact: Genevieve Marcus PhD, Pres.
Founded: 1972. **Staff:** 7. **Regional Groups:** 2. **Description:** Aims to find innovative solutions to urban deterioration. Works to form a database of innovative approaches to energy, waste disposal, health, city management, decision-making, conflict resolution, education, environmental design, crime and violence, economics, and unemployment. Studies whole-systems applications to social and environmental planning. Sponsors Earthlab research center and conducts tests of promising new environmental inventions. Provides results of research to local, state, and federal groups and to the public through lectures, articles, television shows, and books. Has established the Equal Relationships Institute that studies and implements cooperation and equal relationships between individuals and groups. Activities include lectures, seminars, consulting, and publications. Conducts workshops and consults on cooperative/ equal relationships. Plans to maintain computerized information services. **Publications:** *Dialog*, periodic ● *Equal Time: Maintaining a Balance in Today's Intimate Relationships*. Book ● *New Relationships*, periodic. Newsletter.

16878 ■ National Main Street Center (NMSC)
1785 Massachusetts Ave. NW
Washington, DC 20036
Ph: (202)588-6219
Fax: (202)588-6050
E-mail: mainstreet@nthp.org
URL: http://www.mainstreet.org
Contact: Doug Loescher, Dir.
Founded: 1977. **Members:** 1,300. **Membership Dues:** standard network, $195 (annual) ● allied network, $495 (annual). **Staff:** 24. **State Groups:** 47. **Local Groups:** 800. **Description:** A program of the National Trust for Historic Preservation; cities, towns, downtown development authorities, and companies interested in economic development and historic preservation. Works with communities and states to rekindle downtown entrepreneurship, cooperation, and civic concern through development of preservation-based revitalization programs for traditional commercial areas. Develops methods by which separate groups can work together in a business district, promotes the downtown area, physically improves buildings and public spaces, and diversifies and rebuilds the economic base of the business district. Provides assistance to states in establishing programs at the state level and in implementing programs locally; contracts with state government agencies or private-sector statewide organizations to provide training and technical assistance to state and local program participants. **Libraries: Type:** reference. **Holdings:** 300; audiovisuals, books, clippings, periodicals. **Subjects:** design, organization, promotion, economic restructuring. **Awards:** Great American Main Street Awards. **Frequency:** annual. **Type:** monetary. **Formerly:** (1980) Main Street Project. **Publications:** *Main Street News*, monthly. Newsletter. Contains periodical covering downtown revitalization. **Price:** $195.00. **Circulation:** 1,400. Alternate

Formats: online ● *Main Street News Index*, semiannual ● *Revitalizing Downtown: Board Members Handbook*. Handbooks ● Booklets ● Bulletins ● Manuals ● Makes available audiovisual aids and downtown management computer software package. **Conventions/Meetings:** annual conference, educational conference about downtown revitalization (exhibits).

16879 ■ Project for Public Spaces (PPS)
700 Broadway, 4th Fl.
New York, NY 10003
Ph: (212)620-5660
Fax: (212)620-3821
E-mail: pps@pps.org
URL: http://www.pps.org
Contact: Fred I. Kent, Pres./Chm.
Founded: 1975. **Membership Dues:** individual, $50 (annual) ● senior, student, international, $35 (annual) ● professional, $100 (annual) ● organizational, $150 (annual). **Staff:** 22. **Description:** Aims to: improve the use, design, and management of public spaces such as plazas, parks, downtowns, neighborhoods, public markets, streets and transportation facilities, using data derived from the study of people's behavior in these spaces; encourage designers, government agencies, and other institutions to make observational analysis part of the planning process in the design and management of public spaces. Offers technical assistance services; researches and analyzes the design, use, and management of public spaces. Recommends ways to make public spaces more attractive, safe, comfortable, enjoyable, and economically viable. Offers educational workshops on issues in public space planning, design, and management. Offers student internship program. Conducts community-based planning processes and small scale implementation initiatives. **Libraries: Type:** reference. **Holdings:** photographs. **Subjects:** urban design, public space examples. **Programs:** Building Livable Communities Through Transportation; Lila Wallace Readers Digest Urban Parks Institute; Public Market Collaborative; Transportation. **Publications:** *Making Places*. Newsletter. **Price:** included in membership dues. Alternate Formats: online ● Handbooks. Contains information on urban design, public space improvement, transportation and livability markets. ● Videos ● Books ● Articles. Alternate Formats: online. **Conventions/Meetings:** conference and workshop.

16880 ■ Public Art Fund (PAF)
1 E 53rd St.
New York, NY 10022
Ph: (212)980-4575
Fax: (212)980-3610
E-mail: paforg@publicartfund.org
URL: http://www.publicartfund.org
Contact: Susan K. Freedman, Pres.
Founded: 1977. **Membership Dues:** regular, $50 (annual). **Staff:** 8. **Budget:** $2,000,000. **Description:** Works with artists, architects, city planners, and community groups to explore and develop programs that bring art of both a temporary and permanent nature directly into the public environment. Provides public information and consultation on public art to governmental agencies, private businesses, and community groups, both in New York City and across the country. **Libraries: Type:** reference. **Holdings:** archival material. **Subjects:** public art. **Programs:** Additional Outreach; In the Public Realm; Major Initiatives with Established Artists. **Projects:** Alejandro Diaz; Janet Cardiff; Julian Opie; Little Boy; Semiprecious. **Absorbed:** City Walls; (1977) Public Arts Council. **Publications:** *In Process*, quarterly. Newsletter. Lists and describes events, lectures, essays, photos, upcoming projects, etc. **Price:** included in membership dues. ISSN: 1060-6734. **Circulation:** 3,000 ● Books ● Catalogs ● Makes available postcards and brochures of events.

16881 ■ Sculpture in the Environment (SITE)
25 Maiden Ln.
New York, NY 10038
Ph: (212)285-0120
Fax: (212)285-0125

E-mail: info@siteenvirodesign.com
URL: http://www.siteenvirodesign.com
Contact: James Wines, Pres./Creative Dir./Founder
Founded: 1970. **Members:** 12. **Staff:** 10. **Budget:** $250,000. **State Groups:** 2. **Languages:** English, German, Italian. **Description:** Artists, writers, and architects united to explore and develop new concepts for architecture and public spaces. Serves as an extension of the physical, psychological, and phenomenological characteristics of a particular context. Provides projects that are intended to change the public attitude toward the constructed environment and architecture while enlarging the role of the architect and visual artist in community planning. Includes solutions such as the original concepts and all plans, elevations, models, and supervisions necessary for realization of each proposal. Provides consultation services to community groups, schools, colleges, universities, and corporations including site analysis, research, and recommendations for visual improvements. Conducts lectures and workshops. Collects and files research data on all aspects of the environmental arts. Operates production studio, environmental arts study center, and educational facilities. **Libraries: Type:** not open to the public. **Holdings:** 8,000; books, periodicals, photographs. **Subjects:** art, architecture, science, fashion, history, cuisine, fiction, reference, business. **Awards:** Chrysler Award for Innovation. **Frequency:** annual. **Type:** monetary. **Recipient:** for design innovation-educational programs. **Divisions:** Education; Projects; Publications. **Publications:** *Report of Projects,* bimonthly. Newsletter. Alternate Formats: online ● Newsletter, semiannual ● Books ● Catalogs ● Monographs. **Conventions/Meetings:** Architectural Sustainability - seminar and convention, with drawings of projects and proposals - 8/year, approximately every six weeks.

Computer Users

16882 ■ Stop Net Abusers
Address Unknown since 2007

Description: Dedicated to victims of stalkers who frequent chat rooms and Internet Relay Chat channels; provides information about perpetrators. **Publications:** Newsletter, periodic.

Computers

16883 ■ NetAction
PO Box 6739
Santa Barbara, CA 93160
Ph: (415)215-9392
E-mail: info@netaction.org
URL: http://www.netaction.org
Contact: Audrie Krause, Exec. Dir.

Founded: 1996. **Description:** Promotes use of the Internet for effective grassroots citizen action campaigns.

16884 ■ Online Policy Group (OPG)
1800 Market St., No. 123
San Francisco, CA 94102
Ph: (415)826-3532
Fax: (928)244-2347
E-mail: support@onlinepolicy.org
URL: http://www.onlinepolicy.org
Contact: Will Doherty, Founder

Founded: 2000. **Staff:** 3. **Description:** Conducts online policy research, outreach, and action on issues such as access, privacy and digital defamation. Provides free internet services by and for non-profits. **Telecommunication Services:** electronic mail, doherty@onlinepolicy.org.

16885 ■ Organizers' Collaborative (OC)
14 Beacon St., Ste.707
Boston, MA 02108
Ph: (617)720-6190

E-mail: oc@oc-tech.org
URL: http://organizerscollaborative.org
Contact: Rich Cowan, Founder/ODB Proj. Dir.
Founded: 1999. **Members:** 250. **Membership Dues:** regular individual, $30 (annual) ● low-income individual, $15 (annual) ● supporting individual or organization, $50 (annual) ● sponsoring, $100 (annual) ● sustaining, $200 (annual). **Staff:** 2. **Budget:** $100,000. **Multinational. Description:** Seeks to further the potential of computers and the Internet to increase communication and collaboration among those working for social change. Collects, classifies and disseminates information about grassroots uses of technology; develops, tests and distributes software applicable to social change organizations free of charge; provides on-line methods of collaboration and resource sharing for organizers; and provides technical assistance. **Programs:** Grassroots Technology Assistance; Information Clearinghouse; Social Change Networking. **Publications:** *OCTECH*, monthly. Newsletter. Alternate Formats: online ● *Online Directory of Social Change Email Lists.* Alternate Formats: online. **Conventions/Meetings:** annual Grassroots Use of Technology - conference.

Conflict

16886 ■ HALO USA
850 7th Ave., Ste.506
New York, NY 10019-5230
Ph: (212)581-0099
Fax: (212)581-2029
E-mail: halo.usa@verizon.net
URL: http://www.halousa.org
Contact: Guy Willoughby, Dir.
Members: 4,850. **National Groups:** 9. **Multinational. Description:** Works to remove all debris of war such as landmines, and provides safe ground and assistance.

16887 ■ International Crisis Group, Washington Office (ICG)
1629 K St. NW, Ste.450
Washington, DC 20006
Ph: (202)785-1601
Fax: (202)785-1630
E-mail: mschneider@crisisgroup.org
URL: http://www.crisisgroup.org
Contact: Mark Schneider, Sr. VP

Multinational. Description: Works to advance the capacity of the international community to anticipate, understand and act to prevent and contain conflict. **Publications:** *Apres six mois de transition au Burundi: poursuivre la guerre ou gagner la paix?.* Report ● *Central Asia: Water and Conflict.* Report ● *Commentary Will Ballots or Bullets Rule? Afghanistan Fate Hinges on the Outcome of This Week's Loya Jirga* ● *CrisisWatch,* monthly. Bulletin. Alternate Formats: online ● *Don't Let Zimbabwe Implode* ● *International Challenges After September 11* ● *No Abandonemos a Asia Central* ● *President Uribe's Columbian Challenge* ● *UNMIK's Kosovo Albatross: Tackling Division in Mitrovica.* Report ● *Wanted: U.S. Leadership* ● *Zimbabwe: What Next?.* Report ● Annual Report. Alternate Formats: online.

16888 ■ Pugwash Conferences on Science and World Affairs
Washington Off.
1111 19th St. NW, No. 1200
Washington, DC 20036
Ph: (202)478-3440
Fax: (202)238-9604
E-mail: pugwashdc@aol.com
URL: http://www.pugwash.org
Contact: Jeffrey Boutwell, Exec. Dir.
Founded: 1957. **Members:** 2,000. **Staff:** 4. **National Groups:** 45. **Multinational. Description:** Seeks to reduce the danger of armed conflict and cooperative solutions for global problems. **Formerly:** (2004) International Pugwash. **Publications:** *A Nuclear-Weapon-Free World: Desirable? Feasible?.* Book ● *A Nuclear Weapon-Free World: Steps Along the Way.* Book ● *Ending War: The Force of Reason.* Book ●

Light Weapons and International Security. Book ● *Nuclear Energy: Promise or Peril?.* Book ● *Nuclear Weapons: The Road to Zero.* Book ● *Pugwash Newsletter,* semiannual ● *Pugwash Occasional Papers* ● *Remember Your Humanity.* Book ● *US-Cuban Medical Cooperation: Effects of the US Embargo (June 2001).* **Conventions/Meetings:** annual Pugwash Conferences ● symposium ● workshop.

Conflict Resolution

16889 ■ Alliance for Peacebuilding
11 Dupont Cir. NW, Ste.200
Washington, DC 20036
Ph: (202)822-6135
Fax: (202)822-6068
E-mail: info@allianceforpeacebuilding.org
URL: http://www.allianceforpeacebuilding.org
Contact: Andrea L. Strimling, Chair
Founded: 1999. **Membership Dues:** organization (with a budget of less than $900,000), $275-$550 (annual) ● organization (with a budget of $900,001 to $10 million), $1,100-$1,300 (annual) ● organization (with a budget of more than $10 million), $1,500-$1,900 (annual). **Multinational. Description:** Aims to build sustainable peace and security worldwide. Initiates, develops and supports collaborative action among governmental, nongovernmental, and intergovernmental organizations to prevent and resolve destructive conflicts. Builds understanding of and support for peacebuilding policies and programs among leaders in government, business, media, philanthropy, religion, and other sectors of civil society. Increases the effectiveness of the peacebuilding field by developing networks, disseminating best practices, and enhancing organizational capacities and professional skills. **Formerly:** (2006) Alliance for International Conflict Prevention and Resolution.

16890 ■ Global Majority
479 Pacific St., Ste.5C
Monterey, CA 93940
Ph: (831)372-5518
Fax: (831)372-5519
E-mail: info@globalmajority.net
URL: http://www.globalmajority.net
Contact: William Monning, Pres.
Multinational. Description: Promotes nonviolent conflict resolution through training, education, networking, publications, mediation services and advocacy. Fosters a network of people and groups devoted to nonviolent conflict resolution. **Publications:** *Global Voice,* quarterly. Newsletter. Alternate Formats: online ● Brochure. Alternate Formats: online.

16891 ■ "Love Yourself" Stop the Violence
PO Box 101054
Brooklyn, NY 11210
E-mail: jamesedavislyst@aol.com
URL: http://www.jedavis-stopviolence.org
Founded: 1990. **Membership Dues:** individual, $30 (annual). **Description:** Seeks to unite inner-city communities and teach themselves self-love and respect in order to become empowered to fight against violence, drugs and poverty. **Publications:** Newsletter, monthly. Provides information on latest trends concerning violence throughout America. **Conventions/Meetings:** annual Stop the Violence March - rally.

Congress

16892 ■ Civilian Congress (CC)
Address Unknown since 2007

Founded: 1964. **Languages:** French, Japanese, Spanish. **Nonmembership. Description:** Nonprofit correspondence network of scholars, writers, journalists, politicians, lawyers, and students. Provides biographical data on the current military affiliations of congressmen which cannot be obtained from standard government or private directories. Educates U.S.

and foreign citizens on the separation-of-powers doctrine of the U.S. Constitution. Maintains collection of legal opinions, lawsuits, books, articles, and correspondence relating to the incompatibility-of-offices clause of the U.S. Constitution. Operates speakers' bureau. **Libraries: Type:** reference. **Holdings:** archival material. **Publications:** *Military Officers in the U.S. Congress,* annual. Directory. **Advertising:** not accepted. **Conventions/Meetings:** annual conference (exhibits) - always on or near Constitution Day, September 17, San Francisco, CA.

16893 ■ National Committee for an Effective Congress (NCEC)
122 C St. NW, Ste.650
Washington, DC 20001
Ph: (202)639-8300
Free: (800)547-5911
E-mail: info@ncec.org
URL: http://www.ncec.org
Contact: Russell D. Hemenway, Natl. Dir.
Founded: 1948. **Members:** 50. **Staff:** 14. **Budget:** $1,200,000. **Description:** Serves as an independent political action committee that raises funds from private citizens and distributes them to its endorsed candidates for the U.S. Senate and House of Representatives. Provides both support and professional technical campaign assistance to candidates. Supports progressive Democrats and Republicans who are genuinely committed to preserving and advancing the liberties and rights of all Americans. Includes recent research and educational programs such as election finance reform, congressional procedures, and military versus domestic items in national budget. Operates speakers' bureau; compiles statistics. **Awards:** Eleanor Roosevelt Public Service Award. **Frequency:** periodic. **Type:** recognition. **Computer Services:** database, electoral and demographic. **Publications:** *Campaign Report,* monthly ● *Election Update,* 10/year. Newsletter ● *109th Congressional Directory.* Contains vital information on House and Senate members. ● Annual Report, annual.

16894 ■ United States Association of Former Members of Congress (USAFMC)
1401 K St. NW, Ste.503
Washington, DC 20005
Ph: (202)222-0972
Fax: (202)222-0977
E-mail: admin@usafmc.org
URL: http://www.usafmc.org
Contact: Peter M. Weichlein, Exec. Dir.
Founded: 1970. **Members:** 550. **Membership Dues:** former member of Congress, $200 (annual) ● individual (over 70 years of age), $100 (annual). **Staff:** 4. **Budget:** $648,900. **Description:** Former members of the U.S. Congress. Works as a nonpartisan group to promote the public understanding of the U.S. Congress as an institution and representative democracy as a system of government; does not take positions on public issues, lobby regarding specific legislation, or engage in political or partisan activity. (Membership is suspended if a member seeks re-election to Congress and terminated if elected and sworn in.) Prepares oral histories of former members of Congress and administers Congress to Campus fellows program in which former members of Congress visit college and high school campuses. Serves as the secretariat for Congressional Study Groups on Germany, Japan, China and Mexico to conduct programs involving current members of Congress with their counterparts in those countries. **Awards:** Distinguished Service Award. **Frequency:** annual. **Type:** recognition. **Recipient:** for outstanding service to the republic ● Statesmanship Award. **Frequency:** annual. **Type:** recognition. **Recipient:** for outstanding service to the republic. **Computer Services:** Online services, directory. **Committees:** Budget; Finance; Membership; Program; Public Relations. **Programs:** Congress to Campus; Congressional Study Group on Germany; Congressional Study Group on Japan. **Formerly:** (1970) Former Members of Congress. **Publications:** *Congressional Alumni News,* annual. Newsletter. Provides news about association's activities. **Price:** free. **Circulation:** 1,000 ● *Inside The House: Former Members Reveal How Congress Really*

Works. Book. **Price:** $32.50 ● Membership Directory, biennial. Lists members of the association. **Price:** $50.00 ● Newsletter. Alternate Formats: online ● Brochure. Alternate Formats: online ● Report. Alternate Formats: online. **Conventions/Meetings:** annual meeting - usually May in Washington, DC.

Congressional

16895 ■ Congressional Arts Caucus
2469 Rayburn House Off. Bldg.
Washington, DC 20515
Ph: (202)225-3615
Fax: (202)225-7822
E-mail: louiseny@mail.house.gov
Contact: Sherrye Henry, Contact
Founded: 1980. **Members:** 186. **Description:** Bipartisan group of House members concerned about Federal funding for the arts in America. **Formerly:** (1998) Congressional Arts Caucus; (2003) Congressional Member Organization for the Arts.

16896 ■ Congressional Automotive Caucus (CAC)
c/o Dale Kildee, Co-Chm.
2107 Rayburn House Off. Bldg.
Washington, DC 20515
Ph: (202)225-3611
Fax: (202)225-6393
E-mail: dkildee@mail.house.gov
URL: http://www.house.gov/kildee
Contact: Dale Kildee, Co-Chm.
Founded: 1983. **Members:** 75. **Staff:** 1. **Description:** Represents members of the U.S. House of Representatives from congressional districts with an economic stake in the automotive industry. Aims to focus congressional attention on problems in the auto industry including trade imbalances, the yen-dollar relationship, and modernization. Works for legislation addressing such problems. **Supersedes:** Congressional Auto Conference. **Conventions/Meetings:** periodic meeting.

16897 ■ Congressional Black Caucus (CBC)
2236 Rayburn Bldg.
Washington, DC 20515-3312
Ph: (202)226-9776
Fax: (202)225-1512
URL: http://www.congressionalblackcaucus.net
Contact: Rep. Melvin L. Watt, Chm.
Founded: 1969. **Members:** 37. **Staff:** 3. **Description:** Black members of the U.S. House of Representatives. Addresses the legislative concerns of black and other underrepresented citizens and to formalize and strengthen the efforts of its members. Works to implement these objectives through personal contact with other House members, through the dissemination of information to individual black constituents, and by working closely with black elected officials in other levels of government. Establishes a yearly legislative agenda setting forth the issues which it supports: full employment, national health development, welfare reform, and international affairs. **Awards: Type:** recognition. **Committees:** Fundraising. **Publications:** *Black Hill Staff Directory,* annual ● *For the People,* quarterly. Newsletter. **Conventions/Meetings:** annual Fundraising/Legislative Conference - meeting - always September, in Washington, DC.

16898 ■ Conservative Opportunity Society (COS)
2418 Rayburn House Off. Bldg.
Washington, DC 20515
Ph: (202)225-3501
Fax: (202)226-2019
E-mail: ron.lewis@mail.house.gov
URL: http://www.house.gov/ronlewis
Contact: Ron Lewis, Member of Congress
Founded: 1982. **Members:** 30. **Staff:** 1. **Description:** Republican members of Congress committed to representing the "conservative agenda" in the House of Representatives and throughout the U.S. Supports "traditional values that made this country great: a

foundation of religion, family, moral integrity and fiscal conservatism.". **Publications:** *A House of Ill Repute.* Book. **Conventions/Meetings:** weekly meeting.

16899 ■ Senate Children's Caucus (SCC)
c/o Hon. Senator Christopher J. Dodd
448 Russell Bldg.
Washington, DC 20510
Ph: (202)224-2823
Fax: (202)224-1083
URL: http://shelby.senate.gov/caucus/main.html
Contact: Hon. Senator Christopher J. Dodd, Contact
Founded: 1983. **Members:** 34. **Description:** U.S. Senators serving on committees addressing the needs of children in America. Seeks to educate Senate members and the public about the problems affecting young people. Holds policy forums and hearings on issues such as: education of the gifted; the effects of dropping out of school; prevention of child sexual abuse; risks faced by latchkey children (young children of working parents who must spend part of the day at home unsupervised). **Additional Websites:** http://dodd.senate.gov.

16900 ■ Senate Tourism Caucus (STC)
c/o Sen. Conrad Burns, Co-Chm.
187 Dirksen Senate Off. Bldg.
Washington, DC 20510
Ph: (202)224-2644 (202)224-8616
Free: (800)344-1513
Fax: (202)224-8594
Contact: Sen. Conrad Burns, Co-Chm.
Founded: 1979. **Members:** 70. **Staff:** 2. **Description:** Bipartisan senators interested in travel and tourism issues. Works to share information concerning travel and tourism industry issues facing Congress. **Conventions/Meetings:** periodic meeting.

Conservation

16901 ■ Center for a New American Dream
6930 Carroll Ave., Ste.900
Takoma Park, MD 20912-4466
Ph: (301)891-3683
Free: (877)68-DREAM
E-mail: newdream@newdream.org
URL: http://www.ibuydifferent.org
Contact: Nancy Smith, Dir. of Administration
Founded: 1997. **Membership Dues:** individual, $30 (annual) ● individual overseas, $45 (annual) ● senior, student, low-income, $15 (annual). **Staff:** 20. **Budget:** $2,000,000. **Description:** Helps Americans consume responsibly to protect the environment, enhance quality of life, and promote social justice. Works with individuals, institutions, communities, and businesses to conserve natural resources, counter the commercialization of the culture, and change the way goods are produced and consumed. **Additional Websites:** http://www.responsiblepurchasing.org, http://www.simplifytheholidays.org, http://www.newdream.org. **Telecommunication Services:** electronic bulletin board, discussion forums. **Publications:** *Good Times Made Simple: The Lost Art of Fun.* Booklet. **Price:** $4.00. Alternate Formats: online ● *Good Times Made Simple & Tips for Parenting in a Commercial Culture.* Booklets. **Price:** $6.00 ● *More Fun, Less Stuff Starter Kit.* Book. **Price:** $10.00 ● *More Fun, Less Stuff: The Challenges and Rewards of a New American Dream.* Film. **Price:** $10.00 ● *Responsible Purchasing Guide for Faith Communities.* Book. **Price:** $5.00 ● *Simplify the Holidays Guide.* Booklet. **Price:** $4.00. Alternate Formats: online ● *Sustainable Planet: Solutions for the 21st Century.* Book. **Price:** $15.50 ● *Tips for Parenting in a Commercial Culture.* Booklet. **Price:** $4.00. Alternate Formats: online ● *What Kids Really Want That Money Can't Buy.* Book. **Price:** $19.00.

Conservative

16902 ■ American Conservative Union (ACU)
1007 Cameron St.
Alexandria, VA 22314

Ph: (703)836-8602
Free: (800)ACU-7345
Fax: (703)836-8606
E-mail: acu@conservative.org
URL: http://www.conservative.org
Contact: David A. Keene, Chm.

Founded: 1964. **Members:** 500,000. **Membership Dues:** basic, $25 (annual) ● Patron's Club, $120 (annual) ● Chairman's Circle, $1,000 (annual) ● regular, $50 (annual) ● Sustainer's Club, $45 (monthly). **Staff:** 5. **Budget:** $760,000. **State Groups:** 30. **Description:** Serves as lobbying organization seeking to mobilize resources of responsible conservative activists across the country and to further the general cause of conservatism. Lobbies and educates in subject areas, such as political activity, foreign and military policy, domestic economic policy, legal policy, social issues, etc. Rates members of Congress on important legislation. **Awards: Type:** recognition. **Computer Services:** Online services, legislative action, conservative battleline. **Committees:** ACU Foundation; ACU Political Action. **Absorbed:** (1966) Political Action Committee of Young Americans for Freedom. **Publications:** *Battleline*, quarterly. Newsletter. **Price:** included in membership dues ● *Conservative Battleline*. Magazine. Alternate Formats: online ● *In Defense of the West: American Values Under Siege*. Book. Contains stories of the Western vision and its American values and institutions. **Price:** $27.00 ● *Ratings of Congress*, annual. Booklet. Contains state-by-state list of members of Congress, vote descriptions, how each voted, and numerical score. **Price:** $2.00/copy. Alternate Formats: online ● *Reagan's Revolution: The Untold Story of the Campaign That Started It All*. Book. **Price:** $10.40 ● Videos. **Conventions/Meetings:** annual Conservative Political Action Conference, with speeches, panels, discussion with key leaders of the conservative movement (exhibits) - usually February.

16903 ■ Center of the American Experiment (CAE)
12 S 6th St.
Minneapolis, MN 55402
Ph: (612)338-3605
Fax: (612)338-3621
E-mail: info@americanexperiment.org
URL: http://www.amexp.org
Contact: Mark S. Larson, Sec.

Founded: 1990. **Members:** 5,000. **Membership Dues:** supporting, $75 (annual) ● sustaining, $250 (annual) ● patron, $1,000 (annual) ● founder, $5,000 (annual) ● trustee, $10,000 (annual). **Staff:** 8. **Budget:** $1,400,000. **Description:** Political conservatives. Promotes "conservative common sense" in public policy. Serves as a clearinghouse on conservative approaches to social, economic, and political issues. Produces print and radio commentaries on current affairs; conducts research and educational programs; maintains speakers' bureau. **Libraries: Type:** by appointment only. **Holdings:** periodicals. **Subjects:** conservative public policies. **Publications:** *American Experiment Quarterly*. Journal. **Price:** $30.00 /year for nonmembers; included in membership dues. ISSN: 1097-1866. **Circulation:** 5,000. **Advertising:** accepted. Alternate Formats: online ● Reports. Alternate Formats: online ● Books. **Conventions/Meetings:** annual dinner ● monthly luncheon.

16904 ■ Christian-Patriots Defense League/Citizen's Emergency Defense System
PO Box 565
Flora, IL 62839
Ph: (618)665-3937
Contact: John Harrell, Founder

Founded: 1950. **Members:** 25,000. **Description:** Conservative Christians and patriots. Believes several nations of the world will invade and plunder the U.S. in the near future. Maintains properties where members may retreat in times of crisis. **Publications:** Brochures ● Newsletter, monthly. **Conventions/Meetings:** periodic meeting.

16905 ■ The Conservative Caucus (TCC)
450 Maple Ave. E
Vienna, VA 22180
Ph: (703)938-9626

Fax: (703)281-4108
E-mail: corndorf@cais.com
URL: http://www.conservativeusa.org
Contact: Howard Phillips, Chm./Founder

Founded: 1974. **Members:** 35,000. **Membership Dues:** basic, $15 (annual). **Staff:** 9. **Budget:** $3,000,000. **Description:** Seeks to build a grass roots "new majority" lobbying coalition in every congressional district, through which conservatives can achieve the strategic capacity to set the agenda for public debate, define issues on their own terms, and develop effective leadership. **Computer Services:** Mailing lists. **Projects:** Constitution Education Program. **Publications:** *The Importance of the Electoral College*. Book ● *Member's Message*, periodic. Newsletter ● Survey. **Conventions/Meetings:** annual Constitution Day - meeting.

16906 ■ The Conservative Caucus Research, Analysis and Education Foundation (TCCF)
c/o The Conservative Caucus
450 Maple Ave. E
Vienna, VA 22180
Ph: (703)281-6782
Fax: (703)281-4108
E-mail: corndorf@cais.com
URL: http://www.conservativeusa.org/TCCFMission.htm
Contact: Howard Phillips, Chm.

Founded: 1976. **Members:** 6,000. **Membership Dues:** individual, $25 (annual). **Staff:** 8. **Budget:** $1,000,000. **Description:** Conservative individuals interested in staying informed of the activities of the federal government. Disseminates information concerning the actions and expenditures of the federal government. Supports Accountability Project to monitor federal moneys given to political activist groups. **Libraries: Type:** reference. **Holdings:** 4,000; books, periodicals. **Subjects:** government, politics. **Departments:** Communications; Research; Resources. **Projects:** The First 100 Days. **Also Known As:** Conservative Caucus Foundation. **Publications:** *Eye on Bureaucracy*, monthly. Newsletter. **Price:** $50.00 ● *Howard Phillips Issues and Strategy*, semimonthly. Bulletin ● Monographs ● Report. **Conventions/Meetings:** periodic meeting.

16907 ■ Conservative Majority for Citizen's Rights (CMCR)
c/o American Gospel Ministries
302 Briarwood Cir. NW
Fort Walton Beach, FL 32548-3904
Ph: (850)862-6211 (850)862-4429
Fax: (850)862-6211
E-mail: jharkins@americangospel.org
URL: http://www.americangospel.org
Contact: James Stanley Harkins Sr., Pres.

Founded: 1981. **Members:** 30,000. **Staff:** 20. **Description:** International and national conservative organizations; individuals promoting a conservative government. Provides on-call citizen aid through political advocacy. Supports and distributes literature on issues such as citizens' rights, separation of church and state, pro-life activities and stances, pro-traditional family, anti-pornography, a strong national defense, and equal rights for women. Conducts research and educational programs. Maintains speakers' bureau; sponsors charitable programs. Compiles statistics. **Libraries: Type:** reference. **Holdings:** 3; periodicals. **Subjects:** government, social, religious, business, professional, national, international security. **Committees:** American Gospel Ministries. **Affiliated With:** Free Congress Research and Education Foundation; High Frontier. **Publications:** *The Angry Samaritan Chronicles*. Book. Consists of three volumes. ● *Conservative Majority Newsletter*, quarterly.

16908 ■ Eagle Forum (EF)
PO Box 618
Alton, IL 62002
Ph: (618)462-5415
Fax: (618)462-8909

E-mail: eagle@eagleforum.org
URL: http://www.eagleforum.org
Contact: Ms. Jessica Echard, Exec. Dir.

Founded: 1972. **Members:** 80,000. **Membership Dues:** regular, $20 (annual). **Staff:** 41. **Budget:** $1,000,000. **State Groups:** 50. **Description:** Men and women advocating issues involving family, education, literacy and national defense through local, state, and federal government. Supports pro-family and conservative philosophy. Promotes traditional morality, family values, private enterprise, and national defense. Calls for tax cuts, preservation of national sovereignty, respect for personal and electronic privacy, and a strong national defense. Strives to strengthen parents' and pupils' rights in education. Maintains a relationship with Eagle Forum Education and Legal Defense Fund and Eagle Forum PAC. **Libraries: Type:** by appointment only. **Holdings:** 5,000. **Awards:** Eagle Award. **Frequency:** annual. **Type:** recognition ● Fulltime Homemaker Award. **Frequency:** annual. **Type:** recognition. **Committees:** Education; Family; National Defense. **Publications:** *Phyllis Schlafly Report*, monthly. Newsletter. Provides commentaries on education, national defense, politics, feminism and family, economics, and social, public, and foreign policy. **Price:** $20.00/year. ISSN: 0556-0152. **Circulation:** 40,000. **Conventions/Meetings:** annual Eagle Council - meeting - fall.

16909 ■ Free Congress Political Action Committee (FCPAC)
717 2nd St. NE
Washington, DC 20002
Ph: (202)546-3000
Fax: (202)543-5605
E-mail: elicht@freecongress.org
URL: http://www.freecongress.org
Contact: Paul Weyrich, Chm./CEO

Founded: 1974. **Staff:** 3. **Budget:** $25,000. **Regional Groups:** 8. **Description:** Bipartisan political action committee dedicated to the election of "conservative, responsible, and realistic leaders" to the U.S. House of Representatives and Senate. Identifying and recruits conservative candidates; trains candidates and personnel in the skills of campaigning. Provides services in primary and general elections. Provides financial support to campaigns. Trains newly elected members of Congress; works with members on key legislative proposals. Assists conservative political candidates in precinct organization and coalition building. Conducts training seminar. **Formerly:** (1985) Committee for the Survival of a Free Congress. **Publications:** *Building for Victory*. Newsletter ● Pamphlets.

16910 ■ Freedom House
1301 Connecticut Ave. NW, 6th Fl.
Washington, DC 20036
Ph: (202)296-5101
Fax: (202)293-2840
E-mail: info@freedomhouse.org
URL: http://www.freedomhouse.org
Contact: Jennifer Windsor, Exec. Dir.

Founded: 1941. **Staff:** 80. **Multinational. Description:** Promotes democracy and freedom worldwide, as well as political and economic freedom. **Programs:** American Volunteers of International Development; NGO Regional Networking Project for Central and Eastern Europe; Rule of Law Initiative/Global Human Rights Training and Support; Visiting Fellows. **Formerly:** (1999) Freedom House/National Forum Foundation. **Publications:** *Freedom House Monitor*. Newsletter. Alternate Formats: online ● *Freedom in the World*. Book. **Price:** $29.95 ● *Nations In Transit*, annual. Book. **Price:** $39.95. **Conventions/Meetings:** periodic conference.

16911 ■ Future of Freedom Foundation (FFF)
11350 Random Hills Rd., Ste.800
Fairfax, VA 22030
Ph: (703)934-6101
Fax: (703)352-8678

E-mail: fff@fff.org
URL: http://www.fff.org
Contact: Jacob G. Hornberger, Pres.

Founded: 1989. **Membership Dues:** subscription, $15 (annual). **Staff:** 3. **Budget:** $350,000. **Description:** Advocates the libertarian philosophy. Conducts seminars. **Telecommunication Services:** electronic mail, jhornberger@fff.org. **Publications:** *Freedom Daily*, monthly. Journal. Includes essays and book reviews. **Price:** $18.00/year. **Circulation:** 5,000.

16912 ■ Intercollegiate Studies Institute (ISI)
3901 Centerville Rd.
PO Box 4431
Wilmington, DE 19807-0431
Ph: (302)652-4600
Free: (800)526-7022
Fax: (302)652-1760
E-mail: info@isi.org
URL: http://www.isi.org
Contact: T. Kenneth Cribb Jr., Pres.

Founded: 1953. **Members:** 50,000. **Membership Dues:** associate, $25 (annual) ● alumni, Young President Club, $100 (annual) ● President Club, $1,000 (annual) ● Leadership Council, $10,000 (annual). **Staff:** 18. **Description:** Nonpartisan, educational organization directed primarily at the college campus. Seeks to develop among college students and professors an understanding of "the conservative philosophy of individual liberty, limited government, free-market economics, the right of private property, and the spiritual and moral underpinnings of this philosophy." Promotes sound scholarship within the disciplines of economics, sociology, literature, political science, history, and philosophy. Arranges lecture tours; provides a forum for students to meet with prominent scholars. Assists in the formation of student discussion groups with ISI-associated clubs. Maintains speakers' bureau. **Awards:** Richard M. Weaver Fellowship. **Frequency:** annual. **Type:** fellowship. **Recipient:** to exceptional students for graduate study. **Programs:** Lecture; Understanding Law Enforcement; Volunteer in the ISA Campus Representative. **Formerly:** (1966) Intercollegiate Society of Individualists. **Publications:** *Campus: America's Student Newspaper*, quarterly. **Price:** $2.50. **Advertising:** accepted ● *Continuity: A Journal of History*, semiannual. Provides a forum for historiographical studies as a counter to those who view history through Marxist or other reductionist ideologies. **Price:** $10.00/year; $5.00/copy. ISSN: 0277-1446. **Advertising:** accepted ● *The Intercollegiate Review: A Journal of Scholarship and Opinion*, 2-4/year. Includes book reviews. **Price:** free for members; $10.00/4 issues, for nonmembers. ISSN: 0020-5249. **Advertising:** accepted ● *Modern Age*, quarterly. Journal. Covers conservative intellectual revival. Includes essays in political science, history, philosophy, and literary and cultural criticism. **Price:** $4.00/copy; $15.00/year; $7.50/year (academic rate). ISSN: 0026-7457. **Advertising:** accepted ● *The Political Science Reviewer*, annual. Journal. Contains reviews of recent studies in law and politics. **Price:** $10.00/issue. **Advertising:** accepted ● Books. **Conventions/Meetings:** periodic conference.

16913 ■ International Freedom Foundation (IFF)
200 G St. NE, Ste.300
Washington, DC 20002-4328
Ph: (202)546-5788
Fax: (202)546-5488
E-mail: katman0@hotmail.com
URL: http://www.iff-ifoundfreedom.com
Contact: Duncan Sellars, Chm.

Founded: 1986. **Staff:** 8. **Description:** Works to foster individual freedom throughout the world by engaging in activities which promote the development of free and open societies based on the principles of free enterprise. Works to develop free institutions in reforming societies. Sponsors international exchanges; maintains speakers' bureau. **Awards: Type:** fellowship.

16914 ■ Jefferson Educational Foundation (JEF)
Address Unknown since 2007

Founded: 1979. **Staff:** 6. **Budget:** $350,000. **Description:** Recruits and trains young conservative political and diplomatic leaders through educational projects, academic scholarships, and leadership conferences. Conducts briefings for students and business, political, and community leaders. Sponsors domestic and foreign policy conferences, lectures, and tours. The foundation is named for Thomas Jefferson (1743-1826), third president of the U.S., signatory to the Declaration of Independence, and noted scholar, naturalist, and architect. **Publications:** *Issues for Young Americans*, periodic. **Conventions/Meetings:** seminar.

16915 ■ John Birch Society (JBS)
PO Box 8040
Appleton, WI 54912
Ph: (920)749-3784
Free: (800)727-TRUE
Fax: (920)749-3785
E-mail: lgreenley@jbs.org
URL: http://www.jbs.org
Contact: Arthur R. Thompson, CEO

Founded: 1958. **Members:** 50,000. **Membership Dues:** individual, $48 (annual) ● married couple, $60 (annual) ● youth, $24 (annual) ● life, $4,000. **Staff:** 90. **Budget:** $6,000,000. **Description:** Individuals who believe that the American system of government (Constitutional Republic) is the "finest yet developed by man." Believes in the traditional moral values of a Judeo-Christian heritage, and that it is the cornerstone to western civilization. Provides action programs, professional leadership training, educational information, youth program, and book and video production. **Libraries: Type:** not open to the public. **Holdings:** 18,000. **Subjects:** politics, history. **Computer Services:** Mailing lists. **Publications:** *The John Birch Society Bulletin*, monthly. **Price:** $60.00/year. **Circulation:** 50,000 ● *The New American*, biweekly. Magazine. **Price:** $39.00/year. **Circulation:** 65,000. **Advertising:** accepted ● Brochure. **Price:** free for individuals in U.S.; $5.00 outside U.S. **Conventions/Meetings:** annual dinner, 4 to 6 council dinners in various locations nationwide.

16916 ■ LibertyTree
100 Swan Way
Oakland, CA 94621-1428
Ph: (510)568-6047
Free: (800)927-8733
Fax: (510)568-6040
E-mail: info@liberty-tree.org
URL: http://www.liberty-tree.org
Contact: David J. Theroux, Pres.

Founded: 1986. **Members:** 1,100. **Staff:** 12. **Description:** Educational organization promoting the history and practice of individual liberty, with emphasis on limited government intervention. Assembles, reviews, and distributes books and other educational materials in areas including: American history and politics; the Constitution; world history and politics; economic and civil liberties; personal finance; free markets; privacy; self-defense and the right to bear arms. Conducts seminars, tours, and receptions for authors; maintains speakers' bureau; provides children's educational services. **Libraries: Type:** not open to the public. **Holdings:** 4,000; articles, books, periodicals. **Subjects:** social sciences. **Computer Services:** Mailing lists, membership. **Subgroups:** Russian Sister Institute. **Formerly:** (2003) LibertyTree Network. **Publications:** *LibertyTree: Review and Catalog*, semiannual. Contains review of books, audio tapes, video tapes, and collectibles on liberty. **Price:** free. ISSN: 1048-4922. **Circulation:** 550,000. **Advertising:** accepted. Alternate Formats: online ● Audiotapes ● Books ● Videos ● Also issues games and collectibles.

16917 ■ National Traditionalist Caucus (NTC)
PO Box 971, GPO
New York, NY 10116-0971
Ph: (212)685-4689

E-mail: info@ntcamerica.org
URL: http://www.ntcamerica.org
Contact: Donald P. Rosenberg, Chm./Founder

Founded: 1970. **Members:** 2,000. **Membership Dues:** student, $5 (annual) ● young adult, $10 (annual) ● adult, $15 (annual). **Description:** Conservative youth organization primarily concerned with the political education of high school, junior high school, and college students. Teachings are "of a constitutional, patriotic, conservative, anticommunist, pro-free enterprise nature and moral orientation." Activities include seminars, receptions, letter-writing campaigns, lobbying, and demonstrations. Petitions Congress, state legislatures, municipal councils, and boards of education concerning pending legislation and policy. Distributes literature; sponsors speech and essay contests. Maintains speakers' bureau. **Libraries: Type:** not open to the public. **Subjects:** history, political science, education. **Awards:** Advancement and Preservation of Civilization Award. **Frequency:** semiannual. **Type:** recognition. **Recipient:** for individuals who have contributed significantly to the pro-family cause and/or to the national strength and independence ● Reach for the Stars Award. **Type:** recognition. **Recipient:** for young Hollywood entertainers who act as positive role models for children. **Publications:** *EXCALIBUR*, periodic. Magazine. **Advertising:** accepted. **Conventions/Meetings:** semiannual meeting - usually New York City.

16918 ■ Students for America (SFA)
Address Unknown since 2007

Founded: 1984. **Membership Dues:** charter, $10 (annual) ● non student, $25 (annual). **Staff:** 3. **Budget:** $90,000. **Description:** Composed of Christian college students. Promotes liberty, free enterprise, limited government, fiscal responsibility, rule of law, strong national defense, and Judeo-Christian ethics. Encourages Generation Xers to pray for national leaders. **Libraries: Type:** reference. **Holdings:** 150. **Subjects:** current public policy topics, founding principles literature. **Awards:** Victory Award. **Frequency:** annual. **Type:** recognition. **Recipient:** to a member. **Boards:** Education. **Committees:** Programs. **Publications:** *Future's Forum*, periodic. Newsletter. **Price:** free. **Advertising:** accepted ● Pamphlets. **Conventions/Meetings:** annual conference (exhibits) ● periodic regional meeting.

16919 ■ Third Generation (3G)
c/o Heritage Foundation
214 Massachusetts Ave. NE
Washington, DC 20002-4999
Ph: (202)546-4400
Fax: (202)546-8328
E-mail: info@heritage.org
URL: http://www.heritage.org
Contact: Edwin J. Feulner PhD, Pres.

Founded: 1984. **Members:** 150. **Staff:** 2. **Description:** Conservative individuals and political activists under 35 years of age. Provides a forum for members to discuss current political issues and devise strategies to advance free market economic principles and a strong national defense. Provides speakers who analyze national political trends and defend conservative principles in economic, national defense, social and cultural issues. **Publications:** none. **Telecommunication Services:** electronic mail, staff@heritage.org. **Affiliated With:** The Heritage Foundation. **Conventions/Meetings:** annual meeting ● monthly seminar, to discuss current political issues.

16920 ■ Young Americans for Freedom (YAF)
8116 Arlington Blvd., No. 263
Falls Church, VA 22042-1002
Free: (877)YAF-2170
Fax: (703)249-0779
E-mail: info@yaf.com
URL: http://www.yaf.com
Contact: Jason Harding, Exec. Dir.

Founded: 1960. **Members:** 55,000. **Staff:** 4. **Local Groups:** 200. **Description:** Represents nonpartisan, political youth (up to age 39). Seeks to promote a conservative philosophy of free enterprise and strong national defense. Acts as a clearinghouse for speakers' bureaus and placement services. Conducts research programs and compiles statistics. **Libraries: Type:** reference. **Committees:** Sharon Foundation; YAF-Political Action. **Publications:** *Dialogue on Liberty*, quarterly ● *New Guard*, quarterly. Magazine. Includes national activism reports and book reviews. **Price:** $2.50. **Circulation:** 10,000. **Advertising:** accepted. Alternate Formats: microform ● *YAF in the News*, annual. Newsletter ● Reports. **Conventions/ Meetings:** annual Conservative Political Action Conference - meeting - always winter, Washington, DC ● biennial convention.

16921 ■ Young America's Foundation (YAF)
F.M. Kirby Freedom Ctr.
110 Elden St.
Herndon, VA 20170
Ph: (703)318-9608
Free: (800)USA-1776
Fax: (703)318-9122
E-mail: yaf@yaf.org
URL: http://www.yaf.org
Contact: Ron Robinson, Pres.
Founded: 1969. **Staff:** 32. **Budget:** $10,800,000. **State Groups:** 50. **Description:** Works to acquaint American youth with the principles of American government in order that they may have a fuller understanding of contemporary public policy questions. Promotes conservative ideas among high school and college students. Accepts tax-deductible contributions from individuals, corporations and other foundations. Maintains Ronald Reagan ranch in Santa Barbara, CA. **Libraries: Type:** reference. **Holdings:** 1,000. **Subjects:** conservative topics. **Projects:** National Journalism Center. **Publications:** *Campus Leader*, 9/year ● *Libertas*, bimonthly. Alternate Formats: online ● Books ● Films ● Manual. Contains the conservative argument for the national debate topic selected each year for high school students. ● Monographs ● Reprints. **Conventions/ Meetings:** annual meeting - always Washington, DC.

Conservative Traditionalists

16922 ■ American Decency Association (ADA)
PO Box 202
Fremont, MI 49412
Ph: (231)924-4050
Fax: (231)924-1966
E-mail: info@americandecency.org
URL: http://www.americandecency.org
Contact: Bill Johnson, Pres./Founder
Founded: 1999. **Description:** Educates members and the general public on matters of decency. Initiates, promotes, encourages, and coordinates activities designed to safeguard and advance public morality consistent with biblical Christianity. Conducts boycotts of shows and advertisers who "indirectly advocate immorality on television and in other media". **Telecommunication Services:** electronic mail, bjohnson@americandecency.org. **Publications:** *American Decency Update*, monthly. Bulletin. Contains updates on the campaigns the association is involved in. ● *Frontline*, monthly. Newsletter. Provides updates and commentaries on salient issues facing Christians across the nation. Alternate Formats: online.

16923 ■ Americans for Decency (AFD)
3431 W Thunderbird Rd., No. 13-275
Phoenix, AZ 85053-5641
Ph: (602)993-4353
E-mail: afd-bundy@cox.net
URL: http://www.americansfordecency.com
Contact: Rev. T.C. Bundy, Pres.
Founded: 1975. **Description:** Concerned individuals and organizations whose purpose is to educate about the harm of pornography and sexual victimization. Promotes the importance of family unity and family issues. Seeks to improve and unify families through counseling and education. **Awards:** Decency Award. **Frequency:** periodic. **Type:** recognition. **Recipient:** to companies or individuals who do exemplary work

to protect people from sexual victimization and abuse. **Publications:** *Americans for Decency Flyers*, periodic ● *Hope for the Family News*, monthly. Newsletters. Small education publication to encourage and educate members. **Price:** $2.00. **Advertising:** accepted. Alternate Formats: online ● Also publishes flyers and distributes copies of articles.

16924 ■ Care Net (CN)
44180 Riverside Pkwy., Ste.200
Lansdowne, VA 20176
Ph: (703)478-5661
Free: (800)395-HELP
Fax: (703)478-5668
E-mail: info@care-net.org
URL: http://www.care-net.org
Contact: Kurt Entsminger, Pres.
Founded: 1975. **State Groups:** 550. **Description:** A Christian, pro-life network of pregnancy care centers and churches. Proclaims the Gospel and provides practical help to women, men, and unborn children threatened by abortion in the United States and Canada. **Telecommunication Services:** electronic mail, etlanna@ix.net.com. **Formerly:** (1995) Christian Action Council. **Publications:** *Center of Tomorrow*, quarterly. Journal. Contains reports on emerging programs, services and methods within the pregnancy center movement. **Price:** $29.95/year; $9.95 single issue ● *Faces of Care Net*, quarterly. Newsletter. Describes what Care Net is doing and gives crisis pregnancy center stories. ● Report, bimonthly. Contains information about the issues surrounding abortion and the sanctity of human life. Alternate Formats: online ● Manual ● Also publishes brochures. **Conventions/Meetings:** annual conference (exhibits).

16925 ■ Christian Coalition of America (CCA)
PO Box 37030
Washington, DC 20013-7030
Ph: (202)479-6900
Free: (877)809-1659
Fax: (202)479-4260
E-mail: coalition@cc.org
URL: http://www.cc.org
Contact: Roberta Combs, Pres.
Founded: 1989. **Staff:** 20. **Description:** Serves as grass roots political organization working to "stop the moral decay of government"; promotes the election of "moral" legislators and legislation. **Formerly:** (2004) Christian Coalition. **Publications:** *Christian American*, bimonthly. **Price:** free. **Advertising:** accepted ● *Washington Weekly Review*. Newsletter. Alternate Formats: online ● Newsletter, monthly. **Price:** free. **Conventions/Meetings:** periodic meeting.

16926 ■ Christian Heritage Center (CHC)
10 Croyden Ln.
Staunton, VA 24401
Ph: (540)885-7333
E-mail: bill@godshistory.com
URL: http://www.christianheritageworks.com
Contact: Bill Dolack, Gen. Mgr.
Founded: 2000. **Members:** 750. **Staff:** 3. **Description:** Serves as a free Christian lending library and museum specializing in the religious history of the United States from 1730 through the Civil War. **Libraries: Type:** reference. **Holdings:** 30,000. **Subjects:** Christian, cults, history, missions, apologetics, prayer, evangelism, classic authors, end times, charismatic, social issues, commentaries, bible studies, bibles, pastoral study aids, sermons, preaching, church history, financial, Israel. **Additional Websites:** http://www.godshistory.com. **Conventions/Meetings:** annual meeting.

16927 ■ Coalitions for America (CA)
Address Unknown since 2006
Description: Nonpartisan lobbying organization that acts as a coordinating council for the promotion of the free enterprise system, a limited government, a strong national defense, and traditional values. Seeks to develop a common strategy on political, legislative, and regulatory issues. Has organized task forces to prepare the conservative legislative agenda on is-

sues such as economics, the judiciary, consumer affairs, education, child care, health and welfare, budgetary reform, and taxes. Has initiated the Family Protection Act to help low- and middle-income families survive economically and to perpetuate traditional values in homes and schools without federal intervention. Seeks to coordinate various conservative business and single-issue groups to combat liberal initiatives at all governmental levels. Maintains: Kingston Group, a coalition seeking to organize activities of organizations involved with economics and budgetary reform; Library Court Group, which works to protect the family and promote social policies supporting traditional values; Stanton Group, which promotes strong national defense programs; 721 Group, an anticrime coalition that seeks judicial reform; Jewish/Conservative Alliance, to identify areas of agreement between Jewish and conservative organizations.

Constitution

16928 ■ Academics for the Second Amendment (A2A)
c/o Hamline University
School of Law
1536 Hewitt Ave.
St. Paul, MN 55104
Ph: (651)523-2142 (651)523-2076
Fax: (651)523-2236
E-mail: jolson@gw.hamline.edu
URL: http://www.hamline.edu/law/school_of_law.html
Contact: Dr. Joseph Olson, Pres.
Founded: 1992. **Members:** 500. **Membership Dues:** contributor, $25 (annual). **Budget:** $50,000. **Description:** Law school teachers, historians, political scientists, government philosophers, and individuals supporting the right to keep and bear arms. Challenges the legal profession and the public to appreciate the place of the individual right to keep and bear arms as granted by the second amendment of the American Constitution. Sponsors academic symposia, support research, and publications. **Conventions/ Meetings:** Scholarship Conference.

16929 ■ Americans United for God and Country (AUGC)
Address Unknown since 2007
Founded: 1977. **Members:** 10,422. **Regional Groups:** 3. **Description:** "To promote patriotism and the love of God and country in accordance with the principles and purposes of the framers of the Constitution of the United States, and the amendments known as the Bill of Rights." Seeks to revitalize the Judeo-Christian concepts in America with the use of federal tax credits and grants to help finance private schools. Believes that since Judeo-Christian citizens provide support for public schools through their tax funds, their concepts should be taught in these schools. **Conventions/Meetings:** annual conference - always July 4.

16930 ■ Citizens for Governmental Restraint (CGR)
3541 Robinwood Terr.
Minnetonka, MN 55305-4327
Ph: (952)938-6472
Fax: (952)935-9235
Contact: M. Jacquelin Stevenson, Sec.-Treas.
Founded: 1967. **Description:** Maintains that Presidents Johnson and Nixon were "guilty of violations of executive power in the war-making areas." According to the organization, "the Constitution permits the imposition of a state of military slavery on our people only in time of serious insurrection or actual invasion" and that these constitutional restrictions were evaded in Southeast Asia during the Johnson and Nixon administrations. Have circulated petitions for impeachment because of the alleged presidential violations.

16931 ■ Committee on the Constitutional System (CCS)
1400 20th St. NW, No. 912
Washington, DC 20036
Ph: (202)387-8787

Fax: (202)822-8766
Contact: Peter Schauffler, Coor.
Founded: 1984. **Members:** 300. **State Groups:** 12.
Description: Former government officials, members of Congress, academicians, and others interested in discussing ways to improve governmental performance, including legislation, party rules, and structural amendments to the U.S. Constitution. Examines options such as synchronizing terms and allowing members of Congress to serve in the cabinet. **Publications:** Workbook examining the structural problems of the Constitution. **Conventions/Meetings:** annual meeting.

16932 ■ Committee to Restore the Constitution (CRC)
2218 W Prospect Rd.
PO Box 986
Fort Collins, CO 80522
Ph: (970)484-2575
E-mail: comminc@webaccess.net
Contact: Col. Archibald E. Roberts, Dir.
Founded: 1965. **Members:** 10,000. **Membership Dues:** individual, $25 (annual) ● outside U.S., $25. **Staff:** 5. **State Groups:** 100. **Description:** Individuals united for: motivating Americans to act within authority of the Constitution to restore interest-free money, repudiate unpayable national debt, and eliminate federal deficits. Seeks to provide public education on the facts "behind the constitutional crisis"; organization of conscientious citizens in patriotic action centers; motivation of elected officials at county and state levels of government to correct excesses of federal agents. Seeks to end the fraud it claims is being perpetuated by the Federal Reserve System. Areas of interest include federal regionalism and land control edicts, new federal constitution, United Nations, and "other threats to the Republic." Conducts public rallies; gives testimony before county commission and state legislatures; sponsors training of local leaders at state seminars; conducts public information programs. **Publications:** CRC Bulletin, monthly. Explains constitutional authority in hopes of halting economic/political exploitation. **Price:** included in membership dues ● Books ● Brochures ● Manuals ● Pamphlets ● Also makes available videotapes and audiocassettes. **Conventions/Meetings:** annual meeting.

16933 ■ Constitutional Rights Foundation (CRF)
601 S Kingsley Dr.
Los Angeles, CA 90005
Ph: (213)487-5590
Fax: (213)386-0459
E-mail: crf@crf-usa.org
URL: http://www.crf-usa.org
Contact: Todd Clark, Exec. Dir.
Founded: 1962. **Staff:** 23. **Budget:** $2,800,000. **Description:** Helps young people to better understand the workings of the democratic system and encourage them to undertake a positive role in American society. Strives to empower a new generation of engaged citizens, urging them to familiarize themselves with the substance of the Constitution and civil institutions. Provides mentoring programs, professional internships, leadership development, community problem solving, teacher training and educational materials. Works to lead young Americans towards a future based on democratic values and responsible action. **Awards:** Maurice R. Robinson Mini-Grants. **Frequency:** annual. **Type:** grant. **Recipient:** for funding of service learning projects. **Councils:** Lawyers Advisory; Sports and the Law Advisory. **Programs:** Active Citizen Today; Mock Trial; Youth for Justice; Youth Internship. **Publications:** Bill of Rights in Action, quarterly. Newsletter. Describes law-related civics, history, and government readings, activities, and questions suitable for classroom use. **Price:** free. **Circulation:** 40,000 ● Catalogs. **Price:** free ● Also publishes curriculum material for students and teachers on criminal and civil justice, history, political science, and international subjects; makes available role-playing simulation games. **Conventions/Meetings:** semiannual Student Conference.

16934 ■ Constitutionists Networking Center (CNC)
442 E 1250 Rd.
Baldwin City, KS 66006
Ph: (785)594-3367
E-mail: cnc@idir.net
URL: http://www.idir.net/~cnc
Contact: Evan Mecham, Chm.
Founded: 1993. **Members:** 8. **Staff:** 2. **Description:** Leaders of national organizations, judges, and legislators. Seeks to return the United States government to the limits prescribed by the Constitution by providing leadership for and communications between persons who subscribe to the organization's goals. Maintains speakers' bureau. **Working Groups:** Objective Pursuit Teams. **Publications:** Media Bypass Magazine. **Conventions/Meetings:** periodic meeting.

16935 ■ Foundation for Rational Economics and Education (FREE)
PO Box 1776
Lake Jackson, TX 77566
Ph: (409)265-3034
Fax: (409)265-7378
E-mail: jhardin@mindspring.com
URL: http://freedompage.home.mindspring.com/free.htm
Contact: Lori Pyatt, Exec. Off.
Founded: 1976. **Description:** Represents individuals interested in studying the Constitution and subjects such as economic freedom, personal liberty, and foreign policy. Maintains National Endowment for Liberty which produces the "At Issue" educational television series. **Additional Websites:** http://www.free-nefl.com. **Projects:** National Endowment for Liberty. **Formerly:** Foundation for Research in Economics and Education. **Publications:** Abortion and Liberty. **Price:** $3.95 ● Challenge to Liberty. Covers the abortion controversy. **Price:** $10.00 ● Freedom Report, monthly. Newsletter ● Gold, Peace, and Prosperity. Introduces the history of money. Covers inflation and the business cycle. **Price:** $2.00 ● The New Money Survival Handbook. **Price:** $50.00 ● Ten Myths About Paper Money. Argues against fiat paper money and answers common objections to a gold standard. **Price:** $1.00 ● Videos.

16936 ■ Independent Americans (IA)
704 W 1100 S
Payson, UT 84651
Ph: (801)465-3228
E-mail: sovereign50@independentamericans.org
URL: http://www.independentamericans.org
Contact: Robert Marck, Natl. Coor.
Founded: 1973. **State Groups:** 50. **Description:** Promotes the proper role of government and educates the American people on the principles of constitutional law and liberty; preserves the Constitution of the U.S. as a stronghold of freedom and truth among individuals worldwide. Supports a free enterprise economic system that includes the right to possess private property and the right to exchange and profit; opposes mandatory government charity and income tax levying; promotes a currency backed by precious metals such as gold and silver. Maintains collection of pamphlets, letters, and papers. **Publications:** The American Dream. Book. Covers the role of government and many other vital issues for today. **Price:** $6.95 ● Brochures ● Newsletter, periodic. **Conventions/Meetings:** semiannual conference.

16937 ■ Jefferson Foundation (JF)
809 Quail St., Bldg. No. 1
Lakewood, CO 80215
Ph: (303)982-2210
Fax: (303)982-2209
E-mail: monasandoval@jeffersonfoundation.org
URL: http://www.jeffersonfoundation.org
Contact: Mona Sandoval, Exec. Dir.
Founded: 1983. **Staff:** 2. **Budget:** $550,000. **Description:** Participants conduct nonpartisan research and citizen education on constitutional reforms designed to improve government structure and functioning. Sponsors Jefferson Meetings on the Constitution, a series of citizen debates. **Libraries:**

Type: reference. **Holdings:** 250. **Subjects:** constitution, structural reform of government. **Committees:** School Programs Advisory. **Funds:** Second Wind Walk/Run. **Affiliated With:** National Council for the Social Studies. **Supersedes:** Foundation for the Study of Presidential and Congressional Terms. **Publications:** Jefferson Foundation News, semiannual ● Also publishes guides on constitutional issues.

16938 ■ Liberty Amendment Committee of the U.S.A. (LACUSA)
PO Box 188785
Sacramento, CA 95818
Ph: (916)443-7769
Fax: (916)443-7769
URL: http://libertyamendment.com
Contact: John Rakus Esq, Natl. Chm.
Founded: 1949. **Members:** 2,100. **Membership Dues:** Advisory Board, $2,000 ● life, $1,000 ● participating, $150 (annual) ● family, $100 (annual) ● associate, $50 (annual) ● senior citizen (over 65), $30 (annual) ● student (under 21), $30 (annual). **Staff:** 2. **State Groups:** 50. **Description:** Promotes the passage of the Liberty Amendment (repeatedly introduced in Congress as H.J. Res. 23) and "to reduce the size and cost of federal government to those functions specified in the U.S. Constitution." According to the committee, nine state legislatures have endorsed the proposed amendment: Arizona, Georgia, Indiana, Louisiana, Mississippi, Nevada, South Carolina, Texas, and Wyoming. Initiates campaign to obtain additional state endorsements. Conducts research; compiles statistics. **Libraries:** **Type:** not open to the public. **Subjects:** free enterprise, monetary policy, fiscal policy. **Awards:** Friends of Liberty. **Frequency:** annual. **Type:** recognition. **Recipient:** for free market principles. **Formerly:** National Committee for Economic Freedom. **Publications:** Yes On 23/Liberty Amendment News, semimonthly. Reports. Contains information on liberty and justice times. **Price:** included in membership dues. **Advertising:** accepted. **Conventions/Meetings:** annual board meeting.

16939 ■ National Center for Constitutional Studies (NCCS)
37777 W Juniper Rd.
Malta, ID 83342
Ph: (208)645-2625
Free: (800)388-4512
Fax: (208)645-2667
E-mail: zeldon@nccs.net
URL: http://www.nccs.net
Contact: Zeldon Nelson, CEO
Founded: 1971. **Members:** 45,000. **Membership Dues:** regular, $10 (monthly). **Staff:** 30. **Description:** Researches, develops, and produces programs that teach constitutional principles "in the tradition of America's Founding Fathers." Believes in a strict interpretation of the Constitution whereby states rights are not denied by the evolution of a strong central government. Participates in seminars on the above topics and on current issues in relation to constitutional questions. Maintains research file and speakers' bureau. **Libraries:** **Type:** reference. **Holdings:** 5,000; archival material, books. **Awards:** **Type:** recognition. **Formerly:** (1984) Freemen Institute. **Publications:** The Constitution of the United States. Booklet. **Price:** $1.00/copy ● The Constitution: Special Reports, periodic. Reviews current tax and defense issues. Discusses related problems and offers constitutional solutions. ● Principles of Good Government, monthly. Newsletter. **Price:** available through donation ● Audiotapes ● Books ● Videos. **Conventions/Meetings:** competition ● monthly meeting.

16940 ■ National Justice Foundation of America (NJFA)
1617 16th St.
Sacramento, CA 95814
Ph: (916)442-0537 (916)443-7769
Fax: (916)443-7769
Contact: John Rakus Esq., CFP Pres.
Founded: 1970. **Membership Dues:** $30 (annual) ● life, $2,000. **Description:** U.S. citizens who believe

in the ownership of private property and the American government as a constitutional republic. Promotes by educational and legal means the balanced representation of opinion in the courts and legal tribunals of our nation. Promotes issues such as the right to keep arms, fair tax practices, health freedom, and freedom of choice and association in education and business. Maintains speakers' bureau. Sponsors research programs. **Libraries: Type:** reference. **Holdings:** 400. **Subjects:** constitutional rights. **Awards:** Justice Attorney of the Year Award. **Frequency:** annual. **Type:** recognition. **Recipient:** for outstanding representative of a constitutional issue resulting in freedom. **Computer Services:** database, ALPHA 5 ● online services. **Committees:** Education; Justice. **Also Known As:** Justice Foundation; Liberty Foundation; American Monetary Foundation. **Publications:** *Are You a Freeman? Test Yourself!.* Brochure. Features a 21 question Constitutional I.Q. test. ● *Citizens Rule Book.* Reports. Contains the Declaration of Independence, Constitution, Bill of Rights, Ten Commandments, Communist Manifesto, etc. **Price:** free for members; $2.00/copy including shipping and handling; $1.70 two - ten copies including shipping and handling ● *Declaration by the Justice Foundation.* Brochure ● *Highlights Sheet Quarterly,* bimonthly. Newsletter. Covers news and activities of the organization. Alternate Formats: online ● *Liberty and Justice Times.* Newsletter ● *Political Subversion of Our Constitutional Republic.* Booklet. **Price:** included in membership dues. **Conventions/Meetings:** biennial convention (exhibits) ● Legislative Awards Luncheon ● periodic seminar.

16941 ■ Third Continental Congress (3CC)
c/o William D. Day, Membership Committee Chm.
3003 Short Cherry St.
Vicksburg, MS 39180
E-mail: ceo@3telecom.net
Contact: Hon. John M. Smith, Interim Pres.
Founded: 1961. **Description:** Promotes the "restoration of a limited constitutional government" in the U.S. "based on the principles of the Founding Fathers" and on observance and execution of the Bill of Rights to the exclusion of all subsequent amendments to the Constitution. Establishes councils comprised of Christian men from various states; these councils work to inform the public about the "excesses" of the federal government and engage in grass roots efforts to repeal all Constitutional amendments beyond the Bill of Rights. **Supersedes:** Constitution Parties of the U.S.

Constitutional Law

16942 ■ Citizens Flag Alliance (CFA)
PO Box 7197
Indianapolis, IN 46207-7197
Ph: (317)630-1384
Fax: (317)630-1385
E-mail: cfa@cfa-inc.org
URL: http://www.cfa-inc.org
Contact: Maj. Gen. Patrick H. Brady, Chm.
Founded: 1994. **Members:** 145. **State Groups:** 50. **National Groups:** 149. **Description:** Seeks to protect the American flag from physical desecration. **Publications:** *Old Glory News,* periodic. Newsletter. **Price:** free. **Circulation:** 6,000. Alternate Formats: online.

Consumers

16943 ■ AFSA Education Foundation (AFSAEF)
919 18th St. NW
Washington, DC 20006
Ph: (202)296-5544
Fax: (202)223-0321
E-mail: info@afsaef.org
Contact: M. Susie Irvine, Exec. Dir.
Founded: 1990. **Staff:** 1. **Budget:** $177,300. **Description:** Promotes public education about personal finance and consumer credit issues. Develops

educational materials and disseminates information. **Convention/Meeting:** none. **Formerly:** Consumer Credit Education Foundation. **Publications:** *Consumer Budget Planner.* **Price:** $10.00 ● *Consumer Finance Bulletin,* monthly. **Circulation:** 1,200 ● *Consumer's Almanac.* **Price:** $18.75 ● *How to Be Credit Smart●* *Money and Your Marriage* ● Videos.

16944 ■ Alliance Against Fraud in Telemarketing and Electronic Commerce (AAFT)
c/o National Consumers League
1701 K St. NW, Ste.1200
Washington, DC 20006
Ph: (202)835-3323
Free: (800)876-7060
Fax: (202)835-0747
E-mail: info@nclnet.org
URL: http://www.fraud.org/aaft/aaftinfo.htm
Contact: Susan Grant, VP of Public Policy/Dir. of NFIC
Founded: 1989. **Members:** 100. **Membership Dues:** nonprofit, education institution, labor organization, $35 (annual) ● government consumer protection, law enforcement agency, $65 (annual) ● business, trade group, $350 (annual). **Staff:** 2. **Budget:** $84,000. **Description:** Consumer groups, trade associations, labor unions, industry, educational institutions and government agencies involved in educational strategies to prevent telemarketing and Internet fraud. Provides information on fraud practices to increase public awareness. Distributes consumer education materials; provides alerts to members. Coordinated by the National Consumers League. **Publications:** *Focus on Fraud,* quarterly. Newsletter. Includes information on educational developments, new publications, and state and federal legislative/regulatory activities. **Price:** $9.00 in U.S.; $12.00 outside U.S. ISSN: 1055-4491. Alternate Formats: online. **Conventions/Meetings:** quarterly meeting.

16945 ■ Alliance for Consumer Rights (ACR)
c/o New York State Trial Lawyers Association
132 Nassau St., 2nd Fl.
New York, NY 10038
Ph: (212)349-5890
Fax: (212)608-2310
E-mail: info@nystla.org
URL: http://nystla.org
Contact: Daniel L. Fieldman, Exec. Dir./Gen. Counsel
Founded: 1985. **Budget:** $500,000. **Description:** Works to preserve the rights of people who have been injured by faulty products and seek compensation through the courts; and to protect and expand the U.S. tort system. Conducts lobbying, educational, and outreach programs on tort laws covering environmental, product liability, medical malpractice, and other areas. **Libraries: Type:** reference. **Publications:** *ACR Bulletin,* quarterly ● Also publishes reports.

16946 ■ American Consumers Association (ACA)
2633 Flossmoor Rd.
Flossmoor, IL 60422
Ph: (708)957-2900
Fax: (708)957-4155
E-mail: amerconassn@ameritech.net
Contact: James Scott Tiernan, Exec. Dir..
Founded: 1984. **Staff:** 2. **Description:** Provides information on consumer goods and services, including product quality, cost, safety, and effectiveness. Promotes exchange of information beneficial to the health and welfare of the American consumer. Cooperates with individual or group efforts with the same goals. Offers a group insurance program and referrals on questions related to health and welfare. Issues public service announcements; conducts radio and direct mail advertising; endorses products. Compiles statistics; plans to establish a library. **Publications:** Pamphlets. Provides information on discount eyewear and prescription drugs. **Conventions/Meetings:** annual conference.

16947 ■ American Council on Consumer Interests (ACCI)
415 S Duff Ave., Ste.C
Ames, IA 50010-6600
Ph: (515)956-4666
Fax: (515)233-3101
E-mail: info@consumerinterests.org
URL: http://www.consumerinterests.org
Contact: Terri Haffner, Exec. Dir.
Founded: 1953. **Members:** 750. **Membership Dues:** individual, $110 (annual) ● student/retired, $55 (annual). **Staff:** 3. **Budget:** $175,000. **Description:** Teachers, researchers, counselors, and others working in information media and for the government who are concerned with problems of the economy from the point of view of the consumer. Works to: stimulate an exchange of ideas among consumer groups and between them and other groups in the economy; contribute to a better understanding of the role of the consumer in the economy as well as of the producer and distributor; contribute to more effective research and fact finding; disseminate information on consumer problems; promote better consumer education. **Awards: Type:** recognition. **Recipient:** for outstanding research in any topic of relevance to consumer welfare. **Committees:** Award; Career Opportunities; Consumer Education; Future Directions; International Consumer Affairs; Research; Student Section. **Formerly:** (1969) Council on Consumer Information. **Publications:** *Consumer Interests Annual,* annual. Proceedings ● *Journal of Consumer Affairs,* semiannual. **Conventions/Meetings:** annual conference, consumer protection and regulation (exhibits) - always March or April.

16948 ■ Association for Consumer Research (ACR)
c/o Rajiv Vaidyanathan, Exec. Dir.
Univ. of Minnesota Duluth
Labovitz School of Bus. and Economics
11 E Superior St., Ste.210
Duluth, MN 55802
Ph: (218)726-7853
Fax: (218)726-6338
E-mail: acr@acrweb.org
URL: http://www.acrwebsite.org
Contact: Rajiv Vaidyanathan, Exec. Dir.
Founded: 1969. **Members:** 1,800. **Membership Dues:** retired, student, $20 (annual) ● regular, $60 (annual). **Multinational. Description:** Individuals in academia, government, and business interested in consumer research. Facilitates the exchange of scholarly information among members of academia, industry, and government worldwide. **Councils:** Advisory. **Publications:** *Advances in Consumer Research,* annual. Proceedings. Contains papers presented at the October conference. **Price:** $59.00. **Conventions/Meetings:** biennial Asia Pacific - conference, co-sponsored by an academic institution in one of the Asia Pacific countries ● annual conference, competitively judged papers presented - always October.

16949 ■ Automotive Consumer Action Program (AUTOCAP)
c/o National Automobile Dealers Association
8400 Westpark Dr.
McLean, VA 22102
Ph: (703)821-7000
E-mail: autocap@wanada.org
URL: http://www.wanada.org/autocap.html
Founded: 1973. **Members:** 31. **State Groups:** 19. **Local Groups:** 12. **Description:** Participating new car dealers' associations and automobile manufacturers complying with standards administered through the National Automobile Dealers Association. Acts as a public service program providing dealers and their customers with consumer dispute resolution assistance. Act as "mini-juries" through panels of volunteers (usually 3 dealers and 3 consumer representatives) in cases of customer dissatisfaction with dealers, when direct contact fails to resolve the problem. **Affiliated With:** National Automobile Dealers Association. **Publications:** *Automotive Customer Relations Directory.*

16950 ■ Aviation Consumer Action Project (ACAP)
529 14th St. NW, No. 923
Washington, DC 20045
Ph: (202)638-4000
Free: (800)588-ACAP
Fax: (202)638-0746
Contact: Paul Hudson, Exec.Dir.
Founded: 1971. **Members:** 1,500. **Membership Dues:** individual, $35 (annual). **Staff:** 2. **Budget:** $65,000. **Description:** Promotes the interests of consumers in improved ground and air safety, environmental protection, affordable air fares, and expanded passenger rights. Activities include distributing passenger information leaflets and advocating passenger interests before federal regulatory agencies and the courts. Seeks: lower fares and increased competition in domestic and international air transportation; improved airline crash survivability; enhanced standards and equipment for crash prevention; elimination of unfair consumer practices; increased government accessibility. **Libraries:** Type: reference. **Holdings:** 3; books. **Subjects:** consumer airline issues, victims of air crash incidents, aviation security. **Publications:** *Facts and Advice for Airline Passengers.* ■

16951 ■ BBB Wise Giving Alliance
4200 Wilson Blvd., Ste.800
Arlington, VA 22203-1838
Ph: (703)276-0100
Fax: (703)525-8277
E-mail: give@cbbb.bbb.org
URL: http://www.give.org
Contact: Herman A. Taylor, Pres./CEO
Founded: 2001. **Membership Dues:** business, $2,500 (annual). **Staff:** 10. **Multinational. Description:** Supported by companies and local Better Business Bureaus operated autonomously in the United States and Puerto Rico, which are in turn supported by 270,000 local business members. Seeks to promote and foster the highest ethical relationship between businesses and the public through voluntary self-regulation, consumer and business education, and service excellence. Provides support to local Better Business Bureaus. Administers the advertising industry's self-regulatory program that monitors and investigates the truth and accuracy of national advertising claims; monitors and pre-screens advertising directed towards children. Develops information on national charitable organizations and whether they meet voluntary ethical standards for soliciting organizations. Provides information to help consumers and businesses make informed purchasing decisions and avoid costly scams and frauds; and settles consumer complaints through arbitration and other means. Operates BBB AUTO LINE, a national mediation and arbitration service providing an independent forum to resolve consumer complaints involving 32 participating auto manufacturers; Local Better Business Bureaus respond to more than 23 million requests for service annually, fielding 20 million pre-purchase inquiries and 3 million complaints. **Awards:** BBB National Torch Award for Marketplace Ethics. **Frequency:** annual. **Type:** trophy. **Recipient:** for demonstrated compliance with ethical business practices towards employees, customers, suppliers, stockholders and communities. **Formed by Merger of:** (1970) National Better Business Bureau; (2001) Council of Better Business Bureaus Foundation; (2001) National Charities Information Bureau; Association of Better Business Bureaus. **Publications:** *BBB Wise Giving Guide,* quarterly. Magazine. Includes a variety of articles and features about charity accountability issues. ● Annual Report, annual. Alternate Formats: online ● Reports. Alternate Formats: online ● Also publishes arbitration forms and pamphlets, consumer education leaflets, and parent guides for advertising aimed at children. **Conventions/Meetings:** annual general assembly and workshop (exhibits) - usually September or October.

16952 ■ Care USA
151 Ellis St. NE
Atlanta, GA 30303-2420
Ph: (404)681-2552
Free: (800)521-CARE

Fax: (404)577-5977
E-mail: info@care.org
URL: http://www.care.org
Contact: Helene Gayle, Pres./CEO
Founded: 1985. **Description:** Focuses on designing and furnishing benefit programs for affiliated consumer associations. **Libraries:** **Type:** reference. **Committees:** Benefit Development; Legal. **Affiliated With:** Federation of American Consumers and Travelers; United Savers Association. **Publications:** Bulletin, periodic. **Conventions/Meetings:** annual meeting.

16953 ■ Cemetery Consumer Service Council (CCSC)
c/o International Cemetery and Funeral Association
107 Carpenter Dr., Ste.100
Sterling, VA 20164
Ph: (703)391-8400
Free: (800)645-7700
Fax: (703)391-8416
E-mail: rfells@icfa.org
URL: http://www.icfa.org
Contact: Robert M. Fells, External COO/Gen.
  Counsel
Founded: 1979. **Members:** 7. **Staff:** 6. **Description:** Council members are: the International Cemetery and Funeral Association, Cremation Association of North America, (see separate entries), Southern Cemetery Association, and Central States Cemetery Association. Acts as a central clearinghouse for consumer inquiries and complaints concerning the cemetery industry, including cremation. Establishes uniform standards and guidelines for the handling of these inquiries and complaints on a national, state, and local basis. Publicizes the availability and mechanics of the council's services to consumer groups, governmental agencies, and other interested parties; seeks, through cooperative efforts within the various segments of the cemetery industry, the correction of unfair and unbusinesslike procedures. **Conventions/Meetings:** annual meeting.

16954 ■ Center for Consumer Affairs, University of Wisconsin-Milwaukee (CCA-UWM)
c/o UWM School of Continuing Education
161 W Wisconsin Ave., Ste.6000
Milwaukee, WI 53203-2602
Ph: (414)227-3200 (414)227-3252
Free: (800)222-3623
Fax: (414)227-3146
E-mail: jbrown@uwm.edu
URL: http://cfprod.imt.uwm.edu/sce/dci_long.
  cfm?id=7
Contact: Prof. James L. Brown, Dir.
Founded: 1964. **Staff:** 4. **Budget:** $500,000. **Description:** Develops consumer leadership skills through adult education programs. Provides referral service to appropriate agencies for the handling of consumer complaints. Makes available lecturers and resource persons for community group meetings and programs. Holds conferences, seminars, institutes, and meetings. Conducts extensive research on consumer issues. **Convention/Meeting:** none. **Committees:** Advisory. **Publications:** *Wisconsin Funeral Service: A Consumer's Guide* ● Booklets ● Manuals ● Pamphlets.

16955 ■ Center for Science in the Public Interest (CSPI)
1875 Connecticut Ave. NW, Ste.300
Washington, DC 20009
Ph: (202)332-9110
Fax: (202)265-4954
E-mail: cspi@cspinet.org
URL: http://www.cspinet.org
Contact: Michael F. Jacobson PhD, Founder/Exec.
  Dir.
Founded: 1971. **Members:** 9,000,000. **Membership Dues:** individual, $25 (annual). **Staff:** 60. **Budget:** $14,000,000. **Description:** Scientists, nutrition educators, and lawyers concerned with the effects of science and technology on society. Past work has centered primarily on food safety and nutrition problems at the national level. Monitors current

research and federal agencies that oversee food safety, trade, antibiotics, alcoholic beverages, biotechnology, and nutrition. Has initiated legal actions to ban unsafe and poorly tested food additives; has petitioned federal agencies for better food labeling and action against deceptive food advertising, especially advertising directed at children. Produces educational materials and attempts to influence policy decisions with regard to the American health and diet. between 1975 and 1977. **Programs:** Public Interest Internship. **Projects:** Alcohol Policies. **Publications:** *Nutrition Action HealthLetter,* 10/year. Newsletter. Promotes public education concerning food and nutrition, the food industry, and relevant government regulations and legislation. **Price:** $24.00 /year for individuals. ISSN: 0885-7792. **Circulation:** 800,000 ● Videos ● Also publishes press releases, leaflets and posters.

16956 ■ Center for Study of Responsive Law (CSRL)
PO Box 19367
Washington, DC 20036
Ph: (202)387-8030
Fax: (202)234-5176
E-mail: csrl@csrl.org
URL: http://www.csrl.org
Contact: Ralph Nader, Contact
Founded: 1968. **Staff:** 20. **Description:** Seeks to raise public awareness of consumer and environmental issues. Conducts research and educational projects to encourage public and private institutions to be more responsive to the needs of citizens and consumers. Areas of interest include: Energy conservation; government procurement; environmental concerns; management of taxpayer assets; health and safety issues. Sponsors Freedom of Information Clearinghouse.

16957 ■ Coalition for Auto-Insurance Reform (CAR)
7310 Stafford Rd.
Alexandria, VA 22307
Ph: (703)660-0799
Fax: (703)660-0799
E-mail: pkinzler@cox.net
URL: http://www.autoreform.org
Contact: Peter Kinzler, Pres.
Founded: 1997. **Staff:** 1. **Description:** Individuals and organizations with an interest in automobile insurance reform. Seeks adoption of federal and state legislation to lower automobile insurance premiums, promote greater medical and rehabilitation benefits, more prompt payment of economic loss, and more stringent punishment of individuals convicted of driving while under the influence of alcohol or drugs. Serves as a clearinghouse on automobile insurance reform; conducts lobbying campaigns. **Libraries:** **Type:** reference. **Holdings:** archival material, audio recordings, video recordings. **Subjects:** automobile insurance reform.

16958 ■ Commission for the Advancement of Public Interest Organizations (CAPIO)
PO Box 53305
Washington, DC 20009
Ph: (202)462-0505
Founded: 1974. **Description:** Investigates ways of enlarging the constituency and capabilities of the public interest movement. Goals are to promote cooperation among groups and individuals in order to develop common strategies for resolving specific current public interest problems; to make known the results of public interest work to individual citizens, public interest groups, and the media, both nationally and internationally. Conducts workshops on selected public interest issues in order to identify areas for cooperation. Acts as information resources clearing house. Maintains public interest reference collection. **Publications:** *Conference Proceedings,* periodic ● *The Federal Advisory Committee System, An Assessment* ● *Notes on Public Interest Resources* ● *Periodicals of Public Interest Organizations: A Citizen's Guide.* **Conventions/Meetings:** periodic conference.

16959 ■ Committee for a Constructive Tomorrow (CFACT)

PO Box 65722
Washington, DC 20035
Ph: (202)429-2737
E-mail: info@cfact.org
URL: http://www.cfact.org
Contact: David Rothbard, Pres./Co-Founder
Founded: 1985. **Members:** 35,000. **Membership Dues:** subscriber, $18 (annual). **Staff:** 5. **Description:** Works to "balance the public debate of consumer and environmental issues". Produces a daily radio commentary. Conducts education programs. **Boards:** Academic and Scientific Advisors. **Publications:** *Citizen Outlook*, bimonthly. Newsletter ● Articles. Alternate Formats: online.

16960 ■ Consumer Action (CA)

221 Main St., Ste.480
San Francisco, CA 94105
Ph: (415)777-9635
E-mail: info@consumer-action.org
URL: http://www.consumer-action.org
Contact: Ken McEldowney, Exec. Dir.
Founded: 1971. **Languages:** Chinese, English, Spanish. **Description:** Consumer advocacy organization. Provides free, non-legal advice and referrals on a wide range of issues, in Chinese, English and Spanish. **Libraries: Type:** reference. **Conventions/Meetings:** workshop, training.

16961 ■ Consumer Alert (CA)

3050 K St. NW, Ste.400
Washington, DC 20007
Ph: (202)467-5809
E-mail: consumer@consumeralert.org
URL: http://www.consumeralert.org
Contact: Mr. William MacLeod, Chm.
Founded: 1977. **Membership Dues:** regular, $35 (annual). **Description:** Public interest group opposing excessive regulations and supporting free enterprise, consumer rights, and freedom of choice for individual consumers. Examines current and proposed regulations in terms of demonstrated need and ultimate cost in areas where CA believes consumer interests are being abused; if the regulation is deemed excessive, CA develops proposals to change or abolish it or inform the public about its cause and effects. Works with other public interest groups to take legal action to remedy consumer abuse. Current activities include: lowering taxes; preventing public interest organizations from using tax revenues from students to further their own legislative objectives and goals; disseminating risk data. Conducts lectures nationwide; maintains Speaker's Bureau; provides educational programs. **Libraries: Type:** reference. **Awards: Type:** recognition. **Computer Services:** Mailing lists, of members. **Publications:** *Consumer Alert Consumer Comments*, quarterly. Newsletter. Covers activities and issues of CA. **Price:** $35.00/year; $35.00 included in membership dues. **Circulation:** 3,000. Alternate Formats: online. **Conventions/Meetings:** periodic meeting.

16962 ■ Consumer Federation of America (CFA)

1620 I St. NW, Ste.200
Washington, DC 20006
Ph: (202)387-6121
Fax: (202)265-7989
E-mail: cfa@consumerfed.org
URL: http://www.consumerfed.org
Contact: Stephen J. Brobeck, Exec. Dir.
Founded: 1967. **Members:** 300. **Staff:** 30. **Budget:** $3,500,000. **Description:** National, regional, state, and local consumer groups; consumer cooperatives; public utilities and labor organizations; state and local protection agencies. Supports activities of members. Gathers and disseminates information on consumer issues. Serves as an advocate of pro-consumer policies before Congress, regulatory agencies, and the courts. **Awards:** Distinguished Consumer Service. **Frequency:** annual. **Type:** recognition ● Distinguished Media Achievement. **Frequency:** annual. **Type:** recognition ● Distinguished Public Service. **Frequency:** annual. **Type:** recognition. **Committees:**

Antitrust; Communications; Credit; Education; Energy and Natural Resources; Environment; Food Health; Housing; Insurance; Needs of Low Income Consumers; Political Action; Taxation; Transportation. **Divisions:** State and Local Consumer Resource Center. **Absorbed:** Electric Consumers Information Committee. **Publications:** *Annual Voting Record of U.S. Congress* ● *CFA News*, bimonthly. Newsletter. Provides information about CFA advocacy, conferences and publications. ● Also prepares legislative fact sheets and testimony on consumer issues. **Conventions/Meetings:** annual assembly (exhibits) ● annual banquet, includes awards presentation ● periodic conference.

16963 ■ Consumer Web Watch

c/o Consumers Union
101 Truman Ave.
Yonkers, NY 10703-1057
Ph: (914)378-2600
E-mail: consumerwebwatch@cu.consumer.org
URL: http://www.consumerwebwatch.org
Contact: Beau Brendler, Dir.
Description: Provides unbiased and practical research on consumer behavior trends and business practices on the Web to help devise guidelines for credibility. Promotes consumer awareness of important issues through information and advocacy. **Computer Services:** Information services, list of consumer groups and websites ● online services, media center. **Affiliated With:** Consumers Union of United States.

16964 ■ Consumers Education and Protective Association (CEPA)

6048 Ogontz Ave.
Philadelphia, PA 19141-1347
Ph: (215)424-1441
Fax: (215)424-8045
E-mail: info@jewishceliacs.com
URL: http://www.cepa.us
Contact: Tina Nelson, Exec. Dir.
Founded: 1966. **Membership Dues:** individual, $15 (annual). **Local Groups:** 2. **Description:** Seeks to educate the consumer, combat fraud and other unscrupulous business activities, and strengthen the power of consumers to deal with economic problems affecting their interests. Engages in direct action, such as peaceful picketing, to expose consumer grievances. **Conventions/Meetings:** annual conference.

16965 ■ Consumers Union of United States (CU)

101 Truman Ave.
Yonkers, NY 10703-1057
Ph: (914)378-2000
Free: (800)333-0663
Fax: (914)378-2900
URL: http://www.consumerreports.org
Contact: James A. Guest, Pres./CEO
Founded: 1936. **Staff:** 420. **Description:** Testing, rating, and reporting organization providing information on competing brands of appliances, automobiles, food products, and household equipment. Aims to provide consumers with information and advice on consumer goods and services; to give information and assistance on all financial matters affecting consumers; to initiate and to cooperate with individual and group efforts seeking to create, maintain, and enhance the quality of life for consumers. Regional offices represent consumer interests in the legislature, courts, and administrative agencies. Derives income from sale of its publication, *Consumer Reports*, and other publications. All subscribers may become members. Produces a syndicated radio program, Report to Consumers; a syndicated newspaper column, *From Consumer Reports*; and television series for cable television, Consumer Reports Presents. **Additional Websites:** http://www.consumersunion.org. **Publications:** *Consumer Reports*, monthly. Magazine. Includes annual buying guide issue. Alternate Formats: online ● *On Health*, monthly. Newsletter. Alternate Formats: online ● *Travel Letter*, monthly. Newsletter. Provides an in-depth information on health and travel. ● *Zillions*, bimonthly. Magazine.

For young consumers. Alternate Formats: online ● Also publishes special reports and books on particular fields of consumer interest such as automobiles, food, insurance, health, and consumer services; produces educational films. **Conventions/Meetings:** annual meeting.

16966 ■ Consumers for World Trade (CWT)

1707 L St. NW, Ste.570
Washington, DC 20036
Ph: (202)293-2944
Fax: (202)293-0495
E-mail: cwt@cwt.org
URL: http://www.cwt.org
Contact: Maureen Smith, Pres.
Founded: 1978. **Membership Dues:** sustaining, $50 (annual). ● patron, $500 (annual). **Staff:** 3. **Budget:** $100,000. **Description:** Economists, educators, students, trade experts, consumer specialists, civic and political leaders, legal consultants, and concerned citizens. Represents the consumer interest in U.S. trade policy. Lobbies against protectionism and for expanded overseas markets for U.S. goods and services in order to give consumers more choices, to counter inflationary prices, and to promote healthy and stable economic growth. Has established an education fund to conduct seminars and forums in various cities, and to carry out other research projects designed to educate consumers on trade issues and maintain communication with the federal government. Maintains Speaker's Bureau. **Awards:** CWT Award. **Frequency:** annual. **Type:** recognition. **Recipient:** for distinguished service on behalf of open trade ● CWT's Hall of Fame. **Frequency:** annual. **Type:** recognition. **Recipient:** for lifelong contributions to the cause of free and open markets ● Doreen L. Brown CWT Trade Leadership Award. **Frequency:** annual. **Type:** recognition. **Recipient:** for a leader who has made an outstanding and lasting contribution. **Committees:** Awards; Program. **Publications:** *World Trade Connections*, semimonthly. Newsletter ● Pamphlets ● Also publishes occasional papers, and Action Alerts. **Conventions/Meetings:** biennial conference ● annual Congressional - seminar and luncheon ● annual dinner and seminar, includes awards ceremony.

16967 ■ Council for the Advancement of Consumer Policy (CACP)

Address Unknown since 2007
Founded: 1979. **Staff:** 4. **Description:** Individuals and corporations whose purposes are to promote the rights of consumers through the study and analysis of consumer issues; stimulate public awareness of these issues through distribution of study results to educational institutions, study groups, and business and news media; work for the ordering of consumer priorities at the international, national, state, and local levels. Council is founded on "five basic consumer rights": the right to safety, to choice, to information, to be heard, to consumer education. **Libraries: Type:** open to the public. **Subjects:** aspartame, mercuruy free dentistry.

16968 ■ Coupon Exchange Club (CEC)

Box 250960
Milwaukee, WI 53225
Ph: (414)453-9803
Fax: (414)453-9834
Contact: Becky Thompson, Membership Dir.
Founded: 1972. **For-Profit. Description:** Seeks to help members reduce the cost of household, grocery, and drugstore items by supplying them with money-off store coupons. Members select coupons for desired products from a list of 1000 items; $8.00 worth of coupons are provided for a $2.50 service fee. Club buys coupons from individuals and charitable organizations through Cash-for-Cash-Off Program.

16969 ■ Food and Water (F&W)

PO Box 543
Montpelier, VT 05601
Ph: (802)229-6222

E-mail: info@broadsides.org
URL: http://www.broadsides.org
Contact: Michael Colby, Dir.
Founded: 1986. **Members:** 4,000. **Membership Dues:** individual, $25 (annual) ● non-profit/co-op, $50 ● all other, $100. **Staff:** 4. **Description:** Educates the public about various threats to the nutritional integrity of the food and water supply. Researches and publicizes environmental and health impacts of food irradiation and other food treatments, before and after harvest. Exposes what it considers to be the critical interconnections between health and environmental problems and challenges the need for technologies, processes, or additives which threaten both. Focuses on the issue of food irradiation and the possible dangers which this technology poses. Delves into the radical, underlying philosophies of those movements seeking substantive change. **Absorbed:** (1991) National Coalition to Stop Food and Water Irradiation. **Publications:** *Food and Water Journal*, quarterly. **Price:** $25.00/year. **Circulation:** 25,000.

16970 ■ Foundation Aiding the Elderly (FATE)
PO Box 254849
Sacramento, CA 95865-4849
Ph: (916)481-8558
Free: (877)481-5558
Fax: (916)481-8329
E-mail: caroleh@4fate.org
URL: http://www.4fate.org
Contact: Carole Herman, Pres./Chair
Founded: 1982. **Staff:** 2. **Budget:** $100,000. **Non-membership. Description:** Assists the public with relatives and friends in long-term care nursing homes. Provides awareness of the existence of, and potential for, abuse, neglect, and lack of dignity of the elderly in nursing homes. Initiates action to make improvements. Raises funds to bring about nursing home reform. Offers referrals for senior issues and advocates for legislation. **Convention/Meeting:** none. **Affiliated With:** National Citizens Coalition for Nursing Home Reform. **Formerly:** (1991) Americans for Better Care. **Publications:** Newsletter.

16971 ■ Funeral Service Consumer Assistance Program (FSCAP)
13625 Bishop Dr.
Brookfield, WI 53005-6607
Free: (877)402-5900
Fax: (262)789-6977
E-mail: info@funeralservicefoundation.org
URL: http://www.FuneralServiceFoundation.org
Contact: Bob Horn, Chm.
Founded: 1982. **Staff:** 3. **Description:** Assists consumers in matters involving funeral service including concerns regarding delivery of services, bereavement, grief, mourning, preplanning and preneed. Provides free information, resources and recommendations to steer consumer in right direction to resolve concerns or complaints. Offers hotline and services of an intervener. Recognizes consumers right to accurate, clear, and compassionate information about funeral service. **Awards:** Children's Fund. **Frequency:** annual. **Type:** grant. **Recipient:** for highly credible national children's organizations ● Joseph Hagan. **Frequency:** annual. **Type:** scholarship. **Recipient:** to outstanding students at schools accredited by the American Board of Funeral Service Education. **Formerly:** (1988) ThanaCAP; (1991) General Service Consumer Arbitration Program. **Publications:** Annual Report, annual.

16972 ■ Green Seal
1001 Connecticut Ave. NW, Ste.827
Washington, DC 20036-5525
Ph: (202)872-6400
Fax: (202)872-4324
E-mail: greenseal@greenseal.org
URL: http://www.greenseal.org
Contact: Dr. Arthur Weissman PhD, Pres./CEO
Founded: 1989. **Members:** 250. **Membership Dues:** environmental partners program, $169 (annual). **Staff:** 6. **Budget:** $600,000. **Description:** Serves as an environmental certification and consumer educa-

tion organization. Establishes criteria and standards for consumer products, conducts product testing, and awards a seal of approval to products meeting standards. Offers membership program; Environmental Partners in which organizations receive assistance with green procurement. **Telecommunication Services:** electronic mail, aweissman@greenseal.org. **Publications:** *Campus Green Buying Guide*. Provides focus on implementing and maintaining green procurement plan, index of product lists. ● *Choose Green Report*, monthly. Newsletter. Contains product reports, general impacts of product, and brand name recommendations. **Price:** $169.00/year; $25.00/copy. **Circulation:** 1,000 ● *Office Green Buying Guide*. Provides focus on implementing and maintaining green procurement plan, index of product lists.

16973 ■ Heirs
PO Box 292
Villanova, PA 19085
Ph: (610)525-4442
Fax: (610)525-8251
E-mail: stancedar@comcast.net
URL: http://www.heirs.net
Contact: Standish Smith, Founder
Founded: 1991. **Members:** 2,400. **Membership Dues:** individual, $95 (annual). **Staff:** 1. **Budget:** $30,000. **Description:** Beneficiaries and creators of irrevocable trusts, and interested individuals. Acts as a support group primarily for beneficiaries of irrevocable trusts. Offers counseling and practical suggestions to beneficiaries seeking to improve relationships with their corporate fiduciary or to others considering establishing an irrevocable trust with an independent trustee or corporate entity such as a bank as fiduciary. Advocates reform of trust/estate administration regulations. Supports remedial legislation in Pennsylvania. Does not offer legal counsel. Maintains Speaker's Bureau. **Libraries:** **Type:** reference. **Holdings:** 2,000; books, clippings, monographs, periodicals. **Subjects:** trust/estate issues. **Telecommunication Services:** hotline, (610)527-6260. **Publications:** *Barristers, Banks and Beneficiaries*. Book. Chronicles the decimation of a $17 million dollar estate. ● *Fiduciary Fun - Newsletter*, semiannual. Provides practical advice to trust/estate beneficiaries and creators of trust. **Price:** included in membership dues. **Circulation:** 500. Alternate Formats: online ● *Heirs Personal Trust Handbook*. **Price:** included in membership dues ● Monographs.

16974 ■ International Anticounterfeiting Coalition (IACC)
1725 K St. NW, Ste.411
Washington, DC 20006
Ph: (202)223-6667
Fax: (202)223-6668
E-mail: rwynne@iacc.org
URL: http://www.iacc.org
Contact: Nils Montan, Pres.
Founded: 1978. **Members:** 150. **Membership Dues:** government official (per office or department), $100 (annual) ● investigative firm (with 25 or less investigators), $2,500 (annual) ● law firm (with 26 or more attorneys), brand owner (with annual revenues over $500 million), $7,000 (annual). **Staff:** 3. **Budget:** $500,000. **Description:** Works to eliminate counterfeiting of merchandise such as aircraft and auto parts, medical devices, chemicals, apparel, and watches. Maintains that counterfeiting hurts everyone because manufacturers lose money and consumers get low-quality, often dangerous merchandise. Helped secure more strict U.S. customs restrictions on counterfeits and passage of the Trademark Counterfeiting Act of 1984, and the Anti-counterfeiting Consumer Protection Act of 1996 providing strong criminal sanctions against counterfeiters. Promotes the development of innovative anti-counterfeiting technologies to authenticate products. Conducts legislative action programs. Promotes information exchange, provides speakers and compiles statistics. **Committees:** Legislative and Enforcement Policy. **Publications:** *Reality Check*, monthly. Newsletters. Includes complete update of all IACC activities. Alternate Formats: online. **Conven-**

tions/Meetings: annual conference, updates to educate members and non-members (exhibits) - spring/fall.

16975 ■ National Association of Consumer Advocates (NACA)
1730 Rhode Island NW, Ste.710
Washington, DC 20036
Ph: (202)452-1989
Fax: (202)452-0099
E-mail: info@naca.net
URL: http://www.naca.net
Contact: Ian Lyngklip, Co-Chm.
Founded: 1994. **Members:** 600. **Membership Dues:** law student, $50 (annual) ● public interest attorney, $100 (annual) ● public interest organization, $250 (annual) ● private attorney, $150-$250 (annual) ● advocate, $500-$999 (annual) ● patron, $1,000-$1,499 (annual) ● benefactor, $1,500-$2,499 (annual) ● Platinum Club (minimum), $25,000 (annual) ● Gold Club (maximum), $24,999 (annual) ● Silver Club, $5,000-$9,999 (annual) ● Bronze Club, $2,500-$4,999 (annual). **Staff:** 2. **Budget:** $250,000. **Description:** Consumer advocates and attorneys. Works to promote justice for all consumers and combat unfair, fraudulent, and abusive business practices. Provides information and resources, litigation support, consulting services, and educational programs. **Libraries:** **Type:** not open to the public. **Awards:** Distinguished Service to Consumers Award. **Frequency:** annual. **Type:** recognition ● Media Awards. **Frequency:** annual. **Type:** recognition. **Recipient:** for strong investigative reporting on consumer protection issues. **Publications:** *Consumer Advocate*, bimonthly. Newsletter. **Price:** included in membership dues. **Conventions/Meetings:** annual board meeting.

16976 ■ National Citizens Coalition for Nursing Home Reform (NCCNHR)
1828 L St. NW, Ste.801
Washington, DC 20036
Ph: (202)332-2275 (202)332-2276
Fax: (202)332-2949
E-mail: coalitiontoprotect@comcast.net
URL: http://www.nursinghomeaction.org
Contact: Alice H. Hedt, Exec. Dir.
Founded: 1975. **Members:** 1,250. **Membership Dues:** individual nursing (board and care home/assisted living resident), $2 (annual) ● individual (persons age 65 and over), $25 (annual) ● licensed professional, $65 (annual) ● student/nursing assistant, $10 (annual) ● group (budget under $25000 and over $2 million), $45-$500 (annual) ● Family Council, $35 (annual) ● Resident Council, $5 (annual) ● regular, $40 (annual). **Staff:** 14. **Budget:** $1,400,000. **Description:** National, state and local consumer/citizen groups and individuals seeking nursing home and board and care reform. Seeks to provide a consumer voice at the national, state, and local levels in the development and implementation of the long-term care system. Provides a platform through which groups can keep informed of current movements for change and can make their views known. Conducts seminars and training programs and utilizes a speakers' bureau consisting of advocates from around the country. Serves as a clearinghouse for information on nursing home and board care issues, and publishes consumer books and pamphlets. Maintains Speaker's Bureau; conducts research and advocacy programs. **Libraries:** **Type:** reference. **Holdings:** archival material, audiovisuals, books, clippings, periodicals. **Subjects:** nursing home residents' rights. **Programs:** Jackie Koenig Memorial Summer Internship. **Projects:** Campaign for Quality Care; Long Term Care Ombudsman Resource Center. **Also Known As:** Nursing Home Reform Coalition. **Publications:** *Avoiding Drugs Used as Chemical Restraints: New Standards in Care*. Booklet ● *Avoiding Physical Restraint Use: New Standards in Care*. Booklet ● *Nursing Home Staffing: A Guide for Residents, Families, Friends, and Caregivers*. Booklet ● *Nursing Homes: Getting Good Care There*, bimonthly. Book ● *Quality Care Advocate*, quarterly. Newsletter. **Price:** free for members; $45.00 for nonmembers. Alternate Formats: online ● *Where Do I Go From*

Here? A Guide for Nursing Home Residents, Families, and Friends a Consulting on Attorney. Booklet. **Conventions/Meetings:** annual conference (exhibits) - always Washington, DC.

16977 ■ National Coalition for Consumer Education (NCCE)
c/o National Consumers League
1701 K St. NW, Ste.1200
Washington, DC 20006
Ph: (202)835-3323
Fax: (202)835-0747
E-mail: lifesmarts@nclnet.org
URL: http://www.nclnet.org
Contact: Linda Golodner, Pres./CEO
Founded: 1981. **Members:** 500. **Staff:** 4. **Budget:** $350,000. **For-Profit. Description:** State representatives who coordinate consumer education programs in a 50-state network. Promotes consumer education at the local, state, and national levels. Sponsors consumer education activities in local communities, through the news media, and within the public sector. Seeks to motivate the public to become more involved in consumer education issues. Sponsors contests. **Additional Websites:** http://www.lifesmarts.org. **Publications:** *Coalition Exchange,* quarterly. Newsletter. Reports on consumer education programs and projects. ● Brochures. **Conventions/Meetings:** annual conference (exhibits).

16978 ■ National Consumer Affairs Internship Program (NCAIP)
Address Unknown since 2007
Founded: 1976. **Description:** Graduate and undergraduate students and faculty members at American colleges and universities with career interests in consumer affairs are eligible to participate. Internships are sponsored by businesses, government agencies, and nonprofit associations with consumer affairs offices. Students must have a career interest in consumer affairs and be a candidate for a degree. Thirty internships are available for each of three 13-week classes, beginning January, May, and August. Interns work full-time for sponsoring organizations and earn college credit. **Convention/Meeting:** none. **Affiliated With:** American Council on Consumer Interests; Society of Consumer Affairs Professionals in Business.

16979 ■ National Consumers League (NCL)
1701 K St. NW, Ste.1200
Washington, DC 20006
Ph: (202)835-3323
Fax: (202)835-0747
E-mail: info@nclnet.org
URL: http://www.nclnet.org
Contact: Linda Golodner, Pres./CEO
Founded: 1899. **Membership Dues:** individual, $20 (annual). **Staff:** 19. **Budget:** $1,600,000. **State Groups:** 2. **Description:** Identifies, protects, represents, and advances the economic and social interests of consumers and workers. Addresses issues including healthcare, food and drug safety, and consumer fraud. Promotes fairness and safety at the marketplace and in the workplace. Coordinates the Alliance Against Fraud in Telemarketing and the Child Labor Coalition. Administers the National Fraud Information Center and Internet Fraud Watch. **Awards:** Florence Kelley Consumer Leadership Award. **Frequency:** annual. **Type:** recognition. **Recipient:** for consumer leaders who have emulated Kelley's approach to advocacy ● Trumpeter Award. **Frequency:** annual. **Type:** recognition. **Recipient:** for national leaders who have made significant contributions to consumerism. **Publications:** *Focus on Fraud,* quarterly. Presents online update for professionals and education on fraud. **Price:** $9.00 in U.S.; $12.00 outside U.S. ● *NCL Bulletin,* bimonthly. Newsletter. **Price:** $20.00 for nonmembers; $25.00 non-profit; $100.00 for profit; included in membership dues ● *Online Child Labor Monitor,* weekly. **Price:** free ● Bulletin. **Price:** included in membership dues ● Also publishes consumer guides, fact sheets and brochures. **Conventions/Meetings:** annual Consumer Conference, on consumer issues (exhibits).

16980 ■ National Fraud Information Center/Internet Fraud Watch (NFIC/IFW)
c/o National Consumers League
1701 K St. NW, Ste.1200
Washington, DC 20006
Ph: (202)835-3323
Free: (800)876-7060
Fax: (202)835-0747
E-mail: info@nclnet.org
URL: http://www.fraud.org
Founded: 1992. **Languages:** English, Spanish. **Description:** Works to end telemarketing and Internet fraud by improving prevention and enforcement.

16981 ■ Process Gas Consumers Group (PGC)
1275 Pennsylvania Ave.
Washington, DC 20004-2415
Ph: (202)383-0444
Fax: (202)637-3593
E-mail: dena.wiggins@sablaw.com
URL: http://www.pgcg.com
Contact: Dena Wiggins, Gen. Counsel
Founded: 1978. **Members:** 15. **Description:** Industrial consumers of natural gas who require it for processes which cannot technically or economically use an alternate (non-gaseous) fuel. Members represent a wide variety of industries. Promotes the development and adoption of coordinated, rational, and consistent federal and state policies concerning industrial process gas users. **Committees:** Government Relations. **Conventions/Meetings:** quarterly meeting.

16982 ■ Public Citizen (PC)
1600 20th St. NW
Washington, DC 20009
Ph: (202)588-1000
E-mail: member@citizen.org
URL: http://www.citizen.org
Contact: Joan Claybrook, Pres.
Founded: 1971. **Members:** 125,000. **Membership Dues:** basic, $20 (annual) ● combination, $35 (annual). **Staff:** 120. **Budget:** $7,000,000. **Regional Groups:** 2. **Description:** Formed by Ralph Nader to support the work of citizen advocates. Areas of focus include: consumer rights in the marketplace, safe products, a healthful environment and workplace, clean and safe energy sources, corporate and government accountability, and citizen empowerment. Methods for change include lobbying, litigation, monitoring government agencies, research, and public education including special reports, periodicals, expert testimony, and news media coverage. Acquires funding primarily through direct mail and also through payment for publications and court awards. **Computer Services:** database ● mailing lists. **Publications:** *Buyers Up News.* Newsletter ● *Health Letter,* monthly. Newsletter. Covers consumer health issues including drugs, doctor discipline, Medicare, occupational safety and health, and medical devices. **Price:** $18.00/year. **Circulation:** 80,000 ● *Public Citizen News,* bimonthly. Magazine. Covers consumer issues including nuclear power and nuclear safety, banking, pesticides, pollution and separation of power. **Price:** included in membership dues; $20.00 /year for nonmembers. ISSN: 0738-5927. **Circulation:** 150,000. **Advertising:** accepted ● *Worst Pills/ Best Pills.* Magazine. Provides information on prescription drugs and medication. **Price:** $20.00/year ● Books ● Monographs ● Papers ● Reports. **Conventions/Meetings:** periodic conference.

16983 ■ Public Citizen Litigation Group (PCLG)
1600 20th St. NW
Washington, DC 20009
Ph: (202)588-1000
E-mail: weblitigationmail@citizen.org
URL: http://www.citizen.org/litigation
Contact: Brian Wolfman, Dir.
Founded: 1971. **Members:** 105,000. **Membership Dues:** individual, $20 (annual). **Staff:** 103. **Budget:** $11,000,000. **Description:** Serves as the litigating arm of Public Citizen and specializes in cases involving health and safety regulation, consumer rights, ac-

cess to the courts, open government, and the First Amendment, including internet free speech. Litigates cases at all levels of the federal and state judiciaries and has a substantial practice before federal regulatory agencies; efforts are also pursued through programs such as the Alan Morrison Supreme Court Assistance Project and the Freedom of Information Clearinghouse. Aims to promote consumer rights, open government, clean energy, fair trade, environmental protection, and work place safety. **Awards:** Supreme Court Assistance Project Fellowship. **Frequency:** annual. **Type:** fellowship. **Recipient:** for recent law school graduates. **Affiliated With:** Public Citizen. **Publications:** *Health Letter,* monthly ● *Public Citizen News,* bimonthly. Newsletter ● *Worst Pills/ Best Pills.* Book ● *Worst Pills Best Pills News,* monthly. Magazine. **Price:** $20.00/year.

16984 ■ Public Citizen's Congress Watch (PCCW)
1600 20th St. NW
Washington, DC 20009
Ph: (202)588-1000
Fax: (202)547-7392
E-mail: congress@citizen.org
URL: http://www.citizen.org/congress
Contact: Frank Clemente, Dir.
Founded: 1971. **Members:** 150,000. **Membership Dues:** regular, $35 (annual). **Staff:** 15. **Budget:** $800,000. **Description:** Congressional lobby representing consumer interests, specifically citizens' access to government decision-making, campaign finance reform, product safety, product liability health care, and medical malpractice issues and reducing corporate subsidies. **Convention/Meeting:** none. **Libraries: Type:** reference. **Holdings:** 500. **Subjects:** congressional documents. **Formerly:** (1998) Congress Watch. **Publications:** *Congressional Voting Index,* annual. Records and ratings of how Representatives and Senators voted on various consumer issues. ● *Public Citizen News,* bimonthly. Newsletter ● Also Publishes research reports.

16985 ■ Society for Consumer Psychology (SCP)
c/o Larry D. Compeau, Exec. Off.
Box 5795
Potsdam, NY 13699
Ph: (315)268-6605 (212)998-0428
E-mail: haugtvedt.1@osu.edu
URL: http://fisher.osu.edu/marketing/scp
Contact: Laura A. Peracchio, Pres.
Membership Dues: retired, $25 (annual) ● student, $30 (annual) ● academic, practitioner, $50 (annual). **Description:** Represents the interests of behavioral scientists in the fields of psychology, marketing, advertising, communication, consumer behavior and other related areas. Encourages members to share their knowledge and contribute to the discipline of consumer psychology. Generates applied knowledge to solve specific marketing related problems. **Telecommunication Services:** electronic mail, dmaheshwaran@stern.nyu.edu ● electronic mail, compeau@ clarkson.edu. **Publications:** *The Communicator.* Newsletter. **Price:** included in membership dues. Alternate Formats: online ● *Journal of Consumer Psychology,* annual. Focuses on consumer phenomena at intrapersonal and interpersonal level. **Price:** included in membership dues. Alternate Formats: online. **Conventions/Meetings:** annual Advertising and Consumer Psychology - conference.

16986 ■ Southwest Research and Information Center (SRIC)
PO Box 4524
Albuquerque, NM 87106
Ph: (505)262-1862
Fax: (505)262-1864
E-mail: info@sric.org
URL: http://www.sric.org
Contact: Don Hancock, Dir.
Founded: 1971. **Budget:** $275,000. **Description:** Provides educational and scientific information to citizens and community groups on subjects of public interest; current emphasis is on the health effects of: nuclear waste disposal, mining, waste management,

toxics, oil and gas, water, and uranium mining issues in the Southwest. Acts as a consultant to community organizations. Sponsors National Campaign for Radioactive Waste Safety (see separate entry) and Health and Radiation Projects. **Libraries: Type:** reference. **Holdings:** 10,000; books, clippings, periodicals. **Subjects:** environmental, consumer related. **Affiliated With:** National Campaign for Radioactive Waste Safety. **Publications:** *How Safe is Mexico's Atomic City.* **Advertising:** accepted ● *Public Land Private Profit* ● *Uranium Mining and Milling: A Primer.* **Advertising:** accepted ● *Voices From The Earth,* quarterly. Journal. **Price:** $15.00 /year for individuals; $30.00 /year for institutions; $10.00/year for students and senior citizens ● Also publishes testimonies and legal briefs.

16987 ■ TeleTruth: The Alliance for Customers' Telecommunications Rights
568 Broadway, Ste.404
New York, NY 10012
Free: (800)870-1939
E-mail: bruce@teletruth.org
URL: http://teletruth.org
Contact: Bruce Kushnick, Chm.
Description: Defends the public's interests in telecommunications and broadband issues. Educates and informs the public to combat monopoly control of critical telecommunications infrastructure. Promotes fairness, innovation and competition. Accelerates the deployment of advanced networks and new forms of communications. **Computer Services:** Information services, DSL headaches ● information services, phone bill problems.

Corporate Economics

16988 ■ American Council for Capital Formation (ACCF)
1750 K St. NW, Ste.400
Washington, DC 20006-2302
Ph: (202)293-5811
Fax: (202)785-8165
E-mail: info@accf.org
URL: http://www.accf.org
Contact: Mr. Mark Bloomfield, Pres./CEO
Founded: 1973. **Members:** 200. **Staff:** 10. **Budget:** $1,500,000. **Description:** Supported by individuals, businesses, foundations, and associations. Purposes are: to communicate the capital formation issue to the public, national opinion leaders, and members of Congress; "to actively encourage saving and investment, which are essential for a strong economy, by advocating sound tax, regulatory, environmental policies that do not hinder economic growth and capital formation." Prepares and submits testimony before congressional committees; prepares articles, books, and reports on issues of importance to capital formation. **Subgroups:** Center for Policy Research. **Formerly:** (1975) American Council on Capital Gains and Estate Taxation. **Publications:** *Capital Formation,* bimonthly. Newsletters. Alternate Formats: online ● Annual Report, annual. **Conventions/Meetings:** periodic symposium.

16989 ■ Private Sector Council (PSC)
c/o Partnership for Public Service
1725 Eye St. NW, Ste.900
Washington, DC 20006
Ph: (202)775-9111
Fax: (202)775-8885
E-mail: hweizmann@ourpublicservice.org
URL: http://www.ourpublicservice.org/psc
Contact: Howard Weizmann, Pres.
Founded: 1983. **Members:** 42. **Staff:** 5. **Budget:** $500,000. **Description:** Serves as a nonpartisan, public service organization dedicated to improving the productivity, efficiency, and management of the federal government through a cooperative sharing of knowledge between the public and private sectors. **Awards:** Private Sector Council Leadership Award. **Frequency:** annual. **Type:** recognition. **Recipient:** for the most outstanding leader ● Public Sector Leadership Award. **Frequency:** annual. **Type:** recog-

nition. **Publications:** *Communicator,* quarterly. Newsletter. **Conventions/Meetings:** semiannual CFO Task Force Meeting - always fall and spring.

16990 ■ Rebuild America
c/o U.S. Department of Energy
Off. of Energy Efficiency and Renewable Energy
1000 Independence Ave. SW
Washington, DC 20585-0121
Ph: (202)586-9424
Fax: (202)586-1233
E-mail: mark.bailey@ee.doe.gov
URL: http://www.rebuild.gov
Contact: Mark Bailey, CEO
Founded: 1987. **Members:** 60. **Membership Dues:** general, $1,000 (annual). **Staff:** 1. **Budget:** $100,000. **Description:** Coalition of public and private organizations committed to reversing the decline in America's investment in infrastructure. Promotes investment in improving and rebuilding America's highways, bridges, mass transit facilities, airports, wastewater treatment plants, and solid waste disposal facilities. Maintains speakers' bureau; compiles statistics; provides technical assistance and public information programs. **Publications:** *Infrastructure News Brief,* monthly. Newsletter ● *White Papers.*

16991 ■ Small Business Council of America (SBCA)
PO Box 2283
Wilmington, DE 19899
Ph: (302)691-7222
Free: (877)404-1329
E-mail: calimafd@paleyrothman.com
URL: http://www.sbca.net
Contact: Paula Calimafde, Chair
Founded: 1979. **Members:** 1,480. **Membership Dues:** individual, $180 (annual) ● business, $315 (annual) ● institutional, $500 (annual) ● contributing sponsor, $1,000-$2,500 (annual) ● corporate sponsor, $3,000 (annual) ● national corporate sponsor, $5,000 (annual) ● silver club, $7,500 (annual) ● gold club, $10,000 (annual) ● diamond club, $20,000 (annual). **State Groups:** 1. **Local Groups:** 5. **Description:** Small business and professional organizations. Goals are to keep federal tax and employee benefit legislation from becoming burdensome, and to support legislation creating economic incentives for small businesses. Lobbies Congress on behalf of members; alerts members to proposed legislation so that opposition or support can be mustered before a bill becomes law; operates ad hoc committees on specific legislation. Maintains speakers' bureau; compiles statistics. **Committees:** Congressional Award; Legislative. **Absorbed:** (1988) National Association of Pension Consultants and Administrators. **Publications:** *News Flashes,* periodic. Contains legislative updates. ● *SBCA Member and Congressional Directory,* annual ● *Tax Report,* monthly. Newsletter ● Articles. Alternate Formats: online. **Conventions/Meetings:** annual Congressional Awards Ceremony - conference - always May, Washington, DC.

Corporate Responsibility

16992 ■ Fund for Stockowners Rights
c/o Carl Olson, Chm.
PO Box 65398
Washington, DC 20035
Ph: (703)241-3700 (818)223-8080
E-mail: sdw@statedepartmentwatch.org
URL: http://www.statedepartmentwatch.org
Contact: Carl Olson, Chm.
Founded: 1984. **Description:** Stockowners in corporations united to: improve election methods of corporations' boards of directors; encourage companies to conduct secret votes at annual meetings; prevent anti-takeover abuses, such as greenmail and golden parachutes. (Greenmail is a term used to describe the repurchase of stock, at a premium above the stock's market value. Golden parachutes is defined as lucrative payments to departing management in a takeover if one should occur where

management is dismissed.) Advocates corporations' adoption of anti-slave labor policies by companies engaged in transactions with communist countries. Promotes reporting of total taxation and other government burdens on the corporation. Disseminates information and offers advice to stockowners. Compiles statistics on stockholder votes and tax burdens on corporations. **Formed by Merger of:** (1992) Stockholders Sovereignty Society; (1992) Stockholders Against the Government Burden; Stockholders for World Freedom.

16993 ■ Hispanic Association on Corporate Responsibility (HACR)
1444 I St. NW, Ste.850
Washington, DC 20005
Ph: (202)835-9672
Fax: (202)457-0455
E-mail: hacr@hacr.org
URL: http://www.hacr.org
Contact: Rima K. Matsumoto, Exec. Dir.
Founded: 1986. **Membership Dues:** generation, $25,000 (annual) ● associate, $10,000 (annual) ● vision, $50,000 (annual). **Staff:** 7. **Budget:** $500,000. **National Groups:** 11. **Description:** Coalition of the ten most prominent national Hispanic organizations. Aims to include Hispanics in Corporate America at a level commensurate with their economic contributions. **Awards:** Corporate Vision Award. **Frequency:** annual. **Type:** recognition. **Telecommunication Services:** electronic mail, rmatsumoto@hacr.org. **Publications:** *HACR Corporate Observer,* quarterly. Newsletter. **Circulation:** 5,000. Alternate Formats: online ● Annual studies on corporate philanthropy, governance, and employment. **Conventions/Meetings:** annual symposium.

16994 ■ Interfaith Center on Corporate Responsibility (ICCR)
475 Riverside Dr., Rm. 1842
New York, NY 10115
Ph: (212)870-2295 (212)870-2294
Fax: (212)870-2023
E-mail: info@iccr.org
URL: http://www.iccr.org
Contact: Fr. Michael Hoolahan, Interim Exec. Dir.
Founded: 1971. **Staff:** 10. **Budget:** $1,000,000. **Description:** Religious agencies and their representatives, including 25 Protestant denominations and Jewish agencies and over 250 Roman Catholic orders, pension funds, healthcare corporations and dioceses. Assists members in coordinating their corporate responsibility programs and expressing social responsibility with their investments by facilitating exchange of views, sharing research and information, and developing strategies. Conducts research in the areas of sweat shops, equal employment opportunity, nuclear weapons production, infant formula, tobacco marketing, board diversity, land mines, energy, environment and alternative investments among others. Provides channel for cooperating with other institutions and coalitions; encourages education and interpretation efforts in the field of socially responsible investment. Sponsors research on specific corporations; maintains contact with other corporate responsibility action groups; conducts discussions with representatives of government, business and industry, foundations, and universities; develops information related to the concern for social criteria in investment policy. Maintains subscriber service of topical materials on corporate responsibility. **Libraries: Type:** not open to the public. **Telecommunication Services:** electronic mail, mhoolahan@iccr.org. **Working Groups:** Access to Health Care; Contract Suppliers; Corporate Governance; Enabling Access to Capital; Environment Justice; Global Warning; Militarism and Violence in Society; Promoting Human Rights. **Affiliated With:** National Council of Churches of Christ in the U.S.A. **Absorbed:** Church Project on United States Investments in Southern Africa. **Formed by Merger of:** (1974) Interfaith Committee on Social Responsibility in Investments; Corporate Information Center. **Publications:** *Corporate Examiner,* 10/year. Newsletter. Includes opinions of corporate responsibility leaders and publication reviews. **Price:** $50.00/year. ISSN: 0361-2309 ● Also

publishes proxy resolutions, research papers, briefs. **Conventions/Meetings:** annual meeting.

16995 ■ Public Affairs Council (PAC)
2033 K St. NW, Ste.700
Washington, DC 20006
Ph: (202)872-1790
Fax: (202)835-8343
E-mail: pac@pac.org
URL: http://www.pac.org
Contact: Douglas G. Pinkham, Pres.

Founded: 1954. **Members:** 550. **Membership Dues:** corporation (with annual sales of up to $1 billion), $1,800 (annual) ● corporation (with annual sales of $2-$3 billion), $2,000-$3,000 (annual) ● corporation (with annual sales of $4-$5 billion), $3,000-$5,000 (annual) ● corporation (with annual sales of $6-$10 Billion), $5,000-$7,500 (annual) ● corporation (with annual sales of $11 billion and above), $7,500-$12,000 (annual) ● association, consulting, law firm, $1,800-$3,000 (annual). **Staff:** 18. **Budget:** $3,000,000. **Description:** Public affairs executives representing member corporations associations. Encourages members of the business community to be active and informed participants in political affairs and to provide thoughtful leadership in the fields of corporate citizenship and social responsibility. Conducts clinics; sponsors Public Affairs Institute each January. Offers counseling services to individual corporations and associations that are initiating or expanding programs in government relations or public affairs. **Awards:** Grassroots Innovator Award. **Frequency:** annual. **Type:** recognition. **Affiliated With:** Foundation for Public Affairs. **Formerly:** (1967) Effective Citizens Organization. **Publications:** *National Directory of Corporate Public Affairs.* Contains information on the public functions of 1,700 major U.S. corporations and descriptions of their PACs, foundation and charitable funds. **Price:** $159.00 for nonmembers ● *Public Affairs Council—Impact,* monthly. Newsletter. Includes calendar of events and personnel changes in the field. **Price:** included in membership dues; $15.00 /year for nonmembers ● *Public Affairs News Monitor,* biweekly. Newsletter. Provides summaries of major national news stories dealing with public affairs issues. **Price:** free for members ● *Public Affairs Review,* annual. Annual Report. Contains challenging articles and the annual reports of the Public Affairs Council and the Foundation for Public Affairs. **Price:** free; $5.00 for additional copy. Alternate Formats: online ● Brochures ● Book. **Conventions/Meetings:** annual Public Affairs Institute - seminar, on public affairs training - always January.

Creative Education

16996 ■ National Center for Creativity (NCCI)
Address Unknown since 2007
Founded: 1993. **Members:** 200. **Membership Dues:** individual, $60 (annual). **Staff:** 3. **Budget:** $60,000. **Description:** Dedicated to provide techniques and concepts that help in creativity and innovative thinking in various business and civic settings. **Committees:** City Lights Volunteers. **Publications:** *Bright Points,* quarterly. Newsletter.

Credit

16997 ■ American Credit Card Collectors Society (ACCCS)
PO Box 2465
Midland, MI 48641
E-mail: info@creditcollectibles.com
URL: http://www.creditcollectibles.com
Contact: Jerry Ballard, Contact

Founded: 1994. **Membership Dues:** regular in U.S. and Canada, $30 (annual) ● regular outside U.S. and Canada, $40 (annual). **Description:** Represents credit card collectors. **Conventions/Meetings:** convention.

16998 ■ Consumer Credit Counseling Services (CCCS)
9009 West Loop S, Ste.700
Houston, TX 77096
Ph: (713)923-2227
Free: (800)873-2227
E-mail: jbrient@piercom.com
URL: http://www.cccsintl.org
Contact: Jordan Brient, Contact

Description: Promotes financial education as an investment in the community. **Programs:** Budgeting Basics; Credit Usage; Debt Management; First Time Homebuyers; Holiday Survival Skills; Understanding Your Credit Report; When The Income Decreases But The Bills Don't.

Criminal Justice

16999 ■ African American Criminal Justice Society (AACJS)
PO Box 11284
Wilmington, DE 19850
Ph: (302)838-3583
Free: (877)485-6422
URL: http://www.aacjs.org
Contact: Darrell A. Hervey, Founder/CEO

Membership Dues: active, retired, $25 (annual) ● associate, student, $20 (annual) ● agency/affiliate, $100 (annual). **Description:** Increases awareness of the criminal justice system. Enhances the quality of life in the African-American community. Improves criminal justice through educational activities. Promotes professional, academic and public awareness of criminal justice issues. **Affiliated With:** National Black Police Association.

17000 ■ Life After Exoneration Program (LAEP)
PO Box 10208
Berkeley, CA 94709
Ph: (510)292-6010 (510)526-2168
E-mail: info@exonerated.org
URL: http://www.exonerated.org
Contact: Lola Vollen MD, Founder/Exec. Dir.

Description: Addresses the injustice of wrongful conviction and incarceration by assisting exonerees and their family members in rebuilding their lives. Works to secure exonerees' physical, spiritual, psychological, social and economic well-being. Coordinates direct services to exonerees. Helps to build a community of the exonerated. Supports legislative and policy change. **Telecommunication Services:** electronic mail, lola@exonerated.org. **Publications:** *The Exoneree Times.* Newsletter. Covers recent events and program activities. Alternate Formats: online.

Criminal Law

17001 ■ Coalition for an International Criminal Court (CICC)
c/o World Federalist Movement
708 3rd Ave., 24th Fl.
New York, NY 10017
Ph: (212)687-2863
Fax: (212)599-1332
E-mail: cicc@iccnow.org
URL: http://www.iccnow.org
Contact: William R. Pace, Convenor

Founded: 1995. **Members:** 2,000. **Languages:** English, French, Spanish. **Multinational. Description:** Advocates for a fair, effective and independent International Criminal Court (ICC). Raises awareness of the ICC at the national, regional and global level. Monitors and supports the work of the Assembly of States Parties. Facilitates involvement and capacity building of NGOs in the ICC process. Provides technical expertise to governments, the ICC, and other institutions. **Publications:** *Agenda CPI* (in English and Spanish), monthly. Newsletter. Provides updates and information on issues concerning the ICC in Ibero-America. Alternate Formats: online ● *European Newsletter,* bimonthly. Covers the latest develop-

ments, resources, and events in Europe. Alternate Formats: online ● *ICC Monitor* (in English, French, and Spanish), quarterly. Newspaper. Contains information on the current status of ICC developments. Alternate Formats: online ● *ICC Update* (in English and French), monthly. Bulletin. Reports on regional updates on ratification and implementation, media coverage, upcoming meetings, and resources. Alternate Formats: online ● *Insight on the ICC* (in English and French), quarterly. Newsletter. Focuses on important developments at the International Criminal Court and in The Hague. Alternate Formats: online.

Croatian

17002 ■ National Federation of Croatian Americans (NFCA)
2401 Res. Blvd., Ste.115
Rockville, MD 20850
Ph: (301)208-6650
Fax: (301)208-6659
E-mail: nfcahdq@aol.com
URL: http://www.nfcaonline.com
Contact: Edward Anthony Andrus, Pres.

Membership Dues: individual, $35 (annual) ● organization, $500 (annual). **Description:** Maintains a national infrastructure and network linking Croatian-American organizations and individual activists. Advocates for the enhancement of the Croatian image in the United States. Promotes programs that strengthen and support the cultural, educational, humanitarian, public relations, and social and political activities of the Croatian American community. **Publications:** *Croatian American Advocate.* Newsletter. Alternate Formats: online.

Cuba

17003 ■ Alpha-66 (A-66)
PO Box 420067
Miami, FL 33142
Ph: (305)541-5433
E-mail: pedroa@shadownet.net
URL: http://www.alpha66.org
Contact: Nazario Sargen, Sec. Gen.

Founded: 1961. **Members:** 5,000. **Languages:** English, Spanish. **Description:** Cuban exiles in the U.S. and their sympathizers in Cuba. Objective is to "liberate Cuba from the communists" and to bring to the island a democratic, free enterprise system modeled on that of the U.S. Trains and has sent commandos to Cuba to fight Premier Fidel Castro's troops. The group's general assembly, comprised of delegates from throughout the U.S., has formulated ideological principles which it hopes to see implemented upon overthrow of the present government. Sponsors radiobroadcasts to Cuba. **Publications:** Newsletter, monthly. **Conventions/Meetings:** quadrennial convention ● biennial general assembly.

17004 ■ Cuban American National Foundation (CANF)
1312 SW 27th Ave.
Miami, FL 33145
Ph: (305)592-7768
Fax: (305)592-7889
E-mail: hq@canf.org
URL: http://www.canf.org
Contact: Francisco J. Hernandez, Pres.

Founded: 1981. **Members:** 30,000. **Staff:** 14. **Languages:** English, Spanish. **Description:** Americans of Cuban descent and others with an interest in Cuban affairs. Serves as a grass roots lobbying organization promoting freedom and democracy in Cuba and worldwide. Maintains speakers' bureau; offers educational and research programs. **Libraries: Type:** by appointment only. **Holdings:** 1,035. **Subjects:** Cuba. **Awards:** Mas Family Scholarships. **Frequency:** annual. **Type:** scholarship. **Recipient:** for merit and financial need. **Computer Services:** database ● mailing lists. **Formerly:** (1983) Cuban American Public Affairs Committee; (1987) Cuban

American Freedom Coalition; (1997) Cuban American Foundation. **Publications:** *Cuban Monitor*, 8/year. Newsletter. **Conventions/Meetings:** periodic meeting - always in Washington, DC.

17005 ■ Directorio Democratico Cubano
PO Box 110235
Hialeah, FL 33011
Ph: (305)220-2713
E-mail: info@directorio.org
URL: http://www.directorio.org
Contact: Javier de Cespedes, Pres./Co-Founder

Founded: 1990. **Languages:** English, Spanish. **Multinational. Description:** Strives for liberation of Cuba from totalitarian dictatorship by identifying, contacting and supporting civic and democratic associations in Cuba; seeks and obtains support for Cuba's internal opposition from international organizations and institutions worldwide; compiles, analyzes and disseminates information on the tradition of Cuban civic and democratic thought. Conducts research on democratic philosophy and practice in world history. **Also Known As:** Cuban Democratic Directorate. **Formerly:** (2002) Directorio Revolucionario Democratico Cubano.

17006 ■ Junta Civico-Militar Cubana (JCMC)
Address Unknown since 2007
Founded: 1969. **Members:** 200. **Staff:** 14. **Languages:** Spanish. **Description:** Military professionals and civilians interested in the restoration of democracy in Cuba. Activities of JCMC are conducted within the bounds of U.S. and international law, and are of a pacific nature. **Awards:** Honor Al Merito. **Type:** recognition. **Recipient:** for services to the organization. **Publications:** *Organo Oficial de la Junta Civico Militar Cubana*, annual ● Newsletter, quarterly. **Conventions/Meetings:** monthly general assembly and meeting - first Sunday of the month. Los Angeles, CA - **Avg. Attendance:** 30.

17007 ■ Movement for an Independent and Democratic Cuba (CID)
10020 SW 37th Terr.
Miami, FL 33165
Ph: (305)221-3820
Fax: (305)551-0271
Contact: Cmdr. Huber Matos, Sec. Gen.

Founded: 1980. **Members:** 1,000. **Staff:** 35. **Regional Groups:** 75. **Description:** Political scientists, educators, economists, and other interested individuals. Organized to "denounce the aggressive nature of Castro's satellite government, and to establish the need for a joint strategy which will prevent the large majorities of the peoples of the Americas from succumbing to minority groups directed from Havana and Moscow." Objectives are defined by the movement's five "ideological-programmatical points": national independence; political democracy; economic democracy; social justice; Latin American integration. Maintains that at the "end of Soviet occupation and the Castro dictatorship we will see the rebirth of Cuban democracy." Urges support from other democratic forces of the continent and the western world. Operates Institute for Economic Development of Cuba project, which publishes reports on the Cuban economy and maintains four 24-hour shortwave radio stations broadcasting to Cuba. Compiles statistics on Cuban economics, sugar harvest, and education. Operates 58 committees. **Libraries: Type:** reference. **Holdings:** 500. **Subjects:** economics and politics in Cuba. **Also Known As:** Cuba Independiente y Democratica. **Publications:** *NewsCuba*, monthly. Newsletter. Provides information about Cuba and its communist regime. **Price:** free. **Circulation:** 15,000 ● *Pueblo Unido* (in English and Spanish), monthly. Newsletter. Provides uncensored news and information for Cubans. **Price:** free. **Circulation:** 10,000 ● Newspaper (in English and Spanish), bimonthly. Covers organization activities and world news related to Cuba. **Price:** included in membership dues; $15.00 /year for nonmembers (donation requested). **Circulation:** 40,000. **Conventions/Meetings:** annual meeting.

Cults

17008 ■ International Cultic Studies Association (ICSA)
PO Box 2265
Bonita Springs, FL 34133
Ph: (239)514-3081
Fax: (305)393-8193
E-mail: aff@affcultinfoserve.com
URL: http://www.culticstudies.org
Contact: Michael D. Langone PhD, Exec. Dir.

Founded: 1979. **Budget:** $290,000. **Description:** Educational research organization seeking to understand and alleviate the problems caused to individuals, families, and society at large by people and groups that employ unethical forms of social influence. Reports on legal, medical, psychological, and social issues raised by cultism. **Projects:** Alert; Discover; Recovery. **Formerly:** (2004) American Family Foundation. **Publications:** *Cult Observer*, quarterly. Magazine ● *Cultic Studies Journal*, annual ● Books ● Catalogs ● Reports.

Cultural Exchange

17009 ■ American Institute for Managing Diversity (AIMD)
1155 Peachtree St., Ste.6B
Atlanta, GA 30303
Ph: (404)575-2131
Fax: (404)575-2139
E-mail: mharrington@aimd.org
URL: http://aimd.org
Contact: Melanie Harrington, Exec. Dir.

Founded: 1984. **Membership Dues:** multi-year founding charter, $30,000 (triennial) ● 20th anniversary charter, $10,000 (annual) ● corporate, $5,000 (annual). **Description:** Aims to advance the field of diversity management through research, education, and public outreach. **Councils:** Public Outreach Advisory. **Divisions:** Diversity Leadership Academy. **Publications:** *A Guide to Culture Audits: Analyzing Organizational Culture for Managing Diversity*. Book. **Price:** $395.00 ● *Beyond Race and Gender: Unleashing the Power of Your Total Work Force by Managing Diversity*. Book. **Price:** $15.95 ● *Building a House for Diversity*. Book. **Price:** $27.95 ● *Cultural Manifestations of Diversity: The Impact of Recruitment, Selection, Promotion and Compensation Policies and Practices on the Glass Ceiling*. Report. **Price:** $50.00 ● *Designing a House for Diversity*. Book. **Price:** $85.00 ● *Diversity Practitioner Study: A Job and Skill Analysis*. Report. **Price:** $15.00 ● *Elements of a Successful Diversity Process - Parts 1 and 2*. Article. **Price:** $5.00 for each part ● *Giraffe and Elephant: A Diversity Fable*. Book. **Price:** $24.95 ● *Lessons from Archie Bunker*. Article. **Price:** $5.00.

17010 ■ CEC ArtsLink
435 Hudson St., 8th Fl.
New York, NY 10014
Ph: (212)643-1985
Fax: (212)643-1996
E-mail: info@cecartslink.org
URL: http://www.cecartslink.org
Contact: Michael C. Brainerd, Pres.

Founded: 1962. **Staff:** 8. **Budget:** $1,100,000. **Description:** Provides opportunities for individuals and groups involved in the arts to collaborate as partners in East/Central Europe and Eurasia for mutual benefit. **Awards:** ArtsLink Awards. **Frequency:** annual. **Type:** recognition. **Recipient:** for artists, arts managers and non-profit organizations. **Committees:** Advisory. **Departments:** Artslink. **Projects:** VisArt. **Formerly:** (1965) Peace Hostage Exchange Foundation; (1980) Citizen Exchange Corps; (1995) Citizen Exchange Council; (2004) CEC International Partners.

17011 ■ Panamerican/PanAfrican Association (PA/PA)
London Park Towers
5375 Duke St., Ste.1210
Alexandria, VA 22304

Ph: (703)567-1441 (202)487-4142
Fax: (703)567-1441
E-mail: papaassociation@yahoo.com
URL: http://www.papausa.org
Contact: Dr. Robert Starling Pritchard II, Chm./ Founder

Founded: 1967. **Description:** Supporters include scholars, diplomats, denominations, African-American and inter-American cultural exchange organizations, and persons who promote intercultural, interracial, and inter-group understanding. Coordinated the 7th International Panafricanist congress in Cotonou, Benin, February 1991. Sponsors Inter-American, African-American, and Asian-American educational, cultural, and economic exchange. Maintains public diplomacy program; promotes artistic endeavors including concerts and recitals; conducts public interest civil and human rights litigation activities; promotes Third World economic development. Administers the Papa International Trade Consultants group. Administers National and International Black History Month observances each February. **Libraries: Type:** reference. **Holdings:** 2,000. **Subjects:** Afro-Brazilian ecclesiastical music, multiethnic/multicultural education and curriculum development. **Awards:** Artist and Scholars Award. **Frequency:** periodic. **Type:** scholarship. **Recipient:** for artists and scholars in residency ● Kenneth David Kaunda Award for Humanism. **Frequency:** periodic. **Type:** scholarship. **Recipient:** for career and student interns. **Programs:** Inter-American/African-American Cultural, Educational and Economic Exchange; International Trade Consultants Group; New World Festival Concerts and Lectures Bureau; Resident and Non-Resident Student-Intern; Roland Hayes Observances. **Projects:** Minas Gerais Brazilian Masterworks Performance; National Demonstration Project to Study Extremism. **Publications:** *Panamerican/Panafrican Association—Notes*, periodic. Newsletter. Covers association activities and international ethnic and cultural topics. Includes commentary. **Price:** free. **Circulation:** 1,000. **Advertising:** accepted. **Conventions/Meetings:** periodic National/International Conferences.

Defense

17012 ■ Alliance Defense Fund (ADF)
15333 N Pima Rd., Ste.165
Scottsdale, AZ 85260
Free: (800)835-5233
Fax: (480)444-0025
E-mail: asears@alliancedefensefund.org
URL: http://www.alliancedefensefund.org
Contact: Alan E. Sears Esq., Pres./CEO/Gen. Counsel

Founded: 1993. **Staff:** 10. **Budget:** $5,000,000. **Description:** Works to promote religious civil liberties, the sanctity of life, and family values. Offers training for attorneys; funds legal battles; provides strategic planning; conducts educational programs. **Programs:** National Litigation Academy. **Projects:** National Campaign to Stop the American Civil Liberties Union. **Publications:** *ADF Briefing*, monthly. Newsletter. **Conventions/Meetings:** annual seminar.

17013 ■ American Defense Institute (ADI)
1055 N Fairfax St., Ste.200
Alexandria, VA 22314
Ph: (703)519-7000
Fax: (703)519-8627
E-mail: rdt2@americandefinst.org
URL: http://www.ojc.org/adi
Contact: Eugene McDaniel, Pres.

Founded: 1983. **Members:** 15,000. **Staff:** 5. **Budget:** $900,000. **Description:** Non-partisan public policy foundation promoting a strong national defense. Analyzes and reports on key defense issues. Maintains liaison with members of Congress; operates Speaker's Bureau; offers graduate fellowships and undergraduate internships. **Convention/Meeting:** none. **Libraries: Type:** not open to the public. **Awards:** National Security Studies Fellowship. **Type:** monetary. **Recipient:** for graduate students in National Security and the Foreign Affairs field. **Pro-**

grams: Military Voter. **Publications:** *ADI Briefing,* monthly ● *ADI News,* quarterly. Newsletter. **Circulation:** 15,000 ● *After the Hero's Welcome* ● *Scars and Stripes.*

17014 ■ British American Security Information Council (BASIC)

110 Maryland Ave. NE, Ste.205
Washington, DC 20002
Ph: (202)546-8055
Fax: (202)546-8056
E-mail: basicus@basicint.org
URL: http://www.basicint.org
Contact: Ian Davis, Exec. Dir.
Founded: 1987. **Staff:** 12. **Nonmembership. Description:** Promotes public awareness of defense, disarmament, military strategy, and nuclear policies of the United States and Britain. Facilitates exchange of information and analysis among military observers in the U.S. and Britain; sponsors research and educational programs. **Publications:** Reports ● Papers ● Newsletter, bimonthly.

17015 ■ Center for Defense Information (CDI)

1779 Massachusetts Ave. NW
Washington, DC 20036-2109
Ph: (202)332-0600
Fax: (202)462-4559
E-mail: info@cdi.org
URL: http://www.cdi.org
Contact: Bruce G. Blair PhD, Pres.
Founded: 1972. **Staff:** 25. **Budget:** $2,100,000. **Description:** Aims to strengthen security through international cooperation; reduced reliance on unilateral military power to resolve conflict; reduced reliance on nuclear weapons; a transformed and reformed military establishment; and prudent oversight of, and spending on, weapons programs. Seeks to contribute alternative views on security to promote wide-ranging discourse and debate. Educates the public and informs policy-makers about issues of security policy, strategy, operations, weapons systems and defense budgeting, and pursues creative solutions to the problems of today and tomorrow. Aims to improve understanding between the United States and key nations on security matters through new media initiatives that inform and educate opinion-makers, policy-makers and the general public. Accepts no government or defense industry funding, and does not hold organizational positions. Believes on the concept that the public and political leaders "can, and will, make wise choices on complex security matters when provided with facts, and practical alternatives". **Programs:** Arms Control Advocacy Collaborative; Chemical and Biological Warfare; Children and Armed Conflict; Eye on Iraq; Failed States; Insights; Peacekeeping; Terrorism. **Publications:** *Defense Monitor,* bimonthly. Newsletter. Seeks to strengthen security through international cooperation; reduced reliance on unilateral military power to resolve conflict. **Price:** $45.00/year. **Circulation:** 25,000. Alternate Formats: online. **Conventions/Meetings:** periodic conference and meeting ● annual meeting.

17016 ■ Defense Forum Foundation (DFF)

3014 Castle Rd.
Falls Church, VA 22044
Ph: (703)534-4313
Fax: (703)538-6149
E-mail: skswm@aol.com
URL: http://defenseforum.org
Contact: Suzanne Scholte, Pres.
Founded: 1987. **Staff:** 3. **Description:** Promotes increased public awareness of national defense issues, foreign affairs, and human rights issues. Conducts educational forums on defense, foreign policy and human rights issues for Congressional staff and the public. Conducts fact-finding missions in Africa. **Study Groups:** Educational Project. **Subgroups:** U.S. Western Sahara Foundation. **Working Groups:** North Korea Freedom Coalition. **Publications:** *Life and Human Rights in North Korea* (in English, Japanese, and Korean), quarterly. Booklet. **Circulation:** 300.

17017 ■ Family Defense Council (FDC)

PO Box 310478
Jamaica, NY 11431-0478
Contact: Howard L. Hurwitz PhD, Chm.
Founded: 1991. **Membership Dues:** regular, $25 (annual). **Description:** Seeks to promote public morality and combat "virulent attacks on traditional family values by radical homosexuals abetted by the liberal media". Conducts media and political activities against pro-homosexual school curriculums, sex education, abortion, drug abuse and out-of-wedlock pregnancies.

17018 ■ Inter-American Defense Board (IADB)

2600 NW 16th St.
Washington, DC 20441
Ph: (202)939-6041
Fax: (202)387-2880
E-mail: iadc-personnel@jid.org
URL: http://www.jid.org
Contact: Major Gen. Keith M. Huber, Pres./Chm.
Founded: 1942. **Members:** 200. **Budget:** $2,228,000. **Languages:** English, French, Portuguese, Spanish. **Description:** Government-appointed military officers and advisers of North, Central, and South America. Studies and recommends measures concerning the collective self-defense of the American continent and the standardization of military organizations and operations. Promotes close military collaboration among governments of the Western Hemisphere. Operates the Inter-American Defense College. **Libraries: Type:** not open to the public. **Councils:** Delegates. **Subcommittees:** Administration; College Curriculum; Objectives and Administration; Public Relations. **Affiliated With:** Organization of American States. **Conventions/Meetings:** bimonthly Council Sessions - meeting.

17019 ■ International Strategic Studies Association (ISSA)

PO Box 20407
Alexandria, VA 22320
Ph: (703)548-1070
Fax: (703)684-7476
E-mail: grcopley@strategicstudies.org
URL: http://www.strategicstudies.org
Contact: Gregory R. Copley, Pres.
Founded: 1982. **Members:** 500. **Membership Dues:** individual, $165 (annual) ● institutional, $1,000 (annual) ● sponsoring, $5,000-$10,000 (annual) ● life, $1,000. **Staff:** 1. **Description:** Individuals in industry and government. Focuses on regular discussion of strategic issues including: defense; transfer of international technology; geopolitical and psychological strategies; military doctrine and operations; new technology and intelligence matters; defense of industrial concerns. Research and educational programs include workshops and seminars. **Libraries: Type:** reference. **Holdings:** 10,000. **Subjects:** strategic, political, defense and sociological issues. **Awards: Type:** recognition. **Publications:** *Defense and Foreign Affairs: Strategic Policy,* monthly. Journal. **Price:** $139.00/year. ISSN: 0277-4933 ● *Study Group Reports,* periodic ● Newsletter, quarterly. **Conventions/Meetings:** semiannual meeting.

17020 ■ Jewish Institute for National Security Affairs (JINSA)

1779 Massachusetts Ave. NW, Ste.515
Washington, DC 20036
Ph: (202)667-3900
Fax: (202)667-0601
E-mail: info@jinsa.org
URL: http://www.jinsa.org
Contact: Mark Broxmeyer, Chm.
Founded: 1976. **Members:** 17,000. **Membership Dues:** basic, $100 (annual) ● premier, $500 (annual) ● sustaining, $1,000 (annual) ● benefactor, $2,500 (annual) ● patron, $5,000 (annual) ● sponsor, $10,000 (annual) ● platinum, $25,000 (annual). **Staff:** 7. **Budget:** $1,300,000. **Regional Groups:** 6. **Description:** Aims to inform the American public of "the vital necessity for an adequate American defense program"; inform the defense and national security community of the value of strategic cooperation

between the U.S. and Israel. Offers internships. **Awards:** Henry M. Jackson Distinguished Service Award. **Frequency:** annual. **Type:** recognition. **Recipient:** for dedication to programs fostering a strong U.S. national defense and strong U.S.-Israel security cooperation. **Committees:** Defense Studies; Editorial Review. **Publications:** *The Journal of International Security Affairs,* semiannual. Covers U.S. national security and topics in international affairs. **Price:** $8.00/issue. ISSN: 1532-4060. **Circulation:** 5,000. **Advertising:** accepted. Alternate Formats: online ● *Profiles in Terror: A Guide to Middle East Terrorist Organizations.* Book. **Price:** $18.87/item. Alternate Formats: online. **Conventions/Meetings:** semiannual board meeting.

17021 ■ Leonard Peltier Defense Committee (LPDC)

2626 N Mesa, No. 132
El Paso, TX 79902
Ph: (915)533-6655
E-mail: info@leonardpeltier.net
URL: http://www.freepeltier.org
Founded: 1976. **Membership Dues:** individual, $25 ● neighborhood, $50 ● area, $100. **Staff:** 2. **Budget:** $60,000. **Multinational. Description:** Seeks to gain justice for Leonard Peltier through promotion, education, and public speaking. Works to improve the lives of American Indians and prisoners. Provides information on social, judicial and cultural issues. **Libraries: Type:** reference; open to the public. **Holdings:** clippings. **Subjects:** Native Americans, environment, prison, court/legal materials. **Additional Websites:** http://www.leonardpeltier.net. **Publications:** *The Case of Leonard Peltier, Evidence and Documentation of A Wrongful Conviction.* Book. **Price:** $24.85 single copy; $13.00 bulk order ● *Have You Thought of Leonard Peltier Lately?.* Book. **Price:** $28.00 soft cover. Alternate Formats: online ● *Prison Writings: My Life is My Sundance.* Book. **Price:** $30.00 hard cover; $18.85 soft cover ● *Spirit of Crazy Horse,* bimonthly. Newsletter. **Price:** $20.00/year in U.S.; $30.00/year outside U.S.; $10.00/year for seniors; free to prisoners. **Circulation:** 3,000. **Advertising:** accepted. **Conventions/Meetings:** semiannual regional meeting ● support group meeting.

17022 ■ Missile Defense Advocacy Alliance (MDAA)

515 King St., Ste.320
Alexandria, VA 22314
Ph: (703)299-0060
Fax: (703)299-0132
E-mail: info@missiledefenseadvocacy.org
URL: http://www.missiledefenseadvocacy.org
Contact: Riki Ellison, Pres./Founder
Founded: 2002. **Members:** 9,000. **Description:** Seeks to raise public support for the development of a missile defense system for the promotion of safety and protection of the U.S. and its allied nations. Encourages the development, testing, deployment, and evolution of a robust missile defense system. Conducts public surveys concerning missile defense issues. **Telecommunication Services:** electronic mail, rikiellison@missiledefenseadvocacy.org. **Publications:** Brochure. Alternate Formats: online.

17023 ■ National Strategy Information Center (NSIC)

1730 Rhode Island Ave. NW, Ste.500
Washington, DC 20036-3117
E-mail: info@strategycenter.org
URL: http://www.strategycenter.org
Contact: Dr. Roy Godson, Pres.
Founded: 1962. **Staff:** 11. **Budget:** $1,000,000. **Description:** Seeks to educate leaders of public opinion about national defense and emerging security challenges through postdoctoral seminars, policy workshops, and briefing sessions for business, labor, professional, and military groups in the U.S. and abroad; academic and mass media; governmental schools; colleges and universities. **Publications:** *Trends in Organized Crime,* quarterly. Journal. **Price:** $45.00/year. **Advertising:** accepted ● *Working Group on Organized Crime,* quarterly. Monograph. Presents a series on strategic approaches to orga-

nized crime. **Price:** $7.00/copy. **Conventions/Meetings:** periodic conference and seminar, for teaching faculty.

17024 ■ Naval Submarine League (NSL)
PO Box 1146
Annandale, VA 22003
Ph: (703)256-0891
Fax: (703)642-5815
E-mail: nslmem@cavtel.net
URL: http://www.navalsubleague.com
Contact: Capt. C. Michael Garverick, Exec. Dir.
Founded: 1982. **Members:** 4,300. **Membership Dues:** regular (including retired military), $35 (annual) ● active duty, naval reserve active status, student, $15 (annual) ● life (based on age), $230-$750. **Staff:** 5. **Budget:** $500,000. **Regional Groups:** 10. **Description:** Active and retired submariners, submarine industry employees, and other individuals interested in promoting a strong submarine force. Provides service and support to the active duty submarine force personnel. Seeks to educate the public on the need for a strong submarine force. Provides speakers, films, and slides to civic groups. Conducts annual closed sessions for members. Sponsors writing competitions and special awards. **Libraries: Type:** reference. **Holdings:** 1,000; books, video recordings. **Subjects:** submarine related material. **Awards: Frequency:** annual. **Type:** recognition. **Recipient:** based on merit. **Publications:** *NSL Directory of Membership.* Membership Directory. Contains names and addresses of members. **Price:** free, for members only. **Circulation:** 4,100. Alternate Formats: online ● *NSL Fact Book*, periodic ● *Submarine Review*, quarterly. Journal. Covers submarine history and current Soviet and American nuclear submarine forces and strategy. Includes annual index and book review. **Price:** included in membership dues. **Circulation:** 5,000. **Advertising:** accepted ● Annual Report, annual. Alternate Formats: online. **Conventions/Meetings:** annual Submarine Technology Symposium, technical papers (exhibits) ● annual symposium and meeting (exhibits) - three days in June.

17025 ■ Project on Defense Alternatives (PDA)
c/o The Commonwealth Institute
PO Box 398105
Inman Sq. Post Off.
Cambridge, MA 02139
Ph: (617)547-4474
Fax: (617)868-1267
E-mail: pda@comw.org
URL: http://www.comw.org/pda/index.html
Contact: Carl Conetta, Co-Dir.
Founded: 1991. **Description:** Seeks to adapt security policy to the challenges of the post-Cold War era; promotes consideration of the broadest range of defense options. **Computer Services:** database, Gulf War, Air Power, multinational security operations including those of the U.N. **Telecommunication Services:** electronic mail, cconetta@comw.org. **Publications:** *Disappearing the Dead: Iraq, Afghanistan, and the Idea of a "New Warfare".* Monograph ● *Operation Enduring Freedom: Why a Higher Rate of Civilian Bombing Casualties.* Monograph. Contains the PDA Briefing Report No. 11, 18 January 2002. ● *Radical Departure: Toward a Practical Peace in Iraq.* Reprint ● *Strange Victory: A Critical Appraisal of Operation Enduring Freedom and the Afghanistan War.* Monograph. Contains the PDA Research Monograph No. 6, 30 January 2002.

17026 ■ Women in Defense, a National Security Organization
2111 Wilson Blvd., Ste.400
Arlington, VA 22201-3061
Ph: (703)247-2552
Fax: (703)522-1885
E-mail: wid@ndia.org
URL: http://wid.ndia.org
Contact: Jane Walter, Pres.
Founded: 1985. **Members:** 530. **Membership Dues:** individual, $35 (annual) ● life, $500. **Budget:** $30,000. **Local Groups:** 4. **Description:** Professional organization for individuals whose careers are related to the defense of the United States and national security. Provides its members with opportunities for professional development, a forum for exchanging ideas and experiences, a vehicle for expanding their network, opportunities for members to meet and interact with distinguished officials from government and industry in open discussions on key issues. **Awards:** Horizons Foundation Scholarship. **Frequency:** semiannual. **Type:** scholarship. **Recipient:** for women pursuing careers in national defense. **Telecommunication Services:** electronic mail, walter_jane@bah.com. **Affiliated With:** National Defense Industrial Association. **Formerly:** (1999) Women in Defense. **Publications:** *Network Notes.* Newsletter.

Democracy

17027 ■ America's Development Foundation (ADF)
101 N Union St., Ste.200
Alexandria, VA 22314
Ph: (703)836-2717
Fax: (703)836-3379
E-mail: mmiller@adfusa.org
URL: http://www.adfusa.org
Contact: Mr. Michael D. Miller, Pres.
Founded: 1980. **Description:** Assists in the "international development of democracy and respect for human rights." Provides training, technical assistance, and financial support to non-governmental organizations working to build civil societies based on respect for human rights and the rule of law worldwide. Maintains field offices in Croatia, Haiti, Mozambique, Angola, Egypt, and the West Bank and Gaza Strip.

17028 ■ Center for the Study of Democratic Institutions (CSDI)
Address Unknown since 2006
Founded: 1959. **Members:** 15,000. **Membership Dues:** Association, $55 (annual). **Staff:** 4. **Languages:** English, French, Spanish, Turkish. **Description:** Educational corporation. Investigates critical issues confronting the world today. Publishes New Perspectives Quarterly (NPQ) on social and political issues. Sponsors Global Viewpoint syndicated service, which engages world leaders involved in government, academia, literature, and the media in discussions about the most important issues of our time. **Libraries: Type:** open to the public. **Holdings:** 13; periodicals. **Subjects:** global, social, and political issues. **Publications:** *New Perspectives Quarterly* (in English, Spanish, and Turkish). Journal. Covers current Global issues of trade, international relations, economics, religion, and social change. **Price:** $55. 00/year. ISSN: 0893-7850. **Circulation:** 15,000. **Advertising:** not accepted. Alternate Formats: microform; online; CD-ROM.

17029 ■ Center for the Study of Democratic Societies (CSDS)
Box 475
Manhattan Beach, CA 90267-0475
Ph: (310)798-2737
Fax: (310)374-0440
E-mail: georgecsds@aol.com
URL: http://www.centersds.com
Contact: Robley Evans George, Dir.
Founded: 1969. **Multinational. Description:** Research and educational institution dedicated to the necessary examination and explanation of the properties and possibilities of democratic societies. Aims to devise rational, humanistic, just, and democratic solutions to existing societal problems and to analyze the procedures required to improve societal systems. Originates and develops new political economy known as Socioeconomic Democracy. Conducts short courses and research programs. Offers research, writing, and consulting services. Maintains speakers' bureau. **Libraries: Type:** reference. **Holdings:** 500. **Subjects:** democracy, economics, political science, future research, philosophy, Utopian studies. **Publications:** *Socioeconomic Democracy: An Advanced Socioeconomic System.* Book ● Audiotapes ● Videos. **Conventions/Meetings:** periodic conference ● lecture ● seminar.

17030 ■ Coalition for Democracy in Iran (CDI)
PO Box 65763
Washington, DC 20035
Ph: (202)347-3257
Fax: (202)393-7006
E-mail: cdi_org@hotmail.com
Description: Mobilizes the efforts of groups and individuals across the United States, including Iranian-Americans, who support the aspirations of the Iranian people for democracy and respect for human rights in Iran. **Computer Services:** Information services, information and articles about Iran. **Publications:** Articles. Alternate Formats: online.

17031 ■ Democracy Project (DP)
PO Box 9316
Wilmington, DE 19809
E-mail: info@democracy-project.com
URL: http://www.democracy-project.com
Contact: Brent S. Tantillo,,CEO
Founded: 1981. **Staff:** 5. **Budget:** $250,000. **Description:** Critiques conservative public and political policy and develops progressive alternatives. Includes areas of interest such as economics and democracy, citizens' access to government, health and safety regulations, and crime. Works with key political and policymaking figures in developing new policies. Conducts research projects and seminars. **Publications:** *Challenge of Hidden Profits* ● *The Challenge of Hidden Profits: Reducing Corporate Bureaucracy and Waste* ● *Ideas That Work* ● *Reagan's Reign of Error* ● *Transition '89* ● *Winning Back America.* **Conventions/Meetings:** periodic conference.

17032 ■ Global Exchange
2017 Mission St., No. 303
San Francisco, CA 94110
Ph: (415)255-7296
Fax: (415)255-7498
E-mail: admin@globalexchange.org
URL: http://www.globalexchange.org
Founded: 1988. **Members:** 10,000. **Membership Dues:** student/low income, $25 (annual) ● individual, $35 (annual) ● partner, $500 (annual) ● supporting, $50 (annual) ● benefactor, $250 (annual) ● contributing, $100 (annual) ● leader, $1,000 (annual). **Staff:** 30. **Budget:** $850,000. **Languages:** English, Portuguese, Spanish. **Description:** Promotes democracy around the world by facilitating communication between grassroots pro-democracy groups. Sponsors study seminar trips to areas of interest such as Cuba, South Africa, Haiti, and Mexico. Provides resources and information on Third World issues. Maintains speakers' bureau; conducts charitable and educational programs; holds art shows and craft sales. **Publications:** *Democratizing the Global Economy: The Battle Against the World Bank and the IMF* ● *Globalize This! The Battle Against the World Trade Organization and Corporate Rule* ● *Know Justice, Know Peace: A Program for Building Global Security* ● *The Peace Corps and More: 120 Ways to Work, Study, Travel Overseas.* **Price:** $8.95 plus shipping and handling ● *Still Waiting for Nike to Do It* ● *Ten Reasons to Abolish the Work Bank* ● Newsletter, quarterly. **Price:** free for members. **Circulation:** 10,000 ● Corporations are gonna get your Mama, Kevin Danaher editor.

17033 ■ Institute on Religion and Democracy (IRD)
1023 15th St. NW, Ste.601
Washington, DC 20005-2601
Ph: (202)682-4131
Fax: (202)682-4136
E-mail: mail@ird-renew.org
URL: http://www.ird-renew.org
Contact: Alan Wisdom, VP
Founded: 1981. **Members:** 5,000. **Membership Dues:** regular, $25 (annual). **Staff:** 7. **Budget:** $800,000. **Description:** Churches, ministers, and church members dedicated to restoring democratic values to churches. Examines the connection between religion and the promotion of democratic

institutions worldwide. Opposes efforts by some American churches to provide international financial and ideological support to movements the institute believes are neglectful of democratic values, promote leftist views in the U.S., and are wrongfully silent about violations of religious freedoms abroad. Demands accountability of church groups for aid rendered for political purposes. Sponsors regional seminars dealing with international issues; maintains information service and speakers' bureau. **Awards:** Religious Freedom Award. **Frequency:** periodic. **Type:** recognition. **Committees:** Ecumenical Coalition on Women and Society; Episcopal Action; Presbyterian Action; United Methodist Action. **Publications:** *Episcopal Action Briefing*, quarterly. **Price:** included in membership dues ● *Faith & Freedom*, quarterly. Newsletter. **Price:** $25.00/year. **Circulation:** 15,000 ● *Presbyterian Action Briefing*, quarterly. **Price:** included in membership dues ● *Prophets and Politics* ● *Re-Imaging Resource Packet* ● *Sudan Resource Packet* ● *United Methodist Action Briefing*, quarterly. **Price:** included in membership dues ● Pamphlets, 2-3/year. Includes briefings. **Conventions/Meetings:** periodic conference.

17034 ■ Inter-American Conference of Ministers of Labor (IACML)
c/o Organization of American States
1889 F St. NW, 6th Fl.
Washington, DC 20006-4401
Ph: (202)458-3000
Fax: (202)458-3280
E-mail: mcamacho@oas.org
URL: http://www.oas.org/dsd
Contact: Cesar Gaviria, Sec. Gen.
Founded: 1898. **Members:** 34. **Staff:** 650. **Budget:** $7,600,000. **Multinational. Description:** Promotes peace, security, democracy, human rights, economic and social development throughout the Americas. **Libraries: Type:** open to the public. **Subjects:** political, economic, social.

17035 ■ International People's Democratic Uhuru Movement (InPDUM)
1245 18th Ave. S
St. Petersburg, FL 33705
Ph: (727)502-0575
E-mail: info@inpdum.org
URL: http://www.inpdum.org
Contact: Chimurenga Waller, Pres.
Founded: 1991. **Membership Dues:** general, $15 (annual). **Local Groups:** 12. **Multinational. Description:** Advances the welfare of African people around the world. Defends the international democratic rights of all colonized African communities. Works to fight for the rights of African people to have freedom of speech, freedom of assembly, freedom to live without the constant threat of police violence and the right to access to adequate food, shelter and clothing.

17036 ■ International Republican Institute - USA (IRI)
1225 Eye St. NW, Ste.700
Washington, DC 20005
Ph: (202)408-9450
Fax: (202)408-9462
E-mail: volunteer@iri.org
URL: http://www.iri.org
Contact: Lorne Craner, Pres.
Founded: 1983. **Staff:** 60. **Budget:** $13,000,000. **Description:** Conducts programs outside the United States to promote democracy and strengthen free-markets, and the rule-of-law. Conducts programs in Afghanistan, Albania, Angola, Azerbaijan, Belarus, Bulgaria, Burma, Burundi, Cambodia, China, Cuba, Djibouti, El Salvador, Georgia, Guatemala, Haiti, Indonesia, Kenya, Liberia, Macedonia, Malaysia, Mexico, Mongolia, Morocco, Nicaragua, Nigeria, Peru, Pakistan, Poland, Romania, Russia, Serbia, Slovakia, Somaliland, South Africa, Sudan, East Timor, Turkey, Ukraine, Venezuela, West Bank and Gaza Strip, Western Sahara, and Zimbabwe. **Libraries: Type:** open to the public. **Awards:** Freedom Award. **Type:** recognition. **Computer Services:** database ● mailing lists ● online services. **Subgroups:** Regional Advisory Working. **Formerly:** (1991) National Republican Institute for International Affairs. **Publications:** *Country Specific Reports*, periodic ● *IRI Newsletter*, quarterly. Features current news and activities of the organization. **Circulation:** 7,500 ● Annual Report, annual. **Conventions/Meetings:** periodic meeting, foreign policy, national security forum.

17037 ■ National Endowment for Democracy (NED)
1025 F St. NW, Ste.800
Washington, DC 20004
Ph: (202)293-9700
Fax: (202)378-9407
E-mail: info@ned.org
URL: http://www.ned.org
Contact: Carl Gershman, Pres.
Founded: 1983. **Staff:** 60. **Budget:** $31,000,000. **Description:** A private, grant-making, government-financed effort promoting worldwide development of democratic values and human rights and freedoms through private sector initiatives. Provides the opportunity for exchange between democratic groups abroad and U.S. private sector groups such as the two major political parties, labor, and business. Encourages U.S. nongovernmental participation in democratic training programs and institution-building abroad; seeks to strengthen democratic electoral processes abroad. Supports programs in the areas of pluralism; democratic governance and political processes; education, culture, and communications; international cooperation. **Libraries: Type:** open to the public. **Holdings:** 15,000. **Subjects:** democracy, international affairs, human rights, civil education. **Awards:** Democracy Award. **Frequency:** annual. **Type:** recognition. **Recipient:** for NED grantees ● Democracy Service Award. **Frequency:** annual. **Type:** medal. **Recipient:** to individuals who have made significant contributions to the progress of democracy around the world. **Computer Services:** database, democracy projects ● online services, OCLC, Internet access, First Search. **Committees:** International; Research Center. **Publications:** *Journal of Democracy*, quarterly. Monitors and analyzes democratic regimes and movements in scores of countries around the world. **Price:** $30.00 /year for individuals; $85.50 /year for institutions (online only); $95.00 /year for institutions. ISSN: 1045-5736. **Circulation:** 5,000. **Advertising:** accepted. Alternate Formats: online ● *National Endowment for Democracy Newsletter*, annual. Features current issues and activities of the organization. ● Annual Report, annual. Alternate Formats: online. **Conventions/Meetings:** biennial World Movement for Democracy - general assembly, brings together democratic activists from around the world.

17038 ■ ReclaimDemocracy.org
222 S Black Ave.
Bozeman, MT 59715
Ph: (406)582-1224
E-mail: info@reclaimdemocracy.org
URL: http://reclaimdemocracy.org
Contact: Jeff Milchen, Exec. Dir./Founder
Founded: 1999. **Description:** Strives to revoke the power of money and corporations to control government and civic society. Aims to reverse the precedent of granting Bill of Rights protections to corporations. **Computer Services:** database, primers ● information services, issues resources. **Publications:** *The Insurgent*, quarterly. Newsletter. Contains significant news in the democracy movement.

Democratic Party

17039 ■ Association of State Democratic Chairs (ASDC)
430 S Capitol St. SE
Washington, DC 20003
Ph: (202)479-5121
E-mail: info@stateparty.org
Contact: Ann Fishman, Exec.Dir.
Founded: 1969. **Members:** 168. **Staff:** 3. **Regional Groups:** 4. **State Groups:** 56. **Description:** State chairs and vice chairs of the Democratic party. Works with the Democratic National Committee (see separate entry) and other top party leaders to strengthen the state parties' structures around the country. Compiles statistics; gives seminars and training workshops; consults with state party offices; provides speakers from national offices. Provides legal assistance, technical assistance, and informational services to state parties. Administers and disburses funds to state parties from small donor telemarketing programs. Conducts other fundraising. **Libraries: Type:** not open to the public. **Subjects:** campaign operations, state party management. **Computer Services:** database ● mailing lists, available to public. **Committees:** Fundraising; Grassroots Party Building; Technology. **Affiliated With:** Democratic National Committee. **Formerly:** (1982) Association of State Democratic Chairmen. **Publications:** *The ASDC Party Faxline*, weekly. Newsletter. **Circulation:** 200 ● *Directory of State Chairs, Vice Chairs, Executive Directors and State Headquarters*, monthly. **Circulation:** 200 ● *State Chairs Manual*, annual ● *State Party Operations Handbook*, annual. **Conventions/Meetings:** semiannual meeting (exhibits).

17040 ■ College Democrats of America (CDA)
430 S Capitol St. SE
Washington, DC 20003-4024
Ph: (202)863-8018
E-mail: director@collegedems.com
URL: http://www.collegedems.com
Contact: LaToia Jones, Exec. Dir.
Founded: 1932. **Members:** 80,000. **Membership Dues:** chapter charter, $25 (annual). **Staff:** 2. **Regional Groups:** 12. **State Groups:** 50. **National Groups:** 1,500. **Description:** National chapters on college campuses comprising students, both undergraduate and graduate. Seeks to stimulate in young people an active interest in government affairs; to encourage involvement in the political process; to promote the principles of the Democratic Party; and to elect Democrats to all levels of office. **Affiliated With:** Democratic National Committee; Young Democrats of America. **Formerly:** (1959) College Democrats; (1987) College Young Democrats of America. **Publications:** *Action*, monthly. Legislative alerts. ● *CDA News*, monthly. Newsletter. **Price:** free. **Circulation:** 5,000. **Advertising:** accepted ● Brochure, annual. **Conventions/Meetings:** annual convention and conference - always June in Washington, DC.

17041 ■ Committee for a Democratic Majority (CDM)
301 4th St. NE, Ste.202
Washington, DC 20002
E-mail: democraticmajority@democraticmajority.com
URL: http://www.democraticmajority.com
Contact: Sen. Edward M. Kennedy, Founder
Founded: 1981. **Members:** 200,000. **Staff:** 5. **Budget:** $1,500,000. **Description:** National political action committee formed to assist Democratic candidates in upcoming U.S. House and Senate races. **Convention/Meeting:** none. **Departments:** Political Finance; Political Research. **Formerly:** (1998) Fund for a Democratic Majority. **Publications:** Newsletter, annual.

17042 ■ Democratic Congressional Campaign Committee (DCCC)
430 S Capitol St. SE
Washington, DC 20003
Ph: (202)863-1500
Fax: (202)485-3436
E-mail: dccc@dccc.org
URL: http://www.dccc.org
Contact: Rahm Emanuel, Chm.
Founded: 1882. **Members:** 51. **Staff:** 60. **Description:** Represents democrats who are members of the U.S. House of Representatives. Aims to increase the number of Democrats in the U.S. House of Representatives. Conducts fundraising activities, research, communications, and a variety of political support programs.

17043 ■ Democratic Leadership Council (DLC)
600 Pennsylvania Ave. SE, Ste.400
Washington, DC 20003-4350
Ph: (202)546-0007
Free: (800)546-0027
Fax: (202)544-5002
E-mail: donations@dlcppi.org
URL: http://www.dlc.org
Contact: Al From, Founder/CEO

Founded: 1985. **Members:** 400. **Membership Dues:** mainstream movement, $50 (annual) ● student, $25 (annual) ● fund, $500 (annual) ● new democrat forum, $2,500 (annual). **Staff:** 40. **State Groups:** 10. **Description:** Elected Democrats from all government levels. Seeks to serve as a catalyst for the development of progressive ideas and policy innovation beneficial to the Democratic Party. Believes that "Democrats should be the party that embraces change, that risks new departures, and that speaks to broad, national purposes." Sponsors public forums, town hall meetings, and seminars. **Publications:** *Blueprint: Ideas for a New Century*, bimonthly. Magazine. **Price:** included in membership dues; $25.00 /year for nonmembers. ISSN: 1045-8441 ● *New Democrat*. Magazine. **Price:** $25.00/year in U.S.; $75.00 overseas ● Also publishes policy/position papers. **Conventions/Meetings:** annual National Conversation - conference.

17044 ■ Democratic National Committee (DNC)
430 S Capitol St. SE
Washington, DC 20003
Ph: (202)863-8000
Free: (877)336-7200
Fax: (202)863-8081
URL: http://www.democrats.org/index.html
Contact: Gov. Howard Dean, Chm.

Founded: 1848. **Members:** 440. **Staff:** 125. **Regional Groups:** 4. **State Groups:** 57. **Languages:** English, Spanish. **Description:** Political organization formed to promote and teach Democratic interests and beliefs. Maintains liaison between the state organizations and national officers and administration; organizes and sponsors national political activities; provides technical assistance to political candidates; assembles representative groups from home states to attend national functions. Sponsors Democratic candidate training seminars. **Committees:** Credentials; Democratic Congressional Campaign; Democratic Legislative Campaign; State Participation. **Councils:** Communications; Computer; Direct Mail; Fundraising; Judicial; National Education and Training; Policy and Information; Political. **Affiliated With:** Association of State Democratic Chairs. **Publications:** *Delegate Selection Rules for Conventions* ● *Democratic National Committee Membership List*, 6-12/year. Membership Directory ● *Final Calls to Conventions* ● *Official Proceedings of National Convention*, quadrennial. **Conventions/Meetings:** quadrennial convention.

17045 ■ Democratic Senatorial Campaign Committee (DSCC)
PO Box 96047
Washington, DC 20077
Ph: (202)224-2447
Fax: (202)969-0354
E-mail: info@dscc.org
URL: http://www.dscc.org
Contact: Sen. Charles Schumer, Chm.

Founded: 1916. **Staff:** 25. **For-Profit. Description:** Provides financial and political support to Democratic U.S. Senatorial candidates. **Publications:** none. **Convention/Meeting:** none.

17046 ■ Democrats Abroad (DA)
430 S Capitol St. SE
Washington, DC 20003
Ph: (202)488-5073
Fax: (202)863-8174

E-mail: info@democratsabroad.org
URL: http://www.democratsabroad.org
Contact: Alexandra Chalupa, Exec. Dir.

Founded: 1964. **Members:** 11,000. **Staff:** 1. **Regional Groups:** 32. **Description:** American citizens living outside the U.S. who seek to nominate and elect Democratic party candidates to public office in the U.S. Works to insure the voting rights of Americans abroad and the citizenship rights of American children born overseas; seeks fair taxation and health care insurance for American residents abroad. Stimulates voter registration; elects delegates to U.S. national party conventions; provides grassroots feedback on the impact of U.S. foreign policy decisions. Disseminates political information; conducts worldwide primaries; raises funds. Maintains committees in 30 countries; administered by the Democratic Party Committee Abroad. **Affiliated With:** Democratic National Committee. **Also Known As:** Democratic Party Committee Abroad. **Publications:** *Democrats Abroad Report*, periodic. Directory ● *Letter From Washington*, monthly. Newsletter. Provides analysis of Washington politics. **Price:** $35.00. Alternate Formats: online ● *Overseas Democrat*, quarterly. Newsletter. **Advertising:** accepted. **Conventions/Meetings:** quadrennial World Nominating Convention.

17047 ■ National Democratic Club (NDC)
30 Ivy St. SE
Washington, DC 20003
Ph: (202)543-2035
Fax: (202)479-4273
E-mail: club@natdemclub.org
URL: http://www.natdemclub.org
Contact: Christine Hilty, Gen. Mgr.

Founded: 1834. **Members:** 1,200. **Membership Dues:** resident $80 (monthly) ● non-resident, $20 (monthly) ● government, $35 (monthly) ● regular of Congress, $25 (monthly) ● retired, $130 (annual) ● life, $5,000 ● associate (ages 21-29), $5 (monthly). **Description:** Serves as a democratic social and political club. **Telecommunication Services:** electronic mail, chilty3@earthlink.net. **Committees:** Election. **Publications:** *Inside*. Newsletter. Alternate Formats: online ● Bulletin, monthly.

17048 ■ National Federation of Democratic Women (NFDW)
c/o Barbara Mansfield, Pres.
PO Box 72
Bastrop, LA 71221
Ph: (318)281-2356
Fax: (318)281-2736
E-mail: president@nfdw.com
URL: http://nfdw.com
Contact: Barbara Mansfield, Pres.

Founded: 1972. **Members:** 300,000. **Budget:** $50,000. **Regional Groups:** 4. **State Groups:** 42. **Description:** Acts as democratic women's organization; state, local, and regional clubs; individuals. Works to develop leadership among women locally and nationally, both as party workers and elected public officials. Aims to unite the women of the party and to encourage full participation of women on every level of the party structure by promoting the exchange of ideas and communication. Maintains biographical archives and special study groups; conducts specialized education programs; offers an internship. **Awards: Type:** recognition. **Committees:** Legislative; Status of Women. **Affiliated With:** Democratic National Committee. **Publications:** *The Communicator*, quarterly. Includes president's message and regional reports. **Price:** $10.00/year. **Circulation:** 500. **Advertising:** accepted ● Directory, semiannual. **Conventions/Meetings:** annual convention (exhibits).

17049 ■ New Democratic Dimensions (NDD)
152 Madison Ave., Ste.804
New York, NY 10016-5424
Ph: (212)481-7251
Fax: (212)481-9015

E-mail: nddmain@newdd.org
URL: http://newdd.org
Contact: Thomas Acosta, Chm.

Founded: 1981. **Members:** 2,000. **Membership Dues:** president's club, $1,000 (annual) ● liberty club, $250 (annual) ● regular, $100 (annual). **State Groups:** 2. **Description:** Democrats from all walks of life united to foster unity and new leadership within the Democratic Party. Provides members with the opportunity to meet candidates and elected party officials. Encourages members' involvement in Democratic Party activities between elections as well as at election time. Sponsors registration drives and televised and nontelevised debates. Works with student political groups. Conducts research and fundraisers for candidates. Offers lecture series and educational programs; state groups hold bimonthly issue forums. Bestows citizen's achievement awards; maintains speakers' bureau. **Committees:** Campaign; New Democratic Dimensions. **Publications:** *America's Future*, quarterly. Newsletter. Covers Democratic policies on issues of the future. **Price:** included in membership dues. **Advertising:** accepted.

17050 ■ Woman's National Democratic Club (WNDC)
1526 New Hampshire Ave. NW
Washington, DC 20036
Ph: (202)232-7363
Fax: (202)986-2791
E-mail: info@democraticwoman.org
URL: http://www.democraticwoman.org
Contact: Sandra Bieri, Contact

Founded: 1922. **Members:** 1,000. **Membership Dues:** individual, $540 (annual) ● family, $816 (annual) ● young Democrat, $276 (annual) ● non-resident, $144 (annual) ● friend, $70 (annual). **Staff:** 20. **Budget:** $1,300,000. **Description:** Democratic party members concerned with analyzing educational, social, and political issues to affect an informed democratic opinion. Works to study the processes of democracy and procedures of government. Renders educational and social services to the community. Educates members in political science, economics, and the arts; activities include travel events and panel discussions. Maintains Public Policy Committee composed of task force committees on subjects such as foreign policy, the economy, social security, education, energy, the environment, and human rights. **Libraries: Type:** reference. **Holdings:** 1,500; books. **Subjects:** prominent Democrats, political leaders in the nation's history. **Awards:** Democratic Woman of the Year. **Frequency:** annual. **Type:** recognition. **Recipient:** to an outstanding Democratic woman. **Publications:** *Democratic Women: An Oral History of the Woman's National Democratic Club*. Book. **Price:** $19.95 ● *WNDC News*, monthly. Newsletter. Includes calendar of events. **Price:** included in membership dues. **Conventions/Meetings:** biweekly luncheon and dinner ● seminar.

17051 ■ Women's Leadership Forum (WLF)
c/o The Democratic Party Headquarters
430 S Capitol St. SE
Washington, DC 20003
Ph: (202)479-5103 (202)863-8000
Free: (877)336-7200
Fax: (202)479-5149
E-mail: wlf@dnc.org
URL: http://www.democrats.org/a/communities/women/womens_leadership_forum
Contact: Emily Berman, Dir.

Founded: 1993. **Membership Dues:** individual, $1,000 (annual). **State Groups:** 14. **Description:** Women supporting the public policies of the Democratic Party. Promotes increased participation by women in the Party; seeks to advance the electoral prospects of Democratic candidates. Conducts educational and fundraising activities; works to influence Party positions on issues of interest to women. Assists in the formation of grass roots organizations of Democratic women. **Publications:** *Week in Review*, weekly. Newsletter. **Conventions/Meetings:** annual National Issues Conference.

17052 ■ Young Democrats of America (YDA)
PO Box 77496
Washington, DC 20013-8496
Ph: (202)639-8585
Free: (877)639-8585
Fax: (202)318-3221
E-mail: office@yda.org
URL: http://www.yda.org
Contact: Chris Gallaway, Pres.
Founded: 1932. **Members:** 100,000. **Staff:** 1. **Regional Groups:** 8. **State Groups:** 50. **Local Groups:** 2,000. **Description:** A division of the Democratic National Committee (see separate entry); official youth (35 and under) organization of the Democratic Party. Seeks to encourage young men and women to take an active part in politics and to become members of the Democratic Party. Acts as a forum for discussion of important issues. Provides opportunity to become acquainted with candidates for office and to gain experience necessary for future leadership in politics and government. Conducts such activities as voter registration, preparation and distribution of campaign literature, organization of rallies and caravans, collegiate political activity, political workshops, fundraising, poll watching, recruitment of new members, study sessions, and political publicity. **Awards: Type:** recognition. **Computer Services:** Mailing lists. **Caucuses:** Disabilities Issues; Gay, Lesbian, and Bisexual; Labor; Minorities; Women. **Committees:** Affirmative Action; Campaign; Credentials; Resolutions; Rules and Charter; Site Selection. **Councils:** Judicial. **Affiliated With:** American Council of Young Political Leaders; Democratic National Committee. **Formerly:** (1978) Young Democratic Club of America. **Publications:** *Convention Program State Offices Directory*, semiannual ● *The Young Democrat*, quarterly ● Manuals. Contains information on voter registration. **Conventions/Meetings:** competition ● quarterly meeting.

Disabled

17053 ■ American Disabled for Attendant Program Today (ADAPT)
201 S Cherokee St.
Denver, CO 80223
Ph: (303)733-9324
Fax: (303)733-6211
E-mail: adapt@adapt.org
URL: http://www.adapt.org
Contact: Babs Johnson, Contact
Founded: 1983. **Members:** 5,000. **State Groups:** 34. **Local Groups:** 50. **Description:** Promotes federal funding of in-home support services for the elderly and disabled in an effort to decrease the number of individuals being placed in nursing homes. **Telecommunication Services:** TDD, (303)733-0047. **Formerly:** (1991) American Disabled for Accessible Public Transit. **Publications:** *Incitement*, periodic. Newsletter. **Circulation:** 4,000. Alternate Formats: magnetic tape; online. **Conventions/Meetings:** semiannual meeting.

17054 ■ APSE: The Network on Employment
1627 Monument Ave.
Richmond, VA 23220
Ph: (804)278-9187
Fax: (804)278-9377
E-mail: apse@apse.org
URL: http://www.apse.org
Contact: Celane McWhorter, Exec. Dir.
Founded: 1988. **Membership Dues:** professional, $55-$100 ● non-professional family, student, $40 ● basic organizational, $640 ● contributing, $840 ● gold contributing, $1,050 ● supported employee, $20. **Multinational. Description:** Committed to supported employment, which enables people with disabilities who have not been successfully employed to work and contribute to society. **Formerly:** (2006) Association for Persons in Supported Employment. **Publications:** *The Advance*, quarterly. Newsletter. **Price:** included in membership dues; $140.00 for nonmembers. **Advertising:** accepted. Alternate Formats: online ● *Journal of Vocational Rehabilitation*. **Price:**

included in membership dues; $453.00 for nonmembers. Alternate Formats: online. **Conventions/Meetings:** annual conference.

17055 ■ Challenge International
1204 Ina Ln.
McLean, VA 22102-1704
Ph: (703)821-3385
Fax: (703)790-1791
E-mail: mndoremus@msn.com
Contact: Mary Nemec Doremus, Founding Pres.
Founded: 1983. **Budget:** $250,000. **Description:** A media awareness campaign designed to make disability a familiar and comfortable issue by closing the communication gap between the public and the disabled community. Purposes are to: serve the disabled community by changing the way in which Americans perceive disability and disabled individuals; promote positive images of disabled persons in the media through newspaper articles, radio and television news reports, television shows, motion pictures, and advertisements; educate the public about disability issues; serve as clearinghouse on the needs of the disabled and the organizations that represent them; assist the media so that they report realistically and positively on disability and disabled persons; encourage the acceptance of people with disabilities, thus enabling them to become more productive, contributing members of society. Other activities include: providing internships for qualified disabled persons to pursue careers in media-related fields; establishing a speakers' bureau; designing school programs and educational materials. **Convention/Meeting:** none. **Formerly:** (1985) National Challenge Committee of the Disabled; (1988) National Challenge Committee on Disability.

17056 ■ Consortium for Citizens with Disabilities (CCD)
1660 L St. NW, Ste.700
Washington, DC 20036
Ph: (202)783-2229
Fax: (202)783-8250
E-mail: info@c-c-d.org
URL: http://www.c-c-d.org
Contact: Marty Ford, Chm.
Founded: 1973. **Members:** 100. **Description:** Advocates for national policy that ensures self-determination, independence, empowerment, integration and inclusion of children and adults with disabilities. **Task Forces:** Child Abuse; Developmental Disabilities; Education; Employment and Training; Fiscal Policy; Health; Housing; Long Term Services and Supports; Prevention; Rights; Social Security; Technology and Telecommunications; Transportation; Work Incentives Implementation.

17057 ■ Inter-National Association of Business, Industry and Rehabilitation (I-NABIR)
PO Box 15242
Washington, DC 20003
Ph: (202)543-6353
E-mail: harles@inabir.org
URL: http://www.inabir.org
Contact: Charles Harles, Exec. Dir.
Founded: 1985. **Members:** 100. **Description:** Businesses, rehabilitation service providers, schools and universities, trade unions, and associations placing people with disabilities into employment using a model of partnership with community business and employers. **Publications:** Newsletter. **Conventions/Meetings:** annual meeting.

17058 ■ National Black Deaf Advocates (NBDA)
c/o Cory L. Parker, Sec.
PO Box 1126
Asheville, NC 28802-1126
E-mail: president@nbda.org
URL: http://www.nbda.org
Contact: Thomas Samuels, Pres.
Founded: 1982. **Membership Dues:** associate, $15 (annual) ● sponsor, $100 (annual) ● organization, $250 (annual) ● corporate/professional, $500 (annual). **Local Groups:** 20. **Description:** Advocates

for the rights of African-American deaf and hearing impaired people. Seeks to promote the well-being, culture and empowerment of African-Americans who are deaf or hard of hearing. Conducts educational outreach programs; offers leadership training and training for interpreters and transliterators of color. Sponsors pageant. **Awards:** Miss Black Deaf of America. **Frequency:** annual. **Type:** recognition. **Recipient:** for black deaf woman ● NBDA Scholarship. **Frequency:** annual. **Type:** scholarship. **Recipient:** for black deaf or hard of hearing undergraduate or graduate student member of the organization. **Computer Services:** Mailing lists. **Committees:** Archives; Senior Citizen; Training for Interpreters and Transliterators of Color. **Programs:** Black Deaf History; Family Support Network; Scholarships Pledge; Youth Empowerment Summit. **Projects:** Andrew Foster Sculpture and Cultural Recognition. **Publications:** *NBDA Connections*, quarterly. Newsletter. **Price:** included in membership dues. **Advertising:** accepted. **Conventions/Meetings:** annual convention ● workshop.

17059 ■ National Organization on Disability (NOD)
910 16th St. NW, Ste.600
Washington, DC 20006
Ph: (202)293-5960
Fax: (202)293-7999
E-mail: ability@nod.org
URL: http://www.nod.org
Contact: Michael R. Deland, Pres.
Founded: 1982. **Staff:** 20. **Budget:** $1,200,000. **Description:** Works to promote the full and equal participation of people with disabilities in all aspects of life. **Awards:** Accessible American Community Award. **Frequency:** annual. **Type:** recognition ● FDR International Award. **Frequency:** annual. **Type:** recognition ● N.O.D National Partner Organization Awards. **Frequency:** annual. **Type:** recognition. **Computer Services:** Online services, e-newsletter. **Telecommunication Services:** TDD, (202)293-5968. **Programs:** Community Partnership; National Partnership.

17060 ■ Society for Accessible Travel and Hospitality (SATH)
347 5th Ave., Ste.610
New York, NY 10016
Ph: (212)447-7284
Fax: (212)725-8253
E-mail: sathtravel@aol.com
URL: http://www.sath.org
Contact: Jani Nayar, Exec. Coor.
Founded: 1976. **Members:** 2,700. **Membership Dues:** individual, homebased agent, $49 (annual) ● patron, $250 (annual) ● senior/student, $29 (annual) ● life, $1,000 ● agency/organization, $99 (annual) ● corporate sponsor, $2,500 (annual). **Staff:** 5. **Languages:** English, French. **Description:** Travel professionals, consumers with disabilities, other individuals and corporations supporting this mission. Strives to raise awareness of needs of all travelers with disabilities, remove physical and attitudinal barriers to free access and expand travel opportunities in the United States and abroad. Operates speaker's bureau and library. Helps create training programs and materials, improve customer service and develop better outreach and marketing. Performs access audits of hotels, restaurants and attractions; serves as clearinghouse for access information. **Libraries: Type:** reference. **Holdings:** 300. **Subjects:** statistics on potential travel market for various handicapped groups and their locations. **Awards:** Noah Award. **Frequency:** annual. **Type:** recognition. **Recipient:** for role models in matters relating to handicapped travel. **Committees:** Adaptive Equipment; Sports and Adventure Travel. **Affiliated With:** American Society of Travel Agents. **Formerly:** (2005) Society for Accessible Travel for the Handicapped. **Publications:** *Open World*, quarterly. Magazine. Contains articles on travel and related matters of interest to all handicapped persons. **Price:** included in membership dues. **Price:** $13.00 /year for nonmembers, plus shipping and handling; $24.00/2 years for nonmembers, plus shipping and handling; $30.00/3 years for

nonmembers, plus shipping and handling. **Circulation:** 10,000. **Advertising:** accepted ● *SATH Newsletter* ● Information sheets on matter related to travel. The travel related Industries Accessibility Guide. **Conventions/Meetings:** annual World Travel Congress for Travellers with Disabilities and the Mature - congress and trade show, for all items and services related to disability travel (exhibits).

Disarmament

17061 ■ Abolition 2000
215 Lexington Ave., Ste.1001
New York, NY 10016
Ph: (212)726-9161
Fax: (212)726-9160
E-mail: admin@abolition2000.org
URL: http://www.abolition2000.org
Contact: Emma McGregor-Mento, Outreach and Development Coor.
Founded: 1995. **Members:** 2,039. **Staff:** 1. **Budget:** $50,000. **Languages:** English, French, German, Romanian, Russian, Spanish. **Multinational. Description:** Individuals and organizations. Promotes nuclear disarmament. Serves as a clearinghouse on nuclear weapons and disarmament issues; sponsors educational programs. **Publications:** *Abolition 2000 Grassroots*, monthly. Newsletter. **Price:** free for members. Alternate Formats: online. **Conventions/Meetings:** annual meeting.

17062 ■ Arms Control Association/Arms Control Today (ACA)
1150 Connecticut Ave. NW, Ste.620
Washington, DC 20036
Ph: (202)463-8270
Fax: (202)463-8273
E-mail: aca@armscontrol.org
URL: http://www.armscontrol.org
Contact: Daryl G. Kimball, Exec. Dir.
Founded: 1971. **Members:** 1,500. **Membership Dues:** regular, $65 (annual) ● student, $30 (annual) ● contributing, $100 (annual) ● international associate, $80 (annual) ● sustaining, $500 (annual). **Staff:** 9. **Budget:** $650,000. **Description:** Formed by a group of individuals "with extensive backgrounds in the planning, negotiation, and management of arms control and disarmament programs as a means to improve U.S. and world security." Strives to promote public understanding of effective policies and programs in national arms control and disarmament. Conducts research on arms control. Provides information and analysis on request to the media and appropriate officials of the Executive Branch and Congress. Conducts press conferences. **Libraries: Type:** reference. **Holdings:** 3,000. **Computer Services:** Mailing lists, ACA E-Update Listserv. **Publications:** *Arms Control Today*, 10/year. Journal. Includes book reviews, bibliography, editorials, news, analyses and commentary, and bibliography. Double issues occur in Jan./Feb. and June/July. **Price:** $60.00 /year for individuals in U.S.; $80.00 /year for institutions in U.S.; $75.00 /year for individuals outside U.S.; $85.00 /year for institutions outside U.S. ISSN: 0196-125X. **Circulation:** 1,800. **Advertising:** accepted. Also Cited As: *ACT* ● Books ● Reports ● Newsletter. **Conventions/Meetings:** periodic Arms Control Conference ● annual meeting - always January, Washington, DC.

17063 ■ Center for Economic Conversion (CEC)
222 View St.
Mountain View, CA 94041-1344
Ph: (650)968-8798
Fax: (650)968-1126
E-mail: cec@igc.org
URL: http://cec.igc.org/cec
Contact: Joan Holtzman PhD, Exec. Dir.
Founded: 1975. **Members:** 2,000. **Membership Dues:** regular, $35 (annual) ● limited income, $15 (annual). **Budget:** $65,000. **Description:** Works to redirect the economy to meet the human needs and works in harmony with the environment. Focuses on

educating the public about sustainability and sustainable economic development. Activities include: conversion-planning assistance to public officials and community groups, technical assistance on sustainable building practices to non-profit and for-profit developers, producing a variety of educational materials including a newly revised Sustainable Economics Curriculum designed to supplement traditional high school economics courses. **Libraries: Type:** reference. **Holdings:** archival material, books, clippings, periodicals. **Subjects:** conversion, military spending, sustainability. **Formerly:** (1984) Mid-Peninsula Conversion Project. **Publications:** *Converting Cold War Economy* ● *Converting to Sustainability Series* ● *Fact Sheets* ● *Perspectives Newsletter*, quarterly. Provides information about the economic conversion movement. **Price:** included in membership dues; $35.00 /year for nonmembers. **Circulation:** 5,000 ● *Sustainable Economics Curriculum.*

17064 ■ Clear Path International (CPI)
321 High School Rd. NE, No. 574
Bainbridge Island, WA 98110
Ph: (206)780-5964 (802)867-4406
E-mail: west@cpi.org
URL: http://www.cpi.org
Contact: Imbert Matthee, Pres./Co-Founder
Founded: 2000. **Members:** 2,600. **Staff:** 6. **Budget:** $500,000. **State Groups:** 2. **Languages:** English, French, Vietnamese. **Multinational. Description:** Humanitarian mine action in Southeast Asia, including landmine and bomb removal, mine survivor assistance, and hospital support. **Telecommunication Services:** electronic mail, info@clearpathinternational.org. **Publications:** Newsletter, quarterly. Contains information about program activities in Vietnam, Cambodia, and Thailand. **Price:** free. **Circulation:** 3,000. **Advertising:** accepted. **Conventions/Meetings:** Charity Fairs - meeting ● festival - fall.

17065 ■ Council for a Livable World (CLW)
322 4th St. NE
Washington, DC 20002
Ph: (202)543-4100
Fax: (202)543-6297
E-mail: clw@clw.org
URL: http://www.clw.org
Contact: John Isaacs, Pres./Exec. Dir.
Founded: 1962. **Members:** 100,000. **Staff:** 12. **Budget:** $600,000. **Description:** Endorses and raises funds for Senate candidates who support arms control and reduced military spending. Concentrates efforts on the U.S. Senate, "which has unique powers in foreign affairs and military spending". Maintains liaison with Peace Pac, a lobby group for the U.S. House of Representatives. Sends alerts to members outlining key arms control legislation. **Libraries: Type:** reference. **Telecommunication Services:** 24-hour hotline, arms control, (202)543-0006. **Affiliated With:** Peace Pac. **Publications:** *Candidate Profiles*, monthly. Pamphlet. Available during election cycle(s). ● *Election Analysis, Legislation Updates*, periodic. Newsletter ● *Senate National Security Index: 1997-1998 Voting Record*, annual. **Conventions/Meetings:** bimonthly board meeting ● periodic meeting, fundraiser.

17066 ■ Council for a Livable World Education Fund (CLWEF)
c/o Council for a Livable World
322 4th St. NE
Washington, DC 20002
Ph: (202)543-4100
Fax: (202)543-6297
E-mail: clw@clw.org
URL: http://www.clw.org
Contact: Thomas A. Cardamone Jr., Exec. Dir.
Founded: 1980. **Staff:** 16. **Budget:** $981,000. **Description:** Seeks to inform policy-makers, opinion-shapers, and voters about the adverse effects of relying on nuclear weapons for security, exporting excessive amounts of military equipment around the globe, and increasing the military budget for unnecessary weapons systems. Includes three permanent projects: the Project to Eliminate Weapons of Mass Destruction, the Military Spending Monitoring Project, and

the Arms Trade Reduction Project. **Libraries: Type:** reference. **Subjects:** global arms sales, weapons of mass destruction, military budget, non-proliferation. **Awards: Type:** recognition. **Computer Services:** Mailing lists. **Boards:** Directors. **Publications:** *Arms Control Briefing Book: Arms Control & Security in the Post-Cold War Era-104th Congress.* **Price:** $6.00 ● *Arms Trade News*, monthly. Newsletter. Provides information on and analysis of the conventional arms trade. **Price:** free. **Circulation:** 2,000 ● *Behind the Numbers: An Analysis of the Fiscal Year 2001 Defense Budget.* Book. **Price:** free ● *The Briefing Book on Peacekeeping: The U.S. Role in United Nations Peace Operations.* **Price:** free ● *Briefing Book on The Nonproliferation of Nuclear Weapons.* **Price:** $5.00 ● *Pushing the Limits: The Decision on National Missile Defense.* Book. **Price:** free. Alternate Formats: online.

17067 ■ Demilitarization for Democracy (DFD)
2001 S St. NW, Ste.630
Washington, DC 20009
Ph: (202)319-7191
Fax: (202)319-7194
E-mail: pdd@clark.net
Contact: Dr. Caleb Rossiter, Founder/Dir.
Founded: 1992. **Description:** Works as action tank in the fight against arms transfers, training and other U.S. military and financial support for non-democratic governments. **Projects:** Campaign to Ban Landmines; No Arms to Dictators.

17068 ■ Disarm Education Fund (DEF)
113 Univ. Pl., 8th Fl.
New York, NY 10003
Ph: (212)353-9800
Fax: (212)353-9676
E-mail: bschwartz@disarm.org
URL: http://www.disarm.org
Contact: Robert Schwartz, Exec. Dir.
Founded: 1976. **Members:** 18,000. **Budget:** $685,000. **Description:** Promotes international peace, social justice, and self-determination through opposition to military intervention and nuclear arms. Supports a demilitarized foreign policy and believes that freedom from war is a fundamental human right. Stresses that U.S. foreign policy must be carried out with the consent of the American people. Representatives from professional, human rights, and church organizations are sent to various countries to provide information, monitor U.S. military intervention, and brief Congress. Maintains speakers' bureau. **Projects:** Central American Peace Campaign; Cuban Medical. **Publications:** Report, periodic.

17069 ■ Economists for Peace and Security (EPS)
c/o The Levy Institute
PO Box 5000
Annandale-on-Hudson, NY 12504
Ph: (845)758-0917
Fax: (845)758-1149
E-mail: info@epsusa.org
URL: http://www.epsusa.org
Contact: Ms. Thea Harvey, Exec. Dir.
Founded: 1989. **Members:** 800. **Membership Dues:** basic, $35 (annual) ● student, $10 (annual) ● supporting, $50 (annual) ● sustaining donor, $100 (annual) ● major donor, $250 (annual) ● sustaining patron, $1,000 (annual). **Staff:** 3. **Budget:** $175,000. **Multinational. Description:** Represents economists. Has affiliates in Russia, Japan, UK, South Africa, France, Chile, Israel, India, Netherlands, Australia and Canada. Promotes reduction in global military spending. Encourages support for world disarmament. Strives to solve international disputes without war. Encourages writing and publication of books and articles to inform public, students, and political leaders on human welfare and environmental concerns. Conducts seminars to influence governmental policy. **Computer Services:** Mailing lists. **Formerly:** (2005) Economists Allied for Arms Reduction. **Publications:** *EPS Quarterly.* Newsletters. Contains themed issues with in-depth articles relating to its mission. **Price:** $35.00 for nonmembers; free for members. **Circula-**

tion: 1,000. Alternate Formats: online. **Conventions/Meetings:** annual conference (exhibits) ● annual workshop, co-sponsors panels with the Peace Science Society and the American Economic Association on topics of peace economics such as conversion, development and disarmament, arms trades, and resource allocation.

17070 ■ Institute for Defense and Disarmament Studies (IDDS)
675 Massachusetts Ave.
Cambridge, MA 02139
Ph: (617)354-4337
Fax: (617)354-1450
E-mail: info@idds.org
URL: http://www.idds.org
Contact: Ret. Ambassador Jonathan Dean, Pres.
Founded: 1980. **Staff:** 7. **Budget:** $500,000. **Description:** Serves as a clearinghouse to educate the public on alternative defense policies and cooperative security. Conducts research on policies yielding minimum deterrent nuclear arsenals, small defense-oriented conventional forces, military nonintervention, reduced military spending, and limits on weapons trade. Maintains research library; sponsors forums and discussions. Sponsors projects: International Fighter Study, US Force and Budget Cuts, and Multilateral Peacekeeping, Arms Control Reporter. **Libraries: Type:** open to the public. **Holdings:** 5,125; books, periodicals. **Subjects:** international affairs (military), peace, UN, nuclear weapons. **Computer Services:** database, IDDS World Arms. **Councils:** Global Action to Prevent War. **Publications:** *Analysis of US Army RDT&E Funding FY 1980-FY1995.* Book ● *Arms Control Reporter,* 11/year. Journal. Reference service; includes chronology of arms control negotiations and relevant weapon descriptions. **Price:** $799.00 online standard rate; $899.00 CD standard rate; $1,099.00 paper standard rate. ISSN: 0886-3490. **Circulation:** 400. Alternate Formats: online; CD-ROM ● *The Arms Production Dilemma: Contraction and Restraint in the World Combat Aircraft Industry.* Book. **Price:** $17.95 FORFP; $39.95 FORFH ● *Cutting Conventional Forces.* Book ● *IDDS Almanac 1996: World Combat Aircraft Holdings, Production, and Trade,* annual. Reference work focusing on different weapon systems. ● *Nonproliferation Primer.* Book. Contains information on preventing the spread of nuclear, chemical, and biological weapons. **Price:** $30.00 FORJH; $15.00 FORJP ● *Soviet Missiles and Soviet Military Aircraft.* Book ● *Strategic Antisubmarine Warfare and Naval Strategy.* Book ● Papers. Alternate Formats: online ● Also publishes a reprint series, papers, and fact sheets. Makes ViennaFax, Defense and Disarmament News, and Defense and Disarmament Alternatives back issues available.

17071 ■ International Campaign to Ban Landmines (ICBL)
c/o US Campaign to Ban Landmines
Friends Comm. on Natl. Legislation
245 2nd St. NE
Washington, DC 20002
Ph: (202)547-6000
Fax: (202)547-6019
E-mail: icbl@icbl.org
URL: http://www.icbl.org
Contact: Scott Stedjan, Contact
Founded: 1992. **Members:** 1,400. **Staff:** 4. **Budget:** $1,800,000. **Multinational. Description:** Works for a global ban on landmines. **Libraries: Type:** not open to the public. **Subjects:** landmines. **Working Groups:** Mine Action; Mine Awareness; Non-State Actors; Victim Assistance. **Publications:** *Landmine Monitor,* annual. Report.

17072 ■ NGO Committee on Disarmament, Peace and Security
777 UN Plz., Ste.3-B
New York, NY 10017
Ph: (212)687-5340
Fax: (212)687-1643
E-mail: disarmtimes@igc.org
URL: http://disarm.igc.org
Contact: Ann Hallan Lakhdhir, Pres./VP for Program
Founded: 1973. **Members:** 150. **Membership Dues:** student/fixed income in North America, $35 (annual)

● student/fixed income outside North America, $40 (annual) ● individual in North America, $45 (annual) ● individual outside North America/library, $50 (annual) ● organization, $200 (annual). **Staff:** 1. **Budget:** $45,000. **Description:** Representatives of non-governmental organizations at United Nations headquarters concerned with disarmament. Seeks to exert influence on UN disarmament activities and reflect such activities to members' constituencies. Arranges seminars; undertakes educational projects. Sponsors forums. **Libraries: Type:** open to the public. **Holdings:** 100. **Subjects:** disarmament. **Awards:** Pomerance Award. **Frequency:** periodic. **Type:** recognition. **Recipient:** to individuals or groups for service in the field of disarmament in the U.N. context. **Also Known As:** Non-Governmental Organization Committee on Disarmament. **Formerly:** (2003) NGO Committee on Disarmament. **Publications:** *Disarmament Times,* quarterly. Newspaper. Reports on UN activities pertaining to arms control and disarmament. **Price:** $20.00/year in North America; $25.00/year outside North America. ISSN: 0259-3629. **Circulation:** 5,000. Alternate Formats: online ● Also publishes forum proceedings. **Conventions/Meetings:** semiannual Forum - meeting - always in New York City ● quarterly meeting.

17073 ■ Parliamentarians For Global Action (PGA)
211 E 43rd St., Ste.1604
New York, NY 10017
Ph: (212)687-7755
Fax: (212)687-8409
E-mail: info@pgaction.org
URL: http://www.pgaction.org
Contact: Ms. Shazia Rafi, Sec. Gen.
Founded: 1979. **Members:** 1,300. **Membership Dues:** general, $50 (annual). **Staff:** 13. **Budget:** $1,120,000. **National Groups:** 85. **Languages:** English, Spanish. **Description:** Parliamentarians from 95 nations seeking solutions to problems of the environment, uncontrolled population growth, poverty, and war which require the action of the world community. **Awards:** Defender of Democracy Award. **Frequency:** annual. **Type:** recognition. **Recipient:** for individuals who have defended the principles of democracy, peace and justice. **Councils:** International. **Programs:** International Law and Human Rights; Peace and Democracy; Sustainable Development and Population. **Formerly:** (1985) Parliamentarians for World Order; (1991) Parliamentarians Global Action for Disarmament, Development, and World Reform. **Publications:** *Parliamentarians Global Action Update,* quarterly. Newsletter ● Annual Report, annual. **Conventions/Meetings:** annual UN Parliamentary Forum - seminar - usually October in New York City.

17074 ■ Physicians Against Landmines (PALM)
c/o Center for International Rehabilitation
333 E Huron St., Ste.225
Chicago, IL 60611
Ph: (312)926-0030
Fax: (312)926-7662
E-mail: info@cirnetwork.org
URL: http://www.banmines.org
Contact: William K. Smith, Pres.
Founded: 1996. **Staff:** 10. **Description:** Represents physicians who oppose the use of land mines.

17075 ■ Proposition One Committee
PO Box 27217
Washington, DC 20038
Ph: (202)682-4282
E-mail: prop1@prop1.org
URL: http://prop1.org
Contact: Ellen Thomas, Exec. Dir.
Founded: 1990. **Nonmembership. Description:** Seeks implementation of Proposition One, "an initiative that calls for global nuclear disarmament and economic conversion of the war machines to provide for human needs, such as solar panels and windmills, not missiles or bombs." Encourages people to become involved at every level in order to achieve this goal. Supports House legislation and voter initia-

tives. **Libraries: Type:** not open to the public. **Holdings:** archival material, articles, clippings, photographs, video recordings. **Subjects:** war, peace, justice, arms sales, renewable energy versus nuclear power. **Publications:** *NucNews.* Newsletter. Alternate Formats: online ● *Peace Release,* periodic. Newsletter. Contains updates on issues related to Proposition One. **Price:** free. **Circulation:** 5,000. Alternate Formats: online ● *Proposition One - Peace through Reason,* periodic. Video. **Conventions/Meetings:** annual Hiroshima Week - meeting, in conjunction with Gray Panthers Hiroshima/Nagasaki Committee - always August 5 through 9 ● Peace Park Antinuclear Vigil - assembly, continuously held outside the White House.

17076 ■ Reaching Critical Will
c/o Women's International League for Peace and Freedom
777 UN Plz.
New York, NY 10017
Ph: (212)682-1265
Fax: (212)286-8211
E-mail: info@reachingcriticalwill.org
URL: http://www.reachingcriticalwill.org
Contact: Jennifer Nordstrom, Proj. Assoc.
Founded: 1999. **Description:** Encourages the participation of civil society at international disarmament fora, such as those that take place at the UN. Maintains a centralized electronic repository of information on disarmament. Believes that nuclear disarmament requires coordinated and sustained efforts on the part of governments, non-governmental organizations, and the United Nations. **Computer Services:** database, disarmament index, non-governmental organizations ● information services, disarmament resources ● mailing lists, of members ● online services, search engine. **Projects:** The Dirty Dozen. **Publications:** *First Committee Monitor,* weekly. Newsletter. Alternate Formats: online ● *News in Review,* daily. Newsletter. Includes NGO critique of energy, transport, mining and waste issues. Alternate Formats: online ● *NGO Shadow Report: Accountability is Democracy, Transparency is Accountability.* Features a comprehensive guideline by which States can report on their nuclear holdings, both military and civilian. Alternate Formats: online ● *Nuclear Disarmament: What Next?.* Booklet. Features NGO analysis of the 13-point action plan from the 2000 Review Conference of the Non-Proliferation Treaty. Alternate Formats: online.

Divorce

17077 ■ Ex-Partners of Service Members for Equality (EX-POSE)
PO Box 11191
Alexandria, VA 22312-0191
Ph: (703)941-5844
Fax: (703)212-6951
E-mail: ex-pose@juno.com
URL: http://www.ex-pose.org
Contact: Ms. Nancy Davis, Office Admin.
Membership Dues: individual, $20 (annual) ● life (individual), $200 ● attorney, $50 (annual) ● life (attorney), $500. **Description:** Promotes the interests of former spouses of all Armed Services personnel; advocates the enactment of laws to protect such interests; provides education and information on issues of separation and divorce from military service members. **Publications:** Newsletter, quarterly. **Price:** $5.00 for members; $10.00 for nonmembers. **Conventions/Meetings:** annual conference.

Draft

17078 ■ Center on Conscience and War (CCW)
1830 Connecticut Ave. NW
Washington, DC 20009-5732
Ph: (202)483-2220
Free: (800)379-2679
Fax: (202)483-1246

E-mail: ccw@centeronconscience.org
URL: http://www.centeronconscience.org
Contact: J.E. McNeil, Exec. Dir.
Founded: 1940. **Staff:** 5. **Budget:** $200,000. **National Groups:** 30. **Nonmembership. Description:** International service agency for individual conscientious objectors, churches, religious groups, and organizations interested in conscientious objectors. Provides professional counseling and current literature on every facet of the conscientious objector's claim and appeal procedures; maintains extensive referral service; provides speakers; serves as major source of information about conscription and proposals for national service. Also aids persons who have become conscientious objectors after entering the military. Staff members are constantly alert to legislative and administrative changes affecting conscientious objectors and are in regular contact with government personnel and constituent agencies on behalf of conscientious objectors. Maintains the Fund for Education and Training to assist individuals who believe it is wrong to register for the draft. Conducts research and educational programs. **Libraries: Type:** reference; by appointment only. **Holdings:** 800; archival material, books, papers, periodicals, photographs. **Subjects:** conscientious objection, selective service system. **Formerly:** National Service Board for Religious Objectors; (1999) National Interreligious Service Board for Conscientious Objectors. **Publications:** *Directory of Civilian Public Service - May 1941 to March 1947.* Contains list of the participants in the Civilian Public Service. **Price:** $25.00/copy ● *Draft Counselor's Manual.* Book. **Price:** $25.00 ● *National Service and Religious Values* ● *Report on 210 Conscientious Objectors from World War II* ● *Reporter for Conscience Sake,* quarterly. **Price:** $20.00 /year for individuals. **Circulation:** 3,000 ● *Words of Conscience: Religious Statements on Conscientious Objection.* Book. **Price:** $15.00. **Conventions/Meetings:** annual Advisory Council - meeting - usually May, Washington DC.

17079 ■ Central Committee for Conscientious Objectors (CCCO)
1515 Cherry St.
Philadelphia, PA 19102
Ph: (215)563-8787 (510)465-1617
Fax: (215)567-2096
E-mail: info@objector.org
URL: http://www.objector.org
Contact: Steve Morse, Program Coor.
Founded: 1948. **Staff:** 6. **Budget:** $300,000. **Regional Groups:** 1. **Description:** Supports and promotes individual and collective resistance to war and preparations for war. Works to demilitarize schools; provides draft and military counseling; trains counselors; assists counselors with draft and military cases; provides speakers for groups. **Telecommunication Services:** electronic mail, steve@objector.org. **Programs:** AWOL! Youth for Peace and Revolution; The GI Rights Hotline; Military Out of Our Schools; Third World Outreach. **Also Known As:** CCCO/An Agency for Military and Draft Counseling. **Publications:** *Advice for Conscientious Objectors in the Armed Forces.* Book. **Price:** $20.00. Alternate Formats: online ● *AWOL Magazine: Revolutionary Artists Workshop* ● *Choosing Peace.* Handbook. Serves as the 14th edition of the *Handbook for Conscientious Objectors.* **Price:** $10.00 ● *Helping Out: A Guide to Military Discharges and GI Rights.* Books ● *Military Out of Our Schools Organizing Kit,* quarterly. **Price:** $7.00 ● *The Objector: A Magazine of Conscience and Resistance,* semiannual. Newsletter. **Price:** $2.00. Alternate Formats: online ● Pamphlets.

Drunk Driving

17080 ■ Towing Operators Working to Eliminate Drunk Driving (TOWED)
Address Unknown since 2006
Founded: 1986. **Description:** Towing operators. Dedicated to saving lives, by providing a ride home and free vehicle tow to intoxicated drivers.

E-Commerce

17081 ■ Americans for Fair Electronic Commerce Transactions (AFFECT)
1615 New Hampshire Ave. NW
Washington, DC 20009
E-mail: cashworth@alawash.org
Contact: Carol Ashworth, Contact
Founded: 1999. **Description:** Represents consumers, retail and manufacturing businesses and technology professionals working to oppose the Uniform Computer Information Transactions Act (UCITA). Educates the public and policy makers about the dangers of UCITA. Monitors state legislatures for UCITA. Supports the growth of fair and competitive markets in the United States.

East Timor

17082 ■ East Timor and Indonesia Action Network/US (ETAN/US)
PO Box 21873
Brooklyn, NY 11202-1873
Ph: (212)596-7668
E-mail: etan@etan.org
URL: http://www.etan.org
Founded: 1991. **Members:** 3,000. **Staff:** 2. **Budget:** $100,000. **Description:** Works in solidarity with the people of East Timor and Indonesia. Educates, organizes, and advocates for justice for historic and ongoing crimes against humanity, war crimes, and human rights violations in East Timor and Indonesia. Supports democratic reconstruction of East Timor. Supports restrictions on military assistance to Indonesia in order to support democracy and justice in both countries. **Telecommunication Services:** electronic mail, john@etan.org. **Formerly:** (2005) East Timor Action Network/US. **Publications:** *East Timor ESTAFETA.* Newsletter. Serves as the voice of the East Timor and Indonesia Action Network/US. **Price:** $25.00 /year for institutions. Alternate Formats: online.

Eastern Europe

17083 ■ Action for Post-Soviet Jewry (APSJ)
24 Crescent St., Ste.306
Waltham, MA 02453-4089
Ph: (781)893-2331
Fax: (781)647-9474
E-mail: actionpsj@aol.com
URL: http://www.actionpsj.org
Contact: Judith K. Patkin, Exec. Dir.
Founded: 1975. **Members:** 1,200. **Membership Dues:** individual, family, $36 (annual). **Staff:** 3. **Budget:** $135,000. **Description:** Human rights organization working on behalf of Jews in the former Soviet Union. Has main program, the Adopt-a-Bubbe, which provides direct support with food, medicine, clothing, and more for needy pensioners in Ukraine, Belarus and Moldova. Supports medical clinics for pensioners and others. Maintains speaker's bureau; conducts charitable and educational programs; compiles statistics. Provides pen pals with pensioners in FSU. **Libraries: Type:** reference; by appointment only. **Holdings:** audiovisuals, books, clippings. **Awards:** Freedom Award. **Type:** recognition. **Recipient:** for significant work on behalf of Jews in the former Soviet Union. **Computer Services:** Online services. **Committees:** Governing Board; Nominating; Research; Speakers' Bureau; Task. **Affiliated With:** Union of Councils for Jews in the Former Soviet Union. **Formerly:** Action for Soviet Jewry. **Publications:** *Bar/Bat Mitzvah Twinning.* Brochure ● *Post-Soviet Jewry Report,* 3/year. **Circulation:** 5,000 ● *Yad l'Yad,* semimonthly. Brochure. Describes program to reach out to Jews in the former Soviet Union. **Conventions/Meetings:** semiannual meeting.

17084 ■ Chicago Action for Jews in the Former Soviet Union
555 Vine St., Ste.111
Highland Park, IL 60035
Ph: (847)433-0144
Fax: (847)433-5530
E-mail: officecasj@ameritech.net
URL: http://www.chicagoaction.org
Contact: Marillyn Tallman, Chair
Founded: 1972. **Staff:** 10. **Languages:** English, Russian. **Multinational. Description:** Seeks to give humanitarian aid to Jews in the former Soviet Union; funds soup kitchens, meals on wheels, medicine, visiting nurses, meals for school children, heating for homes and schools, and security systems for synagogues. Communicates daily with Jewish communities in towns and villages in the former Soviet Union for information, and also informs members in the U.S. of anti-Semitic incidents there; created and supervised a program, Yad L'Yad (Hand to Hand), which pairs synagogues in the Chicago area and the Midwest with Jewish communities in the former Soviet Union. **Telecommunication Services:** electronic mail, chicagoaction@ameritech.net. **Formerly:** (1998) International Physicians Commission. **Publications:** *Lifeline,* periodic. Newsletter. Alternate Formats: online.

17085 ■ Civil Society International (CSI)
38 Miller Ave., No. 155
Mill Valley, CA 94941
E-mail: csi@civilsoc.org
URL: http://www.civilsoc.org
Contact: Holt Ruffin, Exec. Dir.
Founded: 1992. **Staff:** 3. **Budget:** $100,000. **Languages:** English, Russian. **Nonmembership. Description:** Produces information that supports the growth of democratic citizen organizations and citizen participation in countries where these traditions are weak or actively repressed. **Convention/Meeting:** none. **Awards:** GKP Youth Award. **Type:** monetary. **Recipient:** to the outstanding work of young people who used information communication technologies for the promotion of development in their communities ● Transparency International Integrity Awards. **Type:** recognition. **Recipient:** for journalists, civil society activists, government and corporate whistleblowers who work to investigate and unmask corruption. **Additional Websites:** http://www.civilsocietyinternational.org. **Formerly:** (2002) Center for Civil Society International. **Publications:** *Civil Society in Central Asia.* Book. **Price:** $19.95/copy ● *Internet Resources for Eurasia,* periodic. Handbook. **Price:** $9.95/copy ● *Post-Soviet Handbook,* periodic. **Price:** $19.95/copy.

17086 ■ Institute for Democracy in Eastern Europe (IDEE)
1718 M St. NW, No. 147
Washington, DC 20036
Ph: (202)466-7105
Fax: (202)387-6466
E-mail: idee@idee.org
URL: http://www.idee.org
Contact: Mr. Eric Chenoweth, Co-Dir.
Founded: 1986. **Staff:** 2. **Budget:** $500,000. **Languages:** English, French, German, Polish, Russian. **Description:** Supports independent social, political, and human rights movements and publications independent of government control in Central and Eastern Europe and countries of the former Soviet Union. Coordinates Centers for Pluralism program involving Centers in 16 countries of the region that work within and across borders to promote development of civil society in former communist countries. Organizes a Network of Independent Journalists to promote cross-border coverage of events in Eastern Europe and coordinates media support programs especially for local and regional press. **Libraries: Type:** by appointment only. **Holdings:** 1,000; archival material, articles, books, periodicals, photographs, reports. **Subjects:** Central and Eastern Europe and the former Soviet Union (former communist countries). **Absorbed:** (1988) Committee in Support of Solidarity. **Publications:** *Cuba Chronicle of Events* (in English, Russian, and Spanish), semimonthly. Pamphlet. Features news concerning the Cuban democracy movement.

17087 ■ Jamestown Foundation (JF)
1111 16th St. NW, Ste.No. 320
Washington, DC 20036
Ph: (202)483-8888
Fax: (202)483-8337
E-mail: pubs@jamestown.org
URL: http://www.jamestown.org
Contact: Glenn E. Howard, Pres.
Founded: 1983. **Staff:** 6. **Budget:** $1,000,000. **Description:** Improves Western understanding of the former Soviet Union, China, and terrorism. Promotes the understanding of the Commonwealth of Independent States. Utilizes information and experiences of analysts from the region. Disseminates information to policymakers, journalists, community, and academia. **Libraries: Type:** reference. **Subjects:** former Soviet Union. **Boards:** Advisory. **Publications:** *Chechnya Weekly.* Alternate Formats: online ● *China Brief,* biweekly. Contains timely information and cutting-edge analysis. Alternate Formats: online ● *Eurasia Daily Monitor.* Provides a chronicle of events in the former Soviet Union. **Price:** included in membership dues. **Circulation:** 2,000. Alternate Formats: online ● *Terrorism Focus,* weekly. Articles ● *Terrorism Monitor,* biweekly. Articles.

17088 ■ NCSJ: Advocates on Behalf of Jews in Russia, Ukraine, the Baltic States and Eurasia (NCSJ)
2020 K St. NW, Ste.7800
Washington, DC 20006
Ph: (202)898-2500
Fax: (202)898-0822
E-mail: ncsj@ncsj.org
URL: http://www.ncsj.org
Contact: Mark Levin, Exec. Dir.
Founded: 1971. **Staff:** 6. **Budget:** $790,000. **State Groups:** 200. **Local Groups:** 300. **National Groups:** 49. **Description:** Works as coordinating agency of the organized Jewish community for policy and activities and behalf of the estimated 1.5 million Jews in the former Soviet Union (FSU.) Comprises nearly 50 national organizations and over 300 local federations, community councils and committees. Mission is to safeguard the individual and communal political rights of Jews living in the former Soviet Union and to secure their religious and political freedoms. **Libraries: Type:** reference. **Holdings:** biographical archives. **Awards: Frequency:** annual. **Type:** recognition. **Committees:** Community Services; Cultural; Helsinki; Interreligious; Legal. **Formerly:** (1971) American Jewish Conference on Soviet Jewry; (2001) National Conference on Soviet Jewry. **Publications:** *NCSJ—Community Reports,* periodic ● *NCSJ—Newswatch,* monthly ● Bibliographies ● Monographs ● Pamphlets ● Reports. **Conventions/Meetings:** semiannual board meeting ● annual meeting.

17089 ■ Raoul Wallenberg Committee of the United States (RWCUS)
230 Park Ave., 7th Fl.
New York, NY 10169
Ph: (212)499-2695
Fax: (212)499-2671
E-mail: rachel@raoulwallenberg.org
URL: http://www.raoulwallenberg.org
Contact: Rachel Oestreicher Bernheim, Chair
Founded: 1981. **Members:** 11,000. **Membership Dues:** individual, $50 (annual). **Staff:** 5. **Budget:** $250,000. **State Groups:** 50. **Description:** Educates the American public about the life and deeds of Raoul Wallenberg (1912-), a Swedish diplomat and honorary citizen of the United States responsible for saving over 100,000 Jews in Budapest, Hungary from the Nazi concentration camps during World War II. (Wallenberg disappeared in 1945 at the hands of the Soviet forces but has reportedly been seen in Soviet Gulag prisons and mental institutions and is believed to be alive.) Works to secure Wallenberg's freedom or to establish the truth of his fate. Serves as an information clearinghouse and provides background materials on Wallenberg to schools, universities, churches, and synagogues. Sponsors an exhibit and helps with research programs. Maintains speakers' bureau; offers children's educational services. **Libraries: Type:** reference. **Holdings:** 3,000; archival

material, periodicals, video recordings. **Subjects:** Raoul Wallenberg. **Awards:** The Raoul Wallenberg A Hero for Our Time Award. **Type:** recognition. **Recipient:** to an individual who reflects the ideals of Raoul Wallenberg ● The Raoul Wallenberg Civil Courage Award. **Type:** recognition. **Recipient:** for a community showing courage in the face of adversity ● The Raoul Wallenberg Educational Excellence Award. **Type:** recognition. **Recipient:** for individuals strongly identified with educational awareness and opportunities. **Telecommunication Services:** electronic mail, betty@raoulwallenberg.org. **Committees:** Awards; Benefit and Fundraising; Education; Policy. **Formerly:** (1981) Raoul Wallenberg Working Group. **Publications:** *A Study of Heroes.* Serves as an educational resource for grades K-12. **Price:** $495.00/copy ● *Chronology of the Raoul Wallenberg Case.* Booklet. Features an eight-page compendium following all available information on the case. ● *Chronology of the Raoul Wallenberg Case,* 1-2/year. Newsletter. Alternate Formats: online ● *Raoul Wallenberg: A Hero For Our Times.* Booklet. **Conventions/Meetings:** board meeting, to discuss the work accomplishments, and the challenges facing the organization ● annual meeting ● annual meeting, includes reception - usually October in New York City.

17090 ■ SMOLOSKYP, Ukrainian Information Service (SUIS)
PO Box 8041
Bridgewater, NJ 08807
Ph: (908)725-5322
Fax: (908)725-5322
E-mail: mbf@smoloskyp.kiev.ua
URL: http://www.smoloskyp.kiev.ua/docs/englishe.htm
Contact: Oleksiy Shevchenko, Chm.
Founded: 1967. **Members:** 16. **Budget:** $30,000. **Description:** Monitors violations of human, national, and religious rights in Ukraine and the former USSR. Compiles list of political and religious prisoners in Eastern Europe; encourages writing letters of support to prisoners. Collects and disseminates information. **Libraries: Type:** reference. **Holdings:** 10,000; biographical archives. **Subjects:** Ukraine, Eastern Europe, communism. **Publications:** *Smoloskyp Ukrayiny,* monthly. Newsletter ● Catalogs (in Ukrainian) ● Journal (in Ukrainian) ● Bulletin (in Ukrainian).

17091 ■ Student Struggle for Soviet Jewry (SSSJ)
c/o Jacob Birnbaum
240 Cabrini Blvd., No. 5B
New York, NY 10033-1118
Ph: (212)928-7451
Fax: (212)795-8867
Contact: Jacob Birnbaum, Dir.
Founded: 1964. **Description:** Organization concerned with "the precarious status of Jews in the former Union of Soviet Socialist Republics." Seeks to protest this situation. Coordinates joint action with student and community groups throughout the world. Operates a continual educational campaign to achieve "a responsible public outcry" in the hope that the difficult conditions of Jews in the former Soviet Union will be relieved, freer emigration permitted, support for rebuilding of Jewish life expanded, and anti-semitism combatted. Conducts study groups, public hearings, and demonstrations. Engages in research and guides researchers to available sources. Provides speakers' bureau and programming services. **Libraries: Type:** reference. **Holdings:** audio recordings. **Subjects:** Soviet Jewry.

17092 ■ Union of Councils for Jews in the Former Soviet Union (UCSJ)
PO Box 11676
Cleveland Park
Washington, DC 20008
Ph: (202)237-8262
Fax: (202)237-2236
E-mail: mnaftalin@ucsj.com
URL: http://www.fsumonitor.com
Contact: Micah H. Naftalin, Natl. Dir./Sec.
Founded: 1970. **Members:** 100,000. **Staff:** 6. **Budget:** $750,000. **Local Groups:** 38. **Languages:**

English, Russian. **Description:** Acted as the voice of Russia's Refuseniks throughout the 1970s and 1980s. Today, it stands alone in providing anti-Semitism, xenophobia and human rights monitoring and advocacy through its seven bureaus across the former Soviet Union, and by providing a bridge between vital Jewish interests and the mainstream human rights NGO community there, especially in the Russian Federation. Also has a flourishing "Yad L'Yad" (hand to hand) partnership program which provides humanitarian, religious, and cultural aid to FSU Jewish communities through the volunteer participation of member councils and participating synagogues and school in the U.S. Also educates the American public about the situation facing Jews and human rights activists in the former Soviet Union, briefs administration officials, congressmen, and senators. **Libraries: Type:** reference; open to the public. **Holdings:** articles, books, periodicals. **Subjects:** Soviet Jewry, human rights. **Awards:** Henry Scoop Jackson Award. **Frequency:** semiannual. **Type:** recognition ● Michael Tryson Award. **Type:** recognition. **Recipient:** for attorneys ● Scharansky Freedom Award. **Frequency:** semiannual. **Type:** recognition. **Programs:** Congressional Call to Conscience. **Subgroups:** Yad L'Yad. **Affiliated With:** Chicago Action for Jews in the Former Soviet Union; Student Struggle for Soviet Jewry. **Formerly:** (1993) Union of Councils for Soviet Jews; (2002) Union of Councils. **Publications:** *Anti-Semitism, Xenophobia and Religious Persecution in Russia's Regions,* annual. Manual ● *Bigotry Monitor,* weekly. Newsletter. **Circulation:** 1,000. Alternate Formats: online. **Conventions/Meetings:** annual conference, board and councils.

Economic Development

17093 ■ Bretton Woods Committee (BWC)
1726 M St. NW, Ste.200
Washington, DC 20036
Ph: (202)331-1616
Fax: (202)785-9423
E-mail: info@brettonwoods.org
URL: http://www.brettonwoods.org
Contact: James C. Orr, Exec. Dir.
Founded: 1984. **Members:** 600. **Description:** Corporate CEOs, university administrators, former government officials, state governors, association and trade union executives, and bankers. Seeks to inform and educate the public regarding the activities of the World Bank, International Monetary Fund, and other Multinational Development Banks (MDB). Promotes U.S. participation in MDBs. **Publications:** Newsletter, quarterly ● Also publishes reports. **Conventions/Meetings:** annual conference.

17094 ■ Cliometric Society
Dept. of Economics
Campus Box 8110
North Carolina State Univ.
Raleigh, NC 27695-8110
Ph: (919)513-2870
Fax: (919)515-5613
E-mail: csociety@eh.net
URL: http://eh.net/Clio
Contact: Lee A. Craig, Exec. Dir.
Founded: 1983. **Members:** 500. **Membership Dues:** regular, $22 (annual) ● student, $12 (annual) ● sustaining, $32 (annual). **Staff:** 1. **Description:** Represents those interested in the application of economic theory and quantitative techniques to describe and explain historical economic events. **Computer Services:** Online services, membership information. **Publications:** *The Newsletter of the Cliometric Society,* 3/year. Features interviews with individuals in the field. **Price:** included in membership dues. **Circulation:** 415. **Advertising:** accepted ● Membership Directory, semiannual. **Conventions/Meetings:** annual conference.

17095 ■ Committee for Economic Development (CED)
2000 L St. NW, Ste.700
Washington, DC 20036

Ph: (202)296-5860
Free: (800)676-7353
Fax: (202)223-0776
E-mail: info@ced.org
URL: http://www.ced.org
Contact: Charles E.M. Kolb, Pres.

Founded: 1942. **Members:** 200. **Staff:** 24. **Budget:** $4,400,000. **Description:** Trustees are heads of major corporations or university presidents. Works with expert advisers. Conducts research and formulates policy recommendations on national and international economic issues, including education, trade policy, U.S.-Japan economic relations, and problems of the inner city. Seeks to contribute to full employment, higher living standards, and increased opportunities for all through its studies and works; promote economic growth and stability; strengthen the concepts and institutions essential to progress in a free society. **Telecommunication Services:** electronic mail, charles.kolb@ced.org. **Committees:** Research and Policy. **Subcommittees:** Campaign Finance Reform; The Employer's Role in Linking School to Work; Legal Reform; Science and Technology/Basic Research; The United States in the World Economy; Welfare Reform. **Publications:** *Statements on National Policy* ● Films ● Papers ● Reports. **Conventions/Meetings:** annual board meeting.

17096 ■ Concord Coalition (CC)

1011 Arlington Blvd., Ste.300
Arlington, VA 22209
Ph: (703)894-6222
Free: (888)333-4248
Fax: (703)894-6231
E-mail: concordcoalition@concordcoalition.org
URL: http://www.concordcoalition.org
Contact: Robert Bixby, Exec. Dir.

Founded: 1992. **Members:** 200,000. **Membership Dues:** regular, $25 (annual). **Staff:** 17. **Budget:** $1,900,000. **Regional Groups:** 8. **State Groups:** 50. **Description:** Individuals and organizations. Promotes development of "a sound economy for future generations." Conducts educational programs; maintains speakers' bureau. **Awards:** Paul E. Tsongas Economic Patriot Award. **Frequency:** annual. **Type:** recognition. **Recipient:** for outstanding leadership and commitment to Concord's goals of fiscal and generational responsibility. **Telecommunication Services:** electronic bulletin board. **Publications:** *Concord Courier*, quarterly. Newsletter. Alternate Formats: online ● *Congressional Scorecard*, periodic. Report. Alternate Formats: online ● *Facing Facts Quarterly*. Report. Contains information on a variety of fiscal policy issues. Alternate Formats: online. **Conventions/Meetings:** periodic board meeting ● periodic conference ● periodic regional meeting.

17097 ■ Corporation for Enterprise Development (CFED)

777 N Capital St. NE, Ste.800
Washington, DC 20002
Ph: (202)408-9788
Fax: (202)408-9793
E-mail: info-dc@cfed.org
URL: http://www.cfed.org
Contact: Andrea Levere, Pres.

Founded: 1979. **Staff:** 11. **Description:** Provides assistance to public and private organizations concerned with increasing economic opportunity for individuals through the encouragement and support of enterprise development; serves as a forum for the exchange of ideas. Strives to research, develop, and disseminate entrepreneurial policy initiatives at the local, state, and federal levels. Conducts consulting services and compiles statistics. **Computer Services:** Mailing lists. **Telecommunication Services:** electronic mail, alevere@cfed.org. **Publications:** *Accountability Newsletter*, monthly. Critiques the common practice of offering tax incentives to attract and retain businesses. **Price:** available for free download. Alternate Formats: online ● *Assets*, quarterly. Newsletter. Highlights developments in the IDA field. **Price:** free to download. Alternate Formats: online ● *The Development Report Card for the States*, annual. Book. Includes economic benchmarks for state and

corporate decision makers. ISSN: 1045-4691 ● *Effective State Policy and Practice*, quarterly. Bulletin. Considers current issues in microenterprise and offers concrete tips to increase effectiveness. **Price:** free to download. Alternate Formats: online ● Also publishes books and monographs.

17098 ■ Council of Development Finance Agencies (CDFA)

815 Superior Ave., Ste.1301
Cleveland, OH 44114
Ph: (216)920-3073
Fax: (216)771-4938
E-mail: info@cdfa.net
URL: http://www.cdfa.net
Contact: Toby Rittner, Exec. Dir.

Founded: 1982. **Members:** 180. **Staff:** 3. **Description:** Works for the advancement of development finance concerns and interests. Represents the nation's leading and most knowledgeable members of the development finance community from the public, private and non-profit sectors. **Awards:** Practioners Showcase. **Type:** recognition. **Recipient:** for outstanding development finance programs and success stories. **Computer Services:** database, online resource database of topics related to development finance. **Formerly:** (1992) Council of Industrial Development Bond Issuers. **Publications:** *CDFA Update*, monthly. Newsletters. Contains information related to development finance. **Conventions/Meetings:** annual conference, gathering of leaders and innovators in the development finance industry (exhibits).

17099 ■ Economic and Social Council (ECOSOC)

c/o Mr. Nikhil Seth, Dir.
Off. for ECOSOC Support and Coordination
1 UN Plz.
New York, NY 10017
Ph: (212)963-1811 (212)963-2184
Fax: (212)963-1712
E-mail: ecosocinfo@un.org
URL: http://www.un.org/docs/ecosoc
Contact: Ali Hachani, Pres.

Founded: 1965. **Members:** 54. **Multinational. Description:** Representatives from United Nations (see separate entry) member countries. Coordinates and makes recommendations on the economic and social activities of the U.N. and related agencies. Conducts and initiates studies on current problems and concerns including world trade, industrialization, natural resources, human rights, the status of women, population, social welfare, science and technology, and crime prevention. Fosters the observance of human rights and fundamental freedoms; provides consulting and negotiating services. Maintains regional groups to assist in solving economic and social problems, including Economic Commission for Africa, Economic Commission for Latin America and the Caribbean, Economic and Social Commission for Asia and the Pacific, Economic and Social Commission for Western Asia, and Economic Commission for Europe. **Commissions:** Economic and Social Commission for Asia and the Pacific; Economic Commission for Africa; Human Rights; Human Settlements; Narcotic Drugs; Population and Development; Social Development; Statistical; Status of Women; Sustainable Development. **Committees:** Crime Prevention and Control; Natural Resources; Negotiations with Intergovernmental Agencies; Non-Governmental Organizations; Programme and Coordination; Science and Technology for Development. **Conventions/Meetings:** periodic conference ● annual meeting - always in New York City or Geneva, Switzerland.

17100 ■ Inter-American Development Bank (IDB)

1300 New York Ave. NW
Washington, DC 20577
Ph: (202)623-1000
Fax: (202)623-3096
E-mail: webmaster@iadb.org
URL: http://www.iadb.org
Contact: Luis Alberto Moreno, Pres.

Founded: 1959. **Members:** 47. **Staff:** 1,500. **Multinational. Description:** Western Hemisphere coun-

tries; other interested countries. Seeks to help accelerate the economic and social development of members in Latin America and the Caribbean. Works to: promote the investment of public and private capital in the region; use its own capital, as well as funds raised in financial markets and other available resources, for financing high-priority projects; supplement private investment when capital is not available on reasonable terms and conditions; encourage members to direct their policies toward better use of their natural resources while fostering growth of their foreign trade and development of complementary economies in Latin America; provide technical cooperation for the preparation, financing, and execution of development plans and projects, including the study of priorities and formulation of specific project proposals; contribute to the strengthening of the institutional base of lesser-developed member countries. Fosters equitable distribution of benefits of development. Sponsors projects which alleviate poverty, expand agricultural production, finance energy projects, promote modernization, develop industry, urban renewal, and health and education, and improve development institutions. Operates Fund for Special Operations, which is used to make long-term, low-interest loans to less-developed Latin American countries and a microenterprise division, which provides financing and technical support to low-income individuals and groups who ordinarily do not have access to public or commercial credit. Also administers the Venezuelan Trust Fund and the Social Progress Trust Fund. Cooperates with other development and financial institutions with similar goals. Offers technical training and seminars. Operates Speakers' Bureau. **Libraries: Type:** reference. **Holdings:** 135,000. **Computer Services:** Information services ● online services, loan operations of members. **Committees:** Environmental Management. **Departments:** Administrative; Economic and Social Development; Legal; Operations; Project Analysis; Secretariat. **Also Known As:** Banco Interamericano de Desarrollo; Banco Interamericano de Desenvolvimento; Banque Interamericaine de Developpement. **Publications:** *Economic and Social Progress Report* (in English, French, Portuguese, and Spanish), annual ● *IDB News* (in English, French, Portuguese, and Spanish), monthly ● *Proceedings of Annual Meeting* (in English, French, Portuguese, and Spanish) ● Annual Report (in English, French, Portuguese, and Spanish). Alternate Formats: online ● Newsletters. Alternate Formats: online ● Also publishes reports and brochures. **Conventions/Meetings:** annual meeting.

17101 ■ International Finance Corporation (IFC)

2121 Pennsylvania Ave. NW
Washington, DC 20433
Ph: (202)473-1000 (202)473-3800
Fax: (202)974-4384
E-mail: webmaster@ifc.org
URL: http://www.ifc.org
Contact: Lars Thunell, Exec. VP/CEO

Founded: 1956. **Members:** 178. **Languages:** English, French, Portuguese, Russian, Spanish. **Description:** Promotes sustainable private sector investments in developing countries, as a way to reduce poverty and improve people's lives. **Libraries: Type:** reference. **Affiliated With:** International Bank for Reconstruction and Development; World Bank Group. **Conventions/Meetings:** annual meeting, publications (exhibits).

17102 ■ International Monetary Fund (IMF)

700 19th St. NW
Washington, DC 20431
Ph: (202)623-7000 (202)623-7300
Fax: (202)623-4661
E-mail: publicaffairs@imf.org
URL: http://www.imf.org
Contact: Rodrigo de Rato y Figaredo, Managing Dir.

Founded: 1945. **Members:** 184. **Staff:** 2,500. **Multinational. Description:** Comprises 184 national governments. Works to: facilitate monetary cooperation through consultation and collaboration among member nations; assist in the balanced expansion of trade and thus contribute to the internal development and prosperity of member nations; maintain stability in monetary exchange arrangements, particularly to avoid exchange depreciations; participate in establishing a multilateral system of payments between member nations and in eliminating exchange restrictions that hamper trade; make available the resources of the fund to provide member nations with a means of assuaging economic difficulties. Maintains the IMF Institute, which conducts training courses and seminars and provides lecturers on subjects such as compilation of statistics and formulation and execution of balance of payment policies. Offers technical assistance on monetary matters to member nations and their dependencies and to multinational institutions. Acts as a depository of information and statistical data regarding the economic affairs of member nations. Operates library, in conjunction with the World Bank, on finance and economic development. **Departments:** African; Asia and Pacific; European; External Relations; Fiscal Affairs; International Capital Markets; Legal; Middle East and Central Asia; Monetary and Financial Systems; Policy Development and Review; Research; Secretary's; Statistics; Western Hemisphere. **Publications:** *Annual Report of Executive Board*, annual ● *Annual Report on Exchange Arrangements and Exchange Restrictions*, annual ● *Balance of Payments Statistics*, annual ● *Direction of Trade Statistics*, annual ● *Finance and Development*, quarterly. Magazine ● *Government Finance Statistics Yearbook*, annual ● *IMF Survey*, 23/year ● *International Financial Statistics*, annual ● *Staff Papers*, quarterly. Journal ● *Summary Proceedings*, annual ● *World Economic Outlook*, semiannual ● Also publishes pamphlet and working paper series and books. **Conventions/Meetings:** annual meeting.

17103 ■ National Congress for Community Economic Development (NCCED)
1030 15th St. NW, Ste.325
Washington, DC 20005
Ph: (202)289-9020
Free: (877)44N-CCED
Fax: (202)289-7051
E-mail: pmckee@ncced.org
URL: http://www.ncced.org
Contact: Pamela McKee, Interim Pres./CEO
Founded: 1970. **Members:** 850. **Membership Dues:** regular, $150-$1,000 (annual) ● corporate, $10,000 (annual) ● associate, $200 (annual). **Staff:** 27. **Budget:** $6,500,000. **State Groups:** 33. **Description:** Community development corporations, community action agencies, and rural co-ops involved in community economic development. Provides a national program of promotion, partnership, and assistance for organizations in community-based economic development; monitors legislative issues. Provides information to newly formed community-based economic development organizations. Compiles information on new programs in community economic development. **Awards: Frequency:** annual. **Type:** recognition. **Recipient:** for outstanding organization, staff person, and public advocate. **Programs:** AmeriCorpsVISTA; Community Development Leadership Association; Family Strengthening Awards; Forum for Reentry and Community Economic Development. **Projects:** Corporate Program; Faith Based Initiative; Human Capital; State Associations. **Absorbed:** (1998) National Training Institute for Community Economic Development. **Status Note:** (2006) Defunct. **Publications:** *Coming of Age*. Reprint. Data from national census of SDCs. **Price:** $8.00 for members; $10.00 for nonmembers ● *Development Times*, bimonthly. Newsletter. **Price:** included in membership dues ● *Empower Magazine*. Newsletter. **Price:** included in membership dues ● *NCCED Newsnotes*, bimonthly. Newsletter. **Price:** included in membership dues ● *Resources*, quarterly. Magazine. **Price:** included in membership dues. **Conventions/Meetings:** annual conference, includes public policy forum (exhibits).

17104 ■ National Development Council (NDC)
708 Third Ave., Ste.710
New York, NY 10017
Ph: (212)682-1106

Fax: (212)573-6118
E-mail: training@nationaldevelopmentcouncil.org
URL: http://www.nationaldevelopmentcouncil.org
Contact: Robert W. Davenport, Pres.
Founded: 1969. **Staff:** 35. **State Groups:** 20. **Description:** Brings innovative economic development financing programs to urban and rural communities interested in local business and industrial growth, commercial revitalization, and permanent job creation. Finances professionals' work with cities, counties, and states to: build permanent systems for developing financing; train local staff; structure and negotiate financing for development projects, local business development, and industrial expansion. Conducts intensive training program for economic development professionals with courses in business credit analysis, real estate financing, loan packaging, federal financing, and program management and implementation; has provided advice to Congress and federal agencies that has helped create lending programs for job creation and small business investment; has initiated and managed presidential programs for Presidents Nixon, Ford, Carter, and Reagan. **Publications:** *Developments Newsletter*, quarterly.

17105 ■ National Economic Development and Law Center (NEDLC)
2201 Broadway, Ste.815
Oakland, CA 94612
Ph: (510)251-2600
Fax: (510)251-0600
E-mail: roger@nedlc.org
URL: http://www.nedlc.org
Contact: Roger A. Clay Jr., Pres.
Founded: 1969. **Staff:** 30. **Languages:** Cantonese, English, Filipino, French, Portuguese, Samoan, Spanish, Vietnamese. **Description:** Offers assistance to Community Development Corporations (CDCs), other community organizations, state and local governments, co-ops, and legal services attorneys working in the field of economic development. Provides counseling and representation in connection with: establishment and financing of activities; business, corporate, and commercial transactions; tax exemptions; security offerings; comprehensive planning assistance related to economic and community development. Seeks to create a uniform and comprehensive community economic development policy through continuing planning assistance and training and legal education, with special emphasis on integrating development of business, jobs, health care, and housing interests. Acts as liaison in counseling research and representation; recommends administrative, legal, and legislative solutions on economic development issues to federal agencies, and state and local governments and agencies. Sponsors seminars and workshops on legal and tax issues. **Libraries: Type:** reference. **Holdings:** 10,000. **Programs:** Children, Youth and Families; Community Infrastructure; Jobs, Income and Assets. **Projects:** Californians for Family Economics Self-Sufficiency; Car Ownership Program Clearinghouse; National Network of Sector Partners. **Publications:** *Economic Development Law Center Report*, quarterly ● Manuals ● Reports. Alternate Formats: online. **Conventions/Meetings:** annual conference.

17106 ■ United States National Committee for Pacific Economic Cooperation (USNCPEC)
1819 L St. NW, 2nd Fl.
Washington, DC 20036
Ph: (202)293-1093 (202)293-3995
Fax: (202)293-1402
E-mail: info@usapc.org
URL: http://www.pecc.org
Contact: Dr. Mark Borthwick, USAPC Dir.
Founded: 1984. **Multinational. Description:** Business executives. Works to provide the Asia Pacific Economic Cooperation with information and analysis of major trade and investment in the Asia-Pacific region.

17107 ■ U.S.A. - Business and Industry Advisory Committee to the OECD (USA-BIAC)
c/o United States Council for International Business
1212 Ave. of the Americas
New York, NY 10036
Ph: (212)354-4480
Fax: (212)575-0327
E-mail: info@uscib.org
URL: http://www.uscib.org
Contact: Thomas Niles, Pres.
Founded: 1962. **Membership Dues:** business (minimum; based on revenue), $10,000 (annual) ● association (minimum; based on budget), lawfirm (minimum; based on number of attorneys), $5,000 (annual). **Description:** Sponsored by United States Council for International Business. Represents the United States on the Business and Industry Advisory Committee to the Organisation for Economic Co-Operation and Development. Acts as the official channel for conveying the views of the business community to the OECD in the fields of economics, finance, international trade, industrial relations, information and telecommunications policy investment, and taxation. **Telecommunication Services:** electronic mail, membership@uscib.org. **Committees:** BIAC Policy; Chemicals; Competition Law and Policy; Economic Policy; Education; Environment; Information, Computing and Communications Policies; International Investment and Multinational Enterprises; Manpower and Social Affairs; Maritime Transport; Taxation and Fiscal Policy; Technology; Trade. **Affiliated With:** United States Council for International Business. **Publications:** Pamphlets ● Also distributes information on OECD activities.

17108 ■ USA Engage
c/o Jake Colvin, Dir.
1625 K St. NW, Ste.200
Washington, DC 20006
Ph: (202)464-2025
E-mail: usaengage@nftc.org
URL: http://www.usaengage.org
Contact: Jake Colvin, Dir.
Founded: 1997. **Members:** 647. **Description:** Promotes economic strength in America as integral to the nation's security and worldwide leadership. **Computer Services:** Mailing lists.

Economics

17109 ■ Athena Alliance
c/o Kenan Patrick Jarboe, Pres.
911 E Capitol St. SE
Washington, DC 20003-3903
Ph: (202)547-7064
E-mail: info@athenaalliance.org
URL: http://www.athenaalliance.org
Contact: Kenan Patrick Jarboe, Pres.
Description: Promotes public education and research on the emerging global information economy. Seeks to bring together organizations and individuals to help meet the challenges posed by the emerging information economy. Undertakes outreach activities to better understand the issues and craft policies and programs. **Telecommunication Services:** electronic mail, kpjarboe@athenaalliance.org. **Publications:** Papers. Alternate Formats: online.

17110 ■ Center for Economic and Policy Research (CEPR)
1611 Connecticut Ave. NW, Ste.400
Washington, DC 20009
Ph: (202)293-5380
Fax: (202)588-1356
E-mail: cepr@cepr.net
URL: http://www.cepr.net
Contact: Dean Baker, Co-Dir.
Founded: 1999. **Languages:** English, Portuguese, Spanish. **Description:** Promotes democratic debate on the most important economic and social issues that affect people's lives. **Publications:** Papers.

17111 ■ Economic Security Project (ESP)
Address Unknown since 2006
Description: Seeks to advance personal growth, mutual support, spiritual enrichment, and economic security. **Publications:** *Economic Security for All.* Alternate Formats: online ● *Economic Security for All: How To End Poverty in the United States.*

17112 ■ Institute on Taxation and Economic Policy (ITEP)
Washington Off.
1616 P St. NW, Ste.200
Washington, DC 20036
Ph: (202)299-1066
Fax: (202)299-1065
E-mail: itep@itepnet.org
URL: http://www.ctj.org/itep
Contact: Richard Pomp, Pres.
Founded: 1980. **Membership Dues:** regular, $35 (annual) ● supporter, $50 (annual) ● patron, $100 (annual) ● benefactor, $250 (annual). **Description:** Conducts research and education into government taxation and spending policy issues. **Publications:** Reports.

17113 ■ More Than Money
PO Box 1002
Concord, MA 01742
Ph: (978)371-1726
Free: (866)306-8200
Fax: (978)371-1465
E-mail: info@morethanmoney.org
URL: http://www.morethanmoney.org
Contact: Bob Kenny, Exec. Dir.
Membership Dues: full, $150 (annual) ● professional associate, $275 (annual). **Description:** Commits to change the way society understands the purpose, potential and challenges of money. **Libraries: Type:** reference. **Subjects:** money. **Computer Services:** Online services, discussions. **Programs:** Coaching. **Publications:** *More Than Money Ezine*, bimonthly. Magazine. **Price:** free. Alternate Formats: online ● *Taking Charge*. Book ● Journal, quarterly. **Price:** included in membership dues; $45.00 for nonmembers. **Conventions/Meetings:** conference.

17114 ■ Society for the Advancement of Socio-Economics (SASE)
PO Box 39008
Baltimore, MD 21212
Ph: (410)435-6617
Fax: (410)377-7965
E-mail: office@sase.org
URL: http://www.sase.org
Contact: Mary H. Grossman, Exec. Dir.
Founded: 1989. **Members:** 1,500. **Membership Dues:** regular, $70 ● student, $45. **Staff:** 2. **Description:** Offers educational and research programs and competitions. **Awards:** Founders Prize. **Type:** grant. **Recipient:** for conference paper submittals. **Publications:** Newsletter. **Conventions/Meetings:** annual meeting.

17115 ■ United for a Fair Economy (UFE)
29 Winter St.
Boston, MA 02108
Ph: (617)423-2148
Free: (888)JOI-NUFE
Fax: (617)423-0191
E-mail: info@faireconomy.org
URL: http://www.faireconomy.org
Contact: Meizhu Lui, Exec. Dir.
Founded: 1995. **Members:** 5,000. **Membership Dues:** individual, $30 (annual). **Staff:** 17. **Budget:** $1,100,000. **Languages:** English, Spanish. **Description:** Individuals concerned about "the excessive inequality of income and wealth in the United States." Promotes a more equitable distribution of wealth; seeks to empower the economically disenfranchised. Conducts grassroots economic education courses; maintains theater troupe and arts programs; sponsors public education programs to raise awareness of economic inequality. **Additional Websites:** http://www.responsiblewealth.org. **Telecommunication Services:** electronic mail, mlui@faireconomy.org. **Programs:** Creative Action; Education for Action;

Media; Research Publications and Books. **Projects:** Responsible Wealth. **Also Known As:** Responsible Wealth. **Publications:** *Fair Play*, semiannual. Newsletter. Alternate Formats: online ● Annual Report, annual. Alternate Formats: online ● Reports. Alternate Formats: online.

17116 ■ William E. Simon Foundation
310 S St.
PO Box 1913
Morristown, NJ 07962-1913
Ph: (212)661-8366
E-mail: roriolo@wesandsons.com
URL: http://www.wesimonfoundation.org
Contact: Mary Simon Streep, Dir.
Description: Works to support programs that are intended to strengthen education, family, and faith. **Awards:** William E. Simon Prize in Philanthropic Leadership. **Frequency:** annual. **Type:** grant. **Recipient:** by invitation only ● William E. Simon Prize in Social Entrepreneurship. **Frequency:** annual. **Type:** grant. **Recipient:** by invitation only. **Programs:** William E. Simon Prize.

17117 ■ Women's International Coalition for Economic Justice (WICEJ)
12 Dongan Pl., No. 206
New York, NY 10040
E-mail: info@wicej.org
URL: http://www.wicej.addr.com
Contact: Carol Barton, Coor.
Multinational. Description: Works to link gender with macro-economic policy in international intergovernmental policy-making arenas, from a human rights perspective. Seeks to bring a stronger economic analysis to women's issues and a stronger gender analysis to social and economic issues in the international arena. **Publications:** Pamphlets. Alternate Formats: online.

Education

17118 ■ Character Education Partnership (CEP)
1025 Connecticut Ave. NW, Ste.1011
Washington, DC 20036
Ph: (202)296-7743
Free: (800)988-8081
Fax: (202)296-7779
E-mail: geninfo@character.org
URL: http://www.character.org
Contact: Joseph W. Mazzola, Exec. Dir.
Membership Dues: student, $40 (annual) ● individual, $75 (annual) ● organization, $300 (annual). **Description:** Non-partisan organizations and individuals. Seeks to develop moral character and civic virtue in youth. Sponsors a media campaign to raise public awareness of effective character and civic education programs. **Awards:** National Schools of Character Awards Program. **Frequency:** annual. **Type:** recognition. **Recipient:** for schools and districts that exemplify CEP's Eleven Principles of Effective Character Education. **Publications:** *Character Educator*, quarterly. Newsletter. Contains information pertaining to character education.

17119 ■ Thomas B. Fordham Foundation
1701 K St. NW, Ste.1000
Washington, DC 20006
Ph: (202)223-5452
Free: (888)823-7474
Fax: (202)223-9226
E-mail: backtalk@edexcellence.net
URL: http://www.edexcellence.net
Contact: Chester E. Finn Jr., Pres.
Founded: 1959. **Description:** Supports research, publications, and action projects of national significance in elementary/secondary education reform, as well as significant education reform projects in Dayton, Ohio and vicinity. **Awards:** Fordham Prizes. **Frequency:** annual. **Type:** scholarship. **Recipient:** for a scholar who has made major contributions to education ● Thomas B. Fordham Prize for Valor. **Frequency:** annual. **Type:** monetary. **Recipient:** for

a leader who has made major contributions to education. **Projects:** Dayton. **Publications:** *Education Gadly*, weekly. Bulletin. Alternate Formats: online ● *Politicizing Science Education*. Report. Explores four case studies of threats to the integrity of science education. ● *The State of State Standards 2000*. Report. Addresses the fact that only five states combine solid academic standards with strong accountability.

17120 ■ World Care
3538 E Ellington Pl.
Tucson, AZ 85713
Ph: (520)514-1588
Fax: (520)514-1589
E-mail: hope@worldcare.org
URL: http://www.worldcare.org
Contact: Lisa Hopper, Founder/Pres.
Founded: 1994. **Staff:** 6. **Budget:** $294,000. **Non-membership. Multinational. Description:** Raises consciousness in education, health, environmental and community service arenas, both locally and internationally. Committed to Recycler's of Earth Resources to support Humanitarian and Animalitarian Relief.

Educational Funding

17121 ■ Bill Raskob Foundation
PO Box 507
Crownsville, MD 21032-0507
Ph: (410)923-9123
Fax: (410)923-9124
E-mail: ed@billraskob.org
URL: http://www.billraskob.org
Contact: Edward H. Robinson, Exec. Dir./Corporate Sec.
Founded: 1928. **Members:** 15. **Description:** Works to support students in USA by providing undergraduate, postgraduate, and graduate loans that are interest free.

17122 ■ Henry M. Jackson Foundation
1001 4th Ave., Ste.3117
Seattle, WA 98154-1101
Ph: (206)682-8565
Fax: (206)682-8961
E-mail: foundation@hmjackson.org
URL: http://www.hmjackson.org
Contact: Lara Iglitzin, Exec. Dir.
Founded: 1983. **Description:** Provides grants in Education and Advanced Research in International Affairs, Environment and Natural Resources Management, Public Service, and Human Rights.

Egypt

17123 ■ American Egyptian Cooperation Foundation (AECF)
235 E 40th St., Ste.22A
New York, NY 10016
Ph: (212)867-2323
Fax: (212)697-0465
E-mail: aecf32@aol.com
URL: http://www.americanegyptiancoop.org
Contact: Abdel Fattah Zaki, Pres./CEO
Founded: 1987. **Membership Dues:** academic institution/sponsoring individual, $100 (annual) ● corporate/not-for-profit organization, $200 (annual). **Description:** Companies, organizations, and individuals having an interest in promoting commercial, investment, tourism, and closer relations between Egypt and the United States. Focuses on efforts that increase international understanding. Provides American suppliers to Egypt with required certifications and related documents. Organizes trade missions between the two countries. Prepares and disseminates business information to improve trade, investment, and industrial opportunities. Organizes study missions to Egypt for members of Congress and their staffs. Sponsors cultural events and exchange programs; fosters cooperation between educational and scientific institutions in both coun-

tries. **Libraries: Type:** reference. **Computer Services:** database, available to members only ● mailing lists, available to members only. **Committees:** Culture; Education; Media; Medical Cooperation; Public Relations; Tourism; Trade and Investment. **Publications:** *United States-Egypt-Canada Today*, quarterly. Newsletter. **Price:** available to members only. **Circulation:** 2,000. **Advertising:** accepted. **Conventions/Meetings:** periodic conference ● seminar.

El Salvador

17124 ■ COAR Peace Mission (COAR)
4395 Rocky River Dr.
Cleveland, OH 44135
Ph: (216)252-5572
Fax: (216)252-5573
E-mail: coarpm@sbcglobal.net
URL: http://www.coarpeacemission.org
Contact: Mary Stevenson, Exec. Dir.
Founded: 1980. **Staff:** 2. **Budget:** $400,000. **Languages:** English, Spanish. **Description:** Provides housing, education, and health care to orphaned, abandoned and street children in Zaragoza, El Salvador, Central America. The Children's Village can house up to 120 children under supervision and guidance of a housemother in fifteen home-like cottages. Provides a kindergarten to grade twelve school education to about 800 children from Zaragoza and neighboring villages. Offers state approved vocational training to high school students. The Santa Teresita Clinic, a quality medical clinic in an area with little other access to health care, serves the health and dental needs of up to 75-100 patients (adults and children) weekly. The Sisters of Charity of the Incarnate Word administer the Children's Village. Supports the Children's Village in El Salvador. Strives to be "the tangible and real expression of the Gospel to promote justice, community and peace in El Salvador through the support of effective programs in health, education and welfare, which assist children and others, not only to develop their full human potential, but also to contribute to the improvement of the world in which they live". **Affiliated With:** National Catholic Development Conference. **Also Known As:** Comunidad Oscar A. Romero Peace Mission. **Publications:** *COAR News*, bimonthly. Newsletter. Provides updates of activities. **Price:** free. **Circulation:** 3,000. **Advertising:** accepted. Alternate Formats: online. **Conventions/Meetings:** annual luncheon, a fundraising activity.

17125 ■ Committee in Solidarity With the People of El Salvador (CISPES)
PO Box 8560
New York, NY 10116
Ph: (212)465-8115
Fax: (212)465-8998
E-mail: cispes@cispes.org
URL: http://www.cispes.org
Contact: Burke Stansbury, Exec. Dir.
Founded: 1980. **Regional Groups:** 4. **Local Groups:** 125. **Description:** Grass roots organization in favor of self-determination for Salvadorans. Seeks to: halt U.S. intervention in El Salvador and Central America; educate the public on the realities of the Salvadoran situation; denounce human rights violations; support Salvadoran people through material aid. Has organized demonstrations in 50 cities. Sponsors tours to U.S. cities by Salvadoran labor, religious, and human rights activists. Publishes monthly newsletter "El Salvador Watch". **Formerly:** (1987) U.S. Committee in Solidarity With the People of El Salvador. **Publications:** *El Salvador Watch*, quarterly. Newsletter. Alternate Formats: online. **Conventions/Meetings:** biennial meeting.

17126 ■ SHARE Foundation: Building a New El Salvador Today (SHARE)
598 Bosworth St., No. 1
San Francisco, CA 94131
Ph: (415)239-2595
Fax: (415)239-0785

E-mail: sharesf@share-elsalvador.org
URL: http://www.share-elsalvador.org
Contact: Jose Artiga, Exec. Dir.
Founded: 1981. **Members:** 800,000. **Staff:** 18. **Budget:** $1,300,000. **Regional Groups:** 1. **Local Groups:** 55. **Languages:** Spanish. **Description:** Supports the empowerment of historically impoverished and marginalized communities, as they strive to meet both their most immediate needs and construct long-term sustainable solutions to the problems of poverty, underdevelopment and social injustice; the communities that the Foundation work with in El Salvador are changing the structures that keep people poor through an integrated effort that is reactivating sustainable local economies, creating viable rural policies that aid subsistence farmers, and financing projects that provide for the empowerment of women, development of leadership and community organizing. Has a dynamic sister parish and community program where a relationship of accompaniment is created with communities in the U.S. and El Salvador. **Awards: Frequency:** annual. **Type:** recognition. **Divisions:** Major Donor Program; Sister Parish Program. **Formed by Merger of:** (1992) Share Foundation; New El Salvador Today. **Publications:** *SHARE: Building a New El Salvador Report*, semiannual. Newsletter. Covers association projects and activities. **Price:** available to donors. **Conventions/Meetings:** National Sister Relations Conference.

Elections

17127 ■ Honest Ballot Association (HBA)
272-30 Grand Central Pkwy.
Floral Park, NY 11005
Free: (800)541-1851
E-mail: info@honestballot.com
URL: http://www.honestballot.com
Contact: Linda Gibbs, Pres.
Founded: 1909. **Description:** Serves as a nonpartisan union of citizens organized to insure clean elections, and to prevent honest votes from being offset by trickery and fraud. Investigates and prevents colonization of voters, fraudulent registrations, repetitious voting, intimidation of voters, and unsuitable polling places. Conducts studies of the adequacy of existing election laws; instructs qualified persons to serve as watchers at polling places. Prints pamphlets summarizing essential facts of election law and make them available to political parties, schools, colleges, and other groups. Sponsors research, polling, and arbitration. In addition to general public elections, supervises elections involving labor, management, municipalities, school boards, corporations, governments, and other organizations. **Conventions/Meetings:** annual meeting.

17128 ■ International Foundation for Election Systems (IFES)
1101 15th St. NW, 3rd Fl.
Washington, DC 20005
Ph: (202)350-6700
Fax: (202)452-0804
E-mail: info@ifes.org
URL: http://www.ifes.org
Founded: 1987. **Staff:** 200. **Description:** Works to support and improve the management of the election process to help assure free, fair, and credible elections in countries that request such assistance. Provides technical assistance to designated election officials in: establishing an electoral commission and body of laws; establishing a voter registry; designing voting station procedures; recruiting and training poll workers; acquiring transportation; acquiring voting materials; establishing security; aiding in counting, reporting, and certification of votes; aiding in system management; and promoting voter education and motivation. Engages in international election observation and organizes elections conferences. Promotes active citizen involvement in all aspects of the political process and respect for the rule of law. **Libraries: Type:** reference. **Holdings:** 6,000. **Subjects:** elections, political development. **Formerly:** International Foundation for Electoral Systems. **Publications:** *De-*

mocracy at Large, quarterly. Magazine. Designed for professionals interested in democracy development worldwide. **Price:** $22.00 local; $32.00 international. ISSN: 1552-9606. **Circulation:** 10,000. **Advertising:** accepted. Alternate Formats: online ● *Elections Today*, quarterly. Newsletter. Reports on election assistance projects, election calendar, election results, and technical topics in field of election administration. ISSN: 1073-6719. **Circulation:** 5,000. **Advertising:** accepted ● *IFES Buyer's Guide to Election Suppliers*, biennial. Catalog. Lists companies selling election supplies, equipment and services to those responsible for managing public and private elections. **Price:** $10.00. ISSN: 1092-5406. **Advertising:** accepted. Alternate Formats: online.

17129 ■ Open Debates
PO Box 18881
Washington, DC 20036
Ph: (202)628-9195
E-mail: info@opendebates.org
URL: http://www.opendebates.org
Contact: George Farah, Exec. Dir.
Description: Seeks to reform the presidential debate process. Works to inform the public, the news media and the policy makers about the fundamental problems with the bipartisan Commission on Presidential Debates. Advocates for an alternative presidential debate sponsor. **Computer Services:** Information services, presidential debates resources.

17130 ■ Open Voting Consortium (OVC)
9560 Windrose Ln.
Granite Bay, CA 95746
Ph: (916)791-0456 (916)772-5360
E-mail: mail@openvotingconsortium.org
URL: http://openvotingconsortium.org
Contact: Alan Dechert, Pres./CEO
Founded: 2000. **Membership Dues:** supporting, $10 (monthly). **Staff:** 40. **Languages:** English, French, Spanish. **Multinational. Description:** Aims to develop, maintain, and deliver open voting systems for use in public elections. Seeks the involvement of developers and users of voting equipment, including vendors, integrators, government agencies, standards organizations, and academia in collaborative development of open source voting system software, technology specifications, and uniform election codes. **Computer Services:** Information services, open voting resources ● mailing lists, announcements list ● online services, web ballot demo. **Programs:** Climate Change; International Waters; Multifocal Area. **Projects:** Electronic Voting Machine.

17131 ■ Voter Rights March
PO Box 3275
New York, NY 10167
E-mail: director@votermarch.org
URL: http://www.votermarch.org
Contact: Louis Posner Esq., Founder/Dir.
Founded: 2000. **Membership Dues:** $20 (annual). **Description:** Promotes voter rights, electoral reform and a progressive agenda.

Employee Rights

17132 ■ National Association for Employee Recognition (NAER)
1801 N Mill St., Ste.R
Naperville, IL 60563
Ph: (630)369-7783
Fax: (630)369-3773
E-mail: naer@recognition.org
URL: http://www.recognition.org
Contact: Steve Richardson, Pres.
Membership Dues: recognition practitioner, $250 ● resource provider, $350 ● corporate practitioner, corporate resource provider, $2,000. **Description:** Aims to enhance employee performance through recognition, including its strategies and related initiatives. Provides a medium for information, sharing, and resources to aid employees in establishing a better work environment. **Conventions/Meetings:** annual conference.

Employment

17133 ■ American Contract Compliance Association (ACCA)
PO Box 65586
St. Paul, MN 55165-0586
Free: (866)222-2298
E-mail: bjohnson@ebmud.com
URL: http://www.acca298.org
Contact: Beverly Johnson, Pres.
Founded: 1986. **Membership Dues:** general, $100 (annual) ● retired, $50 (annual). **Description:** Ensures equitable employment and contracting practices with public and private sector institutions. Promotes uniform standards and professionalism in the administration of contract compliance programs. Provides ongoing professional training to individuals. Facilitates networking and exchange of information among members. **Publications:** Membership Directory.

17134 ■ POWER: People Organized to Win Employment Rights
32 7th St.
San Francisco, CA 94103
Ph: (415)864-8372
Fax: (415)864-8373
E-mail: power@unite-to-fight.org
URL: http://www.unite-to-fight.org
Contact: Steve Williams, Exec. Dir./Co-Founder
Founded: 1997. **Description:** Low-wage workers committed to economic and social justice in order to eliminate poverty and oppression. **Committees:** Steering; Working Class Leadership and Strategy. **Projects:** Women Workers.

Energy

17135 ■ Americans for Balanced Energy Choices (ABEC)
PO Box 1638
Alexandria, VA 22313
Ph: (703)684-7473
Free: (877)358-6699
E-mail: membership@balancedenergy.org
URL: http://www.balancedenergy.org
Contact: Joe Lucas, Exec. Dir.
Description: Promotes a dialogue with community leaders on issues involving America's growing demand for electricity. Advocates for the proper balance between protecting the environment and providing for continued economic growth and prosperity for America's working families. **Computer Services:** database, states' electricity portfolio.

17136 ■ Consumer Energy Council of America Research Foundation (CECA/RF)
2000 L St. NW, Ste.802
Washington, DC 20036
Ph: (202)659-0404
Fax: (202)659-0407
E-mail: outreach@cecarf.org
URL: http://www.cecarf.org
Contact: Ellen Berman, Pres.
Founded: 1973. **Staff:** 8. **Budget:** $1,000,000. **Description:** Focuses on network industries. Strives to establish arenas in which domestic and international policymakers and business leaders can forge innovative solutions to economic, environmental, and educational challenges worldwide. Works for constructive involvement of government and private organizations in broad educational initiatives and in the creation of self-sustaining and socially responsible markets for essential services. Provides expertise in how government and corporate policies affect the public, and how public response will affect legislation and the vibrancy of new markets. **Libraries: Type:** reference. **Holdings:** 10,000; articles, books, periodicals. **Subjects:** energy, policy, demand side management, energy efficiency, renewable, petroleum, natural gas, transportation, public utilities, conservation. **Computer Services:** database, utility appliance rebate programs. **Committees:** Advisory. **Publications:** *A Compendium of Utility Sponsored Energy*

Efficient Rebate Programs. **Price:** $75.00 ● *Bidding for Power.* **Price:** $75.00 ● *The Convergence Phenomenon: A Consumer Prospective.* Report. **Price:** $20.00 ● *Findings of the Ceca Broadband Access Summit.* Report. **Price:** $100.00. Alternate Formats: online ● *Incorporating Environmental Externalities Annotated Bibliography: Final Edition.* **Price:** $125.00 ● *Oil, Gas, or .?.* Report. Features technical support documents. **Price:** $35.00.

17137 ■ National Energy Education Development Project (NEED)
8408 Kao Cir.
Manassas, VA 20110
Ph: (703)257-1117
Free: (800)875-5029
Fax: (703)257-0037
E-mail: info@need.org
URL: http://www.need.org
Contact: Paul Loeffelman, Chm.
Founded: 1980. **Members:** 5,000. **Membership Dues:** educator/school, $35 (annual). **Staff:** 3. **Budget:** $975,000. **State Groups:** 38. **Description:** Students and educators; community, industry, and government leaders. Seeks to educate individuals so that they are capable of making informed decisions regarding energy use and policy through the development of a grassroots energy education network. Provides assistance in the development of energy education programs for schools; these programs encourage students to work in small groups while fostering development of their critical thinking and problem solving skills. Compiles statistics. **Awards:** Youth Award for Energy Achievement. **Frequency:** annual. **Type:** recognition. **Recipient:** for submission of scrapbook highlighting energy education activities. **Also Known As:** Need Project. **Formerly:** (1988) National Energy Education Day Project. **Publications:** *Career Currents,* periodic. Newsletter. Explores careers in the hydropower industry. ● *Energy Around the World* ● *Energy Carnival* ● *Energy Conservation Contract* ● *Energy Enigma* ● *Energy Exchange,* semiannual. Magazine. **Price:** included in membership dues ● *Energy Jeopardy* ● *Energy Plays* ● *The Great Energy Debate Game* ● *Great Energy Rock Performances* ● *Local Participation Kit.* Includes resource and activities guides, fact sheets, and reports. ● *Museum of Solid Waste and Energy* ● *The Nation's Energy Education Report Card,* annual. Includes results of poll taken by students in grades 4-12. ● *NEED Project Annual Report and National Recognition Ceremonies* ● *Science of Energy Guide.* **Conventions/Meetings:** annual National Leadership Training Conference (exhibits) - every summer ● annual National Recognition Ceremonies - conference - always June, Washington, DC ● workshop, for training regionally.

17138 ■ Redwood Alliance (RA)
PO Box 293
Arcata, CA 95518
Ph: (707)822-7884
E-mail: info@redwoodalliance.org
URL: http://www.redwoodalliance.org
Contact: Michael Welch, Contact
Founded: 1978. **Members:** 4,000. **Staff:** 1. **Budget:** $20,000. **Description:** Promotes safe and efficient energy use and development. Supports: anti-nuclear energy work; renewable energy promotion; climate protection; consumer activism; environmental education; and progressive local, regional, and national policies. Influences the government for environmentally sound laws. Offers a referral service to other groups. Conducts research and educational programs. **Libraries: Type:** reference; open to the public. **Holdings:** 400; archival material, books, video recordings. **Subjects:** renewable energy, nuclear, climate protection. **Telecommunication Services:** electronic bulletin board, (707)822-8640 ● electronic mail, redwood.alliance@homepower.com. **Programs:** Solar-electric Demonstration. **Projects:** Climate Action.

Entertainment

17139 ■ Black Rock Coalition (BRC)
PO Box 1054, Cooper Sta.
New York, NY 10276

Ph: (212)713-5097
E-mail: ldavis@blackrockcoalition.org
URL: http://www.blackrockcoalition.org
Contact: LaRonda Davis, Pres.
Founded: 1985. **Members:** 400. **Membership Dues:** individual, $25 (annual) ● band, $100 (annual). **Staff:** 10. **Description:** Artists, musicians, writers, and supporters of alternative/black music. (Alternative/black music refers to popular musical styles, such as rock, that are usually not performed or recorded by black artists and musicians.) Works to foster change in the conventional operation and classification of black music and musicians within the entertainment industry. Seeks to counteract competition among musicians through networking programs and the sharing of resources. Opposes what the group terms the American "apartheid-oriented" rock circuit, which perpetuates racism, commercial restrictions, and double standards within the music industry that may deter black artists from receiving the same musical freedom of expression and marketing privileges afforded white artists. Promotes, produces, and distributes alternative/black music and provides information, technical expertise, and performance and recording opportunities for "musically and politically progressive musicians". Works to increase the visibility of black rock artists in music media and on college radio stations. Conducts seminars on all aspects of music, musical technology, and the entertainment industry. Offers concert promotion services. Plans to develop videotape recording opportunities for the archival documentation of cultural events. Conducts music workshops for children and adults. **Libraries: Type:** open to the public. **Subjects:** music by member bands. **Computer Services:** Mailing lists, of members. **Subgroups:** Orchestra. **Also Known As:** The BRC. **Publications:** *BRC Newsletter,* monthly. Contains arts and education information, reviews and updates on organizational activities and musical artists. **Price:** free for members; $12.00 /year for nonmembers. **Circulation:** 450. **Advertising:** accepted. **Conventions/Meetings:** meeting - seasonally, second Saturday of each third month.

Environment

17140 ■ American Public Information on the Environment
PO Box 676
Northfield, MN 55057-0676
Free: (800)320-2743
Fax: (507)645-5724
E-mail: info@americanpie.org
URL: http://www.AmericanPIE.org
Contact: Brad Easterson, Exec. Dir.
Founded: 1993. **Members:** 700. **Membership Dues:** regular, $25 (annual) ● regular, $45 (biennial) ● advocate, $100 (quinquennial) ● patron - life, $1,000. **Staff:** 7. **Description:** Individuals, organizations, and businesses. Promotes "development of a land ethic and ecological consciousness essential to sustaining the environment". Gathers and disseminates information on "environmental quality, protection of natural resources and promotion of environmental health for all elements of the biotic community". **Also Known As:** American PIE.

17141 ■ Network for Environmental Policy Awareness (NEPA)
c/o Paula P. Easley, Coor.
2134 Crataegus Ave.
Anchorage, AK 99508-4028
Ph: (907)274-6800
E-mail: peasley@gci.net
Contact: Paula P. Easley, Coor.
Founded: 1991. **Staff:** 1. **Description:** Works to collect and disseminate by fax and e-mail information on federal policies, regulations and legislation. Conducts research on regulatory reform issues; offers educational programs; maintains speakers' bureau. **Libraries: Type:** by appointment only. **Holdings:** articles, audiovisuals, books, clippings, periodicals.

17142 ■ Political Ecology Group (PEG)
Address Unknown since 2007
Founded: 1990. **Members:** 300. **Membership Dues:**
general, $35 (annual). **Staff:** 4. **Budget:** $200,000.
Description: Individuals with an interest in environmental justice and immigrant rights. Promotes adoption of more effective public environmental and immigration policies. Conducts leadership development
and educational programs to raise public awareness
of environmental and immigration issues. **Libraries:**
Type: by appointment only. **Holdings:** books, clippings, periodicals. **Subjects:** Environmental justice,
immigrant rights, population. **Awards:** Poetry in Action Awards. **Frequency:** periodic. **Type:** monetary.
Recipient: outstanding urban poets.

Environmental Health

17143 ■ Towards Freedom
2116 Pico Blvd., No. B
Santa Monica, CA 90405
Ph: (310)866-6116
E-mail: info@towardsfreedom.com
URL: http://www.towardsfreedom.com
Contact: Nanci Rose, Volunteer Coor.
Description: Promotes issues relating to environ-
ment, education, nutrition, ways to live and changes
needed to live in a changing world. **Computer**
Services: Electronic publishing, e-newsletters.

Environmental Law

17144 ■ National Endangered Species Act
Reform Coalition (NESARC)
1050 Thomas Jefferson St., 7th Fl.
Washington, DC 20007
Ph: (202)333-7481
Fax: (202)338-2416
E-mail: nesarc@vnf.com
URL: http://www.nesarc.org
Contact: Nancy Macan McNally, Exec. Dir.
Founded: 1991. **Description:** Represents rural ir-
rigators, municipalities, farmers, electric utilities,
organizations, and businesses that are supportive of
updating the ESA to achieve the ultimate goal of species recovery. Seeks to achieve improvements to the
Endangered Species Act (ESA). Works with both parties of the U.S. Congress on their proposals to
improve the ESA. **Publications:** *ESA Update.* Newsletter ● *NESARC News,* periodic. Report. Issues and
updates on events surrounding the implementation of
the Endangered Species Act. Alternate Formats: online.

Ethics

17145 ■ Joseph and Edna Josephson
Institute of Ethics
9841 Airport Blvd., Ste.300
Los Angeles, CA 90045-5415
Ph: (310)846-4800
Free: (800)711-2670
Fax: (310)846-4857
E-mail: ji@jiethics.org
URL: http://www.josephsoninstitute.org
Contact: Michael S. Josephson, Founder/Pres.
Founded: 1987. **Description:** Works to improve the
ethical quality of society by advocating principled
reasoning and ethical decision-making. **Projects:**
Character Counts. **Publications:** Newsletter. Alter-
nate Formats: online ● Reports ● Surveys. **Conven-**
tions/Meetings: workshop.

17146 ■ Joseph P. and Rose F. Kennedy
Institute of Ethics
Box 571212
Georgetown Univ.
Healy Hall, 4th Fl.
Washington, DC 20057-1212
Ph: (202)687-8099 (202)687-6821
Fax: (202)687-8089

E-mail: kicourse@georgetown.edu
URL: http://kennedyinstitute.georgetown.edu/index.
htm
Contact: Madison Powers JD, Dir./Sr. Research
Scholar
Founded: 1971. **Membership Dues:** regular, $55
(annual) ● student, $35 (annual) ● institutional, $169
(annual) ● pension, $43 (annual). **Description:** Acts
as a teaching and research center offering ethical
perspectives on policy issues. **Libraries: Type:** reference. **Subjects:** ethics. **Programs:** Asian Bioethics;
European Program in Professional Ethics; Visiting
Researchers; Visiting Scholars. **Publications:** *Bibliography of Bioethics* ● *Bioethics Thesaurus* ● *Encyclopedia of Bioethics* ● *Kennedy Institute of Ethics
Journal.* **Price:** included in membership dues ● *New
Titles in Bioethics,* quarterly. Book ● *Newsletter of
the Network on Ethics and Intellectual Disabilities* ●
Scope Note Series. **Price:** $5.00 in U.S.; $8.00
outside U.S. **Conventions/Meetings:** lecture ● annual symposium, held at Georgetown University.

Europe

17147 ■ European Union - Delegation of the
Commission to the United States
2300 M St. NW
Washington, DC 20037
Ph: (202)862-9500
Fax: (202)429-1766
E-mail: relex-delusw-help@cec.eu.int
URL: http://www.eurunion.org
Contact: John Bruton, Ambassador
Founded: 1954. **Members:** 15. **Staff:** 80. **Lan-
guages:** English, French. **Description:** Diplomatic
delegation of the European Commission in the United
States for the European Union, comprising European
Community (Common Market); European Coal and
Steel Community; and European Atomic Energy
Community. Distributes official documents and
information brochures of the European Union. Pro-
vides Speaker's Bureau and reference service.
Represents the EU to U.S. government, international
organizations, trade associations, academia, U.S.
industry and the general public. Responds to all
public inquiries. **Libraries: Type:** reference. **Holdings:** 50,000. **Subjects:** EU law and policies. **Formerly:** European Community Office of Press and
Public Affairs; (1993) European Community Information Service; (1998) European Commission Office of
Press and Public Affairs; (2001) European Union Office of Press and Public Affairs. **Publications:**
Newsletters. Alternate Formats: online ● Brochures.

Families

17148 ■ American Family Rights Association
(AFRA)
c/o Nev Moore, Co-Founder
PO Box 1560
Cotuit, MA 02635
E-mail: secretgarden53@hotmail.com
URL: http://familyrightsassociation.com
Contact: Dennis Hinger, Exec. VP
Description: Promotes the fundamental liberty, rights
and privileges of families. Assists families and
children by providing educational materials, news,
support and information on sovereign rights and liber-
ties of families. **Computer Services:** database,
services directory. **Departments:** Advocacy; Cam-
paigns and Activism; Elders and Grandparents;
Investigations; Kids; Military Concerns; Parent News;
Statistics.

17149 ■ Kids Need Both Parents
PO Box 6481
Portland, OR 97228-6481
Ph: (503)727-3686 (503)224-9477
E-mail: jpwhinston@aol.com
URL: http://www.kidsneedbothparents.org
Contact: James P. Whinston, Contact
Description: Promotes fairness, equality, and family
in the best interests of children; encourages parents

to stand and work together. **Conventions/Meetings:**
weekly Support Groups - meeting.

17150 ■ National Fatherhood Initiative (NFI)
101 Lake Forest Blvd., Ste.360
Gaithersburg, MD 20877
Ph: (301)948-0599
Fax: (301)948-4325
E-mail: info@fatherhood.org
URL: http://www.fatherhood.org
Contact: Mr. Roland Warren, Pres.
Founded: 1994. **Membership Dues:** individual, $30
● organizational, $100. **Description:** Promotes
fatherhood; conducts public awareness campaigns
encouraging responsible fatherhood; provides re-
source materials to organizations; conducts research;
works to improve the effectiveness of public policies
that encourages responsible fatherhood; disseminates information to men seeking to become better
fathers. Conducts community fatherhood forums. **Programs:** Best Practices in Fatherhood; Building
Systems That Support Marriage in Fatherhood;
Deployed Fathers and Families; Doctor Dad; Long
Distance Dads; Social Marketing for Fatherhood; 24/7
Dad; 24/7 Dad Christian-based. **Publications:** *Fatherhood Today,* quarterly. Newsletter ● Brochures.
Conventions/Meetings: National Summit on Fatherhood - conference.

Federal Government

17151 ■ National Priorities Project (NPP)
17 New South St., Ste.302
Northampton, MA 01060
Ph: (413)584-9556
Fax: (413)586-9647
E-mail: info@nationalpriorities.org
URL: http://www.nationalpriorities.org
Contact: Greg Speeter, Exec. Dir.
Founded: 1982. **Staff:** 9. **Budget:** $350,000. **De-
scription:** Offers citizen and community groups' tools
and resources to shape federal budget and policy
priorities promoting social and economic justice.
Computer Services: database, Congressional
District Profiles. **Telecommunication Services:** elec-
tronic mail, pschwartz@nationalpriorities.org ●
electronic mail, philk@nationalpriorities.org. **Publications:** *Factbook* ● *Grassroots Factbook.* Provides
updates on impact of current spending proposals and
debate on nation's states and cities.

Feminism

17152 ■ 9 to 5, National Association of
Working Women
207 E Buffalo St., No. 211
Milwaukee, WI 53202
Ph: (414)274-0925
Free: (800)522-0925
Fax: (414)272-2870
E-mail: 9to5@9to5.org
URL: http://www.9to5.org
Contact: Ellen Bravo, Co-Dir.
Founded: 1973. **Members:** 13,000. **Membership
Dues:** regular, $25 (annual) ● sisterhood, organiza-
tion, $40 (annual). **Staff:** 14. **Budget:** $600,000. **Local Groups:** 25. **Description:** Represents women
office workers. Seeks to build a national network of
local office worker chapters that strives to gain better
pay, proper use of office automation, opportunities for
advancement, elimination of sex and race discrimination, and improved working conditions for women office workers. Works to introduce legislation or regulations at state level to protect video display terminal
operators. Produces studies and research in areas
such as reproductive hazards of Video Display
Terminals (VDTs), automation's effect on clerical
employment, family and medical leaves, and stress.
Conducts annual summer school for working women.
Maintains speakers' bureau. **Telecommunication
Services:** electronic mail, hotline@9to5.org. **Funds:**
9to5 Working Women. **Formerly:** (1978) Working
Women Organizing Project; (1982) Working Women,

National Association of Office Workers. **Supersedes:** National Women's Employment Project. **Publications:** *The 9 to 5 Guide to Combating Sexual Harassment.* **Price:** $15.00 ● *9 to 5 Newsline,* 5/year. Newsletter. **Price:** included in membership dues; $25.00 /year for individuals; $40.00 /year for institutions. **Circulation:** 12,000 ● *9 to 5: Working Women's Guide to Office Survival* ● Videos. **Conventions/Meetings:** annual conference.

17153 ■ 9 to 5 Working Women Education Fund (WWEF)
207 E Buffalo St., No. 211
Milwaukee, WI 53202
Ph: (414)274-0925
Free: (800)522-0925
Fax: (414)272-2870
E-mail: 9to5@9to5.org
URL: http://www.9to5.org
Contact: Donna Skenadore, Chair
Founded: 1973. **Members:** 20,000. **Membership Dues:** $25 (annual). **Staff:** 17. **Budget:** $900,000. **Regional Groups:** 28. **Description:** Conducts research on the concerns of women workers. Includes topics such as: work/family, anti-discrimination, welfare/workfare, contingent work. Conducts public presentations and seminars upon request; provides speakers and trainers on sexual harassment. Compiles statistics of women in the workforce. **Libraries: Type:** open to the public. **Awards:** Scholarships to Annual Leadership Conference. **Frequency:** annual. **Type:** scholarship. **Recipient:** based on need or activity within organization. **Subgroups:** 9 to 5 National Association of Working Women. **Affiliated With:** 9 to 5, National Association of Working Women. **Formerly:** (1989) Working Women Education Fund. **Publications:** *Balancing Job/Family Challenge: Not for Women Only.* Reports. **Price:** $13.00. **Conventions/Meetings:** annual National Leadership Conference - conference and workshop, public policy and leadership issues - usually in Washington, DC.

17154 ■ ALA Social Responsibilities Round Table Feminist Task Force
c/o American Library Association
50 E Huron St.
Chicago, IL 60611
Free: (800)545-2433
E-mail: jenny_baltes@hotmail.com
URL: http://libr.org/FTF
Contact: Jennifer Baltes, Coor.
Founded: 1971. **Description:** Members of the American Library Association interested in Feminist issues. **Additional Websites:** http://www.ala.org. **Telecommunication Services:** additional toll-free number, (888)814-7692. **Affiliated With:** American Library Association. **Publications:** *Women in Libraries,* quarterly. Newsletter. **Price:** $10.00 /year for individuals; $15.00 /year for institutions. **Circulation:** 300. **Conventions/Meetings:** semiannual conference, held in conjunction with the American Library Association (exhibits).

17155 ■ Business and Professional Women USA (BPW/USA)
1900 M St. NW, Ste.310
Washington, DC 20036
Ph: (202)293-1100
Fax: (202)861-0298
E-mail: memberservices@bpwusa.org
URL: http://www.bpwusa.org
Contact: Deborah L. Frett, CEO
Founded: 1919. **Members:** 35,000. **Membership Dues:** member-at-large, $100 (annual). **Staff:** 13. **Budget:** $3,000,000. **Regional Groups:** 53. **Local Groups:** 2,000. **Description:** Represents men and women of every age, religion, political party, and socioeconomic background. Works to achieve equity for all women in the workplace through advocacy, education, and information. Provides professional development, networking, and career advancement opportunities for working women. Sponsors a grass roots action team to influence elected officials on issues concerning women. Sponsors National Business Women's Week during the third week of October. **Awards:** Women Mean Business Awards.

Frequency: annual. **Type:** recognition. **Recipient:** for outstanding achievements. **Formerly:** (2000) National Federation of Business and Professional Women's Clubs. **Publications:** *BusinessWoman,* quarterly. Magazine. Covers women's socioeconomic issues such as pay equity and child care; includes association news. **Price:** included in membership dues; $20.00 /year for nonmembers. ISSN: 0027-8831. **Circulation:** 80,000. **Advertising:** accepted ● *Making Workplaces Work: Quality Work Policies for Small Business,* annual. Video. Details working family values. **Price:** $29.95 for members; $295.00 for businesses ● *Work and Family Policies: Options for the 90's and Beyond.* Paper. **Conventions/Meetings:** annual conference and workshop (exhibits) ● periodic meeting.

17156 ■ Center for American Women and Politics (CAWP)
Eagleton Inst. of Politics
Rutgers Univ.
191 Ryders Ln.
New Brunswick, NJ 08901-8557
Ph: (732)932-9384
Fax: (732)932-0014
E-mail: walsh@rci.rutgers.edu
URL: http://www.cawp.rutgers.edu
Contact: Debbie Walsh, Dir.
Founded: 1971. **Staff:** 10. **Description:** Serves as a university-based research, education and public service center. Aims to promote greater understanding and knowledge about women's changing relationship to politics and government and to enhance women's influence and leadership in public life. **Libraries: Type:** reference. **Holdings:** books, papers, periodicals. **Subjects:** women's political participation. **Computer Services:** database, National Information Bank of Women in Public Office (lists women elected officials). **Conventions/Meetings:** periodic conference ● workshop.

17157 ■ Center for Community Solutions (CCS)
4508 Mission Bay Dr.
San Diego, CA 92109
Ph: (858)272-5777
E-mail: info@ccssd.org
URL: http://www.ccssd.org
Contact: Verna Griffin-Tabor, Exec. Dir.
Founded: 1969. **Staff:** 55. **Budget:** $1,800,000. **Local Groups:** 2. **Description:** Offers: counseling on a one-to-one basis or in groups; crisis hotline for victims of sexual assault and family violence; shelter for battered women; family and relationship counseling; legal counseling and assistance for battered individuals; information on and referral to other programs and organizations and to human service agencies. Conducts classes in the community and special workshops (Sexual Assault Prevention, Family Violence, and Assertiveness Training). Includes projects such as: Dissolution Clinic - Uncontested Divorces, Rape Crisis Center, Shelter for Battered Women and Their Children, and Temporary Restraining Order Legal Clinic. Maintains speakers' bureau. **Telecommunication Services:** 24-hour hotline, crisis line, (888)385-4657. **Programs:** Counseling Center; Domestic Violence Services; Legal Clinic; Prevention and Education; Rape Crisis Center; Youth To Youth Helpline. **Formerly:** (1971) Center for Women's Studies; (1998) Center for Women's Studies and Services. **Publications:** *Bylines by Women* ● *CCS Connections.* Newsletter. Alternate Formats: online.

17158 ■ Center for Women Policy Studies (CWPS)
1776 Massachusetts Ave. NW, Ste.450
Washington, DC 20036
Ph: (202)872-1770
Fax: (202)296-8962
E-mail: cwps@centerwomenpolicy.org
URL: http://www.centerwomenpolicy.org
Contact: Leslie R. Wolfe, Pres.
Founded: 1972. **Staff:** 13. **Languages:** English, Spanish. **Description:** Independent feminist policy research and advocacy institution. Believes that all issues affecting women are interrelated, and that sex,

race, and class biases in society must be addressed simultaneously. Works for reform of public health, education, and economic policies to make society more open to the advancement of women. Conducts research programs in areas including educational equity, family and workplace diversity, economic opportunity for low-income women, violence against women, women's health, reproductive rights, and operates the National Resource Center on Women and AIDS Policy. Makes available policy internships. **Programs:** Contract With Women of the USA State Legislators Initiative; Foreign Policy Institute for State Legislators; National Resource Center on Women and AIDS; Project EMPOWER - Access to College for Low Income Women; State Policy on Reproductive Rights and Health; US PACT (Policy Advocacy to Combat Trafficking); Work/Family and Workplace Diversity. **Publications:** Books ● Monographs ● Reports.

17159 ■ Clearinghouse on Women's Issues (CWI)
PO Box 70603
Friendship Heights
Bethesda, MD 20813
Ph: (202)362-5717
E-mail: cwi@womensclearinghouse.org
URL: http://www.womensclearinghouse.org
Contact: Ellen S. Overton, Pres.
Founded: 1972. **Members:** 400. **Membership Dues:** individual, $25 (annual) ● organization, $35 (annual). **Description:** Nonpartisan clearinghouse for national, regional, state, and local women's and civil rights. Aims to exchange and disseminate educational information and materials on issues related to discrimination on the basis of race, sex, age, or marital status, with particular emphasis on public policies affecting the economic and educational status of women. **Publications:** *CWI Newsletter,* monthly. **Price:** included in membership dues. **Circulation:** 400. **Conventions/Meetings:** meeting - every 4th Tuesday, Washington, DC.

17160 ■ Coalition for Women's Appointments (CWA)
1634 Eye St. NW, Ste.310
Washington, DC 20006
Ph: (202)785-1100
Fax: (202)785-3605
E-mail: info@nwpc.org
URL: http://www.nwpc.org
Contact: Jenny Johnson, Contact
Founded: 1976. **Members:** 84. **Staff:** 2. **Description:** Organization coordinated by the National Women's Political Caucus. Seeks to promote the appointment and promotion of women to high level government positions and to assist women seeking appointment or election to the state or federal bench. The coalition evaluates and monitors appointments to determine their impact on issues affecting women. Compiles statistics and maintains biographical archives.

17161 ■ Commission on the Status of Women (CSW)
c/o Department of Economic and Social Affairs
Div. for the Advancement of Women
2 UN Plz., DC2-12th Fl.
New York, NY 10017
Ph: (212)963-3463
Fax: (212)963-3463
E-mail: daw@un.org
URL: http://www.un.org/womenwatch/daw/csw
Contact: Ms. Carmen Maria Gallardo, Chair
Founded: 1946. **Members:** 45. **Staff:** 15. **Budget:** $202,400. **Regional Groups:** 5. **Languages:** Arabic, Chinese, English, French, Russian, Spanish. **Description:** 45 Representatives from United Nations member States. Promotes women's rights in political, economic, civil, social, and educational fields. Encourages cooperation between organizations seeking to advance the status of women, and advises the U.N. and member bodies on situations requiring immediate attention. Acts as a preparatory body for the world conference on women. **Working Groups:** Communications on the Status of Women.

17162 ■ Commission for Women's Equality (CWE)

c/o American Jewish Congress
825 3rd Ave., Ste.1800
New York, NY 10022
Ph: (212)879-4500
Fax: (212)758-1633
E-mail: hkurlander@ajcongress.org
URL: http://www.ajcongress.org
Contact: Harriet Kurlander, Dir.
Founded: 1984. **Members:** 200. **Staff:** 2. **Regional Groups:** 15. **Description:** Represents feminists, elected officials, professionals, academics, and Jewish communal leaders working to define feminism within a context compatible with Judaism. Areas of concern include: reproductive freedom, economic equity, child care, equality in religious life, and the empowerment of women in politics and in Jewish communal life. Serves as a commission of the American Jewish Congress. **Libraries: Type:** reference. **Holdings:** archival material, books, business records, clippings, periodicals. **Subjects:** feminism, women's health issues, Judaism, feminism. **Affiliated With:** American Jewish Congress. **Formerly:** (1991) National Commission for Women's Equality. **Publications:** *International Jewish Feminist Directory* ● Brochure ● Newsletter, monthly. **Conventions/Meetings:** periodic international conference ● quarterly meeting.

17163 ■ Committee on the Elimination of Discrimination Against Women (CEDAW)

c/o United Nations Division for the Advancement of Women
2 United Nations Plz., DC 2-12th Fl.
New York, NY 10017
Fax: (212)963-3463
E-mail: daw@un.org
URL: http://www.unhchr.ch/html/menu2/6/cedw.htm
Multinational. Description: A program of the United Nations Division for the Advancement of Women. Individuals and organizations with an interest in the civil and human rights of women. Works to strengthen and expand legal protection of women's rights worldwide. Sponsors studies and conferences; gathers and disseminates information. **Additional Websites:** http://www.un.org/womenwatch/daw/cedaw. **Publications:** Report. Alternate Formats: online. **Conventions/Meetings:** annual meeting.

17164 ■ Committee on South Asian Women (COSAW)

c/o Dr. Jyotsna Vaid, Ed.
Texas A&M Univ.
Dept. of Psychology
College Station, TX 77843-4235
Ph: (979)845-2576
Fax: (979)845-4727
E-mail: jxv@psyc.tamu.edu
URL: http://people.tamu.edu/~jvaid/cosaw.html
Contact: Dr. Jyotsna Vaid, Ed.
Founded: 1982. **Staff:** 5. **Description:** Network of women of South Asian origin or interests. Publicizes efforts of South Asian and North American women's groups. Publishes writings by South Asian women on the living and working conditions of women in and from South Asia, including Bangladesh, India, Nepal, Pakistan, and Sri Lanka. Supports research on issues of interest to South Asian women settled abroad. Sponsors films. Maintains speakers' bureau. **Libraries: Type:** reference. **Publications:** *COSAW Bulletin*, semiannual. Includes essays, creative writing, book and film reviews, news from South Asian women's groups, a research index, and a directory of organizations. **Price:** $7.00/issue; $14.00/year for students; $18.00 /year for individuals; $30.00/year for organizations. ISSN: 0885-4319. **Circulation:** 300. **Advertising:** accepted ● *South Asian Women at Home and Abroad: A Guide to Resources* ● Audiotapes ● Monographs ● Videos. **Conventions/Meetings:** lecture ● seminar ● workshop.

17165 ■ Congressional Caucus for Women's Issues (CCWI)

c/o Carolyn B. Maloney, Co-Chair
2331 Rayburn HOB
Washington, DC 20515-3214
Ph: (202)225-7944
Fax: (202)225-4709
URL: http://www.house.gov/pelosi/womcauc.htm
Contact: Carolyn B. Maloney, Co-Chair
Founded: 1977. **Members:** 55. **Staff:** 2. **Description:** Bipartisan legislative service organization of the U.S. House of Representatives with the goal of improving the status of American women and eliminating discrimination "built into many federal programs and policies". Supports legislation to improve women's status. Focuses on equal treatment of women with regard to violence, health care, safe motherhood, education, opportunity, retirement, children and child care, military and veteran women, and tax policy. **Formerly:** (1982) Congresswomen's Caucus.

17166 ■ Coordinating Council for Women in History (CCWH)

211 Marginal Way, No. 733
PO Box 9715
Portland, ME 04104-5015
E-mail: jscanlon@bowdoin.edu
URL: http://www.theccwh.org
Contact: Jennifer R. Scanlon, Exec. Dir.
Founded: 1969. **Members:** 800. **Membership Dues:** income over $75,000, $75 (annual) ● full-time employee, $50 (annual) ● student, part-time/low income, $20 (annual) ● institution, $50 (annual). **Staff:** 1. **Budget:** $20,000. **Regional Groups:** 14. **Description:** Represents women historians and others interested in women's history. Works to encourage and help develop research and instruction in the field of women's history, advance the status of women at all levels and increase their numbers, and to oppose discrimination against women in the profession. Assists members in establishing panels in different conferences; promotes networking. **Awards:** Catherine Prelinger Award. **Frequency:** annual. **Type:** monetary. **Recipient:** for scholarly excellence to a non-traditional scholar ● Graduate Student Award. **Frequency:** annual. **Type:** monetary. **Recipient:** for scholarly excellence ● Ida B. Wells. **Frequency:** annual. **Type:** monetary. **Recipient:** for scholarly excellence. **Committees:** Catherine Prelinger Non-Traditional Scholar Award; Graduate Student Award. **Formerly:** (1995) Coordinating Committee on Women in the Historical Profession/Conference Group on Women's History. **Publications:** Newsletter, semiannual. **Price:** included in membership dues. **Circulation:** 1,000. **Advertising:** accepted ● Also publishes courses and job advertisements. **Conventions/Meetings:** annual meeting, in conjunction with American Historical Association (exhibits) - always in January.

17167 ■ DC Feminists Against Pornography (DCFAP)

Address Unknown since 2007
Founded: 1978. **Membership Dues:** activist, $25 (annual). **Description:** Works to address the impact of sexism, racism and violence in the media, advertising and pornography. Advocates community action instead of censorship; conducts educational and research programs; sponsors protest actions; offers slide shows and speakers' bureau. **Libraries: Type:** reference; by appointment only. **Holdings:** archival material, articles, audiovisuals, books, clippings, periodicals. **Subjects:** sexism and racism in media, pornography industry, violence against women, community organizing strategies.

17168 ■ Delegation for Friendship Among Women (DFW)

1630 Edgecumbe Rd.
St. Paul, MN 55116
URL: http://www.friendshipamongwomen.org
Contact: Mary Pomeroy, Sec.-Treas.
Founded: 1962. **Members:** 144. **Budget:** $72,000. **Description:** Women who have displayed leadership qualities in the fields of academia, architecture, business, journalism, law, and science. Promotes better understanding between women and women's organizations in developing nations and American women. Sponsors networks for the health, education, and welfare of women and children. Arranges programs for women visiting the U.S. from developing countries; provides speakers for women's activities. **Libraries: Type:** reference. **Holdings:** 600; archival material. **Publications:** Bulletin, periodic ● Newsletter, periodic. **Conventions/Meetings:** annual meeting.

17169 ■ Eleanor Foundation (EF)

325 W Huron St., Ste.706
Chicago, IL 60610
Ph: (312)337-7766
Fax: (312)337-7762
E-mail: info@eleanorfoundation.org
URL: http://www.eleanorfoundation.org
Contact: Rosanna A. Marquez, Pres.
Founded: 1898. **Staff:** 25. **Budget:** $950,000. **Description:** Promotes the advancement of women. Sponsors affordable residence for working women and full-time students in Chicago, IL, social and philanthropic club for mature women. **Committees:** Marketing; Physical Facilities; Resource Development. **Programs:** Education; Housing. **Formerly:** (1993) Eleanor Association; (2006) Eleanor Women's Foundation. **Publications:** *CEC Bulletin*, monthly. **Price:** $27.50/year. **Circulation:** 100 ● *The Eleanor Record*, quarterly. Newsletter. **Price:** free. **Circulation:** 300 ● Brochures.

17170 ■ Federally Employed Women (FEW)

1666 K St. NW, Ste.440
Washington, DC 20006
Ph: (202)898-0994
Fax: (202)898-0994
E-mail: few@few.org
URL: http://www.few.org
Contact: Ms. Rhonda Trent, Pres.
Founded: 1968. **Membership Dues:** member-at-large, $35 (annual) ● chapter, $25 (annual) ● life, $250. **Regional Groups:** 11. **Local Groups:** 200. **Description:** Represents men and women employed by the federal government. Seeks to end sexual discrimination in government service; to increase job opportunities for women in government service and to further the potential of all women in the government; to improve the merit system in government employment; to assist present and potential government employees who are discriminated against because of sex; to work with other organizations and individuals concerned with equal employment opportunity in the government. Provides speakers and sponsors seminars to publicize the Federal Women's Program; furnishes members with information on pending legislation designed to end discrimination against working women; informs and provides members opportunities for training to improve their job potential; issues fact sheets interpreting civil service rules and regulations and other legislative issues; provides annual training conference for over 3,000 women and men. **Awards:** Distinguished Service Award. **Frequency:** annual. **Type:** recognition. **Recipient:** for most outstanding person during the year to advance equality of opportunity for women ● **Type:** recognition. **Committees:** Awards; Bylaws and Resolution; Credentials; Legal; Publications, Policy and Review. **Programs:** Diversity; Legislative; Training. **Publications:** *A Handbook For Agency Visits*, periodic. Alternate Formats: online ● *Annual Report to the Membership*, annual. Alternate Formats: online ● *FEW's News and Views*, bimonthly. Newsletter. **Price:** included in membership dues. **Circulation:** 12,000. **Advertising:** accepted. Alternate Formats: online ● *National Policy and Procedures Manual*, annual. Alternate Formats: online ● Brochures, periodic. **Conventions/Meetings:** annual National Training Program - conference (exhibits) - always July. 2008 July 14-18, Anaheim, CA; 2009 July 19-24, Orlando, FL.

17171 ■ Feminist Majority Foundation (FMF)

1600 Wilson Blvd., Ste.801
Arlington, VA 22209
Ph: (703)522-2214 (310)556-2500
Fax: (703)522-2219
E-mail: volunteer@feminist.org
URL: http://www.feminist.org
Contact: Eleanor Smeal, Pres.
Founded: 1987. **Membership Dues:** regular, $25-$250 (annual). **Description:** Serves as a cutting edge

organization dedicated to women's equality, reproductive health, and non-violence. Utilizes action and research to empower women economically, socially, and politically. Believes that feminists, both women and men, who believe in women's equality are the majority, but this majority must be empowered. Focuses on advancing the legal, social, and political equality of women with men, countering the backlash to women's advancement, and recruiting/training young feminists to encourage future leadership for the feminist movement. Engages in research and public policy development, public education programs, grassroots organizing projects, leadership training and development programs. Participates in and organizes forum on issues of women's equality and empowerment. **Libraries: Type:** not open to the public. **Holdings:** 1,000; books, periodicals. **Subjects:** feminism. **Subgroups:** Feminization of Power Campaign. **Formerly:** Fund for the Feminist Majority. **Publications:** *Feminist Majority*, quarterly. Newsletter. **Price:** included in membership dues. Alternate Formats: online ● Also makes available organizing kits, fact sheets, videos, and books. **Conventions/Meetings:** Feminist Expo for Women's Empowerment - show (exhibits).

17172 ■ Feminists Concerned for Better Feminist Leadership (FCBFL)
Address Unknown since 2007
Founded: 1986. **Description:** Participants include women's groups and individuals in the worldwide feminist community. Seeks to develop feminist citizenship and leadership roles. Distributes nationalist feminist educational literature. **Libraries: Type:** reference. **Holdings:** archival material. **Publications:** *Feminism: Freedom from Wifism.* Book ● *Gold Flag Bulletin* ● Audiotapes ● Books ● Pamphlets. **Conventions/Meetings:** seminar ● workshop.

17173 ■ Feminists for Free Expression (FFE)
2525 Times Square Sta.
New York, NY 10108-2525
Ph: (718)651-1232
Fax: (718)651-1232
E-mail: freedom@well.com
URL: http://www.ffeusa.org
Contact: Jamye Waxman, Pres.
Founded: 1992. **Membership Dues:** regular, $35 (annual) ● couple/family, $60 (annual) ● supporting, $100 (annual) ● sustaining, $250 (annual) ● limited income/student, $10 (annual). **Description:** Represents feminists dedicated to preserving the individual's right and responsibility to read, listen, view and produce materials of her choice without the intervention of the state. **Publications:** *Free Speech Pamphlet Series.* Pamphlets. Includes arts censorship, the Internet, sexual harassment, and pornography.

17174 ■ General Commission on the Status and Role of Women (GCSRW)
77 W Washington St., Ste.1009
Chicago, IL 60602
Ph: (312)346-4900
Free: (800)523-8390
Fax: (312)346-3986
E-mail: gcsrw@gcsrw.org
URL: http://gcsrw.org
Contact: M. Garlinda Burton, Gen. Sec.
Founded: 1972. **Members:** 43. **Staff:** 5. **Budget:** $600,000. **Description:** Represents both sexes and various ethnic groups within the United Methodist church. Aims to challenge the church to make a continuing commitment to the full and equal responsibility and participation of women in the total life and mission of the church, sharing fully in the power and policymaking at all levels of the church. Believes that the church cannot be an effective witness to society until it has examined its own faithfulness to the full inclusiveness of all persons. Works to foster an awareness of issues, problems, and concerns related to the status and role of women within the denomination; deals with issues such as sexual harassment/misconduct and sex discrimination. Holds leadership training sessions with annual conference constituency, cabinets, Boards of Ordained Ministry, and other United Methodist Church groups. **Programs:**

Education and Advocacy; Issue Development; Monitoring and Research. **Publications:** *EFlyer.* Newsletter. Alternate Formats: online ● *The Flyer*, quarterly. Newsletter. Provides a link between national and local commissions on the status and role of women in the United Methodist Church in general, and in society. **Price:** $10.00/year; $18.00 for two years. **Circulation:** 13,000. Alternate Formats: online ● Books ● Also publishes brochures, including guidelines and procedures to be used in responding to the grievances of women who are members or employees of the church. **Conventions/Meetings:** annual meeting.

17175 ■ Global Fund for Women
1375 Sutter St., Ste.400
San Francisco, CA 94109
Ph: (415)202-7640
Fax: (415)202-8604
E-mail: gfw@globalfundforwomen.org
URL: http://www.globalfundforwomen.org
Contact: Ms. Lillian Cincone, Special Projects Coor.
Founded: 1987. **Staff:** 37. **Budget:** $7,100,000. **Languages:** English, French, Portuguese, Spanish. **Description:** Grant making organization providing support to women's groups working on emerging, controversial, or difficult issues. Supports overseas groups working on projects related to female human rights. Provides funds to seed, strengthen, and link groups that are committed to women's well being and that work for their full participation in society. **Libraries: Type:** open to the public. **Subjects:** female human rights. **Awards: Frequency:** triennial. **Type:** grant. **Programs:** Beijing 10: Defending Women's Empowerment; The Global Fund for Women on Ending Trafficking; How the Global Fund is Responding to the Tsunami Disaster; Imagining Peace: Reflections from Istanbul; Ongoing Support for Women in Afghanistan and Pakistan; Outreach Trip to Central America; Preston Education Fund for Girls; Young Women's Declaration in the Asia Pacific. **Publications:** *Investing in Women: Beyond the Rhetoric*, annual. Annual Report. Includes stories of the extraordinary leadership shown by women's groups around the world while confronting tremendous challenges. Alternate Formats: online ● *Raising Our Voices* (in English and Spanish), semiannual. Newsletter. Contains news on grantee groups, working on women's rights issues. Alternate Formats: online ● *Women's Fundraising Handbook* (in English, French, and Spanish). Explores key ideas about raising money to fund women's rights work. Alternate Formats: online ● Brochure ● Bulletin, bimonthly. Alternate Formats: online. **Conventions/Meetings:** semiannual board meeting.

17176 ■ Guam Women's Club
Address Unknown since 2007
Founded: 1952. **Members:** 80. **Membership Dues:** $30 (annual). **Description:** Women working to improve the education, health, and standard of living in Guam. Researches health issues, economic conditions, and educational methods. Supports and promotes similar organizations. Conducts fundraising activities to assist charitable projects. **Awards:** Guam Women's Club Scholarship. **Frequency:** annual. **Type:** scholarship. **Projects:** Guam Women's Club History. **Publications:** *Plumeria Press*, monthly. Newsletter. **Price:** free. **Advertising:** not accepted. **Conventions/Meetings:** monthly meeting - always last Friday of the month.

17177 ■ Institute of Women Today (IWT)
7315 S Yale Ave.
Chicago, IL 60621
Ph: (773)651-8372
Fax: (773)783-2673
E-mail: iwt7315@aol.com
URL: http://instituteofwomentoday.org
Contact: Donna Quinn OP, Exec. Dir.
Founded: 1974. **Members:** 1,500. **Staff:** 25. **Budget:** $650,000. **Description:** Sponsored by church-related Protestant, Catholic, and Jewish women's organizations to examine religious and historical origins of women's liberation. Endeavors to bring church-related women into the women's movement so that

the principles of faith will be reflected in the women's struggle for equality. Sponsors two shelters for homeless women and children. Conducts research. Provides legal services to women in prisons. **Libraries: Type:** reference. **Holdings:** archival material. **Conventions/Meetings:** annual meeting ● workshop.

17178 ■ Institute for Women's Policy Research (IWPR)
1707 L St. NW, Ste.750
Washington, DC 20036
Ph: (202)785-5100
Fax: (202)833-4362
E-mail: iwpr@iwpr.org
URL: http://www.iwpr.org
Contact: Heidi Hartmann PhD, Pres./CEO
Founded: 1987. **Members:** 1,000. **Membership Dues:** graduate student, $35 (annual) ● friend, $75 (annual) ● sustainer, $175 (annual) ● affiliate, $350 (annual) ● partner, $250 (annual) ● corporate affiliate, $1,000 (annual). **Staff:** 22. **Description:** Individuals and organizations concerned with economic and social justice for women and families. Designs, executes, and disseminates research findings that illuminate policy issues affecting women and families. Works to addressing complex issues engendered by race, ethnicity, and class. Focuses on survival issues such as welfare reform, family and medical leave, childcare, pay equity and the wage gap, the glass ceiling, labor law reform, and equal opportunity for women of all race and ethnic backgrounds. Builds a network of individuals and organizations that conduct and use women-oriented policy research. **Publications:** *Research News Reporter*, monthly. **Price:** included in membership dues ● Papers ● Reports. **Conventions/Meetings:** biennial conference.

17179 ■ Inter-American Commission of Women (CIM)
c/o Organization of American States
17th St. and Constitution Ave. NW
Washington, DC 20006
Ph: (202)458-3000
E-mail: spcim@oas.org
URL: http://www.oas.org/cim
Contact: Carmen Lomellin, Exec. Sec.
Founded: 1928. **Members:** 34. **Staff:** 7. **Budget:** $1,500,000. **Languages:** English, French, Portuguese, Spanish. **For-Profit. Description:** Specialized agency of the Organization of American States, dealing with issues concerning women. Composed of one presidentially-appointed delegate for each member country of OAS: 34 democracies of the Western Hemisphere. Mobilizes, trains, and organizes women "so that they may fully participate in all fields of human endeavor, on a par with men, as two beings of equal value, responsible for the destiny of humanity." Serves as liaison for women's groups throughout the hemisphere and conducts research on laws affecting women. Operates a regional information center in Santiago, Chile; finances development projects in Latin America and the Caribbean. **Libraries: Type:** reference. **Holdings:** 9,000. **Affiliated With:** Organization of American States. **Publications:** *Final Report-Assembly of Delegates*, biennial ● *Series: Studies*, periodic ● Reports. Includes proceedings of technical meetings.

17180 ■ International Association for Women of Color Day (IAWOCDay)
3325 Northrop Ave.
Sacramento, CA 95864
Ph: (916)483-9804
Fax: (916)483-9805
E-mail: iawocday@aol.com
URL: http://www.womenofcolorday.com
Contact: Suzanne Brooks, CEO/Pres.
Founded: 1986. **Staff:** 2. **Budget:** $20,000. **Non-membership. For-Profit. Multinational. Description:** Social entrepreneurship-a business operating in the public interest and established to promote the worldwide observance of Women of Color Day-a day in which the contributions of Women of Color-now including Aboriginal, African/African Diaspora, Alaska Native, Asian, Caribbean, Latin American, Maori, Native American Indian, South Sea and Pacific Island,

and Indigenous heritages throughout the world-are recognized and honored. Serves as a network for those who wish to conduct Women of Color Day observances. Provides guidelines, suggestions, and encouragement. There are no meetings or dues. "Networkers" are asked to supply information regarding their events, which will be posted online. This work is supported through the sale of related and associated products, a speaker's bureau, diversity training and other services. Of course, one need not be a woman of color to have the spirit of women of color which includes a willingness to cooperate and collaborate, a love of culture and the desire to honor women of color for their contributions and achievements. **Libraries: Type:** not open to the public. **Holdings:** 15. **Subjects:** program booklets from Sacramento and Stockton events and from Fresno event. **Awards:** Outstanding Woman of Color Award. **Frequency:** annual. **Type:** recognition. **Recipient:** to women in categories and fields selected by community groups, businesses and individuals. **Telecommunication Services:** electronic mail, suzanne@womenofcolorday.com. **Formerly:** (2003) National Institute for Women of Color. **Publications:** *Brown Papers*. **Conventions/Meetings:** periodic conference.

17181 ■ International Black Women's Congress (IBWC)

555 Fenchurch St., Ste.102
Norfolk, VA 23510
Free: (800)280-0122
E-mail: ibwc1069@cs.com
URL: http://www.ibwc.info
Contact: Sharon Bailey PhD, Natl. Pres.

Founded: 1983. **Members:** 1,500. **Membership Dues:** life, $500 ● organizational, $100 (annual) ● regular, $50 (annual) ● student/senior, $50 (annual). **Staff:** 20. **Budget:** $450,000. **Regional Groups:** 5. **State Groups:** 1. **Local Groups:** 1. **National Groups:** 25. **Multinational. Description:** Women of African ancestry; interested individuals. Aims to unite members for mutual support and socioeconomic development through: annual networking tours to Africa; establishing support groups; addressing health issues; assisting women in starting their own businesses; assisting members in developing resumes and other educational needs; offering to answer or discuss individual questions and concerns. Conducts educational, research, and charitable programs; compiles statistics. Operates speakers' bureau and rites of passage programs for girls and adult women. **Libraries: Type:** reference. **Holdings:** 375. **Subjects:** African history, African culture, African-American studies, women's issues, health of African Americans. **Awards:** Alma "Nomsa" John Inspirational Award. **Frequency:** annual. **Type:** recognition ● Elwood R. Clough and James T. Rodgers "Encircle" Award. **Frequency:** annual. **Type:** recognition ● Oni Award. **Frequency:** annual. **Type:** recognition. **Recipient:** for the person identified as "someone who protects, defends and enhances the general well being of African people" ● Wytonya Thompson "Yes I Can" Scholarship. **Type:** scholarship. **Computer Services:** Online services, Community Services-Outreach. **Committees:** Business Development; Health; Rites of Passage; Support Group Network; Undergraduate. **Task Forces:** Health; Marketing/Communications. **Affiliated With:** National Black United Fund. **Publications:** *Black Women's Health and Social Policy*, quarterly. Newsletter. **Price:** for members. **Circulation:** 1,500. **Advertising:** accepted. Alternate Formats: online ● *Every Black Woman Should Wear a Red Dress*, periodic. Directory ● *International Black Women's Directory*, periodic ● *Oni Newsletter*, quarterly ● *The Political Socialization of Black Women: Empowerment* ● *River of Tears: Politics of Black Women's Health*. **Conventions/Meetings:** annual Wholistic Preventive Health Care: Strategies for Wellness - conference (exhibits) ● workshop.

17182 ■ International Center for Research on Women (ICRW)

1717 Massachusetts Ave. NW, Ste.302
Washington, DC 20036
Ph: (202)797-0007
Fax: (202)797-0020
E-mail: info@icrw.org
URL: http://www.icrw.org
Contact: Dr. Geeta Rao Gupta, Pres.

Founded: 1976. **Staff:** 45. **Budget:** $3,500,000. **Multinational. Description:** Aims to promote social and economic development with women's full participation. Conducts research programs and provides technical services for the design, implementation, and evaluation of development projects that integrate women into mainstream economic roles. Disseminates research findings to policymakers and others throughout the world concerned with economic and socioeconomic issues of developing countries. Conducts policy roundtables. **Libraries: Type:** by appointment only; open to the public. **Holdings:** 15,000; books, papers, periodicals. **Subjects:** women in development. **Computer Services:** Mailing lists, of members ● online services, discussion forums. **Publications:** *Information Bulletins* (in English, French, and Spanish), periodic. Contains information on ICRW projects and programs. ● *International Center for Research on Women—Papers* (in English, French, and Spanish), periodic. Covers women's socioeconomic status, health, and nutrition in developing countries and women's participation in development. ● Reports. **Conventions/Meetings:** periodic seminar and roundtable.

17183 ■ International Women's Tribune Centre/Women, Ink (IWTC)

777 United Nations Plz.
New York, NY 10017
Ph: (212)687-8633
Fax: (212)661-2704
E-mail: iwtc@iwtc.org
URL: http://www.iwtc.org
Contact: Vicki J. Semler, Exec. Dir.

Founded: 1976. **Staff:** 14. **Budget:** $800,000. **Languages:** English, Spanish. **Description:** Women's development communications service responding to requests for information and technical assistance from individuals around the world who are involved in women's projects in Africa, Asia, Latin America, West Asia, Pacific, and Caribbean. Seeks to develop communication methods and educational materials in collaboration with regional women's groups. Acts as a clearinghouse for and about women in development activities; conducts workshops; provides advisory services in low-cost media, women's resource centers, communications techniques, and organizational developments; compiles resource books. **Libraries: Type:** reference. **Holdings:** 4,000; audiovisuals, books, clippings, monographs, periodicals, reports. **Subjects:** women and developmental issues and activities. **Telecommunication Services:** electronic mail, wink@womenink.org. **Foreign language name:** Centro Tribuna Internacional de la Mujer; Centre Tribune Internationale de la Femme. **Formerly:** (1978) International Women's Year/Tribune Project. **Publications:** *Rights of Women*. Manual. Includes effective strategies for using international law to better women's human rights. ● *The Tribune* (in English, French, and Spanish), periodic. Newsletter. Provides practical information on issues, activities, and programs by, and for women in the global south. **Price:** $12.00/year in North America; $16.00/year in Europe, Australia, Japan, and New Zealand; free in Asia, Africa, and Latin America. ISSN: 0738-9779. **Circulation:** 16,000 ● Also publishes information on small business activities, appropriate technology for women, UN resolutions of interest to women, and networking activities linking women worldwide.

17184 ■ Know, Inc. (KI)

807 Penn Ave.
Wilkinsburg, PA 15221
Ph: (412)241-4844
E-mail: pwetherby@aol.com
Contact: Phyllis Wetherby, Pres.

Founded: 1969. **Members:** 1,000. **Description:** "All members are dedicated to human equality." Aims to publish articles about human rights. Discusses problems of discrimination where they exist. Investigates problems in human rights, particularly those unique to women's changing role in society. Educates

with regard to changing roles of men and women. **Publications:** *Know News Service*, periodic.

17185 ■ Legal Momentum: Advancing Women's Rights

395 Hudson St.
New York, NY 10014
Ph: (212)925-6635
Fax: (212)226-1066
E-mail: policy@legalmomentum.org
URL: http://www.legalmomentum.org
Contact: Kathy J. Rodgers, Pres.

Founded: 1970. **Staff:** 55. **Budget:** $6,000,000. **Nonmembership. Description:** Aims to achieve equality for women and girls by transforming the institutions and values of the society through legal advocacy, public policy development, education and strategic alliances. Current areas of focus are economic empowerment, child care, physical safety, the inclusion of women's voices and perspectives in the media and the elimination of gender bias in the justice system. **Programs:** Employment and Housing Rights for Survivors of Abuse; Family Initiative; Immigrant Women; National Judicial Education; Women Rebuild. **Formerly:** (2004) NOW Legal Defense and Education Fund; (2004) Legal Momentum. **Supersedes:** NOW Legal Committee. **Publications:** *An Annotated Summary of the Regulations for Title IX of the Education Amendments of 1972*. Booklet ● *Drawing the Line: A Handbook for Creating Residential Picketing and Buffer Zone Laws in Your Community* ● *In Brief*, quarterly. Newsletter. Updates on current cases and projects. ● *Manual for Survival for Women in Nontraditional Employment* ● *What Congress Didn't Tell You: A State-by-State Guide to the Welfare Law's Hidden Reproductive Rights Agenda*. Report ● Annual Report, annual. Alternate Formats: online ● Legal resource kits on incest, sexual harassment in the workplace and school, divorce and separation, lesbian rights, and other related issues.

17186 ■ Lucy Stone League (LSL)

PO Box 390
Newcastle, ME 04553-0390
Ph: (207)586-6078
Fax: (207)586-6080
E-mail: morrison@lucystoneleague.org
URL: http://www.lucystoneleague.org
Contact: Morrison Bonpasse, Pres.

Founded: 1921. **Members:** 100. **Membership Dues:** life, $18. **Description:** Individuals. Promotes gender equality, particularly in the matter of names (the organization derives its name from Lucy Stone, the 19th century feminist who decided to retain her birth surname following her marriage to Henry Blackwell in 1855). Seeks to raise public awareness of the choices available to women regarding the retention of their birth surnames following marriage, and the use of the mother's birth surname in the naming of children. Conducts research; maintains speakers' bureau. **Libraries: Type:** by appointment only. **Holdings:** clippings. **Subjects:** names, feminism. **Publications:** Newsletter, periodic.

17187 ■ MANA, A National Latina Organization

1725 K St. NW, Ste.201
Washington, DC 20006
Ph: (202)833-0060
Fax: (202)496-0588
E-mail: hermana2@aol.com
URL: http://www.hermana.org
Contact: Alma Morales Riojas, Pres./CEO

Founded: 1974. **Members:** 4,000. **Membership Dues:** regular, $35 (annual) ● senior citizen, student, $15 (annual) ● friend, $100 (annual) ● life, $250 ● chapter, $50 (annual). **Staff:** 3. **Local Groups:** 12. **National Groups:** 19. **Description:** Promotes leadership and economic and educational development for Mexican-American and other Latina women. Includes areas of concern: pay equity, adolescent pregnancy, and children in poverty health and education. Offers leadership development course, which includes training at the national and local levels; operates Hermanitas Project, an annual conference on self-image building and career counseling for high school

Hispanic girls. **Awards:** Corporation of the Year Award. **Frequency:** annual. **Type:** recognition. **Recipient:** to a corporation that demonstrates long term, consistent support to and inclusion of the Hispanic community in their corporate practice ● HerMANO/HerMANA Award. **Frequency:** annual. **Type:** recognition. **Recipient:** for individuals who have supported the issues of the Hispanic Community, especially Latinas ● Las Primeras Awards. **Frequency:** annual. **Type:** recognition. **Recipient:** for Latinas who have accomplished firsts at its annual Las Primeras event ● MANA Scholarships. **Frequency:** annual. **Type:** scholarship. **Recipient:** for United States citizens enrolled in a college or university. **Councils:** National Corporate Partnership. **Programs:** AvanZamos; HERMANITAS. **Formerly:** (1994) Mexican American Women's National Association. **Publications:** *Issue Updates* (in English and Spanish), quarterly. Newsletter. **Advertising:** accepted ● Newsletter, quarterly. **Price:** included in membership dues. Alternate Formats: online ● Manual. **Price:** included in membership dues ● Papers. **Price:** included in membership dues. **Conventions/Meetings:** biennial Training Conference, leadership conference (exhibits).

17188 ∎ Ms. Foundation for Women (MFW)

120 Wall St., 33rd Fl.
New York, NY 10005
Ph: (212)742-2300
Fax: (212)742-1653
E-mail: info@ms.foundation.org
URL: http://www.ms.foundation.org
Contact: Sara K. Gould, Pres./CEO
Founded: 1972. **Staff:** 40. **Budget:** $11,000,000. **Description:** Supports the efforts of women and girls to govern their own lives and influence the world around them. Funds and assists women's self-help organizing efforts, and pursues changes in public consciousness, law, philanthropy, and social policy. Directs resources to break down barriers based on race, class, age, disability, sexual orientation, and culture. Sponsors Take Our Daughters to Work, a public education campaign to broaden girls' horizons and increase their self-esteem by bringing them to the workplace. **Awards:** Gloria Awards. **Frequency:** annual. **Type:** recognition. **Recipient:** for remarkable women from across the country. **Additional Websites:** http://www.daughtersandsonstowork.org. **Funds:** Reproductive Rights Coalition and Organizing; Women and AIDS. **Programs:** Democracy Funding Circle; Peer-to-Peer Education; Public Voices; Public Policy; Rapid Response Policy Fund; Safety; TODAS. **Publications:** *Voices*, quarterly. Newsletter. Alternate Formats: online ● Annual Report, annual. Contains information on MFW programs, grants given, and funds received. **Price:** free ● Brochure. Alternate Formats: online ● Books ● Also publishes periodic grant listings and summary brochures. **Conventions/Meetings:** Institute on Women and Economic Development - meeting, with training for economic security practitioners - 18-month intervals.

17189 ∎ National Association of Commissions for Women (NACW)

401 N Washington St., Ste.100
Rockville, MD 20850-1737
Ph: (240)777-8308
Free: (800)338-9267
Fax: (301)279-1318
E-mail: info@nacw.org
URL: http://www.nacw.org
Contact: Bonnie Coffey, Pres.
Founded: 1970. **Members:** 128. **Membership Dues:** official, $75-$250 (annual) ● affiliate - platinum, $25,000 (annual) ● affiliate - gold, $15,000 (annual) ● affiliate - silver, $10,000 (annual) ● affiliate - bronze, $5,000 (annual) ● affiliate - corporate, $1,000 (annual) ● affiliate - sustaining, $250 (annual) ● affiliate - regular (college and university women's commission, center, committee, study program), $50 (annual) ● affiliate - regular (individual, group, nongovernmental organization), $30 (annual). **Staff:** 2. **Budget:** $50,000. **Regional Groups:** 33. **State Groups:** 40. **Local Groups:** 200. **Description:** Represents state, city, and county commissions that focus on the status of women. Aims to strengthen and coordinate the vital work of the state and local commissions, in seeking to further the legal, social, political, economic, and educational equality of American women, that they may make their fullest contribution in the nation. Works to: eliminate discrimination based on sex, race, age, religion, national origin, or marital status in all phases of American society; foster the dissemination of information and provide counsel on opportunities for the effective participation of women in the private and public sector; create greater public awareness of the role and function of commissions on the status of women and provide a national focus on issues affecting women; strengthen commissions, coordinate their efforts nationwide, and provide a unified voice; act as a central clearinghouse and networking resource for information and activities of commissions across the country; foster a closer relationship and fuller exchange of ideas among members. Offers guidance in the designing of new strategies and programs on critical contemporary issues of concern to women; assists efforts to broaden the base of involvement of women of color and those of different backgrounds; works with other national women's groups on issues requiring collective action. Presents testimony at public hearings; monitors legislation of special interest to women. Maintains speakers' bureau; compiles statistics. Conducts research, workshops, and leadership training programs. **Libraries:** Type: reference. **Committees:** Awards; By-Laws; Convention Planning and Protocol; Finance and Fundraising; Legislation; Nominating; Public Relations; Resolutions. **Publications:** *Breakthrough*, quarterly. Newsletter. Reports on news and activities of regional, state, and local commissions; includes legislative updates. **Price:** free. **Circulation:** 3,000. **Advertising:** accepted. Alternate Formats: online ● *Directory of National, Regional, State and Local Commissions*, periodic ● *Women's Health Connection*, quarterly. Newsletter. **Price:** free. **Circulation:** 800. Alternate Formats: online ● Brochures ● Articles. Alternate Formats: online ● Also publishes informational pamphlets, organizational handbook, and federal legislative alerts. **Conventions/Meetings:** annual conference and convention (exhibits).

17190 ∎ National Black Women's Consciousness Raising Association (BWCR)

1906 N Charles St.
Baltimore, MD 21218
Ph: (410)727-8900
Fax: (410)230-2964
E-mail: elainesimon1@aol.com
Contact: Dr. Elaine Simon, Exec. Dir.
Founded: 1975. **Members:** 800. **State Groups:** 2. **Local Groups:** 4. **National Groups:** 7. **Description:** Black women interested in women's rights and women's issues. Acts as a support group for women. Provides educational and informational workshops and seminars on subjects of concern to black women and women in general. **Awards:** **Frequency:** annual. **Type:** recognition. **Recipient:** for individuals with academic achievement. **Publications:** Newsletter, semiannual. **Conventions/Meetings:** annual meeting (exhibits) - always in Baltimore, MD.

17191 ∎ National Coalition of 100 Black Women (NCBW)

1925 Adam C. Powell Jr. Blvd., Ste.1-L
New York, NY 10026
Ph: (212)222-5660
Fax: (212)222-5675
E-mail: nc100bw@aol.com
URL: http://www.ncbw.org
Contact: Leslie A. Mays, Pres.
Founded: 1981. **Members:** 7,000. **Staff:** 4. **State Groups:** 65. **Description:** Represents African-American women actively involved with issues such as economic development, health, employment, education, voting, housing, criminal justice, the status of black families, and the arts. Seeks to provide networking and career opportunities for African-American women in the process of establishing links between the organization and the corporate and political arenas. Encourages leadership development; sponsors role-model and mentor programs to provide guidance to teenage mothers and young women in high school or who have graduated from college and are striving for career advancement. **Awards:** Candace Awards. **Type:** recognition. **Recipient:** for outstanding African-American women and men. **Committees:** Arts and Culture; Community Action; Economic Development; Education; Employment; Health; Political Action. **Publications:** *National Coalition of 100 Black Women—Statement*, quarterly. Newsletter. Reports on the activities and achievements of black women. **Price:** included in membership dues. **Circulation:** 7,000. **Advertising:** accepted. **Conventions/Meetings:** biennial convention.

17192 ∎ National Committee on Pay Equity (NCPE)

555 New Jersey Ave. NW
Washington, DC 20001-2029
Ph: (703)920-2010
Fax: (703)979-6372
E-mail: fairpay@pay-equity.org
URL: http://www.pay-equity.org
Contact: Michele Leber, Chair
Founded: 1979. **Members:** 85. **Description:** Individuals and organizations such as women's groups, labor unions, professional associations, minority and civil rights groups, and governmental and educational groups. Educates the public about the historical, legal, and economic basis for pay inequities between men and women and white people and people of color. Promotes grassroots activism. **Awards:** The Winn Newman Pay Equity Award. **Frequency:** annual. **Type:** recognition. **Recipient:** for exemplary contribution to pay equity movement. **Task Forces:** Equal Pay Day; Legislative. **Publications:** *Bargaining for Pay Equity: A Strategy Manual* ● *Briefing Paper: The Wage Gap* ● *Erase the Bias: A Pay Equity Guide to Eliminating Race and Sex Bias from Wage Setting Systems* ● *The Intersection Between Pay Equity and Workplace Representation* ● *Pay Equity Activity in the Public Sector, 1979-1989* ● *Pay Equity: An Issue of Race, Ethnicity, and Sex* ● *Pay Equity Bibliography and Resource Listing* ● *Pay Equity Makes Good Business Sense.* **Conventions/Meetings:** annual Equal Pay Day - meeting - always April ● annual meeting.

17193 ∎ National Conference of Puerto Rican Women (NACOPRW)

1220 L St. NW, Ste.No. 177
Washington, DC 20005-4018
E-mail: vannym@erols.com
URL: http://www.nacoprw.com
Contact: Anaida Colon-Muniz, Pres.
Founded: 1972. **Members:** 3,000. **Membership Dues:** active, $30 (annual) ● student, $15 (annual). **Staff:** 1. **Budget:** $50,000. **State Groups:** 17. **Languages:** English, Spanish. **Description:** Promotes equal participation of Puerto Rican and other Hispanic women in the economic, social, and political life of the U.S. and Puerto Rico. Collaborates with other national organizations committed to equal rights for all. Encourages the formation of local chapters in all Puerto Rican communities and fosters closer ties among them. **Awards:** Special Achievement. **Frequency:** annual. **Type:** recognition ● Woman of Achievement. **Frequency:** annual. **Type:** recognition ● Woman of the Year. **Frequency:** annual. **Type:** recognition. **Publications:** *Ecos Nacionales*, 3/year. Newsletter. Includes association news, book reviews, chapter news, employment opportunity listings. **Price:** included in membership dues; $25.00 /year for nonmembers ● *Fact Sheets*, periodic ● Books ● Membership Directory, annual. **Conventions/Meetings:** competition ● annual conference (exhibits).

17194 ∎ National Council of Negro Women (NCNW)

633 Pennsylvania Ave. NW
Washington, DC 20004
Ph: (202)737-0120
Free: (866)234-NCNW
Fax: (202)737-0476

E-mail: ncnwinfo@ncnw.org
URL: http://www.ncnw.org
Contact: Dr. Dorothy I. Height, Chair
Founded: 1935. **Members:** 40,000. **Membership Dues:** student, $10 (annual) ● regular/associate (men), $30 (annual) ● partner, $50 (annual) ● advocate, $75 (annual) ● Leadership Circle, $150 (annual) ● life, $500 ● group life, $750 ● legacy life, $1,000. **Staff:** 53. **Budget:** $1,500,000. **Local Groups:** 240. **Description:** A coalition of 31 national organizations and concerned individuals. Assists in the development and utilization of the leadership of women in community, national, and international life. Provides a center of information for and about women in the black community; stimulates cooperation among women in diverse economic and social interests; acts as a catalyst for constructive advocacy on a number of women's issues. Maintains Women's Center for Education and Career Advancement in New York City, which offers programs designed to aid minority women pursuing nontraditional careers; also maintains the Bethune Museum and Archives for Black Women's History. Operates offices in west and southern Africa, which serve NCNW's international projects and which were deigned to improve the social and economic status of rural women in Third World countries. Founded by Mary Mcleod Bethune (1875-1955), black American educator and presidential advisor. **Awards:** Uncommon Height Award. **Frequency:** annual. **Type:** recognition. **Recipient:** for persons who render lifetime service to others. **Programs:** African American Women As We Age; Black Family Reunion Celebration; International Development Center; International Visitors; Mary McLeod Bethune Recognition; Partnership for Academic Achievement; Young Women's Leadership. **Publications:** *Black Woman's Voice*, periodic ● *Sisters Magazine*, quarterly ● Newsletter. **Conventions/Meetings:** biennial meeting (exhibits) - usually last week in November, Washington, DC.

17195 ■ National Council for Research on Women (NCRW)

11 Hanover Sq., 24th Fl.
New York, NY 10005
Ph: (212)785-7335
Fax: (212)785-7350
E-mail: ncrw@ncrw.org
URL: http://www.ncrw.org
Contact: Linda G. Basch PhD, Pres.
Founded: 1982. **Members:** 97. **Staff:** 6. **Budget:** $1,000,000. **Description:** Serves as a national network of organizations representing the academic community, policy makers, and others interested in women's issues. Works to bring institutional resources to bear on feminist research, policy analysis, and educational programs addressing legal, economic, and social inequities. Promotes collaborative research on issues affecting women; acts as clearinghouse. Houses the National Network of Women's Caucuses and Committees in the Disciplinary and Professional Associations. **Computer Services:** Mailing lists. **Publications:** *Directory of Women's Media*, periodic. Price: $20.00 ● *The Girls Report*. Price: $20.00 ● *International Centers for Research on Women*. Price: $10.00 ● *Issues Quarterly*. Newsletter. Synthesizes current research on issues affecting women and girls. Price: $20.00/year ● *Mainstreaming Minority Women's Studies* ● *Opportunities for Research and Study 1996-97* ● *Sexual Harassment: Research and Resources* ● *Who Benefits, Who Decides? An Agenda for Improving Philanthropy: The Case for Women and Girls*. Price: $12.00 ● *Who's Where and Doing What*, periodic. Directory. Lists individual affiliates, researchers, and staff of council member centers. Price: free to council affiliates; $10.00 to non-affiliates ● *Women in Academe: Progress and Prospects, A Task Force Report* ● *Women of Color and the Multicultural Curriculum: Transforming the College Classroom*. Price: $22.00 ● *Women's Mailing List Directory*, periodic. Price: $10.00 ● *Women's Research Network News*, 3-4/year. Newsletter. Reports on member centers' activities, women's caucuses, and research; includes information on new books, fellowships, and job opportunities. Price: $35.00 for individuals; $100.00 for

institutions ● *Women's Thesaurus: An Index of Language Used to Describe and Locate Information By and About Women*. **Conventions/Meetings:** annual conference.

17196 ■ National Council of Women of the United States (NCW/US)

777 United Nations Plz.
New York, NY 10017
Ph: (212)697-1278
Fax: (212)972-0164
E-mail: info@ncw-us.org
URL: http://www.ncw-us.org
Contact: Mary E. Singletary, Pres.
Founded: 1888. **Members:** 233. **Membership Dues:** student, $30 (annual) ● bronze-supporting, $60 (annual) ● silver-sponsoring, $150 (annual) ● gold-sustaining, organization, $250 (annual). **Staff:** 1. **Budget:** $100,000. **State Groups:** 33. **Local Groups:** 3. **National Groups:** 31. **Description:** Works for the education, participation, and advancement of women in all areas of society. Serves as information center and clearinghouse for affiliated women's organizations. Conducts projects and sponsors conferences on national and international problems and matters of concern to women and shares the results with affiliated groups. Has observer status at the United Nations. **Awards:** Corporate Advancement of Women. **Frequency:** biennial. **Type:** recognition. **Recipient:** for corporations providing fair promotion and equal opportunities for women ● Women of Conscience. **Frequency:** biennial. **Type:** recognition. **Committees:** Arts and Letters; Development; Environment and Habitat; Family; Health; Human Rights; International Hospitality; Migration; Population; Public Policy; Social Welfare; United Nations Representation; Women and Employment. **Projects:** Parents Mentoring Parents (on antiviolence); Racial and Ethnic Harmony. **Affiliated With:** International Council of Women. **Publications:** *National Council of Women of the U.S.—Bulletin*, semiannual. Newsletter. Reports on council programs and activities of member organizations. Includes awards announcements, book reviews, and news on women's issues. Price: $10.00/year. Circulation: 1,200. Advertising: accepted ● Annual Report, annual. **Conventions/Meetings:** semiannual board meeting and executive committee meeting ● monthly executive committee meeting.

17197 ■ National Council of Women's Organizations (NCWO)

1050 17th St. NW, Ste.250
Washington, DC 20036
Ph: (202)293-4505
Fax: (202)293-4507
E-mail: ncwo@ncwo-online.org
URL: http://www.womensorganizations.org
Contact: Susan Scanlan, Chair
Founded: 1980. **Members:** 150. **Membership Dues:** organization (based on annual operating budget), $50-$200 (annual) ● individual, $35 (annual). **Staff:** 5. **Description:** Presidents or executive directors of more than 100 national women's organizations, including the National Organization for Women, American Association of University Women, American Nurses Association, Center for Women Policy Studies, and National Council for Negro Women. Addresses women's rights issues before the government, through the development of a Women's Agenda; works for the passage of the Equal Rights Amendment. Advocates that women and girls should be trained and educated on a level equal to men in order to strengthen the American workforce. Presents issues being addressed includes: family policies assuring access to housing, child and elder care, and family and medical leave; occupational opportunity, including pay equity, raising the minimum wage, and welfare reform; comprehensive health care and safety, including reproductive health care; legal equality, including protection of civil rights and reproductive choice. **Telecommunication Services:** electronic mail, staff@ncwo-online.org ● electronic mail, scanlan@ncwo-online.org. **Also Known As:** Council of Presidents of Women's National Organizations. **For-**

merly: (1998) Council of Presidents. **Conventions/Meetings:** periodic Women's Agenda Conference.

17198 ■ National Hook-Up of Black Women (NHBW)

1809 E 71st St., Ste.205
Chicago, IL 60649-2000
Ph: (773)667-7061
Fax: (773)667-7064
E-mail: info@nhbwine.com
URL: http://www.nhbwinc.com
Contact: Dr. Wynetta A. Frazier, Natl. Pres.
Founded: 1973. **Members:** 300. **Membership Dues:** individual, at-large, contributing, $50 (annual) ● life, $1,000. **Staff:** 1. **Budget:** $60,230. **Regional Groups:** 4. **Local Groups:** 11. **Description:** Black women from business, professional, and community-oriented disciplines representing all economic, educational, and social levels. Provides a communications network in support of black women who serve in organizational leadership positions, especially those elected or appointed to office and those wishing to elevate their status through educational and career ventures. Works to form and implement a Black Women's Agenda that would provide representation for women, families, and communities and that would help surmount economic, educational, and social barriers. Supports efforts of the Congressional Black Caucus (see separate entry) in utilizing the legislative process to work toward total equality of opportunity in society. Seeks to highlight the achievements and contributions of black women. Operates speakers' bureau. **Awards:** Arnita Y. Boswell Award. **Frequency:** annual. **Type:** scholarship. **Recipient:** for outstanding African-American student ● Distinguished Community Service Award. **Frequency:** annual. **Type:** recognition ● Distinguished Family Service Award. **Type:** recognition ● Hook-Up VIP of the Year Award. **Frequency:** annual. **Type:** recognition ● Outstanding Leadership Award. **Type:** recognition ● Wynetta A. Frazier Award. **Frequency:** annual. **Type:** recognition. **Recipient:** for outstanding contribution to society by a mature African-American woman. **Committees:** Education; Health; Membership; Program; Scholarship. **Affiliated With:** Congressional Black Caucus. **Publications:** *Hook-Up News and Views and Healthy Hook-Up*, quarterly. Newsletter. Price: free. Circulation: 200. Advertising: accepted. Alternate Formats: CD-ROM; diskette. **Conventions/Meetings:** annual meeting ● workshop.

17199 ■ National Organization for Women (NOW)

1100 H St. NW, 3rd Fl.
Washington, DC 20005
Ph: (202)628-8669 (202)331-9002
Fax: (202)785-8576
E-mail: now@now.org
URL: http://www.now.org
Contact: Kim Gandy, Pres.
Founded: 1966. **Members:** 500,000. **Membership Dues:** individual, $35 (annual) ● individual in AZ, CA, CT, IL, MI, NY, IN, MO, and TX, $40 (annual) ● life, $1,000. **Staff:** 30. **Regional Groups:** 9. **State Groups:** 50. **Local Groups:** 500. **Description:** Men and women who support "full equality for women in truly equal partnership with men." Seeks to end prejudice and discrimination against women in government, industry, the professions, churches, political parties, the judiciary, labor unions, education, science, medicine, law, religion, "and every other field of importance in American society." Promotes passage of a constitutional equality amendment and enforcement of federal legislation prohibiting discrimination on the basis of sex. Engages in lobbying and litigation. Works to increase the number of women elected to local, county, and state offices, the House of Representatives, and the Senate. **Committees:** Advisory; Composition; Nominating Committee for the Election of Officers; Political Action; Standing. **Publications:** *National Now Times*, bimonthly. Newspaper. Price: free, for members only. **Advertising:** accepted. Alternate Formats: online. **Conventions/Meetings:** annual conference (exhibits) - usually June or July.

17200 ■ National Partnership for Women and Families

1875 Connecticut Ave. NW, Ste.650
Washington, DC 20009
Ph: (202)986-2600
Fax: (202)986-2539
E-mail: info@nationalpartnership.org
URL: http://www.nationalpartnership.org
Contact: Debra L. Ness, Pres.

Founded: 1971. **Members:** 2,500. **Membership Dues:** student, young professional, $35 (annual) ● action council, $100 (annual) ● sustaining, $500 (annual) ● presidential partner, $1,000 (annual) ● executive partner, $2,500 (annual) ● capital partner, $5,000 (annual) ● trustee, $10,000 (annual) ● basic, $45 (annual). **Staff:** 30. **Budget:** $4,300,000. **Description:** Represents attorneys, administrators, publicists, and secretaries. Aims to secure equal rights for women through advocacy and monitoring, and public education. Works to promte women's rights in family law, employment, women's health, and other areas. Maintains speakers' bureau. **Libraries: Type:** reference. **Subjects:** genetic discrimination, judicial nominations. **Computer Services:** Mailing lists. **Divisions:** Health Care. **Programs:** Work and Family. **Formerly:** (1998) Women's Legal Defense Fund. **Publications:** *Expecting Better: A State-by-State Analysis of Parental Leave Programs.* Report. Alternate Formats: online ● *Guide to HIPAA: What the Health Insurance Reform Law Means for Women and Families.* Brochures ● *Guide to the Family & Medical Leave Act: Questions & Answers* (in English and Spanish). Brochures ● *National Partnership News,* quarterly. Newsletter. Reports on women's legal rights in the areas of employment and family law, including Supreme Court decisions and legislative developments. **Price:** included in membership dues; single issues available free to the public. ISSN: 0736-9433. **Circulation:** 12,000 ● Manuals ● Also publishes Fact Sheets, testimony, reports. **Conventions/Meetings:** annual luncheon, with awards presentation.

17201 ■ National Woman's Party (NWP)

Sewall-Belmont House & Museum
144 Constitution Ave. NE
Washington, DC 20002-5608
Ph: (202)546-1210
Fax: (202)546-3997
E-mail: conroy@sewallbelmont.org
URL: http://www.sewallbelmont.org
Contact: Audrey Sheppard, Pres.

Founded: 1916. **Members:** 200. **Membership Dues:** $25 (annual). **Staff:** 12. **Budget:** $250,000. **Description:** Promotes and educates the public about equality for women through interpretation of collection of artifacts from the suffrage and equal rights movement. (Sewall-Belmont House and Museum open five days per week.). **Awards:** Alice Award. **Frequency:** annual. **Type:** recognition. **Recipient:** to a woman who made an outstanding contribution for other women. **Councils:** National. **Affiliated With:** National Council of Women of the United States. **Publications:** *The Sewall-Belmont News,* quarterly. Newsletter. **Price:** included in membership dues. **Conventions/Meetings:** annual meeting - usually December, in Washington, DC.

17202 ■ National Women's Conference (NWC)

2020 Pennsylvania Ave., No. 267
Washington, DC 20006
Ph: (703)922-4468 (715)831-9193
Fax: (703)922-8139
E-mail: harderss@uwec.edu
Contact: Mal Johnson, Co-Chair

Founded: 1978. **Members:** 470. **Membership Dues:** individual, $25 (annual) ● organization, $50 (annual). **Staff:** 3. **Budget:** $4,000. **State Groups:** 34. **Description:** Established by a mandate from the federally sponsored 1977 National Women's Conference held in Houston, TX. Seeks to mobilize support and initiatives for implementing the National Plan of Action, the resulting document of the conference; builds networks addressing legal, economic, and social changes, and participates in UN World Conference activities. Maintains speakers' bureau; sponsors workshops and seminars; coalesces with National Council of Women's Organizations and other issue-oriented women's organizations. **Telecommunication Services:** electronic mail, maljp@msn.com. **Roundtables:** American Women's. **Task Forces:** Decade of Women; ERA Summit. **Affiliated With:** National Council of Women's Organizations. **Formerly:** (1981) Continuing Committee of the National Women's Conference; (1996) National Women's Conference Committee. **Publications:** *Decade of Achievement: 1977-1987* ● *ERA Facts and Action Guide* ● *Moving History Forward: An Update of 1977 U.S. National Plan of Action for Women (1997)* ● Also publishes survey report and monographs. **Conventions/Meetings:** annual conference.

17203 ■ National Women's Conference Center

Address Unknown since 2007

Founded: 1980. **Membership Dues:** individual, $25 (annual) ● contributing, $35 (annual) ● sustaining, $50 (annual) ● patron, $100 ● advocate, $250 ● sponsor, $500 ● lifetime, $1,000. **State Groups:** 26. **Description:** Currently Inactive. National Women's Conference board members, delegates, and advisory committee of past presidents. Promotes equality for women in every aspect of life. Provides public information and leadership development to build a well-informed and growing constituency around women's issues. Develops partnerships with educational institutions, government agencies, and the private sector. Disseminates information; maintains a speakers' bureau; participates in world conferences. **Awards: Type:** scholarship. **Recipient:** for NWC members to attend conferences. **Publications:** *Network Exchange.* Newsletter. **Price:** included with membership dues; $25.00/year for nonmembers. **Conventions/Meetings:** annual conference.

17204 ■ National Women's Law Center (NWLC)

11 Dupont Cir. NW, Ste.800
Washington, DC 20036
Ph: (202)588-5180
Fax: (202)588-5185
E-mail: action@nwlc.org
URL: http://www.nwlc.org
Contact: Nancy Duff Campbell, Co-Pres.

Founded: 1972. **Staff:** 40. **Budget:** $5,500,000. **Nonmembership. Description:** Has "expanded the possibilities for women and girls in our country". Uses the law in all its forms: getting new laws on the books; litigating ground-breaking lawsuits all the way to the Supreme Court; and educating the public about how to make the law and public policies work for women and their families. "Takes on the issues that cut to the core of women's and girls' lives" in health, education, employment, and family economic security, with special priority given to the needs of low-income women and their families. **Formerly:** (1981) Women's Rights Project of the Center for Law and Social Policy. **Publications:** *Be All That We Can Be: Lessons From the Military for Improving Our Nation's Child Care System.* Report ● *Check It Out: Is the Playing Field Level for Women and Girls at Your School?* ● *Hospital Mergers and the Threat to Women's Reproductive Health Services: Using Charitable Assets Laws to Fight Back.* Report ● *Making the Grade on Women's Health: A National and State-By-State Report Card 2001* ● *The Supreme Court and Women's Rights: Fundamental Protections Hanging in the Balance.* Report ● *Take Action: Get Your Prescription Contraceptives Covered—A Practical Guide for Employees* ● *Update,* quarterly. Newsletter. **Circulation:** 3,500 ● Also publishes fact sheets and testimonies.

17205 ■ National Women's Political Caucus (NWPC)

1712 I St. NW, Ste.503
Washington, DC 20006
Ph: (202)785-1100
Fax: (202)370-6306
E-mail: info@nwpc.org
URL: http://www.nwpc.org
Contact: Llenda Jackson-Leslie, Pres.

Founded: 1971. **Members:** 75,000. **Membership Dues:** full, $65 (annual) ● limited resource, $20 (annual). **Staff:** 10. **Regional Groups:** 300. **State Groups:** 30. **Local Groups:** 69. **Description:** Represents individuals that are supporting increased political influence of women. Serves as multipartisan caucus seeking to gain an equal voice and place for women in the political process at local, state, and national levels. Supports women candidates for elective and appointive political offices. Raises women's issues in elections and seeks to ensure that women hold policymaking positions in political parties. Has lobbied in state legislatures to pass the Equal Rights Amendment, to protect women's rights of reproductive freedom, and to secure comparable worth on the job. Works for affirmative action within the major political parties. Compiles statistics. **Awards:** Exceptional Merit Media Awards. **Frequency:** biennial. **Type:** recognition. **Recipient:** for exceptional coverage of women in the news ● Good Guys Award. **Frequency:** biennial. **Type:** recognition. **Computer Services:** database. **Committees:** Campaign Support; Leadership Development Education and Research Fund; Political Action. **Programs:** National Women's Political Caucus Training. **Publications:** *Campaigning to Win* ● *Fact Sheet on Women's Political Progress* ● *National Directory of Women Elected Officials* ● *Weekly Political Report.* **Price:** included in membership dues. Alternate Formats: online ● *Women's Political Times,* quarterly. Newsletter. Covers political issues from a feminist viewpoint. Includes book reviews and legislative updates. **Price:** included in membership dues. ISSN: 0195-1688. **Circulation:** 30,000. **Advertising:** accepted. **Conventions/Meetings:** biennial conference (exhibits).

17206 ■ Organization of Chinese American Women (OCAW)

4641 Montgomery Ave., Ste.208
Bethesda, MD 20814
Ph: (301)907-3898
Fax: (301)907-3899
E-mail: ocawwomen@aol.com
URL: http://www.ocawwomen.org
Contact: Ms. Rosetta Lai, Natl. Pres.

Founded: 1977. **Members:** 2,000. **Membership Dues:** individual, $30 (annual) ● joint, $50 (annual) ● full time student, $20 (annual) ● century club, $100 (annual) ● affiliate, $500 (annual) ● corporate, $1,000 (annual). **National Groups:** 8. **Languages:** Chinese, English. **Description:** Advances the cause of Chinese American women in the U.S. and fosters public awareness of their special needs and concerns. Seeks to integrate Chinese American women into the mainstream of women's activities and programs. Addresses issues such as equal employment opportunities at both the professional and nonprofessional levels; overcoming stereotypes; racial and sexual discrimination and restrictive traditional beliefs; assistance to poverty-stricken recent immigrants; access to leadership and policymaking positions. Serves as networking for Chinese American women. Sponsors annual opera and Mother's Day and Award Banquet. Establishes scholarships for middle school girls in rural China. **Awards:** Presidential Classroom Scholarships. **Frequency:** annual. **Type:** scholarship. **Recipient:** recommendations by chapters and members. **Programs:** Communication; Cultural Events; Research; Technical Assistance; Women to Women's Exchange. **Affiliated With:** National Council of Women's Organizations. **Publications:** *OCAW Women Today,* semiannual. Newsletter. **Conventions/Meetings:** biennial National Training Conference.

17207 ■ Priests for Equality (PFE)

c/o Rea Howarth
PO Box 5206
Hyattsville, MD 20782
Ph: (301)699-0042
Fax: (301)864-2182

E-mail: cso@quixote.org
URL: http://www.quixote.org/pfe
Contact: Rea Howarth, Contact
Founded: 1975. **Members:** 2,300. **Staff:** 1. **Description:** Represents Catholic priests seeking to achieve full equality for women both in the Catholic Church and in society. Believes that women can and should be ordained as priests; that women and men are "equally precious to a loving Creator, equally bearing the image of that Creator, equally called to develop his or her human rights." Engages in sociological studies and surveys. Sponsors research studies, reports, and other activities designed to raise the consciousness of individuals and strengthen their commitment to equality. **Publications:** *The Living Mosaic*, quarterly. Newsletter. Alternate Formats: online ● Also publishes pamphlets and papers.

17208 ■ Radical Women (RW)
New Valencia Hall
1908 Mission St.
San Francisco, CA 94103
Ph: (415)864-1278
Fax: (415)864-0778
E-mail: natradicalwomen@aol.com
URL: http://www.radicalwomen.org
Contact: Anne Slater, Organizer
Founded: 1967. **Local Groups:** 9. **Languages:** English, Spanish. **Description:** Represents women with a socialist-feminist political orientation who believe that women's leadership is decisive for basic social change. Works toward reform in the areas of reproductive rights, childcare, affirmative action, divorce, police brutality, rape, women of color, lesbians, and working women. Opposes efforts of conservative anti-feminist groups. **Publications:** Papers, quarterly. **Price:** $1.00 each; $5.00/year. **Conventions/Meetings:** annual conference.

17209 ■ St. Joan's International Alliance U.S. Section (SJIA-USA)
1545 W Armour Ave.
Milwaukee, WI 53221
Ph: (414)282-6943
E-mail: ginnfinn@sbcglobal.net
Contact: C. Virginia Finn, Pres.
Founded: 1965. **Membership Dues:** individual, regular, $25 (annual). **Languages:** French. **Description:** Objectives are to secure legal and de facto equality between women and men in society, church, and state. Has worked for the passage of the Equal Rights Amendment since 1966. The International Alliance, founded in 1911, has worked with the United Nations (and earlier with the League of Nations) for: the abolition of child and forced marriages and slavery traffic and traffic in persons; the political rights of women; equal access to education and vocational training and economic opportunities; family law; elimination of discrimination against women. In the church, the alliance has petitioned for lay men and women observers and women auditors at the Second Vatican Council, for the revision of the nuptial liturgy, revision of those canons of the code that adversely affect women, and admission of women to the diaconate and priesthood on the same terms and under the same conditions as men. Seeks dialogue with bishops regarding the status of women in the church. **Libraries:** Type: not open to the public. **Subjects:** Women's Status Rights. **Publications:** *Catholic Citizen*, semiannual. Journal. **Price:** included in membership dues. Also Cited As: *Alleanza and L'Alliance* ● *President's Newsletter*, periodic. **Conventions/Meetings:** biennial International Council Assembly - general assembly.

17210 ■ United Nations Development Fund for Women (UNIFEM)
304 E 45th St., 15th Fl.
New York, NY 10017
Ph: (212)906-6400
Fax: (212)906-6705
URL: http://www.unifem.org
Contact: Ms. Noeleen Heyzer, Exec. Dir.
Founded: 1976. **Staff:** 18. **Budget:** $13,000,000. **Regional Groups:** 5. **Languages:** English, French, Spanish. **Description:** Autonomous fund operating in

association with the United Nations Development Programme (see separate entry) and created by the UN General Assembly following the International Women's Year, 1975. Supports the efforts of women in the developing world to achieve their objectives for economic and social development and for equality, and by doing so, to improve the quality of life for all. Works in three key program areas of strategic importance to women: Agriculture, Trade and Industry, and Macro Policy and National Planning. Initiatives are complemented by technical support for credit, technology transfer, small business development, and training. The approach stresses capacity-building, empowerment and collaboration with appropriate partners. Addresses issues which are on the international agenda, and which critically affect women as beneficiaries and contributors to the development process. **Affiliated With:** United Nations Development Programme. **Formerly:** (1985) Voluntary Fund for the United Nations Decade for Women. **Publications:** *A Guide to Community Revolving Loan Funds* (in English, French, and Spanish) ● *Aceh Tsunami Response*. Newsletter. Provides an overview of the achievements of UNIFEM and its partners in response to the tsunami that hit Aceh, Indonesia. Alternate Formats: online ● *Development Review* (in English, French, and Spanish), semiannual ● *Information Booklets* (in English, French, and Spanish), periodic ● *UNIFEM Currents*, bimonthly. Bulletin. Alternate Formats: online ● *UNIFEM News* (in English, French, and Spanish), quarterly. Newsletter ● Papers (in English, French, and Spanish). **Conventions/Meetings:** semiannual Intergovernmental Committee Meeting.

17211 ■ The Woman Activist (TWA)
Address Unknown since 2007
Founded: 1975. **Staff:** 1. **Nonmembership.** **Description:** Consulting firm specializing in service on issues of political concern to women. Activities include research, program development, issue analysis, report writing, and statistics compilation. Rates members of Congress on women's issues and compares voting patterns of congressmen and congresswomen on civil and social rights issues. Compiles Woman Activist Mailing List of political feminists. Maintains library of feminist books and information. **Convention/Meeting:** none. **Affiliated With:** The Woman Activist Fund. **Publications:** *The Woman Activist*, 10/year. **Price:** $17.00/year.

17212 ■ The Woman Activist Fund (TWAF)
PO Box 6530
Alexandria, VA 22306-6530
Ph: (571)216-4107
URL: http://www.almanacvapolitics.org
Contact: Jeanne O'Hara, Ed.
Founded: 1977. **Members:** 11. **Description:** Compiles information on representatives of individuals and groups in elected and appointed governmental bodies at local, state, and national levels, especially as such information affects women and minorities. Analyzes and publishes findings; conducts polls and surveys; educates the public, especially women and minorities, through programs and reports. **Affiliated With:** The Woman Activist. **Publications:** *Almanac of Virginia Politics*. Book ● *The Wisteria Acres Cookbook*. **Price:** $15.62.

17213 ■ Women, Law and Development International (WLDI)
Address Unknown since 2006
Founded: 1993. **Staff:** 4. **Budget:** $350,000. **Languages:** Arabic, English, French, Hindi Suriname Hindustanti, Spanish, Urdu. **Description:** Committed to the defense and promotion of women's rights globally. Links individuals from activist groups, research institutions, and advocacy and human rights organizations throughout the world in order to: discern a global consensus on fundamental gender rights; develop the legal and political skills women need to transform this consensus into concrete action for change; advocate favorable UN and governmental policies affecting women's rights; and expand and strengthen the women's rights network. Conducts educational and training programs. **Libraries:** Type:

reference. **Subjects:** human rights, violence against women, United Nations, economic rights. **Awards:** Type: grant. **Formerly:** (1980) Overseas Education Fund of the League of Women Voters; (1984) Overseas Education Fund; (1993) OEF International; (1995) Institute for Women, Law, and Development. **Publications:** Brochures ● Handbooks ● Reports.

17214 ■ Women and Philanthropy
c/o Council on Foundations
1828 L St. NW, Ste.300
Washington, DC 20036
Free: (877)293-8809
Fax: (202)887-6240
E-mail: info@womenphil.org
URL: http://www.womenphil.org
Contact: Gwen I. Walden, Chair
Founded: 1977. **Members:** 600. **Membership Dues:** regular, $150 (annual). **Staff:** 5. **Budget:** $400,000. **Description:** Represents staff and trustees of grant-making organizations. Seeks to increase the amount of money for programs on behalf of women and girls and to enhance the status of women as decision-makers within private philanthropy. Builds regional networks of women and men in philanthropy; conducts research on grant-making patterns in the funding of programs; disseminates information to promote thoughtful decision-making with regard to the funding of programs that meet the needs of women. **Awards:** LEAD Award. **Frequency:** annual. **Type:** recognition. **Caucuses:** Gender and Education Initiative; Women of Color Leadership. **Affiliated With:** Council on Foundations. **Formerly:** (1994) Women and Foundations/Corporate Philanthropy. **Publications:** Annual Report, annual ● Brochure ● Newsletter, 3/year. **Price:** included in membership dues ● Papers, 1-2/year ● Also publishes research studies and special publications on needs of women and girls. **Conventions/Meetings:** annual conference, business meeting with speakers - usually April ● annual meeting.

17215 ■ Women's Campaign Fund (WCF)
734 15th St. NW, Ste.500
Washington, DC 20005
Ph: (202)393-8164
Fax: (202)393-0649
E-mail: info@wcfonline.org
URL: http://www.wcfonline.org
Contact: Ilana Goldman, Pres.
Founded: 1974. **Staff:** 5. **Budget:** $1,200,000. **Description:** Seeks to foster and support the election of qualified, pro-choice women to public offices. Raises funds; makes direct cash contributions to the campaigns of endorsed candidates; provides campaign counsel and services (media, field organization, and polling) to candidates; recruits and develops pro-choice candidates; stimulates support for endorsed candidates by other groups and individuals; promotes public awareness of the need for more women in public office. **Publications:** *Charge for Choice*, quarterly. Newsletter. **Circulation:** 6,000. Alternate Formats: online.

17216 ■ Women's Environment and Development Organization (WEDO)
355 Lexington Ave., 3rd Fl.
New York, NY 10017
Ph: (212)973-0325
Fax: (212)973-0335
E-mail: wedo@wedo.org
URL: http://www.wedo.org
Contact: June Zeitlin, Exec. Dir.
Founded: 1990. **Multinational.** **Description:** Works to make women more visible as participants, policymakers, and leaders in fate-of-the-earth decisions. Campaigns for gender balance by the year 2001 in all governmental and non-governmental bodies, commissions, committees, and boards that deliberate on environment, development, and women's rights issues. Monitors implementation of governments' Earth Summit ICPD, Social Summit and Women's Conference commitments. Participates in United Nations conferences and facilitates the women's caucus for NGO advocacy. Undertakes Women, Health and the Environment: Action for Cancer Prevention Campaign, public hearings, activities, conferences, and

public education. **Libraries: Type:** reference. **Holdings:** 300; articles, biographical archives, books, papers, photographs, reports. **Subjects:** women, environment, government, United Nations, MDGs, global policy, U.S. policy, activism, water, human rights, sustainable development, governance, economic and social justice, development, trade, finance, feminism, grassroots. **Computer Services:** Online services, library. **Programs:** Economic and Social Justice; Gender and Governance; Sustainable Development; U.S. Global Policy. **Publications:** *News and Views.* Newsletter. Alternate Formats: online ● Brochures ● Reports ● Promotes action through action alert mailings, primers, press and political briefings, advertising, flyers and postcards. Also produces a video and radio documentaries. **Conventions/Meetings:** periodic workshop and seminar.

17217 ■ Women's International Network (WIN)
c/o WIN News
187 Grant St.
Lexington, MA 02420-2126
Ph: (781)862-9431
Fax: (781)862-1734
E-mail: winnews@igc.org
URL: http://www.feminist.com/win.htm
Contact: Fran P. Hosken, Ed.
Founded: 1975. **Staff:** 2. **Description:** Encourages cooperation and communication between women of all backgrounds, beliefs, nationalities, and age groups through the compilation and dissemination of information on women's development. Participants voluntarily contribute news and information on women and health, environment, media, violence, female genital mutilation, and United Nations events of concern to women. The network's Women and International Affairs Clearinghouse surveys career opportunities for women interested in working in international and development agencies. Conducts research on women's health, on female genital mutilation, and on women's development throughout the world. **Publications:** *The Childbirth Picture Book Program* (in Arabic, English, French, Somali, and Spanish). Flexible, adaptable, multi-ethnic teaching aid on reproduction. Includes a separate text, a teacher's discussion guide, a glossary, and resource list. **Price:** $7.00 prepaid; $11.00 airmail overseas ● *Hosken Report: Genital/Sexual Mutilation of Females, 4th Edition, 1994.* Book. Contains research work with historical and political perspectives; includes case histories, background and economic facts, and bibliography. **Price:** $45.00 for institutions, plus shipping and handling; $35.00 for individuals, plus shipping and handling ● *Stop Female Genital Mutilation: Women Speak 1995.* Book. Based on the Hosken Report with chapters on health facts, human rights, politics of FGM, actions for change, and grassroots initiatives. **Price:** $15.00 prepaid; $20.00 overseas; $3.00 priority mail. ISSN: 0145-7985 ● *WIN News* (in Arabic, English, French, Somali, and Spanish), quarterly. Journal. Provides information on women and women's groups worldwide. **Price:** $35.00 /year for individuals, plus postage overseas; $48.00 /year for institutions, plus postage overseas. ISSN: 0145-7985.

17218 ■ Women's Law Project (WLP)
125 S 9th St., No. 300
Philadelphia, PA 19107
Ph: (215)928-9801
Fax: (215)928-9848
E-mail: info@womenslawproject.org
URL: http://www.womenslawproject.org
Contact: Carol E. Tracy, Exec. Dir.
Founded: 1974. **Staff:** 8. **Budget:** $700,000. **Description:** Serves as feminist law firm working to challenge sex discrimination in the law and in legal and social institutions through litigation, public education, research and writing, representation of women's groups, and individual counseling. Specializes in the areas of family law, education, employment, reproductive rights, violence against women, and sex-based insurance rates. **Publications:** *Child Custody & Family Violence Handbook* ● *Interstate Child Support.* Handbook ● *Justice in the Domestic Relations Division of Philadelphia Family Court: A Report to the*

Community. Alternate Formats: online ● *Laura's Circle: Pennsylvanians for Choice*, quarterly. Newsletter. Contains LC telephone counseling service PFC prochoice advocates. ● *Pennsylvania Abortion Law for Teenagers* ● *Responding to the Needs of Pregnant and Parenting Women With Substance Use Disorders in Philadelphia.* Report. Alternate Formats: online ● Brochures. Alternate Formats: online.

17219 ■ Women's Research and Education Institute (WREI)
3300 N Fairfax Dr., Ste.218
Arlington, VA 22201
Ph: (703)812-7990
Fax: (703)812-0687
E-mail: wrei@wrei.org
URL: http://www.wrei.org
Contact: Susan Scanlan, Pres.
Founded: 1977. **Staff:** 6. **Description:** Acts as a nonpartisan policy research organization. Provides information to policymakers, legislators, women's research centers, and the media concerning issues of importance to women and families. Sponsors Congressional Fellowships on Women and Public Policy. Conducts research projects on women's access to health care and women in the military. Compiles statistics on education, health, employment, earnings, population, marriage, divorce, and politics. **Awards:** American Woman Award. **Frequency:** annual. **Type:** recognition. **Councils:** Advisory. **Programs:** Congressional Fellowship. **Projects:** The American Woman Series; Crossing Borders; Women in the Military; Women Writing Africa; Women's Health. **Formerly:** (1980) Congresswomen's Caucus Corporation. **Publications:** *American Woman Series*, biennial. Books. Alternate Formats: online ● *The American Women 2004-05: Daughters of a Revolution-Young Women Today.* Book. **Price:** $24.95/copy ● *The Health of Mid-Life Women in the States.* Report. **Price:** $6.50/copy ● *Older Women: The Economics of Aging*, periodic. Report. **Price:** $6.95/copy ● *Women in the Military: Where They Stand* (5th edition), periodic. Booklet. **Price:** $5.00/copy ● *WREI Update.* Newsletter. Contains information on the association's projects, publications and upcoming events. Alternate Formats: online ● Reports.

17220 ■ Women's Rights Committee (WRC)
c/o American Federation of Teachers
Human Rights Dept.
555 New Jersey Ave. NW
Washington, DC 20001
Ph: (202)879-4400
E-mail: assocmbr@aft.org
URL: http://www.aft.org
Contact: Edward McElroy, Pres.
Founded: 1970. **Description:** Carries out policy resolutions of the American Federation of Teachers (see separate entry) in the area of women's rights. Encourages programs on the local level that implement these policies; works with other feminist groups with the same views. Conducts research and education programs; maintains speakers' bureau; compiles statistics. **Affiliated With:** American Federation of Teachers. **Publications:** *Action*, weekly ● *American Educator*, quarterly ● *American Teacher*, monthly. **Conventions/Meetings:** annual conference ● biennial meeting.

17221 ■ Women's Rights Project (WRP)
c/o American Civil Liberties Union
125 Broad St., 18th Fl.
New York, NY 10004
Ph: (212)549-2644
Fax: (212)549-2580
E-mail: womensrights@aclu.org
URL: http://www.aclu.org/WomensRights/Women-sRightsMain.cfm
Contact: Lenora M. Lapidus, Dir.
Founded: 1972. **Members:** 400,000. **Staff:** 7. **Languages:** English, Spanish. **Description:** Works to advance the rights and interests of women, with a particular focus on issues affecting low-income women and women of color. Implements ACLU policy in the area of gender discrimination through litigation, legislative advocacy and public education. **Publica-**

tions: Annual Report, annual. Alternate Formats: online. **Conventions/Meetings:** biennial meeting, held in conjunction with the American Civil Liberties Union.

Finance

17222 ■ Finance Project
1401 New York Ave. NW, Ste.800
Washington, DC 20005
Ph: (202)628-4200
Fax: (202)628-1293
E-mail: info@financeproject.org
URL: http://www.financeproject.org
Contact: Cheryl Hayes, Exec. Dir.
Description: Develops and disseminates information, knowledge, tools, technical assistance for improved policies, programs, financing strategies that will benefit children, families and communities. **Computer Services:** Mailing lists, of members.

17223 ■ International Open Finance Association (IOFASOC)
10201 Hammocks Blvd., No. 153
Miami, FL 33196
Ph: (305)773-7663
E-mail: jkromano@bellsouth.net
URL: http://www.iofasoc.org
Contact: John K. Romano, Exec. Dir.
Founded: 2002. **Members:** 50. **Membership Dues:** individual, $50 (annual). **Staff:** 3. **Budget:** $35,000. **Multinational. Description:** Supports capital formation for economic development. **Libraries: Type:** not open to the public. **Holdings:** archival material, articles, books. **Subjects:** microfinance, small business capital formation, direct public offerings.

Financial Aid

17224 ■ Jubilee USA Network
222 E Capitol St. NE
Washington, DC 20003
Ph: (202)783-3566
Fax: (202)546-4468
E-mail: coord@jubileeusa.org
URL: http://www.jubileeusa.org
Contact: Neil Watkins, Natl. Coor.
Multinational. Description: Provides relief to countries suffering from debt. **Computer Services:** Mailing lists. **Publications:** *Jubilee Newsletter.* Alternate Formats: online ● *Jubilee USA Network's Email News and Action Alerts.* **Price:** free for members. Alternate Formats: online ● Articles. Alternate Formats: online.

Firearms

17225 ■ Armed Females of America (AFA)
2702 E Univ. Dr., Ste.103
PMB 213
Mesa, AZ 85213
Ph: (480)924-8202
E-mail: afa@armedfemalesofamerica.com
URL: http://www.armedfemalesofamerica.com
Contact: Carma Lewis, Exec. Dir.
Membership Dues: regular, $20 (annual) ● senior, $15 (annual) ● family (two adults plus children up to 18 years of age), $50 (annual) ● life, $300. **Description:** Defends rights to keep and bear arms guaranteed by U.S. Second Amendment of the Bill of Rights. **Publications:** Newsletter.

17226 ■ Brady Campaign to Prevent Gun Violence (HCI)
1225 Eye St. NW, Ste.1100
Washington, DC 20005
Ph: (202)898-0792

Fax: (202)371-9615
URL: http://www.bradycampaign.org
Contact: Michael D. Barnes, Pres. Emeritus/Sr. Advisor
Founded: 1974. **Members:** 400,000. **Membership Dues:** individual, $15 (annual). **Staff:** 60. **Budget:** $7,500,000. **Description:** Public citizens' lobby working for legislative controls and governmental regulations on the manufacture, importation, sale, transfer, and civilian possession of guns. Compiles up-to-date information on the gun issue, including approaches, statistics, legislation, and research. Maintains speakers' bureau. **Awards: Type:** recognition. **Committees:** Brady Campaign; Voter Education Fund. **Councils:** Brady Leadership. **Projects:** The Legal Action. **Formerly:** (1979) National Council to Control Handguns; (2002) Handgun Control. **Publications:** *Guns Don't Die - People Do.* Book ● *Progress Report*, 3/year. Newsletter. Includes calendar of events. **Price:** included in membership dues. **Circulation:** 250,000 ● Pamphlets ● Reports ● Also publishes fact sheets and report cards. **Conventions/Meetings:** annual meeting.

17227 ■ **Brady Center to Prevent Gun Violence (BCPGV)**
1225 Eye St. NW, Ste.1100
Washington, DC 20005
Ph: (202)289-7319
Fax: (202)408-1851
URL: http://www.bradycenter.org
Contact: Sarah Brady, Chair
Founded: 1983. **Staff:** 20. **Budget:** $3,400,000. **Description:** Serves as the education, legal advocacy, and research affiliate of Handgun Control, Inc. Sponsors prevention programs for parents and youth on the risks associated with guns; legal representation for gun violence victims; and out reach to the entertainment community to encourage deglamorization of guns in the media. **Libraries: Type:** not open to the public. **Holdings:** 3,000. **Subjects:** gun violence prevention. **Departments:** Law Enforcement Relations. **Programs:** A Day in the Neighborhood; Linking with Victims for Change; Steps to Prevent Firearm Injury In The Home. **Projects:** The Legal Action. **Absorbed:** (1985) American Alliance Against Violence. **Formerly:** (1986) Handgun Information Center; (2003) Center to Prevent Handgun Violence. **Publications:** *Legal Action Report*, quarterly. Newsletter. Contains updated information on gun industry reform and gun violence prevention litigation. Alternate Formats: online ● Also issues news releases and studies.

17228 ■ **Citizens for Safe Government (CSG)**
Address Unknown since 2006
Description: Defends Second Amendment Rights of Americans to keep and bear arms.

17229 ■ **Coalition to Stop Gun Violence (CSGV)**
1023 15th St. NW, Ste.301
Washington, DC 20005
Ph: (202)408-0061
E-mail: development@csgv.org
URL: http://www.csgv.org
Contact: Joshua Horwitz Esq., Exec. Dir.
Founded: 1975. **Members:** 120,000. **Staff:** 7. **Budget:** $600,000. **National Groups:** 40. **Description:** National educational, professional, and religious organizations, representing 120,000 individuals, united to seek a ban on the private sale and possession of handguns in America. (Exceptions to the ban would include the police, active military personnel, federally licensed collectors, and target shooters whose handguns are used and kept only at shooting clubs) Works to enact restrictive handgun controls at the national, state, and local levels; assists state and local handgun control organizations. Conducts research and compiles statistics on subjects such as: suicide, homicide, and accidents involving handguns; handguns and self-defense; handgun production and the marketing tactics of manufacturers; efficacy of restrictive handgun laws; lobbying tactics employed by pro-handgun organizations. Develops original educational materials; provides information to the

news media. Maintains speakers' bureau. **Libraries: Type:** open to the public. **Holdings:** 5,000; articles, books, papers, periodicals. **Subjects:** gun industry, public health, research, product liability. **Awards:** Kennedy-King Award. **Frequency:** annual. **Type:** recognition. **Recipient:** for political leadership on gun violence. **Affiliated With:** Educational Fund to Stop Gun Violence. **Formerly:** (1990) National Coalition to Ban Handguns. **Publications:** *Citizens Conference to Stop Gun Violence Briefing Book.* Contains reference materials on gun violence statistics, legislation, litigation, the second amendment, and organizing for change. **Price:** $10.00 each. Alternate Formats: online.

17230 ■ **Drums No Guns (DNG)**
PO Box 1455
New Haven, CT 06510
Ph: (203)467-7344 (336)449-0730
URL: http://www.vegetarianusa.com/drumsnoguns
Contact: Michael Mills, Exec. Dir.
Founded: 1995. **Description:** Aims to promote the prevention of handgun violence through a national campaign of educational concerts. **Programs:** Community Works; Operation Y.E.S. **Projects:** Art Gallery.

17231 ■ **Educational Fund to Stop Gun Violence**
1023 15th St. NW, Ste.301
Washington, DC 20005-2602
Ph: (202)408-0061
URL: http://www.efsgv.org
Contact: Joshua Horwitz, Exec. Dir.
Founded: 1978. **Staff:** 6. **Budget:** $400,000. **Description:** Examines and offers public education on handgun violence in the U.S., particularly as it affects children. Maintains Firearms Litigation Clearinghouse that provides assistance to litigants, victims, attorneys, and legal scholars. Participates in the development of materials and educational programs in an effort to promote youth alternatives to gun violence. Examines the impact of handguns on public health. Conducts research on handgun violence, firearms marketing and production, and the design of firearms. Maintains speakers' bureau; compiles statistics. **Libraries: Type:** reference. **Holdings:** 2,000; books, periodicals. **Subjects:** firearms, gun violence. **Computer Services:** database, firearms litigation. **Formerly:** (1988) Foundation for Handgun Education; (2001) Educational Fund to End Handgun Violence. **Publications:** *Firearm Litigation Reporter*, quarterly. Newsletter. Contains summary of important firearms liability cases, recent studies in medical and public health magazines, and firearms industry updates. **Price:** $80.00/year. **Circulation:** 325 ● *Grass Roots Organizing*, Manual ● *Kids and Guns: A National Disgrace*. Booklet ● *Stop Gun Violence News*, bimonthly. Newsletter. Provides information and advice for citizens to reduce gun violence in their communities. **Price:** free. **Circulation:** 2,000. **Conventions/Meetings:** annual Citizens Conference to Stop Gun Violence - conference and workshop, includes grassroots antiviolence groups (exhibits).

17232 ■ **Firearms Research and Identification Association (FRIA)**
PO Box 620
Wrightwood, CA 92397-0620
Ph: (760)249-6837
Fax: (760)249-1098
E-mail: info@jacaudron.com
URL: http://www.jacaudron.com
Contact: John Armand Caudron, Pres.
Founded: 1978. **Members:** 16. **Staff:** 2. **Budget:** $1,000. **State Groups:** 1. **Languages:** English, French, Japanese. **Description:** Represents engineers, curators, safety professionals, insurance, finance, and business consultants, and medical technicians. Conducts research on the authenticity, history and development, and accident analysis of firearms. Submits reports on defective weapons. Issues firearm certificates of authenticity and identification. Provides expert witnesses. Develops a certification test for firearm professionals. **Libraries: Type:** not open to the public. **Holdings:** 150. **Subjects:**

militaria, military history, firearms. **Publications:** *A Metered Stride.* Book. **Price:** $15.00. **Circulation:** 125 ● *The C-3/1 Papers*, bimonthly. Book. **Price:** $15.00. **Circulation:** 125. **Conventions/Meetings:** annual meeting and symposium - first weekend in May.

17233 ■ **Guns Save Lives (GSL)**
7481 Huntsman Blvd., Ste.525
Springfield, VA 22153
Ph: (720)435-9964
E-mail: train@therange.com
URL: http://www.gunssavelives.com
Description: Works to spread the facts that show firearms are beneficial.

17234 ■ **HELP Network**
c/o Children's Memorial Hospital
2300 Children's Plz., No. 88
Chicago, IL 60614
Ph: (773)880-3993 (773)880-3826
E-mail: alhill@childrensmemorial.org
URL: http://www.helpnetwork.org
Contact: Katherine Kaufer Christoffel MD, Founder/Pres.
Founded: 1993. **Members:** 127. **Membership Dues:** large organization (with 150 or more members), $500 (annual) ● small organization (with less than 150 members), $175 (annual) ● chapter of large organization, $175 (annual) ● supporting organization/individual, $60 (annual) ● student, $20 (annual). **Multinational. Description:** Aims to reduce firearm injuries and deaths. **Affiliated With:** American Academy of Child and Adolescent Psychiatry; American Academy of Pediatrics; American College of Physicians-American Society of Internal Medicine; American Medical Association; Center for Food Safety. **Publications:** *Disabilities from Guns: The Untold Costs of Spinal Cord and Traumatic Brain Injuries.* Manual. **Price:** $8.00 ● *Gun Injury Prevention* (in English and Spanish). Brochure. Brochure and poster. **Price:** $1.00 ● *Guns and Domestic Violence: A Deadly Combination.* Manual ● *The HELP Handgun Disposal Handbook: A Prescription for Safety.* **Price:** free ● *HELP Nation Status Reports (International Mortality Data).* **Price:** $10.00 ● *Missing in Action.* Manual ● *Old GUNS.* Brochure ● *School-Based Curricula to Prevent Gun Violence.* Manual ● *State Status Reports.* Alternate Formats: online ● *The Unrecognized Injury Toll of Non-Powder Guns: These Guns Aren't Toys.* Manual. **Price:** $8.00 ● Newsletters, quarterly. Alternate Formats: online. **Conventions/Meetings:** conference.

17235 ■ **Million Mom March**
1225 Eye St. NW, Ste.1100
Washington, DC 20005
Ph: (202)898-0792
Free: (888)989-MOMS
Fax: (202)408-1851
URL: http://www.millionmommarch.org
Description: Dedicated to eliminating gun violence in America.

17236 ■ **St. Gabriel Possenti Society**
PO Box 2844
Arlington, VA 22202-0844
Ph: (703)212-9860
Fax: (703)212-9861
E-mail: info@possentisociety.com
URL: http://www.possentisociety.com
Contact: John Michael Snyder, Chm./Founder
Founded: 1989. **Nonmembership. Multinational. Description:** Promotes public recognition of St. Gabriel Possenti as Patron Saint of Handgunners. Underscores historical, philosophical and theological bases for the doctrine of legitimate self-defense. **Awards:** St. Gabriel Possenti Society Medallion. **Type:** medal. **Additional Websites:** http://www.gun-saint.com. **Publications:** *Self Defense and the Bible.* Booklet. **Price:** $10.00 contribution.

17237 ■ Second Amendment Sisters (SAS)
900 RR 620 S, Ste.C-101
PMB 228
Lakeway, TX 78734
Free: (877)271-6216
E-mail: inquire@2asisters.org
URL: http://www.2asisters.org
Contact: Marinelle W. Thompson, Pres./Founder
Founded: 1999. **Membership Dues:** youth, associate, $15 (annual) ● full, $25 (annual) ● family, $50 (annual) ● life (associate), $350 ● life, $500. **Description:** Supports gun ownership, directed mostly towards women.

17238 ■ Silent March: Americans Against Violence
Address Unknown since 2007
Description: Works for elected officials to end gun violence through regulating the firearm industry. **Projects:** Shoes.

17239 ■ Sportsmen's Association for Firearms Education (SAFE)
PO Box 343
Commack, NY 11725
Ph: (631)475-8125
E-mail: jcushman@juno.com
URL: http://www.nysafe.org
Contact: John L. Cushman, Pres.
Founded: 1992. **Members:** 600. **Membership Dues:** individual, $25 (annual) ● junior, $15 (annual) ● sponsor, club, $50 (annual). **Description:** Promotes lawful firearms ownership in the U.S. **Affiliated With:** Citizens Committee for the Right to Keep and Bear Arms; National Rifle Association of America. **Publications:** SAFE Legislative Report, monthly. **Price:** free, for members only ● Newsletter, monthly ● Reports. **Conventions/Meetings:** annual CCW Conference ● meeting, educational.

17240 ■ Student Pledge Against Gun Violence
112 Nevada St.
Northfield, MN 55057
Ph: (507)645-5378
Fax: (507)663-1207
E-mail: mlgrow@pledge.org
URL: http://www.pledge.org
Contact: Mary Lewis Grow, Natl. Coor.
Description: Works to end gun violence among young people. Provides information; conducts events, programs, and activities for the youth. **Conventions/Meetings:** Day of National Concern about Young People and Gun Violence Pledge - meeting.

17241 ■ Students for the Second Amendment (SF2A)
9624 Braun Run
San Antonio, TX 78254
Ph: (210)674-5559
Fax: (210)674-5559
E-mail: info@sf2a.org
URL: http://www.sf2a.org
Contact: Ryan T. Bragg, Co-Founder/Chm.
Founded: 2000. **Description:** Educates youth about rights guaranteed under U.S. Constitution, especially Second Amendment. **Conventions/Meetings:** workshop, with speakers.

Fishing

17242 ■ Recreational Fishing Alliance (RFA)
PO Box 3080
New Gretna, NJ 08224
Ph: (609)404-1060
Free: (888)564-6732
Fax: (609)404-1968
E-mail: rfa@joinrfa.org
URL: http://www.joinrfa.org
Contact: James A. Donofrio, Exec. Dir.
Membership Dues: general, $35 (annual) ● general, $90 (triennial). **State Groups:** 6. **Local Groups:** 1. **Description:** Strives to safeguard the rights of saltwater anglers. Protects marine, boat and tackle

industry jobs. Ensures the long-term sustainability of the nation's fisheries. **Publications:** Making Waves. Newsletter. **Price:** free for members. Alternate Formats: online.

Food

17243 ■ Campaign to Label Genetically Engineered Foods
PO Box 55699
Seattle, WA 98155
Ph: (425)771-4049
Fax: (425)740-8967
E-mail: label@thecampaign.org
URL: http://www.thecampaign.org
Contact: Alexander Schauss PhD, Pres.
Founded: 1999. **Description:** Represents food manufacturers who is committed to mandatory labeling of genetically engineered foods; promotes letter writing campaign to implement a moratorium on growing genetically engineered corn because the pollen is polluting organic cornfield; provides educational materials. **Publications:** The Campaign Reporter. Newsletter. Alternate Formats: online.

17244 ■ International Food Safety Council (IFSC)
c/o National Restaurant Association Educational
  Foundation
175 W Jackson Blvd., Ste.1500
Chicago, IL 60604-2814
Ph: (312)715-1010
Free: (800)765-2122
E-mail: info@nraef.org
URL: http://www.nraef.org
Contact: John R. Farquharson, Pres.
Founded: 1993. **Description:** Seeks to heighten the awareness of the importance of food safety education throughout the restaurant and foodservice industry. **Programs:** Food Safety Seal of Commitment. **Publications:** Food Safety Illustrated, quarterly. Focuses on ways to enhance food safety practices and procedures. **Conventions/Meetings:** conference.

Food and Drugs

17245 ■ Food and Drug Administration Alumni Association (FDAAA)
5600 Fishers Ln., Rm. 11-101
Rockville, MD 20857
E-mail: mail@fdaaa.org
URL: http://www.fdaaa.org
Contact: John C. Villforth, Chm.
Founded: 2001. **Membership Dues:** associate, $20 (annual) ● alumni, $35 (annual). **Description:** Represents the interests of individuals dedicated to serving those who have supported the consumer protection mission of the U.S. Food and Drug Administration (FDA). Enables former colleagues to stay current on major scientific and regulatory issues facing FDA. Educates the public about the work of the FDA. Promotes interest among America's youth in national service careers and public health opportunities at FDA. **Awards:** FDA Distinguished Alumni Award. **Frequency:** annual. **Type:** recognition. **Recipient:** to individuals who have outstanding commitment to meeting the FDAAA's mission of protecting public health ● FDAAA Volunteer of the Year Award. **Frequency:** annual. **Type:** recognition. **Recipient:** to individuals who have made extraordinary contributions to the growth and image of the FDAAA. **Publications:** Connections, quarterly. Newsletter. **Price:** included in membership dues.

Foreign Policy

17246 ■ Asian Speakers' Bureau (ASB)
18600 Walkers Choice Rd., Ste.4
Montgomery Village
Gaithersburg, MD 20886

Ph: (301)990-8831
Fax: (301)990-8831
E-mail: bi@speakersonasiantopics.org
URL: http://www.speakersonasiantopics.org
Contact: Dr. E. Bing Inocencio, Pres.
Founded: 1996. **Members:** 36. **Staff:** 2. **Description:** Maintains speaker's bureau comprised of English-speaking Asian professors and experts who discuss Far East political and cultural affairs, Asian mores, customs and phenomena such as Chigong, Feng Shui, alternative medicine, origami, ikebana art of flower arrangements, Kabuki theatre, mahjongg, cuisines, tai chi, acupuncture, yoga, and Zen Buddhism, among many others. **Also Known As:** SpeakersOnAsianTopics.org.

17247 ■ Council on Foreign Relations (CFR)
The Harold Pratt House
58 E 68th St.
New York, NY 10021
Ph: (212)434-9400
Fax: (212)434-9800
E-mail: communications@cfr.org
URL: http://www.cfr.org
Contact: Elise Carlson Lewis, VP/Dir.
Founded: 1921. **Members:** 3,800. **Staff:** 175. **Budget:** $30,000,000. **Description:** Individuals with specialized knowledge of and interest in international affairs. Studies the international aspects of American political, economic, and strategic problems; research projects are carried out by professional staff advised by study groups of selected leaders in education, public service, business, and the media. **Libraries: Type:** reference. **Holdings:** 20,000. **Awards:** International Affairs Fellowship. **Frequency:** annual. **Type:** grant. **Recipient:** for advanced international relations research or government experience by Americans between the ages of 27 and 35. **Telecommunication Services:** electronic mail, elewis@cfr.org. **Programs:** International Affairs Fellowship. **Publications:** Foreign Affairs, bimonthly. Journal. Includes book reviews. **Price:** $38.00/year; $7.95/copy. ISSN: 0015-7120. **Circulation:** 100,000. **Advertising:** accepted. Alternate Formats: microform ● Globalization: What's New?. Book. Contains information about globalization. **Price:** $64.50 ● Losing Iraq: Inside the Postwar Reconstruction Fiasco. Book. Contains information and views of war in Iraq. **Price:** $16.50 ● The Opportunity: America's Moments to Alter History's Course. Book. Describes an unprecedented moment in which the U.S. has a chance to bring about a world where most people can enjoy a decent standard of living. **Price:** $25.00 ● Understanding the War on Terror. Book. **Price:** $19.95 ● Unsilencing the Past: Track Two Diplomacy and Turkish-Armenian Reconciliation. Book. **Price:** $39.95 ● Annual Report, annual ● Books ● Also publishes specialized studies on U.S. foreign policy. **Conventions/Meetings:** annual meeting - always fall.

17248 ■ Foreign Bases Project (FBP)
48 Duffield St.
Brooklyn, NY 11201
Ph: (718)596-7668
E-mail: fbp@igc.org
Contact: John M. Miller, Dir.
Founded: 1988. **Description:** Examines the social, political, military, and environmental impact of the U.S. military presence around the world.

17249 ■ Foreign Policy Association (FPA)
470 Park Ave. S
New York, NY 10016
Ph: (212)481-8100
Free: (800)628-5754
Fax: (212)481-9275
E-mail: info@fpa.org
URL: http://www.fpa.org
Contact: Noel V. Lateef, Pres./CEO
Founded: 1918. **Members:** 500. **Staff:** 25. **Description:** Nonpartisan educational organization established to educate American citizens on foreign policy. Seeks to stimulate wider interest, more effective participation in and greater understanding of world affairs among American citizens. Sponsors the "Great Decisions Discussion Group Program, the oldest and

largest international affairs community discussion group program in the country". **Libraries: Type:** not open to the public. **Subjects:** foreign policy. **Awards:** Nancy Hoepli-Phalon Scholarship. **Frequency:** annual. **Type:** scholarship. **Programs:** Great Decisions. **Absorbed:** (1960) World Affairs Center for the United States. **Formerly:** (1921) League of Free Nations Association. **Publications:** *A Cartoon History of U.S. Foreign Policy: From 1945 To The Present.* Book. **Price:** $12.95/copy ● *A Cartoon History of United States Foreign Policy: 1776-1976.* Book. **Price:** $9. 95/copy ● *Citizen's Guide to U.S. Foreign Policy Issues,* published in presidential election years. Contains foreign policy issues. **Price:** $9.95/copy ● *Great Decisions,* annual. Provides impartial background and analysis of eight critical U.S. foreign policy issues. Includes ballot for tabulation on U.S. foreign policy issues. **Price:** $15.00/issue. **ISSN:** 0072-727X. **Circulation:** 50,000 ● *Great Decisions National Opinion Ballot Report,* annual. **Price:** free ● *Great Decisions Teacher's Guide,* annual. Book. Provides materials for teachers and discussion leaders intended to reinforce concepts and promote critical thinking skills; includes glossary. **Price:** $19.00/issue ● *Headline Series,* quarterly. Contains global issues. **Price:** $20.00/year. **ISSN:** 0017-8780. **Circulation:** 8,000 ● Distributes audio- and videocassettes. **Conventions/Meetings:** annual World Leadership Forum - conference, on economic and political global trends - always September in New York.

17250 ■ Foreign Policy In Focus (FPIF)
1112 16th St. NW, Ste.200
Washington, DC 20036
Ph: (202)234-9382
Fax: (202)387-7915
E-mail: infocus@fpif.org
URL: http://www.fpif.org
Contact: Tom Barry, Policy Dir.
Founded: 1996. **Members:** 650. **Description:** Think tank committed to advancing a citizen-based foreign policy agenda, rooted in citizen initiatives and movements. **Computer Services:** Information services, Self-Determination Crisis Watch listserv. **Telecommunication Services:** electronic mail, tom@irc-online.org. **Committees:** Advisory. **Projects:** Foreign Policy In Focus. **Publications:** *GLOBAL FOCUS: Foreign Policy at the Turn of the Millennium.* Book. **Price:** $19.95 paperback, plus shipping and handling ($3) ● *Global Perspectives: A Media Guide to Progressive Foreign Policy Experts.* Book ● *In Focus Briefs,* usually one/week. Paper. Features information and analysis on a regular basis. **Price:** $20.00 each. Alternate Formats: online ● *The Next Fifty Years: The United Nations and the United States.* Book. **Price:** $11.95 plus shipping and handling ($3) ● *Progressive Response,* weekly. Bulletin. Contains information about U.S. foreign policy. Alternate Formats: online.

17251 ■ Institute for Foreign Policy Analysis (IFPA)
Central Plz. Bldg., 10th Fl.
675 Massachusetts Ave.
Cambridge, MA 02139-3309
Ph: (617)492-2116
Fax: (617)492-8242
E-mail: mail@ifpa.org
URL: http://www.ifpa.org/home.htm
Contact: Dr. Robert L. Pfaltzgraff Jr., Pres.
Founded: 1976. **Description:** Provides research and strategic planning for issues of national security, foreign policy, political economics, and government-industrial relations. **Publications:** *Point Papers* ● Reports. **Conventions/Meetings:** annual conference ● seminar ● workshop.

17252 ■ International Center
731 8th St. SE
Washington, DC 20003
Ph: (202)547-3800
Fax: (202)546-4784
E-mail: icnfp@erols.com
URL: http://www.theinternationalcenter.org
Contact: Virginia B. Foote, Exec. Dir.
Founded: 1977. **Staff:** 12. **Languages:** English, Russian, Spanish. **Description:** Public interest group

established to review current events in Asia, Africa, and Latin America and to analyze current U.S. policy toward developing countries. Seeks to provide alternative political, economic, and military policies that further democratic development and the resolution of regional conflict. Sends U.S. delegates to Asia, Africa, Latin America, and Russia to inform the public on current developments. Sponsors intern program and senior and visiting fellows. Active in tree-planting in 80 countries and starting solar PV program for micro-credit groups. **Libraries: Type:** reference. **Holdings:** 4,500. **Subjects:** Third World development and foreign policy. **Formerly:** (1986) Center for Development Policy; (1992) International Center for Development Policy. **Publications:** Newsletters ● Also publishes periodic briefing books.

17253 ■ Jewish Peace Lobby (JPL)
817 Silver Spring Ave., Ste.301
Silver Spring, MD 20910
Ph: (301)589-8764
Fax: (301)589-2722
E-mail: jplhome@peacelobby.org
URL: http://www.peacelobby.org
Contact: Dr. Jerome M. Segal, Pres.
Founded: 1989. **Members:** 4,000. **Membership Dues:** general, $100 (annual). **Staff:** 4. **Budget:** $150,000. **Description:** American Jews working to affect U.S. foreign policy regarding the Israeli-Palestinian conflict. Promotes a peaceful resolution based on the Israeli right to peace and security and the Palestinian right to self-determination. Conducts lobbying activities at the federal level; organizes and supports local lobbying efforts. Maintains speakers' bureau; operates Telephone Urgent Action network. **Publications:** *Washington Action Alert,* bimonthly. Describes pending legislation, provides background information, and suggests action. **Price:** included in membership dues.

17254 ■ National Committee on American Foreign Policy (NCAFP)
320 Park Ave., 8th Fl.
New York, NY 10022-6839
Ph: (212)224-1120
Fax: (212)224-2524
E-mail: contact@ncafp.org
URL: http://www.ncafp.org
Contact: Daniel Morris, Program Dir.
Founded: 1974. **Members:** 300. **Membership Dues:** corporate, $5,000 (annual) ● academic institution, $1,500 (annual) ● patron, $1,000 (annual) ● benefactor, $750 (annual) ● sponsor, $500 (annual) ● general, $300 (annual) ● academic, $150 (annual) ● student, $100 (annual). **Staff:** 7. **Budget:** $750,000. **Local Groups:** 1. **Description:** Individuals from all areas of American life who are interested in foreign affairs. Stimulates citizen interest in American foreign policy with regard to the immediate and long-range national and security interests of the U.S. **Awards:** George F. Kennan Award. **Frequency:** annual. **Type:** recognition. **Recipient:** for individuals who have served their country or who have made a contribution to the U.S. ● Hans J. Morgenthau Award. **Frequency:** annual. **Type:** recognition ● William J. Flynn Initiative for Peace Award. **Frequency:** annual. **Type:** recognition. **Recipient:** for individuals with remarkable efforts to preserve peace in United States. **Publications:** *American Foreign Policy Interests,* bimonthly. Describes the committee's positions on relevant questions. **Price:** $65.00 /year for individuals; $185.00 /year for institutions. **ISSN:** 1080-3920. **Circulation:** 2,000 ● Monographs ● Books. Features topics about foreign policy. ● Pamphlets. Includes foreign policy reports with policy recommendations. **Conventions/Meetings:** annual Angier Biddle Duke Lecture, with speakers who have played key roles in formulating and implementing foreign policy ● monthly The George D. Schwab Foreign Policy Briefings - meeting, briefings by American and foreign experts on foreign policy issues.

17255 ■ Nixon Center
1615 L St. NW, Ste.1250
Washington, DC 20036
Ph: (202)887-1000

Fax: (202)887-5222
E-mail: mail@nixoncenter.org
URL: http://www.nixoncenter.org
Contact: Dimitri K. Simes, Pres.
Founded: 1994. **Staff:** 10. **Budget:** $1,600,000. **Nonmembership. Description:** Aims to explore ways to enhance American security and prosperity while taking into account the legitimate perspectives of other nations. **Awards:** Distinguished Service Award. **Frequency:** annual. **Type:** recognition. **Programs:** Chinese Studies; Immigration and National Security; International Security and Energy; National Security Studies; Regional Strategy (Middle East, Caspian Basin, and South Asia); U.S.-Russia Relations. **Formerly:** (1998) Nixon Center for Peace and Freedom. **Publications:** *Center Monographs: Detailed Analysis of Key Foreign Policy Issues by Center Scholars* ● *Nixon Center Perspectives: Longer Policy Speeches and Essays by Center Guests* ● *Program Briefs and Transcripts: Summaries of Panel Discussions and Lectures Held at the Center* ● Articles. **Conventions/Meetings:** conference ● annual Distinguished Service Award - dinner - fall ● lecture ● seminar.

17256 ■ Secretary's Open Forum
US Dept. of State
S/OF, Rm. 5312A
2201 C St. NW
Washington, DC 20520
Ph: (202)647-0819
Fax: (202)647-4040
E-mail: openforum@state.gov
URL: http://www.state.gov/s/p/of
Contact: Dr. Stephen Krasner, Dir. of Policy Planning
Founded: 1967. **Members:** 1,500. **Staff:** 2. **Description:** Employees of the U.S. Department of State, the Agency for International Development, United States Information Agency, and Arms Control and Disarmament Agency. Initiated in 1967 by Secretary of State Dean Rusk who established it as a permanent institution. Successive secretaries have committed themselves to supporting the forum, which brings new or alternative foreign policy views to the attention of the Secretary of State and senior officials. Conducts a program of meetings with speakers on foreign policy issues; sponsors working groups on a variety of topics; and oversees arrangements enabling employees to communicate to the secretary new or dissenting suggestions on policy. Takes no position on issue. **Awards:** Distinguished Public Service Award. **Type:** recognition. **Recipient:** to distinguished scholars and public servants for their contributions to national and international affairs; for invited speakers to participate in the open forum's distinguished lecture series. **Special Interest Groups:** Friends of the Open Forum. **Working Groups:** Conflict Resolution; International Economics; International Security Studies; Science & Technology Policy; U.S.-China Relations.

17257 ■ State Department Watch
PO Box 65398
Washington, DC 20035-5398
E-mail: sdw@statedepartmentwatch.org
URL: http://www.statedepartmentwatch.org
Contact: Carl Olson, Chm.
Founded: 1984. **Staff:** 1. **Budget:** $200,000. **Description:** Nonpartisan, public interest, foreign policy watchdog group concerned with U.S. State Department and other governmental bodies and their actions regarding American foreign policy. Conducts campaigns to stop the U.S. State Department from "giving away" five Alaskan Islands and oil-rich seabeds to the former Soviet Union; to collect World War I and II debts from the former Soviet Union; and to stop the importing of slave-made goods from China and the former Soviet Union. **Convention/Meeting:** none. **Publications:** Newsletter, monthly. **Price:** $15. 00/year.

17258 ■ William Penn House (WPH)
515 E Capitol St. SE
Washington, DC 20003
Ph: (202)543-5560
Fax: (202)543-3814

E-mail: info@wmpennhouse.org
URL: http://www.williampennhouse.org
Contact: Byron Sandford, Exec. Dir.
Founded: 1966. **Staff:** 5. **Budget:** $169,000. **Description:** Conducts seminars to enable adult and student groups to better understand U.S. government policy, current events, and ways to bring about change in the world. Provides low-cost group and individual lodging. **Computer Services:** database ● mailing lists. **Committees:** National Consultative. **Absorbed:** Washington Friends Seminar Program. **Publications:** *Penn Notes*, quarterly. Newsletter. Contains summary of past seminars and description of upcoming events. **Price:** free. **Circulation:** 2,000. Alternate Formats: online. **Conventions/Meetings:** annual meeting ● monthly meeting.

17259 ■ World Policy Institute (WPI)
66 5th Ave., 9th Fl.
New York, NY 10011
Ph: (212)229-5808
Fax: (212)229-5579
E-mail: wpi@newschool.edu
URL: http://www.worldpolicy.org
Contact: Stephen Schlesinger, Dir.
Founded: 1948. **Staff:** 5. **Budget:** $650,000. **Description:** Formulates and promotes practical policy recommendations on U.S. and world economic and security issues; develops positive initiatives that reflect the shared needs and interests of all nations. Conducts ongoing research program on U.S. international policy. Offers seminars, briefings, research reports, and lectures. **Computer Services:** Mailing lists, 3,500 names of people interested in foreign affairs. **Boards:** Advisory; World Policy Journal Advisory. **Formerly:** (1952) Association for Education in World Government; (1954) Institute for International Government; (1973) Institute for International Order; (1983) Institute for World Order. **Publications:** *World Policy Journal*, quarterly. Examines the complex cultural, political, and historical issues that are coming to shape people's lives. **Price:** $30.00 /year for individuals; $37.00 /year for institutions. ISSN: 0740-2775. **Circulation:** 7,000. **Advertising:** accepted. Alternate Formats: microform; online.

France

17260 ■ Conference Group on French Politics and Society (CGFPS)
Center for European Stud.
27 Kirkland St.
Cambridge, MA 02138
Ph: (617)495-4303
Fax: (617)495-8509
E-mail: gross@brandeis.edu
Contact: Prof. George Ross, Exec. Dir.
Founded: 1974. **Members:** 300. **Languages:** English, French. **Description:** Independent association of scholars concerned with the study of contemporary French political and social issues. Holds conferences on French problems in conjunction with other specialized groups. **Awards:** Georges Lavau Prize. **Frequency:** annual. **Type:** recognition ● **Type:** recognition. **Recipient:** for best doctoral dissertation on contemporary French politics and social problems submitted during the previous two years. **Publications:** *French Politics, Culture and Society*, 3/year. Journal. Academic journal on French history, politics and society. **Price:** $10.00 each; $40.00/year. ISSN: 0882-1267. **Circulation:** 350. **Advertising:** accepted ● *Research and Teaching Register*, periodic. Includes directory. **Conventions/Meetings:** annual meeting, held in conjunction with American Political Science Association - Labor Day weekend.

Free Enterprise

17261 ■ American Business Conference (ABC)
1828 L St. NW, Ste.908
Washington, DC 20036
Ph: (202)822-9300

Fax: (202)467-4070
E-mail: abc@americanbusinessconference.org
URL: http://www.americanbusinessconference.org
Contact: John Endean, Pres.
Founded: 1981. **Members:** 100. **Staff:** 3. **Budget:** $1,600,000. **Description:** Represents chief executive officers of midsize, high-growth companies. Concerns itself with tax policy, regulatory reform, and international trade issues; works to preserve the free enterprise system. **Task Forces:** International Trade; Tax Policy. **Publications:** *Capital Gains: Economic Growth and Jobs* ● *Commitment to Growth: American Business Conference and Challenge of Economic Policy* ● *Overconsumption: The Challenge to U.S. Economic Policy* ● *Winning in the World Market* ● *Winning Performance of Midsize, High Growth Companies*. **Conventions/Meetings:** semiannual conference - always in Washington, DC.

17262 ■ Americanism Educational League (AEL)
PO Box 1287
Monrovia, CA 91017
Ph: (626)357-7733
URL: http://www.americanism.org
Contact: Thomas L. Flattery, Sec.
Founded: 1927. **Members:** 5,000. **Staff:** 4. **Budget:** $250,000. **Description:** Represents individuals, business firms, and foundations concerned with free enterprise and America's heritage and traditional values. Aims to: conduct a sustained campaign of public education; promote constitutional principles advocating a drastic reduction in the size of bureaucratic government at all levels; advance the private enterprise system; protect and enhance the freedom of citizens from external and internal threats. Maintains a news bureau that provides weekly feature articles to 285 newspapers, and a youth economics education program. Holds civic luncheons and dinners. Sponsors annual essay contest for college students. **Convention/Meeting:** none. **Libraries:** **Type:** reference. **Holdings:** 400; films, video recordings. **Subjects:** free enterprise, American heritage. **Awards:** American Patriot Award. **Frequency:** annual. **Type:** recognition. **Publications:** Brochures ● Catalogs ● Newsletter, bimonthly ● Pamphlets.

17263 ■ America's Future (AF)
7800 Bonhomme Ave.
St. Louis, MO 63105
Ph: (314)725-6003
Fax: (314)721-3373
E-mail: frd@politickles.com
URL: http://www.americasfuture.net
Contact: F.R. Duplantier, Editorial Dir.
Founded: 1946. **Membership Dues:** individual, $15 (annual). **Staff:** 1. **Budget:** $100,000. **Description:** Seeks to educate Americans on the history, character, importance, and value of the U.S. constitutional republic and institutions and the social, economic, and political principles upon which such government and institutions are founded, emphasizing the advantages of the free enterprise system. **Convention/Meeting:** none. **Publications:** Newsletter, bimonthly. Features a review of news, books and public affairs. **Price:** $15.00/year; free for libraries. ISSN: 0003-3593 ● Also publishes a newspaper column; produces *Behind the Headlines* (radio program).

17264 ■ Center for the Defense of Free Enterprise (CDFE)
Liberty Park
12500 NE 10th Pl.
Bellevue, WA 98005
Ph: (425)455-5038
Fax: (425)451-3959
E-mail: ron@cdfe.org
URL: http://www.cdfe.org
Contact: Ron Arnold, Exec. VP
Founded: 1976. **Members:** 15,000. **Membership Dues:** standard, $15 ● special insider notice, $25. **Budget:** $70,000. **Description:** Defends and promotes the principles of the American free enterprise system and relates their application to contemporary American society. Engages in and conducts research on issues relating to economics and economic trends,

and governmental regulatory bodies and their interaction with the free market. Defends the right of individual Americans and American businesses to participate in the free market without government hindrance. Seeks to develop an efficient mass-media approach to public education consisting of public service announcements for radio and television and production and distribution of radio programming through its in-house American Broadcasting Network, and publication of newspaper columns and feature stories on the economy through its in-house American Press Syndicate. **Libraries:** **Type:** reference. **Holdings:** 1,500. **Subjects:** economics, government. **Awards:** **Type:** grant ● Lifetime Industrial Achievement Award. **Frequency:** periodic. **Type:** recognition ● Lifetime Policy Achievement Award. **Frequency:** periodic. **Type:** recognition ● **Type:** recognition. **Recipient:** for journalists, reporters, and commentators for their objective and accurate reporting of economic activities through the mass media ● **Type:** scholarship. **Computer Services:** Mailing lists. **Divisions:** Communications; Free Enterprise Legal Defense Fund. **Projects:** Ecoterror Response Network. **Publications:** *Battered Communities, Power to Hurt, Autocrats and Activists, Subverting Development*. Reports ● *Brother Against Brother: America's New War Over Land Rights*. Book. Features the culture war over land rights and water rights in America. **Price:** $12.75/copy ● *Eco-Imperialism: Green Power, Black Death*. Book. Contains issues on developing countries. **Price:** $10.20/copy ● *EcoTerror: The Violent Agenda to Save Nature*. Book. Contains information on eco-violence. **Price:** $14.41/copy ● *Rules for Corporate Warriors*. Book. Contains views about defending a company or association from the campaigns of extortion, denigration, and false claims. **Price:** $21.25/copy ● *Undue Influence*. Book. Contains exposes on wealthy foundations. **Price:** $14.41/copy.

17265 ■ Committee to Support the Antitrust Laws (COSAL)
c/o Cuneo Gilbert & LaDuca, LLP
507 C St. NE
Washington, DC 20002
Ph: (202)789-3960
Fax: (202)789-1813
E-mail: contact@cuneolaw.com
URL: http://www.cuneolaw.com/areas/cosal.cfm
Contact: Jonathan W. Cuneo, Gen. Counsel
Founded: 1985. **Members:** 26. **Description:** Individuals and firms that support federal and state antitrust laws. Seeks to promote a competitive and fair economy. **Telecommunication Services:** electronic mail, jonc@cuneolaw.com.

17266 ■ Entrepreneurial Leadership Center (ELC)
1000 Galvin Rd. S
Bellevue Univ.
Bellevue, NE 68005
Ph: (402)293-3743
Fax: (402)293-3819
E-mail: jpatton@bellevue.edu
Contact: Dr. Judd Patton, Dir. for Economic Education
Founded: 1982. **Staff:** 1. **Description:** Promotes worldwide understanding of the free enterprise system. Conducts lecture series. **Libraries:** **Type:** reference. **Awards:** Kountze Award. **Frequency:** annual. **Type:** recognition. **Recipient:** for entrepreneurial excellence ● McDonald's Scholarship. **Frequency:** annual. **Type:** scholarship. **Boards:** Entrepreneurial. **Publications:** *Jefferson's "Bible" - The Life and Morals of Jesus and Nazareth*. Book ● *The Maker's Economics*, 7/year. Book. Contains biblical economic worldview of economic science. **Price:** $30.00 ● *Missing Dimensions in Economics*. Book. **Conventions/Meetings:** seminar.

17267 ■ Fisher Institute for Medical Research (FI)
PO Box 530689
Grand Prairie, TX 75051
Ph: (972)660-3219
Fax: (972)660-1245

E-mail: helen@fisherinstitute.org
URL: http://www.fisherinstitute.org
Contact: Dr. H. Reg McDaniel, Contact

Founded: 1977. **Members:** 50. **Staff:** 4. **Budget:** $2,500,000. **Description:** Seeks to promote wellness, healing, and hope for those in compromised states of health by providing research into the benefits of glyconutrients, phytochemicals, and functional foods that have been scientifically validated to provide optimum immune system support. **Formerly:** (2001) Fisher Institute. **Publications:** *Colostrum: Nature's Gift to the Immune System.* Book. Includes information about colostrum. **Price:** $6.00/copy ● *Discover the Beta Glucan Secret.* Book. Features information on immune enhancement, cancer prevention and treatment. **Price:** $4.00/copy ● *Real Truth About Vitamins and Antioxidants.* Book. Includes teachings on more accurate approach to nutritional therapy. ● *What the Bible Says About Healthy Living.* Book. Features three Biblical Principles on diet and improved health. **Price:** $18.00/copy ● *The Wonderful World Within You.* Book. Contains topics on biology and chemistry. **Price:** $15.00/copy. **Conventions/Meetings:** periodic conference.

17268 ■ Free the Eagle (FTE)

3902 Pender Spring Dr.
Fairfax, VA 22033
Ph: (703)385-0600
Fax: (703)691-7889
E-mail: tjlyles@aol.com
Contact: Tammy J. Lyles, Exec. Dir.

Founded: 1980. **Members:** 265,000. **Staff:** 6. **Description:** Serves as a citizen's lobbying organization to encourage legislation in Congress to maintain and encourage free enterprise and individual freedom. Supports legislation to reduce government waste and to assist and recognize the legitimacy of antidictatorship democratic resistance movements throughout the world. Initiates campaigns to reform Congressional policies toward multilateral lending institutions which support developing countries. Campaigns against loans to communist governments. Conducts legislative research and instruction on lobbying techniques. **Publications:** *Eye on Washington*, periodic. Newsletter. **Circulation:** 20,000.

17269 ■ Free Enterprise Legal Defense Fund (FELDF)

c/o Center for the Defense of Free Enterprise
Liberty Park
12500 NE 10th Pl.
Bellevue, WA 98005
Ph: (425)455-5038
Fax: (425)451-3959
E-mail: alan@cdfe.org
URL: http://www.cdfe.org
Contact: Alan M. Gottlieb, Pres.

Founded: 1976. **Budget:** $100,000. **Description:** Engages in legal action to defend the right of individuals and businesses to operate unhindered in the free market. Enters legal disputes that individuals may have with government agencies by filing amicus curiae or "friends of the court" briefs. Initiates test cases by challenging various laws and government regulations through the filing of suits questioning the legitimacy of such laws and regulations and offers financial assistance to individuals and small businesses engaged in litigation with the government. Provides legal referral services to help locate, and in some cases pay for, competent attorneys; a division of the Center for the Defense of Free Enterprise (see separate entry). **Affiliated With:** Center for the Defense of Free Enterprise. **Conventions/Meetings:** annual meeting.

17270 ■ The Heritage Foundation (THF)

214 Massachusetts Ave. NE
Washington, DC 20002-4999
Ph: (202)546-4400
Fax: (202)546-8328

E-mail: info@heritage.org
URL: http://www.heritage.org
Contact: Edwin J. Feulner PhD, Pres.

Founded: 1973. **Staff:** 188. **Budget:** $32,000,000. **Description:** Public policy research institute dedicated to the principles of free competitive enterprise, limited government, individual liberty, and a strong national defense. Programs include analysis of current public policy subjects. Maintains Heritage Resource Bank, which provides for communication among 2,000 academics and several hundred other policy research groups. Sponsors research; operates speakers' bureau. **Libraries:** Type: reference. **Subjects:** public policy. **Departments:** B. Kenneth Simon Center For American Studies; Communication and Marketing; Development; Domestic Policy; External Relation; Government Relations; Information Technology; Kathryn And Shelby Cullom Davis Institute For International Studies. **Publications:** *Backgrounder/Issue Bulletin*, weekly ● *Business-Education Insider*, monthly ● *Heritage Members' News*, quarterly. Newsletter ● *Heritage Today*, bimonthly. Newsletter ● *Insider Newsletter*, monthly ● *Policy Review*, quarterly. Journal. Covers current political issues from a conservative point of view. Includes book reviews. **Price:** $18.00/year. ISSN: 0146-5945 ● *Publications Catalog*, annual ● *Reforming Congress*, monthly ● Books ● Monographs ● Papers ● Also publishes studies. **Conventions/Meetings:** conference.

17271 ■ National Center for Construction Education and Research (NCCER)

PO Box 141104
Gainesville, FL 32614-1104
Ph: (352)334-0911
Free: (888)622-3720
Fax: (352)334-0932
URL: http://www.nccer.org
Contact: Ronald McKenzie, Chm.

Founded: 1995. **Staff:** 38. **Description:** Education foundation committed to the development and publication of Contren(TM) Learning Series, the source of craft training, management education and safety resources for the construction industry. **Publications:** *Construction Education Newsline.* Newsletter. Provides the association's latest news and information. Alternate Formats: online. **Conventions/Meetings:** annual meeting (exhibits).

17272 ■ National Council for Public-Private Partnerships (NCPPP)

1660 L St. NW, Ste.510
Washington, DC 20036
Ph: (202)467-6800
Fax: (202)467-6312
E-mail: ncppp@ncppp.org
URL: http://www.ncppp.org
Contact: Chastity Nelson, Office Mgr.

Founded: 1985. **Members:** 180. **Membership Dues:** individual/public, $35 (annual) ● general/public, $250 (annual) ● general/small business (less than $10 million in annual revenue), $1,000 (annual) ● corporate, sponsor/public agency, $2,000 (annual) ● sponsor/small business (less than $10 million in annual revenue), $5,000 (annual) ● sponsor/corporate, $7,500 (annual) ● sustaining, $12,000 (annual). **Staff:** 3. **Budget:** $400,000. **Description:** Corporations, private industries, municipalities, and non-profit organizations. Aims to inform the public about the benefits of private participation in the ownership, operation, or management of public services and projects. Sponsors referral network among privatization industry leaders. Provides testimony to legislative bodies; conducts workshops and symposia. Offers publications and consulting services to city, state, and local governments. Maintains speakers' bureau. **Awards:** Public - Private Partnership Awards. **Frequency:** annual. **Type:** recognition. **Recipient:** for outstanding projects and leadership in the exemplary promotion and demonstration of public and private partnerships. **Task Forces:** Environment; Federal; Legislative Issues; Real Estate; Transportation. **Formerly:** (1993) Privatization Council, Inc. **Publications:** *Case Studies from Across the United States.* Book. **Price:** $40.00 for members; $50.00 for non-members; $10.00 plus shipping and handling ● *Com-*

pendium of Privatization Laws, biennial. Enables legislation for private participation in public series provision. **Price:** $375.00 ● *Council Insights*, quarterly. Newsletter. Alternate Formats: online ● Membership Directory, annual. Contains list of members and their activities. **Price:** $25.00 private sector; $15.00 public sector; included in membership dues ● Annual Report, annual. Alternate Formats: online ● Papers. Alternate Formats: online. **Conventions/Meetings:** annual conference (exhibits) - usually October ● regional meeting.

17273 ■ National Journalism Center (NJC)

110 Elden St.
Herndon, VA 20170
Free: (800)872-1776
Fax: (703)318-9122
E-mail: amooney@yaf.org
URL: http://njc.yaf.org
Contact: Mr. Alex Mooney, Exec. Dir.

Founded: 1977. **Staff:** 4. **Description:** Advances awareness and understanding of America's traditional values and free enterprise system through the publication and distribution of studies on major issues of public policy. Conducts educational programs for youth and trains college students in journalistic skills. Sponsors internship program that features research projects, writing assignments, and weekly seminars with professional journalists. Operates a job bank to match potential candidates with media-related jobs. **Libraries:** Type: reference. **Holdings:** clippings. **Subjects:** free enterprise system. **Formerly:** (1982) ACU Education Research Institute; (2006) Education and Research Institute. **Conventions/Meetings:** annual meeting and symposium.

17274 ■ Private Enterprise Research Center (PERC)

Texas A&M Univ.
4231 TAMU
College Station, TX 77843-4231
Ph: (979)845-7722 (979)845-7559
Fax: (979)845-6636
E-mail: perc@tamu.edu
URL: http://www.tamu.edu/perc
Contact: Dr. Thomas R. Saving, Dir.

Founded: 1977. **Staff:** 7. **Budget:** $500,000. **Description:** Conducts research on Social Security, Medicare reform, government tax and debt policy. Promotes individual freedom to strengthen U.S. economy. **Formerly:** (1992) Center for Education and Research in Free Enterprise. **Publications:** *PERCspectives on Research.* Newsletter ● Brochures ● Monographs. **Conventions/Meetings:** lecture ● seminar ● symposium ● workshop.

17275 ■ Professional Services Council (PSC)

2101 Wilson Blvd., Ste.750
Arlington, VA 22201
Ph: (703)875-8059
Fax: (703)875-8922
E-mail: chvotkin@pscouncil.org
URL: http://www.pscouncil.org
Contact: Alan Chvotkin, Sr. VP and Counsel

Founded: 1972. **Members:** 140. **Membership Dues:** regular (less than 2.8 million annual gross), $750 (annual) ● trade/professional association, $100 (annual) ● financial institution/law firm, $2,650-$5,300 (annual). **Staff:** 8. **Budget:** $950,000. **For-Profit. Description:** Provides professional and technical services for local, state, and federal government, as well as commercial clients; companies that conduct research and development and scientific and technical laboratory work or provide architectural and engineering services, systems analyses, and computer software services. Conducts seminars and educational programs. **Awards:** Outstanding Achievement Award. **Frequency:** annual. **Type:** recognition. **Recipient:** to individuals with outstanding contribution to the professional services industry. **Computer Services:** Mailing lists, of media. **Committees:** Government Affairs; Membership Development; Membership Services; Public Relations. **Absorbed:** (1972) Council for Private Enterprise. **Formerly:** (1982) National Council of Professional Services Firms. **Pub-**

lications: *Action Update*, bimonthly. Newsletter ●
Papers. **Conventions/Meetings:** annual conference.

17276 ■ Students in Free Enterprise (SIFE)
The Jack Shewmaker SIFE World HQ
1959 E Kerr St.
Springfield, MO 65803-4775
Ph: (417)831-9505
Free: (800)677-7433
Fax: (417)831-6165
E-mail: sifehq@sife.org
URL: http://www.sife.org
Contact: Mr. Leonard H. Roberts, Chm.
Founded: 1975. **Members:** 40,000. **Staff:** 34. **Budget:** $5,813,148. **Local Groups:** 700. **National Groups:** 15. **Description:** Supports student teams on over 1,000 college campuses and universities in 20 countries worldwide, providing students the opportunity to make a difference through free enterprise education. **Awards: Type:** recognition. **Publications:** *SIFE Yearbook*, annual ● Books ● Pamphlets ● Booklets. **Conventions/Meetings:** annual National Exposition - international conference ● Regional Exposition and Career Opportunity Fair - competition - 20/year, in March/April.

17277 ■ United Savers Association (USA)
Address Unknown since 2007
Founded: 1983. **Description:** Devoted to preserving the free enterprise system, and to making that system work for the so-called "little guy". Provides information and assistance to members who are (or who want to be) self-employed, but who may be facing up-hill battles in this age of corporate "megaliths" and conglomerates. Helps members understand and contend with relevant government policies and regulations; does research to determine whether and how small businesses can survive in today's world; defines and/or develops ways to save money on legal services, property management, marketing, accounting, and other elements which are necessary to success. **Committees:** Education; Legal Aid Adisory. **Programs:** Legal and Regulatory Assistance.

17278 ■ United States Business and Industry Council (USBIC)
910 16th St. NW, Ste.300
Washington, DC 20006
Ph: (202)728-1990 (202)728-1980
Free: (800)767-2267
Fax: (202)728-1981
E-mail: council@usbusiness.org
URL: http://www.usbusiness.org
Contact: Kevin L. Kearns, Pres.
Founded: 1933. **Members:** 1,500. **Membership Dues:** domestic manufacturer, $500 (annual). **Staff:** 5. **Budget:** $750,000. **Description:** Business and industrial leaders. Conservative national business organization promoting fair trade, private enterprise, less intrusive government, strong national security, and a vibrant national economy led by manufacturing and technology industries. Conducts press campaigns, seminars and speeches, and lobbying activities. **Awards:** American Values Award. **Frequency:** annual. **Type:** recognition. **Recipient:** to a public official who best embodies the values of the organization in his work or writing ● Defender of the National Interest. **Frequency:** annual. **Type:** recognition. **Recipient:** to a public official or business leader who has made prominent efforts to protect the security and future of the American nation ● Fighting Congressional Frosh. **Frequency:** annual. **Type:** recognition. **Recipient:** to the most promising freshman member of Congress. **Additional Websites:** http://www.AmericanEconomicAlert.org. **Formerly:** (1973) Southern States Industrial Council; (1983) United States Industrial Council; (1998) United States Business and Industrial Council. **Publications:** *Business Voice Monographs*. Features business related topics. **Conventions/Meetings:** annual meeting.

Freedom

17279 ■ Action Without Borders/Idealist.org
360 W 31st St., Ste.1510
New York, NY 10001

Ph: (212)843-3973
Fax: (212)564-3377
E-mail: info@idealist.org
URL: http://www.idealist.org
Contact: Ami Dar, Exec. Dir.
Founded: 1995. **Staff:** 20. **Languages:** English, French, Spanish. **Multinational. Description:** Works to build a world where all people can live free, dignified and productive lives. **Computer Services:** database, online nonprofit directory ● mailing lists, nonprofit job listserv. **Absorbed:** (2004) Campus Outreach Opportunity League. **Formerly:** (2001) Idealist and Action Without Borders. **Conventions/Meetings:** Nonprofit Career Fairs - meeting, held in US and Canada - spring/fall.

17280 ■ American Booksellers Foundation for Free Expression (ABFFE)
275 7th Ave., 15th Fl.
New York, NY 10001
Ph: (212)587-4025
Fax: (212)587-2436
E-mail: chris@abffe.com
URL: http://www.abffe.org
Contact: Chris Finan, Pres.
Founded: 1990. **Members:** 700. **Membership Dues:** friend, $50 (annual) ● supporter, $75 (annual) ● benefactor, $100 (annual). **Staff:** 2. **Budget:** $300,000. **Description:** Committed to fight against censorship. Seeks to defend the First Amendment rights of booksellers, their customers, and others concerned about defending First Amendment Rights. Defends the privacy of customer records from unwarranted subpoenas. Files amicus curiae briefs and participates in trials involving First Amendment issues; acts as spokesperson for booksellers on censorship, freedom of speech, and related matters. **Publications:** *ABFFE Update*, monthly. Newsletter. **Price:** free. **Circulation:** 1,000. Alternate Formats: online ● *Censorship and First Amendment Rights*. Handbook.

17281 ■ The American Cause (TAC)
501 Church St., Ste.217
Vienna, VA 22180
Ph: (703)255-2632
Fax: (703)255-2219
E-mail: webmaster@theamericancause.org
URL: http://www.theamericancause.org
Contact: Patrick J. Buchanan, Chm./Founder
Founded: 1993. **Membership Dues:** regular, $30 (annual) ● student, $15 (annual). **Description:** Seeks to advance and promote traditional American values that are rooted in conservative principles of national sovereignty, economic patriotism, limited government, and individual freedom. Promotes the professional, social, and economic interests of the American citizen. **Publications:** *The American*, monthly. Newsletter. Alternate Formats: online.

17282 ■ Center For Inquiry (CFI)
PO Box 741
Amherst, NY 14228
Ph: (716)636-7571
E-mail: director@campusfreethought.org
URL: http://www.campusfreethought.org
Contact: D.J. Grothe, Dir.
Founded: 1996. **Description:** Promotes free thought, skepticism, secularism, humanism, philosophical naturalism, rationalism, and atheism on campuses worldwide. **Formerly:** (2004) Campus Freethought Alliance.

17283 ■ Freedoms Foundation at Valley Forge (FFVF)
PO Box 706
Valley Forge, PA 19482-0706
Ph: (610)933-8825
Free: (800)896-5488
Fax: (610)935-0522
E-mail: ffvf@ffvf.org
URL: http://www.ffvf.org
Contact: Aaron Siegel, Pres./CEO
Founded: 1949. **Members:** 4,000. **Membership Dues:** national/chapter, $25. **Staff:** 15. **Budget:** $2,500,000. **State Groups:** 29. **Description:** Chal-

lenges individuals to become active and responsible Americans through an array of education and awards programs. Aims to "Teach Americans About America". **Libraries: Type:** reference. **Holdings:** 40,000; books, periodicals. **Subjects:** democracy, rights and responsibilities, free enterprise. **Awards:** Distinguished Award. **Frequency:** annual. **Type:** recognition. **Recipient:** for outstanding individuals who inspire and encourage others ● Leavey Award for Excellence in Private Enterprise Education. **Frequency:** annual. **Type:** recognition. **Recipient:** for innovation and excellence in private enterprise education ● National Award. **Frequency:** annual. **Type:** recognition. **Recipient:** for individuals with outstanding contributions to their communities ● President's Medal. **Frequency:** annual. **Type:** medal. **Recipient:** for a corporate leader who has provided the youth with the tools for achieving success in the 21st century. **Absorbed:** (1983) Enterprise America. **Formerly:** (1953) Freedoms Foundation. **Publications:** *The Patriot*, quarterly. Newsletter. Covers current programs and activities. **Price:** free. **Circulation:** 10,000. Alternate Formats: online. **Conventions/Meetings:** seminar, for teachers and professionals on various topics such as the American Legislative Process ● weekly Spirit of America Leadership Program - conference, created "by the students for the students" where participants examine their responsibilities while seeking their identity as Americans ● workshop, participants visit selected historical sites and are presented the opportunity to review the events that shaped the nation.

17284 ■ Toward Freedom (TF)
PO Box 468
Burlington, VT 05402
Ph: (802)657-3733
E-mail: admin@towardfreedom.com
URL: http://www.towardfreedom.com
Contact: Robin Lloyd, Publisher
Founded: 1952. **Members:** 3,000. **Membership Dues:** subscriber, $25 (annual). **Staff:** 2. **Budget:** $80,000. **Description:** Primary purpose is to publish an international newsletter with a progressive perspective on politics, news, culture, and global transformation. **Affiliated With:** United Nations. **Publications:** Magazine, 8/year. Contains political, cultural, and environmental information from a progressive, international perspective. Focuses on human rights and freedom. **Price:** $25.00/year; $35.00/year outside U.S. ISSN: 0048-9898. **Circulation:** 4,000. **Advertising:** accepted ● Newsletter, weekly. Alternate Formats: online. **Conventions/Meetings:** quarterly board meeting.

Fundraising

17285 ■ Ludwick Family Foundation
PO Box 1796
Glendora, CA 91740
Ph: (626)852-0092
Fax: (626)852-0776
E-mail: ludwickfndn@ludwick.org
URL: http://www.ludwick.org
Contact: Patrick Bushman PhD, Exec. VP/CEO
Founded: 1990. **Description:** Seeks opportunities to encourage new and expanded projects and programs by providing grants to non-profit organizations for new equipment, improvements, and educational resources. **Awards:** Ludwick Family Foundation Grant. **Frequency:** semiannual. **Type:** grant. **Recipient:** for charitable, scientific, literary and educational purposes.

Future

17286 ■ Millennium Institute (MI)
2200 Wilson Blvd., Ste.650
Arlington, VA 22201-3357
Ph: (703)841-0048
Fax: (703)841-0050

E-mail: info@millennium-institute.org
URL: http://www.millennium-institute.org
Contact: Dr. Hans R. Herren, Pres.
Founded: 1983. **Staff:** 7. **Description:** Provides integrated national development planning tools that promotes systems analysis and empowers people and governments to build societies that are peaceful, equitable and sustainable. **Libraries: Type:** reference. **Holdings:** 300. **Subjects:** sustainable development, strategic studies, millennium. **Councils:** Millennium Council for the Future. **Formerly:** (1987) Global Studies Center; (1993) Institute for 21st Century Studies. **Publications:** *Electronic Newsletter*. Alternate Formats: online ● *Global 2000 Revisited: What Shall We Do?*. Book. **Price:** $20.00 plus $3 shipping and handling. Alternate Formats: online ● *Handbook: Preparing a 21st Century Study* ● *Managing a Nation: The Microcomputer Software Catalog*. Book ● *Studies for the 21st Century*. Book. **Conventions/Meetings:** periodic International Meeting ● periodic Millennium Conference ● periodic Millennium Roundtable.

Gambling

17287 ■ National Coalition Against Legalized Gambling (NCALG)
100 Maryland Ave. NE, Rm. 311
Washington, DC 20002
Ph: (307)587-6568 (307)899-4852
Free: (800)664-2680
E-mail: ncalg@ncalg.org
URL: http://www.ncalg.org
Contact: Guy C. Clark DDS, Chm.
Founded: 1994. **Description:** Exists to "oppose the gambling industry in every forum at every level with every educational tool available". **Libraries: Type:** reference. **Holdings:** reports. **Publications:** *The Bet's-Off Bulletin*. Alternate Formats: online ● *Director's Newsletter*. Alternate Formats: online ● *Legalized Gambling (The Inside Story)*. Brochure. Alternate Formats: online ● Reports ● Audiotapes. Alternate Formats: online ● Videos. Alternate Formats: online.
Conventions/Meetings: conference.

Gay/Lesbian

17288 ■ African Asian Latina Lesbians United (AALLU)
PO Box 5412
Hillside, NJ 07205
Ph: (732)679-7687
E-mail: info@celebratesisterhood.org
URL: http://www.celebratesisterhood.org
Contact: Tiye Lasley, Exec. Dir./Co-Founder
Founded: 2003. **Description:** Provides "womyn" of color with educational and networking opportunities. Seeks to address and focus on health, educational, political, economical, social and emotional issues that affect the lives of African Asian Latina "womyn". **Telecommunication Services:** electronic mail, tyaallu@yahoo.com. **Conventions/Meetings:** monthly meeting - every 4th Thursday in New Brunswick, NJ.

17289 ■ Couples National Network
PO Box 500699
Marathon, FL 33050-0699
Free: (800)896-0717
E-mail: couples@couples-national.org
URL: http://www.couples-national.org
Contact: Mr. Jorg Gobel-Staib, Chm.
Founded: 1984. **Members:** 950. **Membership Dues:** couple; varies per local affiliate, $40 (annual). **Budget:** $4,500. **Local Groups:** 10. **Description:** Provides a social, educational, and humanitarian forum for gay couples and lesbian couples. Promotes the validity of same-gender relationships. **Publications:** *The Duet*, quarterly. Newsletter. Includes network and affiliate news. **Price:** included in membership dues. **Advertising:** accepted. Alternate Formats: on-

line. **Conventions/Meetings:** annual convention, social gathering, education and membership meeting.

17290 ■ Families Like Mine
1730 New Brighton Blvd.
PMB 175
Minneapolis, MN 55413
Free: (866)245-4281
E-mail: info@familieslikemine.com
URL: http://www.familieslikemine.com
Contact: Abigail Garner, Founder
Description: Strives to decrease the isolation for children with parents who are gay, lesbian, bisexual or transgender. **Publications:** *Families Like Mine: Children of Gay Parents Tell It Like It Is*. Book.

17291 ■ Gay Lesbian Alliance Against Defamation (GLAAD)
5455 Wilshire Blvd., Ste.1500
Los Angeles, CA 90036
Ph: (323)933-2240
Fax: (323)933-2241
E-mail: wilks@glaad.org
URL: http://www.glaad.org
Contact: Neil G. Giuliano, Pres.
Founded: 1985. **Members:** 20,000. **Membership Dues:** ordinary, $35 (annual). **Staff:** 50. **Budget:** $8,500,000. **Regional Groups:** 5. **Description:** Promotes fair, accurate and inclusive representation of individuals and events in all media as a means of combating homophobia and all forms of discrimination based on sexual orientation and identity. Organizes the lesbian, gay, bisexual and transgender community to respond to negative and positive portrayals of the community in media through its Monitoring and Mobilization program. Works directly with media professionals to improve their understanding of the lesbian, gay, bisexual and transgender community by providing accurate information and offering seminars as part of its Outreach to Media Professionals program. Works continually with lesbian, gay, bisexual and transgender organizations and individuals to refine and expand their understanding of the media and skills needed to work with them by offering training interventions and technical assistance through its Community Relations program. Studies and articulates cultural and media-specific trends issues and controversies to inform the work of the Alliance and other organization through its Research and Analysis program; and to promote lesbian, gay, bisexual and transgender Visibility by designing and implementing public education campaigns with positive lesbian, gay, bisexual and transgender images. **Awards:** GLAAD Media Award. **Frequency:** annual. **Type:** recognition. **Programs:** People of Color Media. **Formerly:** (1998) Gay and Lesbian Alliance Against Defamation New York. **Publications:** *GLAAD Alert*, weekly. **Circulation:** 90,000. Alternate Formats: online ● *Images*, quarterly. Magazine ● *Media Guide to the Lesbian and Gay Community* ● Brochures.

17292 ■ Human Rights Campaign (HRC)
1640 Rhode Island Ave. NW
Washington, DC 20036-3278
Ph: (202)628-4160
Free: (800)777-4723
Fax: (202)347-5323
E-mail: hrc@hrc.org
URL: http://www.hrc.org
Contact: Joe Solmonese, Exec. Dir.
Founded: 1980. **Members:** 400,000. **Membership Dues:** basic, $35 (annual). **Staff:** 90. **Budget:** $15,000,000. **Description:** Aims to lobby Congress to prevent enactment of national legislation adversely affecting the civil rights of gay and lesbian individuals and people living with AIDS/HIV; to encourage funding for AIDS education, patient care, and research; to support legislation favorable to gays, lesbians, and AIDS patients. Directs messages to senators and representatives prior to legislative action on gay/lesbian, AIDS or choice issues; organizes a support network on the state, congressional district, and local levels; maintains a congressional alert system to inform local leaders and organizations about legislative developments. **Telecommunication Services:**

additional toll-free number, membership, (800)727-4723. **Formerly:** (1988) Fairness Fund; (1988) Human Rights Campaign Fund's Mobilization Project. **Publications:** *Equality*, quarterly. Magazine. Contains political news affecting the lesbian and gay community. **Price:** free for members. **Circulation:** 250,000. **Advertising:** accepted. **Conventions/Meetings:** annual OutVote - convention (exhibits).

17293 ■ Momazons
Address Unknown since 2006
Membership Dues: $25 (annual). **Description:** Promotes issues of importance to lesbian mothers, their friends and families. **Publications:** *Momazon Letters* ● *momma'zine*, 6/year. Magazine. Celebrates lesbian families and families-to-be. ● Directory. Contains resources for lesbian mothers. ● Membership Directory ● Articles.

17294 ■ Partners Task Force for Gay and Lesbian Couples (PARTNERS)
Box 9685
Seattle, WA 98109-0685
Ph: (206)935-1206
E-mail: demian@buddybuddy.com
URL: http://www.buddybuddy.com
Founded: 1986. **Description:** Serves as a national resource for same-sex couples, supporting the diverse community of committed gay and lesbian partners through a variety of media. Maintains web site that contains more than 250 essays, surveys, legal articles, and resources on legal marriage, ceremonies, domestic partner benefits, relationship tips, parenting, and immigration.

17295 ■ Presbyterian Parents of Gays and Lesbians (PPGL)
PO Box 191084
Dallas, TX 75219-8084
Ph: (972)219-6063
E-mail: ppglinfo@presbyterianparents.org
URL: http://www.presbyterianparents.org
Contact: Rev. Lander Bethel, Board Pres.
Founded: 1994. **Description:** Parents of gay and lesbian children, elders and clergy. Created to provide a support network to the parents of gay sons and lesbian daughters regardless of faith. **Publications:** Brochure. Alternate Formats: online.

17296 ■ Queer Nation (QN)
c/o The Online Gay Comic
PO Box 447
New York, NY 10159-0447
E-mail: queernation@queernation.com
Contact: Chris Cooper, Contact
Founded: 1991. **Members:** 120. **Regional Groups:** 50. **State Groups:** 3. **Local Groups:** 20. **Description:** Focuses on the "subversion of heterosexism and homophobia in all of its various cultural, political, and economic manifestations." Uses nonviolent actions to "celebrate and flaunt sexual diversity." Organizes press conferences, candlelight vigils, marches, and protests. Conducts charitable, educational, and research programs. Has no elected officials or hierarchy of power. **Computer Services:** database, queer resources (for members only). **Committees:** Political Action. **Divisions:** Queer Scouts. **Projects:** Sodomy Repeal. **Conventions/Meetings:** semimonthly meeting - first and third Monday.

17297 ■ Soulforce
PO Box 3195
Lynchburg, VA 24503-0195
Ph: (434)384-7696
Free: (877)705-6393
Fax: (434)384-9333
E-mail: info@soulforce.org
URL: http://www.soulforce.org
Contact: Rev. Dr. Mel White, Co-Founder/Pres.
Local Groups: 26. **Description:** Advocates for an end to spiritual violence perpetuated by religious policies and teachings against gay, lesbian, bisexual and transgender people. Promotes and employs the nonviolent principles of Mahatma Gandhi and Martin Luther King, Jr. to the liberation of sexual and gender minorities. **Computer Services:** Information services,

denominational pages, emergency numbers, resources ● mailing lists, of members ● online services, bulletin board. **Telecommunication Services:** electronic mail, mel@soulforce.org. **Publications:** *How Can I Be Sure That God Loves Me, Too.* Video. Features Soulforce founder Mel White's response to those who would misuse the Biblical record to condemn lesbians, gays, bisexuals, and transgenders. **Price:** $15.00 suggested donation ● *The Rhetoric of Intolerance.* Video. **Price:** $15.00 suggested donation ● *Stranger at the Gate: To Be Gay and Christian in America.* Book. Serves as an autobiography of the founder of Soulforce, Mel White and his fight for justice and understanding for God's gay and lesbian children. **Price:** $23.00 hard copy first edition; $15.00 autographed quality paperback ● *The Trials of Jimmy Creech.* Video. **Price:** $15.00 suggested donation ● *What the Bible Says and Doesn't Say About Homosexuality.* Booklet. **Price:** free. Alternate Formats: online.

17298 ■ An Uncommon Legacy Foundation
c/o Kim Hoover, Mgr.
PO Box 33727
Washington, DC 20033
Ph: (202)309-5209
E-mail: kimhoover@hooverpartners.com
URL: http://www.lgbtgiving.org/foundations/legacy.htm
Contact: Kim Hoover, Mgr.
Description: Committed to enhancing the visibility, strength and vitality of the lesbian community; addresses lesbian issues; promotes lesbian anthropology. Conducts fundraising. **Awards: Type:** grant. **Recipient:** to projects or organizations that address lesbian issues and promote lesbian anthropology ● **Type:** scholarship. **Recipient:** to lesbian students.

17299 ■ We Are Family
PO Box 30734
Charleston, SC 29417
Ph: (843)762-3275
Fax: (843)762-3274
E-mail: administrator@waf.org
URL: http://www.waf.org
Founded: 1994. **Membership Dues:** friend, $50 (annual) ● partner, $51-$100 (annual) ● sponsor, $101-$200 (annual). **Description:** Advocates of informed straight, lesbian and gay people. Encourages straight and gay/lesbian community members to value one another through education. Promotes and distributes educational resources; works for the acceptance of gays and lesbians as full members of society; focuses on gay and lesbian children.

Genocide

17300 ■ Genocide Watch
PO Box 809
Washington, DC 20044
Ph: (703)448-0222
E-mail: info@genocidewatch.org
URL: http://www.genocidewatch.org
Contact: Dr. Gregory H. Stanton, Pres.
Multinational. Description: Works to predict, prevent, stop and punish genocide and other forms of mass murder. Seeks to raise awareness and consciousness of genocide as a global problem and to influence public policy concerning potential and actual genocide. Addresses political mass murder, ethnic cleansing and other genocide-like crimes. Prepares options papers for policy makers, recommending specific actions to prevent genocide in high-risk areas. **Telecommunication Services:** electronic mail, genocidewatch@aol.com.

17301 ■ International Association of Genocide Scholars (IAGS)
c/o Dr. Steven Leonard Jacobs, Sec.-Treas.
Univ. of Alabama
Dept. of Religious Stud.
212 Manly Hall
Box 870264
Tuscaloosa, AL 35487-0264

Ph: (205)348-0473
Fax: (205)348-6621
E-mail: info@isg-iags.org
URL: http://www.isg-iags.org
Contact: Prof. Israel W. Charny PhD, Pres.
Founded: 1994. **Membership Dues:** regular (annual income $30,000 and above), $80 (annual) ● graduate student, retired, regular (annual income below $30,000), $60 (annual). **Multinational. Description:** Furthers and supports research and teaching on the causes, parameters and effects of genocide. Aims to advance policy studies on the prevention and intervention of genocide. Encourages communication and interdisciplinary conversation about the causes, prevention and consequences of genocide. **Telecommunication Services:** electronic mail, sjacobs@bama.ua.edu. **Publications:** *Genocide Studies and Prevention.* Journal. **Price:** included in membership dues ● Newsletter. **Price:** included in membership dues. Alternate Formats: online. **Conventions/Meetings:** biennial Responding to Genocide Before It's Too Late: Genocide Studies and Prevention - meeting.

Germany

17302 ■ German Politics Association (GPA)
c/o Jonathan Olsen, Sec.-Treas.
Univ. of Wisconsin-Parkside
Dept. of Political Sci.
Kenosha, WI 53141-2000
Ph: (262)595-2377
E-mail: olsenj@uwp.edu
URL: http://cmclem.people.wm.edu/cggp.html
Contact: Jonathan Olsen, Sec.-Treas.
Founded: 1968. **Members:** 60. **Languages:** English, German. **Description:** Political scientists, historians, sociologists, economists, and other scholars conducting research on German politics and other topics related to contemporary ideas and European affairs. Encourages contact between members and German academicians and political leaders. **Publications:** *Directory of Current Research,* periodic ● Newsletter, periodic. **Conventions/Meetings:** periodic conference ● annual meeting.

Government

17303 ■ Citizens United
1006 Pennsylvania Ave., SE
Washington, DC 20003
Ph: (202)547-5420
Free: (800)362-4788
Fax: (202)547-5421
E-mail: info@citizensunited.org
URL: http://www.citizensunited.org
Contact: David N. Bossie, Pres.
Membership Dues: general, $15 (annual). **Description:** Aims to "restore the government to citizens control. Seeks to reassert the traditional American values of limited government, freedom of enterprise, strong militaries and national sovereignty and security". **Computer Services:** Mailing lists, of members. **Projects:** American Sovereignty; Citizens United for the Bush Agenda.

17304 ■ Council for Government Reform (CGR)
c/o Center for Government Reform
2915 Hunter Mill Rd., Ste.23
Oakton, VA 22124-1716
Ph: (703)319-0009
E-mail: info@govreform.org
URL: http://www.govreform.org
Contact: Charles Hardin, Pres.
Founded: 1991. **Members:** 500,000. **Description:** Works to educate Americans about the concept of "Privatization". Believes government services can be performed more efficiently and effectively within the private sector, thereby eliminating considerable government waste. Conducts grassroots lobbying and public information campaigns. **Formerly:** (2003) National Center for Privatization.

17305 ■ National Organization for the Repeal of the Federal Reserve Act and the Internal Revenue Code (NORFED)
225 N Stockwell Rd.
Evansville, IN 47715-2456
Ph: (812)473-5250
Free: (888)421-6181
Fax: (775)218-1847
E-mail: truth@libertydollar.org
URL: http://www.libertydollar.org
Contact: Bernard von Nothaus, Contact
Founded: 1998. **Members:** 3,000. **Membership Dues:** association, one time fee, $250. **Staff:** 6. **Regional Groups:** 50. **State Groups:** 50. **Description:** Dedicated to changing the current monetary system in the United States. **Additional Websites:** http://www.norfed.org. **Publications:** *Liberty Dollar News Alerts!,* monthly. Newsletter. **Price:** free for members. **Circulation:** 6,000.

Government Accountability

17306 ■ Center for Public Integrity
910 17th St. NW, Ste.700
Washington, DC 20006
Ph: (202)466-1300
Fax: (202)466-1101
E-mail: contact@publicintegrity.org
URL: http://www.publicintegrity.org
Contact: Bill Buzenberg, Exec. Dir.
Founded: 1989. **Members:** 4,500. **Membership Dues:** individual, $35 (annual). **Staff:** 22. **Budget:** $1,800,000. **Languages:** English, German. **Description:** Promotes a higher standard of integrity in the American political process and in government. Investigates, analyzes, and reports about public service issues. **Computer Services:** database. **Publications:** *For Their Eyes Only: How Presidential Appointees Treat Public Documents as Personal Property.* Report. **Price:** $10.00 ● *Limited Partners: An Examination of Elizabeth and Robert Dole's Investment in the Altenn Associates Tax Shelter.* Newsletter. **Price:** $5.00 ● *Place Your Bets: The Gambling Industry and the 1996 Presidential Elections.* Report. **Price:** $10.00 ● *Presidential Frequent Fliers.* Newsletter. **Price:** $5.00 ● *Private Parties: Political Party Leadership in Washington's Mercenary Culture.* Report. **Price:** $10.00 ● *The Public i.* Newsletter. Alternate Formats: online ● *Saving for a Rainy Day: How Congress Turns Leftover Campaign Cash Into Golden Parachutes.* Report. **Price:** $5.00 ● *Saving for a Rainy Day II: How Congress Spends Leftover Campaign Cash.* Report. **Price:** $10.00 ● *Short-Changed: How Congress and Special Interests Benefit at the Expense of the American People.* Report. **Price:** $5.00 ● *Silence of the Laws: How America's Leading Defense Companies Employ Women and Minority Executives.* Report. **Price:** $10.00 ● *Sleeping With the Industry: The U.S. Forest Service and Timber Interests.* Report. **Price:** $10.00 ● *Squeeze Play: The United States, Cuba, and the Helms-Burton Act.* Report. **Price:** $10.00 ● *The Torturers' Lobby: How Human Rights-Abusing Nations are Represented in Washington.* Report. **Price:** $5.00 ● *Toxic Deception.* Book. **Price:** $24.95 ● *Toxic Temptation: The Revolving Door, Bureaucratic Inertia and the Disappointment of the EPA Superfund Program.* Report. **Price:** $10.00 ● *The Trading Game: Inside Lobbying for the North American Free Trade Agreement.* Report. **Price:** $10.00 ● *Under Fire: U.S. Military Restrictions on the Media from Grenada to the Persian Gulf.* Report. **Price:** $15.00 ● *Under the Influence: Presidential Candidates and their Campaign Advisers.* Report. **Price:** $10.00 ● *Well-Healed: Inside Lobbying for Health Care Reform.* Report. **Price:** $20.00.

17307 ■ Citizens Against Government Waste (CAGW)
1301 Connecticut Ave. NW, Ste.400
Washington, DC 20036
Ph: (202)467-5300
Free: (800)BE-ANGRY
Fax: (202)467-4253

E-mail: membership@cagw.org
URL: http://www.cagw.org
Contact: Thomas A. Schatz, Pres.
Founded: 1984. **Members:** 600,000. **Membership Dues:** donation, $25-$250 (annual) ● President's Club, $500 (annual) ● President's Club Executive Committee, $1,000 (annual). **Staff:** 18. **Budget:** $1,000,000. **Local Groups:** 436. **Description:** Serves as nonpartisan organization that seeks to educate the public, individuals in public administration, and Congress on eliminating waste, mismanagement, and inefficiency in government spending. Promotes the need to reduce the federal deficit and seeks to create public support for programs designed to reduce waste in spending. Seeks to expose cases of mismanagement that may occur at any level of government. Develops national advertising and distributes educational literature. Supports recommendations to improve government spending and operations, such as those proposed by the Grace Commission. **Telecommunication Services:** electronic mail, media@cagw.org. **Publications:** *Congressional Pig Book Summary*, annual. Booklet. Includes list of pork-barrel spending in congressional appropriations' bills. ● *Government Wastewatch*, quarterly. Newsletter. **Price:** free for members. **Circulation:** 600,000 ● *Prime Cuts*, annual. Booklet. Includes list of budget-cutting proposals from public and private sources; catalog of recommended budget cuts from various sources. ● Also issues briefs and studies. **Conventions/Meetings:** semiannual Taxpayer's Education Conference.

17308 ■ Fund for Constitutional Government (FCG)
122 Maryland Ave. NE
Washington, DC 20002
Ph: (202)546-3799
Fax: (202)543-3156
E-mail: funcongov@aol.com
URL: http://www.epic.org/fcg
Contact: Russell D. Hemenway, Chm.
Founded: 1974. **Members:** 14. **Budget:** $325,000. **Description:** Publicly-supported foundation that seeks to expose and correct corruption, illegal activities, or lack of accountability in the federal government. Conducts research, public education, and litigation in cases with a large public impact, of precedent-setting value, and which, if rectified, will help preserve an open and accountable government. **Sponsors:** Project on Military Procurement, which seeks to expose fraudulent and wasteful weapons systems of the Department of Defense; the Investigative Journalism Project, which provides financial support for investigative projects; the Government Accountability Project, which furnishes the needs of "whistleblowers" by furnishing legal counsel and referral services and by exposing harassment and retaliation; the KAL Project, which supports the investigation of the 1983 incident in which a Korean airliner was shot down over the Soviet Union. **Committees:** Journalism; Litigation; Technical. **Publications:** *More Bucks, Less Bang.* **Conventions/Meetings:** quarterly meeting.

17309 ■ Government Accountability Project (GAP)
1612 K St. NW, Ste.1100
Washington, DC 20006
Ph: (202)408-0034
E-mail: gapdc@whistleblower.org
URL: http://www.whistleblower.org
Contact: Mary Brumder, Exec. Dir.
Founded: 1977. **Members:** 5,000. **Membership Dues:** individual, $35 (annual). **Staff:** 19. **Budget:** $1,300,000. **Description:** Provides legal and advocacy assistance to concerned citizens who witness dangerous, illegal or environmentally unsound practices in their own workplaces and communities and choose to "blow the whistle". **Libraries: Type:** reference. **Holdings:** 1,300; books. **Subjects:** federal law. **Telecommunication Services:** electronic mail, gap@whistleblower.org. **Publications:** *Bridging the Gap*, quarterly. Newsletter. Contains updates on programs and activities. **Price:** included in membership dues ● *Courage Without Martyrdom: A Survival Guide for Whistleblowers* ● *Protecting Environmental*

and Nuclear Whistleblowers: A Litigation Manual ● *Study of Whistleblower Protections for Federal Employees* ● *Whistleblowers Guide to Federal Bureaucracy* ● *Whistleblowers Protection - the GAP Between the Law and Reality* ● Also publishes reprints of law review articles. **Conventions/Meetings:** seminar, provides training for lawyers representing environmental whistle-blowers and citizen activists dealing with environmental concerns.

17310 ■ National Legal and Policy Center (NLPC)
107 Park Washington Ct.
Falls Church, VA 22046
Ph: (703)237-1970
Fax: (703)237-2090
E-mail: nlpc@nlpc.org
URL: http://www.nlpc.org
Contact: Kenneth Boehm, Co-Founder
Founded: 1991. **Members:** 30,000. **Staff:** 6. **Budget:** $1,000,000. **Description:** Legal foundation promoting ethics in government. Distributes code of ethics to government workers and federal employees. Engages in litigation when it believes the government has done something unethical. **Libraries: Type:** reference. **Holdings:** books. **Subjects:** legal topics associated with ethical questions in government. **Awards: Type:** recognition. **Recipient:** for individuals who promote ethics in government. **Projects:** Corporate Integrity; Government Integrity; Legal Services Accountability; Organized Labor Accountability. **Publications:** *Ethics Watch*, quarterly. Newsletter ● *Union Corruption Update*, biweekly. Newsletter. Alternate Formats: online. **Conventions/Meetings:** board meeting.

17311 ■ OMB Watch (OMBW)
1742 Connecticut Ave. NW
Washington, DC 20009
Ph: (202)234-8494
Fax: (202)234-8584
E-mail: ombwatch@ombwatch.org
URL: http://www.ombwatch.org
Contact: Gary D. Bass PhD, Exec. Dir.
Founded: 1983. **Members:** 1,000. **Membership Dues:** basic, $35 (annual) ● sustaining, $100 (annual). **Staff:** 13. **Budget:** $1,000,000. **Description:** Collects, researches, and disseminates information on the federal Office of Management and Budget (OMB), particularly information affecting non-profit and community-based organizations. Advocates for more public accountability and increased public knowledge of administrative government issues. Serves as a reaction to events that OMB Watch feels have provided the OMB with unprecedented powers and "allow it to remain unaccountable to Congress and the American people". **Libraries: Type:** not open to the public. **Subjects:** federal registrars. **Computer Services:** Mailing lists, of members ● online services, data bank on toxic emissions and housing data. **Additional Websites:** http://www.rtk.net. **Publications:** *Government Information Insider*, bimonthly. Magazine. Focuses on federal information policy. **Price:** $35.00 /year for individuals; $75.00 /year for libraries, community groups, businesses ● *Living with A-122* ● *OMB Watcher*, biweekly. Newsletter. Includes summary of OMB initiatives. **Price:** $35.00 /year for individuals, community groups, libraries; $100.00/ year for businesses. Alternate Formats: online ● *Playing the Numbers—OMB a Paperwork Reduction* ● *So You Want to Make a Difference: A Key to Advocacy* ● *Through the Corridors of Power—A Guide to Federal Rulemaking* ● *Using Community Right-to-Know—A Guide to a New Federal Law* ● Report, biennial. Alternate Formats: online.

17312 ■ Third Millennium: Advocates for the Future (TM)
330 W 38th St., Ste.1705
New York, NY 10018
Ph: (212)760-4240
E-mail: thirdmil@juno.com
Contact: Richard Thau, Pres./Exec.Dir.
Founded: 1993. **Members:** 4,000. **Staff:** 3. **Budget:** $750,000. **Description:** Young adults. Offers solutions to long-term problems facing the U.S. Focus is

to balance the federal budget and reform programs such as social security and Medicare. Offers educational programs, statistics, and a speakers' bureau.

Government Relations

17313 ■ US-Cuba Reconciliation Initiative
c/o Fund for Reconciliation & Development
355 W 39th St.
New York, NY 10118
Ph: (212)760-9903
Fax: (212)760-9906
E-mail: cuba@ffrd.org
URL: http://www.ffrd.org/cuba
Contact: John McAuliff, Exec. Dir.
Founded: 1999. **Multinational. Description:** Provides opportunities for personal travel for Americans to see Cuba and make decisions regarding U.S. policy and the human impact of the embargo. **Publications:** Reports.

17314 ■ Women in Government Relations (WGR)
801 N Fairfax St., Ste.211
Alexandria, VA 22314-1757
Ph: (703)299-8546
Fax: (703)299-9233
E-mail: info@wgr.org
URL: http://www.wgr.org
Contact: Lauren E. Beck, Pres.
Founded: 1975. **Members:** 600. **Membership Dues:** regular, vendor, supplier, $195 (annual) ● public, $45 (annual) ● associate, $100 (annual) ● student, $25 (annual). **Staff:** 4. **Budget:** $265,000. **Description:** Professional women and men who have legislative or regulatory responsibilities involving federal, state, and local governmental bodies; members represent corporations, trade associations, the executive and legislative branches of government, and non-profit organizations. Promotes the professional status of women; provides a forum for discussion of issues of national importance with political and business leaders; gives members the opportunity to develop contacts in the government relations field. Maintains speakers' bureau and job bank for government relations positions; compiles statistics. Sponsors Women in Government Relations LEADER Foundation (see separate entry). **Awards:** Distinguished Member Award. **Frequency:** annual. **Type:** recognition. **Telecommunication Services:** electronic mail, lauren. beck@unilever.com. **Committees:** Awards; Career Services; Congressional Relations; Executive Branch Liaison; Foreign Relations; Job Bank; Member Relations; Professional Development; Public Relations; Regulatory Relations; Skills Development. **Task Forces:** Banking and Financial Services; Budget and Tax; Energy; Environment; Grassroots Lobbying; Health Services; International Relations; PACs and Politics; State Affairs; Telecommunications. **Affiliated With:** Women in Government Relations LEADER Foundation. **Publications:** *Women in Government Relations—Newsletter*, weekly. **Circulation:** 1,000. **Advertising:** accepted ● Membership Directory, annual. **Price:** available to members only. Alternate Formats: online. **Conventions/Meetings:** annual Anniversary Gala - conference ● workshop and seminar, topics include improving communication skills, establishing professional credentials, achieving career objectives, and developing management techniques.

17315 ■ Women in Government Relations LEADER Foundation (WGR)
PO Box 66812
Washington, DC 20035-6812
Ph: (202)347-0437
Fax: (202)508-6083
E-mail: leaderfoundation@hotmail.com
URL: http://www.leaderfoundation.org
Contact: Tiffany N. Adams, Pres./Chair
Founded: 1979. **Staff:** 1. **Description:** Creates scholarships, educational programs and events for women of all ages to strengthen management and other skills critical to leadership in public policy and

business. Seeks to enhance the ability of women to excel and make distinguished professional and civic contributions to their field by increasing their access to vital resources, knowledge and opportunities. **Awards:** Award of Achievement. **Frequency:** annual. **Type:** recognition. **Recipient:** for outstanding contributions and achievements toward women's career development and education ● Shared Vision Award. **Frequency:** annual. **Type:** recognition.

Greyhound

17316 ■ American-European Greyhound Alliance (AEGA)
c/o Louise Coleman, Pres.
167 Saddle Hill Rd.
Hopkinton, MA 01748
Ph: (508)435-5969
E-mail: greyhndfds@aol.com
URL: http://www.ameurogreyhoundalliance.org
Contact: Louise Coleman, Pres.

Multinational. Description: Works for the welfare of greyhounds in the U.S. and abroad, through on-going monitoring of existing and proposed racing venues; liaises with racing industry and adoption groups; provides a source of collection and dissemination of information; educates the public as to the suitability of the greyhound as an adopted companion animal. Rehabilitates greyhounds with special needs, i.e. broken legs, medical problems, etc., and prepares them for adoption.

Guatemala

17317 ■ Guatemala Human Rights Commission/U.S.A. (GHRC/USA)
3321 12th St. NE
Washington, DC 20017
Ph: (202)529-6599
Fax: (202)526-4611
E-mail: ghrc-usa@ghrc-usa.org
URL: http://www.ghrc-usa.org
Contact: Patricia Davis, Contact

Founded: 1982. **Staff:** 5. **Budget:** $200,000. **Languages:** English, Spanish. **Description:** Promotes public awareness of human rights violations in Guatemala. Participates in forums involving human rights and humanitarian issues. Maintains speakers' bureau; compiles statistics. **Libraries: Type:** reference. **Holdings:** reports. **Subjects:** human rights violations. **Computer Services:** Online services, publication. **Publications:** *Alerts* (in English and Spanish), periodic. Contains information on human rights violations in Guatemala. **Circulation:** 300. Alternate Formats: online ● *Confronting the Heart of Darkness.* Report. Contains information on human rights violations in Guatemala. **Circulation:** 300. Alternate Formats: online ● *The Dark Light of Dawn.* Video. Features symposium on torture in Guatemala. ● *Human Rights Update,* bimonthly. **Price:** $35.00/copy; $20.00 online. ISSN: 1085-0864. **Circulation:** 400. Alternate Formats: online ● *Press Releases,* bimonthly. **Price:** $35.00/copy; $20.00 online. ISSN: 1085-0864. **Circulation:** 400. Alternate Formats: online ● *Special Report,* periodic ● *Annual Report,* periodic. Contains statistics and analysis. **Price:** $10.00/year. **Circulation:** 1,500 ● Brochures, annual. Contains statistics and analysis. **Price:** $10.00/year. **Circulation:** 1,500. **Conventions/Meetings:** annual Commemoration for Torture Victims and Survivors - meeting, twenty-four hour vigil in front of the White House for torture survivors and supporters of survivors - always in June 26.

17318 ■ Guatemala News and Information Bureau (GNIB)
3181 Mission St.
Box 12
San Francisco, CA 94110
Ph: (415)826-3593
Fax: (415)826-3593

E-mail: gnib@igc.apc.org
Contact: Christina Albo, Ed.
Founded: 1978. **Budget:** $15,000. **Languages:** English, Spanish. **Description:** Provides news and analysis of political, economic, and social developments in Guatemala. Presents speakers' bureaus and educational forums. Advocates for human rights and social justice in Guatemala. Conducts research. **Libraries: Type:** reference. **Holdings:** archival material, audiovisuals, books, clippings, periodicals. **Subjects:** Guatemala. **Affiliated With:** Network in Solidarity With the People of Guatemala. **Publications:** *Resource Guide.*

17319 ■ Network in Solidarity With the People of Guatemala (NISGUA)
1830 Connecticut Ave. NW
Washington, DC 20009
Ph: (202)518-7638
Fax: (202)223-8221
E-mail: info@nisgua.org
URL: http://www.nisgua.org
Contact: Kaaren Johnson, Pres.

Founded: 1981. **Members:** 3,800. **Staff:** 7. **Budget:** $350,000. **Regional Groups:** 6. **Local Groups:** 40. **Languages:** English, Spanish. **Description:** Builds mutually beneficial grassroots ties between the people of the U.S. and Guatemala and advocates for grassroots alternatives to challenge elite power structures and oppressive U.S. economic and foreign policy. **Libraries: Type:** open to the public; by appointment only. **Holdings:** books, video recordings. **Subjects:** Guatemala. **Publications:** *Report on Guatemala,* quarterly. Newsletter. Includes legislative updates, political analysis, interviews, and resource information. **Price:** $25.00 /year for individuals in North America; $20.00/year for low income; $30.00/year outside North America; $30.00 /year for institutions. ISSN: 1043-3856. **Circulation:** 750 ● *Solidarity Update,* bimonthly. Newsletter.

Haiti

17320 ■ Haiti Support Network (HSN)
c/o International Action Center
39 W 14th St., Rm. 206
New York, NY 10011
Ph: (212)633-6646
Fax: (212)633-2889
E-mail: haiticom@nyxfer.blythe.org
URL: http://www.iacenter.org/Haitifiles/haiti.htm
Contact: Kim Ives, Co-Dir. of Haiti Progress
Founded: 1971. **Description:** Volunteers interested in generating political and material support in the U.S. for the Haitian national liberation struggle, particularly the Mouvement Haitien de Liberation, an anti-imperialist, national liberation movement based in Haiti. Works to disseminate information on the Haitian social structure and the liberation process, with an emphasis on U.S. economic, political, and military involvement. Activities include conducting research and fundraising. Maintains data center on Haiti and the Caribbean and library of 3000 volumes. **Formerly:** (2001) Friends of Haiti.

17321 ■ Haitian Studies Association (HSA)
c/o University of Massachusetts Boston
100 Morrissey Blvd.
McCormack Hall Rm. 2-211
Boston, MA 02125-3393
Ph: (617)287-7138
Fax: (617)287-6797
E-mail: hsa@umb.edu
URL: http://www.haitianstudies.umb.edu/index.html
Contact: Florence Bellande-Robertson, Pres.
Founded: 1989. **Members:** 350. **Membership Dues:** regular (with JOHS), $60 (annual) ● student (with JOHS), $50 (annual) ● regular (no JOHS), $20 (annual) ● student (no JOHS), $10 (annual). **Staff:** 3. **Budget:** $100,000. **Languages:** English, Spanish. **Description:** Encourages research and interest in Haiti, the Haitian people, and their culture. Provides statistics and relevant information. **Libraries: Type:** reference. **Holdings:** 100; articles, periodicals. **Sub-**

jects: politics, economic development, historical, linguistic, religion, engineering, environmental and cultural studies. **Computer Services:** Mailing lists. **Task Forces:** Educational; Environmental. **Publications:** *Journal of Haitian Studies* (in English, French, and Spanish), semiannual. **Price:** $30.00/copy; $65.00 /year for institutions. ISSN: 1090-3488. **Circulation:** 103. **Conventions/Meetings:** annual The Road to Social, Political and Economic Development in Haiti - convention, book display (exhibits) - always October.

Handguns

17322 ■ Handgun Safety and Education Council (HSEC)
212 1st Ave. SW
Rochester, MN 55902
Ph: (507)280-3860
Fax: (509)271-9008
E-mail: info@hsec.org
Founded: 1993. **Description:** Dedicated to firearms safety through education and training.

17323 ■ Women Against Gun Control (WAGC)
PO Box 95357
South Jordan, UT 84095
Ph: (801)328-9660
E-mail: info@wagc.com
URL: http://www.wagc.com
Contact: Janalee Tobias, Pres./Founder
Founded: 1994. **Languages:** English, Italian. **Multinational. Description:** Women opposing tighter gun controls; promotes firearms instruction and gun safety training. Members are active in tracking and reporting on legislation at all levels of government, which impacts on the right of gun ownership. Members also boycott businesses that discriminate against gun owners. **Publications:** *The BULLETin,* quarterly. Newsletter. Highlights current and future projects and successes.

Health

17324 ■ Ad Hoc Group for Medical Research Funding (AHGMRF)
c/o Association of American Medical Colleges
2450 N St. NW
Washington, DC 20037-1126
Ph: (202)828-0525
Fax: (202)862-6218
E-mail: adhoc@aamc.org
URL: http://www.aamc.org/research/adhocgp/start. htm
Contact: Richard M. Knapp PhD, Chm.
Founded: 1982. **Members:** 300. **Description:** Organizations engaged in or supporting biomedical and behavioral research. Aims to assess federal funding for biomedical and behavioral research and advocate appropriate funding for the National Institutes of Health. **Publications:** *Annual Funding Proposal,* annual. Brochure ● *NIH Resource Guide,* biennial. Directory ● Annual Report, annual. **Price:** free. **Conventions/Meetings:** monthly meeting, membership briefings.

17325 ■ Alliance for Health Reform (AHR)
1444 Eye St. NW, Ste.910
Washington, DC 20005
Ph: (202)789-2300
Fax: (202)789-2233
E-mail: info@allhealth.org
URL: http://www.allhealth.org
Contact: Edward F. Howard, Exec. VP
Founded: 1991. **Description:** Individuals and organizations with an interest in health care. Promotes increased public awareness of health care issues and proposals for health care reform in the United States. Serves as a clearinghouse on health care reform.

17326 ■ Family Research Institute (FRI)
PO Box 62640
Colorado Springs, CO 80962-2640
Ph: (303)681-3113
Fax: (303)681-3427
URL: http://familyresearchinst.org
Contact: Dr. Paul Cameron, Chm.
Founded: 1982. **Members:** 1,900. **Membership Dues:** regular, $25 (annual). **Staff:** 6. **Description:** Promotes information about sexual, family, and substance abuse issues. Conducts research and educational programs. Maintains speakers' bureau; compiles statistics. **Libraries: Type:** reference. **Holdings:** 500; archival material, books, periodicals. **Subjects:** sexuality, drug use. **Publications:** *Family Research Report*, 8/year. Newsletter. **Price:** $25.00/year in U.S.; $40.00/year outside U.S. **Circulation:** 2,000 ● *The Gay 90's.* Book. **Price:** $10.00 ● Pamphlets ● Articles. **Price:** $5.00.

17327 ■ Forum for State Health Policy Leadership
444 N Capitol St. NW, Ste.515
Washington, DC 20001
Ph: (202)624-5400
Fax: (202)737-1069
E-mail: donna.folkemer@ncsl.org
URL: http://www.ncsl.org/programs/health/forum
Contact: Donna Folkemer, Dir.
Founded: 1995. **Staff:** 10. **Budget:** $1,500,000. **Description:** Represents health policy researchers. Provides information on state health legislation and programs to state executive officials, legislators, legislative staff, and others. Serves as information clearinghouse; responds to specific information requests on state programs. Compiles statistics. Offers a customized legislative tracking service to customers. **Libraries: Type:** reference. **Subjects:** health. **Formerly:** Intergovernmental Health Policy Project. **Publications:** *State Health Notes*, biweekly. Newsletter. Contains information on health policy trends. **Price:** $237.00 for non-profits; $307.00 others. **Circulation:** 2,000 ● Newsletter, bimonthly ● Newsletter, 10/year ● Monograph, annual. Summarizes state legislation relating to health care. **Conventions/Meetings:** periodic conference and meeting, about health care.

17328 ■ Medicare Rights Center (MRC)
1460 Broadway, 17th Fl.
New York, NY 10036-7306
Ph: (212)869-3850
Fax: (212)869-3532
E-mail: info@medicarerights.org
URL: http://www.medicarerights.org
Contact: Atty. Robert M. Hayes, Pres./Gen. Counsel
Founded: 1989. **Members:** 29. **Membership Dues:** professional, $225 (annual). **Staff:** 20. **Budget:** $3,000,000. **Languages:** English, Spanish. **Description:** Seeks to ensure the rights of senior citizens and people with disabilities to quality, affordable health care. Provides counseling services to people with Medicare with health insurance problems and questions; compiles information on inquiries to detect issues and systemic problems in Medicare claims administration. Educates consumers, advocates, providers, and social workers about developments in Medicare law and how to handle problems. Monitors trends and changes in Medicare laws, regulations, and guidelines. **Telecommunication Services:** hotline, consumer, (800)333-4114. **Boards:** Consumer Action. **Committees:** Media Advisory; Policy Advisory. **Formerly:** (1997) Medicare Beneficiaries Defense Fund. **Publications:** *"Lets Learn Medicare!" Training and Reference Manual.* Contains medicare educational materials for consumers and professionals. **Price:** $150.00 plus $15 for handling and shipping ● *The Medicare Survival Kit: Medicare Answers.* Contains medicare educational materials for consumers and professionals. **Price:** $25.00 plus $6 for handling and shipping.

17329 ■ National Coalition for Cancer Research (NCCR)
2300 N St. NW
Washington, DC 20004
Ph: (202)544-1880

Fax: (202)543-2565
E-mail: md@capitolassociates.com
Contact: Carolyn R. Aldige, Pres./Founder
Founded: 1986. **Members:** 19. **Budget:** $150,000. **Description:** Lay and professional organizations committed to the eradication of cancer. Dedicated to strengthening the National Cancer Program through public education and communication about the value of cancer research, treatment, and prevention. **Conventions/Meetings:** annual meeting - always January or February, Washington, DC.

17330 ■ National Council Against Health Fraud (NCAHF)
119 Foster St., Bldg. R, 2nd Fl.
Peabody, MA 01960
Ph: (978)532-9383
Fax: (978)532-9450
E-mail: ncahf.office@verizon.net
URL: http://www.ncahf.org
Contact: Dr. Robert S. Baratz MD, Pres.
Founded: 1977. **Members:** 500. **Membership Dues:** individual, $20 (annual) ● professional, $30 (annual) ● supporting, $100 (annual) ● student, $15 (annual) ● patron, $1,000 (annual). **Regional Groups:** 13. **State Groups:** 12. **Local Groups:** 1. **Description:** Health professionals, researchers, legal professionals, and other interested individuals. Seeks to educate the public on fraud and quackery in health care. Offers advice to consumers. Provides witnesses for health fraud trials. Assists law enforcement officials with health fraud cases. Sponsors speaker's bureau and research programs. Offers aid to victims in the form of free legal screening. **Libraries: Type:** reference. **Holdings:** archival material, audiovisuals, books, business records, clippings, periodicals. **Subjects:** health fraud, quackery, health misinformation. **Awards:** Consumer Service Awards. **Frequency:** annual. **Type:** recognition. **Recipient:** for providing reliable information on controversial health practices. **Computer Services:** Information services, quackery resources ● online services, health fraud discussion lists. **Task Forces:** Acupuncture; Addiction Therapy; AIDS Quackery; Anthroposophical Medicine; Broadcast Media Abuse; Children's Health Threats; Chiropractic; Diet and Behavior; Dietary Supplement Abuse; Dubious Healthcare Credentials; Ergogenic Aids; Health Information; Health Publications; Herbal Remedies; Homeopathy; Internet Misinformation; Local Consumer Activism; Nutrition Quackery and Dentistry; Prostate Remedies; Questionable Arthritis Remedies; Questionable Methods of Cancer Management; Questionable Nursing Practices; Veterinary Pseudosciences; Vision Care; Weight Loss Abuse. **Also Known As:** (2003) Quackwatch. **Formerly:** California Council Against Health Fraud; (1998) National Council Against Health Fraud; (2004) National Council for Reliable Health Information. **Publications:** *Consumer Health Digest*, weekly. Newsletter. Alternate Formats: online ● Also publishes position statement on various topics. **Conventions/Meetings:** annual convention, in conjunction with the FASEB Convention.

17331 ■ National Health Policy Forum (NHPF)
2131 K St. NW, Ste.500
Washington, DC 20037
Ph: (202)872-1390
Fax: (202)862-9837
E-mail: nhpf@gwu.edu
URL: http://www.nhpf.org
Contact: Judith Miller Jones, Dir.
Founded: 1971. **Staff:** 16. **Budget:** $2,300,000. **Nonmembership. Description:** Nonpartisan education program serving primarily senior federal legislative and executive branch health staff but also addressing the interests of state officials and their Washington representatives. Seeks to foster more informed government decision-making. Helps decision makers forge the personal acquaintances and understanding necessary for cooperation among government agencies and between government and the private sector. **Publications:** *Background Papers.* Includes issues that synthesize market analysis or research findings. ● *Basics*, periodic. Paper ● *Issue Briefs*, 25-30/year. Contains information on health

policy issues. ● *Site Visit Reports*, periodic. **Conventions/Meetings:** seminar, with guest speakers from the health sector, private industry, and academia ● workshop.

17332 ■ People's Medical Society (PMS)
PO Box 868
Allentown, PA 18105-0868
Ph: (610)770-1670
Free: (800)624-8773
Fax: (610)770-0607
E-mail: cbi@peoplesmed.org
URL: http://www.peoplesmed.org
Contact: Pamela Maraldo PhD, Chair
Founded: 1983. **Members:** 80,000. **Membership Dues:** regular, $20 (annual). **Staff:** 5. **Description:** Promotes citizen involvement in the cost, quality, and management of the American health care system. Seeks to: train and encourage individuals to study local health care systems, practitioners, and institutions and promote preventive health care and medical cost control by these groups; address major policy issues and control health costs; encourage more preventive practice and research; promote self-care and alternative health care procedures; launch an information campaign to assist individuals in maintaining personal health and to prepare them for appointments with medical professionals. **Convention/Meeting:** none. **Commissions:** Online and Mailing List Services. **Publications:** *Allergies: Questions You Have.Answers You Need* ● *Alzheimer's and Dementia: Questions You Have.Answers You Need* ● *Arthritis: Questions You Have, Answers You Need* ● *Asthma: Questions You Have, Answers You Need* ● *Breathe Better, Feel Better* ● *The Consumer's Medical Desk Reference* ● *Depression: Questions You Have, Answers You Need* ● *Headaches: 47 Ways to Stop the Pain* ● *Hearing Loss: Questions, You Have, Answers You Need* ● *Long-Term Care and Alternatives* ● *Medicare Made Easy* ● *Medicine on Trial* ● *Misdiagnosis: Woman as a Disease* ● *Natural Recipes for the Good Life* ● *150 Ways to Be a Savvy Medical Consumer* ● *People's Medical Society Newsletter*, bimonthly. Includes membership activities information. **Price:** included in membership dues. ISSN: 0736-4873. **Circulation:** 65,000 ● *Prostate: Questions You Have.Answers You Need* ● *77 Ways to Beat Colds and Flu* ● *Take This Book to the Gynecologist With You* ● *Take This Book to the Hospital With You.*

Health Care

17333 ■ Citizen Advocacy Center (CAC)
1400 16th St. NW, Ste.101
Washington, DC 20036
Ph: (202)462-1174
Fax: (202)265-6564
E-mail: cac@cacenter.org
URL: http://www.cacenter.org
Contact: David A. Swankin, Pres./CEO
Founded: 1994. **Description:** Provides training and support for public members serving on healthcare regulatory agencies, governing boards, and advisory bodies representing consumer interests. **Publications:** *Citizen Advocacy News and Views*, quarterly. Newsletter. **Price:** $40.00/copy; $195.00/year; $330.00 8 issues ● Reports. **Conventions/Meetings:** annual conference - in November ● seminar.

17334 ■ Citizens' Council on Health Care (CCHC)
1954 Univ. Ave. W, Ste.8
St. Paul, MN 55104-3460
Ph: (651)646-8935
Fax: (651)646-0100
E-mail: info@cchconline.org
URL: http://www.cchconline.org
Contact: Twila J. Brase RN, Pres.
Founded: 1988. **Description:** Opposes universal public health insurance; promotes a free-market resource for future health care design. **Publications:** *Insider Report*, quarterly. Newsletter. Alternate Formats: online ● Articles. Alternate Formats: online.

17335 ■ National Coalition on Health Care
1200 G St. NW, Ste.750
Washington, DC 20005
Ph: (202)638-7151
E-mail: cfitzpatrick@nchc.org
URL: http://www.nchc.org
Contact: Catherine A. Fitzpatrick, Public Affairs Asst.
Founded: 1990. **Members:** 100,000,000. **Regional Groups:** 96. **Description:** Large and small businesses, labor unions, consumer groups, religious groups, and primary care providers. Aims to achieve better and more affordable health care for all Americans. **Publications:** *Building a Better Health Care System: Specifications for Reform.* Report. Alternate Formats: online.

Hispanic

17336 ■ Center for U.S.-Mexican Studies
c/o University of California, San Diego
9500 Gilman Dr., Dept. 0510
La Jolla, CA 92093-0510
Ph: (858)534-4503
Fax: (858)534-6447
E-mail: usmex@ucsd.edu
URL: http://www.usmex.ucsd.edu
Contact: Chriss Woodruff, Dir.
Founded: 1979. **Staff:** 10. **Budget:** $1,100,000. **Languages:** English, Spanish. **Description:** Research institute that conducts studies on the relationship between Mexico and the United States. Conducts seminars and educational programs. **Libraries: Type:** reference. **Holdings:** books, monographs, periodicals. **Subjects:** Mexico, U.S.-Mexican relations, Latin America. **Awards:** Center for U.S.-Mexican Studies' Fellowships. **Frequency:** annual. **Type:** grant. **Recipient:** postdocs and PhD candidates; for the write-up of advanced research project within the social sciences and history. **Boards:** Advisory. **Programs:** Post Doctoral; Visiting Fellows. **Projects:** Border Water. **Publications:** *Center for U.S. - Mexican Publications Series,* 5/year. Reports. Published research on Mexican studies and U.S. - Mexican relations. ● *Enfoque Newsletter,* 3/year ● Papers. Alternate Formats: online. **Conventions/ Meetings:** periodic conference and workshop.

17337 ■ Chicano Family Center (CFC)
7524 Ave. E
Houston, TX 77012
Ph: (713)923-2316
Fax: (713)923-4243
Contact: Dr. Elena R. Vergara, Exec.Dir.
Founded: 1971. **Staff:** 37. **Budget:** $900,000. **Description:** Provides mental health and social work services designed to enhance the quality of life in the Chicano community. Promotes improved understanding of culturally relevant intervention; fosters interpersonal and intergroup relationships; supports optimal functioning of individuals and families. Conducts community education programs covering nutrition, citizenship, interpersonal skills, and English. Operates Huellas (footprints) program for sixth grade students to encourage value exploration, building of self esteem, and assertiveness. Conducts institutes for and provides consultation to institutions, agencies, and organizations that extend services to the Chicano community. Maintains referral service. **Libraries: Type:** reference. **Programs:** Adult Drug Treatment; AIDS/Drama Education and Prevention; Bilingual/ Bicultural Family Group and Individual Counseling; Drug Abuse Treatment; Drug Prevention, Women; Emergency Food Assistance; HRSA/AIDS Education and Prevention; Substance Abusing Youth; Tangible Services; Young, Pregnant Females. **Formerly:** (1983) Chicago Training Center. **Publications:** *Curriculum Schema.* **Conventions/Meetings:** seminar ● workshop.

17338 ■ Congressional Hispanic Caucus (CHC)
1609 Longworth HOB
Washington, DC 20515
Ph: (202)225-2410
Fax: (202)225-0027
URL: http://www.napolitano.house.gov/chc
Contact: Congresswoman Grace Flores Napolitano, Chair
Founded: 1976. **Members:** 21. **Staff:** 3. **Description:** Members of Congress of Hispanic descent. Dedicated to voicing and advancing, through the legislative process, issues affecting Hispanic Americans in the United States and insular areas.

17339 ■ Hispanas Organized for Political Equality (HOPE)
634 S Spring St., Ste.920
Los Angeles, CA 90014
Ph: (213)622-0606
Fax: (213)622-0007
E-mail: latinas@latinas.org
URL: http://www.latinas.org
Contact: Elmy Bermejo, Chair
Founded: 1989. **Membership Dues:** student, $20 (annual) ● senior, $25 (annual) ● advocate, $50 (annual) ● patron, $100 (annual) ● guardian, $250 (annual). **Description:** Ensures political and economic parity for Latinas. Provides leadership, advocacy and education to benefit the communities and the status of women. **Computer Services:** Online services, bulletin boards ● online services, forum. **Programs:** Glass Ceiling Initiative; HOPE Leadership Institute; Latina Action Day; Voter Empowerment.

17340 ■ Hispanic Policy Development Project (HPDP)
122 E 42nd St., 42nd Fl.
New York, NY 10168
Ph: (646)723-0750
Fax: (646)723-0752
E-mail: siobhan96@aol.com
Contact: Siobhan Oppenheimer-Nicolau, Pres.
Founded: 1982. **Staff:** 9. **Budget:** $500,000. **Languages:** English, Spanish. **Description:** Seeks to: correct what the project calls the long-standing neglect of the Hispanic population; address and arouse public interest in Hispanic concerns including employment and secondary education; improve communications among Hispanics and non-Hispanics. Works to increase participation of Hispanics in policy debates and to provide opportunities for young Hispanic policy analysts. Conducts research. Has sponsored National Commission on Secondary Schooling for Hispanics. **Publications:** *Handsome Dividends - Handbook to Demystry The Hispanic Market.* Reports ● *Hispanic Almanac,* periodic ● *Preschool Bilingual Children's Book* ● *Research Bulletin,* periodic ● *Together is Better - Handbook for Teachers.* Monographs ● Books. **Conventions/Meetings:** semiannual board meeting ● competition ● seminar.

17341 ■ Mexican American Legal Defense and Educational Fund (MALDEF)
634 S Spring St.
Los Angeles, CA 90014
Ph: (213)629-2512
Fax: (213)629-0266
URL: http://www.maldef.org
Contact: John Trasvina, Interim Pres./Gen. Counsel
Founded: 1968. **Staff:** 75. **Budget:** $5,400,000. **Regional Groups:** 4. **Description:** Funded through a range of sources including foundations, corporations, and individuals. Aims to protect the civil rights of Latinos, including Mexican-Americans. Has offices in Sacramento and Los Angeles, San Antonio, TX; Chicago, IL; and Washington, DC. Has been responsible for civil rights class-action litigation affecting Latinos. Areas of focus include education, employment, immigration, voting rights and public resource equity. Offers leadership training, parent leadership programs and higher education scholarships. **Libraries: Type:** reference. **Holdings:** 2,000. **Subjects:** legal issues. **Awards:** Law School Scholarship Program. **Frequency:** annual. **Type:** scholarship. **Recipient:** for promising and committed students entering the legal profession ● **Frequency:** annual. **Type:** recognition. **Publications:** *Leadership Program Newsletter,* 3/year ● Annual Report, annual. **Conventions/Meetings:** annual board meeting - always April.

17342 ■ National Association of Latino Elected and Appointed Officials (NALEO)
1122 W Washington Blvd., 3rd Fl.
Los Angeles, CA 90015-3316
Ph: (213)747-7606
Fax: (213)747-7664
E-mail: info@naleo.org
URL: http://www.naleo.org
Contact: Dr. Arturo Vargas, Exec. Dir.
Founded: 1976. **Members:** 628. **Staff:** 30. **Description:** Hispanic elected and appointed officials and people who support them, including both individuals and corporate members; associate members are others interested in furthering association's goals. Serves as an advocacy and leadership network dedicated to the advancement of the Hispanic people. Works as a vehicle through which Hispanic needs and concerns may be articulated, particularly in Washington, DC and the Southwestern U.S., on issues such as economic development, U.S. citizenship, legalization, and Latino child poverty. Serves as a clearinghouse on citizenship information; compiles Hispanic voting statistics. **Computer Services:** database, citizenship service providers ● database, Hispanic businesses in the 8(a) minority procurement program ● mailing lists, Latino elected officials in the United States. **Formerly:** (1978) National Association of Latino Appointed Democratic Officials. **Publications:** *Background Paper Series,* quarterly ● *National Directory of Latino Elected Officials,* annual ● *National Report,* quarterly ● *Politica,* bimonthly. Newsletter. **Conventions/Meetings:** annual conference (exhibits) ● seminar.

17343 ■ National Hispana Leadership Institute (NHLI)
1601 N Kent St., Ste.803
Arlington, VA 22209
Ph: (703)527-6007
Fax: (703)527-6009
E-mail: nhli@nhli.com
URL: http://www.nhli.org
Contact: Marisa Rivera-Albert, Pres.
Founded: 1987. **Members:** 450. **Staff:** 3. **Budget:** $1,100,000. **Languages:** English, Spanish. **Description:** Promotes the leadership education and potential of Hispanic women. Conducts annual month-long program for selected participants. **Awards:** Mujer Award. **Frequency:** annual. **Type:** recognition. **Committees:** Alumnae Association. **Publications:** *NHLI News,* quarterly. Newsletter. Features information on Hispanic women leaders and issues affecting Hispanic women. **Circulation:** 5,000. **Advertising:** accepted. Alternate Formats: online.

17344 ■ National Hispanic Leadership Agenda (NHLA)
c/o National Puerto Rican Coalition, Inc.
1901 L St. NW, Ste.802
Washington, DC 20036
Ph: (202)223-3915
Fax: (202)429-2223
E-mail: nprc@nprcinc.org
URL: http://www.bateylink.org/nhla.htm
Contact: Ronald Blackburn-Moreno, Chm.
Founded: 1991. **Members:** 32. **Membership Dues:** board, $500 (annual). **Staff:** 1. **Budget:** $150,000. **Description:** Promotes knowledge and understanding of issues of concern to Hispanic Americans. Offers policy recommendations. **Publications:** *Congressional Scorezaro,* periodic. Reports. Discusses policy recommendations. ● *NHLA Policy Summary.* Book.

17345 ■ National Organization for Mexican American Rights (NOMAR)
c/o Mary Louise Garcia, Sec.
PO Box 4468
Fairview, NM 87533
Ph: (505)852-2278
E-mail: secretary@nomarinc.org
URL: http://www.nomarinc.org
Contact: Dan J. Solis, Chm.
Founded: 1998. **Membership Dues:** general, $20 (annual). **Description:** Defends the civil rights of

Mexican-Americans and their right to equal employment and educational opportunities.

Historic Preservation

17346 ■ Hollywood Sign Trust
PO Box 480314
Los Angeles, CA 90048
Ph: (323)939-1191
Contact: Chris Baumgart, Chm.
Founded: 1978. **Description:** Committed to preserving the Hollywood Sign as a monument.

Historical Revisionism

17347 ■ Institute for Historical Review (IHR)
PO Box 2739
Newport Beach, CA 92659
Ph: (949)631-1490
Fax: (949)631-0981
E-mail: ihr@ihr.org
URL: http://www.ihr.org
Contact: Mark Weber, Dir.
Founded: 1978. **Staff:** 3. **Budget:** $250,000. **Non-membership. Description:** Promotes greater public awareness of the past, and especially socially-politically relevant aspects of 20th century history. Strives in particular to increase understanding of the causes, nature and consequences of war and conflict; provides special focus on World War II, The Holocaust, and Zionism. **Libraries: Type:** not open to the public; reference. **Holdings:** 2,000. **Subjects:** history, politics, current affairs, economics. **Computer Services:** database, newsletter via email. **Telecommunication Services:** electronic mail, news@ihr.org. **Publications:** *IHR Update*, 3/year. Newsletter. **Price:** free to donors. **Circulation:** 12,000. **Conventions/Meetings:** conference.

Holocaust

17348 ■ American Gathering of Jewish Holocaust Survivors (AGJHS)
122 W 30th St., Ste.205
New York, NY 10001
Ph: (212)239-4230
E-mail: info@americangathering.com
URL: http://www.americangathering.com
Contact: Max K. Liebmann, Treas.
Founded: 1980. **Members:** 180,000. **Membership Dues:** individual, $50 (annual) ● family, $72 (annual). **Staff:** 7. **Description:** Holocaust survivors; related associations. Perpetuates the remembrance of the Holocaust and of responsibility for Nazi crimes against the Jews; combats anti-Semitism. Holds commemorative programs and gatherings periodically. Organizes teacher education programs. Presents articles; holds public assemblies; gathers names and histories of survivors for the National Registry of Jewish Holocaust Survivors. **Computer Services:** database, national directory of information on Holocaust survivors and their children in the U.S. **Commissions:** Cultural. **Affiliated With:** World Jewish Congress, American Section. **Formerly:** (1982) World Gathering of Jewish Holocaust Survivors. **Publications:** *Together*, quarterly. Newspaper. **Circulation:** 180,000.

17349 ■ Anne Frank Center U.S.A. (AFC USA)
38 Crosby St., 5th Fl.
New York, NY 10013
Ph: (212)431-7993
Fax: (212)431-8375
E-mail: afcenter@annefrank.com
URL: http://www.annefrank.com
Contact: Paul D. Kaplan, Chm.
Founded: 1977. **Members:** 4,000. **Membership Dues:** basic, $40 (annual) ● student, $25 (annual) ● supporting, $100 (annual) ● sustaining, $250 (annual) ● distinguished, $500 (annual) ● patron, $1,000

(annual) ● benefactor, $5,000 (annual). **Staff:** 3. **Budget:** $500,000. **Multinational. Description:** Promotes the universal message of tolerance, by developing and disseminating a variety of educational programs, including exhibitions, workshops, speakers and special events. "Based on the power of Anne Frank's diary, aims to inspire the next generation to build a world of compassion, mutual respect and social justice". Runs the Exhibition and Education Center, which contains a small permanent exhibit gallery, a library of books and videos, a book shop, a virtual tour of the Anne Frank House and secret annex, free of charge. **Libraries: Type:** reference. **Holdings:** 650; archival material, artwork, audiovisuals, books, clippings. **Subjects:** Holocaust, Anne Frank, human rights. **Awards:** Spirit of Anne Frank Award. **Frequency:** annual. **Type:** monetary. **Recipient:** for contributions to humanitarian causes and promotion of social justice. **Computer Services:** database ● mailing lists ● online services. **Divisions:** Anne Frank: A History for Today; Anne Frank: A Private Photo Album; Anne Frank in the World: 1929-1945; The Anne Frank Story; Bilingual Exhibitions; Community Projects; Educational Programming; Special Events. **Formerly:** (1993) American Friends of the Anne Frank Center. **Publications:** *A House With A Story*. Alternate Formats: CD-ROM ● *The Anne Frank Center USA Newsletter*, biennial. Contains current news and events. ● *Anne Frank in the World 1929-1945 Exhibition Catalog*. **Price:** $15.00/copy ● *Just a Diary*. Video ● *The Short Life of Anne Frank*. Video.

17350 ■ Association of Holocaust Organizations (AHO)
PO Box 230317
Hollis, NY 11423
Ph: (516)582-4571
E-mail: ahoinfo@att.net
URL: http://www.ahoinfo.org
Contact: Dr. William L. Shulman, Pres.
Founded: 1985. **Members:** 250. **Membership Dues:** individual, $50 (annual) ● organization, $200 (annual). **Regional Groups:** 2. **State Groups:** 1. **Multinational. Description:** Serves as a network of organizations and individuals to advance programming, awareness, education, and research on the Holocaust. **Publications:** *AHO Directory*, annual. Lists Holocaust organizations in the U.S., Canada, and worldwide. **Price:** free for members. **Conventions/Meetings:** annual meeting (exhibits).

17351 ■ Braun Holocaust Institute (BCHS)
c/o Anti-Defamation League
PO Box 96226
Washington, DC 20090-6226
E-mail: webmaster@adl.org
URL: http://www.adl.org/braun/start.html
Contact: Abraham H. Foxman, Natl. Dir.
Founded: 1984. **Staff:** 4. **Regional Groups:** 30. **Description:** A program of the Anti-Defamation League of B'nai B'rith. Serves as a central resource for information on the Holocaust. Develops curricula; organizes teacher-training workshops. Administers the Hidden Child Foundation. Maintains speakers' bureau; conducts research programs. **Libraries: Type:** reference. **Holdings:** 3,000; archival material, books, clippings, films. **Awards:** Courage to Care Award. **Type:** recognition. **Recipient:** for rescuers of Jews during the Holocaust. **Boards:** Advisory; Editorial. **Formerly:** (1984) Center for Studies on the Holocaust; (1990) International Center for Holocaust Studies; (2003) Braun Center for Holocaust Studies. **Publications:** *Dimensions: A Journal of Holocaust Studies*, semiannual. Alternate Formats: online ● *The End of Innocence: Anne Frank and the Holocaust* ● *The Holocaust: Catalog of Publications and Audio-Visual Materials*, semiannual ● *Nazism: A Study of Racial Tyranny* ● *The Record: The Holocaust in History* ● *To Know Where They Are* ● *Witness to the Holocaust* Videos. **Conventions/Meetings:** symposium - 2-4/year.

17352 ■ Group Project for Holocaust Survivors and Their Children (GPHSC)
211 W 56th St., Ste.7K
New York, NY 10019
Ph: (212)724-2161 (212)315-5872

Fax: (212)877-9054
Contact: Eva Fogelman, Exec. Off.
Founded: 1975. **Description:** Holocaust survivors and their children; psychotherapists and educators. Aims to provide preventive and reparative therapeutic work with Holocaust survivors and their children by counteracting their sense of isolation and alienation. Is formed in response to survivor complaints of neglect and avoidance of Holocaust experiences by mental health professionals. Believes that awareness of the possibility that a survivor can transmit trauma to his or her children will inhibit such transmission. Has project that aided in compensating for counter-transference reactions by allowing individuals to discuss Holocaust experiences outside the family. Provides supervision and training for professionals working with Holocaust survivors. Provides community interaction to rebuild a sense of extended family and community lost to these individuals during the Holocaust. Maintains contact with other Holocaust-related organizations and participates in their activities. Serves as a data bank for clinical and research information on Holocaust survivors and their children, and studies in the field of victimology. Holds gathering with International Network of Children of Jewish Holocaust Survivors. Sponsors psychoanalytic institutes that have held study groups on children of Holocaust survivors and children of Nazis. **Publications:** Newsletter, annual. Includes list of mental health professionals involved in therapeutic and research work with survivors and their children. **Conventions/Meetings:** periodic conference.

17353 ■ Holocaust Documentation and Education Center (HDEC)
13899 Biscayne Blvd., Ste.404
North Miami Beach, FL 33181
Ph: (305)919-5690
Fax: (305)919-5691
E-mail: info@hdec.org
URL: http://www.hdec.org
Contact: Rositta E. Kenigsberg, Exec. VP
Founded: 1980. **Staff:** 5. **Budget:** $300,000. **Description:** Preserves the memory of the Holocaust by conducting oral histories and compiling documentation. Conducts interviews with Holocaust survivors and others including partisans, concentration camp liberators, and individuals who sheltered Holocaust victims; transcribes taped interviewer. Maintains speakers' bureau. Conducts volunteer interview training programs; assists in establishing Holocaust documentation centers in local communities. Sponsors film and lecture series. Promotes Student Awareness Days and Holocaust Awareness Week. Sponsors charitable programs benefitting Holocaust survivors and other civilians who resisted Nazism. **Libraries: Type:** reference. **Holdings:** archival material, audio recordings, books, video recordings. **Subjects:** Holocaust. **Formerly:** Southeastern Florida Holocaust Memorial Center. **Publications:** Proceedings. **Conventions/Meetings:** competition, for visual arts and writing ● annual Memorial Program - meeting ● seminar, for teachers.

17354 ■ Holocaust Resource Center (HRC)
Kean Univ. Lib., 2nd Fl.
Union, NJ 07083
Ph: (908)737-4660
Fax: (908)737-4664
E-mail: keanhrc@kean.edu
URL: http://www.kean.edu/~hrc
Contact: Helen Walzer, Asst. Dir.
Founded: 1982. **Staff:** 4. **Description:** Promotes open use of research facilities for students, teachers, and others interested in studying the Holocaust and related subjects. Gathers and disseminates information about the Holocaust; conducts tuition-free educational courses for primary and secondary school teachers; sponsors lecture series. Makes available children's services; sponsors research programs. Conducts oral history project consisting of more than 220 audio and videotaped interviews with Holocaust survivors and liberators. Offers film series and diversity programs. **Libraries: Type:** reference. **Holdings:** 4,500; archival material, audio recordings, films, video recordings. **Subjects:** genocide, preju-

dice reduction, holocaust, diversity programs. **Affiliated With:** Association of Holocaust Organizations; Yad Vashem, The Holocaust Martyrs' and Heroes' Remembrance Authority. **Publications:** *Audio Visual Materials Catalog*, annual ● *Diversity 2000 Newsletter And Voices*, quarterly. **Conventions/Meetings:** annual Holocaust Memorial Observance - meeting and lecture.

17355 ■ Holocaust Survivors and Friends in Pursuit of Justice (HSFPJ)

800 New Loudon Rd., Ste.400
Latham, NY 12110
Ph: (518)785-0035
Fax: (518)783-1557
E-mail: hsfec@crisny.org
URL: http://www.holocausteducation.org
Contact: Shelly Zima Shapiro, Dir.
Founded: 1978. **Members:** 10,000. **Staff:** 2. **Budget:** $18,000. **Description:** Educational organization dedicated to increasing public awareness of the presence of Nazi collaborators and war criminals in the U.S. Supports bringing Holocaust perpetrators to justice through legal means, including extradition in accordance with the Moscow Declaration. Makes available curricula and audiovisual materials covering the Holocaust and contemporary anti-Semitism in the U.S; conducts lectures, seminars, and multimedia presentations on the Holocaust, genocide as a result of racial prejudice, and legal issues encountered in the prosecution of Nazi war criminals. Maintains research center and library on the lives of Nazi war criminals living in the U.S. Distributes photographs of Holocaust perpetrators residing in the U.S; maintains speakers' bureau; compiles statistics. **Libraries: Type:** by appointment only. **Holdings:** 8,000. **Subjects:** Holocaust, hate, denial, Judaism, race relations. **Computer Services:** database. **Formerly:** (1984) Ad Hoc Committee to Bring Nazi War Criminals to Justice. **Publications:** *Holocaust Survivors and Friends in Pursuit of Justice Newsletter*, quarterly ● *Justice*, semiannual. Contains historical photographs, reprints of original documents, book and film reviews, and coverage of the trials of Nazi war criminals. **Price:** $5.00/issue, plus $1.50 shipping ● *Kristallnacht Annotated Bibliography* ● *Select Seminar on the Holocaust*. **Conventions/Meetings:** periodic international conference.

17356 ■ International Network of Children of Jewish Holocaust Survivors (INCJHS)

c/o Rositta Kenigsberg, Exec. VP
13899 Biscayne Blvd., Ste.404
North Miami Beach, FL 33181
Ph: (305)919-5690
Fax: (305)919-5691
E-mail: info@hdec.org
Contact: Rositta Kenigsberg, Exec. VP
Founded: 1981. **Members:** 250,000. **Local Groups:** 67. **Description:** Seeks to provide a liaison among organizations of children of Holocaust survivors and coordinate their activities; provide these groups with a unified voice on issues including the rise of neo-Nazism, anti-Semitism, and desecration of the Holocaust. **Committees:** Documentation; Education; Psycho-Social Issues; Social Action; Speakers' Bureau. **Conventions/Meetings:** conference - every 2-3 years.

17357 ■ Jewish Foundation for the Righteous (JFR)

305 7th Ave., 19th Fl.
New York, NY 10001-6008
Ph: (212)727-9955
Fax: (212)727-9956
E-mail: jfr@jfr.org
URL: http://www.jfr.org
Contact: Stanlee Joyce Stahl, Exec. VP
Founded: 1986. **Staff:** 8. **Budget:** $2,500,000. **Languages:** English, German, Hebrew, Polish, Russian, Yiddish. **Multinational. Description:** Provides monthly financial assistance to more than 1,700 aged and needy non-Jews who rescued Jews during the Holocaust. Conducts educational programs that use the stories of Christian rescuers to teach the Holocaust. Maintains speaker's bureau. **Libraries: Type:**

reference. **Holdings:** 500. **Subjects:** rescue during Holocaust, Holocaust history, literature. **Awards:** Recognition of Goodness. **Frequency:** annual. **Type:** recognition. **Recipient:** for individuals who have demonstrated their commitment to improving the society ● Schulweis Award. **Frequency:** annual. **Type:** recognition. **Recipient:** to individuals who have demonstrated a commitment to be a righteous Gentile. **Boards:** Board of Trustees. **Committees:** Allocation; Education. **Programs:** Bar/Bat Mitzvah. **Formerly:** (1996) The Jewish Foundation for Christian Rescue. **Publications:** *At the JFR*, semiannual. Newsletter ● *Schools as Moral Communities*. **Price:** $9.95. **ISSN:** 0884-6416 ● *Voices and Views: A History of the Holocaust*. **Price:** $44.95 paper.

17358 ■ Masada the Holocaust Survivors Organization (MHSO)

2615 Brown St.
Brooklyn, NY 11235
Ph: (718)332-8771 (718)743-7598
Fax: (718)332-8771
Contact: Isaac Pulvermacher, Sec.
Founded: 1951. **Members:** 475. **Membership Dues:** $30 (annual). **Description:** Survivors of the Holocaust. Conducts educational, fraternal, charitable, and other voluntary activities. Conducts fundraising for Jewish education. Sponsors charitable programs. **Awards: Frequency:** annual. **Type:** recognition. **Recipient:** for best book in Yiddish about the Holocaust. **Conventions/Meetings:** monthly meeting ● semiannual seminar.

17359 ■ National Liberty Museum

321 Chestnut St.
Philadelphia, PA 19106
Ph: (215)925-2800
Fax: (215)925-3800
E-mail: liberty@libertymuseum.org
URL: http://www.libertymuseum.org
Contact: Gwen Borowsky, Exec. Dir.
Founded: 1996. **Members:** 7,000. **Membership Dues:** family, $60 (annual) ● supporter, $100 (annual) ● patron, $250 (annual) ● benefactor, $500 (annual) ● founder's committee, $1,000 (annual) ● chairman's circle, $2,000 (quinquennial) **Staff:** 20. **Budget:** $1,800,000. **Description:** Dedicated to honoring heroes from the ancient past to the present who sought to prevent violence and bigotry. Galleries and programs inspire visitors to participate in a hate-free society which will lead to a reduction in violence; training for teachers; a replica of the Amsterdam attic in which Anne Frank hid; visual educational experiences for students and visitors. Maintains speakers' bureau. **Libraries: Type:** reference. **Holdings:** 200. **Subjects:** freedom. **Awards:** Anne Frank Yough Award. **Frequency:** annual. **Type:** recognition ● Eternal Flame Award. **Frequency:** annual. **Type:** recognition. **Affiliated With:** U.S. Holocaust Memorial Council. **Formerly:** (1984) National Institute on the Holocaust; (1997) Anne Frank Institute of Philadelphia; (1999) Liberty Museum and Education Center. **Publications:** *Anne Frank Day Program*, annual ● *Conference Scholars*, annual ● *Faith and Freedom* ● *Holocaust Education: A Resource Book for Teachers and Professional Leaders* ● *Kristallnacht Program*, annual ● *Liturgies on the Holocaust: An Index for the Anthology* ● *Yom Ha Shoah Program*, annual ● Newsletter, quarterly. **Conventions/Meetings:** annual conference.

17360 ■ Simon Wiesenthal Center (SWC)

1399 S Roxbury Dr.
Los Angeles, CA 90035
Ph: (310)553-9036
Free: (800)900-9036
Fax: (310)553-4521
E-mail: information@wiesenthal.net
URL: http://www.wiesenthal.com
Contact: Rabbi Meyer May, Exec. Dir.
Founded: 1977. **Members:** 400,000. **Regional Groups:** 6. **Description:** An international center for Holocaust remembrance, the defense of human rights and the Jewish people. Maintains offices in Los Angeles, New York, Chicago, Toronto, Miami, Jerusalem and Paris. Dedicated to the preservation of the

memory of the Holocaust through education and awareness, with the goal that "no people shall ever again fall victim to an atrocity of such magnitude". Develops programs in the areas of Holocaust Studies and Research, Educational Outreach to schools and various organizations, International Social Action and Media. Operates the Museum of Tolerance focusing on "racism and prejudice in America and the Nazi Holocaust". **Awards:** Simon Wiesenthal Humanitarian Award. **Type:** recognition. **Additional Websites:** http://motlc.wiesenthal.com. **Departments:** Holocaust Studies and Research; Library/Archives; Media; Public Relations; Social Action. **Publications:** *Commitment*, quarterly ● *Genocide: Critical Issues of the Holocaust* ● *Museum Update*, quarterly. Reports on the Beit Hashoah-Museum of Tolerance. ● *Response*, quarterly. Newsletter. **Price:** included in membership dues. **Circulation:** 386,200 ● *Simon Wiesenthal Center Annual*. Provides a scholarly study of the Holocaust, including Nazi Germany and the Final Solution, European Jewry during World War II and refugees. **ISSN:** 0741-8450 ● Also publishes a continuing monograph series. **Conventions/Meetings:** annual Leadership Conference - meeting.

17361 ■ U.S. Holocaust Memorial Council (USHMC)

100 Raoul Wallenberg Pl. SW
Washington, DC 20024-2126
Ph: (202)488-0400 (202)488-0406
URL: http://www.ushmm.org
Contact: Sara J. Bloomfield, Dir.
Founded: 1980. **Members:** 65. **Description:** Represents presidential appointees including ten members of Congress. Works to implement the recommendations of the President's Commission on the Holocaust. Has implemented the construction in Washington, DC of a national Holocaust Memorial Museum; works for an annual civic commemoration of the Holocaust, to be known as the Days of Remembrance, and serves to support and encourage such commemoration throughout the U.S. Encourages educational programs on the Holocaust. **Publications:** *Days of Remembrance Guidebook* ● *Directory of Holocaust Resource Centers, Institutions, and Organizations in North America*, periodic ● Also publishes teacher's guides, lesson plans, and a poster series.

17362 ■ World Federation of Bergen-Belsen Associations (WFBBA)

PO Box 288
New York, NY 10021
Ph: (212)339-6022
Fax: (212)318-6176
Contact: Sam E. Bloch, Pres.
Founded: 1965. **Regional Groups:** 7. **National Groups:** 3. **Description:** Associations of survivors of the Bergen-Belsen (Germany) World War II concentration camp. Conducts fraternal activities that include the care of monuments and memorial programs throughout the world to perpetuate the memory of the Holocaust and its victims. **Publications:** Books. **Conventions/Meetings:** annual Memorial Meeting.

17363 ■ Yad V'Kidush Hashem, House of Martyrs (KH-M)

Address Unknown since 2006
Founded: 1947. **Members:** 400. **Staff:** 7. **Budget:** $200,000. **Regional Groups:** 4. **Languages:** English, German, Hebrew, Hungarian, Yiddish. **Description:** Persons involved in research concerning the Holocaust, especially religious acts of martyrdom. Honors victims of the Holocaust; assists in maintenance of burial sites of Jewish dead. Sponsors charitable program. Compiles statistics. **Libraries: Type:** open to the public. **Holdings:** 600; periodicals. **Subjects:** Holocaust, Torah Responsa, H. C. Research. **Computer Services:** Online services. **Programs:** Beth Medrash Kidush Hashem; Cong. & Yesheva Yeshurin; Kolel Kidush Hashem. **Also Known As:** Kidush Hashem; Kidush Hashem Institute. **Publications:** *The Final Solution is Life*. Book ● *Word and Opinion* (in English and Hebrew), periodic. Newsletter. **Price:** free. **Circulation:** 2,000. **Advertising:** accepted. **Conventions/Meetings:** semiannual meeting; **Avg. Attendance:** 25.

Home

17364 ■ American Homeowners Grassroots Alliance (AHGA)

6776 Little Falls Rd.
Arlington, VA 22213-1213
Free: (800)489-7776
Fax: (703)536-7079
E-mail: ahga@americanhomeowners.org
URL: http://www.americanhomeowners.org
Contact: Mr. Bruce Hahn CAE, Pres.
Founded: 1984. **Members:** 5,000. **Membership Dues:** individual, $19 (annual). **Staff:** 3. **Budget:** $200,000. **Description:** Serves as national grass-roots advocacy organization for homeowners and prospective homeowners; lobbies at federal, state and local levels. **Publications:** *A 2004 Policy Guide for Federal, State, and Local Legislators.* Brochure ● *The Complete Home Buyers Guide.* Book. **Price:** $13.00 ● *How To Sell Your Home Fast!.* Book ● *Testimony on Home Related Issues.*

Honduras

17365 ■ Honduras Outreach, Inc. (HOI)

150 E Ponce De Leon Ave., Ste.270
Decatur, GA 30030-2547
Ph: (404)378-0919
Fax: (404)378-8429
E-mail: askhoi@hoi.org
URL: http://www.hoi.org
Contact: Beth Barnwell, Exec. Dir.
Languages: English, Spanish. **Description:** Development and social welfare organizations operating in Honduras. Promotes appropriate and sustainable social, political, and economic development in Honduras. Conducts educational and development programs; makes available social services. **Telecommunication Services:** electronic mail, bbarnwell@hoi.org. **Publications:** Newsletter. **Price:** free. Alternate Formats: online.

Horses

17366 ■ For the Love of Horses

7371 Sterrettania Rd.
Fairview, PA 16415
Ph: (814)654-9733 (814)474-5382
Fax: (814)654-2178
E-mail: loveofhorses@earthlink.net
URL: http://www.loveofhorses.org
Contact: Mary Wisniewski, Contact
Founded: 2001. **Description:** Provides foal recovery program which dedicated to the adoption and placement of PMU/Premarin foals.

17367 ■ Horse Lovers United (HLU)

PO Box 2744
Salisbury, MD 21802-2744
Ph: (410)749-3599
Fax: (410)749-7297
E-mail: horse@intercom.net
URL: http://www.horseloversunited.com
Contact: Lorraine Truitt, Pres.
Founded: 1992. **Members:** 55. **Membership Dues:** individual, $10 (annual) ● life, $100. **Staff:** 1. **Description:** Seeks to find new and lifetime homes for unwanted horses, and establish a retirement farm.

17368 ■ ReRun

PO Box 113
Helmetta, NJ 08828
Ph: (732)521-1370 (215)272-6716
E-mail: rerunnj@verizon.net
URL: http://www.rerun.org
Contact: Laurie Condurso-Lane, Pres./Adoption Coor.
Founded: 1996. **Staff:** 3. **State Groups:** 7. **Description:** Aims to provide new homes for ex-racehorses. Conducts fundraisings. **Publications:** *ReViews,* quarterly. Newsletter.

17369 ■ United Pegasus Foundation (UPF)

120 S 1st Ave.
Arcadia, CA 91006
Ph: (626)279-1306 (661)823-9672
Fax: (626)452-8620
E-mail: unitedpegasus@yahoo.com
URL: http://www.unitedpegasus.com
Contact: Helen Meredith, Pres.
Founded: 1994. **Description:** Seeks to identify and rescue abused and/or slaughter bound equines, facilitates adoption; promotes education regarding alternatives to slaughter and abuse. **Conventions/Meetings:** annual Benefit Stallion Auction - meeting - held 3rd week of November.

Housing

17370 ■ National Fair Housing Alliance (NFHA)

1212 New York Ave. NW, Ste.525
Washington, DC 20005
Ph: (202)898-1661
Fax: (202)371-9744
E-mail: nfha@nationalfairhousing.org
URL: http://www.nationalfairhousing.org
Contact: Shanna Smith, Pres./CEO
Founded: 1988. **Description:** Works to eliminate housing discrimination. Promotes equal housing, lending and insurance opportunities. Advocates for fair housing action in Congress, state legislatures, federal, state and local regulatory agencies, court and communities. **Computer Services:** Information services, employment opportunities ● information services, housing resources.

Human Relations

17371 ■ Initiatives of Change (IC)

1156 15th St. NW, Ste.910
Washington, DC 20005-1704
Ph: (202)872-9077
Fax: (202)872-9137
URL: http://www.us.initiativesofchange.org
Contact: Mr. Don Cowles, Exec. Dir.
Founded: 1941. **Staff:** 25. **Budget:** $1,500,000. **Nonmembership. Description:** A worldwide network of people of diverse races, nations, creeds and backgrounds, who are committed to transformation in society based on change in individuals, starting with themselves. Works to promote change in the world through the strengthening of the moral and spiritual foundations of democracy. **Formerly:** Oxford Group - Moral Re-Armament; (2002) Moral Re-Armament. **Publications:** *Breakthroughs,* bimonthly. Newsletter. **Price:** free. Alternate Formats: online ● *Breakthroughs in Peacemaking.* Pamphlet ● *Faith In Diplomacy.* Book ● *For a Change,* bimonthly. Magazine. Provides analysis and news on issues from a moral and spiritual perspective. Includes profiles and book reviews. **Price:** $25.00/year. **Circulation:** 6,000 ● *The Forgiveness Factor.* Book. **Price:** $19.95/copy ● *Forgiveness in International Affairs.* Pamphlet ● *Healing the Heart of America.* Video. Features a documentary of a walk through historic Richmond, Virginia's racial history. ● *How to Listen to the Inner Voice.* Pamphlet ● *It Started Right There: AA & MRA.* Pamphlet ● *On the Tail of a Comet.* Book. Tells about the life of Frank Buchman, founder of Moral Re-Armament, and the story of Moral Re-Armament. ● Audiotapes. **Conventions/Meetings:** annual assembly - always summer in Caux, Switzerland.

17372 ■ International Peace Academy (IPA)

777 UN Plz., 4th Fl.
New York, NY 10017-3521
Ph: (212)687-4300
Fax: (212)983-8246
E-mail: ipa@ipacademy.org
URL: http://www.ipacademy.org
Contact: Terje Roed-Larsen, Pres.
Founded: 1970. **Staff:** 32. **Budget:** $4,500,000. **Description:** Promotes the prevention and settlement of armed conflicts between and within states. Works closely with the United Nations, regional and other international organizations, governments and parties to conflicts. Activities are enhanced by its ability to draw on a worldwide network of statesmen, scholars, business leaders, diplomats, military officers, and leaders of civil society. **Libraries: Type:** not open to the public. **Holdings:** 800. **Subjects:** peace. **Publications:** *International Peacekeeping,* quarterly. Journal. Examines theory and practice of peacekeeping. **Price:** $45.00 /year for individuals; $170.00 /year for institutions. ISSN: 1353-3312 ● *IPA Initiatives,* semiannual. Newsletter ● *Keeping the Peace: Lessons from Multidimensional UN Operations in Cambodia and El Salvador.* Books. Compares the strength and weaknesses of the UN peacekeeping operations. **Price:** $37.99 ● *Occasional Paper Series,* periodic ● *Peacemaking and Peacekeeping for the New Century.* Book ● *Rights & Reconciliation: UN Strategies in El Salvador* ● Reports. **Conventions/Meetings:** annual dinner and seminar ● periodic workshop.

17373 ■ Interns for Peace (IFP)

c/o Middle East Peace Dialogue Network
The Ellipse Bldg.
4201 Church Rd., Ste.13
Mount Laurel, NJ 08054-2240
Ph: (856)235-3111
Fax: (856)235-4674
E-mail: pearleldridge@cs.com
URL: http://mpdn.org/interns.htm
Contact: Richard Goodwin, Founder
Founded: 1976. **Staff:** 20. **Budget:** $500,000. **Regional Groups:** 3. **State Groups:** 1. **Languages:** Arabic, English, Hebrew. **Description:** Human relations training program providing an opportunity to live and work in communities in Israel and develop joint activities between neighboring Jewish, Palestinian and Arab communities. Works to bring together Jewish and Arab citizens of Israel on a grass roots level to establish mutual trust, understanding, and continuing cooperation; trains professional community workers for a career in human relations; encourages Jews and Arabs in Israel and the Diaspora to conduct cooperative economic, social, and educational projects for the promotion of peace; uses these projects as models of positive cross-cultural and majority-minority interaction that can be incorporated into a variety of cultures. Believes that understanding and trust will evolve from people working, learning, and interacting to achieve shared goals. Sponsors intern training seminars on Israeli society, the Israeli Jewish community, Jewish-Arab relations, and the history of Israel and Israeli Arab-Jewish relations. Organizes annual public Jewish-Arab activities including summer camps, sports events, cultural fairs, family picnics, and historic landmark projects. Supports the networking of organizations active in inter-ethnic relations. Conducts recruitment program. Plans to develop a multinational youth agricultural corps camp to teach the principles of agroforestry to youth from drought-stricken countries. Also hopes to develop an Education for Tolerance Pilot Project for replication in the United States school systems modeled on Jewish-Arab Education for Democracy project in Israel. **Task Forces:** International. **Publications:** *IFP Reports,* triennial. Newsletter. Contains Multi-religious art and photography and a peace calendar. **Conventions/Meetings:** periodic Educational Meeting, located in churches, synagogues, mosques and universities throughout North America; includes a video presentation ● triennial meeting.

17374 ■ Lucis Trust (LT)

120 Wall St., 24th Fl.
New York, NY 10005
Ph: (212)292-0707
Fax: (212)292-0808
E-mail: newyork@lucistrust.org
URL: http://www.lucistrust.org
Contact: Sarah McKechnie, Pres.
Founded: 1922. **Staff:** 15. **Budget:** $360,000. **Languages:** Danish, English, French, German, Greek, Italian, Russian, Spanish. **Nonmembership. Multinational. Description:** Dedicated to the establishment of positive human relations. Promotes recognition and practice of the spiritual principles and values

upon which a stable and interdependent world society may be based. Objectives are to: encourage the study of comparative religion, philosophy, science, and art; promote the broadening of human sympathies and interests and the expansion of ethical, religious, and educational literature; assist or engage in activities for the relief of suffering and human betterment; further worthy efforts for humanitarian and educational ends. Activities include the Arcane School, the Lucis Publishing Companies, World Goodwill, Triangles, and Lucis Productions. **Libraries: Type:** reference. **Holdings:** 3,500. **Subjects:** ethics, religion. **Publications:** *The Beacon*, bimonthly. Magazine. **Price:** $22.00/year; $4.00/issue. **Circulation:** 1,800 ● *Triangles Bulletin*, quarterly ● *World Goodwill Newsletter*, quarterly ● Has also published the works of Alice A. Bailey and Foster Bailey. **Conventions/Meetings:** annual conference, arcane school conference - always spring, in New York City.

17375 ■ New Dimensions Radio (NDR)
PO Box 569
Ukiah, CA 95482
Ph: (707)468-5215
Free: (800)935-TAPE
E-mail: info@newdimensions.org
URL: http://www.newdimensions.org
Contact: Justine Toms, Co-Pres./Co-Founder
Founded: 1973. **Members:** 4,000. **Membership Dues:** individual, $45 (annual) ● family/sponsor, $60-$99 (annual) ● sustaining, $100-$249 (annual) ● radio underwriter, $250-$499 (annual) ● satellite sponsor, $500-$999 (annual) ● benefactor, $1,000 (annual). **Staff:** 12. **Budget:** $1,200,000. **Description:** Educational organization that presents information about changing human values and their effect on people and the world. Asserts that a positive, constructive media is a powerful tool for the communication of new possibilities, choices, methods, and priorities based on essential human values and a greater understanding of the human potential and betterment of the human condition. Produces audiotapes featuring speakers from a variety of fields such as community action ecology, spirituality, economics, education, health, the arts, humanities, politics, psychology, and science. Programming covers topics including quantum physics, green politics, the exploration of space, appropriate technology, and holistic medicine. **Libraries: Type:** reference. **Holdings:** 10,000; audio recordings, books. **Subjects:** media. **Awards:** New Dimensions Broadcaster. **Frequency:** annual. **Type:** recognition. **Recipient:** for contributions to the betterment of society. **Also Known As:** New Dimensions Foundation. **Publications:** *An Open Life: Joseph Campbell in Conversation with Michael Toms*. Book ● *Anne Wilson Schaef in Conversation with Michael Toms* ● *At the Leading Edge: New Visions of Science, Spirituality, and Society*. Book ● *Fritjof Capra in Conversation with Michael Toms*. Book ● *Larry Dossey in Conversation with Michael Toms* ● *Lynn Andrews in Conversation with Michael Toms* ● *Marsha Sinetar in Conversation with Michael Toms*. Book ● *New Dimensions Journal*, bimonthly. **Price:** included in membership dues. **Circulation:** 25,000. **Advertising:** accepted. Alternate Formats: online. Also Cited As: *New Dimensions Radio Network News* ● *Radio Calendar*, bimonthly ● Also makes available free listing of audiotapes.

17376 ■ World Goodwill - USA (WG)
120 Wall St., 24th Fl.
New York, NY 10005
Ph: (212)292-0707
Fax: (212)292-0808
E-mail: newyork@lucistrust.org
URL: http://www.lucistrust.org/goodwill
Contact: Sarah McKechnie, Pres.
Founded: 1932. **Staff:** 3. **Languages:** Danish, English, French, German, Greek, Italian, Russian, Spanish. **Nonmembership. Description:** Promotes the constructive power of goodwill as a means to establish successful human relations and to solve problems worldwide. "Aims to help mobilize the energy of goodwill; prepare for the reappearance of Christ; educate the public on the causes of the major

world problems and to help create solutions." Provides educational resources, study courses, and information. **Affiliated With:** Lucis Trust. **Formerly:** (1950) Men of Goodwill. **Publications:** *Commentary* (in English and Spanish), periodic. Focuses on current world affairs and problems. ● Newsletter, quarterly ● Distributes pamphlets worldwide. **Conventions/Meetings:** annual seminar and symposium - always in fall ● annual World Goodwill Symposium - conference - always fall, in New York, NY, London, UK, and Geneva, Switzerland.

Human Rights

17377 ■ Africa Network (AN)
310 Auditorium Bldg.
Michigan State Univ.
East Lansing, MI 48824
Ph: (517)355-9300 (517)432-5134
Fax: (517)355-8363
E-mail: hbooks@mail.h-net.msu.edu
URL: http://www.h-net.org/~africa
Contact: Dr. Jay Spaulding, Ed.
Founded: 1981. **Description:** Represents professors, students, writers, and individuals working to defend just law, freedom, and human rights. Opposes "the crime of racist, apartheid law." Provides resource materials and information on South Africa; offers educational outreach program. Sponsors programs commemorating important historical events of South Africa, including Sharpeville Memorial Day and Soweto Anniversary Commemoration. (Group was originally named for Dennis Brutus, former political prisoner, South African poet, scholar, and anti-apartheid activist. Brutus was granted political asylum in the U.S. in 1983). **Awards:** Kwanzaa Awards for Literature, Film, and Video. **Type:** recognition. **Absorbed:** (1987) Dennis Brutus Defense Committee. **Formerly:** (1988) African National Network. **Publications:** *Africa Network Directory of Resources*, periodic ● Newsletter, periodic.

17378 ■ American Association for the International Commission of Jurists (AAICJ)
280 Madison Ave., Ste.1102
New York, NY 10016
Ph: (212)972-0883
Fax: (212)972-0888
E-mail: aaicj@mindspring.com
URL: http://www.icj.org
Contact: William J. Butler, Pres.
Founded: 1967. **Description:** Jurists and academics in international law, human rights, and international affairs. Supports the maintenance of the Rule of Law and protection of human rights alone and in cooperation with other organizations, principally the International Commission of Jurists sponsors conferences on a variety of topics and intergovernmental briefings on human rights and foreign policy. Provides documentation service and internship program. **Publications:** *CIJL Yearbook*, annual ● *International Commission of Jurists Newsletter/Quarterly Report* ● *International Commission of Jurists Review*, semiannual ● Also publishes special studies and reports of inquiries of its observers at trials, of its international congress, and regional conferences.

17379 ■ American Homeowners' Resource Center (AHRC)
PO Box 97
San Juan Capistrano, CA 92693
Ph: (949)366-2125
E-mail: ahrc@ahrc.com
URL: http://www.ahrc.com
Contact: Ms. Elizabeth McMahon, Contact
Founded: 1992. **Members:** 4,000. **Staff:** 20. **Description:** Promotes individual human rights and fosters an awareness of the intrinsic dignity of all human beings. Gathers, assembles, and organizes research related to human rights for individuals or organizations. Works to preserve and protect the right of every individual to a home. Offers educational programs; provides charitable programs and children's services; maintains speakers' bureau. **Librar-**

ies: Type: lending; reference; not open to the public. **Holdings:** articles, audiovisuals, books, clippings. **Subjects:** housing, human rights. **Awards:** AHRC Awards. **Frequency:** annual. **Type:** grant. **Computer Services:** database, housing related complaints, reports, news articles on business, politicians and others ● electronic publishing, chat programs ● online services, helpline ● record retrieval services, complaints and lawsuits, legislation, news articles, reports on housing. **Divisions:** AHRC News Services. **Publications:** *Homeowner Advocate*, annual. Newsletter. **Advertising:** accepted ● Also produces the radio and television shows Homeowner Forum. **Conventions/Meetings:** board meeting ● competition.

17380 ■ Americans for Human Rights in Ukraine (AHRU)
43 Midland Pl.
Newark, NJ 07106
Ph: (973)373-9729
Fax: (973)373-4755
Contact: Ms. Bozhena Olshaniwsky, Pres.
Founded: 1979. **Members:** 4,000. **Budget:** $35,000. **Local Groups:** 20. **Description:** Organizations and individuals whose goals are to: pursue, expose, and combat violations of human rights and racial and ethnic prejudice in Ukraine; disseminate information among U.S. officials, governmental agencies, and concerned citizens regarding what the AHRU calls the non-observance of human rights in the region; promote the welfare of political prisoners and their families both in Ukraine and in exile. Supports individuals who defend religious, national, and human rights in Ukraine. Group also contends there is a close relationship between human rights in Ukraine and other countries and the security of the U.S. Initiated and successfully lobbied for U.S. congressional passage of the Ukraine Famine Bill, which called for the creation of the Commission on the Ukraine Famine Act for studying the causes and effects of the famine in Ukraine. Operates speakers' bureau and charitable program. **Libraries: Type:** reference. **Holdings:** archival material, clippings. **Awards: Type:** recognition. **Recipient:** for human rights activism above and beyond the call of duty. **Computer Services:** database ● mailing lists. **Publications:** *AHRU Newsletter*, 4/year. **Circulation:** 4,000 ● *Newsbriefs*, quarterly ● Annual Report (in English and Ukrainian). **Conventions/Meetings:** annual conference ● seminar.

17381 ■ Amnesty International - Puerto Rico
Calle Robles, No. 54 - Altos
Oficina 11
Rio Piedras, PR 00925
Fax: (787)763-5096
URL: http://web.amnesty.org/contacts/index/eng-pri
Multinational. Description: Puerto Rican section of Amnesty International. Works for the release of nonviolent prisoners of conscience. Promotes human rights. **Libraries: Type:** open to the public. **Holdings:** archival material, reports.

17382 ■ Amnesty International of the U.S.A. (AIUSA)
5 Penn Plz.
New York, NY 10001
Ph: (212)807-8400
Fax: (212)627-1451
E-mail: aimember@aiusa.org
URL: http://www.amnesty-usa.org
Contact: Larry Cox, Exec. Dir.
Founded: 1961. **Members:** 320,000. **Membership Dues:** individual, $25 (annual) ● student, senior, limited income, $15 (annual). **Staff:** 140. **Budget:** $35,000,000. **Description:** Undertakes research and action focused on preventing and ending grave abuses of the rights to physical and mental integrity, freedom of conscience and expression, and freedom from discrimination within the context of its work to promote all human rights. Has consultative status with the United Nations and the Council of Europe, has cooperative relations with the Inter-American Commission on Human Rights, and has observer status with the Organization of African Unity. Was the recipient of the 1977 Nobel Prize for Peace. Volun-

teers participate in networks: Educators; Freedom Writers; Health Professionals; Legal Professionals; Urgent Action; Women; gays and lesbians. **Additional Websites:** http://www.amnesty.org. **Affiliated With:** Amnesty International - United Kingdom. **Publications:** *Amnesty Action*, 3/year. Newsletter. **Price:** included in membership dues. **Circulation:** 308,000 ● *Amnesty International Magazine*, 3/year. **Price:** included in membership dues ● *Amnesty International Report*, annual. Covers human rights abuses in 151 countries. **Price:** $20.00/copy for individuals; $15.00/copy for libraries ● Also publishes country briefing papers, mission reports, and other special reports. **Conventions/Meetings:** annual meeting - always in June.

17383 ■ Center of Concern

1225 Otis St., NE
Washington, DC 20017-2516
Ph: (202)635-2757
Fax: (202)832-9494
E-mail: coc@coc.org
URL: http://www.coc.org
Contact: James E. Hug PhD, Pres.

Founded: 1971. **Staff:** 18. **Budget:** $1,300,000. **Description:** Promotes social analysis, theological reflection, policy advocacy, research, and public education on global and local issues such as poverty, hunger, women's rights, economic justice and social development, human rights, and private sector in development and international financial institutions. **Libraries: Type:** reference. **Holdings:** 1,000; books, periodicals. **Subjects:** development, ecology, debt, Africa, social justice. **Projects:** Catholic Social Teaching; Food Security; Gender and Trade; Rethinking Bretton Woods; Social Theology and Social Justice; Third World Development; Women in Global Leadership. **Publications:** *Catholic Social Teaching: Our Best Kept Secret*. Book ● *Center Focus*, quarterly. Newsletter. **Price:** $35.00/year. **Circulation:** 10,000 ● *Opting for the Poor: The Challenge for the Twenty-First Century*. Book ● *Rethinking Bretton Woods*. Books. Contains information on international financial institutions.

17384 ■ Center for International Policy (CIP)

1717 Massachusetts Ave. NW, Ste.801
Washington, DC 20036
Ph: (202)232-3317
Fax: (202)232-3440
E-mail: cip@ciponline.org
URL: http://www.ciponline.org
Contact: Robert E. White, Pres.

Founded: 1975. **Staff:** 18. **Budget:** $1,700,000. **Description:** Monitors security assistance in Latin America and Africa and examines the impact of U.S. foreign policy on human rights in the Third World. Studies and reports on the implications of U.S. foreign assistance. **Formerly:** (1976) Institute for International Policy. **Publications:** *International Policy Reports*, bimonthly. **Price:** $2.50/copy, for single purchase; $1.00/copy, for 20 or more purchase. Alternate Formats: online ● Monographs ● Reprints ● Also publishes books and monographs.

17385 ■ Center for Religious Freedom, Freedom House

1319 18th St. NW
Washington, DC 20036
Ph: (202)296-5101
Fax: (202)296-5078
E-mail: religion@freedomhouse.org
URL: http://crf.hudson.org
Contact: Nina Shea, Dir.

Founded: 1983. **Membership Dues:** individual, $25 (annual). **Staff:** 3. **Description:** A self-sustaining division of Freedom House. Defends against religious persecution of all groups throughout the world and insists that U.S. foreign policy defend Christians and Jews, Muslim dissidents and minorities, and other religious minorities in countries such as Indonesia, Pakistan, Nigeria, Iran and Sudan. Works to "fight the imposition of harsh Islamic law in the new Iraq and Afghanistan and opposes blasphemy laws in Muslim countries that suppress more tolerant and pro-American Muslim thought." Also sponsors investiga-

tive field missions. **Libraries: Type:** open to the public. **Holdings:** archival material, articles. **Formerly:** (2001) Puebla Institute. **Publications:** *Endangered Christians Report*. Alternate Formats: online ● *The First Freedom*, bimonthly. Newsletter. Covers religious persecution worldwide. **Price:** included in membership dues. **Circulation:** 4,000. **Advertising:** accepted. Alternate Formats: online ● *Massacre at the Millennium: A Report on the Murder of 21 Christians in Al-Kosheh, Egypt in January 2000 and the Failure of Justice* ● *Religious Freedom in the World: A Global Report on Freedom and Persecution*. Survey ● *The Rise of Hindu Extremism and the Repression of Christians and Muslims in India*. Report ● *The Talibanization of Nigeria: Sharia Law and Religious Freedom*. Report. Alternate Formats: online.

17386 ■ Center for the Study of Human Rights (CSHR)

Columbia Univ., Mail Code: 3365
420 W 118th St., Rm. 1108 IAB
New York, NY 10027
Ph: (212)854-2479
Fax: (212)316-4578
E-mail: cshr@columbia.edu
URL: http://www.columbia.edu/cu/humanrights
Contact: Dr. J. Paul Martin, Exec. Dir.

Founded: 1978. **Members:** 34. **Staff:** 15. **Description:** Academic advisers and directors. Promotes teaching and research in the field of human rights. Sponsors interdisciplinary human rights research. Offers advice, fellowships, training and other assistance in conducting and financing such research; provides assistance in teaching and curriculum development. Offers consultation service, which provides information on human rights research, resources, and education and training programs at other institutions. **Libraries: Type:** reference. **Subjects:** human rights. **Awards:** Gitelson/Meyerowitz Human Rights Essay Award. **Frequency:** annual. **Type:** monetary. **Publications:** *Center for the Study of Human Rights—Newsletter*, quarterly. Includes bibliographies, calendar of events, course listings, and information on funding opportunities. **Price:** free. **Circulation:** 800 ● *Conference Proceedings*, annual ● *Human Rights: A Topical Bibliography* ● *Human Rights Syllabi* ● Annual Report, annual ● Papers ● Also publishes human rights documents. **Conventions/Meetings:** annual meeting and symposium - always in June.

17387 ■ Coalition Against Trafficking in Women (CATW)

c/o Dr. Janice Raymond, Co-Exec. Dir.
PO Box 9338
North Amherst, MA 01059
Fax: (413)367-9262
E-mail: info@catwinternational.org
URL: http://www.catwinternational.org
Contact: Dr. Janice Raymond, Co-Exec. Dir.

Founded: 1988. **Languages:** English, French, Spanish. **Multinational. Description:** Serves as a clearinghouse on violations of women's human rights worldwide, particularly those arising from prostitution and sex trafficking. Works with international policy makers, women's rights and human rights advocates, and the United Nations to promote women's right to be free from sexual exploitation. Creates a new U.N. Convention Against Sexual Exploitation and seeks governmental and non-governmental endorsement for establishing it as international legislation. **Publications:** *The Penn State Report* (in English and French). Contains analysis of sexual exploitation and a U.N. legislative history of prostitution and trafficking in women. ● Newsletter.

17388 ■ Committee of Concerned Scientists (CCS)

145 W 79th St., Ste.4D
New York, NY 10024
Ph: (212)362-4441
E-mail: mnk.ccs@verizon.net
URL: http://www.libertynet.org/ccs
Contact: Maud Kozodoy, Exec. Dir.

Founded: 1972. **Members:** 5,000. **Membership Dues:** individual, $35 (annual) ● student, $10 (an-

nual). **Staff:** 1. **Description:** Scientists and scholars united for "the protection and advancement of the scientific and human rights of scientists throughout the world.". **Divisions:** Astronomy; Biology; Chemistry; Computer Science; Dental Sciences; Engineering; Industrial Labs; Mathematics; Medical Sciences; Physics; Psychology and Psychiatry; Social Sciences. **Conventions/Meetings:** annual board meeting - always February or March, in New York City.

17389 ■ Committee on Human Rights

c/o The National Academies
500 5th St. NW
Washington, DC 20001
Ph: (202)334-3043
Fax: (202)334-2225
E-mail: chr@nas.edu
URL: http://www7.nationalacademies.org/human-rights/index.html
Contact: Carol Corillon, Dir.

Founded: 1976. **Members:** 16. **Staff:** 4. **Description:** Uses the "influence and prestige of the institutions it represents in behalf of scientists, engineers, and health professionals anywhere in the world who are unjustly detained or imprisoned for exercising their basic human rights as promulgated by the U.N. Declaration". Activities of the committee include private inquiries, appeals to governments, moral support to prisoners and their families, and consciousness-raising efforts such as workshops and symposia. **Affiliated With:** Institute of Medicine; National Academy of Engineering; National Academy of Sciences. **Formerly:** Committee on Human Rights of the U.S. National Academy of Sciences; (2004) Committee on Human Rights of the U.S. National Academy of Sciences, National Academy of Engineering, and Institute of Medicine. **Publications:** *The Myrna Mack Case: An Update*. Book. **Price:** $9.00. Alternate Formats: online ● *Science and Human Rights*. Book. Alternate Formats: online ● *Scientists and Human Rights in Chile*. Book. Alternate Formats: online ● *Scientists and Human Rights in Guatemala*. Book. Presents a history of violence and research findings and conclusions of a 1992 delegation to Guatemala. **Price:** $18.00. Alternate Formats: online ● *Scientists and Human Rights in Somalia*. Book ● *Scientists and Human Rights in Syria*. Book. Alternate Formats: online.

17390 ■ Concerned Citizens for Racially Free America (CCfRFA)

PO Box 320497
Birmingham, AL 35232-0497
Ph: (205)856-0481
Fax: (205)856-2244
E-mail: civilrights@bellsouth.net
URL: http://www.concernedcitizensnews.org
Contact: Richard A. Peters, Dir.

Founded: 1992. **Membership Dues:** individual, $25 (annual) ● corporate, $100 (annual) ● life (corporate), $1,000 ● life (individual), $250. **Staff:** 11. **State Groups:** 10. **Local Groups:** 3. **Description:** Individuals and organizations. Promotes respect for the rights of the individual and the rule of law; opposes racial discrimination. Provides consulting and legal services to individuals whose rights have been violated. **Publications:** *NEWS Magazine*, quarterly. **Circulation:** 5,000.

17391 ■ Congressional Human Rights Caucus (CHRC)

c/o Hans Hogrefe, Dir.
Off. of Congressman Tom Lantos
2413 Rayburn HOB
Washington, DC 20515
Ph: (202)225-3531
E-mail: hans.hogrefe@mail.house.gov
URL: http://lantos.house.gov/HoR/CA12/Human-RightsCaucus
Contact: Hans Hogrefe, Dir.

Founded: 1983. **Members:** 150. **Staff:** 3. **Description:** Bipartisan congressional members organization of the House of Representatives concerned with human rights abuses around the world. Coordinates efforts of the members of Congress to end these abuses and to secure freedom from religious, ethnic, cultural, or political persecution for all people. Provides information on specific human rights cases; sponsors forums; serves as a congressional liaison with human rights organizations. Conducts briefings and press conferences for congresspersons and their staffs. Writes letters to heads of state protesting the imprisonment of people around the world for their political beliefs, religious practices, or ethnic origins. **Libraries: Type:** reference. **Subjects:** human rights. **Computer Services:** Bibliographic search, tracking system for monitoring congressional action on individual cases of human rights abuses. **Publications:** *Congressional Human Rights Caucus Annual Report,* annual. Contains summary of Caucus Members' activities in Congress to protect human rights around the world. ● *Human Rights Newsline,* monthly. Contains news articles on the issue of human rights. ● Newsletter, quarterly. **Conventions/Meetings:** meeting ● seminar.

17392 ■ CorpWatch (CW)

1611 Telegraph Ave., No. 702
Oakland, CA 94612
Ph: (510)271-8080
URL: http://www.corpwatch.org
Contact: Pratap Chatterjee, Managing Ed.
Founded: 1996. **Staff:** 5. **Budget:** $359,000. **Languages:** English, Spanish. **Multinational. Description:** Strives to counter corporate-led globalization through education and activism; works to foster democratic control over corporations by building grassroots globalization, including human rights, labor rights, and environmental justice. Hosts the Climate Justice Initiative and the UN and Corporations Project. Produced five one-hour radio broadcasts. **Publications:** *Greenhouse Gangsters vs. Climate Justice.* Report. **Price:** $2.00 each, bulk discounts available. Alternate Formats: online ● *Tangled Up in Blue: Corporate Partnerships at the United Nations.* **Price:** $2.00 each, bulk discounts available ● Annual Report, annual. Alternate Formats: online.

17393 ■ Falun Data Information Center (FDI)

331 W 57th St., PMB 409
New York, NY 10019
Ph: (646)533-6147
Free: (888)842-4797
E-mail: contact@faluninfo.net
URL: http://www.faluninfo.net
Contact: Erping Zhang, Spokesperson
Languages: Bulgarian, Chinese, Dutch, English, French, German, Hebrew, Japanese, Korean, Russian, Spanish, Swedish. **Multinational. Description:** Works to compile, cross-check, organize and publish Falun Gong reports. Provides reports to government officials, international media, human rights organizations and the general public. Informs fellow citizens about the systematic persecution of Falun Gong practitioners. **Telecommunication Services:** electronic mail, feedback@faluninfo.net. **Publications:** *Falun Gong News Bulletin,* weekly. Newsletter. Alternate Formats: online.

17394 ■ Global Rights

1200 18th St. NW, Ste.602
Washington, DC 20036
Ph: (202)822-4600
Fax: (202)822-4606
E-mail: media@globalrights.org
URL: http://www.hrlawgroup.org
Contact: Salih Booker, Exec. Dir.
Founded: 1978. **Staff:** 100. **Budget:** $4,000,000. **Languages:** English, French, Spanish. **Description:** Human rights and legal professionals engaged in human rights advocacy, litigation and training around the world. Supports and helps empower advocates expanding the scope of human rights protection for men and women and promotes broad participation in building human rights standards and procedures at the national, regional and international levels. **Libraries: Type:** not open to the public. **Subjects:** human rights. **Awards:** Human Rights Award. **Frequency:** annual. **Type:** recognition. **Boards:** Directors. **Councils:** Advisory; International. **Formerly:** (2005)

International Human Rights Law Group. **Conventions/Meetings:** periodic conference, includes briefing.

17395 ■ Human Rights First

333 7th Ave., 13th Fl.
New York, NY 10001-5108
Ph: (212)845-5200
Fax: (212)845-5299
E-mail: feedback@humanrightsfirst.org
URL: http://www.humanrightsfirst.org
Contact: Michael H. Posner, Pres.
Founded: 1978. **Members:** 800. **Staff:** 35. **Budget:** $3,000,000. **Languages:** English, Spanish. **Description:** Public interest law center that works to promote international human rights and refugee law and legal procedures. Focuses on cases where volunteer lawyers may help promote international human rights standards. Involves in the pro bono representation of indigent political asylum applicants in the US. Investigates human rights issues in the justice system for follow-ups with local lawyers, U.S. foreign policy issues in markers, and intergovernmental organizations. Conducts training sessions and educational workshops for attorneys on international human rights and refugee law. **Awards:** Roger Baldwin Medal of Liberty. **Frequency:** biennial. **Type:** medal. **Recipient:** to individuals and organizations making a significant contribution to human rights in any part of the world. **Formerly:** Lawyers Committee for International Human Rights; (2004) Lawyers Committee for Human Rights. **Publications:** *Lawyers Committee for Human Rights—Newsbriefs,* quarterly. Newsletter. Reports on committee activities and developments in asylum law. Includes obituaries. **Price:** included in membership dues. **Circulation:** 2,000 ● Also publishes periodic reports on human rights abuses, refugee law, and related topics.

17396 ■ Human Rights Resource Center (HRRC)

Univ. of Minnesota Law School
Mondale Hall
229 19th Ave. S, Ste.N-120
Minneapolis, MN 55455
Ph: (612)626-0041
Free: (888)HRE-DUC8
Fax: (612)625-2011
E-mail: humanrts@umn.edu
URL: http://www1.umn.edu/humanrts/hrcenter.htm
Contact: Ms. Kristi Rudelius-Palmer, Co-Dir.
Founded: 1988. **Multinational. Description:** Works to create and distribute human rights education resources. **Libraries: Type:** open to the public. **Holdings:** 23,000; archival material, articles, books, papers, reports. **Subjects:** human rights. **Awards:** Internships. **Type:** scholarship ● Upper Midwest Human Rights Fellowship Program. **Frequency:** annual. **Type:** scholarship. **Recipient:** for residents of the Upper Midwest including students, teachers, lawyers, health professionals, community leaders and others. **Computer Services:** Online services, Global Human Rights Education Listserv. **Additional Websites:** http://www.umn.edu/humanrts, http://www.hrusa.org, http://www.humanrightsandpeacestore.org. **Also Known As:** (2005) University of Minnesota Human Rights Center. **Conventions/Meetings:** Human Rights Training Workshops - seminar ● workshop.

17397 ■ Human Rights Watch (HRW)

350 5th Ave., 34th Fl.
New York, NY 10118-3299
Ph: (212)290-4700
Fax: (212)736-1300
E-mail: hrwnyc@hrw.org
URL: http://www.hrw.org
Contact: Kenneth Roth, Exec. Dir.
Founded: 1978. **Members:** 8,000. **Staff:** 120. **Budget:** $12,000,000. **Regional Groups:** 5. **Languages:** English, French, Portuguese, Spanish. **Multinational. Description:** Promotes and monitors human rights worldwide. Evaluates the human rights practices of governments in accordance with standards recognized by international laws and agreements including the United Nations Declaration of Human Rights and the Helsinki Accords. Identifies government abuses

of human rights such as kidnapping, torture, and imprisonment for nonviolent association, exile, psychiatric abuse, and censorship; publicizes and protests against these violations. Also observes the human rights practices of nongovernmental groups, such as guerrilla groups, that are in sustained armed conflict with governments and measures these practices against internal war standards set forth in the Geneva Conventions and Protocols. Sponsors missions to countries accused of human rights abuses; meets with government officials, local human rights and relief groups, church officials, labor leaders, journalists, and others with information on human rights practices. Testifies before congressional hearings. **Computer Services:** Mailing lists, of members. **Publications:** *Human Rights Watch Publications Catalog,* semiannual. Alternate Formats: online ● *Human Rights Watch Quarterly Newsletter.* **Price:** $20.00. **Circulation:** 15,000 ● *Human Rights Watch: Questions and Answers.* Brochure ● *Human Rights Watch World Report,* annual. Book. **Price:** $25.00. ISSN: 1054-948X ● Reports. Alternate Formats: online ● Papers. Alternate Formats: online.

17398 ■ Human Rights Watch Asia (AsW)

350 5th Ave., 34th Fl.
New York, NY 10118-3299
Ph: (212)290-4700
Fax: (212)736-1300
E-mail: hrwnyc@hrw.org
URL: http://hrw.org/doc/?t=asia
Contact: Kenneth Roth, Exec. Dir.
Founded: 1978. **Staff:** 185. **Budget:** $21,000,000. **Description:** Promotes and monitors human rights with respect to laws requiring human rights considerations in foreign policymaking. **Affiliated With:** Human Rights Watch. **Formerly:** (1994) Asia Watch Committee. **Publications:** *Human Rights Watch World Report,* annual ● Reports, periodic.

17399 ■ Human Rights Watch - Helsinki (HRWH)

350 5th Ave., 34th Fl.
New York, NY 10118-3299
Ph: (212)290-4700
Fax: (212)736-1300
E-mail: hrwnyc@hrw.org
Contact: Kenneth Roth, Exec. Dir.
Founded: 1979. **Staff:** 22. **Multinational. Description:** A division of Human Rights Watch. Seeks to monitor domestic and international compliance with the human rights provisions of the 1975 Helsinki Final Act. Commissions reports; holds briefings and discussions with government officials and private citizens; organizes meetings, receptions, and conferences. Issues press releases and public statements; sends letters to government officials and newspapers. Maintains contact with Helsinki monitoring groups in Eastern and Western Europe. **Affiliated With:** Human Rights Watch; Human Rights Watch Asia. **Formerly:** Helsinki Watch; (1993) U.S. Helsinki Watch. **Publications:** Newsletters ● Reports.

17400 ■ Institute for the Study of Genocide (ISG)

899 10th Ave., Rm. 325
New York, NY 10019
E-mail: info@isg-iags.org
URL: http://www.isg-iags.org
Contact: Prof. Orlanda Brugnola, Pres.
Founded: 1982. **Members:** 50. **Membership Dues:** general, $30 (annual) ● supporter, $50 (annual) ● sponsor, $100 (annual). **Description:** Unites to further research and scholarship on the causes, prevention, and consequences of genocide. Aims to sponsor historical, contemporary, and predictive research on the causes of genocide, mass political killing, and other violations of human rights; research and evaluate responses to genocide; monitor contemporary reports of human rights violations; considers deterrents to genocide and strategies to impede genocide and to assist the potential victims. Establishes liaison with international related groups and with archives and libraries specializing in the history of indigenous peoples. **Awards:** Lemkin Award. **Frequency:** biennial. **Type:** monetary. **Recipient:** for

best scholarly book. **Computer Services:** Online services, listserv for members. **Subcommittees:** Academic Scholars. **Publications:** *ISG Newsletter*, semiannual. **Price:** $20.00 for libraries. ISSN: 1078-1706. Alternate Formats: online. **Conventions/Meetings:** semiannual conference (exhibits) ● symposium and lecture.

17401 ■ Inter-American Commission on Human Rights (IACHR)
1889 F St. NW
Washington, DC 20006
Ph: (202)458-6002
Fax: (202)458-3992
E-mail: cidhoea@oas.org
URL: http://www.cidh.oas.org/DefaultE.htm
Contact: Jose Zalaquett, Pres.
Founded: 1960. **Members:** 7. **Staff:** 45. **Budget:** $3,200,000. **Languages:** English, French, Portuguese, Spanish. **Description:** Citizens of member nations of the Organization of American States. Promotes and protects human rights in the Caribbean, and North, Central, and South America. **Libraries: Type:** reference. **Holdings:** 5,000. **Subjects:** human rights, humanitarian law. **Publications:** *Special County Reports* ● Annual Report (in English, French, and Spanish), annual ● Reports. Covers all member states of the Organization of American States (OAS). **Conventions/Meetings:** meeting - 2-3/year.

17402 ■ International Association of Former Soviet Political Prisoners and Victims of the Communist Regime (IASPPV)
1310 Ave. R, Ste.6-F
Brooklyn, NY 11229
Ph: (718)339-4563
Fax: (718)339-4563
E-mail: abolonkin@juno.com
URL: http://iasppv.narod.ru
Contact: Dr. Alexander Bolonkin PhD, Pres.
Founded: 1989. **Members:** 32,000. **Membership Dues:** victim of the former USSR, $35 (annual) ● unemployed, $15 (annual). **Staff:** 8. **State Groups:** 15. **Local Groups:** 20. **National Groups:** 12. **Languages:** English, Russian. **Description:** Works to protect former Soviet political prisoners and victims of the Communist regime from human rights abuses. Collects and disseminates information. Fights for compensation to victims of the Communist regime. **Libraries: Type:** not open to the public. **Holdings:** 250; books, periodicals. **Subjects:** problems of former soviet political prisoners and victims of communist regime. **Additional Websites:** http://www.geocities.com/iasppv, http://bolonkin.narod.ru. **Telecommunication Services:** electronic mail, bolonkin@narod.ru. **Formed by Merger of:** American Association of Former Soviet Political Prisoners. **Publications:** *Alexander Bolonkin "Notes of Political Prisoner," New York 1991* (in English and Russian). Book. **Price:** $9.00/copy. ISSN: 9307-7199. **Circulation:** 1,000 ● *Vestnik of the IASPPV* (in English and Russian), quarterly. Magazine. **Price:** $23.00/year. ISSN: 1067-4179. **Circulation:** 1,000. **Advertising:** accepted ● Newsletter ● Also publishes articles about problems in newspapers and magazines in the USA, Russia and Israel. **Conventions/Meetings:** annual regional meeting.

17403 ■ International Center for Transitional Justice (ICTJ)
5 Hanover Sq., 24th Fl.
New York, NY 10004
Ph: (917)438-9300
Fax: (212)509-6036
E-mail: info@ictj.org
URL: http://www.ictj.org
Contact: Ms. Suzana Grego, Dir. of Communications
Founded: 2000. **Multinational. Description:** Assists countries pursuing accountability for past mass atrocity or human rights abuse. Works in societies emerging from repressive rule or armed conflict, as well as in established democracies where historical injustices or systemic abuse remain unresolved. Provides comparative information, legal and policy analysis, documentation, and strategic research to justice and

truth-seeking institutions, nongovernmental organizations, governments and others. **Publications:** *Transitional Justice in the News*. Newsletter. Alternate Formats: online.

17404 ■ International Federation for the Protection of the Rights of Ethnic, Religious, Linguistic and Other Minorities
11-25 30th Ave.
Long Island City, NY 11102
Ph: (718)728-3330
Fax: (718)956-9583
Contact: Mr. Menelaos G. Tzelios, Sec.Gen.
Founded: 1984. **Membership Dues:** individual, $50 (annual). **Staff:** 5. **Description:** Individuals united in protecting the human rights of ethnic, religious, and linguistic minorities. Reports human rights violations. **Libraries: Type:** reference. **Publications:** Newsletter, quarterly. **Price:** free. **Circulation:** 2,000 ● Reports. **Conventions/Meetings:** semiannual workshop and seminar, presented before Human Rights Commission and Subcommission - always Geneva, Switzerland.

17405 ■ International League for Human Rights (ILHR)
228 E 45th St., 5th Fl.
New York, NY 10017
Ph: (212)661-0480
Fax: (212)661-0416
E-mail: info@ilhr.org
URL: http://www.ilhr.org
Contact: Ms. Mindy Downey, Admin. Off.
Founded: 1942. **Staff:** 4. **Budget:** $1,000,000. **Regional Groups:** 35. **Nonmembership. Multinational. Description:** Individuals and national affiliates promoting human rights, including political and civil rights, racial and religious freedom, and the implementation of the Universal Declaration of Human Rights. Serves as a nongovernmental agency accredited by the United Nations, International Labor Organization, United Nations Educational, Scientific and Cultural Organization, and Council of Europe. Participates in studies and programs on human rights. Advocates effective procedures to protect human rights, including protection of minorities; deals with issues of torture, political imprisonment, due process of law, racial discrimination, genocide, apartheid, treatment of prisoners, status of women, and religious freedom; promotes ability of local human rights groups to exist and work unimpeded by government. **Libraries: Type:** not open to the public. **Holdings:** 2,000; archival material, articles, books, periodicals. **Subjects:** human rights. **Awards:** Human Rights Award. **Frequency:** annual. **Type:** recognition ● Human Rights in Business. **Type:** recognition ● Human Rights in Media Award. **Type:** recognition. **Formerly:** (1976) International League for the Rights of Man. **Publications:** *Crime and Servitude*. Report. Contains expose of the traffic in women for prostitution from the newly independent states. ● *In Brief*, 10-15/year. **Price:** $20.00/copy ● *Petitions Before the UN Trusteeship Council* ● *Report of a Medical Fact-Finding Mission to El Salvador* ● Booklets ● Books ● Pamphlets ● Reports. Covers special reports on worldwide human rights.

17406 ■ International Women's Rights Action Watch (IWRAW)
c/o Human Rights Center
Univ. of Minnesota
229-19th Ave. S
Minneapolis, MN 55455
Ph: (612)625-4985
Fax: (612)625-2011
E-mail: mfreeman@umn.edu
URL: http://iwraw.igc.org
Contact: Marsha Freeman, Contact
Founded: 1985. **Multinational. Description:** Resource and communication center for an international network of over 5,300 individuals and groups concerned with implementation of the Convention on the Elimination of Discrimination Against Women (CEDAW). Works closely with Non Governmental Organizations (NGOs) in developing countries and with the CEDAW secretariat and the members of the

CEDAW Committee. Attends the CEDAW session and reports on the Committees work. Conducts on the status of women in countries under review each session and provide the Committee with additional information to use in its review. Provides a great deal of information to NGO activist around the world, not only on the Convention but on what others are doing and developments in law and policy concerning women. **Publications:** *Assessing the Status of Women: A Guide to Reporting Under the Convention on the Elimination of All Forms of Discrimination Against Women* (in English, French, and Spanish). Book. **Price:** $15.00 ● *From the Fourth World Conference on Women: The Beijing Declaration and Platform for Action*. **Price:** $14.00 ● *Implementing the International Right to Sexual Nondiscrimination*. Bibliography ● *IWRAW Consultation Reports*, annual. Features key points of discussion from IWRAW's annual meeting. ● *Women's Human Rights and Reproductive Rights: Capacity and Choice* (in English, Portuguese, and Spanish) ● *Women's Watch* (in English and Spanish), quarterly. Newsletter. **Price:** $25.00/year ● Also publishes books, videos, and bulletins about women's rights. **Conventions/Meetings:** annual conference and seminar, held in conjunction with Committee to Eliminate Discrimination Against Women - always in New York City.

17407 ■ Jacob Blaustein Institute for the Advancement of Human Rights (JBI)
c/o American Jewish Committee
PO Box 705
New York, NY 10150
Ph: (212)751-4000
Fax: (212)891-1450
E-mail: prf@ajc.org
URL: http://www.ajc.org
Contact: Richard Sideman, Pres.
Founded: 1971. **Description:** A specialized program of the American Jewish Committee. Works to advance human rights and to promote interreligious understanding. Seeks to increase awareness and knowledge of human rights concepts and to encourage education on international human rights in learning institutions of all levels. Supports and strengthens existing human rights efforts by providing international legal tools and strategies for human rights advocacy. Works through a network of human rights organizations, legal groups, and academic institutions. Has initiated or cosponsored activities on subjects including: an individual's right to leave and return to his/her home country; the International Covenant on Civil and Political Rights; education and human rights; incorporating the tenets of international human rights into U.S. constitutional and criminal law; civil rights in Israel; the Helsinki Process; and regional human rights. Is developing a legal guide to the UN Declaration of Religious Intolerance, the Convention on the Prevention of Genocide, and the Right to Leave and Return. Bestows Andrei Sakharov Fellowship; offers internships and grants. The institute is named for Jacob Blaustein (1892-1970), a life-long advocate of human rights, a member of the U.S. Delegation to the United Nations, and former president of the AJC. **Publications:** *The Right to Know One's Human Rights*.

17408 ■ Laogai Research Foundation (LRF)
1925 K St. NW, Ste.400
Washington, DC 20006
Ph: (202)833-8770
Fax: (202)833-6187
E-mail: laogai@laogai.org
URL: http://www.laogai.org
Contact: Mr. Harry Wu, Exec. Dir.
Founded: 1992. **Nonmembership. Description:** Collects information about China's system of forced labor camps. Publishes special investigative reports. **Publications:** *Laogai Handbook* (in Chinese and English), biennial. **Price:** $25.00 ● *LRF Newsletter* (in Chinese and English). Alternate Formats: online.

17409 ■ Magnus Hirschfeld Center for Human Rights (MHCHR)
c/o Crosswicks House
PO Box 1974
Bloomfield, NJ 07003-1974

Ph: (862)823-1767
Fax: (862)823-1767
E-mail: humanrights@post.com
URL: http://come.to/humanrights
Contact: William A.M. Courson, Exec. Dir.
Founded: 1995. **Members:** 6. **Staff:** 3. **Budget:** $750,000. **Regional Groups:** 13. **Local Groups:** 2. **National Groups:** 7. **Languages:** English, French, Spanish. **Description:** Promotes respect for the civil and human rights of the individual worldwide, with particular emphasis on protecting the rights of gay, lesbian, bisexual and transgendered people. Documents cases involving abuse of human rights; conducts legal research and educational programs and works with international organizations to address human rights abuses. Makes available legal services, with respect to legal representation of victims of human rights abuses before international and regional forum. **Libraries: Type:** open to the public. **Holdings:** 500. **Subjects:** human rights, law, international relations, gay and lesbian issues. **Committees:** Casework; Inquiry on Academic Responsibility; Inquiry on Crimes Against the Gay and Lesbian Communities; Liaison Committee. **Affiliated With:** International Gay and Lesbian Human Rights Commission; International Lesbian and Gay Association. **Also Known As:** The Hirschfeld Centre. **Publications:** *Occasional Papers*, quarterly. Newsletter. Includes copies of legal pleadings. **Circulation:** 100.

17410 ■ Middle East Children's Alliance (MECA)
901 Parker St.
Berkeley, CA 94710
Ph: (510)548-0542
Fax: (510)548-0543
E-mail: meca@mecaforpeace.org
URL: http://www.mecaforpeace.org
Multinational. Description: Works for justice in the Middle East, focusing on the occupied Palestinian territories, Israel, and occupied Iraq. Protects the rights of all people, especially children from all forms of oppression and discrimination. **Computer Services:** Information services, human rights, international law, global peace and justice and other related resources ● mailing lists, of members.

17411 ■ Mind Justice
c/o Cheryl Welsh, Pres.
915 Zaragoza St.
Davis, CA 95618
Ph: (530)758-1626
E-mail: welsh@mindjustice.org
URL: http://www.mindjustice.org
Contact: Cheryl Welsh, Pres.
Founded: 1996. **Multinational. Description:** Represents human rights group working for the rights and protections of mental integrity and freedom from new technologies and weapons which target the mind and nervous system. Uses educational, nonpolitical, research, human rights reports, public awareness, victim support, and networking programs. **Formerly:** (2004) Citizens Against Human Rights Abuse. **Conventions/Meetings:** biennial conference and board meeting ● annual Senior Management - meeting.

17412 ■ MindFreedom International (MFI)
PO Box 11284
Eugene, OR 97440
Ph: (541)345-9106
Free: (877)MAD-PRIDE
Fax: (541)345-3737
E-mail: office@mindfreedom.org
URL: http://www.mindfreedom.org
Contact: David Oaks, Dir.
Founded: 1986. **Members:** 10,000. **Membership Dues:** individual, $35 (annual). **Staff:** 2. **Regional Groups:** 2. **Local Groups:** 100. **National Groups:** 5. **Multinational. Description:** Coalition of human rights, support, and advocacy groups. Works to expose and stop psychiatric human rights violations such as involuntary drugging and use of electroshock. Supports emotional support as an alternative to psychiatric coercion. Maintains Speaker's Bureau. **Libraries: Type:** open to the public. **Holdings:** 200; books. **Subjects:** human rights in mental health.

Computer Services: Mailing lists. **Formerly:** (1992) The Support-In; (2005) Support Coalition International. **Publications:** *Dendron News*, periodic. Newspaper. **Price:** $20.00/year. ISSN: 1073-7138. **Circulation:** 20,000. **Advertising:** accepted. Alternate Formats: online. **Conventions/Meetings:** semiannual conference, includes protest of psychiatry (exhibits).

17413 ■ Mission for Establishment of Human Rights in Iran (MEHR)
PO Box 2037
Palos Verdes Peninsula, CA 90274
Ph: (310)377-4590 (818)831-4938
Fax: (310)377-3103
E-mail: mehr@mehr.org
URL: http://www.mehr.org
Contact: Mohammad Parvin PhD, Pres.
Founded: 1997. **Membership Dues:** student, $25 (annual) ● standard, $50 (annual) ● active, $25 (monthly). **Languages:** English, Persian. **Multinational. Description:** Provides better understanding of the universality of human rights. Brings the human rights issues in Iran to the attention of the world community. Encourages the Iranian-American community to participate in the democratic processes of the United States. Promotes awareness of the International Criminal Court and other international avenues to seek justice. Encourages the Iranian Community to seek the separation of religion and state and the abolition of capital punishment. **Publications:** Newsletter. Alternate Formats: online.

17414 ■ National Economic and Social Rights Initiative (NESRI)
90 John St., Ste.308
New York, NY 10038
Ph: (212)253-1710
E-mail: info@nesri.org
URL: http://www.nesri.org
Contact: Catherine Albisa, Exec. Dir.
Description: Promotes a human rights vision for the United States that ensures access to the basic resources needed for human development and civic participation. Works with organizers, policy advocates and legal organizations to incorporate a human rights perspective into their work and build human rights models tailored for the US. Provides human rights training within the social justice community. **Telecommunication Services:** electronic mail, cathy@nesri.org.

17415 ■ National Organization for Men Against Sexism (NOMAS)
PO Box 455
Louisville, CO 80027-0455
Ph: (303)666-7043
E-mail: info@nomas.org
URL: http://www.nomas.org
Contact: Moshe Rozdzial, Co-Chm.
Founded: 1982. **Membership Dues:** general, $50 (annual) ● non-profit, $15-$100 (annual) ● supporting, corporation/organization, $100 (annual). **State Groups:** 7. **Description:** Supports positive changes for men; advocates pro-feminist, gay-affirmative, anti-racist perspective. Committed to justice of social issues including class, age, religion, and physical abilities. **Divisions:** Ending Men's Violence Network; Men's Studies Association. **Task Forces:** Adult Supremacy; Bisexuality; Child Custody; Eliminating Racism; Ending Men's Violence; Homophobia; Men and Mental Health; Men and Prisons; Men and Spirituality; Men's Culture; Men's Studies; Pornography and Prostitution; Sexual Harassment. **Formerly:** (1990) National Organization for Changing Men. **Publications:** *Brother*, quarterly. Magazine. Alternate Formats: online ● Reports ● Videos. **Conventions/Meetings:** annual National Conference on Men and Masculinity.

17416 ■ OneWorld International Foundation (OWIF)
c/o OneWorld United States
3201 New Mexico Ave. NW, Ste.395
Washington, DC 20016
Ph: (202)885-2679

Fax: (202)885-1309
E-mail: us@oneworld.net
URL: http://www.oneworld.net/about
Contact: Rajendre Khargi, Chm. of Trustees
Founded: 1999. **Multinational. Description:** Aims to promote the democratic potential of the Internet; strengthen bonds, creative synergy and mutual learning across the network; and maximize network advantage.

17417 ■ Owen M. Kupferschmid Holocaust and Human Rights Project (H/HRP)
Boston Coll. Law School
885 Centre St.
Newton, MA 02459
Ph: (617)552-8285
E-mail: eggersa@bc.edu
URL: http://www.bc.edu/schools/law/services/studentorgs/hhrp
Contact: Siobhan Beasley, Pres.
Founded: 1985. **Members:** 53. **Description:** Seeks to create government accountability for contemporary human rights violations and state-sponsored abuses using the precedent of the Holocaust. Explores alternate methods of assessing accountability such as documentation and public commissions of inquiry when judicial avenues are ineffective or unavailable. Conducts research and educational programs. Maintains speaker's bureau, including annual lecture. **Libraries: Type:** reference. **Holdings:** archival material, video recordings. **Awards:** Owen M. Kupferschmid Award. **Type:** recognition. **Recipient:** for activity in areas of interest to HHRP. **Computer Services:** database. **Committees:** Political Action. **Formerly:** (1993) Holocaust/Human Rights Research Project. **Conventions/Meetings:** annual conference ● biennial international conference.

17418 ■ People's Decade of Human Rights Education (PDHRE)
211 E 43rd St., Ste.1104
New York, NY 10017
Ph: (212)749-3156
Fax: (212)666-6325
E-mail: pdhre@igc.org
URL: http://www.pdhre.org
Contact: Shulamith Koenig, Founder/Exec.Dir.
Founded: 1988. **Multinational. Description:** Develops and advances pedagogies for human rights education. Cooperates with educators, human rights experts, UN officials, advocates and activists who conceive, initiate and facilitate service projects on education in human rights for social and economic transformation. Disseminates human rights training manuals and teaching materials.

17419 ■ Physicians for Human Rights (PHR)
2 Arrow St., Ste.301
Cambridge, MA 02138
Ph: (617)301-4200
Fax: (617)301-4250
E-mail: phrusa@phrusa.org
URL: http://www.phrusa.org
Contact: Leonard Rubenstein JD, Exec. Dir.
Founded: 1986. **Members:** 3,000. **Membership Dues:** advocate, $50 (annual) ● student, $15 (annual) ● associate, $100 (annual) ● sponsor, $250 (annual) ● sustainer, $500 (annual) ● benefactor, $1,000 (annual) ● patron, $2,500 (annual). **Staff:** 24. **Budget:** $3,000,000. **Multinational. Description:** Mobilizes the health professions and enlists the support of the general public to protect and promote the human rights of all people. **Libraries: Type:** reference. **Holdings:** 1,000; archival material, audiovisuals, books, clippings, monographs, periodicals. **Subjects:** medicine, human rights, land mines, torture treatment. **Committees:** Communications; Constituency Outreach; Development; Public Policy; Research and Investigations. **Formerly:** (1987) American Committee for Human Rights. **Publications:** *Medical Action Alert*, periodic. Encourages letter writing by readers on cases of imprisoned health professionals. **Price:** included in membership dues. **Circulation:** 8,000 ● News from PHR, biweekly. Newsletter. **Price:** free for members. Alternate Formats: online ● *Record*, 3/year. Newsletter. **Price:** free for

members. ISSN: 1054-1675. **Circulation:** 8,000 ● Also publishes special reports on investigative findings. **Conventions/Meetings:** periodic meeting, continuing education courses; in conjunction with American Nurses Association, American Public Health Association, and American Psychiatric Association.

17420 ■ Polaris Project Combating Trafficking of Women and Children
PO Box 77892
Washington, DC 20013
Ph: (202)745-1001
Free: (866)878-4754
Fax: (202)745-1119
E-mail: info@polarisproject.org
URL: http://www.polarisproject.org/polarisproject
Contact: Katherine Chon, Co-Exec. Dir./Co-Founder
Founded: 2002. **Staff:** 100. **Languages:** English, Japanese. **Multinational. Description:** Works to advance the anti-trafficking movement to end the practice of modern slavery. **Awards:** FreeWeb Technical Assistant Grant. **Type:** grant. **Additional Websites:** http://HumanTrafficking.com. **Programs:** Fellowship; Japan Anti-Trafficking Campaign; National Trafficking Alert System; U.S. Research; U.S. State Policy. **Task Forces:** Greater DC Community Task Force Against Trafficking in Persons. **Publications:** Brochure. Alternate Formats: online.

17421 ■ Project on Ethnic Relations (PER)
15 Chambers St.
Princeton, NJ 08542-3707
Ph: (609)683-5666
Fax: (609)683-5888
E-mail: per@per-usa.org
URL: http://www.per-usa.org
Contact: Alfred H. Moses, Chm.
Founded: 1991. **Description:** Promotes and supports peaceful resolution of ethnic conflicts in Central and Eastern Europe and the Russian Federation. Initiates dialogues between majority and minority leaders on sensitive issues of ethnic relations. **Affiliated With:** Carnegie Corporation of New York; Pew Charitable Trusts. **Publications:** Bulletin, quarterly. Alternate Formats: online ● Also distributes bulletins.

17422 ■ Torture Abolition and Survivors Support Coalition International (TASSC)
4121 Harewood Rd., Ste.B
Washington, DC 20017
Ph: (202)529-2991
Fax: (202)529-8334
E-mail: info@tassc.org
Founded: 1998. **Multinational. Description:** Works for the abolition of torture. Protects and defends the rights of all torture survivors. Creates international communities of healing for torture survivors and their families. Influences domestic and international policy through advocacy, social action, public testimony and targeted media campaigns. Monitors human rights violations in nations where TASSC members may be at risk.

17423 ■ U.S. Council for Human Rights in the Balkans (USCHRB)
Address Unknown since 2007
Founded: 1987. **Members:** 100. **Staff:** 1. **Budget:** $50,000. **Description:** Works to promote the advancement and recognition of human rights in the Balkans, the new central Asian republics, Cyprus and other regions within the framework of the 1975 Helsinki Accords, the Universal Declaration of Human Rights, and other United Nations documents. Monitors human rights violations and disseminates information to human rights organizations, U.S. government and congressional authorities, and the media. Participates in public hearings; sponsors speakers on the culture, human rights, and religious freedom of the Turkish people around the world. Compiles statistics. Sponsors briefing and discussions. **Committees:** Anti-Defamation; Cyprus; East Turkistan (China); Public Affairs; Western Thrace Turks in Greece. **Publications:** ECHO: Quarterly Review of Human Rights. Newsletter. **Circulation:** 600. **Advertising:** not accepted ● News Bulletin,

bimonthly ● Also issues press releases. **Conventions/Meetings:** annual meeting ● symposium.

17424 ■ Uyghur American Association (UAA)
1700 Pennsylvania Ave. NW, Ste.400
Washington, DC 20006
Ph: (202)349-1496
Fax: (202)349-1491
E-mail: info@uyghuramerican.org
URL: http://uyghuramerican.org
Contact: Mr. Alim Seytoff JD, Gen. Sec.
Founded: 1998. **Membership Dues:** general, $5 (monthly). **Staff:** 3. **Budget:** $215,000. **Languages:** Chinese, English. **Multinational. Description:** Promotes improved human rights conditions for Uyghurs and other indigenous groups in East Turkistan. Supports the right of the Uyghur people to determine their political future. Monitors and exposes harmful development projects in the Uyghur region. **Computer Services:** Information services, Uyghur resources ● online services, features ● online services, message board. **Projects:** Uyghur Human Rights.

17425 ■ WITNESS
80 Hanson Pl., 5th Fl.
Brooklyn, NY 11217
Ph: (718)783-2000
Fax: (718)783-1593
E-mail: witness@witness.org
URL: http://www.witness.org
Contact: Gillian Caldwell, Exec. Dir.
Founded: 1992. **Membership Dues:** i-witness, $40 (annual) ● key witness, $100 (annual). **Staff:** 23. **Budget:** $1,200,000. **Description:** Seeks to promote international human rights through partnerships as a provider of video equipment and distributor of documentaries. **Libraries: Type:** by appointment only. **Holdings:** films, video recordings. **Subjects:** human rights. **Awards:** Ford Foundation Grant. **Type:** grant. **Affiliated With:** Physicians for Human Rights. **Publications:** Rights Alert, quarterly. Video. Alternate Formats: online.

Humanism

17426 ■ Secular Student Alliance (SSA)
PO Box 3246
Columbus, OH 43210
Free: (877)842-9474
E-mail: ssa@secularstudents.org
URL: http://www.secularstudents.org
Contact: August E. Brunsman IV, Exec. Dir.
Founded: 2000. **Membership Dues:** student, low income, $10 (annual) ● joint student, $15 (annual) ● faculty/professional university staff, $25 (annual) ● non-student, $35 (annual) ● joint academic, $40 (annual) ● joint non-student, $50 (annual) ● supporting, $100 (annual) ● sustaining, $250 (annual) ● silver sponsor, $500 (annual) ● gold sponsor, $750 (annual) ● platinum sponsor, $1,000 (annual) ● life, $1,000. **Description:** Promotes the value of scientific reason and the intellectual basis of secularism in its atheistic and humanistic manifestations to high school and college students. **Libraries: Type:** reference. **Publications:** SSA Bulletin, monthly. Includes highlights of the SSA's development and articles by students and guest columnist. Alternate Formats: online ● SSA Update. Newsletter. Consists of periodical reports on the growth and achievement of SSA. Alternate Formats: online.

Hungary

17427 ■ Hungarian Freedom Fighters Federation U.S.A. (HFFF)
Alba Regia Chapel, Memorial Park
PO Box 867
Berkeley Springs, WV 25411
Ph: (304)258-4051
Fax: (304)258-1352

E-mail: hfff@hungaria.org
URL: http://hungaria.org/hfff
Contact: Mrs. Ilona M. Gyorik, Sec.
Founded: 1958. **Members:** 350. **Membership Dues:** individual, $10 (annual) ● family, $15 (annual). **Budget:** $20,000. **Regional Groups:** 2. **State Groups:** 5. **Languages:** English, Hungarian. **Description:** Participants in the 1956 Hungarian Revolution and others interested in freedom, liberty, and national independence for Hungary. Sponsors charitable programs; maintains speakers' bureau; compiles statistics. Maintains chapel and cemetery. **Libraries: Type:** reference. **Holdings:** articles, books. **Subjects:** chapel, Hungarian history in painting, folk art in wood and iron at the chapel park, Hungarian immigrants in the U.S. **Awards:** Freedom Award. **Frequency:** periodic. **Type:** recognition. **Recipient:** for outstanding service on behalf of freedom and independence for Hungary. **Committees:** Alba Regia Chapel Memorial Park. **Also Known As:** (2001) Alba Regia Chapel Memorial Park. **Publications:** Freedom Fighter, monthly. Bulletin ● H.F.F.F. Newsletter (in English and Hungarian), quarterly. **Price:** free distribution. **Circulation:** 500. **Advertising:** accepted. **Conventions/Meetings:** semiannual conference, with book sales, Hungarian objects and gifts (exhibits) ● monthly meeting - always second Sunday.

Hunger

17428 ■ Bread for the World (BFW)
50 F St. NW, Ste.500
Washington, DC 20001
Ph: (202)639-9400
Free: (800)822-7323
Fax: (202)639-9401
E-mail: bread@bread.org
URL: http://www.bread.org
Contact: David Beckmann, Pres.
Founded: 1973. **Members:** 55,000. **Membership Dues:** individual, church, $25 (annual). **Staff:** 60. **Budget:** $4,000,000. **Description:** "Seeks justice for the world's hungry people by lobbying the nation's decision makers." Engages in research and education on policies related to hunger and development. **Libraries: Type:** reference. **Holdings:** 5,000; periodicals. **Subjects:** hunger, third world development, poverty, agriculture, social justice. **Telecommunication Services:** electronic mail, institute@bread.org. **Divisions:** Church Relations; Communications; Development; Government Relations; Organizing. **Publications:** Bread, monthly. Newsletter. Reports on current hunger-related legislation and member activities. **Price:** included in membership dues. ISSN: 1045-1005. **Circulation:** 55,000 ● Hunger Sunday, monthly. Newsletter. Contains issues of hunger and poverty in the world. Alternate Formats: online ● Offering of Letters Kit, annual. Handbook. Includes materials needed to organize letter writing campaign on BFW main legislation. **Price:** $7.00 for members; $9.00 for nonmembers. **Circulation:** 12,000. Alternate Formats: CD-ROM. **Conventions/Meetings:** biennial meeting (exhibits) ● periodic regional meeting.

17429 ■ End Hunger Network
PO Box 3032
Santa Monica, CA 90408-3032
Ph: (310)454-3716
E-mail: staff@endhunger.com
URL: http://www.endhunger.com
Contact: Michael Robitalle, Exec. Dir.
Founded: 1982. **Staff:** 3. **Budget:** $235,000. **Description:** Seeks to end hunger. Aims to: involve the media and entertainment industry in efforts to end hunger; educate the public on hunger issues; create resources and support for hunger organizations; act as a catalyst both for individual and combined community action. Works to develop coalitions of agencies, businesses, educators, service groups, and government to produce media events, programs, and audiovisual materials. Is nonpartisan and nonsectarian. **Awards:** U.S. Mayors' End Hunger Award. **Type:** recognition. **Committees:** Entertainment Industry;

Events. **Affiliated With:** Interaction/American Council for Voluntary International Action. **Conventions/ Meetings:** board meeting - 3/year.

17430 ■ The Hunger Project (THP)
15 E 26th St., No. 1401
New York, NY 10010
Ph: (212)251-9100
Free: (800)228-6691
Fax: (212)532-9785
E-mail: info@thp.org
URL: http://www.thp.org
Contact: Dr. John Coonrod PhD, VP/COO

Founded: 1977. **Staff:** 21. **Budget:** $10,200,000. **Languages:** Dutch, English, French, German, Hindi, Japanese, Portuguese, Spanish, Swedish. **Nonmembership. Multinational. Description:** In 13 countries of Asia, Africa and Latin America, implements programs that empower millions of grassroots people to achieve lasting progress in health, education, nutrition, food production, family income, environmental sustainability and the status of women. **Affiliated With:** Interaction/American Council for Voluntary International Action. **Publications:** *African Farmer* (in English and French), periodic. Magazine ● *Investor Newsletter*, monthly ● Newspaper, periodic ● Also publishes assorted informational material.

17431 ■ Institute for Food and Development Policy (IFDP)
398 60th St.
Oakland, CA 94618
Ph: (510)654-4400
Fax: (510)654-4551
E-mail: foodfirst@foodfirst.org
URL: http://www.foodfirst.org
Contact: Ms. Marilyn Borchardt, Development Dir.

Founded: 1975. **Members:** 17,000. **Membership Dues:** basic, $35 (annual). **Staff:** 12. **Budget:** $1,000,000. **Languages:** English, Spanish, Tagalog. **Description:** Research, documentation, and public educational center focusing on the social and economic causes of world hunger. Investigates the root causes of hunger and food problems in the U.S. and abroad. Aims to transform the American economic system into a democratic order where all citizens can participate in planning for the well-being of others and everyone can benefit equitably from their labor. Works to cut through popular myths about hunger using radio and television, slide/tape shows, and publications. Seeks to find appropriate responses to world hunger. Helps people weigh alternative long-term strategies to end hunger and build networks of progressive groups worldwide by contacting people in all parts of the world who are working to end hunger in their countries. **Libraries: Type:** reference; open to the public. **Holdings:** articles, books, periodicals. **Subjects:** food policy, environment, Third World development, hunger, structural adjustment, GATT, WTO, alternative agriculture, economic human rights. **Computer Services:** Mailing lists. **Also Known As:** Food First. **Publications:** *Alternatives to the Peace Corps*, semiannual. Directory. Lists volunteer opportunities in the Third World and the U.S. **Price:** $9.95 plus shipping and handling ● *Education for Action: Undergraduate and Graduate Programs that Focus on Social Change*, 3/year. Directory ● *Food First Backgrounders*, quarterly. Pamphlets ● *Food First Books* ● *Food First Development Reports and Policy Briefs*, periodic. Book ● *Food First News and Views*, quarterly. Newsletter. Covers membership activities. Provides calendar of events and research updates. **Price:** included in membership dues. ISSN: 0749-9825. **Circulation:** 17,000 ● *World Hunger: 12 Myths*. Book ● Distributes audiovisual materials.

17432 ■ International Food Policy Research Institute (IFPRI)
2033 K St. NW, 4th Fl.
Washington, DC 20006-1002
Ph: (202)862-5600
Fax: (202)467-4439
E-mail: ifpri@cgiar.org
URL: http://www.ifpri.org
Contact: Joachim von Braun, Dir. Gen.

Founded: 1974. **Staff:** 190. **Budget:** $34,000,000. **Multinational. Description:** Research center established to analyze alternative national and international strategies and policies for meeting the food needs in developing countries with a view toward reducing hunger and malnutrition. Conducts policy research on the problems of food production, consumption, and trade in developing countries. Addresses issues of increasing sustainable food production and improving the equity of its distribution. Seeks to develop new options for policymakers and to assess the efficacy of existing policies. Funded by the Consultative Group on International Agricultural Research. Agricultural Research (see separate entry). **Libraries: Type:** reference; open to the public. **Holdings:** 9,500; articles, monographs, papers, periodicals, reports. **Subjects:** food policy, water resources and management, agricultural economics, poverty reduction, nutrition/malnutrition, HIV/AIDS, food security, sustainable agriculture, natural resources management, common property, governance, trades and markets, education. **Computer Services:** Bibliographic search ● database. **Divisions:** Communications Strategy; Governance Environment; ISNAR; Markets, Trade, Institutions; Production Technology Food Consumption; 2020 Vision Initiative. **Affiliated With:** Consultative Group on International Agricultural Research. **Publications:** *Food Policy Review*, monthly. Monograph. Contains information regarding academic monograph. ● *IFPRI at a Glance*. Brochures ● *IFPRI Forum*, quarterly. Newsletters ● *Research Report and Abstract*, 5-10/year. Monograph. Contains information regarding academic monograph. ● *2020 Focus Briefs*, 1-2/year. Reports. Contains information regarding research. ● *2020 Vision Discussion Papers*, 3-4/year. Monograph. Contains information regarding policy research monograph. **Conventions/Meetings:** semimonthly Policy Seminars Series - meeting and seminar, with guest lecturers; topics on food and agricultural policy research.

17433 ■ RESULTS
750 First St. NE, Ste.1040
Washington, DC 20002
Ph: (202)783-7100
Fax: (202)783-2818
E-mail: results@results.org
URL: http://www.results.org
Contact: Barbara Wallace, Exec. Dir./Dir. of Development

Founded: 1980. **Members:** 8,000. **Membership Dues:** regular, $35 (annual). **Staff:** 13. **Budget:** $750,000. **Local Groups:** 100. **Multinational. Description:** Works to foster the political will to end world hunger. Seeks to instill the notion that individuals can make a difference toward ending world hunger and to heal the break between people and government. Identifies programs and policies that are most effective in reducing hunger and poverty, and seeks to be funded or replicated. Conducts grass roots citizen lobbying. Sponsors monthly campaigns intended to have governmental representatives step forward as leaders and spokespersons for abolishing world hunger. Conducts monthly conference call among members, hunger experts, leaders of international organizations, and members of Congress. Coordinates work with the Results Educational Fund and maintains speakers' bureau. Offers educational programs and internships. **Awards:** Cameron Duncan Media Award. **Frequency:** annual. **Type:** recognition. **Recipient:** for best print media on hunger/ poverty issues ● Congressional Leadership Award. **Frequency:** annual. **Type:** recognition. **Recipient:** for outstanding leadership in Congress. **Computer Services:** Mailing lists. **Telecommunication Services:** electronic mail, bwallace@results.org. **Funds:** Results Educational. **Publications:** *Action Sheet*, monthly ● *Integrating HIV/AIDS and TB Efforts: The Challenge for the President's AIDS Initiative*. Report. Alternate Formats: online ● *Results Quarterly*. Newsletter. **Price:** included in membership dues. Alternate Formats: online ● Annual Report, annual.

Alternate Formats: online ● Brochures. **Conventions/Meetings:** annual international conference, for volunteers.

17434 ■ World Hunger Education Service (WHES)
PO Box 29056
Washington, DC 20017
Ph: (202)269-6322
E-mail: hungernotes@verizon.net
URL: http://www.worldhunger.org
Contact: Mr. Lane Vanderslice, Managing Ed., Hunger Notes

Founded: 1976. **Members:** 570. **Membership Dues:** regular, $25 (annual) ● associate, $50 (annual). **Staff:** 2. **Budget:** $20,000. **Description:** Studies Third World development and economic justice issues like poverty and hunger issues in the United States and developing countries. **Convention/Meeting:** none. **Publications:** *Hunger Notes*, quarterly. Journal. Offers information exchange on world hunger, domestic hunger, and economic development. **Price:** $18.00 /year for individuals; $45.00 /year for institutions. ISSN: 0740-1116. **Circulation:** 500 ● *Who's Involved with Hunger: An Organization Guide for Education and Advocacy*.

17435 ■ World Hunger Year (WHY)
505 Eighth Ave., Ste.2100
New York, NY 10018
Ph: (212)629-8850
Free: (866)348-6479
Fax: (212)465-9274
E-mail: development@worldhungeryear.org
URL: http://www.worldhungeryear.org
Contact: Bill Ayres, Co-Founder/Exec. Dir.

Founded: 1975. **Staff:** 17. **Budget:** $1,200,000. **Description:** Attacks the root causes of hunger and poverty by promoting effective and innovative community-based solutions that create self-reliance economic justice and food security. **Libraries: Type:** reference. **Holdings:** 1,000. **Subjects:** hunger, poverty, food, agriculture. **Awards:** Harry Chapin Media Award. **Frequency:** annual. **Type:** recognition. **Recipient:** for outstanding coverage of hunger and poverty issues ● Harry Chapin Self-Reliance Award. **Frequency:** annual. **Type:** recognition. **Recipient:** for model grassroots group focusing on self-reliance. **Computer Services:** database, Reinvesting in America Model Programs, Policies National Hunger Clearinghouse. **Publications:** *WHY Connections*, quarterly. Newsletter. Covers and domestic issues of hunger and poverty. **Circulation:** 6,000. Alternate Formats: online ● Also publishes educational materials about food and hunger issues.

Immigration

17436 ■ American Immigration Control Foundation (AIC)
PO Box 525
222 W Main St.
Monterey, VA 24465
Ph: (540)468-2022
Fax: (540)468-2024
E-mail: aicfndn@ntelos.net
URL: http://www.aicfoundation.com
Contact: John Vinson, Pres.

Founded: 1983. **Staff:** 2. **Budget:** $500,000. **Description:** American citizens concerned about uncontrolled immigration into the U.S. Aims to educate Americans and their leaders about the need for immigration control and problems the caused by illegal immigration. Seeks to resolve current crisis caused by illegal immigration practices. Commissions research projects on immigration policies and related issues. **Libraries: Type:** reference. **Holdings:** 2,000; books, video recordings. **Subjects:** immigration control and practices, illegal immigration. **Publications:** *Immigration by Numbers*. Video. **Price:** $7.00 ● Books ● Monographs. **Conventions/Meetings:** periodic seminar.

17437 ■ Americans for Better Immigration (ABI)

c/o Roy Beck, Pres.
1601 N Kent St., Ste.1100
Arlington, VA 22209
Ph: (703)816-8820
Fax: (703)816-8824
E-mail: info@betterimmigration.com
URL: http://www.betterimmigration.com
Contact: Roy Beck, Pres.
Description: Seeks better immigration policy by lobbying Congress for reductions in immigration numbers.

17438 ■ Americans for Immigration Control (AIC)

PO Box 738
Monterey, VA 24465
Ph: (540)468-2023
Fax: (540)468-2026
E-mail: aic@immigrationcontrol.com
URL: http://www.immigrationcontrol.com
Contact: Robert Goldsborough, Pres.
Founded: 1983. **Members:** 250,000. **Budget:** $5,000,000. **Description:** Lobbies for: an increase in the budget of the U.S. Immigration and Naturalization Service in an effort to increase the effectiveness of border patrols; advocates using military forces to assist border patrol; no amnesty for illegal immigrants in the U.S; sanctions against employers who knowingly hire illegal immigrants. **Convention/Meeting:** none. **Libraries: Type:** reference. **Holdings:** archival material, video recordings. **Publications:** *America Extinguished.* Book. **Price:** $4.00 ● *Immigration Watch*, bimonthly. Newsletter.

17439 ■ Center for Immigration Studies

1522 K St. NW, Ste.820
Washington, DC 20005-1202
Ph: (202)466-8185
Fax: (202)466-8076
E-mail: center@cis.org
URL: http://www.cis.org
Founded: 1985. **Description:** Promotes the need for immigration policy with priority to broad national interest. **Awards:** Katz Award for Excellence in the Coverage of Immigration. **Frequency:** annual. **Type:** recognition. **Recipient:** to a journalist challenging the norm of immigration reporting. **Computer Services:** Online services, listservs covering immigration news worldwide. **Publications:** Papers ● Reports.

17440 ■ Emerald Isle Immigration Center (EIIC)

59-26 Woodside Ave.
Woodside, NY 11377
Ph: (718)478-5502 (718)324-3039
Fax: (718)446-3727
E-mail: siobhand@eiic.org
URL: http://www.eiic.org
Contact: Siobhan Dennehy, Exec. Dir.
Founded: 1988. **State Groups:** 25. **Local Groups:** 6. **Languages:** English, Spanish. **Description:** Immigrants, including Irish immigrants, and U.S. citizens of Irish descent. Provides immigration counseling and citizenship application advice and assistance. Provides employment and education advice and assistance, including computer training. **Computer Services:** Mailing lists. **Telecommunication Services:** electronic mail, mkerins@eiic.org. **Programs:** Citizenship. **Formerly:** (1993) Irish Immigration Reform Movement. **Publications:** *EIIC News*, quarterly. Newsletter. **Price:** free. Alternate Formats: online.

17441 ■ Federation for American Immigration Reform (FAIR)

1666 Connecticut Ave. NW, Ste.400
Washington, DC 20009
Ph: (202)328-7004
Free: (877)627-3247
Fax: (202)387-3447
E-mail: fair@fairus.org
URL: http://www.fairus.org
Contact: Nancy S. Anthony, Chair
Founded: 1979. **Members:** 70,000. **Membership Dues:** American Sycamore, $20-$99 (annual) ● Live Oak, $100-$499 (annual) ● Silver Maple, $500-$999 (annual). **Staff:** 22. **Budget:** $4,000,000. **Description:** Advocates comprehensive reform of immigration policies to conform with present-day demographic, environmental security, and labor-force realities; promotes active enforcement of laws against illegal immigration. Seeks to establish a five-year moratorium on all legal immigration, excluding spouses and minor children of U.S. citizens; enforce the prohibition of employment of illegal immigrants; establish better enforcement of U.S. borders and more efficient recording of visitors and guests in the U.S. to prevent visa abuses. Encourages diplomatic and economic efforts to help leaders in source countries deal with the overpopulation and underdevelopment that result in emigration pressures. **Libraries: Type:** reference. **Holdings:** books, video recordings. **Subjects:** immigration, population, labor economics, government. **Publications:** *FAIR Immigration Report*, monthly. Newsletter. Summarizes major developments in U.S. immigration law and policy. **Price:** included in membership dues; $20.00/year for student ● *FAIR Papers*. Monographs ● Brochures. **Conventions/Meetings:** regional meeting ● seminar.

17442 ■ National Immigration Forum

50 F St. NW, Ste.300
Washington, DC 20001
Ph: (202)347-0040
Fax: (202)347-0058
URL: http://www.immigrationforum.org
Contact: Frank Sharry, Exec. Dir.
Founded: 1982. **Members:** 200. **Staff:** 13. **Budget:** $1,100,000. **Description:** Dedicated to extending and defending America's tradition as a nation of immigrants. Supports the reunification of families, the rescue and resettlement of refugees fleeing persecution, and the equitable treatment of immigrants under the law. Encourages immigrants to become U.S. citizens and promote cooperation and understanding between immigrants and other Americans. **Libraries: Type:** reference. **Holdings:** 1,100. **Subjects:** naturalization, immigration policy, refugee. **Absorbed:** American Immigration and Citizenship Conference. **Formerly:** (1993) National Immigration Refugee Citizenship Forum. **Publications:** *A Fiscal Portrait of the Newest Americans*. Reviews the fiscal impact of the 25 million immigrants living in the U.S. Includes findings of more than two dozen national studies. **Price:** $10.00 plus shipping ● *Action Alerts*, periodic ● *Basic Immigration Facts*. Contains information on immigrants in the U.S. **Price:** free. Alternate Formats: online ● *Finding Common Ground: A Primer for Environment and Population Advocates Concerned About Immigration*. Pamphlet. Contains 16 pages discussing environmental and population issues as they relate to immigration and global migration. **Price:** $3.00 plus shipping ● *From Newcomers to New Americans: The Successful Integration of Immigrants into American Society*. Study that explodes the myth that immigrants resist integrating into our Society; examines data from 1990 US Census for several indices of assimilation. **Price:** $10.00 plus shipping ● *Houston: Diversity Works*. Magazine. Highlights the extent of cooperation between new immigrants and established residents. **Price:** $5.00 plus shipping ● *Immigration Basics 2005*. Contains information on immigrants in the U.S. **Price:** free. Alternate Formats: online ● *Immigration Policy Handbook*, annual. Contains an overview of immigration policy, facts, issues, statistics and history. **Price:** $40.00 plus shipping, non Forum Associates; $25.00 plus shipping, for Forum Associates ● *Miami: Cosmopolitan Capitol of the Americas*. Magazine. **Price:** $5.00 plus shipping ● *Together in our Differences: How Newcomers and Established Residents are Rebuilding America's Communities*. **Price:** $12.95 plus shipping. **Conventions/Meetings:** periodic regional meeting.

17443 ■ National Immigration Law Center (NILC)

3435 Wilshire Blvd., Ste.2850
Los Angeles, CA 90010
Ph: (213)639-3900
Fax: (213)639-3911
E-mail: info@nilc.org
URL: http://www.nilc.org
Contact: Linton Joaquin, Exec. Dir./Dir. of Programs
Founded: 1979. **Staff:** 22. **Languages:** English, Spanish. **Description:** Serves as a national center and clearinghouse on immigration and refugee issues for church, community, and other nonprofit organizations. Conducts class action litigation, training and policy analysis on immigration, public benefits, and employment issues for low-income immigrants; seeks to impact federal and state policies in the area of immigrants' rights; acts as advocate for the legal rights of immigrants in the U.S. Distributes information to networks of immigrant and refugee advocates. **Telecommunication Services:** electronic mail, joaquin@nilc.org. **Formerly:** (1990) National Center for Immigrants' Rights. **Publications:** *Advocate's Guide to Immigration - Related Employment Discrimination*. Directory ● *Directory of Nonprofit Agencies that Assist Persons in Immigration Matters*, annual ● *Immigrants and Welfare Resource Manual* ● *Immigrants' Rights Manual*. Newsletter ● *Immigrants' Rights Update*, 8/year. Newsletter. **Price:** $50.00/year ● *Worker's Rights Curriculum*. **Conventions/Meetings:** periodic conference.

17444 ■ National Network for Immigrant and Refugee Rights (NNIRR)

310 8th St., Ste.303
Oakland, CA 94607
Ph: (510)465-1984
Fax: (510)465-1885
E-mail: nnirr@nnirr.org
URL: http://www.nnirr.org
Contact: Catherine Tactaquin, Exec. Dir.
Founded: 1986. **Membership Dues:** regular individual, $25 (annual) ● low income individual, $15 (annual) ● fixed/unemployed, $5 (annual) ● organization (based on annual budget), $35-$200 (annual). **Description:** Represents immigrant and refugee rights advocates, organizers, and supporters. Promotes fair immigration policy and defends immigrant and refugee rights. Coordinates national campaigns and projects. Provides information, analysis, educational and organizing resources. **Libraries: Type:** reference. **Holdings:** archival material, books, clippings, periodicals. **Subjects:** employer sanctions, border issues, anti-immigrant activity, women. **Computer Services:** Information services, key updates, information alerts. **Departments:** BRIDGE Curriculum Project; International Networking; Legalization Initiative. **Publications:** *Network News*, quarterly. Newsletter. Includes updates, analyses, and articles. **Price:** $25.00 /year for institutions; $5.00/year for fixed-income; $20.00 /year for nonmembers; included in membership dues. **Circulation:** 2,500. **Conventions/Meetings:** biennial conference.

17445 ■ ProjectUSA

PO Box 15641
Washington, DC 20003
Ph: (202)543-2323
E-mail: contact@projectusa.org
URL: http://www.projectusa.org
Contact: Craig Nelson, Founder
Founded: 1999. **Description:** Advocates for ending illegal immigration and reducing legal immigration to traditional, sustainable levels. Works for a moderate and democratic immigration policy.

17446 ■ U.S. Border Control (USBC)

8180 Greensboro Dr., No. 1070
McLean, VA 22102
Ph: (703)356-6567
Fax: (202)478-0254
E-mail: info@usbc.org
URL: http://www.usbc.org
Contact: Edward I. Nelson, Chm.
Founded: 1988. **Description:** Seeks to end illegal immigration by securing the nation's borders and reforming immigration policies. **Libraries: Type:** reference. **Holdings:** archival material, articles, monographs, papers, reports. **Subjects:** immigration, birthright citizenship, amnesty for illegal aliens, social

security treaties, job statistics. **Computer Services:** Online services, forums and chat rooms ● online services, key word search of all data spanning 10 years ● online services, polls and survey data. **Publications:** *Border Alert*, periodic. Newsletter. Includes reviews and reports on America's border and immigration policies. **Price:** free for members. Alternate Formats: online; CD-ROM.

India

17447 ■ India Partners
PO Box 5470
Eugene, OR 97405-0470
Ph: (541)683-0696
Free: (877)874-6342
E-mail: info@indiapartners.org
URL: http://www.indiapartners.org
Contact: Brent Hample, Pres./CEO
Founded: 1984. **Staff:** 4. **Budget:** $400,000. **Description:** Empowers grassroots self-help programs in India through development assistance, disaster relief, training local leaders, and education. Manages mission teams, speakers, and a child sponsorship program. **Publications:** *Partners*, 8/year. Newsletter. Contains Christianity and social issues in India. Includes project information. **Price:** free to donors. **Circulation:** 1,500. **Advertising:** accepted. Alternate Formats: online. **Conventions/Meetings:** annual banquet, photo exhibit, speaker, video (exhibits).

Indigenous Peoples

17448 ■ Center for World Indigenous Studies (CWIS)
PMB 214
1001 Cooper Point Rd. SW, Ste.140
Olympia, WA 98502-1107
Ph: (360)586-0656
Fax: (253)276-0084
URL: http://www.cwis.org
Contact: Rudolph C. Ryser PhD, Chm./Exec. Dir.
Founded: 1984. **Staff:** 12. **Budget:** $450,000. **Languages:** English, Spanish. **Multinational. Description:** Research and education organization dedicated to wider understanding and appreciation of the ideas and knowledge of indigenous peoples. Fosters a better understanding between people through the publication of literature written and voiced by leading contributors from Fourth World nations. Seeks to establish cooperation between nations and to democratize relations between nations and states. Sponsors educational and research programs. **Libraries: Type:** reference. **Holdings:** archival material, articles, clippings. **Subjects:** indigenous nations and peoples, international relations, United Nations, traditional medicine, healing arts and science, Fourth World geopolitics. **Awards:** Chief George Manuel Leadership Award. **Frequency:** annual. **Type:** recognition. **Computer Services:** database ● electronic publishing ● online services, archives, seminar registration, CWIS Bookstore ● record retrieval services. **Telecommunication Services:** electronic bulletin board, The Quatro Mundista BBS. **Programs:** Education; Forum for Global Exchange; Fourth World Documentation; Fourth World Papers. **Projects:** Fourth World Atlas. **Publications:** *Anti-Indian Movement on the Tribal Frontier* ● *Fourth World Eye*. Newsletter. Alternate Formats: online ● *Fourth World Geopolitical Reader I* ● *Fourth World Journal*, semiannual. Contains essays, articles, and commentaries by leading contributors about Fourth World nations. Alternate Formats: online ● *Fourth World Papers Series*, up to 6/year. Monographs ● *Indian Self-Governance* ● *Indian War and Peace in Nicaragua* ● *Somatic Energy* ● Also publishes research papers. **Conventions/Meetings:** annual board meeting ● periodic seminar, on traditional medicine, energy medicine, collapsing studies and reemergent nations, and faculty development ● periodic seminar and workshop, with certification in Healing Arts and Sciences and 4th World Geopolitics ● periodic symposium, about cultural

property rights, community trauma, and ecotourism in Fourth World nations.

17449 ■ For Mother Earth
c/o Mark Stansbery
1101 Bryden Rd.
Columbus, OH 43205
Ph: (614)252-9255
E-mail: usa@motherearth.org
URL: http://www.motherearth.org/archive/archive/usa
Contact: Mark Stansbery, Contact
Founded: 1989. **Membership Dues:** $19. **Staff:** 2. **Budget:** $17,000. **Regional Groups:** 87. **State Groups:** 24. **Languages:** Czech, English, Flemish, German, Japanese, Korean, Russian, Somali, Spanish. **Description:** Sponsors Walk Across America and Europe to increase public awareness of injustice to indigenous people, especially Native Americans. Works to: repeal Public Law 93-531 which advocates forced relocation of the Dine (Navajo) from their homelands; end nuclear testing, which occurs on the land of indigenous persons; support the inclusion of indigenous nations into the United Nations; train community organizers; conduct educational series on interrelated issues. Offers children's services. Conducts educational, charitable, and research programs. Compiles statistics. Maintains speakers' bureau and museum; operates placement service. Affiliated with the Ohio Peace March for Global Nuclear Disarmament. **Libraries: Type:** reference. **Holdings:** archival material, artwork, audiovisuals, books, clippings, periodicals. **Subjects:** human rights, native rights, disarmament, environmental and economic justice. **Task Forces:** Finance and Budget; Site. **Publications:** *For Mother Earth Newsletter*, periodic. **Circulation:** 6,700. **Advertising:** accepted. Alternate Formats: online ● *Ohio Peace March for Global Nuclear Disarmament*. **Conventions/Meetings:** Faith and a Just Peace: Is this Possible? Education and Action Series - convention ● Faith and Colonialism Series: Education and Action - convention ● annual 510: Indigenous Peoples' Convention (exhibits) ● Indigenous Peoples Convention and Observance.

17450 ■ Fourth World Documentation Project (FWDP)
c/o Center for World Indigenous Studies
Chief George Manuel Memorial Lib.
Fourth World Documentation
1001 Cooper Point Rd. SW, Ste.140
PMB 214
Olympia, WA 98502-1107
Ph: (360)586-0656
Fax: (253)276-0084
E-mail: usaoffice@cwis.org
URL: http://www.cwis.org
Contact: Rudolph C. Ryser PhD, Exec. Dir./Chm.
Founded: 1992. **Description:** A project of the Center for World Indigenous Studies Chief George Manuel Memorial Library. Gathers documents pertaining to Fourth World nations and the global economy and international development, traditional medicine, culture including essays, position papers, government reports, treaties, and United Nations documents as an online archive. **Libraries: Type:** open to the public. **Holdings:** 3,000. **Subjects:** includes Harper photo collection; indigenous peoples culture, education, history, politics, traditional medicines. **Publications:** *Fourth World Eye*. Newsletter. Alternate Formats: online ● *Fourth World Journal*. Contains analysis, ideas and thorough scholarship that explains world events. Alternate Formats: online.

17451 ■ Hmong National Development (HND)
1112 16th St. NW, Ste.110
Washington, DC 20036
Ph: (202)463-2118
Fax: (202)463-2119
E-mail: info@hndinc.org
URL: http://www.hndlink.org
Contact: Paul Lo Esq., Pres.
Founded: 1993. **Membership Dues:** student, $10 ● individual, $20 ● organization, $100. **Description:** Ensures the full participation of the Hmong people in society. Promotes, increases and develops educational opportunities, community capacity and re-

sources for the well-being, growth and full participation of the Hmong people in society. Advocates on issues of concern to the Hmong across the country including the areas of citizenship, farming, immigration, education and welfare reform. **Programs:** Community Strengthening; Economic and Community Development; HND Educational Scholarship; Internship. **Publications:** *HNDFlash*, bimonthly. Newsletter. Alternate Formats: online ● *HNDLink*, quarterly. Newsletter. Contains feature articles and announcements of HND activities. **Price:** for members.

17452 ■ International Indian Treaty Council (IITC)
2390 Mission St., Ste.301
San Francisco, CA 94110
Ph: (415)641-4482
Fax: (415)641-1298
E-mail: iitc@treatycouncil.org
URL: http://www.treatycouncil.org
Contact: Francisco Cali, Board Pres.
Founded: 1974. **Staff:** 5. **Languages:** English, Spanish. **Multinational. Description:** Organization of traditional Indian nations formed to draw attention to Indian problems and Indian rights. Maintains NGO status with the United Nations; makes regular presentations to the United Nations Commission on Human Rights; cosponsored a conference in Geneva, Switzerland in 1981 on Indigenous People and the Land. Cooperates with other human rights organizations. **Libraries: Type:** reference. **Holdings:** archival material, artwork, audiovisuals, books, clippings, periodicals. **Subjects:** indigenous issues. **Awards:** Bill Wahpepah Memorial Human Rights Award. **Frequency:** annual. **Type:** recognition. **Publications:** *Treaty Council News*, quarterly. Newsletter. **Price:** $15.00 /year for individuals. **Conventions/Meetings:** annual conference.

17453 ■ National Haitian Society (NHS)
PO Box 3003
Garden City, NY 11531
E-mail: nhsemail@hotmail.com
URL: http://www.nationalhaitiansociety.org
Contact: Ms. Paule D. Borgella, Exec.Dir./Founder
Multinational. Description: Works to develop and implement programs that address the physical, psychological and socio-economic conditions that concern indigent Haitians in the United States and Haiti. Provides immediate medical assistance. **Telecommunication Services:** electronic mail, projects@nationalhaitiansociety.com ● electronic mail, events@nationalhaitiansociety.com. **Programs:** Haitian Cultural Awareness; Hot Lunch. **Projects:** Community Rebuilding; Computers In Classrooms; Educational Facility Development; Health; School Reform.

17454 ■ South and Meso-American Indian Rights Center (SAIIC)
PO Box 7829
Oakland, CA 94601
Ph: (510)534-4882 (510)834-4263
Fax: (510)834-4264
E-mail: indian@igc.org
URL: http://saiic.nativeweb.org
Contact: Soledad Jerez, Interim Exec. Dir.
Founded: 1983. **Members:** 1,500. **Membership Dues:** low income, $15 (annual) ● individual, Indian/social justice group, $25 (annual) ● organization/library, $40 (annual). **Staff:** 2. **Budget:** $98,000. **National Groups:** 4. **Description:** Provides information about the problems currently facing Indians in South and Central America and Mexico. (These problems include the increasing control of agriculture in the region by large corporations and the damage done to the Amazonian rainforest environment by developers and others.) Encourages interchange between Indian organizations in North, Central and South America; coordinates visits of leaders of Indian nations of Mexico, South and Central America. Broadcasts South and Central American Indian Update (radio program). **Libraries: Type:** reference. **Holdings:** 120; books, clippings, periodicals. **Subjects:** indigenous peoples, environment, human rights, Latin America. **Computer Services:** Mailing lists. **Committees:** Communications; Issues; Women's Project.

Formerly: (1985) South American Indian Information Center; (1988) South and Central American Indian Information Center; (1998) South and Meso-American Indian Information Center. Publications: *Abya Yala News* (in English and Spanish), biennial. Journal. Contains information on the indigenous movement in Mexico, Central and South America. Price: included in membership dues; $25.00 /year for nonmembers. Advertising: accepted. Also Cited As: *AYN* ● *Daughters of Abya Yala: Testimonies of Indian Women Organizing Throughout the Continent*. Book. Includes directory of Indian women organizations; statements from grass-roots Indian women leaders from South and Meso America. Price: $8.00 plus shipping and handling ● *1992 International Directory and Resource Guide for 500 Years of Resistance*. Price: $5.00 plus shipping and handling ● Film. Features land conflicts in Amazonia. ● Reports. Conventions/Meetings: periodic conference.

Integration

17455 ■ Fund for an OPEN Society
The Map Bldg.
515 Valley St., Ste.170
Maplewood, NJ 07040
Ph: (973)821-4198 (215)546-0511
Fax: (973)313-9712
E-mail: open@opensoc.org
URL: http://www.opensoc.org
Contact: Barbara Heisler Williams, Exec. Dir.
Founded: 1975. Members: 10,000. Staff: 3. Budget: $193,000. Description: Promotes integrated and balanced living patterns, one of the original purposes of the nation's fair housing law. Services include: residential mortgage brokering with loan origination discounts, home purchase readiness counseling, Pro-Integrative Consultation (PIC) program for local communities, and education and advocacy for integration. Seeks the support of local institutions, businesses, and community groups. Provides mortgages below the prevailing costs. Convention/Meeting: none. Telecommunication Services: electronic mail, bhw@opensoc.org. Absorbed: Sponsors of Open Housing Investment. Also Known As: OPEN Mortgage. Publications: *OPEN Forum*, annual. Newsletter. Price: free. Alternate Formats: online ● Pamphlets.

17456 ■ National Association for Neighborhood Schools (NANS)
PO Box 14883
Columbus, OH 43214
Ph: (216)398-4667
E-mail: membership@nans.org
URL: http://www.nans.org
Contact: Joyce Haws, Dir. of Communication
Founded: 1976. Members: 4,500. Membership Dues: individual, $10 (annual) ● family, $15 (annual) ● organization, $100 (annual). State Groups: 12. Description: Organizations and activists in 38 states opposed to forced busing for racial balance or other diversity goals in public schools. Seeks to "bring an end to racial control and forced busing of school children and to oppose harmful federal interference in the schools" by encouraging Congress to use its power under the Constitution to challenge the authority of the judiciary and the bureaucracy. Strives to limit specialty schools, which "are designed and located strategically for the purpose of eliminating the opportunity of receiving quality education in one's own neighborhood." Works for school systems under court orders to seek unitary status; advocates modifications which would provide the option of a neighborhood school without racial quotas. Lobbies and distributes information on the busing issue; provides testimony before congressional committees. Compiles data on the effects of busing throughout the U.S. Maintains Speaker's Bureau. Libraries: Type: reference. Subjects: desegregation, integration, racial quotas, education, judicial control, magnet schools, schools, neighborhood schools, goals 2000, outcome-based education, controlled choice, diversity. Telecommunication Services: electronic mail,

joyce_haws@nans.org. Publications: Brochures ● Bulletin, quarterly. Includes legislative updates, information on trends, and specific news of impacted cities. Price: included in membership dues. Circulation: 3,500 ● Also publishes news releases and alerts. Conventions/Meetings: annual conference and board meeting.

Intelligence

17457 ■ Consortium for the Study of Intelligence (CSI)
1730 Rhode Island Ave. NW, Ste.500
Washington, DC 20036-3117
E-mail: info@intelligenceconsortium.org
URL: http://www.intelligenceconsortium.org
Contact: Dr. Richard H. Shultz Jr., Dir. of Research
Founded: 1979. Staff: 4. Description: Represents political scientists, historians, sociologists, and international affairs specialists who promote research and instruction on intelligence. Serves as a nongovernmental resource center for academicians, public policy experts, the media, and government officials interested in the subject of intelligence. Conducts colloquia with academicians and intelligence officers to examine U.S. intelligence requirements; offers courses on intelligence for college teachers; a project of National Strategy Information Center (see separate entry). Publications: *Comparing Foreign Intelligence: The U.S., The USSR, UK, and the Third World* ● *Intelligence Requirements for the 1980s* ● *Intelligence Requirements for the 1990s*.

17458 ■ Nathan Hale Institute (NHI)
24 Harbor River Cir.
PMB 223
St. Helena Island, SC 29920-0192
Ph: (843)838-0191
Fax: (843)838-0192
E-mail: sulc@islc.net
URL: http://www.nathanhaleinstitute.org
Contact: Lawrence B. Sulc, Pres.
Founded: 1977. Staff: 2. Nonmembership. Description: Seeks to increase public awareness of the "need for a strong intelligence community" and to stimulate scholarly pursuit of intelligence-related issues. Conducts research on domestic and foreign intelligence, particularly counterterrorism and the role of intelligence in a free society. Maintains speakers' bureau. Conducts interviews and briefings; provides counseling. Named for Nathan Hale (1755-76), U.S. intelligence officer famed for his comment: I only regret that I have but one life to lose for my country. Libraries: Type: reference. Awards: Type: scholarship. Computer Services: Mailing lists. Publications: *Active Measures, Quiet War, and Two Socialist Revolutions*. Price: $10.00 ● *Conference on Spetsnaz, Soviet Special Purpose Forces*. Out of print; available in photocopy form. Price: $3.00 ● *Deception, a Tool of Soviet Foreign Policy*. Price: $8.00 ● *Fifteen Years of Espionage*. Out of print; available in photocopy form. Price: $2.00 ● *Intelligence in the War of Independence*. Reprint of CIA publication; available in photocopy form. ● *Joint Committee on Intelligence? Yes No*. Price: $2.50 ● *The KGB and the United Nations*. Out of print; available in photocopy form. Price: $2.50 ● *Nathan Hale Institute Newsletter*, periodic. Price: free; contributions welcome. Advertising: accepted ● *1984—Year of the Terrorist?*. Out of print; available in photocopy form. Price: $2.00 ● *The President's Foreign Intelligence Advisory Board*. Pamphlet. Out of print; available in photocopy form. ● *Soviet Active Measures in the United States*. Reprint of FBI report; available in photocopy form. ● *The Terrorist Underground in the United States*. Out of print; available in photocopy form. Price: $5.00 ● *U.S. Counter-intelligence Today*. Out of print; available in photocopy form. Price: $9.95 ● *U.S. Intelligence Requirement for the Late 1980s*. Price: $2.00 ● *Who Is Tracking the Terrorists?*. Pamphlet. Out of print; available in photocopy form. Price: $3.00 ● *The World Peace Council and Soviet Active Measures*. Pamphlet. Price: $5.00 ● Pamphlets.

International Affairs

17459 ■ EastWest Institute (EWI)
700 Broadway, 2nd Fl.
New York, NY 10003
Ph: (212)824-4100 (212)824-4110
Fax: (212)824-4149
E-mail: iews@iews.org
URL: http://www.ewi.info
Contact: John Edwin Mroz, Pres./CEO
Founded: 1981. Multinational. Description: Works to resolve tensions and conflict that threatens geopolitical stability while building democracy, free enterprise and prosperity in Central and Eastern Europe, Russia and other areas of Eurasia. Telecommunication Services: electronic mail, newyork@ewi.info. Programs: Centre for Border Cooperation; Global Security; Leadership; Middle East Bridges; Private Sector Initiative. Formerly: Institute for East West Studies. Publications: *Conference Papers* ● *Policy Briefs* ● *Toward the Common Good: Building a New U.S.-Russian Relationship*. Book ● Reports.

17460 ■ Henry L. Stimson Center
1111 19th St. NW, Ste.1200
Washington, DC 20036
Ph: (202)223-5956
Fax: (202)238-9604
E-mail: info@stimson.org
URL: http://www.stimson.org
Contact: Ellen Laipson, Pres./CEO
Founded: 1989. Description: Works to enhance international peace and security. Publications: *Following the Money: The Bush Administration FY03 Budget Request and Current Funding for Selected Defense, State, and Energy Department Programs*. Report. Analyzes key areas of both the Bush Administration's fiscal year 2003 (FY03) and the FY02 (March) supplemental request. Alternate Formats: online ● *Report 45: Missile Defense and Asian Security*. Contains information on NMD's potential effect upon the China-South Asia nuclear balance. Alternate Formats: online ● *Report 46: The Impact of US Ballistic Missile Defenses on Southern Asia*. Contains information on the possible consequences of prospective US deployment of theater and national ballistic missile defenses. ● *Security and Peace Support in Afghanistan: Analysis and Short to Medium Term Options*. Report. Alternate Formats: online.

17461 ■ International Forum on Globalization (IFG)
1009 Gen. Kennedy Ave., No. 2
San Francisco, CA 94129
Ph: (415)561-7650
Fax: (415)561-7651
E-mail: ifg@ifg.org
URL: http://www.ifg.org
Contact: Ms. Debi Barker, Co-Dir.
Founded: 1994. Membership Dues: basic, $25 (annual) ● friend, $50 (annual) ● patron, $100 (annual) ● benefactor, $500 (annual) ● contributing, $1,000 (annual) ● group of 100, $2,500 (triennial). Staff: 8. Description: Works to expose multiple effects of economic globalization; and seeks to reverse the globalization process and ensure long-term ecological stability. Committees: Corporations; Environmental Impacts of Economic Globalization; Globalization of Water. Programs: Food and Agriculture; Technology and Globalization. Projects: Indigenous Peoples and Globalization. Working Groups: Forest and Globalization. Publications: *Debate: Economic Globalization and the WTO*. Video. Price: $15.00 for members; $18.00 for nonmembers ● *Does Globalization Help the Poor? A Special Report*. Examines the impact of economic globalization on poverty. Price: $8.00 for members; $12.00 for nonmembers ● *Free Trade Area of the Americas: The Threat to Social Programs, Environmental Sustainability & Social Justice*. Booklet. Price: $2.00 ● *Invisible Government: The World Trade Organization*. Price: $5.00 for members; $10.00 for nonmembers ● *Paradigm Wars: Indigenous Peoples' Resistance to Economic Globalization*. Report. Price: $30.00 in U.S. ● Newsletter.

Price: included in membership dues ● Audiotapes.
Price: $10.00 for members; $12.00 for nonmembers.

International Development

17462 ■ African Development Foundation (ADF)
1400 I St. NW, 10th Fl.
Washington, DC 20005-2208
Ph: (202)673-3916
Fax: (202)673-3810
E-mail: info@adf.gov
URL: http://www.adf.gov
Contact: Nathaniel Fields, VP/CEO, Africa Operations
Founded: 1980. **Description:** Individuals and organizations. Seeks to advance social, economic, and community development in Africa. Promotes active participation of indigenous people in development projects. Coordinates community development programs throughout Africa. **Publications:** Report, semiannual. Alternate Formats: online.

17463 ■ Agri-Energy Roundtable (AER)
1312 18th St. NW, Ste.300
Washington, DC 20036
Ph: (202)887-0528 (202)887-0238
Fax: (202)887-9178
E-mail: agenergy@aol.com
URL: http://www.agribusinesscouncil.org/aer.htm
Contact: Nicholas E. Hollis, Exec. Dir.
Founded: 1980. **Members:** 200. **Staff:** 3. **Budget:** $200. **Description:** International association that includes oil company executives and leaders of international agribusinesses. Serves as an information clearinghouse to improve dialogue on cooperative energy-agricultural development among the industrialized and developing nations. Attempts to bridge the gap on food and energy issues through cooperation between the oil exporting countries and western technology in the private sector. Sponsors trade missions. **Awards:** World Food Policy Award. **Type:** recognition. **Task Forces:** Energy and Natural Resources; Food Processing/Storage/Distribution; International Finance; New Food and Energy Technologies; Technology Transfer and Management. **Affiliated With:** Agribusiness Council. **Publications:** Agri-Energy Report, quarterly. Newsletter ● Agri-Enterprise in Development: New Leadership and Technology for Food Security. Book ● Beyond Food and Energy Security: New Agribusiness Markets and Technologies. Book ● Conference Proceedings, annual ● Food and Energy Security: Managing the New Technologies. Book ● Managing Agro-Economic Peacekeeping: Trade and Development Realities for Food Security. Book ● Regional Africa Bulletin ● Books. **Conventions/Meetings:** symposium ● workshop, to foster establishment of autonomous agribusiness associations.

17464 ■ Alliance of Small Island States (AOSIS)
c/o Dr. Julian R. Hunte, Chm.
800 Second Ave., Ste.910
New York, NY 10017
Ph: (212)697-9361
Fax: (212)599-0505
E-mail: slumission@aol.com
URL: http://www.sidsnet.org/aosis
Contact: Dr. Julian R. Hunte, Chm.
Languages: English, French. **Description:** Representatives of Small Island and coastal states. Promotes appropriate and sustainable economic and social development in member countries. Serves as a clearinghouse on island and coastal states; represents members' interests before the United Nations and international trade and development organizations.

17465 ■ Association for the Advancement of Policy, Research and Development in the Third World (AAPRDTW)
Address Unknown since 2007
Founded: 1981. **Members:** 3,450. **Staff:** 10. **Regional Groups:** 7. **State Groups:** 100. **National**

Groups: 10. **Description:** Scholars; private industries; international, national, and local government personnel; interested individuals. Promotes science, technology, and development through exchange and generation of practical solutions to problems facing governments in developing countries. Encourages the effective and improved utilization of resources, including human development and planning institutions. Advocates ethical standards and supports interest in government research and development policies and programs. Facilitates the exchange of experience and ideas between professionals in developing countries. Disseminates information on policy management practices and current research in the field. Compiles statistics; offers consultations; organizes research symposia. Provides placement service, charitable program, and speakers' bureau. Maintains 31 committees and 7 regional sections. **Libraries: Type:** reference. **Holdings:** 2,000; archival material. **Subjects:** science, technology, economic development. **Awards:** International Service Award. **Frequency:** annual. **Type:** recognition. **Recipient:** for outstanding leadership, scholarship, professional service, and community work. **Computer Services:** database. **Publications:** Basic Principles for the Equal Treatment and Protection of Overseas Scholars, periodic. **Price:** $20.00. **Advertising:** not accepted ● Comparative Development and African Administration. Book ● Credential: Journal of Science, Technology and International Development ● Credentials: International Journal of Science, Research and Development, annual. Contains reviews of contemporary development issues and information on research practices and funding for professional institutions. **Price:** included in membership dues; $30.00/year for nonmembers. **Advertising:** accepted. Alternate Formats: microform ● Development Futures: The Coming Challenges. Book ● International Science and Technology. Book ● Perspectives in International Development, and Science, Technology, and Development. Book ● Membership Directory, periodic. **Conventions/Meetings:** competition ● semiannual conference (exhibits) ● annual regional meeting.

17466 ■ Association on Third World Affairs (ATWA)
1629 K St. NW
Washington, DC 20036
Ph: (202)973-0157 (202)234-3201
Fax: (202)775-7465
E-mail: info@atwa.org
Contact: Dr. Lorna Hahn, Exec. Dir.
Founded: 1967. **Members:** 1,000. **Membership Dues:** student, $30 ● individual, $30 ● embassy/corporate, $250. **Staff:** 4. **Budget:** $24,000. **Languages:** English, French. **Multinational. Description:** Diplomats, development specialists, lawyers, academicians, government officials, and government representatives. Promotes cooperation between Americans and groups in developing countries. Provides consultative services, guest speakers, and information. **Libraries: Type:** reference. **Holdings:** 400; books, periodicals. **Subjects:** politics, diplomacy. **Awards: Type:** recognition. **Computer Services:** database. **Publications:** Capitol Hill Conference Report, quarterly. Monographs. Contains reports of Capitol Hill conferences. **Price:** $10.00. **Circulation:** 500 ● Reports. **Conventions/Meetings:** periodic Capitol Hill Conferences on Foreign Policy - conference and seminar, for ambassadors and congressmen and concerned professionals - 4/year ● periodic seminar.

17467 ■ Association of Third World Studies (ATWS)
c/o Dr. William D. Pederson, Exec. Dir.
Intl. Lincoln Center for Amer. Stud.
Louisiana State Univ.
Shreveport, LA 71115-2301
Ph: (318)797-5349 (318)797-5158
Fax: (318)795-4203
E-mail: wpederso@lsus.edu
URL: http://itc.gsw.edu/atws
Contact: Dr. William D. Pederson, Exec. Dir.
Founded: 1983. **Members:** 600. **Membership Dues:** student/Third World resident, $30 (annual) ● regular,

$60 (annual) ● husband and wife, $90 (annual) ● sustainer, $75 (annual) ● patron, $100 (annual) ● Third World resident (life), $150 ● individual (life), $400 ● husband and wife (life), $600 ● institutional (life), $1,000. **Staff:** 1. **National Groups:** 3. **Multinational. Description:** Development specialists and other individuals interested in economic, political and social issues affecting Third World countries. Seeks to increase public awareness of Third World cultures and socioeconomic problems. Promotes Western interest in the developing countries. Conducts educational programs. **Awards:** ATWS Presidential Award. **Frequency:** annual. **Type:** scholarship. **Recipient:** for outstanding achievement in promoting Third World studies ● Cecil B. Currey Book Award. **Frequency:** annual. **Type:** scholarship. **Recipient:** for outstanding book published by an ATWS member ● Lawrence D. Reddick Memorial Award. **Frequency:** annual. **Type:** scholarship. **Recipient:** for a scholar who publishes the best article on Africa in Journal of Third World Studies ● Mario D. Zamora Memorial Award for Excellence in Scholarship on the Third World. **Frequency:** annual. **Type:** scholarship. **Recipient:** for a scholar who publishes the best article in Journal of Third World Studies. **Publications:** ATWS Conference Proceedings, annual. Contains papers presented at the ATWS annual conference. **Price:** $20.00/issue ● ATWS Membership Brochure. **Price:** free ● Journal of Third World Studies, semiannual. Analyzes Third World problems and issues; includes refereed articles, book reviews, and essays. **Price:** included in membership dues; $45.00 /year for nonmembers; $23.00/copy for nonmembers. ISSN: 8755-3449. **Circulation:** 900. **Advertising:** accepted ● JTWS Subscription Order Brochure. **Price:** free ● Newsletter, 3/year. **Price:** free. **Circulation:** 900. Alternate Formats: online. **Conventions/Meetings:** annual conference ● periodic seminar.

17468 ■ Citizens Development Corps (CDC)
1726 M St. NW, Ste.1100
Washington, DC 20036
Ph: (202)872-0933
Free: (800)394-1945
Fax: (202)872-0923
E-mail: info@cdc.org
URL: http://www.cdc.org
Contact: Michael A. Levett, Pres./CEO
Founded: 1990. **Staff:** 30. **Description:** Volunteer organization that works to mobilize U.S. private sector resources to provide assistance to Russia, Ukraine, Central Europe, and developing countries in other regions in building democratic institutions and free market economies. Helps match senior-level American business people with small and medium-sized businesses and business-support institutions seeking specific expertise. Provides assistance to business, municipal, nonprofit, or university management, maintains volunteer registry. **Computer Services:** database. **Programs:** Citizens Volunteer; Enterprise and Economic Development. **Publications:** CDC Update, quarterly. Newsletter. Contains six pages featuring volunteer and organizational news. **Price:** free for members. **Circulation:** 5,500. Alternate Formats: online ● The Corps Report, semimonthly. Newsletter. Alternate Formats: online.

17469 ■ Commission on International Programs (CIA)
c/o National Association of State Universities and Land-Grant Colleges
1307 New York Ave. NW, Ste.400
Washington, DC 20005-4701
Ph: (202)478-6040
Fax: (202)478-6046
E-mail: nancy.zimpher@uc.edu
URL: http://www.nasulgc.org
Contact: Dr. Nancy L. Zimpher, Pres.
Founded: 1962. **Members:** 175. **Staff:** 2. **Description:** Established by the National Association of State Universities and Land-Grant Colleges (see separate entry) to aid in their work of assisting less developed countries in cooperation with the Agency for International Development and the U.S. Department of Agriculture. Seeks to develop a strong partnership between public universities and federal and state

governments. Serves as a forum for discussion and resolution of major issues affecting public higher education. **Awards:** Michael P. Malone International Leadership Award. **Frequency:** annual. **Type:** recognition. **Recipient:** for outstanding contributions. **Boards:** Advisory. **Committees:** Standing. **Subcommittees:** Academic Affairs; Federal, State Private Sector Relations; International Development; International Exchange. **Task Forces:** International Education. **Affiliated With:** National Association of State Universities and Land-Grant Colleges. **Formerly:** International Rural Development Office; Division of International Affairs; (1976) International Program Office; (1977) International Programs and Studies Office; (2002) Commission on International Affairs. **Publications:** Contributes articles to *Newsline*, the newsletter of the National Association of State Universities and Land-Grant Colleges. **Conventions/Meetings:** annual conference (exhibits) - always November.

17470 ■ Consultative Group to Assist the Poor (CGAP)
900 19th St. NW, Ste.300
Washington, DC 20006
Ph: (202)473-9594
Fax: (202)522-3744
E-mail: cgap@worldbank.org
URL: http://www.cgap.org
Contact: Elizabeth Littlefield, Dir./CEO

Members: 34. **Staff:** 23. **Budget:** $10,000,000. **Multinational. Description:** Creates permanent financial services for the poor on a large scale or in microfinance level. Serves as a resource center for the microfinance industry, where it incubates and supports new ideas, innovative products, cutting edge technologies, novel mechanisms for delivering financial services, and concrete solutions to the challenges of expanding microfinance. **Libraries: Type:** reference. **Holdings:** articles, papers, reports. **Subjects:** finance, industry surveys, commercialization, donor issues, savings. **Awards:** Financial Transparency Award. **Frequency:** annual. **Type:** monetary. **Recipient:** for microfinance providers who have presented a comprehensive annual financial report ● Pro-Poor Innovation Challenge Award. **Frequency:** annual. **Type:** recognition. **Recipient:** for organizations who presented promising ideas from all over the world based on depth of outreach and innovation in client identification. **Computer Services:** Information services, microfinance, policy frameworks, poverty outreach ● mailing lists, of members ● online services, links to financial resources. **Committees:** Investment. **Special Interest Groups:** Consultative Group of Member Donors. **Working Groups:** Budget and Administrative Team; Communications Team; Donor Team; End Client Team; Financial Institutions Team; Industry Team. **Publications:** *CGAP III Strategy*. Report. Serves as a guide for the organization in the next four years. ● *Financial Institutions with a Double Bottom Line: Implications for the Future of Microfinance*. Paper. Features survey results of the global outreach of institutions that extend financial services downward. Alternate Formats: online ● *Interest Rate Ceilings and Microfinance: The Story So Far*. Paper. Outlines the rationale for higher microcredit interest rates and the impact of interest rate ceilings on microfinance clients. Alternate Formats: online ● *Key Principles of Microfinance*. Pamphlet. Alternate Formats: online ● Annual Report, annual. Alternate Formats: online.

17471 ■ Counterpart - United States Office
1200 18th St. NW, Ste.1100
Washington, DC 20036-2561
Ph: (202)296-9676
Fax: (202)296-9679
E-mail: communications@counterpart.org
URL: http://www.counterpart.org
Contact: Lelei LeLaulu, Pres./CEO

Description: Promotes sustainable and appropriate global economic development. Serves as a clearinghouse on USAID-sponsored programs worldwide. Gathers and disseminates information on economic development programs; provides technical assistance to selected projects. **Programs:** Civil Society; Community and Humanitarian Assistance. **Projects:** Sri Lanka Redevelopment. **Publications:** Annual Report, annual. Alternate Formats: online.

17472 ■ Development Group for Alternative Policies (Development GAP)
927 15th St. NW, 4th Fl.
Washington, DC 20005
Ph: (202)898-1566
Fax: (202)898-1612
E-mail: dgap@developmentgap.org
URL: http://www.developmentgap.org
Contact: Stephen Hellinger, Pres.

Founded: 1977. **Staff:** 6. **Budget:** $500,000. **Languages:** English, Spanish. **Nonmembership. Multinational. Description:** Coordinates global and national civil-society networks challenging trade and economic adjustment policies imposed by the World Bank, International Monetary Fund and U.S. Government. Assists in the development and promotion of alternative policies that reflect local realities and priorities. **Libraries: Type:** reference. **Holdings:** books, clippings, monographs, periodicals. **Subjects:** structural adjustment.

17473 ■ East Meets West Foundation (EMW)
PO Box 29292
Oakland, CA 94604
Ph: (510)763-7045
Fax: (510)763-6545
E-mail: info@eastmeetswest.org
URL: http://www.eastmeetswest.org
Contact: Peter A. Singer MD, Chm.

Founded: 1988. **Description:** Development organizations. Promotes appropriate and sustainable economic and community development in Eastern Asia and the Pacific Basin. Coordinates members' activities; formulates model development strategies. **Publications:** *EMW Newsletter*, quarterly. Features the latest breaking news, exclusive photos and stories from the association. **Price:** $2.00 back issues, plus shipping and handling ● *Reach Vietnam*, quarterly. Magazine. Contains information on the associations' activities. **Price:** $25.00/year.

17474 ■ Financial Services Volunteer Corps (FSVC)
800 3rd Ave., 11th Fl.
New York, NY 10022
Ph: (212)771-1400
Fax: (212)421-2162
E-mail: fsvc_mail@fsvc.org
URL: http://www.fsvc.org
Contact: J. Andrew Spindler, Pres./CEO

Founded: 1990. **Members:** 3. **Staff:** 40. **Budget:** $5,000,000. **Languages:** Albanian, Czech, English, Hungarian, Indonesian, Polish, Romanian, Russian, Slovak, Ukrainian. **Multinational. Description:** Assists emerging democracies in establishing financial systems. Arranges consultations with industry experts to aid countries in financial development.

17475 ■ Floresta U.S.A.
4903 Morena Blvd., Ste.1215
San Diego, CA 92117
Ph: (858)274-3718
Free: (800)633-5319
Fax: (858)274-3728
E-mail: floresta@xc.org
URL: http://www.floresta.org
Contact: Scott C. Sabin, Exec. Dir.

Founded: 1984. **Staff:** 6. **Budget:** $323,000. **Multinational. Description:** Christians united for Third World economic development and environmental protection. Promotes establishment of tree farms and other locally administered agroforestry enterprises as a means to economic development and self-sufficiency in the developing world. Provides seedlings and technical and financial assistance to agroforestry enterprises; supports reforestation initiatives. **Publications:** *Floresta*, annual. Annual Report. Alternate Formats: online ● Newsletter. Alternate Formats: online.

17476 ■ Global Policy Forum (GPF)
777 UN Plz., Ste.3D
New York, NY 10017
Ph: (212)557-3161
Fax: (212)557-3165
E-mail: gpf@globalpolicy.org
URL: http://www.globalpolicy.org
Contact: Mr. James A. Paul, Exec. Dir.

Founded: 1993. **Membership Dues:** ordinary, $35 (annual) ● student, $10 (annual) ● donor, $100 (annual) ● friend, $250 (annual) ● associate, $500 (annual) ● supporter, $1,000 (annual) ● sustainer, $2,500 (annual) ● major sponsor, $10,000 (annual) ● leader, $25,000 (annual) ● benefactor, $50,000 (annual). **Staff:** 3. **Budget:** $350,000. **Description:** Individuals and organizations with an interest in policy making at the United Nations. Promotes development of "a more open, accountable and democratic global policy process." Seeks to accomplish its mission through informational and advocacy work. Works with partners around the world to strengthen international law and create a more equitable and sustainable global society. Uses a holistic approach, linking peace and security with economic justice and human development, and places a heavy emphasis on networking to build broad coalitions for research, action and advocacy. Puts its energy into well-focused and unique programs in which the organization has a special analytical and organizational edge. **Computer Services:** Mailing lists. **Publications:** Newsletter, weekly. Alternate Formats: online.

17477 ■ Institute for Transportation and Development Policy (ITDP)
127 W 26th St., Ste.1002
New York, NY 10001
Ph: (212)629-8001
Fax: (212)629-8033
E-mail: mobility@itdp.org
URL: http://www.itdp.org
Contact: Dr. Walter Hook, Exec. Dir.

Founded: 1985. **Members:** 3,000. **Membership Dues:** associate, $25 (annual) ● friend, $50 (annual) ● donor, $100 (annual) ● sponsor, $250 (annual) ● patron, $500 (annual) ● benefactor, $1,000 (annual) ● sustaining, $2,500 (annual). **Staff:** 5. **Budget:** $500,000. **Description:** Promotes the use of economically and environmentally sustainable transportation policies and programs in developing countries; promotes non-motorized forms of transportation such as bikes and carts. Organizes Bikes Not Bombs, Bikes for Africa, Mobility Haiti, and Transportation Alternatives, which, in conjunction with other humanitarian organizations, encourages private voluntary agencies, governmental organizations, and international lending institutions to adopt policies benefiting and award funding to projects promoting use of non-motorized forms of transportation. Conducts research and works to educate policymakers and the public about transportation problems in developing countries, as well as opportunities and solutions. Fosters development of bicycle assembly and repair workshops and bicycle mechanic training programs in developing countries. Maintains speakers' bureau. **Libraries: Type:** reference; lending; open to the public. **Holdings:** 10,000; audiovisuals, books, clippings, periodicals. **Subjects:** transportation policy, urban planning, bicycling. **Computer Services:** Mailing lists. **Affiliated With:** Bikes Not Bombs. **Publications:** *Informart*, annual. Lists publications that address alternative non-motorized transportation issues. **Price:** free ● *Sustainable Transport*, annual. Magazine. **Price:** free; available upon request. Alternate Formats: online ● Annual Report. Alternate Formats: online. **Conventions/Meetings:** annual meeting.

17478 ■ International Bank for Reconstruction and Development (IBRD)
1818 H St. NW
Washington, DC 20433
Ph: (202)473-1000
Fax: (202)477-6391
E-mail: pic@worldbank.org
URL: http://www.worldbank.org
Contact: Mr. Paul Wolfowitz, Pres.

Founded: 1945. **Description:** Member governments of the International Monetary Fund. Assists the reconstruction and productive growth of Third World nations by facilitating the investment of capital in development projects and activities. Encourages foreign investment and the balanced growth of international trade. Provides financial aid for specified programs. Works in conjunction with the International Development Association and the International Finance Corporation to carry out policies and strategies of the World Bank. **Also Known As:** (2006) The World Bank.

17479 ■ International Development Association (IDA)
The World Bank
1818 H St. NW
Washington, DC 20433
Ph: (202)473-1000
Fax: (202)477-6391
URL: http://www.worldbank.org
Contact: Paul Wolfowitz, Pres.
Founded: 1960. **Members:** 134. **Multinational. Description:** Functional member of the World Bank (see separate entry); membership is open to countries of the World Bank. Promotes the economic development of the World Bank's poorer member countries by extending credits on easier terms than are normally available. Makes loans for projects aimed at strengthening the economies of developing countries in Asia, the Middle East, Africa, and the Western Hemisphere. Provides economic advice. **Publications:** *Annual Report: Bank/IDA-IFC*, annual ● *World Bank Atlas*, annual. Book. Provides easy-to-read colorful world maps, tables, and graphs highlighting key social, economic, and environmental data for 208 countries. ● *World Development Report*, annual. Contains information on the economic and social state of the world. **Price:** $26.00. **Conventions/ Meetings:** annual meeting.

17480 ■ Pacific Basin Development Council (PBDC)
711 Kapiolana Blvd., Ste.1075
Honolulu, HI 96813-5214
Ph: (808)596-7229
Fax: (808)596-7249
E-mail: pbdc@elele.peacesat.hawaii.edu
Contact: Carolyn K. Imamura, Exec. Dir.
Founded: 1980. **Members:** 3. **Budget:** $80,000. **Regional Groups:** 1. **Description:** Governors of Guam, Commonwealth of the Northern Mariana Islands, American Samoa, and Hawaii. Seeks to: identify economic development needs in the Pacific Basin; provide for research efforts to address developmental issues. Fosters economic cooperation among member entities, the U.S. government, and the private sector; promotes collective actions that improve the quality of life in the region. Compiles statistics; operates speakers' bureau. **Libraries: Type:** reference. **Holdings:** 800; books, monographs. **Computer Services:** database, Pacific Basin. **Conventions/ Meetings:** annual meeting.

17481 ■ Partners for Democratic Change (PDC)
2121 K St. NW, Ste.700
Washington, DC 20037
Ph: (202)942-2166
Fax: (202)785-5886
E-mail: partners@partnersglobal.org
URL: http://www.partnersglobal.org
Contact: Raymond Shonholtz, Pres.
Founded: 1989. **Staff:** 10. **Budget:** $1,800,000. **Regional Groups:** 11. **Multinational. Description:** Works to advance the democratic management of conflict and the building of civil society in transitioning democracies through developing indigenous capacities to address in-country conflicts. Provides training services to government ministries, local government officials, environmental groups, schools, and private enterprises. Offers third-party facilitation for meetings, disputes, and strategic planning sessions. **Convention/Meeting:** none. **Libraries: Type:** reference. **Holdings:** articles, books, clippings, periodicals. **Subjects:** conflict resolution. **Also Known As:** Partners; PDCI. **Publications:** *PDC International Quarterly*, biennial. Newsletter. Contains

information on events and training at all centers. **Price:** free. **Alternate Formats:** online.

17482 ■ Pax World Service (PWS)
c/o Mercy Corps.
Dept. Pax
PO Box 2669
Portland, OR 97208-2669
Ph: (503)796-6800 (202)463-0486
Free: (800)292-3355
E-mail: info@paxworld.org
URL: http://www.paxworld.org
Contact: Dr. Landrum Bolling, Pres.
Founded: 1971. **Staff:** 2,000. **Budget:** $130,000,000. **National Groups:** 35. **Nonmembership. Multinational. Description:** Promotes peaceful resolution of conflict, strengthened civil society, sustainable development, promotion of small business, and humanitarian relief and development. **Affiliated With:** Mercy Corps. **Also Known As:** (1988) Mercy Corps. **Formerly:** (1992) Pax World Foundation. **Publications:** *Pax Facts*, quarterly. Newsletter. **Price:** free.

17483 ■ Planning Assistance (PA)
50 F St. NW, Ste.1100
Washington, DC 20001
Ph: (202)879-0612
Fax: (202)638-0026
E-mail: rlearmonth@planasst.org
URL: http://www.planningassistance.org
Contact: Robert Learmonth, Exec. Dir.
Founded: 1973. **Staff:** 19. **Budget:** $3,500,000. **Languages:** English, French, Spanish. **Multinational. Description:** Assists voluntary and governmental organizations in developing countries and the U.S. in improving the planning and management of their economic and social development programs and in establishing the programs most appropriate to their resources and populations. Assists organizations from a given geographical area in achieving common goals by establishing collaborative planning and management of their programs; provides management training programs for program and organization directors. Prepares reports on programs and projects. **Libraries: Type:** reference. **Holdings:** archival material, books, clippings, monographs, periodicals. **Subjects:** economic and social development. **Sections:** Food for Development; Nutrition/Health; Population Program Planning; Private Enterprise; Rural Development; Voluntary Agencies.

17484 ■ Sabre Foundation (SF)
872 Massachusetts Ave., Ste.2-1
Cambridge, MA 02139
Ph: (617)868-3510
Fax: (617)868-7916
E-mail: inquiries@sabre.org
URL: http://www.sabre.org
Contact: Tania Vitvitsky, Exec. Dir.
Founded: 1969. **Description:** Distributes in-kind donations of new books, CD-Roms, and other educational materials to support education, private sector growth, research and higher learning in Africa, the former Soviet Union, and select countries in other regions of the world through non-governmental partner organizations. Sabre also provides Internet and related information technology training, targeted to these regions, through workshops in the U.S. and overseas. Sabre's Philosophy of Institutions Project explores the nature and accountability of free institutions. **Publications:** *Update*, quarterly. Newsletter. Alternate Formats: online.

17485 ■ Society for International Development - USA (SID)
1875 Connecticut Ave. NW, Ste.720
Washington, DC 20009-5728
Ph: (202)884-8590
Fax: (202)884-8499
E-mail: sid@aed.org
URL: http://www.sidw.org
Contact: Asif Shaikh, Pres./CEO
Membership Dues: additional household, full time student, $35 (annual) ● young professional, $45 (annual) ● retired, $60 (annual) ● employee (institu-

tional), $65 (annual) ● regular, $75 (annual). **Description:** Conducts economic and community development programs on an international basis. Promotes sustainable development tailored to local needs and capacities. Provides technical support and other services to development projects. **Computer Services:** Mailing lists. **Working Groups:** Civil Society; Corporate Responsibility; Crisis, Conflict and Transition; Development Education; Development Finance; Development Information; Education for Development; Energy and Infrastructure; Environment; Food and Agriculture; Governance and Rule of Law; Human Resource Development and Institution Strengthening; Information Technology; International Health and Nutrition; Urban Development; Young Professionals in Development; Youth Development.

17486 ■ TechnoServe (TNS)
1800 M St. NW, Ste.1066, South Tower
Washington, DC 20036
Ph: (202)785-4515
Free: (800)99-WORKS
Fax: (202)785-4544
E-mail: technoserve@tns.org
URL: http://www.technoserve.org
Contact: Bruce McNamer, Pres./CEO
Founded: 1968. **Members:** 99. **Staff:** 300. **Budget:** $20,000,000. **Languages:** English, Spanish. **Multinational. Description:** Works to improve the economic and social well-being of low-income people in Latin America, Africa, and Eastern Europe. Provides agriculture and business training to help the poor build their own self-sustaining enterprises. Works with more than 175 enterprises and institutions. Provides feasibility assessment; design and implementation of management, production and financial systems and controls; monitoring and evaluating enterprise performance and impact. **Additional Websites:** http://www.believe-begin-become.com. **Divisions:** Africa; Latin America. **Publications:** *E-News Alerts*, monthly. Newsletters. Electronic newsletters sent via email. Alternate Formats: online ● *Learning Solutions*, periodic. Newsletter. Releases best practice and thought leadership pieces produced by TechnoServe. Alternate Formats: online ● *World Newsletter*, quarterly ● Annual Report, annual. Includes membership listing. ● Also publishes research findings, case histories, and sector studies. **Conventions/Meetings:** semiannual board meeting - always May and November, New York City.

17487 ■ Third World Conference Foundation (TWCF)
1525 E 53rd St., Ste.437
Chicago, IL 60615-4509
Ph: (773)241-6688
Fax: (773)241-7898
E-mail: inquiries2@twcfinternational.org
URL: http://www.twcfinternational.org
Founded: 1973. **Membership Dues:** student, $35 (annual) ● individual, $90 (annual) ● international, $100 (annual) ● institution, $500 (annual) ● donor, $2,000 (annual). **Description:** Individuals interested in issues concerning Third World nations. Promotes interdisciplinary research on political, cultural, and economic issues facing Third World countries and emigrants from these' areas living in Europe and North America. Conducts educational programs for college/university and secondary schools. Sponsors research programs. **Awards: Type:** grant. **Recipient:** for student members who attend the annual conference ● **Type:** recognition. **Recipient:** for outstanding service on behalf of Third World community development projects. **Telecommunication Services:** electronic mail, twcfusa@aol.com. **Publications:** *Annual Third World Conference Proceedings*, annual. Includes articles on critical understanding of complex development problems in changing global systems. **Price:** $175.00/copy (plus $7.50 shipping & handling). ISSN: 0885-2316. **Advertising:** accepted ● *Third World Briefings*, quarterly. Newsletter. Focuses on activities of the foundation and Third World/Diaspora issues. **Price:** included in membership dues ● *Third World in Perspective*. Journal. Features interdisciplinary analyses of major issues facing Third World countries in the 21st century.

Price: $120.00 /year for institutions. **Advertising:** accepted. **Conventions/Meetings:** annual conference, with educational materials and ethnic artifacts (exhibits).

17488 ■ United Nations Development Programme (UNDP)

1 United Nations Plz.
New York, NY 10017
Ph: (212)906-5000 (212)963-1234
Fax: (212)906-5364
URL: http://www.undp.org
Contact: Kemal Dervis, Admin.

Founded: 1965. **Budget:** $1,000,000,000. **Languages:** English, French, Spanish. **Description:** Enhances self-reliance and promotes sustainable human development. Gives priority to the fields of poverty alleviation and grassroots development, environment and natural resources, management development, technical cooperation among developing countries, transfer and adaptation of technology, and women in development. Operates the Global Environment Facility in cooperation with the World Bank and the United Nations Environment Programme, which provides grants to enable developing countries to address the global dimensions of their environmental problems. **Publications:** *Choices* (in English, French, Japanese, and Spanish), 3/year. Magazine. **Price:** free ● *Compendium of Approved Projects*, annual ● *Cooperation South*, periodic. Journal. Features critical analysis and discussion of development issues relevant to the South. Alternate Formats: online ● *Flash* (in Arabic, English, French, Russian, and Spanish), weekly ● *UNDP Annual Report of the Administrator* (in Arabic, English, French, Japanese, and Spanish), annual. Features a concise picture of the new UNDP, its missions and its achievements. Alternate Formats: online ● *UNDP Human Development Report*, annual. Contains analyses of major issues and updated Human Indicators that compare the relative levels of human development in over 175 countries. Alternate Formats: online. **Conventions/Meetings:** annual board meeting - always June, either New York, NY or Geneva, Switzerland.

17489 ■ United Nations Development Programme - Regional Bureau for Asia and the Pacific (UNDP-RBAP)

c/o United Nations Development Programme
One United Nations Plz.
New York, NY 10017
Ph: (212)906-5800
Fax: (212)906-6576
E-mail: nay.htun@undp.org
URL: http://www.undp.org
Contact: Mr. Nay Htun, Regional Dir.

Description: Promotes communication and cooperation among members. Assists members in their interactions with nongovernmental and community organizations. **Publications:** *Lao PDR National Human Development Report*. Includes chapters on ecology and the ethnic diversity of Lao PDR. ● *Pacific Human Development Report*. Includes updated calculations of the Human Development Index (HDI) and Human Poverty Index (HPI). ● *Promoting the Millennium Development Goals in Asia and the Pacific: Meeting the Challenges of Poverty Reduction*. Report. Contains an assessment on the status of the Millennium Development Goals (MDGs) in Asia and the Pacific.

17490 ■ Water for People (WFP)

6666 W Quincy Ave.
Denver, CO 80235-3098
Ph: (303)734-3490
Fax: (303)734-3499
E-mail: swerner@waterforpeople.org
URL: http://www.waterforpeople.org
Contact: Steve Werner, Exec. Dir.

Founded: 1991. **Staff:** 7. **Budget:** $1,000,000. **Description:** Works to receive, administer, and expend funds to assist developing countries organize and implement drinking water and sanitation projects that improve the health and welfare of the population. Provides related technical referral and technical literature distribution services. Aids poor people in developing countries improve their quality of life by funding and facilitating sustainable drinking water sanitation and hygiene education projects. Conducts training programs, technical assistance services, information exchange, charitable and educational programs. **Convention/Meeting:** none. **Libraries: Type:** reference. **Holdings:** audio recordings, business records, video recordings. **Subjects:** water and sanitation in developing countries. **Computer Services:** database, volunteers and donors. **Committees:** Bylaws; Nominating; Project Selection. **Councils:** Fundraising Advisory. **Publications:** *Special Report*. Alternate Formats: online ● *Voices from the Field*. Newsletter. Alternate Formats: online ● Newsletter, quarterly. **Price:** free. **Circulation:** 6,100 ● Annual Report, annual. Alternate Formats: online.

17491 ■ William J. Clinton Foundation (WCF)

1200 Pres. Clinton Ave.
Little Rock, AR 72201
Ph: (501)370-8000
Fax: (501)375-0512
E-mail: operationslr@clintonfoundation.org
URL: http://www.clintonfoundation.org
Contact: William J. Clinton, Founder

Multinational. Description: Promotes the values of fairness and opportunity for all. Strengthens the capacity of people in the United States and throughout the world to meet the challenges of global interdependence. Develops programs and partnerships in the areas of health security, economic empowerment, leadership development and citizen service, and racial, ethnic and religious reconciliation. **Publications:** Newsletter. Alternate Formats: online ● Annual Report, annual. Alternate Formats: online.

17492 ■ World Bank Group (WBG)

1818 H St. NW
Washington, DC 20433
Ph: (202)473-1000
Fax: (202)477-6391
E-mail: newsbureau@worldbank.org
URL: http://www.worldbank.org
Contact: Paul Wolfowitz, Pres.

Founded: 1944. **Staff:** 10,713. **Languages:** Arabic, English, French, Russian, Spanish. **Multinational. Description:** Comprises the International Bank for Reconstruction and Development, the International Development Association, International Finance Corporation and the Multilateral Investment Guarantee Agency. Established by the United Nations to assist in raising the standards of living in developing countries by channeling financial resources from developed countries. Emphasis is placed on investments which foster active participation in the development process. Programs concentrate on rural and urban development, agriculture, and education. Activities include improving water and sewage facilities, building low-cost housing, and increasing the productivity of small industries. Assists organizations with identifying, designing, and executing development projects; offers financial aid to national development institutions. Encourages discussion on common development problems such as income distribution, rural poverty, unemployment, excessive population growth, and rapid urbanization. Conducts research programs on topics including economic planning and public utilities. Works in association with the United Nations Development Program and executes many UNDP projects. **Computer Services:** database, projects ● mailing lists, for subscription. **Publications:** *World Bank Weekly Update*. Newsletter. Alternate Formats: online ● Annual Report, annual. Alternate Formats: online.

International Relations

17493 ■ American Ditchley Foundation (ADF)

445 Park Ave., 9th Fl.
New York, NY 10022
Ph: (212)541-3791
Fax: (212)541-3751
E-mail: americanditchley@aol.com
URL: http://www.ditchley.co.uk/page/43/american-ditchley.htm
Contact: Mr. John J. O'Connor, Exec. Dir.

Founded: 1972. **Staff:** 3. **Budget:** $225,000. **Description:** The American affiliate of the Ditchley Foundation. Sponsors 15 conferences each year on international political, military, economic, and cultural issues of concern to North America and Western Europe. **Awards:** Travel Grants. **Frequency:** monthly. **Type:** recognition. **Recipient:** for conference participants. **Affiliated With:** American Ditchley Foundation. **Publications:** Newsletter, 3/year. **Conventions/Meetings:** annual meeting.

17494 ■ American Peace Society (APS)

c/o Walter Beach
1319 18th St. NW
Washington, DC 20036-1802
Ph: (202)296-6267
Fax: (202)296-5149
Contact: Douglas Kirkpatrick, Contact

Founded: 1828. **Members:** 110. **Staff:** 2. **Description:** Advances judicial methods and other peaceful means of avoiding and adjusting differences among nations. **Publications:** *World Affairs*, quarterly. **Conventions/Meetings:** annual meeting.

17495 ■ American Sovereignty Task Force (ASTF)

c/o State Department Watch
PO Box 65398
Washington, DC 20035
Ph: (818)223-8080
E-mail: sdw@statedepartmentwatch.org
URL: http://www.statedepartmentwatch.org
Contact: Carl Olson, Chm.

Founded: 1984. **Description:** Conducts research on governmental sovereignty and related matters. Examines issues concerning boundaries, jurisdiction, sovereignty within a federal system, territorial claims, maritime law, exclusive economic zones, rights of strait passage, and seabed and outcontinental shelf policies. Involves current research such as the issue of U.S. sovereignty over the Alaskan islands of Wrangell, Herald, Bennett, Henrietta, and Jeannette. Compiles statistics; maintains speakers' bureau. **Convention/Meeting:** none.

17496 ■ American Task Force on Palestine (ATFP)

815 Connecticut Ave., Ste.200
Washington, DC 20006
Ph: (202)887-0177
Fax: (202)887-1920
E-mail: atfp@atfp.net
URL: http://www.americantaskforce.org
Contact: Ziad J. Asali, Pres.

Description: Advocates for the establishment of a democratic state of Palestine living in peace and security. Enhances national security, regional peace and stability. Proliferates American values of freedom and democracy through the creation of a democratic and constitutional state for the Palestinian people.

17497 ■ Bridging Nations

1800 K St. NW, Ste.622
Washington, DC 20006
Ph: (202)741-3870
Fax: (202)741-3871
E-mail: info@bridgingnations.org
URL: http://www.bridgingnations.org
Contact: Dr. Prakash Ambegaonkar, Founder/CEO

Multinational. Description: Promotes an informed, multifaceted channel of communication and forum of exchange on technological innovation and responsible leadership. Assists in the development of innovative international policy making to ensure the collective security and well-being of every nation. **Computer Services:** Online services, discussion forum ● online services, interactive poll. **Projects:** Measuring the India Caucus; National India Center; Profiles in Leadership - Prime Minister Vaypayee.

17498 ■ Business Council for International Understanding (BCIU)
1212 Ave. of the Americas, 10th Fl.
New York, NY 10036
Ph: (212)490-0460
Fax: (212)697-8526
E-mail: hr@bciu.org
URL: http://www.bciu.org
Contact: Peter J. Tichansky, Pres./CEO
Founded: 1958. **Members:** 156. **Staff:** 9. **Budget:** $909,000. **Description:** Comprised of U.S. corporations engaged in international business. Works with U.S. and foreign governments in arranging briefings with U.S. industry executives. Cooperates with these governments on problems of democratic, economic, and social development by organizing schedules of one-on-one briefings as well as small discussion groups for heads of state, their ministers, and foreign industry missions. Collaborates with many other business-related associations. Maintains comprehensive company-country research. Provides area intensive study courses and special cross-cultural programs, which include familiarization with foreign institutions and viewpoints, private briefings with U.S. and foreign government specialists, and language study and orientation for spouses and older children. **Publications:** Papers, periodic. **Conventions/Meetings:** annual general assembly and board meeting.

17499 ■ Carnegie Endowment for International Peace (CEIP)
1779 Massachusetts Ave. NW
Washington, DC 20036-2103
Ph: (202)483-7600
Fax: (202)483-1840
E-mail: info@carnegieendowment.org
URL: http://www.carnegieendowment.org
Contact: Jessica T. Mathews, Pres.
Founded: 1910. **Staff:** 100. **Nonmembership. Description:** Conducts research, discussion, publication, and education programs in international affairs and American foreign policy. Activities change periodically and cover a broad range of military, political, and economic issues. Maintains office in Moscow. **Libraries: Type:** reference. **Holdings:** books. **Subjects:** international affairs. **Telecommunication Services:** information service, Carnegie Non-proliferation Network; Carnegie e-News, FP e-Alert. **Publications:** *Arab Reform Bulletin* (in Arabic and English), monthly. Contains analysis, news synopsis and annotated resource guides. Alternate Formats: online ● *Carnegie Endowment*, biweekly. Newsletter. Contains information on the latest conferences, books and policy briefs. Alternate Formats: online ● *Foreign Policy*, bimonthly. Magazine. Covers international affairs topics. **Price:** $20.00 /year for individuals. ISSN: 0015-7228. **Circulation:** 34,000. **Advertising:** accepted. Alternate Formats: online. **Conventions/Meetings:** annual Carnegie Non-Proliferation Conference.

17500 ■ Center for New National Security (CNNS)
664 Cherry Run Rd.
Harpers Ferry, WV 25425
Ph: (304)876-9400
Fax: (304)876-9400
E-mail: nhuddle@frontiernet.net
URL: http://www.bestgame.org
Contact: Norie Huddle, Pres.
Founded: 1979. **Budget:** $25,000. **Description:** Promotes national and global security through the design of a global security system, also emphasizes new concepts in global economic and financial systems, in health, education, and interactive media. (Researches and writes books; produces audio and video educational materials.) Functions as an international nonprofit think tank and consulting service to catalyze and support high leverage projects that will create constructive attitudes and positive alternatives for the future. Committed to nonviolence and improving the quality of diplomacy. Maintains that both personal and social systems transformation are necessary to ensure the quality survival of humanity. Conducts lectures, lay sermons, seminars and training programs on goal setting, values clarification, team build-

ing, creative problem solving, and new global perspectives. Established The Best Game on Earth (interactive global game using television, radio and video, computer networking, and educational programs). **Libraries: Type:** reference. **Holdings:** 2,000. **Subjects:** security issues, environment, economics, future studies. **Additional Websites:** http://www.butterflyspirit.org. **Publications:** *Butterfly: A Tiny Tale of Great Transformation.* Book. Features a story of global transformation told through the story of how a caterpillar turns into a butterfly. **Price:** $18.00 plus shipping and handling ● *Huggles.* Book. Coloring book. ● *If the World Became a Butterfly.* Book. **Price:** $15.00 ● *Island of Dreams: Environmental Crisis in Japan.* Book. Features a holistic analysis of Japan's environmental crisis and its global implications. ● *Surviving: The Best Game on Earth.* Book. Includes interviews. **Price:** $17.00 plus shipping and handling.

17501 ■ Center for War/Peace Studies (CW/PS)
330 E 38th St., Ste.19Q
New York, NY 10016
Ph: (212)490-6494
E-mail: lucywebster@vistas.net
URL: http://www.cwps.org
Contact: Lucy Law Webster, Exec. Dir.
Founded: 1977. **Members:** 2,000. **Staff:** 3. **Budget:** $100,000. **Description:** Carries out independent studies on global problems in the hope of proposing solutions. Primary areas of concern include: creation of global structures that will "move the world toward cooperation under law rather than violent conflict"; arms control and disarmament; the need for a general settlement in the Middle East. Gives priority to research and development of its Binding Triad proposal for global decision-making which would introduce a weighted voting system into the United Nations General Assembly based on three factors: one nation, one vote; population; contributions to the regular UN budget. At the same time, General Assembly resolutions would become binding, not simply recommendations as at present. **Publications:** *Global Report: Progress Toward a World of Peace with Justice,* quarterly. Newsletter. Covers global problems, particularly in the United Nations. **Price:** $35.00 /year for nonmembers; $20.00 /year for members. ISSN: 0730-9112. **Circulation:** 5,000.

17502 ■ Citizens Network for Foreign Affairs (CNFA)
1828 L St. NW, Ste.710
Washington, DC 20036
Ph: (202)296-3920
Fax: (202)296-3948
E-mail: info@cnfa.org
URL: http://www.cnfa.org
Contact: John H. Costello, Pres./CEO
Founded: 1985. **Staff:** 45. **Budget:** $12,000,000. **Description:** Committed to stimulating international economic growth and development. Builds partnerships between the public and private sectors to achieve the dual goals of providing foreign aid and positioning U.S. enterprises in growing markets. Seeks to leverage a limited amount of government resources with the technology, creativity, and capital investment of U.S. private enterprise. Aims to create lasting and effective opportunities worldwide. **Computer Services:** database. **Publications:** *Farm Inputs Exhibition.* Magazine. Highlights the purpose, impact and the outcome of the Farm Input Exhibition. ● *Global Focus Facts,* monthly. Report ● *Global Focus Report,* quarterly. **Conventions/Meetings:** annual meeting.

17503 ■ Coalition for American Leadership Abroad (COLEAD)
2101 E St. NW
Washington, DC 20037
Ph: (202)944-5519
Fax: (202)338-6820
E-mail: colead@afsa.org
URL: http://www.colead.org
Contact: Harry C. Blaney III, Pres./CEO
Founded: 1995. **Members:** 50. **Membership Dues:** associate, $20 (annual). **Description:** Organizations

with an interest in international issues affecting the United States and promoting American Engagement in world affairs. Seeks to further "well-informed debate about international issues". Promotes development of "new ways for the foreign affairs community to work together". Monitors federal legislative and State Department activities and conducts lobbying campaigns; serves as a clearinghouse on international issues affecting the United States. **Publications:** *Restoring America's International Engagement.* Paper. Alternate Formats: online.

17504 ■ Hispanic Council on International Relations (HCIR)
1111 19th St. NW, Ste.403
Washington, DC 20036
Ph: (202)785-5384
Fax: (202)785-0265
E-mail: hispaniccouncil@hcir.org
Contact: Marco Vinicio Aguilar, Exec.Dir.
Multinational. Description: Increases the voice of Hispanic Americans in U.S. foreign affairs. Fosters greater awareness of global affairs and encourages Hispanic American participation in international relations. **Awards:** International Leadership Award. **Frequency:** annual. **Type:** recognition. **Recipient:** for an individual who has promoted increased US Hispanic participation in international affairs.

17505 ■ National Democratic Institute for International Affairs (NDI)
2030 M St. NW, 5th Fl.
Washington, DC 20036-3306
Ph: (202)728-5500
Fax: (202)728-5520
E-mail: contact@ndi.org
URL: http://www.ndi.org
Contact: Kenneth D. Wollack, Pres.
Founded: 1983. **Staff:** 170. **Languages:** Arabic, English, French, Russian, Spanish. **Description:** Works to strengthen and expand democracy worldwide. Provides practical assistance to civic and political leaders advancing democratic values, practices and institutions. Works with democrats in every region of the world to build political and civic organizations, safeguard elections, and promote citizen participation, openness and accountability in government. **Libraries: Type:** open to the public; by appointment only. **Holdings:** 2,000. **Subjects:** international relations, democratization, election monitoring. **Awards:** H. Averell Harriman Democracy Award. **Frequency:** annual. **Type:** recognition. **Recipient:** to an individual or organization that has demonstrated a commitment to democracy and human rights. **Also Known As:** National Democratic Institute. **Publications:** *National Democratic Institute for International Affairs Activities,* annual. Report. Contains report of activities. ● *NDI Reports,* quarterly. Newsletter. Features current issues and activities of the organization. ● Also publishes reports on international election observing, topical democratization issues, and NDI programs.

17506 ■ Open Society Institute (OSI)
400 W 59th St.
New York, NY 10019
Ph: (212)548-0600
Fax: (212)548-4600
E-mail: info@sorosny.org
URL: http://www.soros.org
Contact: Aryeh Neier, Pres.
Founded: 1993. **Staff:** 268. **Budget:** $450,000,000. **Description:** Promotes development of open societies around the world; part of an informal network of foundations and organizations active in more than fifty countries worldwide that support a range of programs in education, civil society, media and human rights. Supports social, legal and economic reforms that provide alternative solutions to complex problems. Provides administrative support, technical assistance, and programmatic advice to foundations in Central and Eastern Europe and the former Soviet Union, Southern and West Africa, Guatemala, Haiti, Mongolia, and the United States. **Libraries: Type:** reference. **Holdings:** archival material. **Subjects:** social reform. **Awards:** Community Fellowships. **Fre-**

quency: annual. **Type:** fellowship. **Recipient:** for individuals who wish to employ their educational and professional attainments in service to disadvantaged communities. **Programs:** Judicial Independence. **Projects:** Community Advocacy; Death in America; Gideon. **Publications:** *Open Society News*, quarterly. Newsletter. **Price:** free. Alternate Formats: online ● Annual Report, annual. Alternate Formats: online.

17507 ■ Project South: Institute for the Elimination of Poverty and Genocide
9 Gammon Ave.
Atlanta, GA 30315
Ph: (404)622-0602
Fax: (404)622-6618
E-mail: general-info@projectsouth.org
URL: http://www.projectsouth.org
Contact: Jerome Scott, Exec. Dir.
Membership Dues: part-time/temporary, $10 (annual) ● full, $25 (annual). **Multinational. Description:** Creates education tools and conducts action research to build grassroots leaders. Provides opportunities for organizers to learn and develop movement building tools. Strives to build movement for social and economic justice by connecting local organizing efforts to consciousness, vision and strategy. **Publications:** *As The South Goes*, semiannual. Newsletter. Includes articles, educational materials and updates. **Price:** included in membership dues.

17508 ■ Sovereignty International
PO Box 191
Hollow Rock, TN 38342
Ph: (731)986-0099
E-mail: webmaster@sovereignty.net
URL: http://www.sovereignty.net
Contact: Michael S. Coffman PhD, CEO
Nonmembership. Multinational. Description: Advocates for individual freedom, private property ownership, free markets and national sovereignty. Advocates for the free and open elections of officials who are exclusively responsible for enacting public policy. Promotes respect for the sovereignty of individual citizens and independent nations. **Publications:** *World Concerns*, periodic. Newsletter.

17509 ■ Transnational Diplomatic Network (TDN)
4201 Wilson Blvd. 110312
Arlington, VA 22203
Ph: (202)288-9997
E-mail: info@transnationaldiplomacy.com
URL: http://www.transnationaldiplomacy.com
Contact: Paul Hickman, Founder/Exec.Dir.
Membership Dues: national, $5,000 (annual) ● corporate, $2,500 (annual) ● individual/honorary, $250 (annual). **Multinational. Description:** Works to empower nonprofit organizations through the promotion and facilitation of constructive international interaction. Provides a forum through which internationally orientated nonprofit organizations can better communicate and interact with international partners. **Computer Services:** Online services, chat ● online services, diplomacy poll. **Telecommunication Services:** electronic mail, director@transnationaldiplomacy.com. **Publications:** *The International Non-Profit Review*, quarterly. Journal. **Price:** included in membership dues ● Newsletter.

17510 ■ Trilateral Commission (TC)
1156 15th St. NW
Washington, DC 20005
Ph: (202)467-5410
Fax: (202)467-5415
E-mail: contactus@trilateral.org
URL: http://www.trilateral.org
Contact: Thomas S. Foley, North American Group Chm.
Founded: 1973. **Members:** 330. **Staff:** 13. **Regional Groups:** 3. **Description:** Distinguished private citizens from North America, Western Europe, and Japan, including academic, business, labor, and media professionals. Encourages closer cooperation among these three democratic industrialized regions. Meets annually to analyze major issues confronting

the "trilateral" area; seeks to improve public understanding of these issues. Works to develop proposals for joint action and to nurture habits of working together. **Telecommunication Services:** electronic mail, trilateral.sisk@verizon.net. **Publications:** *Trialogue*, annual. Magazine. Contains opening presentations of speakers at TC annual meetings. Alternate Formats: online ● *Triangle Papers*, annual. Reports. Contains topics such as monetary matters, trade, energy security institution reform, and international cooperation. ● Also publishes brochure. **Conventions/Meetings:** annual meeting.

17511 ■ Washington Institute of Foreign Affairs (WIFA)
2121 Massachusetts Ave. NW
Washington, DC 20008
Ph: (202)332-1616
Fax: (202)332-0108
E-mail: wifa@erols.com
URL: http://wifadc.org
Contact: Marina G. Fischer, Exec. Sec.
Founded: 1961. **Members:** 362. **Staff:** 1. **Description:** Represents former directors of the Central Intelligence Agency; retired officials of the U.S. Defense Department; military leaders and personnel; former Assistant Secretaries of State, ambassadors, and retired Cabinet officials; former congresspersons; educators, economists, journalists, lawyers, and businesspersons presently or formerly engaged in foreign affairs. Promotes greater knowledge and understanding of foreign affairs by Americans and those involved in international activities, including foreign officials, dignitaries, and leaders of thought in other countries. Provides a means whereby persons involved in foreign affairs, international organizations responsible for the conduct of foreign affairs, and government individuals may consider international problems and exchange views. Encourages creative thinking on current and long-term problems in the area of foreign affairs. Sponsors 28-30 sessions each year at which officials and notables in the field of international affairs lecture or participate in discussions.

17512 ■ Weatherhead Center for International Affairs (WCFIA)
Harvard Univ.
1737 Cambridge St.
Cambridge, MA 02138
Ph: (617)495-4420
Fax: (617)495-8292
E-mail: cputnam@wcfia.harvard.edu
URL: http://www.wcfia.harvard.edu
Contact: Steven B. Bloomfield, Exec. Dir.
Founded: 1958. **Members:** 250. **Staff:** 33. **For-Profit. Description:** Individuals with interest in international relations. Seeks to increase understanding of diplomatic issues worldwide. Conducts research and educational programs. **Libraries: Type:** not open to the public. **Holdings:** 20,000; books, periodicals. **Subjects:** international affairs. **Awards:** Post and Pre-doctoral Fellowships. **Frequency:** annual. **Type:** grant. **Formerly:** (2002) Center for International Affairs. **Publications:** *Working Paper Series*, monthly. Contains academic works in progress.

International Understanding

17513 ■ Center for Citizen Initiatives (CCI)
c/o The Presidio of San Francisco
PO Box 29912
San Francisco, CA 94129
Ph: (415)561-7777
Free: (888)729-7071
Fax: (415)561-7778
E-mail: info@ccisf.org
URL: http://www.ccisf.org
Contact: Sharon Tennison, Pres.
Founded: 1984. **Staff:** 28. **Regional Groups:** 7. **Languages:** English, Russian. **Description:** Implements programs that assist Russian citizens in securing economic and political reforms. Fosters cooperative partnerships and relations between U.S. and

Russia. **Computer Services:** Mailing lists, of members. **Programs:** Next Steps; Productivity Enhancement. **Projects:** Angels for Angels; Leaders Institute; St. Petersburgh School of Management; Schultz Awards; Travel Program. **Formerly:** (1992) Center for U.S.-USSR Initiatives. **Publications:** Newsletter, quarterly.

17514 ■ Crosscurrents International Institute (CCII)
7122 Hardin-Wapak Rd.
Sidney, OH 45365
Ph: (937)492-0407
Fax: (937)492-0497
E-mail: cci@bright.net
URL: http://www.crosscurrentsinstitute.org
Contact: Dr. William P. Shaw, Pres.
Founded: 1984. **Staff:** 3. **Budget:** $150,000. **Languages:** English, French, Russian, Spanish. **Multinational. Description:** Seeks to reduce tensions among countries by increasing knowledge and understanding. Encourages unofficial dialogue between leaders from different nations on world issues. Conducts field research on the social and economic impact of new technologies applied to other countries. Studies management skills and governance in different cultures. Offers educational programs and interpretation services in Russian; conducts educational tours for local leaders. Conducts long-term education programs in agriculture. Maintains Speaker's Bureau.

17515 ■ Delphi International Program of World Learning (DI)
1015 18th St. NW, Ste.1000
Washington, DC 20036-5272
Ph: (202)898-0950
Free: (800)826-0196
Fax: (202)842-0885
E-mail: delphi@worldlearning.org
URL: http://www.worldlearning.org/wlid/tande/delphi/index.html
Contact: Peter Simpson PhD, Program Dir.
Founded: 1976. **Staff:** 24. **Budget:** $6,500,000. **Description:** Assists leaders in the U.S. and abroad to meet social, political, and economic challenges at the local, regional and global levels. Core programs and international service areas include: professional exchanges, design and administration of observational study tours, and educational exchanges. Major program topics are: U.S. Government System, U.S. Political Systems, U.S. Foreign Policy, Business and Economic Development, Education and Training, Media, Science and Technology, Agriculture, Arts, and U.S. Social Concerns such as environment, health, justice/law, labor issues, narcotics issues, non-governmental organizations, urban planning, and women's issues. **Libraries: Type:** not open to the public. **Holdings:** 1,000. **Publications:** *This Month at Delphi*, monthly. Newsletter. Alternate Formats: online.

17516 ■ East-West Center (EWC)
1601 East-West Rd.
Honolulu, HI 96848
Ph: (808)944-7111
Fax: (808)944-7376
E-mail: ewcinfo@eastwestcenter.org
URL: http://www.eastwestcenter.org
Contact: Charles E. Morrison, Pres.
Founded: 1960. **Staff:** 160. **Budget:** $20,000,000. **Multinational. Description:** Established by congress as a national education and research organization to promote US-Asia-Pacific relations and understanding through cooperative study, training and research. Assists in "building an Asia Pacific community in which the United States is a natural, valued and leading partner". Provides awards annually to scholars, researchers, graduate students, and professionals in business and government. Holds seminars and workshops in conjunction with long-term research projects and research grants. Education and dialogue programs seek to prepare Americans for an era in which the Asia-Pacific region is vastly more important to the United States. **Libraries: Type:** not open to the public. **Programs:** Dialogue; Education. **Also**

Known As: Center for Cultural and Technical Interchange Between East and West. **Publications:** *Asia Pacific Issues*, periodic ● *Asia-Pacific Population Forum*, quarterly. Newsletter ● *East West Center Special Reports*, periodic ● Annual Report, annual ● Also publishes research reports, program reports, case studies, and educational materials. **Conventions/Meetings:** periodic meeting ● seminar ● workshop.

17517 ■ Educators for Social Responsibility (ESR)
23 Garden St.
Cambridge, MA 02138
Ph: (617)492-1764
Free: (800)370-2515
Fax: (617)864-5164
E-mail: educators@esrnational.org
URL: http://www.esrnational.org
Contact: Larry Dieringer, Exec. Dir.
Founded: 1982. **Membership Dues:** individual, $35 (annual) ● low-income, $20 (annual) ● family, $50 (annual) ● institutional, $100 (annual). **Staff:** 25. **Budget:** $3,200,000. **Local Groups:** 15. **Description:** Helps young people develop the convictions and skills to shape a safe, sustainable, and just world. Promotes children's ethical and social development through leadership in conflict resolution, violence prevention, social and emotional learning, and diversity awareness. **Publications:** *Adventures in Peacemaking: A Conflict Resolution Activity Guide for School-age Programs* ● *Conflict Resolution in the High School* ● *Conflict Resolution in the Middle School* ● *Early Childhood Adventures in Peacemaking* ● *Elementary Perspectives: Teaching Concepts of Peace and Conflict* ● *Forum*, monthly. Newsletter. Alternate Formats: online ● *Making Choices about Conflict, Security, and Peacemaking* ● *Making History: A Social Studies Curriculum* ● *The Power of Numbers: A Teacher's Guide to Mathematics in a Social Studies Context* ● *Teaching Young Children in Violent Times: Building a Peaceable Classroom* ● *Trash Conflicts: A Science and Social Studies Curriculum on the Ethics of Disposal*. **Conventions/Meetings:** workshop, professional development for educators.

17518 ■ Eisenhower Fellowships (EF)
256 S 16th St.
Philadelphia, PA 19102
Ph: (215)546-1738
Fax: (215)546-4567
E-mail: ike@eisenhowerfellowships.org
URL: http://eisenhowerfellowships.org
Contact: John S. Wolf, Pres.
Founded: 1953. **Members:** 1,600. **Staff:** 22. **Budget:** $3,000,000. **Description:** Works as a nonpartisan tribute to former U.S. President Dwight D. Eisenhower (1890-1969) to foster international development and understanding. Offers grants providing 3 months of travel, professional discussions, seminars, field trips, and observation in the United States for men and women from other countries who are currently in mid-career and who have already demonstrated outstanding leadership potential. Enables individuals, who often become top business, government, and professional leaders in their own countries, to meet their professional counterparts and people from all walks of life in the U.S., and to acquire an understanding of American institutions, accomplishments, and aspirations; activities include 2 group seminars and an individually tailored program for each Fellow; a special program enables Americans to pursue professional interests in selected areas overseas; nominations must come from potential Fellows' respective countries. **Awards:** Dr. Eisenhower Medal. **Frequency:** annual. **Type:** medal. **Formerly:** (2002) Eisenhower Exchange Fellowships. **Conventions/Meetings:** periodic Special Forum - meeting.

17519 ■ English in Action (EiA)
144 E 39th St.
New York, NY 10016
Ph: (212)818-1200
Fax: (212)867-4177

E-mail: info@esuus.org
URL: http://www.esuus.org
Contact: Alice Boyne, Pres./Exec. Dir.
Founded: 1960. **Members:** 10,000. **Membership Dues:** registration, $195 (annual). **Staff:** 3. **Regional Groups:** 7. **Local Groups:** 18. **Description:** Program administered by the English-Speaking Union of the United States. Volunteers and individual contributors; corporations, foundations, churches, and other institutions. Helps immigrants, international visitors, students, and professionals with conversational English practice through weekly person-to-person meetings with American volunteers; through this program, volunteer tutors help newcomers in their adjustment to a new language and culture in the U.S. Individuals are referred to the program by universities, corporations, hospitals, consulates, and other international organizations and referral agencies. **Libraries: Type:** reference. **Holdings:** 500. **Subjects:** English as a second language. **Formerly:** (1966) Greater New York Council for Foreign Students -English in Action. **Publications:** *Here and There*, monthly. Newsletter. **Price:** free. **Circulation:** 800 ● *Tips on Tutoring English*. **Conventions/Meetings:** biennial workshop, with tutor workshops.

17520 ■ French-American Foundation (FAF)
28 W 44th St., Ste.1420
New York, NY 10036
Ph: (212)829-8800
Fax: (212)829-8810
E-mail: info@frenchamerican.org
URL: http://www.frenchamerican.org
Contact: Nicholas W. Dungan, Pres.
Founded: 1976. **Membership Dues:** council-benefactor, associate, $1,000 (annual) ● council-senior fellow, corporate individual, $5,000 (annual) ● council-national fellow, corporate partner, $10,000 (annual) ● corporate leader, $50,000 (annual) ● corporate benefactor, $25,000 (annual) ● young fellow, $75 (annual) ● student, $15 (annual). **Staff:** 7. **Budget:** $1,500,000. **Languages:** English, French. **Description:** Works to strengthen relations between the United States and France by creating opportunities for French and American professionals to discuss and address problems of major concern to both societies and to stimulate change through cooperation. Projects include exchange of specialists, internships, study tours, conferences, fellowships, surveys, and special studies. Sponsors bicentennial fellowships for U.S. doctoral candidates, a continuing Chair in American Civilization at a university in Paris, and a two-month professional exchange for American and French journalists. **Awards: Type:** scholarship. **Publications:** *End of Year Report*, annual, always December ● *Project Reports*, periodic.

17521 ■ Friends of Togo (FOT)
(Les Amis du Togo)
PO Box 9436
Washington, DC 20016
E-mail: rreeder@bellatlantic.net
URL: http://www.friendsoftogo.org
Contact: Ruth Reeder, Co-Pres.
Founded: 1981. **Members:** 360. **Membership Dues:** individual, $25 (annual) ● overseas, $35 (annual). **Languages:** English, French. **Description:** Peace Corps participants who served in Togo; other individuals with an interest in Togo. Seeks to increase public awareness of the Republic of Togo in the United States. Provides assistance to community development and educational programs operating in Togo; conducts educational and fundraising activities in the United States. Sponsors cultural projects including recording of oral histories and development of language educational materials. Distributes Togolese art and craft products. **Affiliated With:** Peace Corps. **Publications:** Newsletter, annual. **Conventions/Meetings:** annual meeting.

17522 ■ Friendship Ambassadors Foundation (FAF)
299 Greenwich Ave.
Greenwich, CT 06830
Ph: (203)542-0652 (203)622-7420
Free: (800)526-2908

Fax: (203)542-0661
E-mail: friendlyam@faf.org
URL: http://www.faf.org
Contact: Patrick L. Sciarratta, Exec. Dir.
Founded: 1973. **Staff:** 7. **Budget:** $1,000,000. **State Groups:** 1,250. **Languages:** English, French, Spanish. **Multinational. Description:** Groups active in culture and the performing arts (choral groups, jazz ensembles, orchestras, and dance groups) united to promote international understanding. Develops cultural exchanges (performing and concert tours) between the U.S., Europe, Latin America and Asia. **Awards:** Short Term Travel Grants. **Frequency:** annual. **Type:** monetary. **Recipient:** to group leaders only. **Computer Services:** Online services, example itineraries. **Telecommunication Services:** electronic mail, psglobal@faf.org. **Affiliated With:** Chorus America. **Also Known As:** Ambassadors for Friendship. **Publications:** *Friendship Ambassador*, monthly. Newsletter. Contains information on group cultural exchange programs. **Price:** free. **Advertising:** accepted. Alternate Formats: online ● Report, annual. **Conventions/Meetings:** biennial Balkan Youth Reconciliation Seminar Series - conference ● International Choral Festival.

17523 ■ Friendship Force International (FFI)
34 Peachtree St., Ste.900
Atlanta, GA 30303
Ph: (404)522-9490 (404)965-4335
Fax: (404)688-6148
E-mail: info@friendshipforce.org
URL: http://www.friendshipforce.org
Contact: Dr. George T. Brown Jr., Pres.
Founded: 1977. **Members:** 12,000. **Staff:** 20. **Budget:** $1,300,000. **Local Groups:** 375. **Multinational. Description:** Private organization, with members in over 50 countries and throughout the U.S., whose purpose is promoting understanding in the world through the "force of friendship" accomplished by creating an environment for establishing friendships through exchange visits. A group of citizens travel to a city in another nation to stay in private homes for an exchange period of approximately one to two weeks. Aims to exchange a cross-section from each community, representative of occupation, race, age and sex. Ambassadors are interviewed and selected by a local committee. Individuals, families, and couples are encouraged to participate. Local organizations maintain speakers' bureaus and libraries, and arrange meetings and educational programs for their members. **Awards: Type:** recognition. **Computer Services:** database, email list of programs. **Telecommunication Services:** electronic mail, gbrown@friendshipforce.org. **Affiliated With:** Alliance for International Educational and Cultural Exchange. **Publications:** *Friendship*, quarterly. Magazine. Provides news of the organization and its programs. **Price:** $15.00 /year for individuals. **Circulation:** 5,000. **Conventions/Meetings:** annual international conference.

17524 ■ German Marshall Fund of the United States (GMF)
1744 R St. NW
Washington, DC 20009
Ph: (202)745-3950
Fax: (202)265-1662
E-mail: info@gmfus.org
URL: http://www.gmfus.org
Contact: Craig Kennedy, Pres.
Founded: 1972. **Multinational. Description:** Works to promote cooperation between the U.S. and Europe in the spirit of the postwar Marshall Plan.

17525 ■ Global Education Associates (GEA)
475 Riverside Dr., No. 1850
New York, NY 10115
Ph: (212)870-3290
Fax: (212)870-2729
E-mail: gea475@aol.com
URL: http://www.globaleduc.org
Contact: Dr. Patricia Mische, Pres.
Founded: 1973. **Members:** 3,000. **Membership Dues:** associate, $35 (annual) ● supporter, $100 (annual) ● sustainer, $500 (annual). **Staff:** 3. **Budget:**

$500,000. **Multinational. Description:** International organization which "facilitates the efforts of concerned people of diverse cultures, talents, and experience in contributing to a more humane and just world order." Hopes to change international competition over weapons, money, and scarce natural resources to international cooperation through education; has held over 2000 workshops and conferences in North and South America, Europe, East Asia, Latin America, Africa, and India. Programs include: Religious Orders Partnership, Global Action to Prevent War, Engaged Cosmology, Conflict Resolution, and Global Citizenship. **Libraries: Type:** reference. **Holdings:** 2,200; books. **Subjects:** global issues, alternative futures, education, United Nations, spirituality, religions. **Awards:** Jerry Mische Global Service Award. **Frequency:** annual. **Type:** recognition. **Recipient:** for service to global community. **Computer Services:** database ● mailing lists ● online services. **Programs:** Books for African Children; Conflict Resolution; Diversity Workshops; Engaged Cosmology; Global Action to Prevent War; Global Citizenship; Religious Orders Partnership. **Publications:** *Breakthrough News*, 3/year. Newsletter. Promotes the movement toward a global community. Contains book reviews and research updates. **Price:** included in membership dues; $25.00 /year for nonmembers. ISSN: 0889-3942. **Circulation:** 3,000 ● *Star Wars and the State of Our Souls.* Monographs. Explores the linkage between local and global concerns. ● *Toward a Global Civilization: The Contribution of Religions,* 3/year. Newsletter. Promotes the movement toward a global community. Contains book reviews and research updates. **Price:** included in membership dues; $25.00 /year for nonmembers. ISSN: 0889-3942. **Circulation:** 3,000 ● *Toward a Human World Order.* Monographs. Explores the linkage between local and global concerns. ● *Whole Earth Papers.* Monographs. Explores the linkage between local and global concerns. ● Environmental Security and the United Nations System, Past, Present and Future, Patricia Mische, Global Education Associates, 1998. **Conventions/Meetings:** monthly Enhancing Leadership Through Conflict Resolution - workshop - every 3rd Thursday.

17526 ■ Global Nomads International (GNI)
PO Box 8066
Reston, VA 20191
E-mail: info@gnvv.org
URL: http://www.gnvv.org/GNI
Founded: 1986. **Membership Dues:** individual, $35 ● full time student, $15. **Description:** Persons who have lived outside their passport countries. Explores the lifelong impact of the internationally-mobile childhood. Conducts presentations, workshops and seminars, as well as annual conferences. **Libraries: Type:** by appointment only. **Holdings:** 200; articles, biographical archives, books, business records, photographs, video recordings. **Subjects:** global nomads, third culture children, globalization, international mobility. **Computer Services:** Information services, global community, research. **Publications:** *GNI Perspectives.* Magazine. **Conventions/Meetings:** annual workshop.

17527 ■ Global Volunteers
375 E Little Canada Rd.
St. Paul, MN 55117-1628
Ph: (651)407-6100
Free: (800)487-1074
Fax: (651)482-0915
E-mail: email@globalvolunteers.org
URL: http://www.globalvolunteers.org
Contact: Bud Philbrook, CEO
Founded: 1984. **Membership Dues:** regular, $35 (annual). **Staff:** 50. **Budget:** $2,500,000. **Description:** Seeks to establish global understanding through volunteer work experience. Organizes both continental and overseas trips to assist developing communities. **Publications:** *Adventures in Service,* annual. Catalog. Gives descriptions of volunteer programs. **Price:** free. **Circulation:** 25,000 ● *Adventures in Service Update.* Newsletter. **Price:** free. Alternate Formats: online ● Annual Report. Alternate Formats: online.

17528 ■ Ground Zero Pairing Project (GZPP)
7135 SW 36th Ave.
Portland, OR 97219
Ph: (503)245-3403
E-mail: emolander@yahoo.com
Contact: Earl A. Molander, Exec. Dir.
Founded: 1982. **Staff:** 1. **Description:** Promotes community-to-community links between the U.S., Russia, and other emerging market countries. Conducts business education programs in these target countries. **Publications:** Russian/English business education course packages.

17529 ■ Hospitality Committee for United Nations Delegations (HCUND)
PO Box 1201
New York, NY 10164
Ph: (212)963-8753
Fax: (212)963-1320
E-mail: hcund@un.org
URL: http://www.hcund.org
Contact: Ms. Lillian Liccardi, Pres.
Founded: 1954. **Staff:** 3. **Languages:** English, French, Russian, Spanish. **Description:** Introduces United Nations delegates and their families from abroad to America and American institutions. Assists delegates in and around New York City. **Committees:** Executive. **Councils:** Advisory. **Publications:** Newsletter, annual. **Conventions/Meetings:** annual Ambassador's Ball - dinner, fundraiser with dancing.

17530 ■ The Hospitality and Information Service (THIS)
Meridian House
1630 Crescent Pl. NW
Washington, DC 20009
Ph: (202)232-3002
Fax: (202)667-1475
E-mail: this@meridian.org
URL: http://www.this4diplomats.org
Contact: Sarah Thompson, Exec.Dir.
Founded: 1961. **Members:** 400. **Staff:** 3. **Budget:** $150,000. **Description:** Volunteer organization serving foreign diplomatic residents and their families living in the Washington, DC area. Organized upon a request from the Office of the Chief of Protocol of the U.S. Department of State. Activities include: providing information about Washington and the United States; English and foreign language conversation practice; informal home hospitality; special events; tours in Washington and out of town; welcoming of new arrivals. **Affiliated With:** Meridian International Center. **Publications:** *Calendar of Events,* bimonthly. Provides descriptions of programs offered for that time period -tours, lectures, demonstrations, outings, etc. **Circulation:** 3,600 ● *THIS Newsletter,* bimonthly. **Price:** included in membership dues. **Circulation:** 400 ● Newsletter. **Price:** included in membership dues. **Circulation:** 400 ● Also publishes material about English language schools in the Washington, DC area, a reading list on Washington and household guide books, list of emergency telephone numbers, gourmet grocers, and domestic and baby-sitting services. **Conventions/Meetings:** annual meeting.

17531 ■ International Center in New York (ICNY)
50 W 23rd St., 7th Fl.
New York, NY 10010-5205
Ph: (212)255-9555
Fax: (212)255-0177
E-mail: icny@intlcenter.org
URL: http://www.intlcenter.org
Contact: Joanne Heyman, Exec. Dir.
Founded: 1961. **Members:** 2,000. **Membership Dues:** individual, $350 (annual). **Staff:** 17. **Budget:** $950,000. **Description:** International students and business professionals; immigrants and refugees. Volunteers assist recently arrived foreigners (members) in adjusting to American life through programs including: English conversation practice; social and cultural activities; tours of the New York area; home hospitality; education, housing, and employment referrals. **Libraries: Type:** reference. **Holdings:** 1,000. **Subjects:** English as a second language. **Formerly:** (1967) Midtown International Center. **Publica-**

tions: *Center News,* monthly. Newsletter ● *International Center in New York—Annual Report* ● *International Yours.*

17532 ■ International Multiracial Shared Cultural Organization (IMSCO)
PO Box 3865
New York, NY 10163
Ph: (212)532-5449
Fax: (212)532-4680
E-mail: westimsco@aol.com
URL: http://www.globalimsco.com
Contact: Roger Chapman, Sec.
Founded: 1979. **Languages:** Arabic, English, French, Portuguese, Spanish. **Description:** Promotes mutual cultural appreciation and cooperation in economic and social development among all peoples. Seeks to eliminate what the group feels is "economic apartheid between the North and South." Develops business and cultural exchange programs; encourages creation and implementation of nondiscriminatory economic development strategies. Plans to establish an institution for deciding global humanitarian, social, and economic issues in a nondiscriminatory manner.

17533 ■ ISAR: Resources for Environmental Activists
PO Box 70029
Washington, DC 20024-0029
Ph: (202)966-0880
Fax: (202)667-3291
E-mail: eliza@isar.org
URL: http://www.isar.org
Contact: Harriett Crosby, Pres./Co-Founder
Founded: 1983. **Members:** 300. **Membership Dues:** friend, $99 (annual) ● advocate, $100-$249 (annual) ● sponsor, $250-$499 (annual) ● patron, $500-$999 (annual) ● champion, $1,000 (annual). **Staff:** 35. **Budget:** $2,500,000. **Languages:** English, Russian. **Multinational. Description:** Promotes citizen participation and the development of the non-governmental sector in the countries of the former Soviet Union. Supports citizen activists and grassroots nongovernmental organizations(NGOs) in their efforts to create just and sustainable societies. Programs emphasize information exchange, cooperative activities and networking. **Libraries: Type:** open to the public. **Holdings:** 500; books, periodicals. **Subjects:** general environmental info, environment in the former Soviet Union. **Formerly:** (1992) Institute for Soviet American Relations; (1998) ISAR: Clearinghouse on Grassroots in Eurasia; (2005) ISAR: Initiative for Social Action and Renewal in Eurasia. **Publications:** *Give and Take: A Journal on Civil Society in Eurasia,* quarterly. Environmental protection, alternative energy, sustainable economics and agriculture, health and women's issues. **Price:** $35.00 for individuals; $50.00 for universities/nonprofit; $65.00 for corporate. ISSN: 0859-6286. **Circulation:** 500. Alternate Formats: online ● *In Focus,* semiannual. Newsletter. Includes annual report. Alternate Formats: online.

17534 ■ Japan Center for International Exchange - USA (JCIE/USA)
274 Madison Ave., Ste.1102
New York, NY 10016
Ph: (212)679-4130
Fax: (212)679-8410
E-mail: info@jcie.org
URL: http://www.jcie.org
Contact: James Gannon, Exec. Dir.
Founded: 1975. **Staff:** 3. **Description:** Participants are U.S. and Japanese policy makers and opinion leaders. Promotes improved communications between the U.S. and Japan. Encourages Japanese private philanthropy and good corporate citizenship in the United States. Conducts policy-related exchange, dialogue, and research programs including: U.S.-Japan Parliamentary Exchange Program, which facilitates visits to Japan by U.S. Members of Congress and visits to the U.S. by Japanese parliamentarians; exchange program for legislative staff members and state and local officials, in cooperation with the American Council of Young Political Leaders. **Telecommunication Services:** electronic mail, jgan-

non@jcie.org. **Publications:** *Emerging Civil Society in the Asia Pacific Community.* Book. **Price:** $35.00 soft cover; $50.00 hard cover ● *GrassNet* (in English and Japanese), monthly. Magazine. Reports on new trends, issues, and developments in the field of local-level international exchange and cooperation activities in Japan. Alternate Formats: online.

17535 ■ Meridian International Center (MHI)
1630 Crescent Pl. NW
Washington, DC 20009
Ph: (202)667-6800
Fax: (202)667-1475
E-mail: info@meridian.org
URL: http://www.meridian.org
Contact: Stuart W. Holliday, Pres.
Founded: 1960. **Membership Dues:** Meridian Circle, $100 (annual) ● Diplomat's Circle, $175 (annual) ● Linden Circle, $50 (annual) ● Envoy's Circle, $250 (annual) ● Ambassador's Circle, $500 (annual) ● President's Circle, $1,000 (annual) ● Chairman's Circle, $5,000 (annual) ● Visionary's Circle, $10,000 (annual). **Staff:** 100. **Description:** Cultural and educational organization in the field of international affairs dedicated to the promotion of international understanding through the exchange of people, ideas, and the arts. Provides services to international visitors, diplomats, and Americans interested in international issues. Owns and operates Meridian House and White-Meyer House, both listed in the National Register of Historic Places. Offers art exhibitions, international cultural presentations, and educational programs. **Boards:** Trustees. **Subcommittees:** Arts and Cultural Affairs; Marketing; Programming. **Formerly:** (1972) Meridian House Foundation; (1992) Meridian House International. **Publications:** *The Meridian Exchange,* semiannual. Newsletter ● *There is a Difference.* Book ● Catalogs ● Pamphlets. **Conventions/Meetings:** periodic seminar and conference ● symposium.

17536 ■ Meridian International Center Programming Division
1630 Crescent Pl. NW
Washington, DC 20009
Ph: (202)667-6800
Fax: (202)667-1475
E-mail: info@meridian.org
URL: http://www.meridian.org
Contact: Stuart W. Holliday, Pres.
Founded: 1950. **Membership Dues:** individual, $100 (annual) ● family, .$175 (annual). **Staff:** 50. **Description:** Promotes international understanding by introducing distinguished foreign visitors to American life and culture. Develops professional programs of study for approximately 1800 visitors to the U.S. each year, in conjunction with the U.S. government's International Visitors Program. **Affiliated With:** Meridian International Center. **Formerly:** (1957) Governmental Affairs Institute; (1992) Visitor Program Service of the Meridian House International. **Publications:** *The Meridian Exchange.* Newsletter. Alternate Formats: online.

17537 ■ National Council for International Visitors (NCIV)
1420 K St. NW, Ste.800
Washington, DC 20005
Ph: (202)842-1414
Free: (800)523-8101
Fax: (202)289-4625
E-mail: smueller@nciv.org
URL: http://www.nciv.org
Contact: Sherry L. Mueller PhD, Pres.
Founded: 1961. **Members:** 128. **Membership Dues:** individual, $60 (annual) ● community associate, $150 (annual) ● national associate, $250 (annual) ● student, $25 (annual). **Staff:** 8. **Local Groups:** 98. **National Groups:** 30. **Description:** Promotes excellence in citizen diplomacy. Provides services including training, networking opportunities, and publications to build leadership skills and capacity to organize professional and cultural experiences for participants in the U.S. Department of State's International Visitor Leadership Program and other international professional exchange programs.

Awards: Citizen Diplomat Award. **Frequency:** periodic. **Type:** recognition ● NCIV Excellence in Advocacy Award. **Frequency:** annual. **Type:** recognition. **Recipient:** to an individual who has rendered exceptional service to the NCIV network ● NCIV Lorinne Emery Award for Outstanding Volunteer Service. **Frequency:** annual. **Type:** recognition ● NCIV Phyllis Layton Perry Educator of the Year Award. **Frequency:** annual. **Type:** recognition. **Recipient:** to an outstanding educator who has helped to increase global awareness in his or her classroom and community ● Programming Awards. **Frequency:** annual. **Type:** recognition. **Recipient:** to outstanding achievers within the NCIV network who have given tirelessly of their energies and creativity to the success of the international visitor leadership program. **Affiliated With:** Academy for Educational Development; Delphi International Program of World Learning; Institute of International Education; Meridian International Center Programming Division; Phelps-Stokes Fund. **Formerly:** National Council for Community Services to International Visitors. **Publications:** *NCIV Network News,* monthly. Newsletter ● Membership Directory, annual ● Membership Directory listing 130 member organizations is published annually. **Conventions/Meetings:** annual Regional and National Conferences, attended by volunteers and professional staff of community organizations and related federal and private agencies (exhibits).

17538 ■ Organization for International Cooperation (OIC)
100 Conestoga Dr.
Bldg. C, Ste.196
Marlton, NJ 08053
Ph: (856)596-6679
Fax: (732)838-0747
E-mail: ak@oicworldpeace.org
URL: http://www.oicworldpeace.org
Contact: Arnold Keiser, Pres.
Founded: 1984. **Members:** 86,770. **Staff:** 3. **Budget:** $1,000,000. **Regional Groups:** 5. **State Groups:** 12. **Local Groups:** 30. **Description:** Citizen diplomats committed to improving cooperation in U.S. foreign relations through programs related to conflict reduction, international friendship and support for the United Nations. **Publications:** *OIC Newsletter,* semiannual.

17539 ■ Organization for International Professional Exchanges (IPEX)
Address Unknown since 2007
Founded: 1980. **Members:** 15. **Membership Dues:** $35 (annual). **Staff:** 3. **Languages:** English, Russian. **Description:** Promotes professional exchanges and tours between the U.S. and other countries throughout the world, professional, citizens', and scientific groups. Offers public education program on U.S.-Russian relations. Provides consulting, interpretation, research, and translation services. Conducts two-way travel programs. Maintains speakers' bureau; offers children's services; conducts educational programs. **Convention/Meeting:** none. **Formerly:** (1993) Organization for American-Soviet Exchanges. **Publications:** Brochures, annual. **Price:** free ● Newsletter, annual. **Price:** free.

17540 ■ Our Developing World (ODW)
13004 Paseo Presada
Saratoga, CA 95070-4125
Ph: (408)379-4431
Fax: (408)376-0755
E-mail: odw@magiclink.net
URL: http://www.magiclink.net/~odw
Contact: Ms. Barby Ulmer, Founder/Co-Dir.
Founded: 1974. **Membership Dues:** regular, $10. **Budget:** $40,000. **Description:** Serves as an educational project designed to make North Americans aware of the life, and socio-economic and political realities faced by people living in developing countries. Conducts Eco-reality tours to Central America, Southern Africa, and Southeast Asia to promote understanding between the participants and the people of the region. Develops curricula and offers teacher training courses on global education, world hunger, interdependence, and sustainable develop-

ment. Organizes weekend retreats. **Libraries: Type:** reference; lending. **Computer Services:** Mailing lists. **Publications:** *Our Developing World's Voices,* 3/year. Newsletter. **Price:** free to mailing list's members.

17541 ■ Pan-Pacific and Southeast Asia Women's Association of the U.S.A. (PPSEAWA-USA)
PO Box 1531
Madison Sq. Sta.
New York, NY 10159
Ph: (212)228-5307
Fax: (212)473-0942
E-mail: info@ppseawa.org
URL: http://www.ppseawa.org/USA
Contact: Ms. Shirley Munyan, Rep.
Founded: 1928. **Members:** 350. **Membership Dues:** $35 (annual). **Budget:** $50,000. **State Groups:** 5. **Local Groups:** 5. **Description:** Seeks to strengthen peaceful ties by fostering international understanding and friendship among the women of Asia and the Pacific and women of the U.S.A. Promotes cooperation among women of these regions for the study and improvement of social, economic, and cultural conditions. Engages in studies on Asian and Pacific affairs; offers friendship, hospitality, and assistance to Asian and Pacific area women; presents programs of educational and social interest, dealing with the customs and cultures of Asian and Pacific countries. Conducts lectures, panels, and workshops. **Awards: Frequency:** monthly. **Type:** scholarship. **Affiliated With:** Pan-Pacific and South-East Asia Women's Association. **Publications:** *International Bulletin,* semiannual. Provides information of significant activities in member countries and interest areas. Alternate Formats: online ● *International Conference Reports,* triennial ● *USA Bulletin.* **Conventions/Meetings:** triennial international conference ● annual meeting.

17542 ■ People to People Ambassador Program (PPAP)
110 S Ferrall St.
Dwight D. Eisenhower Bldg.
Spokane, WA 99202-4800
Ph: (509)534-0430
Fax: (877)284-4517
E-mail: info@studentambassadors.org
URL: http://www.studentambassadors.org
Contact: Dawn M. Davis, Managing Dir.
Founded: 1978. **Description:** A program of People to People International. Coordinates the international exchange of professionals working in scientific and technical fields; sends delegations of those in specialized disciplines to other countries. **Convention/Meeting:** none. **Affiliated With:** People to People International. **Also Known As:** Ambassador Programs. **Formerly:** (2003) People to People Citizen Ambassador Program. **Publications:** *Project Synopsis,* annual.

17543 ■ People to People International (PTPI)
501 E Armour Blvd.
Kansas City, MO 64109-2200
Ph: (816)531-4701
Fax: (816)561-7502
E-mail: ptpi@ptpi.org
URL: http://www.ptpi.org
Contact: Mary Jean Eisenhower, Pres./CEO
Founded: 1956. **Members:** 80,000. **Membership Dues:** individual, $20 (annual) ● family, $35 (annual) ● student, $15 (annual). **Staff:** 16. **Multinational. Description:** Professionals and university and secondary school students. Founded by President Dwight D. Eisenhower to promote international understanding through direct people-to-people contacts. Offers programs including the Adult International Exchange Program, the International Visitor Program, the Collegiate and Professional Studies Program, and the Student Ambassador Program. Also offers modest scholarships and loans to facilitate travel or defray college tuition costs. **Awards:** Adult Chapter Matching Grant. **Frequency:** annual. **Type:** grant. **Recipient:** for promoting the mission of the organization ● Best Chapter Newsletter Award. **Frequency:** annual. **Type:** monetary. **Recipient:** for a

chapter with the most creative, informative and accurate presentation ● Eisenhower Medallion. **Frequency:** annual. **Type:** medal. **Recipient:** to individuals who have made outstanding contributions to international understanding ● James and Eunice Doty PTPI/Congressional Award Scholarship. **Frequency:** annual. **Type:** scholarship. **Recipient:** for students who have earned the Congressional Award ● Lifetime Achievement Recognition Award. **Frequency:** annual. **Type:** recognition. **Recipient:** for dedication and longevity of service ● Make a Difference Award. **Frequency:** annual. **Type:** trophy. **Recipient:** for significant impact on improving peoples' lives. **Committees:** Disability. **Publications:** *On Track*, monthly. Bulletin. **Price:** included in membership dues. Alternate Formats: online ● *People*, annual. Magazine. Highlights new programs, chapter activities and news from around the world. ● *PTPI Calendar*, annual. Includes memorable moments, international holidays and inspirational quotes. **Price:** included in membership dues ● *World Wide Newsletter and Magazine*, quarterly. **Price:** included in membership dues. **Conventions/Meetings:** annual Global Youth Forum - conference, with dynamic speakers, interactive workshops and rewarding activities (exhibits) ● biennial Worldwide Conference.

17544 ■ Perhaps Kids Meeting Kids Can Make a Difference

380 Riverside Dr.
Box 8H
New York, NY 10025
Ph: (212)662-2327
Fax: (212)222-1416
E-mail: kidsmtgkids@igc.org
URL: http://kidsmeetingkids.org
Contact: Mary Sochet, Co-Chair

Founded: 1982. **Staff:** 20. **Budget:** $650,000. **Languages:** English, French, Spanish. **Multinational. Description:** Run by youth. Works toward peace, social justice, and children's rights worldwide. Sponsors letter-writing project, international computer exchange, and international children's congress. Conducts children's exchange program. Organizes days against violence at both the local and international level. **Affiliated With:** Non-Governmental Organizations Committee on UNICEF; United Nations. **Also Known As:** Kids Meeting Kids. **Publications:** Newsletter, seasonal. Contains writings by young writers. **Circulation:** 100,000. **Conventions/Meetings:** annual International Children's Congress, on disarmament, violence, and children's rights issues.

17545 ■ Project Handclasp (PH)

c/o Commander M.C. Tevelson, Dir.
Naval Base
San Diego, CA 92132
Ph: (619)532-1492
URL: http://www.sabre.org/books/bookorg/bkdn_phc.htm
Contact: Commander M.C. Tevelson, Dir.

Description: A service provided by the U.S. Navy as an overseas community relations program. Provides donated humanitarian materials to U.S. Navy ships for distribution overseas.

17546 ■ The Russian-American Center/Track Two Institute for Citizen Diplomacy (TRAC)

2670 Leavenworth
San Francisco, CA 94133
Ph: (415)563-4731 (415)292-8922
Fax: (415)563-1566
E-mail: trac@dnai.com
Contact: Dulce Murphy, Exec. Dir.

Founded: 1979. **Staff:** 2. **Budget:** $750,000. **Description:** Seeks to expand opportunities to improve relations between the nations by developing innovative approaches to U.S.-Russian cooperation. Seeks to improve U.S.-Russian relations by: furthering communication between U.S. and Russian professionals; providing the American public with a better understanding of similarities and differences between the two countries; helping leaders in both countries channel interaction into constructive projects. Sponsors informal dialogues between U.S. and Russian scien-

tists, political leaders, and scholars. Emphasizes the impact of citizen diplomacy through the promotion of activities that are not possible on a government-to-government basis. Projects include: live interactive satellite educational events between the U.S. and the former USSR; interdisciplinary working seminars on U.S.-Russian relations; writing exchange and cooperative exchanges in the field of health promotion; public seminars to better inform Americans about the former Soviet Union. **Affiliated With:** Esalen Institute. **Formerly:** (1980) Escalen Institute Soviet-American Exchange Program; (1992) Escalen Institute Russian-American Exchange Center; (1994) The Russian-American Center. **Conventions/Meetings:** annual conference.

17547 ■ Sister Cities International (SCI)

1301 Pennsylvania Ave. NW, Ste.850
Washington, DC 20004
Ph: (202)347-8630
Fax: (202)393-6524
E-mail: info@sister-cities.org
URL: http://www.sister-cities.org
Contact: Tim Honey, Exec. Dir.

Founded: 1967. **Members:** 675. **Membership Dues:** individual, $25-$50 (annual) ● global, $140 (annual) ● embassy, $500 (annual) ● non-profit, $600 (annual) ● corporate/municipal association, $1,000 (annual) ● state, $1,200 (annual) ● city and county, $140-$1,865 (annual). **Staff:** 11. **Budget:** $1,042,430. **Description:** U.S. cities, towns, and communities. Seeks to affiliate communities in the U.S. with communities in other nations, in the hopes of encouraging international understanding. The long-term, sustainable partnerships focus on education, cultural, and economic exchanges. Provides advice to American cities in choosing a sister city; distributes publications, reports, and surveys of general or specific interest to member communities. Sponsors technical assistance program that sends U.S. technicians to developing countries. Aids members who wish to undertake specific projects, such as sending equipment abroad or participating in student exchange group tours. **Libraries:** Type: reference. **Subjects:** education, cultural and economic exchanges. **Awards:** Young Artist Program. **Frequency:** annual. **Type:** monetary. **Telecommunication Services:** electronic mail, thoney@sister-cities.org. **Committees:** Disabilities Awareness; Organizational Relationships; Public Officials; Special Programs; Youth Programs. **Also Known As:** Town Affiliation Association of the United States, Inc. **Publications:** *Inside SCI*, annual. Magazine. **Circulation:** 2,500 ● *Sister City News*, semiannual. Newspaper. **Circulation:** 13,000 ● Annual Report, annual ● Membership Directory, annual ● Handbook. **Conventions/Meetings:** annual conference (exhibits) - always July. 2008 July 16-19, Kansas City, MO ● annual Young Artist Program Contest - competition.

17548 ■ U.S. Servas (SI)

1125 16th St., Ste.201
Arcata, CA 95521-5585
Ph: (707)825-1714
Fax: (707)825-1762
E-mail: info@usservas.org
URL: http://www.usservas.org
Contact: Gran Barnes, Board Chair

Founded: 1949. **Members:** 4,000. **Membership Dues:** regular/day host, contributor, $40 (annual) ● international traveler, $85 (annual) ● domestic traveler, $50 (annual). **Staff:** 3. **Budget:** $150,000. **State Groups:** 50. **Description:** Hosts and travelers in over 130 countries working to build world peace, goodwill, and understanding by providing opportunities for deeper, more personal contacts among people of diverse cultures and backgrounds. **Computer Services:** Electronic publishing, e-newsletter ● online services, talk forum for hosts and travelers. **Sections:** American Family; Domestic Travel Programs; Host; International Student; Travel. **Formerly:** (1952) Peace Builders; (1993) Servas International. **Publications:** *National Host Directory*, annual. Lists hosts in various countries. ● *Servas International News*, annual. Newsletter ● *U.S. Servas News*, quarterly. Newsletter. Covers membership activities.

Price: included in membership dues. Alternate Formats: online. **Conventions/Meetings:** annual conference.

17549 ■ Uniterra Foundation (UF)

16 Gowell Ln.
Weston, MA 02493
Ph: (781)647-5295
Fax: (781)647-5295
Contact: Mark Horowitz, Dir.

Founded: 1981. **Members:** 600. **Description:** Individuals who promote unity among people throughout the world. Fosters an awareness that humans share a common future, and that this link is a unifying factor that transcends individual differences. Believes that creative expressions that affirm world unity will serve as inspiration for solving global problems such as hunger, poverty, and the threat of nuclear attack. Encourages personal creative activity and projects that promote the theme of "One Earth, One Humanity, One Future." Maintains film and video library on global concerns. **Publications:** Newsletter, periodic.

17550 ■ Unity-and-Diversity World Council (UDC)

c/o Leland P. Stewart, BSE, Founder/Coor.
PO Box 661401
Los Angeles, CA 90066-9201
Ph: (310)391-5735
Fax: (310)827-9187
E-mail: udcworld1@yahoo.com
URL: http://www.udcworld.org
Contact: Leland P. Stewart BSE, Founder/Coor.

Founded: 1965. **Members:** 200. **Membership Dues:** individual, $25 (annual) ● organization, $60 (annual) ● student, senior citizen, $15 (annual) ● professional, $40 (annual). **Staff:** 1. **Budget:** $25,000. **Regional Groups:** 100. **Multinational. Description:** Works to establish and sustain a local-to-global body of individuals, groups, and networks on a moral and spiritual foundation for cooperation on peace, justice and on environmentally sustainable future for all races, cultures, and religions. **Libraries:** Type: reference. **Holdings:** 1,000; articles, audio recordings, books, periodicals, video recordings. **Subjects:** philosophy, education, religion, science, arts, politics. **Awards:** Heart of Humanity Award. **Frequency:** annual. **Type:** recognition. **Recipient:** for an outstanding individual. **Computer Services:** database, referrals and clearinghouse ● mailing lists, individuals and organizations. **Boards:** Advisory; World. **Committees:** Peace Sunday Steering. **Departments:** Administration; Central Coordination; Geographic Councils; Program; Public Relations; Specialized Affiliates. **Projects:** Arts; Education; Environment; Health; Interfaith Network; Media; Peace and Justice; Pilot; Unity-and-Diversity Education in Public and Private Schools; Unity-and-Diversity Spiritual Group; Worldview Exploration Seminar. **Absorbed:** (1965) Conference on Science and Religion. **Formerly:** (1965) Pageant for Peace; (1979) International Cooperation Council; (1980) Unity in Diversity Council; (1988) Unity and Diversity World Organization. **Publications:** *General Assembly Bulletin* ● *Interfaith Celebration*, monthly. Bulletin ● *Spectrum*, quarterly. Magazine. Alternate Formats: online ● *Spectrum Update*, monthly. Newsletter. Alternate Formats: online ● *Unity-and-Diversity Spiritual Celebration Guide* ● *Unity and Diversity Worship*, weekly. Bulletin. Announces weekly celebrations and other meetings. **Price:** free ● *Worldview Exploration Publications*. **Conventions/Meetings:** monthly general assembly, group reports, dialogues, action; includes all interested fields ● monthly Interfaith Celebration - meeting, music, prayer and meditation, messages from the faiths, dialogue ● annual Peace Sunday - meeting, celebration featuring speakers, performers, choirs, interfaith candlelighting, and table displays - November or December ● quarterly Worldview Exploration Seminar, with papers and dialogue.

17551 ■ Venceremos Brigade (VB)

PO Box 5202
Englewood, NJ 07631-5202
Ph: (212)560-4360

E-mail: vbrigade@yahoo.com
URL: http://www.venceremosbrigade.org
Founded: 1969. **Multinational. Description:** Promotes friendship between the U.S. and Cuba by sponsoring U.S. contingents to Cuba to visit schools and factories, attend cultural programs, and experience Cuban life. Encourages U.S. dialogue and relations with Cuba. Works to improve information-sharing and travel between the U.S. and Cuba. Also works towards social change in the U.S. through participation in the peace movement, civil rights, and labor relations.

17552 ■ Veterans for America (VFA)
1025 Vermont Ave. NW, 7th Fl.
Washington, DC 20005
Ph: (202)483-9222
Fax: (202)483-9312
E-mail: immap@vi.org
URL: http://www.veteransforamerica.org
Contact: Robert O. Muller, Chm.
Founded: 1980. **Multinational. Description:** Works to address the causes, conduct and consequences of war through programs of advocacy and service for victims of conflict. Works in more than a dozen countries providing services such as physical rehabilitation, information mapping and management, children and family development, refugee assistance, nuclear threat reduction and sport therapy and rehabilitation. **Funds:** Cambodia. **Programs:** Information Management and Mine Action; Nuclear Threat Reduction Campaign; Post Conflict Rehabilitation; Sports For Life; War Kids Relief. **Affiliated With:** Vietnam Veterans of America. **Absorbed:** (1990) Vietnam Project. **Also Known As:** (2006) Veterans International. **Formerly:** (2007) Vietnam Veterans of American Foundation. **Publications:** *The Humanitarian*, quarterly. Newsletter. Alternate Formats: online ● Brochure ● Annual Report, annual. Alternate Formats: online ● Reports. Alternate Formats: online. **Conventions/Meetings:** periodic international conference - always Washington, DC ● periodic luncheon and seminar.

17553 ■ Volunteers for Peace (VFP)
1034 Tiffany Rd.
Belmont, VT 05730
Ph: (802)259-2759
Fax: (802)259-2922
E-mail: vfp@vfp.org
URL: http://www.vfp.org
Contact: Peter R. Coldwell, Pres.
Founded: 1982. **Members:** 5,000. **Membership Dues:** individual, $20 (annual). **Staff:** 3. **Budget:** $300,000. **Multinational. Description:** Offers over 2,000 short-term (2-3 week) voluntary service placements in over 80 different countries. Placed more than 12,000 volunteers in international workcamps abroad. Programs are an affordable way to complete meaningful community service while living and interacting in an international environment. Participants live and work with an international group from 4 or more countries for 2-3 weeks, providing a diverse cultural exchange with the other volunteers as well as the local hosts. **Awards:** Registration Scholarship. **Type:** scholarship. **Recipient:** for US or Canadian residents. **Publications:** *The International Volunteer*, annual. Newsletter. Includes information on work camps worldwide. **Price:** included in membership dues ● *International Workcamp Directory*, annual. Lists over 1,500 work camp programs in 70 countries. **Price:** included in membership dues. **Circulation:** 4,000. **Conventions/Meetings:** semiannual meeting.

17554 ■ Wisconsin Coordinating Council on Nicaragua (WCCN)
PO Box 1534
Madison, WI 53701
Ph: (608)257-7230 (608)742-8408
Fax: (608)257-7904
E-mail: wccn@wccnica.org
URL: http://www.wccnica.org
Contact: Carlos Arenas, Exec. Dir.
Founded: 1984. **Members:** 1,100. **Membership Dues:** regular, $35 (annual). **Staff:** 6. **Budget:** $350,000. **Languages:** English, Spanish. **Descrip-**

tion: Serves as an organization working in partnership with Nicaraguans to promote social and economic justice through alternative models of development and activism. **Telecommunication Services:** electronic mail, exdir@wccnica.org. **Committees:** Loan Fund Oversight; Outreach; Women's Empowerment Project. **Projects:** NICA Fund; US-Nicaragua Women's Empowerment. **Publications:** *Bibliography on Alternative Credit in Nicaragua*. Alternate Formats: online ● *Friends in Deed: The Story of U.S. Nicaragua Sister Cities*, quarterly. Book. **Price:** $10.00 ● *Nicaraguan Developments*, quarterly. Newsletter. **Price:** included in membership dues. Alternate Formats: online ● Annual Reports, annual. Includes financial statements, activities reports and projects for the year, and lists of valued volunteers and financial supporters. Alternate Formats: online ● Reports. Alternate Formats: online. **Conventions/Meetings:** annual meeting.

17555 ■ World Neighbors (WN)
4127 NW 122nd St.
Oklahoma City, OK 73120-9933
Ph: (405)752-9700
Free: (800)242-6387
Fax: (405)752-9393
E-mail: info@wn.org
URL: http://www.wn.org
Contact: Melanie Macdonald, Pres./CEO
Founded: 1951. **Staff:** 34. **Budget:** $6,172,513. **Local Groups:** 35. **Multinational. Description:** Seeks to eliminate hunger, disease, and poverty in Asia, Africa, and Latin America. Helps people to analyze and solve their own problems by developing and testing simple technologies at the community level and training local leaders to spread successful methods. Programs focus on food production, community-based health, family planning, water and sanitation, environmental conservation, and small business. Provides speakers, videocassettes, films, filmstrips, literature, and other training materials on long-term economic development and causes of poverty and hunger to schools, religious and study groups, and other organizations. **Libraries: Type:** open to the public. **Holdings:** 1,000; artwork, books, periodicals. **Subjects:** developers. **Additional Websites:** http://www.workofwomen.org. **Telecommunication Services:** electronic mail, mmacdonald@wn.org. **Boards:** Trustees. **Departments:** Marketing Communications. **Absorbed:** World Assistance. **Publications:** *From the Roots Up - Strengthening Organizational Capacity through Guided Self-Assessment*. Handbook ● *Neighbors*, quarterly. Newsletter. **Price:** free. **Circulation:** 13,250 ● *Training Materials Catalog* ● *Two Ears of Corn - A Guide to People-Centered Agricultural Improvement* ● Annual Report, annual. **Price:** free.

17556 ■ World Peace Foundation (WPF)
79 John F. Kennedy St.
Cambridge, MA 02138
Ph: (617)496-9812
Fax: (617)491-8588
E-mail: world_peace@harvard.edu
URL: http://www.worldpeacefoundation.org
Contact: Robert I. Rotberg, Pres.
Founded: 1910. **Staff:** 4. **Description:** Seeks to advance the cause of world peace through study, analysis, and the advocacy of wise action. Includes interests such as: international relations and foreign affairs, regional security, international economic issues, preventive diplomacy, and the creation of early warning systems. **Computer Services:** database ● mailing lists. **Publications:** *Africa's Discontent: Coping with Human and Natural Disasters*. Report. Explains how and why many of the important countries across the great swath of Middle Africa became problems. **Price:** $13.57/copy ● *Combating Terrorism in the Horn of Africa and Yemen*. Report ● *Cyprus After Annan: Next Steps Toward a Solution*. Report ● *Diamonds In Peace and War: Severing the Conflict-Diamond Connection*. Report. Contains latest word on conflict diamonds and their contribution to the wars of Middle Africa. **Price:** $13.57/copy ● *The Good Governance Problem: Doing Something About It*. Report ● *Haiti's Turmoil: Politics and Policy*

Under Aristide and Clinton. Report. Contains comments on Haiti's recent vicissitudes and the policy choices that was made before and during the Clinton and Aristide presidencies. **Price:** $13.57/copy ● *Preventing Conflict in Africa: Possibilities of Peace Enforcement*. Report ● *Sudan: Policy Options Amid Civil War*. Report. Discusses the long-running civil war in Sudan. **Price:** $19.95/copy ● *Sudan: Policy Options Amid Civil War: Postscript*. Report ● *To Rid the Scourge of War: UN Peacekeeping Operations & Today's Crises*. Report. Examines the UN's capacity for peacekeeping, peace enforcement, and peace building. **Price:** $13.57/copy ● *Zimbabwe Before and After the Elections: a Concerned Assessment*. Report ● Also publishes a variety of reports and books available from their individual publishers. **Conventions/Meetings:** conference - 2-3/year.

Internet

17557 ■ Enough Is Enough (EIE)
746 Walker Rd., Ste.116
Great Falls, VA 22066
Free: (888)744-0004
Fax: (571)333-5685
E-mail: webpk@cox.net
URL: http://www.enough.org
Contact: Donna Rice Hughes, Chair/Pres.
Founded: 1992. **Description:** Seeks to make the Internet safer for children and families. Raises public awareness of the dangers of Internet pornography and sexual predators. Advances solutions that promote equality, fairness and respect for human dignity with shared responsibility between the public, technology and the law. **Telecommunication Services:** electronic mail, pkwebmaster@cox.net ● electronic mail, eieiwong@aol.com.

Iran

17558 ■ Iran Freedom Foundation (IFF)
PO Box 422
Bethesda, MD 20817
Ph: (301)215-6677
Fax: (301)907-8877
E-mail: mrtabatabai@iffmrt.org
URL: http://iffmrt.org
Contact: M.R. Tabatabai, Pres.
Founded: 1979. **Staff:** 4. **Description:** Opposes the Islamic Republic of Iran. Promotes and protects the human rights of the Iranian people. Promotes the establishment of a secular, constitutional democracy in Iran. Organizes demonstrations and gatherings. Provides information and opinions for the media, universities and political institutions in the form of interviews, articles, and analyses concerning Iranian social and political affairs. **Awards: Type:** recognition. **Recipient:** for outstanding contribution to human rights. **Committees:** Human Rights; National Resources; Strategy.

Iranian

17559 ■ American Iranian Council (AIC)
20 Nassau St., Ste.111
Princeton, NJ 08542
Ph: (609)252-9099
Fax: (609)252-9698
E-mail: aic@american-iranian.org
URL: http://www.american-iranian.org
Contact: Hooshang Amirahmadi PhD, Founder/Pres.
Founded: 1997. **Membership Dues:** individual, $100 ● supporter (individual), $500 ● supporter (organization), $1,000 ● sponsor (organization), $2,500 ● sponsor (corporation), $5,000 ● patron, $10,000 ● benefactor, $20,000. **Multinational. Description:** Promotes a peaceful relationship between Iran and the United States. Seeks to improve U.S.-Iran relations through understanding, dialogue, and constructive engagement. Acts as a platform for dialogue on U.S.-Iran relations. Serves as a forum for discussion

of issues of importance in Iranian society. **Publications:** *AIC Insight*, quarterly. Newsletter. Addresses the issues preventing rapprochement in the absence of accurate information and direct communication between the US and Iran. **Price:** included in membership dues. Alternate Formats: online ● *AIC Update*. Newsletter. Promotes policy commentary and responds to events surrounding U.S.-Iran relations. **Price:** free. Alternate Formats: online ● Books.

Iraq

17560 ■ Education for Peace in Iraq Center (EPIC)

1101 Pennsylvania Ave. SE
Washington, DC 20003
Ph: (202)543-6176
Fax: (202)543-0725
E-mail: info@epic-usa.org
URL: http://www.epic-usa.org
Contact: Erik Gustafson, Exec. Dir.
Founded: 1998. **Multinational. Description:** Works to improve humanitarian conditions in Iraq. **Programs:** EPIC Advocacy; Epic Dispatches; Faces of Iraq Exhibition; Iraq Culture Nights; Reports from the Field; Speakers Bureau.

17561 ■ Iraq Action Coalition

7309 Haymarket Ln.
Raleigh, NC 27615
Fax: (919)846-7422
E-mail: iac@leb.net
URL: http://iraqaction.org
Multinational. Description: Serves as an online media activists' resource center for groups and activists who are working to end the war against the people of Iraq. Maintains listserv. **Computer Services:** Mailing lists. **Publications:** *Iraq Under Siege: The Deadly Impact of Sanctions and War*. Book. **Price:** $16.00/copy ● *Starving Iraq: One Humanitarian Disaster We Can Stop*. Pamphlet.

Ireland

17562 ■ American Ireland Fund (AIF)

211 Cong. St.
Boston, MA 02110
Ph: (617)574-0720
Fax: (617)574-0730
E-mail: info@irlfunds.org
URL: http://www.irlfunds.org
Contact: Kingsley Aikins, Pres./CEO
Founded: 1976. **Membership Dues:** gold, $1,000 (annual) ● silver, $500 (annual) ● bronze, $100 (annual). **Staff:** 30. **Budget:** $10,000,000. **Multinational. Description:** Individuals of Irish ancestry and friends of Ireland dedicated to raising funds to support programs of peace and reconciliation, arts and culture, education and community development. **Awards:** Peace Award. **Frequency:** annual. **Type:** recognition. **Recipient:** for outstanding leadership in promoting the peace process. **Publications:** *Connect*, semiannual, every June and December. Magazine. **Circulation:** 45,000. **Advertising:** accepted.

17563 ■ Christian Ireland Ministries (CIM)

PO Box 11057
Albany, NY 12211
Ph: (518)634-7021
E-mail: frfrancis@scripturewall.com
URL: http://www.scripturewall.com
Contact: Rev. Francis G. McCloskey, Pres.
Founded: 1981. **Staff:** 3. **Nonmembership. Multinational. Description:** Promotes and monitors Ireland's "ancient Christian tradition vs. current attempts to devalue that tradition, with emphasis on the sanctity of human life.". **Formerly:** (1984) Columba House Fund. **Publications:** *Scripture Wall Bulletin*, periodic. Alternate Formats: online. **Conventions/Meetings:** annual Oh Saratoga! - conference, with prayer and witness (exhibits).

17564 ■ Doors of Hope (DH)

PO Box 485
Ho Ho Kus, NJ 07423
Ph: (201)444-4786
Fax: (201)444-7588
E-mail: tony@doorsofhope.com
URL: http://www.doorsofhope.com
Contact: Elizabeth Logue, Sec.
Founded: 1987. **Members:** 1,300. **Description:** Individuals concerned with "the oppression and deprivation of the people of Northern Ireland." Supports self-help projects in Northern Ireland through dances, concerts, and mail appeals. Provides education and job training. **Convention/Meeting:** none. **Computer Services:** Mailing lists, of members. **Also Known As:** Doirse Dochais. **Publications:** *Nation*, monthly. Newsletter.

17565 ■ Irish American Unity Conference (IAUC)

611 Pennsylvania Ave. SE, No. 4150
Washington, DC 20003
Free: (800)947-4282
E-mail: iauc@iauc.org
URL: http://www.iauc.org
Contact: Dr. Robert C. Linnon, Pres.
Founded: 1983. **Members:** 10,000. **Membership Dues:** regular, $25 (annual) ● senior citizen/student, $15 (annual) ● family, $35 (annual). **Staff:** 2. **Budget:** $50,000. **Regional Groups:** 17. **State Groups:** 35. **Description:** American human rights organization working for peace with justice in a united Ireland. Promotes U.S. awareness of human rights violations in Northern Ireland. Coordinates fact-finding missions to Northern Ireland for attorneys and U.S. legislators, sponsors speaking tours throughout the U.S., holds briefings before the U.S. Congress on issues important to Irish-Americans. Promotes the passage of federal legislation in support of the MacBride principles, nine guidelines for fair employment practices in Northern Ireland. Issues affecting Ireland, north and south. **Committees:** Cultural; Education; Fundraising; Human Rights; Political Action; Press and Publicity. **Publications:** *IAUC National Newsletter*, monthly. **Price:** $25.00/year. **Conventions/Meetings:** annual convention (exhibits).

17566 ■ Irish National Caucus (INC)

PO Box 15128
Washington, DC 20003-0849
Ph: (202)544-0568
Fax: (202)488-7537
E-mail: info@irishnationalcaucus.org
URL: http://www.irishnationalcaucus.org
Contact: Fr. Sean McManus, Pres.
Founded: 1974. **Members:** 50,000. **Description:** Persons concerned with the protection of human rights in Northern Ireland. Through lobbying and public education efforts, seeks to make human rights in Ireland an American issue, both legally and morally. Promotes just and lasting peace in Ireland. Initiated and launched the MacBride Principles a corporate code of conduct for U.S. companies doing business in Northern Ireland. **Publications:** *Irish Lobby*, periodic. Newsletter ● *The MacBride Principles: Genesis and History*. Book.

17567 ■ Irish Northern Aid Committee (NORAID)

252 W 38th St., Ste.1404
New York, NY 10018
Ph: (212)736-1916
Free: (800)IRE-LAND
E-mail: noriad@inac.org
URL: http://inac.org
Contact: Paul Doris, Natl. Chm.
Founded: 1970. **Staff:** 2. **Local Groups:** 105. **Description:** Aims are to: raise money to support families of Irish political prisoners; generate support for a free, independent, reunited Ireland of 32 counties; heighten awareness among Americans of the nature of British colonial rule in Ireland and the resulting conflicts. Organizes protest demonstrations; acts as a political lobby. Offers tours to Northern Ireland. Collects and disseminates information; operates speakers' bureau. **Publications:** Books ● Pamphlets. **Conventions/Meetings:** periodic meeting.

Israel

17568 ■ Americans for Peace Now (APN)

1101 14th St. NW, 6th Fl.
Washington, DC 20005
Ph: (202)728-1893
Fax: (202)728-1895
E-mail: apndc@peacenow.org
URL: http://www.peacenow.org
Contact: Debra DeLee, Pres./CEO
Founded: 1981. **Staff:** 15. **Budget:** $2,400,000. **Description:** A support group of American Jews representing the Peace Now movement in Israel. (Peace Now, also known as Shalom Achshav, is an Israeli peace movement that supports a negotiated peace settlement between the Israeli government and Palestinian leaders based on exchanging territories for peace and security.) Helps familiarize American Jews with Peace Now, its history and goals, and its impact on the peace struggle in Israel. Promotes solidarity with Israel. **Programs:** Advocacy Action Network; Media Outreach and Monitoring; Peace Messengers from the Middle East; Public Campaigns; Shalom Achshav (Peace Now in Israel); Speakers Bureau/Policy Briefings. **Formerly:** (1990) Friends of Peace Now. **Publications:** *Peace Now: A Newsletter for Our Friends in North America*, semiannual. Reports on organizational activities and events. ● Pamphlets ● Videos ● Also publishes a platform statement. **Conventions/Meetings:** annual conference.

17569 ■ Christians' Israel Public Action Campaign (CIPAC)

PO Box 18173
Washington, DC 20036-8173
Ph: (202)234-3600
Fax: (202)332-3221
E-mail: info@cipaconline.org
URL: http://www.cipaconline.org
Contact: Richard A. Hellman, Founder/Pres.
Founded: 1989. **Members:** 3,000. **Description:** Represents Christians and other interested individuals lobbying on behalf of a strong relationship between the U.S. and Israel. Organizes and informs the Christian community of legislative and policy issues pertaining to Israel. Communicates with legislators, policymakers, and the American public about support for Israel. Opposes the creation of a Palestinian Arab state in the "biblical" areas of Judea, Samaria, Gaza, the Golan, and all of Jerusalem. Hosts programs and events to prepare the Christian community to effectively demonstrate political action. Operates speakers' bureau. **Libraries: Type:** reference. **Publications:** Newsletter, quarterly. **Price:** free. **Circulation:** 3,000.

17570 ■ Kibbutz Program Center (KPC)

114 W 26th St., Ste.1004
New York, NY 10001
Ph: (212)462-2764
Fax: (212)462-2765
E-mail: mail@kibbutzprogramcenter.org
URL: http://www.kibbutzprogramcenter.org
Contact: Eytan Peer, Dir.
Founded: 1971. **Members:** 250. **Staff:** 4. **Budget:** $42,000. **Regional Groups:** 8. **State Groups:** 1. **Local Groups:** 3. **National Groups:** 72. **Languages:** English, Hebrew. **Description:** Represents individuals who have had experience in kibbutz and are either considering immigrating to Israel to kibbutz in the future, or wish to remain in contact with others who have experienced kibbutz. Provides programming for returnees, including lectures, films, seminars, summer workshops, and discussion panels. Sends groups of immigrants to kibbutz each year. **Telecommunication Services:** electronic mail, kibbutzdsk@aol.com. **Formerly:** (1997) Garin Yarden - Young Kibbutz Movement. **Publications:** *New Horizons News Magazine*, monthly ● Newsletter, monthly ● Also publishes membership directory and pamphlets. **Conventions/Meetings:** quarterly conference.

17571 ■ Kolel Shomre Hachomos/Reb Meir Baal Haness (KSH/RMBH)
18 Heyward St.
Brooklyn, NY 11211
Ph: (718)243-2495
Fax: (718)243-2499
Contact: Rabbi P. Weinberger, Exec. Officer
Description: Purpose is to raise funds for the Holy Land. Conducts Torah education and charitable programs. **Formerly:** (1985) Kolel Shomre Hachomos. **Publications:** *Hakolel*, annual. Journal. **Advertising:** accepted. **Conventions/Meetings:** annual dinner - Brooklyn, NY.

17572 ■ National Christian Leadership Conference for Israel (NCLCI)
43422 W Oaks Dr., No. 300
Novi, MI 48377
Ph: (248)557-4540
Fax: (248)557-4527
E-mail: nclci@msn.com
URL: http://www.nclci.org
Contact: Dr. David Blewett, Pres.
Founded: 1978. **Membership Dues:** regular, $50 (annual) ● student, $25 (annual) ● patron, $100 (annual) ● individual benefactor, $250 (annual) ● family benefactor, $500 (annual) ● sponsor (minimum), $1,000 (annual). **Staff:** 4. **Regional Groups:** 35. **Description:** Christian clergy and laity with a concern in reaffirming American Christian support for "the people, land, and State of Israel." Efforts are aimed toward helping coordinate, unify, and support the activities of many local and regional Christian groups in the U.S. working on behalf of Israel. Acts as clearinghouse for American Christian organizations advocating support to Israel through their educational programs. Encourages other Christians to support Israel. Conducts research; maintains speakers' bureau. Maintains organizational files on Christian activities and programs on Israel and the Middle East. **Libraries:** Type: reference. **Supersedes:** Christians Concerned for Israel. **Publications:** *Backgrounder*, quarterly. Newsletter. **Circulation:** 1,000 ● *Honor the Promise*, semiannual. Newsletter. **Circulation:** 6,000 ● Brochure. **Conventions/Meetings:** semiannual executive committee meeting - spring and fall.

17573 ■ New Israel Fund (NIF)
1101 14th St. NW, 6th Fl.
Washington, DC 20005-5639
Ph: (202)842-0900
Free: (888)988-3863
Fax: (202)842-0991
E-mail: info@nif.org
URL: http://www.nif.org
Contact: Larry Garber, Exec. Dir./CEO
Founded: 1979. **Members:** 12,000. **Staff:** 65. **Budget:** $12,200,000. **Regional Groups:** 7. **National Groups:** 4. **Languages:** English, Hebrew. **Description:** International philanthropic partnership of North Americans, Israelis, and Europeans, which supports activities in Israel that defend civil and human rights, promote Jewish-Arab equality and coexistence, advance the status of women, nurture tolerance and religious pluralism, reduce social and economic gaps, pursue environmental justice and promote government accountability. Operates SHATIL, technical assistance agency, provides grants and technical assistance to some 700 Israeli public interest groups, trains Israeli civil-rights and environmental lawyers, and conducts study tours and public education in North America and Israel about the challenges to Israeli democracy. **Publications:** Annual Report, annual. **Circulation:** 12,000.

17574 ■ StandWithUs (SWU)
PO Box 341069
Los Angeles, CA 90034-1069
Ph: (310)836-6140
E-mail: info@standwithus.com
URL: http://www.standwithus.com
Contact: Roz Rothstein, Natl. Dir.
Founded: 2001. **Multinational. Description:** Promotes education and understanding that will bring a secure future for Israel. Works to ensure that Israel's side of the story is told in communities, campuses, libraries, the media and churches. Encourages communities all over the world to meet in support of Israel. **Telecommunication Services:** electronic mail, campus@standwithus.com. **Also Known As:** (2006) Israel Emergency Alliance. **Publications:** Brochure (in English, French, and Spanish).

17575 ■ Volunteers for Israel (VFI)
330 W 42nd St., Ste.1618
New York, NY 10036
Ph: (212)643-4848
Free: (866)514-1948
E-mail: new-york@vfi-usa.org
URL: http://www.vfi-usa.org
Contact: Josef Herz, Natl. Pres.
Founded: 1982. **Membership Dues:** student/returning volunteer, $50 (annual) ● regular, $80 (annual). **Staff:** 2. **Budget:** $100,000. **Regional Groups:** 8. **Description:** Fosters friendship between diaspora Jews and Israelis by recruiting volunteers to work in Israel. Volunteers work on Israel Defense Force bases, and serve in warehousing, supply, and maintenance and in hospitals and social services areas supplying geriatric care and other services. Volunteers participate in tours and attend lectures and cultural events while in Israel. **Computer Services:** database ● mailing lists. **Committees:** College Campus; Dinner and Holiday Event. **Conventions/Meetings:** periodic International Congress.

Jewish

17576 ■ American Committee for Rescue and Resettlement of Iraqi Jews (AMCORR)
1125 Park Ave.
New York, NY 10028
Ph: (212)427-1246
Fax: (212)360-7009
URL: http://www.wojac.com
Contact: Dr. Heskel M. Haddad MD, Pres.
Founded: 1969. **Members:** 1,000. **Languages:** Arabic, English, Hebrew. **Description:** Aims to rescue the Jews of Iraq. Disseminates information to arouse public opinion regarding "the persecution of Jews in Iraq" and raises funds to help in their rescue and resettlement. A committee advertisement in the New York Times of Jan. 29, 1970 asked for immediate restoration of fundamental human rights of Jews in Iraq, release of Jews in prisons there, and permission for the emigration of those Jews who wished to leave Iraq. As a result of pressure by other governments, the Iraqi government released all Jewish detainees held in Iraqi prisons and allowed a limited number of Jewish families to leave Iraq. **Publications:** *AMCORR-HOPE*, periodic ● *Born in Baghdad*. Book ● *Flight from Babylon*. Book ● *Iraq-Quo Vadis*. Book ● *Jews of Arab*. Book. **Conventions/Meetings:** annual meeting.

17577 ■ American Federation of Jews From Central Europe (AFJCE)
570 7th Ave.
New York, NY 10018
Ph: (212)921-3871
Fax: (212)575-1918
Contact: Dr. Fritz Weinschenk, Pres.
Founded: 1941. **Staff:** 2. **Languages:** English, German. **Description:** Acts as a liaison and coordinating agency for all social, cultural, and welfare organizations founded by German-speaking Jewish immigrants from Central Europe in the U.S. Seeks to protect the rights and represent the interests of its members through such means as aid in the fields of restitution and indemnification; support of liberalized immigration program; analysis and interpretation of laws, government decrees, and legal decisions that affect constituents; cultural activities, public conferences, and migration history research. **Awards:** Type: recognition. **Affiliated With:** Jewish Philanthropic Fund of 1933; Research Foundation for Jewish Immigration. **Publications:** Booklets ● Books. **Conventions/Meetings:** annual meeting - always New York City.

17578 ■ Center for Jewish Community Studies
Baltimore Hebrew Univ.
5800 Park Heights Ave.
Baltimore, MD 21215
Ph: (410)664-5222
Fax: (410)664-1228
E-mail: cjcs@cjcs.net
URL: http://www.jcpa.org
Contact: Prof. Allan Mittleman, Proj. Dir.
Founded: 1976. **Members:** 5,000. **Membership Dues:** sponsor, $5,000 (annual) ● patron, $1,000 (annual) ● sustaining, $250 (annual) ● contributing, $100 (annual). **Staff:** 25. **Languages:** English, Hebrew. **Description:** Action oriented research center serving Israel and the Jewish people. Believes that ideas have consequences, and accordingly provides knowledge, insight and creative alternatives and solutions where appropriate in relation to the issues and concerns outlined below. Focuses on issues relating to the Israeli government and politics, Israel-Diaspora relations, World Jewish communities, inter and intra-governmental relations in Israel, the roles and functions of the Jewish Agency, the World Zionist organization and related organizations, Israel-Arab peace, educational systems and the federated governance and fundraising mechanisms throughout the Jewish and general worlds. **Libraries:** Type: not open to the public. **Holdings:** 1,000; articles, books, periodicals. **Subjects:** Israel, Jewish Diaspora related. **Additional Websites:** http://www.cjcs.net. **Publications:** *Jerusalem Letter/Viewpoints*, bimonthly. Newsletter. Covers vital issues and developments in Israel, the Jewish world, and the Middle East. **Price:** $40.00 /year for individuals; $55.00/year for organizations. ISSN: 0334-4096 ● *Jewish Political Studies Review*, semiannual. Journal. Focuses on Jewish political institutions and behavior, political thought, and public affairs. **Price:** $18.00/year for students; $24.00 /year for individuals; $38.00 /year for libraries and organizations.

17579 ■ Center for Russian and East European Jewry (CREEJ)
c/o Jacob Birnbaum
240 Cabrini Blvd., No. 5B
New York, NY 10033-1118
Ph: (212)928-7451
Fax: (212)795-8867
Contact: Jacob Birnbaum, Dir.
Founded: 1966. **Description:** Assists Jews in the former USSR in their "struggle to emigrate and to achieve a cultural and religious renaissance." Emphasizes the plight of the "prisoners of conscience" and refuseniks and provides their families with material aid. Is also concerned with the emigration problems of Romanian Jews. Conducts educational campaigns in the U.S., Europe, and Israel. **Affiliated With:** Student Struggle for Soviet Jewry. **Publications:** *Samizdat*, periodic. Underground literature with particular reference to Jewish culture in the former USSR.

17580 ■ Consultative Council of Jewish Organizations (CCJO)
c/o Friends of the Alliance Israelite Universelle
15 W 16th St., 6th Fl.
New York, NY 10011
Ph: (917)606-8260
Fax: (212)294-8348
E-mail: afaiu@cjh.org
URL: http://www.ccjo.org
Contact: Clemens Nathan, Co-Chm.
Founded: 1946. **Members:** 3. **Languages:** English, French. **Description:** Representatives from the Alliance Israelite Universelle in Paris, France, the Anglo-Jewish Association in London, England, and the Canadian Friends of the Alliance Israelite Universelle in Montreal, PQ, Canada. Promotes and advances human rights and freedom accomplished through cooperation with the United Nations (see separate entry) and its specialized agencies. **Convention/Meeting:** none. **Affiliated With:** United Nations. **Publications:** *Alliance Review*, annual. Magazine. Covers activities included in the annual journal of the American Friends of the Alliance.

17581 ■ Jewish Defense Organization (JDO)
PO Box 159
FDR Sta.
New York, NY 10150
Ph: (212)252-3383
E-mail: judeam@jdo.org
URL: http://www.jdo.org
Contact: Mordechai Levy, Founder
Founded: 1982. **Members:** 3,500. **Staff:** 5. **Regional Groups:** 15. **State Groups:** 10. **Local Groups:** 25. **National Groups:** 10. **Languages:** English, Hebrew, Spanish. **Multinational. Description:** Militant Jews concerned about anti-Semitism. Promotes Zionism and encourages Aliyah (immigration to Israel). Promises to "defend Jews by any means necessary." Advocates the use of violence. Conducts classes in self-defense, including firearms and weaponry training. Provides religious and historical instruction concerning the Holocaust, Israel and Zionism, Jewish resistance; the areas where the organization believes Jews are threatened. Protests persecution of Jews in the former Soviet Union, Iraq, and Syria. Operates Jewish Defense Organization Youth Movement and training camp for Jews to learn self-defense. Conducts research on anti-Semitic extremist groups. Sponsors speakers' bureau; compiles statistics. **Libraries: Type:** reference. **Holdings:** 1,000. **Subjects:** the Holocaust, Jewish resistance, Judaism, the Torah. **Awards:** Jabotinsky Award. **Frequency:** annual. **Type:** scholarship. **Recipient:** for courage by Jews in defending Jews ● Stern Award. **Frequency:** annual. **Type:** scholarship. **Committees:** Aliyah; Nazi War Criminals; Soviet Jewry. **Sections:** Firearms; Karate; Patrols. **Subgroups:** Jewish Defense Organization Youth Movement. **Affiliated With:** Jewish Defense Organization Youth Movement. **Publications:** By Any Means Necessary. Booklet ● Ideology of JDO. Booklet ● Jewish Resistance, monthly. **Conventions/Meetings:** annual convention - always in New York City.

17582 ■ Jewish Defense Organization Youth Movement (JDOYM)
PO Box 159
FDR Sta.
New York, NY 10150
Ph: (212)252-3383
E-mail: judeam@jdo.org
URL: http://jdo.org
Contact: Mordechai Levy, Founder
Founded: 1986. **Members:** 1,000. **Regional Groups:** 10. **State Groups:** 13. **Local Groups:** 13. **Languages:** English, Hebrew. **Description:** Youth branch of the Jewish Defense Organization. Jewish youths 13-21 years of age who are concerned with anti-Semitism. Sponsors rallies, demonstrations, and sit-ins; conducts self-defense training camps. **Libraries: Type:** open to the public. **Holdings:** 1,000. **Subjects:** Torah-Jewish assistance in Holocaust and Modern Israel. **Affiliated With:** Jewish Defense Organization. **Publications:** Jewish Power, monthly. Newsletter. **Price:** $25.00/year. **Circulation:** 5,000 ● Jewish Resistance, periodic. Magazine. **Conventions/Meetings:** semiannual Youth Conference - always February 1 and November 1, New York City.

17583 ■ Jewish Labor Committee (JLC)
25 E 21st St.
New York, NY 10010
Ph: (212)477-0707
Fax: (212)477-1918
E-mail: jlcexec@aol.com
URL: http://www.jewishlabor.org
Contact: Avram Lyon, Exec. Dir.
Founded: 1934. **Membership Dues:** sustaining, $200 (annual) ● supporting, $100 (annual) ● couple, $60 (annual) ● individual, $40 (annual) ● retired couple, $35 (annual) ● retired individual/student, $20 (annual). **Staff:** 11. **Budget:** $700,000. **Regional Groups:** 8. **State Groups:** 1. **Languages:** English, Yiddish. **Description:** Serves as a federation of organizations including fraternal bodies, labor Zionists, and trade unions together with local committees throughout the U.S. Acts as a liaison between the Jewish community and the trade union movement. Seeks to support the State of Israel, counter anti-

Semitism, and ethnic and religious discrimination in cooperation with organized labor and other groups; supports trade unions and progressive economic and social programs as well as Yiddish cultural development; works to maintain cooperation and contact between the labor movement and the organized Jewish community. **Awards:** Human Rights Award. **Frequency:** annual. **Type:** recognition. **Recipient:** for prominent trade unionists and community leaders. **Affiliated With:** Labor Zionist Alliance; Workmen's Circle. **Publications:** Alumni Newsletter, semiannual. **Circulation:** 5,000 ● Jewish Labor Committee Review, quarterly. **Conventions/Meetings:** biennial convention.

17584 ■ Jewish Telegraphic Agency (JTA)
330 7th Ave., 17th Fl.
New York, NY 10001
Ph: (212)643-1890
Fax: (212)643-8498
E-mail: info@jta.org
URL: http://www.jta.org
Contact: Mark J. Joffe, Exec. Ed./Publisher
Founded: 1917. **Staff:** 18. **Budget:** $2,000,000. **Multinational. Description:** Aims to report worldwide news concerning Jewish issues. **Publications:** Community News Reporter, monthly. Newsletter. Contains articles on Jewish community and calendar of events. **Price:** $50.00 /year for individuals. **Circulation:** 2,000 ● Daily E-Mail Edition. **Price:** $180.00 /year for individuals; $250.00 /year for institutions ● Daily News Bulletin. **Price:** $295.00/year mailing ● JTA World Report, weekly. Features the latest news coverage and developments. **Price:** $180.00 /year for individuals. Alternate Formats: online ● Weekly News Digest. **Price:** $100.00/year mailing; $150.00/year fax.

17585 ■ Jews Against the Occupation (JATO)
PO Box 494
Prince St. Sta.
New York, NY 10012
Ph: (212)539-6683
E-mail: jatonyc@yahoo.com
URL: http://www.jatonyc.org
Description: Advocates for peace through justice for Palestine and Israel.

17586 ■ North American Conference on Ethiopian Jewry (NACOEJ)
132 Nassau St., Ste.412
New York, NY 10038-2434
Ph: (212)233-5200
Fax: (212)233-5243
E-mail: nacoej@nacoej.org
URL: http://www.nacoej.org
Contact: Barbara Ribakove Gordon, Exec. Dir.
Founded: 1982. **Staff:** 5. **Budget:** $1,500,000. **Description:** Works for the welfare and advancement of the Ethiopian Jewish community in Israel. Sponsors educational, vocational, and cultural preservation programs in Israel. Assists Jews still in Ethiopia. Conducts research; maintains speakers' bureau; offers exhibits on Ethiopian Jewry. **Publications:** Lifeline, quarterly. Newsletter. Contains updates on the Ethiopian Jewish community. **Price:** free. **Circulation:** 60,000. Alternate Formats: online. **Conventions/Meetings:** annual board meeting.

17587 ■ Religious Action Center of Reform Judaism (RAC/RJ)
Arthur and Sara Jo Kobacker Bldg.
2027 Massachusetts Ave. NW
Washington, DC 20036
Ph: (202)387-2800
Fax: (202)667-9070
E-mail: rac@urj.org
URL: http://www.rac.org
Contact: Rabbi David Saperstein, Dir./Counsel
Founded: 1961. **Members:** 850. **Staff:** 10. **Regional Groups:** 13. **Description:** Serves as a government liaison between synagogues comprising the Union of American Hebrew Congregations and the rabbis who comprise the Central Conference of American Rabbis (see separate entries). Represents the official positions of the UAHC and CCAR to the federal govern-

ment; informs congregations and rabbis of important developments; monitors federal legislation. Conducts seminars and conferences in Washington, DC on social justice issues for lay leaders, rabbinic students, and undergraduate (credit program) and graduate students. Maintains: library of books and papers on Jewish social justice themes and general public policy issues; Chai/Impact Legislative Alert Network; speakers' bureau. **Computer Services:** Mailing lists. **Commissions:** Social Action. **Formerly:** (1986) Religious Action Center of the Union of American Hebrew Congregations. **Publications:** Chai/Impact Newsletter, 30/year. Represents the official positions of the UAHC and the CCAR. Informs congregations and rabbis of important developments. ● The Challenge of the Religious Right: A Jewish Response ● Preventing the Nuclear Holocaust: A Jewish Response ● Social Action Briefings, 5/year ● Social Action Manual. **Conventions/Meetings:** biennial meeting.

17588 ■ World Jewish Congress, American Section (WJC)
501 Madison Ave., 17th Fl.
New York, NY 10022
Ph: (212)755-5770
Fax: (212)755-5883
E-mail: americansection@wjcmail.org
URL: http://www.worldjewishcongress.org
Contact: Evelyn Sommer, Chair
Founded: 1936. **Regional Groups:** 4. **Languages:** English, French, Hebrew, Spanish. **Multinational. Description:** National Jewish organizations representing 3,000,000 individuals in 90 countries. Seeks to secure and safeguard the rights, status, and interests of Jews and Jewish communities throughout the world. Commits in supporting national and international protection of human rights, without distinction on grounds of race or religion. **Committees:** Anti-Semitism; East-West Relations; Interreligious Affairs; Small Communities; Third World. **Publications:** Batefutsot (in Hebrew), monthly ● Boletin Informative OJI (in Spanish), biweekly. Bulletin ● Christian Jewish Relations, quarterly ● Coloquio (in Spanish), quarterly ● Gesher (in Hebrew), quarterly ● Report, quarterly ● Also publishes books and research reports. **Conventions/Meetings:** monthly meeting.

Judicial Reform

17589 ■ Center for Judicial Accountability (CJA)
PO Box 8220
White Plains, NY 10602
Ph: (914)421-1200 (914)997-8105
Fax: (914)428-4994
E-mail: judgewatch@aol.com
URL: http://www.judgewatch.org
Contact: Doris L. Sassower JD, Co-Founder/Admin.
Founded: 1994. **Membership Dues:** regular, $25 (annual) ● friend, $100 ● sponsor, $250 ● benefactor, $500 ● patron, $1,000. **Description:** Strives to improve the quality of the judiciary by removing political considerations from the judicial selection process and by ensuring that the process of disciplining and removing judges is effective and meaningful. Educates the public about the importance of the judiciary. Works to document, track, testify at public hearings, and initiate legal action in the public interest to advance the goal of a quality judiciary, free from political influence.

17590 ■ Citizens for Impartial Justice (CIJ)
c/o David B. Jackson, Chm.
2725 Turtle Creek Blvd., Ste.200
Dallas, TX 75219
Ph: (214)855-5300
Fax: (214)855-1478
E-mail: d.b.jackson@charter.net
URL: http://www.cijonline.org
Contact: David B. Jackson, Chm.
Founded: 1997. **Description:** Opposes the practice under which private parties in litigation directly enter into long-term contracts with court reporters. Con-

ducts educational programs to raise public awareness of contracting with court reporters; lobbies for legislation to abolish this practice at the state and federal levels. **Libraries: Type:** reference. **Holdings:** clippings. **Subjects:** contracting of court reporters. **Publications:** Papers. Alternate Formats: online.

17591 ■ Citizens for Law and Order (CLO)
PO Box 412
Carlsbad, CA 92018
Ph: (760)631-2028
Fax: (760)724-0341
E-mail: info@cloinc.org
URL: http://www.cloinc.org/about_clo.htm
Contact: Susan Fisher, Contact
Founded: 1970. **Members:** 1,300. **Membership Dues:** general, $25 (annual) ● supporting, $35 (annual) ● sponsoring, $50 (annual) ● sustaining, $100-$1,000 (annual). **Staff:** 2. **Budget:** $45,000. **Description:** Individuals interests in criminal justice. Seeks to support crime victims and reform the criminal justice system. Monitors judicial performance and issues endorsements in races affecting criminal justice. **Publications:** *CLO News*, 4-6/year. Newsletter. **Price:** included in membership dues. **Conventions/Meetings:** annual meeting.

17592 ■ Criminal Justice Policy Foundation (CJPF)
8730 Georgia Ave., Ste.400
Silver Spring, MD 20910
Ph: (301)589-6020
Fax: (301)589-5056
E-mail: info@cjpf.org
URL: http://www.cjpf.org
Contact: Eric E. Sterling, Pres.
Founded: 1988. **Description:** Non-partisan educational group which promotes solutions to problems facing the criminal justice system. Promotes the use of community-based problem-solving techniques which deal with the societal causes of crime instead of the present offender-oriented, incarceration-as-deterrent methods. Supports the National Drug Strategy Network, which is composed of people and organizations that are working for effective approaches to the nation's drug problems. It is primarily an information exchange. **Convention/Meeting:** none. **Libraries: Type:** reference. **Holdings:** 1,600; books, clippings. **Subjects:** drug policy, criminal justice. **Affiliated With:** National Drug Strategy Network. **Publications:** *On Balance*, quarterly. Newsletter. Reviews a current topic in criminal justice. **Price:** free. Alternate Formats: online ● Reports.

17593 ■ Fully Informed Jury Association (FIJA)
PO Box 5570
Helena, MT 59604-5570
Ph: (406)442-7800
Free: (800)TEL-JURY
Fax: (406)442-9332
E-mail: fijamail@earthlink.net
URL: http://www.fija.org
Contact: Ms. Iloilo Marguerite Jones, Exec. Dir.
Founded: 1992. **Members:** 3,750. **Membership Dues:** senior, $20 (annual) ● standard, $30 (annual) ● sustaining, $35 (annual) ● FIJActivist, $50 (annual) ● defender, $100 (annual) ● sponsor, $250 (annual) ● benefactor, $500 (annual) ● guardian, $1,000 (annual) ● founder, $5,000 (annual). **Staff:** 3. **Budget:** $130,000. **Regional Groups:** 3. **State Groups:** 48. **National Groups:** 3. **Description:** Works to increase the effectiveness of the institution of trial by jury by educating all potential jurors of their authority and obligations when serving on juries. Jurors—and defendants as well—must know that the jury has the authority and the obligation to the defendant to "judge both the law and facts in reaching a verdict." Promotes the right of the defense to tell the jury of their power to judge the law. Maintains Speaker's Bureau. **Committees:** Education; Fundraising; Legal Advisory. **Publications:** *The FIJActivist*, quarterly. Newsletter. **Price:** $25.00. **Circulation:** 4,000. Alternate Formats: CD-ROM; online. Also Cited As: *FIJA Newsletter* ● *Jury Power Information Kit*. Brochure ● *Jury Primer*. Brochure ● *True/False*. Brochure. **Conventions/**

Meetings: triennial conference ● periodic Continuing Legal Education Seminar, for defense attorneys, public defenders, and other interested parties.

17594 ■ HALT - An Organization of Americans for Legal Reform (HALT)
1612 K St. NW, Ste.510
Washington, DC 20006
Ph: (202)887-8255
Free: (888)FOR-HALT
Fax: (202)887-9699
E-mail: halt@halt.org
URL: http://www.halt.org
Contact: James C. Turner, Exec. Dir.
Founded: 1978. **Members:** 50,000. **Membership Dues:** regular, $25 (annual). **Staff:** 6. **Budget:** $750,000. **Description:** Serves as a nonpartisan public interest group. Believes to the principle that "all Americans should be able to handle their legal affairs simply, affordably and equitably, reform projects challenge the legal establishment to improve access and reduce costs in our civil justice system at both the state and federal levels". Provides self-help books and educational materials to help citizens understand the legal process and better manage their legal affairs. **Libraries: Type:** open to the public. **Holdings:** 500; articles, books, periodicals. **Subjects:** legal reform. **Awards: Type:** recognition. **Computer Services:** Mailing lists, of members. **Projects:** Freedom of Legal Information; Judicial Integrity; Lawyer Accountability; Legal Consumers Bill of Rights; Small Claims Reform. **Formerly:** (1979) HALT - Help Abolish Legal Tyranny; (2002) HALT - Americans for Legal Reform. **Publications:** *Do-It-Yourself Law: HALT's Guide to Self-Help Books, Kits and Software*. Manual ● *The Easy Way to Probate*. Manual ● *Everyday Contracts*. Manual ● *If You Want to Sue a Lawyer: A Directory of Legal Malpractice Attorneys* ● *The Legal Reformer*, quarterly. Newsletter. Alternate Formats: online ● *Legal Resource Directory*. Manual ● *Real Estate*. Manual ● *Small Claims Courts: Making Your Way Through the System*. Manual ● *Using a Lawyer. And What to Do If Things Go Wrong*. Manual ● *Your Guide to Living Trusts and Other Trusts*. Manual ● Annual Report, annual. Alternate Formats: online.

17595 ■ Lawyers for Civil Justice (LCJ)
1140 Connecticut Ave. NW, Ste.503
Washington, DC 20036
Ph: (202)429-0045
Fax: (202)429-6982
E-mail: bbauman@lfcj.com
URL: http://www.lfcj.com
Contact: Barry H. Bauman, Exec. Dir.
Founded: 1987. **Members:** 58. **Staff:** 3. **Budget:** $200,000. **Description:** Defense trial attorneys, defense bar organizations, and concerned business leaders. Promotes legislative and judicial reform by: furthers public education; gathers and exchanges information on judicial and legislative developments; maintains a resource bank of defense trial lawyers to provide legal expertise nationwide; files amicus briefs in tort reform cases to encourage countering of the plaintiff's bar. Seeks to: contain litigation costs; reestablish fault-based standards of liability; reform joint and several liability; control punitive and non-economic damage awards; and eliminate double recoveries from collateral sources. Encourages state legislatures to enact tort reform by stressing responsible legislation. **Publications:** *Briefs Notes*, quarterly ● Brochure. Alternate Formats: online. **Conventions/Meetings:** semiannual meeting.

17596 ■ National Committee for Judicial Reform (NCJR)
c/o Eustace Mullins, Exec.Dir.
1247 Mt. Torrey Rd.
Lyndhurst, VA 22952
E-mail: info@eustacemullins.com
Contact: Eustace Mullins, Exec.Dir.
Founded: 1982. **Members:** 180. **Staff:** 4. **Budget:** $300,000. **Description:** Works to provide information on legal issues worldwide. Conducts seminars on legal problems. **Libraries: Type:** reference. **Holdings:** articles, books. **Subjects:** history of law,

international law, tax and banking law, civil and criminal procedures.

17597 ■ National Judicial Education Program (NJEP)
395 Hudson St.
New York, NY 10014-3669
Ph: (212)925-6635
Fax: (212)226-1066
E-mail: njep@legalmomentum.org
URL: http://www.legalmomentum.org/legalmomentum/programs/njep
Contact: Mary Mitchell, Contact
Founded: 1980. **Staff:** 5. **Description:** Serves as a project of the Legal Momentum in cooperation with the National Association of Women Judges. Works to eliminate gender bias in the courts by making judges aware of stereotypes, myths, and biases pertaining to the roles of men and women, and how those biases can affect judicial decision-making and the courtroom environment. Serves as a clearinghouse for data on gender bias in the courts. Conducts courses and other educational programs for judges, lawyers, and the public. Collaborates with state and national judicial colleges and state task forces; participates in legal conferences, law school programs, and continuing education projects. **Affiliated With:** Legal Momentum: Advancing Women's Rights. **Formerly:** (2004) National Judicial Education Program to Promote Equality for Women and Men in the Courts. **Publications:** *Adjudicating Allegations of Child Sexual Abuse When Custody is in Dispute* ● *Understanding Sexual Violence: Prosecuting Adult Rape and Sexual Assault Cases* ● *Understanding Sexual Violence: The Judicial Response to Stranger and Nonstranger Rape and Sexual Assault* ● *When Bias Compounds: Insuring Equal Justice for Women of Color in the Courts* ● Videos. **Conventions/Meetings:** seminar.

Korea

17598 ■ Korea Economic Institute (KEI)
1201 F St. NW, Ste.910
Washington, DC 20004
Ph: (202)464-1982
Fax: (202)464-1987
E-mail: jp@keia.org
URL: http://www.keia.org
Contact: Charles L. Pritchard, Pres.
Founded: 1982. **Staff:** 8. **Description:** Participants are politicians, academics, trade organizations, banks, and other individuals and institutions concerned with Korean economics. Aims to promote mutually beneficial economic relations between the U.S. and the Republic of Korea through public information programs. Seeks to place bilateral issues in broader regional and global contexts. Sponsors speeches and seminars. Compiles statistics. **Libraries: Type:** open to the public. **Holdings:** articles, biographical archives, books, papers. **Formerly:** (2005) Korea Economic Institute of America. **Publications:** *Korea Economic Update*, quarterly. Newsletter. Includes statistics. **Price:** free. **Circulation:** 9,000 ● *Korea's Economy*, annual. Journal. Includes statistics. ISSN: 0894-6302. Alternate Formats: online ● Also publishes books and statistical tables. **Conventions/Meetings:** Academic Conference ● annual Business Conference - meeting.

17599 ■ Korean American Peace Institute
60 Cedar St.
Ridgefield Park, NJ 07660
Ph: (973)200-0071
Fax: (201)229-0072
Contact: Rev. Paul Kim, Exec. Dir.
Founded: 1991. **Staff:** 3. **Budget:** $105,000. **Local Groups:** 1. **Description:** Works for peace, human rights, and the reunification of Korea. Promotes political, social, and economic justice in Korea; seeks to influence U.S. policy towards Korea. Conducts educational programs. Maintains speakers' bureau; compiles statistics. **Libraries: Type:** reference. **Awards: Type:** recognition. **Working Groups:** Edu-

cation; Fundraising/Membership; Networking/ Mobilization; Policy Advocacy. **Formed by Merger of:** North American Coalition for Human Rights in Korea; Campaign for the Peace and Reunification of Korea. **Formerly:** (1998) Korea Church Coalition for Peace, Justice and Reunification. **Publications:** *Korea/Update*, quarterly. Newsletter. Includes book reviews and statistics. **Price:** $20.00/year in North America; $25.00/year outside North America. **Circulation:** 1,600 ● Also publishes resource papers, reprints, and documents from Korea; makes available videotapes. **Conventions/Meetings:** annual meeting.

Kurdish

17600 ■ American Kurdish Information Network (AKIN)
c/o Kani Xulam, Dir.
2722 Connecticut Ave. NW, No. 42
Washington, DC 20008-5316
Ph: (202)483-6444
Fax: (202)483-6476
E-mail: akin@kurdistan.org
URL: http://www.kurdistan.org
Contact: Kani Xulam, Dir.
Founded: 1993. **Staff:** 2. **Budget:** $50,000. **Regional Groups:** 2. **Description:** Promotes increased public awareness of political developments in the Kurdish regions of Turkey, Iran, Syria, Armenia, and Iraq; seeks to improve mutual understanding among the people of the United States and the Kurds. Serves as a clearinghouse. **Libraries: Type:** by appointment only. **Holdings:** archival material, articles, books, clippings, periodicals. **Publications:** *Kurdish News*, quarterly. Newsletter. ISSN: 1091-8523. **Advertising:** accepted.

Labor

17601 ■ American Rights at Work
1100 17th St. NW, Ste.950
Washington, DC 20036
Ph: (202)822-2127
Fax: (202)822-2168
E-mail: info@americanrightsatwork.org
URL: http://www.americanrightsatwork.org
Contact: David Bonior, Chm.
Founded: 2003. **Staff:** 12. **Description:** Advances democracy in the American workplace. Seeks to investigate and expose workers' rights abuses and the inadequacy of U.S. labor law. Stimulates debate about the state of workers' rights. Promotes public policies that protect workers. **Computer Services:** database, lists of cases of workers ● mailing lists.

17602 ■ California Public Employee Relations Program (CPER)
c/o Institute of Industrial Relations
2521 Channing Way, No. 5555
Berkeley, CA 94720-5555
Ph: (510)643-7096
E-mail: cvendril@uclink.berkeley.edu
URL: http://cper.berkeley.edu
Contact: Carol Vendrillo JD, Dir./Ed.
Founded: 1969. **Membership Dues:** individual, $250 (annual). **Staff:** 6. **State Groups:** 1. **Description:** Works to serve the changing needs of those involved in public sector employment relations and public policymaking. Conducts public sector labor relations research; provides reference and consultation services; maintains collection of primary and secondary source data. **Libraries: Type:** reference. **Holdings:** archival material, clippings, monographs, periodicals. **Subjects:** California public employer-employee relations. **Computer Services:** Mailing lists, of members. **Publications:** *CPER Journal*, bimonthly. **Price:** $250.00 /year for institutions. ISSN: 0194-3073. Alternate Formats: online ● *CPER Pocket Guide Series*. Booklets. Includes a concise review of several public sector laws. **Price:** $15.00 plus shipping and handling.

17603 ■ Center for Labor and Community Research (CLCR)
3411 W Diversey Ave., Ste.10
Chicago, IL 60647-6207
Ph: (773)278-5418
Fax: (773)278-5918
E-mail: dswinney@clcr.org
URL: http://www.clcr.org
Contact: Dan Swinney, Exec. Dir.
Founded: 1982. **Staff:** 8. **Budget:** $800,000. **Description:** Represents academicians, labor organizers, community organizers, and church leaders united to provide independent research, technical assistance, and consulting expertise to the labor movement. Seeks the creation of sustainable jobs in industrial communities; assists in the formation of coalitions among businesses, communities, and labor groups to prevent plant closures; promotes economic development and worker ownership projects. Maintains speakers' bureau. Activities are national, although currently concentrated in the Midwestern U.S. **Committees:** Education. **Formerly:** (2000) Midwest Center for Labor Research. **Publications:** *CLCR News*. Newsletter. Alternate Formats: online ● *MCLR Working Paper*, periodic ● Articles. Alternate Formats: online ● Papers. Alternate Formats: online.

17604 ■ Concerned Educators Against Forced Unionism - A Special Project of the National Right to Work Legal Defense Foundation (CEAFU)
8001 Braddock Rd.
Springfield, VA 22160
Ph: (703)321-8519
Free: (800)336-3600
Fax: (703)321-9319
E-mail: clj@nrtw.org
URL: http://www.nrtw.org/ceafu
Contact: Cathy Jones, Dir.
Founded: 1975. **Members:** 6,500. **Staff:** 1. **Description:** Special project of the National Right to Work Legal Defense & Education Foundation, Inc. Provides free legal aid to employees whose human or civil rights have been violated by .abuses of compulsory unionism. **Affiliated With:** National Right to Work Committee. **Publications:** *Compulsory Unionism in Education — Insider's Report*, quarterly. Pamphlets ● *Concerned Educators Against Forced Unionism— Insider's Report*, 3/year. Newsletter. Covers legislation, court cases, and general information concerning forced unionism. **Price:** free. **Circulation:** 6,000 ● *Insider's Report*. Films ● News, quarterly. Newsletter. **Conventions/Meetings:** annual conference and seminar, with speakers/discussion about compulsory unionism in education - last weekend in June ● annual seminar and workshop (exhibits) - always July in Washington, DC.

17605 ■ HR Policy Association
1015 15th St. NW, Ste.1200
Washington, DC 20005-2605
Ph: (202)789-8670
Fax: (202)789-0064
E-mail: info@hrpolicy.org
URL: http://www.hrpolicy.org
Contact: Jeffrey C. McGuiness, Pres.
Members: 200. **Staff:** 12. **Description:** Senior human resource executives of Fortune 500 companies. Conducts research and publishes findings on matters relating to federal human resources policy and its application and effects. Maintains task forces to study pending employment issues; conducts seminars, and offers a suite of labor relations and HR effectiveness training courses. **Boards:** Executive Compensation Advisory. **Councils:** Aerospace Human Resource. **Formerly:** (2003) Labor Policy Association. **Publications:** *NLRB Watch*, bimonthly. Newsletter. Reviews the actions of the National Labor Relations Board. **Price:** $225.00/year. **Advertising:** accepted. Alternate Formats: online. **Conventions/Meetings:** annual HR Summit - conference - always March, in Boca Raton, FL ● annual Washington Policy Conference - always September, Washington, DC.

17606 ■ International Labor Rights Fund (ILRF)
2001 South St. NW, No. 420
Washington, DC 20009
Ph: (202)347-4100
Fax: (202)347-4885
E-mail: laborrights@ilrf.org
URL: http://www.laborrights.org
Contact: Bama Athreya, Exec. Dir.
Founded: 1986. **Membership Dues:** advocate, $35 (annual). **Staff:** 7. **Budget:** $1,100,000. **Languages:** Chinese, Creole, English, French, Indonesian, Korean, Spanish. **Multinational. Description:** Seeks to ensure that labor laws are understood and adequately implemented and enforced worldwide. Promotes education and research in labor, business, human rights, religious, and other communities in order to facilitate the advancement of labor rights. Fosters respect for international labor rights and the expansion of the number of people benefiting from U.S. trade and investment in other countries. Encourages participation by individuals and organizations in the formulation of U.S. trade and investment policies. Supports identification and research into trade, investment, taxation, finance, and foreign aid actions that the U.S. government could take in order to promote "economic justice for all workers". **Libraries: Type:** reference. **Holdings:** 1,500; books, clippings, monographs, periodicals. **Subjects:** labor conditions, international labor law, trade, economic, social rights. **Awards:** International Labor Rights Advocate Award. **Frequency:** periodic. **Type:** recognition. **Recipient:** for pioneering or outstanding contribution to extension of labor rights. **Subgroups:** Advocates Group of Lawyers; International Labor Rights Advocates. **Formerly:** International Labor Rights Education and Research Fund. **Publications:** *Global Village vs. Global Pillage.* Book. **Price:** $3.75 plus shipping and handling (1) ● *Labor Rights in Haiti.* Book. **Price:** $5.00 plus shipping and handling (1) ● *Mask of Democracy: Labor Suppression in Mexico Today.* Book. Highlights the plight of workers in the maquiladoras. **Price:** $14.00 plus shipping and handling (2) ● *North American Trade as if Democracy Mattered.* Book ● *Rugmark After One Year.* Report ● *Workers in the Global Economy.* Book. **Conventions/Meetings:** periodic conference.

17607 ■ National Institute for Work and Learning (NIWL)
1825 Connecticut Ave. NW
Washington, DC 20009
Ph: (202)884-8185
Fax: (202)884-8422
E-mail: niwl@aed.org
URL: http://www.niwl.org
Contact: Ivan Charner, VP/Dir.
Founded: 1971. **Staff:** 12. **Budget:** $1,000,000. **Description:** Represents corporate representatives, educators, labor and government officials, and researchers concerned with providing a better integration of education and work throughout Americans' lives. Promotes the fullest and best use of the human potential. Works to develop and implement education-work policy and rational integration of education, human resource, and economic policy. Emphasizes educational preparation for youth, employees in their middle years, and senior citizens. **Libraries: Type:** reference. **Holdings:** 1,000. **Programs:** Bridge to Employment; Central Educational Center Evaluation; Community College Labor Market Responsiveness Initiative; Contextual Teaching and Learning; Coordination Services for the Grantmakers Evaluation Network; Curriculum Integration Study; National Adult Literacy and Learning Disabilities Center. **Projects:** Lansing Area Manufacturing Partnership. **Formerly:** (1974) The Manpower Institute; (1980) National Manpower Institute. **Publications:** *NALLDC Tool Kit.* Monographs ● *Preparing to Serve Adults with Learning Disabilities.* Book ● *School-to-Work Series.* Books. **Price:** $12.00/copy; $80.00 for 8 book series. Alternate Formats: online ● Brochures. **Conventions/Meetings:** monthly conference and convention (exhibits).

17608 ■ National Mobilization Against Sweatshops (NMASS)
PO Box 130293
New York, NY 10013-0995
Ph: (718)625-9091
Fax: (718)625-8950
E-mail: nmass@yahoo.com
URL: http://www.nmass.org
Contact: JoAnn Lum, Exec. Dir.
Founded: 1996. **Membership Dues:** student, $10 (annual) ● general, $25 (annual). **Description:** Fights for the right of working people to compensation and medical benefits. Strives to develop a positive identity of youth and students as future workers, agents of change, and leaders in confronting the sweatshop system. Recognizes and supports the work of women, including the work of mothering. **Publications:** Sweatshop Nation (in English and Spanish). Newsletter. Alternate Formats: online.

17609 ■ Public Service Research Council (PSRC)
320-D Maple Ave. E
Vienna, VA 22180-4742
Ph: (703)242-3575
Fax: (703)242-3579
E-mail: info@psrconline.org
URL: http://psrconline.org
Contact: David Y. Denholm, Pres.
Founded: 1973. **Members:** 3,000. **Membership Dues:** regular, $20 (annual). **Staff:** 3. **Description:** Conducts research, education, and public affairs programs in the area of public sector employer-employee relations, including issues such as strikes, growth of unionism, legislation, and political spending. Sponsors Americans Against Union Control of Government. **Convention/Meeting:** none. **Affiliated With:** Americans Against Union Control of Government. **Publications:** Pamphlets.

17610 ■ Sweatshop Watch (SW)
1250 S Los Angeles St., Ste.212
Los Angeles, CA 90015
Ph: (213)748-5945
Fax: (213)748-5955
E-mail: sweatinfo@sweatshopwatch.org
URL: http://www.sweatshopwatch.org
Contact: Rini Chakraborty, Exec. Dir.
Description: Labor, community, civil rights, and women's organizations and attorneys and advocates. Seeks to eliminate "the exploitation that occurs in sweatshops." Conducts public education and public advocacy programs; works to build coalitions among organizations opposing sweatshop working conditions. **Programs:** Globalization and Economic Justice. **Projects:** Corporate Accountability Campaign.

17611 ■ U.S./Labor Education in the Americas Project (US/LEAP)
PO Box 268-290
Chicago, IL 60626
Ph: (773)262-6502
Fax: (773)262-6602
E-mail: info@usleap.org
URL: http://www.usleap.org
Contact: Charity Ryerson, Campaign Coor.
Founded: 1987. **Members:** 2,500. **Membership Dues:** ordinary (minimum), $35 (annual). **Staff:** 4. **Budget:** $200,000. **Multinational. Description:** Works to build U.S. support for Latin American workers. **Formerly:** (1999) U.S./Guatemala Labor Education Project. **Publications:** US/LEAP Update, quarterly. Newsletter. **Price:** included in membership dues ● Updates on education campaigns.

Labor Reform

17612 ■ Americans Against Union Control of Government (AAUCG)
c/o Public Service Research Council
320-D Maple Ave. E
Vienna, VA 22180-4742
Ph: (703)242-3575
Fax: (703)242-3579

E-mail: info@psrconline.org
URL: http://www.psrconline.org
Contact: David Y. Denholm, Pres.
Founded: 1973. **Members:** 8,000. **Staff:** 4. **Description:** Division of the Public Service Research Council. Individual citizens united: to reverse the trend toward compulsory public sector bargaining in America; for research, education, and legislation relating to public sector unionism; to alert the public to the need for action on specific legislative proposals. Maintains State Political Fund. **Affiliated With:** Public Service Research Council. **Publications:** Pamphlets ● Also publishes position papers as needed. **Conventions/Meetings:** annual board meeting.

17613 ■ Center on National Labor Policy (CNLP)
5211 Port Royal Rd., Ste.103
North Springfield, VA 22151
Ph: (703)321-9180
Fax: (703)321-9325
Contact: Michael Avakian, Contact
Founded: 1975. **Budget:** $300,000. **Description:** Nonpartisan public interest foundation. Protects employees, employers, and consumers whom the center believes have been deprived of their individual rights through excesses of union and government power. Objectives are to prevent the use of violence and coercion as a union organizing tool; promote free enterprise as the guiding force in labor policy; stop the flow of government grants to unions; establish union liability for monopoly behavior; protect the public against illegal public employee strikes; prevent government interference with employee and employer freedom of choice; prevent union control of pension funds for coercive purposes; overturn bureaucratic procedures and regulations that limit individual rights; apply civil rights laws equally against union officials. Promotes free enterprise in U.S. labor policy. Offers free legal aid; works to set legal precedents in key labor-related cases; advocates elimination of complexity and bias in regulations and regulatory hearings; distributes editorials and sponsors public addresses to educate the public on key labor issues from a free enterprise, individual rights standpoint. Sponsors NLRB Watch, which monitors activities of the National Labor Relations Board; maintains Task Force on Government Grants to identify and expose cases of union mishandling of public funds. **Publications:** Insider's Report, quarterly ● News, quarterly ● Films ● Pamphlets ● Also publishes classroom materials. **Conventions/Meetings:** annual meeting and seminar.

17614 ■ National Association of Orchestra Leaders (NAOL)
Address Unknown since 2007
Founded: 1967. **Members:** 5,000. **Membership Dues:** individual, $100 (annual). **State Groups:** 3. **Description:** Self-employed orchestra leaders, musical groups, and individual performers; buyers of musical services. Purpose is to actively oppose legislation assigning the status of "employee" to independent musicians currently classified as independent contractors. Such legislation would enable entertainment industry unions, such as the American Federation of Musicians of the U.S. and Canada, to picket or otherwise exert pressure on independent contractors and establishments employing nonunion performers. Engages in legal proceedings against entertainment industry unions, including American Guild of Variety Artists and American Federation of Television Recording Artists. **Convention/Meeting:** none. Presently inactive. **Publications:** National Association of Orchestra Leaders, periodic ● Also publishes news releases.

17615 ■ National Right to Work Committee (NRTWC)
8001 Braddock Rd., Ste.500
Springfield, VA 22160
Ph: (703)321-9820
Free: (800)325-7892
Fax: (703)321-7342

E-mail: members@nrtw.org
URL: http://www.right-to-work.org
Contact: Mark A. Mix, Pres.
Founded: 1955. **Members:** 2,000,000. **Staff:** 131. **Budget:** $6,887,544. **Description:** Individuals seeking to promote the principle that "everyone must have the right but not be compelled to join labor unions." Lobbies; maintains speakers' bureau; conducts research and educational programs. **Convention/Meeting:** none. **Publications:** National Right to Work Newsletter, monthly. **Price:** free for members ● Brochures ● Also issues briefing papers.

17616 ■ National Right to Work Legal Defense and Education Foundation (NRTWLDEF)
8001 Braddock Rd.
Springfield, VA 22160
Ph: (703)321-8510
Free: (800)336-3600
Fax: (703)321-9613
E-mail: info@nrtw.org
URL: http://www.nrtw.org
Contact: Mark A. Mix, Pres.
Founded: 1968. **Staff:** 52. **Budget:** $6,900,000. **Description:** Assists employees whose human and civil rights are being violated under compulsory union membership arrangements. Provides free legal aid to individual workers and conducts in-depth research aimed at developing new legal theories based on existing law and legal precedents which may be effectively utilized to assist employees whose rights have been infringed by compulsory unionism. **Convention/Meeting:** none. **Also Known As:** National Right to Work Legal Defense Foundation; National Right to Work Foundation. **Publications:** Foundation Action, bimonthly. Newsletter. **Price:** free. Alternate Formats: online.

17617 ■ Rescue American Jobs
c/o United Steelworkers of America
5 Gateway Ctr.
Pittsburgh, PA 15222
Ph: (614)888-6052
Free: (866)879-2937
E-mail: info@rescueamericanjobs.org
URL: http://www.rescueamericanjobs.org
Contact: Carla Henthorn, Coor.
Membership Dues: unemployed/student, $20 (annual) ● individual, $40 (annual). **Description:** Aims to protect American jobs and American workers. Educates, organizes and mobilizes American workers across traditional occupational boundaries for the common good of all Americans. Conducts awareness programs, projects, activities, events and campaigns. **Telecommunication Services:** electronic mail, chenthorn@steelworkers-usw.org. **Publications:** American Jobs Journal, weekly. Alternate Formats: online.

Land Control

17618 ■ League of Private Property Voters (LPPV)
PO Box 423
Battle Ground, WA 98604
Ph: (360)687-2471
Fax: (360)687-2973
E-mail: ccushman@pacifier.com
URL: http://www.landrights.org/_private/lppvhome.htm
Contact: Charles Cushman, Exec. Dir.
Founded: 1990. **Members:** 600. **Description:** Land use groups. Provides information to the public on how each Congressman and Senator voted on important land-use issues. **Publications:** Private Property Congressional Vote Index.

Latin America

17619 ■ Community Action on Latin America (CALA)
731 State St.
Madison, WI 53705
Ph: (608)251-3241

Fax: (608)251-3267
E-mail: info@calamadison.org
URL: http://www.calamadison.org
Contact: Carol Bracewell, Pres.
Founded: 1970. **Members:** 30. **Budget:** $4,000. **Local Groups:** 1. **Languages:** English, Spanish. **Description:** Seeks to educate people in the United States about the nature and effects of U.S. intervention in Latin America; promotes "peaceful opposition" to U.S. intervention. Works with and sends humanitarian aid to people and organizations that are seeking fundamental social change in Latin America. Offers speakers; makes available slide shows. **Committees:** Chiapas Solidarity. **Conventions/Meetings:** weekly meeting, general coordination of activities - always Wednesday, in Madison, WI.

17620 ■ Ecumenical Program on Central America and the Caribbean (EPICA)
1470 Irving St. NW
Washington, DC 20010
Ph: (202)332-0292
Fax: (202)332-1184
E-mail: epicainfo@epica.org
URL: http://www.epica.org
Contact: Olivia Burlingame Goumbri, Dir.
Founded: 1968. **Languages:** English, Spanish. **Description:** Conducts public education projects on socioeconomic problems in the Caribbean and Central America by preparing educational materials and by developing programs to increase awareness among U.S. organizations and individuals. Organizes educational tours of the region. **Formerly:** (1988) Ecumenical Program for Inter American Communication and Action. **Publications:** *Beyond the Mountains.* Report ● *Caribbean Connections* ● *Caribbean: Survival, Struggle and Sovereignty* ● *Challenge: Faith & Action in the Americas,* quarterly ● *El Salvador: A Spring* ● *Esta Esperanza/Hope for El Salvador.* Video ● *Guatemala: The Certainty of Spring.* Book ● *Guatemala: The Right to Dream.* Book ● *Guatemalan Women Speak* ● *Historia de un Gran Amor* (in Spanish). Book ● *Martires de la UCA.* Book ● *Monuments to Truth: Against Forgetting.* Video ● *The New Politics of Survival.* Book ● *The Peoples Church.* Book ● *Piezas para un Retrato* (in Spanish). Book ● *Promised Land: Death & Life in El Salvador.* Book ● *Threatened with Resurrection.* Book ● *Unearthing the Truth.* Report.

17621 ■ Fellowship of Reconciliation Task Force on Latin America and Caribbean (FOR TFLAC)
PO Box 271
Nyack, NY 10960
Ph: (845)358-4601
Fax: (845)358-4924
E-mail: for@forusa.org
URL: http://www.forusa.org/programs/tflac/tflac.html
Contact: Mark C. Johnson, Exec. Dir.
Founded: 1983. **Staff:** 2. **Local Groups:** 75. **Languages:** English, Spanish. **Description:** Organizations, and individuals who support work for nonviolent social change in Latin America and the Caribbean. Seeks to strengthen communication and collaboration among nonviolent movements and to enhance the U.S. and international network of peace. Sponsors: delegations to Panama and other Latin American nations to assess the political, military, and human impact of U.S. policy in the region; speaking tours for visiting Latin American and U.S. nonviolent activists; Urgent Action Network, which appeals for letters in support of people suffering human rights abuses in Latin America. Maintains an exchange residency program between Latin American and U.S. activists. **Convention/Meeting:** none. **Affiliated With:** Fellowship of Reconciliation - USA; International Fellowship of Reconciliation - Netherlands. **Publications:** *Panama Update,* quarterly. Newsletter. **Price:** $15.00/year. **Circulation:** 750 ● *Urgent Action Appeals,* semiannual.

17622 ■ Human Rights Documentation Exchange (HRDE)
PO Box 2327
Austin, TX 78768
Ph: (512)476-9841

Fax: (512)476-0130
E-mail: mail@hrde.org
URL: http://www.handplant.com/mockups/hrde/default.htm
Contact: Rebecca Hall, Exec. Dir.
Founded: 1983. **Staff:** 7. **Description:** Serves as clearinghouse for information and reference materials on refugees, immigration, and U.S. policy. Helps North Americans understand the economic, political, and social contexts of human rights issues around the world. Contributes to the development of U.S. policies that respect the integrity and security of each country and its people. Protects the human and legal rights of refugees who seek asylum in the United States. Maintains Refugee Legal Support Service to provide defense lawyers with documentation for use in political asylum cases for refugees worldwide. **Libraries: Type:** reference. **Holdings:** 2,000; clippings. **Subjects:** human rights reports, government reports on refugee issues worldwide. **Computer Services:** database, human rights abuses. **Programs:** Public Education; Refugee Legal Support Service. **Formerly:** (1993) Central America Resource Center; (1997) Documentation Exchange. **Publications:** *Central America Newspak,* biweekly. Compilation of current news articles from ten major U.S. and Mexican newspapers on topics relating to Central America. **Price:** $42.00/year; $54.00/year in Caribbean, Central and South America; $60.00/year in Asia, Africa and Pacific Rim. ISSN: 0887-0594. **Circulation:** 500 ● *Mexico NewsPak,* biweekly. **Price:** $42.00/year; $46.00/year in Canada; $48.00/year in Mexico; $58.00/year in Europe. ISSN: 1068-2074. **Circulation:** 200.

17623 ■ Information Services on Latin America (ISLA)
PO Box 6103
Albany, CA 94706
Ph: (510)996-2318
Fax: (510)835-3017
E-mail: isla@lmi.net
URL: http://isla.igc.org
Contact: Karen Crump, Dir.
Founded: 1970. **Staff:** 3. **Description:** Collects and disseminates information on Latin America. Selects key articles on Latin American events from nine English-language daily newspapers and organizes the information for dissemination to the public. Serves scholars, journalists, government officials, business people, and church leaders in need of comprehensive analyses of Latin American events. **Publications:** *Articles,* monthly. Reprints articles from English-language newspapers on Latin America. **Price:** $750.00/year for full publication; $245.00/year for regional section. ISSN: 0046-8401. **Circulation:** 250 ● Also publishes annual index.

17624 ■ Latin America Data Base (LADB)
1 Univ. of New Mexico
MSC 02 1690
Albuquerque, NM 87131-1016
Ph: (505)277-6839
Free: (800)472-0888
Fax: (505)277-6837
E-mail: info@ladb.unm.edu
URL: http://ladb.unm.edu
Contact: Rebecca R. Bannister, Dir.
Founded: 1986. **Staff:** 8. **Languages:** English, Spanish. **Description:** Produces database containing newsletters on Central America, the Latin American economy, the Mexican economy, and South American and Caribbean politics and searchable archive available via website by subscription. **Computer Services:** Online services, news and news archive about Latin America. **Publications:** *Noticen,* weekly. Newsletter. Provides news on Central America and the Caribbean. ISSN: 1054-8882. Alternate Formats: online ● *Notisur,* weekly, every Friday. Bulletin. Provides news on South American economic and political affairs. Alternate Formats: online ● *SourceMex,* weekly, every Wednesday. Bulletin. Contains economic and political news and analyses on Mexico. ISSN: 1054-8890. Alternate Formats: online.

17625 ■ Latin America Working Group (LAWG)
424 C St. NE
Washington, DC 20002
Ph: (202)546-7010
Fax: (202)543-7647
E-mail: lawg@lawg.org
URL: http://www.lawg.org
Contact: Lisa Haugaard, Exec. Dir.
Founded: 1983. **Members:** 60. **Multinational.** **Description:** Religious, human rights, policy, grassroots and development organizations. Strives for U.S. policies that promote peace, justice and sustainable development in the Latin American region; assists organizations in designing and implementing coordinated advocacy efforts and public education campaigns; disseminates information to non-governmental organizations, congressional offices, the media and citizens concerned about U.S. policy towards Latin America. **Also Known As:** Latin America Working Group Education Fund. **Publications:** *The Advocate,* 8/year. Newsletter. Alternate Formats: online ● Annual Report, annual. Alternate Formats: online. **Conventions/Meetings:** monthly meeting, to analyze developments in Washington and the hemisphere and develop common positions and effective strategies for action.

17626 ■ Letelier-Moffitt Memorial Fund for Human Rights (LMMFHR)
c/o Institute for Policy Studies
1112 16th St. NW, Ste.600
Washington, DC 20036
Ph: (202)234-9382
Fax: (202)387-7915
E-mail: robin@ips-dc.org
URL: http://www.tni.org/letelier-docs/lmfund.htm
Contact: Robin Weiss-Castro, Contact
Founded: 1976. **Members:** 4,000. **Budget:** $50,000. **Description:** Established in commemoration of Chilean exile Orlando Letelier and his co-worker, Ronni Karpen Moffitt, who were assassinated in Washington, DC (allegedly by Chilean intelligence agents). Investigates and seeks to inform the public of human rights violations and state sponsored terrorism in Latin America, particularly Chile. Conducts research programs, including Women's Project to examine the status of women in Third World countries, and Indigenous Affairs and Human Rights Project to examine the relationship between economic policy and human rights. **Awards:** Letelier-Moffitt Memorial Human Rights Award. **Frequency:** annual. **Type:** grant. **Recipient:** for individuals for distinguished service in defense of human rights. **Additional Websites:** http://www.ips-dc.org. **Publications:** *Proceedings from Annual Ceremony.* **Advertising:** accepted ● Also publishes material on Latin American human rights policy; offers film rental service. **Conventions/Meetings:** annual meeting, includes memorial service at Sheridan Circle - always September in Washington, DC.

17627 ■ Reach-Out International (ROI)
1968 Wooddale Ct.
Baton Rouge, LA 70806-1526
Ph: (225)928-3123
Fax: (225)924-1512
E-mail: reachoin@aol.com
URL: http://www.reach-out-international.org
Contact: Catalina Lopez-Galvez, VP/Sec.
Founded: 1996. **Members:** 60. **Membership Dues:** individual, $25 (annual) ● sponsor, $250 (annual) ● friend, $50 (annual) ● contributor, $100 (annual) ● sustaining, $1,500 (annual) ● supporting, $1,000 (annual) ● associate, $500 (annual). **Staff:** 3. **Budget:** $25,000. **Languages:** English, Spanish. **Multinational.** **Description:** Individuals, corporations, and organizations with an interest in the economic development of Latin America and the Caribbean. Promotes socially equitable and environmentally sustainable economic development in the region. Operates small business development center in Guatemala; plans to establish a research and training center to increase indigenous environmental and business management resources in Latin America and the Caribbean. **Telecommunication Services:**

electronic mail, cathylopez@reach-out-international. org. **Publications:** *1999 Report,* quarterly. Newsletter. Contains overview of the organization, programs and projects. **Price:** free. **Advertising:** accepted. Alternate Formats: online. **Conventions/Meetings:** annual general assembly.

17628 ■ Washington Office on Latin America (WOLA)
1630 Connecticut Ave. NW, Ste.200
Washington, DC 20009
Ph: (202)797-2171
Fax: (202)797-2172
E-mail: wola@wola.org
URL: http://www.wola.org
Contact: Joy Olson, Exec. Dir.
Founded: 1974. **Staff:** 20. **Budget:** $2,000,000. **Languages:** English, Spanish. **Description:** Nonpartisan organization concerned with the economic, political, and social conditions in Latin America. Monitors human rights practices and political developments in Latin America and the formulation of U.S. policy toward the area. Serves as liaison between Latin Americans and U.S. institutions affecting foreign policy such as churches, the press, nongovernmental organizations, and the executive and legislative branches of government. Sponsors up to 100 seminars and symposia/year; holds briefings on human rights situations in particular countries and expositions by Latin American political and religious leaders. Compiles and organizes documentation on violations of human rights. **Subgroups:** Central America; Management; South America. **Publications:** *Cross Currents* (in English and Spanish). Newsletter. **Price:** $35.00/year ● *Enlace* (in Spanish), quarterly. Bulletin. Examines U.S. foreign policy formation and its impact on human rights in the region. **Price:** $35.00 /year for individuals. ISSN: 1059-6402. **Circulation:** 1,000 ● Books ● Reports (in English and Spanish) ● Also publishes statements on human rights violations. **Conventions/Meetings:** periodic conference (exhibits).

Latin American

17629 ■ National Latina/Latino Law Student Association (NLLSA)
c/o Andrea Maldonado, Treas.
535 S Curson Ave., Apt. 6B
Los Angeles, CA 90036
E-mail: treasurer@nllsa.org
URL: http://www.nllsa.org
Contact: Andrea Maldonado, Treas.
Founded: 2003. **Membership Dues:** chapter (based on number of students), $20-$200 (annual). **Description:** Serves as a medium for a collective Latina/ Latino law student voice. Protects and advances the civil rights of Latinas and Latinos in law school and in the communities. Promotes and sustains the academic success of Latina and Latino law students. **Publications:** Newsletter.

Latvia

17630 ■ World Federation of Free Latvians (WFFL)
400 Hurley Ave.
Rockville, MD 20850
Ph: (301)340-7646
Fax: (301)762-5938
E-mail: pbla@erols.com
URL: http://www.pbla.lv
Contact: Janis Kukainis, Pres.
Founded: 1956. **Members:** 5. **Staff:** 3. **Budget:** $250,000. **Languages:** English, Latvian. **Multinational. Description:** Works to assist the development of free Latvia; monitors political, cultural, and social life in Latvia. Maintains contact with governments and international organizations; gathers and distributes information about the situation in Latvia. Operates information bureau; compiles statistics.

Committees: Cultural Fund; Educational; Human Rights; Information. **Conventions/Meetings:** annual conference.

Law

17631 ■ Advocates International
8001 Braddock Rd., Ste.300
Springfield, VA 22151-2110
Ph: (703)894-1084
Fax: (703)894-1074
E-mail: info@advocatesinternational.org
URL: http://www.advocatesinternational.org
Contact: Samuel E. Ericsson, Pres./CEO
Founded: 1991. **Multinational. Description:** Works relationally, professionally, and spiritually with people involved in law and related professions. Encourages and enables a global network of skilled advocates committed to religious liberty, human rights, conflict resolution, reconciliation, professional ethics, and the integration of faith and practice. Seeks local partners to take responsibility for their nation or region. **Publications:** Newsletter. Alternate Formats: online.

Law Enforcement

17632 ■ Law Enforcement Against Prohibition (LEAP)
121 Mystic Ave.
Medford, MA 02155
Ph: (781)393-6985
Fax: (781)393-2964
E-mail: info@leap.cc
URL: http://www.leap.cc
Contact: Jack A. Cole, Exec. Dir.
Founded: 2002. **Multinational. Description:** Seeks to educate the public, the media and the policy makers about the failure of current drug policies. Seeks to end drug prohibition. Advocates for a system of regulation and control. **Computer Services:** database, audio/video presentations ● database, speakers bureau. **Telecommunication Services:** electronic mail, jackacole@leap.cc. **Publications:** Articles. Alternate Formats: online.

Leadership

17633 ■ American Council of Young Political Leaders (ACYPL)
1717 K St. NW, Ste.500
Washington, DC 20036
Ph: (202)857-0999
Fax: (202)857-0027
E-mail: info@acypl.org
URL: http://www.acypl.org
Contact: Brad Minnick, CEO
Founded: 1966. **Members:** 2,000. **Membership Dues:** life, $1,000 ● individual, $100 (annual). **Staff:** 10. **Budget:** $1,500,000. **Multinational. Description:** A bipartisan educational organization founded to promote understanding and cooperation among young (ages 25-41) political leaders of all countries. Sponsors multilateral and bilateral study tours between U.S. political leaders and their counterparts around the world. Sets up meetings and conferences with government officials, businessmen, academicians, and practicing politicians to give visiting young political leaders a practical understanding of American politics. Is governed by a board of trustees comprising elected officials, corporate representatives, and other political leaders; is supported by funding from corporations, foundations, and the U.S. Department of State. **Publications:** *Navigator,* quarterly. Newsletter. Provides information on the group's activities and articles written by experts on specific foreign policy topics. Includes calendar of events. **Price:** free for members. **Circulation:** 2,500. **Advertising:** accepted. Alternate Formats: online.

17634 ■ American Leadership Forum (ALF)
3101 Richmond Ave., Ste.140
Houston, TX 77098
Ph: (713)807-1253
Fax: (713)807-1064
E-mail: information@alfnational.org
URL: http://www.alfnational.org
Contact: Joe Synan, Chm.
Founded: 1980. **Members:** 1,700. **Staff:** 2. **Budget:** $250,000. **State Groups:** 8. **Description:** Seeks to join and strengthen "established leaders in order to serve the public good." Facilitates coordination of members' activities and communication among community leaders. Conducts leadership development programs emphasizing the strengths of social diversity and the use of collaborative problem-solving within communities.

17635 ■ Center for Visionary Leadership
PO Box 2241
Arlington, VA 22202
Ph: (202)237-2800
E-mail: cvldc@visionarylead.org
URL: http://www.visionarylead.org
Contact: Gordon Davidson, Pres./Co-Founder
Founded: 1996. **Membership Dues:** student, $20 (annual) ● associate, $35-$99 (annual) ● supporting, $100-$999 (annual) ● life, $1,000. **Description:** Helps people develop their inner resources to be effective leaders and respond creatively to change. Provides leadership training, consulting and coaching services based on core values and clear vision. Promotes the application of universal and spiritual values in business and politics. **Boards:** International Advisory. **Publications:** *Soul Light.* Newsletter. Alternate Formats: online.

17636 ■ Network 20/20
850 Seventh Ave., Ste.1200
New York, NY 10019
Ph: (212)582-1870
Fax: (212)586-3291
E-mail: info@network2020.org
URL: http://www.network2020.org
Contact: Patricia Huntington, Pres./Founder
Founded: 2003. **Description:** Helps prepare next generation leaders in the U.S. to participate in public diplomacy and in the creation and execution of policies promoting global public security. Provides lectures, educational initiatives and series of trips and exchanges abroad. **Committees:** International Trips and Exchanges; Legal; Planning and Development. **Councils:** Advisory. **Publications:** Newsletter.

17637 ■ Rising Leaders
Congressional House Bldg.
236 Massachusetts Ave. NE, Ste.207
Washington, DC 20002
Ph: (202)675-2004
Fax: (202)675-2006
E-mail: risingleaders@gmail.com
URL: http://www.risingleaders.org
Contact: Sadia Sindhu, Exec. Dir.
Membership Dues: general, $10 (annual). **Description:** Seeks to promote a sense of Pakistani-American identity. Encourages leadership, activism and community involvement among Pakistani-Americans. Educates members about the importance of communicating their thoughts and concerns to their local congressional representatives and media.

Lebanese

17638 ■ United States Committee for a Free Lebanon (USCFL)
445 Park Ave., 9th Fl.
New York, NY 10022
Fax: (212)202-6166
E-mail: info@freelebanon.org
URL: http://freelebanon.org
Contact: Ziad K. Abdelnour, Pres.
Founded: 1997. **Membership Dues:** regular, $100 ● contributing, $500 ● Golden Circle, $1,000. **Description:** Educates the American public about Lebanon's

strategic and moral significance as an ally to the U.S. and an outpost of Western values in the Middle East.

Legal Services

17639 ■ Identity Theft Resource Center (ITRC)
PO Box 26833
San Diego, CA 92196
Ph: (858)693-7935
E-mail: itrc@idtheftcenter.org
URL: http://www.idtheftcenter.org
Contact: Linda Goldman-Foley, Co-Exec. Dir./ Founder
Founded: 1999. **Description:** Dedicated to the development and implementation of a comprehensive program against identity theft. **Libraries: Type:** reference. **Holdings:** articles. **Subjects:** identity theft. **Computer Services:** database, Victim Resource. **Programs:** Local Assistance. **Publications:** *Identity Theft: The Aftermath 2003.* Survey. Alternate Formats: online.

17640 ■ Lawyers Without Borders (LWOB)
330 Main St.
Hartford, CT 06106
Ph: (860)541-2288
Fax: (860)525-0287
E-mail: cstorm@lwob.org
URL: http://www.lawyerswithoutborders.org
Contact: Christina M. Storm, Founder/Exec. Dir.
Founded: 2000. **Membership Dues:** individual, $100 (annual) ● law firm - minimum (based on number of lawyers), $500 (annual) ● law firm - maximum (based on number of lawyers), $15,000 (annual). **Multinational. Description:** Creates a global association of lawyers dedicated to the promotion and protection of human justice by providing free legal services. Supports capacity building of non-governmental organizations worldwide. Protects the integrity of legal process through neutral observation. Serves as a law oriented clearinghouse linking needs with the legal resources to meet them. **Computer Services:** Information services, non-profit resource page ● online services, job board ● online services, lawyer survey ● online services, merchandise. **Projects:** Law School - NGO Linkage; Lawyer to Lawyer; Lawyers At Risk; Neutral Independent Court Trial Observer; Quarter-Backs Observer Teams for ABA INS Detainee Observation. **Publications:** *Borderlines.* Newsletter. Features articles about Lawyer's experiences in the field of conflicts, projects and highlights of issues in regions with human rights concerns. Alternate Formats: online.

Liberalism

17641 ■ Americans for Democratic Action (ADA)
1625 K St. NW, Ste.210
Washington, DC 20006
Ph: (202)785-5980
Fax: (202)785-5969
E-mail: info@adaction.org
URL: http://www.adaction.org
Contact: Amy Isaacs, Natl. Dir.
Founded: 1947. **Members:** 50,000. **Membership Dues:** individual, $55 (annual) ● family, $80 ● limited income, $30 ● student, $20. **Staff:** 8. **Budget:** $150,000. **State Groups:** 15. **Description:** Professionals and businesspersons, labor leaders, educators, students, political leaders, and other individuals interested in liberal political ideas. Aims to formulate liberal domestic and foreign policies based on the changing needs of American democracy, enlist public understanding and support of these policies, and put them into effect through the political process. Sponsors conferences and campus outreach. **Libraries: Type:** reference; by appointment only. **Holdings:** 52. **Committees:** Economics; Energy and the Environment; Foreign Policy; Labor; Political Action; Social and Domestic; Workers' Rights. **Divisions:** Communications; Legislative; Political. **Publications:** *ADA*

Today, quarterly. Newsletter. Provides information of legislation on Capitol Hill and actions taken by the executive branch; includes chapter news. **Price:** included in membership dues; $20.00 /year for nonmembers. ISSN: 0896-3134. **Circulation:** 20,000. Alternate Formats: online. Also Cited As: *ADA World* ● *ADA Voting Record,* annual ● *ADAction News and Notes,* weekly, when Congress is in session. Newsletter. Contains news about the weeks' happenings on the Hill. ● *Legislative and Membership Alerts,* periodic. **Conventions/Meetings:** annual convention and meeting (exhibits) - always June.

17642 ■ Foundation for the Study of Independent Social Ideas (FSISI)
310 Riverside Dr., Ste.2008
New York, NY 10025
Ph: (212)316-3120
Fax: (212)316-3145
E-mail: inquires@dissentmagazine.org
URL: http://www.dissentmagazine.org
Contact: Michael Walzer PhD, Pres.
Founded: 1980. **Staff:** 3. **Description:** Aims to "defend democratic values and to question the status quo" through its publications. Conducts research in connection with publications. **Publications:** *Dissent Magazine,* quarterly. Journal. Covers and analyzes social issues, politics, and current events from a socialist perspective; includes book reviews. **Price:** $24.00 /year for individuals; $34.00 /year for institutions; $17.00/year for students. ISSN: 0012-3846. **Circulation:** 9,000. **Advertising:** accepted ● *The HMO Revolution: How It Happened, What It Means and What to Do About It* ● *Organizing Graduate Students.* **Conventions/Meetings:** periodic conference.

17643 ■ Trusteeship Institute (TI)
61 Baker Rd.
Shutesbury, MA 01072
Ph: (413)584-8191
Fax: (413)584-4310
E-mail: terry@trusteeship.org
Contact: Terry Mollner, Pres.
Founded: 1973. **Staff:** 3. **Description:** Professional writers, educators, and lawyers. Conducts seminars on subjects such as workers' ownership of business, community land trust, socially responsible investments, Gandhian philosophy, and consensus decision-making. Consults with businesses and groups that wish to form worker-owned businesses, employee stock ownership plans, community land trusts, and nonprofit, tax-exempt organizations. **Formerly:** (1984) New England Foundation for Cooperative Living.

Libertarianism

17644 ■ Advocates for Self-Government
Liberty Bldg.
213 S Erwin St.
Cartersville, GA 30120
Ph: (770)386-8372
Free: (800)932-1776
Fax: (770)386-8373
E-mail: info@theadvocates.org
URL: http://www.theadvocates.org
Contact: Sharon Harris, Pres.
Founded: 1985. **Members:** 9,500. **Staff:** 6. **Budget:** $225,000. **Description:** Individuals interested in the libertarian ideal of individual freedom and the goal of self-government. Seeks to educate the public on and promote the value of self-government. Provides communication and outreach tools and training. **Libraries: Type:** reference. **Subjects:** liberty, libertarianism. **Awards:** Light of Liberty Award. **Frequency:** annual. **Type:** recognition. **Recipient:** letters to the editor, public speaking, outreach booth work. **Computer Services:** Online services, catalog. **Programs:** Libertarian Newsstand; Lights of Liberty; Operation Politically Homeless; World's Smallest Political Quiz. **Formerly:** (1985) Self-Government Advocates. **Publications:** *Discovering Self-Government: A Bible Based Study Guide.* Book. Price: $3.95 ● *Liberator*

Online, semimonthly. Newsletter. **Price:** free. Alternate Formats: online ● *The Libertarian Communicator,* quarterly. Magazine. Includes articles from famous libertarian authors. **Price:** $15.00/year ● *Liberty A-Z.* Book. **Price:** $13.95 ● *Minimum Wage, Maximum Damage.* Book. **Price:** $5.00 ● *OPH Manual.* **Price:** $20.00 ● *Secrets of Libertarian Persuasion.* Book. **Price:** $15.00 ● *The World's Smallest Political Quiz.* Alternate Formats: online. **Conventions/Meetings:** quinquennial conference, with focus on communication skills ● workshop, training.

17645 ■ Association of Libertarian Feminists (ALF)
484 Lake Park Ave., No. 24
Oakland, CA 94610-2730
Ph: (925)228-0565
Fax: (925)891-3515
E-mail: membership@alf.org
URL: http://www.alf.org
Contact: Sharon Presley, Natl. Coor.
Founded: 1975. **Members:** 200. **Membership Dues:** individual, $10 (biennial). **Staff:** 3. **Description:** Women and men who are both libertarians and feminists. Seeks to provide a libertarian alternative to those aspects of the women's movement that discourage independence and individuality; encourage women to become economically self-sufficient and psychologically independent; oppose the abridgment of individual rights by any government on the basis of sex; work toward changing sexist attitudes and behavior; publicize and promote realistic attitudes toward female competence, achievement, and potential. Distributes literature. **Committees:** Coordinating. **Publications:** *ALF News,* quarterly. Newsletter. Alternate Formats: online ● Papers. Alternate Formats: online ● Articles. Alternate Formats: online ● Also publishes occasional essays. **Conventions/Meetings:** periodic meeting.

17646 ■ Center for Libertarian Studies (CLS)
851 Burlway Rd., Ste.202
Burlingame, CA 94010
Free: (800)325-7257
Fax: (650)401-5530
E-mail: info@libertarianstudies.org
URL: http://www.lewrockwell.com
Contact: Burton S. Blumert, Publisher
Founded: 1976. **Description:** Promotes scholarly analysis of social, economic, political, and philosophical problems from a Libertarian perspective. Encourages interdisciplinary study of the "science of liberty." Maintains speakers' bureau. Sponsors Libertarian Heritage Lectures, Urban Studies Lectures, Libertarian Scholars Conferences, and various interdisciplinary colloquia. **Libraries: Type:** reference. **Holdings:** 500. **Awards:** Mises Fellowship in the Humanities. **Type:** fellowship ● **Type:** recognition. **Publications:** *In Pursuit of Liberty Newsletter,* periodic ● *Journal of Libertarian Studies,* semiannual ● *Occasional Papers,* periodic. **Conventions/Meetings:** annual meeting.

17647 ■ International Society for Individual Liberty (ISIL)
836-B Southampton Rd., No. 299
Benicia, CA 94510
Ph: (707)746-8796
Fax: (707)746-8797
E-mail: isil@isil.org
URL: http://www.isil.org
Contact: Vincent H. Miller, Pres./Ed.
Founded: 1989. **Members:** 3,000. **Membership Dues:** basic, $35 (annual) ● student/retired/fixed income, $15 (annual) ● sustaining, $50 (annual) ● benefactor, $100 (annual) ● donor, $300 (annual) ● patron, $500 (annual) ● supporting, $200 (annual) ● life, $1,500. **Staff:** 3. **Budget:** $250,000. **Regional Groups:** 25. **Multinational. Description:** Individuals and organizations which seek to establish a free and peaceful world through libertarian doctrine. Advocates free market economics and individual liberty; exchanges ideas and strategies with fellow members. Conducts charitable programs. **Awards:** Freedom Torch Award. **Frequency:** biennial. **Type:** recognition. **Recipient:** for outstanding contribution to liberty.

Computer Services: database, international contact ● online services, membership networking service ● online services, research. **Additional Websites:** http://www.free-market.net. **Formed by Merger of:** (1989) Society for Individual Liberty; (1989) Libertarian International. **Publications:** *Educational Outreach* (in English and Spanish). Brochures. **Circulation:** 5,000. **Advertising:** accepted. Alternate Formats: online ● *Freedom Network News*, bimonthly. Journal. **Price:** $35.00. **Circulation:** 3,000. **Conventions/ Meetings:** annual international conference (exhibits) - usually July or August.

17648 ■ Libertarian Futurist Society (LFS)
650 Castro St., Ste.120-433
Mountain View, CA 94041
E-mail: dtuchman@gmail.com
URL: http://www.lfs.org
Contact: Fran Van Cleave, Dir.
Founded: 1982. **Members:** 150. **Membership Dues:** full, $50 (annual) ● basic, $25 (annual) ● basic (overseas), $30 (annual) ● sponsor, $100 (annual) ● benefactor, $200 (annual). **Staff:** 2. **Description:** Futurists and science fiction fans who share a concern for individual freedom. Stresses the doctrine of free will in its efforts to promote a decentralized power structure; encourages voluntary cooperation among the peoples of the world. Views the cultural and technological innovations presented in science fiction as a means toward a freer society. **Awards:** Hall of Fame Award. **Frequency:** annual. **Type:** recognition ● Prometheus Award. **Frequency:** annual. **Type:** recognition. **Publications:** *LFS News*, quarterly. Newsletter. Includes book reviews on publications of favorite authors. **Price:** $20.00/year ● *Prometheus*, quarterly. Journal. Features articles and reviews about futurism and science fiction. Includes book reviews, calendar of events, news of members, and research updates. **Price:** $20.00/year. **Circulation:** 300. **Conventions/Meetings:** annual meeting, held in conjunction with World Science Fiction Convention or North American Science Fiction Convention - always Labor Day weekend.

17649 ■ Libertarians for Life (LFL)
13424 Hathaway Dr.
Silver Spring, MD 20906
Ph: (301)460-4141
E-mail: dorisgordon@comcast.net
URL: http://www.L4L.org
Contact: Doris Gordon, Founder/Natl. Coor.
Founded: 1976. **Nonmembership. Description:** "Founded to show why abortion is aggression, not a right. Reasoning is expressly philosophical and scientific - rather than either religious or pragmatic, or merely political or emotional. Holds to libertarianism's basic principle that each of us has the obligation not to aggress against (violate the rights of) anyone else - for any reason (personal, social, or political), however worthy. When the government legalizes aggression, it is still aggression". **Libraries: Type:** reference. **Computer Services:** Online services, publication. **Telecommunication Services:** electronic mail, lfl-discuss-subscribe@topica.com ● electronic mail, lfl-discuss@topica.com. **Publications:** *A False Assumption*. Article ● *A Libertarian Atheist Answers Pro-Choice Catholics*. Article ● *A Wrong, Not a Right: An Atheist Libertarian Looks at Abortion*. Article ● *Abortion and Libertarianism's First Principles*. Article ● *Abortion and Rights: Applying Libertarian Principles Correctly*. Article ● *Abortion and the Question of the Person*. Article ● *Abortion and Thomson's Violinist: Unplugging a Bad Analogy*. Article ● *Abortion, Choice, and Libertarian Principles*. Article ● *Abortion, Choice, and the Future of the Libertarian Party*. Article ● *Abortion Choice: in Harmony or in Conflict with the Rest of the Libertarian Party Platform?*. Article ● *Abortion in the Case of Pregnancy Due to Rape*. Article ● *An Exchange Between David F. Nolan and Doris Gordon on Abortion and the Libertarian Party Platform*. Article ● *An Open Letter to Murray Rothbard*. Article ● *Being Pro-Life Is Necessary to Defend Liberty*. Article ● *Beneath the Pro-Abortion Logic*. Article ● *Comments on the LP Platform's Abortion Plank*. Article ● *How I Became Pro-Life: Remarks on Abortion, Parental Obligation*

and the Draft. Article ● *If the Unborn Child is a Person Entitled to Rights, Abortion is Aggression*. Article ● *Introduction*. Article ● *Is It Just to Impose the Death Penalty?*. Article. **Conventions/Meetings:** periodic meeting.

17650 ■ The Voluntaryists (TV)
PO Box 275-D
Gramling, SC 29348
Ph: (864)472-2750
E-mail: vlntryst@aol.com
URL: http://members.aol.com/vlntryst
Contact: Carl Watner, Co-Organizer
Founded: 1982. **Description:** Participants are libertarians who reject all political activity, including attempts to elect libertarians to political office, in the belief that such activity conflicts with libertarian principles and bestows "the illusion of moral legitimacy upon political power." Voluntaryists, a term used to describe libertarians in the 19th century, distinguish themselves from advocates of the Libertarian Party (see separate entry). Aims to explore and promote nonpolitical strategies in achieving a free society. Seeks to delegitimize the state through education, nonviolent resistance, and counter-economics. **Libraries: Type:** reference. **Holdings:** 450. **Subjects:** anarchism, nonviolence, libertarianism. **Publications:** *A Personal Declaration of Independence*. Book ● *A Voluntary Political Government*. Book ● *Bearing Witness for Silence*. Book ● *I Must Speak Out: The Best of the Voluntaryist 1982-1999*. Book ● *Neither Bullets Nor Ballots*. Book ● *Truth Is Not a Half-Way Place*. Book ● Newsletter, quarterly. **Price:** $20.00/ year. **Conventions/Meetings:** periodic regional meeting.

17651 ■ World Libertarian Order (WLO)
PO Box 40608
Reno, NV 89504
E-mail: wlo418@yahoo.com
URL: http://wlo418.tripod.com/worldlibertarianorder
Contact: Eric F. Magnuson, Dir.
Founded: 1983. **Membership Dues:** life, $10. **Description:** International fraternal organization. Promotes permanent peace, full employment and prosperity everywhere on Earth without injustice or sacrifice for anyone. Seeks to educate the world about "the superior workability of Libertarian principles in order to save this planet from the destructive effects of collectivist governments." Works for a "World Libertarian Order" of separate nations interacting in a free world market. **Publications:** *Evolutionary Psychology and the Liberation of the Higher Self*. Book ● *Introduction to the World Libertarian Order*. Book ● *World Libertarian Revolution and the Fulfillment of Evolutionary Destiny*. Book.

Literacy

17652 ■ Family Literacy Alliance (FLA)
325 W Main St., Ste.300
Louisville, KY 40202-4237
Ph: (502)584-1133
Free: (877)FAMLIT-1
Fax: (502)584-0172
E-mail: dnichols@famlit.org
URL: http://www.famlit.org/ProgramsandInitiatives/ FLA/index.cfm
Contact: Debbie Nichols, Dir.
Description: Promotes family literacy. **Awards:** FLA Advocacy Champion Award. **Frequency:** annual. **Type:** recognition. **Recipient:** for family literacy programs demonstrating exemplary advocacy efforts. **Affiliated With:** National Center for Family Literacy. **Publications:** *Connecting*, quarterly. Magazine. **Price:** included in membership dues. Alternate Formats: online ● *FLA Member Directory*. Membership Directory.

Lithuania

17653 ■ Lithuanian National Foundation (LNF)
307 W 30th St.
New York, NY 10001-2703

Ph: (212)868-5860
Fax: (212)868-5815
E-mail: tautfd@aol.com
URL: http://www.tautfd.org
Contact: Giedre M. Kumpikas PhD, Pres.
Founded: 1922. **Members:** 15. **Staff:** 2. **Languages:** English, Lithuanian. **Multinational. Description:** Collects, researches, analyzes, and disseminates information on Lithuania and the Lithuanian nation. Provides documentation on the human rights situation in Lithuania. Conducts seminars. **Libraries: Type:** reference. **Holdings:** 1,000. **Subjects:** Lithuanistica, international affairs. **Publications:** *ELTA Information Bulletin*, monthly. Reports on the current situation in Lithuania and other Baltic countries. Covers human rights violations and related topics. **Price:** free. **Circulation:** 4,000 ● Books (in English, French, Italian, and Lithuanian) ● Bulletins (in English, French, Italian, and Lithuanian) ● Pamphlets (in English, French, Italian, and Lithuanian). **Conventions/Meetings:** annual meeting - always November/ December.

Marijuana

17654 ■ Drug Peace Campaign
PO Box 323
Middletown, CA 95461
Ph: (415)971-3573
E-mail: comments@drugpeace.org
URL: http://www.drugpeace.org
Contact: Julia Bono, Chair
Founded: 1999. **Description:** Seeks a peaceful end to enforcement of prohibitionist drug policies. **Boards:** Campaign.

17655 ■ Friends and Families of Cannabis Consumers (FFCC)
PO Box 1716
El Cerrito, CA 94530
Ph: (510)215-8326
Fax: (510)215-8326
E-mail: chris@fcda.org
URL: http://www.equalrights4all.org/ffcc/ffcc.html
Contact: Chris Conrad, Dir.
Membership Dues: token, $10 (annual) ● basic, $25 (annual). **Description:** Committed to changing marijuana laws; in favor of legalization.

Marriage

17656 ■ Alternatives to Marriage Project (AtMP)
PO Box 320151
Brooklyn, NY 11232
Ph: (718)788-1911
E-mail: atmp@unmarried.org
URL: http://www.unmarried.org
Founded: 1998. **Multinational. Description:** Advocates for equality and fairness for unmarried people, including people who choose not to marry, cannot marry, or live together before marriage. Stands in the vital intersection of the shared values and interests of widely diverse people: America's rapidly growing unmarried constituency includes those who identify as GLBT and as straight, seniors and young adults, people trying to plan their estates and people trying to pay the rent. Embraced equally by people boycotting marriage and by people trying to establish their common law status. Works by responding to daily requests for information from the public, students and media, issuing policy statements, and moderating listservs. Represents unmarried people and responding to the marriage-only movement. **Libraries: Type:** reference. **Subjects:** unmarried relationships. **Publications:** *Alternatives to Marriage Update*, quarterly. Newsletter. Features short reviews of books relating to marriage and its alternatives. **Circulation:** 7,000. Alternate Formats: online ● *Let Them Eat Wedding Rings: The Role of Marriage Promotion in Welfare Reform*. Reports. Gives an explanation on the effects of marriage-promoting policies to the family life. **Price:** $5.00 plus shipping and handling ● *Unmarried*

To Each Other: The Essential Guide to Living Together as an Unmarried Couple. Book ● Annual Report, annual. Alternate Formats: online ● Articles.

Media

17657 ■ Action Coalition for Media Education (ACME)
2808 El Tesoro Escondido NW
Albuquerque, NM 87120
Ph: (505)893-9702
Fax: (505)828-3142
E-mail: aokb@umich.edu
URL: http://www.acmecoalition.org
Contact: Alison Brzenchek, Communications Dir.

Founded: 2002. **Membership Dues:** individual, professional, $50 (annual) ● student, senior, $25 (annual) ● organization, $100 (annual). **Regional Groups:** 3. **Description:** Serves as a strategic network linking media educators, health advocates, media reformers, independent media makers, community organizers, and others. Works for the democratization of media system by advocating media education and independent media production. **Computer Services:** Information services, election, democracy and media education resources. **Boards:** Advisory. **Committees:** Planning. **Publications:** *BACME*, bimonthly. Newsletter. Contains news and information about media literacy related curricula, conferences, and initiatives. Alternate Formats: online.

17658 ■ Internews Network
PO Box 4448
Arcata, CA 95518-4448
Ph: (707)826-2030
Free: (877)247-8819
Fax: (707)826-2136
E-mail: info@internews.org
URL: http://www.internews.org
Contact: David Hoffman, Pres.

Founded: 1982. **Budget:** $19,800,000. **National Groups:** 45. **Multinational. Description:** Supports and encourages open media worldwide. Fosters independent media in emerging democracies. Offers training to journalists and station managers in the standards and practices of professional journalism. Produces innovative television and radio programming and internet content. Uses media to reduce conflict within and between countries. **Computer Services:** Information services, access to online articles and reports ● mailing lists, of members. **Programs:** Local Voices. **Projects:** Global Internet Policy Initiative; Open Skies/Culture for the New Millennium. **Publications:** *Flashes*. Bulletin. Contains news and information on activities of Internews. Alternate Formats: online ● *Freedom of Journalism in Afghanistan.* Newsletter. Contains articles about freedom of journalism in Afghanistan. Alternate Formats: online ● *Internet Governance: A Discussion Document.* Report. Alternate Formats: online ● *Media Monitor.* Newsletter. Contains information on Afghan media. Alternate Formats: online ● *National Radio Frequency Survey.* Alternate Formats: online ● Annual Reports, annual. Alternate Formats: online ● Brochure. Alternate Formats: online.

17659 ■ May I Speak Freely Media (MISF)
20 Greenleaf Ave.
Medford, MA 02155
Ph: (781)393-0906
E-mail: speak@mayispeakfreely.org
URL: http://www.mayispeakfreely.org
Contact: Roz Dzelzitis, Exec. Dir./Producer

Description: Produces and distributes media on issues of social, environmental and economic justice. Works closely with activists, international NGOs and grassroots organizations to research and document threats to human and civil rights. Educates the public about global issues and builds awareness of how historical events are relevant to contemporary political issues. Encourages democratic participation and motivates individuals to hold media, corporations and

government officials accountable to the people they serve. Creates forums for public education and discussion.

17660 ■ Media Action Network for Asian Americans (MANAA)
PO Box 11105
Burbank, CA 91510
Ph: (213)486-4433
Free: (888)906-2622
E-mail: manaaletters@yahoo.com
URL: http://www.manaa.org
Contact: Guy Aoki, Founding Pres.

Founded: 1992. **Membership Dues:** general, $50 (annual) ● student, $35 (annual) ● sustaining, $100 (annual) ● corporate (gold), $500 (annual) ● corporate (silver), $250 (annual). **Description:** Advocates for the balanced portrayal of Asian-Americans in the media. Monitors depictions in the media of persons of Asian Pacific descent. Encourages increased news coverage of significant issues concerning Asian-Americans. **Awards:** MANAA Media Scholarship. **Frequency:** annual. **Type:** scholarship. **Recipient:** for college and graduate students interested in pursuing careers in filmmaking and in television production. **Computer Services:** database, media contact ● online services, Yahoo groups discussion page. **Publications:** *Eyes and Ears*, quarterly. Newsletter. **Price:** included in membership dues.

17661 ■ MediaChannel.org
575 8th Ave.
New York, NY 10018
Ph: (212)246-0202
Fax: (212)246-2677
E-mail: info@mediachannel.org
URL: http://www.mediachannel.org
Contact: Danny Schechter, Exec. Ed.

Description: Public interest Web site dedicated to global media issues; concerned with the political, cultural and social impacts of the media; provides information and perspectives for debate, collaboration, action, and citizen engagement. Offers thematic special reports, action toolkits, forums for discussion, indexed directory, and search engine. **Telecommunication Services:** electronic mail, danny@mediachannel.org. **Publications:** Newsletters. Alternate Formats: online.

17662 ■ Mediascope
100 Universal City Plz., Bldg. 6159
Universal City, CA 91608
Ph: (818)733-3180
Fax: (818)733-3181
E-mail: facts@mediascope.org
URL: http://www.mediascope.org
Contact: Donna Mitroff PhD, Pres.

Founded: 1992. **Description:** Works with issues of social relevance within the entertainment industry, especial issues affecting children and society at large. **Publications:** *Building Blocks: A Guide for Creating Children's Educational Television.* Book. Provides guidance for creating educational programs. **Price:** $18.95 ● *Children, the Media, and Drugs: A Parent's Guide.* Book. Provides advice on how to protect children from the effects of problematic media portrayals of tobacco, alcohol and illicit drugs. **Price:** $4.95 ● *From Parents to Pop Stars: Role Models and Heroes in the Third Millennium.* Report. Contains a review of the literature of heroes and role models. **Price:** $20.00. Alternate Formats: online ● *The Kids Are Watching.* Video. Contains visual exploration into violence in the lives of children. **Price:** $20.00 for students and non-profits; $40.00 ● Newsletter. Alternate Formats: online.

17663 ■ Mobile Voter
44 Elsie St.
San Francisco, CA 94110
Ph: (415)641-4921
E-mail: info@mobilevoter.org
URL: http://www.mobilevoter.org
Contact: Ben Rigby, Co-Exec. Dir./Founder

Founded: 2004. **Description:** Seeks to facilitate the process of civic participation through web and mobile technologies. Utilizes technology to connect with and

mobilize voters. Communicates with voters about matters relating to youth voting, voter registration, text messaging and web technology.

17664 ■ Public Media Foundation (PMF)
351 Ryder Hall
Coll. of Arts & Sciences
Northeastern Univ.
Boston, MA 02115-5000
Ph: (617)373-4698
E-mail: publicmedia@neu.edu
URL: http://www.scribblingwomen.org
Contact: Valerie Henderson, Exec. Dir.

Founded: 1979. **Description:** Promotes the media industry. Sponsors the Scribbling Women project, a web site dedicated to American women writers for national radio broadcast; provides classroom resources for teaching and learning the tradition of American literature by women. **Publications:** *Scribbling Women.* Newsletter. Alternate Formats: online.

17665 ■ We Interrupt This Message
1215 York St.
San Francisco, CA 94110
Ph: (415)621-3302
E-mail: we@interrupt.org
URL: http://www.interrupt.org
Contact: Hunter Cutting, Co-Founder

Founded: 1996. **Description:** Dedicated to building capacity in grassroots and public interest organizations to conduct traditional media work and reframe public debate and interrupt media stereotypes. **Programs:** Help Desk-Technical Assistance, Media Services and Consultation; Media Activism Campaigns; Media Messaging; Media Training and Consultation; 911 Peace and Justice; Tool Kits; Voices for the Silenced; Youth Media Council. **Projects:** Talking the Walk: Race and Media. **Publications:** *Speaking for Ourselves: Youth Assessment of Local News Coverage.* Report. Alternate Formats: online ● *Talking the Walk: A Communications Guide for Racial Justice.* Book. Alternate Formats: online.

17666 ■ World Media Association (WMA)
3600 New York Ave. NE, 3rd Fl.
Washington, DC 20002
Ph: (202)636-3124
Fax: (202)635-9227
E-mail: wma@wmassociation.com
URL: http://www.wmassociation.com
Contact: Larry Moffitt, Exec. Dir.

Membership Dues: individual, $60 (annual). **Multinational. Description:** Media professionals and opinion leaders. Dedicated to advancing standards of journalistic ethics; promotes press freedom where it does not exist, encourages the responsible use of that freedom where it does. **Computer Services:** Mailing lists. **Publications:** Proceedings. Alternate Formats: online. **Conventions/Meetings:** annual conference.

Men's Rights

17667 ■ American Union of Men (AUM)
PO Box 80131
Santa Barbara, CA 93117
E-mail: aum@yahoogroups.com
URL: http://groups.yahoo.com/group/aum
Contact: Tom Smith, Founder/Pres.

Founded: 1983. **Members:** 125. **Membership Dues:** full, $25 (annual). **Staff:** 6. **Description:** Works to further the interests and rights of men. Group believes that men have been suppressed by the "powerful female majority" and that men have been forced to "serve" that majority. Conducts speakers' bureau. Sponsors political action committee. **Telecommunication Services:** electronic mail, qimnews@yahoo.com. **Publications:** Newsletter, quarterly. Features Men's Movement Internet News. **Price:** free, for members only. **Advertising:** accepted. Alternate Formats: online.

17668 ■ Male Liberation Foundation (MLF)
701 NE 67th St.
Miami, FL 33138
Ph: (305)756-6249
Fax: (305)756-6006
URL: http://malelib.org
Contact: Natasha Wolf-Cohen, VP Foundation Relations

Founded: 1965. **Members:** 39,250. **Membership Dues:** $25 (annual). **Staff:** 12. **Budget:** $14,000. **Regional Groups:** 350. **State Groups:** 35. **Local Groups:** 850. **Description:** Individuals who seek to publicize the "new discrimination" against white men, including discrimination which caused "white boys to become the coffee boys, floor sweepers, and delivery boys in the 1990s." Believes that men and women have real biological and psychological differences and that public awareness, education, and acceptance of these differences will reduce the divorce rate. Seeks to educate men about their economic and political losses and solutions; supports joint custody and paternal leave for fathers of newborn children. Seeks to defend homemakers (traditional women) from "screaming radical feminists." Lobbies for changes in Affirmative Action policies, abortion laws, divorce inequities, and sexual harassment rulings. Offers legal referrals. Compiles statistics; operates speakers' bureau; conducts children's services, research programs, and educational programs. **Libraries: Type:** reference. **Holdings:** artwork, audio recordings, books, clippings, periodicals, video recordings. **Subjects:** gender relations, gender discrimination. **Awards:** Humanitarian Award. **Frequency:** monthly. **Type:** recognition. **Recipient:** for outstanding work toward educating the genders to get back together again. **Committees:** Political Action. **Publications:** *The First Book on Male Liberation and Sex Equality*. Historic issue. **Price:** included in membership dues; $25.00/copy. **Advertising:** accepted ● *Make Love.Not Gender Wars*. Video. **Price:** $25.00 each ● *Male Lib Audios*, monthly. Audiotapes. Includes the MLF position on current issues. **Price:** $10.00 each. **Circulation:** 15,000. **Advertising:** accepted ● *The Male Lib News*, monthly. Newsletter. Includes the MLF position on current issues. **Price:** $24.95/12 issues. **Circulation:** 15,000. **Advertising:** accepted ● *101 Reasons Why Men Need Liberating*. **Price:** included in membership dues ● *Pennsylvania University Celebrity Lecture*. Video. **Price:** $10.00 available to groups ● *20 Constitutional Violations of Men, Via Feminism*. Papers. Includes 250 MLF position papers. **Price:** included in membership dues ● Papers. Includes 250 MLF position papers. **Conventions/Meetings:** annual congress - always fall, England.

17669 ■ Men and Fathers Resource Center (MFRC)
807 Brazos St., Ste.315
Austin, TX 78701-2508
Ph: (512)472-3237
Fax: (512)499-8056
E-mail: dads@fathers.org
URL: http://www.fathers.org
Contact: Sula Milstead, Exec. Dir.

Founded: 1992. **Members:** 500. **Membership Dues:** regular, $100 (annual). **Staff:** 3. **Budget:** $65,000. **Local Groups:** 1. **Languages:** English, Spanish. **Description:** Refers calls to programs that can assist with their individual problems. Provides services on how to represent yourself in court class. Sponsors research and statistical data. Provides community services. Provides free and low-cost counseling and legal services to the greater central Texas community, as well as low-cost DNA testing. **Libraries: Type:** reference. **Holdings:** 250. **Doing business as:** Lonestar Fatherhood Initiative. **Formerly:** (2000) Men/Fathers Hotline. **Publications:** *Men's Issues Distribution List*, weekly. Newsletter. **Advertising:** accepted. Alternate Formats: online.

17670 ■ Men's Defense Association (MDA)
17854 Lyons
Forest Lake, MN 55025
Ph: (651)464-7887

Fax: (651)464-7135
URL: http://www.mensdefense.org
Contact: Richard F. Doyle, Pres.

Founded: 1972. **Members:** 15,000. **Membership Dues:** individual (one-time fee), $20. **Staff:** 2. **Budget:** $20,000. **Description:** Male victims of sex discrimination, actual or potential. Purposes are: to preserve the traditional, nuclear family through restoration of equal dignity and equal rights under the law for all male persons; to promote and foster the just and competent administration of government, especially of the judicial branch; to educate officialdom and the public regarding these and other issues pertaining to gender. Conducts extensive informal research; plans to conduct scholarly research. Compiles statistics. Offers attorney and local organization referral service to members. **Convention/Meeting:** none. extensive informal research; plans to conduct scholarly research. Compiles statistics. Offers attorney and local organization referral service to members. **Convention/Meeting:** none. **Computer Services:** database ● mailing lists. **Affiliated With:** Men's Equality Now International. **Formerly:** (1971) Aid to Divorced and Separated Men; (1993) Men's Rights Association. **Publications:** *Divorce What Everyone Should Know to Beat the Racket*. Booklet. **Price:** $4.00 ● *The Liberator*, semimonthly. Newsletter. **Price:** $24.00/year. ISSN: 1040-3760. **Circulation:** 2,500. **Advertising:** accepted ● *The Men's Manifesto*. Booklet. **Price:** $4.00 each.

17671 ■ Men's Equality Now International
17854 Lyons St.
Forest Lake, MN 55025
Ph: (651)464-7663
Fax: (651)464-7135
Contact: Richard F. Doyle, Chm.

Founded: 1977. **Members:** 18. **Staff:** 3. **Budget:** $500. **Local Groups:** 137. **Description:** Coalition of men's rights and divorce reform organizations. Works to obtain equal rights for men in all areas of law; to obtain just and competent administration of domestic relations; to combat anti-male discrimination; and to strengthen the family. Works to strengthen the male image, especially in the role of father. Assists men who have been falsely accused of child abuse or rape. Serves as clearinghouse and resource center. **Affiliated With:** Men's Defense Association. **Absorbed:** (1990) Parents and Children's Equality. **Formerly:** (1982) Men's Equality Now International. **Publications:** *The Liberator*, monthly. Newsletter. **Price:** $24.00/year. **Circulation:** 8,000. **Advertising:** accepted. **Conventions/Meetings:** annual general assembly.

17672 ■ Men's Rights (MR)
PO Box 163180
Sacramento, CA 95816
Ph: (916)484-7333
Fax: (916)484-7333
Contact: Fredric Hayward, Exec.Dir.

Founded: 1977. **Members:** 1,000. **Membership Dues:** $26 (annual). **Description:** Seeks to end sexism in a way that recognizes the social, psychological, physical, legal, and economic problems of men; to correct low standards of male self-image and male health; to encourage women to share the burdens of taking the romantic initiative; to eliminate "the dictum that the worst failure a man can commit is the failure to live up to the male role." Seeks to achieve equal opportunity for male parents; believes that "the provider and protector roles have dehumanized, damaged, and limited men." Has initiated legal actions designed to focus attention on men's issues. Maintains speakers' bureau; compiles statistics; conducts programs and demonstrations. **Convention/Meeting:** none. **Libraries: Type:** reference. **Holdings:** 1,000. **Projects:** ERA; Media Watch; Parental Leave; Pro-Choice for Men-Too. **Absorbed:** National Coalition for a Just Draft. **Publications:** Distributes periodic news releases to the media, and literature to members.

17673 ■ National Center for Men (NCM)
PO Box 555
Old Bethpage, NY 11804
Ph: (516)938-3075

E-mail: info@nationalcenterformen.org
URL: http://www.nas.com/c4m
Contact: Mel Feit, Exec. Dir.

Founded: 1987. **Members:** 3,000. **Membership Dues:** unemployed, low income, $30 (annual) ● individual, $40 (annual) ● sustaining, $60 (annual). **Description:** Individuals dedicated to eliminating the sexism which the group believes is directed against men. Works to address such men's rights issues as sexual harassment, fathers' rights, gender quotas, divorce law, men's reproductive rights, paternity suits, and feminism. **Libraries: Type:** reference. **Subjects:** gender issues, men's issues, men's rights. **Additional Websites:** http://www.nationalcenterformen.org. **Publications:** *Men's Rights Report*, quarterly. Contains reports on the association's activities, articles, and letters. **Conventions/Meetings:** monthly meeting.

17674 ■ National Coalition of Free Men (NCFM)
PO Box 582023
Minneapolis, MN 55458-2023
Ph: (516)482-6378
Free: (888)223-1280
E-mail: ncfm@ncfm.org
URL: http://www.ncfm.org
Contact: Mr. Michael Rother, Pres.

Founded: 1977. **Members:** 2,000. **Membership Dues:** individual, $30 (annual). **Local Groups:** 2. **Description:** Men seeking a "fair and balanced perspective to gender issues." Advocates the legal rights of males in abortion issues, divorce and child custody law, the draft, "false accusation" of rape, divorce, and sexual harassment, sex discrimination, and abuse of men. Conducts research; sponsors educational programs; operates speakers' bureau on men's issues, and some men's rights activities. **Awards:** Award for Excellence in Promoting Gender Fairness in the Media. **Frequency:** annual. **Type:** recognition. **Recipient:** for media sources ● Excellence in Advancement of Men's Issues. **Frequency:** annual. **Type:** recognition ● NCFM Award of Honor. **Frequency:** annual. **Type:** recognition. **Recipient:** for those working hard behind the scenes. **Computer Services:** database, contains library of men's issues. **Committees:** Letter Writing; William Hethering Defense. **Also Known As:** Men's Resources Hot Line. **Publications:** *Transitions: Journal of Men's Perspectives*, bimonthly. Newsletter. Features articles on men's issues, movie and book reviews, and research results. **Price:** included in membership dues. ISSN: 0886-826X. **Advertising:** accepted. **Conventions/Meetings:** periodic conference.

17675 ■ National Men's Resource Center (NMRC)
PO Box 1080
Brookings, OR 97415-0024
E-mail: menstuff@menstuff.org
URL: http://www.menstuff.org
Contact: Gordon Clay, Pres.

Founded: 1982. **Staff:** 1. **Budget:** $20,000. **Description:** Works to "end men's isolation." Gathers and disseminates information on legal and social issues of relevance to men. Conducts bookmobile tours. **Libraries: Type:** reference. **Holdings:** 3,400; books. **Subjects:** men's issues. **Telecommunication Services:** electronic mail, gordonclay@aol.com. **Formerly:** The Fathers' Network. **Publications:** *Menstuff*. Directory. Provides information on hundreds of men's issues regarding positive change in male roles and relationships. Alternate Formats: online.

17676 ■ National Organization for Men (NOM)
30 Besey St.
New York, NY 10007
Ph: (760)753-5000 (510)655-2777
E-mail: warren@warrenfarrell.com
URL: http://www.orgformen.org
Contact: Dr. Warren Farrell, Co-Pres.

Founded: 1983. **Members:** 13,800. **Membership Dues:** $25 (annual). **Regional Groups:** 26. **Local Groups:** 30. **Description:** Men and women united in efforts to promote and advance the equal rights of men in matters such as affirmative action programs, alimony, child custody, men's health, child abuse, battered husbands, divorce, educational benefits, military conscription, and veterans' benefits. Maintains Institute for the Study of Matrimonial Laws, established as a research and education foundation for the study of the nation's divorce, alimony, and custody and visitation laws. Offers support group; lobbies for equal rights for men; compiles statistics. **Libraries: Type:** reference. **Holdings:** 30,000; clippings. **Subjects:** "battle of the sexes", divorce, custody cases. **Awards:** Wimp Award. **Frequency:** annual. **Type:** recognition. **Recipient:** for any public figure who denigrates the male gender. **Computer Services:** database, membership list. **Absorbed:** (1993) National Committee for Fair Divorce and Alimony Laws. **Publications:** *The Quest*, bimonthly. Newsletter. **Price:** included in membership dues. **Circulation:** 15,000. **Advertising:** accepted. **Conventions/Meetings:** periodic meeting and seminar (exhibits) ● semiannual symposium.

Mental Health

17677 ■ Association for Happiness Advancement (AHA)
Address Unknown since 2007
Description: Promotes happiness through science.
Conventions/Meetings: lecture.

Middle East

17678 ■ America-Israel Council for Israeli-Palestinian Peace (AICIPP)
224 Lake Dr.
Kensington, CA 94708
Ph: (510)526-8449
Fax: (866)549-4649
E-mail: aicipp@igc.org
URL: http://otherisrael.home.igc.org
Contact: Mary Appelman, Chair
Founded: 1982. **Budget:** $10,000. **Nonmembership. Description:** Supports a peaceful solution to the Israeli-Palestinian conflict based on withdrawal of Israeli forces from the territories occupied in the 1967 war and creation of a Palestinian state in the West Bank and Gaza Strip that will live in peace with Israel. Helps with distribution in the U.S. of ICIPP's newsletter, The Other Israel, (which chronicles the many Israeli and Palestinian efforts directed toward achieving Israeli-Palestinian peace). **Libraries: Type:** reference. **Subjects:** Israeli-Palestinian peace. **Telecommunication Services:** electronic mail, aicipp@igc.apc.org. **Affiliated With:** Israeli Council for Israeli-Palestinian Peace. **Publications:** *The Other Israel*, periodic. Newsletter. Contains commentaries on events in Israel and the Middle East. **Price:** $30.00 for individuals; $50.00 for institutions; $15.00 limited income. ISSN: 0792-4615. **Circulation:** 3,000 ● Periodic supplemental briefings are distributed by e-mail to subscribers on request and without additional charge.

17679 ■ America-MidEast Educational and Training Services (AMIDEAST)
1730 M St. NW, Ste.1100
Washington, DC 20036
Ph: (202)776-9600
Fax: (202)776-7000
E-mail: inquiries@amideast.org
URL: http://www.amideast.org
Contact: Ambassador Theodore H. Kattouf, Pres./ CEO
Founded: 1951. **Members:** 204. **Membership Dues:** institutional, $365 (annual). **Staff:** 202. **Budget:** $24,000,000. **Languages:** Arabic, English, French. **Multinational. Description:** Works to strengthen mutual understanding between Americans and the people of the Middle East and North Africa. Offers educational advising and testing services for Arab students and institutions interested in U.S. educational opportunities. Administers educational and training programs for a variety of government, corporate, and institutional sponsors of Arab students.

Operates English-language programs for the general public and corporate and government agency clients in Egypt, Jordan, Kuwait, Lebanon, Morocco, Syria, West Bank and Gaza, Tunisia, and Yemen. Provides public outreach services in the form of publications and videotapes to support educational exchanges and materials to improve teaching about the Arab world in American secondary schools and colleges. **Formerly:** (1977) American Friends of the Middle East. **Publications:** *The Advising Quarterly*. Newsletter. Contains resource reviews, training and academic news listings. **Price:** $40.00 /year for individuals in U.S.; $50.00 /year for individuals outside U.S. ISSN: 0895-1101. **Circulation:** 1,200. **Advertising:** accepted. Alternate Formats: online ● *AMIDEAST Today*, quarterly. Newsletter. Contains project activities updates and current news on AMIDEAST. **Circulation:** 5,000 ● *Bridging Cultures, Building Understanding*. Annual Report. Includes program review, membership list, project descriptions, and financial statement. ● *Education in the Arab World*. Describes the educational systems of Algeria, Bahrain, Egypt, Jordan, Kuwait, Lebanon, and Morocco. **Price:** $50.00 /year for individuals ● *Planning Your Future: Resources on Careers and Higher Education*. Lists over 1000 field-of-study resources providing the most current information on career and educational advising books, videos and software. **Price:** $15.00 /year for individuals ● *Young Voices from the Arab World: The Lives and Times of Five Teenagers*. Video. Introduces the diversity and unity, cultural traditions, and contemporary concerns of the Arab world, through the lives of five teenagers. **Price:** $35.00 each ● Various educational resources on the Arab world.

17680 ■ American Educational Trust (AET)
PO Box 53062
Washington, DC 20009
Ph: (202)939-6050
Free: (800)368-5788
Fax: (202)265-4574
E-mail: webmaster@wrmea.com
URL: http://www.wrmea.com
Contact: Andrew I. Killgore, Publisher/Pres.
Founded: 1982. **Membership Dues:** subscriber, $29 (annual). **Staff:** 5. **Description:** Attempts to disseminate unbiased and accurate information and analysis on the Middle East and on United States relations in the area. Supports the solutions presented in the United Nations charter and traditional United States views on human rights, self-determination, and "fair play". **Convention/Meeting:** none. **Computer Services:** Mailing lists, e-mail distribution list ● online services, subscriptions and book orders. **Publications:** *AET Book Club*, 10/year. **Advertising:** accepted. Alternate Formats: online ● *Washington Report on Middle East Affairs*, 9/year. Magazine. **Price:** $3.50/issue; $29.00/year. **Circulation:** 30,000. **Advertising:** accepted ● Seeing the Light: Personal Encounters with the Middle East & Islam by Richard Curtiss & Janet McMahon, eds. Stealth PACS: Lobbying Congress for control of US Middle East Policy by Richard Curtiss.

17681 ■ American Israel Public Affairs Committee (AIPAC)
440 1st St. NW, Ste.600
Washington, DC 20001
Ph: (202)639-5200
Fax: (202)347-4918
E-mail: update@aipac.org
URL: http://www.aipac.org
Contact: Howard Kohr, Exec. Dir.
Founded: 1954. **Description:** Registered lobby. Lobbies Congress and the Administration on issues affecting U.S.-Israel relations. Provides services and information on American foreign policy in the Middle East. Seeks to maintain and improve strong bi-lateral relations between the U.S. and Israel. **Formerly:** (1959) American Zionist Committee for Public Affairs. **Conventions/Meetings:** annual meeting - always spring, in Washington, DC.

17682 ■ Americans for Middle East Understanding (AMEU)
475 Riverside Dr., Rm. 245
New York, NY 10115-0245

Ph: (212)870-2053
Fax: (212)870-2050
E-mail: info@ameu.org
URL: http://www.ameu.org
Contact: John F. Mahoney, Exec. Dir.
Founded: 1967. **Staff:** 5. **Budget:** $310,000. **Description:** Fosters better understanding in America about the history, goals, and values of Middle East people as well as an understanding of the forces that are shaping American policy there. Distributes educational material to churches, schools, and libraries. Maintains speakers' bureau. Holds nongovernmental organization status with the United Nations. **Computer Services:** Mailing lists. **Affiliated With:** United Nations. **Publications:** *Americans for Middle East Understanding—Book Catalogue*, annual. Lists U.S.- and foreign-published books dealing with the Middle East, particularly the Arab-Israeli conflict. **Circulation:** 50,000 ● *The Link*, bimonthly. Magazine. Covers the history, culture, and current events of the Middle East, with special focus on Arab-Israeli conflict. Includes book reviews. **Price:** $35.00/year. ISSN: 0024-4007. **Circulation:** 50,000. Alternate Formats: online ● *The Loss of Liberty*. Video. Contains information on Israel's 1967 attack on the USS Liberty. **Price:** $20.00 ● *Public Affairs Pamphlet Series*, 3/year ● *Unlocking the Middle East*. Book. **Price:** $16.95.

17683 ■ Americans for a Safe Israel (AFSI)
1623 3rd Ave., Ste.205
New York, NY 10128
Ph: (212)828-2424
Free: (800)235-3658
Fax: (212)828-1717
E-mail: afsi@rcn.com
URL: http://afsi.org
Contact: Herbert Zweibon, Chm.
Founded: 1971. **Members:** 15,000. **Membership Dues:** regular, $50 (annual) ● student, $20 (annual) ● sustaining, $100 (annual) ● sponsor, $500 (annual) ● advisory council, $1,000 (annual) ● national council, $2,500 (annual). **Budget:** $250,000. **Regional Groups:** 11. **Local Groups:** 22. **National Groups:** 2. **Description:** Provides and disseminates information to concerned American citizens regarding the nature of the conflict in the Middle East, based on the belief that a strong Israel is vital to American security interests. Holds frequent seminars and press conferences. Is involved in research regarding the Middle East conflict and relevant issues in other parts of the world. Plans semi-annual trips to Israel, visiting Judea, Samaria, Gaza, the Golan, including Hebron and Jerusalem. Maintains speakers' bureau. **Libraries: Type:** reference. **Holdings:** archival material, clippings, monographs. **Subjects:** Middle East. **Awards:** AFSI Annual Award. **Frequency:** annual. **Type:** recognition. **Publications:** *AFSI Advocate*, bimonthly. Newsletter. Alternate Formats: online ● *Outpost*, monthly. Journal. Alternate Formats: online ● Articles ● Books ● Pamphlets ● Videos ● Also publishes and distributes news updates, and other material on the Middle East. **Conventions/Meetings:** annual conference ● semiannual tour.

17684 ■ Bethlehem Association
PO Box 1111
Media, PA 19063
Ph: (610)353-2010
Fax: (973)942-0876
E-mail: betsoc@comcast.net
URL: http://www.bethlehemassoc.org
Contact: Mr. David D. Handal, Pres.
Founded: 1985. **Members:** 8,000. **Membership Dues:** single, $30 ● family, $50. **Staff:** 18. **Budget:** $120,000. **Regional Groups:** 5. **Description:** Promotes understanding by the American public of the Arab people, and especially the Palestinian culture. Perpetuates close ties between the people of the Bethlehem region living in the U.S., Canada, and Latin American countries, and the people of the Bethlehem area in Palestine. Raises funds; conducts social and cultural activities; educates and informs members about civil, social, and religious history, customs, traditions, folklore, and current events in the Bethlehem region; conducts outreach projects; and main-

tains an educational fund. **Awards: Frequency:** annual. **Type:** scholarship. **Recipient:** to students at Bethlehem University. **Publications:** Newsletter, quarterly. **Price:** free. **Advertising:** accepted. Alternate Formats: online. **Conventions/Meetings:** annual convention.

17685 ■ Catholic Near East Welfare Association (CNEWA)
1011 1st Ave.
New York, NY 10022-4195
Ph: (212)826-1480
Free: (800)442-6392
Fax: (212)826-8979
E-mail: cnewa@cnewa.org
URL: http://www.cnewa.org
Contact: Msgr. Archimandrite Robert L. Stern, Sec. Gen.
Founded: 1926. **Staff:** 60. **Budget:** $22,000,000. **Regional Groups:** 4. **Languages:** Arabic, English, French, Hindi, Italian, Kannada, Malayalam, Marathi, Tamil. **Multinational. Description:** Catholic organization of individuals and unrelated groups. Raises funds to assist humanitarian projects in 28 countries, primarily in the Near and Middle East, as well as northeast Africa, India, and eastern Europe; pays costs of education for native priests and sisters and provides money for chapels and rectories, orphanages, convents, and schools. Sponsors health care programs and maintains clinics. Promotes interest in the Eastern Rites and issues related to church unity. Participates in interfaith dialogue with non-Christian religions. Maintains speakers' bureau. Compiles statistics. **Libraries: Type:** not open to the public. **Holdings:** 900. **Subjects:** Middle East, Eastern religions, India, northeast Africa, eastern Europe. **Computer Services:** database, donors. **Boards:** Management. **Divisions:** Administrative Services; Communications/Development; Programs. **Affiliated With:** Pontifical Mission for Palestine. **Publications:** *ONE*, bimonthly. Magazine. Includes coverage of the events and activities of projects throughout the Near and Middle East. **Price:** $12.00 /year for individuals. **Circulation:** 90,000. Alternate Formats: online ● Brochures ● Also publishes resource materials guides and instructional work sheets.

17686 ■ Committee for Accuracy in Middle East Reporting in America
PO Box 35040
Boston, MA 02135-0001
Ph: (617)789-3672
Fax: (617)787-7853
E-mail: feedback@camera.org
URL: http://www.camera.org
Founded: 1982. **Members:** 41,000. **Membership Dues:** ordinary, $50 (annual) ● fellow, $2,500 (annual) ● senior/student, $30 (annual) ● sponsor, $1,000 (annual) ● associate, $250 (annual) ● friend, $500 (annual) ● sponsor, $1,000 (annual) ● patron, $5,000 (annual) ● founder, $10,000 (annual). **Staff:** 13. **Regional Groups:** 2. **Description:** Promotes accurate and balanced coverage of Israel and the Middle East. Works to ensure more "balanced reports in the future by providing information to journalists, publishing monographs on Middle East topics of media interest.". **Libraries: Type:** not open to the public. **Holdings:** 1,200. **Committees:** Community Outreach; Research; Speaker's Bureau. **Also Known As:** CAMERA. **Publications:** *CAMERA Media Report*, quarterly. Newsletter. Highlights subjects of concern in key media, focusing on both instances of distortion and sound reporting on Middle East subjects. ISSN: 1086-7503 ● *CAMERA on Campus*, periodic. Newsletter. Provides strategies for action and basic facts to counter misinformation and distortion about Israel and Middle East. ISSN: 1086-7511. **Conventions/Meetings:** periodic conference.

17687 ■ Council for the National Interest (CNI)
1250 4th St. SW, Ste.WG-1
Washington, DC 20024
Ph: (202)863-2951
Free: (800)296-6958
Fax: (202)863-2952

E-mail: inform@cnionline.org
URL: http://www.cnionline.org
Contact: Paul Findley, Chm.
Founded: 1988. **Members:** 6,500. **Membership Dues:** regular, $35 (annual). **Staff:** 3. **Regional Groups:** 5. **Description:** Individuals interested in issues concerning the Middle East. Lobbies for foreign policy and public interest in the Middle East. **Awards:** They Dare to Speak Out. **Frequency:** annual. **Type:** recognition. **Recipient:** for individual who contributes to the community for increasing awareness on America's ME policy/relations. **Additional Websites:** http://www.rescuemideastpolicy.com. **Publications:** Newsletter, annual. **Conventions/Meetings:** annual conference (exhibits) ● regional meeting.

17688 ■ Facts and Logic About the Middle East (FLAME)
PO Box 590359
San Francisco, CA 94159
Ph: (415)356-7801
Fax: (415)356-7804
E-mail: kadeemah@aol.com
URL: http://www.factsandlogic.org
Contact: Gerardo Joffe, Pres.
Description: Researches and makes available information about the Middle East in order to expose "false propaganda that might harm the interests of the United States and its allies". Publishes "clarifying messages" in U.S. national newspapers and magazines.

17689 ■ Foundation for Middle East Peace (FMEP)
1761 N St. NW
Washington, DC 20036
Ph: (202)835-3650
Fax: (202)835-3651
E-mail: info@fmep.org
URL: http://www.fmep.org
Contact: Ambassador Philip C. Wilcox Jr., Pres.
Founded: 1979. **Staff:** 3. **Budget:** $600,000. **Description:** Seeks to educate the public, government, and other interested parties to foster an understanding of the Israeli-Palestinian conflict, including the identification of U.S. interests in that conflict. Works to contribute to a just and peaceful resolution of the conflict with security for both peoples through grants, educational programs and conferences. **Libraries: Type:** not open to the public. **Holdings:** 400. **Awards: Type:** grant. **Recipient:** to groups that contribute to peace in the Middle East, specifically for the Israeli-Palestinian conflict. **Formerly:** (1980) Merle Thorpe, Jr. Foundation. **Publications:** *A Policy for the Moment of Truth*, bimonthly. Magazine. Reports on Israeli settlement activities in the Occupied Territories. **Circulation:** 4,500. Alternate Formats: online ● *Error and Betrayal in Lebanon* ● *Facing the PLO Question* ● *Prescription for Conflict* ● *Report on Israeli Settlement Activities in the Occupied Territories*, bimonthly. **Conventions/Meetings:** periodic lecture - 4-6/year.

17690 ■ Givat Haviva Educational Foundation (GHEF)
114 W 26th St., Ste.1001
New York, NY 10001
Ph: (212)989-9272
Free: (800)385-3536
Fax: (212)989-9840
E-mail: info@givathaviva.org
URL: http://www.givathaviva.org
Contact: Judith Scheuer, Sec.
Founded: 1966. **Members:** 2,000. **Staff:** 4. **Budget:** $285,000. **State Groups:** 10. **Local Groups:** 16. **Description:** Trade unionists, progressive Jews, and others of various backgrounds, particularly those affiliated with Israel's kibbutzim (collective farms or settlements) and other progressive causes. Supports programs aimed at furthering Jewish-Arab rapprochement, with the goal of creating a more egalitarian society, and one of equality with respect to social, political, and economic rights and privileges for all citizens of Israel. Sponsors projects designed to narrow social gaps such as a fund for Arab students, cooperative programs between Jews and Arabs,

vocational school training, building renovations, and a mobile education unit. Organizes fundraising events; operates speakers' bureau. **Awards: Type:** recognition. **Publications:** *Givat Haviva Newsletter*, semiannual. Alternate Formats: online ● Brochures. Alternate Formats: online. **Conventions/Meetings:** periodic meeting.

17691 ■ Jewish Committee on the Middle East (JCOME)
PO Box 18367
Washington, DC 20036
Ph: (202)362-5266
Fax: (202)362-6965
E-mail: jcome@middleeast.org
URL: http://www.middleeast.org/archives/jcome.htm
Contact: Mark A. Bruzonsky, Founder
Description: American Jews and other concerned individuals. Encourages the U.S. to reduce shipments of arms and money to Israel until Israel accepts the right of self-determination of the Palestinian people. Fosters the ideas that: the U.S. should oppose occupation and encourage human rights throughout the Middle East; the U.S. should recognize both Israel's and Palestine's right to statehood and national security; the U.S. should insist that Israel stop the violence against the Palestinian people; the U.S. should not allow foreign policy to be dictated by political and financial pressure applied by the Israeli lobby. **Telecommunication Services:** electronic mail, mark@middleeast.org.

17692 ■ Lebanese Information Center (LIC)
4900 Leesburg Pike, Ste.203
Alexandria, VA 22302
Ph: (703)578-4214
Fax: (703)578-4615
E-mail: info@licus.org
URL: http://www.licus.org
Contact: Youssef Haddad, Staff Writer
Founded: 1978. **Staff:** 10. **Languages:** Arabic, English, French. **Description:** Researches the situation in Lebanon and disseminates the information, on a daily basis, to the American media and administration, Lebanese-American communities, and the general public. Sponsors Operation Roots, an annual trip to Lebanon for young Lebanese-Americans to explore Lebanon and its people, culture, aspirations, and values. Maintains speakers' bureau; compiles statistics. Makes available audiovisual information to community and educational groups on the situation in Lebanon. **Libraries: Type:** reference. **Holdings:** 1,000; archival material. **Subjects:** Lebanon, Middle-East. **Computer Services:** database ● mailing lists, of members. **Departments:** Editorials; Public Affairs and Media Relations; Subscriptions. **Publications:** *Issue Papers*, periodic. Booklets. Discusses wide variations on Lebanon, Political and Economics. ● *Lebanon News English*, monthly. Newsletter. Provides a day-to-day description of political, historical, cultural, and economic events in Lebanon. **Price:** included in membership dues; $30.00 for nonmembers. ISSN: 0742-9665. **Circulation:** 8,000 ● *Press Releases*, periodic. **Price:** free. **Conventions/Meetings:** seminar ● workshop.

17693 ■ Middle East Institute (MEI)
1761 N St. NW
Washington, DC 20036-2882
Ph: (202)785-1141
Fax: (202)331-8861
E-mail: mideasti@mideasti.org
URL: http://www.mideasti.org
Contact: David L. Mack, Acting Pres.
Founded: 1946. **Members:** 3,000. **Membership Dues:** associate, $50 (annual) ● full, $100 (annual) ● contributing, $250 (annual) ● sustaining, $500 (annual) ● patron, $1,000 (annual) ● corporate, $25,000 (annual). **Staff:** 24. **Budget:** $2,000,000. **Languages:** Arabic, English, Hebrew, Persian, Turkish. **Description:** Government officials, scholars, business executives, students, and others interested in the Middle East. Promotes interest in the history, culture, politics, economy, and languages of the Middle East through lectures, publications, conferences, and programs. Seeks to provide up-to-date, complete, and objective

information about the Middle East. Sponsors Sultan Qaboos bin Said Research Center, which works to promote understanding among Americans and peoples of the Middle East. Offers classes in modern Middle Eastern languages; conducts Islamic Affairs Program. **Libraries: Type:** reference; by appointment only. **Holdings:** 25,000; audiovisuals, books, periodicals. **Subjects:** Middle Eastern countries, Islam, Islamic art. **Computer Services:** database, Middle Eastern Information. **Boards:** Governors. **Departments:** Language and Regional Studies; Programs and Events. **Programs:** Leadership Development Internship. **Subgroups:** Development and Corporate Relations; Media, Outreach and Congressional Relations; The Middle East Journal and Publications; Public Policy Center. **Absorbed:** (1987) American Institute for Islamic Affairs. **Publications:** *Middle East Institute Bulletin*, bimonthly. Newsletter ● *The Middle East Journal*, quarterly. Provides original and objective research and analysis. **Price:** included in membership dues; $115.00 for institutions; $133.00 for international institutions. **Advertising:** accepted. Also Cited As: *TMEJ* ● *Middle East Organizations in Washington, DC.* Directory ● Books. **Conventions/Meetings:** annual conference (exhibits) - usually September/October, in Washington, DC.

17694 ■ Middle East Policy Council

1730 M St. NW, Ste.512
Washington, DC 20036
Ph: (202)296-6767
Fax: (202)296-5791
E-mail: info@mepc.org
URL: http://www.mepc.org
Contact: Mrs. Anne Joyce, VP/Ed. of Middle East Policy

Founded: 1981. **Staff:** 9. **Budget:** $720,000. **Description:** Individuals dedicated to better acquainting Americans with Middle East political and economic issues, and improving U.S. Middle East relations through publications, symposia, and other projects. **Formerly:** (1991) American Arab Affairs Council. **Publications:** *A Century in Thirty Years: Shaykh Zayed and the United Arab Emirates*. Book ● *The Gulf, Cooperation and the Council An American Perspective*. Book. **Price:** $15.95 ● *Middle East Policy*, quarterly, March, June, September and December. Journal. Analyzes U.S. foreign policy in the Middle East, the Arab-Israeli conflict, the Persian Gulf, and economic relations between U.S.-Middle East. **Price:** $54.00 /year for individuals, Americas; $187.00 /year for institutions, Americas; EUR 69.00 /year for individuals, Europe; EUR 149.00 /year for institutions, Europe. ISSN: 1061-1924. **Circulation:** 7,500. **Advertising:** accepted. Alternate Formats: microform ● *Selected Documentation Pertaining to U.S.-Arab Relations*. Book ● Newsletter. Alternate Formats: online.

17695 ■ Middle East Research and Information Project (MERIP)

1500 Massachusetts Ave. NW, Ste.119
Washington, DC 20005
Ph: (202)223-3677
Fax: (202)223-3604
E-mail: ctoensing@merip.org
URL: http://www.merip.org
Contact: Chris Toensing, Exec. Dir.

Founded: 1971. **Staff:** 4. **Budget:** $300,000. **Nonmembership. Description:** Editorial committee of part- or full-time researchers in Middle East studies. Provides information, research, and analysis on U.S. involvement in the Middle East and cultural, political, social, and economic developments. Maintains speakers' bureau. **Awards:** Philip Shehadi New Writers Award. **Frequency:** annual. **Type:** monetary. **Recipient:** for individuals who are not professional journalists. **Committees:** Development; Editorial. **Publications:** *Middle East Report*, quarterly. Magazine. Includes columns, articles, photographs, reviews, and interviews contributed by journalists and scholars worldwide. **Price:** $37.00 /year for individuals in U.S.; $42.00 /year for individuals in Canada; $55.00 /year for individuals outside U.S. and Canada; $107.00 /year for institutions outside U.S. ISSN: 0899-2851. **Circulation:** 6,000. **Advertising:** ac-

cepted. Alternate Formats: online. Also Cited As: *MERIP Reports.*

17696 ■ Middle East Studies Association of North America (MESA)

1219 N Santa Rita Ave.
Univ. of Arizona
Tucson, AZ 85721
Ph: (520)621-5850
Fax: (520)626-9095
E-mail: mesana@u.arizona.edu
URL: http://mesa.wns.ccit.arizona.edu
Contact: Mark J. Lowder, Asst. Dir.

Founded: 1966. **Members:** 2,600. **Staff:** 5. **Budget:** $500,000. **Description:** Aims to bring together scholars, educators, and those interested in the study of the region from all over the world. Seeks to advance learning, facilitate communication and promote cooperation among persons and organizations concerned with the scholarly study of the Middle East. Is governed by a nine-member Board of Directors elected by the membership. **Awards:** Academic Freedom Award. **Frequency:** annual. **Type:** recognition. **Recipient:** for contributions in support of academic freedom ● Albert Hourani Book Award Competition. **Frequency:** annual. **Type:** recognition. **Recipient:** for published book in Middle East studies ● Graduate Student Paper Prize. **Frequency:** annual. **Type:** recognition. **Recipient:** for best paper work by current graduate students ● Jere L. Bacharach Service Award. **Frequency:** annual. **Type:** recognition. **Recipient:** for outstanding service to the profession ● Malcolm H. Kerr Dissertation Award Competition. **Frequency:** annual. **Type:** recognition. **Recipient:** for dissertation in the humanities and social sciences field ● Mentoring Award. **Frequency:** annual. **Type:** recognition. **Recipient:** for exceptional contributions of a retired faculty. **Computer Services:** database, access ● mailing lists, provided in excel; price varies ● online services, publication. **Committees:** Academic Freedom in the Middle East and North Africa; Albert Hourani Book Award; Canadian; Conflict of Interest Statement; Finance; Malcolm H. Herr Dissertation Awards. **Publications:** *Directory of Graduate and Undergraduate Programs and Courses in Middle East Studies in the U.S., Canada and Abroad*, periodic. Contains descriptions of programs and courses of Middle East studies in universities worldwide. **Price:** free. Alternate Formats: online ● *International Journal of Middle East Studies*, quarterly. **Price:** included in membership dues ● *International Journal of Middle East Studies Index*, periodic ● *MESA Bulletin*, semiannual. **Advertising:** accepted ● *MESA Bulletin Index*, periodic ● *MESA Newsletter*, quarterly. **Advertising:** accepted. Alternate Formats: online ● *Roster of Members*, biennial. Membership Directory. **Conventions/Meetings:** annual conference, for scholarship, intellectual exchange, and pedagogical innovation (exhibits).

17697 ■ National Council on U.S.-Arab Relations (NCUSAR)

1730 M St. NW, Ste.503
Washington, DC 20036
Ph: (202)293-6466
Fax: (202)293-7770
E-mail: info@ncusar.org
URL: http://www.ncusar.org
Contact: Dr. John Duke Anthony, Pres./CEO/Founder

Founded: 1983. **Staff:** 14. **State Groups:** 16. **Description:** Assists programs that improve the understanding, dialogue, and friendship between the peoples of the U.S. and the Arab world. Acts as clearinghouse to strengthen current and emerging programs dealing with U.S.-Arab relations. Cosponsors outreach programs at university centers for Middle Eastern studies. Provides speakers on: politics, development, economics, society and culture, security, and regional studies. Conducts travel-study tours for educators, public leaders, journalists, and students. **Awards: Type:** grant. **Recipient:** for educational and cultural projects including conferences, teacher training institutes, and travel-study tours.

17698 ■ National PAC

600 Pennsylvania Ave. SE, Ste.207
Washington, DC 20003
Ph: (202)879-7710
Fax: (202)879-7728
Contact: Charles D. Brooks, Exec. Dir.

Founded: 1982. **Members:** 58,000. **Staff:** 3. **Description:** Encourages support for improved U.S.-Israel relations. Supports Congressional candidates who view Israel as a strategic asset and valuable ally in the Middle East. Works against political anti-Semitism. **Convention/Meeting:** none. **Formerly:** National PAC; NATPAC.

17699 ■ Near East Foundation (NEF)

90 Broad St., 15th Fl.
New York, NY 10004
Ph: (212)425-2205
Fax: (212)425-2350
E-mail: nef-hq@neareast.org
URL: http://www.neareast.org
Contact: Linda K. Jacobs PhD, Pres.

Founded: 1915. **Members:** 33. **Staff:** 25. **Budget:** $4,200,000. **Languages:** Arabic, English, French. **Multinational. Description:** Works in the Middle East and Africa on projects to increase food production, with related activities in rural and community development and primary health cares; provides start-up funds for projects until support is available from local sources. Assigns qualified specialists overseas to assist with transfer of technical skills and human resources development. Countries and areas of operation include Egypt, Jordan, Lebanon, Lesotho, Mali, Morocco, Sudan, Swaziland, and West Bank/Gaza. **Computer Services:** database. **Councils:** International. **Affiliated With:** Interaction/ American Council for Voluntary International Action. **Formerly:** (1930) Near East Relief. **Publications:** *Near East Foundation—Annual Report*. Contains an overview of NEF program activities of the past year. **Price:** free. **Circulation:** 2,500. Alternate Formats: online ● *NEF Newsletter* ● *Reports From the Field*. Alternate Formats: online ● Brochure. Alternate Formats: online. **Conventions/Meetings:** semiannual meeting - always June and October, in New York City.

17700 ■ Palestine Liberation Organization (PLO)

c/o Federation of American Scientists
1717 K St. NW, Ste.209
Washington, DC 20036
Ph: (202)546-3300
Fax: (202)675-1010
URL: http://www.fas.org/irp/world/para/plo.htm
Contact: Hasan Abdel Rahman, Chief Rep.

Founded: 1988. **Membership Dues:** regular, $50 (annual). **Staff:** 7. **Languages:** Arabic, English, Spanish. **Description:** Informs the American public about the social, economic, and political affairs of the Palestinian people. Disseminates literature. Maintains Speaker's Bureau; compiles statistics. **Convention/Meeting:** none. **Formerly:** (1998) Palestine Affairs Center. **Supersedes:** Palestine Information Office. **Publications:** *Palestine Affairs*, periodic ● Books ● Also publishes periodicals.

17701 ■ Scholars for Peace in the Middle East (SPME)

c/o Susquehanna Industry
624 Sandra Ave.
Harrisburg, PA 17109
E-mail: scholarsforpeace@aol.com
URL: http://www.spme.net
Contact: Edward S. Beck EdD, Pres.

Members: 700. **Membership Dues:** student, $18 (annual) ● retiree, $25 (annual) ● adjunct, part-time faculty, $45 (annual) ● full time faculty, professional, community, $50 (annual). **Multinational. Description:** Informs, motivates, and encourages faculty to use their academic skills and disciplines on campus, in classrooms, and in academic publications to develop effective responses to the "ideological distortions that poison debate and work against peace.". **Publications:** *SPME Faculty Forum*. Newsletter.

Price: included in membership dues. Alternate Formats: online ● Papers. Alternate Formats: online.

17702 ■ Search for Justice and Equality in Palestine/Israel (SEARCH)
PO Box 3452
Framingham, MA 01705-3452
Ph: (508)879-0777
Fax: (508)877-2611
E-mail: info@searchforjustice.org
URL: http://searchforjustice.org
Contact: Edmund R. Hanauer, Exec. Dir.
Founded: 1972. **Members:** 500. **Staff:** 1. **Budget:** $80,000. **Description:** Promotes a just Israeli-Palestinian peace based on the inalienable rights of both peoples. Advocates a U.S. policy which supports Palestinian rights as well as Israeli rights. Seeks to improve media coverage of Palestine and Israel, and encourage editorial support of Palestinian rights. Maintains Speaker's Bureau. **Telecommunication Services:** electronic mail, hanauer@searchforjustice. org. **Formerly:** (1984) Search for Justice and Equality in Palestine. **Conventions/Meetings:** board meeting - 4-5/year ● workshop, on media advocacy for peace, human rights, and Middle East related groups.

17703 ■ Writers and Artists for Peace in the Middle East (WAPME)
310 Lexington Ave., Apt. 12-F
New York, NY 10016
Ph: (212)687-0121
E-mail: swimbook@nyc.rr.com
Contact: Ellyne Rose, Contact
Description: Writers and artists concerned with educating the public on the Middle East situation. Members have included well-known writers and artists, including Saul Bellow, Lionel Hampton, John Hersey, Zubin Mehta, Arthur Miller, Estelle Parsons, Beverly Sills, Shelley Winters, and Herman Wouk. **Awards:** Distinguished Achievement Award. **Type:** recognition. **Publications:** Newsletter. **Advertising:** accepted. **Conventions/Meetings:** quarterly meeting.

17704 ■ Youth Institute for Peace in the Middle East (YIPME)
Address Unknown since 2007
Founded: 1969. **Members:** 9,500. **Description:** Seeks to rally youth support for a lasting peace in the Middle East and to counter propaganda of those who call for Israel's destruction. Maintains speakers' bureau. Sponsors essay contests and internship program for undergraduate and graduate students. Conducts research on Middle East issues. **Formerly:** (1971) Youth Committee for Peace and Democracy in the Middle East. **Publications:** Crossroads, quarterly ● Policy Analysis Middle East - Myth and Reality, bimonthly.

Migrant Workers

17705 ■ Global Workers Justice Alliance
113 Univ. Pl., 8th Fl.
New York, NY 10003
Ph: (917)238-0979
E-mail: info@globalworkers.org
URL: http://www.globalworkers.org
Contact: Cathleen Caron, Founder/Exec. Dir.
Multinational. Description: Represents migrant workers. Advocates against migrant worker exploitation. Promotes justice for transnational migrants through a cross-border network of worker advocates and resources. **Publications:** Clearinghouse Review Journal of Poverty Law and Policy. Alternate Formats: online.

Military

17706 ■ Center for Strategic and Budgetary Assessments (CSBA)
1730 Rhode Island Ave. NW, Ste.912
Washington, DC 20036
Ph: (202)331-7990

Fax: (202)331-8019
E-mail: info@csbaonline.org
URL: http://www.csbaonline.org
Contact: Dr. Andrew F. Krepinevich, Exec. Dir.
Founded: 1983. **Staff:** 7. **Budget:** $500,000. **Description:** Serves as nonpartisan independent research organization that analyzes military spending and national security policy issues. Provides timely, independent analyses of military budget and defense issues to the media, citizens' organizations, policymakers, and advocacy groups. Conducts research and educational programs. Sponsors briefings and discussions on defense and military issues. Analyzes issues such as the impact of the defense budget on other national spending priorities, the American economy, and the federal deficit; the relationship between defense spending, national security, and the development of alternatives to present national security policies. Maintains internship program. **Formerly:** (2002) Defense Budget Project. **Publications:** Analysis for Fiscal Year Defense Budget, annual. Includes tables and graphs highlighting budgetary trends. **Price:** $75.00/year for nonprofit organizations; $150.00/year for corporations. **Circulation:** 3,000. Also Cited As: Budget Analysis; Defense Budget Analysis ● Also publishes issue briefs and reports.

17707 ■ International Action Center (IAC)
5C Solidarity Center
55 W 17th St.
New York, NY 10011
Ph: (212)633-6646
Fax: (212)633-2889
E-mail: iacenter@action-mail.org
URL: http://www.iacenter.org
Contact: Ramsey Clark, Founder
Founded: 1992. **Languages:** English, Spanish. **Description:** Opposes U.S. militarism. Organizes opposition to U.S. intervention abroad and to racism and political repression at home. Sponsors educational activities and research. **Telecommunication Services:** electronic mail, iac-cai@action-mail.org. **Publications:** Books ● Videos ● Also publishes press releases and information packets.

17708 ■ Project on Government Oversight (POGO)
666 11th St. NW, Ste.500
Washington, DC 20001-4542
Ph: (202)347-1122
Fax: (202)347-1116
E-mail: info@pogo.org
URL: http://www.pogo.org
Contact: Danielle Brian, Exec. Dir.
Founded: 1981. **Staff:** 9. **Budget:** $700,000. **Description:** Promotes accountability in government; monitors governmental agencies; exposes abuses of power, and waste and fraud committed by the government and its contractors. **Convention/Meeting:** none. **Telecommunication Services:** electronic mail, pogo@pogo.org. **Formerly:** (1990) Project on Military Procurement. **Publications:** A Partial Approach to Clean-Up: EPA Mishandles Superfund Investigations, 2002 Report ● The Art of Anonymous Activism: Serving the Public While Surviving Public Service (A Guide for Whistleblowers). Book. **Price:** $10.00 ● At the Federal Election Commission: Things Just Don't Add Up, 2001 Report ● Big Dreams Still Need Oversight: Missile Defense Testing & Financial Accountability Are Being Circumvented, 2002 Report ● Children's Ears and Antibiotics: Gold Mine for Pharmaceutical Companies, Land Mine for Children ● Corporate Welfare for Arms Merchants ● Defense Waste & Fraud Camouflaged as Reinventing Government, 1999 Report ● Federal Contractor Misconduct: Failures of the Suspension & Debarment System 2002 Report ● Fill 'Er Up: Back Door Deal for Boeing Will Leave the Taxpayer on Empty, 2002 Report ● The Government's Slick Deal for the Oil Industry ● Heavy Lifting for Boeing: Sweetheart Deal Helps Defense Contractor & Hurts Taxpayer, 2001 Report ● No Light at the End of this Tunnel: Boston's Central Artery/Third Harbor Tunnel Project, periodic. Report ● NRS Sells the Environment Down the River: Radiation Flows Unchecked into the Colorado River. Report ● Nuclear Power Plant Security: Voices from Inside

the Fences, 2002 Report ● Pick Pocketing the Taxpayer: The Insidious Effects of Acquisition Reform, 2002 Report ● Re-Establishing Institutional Integrity at the FEC: Ten Common Sense Campaign Finance Disclosure Reforms. Report ● U.S. Nuclear Weapons Complex: Security at Risk, 2001 Report ● Newsletter, quarterly. Alternate Formats: online ● Also publishes With a Wink and a Nod: How the Oil Industry and the Department of Interior are Cheating the American Public and California School Children.

17709 ■ Women Against Military Madness (WAMM)
310 E 38th St., Ste.222
Minneapolis, MN 55409-1337
Ph: (612)827-5364
Fax: (612)827-6433
E-mail: wamm@mtn.org
URL: http://www.worldwidewamm.org
Contact: Mary Beaudoin, Dir.
Founded: 1982. **Members:** 2,200. **Membership Dues:** general, $40 (annual) ● household, $60 (annual) ● sustainer, $100 (annual) ● low income, student, $15 (annual). **Staff:** 2. **Budget:** $149,000. **Description:** Advocates a "radical shift in our nations priorities away from militarism, military spending, arms trade, military intervention, and the militarization of schools.". **Computer Services:** Mailing lists. **Committees:** Asia-Pacific; Depleted Uranium; Intercultural Action for Peace; Iraq; Middle East; Yugoslavia. **Publications:** WorldwideWAMM, 10/year. Newsletter. Includes analysis, action alerts, and calendar. **Price:** included in membership dues; $35.00 /year for nonmembers. **Circulation:** 1,800. **Advertising:** accepted. Alternate Formats: online. Also Cited As: WAMM Newsletter. **Conventions/Meetings:** bimonthly meeting ● annual meeting, peace and justice (exhibits).

Mining

17710 ■ Project Underground
1916A MLK Jr. Way
Berkeley, CA 94704
Ph: (510)705-8981
Fax: (510)705-8983
E-mail: project_underground@moles.org
URL: http://www.moles.org
Contact: M.E. Dueker, Dir.
Founded: 1996. **Description:** Provides informational, technical, legal and scientific support to communities facing oil, gas and mining operations; informs communities of environmental impacts of oil and mining activities, their rights under international and national law, and supplies corporate data, history and examples of best-practice to communities. **Publications:** Drillbits and Tailings (in English and Spanish), monthly. Newsletter. **Price:** $500.00/year for corporations; $60.00 /year for institutions; $35.00/year for non-profit organizations; $25.00 /year for individuals. Alternate Formats: online.

Minorities

17711 ■ Minority Health Professions Foundation (MHPF)
100 Edgewood Ave., Ste.1020
Atlanta, GA 30303
Ph: (678)904-4217
Free: (877)895-0902
Fax: (678)904-4518
E-mail: tadams@minorityhealth.org
URL: http://www.minorityhealth.org
Contact: Phyllis Champion, Exec. Dir.
Description: Promotes research for the advancement of knowledge and treatment of diseases, disabilities and adverse health problems affecting minority populations. Supports improvement of healthcare to black and other minority under-served populations. Furthers public education to prevent health problems and promotes healthy lifestyles among the black and other minorities. Identifies and facilitates new directions in the area of minority health by supporting

scholarly exchange of scientific and clinical information. Facilitates an increase in representation and recognition of blacks and other under-represented minorities in the health professions of medicine, dentistry, pharmacy, and veterinary medicine. **Formerly:** (2004) Minority Health Professionals Foundation.

Missing-in-Action

17712 ■ National League of Families of American Prisoners and Missing in Southeast Asia

1005 N Glebe Rd., Ste.170
Arlington, VA 22201
Ph: (703)465-7432
Fax: (703)465-7433
E-mail: info@pow-miafamilies.org
URL: http://www.pow-miafamilies.org
Contact: Ann Mills Griffiths, Exec. Dir.
Founded: 1970. **Members:** 1,000. **Membership Dues:** associate/family, $25 (annual). **Staff:** 2. **Budget:** $300,000. **Regional Groups:** 8. **State Groups:** 50. **Multinational. Description:** Family members of American servicemen who are missing and/or prisoners in Southeast Asia as a result of the Vietnam War; returned prisoners of war. Works to determine the status of servicemen still listed as unaccounted for in Southeast Asia, secure the release and return of all POWs, secure the return of the remains of American servicemen who died during the Vietnam War, and educate the public on these issues. Acts as liaison among the families of POW/MIAs and the U.S. government. Conducts educational programs. **Formerly:** National League of POW/MIA Families. **Publications:** Newsletter, bimonthly. Provides current status updates on all efforts and activities. **Price:** included in membership dues. **Circulation:** 2,500. Alternate Formats: online ● Annual Report. **Conventions/Meetings:** annual meeting - always in Washington, DC.

Monarchy

17713 ■ Society of American Royalty (SAR)

PO Box 190313
Dallas, TX 75219
Ph: (972)224-6881
E-mail: cherokeelee@cowtown.net
URL: http://www.geocities.com/Heartland/Oaks/8010/thesocietya.htm
Contact: Lee MacDonald, Chief Genealogist
Founded: 1997. **Members:** 300. **Staff:** 3. **Regional Groups:** 1. **Description:** Individuals able to trace their lineage to Cherokee or Hawaiian royalty. Promotes knowledge of Native American royal families and their histories. Conducts genealogical research and educational programs. Produces teaching materials. Membership is by invitation only.

Muslim

17714 ■ Free Muslims Coalition (FMC)

2560 Virginia Ave. NW, Ste.171
Washington, DC 20037
Ph: (202)776-7190 (301)905-6438
E-mail: info@freemuslims.org
URL: http://www.freemuslims.org
Contact: Kamal Nawash, Pres.
Multinational. Description: Promotes a modern, secular interpretation of Islam as peace-loving, democracy-loving and compatible with other faiths and beliefs. Seeks to eliminate broad support for Islamic extremism and terrorism. Strives to strengthen secular democratic institutions in the Middle East and the Muslim world by supporting Islamic reformation efforts. **Telecommunication Services:** electronic mail, media@freemuslims.org ● electronic mail, president@freemuslims.org.

17715 ■ Muslim Public Affairs Council (MPAC)

110 Maryland Ave. NE, Ste.304
Washington, DC 20002
Ph: (202)547-7701
Fax: (202)547-7704
E-mail: mpac-contact@mpac.org
URL: http://www.mpac.org
Contact: Salam Al-Marayati, Exec. Dir.
Description: Committed to the establishment of the American Muslim community in order to enrich American society through promotion of Islamic values of mercy, justice, peace, human dignity, freedom, and equality for all.

National Sovereignty

17716 ■ Armenian Revolutionary Federation (ARF)

80 Bigelow Ave.
Watertown, MA 02472
Ph: (617)926-3685
Fax: (617)926-5525
E-mail: info@arf.am
URL: http://www.arfd.am
Contact: Asbed Kotch, Exec. Sec.
Founded: 1890. **Description:** Promotes social justice, democracy, and national self-determination for the Armenian people. **Libraries: Type:** reference. **Holdings:** audiovisuals, books, clippings, periodicals. **Subjects:** Armenian history, genocide. **Committees:** Central; Marzayin. **Formerly:** Armenian Revolutionary Federation of America. **Publications:** Armenian Weekly. Covers Armenian community political, cultural, social, and religious issues, and youth activities. Includes book reviews and calendar of events. **Circulation:** 3,000. Alternate Formats: microform ● Hairenik Daily: The Oldest Armenian Language Newspaper. Covers Armenian cultural, political, religious, social, and youth athletic activities. Includes book reviews and calendar of events. **Price:** $75.00/year. **Circulation:** 3,000. **Advertising:** accepted. Alternate Formats: microform. **Conventions/Meetings:** annual conference.

17717 ■ Armenian Youth Federation - Youth Organization of the ARF (AYF-YOARF)

80 Bigelow Ave.
Watertown, MA 02472
Ph: (617)923-1933
Fax: (617)924-1933
E-mail: info@ayf.org
URL: http://www.ayf.org
Contact: Aremin Hacobian, Chm.
Founded: 1933. **Members:** 1,500. **Membership Dues:** non-discriminatory, $35 (annual). **Local Groups:** 17. **Languages:** Armenian, English. **Description:** Committed in efforts to provide Armenian youth with an understanding and appreciation of their ethnic heritage. Conducts educational program; offers internships in America and Armenia, and scholarships. Sponsors AYF junior organization (for youths 10 to 16 years of age); operates Camp Haiastan for children and youth of Armenian descent; sponsors athletic competitions. **Awards:** AYF Hagopian and Bozoian Scholarships. **Frequency:** annual. **Type:** scholarship. **Recipient:** for members of AYF. **Formerly:** ARF Tzeghagrons; (1980) Armenian Youth Federation of America. **Publications:** Haytoug/Hoki (in Armenian and English), quarterly. Journal. Discusses cultural and educational topics. **Price:** free. **Advertising:** accepted. Alternate Formats: online.

17718 ■ National Captive Nations Committee (NCNC)

PO Box 1171
Washington, DC 20013
Ph: (202)547-0018 (703)354-4036
Fax: (202)543-5502
Contact: Amb. Lev E. Dobriansky PhD, Chm.
Founded: 1959. **Description:** Leaders in government, churches, education, labor, and industry; civic, veterans, women's, and fraternal groups. Conducts research and disseminates information on captive

nations in Central and Eastern Europe, those within the former USSR, and those in Asia and the Caribbean. Monitors independence drives and movements toward full liberation in Europe and Asia. Advises the U.S. government regarding its policies toward captive nations. Initiates a "liberation countdown" in captive nations. Acts as coordinator for many local, state, and international organizations. Advocates a policy of human rights, democracy, and national self-determination. Attempts to reinforce the Voice of America, Radio Free Europe/Radio Liberty as "genuine projectors of the American image in both the liberated and remaining captive nations." Also supports a Radio Free Asia. Sponsors National Captive Nations Week, the third week in July, on the basis of the Captive Nations Week Resolution passed by the U.S.(P.I. 86-90) Advances victims of Communism International Memorial in nation's capital (P.I.103-199) and U.N. Year of Remembrance for over 100 million victims of Communism. **Libraries: Type:** open to the public. **Subjects:** captive nations, communism, U.S. foreign policy. **Awards:** Freedom Awards. **Type:** recognition. **Publications:** Congressional House Documents, periodic ● Congressional Record Reprints, periodic ● Also publishes news releases and distributes books. **Conventions/Meetings:** annual meeting.

Nationalism

17719 ■ Nationalist Foundation

Address Unknown since 2006
URL: http://www.angelfire.com/ms/unabuilder
Founded: 1996. **Membership Dues:** individual, $20 (annual). **Description:** Sponsors educational and charitable programs as well as a speakers bureau. A pro-majority legal and educational arm. Uses private attorney-general in defense of the First Amendment, Constitutional, and Patriotic methodology. **Libraries: Type:** reference; not open to the public. **Holdings:** archival material. **Subjects:** First Amendment, free speech, freedom of assembly. **Computer Services:** database. **Publications:** Unabuilder. Newsletter. **Advertising:** not accepted. Alternate Formats: online. **Conventions/Meetings:** annual board meeting - always March in Jackson, MS.

Native American

17720 ■ All Indian Pueblo Council (AIPC)

2401 12th St. NW
Albuquerque, NM 87104-2302
Ph: (505)975-4100 (505)975-4094
Fax: (505)883-7682
Contact: Amadeo Shije, Chm.
Founded: 1598. **Members:** 19. **Staff:** 60. **Budget:** $3,000,000. **Description:** Indian tribes. Serves as advocate on behalf of 19 Pueblo Indian tribes on education, health, social, and economic issues; lobbies on those issues before state and national legislatures. Activities are centered in New Mexico. Operates boarding school, Indian Pueblo Cultural Center, museum, and theater in Albuquerque, NM. Maintains Business Development Center. Offers placement service and charitable program; conducts children's services. **Libraries: Type:** reference. **Holdings:** 618; archival material. **Awards: Type:** recognition. **Committees:** Economic Development; Education; Legislation; Natural Resources; Political Action. **Divisions:** Education; Employment and Training; Highway Safety; Scholarships; Speech and Hearing. **Programs:** Alcoholism; Children; Computer-Based Partnership Act; Teacher Training. **Projects:** Indian Business Development Corporation; Social Economic Development Strategies. **Affiliated With:** National Congress of American Indians. **Publications:** Governors 19 Indian Pueblos, annual. Directory ● Brochure ● Pamphlet. **Conventions/Meetings:** annual Charity Benefit Ball - meeting ● biennial Political Caucus - always fall. Albuquerque, NM.

17721 ■ American Indian Movement (AIM)

Grand Governing Coun.
PO Box 13521
Minneapolis, MN 55414

Ph: (612)721-3914
Fax: (612)721-7826
E-mail: aimggc@worldnet.att.net
URL: http://www.aimovement.org
Founded: 1968. **Members:** 5,000. **Description:** Works to encourage self-determination among American Indians. Establishes international recognition of American Indian treaty rights; Membership limited to American Indians. Founded Heart of the Earth Survival School, which enrolls 600 students in preschool to adult programs. Maintains historical archives. Offers charitable, educational, and children's services; maintains speakers' bureau; conducts research; compiles statistics. **Publications:** *Survival News*, quarterly. **Conventions/Meetings:** annual meeting, held in conjunction with the International Indian Treaty Council.

17722 ■ American Indian Ritual Object Repatriation Foundation (AIRORF)
463 E 57th St.
New York, NY 10022-3003
Ph: (212)980-9441
Fax: (212)421-2746
E-mail: circle@repatriationfoundation.org
URL: http://www.repatriationfoundation.org
Contact: Elizabeth A. Sackler PhD, Pres./Founder
Founded: 1992. **Staff:** 2. **Description:** Intercultural partnership assisting in the return of sacred ritual material to American Indian nations. Conduits ritual objects from the private sector back to their Nation of origin. Offers speakers and educational programs to make the public aware of the importance of repatriation materials. Conducts research for nations, museums, and private collectors. **Libraries: Type:** not open to the public. **Holdings:** articles. **Publications:** *Mending the Circle: A Native American Repatriation Guide.* Book. Written by and for Native Americans dealing with NAGPRA, the Smithsonian Institution and the private sector. **Price:** $40.00 in U.S. Alternate Formats: online ● *News and Notes*, semiannual. Newsletter. **Price:** free. Alternate Formats: online.

17723 ■ Association on American Indian Affairs (AAIA)
966 Hungerford Dr., Ste.12-B
Rockville, MD 20850
Ph: (240)314-7155 (605)698-3998
Fax: (240)314-7159
E-mail: general.aaia@verizon.net
URL: http://indian-affairs.org
Contact: Jack F. Trope, Exec. Dir.
Founded: 1923. **Members:** 20,000. **Membership Dues:** $25 (annual). **Staff:** 8. **Budget:** $900,000. **Description:** Aims to promote the welfare of American Indians and Alaska natives by supporting efforts to sustain and perpetuate cultures and languages; protect sovereignty, constitutional, legal and human rights and natural resources; and improve health, education, economic and community development. **Libraries: Type:** open to the public; reference. **Holdings:** 200; archival material, articles, books, business records, papers, photographs. **Subjects:** Indian affairs, Indian history. **Awards:** Allogan Slagle Memorial Scholarship. **Frequency:** annual. **Type:** scholarship. **Recipient:** for students from tribes that are state recognized, not federally recognized ● Displaced Homemakers Scholarships. **Frequency:** annual. **Type:** scholarship. **Recipient:** to men and women who were not able to complete their educational goals due to family responsibilities ● Elizabeth and Sherman Asche Scholarships. **Frequency:** annual. **Type:** scholarship. **Recipient:** to graduate and undergraduate students pursuing a major in Public Health ● Emilie Hesemeyer Memorial Scholarship. **Frequency:** annual. **Type:** scholarship. **Recipient:** to students pursuing a major in Education. **Computer Services:** Mailing lists. **Councils:** Advisory. **Departments:** Direct Mail and Member Services; Language Preservation; Sacred Land Protection. **Formed by Merger of:** National Association of Indian Affairs; American Indian Defense Association. **Formerly:** (1946) American Association on Indian Affairs. **Publications:** *Indian Affairs*, semiannual, in May and September. Newsletter. Contains organizational updates. **Price:** $25.00/year. **Circulation:** 40,000: **Conventions/**

Meetings: annual conference - always December, New York City.

17724 ■ Council of Energy Resource Tribes (CERT)
695 S Colorado Blvd., Ste.10
Denver, CO 80246
Ph: (303)282-7576
Fax: (303)282-7584
E-mail: info@certredearth.com
URL: http://www.certredearth.com
Contact: A. David Lester, Exec. Dir.
Founded: 1975. **Members:** 57. **Staff:** 20. **Budget:** $1,500,000. **Description:** American Indian tribes owning energy resources. Promotes the general welfare of members through the protection, conservation, control, and prudent management of their oil, coal, natural gas, uranium, geothermal, oil shale, and other resources. Provides on-site technical assistance to tribes in all aspects of energy resource management, economic development, human resource development, and environmental protection. Conducts youth education and professional/technical training programs aimed at enhancing tribal planning and management capacities. **Publications:** *CERT Report*, quarterly. Newsletter. Contains articles about Tribes' programs, projects, events and campaigns. **Circulation:** 2,000 ● *D.C. Update*, periodic. Newsletter. **Circulation:** 2,000 ● *Discover Indian Reservations U.S.A.*. Book. Contains profiles on 350 U.S. Indian tribes - their location, industries, cultural events, historic sites, and recreational opportunities. **Conventions/Meetings:** annual conference (exhibits) - always fall, Denver, CO ● annual rally.

17725 ■ Indian Law Resource Center (ILRC)
602 N Ewing St.
Helena, MT 59601
Ph: (406)449-2006
Fax: (406)449-2031
E-mail: mt@indianlaw.org
URL: http://www.indianlaw.org
Contact: Robert T. Coulter, Exec. Dir.
Founded: 1978. **Staff:** 10. **Budget:** $1,000,000. **Description:** Serves as a legal, environmental, and human rights organization for Indian tribes and other indigenous peoples in the Western Hemisphere. Works to enable Indian people to survive as distinct peoples with unique cultures. Combats discrimination and injustice in the law and in public policy. Engages in human rights advocacy and environmental protection on behalf of Indians in the UN and U.S. courts; holds consultative status as a nongovernmental organization with the UN Economic and Social Council; offers free legal help. Conducts research and educational programs. **Publications:** *Indian Rights-Human Rights.* Handbook ● *Indian Rights, Human Rights*, quarterly. Newsletter ● Annual Report, annual ● Articles ● Reports ● Reprints. **Conventions/Meetings:** periodic conference.

17726 ■ Institute for the Development of Indian Law (IDIL)
Address Unknown since 2007
Founded: 1971. **Staff:** 5. **Budget:** $100,000. **Description:** Public interest law firm that functions as a research training center on federal Indian law. The institute places special emphasis on three areas: Indian sovereignty; encouragement of Indian self-confidence and self-government; clarification of historical and legal foundations of modern Indian rights. Activities include: research and analysis; training and technical assistance; dissemination of educational materials relating to federal Indian law, Indian Treaties, curriculum and community development, and other subjects. Conducts educational programs for Indians and non-Indians. Holds seminars on federal Indian law, taxation, and the role of Indians in the development of the U.S. constitution. **Libraries: Type:** reference. **Holdings:** 1,500. **Subjects:** law. **Divisions:** Educational; Research; Services. **Programs:** American Indian Legal Studies; American Indian Life Coping Skills; Indian Legal Curriculum and Training. **Publications:** *American Indian Journal*, quarterly ● *Annual Publications Catalogue* ● *The Indians and the U.S. Constitution* ● *Publications*

and Materials List, semiannual ● Also makes available films, videotapes, and filmstrips.

17727 ■ National Congress of American Indians (NCAI)
1301 Connecticut Ave. NW, Ste.200
Washington, DC 20036
Ph: (202)466-7767
Fax: (202)466-7797
E-mail: ncai@ncai.org
URL: http://www.ncai.org
Contact: Jacqueline L. Johnson, Exec. Dir.
Founded: 1944. **Members:** 2,685. **Membership Dues:** native individual - voting, associate individual - non voting, $40 (annual) ● associate organization, $500 (annual) ● life, $1,000. **Staff:** 15. **Budget:** $1,400,000. **Description:** Tribes representing over 225 tribes and individuals (2500). Seeks to protect, conserve, and develop Indian natural and human resources. Serves legislative interests of Indian tribes. Improves health, education, and economic conditions. Administers NCAI Fund for educational and charitable purposes. Conducts research on Indian problems as a service to Indian tribes. Compiles statistics. Advocates the interest of American Indians and Alaskan Natives. **Awards:** Congressional Awards. **Type:** recognition. **Computer Services:** database ● mailing lists ● online services. **Telecommunication Services:** electronic mail, jjohnson@ncai.org. **Committees:** Economic Development; Education; Health and Housing; Human Resources; Indian Elders; Indian Veterans; Jobs, Training and Indian Preference; Legislation and Litigation; National Indian Nuclear Waste Policy; Natural Resources; Political Resources; Treaty and Land Rights. **Publications:** *Sentinel*, quarterly. Newsletter. Provides information on political and legislative news. Includes survey results, calendar of events, and federal register notices. **Price:** included in membership dues. **Circulation:** 3,000. **Advertising:** accepted ● Annual Report, annual ● Brochure. Contains information on the association and the NCAI Youth Commission. **Conventions/Meetings:** annual conference - usually June. 2008 June 1-4, Reno, NV ● annual convention (exhibits) - always fall. 2007 Nov. 11-16, Denver, CO; 2008 Sept. 19-2007 Sept. 24, Phoenix, AZ.

17728 ■ National Tribal Environmental Council (NTEC)
2501 Rio Grande Blvd. NW, Ste.A
Albuquerque, NM 87104
Ph: (505)242-2175
Fax: (505)242-2654
E-mail: info@ntec.org
URL: http://www.ntec.org
Contact: Bob Gruenig, Interim Exec. Dir.
Founded: 1991. **Members:** 108. **Membership Dues:** individual (associate), $35 (annual) ● community based (associate), $75 (annual) ● national/nonprofit (associate), $1,000 (annual) ● corporation (associate), $2,500 (annual). **Staff:** 7. **Budget:** $400,000. **Description:** Native American tribes. Focuses on the environmental concerns of Native Americans. Seeks to strengthen environmental management of lands by Native American tribes. Acts as a clearinghouse for environmental information. Monitors legislation related to the environment. Maintains Speaker's Bureau. **Libraries: Type:** reference; open to the public. **Holdings:** clippings, periodicals. **Subjects:** environmental issues, legislative analysis. **Programs:** Air; Water. **Working Groups:** Superfund. **Publications:** *Tribal Vision*, quarterly. Newsletter. Provides tribal environmental news. **Circulation:** 1,500. **Conventions/Meetings:** annual conference.

17729 ■ Native American Rights Fund (NARF)
1506 Broadway
Boulder, CO 80302
Ph: (303)447-8760
Fax: (303)443-7776
URL: http://www.narf.org
Contact: Atty. John E. Echohawk, Exec. Dir.
Founded: 1970. **Staff:** 36. **Budget:** $7,590,652. **Description:** Provides legal representation and technical services to individuals, tribes and organizations in

matters of Indian law. **Libraries: Type:** reference. **Holdings:** 12,000. **Subjects:** Indian law cases, studies, hearings, tribal constitutions and codes. **Affiliated With:** Colorado Nonprofit Association. **Publications:** *Landmark Indian Law Cases*, every 2-3 years. Book. Contains a fully-indexed compilation of important Indian law cases. **Price:** $95.00 ● *NARF Legal Review*, biennial. Newsletter. Provides information on NARF's work in Indian law. Includes a publication list. **Price:** free. **ISSN:** 0739-862X. **Circulation:** 10,000. Alternate Formats: online ● Annual Report, annual. Alternate Formats: online. **Conventions/Meetings:** semiannual board meeting - always April and November, Boulder, CO.

17730 ■ Seventh Generation Fund for Indian Development (SGF)
PO Box 4569
Arcata, CA 95518
Ph: (707)825-7640
Fax: (707)825-7639
E-mail: of7gen@pacbell.net
Contact: Christopher Peters, CEO/Pres.
Founded: 1977. **Staff:** 7. **Budget:** $1,000,000. **Languages:** English, Spanish. **Description:** Provides seed grants and technical assistance in order to increase self-reliance in Indian communities and decrease government dependency. Aims to: reclaim and live on aboriginal lands; protect tribal lands and natural resources; redevelop self-sufficient communities through food production, appropriate technologies, and alternative energy use; restore traditional indigenous forms of political organization or to modify existing governments along traditional lines. Supports and promotes the spiritual, cultural, and physical well-being of the Native family. Reports on such subjects as Native American rights, Indian family life, and judicial issues and cases affecting American Indians. Maintains small library on appropriate technologies, fundraising, and resource materials; the fund's title is drawn from the Hau de no sau nee (Six Nations) principle of considering the impact upon the seventh generation in the decision-making process. **Formerly:** (1984) Tribal Sovereignty Program. **Publications:** *Sovereignty*, quarterly. Newsletter ● Annual Report, annual. **Conventions/Meetings:** Keeping the Homefires Burning - meeting.

17731 ■ United Indians of All Tribes Foundation (UIATF)
Discovery Park
PO Box 99100
Seattle, WA 98199
Ph: (206)285-4425
E-mail: info@unitedindians.com
URL: http://www.unitedindians.com
Founded: 1970. **Members:** 13. **Staff:** 100. **Budget:** $4,000,000. **Description:** Provides a wide range of social, cultural, and educational services to the urban Native American Community owns and operates the Daybreak Star Indian Cultural Center which houses the permanent art collection of the foundation. Hosts yearly cultural activities for the native and non-native American community. **Convention/Meeting:** none. **Affiliated With:** National Congress of American Indians. **Publications:** *Daybreak Star Press*, monthly. Magazine. Contains native American curriculum materials for public schools.

Natural Resources

17732 ■ Rocky Mountain Institute (RMI)
1739 Snowmass Creek Rd.
Snowmass, CO 81654-9199
Ph: (970)927-3851
Fax: (970)927-4510
E-mail: ablovins@rmi.org
URL: http://www.rmi.org
Contact: Amory B. Lovins, CEO
Founded: 1982. **Staff:** 45. **Budget:** $7,000,000. **Description:** Serves as an entrepreneurial organization fostering efficient and restorative use of resources to create a more secure, prosperous, and life-sustaining world. **Publications:** *Cleaner Energy, Greener Prof-*

its. Alternate Formats: online ● *Cool Citizens: Everyday Solutions to Climate Change.* **Price:** free. Alternate Formats: online ● *The New Business Climate.* **Price:** free. Alternate Formats: online ● *RMI Solutions.* Newsletter. Alternate Formats: online ● Annual Report, annual. Alternate Formats: online.

Newspapers

17733 ■ North American Street Newspaper Association (NASNA)
c/o Timothy Harris, Pres.
2129 2nd Ave.
Seattle, WA 98121
Ph: (206)441-3247
E-mail: rchange@speakeasy.org
URL: http://www.nasna.org
Contact: Timothy Harris, Pres.
Founded: 1996. **Multinational. Description:** Builds and promotes the street newspaper movement in North America. Offers technical assistance to new and growing street newspapers. Strives to support a street newspaper movement that creates and upholds journalistic and ethical standards while promoting self-help and empowerment among people living in poverty. **Publications:** Manual.

Nicaragua

17734 ■ Bikes Not Bombs (BNB)
284 Amory St.
Jamaica Plain, MA 02130
Ph: (617)522-0222
Fax: (617)522-0912
E-mail: mail@bikesnotbombs.org
URL: http://www.bikesnotbombs.org
Contact: Lara Soul Brown, Exec. Dir.
Founded: 1984. **Membership Dues:** youth 16 and under, $5 (annual) ● low income, $10 (annual) ● individual, $35 (annual) ● household/family, $50 (annual). **Staff:** 8. **Budget:** $180,000. **Languages:** English, Spanish. **Description:** Bicyclists, environmentalists, teachers, and young people who are opposed to "the prioritization of spending on the military over basic human needs." Promotes bicycles as a pollution-free means of transportation; is concerned about the personal and economic empowerment of inner-city youth; works to collect and ship donated bicycles and spare parts to top-creation development projects in Nicaragua and in Haiti; also uses them in innovative education programs in inner-city Boston neighborhoods; has established 5 bicycle mechanic training centers in 3 cities in Nicaragua, one in the Dominican Republic, and one in Haiti. Sponsors slide shows and public forums. Runs a Bicycle Recycling and Youth Training Center in Roxbury, a majority African-American and Latino neighborhood of Boston, MA. (At the Center, young people can earn bicycles through participating in training programs and doing community service work.). **Affiliated With:** Transportation Alternatives. **Publications:** *Spoke and Word*, semiannual. Newsletter. Alternate Formats: online ● Also publishes Earn-A-Bike lesson plans and course outline a packet for the instruction of 11-16 year olds who are enrolled in experimental education programs where they earn bicycles while learning bike safety, bike mechanics and higher order thinking skills.

17735 ■ Latinas and Latinos for Social Change (LFSC)
PO Box 1279
Cambridge, MA 02238
Ph: (617)290-5614 (857)829-1496
E-mail: lfsc@lfsc.org
URL: http://www.lfsc.org
Founded: 1979. **Members:** 1,800. **Membership Dues:** $25 (annual). **Budget:** $25,000. **Languages:** English, Spanish. **Description:** Grassroots organization working to change the "oppressive policies" of the United States government and U.S.-based corporations toward the countries of Latin America and the Caribbean. LACASA is a project of the Central America Education Fund. **Libraries: Type:**

reference. **Subjects:** Latin American politics, history, culture, U.S. foreign policy. **Caucuses:** Cuba. **Committees:** Cuba. **Programs:** July 26th Coalition. **Formerly:** Caribbean Solidarity Association; (1994) Latin American and Caribbean Solidarity Association. **Publications:** *The Reporter*, bimonthly. Newsletter. Covers Latin America events and solidarity movement in U.S. **Conventions/Meetings:** annual meeting.

17736 ■ Nicaragua Network Education Fund (NN)
1247 E St. SE
Washington, DC 20003
Ph: (202)544-9355
E-mail: nicanet@afgj.org
URL: http://www.nicanet.org
Contact: Chuck Kaufman, Co-Coor.
Founded: 1979. **Members:** 250. **Membership Dues:** committee, individual supporter (non-voting), $50 (annual). **Staff:** 7. **Budget:** $215,000. **Description:** Network of organizations and individuals united in opposition to U.S. intervention in the Central American/Caribbean region and in support of the Nicaraguan revolution. Seeks to create a peaceful and friendly relationship between the U.S. and Nicaragua through public education. Sponsors educational activities. Raises funds for grass roots education and economic development projects in Nicaragua. Protests U.S. policies toward Nicaragua; facilitates establishment of sister-city relationships between U.S. and Nicaraguan cities. Organizes speaking tours of Nicaraguans to the U.S. and delegations of U.S. citizens to Nicaragua. Responds to human rights violations in Nicaragua through its Emergency Response Network. Maintains speakers' bureau. **Libraries: Type:** reference. **Holdings:** audiovisuals, books, clippings, periodicals. **Subjects:** Nicaragua and U.S. policy on Central America. **Formerly:** National Network in Solidarity With the Nicaraguan People; (1989) Nicaragua Network. **Publications:** *An Activist's Introduction to Nicaragua.* Brochure. **Price:** free for members ● *Nicaragua Monitor*, 10/year. Newsletter. Contains news and analysis of developments in Nicaragua and U.S. Nicaraguan policy. Reports on programs and activities of the Association. **Price:** $20.00 /year for individuals; $50.00 /year for institutions ● *Unbinding the Ties: The Popular Organizations and the FSLN in Nicaragua.* Book. **Price:** $4.67.

17737 ■ Quest for Peace (QP)
PO Box 5206
Hyattsville, MD 20782
Ph: (301)699-0042
Fax: (301)864-2182
E-mail: quest@quixote.org
URL: http://quest.quixote.org
Contact: Tom Loudon, Contact
Founded: 1984. **Members:** 25,000. **Staff:** 6. **Budget:** $300,000. **Description:** Serves as project of the Quixote Center. Represents religious, human rights, and social justice organizations and individuals interested in providing development and humanitarian aid to the people of Nicaragua and Haiti, including items such as vegetable seeds, clothing, and school supplies. Provides packing and shipping services for groups interested in sending humanitarian aid to Nicaragua. Conducts educational programs on U.S. foreign policy and the political situation in Nicaragua and Haiti. **Convention/Meeting:** none. **Affiliated With:** Quixote Center. **Publications:** *Quest for Peace News*, bimonthly. Newsletter. **Circulation:** 15,000 ● Videos.

17738 ■ Witness for Peace (WFP)
3628 12th St. NE, 1st Fl.
Washington, DC 20017
Ph: (202)547-6112
Fax: (202)536-4708
E-mail: melinda@witnessforpeace.org
URL: http://www.witnessforpeace.org
Contact: Melinda St. Louis, Exec. Dir.
Founded: 1983. **Members:** 16,000. **Membership Dues:** basic, $35 (annual) ● peace circle, $250 (annual). **Staff:** 11. **Budget:** $700,000. **Regional**

Groups: 6. **Languages:** English, French, Spanish. **Multinational. Description:** Grass roots movement working through nonviolent action to change those U.S. foreign and economic policies that lead to poverty and oppression in Latin American and the Caribbean, and to offer just alternatives. Activists and volunteers engage in direct action to affect positive policy changes. **Also Known As:** (2000) Accion Permanente Por la Paz. **Publications:** *Bitter Medicine: Structural Adjustment.* Journal. **Price:** $2.50/copy ● *High Price to Pay: Structural Adjustment and Women in Nicaragua.* Newsletter. **Price:** $5.00/copy ● *WFP Newsletter*, 3/year. Provides an ongoing source of spiritual reflection, resource sharing, organizational information, and political analysis. **Price:** $35.00/year suggested donation. **Circulation:** 15,000. **Conventions/Meetings:** annual board meeting and workshop.

Nonviolence

17739 ■ Albert Einstein Institution (AEI)
PO Box 455
East Boston, MA 02128
Ph: (617)247-4882
Fax: (617)247-4035
E-mail: einstein@igc.org
URL: http://www.aeinstein.org
Contact: Bob Helvey, Pres.
Founded: 1983. **Staff:** 2. **Description:** Supports and conducts basic and problem solving research, policy studies, and public education programs on the nature and potential of nonviolent forms of struggle. Assesses the possible role of nonviolent sanctions in present and emerging conflicts worldwide; works to preserve primary sources of information covering contemporary nonviolent struggles.. **Awards: Type:** fellowship. **Recipient:** for significant contributions to the study of nonviolent sanctions. **Computer Services:** Information services, nonviolent action resources ● mailing lists. **Programs:** Policy and Outreach. **Publications:** *Nonviolent Sanctions*, quarterly. Newsletter. Includes reports on current nonviolent protests worldwide. **Price:** free ● Articles ● Books ● Monographs ● Pamphlets. **Conventions/Meetings:** periodic conference.

17740 ■ Catholic Worker Movement (CW)
36 E 1st St.
New York, NY 10003
Ph: (212)777-9617 (212)254-1640
URL: http://www.catholicworker.org
Founded: 1933. **Description:** Radical Christian pacifist movement that "works directly with the poor and victims of injustice, while offering a critique of the causes of oppression". Espouses decentralism, personal responsibility, voluntary poverty, and opposition to war by nonpayment of federal taxes, refusal to cooperate with conscription, and other nonviolent means. Opposes capitalism and communism "because both serve to undermine human rights and the common good". **Publications:** *Catholic Worker*, 7/year. Newspaper. ISSN: 0008-8463. Alternate Formats: microform.

17741 ■ Center for Nonviolent Communication (CNVC)
2428 Foothill Blvd., Ste.E
La Crescenta, CA 91214
Ph: (818)957-9393
Free: (800)255-7696
Fax: (818)957-1424
E-mail: cnvc@cnvc.org
URL: http://cnvc.org
Contact: Jori Manske, Interim Exec. Dir.
Founded: 1984. **Members:** 200. **Membership Dues:** regular, $35 (annual). **Staff:** 8. **Regional Groups:** 3. **Local Groups:** 24. **Languages:** English, German, Spanish. **Description:** Works to help people liberate themselves from thought and communication patterns that contribute to their being psychologically and physically violent to themselves and others; to strengthen skills that help people resolve differences peacefully. Conducts continuing and in-service

education classes and consulting services. Sponsors workshop that demonstrates a model for nonviolent communication and provides opportunities for participants to practice applying the model in relevant situations. Maintains Speaker's Bureau. **Libraries: Type:** reference. **Formerly:** (1983) Center for Nonviolent Persuasion. **Publications:** *A Model for Nonviolent Communication.* Book ● *The Basics of Nonviolent Communication.* Video. Set of two tapes. ● *Connecting Compassionately.* Audiotapes ● *Making Life Wonderful.* Video. Set of 4 tapes. ● *Network News*, annual ● *Nonviolent Communication: A Language of the Heart.* Video ● *Resolving Conflicts Between Children and Adults.* Videos ● Also has produced two records.

17742 ■ Conflict Resolution Program
c/o Laurence Berg, Program Dir.
15 Rutherford Pl.
New York, NY 10003
Ph: (212)598-0950
Fax: (212)529-4603
E-mail: lberg@afsc.org
URL: http://www.afsc.org/nymetro/conflictresolution/default.htm
Contact: Laurence Berg, Program Dir.
Founded: 1992. **Staff:** 2. **Description:** Sponsored by the American Friends Service Committee. Promotes peaceful resolution of intergroup conflict, particularly when based on ethnic, racial, and religious identification. Works directly with those in neighborhoods at risk, as well as those in wars. **Libraries: Type:** not open to the public. **Holdings:** 2,000. **Subjects:** disarmament, nonviolence, international affairs, social analysis. **Projects:** Expatriate Dialogue; Partnership for Youth. **Affiliated With:** American Friends Service Committee.

17743 ■ Fourth Freedom Forum
803 N Main St.
Goshen, IN 46528
Ph: (574)534-3402
Free: (800)233-6786
Fax: (574)534-4937
E-mail: info@fourthfreedom.org
URL: http://www.fourthfreedom.org
Contact: Jennifer Glick, Dir. of Information Services
Founded: 1982. **Staff:** 8. **Nonmembership. Multinational. Description:** Works to find options for nonviolent resolution to international conflict. **Libraries: Type:** reference. **Holdings:** 3,000. **Subjects:** Iraq, international diplomacy, sanctions, incentives, nonproliferation. **Computer Services:** Online services, information/consulting services. **Telecommunication Services:** electronic mail, jglick@fourthfreedom.org. **Programs:** Counter-Terrorism Evaluation; Nonproliferation; Nonviolent Social Change; Sanctions and Security. **Affiliated With:** Joan B. Kroc Institute for International Peace Studies. **Formerly:** (1985) Alternative World Organization. **Publications:** *A Peaceful Superpower: The Movement Against War in Iraq.* Books ● *Contested Case: Do the Facts Justify the Case for War in Iraq?.* Report. Explores the case for war in Iraq. **Price:** free. **Circulation:** 20,000. Alternate Formats: online ● *The End Game: Removing Sanctions in Iraq.* Report. Alternate Formats: online ● *Grading Iraqi Compliance.* Report. Alternate Formats: online ● *Hidden Costs of War.* Report. Alternate Formats: online ● *Political Gain & Civilian Pain: Humanitarian Impacts of Economic Sanctions.* Book. **Price:** $28.95 paperback; $82.00 cloth ● *The Price of Peace: Incentives & International Conflict* ● *The Progress of UN Disarmament in Iraq: An Assessment Report.* Alternate Formats: online ● *The Sanctions Decade: Assessing UN Strategies in the 1990s.* Book. **Price:** $18.95 paperback; $48.00 hardcover ● *Sanctions, Inspection, and Containment: Viable Policy Options in Iraq.* Report. Alternate Formats: online ● *Sanctions & the Search for Security: Challenges to UN Action.* Book. **Price:** $49.95 hardcover; $18.95 paperback ● *Smart Sanctions: Restructuring UN Policy in Iraq.* Report. Alternate Formats: online ● *Smart Sanctions: Targeting Economic Statecraft.* Book. **Price:** $25.46 paperback; $64.60 hardcover ● *Toward a More Secure America.* Report. Alternate Formats: online ● *Toward*

a Strategy for Success in Iraq Policy Brief ● *Towards UN Administration of Iraq's Internal Security & Political Transition.* Alternate Formats: online ● *Uncovered Nukes: Arms Control & the Challenge of Tactical Nuclear Weapons.* Report. Alternate Formats: online ● *Unproven: The Flawed Case for War in Iraq.* **Conventions/Meetings:** conference ● symposium ● workshop.

17744 ■ Global Action to Prevent War
675 Third Ave., Ste.315
New York, NY 10017
Ph: (212)818-1815
Fax: (212)818-1857
E-mail: coordinator@globalactionpw.org
URL: http://www.globalactionpw.org
Contact: Dr. Randall Caroline Forsberg, Dir.
Multinational. Description: Commits to "a world where deadly conflict is rare, brief, and small in scale, working toward the abolition of war". **Working Groups:** UN. **Publications:** Newsletters. Alternate Formats: online.

17745 ■ Guitars Not Guns (GNG)
PO Box 9602
San Jose, CA 95157
Ph: (408)251-5775
E-mail: guitarsnotguns@msn.com
URL: http://www.guitarsnotguns.org
Contact: Ray Nelson, Pres./CEO
Founded: 2000. **Multinational. Description:** Aims to stop violence in schools and in the streets which result in self-destructive behaviors of drugs, alcohol and gang activities. Cultivates the creative musical potential in foster children, youth at risk and other deserving children around the world by providing them with guitars and lessons. **Telecommunication Services:** electronic mail, guitarsnotguns@aol.com ● electronic mail, ray@guitarsnotguns.org.

17746 ■ International Nonviolent Initiatives (INI)
Address Unknown since 2007
Founded: 1975. **Staff:** 2. **Description:** Promotes use of nonviolent means to resolve disputes. Member of War Resisters International (see separate entry, *International Organizations*). Conducts research and educational programs. **Libraries: Type:** reference. **Affiliated With:** War Resisters' International. **Formerly:** (1987) International Seminars on Training for Nonviolent Action.

17747 ■ Martin Luther King, Jr. Center for Nonviolent Social Change (MLKCNSC)
449 Auburn Ave. NE
Atlanta, GA 30312
Ph: (404)526-8900 (404)526-8911
Fax: (404)526-8969
E-mail: information@thekingcenter.org
URL: http://www.thekingcenter.org
Contact: Mr. Dexter Scott King, Chm./Pres./CEO
Description: Participants are individuals interested in the philosophy and actions of Rev. Martin Luther King, Jr. (1929-68), American clergyman, civil rights leader, and Nobel Peace Prize winner (1964). Encourages individuals, organizations, institutions, and nations to settle disputes by nonviolent means. Works to continue Dr. King's work through study, education, training, research, and constructive action. The U.S. Congress has established the 23.5 acres that accommodate the physical facilities of the center as a Martin Luther King, Jr. National Historic Site. **Formerly:** (1980) Martin Luther King, Jr. Center for Social Change.

17748 ■ National Association of Students Against Violence Everywhere (SAVE)
322 Chapanoke Rd., Ste.110
Raleigh, NC 27603
Ph: (919)661-7800
Free: (866)343-SAVE
Fax: (919)661-7777

E-mail: cwray@nationalsave.org
URL: http://www.nationalsave.org
Contact: Dr. Pamela L. Riley, Exec. Dir.
Founded: 1989. **Members:** 185,000. **Membership Dues:** chapter, $100 (annual). **Staff:** 3. **Local Groups:** 1,600. **Multinational. Description:** Strives to decrease the potential for violence in schools and communities by promoting student involvement in crime prevention, conflict management, and service activities. **Awards:** Advisor of the Year. **Frequency:** annual. **Type:** recognition ● Chapter of the Year. **Frequency:** annual. **Type:** recognition ● Student of the Year. **Frequency:** annual. **Type:** recognition. **Computer Services:** Information services, press room, resources ● online services, student forum. **Telecommunication Services:** electronic mail, drpriley@nationalsave.org. **Boards:** Ambassadors; Youth Advisory. **Programs:** Sister Chapter. **Projects:** Conflict Management; Crime Prevention. **Publications:** *Ernie the Elephant Learns About Communication.* Book. **Price:** $1.00 ● *Save eSource,* monthly. Newsletter. **Advertising:** accepted. Alternate Formats: online ● *SAVE Essentials.* Manual. Assists adults and SAVE chapters in their violence prevention efforts. **Price:** $79.00 for members; $65.00 for registered SAVE chapters ● *SAVE SOURCE.* Newsletter. Alternate Formats: online ● *Youth Voices, Grown-Up Choices.* Video. Includes SAVE's history, mission, vision, and three essential elements: crime prevention, conflict management, and service projects. **Price:** $20.00 ● Brochure. Provides an overview of the SAVE program. Alternate Formats: online. **Conventions/Meetings:** annual conference (exhibits) ● annual meeting, raises awareness in the school/community about safety measures using posters or assemblies or a safety course (exhibits).

17749 ■ National Conference on Peacemaking and Conflict Resolution (NCPCR)
1718 E Speedway Blvd., No. 305
Tucson, AZ 85719
Ph: (520)670-1541
Fax: (520)884-9676
E-mail: azyellott@aol.com
URL: http://www.apeacemaker.net
Contact: Ann Yellott, Admin./Network Coor.
Founded: 1982. **Staff:** 3. **Description:** Promotes the use and acceptance of nonviolent solutions to conflict resolution and peacemaking. Works as a liaison between national and international groups with similar goals. Sponsors educational programs and training in methods of nonviolent conflict resolution. **Awards:** Margaret Herrman Award. **Frequency:** biennial. **Type:** recognition. **Recipient:** for contribution to the field. **Telecommunication Services:** electronic mail, ncpcr@apeacemaker.net. **Also Known As:** Network of Communities for Peacemaking and Conflict Resolution; PeaceWeb. **Publications:** *The Peacemaker,* annual. Newsletter. **Price:** free. **Advertising:** accepted. **Conventions/Meetings:** biennial conference (exhibits).

17750 ■ Nonviolence International (NI)
PO Box 39127
Washington, DC 20016
Ph: (202)244-0951
Fax: (202)244-6396
E-mail: info@nonviolenceinternational.net
URL: http://www.nonviolenceinternational.net
Contact: Mubarak Awad, Founder
Founded: 1989. **Members:** 5,000. **Membership Dues:** student, $10 (annual) ● individual, organization, $25 (annual). **Staff:** 5. **Regional Groups:** 4. **Languages:** Arabic, English, French, Indonesian, Russian, Spanish, Thai. **Description:** Individuals interested in bringing about social and political change through nonviolent means. Provides training and educational programs. Coordinates internship/volunteer program. **Libraries: Type:** reference. **Holdings:** books, periodicals. **Subjects:** nonviolence, nonviolence training. **Computer Services:** database, nonviolence trainers. **Publications:** *Frontline,* quarterly. Newsletter. **Price:** $16.00. **Advertising:** accepted ● *International Journal of Nonviolence,* annual. **Price:** $10.00/year for students; $15.00 /year

for individuals; $25.00 /year for institutions and organizations. ISSN: 1069-2541. **Advertising:** accepted ● *Trainer's Database* (in Arabic and English), annual. Booklets. Consists of a series on nonviolent action. **Price:** $3.00 each. **Conventions/Meetings:** conference and seminar, on nonviolent action ● seminar.

17751 ■ Nonviolent Peaceforce (NP)
425 Oak Grove St.
Minneapolis, MN 55403
Ph: (612)871-0005
Fax: (612)871-0006
E-mail: info@nonviolentpeaceforce.org
URL: http://www.nonviolentpeaceforce.org
Contact: Mel Duncan, Exec. Dir.
Founded: 1999. **Staff:** 25. **Budget:** $2,400,000. **Regional Groups:** 47. **Local Groups:** 10. **National Groups:** 7. **Multinational. Description:** Works to "protect human rights and prevent death and destruction, and seeks peaceful resolution to conflict". **Libraries: Type:** open to the public. **Holdings:** 150; articles, books, periodicals. **Subjects:** peace, civil rights, justice, nonviolence. **Computer Services:** Mailing lists. **Telecommunication Services:** electronic mail, mduncan@nonviolentpeaceforce.org. **Publications:** *Rumors of Peace* (in English, French, and Spanish), annual. Newsletter. **Circulation:** 6,000. Alternate Formats: online. **Conventions/Meetings:** conference.

17752 ■ Pax Christi - U.S.A. (PC-USA)
532 W 8th St.
Erie, PA 16502
Ph: (814)453-4955
Fax: (814)452-4784
E-mail: info@paxchristiusa.org
URL: http://www.paxchristiusa.org
Contact: Dave Robinson, Exec. Dir.
Founded: 1972. **Members:** 14,000. **Membership Dues:** regular, $35 (annual) ● student, $10 (annual) ● parish sponsor, corporate sponsor, $150 (annual) ● bishop sponsor, $50 (annual) ● university/campus sponsor, $100 (annual). **Staff:** 16. **Budget:** $800,000. **Regional Groups:** 18. **State Groups:** 13. **Local Groups:** 500. **Description:** Represents Roman Catholics and others committed to the Christian ideal of nonviolence. Works for disarmament and demilitarization, economic and interracial justice, human rights and global restoration, education for peace, and alternatives to violence. Maintains Speaker's Bureau; conducts charitable and educational programs. **Libraries: Type:** open to the public. **Holdings:** 1,000; articles, books, periodicals. **Subjects:** peace movement, non-violence, human rights. **Awards:** Paul VI Award. **Frequency:** annual. **Type:** recognition. **Recipient:** for outstanding teacher of peace ● Pax Christi Book Award. **Frequency:** annual. **Type:** recognition. **Recipient:** to an author who writes an outstanding book in the area of peace making. **Computer Services:** Mailing lists. **Committees:** Peace Studies. **Task Forces:** Haiti; Youth and Young Adult Forum. **Absorbed:** (1973) American Pax Association. **Publications:** *Catholic Peace Voice,* bimonthly. Newspaper. **Price:** free for members. **Advertising:** accepted. Alternate Formats: online ● Also publishes adult peace education materials. **Conventions/Meetings:** annual assembly (exhibits) ● periodic conference ● periodic regional meeting and conference.

17753 ■ Resource Center for Nonviolence (RCNV)
515 Broadway
Santa Cruz, CA 95060
Ph: (831)423-1626
Fax: (831)423-8716
E-mail: information@rcnv.org
URL: http://www.rcnv.org
Contact: Bob Fitch, Contact
Founded: 1974. **Members:** 2,400. **Staff:** 7. **Budget:** $150,000. **Multinational. Description:** Offers the public a broad educational program on the history, theory, and practice of nonviolence as a force for personal and social change. Conducts: study groups and workshops on non-violence as espoused by

Mahatma Gandhi and Martin Luther King Jr; training for participants in nonviolent direct actions such as demonstrations at nuclear power plants and endangered environmental sites, and labor strikes. Special projects include: Middle East Project, which sends educational and political delegations to the Middle East to promote nonviolent solutions to the region's conflicts, and Racial and Economic Justice Program which deals with local issues. Offers unpaid internships; invites prominent activists to spend a brief period in residency at the center. Provides conscientious objection and draft counseling. Coordinates speaking tours and provides speakers; offers films and books for rental or sale. **Libraries: Type:** reference. **Holdings:** 2,000. **Awards:** Drawing the Line Award. **Frequency:** annual. **Type:** recognition. **Recipient:** for individuals or groups performing outstanding social service. **Publications:** *Calendar,* quarterly. Alternate Formats: online ● *Dana Doesn't Like Guns Anymore.* Book. **Price:** $10.00 ● *The Dark.* Book. **Price:** $4.95 ● *The Great Peach March.* Book. **Price:** $15.95 ● *Judge Rabbit and the Tree Spirit, a Folktale from Cambodia.* Book. **Price:** $13.95 ● *Love You Forever.* Book. **Price:** $4.95 ● *Resource Center for Nonviolence—Center Report,* annual. Reports. **Price:** free. **Circulation:** 2,500. **Conventions/Meetings:** annual dinner, for awards presentation.

17754 ■ War Resisters League (WRL)
339 Lafayette St.
New York, NY 10012
Ph: (212)228-0450
Fax: (212)228-6193
E-mail: wrl@warresisters.org
URL: http://www.warresisters.org
Contact: Judith Atiri, Admin. Coor.
Founded: 1923. **Members:** 9,000. **Staff:** 5. **Budget:** $900,000. **Regional Groups:** 1. **Local Groups:** 20. **Description:** Secular pacifist organization concerned with international, economic, and social cooperation and nonviolent resistance for settling disputes. Conducts organizers' training. Maintains speakers' bureau. **Awards:** Peace Award. **Frequency:** annual. **Type:** recognition. **Telecommunication Services:** electronic mail, juditha@warresisters.org. **Committees:** Disarmament/Peace Conversion; Draft/Counter-Recruitment; Feminism and Nonviolence; International; Racism; War Tax Resistance. **Programs:** Anti-Militarism; ROOTS; War Tax Resistance; Youth and Counter-Militarism. **Projects:** YouthPeace. **Affiliated With:** International Peace Bureau; War Resisters' International. **Absorbed:** (1967) Committee for Nonviolent Action; (1972) New York Workshop in Nonviolence. **Publications:** *Literature List* ● *Militarization of Students.* Pamphlet ● *Military Myth.* Video. **Price:** $20.00 ● *Nonviolent Activist,* bimonthly. Magazine. Provides political analysis from a pacifist perspective; contains articles on feminism, nonviolence, disarmament and war tax resistance. **Price:** included in membership dues; $15.00 /year for nonmembers; $25.00 /year for institutions. ISSN: 8755-7428. **Circulation:** 10,000. **Advertising:** accepted. Alternate Formats: online ● *Organizers Manual.* **Price:** $10.00 ● *Peace Calendar,* annual. **Price:** $12.95 ● *War Tax Resistance.* Book. **Price:** $15.00 ● Brochures. Alternate Formats: online ● Reports. Alternate Formats: online. **Conventions/Meetings:** triennial conference.

17755 ■ Win Without War
1320 18th St. NW, 5th Fl.
Washington, DC 20036
Ph: (202)822-2075
URL: http://www.winwithoutwarus.org
Contact: Trevor Fitzgibbon, Contact
Members: 40. **Description:** Advocates for international cooperation and enforceable international law. Supports initiatives developed by grassroots groups around the country. **Computer Services:** Information services, Iraq news.

Nuclear Energy

17756 ■ Alliance for Nuclear Accountability (ANA)
1914 N 34th St., Ste.407
Seattle, WA 98103-9091

Ph: (206)547-3175
Fax: (206)547-7158
E-mail: susangordon@earthlink.net
URL: http://www.ananuclear.org
Contact: Susan Gordon, Dir.
Founded: 1987. **Members:** 33. **Staff:** 3. **Budget:** $300,000. **Description:** Represents local, regional and national organizations working together to promote education and action in addressing issues pertaining to the U.S. nuclear weapons complex and related facilities, including issues of nuclear weapons production and waste cleanup.

17757 ■ Committee for Nuclear Responsibility (CNR)

PO Box 421993
San Francisco, CA 94142
Ph: (415)776-8299
E-mail: comments@x-raysandhealth.org
URL: http://www.ratical.org/radiation/CNR
Contact: Dr. John William Gofman MD, Chm.
Founded: 1971. **Staff:** 2. **Nonmembership. Multinational. Description:** Offers independent analyses of the aggregate cancer and genetic consequences from nuclear pollution and medical x-ray procedures (which include CT scans, fluoroscopy, mammograms). Provides evidence that aggregate consequences are very large and that harm occurs in proportion to dose, right down to zero dose. Discusses scientific and other reasons for lack of consensus, conflicts of interest in radiation research, and ethics of "permissible" levels of pollution. Offers free written materials to teachers and students at all levels. **Convention/Meeting:** none. **Libraries: Type:** not open to the public. **Additional Websites:** http://www.x-raysandhealth.org. **Study Groups:** Xrays: Doses Down Now. **Formerly:** CNR Books. **Publications:** *Preventing Breast Cancer: The Story of a Major, Proven, Preventable Cause of this Disease.* Book. **Advertising:** accepted ● *Radiation from Medical Procedures in the Pathogenesis of Cancer and Ischemic Heart Disease.* Book ● *Radiation-Induced Cancer from Low-Dose Exposure: An Independent Analysis.* Book ● *X-Rays: Health Effects of Common Exams.* Book ● Offers more than 100 technical and nontechnical essays throughout the year, available free on the two Web sites.

17758 ■ Environmental Coalition on Nuclear Power (ECNP)

433 Orlando Ave.
State College, PA 16803
Ph: (814)237-3900
E-mail: johnsrud@uplink.net
Contact: Dr. Judith H. Johnsrud, Exec. Off.
Founded: 1970. **Description:** Represents individuals and groups concerned about nuclear power and energy policy. Seeks establishment of a safe nonnuclear energy policy in the U.S. Conducts many educational, legal, and political activities at local, state, and national levels. Maintains speakers' bureau and conducts research programs. **Libraries: Type:** reference. **Holdings:** 2,000. **Subjects:** nuclear power, radioactive waste, radiation, health. **Publications:** Newsletter, periodic ● Also publishes papers. **Conventions/Meetings:** quarterly meeting - always in Pennsylvania.

17759 ■ Friends of Hibakusha (FOH)

1765 Sutter St., No. 2
San Francisco, CA 94115
Ph: (415)567-7599
Fax: (415)931-6158
Contact: Geri Handa, Contact
Founded: 1981. **Description:** Supports group for hibakusha, who are U.S. citizens and Japanese-American survivors of radiation exposure resulting from the World War II atomic bombings of Hiroshima and Nagasaki, Japan in 1945; the term hibakusha, or bomb-affected person, also refers to those in utero at the time of the bombings. Primary objectives are to: provide assistance to hibakusha; help hibakusha inform the American public about the effects of nuclear war; encourage research into the medical aspects of radiation exposure and establish medical programs for radiation victims in conjunction with other radiation survivor groups. Serves as a forum for relating experiences of atomic bomb survivors. Works to: survey the social needs of hibakusha and to assist them in the U.S. in organizing support and discussion groups among second- and third-generation atomic bomb survivors; raise awareness of the dangers of radiation exposure and the need for medical assistance for individuals suffering from radiogenic illnesses; train educators in presentation of issues and information related to the atomic bombings; develop educational and classroom materials for community and church schools. Provide and sponsor medical care, health examinations, and consultation for hibakusha; supply emergency travel and housing funds for American hibakusha who need to travel to Japan for free treatment of radiation-related diseases. (The U.S. does not currently offer free medical treatment programs for atomic bomb-affected individuals; Japan does.) Assists in the organization of Hiroshima-Nagasaki commemorations; disseminates information to the media. Cosponsors seminars; co-hosts biennial medical examination and screening teams from Japan; provides speakers and films to schools, churches, and peace and community groups. **Committees:** Medical; Program and Educational. **Projects:** Personal History. **Publications:** *The Paper Crane*, quarterly. Newsletter. Includes articles on individual hibakusha, updates on community events and programs, book and film reviews, and legislative news. **Price:** included in membership dues. **Circulation:** 700.

17760 ■ National Association of Radiation Survivors (NARS)

PO Box 1587
Marysville, CA 95901-0047
Ph: (530)741-9654
Free: (800)798-5102
Fax: (530)741-9654
E-mail: nars@radiationsurvivors.org
URL: http://www.radiationsurvivors.org
Contact: Fred Allingham, Exec. Dir.
Founded: 1982. **Members:** 7,000. **Membership Dues:** survivor/interested individual, $15 (annual). **Staff:** 1. **Budget:** $95,000. **Regional Groups:** 9. **Local Groups:** 50. **Description:** Persons exposed to nuclear radiation including uranium miners, test-site workers, civilian workers at the national laboratories, atomic veterans, "downwind" residents, clinical radiation experiment victims, medical therapy victims, and Japanese-American atom bomb survivors. Objectives are to provide health care, compensation, legal and medical services, genetic research, and support services for survivors and their families. Sponsors conferences for "atomic widows" and parents of genetically-affected children; generates research; reports on experiences of radiation survivors; initiates litigation on behalf of radiation victims and their families. Sponsors seminars, workshops, and slide show. Conducts charitable programs; compiles statistics; operates speakers' bureau. **Libraries: Type:** reference. **Holdings:** 100. **Subjects:** health effects of radiation exposure. **Computer Services:** database, atomic tests ● database, medical and genetic data on 11000 radiation survivors sorted by age and site exposure. **Committees:** Legislation; Litigation; Medical Research. **Publications:** Newsletter, quarterly. **Price:** $15.00/year. **Circulation:** 3,500. **Conventions/Meetings:** biennial conference.

17761 ■ National Campaign for Radioactive Waste Safety (NCRWS)

PO Box 4524
Albuquerque, NM 87106
Ph: (505)262-1862
Fax: (505)262-1864
E-mail: info@sric.org
URL: http://www.sric.org
Contact: Don Hancock, Dir.
Founded: 1979. **Staff:** 2. **Description:** Aims to develop safe nuclear waste disposal programs. Opposes U.S. government's "current unsafe efforts at waste disposal" taking place at the WIPP (Waste Isolation Pilot Plant Project) in Carlsbad, NM and elsewhere. Provides citizens' groups around the country with information on the issues; monitors the development of industry and government programs for nuclear waste disposal in the public interest; offers expert testimony before government committees and other agencies; encourages public concern through public relations programs; consults with organizations that share related goals. Conducts scientific and technical research, currently concentrating on transportation problems and on salt bed disposal. Acts as clearinghouse for data on radioactive waste disposal. Operates speakers' bureau.

17762 ■ Nuclear Energy Information Service (NEIS)

3411 W Diversey Ave., No. 16
Chicago, IL 60647
Ph: (773)342-7650
Fax: (773)342-7655
E-mail: neis@neis.org
URL: http://www.neis.org
Contact: Dave Kraft, Exec. Dir.
Founded: 1981. **Members:** 620. **Membership Dues:** family, organizational, $30 (annual) ● individual, $20 (annual) ● student, low-income, senior, $12 (annual). **Staff:** 1. **Budget:** $57,000. **Regional Groups:** 1. **State Groups:** 1. **Local Groups:** 1. **Description:** Provides information on nuclear power, nuclear waste, radiation hazards, and energy alternatives to nuclear power. Conducts educational programs; maintains speakers' bureau. **Libraries: Type:** reference. **Holdings:** 500; artwork, audio recordings, books, clippings, periodicals, video recordings. **Subjects:** nuclear power, radiation issues, radioactive waste, alternative/renewable energy. **Publications:** *NEIS News*, bimonthly. Newsletter. Contains current nuclear issues. **Price:** $30.00 /year for nonmembers; included in membership dues. **Circulation:** 620. **Advertising:** accepted. Alternate Formats: online. **Conventions/Meetings:** annual meeting (exhibits) - always third Sunday of January.

17763 ■ Nuclear Information and Resource Service (NIRS)

6930 Carroll Ave., Ste.340
Takoma Park, MD 20912
Ph: (301)270-6477
Fax: (301)270-4291
E-mail: nirsnet@nirs.org
URL: http://www.nirs.org
Contact: Michael Mariotte, Exec. Dir.
Founded: 1978. **Members:** 7,000. **Membership Dues:** individual, $35 (annual). **Staff:** 7. **Budget:** $700,000. **Description:** Represents antinuclear grassroots groups and individuals. Seeks to: assist individuals and organizations interested in and concerned about nuclear power issues; provide information, advice, materials, and speakers to people trying to halt the construction of nuclear power plants; promote all alternatives to nuclear power. Works with local activist groups, public officials, and attorneys representing concerned employees at nuclear plants; helps local groups "work their way through the maze of government regulations and roadblocks established to discourage public participation in nuclear decisions". Monitors the Nuclear Regulatory Commission, Congress, the nuclear industry, and legislative, judicial, and regulatory bodies; reports on developing issues and upcoming events. Conducts research; provides technical assistance and referrals to legal aid and technical experts; facilitates Freedom of Information Act requests; answers inquiries for information on nuclear issues. Maintains extensive files on operating nuclear plants as well as nuclear reactors under construction, utility companies, radioactive waste, and general nuclear issues. **Libraries: Type:** reference. **Holdings:** 5,000; periodicals. **Subjects:** nuclear power, radioactive waste, radiation. **Affiliated With:** World Information Service on Energy. **Publications:** *Nuclear Monitor* (in English, Russian, Spanish, and Ukrainian), biweekly. Newsletter. **Price:** $250.00/year; $150.00/year for public and university libraries; $35.00/year for activists. ISSN: 0889-3411. **Circulation:** 3,000. Alternate Formats: online ● Brochure ● Pamphlets. **Conventions/Meetings:** periodic conference.

17764 ■ Nukewatch
PO Box 649
Luck, WI 54853
Ph: (715)472-4185
Fax: (715)472-4184
E-mail: nukewatch@lakeland.ws
URL: http://www.nukewatch.com
Contact: Bonnie Urfer, Co-Dir.
Founded: 1979. **Members:** 3,000. **Membership Dues:** public, organization, $25 (annual). **Staff:** 2. **Budget:** $60,000. **Description:** A public education project of the Progressive Foundation. Works to monitor developments in atomic energy, both military and commercial, and to promote safer and healthier alternatives. Opposes secrecy of the Defense Department in nuclear weapons development; seeks to end the arms race, "skyrocketing military spending," and academic military research. Sponsors public conferences and workshops on nuclear issues. Assists grassroots citizens groups by providing resources, contacts, and other benefits of Nukewatch's experience in environmental, energy, and peace concerns. Conducts research; maintains speaker's bureau. **Libraries: Type:** reference. **Holdings:** 400; books, clippings, periodicals. **Subjects:** peace, nuclear secrecy, nuclear weapons, transportation of bombs and radioactive waste. **Computer Services:** Mailing lists. **Affiliated With:** Progressive Foundation. **Publications:** *Nuclear Heartland: A Guide to the 1000 Missile Sites of the United States.* Book. **Price:** $40.00 each ● *Nukewatch Special Report.* Alternate Formats: online ● *The Pathfinder,* quarterly. Newsletter. Covers news regarding nuclear reactor accidents. Alternate Formats: online ● *Prisoners on Purpose: A Peacemaker's Guide to Jails and Prisons.* Book. **Price:** $10.00 each ● *Radioactive Waste: No End in Sight.* Booklet. **Price:** $2.00 each. **Conventions/Meetings:** periodic meeting.

17765 ■ Public Citizen's Critical Mass Energy and Environment Program
215 Pennsylvania Ave. SE
Washington, DC 20003
Ph: (202)546-4996
E-mail: cmep@citizen.org
URL: http://www.citizen.org/CMEP
Contact: Wenonah Hauter, Dir.
Founded: 1974. **Membership Dues:** individual, $20 (annual). **Staff:** 11. **Budget:** $500,000. **Description:** Energy research and education arm of Public Citizen founded to oppose nuclear power and advocate energy alternatives. Promotes renewable energy and energy efficiency technologies, programs, and policies; prepares and disseminates reports; lobbies Congress; acts as a watchdog of key federal and state energy regulatory agencies; monitors nuclear power issues such as disposal and transport of nuclear waste; provides information and resources (including action alerts, testimony, fact sheets, and other energy policy information via internet) to citizens, activists, grassroots groups, local officials and national press. Works closely with other citizens' groups and individuals across the country, empowering them to participate in pertinent decisions affecting their health, safety, and standard of living. Operates Coalition of Ratepayers for Affordable Green Electricity. **Libraries: Type:** reference. **Holdings:** 2,000; books, periodicals. **Subjects:** consumer affairs, environmental issues. **Affiliated With:** Public Citizen. **Formerly:** (1977) Critical Mass; (1998) Critical Mass Energy Project of Public Citizen; (2001) Public Citizen's Critical Mass Energy and Environment Project. **Publications:** *The Dark at the End of the Tunnel: Federal Clean-up Standards for Nuclear Power Plants.* Examines the Nuclear Regulatory Commission's Enhanced Rulemaking on Residual Radioactivity (ERORR). **Price:** $30.00 ● *Directory of Anti-Nuclear Activists,* semiannual ● *Energy Audit II: A State-by-State Profile of Energy Consumption and Conservation.* Details energy use in all fifty states, ranking each according to its dependence on nonrenewable resources, use of renewable energy, and consumption. **Price:** $40.00 ● *National Directory of Safe Energy Organizations,* annual. Contains the names and addresses of more than 1000 citizen groups which work to promote renewable energy as

alternatives to nuclear power. **Price:** $30.00/year ● *Nuclear Legacy: An Overview of the Places, Problems and Politics of Radioactive Waste in the United States.* Provides a comprehensive, state-by-state analysis of the amounts, radioactivity levels, and types of radioactive waste from nuclear power plants. **Price:** $40.00 ● *Nuclear Lemons: An Assessment of America's Worst Commercial Nuclear Reactors.* Examines each American nuclear power plant based on eleven key indicators of safety and performance. **Price:** $40.00 ● *Payment Due: A Reactor-by-Reactor Assessment of the Nuclear Industry's $25 Billion Decommissioning Bill.* Examines the cost to decommission each of the United States commercial nuclear reactors, the funds already set aside, and the amount still needed. **Price:** $40.00 ● *Renewable Energy: A National Directory of Resources, Contacts, and Companies.* Lists more than 1,650 domestic organizations working to promote, buy, sell, develop, and research renewable-energy technologies. **Price:** $40.00 ● *Renewable Energy Research and Development: An Alternative Budget for FY'1993 1995.* Outlines proposed expanded levels of federal funding for 1993-95 and redirected programs for the further development of solar and other energies. **Price:** $30.00. **Conventions/Meetings:** periodic meeting.

17766 ■ Task Force Against Nuclear Pollution (TFANP)
PO Box 564
Greenbelt, MD 20768
Ph: (301)474-8311 (703)869-8434
Fax: (301)474-8311
Contact: John W. Gofman MD, Pres.
Founded: 1971. **Description:** Objectives are to: educate the public and influence the government to deal with problems of nuclear pollution; stop development and construction of nuclear power plants; promote energy efficiency; encourage development and use of solar power. Conducts petition drive according to congressional districts to be presented to Congress. Provides research sources on nuclear power issues. **Publications:** *An Irreverent, Illustrated View of Nuclear Power.* Book ● *Energy Bibliography.* Book ● *Task Force Against Nuclear Pollution—Progress Report,* semiannual ● Reprints.

17767 ■ Three Mile Island Alert (TMIA)
4100 Hillsdale Rd.
Harrisburg, PA 17112-1419
Ph: (717)541-1101
Fax: (717)233-3261
E-mail: tmia@tmia.com
URL: http://www.tmia.com
Contact: Kay Pickering, Sec.
Founded: 1977. **Members:** 400. **Membership Dues:** individual, $20 (annual) ● nonprofit organization, $25 (annual) ● student, low income, $5 (annual) ● sustaining, $50 (annual) ● institutional or corporate, $100 (annual). **Staff:** 1. **Budget:** $5,000. **Description:** Represents individuals concerned about the potentially hazardous effects of Three Mile Island. Seeks to facilitate the safe clean up of the TMI Unit-2 nuclear reactor that developed the leak in 1979, and to close the TMI Unit-1 plant as a nuclear facility. Researches and disseminates information about the conditions and management at TMI, evacuation procedures, and health hazards of nuclear plants. Raises money for legal intervention; assists groups in monitoring the transportation of radioactive waste; testifies before governmental bodies at all levels. Maintains speakers' bureau and archives. Conducts local seminars. **Telecommunication Services:** electronic mail, tmi-alert@tmia.com. **Committees:** Legal; Radiation Monitoring; Radioactive Waste Disposal; Research. **Publications:** *Decade of Delay, Deceit, and Danger: TMI,* quarterly. Newsletter. **Price:** $3.00/issue ● Brochure, quarterly. Covers the Three Mile Island reactor. **Price:** included in membership dues; $10.00 /year for nonmembers ● Brochure. Describes TMIA's activities and purpose. Provides information on joining the association. **Conventions/Meetings:** annual meeting.

17768 ■ Union of Concerned Scientists (UCS)
2 Brattle Sq.
Cambridge, MA 02238-9105

Ph: (617)547-5552
Fax: (617)864-9405
URL: http://www.ucsusa.org
Contact: Kathleen M. Rest, Exec. Dir.
Founded: 1969. **Members:** 60,000. **Membership Dues:** regular, $25 (annual). **Staff:** 70. **Budget:** $7,000,000. **Description:** Advocacy organization concerned about the impact of advanced technology on society. Conducts research on energy policy, global environmental problems, transportation, biotechnology, and arms control. Disseminates research results to the public and assists members and the public in presenting their views before administrative agencies and the courts. Conducts public education programs including nationwide events, television and radio appearances, and speaking engagements. Sponsors annual nationwide educational campaign. **Libraries: Type:** reference. **Holdings:** 1,500; reports. **Subjects:** food and environment, global environment, global security, clean energy, clean vehicles. **Programs:** Clean Energy; Clean Vehicles; Food and Environment; Global Environment; Global Security. **Publications:** *A Growing Concern: Protecting the Food Supply in an Era of Pharmaceutical and Industrial Crops.* Report. **Price:** $20.00 each ● *Catalyst,* semiannual. Magazine. Includes updates on UCS issues, new reports, and new projects/campaigns. **Price:** included in membership dues. **Circulation:** 700,000. Alternate Formats: online ● *Earthwise,* quarterly. Newsletter. Provides updates on current UCS research and advocacy. Alternate Formats: online ● *The Economics of Pharmaceutical Crops.* Report. **Price:** $10.00 each ● *Gone to Seed: Transgenic Contaminants in the Traditional Seed Supply.* Report. **Price:** $15.00 each ● *Greener Pastures: How Grass-fed Beef and Milk Contribute to Healthy Eating.* Report. **Price:** $15.00 each ● *Legislative Alert,* periodic ● *United States Nuclear Plants in the 21st Century: The Risk of a Lifetime.* Report. **Price:** $10.00 each. Alternate Formats: online ● *Walking a Nuclear Tightrope: Unlearned Lessons of Year-plus Reactor Outages.* Report. **Price:** $10.00 each. Alternate Formats: online. **Conventions/Meetings:** periodic conference.

17769 ■ We the People
200 Harrison St.
Oakland, CA 94607
Ph: (510)836-3273
Fax: (510)836-3063
E-mail: wtp@wtp.org
URL: http://www.wtp.org
Contact: Edmund G. Brown Jr., Contact
Founded: 1987. **Membership Dues:** individual, $25 (annual). **Description:** Promotes safety in the nuclear power plant industry. Works to reveal what the group feels is corruption in the Nuclear Regulatory Commission, which sets and enforces standards of safety within the industry. Provides assistance to "whistleblowers" (individuals from within the industry who are willing to testify that nuclear power plants are unsafe). Lobbies the government to provide better safety regulation of the nuclear power plant industry. **Awards: Frequency:** annual. **Type:** recognition. **Publications:** Newsletter. **Conventions/Meetings:** annual convention and workshop, includes a meeting of the general assembly.

17770 ■ Western Interstate Energy Board/WINB (WIEB/WINB)
c/o Douglas C. Larson, Exec. Dir.
1515 Cleveland Pl., Ste.200
Denver, CO 80202-5114
Ph: (303)573-8910
Fax: (303)534-7309
E-mail: dlarson@westgov.org
URL: http://www.westgov.org/wieb
Contact: Douglas C. Larson, Exec. Dir.
Founded: 1969. **Members:** 16. **Staff:** 4. **Budget:** $350,000. **State Groups:** 16. **Description:** States of the Western U.S. Works to assist western state governors and legislatures in achieving optimum influence with federal government activities affecting the western region. Seeks to foster the orderly development of all energy resources in the West consistent with regional economic, social, and environmental

goals. Develops a proper balance of performance and responsibility between the states and the federal establishment. Provides mutual aid among member states and between federal agencies and state and regional programs. Maintains library. Programs and activities include: provision of technical and administrative services, advice, and information; sponsorship of conferences; research studies; acting as fiscal and administrative agency for organization and implementation of cooperative projects. **Committees:** Federal Lands and Energy Resources; High Level Radioactive Waste; Reclamation; Regional Electric Power Cooperation. **Projects:** Alternative Vehicle Fuels and Air Quality; Energy Conservation; Energy Emergency Planning; Federal Energy Mineral Leasing and Development; Impact of Federal Legislation; Power Plant Siting; Radioactive Waste Management and Transportation; Regional Electric Power Supplies; Renewable Resources; Rules and Regulations of Member States. **Formerly:** (1977) Western Interstate Nuclear Compact. **Publications:** Annual Report ● Newsletter, biweekly ● Also publishes staff analyses and special reports.

Nuclear War and Weapons

17771 ■ Accidental Nuclear War Prevention Project (ANWPP)
c/o Nuclear Age Peace Foundation
PMB 121
1187 Coast Village Rd., Ste.1
Santa Barbara, CA 93108-2794
Ph: (805)965-3443
Fax: (805)568-0466
E-mail: dkrieger@napf.org
URL: http://www.wagingpeace.org
Contact: David Krieger, Foundation Pres.
Founded: 1984. **Members:** 2,500. **Description:** Scientists, engineers, researchers, and others interested in reversing the nuclear arms race and preventing an accidental outbreak of nuclear war. Seeks to raise public awareness of the possibility of accidental nuclear war. Disseminates information on events that the group feels nearly triggered a nuclear exchange. Informs members of meetings and projects that address reduction and world peace and that work to lessen the chance of nuclear war. Is a project of the Nuclear Age Peace Foundation (see separate entry). **Additional Websites:** http://www.nuclearfiles.org. **Affiliated With:** Nuclear Age Peace Foundation. **Conventions/Meetings:** periodic meeting.

17772 ■ ALEPH: Alliance for Jewish Renewal
7000 Lincoln Dr., Ste.B2
Philadelphia, PA 19119-3046
Ph: (215)247-0210
Fax: (215)247-9703
E-mail: alephajr@aol.com
URL: http://www.aleph.org
Contact: Debra Kolodny, Exec. Dir.
Founded: 1978. **Members:** 4,000. **Membership Dues:** contribution, $36 (annual). **Staff:** 10. **Budget:** $350,000. **Local Groups:** 60. **Multinational. Description:** Works toward the spiritual renewal of Judaism. Serves as resource center for Jewish perspectives. **Publications:** ALEPH Resources. Catalog. Offers books and CDs. Alternate Formats: online ● Kol ALEPH, 3/year. Newsletter. **Price:** included in membership dues; $36.00 /year for institutions ● Kol Koreh. Book. Prayerbook. **Price:** $26.00. **Conventions/Meetings:** biennial conference (exhibits) - summer; odd numbered years.

17773 ■ Architects/Designers/Planners for Social Responsibility (ADPSR)
PO Box 9126
Berkeley, CA 94709
Ph: (510)845-1000
E-mail: response@adpsr.org
URL: http://www.adpsr.org
Contact: Raphael Sperry, Natl. Pres.
Founded: 1982. **Members:** 2,000. **Membership Dues:** individual, $50 (annual) ● steward, $85 (annual) ● contributor/small firm, $100 (annual) ● sus-

tainer/large firm, $250 (annual) ● patron/institution, $500 (annual) ● donor, $1,000 (annual) ● student, $35 (annual). **Staff:** 2. **Budget:** $324,000. **Regional Groups:** 6. **Description:** Architects, designers, planners, and persons employed in construction and real estate. Informs the public of the danger of nuclear war. Plans include: development of a poster that expresses the concerns of architects regarding nuclear war; a traveling exhibit that will communicate members' concerns in detail; organization of a speakers and information bureau to assist community planning boards and other citizens' groups in equating their capital improvement needs with nuclear weapons costs; a program to examine and make the public aware of Federal Emergency Management Administration's Summer Shelter Program and to study the feasibility of the FEMA community emergency evacuation plans. Has produced a cost equivalency study comparing the cost of the Department of Defense appropriation for a nuclear armed naval fleet at Stapleton, Staten Island, NY with the proposed public works budget to rebuild the city's infrastructure. Conducts seminars; sponsors student design competitions; maintains speakers' bureau. **Awards:** Mumford Awards. **Frequency:** annual. **Type:** recognition. **Computer Services:** Mailing lists, national and chapter listservs. **Additional Websites:** http://www.newvillage.net, http://www.newvillagepress.net. **Formerly:** Architects for Social Responsibility. **Publications:** ADPSR News, 2-3/year. Newsletter. Lists architects, designers, and planners concerned with peace, disarmament, and social welfare issues. Includes book reviews and calendar of events. **Price:** free. **Circulation:** 800 ● New Village Journal, annual. Magazine. Mixes views of sociologists, economists, citizen activists, educators and designers of the built environment. **Price:** $8.00/issue; $15.00 2 issues; $25.00 4 issues. Alternate Formats: online ● Plans to publish brochure. **Conventions/Meetings:** annual conference.

17774 ■ Campaign to Boycott SDI
c/o John B. Kogut, Co-Founder
1110 W Green St.
Univ. of Illinois
Urbana, IL 61801
Ph: (217)333-1060
Fax: (217)333-4990
E-mail: j-kogut@uiuc.edu
Contact: John B. Kogut, Co-Founder
Founded: 1985. **Members:** 12,000. **Regional Groups:** 110. **Description:** Scientists and engineers in applied physics, astronomy, chemistry, computer science, engineering, mathematics, and physics departments at universities, who affirm that they will not accept government contracts to perform research on the Strategic Defense Initiative, known colloquially as Star Wars. Believes that it is not possible to build a reliable SDI system; that building the SDI system will spur the arms race, prevent meaningful arms control negotiations, and violate existing arms control agreements; and that the SDI system will encourage nuclear war. Seeks to curtail the development of the SDI system; educates the scientific community on the role it has been asked to play in increasing support for the SDI system. Maintains speakers' bureau; compiles statistics. **Convention/Meeting:** none. **Publications:** A Status Report on the Boycott of Star Wars Research by Academic Scientists and Researchers.

17775 ■ Committee of Atomic Bomb Survivors in the U.S. (CABSUS)
1759 Sutter St.
San Francisco, CA 94115
Ph: (562)698-0855
Fax: (562)698-0855
Contact: Mitsuo Tomozawa, Pres.
Founded: 1971. **Members:** 300. **Membership Dues:** atomic bomb survivor of Hiroshima and Nagasak, $20 (annual). **Local Groups:** 6. **Languages:** English, Japanese, Korean. **Description:** Nagasaki and Hiroshima atomic bomb survivors of World War II who are American citizens and permanent U. S. residents. Aims to identify other survivors (the committee estimates there are over 1,100 survivors in the U.S.)

and offer support and assistance to relieve their fears of ostracism from the community as well as possible loss of employment and insurance policies. Offers some medical assistance to survivors in dealing with the long-term effects and consequences of radiation exposure. Presses for legislation to provide U.S. survivors with the same benefits the Japanese government provides its citizens, including medical and insurance aid and counseling. Raises funds to send victims to Japan for specialized treatment. **Affiliated With:** Friends of Hibakusha. **Publications:** American Atomic Bomb Survivors - A Plea for Medical Assistance. Booklet. Contains survivors' stories and committee history. **Conventions/Meetings:** biennial conference - usually September.

17776 ■ Committee to Bridge the Gap (CBG)
1637 Butler Ave., Ste.203
Los Angeles, CA 90025
Ph: (310)478-0829
Fax: (310)478-0820
E-mail: ctbtg@aol.com
URL: http://www.committeetobridgethegap.org
Contact: Daniel Hirsch, Pres.
Founded: 1970. **Description:** Addresses issues such as nuclear nonproliferation, control of weapons-grade materials, nuclear power in space, nuclear reactor safety and regulation, nuclear weapons, and radioactive waste. **Convention/Meeting:** none. **Formerly:** Campus Committee to Bridge the Gap.

17777 ■ Computer Professionals for Social Responsibility (CPSR)
1370 Mission St., 4th Fl.
San Francisco, CA 94103
Ph: (415)839-9355
Fax: (415)839-8617
E-mail: cpsr@cpsr.org
URL: http://www.cpsr.org
Contact: Mr. Daniel Krimm, Communications Dir.
Founded: 1981. **Members:** 800. **Membership Dues:** regular, $75 (annual) ● student, low income, $20 (annual) ● basic, $50 (annual) ● supporting, $200 (annual) ● life, $1,250. **Staff:** 1. **Local Groups:** 22. **Multinational. Description:** Welcomes everyone who uses or is concerned about the role of information technology in the society. Works to educate policymakers, the public, and those in the computer science field about the social implications of computer use, particularly in regard to computers and nuclear weapons, computers and privacy/civil liberties, computers in the workplace, and the national information infrastructure. Encourages discussion and critical examination of social and technical issues by those within the computer profession; advocates public responsibility for decisions involving computer use in societal systems. Works to refute the beliefs that technological systems are infallible, that expert judgments are inviolable, and that it is appropriate to resolve political and social problems with technological solutions. Maintains speakers' bureau; conducts educational and research programs. **Libraries: Type:** reference. **Awards:** Norbert Wiener Award for Social and Professional Responsibility. **Frequency:** annual. **Type:** recognition. **Recipient:** for demonstration of a deep commitment to the socially responsible use of computing technology. **Computer Services:** Mailing lists. **Telecommunication Services:** electronic mail, listserv@cpsr.org ● electronic mail, admin@cpsr.org. **Boards:** Advisory. **Committees:** Board Development; Fundraising; Personnel; Program; Publications. **Projects:** Privaterra; Public Sphere. **Working Groups:** Community Networking and Workplace Issues; Computers and Civil Liberties; Computers and Environment; Education; Gender; Intellectual Property; International Concerns; National Information Infrastructure; Peace and Social Justice; Workplace. **Publications:** CPSR Journal, quarterly. Contains articles on computer technology and its impact on the military, economy, civil liberties, social justice, and professional ethics. **Price:** included in membership dues. **Circulation:** 2,500. Alternate Formats: online ● CSPR Compiler, monthly. Newsletter. Alternate Formats: online ● PING!, quarterly. Newsletter. Alternate Formats: online ● Proceedings of DIAC and Participatory Design Conferences ● Brochure.

Describes the mission, history, membership benefits, projects, and electronic services of the organization. ● Annual Report, annual. Alternate Formats: online ● Papers. Alternate Formats: online ● Also distributes a variety of publications on civil liberties, participatory design and workplace issues, computers and environment, community computing, computers and education, and reliability and risk; proceedings; transcripts; books; and other educational materials. **Conventions/Meetings:** annual conference - usually October ● biennial Directions and Implications of Advanced Computing Conference ● biennial Participatory Design Conference.

17778 ■ Concerned Citizens for Nuclear Safety (CCNS)
107 Cienega
Santa Fe, NM 87501
Ph: (505)986-1973 (505)982-5611
Free: (800)456-8863
Fax: (505)986-0997
E-mail: ccns@nuclearactive.org
URL: http://www.nuclearactive.org
Contact: Joni Arends, Exec. Dir.
Founded: 1988. **Membership Dues:** sustaining, $250-$1,000 (annual) ● supporting, $50-$100 (annual). **Description:** Works to provide public information about environmental and economic impact of production, handling, transportation, and disposal of radioactive materials. **Affiliated With:** Alliance for Nuclear Accountability. **Publications:** *New Mexico's Right to Know: The Impacts of the Los Alamos National Laboratory Operations on Public Health and the Environment.* Report. Alternate Formats: online ● *New Mexico's Right to Know: The Potential for Groundwater Contaminants from Los Alamos National Laboratory to Reach the Rio Grande.* Report. Alternate Formats: online.

17779 ■ Concerned Educators Allied for a Safe Environment (CEASE)
55 Frost St.
Cambridge, MA 02140
Ph: (617)661-8347
E-mail: info@peaceeducators.org
URL: http://www.peaceeducators.org
Contact: Lucy Stroock, Coor.
Founded: 1979. **Members:** 850. **Membership Dues:** regular, $10 (annual) ● student, $5 (annual) ● individual, $10 (annual). **State Groups:** 3. **Local Groups:** 4. **Description:** Early childhood educators and parents concerned with the danger of nuclear arms production, nuclear power, and the environmental consequences of nuclear war. Seeks to inform the public on issues involving nuclear warfare and peaceful alternatives. Works to aid in the redirection of funds allocated for the military to develop human service programs for children and their families. Offers college classes and parent groups. Has submitted petitions to congress to advocate funding for child day care programs instead of nuclear warfare and to toy manufacturers to protest the production of war toys. **Publications:** *Annual CEASE Packet,* annual. Bulletin. Information about activities, participation in NAEYC Annual Conference, informational fliers, and articles. **Price:** free for members. Alternate Formats: online ● *CEASE News,* annual. Newsletter. Reports member activities, opinions, articles, and reviews, resources and links with other like-minded organizations. **Price:** free for members. Alternate Formats: online. **Conventions/Meetings:** annual conference, held in conjunction with NAEYC ● annual meeting, planning ● workshop, held in conjunction with National Association for Education of Young Children.

17780 ■ Corporate Accountability International
46 Plympton St.
Boston, MA 02118
Ph: (617)695-2525
Free: (800)688-8797
Fax: (617)695-2626
E-mail: info@stopcorporateabuse.org
URL: http://www.stopcorporateabuse.org/cms/index. cfm?group_id=1000
Contact: Kathryn Mulvey, Exec. Dir.
Founded: 1977. **Members:** 25,000. **Membership Dues:** international, $25 (annual). **Staff:** 10. **Budget:**

$1,300,000. **Multinational. Description:** Works to expose life-threatening abuses by transnational corporations and organizing successful grassroots campaigns to hold corporations accountable to consumers and society at large. Conducts broad-based consumer campaigns and the Corporate Hall of Shame. **Departments:** Campaign; Development; International; Media; Research. **Formerly:** (2004) Infact. **Publications:** *Bringing GE to Light: How General Electric Shapes Nuclear Weapons Policies for Profits.* Book ● *Deadly Deception: General Electric, Nuclear Weapons and Our Environment.* Video. **Price:** $25.00 for individuals ● *Handbook for FCTC Ratification Campaigns* (in Arabic, English, French, and Spanish). Includes history and precedents of the global tobacco treaty. Alternate Formats: online ● *INFACT Update,* quarterly. **Price:** $25.00/ year. **Circulation:** 25,000 ● *Making A Killing: Philip Morris, Kraft, and Global Tobacco Addiction.* Video. **Price:** $25.00 for individual; $50.00 for nonprofit; $75.00 for institution ● *Toxics Report* ● Annual Report, annual. Alternate Formats: online. **Conventions/Meetings:** periodic regional meeting.

17781 ■ Downwinders
254 W 500 N
Malad City, ID 83252
Ph: (208)766-5649
E-mail: hermit@downwinders.org
URL: http://www.downwinders.org
Contact: Preston J. Truman, Dir.
Founded: 1978. **Multinational. Description:** Works to protect the rights of residents exposed to radioactive fallout, fights for immediate end to all nuclear testing. **Publications:** Articles.

17782 ■ Global Issues Resource Center (GIRC)
East 1, Cuyahoga Community Coll.
4250 Richmond Rd.
Cleveland, OH 44122
Ph: (216)987-2224
Fax: (216)987-2133
E-mail: joanne.lewis@tri-c.edu
URL: http://www.global-issues.org
Contact: Joanne M. Lewis, Founder/Dir.
Founded: 1985. **Members:** 150. **Staff:** 4. **Budget:** $150,000. **Description:** Works to provide balanced information on issues that threaten global security. Strives to bridge the information gap between experts and citizens. Conducts lectures and workshops; develops programs and curricula for teachers, community groups, and professional organizations. **Libraries: Type:** open to the public. **Holdings:** 2,000; audio recordings, books, clippings, periodicals, video recordings. **Subjects:** nuclear weapons, energy resources, arms control, international and interpersonal conflict resolution, environmental issues, global education. **Awards:** SIRS Peace Award. **Frequency:** annual. **Type:** monetary. **Recipient:** for one's role in the advancement of knowledge on the issues of international peace and security. **Computer Services:** Online services, CLEVNET. **Formerly:** (1994) Nuclear Age Resource Center. **Publications:** *Update,* quarterly. Newsletter. Alternate Formats: online.

17783 ■ Global Network Against Weapons and Nuclear Power in Space
c/o Bruce K. Gagnon, Sec./Coor.
PO Box 652
Brunswick, ME 04011
Ph: (207)443-9502
E-mail: globalnet@mindspring.com
URL: http://www.space4peace.org
Contact: Bruce K. Gagnon, Sec./Coor.
Founded: 1992. **Membership Dues:** individual, $10-$100 (annual). **Staff:** 1. **Budget:** $60,000. **Regional Groups:** 165. **Description:** Works against nuclearization and weaponization of space. **Awards:** Peace in Space Award. **Frequency:** annual. **Type:** recognition. **Also Known As:** Global Network. **Publications:** *Space Alert!,* quarterly. Newsletter. Alternate Formats: online. **Conventions/Meetings:** annual International Conference for Peace in Space.

17784 ■ Global Security Institute (GSI)
GSB Bldg., Ste.400
One Belmont Ave.
Bala Cynwyd, PA 19004
Ph: (610)668-5488
Fax: (610)668-5489
E-mail: info@gsinstitute.org
URL: http://www.gsinstitute.org
Contact: Jonathan Granoff, Pres.
Founded: 1999. **Staff:** 5. **Budget:** $700,000. **Languages:** English, French, German, Italian, Portuguese, Spanish. **Multinational. Description:** Works to promote steps that enhance security and lead to global elimination of nuclear weapons. **Awards:** Alan Cranston Peace Award. **Frequency:** annual. **Type:** recognition. **Recipient:** for leaders who demonstrated the principles for which Senator Cranston devoted his life. **Telecommunication Services:** electronic mail, granoff@gsinstitute.org. **Study Groups:** Bipartisan Security; Middle Powers Initiative; Parliamentary Network for Nuclear Disarmament. **Publications:** Newsletter, monthly. Alternate Formats: online ● Reports. Alternate Formats: online ● Papers. Alternate Formats: online.

17785 ■ Grandmothers for Peace International (GPI)
PO Box 580788
Elk Grove, CA 95758
Ph: (916)685-1130
E-mail: lorraine@grandmothersforpeace.org
URL: http://www.grandmothersforpeace.org
Contact: Lorraine Krofchok, Dir.
Founded: 1982. **Members:** 2,000. **Membership Dues:** senior, $15 (annual) ● men's auxiliary, regular, $25 (annual) ● sponsor, $100 (annual) ● family, $30 (annual) ● patron, $50 (annual). **Local Groups:** 1. **National Groups:** 11. **Multinational. Description:** Grandmothers and other individuals worldwide. Seeks an end to the nuclear arms race. Supports other "peace-loving groups which promote the elimination of all nuclear weapons and violence in our communities, our nation, and around the world." Encourages public involvement in campaigns against nuclear weapons, including vigils at military installations, armaments factories, and the Nevada nuclear weapons test site. Supports nonviolent resistance and efforts toward peaceful coexistence with all nations. Corresponds with women sharing similar beliefs worldwide. Favors development of peace curricula for use in secondary schools; provides educational programs on peace and human rights issues. Maintains speakers' bureau. **Awards:** Barbara Wiedner and Dorothy Vandercook Memorial Peace Scholarship. **Frequency:** annual. **Type:** scholarship. **Recipient:** for high school seniors or first year college students ● Peace and Justice Scholarship. **Frequency:** annual. **Type:** scholarship. **Recipient:** for high school seniors entering college. **Formerly:** (1991) Grandmothers for Peace. **Publications:** *Grandmothers for Peace Newsletter,* semiannual. Alternate Formats: online ● Also makes available buttons and t-shirts.

17786 ■ Institute for Space and Security Studies (ISSS)
5115 S A1A Hwy.
Melbourne, FL 32951
Ph: (407)952-0601
E-mail: isss@rmbowman.com
URL: http://rmbowman.com/isss
Contact: Dr. Robert Bowman, Pres.
Founded: 1983. **Members:** 8,500. **Staff:** 2. **Budget:** $70,000. **Description:** An independent organization devoted to research and educational activities in science and strategy relating to space and other high-technology areas. Works to prevent nuclear war and promotes comprehensive security. Seeks to educate the public and Congress about what ISSS feels is the truth about National Missile Defense (Star Wars), a partly space-based anti-satellite, anti-ballistic missile system being developed whereby enemy missiles can be shot down with energy weapons such as laser beams or impact weapons before they explode over American territory, and other proposed systems. Conducts research into the latest proposals for weap-

onizing space, and provides an independent, credible view of the alternatives to the American people, Congress, and the executive branch. Supports the use of space for early warning and communications, and for environmental monitoring. Promotes the application of space technology to energy and transportation, such as solar cars. Sponsors workshops, news conferences, congressional briefings, speeches, and television productions, and provides educational videotapes. **Libraries:** Type: reference; not open to the public. **Holdings:** 400; articles. **Subjects:** space, national security. **Computer Services:** database ● mailing lists. **Publications:** *Space and Security News*, quarterly. Newsletter. ISSN: 1071-2569. **Circulation:** 10,000. **Advertising:** accepted. Alternate Formats: online ● Annual Report ● Also publishes news releases, issue papers and briefs, articles, and books.

17787 ■ International Philosophers for the Prevention of Nuclear Omnicide (IPPNO)

c/o Ms. Shireen Parsons, Treas.
306 Miller St.
Christiansburg, VA 24073
E-mail: horizon@wsva.net
URL: http://www.radford.edu/~peace/ippno/who.html
Contact: Prof. Margit J. Horvath, Exec. Sec.
Founded: 1983. **Membership Dues:** regular, $30 (annual) ● student, individual from developing country, $10 (annual). **Description:** Philosophers and other professionals interested in the prevention of "omnicide", the ending of sentient life by humans. Seeks to bring the resources of philosophers to bear upon the problem of preventing omnicide; works to define and analyze the specifics of preventing omnicide through direct and responsible dialogue among philosophers of all countries. **Telecommunication Services:** electronic mail, nomads@golden.net. **Publications:** *IPPNO Newsletter*, periodic. Covers news of, and for, membership. **Price:** included in membership dues ● *Journal of International Dialogue*, quarterly ● Papers. **Conventions/Meetings:** conference, held nationally in conjunction with the American Philosophical Association ● biennial international conference ● workshop, held internationally in conjunction with the World Congress of Philosophy.

17788 ■ International Physicians for the Prevention of Nuclear War (IPPNW)

727 Massachusetts Ave.
Cambridge, MA 02139
Ph: (617)868-5050
Fax: (617)868-2560
E-mail: ippnwbos@ippnw.org
URL: http://www.ippnw.org
Contact: Michael Christ, Exec. Dir.
Founded: 1980. **Members:** 200,000. **Staff:** 12. **Budget:** $1,600,000. **Description:** Non-partisan, global Federation of National medical Organizations in more than 60 countries dedicated to research, education, and advocacy relevant to the prevention of nuclear war. Seeks to prevent all wars, to promote non-violent conflict resolution, and to minimize the effects of war and preparations for war on health, development, and the environment. Works toward the abolition of all nuclear weapons, demilitarization of the global economy, and an end to the arms trade. Seeks to reallocate resources from military to civilian needs, especially to basic health care and human necessities. Works on projects to end the threats posed by landmines, small arms and light weapons, chemical and biological weapons, and the burden of debt on developing nations. **Libraries:** Type: reference. **Holdings:** audiovisuals, books, clippings, periodicals. **Subjects:** peace, militarism, development, environment. **Departments:** Development; Program; Publications. **Publications:** *Abolition 2000: Handbook for a World Without Nuclear Weapons*. Contains useful facts and figures about arms control victories. **Price:** $10.00/issue ● *Affiliate Directory*, semiannual ● *Crude Nuclear Weapons: Proliferation and the Terrorist Threat Report* ● *Nuclear Wastelands*. Book. Features a global guide to nuclear weapon production and its health and environmental effects. **Price:** $55.00/issue ● *Opportunities for International Control of Weapons-Usable Fissile Materials*. Report ● *Pluto-*

nium: Deadly Gold of the Nuclear Age. Book. Examines the huge risks of plutonium. **Price:** $10.00/issue ● *Radioactive Heaven and Earth: The Health and Environmental Effects of Nuclear Weapons Testing In, On, and Above the Earth*. Report. Assesses the legacy of nuclear testing and its consequences. **Price:** $10.00/issue ● *Vital Signs*, quarterly. Newsletter. **Price:** $25.00/issue. **Circulation:** 30,000. Alternate Formats: online ● *The War in Nicaragua: The Effects of Low-Intensity Conflict on an Underdeveloped Country*. Report ● Annual Report. **Conventions/Meetings:** biennial congress, jointly organized by Physicians for Social Responsibility ● periodic regional meeting and symposium.

17789 ■ Lawyers Alliance for World Security (LAWS)

c/o Center for Defense Information
1779 Massachusetts Ave. NW
Washington, DC 20036-2109
Ph: (202)745-2450 (202)332-0600
Fax: (202)667-0444
E-mail: swelsh@cdi.org
URL: http://www.cdi.org/LAWS
Contact: Jack Mendelsohn, VP/Exec. Dir.
Founded: 1981. **Members:** 1,500. **Membership Dues:** $50 (annual). **Staff:** 4. **Budget:** $304,000. **Regional Groups:** 7. **State Groups:** 6. **Local Groups:** 1. **Description:** Judges, lawyers, law professors and students, paralegals, and other members of the legal profession. Seeks to educate members of the legal profession and others on the key issues of nuclear weapons policy including the history, successes, and weaknesses of previous arms control measures, and to establish arms control as the highest national priority; to elicit viable alternative proposals from the legal community for reducing the chances of a nuclear war while maintaining national security. Has conducted major symposia which featured internationally known experts in the field of nuclear arms and arms control from the U.S. and the former Soviet Union. Offers educational programs to train members to speak publicity on arms control issues; sponsors media appeals. **Libraries:** Type: reference. **Holdings:** archival material, books, clippings. **Subjects:** law and arms control, related groups and media sources. **Awards:** W. Averell Harriman Award. **Frequency:** annual. **Type:** recognition. **Recipient:** for significant contribution to the cause of peace. **Committees:** Comprehensive Test Ban Treaty; Law Professors Outreach; Lawyers Outreach. **Formerly:** (1990) Lawyers Alliance for Nuclear Arms Control. **Publications:** *Lawyers Alliance for World Security Newsletter*, quarterly ● *Reprints*, periodic ● Bibliographies ● Brochures ● Also publishes papers on the history and status of arms control, export controls, security assurances, treaties, and briefs and letters. **Conventions/Meetings:** semiannual conference ● annual W. Averell Harriman Award Dinner.

17790 ■ Lawyers' Committee on Nuclear Policy (LCNP)

675 Third Ave., Ste.315
New York, NY 10017
Ph: (212)818-1861
Fax: (212)818-1857
E-mail: lcnp@lcnp.org
URL: http://www.lcnp.org
Contact: John Burroughs, Exec. Dir.
Founded: 1981. **Members:** 2,500. **Membership Dues:** individual, $25 (annual) ● sustainer, $100 ● low income, $15. **Staff:** 4. **Description:** Lawyers, legal scholars and citizens dedicated to the abolition of nuclear weapons and war. Works to educate lawyers and the public on nuclear weapons and disarmament from the standpoint that nuclear weapons are illegal under existing international law. Maintains speakers' bureau; conducts research. Sponsors antinuclear litigation; conducts legal symposia; communicates with United Nations agencies concerned with disarmament and nuclear weapons. **Computer Services:** database. **Telecommunication Services:** electronic mail, johnburroughs@lcnp.org. **Affiliated With:** International Association of Lawyers Against Nuclear Arms. **Publications:** *Bombs Away*, semiannual. Newsletter.

Provides information on nuclear disarmament and international law. **Price:** $20.00 for nonmembers; included in membership dues. ISSN: 1059-6585. **Circulation:** 5,000. **Advertising:** accepted. Alternate Formats: online. Also Cited As: *LCNP Newsletter* ● *Ending the Nuclear Nightmare: A Strategy for the Bush Administration*. Article ● *The (IL) Legality of Threat or Use of Nuclear Weapons by John Burroughs*. Book. **Price:** $24.95 plus shipping and handling ● *International Law, the International Court of Justice and Nuclear Weapons*. Article ● *Rule of Power or Rule of Law?*. Book. Examines "U.S. undermining of multilateral treaty regimes from nuclear, chemical, and biological weapons to global warming to international justice". ● Reports. Alternate Formats: online ● Also distributes reprints of articles on arms control, nuclear disarmament, and the law. **Conventions/Meetings:** periodic workshop.

17791 ■ National No-Nukes Prison Support Collective (NNNPSC)

c/o Felice Cohen-Joppa, Co-Ed.
PO Box 43383
Tucson, AZ 85733
Ph: (520)323-8697
E-mail: nukeresister@igc.org
URL: http://www.serve.com/nukeresister
Contact: Felice Cohen-Joppa, Co-Ed.
Founded: 1980. **Members:** 800. **Membership Dues:** $15 (annual). **Staff:** 2. **Budget:** $35,000. **Multinational. Description:** Correspondents and newsletter subscribers who supply information and write to jailed anti-nuclear and anti-war activists. Maintains speakers' bureau. Compiles statistics and disseminates information about nationwide anti-nuclear and anti-war arrests. **Publications:** *Nuclear Resister: Information About and Support for Jailed and Imprisoned Anti-Nuclear Activists*, bimonthly. Newspaper. Covers anti-nuclear and anti-war civil disobedience in the U.S., with an emphasis on jailed and imprisoned anti-nuclear and anti-war activists. **Price:** included in membership dues; $15.00 /year for nonmembers. ISSN: 0883-9875. **Circulation:** 800. Alternate Formats: microform ● Brochures. **Conventions/Meetings:** periodic workshop, on nonviolent resistance to nuclear power and weapons.

17792 ■ Nevada Desert Experience (NDE)

1420 W Bartlett Ave.
Las Vegas, NV 89106-2226
Ph: (702)646-4814
E-mail: info@nevadadesertexperience.org
URL: http://www.nevadadesertexperience.org
Contact: Amy Schultz, Dir.
Founded: 1984. **Members:** 4,500. **Staff:** 4. **Budget:** $100,000. **Languages:** English, French. **Description:** Protests the nuclear arms race and testing of nuclear weapons. Sponsors: annual Lenten Desert Experience, a spring vigil characterized by fasting, praying, and nonviolent action and held at the Nevada Test Site; Peace Walk (65 miles) from Las Vegas to Nevada test site for Good Friday. Conducts other protest activities at the site throughout the year. Maintains speakers' bureau. **Formerly:** (1984) Lenten Desert Experience. **Publications:** *Desert Voices*, quarterly. Newsletter. Explores spiritual dimensions of nonviolence and the campaign to end nuclear testing. Includes news notes, poetry, and calendar of events. **Price:** free. **Circulation:** 4,600 ● *Nevada Desert Experience in the Nuclear Age*. Video.

17793 ■ Never Again Campaign

c/o Prof. Donald N. Lathrop, Coor.
Berkshire Community Coll.
1350 West St.
Pittsfield, MA 01201-5720
Ph: (413)499-4660
Fax: (413)447-7840
E-mail: dlathrop@berkshirecc.edu
Contact: Prof. Donald N. Lathrop, Coor.
Founded: 1985. **Multinational. Description:** Nonpolitical, nonpartisan volunteer organization. Seeks Japanese volunteers to spread the peace message of the atomic bomb survivors of Hiroshima and Nagasaki and to share Japanese culture with American and Canadian audiences in order to promote interna-

tional understanding. Locates families and groups in the United States and Canada to host Japanese volunteer speakers in their homes during the program. (Japanese volunteers pay for their own transportation to and from the United States as well as any personal or medical expenses; American host families provide free room and board for up to six months.) Japanese volunteers use documentary films, videos, and slides to provide information about Hiroshima and Nagasaki. Volunteers also present and demonstrate such Japanese cultural activities as origami, traditional songs and instrumental music, dance, tea ceremonies, and martial arts. **Convention/Meeting:** none. **Publications:** Brochure. Describes the purpose, activities, origins, and funding of the Never Again Campaign.

17794 ■ Nuclear Control Institute (NCI)
1000 Connecticut Ave. NW, Ste.400
Washington, DC 20036
Ph: (202)822-8444
Fax: (202)452-0892
E-mail: mail@nci.org
URL: http://www.nci.org
Contact: Paul Leventhal, Pres./Founder
Founded: 1981. **Staff:** 6. **Description:** Citizens concerned with the proliferation of nuclear weapons. Objectives are to: alert the public, Congress, and public interest groups to U.S. and foreign nuclear programs that promote the spread of nuclear weapons; propose positive alternatives to proliferation-prone nuclear policies; monitor nuclear programs worldwide; develop grass roots support for strategies to ban all commerce in nuclear weapons materials worldwide. Maintains reference library containing files on all countries with nuclear power and research programs. **Formerly:** (1982) Nuclear Club. **Publications:** Brochures ● Pamphlets.

17795 ■ Nuclear Threat Initiative (NTI)
1747 Pennsylvania Ave. NW, 7th Fl.
Washington, DC 20006
Ph: (202)296-4810
Fax: (202)296-4811
E-mail: contact@nti.org
URL: http://www.nti.org
Contact: Charles B. Curtis, Pres./COO
Founded: 2001. **Description:** Works to strengthen the global security by reducing the risk of use and preventing the spread of nuclear, biological, and chemical weapons. **Libraries: Type:** reference. **Holdings:** papers, reports. **Subjects:** global security. **Awards: Type:** grant. **Computer Services:** database, nonproliferation. **Programs:** Biological; Communications and Education; Regional; Russia/New Independent States; United States. **Publications:** Annual Report, annual.

17796 ■ Nuclear Threat Reduction Campaign (NTRC)
c/o Vietnam Veterans of America Foundation
1025 Vermont Ave. NW, 7th Fl.
Washington, DC 20006-2412
Ph: (202)638-5855 (202)483-9222
Fax: (202)483-9312
E-mail: ntrc@vi.org
URL: http://www.vvaf.org/programs/ntrc
Contact: Brian D. Finlay, Dir.
Founded: 2001. **Description:** Works to mitigate threats associated with weapons of mass destruction, nuclear and biological materials, and weapons expertise.

17797 ■ Peace Action
1100 Wayne Ave., Ste.1020
Silver Spring, MD 20910
Ph: (301)565-4050
Fax: (301)565-0850
E-mail: kmartin@peace-action.org
URL: http://www.peace-action.org
Contact: Kevin Martin, Exec. Dir.
Founded: 1957. **Members:** 90,000. **Membership Dues:** individual, $35 (annual) ● family, $52 (annual) ● partner for peace, $250 (annual). **Staff:** 14. **Budget:** $1,000,000. **State Groups:** 28. **Local Groups:** 150. **Description:** Seeks a comprehensive nuclear

test ban treaty, an end to the global arms trade, deep reductions in nuclear weapons and U.S. military intervention abroad, and a shift in federal priorities from military to human needs. Lobbies on Capitol Hill and coordinates grassroots lobbying by members. **Formed by Merger of:** (1987) Committee for a SANE Nuclear Policy; (1987) Nuclear Weapons Freeze Campaign. **Formerly:** (1988) SANE/FREEZE: Campaign for Global Security. **Publications:** Action Report, quarterly. Newsletter. Covers nuclear disarmament, arms control, military intervention, legislative news on military budget, and other arms issues. ISSN: 0036-4304. **Circulation:** 70,000 ● Grassroots Organizer, semimonthly. Newsletter. Provides organizing ideas and legislative information. **Price:** $40.00/year. **Circulation:** 200 ● Pamphlets. **Conventions/Meetings:** annual conference, for members, activists, supporters (exhibits).

17798 ■ Peace Action Education Fund (PAEF)
1100 Wayne Ave., Ste.1020
Silver Spring, MD 20910-5643
Ph: (301)565-4050
Fax: (301)565-0850
E-mail: kmartin@peace-action.org
URL: http://www.peace-action.org/edfund.html
Contact: Kevin Martin, Exec. Dir.
Founded: 1987. **Staff:** 5. **Budget:** $400,000. **Description:** Aims to conduct educational activities on the political, economic, and environmental consequences of the arms race and to explore peaceful alternatives to the arms race. Maintains peace program which examines the harmful effects of excessive military spending and the need for economic conversion planning. Operates Disarmament and Arm Trade Campaign which aims to reduce nuclear arms and international trade of weapons. **Affiliated With:** Peace Action. **Formerly:** (1993) SANE/FREEZE Education Fund. **Publications:** Peace Action/Peace Educational Fund, quarterly. Newsletter. ISSN: 0036-4304. **Circulation:** 40,000 ● Publishes fact sheets and briefing papers.

17799 ■ Peace Pac (PP)
c/o Council for a Livable World
322 4th St. NE
Washington, DC 20002
Ph: (202)543-4100
E-mail: clw@clw.org
URL: http://www.clw.org
Contact: Beth Cohen DeGrasse, Accounting Exec. Dir.
Founded: 1982. **Description:** Grass roots political action committee. Aims to elect a Congress committed to prevention of nuclear war. Supports candidates for the U.S. House of Representatives who are committed to specific nuclear arms control measures and the prevention of nuclear war, recognizing the importance of the House on measures to freeze nuclear arms and military spending. Conducts research and reviews congressional races to choose appropriate candidates for support, regardless of party; provides approved candidates with campaign contributions, research and speech material, and organizational support in reaching and organizing constituents. **Affiliated With:** Council for a Livable World. **Publications:** Peace Pac—Congressional Update, quarterly. Newsletter. Includes calendar of events, reports on organization news, and research news. ● Peace Pac—Election Report, periodic.

17800 ■ Physicians for Social Responsibility (PSR)
1875 Connecticut Ave. NW, Ste.1012
Washington, DC 20009
Ph: (202)667-4260 (202)587-5225
Fax: (202)667-4201
E-mail: psrnatl@psr.org
URL: http://www.psr.org
Contact: Mike McCally, Exec. Dir.
Founded: 1961. **Members:** 15,000. **Membership Dues:** sponsoring, $125 (annual) ● supporting, $50 (annual) ● retired, $35 (annual) ● student, $15 (annual). **Staff:** 15. **Budget:** $3,000,000. **Local Groups:** 65. **Description:** Medical professionals and others

with doctoral degrees and medical students concerned with the threat of nuclear war, environmental degradation, and violence in the society; others supporting the work of PSR. Educates the public on the medical effects of nuclear war and nuclear weapons and on the implications of national policy and legislative actions on arms control and environmental issues. Conducts media outreach and voter education programs. Supports the negotiation of comprehensive test ban treaty and opposes nuclear attack-related civilian defense. Engages in lobbying; researches legislative alternatives and disseminates legislative information. **Awards: Type:** recognition. **Committees:** Chapter Development; Environment; International; Policy and Legislation. **Task Forces:** Health Risks of Nuclear Weapons Production. **Affiliated With:** International Physicians for the Prevention of Nuclear War. **Publications:** Briefing Papers, periodic ● PSR Report, quarterly. Newsletter. Informs the public of the medical consequences of nuclear war and the testing of nuclear weapons. Focuses on environmental issues and disarmament. **Price:** included in membership dues. **Circulation:** 3,000. **Conventions/Meetings:** periodic regional meeting.

17801 ■ Progressive Foundation (PF)
PO Box 649
Luck, WI 54853-0649
Ph: (715)472-4185
Fax: (715)472-4184
E-mail: nukewatch@lakeland.ws
URL: http://www.nukewatch.com
Contact: Bonnie Urfer, Co-Dir.
Founded: 1979. **Members:** 2,300. **Membership Dues:** regular, $25 (annual). **Staff:** 3. **Budget:** $60,000. **Description:** Works to promote awareness and debate on issues of public concern. Focuses on the dangers of nuclear power and weapons, nuclear waste, ionizing radiation, the nuclear industry, and the chilling effect of nuclear secrecy that prevents informed public decision-making on arms and energy issues. Maintains speakers' bureau. Sponsors Nukewatch, a public education and non-violent action project. **Libraries: Type:** open to the public. **Holdings:** 100. **Subjects:** nuclear industry, weapons statistics, radioactive waste. **Affiliated With:** Nukewatch. **Publications:** Crossing the Line. Book. **Price:** $15.00 each. **Circulation:** 3,000 ● Nuclear Heartland: A Guide to the 1000 Missile Sites of the United States. Book. **Price:** $40.00 each ● The Pathfinder, quarterly. Newsletter. Alternate Formats: online ● Prisoners on Purpose: A Peacemaker's Guide to Jails and Prisons. Book. **Price:** $10.00 each ● Radioactive Waste: No End in Sight. Booklet. **Price:** $2.00 each. **Conventions/Meetings:** symposium, on nuclear issues.

17802 ■ Psychologists for Social Responsibility (PsySR)
208 I St. NE
Washington, DC 20002-4340
Ph: (202)543-5347
Fax: (202)543-5348
E-mail: psysr@psysr.org
URL: http://www.psysr.org
Contact: Colleen Cordes, Exec. Dir.
Founded: 1982. **Members:** 2,000. **Membership Dues:** regular, $45 (annual) ● student, $15 (annual) ● limited income, $20 (annual) ● life, $1,000. **Staff:** 1. **Budget:** $50,000. **State Groups:** 20. **Local Groups:** 30. **Description:** Represents psychologists who participate in the antinuclear arms movement. Seeks to develop psychologically sound alternatives to the arms race. Promotes research in arms control; sponsors workshops and public forums for discussion of alternatives to the arms race and private discussion sessions; takes part in demonstrations; compiles reading lists. Maintains speakers' bureau. **Awards: Type:** recognition. **Telecommunication Services:** electronic mail, ccordes@psysr.org. **Task Forces:** Briefing Papers; Curriculum; Research. **Publications:** Dismantling the Mask of Enmity: An Educational Resource Manual on the Psychology of Enemy Images ● Psychologists for Social Responsibility—Newsletter, quarterly. Includes membership news and psychological analysis of the arms race;

also includes book reviews, regional news, and resources. **Price:** included in membership dues. **Circulation:** 1,000 ● *Research Directory*, annual. **Price:** $18.00. **Conventions/Meetings:** annual meeting, in conjunction with American Psychological Association.

17803 ■ Students for Social Responsibility (SSR)
c/o Student Center
450 Clarkson Ave.
PO Box 3010
Brooklyn, NY 11203-2098
Ph: (718)270-3160
URL: http://www.downstate.edu/sc/student%20organizations/studentorgs/organ29.html
Founded: 1977. **Members:** 24. **Description:** College and university students. Works to promote nuclear disarmament and world peace. Holds seminars on nuclear issues; sponsors public awareness campaigns. Maintains speakers' bureau and library of 350 peace-related monographs. Conducts research and educational programs on the environmental impact of offshore drilling. Sponsors charitable program and symposia; bestows Peace Teacher Award. **Computer Services:** database, membership list ● mailing lists. **Publications:** Bulletin, annual. **Conventions/Meetings:** annual meeting ● weekly meeting, action planning.

17804 ■ UrgentCall.org
c/o Institute for Defense and Disarmament Studies
675 Massachusetts Ave.
Cambridge, MA 02139
Ph: (617)354-4337
Fax: (617)354-1450
E-mail: forsberg@urgentcall.org
URL: http://www.idds.org/EDUrgentcall.html
Contact: Randall Caroline Forsberg PhD, Dir.
Founded: 2002. **Description:** Committed to changing U.S. military and foreign policy to promote national security. **Affiliated With:** Institute for Defense and Disarmament Studies; Nation Institute.

17805 ■ WAND Education Fund (WAND EF)
691 Massachusetts Ave.
Arlington, MA 02476
Ph: (781)643-6740
Fax: (781)643-6744
E-mail: peace@wand.org
URL: http://www.wand.org/wand_edfund_home.htm
Contact: Susan Shaer, Exec. Dir.
Founded: 1982. **Staff:** 6. **Budget:** $162,500. **Description:** Seeks to improve public understanding of nuclear disarmament and other military issues. Sponsors lectures on nuclear disarmament and national security. Works to enhance the political influence of women in the U.S. Promotes registration of female voters. Maintains Speakers' Bureau. **Awards: Type:** recognition. **Affiliated With:** Women's Action for New Directions. **Publications:** Brochures ● Manuals ● Also publishes fact sheet. **Conventions/Meetings:** workshop, on developing skill in speaking, lobbying, and grass roots organizing.

17806 ■ Women's Action for New Directions (WAND)
691 Massachusetts Ave.
Arlington, MA 02476
Ph: (781)643-6740
Fax: (781)643-6744
E-mail: info@wand.org
URL: http://www.wand.org
Contact: Susan Shaer, Exec. Dir.
Founded: 1982. **Members:** 2,500. **Membership Dues:** standard, $35 (annual). **Staff:** 14. **Budget:** $211,000. **Local Groups:** 12. **Description:** Women's initiative uniting women and men in an effort to halt and reverse the nuclear arms race and redirect spending to meet human and environmental needs. Works to empower women to act politically; to raise public awareness about nuclear issues; to support grass roots organizing for educational and political activities across the country; to monitor legislative activities that have an impact on nuclear weapons policy; to organize congressional district lobbying networks to be mobilized before key nuclear weapons

votes. Compiles statistics; has established WAND Education Fund. **Libraries: Type:** reference. **Holdings:** audiovisuals. **Subjects:** nuclear war, civil defense, nuclear weapons, testing, military budget, landmines. **Telecommunication Services:** electronic mail, shaer@wand.org. **Affiliated With:** WAND Education Fund. **Formerly:** Women's Party for Survival; (1992) Women's Action for Nuclear Disarmament. **Publications:** *WAND Bulletin*, quarterly. **Price:** $35.00/year. Alternate Formats: online ● Offers fact sheets and publications on issues of nuclear arms, the federal budget and effective organizing and lobbying. **Conventions/Meetings:** workshop.

17807 ■ World Peacemakers (WP)
11427 Scottsbury Terr.
Germantown, MD 20876-6010
Ph: (301)972-4041
E-mail: worldpeacemakers@worldpeacemakers.org
URL: http://www.worldpeacemakers.org
Contact: Dr. William J. Price, Dir.
Founded: 1978. **Budget:** $20,000. **Regional Groups:** 75. **Description:** Promotes an understanding of what true security is and how to move toward it. Emphasizes the ethical, spiritual, economic, and political dimensions of the "growing threat of nuclear war and the overall degradation of our security as the arms race continues." Works to increase public understanding of the "unprecedented dangers" facing mankind and publicize the need for the U.S. to stop the arms race and concentrate on solving global problems such as unemployment and the protection of cities and rural communities. Activities include developing a network of peacemaking groups to pursue peace by questioning the war system and offering alternatives. Provides speakers for workshops and seminars on disarmament. **Libraries: Type:** reference. **Holdings:** 200. **Also Known As:** World Peacemakers - A Division of Every Church A Peace Church. **Publications:** *World Peace Papers* ● *World Peacemaker Quarterly*. Newsletter ● Also publishes pamphlets and handbook; offers cassettes. **Conventions/Meetings:** Peace One Day through Small Peace Groups - workshop, for small Inward/Outward Journey Leaders.

Obesity

17808 ■ Largely Positive
c/o Carol A. Johnson, MA, Founder/Pres.
PO Box 170223
Milwaukee, WI 53217-8021
Ph: (414)299-9295
Fax: (414)224-0243
E-mail: carol@largelypositive.com
URL: http://www.largelypositive.com
Contact: Carol A. Johnson MA, Founder/Pres.
Description: Promotes health and self-esteem for individuals of all sizes. **Publications:** *On A Positive Note*, quarterly. Newsletter. **Price:** free. Alternate Formats: online ● *Self-esteem Comes in All Sizes*. Book. **Price:** $15.00 plus shipping and handling for US destinations; $18.00 plus shipping and handling for Canadian destinations; $22.00 plus shipping and handling for other foreign destinations ● *Starting a Largely Positive Discussion Group*. Manual. **Price:** $15.00 plus shipping and handling for US destinations; $18.00 plus shipping and handling for Canadian destinations; $22.00 plus shipping and handling for other foreign destinations.

Pacific

17809 ■ Pacifica Foundation (PF)
1925 Martin Luther King Jr. Way
Berkeley, CA 94704
Ph: (510)849-2590
E-mail: contact@pacifica.org
URL: http://www.pacifica.org
Contact: Greg Guma, Exec. Dir.
Founded: 1946. **Members:** 75,000. **Staff:** 150. **Budget:** $10,500,000. **Description:** Aims to: "contribute to lasting understanding between nations and be-

tween individuals; promote the study of political and economic problems and of causes of religious, philosophical, and racial antagonisms; obtain access to sources of news not commonly brought together in the same medium and to employ such varied sources in the public presentation of accurate, objective, and comprehensive news on all matters vitally affecting the community." The Pacifica Program Service and Radio Archives supplies programs to schools, organizations, radio stations, and individuals. **Computer Services:** Mailing lists. **Publications:** *Program Folio*, monthly. Serves as a program guide published by each station. ● *Tape Brochures*, monthly ● *Tape Catalog*, semiannual ● Reports.

Parents

17810 ■ Father Matters
PO Box 612473
San Jose, CA 95161-2473
Free: (888)648-0718
E-mail: fathermatters@hotmail.com
URL: http://www.fathermatters.com
Contact: Vance Simms, Founder/CEO
Founded: 1997. **Description:** Seeks to make fathers more effective, more active and more involved in their role as fathers. Provides an opportunity for fathers to commit to encouragement, support and accountability with other fathers, as well as themselves. **Telecommunication Services:** electronic mail, vjsimms@yahoo.com. **Programs:** Young Adult/Teen Dad. **Publications:** *Father Matters Newsgram*. Newsletter.

17811 ■ National Center for Fathering (NCF)
PO Box 413888
Kansas City, MO 64141
Ph: (913)384-4661
Free: (800)593-DADS
Fax: (913)384-4665
E-mail: dads@fathers.com
URL: http://www.fathers.com
Contact: Ken R. Canfield PhD, Founder/Pres.
Founded: 1990. **Staff:** 17. **Budget:** $2,000,000. **Multinational. Description:** Inspires and equips men to be better fathers. **Publications:** *fathers.com*, weekly. Offers challenging perspectives and concrete actions for becoming a better father. **Price:** free. Alternate Formats: online ● *Today's Father*, semiannual. Features practical tips for dads. **Price:** $15.00 in U.S.; $20.00 in Canada and Mexico. **Conventions/Meetings:** seminar.

17812 ■ Slowlane/Stay At Home Dads (SAHD)
c/o Jay Massey, Admin.
1216 E Lee St.
Pensacola, FL 32503
Ph: (850)434-2626
Fax: (850)434-7937
E-mail: jay@slowlane.com
URL: http://www.slowlane.com
Contact: Jay Massey, Admin.
Founded: 1997. **Description:** Helps dads connect with other dads in their community and around the world. Compiles collection of online resources and references dealing with issues of fathering, family and being a stay-at-home dad. Helps support not-for-profit web sites for stay-at-home dad groups and organizations. **Publications:** Articles. Alternate Formats: online ● Books.

17813 ■ Welfare Warriors
2711 W Michigan Ave.
Milwaukee, WI 53208
Ph: (414)342-6662
Fax: (414)342-6667
E-mail: wmvoice@execpc.com
URL: http://www.welfarewarriors.org
Contact: Pat Gowens, Dir.
Founded: 1986. **Members:** 500. **Membership Dues:** regular, $15 (annual). **Staff:** 3. **Budget:** $50,000. **Local Groups:** 1. **Languages:** English, Spanish. **Multinational. Description:** Works to create a voice for mothers and children in poverty to fight for economic justice. **Publications:** *Mother Warriors Voice* (in

English and Spanish), quarterly. Newspaper. Features Mother Warriors report on activism worldwide and mother's stories. **Price:** $15.00 /year for individuals; $25.00 /year for institutions; $5.00/year for victims of poverty. **Circulation:** 17,000. **Advertising:** accepted. Alternate Formats: online. **Conventions/Meetings:** monthly Forum - meeting - every 2nd Wednesday.

Parks and Recreation

17814 ■ City Parks Alliance (CPA)
1111 16th St. NW, Ste.310
Washington, DC 20036
Ph: (202)223-9111
Fax: (202)223-9112
E-mail: info@cityparksalliance.org
URL: http://www.cityparksalliance.org
Contact: Catherine Nagel, Exec. Dir.
Founded: 2002. **Membership Dues:** individual, $50-$250 ● group, $50-$2,500 ● foundation, $2,500. **Description:** Organizes, builds and enhances a national network of city parks groups throughout the country. Shares information on best practices and creative public-private partnerships. Advocates for greater federal, state and municipal funding of city parks. Collects, disseminates and promotes information that makes the case for greater investment in city parks. **Publications:** *Benchmarks*, quarterly. Newsletter. **Price:** included in membership dues. Alternate Formats: online.

Patriotism

17815 ■ National Congress of Patriotic Organizations (NCPO)
c/o James A. McCafferty, Pres.
613 Rosier Rd.
Fort Washington, MD 20744-5554
E-mail: jirma@aol.com
Contact: James A. McCafferty, Pres.
Founded: 1990. **Membership Dues:** individual fellow, $10 (annual) ● life, $100. **Description:** Represents patriotic and heredity institutions and individuals who believe in and uphold the Declaration of Independence and the Constitution of the U.S. **Conventions/Meetings:** annual meeting.

17816 ■ Patriots for the Defense of America
527 3rd Ave., No. 239
New York, NY 10016
E-mail: info@defenseofamerica.org
Contact: Jason Crawford, Pres./Founder/Chm.
Founded: 2001. **Description:** Promotes "America's sovereign right to self-defense." Founded on the ideals that "freedom is the political ideal; all forms of tyranny are evil; America is a great nation, based on the values of freedom, productivity and happiness; tyranny is the greatest threat to the free world, the cause of war and of terrorism; a free nation has the right and responsibility of self-defense against foreign threats; a free nation has the right and responsibility to act alone in its defense; a free nation must not compromise with, negotiate, or appease dictatorships and other forms of tyranny.". **Computer Services:** Online services, facts & ideas center, patriots center. **Telecommunication Services:** electronic mail, president@defenseofamerica.org ● electronic mail, member-inquiry@defenseofamerica.org. **Sections:** News & Analysis.

Peace

17817 ■ A. J. Muste Memorial Institute
339 Lafayette St.
New York, NY 10012
Ph: (212)533-4335
Fax: (212)228-6193
E-mail: info@ajmuste.org
URL: http://www.ajmuste.org
Contact: Murray Rosenblith, Exec. Dir.
Staff: 2. **Languages:** English, Spanish. **Multinational. Description:** Works to keep the legacy of

U.S. pacifist leader A.J. Muste alive through ongoing support of the nonviolent movement for social change. Provides grants and sponsorships to grassroots groups throughout the U.S. and the world, and provides subsidized office space to social justice organizations. **Awards:** International Nonviolence Training Grant. **Type:** grant. **Recipient:** for US residents or within native nations in US ● Small Grants Program. **Frequency:** quarterly. **Type:** grant. **Funds:** International Nonviolence Training. **Programs:** Freeman Internship. **Publications:** *Essay Series* (in English and Spanish). Pamphlets. Contains historical and contemporary essays on issues of social change. **Price:** $2.00/copy; $1.40 each (for 20 or more copies) ● *Muste Notes*, quarterly. Newsletter. Contains information about the work of the A.J. Muste Memorial Institute. Alternate Formats: online.

17818 ■ Academy for Peace Research (APR)
PO Box 514
Soquel, CA 95073-0514
Ph: (831)425-3324
Contact: Dr. Buryl Payne, Pres./Founder
Founded: 1982. **Members:** 100. **Staff:** 4. **Budget:** $18,000. **Description:** Seeks to educate the public about peace, causes of war, and alternative methods of conflict resolution; conducts educational, scientific, cultural, and charitable activities aimed at enhancing the likelihood of peace. Offers consultation services to organizations and individuals developing creative solutions to social problems and issues. Organizes world meditations for healing the planet. **Libraries: Type:** open to the public. **Subjects:** solar activity predictions. **Committees:** Research. **Conventions/Meetings:** annual conference.

17819 ■ American Committee for Peace In Chechnya (ACPC)
1319 18th St. NW
Washington, DC 20036
Ph: (202)296-2861
Fax: (202)296-3980
E-mail: acpc@peaceinchechnya.org
URL: http://rightweb.irc-online.org/profile/1429
Contact: Glen E. Howard, Exec. Dir.
Founded: 1999. **Multinational. Description:** Promotes peaceful resolution to the Russo-Chechen war. Advocates the advancement of public awareness of the Chechen war, including its broader implications for democracy, human rights, and regional stability in the former Soviet Union. Organizes educational programs for the public and develops policy recommendations for lawmakers. Operates speakers' bureau. **Publications:** *Chechnya's Suicide Bombers: Desperate, Devout, or Deceived*. Report. Contains information on suicide terrorism. Alternate Formats: online.

17820 ■ Athletes United for Peace (AUP)
712 Peralta Ave.
Berkeley, CA 94707
Ph: (510)273-9235
E-mail: dharris@athletesunitedforpeace.org
URL: http://www.athletesunitedforpeace.org
Contact: Dr. Phil Shinnick, Chm.
Founded: 1982. **Members:** 300. **Budget:** $50,000. **Local Groups:** 3. **Description:** Professional and amateur athletes and athletic advisers interested in promoting sports, health, and athletics as a means for peace and friendship. Seeks to: promote peaceful, controlled competition between the U.S., USSR, and other countries; demonstrate, by sports exchanges and related activities, that through athletic competition, athletes form common bonds that lead to cooperation and respect for differences; uphold the two basic principles of the Olympic Charter, which are the promotion of physical and moral qualities that are the basis of sport, and the education of young people, through sport, regarding mutual understanding and friendship, thereby creating a more peaceful world. Works for the cause of peace through: sponsoring radio, television, and public service peace athletic activity announcements; cooperating with public officials; visiting and lecturing at schools, community centers, and civic organizations; attending social functions, benefits, and athletic activities.

Sponsors competitions. Operates children's services; maintains speakers' bureau. **Computer Services:** Mailing lists. **Committees:** Nicaraguan; Soviet. **Publications:** *Athletes United for Peace—Newsletter*, semiannual. Includes program calendar of events for team participation in sports in foreign countries and book reviews. **Price:** included in membership dues. **Circulation:** 2,000 ● Also publishes brochure.

17821 ■ Baptist Peace Fellowship of North America (BPFNA)
4800 Wedgewood Dr.
Charlotte, NC 28210
Ph: (704)521-6051
Fax: (704)521-6053
E-mail: gary@bpfna.org
URL: http://www.bpfna.org
Contact: Wendy Scott, Pres.
Founded: 1984. **Members:** 2,000. **Membership Dues:** low income and student, $15 (annual) ● individual, $30 (annual) ● family/household, $40 (annual) ● church/institution, $50 (annual). **Staff:** 7. **Budget:** $360,000. **Description:** Baptists from various conventions interested in focusing attention on peace and justice issues. Conducts educational and charitable programs; offers programs on conflict transformation, Jubilee economics, and restorative justice. **Publications:** *Baptist Peacemaker*, quarterly. Journal. Contains articles on peace and justice issues. **Price:** free. ISSN: 0735-5815. **Circulation:** 8,000. **Advertising:** accepted ● *Peace Primer: Quotes from Christian and Islamic Scripture and Tradition*. Book. Contains collection of quotes on justice and peace from the Qur'an, the Bible and other Islamic and Christian sources. **Price:** $3.50 ● *Peacework*, bimonthly. Newsletter. **Price:** included in membership dues. **Circulation:** 2,000 ● *Pursuing Justice: A social justice curriculum for churches*. Book ● *Recipe for Peacemaking*. Book ● *Rightly Dividing the Word of Truth: a resource for congregations in dialogue on sexual orientation*. Book. **Price:** $25.00 in U.S.; $36.00 outside U.S. ● Also publishes Bible studies; makes available posters, worship resources; position statements on various current issues. **Conventions/Meetings:** annual Peace Camp - conference, gathering for all concerned with peace and justice issues (exhibits).

17822 ■ Boise Peace Quilt Project (BPQP)
PO Box 6469
Boise, ID 83707
Ph: (208)378-0293 (208)384-1155
E-mail: email@dotster.com
URL: http://www.boisepeacequilt.org
Founded: 1981. **Members:** 50. **Staff:** 2. **Budget:** $12,000. **Description:** Individuals working to produce peace quilts as gestures of international goodwill and as awards for peacemakers; local project has produced Soviet friendship quilts sent to the national Soviet Women's Committee as a symbol of goodwill, hope, and peace; a joint Soviet-American Peace Quilt was made in cooperation with Soviet women and presented at the bilateral arms talks in Geneva, Switzerland. Sponsors the National Peace Quilt Project, a patchwork quilt made with 50 squares (one representing each state) based on children's drawings. Provides quilting training; maintains a "peace bank" of information on peacemakers who have been nominated to receive peace quilts. Provides speakers for adult and youth audiences. **Awards:** Peace Quilt Award. **Type:** recognition. **Recipient:** for peacemakers. **Publications:** *A Stitch for Time*. Video ● *How to Start a Peace Quilt Project in Your Own Community* ● Also produces greeting cards, postcards, and posters. **Conventions/Meetings:** weekly meeting, quilting ● workshop.

17823 ■ Buddhist Peace Fellowship (BPF)
PO Box 3470
Berkeley, CA 94703
Ph: (510)655-6169
Fax: (510)655-1369
E-mail: maia@bpf.org
URL: http://www.bpf.org
Contact: Maia Duerr, Exec. Dir.
Founded: 1978. **Members:** 4,500. **Membership Dues:** low income, $20 (annual) ● individual, $45

(annual) ● international, $55 (annual) ● low income (international), $30 (annual). **Staff:** 8. **Budget:** $400,000. **Regional Groups:** 43. **Description:** Devoted to the cultivation of worldwide peace, social justice, nonviolence, and environmental activism. Objectives include witnessing to the Buddhist commitment to nonviolence as a means of social change, and promoting national and international Buddhist peace projects. Members' work in disarmament and environmental campaigns, and provide support for homeless people and Buddhist prisoners. Supports peace and relief efforts worldwide. **Awards:** Young Writers Award. **Frequency:** annual. **Type:** recognition. **Recipient:** for writers 30 years old or younger. **Boards:** International Advisory. **Committees:** Buddhist Alliance for Social Engagement. **Programs:** Prison. **Affiliated With:** Fellowship of Reconciliation - USA; International Fellowship of Reconciliation - Netherlands. **Publications:** *Turning Wheel*, quarterly. Journal. Contains issues on peace, social justice and environmental activism. **Price:** included in membership dues. ISSN: 1065-058X. **Circulation:** 6,500. **Advertising:** accepted. Alternate Formats: online ● Also publishes texts on the historical and scriptural roots of Buddhist activism. **Conventions/Meetings:** annual conference.

17824 ■ Catholic Peace Fellowship (CPF)
PO Box 4232
South Bend, IN 46634
Ph: (574)232-2295
E-mail: staff@catholicpeacefellowship.org
URL: http://www.catholicpeacefellowship.org
Contact: Fr. Michael J. Baxter CSE, Natl. Sec.
Founded: 1964. **Members:** 3,000. **Staff:** 4. **Regional Groups:** 4. **Local Groups:** 10. **Description:** Represents Catholics including laity, priests, nuns, seminarians, teachers, and students (graduate and undergraduate) who are involved in peace and justice work. Seeks to initiate educational and action programs for peace and social change and to acquaint the American Catholic community with the teaching of the Roman Catholic Church in regards to war, peace, and conscience. Counsels conscientious objectors, particularly Catholic objectors and resisters. Promotes disarmament and civil disobedience. Maintains a small library. **Computer Services:** Mailing lists. **Affiliated With:** Fellowship of Reconciliation - USA. **Publications:** *The Sign of Peace*, quarterly. Journal. Includes theological articles on war, peace and conscience; practical information on the military; reflection on Church teaching and tradition, etc. **Price:** $20.00 donation per year. ISSN: 0008-8277. **Circulation:** 2,000. Alternate Formats: online ● Also publishes booklets and reprints. **Conventions/Meetings:** annual conference ● annual retreat - in spring ● annual Summer Institute - meeting - one week.

17825 ■ Center for Campus Organizing (CCO)
Box 748
Cambridge, MA 02142
Ph: (617)354-9363
E-mail: cco@igc.apc.org
URL: http://organizenow.net/cco
Contact: Bill Capowski, Exec. Dir.
Founded: 1991. **Members:** 750. **Membership Dues:** individual, $25 (annual) ● student activist, $20 (annual). **Staff:** 2. **Budget:** $200,000. **Local Groups:** 500. **Description:** Promotes progressive activism and investigative journalism on campus; seeks to help students examine right-wing and military funding; develops resources to challenge military, right wing, and corporate influence on campus and to promote socially responsible alternatives. Offers a 16-page "Campus Organizing Guide for Peace and Justice Groups" ($1), "Guide to Uncovering the Right on Campus" ($7), and other resources. Conducts educational programs. **Libraries:** Type: reference. **Holdings:** 250; books, periodicals. **Subjects:** military funding and influence on academia and society. **Awards:** Campus Alternative Journalism Award. **Frequency:** annual. **Type:** monetary. **Publications:** *Infusion: The National Magazine of Progressive Student Activism*, bimonthly. Bulletin. **Price:** $25.00 /year for

individuals; $35.00 /year for institutions. ISSN: 1084-659X. **Circulation:** 1,000. **Advertising:** accepted.

17826 ■ Children as the Peacemakers (CATP)
1243 Lago Vista Dr.
Beverly Hills, CA 90210
Ph: (310)859-1325
E-mail: info@peace-kids.org
URL: http://www.peace-kids.org
Contact: Patricia Montandon, Founder/Pres.
Founded: 1982. **Members:** 4,000. **Staff:** 4. **Description:** Individuals interested in fostering world peace through cultural exchange. Makes arrangements for children to speak to world leaders about peace. Operates four major international programs: Peace Mission, which brings together children from every continent to meet with world leaders on the subject of peace; Banner Project, which coordinates efforts in research and represents children who are victims of war since 1930; Peace to the Planet Workshops, which bring together youths from 50 countries to work together on environmental issues; Pat's Peace Kids International Peace Clubs, which offer peace education programs to children. Other projects include Stop the Clock of Violence, Killing America's Children and the California Banner of Hope, memorializing 8000 children who were murdered in California between 1982 and 1992. Maintains Speaker's Bureau. **Libraries:** Type: reference. **Subjects:** world peace. **Also Known As:** Children as the Peacemakers Foundation. **Formerly:** Roundtable Foundation; (1985) Children as Teachers of Peace. **Publications:** *Making Friends*. Book ● *Peace Club Booklets*.

17827 ■ The Children of War (TCOW)
1608 Washington Plz. N, 3rd Fl.
Reston, VA 20190
Ph: (703)923-0455 (703)625-9147
Fax: (703)923-0456
E-mail: info@thechildrenofwar.org
URL: http://www.thechildrenofwar.org
Contact: Mr. Najib Aziz, Pres./Founder
Founded: 1984. **Staff:** 5. **Local Groups:** 5. **Multinational. Description:** A project of the Religious Task Force. Youth aged 15-20 from both the U.S. and "conflict zones" worldwide who act as role models to help other children deal with violence, racism, and war in their lives. Denounces glamorization and acceptance of violence. Offers peer counseling, tours, and leadership training workshops to educate and unify troubled youth. Creates action activities on community and international issues. Maintains Speaker's Bureau. **Libraries:** Type: reference. **Affiliated With:** Church Women United; World Alliance of Reformed Churches. **Conventions/Meetings:** periodic meeting.

17828 ■ Coalition for Harmony of Races in the U.S. (CHORUS)
2 Gienhurst Ct.
Darnestown, MD 20878
Ph: (301)948-7272
E-mail: mvosburgh1@aol.com
Contact: Mimi Vosburgh-Segal, Founder
Founded: 1992. **Members:** 500. **State Groups:** 2. **Local Groups:** 1. **National Groups:** 2. **Languages:** English, Spanish. **Description:** Works to communicate and learn from each member's different experiences and perceptions about strained race relations and their solutions; in this way, the association intends to emerge with effective, practical ways in which members can improve race relations in their personal lives. Conducts self-help discussions using group structures to promote open communication across and about ethnic, cultural, and racial lines. Maintains speakers' bureau and free book loan library. **Conventions/Meetings:** annual Racial Harmony Ribbons Day - meeting (exhibits) - always second Sunday of June in Washington, DC; Maryland; Colorado; and Alabama.

17829 ■ Code Pink Women's Pre-Emptive Strike for Peace
2010 Linden Ave.
Venice, CA 90291
Ph: (310)827-4320

Fax: (310)827-4547
E-mail: info@codepinkalert.org
URL: http://www.codepinkalert.org
Contact: Jodie Evans, Co-Founder
Founded: 2002. **Members:** 35,000. **Staff:** 2. **Budget:** $150,000. **Local Groups:** 100. **Multinational. Description:** Represents women devoted to global peace. Works to end the war in Iraq, stop new wars, and redirect resources into healthcare, education and other life-affirming activities. **Affiliated With:** United for Peace and Justice. **Publications:** *Stop the Next War Now! Effective Responses to Violence and Terrorism*. Book. **Price:** $20.00/copy ● *Twilight of Empire: Responses to Occupation*. Book.

17830 ■ Consistent Life (CL)
c/o Seamless Garment Network
PO Box 9295
Silver Spring, MD 20916-9295
Ph: (641)985-5700
Fax: (603)908-0730
E-mail: mail@consistent-life.org
URL: http://www.consistent-life.org
Contact: Mr. Bill Samuel, Pres.
Founded: 1987. **Members:** 140. **Staff:** 3. **State Groups:** 6. **Local Groups:** 41. **National Groups:** 83. **Description:** Organizations opposing violence. Opposes the "violence of abortion, war, poverty, the death penalty, racism, euthanasia" and the aims race. Encourages a "consistent ethic of life" and urges individuals to "work together in the spirit of reconciliation and respect in protecting the unprotected." Solicits and publicizes the support of national and international figures on these issues. Maintains Speaker's Bureau. **Programs:** Institute for Integrated Social Analysis. **Affiliated With:** Evangelical Social Action Commission; Feminists for Life of America; Pax Christi - U.S.A.; Sojourners. **Formerly:** (2003) Seamless Garment Network. **Publications:** *Consistent Ethic Resources*, periodic. Directory. Lists organizations, speakers, and publications. **Price:** $2.00/copy ● *The Garment Bag*. Newsletter. **Price:** free. **Conventions/Meetings:** annual board meeting - usually March or April.

17831 ■ Disciples Peace Fellowship (DPF)
c/o Disciples Home Missions
PO Box 1986
Indianapolis, IN 46206-1986
Ph: (317)713-2679 (317)713-2678
Free: (888)346-2631
Fax: (317)635-4426
E-mail: mail@dhm.disciples.org
URL: http://www.homelandministries.org/DPF
Contact: Rev. Bruce Patton, Office Coor.
Founded: 1935. **Members:** 2,200. **Membership Dues:** individual, $30 (annual). **Budget:** $30,000. **State Groups:** 6. **Description:** Members of the Christian Church (Disciples of Christ) who are determined to "keep alive the passion for peace." Believes that war is "pagan, futile and destructive of the values for which the Christian faith stands"; supports a positive nonviolent approach to human conflicts. Supports disarmament and disarmament negotiations. Conducts specialized education and youth programs focusing upon the recognizable effects of violence. Organizes local groups on a city or area basis for study, education, and action. **Awards:** Will Wittkamper Peace Award. **Frequency:** biennial. **Type:** recognition. **Computer Services:** Mailing lists. **Affiliated With:** Fellowship of Reconciliation - USA. **Publications:** *DPF News Notes*. Newsletter. Reports on world order, peace, and justice; discusses disarmament, arms control, war and warlike events worldwide, and the peace program. **Price:** free. **Circulation:** 2,200. **Conventions/Meetings:** annual competition, for peace sermons and peace essays ● biennial conference.

17832 ■ Fellowship of Reconciliation - USA (FOR)
521 N Broadway
Nyack, NY 10960
Ph: (845)358-4601
Fax: (845)358-4924

E-mail: for@forusa.org
URL: http://www.forusa.org
· Contact: Rachel Pfeffer, Interim Exec. Dir.
Founded: 1914. **Members:** 20,000. **Membership Dues:** individual, $35 (annual). **Staff:** 33. **Budget:** $1,800,000. **Regional Groups:** 3. **State Groups:** 20. **Local Groups:** 80. **National Groups:** 40. **Description:** Interfaith organization. Committed to creating peace and justice, locally and globally, using education, training, coalition-building, and nonviolent action. **Libraries: Type:** reference. **Holdings:** archival material, artwork, books, clippings, monographs, periodicals. **Subjects:** nonviolence, war, religion, social ethics, peace and justice activism, history. **Awards:** Martin Luther King, Jr. Award. **Frequency:** annual. **Type:** monetary. **Recipient:** for carrying on the work and spirit of King ● Pfeffer Peace Prize. **Frequency:** annual. **Type:** monetary. **Recipient:** for individual or group achievements. **Affiliated With:** Baptist Peace Fellowship of North America; Buddhist Peace Fellowship; Catholic Peace Fellowship; Disciples Peace Fellowship; Episcopal Peace Fellowship; Jewish Peace Fellowship; Lutheran Peace Fellowship; Presbyterian Peace Fellowship. **Publications:** *Fellowship*, bimonthly. Magazine. Contains articles and information about peace, justice and compassion. **Price:** $25.00 /year for individuals in U.S.; $35.00 /year for individuals in Canada and Mexico; $40.00 /year for institutions outside U.S. ISSN: 0014-9810. **Circulation:** 8,100. **Advertising:** accepted ● *Peace is the Way*. Books. **Price:** $20.00/ issue ● *Steps to Nonviolence*. Booklets ● Brochures ● Pamphlets ● Also publishes greeting cards. **Conventions/Meetings:** biennial conference, with plenary speakers, workshop, cultural events (exhibits).

17833 ■ Foundation for Global Community (FGC)
251 High St., Ste.B
Palo Alto, CA 94301
Ph: (650)328-7756
Free: (800)707-7932
Fax: (650)328-7785
E-mail: trustees@globalcommunity.org
URL: http://www.globalcommunity.org
Contact: Joseph Kresse, Contact
Founded: 1968. **Staff:** 20. **Budget:** $750,000. **Local Groups:** 10. **Description:** Nonpartisan, educational movement who aims to discover, live, and communicate on what is needed to build a world that functions for the benefit of all life. **Libraries: Type:** reference. **Absorbed:** Creative Initiative. **Formerly:** (1991) Beyond War Foundation. **Publications:** *Timeline*, bimonthly. Magazine. Covers leading-edge thinking. **Price:** $15.00/year. ISSN: 0887-9567. **Circulation:** 5,000. Alternate Formats: online.

17834 ■ Foundation for P.E.A.C.E. (FFP)
PO Box 15922
Asheville, NC 28813-0922
Ph: (828)296-0194
E-mail: fdn4peace@aol.com
URL: http://www.promotingpeace.org
Contact: James L. Roush, Pres.
Founded: 1979. **Staff:** 1. **Nonmembership. Description:** Individuals who work to achieve peace at community and international levels. The group believes that only by developing institutions for preventing and resolving conflict can the world move toward disarmament and lasting peace. Promotes improved interpersonal and international communications; fosters nonviolent solutions to individual, family, community, and world problems; encourages people to "think globally, act locally." Publicizes conflict resolutions reached without military force; supports conflict-resolution institutions. Proposes an international conflict management service; offers consulting services in conflict resolution. Encourages participation in the International Decade for the Culture of Peace. **Also Known As:** Foundation for a Peaceful Environment Among Communities Everywhere. **Publications:** *PEACE in Action: Peacemaking and Conflict Resolution*, annual. Magazine. Focuses on conflicts resolution/prevention, peace education, nuclear weapon elimination, and building community.

ISSN: 0893-5920. **Circulation:** 3,000. **Advertising:** accepted ● Brochure.

17835 ■ Friends of Sabeel - North America (FOSNA)
PO Box 9186
Portland, OR 97207
Ph: (503)653-6625
E-mail: friends@fosna.org
URL: http://www.fosna.org
Contact: Rev. Richard K. Toll, Chm./Sec.
Multinational. Description: Seeks justice and peace in the Holy Land through non-violence and education. Supports the vision of Sabeel (an international peace movement initiated by Palestinian Christians in the Holy Land). Promotes awareness and understanding of the conflict between the Palestinians and the State of Israel through educational programs for North American Christians. **Telecommunication Services:** electronic mail, rtoll41439@aol.com. **Publications:** *Cornerstone*, quarterly. Journal. Alternate Formats: online ● Newsletter. Alternate Formats: online ● Brochure. Alternate Formats: online.

17836 ■ Friends World Committee for Consultation (FWCC)
c/o Margaret Fraser, Exec. Sec.
1506 Race St.
Philadelphia, PA 19102
Ph: (215)241-7250
Fax: (215)241-7285
E-mail: americas@fwccamericas.org
URL: http://www.fwccamericas.org
Contact: Margaret Fraser, Exec. Sec.
Founded: 1937. **Staff:** 5. **Regional Groups:** 9. **Languages:** English, Spanish. **Description:** Representatives from the Americas only from the Religious Society of Friends (Quakers). Seeks to maintain understanding and unity among Friends and to conduct consultations on issues of peace and justice. **Committees:** Administrative; Program. **Publications:** *Friends World News*, semiannual. Newsletter. **Price:** free. Alternate Formats: online ● *FWCC Friends Directory*, biennial. **Price:** $13.00 ● *Newsletter of the Americas*, semiannual. Alternate Formats: online ● Books ● Reports, annual. Alternate Formats: online. **Conventions/Meetings:** annual meeting, with information about Quaker programs and projects (exhibits).

17837 ■ Global Vision for Peace
5419 Hollywood Blvd., Ste.C208
Los Angeles, CA 90027
E-mail: info@globalvisionforpeace.org
URL: http://www.globalvisionforpeace.org
Contact: Heathcliff Rothman, Co-Chm./Co-Founder
Founded: 2003. **Description:** Serves as a high-profile collaboration between entertainment, business, and government that works for peace worldwide. Runs "Artists for the United Nations" to recruit artists of letters, philosophy, visual arts, and entertainment to affirm the UN as a global peacekeeper. **Telecommunication Services:** electronic mail, cliff@globalvisionforpeace.org ● electronic mail, xorin@globalvisionforpeace.org.

17838 ■ GlobalSecurity.org
300 N Washington St., Ste.B-100
Alexandria, VA 22314
Ph: (703)548-2700
Fax: (703)548-2424
E-mail: info@globalsecurity.org
URL: http://www.globalsecurity.org
Contact: John E. Pike, Dir.
Founded: 2000. **Description:** Works to "reduce reliance on nuclear weapons and the risk of their use, including existing nuclear weapons states and those states seeking to acquire such capabilities". **Publications:** Reports. Alternate Formats: online.

17839 ■ Institute for Peace and Justice (IPJ)
475 E Lockwood Ave.
St. Louis, MO 63119
Ph: (314)918-2630
Fax: (314)918-2643

E-mail: ppjn@aol.com
URL: http://www.ipj-ppj.org
Contact: James McGinnis, Founder/Program Dir.
Founded: 1970. **Members:** 500. **Staff:** 11. **Description:** Represents educators, fundraisers, lecturers, and authors. Encourages study in the areas of peace and justice by providing educational resources including books, workshops, and audiovisual materials on the topics of world hunger and global economics, sexism, racism, parenting for peace and justice, and faith and justice. Conducts research and provides curricula in multicultural studies. **Libraries: Type:** reference. **Holdings:** audio recordings, books, films. **Subjects:** peace, justice. **Formerly:** Institute for Education in Peace and Justice. **Publications:** *IPJ Newsletter*, 3/year. **Price:** included in membership dues ● *Parenting for Peace and Justice Newsletter*, bimonthly. Contains articles for parents on conflict resolution, sexism, racism, multicultural awareness, peace, and spirituality. **Price:** included in membership dues; $25.00 for nonmembers. **Circulation:** 2,500. Also Cited As: *PPJN Newsletter* ● *Resource Catalog* ● Audiotapes ● Books ● Brochures ● Videos ● Makes available education kits.

17840 ■ International A.N.S.W.E.R. Coalition - Act Now to Stop War and End Racism
1247 E St. SE
Washington, DC 20003
Ph: (202)544-3389
E-mail: info@internationalanswer.org
URL: http://www.internationalanswer.org
Contact: Sarah Sloan, Contact
Founded: 2001. **Description:** Encourages citizens to grass roots organize for the prevention of war and to protect civil liberties.

17841 ■ International Association of Educators for World Peace - USA (IAEWP)
PO Box 3282
Mastin Lake Sta.
Huntsville, AL 35810-0282
Ph: (256)534-5501
Fax: (256)536-1018
E-mail: info@iaewp.org
URL: http://www.earthportals.com/Portal_Messenger/mercieca.html
Contact: Dr. Charles Mercieca, Pres.
Founded: 1969. **Members:** 55,000. **Membership Dues:** educator, $40 (annual) ● graduate, $45 (annual) ● undergraduate, $25 (annual) ● senior, $15 (annual) ● librarian, $75 (annual) ● associate, $50 (annual). **Staff:** 40. **Languages:** English, French, Russian, Spanish. **Description:** Teachers, students, attorneys, medical doctors, social workers, clergy, business people, and other individuals united to achieve world peace and better international relations through education. Promotes improved curriculum and methods of instruction in schools and seeks to implement the United Nations Universal Declaration of Human Rights. Cooperates with programs organized by the United Nations Educational, Scientific, and Cultural Organization. Maintains speakers' bureau and children's services. **Libraries: Type:** reference. **Holdings:** 100,000. **Subjects:** world peace. **Awards:** Diploma of Honor. **Frequency:** periodic. **Type:** recognition. **Recipient:** for distinguished service for peace ● Fountain of Universal Peace Award. **Frequency:** periodic. **Type:** recognition. **Recipient:** for distinguished service for peace ● World Peace Academy Diploma. **Frequency:** periodic. **Type:** recognition. **Recipient:** for distinguished service for peace. **Additional Websites:** http://user.transit.ru/~maria/s2-2.htm, http://www.iaewp.net. **Telecommunication Services:** electronic mail, mercieca@knology.net. **Boards:** Advisory. **Councils:** Executive. **Affiliated With:** United Nations. **Publications:** *Circulation Newsletter*, monthly. Provides updates on the association's worldwide chapter events, (presently active in 97 countries), including professional meetings and seminars. **Price:** $15.00. **Advertising:** accepted. Also Cited As: *IAEWP Newsletter* ● *International Association of Educators for World Peace—Directory of International Officers*, biennial. Membership Directory. Includes biographical data. **Price:** $10.00 /year for members ● *Mismanage-*

ment in *Higher Education.* Book. **Price:** $25.00 ●
Peace Education Journal, biennial. Contains articles
on the philosophy and techniques in promotion of
peace Education. ● *Peace Progress Journal*, semiannual. Publishes articles on ideas, studies and activities that promote international understanding and
world peace. ● *UN NEWS* (in English, Korean, and
Portuguese), monthly. Newspaper. **Price:** $35.00
/year for individuals ● *World and Spirituality in the
Third Millennium* (in English and Russian). Book.
Price: $25.00. **Conventions/Meetings:** annual
Continental Convention ● annual World Congress.

**17842 ■ International Mothers' Peace Day
Committee**
PO Box 102
West Liberty, WV 26074
Ph: (304)336-7159
Fax: (304)336-7893
E-mail: j_v_schramm@hotmail.com
Contact: Jeanne V. Schramm, Chair
Founded: 1982. **Description:** Seeks to unite moth-
ers and others worldwide to promote the establish-
ment of the first Sunday in June as International
Mothers' Peace Day, originated as Mothers' Peace
Day, a day of observance established in 1872 by Julia
Ward Howe (1819-1910), peace advocate and
composer of The Battle Hymn of the Republic. Stages
letter-writing campaigns and peace demonstrations.
Observance based upon the motto, "Those who
nurture life on earth are of one mind in their opposition to those who would destroy it".

**17843 ■ International Peace Operations
Association (IPOA)**
1900 L St. NW, Ste.320
Washington, DC 20036
Ph: (202)464-0721
Fax: (202)464-0726
E-mail: ipoa@ipoaonline.org
URL: http://ipoaonline.org
Contact: Mr. Doug Brooks, Pres./Founder
Founded: 2001. **Membership Dues:** security company, $15,000 (annual) ● product company, $10,000
(annual) ● supply and logistics company, $5,000 (an-
nual) ● friend, $30 (annual). **Multinational. Descrip-
tion:** Promotes high operational and ethical standards
of firms involved in the peace and stability industry.
Strives to raise the industry standards by ensuring
that sound and ethical professionalism and transparency be conducted in peacekeeping and post-conflict
reconstruction activities. Engages in constructive
dialogues with policy makers about the growing and
positive contribution of firms to the enhancement of
international peace, development and human security. **Publications:** *Journal of International Peace Operations*, bimonthly. **Price:** $30.00 in U.S.; $35.00
outside U.S.; $15.00 registered friend. **Advertising:**
accepted. Alternate Formats: online ● Papers.
Alternate Formats: online.

**17844 ■ Interreligious and International
Federation for World Peace (IIFWP)**
155 White Plains Rd., Ste.222
Tarrytown, NY 10591
Ph: (914)631-1331
Fax: (914)631-1308
E-mail: info@peacefederation.org
URL: http://www.iifwp.org
Contact: Dr. Thomas G. Walsh, Sec. Gen.
Founded: 1999. **Multinational. Description:** Aims
to build a unified world of peace. **Publications:** *The
Millennium Declaration of the United Nations: A
Response from Civil Society.* Book. Includes a copy
of the United Nations Millennium Declaration in the
appendix. **Price:** $10.00 ● Newsletter. Alternate
Formats: online ● Journals. **Conventions/Meetings:**
seminar.

**17845 ■ Jane Addams Peace Association
(JAPA)**
777 United Nations Plz., 6th Fl.
New York, NY 10017
Ph: (212)682-8830
Fax: (212)286-8211

E-mail: japa@igc.org
URL: http://www.janeaddamspeace.org
Contact: Linda B. Belle, Exec. Dir.
Founded: 1948. **Membership Dues:** life, $100.
Staff: 2. **Budget:** $102,000. **Description:** Empowers
women in 45 countries to work for human needs,
equity, social justice, and disarmament. Offers
programs both internationally and nationally including
international training for women in conflict resolution
and preventative diplomacy, peace education camps
for children, and internships for women in disarmament, development, and human rights. **Awards:** Jane
Addams Children's Book Award. **Frequency:** annual.
Type: monetary. **Recipient:** for children's book that
best combines literary merit with themes of world
community and social justice. **Conventions/Meet-
ings:** semiannual board meeting.

17846 ■ Jewish Peace Fellowship (JPF)
Box 271
Nyack, NY 10960-0271
Ph: (845)358-4601
Fax: (845)358-4924
E-mail: jpf@forusa.org
URL: http://www.jewishpeacefellowship.org
Contact: Murray Polner, Chm./Ed.
Founded: 1941. **Members:** 3,100. **Membership
Dues:** individual, $25 (annual). **Staff:** 1. **Budget:**
$28,000. **Local Groups:** 3. **Description:** Represents
persons who believe that Jewish ideals and experience provide inspiration for a nonviolent philosophy
of life. Advises Jewish conscientious objectors of their
rights under the Selective Service Act. Promotes
peace education in the Jewish community. Maintains
speakers' bureau. **Awards:** Rabbi Abraham Joshua
Heschel Award. **Frequency:** semiannual. **Type:**
recognition. **Recipient:** for outstanding Jewish group
or individual making a contribution to peace in the
tradition of Rabbi Haschel. **Affiliated With:** Fellowship of Reconciliation - USA. **Publications:** *The
Challenge of Shalom.* Book ● *Jewish Peace Letters*,
quarterly. Newsletter. Includes information about fellowship activities, ideas for peace activists, and news
of the progress of peace initiatives in the U.S. and
Israel. ● *Shalom*, quarterly. Newsletter. Covers
organization activities and issues related to peace in
the Jewish tradition. **Price:** included in membership
dues; $5.00 /year for nonmembers. ISSN: 0197-9115.
Circulation: 3,300. Alternate Formats: online. **Con-
ventions/Meetings:** monthly executive committee
meeting.

**17847 ■ Joan B. Kroc Institute for
International Peace Studies**
PO Box 639
Notre Dame, IN 46556-0639
Ph: (574)631-6970
Fax: (574)631-6973
E-mail: krocinst@nd.edu
URL: http://www.nd.edu/~krocinst
Contact: Scott Appleby, Dir.
Founded: 1986. **Description:** Conducts research,
education, and outreach programs on the causes of
violence and the conditions for sustainable peace.
Programs: Master of Arts in Peace Studies; Religion,
Conflict and Peacebuilding; Undergraduate in Peace
Studies; Visiting Fellowship. **Projects:** Research
Initiative on the Resolution of Ethnic Conflict; Sanc-
tion and Security. **Publications:** *Peace Colloquy*,
semiannual. Alternate Formats: online ● Papers.
Alternate Formats: online ● Annual Report, annual.
Alternate Formats: online ● Videos. Alternate For-
mats: online. **Conventions/Meetings:** periodic
workshop.

17848 ■ Laucks Foundation (LF)
Address Unknown since 2006
Founded: 1969. **Description:** Educational organization that encourages efforts toward world peace,
environmental responsibility, and equity. Disseminates reprints of published materials the foundation
feels might contribute to clarification of issues affecting world peace. Does not make grants to individuals
for study, research, or travel.

17849 ■ Lentz Peace Research Association
c/o University of Missouri-St. Louis
One Univ. Blvd.
St. Louis, MO 63121-4400
Ph: (314)516-5000 (314)516-5753
Fax: (314)516-6757
E-mail: twilliams@umsl.edu
URL: http://www.umsl.edu/services/cis/research/the-
odore_lentz.html
Contact: Ms. Miranda Duncan, Contact
Founded: 1930. **Members:** 50. **Membership Dues:**
individual, $25 (annual). **Budget:** $20,000. **Descrip-
tion:** Seeks to promote peace research and educa-
tion. Focuses on understanding reasons for conflict
and identifies strategies successful in resolving
conflict. **Awards:** Lentz Fellowship in Peace and
Conflict Resolution Research. **Frequency:** annual.
Type: fellowship ● Lentz International Peace Research Award. **Type:** recognition. **Recipient:** for
contribution in the field of peace research. **Committees:** Research. **Formerly:** (1986) Peace Research
Laboratory. **Publications:** *Peace Research*, quarterly.
Reports ● Annual Report, annual ● Also publishes
manual, books, and monographs. **Conventions/
Meetings:** biennial seminar and dinner.

17850 ■ Lutheran Peace Fellowship (LPF)
1710 11th Ave.
Seattle, WA 98122-2420
Ph: (206)720-0313
E-mail: lpf@ecunet.org
URL: http://www.lutheranpeace.org
Contact: Grace Hanson, Youth Trainer
Founded: 1941. **Members:** 1,600. **Membership
Dues:** regular, $35 (annual) ● supporter, $52 (annual) ● sustainer, congregation, $100 (annual) ●
student, low income, $9 (annual) ● new to LPF, $19
(annual). **Budget:** $60,000. **Description:** Lutheran
clergy and laity, many of who accept the pacifist position. Seeks to work for world peace. Publicizes the
fact that the pacifist position is one recognized by the
Lutheran church. Provides counseling and materials
to Lutheran conscientious objectors and others
whose commitment to disarmament places them in
legal jeopardy. Advocates a military chaplaincy that is
more independent of government control. Supports
Lutheran war tax resisters. Calls individuals to pursue
ministries of peacemaking within their own lives; witnesses to the Lutheran community, calling the church
to follow its biblical vocation of loving enemies, waging peace, and representing hope in God's future.
Maintains speakers bureau and cooperative relationship with Fellowship of Reconciliation (see separate
entry). Provides training in nonviolent conflict resolution. Conducts educational programs. **Affiliated
With:** Fellowship of Reconciliation - USA. **Publications:** *Peace Notes*, quarterly. Newsletter. Provides
education, advocacy, and witnesses to developments
in the peace movement. Includes calendar of events,
fellowship reports, and member news. **Price:** included
in membership dues. **Circulation:** 2,200 ● Annual
Report, annual. Alternate Formats: online. **Conven-
tions/Meetings:** annual meeting.

**17851 ■ Mennonite Central Committee
Overseas Peace Office (MCCPO)**
21 S 12th St.
PO Box 500
Akron, PA 17501-0500
Ph: (717)859-1151
Free: (888)563-4676
Fax: (717)859-2171
E-mail: mailbox@mcc.org
URL: http://www.mcc.org/peace/pon
Contact: Mr. Robert Herr, Co-Dir.
Founded: 1943. **Multinational. Description:** Mem-
bers of the Mennonite and Brethren in Christ
churches. Addresses and interprets international
justice and peace issues from a peace church
perspective. Promotes peaceful resolution of conflict
and advocates a biblical model of peace. Administers
and participates in peacemaking missions and
seminars, promoting ecumenical dialogue in peace
theology. Provides training in peacemaking skills; offers consulting services; conducts research programs.
Sponsors charitable programs; assists in establishing

peace libraries. **Publications:** *Peace Office Newsletter*, quarterly. Features international peace and justice topics from a Christian perspective. **Price:** $10.00/year. **Circulation:** 2,500. Alternate Formats: online ● Also distributes peace and justice literature.

17852 ■ Men's International Peace Exchange (MIPE)
612 Kenney Ln.
Brookhaven, PA 19015
Ph: (610)872-8178
E-mail: mipe00@aol.com
URL: http://www.peaceexchange.org
Contact: Mordecai S. Jackson, Dir./Co-Founder
Founded: 1991. **Description:** Brings together women and men to foster peaceful beliefs, attitudes and behaviors to move from cultures, which support men in being violent to ones which support men in being peaceful. Aims to build Peace Communities internationally. **Publications:** *The Peace Exchange*, quarterly. Newsletter. Contains prose and poetry in support of men becoming more peaceful. **Circulation:** 500. **Conventions/Meetings:** annual Changing A Culture - conference, share skills and values, exchange ideas, network (exhibits) - always in October.

17853 ■ Mothers Against War (MAW)
PO Box 3048
Amherst, MA 01004
Ph: (413)253-3354
E-mail: mothrsagainstwar@aol.com
URL: http://mothersagainstwar.info
Contact: Daphne Reed, Founder
Description: Advocates for an end to the Iraq War and the complete withdrawal of American troops in Iraq.

17854 ■ Mt. Diablo Peace Center (MDPC)
55 Eckley Ln.
Walnut Creek, CA 94596
Ph: (925)933-7850
E-mail: info@mtdpc.org
URL: http://www.mtdpc.org
Contact: Andy Baltzo, Founder
Founded: 1969. **Members:** 2,300. **Staff:** 3. **Budget:** $65,000. **Description:** A Committee of the Mount Diablo Unitarian Universalist Church. Aims to promote world peace, world disarmament, and world law. Trains peace activists and conducts draft counseling and referral services for churches wishing to support sanctuary for Central American refugees; projects include Peace in Central America, Peace Action in Contra Costa County, CA, and Children's Peace Camp. Conducts educational programs on racism, the Pacific Nations, the Hiroshima and Nagasaki bombings, and conversion from military production to a "peace economy". Operates speakers' bureau; compiles statistics. **Libraries: Type:** reference. **Holdings:** 700. **Subjects:** peace, freedom. **Awards: Type:** recognition. **Committees:** Draft Counseling; Economic Conversion; Fundraising. **Programs:** Race Awareness; Raising Nonviolent Children. **Projects:** Central America. **Publications:** *Peace Gazette*, monthly. Newsletter. Provides information about the center's activities, international relations, and local political issues. Includes book reviews and calendar. **Price:** included in membership dues. **Circulation:** 2,300. **Advertising:** accepted. **Conventions/Meetings:** semiannual Peace Celebration - meeting ● seminar.

17855 ■ Musicians' Alliance for Peace (MAP)
c/o Music Dept.
Stony Brook Univ.
3304 Staller Ctr.
Stony Brook, NY 11794-5475
E-mail: info@m4p.org
URL: http://www.m4p.org
Founded: 2001. **Multinational. Description:** Promotes the use of music for peace. Fosters an active local and global peace community. Promotes empathy, ethical thought and critical social involvement through music. **Computer Services:** Online services, bulletin board. **Projects:** Music for Peace.

17856 ■ National Association of Peace Education
Address Unknown since 2006
Membership Dues: $30 ● student, $15. **Description:** Promotes peace education and anti-violence. **Conventions/Meetings:** conference.

17857 ■ National Campus Antiwar Network (NCAN)
Address Unknown since 2006
Founded: 2002. **Members:** 200. **Regional Groups:** 8. **Multinational. Description:** Campus-based antiwar coalitions and committees; works to end racism, promotes civil liberties.

17858 ■ National Peace Foundation (NPF)
666 11th St. NW, Ste.202
Washington, DC 20001
Ph: (202)783-7030
Free: (800)23-PEACE
Fax: (202)783-7040
E-mail: npf@nationalpeace.org
URL: http://www.nationalpeace.org
Contact: Sarah Harder, Pres./Chair
Founded: 1982. **Members:** 8,000. **Membership Dues:** basic, $35 (annual) ● student, $25 (annual). **Staff:** 6. **Budget:** $495,000. **Description:** Individuals and organizations seeking to advance conflict resolution and peace education; supports the efforts of the U.S. Institute of Peace. Provides information and education regarding the management and resolution of conflict. Seeks to create an effective working relationship among individuals, organizations, and educational institutions interested in conflict resolution and peacemaking. Provides networking for those interested in peacemaking and conflict resolutions. Facilitates training in conflict resolution and shared decision-making. **Awards:** Peacemaker/Peacebuilder Award. **Frequency:** periodic. **Type:** recognition. **Recipient:** for lifetime achievements and dedication to peace. **Absorbed:** (1985) National Peace Academy Campaign. **Formerly:** (1982) National Peace Academy Fund; (1985) National Peace Academy Foundation; (1991) National Peace Institute Foundation. **Publications:** *Conflict Resolution in Urban American School System*. Report. **Price:** $10.00 ● *Inventory of International Conflict Resolution Program*. Directory. **Price:** $15.00 ● *Organizations Concerned with Peaceful Resolution of Arab-Israelite-Palestinian Conflicts*, periodic. Directory. **Price:** $10.00. Alternate Formats: online ● *Peacemaking Behavior: Major Research Areas* ● *U.S. Academy of Peace: Long Step Toward Security*.

17859 ■ National Peace Garden Foundation
Address Unknown since 2007
Founded: 1986. **Members:** 36. **Staff:** 2. **Description:** Established by an act of Congress (PL 100-63), group is working to create a National Memorial in Washington, DC, to symbolize and honor the United States commitment to world peace. Memorial will be located at Hain's Point in the East Potomac Park. Fund raising for construction is currently in progress. **Formerly:** (1990) Peace Garden Project; (1994) National Peace Garden. **Publications:** *National Peace Garden Newsletter*, semiannual. **Price:** free. **Advertising:** not accepted ● Brochures.

17860 ■ National Youth and Student Peace Coalition (NYSPC)
PO Box 3674
Washington, DC 20027-0174
Free: (800)228-1228
E-mail: nyspcinfo@gmail.com
URL: http://www.nyspc.org
Founded: 2003. **Description:** Represents student and youth opposed to war, racism, cuts to education, and freedom-limiting anti-terrorism policies.

17861 ■ No Peace Without Justice (NPWJ)
c/o United Nations
866 UN Plz., No. 408
New York, NY 10017
Ph: (212)980-2558
Fax: (212)980-1072

E-mail: epolizzottono@spamnpwj.org
URL: http://www.npwj.org
Contact: Elio Polizzotto, Contact
Founded: 1993. **Multinational. Description:** Works for the protection and promotion of human rights, democracy, the rule of law and international justice. Maps and documents wide scale violations of the laws of war. Promotes democratic reform in the broader Middle East and North Africa through constructive dialogue between governments, parliaments and civil society. Advocates for the strengthening of an effective international criminal justice system for the prevention, deterrence and prosecution of war crimes, crimes against humanity and genocide. **Telecommunication Services:** electronic mail, webmasterno@spamnpwj.org. **Publications:** Reports. Alternate Formats: online ● Newsletter. Alternate Formats: online.

17862 ■ Nonviolence.Org
c/o Martin Kelley, Founder
PO Box 38504
Philadelphia, PA 19104
Ph: (215)681-0783
E-mail: nvweb@nonviolence.org
URL: http://www.nonviolence.org
Contact: Martin Kelley, Founder
Founded: 1995. **Description:** Web portal created for the nonviolence movement. **Computer Services:** Online services, discussion board.

17863 ■ Nuclear Age Peace Foundation (NAPF)
PMB 121
1187 Coast Village Rd., Ste.1
Santa Barbara, CA 93108-2794
Ph: (805)965-3443
Fax: (805)568-0466
E-mail: dkrieger@napf.org
URL: http://www.wagingpeace.org
Contact: David Krieger, Pres.
Founded: 1982. **Members:** 8,500. **Staff:** 10. **Budget:** $13,000,000. **Description:** Nonpartisan international educational and advocacy organization. Provides leadership toward achieving a nuclear-weapons-free world, strengthening international law and institutions, teaching peace, empowering youth, using technology responsibly and sustainably, and creating a world based upon liberty, justice, and human dignity. Works to play an important role in making the Twenty-First Century a time of peace and justice, and a time in which the rights of all individuals to peace, security and a healthy environment will be realized. Maintains consultative status with the Economic and Social Council of the United Nations. **Libraries: Type:** reference. **Holdings:** 3,000; audio recordings, books, periodicals, video recordings. **Subjects:** war, peace, international law, nuclear weapons, Hiroshima, Nuclear Energy, disarmament, nonviolence, United Nations, International Relations, human rights. **Awards:** Barbara Mandigo Kelly Peace Poetry Awards. **Frequency:** annual. **Type:** monetary. **Recipient:** for poets ● Distinguished Peace Leadership Award. **Frequency:** annual. **Type:** recognition ● Lena Chang Internships. **Frequency:** annual. **Type:** monetary. **Recipient:** for ethnic minority students enrolled in undergraduate or graduate course work ● Swackhamer Peace Essay Contest. **Frequency:** annual. **Type:** monetary. **Recipient:** for high school students ● World Citizenship Award. **Frequency:** annual. **Type:** recognition. **Computer Services:** Online services, publications. **Additional Websites:** http://www.nuclearfiles.com. **Programs:** Nuclear Dangers; Youth Outreach. **Projects:** Auxiliary; Nuclear Files. **Affiliated With:** Abolition 2000; International Network of Engineers and Scientists for Global Responsibility; International Peace Bureau. **Absorbed:** (1998) International Accidental War Information Sharing Project; (1998) Accidental Nuclear War Prevention Project. **Publications:** *A Maginot Line in the Sky: International Perspectives on Ballistic Missile Defense*. Book ● *An Unacceptable Risk: Nuclear Weapons in a Volatile World*. Book ● *The Sunflower*, monthly. Newsletter. Provides educational information on nuclear weapons abolition and other issues relating to global security. **Price:** free. Alternate

Formats: online ● *Waging Peace II, Vision and Hope for the 21st Century.* Book ● *Waging Peace in the Nuclear Age: Ideas for Action.* Book ● *Waging Peace Report,* annual. Annual Report. Provides information on issues of peace and international law and information on foundation activities. Alternate Formats: online ● *Waging Peace Series,* semiannual. Booklets. **Price:** $5.00/copy. **Circulation:** 2,500 ● Brochure. **Conventions/Meetings:** annual Evening For Peace - dinner, with awards presentation ● annual Peace Retreat/Summit for Humanity.

17864 ■ Partners for Peace
1250 4th St. SW, Ste.WG-1
Washington, DC 20024
Ph: (202)863-2951
Fax: (202)863-2952
E-mail: info@partnersforpeace.org
URL: http://www.partnersforpeace.org
Contact: Jerri Bird, Pres./Founder
Founded: 1990. **Multinational. Description:** Raises public awareness of the issues in the quest for peace and justice in the Middle East. Promotes settlement of the Israeli-Palestinian conflict by engaging existing networks and unaffiliated individuals who share this concern. Advocates for human rights in the Middle East. Assists other organizations working on these issues to enhance their media relation skills. **Libraries: Type:** reference. **Holdings:** articles, papers.

17865 ■ Peace Brigades International - U.S.A. (PBI-USA)
1326 9th St. NW
Washington, DC 20001
Ph: (202)232-0142
Fax: (202)232-0143
E-mail: info@pbiusa.org
URL: http://www.peacebrigades.org/usa.html
Contact: Michael Joseph, Co-Dir.
Founded: 1981. **Members:** 7,500. **Membership Dues:** regular, $30 (annual). **Staff:** 3. **Budget:** $250,000. **Languages:** English, French, Spanish. **Description:** Promotes nonviolent social change and human rights protection worldwide. Encourages the establishment of international, nonpartisan approaches to peacemaking. Sponsors unarmed volunteer peace teams, when invited, provides protective accompaniment to threatened members of civil society—such as human rights defenders and civilian peace initiatives—in the midst of internal armed conflicts. Currently maintains teams in Colombia, Guatemala, Indonesia, Mexico and Nepal. Maintains Emergency Response Network to exert pressure when a crisis occurs. Maintains speakers' bureau of returned field volunteers; operates placement services for volunteers in field projects; sponsors delegations. **Publications:** *PBI/USA Report,* quarterly. Newsletter ● Brochures. **Conventions/Meetings:** biennial National Gathering - meeting.

17866 ■ Peace Development Fund (PDF)
44 N Prospect St.
PO Box 1280
Amherst, MA 01004
Ph: (413)256-8306
Fax: (413)256-8871
E-mail: info@peacefund.org
URL: http://www.peacedevelopmentfund.org
Contact: Paul Haible, Exec. Dir.
Founded: 1981. **Staff:** 11. **Budget:** $2,000,000. **Description:** Works to strengthen a broad-based social justice movement that embodies, embraces, and honors many cultures to create the new systems and institutions essential to building a peaceful, just, and equitable world. Provides grants, training, and other resources in partnership with communities, organizations, trainers, and donors with whom is shared a common vision for change. **Telecommunication Services:** electronic mail, pdf@peacefund.org ● electronic mail, paul@peacefund.org. **Publications:** *Peace Developments,* 3/year. Newsletter.

17867 ■ Peace and Justice Studies Association (PJSA)
Univ. Ctr., 5th Fl.
2130 Fulton St.
San Francisco, CA 94117-1080
Ph: (415)422-5238
E-mail: pjsa@usfca.edu
URL: http://www.peacejusticestudies.org
Contact: Joy Snyder, Exec. Dir.
Founded: 2003. **Membership Dues:** student (without journal), $15 (annual) ● student (with journal), $30 (annual) ● low income, $40 (annual) ● individual, $80 (annual) ● contributing, $200 (annual) ● life, $1,500 ● small program, low income organization, student organization, $120 (annual) ● library institutional, $200 (annual) ● large program, organization, $250 (annual) ● sponsoring institution, $450 (annual) ● institutional leader, $2,000 (annual). **Description:** Academic institutions, foundations, and program organizations and individuals connected with national and international peace research/education movements. Conducts educational and research programs; offers children's services. Maintains Speaker's Bureau. **Libraries: Type:** reference; open to the public. **Holdings:** 500; artwork, audiovisuals, books, clippings, monographs, periodicals. **Subjects:** economics of poverty, disarmament, peace conflict research race relations, human-civil rights, sustainable development, peacekeeping, conflict resolution, media. **Awards:** Social Courage. **Frequency:** annual. **Type:** recognition. **Recipient:** for social courage through nonviolent methods ● Teacher of the Year Award. **Frequency:** annual. **Type:** recognition. **Recipient:** for individuals who have contributed to the peaceful education of youth. **Computer Services:** database, global directory of studies programs ● mailing lists. **Affiliated With:** International Studies Association; Peace History Society. **Formerly:** (1998) Peace Research Network; (2000) Copred Consortium: Peace Research and Educational Development; (2003) Consortium on Peace Research, Education and Development. **Publications:** *Global Directory of Peace Studies and Conflict Resolution Programs,* periodic. **Price:** $25.00 ● *Peace and Change: A Journal of Peace Research,* quarterly ● *Peace Chronicle,* 3/year. Newsletter. Contains network reports, book reviews, essays and a calendar. **Circulation:** 250. **Advertising:** accepted. Alternate Formats: online ● *Peace Education Packet.* Contains a collection of K-12 resources. ● Also publishes peace studies materials. **Conventions/Meetings:** annual conference, provides a central meeting place for activists, academics, and educators to exchange ideas, teaching methods, and materials (exhibits) ● conference.

17868 ■ Peace Museum (PM)
PO Box 803887
Chicago, IL 60680-3887
Ph: (773)638-6450
URL: http://www.peacemuseum.org
Contact: Melissa Sue McGuire MPH, Exec. Dir.
Founded: 1981. **Members:** 3,500. **Membership Dues:** student/senior, $45 ● individual or family, $80 ● non-profit organization, $200 ● sponsor, $300 ● donor, $500 ● business, $700 ● peace lover, $1,000 ● dove, $3,000. **Staff:** 2. **Budget:** $250,000. **Description:** Provides peace education through the arts and humanities; promotes research and study of peace, conflict resolution and political graphics; disseminates peace education materials in schools and communities; explores and celebrates the cultural heritage of peacemaking and peacemakers through special programs and exhibitions. Has created exhibits on topics including the life of Dr. Martin Luther King, Jr., artifacts from peace movements of the 20th century; alternatives to "war toys," and a collection of drawings by survivors of the Hiroshima and Nagasaki, Japan atomic bombings. Sponsors 15 different traveling exhibits (available for loan to other organizations), film showings, and lectures. Offers student internships. **Libraries: Type:** open to the public. **Holdings:** 1,000. **Subjects:** war, peace, civil rights, domestic peace. **Awards:** Community Peacemaker Award. **Frequency:** annual. **Type:** recognition. **Recipient:** for contributions to community peace. **Departments:** Education; Traveling Exhibits. **Publications:** *Drive-By Peace.* Contains educational curriculum. ● *Handbill of the Peace Museum* ● *The Peace Release: A Handbill of the Peace Museum,* quarterly. Newsletter. **Price:** included in membership

dues. **Circulation:** 4,000. **Advertising:** accepted. **Conventions/Meetings:** monthly workshop.

17869 ■ Peace Run (SCPR)
Address Unknown since 2006
Founded: 1986. **Members:** 500. **Regional Groups:** 50. **State Groups:** 25. **National Groups:** 50. **Description:** Organizes biennial international relay run in 12 countries, featuring a lighted torch in the Olympic tradition, to support world peace and to demonstrate the power of individuals working together toward a common goal. Maintains speakers' bureau; sponsors educational programs. **Computer Services:** database, runners. **Formerly:** (2003) Sri Chinmoy Oneness-Home Peace Run. **Publications:** *America's Heroes and You* ● *Welcome to the Peace Run* ● Brochures ● Directory, periodic ● America's Heroes and You. **Conventions/Meetings:** annual workshop (exhibits).

17870 ■ Peace Science Society (International) (PSS-I)
c/o Prof. Glenn Palmer, Exec. Dir.
Dept. of Political Sci.
202 Pond Bldg.
Pennsylvania State Univ.
University Park, PA 16802
Ph: (814)865-5594
Fax: (814)863-8979
E-mail: gpalmer@psu.edu
URL: http://pss.la.psu.edu
Contact: Prof. Glenn Palmer, Exec. Dir.
Founded: 1963. **Members:** 250. **Membership Dues:** regular, $42 (annual) ● student, $10 (annual). **Staff:** 2. **Budget:** $20,000. **Multinational. Description:** Individuals worldwide concerned with the advancement of peace research and related studies; libraries and other institutions are subscribers. Operates as a scientific organization, free of political, social, and nationalistic alliances. Fosters exchange of ideas and discussion among members and scholars from all fields. Conducts peace studies utilizing analytical methods and theoretical frameworks of peace science as well as methods designed for engineering, law, and social or natural science research. Avoids activities involving propaganda or attempts to influence legislation or domestic or international deliberations. **Awards:** Founders' Medal. **Frequency:** annual. **Type:** recognition. **Recipient:** for significant and distinguished lifelong scientific contributions ● Stuart A. Bremer Award for Best Graduate Student Paper. **Frequency:** annual. **Type:** recognition. **Recipient:** for the best graduate student paper ● Walter Isard Award for the Best Dissertation in Peace Science. **Frequency:** biennial. **Type:** recognition. **Recipient:** for outstanding contributions to the scientific knowledge of peace. **Formerly:** (1972) Peace Research Society - International. **Publications:** *Conflict Management and Peace Science,* quarterly. Journal. Contains manuscripts. **Price:** $25.00/volume. ISSN: 0738-8942. **Circulation:** 1,000. Also Cited As: *CMPS* ● *Journal of Conflict Resolution,* 6/year. Contains issues on international conflict. **Price:** $551.00 /year for institutions; $97.00 for individuals; $40.00 /year for members. **Advertising:** accepted. Also Cited As: *JCR.* **Conventions/Meetings:** annual North American Meeting.

17871 ■ Peace Through Law Education Fund (PTLEF)
PO Box 44354
Washington, DC 20026-4354
Ph: (202)686-4600
E-mail: ptlef@aol.com
URL: http://www.ptlef.org
Contact: Beth C. DeGrasse, Exec. Dir.
Founded: 1975. **Staff:** 3. **Budget:** $50,000. **Nonmembership. Description:** Engages in nonpartisan, independent and objective research of issues relevant to international peace and security, primarily for members of the US Congress. **Publications:** *A Force for Peace: U.S. and Allied Commanders' Views of the Military's Role in Peace Operations and the Impact of Terrorism of States in Conflict,* annual. Reprint. Alternate Formats: online ● *The Briefing Book on the Former Soviet Union* ● *Congressional*

Roundtable on Post-Cold War Relations, annual. Report ● *The Lessons of Bosnia*. Report ● *World Military and Social Expenditures*.

17872 ■ Peace X Peace (PXP)
1601 Connecticut Ave. NW
Washington, DC 20009
Ph: (703)391-8932
Fax: (202)745-0017
E-mail: info@peacexpeace.org
URL: http://www.peacexpeace.org
Contact: Patricia Smith Melton, Founder/Exec. Dir.
Multinational. Description: Empowers women to connect across cultural divides through technology, education and action for sustainable peace. **Libraries: Type:** reference. **Holdings:** articles, papers, video recordings. **Computer Services:** Information services, peace resources ● mailing lists ● online services, e-mail discussion groups. **Programs:** Educational Outreach; Global Network. **Publications:** *Peace Times*, monthly. Newsletter. Alternate Formats: online.

17873 ■ Peacework Volunteer Organization
209 Otey St.
Blacksburg, VA 24060-7426
Ph: (540)953-1376
Free: (800)272-5519
Fax: (540)953-0300
E-mail: mail@peacework.org
URL: http://www.peacework.org
Multinational. Description: Provides volunteer programs that promote peaceful cooperation, understanding and service.

17874 ■ Peaceworkers Nonviolent Peaceforce
425 Oak Grove St.
Minneapolis, MN 55403
Ph: (612)871-0005
Fax: (612)871-0006
E-mail: info@nonviolentpeaceforce.org
URL: http://www.nonviolentpeaceforce.org
Contact: Mel Duncan, Exec. Dir.
Founded: 1999. **Members:** 85. **Staff:** 10. **Budget:** $2,539,600. **Regional Groups:** 6. **Local Groups:** 20. **Languages:** English, French, German, Russian, Spanish. **Multinational. Description:** Promotes the widespread implementation of effective nonviolent peacemaking in conflict areas around the world. Currently working to create the Nonviolent Peaceforce, an international organization to send hundreds and eventually thousands of trained peacemakers to work in areas of conflict at the invitation of local peacemakers or human rights workers. The Peace Force will be sent to conflict areas to prevent death and destruction, and protect human rights, thus creating the space for local groups to struggle nonviolently, enter into dialogue, and seek peaceful resolution. **Libraries: Type:** open to the public. **Holdings:** 100; articles, books, periodicals, video recordings. **Subjects:** nonviolence, focused change. **Subgroups:** Affinity. **Formerly:** (2002) Peaceworkers. **Supersedes:** Volunteers for International Development. **Publications:** *Rumors of Peace* (in English, French, and Spanish), 3/year. Newsletter. Updates on the development of the nonviolent peaceforce. **Circulation:** 7,000. Alternate Formats: online.

17875 ■ Plowshares Institute (PI)
809 Hopmeadow St.
PO Box 243
Simsbury, CT 06070-0243
Ph: (860)651-4304
Fax: (860)651-4305
E-mail: plowshares@plowsharesinstitute.org
URL: http://www.plowsharesinstitute.org
Contact: Rev. Dr. Robert A. Evans, Exec. Dir.
Founded: 1981. **Staff:** 8. **Description:** Individuals interested in creating more just, sustainable, and peaceful world community. Promotes increased understanding of international issues among people in North America; works to insure that conflicts, whether arising at the local or international level, are resolved nonviolently. Conducts research and educational programs; sponsors charitable initiatives. **Li-**

braries: Type: reference. **Holdings:** audio recordings, books, video recordings. **Subjects:** community development, peace, pedagogy, case studies. **Telecommunication Services:** electronic mail, bobevans@plowsharesinstitute.org. **Publications:** Brochures ● Newsletter, periodic. **Conventions/Meetings:** semiannual board meeting.

17876 ■ Presbyterian Peace Fellowship (PPF)
PO Box 271
Nyack, NY 10960
Ph: (845)358-4601
E-mail: ppf@forusa.org
URL: http://www.presbypeacefellowship.org
Contact: Annabelle Dirks, Corresponding Sec.
Founded: 1983. **Members:** 2,000. **Staff:** 1. **Budget:** $12,000. **Description:** Voluntary group of ministers and laypersons of the Presbyterian Church U.S.A. "Works throughout all areas of faith and life for the principles of reconciliation and peace." Seeks the goal of universal peace and justice; testifies against military conscription, particularly universal military training; provides friendship and counsel for Presbyterian conscientious objectors; relates Presbyterians with inclusive interdenominational peace groups; and works to strengthen official forces within the church that witness to peace. **Awards:** Presbyterian Peace Seeker of the Year Award. **Frequency:** annual. **Type:** recognition. **Committees:** Coordinating. **Affiliated With:** Fellowship of Reconciliation - USA. **Formed by Merger of:** Southern Presbyterian Peace Fellowship; United Presbyterian Peace Fellowship. **Publications:** *Briefly*, quarterly. Newsletter. Alternate Formats: online ● Brochure, annual ● Papers. **Conventions/Meetings:** annual meeting and general assembly.

17877 ■ Program on the Analysis and Resolution of Conflicts (PARC)
Syracuse Univ.
400 Eggers Hall
Syracuse, NY 13244-1090
Ph: (315)443-2367
Fax: (315)443-3818
E-mail: parc@maxwell.syr.edu
URL: http://www.maxwell.syr.edu/parc/parcmain.htm
Contact: Dr. Robert A. Rubinstein, Dir.
Founded: 1983. **Members:** 500. **Description:** Anthropologists. Fosters research on the social and cultural dynamics of peace and war. Provides curricular services; operates speakers' bureau and placement service; compiles statistics. Sponsors seminars and professional workshops. **Telecommunication Services:** electronic mail, rar@syr.edu. **Working Groups:** Conflict Resolution/Social Movements; PLACA/PARC Colombia; Student Association on Terrorism and Security Analysis. **Affiliated With:** International Union of Anthropological and Ethnological Sciences. **Formerly:** (1999) Commission on the Study of Peace; (2003) Commission on Peace and Human Rights. **Publications:** *Directory of Anthropologists Working on Topics of Peace, Conflict Resolution, and International Security*, periodic ● *PARC News*, semiannual. Newsletter. Alternate Formats: online ● *Social Justice, Anthropology, Peace and Human Rights*, quarterly ● *25-Hour Meditation Manual*. **Price:** $20.00 plus shipping and handling ($2) ● Annual Report, annual. Alternate Formats: online ● Also publishes books. **Conventions/Meetings:** annual meeting.

17878 ■ Promoting Enduring Peace (PEP)
66 Edgewood Ave.
New Haven, CT 06511
Ph: (203)624-4034
Fax: (203)624-0339
E-mail: phodel@pepeace.org
URL: http://www.pepeace.org
Contact: Yael Martin, Exec. Dir.
Founded: 1952. **Members:** 5,000. **Staff:** 1. **Budget:** $60,000. **Description:** Peace educational organization that makes available articles relating to international peace and goodwill. Seeks to stimulate thought and discussion on national and international problems. Works with other peace organizations. **Libraries: Type:** reference. **Awards:** Gandhi Peace Award.

Frequency: annual. **Type:** recognition. **Recipient:** to individuals who have made significant contributions toward world peace and international understanding. **Conventions/Meetings:** meeting, with prominent speakers from throughout the U.S. ● seminar, on peace for ministers, professors, teachers, social workers, physicians, and attorneys ● tour, citizen exchanges to other countries.

17879 ■ Roots of Peace
1299 Fourth St., Ste.200
San Rafael, CA 94901
Ph: (415)455-8008
Free: (888)766-8731
Fax: (415)455-9086
E-mail: info@rootsofpeace.org
URL: http://www.rootsofpeace.org
Contact: Heidi Kuhn, Founder/Chair
Founded: 1997. **Nonmembership. Description:** Works to rid the world of landmines by transforming toxic minefields into thriving farmland. Coordinates projects in Afghanistan, Angola, Croatia, Cambodia, and Iraq. **Publications:** *Report*. Newsletter. Alternate Formats: online.

17880 ■ Seeds of Peace (SOP)
370 Lexington Ave., Ste.401
New York, NY 10017
Ph: (212)573-8040 (212)573-6049
Fax: (212)573-8047
E-mail: info@seedsofpeace.org
URL: http://www.seedsofpeace.org
Contact: Janet Wallach, Pres.
Founded: 1993. **Description:** Promotes peace among children who have grown up around war. **Programs:** Beyond Boarders; Center for Coexistence; Delegation Leaders; Global Programming; International Camp; Leadership; Media and Technology; Youth Conferences. **Publications:** Bulletin ● Annual Report, annual. Alternate Formats: online.

17881 ■ Service for Peace (SFP)
2838 Fairfield Ave.
Bridgeport, CT 06605
Ph: (203)610-6745
E-mail: info@serviceforpeace.org
URL: http://www.serviceforpeace.org
Contact: Philbert Seka, Exec. Dir.
Description: Promotes a lifestyle of service leading to a culture of peace. **Libraries: Type:** reference. **Holdings:** video recordings. **Subjects:** practical documents, service project. **Programs:** Leadership Training. **Publications:** *Summer of Service*. Video. **Price:** $15.00/copy for members, plus shipping and handling; $20.00/copy for nonmembers, plus shipping and handling ● Reports ● Newsletter.

17882 ■ Traprock Peace Center
103A Keets Rd.
Deerfield, MA 01342
Ph: (413)773-7427
Fax: (413)773-7507
E-mail: info@traprockpeace.org
URL: http://traprockpeace.org
Contact: Sunny Miller, Exec. Dir.
Founded: 1979. **Description:** Provides peace education programs regionally and nationally.

17883 ■ United for Peace and Justice (UFPJ)
PO Box 607
Times Square Sta.
New York, NY 10108
Ph: (212)868-5545
Fax: (646)723-0996
E-mail: webmaster@unitedforpeace.org
URL: http://www.unitedforpeace.org
Contact: Leslie Kielson, Contact
Founded: 2002. **Membership Dues:** local organization with no paid staff, $50 (annual) ● local organization with paid staff, $100 (annual) ● national organization with no paid staff, $200 (annual) ● national organization with one paid staff, $300 (annual) ● national organization with more than one paid staff, $500 (annual). **Multinational. Description:** Peace and social justice organizations committed to a peaceful world. **Libraries: Type:** open to the public;

reference. **Holdings:** articles. **Subjects:** activism. **Computer Services:** Mailing lists. **Committees:** Steering. **Formerly:** (2004) United for Peace.

17884 ■ United States Institute of Peace (USIP)
1200 17th St. NW
Washington, DC 20036
Ph: (202)457-1700 (202)429-4144
Fax: (202)429-6063
E-mail: usiprequests@usip.org
URL: http://www.usip.org
Contact: Richard H. Solomon, Pres.

Founded: 1984. **Staff:** 60. **Budget:** $16,000,000. **Multinational. Description:** Federally funded institute created by the United States Congress; board is appointed by the United States President with Senate approval. Promotes and supports peace scholarships and research; facilitates training in negotiation and conflict resolution; compiles statistics. Maintains speakers' bureau. Sponsors grant competitions and research. Conducts study groups and other research analysis projects, convenes public events. **Libraries: Type:** reference. **Holdings:** 11,000; books, periodicals. **Subjects:** conflict management, resolution, diplomacy, negotiations, mediation. **Awards:** Solicited Grant. **Frequency:** semiannual. **Type:** grant. **Recipient:** for nonprofit institutions and individuals ● Unsolicited Grant. **Frequency:** semiannual. **Type:** grant. **Recipient:** for nonprofit institutions and individuals. **Computer Services:** Information services, peace resources ● mailing lists, of members ● online services. **Programs:** Education and Training; Fellowships; Grants; Jeannette Rankin Library; Religion and Peacemaking; Research and Studies; Rule of Law; Virtual Diplomacy. **Publications:** *Peace Watch*, 5/year. Newsletter. **Price:** free ● *Peaceworks/Special Reports* ● Report, biennial ● Books ● Monographs. **Conventions/Meetings:** bimonthly board meeting.

17885 ■ United States Peace Government
2000 Capital Blvd.
Fairfield, IA 52556
Free: (877)424-3546
Fax: (641)472-1165
E-mail: info@uspeacegovernment.org
URL: http://www.uspeacegovernment.org
Contact: John Hagelin PhD, Founder/Pres.

Description: Dedicated to permanently ending terrorism and war through scientific process. **Computer Services:** Information services, periodic news updates and activities.

17886 ■ Veterans for Peace (VFP)
216 S Meramec Ave.
St. Louis, MO 63105
Ph: (314)725-6005
Fax: (314)725-7103
E-mail: vfped@veteransforpeace.net
URL: http://www.veteransforpeace.org
Contact: Mr. Michael T. McPhearson, Exec. Dir.

Founded: 1985. **Members:** 2,500. **Membership Dues:** regular, $25 (annual) ● supporting, $50 (annual) ● sustaining, $100 (annual) ● life, $1,000. **Staff:** 2. **Budget:** $100,000. **State Groups:** 55. **Local Groups:** 50. **Description:** Veterans and supporters. Works to educate the public on: the cost of war; nuclear and U.S. foreign policy issues; the need to abolish war as an instrument of international policy. Works in conjunction with veterans' groups in Canada, France, Great Britain, El Salvador, Israel, Japan, and Russia "to abolish war." Maintains Speaker's Bureau. **Libraries: Type:** reference. **Holdings:** 300; artwork, audiovisuals, books, business records, clippings, periodicals. **Awards:** VFP Medal. **Frequency:** annual. **Type:** medal. **Recipient:** for courage and personal sacrifice in peace work. **Publications:** *VFP Newsletter*, quarterly. Alternate Formats: online ● *Why We Are Veterans for Peace*. Brochure. **Conventions/Meetings:** annual conference - always August.

17887 ■ Voices in the Wilderness (VITW)
1460 W Carmen Ave.
Chicago, IL 60640
Ph: (773)784-8065
Fax: (773)784-8837
E-mail: info@vitw.org
URL: http://vitw.org
Contact: Scott Blackburn, Contact

Founded: 1996. **Multinational. Description:** Aims to end economic and military warfare against the Iraqi people. Promotes nonviolent education and action by developing and practicing ways of nonviolent resistance. **Libraries: Type:** reference. **Holdings:** articles. **Computer Services:** Mailing lists. **Programs:** Counter Terror; Life Under Occupation; Wheels of Justice.

17888 ■ War and Peace Foundation (WP)
20 E 9th St., No. 23E
New York, NY 10003
Ph: (212)228-5836
Fax: (212)228-5791
E-mail: info@warpeace.org
URL: http://www.warpeace.org
Contact: Selma Brackman, Pres./Exec. Dir.

Founded: 1982. **Members:** 1,700. **Staff:** 4. **Budget:** $80,000. **Regional Groups:** 170. **Multinational. Description:** Promotes awareness of issues such as disarmament, poverty, health care, environment, and international cooperation and works with citizens groups to effect change. Supports the role of the United Nations in peaceful conflict resolution. Is concerned with media accountability and facilitating peace and understanding within and between nations. Conducts lobbying. Operates War and Peace Foundation for Education, which distributes materials on issues of peace, environment, and international cooperation. **Libraries: Type:** reference. **Holdings:** 14,000. **Subjects:** government, environment. **Committees:** Advisory; Development; Nobel Laureates. **Publications:** *War and Peace Digest*, bimonthly. Newsletter. **Price:** $15.00/year. **Circulation:** 10,000.

17889 ■ Women in Black (WIB)
PO Box 20554
New York, NY 10021
Ph: (212)560-0905
E-mail: 074182@newschool.edu
URL: http://www.womeninblack.org
Contact: Indira Kajosevic, Contact

Founded: 1988. **Languages:** English, French. **Multinational. Description:** Committed to mobilizing women to protest war; promotes peace. **Additional Websites:** http://www.womeninblack.net. **Telecommunication Services:** electronic mail, womeninblacknyc@yahoo.com. **Conventions/Meetings:** annual international conference.

17890 ■ Women's International League for Peace and Freedom, U.S. Section (WILPF-US)
1213 Race St.
Philadelphia, PA 19107-1617
Ph: (215)563-7110
Fax: (215)563-5527
E-mail: wilpf@wilpf.org
URL: http://www.wilpf.org
Contact: Mary Day Kent, Exec. Dir.

Founded: 1915. **Members:** 7,000. **Membership Dues:** limited income, $15 (annual) ● individual, $35 (annual) ● household, $40 (annual) ● life, $500. **Staff:** 8. **Budget:** $500,000. **Local Groups:** 100. **Description:** Women working, through nonviolent means, to: promote a world free from war, poverty, and violence and to promote economic and social justice for all peoples by working toward the elimination of sexism, racism, classism, and homophobia. International headquarters are in Geneva, Switzerland. **Awards:** Jane Addams Children's Book Award. **Frequency:** annual. **Type:** monetary. **Recipient:** for a youth oriented book that best promotes ideals of international friendship and understanding geared towards youth. **Computer Services:** database ● online services. **Committees:** Africa; Asia/Pacific; CEDAW; Civil Liberties; Death Penalty; Drug Policy; Middle East; Queer Concerns (LGBT); United Nations. **Projects:** Challenge for Corporate Power; Disarm!; Reaching Critical Will; Uniting for Racial Justice; Women and Cuba. **Affiliated With:** Jane Addams Peace Association; Women's International League for Peace and Freedom - Switzerland. **Formerly:** (1919) Women's Peace Party. **Publications:** *International Peace Update*, quarterly. Newsletter. Includes reports from WILPF's international sections, worldwide peace activities with an emphasis on women United Nations events, and book reviews. **Price:** $15.00 /year for individuals. **Circulation:** 5,000. Also Cited As: *IPU* ● *Peace and Freedom*, semiannual. Magazine. Contains news of the organization's activities. Includes book reviews and legislative news. **Price:** included in membership dues; $15.00 /year for nonmembers. **Circulation:** 8,500. **Advertising:** accepted ● *Women for All Seasons*. Book. Contains history of the organization from 1915 to 1985. **Price:** $10.00/issue. **Conventions/Meetings:** triennial congress - usually the 3rd week of June.

17891 ■ World Conference of Religions for Peace (WCRP/USA)
777 UN Plz.
New York, NY 10017
Ph: (212)687-2163
Fax: (212)983-0566
E-mail: info@wcrp.org
URL: http://www.wcrp.org
Contact: Dr. William F. Vendley, Sec. Gen.

Founded: 1970. **Members:** 10,000. **Membership Dues:** individual, $25 (annual) ● institution, $100 (annual). **Staff:** 17. **Budget:** $1,500,000. **Regional Groups:** 2. **National Groups:** 35. **Description:** Works to promote cooperation among the world's religions for peace, while maintaining respect for religious differences. Provides a potent base of local, national, regional, and global levels for a variety of peace-related activities. **Boards:** International Governing. **Programs:** Action and Advocacy for Children; Women's Mobilization. **Formerly:** National Inter-religious Conference on Peace; (1976) United States Interreligious Committee on Peace. **Publications:** *Religion for Peace: A Newsletter on Inter-Religious Dialogue and Action for Peace Issued by the World Conference on Religion and Peace*, 3/year. Focuses on the activities of the conference. Publicizes problems facing the developed and the developing world such as poverty and malnutrition. **Circulation:** 10,000. Alternate Formats: online ● *WCRP/USA Occasional Papers*, periodic ● Brochures ● Monographs. **Conventions/Meetings:** periodic assembly.

17892 ■ World Peace Prayer Society (WPPS)
c/o The World Peace Sanctuary
26 Benton Rd.
Wassaic, NY 12592
Ph: (845)877-6093
Free: (800)PEACELINE
Fax: (845)877-6862
E-mail: info@worldpeace.org
URL: http://www.worldpeace.org
Contact: Ms. Fumi Johns-Stewart, Exec. Dir.

Founded: 1955. **Members:** 300,000. **Staff:** 50. **Languages:** English, Japanese. **Multinational. Description:** Persons advocating world peace. Works to unite people worldwide through the universal message and prayer: "May Peace Prevail on Earth." Plants peace poles, 4-sided pillars with the message of peace inscribed on every side. Performs the World Peace Prayer Ceremony with the flags of all nations. **Programs:** Peace Pals. **Projects:** Peace Pole. **Formerly:** (1992) Society of Prayer for World Peace. **Publications:** *Global Link Newsletter*, semiannual. Alternate Formats: online ● *The Peace Pole Project*. Brochure. Alternate Formats: online. **Conventions/Meetings:** annual Armenia World Peace Festival - meeting, celebration of peace through multicultural entertainment, crafts, food and prayer (exhibits) - around the International Day of Peace in September.

17893 ■ World Without War Council (WWWC)
1730 Martin Luther King, Jr. Way
Berkeley, CA 94709
Ph: (510)845-1992

Fax: (510)845-5721
E-mail: wwwc@wwwc.org
URL: http://www.wwwc.org
Contact: Robert Pickus, Pres.
Founded: 1958. **Staff:** 5. **Budget:** $205,000. **Regional Groups:** 2. **Nonmembership. Description:** Represents program and policy consultant for American independent sector organizations. Offers specialized leadership training and program development to resolve mass political conflict without war that aids in national security and ultimately a stable peace. **Libraries: Type:** reference. **Holdings:** 2,000. **Subjects:** U.S., world affairs, conscience and war, civic education. **Formerly:** (1961) Acts for Peace; (1963) Turn Toward Peace; (1967) World Without War Education Fund. **Publications:** *Christian Pacifism in History, 1971, Nutall, Geoffrey.* Report ● *Governance in World Politics,* Sept. 2001. Books ● *Peace Archives: A Guide to Library Collections, 1986 Green, Marguerite Edition.* Article ● *World Affairs Organizations in Northern California: A Guide to the Field & Related Guides in other Metropolitan Areas,* periodic. Directory ● Brochures ● Also: Camus, Albert, "Neither Victims Nor Executioners," 1972 and Dougall, Lucy, Compiler, "War and Peace in Literature," 1982. **Conventions/Meetings:** periodic conference ● semiannual meeting.

Peace Corps

17894 ■ Lesbian, Gay, Bisexual and Transgender US Peace Corps Alumni (LGBRPCV)
PO Box 14332
San Francisco, CA 94114-4332
Free: (800)424-8580
E-mail: lgbrpcv@lgbrpcv.org
URL: http://www.lgbrpcv.org
Contact: Mike Learned, Natl. Coor./Ed.
Founded: 1991. **Members:** 600. **Membership Dues:** general, $15 (annual). **Regional Groups:** 5. **Description:** Individuals with gay, lesbian, or bisexual sexual orientation who have served in the Peace Corps. Promotes worldwide acceptance of individuals with differing sexual orientation. Conducts charitable and educational programs; maintains speakers' bureau. **Computer Services:** Online services, publication. **Telecommunication Services:** electronic mail, lgbrpcv-news@lgbrpcv.org. **Formerly:** (2004) Lesbian, Gay and Bisexual Returned Peace Corps Volunteers. **Publications:** *LGBRPCV Newsletter,* quarterly. **Circulation:** 600. Alternate Formats: online.

17895 ■ Minority Peace Corps Association (MPCA)
PO Box 244
Village Sta.
New York, NY 10014
Ph: (212)352-5452
Fax: (212)352-5441
E-mail: info@minoritypca.org
URL: http://www.minoritypca.org
Contact: Leslie Jean-Pierre, Pres.
Membership Dues: individual, $15 (annual) ● household, $25 (annual) ● life, $250. **Description:** Promotes community service. Provides support and assistance to Peace Corps volunteers and applicants of color. Enhances the awareness and participation of Americans of color in international experience, international careers and international affairs. **Awards:** Franklin H. Williams Award. **Frequency:** annual. **Type:** recognition. **Recipient:** for dedication to community service and community leadership. **Telecommunication Services:** electronic mail, ljeanpierre@minoritypca.org. **Publications:** Newsletter, quarterly. **Price:** included in membership dues ● Annual Report.

17896 ■ National Peace Corps Association (NPCA)
1900 L St. NW, Ste.205
Washington, DC 20036-5028
Ph: (202)293-7728
Fax: (202)293-7554

E-mail: npca@rpcv.org
URL: http://www.rpcv.org
Contact: Kevin F.F. Quigley PhD, Pres.
Founded: 1979. **Members:** 15,000. **Membership Dues:** individual, $35 (annual) ● affiliate, $15 (annual). **Staff:** 12. **Budget:** $1,400,000. **Local Groups:** 132. **Description:** Former Peace Corps staff and Peace Corps volunteers who have returned to the U.S. from duty overseas; associate members are interested individuals who have not served in the Peace Corps. Seeks to further international understanding and the goals of the Peace Corps by educating and informing U.S. citizens about developing nations. Informs returned volunteers about international affairs and educational and employment opportunities. Sponsors informational fairs. Maintains nationwide network of 76 community based groups and 59 national groups based on third world countries of Peace Corps service to engage returned volunteers in educating Americans about problems of developing nations. Conducts educational programs; coordinates organizations to improve quality of American global education, maintains Speaker's Bureau. Maintains databank to refer members to relief and development agencies for emergency and short-term projects. **Awards:** Continuation of Service Grants. **Frequency:** annual. **Type:** monetary. **Recipient:** for affiliated groups ● Loret Miller Ruppe Award for Outstanding Community Service. **Frequency:** annual. **Type:** recognition. **Recipient:** to an outstanding affiliated group ● Newsletter Award. **Frequency:** annual. **Type:** recognition. **Recipient:** for the best newsletter ● NPCA Website Award. **Frequency:** annual. **Type:** recognition. **Recipient:** to an outstanding group ● Shriver Award for Humanitarian Service. **Frequency:** annual. **Type:** recognition. **Recipient:** for outstanding contribution to humanitarian causes. **Computer Services:** Mailing lists, of former Peace Corps volunteers. **Committees:** Audit; Awards; Communications; Conference; Development; Finance; Government Relations; Program. **Programs:** Advocacy; Global Education; Volunteerism. **Formerly:** National Peace Corps Association; National Council of Returned Peace Corps Volunteers. **Publications:** *Group Leaders Digest,* quarterly. **Circulation:** 750 ● *Hot Line,* biweekly. Newsletter. **Circulation:** 2,000 ● *3/1/61,* quarterly. Newsletter. **Circulation:** 15,000. **Advertising:** accepted ● *World View Magazine,* quarterly. **Price:** $25.00 /year for individuals; $35.00 /year for libraries and institutions. **Circulation:** 20,000. **Advertising:** accepted. Alternate Formats: online ● Annual Reports, annual. Alternate Formats: online. **Conventions/Meetings:** biennial conference, includes speakers, workshops, and social activities (exhibits).

17897 ■ Peace Corps (PC)
c/o Paul D. Coverdell Peace Corps Headquarters
1111 20th St. NW
Washington, DC 20526
Ph: (202)692-2170
Free: (800)424-8580
Fax: (202)692-2171
E-mail: webmaster@peacecorps.gov
URL: http://www.peacecorps.gov
Contact: Gaddi H. Vasquez, Dir.
Founded: 1961. **Members:** 7,400. **Budget:** $241,000,000. **Regional Groups:** 11. **Languages:** English, French, Spanish. **Description:** Independent federal government agency; area offices, recruitment centers, and overseas operations. Seeks to: promote world peace and friendship; help people in other countries meet trained manpower needs; further mutual understanding among Americans and people from other countries. Volunteers are trained in language, technical, and cross-cultural skills. Service lasts for two years, during which the volunteer becomes a part of an overseas community. Projects are primarily in the areas of agricultural and rural development, small business assistance, urban development, health, and education. Serves 80 countries. Sponsors Peace Corps Partnership Program, which provides financial support to selected programs; World Wise Schools program linking U.S. classrooms and overseas volunteers; Fellows/USA program, returning former volunteers to high-need

U.S. communities. **Libraries: Type:** reference. **Holdings:** 26,000. **Divisions:** Africa; Domestic Education; InterAmerica; Pacific Rim, Asia, Central Europe, and Mediterranean. **Formerly:** (1991) United States Peace Corps; (1999) Peace Corps of the United States. **Publications:** *Passport.* Newsletter. Alternate Formats: online ● *U.S. Peace Corps—Annual Report.*

17898 ■ Peace Corps Partnership Program (PCPP)
1111 20th St. NW, 8th Fl.
Washington, DC 20526
Ph: (202)692-2170
Free: (800)424-8580
Fax: (202)692-2171
E-mail: pcpp@peacecorps.gov
URL: http://www.peacecorps.gov
Contact: Gaddi H. Vasquez, Dir.
Founded: 1964. **Staff:** 2. **Languages:** English, French, Spanish. **Description:** Facilitates the active participation of Americans in the development process, promotes community action and involvement both overseas and in the United States, and fosters greater international understanding through opportunities for cross-cultural exchange. **Formerly:** (1965) Peace Corps School to School Program; (1975) Peace Corps School Partnership Program. **Publications:** *Educating through the Peace Corps Partnership Program.* Newsletter ● *Peace Corps Partnership Program Project Listing,* monthly. Newsletter. Contains abstracts on projects in need of support. **Price:** free. **Circulation:** 500 ● *Program Brochure.*

Performing Arts

17899 ■ Return to Unity (RTU)
PO Box 91480
Phoenix, AZ 85066
Ph: (480)892-9223
E-mail: theswingkids@cox.net
URL: http://www.swingkidsusa.org
Contact: Bill Clinton, Pres.
Founded: 1999. **Members:** 28. **Staff:** 5. **Budget:** $22,000. **State Groups:** 1. **Local Groups:** 1. **Description:** Serves as youth program providing WWII USO-style shows for all types of events and locations, focusing on patriotism and seniors. **Libraries: Type:** open to the public. **Holdings:** articles, audio recordings, audiovisuals, clippings, photographs, video recordings. **Awards:** RTU EE Scholarship Bonds. **Frequency:** annual. **Type:** scholarship. **Recipient:** for the youth.

Philanthropy

17900 ■ Arcus Foundation
402 E Michigan Ave.
Kalamazoo, MI 49007
Ph: (269)373-4373
E-mail: contact@arcusfoundation.org
URL: http://www.arcusfoundation.org
Contact: Urvashi Vaid, Exec. Dir.
Founded: 2000. **Languages:** English, Spanish. **Description:** Seeks to "contribute to a pluralistic society that celebrates diversity and dignity, invests in youth and justice, and promotes tolerance and compassion. Promotes and supports the rights of animals to live free of human cruelty and abuse. Supports programs and organizations which recognize that members of the Gay, Lesbian, Bisexual and Transgender (GLBT) community deserve to be welcomed and celebrated.". **Funds:** Arcus; Gay and Lesbian; Great Apes; National. **Publications:** *Ascent.* Newsletter. Alternate Formats: online ● Annual Report. Alternate Formats: online.

17901 ■ Association of Small Foundations (ASF)
1720 N St. NW
Washington, DC 20036
Ph: (202)580-6560
Free: (888)212-9922

Fax: (202)580-6579
E-mail: asf@smallfoundations.org
URL: http://www.smallfoundations.org
Contact: Tim Walter, CEO
Founded: 1995. **Members:** 3,000. **Membership Dues:** foundation, $450 (annual). **Staff:** 15. **Description:** Represents foundations with few or no staff. Provides assistance and education to small foundations. **Additional Websites:** http://www.foundation-inabox.org. **Publications:** *Foundation Operations and Management Survey*, annual. Includes tools for finding benchmark practices for foundations. ● *The Professional Directory for Foundations*, biennial ● Newsletter, quarterly. Alternate Formats: online. **Conventions/Meetings:** biennial conference.

17902 ■ BAPS Care International
81 Suttons Ln., Ste.103
Piscataway, NJ 08854
Ph: (732)777-1818
Free: (800)CAR-E881
Fax: (732)777-1919
E-mail: info@bapscare.org
URL: http://www.bapscare.org
Contact: Mr. Nilesh Dave, Office Admin.
Multinational. Description: Serves the world by caring for societies, families and individuals, including disaster relief, medical care, social care, cultural care, moral care, environmental care, and educational care.

17903 ■ Women in Philanthropy
c/o University of Michigan
Off. of Development
3003 S State St., Ste.9000
Ann Arbor, MI 48109-1288
Ph: (734)647-6000
Fax: (734)647-6100
E-mail: wpresearch@umich.edu
URL: http://www.women-philanthropy.umich.edu
Description: Carries on the work of Ann Castle in cataloging the vital role of women in philanthropy. **Publications:** Newsletters.

Philippines

17904 ■ Filipinos for Affirmative Action (FAA)
310 8th St., Ste.306
Oakland, CA 94607
Ph: (510)465-9876 (510)487-8552
Fax: (510)465-7548
E-mail: faa@filipinos4action.org
URL: http://www.filipinos4action.org
Contact: Lillian Galedo, Exec. Dir.
Founded: 1973. **Members:** 300. **Membership Dues:** kaakbay, $500 (annual) ● kaibigan, $100 (annual) ● kababayan, $50 (annual) ● kasapi, $25 (annual) ● student, senior, unemployed, $15 (annual) ● kapatiran (organizational Ninong and Ninang), $10,000 (annual) ● kapatiran (organizational Lolo and Lola), $5,000 (annual) ● kapatiran (organizational Kuya and Ate), $500 (annual) ● kapatiran (organizational Bunso), $250 (annual). **Staff:** 11. **Budget:** $600,000. **Languages:** English, Tagalog. **Description:** Strives to build a self-sufficient Filipino community; addresses the needs of the most vulnerable in the Filipino community. Provides newcomer assistance, youth development, advocacy and community service, and civil rights advocacy. **Projects:** Bayanihan.

Philosophy

17905 ■ Center for Philosophy, Law, Citizenship (CPLC)
SUNY
Knapp Hall 15
Farmingdale, NY 11735
Ph: (631)420-2047
Contact: Prof. James P. Friel, Pres./Dir.
Founded: 1972. **Members:** 10,000. **Membership Dues:** individual, $20 (annual). **Staff:** 15. **Budget:** $10,000. **Description:** Students, faculty, instructors, and other interested individuals. Seeks recognition of

the person as the focus of the community. Believes that social structures, within which the individual must function in order to participate in society, are necessary in order for the individual to maintain an active role of citizenship and therefore control his or her own life. States that "the law is the basic structure on which citizenship rests"; offers instruction and practice in skills necessary for dealing successfully with the law. Encourages participation in other social structures such as government hearings, consumer groups, juries, and elections. Examines the influence of various cultures on American legal thinking; studies the role of law in success fully maintaining a community or culture. Conducts research and educational programs that help students prepare for college. **Awards:** Citizen of the Year. **Frequency:** annual. **Type:** recognition. **Recipient:** for outstanding leadership. **Publications:** *Humanities Magazine*, 3/year. Dedicated to the integration of the humanities with other fields and to the application of philosophy to humanistic education. Includes book reviews. **Price:** included in membership dues. **Circulation:** 2,000. **Advertising:** accepted ● *Perspectives in Philosophy*, periodic ● Brochure ● Also publishes fact sheet. **Conventions/Meetings:** annual meeting (exhibits) - always Farmingdale, NY.

17906 ■ Lonergan Philosophical Society (LPS)
c/o Dr. Elizabeth A. Murray, Founder/Pres.
Dept. of Philosophy
Loyola Marymount Univ.
1 LMU Dr., Ste.3600
Los Angeles, CA 90045-2659
E-mail: emurray@lmu.edu
URL: http://www.lmu.edu/lonergan/lps.htm
Contact: Dr. Elizabeth A. Murray, Founder/Pres.
Members: 65. **Membership Dues:** general, $10 (annual). **Multinational. Description:** Represents those interested in the philosophy of Bernard Lonergan. Promotes scholarly fellowship through activities and exchange. **Conventions/Meetings:** annual meeting, in conjunction with the American Catholic Philosophical Association.

17907 ■ Radical Philosophy Association (RPA)
c/o Harry van der Linden, Treas.
Philosophy and Religion Dept.
Butler Univ.
4600 Sunset Ave.
Indianapolis, IN 46208
E-mail: hvanderl@butler.edu
URL: http://home.grandecom.net/~jackgm/RPA.html
Contact: Harry van der Linden, Treas.
Founded: 1982. **Membership Dues:** institutional, $69 (annual) ● individual, $42 (annual) ● student, $25 (annual). **Multinational. Description:** Works in opposition to capitalism, racism, sexism, homophobia, disability discrimination, environmental ruin, and all forms of domination. **Computer Services:** Online services, email listserv. **Committees:** Advisory; Cross-Cultural; Internet. **Projects:** Anti-Death Penalty; Anti-Intervention; Anti-Racist Classroom; Disabilities; Prison. **Subgroups:** Latin American Solidarity. **Formerly:** Radical Caucus. **Publications:** *Radical Philosophy Review*, semiannual. Journal. Features original articles, special discussions, and reviews. **Price:** included in membership dues; $69.00 /year for nonmembers (institution); $42.00 /year for nonmembers (individual). ISSN: 1388-4441. Also Cited As: *RPR* ● Membership Directory ● Newsletter, quarterly. **Conventions/Meetings:** conference ● annual meeting, with paper-reading sessions.

17908 ■ Society for Philosophy in the Contemporary World (SPCW)
PO Box 7147
Charlottesville, VA 22906-7147
Ph: (434)220-3300
Free: (800)444-2419
Fax: (434)220-3301
E-mail: afiala@csufresno.edu
URL: http://www.spcw.info
Contact: Trudy Conway PhD, Dir.
Founded: 1993. **Membership Dues:** regular, $50 (annual) ● limited income, $20 (annual) ● life, $1,000.

Description: Committed to the application of philosophy to understanding and solving contemporary social problems. **Publications:** *Philosophy in the Contemporary World*. Journal. Price: included in membership dues. **Conventions/Meetings:** annual conference, includes recreational activities for members and family.

Planning

17909 ■ National Association of Planning Councils (NAPC)
11118 Ferndale Rd.
Dallas, TX 75238
Ph: (214)342-2638
Free: (800)795-9834
E-mail: napc@communityplanning.org
URL: http://www.communityplanning.org
Contact: Pam Kestner-Chappelear, Pres.
Membership Dues: sustaining, $1,500 (annual) ● contributing, $750 (annual) ● supporting, $500 (annual) ● organization, $150-$350 (annual) ● individual, $100 (annual). **Description:** Promotes quality community planning. Provides leadership for community-based human services and health planning and action. Brings people together to identify needs and work toward solutions, mobilizing community involvement, developing and coordinating services and linking people with community resources. **Computer Services:** Information services, community planning resources. **Publications:** Newsletter. Alternate Formats: online.

Policy

17910 ■ PolicyLink
101 Broadway
Oakland, CA 94607
Ph: (510)663-2333
Fax: (510)663-9684
E-mail: info@policylink.org
URL: http://www.policylink.org
Contact: Angela Glover Blackwell, Founder/CEO
Founded: 1999. **Description:** Works to advance policies to achieve economic and social equity. Implements strategies to ensure that everyone, including those from low-income communities of color, can contribute to and benefit from economic growth and prosperity. Strives to bridge the traditional divide between local communities and policymaking at the local, regional, state and national levels.

Political Action

17911 ■ 20/20 Vision National Project
8403 Colesville Rd., Ste.860
Silver Spring, MD 20910
Ph: (301)587-1782
Fax: (301)587-1848
E-mail: vision@2020vision.org
URL: http://www.2020vision.org
Contact: Tom Z. Collina, Exec. Dir.
Founded: 1986. **Members:** 10,000. **Membership Dues:** individual, $20 (annual). **Staff:** 7. **Budget:** $600,000. **Local Groups:** 30. **Description:** Promotes citizen involvement in influencing public policies that endorse protection of the environment, an increase in national and global security, reduction of military spending, and the support of individual economic and social needs. Encourages individual political activism by providing convenient, simple, effective activities designed to take less than 20 minutes to complete. (Organization name is derived from the belief that an individual's contribution of 20 minutes a month and $20 a year can have a significant impact on public policy.) Maintains network of local lobbying groups; provides training and promotional materials to local organizers. **Publications:** *Viewpoint*, quarterly. Newsletter. Tracks status of peace and environmental policy. **Price:** $30.00 for individuals; $50.00 for organizations. **Circulation:** 500.

17912 ■ AIDS Action Council (AAC)
1730 M St. NW, Ste.611
Washington, DC 20036
Ph: (202)530-8030
Fax: (202)530-8031
E-mail: aidsaction@aidsaction.org
URL: http://www.aidsaction.org
Contact: Katy Caldwell, Chair
Founded: 1984. **Members:** 125. **Membership Dues:** affiliate, $500 (annual). **Staff:** 15. **Budget:** $1,500,000. **Description:** Serves as a representative in Washington, DC, of community-based AIDS service organizations. Advocates, at the federal level, for more effective AIDS policy, legislation, and funding. Works collaboratively with AIDS Action Foundation, a national public policy research organization. **Publications:** *AIDS Action Legislative Updates & Action Alerts*, periodic. Brings timely information on HIV/AIDS-related issues to policy makers, community-based organizations, students, researchers, and the public. ● *AIDS Action Policy Briefs*, monthly ● *AIDS Action State Fact Sheets*, annual. Contains fact sheets detailing HIV/AIDS statistics per state. ● *The Weekly Update*. Newsletter. Contains up-to-date information about Washington hearings, debates and decisions, the latest national and international news, etc. **Circulation:** 3,000. Alternate Formats: online.

17913 ■ American Medical Political Action Committee (AMPAC)
1101 Vermont Ave. NW
Washington, DC 20005
Ph: (202)789-4587
Free: (800)262-3211
Fax: (202)789-7449
E-mail: ampaconline@ama-assn.org
URL: http://www.ampaconline.org
Contact: David M. Selby MD, Chm.
Founded: 1961. **Members:** 68,000. **State Groups:** 51. **Description:** Represents physicians, their spouses, and others interested in political action and participation in public affairs. Seeks to further political knowledge of its members and to provide them with means for concerted political action. **Departments:** Political Action; Political Education. **Publications:** *Political Stethoscope*, periodic. Journal ● Also publishes material on campaign techniques.

17914 ■ American Renewal Foundation
PO Box 54
Corbin, VA 22446
Ph: (703)758-4600
E-mail: info@americanrenewal.org
URL: http://www.americanrenewal.org
Contact: Steve Myers, Pres.
Founded: 1995. **Nonmembership. Description:** Explores opportunities for renewal; seeks to provide a voice in the national conversation as well as the vision of the nation's founders, through research and promotion of Christian, ethical solutions to national and global issues. Broadcasts a daily radio news show, The World from Washington, and a weekly radio show for teens called SpeakOut. Runs the web newspaper, Page One Daily. Maintains a large student program; new members are always invited to apply. Provides internship opportunities. **Awards:** Student of the Year. **Frequency:** annual. **Type:** scholarship. **Recipient:** for young people who display virtues in their daily lives. **Programs:** Scholars'; Student. **Conventions/Meetings:** meeting, for the public.

17915 ■ BANKPAC
Amer. Bankers Assn.
1120 Connecticut Ave. NW
Washington, DC 20036
Ph: (202)663-5129 (202)663-5121
Free: (800)BANKERS
Fax: (202)828-6071
E-mail: custserv@aba.com
URL: http://www.aba.com
Contact: Gary Fields, Dir.
Founded: 1970. **Description:** Members of the banking community united to help elect to the U.S. Congress, without regard to party affiliation, those who have shown an interest, understanding, and a concern for banking business and a free economic system in which it can function properly. Acts as the political action committee of the American Bankers Association (see separate entry); makes contributions for campaign expenditures in political contests for seats in the House of Representatives and the Senate; does not make contributions in presidential contests or in contests for state and local offices. **Affiliated With:** American Bankers Association. **Formerly:** (1971) Bankers Political Action Committee; (1976) Banking Profession Political Action Committee. **Conventions/Meetings:** semiannual executive committee meeting.

17916 ■ Better Government Association (BGA)
11 E Adams St., Ste.608
Chicago, IL 60603
Ph: (312)427-8330
Fax: (312)386-9203
E-mail: info@bettergov.org
URL: http://bettergov.org
Contact: Mr. Jay E. Stewart, Exec. Dir.
Founded: 1923. **Members:** 3,000. **Membership Dues:** citizen, $50 (annual) ● advocate, $100 (annual) ● investigator, $250 (annual) ● policy maker, $500 (annual) ● whistleblower, $1,000 (annual). **Staff:** 8. **Budget:** $500,000. **Description:** Individuals and corporations concerned with major public policy questions and dedicated to promoting efficient use of tax dollars and high standards of public service. Encourages a responsive and economical government by improving government institutions' performance and maintaining high ethical standards among public officials. Uses official documents, on-the-record interviews, undercover operations, and sophisticated techniques of investigative reporting to uncover corruption. Works closely with national and local media to expose waste, inefficiency, and corruption and to educate the public on the inner workings of the government. Sponsors intern programs for students in law and investigative research. **Awards:** Civic Achievement. **Frequency:** annual. **Type:** recognition ● George Bliss Award. **Frequency:** annual. **Type:** recognition. **Recipient:** for excellence in investigative reporting. **Boards:** Advisory; Junior. **Programs:** Alumni; Annual Awards; Internship; Investigative. **Publications:** *Consumer's Guide to Long Term Health Care Facilities.* **Price:** $74.50/set; $26.50/book. **Advertising:** accepted ● *Watch*, quarterly. Newsletter ● Annual Report, annual ● Also publishes special reports. **Conventions/Meetings:** annual Benefit - meeting, awards benefit (exhibits) - in September.

17917 ■ Business Alliance for Commerce in Hemp (BACH)
PO Box 1716
El Cerrito, CA 94530
Ph: (510)215-8326
Fax: (510)234-4460
E-mail: chris@chrisconrad.com
URL: http://www.equalrights4all.org/bach/BACHcore.html
Contact: Chris Conrad, Dir.
Founded: 1989. **Description:** Businesses, consumers, and other individuals and organizations with an interest in hemp and hemp products. Promotes "full and unrestricted restoration of hemp as a sustainable farm crop and industrial resource;" seeks to legalize therapeutic use of marijuana and regulate adult consumption. Conducts lobbying, community organization, and outreach activities supporting hemp producers and consumers; consulting services; disseminates information on the commercial and industrial uses of hemp and the therapeutic benefits of marijuana. **Publications:** *Cannabis Yields and Dosage.* Booklet. Features practical review of the basics of cultivating and using cannabis for medical purposes. Includes CA and other state laws on the subject. **Price:** $5.99 plus shipping and handling ($3). **Circulation:** 8,000. Alternate Formats: CD-ROM; online ● *Hemp for Health.* Book. **Price:** $14.95 plus shipping and handling; $20.00 in Canada; $25.00 outside U.S. Alternate Formats: online ● *Hemp,*

Lifeline to the Future. Book. **Price:** $12.95 plus shipping and handling. Alternate Formats: online.

17918 ■ Business-Industry Political Action Committee (BIPAC)
888 16th St. NW, Ste.305
Washington, DC 20006
Ph: (202)833-1880
Fax: (202)833-2338
E-mail: info@bipac.org
URL: http://www.bipac.org
Contact: Gregory S. Casey, Pres./CEO
Founded: 1963. **Members:** 400. **Membership Dues:** corporate, $20,000 (annual). **Staff:** 12. **Budget:** $1,600,000. **Regional Groups:** 6. **Description:** Works as independent, bipartisan organization that works to elect pro-business candidates to Congress; has group's Business Institute for Political Analysis that carries out extensive programs of political analysis, research, and communication on campaigns and elections, and fosters business participation in the political process. **Awards:** The Adam Smith Award. **Frequency:** annual. **Type:** recognition. **Recipient:** to a federal elected official and a leading member of the business community for outstanding contributions to the principles of free enterprise. **Additional Websites:** http://www.politikit.com. **Publications:** *Action Report*, quarterly. Newsletter. Contains information about BIPAC. Alternate Formats: online ● *Elections Insight*, semimonthly. Journal. Provides the American business community with objective political research and analysis on campaigns and candidates. **Price:** free ● Also publishes research studies and voting records. **Conventions/Meetings:** monthly PAC Workshops - workshop and roundtable, informal discussions focused on the topics associated with Organization's mission ● monthly Washington Briefing - meeting, political briefing.

17919 ■ Campaign for America
Address Unknown since 2007
Description: Political fund organization.

17920 ■ Campaign for Working Families (CWF)
PO Box 97163
Washington, DC 20090-7163
Ph: (703)671-8800
Fax: (703)671-8899
E-mail: info@cwfpac.com
URL: http://www.cwfpac.com
Contact: Gary L. Bauer, Chm.
Founded: 1996. **Description:** Represents the interests and values of America's traditional families in the political arena. Works on electing pro-family, pro-life and pro-free enterprise candidates to federal and state offices. Conducts extensive media campaigns and distribution of literature.

17921 ■ Common Cause (CC)
1133 19th St. NW, 9th Fl.
Washington, DC 20036
Ph: (202)833-1200
Free: (800)926-1064
E-mail: grassroots@commoncause.org
URL: http://www.commoncause.org
Contact: Chellie Pingree, Pres./CEO
Founded: 1970. **Members:** 220,000. **Membership Dues:** individual, $20 (annual) ● family, $30 (annual). **Staff:** 85. **Budget:** $10,000,000. **State Groups:** 41. **Description:** Nonpartisan citizens' lobby. Dedicated to fighting for open, honest, and accountable government at the national, state, and local levels. Gathers and disseminates information on the effects of money in politics; lobbies for political finance and other campaign reforms. **Awards:** Public Service Achievement Award. **Frequency:** annual. **Type:** recognition. **Recipient:** for individuals who have made outstanding contributions to the public interest in the areas of government performance and integrity. **Funds:** Common Cause Education. **Formerly:** (1970) Urban Coalition Action Council. **Conventions/Meetings:** board meeting - 3/year.

17922 ■ Congressional Agenda: Millennium (CA: 90's)
3220 N St. NW, Ste.178
Washington, DC 20007
Ph: (202)342-9192
Contact: John R. Wagley, Treas.
Founded: 1982. **Staff:** 2. **Description:** Raises funds for congressional representatives working to alter current administration policy trends so that programs developed in the 1970s can be adapted to present needs. Areas of specific attention include the economy, nuclear arms, and environmental preservation. Seeks to reduce interest rates, defer some proposed tax cuts, eliminate unnecessary defense expenditures, and end cuts in domestic programs that are seen as investments in future growth, such as employment training, education, transport, housing, utilities, and water systems. Works toward restoration of funding and governmental support for environmental preservation programs. **Formerly:** Congressional Agenda: 80's; (2003) Congressional Agenda: 90's. **Supersedes:** Committee for 10; Committee for 12; Committee for 15; Class of '74.

17923 ■ Consumers United for Rail Equity (CURE)
1050 Thomas Jefferson St. NW, 6th Fl.
Washington, DC 20007
Ph: (202)298-1844
Fax: (202)338-2416
E-mail: rcw@vnf.com
URL: http://www.railcure.org
Contact: Robert S. Szabo, Chief Counsel
Founded: 1983. **Membership Dues:** company, $25,000 (annual) ● trade association, $20,000 (annual). **Description:** Coalition of railroad shippers that are captive to a single railroad for their transportation needs. **Publications:** *Rail Report*, monthly. Newsletter. Alternate Formats: online.

17924 ■ The Creative Coalition (TCC)
665 Broadway, Ste.804
New York, NY 10012
Ph: (212)614-2121 (212)614-2143
Fax: (212)614-2142
E-mail: info@thecreativecoalition.org
URL: http://www.thecreativecoalition.org
Contact: Robin Bronk, Exec. Dir.
Founded: 1989. **Membership Dues:** individual, $250 (annual) ● couple, $450 (annual) ● non-profit organization, $500 (annual) ● corporation, $1,000 (annual). **Description:** Actors, writers, directors and other arts and entertainment professionals. Aims to educate members about social and political issues, particularly in the areas of the First Amendment, arts advocacy and public education. **Awards:** Christopher Reeve First Amendment Award. **Frequency:** annual. **Type:** recognition. **Recipient:** for individuals who are dedicated to the sanctity of the first amendment and its free speech provision ● Spotlight Award. **Frequency:** periodic. **Type:** recognition. **Recipient:** for individuals/organizations who are dedicated to improving the quality of life for all Americans and have exhibited a long standing commitment to the arts. **Telecommunication Services:** electronic mail, robin@tcconline.org.

17925 ■ Democracy International (DI)
4802 Montgomery Ln., Ste.200
Bethesda, MD 20814
Ph: (301)961-1660
Fax: (301)961-6605
E-mail: info@democracyinternational.us
URL: http://www.democracyinternational.us
Contact: Eric Bjornlund, Pres.
Founded: 1979. **Members:** 1,000. **Description:** Seeks to build a movement of individuals dedicated to practical action on behalf of common commitments to human rights and pluralistic democracy including freedom of speech and press, religious liberty, free political parties, and the right to contest elections. Works to develop political and economic self-determination of citizens allowing them to control their resources, choose their social systems, and end discrimination. Aims to: revive democracy where it has been destroyed; encourage and sustain demo-

crats trying to bring democracy to dictatorships. Calls upon democracies to: increase help for democratic leaders and politicians in the Third World; provide economic sustenance to relieve human suffering; strengthen democracy where it exists. Provides a forum for democrats to express solidarity and to help each other; encourages membership in an effort to build an international force of people working to make the cause of democracy an enduring ideal. Publicizes the efforts of democratic movements in dictatorships; attempts to increase the amount of uncensored information to closed societies. **Convention/Meeting:** none. **Publications:** *The Pluralist*, semiannual. Bulletin.

17926 ■ Dredging Industry Size Standard Committee (DISSC)
c/o James A. Reeder
Patton, Boggs
2550 M St. NW
Washington, DC 20037
Ph: (202)457-6000
Fax: (202)457-6315
E-mail: info@pattonboggs.com
URL: http://www.pattonboggs.com
Description: Provides a legislative forum for the dredging industry. Represents the interests of the industry; lobbies for favorable federal legislation.

17927 ■ EMILY's List (EL)
1120 Connecticut Ave. NW, Ste.1100
Washington, DC 20036-3949
Ph: (202)326-1400
Free: (800)68-EMILY
Fax: (202)326-1415
E-mail: information@emilyslist.org
URL: http://www.emilyslist.org
Contact: Ellen R. Malcolm, Pres./Founder
Founded: 1985. **Members:** 73,000. **Staff:** 60. **Description:** Political network for Democratic women. Seeks to raise campaign funds for the election of pro-choice Democratic women to political office. (EMILY stands for Early Money is Like Yeast.) **Convention/Meeting:** none. **Programs:** Political Opportunity. **Publications:** *Notes from EMILY*, quarterly. Newsletter. Alternate Formats: online.

17928 ■ Free Congress Research and Education Foundation (FCREF)
c/o Free Congress Foundation
717 2nd St. NE
Washington, DC 20002
Ph: (202)546-3000
Fax: (202)543-5605
E-mail: jborda@freecongress.org
URL: http://www.freecongress.org
Founded: 1977. **Members:** 80,000. **Staff:** 10. **Budget:** $100,000,000. **Description:** Brings messages of traditional values, conservative government, and institutional reform to America through publications and TV programs on America's Voice network. Includes projects such as: Judicial Selection Monitoring Project, "Taking Back Our Constitution" seminar services and the Center for Technology Policy's privacy papers. **Publications:** *Essays on our Times*, monthly. Addresses cultural and political issues from a conservative perspective. ● *The Judicial Selection Monitor*. A regular look at issues involving the selecting of federal judges. **Price:** $50.00/year ● *Policy Insights*. Examines political issues. ● *The Weyrich Insider*, monthly. Features an inside look at politics by one of the foremost strategists of the conservative movement. **Price:** $50.00/year. **Conventions/Meetings:** periodic Council on the Constitution - meeting, small group of conservative philanthropists dedicated to constitutional principles.

17929 ■ FreedomWorks
1775 Pennsylvania Ave. NW, 11th Fl.
Washington, DC 20006-5805
Ph: (202)783-3870
Free: (888)564-6273
Fax: (202)942-7649

E-mail: ckinnan@freedomworks.org
URL: http://www.empoweramerica.org
Contact: Matt Kibbe, Pres./CEO
Founded: 1993. **Description:** Devoted to ensuring that government actions foster growth, economic well being and individual responsibility. Sponsors an internship program, introducing its participants to the Washington policy world, giving them a broader base of knowledge about the organization and its inner operations. **Additional Websites:** http://www.freedomworks.org. **Conventions/Meetings:** semiannual conference.

17930 ■ Fund for New Priorities in America (FFNPA)
171 Madison Ave.
New York, NY 10016
Ph: (212)685-8848
Fax: (212)685-8970
E-mail: info@fundfornewpriorities.org
Contact: Stanley Weithorn, Pres.
Founded: 1969. **Membership Dues:** individual, $50 (annual) ● supporter, $250 (annual) ● family, $100 (annual) ● sustainer, $500 (annual). **Staff:** 3. **Description:** Believes that the United States must reorder its national priorities. Works to inform the public, to build active networks and coalitions, and to enhance participatory democracy, in pursuit of a more just, peaceful, open, and humane society. Sponsors public forums. **Awards:** New Priorities Award. **Frequency:** annual. **Type:** recognition. **Recipient:** for an individual or organization that has worked to further the vision of a more just and peaceful society in a manner consistent with the mission of the association. **Projects:** Business, Labor, and Community Coalition; Congressional Conferences; Foreign Relations Watch; Foundation for Social Change; Social Action and Leadership School for Activists (SALSA); Worldwide Anti-Nuclear Campaign. **Publications:** *Congressional Conference Reports*, periodic ● *New Priorities Report*, quarterly ● Books ● Also makes available videotapes of congressional conferences and seminars. **Conventions/Meetings:** annual Awards Dinner - meeting ● periodic Congressional Conference.

17931 ■ International Union, UAW - Community Action Program (National CAP)
8000 E Jefferson Ave.
Solidarity House
Detroit, MI 48214
Ph: (313)926-5000
Free: (800)243-8829
Fax: (313)824-5750
E-mail: uaw@uaw.org
URL: http://www.uaw.org/about/works/community.html
Contact: Mr. Ron Gettelfinger, Pres.
Founded: 1969. **Staff:** 40. **Regional Groups:** 12. **Local Groups:** 155. **Description:** Serves as a program of the International Union, United Automobile, Aerospace and Agricultural Implement Workers of America (UAW) (see separate entry). Informs UAW members through political education programs on topics including lobbying, the relationship between collective bargaining and the ballot box, and voluntary fundraising for political contributions. Maintains speakers' bureau; compiles statistics. **Councils:** State CAP. **Formerly:** (2002) United Auto Workers Community Action Program. **Publications:** *Skill*, quarterly. Magazine. For skilled-trade workers, technicians and engineers of the UAW. **Price:** $5.00 /year for nonmembers. Alternate Formats: online ● *Solidarity*, bimonthly. Magazine. **Price:** $60.00 /year for members; $5.00 /year for nonmembers. Alternate Formats: online. **Conventions/Meetings:** annual conference ● seminar.

17932 ■ League of Revolutionaries for a New America (LRNA)
PO Box 477113
Chicago, IL 60647
Ph: (773)486-0028
Free: (800)691-6888
Fax: (773)486-1728

E-mail: info@lrna.org
URL: http://www.lrna.org
Contact: Laura Garcia, Ed.
Membership Dues: employed, $50 (annual) ● unemployed, $20 (annual). **Languages:** English, Spanish. **Description:** Works toward a vision of a cooperative world where the full potential of all can contribute to the good of everyone. **Publications:** *People's Tribune.* Newspaper. Alternate Formats: online.

17933 ■ National Association of Business Political Action Committees (NABPAC)

101 Constitution Ave. NW, Ste.800-West
Washington, DC 20001
Ph: (202)341-3780
Fax: (202)478-0342
E-mail: nabpac@nabpac.org
URL: http://www.nabpac.org
Contact: Geoffrey C. Ziebart, Exec. Dir.
Founded: 1977. **Members:** 150. **Membership Dues:** regular (based on total PAC receipts for the previous two-year election cycle), $1,750-$5,000 (annual). **Staff:** 2. **Budget:** $350,000. **Description:** Political action professionals and government affairs representatives interested in campaign finance reform issues and innovations in political action committee management. **Libraries: Type:** reference. **Holdings:** audiovisuals. **Publications:** *NABPAC Campaign Finance Reform Principles Restoring the Public Trust: Preserving and Enhancing Political Participation for All Americans.* Paper. Alternate Formats: online ● *NABPAC Newsmemo on Campaign Finance and Election Law,* monthly. **Circulation:** 200 ● *The Pac Professional,* weekly. Newsletter. Provides information on campaign finance law revisions and other matters relating to PAC development, with news summaries and legislative updates. **Price:** included in membership dues. **Circulation:** 200. **Advertising:** accepted. Alternate Formats: online. **Conventions/Meetings:** periodic conference, vendors to political action committees (exhibits) ● semiannual seminar.

17934 ■ Paul Revere Society (PRS)

150 Shoreline Hwy., Bldg. E
Mill Valley, CA 94941
Fax: (415)339-9383
E-mail: paulreveresociety@yahoo.com
URL: http://www.homestead.com/prosites-prs/frontpage.html
Contact: Michael Savage, Founder
Founded: 1996. **Membership Dues:** individual, $40 (annual) ● individual, $70 (biennial). **Description:** Seeks to have a strong voice to the political arena; strives for the reassertion of America's borders, language and culture. Opposes the viewpoint that English is only one of many languages in the new "Multicultural America" and that Americans share no common history or values; believes in the Sovereignty of America, that English is the national "glue", that all Americans do share in the pillars of the Bible, the U.S. Constitution, and the Bill of Rights, and that these documents stand for American's common cultural heritage. **Publications:** *The Best of the Savage Nation.* Book. **Price:** included with two-year membership. Alternate Formats: CD-ROM ● *The Death of the White Male.* Booklet. **Price:** included in membership dues; $9.00 for nonmembers.

17935 ■ Pay for Schools by Regulating Cannabis

PO Box 86741
Portland, OR 97286
Ph: (503)229-0428
E-mail: treefreeeco@igc.apc.org
URL: http://www.erowid.org/psychoactives/law/bills/psychoactive_bills2.shtml
Contact: D. Paul Stanford, Dir.
Founded: 1990. **Members:** 10,000. **Membership Dues:** PAC, $50 (annual). **Staff:** 7. **Budget:** $1,200,000. **State Groups:** 1. **Local Groups:** 12. **Description:** Concerned citizens who believe in hemp's environmental benefits. Seeks to regulate cannabis sales in state liquor stores to fund education and drug treatment programs. Promotes hemp manufacture for paper, fabrics, oil and pharmaceuti-

cal prescriptions. Conducts educational programs; compiles statistics; maintains Speaker's Bureau. **Libraries: Type:** reference. **Holdings:** clippings. **Computer Services:** Electronic publishing, news stories on hemp. **Publications:** *Hemp News.* Bulletin ● *Regulate It!,* monthly. Newsletter. **Price:** included in membership dues. **Circulation:** 10,000. **Advertising:** accepted. **Conventions/Meetings:** weekly conference ● annual convention (exhibits).

17936 ■ Political Department of the AFL-CIO

815 16th St. NW, 7th Fl.
Washington, DC 20006
Ph: (202)637-5000
Fax: (202)637-5058
E-mail: feedback@aflcio.org
URL: http://www.aflcio.org
Contact: John J. Sweeny, Pres.
Founded: 1955. **State Groups:** 50. **Description:** AFL-CIO members and others interested in helping to elect progressive and pro-labor candidates to public office. **Departments:** Public Relations; Research. **Formed by Merger of:** Labor's League for Political Education; Political Action Committee. **Formerly:** (1998) Committee on Political Education, AFL-CIO.

17937 ■ Refuse and Resist

305 Madison Ave., Ste.1166
New York, NY 10165
Ph: (212)713-5657
E-mail: info@refuseandresist.org
URL: http://www.refuseandresist.org
Contact: Robert Rockwell, Sec.
Founded: 1987. **Membership Dues:** basic, $35-$100 (annual) ● student/youth, $20. **Local Groups:** 15. **Description:** Participants seek to build mass resistance to the "entire agenda of repression in the U.S." Works to unite grassroots activists, prominent entertainers, teachers, plumbers, artists, student, etc. in opposition to the fundamentalist right-wing agenda. Opposes racism, restrictions on abortion rights, the escalation of the "war on women", censorship, homophobia, xenophobia, and the execution of Mumia Abu-Jamal. Has demonstrated to prevent the closing of abortion clinics and the incarceration of immigrants. Participates in debates; maintains Speaker's Bureau. **Awards:** Courageous Resister Awards. **Frequency:** biennial. **Type:** recognition. **Recipient:** for notable individual resistance to repressive measures. **Projects:** Philadelphia Freedom Counteroffensive Summer. **Subgroups:** Artists Network; Youth Network. **Task Forces:** Reproductive Freedom. **Working Groups:** Mumia Abu-Jamal; Reproductive Freedom. **Publications:** *Counterattack,* quarterly. Newsletter. Includes news of local actions and new campaigns and info about current repressive measures around the country. **Price:** free for members; $1.00 for nonmembers. Alternate Formats: online ● *Refuse and Resist! E-News and Alerts.* Newsletter. Alternate Formats: online. **Conventions/Meetings:** semiannual conference.

17938 ■ Resist

259 Elm St.
Somerville, MA 02144
Ph: (617)623-5110
E-mail: resistinc@igc.org
URL: http://www.resistinc.org
Contact: Robin Carton, Grant and Fiscal Mgr.
Founded: 1967. **Staff:** 3. **Description:** Provides grants to small progressive groups in all parts of the country; has aided groups that have organized for reproductive rights for women, gay rights, nuclear disarmament, the rights of Third World people, and work for social and economic justice. **Libraries: Type:** reference. **Computer Services:** Mailing lists. **Publications:** *Finding Funding: A Beginner's Guide to Foundation Research, 5th Edition.* Alternate Formats: online ● *Resist Newsletter: A Call to Resist Illegitimate Authority,* bimonthly. Concerned with social change on a national and international scale. Focuses on peace and justice issues such as disarmament and anti-intervention. **Price:** included in membership dues; $20.00 /year for libraries and institutions. ISSN: 0897-2613. **Circulation:** 10,000.

Alternate Formats: online. **Conventions/Meetings:** bimonthly meeting.

17939 ■ Social Democrats, U.S.A. (SDUSA)

815 15th St. NW, Ste.921
Washington, DC 20005
Ph: (202)638-1515
Fax: (202)457-0029
E-mail: info@socialdemocrats.org
URL: http://www.socialdemocrats.org
Contact: David Jessup, Pres.
Founded: 1972. **Staff:** 6. **Local Groups:** 25. **Description:** Serves as political action and education organization of young people, students, and trade unionists. Supports Independent and Democratic liberal-labor candidates for public office. Seeks realignment of the major political parties in the U.S. Maintains Speaker's Bureau. Supports "greater democratic decision-making over the social forces that control our everyday economic lives." Recommends democratic economic planning to ease pains of the economic crisis and to allocate resources in the public interest. Favors public aid to education and increased public investment in such areas as national health care, mass transit, low-cost housing, and new sources of energy. Supports trade unionism. Believes in foreign policy that supports democratic movements and governments. **Awards:** Eugene V. Debs Award. **Frequency:** annual. **Type:** recognition. **Committees:** National; National Action. **Councils:** National Advisory. **Formed by Merger of:** Socialist Party, U.S.A.; Democratic Socialist Federation. **Formerly:** (1973) Socialist Party-Democratic Socialist Federation; (1977) Young Peoples Socialist League; (1998) Young Social Democrats. **Publications:** *The American Challenge* ● *Does America Need a Social Democratic Movement?* ● *New America,* monthly ● *The Social Democrat,* periodic. **Price:** free ● *The Social Democratic Prospect* ● *Socialist Currents,* quarterly ● *Why America Needs a Social Democratic Movement* ● *YSD Bulletin,* monthly ● Pamphlets ● Papers ● Proceedings. **Price:** $7.95. **Conventions/Meetings:** semiannual convention.

17940 ■ U.S.English (USE)

1747 Pennsylvania Ave. NW, Ste.1050
Washington, DC 20006
Ph: (202)833-0100
Free: (800)873-4547
Fax: (202)833-0108
E-mail: info@usenglish.org
URL: http://www.us-english.org
Contact: Mr. Mauro E. Mujica, CEO/Chm.
Founded: 1983. **Members:** 1,600,000. **Staff:** 10. **Budget:** $2,000,000. **Description:** Aims to preserve the common bond by making English the official language of government in the U.S. Promotes opportunities for people living here to learn English. **Libraries: Type:** reference. **Holdings:** 5,000. **Publications:** *Democracy or Babel.* Book ● *English in America: A Study of Linguistic Integration.* Report ● *English: The Global Language.* Book. Explores the phenomenal spread of the English language. ● *Many Languages, One America.* Report ● *Report Card on Bilingual Education in the United States 1993-1994* ● *U.S. English Report,* quarterly. Newsletter. Includes status of pertinent legislation. **Price:** included in membership dues.

Political Federations

17941 ■ Ashburn Institute for Global Studies in Federalism and Democracy (AI)

PO Box 77164
Washington, DC 20013-7164
Ph: (202)220-1388
Fax: (202)220-1389
E-mail: info@ashburninstitute.org
URL: http://www.ashburninstitute.org
Contact: Marielle Reiss, Exec. Dir.
Founded: 1940. **Membership Dues:** small business, $125 ● sustaining small business, $250 ● large business, $300 ● sustaining large business, $500. **Staff:** 4. **Budget:** $331,500. **Regional Groups:** 2. **State**

Groups: 2. **Nonmembership. Description:** Promotes Euro-Atlantic cooperation and the enlargement of the Euro-Atlantic community where newly democratic nations can find support in sustaining strong democracies through educational and cultural exchange among the representatives of the global community, academic conferences and student conferences, roundtable discussions, meetings, publications, distance learning programs, and scholarship grants. **Libraries: Type:** reference. **Holdings:** 300; archival material. **Subjects:** international federalism. **Awards:** Frank Educational Fund. **Frequency:** semiannual. **Type:** scholarship. **Recipient:** for graduate students in international affairs and political science. **Committees:** Frank Scholarship Fund. **Formerly:** (1940) Federal Union; (2004) Association to Unite the Democracies. **Publications:** *Unite!*, quarterly. Newsletter. Covers economic, political, military, and diplomatic interaction among industrial democracies. **Price:** included in membership dues; $20.00 /year for nonmembers. **Circulation:** 2,500. Alternate Formats: online ● Also publishes information kits and pamphlets. **Conventions/Meetings:** semiannual board meeting, citizens constitutional convention - usually January and July ● quarterly Global Governance: A Tripartite Approach to Government Relations - roundtable ● annual Redefining Europe Series - conference - in March.

17942 ■ Council of Volunteer Americans (CVA)
c/o Citizens' Investigative Commission
PO Box 1222
Sterling, VA 20167
Ph: (703)379-9188
E-mail: info@conservativeaction.org
URL: http://conservativeaction.org
Contact: Jack Clayton, VP
Founded: 1981. **Members:** 100,000. **Staff:** 5. **Description:** Individuals opposed to the policies of former President Bill Clinton and Senator Hillary Clinton Seeks to "hold the Clinton White House accountable" for what the group believes are "numerous improprieties and wrongdoings". Advocates the "investigation, impeachment and prosecution of former President Clinton and Senator Hillary Clinton and other administration officials." Operates Clinton Investigative Commission. Conducts petition drives, rallies, and protests against liberal policies in the George W. Bush White House. **Computer Services:** Online services, publication. **Publications:** *Report to Congress*, monthly. Newsletter. Alternate Formats: online. **Conventions/Meetings:** quarterly board meeting.

17943 ■ Crusade to Abolish War and Armaments by World Law (CAWAWL)
Address Unknown since 2007
Founded: 1980. **Members:** 100. **Description:** Supporters in 30 countries united to establish a democratically-elected federal world government with the authority to outlaw war and armaments. Plans to: buy media advertising to urge the abolition of war; file a citizen's suit against national governments for wars and actions related to war; research ways to unite multinational corporations, international trade unions, and the World Council of Churches (see separate entry) and other religious groups into one coalition that will strive for "a world without war"; appeal to national governments to introduce measures calling for world government and establishing ministries of peace. Issues flyers and petitions; maintains speakers' bureau. **Convention/Meeting:** none. Presently inactive.

17944 ■ Independent Women's Forum (IWF)
1726 M St. NW, 10th Fl.
Washington, DC 20036-4527
Ph: (202)419-1820
Free: (800)224-6000
Fax: (703)558-4994
E-mail: info@iwf.org
URL: http://www.iwf.org
Contact: Michelle D. Bernard, Pres./CEO
Founded: 1992. **Membership Dues:** junior, $25 (annual) ● associate, $35 (annual) ● silver club, $100

(annual) ● gold club, $500 (annual) ● president's club, $1,000 (annual). **Staff:** 13. **Description:** Individuals and organizations. Promotes "individual responsibility, limited government, and economic opportunity". Conducts lobbying and advocacy activities. **Publications:** Booklet, annual ● Reports ● Articles. Alternate Formats: online.

17945 ■ League of Conservation Voters (LCV)
1920 L St. NW, Ste.800
Washington, DC 20036
Ph: (202)785-8683
Fax: (202)835-0491
E-mail: lcv@lcv.org
URL: http://www.lcv.org
Contact: Gene Karpinski, Pres.
Founded: 1970. **Members:** 40,000. **Membership Dues:** regular, $25 (annual). **Staff:** 50. **Budget:** $2,627,000. **Description:** Seeks to protect the environment through political action, by helping to elect pro-conservation candidates to Congress and holding members accountable for their actions. **Publications:** *LCV Insider*, quarterly. Newsletter ● *The National Environmental Scorecard*, annual. Provides the environmental scores for the last session of the Congress. Alternate Formats: online ● *Presidential Profiles*. Contains information about the candidates. ● Newsletter, weekly. Covers the environment and politics. ● Also publishes elections reports every election year.

17946 ■ Physicians for a National Health Program (PNHP)
29 E Madison St., Ste.602
Chicago, IL 60602
Ph: (312)782-6006
Fax: (312)782-6007
E-mail: info@pnhp.org
URL: http://www.pnhp.org
Contact: Dr. Ida Hellander, Exec. Dir.
Founded: 1987. **Members:** 10,000. **Membership Dues:** regular, $120 (annual) ● medical resident/low income physician/other health professional, health reform advocate, $40 (annual) ● sustaining, $250 (annual) ● student, $20 (annual). **Staff:** 5. **Budget:** $320,000. **State Groups:** 35. **Description:** Physicians and health care workers supporting universal access to health care. Promotes adoption of a comprehensive, single-payer national health care system. Serves as a clearinghouse on strategies for health care reform. Conducts educational programs to raise public awareness of need for single-payer national health care reform; research. **Awards:** Dr. Quentin Young Health Activist Award. **Frequency:** annual. **Type:** recognition. **Recipient:** for activism. **Publications:** *Action Alerts*. Includes e-mail news. ● *Health Policy "Quote of the Day"*. Includes e-mail news. ● Newsletter, quarterly. Features update on health care issues. **Price:** included in membership dues. **Circulation:** 10,000 ● Periodic Press Releases. **Conventions/Meetings:** semiannual convention and meeting, with discussions and strategy planning sessions - every fall and spring.

17947 ■ Semisocialist Coalition of Earth
PO Box 4051
Bluefield, WV 24701
Ph: (304)327-6265
E-mail: semisocialist@excite.com
URL: http://semisocialist.bizland.com
Founded: 1997. **Staff:** 1. **Description:** Members are people of all races, religions, ages and sexual preferences. Seeks to end poverty, racism, environmental destruction and to establish a global socioeconomic network independent of "the existing elitist world order". Semisocialism is defined as the socialist distribution of essential resources, services and the free-market distribution of non-essentials. Supports charitable activities concerning environmental preservation, population control, and social and economic justice.

17948 ■ United Fascist Union (UFU)
PO Box 2209
Elkton, MD 21922

E-mail: joanne_parker20@hotmail.com
URL: http://www.ufu.gq.nu
Contact: Jesus Peterson, Contact
Founded: 1989. **Members:** 1,800. **Membership Dues:** supporter, $10 (monthly). **Staff:** 4. **Regional Groups:** 18. **State Groups:** 2. **Local Groups:** 1. **Description:** Individuals interested in preserving law and order and in guiding "humanity into a new age of peace, plenty and prosperity." Promotes a revival of the Roman Empire and of "culture and traditions of ancient Babylon." Conducts educational and charitable programs; maintains speakers' bureau. **Additional Websites:** http://joanne21921.tripod.com. **Telecommunication Services:** electronic mail, jesus_with_a_gun@yahoo.com. **Subgroups:** Grand Council; Great Babylonian Sisterhood; One Order Militia. **Publications:** *Corporate Statement*, quarterly. Newsletter ● *Dawn of the New Millennium*. Video. **Price:** $18.00 ● *New World Order for the New Millennium*. Book. **Price:** $45.00. **Conventions/Meetings:** quarterly board meeting, convention of the corporate collective ● biweekly board meeting ● annual meeting.

17949 ■ U.S. Term Limits Foundation (USTL)
73 Spring St., Ste.408
New York, NY 10012
E-mail: info@ustl.org
URL: http://www.ustl.org
Contact: Howard Rich, Pres.
Founded: 1992. **Members:** 175,000. **Staff:** 12. **Budget:** $1,400,000. **Description:** Individuals and organizations. Seeks to "restore citizen control of government by rallying Americans to limit congressional, state, and local terms". Conducts promotional and educational activities. **Computer Services:** Mailing lists, of members. **Telecommunication Services:** electronic mail, info@ustermlimits.org. **Publications:** *No Uncertain Terms/The Legal Limit*, monthly. Newsletter. **Circulation:** 50,000. **Conventions/Meetings:** annual board meeting ● annual conference.

17950 ■ Unrepresented Nations and Peoples Organization (UNPO)
444 N Capitol St., Ste.846
Washington, DC 20001-1570
Ph: (202)637-0475
Fax: (202)637-0585
URL: http://www.unpo.org
Contact: Krishanu Sengupta, Asst.
Founded: 1991. **Membership Dues:** student, $20 (annual) ● individual, $40 (annual) ● organization, $60 (annual) ● life, $400. **Description:** Seeks to provide a voice to those nations not represented in the United Nations and other established international fora. Upholds the principles of self-determination, democracy, non-violence, and environmental protection. Works to protect citizens from the human rights abuses of government. Conducts fact-finding missions and election monitoring. Provides education and training in diplomacy, conflict management, and democratic processes. **Awards:** UNPO Human Rights Award. **Frequency:** biennial. **Type:** recognition. **Councils:** Peace Action. **Publications:** *A UNPO Report on the National and Human Rights Situation of the Albanians in Kosovo*. **Price:** $5.00/copy, plus $3 shipping and handling ● *Human Rights Dimensions of Population Transfer*. Includes the conference report on UNPO International Conference held in Tallinn, Estonia. **Price:** $5.00/copy, plus $3 shipping and handling ● *The Position of UNPO in the International Legal Order* ● *The Reemergence of Self-Determination* ● *Report of a UNPO Mission to Abkhazia, Georgia, and the Northern Caucasus*. **Price:** $5.00/copy, plus $3 shipping and handling ● *Self-Determination in Relation to Individual Human Rights, Democracy, and the Protection of the Environment*. **Price:** $5.00/copy, plus $3 shipping and handling ● *Summary Report of the UNPOI Mission to Kosovo to Monitor Parliamentary and Presidential Elections*. **Price:** $5.00/copy, plus $3 shipping and handling ● *UNPO Members Fact Book*. Contains geographic data, and information on religion, human rights violations, language, and political systems. **Price:** $5.50/ copy, plus $3 shipping and handling ● *UNPO News*, 3/year. Magazine. **Price:** $20.00 /year for individuals;

$40.00 /year for institutions. **Conventions/Meetings:** general assembly and conference.

17951 ■ World Constitution and Parliament Association (WCPA)

8800 W 14th Ave.
Lakewood, CO 80215
Ph: (303)233-3548
Fax: (303)237-7685
E-mail: wcparliament@qwest.net
URL: http://www.worldparliamentgov.net
Contact: Henry Philip Isely, Sec. Gen.
Founded: 1959. **Members:** 2,000. **National Groups:** 15. **Description:** Individuals and organizations in 150 countries interested in implementing a world constitution establishing a federal world government that would "achieve world peace and solve problems for the good of humanity." Promotes national ratification of the Constitution for the Federation of Earth; hopes to sponsor a popular referendum on this issue. **Formerly:** World Committee for a World Constitutional Convention. **Publications:** *Across Frontiers*, bimonthly. Newsletter. **Price:** free ● *Constitution for the Federation of Earth.* Book ● *Design and Action for a New World.* Book ● *Quantum Leap for Survival.* Book ● Pamphlets. **Conventions/Meetings:** annual meeting ● biennial Provisional World Parliament - meeting.

17952 ■ World Service Authority (WSA)

World Off.
1012 14th St. NW, Ste.205
Washington, DC 20005
Ph: (202)638-2662
Fax: (202)638-0638
E-mail: info@worldservice.org
URL: http://www.worldservice.org
Contact: Garry Davis, Founder/World Coor.
Founded: 1954. **Staff:** 15. **Budget:** $500,000. **Languages:** Arabic, Bulgarian, Chinese, Creole, English, Esperanto, Estonian, French, German, Japanese, Russian, Spanish. **Multinational. Description:** Administrative Branch of the World Government of World Citizens. Commits to establish social, economic, environmental, and political justice throughout the world in accordance with the fundamental moral codes of all major religions, and sanctioned by the Universal Declaration of Human Rights, which views the human population as globally interdependent and sovereign. Advocates world peace, generous relations among humans, and a system of just and equitable world law. Fosters better understanding and protection of different cultures, ethnic groups, and language communities and use of a neutral, global language such as Esperanto. Promotes world citizen political involvement and formation of programs dealing with housing, jobs, food, and education on a global basis. Has registered more than 1,000,000 individuals as world citizens, and has issued world birth certificates, passports, identification cards, political asylum cards, and marriage certificates, when applicable. Maintains the World Refugee Fund to finance the issuing of passports to refugees in camps or detention. Sponsors registrant education. **Libraries: Type:** reference. **Holdings:** 1,000; articles, books, clippings, periodicals. **Subjects:** world law, disarmament, economics, conflict resolution, human rights. **Computer Services:** database, legal advocacy and education regarding claiming and exercising human rights; legal assistance for victims of human rights violations ● database, legal clients ● database, omnis, list and files of document holders ● database, World Citizen ● mailing lists, subscribers to World Citizen News and individuals throughout the world who have registered as world citizens. **Commissions:** Communications; Cultural; Cybernetics; Documentation; Economics; Education; Environment; Forestry; Health; Industrial Cybernetics; Judicial; Ocean; Political Asylum; Space; Women; World Court of Human Rights; World Design-Science; World Peace Guards; World Postal Service. **Formerly:** (1992) World Service Authority of the World Government of World Citizens. **Publications:** *Anatomy of Peace.* Book. **Price:** $5.00 plus $5 postage ● *Collated Statements of Importance from the World Syntegrity Project,* biennial. Booklet. Contains compiled

resolutions generated consensually in response to the question, "How can we, as sovereign world citizens, govern our world?". **Price:** $15.00 plus $5 postage. Alternate Formats: online ● *Dear World: A Global Odyssey.* Book. Features one man's continuing personal crusade to live one world and one humanity. **Price:** $20.00 plus $5 postage; $16.00 for paperback; $29.00 for hardbound ● *Ellsworth Declaration.* Pamphlet. **Price:** $5.00 ● *My Country is the World.* Book. Features Garry Davis' exciting autobiography. **Price:** $5.00 ● *Passport to Freedom: A Guide for World Citizens.* Book. **Price:** $15.00 for paperback; $25.00 for hardbound ● *Passport to Freedom and A World Citizen in Rio.* Videos. **Price:** $24.95 plus $5 postage ● *World Government, Ready or Not!.* Book. **Price:** $35.00 plus $10 postage; $20.00 for paperback; $31.00 for hardbound. **Conventions/Meetings:** periodic World Syntegrity Project Syntegration - meeting.

Political Parties

17953 ■ American Nationalist Union (ANU)

PO Box 426
Allison Park, PA 15101-0426
Ph: (412)443-7300
Fax: (724)443-4240
E-mail: mail@anu.org
URL: http://www.anu.org
Contact: Donald B. Wassall, Exec. Dir.
Founded: 1987. **Members:** 35,000. **Membership Dues:** regular (without newspaper), $25 (annual) ● regular (with newspaper), $44 (annual). **Staff:** 4. **State Groups:** 42. **Description:** Seeks to influence the political process by making nationalist solutions to America's problems better known and accepted. **Telecommunication Services:** hotline, message line, (900)370-3709. **Committees:** Grassroots; Platform. **Formerly:** (2000) Populist Party of America. **Publications:** *The Populist Insider,* monthly. Newsletter. **Price:** $60.00/year ● *The Populist Observer,* monthly. Newspaper. Covers national and international news and politics, from a populist perspective. **Price:** $25.00/year. **Circulation:** 10,000. **Advertising:** accepted ● Also publishes pamphlets, stickers, bumper stickers, and calling cards. **Conventions/Meetings:** annual meeting.

17954 ■ Campus Greens

PO Box 536
Lombard, IL 60148
Ph: (630)981-1737
E-mail: info@campusgreens.org
URL: http://www.campusgreens.org
Description: Works to build broad-based movement for radical democracy on high school and college campuses in U.S; acts in solidarity with the Ten Key Values of the Green Party. **Committees:** Bylaws; Coalition-building; Fundraising/Finance; High School Organizing; International; Media; Mobilization; Resources/Clearinghouse; Webteam. **Councils:** Advisors; Alumni; Educators. **Affiliated With:** Green Party of the United States.

17955 ■ Committee for a Unified Independent Party (CUIP)

225 Broadway, Ste.2010
New York, NY 10007
Ph: (212)609-2800
Free: (800)288-3201
Fax: (212)609-2801
E-mail: nross@cuip.org
URL: http://www.independentvoting.org
Contact: Lenora B. Fulani PhD, Chair
Founded: 1994. **Description:** Serves as an independent political party lobbyists. Provides strategy workshops, information, training and support.

17956 ■ Communist Party of the United States of America (CPUSA)

235 W 23rd St.
New York, NY 10011
Ph: (212)989-4994
Fax: (212)229-1713

E-mail: cpusa@cpusa.org
URL: http://www.cpusa.org
Contact: Sam Webb, Natl. Chm.
Founded: 1919. **Membership Dues:** individual, $12 (annual). **State Groups:** 40. **Description:** Works as a political party of the working class dedicated to the interests of all working people-black, brown and white, male and female, younger and older. Seeks to achieve a socialist society. Works in coalition with the people's movement. **Publications:** *People's Weekly World.* Newspaper. **Price:** $30.00 /year for individuals; $75.00 /year for institutions. Alternate Formats: online ● *Political Affairs,* monthly. Journal. **Price:** $18.00 /year for individuals. Alternate Formats: online ● Articles. Alternate Formats: online. **Conventions/Meetings:** conference - midterm ● quadrennial convention.

17957 ■ Conservative Party (CP)

486 78th St.
Brooklyn, NY 11209
Ph: (718)921-2158
Fax: (718)921-5268
E-mail: cpnys@nycap.rr.com
URL: http://www.cpnys.org
Contact: Michael R. Long, Chm.
Founded: 1962. **Members:** 173,000. **Staff:** 6. **Budget:** $130,000. **Local Groups:** 200. **Description:** Political organization in New York State dedicated to "individual liberty, limited constitutional government, and defense of the Republic against its enemies." Seeks to "restore respect for individual responsibility and individual effort as the key feature of the national system." Maintains speakers' bureau; sponsors research and specialized education programs; compiles statistics. **Awards: Type:** recognition. **Conventions/Meetings:** quarterly meeting.

17958 ■ Expansionist Party of the United States (XP)

295 Smith St.
Newark, NJ 07106-2517
Ph: (973)416-6151
E-mail: xpus@aol.com
URL: http://members.aol.com/XPUS
Contact: L. Craig Schoonmaker, Chm.
Founded: 1977. **Members:** 650. **Membership Dues:** individual, $36 (annual) ● student and senior, $18 (annual). **Staff:** 1. **Languages:** English, French, Portuguese, Spanish. **Multinational. Description:** Individuals interested in expanding the U.S. geographically. Seeks annexation to the U.S. of as many countries as are willing to abide by the Constitution, culminating in world union. Urges a larger role in society for ethnic and sexual minorities; areas of interest include Australia, Canada, Latin America, Caribbean, Europe, New Zealand, Philippines, Oceania, Russia, South Asia, and South Africa. Maintains speakers' bureau. Conducts letter-writing campaigns. **Convention/Meeting:** none. Charter member, United States International. **Libraries: Type:** not open to the public. **Holdings:** archival material, articles, audio recordings, books, clippings, video recordings. **Awards:** Expansionist of the Year. **Frequency:** periodic. **Type:** recognition. **Recipient:** for making the public aware of expansionist's ideas and goals. **Additional Websites:** http://www.geocities.com/us_int.

17959 ■ Green Party of the United States (GPUS)

PO Box 57065
Washington, DC 20037
Ph: (202)319-7191 (202)319-7192
Free: (866)41GREEN
Fax: (202)319-7193
E-mail: info@gp.org
URL: http://www.gp.org
Contact: Starlene Rankin, Media Coor.
Founded: 2001. **Members:** 300,000. **Staff:** 2. **Budget:** $1,000,000. **State Groups:** 47. **National Groups:** 90. **Description:** Operates Greens Clearinghouse, which distributes lists of local and regional Green movement contacts and makes available periodicals on the Green movement, ecological awareness, and grassroots politics. Local groups

engage in nonviolent activism including political initiatives, demonstrations, dissemination of information, and campaigns against environmental destruction, racism, sexism, heterosexism, and government repression. Maintains speakers' bureau; conducts educational programs. **Libraries: Type:** reference. **Holdings:** archival material, books, business records, clippings, periodicals. **Subjects:** environment, politics, proportional representation, green movements. **Computer Services:** database. **Telecommunication Services:** electronic mail, gpusa@igc.org. **Subgroups:** Lesbian/Bi/Gay/Transsexual Caucus; People of Color Caucus; People w/Disabilities/Seniors Caucus; Women's Caucus. **Also Known As:** Green Party; American Green Movement; United States Green Network. **Formerly:** (1991) Green Committees of Correspondence. **Publications:** *Green Politics*, quarterly. Newspapers. **Price:** $25.00 for bundles of 100 copies. **Circulation:** 6,000. Alternate Formats: online ● Bibliographies. **Conventions/Meetings:** annual meeting.

17960 ■ La Raza Unida Party (LRUP)
11663 Herrick Ave.
PO Box 13
San Fernando, CA 91340
Ph: (619)420-3826 (818)365-6534
Fax: (818)365-6534
E-mail: pnlru@yahoo.com
URL: http://larazaunida.tripod.com
Contact: Xenaro G. Ayala, Chm.
Founded: 1972. **Budget:** $30,000. **State Groups:** 4. **Local Groups:** 100. **Languages:** English, Spanish. **Description:** Individuals of various backgrounds dedicated to achieving self-determination and greater government representation for Latinos through electoral processes. Concentrates on political issues that involve Chicanos and Mexicans and the working classes. ("La raza" is Spanish for "the people.") Sponsors presentations and study and training sessions. Maintains library of photos, slides, and publications. Compiles statistics. Maintains speakers' bureau; conducts research programs. **Committees:** Student; Youth. **Publications:** *El Sembrador*, monthly. Newspaper ● *La Nacion*, monthly. Newspaper ● *La Semilla*, quarterly. Newspaper ● Pamphlet. **Conventions/Meetings:** biennial congress (exhibits) - always April ● annual meeting ● annual State Convention.

17961 ■ Libertarian National Committee
2600 Virginia Ave. NW, Ste.200
Washington, DC 20037
Ph: (202)333-0008
Free: (800)682-1776
Fax: (202)333-0072
E-mail: info@lp.org
URL: http://www.lp.org
Contact: Shane Cory, Exec. Dir.
Founded: 1971. **Members:** 31,000. **Membership Dues:** individual, $25 (annual). **Staff:** 6. **Budget:** $3,000,000. **Regional Groups:** 8. **State Groups:** 51. **Local Groups:** 300. **Description:** Serves as political party that aims to bring Libertarian ideas to the American public via political campaigns, to elect Libertarians to office and to pressure major-party candidates into taking more Libertarian stands. Believes that "each individual has the absolute right to exercise sole dominion over his or her own life, liberty and property so long as he or she also respects the equal right of all others to live their lives by the same principle." Opposes censorship, the draft, victimless crime laws, and government regulation on personal matters; supports property rights, free trade, and eventual elimination of taxation. Conducts candidate training. **Computer Services:** Mailing lists, available for rent. **Committees:** Affiliate Parties; Libertarian National. **Also Known As:** Libertarian Party. **Publications:** *Issue Papers*, periodic ● *Libertarian Party News*, monthly. Newspaper. **Price:** included in membership dues; $10.00 /year for libraries; $25.00 /year for individuals. **Circulation:** 25,000. **Advertising:** accepted ● *The Libertarian Volunteer*, monthly. Newsletter. **Circulation:** 1,500 ● *Liberty Pledge News*, monthly. Newsletter. **Circulation:**

2,500. **Conventions/Meetings:** periodic board meeting ● biennial convention (exhibits) ● quarterly meeting.

17962 ■ National Hamiltonian Party (NHP)
1901 Montclair Ave.
Flint, MI 48503
Ph: (810)234-3771
E-mail: mkelly@mcc.edu
Contact: Mr. Michael Kelly, Exec. Dir.
Founded: 1965. **Members:** 334. **Staff:** 1. **Regional Groups:** 4. **State Groups:** 43. **National Groups:** 3. **Description:** Seeks to bring nobility, ability and dignity back to American government by either electing Hamiltonians to public office or electing those Democrats and Republicans who is capable of maintaining the dignity and qualifications which their offices demand. Maintains a collection of Hamilton memorabilia. Sponsors Students for Sebastian, National Hamiltonian Women, and League of Voluntary Disenfranchisement. **Libraries: Type:** reference; by appointment only. **Holdings:** 6,700; archival material, articles, artwork, books, clippings, periodicals. **Subjects:** American political history. **Awards:** Gaius Petronius Award. **Frequency:** annual. **Type:** recognition. **Recipient:** for general retention of sanity while in government service. **Committees:** Information; Issues; National Hamiltonian Elections. **Publications:** *The Hamiltonian*, periodic. Newsletter. **Price:** included in membership dues. **Conventions/Meetings:** annual meeting - always August.

17963 ■ NSDAP Auslands-Und Aufbauorganisation (NSDAP/AO)
Box 6414
Lincoln, NE 68506
URL: http://www.nazi-lauck-nsdapao.com
Contact: F. Hansing, Sec.
Founded: 1972. **Languages:** English, German, Italian, Japanese, Portuguese, Romany, Spanish. **Multinational. Description:** National Socialist propaganda machine. Supplier of Nazi underground in Germany. Promotes free speech and non-violent political activism in Germany and elsewhere. Demands for its legalization. Seeks a National Socialist Reich and worldwide pan-Aryan solidarity. Publishes newspapers and other items in over a dozen languages. **Formerly:** (1979) NSDAP Auslandsorganisation. **Publications:** *The New Order*, bimonthly. Newspaper. Traditional National Socialism- White Power. **Price:** $30.00/12 issues in U.S. and Canada; $50.00/12 issues outside U.S. and Canada. ISSN: 0740-3283. Also Cited As: `NS Report ● Ns Kampfruf (in German), bimonthly ● NS News Bulletin (in Danish, Dutch, English, Finnish, French, German, Hungarian, Italian, Norwegian, Portuguese, Spanish, and Swedish), quarterly. Newspapers ● Booklets (in English and German) ● Also publishes leaflets, stickers, posters, and other materials in over 12 languages.

17964 ■ Peace and Freedom Party (PFP)
PO Box 24764
Oakland, CA 94623
Ph: (510)465-9414
E-mail: what_is@peaceandfreedom.org
URL: http://www.peaceandfreedom.org
Founded: 1967. **Members:** 70,000. **Membership Dues:** general, $10 (annual). **Staff:** 1,500. **Budget:** $100,000. **Regional Groups:** 54. **State Groups:** 54. **Local Groups:** 150. **Description:** Consists of "activist union members, professionals, students, environmental activists, women, teenagers, minorities, gays, and other activists who work for world socialism; also includes former church members and former members of such groups as La Raza Unida Party, Christic Institute, National Rainbow Coalition, Students for a Democratic Society, and the Black Panther Party." Objectives are to: "provide safe, natural health care to all people; release the Nixon Watergate tape, jail George Bush for the J.F.K. assassination, reduce the Pentagon budget by 50 percent, establish a 4 day work week; cancel the national debt by a 50&percent; capital tax on the 1000 richest families; end poverty, racism, and sexism; fight organized crime; abolish individual taxes and the IRS; lower present voting age to 13; provide chiropractic adjustments to all ad-

dicted to tobacco, alcohol and drugs to cure addictions; distribute condoms to youths as a disease-prevention measure; promote the French abortion pill RU-486; create a free education system; free all political prisoners, especially Sirhan Sirhan." Works to eliminate oppression and discrimination based on sex and sexual preference, class, race, age, or nationality. Believes the public should be made aware of how "drug profits control state legislature, banks, and the White House." Supports a "feminist-socialist platform that advocates issues such as: a socialist economic system run by and for workers and consumers; abolition of the Federal Reserve; a socialist medical system providing free, quality health care for children under 18 and seniors over 60 years of age; teaches classes on how selenium cures cancer, heart disease, and AIDS; legal guarantees of employment and housing for persons under 25 years of age; support for human liberties and rights; abolition of the CIA and an end to U.S. military invasion of foreign nations." Activities also include: setting up child care centers, medical testing clinics, food co-ops, and community newspapers; picketing with striking workers, rent strikers, and United Farm Workers boycotters; housing development projects; abolishment of oil depletion allowance; demonstrating against nuclear power plants. Maintains speakers' bureau; compiles statistics. **Libraries: Type:** reference. **Holdings:** 5,000. **Subjects:** economics, AIDS, automation, child care, ecology, sexism, abortion, drug legalization, ballot initiatives, Marxism, Zionism, racism, the ruling class, John F. Kennedy assassination, Martin Luther King assassination. **Awards: Type:** recognition. **Committees:** Addiction Treatment; Asthma; Central America; Civil Rights; Drug Legalization; Elections; Gay; JFK/King Assassinations; Labor; Media; Mid-East; Military Draft; Multiple Sclerosis; Seniors; Teens; Women. **Affiliated With:** La Raza Unida Party. **Publications:** *Leaflets*, monthly. **Advertising:** accepted. Alternate Formats: online ● *Nixon and Bush: How the CIA Ambushed JFK*. Video ● *The Partisan*, monthly. Newspaper. Alternate Formats: online. **Conventions/Meetings:** semiannual convention (exhibits) ● monthly meeting.

17965 ■ Progressive Labor Party (PLP)
PO Box 808
Brooklyn, NY 11202
Ph: (212)255-3959 (718)630-9440
Fax: (212)255-0685
E-mail: plp@plp.org
URL: http://www.plp.org
Contact: Milton Rosen, Chm.
Founded: 1962. **Description:** Works to establish communism in the U.S. Seeks to guide the working class to revolt and build a new, egalitarian society, and to apply the principles of Marxism-Leninism to world revolution. **Telecommunication Services:** electronic mail, cd188@juno.com. **Publications:** *Al Tahadi* (in Arabic and English), bimonthly. Newspaper ● *Challenge/Desafio* (in English and Spanish), weekly. Newspaper. Alternate Formats: online ● *The Communist*. Journal. Alternate Formats: online ● *The Communist Magazine* (in English and Spanish), quarterly. Alternate Formats: online ● *Le Defi* (in English and French), monthly. Newspaper ● *PL Magazine*. Journal. Contains information on Communist theory and practice. Alternate Formats: online ● *Vietnam: Defeat U.S. Imperialism*. Pamphlet. Explains the history of the Vietnam War. Alternate Formats: online ● Pamphlets. Alternate Formats: online. **Conventions/Meetings:** annual meeting - always May Day ● quinquennial meeting.

17966 ■ Prohibition National Committee (PNC)
PO Box 2635
Denver, CO 80201
Ph: (303)237-4947
E-mail: earldodge@dodgeoffice.net
URL: http://www.prohibition.org
Contact: Earl F. Dodge, Chm.
Founded: 1869. **Membership Dues:** regular, $20 (annual). **Staff:** 2. **Budget:** $50,000. **Description:** Administrative body of the Prohibition Party, a national political organization that meets quadrenni-

ally to nominate candidates for the U.S. presidency and vice-presidency. Nominees for offices of governor, U.S. senator and representatives, and others are chosen by state conventions. Party platform urges repeal of all laws that legalize liquor and the enactment and enforcement of new laws that prohibit the manufacture, distribution and sale of alcoholic beverages. Takes a conservative stand on most aspects of domestic and foreign policy; calls for civil rights but opposes proposals that "would destroy our neighborhood schools through forced integration"; criticizes the income tax and federal aid to education; questions the soundness of the Social Security system. Maintains historical collection of books, records, and papers in Denver, CO, and at the University of Michigan in Ann Arbor, MI. **Libraries: Type:** open to the public. **Holdings:** 1,700. **Affiliated With:** Partisan Prohibition Historical Society. **Publications:** *National Statesman*, monthly. Newsletter. **Price:** $10.00/year. Alternate Formats: online. **Conventions/Meetings:** biennial convention (exhibits).

17967 ■ Republicans Abroad International
1275 K St. NW, Ste.102
Washington, DC 20005
Ph: (202)608-1423
E-mail: chairman@republicansabroad.org
URL: http://www.republicansabroad.org
Contact: Mr. Christopher Fussner, Chm.
Founded: 1977. **Members:** 1,000,000. **Membership Dues:** presidential, $5,000 (annual) ● ambassador, $1,000 (annual) ● diplomat, $500 (annual) ● envoy, $250 (annual) ● sponsor, $100 (annual) ● international, $50 (annual). **Staff:** 3. **State Groups:** 150. **Description:** Represents Americans living abroad, their spouses, and their dependents. Objectives are to: promote active participation of nonresident Americans in Republican political activities; facilitate voter registration and absentee voting; represent the Republican Party and its supporter's abroad. Disseminates information concerning the Republican Party and its candidates. **Publications:** *The Political Report*, weekly ● *The Republican Ambassador*, quarterly. Newsletter. **Conventions/Meetings:** annual meeting - always January, Washington, DC.

17968 ■ Socialist Labor Party of America (SLP)
PO Box 218
Mountain View, CA 94042-0218
Ph: (408)280-7266
Fax: (408)280-6964
E-mail: socialists@slp.org
URL: http://www.slp.org
Contact: Robert Bills, Natl. Sec.
Founded: 1876. **Staff:** 2. **Local Groups:** 8. **Description:** Serves as political party whose goal is to establish a classless, socialist, industrial democracy in which the political state is abolished and the industries and services are under social ownership and rank-and-file control. Sponsors study classes, discussion groups and speakers. (Emblem is an uplifted arm holding a hammer). **Programs:** Socialist Industrial Union. **Formerly:** (1876) Workingmen's Party; (1877) Socialistic Labor Party. **Publications:** *National Convention Reports*, biennial ● *The People*, bimonthly. Journal. **Price:** $5.00/year. ISSN: 0199-350X ● Books, periodic ● Pamphlets. **Conventions/Meetings:** biennial convention.

17969 ■ Socialist Party U.S.A. (SP-USA)
339 Lafayette St., Ste.303
New York, NY 10012
Ph: (212)982-4586
Fax: (212)982-4586
E-mail: natsec@sp-usa.org
URL: http://www.sp-usa.org
Contact: Greg Pason, Natl. Sec.
Founded: 1973. **Members:** 3,000. **Membership Dues:** full-time student, $15 (annual) ● individual (based on annual income), $25-$250 (annual). **Staff:** 3. **Budget:** $75,000. **State Groups:** 24. **Local Groups:** 34. **Description:** A democratic socialist political party encompassing a wide range of opinions within its ranks instead of a rigid "party line." Seeks radical and fundamental change in the structure and

quality of economic, political, and social relationships in America, through education, grass roots organizing, and electoral action; established originally in 1901 by a merger of the Social-Democratic Party of America and a faction of the older Socialist Labor Party, the party merged in 1972 with the Democratic Socialist Federation becoming the Socialist Party-Democratic Socialist Federation (SP-DSF); in 1972, the majority faction ("Realignment Caucus") of the SP-DSF changed the party's name to Social Democrats, U.S.A. **Affiliated With:** International Peace Bureau. **Publications:** *The Organizer*, periodic. Newsletter. Alternate Formats: online ● *The Socialist*, bimonthly. Newsletter. Covers social and political issues from a socialist perspective. Includes book reviews. **Price:** $9.00/year; $20.00 for bulk copies. ISSN: 0884-6154. Alternate Formats: online. **Conventions/Meetings:** biennial convention.

17970 ■ Socialist Workers Party (SWP)
306 W 37th St., 10th Fl.
New York, NY 10018
Ph: (212)244-4094
E-mail: swpno@mac.com
Founded: 1938. **Description:** Political party whose goal is to educate and organize the working class in order to establish a "workers' and farmers' government," which will "abolish capitalism in the U.S. and join in the worldwide struggle for socialism". Strives to advance the unity of working people by participating in activities that call for: jobs through reducing the workweek with no cut in pay; equality in employment and education for Blacks, Latinos, and women through affirmative action; cancellation of the foreign debt of semicolonial countries; an end to farm foreclosures and guaranteed income to working farmers. Promotes and supports defense of women's right to abortion, defense of the Cuban revolution and an end to imperialist wars.

17971 ■ United States Pacifist Party (USPP)
5729 S Dorchester Ave.
Chicago, IL 60637
Ph: (773)324-0654
Fax: (773)324-6426
E-mail: blyttle@igc.org
URL: http://www.uspacifistparty.org
Contact: Bradford Lyttle, Acting Sec.
Founded: 1983. **Members:** 45. **Staff:** 1. **Regional Groups:** 1. **State Groups:** 1. **Description:** Individuals who believe that "military traditions and institutions are the primary sources of war, impede solutions to social problems such as poverty and political oppression, and contradict many religious and philosophic principles." Platform planks include: zero military budget; immediate and complete nuclear weapons disarmament; an end to hunger and poverty through aid administered by the United Nations; preparation for nonviolent resistance against possible invasion and occupation attempts; "shutdown of nuclear power plants pending international evaluation of the safety of nuclear energy"; promotion of solar, wind, and other sources of low pollution energy; full employment through private and worker-controlled enterprise and federally administered public projects; passage of the Equal Rights Amendment; abolition of the death penalty. **Convention/Meeting:** none. **Computer Services:** Mailing lists. **Publications:** *U.S. Pacifist Party Report*, monthly. Newsletter. **Price:** free. **Circulation:** 600.

17972 ■ Working Families Party (WFP)
2-4 Nevins St., 3rd Fl.
Brooklyn, NY 11217
Ph: (718)222-3796
Fax: (718)246-3718
E-mail: wfp@workingfamiliesparty.org
URL: http://www.workingfamiliesparty.org
Contact: Bertha Lewis, Exec. Dir.
Founded: 1998. **Members:** 15,000. **Membership Dues:** sustainer, $10-$50 (monthly). **Staff:** 30. **State Groups:** 15. **Languages:** English, Spanish. **Description:** A progressive, independent political party working at the grassroots level. **Formerly:** (2004) New Party. **Publications:** *Working Families News*, quar-

terly. Newsletter. **Circulation:** 15,000. **Conventions/Meetings:** annual meeting - always in Albany, NY.

17973 ■ World Socialist Party of the United States (WSPUS)
PO Box 440247
Boston, MA 02144
Ph: (617)628-9096
E-mail: wspusa@worldsocialism.org
URL: http://www.worldsocialism.org/usa
Contact: Ms. Karla Ellenbogen, Postal Correspondent
Founded: 1916. **Members:** 50. **Membership Dues:** ordinary, $5 (monthly). **Regional Groups:** 3. **State Groups:** 1. **Local Groups:** 2. **Languages:** English, Spanish. **Description:** Advocates for the establishment of a system of society based upon common ownership and democratic control of the means and instruments for producing and distributing wealth by and in the interest of society as a whole; this means that communities around the world must return to being not only the sites of production but the owners of the product. Conducts group discussions and propaganda meetings; maintains a speaker's bureau and distributes print and electronic media. **Libraries: Type:** reference. **Holdings:** 300; audio recordings, books, periodicals. **Subjects:** Marxian economics, socialism, anthropology, sociology, political analysis, history. **Computer Services:** Mailing lists. **Telecommunication Services:** electronic mail, comradeh@yahoo.com. **Committees:** Editorial; National Administrative. **Formerly:** Socialist Educational Society; (1948) Worker's Socialist Party. **Publications:** *The Futility of Reformism*. Book ● *News from Nowhere*, monthly. Newsletter ● *Socialism or Your Money Back*. Book. Reprints of 100 years of Socialist Standard articles (published by the Socialist Party of Great Britain). ● *Socialist Standard: Journal of the Socialist Party of Great Britain*, monthly. Advocates the immediate worldwide elimination of production for profit and its replacement by production for use. **Price:** $16.50 /year for individuals; $30.00 /year for institutions. Alternate Formats: online ● *World Socialist Review: Journal of World Socialism in the U.S.*, quarterly. Focuses on the struggle between workers and capitalists to show how elimination of capital and wages is the issue in all crises of class society. **Price:** $3.00/issue for individuals; $1.50/issue for institutions; $8.80 /year for individuals; $20.00 /year for institutions ● *World Without Wages*. Book ● *Yes, Utopia - We Have the Technology*. Book. Contains details on how a socialist society could run. **Conventions/Meetings:** annual conference ● monthly National Administrative Committee Meeting.

Political Reform

17974 ■ CIVICUS: World Alliance for Citizen Participation
1112 16th St. NW, Ste.540
Washington, DC 20036
Ph: (202)331-8518
Fax: (202)331-8774
E-mail: info@civicus.org
URL: http://www.civicus.org
Contact: Kumi Naidoo, Sec. Gen.
Founded: 1993. **Members:** 604. **Membership Dues:** citizen organization, $50-$500 (annual) ● individual associate, $50-$100 (annual) ● youth, $10-$20 (annual) ● corporate, $500 (annual). **Staff:** 15. **Budget:** $1,500,000. **Languages:** English, French, Spanish. **Multinational. Description:** Strengthens citizen action and civil society throughout the world. **Libraries: Type:** open to the public. **Holdings:** 700; books, periodicals. **Subjects:** regional, civil society, directories. **Computer Services:** database ● mailing lists ● online services. **Publications:** *Building Civil Society Worldwide: Strategies for Successful Communications*. Book ● *Citizens*. Book ● *CIVICUS World*, bimonthly. Journal. **Price:** $29.00/year. **Circulation:** 1,500 ● *Civil Society at the Millennium*. Book ● *e-CIVICUS*, weekly. Newsletter. Alternate Formats: online ● *Legal Principles for Citizen Participation: Toward a Legal Framework for Civil Society Organi-

zations. Book ● *New Civic Atlas: Profiles of Civil Society in 60 Countries*. Book ● *Promoting Corporate Citizenship: Opportunities for Business and Civil Society Engagement*. Book. **Price:** $15.00 ● *Sustaining Civil Society! Strategies for Resource Mobilization*. Book. **Price:** $30.00. **Conventions/Meetings:** biennial World Assembly - general assembly (exhibits).

17975 ■ Committee to Support the Revolution in Peru (CSRP)
PO Box 1246
Berkeley, CA 94701
Ph: (415)252-5786
Fax: (415)252-7414
URL: http://www.csrp.org
Founded: 1984. **Membership Dues:** general, $25 (annual). **Languages:** English, Spanish. **Description:** Works to create political support in the U.S. for the People's war led by the Communist Party of Peru. Conducts educational programs; compiles statistics; maintains speakers' bureau. **Computer Services:** Electronic publishing. **Publications:** *Peru Action and News*, quarterly. Newsletter. Alternate Formats: online.

Politics

17976 ■ American Association of Political Consultants (AAPC)
600 Pennsylvania Ave. SE, Ste.330
Washington, DC 20003
Ph: (202)544-9815
Fax: (202)544-9816
E-mail: info@theaapc.org
URL: http://www.theaapc.org
Contact: Martha Lockwood, Exec. Dir.
Founded: 1969. **Members:** 800. **Membership Dues:** platinum, $1,000 (annual) ● gold, $500 (annual) ● individual, $250 (annual) ● associate, academic, $100 (annual) ● student, $60 (annual). **Staff:** 1. **Budget:** $200,000. **Regional Groups:** 2. **Description:** Regular members are corporations and individuals who devote a major portion of their time to or earn a major portion of their livelihood from political counseling and related activities; associate members are persons who devote part of their time to or earn part of their living from political counseling, have an interest in the political process, are teachers of political science, or intend to become actively involved in political activities. Provides a vehicle for the exchange of information, resources, and ideas among persons involved in political activity. Arranges seminars and holds biennial updates on campaign techniques and professional advances. **Awards:** Lifetime Achievement Award. **Frequency:** biennial. **Type:** recognition. **Recipient:** to professionals ● Pollie Awards. **Frequency:** annual. **Type:** recognition. **Telecommunication Services:** electronic mail, mlockwood@theaapc.org. **Affiliated With:** American League of Lobbyists; American Political Science Association. **Publications:** *AAPC News*, monthly. Newsletter ● *AAPC Update*, biweekly. Newsletter. Alternate Formats: online ● *Membership Roster*, annual. Membership Directory. Offers a political resource directory. **Price:** $90.00. **Advertising:** accepted ● *Political Pages Directory* ● Reports. Alternate Formats: online ● Booklets ● Booklet. Alternate Formats: online. **Conventions/Meetings:** annual Academic Outreach Conference (exhibits).

17977 ■ American League of Lobbyists (ALL)
PO Box 30005
Alexandria, VA 22310
Ph: (703)960-3011
Fax: (703)960-4070
E-mail: alldc.org@erols.com
URL: http://www.alldc.org
Contact: Patti Jo Baber, Exec. Dir.
Founded: 1978. **Members:** 650. **Membership Dues:** resident in Washington, DC Metro area, $250 (annual) ● organization, $750 (annual) ● non-resident, $125 (annual) ● government/academic, $100 (annual) ● young leadership network, $99 (annual) ●

associate, $500 (annual) ● student, $30 (annual). **Staff:** 1. **Budget:** $125,000. **Description:** Registered lobbyists and other professionals interested in the lobbying profession. Conducts professional development education programs, seminars, and programs to improve public understanding and recognition of the role of lobbyists in the legislative process. **Telecommunication Services:** electronic mail, info@alldc.org. **Committees:** Access and Security; Budget and Finance; Education; History Project; Professional Ethics and Standards; Programs; Strategic Planning; Website. **Conventions/Meetings:** weekly meeting - always Washington, DC.

17978 ■ Arab American Institute (AAI)
1600 K St. NW, Ste.601
Washington, DC 20006
Ph: (202)429-9210
Fax: (202)429-9214
E-mail: jzogby@aaiusa.org
URL: http://www.aaiusa.org
Contact: Dr. James Zogby, Pres./Founder
Founded: 1985. **Members:** 9,000. **Membership Dues:** general, $25 (annual) ● student, $15 (annual) ● supporting, $150 ● patron, $500 ● President's Circle, $1,500 ● Chairman's Club, $10,000. **Staff:** 15. **State Groups:** 12. **Local Groups:** 15. **Description:** Those interested in promoting political empowerment of the Arab American community. Represents the concerns of Arab Americans to government, media, the general public, and the international community, through leadership training, community service and policy development. **Libraries:** Type: open to the public. **Holdings:** 1,000; periodicals. **Subjects:** politics, policy, events associated with Arab Americans. **Awards:** Kahlil Gibran Spirit of Humanity Award. **Frequency:** annual. **Type:** recognition. **Recipient:** for individuals, corporations, organizations, and communities whose work, commitment, and support made a difference in promoting co-existence and inclusion in all walks of life ● Najeeb Halaby Award. **Frequency:** annual. **Type:** recognition. **Recipient:** for excellence in public service. **Telecommunication Services:** electronic mail, aai@arab-aai.org. **Publications:** *Countdown*, weekly. Newsletter. Alternate Formats: online ● *Issues*, quarterly. Newsletter. Contains community news information. **Price:** free. **Circulation:** 8,000. Alternate Formats: online ● Reports. Alternate Formats: online. **Conventions/Meetings:** annual Kahlil Gibran Humanitarian Awards Ceremony - dinner ● semiannual National Leadership Conference.

17979 ■ Asian and Pacific Islander American Vote (APIAVote)
1666 K St. NW, Ste.440
Washington, DC 20006
Ph: (202)223-9170
Fax: (202)457-0549
E-mail: info@apiavote.org
URL: http://www.apiavote.org
Contact: Christine Chen, Exec. Dir.
Founded: 1996. **Description:** Encourages and promotes civic participation of Asian Pacific Islander Americans (APIA) in the electoral and public policy processes at the national, state and local levels. Works for an accessible democratic process for Asian Pacific Islander Americans. Helps mobilize the APIA community in a political sense. **Publications:** *Starter Training Manual*. Provides community leaders and volunteers basic information on how to register their family, friends and community. Alternate Formats: online.

17980 ■ Black Women's Roundtable on Voter Participation (BWRVP)
c/o National Coalition on Black Civic Participation
1900 L St. NW, Ste.700
Washington, DC 20036
Ph: (202)659-4929
Fax: (202)659-5025
E-mail: ncbcp@ncbcp.org
URL: http://www.bigvote.org
Contact: Melanie L. Campbell, Exec. Dir./CEO
Founded: 1983. **Budget:** $50,000. **Description:** A program of the National Coalition on Black Voter

Participation (see separate entry). Works as a black women organization committed to social justice and economic equity through increased participation in the political process. Organizes voter registration, education, and empowerment programs in the black community; emphasizes the importance of the women's vote. Seeks to develop women's leadership skills through nonpartisan political participation. Encourages black women's involvement in discussions concerning the influence of the women's vote in elections. Supports volunteer coalitions that work on voter registration, voter education, and get-out-the vote efforts. Conducts series of forums. **Affiliated With:** National Coalition on Black Civic Participation.

17981 ■ Center for Responsive Politics (CRP)
1101 14th St. NW, Ste.1030
Washington, DC 20005-5635
Ph: (202)857-0044
Fax: (202)857-7809
E-mail: info@crp.org
URL: http://www.opensecrets.org
Contact: Sheila Krumholz, Acting Exec. Dir./ Research Dir.
Founded: 1983. **Staff:** 14. **Budget:** $1,500,000. **Description:** Research group that tracks money in politics, and its effect on elections and public policy. Conducts computer-based research on campaign finance issues for the news media, academics, activists, and the public at large. Aimed at creating a more educated voter, an involved citizenry and a more responsive government. **Computer Services:** database, campaign finance ● database, financial disclosure ● database, lobbyists ● database, soft money. **Publications:** *The Big Picture*. Price: $10.00 ● *Congressional Preview Package* ● *Digital Democracy* ● *Do-It-Yourself Congressional Investigation Kit* ● *Influence, Inc.*. Price: $20.00 ● *Sex, Money and Politics* ● *Tracking the Cash* ● *Who Paid for This Election?* ● *Who's Paying* ● *Why Do Donors Give?*. **Conventions/Meetings:** seminar.

17982 ■ Center for Voting and Democracy
6930 Carroll Ave., Ste.610
Takoma Park, MD 20912
Ph: (301)270-4616
Fax: (301)270-4133
E-mail: info@fairvote.org
URL: http://www.fairvote.org
Contact: Robert Richie, Exec. Dir.
Founded: 1992. **Members:** 1,200. **Membership Dues:** low-income and student, $15 (annual) ● basic, $20 (annual) ● supporting, $50 (annual) ● sustaining, $100 (annual) ● patron, $1,000 (annual). **Staff:** 8. **Budget:** $600,000. **State Groups:** 6. **Description:** Researches and promotes fair elections. Focuses on: securing the right to vote; researching problems with winner-take-all elections; instant runoff voting when electing one candidate; presidential election reform; and systems of full/proportional representation-full representation, the most widely used voting system in the world, ensures that parties and candidates receive legislative seats in proportion to their percentage of the popular vote and promotes fairer levels of representation for women, people of color, and ideological minorities. Advocates national and state commissions on voting system reform. Compiles statistics; maintains speakers' bureau; conducts educational and research programs. Pursues litigation in Voting Rights Act cases. **Libraries:** Type: reference; by appointment only. **Holdings:** books, clippings, periodicals. **Subjects:** voting systems. **Awards:** Champion of Democracy Award. **Frequency:** annual. **Type:** recognition. **Recipient:** for international and U.S. leaders who have most effectively promoted consideration of alternatives to winner-take-all voting systems. **Computer Services:** Online services, voting. **Committees:** Communication; Education; International Affairs; Outreach; Voting Rights/Legal. **Formerly:** (1993) Citizens for Proportional Representation. **Publications:** *Monopoly Politics*, semiannual. Report. Price: $10.00 ● *Perspectives on Democracy*, 11/year. Report ● *Voting and Democracy Report*, quinquennial. Survey. Price: $12.00 ● *Voting and Democracy Review*, quarterly. Newsletter. Contains up-to-date news on

voting system reform developments. **Price:** $15.00/year. **Circulation:** 4,000 • Pamphlets. **Conventions/Meetings:** biennial convention and meeting.

17983 ■ Citizens' Research Foundation (CRF)
104 Moses Hall
Inst. of Governmental Stud.
Univ. of California
Berkeley, CA 94720-2370
Ph: (510)642-5158
E-mail: jlubenow@uclink4.berkeley.edu
URL: http://www.igs.berkeley.edu/research_programs/CRF
Contact: Gerald C. Lubenow, Program Off.
Founded: 1958. **Staff:** 3. **Budget:** $200,000. **Description:** Scholars, lawyers, and others interested in research on significant aspects of money in politics. Helps increase participation in democracy through better understanding of political finance. Current studies include: financing use of broadcasting facilities for political candidates; public funding of political campaigns; election reform at the federal and state levels; survey of the conditions of successful fundraising. **Libraries:** Type: reference. **Holdings:** 2,000. **Subjects:** state and federal campaign finance regulation, scholarly research on campaign finance reform. **Formerly:** Political Research Foundation; (1959) Research on Self-Government. **Publications:** *Financing the 1996 Election*, quadrennial. Book • Publishes studies on money in politics and the financing of presidential elections. **Conventions/Meetings:** annual board meeting.

17984 ■ Commission on Presidential Debates (CPD)
1200 New Hampshire Ave. NW
PO Box 445
Washington, DC 20036
Ph: (202)872-1020
Fax: (202)783-5923
E-mail: hbalas@debates.org
URL: http://www.debates.org
Contact: Frank J. Fahrenkopf Jr., Co-Chm.
Founded: 1987. **Description:** Nonpartisan commission which sponsors debates during the U.S. presidential election year; seeks to make debates between presidential candidates a permanent part of the election process. Conducts voter education programs. Makes available news packet.

17985 ■ Free Territory of Ely-Chatelaine (FTEC)
Royal Post FTEC
PO Box 7075
Laguna Niguel, CA 92607
E-mail: chancery@worldfreeinternet.net
URL: http://www.worldfreeinternet.net/ftec
Contact: Marc E. Ely-Chaitlin, Contact
Founded: 1975. **Members:** 200. **Description:** Serves as an alliance of households that aims to revitalize and restore royalism as a viable socioeconomic and political force; seeks to educate the public in the art and science of self-government. Stresses nonviolence in all human interactions. **Publications:** *The Constitution Papers*. Book. Features history and politics. **Price:** $16.00 each • *The Inevitable Civil War Looming on the Street in America* • *Royal Post Directory*, annual • *The Royalist Standard* • *The Royalist Tradition*. **Conventions/Meetings:** annual banquet.

17986 ■ Indian American Forum for Political Education (IAFPE)
Address Unknown since 2007
URL: http://www.iafpe.org
Founded: 1982. **Members:** 500. **Staff:** 1. **Budget:** $10,000. **Regional Groups:** 26. **State Groups:** 40. **Description:** Individuals from India; interested others. Serves as a catalyst in the development of civic consciousness and political awareness among Indian Americans; facilitates the exchange of ideas between Indian Americans and U.S. political leaders and public officials; promotes voter registration among Indian American citizens and responsible voting through the study of political issues; educates Indian Americans on individual civic and social responsibilities. Con-

ducts educational lectures, discussions, seminars, symposia, and workshops. **Publications:** *Annual Conference Souvenirs* • *The Indian American*, quarterly • *News Letter*, bimonthly. **Price:** free. **Circulation:** 1,000. **Advertising:** accepted. **Conventions/Meetings:** annual conference (exhibits) - always first weekend in May.

17987 ■ Institute for America's Future (IAF)
c/o Campaign for America's Future
1025 Connecticut Ave. NW, Ste.205
Washington, DC 20036
Ph: (202)955-5665
Fax: (202)955-5606
E-mail: iaf@ourfuture.org
URL: http://www.ourfuture.org/institute
Contact: Robert L. Borosage, Pres.
Description: Fosters robust and democratic debate about the ideas and politics that will shape the nation's future in the new century; focused on policy debates that will affect the future well being and economic progress of working Americans and their families. Carries out research, education and public outreach programs. Networks with progressive leaders, analysts and activists; provides facts and analyses; identifies policy solutions and makes advocates available for media coverage and for empowering citizen discussions of issues. **Affiliated With:** Campaign for America's Future. **Publications:** *On-Line Speaker's Directory*. Alternate Formats: online.

17988 ■ Laborers' Political League (LPL)
905 16th St. NW
Washington, DC 20006
Ph: (202)737-8320
E-mail: rgreer@liuna.org
URL: http://www.liuna.org
Contact: Terence M. O'Sullivan, Gen. Pres./Ed.
Founded: 1964. **Members:** 600,000. **Description:** Seeks to inform the laborers of the U.S. of the need to exercise their right to vote; supports candidates for office who demonstrate concern for the working person and for the aims and objectives of the trade union movement; works for the passage of favorable legislation and the repeal of unfavorable legislation; conducts a program of education about such laws and their opponents and supporters. **Convention/Meeting:** none.

17989 ■ League of Women Voters of the United States (LWVUS)
1730 M St. NW, Ste.1000
Washington, DC 20036-4508
Ph: (202)429-1965
Free: (888)287-7424
Fax: (202)429-0854
E-mail: lwv@lwv.org
URL: http://www.lwv.org
Contact: Mary G. Wilson, Pres./Chair
Founded: 1920. **Members:** 110,000. **Membership Dues:** individual, $55 (annual) • household, $75 (annual). **Staff:** 50. **Budget:** $3,550,000. **Regional Groups:** 32. **State Groups:** 50. **Local Groups:** 1,250. **Description:** Voluntary organization of citizens (men and women) 18 years old or over. Promotes political responsibility through informed and active participation of citizens in government and acts on selected governmental issues. Selects and studies public policy issues at local, state, and national levels and take political action on these issues. Distributes information on candidates, issues, and campaign to encourage registration and voting. Does not support or oppose candidates or political parties. Includes national concerns such as government, international relations, natural resources, and social policy. Has evolved from the National American Woman Suffrage Association, following the fight for woman suffrage. **Formerly:** (1946) National League of Women Voters. **Publications:** *National Voter*, bimonthly • Annual Report, annual • Handbooks. **Conventions/Meetings:** biennial convention (exhibits) - always even-numbered years • biennial meeting - always odd-numbered years in Washington, DC.

17990 ■ League of Young Voters
45 Main St., Ste.628
Brooklyn, NY 11201
Ph: (718)305-4245
E-mail: contactus@indyvoter.org
URL: http://www.indyvoter.org
Contact: Billy Wimsatt, Exec. Dir.
Founded: 2004. **Description:** Supports young people striving to solve problems in the communities. Works with young people who have been shut out of the political process to make politics fun, engaging, relevant, and meaningful. Registers voters, writes and distributes voter guides, and lobbies elected officials.

17991 ■ National Association of Minority Political Families USA (NAMPF)
6120 Oregon Ave. NW
Washington, DC 20015
Ph: (202)686-1216
Fax: (202)686-0598
Contact: Mary E. Ivey, Pres./CEO
Founded: 1983. **Members:** 500. **Description:** Men, women and children of all ages interested in the political process. Conducts research, education, and service programs. **Publications:** newsletters. **Awards:** Diamond Award. **Frequency:** annual. **Type:** recognition • **Type:** scholarship. **Boards:** NAMPF Advisory Board. **Formerly:** (1997) National Association of Minority Political Families. **Conventions/Meetings:** annual meeting.

17992 ■ National Coalition on Black Civic Participation (NCBCP)
1900 L St. NW, Ste.700
Washington, DC 20036
Ph: (202)659-4929
Fax: (202)659-5025
E-mail: ncbcp@ncbcp.org
URL: http://www.bigvote.org
Contact: Melanie L. Campbell, Exec. Dir./CEO
Founded: 1976. **Members:** 86. **Membership Dues:** organization, $500 (annual). **Staff:** 5. **Budget:** $700,000. **State Groups:** 12. **Description:** Works to increase African American participation in civil society. Includes program such as Operation Big Vote!, Black Youth Vote!, Black Women's Roundtable, Voices of the Electorate, and the Information Resource Center. Aims to train and engage African American leaders and community activists in overcoming institutional barriers that have hindered the growth of Black communities politically, socially and economically. **Committees:** Black Youth Vote; Board and Membership Development; Finance/Resource Development; Operation Big Vote/Voices; Program Development. **Roundtables:** Black Women's. **Formerly:** (2002) National Coalition on Black Voter Participation. **Publications:** *Online Voting and Digital Divide*. Report. Alternate Formats: online • *VOICES*, quarterly. Newsletter. **Conventions/Meetings:** annual seminar.

17993 ■ National Federation of the Grand Order of Pachyderm Clubs (NFGOPC)
PO Box 1602
Great Falls, MT 59403-1602
Free: (888)GOPACHY
Fax: (406)771-3941
E-mail: www@pachyderms.org
URL: http://www.pachyderms.org
Contact: Joe Briggs, Pres.
Founded: 1974. **Members:** 3,500. **Membership Dues:** at large, $25 (annual). **Staff:** 1. **State Groups:** 4. **Local Groups:** 65. **Description:** Federation of clubs supporting ideals and goals of the Republican Party. "Believes that most of the corruption and lethargy in American politics could be eliminated if more 'good citizens' participated in politics." Promotes political education programs and provides a means for individual participation in politics; disseminates information on the American political system. **Awards:** Tough Tusk Award. **Frequency:** annual. **Type:** recognition. **Recipient:** for outstanding Pachyderm member. **Formerly:** (1974) Grand Order of Pachyderms. **Publications:** *Club Handbook*, annual. Serves as a guide for operating a local club. Alternate Formats: online • *Join the Team*. Brochure • *The*

National Pachyderm, quarterly. Newsletter. **Price:** $8.00/year. **Circulation:** 4,000. Alternate Formats: online. **Conventions/Meetings:** biennial National Pachyderm Clubs Conference (exhibits).

17994 ■ National Student Campaign for Voter Registration (NSCVR)

Address Unknown since 2007
Founded: 1984. **Budget:** $50,000. **Description:** A program sponsored by state and local chapters of public interest research groups. Cooperates with student governments, local public interest research group chapters, and other organizations interested in expanding the student vote. Has participated in campus registration drives in 42 states, resulting in over one million new registered voters. Serves as a national clearinghouse for students involved in voter registration by linking student volunteers with local voter registration projects. Operates speakers' bureau and compiles statistics. Presently inactive. **Publications:** *The Student Advocate*, monthly ● *Voter Registration Manual*, biennial ● Newsletter, periodic ● Also publishes posters and brochures. **Conventions/Meetings:** annual board meeting.

17995 ■ National Write Your Congressman (NWYC)

PO Box 830308
Richardson, TX 75083-0308
Ph: (214)342-0299
Fax: (214)324-2455
URL: http://www.nwyc.com
Contact: David N. Adamson, Founder
Founded: 1958. **Membership Dues:** business, $365 (annual). **Staff:** 250. **Budget:** $15,000,000. **Regional Groups:** 6. **State Groups:** 50. **For-Profit. Description:** Encourages and assists individuals in writing public officials. Provides research and tools needed to correspond with officials. Offers pro and con issue information and voting records of members' legislators; conducts monthly polls on timely issues and reports results to its members, to Congress and to the President; offers research service whereby members may request information on specific issues before Congress also provide legislative information to members of other associations and PAC members of large corporations. **Awards: Type:** recognition. **Computer Services:** database ● online services. **Divisions:** Corporate. **Programs:** Student Governmental Affairs. **Also Known As:** National Write Your Congressman Club. **Publications:** *Congressmen's Voting Records*, annual. Newsletter. Includes opinion ballot. Alternate Formats: online ● *Legislative Update*, bimonthly. Newsletter. Covers major issues before Congress, the Courts and Executive. **Price:** included in membership dues ● *Opinion Ballot*, monthly ● *R&P Report*, weekly. Alternate Formats: online ● *Voters Voice*, monthly. Includes a state opinion ballot for every state in the union. **Conventions/Meetings:** semiannual meeting.

17996 ■ Operation Big Vote (OBV)

c/o National Coalition on Black Civic Participation
1900 L St. NW, Ste.700
Washington, DC 20036
Ph: (202)659-4929
Fax: (202)659-5025
E-mail: ncbcp@ncbcp.org
URL: http://www.bigvote.org
Contact: Melanie L. Campbell, Exec. Dir./CEO
Founded: 1976. **Budget:** $500,000. **Description:** Serves as a program of the National Coalition on Black Voter Participation. Seeks to increase black voter participation. Organizes coalitions in communities that have large black populations or histories of low black voter participation. Promotes interest among eligible voters; provides printed materials, onsite training, and technical assistance with an emphasis on local fundraising and self-sufficiency. Conducts community-based programs in 31 states. Provides grants to support nonpartisan local voter participation and citizen empowerment projects. Sponsors Operation Big Vote Rap, a public service announcement program. **Publications:** Handbooks ● Manuals. **Conventions/Meetings:** annual seminar.

17997 ■ People's Lobby (PL)

359 Jean St.
Mill Valley, CA 94941
Ph: (415)383-7880
E-mail: attila@myexcel.com
URL: http://ni4d.us/peopleslobby
Contact: Mike Gravel, Pres.
Founded: 1968. **Description:** Serves as a citizens' action group. Seeks to encourage, educate, and assist individuals and groups in the use of the initiative, referendum, and recall processes. Works to adopt a federal constitutional amendment providing for a national initiative process. Maintains speakers' bureau; offers consultation for political campaigns. **Additional Websites:** http://www.ni4d.org, http://peopleslobby.hypermart.net. **Publications:** *Direct Democracy*. Book ● *Ordinary People Doing the Extraordinary.(The Story of Ed & Joyce Koupal & the Initiative Process)*. Book.

17998 ■ Project Vote!

739 8th St. SE, Ste.202
Washington, DC 20003
Free: (800)546-8683
E-mail: info@projectvote.org
URL: http://www.projectvote.org
Contact: Zach Polett, Exec. Dir.
Founded: 1982. **Staff:** 10. **Budget:** $1,000,000. **Local Groups:** 3. **Nonmembership. Description:** Serves as a nonpartisan organization working to increase electoral participation among low-income, minority, and unemployed citizens. Organizes local coalitions and hires local staffs and interns; conducts voter registration and education in order to increase turnout; registers individuals door-to-door as they wait in food stamp and unemployment lines. Sponsors voter education and training programs. **Also Known As:** Americans for Civic Participation. **Publications:** *How to Develop a Voter Registration Plan* ● *How to Register Voters at a Central Site* ● *Project Vote Newsletter* ● Videos.

17999 ■ Reagan Alumni Association (RAA)

122 S Royal St.
Alexandria, VA 22314-3328
Ph: (703)461-7250
Fax: (703)461-7251
E-mail: lou@cordia.com
URL: http://www.reaganalumni.org
Contact: Louis J. Cordia, Exec. Dir.
Founded: 1987. **Members:** 4,500. **Membership Dues:** regular, $25 (annual). **Description:** Political appointees in the Reagan/Bush administration and full-or-part-time staff in the campaigns. Seeks to advance the "Reagan agenda" and to provide knowledge and expertise on national government programs to government, media, and groups interested in public policy. Offers job placement service for members. **Formerly:** (1990) Reagan Appointees Alumni Association. **Publications:** *Reagan Alumni Directory*, annual ● *Reagan Alumni Newsletter*, quarterly. **Conventions/Meetings:** annual meeting - always in Washington, DC ● periodic meeting, events, briefings and receptions.

18000 ■ South Asian American Voting Youth (SAAVY)

1718 M St. NW, Ste.290
Washington, DC 20036
E-mail: info@saavy.org
URL: http://www.saavy.org
Contact: Taz Ahmed, Contact
Description: Empowers South Asian American youth 18-25 years to be a unified political voice. Seeks to encourage politicians to include South Asian Americans in the democratic process. Aspires to bring skills from the progressive movement to the South Asian community. **Telecommunication Services:** electronic mail, taz@saavy.org.

18001 ■ Southwest Voter Registration Education Project (SVREP)

Kelly USA, Bldg. 1670
206 Lombard St., 2nd Fl.
San Antonio, TX 78226

Ph: (210)922-0225 (323)343-9299
Free: (800)404-VOTE
Fax: (210)932-4055
E-mail: agonzalez@svrep.org
URL: http://www.svrep.org
Contact: Antonio Gonzalez, Pres.
Founded: 1975. **Staff:** 16. **Budget:** $1,000,000. **Local Groups:** 200. **Description:** Represents church, civic, labor, and fraternal groups that organize coalitions to register minority voters in the southwest and 13 Western states. Conducts nonpartisan voter education projects and research on Hispanic and Native American political organization participation in the Southwest. Seeks reapportionment of gerrymandered counties and cities. Trains regional coordinators for voter registration campaigns. Compiles statistics. **Computer Services:** database. **Departments:** Communications; Field Operations; Litigation; Research. **Publications:** *Latino Vote Reporter*, bimonthly. Newsletters. Alternate Formats: online ● *National Hispanic Voter Registration Campaign* ● Reports, bimonthly. Alternate Formats: online ● Also publishes research studies. **Conventions/Meetings:** semiannual Latino Vote Banquet/Latino Academy - dinner - June and September ● annual regional meeting.

Polls

18002 ■ American Association for Public Opinion Research (AAPOR)

PO Box 14263
Lenexa, KS 66285-4263
Ph: (913)310-0118
Fax: (913)599-5340
E-mail: aapor-info@goamp.com
URL: http://www.aapor.org
Contact: Michael Flanagan, Exec. Coor.
Founded: 1947. **Members:** 1,600. **Membership Dues:** employer-paid, $105 (annual) ● individual (based on annual income), $55-$130 (annual) ● student, $25 (annual). **Budget:** $480,000. **Regional Groups:** 7. **Description:** Represents individuals interested in the methods and applications of public opinion and social research. **Awards:** AAPOR Award for Exceptionally Distinguished Achievement. **Frequency:** annual. **Type:** recognition. **Recipient:** for outstanding contributions in the field of public opinion research ● Book Award. **Frequency:** annual. **Type:** recognition. **Recipient:** for the most influential book that has stimulated theoretical and scientific research in public opinion ● Innovators Award. **Frequency:** annual. **Type:** recognition. **Recipient:** for outstanding accomplishments in the field of public opinion and survey research that occurred in the past ten years (1994 or later) ● Policy Impact Award. **Frequency:** annual. **Type:** recognition. **Recipient:** for outstanding research that has a clear impact on improving policy decisions, practice and discourse, either on public or private sectors ● Seymour Sudman Student Paper Award. **Frequency:** annual. **Type:** recognition. **Recipient:** to the best paper in any field related to the study of public opinion. **Committees:** Standards. **Publications:** *AAPOR Newsletter*, semiannual. **Price:** included in membership dues. **Circulation:** 1,700 ● *Agencies and Organizations Represented in AAPOR Membership*, annual. Journal ● *Public Opinion Quarterly*. Directory ● Directory, annual. Provides information on membership activities. **Conventions/Meetings:** annual competition and conference ● annual conference.

18003 ■ Council of American Survey Research Organizations (CASRO)

170 N Country Rd., Ste.4
Port Jefferson, NY 11777
Ph: (631)928-6954
Fax: (631)928-6041
E-mail: casro@casro.org
URL: http://www.casro.org
Contact: Diane K. Bowers, Pres.
Founded: 1975. **Members:** 250. **Staff:** 4. **Budget:** $700,000. **Description:** Survey research companies in the U.S. Seeks to provide a vehicle whereby

survey research companies can interact with one another, sharing relevant information and addressing common problems. Promotes the establishment, maintenance, and improvement of professional standards in survey research. **Committees:** Educational and Professional Training; Financial/ Compensation Survey; Government Affairs; International Relations; Public Relations; Publications; Standards; Survey Research Quality; Technology. **Publications:** *CASRO Journal*, annual. Consists of articles submitted by CASRO members and individuals from the global research community. **Price:** $25.00/copy. **Advertising:** accepted. Alternate Formats: online ● *CASRO Quarterly Financial Report*. Alternate Formats: online ● *On the Definition of Response Rates*. Report. Includes reports on the measurements of response rates as an index of survey research data quality. Alternate Formats: online ● Newsletter. Alternate Formats: online. **Conventions/Meetings:** annual conference and seminar (exhibits) - 2007 Oct. 10-12, Scottsdale, AZ.

18004 ■ National Council on Public Polls (NCPP)
c/o Dr. Barbara L. Carvalho, Sec.-Treas.
Marist Inst. for Public Opinion
Marist Coll.
Poughkeepsie, NY 12601
Ph: (845)575-5050
Fax: (845)575-5111
E-mail: info@ncpp.org
URL: http://www.ncpp.org
Contact: Dr. Lee M. Miringoff, Pres.
Founded: 1969. **Members:** 28. **Membership Dues:** public opinion polling organization, $250-$750 (annual). **Description:** Represents organizations conducting regularly published public opinion polls or engaged in the systematic analysis or dissemination of public opinion survey data. Works toward and adhere to standards for the profession. Seeks to give the public a "better understanding and a better basis" for interpreting poll results. Aims to publicize established standards for reporting poll results, inform the public and the news media on the proper interpretation of such findings, and "work toward maximum service to the public in polling operations". **Formerly:** National Committee on Public Polls. **Conventions/Meetings:** annual conference.

18005 ■ World Association for Public Opinion Research (WAPOR)
c/o Dr. Allan L. McCutcheon, Gen. Sec.
Univ. of Nebraska-Lincoln
UNL Gallup Res. Ctr.
200 N 11th St.
Lincoln, NE 68588-0242
Ph: (402)458-2030
Fax: (402)458-2038
E-mail: amccutcheon1@unl.edu
URL: http://www.unl.edu/WAPOR
Contact: Dr. Allan L. McCutcheon, Gen. Sec.
Founded: 1946. **Members:** 433. **Membership Dues:** retired, $80 (annual) ● retired (without journal), $35 (annual) ● student (ID required) $50 (annual) ● life, $2,000 ● individual (tier A), $125 (annual) ● business (tier A), $170 (annual). **Multinational. Description:** Academic survey research scholars and commercial survey researchers. Establishes and promotes contacts between survey researchers on opinions, attitudes, and behaviors of people in various countries. Furthers the use of objective scientific survey research in international affairs. Activities include improving methods and professional standards, training personnel, and coordinating and integrating international polls. **Awards:** Helen Dinerman Award. **Frequency:** annual. **Type:** recognition. **Recipient:** for outstanding contributions and published articles ● Worcester, Nelson and Turner Prizes. **Frequency:** annual. **Type:** recognition. **Recipient:** for outstanding paper. **Publications:** *International Journal of Public Opinion Research*, quarterly. Serves as a source of informed analysis and comment for both professionals and academics. **Price:** included in membership dues. Alternate Formats: online ● Directory, annual ● Newsletter, quarterly. **Conventions/Meetings:** annual Public Opinion and the Challenges of the 21st

Century - conference, held in conjunction with American Association for Public Opinion Research in even-numbered years and European Society for Opinion and Marketing Research in odd-numbered years - 2007 Sept. 19-21, Berlin, Germany ● regional meeting.

Pornography

18006 ■ Foundation for Moral Restoration
PO Box 1009
Ashburn, VA 20146-1009
Ph: (703)724-4141
E-mail: richardenrico@adelphia.net
Contact: Richard J. Enrico, Exec. Dir.
Founded: 1982. **Description:** Faith ministry focusing on "leading people to the true foundation for holy living - Jesus Christ." Distributes free Bibles, tapes, books, literature, and various tracts in an attempt to educate people in the necessity of having a personal relationship with Jesus Christ. **Formerly:** (1993) Citizens Against Pornography. **Publications:** *Foundation for Moral Restoration Newsletter*, monthly. **Price:** free ● *He Is Faithful!*, periodic. Video. **Price:** free ● *Washington Redskins Champions for Christ*. Video. **Price:** free ● *Will You Speak Out to Stop Abortion?*. Video. **Price:** free. **Conventions/Meetings:** periodic meeting and lecture.

18007 ■ Morality in Media (MIM)
475 Riverside Dr., Ste.239
New York, NY 10115
Ph: (212)870-3222
Fax: (212)870-2765
E-mail: mim@moralityinmedia.org
URL: http://www.moralityinmedia.org
Contact: Robert W. Peters, Pres.
Founded: 1962. **Members:** 14,000. **Membership Dues:** individual, $25 (annual) ● organization, $50 (annual). **Staff:** 15. **Budget:** $950,000. **Description:** Works to combat obscenity and to uphold decency standards in the media. Maintains the National Obscenity Law Center, a clearinghouse of legal materials on obscenity law. **Libraries: Type:** reference. **Holdings:** archival material. **Subjects:** obscenity and indecency law, allied subjects. **Additional Websites:** http://www.obscenitycrimes.org. **Publications:** *Cliches: Debunking Misinformation about Pornography and Obscenity Law*. Booklet. Contains information on how to handle the porn-is-harmless arguments. ● *Handbook on the Prosecution of Obscenity Cases* ● *How to Win the War in Your Community*. Handbook. Contains information on how to fight porn in mail, video shops, cable TV, 'Adult' bookstores and nude bars. ● *Morality in Media Newsletter*, bimonthly. **Price:** included in membership dues. ISSN: 1058-3459. **Circulation:** 14,000 ● *Obscenity Law Bulletin*, bimonthly ● *Obscenity Law Reporter* ● *Pornography's Effects on Adults & Children*. Monograph. Features an empirical and clinical evidence of porn's effects. ● *Stranger in the House*. Handbook. Contains information on the effects of TV on children, adults and families. Also Cited As: *TV: The World's Greatest Mind-Bender*.

18008 ■ National Coalition for the Protection of Children and Families (NCPCF)
800 Compton Rd., Ste.9224
Cincinnati, OH 45231
Ph: (513)521-6227
Free: (800)583-2964
Fax: (513)521-6337
E-mail: ncpcf@nationalcoalition.org
URL: http://www.nationalcoalition.org
Contact: Rick Schatz, Pres./CEO
Founded: 1983. **Budget:** $1,900,000. **Description:** Works to unite, train, and assist religious, civic and legal groups and individuals who seek to eliminate obscenity, child pornography, and material harmful to minors. Advocates petitioning elected and law enforcement officials and corporate leaders to strictly uphold existing obscenity and child protection laws. Provides written, video, and audio materials about ways to campaign against illegal pornography, sexual

violence, and child victimization. Conducts research; compiles statistics. Maintains speakers' bureau. **Awards: Type:** recognition. **Computer Services:** Online services, publication. **Formerly:** (1984) National Consultation on Pornography and Obscenity; (1995) National Coalition Against Pornography. **Publications:** *NCPCF Action*, quarterly. Newsletter. **Price:** free. **Circulation:** 10,000. Alternate Formats: online ● *Tips and Talking Points*. Booklet. **Price:** $1.20 ● Annual Report, annual. Alternate Formats: online. **Conventions/Meetings:** annual National City Leaders Conference - meeting (exhibits) ● seminar, for training ● workshop.

Postal Service

18009 ■ Main Street Coalition for Postal Fairness
c/o The Aker Partners, Inc.
2000 K St. NW, Ste.801
Washington, DC 20006
Ph: (202)789-2424
Fax: (202)789-1818
E-mail: info@akerpartners.com
URL: http://www.akerpartners.com
Founded: 1996. **Description:** Works to ensure the needs of all small volume mailers and individuals are addressed by the U.S. Congress and the U.S. Postal Service.

Poverty

18010 ■ Call to Renewal
3333 14th St. NW, Ste.200
Washington, DC 20010
Ph: (202)328-8745
Fax: (202)328-6797
E-mail: ctr@calltorenewal.com
URL: http://www.calltorenewal.org
Contact: Jim Wallis, Pres./Convener
Description: Aims to overcome poverty, dismantle racism, affirm life, rebuild family and community. Develops and supports connections between Evangelicals, mainline Protestants, Catholics, Historic Black Churches, Historic Peace Churches, Pentecostals and major faith based organizations. Provides a voice to influence national and local direction and public policy, and networks churches and faith-based organizations' leaders to build a movement to overcome poverty. **Computer Services:** Online services, Christian Anti-Poverty Online Resource.

18011 ■ Center on Urban Poverty and Community Development
Mandel School of Applied Social Sciences
Case Western Reserve Univ.
10900 Euclid Ave.
Cleveland, OH 44106-7164
Ph: (216)368-6946
Fax: (216)368-5158
E-mail: povcenter@case.edu
URL: http://povertycenter.cwru.edu
Contact: Claudia Coulton, Co-Dir.
Founded: 1988. **Description:** Dedicated to understanding how social and economic changes affect low-income communities and residents. **Computer Services:** database, Northeast Ohio Community and Neighborhood Data for Organizing. **Formerly:** (2006) Center on Urban Poverty and Social Change.

Pro-Life

18012 ■ National Association of Pro-Life Nurses (NAPN)
PO Box 26883
Milwaukee, WI 53226
E-mail: president@nursesforlife.org
URL: http://www.nursesforlife.org
Contact: Sue Meyers RN, Pres.
Membership Dues: individual (renewal), $20 (annual) ● student, $10 (annual) ● individual (new), $30

(annual). **Description:** Promotes respect for every human life from conception to natural death. Seeks to affirm that the destruction of life does not meet the ideals of good nursing practice. **Computer Services:** Online services, Yahoo community. **Publications:** *Pulse-Line.* Newsletter.

Property Rights

18013 ■ American Association of Small Property Owners (AASPO)
4200 Cathedral Ave. NW, Ste.515
Washington, DC 20016
Ph: (202)625-8330
E-mail: jdaines@gmail.com
URL: http://www.aaspo.org
Contact: F. Patricia Callahan, Pres.
Founded: 1993. **Description:** Works for the right of small property owners to prosper freely and fairly. **Publications:** *The Small Property Owner,* monthly. Features information from Washington and around the county.

18014 ■ National Association of Reversionary Property Owners (NARPO)
227 Bellevue Way NE, Ste.719
Bellevue, WA 98004
Ph: (425)646-8812 (760)771-9459
Fax: (425)646-8812
E-mail: dick156@earthlink.net
URL: http://home.earthlink.net/~dick156
Contact: Richard Welsh, Exec. Dir.
Description: Promotes the principle that private property ownership must be maintained in the hands of citizens, not the government. Aims to assist property owners in maintaining their complete land ownership and resisting government confiscation.

18015 ■ Stewards of the Range
PO Box 490
Meridian, ID 83680-0490
Ph: (208)855-0707
Fax: (208)855-0763
E-mail: stewards@stewards.us
URL: http://www.stewardsoftherange.org
Contact: Margaret H. Byfield, Exec. Dir./Sec.
Founded: 1992. **Members:** 6,000. **Membership Dues:** regular, $35 (annual) ● silver, $50 (annual) ● gold, $100 (annual) ● patriot, $250 (annual) ● premier, $500 (annual) ● founding, $1,000 (annual). **Staff:** 6. **Budget:** $500,000. **Description:** National advocate for property rights. Promotes the philosophy "that every person has a right to own property, has the right to cultivate his own land without government interference, and has the right and responsibility to defend the property." Defends property rights in court, including the Hage vs. United States litigation effort. Monitors public policy issues. **Libraries: Type:** open to the public. **Holdings:** articles, artwork, books. **Subjects:** property rights. **Publications:** *Cornerstone,* periodic. Newspaper.

Prostitution

18016 ■ Association of Albanian Girls and Women (AAGW)
c/o Amy L. Sebes, Founder/Dir.
9510 Tirana Pl.
Dulles, VA 20189-9510
Ph: (310)291-9205
E-mail: info@aagw.com
URL: http://www.aagw.org
Contact: Amy L. Sebes, Founder/Dir.
Multinational. Description: Helps former victims of trafficking reintegrate into Albanian society. Educates the general public about trafficking through outreach activities. **Programs:** Handicraft Production. **Publications:** Brochure.

18017 ■ Captive Daughters
3500 Overland Ave., No. 110-108
Los Angeles, CA 90034
Ph: (310)669-4400
Free: (800)320-0476
Fax: (310)815-9197
E-mail: captivedaughters@earthlink.net
URL: http://www.captivedaughters.org
Contact: Sandra Hunnicutt, Founding Dir.
Founded: 1997. **Description:** Aims to end the sexual bondage of female adolescents and children. Seeks to encourage national and international attention to sex trafficking. Informs the general public about the scope and severity of sex trafficking. **Computer Services:** Information services, sex tourism resources ● information services, sex trafficking resources.

Public Affairs

18018 ■ Ad Council
261 Madison Ave., 11th Fl.
New York, NY 10016
Ph: (212)922-1500
Fax: (212)922-1676
E-mail: info@adcouncil.org
URL: http://www.adcouncil.org
Contact: Peggy Conlon, Pres./CEO
Founded: 1942. **Description:** Produces, distributes, and promotes public service campaigns on behalf of non-profit organizations and government agencies in issue areas such as improving the quality of life for children, preventative health, education, community well being, environmental preservation and strengthening of families. **Publications:** *Public Service Advertising Bulletin,* bimonthly. Newsletter. Features articles detailing current news about campaigns and the organization. **Circulation:** 15,000 ● Annual Report, annual.

18019 ■ Alfred P. Sloan Foundation
630 5th Ave., Ste.2550
New York, NY 10111
Ph: (212)649-1649
Fax: (212)757-5117
E-mail: gomory@sloan.org
URL: http://www.sloan.org
Contact: Ralph E. Gomory, Pres.
Founded: 1934. **Description:** Scientists, social scientists, and other individuals and organizations with an interest in science and technology, economics, education, and related national issues. Seeks to improve the quality of life worldwide. Provides support and assistance to research and projects.

18020 ■ Alliance for Democracy (AfD)
PO Box 540115
Waltham, MA 02454-0115
Ph: (781)894-1179
Fax: (781)894-0279
E-mail: afd@thealliancefordemocracy.org
URL: http://www.thealliancefordemocracy.org
Contact: Barbara Clancy, Office Coor.
Description: Seeks to end "the domination of our economy, our government, our culture, our media and the environment by large corporations". **Publications:** *Justice Rising,* quarterly. Newsletter. Alternate Formats: online. **Conventions/Meetings:** convention.

18021 ■ Business Leaders for Sensible Priorities (BLSP)
c/o Greg Corsico, Membership Dir.
460 W 34th St., 17th Fl.
New York, NY 10001-2320
Ph: (212)243-3416
E-mail: greg@sensiblepriorities.org
URL: http://www.sensiblepriorities.org
Contact: Greg Corsico, Membership Dir.
Founded: 1996. **Members:** 500. **Membership Dues:** introductory trial, $100 (annual) ● standard, $250 (annual) ● gold, $500 (annual) ● platinum, $1,000 (annual). **Description:** Aims to change US budget priorities to reflect a national commitment to educa-

tion, healthcare, energy independence, job training and deficit reduction. Strives to eliminate funding for needed Cold War era weapons systems. **Committees:** Military Advisory. **Projects:** Move Our Money.

18022 ■ Campaign for America's Future (CAF)
1025 Connecticut Ave. NW, Ste.205
Washington, DC 20036
Ph: (202)955-5665
Fax: (202)955-5606
E-mail: info@ourfuture.org
URL: http://www.ourfuture.org
Contact: Roger Hickey, Co-Dir.
Members: 100. **Description:** Citizen activists and policy experts concerned about the nation and the world; challenges corporations to debate a new economy and a new future. Maintains an online speakers directory. **Publications:** *The Next Agenda: Blueprint for a New Progressive Movement.* Book.

18023 ■ Carter Center
One Copenhill
453 Freedom Pkwy.
Atlanta, GA 30307
Ph: (404)420-5100
Fax: (404)420-5145
E-mail: carterweb@emory.edu
URL: http://www.cartercenter.org
Contact: Dr. John Hardman, Exec. Dir.
Founded: 1982. **Staff:** 150. **Budget:** $36,000,000. **Multinational. Description:** Is founded by former U.S. President Jimmy Carter and his wife Rosalynn, in partnership with Emory University; works to advance peace and health around the world; seeks to advance democracy, human rights, economic opportunity, disease prevention, improvement in mental health care, and educating farmers to increase crop production. **Libraries: Type:** by appointment only. **Holdings:** archival material, articles, audiovisuals, books, monographs, periodicals. **Subjects:** international relations. **Programs:** Americas; Conflict Resolution; Democracy. **Publications:** *Carter Center News,* semiannual. Magazine. Alternate Formats: online ● Annual Report, annual ● Reports. Alternate Formats: online. **Conventions/Meetings:** annual Conversations at The Carter Center - meeting ● Global Development Initiative Forum - symposium - held in May ● Rosalynn Carter Georgia Mental Health Forum - symposium - held in November ● annual Rosalynn Carter Symposium on Mental Health Policy.

18024 ■ Center for Strategic and International Studies (CSIS)
1800 K St. NW, Ste.400
Washington, DC 20006
Ph: (202)887-0200
Fax: (202)775-3199
E-mail: aschwartz@csis.org
URL: http://www.csis.org
Contact: John J. Hamre, Pres./CEO
Founded: 1962. **Staff:** 190. **Multinational. Description:** Provides global leaders with strategic insights on, and policy solutions to, current and emerging world issues. **Programs:** Young Leaders. **Working Groups:** Caribbean Leadership. **Publications:** *CSIS Panel Reports* ● *Cyberthreats, Information Warfare, and Critical Infrastructure Protection.* Book ● *The Fiscal Challenge of an Aging Industrial World.* Book ● *Global Aging and Financial Markets.* Book ● *Meeting the Challenge of Global Aging.* Book ● *Significant Issues Series.* Books ● *Strategic Threats and National Missile Defenses.* Book ● *The U.S.-Japan Security Alliance.* Book ● *U.S. Armed Forces and Homeland Defense.* Book ● *The Washington Papers.* Monographs ● *Washington Quarterly.* Journal ● Reports, annual. Alternate Formats: online. **Conventions/Meetings:** conference ● meeting ● seminar.

18025 ■ Commercial Alert
PO Box 19002
Washington, DC 20036
Ph: (202)387-8030
Fax: (202)234-5176

E-mail: mark@commercialalert.org
URL: http://www.commercialalert.org
Contact: Gary Ruskin, Exec. Dir.
Founded: 1998. **Members:** 2,000. **Staff:** 1. **Budget:** $120,000. **Description:** Seeks to prevent the commercial culture from exploiting children and subverting the values of family, community, environmental integrity and democracy. **Computer Services:** Information services, listserv. **Telecommunication Services:** electronic mail, gary@commercialalert.org ● information service, free advice to people who want to oppose the commercialization of schools, government or public spaces. **Publications:** Newsletters, semiannual. Contains articles on the commercialization of culture, education and government, along with descriptions of the efforts in opposing it. **Price:** $20.00 for members. **Circulation:** 2,800.

18026 ■ Eisenhower Institute (EI)
915 15th St. NW, 8th Fl.
Washington, DC 20005-2311
Ph: (202)628-4444
Fax: (202)628-4445
E-mail: jkratovil@eisenhowerinstitute.org
URL: http://www.eisenhowerinstitute.org
Contact: Jane Kratovil, Exec. Dir./Treas.
Founded: 1983. **Description:** Works to advance Dwight D. Eisenhower's legacy in foreign and domestic policy. **Awards:** Dwight D. Eisenhower/Ann C. Whitman Scholarship Program. **Frequency:** annual. **Type:** scholarship. **Recipient:** for outstanding graduating senior from Perry High in Perry, Ohio ● Dwight D. Eisenhower/Clifford Roberts Graduate Fellowships. **Frequency:** annual. **Type:** fellowship. **Recipient:** for PhD student ● Dwight D. Eisenhower/Conrad Hilton Scholarship at Gettysburg College. **Frequency:** annual. **Type:** scholarship. **Recipient:** for Gettysburg College senior or junior student ● Dwight D. Eisenhower/Thomas Pappas Graduate Fellowships. **Frequency:** annual. **Type:** fellowship. **Recipient:** for PhD student at Tufts University. **Programs:** America's Relations with Russia and China; Emerging Threats; European security and NATO; Future of Space; National Missile Defense; Weapons of Mass Destruction. **Publications:** *Ballistic Missile Defense in Context: Diplomacy, Deterrence and Defense.* Book ● *Islam and Central Asia: An Enduring Legacy or Evolving Threat?.* Book. **Price:** $20.00 plus shipping and handling ● *The Monks of Tibhirine: Faith, Love and Terror Algeria.* Book ● *NATO at Fifty: Perspectives on the Future of the Atlantic Alliance.* Book. Alternate Formats: online ● *Occasional Papers.*

18027 ■ First Amendment Project (FAP)
1736 Franklin St., 9th Fl.
Oakland, CA 94612
Ph: (510)208-7744
Fax: (510)208-4562
E-mail: fap@thefirstamendment.org
URL: http://www.thefirstamendment.org
Contact: David Greene, Exec. Dir./Staff Counsel
Founded: 1991. **Description:** Serves as a public interest law firm committed to protect, defend, and further the rights to participate in and know about government activities and speak freely about public issues. Offers direct legal representation to individuals, civic organizations, journalists, and media organizations involved in petition and free speech or right-to-know cases; provides litigation support services to other attorneys; promotes public awareness on issues of free speech and access to government; provides education and advice on First Amendment issues. Litigation efforts focus on First Amendment law: anti-SLAPP defense and enforcement of open government laws. **Publications:** Pamphlets. Includes Public Records Act, Brown Act, Access to Court Proceedings and Hearings, Freedom of Information Act, and Strategic Lawsuits Against Public Part.

18028 ■ Ford Foundation
320 E 43rd St.
New York, NY 10017
Ph: (212)573-5000
Fax: (212)351-3677

E-mail: office-secretary@fordfound.org
URL: http://www.fordfound.org
Contact: Mr. Barron M. Tenny, Exec. VP/Sec./Gen. Counsel
Founded: 1936. **Staff:** 504. **Budget:** $9,969,703,000. **Multinational. Description:** Seeks to strengthen democratic values, reduce poverty and injustice, promote international cooperation and advance human achievement. **Publications:** *Current Interests.* Brochure ● *Ford Foundation Report,* quarterly ● Annual Report, annual.

18029 ■ Heart of America Northwest (HOANW)
1314 56th St. NE, Ste.100
Seattle, WA 98105
Ph: (206)382-1014
Fax: (206)382-1148
E-mail: office@heartofamericanorthwest.org
URL: http://www.heartofamericanorthwest.org
Contact: Rebecca Sayre, Field Dir.
Description: Works for the clean up of Hanford Nuclear Reservation, transportation of nuclear waste to the Northwest, and other hazardous waste issues. **Publications:** *Citizen's Guides.* Newsletter. Provides information about giving comments at public hearings on Hanford issues.

18030 ■ International Institute for Strategic Studies - US (IISS-US)
1850 K St. NW, Ste.300
Washington, DC 20006
Ph: (202)659-1490
Fax: (202)296-1134
E-mail: sales@iiss.org
URL: http://www.iiss.org
Contact: Adam Ward, Exec. Dir./Treas.
Founded: 1958. **Members:** 3,000. **Multinational. Description:** Provides information on international strategic issues for politicians and diplomats, foreign affairs analysts, international business, economists, and more. **Publications:** *Adelphi Papers,* 10/year ● *The Military Balance,* annual. Provides annual inventory of the world's armed forces. **Price:** $280.00 for institution; $145.00 for individual ● *Strategic Comments,* monthly. Alternate Formats: online ● *Strategic Survey,* annual. Contains annual retrospective of the year's political and military trends. ● *Survival,* quarterly. Article.

18031 ■ Public Campaign
1320 19th St. NW, Ste.M-1
Washington, DC 20036
Ph: (202)293-0222
Fax: (202)293-0202
E-mail: info@pcactionfund.org
URL: http://www.publicampaign.org
Contact: Nick Nyhart, Exec. Dir./Co-Founder
Description: Campaigns for finance reform. **Publications:** *Clean Money Campaign Reform.*

18032 ■ Public Education Center (PEC)
1100 Connecticut Ave. NW, Ste.1310
Washington, DC 20036-4119
Ph: (202)466-4310
Fax: (202)466-4344
E-mail: info@publicedcenter.org
URL: http://www.storiesthatmatter.org
Contact: Joseph Trento, Pres.
Founded: 1992. **Description:** Works to educate citizens through the major media by developing comprehensive investigations on the environment and national security. **Divisions:** National Security News Service; Natural Resources News Service. **Publications:** Newsletter, monthly. Alternate Formats: online.

18033 ■ School of the Americas Watch (SOA Watch)
PO Box 4566
Washington, DC 20017
Ph: (202)234-3440
Fax: (202)636-4505

E-mail: info@soaw.org
URL: http://www.soaw.org/new
Contact: Fr. Roy Bourgeois, Founder
Description: Aims to close the U.S. Army School of the Americas through vigils and fasts, demonstrations and nonviolent protest, as well as media and legislative work. **Publications:** Newsletter.

18034 ■ W.K. Kellogg Foundation
1 Michigan Ave. E
Battle Creek, MI 49017-4012
Ph: (269)968-1611
Fax: (269)968-0413
URL: http://www.wkkf.org
Contact: Sterling K. Speirn, Pres./CEO
Founded: 1930. **Description:** Social and political scientists and other interested individuals and organizations. Seeks to "help people help themselves." Provides financial support and other assistance to programs operating in areas including: youth; leadership; philanthropy and voluntarism; community-based health services; higher education; food systems; and rural development. Supports operations in the United States, Latin America and the Caribbean, and southern Africa.

Public Finance

18035 ■ Business Council (BC)
PO Box 20147
Washington, DC 20041
Ph: (202)298-7650
Fax: (202)785-0296
URL: http://www.businesscouncil.com
Contact: Philip E. Cassidy, Exec. Dir.
Founded: 1961. **Members:** 180. **Staff:** 2. **Description:** Represents business executives. Aims to serve the national interest, with the primary objectives of developing a constructive point of view on matters of public policy affecting the business interests of the country and by providing a medium for a better understanding of government problems by business. Members are former and present chief executive officers of corporations. **Formerly:** (1933) Business Advisory Council. **Conventions/Meetings:** conference - 3/year.

18036 ■ Business Roundtable (BR)
1717 Rhode Island Ave. NW, Ste.800
Washington, DC 20036
Ph: (202)872-1260
E-mail: info@businessroundtable.org
URL: http://www.businessroundtable.org
Contact: John J. Castellani, Pres.
Founded: 1972. **Members:** 160. **Staff:** 21. **Description:** Chief executive officers of leading U.S. corporations, representing over 10 million employees. The CEOs examine public policy issues that affect the economy and develop positions, which seek to reflect sound economic and social principles. **Programs:** BusinessLinc. **Task Forces:** Civil Justice Reform; Corporate Governance; Education and the Workforce; Energy; Environment, Technology, and the Economy; Fiscal Policy; Health and Retirement; International Trade and Investment; Partnership for Disaster Response; Security. **Publications:** *CEO Economic Outlook Survey Comparison of Results,* quarterly ● *The Wall Street Journal* ● Reports ● Papers ● Also publishes position papers on public issues. **Conventions/Meetings:** annual meeting.

18037 ■ Center on Budget and Policy Priorities (CBPP)
820 1st St. NE, No. 510
Washington, DC 20002
Ph: (202)408-1080
Fax: (202)408-1056
E-mail: center@cbpp.org
URL: http://www.centeronbudget.org
Contact: Robert Greenstein, Founder/Exec. Dir.
Founded: 1981. **Staff:** 40. **Budget:** $3,400,000. **Description:** Promotes better public understanding of the impact of federal and state governmental spending policies and programs primarily affecting low and

moderate income families and individuals; acts as resource center and information clearinghouse for the media, national and local organizations (including major church denominations), and individuals. Includes areas of research: national poverty trends, tax policy, housing affordability, effectiveness and funding for social programs, hunger and nutrition issues, unemployment, minimum wage, and state budget and tax policies. Conducts special studies on minorities and poverty. Organizes educational campaign concerning the Earned Income Tax Credit and Medicaid outreach. **Convention/Meeting:** none. **Libraries: Type:** reference; not open to the public. **Holdings:** 9,000; articles, books, periodicals. **Subjects:** poverty, unemployment, education, hunger, federal and state budgets, welfare, Census Department data, healthcare. **Divisions:** Outreach. **Projects:** International Budget; State Fiscal. **Affiliated With:** Center for Strategic and Budgetary Assessments. **Publications:** *A Hand Up: How State Earned Income Credits Help Working Families Escape Poverty.* Report ● *A New Direction: The Clinton Budget and Economic Plan.* Report ● *A Place to Call Home: The Low Income Housing Crisis in Major Metropolitan Areas.* Report ● *End of the Line? What the End of Emergency Unemployment Benefits Means.* Report ● *Enough to Live On: Setting an Appropriate AFDC Need Standard.* Report ● *Learning for Earning.* Report ● *Making Work Pay: The Unfinished Agenda.* Report ● *National General Assistance Survey, 1992* ● *The States and the Poor: How Budget Decisions Affected Low Income People in 1992.* Report ● *Taxing the Top: Strategies for Increasing State Income Tax Revenue Without Changing Tax Rates.* Report ● *Where Have All the Dollars Gone? A State-by-State Analysis of Income Disparities Over the 1980s.* Report ● *White Poverty in America.* Report ● *Women, Infants, and Children Newsletter,* monthly. Alternate Formats: online ● Articles.

18038 ■ Center for Financial Freedom and Accuracy in Financial Reporting (CFFAFR)
PO Box 37812
Cincinnati, OH 45222
Ph: (513)475-0100
Free: (800)543-0486
Fax: (513)475-6014
E-mail: crimpol@eos.net
URL: http://www.criminalpolitics.com
Contact: Lawrence T. Patterson, Exec. Off./Owner
Founded: 1975. **Members:** 10,000. **Membership Dues:** individual, $25 (annual) ● business, $50 (annual). **Staff:** 10. **For-Profit. Description:** Individuals interested in financial freedom and in reporting on laws that they believe financially hurt the working population. Seeks to protect Social Security retirement benefits against "government confiscation." Advocates a return to the gold standard. Conducts research on IRA accounts and government sponsored programs. **Libraries: Type:** not open to the public. **Holdings:** 10,000; books, periodicals. **Awards:** Literature Award. **Frequency:** annual. **Type:** recognition. **Publications:** *Criminal Politics,* monthly. Magazine. Provides information on how legislation affects investments. Includes book reviews and research reports. **Price:** $187.50/year. ISSN: 1084-8053. **Circulation:** 30,000. **Advertising:** accepted. **Conventions/Meetings:** semiannual seminar (exhibits).

18039 ■ Committee for a Responsible Federal Budget (CRFB)
1630 Connecticut Ave. NW, 7th Fl.
Washington, DC 20009
Ph: (202)986-6599
Fax: (202)986-3696
E-mail: crfb@newamerica.net
URL: http://www.crfb.org
Contact: Maya MacGuineas, Pres.
Founded: 1981. **Members:** 130. **Staff:** 3. **Description:** Serves as bipartisan, non-profit educational organization committed to educate the public regarding the budget process and issues that have significant fiscal policy impact. Sponsors analysis and research, conducts educational symposia, and prepares and distributes educational materials to

Congress, the Administration, the media, and the public. Consists of former members of Congress, former directors of the Office of Management and Budget and the Congressional Budget Office, and other economic and fiscal policy experts. **Publications:** Booklets ● Also publishes symposia compendia. **Conventions/Meetings:** The Exercise in Hard Choices - seminar, full-day exercise on balancing the federal budget - 10/year.

18040 ■ Foundation for Economic Education (FEE)
30 S Broadway
Irvington, NY 10533
Ph: (914)591-7230
Free: (800)960-4FEE
Fax: (914)591-8910
E-mail: fee@fee.org
URL: http://www.fee.org
Contact: Dr. Richard M. Ebeling, Pres.
Founded: 1946. **Members:** 12,000. **Membership Dues:** regular, $39 (annual) ● friend, $100 (annual) ● sponsor, $250 (annual) ● patron, $500 (annual) ● President's Council, $1,000 (annual) ● benefactor, $2,500 (annual) ● entrepreneur, $5,000 (annual). **Staff:** 13. **Budget:** $1,500,000. **Local Groups:** 42. **National Groups:** 12. **Languages:** English, Spanish. **Description:** Sponsors economic studies for those requesting them in the fields of free market theory and limited government. Encourages the study and promotion of private ownership, free exchange, open competition, and limited government. Conducts seminars and maintains speakers' bureau. **Convention/Meeting:** none. **Libraries: Type:** by appointment only. **Holdings:** 8,500. **Subjects:** Henry Hazlitt, Ludwig von Mises, individual rights, private property, history, economics, free markets, government, philosophy. **Computer Services:** Mailing lists. **Telecommunication Services:** electronic mail, comments@fee.org. **Projects:** Scholar Interns. **Publications:** *Economic Sophisms.* Book. Exposes the many fallacies of protectionism. **Price:** $11.95 paperback ● *The Freeman: Ideas on Liberty,* monthly. Magazine. Includes book reviews and annual index. **Price:** $39.00/year. ISSN: 0016-0652. **Circulation:** 31,000. **Advertising:** accepted. Alternate Formats: microform ● *The Law.* Book. **Price:** $3.00 paperback; $12.95 hardcover; $150.00 carton price ● *Mainspring of Human Progress.* Book. **Price:** $9.95 paperback; $438.00 carton price ● Also publishes books and pamphlets.

18041 ■ International Association for Research in Income and Wealth (IARIW)
c/o Jane Forman, Exec. Sec.
48 Morton St.
New York, NY 10014-4021
Ph: (212)924-4386
Fax: (212)366-5067
E-mail: info@iariw.org
URL: http://www.iariw.org
Contact: Jane Forman, Exec. Sec.
Founded: 1947. **Members:** 400. **Membership Dues:** individual, $75 (annual) ● student, $38 (annual). **Staff:** 2. **Multinational. Description:** Specialists in the field of national income accounting. Facilitates communication among members. Disseminates information pertaining to the definition and measurement of national income and wealth and social accounting and their use in economic budgeting, international comparisons, aggregations of national income and wealth, problems of statistical methodology, and related matters. **Libraries: Type:** reference. **Holdings:** articles. **Awards:** Nancy and Richard Ruggles Travel Grant. **Frequency:** biennial. **Type:** grant. **Recipient:** to a scholar aged 35 or under from a developing country or Eastern European country. **Computer Services:** database, online member directory and journals. **Telecommunication Services:** electronic mail, jzforman@msn.com. **Affiliated With:** United Nations. **Publications:** *Bibliography on Income and Wealth.* Covers 1937 to 1960. ● *The Review of Income and Wealth,* quarterly. **Price:** $240.00; 150.00. **Circulation:** 2,000. **Advertising:** accepted. Alternate Formats: online ● Membership Directory, updated continually. Online directory.

Alternate Formats: online. **Conventions/Meetings:** biennial conference, publishers, software (exhibits) - 2008 Aug., Radenji, Slovenia - **Avg. Attendance:** 300; 2010 Aug., St. Gallen, Switzerland - **Avg. Attendance:** 300.

18042 ■ Manhattan Institute for Policy Research (MIPR)
52 Vanderbilt Ave.
New York, NY 10017
Ph: (212)599-7000
Fax: (212)599-3494
E-mail: mi@manhattan-institute.org
URL: http://www.manhattan-institute.org
Contact: Lawrence J. Mone, Pres.
Founded: 1977. **Staff:** 25. **Budget:** $5,000,000. **Description:** Aims to develop and disseminate new ideas that foster greater economic choice and individual responsibility. **Formerly:** (1982) International Center for Economic Policy Studies. **Publications:** *City Journal,* quarterly. Magazine. Discusses public policy and urban affairs. **Price:** $5.95 each; $23.00/year in U.S.; $42.00/2 years; $27.00/year in Canada. ISSN: 1060-8540. **Circulation:** 10,000. **Advertising:** accepted ● Also publishes news releases, books, and brochures.

18043 ■ National Center for Economic and Security Alternatives (NCESA)
2000 P St. NW, Ste.330
Washington, DC 20036
Ph: (202)986-1373 (202)835-1150
Fax: (202)835-1152
E-mail: info@ncesa.org
URL: http://www.ncesa.org
Contact: Carl Helstrom, Chair
Founded: 1977. **Staff:** 10. **Description:** Provides research, education and consultation on innovative solutions to problems that face the American Global economy. The overall effort comprises institutional innovation, new policy directions, value-based political/ economic theory and long term visioning. **Libraries: Type:** not open to the public. **Holdings:** 3,000. **Formerly:** (1999) Exploratory Project for Economic Alternatives.

18044 ■ National Committee to Repeal the Federal Reserve Act (NCRFRA)
Address Unknown since 2007
Founded: 1969. **Members:** 300. **Membership Dues:** $25 (annual). **Staff:** 6. **Description:** "Monetary reformists-realists," economists, research associates, and tax groups. Goals are to: repeal the Federal Reserve Banking Act; restore control over money to Congress in accordance with the U.S. Constitution Article I, section 8, paragraph 5; educate people about the "social evils of the Federal Reserve Banking System;" bring about sound banking based on 100% reserves. Operates speakers' bureau; compiles statistics. **Libraries: Type:** reference. **Holdings:** 150; books, clippings, periodicals. **Subjects:** federal reserve banking, savings and loan association. **Committees:** Tax Groups. **Publications:** *Money-Questions and Answers,* annual. Book. **Price:** $15.00. **Advertising:** accepted ● *News,* quarterly ● *Repeal the Federal Reserve Act.* Book ● *Saving and Loan Unethical Bailouts.* Book. **Conventions/Meetings:** annual conference (exhibits) - always June, Chicago, IL ● seminar.

18045 ■ National Commodity and Barter Association (NCBA)
PO Box 2255
Longmont, CO 80502
Ph: (303)833-3333
Fax: (303)833-3333
E-mail: ncbarpts@boulder.earthnet.net
Contact: John Voss, Dir.
Founded: 1979. **Description:** Individuals interested in constitutional, legal, and political issues relevant to national finances, taxation, and education. "Encourages a main thrust in the abolition of the IRS, the conversion of paper money into precious metals as a precaution against national financial collapse. Feels that the Federal Reserve System is destroying the U.S. and seeks its abolition. Maintains that the U.S.

does not respect the constitutional provision stipulating that the country be governed as a republic." Provides educational materials and legal research assistance to members; organizes seminars and public lectures. **Departments:** Engineering Your Community; Legal Research & Assistance. **Publications:** NCBA Freedom. Book. Contains constitutional taxation and law, home education, administrative procedure, tax court, criminal and civil litigation. **Advertising:** accepted ● NCBA Reports, monthly. Newsletter. Discusses political action, and how to fight IRS abuse. **Advertising:** accepted ● NCBA Reports, NCBA Freedom Books-7 Volumes, monthly. Newsletter. **Price:** included in membership dues; $70.00/year or update services $495/$180. **Advertising:** accepted. **Conventions/Meetings:** annual meeting.

Public Information

18046 ■ DataCenter
1904 Franklin St., Ste.900
Oakland, CA 94612-2923
Ph: (510)835-4692
Free: (800)735-3741
Fax: (510)835-3017
E-mail: datacenter@datacenter.org
URL: http://www.datacenter.org
Contact: Ms. Celia Davis, Researcher

Founded: 1977. **Staff:** 12. **Budget:** $1,000,000. **Languages:** English, Spanish. **Description:** Provides the social justice community with strategic information. Develops original sources and adds value to existing information sources by conducting targeted research and analysis, publishing, accessing progressive publications, and training community-based organizations in the use of information technology. **Telecommunication Services:** electronic mail, celia@datacenter.org.

18047 ■ Freedom of Information Center (FOI)
Univ. of Missouri-Columbia
133 Neff Annex
Columbia, MO 65211-0012
Ph: (573)882-4856
Fax: (573)884-6204
E-mail: edwardsm@missouri.edu
URL: http://foi.missouri.edu
Contact: Kathleen M. Edwards, Mgr.

Founded: 1958. **Staff:** 3. **Description:** Represents advocacy and research center specializing in public education on open governmental information and its role in fostering democracy. **Libraries: Type:** reference. **Holdings:** 200. **Subjects:** First Amendment, freedom of information, privacy. **Telecommunication Services:** electronic mail, foi@missouri.edu. **Publications:** FOI Advocate. Newsletter. **Price:** free. ISSN: 1535-458X. **Circulation:** 346. Alternate Formats: online ● Brochure ● Also distributes Freedom of Information Files Index and back issues of FOI Digests and Reports, which were discontinued in 1985.

18048 ■ Freedom of Information Clearinghouse (FOIC)
Public Citizen Litigation Gp.
1600 20th St. NW
Washington, DC 20009
Ph: (202)588-7783
E-mail: foia@citizen.org
URL: http://www.citizen.org/litigation/free%5Finfo
Contact: Joan Claybrook, Pres.

Founded: 1972. **Description:** A program of the Center for the Study of Responsive Law. Provides legal and technical assistance to public interest groups, citizens, and the press in the effective use of laws granting a right of access to government-held information; also litigates cases under the federal Freedom of Information Act and other access laws in an attempt to reduce illegal secrecy and to secure judicial interpretations in areas where these acts are unclear. Testifies before the U.S. Congress and answers individual requests about how to get information from government agencies. **Publications:** The Freedom of Information Act: A User's Guide. Bro-

chure. **Price:** free ● Litigation Under the Federal Open Government Laws. Book.

18049 ■ Information Council of the Americas (INCA)
Address Unknown since 2007

Founded: 1960. **Members:** 150,000. **Staff:** 18. **Description:** "To manifest truth through the media of communications." Maintains library of 10,000 volumes on communism, fascism, capitalism, and socialism. **Awards: Type:** recognition. **Recipient:** for "patriotic service to freedom". **Publications:** Information Service, bimonthly ● Victory, monthly. **Conventions/Meetings:** annual meeting - always June.

18050 ■ National Anxiety Center (NAC)
28 W 3rd St., Ste.1321
South Orange, NJ 07079
Ph: (973)763-6392
E-mail: acaruba@aol.com
URL: http://www.anxietycenter.com
Contact: Alan Caruba, Founder

Founded: 1990. **Staff:** 1. **For-Profit. Description:** Clearinghouse for information about media-driven scare campaigns. Works to debunk and correct information and dis-information, disseminated to create fear for the purpose of influencing public opinion and policy. Primarily concerned with environmental issues, but also addresses those involving food, energy, immigration, education, property rights, and the Islamic Jihad. **Libraries: Type:** reference. **Subjects:** environmental, health issues, immigration, energy, the Islamic revolution, education, politics. **Publications:** Right Answers, Merril Press, 2006. Book. **Price:** $15.00 ● Warning Signs, weekly. Audiotapes. A syndicated column. ● Warning Signs, Merril Press, 2003. Book. **Price:** $15.00.

Public Policy

18051 ■ Academy for State and Local Government (ASLG)
444 N Capitol St. NW, Ste.345
Washington, DC 20001
Ph: (202)434-4850
Fax: (202)434-4851
Contact: Dawn Hatzer, Coor.

Founded: 1971. **Staff:** 4. **Budget:** $1,000,000. **Description:** Nonprofit public policy center operated by the Council of State Governments, International City/County Management Association, National Association of Counties, National Conference of State Legislatures, National Governors' Association, National League of Cities, and The U.S. Conference of Mayors. Operates State and Local Legal Center. **Formerly:** (1982) Academy for Contemporary Problems. **Publications:** National Associations of State and Local Government Directory, annual ● Papers ● Reports.

18052 ■ American Assembly (AA)
475 Riverside Dr., Ste.456
New York, NY 10115-0456
Ph: (212)870-3500
Fax: (212)870-3555
E-mail: amassembly@columbia.edu
URL: http://www.americanassembly.org
Contact: David H. Mortimer, COO

Founded: 1950. **Staff:** 7. **Description:** Educational institution affiliated with Columbia University in New York City. Holds nonpartisan assemblies of American and international leaders to discuss issues of vital public interest and consider alternatives for national policy. Cosponsors regional, state, municipal, and international assemblies with universities and other educational institutions. Makes available to the public conclusions and recommendations of the assembly. Recent topics include: Public Engagement in U.S. Foreign Policy; Cities and the Nation; After the Soviet Union; The Arts and Government; Preserving the Global Environment; Tort Law and the Public Interest; U.S. Intervention Policy; World Migration and U.S. Policy, U.S. Foreign Policy and the U.N. System; China/U.S. Relations in the Twenty-First Century;

Africa and U.S. National Interest; Community Capitalism; and The Arts and the Public Purpose. **Awards:** Service to Democracy Award. **Frequency:** annual. **Type:** recognition. **Recipient:** for distinguished public service and private sector figures. **Publications:** Beyond the Beltway: Engaging the Public in U.S. Foreign Policy. Book ● Living with China: U.S.-China Relations in the Twenty-First Century. Book ● Threatened Peoples, Threatened Borders: World Migration & U.S. Policy. Books ● U.S. Foreign Policy & the United Nations System. Book ● The United States, Japan & Asia: Challenges for U.S. Policy. Book ● Annual Report, annual. **Price:** free. Alternate Formats: online ● Reports ● Also publishes a publications list. **Conventions/Meetings:** semiannual conference.

18053 ■ American Association of Women (AAW)
337 Washington Blvd., Ste.1
Marina del Rey, CA 90292
Ph: (310)822-4449
Free: (800)867-7777
Fax: (310)822-4577
E-mail: leslie@americanassociationofwomen.org
URL: http://www.americanassociationofwomen.org
Contact: Leslie C. Dutton, Pres.

Founded: 1984. **Staff:** 10. **Description:** Encourages women and the general public to participate in the debate on public policy in order to become involved in community affairs. Provides production and distribution of educational and public affairs television programming covering local, state, and national public policy issues, featuring community representatives, civil servants, representatives from government agencies, social services, industrial experts, elected and appointed officials and newsmakers. "Full Disclosure" program is seen on 37 cable television systems and one satellite system (tele-tv) in Southern California, since March 1992. **Libraries: Type:** open to the public. **Holdings:** 362; video recordings. **Subjects:** government process: criminal justice, special prosecutor process, law enforcement policies, immigration policy, bilingual policy, judicial process, election process and irregularities, health care issues, educational issues, voter fraud and elections, war against terrorism, police chief selection process. **Computer Services:** Online services, transcripts, video, audiotape orders. **Telecommunication Services:** electronic mail, info@americanassociationofwomen.org. **Funds:** Citizen's Protection. **Subgroups:** Citizen's Protection Alliance; Full Disclosure Network. **Formerly:** (1986) American Association of Women Voters. **Publications:** Full Disclosure Network The News Behind the News, weekly/bimonthly transcripts. Videos. Features public affairs cable TV programs (30 minutes). **Price:** $25.00 each ● Transcripts of Full Disclosure Network Program. Brochures. Contains transcripts of public affairs television program. **Price:** $25.00. Alternate Formats: online. **Conventions/Meetings:** periodic conference.

18054 ■ American Enterprise Institute for Public Policy Research (AEI)
1150 17th St. NW
Washington, DC 20036
Ph: (202)862-5800
Fax: (202)862-7177
E-mail: cdemuth@aei.org
URL: http://www.aei.org
Contact: Christopher C. DeMuth, Pres.

Founded: 1943. **Staff:** 125. **Budget:** $12,000,000. **Description:** Private research group which seeks to preserve and improve: open and competitive enterprise; limited and public-oriented government; defense and foreign policies; cultural and political values. Conducts research on domestic and international economic policy; foreign and defense policy; social and political studies. Conducts educational programs. **Libraries: Type:** reference. **Holdings:** archival material, audiovisuals, books, clippings, monographs, periodicals. **Subjects:** economics, political science, public policy. **Awards:** Francis Boyer Award. **Frequency:** annual. **Type:** recognition. **Computer Services:** database, AEI research, 1989-present. **Absorbed:** (1987) Regulation Foundation.

Formerly: American Enterprise Association. **Publications:** *The American Enterprise*, 10/year. Magazine. Covers international and domestic economics; foreign policy and cultural issues; public opinion. **Price:** $38.00/year; $65.00/2 years. ISSN: 1047-3572. **Circulation:** 15,000. **Advertising:** accepted ● Books ● Newsletter, monthly. Contains latest news, events and publications from the Institute. Alternate Formats: online. **Conventions/Meetings:** annual meeting, held in conjunction with AEI World Forum - always June ● monthly seminar.

18055 ■ American Freedom Center (AFC)
2002-A Guadalupe St., Ste.284
Austin, TX 78705
Ph: (512)453-7989
Fax: (512)453-7990
E-mail: amfreedomctr@netscape.net
Contact: Marc Levin JD, Pres.

Description: Dedicated to public education about the economic freedom and individual freedom in America.

18056 ■ American Legislative Exchange Council (ALEC)
1129 20th St. NW, Ste.500
Washington, DC 20036
Ph: (202)466-3800
Fax: (202)466-3801
E-mail: info@alec.org
URL: http://www.alec.org
Contact: Lori Roman, Exec. Dir.

Founded: 1973. **Members:** 3,600. **Membership Dues:** regular, $5,000 (annual) ● Washington Club, $10,000 (annual) ● Madison Club, $25,000 (annual) ● Jefferson Club, $50,000 (annual). **Staff:** 30. **Budget:** $6,000,000. **State Groups:** 50. **Description:** State legislators; business organizations and foundations. Supports the preservation of "individual liberties, productive free enterprise, private property rights and limited representative government". Brings elected representatives together with experts in fields of national interest to share thoughts and legislative proposals in all areas of public policy, with emphasis on sound, imaginative ideas for promoting fiscal responsibility, lowering taxes, encouraging economic growth, safeguarding individual liberties, and fostering federalism. Provides factual analyses, research information, and model legislation on a wide range of issues concerning local, state, and national government. Maintains computer-based research department; monitors legislation; compiles statistics. Maintains Legislator Task Forces on: Civil Justice; Criminal Justice; Education; Environment, Energy and Natural Resources and Agriculture; Tax and Fiscal Policy; Commerce and Economic Development; Health and Human Services; Trade and Transportation; Telecommunications and Information Technology. **Awards:** Legislator of the Year. **Frequency:** annual. **Type:** recognition. **Recipient:** for an outstanding state legislator. **Task Forces:** Commerce, Insurance and Economic Development; Criminal Justice; Federalism; Health and Human Services; Natural Resources; Tax and Fiscal Policy; Telecommunications and Information Technology; Trade and Transportation. **Publications:** *Inside ALEC*, monthly. Newsletter. Contains news on ALEC activities and events. **Circulation:** 4,200. **Advertising:** accepted ● *Issue Analysis*, periodic ● *Leadership Briefing*, periodic. Newsletter. Contains information on activities and projects for the ALEC public and private leadership. ● *State Factor*, periodic. Issue brief. ● Also publishes brochures, monographs, and books. **Conventions/Meetings:** annual meeting (exhibits) - August or July ● annual States & Nations Policy Summit - meeting - December.

18057 ■ Association for Public Policy Analysis and Management (APPAM)
PO Box 18766
Washington, DC 20036-8766
Ph: (202)496-0130
Fax: (202)496-0134

E-mail: appam@appam.org
URL: http://www.appam.org
Contact: Erik Devereux, Exec. Dir.

Founded: 1979. **Members:** 1,900. **Membership Dues:** student, $35 (annual) ● individual (based on income), $60-$100 (annual) ● institutional, $1,500 (annual). **Staff:** 2. **Budget:** $550,000. **Multinational. Description:** Represents public policy analysts, academics, students, and government officials. Improves public policy and management by fostering excellence in research and analysis. **Awards:** PhD Dissertation Award. **Frequency:** annual. **Type:** monetary. **Recipient:** for best PhD dissertation at an APPAM member graduate school. **Computer Services:** Mailing lists. **Publications:** *Journal of Policy Analysis and Management*, quarterly. Includes research in public policy and management; convention and case notes; book reviews. **Price:** included in membership dues. ISSN: 0276-8739. **Circulation:** 3,000. **Advertising:** accepted. Alternate Formats: online. **Conventions/Meetings:** annual Research Conference, book exhibits, publishers, policy web sites (exhibits).

18058 ■ Brookings Institution (BI)
1775 Massachusetts Ave. NW
Washington, DC 20036-2188
Ph: (202)797-6000
Fax: (202)797-6004
E-mail: communications@brookings.edu
URL: http://www.brookings.edu
Contact: Strobe Talbott, Pres.

Founded: 1916. **Staff:** 250. **Budget:** $31,000,000. **Description:** Independent organization devoted to nonpartisan, nonprofit research, education, and publication in the fields of economics, government, and foreign policy. Conducts numerous conferences, forums, and seminars. **Libraries: Type:** reference. **Holdings:** 75,000; periodicals. **Divisions:** Brookings Institutions Press; Brown Center on Education Policy; Center for Northeast Asian Policy Studies; Center for Public Policy Education; Center for Public Service; Center for the United States and France; Center on Urban and Metropolitan Policy; Economic Studies; External Affairs; Foreign Policy Studies; Governmental Studies; Office of Communications; Public Affairs. **Formed by Merger of:** (1927) Institute of Economics, Institute for Government Research; (1927) Robert Brookings Graduate School of Economics and Government. **Publications:** *Brookings Papers on Economic Activity*, semiannual. Journal. Contains articles, reports, and discussion highlights of conferences held by the Brookings Panel on Economic Activity. **Price:** $48.00 /year for individuals (4th class); $60.00 /year for individuals (1st class); $65.00 /year for institutions (4th class); $77.00 /year for institutions (1st class). ISSN: 0007-2303. **Circulation:** 5,500 ● *Brookings Papers on Economic Policy*, annual. Journal. Features the latest thinking from nationally recognized experts on policy issues affecting grades K-12. **Price:** $30.00 /year for individuals (4th class); $36.00 /year for individuals (1st class); $46.00 /year for institutions (4th class); $52.00 /year for institutions (1st class) ● *Brookings Review*, quarterly. Magazine. Includes topics on domestic and foreign policy. **Price:** $17.95/year. ISSN: 0745-1253. **Circulation:** 18,000. **Advertising:** accepted ● *Brookings Trade Forum*, annual. Journal. Features the most authoritative and in-depth analysis available on issues in international trade. **Price:** $30.00 /year for individuals (4th class); $36.00 /year for individuals (1st class); $30.00 /year for institutions (4th class); $36.00 /year for institutions (1st class) ● *Brookings-Wharton Papers on Financial Services*, annual. Journal. Features public policy issues confronting the insurance industry. **Price:** $48.00 /year for individuals (4th class); $54.00 /year for individuals (1st class); $48.00 /year for institutions (4th class); $54.00 /year for institutions (1st class) ● *Brookings-Wharton Papers on Urban Affairs*, annual. Journal. Features forum for cutting-edge, accessible research on urban policy. **Price:** $30.00 /year for individuals (4th class); $36.00 /year for individuals (1st class); $30.00 /year for institutions (4th class); $36.00 /year for institutions (1st class) ● *Economia*, semiannual. Journal. Features forum for influential economists and policymakers to share high-quality

research applied to policy issues within and among those countries. **Price:** $30.00 /year for individuals (4th class); $36.00 /year for individuals (1st class); $46.00 /year for institutions (4th class); $52.00 /year for institutions (1st class) ● *Media Guide/Directory of Scholars*, annual ● Annual Report, annual ● Also publishes research findings in books, staff papers, and reprints. **Conventions/Meetings:** periodic conference.

18059 ■ Cato Institute
1000 Massachusetts Ave. NW
Washington, DC 20001-5401
Ph: (202)842-0200
Fax: (202)842-3490
E-mail: cato@cato.org
URL: http://www.cato.org
Contact: Edward H. Crane III, Pres.

Founded: 1977. **Membership Dues:** basic, $100-$499 (annual) ● sustaining, $500-$999 (annual) ● patron, $1,000-$4,999 (annual) ● benefactor, $5,000-$24,999 (annual) ● Cato Club 200, $25,000 (annual). **Staff:** 100. **Budget:** $13,000,000. **Description:** Serves as public policy research foundation dedicated to increasing policy debate to allow consideration of more options the institute believes are consistent with traditional American principles of limited government, individual liberty, and peace. Conducts research; operates speakers' bureau. Holds policy forums. **Libraries: Type:** reference. **Holdings:** 3,000; audiovisuals, books, clippings, monographs, periodicals. **Subjects:** public policy. **Computer Services:** Mailing lists. **Telecommunication Services:** information service, to order publications, (800)767-1241. **Publications:** *Briefing Papers*, periodic. Report ● *Cato Journal: An Interdisciplinary Journal on Public Policy Analysis*, 3/year. Contains analyses of economic issues from a free market perspective. **Price:** $24.00 /year for individuals; $50.00 /year for institutions. ISSN: 0273-3072. **Circulation:** 3,000. **Advertising:** accepted ● *Cato Policy Report*, bimonthly. Newsletter. Provides analysis and reviews of U.S. policy. ISSN: 0743-605X. **Circulation:** 20,000. Alternate Formats: online ● *Ed Crane's Memo*, bimonthly. Contains information on Cato activities. **Price:** included in membership dues ● *Foreign Policy Briefings*, periodic. Report ● *Policy Analysis Series*, periodic. Report. Covers foreign and domestic policy issues. ● *Regulation*, quarterly. Magazine. Provides commentary from business people, government representatives and scholars on regulatory issues. **Price:** $20.00 /year for individuals; $40.00 /year for institutions. ISSN: 0147-0590. **Circulation:** 5,000. **Advertising:** accepted ● Books, 10/year. Covers various public policy issues. ● Monographs ● Reprints. **Conventions/Meetings:** periodic conference ● annual Constitution Day - conference ● symposium.

18060 ■ Center for Advancement of Public Policy (CAPP)
323 Morning Sun Trail
Corrales, NM 87048
E-mail: capp@capponline.org
URL: http://www.capponline.org
Founded: 1991. **Description:** Fosters equitable, democratic, and humane management in government, corporations and other organizations. Seeks the elimination of prejudice, sexism, and discrimination in the workplace and in society. Promotes democratic government through research, investigation and education.

18061 ■ Center for Governmental Research (CGR)
1 S Washington St., Ste.400
Rochester, NY 14614-1125
Ph: (585)325-6360
Fax: (585)325-2612
E-mail: information@cgr.org
URL: http://www.cgr.org
Contact: Mr. Kent Gardner PhD, Pres./CEO

Founded: 1915. **Members:** 70. **Staff:** 17. **Budget:** $1,500,000. **Description:** A member group of the Governmental Research Association. Represents business leaders and professionals. Analyzes public policy issues; provides information on public concerns to individuals, governments, and businesses. Promotes effective decision-making in the public sector. Compiles statistics. **Libraries: Type:** reference; by appointment only. **Holdings:** 500; archival material, articles, clippings, photographs, reports. **Subjects:** public policy, strategic planning, government management services, census, health human services, education, records management, workforce diversity, economic impact. **Additional Websites:** http://www. newyorkmatters.org. **Affiliated With:** Governmental Research Association. **Formerly:** (1962) Rochester Bureau of Municipal Research. **Publications:** *CGR Close-Up*, quarterly. Newsletter. Disseminates economic and human services information. Includes statistics. **Price:** included in membership dues. **Circulation:** 2,000 ● *Economic Review Letter*, quarterly. Provides economic updates and forecasts. ● *Reports* ● Annual Report, annual. Alternate Formats: online. **Conventions/Meetings:** monthly board meeting.

18062 ■ Center for National Policy (CNP)
1 Massachusetts Ave. NW, Ste.333
Washington, DC 20001
Ph: (202)682-1800
Fax: (202)682-1818
E-mail: info@cnponline.org
URL: http://www.cnponline.org
Contact: Scott Bates, VP/Senior Fellow
Founded: 1981. **Membership Dues:** associate, $50 ● regular, $100 ● newsmaker, $250 ● contributor, $500 ● donor, $1,000. **Staff:** 10. **Budget:** $1,500,000. **Description:** Promotes open discussion of the fundamentals of American public policy, including understanding of the substance of issues, determination of individual and common interests, and assessment of the attitudes, values and opinions of the public. **Awards:** Edmund S. Muskie Distinguished Public Service Award. **Frequency:** annual. **Type:** recognition. **Telecommunication Services:** electronic mail, msteinbruner@cnponline.org. **Programs:** Enhancing National Security; No Child Left Behind; Responsible Budget Policy; Supporting the Economy. **Projects:** Cambodia; Domestic Policy; Post-war U.S. Economy; Vietnam. **Supersedes:** National Democratic Forum. **Publications:** *Adolescence & Poverty.* Book ● *America Tomorrow: The Choices We Face.* Book ● *Center for National Policy—Task Force Reports*, periodic ● *Challenges for the 1990s.* Book ● *CNP Advisory Board Directory*, periodic ● *Democrats and the American Idea.* **Price:** $29.95 ● *Exploring Cambodia.* Book ● *Life in the City.* Report ● *Montana: Steady State in Transition.* Book ● *Passing the Test: The National Interest in Good Schools for All.* Report ● *Regulating for the Future: The Creative Balance.* Book ● *Reports: The Real Story of the U.S. Economy 1950-1990.* Book ● *Smart Stimulus: More Good Jobs.* Book ● *U.S. Agriculture: Myth, Reality and National Policy.* Book ● Annual Report, annual ● Newsletter, quarterly. **Price:** free. **Conventions/Meetings:** annual meeting ● monthly Newsmaker Luncheon.

18063 ■ Center for Policy Alternatives (CPA)
1875 Connecticut Ave. NW, Ste.710
Washington, DC 20009
Ph: (202)387-6030
Free: (800)935-0699
Fax: (202)387-8529
E-mail: info@cfpa.org
URL: http://www.cfpa.org
Contact: Tim McFeeley, Exec. Dir.
Founded: 1975. **Staff:** 12. **Budget:** $2,100,000. **Nonmembership. Description:** State and local government officials and community activists interested in restructuring public policies on the state and local level. Acts as national clearinghouse and forum for ideas on progressive public policy. Offers technical assistance to groups and individuals in developing model legislation. Focuses on critical issues of public policy affecting state and local governments such as: tax reform; voter registration; women's economic issues; investment of public employee pension funds; state and local economic development initiatives; housing; toxic and hazardous wastes; government reform; employment policy; and healthcare. **Awards: Frequency:** annual. **Type:** recogni-

tion. **Recipient:** for outstanding progressive policy leadership. **Programs:** Flemming Leadership Institute. **Formerly:** Conference on Alternative State and Local Policies; (1980) Conference on Alternative State and Local Public Policies; (1990) National Center for Policy Alternatives. **Publications:** *Alternatives*, 10/year. Newsletter. **Price:** $25.00/copy ● *Legislative Briefs*, periodic ● *Policy Memos*, periodic ● *Progressive Victories Report.* Describes 80 proactive and progressive measures that became law in the first half of 2004. Alternate Formats: online ● *Resources*, periodic ● Bibliographies ● Books ● Manuals ● Monographs ● Reports ● Annual Report, annual. Alternate Formats: online. **Conventions/Meetings:** periodic conference ● seminar.

18064 ■ Center for Public Dialogue (CPD)
3152 Gracefield Rd., No. 519
Silver Spring, MD 20904
Ph: (301)890-8578
E-mail: waltrybeck@aol.com
Contact: Walter Rybeck, Dir.
Founded: 1981. **For-Profit. Description:** Promotes correction of flaws in local taxation and land use systems in an effort to ease socioeconomic problems such as lack of affordable housing, sprawl, central city decay, unemployment and poverty. Offers consulting services. Conducts research and educational programs. **Publications:** *Affordable Housing: A Missing Link.* Book ● *From Poverty to Prosperity by 2000: Prospects for Reviving West Virginia's Economy.* Book ● *Land-Value Taxation Around the World, Chapter on US.* Book. Reports on current and historical efforts to apply the principle of collecting community-created land values for community benefit. ISSN: 0002-9246 ● *Look to the Land.* Book ● *Tale of Five Cities: Tax Revolt Pennsylvania Style.* Video. Highlights on how the five cities have increasing revenue while reducing property taxes for majority of homeowners. **Price:** $25.00. Alternate Formats: CD-ROM.

18065 ■ Center for Public Justice (CPJ)
PO Box 48368
Washington, DC 20002-0368
Ph: (410)571-6300
Free: (866)CPJUSTICE
Fax: (410)571-6365
E-mail: inquiries@cpjustice.org
URL: http://www.cpjustice.org
Contact: James W. Skillen, Pres.
Founded: 1977. **Members:** 1,000. **Membership Dues:** associate, $249 (annual) ● supporting, $250 (annual) ● sponsoring, $500 (annual) ● sustaining, $1,000 (annual) ● Center Circle, $2,500 (annual) ● Center Council, $5,000 (annual). **Staff:** 10. **Budget:** $750,000. **Description:** Seeks to provide perspective on public policy and political life from a Biblical standpoint. Believes that justice is revealed through creation and the work of Jesus Christ, and that Biblical revelation can guide citizens in the fulfillment of their responsibility to live justly with all people. Conducts projects on welfare policy, land and resource policy, justice in education, group rights, social pluralism, and just representation in the political system; has presented testimony before the U.S. Congress and state legislatures. Maintains Speaker's Bureau; conducts research programs. **Awards:** Leadership Award. **Frequency:** annual. **Type:** recognition. **Recipient:** for a public servant. **Programs:** Civitas. **Projects:** Saints and Citizens. **Formerly:** Association for Public Justice Education Fund. **Publications:** *Public Justice Report*, quarterly. Journal. Reports on the structure of government, political theory, and significant developments in the spheres of Christian political thought and action. **Price:** $25.00/year. ISSN: 0742-5325. **Circulation:** 1,200. **Advertising:** accepted. Alternate Formats: online ● Books ● Reports. **Conventions/Meetings:** periodic seminar.

18066 ■ Center for the Study of Social Policy (CSSP)
1575 Eye St. NW, Ste.500
Washington, DC 20005
Ph: (202)371-1565
Fax: (202)371-1472

E-mail: judy.meltzer@cssp.org
URL: http://www.cssp.org
Contact: Judith Meltzer, Deputy Dir.
Founded: 1979. **Staff:** 15. **Description:** Serves as research organization that provides analyses on the effects of contemporary policy issues on states, communities, families, and individuals for federal, state, and local decision makers, as well as employers, voluntary agencies, and informal care systems. Seeks to anticipate long-term problems. Analyzes problems using interdisciplinary research techniques. Informs the government and private sector of research findings. Includes issues of concern: poverty and income support programs; long-term care for the elderly and disabled; healthcare for the disadvantaged; children and youth services; disability policy. Seeks to identify policy directions to finance and deliver human services more effectively. **Projects:** Human Resource Management Reform; Non-Adversarial Child Welfare Reform; Policy Matters; Racial Equity in Child Welfare. **Formerly:** Center for the Study of Welfare Policy. **Publications:** *Building Community Ownership in Neighborhood Revitalization.* Report. Alternate Formats: online.

18067 ■ The Century Foundation (TCF)
41 E 70th St.
New York, NY 10021
Ph: (212)535-4441 (212)879-9197
E-mail: info@tcf.org
URL: http://www.tcf.org
Contact: Richard C. Leone, Pres.
Founded: 1919. **Staff:** 25. **Budget:** $3,600,000. **Description:** A research foundation that sponsors and supervises timely analyses of economic policy, foreign affairs, political and governance, and media issues. Endowment was provided by its founder, Edward A. Filene, a Boston merchant and civic leader. **Computer Services:** Electronic publishing ● mailing lists. **Formerly:** (2002) Twentieth Century Fund. **Publications:** Annual Report, annual. Alternate Formats: online. **Conventions/Meetings:** board meeting - 3/year.

18068 ■ Churches' Center for Theology and Public Policy (CCTPP)
c/o Wesley Theological Seminary
4500 Massachusetts Ave. NW
Washington, DC 20016
Ph: (202)885-8648
Fax: (202)885-8559
E-mail: cctpp@wesleysem.edu
URL: http://www.cctpp.org
Contact: Rev. Barbara G. Green, Exec. Dir.
Founded: 1976. **Staff:** 3. **Budget:** $200,000. **Description:** Consulting fellows are individuals from diverse vocations in government, academia, the religious community, and other nongovernmental organizations; visiting fellows are persons on leave from their regular work who pursue special research topics. Aims to: study the bearing of Christian faith on political life and thought; develop humane perspectives on policy issues, especially disarmament, healthcare, urban policy, minority rights, and world political economy; affirm the lay ministry among politicians, bureaucrats, diplomats, judges, lobbyists, and activists; assess the attitudes and behavior of the churches as they affect public life; examine critically the structures, processes, and styles of policymaking in the U.S. Evaluates policy impacts on communities, regions, and cultures. Monitors and interprets research published by other institutions. Sponsors seminars; conducts consultations. **Awards:** James K. Mathews Service Award. **Frequency:** annual. **Type:** recognition. **Programs:** Shape Your World. **Projects:** Nuclear Reduction/Disarmament Initiative. **Publications:** *Center Circles.* Newsletter. Alternate Formats: online ● *Shalom Papers*, periodic. Journal. Features center studies. ● Also publishes articles in scholarly journals.

18069 ■ CitizensLobby.com
PO Box 23037
2020 Pennsylvania Ave. NW, No. 649
Washington, DC 20026

E-mail: comments@citizenslobby.com

Contact: Scott A. Lauf, Exec. Dir.

Description: Advocates for "strong border security and immigration policies; seeks to preserve American sovereignty and traditional values; focuses on an 'America First' foreign and trade policy and the abolition of wasteful government programs like foreign aid.". **Telecommunication Services:** electronic mail, lauf@citizenslobby.com.

18070 ■ Common Sense for Drug Policy (CSDP)

1377-C Spencer Ave.

Lancaster, PA 17603

Ph: (717)299-0600

Fax: (717)393-4953

E-mail: info@csdp.org

URL: http://www.csdp.org

Contact: Kevin B. Zeese, Pres.

Founded: 1995. **Staff:** 2. **Budget:** $700,000. **Description:** Promotes open debate of national drug policies, particularly in the areas of needle exchange programs, mandatory sentencing for drug-related offenses, forfeiture, and marijuana policy. Formulates and advocates the implementation of policies designed to address the root causes of substance abuse and provide avenues for the rehabilitation of substance abusers. Sponsors litigation to challenge policies in need of reform. Current projects include: emphasizing drug policy reform as a human rights issue; development of a national network of harm reduction grantmakers; support for other organizations pursuing similar goals; production of documentaries and other educational programs; sponsorship of media and awareness events. Provides local drug policy reform groups with technical assistance in the areas of management, fundraising, and issues development. Conducts charitable programs; maintains speakers' bureau; compiles statistics. **Awards: Frequency:** periodic. **Type:** grant. **Computer Services:** Online services, publication. **Additional Websites:** http://www.drugwarfacts.org, http://www.medicalmj.org, http://www.addictinthefamily.org. **Publications:** *Drug War Facts*, periodic. Book. Includes data statistics and sources. **Circulation:** 5,000. Alternate Formats: online ● *Health Emergency*, periodic. **Circulation:** 5,000. Alternate Formats: online. **Conventions/Meetings:** periodic meeting.

18071 ■ Communitarian Network

2130 H St. NW, Ste.703

Washington, DC 20052

Ph: (202)994-6118

E-mail: comnet@gwu.edu

URL: http://www.gwu.edu/~ccps/index.html

Contact: Dr. Amitai Etzioni, Founder/Dir.

Founded: 1993. **Staff:** 10. **Budget:** $100,000. **Description:** Works to improve the moral, social, and political environment. **Computer Services:** Mailing lists. **Publications:** *The Responsive Community*, quarterly. Journal. **Price:** $27.00 for individuals; $70.00 for libraries and institutions. ISSN: 1053-0754. **Circulation:** 5,000. **Advertising:** accepted. Alternate Formats: online.

18072 ■ Congressional Economic Leadership Institute (CELI)

201 Massachusetts Ave. NE C-6

Washington, DC 20002

Ph: (202)546-5007

Fax: (202)546-7037

E-mail: joleen@celi.org

URL: http://www.celi.org

Contact: Joleen L. Worsley, Sr. VP

Founded: 1987. **Staff:** 3. **Budget:** $700,000. **Description:** Serves as a neutral bi-partisan, bicameral forum for the consideration of public policy options and the discussion of issues related to U.S. economic competitiveness among representatives of business, labor, Congress, and academia. Disseminates information on such topics as human resources, technology, trade, and capital formation; sponsors educational programs and briefing sessions for members of Congress and congressional staff members. **Conventions/Meetings:** periodic conference.

18073 ■ Coro

c/o Manatt Phelps

700 12th St. NW, Ste.1100

Washington, DC 20005-4075

E-mail: info@coro.org

URL: http://www.coro.org

Contact: Jill F. Hultin, Chair

Founded: 1942. **Members:** 5,000. **Regional Groups:** 5. **Description:** Research and public affairs educational institute supported by annual contributions from individuals, corporations, and philanthropic foundations. Aims "to train dynamic public affairs leaders, emphasizing the complex interrelationships of society's major institutions". Major program is Coro Fellows Program in Public Affairs, a nine-month graduate program for 12 selected college graduates seeking careers in the public affairs fields, offered annually in San Francisco, Los Angeles, St. Louis, New York, and Pittsburgh. A ten-week summer "mini-version" is offered in Kansas City. **Awards: Type:** recognition. **Programs:** Contract; Fellows; Summer. **Formerly:** (2003) Coro Foundation. **Publications:** *Coro Reports*, 3/year. Newsletter.

18074 ■ Council for Social and Economic Studies (CSES)

PO Box 34070

Washington, DC 20043

Ph: (202)371-2700

Fax: (202)371-1523

E-mail: socecon@aol.com

URL: http://www.jspes.org

Contact: Prof. Roger Pearson PhD, Exec. Off./Gen. Ed.

Founded: 1975. **Description:** Publishes academic journals and papers relating to domestic and international economic, social, and political issues. Conducts educational programs. **Libraries: Type:** reference. **Holdings:** 11,000; books, monographs. **Subjects:** sociology, economics, anthropology, psychology. **Formerly:** (1980) Council on American Affairs. **Publications:** *Journal of Social, Political, and Economic Studies*, quarterly. **Price:** $45.00 /year for individuals; $106.00 /year for libraries and institutions. ISSN: 0278-839X. **Circulation:** 1,060. **Advertising:** accepted. Alternate Formats: online. Also Cited As: *Journal of Social and Political Studies* ● *JSPES Monograph Series*. Monographs ● *The Mankind Quarterly*. Journal ● Books ● Papers. **Conventions/Meetings:** periodic seminar.

18075 ■ Economic Policy Institute (EPI)

1333 H St. NW, Ste.300

East Tower

Washington, DC 20005-4707

Ph: (202)775-8810

Fax: (202)775-0819

E-mail: epi@epi.org

URL: http://www.epinet.org

Contact: Lawrence Mishel, Pres.

Founded: 1986. **Membership Dues:** student, $35 (annual) ● friend, $50-$99 (annual) ● partner, $125-$249 (annual) ● sustaining, $250-$499 (annual) ● sponsor, $500-$999 (annual) ● President's Council, $1,000 (annual). **Staff:** 35. **Description:** Conducts research and provides a forum for the exchange of information on economic policy issues. Promotes educational programs to encourage discussion of economic policy and economic issues, particularly the economics of poverty, unemployment, inflation, American industry, international competitiveness, and problems of economic adjustment as they affect the community and the individual. Sponsors seminars for economists and citizens. **Libraries: Type:** by appointment only. **Holdings:** 1,500; books, periodicals. **Subjects:** economics, government policy, trade, taxes. **Awards: Type:** recognition. **Computer Services:** Online services. **Telecommunication Services:** electronic mail, researchdept@epi.org. **Councils:** Research. **Publications:** *Briefing Papers*, periodic ● *EPI Journal*, 3/year. **Price:** free for members. Alternate Formats: online ● *EPI News*, monthly. Newsletter. **Price:** free for members. Alternate Formats: online ● *State of Working America*, biennial. Book. **Price:** $24.95 paperback, plus shipping and handling;

$59.95 cloth, plus shipping and handling. **Conventions/Meetings:** periodic conference.

18076 ■ Eisenhower World Affairs Institute

915 15th St. NW, 8th Fl.

Washington, DC 20005

Ph: (202)628-4444

Fax: (202)628-4445

E-mail: interns@eisenhowerinstitute.org

URL: http://www.eisenhowerinstitute.org

Contact: Ms. Susan Eisenhower, Sr. Fellow/Emeritus Chair

Founded: 1983. **Description:** Admirers and associates of Dwight D. Eisenhower (1890-1969), 34th president of the U.S. Works on contemporary national and international issues that were of primary concern to Eisenhower. Seeks to strengthen public participation in issues related to democratic values and national security. Operates the Eisenhower/Jennings Randolph International Public Works Fellowship. Conducts public dialogue programs; holds luncheon seminars. **Awards:** APWA Jennings Randolph Fellowship. **Type:** fellowship. **Recipient:** to professionals in the public works field for travel and field study overseas ● **Type:** fellowship. **Recipient:** for graduates at one of 13 participating universities ● **Type:** grant. **Recipient:** to scholars using the Eisenhower Library in Abilene, KS ● Leadership Award: Pat Roberts Eisenhower Leadership Award. **Type:** recognition. **Programs:** College Support; Eisenhower Scholarship; Leadership Studies; Public Affairs Dialogues. **Formed by Merger of:** Eisenhower Institute; Gettysburg College. **Publications:** *Dateline*, 3/year. Newsletter. **Circulation:** 2,000. **Conventions/Meetings:** periodic conference ● annual meeting.

18077 ■ Emergency Committee to Defend Constitutional Welfare Rights, U.S.A. (ECDCWRUSA)

c/o Mr. Martin J. Sawma, Exec. Dir./Intl. Rep.

3501 Westwood Dr., Rm. 4

Niagara Falls, NY 14305-3416

Ph: (716)297-7273

Fax: (916)314-8187

E-mail: welfarerights@geocities.com

URL: http://www.welfarerights.org

Contact: Mr. Martin J. Sawma, Exec. Dir./Intl. Rep.

Founded: 1995. **Staff:** 3. **Description:** Political-judicial action committee composed of all persons subscribing to its Mission Statement advocating respect for the obligatory international labor and human rights law in welfare-workforce administration. Opposes legislation, programs and practices depriving the involuntarily unemployed and their families of relief adequate to a dignified life; and opposes any workfare imposition legally constituting involuntary servitude or forced or compulsory labor. Promotes bringing judicial issue over any welfare/workforce violation in all of the several states under the Supremacy Clause to enforce the unimpaired obligatory international law securing right to decent relief and proscribing well-defined forms of forced labor. Testifies before legislative and public hearings, and maintains a speaker's bureau. Aims to post at its website a comprehensive list of attorneys throughout the nation who are committed to pro bono defense of welfare-workfare rights on the federal constitutional and international labor and human rights law. **Libraries: Type:** reference; not open to the public. **Holdings:** archival material, articles, monographs. **Subjects:** law: constitutional, international agreements, statutory, regulatory and case. **Telecommunication Services:** electronic mail, mjsawma@welfarerights.org.

18078 ■ Ethics and Public Policy Center (EPPC)

1015 15th St. NW, Ste.900

Washington, DC 20005

Ph: (202)682-1200

Fax: (202)408-0632

E-mail: ethics@eppc.org

URL: http://www.eppc.org

Contact: M. Edward Whelan III, Pres.

Founded: 1976. **Staff:** 18. **Budget:** $1,500,000. **Description:** Conducts a program of research, writing, publication, and conferences "to encourage reflective debate on major domestic and foreign policy problems." Focuses on the role of organized religion in the public policy arena. Addresses current issues in light of enduring concepts and values. Attempts to clarify the relationship "between the specific and the general, and between political necessity and moral principle." Conducts educational seminars. **Libraries: Type:** reference. **Programs:** The Constitution, the Courts, and the Culture; Economics and Ethics; Evangelicals in Civic Life. **Projects:** Biotechnology and American Democracy; Catholic Studies; Foreign Policy; Law and Society; Religion and Society. **Absorbed:** (1989) James Madison Foundation. **Publications:** *The American Character*, 2-4/year. Newsletter. Includes comments on domestic issues and how they affect the nation's political, social, and moral life. **Price:** free to contributors ● *American Purpose*, 2-4/year. Newsletter. Includes comments on issues relating to peace, freedom, and security. **Price:** free to contributors ● *EPPC Briefly*, biweekly. Newsletter. Alternate Formats: online ● *Ethics and Public Policy Center—Newsletter*, quarterly. Reports on programs and publications relating to the bond between the Judeo-Christian moral tradition and the public debate over domestic issues etc. **Price:** free ● Also publishes books and anthologies. **Conventions/Meetings:** conference and seminar - 10/year.

18079 ■ Federation of American Scientists (FAS)

1717 K St. NW, Ste.209
Washington, DC 20036
Ph: (202)546-3300
Fax: (202)675-1010
E-mail: fas@fas.org
URL: http://www.fas.org
Contact: Henry C. Kelly, Pres.
Founded: 1945. **Members:** 2,500. **Membership Dues:** regular, $50 (annual) ● premier, $250 ● life, $1,000 ● student/retired, $25. **Staff:** 18. **Budget:** $3,000,000. **Description:** Natural and social scientists, engineers, and individuals concerned with problems of science and society. Aims to "act on public issues where the opinions of scientists are relevant, those which affect science or in which the experience or perspective of scientists is a needed guide." Functions through testimony to Congress and government agencies, public statements, and articles. Maintains the Federation of American Scientists Fund, a research and education arm of the association. **Awards:** Hans Bethe Science in Public Service Award. **Frequency:** annual. **Type:** recognition. **Formerly:** (1945) Federation of Atomic Scientists. **Publications:** *FAS Public Interest Report*, bimonthly. Newsletter. Reports on Federation's lobbying activities, proposals, and recommendations. Includes special topic issues. **Price:** $50.00 /year for individuals; $50.00 /year for institutions. **Circulation:** 5,000.

18080 ■ Foundation for National Progress (FNP)

222 Sutter St., Ste.600
San Francisco, CA 94108
Ph: (415)321-1700
Free: (877)GIV-MOJO
Fax: (415)321-1701
E-mail: reynolds@motherjones.com
URL: http://www.motherjones.com/about/admin/index.html
Contact: Jay Harris, Pres.
Founded: 1975. **Members:** 220,000. **Membership Dues:** regular, $24 (annual). **Staff:** 42. **Budget:** $9,000,000. **Description:** Advocates for social justice implemented through first rate investigative reporting. Supports hands-on training for emerging journalists, Mother Jones Internship in Investigative Reporting. **Publications:** *Mother Jones*, bimonthly. Magazine. Political magazine specializing in investigative reporting. **Price:** $10.00/year; $5.00/copy. ISSN: 0362-8841. **Circulation:** 240,000. **Advertising:** accepted. Alternate Formats: online ● *MotherJones.com*, daily. Magazine. Alternate Formats: online.

18081 ■ Foundation for Public Affairs (FPA)

2033 K St. NW, Ste.700
Washington, DC 20006

Ph: (202)872-1790
Fax: (202)835-8343
E-mail: bhawkinson@pac.org
URL: http://www.pac.org/page/FPAOverview.shtml
Contact: Brian P. Hawkinson, Exec. Dir.
Founded: 1964. **Staff:** 3. **Budget:** $340,000. **Description:** Conducts and supports research on emerging public policy issues and trends that affect the practice of public affairs and the ability of organizations to thrive in a dynamic business environment. **Libraries: Type:** reference. **Subjects:** business and public policy, corporate public affairs, public interest groups. **Boards:** Trustees. **Affiliated With:** Public Affairs Council. **Formerly:** (1974) Effective Citizens Organization Foundation. **Publications:** *Corporate Public Affairs Compensation Survey*, biennial. Reports on seven corporate public affairs professional staff positions. **Price:** $100.00 for participants; $250.00 for nonparticipants ● *Corporate Washington Office Compensation Survey*, biennial. Reports on seven Washington-based corporate staff positions, both professional and support. **Price:** $100.00 for participants; $250.00 for nonparticipants ● *Creating a Digital Democracy: The Impact of the Internet on Public Policy-Making*. Report ● *Cyber Activism: Advocacy Groups and the Internet*, periodic. Report ● *Public Affairs Strategies in the Internet Age*, periodic. Report ● *Survey on the State of Corporate Public Affairs*, triennial.

18082 ■ Global Options (GO)

PO Box 40601
San Francisco, CA 94140
Ph: (415)550-1703
Fax: (510)620-0668
E-mail: socialjust@aol.com
URL: http://www.socialjusticejournal.org
Contact: Gregory Shank, Pres.
Founded: 1977. **Membership Dues:** supporting associate, $250 (annual). **Description:** Educates the public on matters such as Central America, East-West relations, the Right Wing, racism, criminology, and international relations. Sponsors seminars; participates in conferences. **Convention/Meeting:** none. **Computer Services:** Mailing lists, buyer's list, 2000 games. **Formerly:** (1986) Institute for the Study of Labor and Economic Crisis. **Publications:** *Social Justice*, quarterly. Journal. Covers criminology, international relations, and world conflict. **Price:** $40.00 /year for individuals; $85.00 /year for institutions. ISSN: 0094-7571. **Circulation:** 2,000. **Advertising:** accepted. Alternate Formats: microform ● Books ● Papers.

18083 ■ Governmental Research Association (GRA)

PO Box 292300
Birmingham, AL 35229
Ph: (205)726-2482
Fax: (205)726-2900
E-mail: rancoble@nccppr.org
URL: http://www.graonline.org
Contact: Ran Coble, Pres.
Founded: 1914. **Members:** 150. **Membership Dues:** individual, $90 (annual) ● organization, $225 (annual). **Description:** Individuals professionally engaged in governmental research. Furthers research that will improve government in the public interest. Encourages development and use of effective methods of administration in government and standards for judging the results. **Awards: Frequency:** annual. **Type:** recognition. **Recipient:** for distinguished research, effective citizen education, and special achievement. **Publications:** *GRA Reporter*, quarterly. Newsletter. Includes bibliography of research publications and index to organizations. **Price:** included in membership dues; $50.00 /year for nonmembers ● *Organizing a Citizen Governmental Research Agency* ● *Professional Directory of Who's Who in Governmental Research*, annual. Includes professionals in public and private agencies that conduct governmental research at the local, state, and federal levels. **Price:** included in membership dues; $50.00 for nonmembers. Also Cited As: *GRA Directory* ● *Your Stake in Governmental Research*. **Conventions/Meetings:** annual conference.

18084 ■ Harry Singer Foundation (HSF)

PO Box 223159
Carmel, CA 93923
Ph: (831)625-4223
Fax: (831)624-7994
E-mail: director@singerfoundation.org
URL: http://www.singerfoundation.org
Contact: Margaret Bohannon-Kaplan, Dir./Co-Founder
Founded: 1987. **Nonmembership. Multinational. Description:** Aims to promote responsibility and community involvement in public policy. Encourages community service and offers recognition and support for productive activities. Provides programs that assists job and career planning; offers investment and saving advice; develops consumer and insurance awareness, and entrepreneurial abilities and skills. **Libraries: Type:** lending; reference; open to the public. **Holdings:** 3,000; articles, audio recordings, books, clippings, periodicals, video recordings. **Subjects:** public policy, responsibility, teens and local communities. **Computer Services:** database, information exchange, links, community services ● online services, essay contests and other interactive projects. **Telecommunication Services:** electronic mail, staff@singerfoundation.org. **Committees:** Another Way; Local Communities. **Publications:** *Alternatives for Local Government*, annual. Book ● *Another Way* ● *Doesn't Anyone Care About the Children?*. Book ● *Excerpts from Essay Contests*, annual. Book. **Price:** $8.00 ● *Kids R Us* ● *Responsibility: Who Has It and Who Doesn't and What That Means to the Nation*. Book ● *White Hats: People Who Are Trying to Make a Difference*. Book.

18085 ■ Hudson Institute (HI)

1015 15th St. NW, 6th Fl.
Washington, DC 20005
Ph: (202)974-2400
Fax: (202)974-2410
E-mail: info@hudson.org
URL: http://www.hudson.org
Contact: Herbert I. London, Pres.
Founded: 1961. **Members:** 300. **Membership Dues:** friend, $50 (annual). **Staff:** 75. **Budget:** $7,000,000. **Languages:** English, French, German, Russian. **Description:** Members of this research center are elected from academic, governmental, and business/industrial sectors. Studies public policy issues in areas of national security, international and domestic economics, education and employment, energy and technology, agriculture and environment, and future studies. Studies are funded through contract or grant from government agencies, private businesses, foundations, associations, and individuals. Sometimes referred to as a "think tank", the institute focuses on "providing policymakers with a broad, workable, conceptual framework within which intelligent and successful policy decisions can be developed"; seeks to determine what issues will have the greatest long-term impact and to identify issues that may become urgent though they are not yet recognized as such. Conducts briefings on policy issues to corporate and other audiences. Distributes research reports to depository libraries. **Libraries: Type:** reference. **Holdings:** 15,300; periodicals, reports. **Subjects:** government and military affairs, current social problems, corporate environment. **Telecommunication Services:** electronic mail, rsvp@hudsondc.org. **Publications:** *Visions*, quarterly. Newsletter ● Annual Report, annual. Alternate Formats: online ● Reports. Alternate Formats: online ● Newsletter, quarterly. Alternate Formats: online ● Also publishes research reports, books, and publication list. **Conventions/Meetings:** periodic meeting.

18086 ■ The Independent Institute (TII)

100 Swan Way
Oakland, CA 94621-1428
Ph: (510)632-1366
Fax: (510)568-6040
E-mail: info@independent.org
URL: http://www.independent.org
Contact: David J. Theroux, Founder/Pres./CEO
Founded: 1986. **Members:** 2,200. **Membership Dues:** introductory, $50 (annual) ● sustaining, $100

(annual) ● sponsor, $500 (annual) ● patron, $1,000 (annual) ● benefactor, $5,000 (annual) ● chairman's circle, $10,000 (annual) ● founder's circle, $25,000 (annual). **Staff:** 20. **Budget:** $2,100,000. **Languages:** English, French, Portuguese, Spanish. **Description:** Research and educational organization conducting studies on the political economy of social and economic problems. Encourages innovative thought to redefine debate over public issues and promote new directions for government reform. Conducts economic, legal, and historical research on domestic and international policies in areas including agriculture, civil liberties, banking, international trade, natural resources and environmental protection, labor relations, education, taxation and government spending, and defense. Maintains speakers' bureau. Sponsors public debates. **Libraries:** Type: reference. **Holdings:** 6,000; articles, books, periodicals. **Subjects:** economics, law, history, political science, sociology, public policy. **Awards:** Alexis de Tocqueville Memorial Award. **Frequency:** annual. **Type:** recognition. **Recipient:** for academic excellence in the study of liberty. **Telecommunication Services:** electronic mail, prose@independent.org. **Boards:** Academic Advisors. **Councils:** Business Advisory; Media Advisory. **Publications:** *The Independent*, quarterly. Newsletter. Contains book reviews and feature articles. **Price:** $12.00/year. ISSN: 1047-7969. **Circulation:** 42,000. **Alternate Formats:** magnetic tape ● *Independent Briefings*, quarterly. Contains policy analyses. ● *Independent Policy Reports*. Monographs ● *The Independent Review*, quarterly. Journal ● *Independent Studies in Political Economy*, 6-8/year. Books ● *LibertyTree: Review and Catalogue*, semiannual ● *The Lighthouse*, weekly. Newsletter ● Audiotapes ● Videos. **Conventions/Meetings:** periodic conference, public policy conference ● semiannual convention ● monthly Independent Policy Forum - lecture ● monthly lecture - in Oakland and San Francisco, CA ● monthly seminar and luncheon ● symposium.

18087 ■ Institute for Contemporary Studies (ICS)

3100 Harrison St.
Oakland, CA 94611-5526
Ph: (510)238-5010
Free: (800)326-0263
Fax: (510)238-8440
E-mail: perenna@icspress.com
URL: http://www.icspress.com
Contact: Robert B. Hawkins Jr., Pres./CEO
Founded: 1974. **Staff:** 10. **Languages:** English, French, Spanish. **Description:** Organizations, corporations, and individuals interested in developing and publishing public policy studies and distributing them to leaders in government, the media, and universities. Undertakes the study of an issue if it has some bearing on free political and economic institutions, is immediately relevant, and has ongoing impact and importance. Maintains the Center for Self-Governance. **Libraries:** Type: not open to the public. **Holdings:** 2,500; books, monographs, periodicals. **Subjects:** public policy. **Publications:** *Crime*. Book. Contains facts and perspectives of the nation's top experts on crime and criminal justice. **Price:** $39.95 ● Books (in English and Spanish).

18088 ■ Institute for Philosophy and Public Policy (IPPP)

Maryland School of Public Affairs
3111 Van Munching
College Park, MD 20742
Ph: (301)405-4753
Fax: (301)314-9346
E-mail: vgehring@umd.edu
URL: http://www.puaf.umd.edu/IPPP
Contact: Verna V. Gehring PhD, Ed.
Founded: 1976. **Budget:** $500,000. **Description:** Educational and research institute engaged in the investigation of conceptual and ethical aspects of public policy formulation and debate. Working groups, composed of philosophers, policymakers, analysts, and other experts from within and without the government, currently conduct studies in such areas as: equality of opportunity and American social policy;

mass media and democratic values; rationality of attitudes toward risk; the teaching of ethics in law schools; ecology as a science. Seeks to develop curricula that will bring philosophical issues before future policy makers and citizens. Offers experimental courses on such topics taken from the research program. Has completed model syllabi on hunger and affluence studies, Philosophical Issues in Public Policy, Ethical Problems in the Legal Profession, Ethics and Energy Policy, Environmental Ethics, Human Rights and Foreign Policy, Racial and Sexual Discrimination, and Ethics, Truth, and the Media. **Convention/Meeting:** none. **Formerly:** (1987) Center for Philosophy and Public Policy. **Publications:** *The New Progressive Era; Toward a Fair and Deliberative Democracy*. Book. **Price:** $19.95/copy ● *Philosophy and Public Policy*, quarterly. **Circulation:** 12,000 ● *Philosophy and Public Policy Quarterly*. Newsletter. Summarizes Institute research on public policy as it relates to philosophy. **Price:** free. **Circulation:** 10,000. **Alternate Formats:** online ● Books. **Alternate Formats:** online ● Monographs ● Papers ● Reports.

18089 ■ Institute for Policy Studies (IPS)

1112 16th St. NW, Ste.600
Washington, DC 20036
Ph: (202)234-9382
Fax: (202)387-7915
E-mail: info@ips-dc.org
URL: http://www.ips-dc.org
Founded: 1963. **Members:** 1,500. **Membership Dues:** regular, $35 (annual). **Staff:** 30. **Budget:** $1,400,000. **Description:** Center for research, education, and social invention. Sponsors critical examination of the "assumptions and policies that define American posture on domestic and international issues and offers alternative strategies." Areas of focus include domestic policy, national security, foreign policy, international economics, and human rights. Established the Transnational Institute (TNI) as its international program in 1973. TNI addresses the "fundamental disparity between the rich and poor peoples and nations of the world, investigates its causes and develops alternatives for its remedy." Also established the Letelier-Moffitt Memorial Fund for Human Rights. Conducts courses; issues films. **Libraries:** Type: not open to the public. **Subjects:** peace and security, global economy. **Awards:** Letelier-Moffitt Human Rights Award. **Frequency:** annual. **Type:** recognition. **Recipient:** for outstanding leaders in human rights activism. **Projects:** Break the Chain Campaign; Bring Pinochet to Justice; Cities for Progress; Drug Policy; Foreign Policy in Focus; Global Economy; New Internationalism; Pathways to the 21st Century; Social Action and Leadership School for Activists; Sustainable Energy and Economy Network. **Affiliated With:** Letelier-Moffitt Memorial Fund for Human Rights. **Absorbed:** (1963) Peace Research Institute. **Publications:** *Atomic Diplomacy Hiroshima and Potsdam*. Book ● *Before and After: US Foreign Policy and the September 11th Crisis*. Book. **Price:** $17.95 ● *IPS Quarterly Report*. Newsletter. **Price:** included in membership dues ● *Nickel and Dimed*. Book ● Brochures ● Papers ● Also publishes reference guides. **Conventions/Meetings:** conference - 4-5/year ● lecture ● seminar.

18090 ■ Institute for Public Accuracy (IPA)

65 9th St., Ste.3
San Francisco, CA 94103
Ph: (415)552-5378
Fax: (415)552-6787
E-mail: institute@igc.org
URL: http://www.accuracy.org
Contact: Norman Solomon, Exec. Dir./Founder
Founded: 1997. **Description:** Seeks to advance public discourse by gaining media access for those whose perspectives are commonly drawn out by corporate-backed think tanks and other influential institutions. **Computer Services:** Mailing lists, open to the public; for journalist. **Telecommunication Services:** electronic mail, dcinstitute@igc.org. **Publications:** *Target Iraq: What the News Media Didn't Tell You*. Book.

18091 ■ Institute for Resource and Security Studies (IRSS)

27 Ellsworth Ave.
Cambridge, MA 02139
Ph: (617)491-5177
Fax: (617)491-6904
E-mail: info@irss-usa.org
URL: http://www.irss-usa.org
Contact: Dr. Gordon Thompson, Exec. Dir.
Founded: 1984. **Staff:** 4. **Budget:** $250,000. **Non-membership. Multinational. Description:** Conducts research and public education related to sustainability of human civilization, protection of natural resources, and global human security. Performs in-depth studies, and prepares and disseminates public-education materials. Works with other organizations to develop, promote and implement feasible solutions to specific problems. **Libraries:** Type: reference.

18092 ■ Institute for SocioEconomic Studies (ISES)

10 New King St.
White Plains, NY 10604-1204
Ph: (914)686-7112
Fax: (914)686-0581
E-mail: mail@socioeconomic.org
URL: http://www.socioeconomic.org
Contact: James B. Bryan, Sr. Economist
Founded: 1974. **Staff:** 14. **Description:** Works with broad research interests on the quality of life, economic development, health care, social motivation, poverty, urban regeneration, and the problems of the elderly. **Awards:** National Service Award. **Type:** recognition. **Publications:** *Socioeconomic Intelligence*, quarterly. Newsletter. Reports on current studies, developments, and legislation affecting socioeconomic subjects, such as health care, taxation, and child support. **Price:** $25.00/year. ISSN: 0194-1011. **Circulation:** 17,500 ● Journal, semiannual. Reports on economic development, social motivation, poverty, urban regeneration, and the quality of life of the elderly. Includes annual index. **Price:** $25.00/year. ISSN: 0364-0779. **Circulation:** 17,500 ● Also publishes monographs and books. **Conventions/Meetings:** annual conference.

18093 ■ League of Women Voters Education Fund (LWVEF)

1730 M St. NW, Ste.1000
Washington, DC 20036-4508
Ph: (202)429-1965
Fax: (202)429-0854
E-mail: lwv@lwv.org
URL: http://www.lwv.org
Contact: Mary Wilson, Pres.
Founded: 1957. **Staff:** 20. **Budget:** $2,000,000. **Description:** Educational arm of the League of Women Voters of the United States (see separate entry). Conducts research on a variety of public policy issues including voter service citizen participation, nuclear and solid waste, social welfare, internal relations, and health care. Encourages more effective citizen participation in government. Organizes seminars. **Departments:** Election Services and Litigation; International Relations; Natural Resources; Social Policy. **Supersedes:** National Woman's Suffrage Association. **Publications:** *LWVEF Publications Catalogue* ● *Motor Voter Status Report* ● *The Nuclear Waste Primer* ● *Presidential Debates: 1988 and Beyond* ● *Safety on Tap: A Citizen's Drinking Water Guide* ● *Understanding Economic Policy* ● Annual Report, annual ● Reports.

18094 ■ Moving Ideas Network

1100 15th St. NW, Ste.600
Washington, DC 20005
Ph: (202)776-0730
Fax: (202)776-0740
E-mail: movingideas@movingideas.org
URL: http://www.movingideas.org
Contact: Diane Greenhalgh, Managing Ed.
Founded: 1995. **Members:** 137. **Staff:** 4. **Description:** Public policy organizations. Strives to provide public policy analysis to the general public. **Formerly:** (2002) Electronic Policy Network. **Publications:** *Moving Ideas News*, weekly. Newsletter. Contains policy

reports, research and action from the progressive community. **Alternate Formats:** online.

18095 ■ Nation Institute (NI)
116 E 16th St., 8th Fl.
New York, NY 10003
Ph: (212)209-5447
E-mail: info@nationinstitute.org
URL: http://www.nationinstitute.org
Contact: Hamilton Fish, Pres.
Founded: 1966. **Staff:** 4. **Description:** Seeks to undertake and support research, conferences, seminars, educational programs, and other projects with an emphasis on social justice, civil liberties, and peace and disarmament. Promotes the fundamental commitment to those rights protected by the speech, press, and assembly clauses of the First Amendment. Develops programs to expand the audience and influence of small, independent journals; promotes the dissemination of ideas and analyses. Conducts internship program. **Awards:** The I. F. Stone Award. **Frequency:** annual. **Type:** recognition. **Recipient:** for student journalism ● Puffin/Nation Prize for Creative Citizenship. **Frequency:** annual. **Type:** monetary. **Recipient:** to an individual who has challenged the status quo through distinctive, courageous, imaginative and socially responsible work of significance ● Robert Masur Fellowship. **Frequency:** annual. **Type:** recognition. **Recipient:** for first year law students pursuing projects in civil liberties ● Ron Ridenhour Award. **Frequency:** annual. **Type:** monetary. **Recipient:** to those who persevere in acts of truth-telling that protect the public interest. **Divisions:** The Centre for Democracy Studies; Cold War Archives Project; The Masur Fellowship in Civil Liberties; Project on Media Ownership; Supreme Court Watch. **Programs:** The Investigative Fund; Journalism Fellows; Nation Books; The Nation Internship; RadioNation. **Publications:** Newsletter, periodic. Contains Nation Institute events. **Alternate Formats:** online. **Conventions/Meetings:** conference ● symposium.

18096 ■ National Center for Policy Analysis (NCPA)
Dallas HQ
12770 Coit Rd., Ste.800
Dallas, TX 75251
Ph: (972)386-6272
Fax: (972)386-0924
E-mail: media@ncpa.org
URL: http://www.ncpa.org
Contact: Mr. Sean R. Tuffnell, Dir. of Communications
Founded: 1983. **Staff:** 14. **Description:** Promotes private alternatives to government regulation and control, including healthcare reform, taxes, Social Security, welfare, education, and energy and environmental regulation. **Publications:** Reports, quarterly.

18097 ■ National Center for Public Policy Research (NCPPR)
501 Capitol Ct. NE
Washington, DC 20002
Ph: (202)543-4110
Fax: (202)543-5975
E-mail: info@nationalcenter.org
URL: http://www.nationalcenter.org
Contact: Amy Moritz Ridenour, Pres.
Founded: 1982. **Staff:** 21. **Budget:** $8,000,000. **Nonmembership. Description:** Educates the public about public policy issues. Conducts research; distributes national policy analysis papers, memorandums, brochures, newsletters, article reprints, and other materials to the public, libraries, and the media. **Libraries: Type:** reference. **Absorbed:** (1989) Coalition for Jobs, Peace, and Freedom in the Americas; (1992) Committee to Stop Chemical Atrocities. **Publications:** In The News, quarterly. Newsletter. Alternate Formats: online ● Legal Briefs, periodic. Newsletter. Alternate Formats: online ● Ten Second Response, periodic. Newsletter. Alternate Formats: online ● What Conservatives Think, periodic. Newsletter. Alternate Formats: online ● Also publishes Political Money Monitor-biweekly campaign finance newsletter; Legal Briefs-biweekly legal reform newsletter.

18098 ■ National Chamber Foundation (NCF)
1615 H St. NW
Washington, DC 20062-2000
Ph: (202)463-5500
Free: (800)638-6582
Fax: (202)463-3129
E-mail: ncf@uschamber.com
URL: http://www.uschamber.com/ncf
Contact: Thomas J. Donahue, Pres.
Founded: 1967. **Staff:** 4. **Description:** Works as public policy research organization concerned with issues vital to the health of the economic system. Provides authoritative information on specific economic problems facing the nation, analyzes the data, and makes recommendations for policy initiatives. Acts as a policy research affiliate of the US Chamber of Commerce. Aims to drive the policy debate on critical national issues by formulating arguments, developing options and influencing thinking in an effort to move the American business Agenda forward. **Libraries: Type:** reference. **Holdings:** 7,000. **Subjects:** business and economics. **Awards:** Dixie Davis Scholarship. **Type:** scholarship. **Committees:** Health Care; International Taxation; Social Cost; Transportation. **Programs:** Corporate Executive Development; Institutes for Organization Management. **Affiliated With:** U.S. Chamber of Commerce. **Publications:** Books ● Monographs ● Reports. **Conventions/Meetings:** periodic conference.

18099 ■ National Defense Council Foundation (NDCF)
1220 King St., Ste.No. 230
Alexandria, VA 22314
Ph: (703)836-3443
Fax: (703)836-5402
E-mail: ndcf@erols.com
URL: http://www.ndcf.org
Contact: Maj. F. Andy Messing Jr., Exec. Dir.
Founded: 1978. **Members:** 19,000. **Membership Dues:** contributor, $15 (annual). **Staff:** 5. **Budget:** $250,000. **Description:** Works to conduct studies on what the group calls low-intensity conflicts (such as those in Angola and Colombia); aid those in the area of conflict; organize fact-finding missions to these conflict areas for congressmen; combat drug trafficking through research and legislation; coordinate studies on energy and the environment. Has sent 198.5 tons of food and medical supplies world wide. **Convention/Meeting:** none. **Libraries: Type:** not open to the public. **Holdings:** 126. **Subjects:** SOLIC (special operations, low intensity conflict), anti-drug operations. **Awards:** American Hero Award. **Frequency:** annual. **Type:** recognition. **Recipient:** for heroic acts done for America. **Computer Services:** Mailing lists. **Programs:** Internship. **Projects:** Refugee Relief. **Publications:** U.S. Drug Control Policy and International Operations ● U.S. Support for Democratic Insurgencies ● Brochures ● Newsletter, monthly. **Price:** included in membership dues ● Papers. Includes national security aspects of The North American Free Trade Agreement (NAFTA). ● Annual Report, annual. **Price:** included in membership dues ● Reports. Alternate Formats: online ● Videos.

18100 ■ National Institute for Public Policy (NIPP)
9302 Lee Hwy., Ste.750
Fairfax, VA 22031
Ph: (703)293-9181
E-mail: amy.joseph@nipp.org
URL: http://www.nipp.org
Contact: Dr. Keith B. Payne, Pres./Chm.
Founded: 1981. **Staff:** 20. **Description:** Focuses on a wide spectrum of rapidly evolving foreign policy and international security issues, including: the "effectiveness of deterrence theory in a post-cold War framework;" U.S./allied measures to counter the proliferation of weapons of mass destruction and the missile delivery systems; and the future of NATO and U.S.-allied security arrangements. **Programs:** European Perspectives on U.S. Ballistic Missile Defense; The Fallacies of Cold War Deterrence and a New Direction; The Future of Ballistic Missiles; National Security Reform in the Republic of Georgia; Rationale and Requirements for U.S. Nuclear Forces and Arms Control; Strategic Offensive Forces and the Nuclear Posture Review's "New Triad"; Understanding "Asymmetric" Threats to the United States. **Publications:** The B-2 Bomber: Air Power for the 21st Century. Book ● Comparative Strategy, quarterly. Journal. Contains international views on contemporary strategic issues. **Circulation:** 1,000 ● Missile Defense for 21st Century: Protection Against Limited Threats ● Nuclear Freeze Controversy and Missiles for the Nineties ● Monographs.

18101 ■ National Issues Forums Institute (NIFI)
PO Box 41626
Dayton, OH 45441
Ph: (937)434-7300 (937)439-9826
Free: (800)433-7834
Fax: (724)443-5942
E-mail: dineenp@msn.com
URL: http://www.nifi.org
Contact: David Mathews, Pres.
Founded: 1989. **State Groups:** 30. **Description:** Promotes the national issues forums of the organization. Primary tasks are: to ensure the ongoing preparation of issue books and other materials that will stimulate serious public deliberation on major issues that Americans face nationally and locally; to encourage collaboration in the NIF network and to provide a legal home for consortia that grow out of this collaboration; to collect and share information about what is going on throughout the NIF network; and to solicit and administer grants for the network. **Formerly:** (1979) Domestic Policy Association; (2004) National Issues Forums. **Publications:** A Nice Place To Live: Creating Communities, Fighting Sprawl. Book. **Price:** $3.90 regular and abridged; $6.00 for video ● Alcohol: Controlling the Toxic Spill. Book. **Price:** $3.90 regular and abridged; $6.00 for video ● At Death's Door: What Are the Choices?. Book. **Price:** $3.90 abridged; $6.00 for video ● Crime & Punishment: Is Justice Being Served?. Book. **Price:** $3.90 regular; $6.00 for video ● Democracy's Challenge: Reclaiming the Public's Role. Booklet. Serves as a deliberative discussion guide. ● Illegal Drugs: What Should We Do Now?. Book. **Price:** $3.90 regular and abridged; $6.00 for video ● Life and Death Decisions: Who Decides?. Booklet. Serves as a deliberative discussion guide. ● Making Ends Meet: Is There a Way to Help Working Americans?. Booklet. Serves as a deliberative discussion guide. ● News Media and Society: How to Restore the Public Trust. Booklets. Serves as a deliberative discussion guide. ● News Media & Society: How to Restore the Public Trust?. Book. **Price:** $3.90 regular and abridged; $12.00 for video ● Public Schools: Are they Making the Grade?. Book. **Price:** $3.90 regular; $6.00 for video ● The Social Security Struggle: Fixing the Retirement System. Booklet. Serves as a deliberative discussion guide. ● Terrorism: What Should We Do Now. Book. **Price:** $3.90 regular; $6.00 for video ● Tokel UnNipi: Community Development on the Rosebud. Book ● Violent Kids: Can We Change the Trend?. Book. **Price:** $3.90 regular and abridged; $6.00 for video ● Booklets, annual. **Conventions/Meetings:** annual meeting.

18102 ■ New America Foundation
1630 Connecticut Ave. NW, 7th Fl.
Washington, DC 20009
Ph: (202)986-2700
Fax: (202)986-3696
E-mail: president@newamerica.net
URL: http://www.newamerica.net
Contact: Ted Halstead, Pres./CEO
Founded: 1999. **Membership Dues:** associate, $100 (annual) ● sponsor, $250 (annual) ● patron, $1,000 (annual) ● benefactor, $5,000 (annual) ● New York Advisory Council, $10,000 (annual) ● Leadership Council, $25,000 (annual). **Staff:** 35. **Description:** Sponsors research, published writing, and events on issues affecting America, ranging from the information age to demographic shifts to economic globalization, and more. **Awards: Type:** fellowship. **Computer Services:** database, staff directory. **Programs:** Asset Building; The Bernard L. Schwartz Fellows; California

Fellows; Fiscal Policy; Global Middle Class; Health Policy; Retirement Security; Strategic Initiatives; Wireless Future. **Publications:** *An American Story.* Book. **Price:** $25.00 ● *The City: A Global History.* Book. **Price:** $21.95 ● *The Coming Anarchy: Shattering the Dreams of the Post Cold War.* Book. **Price:** $21.95 ● *Eastward to Tartary: Travels in the Balkans, Middle East, and the Caucasus.* Book. **Price:** $26.95 ● *Guiding Lights: The People Who Lead Us Toward Our Purpose in Life.* Book. Features evocative stories of memorable people. **Price:** $19.95 ● *Holy War, Inc: Inside the Secret World of Osama bin Laden.* Book. Features insights on the intellectual and religious influences of bin Laden. **Price:** $14.00 ● *The Radical Center: The Future of American Politics.* Book. Features programs of innovative policy ideas adapted to the Information Age. **Price:** $24.95 ● *Silent Theft: The Private Plunder of Our Common Wealth.* Book. **Price:** $18.20 ● *University Inc.: The Corporate Corruption of Higher Education.* Book. **Price:** $17.16 ● *Vietnam The Necessary War: A Reinterpretation of America's Most Disastrous Military Conflict.* Book. **Price:** $17.50 ● *Warrior Politics: Why Leadership Demands a Pagan Ethos.* Book. **Price:** $22.95 ● *What Lincoln Believed: The Values and Convictions of America's Greatest President.* Book ● *What We Owe Iraq: War and the Ethics of Nation Building.* Book. Contains discussion of constitutional aspects of nation building and an account of post-war Iraq. **Price:** $19.95. **Conventions/Meetings:** annual conference.

18103 ■ New Century Policies Educational Programs (NCPEP)

c/o Carla Brooks Johnston, Pres.
One Percy Pl.
Cambridge, MA 02139
Ph: (617)354-5811
Fax: (617)354-5811
E-mail: info@newcenturypolicies.com
Contact: Carla Brooks Johnston, Pres.
Founded: 1981. **Description:** Seeks to educate the public on the options available to individuals and policymakers for dealing with the impact of new technologies on modern life. Focuses on the government's policy of civil defense preparedness and public safety. Concentrates its energies on the media and public policy topics. Works on educational video programs on the environment and on Africa. Sponsors speakers' bureau; offers research and educational programs. (Held 1991 conference on election coverage issues facing journalists in Eastern Europe and the Soviet Union.) **Libraries: Type:** reference. **Holdings:** archival material, audiovisuals, clippings. **Telecommunication Services:** electronic mail, carla-johnston@newcenturypolicies.com. **Supersedes:** (1981) Civil Defense Awareness. **Publications:** *Election Coverage: Blueprint for Broadcasting* ● *International Television Co-Production: From Access to Success* ● *Reversing the Nuclear Arms Race* ● Video.

18104 ■ Newport Institute for Ethics, Law and Public Policy

PO Box 9044
Newport Beach, CA 92658
Free: (800)811-4770
E-mail: info@newportinstitute.org
URL: http://www.newportinstitute.org
Contact: Myron S. Steeves JD, Pres.
Founded: 1978. **Budget:** $50,000. **Description:** Seeks to engage politicians, public officials, leaders, educators, media representatives, and members of the public in examining critical contemporary issues. Organizes seminars, conferences, and meetings in neutral environments to discuss national and international policies. Provides information on public policies and policy alternatives; increases awareness and understanding of consequences of acting on policies. Conducts research on the interaction of political, military, social economic, psychological, religious, and cultural factors and their effect on national tranquility. **Telecommunication Services:** electronic mail, msteeves@newportinstitute.org. **Publications:** *Civilitas,* quarterly. Journal. Features articles and interviews about issues affecting public life. ●

Reports, periodic. **Conventions/Meetings:** board meeting ● annual conference.

18105 ■ Northeast-Midwest Institute (NMI)

50 F St. NW, No. 950
Washington, DC 20001
Ph: (202)544-5200
Fax: (202)544-0043
E-mail: info@nemw.org
URL: http://www.nemw.org
Contact: Joanna Stover, Admin.
Founded: 1977. **Members:** 150. **Membership Dues:** individual, $5,000 (annual). **Staff:** 20. **Budget:** $2,000,000. **Description:** Serves as an independent source of reliable information on the economy of the 18-state region that forms the nation's industrial heartland. Provides nonpartisan research and analysis concerning the national and regional implications of a broad range of federal policy issues including federal spending, taxation, energy, environmental policy, trade, urban and rural policy, economic development, human resources, and defense. Sponsors field hearings and briefings for members of Congress and state officials on these issues. Compiles statistics on a broad range of economic data; maintains an extensive bank of state-by-state and regional information. **Departments:** Brownfields; Economic Development; Economics and Demographics; Energy; Human Resources; Natural Resources; Smart Growth; Tax Policy; Trade and Transportation. **Affiliated With:** Northeast-Midwest Senate Coalition. **Publications:** *Agriculture and Nutrition.* Newsletter. Alternate Formats: online ● *Brownfield Voluntary Cleanup Program Impacts: Reuse Benefits, State by State.* Reprint. Presents a mid-year review of the initiatives in the 50 states. **Price:** $20.00 ● *Brownfields "State of the States",* periodic. Reprint. Presents a mid-year review of the initiatives in the 50 states. **Price:** $20.00/copy, plus shipping and handling. ISSN: 0894-4202 ● *The Budget and the Region: 2002,* annual. Reviews regional impact of the President's budget proposal. State-by-state impacts. **Price:** $25.00 plus shipping and handling ● *Federal Spending in the Northeast-Midwest: Fiscal 2000,* annual. Report. Analyzes a flow of federal funds into the states. **Price:** $50.00 plus shipping and handling ● *Northeast-Midwest Economic Review,* bimonthly. Journal. Covers economic policy. **Price:** $95.00/year. Alternate Formats: online ● Annual Report, annual. Alternate Formats: online. **Conventions/Meetings:** periodic conference.

18106 ■ Northeast-Midwest Senate Coalition (NMSC)

c/o Northeast Midwest Institute
218 D St. SE
Washington, DC 20003-1900
Ph: (202)544-5200 (202)224-0606
Fax: (202)544-0043
URL: http://www.nemw.org/sencoal.htm
Contact: Ari Strauss, Legislative Dir.
Founded: 1977. **Description:** Bipartisan coalition of senators from 18 states in New England, the mid-Atlantic, and the Great Lakes. Informs members of the regional implications of national policies and proposals; seeks to influence federal policy and legislation of regional significance. Issues of concern include economic development, employment, energy, the environment, transportation and infrastructure, and the flow of federal funds. **Task Forces:** Great Lakes; New England; Senate Smart Growth; Senate Task Force on Manufacturing. **Affiliated With:** Northeast-Midwest Institute. **Publications:** Reports.

18107 ■ Organization for International Investment (OFII)

1225 Nineteenth St. NW, Ste.501
Washington, DC 20036
Ph: (202)659-1903
Fax: (202)659-2293
E-mail: tmalan@ofii.org
URL: http://www.ofii.org
Contact: Todd Malan, Pres./CEO
Founded: 1991. **Members:** 52. **Staff:** 4. **Description:** Educational lobbying association of U.S. subsidiaries of foreign companies. Dedicated to

articulating the benefits of international investment to the U.S. economy and ensuring that its members enjoy non-discriminatory treatment in the U.S. **Formed by Merger of:** (1991) Association for International Investment; Organization for Fair Treatment of International Investment. **Conventions/Meetings:** annual meeting.

18108 ■ Pacific Research Institute for Public Policy (PRI)

755 Sansome St., Ste.450
San Francisco, CA 94111
Ph: (415)989-0833
Fax: (415)989-2411
E-mail: info@pacificresearch.org
URL: http://www.pacificresearch.org
Contact: Sally C. Pipes, Pres./CEO
Founded: 1979. **Staff:** 24. **Budget:** $4,300,000. **Description:** Aims to inform the public about issues that affect the free enterprise system and the rights of individuals. Studies public policy issues, including education, environment, technology, economics, health and welfare. Maintains speakers' bureau. Conducts educational programs. **Libraries: Type:** reference. **Holdings:** 50; books, clippings. **Subjects:** environment, education, healthcare, taxes, spending, technology, welfare, women's issues. **Computer Services:** database ● mailing lists ● online services. **Formerly:** (1986) Pacific Institute. **Publications:** *Capital Ideas: Political Commentary,* weekly ● *Contrarian,* bimonthly. Features commentary on women's issues. Alternate Formats: online ● *Impact: Summary of PRI in the News,* monthly. Newsletter ● *Presidents Message,* quarterly. Newsletter. **Circulation:** 8,000. **Conventions/Meetings:** periodic Issues Luncheons - meeting ● annual Privatization Competition - competition and dinner, with awards.

18109 ■ Philadelphia Society

11620 Rutan Cir.
Jerome, MI 49249
Ph: (517)688-5111
Fax: (517)688-5113
E-mail: phillysoc@comcast.net
URL: http://www.phillysoc.org
Contact: Bill Campbell, Sec.
Founded: 1964. **Description:** Works to deepen intellectual foundations for a free and ordered society, focusing on economic, political, cultural and other issues. **Libraries: Type:** reference. **Holdings:** audio recordings. **Telecommunication Services:** electronic mail, wcampbell14@cox.net. **Publications:** *The Ownership Society: Can We Sing and Dance Progressivism and the New Deal Away?.* Bibliography. Alternate Formats: online ● Papers. Alternate Formats: online. **Conventions/Meetings:** meeting.

18110 ■ Planners Network (PN)

Rapson Hall
89 Church St. SE
Minneapolis, MN 55455
Ph: (612)624-3596
Fax: (612)626-0600
E-mail: info@plannersnetwork.org
URL: http://www.plannersnetwork.org
Contact: Tom Angotti, Ed.
Founded: 1975. **Members:** 450. **Membership Dues:** regular, $50 (annual). **Staff:** 1. **Regional Groups:** 4. **Description:** Professionals, activists, academics, and students involved in physical, social, economic, and environmental planning in urban and rural areas. Promotes fundamental change in the American political and economic system. Seeks to create a support network and influence national and local political and economic policies. Believes planning should be a tool for allocating resources and developing the environment in order to eliminate the great inequalities of wealth and power in the society, rather than to maintain and justify the status quo. Opposes the economic structure of American society, which the network says, "values profit and property rights over human rights and needs." Advocates change in the federal budget "to favor human services, social production and environmental protection over military and other nonproductive expenditures." Offers a progressive analysis of planning issues; participates

in debate over public policy issues; proposes and advocates policy and legislative reforms; supports local, regional, and national groups. **Telecommunication Services:** electronic mail, tangotti@hunter.cuny.edu. **Publications:** *Progressive Planning*, quarterly. Magazine. **Price:** included in membership dues. **Advertising:** accepted. **Conventions/Meetings:** annual conference.

18111 ■ Policy Studies Organization (PSO)

1527 New Hampshire Ave. NW
Washington, DC 20036
Ph: (202)483-2512
Fax: (202)483-2657
E-mail: info@ipsonet.org
URL: http://www.ipsonet.org
Contact: Dr. Paul J. Rich, Pres.
Founded: 1971. **Members:** 2,200. **Membership Dues:** regular, $95 (annual) ● life, $1,500. **Staff:** 10. **Description:** Promotes the application of political and social science to important policy problems. Provides activities that are designed to bring academicians and practitioners together on policy problems across disciplinary lines. Acts as a clearinghouse for information. **Awards:** **Frequency:** annual. **Type:** recognition. **Committees:** Editorial. **Formerly:** Policy Studies Group (of the American Political Science Association). **Publications:** *Creativity Plus*, quarterly. Newsletter ● *Developmental Policy*, quarterly. Newsletter ● *Peace, Prosperity and Democracy*, quarterly. Newsletter ● *Policy Evaluation*, quarterly. Newsletter ● *Policy Studies Journal*, quarterly. Includes book reviews and periodic directory. **Price:** $40.00 /year for individuals; $280.00 /year for libraries. ISSN: 0190-292X. **Circulation:** 2,200. **Advertising:** accepted. Alternate Formats: microform ● *Review of Policy Research*, quarterly. Journal. Contains book reviews and periodic directory. **Price:** included in membership dues; $40.00 for nonmembers; $280.00 for libraries. ISSN: 0278-4416. **Circulation:** 2,200. Alternate Formats: microform ● Books ● Directories. **Conventions/Meetings:** periodic conference ● semiannual meeting, held in conjunction with the American Political Science Association and Midwest Political Science Association - always April and September.

18112 ■ Progressive Policy Institute (PPI)

600 Pennsylvania Ave. SE, Ste.400
Washington, DC 20003
Ph: (202)547-0001
Fax: (202)544-5014
E-mail: press@dlcppi.org
URL: http://www.ppionline.org
Contact: Will Marshall III, Pres./Founder
Founded: 1989. **Staff:** 12. **Description:** Strives to define and promote new progressive politics for America in the 21st century, focusing on the Information Age. **Publications:** *Building the Bridge: 10 Big Ideas to Transform America*. Book. **Price:** $10.17 ● *Mandate for Change*. Book.

18113 ■ Public Agenda

6 E 39th St.
New York, NY 10016
Ph: (212)686-6610
Fax: (212)889-3461
E-mail: info@publicagenda.org
URL: http://www.publicagenda.org
Contact: Ruth A. Wooden, Pres.
Founded: 1975. **Staff:** 23. **Budget:** $3,100,000. **Description:** Works to help citizens better understand critical policy issues and to help the nations leaders better understand the public's point of view. Conducts research on how citizens think about policy. Disseminates citizen educational materials. Maintains highly acclaimed non-partisan interactive web site. **Computer Services:** database. **Committees:** Policy Review Board. **Also Known As:** Public Agenda Foundation. **Publications:** *Aggravating Circumstances: A Status Report on Rudeness in America*. Alternate Formats: online ● *Reality Check*, annual. Report. Details the progress of the academic standards movement and the impact of related reforms. ● *Sizing Things Up: What Parents, Teachers and Students Think About Large and Small High Schools.*

Report ● Newsletter, 3/year. Contains summary of recent public agenda research and highlights of PA activities. **Circulation:** 4,000. Alternate Formats: online ● Also publishes reports and focus group studies on: education; welfare; crime and corrections; jobs and productivity; science and technology; saving and retirement; health care and AIDS; the economy and other national policy topics.

18114 ■ Reason Foundation (RF)

3415 S Sepulveda Blvd., Ste.400
Los Angeles, CA 90034
Ph: (310)391-2245
Fax: (310)391-4395
E-mail: feedback@reason.org
URL: http://www.reason.org
Contact: George Passantino, Dir. of Public Affairs
Founded: 1978. **Membership Dues:** individual, $20 (annual). **Staff:** 35. **Budget:** $6,000,000. **Description:** Executives, public officials, media, and other interested individuals. Provides a better understanding of the intellectual basis of a free society and develops new ideas in public policy. Conducts contemporary research on social, economic, urban, and political problems. Promotes individualist philosophy and free market principles. Compiles statistics; operates speakers' bureau. **Libraries:** **Type:** reference. **Holdings:** 3,500. **Subjects:** economics, public policy, related topics. **Additional Websites:** http://www.reason.com, http://www.privatization.org, http://www.newenvironmentalism.org. **Publications:** *Privatization Watch*, monthly. Newsletter. Contains research reports, schedule of events, summaries of privatization activities, and book lists. **Price:** $95.00/ year. **Circulation:** 1,200. **Advertising:** accepted. Also Cited As: *Fiscal Watchdog* ● *Reason Magazine*, 11/year. Contains articles on contemporary social, economic, and political issues. Alternate Formats: online ● Papers ● Annual Report. Alternate Formats: online. **Conventions/Meetings:** annual conference (exhibits).

18115 ■ RESOLVE

1255 23rd St. NW, Ste.275
Washington, DC 20037
Ph: (202)944-2300
Fax: (202)338-1264
E-mail: info@resolv.org
URL: http://www.resolv.org
Contact: Gail Bingham, Pres.
Founded: 1977. **Description:** Works to improve dialogue and negotiation between parties to solve complex public policy issues and advance research and practice in dispute resolution. **Publications:** Papers. Alternate Formats: online ● Articles. Alternate Formats: online. **Conventions/Meetings:** roundtable ● workshop.

18116 ■ Sarah Scaife Foundation

One Oxford Ctre.
301 Grant St., Ste.3900
Pittsburgh, PA 15219-6401
Ph: (412)392-2900
URL: http://www.scaife.com/sarah.html
Contact: Michael W. Gleba, Exec. VP
Founded: 1928. **Multinational. Description:** Works to support public policy programs that address major domestic and international issues. **Awards:** **Type:** grant. **Publications:** Annual Report, annual. Alternate Formats: online.

18117 ■ U.S. Public Interest Research Group (USPIRG)

218 D St. SE
Washington, DC 20003
Ph: (202)546-9707
Fax: (202)546-2461
E-mail: membershipservices@pirg.org
URL: http://www.uspirg.org
Contact: Douglas H. Phelps, Pres.
Founded: 1983. **Members:** 1,000,000. **Membership Dues:** regular, $35 (annual). **Staff:** 30. **State Groups:** 30. **Description:** Individuals who contribute time, effort, or funds toward public interest research and advocacy. Conducts research, monitors corporate and government actions, and lobbies for reforms on

consumer, environmental, energy, and governmental issues. Current efforts include support for: laws to protect consumers from unsafe products and unfair banking practices; laws to reduce the use of toxic chemicals; strengthening clean air laws; efforts to reduce global warming and ozone depletion; energy conservation and use of safe, renewable energy sources. Sponsors internships for college students; provides opportunities for students to receive academic credit for activities such as legislative research, lobbying, and public education and organizing. Offers summer jobs. **Publications:** *Citizen Agenda*, quarterly. Newsletter. Covers federal legislation on environmental, consumer, nuclear, and other public interest issues; reports on USPIRG's lobbying efforts. **Price:** included in membership dues ● Also publishes research reports and studies.

18118 ■ Women's Economic Round Table (WERT)

c/o Dr. Amelia Augustus, Pres./Co-Founder
Knight-Bagehot Fellowship Prog.
School of Journalism, Columbia Univ.
2950 Broadway, Mail Code 3850
New York, NY 10027
Ph: (914)922-1747
Fax: (914)922-1747
E-mail: augustusaa@aol.com
URL: http://www.wert.org
Contact: Dr. Amelia Augustus, Pres./Co-Founder
Founded: 1978. **Members:** 500. **Membership Dues:** regular, $100 (annual) ● supporting, $250 (annual) ● sustaining, $500 (annual) ● benefactor, $1,000 (annual) ● corporate, $2,500 (annual). **Staff:** 1. **Budget:** $200,000. **Description:** Business women who question economic policymakers in a public forum; economists, business executives, unionists and anyone interested in business, economics and financial issues. Consolidates the voice of women in the formation of national and global economic policy and decisions. Conducts seminars; sponsors roundtable discussions to clarify national and global economic business and financial issues and make economic policy leaders accessible to members and the public; acts as resource center for the media and business and other institutions seeking experts and executives. Educates women on how to maintain control over the economic power they hold and stresses the importance of doing so. **Publications:** none. **Libraries:** **Type:** open to the public. **Awards:** Maria and Sidney E. Rolfe Award and Lifetime Achievement in Financial and Entrepreneurship Journalism. **Frequency:** periodic. **Type:** monetary. **Recipient:** for individual or group educating the public about business and economics, or affecting economic and business policy ● Rolfe Award and Financial Journalism Prizes. **Type:** recognition. **Conventions/Meetings:** bimonthly roundtable.

18119 ■ World Priorities (WP)

Box 25140
Washington, DC 20007
Ph: (703)777-4352
Fax: (202)965-1525
E-mail: jimsivard@megapipe.net
Contact: James Sivard, Contact
Founded: 1973. **Multinational. Description:** Public interest organization sponsored by foundations and other nonprofit organizations. Provides independent, balanced and nonpartisan information on social policy issues of world importance. **Libraries:** **Type:** not open to the public. **Subjects:** military and social spending. **Publications:** *Women: A World Survey* ● *World Energy Survey* ● *World Military and Social Expenditures*, biennial ● Reports.

18120 ■ Youth Policy Institute (YPI)

634 S Spring St., Ste.818
Los Angeles, CA 90014
Ph: (213)688-2802
Fax: (213)688-2942
E-mail: info@ypiusa.org
URL: http://www.ypiusa.org
Contact: Dixon Slingerland, Exec. Dir.
Founded: 1978. **Staff:** 30. **Budget:** $500,000. **Description:** Research associates and analysts be-

tween the ages of 17 and 25 who work with experienced professionals. Aims to monitor federal youth and family policy. Provides publications that contains comprehensive updates for youth and family-serving organizations and individuals on the development of policy in the administration, Congress, and public interest groups; encourages students to investigate and report on how such policy initiatives affect their own communities; provides youth and family advocates with an information base for comparing policy initiatives to present and past policy. Gives six-to-12 month internships and training programs to monitor, analyze, and report on policy in areas affecting families and youth for College students and recent graduates. Sponsors interns and contributes funds, expertise, and academic credits to organizations and academic institutions. Sponsors semiannual forum organized around position papers drafted by institute staff addressing federal programs as they relate to family, children's, and youth programs. **Convention/ Meeting:** none. **Computer Services:** database. **Publications:** *Youth Policy.* Magazine. Lists all national youth issues and programs with proposed solutions. **Price:** $127.00 bulk rate monthly; $157.00 first class. ISSN: 8756-0909. **Circulation:** 2,000. **Advertising:** accepted ● *Youth Record,* biweekly. Companion to Youth Policy covering current news of federal legislative and executive actions. **Price:** $127.00 bulk rate; $157.00 first class; $337.00 3/years. ISSN: 1047-7144 ● Also publishes special reports.

Public Relations

18121 ■ Council of Public Relations Firms
317 Madison Ave., Ste.2320
New York, NY 10017
Free: (877)773-4767
Fax: (877)773-2937
E-mail: kcripps@prfirms.org
URL: http://www.prfirms.org
Contact: Kathy Cripps, Pres.
Founded: 1998. **Members:** 125. **Membership Dues:** business (minimum; based on revenue), $2,500 (annual) ● business (maximum; based on revenue), $40,000 (annual). **Staff:** 3. **Budget:** $1,000,000. **Description:** Strives to build the business of public relations by advocating to non-communications business executives, professors, students and media about the validity of public relations as an effective strategic business tool. Works to set standards for the profession. **Publications:** *GAP Study.* Booklet. **Price:** $25.00. Alternate Formats: online.

Public Welfare

18122 ■ Spirit of America
12021 Wilshire Blvd., Ste.558
Los Angeles, CA 90025
Free: (800)691-2209
Fax: (310)356-6015
E-mail: staff@spiritofamerica.net
URL: http://www.spiritofamerica.net
Contact: Jim Hake, Founder/Chm.
Founded: 2001. **Description:** Assists in advancing freedom, democracy and peace abroad. Provides support to American military and civilian personnel and people who call to Americans for help in their struggle for freedom and democracy. Increases the reach, scale and impact of informal humanitarian activities. **Projects:** Friends of Democracy; Gifts for Iraqi Children; Iraqi Orphans; Library Books for Iraqi Children; Operation Snapshot; Re-equip Universities in Baquba, Iraq; Support America - Iraq School Partners; Vests for Afghanistan Police Forces.

Puerto Rico

18123 ■ Committee 51st State for Puerto Rico (COMITE 51)
Address Unknown since 2007
Founded: 1976. **Members:** 25. **Staff:** 5. **Languages:** Spanish. **Description:** Promotes the recognition of

Puerto Rican people in an effort to establish Puerto Rico as the 51st state. Sponsors charitable program; marches in parades; circulates petitions. **Publications:** none.

18124 ■ National Puerto Rican Coalition (NPRC)
1901 L St. NW, Ste.802
Washington, DC 20036
Ph: (202)223-3915
Fax: (202)429-2223
E-mail: nprc@nprcinc.org
URL: http://www.bateylink.org
Contact: Manuel Mirabal, Pres./CEO
Founded: 1977. **Members:** 556. **Membership Dues:** individual, $150 (annual) ● regular, $125 (annual) ● supportive, $25 (annual) ● senior, $75 (annual) ● student, $30 (annual) ● life, $1,000. **Staff:** 15. **Budget:** $1,700,000. **Regional Groups:** 1. **Local Groups:** 51. **Description:** Local and national Puerto Rican organizations and individuals interested in national programs and issues affecting the Puerto Rican community. Objectives are to: foster the social, economic, and political well-being of Puerto Ricans; evaluate the potential impact on Puerto Rican communities of legislative and governmental proposals and policies; represent interests of Puerto Ricans to the public and private sectors; develop a network of Puerto Rican organizations. Conducts public policy analysis, research, and community networking; sponsors educational seminars; collects and compiles statistics on housing, employment, education, and social welfare. Provides technical assistance and training to staff members of developing Puerto Rican agencies in planning and administering social service and community development programs, diagnosing and strengthening organizational management, and developing a stable funding base. Offers public policy fellowship. Maintains placement service and collection of publications, reports, and research works. **Committees:** Business Advisory Council; Legislation; Public Policy. **Departments:** Community Building; Public Policy and Research; Youth Leadership. **Divisions:** Community Development; Public Affairs, Public Policy and Research; Training and Technical Assistance. **Publications:** *Adelante,* quarterly. Newsletter. Alternate Formats: online ● *Mi Casa es Su Casa.* Newsletter. Contains information on vital housing legislation and programming on local and federal level. Alternate Formats: online ● *National Directory of Puerto Rican Organizations,* periodic ● *NPRC Reports,* bimonthly. Newsletter. Contains news about the Puerto Rican communities. ● *Policy Agenda,* semiannual ● *Ponte Al Dia,* monthly. Reports. Contains information on the current legislation affecting the Puerto Rican/Latino community. Alternate Formats: online ● Annual Report, annual ● Bulletin, periodic ● Also publishes research findings. **Conventions/Meetings:** annual conference (exhibits).

18125 ■ Puerto Rico U.S.A. Citizenship Foundation (PRUSA)
600 13th St. NW
Washington, DC 20005
Ph: (202)756-8213
Fax: (202)756-8087
E-mail: prusa@puertoricousa.com
URL: http://www.puertoricousa.com
Contact: Peter Holmes, Exec. Dir.
Founded: 1984. **Members:** 65. **Description:** Coalition supporting preservation of tax incentives for U.S. companies with operations in Puerto Rico. Believes that these tax benefits, initiated in 1921, have encouraged economic development in Puerto Rico by bringing in jobs and investments and raising average personal income. Conducts educational programs and activities to inform U.S. legislative and executive policymakers of the benefits of tax incentives to the continued economic development of Puerto Rico. **Formerly:** Puerto Rico, U.S.A. Foundation. **Conventions/Meetings:** annual meeting.

Racism

18126 ■ Racial Justice 911 (RJ 911)
c/o CAAAV: Organizing Asian Communities
2473 Valentine Ave.
Bronx, NY 10458

Ph: (718)220-7391
Fax: (718)220-7398
E-mail: info@racialjustice911.org
URL: http://www.racialjustice911.org
Contact: Hany Khalil, Coor.
Founded: 2002. **Multinational. Description:** Built a national network of more than 60 community-based racial justice organizations. Participating organizations work on a wide range of issues, including immigrant rights, economic justice, welfare rights, Indigenous environmental issues, LGBT rights, issues facing young people of color, and domestic and sexual violence. The network and its Steering Committee is multigenerational, regionally diverse, and has attracted groups rooted in African American, Latino, Asian Pacific Islander, Arab, and South Asian communities and indigenous nations. **Telecommunication Services:** electronic mail, racialjustice911@riseup.net.

Radio

18127 ■ Mainstream Media Project (MMP)
854 9th St., Ste.B
Arcata, CA 95521
Ph: (707)826-9111
Fax: (707)826-9112
E-mail: info@mainstream-media.net
URL: http://www.mainstream-media.net
Contact: Mark Sommer, Exec. Dir.
Founded: 1995. **Multinational. Description:** Public education organization that places top policy analysts and social innovators on radio stations globally. **Additional Websites:** http://www.aworldofpossibilities.com, http://www.bothand.org.

Real Estate

18128 ■ National Association of Exclusive Buyer Agents (NAEBA)
10725 Lawyers Rd.
Vienna, VA 22181
Ph: (703)920-1095
Free: (800)786-1570
Fax: (703)620-5384
E-mail: naebahq@naeba.us
URL: http://www.naeba.info
Contact: Terry Peters CAE, Exec. Dir.
Founded: 1995. **Membership Dues:** service affiliate, $400 (annual) ● broker/agent, $300-$625 (annual). **Description:** Works to represent real estate buyers. **Publications:** *NAEBA News,* quarterly. Newsletter. Contains news about the association. **Price:** included in membership dues. **Conventions/Meetings:** annual conference.

Refugees

18129 ■ Central American Resource Center (CARECEN)
1459 Columbia Rd. NW
Washington, DC 20009
Ph: (202)328-9799
Fax: (202)328-0023
E-mail: info@carecendc.org
URL: http://www.carecendc.org
Contact: Saul Solorzano, Exec. Dir.
Founded: 1981. **Members:** 13. **Staff:** 12. **Budget:** $750,000. **Languages:** English, Spanish. **Description:** Operates legal, educational and empowerment programs for and in cooperation with the over 300,000-member Central American and Latino community in the Washington D.C. metropolitan area. Aims to help Central Americans/Latinos obtain and/or maintain their legal immigration status and to work with the community to provide the necessary resources to advance self-help and development efforts. Gives educational presentations in local schools where refugees are present. **Telecommunication**

Services: electronic mail, ssolorzano@carecendc. org. **Formerly:** (1998) Central American Refugee Center.

18130 ■ Church World Service, Immigration and Refugee Program (CWS/IRP)

PO Box 968
Elkhart, IN 46515
Ph: (574)264-3102
Free: (800)297-1516
Fax: (574)262-0966
E-mail: info@churchworldservice.org
URL: http://www.churchworldservice.org/Immigration
Contact: Rev. John L. McCullough, Exec. Dir./CEO
Founded: 1946. **Description:** A program of Church World Service. Coordinates the resettlement in the U.S. of refugees from around the world through congregations and offices of participating denominations. Works for the protection of refugees seeking safe haven in the U.S. and abroad. **Telecommunication Services:** electronic mail, awalle@churchworld-service.org. **Affiliated With:** National Council of Churches of Christ in the U.S.A. **Publications:** *Refugee Resettlement Appeal*, periodic.

18131 ■ Haitian Refugee Center (HRC)

Address Unknown since 2006
Founded: 1974. **Staff:** 13. **Budget:** $750,000. **Description:** Provides free legal support and educational services to indigent Haitian aliens in their political asylum proceedings and in federal court litigation designed to protect and establish the basic constitutional and international legal rights of asylum seekers. Works to impede deportations and to publicize the plight of Haitian refugees. Documents U.S. Immigration and Naturalization Service abuses. Represents Haitian refugees in class action lawsuits resulting from violations involving political asylum. During the rule of the Duvalier family more than 1.5 million people have fled Haiti, according to the center. **Publications:** Publishes press releases, legal documents, and briefs.

18132 ■ Humanitarian Law Project - International Education Development

8124 W 3rd St., Ste.105
Los Angeles, CA 90048
Ph: (323)836-6316
Fax: (323)658-6306
E-mail: hlp@igc.org
URL: http://hlp.home.igc.org
Contact: David Lynn, Contact
Founded: 1980. **Staff:** 2. **Description:** Advocacy organization for the enforcement of international humanitarian and human rights law. Consultative status at the United Nations. **Formerly:** (1990) Archbishop Oscar Arnulfo Romero Relief Fund. **Publications:** *Flashpoints*, quarterly. Newsletter. Contains reports on advocacy work, interviews, and features. **Price:** free. **Circulation:** 2,000 ● Reports. Alternate Formats: online. **Conventions/Meetings:** quarterly meeting.

18133 ■ National Coalition for Haitian Rights (NCHR)

275 7th Ave.
New York, NY 10001
Ph: (212)337-0005
Fax: (212)741-8749
E-mail: info@nchr.org
URL: http://www.nchr.org
Contact: Jocelyn McCalla, Exec. Dir.
Founded: 1982. **Members:** 300. **Membership Dues:** individual/institutional, $25 (annual). **Staff:** 6. **Budget:** $600,000. **Languages:** Creole, English, French. **Description:** Seeks to promote the rights of Haitian refugees and Haitian-Americans under U.S. and international law. Advances respect for human rights, the rule of law, and support for civil and democratic society in Haiti. **Telecommunication Services:** electronic mail, jmccalla@nchr.org ● electronic mail, nchr@nchr.org. **Formerly:** (1982) National Coalition for Haitian Refugees; (1983) National Emergency Coalition for Haitian Refugees. **Publications:** Articles ● Reports. Covers human rights issues, specifically

children, immigration, relations between the police and the Haitian community in NY and the state of Haiti.

18134 ■ Refugee Council USA

3211 4th St. NE
Washington, DC 20017-1194
Ph: (202)541-5402 (202)541-5404
Fax: (202)722-8737
E-mail: info@rcusa.org
URL: http://www.refugeecouncilusa.org
Contact: Elizabeth Campbell PhD, Coor.
Multinational. Description: Represents the interests of individuals and U.S. non-governmental organizations focused on refugee protection. Advocates on issues affecting the protection and rights of refugees, asylum seekers, victims of trafficking and torture in the United States and across the world. Serves as the principal consultative forum for the national resettlement and processing agencies. **Publications:** Reports. Alternate Formats: online.

18135 ■ Refugee Women in Development (RefWID)

Robert S. Strauss Bldg.
1333 New Hampshire Ave. NW, No. 547
Washington, DC 20036-1564
Ph: (703)931-6442
E-mail: refwid@erols.com
URL: http://www.refwid.org
Contact: Sima Wali, Pres.
Founded: 1981. **Staff:** 2. **Budget:** $200,000. **Description:** Refugee women who have resettled in the U.S. Seeks to enable refugee women worldwide to attain social and economic independence and security through acculturation, economic security, ethnic preservation, and emotional support. Focuses on low-income working-age refugee women with limited skills and those suffering escape trauma. Sponsors education and research programs; advocates improvements in programs and services for refugee women. Develops program models, training curricula, and community involvement approaches. Programs included leadership development and capacity-building, human rights/protection, domestic violence prevention, and international representation. Priorities include conducting training in domestic violence prevention and intervention; developing practical programs models for leadership development and coalition building; carrying out education and advocacy with refugee and mainstream organizations, policymakers, and the general public. **Publications:** *Leadership Development Model for Refugee Women: A Preliminary Report.* **Price:** $15.00 ● *Leadership Development Model for Refugee Women: A Replication Guide.* Manual ● *The Production and Marketing of Ethnic Handcrafts in the U.S.*. Manual ● *Understanding Family Violence Within U.S. Refugee Communities: A Training Manual.*

18136 ■ South-East Asia Center (SEAC)

5120 N Broadway
Chicago, IL 60640
Ph: (773)989-6927
Fax: (773)989-4871
E-mail: seac1134@yahoo.com
URL: http://se-asiacenter.org
Contact: Peter R. Porr, Exec. Dir.
Founded: 1979. **Members:** 5,000. **Membership Dues:** individual, $65 (annual). **Staff:** 46. **Budget:** $2,000,000. **Languages:** Cantonese, English, Hindi, Mandarin, Tagalog, Thai, Vietnamese. **Description:** Assists Lao, Hmong, Cambodian, Vietnamese, and Chinese refugees and immigrants from Indochina as well as other non and limited English speaking immigrants from Asia, Africa, Eastern Europe and Latin America. Promotes the independence and well-being of immigrants and encourages cooperation and mutual understanding among all minorities. Strives to sensitize people to the plight of immigrants who do not speak English and advocates for sub-linguistic minorities who do not speak English. Promotes equitable allocation of private and public funding, without regard for language ability, educational background, or handicaps. Provides minority advocacy and interethnic/international bridge building

through national and international media; organizes legislative and administrative lobbying and legal action. Offers direct social services and English classes for new refugees. **Libraries: Type:** reference. **Holdings:** 300. **Subjects:** cross-cultural education. **Formerly:** (1986) Association of Chinese from Indochina.

18137 ■ United States Committee for Refugees and Immigrants (USCRI)

1717 Massachusetts Ave. NW, 2nd Fl.
Washington, DC 20036-2003
Ph: (202)347-3507
Fax: (202)347-3418
E-mail: uscr@irsa-uscr.org
URL: http://www.refugees.org
Contact: Lavinia Limon, Pres.
Founded: 1958. **Members:** 13,000. **Membership Dues:** donor, $25 (annual). **Staff:** 56. **Budget:** $21,179,769. **Multinational. Description:** Serves as an information and advocacy center seeking to communicate the plight of the world's millions of refugees, internally displaced persons and asylum seekers to the American people and to provide a non-governmental focal point for humanitarian concern in meeting the needs of a changing world refugee situation. Consults with national and international leaders. Maintains close liaison with voluntary organizations and supports specialized UN agencies working to alleviate refugee problems. Monitors hearings and legislation of the U.S. Congress and policies of the U.S. government on refugee affairs. Conducts research, compiles statistics and produces annual World Refugee Survey. Represents the following languages: Albanian, Amharic, Arabic, Armenian, Bamanakan, Bari, Bassa, Belarussian, Bosnian, Bulgarian, Burmese, Cambodian, Cantonese, Cebuano, Chiluba, Chinese, Creole, Czech/Czech-Slovak, Dari, Dinka, Farsi, French, German, Greek, Guragenya, Hindi, Hmong, Ilocano, Italian, Indonesian, Japanese, Khmer, Korean, Kru, Kuku, Kurdish, Laotian, Lingala, Macedonian, Mandarin, Norwegian, Oromifa, Pashtu, Polish, Punjabi, Portuguese, Romanian, Russian, Serbo-Croatian, Senshoto, Slovene, Slovak, Somali, Spanish, Swahili/Kiswahili, Tagalog, Thai, Turkish, Tigrinya, Urdu, Ukrainian, Vietnamese, Wollof. **Affiliated With:** American Civic Association; Immigration and Refugee Services of America; International Institute of Wisconsin. **Formerly:** (2006) United States Committee for Refugees. **Publications:** *Issue Papers.* Magazine. **Price:** $5.00 ● *Refugee Reports*, monthly. **Price:** $55.00/year in U.S.; $95.00/year outside U.S. **Advertising:** accepted ● *World Refugee Survey*, annual. Accepts sponsorship. **Price:** $25.00. Alternate Formats: CD-ROM ● Also publishes papers on specific refugee situations.

Religion

18138 ■ Center for Reduction of Religious-Based Conflict

649 5th Ave. S, Ste.201
Naples, FL 34102-6601
Ph: (239)821-4850
Fax: (239)263-2824
E-mail: centerrel@center2000.org
URL: http://www.center2000.org
Contact: Terry O. Trowbridge, Founder/Dir.
Founded: 1999. **Languages:** English, French, German, Italian, Portuguese, Spanish. **Multinational. Description:** Focuses on reducing religious-based conflict throughout the world. **Publications:** *The Astonishing Costs of Religious-based Conflict!*. Brochure. **Price:** $1.00 each, plus shipping and handling ● *Beyond Tolerance (Why Tolerance Cannot Solve The Problem Of Religious-Based Conflict And What The Real Answer Is)* (in Dutch, English, and French). Book. **Price:** $21.95. **Advertising:** accepted. Alternate Formats: online ● *Center Report*, annual. Describes conflicts and their causes. **Price:** $1.00 plus shipping and handling ● *Center Updates.* Brochures. **Price:** $1.00 each, plus shipping and handling ● *How Religious-Based Conflict in Far Away Places Affects YOU!*. Brochure. **Price:** $1.00 plus

shipping and handling ● *Religious-Based Violence Reaches America!*. Brochure. **Price:** $1.00 plus shipping and handling ● *What? Why? How? Who?*. Brochure. **Price:** $1.00 plus shipping and handling ● *Why is There Religious Conflict in the World?*. Brochure. **Price:** $1.00 plus shipping and handling.

18139 ■ Foundation for Traditional Values (FTV)
c/o Student Statesmanship Institute
PO Box 80108
Lansing, MI 48908
Ph: (517)321-6233
Free: (877)464-6388
Fax: (517)321-6077
E-mail: ssi@ssi-online.org
URL: http://www.ssi-online.org
Contact: James Muffett, Pres.
Founded: 1993. **Description:** Works to restore and affirm the Judeo-Christian values upon which America was established. Hosts seminars, Student Statesmanship Institute, summer program/on-site program, and high school leadership development.

Religious Freedom

18140 ■ Albanian Catholic Institute (ACI)
Univ. of San Francisco
650 Parker Ave.
San Francisco, CA 94118
Ph: (415)422-6966 (415)422-2188
Fax: (415)387-1867
URL: http://www.albanian-catholic-institute.org
Contact: Raymond Frost, Exec. Dir.
Founded: 1966. **Members:** 250. **Staff:** 2. **Budget:** $15,000. **Languages:** Albanian, English. **Description:** Promotes Albania's religious and cultural heritage. Gathers and disseminates information on the state of religion in Albania; conducts research on Albania's religious and cultural history; maintains collection of materials pertaining to Albanian history. Holds lectures; encourages the formation of prayer groups. Cooperates with religious groups in Albania. **Libraries: Type:** by appointment only. **Awards:** Skanderbeg Medal. **Frequency:** periodic. **Type:** medal. **Recipient:** for contribution to Albanian people and culture. **Formerly:** (1971) American-Albanian Catholic Charity; (1972) Albanian Catholic Information Center. **Publications:** *Albanian Catholic Bulletin*, annual. Journal. **Price:** donation. ISSN: 0272-7250. **Circulation:** 1,000. Alternate Formats: online ● *Ethnic, Religious, and Cultural*, annual. ISSN: 0272-7250. **Circulation:** 1,000 ● *The Fulfilled Promise*. Book. Contains account of religious persecution in Albania. ● *Sacrifice for Albania*. Booklet. **Conventions/Meetings:** periodic conference.

18141 ■ Appeal of Conscience Foundation (ACF)
119 W 57th St.
New York, NY 10019-2401
Ph: (212)535-5800
Fax: (212)628-2513
E-mail: info@appealofconscience.org
URL: http://www.appealofconscience.org
Contact: Rabbi Arthur Schneier, Pres./Founder
Founded: 1965. **Staff:** 3. **Description:** Interfaith coalition of business and religious leaders seeking religious freedom for men and women of all faiths throughout the world. Sponsors international exchange program between religious leaders and educators in the former Soviet Union, Bosnia and the former Yugoslavia, Eastern Europe, People's Republic of China, and Cuba. Conducts research programs. **Awards:** Appeal of Conscience Award. **Frequency:** annual. **Type:** recognition. **Telecommunication Services:** electronic mail, appealofconscience@msn.com. **Publications:** Report, periodic. **Conventions/Meetings:** annual dinner.

18142 ■ Becket Fund for Religious Liberty
1350 Connecticut Ave. NW, Ste.605
Washington, DC 20036
Ph: (202)955-0095

Fax: (202)955-0090
E-mail: khasson@becketfund.org
URL: http://www.becketfund.org
Contact: Kevin J. Hasson Esq., Founder/Chm.
Description: Promotes freedom of religion as a basic human right that no government may lawfully deny. **Publications:** Newsletter, monthly.

18143 ■ Center for Law and Religious Freedom (CLRF)
c/o Christian Legal Society
4208 Evergreen Ln., Ste.222
Annandale, VA 22003
Ph: (703)642-1070
Fax: (703)642-1075
E-mail: clshq@clsnet.org
URL: http://www.clsnet.org
Contact: Gregory S. Baylor, Dir.
Founded: 1976. **Staff:** 6. **Budget:** $560,000. **Description:** Advocacy division of the Christian Legal Society. Defends religious liberty and sanctity of human life through litigation, legislative advocacy, amicus curiae briefs, and educational efforts. **Publications:** *Defender*, quarterly. Newsletter. Included in center partnership. Alternate Formats: online ● *Religious Liberty News*, quarterly. Alternate Formats: online ● Annual Report, annual. Alternate Formats: online. **Conventions/Meetings:** annual conference ● regional meeting.

18144 ■ International Coalition for Religious Freedom (ICRF)
7777 Leesburg Pike, Ste.404 N
Falls Church, VA 22043
Ph: (703)790-1500
Fax: (703)790-5562
E-mail: icrf@aol.com
URL: http://www.religiousfreedom.com
Contact: Dan Fefferman, Exec. Dir.
Founded: 1984. **Members:** 10,000. **Staff:** 3. **Budget:** $150,000. **Description:** Americans of all faiths who are concerned about First Amendment freedoms. Seeks to preserve First Amendment rights protecting the free exercise of religion. Acts as a forum for the religious community of all denominations to effectively deal with the various levels and divisions of government on matters concerning the preservation of religious freedom. Works to educate civic leaders and the public concerning religious freedom; is concerned with matters such as zoning and licensing restrictions on ministries, the application of tax laws to churches and their ministries, curriculum content, and teacher certification in private religious schools. Offers advice to churches. Reports on legislative, judicial, and state and local activities affecting religious institutions. **Task Forces:** Religious Discrimination. **Formerly:** Committee for Religious Freedom; (2001) Coalition for Religious Freedom. **Publications:** *Assault on Religious Freedom* ● *Religious Freedom Alert*, 8-10/year. Newspaper. Provides news and commentary on religious freedom and other church/state issues. **Price:** included in membership dues; $15.00 /year for nonmembers. **Circulation:** 10,000. **Advertising:** accepted ● *Religious Freedom Report*, bimonthly. Newsletter. **Price:** $25.00/year in U.S.; $35.00/year outside U.S. Alternate Formats: online.

18145 ■ International Religious Liberty Association (IRLA)
c/o Carol Rasmussen, Admin. Asst.
12501 Old Columbia Pike
Silver Spring, MD 20904-6600
Ph: (301)680-6686
Fax: (301)680-6695
E-mail: info@irla.org
URL: http://www.irla.org
Contact: Dr. John Graz, Sec. Gen.
Founded: 1893. **Members:** 70,000. **Local Groups:** 5,000. **National Groups:** 70. **Languages:** Croatian, English, French, Indian Dialects, Italian, Japanese, Korean, Portuguese, Ukrainian. **Description:** Seeks to "publish and proclaim the principles of the universal right to religious liberty, promote respect for the religious rights and freedoms of all humankind, minorities as well as majorities, and secure worldwide

recognition of and respect for the basic human right to freedom of conscience and belief.". **Libraries: Type:** open to the public. **Holdings:** periodicals. **Subjects:** religious freedom. **Awards:** IRLA Award. **Frequency:** annual. **Type:** recognition. **Recipient:** for defense and promotion of religious freedom. **Formerly:** (1889) National Religious Liberty Association. **Publications:** *Fides et Libertas* (in English, French, German, Italian, Portuguese, and Spanish), annual. Journal. **Price:** $5.00. **Circulation:** 3,000. **Advertising:** accepted ● *Liberty*, bimonthly. **Circulation:** 150,000 ● *Religion and Human Rights: Basic Documents*. Book. Contains information on human rights. **Conventions/Meetings:** annual Festival of Religious Liberty, includes concert (exhibits) ● meeting ● meeting ● annual Regional Congress - meeting ● quinquennial World Congress on Religious Liberty.

18146 ■ Rutherford Institute (RI)
PO Box 7482
Charlottesville, VA 22906-7482
Ph: (434)978-3888
Fax: (434)978-1789
E-mail: staff@rutherford.org
URL: http://www.rutherford.org
Contact: John W. Whitehead, Founder/Pres.
Founded: 1982. **Staff:** 25. **Budget:** $2,600,000. **Description:** Provides legal and educational services without charge to individuals whose First Amendment freedoms have been threatened or infringed. Areas of primary concern are: freedom of speech; public, private, and home school related issues; parental rights and the expression of family values; freedom of religious institutions and individuals to abide by their beliefs without government interference; the sanctity of all human life; religious persecution in countries outside the United States; the Institute is named for Samuel B. Rutherford, a 17th century Scottish minister who wrote that kings were subject to the civil laws of their realms. **Publications:** *John W. Whitehead Newspaper Commentary Print Columns*, weekly ● *oldSpeak*. Magazine. Contains interviews, articles, and commentaries. Alternate Formats: online ● *Rutherford Newsletter*, quarterly. Alternate Formats: online ● Books ● Papers.

Renting and Leasing

18147 ■ National Alliance of HUD Tenants (NAHT)
42 Seaverns Ave.
Boston, MA 02130
Ph: (617)267-9564
Fax: (617)522-4857
E-mail: naht@saveourhomes.org
URL: http://www.saveourhomes.org
Contact: Carol Driscoll, Pres.
Founded: 1991. **Membership Dues:** associate ($25,000), $50 (annual) ● associate ($25-100,000), $100 (annual) ● associate (over $100,000), $200 (annual) ● tenant association, $25 (annual). **State Groups:** 32. **Description:** Works to preserve affordable housing, protect tenant rights, and promote tenant ownership and control. **Publications:** *Tenants' Rights Manual* ● Newsletter. **Conventions/Meetings:** annual conference ● Save Our Homes Day - meeting.

Reproductive Rights

18148 ■ Catholics for a Free Choice (CFFC)
1436 U St. NW, Ste.301
Washington, DC 20009-3997
Ph: (202)986-6093
Fax: (202)332-7995
E-mail: cffc@catholicsforchoice.org
URL: http://www.catholicsforchoice.org
Contact: Frances Kissling, Pres.
Founded: 1973. **Staff:** 20. **Budget:** $3,500,000. **Languages:** English, Spanish. **Description:** Seeks to shape and advance sexual and reproductive ethics that are based on justice, reflect a commitment to women's well-being, and respect and affirm the moral

capacity of women and men to make sound and responsible decisions about their lives. **Libraries: Type:** reference. **Telecommunication Services:** electronic mail, media@catholicsforchoice.org. **Publications:** *Conscience: The Newsjournal of Catholic Opinion*, quarterly. Serves as a forum for dialogue on ethical questions related to human reproduction; contains book reviews. **Price:** free to donors; $15.00 in U.S.; $25.00 outside U.S. ISSN: 0740-6835. **Circulation:** 15,000. **Advertising:** accepted. Alternate Formats: online ● Monographs. **Conventions/Meetings:** periodic meeting (exhibits).

18149 ■ Center for Reproductive Rights

120 Wall St.
New York, NY 10005
Ph: (917)637-3600
Fax: (917)637-3666
E-mail: info@reprorights.org
URL: http://www.reproductiverights.org
Contact: Ms. Nancy Northup, Pres.

Founded: 1992. **Staff:** 70. **Budget:** $6,500,000. **Languages:** English, French, Spanish. **Description:** Reproductive rights attorneys and activists. Dedicated to securing women's reproductive freedom in the U.S. and around the world. Litigates majority of cases challenging restrictions on women's reproductive health choices, including bans on Medicaid coverage for abortions and mandatory delays for women seeking abortions. Domestic efforts also focus on other aspects of health law, including the rights of pregnant women. International program seeks recognition of health and choice as human rights and encourages U.S. policies that promote women's health and choice as human rights. Disseminates information on maintaining women's reproductive freedom to policy makers, governmental agencies, private institutions, medical and health organizations, and the public. Maintains Speakers' Bureau. **Convention/Meeting:** none. **Libraries: Type:** reference. **Subjects:** reproductive rights. **Formerly:** (2003) Center for Reproductive Law and Policy. **Publications:** *Body and Soul*, periodic. Video. Features the testimonies of Romani women in Slovakia. **Price:** $10.00/copy ● *Legal Grounds: Reproductive and Sexual Rights in African Commonwealth Courts*, periodic. Book. Provides information about decisions and gender-relevant jurisprudence of national courts. **Price:** $15.00/copy. Alternate Formats: online ● *Reproductive Freedom News*, monthly. Newsletter. **Price:** free. **Circulation:** 11,500 ● Papers, periodic. Includes law to reproductive freedom. Alternate Formats: online ● Articles, periodic. Contains discussion and debate on issues of women's reproductive health and rights. ● Also publishes fact sheets, analyses, human rights reports, and special alerts.

18150 ■ NARAL Pro-Choice America

1156 15th St. NW, Ste.700
Washington, DC 20005
Ph: (202)973-3000 (202)973-3018
Fax: (202)973-3096
E-mail: membership@prochoiceamerica.org
URL: http://www.prochoiceamerica.org
Contact: Nancy Keenan, Pres.

Founded: 1969. **Members:** 400,000. **Membership Dues:** minimum, $5 (annual). **Staff:** 40. **Budget:** $4,000,000. **State Groups:** 29. **Description:** Seeks to guarantee every woman the right to make personal decisions regarding a full range of reproductive choices, including preventing unintended pregnancy, bearing healthy children, and choosing legal abortion. Recognizes that genuine reproductive freedom requires the ability to make informed, responsible decisions about sexuality, contraception, abortion, childbirth, and childrearing. **Divisions:** Legal/Research; Political. **Absorbed:** (1974) Abortion Rights Association. **Formerly:** National Abortion Rights Action League; (1973) National Association for Repeal of Abortion Laws; (2003) National Abortion and Reproductive Action League. **Publications:** Newsletter, monthly. Provides updates on legislation regarding abortion and reproductive freedom. **Price:** included in membership dues. **Circulation:** 270,000. Alternate Formats: online.

18151 ■ Religious Coalition for Reproductive Choice (RCRC)

1025 Vermont Ave. NW, Ste.1130
Washington, DC 20005
Ph: (202)628-7700
Fax: (202)628-7716
E-mail: info@rcrc.org
URL: http://www.rcrc.org
Contact: Rev. Carlton Veazey, Pres./CEO

Founded: 1973. **Members:** 39. **Staff:** 18. **State Groups:** 25. **National Groups:** 39. **Description:** Works to educate the media and public that mainstream religions- United Methodist, Presbyterian, Jewish, United Church of Christ, Episcopalian, Unitarian Universalist, and others- support reproductive options, including abortion, family planning, sexuality education, and health care, and oppose antiabortion violence. Works to mobilize pro-choice religious people and clergy to counsel families facing unintended pregnancies, support reproductive health clinics and their staff, and promote pro-choice policy making at the state and federal levels. **Programs:** Black Church Initiative "Keeping It Real"; Breaking the Silence; Clergy for Choice; Latino Initiative; Seminarians for Choice; Spiritual Youth for Reproductive Freedom. **Affiliated With:** Oklahoma Religious Coalition for Reproductive Choice. **Formerly:** (1993) Religious Coalition for Abortion Rights. **Publications:** *Abortion and the Holocaust: Twisting the Language* ● *Faith and Choices*, quarterly. Newsletter. Alternate Formats: online ● *RCRC National Report*, bimonthly. Newsletter. **Price:** included in membership dues. **Circulation:** 60,000. Alternate Formats: online ● Also publishes a fact sheet series and an educational series. **Conventions/Meetings:** annual conference (exhibits).

18152 ■ Republicans for Choice (RFC)

205 S Whiting St., Ste.260
Alexandria, VA 22304
Ph: (703)212-0890
E-mail: gop4choice@rcn.com
URL: http://www.republicansforchoice.com
Contact: Ann Stone, Chair

Founded: 1990. **Members:** 200,000. **Membership Dues:** regular, $35 (annual). **Staff:** 5. **Budget:** $2,000,000. **Description:** Republicans who support a woman's right to choose abortion. Seeks to change the Republican Party platform to reflect the views of pro-choice party members. Supports pro-choice Republican candidates at all levels in primaries and general elections. Maintains the Republicans for Choice Emergency Task Force to counteract pro-life pressure at the state level. **Publications:** *The Choice News*, quarterly. Newsletter. **Price:** free. **Circulation:** 200,000.

18153 ■ Voters for Choice/Friends of Family Planning (VFC)

Address Unknown since 2007

Founded: 1984. **Description:** Independent, bipartisan political committee. Seeks election and reelection of candidates to federal and state office who support the pro-choice position concerning abortion. Provides technical assistance and consulting services for favored candidates; offers direct financial contributions and services. **Formed by Merger of:** Friends of Family Planning; Voters for Choice. **Publications:** *Winning With Choice*.

Republican Party

18154 ■ College Republican National Committee (CRNC)

600 Pennsylvania Ave. SE, Ste.215
Washington, DC 20003
Free: (888)765-3564
Fax: (202)608-1429
E-mail: info@crnc.org
URL: http://www.crnc.org
Contact: Amanda Kathryn Hydro, Exec. Dir.

Founded: 1892. **Members:** 120,000. **Staff:** 7. **State Groups:** 51. **Local Groups:** 1,148. **Description:** Acts as the national coordinating organization for the

Republican youth movement. Works toward the election of Republican candidates as well as the communication of a conservative message to college students. Encourages the individual chapters to organize lectures, debates, and seminars in practical politics; distributes material in the form of manuals, posters, flyers, and buttons, on the organization; provides training for members; acts as a resource for the state federations. **Projects:** Field Program; Fieldman Training. **Affiliated With:** Republican National Committee. **Formerly:** (1964) College Service Committee of the Young Republican National Federation. **Publications:** *College Republican Chapter Manual*. Alternate Formats: online ● Also publishes issue-oriented packages on student-oriented topics and other informational and educational material. **Conventions/Meetings:** College Republican National Convention (exhibits) ● annual meeting.

18155 ■ Log Cabin Republicans (LCR)

1901 Pennsylvania Ave. NW, Ste.902
Washington, DC 20006
Ph: (202)347-5306
Fax: (202)347-5224
E-mail: admin@logcabin.org
URL: http://online.logcabin.org
Contact: Tim Schoeffler, Chm.

Founded: 1978. **Members:** 10,000. **Membership Dues:** student, $25 (annual) ● general, $60 (annual) ● inclusion team, $100 (annual). **Staff:** 6. **Budget:** $500,000. **Local Groups:** 43. **Description:** Partisan organization representing gay and lesbian individuals. Operates at the grass roots level by supporting Republican candidates. Maintains a Washington office with staff devoted to lobbying, candidate tracking, and policy development. **Formerly:** United Republicans for Equality and Privacy; (1995) Log Cabin Federation. **Publications:** *Cabin Talk*, bimonthly. Newsletter ● *Inclusion Wins*. Newsletter. **Price:** included in membership dues. Alternate Formats: online. **Conventions/Meetings:** annual convention, for grass roots activists (exhibits).

18156 ■ National Federation of Republican Women (NFRW)

124 N Alfred St.
Alexandria, VA 22314
Ph: (703)548-9688
Fax: (703)548-9836
E-mail: mail@nfrw.org
URL: http://www.nfrw.org
Contact: Beverly Davis, Pres.

Founded: 1938. **Members:** 95,000. **Membership Dues:** national associate, $50 (annual) ● student associate, $15 (annual). **Staff:** 10. **State Groups:** 52. **Local Groups:** 2,400. **Description:** Provides an organization through which women who share the principles of the Republican Party can join in Republican activities. Distributes political educational materials. Recruits and supports qualified and electable Republican candidates. Encourages more women to seek public office and to provide them with campaign expertise through Campaign Management Schools across the country. Provides research material and legislative information to federation members. **Awards:** Betty Rendel Scholarship. **Frequency:** annual. **Type:** scholarship. **Recipient:** for students majoring in political science ● Kabis Internship. **Frequency:** annual. **Type:** scholarship ● National Pathfinder's Scholarship. **Frequency:** annual. **Type:** scholarship. **Recipient:** for undergraduate or graduate student focusing on substance abuse or related fields. **Committees:** Americanism; Campaign; Candidate Recruitment; Community Relations; Fundraising; Legislation and Research; Membership; Minority Outreach; Party Building; Public Relations. **Formerly:** National Federation of Women's Republican Clubs. **Publications:** *Campaign Management School Manual*. Book. Provides information on how to put together a winning campaign. **Price:** $25.00 ● *Capital Connection*, weekly. Newsletter. Features updates from the White House, Congress and the Republican National Committee. Alternate Formats: online ● *NFRW Member Handbook*. Provides basic information on the NFRW's history, events, programs and communications systems. **Price:** included in membership dues ● *The Republican Woman*, 3/year. Magazine. Contains articles on the Federation and the Republican Party, administrative policies, and legislative activities in Congress. **Price:** included in membership dues; $15.00 /year for nonmembers. **Circulation:** 120,000. **Conventions/Meetings:** annual board meeting and conference ● biennial convention (exhibits).

18157 ■ National Republican Club (NRC)
300 1st St. SE
Washington, DC 20003
Ph: (202)484-4590
Fax: (202)479-9110
Contact: Stan Lawson, Gen. Mgr.
Founded: 1951. **Members:** 4,000. **Description:** Serves as dining and social club for men and women interested in the Republican Party, locally and nationally. **Committees:** Special Events. **Also Known As:** Capitol Hill Club. **Publications:** *Capitol Hill Club Newsletter*, monthly. Includes current events and membership activities. **Price:** free, for members only. **Circulation:** 5,000.

18158 ■ National Republican Congressional Committee (NRCC)
320 1st St. SE
Washington, DC 20003
Ph: (202)479-7000 (202)479-7020
Fax: (202)863-0693
E-mail: website@nrcc.org
URL: http://nrcc.org
Contact: Hon. Sally Vastola, Exec. Dir.
Founded: 1866. **Members:** 229. **Staff:** 50. **Description:** Represents Republican members of Congress; each Republican member of Congress is a member of the Committee. Seeks to elect more Republicans to the U.S. House. Issues materials; produces radio and television ads; provides field representatives to travel to congressional districts; sponsors campaign training seminars for candidates and staff. **Divisions:** Administration; Campaign; Communications; Executive; Finance; Liaison; Research.

18159 ■ National Republican Senatorial Committee (NRSC)
c/o Ronald Reagan Republican Center
425 2nd St. NE
Washington, DC 20002
Ph: (202)675-6000
E-mail: webmaster@gopsenators.com
URL: http://www.nrsc.org
Contact: Sen. Bill Frist, Exec. Dir.
Founded: 1916. **Description:** Republican senators and contributors to the National Republican Senatorial Committee (see separate entry). Aims to coordinate on the elections of Republican senatorial candidates. Provides candidates with public relations services and direct and "in kind" financial assistance. (In kind assistance involves indirect contributions to candidates' campaigns.) Sponsors National Republican Senatorial Inner Circle for contributors of $1000 or more.

18160 ■ National Teen Age Republican Headquarters (TARS)
PO Box 1896
Manassas, VA 20108-1896
Ph: (703)368-4214
Fax: (703)368-0830
E-mail: tars@teenagerepublicans.org
URL: http://www.teenagerepublicans.org
Contact: Barbara Wells, Natl. Dir.
Founded: 1965. **Members:** 100,000. **Staff:** 5. **State Groups:** 50. **Description:** High school students. Promotes involvement of teenagers in the U.S. political process. Conducts educational programs; sponsors Speaker's Bureau; conducts community service projects. **Awards:** Outstanding State TAR Federation in Nation. **Frequency:** annual. **Type:** recognition ● Outstanding TAR Advisor in Nation. **Frequency:** annual. **Type:** recognition ● Outstanding TAR Club in Nation. **Frequency:** annual. **Type:** recognition ● Outstanding TAR in Nation. **Frequency:** annual. **Type:** recognition. **Sections:** STARS. **Publications:** *TARGET*, quarterly. Newsletter. Includes activities of

Teen Age Republicans. **Price:** free. **Circulation:** 100,000 ● Manual ● Papers. **Conventions/Meetings:** annual National TAR Leadership Conference - every summer.

18161 ■ Republican Jewish Coalition (RJC)
50 F St. NW, Ste.100
Washington, DC 20001
Ph: (202)638-6688
Fax: (202)638-6694
E-mail: rjc@rjchq.org
URL: http://www.rjchq.org
Contact: Matthew Brooks, Exec. Dir.
Founded: 1985. **Members:** 24,000. **Membership Dues:** $50 (annual). **Staff:** 20. **Local Groups:** 43. **Description:** Seeks to inform the Jewish community about the Republican Party as it speaks to their needs; seeks to make Senators, Congresspeople, and administration officials aware of the needs and concerns of American Jews. Serves as a clearinghouse of information regarding the Republican Party's position on a wide variety of issues. **Formerly:** (2000) National Jewish Coalition. **Publications:** *RJC Bulletin*, 5/year. Newsletter. Includes reports on world events, Jewish issues, and Republican politics. **Price:** included in membership dues. **Circulation:** 7,000. **Conventions/Meetings:** annual conference ● periodic conference.

18162 ■ Republican Liberty Caucus (RLC)
44 Summerfield St.
Thousand Oaks, CA 91360
Ph: (805)493-4332
Free: (866)752-5423
E-mail: headquarters@rlc.org
URL: http://www.rlc.org
Contact: Mr. William Westmiller, Chm.
Founded: 1987. **Members:** 1,800. **Membership Dues:** regular, $30 (annual) ● premium, $50 (annual) ● sustaining, $100 (annual) ● patron, $250 (annual) ● associate, $500 (annual). **Staff:** 2. **Budget:** $25,000. **State Groups:** 38. **Description:** Libertarian and other liberty-minded Republicans; interested others. Works within the Republican Party to promote individual rights, limited government, and free enterprise. Conducts or assists with political campaigns of Republican candidates whose aims are similar through the RLCUSA-PAC. Operates speakers' bureau, website services, e-groups, newsletter; organizes public forums, demonstrations, and debates. **Libraries: Type:** open to the public. **Holdings:** archival material, articles, periodicals. **Subjects:** libertarian politics. **Awards:** Legislator of the Year. **Frequency:** biennial. **Type:** recognition. **Computer Services:** database, Liberty Index Ratings ● online services, news, organizing materials, Liberty Watch. **Additional Websites:** http://www.republicanlibertycaucus.org, http://www.republicanliberty.org. **Boards:** Academic Advisors; Legislative Advisory. **Publications:** *Republican Liberty*, bimonthly. Newsletter. Includes Libertarian survey of U.S. Congress voting records, interviews with elected Libertarian Republicans, and election coverage and results. **Price:** included in membership dues; $18.00 /year for nonmembers. **Circulation:** 4,000. Alternate Formats: online. **Conventions/Meetings:** biennial convention, held in conjunction with the Republican National Convention during presidential election years; held in various locations during off-election years (exhibits).

18163 ■ Republican Mainstream Committee (RMC)
7620 W 21st Ave.
Kennewick, WA 99338-9163
Ph: (509)528-1265
Free: (877)762-5646
Fax: (202)546-2370
E-mail: info@washingtonmainstream.org
URL: http://www.washingtonmainstream.org
Contact: Alex Hays, Exec. Dir.
Founded: 1984. **Members:** 10,000. **Membership Dues:** $25 (annual). **Staff:** 3. **State Groups:** 12. **Description:** Centrist Republican political committee. Encourages grass roots outreach and organization by moderate and progressive Republicans. Maintains speakers' bureau and placement service. **Computer**

Services: database ● mailing lists. **Publications:** *Progress*, bimonthly. Newsletter. **Price:** $50.00/year. Alternate Formats: online. **Conventions/Meetings:** annual conference.

18164 ■ Republican Majority for Choice (RMC)
1660 L St. NW, Ste.609
Washington, DC 20036-5676
Ph: (202)887-4786
Free: (877)GOP-CHOICE
Fax: (202)887-4994
E-mail: choice@gopchoice.org
URL: http://www.gopchoice.org
Contact: Kellie Rose Ferguson, Exec. Dir.
Founded: 1989. **Membership Dues:** student, senior, $15 (annual) ● supporter, $25 (annual) ● friend, $50 (annual) ● patron, $100 (annual) ● benefactor, $500 (annual) ● GOP Choice Club, $1,000 (annual) ● millennium, $5,000 (annual). **Description:** Works for the Republican principles of individual liberty, freedom and privacy. Supports the Roe vs. Wade Supreme Court ruling of 1973; promotes reproductive health as policy rather than politics; encourages personal responsibility through family planning initiatives; and maintains individual liberty for all women by ensuring access to reproductive health care, regardless of income. Strives to educate and promote the pro-choice position among fellow Republicans, impact legislation at the state and federal levels, influence Republican Party platforms on reproductive health issues, remove anti-choice language from party platforms, and assist in the campaigns of pro-choice Republicans, through its PAC. **Formerly:** (2003) Republican Coalition for Choice; (2005) Republican Pro-Choice Coalition. **Publications:** *Legislative Voting Guide*, annual ● *Voice For Choice*, quarterly. Newsletter. Alternate Formats: online ● Annual Report, annual. **Conventions/Meetings:** board meeting, national - 3/year ● periodic board meeting, state chapter ● annual conference.

18165 ■ Republican National Committee (RNC)
310 1st St. SE
Washington, DC 20003
Ph: (202)863-8500
Fax: (202)863-8820
E-mail: info@gop.com
Contact: Jim Nicholson, Chm.
Founded: 1856. **Members:** 165. **Staff:** 250. **Budget:** $78,000,000. **State Groups:** 55. **Description:** Authorized and recreated every four years by the Republican National Nominating Convention. Under the direction of the Chairman, provides support activities to Republican administrations, members of Congress, governors, state and local office holders, and Republican campaigns at all levels. Operates a field staff to advise state and local party organizations and campaigns; conducts research on current issues; assists the states in their own research and computer operations; seeks to facilitate the drawing of equitable lines in the redistricting and reapportionment process resulting from the decennial census. Maintains files of biographies of major party leaders, historical information, and election statistics. Conducts political education programs. **Divisions:** Communications; Finance; Grassroots; Member Relations; Network Services; Political. **Publications:** *Rising Tide*, quarterly. Magazine ● *Roster*, monthly ● Also publishes pamphlets. **Conventions/Meetings:** semiannual meeting - usually January and July.

18166 ■ Republican National Hispanic Assembly of the United States (RNHA)
1717 Pennsylvania Ave. NW, Ste.650
Washington, DC 20006
Ph: (202)558-5477 (202)281-0891
Fax: (202)903-0933
E-mail: info@rnha.org
URL: http://www.rnha.org
Contact: Pedro Celis PhD, Natl. Chm.
Founded: 1974. **Members:** 11,000. **Membership Dues:** regular, $30 (annual) ● honorary (student, senior citizen), $10 (annual) ● Eagle, $100 (annual). **Staff:** 6. **State Groups:** 20. **Languages:** English,

Spanish. **Description:** Republicans of Hispanic descent. Aims to: educate Hispanics about the political process in the U.S; register voters; recruit Hispanics for the Republican Party. Provides leadership training programs for Hispanics to serve in positions within the Republican Party. Provides recruitment of Hispanic candidates running for political office. Operates speakers' bureau. Serves as an auxiliary of the Republican National Committee with a seat on the GOP National Executive Committee. **Awards:** Hispanic Heritage Leadership Eagle Award. **Frequency:** annual. **Type:** recognition. **Recipient:** based on recommendation. **Computer Services:** database. **Telecommunication Services:** electronic mail, chairman@rnha.org. **Affiliated With:** Republican National Committee. **Publications:** *The American Hispanic*, bimonthly. Newsletter. **Circulation:** 10,000 ● *RNHA Leadership Directory*, annual. **Conventions/Meetings:** annual conference.

18167 ■ Republican Presidential Task Force (RPTF)
Ronald Reagan Republican Center
425 2nd St. NE
Washington, DC 20002
Ph: (202)675-6000 (202)224-6342
E-mail: webmaster@gopsenators.com
Contact: Sen. Elizabeth Dole, Chair
Founded: 1981. **Description:** Serves as a task force of the National Republican Senatorial Committee (see separate entry).

18168 ■ Ripon Society (RS)
1300 L St. NW, Ste.900
Washington, DC 20005
Ph: (202)216-1008
E-mail: info@riponsociety.org
URL: http://www.riponsoc.org
Contact: Hon. Richard Kessler, Pres.
Founded: 1962. **Members:** 10,000. **Membership Dues:** regular, $35 (annual) ● fellow, $75 (annual) ● patron, $250 (annual). **Staff:** 3. **Budget:** $300,000. **State Groups:** 5. **Description:** Moderate Republicans primarily from business, professional, and academic communities. Urges the Republican Party to: adopt a moderate, middle of the road course "since it offers the greatest possibility for constructive achievement"; take a lead in forging a more flexible American foreign policy; develop new initiatives and programs to solve the nation's domestic and urban crises; promote individual civil liberties and equal rights for all under the law; encourage economic opportunity through the expansion of the free enterprise system. Formulates and disseminates Republican positions on domestic and foreign political issues; prepares research papers. Maintains Congressional Advisory Board. (Society is named after Ripon, WI, the birthplace of the Republican Party.). **Awards:** Rough Rider Awards. **Frequency:** annual. **Type:** recognition. **Recipient:** for public office holders. **Publications:** *A Newer World* ● *The Ripon Forum*, bimonthly. Magazine. Covers issues of environmental concern, individual and civil rights, and foreign policy. Contains personality profiles, editorials, and book reviews. **Price:** included in membership dues. ISSN: 0035-5526. **Circulation:** 10,000. **Advertising:** accepted. Alternate Formats: online ● Papers ● Also publishes booklets statement. **Conventions/Meetings:** annual conference.

18169 ■ Women's National Republican Club (WNRC)
3 W 51st St.
New York, NY 10019
Ph: (212)582-5454
E-mail: membership@wnrc.org
URL: http://www.wnrc.org
Contact: Mrs. Evelyn Angevine Silla, Pres.
Founded: 1921. **Members:** 900. **Membership Dues:** resident/suburban, $660 (annual) ● non-resident, $358 (annual) ● junior (ages 18-35), junior associate (ages 18-35), $330 (annual) ● non-resident junior, non-resident junior associate, $275 (annual) ● associate, $605 (annual) ● non-resident associate, non-resident senior, $358 (annual) ● senior (over 65 years of age), senior associate, $468 (annual) ● corporate,

$2,200 (annual) ● life, $10,000. **Staff:** 30. **Description:** Women interested in promoting the programs of the Republican Party and creating interest in political participation. Conducts educational, cultural, social, and political programs. Maintains the Henrietta Wells Livermore School of Politics, which provides political training and education on city, state, national, and international affairs. Operates speakers' bureau. **Libraries: Type:** reference. **Awards:** Distinguished Political Service Award. **Frequency:** annual. **Type:** recognition ● Republican Woman of the Year Award. **Frequency:** annual. **Type:** recognition. **Committees:** Calvin Coolidge Memorial Library; Henrietta Wells Livermore School of Politics; International Affairs; Juniors; Public Relations; Special Events. **Publications:** *Guidon*, quarterly. Newsletter. **Conventions/Meetings:** semiannual meeting - always January and April in New York City.

18170 ■ Young Republican National Federation (YRNF)
PO Box 15293
Washington, DC 20003
Ph: (202)608-1417
E-mail: info@yrnf.com
URL: http://www.yrnf.com
Contact: Jon Woodard, Exec. Dir.
Founded: 1931. **Members:** 156,000. **Staff:** 3. **Regional Groups:** 6. **State Groups:** 50. **Local Groups:** 1,027. **Description:** Men and women between the ages of 18 and 40. Provides the opportunity for young people who are interested in good government under Constitutional principles to become engaged in an active political program. Seeks to further the aims of the Republican Party among young people and to train future candidates, party leaders, and citizens. Works to uphold the principles of individual liberty, free enterprise, and limited and responsible government. **Awards:** Outstanding Local Chapter. **Frequency:** biennial. **Type:** recognition ● Outstanding YR State Chapter. **Frequency:** biennial. **Type:** recognition ● Young Republican Man of the Year. **Frequency:** biennial. **Type:** recognition ● Young Republican Woman of the Year. **Frequency:** biennial. **Type:** recognition. **Computer Services:** Mailing lists, of members. **Publications:** *Executive Committee Memos*, semiannual. Newsletter. **Advertising:** accepted ● *Young Republic*, quarterly. Newsletter. Alternate Formats: online ● Also publishes position papers, platforms, and resolutions. **Conventions/Meetings:** annual Young Republican Leadership Conference (exhibits) ● biennial Young Republican National Convention - convention and conference (exhibits).

Rescue

18171 ■ International Committee for the Rescue of KAL 007 Survivors
408 Parkwood Pl.
Niceville, FL 32578
Ph: (617)780-5088
E-mail: info@rescue007.org
URL: http://www.rescue007.org
Contact: Bert Schlossberg, International Dir.
Multinational. Description: Strives to provide emotional support to victims, families, and survivors of Korean Air Lines (KAL) flight 007 incident. Seeks to uncover and disseminate the truth about the KAL 007 incident. Works to rescue and return home the KAL 007 incident survivors. **Telecommunication Services:** electronic mail, webmaster@rescue007. org ● electronic mail, bert.schlossberg@rescue007. org.

Research

18172 ■ Committee for the Advancement of Stem Cell Research (CASCR)
300 Garden City Plz., Ste.234
Garden City, NY 11530
Ph: (516)294-8607

Fax: (516)294-8623
URL: http://www.cascr.org
Contact: Carl P. McNulty, Co-Exec.Dir.
Description: Supports politicians who support regenerative medical research, which includes all branches of adult stem cell research and all branches of embryonic stem cell research. Ensures that stem cell research is represented in the US legislature.

Retirement

18173 ■ Alliance for Retired Americans
815 16th St. NW, 4th Fl.
Washington, DC 20006
Ph: (202)637-5399
Free: (800)333-7212
E-mail: arawebadmin@retiredamericans.org
URL: http://www.retiredamericans.org
Contact: George J. Kourpias, Pres.
Founded: 2001. **Membership Dues:** individual/couple, $10 (annual). **Description:** Older and retired Americans; members of participating unions affiliated with the AFL-CIO and members of the former National Council of Senior Citizens are automatically members. Advocates a universal health care policy for all Americans; aims to protect and expand Social Security, Medicare, and Medicaid; promotes prescription drug benefit to Medicare; strives to expand job opportunities for people older than 50; aims to improve Older Americans Act programs and financing; clean up political campaign financing; gain patients' rights; and fights for workers' rights. Offers discount program for members.

18174 ■ Alliance for Worker Retirement Security (AWRS)
c/o Derrick A. Max, Exec. Dir.
1331 Pennsylvania Ave. NW, Ste.600
Washington, DC 20004-1751
Ph: (202)637-3453
Fax: (202)637-3182
E-mail: dmax@awrs.org
URL: http://www.retiresecure.org
Contact: Derrick A. Max, Exec. Dir.
Founded: 1998. **Description:** Seeks to reform Social Security so that every American worker has the opportunity to create a secure source of wealth for retirement. Represents the interests of organizations representing large and small employers, corporations and other diverse groups. **Computer Services:** Mailing lists.

Right to Life

18175 ■ American Association of Pro Life Obstetricians and Gynecologists (AAPLOG)
339 River Ave.
Holland, MI 49423
Ph: (616)546-2639
E-mail: info@aaplog.org
URL: http://www.aaplog.org
Contact: Elizabeth Shadigian MD, Pres.
Founded: 1973. **Members:** 2,500. **Membership Dues:** resident, $10 (annual) ● active, retired, $100 (annual). **Staff:** 2. **Regional Groups:** 9. **Description:** Obstetricians and gynecologists who oppose abortions, perform no abortions, and take no part in arranging abortions. Seeks "to draw attention to the value of all human life from the moment of conception." Supports programs that assist unwed mothers who choose to have their babies. Conducts research on complications experienced by women who have had legal abortions and compiles statistics on illnesses and deaths; studies the long-range effects of abortion on fertility and reproductive capability. Offers postgraduate course on the subject of care and concern for women experiencing mental and physical trauma after abortions. **Awards: Type:** recognition. **Recipient:** to congresspersons and physicians who have demonstrated strong support for the protection of human life beginning with conception. **Computer Services:** database, list of area pro-life OB/GYNs when requested. **Publications:** Directory, triennial ●

Newsletter, quarterly. **Conventions/Meetings:** annual conference ● annual symposium, with speakers.

18176 ■ American Association of Pro-Life Pediatricians (AAPLP)
3135 W 111th St.
Chicago, IL 60655
Ph: (773)233-8000
Fax: (708)448-8085
Contact: E. F. Diamond MD, Pres.
Founded: 1978. **Members:** 620. **Membership Dues:** $5 (annual). **State Groups:** 50. **Description:** Members of the American Academy of Pediatrics (see separate entry) interested in issues such as abortion, infanticide, and definition of death. Coordinates member activities; publicizes political trends; educates members. **Affiliated With:** American Academy of Pediatrics; World Federation of Doctors Who Respect Human Life (United States Section). **Publications:** *AAPLP Newsletter*, quarterly ● *The Large Family*. Book ● *Monograph on Fetal Pain* ● *This Curette For Hire*. Book. **Conventions/Meetings:** annual conference ● semiannual meeting and seminar, held in conjunction with AAP.

18177 ■ Center for Bio-Ethical Reform (CBR)
PO Box 219
Lake Forest, CA 92609
Ph: (949)206-0600
Free: (800)848-5683
E-mail: cbr@cbrinfo.org
URL: http://www.abortionno.org
Contact: Gregg Cunningham Esq., Exec. Dir.
Founded: 1990. **Description:** Works "to establish prenatal justice and the right to life for the unborn, the disabled, the infirm, the aged and all vulnerable individuals, through a strictly non-violent agenda". **Awards:** Internships. **Type:** fellowship. **Publications:** *In Perspective*. Newsletter. **Conventions/Meetings:** seminar.

18178 ■ Children of the Rosary (CoR)
PO Box 1028
Scottsdale, AZ 85252-1028
Ph: (480)994-4008
Fax: (715)643-2133
E-mail: cor@childrenoftherosary.org
URL: http://www.childrenoftherosary.org
Contact: Katherine Sabelko, Founder
Founded: 1990. **Description:** Works to educate people about abortion, the pre-born child and the "disclosure of lies of the pro-choice agenda". **Publications:** *CoR Newsletter* ● Newsletter. Alternate Formats: online ● Brochure.

18179 ■ Democrats for Life of America (DFLA)
601 Pennsylvania Ave. NW, South Bldg., Ste.900
Washington, DC 20004
Ph: (202)220-3066
Fax: (202)638-6957
E-mail: information@democratsforlife.org
URL: http://www.democratsforlife.org
Contact: Kristen Day, Exec. Dir.
Membership Dues: charter, $100 (annual) ● individual, $25 (annual) ● senior citizen/student, $15 (annual). **Description:** Members of the Democratic Party who value the life of the unborn child. Works towards the legal protection of the unborn. Elects pro-life Democrats to office and supports people in office with a wide variety of functions.

18180 ■ Dentists for Life (DL)
PO Box 1350
Stafford, VA 22555
Ph: (540)659-4171
Fax: (540)659-2586
E-mail: info@dentistsforlife.org
URL: http://www.all.org/dentists/index.htm
Contact: Dr. Craig Bozzacco DDS, Pres.
Founded: 1989. **Members:** 100. **Membership Dues:** active, $25 (annual). **Local Groups:** 20. **Description:** Dentists opposed to abortion, euthanasia, and "infanticide." Seeks to organize dentists to oppose abortion and euthanasia. Provides free dental care, housing, and other support to unwed expectant moth-

ers. Conducts educational programs to raise public awareness of health care facilities and physicians that perform abortions. Collaborates with other groups pursuing similar goals. Participates in charitable programs; makes available children's services. **Computer Services:** Mailing lists. **Publications:** Brochure.

18181 ■ Eternal Life
902 W Stephen Foster Ave.
Bardstown, KY 40004
Free: (800)842-2871
Fax: (502)348-2224
E-mail: wjsjrnj@bardstowncable.net
URL: http://www.lifeeternal.org
Founded: 1991. **Members:** 25,000. **Membership Dues:** non-profit Apostolate, $10. **Staff:** 3. **Budget:** $210,000. **Description:** Orthodox, lay Catholics. Seeks to organize a Catholic response to "exploitive and sinful sexual behaviors and attitudes" such as abortion, fetal experimentation, euthanasia, sterilization, premarital sex, homosexuality, divorce, pornography, artificial insemination, and contraception. Promotes family-centered sexuality and spirituality by bringing the perspective of Catholic teachings into the prolife movement. **Publications:** *A Prophet for the Priesthood*. Book. **Price:** $8.95 ● *All My Liberty*. Book. **Price:** $9.95 ● *The Catholic Lifetime Reading Plan*. Book. **Price:** $25.00. **Conventions/Meetings:** Make a Moral Miracle Happen - meeting - 3/year.

18182 ■ Feminists for Life of America (FFL)
PO Box 20685
Alexandria, VA 22320
Ph: (703)836-3354
Fax: (703)836-3351
E-mail: info@feministsforlife.org
URL: http://www.feministsforlife.org
Contact: Serrin M. Foster, Pres.
Founded: 1972. **Members:** 5,000. **Membership Dues:** basic, $25 (annual) ● student, $15 (annual). **Staff:** 6. **Budget:** $430,000. **State Groups:** 1. **Description:** Works to secure, through nonviolent means, basic human rights for all people, especially women and children, from first formation until the natural end of life. Aims to eliminate the root causes that drive women to abortion - primarily lack of practical resources and support - through holistic, woman-centered solutions. Seeks real solutions to the challenges that women face. **Libraries:** **Type:** not open to the public. **Publications:** *The American Feminist*, periodic. **Price:** included in membership dues; $35.00 for nonmembers, subscribers only and groups. **Circulation:** 5,000. **Advertising:** accepted ● *Man's Inhumanity to Women Makes Countless Infants Die: The Early Feminist Case Against Abortion*. Booklet ● Booklets ● Also publishes position papers.

18183 ■ Helpers of God's Precious Infants
c/o The Monastery of the Precious Blood
5300 Ft. Hamilton Pkwy.
Brooklyn, NY 11219
Ph: (718)853-2789
Fax: (718)853-0599
E-mail: helpers@helpersbrooklynny.org
URL: http://www.helpersbrooklynny.org
Contact: Msgr. Phillip Reilly, Exec. Dir.
Description: Pro-life Christians. Organizes prayerful presence at abortion clinics and other agencies in an attempt to stop abortions; counsels women on sidewalk who are coming to abortion clinics. Promotes the idea that infants can be saved through the spiritual conversion of their mothers. Uses prayer as a means of spiritual support and in hopes of stopping abortions.

18184 ■ Holy Innocents Reparation Committee (HIRC)
Address Unknown since 2007
Founded: 1972. **Members:** 10. **Description:** Catholic pro-lfe organization that fights the "evil of abortion" through performance of the Holy Sacrifice of the Mass, the Holy Rosary, and Benediction. Distributes educational materials.

18185 ■ Jewish Anti-Abortion League (JAAL)
PO Box 230262 Gravesend Sta.
Brooklyn, NY 11223-0001
Ph: (718)336-0053
Fax: (718)645-0556
Contact: Dr. Arthur Tomases MD, Pres.
Founded: 1979. **Members:** 1,200. **Staff:** 2. **Description:** Religious Jews and other individuals who oppose abortion. Provides counseling, education, and adoption assistance programs. Conducts lobbying activities. Maintains speakers' bureau. **Publications:** none. **Affiliated With:** Jews for Morality. **Conventions/Meetings:** periodic conference.

18186 ■ March for Life Fund (ML)
PO Box 90300
Washington, DC 20090
Ph: (202)543-3377
Fax: (202)543-8202
E-mail: info@marchforlife.org
URL: http://www.marchforlife.org
Contact: Nellie J. Gray, Pres.
Founded: 1974. **Description:** Promotes the right to life of all individuals, born and pre-born. Advocates a mandatory Human Life Amendment to the U.S. Constitution. Sponsors annual March for Life whereby pro-lifers come from across the nation to march in Washington, D.C. in protest to the 1973 U.S. Supreme Court decision legalizing abortion. Sends the President, each member of Congress, and the U.S. Supreme Court a typed message and red roses on behalf of the unborn each year (Jan. 22 - date of march). Conducts lobbying activities and presents testimony from the pro-life viewpoint. Provides seminars; operates speakers' bureau. **Formerly:** (1992) March for Life. **Publications:** *Action Memo*, periodic ● *Student Contests*, annual ● Annual Report, annual ● Also publishes educational materials.

18187 ■ National Committee for a Human Life Amendment (NCHLA)
1500 Massachusetts Ave. NW, Ste.24
Washington, DC 20005
Ph: (202)393-0703
Fax: (202)347-1383
URL: http://www.nchla.org
Contact: Michael A. Taylor, Exec. Dir.
Founded: 1974. **Staff:** 6. **Description:** Seeks to overturn the U.S. Supreme Court decision on abortion by means of a Human Life Amendment. Is also involved in other pro-life legislation and education on the national level. Provides grass roots assistance on the effective organization of congressional districts. **Programs:** National Postcard Campaign; Project Life. **Publications:** Reports. Alternate Formats: online.

18188 ■ National Cops for Life (NCFL)
PO Box 267
Cutchogue, NY 11935
E-mail: ncfl@juno.com
URL: http://members.aol.com/nfofl
Contact: Vincent A. Ciappetta, Founder/Dir.
Founded: 1995. **Members:** 100. **Staff:** 1. **Budget:** $500. **Description:** Active or retired members of various police departments, assistant prosecutors, sheriffs, federal agents, corrections officers and affiliates such as military personnel, also, private security forces recommended by an active member. Works to create a force of active and retired law enforcement professionals who are willing to defend life from the moment of conception to natural death through daily prayer and letter response. **Publications:** *The APB*. Bulletin. **Price:** included in membership dues.

18189 ■ National Federation of Officers for Life (NFOFL)
PO Box 8774
Corpus Christi, TX 78468-8774
Free: (888)ATF-BOMB
E-mail: nfofl@aol.com
Contact: Sgt. Ruben Rodriguez, Dir. & Founder
Founded: 1990. **Members:** 250. **Membership Dues:** professional, $10 (annual) ● associate, $20 (annual). **State Groups:** 5. **Description:** Active, reserve, and retired law enforcement officers and employees from all levels of jurisdiction, public safety officers, and

government officials who oppose abortion and the use of police to escort clients to abortion clinics. Seeks to extend existing conscience clauses which are aimed at protecting officers who for moral reasons refuse to escort women to medical abortion facilities. Maintains speakers' bureau. **Computer Services:** database ● mailing lists. **Affiliated With:** American Life League. **Publications:** The APB, quarterly. Newsletter ● Law or Conscience. Pamphlet. **Conventions/Meetings:** quarterly meeting (exhibits).

18190 ■ National Pro-Life Religious Council (NPLRC)

109 2nd St. NE
Washington, DC 20013
Ph: (718)980-4400
Fax: (413)622-3764
E-mail: mail@nprcouncil.org
URL: http://www.nprcouncil.org
Contact: Rev. Kirk Van der Swaagh, VP
Membership Dues: individual, church, group, $25 (annual). **Description:** Religious individuals supporting the right to life of the unborn. Seeks to "see every denomination or fellowship proclaim and obey the Biblical teaching and religious tradition that affirm the value of all human life". Articulates the "historic Judeo-Christian perspective concerning human life issues" to the public; supports efforts to discourage and prevent abortion and voluntary euthanasia; ministers to people considering abortion or voluntary euthanasia. Serves as a clearinghouse on right to life issues; facilitates communication and cooperation among right to life organizations. **Publications:** Uniting For Life, quarterly. Newsletter. Alternate Formats: online ● Brochure. Alternate Formats: online.

18191 ■ National Right to Life Educational Trust Fund (NRLC)

512 10th St. NW
Washington, DC 20004
Ph: (202)626-8800
Fax: (202)737-9189
E-mail: nrlc@nrlc.org
URL: http://www.nrlc.org
Contact: Wanda Franz PhD, Pres.
Founded: 1973. **Description:** Educational branch of the National Right to Life Committee. Develops factsheets brochures, and other educational materials on issues such as abortion, infanticide, and euthanasia, with the aim of improving personal and societal awareness of and responsibility for human life in all its stages, particularly vulnerable and disadvantaged individuals such as persons with disabilities, the aged, and children both before and after birth. Monitors and researches bioethical issues such as abortion, post abortion syndrome, human embryo and fetal tissue research, infanticide, genetic fetal tissue research, infanticide, genetic engineering, assisted suicide, and euthanasia. Supports overseas life educational and service programs through its membership and financial support of the International Right to Life Federation. **Libraries: Type:** reference. **Holdings:** 1,500; books, periodicals. **Subjects:** abortion, euthanasia, infanticide. **Affiliated With:** National Right to Life Committee. **Publications:** Abortion Information for Classroom Teachers, When Does Life Begin?. Booklets ● Abortion: Some Medical Facts. Booklet ● Abortion: The Hard Cases. Brochure ● LifeCycle, annual. Contains study guides on various contemporary issues in bioethics. ● School-Based Clinics: The Abortion Connection. Books ● The Silent Scream. Video. **Conventions/Meetings:** annual convention and workshop, general sessions, research presentations (exhibits) - always early summer ● seminar.

18192 ■ Operation Save America (OSA)

PO Box 740066
Dallas, TX 75374
Ph: (704)933-3414
Fax: (704)932-3361
E-mail: osa@operationsaveamerica.org
URL: http://www.operationsaveamerica.org
Contact: Rev. Philip L. Benham, Dir.
Founded: 1987. **Description:** "Coalition of pro-life pastors and laypeople of Christian faiths. Organizes

rescues/sit-ins at abortion clinics to block patient entry and save the lives of innocent children; stop the exploitation of mothers from the violence of abortion; call America to repent for allowing 30 million children to be slaughtered since 1973; rescue children and mothers in a way that produces political change. Activities have resulted in over 50000 arrests of participants and over 900 abortions stopped". **Libraries: Type:** open to the public. **Holdings:** archival material, photographs. **Formerly:** (2000) Operation Rescue. **Publications:** Newsletters, monthly. Alternate Formats: online ● Articles. Alternate Formats: online ● Brochures. Alternate Formats: online.

18193 ■ Pharmacists for Life International (PFLI)

PO Box 1281
Powell, OH 43065-1281
Ph: (740)881-5520
Free: (800)227-8359
Fax: (707)667-2447
E-mail: pfli@pfli.org
URL: http://www.pfli.org
Contact: Bogomir M. Kuhar, Exec. Dir.
Founded: 1984. **Members:** 2,000. **Membership Dues:** pharmacist, $45 (annual) ● non-pharmacist, retiree, $25 (annual) ● student/pharmacy tech, $15 (annual). **Regional Groups:** 20. **Multinational. Description:** Pharmacists and interested groups and individuals. Seeks to educate pharmacists, other medical professionals, and the public about the "abortion holocaust." Defends the right to life from conception to natural death, regardless of biological stage, dependency, or residence. Provides medical supplies and vitamins to women and crisis pregnancy centers. Provides children's services; sponsors charitable, educational, and research programs. Maintains speakers' bureau; compiles statistics. **Libraries: Type:** reference. **Holdings:** audiovisuals, books, business records, clippings, monographs, periodicals. **Subjects:** abortion, euthanasia, infanticide, drugs in pregnancy. **Awards:** President's Merit Award. **Frequency:** annual. **Type:** recognition. **Computer Services:** database ● mailing lists ● online services. **Committees:** Communications; Convention; Education; Elections Commission; Executive; Professional Affairs. **Affiliated With:** American Life League. **Formerly:** (1993) Pharmacists for Life. **Publications:** A Consumer's Guide to the Pill and Other Medicines, 2nd Ed. ● Beginnings (in English and Spanish), quarterly. Newsletter. Contains book and literature reviews, guest analyses and editorials, and news on current events. **Price:** included in membership dues. **Circulation:** 1,500. **Advertising:** accepted. Alternate Formats: online ● Can Cancer Pain be Relieved? ● Evidence Which Demands a Conclusion: Norplant ● Gambling with Life: The Birth Control Game ● Infant Homicides Through Contraceptives, 3rd Ed. ● Is Your Pharmacy Prolife? ● IUD: Device of Death ● Model Pharmacists Conscience Clause ● The New Abortionists II: An Update on Chemical and Mechanical Killing ● Norplant: A New Abortifacient ● Norplant Fact Sheet ● The Personality of the Pill ● Pharmaceutical Companies: The New Abortionists ● Pharmacists Code of Ethics ● The Pill Fact Sheet ● RU 486 Fact Sheet. **Conventions/Meetings:** annual convention (exhibits).

18194 ■ Priests for Life

PO Box 141172
Staten Island, NY 10314
Ph: (718)980-4400
Free: (888)735-3448
Fax: (718)980-6515
E-mail: mail@priestsforlife.org
URL: http://www.priestsforlife.org
Contact: Fr. Frank A. Pavone, Dir.
Founded: 1990. **Staff:** 40. **Description:** Provides ongoing training to priests and deacons giving special emphasis to "life issues". Offers audio and video tapes, brochures, and uses the media to spread its message. **Publications:** Newsletter, bimonthly. Alternate Formats: online.

18195 ■ Pro-Life Action League (PLAL)

6160 N Cicero Ave.
Chicago, IL 60646

Ph: (773)777-2900
Fax: (773)777-3061
E-mail: info@prolifeaction.org
URL: http://www.prolifeaction.org
Contact: Joseph M. Scheidler, Natl. Dir./Publisher
Founded: 1980. **Staff:** 8. **Budget:** $600,000. **Languages:** English, Spanish. **Multinational. Description:** Individuals, including doctors, lawyers, business leaders, and students, who are pro-life. Works "to stop abortions now, through effective, legal, nonviolent means" and to lay the groundwork for outlawing all abortions through a constitutional amendment. Conducts demonstrations and picketing against abortion clinics and pro-abortion agencies; appears on radio and television talk shows and demands equal media time to counter pro-abortion views. Lectures student groups; trains volunteers to counsel women in front of clinics. Compiles statistics. **Libraries: Type:** by appointment only. **Holdings:** 2,000; audio recordings, video recordings. **Subjects:** abortion, population control, euthanasia, chastity, Christian ethics, human sexuality. **Awards:** Protector Award. **Frequency:** annual. **Type:** trophy. **Recipient:** to individuals who made outstanding contributions to fight abortion. **Computer Services:** database. **Telecommunication Services:** 24-hour hotline, (773)777-2525, action line to keep pro-life activists informed about abortion related events. **Committees:** Public Demonstration; Public Protest; Street Counselors. **Departments:** Public Relations; Publicity. **Formerly:** (2002) Generations for Life. **Publications:** Abortion: The Inside Story. Video. **Price:** $19.95 ● Action News, quarterly. Newsletter. Covers news on pro-life activism. **Price:** $10.00. **Circulation:** 9,000. **Advertising:** accepted ● Closed: 99 Ways to Stop Abortion. Book. **Price:** $18.00 ● Meet the Abortion Providers. Videos. Covers former abortion providers and sidewalk counseling. **Price:** $19.95 long version; $17.95 short version ● Pro-Life Action News, quarterly. Newsletter. Alternate Formats: online ● Bulletin, periodic. **Conventions/Meetings:** annual Meet the Abortion Providers - conference, former abortion providers speak against abortion (exhibits) ● seminar, for community organizations and pro-life activists ● workshop.

18196 ■ Republican National Coalition for Life (RNC/Life)

PO Box 618
Alton, IL 62002
Ph: (972)387-4160
Fax: (972)387-3830
E-mail: rnclife@swbell.net
URL: http://www.rnclife.org
Contact: Colleen Parro, Exec. Dir.
Founded: 1990. **Members:** 100,000. **Membership Dues:** regular, $15 (annual). **Budget:** $100,000. **State Groups:** 50. **Description:** Members of the Republican Party who believe in the right to life. Seeks to maintain and strengthen the official prolife position of the Republican Party as described in the party platform. Encourages support of public policies upholding the right to life among legislators at all levels of government. **Publications:** Newsletter, bimonthly. **Price:** included in membership dues.

18197 ■ Rock For Life

PO Box 1350
Stafford, VA 22555
Ph: (540)659-4171 (540)659-5855
Fax: (540)659-2586
E-mail: info@rockforlife.org
URL: http://www.rockforlife.org
Contact: Erik Whittington, Dir.
Members: 375,000. **Description:** Offers information about abortion, infanticide, and euthanasia to America's youth through music and ministry. **Telecommunication Services:** electronic mail, erik@rockforlife.org. **Affiliated With:** American Life League. **Conventions/Meetings:** Rock For Life Concerts - show.

18198 ■ STOPP International

PO Box 1350
Stafford, VA 22555
Ph: (540)659-4171

Fax: (540)659-2586
E-mail: jsedlak@all.org
URL: http://www.all.org/stopp
Contact: Jim Sedlak, Exec. Dir.
Founded: 1985. **Local Groups:** 32. **Description:**
Works for the elimination of the organization Planned
Parenthood, its programs, and methods. Endorses
nonviolent activity aimed at hindering the operations
of Planned Parenthood. Acts as a national informa-
tion clearinghouse and coordinates national network
of activists. Conducts research and educational
programs; operates speakers' bureau. **Libraries:**
Type: reference. **Holdings:** books, clippings, periodi-
cals. **Subjects:** Planned Parenthood, sex education,
AIDS education. **Affiliated With:** American Life
League. **Formerly:** Stop Planned Parenthood. **Publi-**
cations: *Parent Power! How Parents Can Gain*
Control of the School Systems That Educate Their
Children. Book. **Price:** $5.00 plus shipping and
handling. **Advertising:** accepted ● *Wednesday*
STOPP Report, weekly. Newsletter. Concentrates on
Planned Parenthood and successful fights against its
programs. **Advertising:** accepted. **Conventions/**
Meetings: biennial conference (exhibits).

18199 ■ Teachers Saving Children National
PO Box 125
Damascus, OH 44619-0125
Ph: (330)821-2747
E-mail: tsc-life@juno.com
URL: http://www.teacherssavingchildren.org
Contact: Ms. Connie Bancroft, Exec. Dir.
Founded: 1994. **Membership Dues:** college student/
retired educator, $10 (annual) ● regular, $25 (an-
nual). **State Groups:** 3. **Description:** Comprised of
educators, college students studying education, and
retired educators. Promotes "respect for all human
life, from conception to natural death." Facilitates
communication among members; seeks to raise
public awareness of right-to-life issues. **Publications:**
Teachers Saving Children, bimonthly. Newsletter.
Alternate Formats: online ● Brochure. Alternate
Formats: online.

Romania

18200 ■ Christian Aid Ministries (CAM)
PO Box 360
Berlin, OH 44610
Ph: (330)893-2428
Fax: (330)893-2305
E-mail: markroth@anabaptists.org
URL: http://www.anabaptists.org/places/cam
Contact: Mark Roth, Ed.
Founded: 1981. **Staff:** 275. **Budget:** $12,665,000.
Description: Supporters include churches, schools,
and volunteers who seek to bring spiritual and mate-
rial aid to Christians in CIS, Romania, Haiti and
Nicaragua, Liberia. Sends parcels of food, clothing,
Christian Literature, and medicine. Operates speak-
ers' bureau. **Convention/Meeting:** none. **Formerly:**
(1991) Christian Aid for Romania. **Publications:**
Newsletter, monthly. **Price:** free.

18201 ■ Hungarian Human Rights
Foundation (HHRF)
PO Box J, Gracie Sta.
New York, NY 10028
Ph: (212)289-5488
Fax: (212)996-6268
E-mail: hamos@hhrf.org
URL: http://www.hhrf.org
Contact: Laszlo Hamos, Pres.
Founded: 1976. **Staff:** 2. **Multinational. Descrip-**
tion: Monitors the human rights situation of ethnic
Hungarian minorities in Romania, Slovakia, Ukraine,
Serbia, Croatia; provides books and other educational
materials to regions. Organizes relief programs that
ship supplies to Romania. Researches, collects, and
disseminates data; presents written and oral testimonies at congressional hearings; organizes demonstrations and initiates letter writing campaigns. Translates
and publishes first hand accounts of minority oppression. Maintains speakers' bureau. **Libraries: Type:**

reference. **Holdings:** 2,000; archival material, books,
clippings, video recordings. **Computer Services:** da-
tabase. **Formerly:** (1984) Committee for Human
Rights in Romania. **Publications:** *Compendium of*
Documents and News Articles, 1-2/year ● *Congres-*
sional Testimony, semiannual ● *Hungarian Minorities*
Monitor, 5/year. Newsletter ● Articles ● Books ●
Newsletter (in English and Hungarian), 2-3/year.

Rural Development

18202 ■ India Development Service (IDS)
PO Box 980
Chicago, IL 60690
Ph: (630)495-4200
E-mail: idsusa@gmail.com
URL: http://www.idsusa.org
Contact: Naimish Shah, Pres.
Founded: 1974. **Members:** 1,800. **Membership**
Dues: general, $25 (annual) ● life, $250. **Budget:**
$100,000. **Multinational. Description:** Individuals
interested in rural development and, in particular, hu-
man development in India. Promotes rural develop-
ment projects in India. Maintains Speaker's Bureau.
Libraries: Type: not open to the public. **Subjects:**
development and economy in India. **Computer**
Services: Mailing lists. **Committees:** Fund Raiser;
Project. **Publications:** *Catalyst,* quarterly. Newsletter. Alternate Formats: online ● *IDS Newsletter,* annual. **Conventions/Meetings:** annual seminar, covers developmental issues (exhibits) - always April or
May in Chicago, IL.

18203 ■ Inter-American Foundation (IAF)
901 N Stuart St., 10th Fl.
Balston
Arlington, VA 22203-1821
Ph: (703)306-4301
Fax: (703)306-4365
E-mail: info@iaf.gov
URL: http://www.iaf.gov
Contact: Ms. Linda Borst-Kolko, VP for Operations
Founded: 1969. **Staff:** 47. **Multinational. Descrip-**
tion: Provides grants to nongovernmental and
community-based organizations in Latin America and
the Caribbean for innovative, sustainable and participatory self-help programs. Primarily funds partnerships among grassroots and nonprofit organizations,
businesses and local governments, directed at
improving the quality of life of poor people and
strengthening participation, accountability and democratic practices. **Libraries: Type:** reference. **Hold-**
ings: articles, artwork, books, monographs. **Pro-**
grams: The Inter-American Network of Corporate
Foundations and Companies for Grassroots Development. **Publications:** *Grassroots Development* (in
English, Portuguese, and Spanish), annual. Magazine. **Price:** $1.00. Alternate Formats: microform; on-
line.

18204 ■ National Rural Economic Developers
Association (NREDA)
431 E Locust St., Ste.300
Des Moines, IA 50309
Ph: (515)284-1421
Fax: (515)243-2049
E-mail: director@nreda.org
URL: http://www.nreda.org
Contact: Stan Rice, Pres.
Founded: 1989. **Membership Dues:** regular/associ-
ate (corporate), $395 (annual) ● regular/associate
(professional), $270 (annual) ● student, $50 (annual).
Description: Promotes rural development opportuni-
ties through electric and telephone cooperatives.
Provides education, advocacy and networking op-
portunities to rural and suburban utilities and affili-
ated organizations. **Committees:** Bylaws and Parliamentarian; Finance and Non-Dues Income; Legislative and Government Affairs; Professional
Development; Strategic Alliances; Strategic Planning.
Councils: Past President. **Conventions/Meetings:**
annual conference.

18205 ■ Rural Coalition (RC)
1012 14th St. NW, Ste.1100
Washington, DC 20005
Ph: (202)628-7160
Fax: (202)628-7165
E-mail: ruralco@ruralco.org
URL: http://www.ruralco.org
Contact: Lorette Picciano, Exec. Dir.
Founded: 1978. **Members:** 145. **Membership Dues:**
individual, $25-$100 (annual) ● organization (based
on annual budget), $100-$1,000 (annual). **Staff:** 4.
Budget: $320,000. **Regional Groups:** 30. **Local**
Groups: 30. **National Groups:** 20. **Description:** Organizations and individuals concerned with issues
directly affecting low income and disadvantaged rural
Americans. Aims to work for effective public policies
and to develop a strong rural constituency for
progressive change to benefit rural people. Sub-
scribes to the following principles: justice and equal
opportunity regardless of sex, race, or place of
residence; availability of goods and services essential
to a decent quality of life; control and use of resources
by rural people; development of rural, community-
based organizations. Promotes policy to achieve
sustainable agriculture, including equity in access to
USDA programs. Provides technical assistance and
information to community-based groups and operates
an online retail website for products of cooperatives.
Additional Websites: http://www.supermarketcoop.
com. **Publications:** *Minority Land Loss Study* ● *Up-*
date, quarterly. Newsletter. **Conventions/Meetings:**
annual assembly.

Russian

18206 ■ Russian American Jews for Israel
2748 Ocean Ave.
Brooklyn, NY 11229
E-mail: forgaber@hotmail.com
URL: http://www.russianamericanjews.org
Contact: Kostya Gaber, Contact
Membership Dues: working professional, $30 (an-
nual) ● working family, $45 (annual) ● student,
senior, $10 (annual). **Description:** Seeks to unite
Russian American Jewish professionals. Assists in
developing and discovering new emigre community
leaders. Strengthens Israeli-American relations by
joining the fight against terrorism and anti-Semitism.
Computer Services: Mailing lists ● online services,
discussion forum ● online services, survey. **Pro-**
grams: Informational Outreach; National Development; Zionist Education/Israel Education.

Safety

18207 ■ Citizens for Reliable and Safe
Highways (CRASH)
c/o Truck Safety Coalition
PO Box 14380
Washington, DC 20044-4380
Free: (888)353-4572
Fax: (202)232-4661
E-mail: crash@trucksafety.org
URL: http://www.trucksafety.org
Contact: Joan Claybrook, Chair
Founded: 1990. **Description:** Dedicated to improv-
ing overall truck safety and eliminating unnecessary
deaths and injuries caused by truck crashes. **Pro-**
grams: First Response; Sorrow to Strength; Survivors
Network. **Projects:** Truck Resource Education
Center. **Publications:** Newsletter, quarterly. Alternate
Formats: online ● Brochure. Alternate Formats: on-
line.

18208 ■ National Program for Playground
Safety (NPPS)
Scholarship of HPELS, WRC 205
Univ. of Northern Iowa
Cedar Falls, IA 50614-0618
Free: (800)554-PLAY
Fax: (319)273-7308

E-mail: playground-safety@uni.edu
URL: http://www.playgroundsafety.org
Contact: Dr. Donna Thompson PhD, Dir.
Founded: 1995. **Description:** Works to address U.S. playground safety issues to reduce playground-related injuries. Provides training and services about outdoor play and safety. **Publications:** *Playground Safety News.* Newsletter.

18209 ■ National Student Safety Program (NSSP)
Highway Safety Center
Indiana Univ. of Pennsylvania
R&P Bldg.
Indiana, PA 15705
Ph: (724)357-4051
Free: (800)896-7703
Fax: (724)357-7595
E-mail: dbowser@hsc.iup.edu
URL: http://www.adtsea.iup.edu/nssp
Contact: Bruce Giles, Pres. of College Division
Founded: 1956. **Membership Dues:** regular, $50 (annual). **Description:** Works to encourage and assist students in their efforts to initiate and implement safety activities within schools and communities on drug, alcohol, safe driving, and health issues. **Conventions/Meetings:** banquet ● conference.

18210 ■ SafetyBeltSafe U.S.A.
PO Box 553
Altadena, CA 91003
E-mail: stombrello@carseat.org
URL: http://www.carseat.org
Contact: Stephanie M. Tombrello, Exec. Dir.
Founded: 1980. **Description:** Dedicated to child passenger safety and helps to reduce the number of serious and fatal traffic injuries suffered by children by promoting the correct, consistent use of safety seats and safety belts. **Publications:** *SafetyBeltSafe News*, bimonthly. Newsletter. **Price:** included in membership dues.

18211 ■ State and Territorial Injury Prevention Directors Association (STIPDA)
2965 Flowers Rd. S, Ste.105
Atlanta, GA 30341
Ph: (770)690-9000
Fax: (770)690-8996
E-mail: email@stipda.cbeyond.com
URL: http://www.stipda.org
Contact: Susan Hardman, Pres.
Founded: 1993. **Description:** Public health injury professionals. Works to promote, sustain and enhance the ability of state and territorial public health departments to reduce death and disability associated with injuries.

18212 ■ World Safety Organization (WSO)
106 W Young Ave., Ste.G
PO Box 518
Warrensburg, MO 64093
Ph: (660)747-3132
Fax: (660)747-2647
E-mail: info@worldsafety.org
URL: http://www.worldsafety.org
Contact: Dr. Vlado Z. Senkovich, Pres./Dir. Gen.
Founded: 1975. **Members:** 5,000. **Membership Dues:** associate, $55 (annual) ● student, $35 (annual) ● affiliate, $80 (annual) ● institutional, $185 (annual) ● corporate, $1,000 (annual). **Staff:** 4. **State Groups:** 8. **National Groups:** 14. **Multinational. Description:** Promotes all safety fields, including occupational and environmental safety and health, accident prevention movement, and others. Aims to internationalize all of these fields and to disseminate throughout the world the practices, skills, arts and technologies of safety and accident prevention professions. **Awards:** WSO Award for Achievement in Scientific Research and Development. **Frequency:** annual. **Type:** recognition. **Recipient:** for outstanding contributions to the advancement of WSO through research and development programs ● WSO Chapter/National Office of the Year Award. **Frequency:** annual. **Type:** recognition. **Recipient:** for exceptional effort on the part of a WSO chapter ● WSO Concerned Citizen Award. **Frequency:** annual. **Type:**

recognition. **Recipient:** to an active member of WSO who has shown above average support and cooperation for the community organizations and programs ● WSO Concerned Company/Corporation Award. **Frequency:** annual. **Type:** recognition. **Recipient:** to a company or corporation with an excellent safety program ● WSO Concerned Company/Corporation Honorable Mention Certificate. **Frequency:** annual. **Type:** recognition. **Recipient:** to a company or corporation with commendable support of environmental, occupational and safety programs ● WSO Concerned Organization Award. **Frequency:** annual. **Type:** recognition. **Recipient:** to an association, society or agency with above average support of safety ● WSO Concerned Professional Award. **Frequency:** annual. **Type:** recognition. **Recipient:** to an individual who has shown above average skills in design, leadership and supervision of environmental/ occupational safety and health programs ● WSO Educational Award. **Frequency:** annual. **Type:** recognition. **Recipient:** for an institution with above average program of educational nature in the fields of safety, environment, public safety and transportation safety ● WSO Environmental/Occupational Safety Person of the Year. **Frequency:** annual. **Type:** recognition. **Recipient:** for an individual working full time in the field of environmental/ occupational safety or an allied field ● WSO International Award. **Frequency:** annual. **Type:** recognition. **Recipient:** for special service in the advancement of the disciplines of WSO in a country other than the United States of America ● WSO James K. Williams Award. **Frequency:** annual. **Type:** recognition. **Recipient:** for an active member of WSO who has shown above average support and cooperation for the organization. **Telecommunication Services:** electronic mail, vlado_senkovich@worldsafety.org. **Committees:** Aviation Transportation; Construction; Highway Transportation; Maritime Transportation; Rail Transportation; Transportation of Dangerous Goods. **Divisions:** Environmental Safety and Health; Governmental Advisory and Research; Occupational Safety and Health; Transportation. **Publications:** *World Safety Journal*, semiannual. **Price:** $5.00. ISSN: 1015-5589. **Advertising:** accepted ● Newsletter, bimonthly. **Price:** free for members. ISSN: 1070-311X. **Advertising:** accepted. **Conventions/Meetings:** annual International Safety and Health Professional Development Conference, with awards banquet (exhibits).

Science

18213 ■ Institute for Science and International Security (ISIS)
236 Massachusetts Ave. NE, Ste.500
Washington, DC 20002
Ph: (202)547-3633
Fax: (202)547-3634
E-mail: isis@isis-online.org
URL: http://www.isis-online.org
Contact: David Albright, Pres./Founder
Founded: 1993. **Multinational. Description:** Works to inform the public about science and policy issues that affect international security. **Awards:** Fellowships. **Type:** fellowship. **Computer Services:** database ● mailing lists. **Telecommunication Services:** electronic mail, albright@isis-online.org. **Projects:** The Nuclear Nonproliferation; The Nuclear Weapons Production. **Publications:** *Algeria: Big deal in the desert?*. Article. Alternate Formats: online ● *Challenges of Fissile Material Control*. Report. **Circulation:** 2,000 ● *Comparison of Drafts of Comprehensive Security Council Resolution on Iraq*. Article. Alternate Formats: online ● *India's and Pakistan's Fissile Material and Nuclear Weapons Inventories, end of 1999*. Article. Alternate Formats: online ● *Iraq's Efforts to Acquire Information about Nuclear Weapons & Nuclear-Related Technologies from the United States*. Article ● *North Korea: It's Taking Too Long*. Paper ● *Plutonium Watch*. Paper. **Circulation:** 2,000 ● *Solving the North Korean Nuclear Puzzle*. Book. **Price:** $29.95 ● *Stay the Course on North Korea*. Paper ● Proceedings. Alternate Formats: online.

Conventions/Meetings: Nuclear Nonproliferation Verification Institute - workshop, 4-day training course.

Scientific Responsibility

18214 ■ Council for Responsible Genetics (CRG)
5 Upland Rd., Ste.3
Cambridge, MA 02140-2717
Ph: (617)868-0870
Fax: (617)491-5344
E-mail: crg@gene-watch.org
URL: http://www.gene-watch.org
Contact: Sujatha Byravan PhD, Pres.
Founded: 1983. **Staff:** 4. **Nonmembership. Description:** Monitors and analyzes the biotechnology industry and discusses the social implications of new developments in genetic technology. Areas of interest include genetic privacy, genetic discrimination, biological weapons, human genetic modification, and genetically engineered food. **Libraries:** Type: reference. **Holdings:** books, clippings, periodicals. **Subjects:** biotech, genetic research, social and ethical issues. **Working Groups:** Biological Weapons; Genetic Discrimination and Privacy; Genetically Engineered Food; Women & Reproductive Technologies. **Affiliated With:** American Medical Writers Association; Biotechnology Industry Organization. **Formerly:** (1989) Committee for Responsible Genetics. **Supersedes:** Coalition for Responsible Genetics. **Publications:** *Fact Sheet*. **Price:** free ● *GeneWatch*, bimonthly. Magazine. Covers the social and ethical issues of genetic engineering and biotechnology. Includes legislative news. **Price:** $35.00 /year for individuals; $50.00/year for nonprofit; $70.00 /year for libraries; $100.00/year for corporate. ISSN: 0740-9737. **Circulation:** 1,000 ● Books ● Magazine, bimonthly ● Papers. **Conventions/Meetings:** annual conference ● periodic meeting.

18215 ■ Public Responsibility in Medicine and Research (PRIM&R)
126 Brookline Ave., Ste.202
Boston, MA 02215-3920
Ph: (617)423-4112
Fax: (617)423-1185
E-mail: info@primr.org
URL: http://www.primr.org
Contact: Leonard Glantz JD, Treas.
Founded: 1974. **Membership Dues:** individual, $125 (annual). **Staff:** 13. **Budget:** $200,000. **Regional Groups:** 1. **Description:** Promotes the advancement of strong research programs and to the consistent application of ethical precepts in both medicine and research. Addresses a broad range of issues in research, clinical practice, ethics and the law through national conferences and published reports; members of the association's affiliate organization, Applied Research Ethics National Association (ARENA), include researchers, clinicians, nurses, research/ health care administrators, subjects/patients, attorneys, and laypersons interested in research, primarily with human subjects and animals. **Libraries:** Type: reference. **Holdings:** 500. **Computer Services:** Mailing lists. **Boards:** Primer. **Councils:** ARENA. **Formerly:** Primer. **Publications:** *Conference Report*, semiannual. Proceedings. Includes educational materials from conferences. **Price:** $30.00/proceeding; $25.00/educational material ● *Guidebook on Institutional Animal Care and Use Committees* ● *Human Subjects Guidebook* ● Membership Directory, annual. Alternate Formats: online ● Also publishes volumes on research and the protection of human subjects. **Conventions/Meetings:** annual conference (exhibits).

Security

18216 ■ American Security Council (ASC)
1237 Pennsylvania Ave., SE
Washington, DC 20003
Ph: (202)546-7348

Fax: (202)546-2100
E-mail: info@ascusa.org
URL: http://www.americansecuritycouncil.org
Contact: Dr. Henry A. Fischer, Pres.
Founded: 1955. **Members:** 325,700. **Staff:** 20. **Description:** Individuals, companies, colleges, labor unions, and others supporting a national research and information center on national security. Maintains Washington bureau. Organizes and serves as program secretariat for Coalition for Peace Through Strength. Conducts annual National Security Issues Polls. Uses polls to rate members of Congress on key national votes. Holds regular national security luncheons for members of Washington press corps. **Committees:** Political Action. **Formerly:** (1956) Mid-American Research Library. **Publications:** *National Security Report*, monthly ● Also publishes studies.

18217 ■ Business Executives for National Security (BENS)
1717 Pennsylvania Ave. NW, Ste.350
Washington, DC 20006-4620
Ph: (202)296-2125
Fax: (202)296-2490
E-mail: bens@bens.org
URL: http://www.bens.org
Contact: Ret.Gen. Charles G. Boyd, Pres./CEO
Founded: 1982. **Members:** 500. **Staff:** 35. **Budget:** $5,000,000. **Regional Groups:** 7. **Description:** Serves as a nonpartisan, non-ideological organization of America's professional and business leaders. Believes that genuine national security is a product of economic strength coupled with an effective, affordable defense. Stands that the employment of proven business practices improves national security. **Publications:** *The BENS Update*, monthly. Newsletter. Features the latest in all of BENS' activities. Alternate Formats: online ● *Trendline*, quarterly. Newsletter. **Circulation:** 7,500. **Conventions/Meetings:** annual meeting, an all day series of discussions on various national security topics - usually May, Washington, DC.

18218 ■ Center for National Security Studies (CNSS)
1120 19th St. NW, 8th Fl.
Washington, DC 20036
Ph: (202)721-5650
Fax: (202)530-0128
E-mail: cnss@gwu.edu
URL: http://www.cnss.org
Contact: Kate Martin, Dir.
Founded: 1974. **Staff:** 3. **Budget:** $300,000. **Description:** Founded to defend civil liberties against violations in the name of national security. Aims to assure that the people are free from government intimidation in exercising their political rights by working to enforce constitutional limits on government surveillance, wiretapping, and collection of information on private individuals. Seeks to strengthen the public right of access to government information, particularity relating to national security issues. Sponsors project to promote Free Trade in Ideas, by eliminating restrictions on the right to travel and legal barriers to the free flow of information and ideas across U.S. borders. Also sponsors a project to assist non-governmental human rights organizations and government officials in emerging democracies seeking to establish oversight and accountability for intelligence, internal security and police agencies.

18219 ■ Center for Security Policy (CSP)
1901 Pennsylvania Ave. NW, Ste.201
Washington, DC 20006
Ph: (202)835-9077
Fax: (202)835-9066
E-mail: info@centerforsecuritypolicy.org
URL: http://www.centerforsecuritypolicy.org
Contact: Dr. Frank J. Gaffney Jr., Pres.
Founded: 1988. **Members:** 100. **Staff:** 4. **Budget:** $850,000. **Description:** Acts as a policy information network serving the executive and legislative branches of the U.S. government, the press, industry, and the public; comprised of a board of advisors who exchange information about national defense and foreign policy issues, develop strategies, and dis-

seminate the results to appropriate decision-makers. Topics of focus include: U.S.-Soviet relations; arms control, compliance, and verification policy; regional security issues; national security decision-making; economic, financial and technological security; and U.S. space policy. Monitors and interfaces with the media to encourage accurate, balanced discussion of national security issues; promotes and facilitates interaction with industry on policy and technology questions; works to educate the public through the use of print and electronic media; testifies before Congress. Sponsors Internship Program to encourage college and graduate students to pursue careers in government. Operates College Campus Speakers' Bureau. **Libraries: Type:** by appointment only. **Holdings:** periodicals. **Subjects:** foreign policy, national security. **Awards:** Freedom Flame Award. **Frequency:** annual. **Type:** recognition ● Keeper of the Flame Award. **Frequency:** annual. **Type:** recognition. **Publications:** Issues weekly press releases and working papers.

18220 ■ Council for Emerging National Security Affairs (CENSA)
1212 New York Ave. NW, Ste.850
Washington, DC 20005
Fax: (202)289-7525
E-mail: query@censa.net
URL: http://www.censa.net
Contact: Michael Fenzel, Chm.
Founded: 1999. **Members:** 185. **Membership Dues:** public sector, $50 (annual) ● private sector, $100 (annual) ● board, $250 (annual) ● associate director, $150 (annual). **Multinational. Description:** Seeks to contribute to national security policy. **Conventions/Meetings:** monthly dinner, with lectures.

18221 ■ Defense Orientation Conference Association (DOCA)
9271 Old Keene Mill Rd., Ste.200
Burke, VA 22015-4202
Ph: (703)451-1200
E-mail: info@doca.org
URL: http://www.doca.org
Contact: Mr. John W. Ohlsen, Exec. Dir.
Founded: 1952. **Members:** 500. **Membership Dues:** individual, $400 (annual). **Staff:** 2. **Budget:** $500,000. **Regional Groups:** 6. **Description:** Citizens from all parts of the country representing the civilian sector. Members either have participated in a Joint Civilian Orientation Conference, an official program of the Department of Defense, consisting of a high-level briefing in the Pentagon and field trips to various military installations (one each for the Army, Navy, Air Force, and Marine Corps), or have been nominated to membership by an existing member. Seeks to provide a means of continuing the education of members in matters pertaining to national security under the direct jurisdiction and supervision of the Departments of Defense and State, and enable dissemination of such information to others, and provide a means of cooperation with the Departments of Defense and State. **Publications:** Annual Report, annual. **Price:** available to members only ● Membership Directory, annual. Includes bimonthly addendum. ● Newsletter, 4-5/year. **Conventions/Meetings:** semiannual international conference.

18222 ■ Mine Warfare Association (MINWARA)
c/o Mr. Lee Hunt, VP
7715 Lookout Ct.
Alexandria, VA 22306-2520
E-mail: huntlah@aol.com
URL: http://www.minwara.org
Contact: Mr. Lee Hunt, VP
Founded: 1995. **Membership Dues:** student, $25 (annual) ● regular, $50 (annual) ● life, $500 ● bronze corporate, $500 (annual) ● silver corporate, $1,000 (annual) ● gold corporate, $2,000 (annual) ● platinum corporate, $5,000 (annual). **Description:** Promotes education and awareness concerning mines; aims to strengthen national security; assists in the attainment of international security and humanitarian objectives.

Publications: *Mine Lines*. Newsletter. Alternate Formats: online. **Conventions/Meetings:** conference ● meeting.

18223 ■ Nautilus Institute
Univ. of San Francisco
2130 Fulton St., LM200
San Francisco, CA 94117-1080
Ph: (415)422-5523
Fax: (415)422-5933
E-mail: nautilus@nautilus.org
URL: http://www.nautilus.org
Contact: Peter Hayes PhD, Co-Founder/Exec. Dir.
Founded: 1992. **Staff:** 12. **Multinational. Description:** Commits to solve interrelated critical global problems by improving processes and outcomes of global governance. **Libraries: Type:** reference. **Subjects:** energy, nuclear issues, security, environment. **Computer Services:** Online services, news services - NAPsNET, SANDNet. **Publications:** *Coastal Ecology and Bay Area Youth*. Papers. Alternate Formats: online ● *Energy Security and Environment*. Papers. Alternate Formats: online ● *Global Peace and Security*. Papers. Alternate Formats: online ● *Globalization and the Environment*. Papers. Alternate Formats: online ● *Government Filings*, annual. Reports. Alternate Formats: online ● *Information Tools*. Papers. Alternate Formats: online. **Conventions/Meetings:** seminar.

18224 ■ OPSEC Professionals Society (OPS)
9200 Centerway Rd.
Gaithersburg, MD 20879
Ph: (301)840-6770
Fax: (301)840-8502
E-mail: zhi@tiac.net
Contact: Zhi Hamby-Nye, Exec. Dir.
Founded: 1988. **Members:** 850. **Membership Dues:** regular, $40 (annual) ● student, $25 (annual). **Description:** Industry and government officials united to advance and enhance the professional image of OPSEC practitioners. (OPSEC, or Operations Security, is a systematic process by which institutions can protect critical information from potential adversaries or competitors.) Provides for the exchange of views, information, and techniques on methods, practices, and procedures for managing OPSEC programs and related activities. Educates corporate and government agencies on the benefits of OPSEC and facilitates personal skills development through seminars and working groups. Provides a professional certification process. **Publications:** *OPS News*, quarterly. Newsletter. **Price:** included in membership dues. **Circulation:** 850. **Advertising:** accepted ● *OPSEC Journal*. **Price:** $15.00 plus shipping and handling ($2). **Conventions/Meetings:** annual conference (exhibits).

18225 ■ Search for Common Ground (SFCG)
1601 Connecticut Ave. NW, Ste.200
Washington, DC 20009-1035
Ph: (202)265-4300
Fax: (202)232-6718
E-mail: search@sfcg.org
URL: http://www.sfcg.org
Contact: John Marks, Pres.
Founded: 1982. **Staff:** 350. **Budget:** $10,000,000. **Languages:** English, French. **Multinational. Description:** Works to change the way the world deals with conflict - away from adversarial confrontation and towards collaborative problem solving. Philosophy is to "understand the differences" but "act on the commonalities." Engaged in a long-term process of incremental transformation, makes long-term commitments. Seek cross-cultural integration of indigenous and international concepts of conflict prevention. Works with partners on the ground to strengthen local capacity to deal with conflict; currently work in ten countries/regions: Angola, Burundi, Indonesia, Iran, Liberia, Sierra Leone, Macedonia, Middle East, Ukraine, and the USA. Methods include mediation/facilitation training, community organizing, radio/TV, journalism, sports, drama and music. **Libraries: Type:** not open to the public. **Awards:** Common Ground Award. **Frequency:** annual. **Type:** recognition. **Recipient:** for outstanding contribution to

peacemaking and conflict resolution in the media, arts community and politics ● Common Ground Middle East Journalism Award. **Frequency:** annual. **Type:** recognition. **Recipient:** for outstanding contribution to peacemaking and conflict resolution in the media, arts community and politics. **Subgroups:** Centre for Common Ground in Angola; Centre for Common Ground in Indonesia; Centre for Common Ground in Ukraine; Common Ground Productions; Search for Common Ground in Burundi; Search for Common Ground in Macedonia; Search for Common Ground in the Middle East; Talking Drum Studio Liberia; Talking Drum Studio Sierra Leone. **Formerly:** (1983) Nuclear Network. **Publications:** *Bulletin of Regional Cooperation in the Middle East* (in English and Hebrew), quarterly. Newsletter. Chronicles nongovernmental conflict resolution activities related to the Middle East. **Price:** $30.00 /year for individuals; $65.00 /year for institutions. ISSN: 1082-3646. **Circulation:** 3,500. **Advertising:** accepted. Alternate Formats: online ● *The Common Ground*, quarterly. Newsletter. Alternate Formats: online ● *Common Ground on Abortion Clinic Activism*. Papers. Includes supporting and respecting the decision-making of women, and rejecting behavior that is coercive or intimidating.

18226 ■ United to Secure America
1301 Pennsylvania Ave. NW, Ste.500
Washington, DC 20004
Ph: (202)742-4251
URL: http://www.secureamerica.info
Description: Believes that "immigration should be in the national interest, and that to protect all Americans, we must restore integrity to America's immigration system and effectively enforce our laws".

18227 ■ United States Congressional Advisory Board (USCAB)
Address Unknown since 2007
URL: http://www.ascf.org
Founded: 1981. **Members:** 5,000. **Staff:** 3. **Description:** A committee of the American Security Council Foundation (see separate entry). Individuals, companies, and corporations. Purpose is to establish and implement a strategy of national foreign policy based on "Peace Through Strength." Works to create a communication network among USCAB members and members of Congress and the Bush Administration. Serves as liaison between state groups and their Congressional representatives. Promotes and assists state groups in implementing educational programs nationwide. Sponsors monthly national security and leadership seminars. Maintains speakers' bureau; bestows annual Congressional Awards. **Publications:** *Briefing Papers*, periodic ● *National Security Report*, monthly. **Conventions/Meetings:** annual meeting.

18228 ■ Women in International Security (WIIS)
Center for Peace and Security Stud.
Edmund A. Walsh School of Foreign Ser.
Georgetown Univ.
3600 N St. NW
Washington, DC 20007
Ph: (202)687-3366
Fax: (202)687-3233
E-mail: wiismembership@georgetown.edu
URL: http://wiis.georgetown.edu
Contact: Marie-Laura Poire, Membership Coor.
Founded: 1987. **Members:** 1,200. **Membership Dues:** patron, $350-$1,000 ● sustaining, $110 ● basic, $60 ● outside Washington, DC area, overseas, $45 ● student, $30 ● nonprofit, $250 ● corporate, $5,000. **Staff:** 4. **Budget:** $250,000. **Multinational. Description:** A project of the Center for International and Security Studies at Maryland. Provides a forum for professional and social contact between women working on international issues in the military, academia, research and business organizations, and governmental and nonprofit groups. Acts as a nonpartisan network and professional development program for women and men. Serves as a clearinghouse for information for and about women, especially those working on international and foreign policy issues.

Sponsors seminars and panel discussions. Maintains a computerized database of women specialists for use by employers and contractors. **Computer Services:** database, women specialists in foreign and defense policy ● mailing lists. **Publications:** *Fellowships in International Affairs*. Directory. **Price:** $17.95 ● *Internships in Foreign and Defense Policy*. Directory. **Price:** $10.95 ● *Jobs Hotline*, biweekly. Contains lists of professional opportunities in the field. ● *WIIS Words*, 3/year. Newsletter. Includes information on seminars and speakers, profiles and accomplishments of members. **Circulation:** 1,500. Alternate Formats: online ● Membership Directory. **Conventions/Meetings:** periodic conference ● monthly seminar ● annual symposium - always June.

Sexual Freedom

18229 ■ National Coalition for Sexual Freedom (NSCF)
822 Guilford Ave.
Box 127
Baltimore, MD 21202-3707
Ph: (410)539-4824
Fax: (410)385-2827
E-mail: ncsfreedom@ncsfreedom.org
URL: http://www.ncsfreedom.org
Contact: Vivienne Kramer, Chair
Founded: 1997. **Membership Dues:** individual, $25 (annual) ● coalition partner, supporting, $100 (annual). **Description:** Aims to advance equal rights of consenting adults practicing alternative sexual expression.

Sleep

18230 ■ Awake In America
PO Box 51601
Philadelphia, PA 19115-1601
Ph: (215)764-6568
E-mail: contact@awakeinamerica.org
URL: http://www.awakeinamerica.org
Description: Focuses on sleep and sleep disorder issues. Educates and increases awareness of sleep disorders among the general public, businesses, corporations, allied health professionals, government and elected officials around the country. Provides support and outreach to individuals who have been diagnosed with sleep disorders. **Publications:** *The Sleep-e Times*, quarterly. Newsletter. **Price:** $4.00/ copy for nonmembers; $14.00 /year for nonmembers; included in membership dues. Alternate Formats: online.

Social Action

18231 ■ ESA
6 E Lancaster Ave.
Wynnewood, PA 19096-3420
Ph: (610)645-9390
Free: (800)650-6600
Fax: (610)649-8090
E-mail: esa@esa-online.org
URL: http://www.esa-online.org
Contact: Dr. Ron Sider, Pres./Founder
Founded: 1978. **Members:** 4,500. **Membership Dues:** student, low/fixed income, $20 (annual) ● basic, $35 (annual) ● international (airmail), $45 (annual) ● regular, in Canada and Mexico, $40 (annual). **Staff:** 11. **Budget:** $720,000. **Multinational. Description:** Christians of all denominations who "share the vision that every Christian be a faithful disciple - marked by service to the poor and powerless, reverence for life, care for creation and a passionate witness to Jesus Christ." Mission accomplished through the integration of Spiritual formation, evangelism, and social engagement at the grass roots level. Advocates that policy changes on issues such as peace, justice, poverty, disarmament, abortion, penal reform, and the environment should be based on holistic biblical discipleship. Directs the Crossroads program, which

engages Christian scholars in biblical public policy analysis. **Awards:** Finney Scholarship. **Frequency:** annual. **Type:** scholarship. **Recipient:** for students at Eastern Baptist Seminary who are concentrating on the Faith/Public Policy MA program. **Formerly:** (1993) Evangelicals for Social Action. **Publications:** *Christian Monographs on Public Policy*, bimonthly. Researches specific public policy issues, includes recommendations. **Price:** $5.00 ● *Creation Care Magazine*, quarterly. Covers environmental issues from a Christian perspective. **Price:** $25.00/year. **Circulation:** 5,000. **Advertising:** accepted ● *Prism*, bimonthly. Magazine. **Price:** included in membership dues. ISSN: 1079-6479. **Circulation:** 5,000. **Advertising:** accepted. Alternate Formats: online.

18232 ■ Starthrowers (SOS)
PO Box 192
Franklin, LA 70538
Ph: (337)828-2375
E-mail: agapebooks2002@yahoo.com
Contact: Bernard Broussard, Exec. Off.
Founded: 1965. **Members:** 50,000. **Membership Dues:** $10 (annual). **Staff:** 25. **Description:** Volunteer individuals advocating peace, social justice, human rights, anti abortion and euthanasia, relations, and the denouncement of the death penalty. Organizes boycotts and petition drives to promote legislative support. Offers home study courses in peace, justice, and environmental spirituality. The group is Catholic in origin but is currently ecumenical. Maintains speakers' bureau and hall of fame. **Libraries: Type:** open to the public. **Holdings:** 5,000; books, periodicals. **Subjects:** social justice, peace, human rights, spirituality, world religion, Catholic faith, civil rights. **Awards:** Ripple of Hope Award. **Frequency:** annual. **Type:** recognition. **Recipient:** for social justice work. **Affiliated With:** Consistent Life. **Formerly:** (1985) Human Dignity Coalition. **Publications:** *Agape*, monthly ● *Caring for Earth* ● *Death Penalty: Ultimate Violence* ● *Nonviolent Love* ● *Ripple of Hope*. Magazine ● *Starthrowers Magazine*, quarterly. **Price:** $8.00/year. **Circulation:** 5,000. **Advertising:** accepted. **Conventions/Meetings:** annual meeting.

Social Change

18233 ■ A. Philip Randolph Institute (APRI)
815-16th St. NW
Washington, DC 20006
Ph: (202)508-3710 (202)508-6954
Fax: (202)508-3711
E-mail: info@apri.org
URL: http://www.apri.org
Contact: Clayola Brown, Pres.
Founded: 1965. **Staff:** 10. **State Groups:** 13. **Local Groups:** 200. **Description:** Promotes cooperation between the labor force and the black community. Advocates for political action through the organization of affiliate groups and the building of coalitions for social change. Includes major areas of activities such as voter registration, labor education, and trade union leadership training. Founded by and named after A. Philip Randolph (1889-1979), founder of the Brotherhood of Sleeping Car Porters (which was absorbed by the Brotherhood of Railway, Airline and Steamship Clerks, Freight Handlers, Express and Station Employees). Conducts research and specialized education programs. Maintains speakers' bureau. **Libraries: Type:** reference. **Awards:** A. Philip Randolph Achievement Award. **Type:** recognition ● A. Philip Randolph/Bayard Rustin Freedom Award. **Type:** recognition ● Bayard Rustin Humanitarian Award. **Type:** recognition ● Rosina Tucker Award. **Type:** recognition. **Telecommunication Services:** electronic mail, cbrown@aflcio.org. **Affiliated With:** AFL-CIO. **Publications:** *News and Notes*, bimonthly ● *Working Paper*, annual ● Annual Report, annual ● Also publishes the Norman Hill column, The Black-Labor Agenda. **Conventions/Meetings:** annual conference ● regional meeting and conference - 5/year.

18234 ■ Alternatives for Simple Living
109 Gaul Dr.
PO Box 340
Sergeant Bluff, IA 51054
Ph: (712)943-6153
Free: (800)821-6153
Fax: (712)943-1402
E-mail: alternatives@simpleliving.org
URL: http://www.simpleliving.org
Contact: Gerald Iversen, Natl. Coor.
Founded: 1973. **Members:** 1,200. **Membership Dues:** downscaler, $500 (annual) ● celebrator, $250 (annual) ● co-operator, $100 (annual) ● nonconformer, $50 (annual) ● simple liver, $35 (annual). **Staff:** 3. **Budget:** $350,000. **Description:** Represents individuals, church, community, and activist organizations who are interested in changing materialistic lifestyles, promoting instead lifestyles of voluntary simplicity. Sponsors national Alternatives Celebrations Campaign, Christmas and Easter, as well as educational and charitable functions. **Libraries: Type:** reference. **Holdings:** 3,000; audio recordings, video recordings. **Subjects:** voluntary simplicity and related topics. **Subgroups:** Slow Down. **Also Known As:** Alternatives. **Publications:** *Break Forth Into Joy.* Video ● *Carols with Justice.* Booklet ● *The Christmas Game.* Booklet ● *Have Yourself a Merry Little Christmas.* Video ● *Living More with Less Study/Action Guide.* Handbook ● *Resource Guide,* quarterly. Catalog. Price: free ● *Simple Living 101: Toolbook for Activists.* Handbook ● *Simply the Best: 30 Years of Alternatives.* Book. Alternate Formats: CD-ROM ● *Spirit of Simplicity: Alternative Quotes and Art.* Book. Alternate Formats: CD-ROM ● *To Celebrate: Reshaping Holiday and Rites of Passage.* Book. **Conventions/Meetings:** semiannual board meeting.

18235 ■ Aquarian Research Foundation (ARF)
5620 Morton St.
Philadelphia, PA 19144
Ph: (215)848-2292
Free: (800)254-8291
E-mail: artr@juno.com
URL: http://www.aquarian.cjb.net
Contact: Judy Rosenblum, Dir.
Founded: 1969. **Staff:** 3. **Description:** Conducts research in discovering ways people can help bring a new age of love and peace into the world. Provides information on natural birth control. **Convention/Meeting:** none. **Libraries: Type:** open to the public. **Holdings:** 230; periodicals. **Subjects:** alternative health, peace, alternative energy. **Publications:** *Best of Aquarian.* Alternate Formats: CD-ROM ● *Grow with Sound and Spray.* Video ● *The Natural Birth Control Book* ● *Where's Utopia.* Video ● Also publishes materials on new developments in the alternative movement.

18236 ■ Behaviorists for Social Responsibility (BFSR)
c/o Dr. Mark Mattaini, Chm.
1040 W Harrison St.
Chicago, IL 60607
Ph: (312)996-4629
Fax: (312)996-2770
E-mail: bfsr@bfsr.org
URL: http://www.bfsr.org
Contact: Dr. Mark Mattaini, Chm.
Founded: 1977. **Members:** 200. **Description:** Serves as a special interest group of the Association for Behavior Analysis. Behavior analysts. Seeks to unite with educators, health care workers, and social service activists to combat social injustices and promote human well-being through the scientific application of individual behavior analysis and analysis of social environment. Maintains Speaker's Bureau; conducts research programs. **Libraries: Type:** reference. **Awards:** Lipson Basic Research Fund Grant. **Type:** grant. **Formerly:** (2001) Behaviorists for Social Action. **Publications:** *Behavior and Social Issues,* semiannual. Journal. Serves as a forum for the discussion of ethical, social, and political issues as they relate to the field of behavior analysis. **Price:** $13.00/year for students; $40.00 /year for individuals; $65.00 /year for institutions. ISSN: 1064-9506. **Circu-**lation: 300. **Advertising:** accepted. Alternate Formats: online. Also Cited As: *Behaviorists for Social Action Journal and Behavior Analysis and Social Action.* **Conventions/Meetings:** annual meeting, in conjunction with ABA.

18237 ■ Brotherhood Organization of a New Destiny (BOND)
PO Box 35090
Los Angeles, CA 90035-0090
Ph: (323)782-1980
Free: (800)411-BOND
Fax: (323)782-0122
E-mail: bond@bondinfo.org
URL: http://www.bondinfo.org
Contact: Rev. Jesse Lee Peterson, Pres./CEO
Founded: 1989. **Multinational. Description:** Works to attain its vision of "rebuilding the family by rebuilding the man". **Awards:** Booker T. Washington Award. **Frequency:** periodic. **Type:** recognition. **Recipient:** for individuals who have served as inspiration to other people. **Publications:** Newsletter, periodic.

18238 ■ Center for Religion, Ethics and Social Policy (CRESP)
117 Anabel Taylor Hall
Cornell Univ.
Ithaca, NY 14853
Ph: (607)255-5027 (607)255-6202
E-mail: akw7@cornell.edu
URL: http://www.cresp.cornell.edu
Contact: Anke K. Wessels PhD, Dir.
Founded: 1971. **Members:** 250. **Staff:** 10. **Budget:** $250,000. **Description:** Educational organization promoting individual, social, and ecological advancement toward a more humane and equitable existence for mankind. Sponsors community projects in areas of peace and justice, world hunger, resource depletion, Latin American relations, sustainability, education for agricultural concerns, and multicultural resources. **Libraries: Type:** reference. **Holdings:** 7,000; audiovisuals, books, periodicals. **Awards:** Jack Taylor Award. **Frequency:** annual. **Type:** recognition. **Recipient:** for a life committed to Social Justice. **Computer Services:** database ● mailing lists ● online services. **Projects:** EcoVillage at Ithaca; Seeds of Simplicity. **Publications:** *CUSLAR Newsletter,* bimonthly ● *EcoVillage at Ithaca,* quarterly. Newsletter ● *Hey!,* annual. Annual Report ● Annual Report, annual. **Conventions/Meetings:** annual conference.

18239 ■ Coalition for Justice in the Maquiladoras (CJM)
4207 Willow Brook Dr.
San Antonio, TX 78228
Ph: (210)732-8957
Fax: (210)732-8324
E-mail: cjm_mojeda@igc.org
URL: http://www.coalitionforjustice.net
Contact: Martha A. Ojeda, Exec. Dir.
Founded: 1989. **Members:** 100. **Membership Dues:** organization, $300 (annual) ● associate, $35 (annual). **Languages:** English, Spanish. **Multinational. Description:** Encourages U.S. corporations to adopt socially responsible practices in their Mexican manufacturing plants. (Maquiladoras is the Spanish term for manufacturing plants.) Conducts educational programs and maintains speakers' bureau. **Libraries: Type:** reference. **Holdings:** audio recordings, clippings, video recordings. **Subjects:** maquiladoras. **Publications:** *Newsletter for Coalition,* quarterly. **Price:** $25.00/year. **Conventions/Meetings:** semiannual conference.

18240 ■ Context Institute (CI)
PO Box 946
Langley, WA 98260
Ph: (360)221-6044
Fax: (360)221-6045
E-mail: ci@context.org
URL: http://www.context.org
Contact: Dr. Robert C. Gilman, Founder/Ed.
Founded: 1979. **Staff:** 2. **Description:** Seeks to facilitate positive cultural change. Acts as a source of information for others interested in creating a "more humane and sustainable culture." Maintains programs intended to increase social and environmental responsibility and promote cooperation between nations. Disseminates information. **Convention/Meeting:** none. **Libraries: Type:** reference. **Programs:** Consulting; Speaking; Sustainability Resource Library. **Publications:** *Eco-Village Report.* Book. Contains ecovillage and sustainable communities case studies and how to develop them. **Price:** $20.00 plus postage ● *In Context, A Journal of Humane Sustainable Culture,* quarterly. **Price:** $6.00 for back issues, plus $2 postage; $5.00 for 2 to 3 orders; $4.00 for 4 to 7 orders; $3.00 for 8 to 15 orders. ISSN: 0741-6180.

18241 ■ Creative Resources Guild (CRG)
PO Box 3397
Santa Monica, CA 90408-3397
Ph: (310)828-0130
Fax: (310)828-0130
E-mail: info@globalartistvillage.org
URL: http://www.globalvisions.org
Contact: John Tibayan, Exec. Dir.
Founded: 1988. **Description:** Assists spiritual and humanitarian projects and organizations get their message out through the Internet by establishing websites and providing an online searchable directory, and calendar of events. **Computer Services:** database, searchable directory of spiritual people, projects and organizations. **Additional Websites:** http://www.globalartistvillage.org. **Also Known As:** Global Visions. **Publications:** Brochures. **Conventions/Meetings:** periodic meeting.

18242 ■ Eco-Justice Working Group (EJWG)
c/o National Council of Churches
110 Maryland Ave. NE
Washington, DC 20002
Ph: (202)544-2350
E-mail: info@nccecojustice.org
URL: http://www.nccecojustice.org
Contact: Cassandra Carmichael, Dir.
Founded: 1984. **Description:** Protestant denominations and related groups. Seeks to provide education about and motivate action leading to "ecological wholeness and social justice." Sponsored by the National Council of the Churches of Christ in the U.S.A. **Telecommunication Services:** electronic mail, mgardner@episcopalchurch.org ● electronic mail, cassandra@toad.net. **Affiliated With:** National Council of Churches of Christ in the U.S.A. **Publications:** *The Egg,* quarterly. Journal. Published in conjunction with the Eco-Justice Project.

18243 ■ Episcopal Peace Fellowship (EPF)
637 S Dearborn St.
Chicago, IL 60605-1839
Ph: (312)922-8628
E-mail: epfnational@ameritech.net
URL: http://www.epfnational.org
Contact: Rev. Barbara K. Armstrong, Sec.
Founded: 1939. **Members:** 1,200. **Membership Dues:** limited income, $10 (annual) ● supporting, $40 (annual) ● sustaining, $70 (annual) ● contributing, $120 (annual) ● benefactor, $250-$1,000 (annual) ● donor, $1,000 (annual). **Staff:** 1. **Budget:** $44,000. **Local Groups:** 55. **Description:** Members of the Episcopal Church and other individuals engaged in the "discovery, advocacy, and practice of personal and social peace". Increases awareness of the peacemaking implications of the gospel. Through its local chapters, and national office works against capital punishment, racism, militarism, nuclear weapons, and the draft. Provides prisoner support and services to conscientious objectors and war or tax resisters. **Libraries: Type:** by appointment only. **Holdings:** 500; books. **Subjects:** peace and justice theology and history. **Awards:** John Nevin Sayre Award. **Frequency:** triennial. **Type:** recognition. **Recipient:** for contributions toward peacemaking. **Boards:** Local Chapters. **Councils:** National Executive. **Special Interest Groups:** Non-Geographic. **Affiliated With:** Fellowship of Reconciliation - USA. **Formerly:** Episcopal Pacifist Fellowship. **Publications:** *Cross Before Flag.* Booklet. Features Resolution of Episcopal Church on peace. **Price:** $1.00 ●

Episcopal Peace Fellowship—Newsletter, quarterly. Covers peace activities around the world, especially in the context of the Episcopal church. **Price:** included in membership dues ● *The Voice of Conscience: A Loud and Unusual Noise? History of EPF 1939-1989.* Paper ● Pamphlets. Contains Series of educational and devotional actions of peace. ● Brochures. Alternate Formats: online. **Conventions/ Meetings:** semiannual board meeting.

18244 ■ Foundation on Economic Trends (FOET)

4520 E West Hwy., Ste.600
Bethesda, MD 20814
Ph: (301)656-6272
Fax: (301)654-0208
E-mail: office@foet.org
URL: http://www.foet.org
Contact: Jeremy Rifkin, Pres.

Founded: 1977. **Description:** Disseminates information through lectures, campaigns, and distribution of educational materials on the economic, social, environmental and ethical impacts of new technologies. Provides speakers for conferences and conventions on the subjects of computer technology's impact on unemployment; biotechnology and genetic engineering. **Libraries: Type:** reference. **Publications:** *Biological Warfare* ● *Deliberate Release of Microorganisms* ● *Reproductive Technology.* **Conventions/ Meetings:** annual conference.

18245 ■ Freedom of Thought Foundation (FTF)

Address Unknown since 2007

Founded: 1994. **Members:** 800. **Membership Dues:** $50 (annual) ● one-time membership fee, $100. **Description:** Individuals with an interest in electronic and other forms of mind control. Seeks to educate the public regarding mind control and the threat posed to individual freedom posed by mind control techniques. Promotes repeal of the National Security Act. Maintains legal advocacy and support programs for victims of mind control; develops countermeasures against mind control; functions as a network linking organizations, professionals, and individuals affected by mind control. Encourages establishment of grass roots freedom of thought organizations. Conducts fundraising activities. **Libraries: Type:** not open to the public. **Holdings:** 10,000. **Subjects:** mind control, DID/MPD, temporal lobe epilepsy. **Awards:** J. Mengele Award. **Type:** recognition. **Recipient:** for experiments on humans or animals without their consent or knowledge. **Publications:** *Freethinking Newsletter*, monthly. **Price:** $50.00/year.

18246 ■ Graduation Pledge Alliance (GPA)

Manchester Coll.
604 E Coll. Ave.
North Manchester, IN 46962
Ph: (260)982-5346
Fax: (260)982-5043
E-mail: njwollman@manchester.edu
URL: http://www.graduationpledge.org
Contact: Neil Wollman, Natl. Coor.

Founded: 1987. **Staff:** 2. **Budget:** $4,000. **Local Groups:** 120. **Multinational. Description:** Participants include students, faculty members, school administrators, and other interested individuals. Promotes social and environmental responsibility by encouraging students to pledge upon graduation that they will investigate and consider the social and environmental consequences of any job opportunity they consider or work at. Seeks to: develop a network of people interested in instituting a graduation pledge program at their respective schools; encourage employers to alter their policies and practices to reflect the social and environmental concerns of their employees; increase the role of school activities in developing an "informed, democratic" citizenry. Holds forums and workshops; sponsors essay contests; maintains speakers' bureau; offers consulting services. **Publications:** *Network Letter*, periodic. Includes lists of GPA contacts.

18247 ■ Groundwork for a Just World (GJW)

c/o Barbara Beesley
11224 Kercheval St.
Detroit, MI 48218
Ph: (313)822-2005
Fax: (313)822-5197
E-mail: groundwork@aol.com
URL: http://www.hkhfdn.org/directory/mi.html
Contact: Barbara Beesley, Contact

Founded: 1976. **Members:** 5,000. **Membership Dues:** individual, $35 (annual) ● group, $150 (annual). **Staff:** 4. **Budget:** $100,000. **Description:** Individuals and organizations, primarily comprising Catholic women, promoting greater understanding of and involvement with global and domestic issues of peace and justice. Participates in campaigns to create what the group feels is a healthier society, including anti-nuclear weapons demonstrations, actions against the use of military power, projects to fight racism and sexism, and efforts to redress economic inequities. Organizes special events concerning racial justice, women's justice, economic justice, environmental concerns, and peace movements. Conducts election workshops; monitors Michigan state and federal legislation; operates clearance retreats and speakers' bureau. **Libraries: Type:** reference; not open to the public. **Awards:** Discipleship Award. **Frequency:** annual. **Type:** recognition. **Committees:** Racial Justice; Testimonial Dinner; Urban Plunge. **Publications:** *Groundwork*, bimonthly. Newsletter. Deals with issues related to peacemaking, racial, economic, and environmental justice, and women's rights. **Price:** included in membership dues. **Circulation:** 3,000 ● *Political Action Guide*, biennial. Handbook. For Michigan and federal governments. **Conventions/Meetings:** quarterly board meeting.

18248 ■ Independent Progressive Politics Network (IPPN)

PO Box 1041
Bloomfield, NJ 07003
Ph: (973)338-5398
E-mail: indpol@igc.org
URL: http://www.ippn.org
Contact: Mr. Ted Glick, Natl. Coor.

Founded: 1995. **Members:** 36. **Staff:** 2. **Budget:** $80,000. **Description:** Individuals, organizations, civil rights groups, women's organizations, peace groups, and other progressive political groups. Seeks to bring together grass roots progressive movements into organized framework in order. Represents the political interests of those often disenfranchised and excluded from the existing political and economic system. **Projects:** Popular Education; Racism Watch. **Publications:** *Independent Politics News*, quarterly. Newspaper. **Price:** $10.00/year. **Circulation:** 5,000.

18249 ■ Interhelp

PO Box 61
Delmar, NY 12054
Ph: (518)439-6065 (518)475-1929
E-mail: info@interhelpnetwork.org
URL: http://www.interhelpnetwork.org
Contact: Sondra Sprinkling, Pres.

Founded: 1980. **Staff:** 1. **Budget:** $10,000. **Regional Groups:** 2. **Local Groups:** 1. **National Groups:** 3. **Multinational. Description:** Nonpartisan network of individuals and groups. Provides forum for individuals to share concerns on issues and conditions threatening human and planetary life. Works to help people overcome feelings of isolation and powerlessness within their communities, thus empowering individuals and connecting them with "the larger web of life." Offers training in Despair and Empowerment, Deep Ecology, and Personal Support Systems; designs programs for professional and community groups, political and environmental organizations, schools, and churches. Maintains speakers' bureau and library. **Telecommunication Services:** electronic mail, interhelp@earthlink.net. **Publications:** *Interhelp: A Networking Newsletter*, quarterly. Includes calendar of events, network news, interviews, poems, art, book reviews and letters. **Price:** $20.00/year. **Circulation:** 500. Alternate Formats: online. Also Cited As: *Interhelp: Awakening in the Nuclear Age.*

Conventions/Meetings: annual Gatherings - meeting - usually in February.

18250 ■ International Society for Panetics (ISP)

PO Box 142
College Park, MD 20741
URL: http://www.paneticsworldwide.org
Contact: Carl F. Stover, Chm. Emeritus

Founded: 1991. **Members:** 100. **Membership Dues:** student, retiree, $15 (annual) ● full, $50 (annual). **Budget:** $22,500. **Description:** Individuals interested in panetics, the effort to "develop a coherent body of data, concepts, and approaches to help reduce the infliction of suffering around the world". Promotes scholarship and action in areas including politics, peace studies, public health, urban violence, and noise abatement. Conducts research and panetic analyses of public policies; sponsors educational programs; provides support and assistance to panetic scholars and researchers worldwide. **Publications:** *Panetics*, quarterly. Journal. **Price:** included in membership dues. Alternate Formats: online ● *Panetics Trilogy.* Book. **Conventions/Meetings:** annual conference and lecture.

18251 ■ International Symbiosis Society (ISS)

c/o Prof. Douglas Zook, Pres./Acting Treas.
Boston Univ.
2 Sherborn St.
Boston, MA 02215
E-mail: iss@bu.edu
URL: http://people.bu.edu/iss
Contact: Prof. Douglas Zook, Pres./Acting Treas.

Founded: 1997. **Membership Dues:** regular, $30 (annual) ● student, $15 (annual) ● pre-college teacher, $20 (annual). **Multinational. Description:** Promotes and advances the science of Symbiology. Provides a forum for biologists interested in symbiosis to communicate with scientists of similar focus and interests. Calls attention to Symbiology as a scientific discipline which requires integration into educational curricula and assists in building those curricula. **Telecommunication Services:** electronic mail, dzook@bu.edu. **Publications:** *Symbiosis*, 9/year. Journal. Seeks to introduce new and unknown symbiosis for research in Symbiology. **Price:** $135.00 /year for members; $110.00/year for students and pre-college teachers; $630.00 /year for nonmembers ● *Symbiosis International*, 3/year. Newsletter. **Price:** free for members. **Conventions/Meetings:** triennial congress.

18252 ■ National Partnership for Social Enterprise

6 Brigade Hill Rd.
Morristown, NJ 07960-4901
Ph: (973)540-1900
Fax: (973)539-1661
Contact: Robert Corman, Pres.

Founded: 1991. **Staff:** 4. **Description:** Works to develop and implement strategies for sustainable social change. Engages in market research, development, business planning and implementation. Works with grass roots groups, government, and businesses. **Libraries: Type:** not open to the public. **Holdings:** 1,000. **Subjects:** banking, health, higher education. **Publications:** Brochure. **Conventions/ Meetings:** periodic conference.

18253 ■ NETWORK, A National Catholic Social Justice Lobby

25 E St. NW, Ste.200
Washington, DC 20001-1630
Ph: (202)347-9797
Fax: (202)347-9864
E-mail: network@networklobby.org
URL: http://www.networklobby.org
Contact: Simone Campbell SSS, Natl. Coor.

Founded: 1971. **Members:** 11,000. **Membership Dues:** regular, $50 (annual) ● limited income, student, $20 (annual). **Staff:** 14. **Description:** Works as a national Catholic social justice lobby that educates, lobbies, and organizes to influence the formation of federal legislation to promote economic and social justice. **Telecommunication Services:** electronic mail, scampbell@networklobby.org. **Programs:** NETWORK Education. **Formerly:** (2001) NETWORK. **Publications:** *Learning About Taxes: Toward a Fair and Just System.* Book. **Price:** $35.00 ● *Legislative Action Fax Program,* biweekly, published only when Congress is in session. **Price:** $40.00 for members; $50.00 for nonmembers ● *NETWORK Connection,* bimonthly. Magazine. Contains feature articles and legislative updates. **Price:** $40.00. **Circulation:** 10,000. Alternate Formats: online ● *Shaping a New World: A Challenge for the 21st Century.* Booklet. **Price:** $6.00 1-9 copies; $5.40 10-30 copies; $5.10 31-99 copies; $4.80 more than 100 copies ● *Shaping A New World Wall Chart.* **Price:** $5.00 folded; $8.50 unfolded ● *Voter Education* (in English and Spanish). Book. **Price:** $75.00 ● Also publishes election materials and videos on globalization, legislative advocacy, etc.

18254 ■ Peace Resource Project (PRP)
PO Box 1122
Arcata, CA 95518-1122
Ph: (707)822-4229
Fax: (707)268-8985
E-mail: peace@peaceproject.com
URL: http://www.peaceproject.com
Contact: Gabriel Day, Coor.
Founded: 1983. **Staff:** 6. **Budget:** $400,000. **For-Profit. Description:** Seeks to create and provide resources for the peace, social justice, and environmental movements. Distributes materials communicating messages for peace, social justice, and environmental concern. Empowers grass root organizations to educate, organize, and raise funds in their communities.

18255 ■ People's Institute for Survival and Beyond (PISB)
PO Box 770175
New Orleans, LA 70177-0175
Ph: (504)301-9292
Fax: (504)301-9291
E-mail: chisom@thepeoplesinstitute.org
URL: http://www.pisab.org
Contact: Ronald Chisom, Exec. Dir.
Founded: 1980. **Staff:** 11. **Description:** Works to combat racism through leadership development and community organization. Conducts workshops and other educational programs; provides technical assistance; maintains speakers' bureau. **Libraries: Type:** reference. **Holdings:** 300; books, periodicals. **Subjects:** civil rights, history, racism. **Committees:** European Dissent; People's Youth Agenda. **Conventions/Meetings:** monthly Undoing Racism/Community Organizing Workshops, 5-8 workshops.

18256 ■ Proutist Universal (UPIF)
PO Box 56533
Washington, DC 20040
Ph: (301)231-0110 (202)468-3004
Fax: (202)829-0462
E-mail: nysector@prout.org
URL: http://www.prout.org
Contact: Prabhat R. Sarkar, Founder
Founded: 1975. **Members:** 750. **Staff:** 3. **Regional Groups:** 13. **State Groups:** 7. **Local Groups:** 29. **Description:** Individuals interested in facilitating social change through promotion of physical, social, moral, intellectual, and spiritual development. Maintains speakers' bureau and charitable program. Organizes leadership training programs. Cosponsors, in conjunction with the Prout Institute, seminars and symposia in Prout theory and its application to current events; offers instruction in meditation and yoga. **Libraries: Type:** reference. **Holdings:** 2,750. **Committees:** Cultural; Service and Relief. **Formerly:** (2000) Universal Proutist Intellectual Federation. **Publications:** *After Capitalism: Prout's Vision for a New World.* Book. **Price:** $14.95 ● *Prout Journal,* quarterly. Alternate Formats: online ● *Proutist America,* quarterly. Newsletter. Carries news and views of a socioeconomic movement based on the ideals of the Progressive Utilization Theory. **Conventions/Meetings:** semiannual meeting.

18257 ■ Quixote Center (QC)
PO Box 5206
Hyattsville, MD 20782-0206
Ph: (301)699-0042
E-mail: quixote@quixote.org
URL: http://www.quixote.org
Contact: Dolores C. Pomerleau, Co-Dir.
Founded: 1976. **Staff:** 14. **Budget:** $1,000,000. **Multinational. Description:** International justice and peace center. Operates: Quest for Peace, funding and humanitarian aid for poor of Nicaragua; Haiti Reborn, which provides education and reforestation and to restore democracy to Haiti; Equal Justice/USA, which works to reform the U.S. criminal justice system by eliminating racism, economic biases and death penalty; Priest for Equality, which promotes gender equality and inclusive language in Roman Catholic Church; Catholics Speak Out, a movement for justice, equality and democracy which encourages Catholics to speak out on issues in church life. **Publications:** *Inclusive Language Lectionaries.* For Roman Catholic mass. ● *The Inclusive Language New Testament* ● *Noisy Contemplation: Prayer for Busy People* ● *Rocinante,* quarterly. Newsletter. Contains reports on the efforts of the center. Alternate Formats: online ● Books ● Pamphlets ● Report, annual. Alternate Formats: online.

18258 ■ Southeast Institute for Group and Family Therapy (SEI)
103 Edwards Ridge Rd.
Chapel Hill, NC 27517-9201
Ph: (919)929-1171
Fax: (919)929-1174
E-mail: vjoines@seinstitute.com
URL: http://www.seinstitute.com
Contact: Vann Joines PhD, Pres./Dir.
Founded: 1969. **Staff:** 5. **Budget:** $25,000. **Description:** Provides training in individual, group, couple and family therapy, organizational effectiveness, and creative group problem-solving. Conducts workshops, seminars, and courses in order to help people identify and solve problems on a personal and institutional level. Trains mental health professionals for certification in the International Transactional Analysis Association, The American Association for Marriage and Family Therapy, and The American Group Psychotherapy Association. Main approach taught is Redecision Therapy. **Formerly:** (1974) Fellowship for Racial and Economic Equality; (1989) Southeast Institute. **Publications:** *Joines Personality Adaptation Questionnaire.* Manual. **Price:** $160.00 ● *Personality Adaptations: A New Guide to Human Understanding for Psychotherapists and Counselors.* Book. Describes the six personality adaptations in detail. **Price:** $29.95 ● *TA Today: A New Introduction to Transactional Analysis.* Book. Features a complete and up to date theory of transactional analysis. **Price:** $21.95 ● Videos. **Conventions/Meetings:** biennial conference.

18259 ■ Technocracy Inc.
c/o Continental Headquarters
2475 Harksell Rd.
Ferndale, WA 98248-9764
Ph: (360)366-1012
Free: (800)797-2711
Fax: (360)366-1409
E-mail: chq111@aol.com
URL: http://www.technocracyinc.org
Contact: Grace Sheldon, Sec.
Founded: 1933. **Membership Dues:** individual, $15 (annual). **Staff:** 5. **Local Groups:** 100. **Description:** Serves as a North American, volunteer membership social movement seeking to inform people about North America's social problems and to find scientific and technological solutions to them. Represents citizens of North American Continent that excludes only aliens (people residing outside of the Continent) and politicians. **Telecommunication Services:** electronic mail, tech-mag@juno.com. **Publications:** *North American Technocrat,* quarterly. Magazine. Reports on current events and social and technological change from a technocratic perspective. **Price:** $6.00/year; $2.00 each. ISSN: 0029-3474. **Conventions/Meetings:** annual meeting.

18260 ■ Universal Proutist Youth Federation (UPYF)
PO Box 56533
Washington, DC 20040
Ph: (301)231-0110
Fax: (202)829-0462
E-mail: yfny@prout.org
Contact: Dada Vimalananda, Sec.
Founded: 1963. **Members:** 1,500. **State Groups:** 12. **Description:** Individuals between the ages of 11 and 45 interested in progressive spiritual and social change for the benefit of all human beings based on the ideas of Prout (the Progressive Utilization Theory). Aims to establish a society that is based on the principles of progressive utilization of all resources and create a socio-economic-political consciousness among all youth. Conducts seminars and study courses; offers classes in meditation and spiritual and social philosophy; sponsors festivals and concerts. Operates children's services and charitable programs. Maintains speakers' bureau. **Libraries: Type:** reference. **Holdings:** 500. **Committees:** Cultural; Relief. **Publications:** *Prout Youth Forum,* monthly ● Books ● Pamphlets. **Conventions/Meetings:** quarterly meeting.

18261 ■ Venus Project
21 Valley Ln.
Venus, FL 33960
Ph: (863)465-0321
Fax: (863)465-1928
E-mail: tvp@thevenusproject.com
URL: http://www.thevenusproject.com
Contact: Roxanne Meadows, Sec.-Treas.
Founded: 1970. **Members:** 250. **Multinational. Description:** Membership represents a cross section of professional and nonprofessional participants. By using the methods of science to serve humankind, the organization calls for a systems-oriented society based upon an energy survey of the earth's resources to determine the available resources and personnel, with a plan for total environmental design. Presently engaged in alternative energy sources research and in redesigning the entire environment of the political, social, and economic institutions toward a humanistically oriented society and in preparing a set of blueprints for a totally integrated environment. Maintains planning center, speakers' bureau, and museum; conducts research programs; presents lectures; prepares videocassettes on alternative futures. **Convention/Meeting:** none. **Libraries: Type:** open to the public. **Committees:** Environmental Studies. **Formerly:** Project Americana; Association Sociocyberneering, Inc. **Publications:** *The Best That Money Can't Buy: Beyond Politics, Poverty and War.* Book. **Price:** $24.95. **Advertising:** accepted ● *Cities in Transition.* Video ● *Designing The Future.* Book. **Price:** $12.00 ● *Self-Erecting Structures.* Video. Presents the fantastic future of the intelligent and humane use of AI and cybernation as they construct the cities, bridges and more. **Price:** $19.95 each ● *The Venus Project: The Redesign of a Culture.* Video. **Price:** $110.80 each ● *Welcome To The Future.* Video. Presents an attainable vision of what the world could be if intelligently apply science and technology with environmental and human concern. **Price:** $29.95 each ● *Welcome To The Venus Project.* Book.

18262 ■ Women Proutists (WP)
PO Box 56533
Washington, DC 20040-6533
Ph: (301)562-8674
E-mail: wpny@prout.org
URL: http://www.prout.org/Womensprout.html
Founded: 1985. **Members:** 10,000. **Regional Groups:** 4. **Local Groups:** 30. **Description:** Enhances the dignity of women through economic independence, cultural renaissance, and lasting social change based on neo-humanism and a universal spiritual outlook. Encourages adherence to ideals outlined in PROUT, the Progressive Utilization Theory, which stresses decentralized economics, world government, and universalism. Sponsors classes, seminars, and a two-month training session in social and spiritual philosophy and organization.

Organizes grass roots social service projects and fundraising events to benefit developing countries. **Also Known As:** Girls' Prout. **Formerly:** Universal Proutists Women. **Publications:** *Rising Sun Newsletter*, monthly ● *Tara: Journal of the Women's Prout Movement*, quarterly. **Price:** $6.00/year. **Circulation:** 10,000 ● Also publishes leaflets, flyers, and local and regional publications. **Conventions/Meetings:** semiannual conference.

18263 ■ Women's Project
55 W End Ave.
New York, NY 10023
Ph: (212)765-1706
E-mail: info@womensproject.org
URL: http://www.womensproject.org
Contact: Leigh A. Giroux, Co-Chair
Founded: 1981. **Members:** 400. **Membership Dues:** low income, $15 (annual) ● general, $25 (annual) ● sustaining, $50 (annual) ● supporting, $100 (annual). **Staff:** 6. **Budget:** $244,000. **Description:** Organization is committed to: the elimination of sexism and racism, particularly violence against women, children, and people of color; women's economic issues, especially those affecting low-income women; social justice issues such as sexism, racism, homophobia, ageism, "ableism", classism, and anti-Semitism. Offers educational programs and community organizing. **Libraries: Type:** reference. **Holdings:** 4,000; books, periodicals, video recordings. **Subjects:** women's, lesbian, gay and African-American literature. **Awards:** Evangeline K. Brown Award for Social Justice. **Frequency:** annual. **Type:** recognition. **Recipient:** for writing a history of the activism in Arkansas. **Telecommunication Services:** TDD, (501)372-6853. **Publications:** *Homophobia: A Weapon of Sexism*. Book. **Price:** $12.00 ● *In the Time of the Right: Reflections on Liberation*. Book ● *Transformation*, quarterly. Newsletter. Contains commentary and analysis on women's and other social issues and occasional book reviews. **Price:** $25.00/year. **Circulation:** 1,500. Alternate Formats: online; magnetic tape.

Social Issues

18264 ■ Applied Research Center (ARC)
900 Alice St., Ste.400
Oakland, CA 94607
Ph: (510)653-3415
Fax: (510)986-1062
E-mail: arc@arc.org
URL: http://www.arc.org
Contact: Gary Delgado PhD, Founder/Exec. Dir.
Founded: 1981. **Description:** Aims to advance social progress and to measure the results. Studies the practice of organizing. **Programs:** Action Education; ERASE; WARP. **Publications:** *Beyond the Politics of Place*. Report. Features topics about the study of community organizing. ● *ColorLines*, quarterly. Magazine. Explores issues of race, culture and action. Alternate Formats: online ● *The Last Stop Sign*. Article. Discusses issues of importance of organizing around the identity of marginalized people. Alternate Formats: online ● *RaceWire*. Articles. Features news and op-ed that focuses on issues of race, politics, and culture. Alternate Formats: online.

18265 ■ Center for Assessment and Policy Development (CAPD)
268 Barren Hill Rd.
Conshohocken, PA 19428.
Ph: (610)828-1063
Fax: (610)828-3718
E-mail: sleiderman@capd.org
URL: http://www.capd.org
Contact: Sally H. Leiderman, Pres.
Founded: 1987. **Description:** Seeks to help institutions, communities and public systems improve outcomes for children, adolescents, and families for positive social change. Issues worked on include: improving the health, positive development and early school success of young children; family support and empowerment; education; adolescent parenting;

violence prevention; community change; reduction in racism, particularly institutional racism; leadership; and civic engagement. Plans, designs and helps to implement community/foundation partnerships, conducts strategic reviews of broad programmatic and issues areas, and provides evaluation and technical assistance to community groups, nonprofit institutions, state and local governments, schools and corporate and private foundations. **Projects:** Change; Children First Initiative; Claremont Cooperative; Community Services Network; Creating the Public Will to Invest in Children; Eureka Communities; Philadelphia Family Centers; Welfare-to-Work.

18266 ■ Simple Society Alliance for Human Empowerment
379 Amherst St., No. 234
Nashua, NH 03063
E-mail: simple@simsoc.org
URL: http://www.simsoc.org
Contact: John M. Watkins, Exec. Dir.
Founded: 1993. **Members:** 470. **Staff:** 2. **Budget:** $100,000. **Description:** Dedicated to creating a "simpler, more humane society in order to help everyone achieve their full potential". The members of The Alliance are non-profit and other cause-related organizations interested in using grassroots strength to simplify the quest for individual human potential. **Also Known As:** (2002) The Alliance for Human Empowerment; (2003) Simple Society. **Publications:** *Alliance Enabler News*, monthly. Newsletter. Provides information to members of the Alliance on news of importance and on how they can use the collaborative fund-raising system. **Price:** free. **Circulation:** 20. Alternate Formats: online.

18267 ■ United States Business and Industry Council Educational Foundation (USBICEF)
910 16th St. NW, Ste.300
Washington, DC 20006
Ph: (202)728-1990
Fax: (202)728-1981
E-mail: usbicef@aol.com
URL: http://www.americaneconomicalert.org
Contact: Kevin L. Kearns, Pres.
Founded: 1968. **Members:** 1,500. **Staff:** 7. **Description:** Serves the Americans to promote entrepreneurship, seeks deregulation of the U.S. economy, pushes for lower taxes and less government spending, and eliminate capital gains and estate taxes on family-owned businesses; promotes the global competitiveness of U.S. businesses. Fights to strengthen American and family values; promotes school choice; strives to combat political correctness and speech control on campus, eliminate multiculturalism in the academic curriculum, and combat all forms of media bias. Strives to define America's international interests, strengthen the economic and technological foundations of U.S. global leadership. Sponsors Campus Newspaper Program, Campus Cartoon Service, Krieble Editorial Service, Campus News Service, and Public Outreach Program. **Awards:** American Values Award. **Frequency:** annual. **Type:** recognition. **Recipient:** for individuals whose professional or private achievements are in line with the policies and goals of the USBIC Educational Foundation. **Affiliated With:** United States Business and Industry Council. **Conventions/Meetings:** annual Campus Lecture Program, held on American college and university campuses - during academic year ● Overseas Lecture Series, tour of campuses with foreign lecturer - usually held during fall semester ● Stranahan American Interests Lecture Series - each academic year.

Social Justice

18268 ■ And Justice for All (AJA)
PO Box 53079
Washington, DC 20009
Ph: (202)547-0508
E-mail: justice@clark.net
URL: http://qrd.tcp.com/qrd/www/orgs/aja
Contact: Jonathan Zucker, Exec. Dir.
Founded: 1995. **Membership Dues:** sustaining, $100 (annual) ● regular, $20 (annual) ● limited

income, $5 (annual) ● student, $1 (annual). **Description:** Seeks equality for everyone regardless of sexual orientation. Aims to increase the visibility and participation of heterosexuals in the lesbian, gay, bisexual and transgender rights movement.

18269 ■ Axis of Justice (AOJ)
1275 N Wilton Pl., Ste.B
Los Angeles, CA 90038
E-mail: info@axisofjustice.org
URL: http://www.axisofjustice.org
Contact: Rosa Romera, Dir.
Multinational. Description: Brings together musicians, fans of music and grassroots political organizations to fight for social justice. Aims to build a bridge between fans of music around the world and local political organizations. Organizes around issues of peace, human rights and economic justice. **Publications:** Newsletter. Alternate Formats: online ● Video. Contains footage of the Palace show as well as some excerpts from past Axis shows. Alternate Formats: CD-ROM.

18270 ■ Citizens for Consumer Justice (CCJ)
117 S 17th St., No. 311
Philadelphia, PA 19103
Ph: (215)569-8220
Fax: (215)569-8229
E-mail: info@ccjustice.org
URL: http://www.ccjustice.org
Contact: Lauren Townsend, Exec. Dir.
Founded: 1997. **Description:** Seeks to promote economic, racial, social, civil and environmental justice through citizen action and campaigns to educate the public. Works for quality healthcare for all and defends Social Security, Medicare and Medicaid. Advocates for the lowering of prescription drug prices. Works for campaign finance reform and clean money elections. Advocates for stronger corporate accountability, dedicated funding of public transportation and democracy in the media and telecommunications industry. **Telecommunication Services:** electronic mail, lauren@ccjustice.org.

18271 ■ International Possibilities Unlimited (IPU)
8403 Colesville Rd., Metro Plaza II
Silver Spring, MD 20910
Ph: (301)562-0883
Fax: (301)562-8084
E-mail: shani@ipunlimited.org
URL: http://www.ipunlimited.org
Contact: Deborah Robinson, Founder/Exec. Dir.
Founded: 1997. **Multinational. Description:** Represents the interests of individuals dedicated to building a global network linking people of African descent within the United States to social justice struggles throughout the world. Strives to increase understanding, participation and activism by Black people in international arenas. Mobilizes national and international networks to participate in international forums. Advocates for social justice, conducts research, provides technical assistance, serves as a clearinghouse for information, and provides avenues for experiential learning. **Programs:** Civic Inclusion and Capacity Building; Environmental Racism and Human Rights; Young Adult Leadership Development. **Publications:** *The Fundamental Human Right To Prosecution And Compensation*. Paper. Alternate Formats: online ● *Shift Happens: Contemporary Racism And African American*. Paper. Alternate Formats: online ● Newsletter. Alternate Formats: online.

18272 ■ National Black Justice Coalition (NBJC)
700 12th St. NW, Ste.700
Washington, DC 20005
Ph: (202)349-3756
E-mail: info@nbjcoalition.org
URL: http://www.nbjcoalition.org
Contact: H. Alexander Robinson, Exec. Dir./CEO
Founded: 2003. **Membership Dues:** student, $20 (annual) ● individual, $35 (annual) ● family, $50 (annual) ● contributing, $100 (annual). **Description:** Fosters equality by fighting racism and homophobia. Advocates for social justice by educating and mobiliz-

ing opinion leaders, including elected officials, clergy and media with focus on Black communities. **Publications:** Brochure.

Social Responsibility

18273 ■ INFORM
120 Wall St., 14th Fl.
New York, NY 10005-4001
Ph: (212)361-2400
Fax: (212)361-2412
E-mail: delayo@informinc.org
URL: http://www.informinc.org
Contact: Katherine Dea, Exec. Dir.
Founded: 1974. **Members:** 500. **Membership Dues:** regular, $35 (annual) ● friend, $50 (annual) ● contributor, $100 (annual) ● supporter, $250 (annual) ● donor, $500 (annual) ● associate, $1,000 (annual) ● benefactor, $5,000 (annual). **Staff:** 14. **Budget:** $1,629,290. **Description:** Examines business practices, technologies and products that threaten the environment, waste the natural resources, or put human health at risk. Works constructively with companies, communities, government agencies, and environmental organizations. Identifies and promotes avenues of innovation that support environmentally sustainable economic growth. Works on: protecting public health against the unsafe use of toxic chemicals; promoting waste prevention and the design of less wasteful products; and advancing the shift to sustainable transportation. Informs public debates worldwide via published reports, expert testimony, conference and workshop presentations, and media and outreach initiatives. **Publications:** *Cleaning for Health: Products and Practices for a Safer Indoor Environment.* Book ● *Greening Garbage Trucks: New Technologies for Cleaner Air.* Book ● *INFORM Reports*, quarterly. Newsletter. Provides updates on research projects and outreach activities. **Price:** $25.00. ISSN: 0275-522X. **Circulation:** 2,000. Alternate Formats: online ● *Waste in the Wireless World: The Challenge of Cell Phones.* Book.

18274 ■ Message! Products
PO Box 700
Edgewood, MD 21040-0700
Free: (800)243-2565
Fax: (800)790-6684
E-mail: helpmp@messageproducts.com
URL: http://www.messageproducts.com
Founded: 1985. **Staff:** 9. **For-Profit. Description:** Prints checks with messages of nonprofit associations, such as Greenpeace, People for the Ethical Treatment of Anis, Mothers Against Drunk Driving, National Organization for Women, Vietnam of America. Company contributes a percentage of its income to these groups as support money. **Affiliated With:** Greenpeace U.S.A.; Mothers Against Drunk Driving; National Organization for Women; People for the Ethical Treatment of Animals; Vietnam Veterans of America.

18275 ■ Social Investment Forum (SIF)
1612 K St. NW, Ste.650
Washington, DC 20006
Ph: (202)872-5319
Fax: (202)822-8471
E-mail: franteplitz@socialinvest.org
URL: http://www.socialinvest.org
Contact: Fran Teplitz, Dir.
Founded: 1981. **Members:** 600. **Membership Dues:** individual financial professional, $300 (annual) ● community investing institution, SRI bank and/or credit union, $350-$4,200 (annual) ● institution with SRI AUM, $350-$16,000 (annual) ● SRI service provider (for-profit), $750-$4,000 (annual) ● institutional investor without distinguished SRI or non-SRI holdings, $1,000-$5,000 (annual) ● non-profit, civil society organization, $350-$600 (annual). **Staff:** 3. **Description:** Consists of investment professionals and institutions promoting socially responsible investment. Provides listings of financial professionals, mutual funds, information sources, and community investments that offer socially responsible investing.

Compiles statistics. **Awards:** Moskowitz Prize. **Frequency:** annual. **Type:** monetary. **Recipient:** for best research on socially responsible investing. **Committees:** Board Nominating; Campaign; Community Investment, Shareholder Action; Conference; Membership; Research. **Publications:** *Connections*, quarterly. Newsletter. Contains news and trends in industry. **Price:** included in membership dues. **Circulation:** 2,200. **Advertising:** accepted ● *Report on Socially Responsible Investing Trends in the US*, biennial. Alternate Formats: online ● *Social Investment Forum Member Directory*, annual. Membership Directory ● Biennial Report on social investment trends; Annual Moskowitz Prize report; Report on Effects of SEC Shareholder Rules; Report on Tobacco Investments for Institutional Investors. **Conventions/Meetings:** annual conference (exhibits) - 2007 Nov. 3-6, Santa Ana Pueblo, NM - **Avg. Attendance:** 640.

Social Security

18276 ■ National Academy of Social Insurance
1776 Massachusetts Ave. NW, Ste.615
Washington, DC 20036-1904
Ph: (202)452-8097
Fax: (202)452-8111
E-mail: nasi@nasi.org
URL: http://www.nasi.org
Contact: Marilyn Moon, Pres.
Founded: 1986. **Members:** 750. **Membership Dues:** honorific, $150 (annual). **Staff:** 15. **Budget:** $3,000,000. **Description:** Experts on social insurance, including Social Security, health care financing, disability, worker's compensation, and unemployment. Furthers research and education in social security and related programs. Promotes informed discussion and debate on social insurance issues and works to increase public understanding of social security. Organizes public forums exploring social insurance issues; offers student internships; provides information clearinghouse, speaker/media referral service, and manuscript review service. Organizes discussion groups and study panels. Provides research consultation and sponsors research projects. **Libraries: Type:** reference. **Holdings:** 2,000; archival material. **Subjects:** social insurance. **Awards:** John Heinz Dissertation Award. **Frequency:** annual. **Type:** recognition. **Recipient:** for outstanding PhD dissertation in the field of social insurance ● Robert M. Ball Award for Outstanding Achievements in Social Insurance. **Frequency:** annual. **Type:** recognition. **Computer Services:** Mailing lists. **Telecommunication Services:** electronic mail, plarson@nasi.org. **Publications:** *NASI Policy Research Conference Proceedings*, annual ● *Social Insurance Update.* Newsletter. Covers new publications and accomplishments by members. **Price:** free. **Circulation:** 1,200. Alternate Formats: online ● *Social Security Briefs, Medicare Briefs* ● Membership Directory, annual ● Also distributes primers, study guides, and educational materials on social insurance and health financing. **Conventions/Meetings:** annual Implementing the Medicare Modernization Act in a Polarized Environment - conference, research - always January, in Washington, DC ● Seminar Series on Social Insurance for Summer Interns ● workshop.

18277 ■ National Association of Disability Representatives (NADR)
1901 Pennsylvania Ave. Nw, Ste.607
Washington, DC 20006
Ph: (202)822-2155
Fax: (202)463-1257
E-mail: chris@andersonmarois.com
URL: http://www.nadr.org
Contact: Chris Marois, Pres.
Founded: 2000. **Membership Dues:** individual, $295 (annual). **Description:** Serves the members' needs in the areas of professional education and political action. Maintains and enhances the skills of members. Conducts conventions and educational seminars to keep practitioners up to date on Social Security rulings, regulatory changes and practice

improvements. Provides a national referral service for claimants.

18278 ■ National Committee to Preserve Social Security and Medicare (NCPSSM)
10 G St. NE, Ste.600
Washington, DC 20002-4215
Ph: (202)216-0420
Free: (800)966-1935
Fax: (202)216-0446
E-mail: general@ncpssm.org
URL: http://www.ncpssm.org
Contact: Barbara B. Kennelly, Pres./CEO
Founded: 1982. **Members:** 3,200,000. **Membership Dues:** individual, $12 (annual). **Staff:** 50. **Budget:** $31,000,000. **Languages:** English, Spanish. **Description:** Grassroots senior citizens' advocacy and education association. Seeks to inform its members and the public through forums, presentations, written correspondence, and telephone communication. Disseminates educational materials. Conducts grassroots lobbying activities. Researches and develops policy on income security and health care issues that effect "seniors of today and tomorrow". **Awards:** Friend of Seniors Award. **Frequency:** annual. **Type:** recognition. **Recipient:** for persons or agencies who demonstrate support of senior issues ● Service to Seniors Award. **Frequency:** annual. **Type:** recognition. **Recipient:** for outstanding assistance to older persons and their families (for individuals or families). **Committees:** Political Action. **Formerly:** (1982) National Committee to Preserve Social Security. **Publications:** Newsletter, quarterly. Covers congressional and executive branch activities regarding Social Security, Medicare, health care, long-term care and other issues of interest. ISSN: 1069-6911.

18279 ■ National Organization of Social Security Claimants' Representatives (NOSSCR)
560 Sylvan Ave.
Englewood Cliffs, NJ 07632
Free: (800)431-2804
Fax: (201)567-1542
E-mail: nosscr@att.net
URL: http://www.nosscr.org
Contact: Nancy Shor, Exec. Dir.
Founded: 1979. **Members:** 2,500. **Staff:** 3. **Description:** Represents attorneys and legal service corporations. Aims to aid members in cases concerning social security disability claims. Collects and disseminates information on social security claim cases; prepares case studies. Operates a referral service to provide legal information and referrals. **Publications:** *The Forum*, monthly. Newsletter. **Conventions/Meetings:** semiannual conference (exhibits) - 2007 Oct. 17-20, St. Louis, MO.

Social Welfare

18280 ■ National Society for Shut-Ins (NSFS)
Address Unknown since 2007
Founded: 1970. **Members:** 25. **Staff:** 20. **Regional Groups:** 2. **Local Groups:** 3. **Description:** Persons united to organize chapters throughout the country in order to educate people to care for and visit shut-ins. Seeks to promote a sense of emotional and spiritual well-being and self-worth in individuals who are confined to their homes or institutions, due to age, sickness, handicap, or imprisonment (inclusively, "shut-ins"). Designates third Sunday in October each year as National Shut-In Day and encourages people to visit the sick, elderly, and imprisoned on that day. Activities include: annual Sunshine Day, providing a day of entertainment and recreation for shut-ins away from the home or institution; National Shut-In Day and Sunshine Week, fostering public recognition of the plight of shut-ins; Sunshine Productions, producing amateur musical performances for the enjoyment and benefit of shut-ins; treating shut-ins to various programs of entertainment. Sponsors Project SUNSHINE, promoting visitation and performance of service by volunteer high school and college students, civic clubs, and church groups to institutionalized and

homebound shut-ins. **Convention/Meeting:** none. **Formerly:** (1982) National Shut-In Day Society.

Socialism

18281 ■ Democratic Socialists of America (DSA)
75 Maiden Ln., Ste.505
New York, NY 10038
Ph: (212)727-8610
Fax: (212)608-6955
E-mail: dsa@dsausa.org
URL: http://www.dsausa.org
Contact: Frank Llewellyn, Natl. Dir.

Founded: 1982. **Members:** 10,000. **Membership Dues:** basic, $35 (annual) ● sustainer, $60 (annual) ● low income, student, $20 (annual). **Staff:** 4. **State Groups:** 4. **Local Groups:** 80. **Description:** Represents individuals who believe on "the realization of the potential of humankind requires many important basic institutional changes, among which are the social ownership and democratic control of the decisive means of production and distribution." Works on "building a society at the service of human needs" and seeks to create a foreign policy "dedicated to the peaceful extension of democratic rule for all the peoples of the world." Works to protect and expand civil liberties, encourage democratic social planning, and distribute the nation's wealth and income more equitably. Maintains youth groups on 40 campuses. **Computer Services:** Bibliographic search. **Commissions:** African-American; Anti-Racism; Feminist; Labor; Latino; Queer; Religion and Socialism. **Committees:** Environmental. **Sections:** Young Democratic Socialists. **Formed by Merger of:** (1981) New America Movement; Democratic Socialist Organizing Committee. **Publications:** *Democratic Left*, quarterly. Newsletter. **Price:** $10.00. **Advertising:** accepted ● *Our Struggle* ● *Religion and Socialism* ● *Socialist Forum*, semiannual. **Conventions/Meetings:** biennial congress (exhibits).

18282 ■ Freedom Socialist Party (FSP)
Natl. Off.
4710 Univ. Way NE, Ste.100
Seattle, WA 98105
Ph: (206)985-4621
Fax: (206)985-8965
E-mail: fspnatl@igc.org
URL: http://www.socialism.com
Contact: Henry Noble, Natl. Sec.

Founded: 1966. **Description:** Serves as socialist feminist organization based on the belief that the international leadership of the exploited - women, people of color, gays, indigenous people - is instrumental to bringing about revolutionary social change. Promotes anti-Nazi organizing on the West Coast and integration of social issues in the labor movement. Calls for creation of an independent Labor Party. Emphasizes grassroots organizing, coalition-building, electoral campaigns, and educational activities. **Affiliated With:** Radical Women. **Publications:** *AIDS Hysteria: A Marxist Analysis* ● *Capitalism's Brutal Comeback in China* ● *The First Decade 1966-1976* ● *Freedom Socialist: Voice of Revolutionary Feminism*, bimonthly. Covers topics on gay resistance, women's role in working class struggles, abortion rights, Native American sovereignty, and global freedom struggles. **Price:** $6.00 /year for individuals; $10.00 /year for institutions. ISSN: 0272-4367. **Circulation:** 8,000 ● *Gay Resistance: The Hidden History* ● *Socialism for Skeptics* ● *Socialist Feminism: The First Decade* ● *Voices of Color* ● *The War on the Disabled* ● *Women of Color: Frontrunners for Freedom* ● Also publishes position papers. **Conventions/Meetings:** biennial convention.

18283 ■ International Socialist Organization (ISO)
PO Box 16085
Chicago, IL 60616-0085
Ph: (773)583-5069
E-mail: contact@internationalsocialist.org
URL: http://www.internationalsocialist.org
Founded: 1977. **Description:** Promotes activities and activism around issues of the labor movement, social and economic justice, the rights of workers and civil rights. Organizing is based on democratic and equitable division of resources and wealth, elimination of poverty and oppression. **Publications:** *The Case for Socialism*. Book. **Price:** $5.00 ● *Socialist Worker*, weekly. Newspaper. Alternate Formats: online. Also Cited As: *SW* ● *Stop the War!*. Pamphlet. Provides necessary background and analysis to expose the U.S.'s real war aims. **Price:** $3.00.

18284 ■ League for the Revolutionary Party (LRP)
PO Box 1936
Murray Hill Sta.
New York, NY 10156
Ph: (212)330-9017
E-mail: lrpcofi@earthlink.net
URL: http://www.lrp-cofi.org
Contact: Sy Landy, Sec.

Founded: 1976. **Languages:** English, German, Russian, Spanish. **Description:** Works to advance socialism through political action and educational activities. Maintains speakers' bureau. **Publications:** *Proletarian Revolution*, 3/year. Journal. **Price:** $7.00 for 8 issues. ISSN: 0894-0754. **Circulation:** 1,000.

18285 ■ News and Letters Committee (NLC)
36 S Wabash, Rm. 1440
Chicago, IL 60603
Ph: (312)236-0799
Fax: (312)236-0725
E-mail: arise@newsandletters.org
URL: http://www.newsandletters.org
Contact: Olga Domanski, Co-Natl. Organizer

Founded: 1955. **Regional Groups:** 6. **Description:** Marxist-Humanists whose aim is to promote "the firmest unity among workers, blacks and other minorities, women, youth, and those intellectuals who have broken with the ruling bureaucracy of both capital and labor." Seeks to abolish capitalism in its private property form as in the U.S., and in its state property form as in Russia or China. Participates in class and freedom struggles, nationally and internationally. Offers specialized education and maintains biographical archives. Operates speakers' bureau. **Libraries:** Type: reference. **Holdings:** 2,000. **Subjects:** political science, philosophy. **Committees:** Internationalist Marxist-Humanist Youth; National Editorial Board; Resident Editorial Board. **Publications:** *Guides to the Raya Dunayevskaya Collection*. **Price:** $5.00. Alternate Formats: microform ● *Marxist-Humanism - A Half-Century of its World Development* ● *News & Letters*, bimonthly. Newspaper. **Price:** $5.00/year. ISSN: 0028-8969. Alternate Formats: online; microform ● *Political-Philosophic Letters of Raya Dunayevskaya: Vols. I and II*. **Conventions/Meetings:** biennial meeting.

18286 ■ Religion and Socialism Commission of the Democratic Socialists of America
536 W 111th St., No. 37
New York, NY 10025
E-mail: religioussocialism@socialist.org
URL: http://www.dsausa.org/rs
Contact: Maxine Phillips, Sec.

Founded: 1977. **Members:** 100. **Membership Dues:** regular, $10 (annual). **Description:** Members of the Democratic Socialists of America who promote socialism from a religious point of view. Supplies speakers for religious and other groups. **Formerly:** (1984) Religion and Socialism Committee of DSA. **Publications:** *Religious Socialism*, quarterly. Magazine. Includes book reviews and guest editorial. **Price:** $10.00/year; $15.00 sustaining; $12.00 in Canada; $158.00 foreign. **Circulation:** 400. **Advertising:** accepted. **Conventions/Meetings:** biennial meeting - usually odd-numbered years.

18287 ■ Socialist Action (SA)
298 Valencia St.
San Francisco, CA 94103
Ph: (415)255-1080
Fax: (415)255-1082
E-mail: socialistact@igc.org
URL: http://www.socialistaction.org
Contact: Jeff Mackler, Natl. Sec.

Founded: 1983. **Membership Dues:** general, $5 (monthly). **Local Groups:** 18. **Description:** Promotes the education and organization of the working class in an effort to abolish capitalism. Works for the establishment of a socialist workers' government. **Publications:** Newspaper, monthly. **Price:** $8.00/year. ISSN: 0747-4237. **Advertising:** accepted. **Conventions/Meetings:** biennial meeting.

18288 ■ Spartacist League (SL)
PO Box 1377
New York, NY 10116
Ph: (212)267-1025
Fax: (212)406-2210
E-mail: vanguard@tiac.net
URL: http://www.icl-fi.org
Contact: Len Myers, Ed.

Founded: 1966. **Regional Groups:** 12. **Description:** Trotskyist organization "committed to the task of building the party that will lead the working class to the victory of the socialist revolution in the U.S." Holds class series on college and university campuses to recruit new membership. **Convention/Meeting:** none. **Libraries:** Type: reference. **Committees:** Political Bureau. **Publications:** *Spartacist*, periodic. Journal. Published by the International Executive Committee of the International Communist League. **Price:** $2.00/issue ● *Workers Vanguard*, biweekly. Covers current affairs from a Marxist, working-class perspective. **Price:** $10.00/year ● Pamphlets ● Also makes available Annual bound edition of *Spartacist* and *Workers Vanguard*.

18289 ■ Workers World Party (WWP)
55 W 17th St., 5th Fl.
New York, NY 10011
Ph: (212)627-2994
Fax: (212)675-7869
E-mail: wwp@workers.org
URL: http://www.workers.org
Contact: Sara Flounders, Contact

Founded: 1959. **Description:** Represents individuals who promotes socialism and fights social injustice. Seeks to secure equal employment, housing, education, and health care for all people. Sponsors educational programs; maintains Speaker's Bureau. **Libraries:** Type: open to the public. **Publications:** *Workers World*, weekly, except first week of January. Newspaper. Contains national and international news concerning socialism. **Price:** $25.00 /year for members; $35.00 /year for institutions. ISSN: 1070-4205.

18290 ■ Young Communist League of the United States of America (YCL-USA)
235 W 23rd St.
New York, NY 10011
Ph: (212)741-2016
Fax: (212)229-1713
E-mail: yclconvention@yclusa.org
URL: http://www.yclusa.org
Contact: Jessica Marshall, Co-Coor.

Founded: 1983. **Membership Dues:** regular, $24 (annual) ● high school, unemployed, $12 (annual). **Staff:** 4. **State Groups:** 25. **Local Groups:** 50. **Description:** Young people "who believe capitalism is the root of all problems confronting youth and that socialism is the next stage of human development." Aims to struggle for the rights of youth to build a movement for social equality against racism and sexism, for free public university education, jobs for all, a clean environment, and an end to the arms race. Fights for full funding of social, recreational, and cultural activities in all communities; socialism. Sponsors educational programs. Offers children's services; operates speakers' bureau. **Libraries:** Type: reference. **Committees:** Arts and Culture; Jobs for Youth; Students. **Formerly:** (1983) Young Workers Liberation League. **Publications:** *Dynamic*, quarterly. Magazine. **Price:** $15.00/year. Alternate Formats: online ● *YCL Mobilizer*, quarterly. Newsletter. **Conventions/Meetings:** biennial convention.

18291 ■ Young Democratic Socialists (YDS)
75 Maiden Ln., Ste.505
New York, NY 10038
Ph: (212)727-8610
Fax: (212)608-6955
E-mail: yds@dsausa.org
URL: http://www.ydsusa.org
Contact: Mr. David Duhalde, Natl. Organizer
Founded: 1982. **Membership Dues:** individual, $20 (annual). **Staff:** 1. **Local Groups:** 40. **Description:** Serves as a diverse collective that informed and inspired by a variety of movements and figures in the long struggle for social justice. From the American labor movement, to the fight for civil rights, from European Social Democracy to women's liberation, the Young Democratic Socialists takes lessons and hope from the wide history of the progressive project. Works in coalitions, as a principled ally of a variety of struggles, and be the socialist voice within the left. Aims to see a progressive, democratic majority in the U.S. and works in good faith to build the majority. **Formerly:** Democratic Socialists of America - Youth Section; (1975) Democratic Socialist Organizing Committee Youth Section. **Publications:** *The Activist*, semiannual. Journal. **Price:** $5.00/year. **Advertising:** accepted. **Conventions/Meetings:** annual conference and convention, includes summer institute.

18292 ■ Youth for International Socialism (YFIS)
c/o Wellred Books
PO Box 4244
St. Paul, MN 55104
E-mail: info@newyouth.com
URL: http://www.newyouth.com
Contact: John Peterson, Contact
Multinational. Description: Fights to end capitalism and promotes democratic socialism. Maintains the specific ideas and principles of Marxism. Works to spread the ideas of genuine Marxism to as many people as possible. Educate and defends the interests of the workers and youth. **Telecommunication Services:** electronic mail, contact@marxist.com. **Publications:** *Socialist Appeal*, 8/year. Newspaper. Provides news, information, and analysis from a youth, labor, and Marxist perspective. **Price:** $10.00 per year (regular price); $15.00 per year (solidarity price); $5.00 4 issues; $20.00 international. Alternate Formats: online. Also Cited As: *SA*.

Sociology

18293 ■ Sociologists Without Borders (SSF)
c/o Cathy Zimmer, Sec.-Treas.
Odum Inst.
Manning Hall
Univ. of North Carolina
Chapel Hill, NC 27599-3355
Ph: (919)929-7885 (919)962-5603
E-mail: jrblau@email.unc.edu
URL: http://www.sociologistswithoutborders.org
Contact: Judith Blau, Pres.
Founded: 2001. **Members:** 500. **Membership Dues:** regular, $30 (annual) ● student, unemployed sociologist, $15 (annual) ● friend, $60 (annual) ● regular (member of the Association of Black Sociologists or of the Latino/a ASA Section), $20 (annual) ● student (member of the Association of Black Sociologists or of the Latino/a ASA Section), $8 (annual). **Budget:** $500. **National Groups:** 8. **Multinational. Description:** Promotes transnational solidarities and justice. Supports the right to peaceful meddling. Opposes practices and programs that advance the State's sovereignty but diminish human rights. Promotes alliances with people in poor countries. **Awards:** Brazilian Student Fellowship. **Frequency:** annual. **Type:** fellowship. **Recipient:** for students who worked collaboratively with faculty at the Federal University of Minas Gerais, Brazil. **Publications:** *Societies without Borders*, biennial. Journal. Explains the interdisciplinary development of human rights understanding and advocacy. **Price:** $85.00. **Advertising:** accepted.

Solar Energy

18294 ■ Enersol Associates
55 Middlesex St., Ste.221
North Chelmsford, MA 01863
Ph: (978)251-1828
Fax: (978)251-5291
E-mail: enersol@igc.org
URL: http://www.enersol.org
Contact: Jessica C. Mace, Exec. Dir.
Founded: 1984. **Multinational. Description:** International development organization that uses clean solar energy to improve the quality of life for people living in rural Latin America while protecting the global environment. Assists rural communities and other nonprofit organizations of the Americas with the application of solar electric technologies in order to improve the health and education of children. **Publications:** *Enersol News*, seasonal. Newsletter. Alternate Formats: online ● Annual Report, annual. Alternate Formats: online ● Articles. Alternate Formats: online.

South Africa

18295 ■ South Africa Partners (SA Partners)
89 South St., Ste.401
Boston, MA 02111
Ph: (617)443-1072
Fax: (617)443-1076
E-mail: info@sapartners.org
URL: http://www.sapartners.org
Contact: Mary Tiseo, Exec. Dir.
Founded: 1997. **Multinational. Description:** Represents the interests of individuals dedicated to the development of institutional partnerships between the United States and South Africa in the areas of health, education and economic development. Identifies and facilitates strategic partnership opportunities that build the capacity of South African organizations and improve their ability to carry out program activities. Offers the potential for long-term collaborations between institutions in the United States and South Africa. **Awards:** Desmond Tutu Award. **Frequency:** annual. **Type:** recognition. **Recipient:** to an individual whose work aspires to the values illuminated by Archbishop Tutu's many years of service. **Computer Services:** Mailing lists. **Programs:** Libraries For South African Schools; Partnerships for Healthy Communities. **Publications:** *Building Bridges*. Newsletter. Alternate Formats: online ● *Building Bridges for Change*. Brochures ● Annual Reports.

Southern Asians

18296 ■ South Asian American Leaders of Tomorrow (SAALT)
6930 Carroll Ave., Ste.400 L
Takoma Park, MD 20912
Ph: (301)270-1855
Fax: (301)270-4000
E-mail: saalt@saalt.org
URL: http://www.saalt.org
Contact: Deepa Iyer, Exec. Dir.
Founded: 2000. **Description:** Works to ensure the full and equal participation by South Asians in the civic and political life of the United States. Provides a uniform and informed voice on issues affecting South Asians that relate to equality and civil rights. Creates opportunities for leadership, service and volunteerism by South Asians in order to foster civic engagement. **Programs:** SAALT Exchange. **Working Groups:** New Jersey South Asian; Pennsylvania South Asian. **Publications:** *American Backlash*. Report ● *The SAALT Connection*. Newsletter. Alternate Formats: online.

Space

18297 ■ Lifeboat Foundation
1638 Esmeralda Ave.
Minden, NV 89423
Ph: (775)783-8443
Fax: (775)783-0803
E-mail: lifeboat@lifeboat.com
URL: http://lifeboat.com/ex
Contact: Eric Klien, Founder/Pres.
Membership Dues: economy, $10 (monthly) ● executive, $25 (monthly) ● first class, $50 (monthly) ● lifeboat 500, $85 (monthly) ● patron, $200 (monthly). **Description:** Dedicated to providing solutions to safeguard humanity from the growing threat of terrorism and technological cataclysm, with emphasis on artificial intelligence and nanotechnology. Seeks to create self-contained space arks. **Publications:** *Lifeboat News*. Newsletter. **Price:** free. Alternate Formats: online.

Spanish

18298 ■ Conquistadores 1492
PO Box 42
Leonia, NJ 07605-0042
Ph: (201)567-7471
Fax: (201)816-9727
E-mail: conquistadors1492@yahoo.com
Contact: Mr. Anthony F. Gonzalez LLb, Pres./CEO
Founded: 2000. **Nonmembership. Description:** Aims to protect the civil and religious rights of white Spanish surnamed American citizens here and abroad. Offers awards, biographical archives, Hall of Fame, speaker's bureau, library, research and educational programs. **Committees:** American Spanish; World Spanish Congress.

Special Days

18299 ■ Committee for National Arbor Day (CNAD)
187 Ridgedale Ave.
East Hanover, NJ 07936
Ph: (973)887-4510
Fax: (973)887-0783
Contact: Harry P. Banker, Chm.
Founded: 1936. **Members:** 50. **State Groups:** 50. **Description:** Tree experts, horticulturists, and interested others. Brings trees into focus as a very necessary part of everyday life, economically, aesthetically, environmentally, and by contributing to the mental and physical well-being of all people. In 1970 and 1972, President Nixon made National Arbor Day Proclamations; in 1988, President Reagan issued a National Arbor Day Proclamation for the last Friday in April; President Bush issued similar proclamations in 1990 and 1991. President Bill Clinton issued a similar proclamation in 1993. **Awards:** Award of Merit. **Frequency:** periodic. **Type:** recognition. **Affiliated With:** American Nursery and Landscape Association; International Society of Arboriculture; Society of Municipal Arborists; Tree Care Industry Association. **Publications:** *Arbor Day Past & Present*. Booklet. **Price:** $5.00 ● *National Arbor Day Review*, periodic. Newsletter ● Also distributes Arbor Day kits for $2 to cover s/h. **Conventions/Meetings:** semiannual meeting, held in conjunction with International Society of Arboriculture in August - always August and November.

18300 ■ Father's Day/Mother's Day Council
47 W 34th St., Ste.534
New York, NY 10001
Ph: (212)594-5977
Fax: (212)594-9349
E-mail: fdcmdc@att.net
URL: http://www.momanddadday.com
Contact: Mr. Joseph Rivers, Pres.
Founded: 1992. **Members:** 2,125. **Staff:** 4. **Regional Groups:** 3. **Description:** Manufacturers of women's and men's gift products. Works to increase the observance of Mother's and Father's Day by advancing public awareness through newspaper, magazine, television, and radio advertising. Conducts attitude and market studies on the changing perceptions of Mother's and Father's Day. Conducts charitable programs. **Awards:** Lifetime Leadership Award. **Frequency:** annual. **Type:** recognition. **Recipient:** for

consistent creative noncommercial promotion of Mother's Day and Father's Day as a family and community event ● Outstanding Mother and Father of the Year Award. **Frequency:** annual. **Type:** recognition. **Committees:** Advertising Awards; Outstanding Mother and Father of the Year Awards; Public Relations. **Formed by Merger of:** Father's Day Council; Mother's Day Council. **Publications:** Membership Directory, annual. **Conventions/Meetings:** annual meeting.

18301 ■ Holiday Institute of Yonkers (HIY)
Address Unknown since 2007
Founded: 1969. **Description:** Seeks to research, study, celebrate, and promote interest in holidays in general. Worked to persuade New York Governor Rockefeller to proclaim July 20 a statewide holiday as Moon Landing Day. Current endeavor is to work for Humanities Day, a proposed international holiday which would fall on Dec. 10. **Telecommunication Services:** electronic mail, hiy@crimeweck.com. **Committees:** Anzac Visitation; Moon Day; Research. **Publications:** *Holidagology Today*, monthly.

18302 ■ National Arbor Day Foundation (NADF)
100 Arbor Ave.
Nebraska City, NE 68410
Ph: (402)474-5555
Free: (888)448-7337
E-mail: member.service@ardorday.org
URL: http://www.arborday.org
Contact: John Rosenow, Pres.
Founded: 1972. **Members:** 1,000,000. **Membership Dues:** regular, $10 (annual). **Languages:** English, Spanish. **Description:** National associations, corporations, communities, state government agencies, and individuals dedicated to tree planting and environmental stewardship. Organized to: properly and officially promote the observance of Arbor Day each year; create an awareness and appreciation among all peoples through all forms of communication of the fundamental role that trees play in day-to-day existence; endorse, support, or otherwise implement education programs that will stimulate and inspire youth to better understand the bounty and joy of trees; recognize achievement among all elements of society through an annual awards program for contributions made to the understanding, appreciation, conservation, and wise use of trees; initiate programs that encourage the planting of trees and create an awareness of those resource programs that will assure the perpetuation and growing abundance of this basic resource; establish and maintain the Arbor Day Farm at Nebraska City, Nebraska, to educate Americans about Arbor Day, trees as a natural resource, and tree planting; raise and collect funds through gifts, contributions, and other funding programs. **Awards:** National Awards Program. **Frequency:** annual. **Type:** recognition. **Recipient:** for corporations, national associations, media, and individuals who have created an awareness and appreciation of America's tree resources. **Programs:** Building With Trees; Celebrate Arbor Day; Conferences and Seminars; Conservation Trees; Rain Forest Rescue; Tree City U.S.A.; Trees for America. **Publications:** *Arbor Day*, bimonthly. Newsletter. Profiles specific trees and reports on the educational efforts of the Foundation. **Price:** included in membership dues. **Circulation:** 1,000,000 ● *Celebrate Arbor Day*. Booklet ● *Conservation Trees*. Booklet ● *Grow Your Own Tree*. Curriculum kit. ● *Keep A Great Thing Growing America*. Booklet ● *Tree City U.S.A.*. Booklet ● *Tree City U.S.A. Bulletin*, bimonthly. Features information on pruning, caring for storm-damaged trees, watering and fertilizing, and wise tree selection. **Price:** included in membership dues ● *Trees are Terrific*. Curriculum kit.

18303 ■ National Father's Day Committee (NFDC)
47 W 34th St., Ste.534
New York, NY 10001
Ph: (212)594-5977
Fax: (212)594-9349

E-mail: fdcmdc@att.net
URL: http://www.momanddaday.com
Contact: Richard Wurtzburg, Chm.
Founded: 1942. **Staff:** 3. **Regional Groups:** 5. **Description:** Individuals and organizations "dedicated to building a permanently free democracy through wise parental influence of the young." The U.S. president, state governors, and former governors cooperate in observances of the committee. Promotes Father's Day as a national holiday by congressional act of April, 1972, to be observed the third Sunday of June. **Awards:** Father of the Year Award. **Frequency:** annual. **Type:** recognition. **Recipient:** for involvement in youth activities and a good personal parental record ● Regional Father of the Year Award. **Frequency:** annual. **Type:** recognition. **Committees:** Father of the Year Advisory; Father of the Year Selection. **Conventions/Meetings:** annual Father of the Year Award Banquet.

18304 ■ National Mother's Day Committee
47 W 34th St., Ste.534
New York, NY 10001
Ph: (212)594-6421
Fax: (212)594-9349
E-mail: fdcmdc@att.net
URL: http://www.momanddaday.com
Contact: Thia Breen, Chair
Founded: 1978. **Description:** Individuals and organizations "dedicated to building a permanently free democracy through wise parental influence of the young." The U.S. president, state governors, and former governors cooperate in observances of the committee. Sponsors annual banquet in New York City to honor Mother of the Year and mothers in special categories. **Awards:** Outstanding Mother Awards. **Frequency:** annual. **Type:** recognition. **Recipient:** for contemporary, involved mothers who are influential role models in today's socio-economic structure. **Affiliated With:** Father's Day/Mother's Day Council. **Formerly:** (1978) National Committee for the Observance of Mother's Day. **Publications:** Newsletter.

18305 ■ Thanks-Giving Foundation
PO Box 131770
Dallas, TX 75313-1770
Ph: (214)969-1977
Free: (888)305-1205
Fax: (214)754-0152
E-mail: tqs@thanksgiving.org
URL: http://www.thanksgiving.org
Contact: Mr. Don M. Glendenning, Chm.
Founded: 1964. **Staff:** 7. **Languages:** English, French, German, Italian, Russian, Spanish. **Multinational. Description:** Preserves and promotes the tradition of Thanksgiving in the United States, with emphasis on the expression of gratitude and praise to God for humankind's blessings. Prepares draft of Presidential Proclamations for National Day of Prayer and Presidential Thanksgiving Proclamations. **Libraries:** Type: reference. **Subgroups:** Interfaith Council. **Formerly:** (1997) National Thanksgiving Commission. **Publications:** *Gratitude: Activities for parents and Educators of Younger Children*. Book. Contains information about moral development in the young child. **Price:** $8.00 includes shipping and handling ● Brochures ● Newsletter, periodic. **Conventions/Meetings:** periodic Convocation of World Thanksgiving - meeting ● annual National Day of Prayer Interfaith Breakfast - meeting ● annual Thanksgiving Dinner - seminar and dinner.

Speech

18306 ■ IDEA: The International Debate Education Association
400 W 59th St.
New York, NY 10019
Ph: (212)548-0185
Fax: (212)548-4610

E-mail: nselegzi@idebate.org
URL: http://www.idebate.org
Contact: Noel Selegzi, Pres.
Members: 73,000. **Membership Dues:** individual (life), $15 ● organizational supporting, $90 (annual). **National Groups:** 27. **Multinational. Description:** Works to create debate clubs that encourage examination of issues affecting communities. **Publications:** *Controversia*, semiannual. Journal. **Price:** $90.00 /year for institutions; $35.00 /year for individuals; free for organizational supporting members ● *iDebate*. Magazine. **Price:** free for organizational supporting members. Alternate Formats: online. **Conventions/Meetings:** annual general assembly.

Standards

18307 ■ American National Metric Council (ANMC)
900 Mix Ave., Ste.1
Hamden, CT 06514-5106
Ph: (203)287-9849
E-mail: anmcmetric@pi-c.com
URL: http://lamar.colostate.edu/~hillger/anmc.htm
Contact: Dan Potts, Pres./CEO
Founded: 1973. **Members:** 200. **Staff:** 2. **Budget:** $190,000. **Description:** Companies, organizations, and individuals interested in keeping up-to-date on all the latest information on the status of metric transition in the U.S. Aims to coordinate metric transition planning activities for all affected segments in the private sector of American society. **Computer Services:** database, metric standards, components, and new product development. **Publications:** *Metric Reporter*, quarterly. Newsletter. Covers metric transition in the United States and in other countries. Includes consumer interests and metric applications in business and industry. **Price:** $100.00/year. **Circulation:** 1,500 ● Also publishes reports, educational materials, and pamphlets. **Conventions/Meetings:** annual conference - always fall in Washington, DC.

18308 ■ Americans for Customary Weight and Measure (ACWM)
PO Box 24A
Wiscasset, ME 04578
URL: http://www.bwmaonline.com/ACWM.htm
Contact: Seaver W. Leslie, Pres.
Founded: 1978. **Description:** Opposes metric conversion by advocating the protection and retention of the "inch-pound-quart" system of measurement. Strongly believes that there should not be U.S. government policy to promote or implement metrics and that conversion would cause widespread confusion, inflation, and an additional burden for U.S. exports. Encourages citizens to write to their representatives in Washington, DC calling for opposition to any metric conversion legislation introduced in Congress. Urges consumers to boycott all American goods produced or packaged in metric sizes. Disseminates information on metric conversion in America. Maintains speakers' bureau. Compiles statistics. **Libraries:** Type: reference. **Holdings:** articles, clippings, periodicals. **Subjects:** metric system, metric conversion, history of measure. **Also Known As:** Miles Ahead. **Publications:** *Footprint* ● *Why America Should Not Go Metric*. **Conventions/Meetings:** annual meeting - usually August 28, Wiscasset, ME.

18309 ■ Data Interchange Standards Association (DISA)
7600 Leesburg Pike, Ste.430
Falls Church, VA 22043
Ph: (703)970-4480
Fax: (703)970-4488
E-mail: info@disa.org
URL: http://www.disa.org
Contact: Jerry C. Connors, Pres.
Founded: 1987. **Members:** 600. **Staff:** 12. **Budget:** $2,000,000. **Description:** Serves as a home for the development of cross-industry electronic business interchange standards. Provides technical and administrative support to e-business, standards and

XML specification development organizations through its affiliate division.

18310 ■ **Global Organization for Multi-Vendor Integration Protocol (GO-MVIP)**
3220 N St. NW, Ste.360
Washington, DC 20007
Ph: (903)769-3717
Free: (800)NOW-MVIP
Fax: (903)769-3818
E-mail: info@mvip.org
Founded: 1990. **Members:** 65. **Membership Dues:** ordinary, $500 (annual). **Description:** Corporations producing and developing computer telephony applications. Promotes standardization in the field of computer telephony. Works with members to develop standards for computer telephony hardware and software; serves as a clearinghouse on multi-vendor integration protocol.

18311 ■ **Metric Opposition Forum (MOF)**
Address Unknown since 2007
Founded: 1995. **Multinational. Description:** Provides for information on why the U.S. should not officially adopt the metric system of measurement. Offers educational programs. **Convention/Meeting:** none. **Publications:** *Let's Not Go Metric.* **Price:** free. **Advertising:** not accepted ● *Save the Inch* ● Also publishes fact finder bulletins.

18312 ■ **Unicode Consortium (UC)**
c/o Magda Danish, Admin. Dir.
1065 L'Avenida St., Microsoft Bldg. 5
Mountain View, CA 94043
Ph: (650)693-3921
Fax: (650)693-3010
E-mail: unicode@unicode.org
URL: http://www.unicode.org
Contact: Magda Danish, Admin. Dir.
Founded: 1991. **Members:** 125. **Staff:** 3. **Description:** Computer software corporations and researchers. Promotes standardization of international character encoding. Has developed the Unicode Standard. Assists corporations wishing to implement the Unicode Standard. **Publications:** *The Unicode Standard v3.0.* Book. **Price:** included in membership dues. **Conventions/Meetings:** semiannual International Unicode Conference.

States Rights

18313 ■ **Council of Conservative Citizens (CofCC)**
PO Box 221683
St. Louis, MO 63122-8683
Ph: (636)940-8474
E-mail: cofcc@cofcc.org
URL: http://www.cofcc.org
Contact: Gordon Lee Baum, CEO
Founded: 1985. **Members:** 100,000. **Membership Dues:** regular, $25 (annual) ● advisory, $100 (annual). **Staff:** 15. **State Groups:** 28. **Local Groups:** 1,000. **Description:** Represents members of state and local councils who are dedicated to "the principles of states' rights." Provides a network of groups and individuals that support the conservative majority. Rejects Affirmative Action programs. Compiles statistics; maintains speakers' bureau; conducts educational and research programs. **Absorbed:** (1989) Citizens' Councils of America. **Publications:** *Citizens' Informer,* quarterly. Newspaper. **Price:** 95/year. ISSN: 0887-3186. **Advertising:** accepted ● *Council Reporter,* semiannual. Newsletter. **Price:** free ● Bulletins ● Newsletters ● Pamphlets. **Conventions/Meetings:** annual seminar, for patriotic vendors (exhibits).

18314 ■ **Public Advocate of the U.S. (PAUS)**
5613 Leesburg Pike, Ste.17
Falls Church, VA 22041
Ph: (703)845-1808
URL: http://www.publicadvocateusa.org
Contact: Eugene A. Delgaudio, Pres.
Founded: 1978. **Members:** 300,000. **Staff:** 4. **Description:** Grass roots educational organization.

Advocates limited federal government. Works to reduce the powers vested in the federal government and reissue control of various programs to state and local levels. **Programs:** Abolish the Department of Education; Abolish the Federal Elections Commission; Abolish the National Institute of Education; Restore Ethics in Congress. **Publications:** *Impact Reports,* periodic ● *Register of Opinion,* periodic. Newsletter. Concerned with transferring powers of the federal government to more local levels. ● *Report to Congress,* semiannual.

Strategic Defense Initiative

18315 ■ **High Frontier Organization**
500 N Washington St.
Alexandria, VA 22314-2314
Ph: (703)535-8774
Fax: (703)535-8776
E-mail: high.frontier@verizon.net
URL: http://www.highfrontier.org
Contact: Maj. Gen. (Ret.) J. Milnor Roberts Jr., Dir.
Founded: 1982. **Description:** Conducts studies and research on the scientific, technical, military and strategic problems associated with foreign policy issues with an emphasis on space. Advocates for the defense against the threat of ballistic missiles and other forms of destructive nuclear arms that threaten the American homeland. **Computer Services:** Information services, guide to missile defense issues. **Publications:** *Confessions of a Cold Warrior.* Book. Features the autobiography of Daniel O. Graham, founder of High Frontier. ● *The Shield,* quarterly. Newsletter. Contains articles and information pertinent to missile defense. **Circulation:** 14,000. Alternate Formats: online.

Substance Abuse

18316 ■ **Drug Free Kids: America's Challenge**
PO Box 60865
Washington, DC 20039
Ph: (301)681-7861
E-mail: info@drugfreekids.org
URL: http://www.ourdrugfreekids.org
Contact: Joyce Nalepka, Pres.
Description: Promotes protection of children against drugs. Hold vigils and rallies. **Publications:** Books.

18317 ■ **Join Together (JTO)**
1 Appleton St., 4th Fl.
Boston, MA 02116-5223
Ph: (617)437-1500
Fax: (617)437-9394
E-mail: info@jointogether.org
URL: http://www.jointogether.org
Contact: David Rosenbloom, Dir.
Founded: 1991. **Description:** Works to reduce, prevent, and treat substance abuse. Offers reports, newsletters, and community action toolkits. Sponsors the National Leadership Fellows program. **Publications:** *Fighting Back Annual Yearbook,* annual. Contains stories of community efforts to reduce demand for illegal drugs and alcohol. ● Newsletter. Alternate Formats: online.

Taiwan

18318 ■ **Center for Taiwan International Relations (CTIR)**
110 Maryland Ave. NE, Ste.206
Washington, DC 20002-5626
Ph: (202)543-6287
Fax: (202)543-2364
E-mail: ctirdwt@erols.com
URL: http://www.taiwandc.org/ctir
Contact: David Tsai PhD, Pres.
Founded: 1988. **Multinational. Description:** Works to uphold the human rights and sovereignty of Taiwan's people. **Roundtables:** Taiwan. **Publications:** *Let Taiwan be Taiwan* (in English and Mandarin

Dialects) ● *National Taiwanese Organization Directory 1996-1997* ● *Taiwangate: Blacklist Policy and Human Rights.* **Conventions/Meetings:** conference.

18319 ■ **Formosan Association for Human Rights (FAHR)**
c/o Ms. Pearl Wang, Pres.
22 Aberdeen Crossing
The Woodlands, TX 77381
Ph: (281)367-1138
E-mail: ptang1@houston.rr.com
URL: http://www.fahr-usa.org
Contact: Ms. Pearl Wang, Pres.
Founded: 1978. **Members:** 120. **Local Groups:** 16. **Description:** Persons concerned with human rights in Taiwan. Promotes respect for the United Nations' Universal Declaration of Human Rights; aids all persons of Formosan birth or heritage who are threatened with denial of, or are actually denied, their fundamental human rights; cooperates with other international organizations on human rights in order to promote common goals. **Awards:** Cheng Nan-Joun Memorial Award. **Frequency:** annual. **Type:** monetary. **Recipient:** for Taiwanese individuals who have been unjustly mistreated, abused or otherwise insulted by the government in Taiwan ● Wang Kan-Lu Human Rights Award. **Frequency:** annual. **Type:** monetary. **Recipient:** for Taiwanese individuals who have promoted and/or contributed to human rights improvement in Taiwan. **Committees:** Caring; Public Relations; Publishing. **Publications:** *FARH Newsletter,* quarterly ● *The Taiwan Confrontation Crisis.* Book ● Books. **Conventions/Meetings:** annual conference - weekend before Human Rights Day.

18320 ■ **Formosan Association for Public Affairs (FAPA)**
552 7th St. SE
Washington, DC 20003
Ph: (202)547-3686
Fax: (202)543-7891
E-mail: home@fapa.org
URL: http://www.fapa.org
Contact: Dr. Wen-Yen Chen, Exec. Dir.
Founded: 1982. **Membership Dues:** basic, $50-$70 (annual) ● student, $25-$35 ● honorary permanent, $1,200-$1,500 ● FAPA-100 club, $100 (monthly). **Description:** Individuals including native Taiwanese (also known as Formosans). Purposes are to: affect the U.S. policy-making process regarding Taiwan through membership education and public information; seek world support for the human rights, freedom, and the right to self-determination of the people of Taiwan; protect and advance the interests, rights, and welfare of Taiwanese communities worldwide. Sponsors leadership and government seminars designed to educate members into an effective movement in American politics. Offers internships; operates speakers' bureau. Conducts research programs. **Libraries:** Type: reference. **Holdings:** articles, audiovisuals, books, papers, periodicals. **Publications:** *Case for Self-Determination* ● *FAPA News,* quarterly. Newsletters. Alternate Formats: online ● *Taiwan: The Silenced Majority.*

18321 ■ **Professor Chen Wen-Chen Memorial Foundation (CWCMF)**
PO Box 6223
Lawrenceville, NJ 08648
Ph: (609)936-1352
Fax: (609)936-1352
E-mail: cwcmf@formosa.org
URL: http://www.cwcmf.org
Contact: Dr. Mark Kao, Chm.
Founded: 1982. **Description:** Taiwanese-Americans who promote, document, and study Taiwanese art, culture, history, education, and human rights. (The foundation is named after Professor Chen Wen-Chen, a professor of statistics at Carnegie-Melon University in Pittsburgh, PA. According to the group, Chen Wen-Chen returned to Taiwan in 1981 and was abducted by police and murdered on July 3, 1981.) Sponsors competitions; offers cultural exchange program. **Awards:** Type: recognition. **Recipient:** for projects ● **Frequency:** annual. **Type:** scholarship. **Committees:** Award and Scholarships; Cultural Center; Taiwan-U.

Publications: *A Memorial for Professor Chen Wen-Chen - A Taiwanese* ● *Taiwan Culture*, bimonthly. **Conventions/Meetings:** semiannual conference.

Tax Reform

18322 ■ Howard Jarvis Taxpayers Association (HJTA)
621 S Westmoreland Ave., Ste.202
Los Angeles, CA 90005
Ph: (213)384-9656
Fax: (213)384-9870
E-mail: info@hjta.org
URL: http://www.hjta.org
Contact: Kris Vosburgh, Exec. Dir.
Founded: 1978. **Members:** 200,000. **Membership Dues:** regular, $15 (annual). **Staff:** 5. **Description:** Dedicated to tax relief for Californians. **Publications:** *Taxing Times*, quarterly. Newsletter. **Price:** included in membership dues.

18323 ■ National Retail Sales Tax Alliance (NRSTA)
2897 N Druid Hills Rd., No. 258
Atlanta, GA 30329
Ph: (404)438-9832
Free: (877)937-6778
E-mail: nwhite@salestax.org
URL: http://www.salestax.org
Contact: Neal White, Pres.
Founded: 1999. **Description:** Community leaders, business people, and ordinary citizens committed to replacing the income tax system. Organization does not "challenge the legality of the federal income tax or the Internal Revenue Service". **Computer Services:** Mailing lists, of members ● online services, petition ● online services, tax reform survey. **Publications:** *Weekly Tax News*. Newsletter.

18324 ■ Policy and Taxation Group
3941 S Bristol St., No. 46
Santa Ana, CA 92704
Ph: (714)641-6913
Fax: (714)641-3128
E-mail: pmsoldano@policyandtaxationgroup.com
URL: http://www.policyandtaxationgroup.com
Contact: Patricia M. Soldano, Pres.
Description: Dedicated to the elimination of the estate and gift taxes (death taxes) and the elimination of the destructive effect those taxes have on families, family businesses, job creation, the national economy and government revenues; coordinates efforts of other tax reform organizations to eliminate duplication of efforts and present consistent data.

18325 ■ ReformAMT
PO Box 915
Cupertino, CA 95015
Ph: (408)482-2400
E-mail: info@reformamt.org
URL: http://www.reformamt.org
Contact: Mr. Jay Cena, Chm.
Founded: 2001. **Regional Groups:** 295. **State Groups:** 48. **Description:** Aims to correct an injustice created by the way in which the Alternative Minimum Tax (AMT) is inappropriately and unjustly imposed upon owners of incentive stock options. Seeks to urge Congress to correct this flawed tax code, through the building of a grassroots tax reform organization, which has resulted in financial devastation for taxpayers obeying this law. Beyond correction of the law, also seeks full redress from the United States Government for those affected. **Computer Services:** Online services, informal poll. **Telecommunication Services:** electronic mail, jay@reformamt.org.

18326 ■ Savers and Investors League
PO Box 210
Mirror Lake, NH 03853-0210
Ph: (603)569-8283
Fax: (603)569-1595

E-mail: tkelly@savers.org
URL: http://www.savers.org
Contact: W. Thomas Kelly, Pres.
Description: Promotes personal saving and investing to foster healthy economic growth in the United States. Works toward the adoption of clear, concise and comprehensible tax laws that promote, rather than deter, increased savings and investments.

18327 ■ Taxpayers for Common Sense (TCS)
651 Pennsylvania Ave. SE
Washington, DC 20003
Ph: (202)546-8500
Free: (800)TAXPAYER
Fax: (202)546-8511
E-mail: info@taxpayer.net
URL: http://www.taxpayer.net
Contact: Jill Lancelot, Pres./Co-Founder
Founded: 1995. **Description:** Independent advocate for the American taxpayer dedicated to cutting wasteful government spending and subsidies in order to achieve a responsible, efficient government. Assists grassroots partners, works with congress, and communicates through the media. **Publications:** Annual Report, annual. **Conventions/Meetings:** annual banquet, fundraiser and awards reception.

Taxation

18328 ■ American Tax Policy Institute (ATPI)
1156 15th St. NW, Ste.900
Washington, DC 20005
Ph: (202)637-3243
Fax: (202)223-9741
E-mail: atpi@americantaxpolicyinstitute.org
URL: http://www.americantaxpolicyinstitute.org
Contact: Kathy Prunty, Admin. Mgr.
Founded: 1989. **Members:** 25. **Staff:** 4. **Budget:** $250,000. **Description:** Works to improve America's tax system. Offers analysis on tax policy issues including: tax legislative processes; the efficiency of tax laws in raising revenue; the administrative process of the Internal Revenue Service; the effect of tax laws on international competitiveness; how taxes affect taxpayers and the economy; the rationality of the tax system; compliance with tax laws. Sponsors research and education programs. **Conventions/Meetings:** periodic conference.

18329 ■ Americans for Tax Reform (ATR)
1920 L St. NW, Ste.200
Washington, DC 20036
Ph: (202)785-0266
Fax: (202)785-0261
E-mail: friends@atr.org
URL: http://www.atr.org
Contact: Grover Norquist, Pres.
Founded: 1985. **Members:** 60,000. **Membership Dues:** individual, $25 ● individual corporate, $10 (annual). **Staff:** 13. **Budget:** $6,000,000. **State Groups:** 750. **Local Groups:** 500. **Description:** Corporations; trade organizations and taxpayer groups. Sponsors the Taxpayer Protection Pledge, a covenant made by incumbents and other candidates for national office who promise to oppose all income tax increases. Conducts the Anti-Vat Coalition and coordinates the anti-VAT caucus in the Congress with 177 members. Opposes any and all tax increase at the federal, state, and local level. Coordinates with local initiative efforts to impose restraint on state and local tax increases. **Awards:** Enemy of the Taxpayer. **Frequency:** monthly. **Type:** recognition ● Friend of the Taxpayer. **Type:** recognition. **Computer Services:** Mailing lists, of members. **Committees:** Citizens Against a National Sales Tax/VAT. **Projects:** Leave Us Alone; Media Freedom; NoDeathTax.org. **Publications:** *Memos*, bimonthly. Reports on the status of tax bills.

18330 ■ Center for Science in the Public Interest - Alcohol Policies Project
1875 Connecticut Ave. NW, Ste.300
Washington, DC 20009-5728
Ph: (202)332-9110

Fax: (202)265-4954
E-mail: alcproject@cspinet.org
URL: http://cspinet.org/booze
Contact: George A. Hacker, Dir., Alcohol Policies Proj.
Founded: 1981. **Description:** Helps focus public and policy maker attention on high-leverage policy reforms to reduce the devastating health and social consequences of drinking; the project has worked with thousands of organizations and individuals to promote a comprehensive, prevention-oriented policy strategy to change the role of alcohol in society. **Telecommunication Services:** electronic mail, ghacker@cspinet.org. **Formerly:** (2002) National Alcohol Tax Coalition. **Publications:** Reports. Alternate Formats: online ● Also publishes fact sheets.

18331 ■ Center for the Study of Economics (CSE)
1518 Walnut St., Ste.604
Philadelphia, PA 19102
Ph: (215)545-6004
Fax: (215)545-4929
E-mail: managers@urbantools.org
URL: http://www.urbantools.org
Contact: Joshua Vincent, Pres./Exec. Dir.
Founded: 1980. **Members:** 200. **Membership Dues:** $35 (annual). **Staff:** 3. **Budget:** $60,000. **Description:** Supporters of land value taxation research. Conducts objective research in property tax reform, land value taxation, and certain aspects of unemployment, recession, and inflation. Compiles statistics. **Libraries:** Type: open to the public. **Holdings:** 60. **Subjects:** land value taxation. **Absorbed:** (1998) Center for Local Tax Research. **Publications:** *Incentive Taxation*, quarterly. Newsletter. Presents research on the two-rate property tax. **Price:** $20.00/year. ISSN: 0896-4556. **Circulation:** 4,600. Alternate Formats: online ● Also publishes studies. **Conventions/Meetings:** annual conference (exhibits) - always October.

18332 ■ Citizens for an Alternative Tax System (CATS)
7825 Sudley Rd., No. 206
Manassas, VA 20109
Free: (800)767-7577
E-mail: mailroom@cats.org
URL: http://www.cats.org
Contact: Vic Krohn, Natl. Chm.
Founded: 1990. **Members:** 20,000. **Membership Dues:** basic, $35 (annual) ● business, $150 (annual) ● sustaining (minimum), $250 (annual). **Staff:** 10. **Regional Groups:** 9. **Local Groups:** 300. **Description:** Individuals, businesses, and corporations in search of a viable alternative to the present income tax system. Promotes the use of a national sales tax as a replacement for income tax. Conducts lobbying activities. **Publications:** *CATS Newsletter*, monthly.

18333 ■ Citizens for Tax Justice (CTJ)
1616 P St. NW, Ste.200
Washington, DC 20036
Ph: (202)299-1066
Fax: (202)299-1065
E-mail: mattg@ctj.org
URL: http://www.ctj.org
Contact: Richard Pomp, Pres.
Founded: 1979. **Members:** 4,100. **Membership Dues:** regular, $35 (annual). **Staff:** 6. **Description:** Labor and other national, state, and local citizens' organizations dedicated to fair taxation. Believes taxes should reflect taxpayers' ability to pay while providing revenues needed to fund government services. Supports federal, state, and local tax relief for unfairly burdened middle and low-income families. Opposes measures shifting tax burdens from upper income groups and large corporations onto average taxpayers. Provides technical assistance and other services. **Libraries:** Type: reference. **Holdings:** clippings, periodicals. **Subjects:** federal, state and local taxation. **Publications:** *CTJ Update*, 9/year. Newsletter. **Price:** $25.00 ● In-Depth studies of state and federal tax systems. **Conventions/Meetings:** annual meeting.

18334 ■ Common Ground - U.S.A. (CGUSA)
PO Box 57
Evanston, IL 60204
Ph: (847)475-0391
Fax: (775)248-8630
E-mail: nadstoner@aol.com
Contact: Sue Walton, Contact

Founded: 1985. **Members:** 170. **Membership Dues:** individual, $36 (annual). **Staff:** 1. **Budget:** $12,850. **Regional Groups:** 1. **State Groups:** 7. **Local Groups:** 2. **Languages:** 2. **Description:** Individuals interested in implementing the theories of Henry George (1839-97), American economist. Promotes "justice and prosperity" through the taxation of land values rather than labor and improvements; is not connected in any way with Ecology Action of the Mid-Peninsula. **Libraries: Type:** open to the public. **Subjects:** land value taxation as relates to property taxes, economic development, environment, etc. **Awards: Frequency:** periodic. **Type:** recognition. **Recipient:** to a member who has conformed the purpose of the Association and its immediate goal. **Computer Services:** database, membership list ● database, membership/subscribers of Common Ground-USA plus contacts from other sources and Internet. **Committees:** Affordable Housing; Electro-Magnetic Spectrum; Federal Deficit Reduction; Mass Transit; Tax Shift Off Workers and Onto Polluters; Undertaxation of Federal, Mineral, Forest and Grazing Lands; Urban Sprawl. **Affiliated With:** Council of Georgist Organizations. **Formerly:** (1988) Common Ground. **Publications:** The Georgist Registry, biennial. Report. Reports to registrants. **Price:** $15.00/year in North America; $20.00/year outside North America. **Circulation:** 200 ● Ground-Swell, bimonthly. Newsletter. **Price:** $15.00/year in North America; $20.00/year outside North America. **Circulation:** 200 ● How to Start and Operate a Chapter of Common Ground-USA, quarterly. Handbook. A pending legislative matter. ● Quarterly Letter Lobby Information Kit. Brochure. A pending legislative matter. ● The Revenue Source is Under Our Feet, biennial. Brochure. Reports to registrants. ● The Revenue Source is Under Our Feet - Lower Taxes to the Ground. Brochure. Contains legislative information. ● Brochure, annual. Lists CG-USA's platform and lists benefits to members. **Price:** free. Alternate Formats: online. **Conventions/Meetings:** annual board meeting, for directors and chapter representatives and committee chairs (exhibits) - between May and October.

18335 ■ Council of Georgist Organizations (CGO)
PO Box 57
Evanston, IL 60204
Free: (888)262-9015
Fax: (775)248-8630
E-mail: shw817@yahoo.com
Contact: Sue Walton, Admin.

Founded: 1979. **Members:** 50. **Membership Dues:** organizational, $50 (annual). **Staff:** 4. **Description:** Organizations and individuals that support the ideas and reforms of American economist Henry George (1839-97), who advocated a single tax on land values, thereby "extending political liberty, economic justice, prosperity, and conservation." Fosters communication and cooperation among Georgist organizations. **Libraries: Type:** reference. **Holdings:** 5,000. **Subjects:** research on Henry George. **Affiliated With:** Common Ground - U.S.A.; International Union for Land Value Taxation and Free Trade. **Absorbed:** (1997) Georgist Registry. **Publications:** CGO Directory, 3/year. Brochure. Contains member organizations. Alternate Formats: online ● The Georgist Journal, quarterly ● Georgist Registry Reports, biennial. Reprint. **Conventions/Meetings:** annual conference (exhibits) - usually summer.

18336 ■ Council On State Taxation (COST)
122 C St. NW, Ste.330
Washington, DC 20001-2109
Ph: (202)484-5222 (202)484-5212
Fax: (202)484-5229

E-mail: dlindholm@statetax.org
URL: http://www.statetax.org/COSTHome.cfm
Contact: Douglas L. Lindholm Esq., Pres./Exec. Dir.
Founded: 1969. **Members:** 570. **Membership Dues:** corporate, $3,000 (annual). **Staff:** 10. **Budget:** $2,500,000. **Description:** Multistate corporate taxpayers. Promotes equitable and nondiscriminatory state and local taxation of multijurisdictional entities. Prepares amicus curiae briefs on state tax issues before state supreme courts and the US Supreme Court. Monitors state tax legislation and conducts lobbying activities. Conducts research and educational programs. Serves as a clearinghouse on state tax legislation. **Awards:** Georgetown University Center Fellowships. **Frequency:** annual. **Type:** fellowship. **Recipient:** to two full-time LLM tax degree candidates with an interest in state and local taxation. **Telecommunication Services:** electronic bulletin board. **Formerly:** (2001) Committee On State Taxation. **Publications:** COST Conscious, biweekly. Newsletter. Alternate Formats: online ● COST Practitioner Connection, biweekly. Newsletter. Alternate Formats: online ● Legislative Update, bimonthly. Newsletter. Alternate Formats: online ● State Tax Report, periodic. Alternate Formats: online ● Membership Directory. Alternate Formats: online. **Conventions/Meetings:** annual Income Tax Conference ● annual meeting ● annual Sales Tax Conference ● periodic seminar.

18337 ■ Henry George Institute - New York (HGI)
121 E 30th St.
New York, NY 10016
Ph: (212)889-8020
E-mail: teacher@henrygeorge.org
URL: http://www.henrygeorge.org/hgi.htm
Contact: Mr. Lindy Davies, Program Dir.
Founded: 1971. **Members:** 175. **Membership Dues:** regular (voting), $20 (annual). **Staff:** 1. **Budget:** $350,000. **Languages:** English, Russian, Spanish. **Description:** Represents individuals interested in the economic theories of American economist Henry George (1839-97), who advocated placing tax burdens on land, rather than buildings and other improvements. Offers educational programs in fundamental economics by correspondence and over the Internet. Maintains speakers' bureau. **Libraries: Type:** open to the public. **Holdings:** 60. **Subjects:** land value taxation. **Computer Services:** Online services, web-based courses in Political Economy and related topics. **Publications:** Georgist Journal, quarterly. Magazine. Features news and commentaries for the international Georgist movement. **Price:** $20.00. ISSN: 0887-6290. **Circulation:** 700.

18338 ■ National Association of Form 1099 Filers (NAF1099)
PO Box 130053
Ann Arbor, MI 48113-0053
Ph: (734)327-9593
Fax: (734)623-1099
E-mail: naf1099@yahoo.com
URL: http://www.naf1099.org
Contact: Candice Hatfield, Pres.
Founded: 1997. **Members:** 450. **Membership Dues:** individual, $95 (annual). **Description:** Individuals who file Internal Revenue Service Form 1099 income tax returns. Seeks to enhance interaction among members of the payer community and to provide additional forums for communication between payer community members and state and federal taxing authorities. Conducts educational and peer networking programs; serves as a clearinghouse on changes in Form 1099 filing requirements and related issues. **Publications:** Journal of the National Association of 1099 Filers, quarterly. **Conventions/Meetings:** annual conference.

18339 ■ National Campaign for a Peace Tax Fund (NCPTF)
2121 Decatur Pl. NW
Washington, DC 20008
Ph: (202)483-3751
Free: (888)732-2382
Fax: (202)986-0667

E-mail: info@peacetaxfund.org
URL: http://www.peacetaxfund.org
Contact: Alan Gamble, Exec. Dir.
Founded: 1971. **Members:** 5,000. **Membership Dues:** regular, $35 (annual). **Staff:** 4. **Budget:** $100,000. **Description:** Represents individuals who support the principle of legal recognition of the right of conscientious objection to taxes being used for war or preparation for war. Seeks to secure passage of legislation establishing a legal right of persons who are against military taxation for reasons of conscience to have the current military portion of their federal taxes redirected into a fund for peacemaking projects. Works to build support for the Peace Tax Fund Bill in Congress. Conducts educational activities and congressional lobbying. **Committees:** Legislative; Networking/Outreach; Personnel. **Formerly:** (1975) World Peace Tax Fund Steering Committee; (1983) National Council for a World Peace Tax Fund; (1984) National Campaign for a World Peace Tax Fund. **Publications:** Peace Tax Fund Newsletter Quarterly Update. Provides information on association activities; includes lobbying update and list of Congressional district contacts. **Price:** included in membership dues. **Circulation:** 5,000 ● Brochures ● Manuals ● Pamphlets. **Conventions/Meetings:** annual meeting.

18340 ■ National Tax-Limitation Committee (NTLC)
151 N Sunrise Ave., Ste.901
Roseville, CA 95661
Ph: (916)786-9400
Fax: (916)786-8163
E-mail: lkuhler@earthlink.net
URL: http://www.limittaxes.org
Contact: Lewis K. Uhler, Founder/Pres.
Founded: 1975. **Members:** 200,000. **Staff:** 4. **Description:** Campaigns for federal and state constitutional amendments which would limit government spending and taxation. Promotes education and research on methods of limiting taxation. Actively supports Tax Limitation/Balanced Budget Constitutional Amendment. Solicits signatures and support from U.S. citizens and coordinates movements in all states. Testifies before state legislative committees; holds national tax limitation conferences; has provided trained personnel, financial assistance, and organizational advice to state petition drives and referendum campaigns. **Publications:** Meeting America's Economic Crisis ● Tax Watch, periodic. Newsletter.

18341 ■ National Taxpayers Union (NTU)
108 N Alfred St.
Alexandria, VA 22314
Ph: (703)683-5700
Fax: (703)683-5722
E-mail: ntu@ntu.org
URL: http://www.ntu.org
Contact: John Berthoud, Pres.
Founded: 1969. **Members:** 335,000. **Membership Dues:** regular, $15 (annual). **Staff:** 20. **Budget:** $3,500,000. **Description:** Seeks to: reduce government spending; cut taxes; protect the rights of taxpayers. Claims to have helped generate federal budget cuts of over 120 billion dollars. Activities include research programs and an intense lobbying campaign in Washington, DC; has been a leader in the fights against government ventures such as: social security tax; guaranteed income; congressional and bureaucratic pay raises; federal subsidies; foreign aid; national health insurance. Works for a balanced federal budget/tax limitation constitutional amendment; federal pension reform; reduction of capital gains and personal income tax; social security reform. Has worked for airline deregulation; indexing of federal income tax, California's Proposition 13, Massachusetts Proposition 2 1/2, and other state tax cutting initiatives. Conducts annual voting study of congressmen and senators, rating their votes on spending and tax issues and presenting awards for best and worst records. **Libraries: Type:** reference. **Holdings:** 250; books, clippings, monographs, periodicals. **Subjects:** federal, state, local tax and spending issues. **Awards:** Taxpayer's Friend Award.

Frequency: annual. **Type:** recognition. **Recipient:** for persons who receive "A" grade on annual rating of congress. **Computer Services:** database, State and Local Taxpayer Groups. **Committees:** Balance the Budget; Campaign Fund (National Political Action Committee); State Victory Fund Political Action. **Publications:** *Dollars and Sense*, bimonthly. Newsletter. Provides updates on important legislation. **Price:** included in membership dues. **Circulation:** 75,000. Alternate Formats: online ● *How to Fight Property Taxes*. Booklet. **Price:** $6.95 ● *Tax Savings Report*, 10/year. Newsletter. Provides income tax advice. **Price:** $39.95/year. **Circulation:** 15,000 ● *Taxpayer's Action Guide* ● *Taxpayers Resource Book*. **Conventions/Meetings:** biennial National Taxpayers Conference, state and national taxpayer groups (exhibits).

18342 ■ National War Tax Resistance Coordinating Committee (NWTRCC)

PO Box 150553
Brooklyn, NY 11215
Ph: (718)768-3420
Free: (800)269-7464
E-mail: nwtrcc@nwtrcc.org
URL: http://www.nwtrcc.org
Contact: Ruth Benn, Coor.

Founded: 1982. **Membership Dues:** local group, $50 (annual) ● regional, $300 ● national group, $500. **Staff:** 1. **Budget:** $30,000. **Regional Groups:** 20. **Local Groups:** 45. **National Groups:** 10. **Description:** Serves as a coalition of national, regional, and local groups working on war tax issues. Works to facilitate the exchange of ideas, enhance networking, and coordinate and build the war tax resistance movement. Supports people who take a nonviolent stand against military taxes and supports redirection of military taxes to alternative funds, escrow accounts, and other life-affirming purposes. Believes that responsible war tax protest and war tax resistance are expressions of individual conscience and a means of creating change in U.S. military and defense policies. Endorses the U.S. Peace Tax Fund Bill in the U.S. Congress; encourages the adjustment of individual lifestyles to a more equitable standard. Sponsors activities including vigils, demonstrations, and war tax clinics. Offers war tax counseling service; sponsors research on the IRS, and the legal and legislative approach to war tax issues. Trains war tax counselors and lawyers. Coordinates a national information and referral network of war tax resistance counselors, attorneys, and activists. Offers workshops; maintains speakers' bureau. **Affiliated With:** Center on Conscience and War; Central Committee for Conscientious Objectors; Fellowship of Reconciliation - USA; Mennonite Central Committee; National Campaign for a Peace Tax Fund; Sojourners; War Resisters League. **Publications:** *Our Telephone Taxes Pay for War!* ● *Practical War Tax Resistance No. 1: Controlling Federal Tax Withholding*. Brochure ● *Practical War Tax Resistance No. 6: Organizational War Tax Resistance: Employers, Contractors, & Financial Institutions*. Brochure. **Price:** $1.00 for non-affiliates ● *Practical War Tax Resistance No. 3: How to Resist Collection, or Make the Most of Collection When It Happens*. Brochure ● *Practical War Tax Resistance No. 2: To File or Not to File an Income Tax Return*. Brochure ● *War Tax Resistance at a Glance: Concise Answers to Frequently Asked Questions About WTR*. Brochure ● *War Tax Resisters and the Internal Revenue Service: An Outline of IRS Practice and Procedure Specific to War Tax Resistance Including Legal Resources*. **Conventions/Meetings:** biennial Coordinating Committee Meetings - executive committee meeting - first full weekends in May and November.

18343 ■ Non-Violent Action Community of Cascadia and the CMTC Escrow Fund (NACC)

4554 12th Ave. NE
Seattle, WA 98105
Ph: (206)547-0952
Fax: (206)547-2631
E-mail: nacc@drizzle.com
URL: http://seanacc.org
Contact: Martin Kelley, Contact

Founded: 1979. **Members:** 5,500. **Staff:** 2. **Budget:** $40,000. **National Groups:** 2. **Description:** Acts to

interrupt and transform militarism and other forms of violence, and to build a society based upon community, economic justice, environmental awareness, personal empowerment, and feminist, queer positive, and anti-racist principles. Uses creative nonviolent direct action, war tax resistance, public education and coalition building towards these ends, creating community and developing empowerment and conflict-resolution skills in the process. Counsels war tax resisters, and administers the Conscience and Military Tax Campaign Escrow Account. **Committees:** Escrow/Legal. **Affiliated With:** National War Tax Resistance Coordinating Committee; War Resisters League. **Formerly:** (1979) Suffolk County Committee for a World Peace Tax Fund; (1998) Conscience and Military Tax Campaign- U.S. **Publications:** *Nonviolent Action*, periodic. Newsletter. **Price:** $10.00. **Conventions/Meetings:** workshop.

18344 ■ Save Our Schools (SOS)

c/o Maureen P. Madden, Founder/CEO
PO Box 175
Annapolis, MD 21404
Ph: (410)552-5331
Free: (877)533-SOS1
E-mail: saveourschools@aol.com
URL: http://www.soschools.org
Contact: Maureen P. Madden, Founder/CEO

Founded: 1980. **Members:** 150,000. **Staff:** 4. **Budget:** $1,100,000. **Description:** Seeks to advance quality of public education; provides necessary tools to schools to enable children to reach full potential, including books, computers, musical instruments, reading specialists, air conditioning, and more; representatives concerning these issues. **Convention/Meeting:** none. **Formerly:** (1982) Taxpayers Education Lobby. **Publications:** *Members' Report*, monthly.

18345 ■ Tax Analysts

400 S Maple Ave., Ste.400
Falls Church, VA 22046
Ph: (703)533-4400
Free: (800)955-2444
Fax: (703)533-4444
E-mail: cservice@tax.org
URL: http://www.tax.org
Contact: Christopher Bergin, Pres.

Founded: 1970. **Staff:** 200. **Budget:** $10,000,000. **Description:** Reviews all tax law developments, federal, state, international comprehensively; compiles statistics. **Convention/Meeting:** none. **Libraries:** **Type:** not open to the public. **Subjects:** current and historical tax information. **Computer Services:** database ● online services, daily tax magazines and full text of tax-related documents. **Telecommunication Services:** electronic mail, techsupport@tax.org. **Committees:** Tax Policy Advisory. **Absorbed:** Taxation With Representation. **Formerly:** (1978) Tax Analysts and Advocates; (1981) Taxation With Representation Fund. **Publications:** *Exempt Organization Tax Review*, monthly. Magazine ● *Highlights and Documents*, daily. Magazine ● *State Tax Notes*, daily. Alternate Formats: online ● *Tax Analysts Microfiche Tax Database*, weekly ● *The Tax Directory*, quarterly. **Price:** $135.00/copy ● *Tax Notes*, weekly. Magazine. Features in-depth articles, special reports, and commentaries analyzing proposed and enacted tax legislation, court decisions, and regulations. Alternate Formats: online ● *Tax Notes International*, daily. Alternate Formats: online ● *Tax Practice*, weekly. Magazine. Delivers comprehensive and concise coverage of federal tax news. **Price:** $366.00/copy ● *Tax-Related Documents*, weekly. Magazine ● *TaxLibrary.com*, weekly.

18346 ■ Taxpayers Against Fraud, The False Claims Act Legal Center (TAF)

1220 19th St. NW, Ste.501
Washington, DC 20036
Ph: (202)296-4826
Free: (800)873-2573
Fax: (202)296-4838

E-mail: taf-info@taf.org
URL: http://www.taf.org
Contact: James W. Moorman, Pres./CEO

Founded: 1986. **Staff:** 9. **Description:** Seeks to combat fraud against the Federal Government through the promotion and use of qui tam provisions under the False Claims Act. Provides litigation assistance to whistleblowers and counsel. Serves as an information clearinghouse and engages in educational and advocacy activities. **Libraries:** **Type:** reference. **Holdings:** articles, monographs, periodicals. **Subjects:** False Claims Act, qui tam cases. **Programs:** Qui Tam Attorney Network. **Publications:** *False Claims Act and Qui Tam Quarterly Review*. Journal. **Price:** $75.00.

18347 ■ Thomas Jefferson Equal Tax Society (TJETS)

c/o Mike Tecton
1469 Spring Vale Ave.
McLean, VA 22101
Ph: (703)356-5800
Fax: (703)893-7945
Contact: Mike Tecton, Founder

Founded: 1974. **State Groups:** 50. **Description:** Individuals united to establish constitutional equal taxation for each individual of voting age and to end "unconstitutional bounties and expenditures". Assists persons "who are inequitiously taxed." Conducts lectures; maintains library. **Publications:** Newspaper, periodic ● Also publishes several books. **Conventions/Meetings:** periodic convention.

18348 ■ TRIM

PO Box 8040
Appleton, WI 54912
Ph: (920)749-3780
Free: (800)775-TRIM
Fax: (920)749-5062
E-mail: trim@jbs.org
URL: http://www.TRIMonline.org
Contact: George Kotalik, Contact

Founded: 1974. **Local Groups:** 225. **Description:** A project of the John Birch Society. Aims to slow and reverse the growth of both federal and state governments. Develops a coordinated program to educate the public in the best ways to stop tax increases, lower taxes, reduce the number of government regulations, and end inflation. Publicizes congressional members' voting records, usually on bills involving one billion dollars or more. Distributes literature and films. Maintains speakers' bureau. **Convention/Meeting:** none. **Libraries:** **Type:** reference. **Holdings:** 5,000. **Computer Services:** database, congressional news ● database, voting and international news ● mailing lists, congressional. **Formerly:** (1998) Tax Reform Immediately. **Publications:** *BRI Congressional Directory*, biennial ● *TRIM Bulletin*, 3/year. Alternate Formats: online.

18349 ■ Urban-Brookings Tax Policy Center (TPC)

2100 M St. NW
Washington, DC 20037
Ph: (202)833-7200
E-mail: lburman@ui.urban.org
URL: http://www.taxpolicycenter.org
Contact: Leonard E. Burman PhD, Co-Dir.

Founded: 2002. **Description:** Provides policymakers and the public with timely and accessible facts and insights on pressing tax policy issues based on state-of-the-art modeling and research. Works to clarify and analyze the nation's tax policy choices; examines social, economic and governance problems in the U.S. **Computer Services:** database, tax facts. **Affiliated With:** Charles Stewart Mott Foundation; Ford Foundation; Open Society Institute. **Publications:** *Discussion Paper Series*. Reports. Contains Tax Policy working paper series that focus on key tax policy issues. Alternate Formats: online ● *Economic Perspective*. Articles. Alternate Formats: online ● *Issues and Options Series*. Reports. Contains policy briefs that are written by Tax Policy Center experts that focus on current tax policy. Alternate Formats: online ● *Tax Break*. Articles. Alternate Formats: online ● *Tax Facts*, semiweekly. Booklets. Alternate

Formats: online ● Newsletter, periodic. Alternate Formats: online ● Annual Report, annual. Alternate Formats: online.

18350 ■ War Tax Resister's Penalty Fund (WTRPF)
c/o Cliff Kindy
PO Box 25
North Manchester, IN 46962
E-mail: kindy@cpt.org
URL: http://www.nonviolence.org/issues/wtrpf
Contact: Cliff Kindy, Contact

Founded: 1982. **Members:** 630. **Description:** A national project of the North Manchester Fellowship of Reconciliation. Provides moral and financial support to individuals who refuse to pay all or part of their federal income taxes because they oppose the expenditure of their tax money on war and preparation for war. Works to collect money from members to reimburse resisters for interest incurred and other penalties imposed by the Internal Revenue Service for nonpayment of taxes. **Formerly:** (1988) Tax Resister's Penalty Fund. **Publications:** *Tax Resisters' Penalty Fund Appeal*, 2-4/year.

Television

18351 ■ Federation Without Television
6282 12th St. N, No. 105
Oakdale, MN 55128
E-mail: fwt@wowmail.com
URL: http://www.orgsites.com/mn/fwt
Contact: Andrew Bushard, Pres.

Founded: 1998. **Local Groups:** 1. **Description:** Provides forums of expression for ideas ignored, suppressed, marginalized, and vilified by the mainstream media; promotes creativity and spontaneity, promotes awareness the effects of mainstream media and television; encourages less mainstream media consumption; promotes intellectual stimulation and critical discourse. Produces audio tapes and gives out audio tapes for free. **Libraries:** Type: reference; open to the public. **Holdings:** 100; audiovisuals. **Also Known As:** Federation W/O TV.

18352 ■ Free Speech TV (FSTV)
PO Box 6060
Boulder, CO 80306
Ph: (303)442-8445 (303)542-4820
Free: (888)550-FSTV
Fax: (303)442-6472
E-mail: viewercomments@freespeech.org
URL: http://www.freespeech.org
Contact: John Schwartz, Pres.

Founded: 1995. **Description:** Works with activists and artists to cultivate an informed and active citizenry to advance progressive social change. **Publications:** Newsletter. Contains programming information.

Terrorism

18353 ■ 9/11 CitizensWatch
c/o Kyle F. Hence
PO Box 1255
Newport, RI 02840
Ph: (401)847-1963
E-mail: kylehence@earthlink.net
Contact: Kyle F. Hence, Contact

Description: Conducts citizen-led oversight process to monitor and constructively engage the Government-sanctioned National Commission on the terrorist attacks on the U.S.

18354 ■ 9/11 Families for a Secure America (9/11 FSA)
PO Box 156
Hawley, PA 18428-0156
Ph: (860)927-3822 (718)948-4108
URL: http://www.911fsa.org
Contact: Bruce DeCell, Contact

Description: Represents relatives of those killed in the September 11 attacks. Informs and educates the American public, elected officials and legislators of issues in America's security. Focuses on the dangers of unsecured borders, visa waiver programs, loose standards for issuing drivers' licenses, and acceptance of matricular cards. Aims to prevent future terrorist attacks and to secure America for generations to come. **Publications:** Newsletter. Alternate Formats: online.

18355 ■ Families of September 11 (FOS11)
1560 Broadway, Ste.305
New York, NY 10036-1518
Ph: (212)575-1878
E-mail: info@familiesofseptember11.org
URL: http://familiesofseptember11.org
Contact: Nikki Stern, Exec. Dir.

Founded: 2001. **Members:** 2,100. **Description:** Promotes public awareness of the effects of terrorism and public trauma. Champions domestic and international policies that respond to the threat of terrorism. Supports the 9/11 Commission Recommendations. **Computer Services:** Information services, legislation/policy resources ● information services, support resources. **Telecommunication Services:** electronic mail, chathelp@familiesofseptember11.org. **Programs:** Chat. **Projects:** Resiliency Album.

18356 ■ Hearts and Minds Network
3074 Broadway
New York, NY 10027
Ph: (212)280-0333
Fax: (212)280-0336
E-mail: vision@heartsandminds.org
URL: http://www.heartsandminds.org
Contact: Dave Peterson, Chm.

Founded: 1996. **Members:** 275. **Multinational.** **Description:** Works to investigate the causes of terrorism, poverty, human rights, the environment, addictions and other important issues; promotes public awareness through a nationwide campaign. **Publications:** Articles. Covers social issues.

18357 ■ International Association for Counterterrorism and Security Professionals (IACSP)
PO Box 10265
Arlington, VA 22210
Ph: (703)243-0993 (201)461-5422
Fax: (703)243-1197
E-mail: iacsp@erols.com
URL: http://www.iacsp.com
Contact: Steven J. Fustero, Dir. of Operations

Founded: 1992. **Membership Dues:** individual, $65 (annual) ● corporate/institution, $75 (annual) ● student, $40 (annual). **State Groups:** 24. **National Groups:** 15. **Multinational.** **Description:** Provides education and information on the threats of terrorism and its counter-measures. Promotes professional ethics and international cooperation in counterterrorism policy. **Awards:** Homeland Security Executive of the Year. **Frequency:** annual. **Type:** recognition. **Recipient:** for individuals who have demonstrated an unwavering commitment to IACSP. **Computer Services:** Information services, terrorism resources ● mailing lists, of members ● online services, message board. **Publications:** *Counterterrorism and Homeland Security Reports*, quarterly. Newsletter. Alternate Formats: online ● *The Journal of Counterterrorism and Security International*, quarterly. Magazine.

18358 ■ International Counter-Terrorism Officers Association (ICTOA)
Empire State Bldg.
350 5th Ave., Ste.3304 - No. 16P
New York, NY 10118
Ph: (212)564-5048
Fax: (718)661-4044
E-mail: info@ictoa.org
URL: http://www.ictoa.org
Contact: Brian J. Corrigan, Exec. Dir.

Membership Dues: general, $45 (annual) ● overseas, $60 (annual). **Multinational.** **Description:** Promotes unity to combat and understand terrorism. Provides training, education and networking to enhance terrorism awareness. Supports members with advanced counter-terrorism measures. Ensures safety and security through international networking. **Computer Services:** Information services, threat level resources. **Publications:** Newsletter, quarterly. **Conventions/Meetings:** annual conference.

18359 ■ Move America Forward (MAF)
PO Box 1497
Sacramento, CA 95812
Ph: (916)441-6197
E-mail: info@moveamericaforward.org
URL: http://www.moveamericaforward.org
Contact: Robert Dixon, Acting Exec. Dir.

Founded: 2004. **Description:** Supports America's efforts to defeat terrorism. Assists the men and women of the United States Armed Forces. Provides medical supplies and equipment to Afghanistan and Iraq. **Computer Services:** Online services, message board ● online services, poll. **Boards:** Advisory. **Programs:** A Call to Home; Coffee for Our Troops.

18360 ■ National Memorial Institute for the Prevention of Terrorism (MIPT)
PO Box 889
Oklahoma City, OK 73101
Ph: (405)278-6300 (405)278-6378
Fax: (405)232-5132
E-mail: research@mipt.org
URL: http://www.mipt.org
Contact: Donald R. Hamilton, Exec. Dir.

Founded: 1999. **Description:** Supports the first responders such as police officers, firefighters, emergency medical technicians and all personnel who are first on the scene in the aftermath of a terrorist activity. Provides focused research on counterterrorism technology and policy recommendations that can better prepare these personnel to face the challenges posed by another terrorist threat. Seeks understanding of the social and political causes and effects of terrorism and the development of technologies to counter biological, nuclear and chemical weapons of mass destruction as well as cyberterrorism. **Libraries:** Type: reference; open to the public. **Holdings:** 3,700; articles, books, papers, reports. **Subjects:** terrorism, weapons of mass destruction, Al Qaeda, aviation security, defense, combating terrorism, political violence against Americans, preparedness, computer security, presidential decision directives, critical infrastructure protection, public health, September 11, World Trade Center, relief organizations, Osama bin Laden, bioterrorism, anthrax, chemical weapons, first responders. **Computer Services:** Bibliographic search, terrorism ● information services, dates of terrorism incidents, terrorism information center ● online services, digital library. **Projects:** Defining First Responder Needs; Detecting Weapons of Mass Destruction; Equipment and Clothing for Emergency Responders; Explosive Forensics and Neutralization; Integrated Terrorism Databases; Promoting Preparedness; Recognizing Bioterrorism in the ER. **Subgroups:** National Emergency Responder Advisory Panel. **Publications:** *Oklahoma City - Seven Years Later: Lessons for Other Communities*. Booklet. Examines the lessons learned from the Oklahoma City bombing. ● *Terrorism Annual*. Yearbook. Alternate Formats: online ● *Terrorism Update*, quarterly. Bulletin. Contains articles on terrorism. Alternate Formats: online ● Annual Report, annual. Alternate Formats: online ● Bibliography. Alternate Formats: online.

18361 ■ September 11 Digital Archive
Center for History and New Media
Dept. of History and Art History, MSN 1E7
George Mason Univ.
4400 Univ. Dr.
Fairfax, VA 22030
Ph: (703)993-4528
E-mail: info@911digitalarchive.org
URL: http://911digitalarchive.org
Contact: Tom Scheinfeldt, Managing Dir.

Description: Works to create a permanent record of the events of September 11, 2001.

18362 ■ Terror Free Tomorrow

5335 Wisconsin Ave. NW, Ste.440
Washington, DC 20015-2052
Ph: (202)274-1800
Fax: (202)274-1821
E-mail: info@terrorfreetomorrow.org
URL: http://www.terrorfreetomorrow.org
Contact: Kenneth Ballen, Contact
Multinational. Description: Seeks to understand and undermine the popular support base that empowers global terrorists. Educates the public on the link between sympathy for anti-American terrorists and national security. **Computer Services:** Information services, Al Qaeda support base. **Projects:** Bridges to Indonesia; Making the Link; Understanding the Terrorist Support Base.

Tibet

18363 ■ International Campaign for Tibet (ICT)

1825 Jefferson Pl. NW
Washington, DC 20036
Ph: (202)785-1515
Fax: (202)785-4343
E-mail: info@savetibet.org
URL: http://www.savetibet.org
Contact: Mary Beth Markey, VP for Advocacy
Founded: 1988. **Members:** 55,000. **Membership Dues:** in U.S., $25 (annual) ● outside U.S., $35 (annual). **Staff:** 13. **Languages:** Chinese, English, Tibetan. **Description:** Promotes human rights and democratic freedoms for the people of Tibet. Proposes the idea that Tibet is occupied by China, that China is stripping Tibet of its natural resources, and that Tibetans have the right self-determination. Organizes fact-finding missions in Tibet; acts as a clearinghouse for information on the political situation in Tibet for the public, the government, and other agencies. Pressures the government of China to stop abuses and violations of human rights. Lobbies the United States Congress to improve the political situation in Tibet. Works with exiled Chinese democracy groups and Chinese language media. Works to protect the right of Tibetan refugees to safely pass through Nepal. Conducts speakers' bureau. Sponsors educational and research programs. **Libraries: Type:** reference; open to the public. **Holdings:** 2,000; audiovisuals, books, clippings, video recordings. **Subjects:** contemporary Tibetan history, politics, culture, religion, Tibet's environment, the Dalai Lama, travel and tourism, refugees, art, photography. **Awards:** Geuzen Medal. **Frequency:** annual. **Type:** medal. **Recipient:** for organizations and individuals who characterize the spirit of resistance against repression. **Publications:** Nuclear Tibet. Handbook. Discusses the Tibetan environment. ● Season to Purge. Reports. Contain information on religious persecution. ● Tibet Press Watch, bimonthly. **Price:** $25.00/year. **Circulation:** 40,000. **Conventions/Meetings:** annual conference.

18364 ■ Project Tibet (PT)

403 Canyon Rd.
Santa Fe, NM 87501
Ph: (505)982-3002
Fax: (505)988-4142
URL: http://www.tibet.org/Resources/TSG/Groups/nmproject.html
Contact: Paljor Thundup, Contact
Founded: 1980. **Members:** 500. **Staff:** 4. **State Groups:** 3. **Local Groups:** 1. **Description:** Tibetan refugees in the U.S. and their friends and sympathizers. Maintains the customs and traditions of Tibet for refugees who fled Tibet after the 1950s Chinese takeover. Helps Tibetan refugees establish handicraft centers and farms as a means of becoming self-sufficient; raises money for educational, religious, medical, and vocational needs until the goal of self-sufficiency is reached. Sponsors Pen Friends, a correspondence/aid program that encourages Westerners to send a letter and small donation each month to a Tibetan refugee. Offers film and slide show on Tibet mediation instructions. Operates retail and wholesale outlet for Tibetan refugee handicrafts. Maintains compound in Santa Fe, NM, that serves as quarters for visiting Tibetans and a site for special events. Offers children's services and speakers. **Awards: Type:** scholarship. **Affiliated With:** U.S.-Tibet Committee. **Publications:** Brochures ● Newsletter, quarterly ● Pamphlets. **Conventions/Meetings:** lecture ● seminar.

18365 ■ Tibet Justice Center (TJC)

2288 Fulton St., Ste.312
Berkeley, CA 94704
Ph: (510)486-0588
Fax: (510)548-3785
E-mail: tibetjustice@tibetjustice.org
URL: http://www.tibetjustice.org
Contact: Robert Sloane, Chm.
Founded: 1989. **Members:** 650. **Membership Dues:** low income, $25 (annual) ● basic, $45 (annual) ● supporter, $100 (annual) ● patron, $250 (annual) ● sponsor, $500 (annual). **Staff:** 2. **Budget:** $100,000. **Description:** Attorneys, concerned individuals, and organizations. Advocates self-determination for Tibetan people. Promotes human rights, environmental protection, and a peaceful solution to the situation in Tibet. Addresses environmental and developmental concerns in Tibet. Is currently reviewing the World Food Program's Project 3357, a project focused on agricultural development in the Lhasa River valley. Works on behalf of political prisoners, filing petitions with the U.N. Working Group on Arbitrary Detention who will then present them to the Chinese government. Offers education and training on individual and collective rights, stress reduction, and legal ethics from a Tibetan Buddhist perspective. Seeks to increase awareness of issues confronting Tibetan women. **Libraries: Type:** reference; open to the public; by appointment only. **Holdings:** articles, audiovisuals, books, clippings, periodicals. **Subjects:** Tibet. **Computer Services:** database ● mailing lists. **Committees:** Article 19; Environment/Sustainable Development; Litigation; Rinchen Project; Trade/Economics; Women's. **Projects:** Asylum and Immigration; Environment and Development. **Publications:** Tibet Brief, quarterly. Newsletter. **Price:** free for members. **Advertising:** accepted ● Also publishes legal, research, and educational materials on issues relevant to Tibet, including: self-determination, population transfer, environment, development, and U.S.-Tibet relations. **Conventions/Meetings:** monthly board meeting - always second Thursday.

18366 ■ U.S.-Tibet Committee (USTC)

241 E 32nd St.
New York, NY 10016
Ph: (212)481-3569
Fax: (212)779-9245
E-mail: ustc@igc.org
URL: http://www.ustibet.org
Contact: Sonam Wangdu, Chm.
Founded: 1977. **Members:** 10,000. **Membership Dues:** regular, $35 (annual). **Staff:** 1. **Regional Groups:** 2. **Description:** Formed by American and Tibetan volunteers to promote the restoration of Tibetan independence. Works on high-profile International campaigns to halt the exploitation of Tibet. Provides the public with information on the history, culture, and plight of the Tibetan people. Sponsors lectures, conferences, demonstrations, and other events to raise public awareness about conditions in Tibet and to help transform that awareness into action. Keeps U.S. politicians informed on the situation in Tibet and press them to take a stand against the Chinese occupation. **Libraries: Type:** open to the public. **Subjects:** Tibetan independence movement.

Tithing

18367 ■ NewTithing Group

1 Market, Steuart Tower, Ste.2105
San Francisco, CA 94105
Ph: (415)274-2754 (415)274-2765
Fax: (415)274-2756
E-mail: general@newtithing.org
URL: http://www.newtithing.com
Contact: Claude N. Rosenberg, Founder/Chm.
Founded: 1998. **Staff:** 6. **Multinational. Description:** Serves as philanthropic research organization committed to increase charitable giving, personal fulfillment, and productivity to the world's charitable sectors. **Publications:** Wealthy & Wise. Book. Demonstrates how many wealthy people can afford to give much more to charity without impairing their investment assets adjusted for inflation. **Price:** $5.00/copy.

Tobacco

18368 ■ American Legacy Foundation

2030 M St. NW, 6th Fl.
Washington, DC 20036
Ph: (202)454-5555
Fax: (202)454-5599
E-mail: info@americanlegacy.org
URL: http://www.americanlegacy.org
Contact: Cheryl Healton, Pres./CEO
Description: Works to build a world where young people reject tobacco and anyone can quit.

18369 ■ International Network of Women Against Tobacco (INWAT)

c/o Pressing Issues
PO Box 224
Metuchen, NJ 08840
Ph: (732)549-9054
Fax: (732)549-9056
E-mail: info@inwat.org
URL: http://www.inwat.org
Contact: Margaret Haglund, Pres.
Founded: 1990. **Members:** 1,200. **Description:** Provides contacts to individuals, particularly women, working in tobacco control; disseminates information about global tobacco issues; develops strategies to counter tobacco advertising; supports the development of women-centered tobacco and cessation programs. **Awards:** Encouragement Award. **Type:** recognition. **Publications:** The Net, semiannual. Newsletter. Features current global initiatives. **Price:** free for members. Alternate Formats: online.

Toxic Exposure

18370 ■ Mercury Policy Project (MPP)

1420 North St.
Montpelier, VT 05602
Ph: (802)223-9000
E-mail: mercurypolicy@mercurypolicy.org
URL: http://www.mercurypolicy.org
Contact: Michael Bender, Exec. Dir./Co-Founder
Founded: 1998. **Description:** Seeks to promote public awareness regarding mercury contamination; promotes policies to eliminate mercury use, reduce the export and trafficking of mercury, and reduce exposures at local, national, and international levels. **Telecommunication Services:** electronic mail, info@mercurypolicy.org.

Traffic

18371 ■ Network of Employers for Traffic Safety (NETS)

8150 Leesburg Pike, Ste.410
Vienna, VA 22182
Ph: (703)891-6005
Fax: (703)891-6010
E-mail: klusby-treber@trafficsafety.org
URL: http://www.trafficsafety.org
Contact: Kathryn A. Lusby-Treber, Exec. Dir.
Founded: 1989. **Staff:** 4. **Budget:** $750,000. **Description:** An employer-led public/private partnership dedicated to improving the safety and health of employees, their families and members of the communities in which they live and work, by reducing the number of traffic accidents that occur on and off the job. Provides employers of all sizes with effective

programs, policies, best practices, and activities related to traffic safety, thereby helping companies to improve employee relations while reducing the cost of doing business. **Programs:** NETS Work-Life. **Publications:** *BeltAmerica: A Seat Belt Program for the Nation's Employers* ● *Drive Safely Work Week Campaign Kit* ● *NETSWork E-Newsletter*, semimonthly. Alternate Formats: online ● *Novice Driver's Road Map: A Guide for Parents* ● *Who's Driving: Distracted Driving, A Lesson in Road Sense.* **Conventions/Meetings:** annual meeting.

Transportation

18372 ■ Association of Pedestrian and Bicycle Professionals (APBP)
957 Rte. 33, Ste.307
Hamilton Square, NJ 08690
Ph: (609)249-0020
Fax: (609)581-8244
E-mail: apbp@hq4u.com
URL: http://www.apbp.org
Contact: Michael Moule PE, Pres.
Founded: 1995. **Membership Dues:** professional, $95 (annual) ● advocate, $75 (annual) ● student, $30 (annual). **Description:** Represents academics, students and professional advocates committed to making bicycling and walking viable transportation options in the United States. Promotes the emerging professional discipline of pedestrian and bicycle transportation. **Publications:** *Footnotes and Bicycle Clips*, bimonthly. Newsletter. Contains current information on bicycle and pedestrian program news. **Price:** for members.

18373 ■ National Safe Skies Alliance
2057 Alcoa Hwy.
McGhee Tyson Airport
Alcoa, TN 37701-3163
Ph: (865)970-0515
Fax: (865)970-0506
E-mail: safeskies@sskies.org
URL: http://www.sskies.org
Contact: Mr. Tom Jensen, Chm./CEO
Founded: 1997. **Members:** 65. **Membership Dues:** national airline, national laboratory, airport (Cat. X or 1 airport), $6,000 (annual) ● regional carrier, university, airport (Cat. 2-4 airports), $3,000 (annual) ● corporation (organization with 250 or more employees), $6,000 (annual) ● corporation (organization with 50-249 employees), association, $4,000 (annual) ● corporation (organization with less than 50 employees), $2,000 (annual). **Staff:** 50. **Budget:** $8,000,000. **Description:** Committed to serve aviation, by providing impartial and effective testing and evaluation of safety and security devices, systems, technologies, policies and deployment, and to provide an impetus for pre-competitive research and development. Funded by the Federal Aviation Administration and administered by the US Transportation Security Administration. **Libraries: Type:** reference. **Subjects:** aviation security testing. **Divisions:** Access Control; Air Cargo; Biometrics; Checked Baggage; Passenger Security Checkpoint; Perimeter Security. **Publications:** *Carpe Diem*, monthly. Newsletter. Available by email only.

18374 ■ National Safe Waterways and Seaports Alliance
c/o McGhee Tyson Airport
2057 Alcoa Hwy.
Alcoa, TN 37701
Ph: (865)970-0515
Fax: (865)970-0506
E-mail: info@sskies.org
Founded: 2003. **Members:** 10. **Membership Dues:** principal, $10,000 (annual) ● seaport operator, university, $3,000 (annual) ● river and terminal operator, $6,000 (annual) ● shipping industry (based on number of employees), vendor, $2,000-$6,000 (annual) ● association, $4,000 (annual). **Staff:** 2. **Description:** Acts on the model of National Safe Skies Alliance to enhance the security of ports and waterways thorough a non-profit alliance of public and private organizations. **Affiliated With:** National Safe Skies Alliance.

18375 ■ Surface Transportation Policy Project (STPP)
1100 17th St. NW, 10th Fl.
Washington, DC 20036
Ph: (202)466-2636
Fax: (202)466-2247
E-mail: stpp@transact.org
URL: http://www.transact.org
Contact: Anne P. Canby, Pres.
Description: Works for transportation policy and investments that conserves energy, protects environmental/aesthetic quality, supports economic improvement, social equity, and community development. **Publications:** *Progress*, bimonthly. Newsletter. Alternate Formats: online ● *Transfer*. Bulletin. Alternate Formats: online.

Turkey

18376 ■ American Friends of Turkey (AFOT)
1111 14th St. NW, Ste.1050
Washington, DC 20005
Ph: (202)783-0483
Fax: (202)783-0511
E-mail: info@afot.us
URL: http://www.afot.us
Contact: George H. Perlman, Acting Pres.
Founded: 1981. **Membership Dues:** Golden Horn Club, $9,500 (annual) ● Bosphorus Club, $3,000 (annual) ● Marmara Club, $750 (annual). **Budget:** $75,000. **Languages:** English, Turkish. **Description:** Serves as a charitable and fundraising organization. **Libraries: Type:** open to the public. **Subjects:** Turkish-U.S. relations, culture, Central Asia. **Conventions/Meetings:** annual conference (exhibits) - first quarter.

18377 ■ American-Turkish Council (ATC)
1111 14th St. NW
Washington, DC 20005
Ph: (202)783-0483
Fax: (202)783-0511
E-mail: atc@the-atc.org
URL: http://www.americanturkishcouncil.org
Contact: Mr. Canan Buyukunsal, Exec. Dir.
Founded: 1992. **Members:** 230. **Membership Dues:** Golden Horn Club, $11,000 (annual) ● Bosphorus Club, $4,000 (annual) ● Marmara Club, $1,500 (annual). **Staff:** 8. **Budget:** $1,500,000. **Languages:** English, Turkish. **Description:** Strives to increase understanding of commercial, defense, and cultural issues involving the U.S. and Turkey. Provides information on historical, economical, and social advancement of Turkey. Conducts educational programs to increase business relations and opportunities between the U.S. and Turkey. **Libraries: Type:** reference. **Subjects:** US Turkish relations, commercial statistics, culture. **Awards:** Commercial and Defense Industry Award. **Frequency:** annual. **Type:** recognition ● Distinguished Citizen Award. **Frequency:** annual. **Type:** recognition ● Education Award. **Frequency:** annual. **Type:** recognition ● Leadership Award. **Frequency:** annual. **Type:** recognition. **Affiliated With:** American Friends of Turkey. **Formerly:** American-Turkish Friendship Council. **Publications:** *Conference Magazine*, annual. **Circulation:** 2,000. **Advertising:** accepted ● *President's Annual Report*, annual. **Conventions/Meetings:** annual conference, provides political and economic briefings, cultural events, and scientific information (exhibits) - during first quarter, Washington, DC.

Ukrainian

18378 ■ Saint Andrew's Ukrainian Orthodox Society (SAUOS)
c/o Michael Heretz, Pres.
95 Orient Way 5B/C
Rutherford, NJ 07070
E-mail: consistory@verizon.net
URL: http://www.uocofusa.org/organizations/StAndrewSociety
Contact: Michael Heretz, Pres.
Founded: 1990. **Members:** 102. **Membership Dues:** individual, $12 (annual). **Staff:** 2. **Budget:** $50,000. **Local Groups:** 1. **Languages:** English, Ukrainian. **Description:** Provides humanitarian assistance to children and the elderly in Ukraine; supports newly formed Ukrainian Orthodox congregations. Promotes growth of the Ukrainian Orthodox faith; works to "reestablish the universal principles of humanity, justice, charity, and tolerance among Ukrainians.". **Awards:** V. Rev. Dr. W. Lewytzkys Theological Scholarship Fund. **Frequency:** annual. **Type:** scholarship. **Recipient:** for academic achievement and active participation in the community. **Computer Services:** Mailing lists. **Committees:** Assistance to Theological Academies and Seminaries in Ukraine; Good Samaritan. **Publications:** *The Book of Needs* (in English and Ukrainian). Contains information for Orthodox Church services. **Price:** free to Orthodox Parishes in Ukraine. Also Cited As: *Festal Minea, Trebnyk* ● *History of the Ukrainian Orthodox Church.* **Conventions/Meetings:** triennial meeting (exhibits).

18379 ■ Ukrainian Congress Committee of America (UCCA)
203 2nd Ave.
New York, NY 10003
Ph: (212)228-6840
Fax: (212)254-4721
E-mail: info@ucca.org
URL: http://www.ucca.org
Contact: Michael Sawkiw Jr., Pres.
Founded: 1940. **Membership Dues:** general, $50 (annual) ● senior citizen, student, $30 (annual). **Staff:** 5. **Local Groups:** 76. **Languages:** English, Ukrainian. **Description:** An umbrella organization of Ukrainian organizations and communities throughout the United States. Maintains the Ukrainian National Information Service in Washington, DC, to keep the U.S. government appraised of Ukrainian-American affairs and of Ukrainian issues in general; also officially opened its Kyiv Bureau in 2002. Since the restoration of Ukraine's national independence in 1991, the Association has focused on aiding Ukraine. Provides educational programs and compiles statistics. **Awards:** Shevchenko Freedom Award. **Frequency:** quadrennial. **Type:** recognition. **Recipient:** for supporters of Ukrainian independence. **Councils:** Aid to Ukrainians; Educational; Ukrainian National Information Service. **Publications:** *Moscow's Russification of Ukraine.* Book ● *The Ukrainian Quarterly.* Journal. **Price:** $30.00/year. ISSN: 0041-6010. **Circulation:** 5,000. **Advertising:** accepted. **Conventions/Meetings:** quadrennial congress (exhibits).

18380 ■ Ukrainian National Information Service (UNIS)
311 Massachusetts Ave. NE
Washington, DC 20002
Ph: (202)547-0018
Fax: (202)543-5502
E-mail: unis@ucca.org
URL: http://www.ucca.org/ucca/unis
Contact: Maria Duplak, Sec.
Founded: 1977. **Membership Dues:** general, $50 (annual) ● senior/student, $30 (annual). **Staff:** 2. **Languages:** English, Ukrainian. **Description:** Informs Ukrainian-Americans about legislation and government policies affecting them. Sponsors Ukrainian Independence Day on January 22 on Capitol Hill in Washington, DC. Arranges itinerary and provides translators to Ukrainian visitors to the U.S. Conducts research and educational programs. Maintains speakers' bureau. **Libraries: Type:** reference. **Subjects:** materials on Euro-ethnic matters in U.S. and Ukraine. **Awards:** Shevchenko Freedom Award. **Frequency:** quadrennial. **Type:** recognition. **Affiliated With:** Ukrainian Congress Committee of America. **Publications:** *Ukrainian Quarterly.* Journal. **Price:** $30.00/year. Alternate Formats: online. Also Cited As: *UQ* ● *UNIS Newsletter*, monthly ● Books ● Brochures ● Also publishes resource list. **Conventions/Meetings:** quadrennial congress, held in

conjunction with Ukrainian Congress Committee of America ● annual seminar.

18381 ■ U.S. - Ukraine Foundation (USUF)
1701 K St. NW, Ste.903
Washington, DC 20006
Ph: (202)223-2228
Fax: (202)223-1224
E-mail: usuf@usukraine.org
URL: http://usukraine.org
Contact: Nadia K. McConnell, Pres.
Founded: 1991. **Staff:** 50. **Budget:** $3,000,000. **Languages:** English, Ukrainian. **Multinational. Description:** Facilitates democratic development, encourages free market reform, and enhances human rights in Ukraine. **Libraries: Type:** not open to the public. **Subjects:** economics, history, culture. **Awards:** Leadership Program. **Frequency:** annual. **Type:** scholarship ● Maryniuk and Kovaluk Scholarships. **Frequency:** annual. **Type:** scholarship. **Programs:** Economic Development; Education; Health Care and Humanitarian Assistance; Public Policy. **Projects:** Community Partnerships; Parliamentary Development; Petrach Community Development. **Publications:** Aspekty Samovriaduvannia (in English and Ukrainian), quarterly. Journal. Includes analysis of issues confronting the reform and development of local government. **Circulation:** 4,000 ● Infolink (in English and Ukrainian), quarterly. Newsletter. Contains information on events, activities, publications and projects of the organization. ● Partners, quarterly. Newsletter. Alternate Formats: online ● Partnery (in English and Ukrainian), monthly. Newsletter. **Circulation:** 4,000 ● Potential (in English and Ukrainian). Journal. **Circulation:** 5,000.

18382 ■ Women's Association for the Defense of Four Freedoms for Ukraine (WADFFU)
Address Unknown since 2007
Founded: 1967. **Regional Groups:** 4. **State Groups:** 25. **Local Groups:** 4. **Description:** American women of Ukrainian descent whose objectives are: to promote human and national rights in the Ukraine; to disseminate information and educate people on the plight of Ukrainians; to support efforts of Ukrainians to secure basic rights of freedom of speech, freedom of conscience, freedom from fear, and freedom from want. Encourages participation in legislative activities denouncing repression and supporting full implementation of the Helsinki Final Act, Human Rights Provision. Holds seminars; sponsors competitions; conducts charitable program. **Awards: Type:** recognition. **Affiliated With:** National Captive Nations Committee; Ukrainian Congress Committee of America. **Publications:** Between Death and Life. **Conventions/Meetings:** annual conference ● triennial convention.

United Nations

18383 ■ Americans for UNESCO
The George Washington Univ.
2131 G St. NW
Washington, DC 20052
Ph: (202)994-0506
Fax: (202)994-0614
E-mail: amunesco@gwu.edu
URL: http://www.americansforunesco.org
Contact: Andre Varchaver, Pres.
Founded: 1985. **Members:** 1,200. **Membership Dues:** voluntary donation, $25. **Description:** Sponsored by U.S. citizens who favor their country's return to membership in the United Nations Educational, Scientific and Cultural Organization (UNESCO) and who support America's presence in international bodies promoting global dialogue and multilateral cooperation. Seeks reform of UNESCO and a reassessment of America's proper role within it; disseminates information regarding recent activities of UNESCO; enlists support for U.S. re-entry into that organization. Provides consultations; carries out educational programs. Maintains speakers' bureau; compiles statistics. Conducts research. Plans to form an advisory council to represent American interests in the international spheres of education, science, culture, and communication. **Libraries: Type:** reference. **Holdings:** 250. **Formerly:** Americans for the Universality of UNESCO. **Publications:** Comprehensive Summary and Assessment of the 25th, 26th, 29th and 30th UNESCO General Conference Sessions ● Re-establishment of the U.S. National Commission for UNESCO (1994) ● Strategies and Policies for the Resumption of U.S. Participation in UNESCO (1996) ● The U.S. National Interest and UNESCO. Booklet ● Newsletter, semiannual. Provides updates and commentary on U.S. multilateral cooperation and the country's return to membership in UNESCO. **Circulation:** 3,000.

18384 ■ Center for U.N. Reform Education (CURE)
211 E 43rd St., Ste.1801
New York, NY 10017
Ph: (212)682-6958
Fax: (212)682-6959
E-mail: inquiries@centerforunreform.org
URL: http://www.centerforunreform.org
Contact: Sir Brian Urquhart, Hon. Pres.
Founded: 1979. **Members:** 27. **Membership Dues:** organization, $150 (annual). **Staff:** 4. **Budget:** $100,000. **National Groups:** 27. **Description:** Organizations working to reform, restructure, and strengthen the United Nations system. Facilitates exchange of information concerning UN reform issues. Sponsors seminars, lectures, media presentations, and research on proposals to improve the UN system. Compiles statistics. Solicits corporate and foundation grants. **Computer Services:** Online services. **Publications:** A Promptbook on Sustainable Development for the World Summit in Johannesburg. Paper ● Additional UN Options to Combat International Terrorism. Paper ● Alternative Voting Systems in International Organizations and the Binding Triad Proposal to Improve the U.N. General Assembly Decision-Taking ● Bridging the Commitment - Capacity Gap. Book ● Globalization and the Challenge of Governance. Monograph. **Price:** $10.00 ● Handbook of Proposals for UN Reform ● Improving on United Nations Human Rights Mechanisms. Monograph. **Price:** $10.00 ● Improving the UN's Peacekeeping Capacity. Monograph ● Improving UN Dispute Settlement Machinery. Monograph ● Outer Space for the Benefit of Humanity. Book. **Price:** $20.00 ● Reader on Second Assembly Parliamentary Proposals. Book. **Price:** $20.00 ● United Nations Electoral Assistance. Monograph ● United Nations Security Council Reform. Monograph ● The World Conference Against Racism: The Adoption and Repeal of the Z=R Resolution and the Implications for UN Reform. **Conventions/Meetings:** annual conference (exhibits).

18385 ■ Citizens for Global Solutions
418 7th St. SE
Washington, DC 20003-2769
Ph: (202)546-3950
Fax: (202)546-3749
E-mail: info@globalsolutions.org
URL: http://www.globalsolutions.org
Contact: Don Kraus, Exec. VP
Founded: 1976. **Members:** 4,400. **Membership Dues:** individual, $15 (annual) ● couple, $30 (annual). **Staff:** 3. **Budget:** $200,000. **Description:** Builds political will within U.S. to support effective, democratic U.N. system to prevent war, protect human rights, and promotes international justice. **Awards:** Global Statesmanship Award. **Type:** recognition. **Recipient:** for congress members who have scored 100 percent in the organization's rankings. **Committees:** Political Action; Political Education. **Absorbed:** Political Education Committee; (1983) U.N. Reform Electoral Campaign Committee. **Formed by Merger of:** (2004) Campaign for U.N. Reform; (2004) World Federalist Association. **Publications:** Candidate Questionnaire, biennial ● Global Statesmanship of America's Senators. Lists "global statesmanship" percentage rating for each member of the U.S. Senate for each congress based on roll call votes relating to world order. **Price:** included in membership dues ● Global Statesmanship of the U.S. Congress. Lists "global statesmanship" percentage rating of U.S. House of Representatives members based on roll call votes relating to world order. **Price:** included in membership dues ● UN Reformer, quarterly. Newsletter. Case for reduction in defense spending via Global Burden sharing. **Price:** included in membership dues ● Booklets ● Brochures. **Conventions/Meetings:** annual meeting, membership assembly ● annual meeting - in Midwest.

18386 ■ Communications Coordination Committee for the United Nations (CCC/UN)
301 E 45th St.
New York, NY 10017
E-mail: cccun@att.net
URL: http://www.ccc-un.org
Contact: Dr. Harry H. Lerner, Pres.
Founded: 1946. **Members:** 200. **Description:** Journalists, lecturers, and other individuals active in the television, radio, film, and computer fields. Aims to inform the public on the value of the United Nations. Projects include: Campaign for a U.N. Global Communications System, consisting of semiweekly satellite programs; International Computer Education Project, promoting computer literacy at the United Nations and in the Third World. Initiated environmental committee and "World Environment Week" programs at the United Nations. Conducts Media Task Force, promoting improved public attitudes towards the United Nations. **Awards: Type:** recognition. **Telecommunication Services:** electronic mail, bobkbogen2@netscape.net. **Formerly:** (1984) Speakers Research Committee for the United Nations. **Publications:** CCC/UN Newsletter, quarterly. Includes calendar of events. **Price:** $12.00/year. **Circulation:** 3,000. **Conventions/Meetings:** annual conference - usually December in New York ● semiannual Forum - meeting.

18387 ■ Emergency Coalition for U.S. Financial Support of the United Nations
110 Maryland Ave. NE, Ste.409
Washington, DC 20002
Ph: (202)546-1572
Fax: (202)543-6297
E-mail: ecun@clw.org
URL: http://www.globalpolicy.org/finance/action/emer-coal.htm
Contact: Linda Jamison, Contact
Founded: 1997. **Description:** Believes on the idea that "the U.S. must pay its legal obligations to the United Nations".

18388 ■ Friends of the United Nations (FUN)
1507 Stanford St., No. 5
Santa Monica, CA 90404
Ph: (310)453-8489
Fax: (310)453-8489
E-mail: info@fotun.org
URL: http://www.fotun.org
Contact: Dr. Noel Brown, Pres.
Founded: 1985. **Budget:** $100,000. **Description:** Promotes and supports the functions of the United Nations. Conducts educational programs. **Convention/Meeting:** none. **Awards: Type:** recognition. **Recipient:** for carrying out the goals of the United Nations.

18389 ■ Non-Governmental Organizations Committee on UNICEF (NGO Committee)
3 UN Plz.
New York, NY 10017
Ph: (212)824-6394
Fax: (212)735-4406
E-mail: ngocommittee@unicef.org
URL: http://www.ngocomunicef.org
Contact: Charles McCormack, Chm.
Founded: 1949. **Members:** 120. **Membership Dues:** voluntary, not-for-profit, $100 (annual). **Budget:** $50,000. **Languages:** English, French. **Multinational. Description:** International nongovernmental organizations (NGOs) on consultive status with UNICEF concerned with promoting the Convention of the Rights of the Child and child survival, protection, well-being and development. Supports United Na-

tions Children's Fund and its goals; supports UNICEF/ NGO program of cooperation. Informs NGOs about child-related issues and works to stimulate their coordinated advocacy, networking, and action. Conducts seminars and cosponsors conferences. **Special Interest Groups:** Rebuilding the Community Around Children. **Subgroups:** Children in Armed Conflict; Exploited Children. **Working Groups:** Children in Especially Difficult Circumstances; Education; Girls; Rights of the Child; World Strategy for Children. **Publications:** *NGO Action for Children* (in English, French, and Spanish), periodic. Newspaper. Covers issues, trends, programs, and other matters affecting the well-being of mothers and children around the world. **Price:** free. **Circulation:** 60,000 ● Booklets ● Reports.

18390 ■ Peoples Assembly for the United Nations (PAUN)

The Delegate
301 E 45th St., Ste.20B
New York, NY 10017
Ph: (212)983-3353
Fax: (212)573-8362
Contact: Dr. Harry H. Lerner, Pres.

Founded: 1978. **Members:** 200. **Description:** Representatives of nongovernmental, public interest organizations participating in various United Nations activities. Sponsors "systematic public discussion and informed democratic action on the issues confronting the United Nations and the Human Race." Originally established by the Association of World Citizens as the Peoples Assembly for the UN Special Session on Disarmament (held in 1978), PAUN is now an ongoing project and has presented additional UN programs, such as: Peoples Assembly for the UN Conference on the Law of the Sea (1978); Peoples Assembly for the UN Disarmament Week (1979 through 1985); Peoples Assembly for the UN Special Session on Disarmament II (1982); Peoples Assembly for World Communications Year (1983). A World Council of 20 organizers was elected in 1978 to form Peoples Assemblies in their respective countries modeled on the Swedish Peoples Parliament. Organized the World Alliance of Non-Governmental Organizations for Disarmament, Development, and Security (Vanguards); assisted in the formation of the International Network for a United Nations Second (Peoples) Assembly. Sponsored Conferences on a More Democratic United Nations (CAMDUN). **Publications:** Newsletter, bimonthly. **Conventions/Meetings:** biennial meeting - usually October, New York City.

18391 ■ UNESCO Association/U.S.A. (UA/USA)

5815 Lawton Ave.
Oakland, CA 94618-1510
Ph: (510)654-4638
Fax: (510)655-1392
E-mail: uausa@pacbell.net
Contact: Dorothy A. Hackbarth, Pres.

Founded: 1973. **Members:** 250. **Membership Dues:** individual, $25 (annual). **Staff:** 2. **Budget:** $15,000. **Description:** Individuals interested in educating the public in the communication, culture, educational, and science programs of United Nations Educational, Scientific and Cultural Organization. Aims to strive for peace among people of the world. Acts constructively to solve global problems concerning literacy, population, scientific investigation, preservation of cultural/ natural heritage, communication technology, and human rights. Operates as a center for distribution and sale of and UNESCO publications. Conducts lectures, film programs, and professional training programs. **Libraries: Type:** reference. **Awards: Type:** recognition. **Boards:** Advisory. **Publications:** *UNESCO Association/U.S.A.—Conference Papers*, quarterly. Includes monographs, reports, and research data of UNESCO conferences, each covering a specific topic. ● *UNESCO Association/U.S.A.—Newsletter*, bimonthly. Provides information about international affairs, with specific information on UNESCO and UA/USA programs. Includes book reviews/research reports. **Price:** included in membership dues. **Conventions/Meetings:** annual Human Rights Day

Conference - seminar, for the public ● annual Literacy Day Conference, literary problems, programs and solutions are recognized ● annual World Telecommunications Conference - workshop, on variety of themes related to international perspectives ● annual Youth Day - seminar, for high school students.

18392 ■ United Nations (UN)

First Ave., 46th St.
New York, NY 10017
Ph: (212)963-4475 (212)963-7555
Fax: (212)963-7055
E-mail: inquiries@un.org
URL: http://www.un.org
Contact: Ban Ki-moon, Sec. Gen.

Founded: 1945. **Members:** 189. **Staff:** 4,500. **Budget:** $1,250,000,000. **Languages:** Arabic, Chinese, English, French, Russian, Spanish. **Multinational**. **Description:** The work of the United Nations is done through six main organs. The General Assembly is the central organ, where every nation can speak up and be heard on any matter including military conflicts and arms race, improving the state of children, youth and women, sustainable development, human rights, budget, etc. The Security Council deals mainly with peace and security, investigates disputes or situations which might lead to international conflicts, recommends actions against any threat or acts of aggression and recommends to the General Assembly the appointment of the Secretary-General. The Economic and Social Council serves as the main forum for international economic and social issues, promotes higher standards of living, full employment and economic and social progress, solutions to international economic, social and health-related problems, as well as international cultural and educational cooperation, respect for human rights and fundamental freedoms. The Trusteeship Council is the organ that supervised the social advancement of the people who lived in "Trust Territories". The International Court of Justice is the organ charged with handing down legal judgments on cases brought before it by countries and clarifying issues of international judicial concern. The Secretariat, the staff of the United Nations, is responsible for carrying out its day-to-day operations, servicing the other organs of the United Nations and administering the programs and policies laid down by them. Maintains the following programs, funds and other UN entities: United Nations Conference on Trade and Development; United Nations Drug Control Program; United Nations Developmental Program; United Nations Environment Program; United Nations Population Fund; Office of the United Nations High Commissioner for Refugees; United Nations Children's Fund; United Nations Development Fund for Women; United Nations Relief and Works Agency for Palestine Refugees in the Near East; United Nations Volunteers; World Food Program; Office of the United Nations High Commissioner for Human Rights; United Nations Centre for Human Settlements; United Nations Office for Project Services; United Nations University. Works with the following autonomous organizations called specialized agencies through the Economic and Social Council: International Labour Organization; Food and Agriculture Organization of the United Nations; United Nations Educational, Scientific, and Cultural Organization; World Health Organization; the World Bank Group: International Bank for Reconstruction and Development, International Development Association, International Finance Corporation, Multilateral Investment Guarantee Agency, International Centre for Settlement of Investment Disputes, International Monetary Fund; International Atomic Energy Agency; International Civil Aviation Organization; International Maritime Organization; International Telecommunication Union; Universal Postal Union; World Meteorological Organization; World Intellectual Property Organization; International Fund for Agricultural Development; United Nations Industrial Development Organization. Conducts research and training activities through the following institutes: International Research and Training Institute for the Advancement of Women; United Nations Institute for Training and Research; United Nations Interregional Crime and Justice Research Institute; United Nations Research

Institute for Social Development; and United Nations Institute for Disarmament Research. Observes United Nations Day every October 24th, the anniversary of the day the United Nations came into being in 1945 after a majority of its original members formally accepted their obligations under the Charter of the United Nations. Maintains the Dag Hammarskjold Library, which also distributes United Nations documents and publications to users around the world through its depository library system. **Libraries: Type:** reference; open to the public. **Councils:** Economic and Social; Security; Trustees. **Affiliated With:** Food and Agriculture Organization of the United Nations - Regional Office for Europe; International Atomic Energy Agency; International Civil Aviation Organization; International Labour Office - Switzerland; International Telecommunication Union; United Nations Educational, Scientific and Cultural Organization; World Trade Organization. **Publications:** *Bulletin on Narcotics*, semiannual. **Price:** $10.00/issue; $20.00/year ● *CEPAL Review* (in English and Spanish), 3/year. Contains essays and studies focusing on economic trends and implementation of reforms, industrialization, income distribution, and monetary systems. **Price:** $10.00/issue; $18.00/year ● *Commodity Trade Statistics*, 28/year. **Price:** $10.00/issue; $180.00/year ● *CTC Reporter*, semiannual. Includes a supplement. Reports on questions about transnational corporations in a governmental and nongovernmental context. **Price:** $10.00/issue; $25.00/year ● *Current Bibliographic Information* (in English and French), monthly. **Price:** $10.00/issue; $75.00/year ● *IRPTC Bulletin*, semiannual. Contains information on hazardous chemicals. **Price:** $30.00/issue; $50.00/ year ● *Monthly Bibliography, Part I* (in English and French), bimonthly. Features subject compilation of newly acquired books, official documents, and periodicals. **Price:** $10.00/issue; $60.00/year ● *Monthly Bibliography, Part II* (in English and French). Lists selected articles on political, legal, economic, financial, and other questions of the day. **Price:** $10. 00/issue; $60.00/year ● *Monthly Bulletin of Statistics* (in English and French), quarterly. Covers population, food, trade, production, finance, and national income. Includes quarterly data on regions. **Price:** $20.00/ issue; $180.00/year ● *Objective Justice*, semiannual. Contains articles on the crucial implications of apartheid, racial discrimination, and colonialism. **Price:** $6.00/issue; $12.00/year ● *Permanent Missions to the United Nations*, semiannual. **Price:** $10. 00/issue; $15.00/year ● *Population and Vital Statistics Report*, quarterly. **Price:** $6.00/issue; $20.00/year ● *Statistical Indicators of Short-Term Economic Changes in ECE Countries*, monthly. **Price:** $6.00/ issue; $45.00/year ● *U.N. Chronicle* (in Arabic, English, French, and Spanish), quarterly. Reports on problems related to food, health, nuclear disarmament, world economy, and other issues. Documents each session of the General Assembly. **Price:** $4.50/ issue; $14.00/year ● *UNDOC: Current Index*, quarterly. Contains UN documents index, with annual cumulative index on microfiche. **Price:** $35.00/issue; $125.00/year ● *Yearbook of the United Nations* (in English and French) ● Books ● Reports ● Also issues daily news releases; sells souvenir items. Committees, councils, departments, institutes, and programs also publish materials.

18393 ■ United Nations Association of the United States of America (UNA-USA)

801 2nd Ave., 2nd Fl.
New York, NY 10017
Ph: (212)907-1300
Fax: (212)682-9185
E-mail: unahq@unausa.org
URL: http://www.unausa.org
Contact: Ambassador William H. Luers, Pres./CEO

Founded: 1964. **Members:** 30,000. **Membership Dues:** student, $10 (annual) ● individual, household, $40 (annual) ● organization, $300 (annual) ● patron, $500 (annual) ● sponsor, $100 (annual) ● life, $1,000. **Staff:** 35. **Budget:** $6,000,000. **Local Groups:** 175. **Description:** Seeks to strengthen the United Nations and the role of the United States in the United Nations to prepare it for the challenges of the future. Carries out research and public education programs on the UN and other multilateral institutions. Promotes annual nationwide observance of UN Day. **Awards:** Arnold Goodman Award. **Frequency:** annual. **Type:** recognition. **Recipient:** for volunteers ● Global Leadership Award. **Frequency:** annual. **Type:** recognition. **Recipient:** for contribution to international cooperation. **Absorbed:** (1965) Conference Group of U.S. National Organizations on the United Nations. **Formed by Merger of:** American Association for the United Nations; United States Committee for the United Nations. **Publications:** *Complete Guide to UN 'Agenda*, annual. Book. **Price:** $26.00 ● *Guide to Delegate Preparation for Model UNs*, annual. Book. Features "How to" model for UN teachers and students. **Price:** $15.00. **Circulation:** 5,000 ● *The Inter Dependent*, quarterly. Magazine. **Price:** $10.00 /year for nonmembers; free for members. ISSN: 0094-5072. **Circulation:** 30,000. **Advertising:** accepted ● *Issues Before the General Assembly*, annual. Book. **Price:** $28.95/3 copies ● *Washington Weekly Report*. Keeps readers informed about developments on Capitol Hill and in the executive branch affecting United States relations with the United Nations. Alternate Formats: online ● Annual Report, annual ● Also publishes fact sheets on UN issues, teaching materials, and reports. **Conventions/Meetings:** convention (exhibits) - twice every five years, in New York City.

18394 ■ United Nations Association of the U.S.A. Council of Organizations

801 2nd Ave., 2nd Fl.
New York, NY 10017
Ph: (212)907-1300 (202)462-3446
Fax: (212)682-9185
E-mail: unahq@unausa.org
URL: http://www.unausa.org
Contact: Jessica Hartl, Contact

Founded: 1965. **Members:** 132. **Membership Dues:** life, $1,000 ● patron, $500 (annual) ● sponsor, $100 (annual) ● individual, household, $40 (annual) ● introductory, $25 (annual) ● student, $10 (annual). **Staff:** 1. **Description:** Represents United Nations observers appointed by national organizations affiliated with the United Nations Association of the U.S.A. Works to advocate for a strong U.S. role in an effective U.N., and exchange information about and report on U.N. issues, and to formulate suggested positions for the U.S. government. Conducts briefings. **Awards:** Eleanore Schnurr. **Frequency:** annual. **Type:** recognition. **Recipient:** to a dedicated NGO representative at the U.N. **Telecommunication Services:** electronic mail, jhartl@unausa.org. **Affiliated With:** United Nations; United Nations Association of the United States of America. **Formerly:** Conference of U.N. Representatives; (1996) Conference of U.N. Representatives, (CUNR), UNA-USA; (1999) Council of Organizations. **Publications:** *Council of Organizations News*, 3/year. Newsletter. **Conventions/Meetings:** annual meeting and symposium - always June ● annual Plenary Meeting ● seminar.

18395 ■ United Nations Commission on the Status of Women

c/o Division for the Advancement of Women
2 United Nations Plz., Rm. DC2, 12th Fl.
New York, NY 10017
Fax: (212)963-3463
E-mail: daw@un.org
URL: http://www.un.org/womenwatch/daw/csw
Contact: Carolyn Hannan, Dir.

Founded: 1956. **Description:** Intergovernmental body focused on the social, economic, and legal status of women worldwide. Facilitates exchange on local, national, and global issues affecting women; gathers and disseminates information; adopts policy recommendations on gender equality and advancement by women. **Conventions/Meetings:** annual assembly.

18396 ■ World Federalist Movement (WFM)

708 Third Ave., 24th Fl.
New York, NY 10017
Ph: (212)599-1320
Fax: (212)599-1332

E-mail: info@wfm.org
URL: http://www.iccnow.org
Contact: Bill Pace, Exec. Dir.

Founded: 1947. **Members:** 30,000. **Staff:** 22. **Regional Groups:** 3. **National Groups:** 24. **Multinational. Description:** Brings organizations together committed to the vision of a "just world order through a strengthened United Nations". Strives to achieve a just world order by strengthening the United Nations. Advocates extending the power of the U.N. to include the authority to make and enforce laws for the peaceful settlement of disputes, to govern the high seas and outer space, and to raise revenue under limited powers of taxation. Calls to improve international cooperation in the areas of the environment, development, and disarmament. Organizes seminars and sponsors educational and research program. **Awards:** Betsy Dana Scholarship. **Frequency:** annual. **Type:** monetary. **Recipient:** for interns. **Computer Services:** Online services, conferences on UN reform, international criminal court. **Additional Websites:** http://www.wfm.org. **Programs:** Creating Lasting Peace; Federalism; Global Economic and Environmental Governance; International Democracy; Promoting Rule of Law. **Projects:** Coalition for the International Criminal Court; Responsibility to Protect - Engaging Civil Society. **Publications:** *International Criminal Court Monitors*, semiannual. Newsletter ● *World Federalist News*, semiannual. Newsletter. **Conventions/Meetings:** annual meeting.

Urban Affairs

18397 ■ Coalition on Urban Renewal and Education (CURE)

6033 W Century Blvd., Ste.950
Los Angeles, CA 90045
Ph: (310)410-9981
Fax: (310)410-9982
E-mail: info@urbancure.org
URL: http://www.urbancure.org
Contact: Star Parker, Pres./Founder

Founded: 1995. **Description:** Strives to strengthen the moral culture of America and rebuild the black family. Develops social policy think tank and research center that specializes in promoting faith-based and free market ideas on issues of race and poverty. **Publications:** *CURE Catalyst*, quarterly. Newsletter. Contains summary of CURE's activities. ● *Policy Research Report*, quarterly.

18398 ■ National Urban Fellows (NUF)

102 W 38th St., Ste.700
New York, NY 10018
Ph: (212)730-1700
Fax: (212)730-1823
E-mail: luisalvarez@nuf.org
URL: http://www.nuf.org
Contact: Luis Alvarez, Pres.

Founded: 1969. **Staff:** 8. **Budget:** $1,900,000. **Description:** Aims to meet the need for competent urban and rural administrators, particularly minority group members and women, by combining a nine-month, on-the-job assignment as special assistant to an experienced practitioner with several kinds of academic work. **Awards:** National Urban Fellows. **Frequency:** annual. **Type:** fellowship. **Recipient:** for individual with post baccalaureate, mid-career and leadership potential. **Committees:** Application Selection; Oral Interview. **Formed by Merger of:** National Urban Fellows; National Rural Fellows. **Formerly:** (2003) National Urban/Rural Fellows. **Publications:** *Bio/Directory of Class*, semiannual. **Price:** free ● Report, semiannual ● Brochures. **Conventions/Meetings:** annual Mid-Year Academic Conference.

18399 ■ Planning and Development Collaborative International (PADCO)

1025 Thomas Jefferson St. NW, Ste.170
Washington, DC 20007
Ph: (202)337-2326
Fax: (202)944-2351

E-mail: padco@padco.aecom.com
URL: http://www.padcoinc.com
Contact: Duanne Kissick, Pres.

Founded: 1965. **Staff:** 130. **Multinational. Description:** Seeks to ensure sustainable economic and social development in urban areas worldwide. Designs case-specific solutions to urban development problems; collaborates with international financing institutions and government agencies to implement urban development strategies. Makes available consulting services.

18400 ■ ULI Foundation

1025 Thomas Jefferson St. NW, Ste.500 W
Washington, DC 20007
Ph: (202)624-7000
Free: (800)321-5011
Fax: (202)624-7140
E-mail: customerservice@uli.org
URL: http://www.uli.org
Contact: Richard Rosan, Pres.

Founded: 1970. **Staff:** 4. **Description:** Raises funds to promote the research, education, and community outreach initiatives of the Urban Land Institute. Emphasizes support for core research on real estate and development issues, innovations in the land use field, and public service activities. Raises funds through annual, capital, planned, and grant giving. **Awards:** Council Leadership Award. **Frequency:** annual. **Type:** recognition. **Recipient:** for ULI councils that raise the most funds or involve the most ULI members in annual giving. **Boards:** Directors; Governors. **Study Groups:** Heritage Society; Skyline Club. **Affiliated With:** Urban Land Institute. **Also Known As:** Urban Land Institute Foundation. **Formerly:** Urban Land Research Foundation; (2003) Urban Land Foundation. **Publications:** *Perspective*, semiannual. Newsletter. **Price:** free ● Annual Report, annual. Reports on sources and uses of the prior year's funds. **Price:** free. **Circulation:** 4,000 ● Newsletter. **Conventions/Meetings:** semiannual meeting.

18401 ■ Urban Institute (UI)

2100 M St. NW
Washington, DC 20037
Ph: (202)833-7200
Fax: (202)261-5709
E-mail: paffairs@ui.urban.org
URL: http://www.urban.org
Contact: Robert D. Reischauer, Pres.

Founded: 1968. **Staff:** 450. **Budget:** $60,000,000. **Nonmembership. Description:** Founded to meet the need for an independent, broadly based, research organization to conduct studies and propose solutions to the nation's social and economic problems. Works closely with government officials and administrators to improve decisions and performance by providing better information and analytic tools; is linked with economic and social researchers in government, universities, and other research organizations. Aims to translate research findings into forms that can be readily understood and used. **Libraries:** **Type:** reference. **Holdings:** 47,500. **Subjects:** social science. **Publications:** *Local Tax Policy*. Book. Provides one-stop reference on profit organizations and their expanding role in the nation's economic and civil life. **Price:** $26.50 ● Annual Report, annual ● Books ● Papers ● Reports. Alternate Formats: online.

Victims

18402 ■ National Victims' Constitutional Amendment Network (NVCAN)

777 S Wadsworth Blvd., Ste.2-100
Lakewood, CO 80226-4334
Ph: (303)832-1522
Free: (800)529-8226
Fax: (303)861-1265
URL: http://www.nvcan.org

Founded: 1984. **Languages:** Dutch, English, French, Italian, Portuguese, Spanish. **Description:** Works to support an amendment to the U.S. Constitution to provide rights of innocent victims of crime. **Conventions/Meetings:** lecture ● meeting ● seminar.

18403 ■ Victim Offender Mediation Association (VOMA)
c/o Doreene Langason, Admin.
Center for Policy, Planning and Performance
2233 Univ. Ave. W, Ste.300
St. Paul, MN 55114
Ph: (612)874-0570
Fax: (612)644-4227
E-mail: voma@voma.org
URL: http://www.voma.org
Contact: Sheri Gatts, Co-Chair
Members: 380. **Membership Dues:** agency, $160 (annual) ● individual, $50 (annual) ● student, $35 (annual) ● institutional, $50 (annual). **Multinational.** **Description:** Promotes and improves restorative justice dialogue, principles, and practices. **Awards:** **Type:** grant. **Recipient:** to members. **Computer Services:** Online services, VOMA-announce listserv ● online services, VOMAlist-I member discussion list. **Telecommunication Services:** electronic mail, sheri. gatts@youthsos.org. **Formerly:** (1997) Association for Victim-Offender Mediation. **Publications:** VOMA Connections, quarterly. Newsletter. Alternate Formats: online ● Directory, annual ● Articles. Alternate Formats: online ● Brochures. Alternate Formats: online. **Conventions/Meetings:** annual International Training Institute and Conference - international conference.

Vietnam Veterans

18404 ■ National Vietnam and Gulf War Veterans Coalition (NV&GWVC)
2020 Pennsylvania Ave., No. 961
Washington, DC 20006
E-mail: veterans-coalition@comcast.net
URL: http://www.veterans-coalition.org
Contact: Ted Streeter, Gen. Sec.
Founded: 1983. **Members:** 90. **Staff:** 7. **Budget:** $10,000. **Description:** Coalition of Vietnam & Gulf War veterans' organizations representing 325,000 Vietnam veterans. Fosters public appreciation for the service of Vietnam veterans; supports maximum relief for Agent Orange and Gulf War syndrome victims. Seeks the return of POWs and accountability for MIAs; encourages the appointment of Vietnam veterans to government policymaking positions. Works to secure meaningful job programs for Vietnam & Gulf War veterans and to obtain political support from the national political parties for Vietnam and Gulf War veterans; promotes judicial review of Veterans Administration benefits decisions. **Libraries:** **Type:** not open to the public. **Holdings:** 30. **Subjects:** veterans' issues. **Awards:** Colt Leadership Award. **Frequency:** annual. **Type:** recognition. **Recipient:** for the best coalition leader in the United States. **Formerly:** (1998) National Vietnam Veterans Coalition. **Publications:** Veterans News Journal, periodic. Newsletter. Features matters of interest to Vietnam veterans. **Price:** $7.99/year. **Circulation:** 4,500. **Advertising:** accepted. **Conventions/Meetings:** annual Coalition Leadership Breakfast - conference - always November.

18405 ■ Saigon Mission Association (SMA)
c/o Homer D. Smith, Admin. Off.
6934 Willow Oak Dr.
San Antonio, TX 78249-1514
Ph: (210)558-6865
Fax: (210)558-9657
E-mail: john.guffey@netzero.net
URL: http://www.saigonmsn.org
Contact: Homer D. Smith, Admin. Off.
Founded: 1975. **Members:** 220. **Membership Dues:** associate, $5 (annual) ● individual, $10 (annual) ● life, $100 ● associate, life, $50. **Staff:** 9. **Description:** Persons who were affiliated with or supported the U.S. government during its involvement in Vietnam, including members of the military, state department officials, other U.S. government employees, and Vietnamese refugees. Seeks to: promote

friendship and cooperation among Americans who served in Vietnam, Vietnamese who worked for contractors, members of the Vietnamese Armed Forces, and their respective families; pool knowledge concerning communications and support of those still in Vietnam; establish a sponsorship program to support Vietnamese families and individuals remaining in Vietnam or living in refugee camps. Provides assistance to Vietnamese persons leaving Vietnam. **Computer Services:** Mailing lists. **Publications:** Newsletter, quarterly. Includes memorial dedications and membership list. **Circulation:** 220. **Conventions/Meetings:** annual conference and meeting - always April or May.

18406 ■ Vietnam Era Veterans in Congress (VVIC)
2211 Rayburn
Washington, DC 20515
Ph: (202)225-5905
Fax: (202)225-5396
E-mail: lane.evans@mail.house.gov
Contact: Lane Evans, Co-Chm.
Founded: 1978. **Members:** 66. **Description:** A bipartisan group of U.S. senators and representatives who served in the armed forces during the Vietnam era. Seeks to enact legislation benefiting Vietnam veterans in the areas of health care, employment, and psychological readjustment needs; notes that official statistics show that Vietnam veterans have significantly higher than average rates of divorce, suicide, alcoholism, and emotional problems. Is currently working for passage of legislation establishing judicial review for veterans. **Also Known As:** Vietnam Veterans in Congress Caucus. **Conventions/Meetings:** annual meeting.

18407 ■ Vietnam Veterans Against the War (VVAW)
PO Box 408594
Chicago, IL 60640
Ph: (773)276-4189 (847)864-3975
E-mail: vvaw@vvaw.org
URL: http://www.vvaw.org
Contact: Pete Zastrow, Co-Coor.
Founded: 1967. **Description:** Works for: improvement of VA conditions and job opportunities; elimination of the possibility of future military conflicts such as Vietnam; no draft or registration; testing and treatment of Agent Orange poisoning. Offers traumatic stress disorder counseling and discharge upgrading; provides Agent Orange self-help information. **Telecommunication Services:** electronic mail, pzastro@aol.com. **Formerly:** (1975) Vietnam Veterans Against the War/Winter Soldier Organization. **Publications:** Agent Orange ● The Draft ● History of the Veterans' Movement ● Post-Traumatic Stress Disorder ● Recollections ● The Veteran, semiannual. Newspaper. Covers topics of interest to Vietnam veterans; includes book reviews. **Price:** $20.00 /year for individuals; $30.00 /year for institutions. **Advertising:** accepted. Alternate Formats: online. **Conventions/Meetings:** annual meeting.

18408 ■ Vietnam Veterans Against the War Anti-Imperialist (VVAWAI)
PO Box 21604
Seattle, WA 98111-3604
Ph: (206)374-2215
Fax: (206)374-2215
E-mail: vvawai@oz.net
URL: http://www.vvawai.org
Founded: 1976. **Membership Dues:** veteran or non-veteran activist, $20 (annual). **Regional Groups:** 8. **Description:** Veterans of all eras and non-veteran activists. Opposes Eastern and Western imperialism. Supports the struggles of world peoples fighting for liberation. Protests all forms of racism, the subjugation of women, and all other forms of oppression. Offers educational programs; maintains Speaker's Bureau. **Libraries:** **Type:** reference. **Subjects:** antiwar, Vietnam War veterans, GI resistance, military recruitment, anti U.S. military intervention. **Publications:** StormWarning!, quarterly. Magazine. **Price:** $20.00 in U.S., 2 years; $30.00 overseas, 2 years.

Circulation: 2,000. Alternate Formats: online. **Conventions/Meetings:** periodic conference.

18409 ■ Vietnam Veterans of America (VVA)
8605 Cameron St., No. 400
Silver Spring, MD 20910
Ph: (301)585-4000
Free: (800)NAM-VETS
Fax: (301)585-0519
E-mail: communications@vva.org
URL: http://www.vva.org
Contact: Mr. John Rowan, Pres.
Founded: 1978. **Members:** 50,000. **Membership Dues:** individual, $20 (annual) ● life, $150-$250 ● individual, $50 (triennial). **Staff:** 30. **Budget:** $5,500,000. **Regional Groups:** 9. **State Groups:** 46. **Local Groups:** 625. **Description:** Acts as congressionally chartered, nationwide veterans service organization formed specifically for Vietnam veterans. Aims to work for the employment, education benefits, improved psychological assistance, and health care of Vietnam veterans. Provides referral services and research and public information programs to help veterans in developing a positive identification with their Vietnam service and with fellow veterans. Offers annual training for veterans service representatives. **Libraries:** **Type:** reference; not open to the public. **Holdings:** 1,000. **Subjects:** Vietnam era and its aftermath. **Formerly:** Council of Vietnam Veterans. **Publications:** The VVA Veteran, bimonthly. Newspaper. **Price:** $20.00. ISSN: 1061-0220. **Circulation:** 55,000. **Advertising:** accepted. **Conventions/Meetings:** biennial convention (exhibits) - always odd-numbered years ● biennial Leadership Conference (exhibits) - always even-numbered years.

Violence

18410 ■ Assassination Archives and Research Center (AARC)
1003 K St. NW, Ste.640
Washington, DC 20001
Ph: (202)393-1921
Fax: (202)393-7310
E-mail: history-matters@history-matters.com
URL: http://www.aarclibrary.org/aarc.htm
Contact: Jim Lesar, Pres.
Founded: 1984. **Members:** 30. **Membership Dues:** individual, in U.S., $30 (annual) ● individual, outside U.S., $40 (annual) ● institution, $100 (annual). **Budget:** $12,000. **Description:** Represents independent researchers, academics, and private citizens' with an interest in political assassinations. Operates research center created for the study of political assassinations throughout American and world history. Focuses on the post World War II era with extensive collections on the John F. Kennedy, Robert F. Kennedy, and Martin Luther King, Jr. assassinations. **Libraries:** **Type:** reference. **Holdings:** 1,800; archival material, audiovisuals, books, clippings, periodicals. **Subjects:** John F. Kennedy, Robert F. Kennedy, Martin Luther King, Jr. assassinations; organized crime; Cuban exiles and Cuban Exile organizations. **Computer Services:** database, persons and events connected with assassinations. **Absorbed:** Committee to Investigate Assassinations; (1985) Assassination Information Bureau. **Publications:** Church Committee Volumes. Contains hearing of the Senate Select Committee to Study Governmental Operations with respect to Intelligence Activities. Alternate Formats: CD-ROM ● Garisson Transcripts, Clayshaw Trial Transcripts and Grand Jury Transcripts. Alternate Formats: CD-ROM ● Russ Holmes Work File. Contains 50,000 pages of CIA records on the John F. Kennedy assassination. Alternate Formats: CD-ROM. **Conventions/Meetings:** annual meeting - always in Washington, DC.

18411 ■ INCITE! Women of Color Against Violence
PO Box 23921
Oakland, CA 94623
Ph: (484)932-3166

E-mail: incite_national@yahoo.com
URL: http://www.incite-national.org
Description: Aims to end all forms of violence against women of color and their communities. Advances a national movement to end violence against women of color through direct action, critical dialogue and grassroots organizing. Campaigns for global peace, justice and liberation. **Publications:** Newsletter. Alternate Formats: online.

18412 ■ Violence Policy Center (VPC)
1730 Rhode Island Ave. NW, Ste.1014
Washington, DC 20036
Ph: (202)822-8200
Fax: (202)822-8205
E-mail: info@vpc.org
URL: http://www.vpc.org
Contact: Josh Sugarmann, Exec. Dir.
Founded: 1988. **Members:** 8. **Staff:** 12. **Budget:** $1,600,000. **Description:** Conducts research on firearms violence in the United States. Coordinates media outreach activities. **Libraries: Type:** reference. **Absorbed:** (1994) Firearms Policy Project. **Formerly:** (1989) New Right Watch. **Publications:** *A .22 for Christmas - How the Gun Industry Designs and Markets Firearms for Children and Youth.* **Price:** $5.00 ● *A Deadly Myth: Women, Handguns and Self-Defense.* **Price:** $3.00 ● *American Roulette: The Untold Story of Murder-Suicide in the United States.* **Price:** $10.00 ● *Closing the Gun Show Loophole: Principles for Effective Legislation.* **Price:** $3.00 ● *Every Handgun is Aimed at You: The Case for Banning Handguns.* **Price:** $25.00 ● *Hispanics and Firearms Violence.* **Price:** $18.00 ● *John Ashcroft: Year One.* **Price:** $3.00 ● *Kids in the Line of Fire: Children, Handguns and Homicide.* **Price:** $3.00 ● *License to Kill IV: More Guns, More Crime.* **Price:** $5.00 ● *No Deal: The Drop in Federally Licensed Firearms Dealers in America.* **Price:** $3.00 ● *Poisonous Pastime: The Health Risks of Shooting Ranges and Lead to Children, Families and the Environment.* **Price:** $15.00 ● *Shot Full of Holes: Deconstructing John Ashcroft's Second Amendment.* **Price:** $10.00 ● *Sitting Ducks: The Threat to the Chemical and Refinery Industry.* **Price:** $5.00 ● *The State of the Gun Industry.* **Price:** $2.00 ● *Unintended Consequences: Pro-Handgun Experts Prove That Handguns Are a Dangerous Choice for Self-Defense.* **Price:** $8.00 ● *The U.S. Gun Industry and Others Unknown* ● *When Men Murder Women: An Analysis of 1999 Homicide Data.* **Price:** $5.00 ● *When Men Murder Women: An Analysis of 2000 Homicide Data.* **Price:** $5.00 ● *Where'd They Get Their Guns? An Analysis of Firearms Used in High-Profile Shootings, 1963-2001.* **Price:** $12.00.

18413 ■ Witness Justice (WJ)
PO Box 475
Frederick, MD 21705-0475
Ph: (301)898-1009
Free: (800)4WJ-HELP
Fax: (301)898-8874
E-mail: info@witnessjustice.org
URL: http://www.witnessjustice.org
Contact: Helga West, Co-Founder/Pres./CEO
Founded: 2001. **Description:** Supports survivors of violent crime with access to information to promote physical, psychological and spiritual healing. **Conventions/Meetings:** National Day of Victim Justice - meeting.

18414 ■ Women Against Gun Violence (WAGV)
PO Box 1501
Culver City, CA 90232-1501
Ph: (310)204-2348
Fax: (310)204-6643
E-mail: info@wagv.org
URL: http://www.wagv.org
Contact: Ann Reiss, Founder/Chair
Founded: 1993. **Membership Dues:** individual, $25 (annual) ● family, $35 (annual). **Staff:** 3. **Description:** Represents women. Provides information, statistics, and current data on gun violence. Raises public awareness. Provides speakers upon request.

Computer Services: Mailing lists, of members. **Publications:** *The Activist.* Newsletter. Alternate Formats: online.

Voluntarism

18415 ■ Cooperative Office for Voluntary Organizations (COVO)
199 W Town St.
Norwich, CT 06360
Ph: (860)886-1986
Fax: (860)889-9639
Contact: Eliot Masters, Exec. Dir.
Founded: 1987. **Description:** Environmental and development organizations. Promotes environmentally sustainable economic and agricultural development worldwide. Seeks to improve the economic viability of small farms and microenterprises. Cooperates with regional development and conservation organizations to formulate and implement sustainable development strategies and programs.

18416 ■ VolunteerMatch
385 Grove St.
San Francisco, CA 94102
Ph: (415)241-6868
Fax: (415)241-6869
E-mail: support@volunteermatch.org
URL: http://www.volunteermatch.org
Contact: Jason Willett, Dir. of Communications
Description: Dedicated to matching individuals with volunteer services. **Telecommunication Services:** electronic mail, jwillett@volunteermatch.org. **Publications:** Annual Report. Alternate Formats: online.

War Resistance

18417 ■ Americans Against World Empire/Americans Against Bombing
3220 N St. NW, Ste.281
Washington, DC 20007
E-mail: info@iraqwar.org
URL: http://www.iraqwar.org
Contact: Peter LaBarbera, Pres.
Description: Works as a conservative/libertarian coalition opposed to military imperialism. **Additional Websites:** http://www.againstbombing.org.

18418 ■ Military Families Speak Out (MFSO)
PO Box 300549
Jamaica Plain, MA 02130
Ph: (617)983-0710
E-mail: mfso@mfso.org
URL: http://www.mfso.org
Contact: Ryan Fletcher, Contact
Founded: 2002. **Description:** Represents people with relatives or loved ones in the military, who are opposed to the war in Iraq.

Waste

18419 ■ Basel Action Network (BAN)
c/o Earth Economics
122 S Jackson, Ste.320
Seattle, WA 98104
Ph: (206)652-5555
Fax: (206)652-5750
E-mail: inform@ban.org
URL: http://www.ban.org
Contact: Mr. Jim Puckett, Secretariat Coor.
Multinational. Description: Works to prevent the globalization of the toxic chemical crisis. Seeks to ensure national self-sufficiency in waste management through clean production and toxic use reduction. **Computer Services:** Information services, Basel Convention resources ● online services, photo gallery ● online services, toxic trade news. **Projects:** Basel Ban Ratification; E-Waste Stewardship; Green Shipbreaking; Zero Mercury Campaign.

White Supremacy

18420 ■ The Creativity Movement (TCM)
c/o Rev. James Logsdon
101 W Tanner St.
Bloomington, IL 61701
E-mail: comes88@yahoo.com
URL: http://www.creatorforum.com
Contact: Rev. Matt Hale, Leader
Founded: 1973. **Members:** 30,000. **Membership Dues:** full, $35 (annual). **Staff:** 5. **Regional Groups:** 24. **State Groups:** 42. **Local Groups:** 24. **National Groups:** 22. **Languages:** English, French, German, Spanish. **Description:** Seeks an "all-white world". **Formerly:** (1995) National Socialist White Americans Party; (2003) World Church of the Creator. **Publications:** *Nature's Eternal Religion.* Book. Contains the full scope and breadth of the beliefs of the religion creativity. **Price:** $18.00 ● *The Struggle*, monthly. Newsletter. Provides news and views of the Creativity Movement. **Price:** $2.00/issue. **Circulation:** 3,000 ● *White Man's Bible.* Book. Includes the commandments and philosophy of the Creativity Movement. **Conventions/Meetings:** annual The Creativity Revival - convention.

18421 ■ Knights of the Ku Klux Klan (KKK)
PO Box 2222
Harrison, AR 72601
Ph: (870)427-3414
E-mail: nationaloffive@theknightsparty.com
URL: http://www.kkk.com
Contact: Rev. Thomas Robb, Dir.
Founded: 1956. **Staff:** 5. **Description:** Political party of white men and women devoted to the preservation and enrichment of the white race. Believes that "White people of America have become an oppressed majority" suffering from discrimination in the awarding of employment, promotions, scholarships, and college entrances; are "victims of massive race-hate propaganda in the mass media"; the "uniqueness, existence, and freedoms of White Americans are threatened by overwhelmingly high non-White birth rates and non-White immigration correlated with non-sustaining, low White birth rates" and that this trend will lead to "increased anti-White discrimination, loss of freedoms, economic dispossession, and escalating racist physical assaults against the White majority turned minority." Believes that "forced integration has caused academic standards to be reduced or discarded", rather than "reveal the inequality between the White and Black races"; the federal government has placed whites "under economic bondage to the privately owned Federal Reserve Corporation"; "Negroes and other non-Whites would have no power to enforce their physical and economic treachery and terror upon Whites if the federal government was faithful to the constitution." Disseminates literature; conducts public gatherings; lobbies Congress. **Libraries: Type:** not open to the public. **Holdings:** 5,000. **Subjects:** history, science, religion, biographies, folklore. **Publications:** *Crusade: Worldwide Voice of the Aryan People*, monthly. **Price:** $20.00/year; $40.00/year in Canada and outside U.S.; $55.00 Europe and elsewhere ● *Group Activity Report* ● *Membership Internal Bulletin*, monthly. **Conventions/Meetings:** annual congress - always Labor Day weekend ● annual Homecoming and White Heritage Craft Festival - meeting - usually third weekend of July.

18422 ■ National Alliance (NA)
PO Box 90
Hillsboro, WV 24946
Ph: (304)653-4600 (304)653-2091
Fax: (304)653-4690
E-mail: national@natvan.com
URL: http://www.natvan.com
Contact: Erich Gliebe, Chm.
Founded: 1970. **Members:** 8,500. **Membership Dues:** $10 (monthly). **Budget:** $250,000. **Description:** White Americans of European descent. Works to develop in other whites "of all ages and walks of life an understanding of and pride in their racial and cultural heritage and an awareness of the present dangers to that heritage." Seeks the unification of

those who share these values "into an effective force for building a new order in American life." Operates speakers' bureau. **Libraries: Type:** not open to the public. **Holdings:** 7,100. **Subjects:** history, prehistory, archaeology, race, anthropology, biology, politics. **Additional Websites:** http://www.natall.com. **Formerly:** (1974) National Youth Alliance. **Publications:** *American Dissident Voices*, weekly. Audiotape of weekly radio show. **Price:** $15.00 ● *Best of Attack and National Vanguard*. Book ● *Free Speech*, monthly. Newsletter. **Price:** $40.00/year ● *Gun Control in Germany, 1925-1945*: Book ● *Hunter*. Book ● *National Vanguard*, bimonthly ● *Serpent's Walk*. Book ● *The Turner Diaries*. Book ● *Who Rules America*. Brochure ● Audiotapes ● Bulletin, monthly ● Catalog. **Conventions/Meetings:** annual meeting.

18423 ■ National Association for the Advancement of White People National (NAAWP)
PO Box 1727
Callahan, FL 32011
Ph: (530)733-3119 (530)684-6328
Fax: (530)884-4460
E-mail: naawp@juno.com
URL: http://www.earstation.com/naawp/02.htm
Contact: Fred Whitehead, Pres.
Founded: 1998. **Membership Dues:** active, $25 (annual). **Staff:** 6. **Budget:** $100,000. **State Groups:** 48. **Description:** Primarily white middle-class persons, including college students and professionals. Objectives are to: promote equal rights for all, including white people; stop "so-called" affirmative action, busing, and anti-white racism on television and in film; limit immigration; reform welfare programs; preserve the heritage and advance the interests of white people. Contacts companies that discriminate against whites; lobbies on white rights issues; sponsors nationwide speakers' program; compiles statistics. **Publications:** *NAAWP National News*, monthly. Newsletter. **Price:** $35.00/year ● *The NAAWP Program* ● Also distributes gift certificate, stickers and business cards. **Conventions/Meetings:** annual conference, with statistics and reports.

18424 ■ National Socialist Movement (NSM)
PO Box 580669
Minneapolis, MN 55458-0669
Ph: (651)659-6307
E-mail: nsmcommander@hotmail.com
URL: http://www.nsm88.com
Contact: Commander Jeff Schoep, Admin. of Propaganda
Founded: 1975. **Members:** 75,000. **Membership Dues:** regular, $10 (monthly) ● life, $600. **Staff:** 10. **Regional Groups:** 4. **State Groups:** 32. **Local Groups:** 100. **Languages:** English, German, Spanish. **Multinational. Description:** White Americans of non-Jewish descent. Primary objective is "National Socialist control of all white homelands, including the U.S., through national self-determination." Conducts information programs on "enlightening people to the threat of communism, Jewish control and racial survival"; also sponsors protest meetings and leaflet distribution. Conducts research on "the truth of Adolf Hitler and Germany." Sponsors Sport Defense Guard, a unit providing training in physical defense and related areas. Maintains speakers' bureau. **Libraries: Type:** reference. **Holdings:** 1,000. **Subjects:** race, Adolf Hitler, national socialism. **Awards:** Rank Promotions. **Type:** recognition. **Computer Services:** database, Nazi. **Councils:** NSM Advisory. **Also Known As:** American Workers Party; National Socialist American Workers Freedom Movement; America's Nazi Party. **Publications:** *Mein Kampf*. Books. Alternate Formats: online ● *The Myth of the Twentieth Century*. Book ● *NSM Magazine*, quarterly. **Price:** $16.00/year; $4.50/issue. **Advertising:** accepted. **Conventions/Meetings:** annual White Unity Gathering - convention, sponsors various rallies throughout the USA (exhibits).

18425 ■ National Socialist Vanguard (NSV)
Address Unknown since 2007
Founded: 1983. **Regional Groups:** 1. **Nonmembership. Description:** Organization whose goal is "to preserve the white race by total geographical separation of all races (by whatever means necessary)." Reports on and supports activities of similar organizations. Conducts charitable program. Compiles statistics; operates speakers' bureau. **Convention/Meeting:** none. **Libraries: Type:** open to the public. **Holdings:** 17; periodicals. **Subjects:** race, economics. **Publications:** *NSV Report*, quarterly. Newsletter. Contains news and philosophy. **Price:** $5.00/year. ISSN: 1083-8384. **Circulation:** 1,000. **Advertising:** not accepted.

18426 ■ The Nationalist Movement (TNM)
PO Box 2000
Learned, MS 39154
Ph: (601)885-2288
E-mail: crosstar@nationalist.org
URL: http://www.nationalist.org
Contact: Richard Barrett, First Off.
Founded: 1987. **Membership Dues:** individual, $20 (annual). **Staff:** 3. **Description:** Individuals united to encourage nationalism and advance the interests of "the working man and the American way of life." Members avow: "freedom as the highest virtue, America as the superlative nation, Christianity as the consummate religion, social justice as the noblest pursuit, English as the premier language, the white race as the supreme civilizer, work as the foremost standard and communism as the paramount foe." Seeks to foster solidarity, honor, and fraternity among members. Promotes "democracy, freedom, and social justice" through charitable, pro-majority, and nationalistic programs. Sponsors pro-majority rallies, patriotic parades, and banquet. Conducts lectures and forums. Maintains computer center, campground, and speakers' bureau. **Libraries: Type:** reference. **Holdings:** 700; archival material. **Subjects:** history of nationalists, the nationalist movement. **Awards:** Nationalist of the Month. **Frequency:** monthly. **Type:** recognition. **Recipient:** for nationalist excellence and achievement ● Patriot of the Nation. **Frequency:** periodic. **Type:** recognition. **Recipient:** for patriotic excellence and achievement. **Computer Services:** database, membership directory. **Telecommunication Services:** electronic bulletin board ● hotline, (601)FREE-TIP. **Committees:** Nationalist Legal Defense Fund. **Divisions:** Nationalist Skinhead Corps; Unixandria: The Nationalist Library; Warrior Training Camp. **Absorbed:** (1988) Forsyth County Defense League. **Publications:** *All the Way*, monthly. Magazine. Presents nationalist news and views. **Price:** $12.00/year. ISSN: 1040-2055. Alternate Formats: microform. **Conventions/Meetings:** annual convention (exhibits) - always summer ● annual Warrior Training Camp - meeting - always fall.

18427 ■ New Order (NO)
Box 270486
Milwaukee, WI 53227
Fax: (414)679-8838
URL: http://www.theneworder.org
Contact: Matt Koehl, Commander
Founded: 1959. **Multinational. Description:** Represents "white men and women of all social backgrounds and age groups who are committed to building a better world for future generations of their race". Seeks to provide a focus for the "moral and spiritual mobilization" of the white race and to build a "separate, all-white society, with its own unique culture and way of life". Believes it is the heir of the worldview and mission of Adolf Hitler, "who has given us a great commission, which it is our duty to discharge". **Libraries: Type:** reference. **Holdings:** 8,500; archival material, audiovisuals, books, periodicals. **Subjects:** national socialism, race, Aryan history and culture, philosophy, religion, World War II, biography. **Awards:** Loyalty Badge. **Type:** recognition. **Recipient:** for demonstrated lifetime loyalty and commitment to the cause of Adolf Hitler. **Formerly:** (1967) American Nazi Party; (1983) National Socialist White People's Party. **Publications:** *Adolf Hitler on America* ● *Beyond Hate*. Alternate Formats: online ● *Dresden: A Real Act of Terrorism*. Alternate Formats: online ● *Faith of the Future* ● *Hitler and We* ● *Hitler: Man and Symbol* ● *NS Bulletin*, quarterly. **Price:** included in membership dues; $35.00/6 issues for nonmembers; $60.00/12 issues for nonmembers. ISSN: 1070-2067 ● *Only One Way!*. Alternate Formats: online ● *Phenomenon of the Age* ● *The Religion of Lincoln Rockwell*. Alternate Formats: online ● *The War Against National Socialism* ● *Who Is Hitler?* ● *The Words of Adolf Hitler*. Alternate Formats: online. **Conventions/Meetings:** periodic meeting.

18428 ■ New Order Legion
PO Box 15259
Portland, OR 97293
E-mail: dave7776@lycos.com
Contact: David Brock, Leader
Founded: 1981. **Membership Dues:** legionary, deputy leader, $10 (monthly). **Description:** Works to form alliances with other groups who share their beliefs, which include: sending people of Jewish descent to Israel, sending people of African descent to Africa or the U.S. Virgin islands, granting independence to Puerto Rico and sending all people of Puerto Rican descent there, allowing Hispanics to live in former Spanish territory such as Florida, and allowing Native Americans to live on autonomous reservations. Plans to establish a parliamentary, quasi-corporatist state with a ceremonial president, prime minister, House of Representatives, Senate, and Supreme Court. Supports independence for Hawaii and reasonable environmental protection. Alters fuel usage in automobiles, etc. **Libraries: Type:** by appointment only; reference. **Holdings:** archival material, audiovisuals, books, clippings, periodicals. **Awards:** Certificate of Merit. **Type:** recognition. **Recipient:** for people who have aided the group in a notable way. **Publications:** Brochures. **Conventions/Meetings:** periodic meeting.

18429 ■ White Confederacy (WC)
c/o National Socialist Movement
PO Box 580669
Minneapolis, MN 55458-0669
Ph: (651)659-6307
E-mail: nsmcommander@hotmail.com
Description: Serves as a coalition of "right wing" conservatives and organizations, including the Nazi Party and Ku Klux Klan, from various countries. **Affiliated With:** National Socialist Movement.

Women

18430 ■ African Women Global Network (AWGN)
c/o Center for African Studies
Ohio State Univ.
314 Oxley Hall
1712 Neil Ave.
Columbus, OH 43210-1219
Ph: (614)292-8169
Fax: (614)292-4273
URL: http://www.osu.edu
Description: Individuals, organizations, and institutions. Seeks to improve the living conditions of women and children in Africa. Coordinates the activities of relief and development organizations working in Africa; facilitates exchange between research institutions and development organizations; provides support services and technical assistance to agricultural development and educational programs targeting African women and children. **Additional Websites:** http://cas.osu.edu. **Conventions/Meetings:** periodic conference and workshop.

18431 ■ Equality Now
PO Box 20646
New York, NY 10023
Fax: (212)586-1611
E-mail: info@equalitynow.org
URL: http://www.equalitynow.org
Founded: 1992. **Multinational. Description:** Works to protect and promote the human rights of women around the world. Coordinates with national human rights organizations and individual activists. Documents violence and discrimination against women and mobilizes international action to support their efforts to stop human rights abuses. Distributes

information about human rights violations, takes action to protest these violations, and brings public attention to human rights violations against women. Commits to voice a worldwide call for justice and equality for women; issues of urgent concern includes rape, domestic violence, reproductive rights, trafficking of women, female genital mutilation, and the denial of equal access to economic opportunity and political participation. **Publications:** *Awaken* (in Arabic, English, and French), 2-3/year. Newsletter ● Annual Report (in Arabic, English, French, and Spanish), annual. Alternate Formats: online.

18432 ■ Every Mother is a Working Mother Network (EMWM)

PO Box 86681
Los Angeles, CA 90086-0681
Ph: (323)292-7405
Fax: (323)292-7405
E-mail: la@crossroadswomen.net
URL: http://www.allwomencount.net
Description: A national multi-racial grassroots network of mothers and other supporters campaigning to establish that raising children is work and that the time mothers spend doing this caring work has economic value, entitling them to welfare and other resources. Opposes welfare reform that denies every mother is a working mother.

18433 ■ International Black Women for Wages for Housework (IBWWH)

PO Box 86681
Los Angeles, CA 90086-0681
Ph: (323)292-7405 (323)221-1968
Fax: (323)292-7405
E-mail: la@crossroadswomen.net
URL: http://www.allwomencount.net
Description: "An independent grassroots network of Black and other women of color. Campaigns for recognition of and compensation for unwaged and low-waged work. Beginning with women of color, we work to make visible the work women do for communities and movements for justice, campaigning against racism and sexism, welfare cuts, rape and other abuse and violence; immigration and asylum laws, police illegalities and other discrimination faced by women and our communities.".

18434 ■ Justice, Economic Dignity and Independence for Women (JEDI)

Address Unknown since 2007
Founded: 1992. **Members:** 1,500. **Membership Dues:** ordinary, $15 (annual). **Staff:** 5. **Budget:** $195,000. **Regional Groups:** 1. **Description:** Individuals with an interest in the economic well-being of women. Seeks to improve the economic prospects of women with low incomes. Represents women with low incomes before businesses, community organizations, and government agencies. Conducts educational programs to raise the income potential of economically disadvantaged women. **Libraries:** **Type:** open to the public; reference. **Holdings:** books. **Subjects:** Self help. **Awards:** Most Courageous Legislator of the Year. **Frequency:** annual. **Type:** recognition.

18435 ■ Matrix Foundation

PO Box 25603
Seattle, WA 98165-1103
E-mail: mail@matrixfoundation.us
URL: http://www.matrixfoundation.us
Contact: Lynn Osborne, Chair
Founded: 1997. **Staff:** 1. **Description:** Promotes the advancement of women in the communications profession; provides funds for education and research.

18436 ■ National Resource and Information Center (NRIC)

U.S. Dept. of Labor
200 Constitution Ave. NW, Rm. S-3002
Washington, DC 20210-0002
Ph: (202)693-6710
Free: (800)827-5335

Fax: (202)693-6725
URL: http://www.dol.gov/wb/programs/nricmain.htm
Contact: Angela Adams, Public Affairs Specialist
Founded: 1989. **Description:** Promotes gender equality and respect for the human and civil rights of women in the workplace. Gathers and disseminates information on issues affecting working women. Provides assistance to employers, workers, unions, and grass roots organizations seeking to eliminate sex discrimination in wage setting policies. **Computer Services:** database. **Formerly:** (1999) Women's Bureau Clearinghouse.

18437 ■ Swiss-American Council of Women (SACW)

100 Park Ave., Ste.1600
New York, NY 10017
Ph: (212)351-5005
E-mail: info@swissamericanwomen.org
URL: http://www.swissamericanwomen.org
Contact: Ally A.C. Gunduz, Founder/Exec. Dir.
Membership Dues: individual - friend, $45 (annual) ● corporate, $150 (annual) ● individual - Helvetia, $75 (annual). **Multinational. Description:** Strengthens and promotes the international role, leadership, and professional visibility and development of women. Serves as a transatlantic platform to create new opportunities for women and foster understanding between Swiss and all women interested in Switzerland. Established as a clearinghouse of information, resources assistance, and contacts for Swiss women in the United States and other women seeking to establish ties with Switzerland. **Awards:** Women of the Year. **Frequency:** annual. **Type:** recognition. **Recipient:** for outstanding contribution to the Swiss-American and international community as well as other areas of recognition. **Computer Services:** database, membership directory ● mailing lists, of members. **Programs:** Community Outreach. **Projects:** Evergreen The Documentary. **Special Interest Groups:** Evergreen Pioneers (mentoring younger women); Small Business Owners and Women in Business; Women in Art and Culture; Women in Science and Technology. **Publications:** *Voice of Helvetia*, quarterly. Newsletter.

18438 ■ Women as Allies (WAA)

PO Box 2193
Los Banos, CA 93635
Ph: (209)826-8710
Fax: (209)826-8710
E-mail: lorene@women-as-allies.org
URL: http://www.women-as-allies.org
Contact: Lorene Garrett-Browder, Exec. Dir.
Founded: 1995. **Membership Dues:** friend, $15 (annual). **Description:** Women "making a conscious effort never to gain social, political, economic, or personal success at the expense of another woman". Seeks to "increase sensitivity among women in organizations and in communities to issues of discrimination and hate involving race, gender, sexism, disability, sexual orientation, religion, culture, class, language, ethnicity, age, immigration, body image, and all issues confronting women on a daily basis". Conducts educational presentations on women's issues, multiculturalism, and racial and gender-based discrimination. **Publications:** Newsletter. **Conventions/Meetings:** annual International Multicultural and Multiracial Conference of Women.

18439 ■ Women Leaders Online (WLO)

PO Box 721066
Jackson Heights, NY 11372
E-mail: wlo@wlo.org
URL: http://www.wlo.org
Contact: Jeanne Clark, Exec. Dir.
Description: Dedicated to empowering women in politics, society, economy, media and cyberspace. **Computer Services:** Online services, members-only interactive email discussion lists. **Telecommunication Services:** electronic mail, comment@wlo.org.

18440 ■ Women Leaders Online/Women Organizing For Change (WLO/WOC)

PO Box 721066
Jackson Heights, NY 11372

E-mail: comment@wlo.org
URL: http://wlo.org
Contact: Jeanne Clark, Exec. Dir.
Description: Seeks to empower women in politics, society, the economy, the media and cyberspace.

18441 ■ Women Work! The National Network for Women's Employment

1625 K St. NW, Ste.300
Washington, DC 20006
Ph: (202)467-6346
Free: (800)235-2732
Fax: (202)467-5366
E-mail: info@womenwork.org
URL: http://www.womenwork.org
Contact: Jill Miller, Pres./CEO
Founded: 1978. **Members:** 2,000. **Membership Dues:** individual, $15 (annual) ● organizational basic, $75 (annual) ● organizational plus, $125 (annual). **Staff:** 15. **Budget:** $1,300,000. **Regional Groups:** 10. **State Groups:** 18. **Description:** Works to "advocate for the economic security of women and families through policies, programs and partnerships". Represents displaced homemakers and single parents, women's training services, persons from related organizations, and supporters. Fosters development of programs and services for women preparing for the workforce. Acts as a clearinghouse to provide communications, technical assistance, public information, data collection, legislative monitoring, funding information, and other services. Compiles statistics. Provides referrals, information on research in progress, and publication distribution. **Awards:** Woman of Vision Award. **Frequency:** annual. **Type:** recognition. **Formerly:** (1993) National Displaced Homemakers Network. **Publications:** *An Advocate's Guide to the Perkins Vocational and Technical Education Act of 2006* ● *An Advocate's Guide to the Workforce Investment Act of 1998* ● *Economic Equity Insider: Women Work! Legislative Bulletin.* Newsletter ● *Expanding Your Expertise: Domestic Violence, Employment, and Self-Sufficiency* ● *Expanding Your Expertise: Substance Abuse, Job Training, and Self-Sufficiency* ● *Getting IT Across!: A Counselor's Guide for Recruiting Women to Information Technology Careers* ● *Jobs That Pay: Nontraditional Occupations for the 21st Century* ● *New Economic Pathways for Young Women: An Advocate's Guide to the School-to-Work Opportunities Act* ● *On the Rights Track: An Empowerment and Workforce Rights Curriculum,* annual. **Price:** $136.95 ● *Satisfaction Guaranteed!* ● *Superstores, Schools and Sewers: A Curriculum for Understanding How Your Local Economy Works.* **Price:** $185.95 ● *We Work! The Voice for Women's Education and Economic Equity,* quarterly. Magazine ● *Work Your Image! Creating a Professional Appearance to Get and Keep a Job.* **Conventions/Meetings:** annual conference ● annual regional meeting.

18442 ■ Women's Foreign Policy Group (WFPG)

1875 Connecticut Ave. NW, Ste.720
Washington, DC 20009-5728
Ph: (202)884-8597 (202)884-8131
Fax: (202)882-8487
E-mail: wfpg@wfpg.org
URL: http://www.wfpg.org
Contact: Patricia Ellis, Exec. Dir.
Founded: 1981. **Members:** 280. **Membership Dues:** individual, $250 (annual) ● institution (based on the budget), $500-$1,000 (annual) ● leadership circle, $1,000 (annual) ● corporate, $3,500 (annual) ● student, $50 (annual). **Multinational. Description:** Individuals interested in participation by women in the formation of foreign policy. Promotes global engagement to increase the number of women employed by national foreign policymaking bodies. Conducts educational programs for women wishing to pursue careers in foreign policy; provides mentoring for female foreign policy-makers; sponsors research on the leadership status of women in international affairs professions. **Computer Services:** Mailing lists. **Publications:** *The Changing Nature of Conflict.* Report. Alternate Formats: online ● Newsletter ● Membership Directory, annual. **Price:** $69.95

for nonmembers; $30.00 for members. **Conventions/ Meetings:** periodic meeting.

18443 ■ Women's Policy, Inc. (WPI)
409 12th St. SW, Ste.310
Washington, DC 20024
Ph: (202)554-2323
Fax: (202)554-2346
E-mail: webmaster@womenspolicy.org
URL: http://www.womenspolicy.org
Contact: Cynthia Hall, Pres.
Founded: 1995. **Staff:** 4. **Budget:** $600,000. **Description:** Promotes increased public awareness of congressional actions affecting women and families. Conducts legislative research; serves as a clearinghouse on public policies and proposed legislation impacting women and families; sponsors congressional briefings. **Libraries: Type:** by appointment only. **Holdings:** archival material, periodicals. **Subjects:** legislative records, women's issues. **Publications:** *The Source on Women's Issues in Congress*, weekly. Newsletter.

18444 ■ Women's World Organization for Rights, Literature and Development (WWORLD)
PO Box 250 891
New York, NY 10025
Ph: (212)947-2915
Fax: (212)947-2973
E-mail: info@wworld.org
URL: http://www.wworld.org
Contact: Meredith Tax, Pres.
Founded: 1994. **Multinational. Description:** Promotes the rights of women writers. Educates the public on the scope and prevalence of gender-based censorship. Mounts international press campaigns on cases and extreme abuses of human rights. **Libraries: Type:** reference. **Also Known As:** (2005) Women's WORLD. **Publications:** *The Power of the Word.* Pamphlet. Alternate Formats: online.

18445 ■ WomensLaw.org
150 Court St., 2nd Fl.
Brooklyn, NY 11201
Ph: (718)923-1400
Fax: (718)923-2869
E-mail: info@womenslaw.org
URL: http://www.womenslaw.org
Contact: Elizabeth Martin, Exec. Dir.
Founded: 2000. **Description:** Provides legal resources to women living with or escaping from domestic violence. **Formerly:** (2005) Women's Law Initiative.

18446 ■ World Connections for Women
c/o Amelia Stinson-Wesley
203 Shady Rest Rd.
Morganton, NC 28655
Ph: (828)437-3697
Contact: Amelia Stinson-Wesley, Contact
Multinational. Description: Focuses on peace and social justice. Provides educational programs to women in Southeast Asia; sponsors rural health care clinic in Jamkhed, India; sells handicrafts made by local women and landmine victims in Southeast Asia; supports the Mosquito Net Campaign in Phnom Penh, Cambodia; and responds to violence against women and children. **Conventions/Meetings:** workshop, for congregations, denominations and judicatories, and direct service providers.

Workers

18447 ■ Jobs with Justice (JwJ)
1325 Massachusetts Ave. NW, Ste.200
Washington, DC 20005
Ph: (202)393-1044
Fax: (202)393-7408
E-mail: info@jwj.org
URL: http://www.jwj.org
Contact: Fred Azcarate, Exec. Dir.
Founded: 1987. **State Groups:** 29. **Local Groups:** 40. **Languages:** English, Spanish. **Description:**

Seeks to improve working people's standard of living, fight for job security, and protect workers' right to organize. **Telecommunication Services:** electronic mail, fred@jwj.org.

18448 ■ Social Accountability International (SAI)
220 E 23rd St., Ste.605
New York, NY 10010
Ph: (212)684-1414
Fax: (212)684-1515
E-mail: info@sa-intl.org
URL: http://www.cepaa.org
Contact: Alice Tepper Marlin, Pres.
Founded: 1997. **Multinational. Description:** Works to improve workplaces and combat sweatshops through the expansion and further development of the currently operative international workplace standard, SA 8000, and its associated verification system. Accredits qualified organizations to verify compliance. Promotes understanding and encourages implementation of such standards worldwide. **Computer Services:** Information services, SA8000 resources. **Programs:** Public Education; Research. **Publications:** Newsletter. Alternate Formats: online.

World Affairs

18449 ■ 50 Years is Enough: U.S. Network for Global Economic Justice
3628 12th St. NE
Washington, DC 20017
Ph: (202)463-2265
E-mail: info@50years.org
URL: http://www.50years.org
Contact: Sameer Dossani, Dir.
Founded: 1994. **Members:** 200. **Multinational. Description:** Organization platform requests: "institutional reform to make openness, full public accountability and the participation of affected populations in decision making standard procedure at the World Bank and the IMF; a shift in the nature of economic-policy reform programs and policies to support equitable, sustainable and participatory development; an end to all environmentally destructive lending and support for more self-reliant, resource-conserving development that preserves biodiversity; the scaling back of the financing, operations, role and hence, power of the World Bank and the IMF and the rechanneling of financial resources thereby made available into a variety of development assistance alternatives; a reduction in multilateral debt to free up additional capital for sustainable development.".

18450 ■ Academy of Arts and Sciences of the Americas (AASA)
9450 Old Cutler Rd.
Miami, FL 33156
Ph: (305)663-9897
Fax: (305)663-5600
Contact: Julia Allen Field, Pres.
Founded: 1965. **Members:** 8. **Staff:** 1. **Budget:** $1,000. **Languages:** English, French, Portuguese, Spanish. **Multinational. Description:** Scientists, thinkers, artists, writers united to pioneer the way toward a global civilization of enlightened biological understanding with a planetary conscience. Seeks an interdisciplinary approach to planning in the 21st century, selectively employing technology to attain and sustain human compatibility with the environment of the planet. Focuses on the global crisis of deforestation and the preservation of the great ecosystems of the rainforests, primarily the Amazon Basin, to promote biological and conceptual models for planet Earth. **Libraries: Type:** not open to the public. **Holdings:** 1,000. **Subjects:** Amazonia; the planet Earth; over-population. **Committees:** Clean Hydrogen Energy Systems, Solar and Wind Energy Systems; Encouragement of Multistrata Agriculture within the Forest Canopy; New Education for Development of Human Intelligence and Ethics. **Publications:** *Amazonia 2000/A World Model* (in English and Spanish), periodic. Papers. Held in Amazonia 2000 Archives, The Frances Loeb Library Special Collec-

tions Graduate School of Design, Harvard University. Contains documentary papers etc. **Conventions/ Meetings:** annual meeting.

18451 ■ Association of World Citizens (AWC)
55 New Montgomery St., Ste.224
San Francisco, CA 94105
Ph: (415)541-9610
Fax: (650)745-0640
E-mail: info@worldcitizens.org
URL: http://www.worldcitizens.org
Contact: Douglas Mattern, Pres.
Founded: 1975. **Members:** 30,000. **Membership Dues:** regular, $25 (annual). **Staff:** 6. **Regional Groups:** 50. **Description:** Individuals united in their concern about the state of the earth and their willingness to accept responsibility as inherent members of the world community. Promotes an end to war and the establishment of a world community; opposes the arms race. Seeks to meet basic human needs, protect the environment, and cooperate with similar groups on human rights issues and other causes. Promotes the idea of "permanent peace through a democratic people-to-people political system of global dimensions." Has established World Citizen Centers throughout the world whose efforts are coordinated through a World Inter-Center Network. Promotes curricula for world consciousness. **Awards:** World Citizens Award. **Frequency:** annual. **Type:** monetary. **Recipient:** for contributions to world peace and understanding. **Commissions:** Alternative Economics; Disarmament; Ecology; Global Institutions; Global Values; Globalization; UN Reform; World Citizenship. **Committees:** Advisory. **Projects:** Let's Abolish War; Peace and Environment; Peoples Assembly at the UN; Political Platform; Students for Peace; World Citizenship Day Celebrations. **Formerly:** (1988) World Citizens Assembly; (1990) World Citizens. **Publications:** *Proceedings of First World Citizens Assembly, 1975* ● *World Citizen*, 2-3/year. Articles. **Conventions/Meetings:** biennial World Citizens Assembly (exhibits).

18452 ■ Council on International and Public Affairs (CIPA)
777 UN Plz., Ste.3C
New York, NY 10017
Ph: (212)972-9877 (914)271-6500
Free: (800)316-2739
Fax: (212)972-9878
E-mail: cipany@igc.org
URL: http://www.cipa-apex.org
Contact: Ward Morehouse, Pres.
Founded: 1954. **Staff:** 4. **Nonmembership. Description:** Research, educational, and publishing group promoting study and public understanding of problems and affairs of peoples worldwide. Areas studied include policymaking, global issues, economics, politics, and the environment. Activities are carried out principally through independent operating programs that publish documents, books, reports, handbooks, guides, directories, and statistics. **Libraries: Type:** open to the public. **Holdings:** articles, books. **Subjects:** unemployment, corporate accountability. **Formerly:** (1976) Conference on World Affairs. **Publications:** *Celebrating Radical Democracy*, periodic. Book. Contains a number of Matt Wuerker's drawing and profiles of CIPA, POCLAD, Pete Seeger and the Public Domain. ● Publishes free catalogue of books on human rights, environment, corporate accountability, and intercultural education annually.

18453 ■ Forum International: International Ecosystems University (IEU)
91 Gregory Ln., No. 21
Pleasant Hill, CA 94523
Ph: (925)946-1500 (925)997-1864
E-mail: info@fieu.edu
URL: http://www.fieu.edu
Contact: Dr. Nicolas D. Hetzer, Dir./Founder
Founded: 1965. **Members:** 48,000. **Staff:** 26. **Budget:** $12,478,000. **Regional Groups:** 6. **State Groups:** 5. **Languages:** English, French, German, Greek, Italian, Portuguese, Romanian, Russian, Spanish, Swedish. **Description:** Works to create a forum for education, research, and action to deal with

problems such as environmental deterioration, socioeconomic change, poverty, overpopulation, and lack of educational opportunity. Sponsors ecosystems field studies in Africa, Europe, Latin America, and North America. **Publications:** *Ecosphere*, bimonthly. Magazine. Describes theory and practice of ecosystemic, whole-world-oriented, transdisciplinary, value-based education, and research. **Price:** $18.00/year. **Advertising:** accepted. Alternate Formats: microform.

18454 ■ Fund for Peace (FFP)
1701 K St. NW, 11th Fl.
Washington, DC 20006
Ph: (202)223-7940
Fax: (202)223-7947
E-mail: comments@fundforpeace.org
URL: http://www.fundforpeace.org
Contact: Pauline H. Baker, Pres.

Founded: 1957. **Staff:** 40. **Budget:** $3,000,000. **Description:** Promotes education and research and proposes practical solutions to global problems that threaten human survival. Fosters security through respect for the principles of constitutional democracy. Conducts core activities and nurtures the development of semi-autonomous projects that promote scholarship, education and action for peace, justice and a secure world. **Computer Services:** Mailing lists. **Programs:** Applied Technologies for Conflict Prevention; Conflict Prevention and Recovery; Regional Responses to Internal War; Visiting Fellows. **Roundtables:** Human Rights and Business. **Formerly:** (1969) Fund for Education in World Order. **Supersedes:** Pierce Butler, Jr. Foundation for Education in World Law. **Publications:** *ACCESS Guide to the Former Soviet Union* ● *ACCESS Issue Briefs* ● *ACCESS Resource Guide* ● *Horn of Africa Reports*, periodic ● *Human Rights and Business Roundtable Newsletter*. Alternate Formats: online ● *Innovations - The FfP Quarterly*. Newsletter. Alternate Formats: online ● *Reality Check: Diverse Voices on Internal Conflict*. Newsletter. Alternate Formats: online ● Annual Report, annual. Alternate Formats: online ● Reports. Alternate Formats: online.

18455 ■ Global Interdependence Center (GIC)
Univ. of Pennsylvania
3701 Chestnut St.
Philadelphia, PA 19104
Ph: (215)898-9453
Fax: (215)898-0893
E-mail: global@pobox.upenn.edu
URL: http://interdependence.org
Contact: Robert Carr, Exec. Dir.

Founded: 1976. **Members:** 200. **Membership Dues:** individual, $200 (annual) ● young professional under 40, academic, international, $100 (annual). **Staff:** 2. **Budget:** $150,000. **Description:** Corporate decision-makers, government policymakers and academic researchers dedicated to exploring key issues in international trade and finance. **Telecommunication Services:** electronic mail, rcarr@pobox.upenn.edu. **Conventions/Meetings:** monthly International Economic Issues - luncheon and dinner, with speakers ● semiannual International Monetary and Trade Conference - held in fall and spring.

18456 ■ Hoover Institution on War, Revolution and Peace (HIWRP)
434 Galvez Mall
Stanford Univ.
Stanford, CA 94305-6010
Ph: (650)723-1754
Free: (877)466-8374
Fax: (650)723-1687
E-mail: horaney@hoover.stanford.edu
URL: http://www.hoover.org
Contact: John Raisian PhD, Dir.

Founded: 1919. **Staff:** 320. **Budget:** $22,000,000. **Description:** Devoted to interdisciplinary scholarship and advanced research in the social sciences and public policy on domestic and international affairs. Maintains archives and library on political, economic, and social change in the 20th century. **Libraries:** **Type:** reference. **Holdings:** 1,600,000; archival material, articles, books, periodicals. **Subjects:** political, social, economic change in the 20th and 21st centu-

ries. **Awards:** National Fellowship. **Frequency:** annual. **Type:** fellowship. **Recipient:** for professional and personal endeavors of members. **Also Known As:** Hoover Institution. **Publications:** *Essay Collection*, quarterly ● *Essays in Public Policy*, monthly. **Price:** free. **Circulation:** 10,000 ● *Hoover Archival Documentaries*, annual. Annual Report ● *Hoover Digest*, quarterly. Journal. Offers informative writing on politics, economics, and history by the scholars and researchers of the Hoover Institution. **Price:** $25.00/year in U.S. ISSN: 1088-5161. Alternate Formats: online ● *Hoover Institution Annual Report*, annual ● *Hoover Institution Newsletter*, quarterly. **Price:** free. **Circulation:** 25,000 ● *Hoover Press Bibliographical Series*. Bibliographies ● *Studies of Nationalities in the Former USSR*. Newsletter.

18457 ■ Institute of Current World Affairs (ICWA)
4 W Wheelock St.
Hanover, NH 03755
Ph: (603)643-5548
Fax: (603)643-9599
E-mail: icwa@icwa.org
URL: http://www.icwa.org
Contact: Steven Butler, Exec. Dir.

Founded: 1925. **Staff:** 3. **Description:** Awards two-year (minimum) fellowships to enable a small number of persons under 36 to observe and study first hand particular foreign areas of contemporary significance; fellowships are not awarded to support work toward academic degrees, nor to underwrite specific studies or programs of research as such, in an attempt to preserve a generalist approach. **Awards:** **Frequency:** semiannual. **Type:** fellowship. **Also Known As:** Crane-Rogers Foundation. **Publications:** Brochure.

18458 ■ Planetary Citizens (PC)
PO Box 1056
Mount Shasta, CA 96067
Ph: (530)926-6424
Fax: (530)926-1245
E-mail: info@planetarycitizens.org·
URL: http://www.planetarycitizens.org
Contact: Purusha Ananda, Contact

Founded: 1971. **Members:** 10,000. **Multinational**. **Description:** Individuals who promote the concept of "global oneness" and the interdependence of all peoples regardless of national origin. Members register as "planetary citizens." Focuses on interspecies and interdimensional communication. Offers a "Planetary Passport" document reflecting the belief in "One Earth, One Humanity, One Destiny." Advocates expanding the authority of the United Nations to act on behalf of humanity. **Affiliated With:** United Nations. **Publications:** *Planet Earth*, quarterly. Journal. **Circulation:** 10,000. **Conventions/Meetings:** biennial World Symposium on Interspecies and Interdimensional Communication (exhibits).

18459 ■ Positive Futures Network (PFN)
PO Box 10818
Bainbridge Island, WA 98110-0818
Ph: (206)842-0216
Free: (800)937-4451
Fax: (206)842-5208
E-mail: info@yesmagazine.org
URL: http://www.futurenet.org
Contact: Rod Arakaki, Operations Mgr.

Founded: 1996. **Description:** Supports people's active engagements in creating a just, sustainable and compassionate world, through communication and networking activities. **Awards:** Fellowships. **Type:** fellowship ● Internships. **Type:** scholarship. **Additional Websites:** http://www.yesmagazine.org. **Publications:** *YES! A Journal of Positive Futures*, quarterly. Focuses on a theme, showing the possibilities and practical steps leading to a more positive future. **Price:** $19.00/year. **Circulation:** 35,000. Alternate Formats: online. **Conventions/Meetings:** semiannual The State of the Possible - retreat.

18460 ■ Renaissance Universal (RU)
3001 58th Ave. S, Apt. 511
St. Petersburg, FL 33712
Ph: (727)867-1813
E-mail: newren@ru.org
URL: http://www.ru.org
Contact: A.V. Avadhuta, Dir.

Founded: 1975. **Members:** 100. **Description:** Represents concerned individuals from all fields striving to create fresh approaches to global problems through integration of personal and spiritual growth with community development and social change. Highlights the role of personal and professional responsibility in creating social institutions that meet basic human needs, promote global unity, enhance environmental quality, insure human rights, and encourage individuals to develop to their fullest potential. Sponsors lectures, conferences, film series, and workshops. Provides general and medical relief and financial aid to poor students. Develops alternative employment service and proposed Research and Community Development Institute. Sponsors workshops and seminars. **Libraries:** **Type:** reference. **Holdings:** 1,500. **Affiliated With:** Renaissance Artists and Writers Association. **Publications:** *New Renaissance*, quarterly. Magazine. Contains journal for social and spiritual awakening. **Price:** $15.00/year; $26.00/2 years; $38.00/3 years. **Circulation:** 1,500. **Advertising:** accepted. Alternate Formats: online ● *New Renaissance News*. Newsletter. **Price:** free. Alternate Formats: online ● Journal, quarterly. **Conventions/Meetings:** annual meeting.

18461 ■ State of the World Forum
PO Box 29434
San Francisco, CA 94129
Ph: (415)561-2345
Fax: (415)561-2323
E-mail: info@worldforum.org
URL: http://www.worldforum.org
Contact: Jim Garrison, Chm./Pres.

Founded: 1995. **Multinational**. **Description:** Works to find solutions to critical global challenges. **Conventions/Meetings:** conference.

18462 ■ Student Pugwash U.S.A. (SPUSA)
1015 18th St. NW, Ste.704
Washington, DC 20036
Ph: (202)429-8900
Free: (800)969-2784
Fax: (202)429-8905
E-mail: spusa@spusa.org
URL: http://www.spusa.org
Contact: Christine Rovner, Exec. Dir.

Founded: 1979. **Members:** 6,000. **Staff:** 3. **Budget:** $300,000. **Description:** Sponsors educational projects in the fields of science, technology, and society at the campus and national levels. Encourages students, early in their professional development, to examine the social and ethical implications of technology on world problems, identify new questions, and discuss these concerns with experts. Topics include: Beyond a Nuclear-Weapons-Free World; Science, Technology, and Culture; Exploring the Social Consequences of Genetics; Evaluating Trends in Communications Technologies; and Rethinking Nuclear Energy. Primary activities are conferences, symposia, and workshops modeled after the International Pugwash Conferences on Science and World Affairs. Produces resources for students seeking practical experience to complement their academic studies. **Libraries:** **Type:** reference. **Formerly:** (1987) International Student Pugwash. **Publications:** *Educational Seminar Newsletter*. Alternate Formats: online ● *Jobs You Can Live With: Working at the Cross Roads of Science, Technology, and Society*, biennial. Directory. Alternate Formats: online ● *Mind-Full*, quarterly. Contains an issue brief. Alternate Formats: online ● *National Conference Newsletter*. Alternate Formats: online ● *Pugwatch*, monthly. Newsletter. Alternate Formats: online ● Proceedings. Presents a student-authored discussion resource. Alternate Formats: online. **Conventions/Meetings:** biennial international conference, with up to 100 students from around the world to look at science, technology, and society issues - always summer ●

annual National Conference on Science and Social Responsibility - meeting, chapter representatives from across the nation gather to discuss cutting edge issues on science, technology and society.

18463 ■ World Affairs Councils of America (WACA)
1800 K St. NW, Ste.1014
Washington, DC 20006
Ph: (202)833-4557
Fax: (202)833-4555
E-mail: waca@worldaffairscouncils.org
URL: http://www.worldaffairscouncils.org
Contact: Dr. Barbara Propes, Pres.
Founded: 1960. **Members:** 102. **Membership Dues:** newly formed council, $200 (annual) ● national association, $200-$2,500 (annual) ● individual council, $25-$75 (annual). **Staff:** 3. **National Groups:** 80. **Description:** Represents local world affairs councils and similar nonpartisan educational organizations in world affairs; membership is composed largely of civic, business, and academic leaders. Aims to: develop and improve the work of its groups; develop a greater sense of responsibility on the part of community leadership; provide means and resources for study and discussion of foreign policy issues; enhance public awareness of the importance of policy issues. Reviews available program resources and informs community groups about it; circulates program ideas to members. Maintains Speaker's Bureau. **Awards:** Carlo Marquis Award for Excellence in School Programs. **Frequency:** annual. **Type:** recognition. **Recipient:** for excellence in school program work over the previous year ● Distinguished International Journalist Award. **Frequency:** annual. **Type:** recognition. **Recipient:** for a journalist voted as the favorite of the 86 councils of the world affairs council system ● Lifetime Achievement Award. **Frequency:** annual. **Type:** recognition. **Recipient:** for outstanding achievements ● President's Awards for Council Excellence. **Frequency:** annual. **Type:** recognition. **Recipient:** to four councils who have made outstanding records of achievement over the previous year. **Formerly:** (1982) National Council of Community World Affairs Organizations; (1998) National Council of World Affairs Organizations. **Publications:** *Directory of the World Affairs Councils of America*, semiannual. Contains geographically arranged list of world affairs councils of America. **Price:** included in membership dues; for members only. **Circulation:** 150 ● *Foreign Policy 500*, biennial. Book. Contains compendium of the most influential individuals living and working in the United States in the field of foreign policy. **Circulation:** 500 ● *Recommended Speakers Book*, annual ● *WACA Bulletin*, monthly. Newsletter. **Circulation:** 150. **Conventions/Meetings:** annual conference (exhibits) - usually fall/winter ● periodic regional meeting.

18464 ■ Worldwatch Institute
1776 Massachusetts Ave. NW
Washington, DC 20036-1904
Ph: (202)452-1999
Free: (877)539-9946
Fax: (202)296-7365
E-mail: worldwatch@worldwatch.org
URL: http://www.worldwatch.org
Contact: Christopher Flavin, Pres.
Founded: 1974. **Members:** 2,300. **Membership Dues:** friend, associate, $50 (annual) ● sustainer, $500 (annual) ● Leadership Circle, $1,000 (annual) ● President's Circle, $5,000 (annual). **Staff:** 30. **Budget:** $4,000,000. **Description:** Research organization that aims to encourage a reflective and deliberate approach to global problem-solving. Seeks to anticipate global problems and social trends and to focus attention on emerging global issues. Takes an international approach that reflects the view that solutions to many of tomorrow's problems are not likely to be found within traditional boundaries. Recent projects include: agriculture; current global trends in population growth, renewable energy options; economic, political, and demographic discontinuities facing the world global climate change, sustainable water strategies, biodiversity, health and environmental justice. **Convention/Meeting:** none. **Libraries:**

Type: reference. **Subjects:** environmental topics, people, energy, nature, economy. **Telecommunication Services:** electronic mail, wwpub@worldwatch.org. **Publications:** *State of the World* (in English, Finnish, French, German, Hungarian, Italian, Portuguese, Romanian, Slovene, Spanish, Swedish, and Turkish), annual. Books. Features a survey dealing with the state of the world's natural resources. **Price:** $18.95. ISSN: 3933-2362 ● *State of the World Library*, annual. Books. Includes state of the world, vital signs and all papers for that year. **Price:** $43.00 /year for institutions in U.S., Canada, and Mexico; $63.00 /year for institutions outside U.S., Canada, and Mexico; $32.00/year for students in U.S., Canada, and Mexico; $41.00 /year for individuals in U.S., Canada, and Mexico. **Circulation:** 15,000 ● *Vital Signs* (in Chinese, English, Finnish, French, German, Hungarian, Italian, Japanese, Romanian, Spanish, Swedish, and Turkish), annual. Books. Features a selection of environmental trends that are shaping the future. **Price:** $16.95 ● *World Watch Magazine*, bimonthly. Features the latest developments in population growth, climate change, species extinction, and the rise of new forms of human behavior and governance. **Price:** $4.00. ISSN: 0896-0615. **Circulation:** 15,000. Alternate Formats: online ● *Worldwatch Books*, bimonthly. Contains articles on global trends. **Price:** $13.95 ● *Worldwatch Papers*, 3-4/year. Includes research reports dealing with global social and environmental issues. **Price:** $7.00/ copy.

Youth

18465 ■ Center for Youth Development and Policy Research (CYDPR)
Acad. for Educational Development
1825 Connecticut Ave. NW
Washington, DC 20009-5721
Ph: (202)884-8267
Fax: (202)884-8404
E-mail: cyd@aed.org
URL: http://www.aed.org/CentersandExperts/acentyouth.cfm
Contact: Bonnie Politz MPA, Dir.
Founded: 1990. **Description:** Devoted to contributing to better futures for all youth in the U.S. Goals are: to make "what works" available in order for youth to be productive and involved citizens; to increase the number of people, places and possibilities available to young people; to strengthen and support local systems in order to build a comprehensive youth development infrastructure; and to increase public will to support positive development for youth. Works on three basic tenets: "problem-free is not fully prepared", "academic skills are not enough", and "competence, in and of itself, is not enough". **Additional Websites:** http://cyd.aed.org/ydmobilization.html. **Publications:** *A New Vision: Promoting Youth Development*. **Price:** $7.00 plus shipping and handling ● *Bridging the Gap: A Rationale for Enhancing the Role of Community Organizations in Promoting Youth Development*. **Price:** $10.00 plus shipping and handling ● *Defining the Fourth R: Promoting Youth Development through Building Relationships*. **Price:** $7.00 plus shipping and handling ● *From Deterrence to Development: Putting Programs for Young African-American Males in Perspective*. **Price:** $7.00 plus shipping and handling ● *Promoting Youth Development: Strengthening the Role of Youth-Serving and Community Organizations*. **Price:** $7.00 plus shipping and handling ● *Pushing the Boundaries of Education: The Implications of a Youth Development Approach to Education Policies*. **Price:** $7.00 plus shipping and handling ● *The Role of Recreational, Cultural, and Other Community Activities and Settings in Preventing Drug Abuse Among Youth*. **Price:** $10.00 plus shipping and handling ● *Violence Prevention and Youth Development: Implications for Medical Clinicians and Community Health Organizations*. **Price:** $7.00 plus shipping and handling ● *Youth and Caring: The Role of Youth Programs in the Development of Caring*. **Price:** $7.00 plus shipping and handling ● *Youth Development and Resil-*

iency Research: Making Connections to Substance Abuse Prevention. **Price:** $7.00 plus shipping and handling.

18466 ■ Center for Youth as Resources (CYAR)
1000 Connecticut Ave. NW, 13th Fl.
Washington, DC 20036
Ph: (202)261-4131 (202)261-4163
Fax: (202)785-0698
E-mail: yar@cyar.org
URL: http://www.yar.org
Contact: Shuan Butcher, Dir.
Founded: 1995. **Staff:** 4. **Budget:** $300,000. **Local Groups:** 80. **Multinational. Description:** Serves as the national and international umbrella organization for Youth as Resources. Fosters the belief that youth are valuable community resources; advocates youth involvement in local, state, and national policy arenas. **Status Note:** (2006) Defunct.

18467 ■ Ewing Marion Kaufman Foundation
4801 Rockhill Rd.
Kansas City, MO 64110-2046
Ph: (816)932-1000
E-mail: cwhite@kauffman.org
URL: http://www.kauffman.org
Contact: Carl J. Schramm PhD, Pres./CEO
Founded: 1966. **Description:** Serves as operating and grant-making foundation working toward the vision of self-sufficient people in healthy communities, focusing on youth development and entrepreneurship. **Additional Websites:** http://www.eventuring.org.

18468 ■ Gay and Lesbian Adolescent Social Services (GLASS)
650 N Robertson Blvd.
West Hollywood, CA 90069
Ph: (310)358-8727
Fax: (310)358-8721
E-mail: info@glassla.org
URL: http://www.glassla.org
Contact: Teresa DeCrescenzo MSW, Exec. Dir.
Founded: 1984. **Staff:** 150. **Budget:** $8,000,000. **Languages:** English, Spanish. **Description:** Strives to help children and adolescents unable to be helped by other social service agencies, with focus on gay, lesbian, HIV-impacted, and other sexual minority youth. **Programs:** Pride Career Academy; Pride Foster Family; Residential Group Homes; Stonewall Day Rehabilitation; Stonewall Outpatient Clinic. **Projects:** Mentoring; Mobile Health Outreach; Scheuer House Transitional Housing Program and High Desert Youth. **Also Known As:** Pride Foster Family Agency; Stonewall Day Program.

18469 ■ Global Action Project (GAP)
4 W 37th St., 2nd Fl.
New York, NY 10018
Ph: (212)594-9577
Fax: (212)594-9574
E-mail: media@global-action.org
URL: http://www.global-action.org
Contact: Diana Coryat, Pres./Co-Founder
Founded: 1991. **Staff:** 5. **Multinational. Description:** Provides media arts and leadership training for young people living in underserved communities. Aims to provide youth with the knowledge, tools, and relationships they need to create powerful, thought-provoking media on local and international issues that concern them, and to use their media as a catalyst for dialogue and social change. **Computer Services:** Mailing lists. **Programs:** Global Voices; New Immigrant/Refugee Youth; The Style; Teen Power; Teens Acting Out; Urban Voices; Youth Empowerment and Human Rights. **Publications:** Newsletter. Alternate Formats: online ● Annual Report. Alternate Formats: online.

18470 ■ Global Youth Action Network (GYAN)
211 E 43rd St., Ste.905
New York, NY 10017
Ph: (212)661-6111
Fax: (212)661-1933

E-mail: gyan@youthlink.org

URL: http://www.youthlink.org

Contact: Mr. Benjamin Quinto, Exec. Dir.

Founded: 1996. **Members:** 1,000. **Staff:** 25. **Regional Groups:** 5. **Multinational. Description:** Aims to create opportunities for young people to be heard and to impact national and global agendas so young people can improve the world. Member organizations become part of this process of empowerment by inclusion into all the activities. **Libraries: Type:** by appointment only. **Holdings:** 10; books. **Subjects:** young people, youth development, HIV/AIDS. **Awards:** Youth in Action Awards. **Frequency:** annual. **Type:** monetary. **Computer Services:** database, shared resources. **Boards:** Youth and Adult Advisory. **Conventions/Meetings:** biweekly Local Jam - Local Gathering - meeting (exhibits).

18471 ■ Global Youth Connect (GYC)

15 Gage St.

Kingston, NY 12401

Ph: (845)338-2220

Fax: (347)412-9779

E-mail: contact@globalyouthconnect.org

URL: http://www.globalyouthconnect.org

Contact: Jennifer Kloes, Exec. Dir.

Founded: 1999. **Languages:** English, Spanish. **Multinational. Description:** Aims to build and support a community of youth who are actively promoting and protecting human rights, and to "educate and inspire the next generation to work for peaceful change". **Computer Services:** Mailing lists. **Programs:** Learning Communities; Take Action for Human Rights.

18472 ■ Just Think

39 Mesa St., Ste.106

San Francisco, CA 94129

Ph: (415)561-2900

Fax: (415)561-2901

E-mail: think@justthink.org

URL: http://www.justthink.org

Contact: Elana Yonah Rosen, Co-Founder/Chair/Exec.Dir.

Founded: 1995. **Budget:** $600,000. **Multinational. Description:** Teaches young people to lead healthy, responsible, independent lives in a culture highly impacted by media. Targets under-resourced populations from low-income communities. Develops and delivers cutting-edge curricula and innovative programs that build skills in critical thinking and creative media production. **Computer Services:** Information services, TV guide for parents ● information services, youth media resources. **Programs:** Family Media Forum; Just Think Mobile; Media Education; Professional Development. **Projects:** Media Education, Arts and Literacy; Peer Health and Media Education. **Publications:** Newsletter. Alternate Formats: online.

18473 ■ JustAct: Youth Action for Global Justice

3307 26th St.

San Francisco, CA 94110

Ph: (415)431-4204

Fax: (415)431-5953

E-mail: info@justact.org

Contact: Liz Suk, Exec.Dir.

Founded: 1983. **Description:** Forum for young people to advance social, economic and environmental justice issues. **Formerly:** Overseas Development Network. **Publications:** Global Links, 3/year. Newsletter. **Conventions/Meetings:** workshop.

18474 ■ National Youth Court Center (NYCC)

c/o American Probation and Parole Association

PO Box 11910

Lexington, KY 40578-1910

Ph: (859)244-8193

Fax: (859)244-8001

E-mail: nycc@csg.org

URL: http://www.youthcourt.net

Contact: Tracy Godwin Mullins, Dir.

Founded: 1999. **Members:** 943. **Staff:** 3. **State Groups:** 14. **Description:** Serves as a central point of contact for youth court programs across the US. Provides training and technical assistance to different youth courts. Educates youth about social issues and creates community service opportunities. **Awards:** Bonner Scholarship. **Frequency:** annual. **Type:** scholarship. **Recipient:** for high financial need and commitment to service ● Truman Scholarship. **Frequency:** annual. **Type:** grant. **Recipient:** for undergraduate students who wish financial support to attend graduate school in preparation for careers in government. **Computer Services:** database, youth courts facts and statistics ● information services, youth issues ● mailing lists, of members ● online services, message board. **Programs:** Implementing and Enhancing Youth Court. **Projects:** Community Service. **Affiliated With:** American Probation and Parole Association. **Publications:** In Session, quarterly. Newsletter. Covers training offered by the organization and current youth court issues. Alternate Formats: online ● Selected Topics on Youth Courts. Monograph. Contains six articles that draw on the ideas and expertise of people who work in youth courts throughout the US. Alternate Formats: online ● Articles. Alternate Formats: online.

18475 ■ National Youth Rights Association (NYRA)

1703 Farragut Ave.

Rockville, MD 20851

Ph: (301)738-6769

E-mail: info@youthrights.org

URL: http://www.youthrights.org

Contact: Alex Koroknay-Palicz, Exec. Dir.

Founded: 1998. **Members:** 150. **Membership Dues:** general, $10 (annual). **Staff:** 1. **State Groups:** 12. **Description:** Protects the civil and human rights of young people. Educates the public on youth rights. Works with public officials to devise policy solutions affecting young people. **Libraries: Type:** reference. **Holdings:** archival material, articles, audio recordings, clippings, video recordings. **Subjects:** youth. **Computer Services:** Information services, youth rights resources ● mailing lists ● online services, discussion forum. **Projects:** Youth Rights Network. **Publications:** NYRA Freedom, monthly. Newsletter. Alternate Formats: online.

18476 ■ Positive Youth Foundation (PYF)

PO Box 64

Greencastle, PA 17225

Ph: (717)597-9065

Fax: (717)597-8818

E-mail: director@positive-youthfoundation.org

URL: http://www.antiracistaction.net

Founded: 2001. **Membership Dues:** individual, $20 (annual). **Description:** Promotes awareness through music and culture concerning bigotry and related issues. **Computer Services:** database, anti-bigotry organizations. **Telecommunication Services:** electronic mail, attitude@epix.net. **Divisions:** Stop Racism Booth. **Publications:** Stop Racism. Includes a benefit musical CD commemorating 9/11. ● Magazine, annual, each summer. Serves as a resource on tours and events. **Price:** free. **Circulation:** 70,000.

18477 ■ Seeking Harmony in Neighborhoods Everyday (SHiNE)

201 Forsyth St.

North Store Front

New York, NY 10002

Ph: (212)777-1303

Free: (877)45SHINE

E-mail: info@shine.com

Contact: Alan Rambam, Founder/Chm.

For-Profit. Description: Seeks to use public events to engage youth in interactive, entertaining and mind-expanding experiences, such as speakouts, town hall meetings, mural paintings, pledge walls and concerts. **Awards:** SHiNE Challenge Grants. **Type:** grant. **Programs:** SHiNE Challenge Grants; SHiNE Clubs; SHiNE Events; SHiNE In-School Activities. **Publications:** Newsletter.

18478 ■ What If Organization

1042 Victory Dr.

Yardley, PA 19067

Ph: (215)321-5558

Fax: (215)321-5167

E-mail: whatif@thewhatif.org

Contact: Heshie Segal, Co-Founder

Description: Mentors. Provide programs for young adults to guide them and increase their future possibilities. **Programs:** Interactive Assembly; Interactive Educational; Partners in Possibility; Resource Network System.

18479 ■ What Kids Can Do (WKCD)

PO Box 603252

Providence, RI 02906

Ph: (401)247-7665

Fax: (401)247-7665

E-mail: info@whatkidscando.org

URL: http://www.whatkidscando.org

Contact: Barbara Cervone, Contact

Founded: 2001. **Description:** Works for the purpose of making public the voices and views of adolescents. Documents young people's lives, learning, work and their partnerships with adults both in and out of school. Collaborates with students around the country on books, curricula and research to expand current views of what constitutes challenging learning and achievement. **Publications:** Kids on the Wire. Bulletin. Alternate Formats: online.

18480 ■ World Youth Alliance (WYA)

228 E 71st St.

New York, NY 10021

Ph: (212)585-0757

Fax: (212)585-0785

E-mail: wya@wya.net

URL: http://www.worldyouthalliance.org

Contact: Anna Halpine, Pres.

Founded: 1999. **Members:** 1,000,000. **Membership Dues:** local partner, $100 ● national partner, $300 ● regional partner, $600 ● continental partner, $1,000 ● global partner, $3,000. **Regional Groups:** 5. **Multinational. Description:** Seeks to develop solidarity and partnership among the youth from different parts of the world. Protects human life and dignity in international agreements. Promotes charitable service projects and innovative cultural events. **Programs:** Global Partnership. **Publications:** Esperanza, published daily during United Nations conferences. Journal. Contains international analysis of developments during the United Nation's meetings. ● Newsletter, monthly. Contains activities and upcoming events that WYA participates in. Alternate Formats: online.

18481 ■ YMCA Earth Service Corps (YESC)

Natl. Rsrc. Center

909 4th Ave.

Seattle, WA 98104

Ph: (206)382-5013

Free: (800)733-YESC

E-mail: info@yesc.org

URL: http://www.yesc.org

Contact: David Kelly-Hedrick, Contact

Founded: 1989. **Regional Groups:** 100. **State Groups:** 40. **Local Groups:** 30. **National Groups:** 150. **Multinational. Description:** Committed to empowering young people to become effective, responsible global citizens by providing opportunities for environmental education and action, leadership development and cross-cultural awareness. **Committees:** Student Advisory. **Formerly:** (1999) Earth Corps. **Conventions/Meetings:** symposium ● annual YMCA Earth Service Corps Environmental Symposium.

African

18482 ■ Abwenzi African Studies
PO Box 1962
Basalt, CO 81621
Fax: (970)927-2690
E-mail: abwenzi@rof.net
URL: http://www.lettersfromafrica.org
Founded: 1989. **Description:** Works to link children in Aspen, Colorado and Malawi, Central Africa as pen pals. Provides African studies, classes, and curriculum materials. Conducts educational programs and grants awards. **Publications:** *Letters from Africa/ Malawi Study Guide.* Handbook. Helps teachers provide African Studies opportunities for grades 3-5, 7-9, and 10-12.

18483 ■ Women's Africa Committee of the African-American Institute (WACAAI)
c/o African-American Institute
Graybar Bldg.
420 Lexington Ave., Ste.1706
New York, NY 10170-0002
Ph: (212)949-5666
Fax: (212)682-6174
E-mail: aainy@aaionline.org
URL: http://www.aaionline.org
Contact: Mora McLean, Pres./CEO
Founded: 1959. **Description:** Volunteer organization of African and American women. Members seek to become better acquainted through social, educational, and cultural activities. **Affiliated With:** Africa-America Institute. **Conventions/Meetings:** monthly meeting.

African-American

18484 ■ 100 Black Men of America
141 Auburn Ave.
Atlanta, GA 30303
Ph: (404)688-5100
Free: (800)598-3411
Fax: (404)688-1028
E-mail: dwayne.crawford@100bmoa.org
URL: http://www.100blackmen.org
Contact: Dwayne Crawford, COO
Founded: 1987. **Description:** Committed to improving the quality of life and enhance educational and economic opportunities for all African Americans. **Awards:** Type: scholarship. **Programs:** Four for the Future.

18485 ■ Black Flight Attendants of America (BFAOA)
1060 Crenshaw Blvd., Ste.202
Los Angeles, CA 90019
Free: (888)682-2322
Fax: (323)932-6099

E-mail: bfaoa@aol.com
URL: http://bfaoa.com
Contact: Jacqueline Jacquet-Williams, Pres.
Founded: 1974. **Membership Dues:** full, $50 (annual) ● associate, $25 (annual) ● organization/ corporation, $200 (annual). **Description:** Aviation professionals. Seeks to expand educational opportunities through travel for at-risk communities; supports and mentors aviation professionals; promotes civic and charitable endeavors in African American communities; assists the corporation in identification of qualified minorities for management and professional positions. Sponsors Career Day in inner-city schools. **Programs:** Career Awareness; Mentor. **Conventions/Meetings:** meeting.

18486 ■ Black Leadership Forum (BLF)
910 17th St. NW, Ste.317
Washington, DC 20006
Ph: (202)689-1965
Fax: (202)689-1954
E-mail: nelam@blackleadershipforum.org
URL: http://www.blackleadershipforum.org
Contact: Joe Leonard Jr., Exec. Dir./COO
Founded: 1977. **Members:** 26. **Description:** Promotes creative, coordinated Black leadership to empower African Americans to improve opportunities in social, economic and political life. **Publications:** Articles. **Conventions/Meetings:** annual Lamplighter Awards Gala - meeting, fundraiser.

18487 ■ Black Radical Congress (BRC)
PO Box 24795
St. Louis, MO 63115
Ph: (314)307-3441
E-mail: brcnatl@blackradicalcongress.org
URL: http://www.blackradicalcongress.org
Contact: Jamala Rogers, Natl. Organizer
Founded: 1998. **Membership Dues:** unemployed, $1 (annual) ● fixed income, $10 (annual) ● general, $25 (annual) ● friend, $25 (annual) ● sustainer, $50 (annual). **Description:** Works to forge African-American activists, scholars, and various black organizations into national movement to rebuild the left presence in Black America. **Publications:** *BRC Today,* quarterly. Newsletter. Alternate Formats: online ● Articles, annual. Alternate Formats: online.

18488 ■ National Black Graduate Student Association (NBGSA)
2400 6th St. NW
Washington, DC 20059
Free: (800)471-4102
E-mail: president@nbgsa.org
URL: http://www.nbgsa.org
Contact: Ivan B. Turnipseed, Pres.
Founded: 1989. **Members:** 500. **Membership Dues:** official - graduate, $25 (annual) ● associate - undergraduate, $15 (annual) ● associate faculty/person, $55 (annual) ● associate (alumni), $45 (annual) ● life, $500. **Staff:** 24. **Regional Groups:** 4. **Description:** Commits to improve status of African Americans in higher education. **Publications:** Membership

Directory ● Newsletter, quarterly. **Conventions/ Meetings:** annual conference and seminar ● annual meeting and general assembly.

Albanian

18489 ■ National Albanian American Council (NAAC)
2021 L St. NW, Ste.402
Washington, DC 20036
Ph: (202)466-6900
Fax: (202)466-5593
E-mail: naac@naac.org
URL: http://www.naac.org
Contact: Avni Mustafaj, Exec. Dir.
Founded: 1996. **Membership Dues:** general, $100 ● donor, $500 ● assembly, $1,000 ● student, $20. **Description:** Provides timely information and analysis of Albanian issues to policy and opinion makers in Washington. **Publications:** *NAAC Bulletin,* monthly. Newsletter ● *NAAC Journal,* quarterly. Report. Alternate Formats: online ● Annual Report, annual. Alternate Formats: online.

Alumni

18490 ■ Alumni Association, Framingham State College (AAFSC)
Development and Alumni Relations Off.
Dwight Hall
100 State St.
PO Box 9101
Framingham, MA 01701-9101
Ph: (508)626-4559 (508)626-4012
Fax: (508)626-4036
E-mail: development@frc.mass.edu
URL: http://www.framingham.edu/alumni
Contact: Ms. Laura J. Lo, Assoc. Dir.
Founded: 1874. **Members:** 32,000. **Staff:** 5. **Budget:** $225,000. **Regional Groups:** 10. **Description:** Graduates of the Framingham State College (FSC). Promotes ongoing communication and good fellowship among members. Provides support and assistance to FSC and its programs; and sponsors social and educational activities. **Libraries:** Type: by appointment only. **Holdings:** archival material, biographical archives, clippings, photographs. **Subjects:** history of college and alumni association. **Awards:** Frequency: periodic. Type: scholarship. **Computer Services:** Online services, directory, career services, chat rooms, class notes. **Publications:** *Framingham State College Magazine,* 3/year. Contains, class notes, faculty and student news, and campus news. **Circulation:** 33,000. Alternate Formats: online. **Conventions/Meetings:** annual Alumni Weekend - reunion ● annual Homecoming Post-Game Reception - reunion.

18491 ■ Alumni Association of the Universidad del Valle (ADSUV)
4712 Richland Ave.
Metairie, LA 70002

Ph: (504)842-3930
E-mail: fhusserl@aol.com
URL: http://www.adsuv.8m.com
Contact: Luis Gabriel Uribe MD, Pres.
Founded: 1989. **Members:** 90. **Languages:** English, Spanish. **Description:** Alumni of the Universidad del Valle.

18492 ■ Alumni Association of the University of Michigan (AAUM)
200 Fletcher St.
Ann Arbor, MI 48109-1007
Ph: (734)764-0384
Free: (800)847-4764
Fax: (734)615-3151
E-mail: m.alumni@umich.edu
URL: http://www.umalumni.com
Contact: Steve Grafton, Pres./CEO
Founded: 1897. **Members:** 100,000. **Membership Dues:** single, joint, parent, $59 (annual) ● recent graduate (within 3 years of graduation), $25 (annual) ● family, $75 (annual) ● life (single), $950 ● life (joint), $1,050 ● life (senior), $475-$525. **Staff:** 50. **Local Groups:** 81. **Description:** Graduates and former students of the University of Michigan. Nurtures lifelong relationships with and among current and future Michigan alumni. Offers programs of relevance and service to alumni and creates support for the University. **Awards:** Distinguished Alumni Service. **Frequency:** annual. **Type:** recognition. **Recipient:** for alumni who have distinguished themselves "by reason of services performed on behalf of the University of Michigan, or in connection with its organized alumni activities" ● Spirit Award. **Frequency:** annual. **Type:** recognition. **Recipient:** for staff who exhibit extraordinary enthusiasm toward their job responsibilities and personal life. **Publications:** e-TrueBlue, weekly. Newsletter ● Michigan Alumnus, quarterly. Magazine. **Advertising:** accepted.

18493 ■ Angelo State University Alumni Association
LeGrand Alumni and Visitors Ctr.
1620 Univ. Ave.
San Angelo, TX 76904
Ph: (325)942-2122
Fax: (325)942-2373
E-mail: alumni@angelo.edu
URL: http://www.angelostatealumni.com
Contact: Louis Gomez, Pres.
Founded: 1978. **Members:** 2,100. **Membership Dues:** individual/friend of ASU, $50 (annual) ● joint, husband and wife, $75 (annual) ● diamond century club, $1,500 (annual) ● platinum century club, $1,000-$1,499 (annual) ● golden century club, $500-$999 (annual) ● silver century club, $200-$499 (annual) ● century club, $100-$199 (annual) ● access ASU silver century club, $400 (annual) ● access ASU century club, $200 (annual). **Staff:** 2. **Budget:** $130,000. **Regional Groups:** 4. **State Groups:** 8. **Description:** Objectives of the Alumni Association of Angelo State University is alumni development and to promote Angelo State University. **Libraries: Type:** open to the public. **Holdings:** 1,000,000. **Subjects:** humanities, arts and sciences, West Texas special collections. **Formerly:** (2002) Angelo State University Ex-Students Association. **Publications:** Alumni Magazine, 3/year. **Advertising:** accepted ● The President's Report, quarterly. **Conventions/Meetings:** annual meeting.

18494 ■ Association of Graduates of the United States Air Force Academy (AOG)
3116 Acad. Dr.
USAF Academy, CO 80840-4475
Ph: (719)472-0300
Fax: (719)333-4194
E-mail: aog@usafa.org
URL: http://www.usafa.org
Contact: James A. Shaw, Pres./CEO
Founded: 1968. **Members:** 18,000. **Membership Dues:** graduate/parent/friend, $50 (annual) ● life (upper class cadet), $700 ● life (fourth-class cadet, freshman, and appointee), $600. **Staff:** 29. **Budget:** $1,600,000. **Local Groups:** 25. **Description:** Gradu-

ates and friends of the U.S. Air Force Academy. Promotes interest in and dedication to the mission, ideals, objectives, activities, and history of the Academy; encourages young people to attend the Academy; encourages and supports fundraising for the Academy; fosters camaraderie among Academy graduates and U.S. armed forces officer corps; professional development of the armed forces officer corps. Sponsors annual class reunions/homecomings. Offers scholarships to graduates of the academy and their dependents; provides placement service. Operates charitable program, including humanitarian support for next-of-kin of academy graduates. Compiles statistics. **Libraries: Type:** reference. **Holdings:** biographical archives. **Awards:** Colonel James Jabara Award. **Frequency:** annual. **Type:** recognition. **Recipient:** for academy graduates whose airmanship contributions are of great significance ● Gerhart Scholarship. **Frequency:** annual. **Type:** scholarship. **Recipient:** for graduates of academy for postgraduate degree ● Graduate Dependent Scholarship. **Frequency:** annual. **Type:** scholarship. **Recipient:** for dependents of graduates ● Graduate Memorial Scholarship. **Frequency:** annual. **Type:** scholarship. **Recipient:** for individuals seeking appointment to academy permitting one-year attendance at private prep school ● Nutter Scholarship. **Frequency:** annual. **Type:** scholarship. **Recipient:** for graduates of academy for postgraduate studies ● Wolfe Scholarship. **Frequency:** annual. **Type:** scholarship. **Recipient:** for graduates of academy for postgraduate studies. **Computer Services:** database, biographical and fund-raising. **Publications:** The Air Force Academy. Book ● Checkpoints, quarterly. Magazine. Contains 136 pages of information about graduates, cadets and the Academy. **Price:** included in membership dues. ISSN: 0274-7391. **Advertising:** accepted ● Register of Graduates, annual. Directory. **Price:** included in membership dues. **Advertising:** accepted. Alternate Formats: online ● United States Air Force Academy, 1954-1979. **Conventions/Meetings:** quinquennial reunion - usually summer, fall.

18495 ■ Auburn University Montgomery Alumni Association (AUMAA)
PO Box 244023
Montgomery, AL 36124-4023
Ph: (334)244-3000 (334)244-3433
Free: (800)227-2649
Fax: (334)244-3837
E-mail: alumni@mail.aum.edu
URL: http://www.aum.edu/alumni
Contact: Connie Theimonge, Asst. Dir.
Founded: 1980. **Members:** 650. **Membership Dues:** individual student, $10 ● student (couple), $17 (annual) ● alumnus (couple), $50 (annual) ● alumnus, $35 (annual). **Staff:** 3. **Local Groups:** 1. **Description:** Students and graduates of Auburn University Montgomery (AUM). Promotes effective education and good citizenship; facilitates communication and good fellowship among members. Supports the AUM and its programs; sponsors social activities. **Libraries: Type:** by appointment only; not open to the public. **Holdings:** archival material, articles, artwork, business records, clippings. **Subjects:** Auburn University Montgomery, alumni activities. **Awards:** Alumni Professorship. **Frequency:** annual. **Type:** monetary. **Recipient:** to an outstanding Auburn University Montgomery professor ● AUM Alumni Association Merit Scholarships. **Frequency:** annual. **Type:** scholarship. **Recipient:** to AUM graduate students ● Community Service Award. **Frequency:** annual. **Type:** recognition. **Recipient:** to an individual who has provided outstanding service to AUM and to the community ● Distinguished Graduate Award. **Frequency:** annual. **Type:** recognition. **Recipient:** for a graduate with outstanding personal achievements ● Faculty Service Award. **Frequency:** annual. **Type:** recognition. **Recipient:** to an outstanding faculty for career contributions to AUM. **Publications:** AUM News, bimonthly. Newsletter. Alternate Formats: online ● AUM Today, semiannual. Magazine. **Price:** free. **Circulation:** 30,000.

18496 ■ Benedict College National Alumni Society (BCAS)
1600 Harden St.
Columbia, SC 29204

Ph: (803)253-5125
Free: (800)868-6598
Fax: (803)255-1751
E-mail: beltona@benedict.edu
URL: http://www.benedict.edu
Contact: Ada Brown Belton, Dir.
Membership Dues: individual, $15 (annual) ● life, $500. **Staff:** 1. **State Groups:** 10. **Local Groups:** 42. **Description:** Graduates and former students of Benedict College. Seeks to advance Benedict College and its programs; promotes ongoing communication and good fellowship among members. Provides voluntary and financial support to Benedict College; sponsors social and educational programs. **Awards:** Distinguished Service Award. **Frequency:** annual. **Type:** recognition ● Lula J. Cambrell Award. **Frequency:** annual. **Type:** recognition. **Recipient:** for Benedict College alumnus identified as "a power for good in society". **Conventions/Meetings:** annual meeting.

18497 ■ Bethune-Cookman College National Alumni Association
640 Dr. Mary McLeod Bethune Blvd.
Daytona Beach, FL 32114-3012
Ph: (386)481-2985
Fax: (386)481-2981
E-mail: whittakc@cookman.edu
URL: http://www2.cookman.edu/Development/media_release/2002/20020710.htm
Contact: Camesha S.C. Whittaker, Contact
Founded: 1942. **Members:** 10,000. **Staff:** 2. **Regional Groups:** 5. **State Groups:** 38. **Local Groups:** 1. **Description:** Perpetuates the history, ideas, and philosophy of Bethune-Cookman College by conducting educational studies. Provides a medium of amicable communication between the college and its graduates as they depart to serve humanity. Renders aid to Bethune-Cookman College, its students and graduates. Maintains speakers' bureau. **Libraries: Type:** reference. **Holdings:** archival material. **Awards: Type:** grant. **Recipient:** for educational purposes. **Publications:** Clarion, quarterly. Magazine. Contains alumni and college news. **Price:** free. **Circulation:** 10,000. **Conventions/Meetings:** annual meeting (exhibits).

18498 ■ Brandeis University Alumni Association (BUAA)
PO Box 549110
Waltham, MA 02454-9110
Ph: (781)736-4100
Free: (800)333-1948
Fax: (781)736-4101
E-mail: office@alumni.brandeis.edu
URL: http://alumni.brandeis.edu/web/aassociation/index.html
Contact: Darlene Green Kamine, Pres.
Members: 30,000. **Membership Dues:** individual, $30 (annual) ● dual, $50 (annual). **Description:** Graduates of Brandeis University. Seeks to advance the University and its programs; facilitates ongoing communication and good fellowship among members. Provides financial support and voluntary assistance to Brandeis University; assists in student recruitment; facilitates development of a network of local and regional alumni associations. **Awards:** Alumni Achievement Award. **Frequency:** annual. **Type:** recognition. **Recipient:** for outstanding alumni ● Service to Association Award. **Frequency:** annual. **Type:** recognition. **Recipient:** for BUAA outstanding activities ● Young Leadership Award. **Frequency:** periodic. **Type:** recognition. **Recipient:** for outstanding alumni.

18499 ■ Brooklyn College of the City University of New York Alumni Association (BCCUNYAA)
2900 Bedford Ave.
1239 Ingersoll Hall
Brooklyn, NY 11210
Ph: (718)951-5065
Fax: (718)951-5962

E-mail: marlag@brooklyn.cuny.edu
URL: http://www.brooklyn.cuny.edu/bc/alumni/alum-frame.htm
Contact: Marla Hasten Schreibman, Dir. of Alumni Affairs
Founded: 1953. **Members:** 145,000. **Regional Groups:** 20. **Description:** Graduates and former students of Brooklyn College. Seeks to strengthen "the lifelong connection between Brooklyn College and its alumni." Sponsors cultural, educational, and social activities; provides services to alumni and financial support to Brooklyn College, its programs and its students. **Libraries: Type:** not open to the public; reference. **Holdings:** archival material, articles, business records, clippings, periodicals. **Subjects:** Brooklyn College, alumni activities, biographical files, yearbooks, commencement programs. **Awards:** Alumna/us of the Year. **Frequency:** annual. **Type:** recognition. **Recipient:** for a work bringing honor to the name of Brooklyn College ● BCAA Student Award. **Frequency:** annual. **Type:** scholarship. **Recipient:** for students ● Distinguished Achievement. **Frequency:** annual. **Type:** recognition ● Distinguished Service. **Frequency:** annual. **Type:** recognition. **Recipient:** for service to the alumni association and all alumni. **Publications:** BCAA Newsletter, annual. **Circulation:** 84,000.

18500 ■ Cal State San Marcos Alumni Association
Off. of Alumni Relations
CSU San Marcos
San Marcos, CA 92096-0001
Ph: (760)750-4405
Fax: (760)750-3240
E-mail: alumni@csusm.edu
URL: http://lynx.csusm.edu/alumni
Contact: Charles Ragland, Pres.
Founded: 1992. **Members:** 540. **Membership Dues:** individual, $30 (annual) ● alumni couple or joint, $40 (annual) ● life, $300. **Staff:** 1. **Budget:** $9,000. **Description:** Graduates and former students of the California State University San Marcos (CSUSM). Seeks to advance the interests of CSUSM and its students and alumni. Provides support and assistance to the University and its programs; makes available career and student mentoring services. **Awards:** CSUSM Alumni Association Scholarship. **Frequency:** annual. **Type:** scholarship. **Recipient:** for alumni of CSUSM returning for credential, graduate degree, or additional bachelor's degree. **Computer Services:** database, Alumni Directory ● database, Business Card Exchange ● online services, message board. **Formerly:** (2002) California State University of San Marcos Alumni Association. **Publications:** Blueprint, semiannual. Magazine.

18501 ■ California College of Arts and Crafts Alumni Association (CCACAA)
c/o Jessica Russell, Alumni Relations Mgr.
5212 Broadway
Oakland, CA 94618
Ph: (510)594-3788
Fax: (415)703-9539
E-mail: alumni@cca.edu
URL: http://www.cca.edu/alumni
Contact: Jessica Russell, Alumni Relations Mgr.
Founded: 1907. **Members:** 12,000. **Staff:** 2. **Budget:** $45,000. **Description:** Graduates and former students of the California College of Arts and Crafts. Seeks to advance members' artistic pursuits; provides support and assistance to the California College of Arts and Crafts and its programs. Works with enrollment services and student affairs to assist with student recruitment, retention, and career advice. **Libraries: Type:** lending; not open to the public; reference. **Holdings:** archival material, artwork, audio recordings, books, periodicals, video recordings. **Subjects:** art, architecture, design. **Awards:** Founder's Day Award. **Frequency:** quadrennial. **Type:** recognition. **Committees:** Archives; Council Agenda; Public Exhibitions; Recruitment. **Councils:** Alumni. **Publications:** CCAC News, quarterly. Newsletter. **Price:** included in membership dues. **Circulation:** 10,000. Alternate Formats: online.

18502 ■ California State University - Northridge Alumni Association (CSUNAA)
18111 Nordhoff St.
Northridge, CA 91330-8385
Ph: (818)677-2137
Fax: (818)677-4823
E-mail: alumni@csun.edu
URL: http://www.csunalumni.com
Contact: D.G. Mounger, Asst. VP
Founded: 1958. **Members:** 120,000. **Membership Dues:** single, $40 (annual) ● joint, $50 (annual) ● life (single), $500 ● life (joint), $600 ● recent graduate, student, $20 (annual). **Staff:** 4. **Budget:** $250,000. **Regional Groups:** 3. **Description:** Graduates and former students of the California State University at Northridge. Seeks to advance the university and its programs; promotes communication and cooperation among members. Sponsors cultural and community events; makes available educational, career network and job search programs to members; provides financial and voluntary assistance to the university. **Computer Services:** database, alumni directory ● mailing lists, of members. **Publications:** Northridge, quarterly. Magazine. Includes current events, class notes and campus news. ● Newsletter, monthly. Alternate Formats: online.

18503 ■ California State University - Stanislaus Alumni Association (CSUSAA)
801 W Monte Vista Ave.
Turlock, CA 95382
Ph: (209)667-3693
Fax: (209)664-7007
E-mail: alumni@csustan.edu
URL: http://csustanalumni.com
Contact: April Dunham-Filson, Sec.
Founded: 1963. **Members:** 783. **Membership Dues:** individual, $40 (annual) ● joint, $60 (annual) ● individual (life), $400 ● joint (life), $500 ● student, $20 (annual). **Staff:** 1. **Regional Groups:** 18. **State Groups:** 2. **Local Groups:** 10. **Description:** Graduates of the California State University at Stanislaus (CSUS), past students, and friends of the university. Promotes ongoing participation by members in the development of CSUS and its programs. Provides voluntary and financial assistance to CSUS; sponsors social and educational activities. **Libraries: Type:** lending; not open to the public; reference. **Holdings:** archival material, audio recordings, books, periodicals, video recordings. **Subjects:** California State University - Stanislaus, alumni activities. **Awards:** Alumni of the Year. **Frequency:** annual. **Type:** recognition. **Recipient:** for exceptional graduates who have excelled in their chosen profession ● Alumni Service Award. **Frequency:** annual. **Type:** recognition. **Recipient:** for exceptional graduates who have excelled in their chosen profession.

18504 ■ Catholic Alumni Clubs, International (CACI)
c/o Mr. Michael Coogan, Pres.
13517 Teakwood Ln.
Germantown, MD 20874-1034
Ph: (301)916-6336
E-mail: cac@caci.org
URL: http://www.caci.org
Contact: Mr. Michael Coogan, Pres.
Founded: 1957. **Members:** 3,000. **Budget:** $250,000. **Regional Groups:** 3. **Local Groups:** 30. **Description:** Single professional Catholics who are free to marry in the Catholic Church. Local chapters conduct religious community service, social, recreational, and cultural activities enabling young and midlife single Catholics to meet others of similar educational and religious backgrounds. **Libraries: Type:** reference. **Holdings:** archival material. **Awards: Type:** recognition. **Telecommunication Services:** electronic mail, tedtri@aol.com. **Committees:** Chapter Development/Grants; Charitable Contributions; Community Service; Newsletter; Special Projects. **Publications:** Communique, semiannual. Newsletter. **Circulation:** 3,000. Alternate Formats: online ● Director's Handbook, annual ● Also publishes committee handbooks and a history of Catholic alumni clubs. **Conventions/Meetings:** annual conference.

18505 ■ Centenary College of Louisiana Alumni Association (CCLAA)
2911 Centenary Blvd.
Shreveport, LA 71104
Ph: (318)869-5151 (318)869-5008
Free: (800)259-6447
Fax: (318)841-7266
E-mail: alumni@centenary.edu
URL: http://www.centenary.edu/alumni
Contact: Ms. Carla E. Alsandor, Dir.
Founded: 1825. **Members:** 10,000. **Staff:** 3. **Regional Groups:** 10. **Description:** Works to develop and strengthen the relationships of alumni with the college and with one another; to initiate and maintain contact with alumni; to utilize traditional and electronic methods of communication; provides ongoing opportunities for social interaction among alumni, faculty, and students. **Libraries: Type:** not open to the public. **Awards:** Alumni Hall of Fame. **Frequency:** annual. **Type:** recognition ● Alumni Loyalty Award. **Frequency:** annual. **Type:** recognition. **Recipient:** for longtime involvement ● Athletic Hall of Fame. **Frequency:** annual. **Type:** recognition. **Recipient:** to an individual out of school for 10 years ● Honorary Alumnus. **Frequency:** annual. **Type:** recognition. **Recipient:** for individuals providing support to Centenary College. **Computer Services:** Online services, monthly newsletter. **Special Interest Groups:** Alumni Athletes; Alumni Clergy; Centenary College Choir; Greek Alumni; MBA Alumni. **Publications:** Centenary Today, semiannual. Newspaper. **Price:** free. **Circulation:** 17,000. **Conventions/Meetings:** annual Homecoming - meeting.

18506 ■ Coastal Carolina University Alumni Association (CCUAA)
Coastal Carolina Univ.
PO Box 261954
Conway, SC 29528-6054
Ph: (843)347-3161
E-mail: alumni@coastal.edu
URL: http://www.coastal.edu/alumni
Contact: Christi Chambers, Dir. of Alumni Relations
Founded: 1976. **Members:** 13,340. **Staff:** 2. **State Groups:** 3. **Local Groups:** 2. **National Groups:** 4. **Description:** Represents the interests of graduates and former students of Coastal Carolina University. Seeks to advance the University and its programs. Facilitates ongoing communication and good fellowship among members. Works with Career Services to provide alumni mentoring program. Conducts networking activities with current/past students and their former faculty members. Sponsors all alumni related social programs. Acts as liaison between University and Alumni Association Board of Directors. **Awards:** Coastal Carolina Alumni Association Endowed Scholarship. **Frequency:** annual. **Type:** scholarship. **Recipient:** for rising senior at Coastal Carolina University ● Will Garland Endowed Scholarship. **Frequency:** annual. **Type:** scholarship. **Recipient:** for nontraditional student aged 25 or older at Coastal Carolina University. **Telecommunication Services:** information service, current news, upcoming events and campus activities. **Special Interest Groups:** Coastal African-American Professionals. **Subcommittees:** Awards; Bylaws and Guidelines; Golf Tournament; Homecoming and Affinity; Legislative; Nominating; Scholarship. **Formerly:** (2005) Coastal Carolina Alumni Association. **Publications:** Beyond Coastal. Newsletter ● Coastal Carolina Magazine, semiannual. **Conventions/Meetings:** annual Homecoming - reunion.

18507 ■ College for Creative Studies Alumni Association
201 E Kirby St.
Detroit, MI 48202-4034
Ph: (313)664-7400 (313)664-7461
Free: (800)952-ARTS
Fax: (313)872-2739
E-mail: alumni@ccscad.edu
URL: http://www.ccscad.edu
Contact: Kimberly Salyers, Dir., Constituency Relations
Founded: 1998. **Members:** 5,000. **Staff:** 1. **Description:** Graduates and former students of the College

for Creative Studies. Seeks to advance the programs of the College for Creative Studies; promotes ongoing communication and good fellowship among members. Keeps members informed regarding current activities at the College for Creative Studies; conducts student recruitment activities; sponsors social and educational programs. **Libraries: Type:** open to the public. **Holdings:** 28,000; books, periodicals. **Subjects:** art specialization. **Awards:** Alumni Scholarships. **Frequency:** annual. **Type:** monetary. **Recipient:** to students with a minimum 3.2 GPA. **Computer Services:** database ● mailing lists ● online services, career services, exhibition, sales, volunteer opportunities. **Councils:** Alumni. **Affiliated With:** Council for Advancement and Support of Education. **Formerly:** (2003) Center for Creative Studies - College of Art and Design Alumni Association. **Publications:** *Centerline*, 3/year. Newsletter. Includes community news, professional work, faculty/student projects, and alumni milestone news. ● Surveys. **Conventions/Meetings:** periodic Alumni Reunion (exhibits).

18508 ■ College of St. Scholastica Alumni Association (CSSAA)
c/o Alumni Relations, The College of St. Scholastica
Tower Hall 1410
1200 Kenwood Ave.
Duluth, MN 55811-4199
Ph: (218)723-6071 (218)723-6016
Free: (800)447-5444
Fax: (218)723-6400
E-mail: alumni@css.edu
URL: http://www.css.edu/x3624.xml
Contact: Mary Gummerson, Pres.
Founded: 1926. **Members:** 13,000. **Staff:** 3. **Description:** Graduates of the College of St. Scholastica. Promotes the advancement of the College of St. Scholastica and its programs; facilitates ongoing communication and good fellowship among members. Works with Volunteer Alumni Board. Sponsors social and educational activities, alumni career network, student alumni association activities. **Awards:** Alumni Recognition Awards. **Frequency:** annual. **Type:** recognition. **Recipient:** for outstanding alumni ● Alumni Scholarship Fund. **Frequency:** annual. **Type:** scholarship ● Faculty Award. **Frequency:** annual. **Type:** recognition. **Recipient:** for outstanding faculty or staff ● St. Scholastica Inspiration Award. **Frequency:** annual. **Type:** recognition. **Recipient:** for outstanding faculty or staff ● Sister Alice Lamb Award. **Frequency:** annual. **Type:** recognition. **Recipient:** for outstanding service of an alumna or alumnus ● Sister Ann Edward Scanlon Award. **Frequency:** annual. **Type:** recognition. **Recipient:** for an alumna or alumnus ● Sr. Timothy Kirby Award. **Frequency:** annual. **Type:** recognition. **Recipient:** for an alumna or alumnus. **Publications:** *TIMES*, 3/year. Magazine. **Price:** free. **Circulation:** 15,000. Alternate Formats: online.

18509 ■ Colorado Christian University Alumni Association
c/o Alumni Relations
8787 W Alameda Ave.
Lakewood, CO 80226
Ph: (303)963-3330
Free: (800)44F-AITH
Fax: (303)963-3331
E-mail: ccualumni@ccu.edu
URL: http://www.ccu.edu/alumni
Contact: Mark Barrington, Pres.
Founded: 1914. **Members:** 12,000. **Regional Groups:** 5. **State Groups:** 3. **Local Groups:** 3. **Description:** Graduates and former students of the Colorado Christian University. Promotes ongoing communication and good fellowship among members; works to advance the programs of the Colorado Christian University. Conducts educational and social activities. **Libraries: Type:** reference; lending. **Holdings:** archival material, articles, books, periodicals. **Subjects:** Colorado Christian University and its alumni. **Awards:** Alumni Scholarships. **Frequency:** annual. **Type:** scholarship. **Publications:** Newsletter, monthly. Alternate Formats: online.

18510 ■ Columbia College of Nursing Alumni Association (CCNAA)
2121 E Newport Ave.
Milwaukee, WI 53211-2952
Ph: (414)961-3530
Fax: (414)961-4121
E-mail: nkressin@ccon.edu
URL: http://www.ccon.edu/Alumni/alumni.htm
Contact: Tracy Blair, Alumni Council Pres.
Description: Graduates of the Columbia College of Nursing. Promotes continuing communication and good fellowship among members. Provides support and assistance to the Columbia College of Nursing and its programs; sponsors social and community service activities.

18511 ■ Defense Intel Alumni Association (DIAA)
PO Box 489
Hamilton, VA 20159
Ph: (571)426-0098
Fax: (703)738-7145
E-mail: diaa@adelphia.net
URL: http://www.dialumni.org
Contact: Dr. Wynfred Joshua, Pres.
Founded: 1998. **Membership Dues:** regular, $30 (annual). **Description:** Employees, retirees, and prospective retirees of the Federal Government and the military services who have been associated with the Defense Intelligence Agency (DIA). Aims to inform members of activities, special accomplishments and whereabouts of other members; provides educational services and information; arranges special activities with the Defense Intelligence Agency, and sponsors social activities to benefit membership. **Publications:** Newsletter. **Conventions/Meetings:** luncheon - always spring ● annual meeting and luncheon ● seminar, covering long-term care.

18512 ■ D'Youville College Alumni Association (DYCAA)
631 Niagara St.
Buffalo, NY 14201-1084
Ph: (716)829-7806
E-mail: alumni@dyc.edu
URL: http://www.dyc.edu/alumni/alumni_association.asp
Contact: Patricia Marino Smyton, Dir.
Founded: 1908. **Members:** 14,000. **Regional Groups:** 13. **Description:** Graduates of D'Youville College. Promotes communication and good fellowship among members; seeks to advance D'Youville College and its programs. Provides voluntary and financial support to D'Youville College; conducts social and fundraising activities. **Awards:** Alumni Service Award. **Frequency:** annual. **Type:** recognition. **Recipient:** for outstanding alumni ● Anne Lum Award. **Frequency:** annual. **Type:** recognition. **Recipient:** for outstanding alumni ● Lee Conroy Higgins Award to Student. **Frequency:** annual. **Type:** monetary. **Recipient:** for an outstanding senior student ● Marguerite D'Youville Honor award. **Frequency:** annual. **Type:** recognition. **Recipient:** for outstanding alumni. **Publications:** *D'Mensions*, 3/year. Magazine. **Circulation:** 13,000. Alternate Formats: online. **Conventions/Meetings:** annual Homecoming Weekend - meeting, for welcoming alumni.

18513 ■ Emerson College Alumni Association (ECAA)
120 Boylston St.
Boston, MA 02116-4624
Ph: (617)824-8500
Free: (800)255-4259
Fax: (617)824-7807
E-mail: alumni@emerson.edu
URL: http://www.emerson.edu/alumni
Contact: Barbara Rutberg, Dir.
Founded: 1880. **Members:** 17,000. **Staff:** 4. **Regional Groups:** 6. **Multinational. Description:** Graduates and former students of Emerson College. Seeks to "foster and maintain the spirit and devotion of the alumni in an effort to promote growth and the reputation of the College as a leader in communications and the performing arts." Provides voluntary

and financial support to Emerson College and its programs; sponsors social and educational activities. **Libraries: Type:** lending; reference. **Holdings:** 190,000; archival material, articles, audio recordings, books, business records, video recordings. **Subjects:** Emerson College, communications, performing arts, all other subjects supporting liberal arts. **Awards:** Alumni Achievement Award. **Frequency:** annual. **Type:** recognition. **Recipient:** for outstanding record of achievement in his or her field. **Publications:** *The Communicator*, semiannual. Newsletter. Alternate Formats: online ● *ECTV Update*, monthly. Newsletter. Contains stories and images about ECTV programs. Alternate Formats: online ● *Emerson Today*, monthly, except for January, July and August. Newsletter. Alternate Formats: online ● *Expression*, 3/year. Magazine. **Price:** free for members. Alternate Formats: CD-ROM; online. **Conventions/Meetings:** annual Alumni Weekend - reunion.

18514 ■ Erskine Alumni Association (EAA)
c/o Erskine Colorado
2 Washington St.
PO Box 608
Due West, SC 29639
Ph: (864)379-2131
Fax: (864)379-3164
E-mail: alumni@erskine.edu
URL: http://www.erskine.edu/alumni/index.shtml
Contact: Ralph Patterson, Dir. of Annual Giving and Alumni Affairs
Founded: 1839. **Members:** 9,000. **Staff:** 2. **Budget:** $125,000. **Regional Groups:** 100. **State Groups:** 30. **Local Groups:** 1. **Description:** Graduates of Erskine College and Seminary. Seeks to perpetuate friendships among members; promotes the welfare of Erskine College and Seminary. Facilitates communication among members; supports and assists Christian higher education. **Awards:** Alumni Distinguished Service. **Frequency:** annual. **Type:** recognition. **Recipient:** for individuals providing long-time service to college, community, or church.

18515 ■ Excelsior College Alumni Association
Excelsior Coll.
7 Columbia Cir.
Albany, NY 12203-5159
Ph: (518)464-8500
Free: (888)647-2388
E-mail: alumni@excelsior.edu
URL: http://www.excelsior.edu
Contact: Mary O'Connor, Pres.
Founded: 1971. **Members:** 79,000. **Staff:** 2. **Budget:** $174,000. **Description:** Graduates and former students of Excelsior (formerly known as Regents) College. Seeks to advance Excelsior College and its programs; facilitates ongoing communication and good fellowship among members. Provides voluntary and financial assistance to the college; sponsors social activities. **Awards:** Alumni Achievement Award. **Frequency:** annual. **Type:** recognition ● C. Wayne Williams Academic Award. **Frequency:** annual. **Type:** recognition. **Recipient:** for outstanding Excelsior College student or graduate making an outstanding contribution to a community service project ● Carrie Lenburg Award. **Frequency:** annual. **Type:** recognition. **Recipient:** for outstanding Excelsior College nursing alumnus ● In Support of Excelsior College as a Graduate Award. **Frequency:** annual. **Type:** recognition. **Committees:** Alumni Activities; Alumni Services; Development; Nominations. **Formerly:** (2003) Alumni Association of Regents College. **Publications:** *Live and Learn*, 3/year. Magazine. **Circulation:** 90,000. **Conventions/Meetings:** annual Alumni Awards Dinner.

18516 ■ Gallaudet University Alumni Association (GUAA)
c/o Sam Sonnenstrahl, Exec. Dir.
Peikoff Alumni House
800 Florida Ave. NE
Washington, DC 20002-3695
Ph: (202)651-5060
Fax: (202)651-5062

E-mail: samuel.sonnenstrahl@gallaudet.edu
URL: http://alumni.gallaudet.edu
Contact: Sam Sonnenstrahl, Exec. Dir.
Founded: 1889. **Members:** 7,300. **Membership Dues:** active/associate/subscribing (life), $75. **Regional Groups:** 52. **Multinational. Description:** Aims to preserve and increase the influence and prestige of Gallaudet University as an institution for deaf people; to promote those concerns affecting the welfare of deaf people; and to perpetuate the friendships formed during college life. **Awards:** Outstanding Young Alumnus. **Frequency:** annual. **Type:** recognition. **Recipient:** for alumnus or alumna who has graduated within the past 15 years and has accomplished some notable achievement ● Service to Others. **Frequency:** annual. **Type:** recognition. **Recipient:** to individuals within the deaf community who have contributed significantly to the community, especially as volunteers. **Telecommunication Services:** electronic mail, alumni.relations@gallaudet.edu. **Formerly:** (1986) Gallaudet College Alumni Association. **Publications:** *Gallaudet Today*, quarterly. Magazine. Includes newsletter.

18517 ■ Hope International University Alumni Association (HIUAA)
2500 E Nutwood Ave.
Fullerton, CA 92831
Ph: (714)879-3901
Fax: (714)681-7420
E-mail: alumni@hiu.edu
URL: http://www.hiu.edu
Contact: Kim Lullo, Dir.
Founded: 1928. **Staff:** 1. **Description:** Graduates and former students of Hope International University. Seeks to advance the University and its programs. **Awards: Frequency:** periodic. **Type:** scholarship. **Telecommunication Services:** electronic mail, klullo@hiu.edu. **Formerly:** (1998) Pacific Christian College Alumni Association.

18518 ■ Indiana State University Alumni Association (ISUAA)
c/o Indiana State University
200 N 7th St.
Terre Haute, IN 47809-9989
Ph: (812)237-3707 (812)237-3132
Free: (800)742-0891
Fax: (812)237-8157
E-mail: alumni@isugw.indstate.edu
URL: http://www.indstate.edu/alum/alum_assoc.htm
Contact: John P. Newton, Exec. Dir.
Founded: 1887. **Members:** 75,000. **Membership Dues:** individual, $40 (annual) ● life, $500. **Staff:** 7. **Budget:** $390,000. **Regional Groups:** 20. **State Groups:** 7. **Local Groups:** 1. **Description:** Graduates of the Indiana State University. Promotes communication and good fellowship among members. Organizes class reunions, homecomings, alumni travel opportunities, and other social activities; provides financial and other support to community and university programs; maintains alumni clubs, alumni career network, and alumni scholars program. **Awards:** Alumni Scholarship. **Frequency:** periodic. **Type:** scholarship ● Distinguished Alumni Award. **Frequency:** periodic. **Type:** recognition. **Boards:** Alumni. **Subgroups:** Student Alumni Association. **Publications:** *Alumni Update*, annual ● *Indiana State University Magazine*, semiannual. **Price:** free. **Circulation:** 72,000.

18519 ■ Iowa Wesleyan College Alumni Association (IWCAA)
601 N Main St.
Mount Pleasant, IA 52641
Ph: (319)385-8021 (319)385-6212
Free: (800)582-2383
E-mail: dstory@iwc.edu
URL: http://www.iwc.edu
Contact: Dennis C. Story, VP, Institutional Relations
Founded: 1842. **Members:** 13,445. **Staff:** 2. **Description:** Graduates and former students of the Iowa Wesleyan College. Seeks to advance the College and its programs; promotes communication among members and between members and current students and faculty. Conducts student recruitment and fundraising activities; maintains career network; sponsors social activities. **Libraries: Type:** not open to the public; reference. **Holdings:** archival material, articles, books, clippings, periodicals. **Subjects:** Iowa Wesleyan College, alumni activities. **Awards:** Distinguished Service Award. **Frequency:** annual. **Type:** recognition ● Service Award. **Frequency:** annual. **Type:** recognition. **Publications:** *The Purple & White*, 3/year. Magazine. Provides alumni news and features. **Circulation:** 10,100. **Conventions/Meetings:** annual reunion.

18520 ■ Jackson State University National Alumni Association (JSUNAA)
PO Box 17144
Jackson, MS 39217
Ph: (601)979-2282
Fax: (601)979-3786
E-mail: mconey@mail1.jsums.edu
URL: http://www.jsums.edu/alumnidev
Contact: Ms. Melvene L. Coney, Interim Dir.
Founded: 1929. **Members:** 58,000. **Membership Dues:** associate/regular, $40 (annual) ● life, $500. **Staff:** 5. **Regional Groups:** 6. **Local Groups:** 63. **Description:** Graduates and former students of Jackson State University. Seeks to advance the University and its programs; facilitates ongoing communication among members. Conducts student recruitment and community relations activities; sponsors social gatherings; provides voluntary and financial support to Jackson State University. Plans to operate alumni bus for group travel. **Libraries: Type:** by appointment only. **Holdings:** books, business records, clippings, periodicals. **Subjects:** Jackson State University, alumni activities, history. **Awards:** JSU Book Loan. **Frequency:** quarterly. **Type:** grant. **Computer Services:** Online services. **Publications:** *Alumni News*, quarterly. Newsletter. **Price:** free. **Advertising:** accepted. **Conventions/Meetings:** biennial reunion.

18521 ■ Kent State University Alumni Association (KSUAA)
Williamson Alumni Center
PO Box 5190
Kent, OH 44242-0001
Ph: (330)672-5368
Free: (888)320-5368
Fax: (330)672-4723
E-mail: alumni@kent.edu
URL: http://www.kent.edu/alumni
Contact: Lori Randorf, Exec. Dir.
Founded: 1910. **Members:** 10,000. **Membership Dues:** individual - life (senior), $250 ● joint - life (senior), $300 ● individual, $35 (annual) ● joint, $50 (annual) ● individual (life), $500 ● joint (life), $600. **Staff:** 12. **Budget:** $1,500,000. **Regional Groups:** 4. **State Groups:** 5. **Local Groups:** 13. **Description:** Graduates of Kent State University. Seeks to advance Kent State University and its programs; facilitates ongoing communication and good fellowship among members. Provides voluntary and financial support to Kent State University; sponsors social activities. **Libraries: Type:** reference. **Holdings:** archival material, audio recordings, video recordings. **Subjects:** Kent State University, alumni activities. **Awards:** Distinguished Alumnus Awards. **Frequency:** annual. **Type:** recognition ● Distinguished Teaching Awards. **Frequency:** annual. **Type:** recognition. **Telecommunication Services:** electronic mail, lrandorf@kent.edu. **Publications:** *Kent State*, quarterly. Magazine. Alternate Formats: online.

18522 ■ Keuka College Alumni Association (KCAA)
Off. of Alumni and Family Relations
Keuka Park, NY 14478
Ph: (315)279-5238
Fax: (315)279-5281
E-mail: alumni@mail.keuka.edu
URL: http://www.keukaalumni.com/alumni/alumni_association.htm
Contact: Patricia Condlin Middlebrook, Pres.
Founded: 1929. **Members:** 7,500. **Staff:** 2. **Description:** Graduates of Keuka College. Seeks to "preserve and strengthen the loyalty of alumni to Keuka Col-

lege, to serve and extend the interest of Keuka College, to contribute in a substantive manner to the governance of the College, to assist in the mission of Keuka College, and to help Keuka College financially whenever possible." Sponsors social activities. **Awards:** Community Service. **Frequency:** annual. **Type:** recognition ● Effective Use of Retirement. **Frequency:** annual. **Type:** recognition ● Professional Achievement. **Frequency:** annual. **Type:** recognition ● Recent Graduate. **Frequency:** annual. **Type:** recognition ● Service to Keuka. **Frequency:** annual. **Type:** recognition. **Publications:** *Keuka Magazine*, quarterly. **Conventions/Meetings:** annual reunion, includes house party.

18523 ■ Lawrence Technological University Alumni Association (LTUAA)
21000 W 10 Mile Rd.
Southfield, MI 48075-1058
Ph: (248)204-2308 (248)204-2309
Free: (800)CALL-LTU
Fax: (248)204-2207
E-mail: alumni@ltu.edu
URL: http://www.ltu.edu/alumni/association.asp
Contact: Angela C. Ruth, Mgr. of Alumni Relations
Founded: 1938. **Members:** 22,000. **Regional Groups:** 4. **State Groups:** 6. **Local Groups:** 3. **Description:** Graduates and former students of Lawrence Technological University and the former Detroit Institute of Technology. Seeks to advance the University and its programs. Serves "as a focus for interaction, networking, and service" among members. **Awards:** Alumni Association Award. **Frequency:** annual. **Type:** recognition ● **Frequency:** annual. **Type:** grant ● **Frequency:** annual. **Type:** scholarship. **Additional Websites:** http://www.lawrencetech.net.

18524 ■ LDS Business College Alumni Association (LDSBCAA)
411 E South Temple
Salt Lake City, UT 84111
Ph: (801)524-8172
Fax: (801)524-1900
E-mail: lbrown@ldsbc.edu
URL: http://www.ldsbcalumni.org
Contact: Gordon B. Hinckley, Pres.
Founded: 1886. **Members:** 55,000. **Description:** Graduates and former students of the Latter Day Saints Business College. Encourages alumni to help improve the college and contribute to the accomplishment of the mission of the LDS Church. Conducts fundraising activities benefiting the college; sponsors social activities. **Awards:** Distinguished Alumnus Award. **Frequency:** annual. **Type:** recognition. **Recipient:** to alumni for making outstanding contributions to their profession, community, family, church, or to the college. **Publications:** *Pathways*, semiannual. Magazine. Features highlights of alumni and accomplishments. **Conventions/Meetings:** annual Founders Day Reunion.

18525 ■ Lincoln University Alumni Association (LUAA)
Memorial Hall
Lincoln Univ.
818 Chestnut St.
Jefferson City, MO 65102-0029
Ph: (573)681-5572
Free: (800)856-3707
Fax: (573)681-5892
E-mail: hdorsey@mindspring.com
Contact: Hardy Dorsey, Pres.
Founded: 1876. **Members:** 17,200. **Membership Dues:** active or associate, $40 (annual) ● life, golden, $400 ● life, silver, $1,000. **Staff:** 3. **Regional Groups:** 4. **State Groups:** 15. **Local Groups:** 1. **Description:** Graduates of Lincoln University. Seeks to advance the University and its programs. Assists in student recruitment; participates in educational, cultural, patriotic, literary, and scientific activities. **Awards: Frequency:** periodic. **Type:** monetary ● **Frequency:** periodic. **Type:** recognition ● **Frequency:** periodic. **Type:** scholarship. **Publications:** *Alumni Line*, 3/year. Magazine.

18526 ■ Long Island University - Southampton College Alumni Association
720 Northern Blvd.
Brookville, NY 11548-1300
Ph: (516)299-4052
Fax: (516)299-3013
E-mail: jane.ferrone@liu.edu
URL: http://www.southampton.liu.edu/admin/alumni/alumni.htm
Contact: Carol Gilbert, Dir. of Alumni Relations
Founded: 1995. **Members:** 6,000. **Staff:** 2. **Regional Groups:** 2. **Local Groups:** 1. **Description:** Graduates of the Long Island University - Southampton College. Promotes communication and good fellowship among members. Makes available professional networking and career services to members; recruits new students for Southampton College; provides financial support to the Southampton College annual fund. **Libraries: Type:** not open to the public. **Holdings:** archival material, books, clippings, periodicals. **Subjects:** Association history. **Awards:** Alumni Award. **Frequency:** annual. **Type:** recognition. **Recipient:** for a graduating senior with record of community service, volunteerism and leadership ● Distinguished Alumni Award. **Frequency:** annual. **Type:** recognition. **Recipient:** for a Southampton College graduate playing a leadership role in a profession, community service, or politics. **Publications:** *Long Island University,* semiannual. Magazine. **Price:** free for alumni. **Circulation:** 115,000. **Conventions/Meetings:** Concert - meeting - October ● annual Homecoming - meeting and reunion - July, August.

18527 ■ Marquette University Alumni Association (MUAA)
c/o Marquette University
PO Box 1881
Milwaukee, WI 53201-1881
Ph: (414)288-7441 (414)351-1998
Free: (800)344-7544
Fax: (414)288-3956
E-mail: muconnect@marquette.edu
URL: http://www.marquette.edu/alumni
Contact: Douglas Kelley, Pres.
Founded: 1893. **Members:** 119,000. **Staff:** 10. **Regional Groups:** 39. **Local Groups:** 12. **Description:** Graduates of Marquette University. Seeks to "help Marquette University, as an urban Catholic, Jesuit institution, become one of the nation's distinguished universities." Facilitates communication among members; provides support and assistance to Marquette University and its programs. **Awards:** **Frequency:** annual. **Type:** recognition ● **Frequency:** annual. **Type:** scholarship.

18528 ■ Montreat College Alumni Association (MCA)
PO Box 1267
Montreat, NC 28757
Ph: (828)669-8012
Free: (800)849-3347
Fax: (828)669-9554
E-mail: alumni@montreat.edu
URL: http://www.montreat.edu/alumni
Contact: Fran Aceto, Pres.
Founded: 1955. **Members:** 6,500. **Staff:** 1. **Description:** Graduates and former students of Montreat College. Supports the aims and ideals of Montreat College; promotes ongoing communication and good fellowship among members. Conducts fundraising and student recruitment campaigns; sponsors social activities. **Awards:** Elizabeth Wilson Scholarship. **Frequency:** annual. **Type:** scholarship. **Recipient:** for students.

18529 ■ National Alumni Council of the United Negro College Fund (NAC)
c/o United Negro College Fund
PO Box 10444
Fairfax, VA 22031-8044
Ph: (703)205-3400 (703)205-3464
Free: (800)331-2244
Fax: (703)205-3574
E-mail: rubyetd@aol.com
URL: http://www.uncf.org/alumni/index.asp
Contact: Mrs. Rubye Taylor-Drake EdD, Pres.
Founded: 1946. **Members:** 300,000. **Staff:** 2. **Description:** Inter-alumni councils, national alumni associations, pre-alumni councils, and students. Purposes are to: stimulate the interest of black college alumni; acquaint the public with the value of black colleges and black higher education; inform students and the public about contributions of black college alumni to civic betterment and community progress; recruit students for UNCF's member colleges; raise funds for United Negro College Fund (see separate entry); encourage and provide a structure for cooperation among black college alumni groups and friends of black higher education. Compiles statistics. **Awards:** Male Scholarship. **Frequency:** annual. **Type:** scholarship ● **Type:** recognition. **Councils:** Inter-Alumni; National Alumni Associations; National Pre-Alumni; Pre-Alumni (Students). **Also Known As:** National Alumni Council of the UNCF. **Publications:** *Conference Journal,* annual. **Price:** free. **Advertising:** accepted ● *Torch,* semiannual. Newsletter ● *Torch Bearer,* quarterly. Newsletter. **Conventions/Meetings:** annual NAC/NPAC-UNCF Conference, includes workshops, seminars, pageant, banquet (exhibits) - always first weekend in February.

18530 ■ National Black College Alumni Hall of Fame Foundation
230 Peachtree St., No. 530
Atlanta, GA 30303
Ph: (404)524-1106
Fax: (404)525-6226
Contact: Thomas W. Dortch Jr., Chm.
Founded: 1984. **Members:** 30. **Staff:** 2. **Description:** Alumni of historical black colleges and universities. Seeks to increase awareness of importance of HBCU. Encourages graduates of black colleges and universities to donate funds to their alma maters. Conducts fund raising activities. **Awards:** Miss National Black College Hall of Fame. **Frequency:** annual. **Type:** scholarship. **Recipient:** for outstanding Queen's of historical black colleges and universities. **Publications:** *Highlights Alumni Achievement & HBCU News* ● *Touchstone,* quarterly. Newsletter. **Conventions/Meetings:** annual Violence and African-American Health Issues - symposium.

18531 ■ Nebraska Christian College Alumni Association (NCCAA)
12550 S 114th St.
Papillion, NE 68046
Ph: (402)935-9400
Fax: (402)935-9500
E-mail: info@nechristian.edu
URL: http://www.nechristian.edu/alumni
Contact: Linda Bigbee, Dir.
Founded: 1969. **Members:** 220. **Membership Dues:** blue, $15 (annual) ● gold, $25 (annual). **Staff:** 1. **Budget:** $5,000. **Local Groups:** 1. **Description:** Graduates of the Nebraska Christian College. Promotes "the cause of Christ through Nebraska Christian College." Facilitates ongoing communication and fellowship among members; provides financial and voluntary support to Nebraska Christian College and its programs; conducts student recruitment campaigns. **Libraries: Type:** lending; reference. **Holdings:** 27,000; archival material, audio recordings, books, clippings, periodicals, video recordings. **Subjects:** Nebraska Christian College, alumni activities. **Awards:** Distinguished Alumni Award. **Frequency:** annual. **Type:** recognition. **Recipient:** to an individual with outstanding service or accomplishment. **Councils:** Alumni. **Publications:** *NCC Newsletter,* annual. Contains information on dues and updates on projects. Alternate Formats: online. **Conventions/Meetings:** Iowa Christian Convention ● Nebraska Christian Convention ● annual North American Christian Convention.

18532 ■ Network of Gay and Lesbian Alumni/ae Associations (NetGALA)
PO Box 53188
Washington, DC 20009
E-mail: netgalacnf@aol.com
URL: http://www.qrd.org/qrd/www/orgs/netgala
Contact: David White, Chm.
Founded: 1985. **Members:** 1,300. **Membership Dues:** individual, $15 (annual) ● group, $100 (annual). **Budget:** $5,000. **Regional Groups:** 6. **Description:** Provides leadership and support to gay, lesbian, and bisexual alum groups. Works to create a greater understanding between academic institutions and gay and lesbian graduates, students, faculty, and staff. Acts as a clearinghouse for information and ideas in the gay and lesbian community. Provides professional and social network. Assists in organizing new gay and lesbian alumni associations. Sponsors charitable and educational programs. Compiles statistics. **Affiliated With:** National Gay and Lesbian Task Force. **Also Known As:** NetGALA. **Formerly:** (1987) Northeastern Gay and Lesbian Alumni/ae Association. **Publications:** *NetGALA News,* quarterly. Newsletter. **Price:** $15.00. ISSN: 1082-9369. **Circulation:** 1,200. **Conventions/Meetings:** semiannual conference and workshop.

18533 ■ North Dakota State University Alumni Association (NDSUAA)
PO Box 5144
Fargo, ND 58105
Ph: (701)231-6800
Free: (800)279-8971
Fax: (701)231-6801
E-mail: office@ndsualumni.com
URL: http://www.ndsualumni.com
Contact: James C. Miller, Exec. Dir.
Founded: 1908. **Members:** 60,000. **Staff:** 31. **Budget:** $1,500,000. **Regional Groups:** 11. **Description:** Graduates and former students of the North Dakota State University. Seeks to advance the university and its programs. Sponsors public relations activities promoting North Dakota State University; facilitates ongoing communication and good fellowship among members; conducts social activities. **Awards:** Alumni Achievement Awards. **Frequency:** annual. **Type:** recognition. **Recipient:** for alumni distinguishing themselves in their professions ● Heritage Award. **Frequency:** annual. **Type:** recognition. **Recipient:** for alumnus providing outstanding service to the university ● Horizon Award. **Frequency:** annual. **Type:** recognition. **Recipient:** for alumnus who graduated within past 10 years and excelled in career and on community service. **Publications:** *Bison Briefs,* 3/year. Newsletter. **Price:** free for members. **Conventions/Meetings:** annual meeting, with homecoming.

18534 ■ Northern Michigan University Alumni Association (NMUAA)
603 Cohodas
Marquette, MI 49855
Ph: (906)227-2610
Free: (877)GRAD-NMU
Fax: (906)227-1301
E-mail: alumni@nmu.edu
URL: http://www.nmu.edu/alumni
Contact: Martha Van Der Kamp, Exec. Dir.
Founded: 1949. **Members:** 4,000. **Membership Dues:** single, $35 (annual) ● couple, $50 (annual) ● life (single), $500 ● life (couple), $750 ● recent graduate (single), $20 (annual) ● recent graduate (couple), $35 (annual). **Staff:** 5. **Budget:** $400,000. **Description:** Graduates of Northern Michigan University (NMU). Cultivates a strong tradition of involvement and loyalty among alumni, students, friends and community, while advancing the interests of the university. Discounts on lodging, auto rentals, alumni events and other services are provided to dues paying members. **Libraries: Type:** reference. **Holdings:** archival material, clippings, periodicals. **Subjects:** NMU and its programs, alumni activities. **Awards:** Alumni Service Award. **Frequency:** annual. **Type:** recognition. **Recipient:** for outstanding service ● Distinguished Alumni Award. **Frequency:** annual. **Type:** recognition. **Recipient:** for outstanding alumni ● Outstanding Young Alumni Award. **Frequency:** annual. **Type:** recognition. **Recipient:** for outstanding alumni under 36 years of age. **Computer Services:** database. **Committees:** Board Development. **Publi-**

cations: *Northern Horizons*, 3/year. Magazine. **Price:** $15.00/year. **Circulation:** 40,000. **Advertising:** accepted. Alternate Formats: online. **Conventions/ Meetings:** board meeting - 3/year.

18535 ■ Northwest Nazarene University Alumni Association (NNUAA)
623 Holly St.
Nampa, ID 83686
Ph: (208)467-8011 (208)467-8843
Free: (800)654-2411
Fax: (208)467-8838
E-mail: alumni@nnu.edu
URL: http://www.nnu.edu
Contact: Darl Bruner, Dir.
Founded: 1913. **Members:** 13,000. **Staff:** 3. **Regional Groups:** 8. **Description:** Seeks to create and enrich relationships among all alumni and the university in order to advance the university's mission of developing the whole person. **Libraries: Type:** reference. **Holdings:** archival material, books. **Subjects:** Northwest Nazarene University and its programs. **Awards:** Alumnus of the Year. **Frequency:** annual. **Type:** recognition ● Distinguished Service Award. **Type:** recognition ● Professional Achievement Award. **Type:** recognition ● Young Alumnus Award. **Type:** recognition. **Boards:** Alumni; Volunteer. **Councils:** Student Alumni. **Subgroups:** Volunteer Student Association. **Conventions/Meetings:** annual reunion.

18536 ■ Oklahoma Baptist University Alumni Association (OBUAA)
Oklahoma Baptist Univ.
500 W Univ.
Shawnee, OK 74804
Ph: (405)275-2850 (405)878-2706
Free: (800)654-3285
Fax: (405)878-2710
E-mail: alumni@okbu.edu
URL: http://www.okbu.edu/alumni/index.html
Contact: Lori Renegar Hagans, Exec. Dir.
Founded: 1910. **Members:** 24,000. **Staff:** 3. **Budget:** $100,000. **Local Groups:** 23. **Description:** Graduates and former students of the Oklahoma Baptist University. Seeks to provide opportunities for "graduates and former students to continue and expand relationships between each other and university personnel." Provides financial and voluntary assistance to the University and its programs; sponsors social activities. **Awards:** Alumni Achievement Award. **Frequency:** annual. **Type:** recognition. **Recipient:** for two individuals who have provided outstanding lifetime service ● Profile in Excellence. **Frequency:** annual. **Type:** recognition. **Recipient:** for 12 individuals who have made outstanding contributions to society through their careers or community service. **Computer Services:** database, alumni directory. **Publications:** *The OBU Anvil*, quarterly. **Price:** free. **Circulation:** 18,200. Alternate Formats: online. **Conventions/Meetings:** annual Homecoming - meeting, plenary meeting.

18537 ■ Oklahoma City University Alumni Office (OCUAO)
2501 N Blackwelder
Oklahoma City, OK 73106-1493
Ph: (405)521-5117 (405)521-5000
Free: (800)872-8984
Fax: (405)521-5191
E-mail: alumni@okcu.edu
URL: http://www.okcu.edu/alumni
Contact: Jacque Fiegel, Pres.
Founded: 1904. **Members:** 20,000. **Description:** Graduates and former students of Oklahoma City University. Promotes ongoing communication among members and between members and current faculty, administration, and students. Provides voluntary and financial support to Oklahoma City University and its programs; sponsors social activities. **Awards:** Distinguished Alumni of the Year. **Frequency:** annual. **Type:** recognition.

18538 ■ Oklahoma University Alumni Association (OUAA)
900 Asp Ave., Ste.427
Norman, OK 73019-4051
Ph: (405)325-1710

Fax: (405)325-1709
E-mail: alumni@ou.edu
URL: http://alumni.ou.edu
Contact: Tripp Hall, Assoc. VP/Exec. Dir.
Founded: 1899. **Members:** 181,000. **Membership Dues:** single - life, $750 ● joint - life, $1,000 ● OU young alumna (less than 4 years), $25. **Budget:** $687,000. **Regional Groups:** 55. **Local Groups:** 30. **National Groups:** 4. **Description:** Graduates and friends of the University of Oklahoma. Seeks to advance the University and its programs; facilitates ongoing communication and good fellowship among members. Conducts fundraising activities benefitting the University of Oklahoma; sponsors student recruitment programs and social activities. **Libraries: Type:** reference. **Holdings:** books. **Subjects:** University of Oklahoma alumni. **Awards:** Alumni Club Matching Scholarship. **Frequency:** annual. **Type:** scholarship ● Generations II. **Frequency:** annual. **Type:** scholarship. **Recipient:** for nonresident-entering students who are descendants of University of Oklahoma alumni ● Regents Alumni Awards. **Frequency:** annual. **Type:** recognition. **Telecommunication Services:** electronic mail, tripp@ou.edu. **Formerly:** (2002) University of Oklahoma Foundation. **Publications:** *Leadership Update*, semiannual. Newsletter ● *OU People*, annual. Magazine ● *Sooner Magazine*, periodic.

18539 ■ Ouachita Baptist University Alumni Association (OBUAA)
410 Ouachita St.
OBU Box 3762
Arkadelphia, AR 71998
Ph: (870)245-5506
Free: (800)342-5628
Fax: (870)245-5500
E-mail: alumni@obu.edu
URL: http://www.obu.edu/alumni
Contact: Dr. Rex M. Horne Jr., Pres.
Founded: 1886. **Members:** 11,000. **Staff:** 3. **National Groups:** 21. **Multinational. Description:** Graduates and former students of Ouachita Baptist University. Promotes ongoing communication and good fellowship among members; seeks to advance the University and its programs. Assists in student recruitment and placement initiatives. **Awards:** Tiger Network Scholarships. **Frequency:** annual. **Type:** scholarship. **Recipient:** for entering students upon the recommendation of alumni who are members of the tiger network within the alumni association; based on high school performance. **Computer Services:** Online services, community. **Working Groups:** Alumni Chapters.

18540 ■ Prescott College Alumni Association (PCAA)
220 Grove Ave.
Prescott, AZ 86301
Ph: (928)350-4502
Free: (800)737-0119
Fax: (928)776-5228
E-mail: alumni@prescott.edu
URL: http://www.prescott.edu/alumni
Contact: Rachel Yoder, Alumni Relations Dir.
Founded: 1996. **Members:** 300. **Staff:** 1. **Description:** Represents graduates of Prescott College in Prescott, Arizona. **Libraries: Type:** open to the public. **Holdings:** 20,000. **Subjects:** liberal arts, environmental education. **Awards:** Alumni Scholarships. **Frequency:** annual. **Type:** scholarship. **Recipient:** for current RDD or ADP students as recommended by financial aid department. **Telecommunication Services:** additional toll-free number, (877)350-2100. **Publications:** *Alumni E-mail Newsletter*, monthly. **Circulation:** 800. Alternate Formats: online ● *Transitions*, 3/year. Magazine. **Price:** free. **Circulation:** 9,500. Alternate Formats: online. **Conventions/Meetings:** reunion (exhibits).

18541 ■ St. Mary's College of California Alumni Association (SMCCAA)
PO Box 3400
Moraga, CA 94575-3400
Ph: (925)631-4200
Free: (800)800-ALUM

Fax: (925)631-4382
E-mail: alumni@stmarys-ca.edu
URL: http://www.stmarys-ca.edu/alumni
Contact: Lloyd V. Schine III, Dir. of Alumni Relations
Founded: 1900. **Members:** 30,000. **Staff:** 4. **Regional Groups:** 12. **State Groups:** 5. **Local Groups:** 8. **Description:** Graduates and former students of St. Mary's College of California. Seeks to advance the College and its programs; facilitates ongoing communication and good fellowship among members. Provides financial and voluntary assistance to St. Mary's College of California; sponsors social activities. **Libraries: Type:** reference. **Holdings:** articles, books, clippings. **Awards:** Alumni Association Awards. **Frequency:** annual. **Type:** recognition. **Computer Services:** database ● mailing lists ● online services. **Telecommunication Services:** hotline, (925)631-4891. **Publications:** *Update*, quarterly. Magazine. **Circulation:** 30,000.

18542 ■ Southern Connecticut State University Alumni Association
501 Crescent St.
New Haven, CT 06515
Ph: (203)392-6501 (203)392-6500
E-mail: alumniinfo@southernct.edu
URL: http://www.southernct.edu/alumni
Contact: Patricia J. Rooney, Dir.
Founded: 1925. **Members:** 72,000. **Membership Dues:** active, $35 (annual). **Staff:** 4. **Budget:** $200,000. **Regional Groups:** 2. **Local Groups:** 4. **Description:** Graduates, former students and friends of Southern Connecticut State University (SCSU). Seeks to establish and maintain a mutually beneficial relationship between SCSU and its alumni, to foster a spirit of loyalty and support among the alumni, and to support the academic mission of the university. **Awards:** Distinguished Alumnus/Alumna. **Frequency:** annual. **Type:** recognition. **Recipient:** for service to university ● **Frequency:** annual. **Type:** scholarship ● Sports Hall of Fame. **Frequency:** annual. **Type:** recognition. **Publications:** *SCAN Alumni News*, 3/year. Newspapers. **Circulation:** 55,000 ● *Southern*, semiannual. Magazine. Contains information on campus events. **Conventions/Meetings:** annual reunion, homecoming for classes ending in 0 or 5.

18543 ■ Spalding University Alumni Association (SUAA)
851 S 4th St.
Louisville, KY 40203-2188
Ph: (502)585-9911
Free: (800)896-8941
Fax: (502)585-7158
E-mail: cschnell@spalding.edu
URL: http://www.spalding.edu/content.
  aspx?id=1876&cid=1600
Contact: Ann Alvey Triplett, Pres.
Founded: 1814. **Members:** 8,000. **Staff:** 1. **Local Groups:** 1. **Description:** Graduates of Spalding University. Seeks to advance Spalding University and its programs. Provides voluntary and financial assistance to Spalding University; facilitates ongoing communication and good fellowship among members. **Libraries: Type:** reference. **Holdings:** archival material, books, periodicals. **Subjects:** Spalding University, alumni activities. **Awards:** Caritas Medal. **Frequency:** annual. **Type:** medal ● Outstanding Alumnus. **Frequency:** annual. **Type:** recognition. **Publications:** *Connections*, biennial. Newsletter. **Conventions/Meetings:** annual reunion.

18544 ■ Stanford Chicano/Latino Alumni Association (SC/LAA)
PO Box 86204
Los Angeles, CA 90086-0204
Ph: (213)473-7528
Fax: (213)473-7511
E-mail: mario.vasquez@lacity.org
Contact: Mario Vasquez, Coor.
Founded: 1991. **Members:** 1,200. **Regional Groups:** 6. **Description:** Encourages alumni participation with Stanford University. Advocates for the needs of past Chicano and Latino students.

18545 ■ Texas A&M University - Commerce Alumni Association (TAMUCAA)
c/o Derryle Peace, Dir.
PO Box 3011
Commerce, TX 75429-3011
Ph: (903)886-5765
Fax: (903)886-5768
E-mail: derryle_peace@tamu-commerce.edu
URL: http://www.tamu-commerce.edu/advancement/
    alumni
Contact: Derryle Peace, Dir.
Founded: 1890. **Members:** 64,000. **Membership Dues:** active, $30 (annual). **Staff:** 3. **Description:** Graduates of Texas A&M University-Commerce. Promotes continuing communication and good fellowship among members. Provides support and assistance to Texas A&M-Commerce and its programs; sponsors social and educational activities. **Awards:** Distinguished Alumnus. **Frequency:** annual. **Type:** recognition ● Gold Blazer. **Frequency:** annual. **Type:** recognition. **Recipient:** for an alumna(ae) who provides outstanding voluntary service to Texas A&M University ● Outstanding Community Service. **Frequency:** annual. **Type:** recognition ● Outstanding Young Alumnus. **Frequency:** annual. **Type:** recognition.

18546 ■ Tufts University Alumni Association (TUAA)
95 Talbot Ave.
Medford, MA 02155
Ph: (617)627-3532
Free: (800)843-2586
Fax: (617)627-3938
E-mail: osherlli@tufts.edu
URL: http://www.tufts.edu/alumni
Contact: Marilyn Blumsack, Dir.
Founded: 1860. **Members:** 72,000. **Staff:** 13. **Budget:** $1,250,000. **Regional Groups:** 40. **Description:** Graduates of Tufts University and former students who completed at least one year of study at the University. Seeks to advance Tufts University and its programs; encourages ongoing communication and good fellowship among members. Provides voluntary and financial support to Tufts University; sponsors social activities. **Awards:** Distinguished Service Awards. **Frequency:** annual. **Type:** recognition ● Senior Awards. **Frequency:** annual. **Type:** recognition. **Committees:** Alumni Career Networking and Internship; Alumni Resources; Alumni Weekend; Awards; Citizenship and Public Service; Communications; Continuing Education; Development; Financial Resources; Homecoming; Regional Programs; Student Issues and Activities; Traditions; Young Alumni. **Publications:** *Tufts Magazine*, quarterly. **Price:** free. **Circulation:** 80,000. Alternate Formats: online. **Conventions/Meetings:** annual Fall Council Meeting.

18547 ■ UERMMMC Nursing Alumni Association U.S.A.
9 Mimosa Ln.
Piscataway, NJ 08854
Ph: (732)463-0504
Fax: (732)463-3869
E-mail: elamor@optonline.net
URL: http://www.uermmmcnursing.com
Contact: Norma C. Rabara, VP
Founded: 1989. **Members:** 500. **Membership Dues:** regular, $30 (annual) ● life, $250. **Regional Groups:** 7. **Description:** Graduates of the UERMMMC College of Nursing who reside in the United States. **Awards:** Outstanding Alumni. **Frequency:** annual. **Type:** recognition. **Recipient:** for excellence in nursing: clinical, administration, research, education, and community service. **Publications:** Newsletter, semiannual. **Price:** free. **Advertising:** accepted. **Conventions/Meetings:** annual reunion, nursing recruitment agencies, health-related products and other services (exhibits).

18548 ■ University of Advancing Computer Technology Alumni Association (UACTAA)
c/o University of Advancing Technology
2625 W Baseline Rd.
Tempe, AZ 85283
Ph: (602)383-8228
Free: (800)658-5744
Fax: (602)383-8222
E-mail: itrep@uat.edu
URL: http://www.uat.edu
Staff: 1. **Description:** Graduates and former students of the University of Advancing Computer Technology. Promotes continuing professional advancement of members. Provides technical support and continuing education courses to members.

18549 ■ University of Alaska Fairbanks Alumni Association (UAFAA)
PO Box 750126
Fairbanks, AK 99775
Ph: (907)474-7081
Free: (800)770-ALUM
Fax: (907)474-6712
E-mail: fyalum@uaf.edu
URL: http://www.uaf.edu/alumni
Contact: Joe Hayes, Exec. Dir.
Founded: 1927. **Members:** 3,126. **Membership Dues:** single, $35 (annual) ● couple, $45 (annual) ● individual - life, $1,000 ● couple - life, $1,200. **Staff:** 2. **State Groups:** 2. **Local Groups:** 1. **Description:** Graduates and former students of the University of Alaska Fairbanks (UAF). Conducts student recruitment campaigns; participates in student social activities; lobbies on behalf of the UAF; makes available career mentoring services to UAF students; provides financial support to UAF programs. Promotes and seeks to advance the UAF and its programs. **Awards:** Alumni Achievement Award. **Frequency:** annual. **Type:** recognition. **Recipient:** for outstanding contributions of graduates and former students of UAF ● Distinguished Alumni Award. **Frequency:** annual. **Type:** recognition. **Recipient:** for distinguished accomplishments in business and professional life ● **Frequency:** annual. **Type:** scholarship. **Programs:** Alumni Benefactor. **Publications:** Newsletter, quarterly. Contains alumni programs, campus activities, and class notes.

18550 ■ University of Colorado Medical Alumni Association (UCHSCMAA)
4200 E 9th Ave., Box A-080
Denver, CO 80262
Ph: (303)315-8832
Free: (877)HSC-ALUM
Fax: (303)315-7729
E-mail: alumni@uchsc.edu
URL: http://www.uchsc.edu/alumni/medicine
Contact: Matthew B. Goodwin, Pres.
Founded: 1941. **Members:** 570. **Membership Dues:** retired/practicing physician, $50 (annual) ● life, $600. **Staff:** 3. **Local Groups:** 1. **Description:** Graduates of the University of Colorado School of Medicine. Promotes communication and good fellowship among members. Participates in voluntary social service and charitable programs; sponsors reunions and other social activities, sponsors student programs. **Awards:** Silver and Gold Alumni Award. **Frequency:** annual. **Type:** recognition. **Recipient:** for outstanding contribution to health care. **Computer Services:** database, advancement partner ● mailing lists, of members. **Publications:** *CU Medicine Today*, semiannual. Magazine. **Circulation:** 10,000. **Conventions/Meetings:** quarterly board meeting.

18551 ■ University of Colorado School of Dentistry Alumni Association (SODAA)
c/o UCHSC Alumni Association
4200 E 9th Ave., A-080
Denver, CO 80262
Ph: (303)315-8832
Free: (877)HSC-ALUM
Fax: (303)315-7729
E-mail: wende.reoch@uchsc.edu
URL: http://www.uchsc.edu/alumni/associations/
    SOD/sod.html
Contact: Wendy Reoch, Dir. of Alumni Relations
Members: 1,130. **Description:** Serves as alumni association for University of Colorado Health Sciences Center, School of Dentistry. **Telecommunication Services:** electronic mail, alumni@uchsc.edu. **Conventions/Meetings:** annual MidWinter Dental Con-

vention ● annual Open-Wider Open Golf Tournament - competition - always 3rd week of May ● Silver and Gold Alumni Days - reunion, homecoming.

18552 ■ University of Iowa Alumni Association (UIAA)
100 Levitt Center for Univ. Advancement
Iowa City, IA 52242-1797
Ph: (319)335-3294
Free: (800)469-2586
Fax: (319)335-1079
E-mail: alumni@uiowa.edu
URL: http://www.iowalum.com
Contact: Vince Nelson, Pres./CEO
Founded: 1869. **Members:** 57,000. **Membership Dues:** individual, $45 (annual) ● Old Capitol Club - bronze, $100-$249 (annual) ● Old Capitol Club - silver, $250-$499 (annual) ● Old Capitol Club - gold, $500-$749 (annual) ● Old Capitol Club - platinum, $750-$999 (annual) ● Director's Club Honor Circle, $1,000 (annual) ● recent graduate (individual who has graduated within the last 5 years), $25 (annual) ● student, $19 (annual) ● life, sustaining, $25-$99. **Staff:** 30. **Budget:** $4,000,000. **State Groups:** 33. **National Groups:** 71. **Multinational. Description:** Graduates of the University of Iowa. Seeks to advance the University of Iowa and its programs; promotes communication and good fellowship among members. Provides services to members including career networking, educational outreach, and discounts on travel, insurance, apparel, and relocation. Sponsors social activities. **Awards:** Alumni Achievement Award. **Frequency:** annual. **Type:** recognition ● Alumni Service Award. **Frequency:** annual. **Type:** recognition ● Faculty - Staff Award. **Frequency:** annual. **Type:** recognition ● Friend of the University Award. **Frequency:** annual. **Type:** recognition ● Hickerson Alumni Recognition Award. **Frequency:** annual. **Type:** recognition ● Young Alumni Award. **Frequency:** annual. **Type:** recognition. **Computer Services:** Mailing lists, of members. **Publications:** *Iowa Alumni Magazine*, bimonthly. **Price:** included in membership dues. **Circulation:** 45,000. **Advertising:** accepted ● *IowaA*, monthly. Newsletter. Updates recipients with news from across the UI campus. Alternate Formats: online.

18553 ■ University of Louisville Alumni Association
Alumni Off.
Malcolm B. Chancey Ctr.
Univ. of Louisville
Louisville, KY 40292
Ph: (502)852-6186
Free: (800)813-8635
Fax: (502)852-6920
E-mail: jimmy.ford@louisville.edu
URL: http://www.alumni.louisville.edu
Contact: Jimmy Ford, Asst. VP
Founded: 1980. **Members:** 96,000. **Staff:** 13. **Budget:** $950,000. **Local Groups:** 10. **National Groups:** 26. **Description:** Graduates and former students of the University of Louisville. Seeks to advance the University and its programs; encourages ongoing communication and good fellowship among members. Provides support and assistance to the University of Louisville; conducts social activities. **Awards:** Rodney Williams Legacy Scholarship. **Frequency:** annual. **Type:** scholarship. **Recipient:** to children and grandchildren of the University of Louisville alumni. **Publications:** *UofL*, quarterly. Magazine. **Circulation:** 126,000. **Advertising:** accepted. Alternate Formats: online.

18554 ■ University of Mary Alumni Association (UMAA)
7500 Univ. Dr.
Bismarck, ND 58504
Ph: (701)255-7500 (701)355-8370
Free: (800)408-6279
Fax: (701)255-7687
E-mail: srdenise@umary.edu
URL: http://www.umary.edu
Contact: Sister Denise Ressler, Dir.
Founded: 1959. **Members:** 10,503. **Staff:** 1. **Regional Groups:** 1. **Description:** Graduates of the

University of Mary. Seeks to advance the University of Mary and its programs, and Benedictine education and community service. Facilitates "continuation of the mission of the University of Mary (formerly called Mary College) and its predecessor, the St. Alexius School of Nursing." Facilitates communication among members; provides voluntary and financial assistance to the University of Mary; sponsors student activities and other social programs. **Libraries: Type:** open to the public. **Holdings:** 70,000; audio recordings, books, periodicals, video recordings. **Subjects:** curriculum topics. **Awards:** University of Mary Bell Banner Award. **Frequency:** annual. **Type:** recognition. **Recipient:** for modeling the values of respect, hospitality, moderation, service, community, and prayer ● University of Mary Harold Schafer Alumni Leadership Award. **Frequency:** annual. **Type:** recognition. **Recipient:** for graduates who have attained distinction as leaders in their professions while exemplifying the value cherished by the University of Mary ● University of Mary Presidential Leadership Award. **Frequency:** annual. **Type:** recognition. **Recipient:** for distinguished achievements as servant leaders regionally or nationally. **Computer Services:** database ● mailing lists ● online services. **Councils:** Alumni. **Divisions:** Alumni Fargo Chapter. **Publications:** *Momentum*, 3-4/year. Magazine. Contains stories of alumni, staff and friends of the University of Mary. Alternate Formats: diskette. **Conventions/Meetings:** annual Christmas Appreciation Party - meeting ● annual Homecoming - party and reunion - September or October, depending on Homecoming dates.

18555 ■ University of Minnesota - Crookston Alumni Association (UMCAA)
2900 Univ. Ave.
Crookston, MN 56716-5000
Ph: (218)281-8434 (218)281-8439
Free: (800)232-6466
Fax: (218)281-8440
E-mail: ckemmer@umn.edu
URL: http://www.umcrookston.edu/alumni
Contact: Mr. Corby Kemmer, Dir. of Development
Founded: 1968. **Members:** 5,500. **Staff:** 3. **Description:** Graduates of the University of Minnesota - Crookston. Promotes continued communication and good fellowship among members; facilitates participation by members in University activities. Provides "a common organization for concerned people with common interests in the University of Minnesota - Crookston.". **Awards:** Distinguished Alumni. **Frequency:** annual. **Type:** recognition. **Recipient:** for individuals contributing to the advancement of the University of Minnesota Crookston and its programs. **Publications:** *The Torch*, 3/year. Magazine. **Circulation:** 5,500. Alternate Formats: online.

18556 ■ University of South Dakota Alumni Association
PO Box 5555
Vermillion, SD 57069-2390
Ph: (605)677-6734 (605)677-6714
Free: (800)655-2586
Fax: (605)677-6717
E-mail: alumni@usd.edu
URL: http://www.usd.edu/alumni
Contact: Courtney M. Marshall, Exec. Dir.
Founded: 1889. **Members:** 40,000. **Membership Dues:** single, $35 (annual) ● life, $500 ● young alumnus, $10 (annual) ● patron, $1,000 (quinquennial) ● household, $50 (annual). **Staff:** 2. **Budget:** $160,000. **Languages:** English, French, German, Lakota, Spanish. **Description:** Graduates and former students of the University of South Dakota. Seeks to "unite the alumni in a close bond of fellowship; to advance the purposes of the University; to foster and stimulate the loyalty of the alumni; and to promote united and constructive action by the alumni on behalf of the University." Sponsors social activities. **Libraries: Type:** reference. **Holdings:** 523,183; books, periodicals. **Subjects:** University of South Dakota, alumni activities. **Awards:** Alumni Achievement Awards. **Frequency:** annual. **Type:** recognition. **Recipient:** for outstanding contribution to the university, community, and the profession. **Computer Services:**

database, Raiser's Edge ● online services, Net donors - Blackbaud. **Telecommunication Services:** electronic mail, courtney.marshall@usd.edu. **Publications:** *The South Dakotan*, 3/year. Newsletter. Contains campus and Alumni news. **Price:** free. **Circulation:** 40,000. **Conventions/Meetings:** annual Dakota Days - meeting ● Homecoming - meeting ● semiannual meeting - spring and fall.

18557 ■ University of Texas at Brownsville and Texas Southmost College Alumni Association
80 Ft. Brown
Brownsville, TX 78520
Ph: (956)982-0106
Fax: (956)983-7990
E-mail: veronica.m.garcia@utb.edu
URL: http://blue.utb.edu/alumni
Contact: Veronica M. Garcia, Program Dir.
Founded: 1998. **Members:** 530. **Membership Dues:** active, $25 (annual). **Description:** Graduates and former students. Seeks to advance the university, the college, and its programs; encourages communication and good fellowship among members. Provides assistance to current students; facilitates continuing involvement of members in the college and the university activities.

18558 ■ University of Texas - Pan-American Alumni Association
1201 W Univ. Dr., UC108
Edinburg, TX 78541
Ph: (956)381-2500 (956)381-3665
Fax: (956)381-2385
E-mail: alumni@utpa.edu
URL: http://ea.panam.edu/alumni
Contact: Dale Winter, Pres.
Founded: 1977. **Members:** 400. **Membership Dues:** ordinary, $30 (annual) ● joint, $45 (annual) ● gold, $125 (annual) ● life, $575 ● life, joint, $675 ● chapter, $35 (annual) ● chapter joint, $50 (annual) ● student, $5 (annual) ● graduating, $10 (annual). **Staff:** 2. **Budget:** $100,000. **Description:** Graduates of the University of Texas - Pan American. Facilitates ongoing communication and good fellowship among members. Provides voluntary and financial support to the University of Texas - Pan American and its programs; sponsors social programs. **Awards:** Alumni Scholarships. **Frequency:** annual. **Type:** scholarship. **Recipient:** for UTPA students. **Publications:** Newsletter, quarterly.

18559 ■ University of Wisconsin - Eau Claire Alumni Association (UWECAA)
216 Schofield Hall
105 Garfield Ave.
PO Box 4004
Eau Claire, WI 54702-4004
Ph: (715)836-3266
Fax: (715)836-4375
E-mail: alumni@uwec.edu
URL: http://www.uwec.edu/alumni
Contact: John Bachmeier, Dir. of Alumni Relations
Founded: 1921. **Members:** 55,000. **Staff:** 2. **Regional Groups:** 2. **Description:** Graduates of the University of Wisconsin - Eau Claire. Seeks to advance the University and its programs; facilitates student development. Sponsors educational, service, cultural, and travel programs; co-sponsors Campus Ambassador program; maintains Connections network linking members with students seeking career and internship opportunities. **Awards:** Alumni Distinguished Service Award. **Frequency:** annual. **Type:** recognition. **Recipient:** for distinguished service to the community, state or nation ● Honorary Alumnus Award. **Frequency:** annual. **Type:** recognition. **Recipient:** to non-alumni who have demonstrated great love of and service to UW-Eau Claire ● Outstanding Recent Alumni Award. **Frequency:** annual. **Type:** recognition. **Recipient:** for special achievement and great promise of alumni ● President's Award. **Frequency:** annual. **Type:** recognition. **Recipient:** for outstanding professional and personal achievements and service to UW-Eau Claire.

18560 ■ University of Wisconsin - Platteville Alumni Association (UWPAA)
Royce Hall
1 Univ. Plz.
Platteville, WI 53818-3099
Ph: (608)342-1181 (608)342-1970
Free: (800)UWP-ALUM
Fax: (608)342-1196
E-mail: alumni@uwplatt.edu
URL: http://www.uwplatt.edu/alumni
Contact: Kim Schmelz, Asst. Dir.
Members: 6,000. **Membership Dues:** individual, $25 (annual) ● individual - life, $400 ● individual, $65 (triennial) ● couple, $40 (annual) ● couple, $100 (triennial) ● couple - life, $640. **Staff:** 4. **Budget:** $45,000. **Description:** Graduates of the University of Wisconsin - Platteville. Seeks to support and promote the University and its faculty, staff, students, and parents. Facilitates communication among members; sponsors social programs. **Awards:** Athletic Hall of Fame. **Frequency:** annual. **Type:** recognition. **Recipient:** for outstanding performance in intercollegiate athletics while a student at UWP; outstanding coaching performance of at least 15 years; or outstanding contributions to UWP intercollegiate athletics ● Distinguished Alumnus. **Frequency:** annual. **Type:** recognition. **Recipient:** for distinguished professional and career achievement and/or distinguished human service ● Outstanding Recent Alumnus. **Frequency:** annual. **Type:** recognition. **Recipient:** for outstanding Alumnus with significant success in profession and/or voluntary service.

18561 ■ Washburn Alumni Association (WAA)
1700 SW Coll. Ave.
Topeka, KS 66621
Ph: (785)670-1641 (785)670-1643
Fax: (785)670-1036
E-mail: wualumni@washburn.edu
URL: http://www.washburn.edu/alumni
Contact: Susie Hoffmann, Dir.
Founded: 1885. **Membership Dues:** individual, $35 (annual) ● couple, $50 (annual) ● student, $10 (annual) ● life - individual, $500 ● life - couple, $650. **Staff:** 4. **Description:** Graduates and former students of Washburn University of Topeka, KS. Promotes ongoing participation by members in the development of Washburn University and its programs. Facilitates communication and good fellowship among members; sponsors social and educational activities. **Awards:** Distinguished Service Award. **Frequency:** annual. **Type:** recognition. **Recipient:** for outstanding alumni who have made personal and professional contributions to society ● GOLD Award. **Frequency:** annual. **Type:** recognition. **Recipient:** for graduates of the last decade who demonstrate leadership in career or civic endeavors and loyalty to Washburn University ● Monroe Award. **Frequency:** annual. **Type:** recognition. **Recipient:** for a woman selected by the alumni board of directors who has given service to the community and/or her chosen profession ● Ruth Garvey Fink Award. **Frequency:** annual. **Type:** recognition. **Recipient:** for individuals who have furthered the mission of the Bradbury Thompson Center. **Publications:** *Ichabod Insider*, monthly. Newsletter. Alternate Formats: online ● Magazine, quarterly. **Price:** included in membership dues. Alternate Formats: online.

18562 ■ Wayland Baptist University Association of Former Students (AFS)
1900 W 7th St., No. 437
Plainview, TX 79072
Ph: (806)291-3600
Fax: (806)291-1966
E-mail: provencej@mail.wbu.edu
Contact: Joe L. Provence, Exec. Dir.
Founded: 1953. **Members:** 32,000. **Staff:** 2. **Description:** Graduates and former students of the Wayland Baptists University. Seeks to advance the university and its programs. Conducts fundraising and student recruitment programs; sponsors continuing professional development courses; compiles statistics. **Libraries: Type:** not open to the public; reference. **Holdings:** archival material, articles, busi-

ness records, clippings, periodicals. **Subjects:** university news, alumni news. **Awards:** Distinguished Alumni Awards. **Frequency:** annual. **Type:** recognition. **Publications:** *Footprints*, 3/year. Magazine. **Circulation:** 27,000. **Conventions/Meetings:** annual meeting, with homecoming.

18563 ■ Western New Mexico University Alumni Association (WNMUAA)
PO Box 680
Silver City, NM 88062
Ph: (505)538-6675
Free: (800)872-9668
Fax: (505)538-6243
E-mail: millerc@wnmu.edu
URL: http://www.wnmu.edu/alumni
Contact: Christy Miller, Alumni Dir.
Founded: 1893. **Members:** 10,000. **Membership Dues:** individual, $15 (annual) ● family, $25 (annual). **Staff:** 3. **Regional Groups:** 5. **State Groups:** 2. **Local Groups:** 1. **Description:** Graduates of Western New Mexico University. Seeks to "establish a mutually beneficial relationship between WNMU and its alumni", and to "promote in every way the best image, interests, and development of the University". Provides support and assistance to Western New Mexico University and its programs; sponsors social activities. **Libraries: Type:** open to the public. **Awards:** Outstanding Alumni Ambassador. **Frequency:** annual. **Type:** recognition ● Outstanding Distinguished Alumni. **Frequency:** annual. **Type:** recognition. **Publications:** *Alumni Bulletin*, semiannual. **Price:** free. **Circulation:** 9,000 ● Newsletter. Alternate Formats: online. **Conventions/Meetings:** semiannual meeting - always held in February.

18564 ■ William Penn University Alumni Association (WPUAA)
201 Trueblood Ave.
Oskaloosa, IA 52577-1799
Ph: (641)673-1046
Free: (800)779-7366
E-mail: eberlinej@wmpenn.edu
URL: http://www.wmpenn.edu
Contact: John Eberline, Dir. of Alumni Relations
Founded: 1873. **Members:** 5,600. **Staff:** 1. **Budget:** $40,000. **Local Groups:** 1. **Description:** Graduates of William Penn University. Promotes William Penn University and its programs; facilitates ongoing communication and good fellowship among members. Provides voluntary and financial support to William Penn University; sponsors social activities. **Awards:** Distinguished Career Award. **Frequency:** annual. **Type:** recognition. **Recipient:** for William Penn University graduate making an outstanding contribution in the chosen field of endeavor ● Distinguished Service Award. **Frequency:** annual. **Type:** recognition. **Recipient:** for individual whose life of service has been exemplary ● The Torch Award. **Frequency:** annual. **Type:** recognition. **Recipient:** for a family of two or more generations of attendance at WPU. **Formerly:** (2001) William Penn College Alumni Association. **Publications:** *Bulletin*, quarterly. Magazine. **Price:** free. **Circulation:** 13,000.

18565 ■ Wofford College National Alumni Association (WCNAA)
429 N Church St.
Spartanburg, SC 29303-3663
Ph: (864)597-4000
Fax: (864)597-4219
E-mail: graych@wofford.edu
URL: http://www.wofford.edu/alumni
Contact: James L. Switzer Jr., Pres.
Founded: 1854. **Members:** 14,000. **Staff:** 3. **Budget:** $61,800. **State Groups:** 2. **Local Groups:** 30. **Description:** Graduates of Wofford College. Seeks to "unite the alumni and friends of Wofford College in good fellowship and cooperative enterprise with the students, faculty, officers, and trustees of Wofford College." Provides voluntary and financial support to Wofford College and its programs; sponsors social activities; maintains alumni career network and alumni educational travel program. **Libraries: Type:** by appointment only. **Holdings:** 262,000; archival material, articles, artwork, books, clippings. **Subjects:**

Wofford College. **Awards:** Distinguished Citizen. **Frequency:** annual. **Type:** recognition. **Recipient:** to a non-alumnus: service to the college/community/country ● Distinguished Service. **Frequency:** annual. **Type:** recognition. **Recipient:** to an alumnus of the college: service to the college/community/country ● Young Alumnus of the Year. **Frequency:** annual. **Type:** recognition. **Recipient:** must be under 40 years of age: service to the college/community/country. **Councils:** Alumni Executive. **Publications:** *Wofford Today*, quarterly. Magazine. **Circulation:** 25,000. **Conventions/Meetings:** annual National Alumni Council Conference - meeting.

18566 ■ Worcester Polytechnic Institute Alumni Association (WPIAA)
100 Inst. Rd.
Worcester, MA 01609-2280
Ph: (508)831-5600
Fax: (508)831-5791
E-mail: alumni-office@wpi.edu
URL: http://alumni.wpi.edu
Contact: Pam DiScipio, Assoc. Dir.
Members: 27,000. **Staff:** 2. **Description:** Alumni and graduate alumni of the Worcester Polytechnic Institute. Seeks to advance the University and its programs. Facilitates communication and good fellowship among members; sponsors social activities. **Formerly:** (2004) Worcester Polytechnic Institute Alumni. **Publications:** *Transformations*, quarterly. Magazine. Contains information on the activities of the alumni. **Price:** free.

American Indian

18567 ■ Affiliated Tribes of Northwest Indians (ATNI)
1827 NE 44th Ave., Ste.130
Portland, OR 97213-1443
Ph: (503)249-5770
Fax: (503)249-5773
E-mail: atni@spiritone.com
URL: http://www.atnitribes.org
Contact: Ernest L. Stensgar, Pres.
Founded: 1953. **Members:** 54. **Membership Dues:** tribal (with 1-500 members), $200 (annual) ● tribal (with 501-1000 members), $400 (annual) ● tribal (with 1001-2000 members), $1,000 (annual) ● tribal (with 2001-3000 members), $1,500 (annual) ● tribal (with 3001 members or over), $2,000 (annual) ● individual, $35 (annual) ● individual (life), $200 ● tribal organization, $100 (annual) ● non-profit organization, $300 (annual) ● corporate, $500 (annual). **Description:** Promotes unity and cooperation among Indian governments and people. **Telecommunication Services:** electronic mail, elstensgar@cdatribe-nsn.gov. **Committees:** Cultural Affairs; Economic Development; Human and Social Services; Law and Justice; Natural Resources and Environment; Tribal Governance. **Publications:** *Native Peoples of the Northwest: A Travelers Guide to Land, Art and Culture*. Book. **Price:** $16.95. **Conventions/Meetings:** conference ● convention ● workshop.

Americans Overseas

18568 ■ American Citizens Abroad (ACA)
1051 N George Mason Dr.
Arlington, VA 22205
Ph: (703)276-0949
Fax: (703)527-3269
E-mail: jacabr@aol.com
URL: http://www.aca.ch
Contact: Jackie Abrams, Dir.
Founded: 1978. **Members:** 2,000. **Membership Dues:** student, $20 (annual) ● senior (over age 60), $30 (annual) ● individual/regular, $40 (annual) ● contributing, $100 (annual) ● life, $350 ● corporate sponsor, $500 (annual). **National Groups:** 45. **Description:** U.S. firms and associations headquartered outside the U.S; U.S. citizens who live and work abroad. Is dedicated to the principle that "the cultural, economic, political, and national security interests of

the U.S. can best be served by a flourishing, proud, and secure community of Americans living and working abroad". Purposes are to: promote a positive image of America overseas; expand foreign trade and exportation; foster American enterprise; inform and assist Americans overseas including teachers, scientists, missionaries, military personnel, writers, artists, engineers, business executives, and students. Works to educate Americans in the U.S. on the activities and concerns of Americans living and working abroad. Provides advice on Americans' rights overseas; monitors issues affecting overseas Americans such as tax policies, entrepreneurial opportunities, citizenship rights, and social security. **Awards:** Eugene Abrams Award. **Frequency:** annual. **Type:** recognition. **Recipient:** for an American volunteer citizen, over 60 years living abroad, who has made outstanding service to his/her community ● Thomas Jefferson Award. **Frequency:** annual. **Type:** recognition. **Recipient:** for state department employees who have made outstanding service to Americans residing abroad. **Computer Services:** Online services, bi-weekly news update. **Publications:** *ACA News Report*, 3-4/year. Newsletter. Provides news and information of interest to Americans living abroad. **Price:** included in membership dues. **Circulation:** 4,500. **Advertising:** accepted ● *Handbook for Overseas Americans* ● Also publishes issues ACA Press Service releases to English language publications overseas. **Conventions/Meetings:** annual general assembly, report of activities, election of directors - May or June.

Appalachian

18569 ■ Melungeon Heritage Association (MHA)
PO Box 4042
Wise, VA 24293
E-mail: mhainc2000@yahoo.com
URL: http://www.melungeon.org
Contact: S.J. Arthur, Pres.
Founded: 1998. **Members:** 1,000. **Description:** Documents and preserves the heritage and cultural legacy of mixed-ancestry peoples in or associated with the Southern Appalachians, with particular interest in those of Melungeon heritage. **Affiliated With:** Assembly of Turkish American Associations. **Publications:** *The Melungeon Heritage Association News*, annual. Newsletter. **Price:** free. **Circulation:** 1,000. **Conventions/Meetings:** semiannual conference, part academic conference, part family reunion.

Arab

18570 ■ Arab American Women's Council
c/o American Arab Chamber of Commerce
12740 W Warren Ave., Ste.101
Dearborn, MI 48126
Ph: (313)945-1700
Fax: (313)945-6697
E-mail: chamber@americanarab.com
URL: http://www.americanarab.com
Contact: Nasser Beydoun, Chm.
Description: Mentors and promotes professional women of Arab descent and women's issues in the marketplace.

Arabic

18571 ■ Arab Community Center for Economic and Social Services (ACCESS)
2651 Saulino Ct.
Dearborn, MI 48120
Ph: (313)842-7010
Fax: (313)842-5150
E-mail: iahmed@accesscommunity.org
URL: http://www.accesscommunity.org
Contact: Ismael Ahmed, Exec. Dir.
Membership Dues: individual, $20 (annual) ● family, $30 (annual). **Description:** Seeks for the develop-

ment of the Arab-American community in all aspects of economic and cultural life. **Programs:** National Arts Network. **Publications:** Newsletter, quarterly.

18572 ■ Association of Arab-American University Graduates (AAUG)
211 E 4th St.
New York, NY 10009
E-mail: khalil@stanford.edu
URL: http://www.aaug-asq.org
Contact: Khalil Barhoum, Pres.
Founded: 1967. **Membership Dues:** regular, $65 (annual) ● student, $35 (annual). **Description:** Promotes knowledge and understanding of cultural, scientific, and educational matters between the Arab and American peoples; establishes links among Arab-American professionals and promotes their professional activities and projects. Assists in the development of the Arab World by providing the professional services of its membership. Sponsors symposia and speakers' bureau. **Awards: Frequency:** annual. **Type:** recognition. **Publications:** *AAUG Newsletter*, quarterly. Covers membership activities. **Price:** included in membership dues. **Advertising:** accepted ● *Arab Studies Quarterly*. Journal. Covers Middle East history, economics, politics, and culture. Contains book reviews. **Price:** included in membership dues; $24.00 /year for nonmembers; $40.00 /year for institutions. ISSN: 0271-3519. **Advertising:** accepted ● *Mideast Monitor*, periodic. Newsletter. Contains analyses and commentary on U.S. foreign policy and Arab affairs. **Price:** included in membership dues. ISSN: 0888-2460 ● Also publishes information papers, books, and monographs on contemporary Arab society, culture, and politics. **Conventions/Meetings:** annual conference (exhibits).

18573 ■ United North Lebanon Society
Address Unknown since 2007
Description: Works to unite immigrants from northern villages of Lebanon; maintains close affiliation with Detroit's Maronite churches. **Conventions/Meetings:** quarterly banquet ● monthly meeting.

Armed Forces

18574 ■ AFBA, The 5Star Association
909 N Washington St.
Alexandria, VA 22314
Ph: (703)549-4455
Free: (800)776-2322
Fax: (703)706-5961
E-mail: info@afba.com
URL: http://www.afba.com
Contact: Gen. Ralph E. Eberhard USAF, Pres.
Founded: 1947. **Members:** 295,000. **Staff:** 125. **Description:** Term and permanent insurance association for commissioned and warrant officers and noncommissioned officers in grades E-1 through E-9 of the U.S. Army, Navy, Air Force, Marine Corps, Coast Guard, Public Health Service, National Oceanic and Atmospheric Administration, cadets and midshipmen at the U.S. service academies, and other candidates in U.S. military officer programs, either on active duty or in the National Guard or Ready Reserve. Affiliates offer banking, mutual funds, and Tricare supplement. **Formerly:** (1993) Armed Forces Relief and Benefit Association; (2003) Armed Forces Benefit Association. **Publications:** *Financial Planning Guide for Military Personnel*, annual. Book. Contains in-depth guidance and detailed benefits available to military personnel and their families. **Price:** free for active duty ● Newsletter, quarterly. Contains president's message and activities of the organization. Alternate Formats: online. **Conventions/Meetings:** annual meeting, for members - always May.

18575 ■ Air Force Aid Society (AFAS)
241 18th St. S, Ste.202
Arlington, VA 22202
Ph: (703)607-3034
Free: (800)769-8951
Fax: (703)607-3022

E-mail: dvosburg@afas.org
URL: http://www.afas.org
Contact: Lt. Gen. John D. Hopper Jr., CEO
Founded: 1942. **Staff:** 24. **Nonmembership. Description:** Collects and holds funds to relieve the distress of active, retired, and selected Reserve Air Force personnel and their dependents, including those of deceased personnel. Operates through local units on all major U.S. Air Force installations worldwide. Education Loan programs are offered to members, to assist in financing postsecondary education; education grants are also offered to dependent children of active duty, retired, and deceased Air Force members. **Programs:** Bundles for Babies; Car Care Because We Care; Child Care for PCS; Child Care for Volunteers; General George S. Brown Spouse Tuition Assistance; Give Parents a Break; Respite Care; Spouse Orientation. **Publications:** Annual Report, annual. Alternate Formats: online.

18576 ■ Army and Air Force Mutual Aid Association (AAFMAA)
102 Sheridan Ave., Bldg. 468
Fort Myer, VA 22211-1110
Ph: (703)522-3060
Free: (866)422-3622
Fax: (703)522-1336
E-mail: info@aafmaa.com
URL: http://www.aafmaa.com
Contact: Ret. Major Walt Lincoln CFP, Pres./Treas.
Founded: 1879. **Members:** 65,315. **Staff:** 37. **Budget:** $4,496,871. **Description:** Provides aid to families of deceased career Army and Air Force service members of all ranks by payment of life insurance benefits, and survivor support. **Formerly:** (1987) Army Mutual Aid Association. **Publications:** *AAFMAA Advantage*. Newsletter. Alternate Formats: online ● *In Your Interest*, quarterly. Newsletter ● Annual Report, annual. Alternate Formats: online. **Conventions/Meetings:** annual meeting - always second Tuesday of April, Ft. Myer, VA.

18577 ■ Army Emergency Relief (AER)
200 Stovall St.
Alexandria, VA 22332-0001
Ph: (703)428-0000
Free: (866)878-6378
Fax: (703)325-7183
E-mail: aer@aerhq.org
URL: http://www.aerhq.org
Contact: Ret. Gen. E.C. Meyer, Pres.
Founded: 1942. **Staff:** 16. **Description:** A private organization whose primary purpose is to relieve distress of members of the Army (active and retired) and their dependents, and to provide assistance to needy spouses and orphans of deceased Army members; a secondary purpose is to make available educational assistance (scholarships) to unmarried dependent children of soldiers (active, retired, or deceased) who need such assistance to pursue undergraduate studies. **Programs:** Dependent Children Education; Spouse Education. **Absorbed:** (1976) Army Relief Society. **Conventions/Meetings:** annual meeting - always second Wednesday of April, in Alexandria, VA.

18578 ■ Military Benefit Association (MBA)
PO Box 221110
Chantilly, VA 20153-1110
Ph: (703)968-6200
Free: (800)336-0100
E-mail: bbarnum@militarybenefit.org
URL: http://www.militarybenefit.org
Contact: G.A. Barnum, Pres.
Founded: 1956. **Members:** 125,000. **Staff:** 28. **Description:** Active reserve and retired U.S. military personnel and U.S. government civilian personnel and their spouses. Provides group life insurance and other benefits. **Awards:** MBA Scholarship. **Frequency:** annual. **Type:** scholarship. **Recipient:** for dependent children of members. **Formerly:** Armed Forces Enlisted Personnel Benefit Association. **Conventions/Meetings:** annual meeting - always third Friday of October, in Washington, DC.

18579 ■ Navy-Marine Corps Relief Society (NMCRS)
875 N Randolph St., Ste.225
Arlington, VA 22203-1767
Ph: (703)696-4904
Fax: (703)696-0144
E-mail: alexande@hq.nmcrs.org
URL: http://www.nmcrs.org
Contact: Ret. Adm. Charles S. Abbot USN, Pres./CEO
Founded: 1904. **Staff:** 300. **Description:** Works to assist, financially and otherwise, Navy and Marine Corps personnel and their dependents in times of need. Provides visiting nurses, budget counseling, thrift shops and food lockers, scholarships and loans for post-secondary education, interest-free loans and outright grants. Provides services that are carried by auxiliaries located at major Naval and Marine Corps stations and branches at minor stations. **Awards:** Admiral Mike Boorda Scholarship Program. **Frequency:** annual. **Type:** grant. **Recipient:** to eligible active duty sailors and marines ● Dependents of Deceased Service Members Scholarship Program. **Frequency:** annual. **Type:** grant. **Recipient:** to students who are military dependents of deceased service members ● USS Tennessee Scholarship Fund. **Frequency:** annual. **Type:** grant. **Recipient:** to dependent children of service members who are serving aboard USS Tennessee ● Vice Admiral E.P. Travers Scholarship and Loan Program. **Frequency:** annual. **Type:** scholarship. **Recipient:** for the dependent children or spouses of active and retired Navy and Marine Corps personnel. **Formerly:** (1991) Navy Relief Society. **Publications:** Annual Report, annual. Alternate Formats: online. **Conventions/Meetings:** annual meeting - always second Thursday in April, Washington, DC.

18580 ■ Navy Mutual Aid Association (NMAA)
Henderson Hall
29 Carpenter Rd.
Arlington, VA 22212
Ph: (703)614-1638
Free: (800)628-6011
Fax: (703)695-4635
E-mail: info@navymutual.org
URL: http://www.navymutual.org
Contact: Ret. Rear Admiral Philip J. Coady CLU, Pres.
Founded: 1879. **Members:** 100,000. **Staff:** 65. **Description:** Veterans' benefits organization providing life insurance and services to Navy, Marine Corps, Coast Guard, National Oceanic and Atmospheric Administration, and Public Health Service personnel. **Libraries: Type:** reference. **Holdings:** reports. **Publications:** *Member Services Handbook*. Alternate Formats: online ● *Navy Mutual Aid News*, quarterly. Newsletter. Alternate Formats: online ● Annual Report, annual. Alternate Formats: online. **Conventions/Meetings:** annual meeting - always April, Arlington, VA.

18581 ■ USO World Headquarters
2111 Wilson Blvd., Ste.1200
Arlington, VA 22201
Ph: (703)908-6400
Free: (800)876-7469
Fax: (703)908-6402
E-mail: info@uso.org
URL: http://www.uso.org
Contact: Edward A. Powell Jr., Pres./CEO
Founded: 1941. **Staff:** 400. **Budget:** $28,600,000. **Regional Groups:** 3. **State Groups:** 83. **Description:** Aims to serve the social, welfare, spiritual, recreational, and community involvement needs of U.S. service persons and their dependents. Seeks to provide through a voluntary civilian agency, programs, and services that enhance the quality of life and improve morale. Operates service facilities and outreach programs in 169 locations throughout the U.S. and overseas. Provides celebrity entertainment to isolated military commands overseas. Maintains biographical and historical archives of annual reports, newsletters, and photos. Operates charitable program and children's services; sponsors competitions. Offers professional staff training and conferences. Major

program services include: family assistance; cultural understanding; community outreach; information and referral; informal counseling and education; recreation. Financed through voluntary contributions from individuals, corporations, United Way International, and Combined Federal Campaigns. **Libraries: Type:** open to the public. **Awards:** Civic Achievement Award. **Frequency:** annual. **Type:** recognition ● Distinguished Service Award. **Frequency:** annual. **Type:** recognition. **Departments:** Administration; Development; Executive; Regional Executive Atlantic; Regional Executive Pacific. **Also Known As:** United Service Organizations. **Publications:** *USO Directory of Locations*, annual ● Annual Report, annual. Alternate Formats: online. **Conventions/Meetings:** board meeting - 3/year.

Armenian

18582 ■ Ararat Foundation
Address Unknown since 2007
Founded: 1985. **Staff:** 3. **Description:** Promotes Armenian culture and Christian faith. Disseminates information on Armenian art, music, history, and crafts. Conducts research on Armenian manuscripts. Conducts educational programs. Maintains speakers' bureau. **Publications:** none.

18583 ■ Armenian General Benevolent Union (AGBU)
55 E 59th St.
New York, NY 10022-1112
Ph: (212)319-6383
Fax: (212)319-6507
E-mail: agbuwb@agbu.org
URL: http://www.agbu.org
Contact: Berge Setrakian, Pres.
Founded: 1906. **Members:** 22,000. **Membership Dues:** individual, $50 (annual) ● family, $100 (annual) ● student, senior, $25 (annual) ● life, $10,000. **Staff:** 500. **Budget:** $36,000,000. **Description:** Humanitarian, cultural, and educational organization established to promote Armenian heritage. Operates 70 schools, chapters, and centers worldwide. Provides summer intern programs, and has established the American University of Armenia, along with other major medical, educational, and cultural institutions in Armenia. **Awards: Type:** scholarship. **Recipient:** to college and university students. **Programs:** New York Summer Intern; Paris Summer Intern. **Formerly:** (1982) Armenian General Benevolent Union of America. **Publications:** *AGBU News*, quarterly. Magazine. Informs the public of the accomplishments, concerns and life of Armenians in over 23 countries. **Price:** free for members; $25.00 /year for nonmembers. **Circulation:** 85,000. **Advertising:** accepted ● *Ararat*, quarterly. Magazine. **Price:** $24.00/year; $7.00/copy. **Circulation:** 1,200 ● *Hoosharar* (in Armenian and English), quarterly. Magazine. Provides news concerning the AGBU. **Price:** free for members; $10.00 /year for nonmembers. **Circulation:** 5,000. **Conventions/Meetings:** biennial general assembly - always November.

18584 ■ Armenian National Committee of America (ANCA)
1711 N St. NW
Washington, DC 20036
Ph: (202)775-1918
Fax: (202)775-5648
E-mail: anca@anca.org
URL: http://www.anca.org
Contact: Aram S. Hamparian, Exec. Dir.
Founded: 1958. **Members:** 5,000. **Staff:** 3. **Budget:** $250,000. **Regional Groups:** 3. **State Groups:** 45. **Languages:** Armenian, English. **Description:** Lobbying arm of the Armenian Revolutionary Federation (see separate entry), which promotes the return of the eastern half of Turkey to the Armenians. Acts as advocate for the Armenian community in America; promotes recognition of the "genocide of Armenians" by the Turkish government; calls for reparations to Armenians for damages and loss of property; supports demands of Armenians in Soviet Armenia for

reunification of their territories in the USSR; disseminates information on current events in Armenia. Conducts research, seminars, lectures, and workshops; sponsors educational programs and forums; operates speakers' bureau for schools and other institutions. Sponsors internship program for work in the offices of elected officials. **Committees:** Communications; Conflict Resolution; Human Rights; Information Systems; Political Action; Post Soviet Issues; Research; Voter Education. **Publications:** Newsletter, quarterly ● Papers. Alternate Formats: online. **Conventions/Meetings:** annual conference.

18585 ■ Armenian Relief Society of Eastern USA (ARSER)
80 Bigelow Ave., Ste.200
Watertown, MA 02472
Ph: (617)926-3801
Fax: (617)924-7238
E-mail: arseastus@aol.com
URL: http://www.ars1910.org
Contact: Ungerouhi Varthouhie Chiloyan, Exec. Sec.
Founded: 1910. **Members:** 14,000. **Staff:** 1. **Regional Groups:** 33. **Description:** Armenian women and men throughout the world; includes 3,200 members in the U.S. and Canada. Raises and distributes money for relief of Armenian people and for advancement of educational and cultural activities. Helps support and operate 50 Armenian language classes in America. Provides support for: Armenian day schools in Easter USA and abroad; clinics; concerts, lectures, and dramatic programs; fresh air camps; orphanages and sanitariums. **Awards:** Undergraduate and Lazarian Graduate. **Frequency:** annual. **Type:** scholarship. **Recipient:** for needy students. **Additional Websites:** http://www.arseastus.com. **Committees:** Annual Fund Drive; Educational; Relief; Scholarship; Summer Studies. **Councils:** Armenian National Educational. **Programs:** Armenian Schools; Camp Haiastan; Essay Contest; Project in Armenia, Karabagh, Javakhk; Sponsor A Child. **Formerly:** (1946) Armenian Red Cross; (1981) Armenian Relief Society. **Publications:** *Hai Sird*, annual. Newsletter. Also Cited As: *Armenian Heart* ● Bulletin, periodic ● Also publishes ethnic heritage materials and produces slides and tapes for bilingual studies. **Conventions/Meetings:** annual workshop and convention.

18586 ■ Armenian Students' Association of America (ASA)
333 Atlantic Ave.
Warwick, RI 02888
Ph: (401)461-6114
E-mail: asa@asainc.org
URL: http://www.asainc.org
Contact: Vartges Saroyan, Pres.
Founded: 1910. **Members:** 1,500. **Membership Dues:** individual, $15 (annual) ● double, $28 (annual) ● student, $10 (annual) ● associate life, $200 ● life, $500. **Regional Groups:** 10. **Description:** Provides financial assistance in the form of scholarships and loans to deserving Armenian students. Develops fellowship and cultivate the spirit of service in the public interest. Acquaints members and the entire American community with Armenian culture. Maintains speakers' bureau. **Awards: Type:** recognition. **Recipient:** for notable Armenian-Americans in the fields of citizenship, humanities, science, and business ● **Frequency:** annual. **Type:** scholarship. **Recipient:** for full time students of Armenian descent attending a four-year accredited college or university in the U.S. **Committees:** Artists' Project; Boyan Award; Dadian Armenian Heritage Award; Gold Medal Awards; Kabakjian Award; Sarafian Award; Scholarship; Silver Medal Awards; Zakian Award. **Programs:** Work For Armenia: Internship. **Publications:** Newsletter, quarterly ● Booklet, annual ● Directory, annual. **Conventions/Meetings:** competition ● annual meeting.

18587 ■ Armenian Women's Welfare Association (AWWA)
PO Box 191
Belmont, MA 02478
Ph: (617)484-2602

Fax: (617)524-7024
E-mail: info@awwa-inc.org
URL: http://www.awwa-inc.org
Contact: Ms. JoAnn Janjigian, Pres.
Founded: 1915. **Members:** 200. **Membership Dues:** individual, $25 (annual) ● life, $500. **Languages:** Armenian, English. **Description:** Women interested in helping with charitable work. Raises funds to maintain highest quality nursing home to care for the aged. Aims to improve quality of life for members of Armenian community through aid, relief or education. Underwrites a project to improve healthcare of elderly in Nagoro Karabagh. **Committees:** Bylaws; Fund Raising; Investment. **Publications:** *AWWA Membership Brochure*. **Circulation:** 3,400 ● *Newsletter of the Armenian Nursing and Rehabilitation Center*, semiannual. **Conventions/Meetings:** annual meeting - always Boston, MA.

18588 ■ Association of Armenian Information Professionals (AAIP)
139 Cedar St.
Cliffside Park, NJ 07010
Ph: (201)941-2266
Fax: (201)941-5110
Contact: Dr. Anie Kalayjian, Sec.
Founded: 1992. **Members:** 50. **Membership Dues:** professional, $25 (annual) ● student, $10 (annual) ● institutional, $50 (annual) ● life, $500. **Languages:** Armenian, English. **Description:** Professionals in various fields, interested in bilingual information science. Promotes the advancement of information professionals concerned with such issues. **Computer Services:** database ● mailing lists. **Publications:** *Journal of the Association of Armenian Information Professionals* (in Armenian and English), semiannual. **Price:** $10.00/issue. ISSN: 1077-2790. **Circulation:** 100. **Advertising:** accepted. Also Cited As: *JAAIP*. **Conventions/Meetings:** quarterly meeting.

18589 ■ Hairenik Association
80 Bigelow Ave.
Watertown, MA 02472
Ph: (617)926-3974 (617)926-3976
Fax: (617)926-1750
E-mail: armenianweekly@hairenik.com
URL: http://www.hairenik.com
Contact: Vahe Habeshian, Mgr.
Founded: 1899. **Membership Dues:** regular, $60 (annual). **Staff:** 10. **Budget:** $500,000. **Languages:** Armenian, English. **Description:** Publishes books; produces videos. Maintains online radio station. **Publications:** *The Armenian Weekly*. Newspaper. **Price:** $75.00/year in U.S.; $95.00/year in Canada; $180.00/year in other countries. ISSN: 0004-2374. **Circulation:** 3,000. **Advertising:** accepted ● *Hairenik Weekly*. Newspaper. **Price:** $60.00. **Circulation:** 1,200. **Advertising:** accepted. **Conventions/Meetings:** annual convention.

Arumanian

18590 ■ Society Farsarotul (SF)
PO Box 753
799 Silver Ln.
Trumbull, CT 06611
Ph: (203)375-0600
Fax: (203)375-5003
E-mail: secretary@farsarotul.org
URL: http://www.farsarotul.org
Contact: William D. Balamaci, Pres.
Founded: 1903. **Members:** 400. **Membership Dues:** regular and supporting (plus $5 initial fee), $18 (annual) ● student (plus $5 initial fee), $9 (annual). **Staff:** 15. **Description:** Persons of Arumanian descent, including Vlachs, Aromanians, Tsintsars, and Macedo-Romanians. Seeks to preserve the history, language, and culture of this ethnic group. Provides information on Arumanians; conducts research on Arumanian history; prepares music, poetry, and language tapes. Maintains scholarship fund for Arumanians; aids members in cases of sickness or distress. Plans to establish museum for the preservation of ethnic artifacts. **Libraries: Type:** reference.

Holdings: 300. **Publications:** *Newsletter of the Society of Farsarotul*, semiannual. Covers Vlachs, Macedo-Romanians, and the Aromanian community in America. **Price:** included in membership dues. ISSN: 1042-3230. **Circulation:** 250 ● Prepares bibliography and other reference materials. Sells, but does not publish additional books covering the Vlachs. **Conventions/Meetings:** annual general assembly - always in Bridgeport, CT.

Asian

18591 ■ Asian/Pacific American Heritage Association (APAHA)
6220 Westpark, Ste.245B
Houston, TX 77057
Ph: (713)784-1112
Fax: (832)201-8228
E-mail: info@apaha.org
URL: http://www.apaha.org
Contact: Linh Doan, Pres.
Founded: 1992. **Membership Dues:** individual, $25 (annual) ● life, $100 ● additional family, $15 (annual) ● life (additional family), $75. **Description:** Promotes awareness of the Asian/Pacific American culture and diversity through education and celebration.

18592 ■ Asian Pacific American Heritage Council (APAHC)
c/o Dr. Mark L. Au, Chm.
8800 Fox Hills Trl.
Potomac, MD 20854-4211
Ph: (301)983-1845 (301)983-0042
E-mail: mlau2@aol.com
Contact: Mary Lau, Pres.
Founded: 1978. **Members:** 17. **Staff:** 10. **Multinational. Description:** Asian/Pacific Islander organizations united to promote a better understanding of Asian/Pacific-Americans. Responsible for the official recognition of Asian Pacific American Heritage Week, held in May. Holds congressional reception, tennis and table tennis tournaments, festival, and poster competition in connection with Heritage Week. Bestows awards; maintains speakers' bureau. **Awards:** Asian Pacific American Heritage Council Award. **Frequency:** annual. **Type:** scholarship. **Publications:** *Heritage Week Booklet*, annual. **Conventions/Meetings:** monthly meeting, for members of the Council.

Asian-American

18593 ■ ASIAN
1167 Mission St., 4th Fl.
San Francisco, CA 94103
Ph: (415)928-5910
Free: (800)359-7998
Fax: (415)921-0182
E-mail: supplier@asianinc.org
URL: http://www.asianinc.org
Contact: Frank Fung, Chm.
Founded: 1971. **Languages:** Cantonese, English, Japanese, Mandarin Dialects, Tagalog, Vietnamese. **Description:** Works to strengthen the infrastructure of Asian-American communities in Northern California; assists in their physical, economic, and social development. Strives to empower Asian-American communities to achieve social equality and obtain their material civil rights. **Libraries: Type:** reference. **Holdings:** 25,000.

Australian

18594 ■ American Australian Association (AAA)
599 Lexington Ave., 18th Fl.
New York, NY 10022
Ph: (212)338-6860
Fax: (212)338-6864

E-mail: information@aaanyc.org
URL: http://www.americanaustralian.org
Contact: Ms. Frances M. Cassidy, Pres.
Founded: 1948. **Members:** 900. **Membership Dues:** individual, $80 (annual) ● family, $120 (annual) ● student, senior, $40 (annual) ● platinum, $10,000 (annual) ● gold, $6,000 (annual) ● silver, $3,000 (annual) ● bronze, $1,000 (annual) ● affiliate, $500 (annual). **Staff:** 6. **Budget:** $1,000,000. **Description:** Acts as an advisory body in the area of Australian-American and New Zealand-American relations, in a non-commercial capacity. Meets with and hosts leading Australian and New Zealand business and political figures visiting the U.S. **Libraries: Type:** not open to the public. **Holdings:** 400. **Subjects:** Australia. **Awards: Frequency:** annual. **Type:** monetary. **Recipient:** to postgraduate students in U.S. or Australia ● Terry Magill Award. **Frequency:** annual. **Type:** recognition. **Recipient:** for contribution to the relationship between Australia/New Zealand and the U.S. **Telecommunication Services:** electronic mail, gabriel.saffioti@aaanyc.org. **Programs:** Corporate; Cultural; Educational; Internship; Philanthropic; Social. **Publications:** *Network*, 8/year. Newsletter. **Price:** included in membership dues. **Circulation:** 2,000. **Advertising:** accepted. Alternate Formats: online ● Annual Report, annual. Alternate Formats: online ● Membership Directory. Alternate Formats: online. **Conventions/Meetings:** annual Australia Day Ball - meeting, for members ● annual Benefit Dinner - usually September/October, New York, NY.

Austrian

18595 ■ American-Austrian Society (A-AS)
c/o Mrs. Urlike Wiesner, Sec.
5618 Dover Ct.
Alexandria, VA 22312
E-mail: american_austrian_society@yahoo.com
URL: http://www.geocities.com/americanaustriansociety
Contact: Hugh Montgomery, Pres.
Founded: 1954. **Members:** 400. **Membership Dues:** single, $20 (annual) ● family, $30 (annual) ● contributor, $50-$99 (annual) ● patron, $100-$499 (annual) ● benefactor/corporate sponsor, $500 (annual). **Description:** Aims to encourage and support the perennial friendship between the United States and Austria. Promotes the understanding of Austrian culture. Assists both American and Austrian institutions in bringing educational programs about Austrian arts, science, and trade to the Washington metropolitan area. Sponsors or supports several cultural events each year that take place at the Embassy of Austria and at other locations in the Washington Metropolitan area; most of these events are open to the general public; its stimulating cultural and educational programs are centered on the artistic, humanistic, and scientific achievements of Austrians and Americans with ties to Austria. **Awards:** Distinguished Membership Citation. **Type:** recognition. **Recipient:** for long-term membership and active support ● Distinguished Service Citation. **Type:** recognition. **Recipient:** for special services rendered to the Society. **Publications:** *A-A Society*, periodic. Newsletter. **Conventions/Meetings:** annual Christmas Ball - party, formal dinner dance ● annual meeting.

Awards

18596 ■ International Gold and Silver Plate Society (IGSPS)
c/o International Foodservice Manufacturers Association
2 Prudential Plz., 180 N Stetson, Ste.4400
Chicago, IL 60601
Ph: (312)540-4400
Fax: (312)540-4401
E-mail: ifma@ifmaworld.com
URL: http://www.ifmaworld.com
Contact: Michael Licata, Trustee
Founded: 1974. **Members:** 175. **Description:** Recipients of Gold and Silver Plate awards bestowed by

the International Foodservice Manufacturers Association (see separate entry). Recipients of awards will, upon request, serve as speakers on their respective area of expertise. **Awards: Type:** recognition. **Recipient:** for outstanding contributions in business and industry, chain fast service, chain full service, colleges and universities, contract food management, elementary and secondary schools, health care hotels and lodgings and independent restaurant operator. **Publications:** *IGSPS Newsletter*, semiannual. Includes IGSPS events. **Circulation:** 1,100 ● *International Gold and Silver Plate Society Roster*, annual. Membership Directory. **Conventions/Meetings:** annual meeting - always spring.

Baltic

18597 ■ Baltic Women's Council (BWC)
c/o Margrita Buss, Coor.
39-65 52nd St.
Woodside, NY 11377
Ph: (718)672-5558
Contact: Helga Ozolins, Pres.
Founded: 1947. **Staff:** 7. **National Groups:** 3. **Description:** Estonian, Latvian, and Lithuanian women's clubs in the U.S. and overseas. To unite the women of Estonian, Latvian, and Lithuanian origin; to preserve native culture; to assist with the development of their countries of birth; to promote the spirit of Baltic solidarity and friendship among the young generations. Sponsors literary, arts, and musical events. Works for reunification of Baltic refugee families. **Divisions:** Estonian Delegation; Latvian Delegation; Lithuanian Delegation. **Affiliated With:** General Federation of Women's Clubs. **Conventions/Meetings:** annual meeting - always March, New York City.

18598 ■ Lithuanian World Community (LWC)
c/o Lithuanian World Center
14911 W 127th St.
Lemont, IL 60439
Ph: (630)257-8787
Fax: (630)257-6887
E-mail: lwcpl@sbcglobal.net
URL: http://www.lithuaniancenter.org
Contact: Vytautas Kamantas, VP
Founded: 1949. **National Groups:** 27. **Languages:** English, French, German, Lithuanian, Polish, Portuguese, Russian, Spanish. **Description:** Represents Lithuanians and individuals of Lithuanian descent living abroad. Coordinates and sponsors activities for Lithuanian communities worldwide. Disseminates information on issues affecting Lithuanian culture. **Affiliated With:** Lithuanian-American Community. **Publications:** *Lithuanian Customs and Traditions* ● *World Lithuanian* (in English and Lithuanian), monthly. Magazine. **Price:** $20.00/year. **Circulation:** 5,000. **Conventions/Meetings:** quadrennial congress.

18599 ■ United Baltic Appeal (UBA)
115 W 183 St.
Bronx, NY 10453-1103
Ph: (718)367-8802
Fax: (718)562-7434
E-mail: pinnis@banet.net
URL: http://www.batun.org
Contact: Margers Pinnis, Pres.
Founded: 1966. **Members:** 1,200. **Membership Dues:** individual, $40 (annual) ● family, $60 ● pensioner, $20 ● organization, $125 ● student, $30. **Staff:** 1. **Budget:** $24,000. **Languages:** English, Estonian, Latvian, Lithuanian. **Multinational. Description:** Individuals of Estonian, Latvian, or Lithuanian descent; professionals interested in the Baltic region. Serves as an information center dealing with events and circumstances pertinent to Estonia, Latvia, and Lithuania. Works with United Nations on behalf of Baltic states; sponsors summer internships and festivals; maintains speakers' bureau. Conducts seminars. **Libraries: Type:** reference. **Holdings:** 500; books. **Subjects:** history and politics. **Also Known As:** Baltic Association to the United Nations. **Publications:** *Baltic Chronology*, annual. Reviews

events in the Baltic states. **Price:** included in membership dues. **Conventions/Meetings:** annual meeting - always in New York City.

18600 ■ World Federation of Estonian Women's Clubs (WFEWCE)
c/o Mrs. Juta Kurman, Pres.
68-50 Juno St.
Forest Hills, NY 11375
Ph: (718)261-9618
Fax: (718)261-9618
Contact: Mrs. Juta Kurman, Pres.
Founded: 1966. **Members:** 50. **Membership Dues:** donation, $10 (annual). **Staff:** 5. **Budget:** $200. **Regional Groups:** 5. **State Groups:** 2. **Local Groups:** 2. **National Groups:** 3. **Languages:** English, Estonian. **Description:** Women's clubs and individuals in Australia, Canada, and the United States. Seeks to preserve Estonian language and ethnic culture; supports the development of independent Estonia. Conducts charitable programs; maintains speakers' bureau; compiles statistics. **Libraries: Type:** reference. **Holdings:** 150; archival material, artwork, books, business records, clippings, monographs. **Subjects:** Estonian, Baltic and American art and literature, specifically Estonian women in perspective at different times, sheet music. **Awards:** Honorary Member. **Frequency:** annual. **Type:** recognition. **Recipient:** for outstanding achievements and services. **Committees:** Cultural; Estonian Women's Clubs; Political Action. **Affiliated With:** General Federation of Women's Clubs. **Formerly:** (1982) Federated Estonian Women's Clubs; (2004) World Federation of Estonian Women's Clubs in Exile. **Publications:** *Shawl of Haapsalu* (in English and Estonian). Booklet. Explains techniques for knitting the shawl of Haapsalu. **Price:** $6.00 ● Also publishes circulars and letters. **Conventions/Meetings:** quinquennial Estonian World Festival.

Belgian

18601 ■ Belgian American Association
Address Unknown since 2007
Founded: 1992. **Members:** 150. **Membership Dues:** individual, $50 (annual) ● couple, $75 (annual). **Budget:** $10,000. **Description:** Individuals and firms united to better the relationship between the U.S. and Belgium, to make Belgium better known in the U.S., and to make Americans more appreciated in Belgium. Activities include cultural presentations, roundtable talks, organization of meetings for businessmen, film showings, and luncheons/dinners in honor of important Belgian visitors. **Publications:** *Belgian American Association Newsletter*, quarterly. **Price:** free to members. **Advertising:** accepted. **Conventions/Meetings:** monthly Executive Committee Meeting; **Avg. Attendance:** 6.

Blood

18602 ■ Associated Health Foundation (AHF)
2347 Jericho Tpke., 2nd Fl.
New Hyde Park, NY 11040
Ph: (516)739-9500
Fax: (516)739-9700
E-mail: ahs4health@aol.com
Contact: Edward Birnbaum, Pres.
Founded: 1937. **Members:** 20,000. **Staff:** 3. **Description:** Extends life-saving services to members through incentive benefits. Contributes to hospitals and institutions that carry on research.

British

18603 ■ British Schools and Universities Club of New York (BSUCNY)
c/o The Williams Club
24 E 39th St.
New York, NY 10016
Ph: (212)713-5713

E-mail: info@bsuc.org
URL: http://207.36.211.87/index.htm
Contact: Joan E. Ward, Pres.
Founded: 1895. **Members:** 155. **Membership Dues:** resident, $80 (annual) ● non-resident, $40 (annual) ● initial, $100 (annual). **Description:** Represents individuals who have studied at British or commonwealth schools or universities. Conducts lectures and sponsors competitions. Holds numerous social activities. **Awards:** Pride of the 20th Century Award. **Frequency:** annual. **Type:** recognition. **Recipient:** for achievement in the field. **Computer Services:** database, membership. **Publications:** *British Schools and University Club: A Brief History*. **Price:** free ● *British Schools and University Club Membership Directory*, annual. **Price:** free. **Conventions/Meetings:** annual meeting - always June, New York City.

18604 ■ National Society, Daughters of the British Empire in the United States of America (DBE)
40575 Calif Oaks Rd., Ste.D2, No. 269
Murrieta, CA 92562
E-mail: organizer@dbesociety.org
URL: http://www.dbesociety.org
Contact: Edwina Clark, Natl. Organizer
Founded: 1909. **Members:** 4,200. **Membership Dues:** individual (varies by state), $30 (annual). **Regional Groups:** 4. **State Groups:** 34. **Local Groups:** 271. **Description:** Women of British or British Commonwealth birth, or who are naturalized subjects of Britain or a Commonwealth country; women with proven British or British Commonwealth ancestry; wives of men born in Britain or the British Commonwealth. Maintains four retirement homes for both men and women. **Affiliated With:** General Federation of Women's Clubs; Victoria League for Commonwealth Friendship. **Publications:** *DBE and the Retirement Homes We Support*. Pamphlets. Contains information on the homes and history of DBE. ● *National Society, Daughters of the British Empire in the United States of America—Yearbook*, annual. **Price:** $8.00/year. **Circulation:** 600. **Conventions/Meetings:** annual convention (exhibits) - always May.

Californian

18605 ■ Native Daughters of the Golden West (NDGW)
543 Baker St.
San Francisco, CA 94117
Ph: (415)563-9091
Free: (800)994-6349
Fax: (415)563-5230
E-mail: ndgwgpo@aol.com
URL: http://www.ndgw.org
Contact: Joan M. Hall, Pres.
Founded: 1886. **Members:** 8,300. **Staff:** 10. **Description:** Represents native born Californian women. Works to promote the history of the State of California, venerate California pioneers, promote child welfare programs, assist in marking and restoring historic landmarks, and participate in civic affairs. Presents annual scholarship. Maintains museum and historical collection. **Libraries: Type:** reference. **Publications:** *California Star*, bimonthly. Newsletter ● Proceedings, annual. **Conventions/Meetings:** annual meeting - always June.

18606 ■ Native Sons of the Golden West (NSGW)
414 Mason St.
San Francisco, CA 94102
Ph: (415)392-1223
Free: (800)337-1875
Fax: (415)392-1230
E-mail: nsgwgp@pacbell.net
URL: http://www.nsgw.org
Contact: J. Michael Anthony, Grand Pres.
Founded: 1875. **Members:** 13,500. **Staff:** 2. **Budget:** $250,000. **State Groups:** 100. **Description:** Serves as a fraternal society of men born in California. Preserves the history and landmarks of California and the West. Gives financial assistance to St. John's

Hospital in Santa Monica, CA, Cleft Palate Clinic at University of California Medical Center, and Sutter Memorial Hospital in Sacramento, CA. **Awards: Type:** monetary. **Recipient:** to winners of public speaking contest. **Publications:** *The Native Son*, bimonthly. Newsletter. Contains information on the activities of NSGW Parlors all over the State. Alternate Formats: online ● *Native Sons of the Golden West Promotional Video/DVD*. **Price:** $10.00 in VHS/DVD ● Brochure. Alternate Formats: online. **Conventions/Meetings:** competition, public speaking contest for high school students ● annual Grand Parlor - meeting - always third Monday of May.

Canadian

18607 ■ Canadian Club of New York (CCNY)
Address Unknown since 2007
Founded: 1903. **Members:** 1,000. **Multinational**. **Description:** Canadian social club. **Publications:** *Maple Leaf*, quarterly.

Caribbean

18608 ■ United Confederation of Taino People (UCTP)
US Regional Coordinating Off.
PO Box 4515
New York, NY 10163
Ph: (212)604-4186
Fax: (775)640-1358
E-mail: uctp_ny@yahoo.com
URL: http://www.uctp.org
Contact: Mr. Roberto Mucaro Borrero, Pres./Chm.
Founded: 1998. **Budget:** $30,000. **Regional Groups:** 8. **State Groups:** 10. **Languages:** English, Spanish. **Description:** Promotes the Taino Native American culture. Promotes heritage information and spiritual traditions. Provides a regional Tribal Registration process. **Libraries: Type:** by appointment only; reference. **Holdings:** articles, artwork, audio recordings, audiovisuals, books, periodicals. **Computer Services:** Information services, tribal enrollment. **Telecommunication Services:** electronic mail, la_voz_taino@yahoo.com. **Publications:** *La Voz del Pueblo Taino (The Voice of the Taino People)*, quarterly. Newsletter. Contains information on the association and its members. **Price:** $12.00/year. Alternate Formats: online.

Catholic

18609 ■ Catholic Aid Association (CAA)
3499 Lexington Ave. N
St. Paul, MN 55126
Ph: (651)490-0170
Free: (800)568-6670
E-mail: caa@catholicaid.com
URL: http://www.catholicaid.com
Contact: Michael F. McGovern, Pres./Chm.
Founded: 1878. **Members:** 80,000. **Staff:** 45. **Description:** Catholics living in Minnesota, North and South Dakota, Iowa and Wisconsin. Supports the financial well-being of its members and providing volunteer and financial resources for the Catholic Church. Offers high-quality financial products, a host of social activities, and a wealth of fraternal opportunities that positively impact Catholic Aid members and their Catholic parishes, schools and religious education programs; is associated with two other organizations, the Catholic Aid Association Foundation and the Catholic Aid Association Credit Union. **Awards:** Matching Grant Program. **Type:** grant. **Recipient:** for Catholic schools and parish educational programs ● **Type:** scholarship. **Recipient:** to member students. **Councils:** Local. **Programs:** Church Sign; Living Assistance; Member Assistance; Student Life Benefit; Youth Parish. **Formerly:** (1923) Deutsche Roemisch Katholisch Unterstuetzungs Gesellschaft von Minnesota. **Publications:** *The Catholic Aid News*, monthly. **Circulation:** 39,000. Alternate Formats: on-

line. **Conventions/Meetings:** annual meeting - always August in Collegeville or St. Paul, MN.

18610 ■ Catholic Association of Foresters (CAOF)
182 Forbes Rd., Ste.119
Braintree, MA 02184-2693
Ph: (781)848-8221
Free: (800)282-CAOF
Fax: (781)848-0311
E-mail: mail@catholicforesters.com
URL: http://www.catholicforesters.com
Contact: John F. Anderson Jr., High Sec.-Treas.
Founded: 1879. **Members:** 6,000. **Membership Dues:** fraternal insurance, life insurance, $3 (annual). **Staff:** 9. **Budget:** $500,000. **Regional Groups:** 40. **State Groups:** 40. **Local Groups:** 40. **Description:** Fraternal benefit life insurance organization of Catholics. Conducts fraternal and religious activities; provides aid to charitable organizations. Sponsors Christmas party for children and family day. **Awards:** Major Gen. Wm. H. Harrison Fund. **Frequency:** annual. **Type:** scholarship. **Recipient:** to a high school student ● Major General Wm. H. Harrison Fund - Educational Grants. **Frequency:** annual. **Type:** grant. **Recipient:** to a high school student. **Affiliated With:** National Fraternal Congress of America. **Formerly:** (1961) Massachusetts Catholic Order of Foresters. **Publications:** *Chips*, bimonthly. Newsletter. Contains fraternal membership news. **Price:** free. **Circulation:** 5,000. Alternate Formats: online. **Conventions/Meetings:** annual banquet and retreat, with weekend business convention for elected delegates - always in June.

18611 ■ Catholic Daughters of the Americas (CDA)
10 W 71st St.
New York, NY 10023
Ph: (212)877-3041
Fax: (212)724-5923
E-mail: cdofanatl@aol.com
URL: http://www.catholicdaughters.org
Contact: Peggy O'Brien, Exec. Dir.
Founded: 1903. **Members:** 95,000. **Staff:** 8. **State Groups:** 35. **Local Groups:** 1,400. **Languages:** English, Spanish. **Description:** Catholic women involved in religious, charitable, and educational projects. Sponsors Operation Morning Star, a legislative program, and Focus 2000, a membership and extension program. **Awards:** Type: scholarship. **Recipient:** to teachers of exceptional children. **Committees:** Apostolate; Community; Renewal; Youth. **Programs:** Circle of Love; Operation Morning Star. **Affiliated With:** National Council of Catholic Women. **Formerly:** (1979) Catholic Daughters of America. **Publications:** *Share Magazine*, quarterly. **Price:** included in membership dues; $4.00 /year for nonmembers. **Circulation:** 113,000. **Advertising:** accepted. **Conventions/Meetings:** biennial meeting and convention (exhibits) - always July.

18612 ■ Catholic Family Life Insurance (CFLI)
PO Box 11563
Milwaukee, WI 53211-0563
Ph: (414)961-0500
Free: (800)227-CFLI
Fax: (414)961-0103
E-mail: mail@cfli.org
URL: http://www.cfli.org
Contact: Bill Eimers, Pres.
Founded: 1868. **Members:** 40,388. **Staff:** 68. **Budget:** $3,000,000. **Local Groups:** 85. **Description:** Fraternal benefit life insurance society for persons of the Catholic faith. Insures women and children, develops a health and accident program, and offers masses for living and deceased members. **Awards:** **Frequency:** annual. **Type:** scholarship. **Recipient:** for students enrolled in Catholic high schools. **Formerly:** (1951) Catholic Family Protective Life Assurance Society. **Publications:** *Family Friend*, quarterly. Magazine. Contains updates about the society's events and programs. **Conventions/Meetings:** quadrennial meeting.

18613 ■ Catholic Knights
1100 W Wells St.
Milwaukee, WI 53233
Ph: (414)273-6266
Free: (800)927-2547
Fax: (414)223-3201
E-mail: web@catholicknights.org
URL: http://www.catholicknights.org
Contact: Mr. William O'Toole Jr., Pres.
Founded: 1885. **Members:** 85,000. **Staff:** 108. **Budget:** $90,000,000. **Local Groups:** 150. **Description:** Fraternal benefit life insurance society for Catholics; local branches carry out educational and social programs and support various Catholic Action activities. Offers fraternal programs, including financial planning seminars, group travel programs, mortgage loans, newborn infant benefits, and access to film library resource; charter member of the Catholic Communications Foundation. Contributes to charitable and educational institutions; conducts Orphan's Monthly Income and Catholic High School and Elementary School Scholarship Program. **Affiliated With:** National Fraternal Congress of America. **Formerly:** (2006) Catholic Knights Insurance Society. **Publications:** *Catholic Knight Magazine*, quarterly. Contains articles on family living and financial matters; also covers member and branch activities. **Price:** included in membership dues. ISSN: 1551-9058. **Circulation:** 85,000. **Advertising:** accepted ● *My Money and More*, 3/year. Newsletters. Covers financial topics and more for consumers. **Price:** $1.00 for nonmembers; free for members and prospects. **Conventions/Meetings:** triennial convention.

18614 ■ Catholic Knights of America (CKA)
4545 Oleatha Ave., Ste.100
St. Louis, MO 63116
Ph: (314)351-1029
Free: (800)844-3728
E-mail: ckoa@ckoa.com
Contact: John F. Kenawell, Pres.
Founded: 1877. **Members:** 14,000. **Membership Dues:** individual, $4 (annual). **Staff:** 22. **Budget:** $8,000,000. **State Groups:** 8. **Local Groups:** 111. **Description:** Fraternal benefit life, annuity, and health insurance society. Supports Pro-Life activities, offers matching gift program for church and community projects. Maintains museum. **Awards:** Type: recognition. **Recipient:** for youth essay contest ● **Type:** recognition. **Recipient:** for policeman of the year ● **Type:** recognition. **Recipient:** for citizen of the year ● **Type:** scholarship. **Recipient:** for seminarians and Catholic high school students. **Programs:** Catholic Action. **Affiliated With:** National Fraternal Congress of America. **Publications:** *The C.K. of A. Journal*, monthly. **Circulation:** 6,000. **Conventions/Meetings:** triennial conference.

18615 ■ Catholic Life Insurance Union (CLIU)
PO Box 659527
San Antonio, TX 78265-9527
Ph: (210)828-9921
Free: (800)262-2548
Fax: (210)828-4629
E-mail: mscenter@cliu.com
URL: http://www.catholiclifeinsurance.com
Contact: Eddie Stolowski, Chm.
Founded: 1901. **Members:** 70,000. **Description:** Serves as fraternal benefit life insurance society. Sponsors competitions. **Awards:** Type: recognition. **Publications:** *Branch Officers Bulletin*, quarterly ● *Catholic Life News*, quarterly ● *Sales Record*, monthly. **Conventions/Meetings:** biennial meeting.

18616 ■ Catholic Order of Foresters (COF)
PO Box 3012
Naperville, IL 60566-7012
Ph: (630)983-4900
Free: (800)552-0145
Fax: (630)983-4057
E-mail: generalbox@catholicforester.com
URL: http://www.catholicforester.com
Contact: Mr. David Huber, High Sec.-Treas.
Founded: 1883. **Members:** 140,000. **Staff:** 90. **State Groups:** 30. **Local Groups:** 490. **Description:** Works as a fraternal benefit legal reserve life insur-

ance society, promoting "friendship, unity and true Christian charity among its members". **Awards:** Legion of Honor Award. **Type:** recognition ● Longevity Award. **Type:** recognition ● Merit Award. **Type:** recognition ● **Type:** scholarship. **Telecommunication Services:** teletype, (800)617-4176. **Programs:** Matching Funds; Orphan Benefits; Pathways; Religious Education Assistance; ScriptSave Prescription Plan; Tuition Assistance. **Absorbed:** (1965) Catholic Central Union; (1981) Forest Rangers and Rangerettes. **Publications:** *Catholic Forester*, bimonthly. Magazine ● Annual Report, annual. **Conventions/Meetings:** quadrennial conference.

18617 ■ Catholic Workman (CW)
1201 1st St. NE
New Prague, MN 56071
Ph: (952)758-2229
Free: (800)346-6231
Fax: (952)758-6221
E-mail: info@catholicworkman.org
URL: http://www.catholicworkman.org
Founded: 1891. **Members:** 16,000. **Staff:** 12. **Budget:** $2,000,000. **State Groups:** 9. **Local Groups:** 90. **Description:** Fraternal benefit life insurance organization of practicing Catholics and their families. Makes available funds to religious and charitable organizations. Provides scholarships and fraternal programs including community service and youth activities. **Awards:** **Frequency:** annual. **Type:** scholarship. **Recipient:** for eligible members for college ● **Type:** scholarship. **Recipient:** for students in seminaries studying to become priests or nuns. **Computer Services:** database, membership. **Telecommunication Services:** electronic mail, mindyr@catholicworkman.org. **Committees:** Educational Funds. **Absorbed:** (1930) Western Bohemian Catholic Union; (1977) Daughters of Columbus. **Formerly:** Katolicky Delnik. **Publications:** *Catholic Workman Voice*, monthly. Journal. Contains membership news, events, and promotes society. **Price:** $8.00 for nonmembers; free for members. **Circulation:** 8,000 ● Brochure. **Conventions/Meetings:** quadrennial convention, with delegates, board assemble to set policy, and elect board.

18618 ■ Columbian Squires (CS)
1 Columbus Plz.
New Haven, CT 06510
Ph: (203)752-4400
Fax: (203)752-4108
E-mail: william.obrien@kofc.org
URL: http://www.kofc.org
Contact: Robert A. Goossens, Dir., Fraternal Services
Founded: 1925. **Members:** 23,482. **Staff:** 6. **State Groups:** 65. **Local Groups:** 1,306. **Languages:** English, French, Spanish. **Multinational. Description:** International fraternity of young Catholic men (12-18 years old) throughout the United States, Canada, Mexico, Philippines, Puerto Rico, the Bahamas, the Virgin Islands and Guam. Promotes leadership building activities for youth. Sponsored by Knights of Columbus. **Awards:** Brother Barnabas Award. **Frequency:** annual. **Type:** recognition ● Corps d'Elite Award. **Type:** recognition. **Committees:** Circle; Service; Spiritual. **Affiliated With:** Knights of Columbus. **Publications:** *Squires Newsletter*, monthly. Includes information for members, counselors, and others. **Price:** included in membership dues; $1.00 for nonmembers. **Circulation:** 51,000. Also Cited As: *Columbian Squires Herald*. **Conventions/Meetings:** competition ● annual State Convention, for states and provinces.

18619 ■ Daughters of Isabella, International Circle (D of I)
PO Box 9585
New Haven, CT 06535
Ph: (203)865-2570
Fax: (203)865-5586
E-mail: info@daughtersofisabella.org
URL: http://www.daughtersofisabella.org
Contact: Elaine Leger, Intl. Regent
Founded: 1897. **Members:** 55,000. **Local Groups:** 730. **Description:** Fraternal society of Catholic

women who seek to emulate the accomplishments and virtues of Queen Isabella (1451-1504), ruler of Aragon and Castile. Promotes friendship and seeks to unite the energies and resources of members "for the advancement of all that is best and truest in life." Sponsors Queen Isabella Foundation, which provides scholarships in Social Service at Catholic University of America. Has established a family center at Catholic University of America. **Formerly:** (1972) Daughters of Isabella, National Circle; (1977) Daughters of Isabella, Supreme Circle. **Conventions/Meetings:** biennial congress.

18620 ■ International Order of Alhambra (OA)
4200 Leeds Ave.
Baltimore, MD 21229
Ph: (410)242-0660
Free: (800)478-2946
Fax: (410)536-5729
E-mail: hq@orderalhambra.org
URL: http://www.orderalhambra.org
Contact: Roger J. Reid, Exec. Sec.
Founded: 1904. **Members:** 5,000. **Membership Dues:** individual, $30 (annual). **Staff:** 3. **Budget:** $250,000. **Regional Groups:** 25. **National Groups:** 100. **Multinational. Description:** Marks Catholic historical places and commemorates Catholic personages and events. Acts in partnership with other groups to assist them in starting Alhambra Houses, which provide housing for approximately six people with special needs. **Awards: Type:** grant. **Recipient:** for research on the causes of Down Syndrome ● **Type:** scholarship. **Recipient:** for teachers of the developmentally disabled. **Telecommunication Services:** electronic mail, salaamone@att.net. **Formerly:** (1969) Order of the Alhambra; (1979) International Order of the Alhambra; (2004) Order of Alhambra. **Publications:** *Alhambra News and Reviews*, semiannual. Newsletter ● *Alhambran*, quarterly. Magazine. Reports on OA's efforts working with developmentally disabled persons. Includes calendar of events and statistics. **Price:** included in membership dues; $5.75 /year for nonmembers. **Circulation:** 6,000. **Advertising:** accepted ● *Order of the Alhambra—Directory*, annual. Lists organization officers. **Price:** included in membership dues. **Conventions/Meetings:** biennial conference (exhibits) ● semiannual meeting.

18621 ■ Junior Daughters of Peter Claver (JDPC)
PO Box 8278
Montgomery, AL 36110-0278
Ph: (334)265-3214
Fax: (334)265-3293
E-mail: info@kofpc.org
URL: http://www.kofpc.org
Contact: H. Bronco Henderson, Exec. Dir.
Founded: 1930. **Members:** 3,600. **Staff:** 8. **Description:** Catholic girls between seven and 17 years of age. Fosters good character and leadership qualities by: supplementing formal religious training received in church, home, and school; cultivating social graces; developing poise and confidence; assisting in the development of physical fitness by organizing activities such as basketball games, bowling, and intramural competitions; heightening members' appreciation of their civic and religious duties via participation in ceremonial work, tours, and political campaigns. Sponsors picnics, fundraisers, dances, discussions, workshops, and folk masses. Presents scholarships. **Affiliated With:** Knights of Peter Claver. **Publications:** *Claverite*, semiannual. Magazine. **Conventions/Meetings:** biennial meeting ● periodic National Convention, Knights of Peter Claver - conference.

18622 ■ Junior Knights of Peter Claver (JKPC)
PO Box 8278
Montgomery, AL 36110-0278
Ph: (334)265-3214
Fax: (334)265-3293

E-mail: info@kofpc.org
URL: http://www.kofpc.org
Contact: H. Bronco Henderson, Exec. Dir.
Founded: 1917. **Members:** 1,800. **Description:** Catholic boys between seven and 17 years of age. Purposes are to: supplement the formal instructional religious training received in church, home, and school; encourage the cultivation of social graces and development of poise and confidence through picnics, fundraising projects, and dances; develop physical fitness through a program of activities such as basketball, baseball, track meets, bowling, and intramural competitions; cultivate interests and tastes that will produce a more profitable use of leisure hours. Sponsors group discussions, workshops, and folk masses. Offers scholarships; bestows awards. **Affiliated With:** Knights of Peter Claver. **Publications:** *Claverite*, semiannual. Magazine. **Conventions/Meetings:** periodic conference ● biennial National Convention, Knights of Peter Claver - meeting.

18623 ■ Knights of Columbus (K of C)
1 Columbus Plz.
New Haven, CT 06510
Ph: (203)752-4000
Free: (800)380-9995
Fax: (203)772-1923
E-mail: info@kofc.org
URL: http://www.kofc.org
Contact: Carl A. Anderson, Supreme Knight
Founded: 1882. **Members:** 1,650,000. **Staff:** 600. **State Groups:** 70. **Local Groups:** 13,272. **Languages:** English, French, Spanish. **Multinational. Description:** Fraternal society of Catholic men, 18 years of age or over. Maintains museum. **Libraries: Type:** reference; lending; open to the public. **Holdings:** archival material, artwork, audiovisuals, books, periodicals. **Subjects:** K of C, church, U.S. history. **Awards:** Gaudium et Spes. **Type:** monetary. **Programs:** Catholic Information Service; Life Insurance. **Absorbed:** (1968) Supreme Council Catholic Benevolent Legion. **Publications:** *Columbia* (in English, French, and Spanish), monthly. Magazine. Features topics of interest to members and Catholic families. **Price:** $6.00/year. ISSN: 0010-1869. **Circulation:** 1,520,000 ● *Knightline*, 18/year. Newsletter. Features the latest news from the Supreme Council office, actions of the Order's Board of Directors, and a message from the Supreme Knight. ● *Squires*, monthly. Newsletter. Provides program information and monthly updates for leaders of Columbian Squires circles. ● Newsletter, quarterly. Contains ideas and suggestions for council leaders on membership recruitment activities. ● Handbooks, periodic. Provides a general overview of the duties and responsibilities of various officer positions within the Order. **Conventions/Meetings:** annual Supreme Council Meeting - convention - first Tuesday - Thursday of August.

18624 ■ Knights of Peter Claver (KPC)
PO Box 8278
Montgomery, AL 36110-0278
Ph: (334)265-3214
Fax: (334)265-3293
E-mail: director@kofpc.org
URL: http://www.kofpc.org
Contact: H. Bronco Henderson, Exec. Dir.
Founded: 1909. **Members:** 35,000. **Staff:** 8. **Regional Groups:** 6. **State Groups:** 22. **Local Groups:** 410. **Description:** Fraternal society of Roman Catholic men. Objectives are to: support local pastors, parishes, and the bishop of the diocese; participate in community activities and civic improvements; encourage Apostolic and Catholic action by laypersons; foster recreational assemblies and facilities; provide social and intellectual fellowship for members, as well as guidance and participation in the ever-changing structure of social and economic life; encourages youth participation. Sponsors workshops, fundraising projects, and educational and recreational activities. Donates to selected charities and organizations. Group derives its name from Peter Claver (1581-1654), a Catholic priest who ministered to slaves in the West Indies and was declared a saint

in 1884. **Awards:** Gold Medal of Merit. **Frequency:** annual. **Type:** recognition. **Recipient:** to individuals with an outstanding contribution to the advancement of mutual understanding and human relations ● **Type:** recognition ● **Type:** scholarship. **Recipient:** for needy students ● Silver Medal of Merit. **Frequency:** annual. **Type:** recognition. **Recipient:** for members of the Order with a significant contribution for the Good of the Order. **Divisions:** Junior; Ladies Auxiliary; Ladies of Grace; Meritorious Fourth Degree. **Also Known As:** Knights and Ladies of Station Peter Claver. **Publications:** *The Claverite*, semiannual. Magazine. **Conventions/Meetings:** annual convention.

18625 ■ Knights of Saint John International
89 S Pine Ave.
Albany, NY 12208-2214
Ph: (518)453-5675
E-mail: jhauser1@nycap.rr.com
URL: http://members.tripod.com/ksji/knights/ksji.html
Contact: Maj. Gen. Joseph Hauser Jr., Supreme Sec.
Founded: 1878. **Members:** 10,000. **Staff:** 3. **Regional Groups:** 4. **State Groups:** 8. **Local Groups:** 90. **National Groups:** 222. **Languages:** English, French. **Description:** Catholic fraternal organization under patronage of St. John the Baptist. Provides honor guards for church activities; assists St. Vincent de Paul Society and charitable organizations. **Awards:** Knight of the Year. **Frequency:** annual. **Type:** monetary. **Recipient:** for priest study for family members. **Committees:** Good of Order; Law; Military Ritual; National Sports. **Formerly:** (2002) Supreme Commandery Knights of Saint John. **Publications:** *Knight of St. John*, quarterly. Newsletter. Includes president's message and new members listing. **Price:** $8.00/year. **Circulation:** 8,000. **Advertising:** accepted. **Conventions/Meetings:** biennial international conference - always July ● annual National Bowling Tournament - competition.

18626 ■ National Catholic Society of Foresters (NCSF)
320 S School St.
Mount Prospect, IL 60056-3334
Ph: (847)342-4500
Free: (800)344-6273
E-mail: info@ncsf.com
URL: http://www.ncsf.com
Contact: Mary Rausch, Pres.
Founded: 1891. **Members:** 38,699. **Staff:** 30. **Budget:** $4,800,000. **National Groups:** 144. **Description:** Fraternal benefit insurance society that insures members of the Roman Catholic Church of all ages and spouses of Catholics. Sponsors Catholic school grants and college scholarships for members as well as membership contests annually. **Formerly:** (1966) Women's Catholic Order of Foresters. **Publications:** *National Catholic Forester*, quarterly. Magazine. Includes message from the president, product information, events, member news, and contests. **Price:** free. **Circulation:** 32,400. **Conventions/Meetings:** quadrennial meeting.

18627 ■ Religious and Military Order of Knights of the Holy Sepulchre of Jerusalem (RMOKHSJ)
c/o The Sovereign Grand Priory
3620 W 10th St., B-150
Greeley, CO 80634-1821
E-mail: ohs@maxalla.net
URL: http://www.greeleynet.com/~maxalla/OKH-SSub/ohs.html
Contact: Duke Lloyd Douglas Worley PhD, Sovereign Grand Master
Founded: 1982. **Members:** 130. **Membership Dues:** regular, $550 (annual). **State Groups:** 3. **Local Groups:** 4. **Description:** Promotes Christian chivalry and godly devotion in everyday life. Encourages members to maintain charitable and philanthropic projects to alleviate the suffering of others; an international knighthood whose Code of Chivalry, the order believes, will strengthen the members' Christian spirituality and make each a "soldier of Christ." Is an ecumenical sepulchre knighthood recognized by

many orders and Royal and Noble Houses. **Libraries: Type:** reference. **Subjects:** religious materials. **Awards:** Order of Merit. **Frequency:** annual. **Type:** recognition. **Recipient:** for outstanding contributions in religious and secular life, including arts and education. **Councils:** Bailiwick. **Publications:** *Gallantry*, periodic. Newsletter. **Price:** included in membership dues. Alternate Formats: online. **Conventions/Meetings:** annual general assembly.

18628 ■ Supreme Ladies Auxiliary Knights of Saint John (SLAKSJ)
c/o Mrs. Ann Friday, Supreme Sec.
2330 Kirby Dr.
Hillcrest Heights, MD 20748-3265
Ph: (301)423-6516
Fax: (301)423-2662
E-mail: christianspirit@starpower.net
URL: http://home.fuse.net/ksji
Contact: Mrs. Ann Friday, Supreme Sec.
Founded: 1900. **Members:** 14,521. **Staff:** 4. **Description:** Fraternal society of Catholic women. Provides children's services; conducts charitable and educational programs. **Committees:** Legislative; Military; Mission; Sports. **Publications:** *Convention Proceedings*, biennial ● *Grand*, annual. Proceedings. **Conventions/Meetings:** competition ● biennial symposium and meeting.

18629 ■ Western Catholic Union (WCU)
510 Maine St.
Quincy, IL 62301
Ph: (217)223-9721
Free: (800)223-4928
Fax: (217)223-9726
E-mail: mail@wculife.org
URL: http://www.wculife.com
Contact: Mark A. Wiewel, Pres.
Founded: 1877. **Members:** 18,927. **Staff:** 12. **Regional Groups:** 7. **Local Groups:** 67. **Description:** Serves as fraternal benefit life insurance society. **Awards:** Catholic High Scholarship. **Frequency:** annual. **Type:** scholarship ● Vocations Award Scholarship. **Frequency:** annual. **Type:** scholarship. **Absorbed:** (1998) North American Union Life Assurance Society. **Formerly:** Supreme Council of the Western Catholic Union. **Publications:** *Western Catholic Union Record*, quarterly. Journal. **Circulation:** 10,000.

Celtic

18630 ■ Celtic League, American Branch (CLAB)
PO Box 20153
Dag Hammarskjold Ctr.
New York, NY 10017
Free: (800)626-CELT
E-mail: stephendevillo@prodigy.net
URL: http://www.celticleague.org
Contact: Margaret Sexton, Sec.
Founded: 1974. **Members:** 250. **Membership Dues:** individual, $30 (annual) ● couple, $35 (annual) ● family, $40 (annual) ● contributing (half price admission to CLAB events), $50 (annual) ● sustaining (half price admission to CLAB events), $100 (annual). **Staff:** 10. **Languages:** Breton, English, Irish, Manx Gaelic, Scottish, Welsh. **Description:** Disseminates information about Celts and their identity, based on culture, politics, economics, and language in the present day Celtic nations, as well as their contribution in the ancient world. Has designed, produced, and distributed a calendar based on the Celtic year. Sponsors Celtic concerts, speakers, and films to stimulate the revival of observances of Celtic holidays. **Committees:** Celtic Calendar; Celtic Languages; Keltoi; Samhan/Celtic New Years. **Affiliated With:** Celtic League. **Publications:** *Guide to Learning Celtic Languages in the U.S. and Canada* ● *Keltoi: A Pan-Celtic Review*, annual. Journal. Addresses the culture and history of the Celtic world. Includes book reviews and biographical sketches of Celtic literary and historical figures. **Price:** $5.00/2 issues, for members; $6.00/2 issues, for nonmembers. **Advertis-**

ing: accepted ● *Six Nations, One Soul*, quarterly. Newsletter. **Conventions/Meetings:** annual Pan-Celtic Conference.

Chinese

18631 ■ Association of Chinese-American Professionals (ACAP)
10303 Westoffice Dr.
Box No. 194
Houston, TX 77042-5306
Fax: (281)545-1308
E-mail: shuang@cs.uh.edu
URL: http://www.acap-usa.org
Contact: Stephen Huang, Pres.
Founded: 1978. **Members:** 260. **Description:** Represents organizations and individuals including scientists, engineers, professors, and students interested in the professional and economic development in the Republic of China or Taiwan. Aims to provide members with opportunities for professional development through the exchange of information and experience. Keeps abreast of technical research and advancement. Assists in the industrial and economic development of the Republic of China or Taiwan. Offers student assistance and placement service. Conducts educational seminars on topics including employment and immigration through the Student Programs Division. Conducts workshops; membership is concentrated in Arkansas, Louisiana, Mississippi, Oklahoma, and Texas; the association is planning to expand nationally. **Libraries: Type:** reference. **Awards: Type:** recognition. **Computer Services:** database, talent. **Committees:** Leadership Scholarship. **Councils:** Control. **Divisions:** Architecture; Chemical Technology; Civil Engineering; Environmental Technology; Information Technology; Mechanical Engineering; Medical Science; Political Science; Social Science. **Formerly:** (1980) Association of Concerned Citizens; (2002) Association of American-Chinese Professionals. **Publications:** *AACP Member Roster*, annual. Membership Directory ● *Science, Engineering, and Technology Seminars Proceedings*, annual. Includes technical papers. **Price:** $50.00. **Advertising:** accepted ● *2005 Diversity Summit Program Brochure*. Alternate Formats: online ● Newsletter, monthly ● Newsletter, periodic ● Also publishes scrapbooks and workshop notes. **Conventions/Meetings:** annual conference (exhibits) ● annual Scientific, Engineering, and Technology Seminar.

18632 ■ Chinese American Citizens Alliance (CACA)
1044 Stockton St.
San Francisco, CA 94108
Ph: (415)434-2222 (323)660-9797
Fax: (323)721-0960
E-mail: skf@pacbell.net
URL: http://www.cacanational.org
Contact: Munson Kwok, Grand Pres.
Founded: 1895. **Members:** 300. **Membership Dues:** regular, $35 (annual). **Local Groups:** 16. **Description:** Represents American citizens of Chinese birth or ancestry. Seeks to practice good citizenship and to encourage the study of the United States. Conducts youth leadership training, essay contest and specialized education programs; maintains speakers' bureau. **Awards: Frequency:** annual. **Type:** scholarship. **Recipient:** for five students in Los Angeles County schools and universities who have met the criteria for scholarship, community activities, and future prospects. **Committees:** Citizenship; Education; Mandarins (social); Scholarship. **Formerly:** (1915) Native Sons of the Golden State. **Publications:** Bulletin, monthly ● Directory, biennial. **Conventions/Meetings:** biennial convention - always August ● monthly meeting - always first Saturday.

18633 ■ Chinese American Civic Council (CACC)
PO Box 166082
Chicago, IL 60616

Ph: (312)225-0234
Contact: Jean Ng, Pres.
Founded: 1951. **Members:** 900. **Membership Dues:** $10 (annual). **Staff:** 1. **Description:** Goals are to become better American citizens and to take an active part in the American way of life. Works to provide a means for Chinese Americans to participate in and contribute to American culture. Seeks to improve housing, business, and educational standards and to develop parental responsibility and responsible behavior among youth. Provides youth career orientation programs. Sponsors a girl scout troop. **Awards: Type:** recognition. **Recipient:** for outgoing presidents. **Committees:** Chinese in America; Community Planning; Education; Miss Chicago Chinatown; Public Information; Senior; Welfare; Youth.

18634 ■ Chinese Consolidated Benevolent Association (CCBA)
62 Mott St.
New York, NY 10013
Ph: (212)226-6280 (212)226-6764
Fax: (212)431-5883
E-mail: ccbany@yahoo.com
URL: http://www.ccbanyc.org
Contact: Mr. Eric Ng, Pres.
Founded: 1883. **Members:** 60. **Staff:** 30. **Local Groups:** 60. **Languages:** Chinese, English. **Description:** Community leadership institution that integrates Chinese family district, and business organizations. Represents the interests of the Chinatown community; monitors business activities and settles disputes. Provides counseling and referrals to immigrants. Maintains the New York Chinese School and adult English language classes. Operates Chinatown Day Care Center. Sponsors the New York City Summer Youth Employment Program and Chinese New Year's Festival.

18635 ■ Sino-American Amity Fund (SAAF)
86 Riverside Dr.
New York, NY 10024
Ph: (212)787-6969
Fax: (212)787-0260
Contact: Rev. Paul Chan, Pres.
Founded: 1956. **Members:** 150. **Membership Dues:** life, $100. **Budget:** $100,000. **Description:** Works to promote better understanding and friendly relations between the Americans and Chinese (Nationalists) through cultural, social, educational, and religious programs. Conducts welfare program for Chinese college students. **Awards: Frequency:** annual. **Type:** scholarship. **Supersedes:** Sino-American Amity. **Conventions/Meetings:** semiannual dinner.

Community Action

18636 ■ Unity Corps
PO Box 29219
Los Angeles, CA 90029-0219
Ph: (323)850-8700
Free: (800)927-0270
E-mail: director@unitycorps.org
URL: http://www.unitycorps.org
Contact: Mr. Angel Tenes, Exec. Dir.
Founded: 1992. **Description:** Seeks out individuals and groups who support the aims of racial, religious and sexual non-discrimination. Promotes peace and human unity through arts, assemblage and literature. Provides rehabilitative services. **Libraries: Type:** reference. **Subjects:** art, music and literature. **Telecommunication Services:** electronic mail, info@unitycorps.org. **Programs:** Art, Literature and Music Development.

Coptic

18637 ■ American Coptic Association (ACA)
582 Bergen Ave.
Jersey City, NJ 07304
Ph: (201)451-0972
Fax: (201)451-3399

E-mail: amcoptic@usa.com
URL: http://www.amcoptic.com
Contact: Mr. Milad Eskander, Pres.
Founded: 1974. **Description:** Copts (Christian Egyptians) who have immigrated to the U.S. Promotes Coptic culture and history; defends human rights of the Copts in Egypt; helps immigrants in the U.S. to be good and productive citizens. Sponsors lectures; conducts research and charitable programs. **Libraries: Type:** reference. **Holdings:** 1,000. **Subjects:** psychology, sociology, history. **Publications:** *Census of the Copts in Egypt.* Report ● *The Copts,* quarterly. Journal ● *The Copts and Muslims.* Report ● *The Copts Since the Arab Conquest.* Report ● *The Copts Since the Arab Invasion: Strangers in Their Own Land.* Report ● *Implications of Applying Islamic Rules in Egypt.* Report ● *Plight of the Copts in Egypt.* Report ● Reports. **Conventions/Meetings:** annual conference.

Cossack

18638 ■ New Kuban Education and Welfare Association (NKEWA)
228 Don Rd.
Buena, NJ 08310-1615
E-mail: atamannk@comcast.net
Contact: Anthony Sienczenko, Pres.
Founded: 1972. **Members:** 50. **Membership Dues:** regular, $50 (annual). **Staff:** 3. **Budget:** $5,000. **Languages:** English, German, Russian, Ukrainian. **Description:** Individuals interested in preserving Cossack history and traditions. Maintains museum. **Publications:** none. **Libraries: Type:** by appointment only. **Holdings:** 5,000. **Subjects:** Cossack history, Russian history, traditions, Russian fiction, Ukrainian history. **Also Known As:** New Kuban Historical Museum. **Formerly:** (1986) All Cossack Association New Kuban. **Conventions/Meetings:** annual meeting - always October in Buena, NJ.

Croatian

18639 ■ Croatian Academy of America (CAA)
PO Box 1767
Grand Central Sta.
New York, NY 10163-1767
E-mail: croatacad@aol.com
URL: http://www.croatianacademy.org
Contact: Karlo Mirth, Managing Ed.
Founded: 1953. **Members:** 265. **Membership Dues:** regular, $30 (annual) ● contributor, $50 (annual) ● life contributor, $1,000. **Local Groups:** 2. **Description:** Persons interested in Croatian history and culture who possess the appropriate academic credentials and who are sponsored by existing members. Sponsors lectures for members and the public on Croatian literature, culture, and history. **Awards: Type:** recognition. **Publications:** *Croatian Medical.* Journal. **Price:** $60.00 /year for individuals; $40.00 /year for institutions ● *Journal of Croatian Studies: Annual Review of the Croatian Academy of America,* annual. Covers Croatian history, sociology, literature, linguistics, fine arts, economics, philosophy, and religion. **Price:** included in membership dues; $20.00 for nonmembers; $30.00 for institutions. ISSN: 0075-4218. **Circulation:** 1,000. **Conventions/Meetings:** annual general assembly.

18640 ■ Croatian Catholic Union of U.S.A. and Canada (CCUAC)
1 E Old Ridge Rd.
PO Box 602
Hobart, IN 46342-0602
Ph: (219)942-1191
Fax: (219)942-8808
E-mail: info@ccu-usa-can.org
Contact: Melchior Masina, Natl. Pres.
Founded: 1921. **Members:** 9,000. **Staff:** 6. **Budget:** $350,000. **Languages:** Croatian, English. **Description:** Serves as a fraternal benefit life insurance society for Croatians and other Roman and Greek Catholics. **Libraries: Type:** open to the public. **Hold-**

ings: 4,000; audio recordings, books, periodicals, video recordings. **Subjects:** Croatia, Catholicism. **Awards: Type:** scholarship. **Formerly:** (1986) Croatian Catholic Union of the U.S.A. **Publications:** *Nasa Nada* (in Croatian and English), monthly. Magazine. Features spiritual, humanitarian, and social topics. **Price:** $20.00/year. **Circulation:** 3,300. Also Cited As: *Our Hope.* **Conventions/Meetings:** quadrennial congress (exhibits).

18641 ■ Croatian Fraternal Union of America (CFU)
100 Delaney Dr.
Pittsburgh, PA 15235
Ph: (412)843-0380
Fax: (412)823-1594
E-mail: cfuofa@usaor.net
URL: http://www.croatianfraternalunion.org
Contact: Bernard M. Luketich, Pres.
Founded: 1924. **Members:** 90,000. **Staff:** 40. **Local Groups:** 769. **Description:** Represents persons of Croatian or Slavic descent or origin and their relatives. Maintains Ethnic Museum. Sponsors: CFU Junior Cultural Federation (see separate entry); CFU Scholarship Foundation. **Libraries: Type:** reference. **Holdings:** 5,000. **Subjects:** history of the Croatian people. **Awards: Type:** recognition. **Absorbed:** (1994) Sloga Fraternal Life Insurance Society. **Formed by Merger of:** Croatian League of Illinois; National Croatian Society. **Publications:** *Junior Magazine,* bimonthly ● *Zajednicar,* weekly. **Conventions/Meetings:** annual Adult Tamburitza Festival ● annual Junior Tamburitza Festival ● National Bowling, Basketball, Golf, Softball and Ski Tournaments - competition.

Cuban

18642 ■ Cuban American Alliance Education Fund (CAAEF)
PO Box 5113
San Luis Obispo, CA 93403
Ph: (805)627-1959
Fax: (805)627-1959
E-mail: caaef@hughes.net
URL: http://www.cubamer.org
Contact: Delvis Fernandez Levy PhD, Exec. Pres.
Description: Educates the public at large on issues related to hardships resulting from current United States-Cuba relations. Serves as a vehicle for the development of mutually beneficial engagements which promote understanding and human compassion. **Programs:** La Gran Familia. **Publications:** *La Alborada* (in English and Spanish). Newsletter. Alternate Formats: online.

Cultural Exchange

18643 ■ United States-Japan Foundation
145 E 32nd St.
New York, NY 10016
Ph: (212)481-8753
Fax: (212)481-8762
E-mail: info@us-jf.org
URL: http://www.us-jf.org
Contact: Dr. George R. Packard, Pres.
Founded: 1980. **Multinational. Description:** Works to support projects that foster knowledge and education, a deepened understanding, create channels of communication, and address problems and concerns relating to the relationships of Americans and the Japanese. **Awards:** Elgin Heinz Outstanding Teacher Award. **Frequency:** annual. **Type:** recognition. **Recipient:** to teachers who further mutual understanding between Americans and Japanese ● **Frequency:** annual. **Type:** grant. **Recipient:** to projects and programs that take advantage of new technology to bring Japanese and American teachers and students together. **Programs:** US-Japan Leadership.

Czech

18644 ■ American Sokol Educational and Physical Culture Organization (ASO)
122 W 22nd St.
Oak Brook, IL 60523-1557
Ph: (630)368-0771 (630)368-0773
Fax: (630)368-0758
E-mail: aso@american-sokol.org
URL: http://www.american-sokol.org
Contact: Larry Laznovsky, Pres.
Founded: 1865. **Members:** 7,000. **Membership Dues:** youth (6-17 years old), $5. **Staff:** 4. **Regional Groups:** 6. **Local Groups:** 60. **Languages:** Czech, English. **Description:** Physical fitness organization/cultural and educational programs for children and adults of all ages. Sponsors gymnastic meets and schools; conducts educational activities; offers lectures and films. Compiles statistics on gymnasts and members. Maintains museum. **Libraries: Type:** reference. **Holdings:** 2,500; periodicals. **Subjects:** technical, educational, historical materials, Czech. **Awards:** American Sokol Merit Award. **Type:** recognition. **Recipient:** for Sokol student ● Citation of Merit. **Frequency:** annual. **Type:** recognition ● Future Leader Scholarship. **Frequency:** annual. **Type:** scholarship. **Boards:** Governors; Instructors. **Committees:** Educational; Foundation; Gymnastic; Public Relations; Scholarship. **Affiliated With:** USA Gymnastics. **Formerly:** (1994) Sokol. **Publications:** *American Sokol,* 10/year. Magazine. **Price:** $8.00 /year for nonmembers. **Circulation:** 5,200. **Advertising:** accepted ● Brochure ● Also Sokol and the Sokol Idea; Our Task, Aim and Goal; Dr. Joseph Scheiner; Sokol Gymnastic Manual; American Sokol - 125 Years; American Sokol Song Book; Highlights of Czech History. **Conventions/Meetings:** quinquennial American Sokol Slet (Physical Fitness Exhibition) - convention (exhibits) ● competition ● quinquennial meeting (exhibits).

18645 ■ CSA Fraternal Life (CSA)
122 W 22nd St.
Oak Brook, IL 60523
Free: (800)543-3272
E-mail: lifecsa@csafraternallife.org
URL: http://www.csafraternallife.org
Contact: Mr. Daniel J. Wenzler Sr., Pres.
Founded: 1854. **Members:** 27,600. **Staff:** 24. **Budget:** $16,000,000. **Regional Groups:** 12. **State Groups:** 14. **Local Groups:** 89. **Languages:** Czech, English, Slovak. **Description:** Fraternal benefit life insurance society. Sponsors sports, photo, poster, and Miss National CSA competitions; coordinates scholarship program and biographical archives. Compiles statistics. **Libraries: Type:** open to the public. **Holdings:** 1,500; archival material, articles, books, periodicals. **Subjects:** Czech/Slovak-American culture history. **Awards:** CSA Scholarship. **Frequency:** annual. **Type:** scholarship. **Recipient:** for a member of at least two years who met all academic standards. **Committees:** Degree Staffs; District Councils; Lodges; Sports. **Absorbed:** (1977) Unity of Czech Ladies and Men. **Formerly:** (1982) Czechoslovak Society of America. **Publications:** *CSA Journal* (in Czech and English), 11/year. Includes chapter news, scholarship report, and calendar of events. **Price:** $12.00/year. ISSN: 0195-9050. **Circulation:** 20,000 ● *Czech and Slovak Connections,* monthly. Magazine. Contains news from Czech and Slovak Republics. **Circulation:** 1,800. **Advertising:** accepted. Alternate Formats: online ● Bulletin, periodic ● Directory, annual. **Conventions/Meetings:** quadrennial congress and convention, includes chief governing body; conducts election of officers and board and amending of bylaws.

18646 ■ Czech Catholic Union (CCU)
5349 Dolloff Rd.
Cleveland, OH 44127
Ph: (216)341-0444 (216)341-0406
Fax: (216)341-0711

E-mail: insurance@czechccu.org
URL: http://www.czechccu.org
Contact: Mary Ann Mahoney, Pres.
Founded: 1879. **Members:** 5,323. **Staff:** 4. **Budget:** $100,000. **Local Groups:** 50. **Languages:** Czech, English. **Description:** Works for persons of Catholic faith. Makes annual donation to the Holy Family Cancer Home. Educates a young man to the priesthood at St. Procopius Abbey. Supports Czech Benedictines in Lisle, IL, and Rome, Italy. Offers children's services; participates in civic and cultural programs on the local level. **Awards:** School Grants. **Frequency:** periodic. **Type:** grant. **Recipient:** for Catholic high schools and colleges. **Publications:** *Posel,* bimonthly. Magazine. **Price:** free. ISSN: 1077-5374. **Circulation:** 2,200. Also Cited As: *Messenger.* **Conventions/Meetings:** quadrennial convention.

18647 ■ Czech Heritage Foundation (CHF)
PO Box 761
Cedar Rapids, IA 52406
Ph: (319)362-5123
Contact: Russell Novotny, Pres.
Founded: 1974. **Members:** 900. **Membership Dues:** $3 (annual). **Description:** Individuals interested in Czech and Slovak heritage and culture. Purpose is to foster interest in Czech and Slovak culture, heritage, language, and the collection of artifacts of Czech and Slovak origin. Works to develop projects, audiovisual educational kits, guidebooks, and museum displays for loan to schools and other organizations. Supplies costumes and representatives to ethnic festivals; organizes trips to Czech and Slovak concerts, polka parties, and other events. Provides support to the Czech Village Association, dedicated to the preservation and restoration of property in the Czech Village historical area of Cedar Rapids, which serves as a monument to the early Czechoslovak settlers who contributed to the development of Cedar Rapids and Linn County, IA. Supports the National Czech and Slovak Museum and Library. Sponsors student exchange program, which sends U.S. students to the Czech Republic each year. Maintains speakers' bureau, offering programs on Czech and Slovak community and heritage, customs, fine arts, history, and travel; provides children's services. **Publications:** *Our Czech Heritage,* quarterly. Newsletter. **Price:** included in membership ● Books. Feature information on Czech language, culture, and folk customs. ● Also publishes materials on topics including history, language, literature, and music. **Conventions/Meetings:** annual meeting - always third Monday in January. Cedar Rapids, IA ● monthly meeting - always second Tuesday of each month. Cedar Rapids, IA.

18648 ■ National Alliance of Czech Catholics (NACC)
PO Box 159
Berwyn, IL 60402
Ph: (630)766-0462 (708)484-0583
Fax: (708)484-0584
Contact: Ms. Frances Uhlir, Sec.
Founded: 1917. **Languages:** Czech, English. **Description:** Seeks to unite Czech-American Catholics for religious, civic, charitable, and educational activities. **Conventions/Meetings:** quadrennial convention - fall.

18649 ■ Western Fraternal Life Association (WFLA)
1900 1st Ave. NE
Cedar Rapids, IA 52402-5372
Ph: (319)363-2653
Free: (877)WFLAINS
Fax: (319)363-8806
E-mail: info@wflains.org
URL: http://www.wflains.org
Contact: Philip J. Torticill, Pres.
Founded: 1897. **Members:** 42,653. **Staff:** 12. **State Groups:** 17. **Description:** Provides burial insurance, social and ethnic activities, and a means to preserve Czech heritage to its members. Offers a wide range of insurance and annuity products to meet the needs of a complex society. **Programs:** Kids Care. **Formerly:** (1971) Western Bohemian Fraternal Association. **Publications:** *Fraternal Herald: Bratrske Vest-*

nik, monthly. Magazine. Features articles on the association. Includes calendar of events, mortuary claims, and obituaries. **Price:** included in membership dues; $10.00 /year for nonmembers. ISSN: 0006-9256. **Circulation:** 24,300. **Conventions/Meetings:** quadrennial meeting.

Danish

18650 ■ Danish Brotherhood in America (DBIA)
c/o Woodmen of the World
9777 S Yosemite St., Ste.200
Lone Tree, CO 80124-3115
Ph: (303)792-9777
Free: (800)345-2827
E-mail: info@denverwoodmen.com
Founded: 1882. **Members:** 8,605. **Regional Groups:** 7. **Local Groups:** 97. **Description:** Fraternal organization of persons of Danish birth or descent; persons who have lived in Denmark six months or more or who speak Danish fluently; persons interested in Danish history and traditions; persons who are friends, spouses, or relatives of members. Encourages members to be faithful to the constitution and laws of the country in which they live; perpetuates memories and traditions from Denmark for the benefit of future generations; aids members and their dependents in cases of illness, disability, or death; assists unemployed members; conducts affairs as a fraternal benefit society. Maintains portfolio of family life insurance products. Sponsors monthly coloring contest. Individual lodges sponsor Danish heritage programs, picnics, dances, and parades. **Libraries: Type:** reference. **Holdings:** archival material, audiovisuals, books. **Awards:** Howard Christensen Award. **Frequency:** annual. **Type:** recognition. **Recipient:** for dedicated DBIA members. **Telecommunication Services:** additional toll-free number, (800)777-9777. **Publications:** *American Dane,* monthly. Magazine. Contains list of new members, articles celebrating Denmark and Danish traditions, lodge news, and recipes. **Price:** included in membership dues; $12.00 /year for nonmembers. ISSN: 0739-9170. **Circulation:** 6,000. **Advertising:** accepted. Alternate Formats: microform ● *Danish Brotherhood in America—Directory of Lodges,* annual ● *Tinder Box,* monthly. Newsletter. **Conventions/Meetings:** quadrennial congress.

18651 ■ Supreme Lodge of the Danish Sisterhood of America (DSA)
c/o Sindy Poremba, Natl. Pres./Ed.
622 Palm Ave.
Penngrove, CA 94951
Ph: (707)794-8430
E-mail: sindyp@comcast.net
URL: http://www.danishsisterhood.org
Contact: Sindy Poremba, Natl. Pres./Ed.
Founded: 1883. **Members:** 2,750. **Membership Dues:** amber, $39 (annual). **Staff:** 7. **Local Groups:** 63. **Description:** Women of, or related to those of, Danish birth or descent or those married to men of Danish descent; individuals interested in the Danish heritage. **Awards:** Outstanding Members. **Frequency:** annual. **Type:** scholarship. **Publications:** *Danish Sisterhood News,* monthly. Newsletter. Includes national and lodge information. **Price:** $9.00. **Circulation:** 3,000. **Advertising:** accepted. **Conventions/Meetings:** quadrennial meeting.

Eagles

18652 ■ Grand Aerie, Fraternal Order of Eagles (FOE)
1623 Gateway Cir. S
Grove City, OH 43123
Ph: (614)883-2200
Fax: (614)883-2201
E-mail: assistance@foe.com
URL: http://www.foe.com
Contact: Mr. Bob Wahls, Grand Sec.
Founded: 1898. **Members:** 1,150,000. **Staff:** 88. **Regional Groups:** 16. **State Groups:** 53. **Local**

Groups: 3,550. **Description:** Fraternal society. Provides grants; maintains hall of fame; conducts charitable program. **Libraries: Type:** reference. **Holdings:** business records. **Awards:** D.D. Dunlap Kidney Fund. **Type:** grant. **Recipient:** for kidney research ● Eagle Hall of Fame Award. **Frequency:** annual. **Type:** recognition. **Recipient:** for dedication to community, family, and organization by a nationally recognized personality ● Eagles Art Ehrmann Cancer Fund. **Type:** grant. **Recipient:** for cancer research ● Eagles Golden Eagle Fund. **Type:** grant. **Recipient:** for senior citizens projects ● Jimmy Durante Children's Fund. **Type:** grant. **Recipient:** for retarded, disabled, and abused children ● Max Baer Heart Fund. **Type:** grant. **Recipient:** for heart research ● Robert W. Hansen Diabetes Fund. **Type:** grant. **Recipient:** for diabetes research. **Publications:** *Eagle Digest,* monthly. Newspaper ● *Eagle Leader,* monthly. Newspaper ● *Eagle Magazine,* bimonthly ● *Mrs. Eagle,* quarterly. **Conventions/Meetings:** periodic competition ● annual convention - 2008 Aug. 11-14, Louisville, KY; 2009 July 13-16, Reno, NV; 2010 Aug. 16-19, Louisville, KY.

Ecuadorean

18653 ■ Ecuadorean American Association (EAA)
30 Vesey St., Ste.506
New York, NY 10007
Ph: (212)233-7776
Fax: (212)233-7779
E-mail: andean@nyct.net
URL: http://www.ecuadoreanamerican.org
Contact: Juana C. Selinger, Pres.
Founded: 1932. **Membership Dues:** student, $85 (annual) ● individual, $150 (annual) ● resident corporate, $350 (annual). **Staff:** 4. **Description:** Represents businesses, financial institutions, organizations, and individuals with investments in Ecuador or those seeking to establish commercial relations with Ecuador. Objectives are to: promote a greater knowledge and understanding of modern Ecuador; encourage commercial and cultural relations and goodwill; disseminate information on current events and on economic and financial matters of concern to investors in Ecuador; sponsor luncheons with guest speakers for business people, government officials, and individuals; increase trade, investments, and travel between Ecuador and the U.S. **Publications:** *Ecuadorean News Digest,* monthly. **Price:** free for members. **Conventions/Meetings:** luncheon - 5/year.

Elks

18654 ■ Benevolent and Protective Order of Elks (BPOE)
2750 N Lakeview Ave.
Chicago, IL 60614-1889
Ph: (773)755-4700
Fax: (773)755-4790
E-mail: grandlodge@elks.org
URL: http://www.elks.org
Contact: Jack M. Jensen, Grand Sec./Chief Operating Off.
Founded: 1868. **Members:** 1,000,000. **State Groups:** 50. **Local Groups:** 2,300. **Description:** Serves as a fraternal and benevolent society. Administers Elks National Foundation, a private charitable trust fund. **Committees:** Americanism; Drug Awareness; Elks National Veterans Service; Government Relations; Lodge Activities; Lodge Development; National Foundation; Ritualistic; State Associations; Youth Activities. **Publications:** *Directory of State Associations,* annual ● *Directory of Subordinate Lodges,* annual ● *Elks Magazine,* 10/year. **Advertising:** accepted ● *Grand Lodge Newsletter,* monthly. **Conventions/Meetings:** annual convention - always July. 2008 July 6-10, Anaheim, CA; 2009 July 5-9, Portland, OR; 2010 July 4-8, Orlando, FL.

18655 ■ Improved Benevolent Protective Order of Elks of the World (IBPOEW)
PO Box 159
Winton, NC 27986
Ph: (252)358-7661
URL: http://northbysouth.kenyon.edu/2000/Fraternal/ibpoew.htm
Contact: Alexander Ashley, Contact
Founded: 1898. **Members:** 500,000. **Description:** International fraternal organization of primarily black membership. Concerned with civil liberties and equal opportunity. **Awards: Type:** scholarship. **Recipient:** for youth of all races. **Divisions:** Civil Liberties; Education; Shrine. **Publications:** Elks News, bimonthly. Newsletter. **Conventions/Meetings:** annual convention (exhibits).

18656 ■ Supreme Emblem Club of the United States of America (SECUS)
c/o Shirley Brigham, Supreme Corresponding Sec.
3608 Redwood Ave.
Los Angeles, CA 90066
Ph: (802)365-7292
E-mail: sbshpr@aol.com
URL: http://www.emblemclub.com
Contact: Barbara Colburn, Supreme Pres.
Founded: 1926. **State Groups:** 26. **Local Groups:** 540. **Description:** Represents women relatives of members of the Benevolent and Protective Order of Elks (see separate entry). Sponsors charitable program; compiles statistics. **Awards: Frequency:** annual. **Type:** scholarship. **Recipient:** to sons and daughters of members. **Committees:** Americanism; Color Guard; Drill; Laws; Publicity; Ritual; Site; Topics; Tract. **Affiliated With:** Benevolent and Protective Order of Elks. **Publications:** Emblem Topics, 10/year. **Circulation:** 41,000. **Advertising:** accepted ● Roster of Affiliated Clubs, annual. Membership Directory ● Manual. **Conventions/Meetings:** annual meeting - always September.

English-Speaking

18657 ■ English-Speaking Union of the United States (ESU)
144 E 39th St.
New York, NY 10016
Ph: (212)818-1200
Fax: (212)867-4177
E-mail: info@esuus.org
URL: http://www.esuus.org/index.htm
Contact: Alice Boyne, Exec. Dir./Pres.
Founded: 1920. **Members:** 20,000. **Staff:** 14. **Regional Groups:** 8. **Local Groups:** 86. **Multinational. Description:** Fosters mutual understanding and friendship among English-speaking people worldwide; seeks to expand channels of communication. Administers information programs and English in Action program. Maintains 7500 volume library of materials pertaining to Britain. Sponsors competitions; maintains speakers' bureau. **Awards:** Ambassador Book Awards. **Frequency:** annual. **Type:** recognition. **Recipient:** to authors who have made exceptional contributions to the life and culture of United States ● **Type:** grant. **Recipient:** for travel ● Luard Scholarship. **Frequency:** annual. **Type:** scholarship. **Recipient:** for outstanding students who are enrolled in a United Negro College Fund schools, Hampton University, or Howard University. **Departments:** Book-Across-the-Sea; Education; English in Action; Speakers Program; Travel. **Publications:** The English Speaker, quarterly. Newsletter. Alternate Formats: online ● Annual Report, annual. Alternate Formats: online. **Conventions/Meetings:** annual meeting.

Entertainment

18658 ■ Showmen's League of America (SLA)
300 W Randolph St.
Chicago, IL 60609
Ph: (312)332-6236
Free: (800)350-9906
Fax: (312)332-6237
E-mail: rick@showmensleague.org
URL: http://www.showmensleague.org
Contact: Tom Davis, Pres.
Founded: 1913. **Membership Dues:** individual, $25 (annual). **Staff:** 3. **Description:** Owners and officials of fairs, expositions, circuses, carnivals, rodeos, auto races, thrill shows, and other indoor and outdoor amusement enterprises. Works to take care of the sick and buries the dead of show business. **Publications:** Showmen's League News Flashes, every 6-8 weeks. Newsletter. **Circulation:** 1,500 ● Also publishes a yearbook. Advertising is accepted. **Conventions/Meetings:** annual meeting and convention - every December.

18659 ■ Tournament of Roses Association
391 S Orange Grove Blvd.
Pasadena, CA 91184
Ph: (626)449-4100
Fax: (626)449-9066
E-mail: rosepr@rosemail.org
URL: http://www.tournamentofroses.com
Contact: Katie McFadden, Dir. of Membership
Founded: 1890. **Members:** 1,400. **Membership Dues:** regular, $55-$100 (annual). **Staff:** 20. **Budget:** $20,000,000. **Description:** Individuals living or working within 15 miles of Pasadena, CA who volunteer their services to help organize and stage the annual Tournament of Roses Parade and Rose Bowl football game (935). Maintains 33 committees including, Community Relations, Coronation, Equestrian, Float Construction, Float Entry, Football, Judging, Music, Press Relations, Television and Radio, and University Entertainment. **Libraries: Type:** reference. **Holdings:** photographs. **Publications:** Rose Bowl Game Official Souvenir Program, annual. **Price:** $10.00. **Circulation:** 100,000. **Advertising:** accepted ● Tournament of Roses Parade Official Souvenir Program, annual. **Price:** $7.00. **Circulation:** 125,000. **Advertising:** accepted ● Tournament Times, annual. Contains Rose Parade and Rose Bowl Game stories and calendar of events. **Price:** included in membership dues. **Circulation:** 3,000.

Estonian

18660 ■ Estonian American National Council (EANC)
9814 Hill St.
Kensington, MD 20895
Ph: (301)587-8353
E-mail: marjura@erols.com
URL: http://www.estosite.org
Contact: Marju Rink-Abel, Pres.
Founded: 1952. **Members:** 35. **Staff:** 2. **Budget:** $110,000. **Regional Groups:** 8. **Languages:** English, Estonian. **Description:** Coordinates activities to preserve the Estonian culture, heritage and language among Estonian-Americans. Promotes the ideas and viewpoints of democracy, human rights and free market economy and propagates and defends such goals. Cooperates with other organizations in achieving its goals and objectives. **Publications:** Estonia and Estonian Americans, periodic. Brochure. **Conventions/Meetings:** annual meeting.

18661 ■ Estonian Educational Society (EHS)
Estonian House
243 E 34th St.
New York, NY 10016
Ph: (212)684-0336
Fax: (212)684-6588
E-mail: info@estonianhousenewyork.com
URL: http://www.estonianhousenewyork.com
Contact: Liisi Lascarro, Mgr.
Founded: 1929. **Members:** 400. **Membership Dues:** full, $50 (annual) ● associate, $35 (annual) ● student, $20 (annual). **Staff:** 5. **Languages:** English, Estonian, Finnish. **Description:** Maintains school of Estonian language and history. **Libraries: Type:** by appointment only. **Holdings:** 1,000. **Divisions:** Bridge Club; Chess Club; Folk Dance; Men's Chorus; Recreational and Modern Gymnastics; Senior Citizen; Theater; Women's Auxiliary; Women's Chorus.

Ethiopian

18662 ■ Ethiopian Community Mutual Assistance Association (ECMAA)
552 Massachusetts Ave., Ste.202
Cambridge, MA 02139
Ph: (617)492-4232
Fax: (617)492-7685
E-mail: btamene@aol.com
URL: http://www.ecmaaonline.org
Contact: Binyam Tamene, Exec. Dir.
Founded: 1981. **Members:** 500. **Description:** Individuals of Ethiopian descent; members reside primarily in New York City metropolitan area. Advances the economic and social welfare of Ethiopians living in the U.S. Identifies the needs of the Ethiopian community, particularly regarding immigration and civil rights, and provides appropriate assistance. Works to strengthen communication among Ethiopians; aims to preserve Ethiopian culture as a source of historical identity; promotes understanding between Ethiopians and non-Ethiopians. Operates refugee assistance project that provides newly-arrived Ethiopian refugees or migrants with access to various educational, health, and other facilities; also offers overall orientation, guidance, and job placement assistance. Conducts a community-wide educational/information program with a view to hastening the acculturation and social adjustment efforts of members. Maintains museum. Plans to establish: cultural/educational center; emergency aid fund; job data bank; referral system. **Conventions/Meetings:** annual meeting - always summer, in New York City.

Ethnic Studies

18663 ■ Ellis Island Medal of Honor Society
c/o National Ethnic Coalition of Organizations
232 Madison Ave., Ste.900
New York, NY 10016-2901
Ph: (212)755-1492
Fax: (212)755-3762
E-mail: ellisislandrose@aol.com
URL: http://www.neco.org
Contact: Rosemarie Taglione, Exec. Dir.
Members: 275. **Description:** Fosters fellowship among medalists; aims to preserve ethnic diversity, promote equality and harmony, combat injustice and bring about unity. **Awards: Type:** recognition. **Recipient:** to prominent luminaries representing business, politics, sports, arts. **Publications:** Heritage Cookbook. **Conventions/Meetings:** annual Gala Dinner.

18664 ■ Inter-University Program for Latino Research (IUPLR)
Univ. of Notre Dame
Inst. for Latino Stud.
230 McKenna Hall
PO Box 764
Notre Dame, IN 46556-5685
Ph: (574)631-3481
Fax: (574)631-3884
E-mail: iuplr@iuplr.nd.edu
URL: http://www.nd.edu/~iuplr
Contact: Dr. Gilberto Cardenas PhD, Exec. Dir.
Founded: 1983. **Languages:** English, Latin. **Description:** Promotes the Latino community at the local, state, regional, national, and international levels. **Telecommunication Services:** electronic mail, cardenas.7@nd.edu.

18665 ■ National Ethnic Coalition of Organizations (NECO)
232 Madison Ave., Ste.900
New York, NY 10016-2901
Ph: (212)755-1492
Fax: (212)755-3762

E-mail: ellisislandrose@aol.com
URL: http://www.neco.org
Contact: Rosemarie Taglione, Exec. Dir.
Description: Seeks to educate and encourage ethnic unity. **Awards:** Ellis Island Medals of Honor. **Frequency:** annual. **Type:** medal. **Recipient:** to U.S. citizens from various ethnic backgrounds.

18666 ■ Project RACE
PO Box 2366
Los Banos, CA 93635
Fax: (209)826-2510
E-mail: projrace@aol.com
URL: http://www.projectrace.com
Contact: Susan Graham, Exec. Dir.
Founded: 1991. **State Groups:** 46. **Multinational.**
Description: Advocates for multiracial children and adults. Promotes a multiracial classification on all identification forms requiring racial data. **Libraries: Type:** reference. **Holdings:** 500; articles, audio recordings, books, papers, reports, video recordings. **Subjects:** race, ethnicity, multiculturalism, data, population, census, black, white, Asian, Hispanic, Native American, Alaska Native, government, Congress. **Divisions:** Teen Project RACE.

Family Name Societies

18667 ■ Morgan Family Club
3120 6th Ave.
Columbus, GA 31904
E-mail: rewoodham@charter.net
URL: http://www.geocities.com/~rewoodham/morgan.html
Contact: R.E. Woodham, Ed.
Membership Dues: general, $15 (annual). **Description:** Gathers and preserves the heritage of all American Morgan families. Serves as the central clearinghouse for information on all the different Morgan families. Provides a forum for family members to share their research efforts and help each other eliminate duplication and errors. **Libraries: Type:** reference. **Holdings:** archival material, articles, clippings. **Publications:** Morgan Family News of the South. Newsletter. Contains current news about all descendants of Morgan families in America. Alternate Formats: online.

Finnish

18668 ■ Finlandia Foundation National (FF)
470 W Walnut St.
Pasadena, CA 91103-3562
Ph: (626)795-2081
Fax: (626)795-6533
E-mail: ffnoffice@mac.com
URL: http://www.finlandiafoundation.org
Contact: John Laine, Pres.
Founded: 1953. **Members:** 5,000. **Membership Dues:** general, $20 (annual). **Staff:** 17. **State Groups:** 19. **Local Groups:** 21. **National Groups:** 24. **Description:** Supports Finnish and Finnish-American cultural and educational programs and projects through grants and scholarships; provides support for chapters located in all sections of the country. **Libraries: Type:** reference. **Holdings:** 100; books, periodicals, video recordings. **Awards: Type:** grant ● **Type:** scholarship. **Formed by Merger of:** Finlandia Foundation. **Publications:** Finlandia Foundation National Newsletter, semiannual. **Conventions/Meetings:** monthly Chapter meetings ● semiannual Trustees Meeting.

18669 ■ Finnish-American Historical Society of the West (FAHSW)
PO Box 5522
Portland, OR 97228-5522
E-mail: info@finamhsw.com
URL: http://www.finamhsw.com
Contact: Gene A. Knapp, Ed.
Founded: 1962. **Members:** 300. **Membership Dues:** individual, $10 (annual) ● family, $15 (annual). **Staff:** 10. **Languages:** English, Finnish. **Description:**

People of Finnish ancestry and friends of Finland interested in discovering, collecting, and preserving material to establish and illustrate the history of persons of Finnish descent in the American West. Maintains Lindgren Log Home, a museum of Finnish-American artifacts from the 1920s. **Libraries: Type:** not open to the public. **Holdings:** archival material. **Publications:** Finish Pioneer Series, annual. Monograph. **Price:** included in membership dues ● FINNAM Newsletter, quarterly. **Price:** included in membership dues ● Also publishes other special publications. **Conventions/Meetings:** annual Commemorative Meeting - always December ● monthly meeting - October through June.

Fraternities and Sororities

18670 ■ International Guild of Nobles
PO Box 7264
Univ. Sta.
Provo, UT 84602-7264
Ph: (801)489-0458
E-mail: jim.williams@ik-fraternity.org
URL: http://www.ik-fraternity.org
Contact: Jim Williams, Contact
Founded: 1989. **Members:** 30,000. **Membership Dues:** participating, $8 (annual). **Staff:** 4. **Multinational. Description:** Promotes the interests of Intercollegiate Knights. Facilitates communication between members and alumni; preserves traditions of the order. **Awards: Type:** recognition ● **Type:** scholarship. **Affiliated With:** Intercollegiate Knights.

18671 ■ Legionarios del Trabajo in America
Grand Lodge
2154 S San Joaquin St.
Stockton, CA 95206
Ph: (209)463-6516
Fax: (209)463-6516
Contact: Gloria Villarta, Sec.
Founded: 1924. **Members:** 812. **Membership Dues:** regular, $15 (annual). **Staff:** 3. **Budget:** $70,050. **Regional Groups:** 43. **State Groups:** 31. **Local Groups:** 9. **Description:** Fraternal organization. Provides specialized education; holds seminars. Operates charitable program; plans to establish a library. **Awards:** Membership Award. **Frequency:** annual. **Type:** recognition ● Scholarship. **Frequency:** annual. **Type:** scholarship ● Trailblazers Award. **Frequency:** annual. **Type:** recognition. **Committees:** Ladies Conference; Supreme Consistory. **Councils:** Life Members. **Publications:** Grand Lodge Membership Directory, triennial ● LDT Circular, monthly ● LDT Membership Directory, triennial ● Bulletin, monthly ● Newsletter, monthly. **Conventions/Meetings:** triennial convention ● annual general assembly - always third weekend in February, Stockton, CA.

18672 ■ Moose International (MI)
Admin. Bldg.
155 S Intl. Dr.
Mooseheart, IL 60539-1169
Ph: (630)966-2209
Fax: (630)859-6616
E-mail: bairey@mooseintl.org
URL: http://www.mooseintl.org
Contact: William B. Airey, Dir. Gen./CEO
Founded: 1888. **Members:** 1,400,000. **Staff:** 200. **Budget:** $20,000,000. **State Groups:** 43. **Local Groups:** 4,000. **Description:** Fraternal organization comprising Lodges (Loyal Order of Moose) and Chapters (Women of the Moose). Operates a school and home in Mooseheart, IL, for qualified children with a need; also operates a home for aging dependent members and their spouses in Moosehaven, Orange Park, FL. **Boards:** Directors. **Councils:** Supreme. **Formerly:** (1991) Supreme Lodge of the World, Loyal Order of Moose. **Publications:** Moose, quarterly. Magazine. Provides members, association, and chapter news. **Price:** $2.00/year. **Circulation:** 1,300,000. Alternate Formats: diskette. **Conventions/Meetings:** annual convention and workshop.

18673 ■ National Association of Latino Fraternal Organizations (NALFO)
PO Box 27322
Tempe, AZ 85285-7322
E-mail: chair@nalfo.org
URL: http://www.nalfo.org
Contact: Ruby Alvarado Hernandez, Chair
Founded: 1998. **Description:** Umbrella organization for Latino Greek Letter Organizations. Promotes positive inter-fraternal relations, communication and development of all Latino Fraternal organizations. **Awards:** Latino Greek Award. **Frequency:** annual. **Type:** recognition. **Publications:** Newsletter. Alternate Formats: online. **Conventions/Meetings:** annual National Latino Greek Awards Convention.

French

18674 ■ ACA Assurance
1750 Elm St., Ste.200
Manchester, NH 03104
Ph: (603)625-8577
Free: (800)222-8577
Fax: (603)625-1214
E-mail: info@aca-assurance.com
URL: http://www.aca-assurance.org
Contact: Pauline Lally, Pres./CEO
Founded: 1896. **Members:** 68,000. **Membership Dues:** regular, $25 (annual). **Staff:** 29. **Budget:** $2,800,000. **Regional Groups:** 9. **State Groups:** 50. **Local Groups:** 53. **Languages:** English, French. **Description:** Fraternal benefit life insurance society of American and Canadian Roman Catholics of French descent. Provides French-language television program entitled Bonjour. **Libraries: Type:** reference. **Holdings:** 40,000; archival material, artwork, books, clippings, monographs, periodicals. **Subjects:** French-Canadians in North America. **Awards: Frequency:** annual. **Type:** scholarship. **Committees:** Archives; Scholarship. **Formerly:** (1999) Association Canado Americaine. **Publications:** Le Canado-Americain (in English and French), quarterly. Magazine. **Price:** available to members only. **Circulation:** 39,000. **Advertising:** accepted ● Repertoire, annual. Directory. **Conventions/Meetings:** board meeting - 3/year.

18675 ■ American Society of the French Legion of Honor (ASFLH)
Address Unknown since 2007
Founded: 1922. **Members:** 300. **Description:** Seeks to: provide a social and fraternal medium for members of the French Order of the Legion of Honor residing in the United States; promote appreciation of French culture in the United States and American culture in France; strengthen the traditional friendship and goodwill existing between the peoples of the two countries. Makes donations to organizations involved in Franco-American exchange. **Awards: Type:** scholarship. **Publications:** French American Review, semiannual. **Price:** free. ISSN: 0270-3793. **Circulation:** 1,000. **Advertising:** not accepted. **Conventions/Meetings:** annual meeting.

18676 ■ Committee of French Speaking Societies (CFSS)
48 W 55th St., No. 3R
New York, NY 10019
Ph: (212)830-4103
Fax: (212)830-4343
E-mail: contact@cafusa.org
URL: http://www.cafusa.org
Contact: Richard Ortoli, Pres.
Founded: 1927. **Members:** 1,500. **Membership Dues:** association, $50 (annual). **Staff:** 10. **Budget:** $25,000. **Regional Groups:** 46. **Description:** Federation of French and French-speaking societies. Sponsors celebrations of French holidays (Bastille Day, Armistice Day). **Publications:** Reports, monthly. **Conventions/Meetings:** meeting - 9/year, always in New York City.

18677 ■ Federation of French American Women (FFFA)

Address Unknown since 2007

Founded: 1951. **Members:** 1,200. **Membership Dues:** Affiliated, $10 (annual). **Staff:** 10. **Regional Groups:** 15. **Local Groups:** 49. **Languages:** English, French. **Description:** Members of French fraternal organizations. Promotes French culture. Conducts oral history program, French speaking contests, youth festivals, ethnic vacations, and reunions. Maintains hall of fame. Compiles statistics. **Awards:** Fonds Irene Levesque. **Frequency:** annual. **Type:** scholarship. **Recipient:** for three outstanding French students. **Also Known As:** Federation Feminine Franco-Americaine. **Conventions/Meetings:** annual conference, with lectures (exhibits) - in October in New England cities ● biennial congress.

18678 ■ French-American Aid for Children (FAAFC)

111 W 58th St., Ste.LL
New York, NY 10019
Ph: (212)486-9593
Fax: (212)486-9594
E-mail: info@faafc.org
URL: http://www.aidforchildren.org
Contact: Ms. Marguerite Mangin, Pres.

Founded: 1939. **Members:** 90. **Membership Dues:** regular, $175 (annual). **Description:** Offers financial aid to organizations helping underprivileged children in France and the U.S.

18679 ■ Union Saint-Jean-Baptiste (USJB)

c/o Saint-Jean-Baptiste Education Foundation
Box F
Woonsocket, RI 02895
Ph: (401)769-0520
Free: (800)225-USJB
Fax: (401)766-3014
E-mail: louisec@csli.org
URL: http://www.sjbef.org
Contact: Louise Champigny, Admin.

Founded: 1900. **Members:** 30,000. **Staff:** 12. **Local Groups:** 75. **Languages:** English, French. **Description:** A division of Catholic Family Life Insurance. Fraternal benefit life insurance society of Roman Catholics of French origin. Conducts charitable and educational activities. **Libraries: Type:** reference. **Holdings:** 6,000; archival material. **Subjects:** Franco-American genealogy, history. **Affiliated With:** Catholic Family Life Insurance. **Publications:** *Jus-forkids*, quarterly. Magazine ● *L'Union* (in English and French), quarterly. **Conventions/Meetings:** annual conference and workshop - usually November.

Genealogy

18680 ■ American/Schleswig-Holstein Heritage Society (ASHHS)

PO Box 506
Walcott, IA 52773-0506
Ph: (563)284-4184 (563)284-6640
Fax: (563)284-4184
E-mail: ashhs@ashhs.org
URL: http://www.ashhs.org
Contact: Lee Muller, Pres.

Founded: 1989. **Members:** 975. **Membership Dues:** individual, $18 (annual) ● joint, $21 (annual) ● foreign, $25 (annual) ● life, individual, $500 ● life, joint, $750 ● life, foreign, $1,000. **Budget:** $20,000. **Languages:** English, German. **Description:** Works to promote the heritage of Schleswig-Holstein, Germany and the immigrants from Schleswig-Holstein to America. Supports genealogical research; encourages the study of the dialects of Schleswig-Holstein; studies the immigration and cultural impact of Schleswig-Holsteiners; conducts educational programs and events. Maintains endowment fund. **Libraries: Type:** open to the public; by appointment only. **Holdings:** 1,000; archival material, articles, books, periodicals. **Subjects:** exclusively Schleswig/Holstein. **Awards: Frequency:** annual. **Type:** grant. **Recipient:** for promotion of Schleswig-Holstein heritage ● **Frequency:** periodic. **Type:** recognition.

Computer Services: database ● mailing lists. **Publications:** Newsletter (in English and German), bimonthly. **Price:** $2.00/copy. ISSN: 1045-0996. **Circulation:** 1,000. Alternate Formats: CD-ROM. **Conventions/Meetings:** monthly board meeting ● biennial meeting ● quarterly regional meeting - always 3rd Sunday of February, May, August, and November.

18681 ■ FAMILIA Ancestral Research Association (FARA)

PO Box 10359
Westminster, CA 92685-0359
Ph: (714)687-0390
E-mail: knwill@juno.com
URL: http://www.rootsweb.com/~cafara
Contact: Elma Valdes, Pres.

Founded: 1997. **Members:** 96. **Membership Dues:** individual, $25 (annual) ● family household, $30 (annual). **Budget:** $2,000. **Languages:** English, Spanish. **Multinational. Description:** Provides research, documentation, and preservation of Mexican American ancestral heritage. **Publications:** *Familia News*, bimonthly. Newsletter. Contains information on FAMILIA events, accounts of research done by fellow members, tips on research and archival sources. **Conventions/Meetings:** monthly meeting and lecture - every 3rd Saturday except July and December.

18682 ■ The Irish Ancestral Research Association (TIARA)

Dept. W
2120 Commonwealth Ave.
Auburndale, MA 02466
E-mail: president@tiara.ie
URL: http://www.tiara.ie
Contact: Mary Choppa, Pres.

Founded: 1983. **Members:** 700. **Membership Dues:** individual and organization in U.S., $20 (annual) ● family in U.S., individual and organization outside U.S. and Canada, $30 (annual) ● individual and organization in Canada, $25 (annual) ● family in Canada, $37 (annual) ● family outside U.S. and Canada, $45 (annual). **Multinational. Description:** People interested in Irish genealogy. Develops and promotes the growth, study and exchange of ideas among people interested in Irish genealogical and historical research and education. **Publications:** Booklets.

Georgian

18683 ■ Georgian Association in the United States of America (GAUSA)

2300 M St. NW, Ste.800
Washington, DC 20037
Ph: (217)698-7071
Free: (877)527-8854
Fax: (217)793-0041
E-mail: georgianassociation@gmail.com
URL: http://www.georgianassociation.org
Contact: Mamuka Tsereteli, Pres.

Founded: 1932. **Membership Dues:** individual of Georgian nationality, $50 (annual). **Staff:** 4. **Regional Groups:** 5. **Languages:** English, French, Russian. **Description:** Provides assistance in hardship cases and information on Georgian history, politics and current affairs. Conducts educational and charitable programs. **Libraries: Type:** reference. **Holdings:** 800; archival material, books, periodicals. **Subjects:** Georgian history and politics. **Awards: Type:** grant ● **Type:** scholarship. **Computer Services:** Mailing lists, members. **Boards:** Directors. **Absorbed:** Georgian National Alliance. **Publications:** *Tsnobis Purtseli*, periodic. Newsletter. Alternate Formats: online ● Newsletter, semiannual. Covers U.S. immigration and events in Georgia. **Price:** $5.00. **Circulation:** 400. **Advertising:** accepted. **Conventions/Meetings:** National Holidays - conference (exhibits) - occasionally.

German

18684 ■ American Aid Society of German Descendants (AASGD)

6540 N Milwaukee Ave.
Chicago, IL 60631-1750

Ph: (773)763-9554
E-mail: wscheffrahn@dls.net
URL: http://www.AmericanAidSociety.com
Contact: Walter Scheffrahn, Press Sec.

Founded: 1944. **Members:** 900. **Membership Dues:** single, $20 (annual) ● couple, $40 (annual). **Budget:** $225,000. **Languages:** English, German. **Description:** Individuals of German descent and those interested in German culture. Seeks to assist ethnic Germans facing persecution in southeastern Europe. Promotes appreciation of German history and culture. Works with government agencies and nongovernmental organizations to insure respect for the civil and human rights of ethnic German minorities. Conducts educational and cultural programs, music exhibitions and soccer clinics. **Libraries: Type:** by appointment only; reference. **Holdings:** 2,000; archival material, artwork, biographical archives, books, maps, photographs. **Subjects:** history, artifacts, German language. **Publications:** *American Aid Society Vereinszeitung* (in English and German), quarterly. Newsletter. Covers organizations, activities, history and culture. **Price:** included in membership dues; $2.50/issue for nonmembers. **Circulation:** 500. **Advertising:** accepted. **Conventions/Meetings:** monthly meeting - held every third Friday.

18685 ■ American Council on Germany (ACG)

14 E 60th St., Ste.1000
New York, NY 10022
Ph: (212)826-3636
Fax: (212)758-3445
E-mail: info@acgusa.org
URL: http://www.acgusa.org
Contact: Garrick Utley, Chm.

Founded: 1952. **Members:** 750. **Membership Dues:** in New York tri-state/New Jersey/Connecticut area, $125 (annual) ● elsewhere, including Europe, $75 (annual) ● corporate contributor, $1,000-$4,999 (annual) ● corporate associate, $5,000-$9,999 (annual) ● corporate leader, $10,000 (annual). **Staff:** 8. **Budget:** $1,400,000. **Regional Groups:** 17. **Languages:** English, German. **Description:** Promotes open communication and mutual understanding between the United States and Germany through ongoing dialogue and exchanges. Organizes conferences and symposia among high-level officials and promising young leaders to discuss issues from economic policy to security; promotes awareness of key transatlantic issues with its ongoing speaker series and occasional papers; sponsors fellowships to facilitate the exchange of experience and information among selected American and German specialists in fields such as agriculture, art, environmental affairs, journalism, and urban affairs; expands the transatlantic dialogue through its 14 Eric M. Warburg Chapters and three pilot programs across the United States. **Awards:** ACG Journalism Fellowship for the Study of German Politics and Society. **Frequency:** annual. **Type:** fellowship. **Recipient:** to mid-level American journalist ● Guido Goldman Fellowship for the Study of German and European Economic and International Affairs. **Frequency:** annual. **Type:** fellowship. **Recipient:** to postgraduate American scholars ● Kellen Fellowship. **Frequency:** annual. **Type:** fellowship. **Recipient:** to accomplished young Berlin journalist ● McCloy Fellowship. **Frequency:** annual. **Type:** fellowship. **Recipient:** to mid-level German and American professionals in fields of agriculture, art, environmental affairs, journalism and urban affairs ● Richard M. Hunt Fellowship for the Study of German Politics, Society, and Culture. **Frequency:** annual. **Type:** fellowship. **Recipient:** to postgraduate American scholars. **Publications:** *Trans-Atlantic Dialogue*, semiannual. Newsletter. **Price:** included in membership dues ● Annual Report, annual ● Also publishes occasional papers on German-American Issues. **Conventions/Meetings:** biennial American-German Conference ● annual American-German Young Leaders Conference - conference and meeting.

18686 ■ American Historical Society of Germans From Russia (AHSGR)

631 D St.
Lincoln, NE 68502-1199
Ph: (402)474-3363

Fax: (402)474-7229
E-mail: ahsgr@ahsgr.org
URL: http://www.ahsgr.org
Contact: Jerome Siebert, Pres.
Founded: 1968. **Members:** 5,000. **Membership Dues:** sustaining, $100 (annual) ● individual, family, institutional, $50 (annual) ● contributing, $75 (annual) ● life, $750 ● youth, $8 (annual) ● student, $15 (annual). **Staff:** 8. **Budget:** $350,000. **Local Groups:** 60. **Languages:** English, German, Polish, Russian, Ukrainian. **Description:** Individuals who are of Russian German ancestry; researchers, historians, libraries, genealogical societies, and historical societies. Records the history of Germans from Russia, encourages research, and assists with genealogical research. Maintains museum. **Libraries: Type:** reference. **Holdings:** 6,000; archival material, books, maps, periodicals. **Subjects:** history, genealogy, folklore, music. **Committees:** Bibliography; Editorial and Publication; Facilities; Finance and Personnel; Folklore; Genealogy; Historical Research; Linguistics; Membership/Public Affairs; Religious History; Research; Strategic Planning; Technology; Translations. **Publications:** *Clues*, annual. Includes Genealogical resource. **Price:** included in membership dues. ISSN: 0149-1725. **Circulation:** 5,500 ● *Journal of the American Historical Society of Germans from Russia*, quarterly. **Price:** $4.00/issue for members; $5.00/issue for nonmembers. ISSN: 0162-8283. **Circulation:** 5,500 ● Newsletter, quarterly. **Price:** included in membership dues. **Advertising:** accepted ● Also publishes maps and books. **Conventions/Meetings:** annual convention (exhibits) ● annual workshop, with folklore, culture, genealogy, religious history, translations, research, and bibliography.

18687 ■ German-American National Congress (DANK)
4740 N Western Ave.
Chicago, IL 60625-2097
Ph: (773)275-1100
Free: (888)872-3265
Fax: (773)275-4010
E-mail: dankoffice-info@yahoo.com
URL: http://www.dank.org
Contact: Ernst Ott, Natl. Pres.
Founded: 1959. **Members:** 4,500. **Membership Dues:** individual/head of household, $30 (annual) ● spouse/college student, $10 (annual). **Budget:** $120,000. **Regional Groups:** 4. **State Groups:** 8. **Local Groups:** 5. **National Groups:** 45. **Languages:** English, German. **Description:** Represents German American interests on local, regional and national levels. Seeks to cultivate the German American heritage. **Funds:** Education. **Also Known As:** Deutsch-Amerikanischer National-Kongress. **Publications:** *The German-American Journal* (in English and German), bimonthly. Newspaper. Includes chapter news, calendar of events, president's report, travel information, and articles of interest to the German community. **Price:** $15.00 for nonmembers. ISSN: 0273-5261. **Circulation:** 7,000. **Advertising:** accepted. Alternate Formats: online. **Conventions/Meetings:** biennial convention - always October.

18688 ■ German Society of the City of New York (GSCNY)
6 E 87th St.
New York, NY 10128
Ph: (212)360-6022
Fax: (212)360-6027
Contact: Wolfgang Hamel, Exec.Dir.
Founded: 1784. **Members:** 600. **Staff:** 6. **Budget:** $3,000,000. **Description:** Individuals and firms interested in assisting German immigrants. Provides German-American families and individuals with welfare services, employment, and professional counseling. Sponsors activities for senior citizens. **Publications:** *The Guardian*, 3-4/year. Newsletter. **Price:** included in membership. **Conventions/Meetings:** annual meeting.

18689 ■ German Society of Pennsylvania (GSP)
611 Spring Garden St.
Philadelphia, PA 19123-3505
Ph: (215)627-2332

Fax: (215)627-5297
E-mail: info@germansociety.org
URL: http://www.germansociety.org
Contact: Hardy von Auenmueller, Pres.
Founded: 1764. **Members:** 1,000. **Membership Dues:** individual, $50 ● student, $25 ● household, $75 ● sponsor, $150 ● corporate, $300 ● life, $1,000. **Staff:** 6. **Budget:** $500,000. **Languages:** English, German. **Description:** Promotes understanding of German and German-American culture and history through exhibits, a public library, educational programs, German and English language courses, and social activities. Arranges lectures, exhibits, and concerts emphasizing German culture. Offers courses in the German language. Offers lecture and concert series. **Libraries: Type:** open to the public. **Holdings:** 90,000; archival material, books. **Subjects:** German-American history, social history, religion, philosophy, literature, arts. **Awards:** Language Proficiency Award. **Frequency:** annual. **Type:** recognition. **Recipient:** to high school students for proficiency in German and to high school teachers for excellence in teaching German ● **Frequency:** annual. **Type:** scholarship. **Recipient:** to full time students majoring in German language and its literature at a four-year college or university. **Committees:** Building; Education; Fundraising; Library; Music; Public Relations. **Publications:** *Der Pennsylvanische Staatsbote* (in English and German), bimonthly. Newsletter. **Price:** included in membership dues.

18690 ■ German-Texan Heritage Society (GTHS)
507 E 10th St.
PO Box 684171
Austin, TX 78768-4171
Ph: (512)482-0927
Free: (866)482-4847
Fax: (512)482-0636
E-mail: info@germantexans.org
URL: http://www.germantexans.org
Contact: Eva Barnett, Office Mgr.
Founded: 1978. **Members:** 1,025. **Membership Dues:** student (society), $15 (annual) ● individual (society), $25 (annual) ● individual (guild and society), $40 (annual) ● family (society), $35 (annual) ● family (guild and society), $50 (annual) ● patron, $75 (annual) ● life, $750 ● student (guild and society), $30 (annual). **Staff:** 1. **Budget:** $100,000. **State Groups:** 1. **Languages:** English, German. **Multinational. Description:** Descendents of all German-speaking peoples, especially those who settled in Texas; researchers, genealogists, history enthusiasts, folklorists, preservationists, and those interested in the German-Texan experience. Promotes awareness and preservation of the German cultural heritage of Texas. Studies and disseminates information on folklore. Conducts research and educational programs. Produces cultural events and social gatherings. Publishes books, a quarterly Journal and a bimonthly newsletter. **Libraries: Type:** reference. **Holdings:** 2,235; archival material, audio recordings, books, periodicals, photographs, video recordings. **Subjects:** German Texana, genealogy, Texas history, German history, German literature, travel in Germany. **Awards:** Ehrenstein Award. **Frequency:** annual. **Type:** recognition. **Recipient:** for outstanding volunteerism. **Computer Services:** Bibliographic search, holdings. **Divisions:** German Free School Guild. **Publications:** *Diary of Hermann Seele*. Book. **Price:** $27.50 plus $4.50 postage/handling ● *Handbook and Registry of German-Texan Heritage*. **Price:** $9.00 plus shipping and handling ● *The Journal*, quarterly. Contains a genealogical section with hints on doing research in German-speaking countries, family histories, activities and events, and book reviews. **Price:** $5.00 for members; $6.00 for nonmembers. ISSN: 0730-3106. **Circulation:** 1,100. **Conventions/Meetings:** annual convention, with books and displays on German heritage and history (exhibits) - usually 2nd Saturday of October.

18691 ■ Germans From Russia Heritage Society (GRHS)
1125 W Turnpike Ave.
Bismarck, ND 58501-8115

Ph: (701)223-6167
Fax: (701)223-4421
E-mail: rachel@grhs.org
URL: http://www.grhs.com
Contact: Rachel Schmidt, Office Mgr.
Founded: 1971. **Members:** 2,300. **Staff:** 4. **Description:** People interested in preserving the heritage of German-Americans who came from Russia. Aims to promote education and social activities and to preserve genealogical records and cultural offerings. Sponsors Oktoberfests, heritage days, food bazaars, travel tours, picnics, songfests, and lectures. Encourages members to write their family histories; collects, translates, indexes, and catalogues genealogical materials and personal documents. Maintains Germans from Russia Heritage Collection archives; makes available papers, books, records, and slides through the Heritage Bookstore; conducts research programs; operates a surname exchange. **Libraries: Type:** reference. **Holdings:** 5,000; books. **Subjects:** Germans from Russia. **Formerly:** (1979) North Dakota Historical Society of Germans from Russia. **Publications:** *Heritage Review*, quarterly. Journal. Contains stories and history of Germans from Russia. Includes ethnic history, passenger lists, other genealogical data, and book lists. **Price:** included in membership dues. **Circulation:** 2,600 ● Newsletter, quarterly. Includes calendar of events. **Price:** included in membership dues. **Circulation:** 2,600 ● Brochures, annual. **Conventions/Meetings:** annual convention.

18692 ■ Schlaraffia Nordamerika (SNA)
c/o Peter Schurig
111 Cidar Ln.
McMurray, PA 15317
Ph: (724)941-0246
Fax: (724)941-8826
Contact: Peter Schurig, Sec.
Founded: 1939. **Members:** 900. **Local Groups:** 32. **Languages:** English, German. **Description:** German language cultural and social fraternity for artists, professionals, and businessmen. **Publications:** *Allschlaraffische Stammrolle* (in German), annual. Directory. **Price:** for members only. **Conventions/Meetings:** quinquennial meeting.

18693 ■ Steuben Society of America (SSA)
6705 Fresh Pond Rd.
Ridgewood, NY 11385-4505
Ph: (718)381-0900
Fax: (718)628-4874
URL: http://www.steubensociety.org
Contact: Randall J. Ratje, Natl. Chm.
Founded: 1919. **Staff:** 3. **Description:** American citizens of Germanic extraction. Named after General Frederick William von Steuben (1730-1794), who came from Germany to fight in the American Revolution. Conducts educational programs. **Libraries: Type:** by appointment only. **Holdings:** 200. **Subjects:** German-Americas, German immigration to US, Steuben Society. **Awards: Frequency:** annual. **Type:** scholarship. **Recipient:** for students enrolled at the U.S. Military Academy and U.S. Naval Academy. **Committees:** Political Action. **Publications:** *The Steuben News*, bimonthly. Newspaper. Alternate Formats: online. **Conventions/Meetings:** biennial meeting.

Good Templars

18694 ■ National Council of the United States, International Organization of Good Templars (NCUSIOGT)
Natl. HQ, IOGT-USA
PO Box 202238
Minneapolis, MN 55420-7238
Ph: (952)210-0382
Fax: (952)435-8093
E-mail: webmaster@iogt.us
URL: http://www.iogt.us
Contact: Ms. Vickie Bakken, Natl. Office Mgr.
Founded: 1852. **Members:** 500. **Membership Dues:** direct, $32 (annual). **Staff:** 10. **Description:** Pro-

motes temperance, peace, and brotherhood, with emphasis on personal abstinence from intoxicating drinks and recreational drugs. Maintains museum; conducts monthly member gatherings and summer children's camps with substance education. **Libraries:** Type: by appointment only; open to the public. **Holdings:** 1,500; archival material, artwork, books, business records, periodicals, photographs. **Subjects:** temperance, organization specific materials. **Committees:** Educational; Historical; Juvenile; Youth. **Formerly:** National Grand Lodge, International Order of Good Templars. **Publications:** *National Good Templar*, 8/year. Newsletter. Features articles on the dangers of drugs and alcohol and trends in society's consumption; also includes research updates. **Price:** included in membership dues; $10.00 /year for nonmembers. **Circulation:** 2,000. **Advertising:** accepted. **Conventions/Meetings:** triennial convention.

Government Employees

18695 ■ National Association of Civilian Conservation Corps Alumni (NACCCA)
16 Hancock Ave.
St. Louis, MO 63125
Ph: (314)487-8666
Fax: (314)487-9488
E-mail: naccca@aol.com
URL: http://www.cccalumni.org
Contact: Vernon E. Schertel, Exec. Dir.
Founded: 1977. **Members:** 6,000. **Membership Dues:** regular, $20 (annual). **Staff:** 3. **Budget:** $150,000. **Regional Groups:** 6. **Local Groups:** 142. **Description:** Individuals associated in any capacity with the original Civilian Conservation Corps, the 1933-1942 Act of Congress Program for conservation of natural resources; membership includes widows, widowers, and close relatives of CCC veterans. Works to revive and preserve the comradeship, nostalgia, history, and accomplishments of CCC. Promotes the establishment of ACC based on the prior program. Works with American youth, participates in efforts to solve problems of senior citizens, and helps members locate old friends. **Libraries:** Type: reference. **Holdings:** archival material. **Awards:** Type: recognition. **Committees:** Publicity; Scholarship; Youth Programs. **Projects:** Museum. **Absorbed:** (1982) Citizens for Conservation. **Publications:** *NACCCA Journal*, monthly. **Conventions/Meetings:** competition ● biennial meeting.

Greek

18696 ■ American Hellenic Educational Progressive Association (AHEPA)
1909 Q St. NW, Ste.500
Washington, DC 20009
Ph: (202)232-6300
Fax: (202)232-2140
E-mail: ahepa@ahepa.org
URL: http://www.ahepa.org
Contact: Mr. Basil N. Mossaidis, Exec. Dir.
Founded: 1922. **Members:** 60,000. **Membership Dues:** regular, $75 (annual). **Staff:** 10. **Regional Groups:** 26. **Local Groups:** 700. **Languages:** English, Greek. **Description:** Composed primarily of persons of Greek descent; U.S. citizenship (or declared intention to achieve citizenship) is required. Conducts charitable, cultural, and social activities in the United States and Canada. Works to educate the American public on issues relating to Greece and Cyprus. Operates senior citizen housing units. **Libraries:** Type: reference. **Holdings:** 1,000; articles, books. **Subjects:** early Americans of Greek descent, Greek history. **Awards:** Athletic Awards. **Type:** recognition ● Educational Scholarships. **Frequency:** annual. **Type:** scholarship. **Recipient:** to 500 eligible students. **Programs:** Athletic; Daughters of Penelope; Hellenic Hall of Fame; Sons of Pericles. **Formerly:** (1992) Order of AHEPA. **Publications:** *The Ahepan*, quarterly. Magazine ● *Headquarters News*. Newsletter. **Conventions/Meetings:** biennial banquet

- held in spring even years, Washington, DC ● annual convention ● quarterly meeting.

18697 ■ Chian Federation of America (CFA)
44-01 Broadway
Astoria, NY 11103
Ph: (718)204-2550
Fax: (718)278-6199
E-mail: chianfed@chianfed.org
URL: http://www.chianfed.org
Contact: Alexandros Doulis, Pres.
Founded: 1974. **Members:** 3,000. **Budget:** $100,000. **Local Groups:** 24. **Languages:** English, Greek. **Description:** Represents Greek-Americans who trace their roots to the island of Chios. Organizes and coordinates patriotic, cultural, educational, charitable, and religious activities for the perpetuation of Greek ethnicity and civilization. Sponsors community events and neighborhood improvement activities. **Libraries:** Type: reference. **Holdings:** 2,000. **Subjects:** Chian and Greek history, Greek literature, history of Greeks in America. **Awards:** Homeric Award. **Frequency:** annual. **Type:** recognition. **Recipient:** for an individual who has worked for human rights and honorable causes of the American and Greek peoples. **Computer Services:** Mailing lists, Chians in the U.S. **Divisions:** Athletic; Cultural; Dance Group; Women's Auxiliary; Youth. **Publications:** *Chios*, quarterly. Magazine ● *Skinos*, quarterly. Magazine ● *Sykousis*, quarterly. Magazine ● Also publishes souvenir journals. **Conventions/Meetings:** annual meeting.

18698 ■ Cretans' Association "Omonoia" (CAO)
32-33 31st St.
Astoria, NY 11106
Ph: (718)721-9172 (718)726-8981
Fax: (718)278-9711
E-mail: info@nycretans.org
URL: http://www.nycretans.org
Contact: Chris E. Fasarakis, Pres.
Founded: 1918. **Members:** 600. **Membership Dues:** individual, $25 (annual). **Languages:** English, Greek. **Description:** Works as a chapter of the Pancretan Association of America (see separate entry). **Libraries:** Type: not open to the public. **Holdings:** 565; books, periodicals. **Subjects:** history, literature, science, music, geography. **Awards:** Cretan Scholarship. **Frequency:** biennial. **Type:** monetary. **Recipient:** for member's children; contingent upon college average and membership in youth chapter. **Computer Services:** Mailing lists. **Committees:** Elections; Supervising. **Conventions/Meetings:** monthly general assembly ● monthly meeting.

18699 ■ Daughters of Evrytania (DE)
121 Greenwich Rd., Ste.212
Charlotte, NC 28211
Ph: (704)366-6571
Free: (800)307-4795
Fax: (704)366-6571
E-mail: velouchi@bellsouth.net
URL: http://www.evrytanianassociation.org
Contact: Stavroula Dallas, Sec.
Founded: 1948. **Members:** 600. **Description:** Represents women with an interest in the province of Evrytania, Greece; especially in helping the schools and hospitals in that area. **Conventions/Meetings:** annual meeting.

18700 ■ Daughters of Penelope (DP)
440 Whitehall Rd.
Albany, NY 12208
Ph: (518)489-4442
E-mail: daughters@ahepa.org
URL: http://daughtersantiques.org
Contact: Helen G. Pappas, Exec. Dir.
Founded: 1929. **Members:** 12,000. **Membership Dues:** philanthropy educational, $20 (annual). **Staff:** 3. **Regional Groups:** 258. **State Groups:** 26. **Local Groups:** 364. **National Groups:** 11,500. **Languages:** English, Greek. **Description:** Promotes educational, philanthropy, civic responsibility, family and individual excellence. Participates in other philanthropic activities. Sponsors Daughters of Pene-

lope Foundation. **Libraries:** Type: not open to the public. **Holdings:** 24; books. **Awards:** Athletic Award. **Frequency:** annual. **Type:** scholarship. **Recipient:** for girls of Greek descent. **Committees:** Charitable; Youth Activities. **Affiliated With:** American Hellenic Educational Progressive Association; General Federation of Women's Clubs. **Publications:** *Penelope Scroll*, quarterly. Bulletin. **Price:** free. **Circulation:** 385. **Conventions/Meetings:** annual Congressional Banquet and Salute to Women (exhibits) ● annual Supreme Council - meeting.

18701 ■ Greek Catholic Union of the U.S.A. (GCU)
5400 Tuscarawas Rd.
Beaver, PA 15009
Ph: (412)495-3400
Free: (800)722-4428
Fax: (724)495-3421
E-mail: info@gcuusa.com
URL: http://www.gcuusa.com
Contact: George N. Juba, Pres./Chm.
Founded: 1892. **Members:** 52,000. **Staff:** 26. **Budget:** $1,500,000. **Regional Groups:** 10. **Local Groups:** 150. **Description:** Provides aid to unemployed individuals and funding for religious education programs. Sponsors competitions. **Awards:** Family of the Year. **Frequency:** annual. **Type:** recognition. **Publications:** *Messenger*, monthly. Magazine. **Price:** free. **Circulation:** 30,000. **Alternate Formats:** online ● Magazine. **Price:** included in membership dues. **Alternate Formats:** online. **Conventions/Meetings:** quadrennial convention - always July.

18702 ■ Maids of Athena (MOA)
1909 Q St. NW, Ste.500
Washington, DC 20009
Ph: (202)232-6300
Fax: (202)232-2140
E-mail: info@maidsofathena.com
URL: http://www.maidsofathena.com
Contact: Maria N. Mastrokyriakos, Pres.
Founded: 1930. **Members:** 1,500. **Membership Dues:** regular, $20 (annual). **Regional Groups:** 26. **State Groups:** 50. **Local Groups:** 272. **Languages:** English, Greek. **Description:** Serves as a junior auxiliary of the Daughters of Penelope. Aims to build character, to guide and prepare young women to lead socially productive lives, and to preserve Hellenic heritage and traditions. Engages in service activities. Offers educational seminars and children's services. Maintains speakers' bureau. **Libraries:** Type: reference; not open to the public. **Holdings:** 100; archival material, articles. **Subjects:** education, Hellenism. **Awards:** Maids of Athena National Scholarship. **Frequency:** annual. **Type:** scholarship. **Recipient:** for members of the Maids of Athena. **Telecommunication Services:** electronic mail, sonsmaids@ahepa. org. **Affiliated With:** American Hellenic Educational Progressive Association; Daughters of Penelope; Sons of Pericles. **Formerly:** (1965) Maids of Athens. **Publications:** *Eleftheri Zoi*, 3/year. Newsletter. **Price:** included in membership dues. **Circulation:** 1,000. **Alternate Formats:** online. **Conventions/Meetings:** annual Athena Family Governor's Conference - meeting and workshop - always September ● annual Miss Athena Pageant - competition ● annual Supreme Ahepa Convention - convention and workshop - always July or August.

18703 ■ Pan Arcadian Federation of America (PFA)
880 N York Rd.
Elmhurst, IL 60126
Ph: (630)833-1900 (630)834-6377
Fax: (630)833-1956
E-mail: headquarters@panarcadian.org
URL: http://www.panarcadian.org
Contact: Demetri J. Poulos, Gen. Sec.
Founded: 1931. **Members:** 4,000. **Membership Dues:** regular, $10 (annual). **Staff:** 20. **Budget:** $40,000. **Regional Groups:** 3. **State Groups:** 14. **Local Groups:** 14. **National Groups:** 31. **Description:** Represents persons of Arcadian ancestry either through birth or marriage. Maintains Panarcadian hospital of Tripolis, Greece. Conducts educational,

social and charitable programs; maintains library and museum. **Libraries: Type:** open to the public. **Awards: Type:** recognition. **Committees:** Foundation; Hospital; Public Relations. **Publications:** *Greek* (in English and Greek), periodic. Newsletter. **Circulation:** 3,000 ● *Pan-Arcadian Newsletter*, periodic. Bulletin. **Circulation:** 8,000 ● Newsletter, quarterly ● Also publishes letters. **Conventions/Meetings:** annual conference - in summer or beginning of fall.

18704 ■ Pan-Dodecanesian Association of America "Xanthos O Philikos" (PAAXOP)
Address Unknown since 2007
Founded: 1977. **Members:** 250. **Membership Dues:** individual, $30 (annual). **Languages:** English, Greek.. **Description:** Persons from the Dodecanese region of Greece or those interested in the affairs of the people of that region. Works to establish, promote, and administer scholarship funds and Hellenic studies programs. Assists people in adjusting to the American way of life and in acquiring citizenship education, Participates in charitable programs and religious and nonprofit institutions. Sponsors English language classes for foreigners and Greek language classes for non-Greek speaking individuals. **Awards:** Pan-Dodecanesian Association Scholarship Award. **Frequency:** annual. **Type:** scholarship. **Recipient:** College students of Dodecanesian descent. **Committees:** Scholarship Funds Administration. **Programs:** Hellenic Studies. **Conventions/Meetings:** annual conference ● annual dinner, with dance ● annual Fundraising Dinner - conference.

18705 ■ Society of Kastorians "Omonoia" (SKO)
150-28 14th Ave.
Whitestone, NY 11357
Ph: (718)746-4505 (718)747-3246
Fax: (718)746-4506
E-mail: kastorians@kastoria.us
URL: http://www.kastoria.us
Contact: Loula Koukoulis, Pres.
Founded: 1910. **Members:** 750. **Staff:** 2. **Languages:** English, Greek. **Description:** Represents persons born in Kastoria (a town in Macedonia, Northern Greece) or of Kastorian descent. Promotes Greek-American relations; assists in bettering conditions in Kastoria; maintains scholarship and hospitalization funds; operates a clubhouse. Conducts charitable and educational programs. **Committees:** Building; Scholarship; Special Fund. **Publications:** *Kastoriana NEA - Kastorian News*, bimonthly. **Circulation:** 3,000. **Advertising:** accepted ● Journal, annual. **Price:** free. **Circulation:** 1,000. **Advertising:** accepted. **Conventions/Meetings:** annual meeting.

18706 ■ Sons of Pericles
1909 Q St. NW, Ste.500
Washington, DC 20009-1007
Ph: (202)232-6300
Fax: (202)232-2140
E-mail: sopsupreme@rogers.com
URL: http://www.sonsofpericles.com
Contact: Elias Papadopoulos, Supreme Pres.
Founded: 1926. **Members:** 2,000. **Membership Dues:** $20 (annual). **Staff:** 2. **Budget:** $50,000. **National Groups:** 25. **Languages:** English, Greek. **Description:** Represents junior auxiliary of the Order of AHEPA (see separate entry) for young men of Greek birth or descent, ages 14-28. Goals are to: promote and instill the spirit of patriotism, allegiance to the American flag, support of the Constitution, and obedience to the laws, history, and traditions of the U.S; foster appreciation of Hellenic culture and ideals; promote high standards of ethics; stimulate education and respect for parents and elders; prepare members for admission into the Order of AHEPA. Engages in numerous charitable and service activities. Sponsors seminars and meetings; operates placement service. Maintains hall of fame. **Libraries: Type:** reference. **Holdings:** 10; archival material, books, clippings, periodicals. **Subjects:** history of the group. **Awards:** Presidential Excellence. **Frequency:** annual. **Type:** recognition ● **Type:** scholarship ● Wall of Honor. **Frequency:** annual. **Type:** recognition. **Computer Services:** database ● mailing lists. **Affili-**

ated With: American Hellenic Educational Progressive Association; Daughters of Penelope; Maids of Athena. **Publications:** *EZ*, biennial. Newsletter. **Price:** free. **Circulation:** 3,000 ● *The Periclean*, 5/year. **Price:** free for members. **Circulation:** 2,000. **Advertising:** accepted ● *Son of Pericles Yearbook*. **Price:** free. **Conventions/Meetings:** annual congress ● annual convention.

18707 ■ United Hellenic American Congress (UHAC)
980 N Michigan Ave., Ste.1210
Chicago, IL 60611
Ph: (312)640-1055
Fax: (312)640-1051
E-mail: info@unitedhellenic.org
URL: http://www.unitedhellenic.org
Contact: Andrew A. Athens, Natl. Chm.
Founded: 1975. **Staff:** 6. **State Groups:** 2. **Languages:** English, Greek. **Description:** Represents business and professional people, clergy, representatives of Hellenic professional societies and Greek-American organizations. Aims to coordinate programs promoting the welfare and defending the ethno-religious legacy of Americans of Greek descent; organize and promote events that project the cultural, civic, educational, and religious heritage and relevance of Greek thought, ideals, and traditions on civilization; promote relations between the U.S. and the Greek government; aid Cyprus and the Cypriot refugees; encourage talented and accomplished persons of Greek heritage and other artistic, intellectual, and social spheres; advocate the establishment of a Hellenic museum and cultural center. **Publications:** *Greek Star* (in English and Greek), weekly. Newspaper. **Price:** $45.00. **Circulation:** 10,000. **Advertising:** accepted.

18708 ■ United Hellenic Voters of America (UHVA)
525 W Lake St.
Addison, IL 60101
Ph: (630)628-0820
Fax: (630)543-7001
E-mail: uhva@smartbiz.net
URL: http://www.smartbiz.net/uhva
Contact: Dr. Dimitrios Kyriazopoulos, Supreme Chm.
Founded: 1974. **Members:** 17,000. **Membership Dues:** life, $100 ● regular, $25 (annual). **Regional Groups:** 6. **State Groups:** 7. **Local Groups:** 2. **National Groups:** 8. **Description:** Persons of Greek descent united to: establish and promote citizenship among people of Hellenic descent; encourage these people to participate in politics or public service, and in the political affairs of their communities; aid members in the exercise of their rights and responsibilities as U.S. citizens. Recommends and supports candidates for elected or appointed office. Helps Greek-Americans in the naturalization process; assists members in learning and becoming fluent in English. Plans to erect and maintain the United Hellenic Cultural Center, Library, and Museum. Maintains hall of fame and placement service; operates youth auxiliary. **Awards:** Man of the Year Award. **Frequency:** annual. **Type:** recognition ● Most Distinguished Greek American Award. **Frequency:** annual. **Type:** recognition. **Computer Services:** Mailing lists, of members. **Committees:** Americanization; Bilingual; Political Action; Press; Property Owners; Voter Registration; Welfare. **Formerly:** (1978) United Hellenic Voters of Illinois. **Publications:** Newsletter (in English and Greek), quarterly. **Price:** free ● Yearbook, annual. **Conventions/Meetings:** monthly conference.

18709 ■ World Council of Hellenes Abroad (SAE)
980 N Michigan Ave., Ste.1210
Chicago, IL 60611
Ph: (312)337-7243
Fax: (312)337-7245
E-mail: hellenes@saeworld.org
URL: http://www.saeworld.org
Contact: Mr. Andrew A. Athens, Pres.
Founded: 1995. **Members:** 3,000. **Multinational.** **Description:** Seeks to unite the Hellenes and Phil-

hellenes worldwide in order to implement projects to further the natural ties among Hellenes. **Funds:** The National Fund (ETO). **Programs:** Primary Health Care Initiative. **Projects:** Adopt a Church. **Conventions/Meetings:** annual conference.

Haiti

18710 ■ National Association for the Advancement of Haitian Descendents (NAAHD)
74 Trinity Pl., Ste.606
Wall St.
New York, NY 10006
Ph: (212)566-4919
E-mail: info@naahd.org
URL: http://www.naahd.org
Contact: Nod Dorcilien, Pres./CEO/Founder
Description: Protects and defends the individual liberties of all Haitians. Improves education, labor, health and human rights to create lasting and impacting change. Brings Haitians together to share knowledge, experience and resources and to create one representative voice throughout the United States and around the world for a better and stronger future for all Haitians. **Telecommunication Services:** electronic mail, nod@naahd.org.

Hispanic

18711 ■ Latino Issues Forum (LIF)
160 Pine St., Ste.700
San Francisco, CA 94111
Ph: (415)284-7220
Fax: (415)284-7222
E-mail: larteaga@lif.org
URL: http://www.lif.org
Contact: Luis Arteaga, Exec. Dir.
Founded: 1987. **Staff:** 15. **Description:** Serves as a public policy and advocacy institute committed to advancing the Latino community, especially on broader issues of access to higher education, economic development, health care, citizenship, regional development, telecommunications issues, and regulatory issues. Acts as a clearinghouse to assist and provide news media with accurate information; addresses public policy issues from a Latino perspective. **Publications:** Reports.

18712 ■ League of United Latin American Citizens (LULAC)
2000 L St. NW, Ste.610
Washington, DC 20036
Ph: (202)833-6130
Free: (877)LUL-AC01
Fax: (202)833-6135
E-mail: bwilkes@lulac.org
URL: http://www.lulac.org
Contact: Brent A. Wilkes, Exec. Dir.
Founded: 1929. **Members:** 115,000. **Membership Dues:** local council or associate, $25 (annual) ● life, $1,000 ● corporate associate, $1,000 (annual). **Staff:** 85. **Regional Groups:** 12. **State Groups:** 43. **Local Groups:** 400. **Description:** Advances the economic condition, educational attainment, political influence, health and civil rights of Hispanic Americans through community-based programs operating at more than 700 LULAC councils nationwide. **Libraries: Type:** reference. **Awards:** LULAC National Scholarship Fund. **Type:** scholarship. **Recipient:** for Hispanic students attending colleges and universities. **Computer Services:** database. **Programs:** Citizenship; Corporate Alliance; Housing; Immigration; Leadership; Literacy. **Projects:** Empower Hispanic America with Technology. **Publications:** *LULAC Civil Rights Manual*. Alternate Formats: online ● *LULAC News*, bimonthly. Magazine. **Price:** $24.00/year; $4.50 each. **Advertising:** accepted. Alternate Formats: online ● Annual Report, annual. Alternate Formats: online. **Conventions/Meetings:** annual convention (exhibits) - usually last week of June, first week of July.

18713 ■ National Association for Hispanic Elderly
234 E Colorado Blvd., Ste.300
Pasadena, CA 91101
Ph: (626)564-1988
Fax: (626)564-2659
E-mail: anppm@aol.com
URL: http://www.anppm.org
Contact: Dr. Carmela G. Lacayo, Pres./CEO
Founded: 1975. **Description:** Promotes services to older Hispanic people; provides a national Hispanic research center, research and consulting services for organizations seeking to reach older Spanish-speaking persons; disseminates written and audiovisual materials in English and Spanish. **Projects:** AYUDA.

18714 ■ National Hispanic Foundation for the Arts (NHFA)
1010 Wisconsin Ave. NW, Ste.650
Washington, DC 20007-3676
Ph: (202)293-8330
Fax: (202)965-5252
E-mail: info@hispanicarts.org
URL: http://www.hispanicarts.org
Contact: Felix Sanchez, Chm.
Founded: 1997. **Staff:** 3. **Description:** Promotes Hispanic talent in the performing arts. Strives to increase access for Hispanic artists and professionals in the entertainment industry. Works to eliminate ethnic stereotypes from the industry. Works closely with the White House, the President's Initiative on Race, the U.S. Congress, the Congressional Hispanic Caucus and the Federal Communications Commission. **Awards:** Raul Juia Award. **Frequency:** annual. **Type:** recognition. **Recipient:** for individuals or organizations whose work epitomize the foundation's ideals ● **Frequency:** annual. **Type:** scholarship.

18715 ■ National Image
PO Box 1368
Bonita, CA 91908-1368
Ph: (619)934-5277
Fax: (858)637-4938
E-mail: nationalchairman@hotmail.com
URL: http://www.nationalimageinc.org
Contact: John Griego, Chm./CEO
Founded: 1972. **Description:** Commits to find positive and creative solutions to the challenges facing the pan-Hispanic community in the U.S. **Publications:** El Noticero de Image, quarterly. Newsletter. Alternate Formats: online.

Hoo-Hoo

18716 ■ Hoo-Hoo International
c/o Beth Thomas, Exec. Sec.
PO Box 118
Gurdon, AR 71743
Ph: (870)353-4997
Free: (800)979-9950
Fax: (870)353-4151
E-mail: info@hoo-hoo.org
URL: http://www.hoo-hoo.org
Contact: David Jones, Chm.
Founded: 1892. **Members:** 98,000. **Staff:** 2. **Budget:** $160,500. **Local Groups:** 72. **Description:** Fraternal society of men involved in forest products and the lumber industry, including lumbermen, foresters, officers of lumber associations, and lumber trade press. Sponsors competitions. **Awards:** Gordon Doman Memorial Trophy. **Frequency:** annual. **Type:** trophy. **Recipient:** to a Supreme Nine members ● Hoo-Hoo International Activity Award. **Frequency:** annual. **Type:** recognition. **Recipient:** for an outstanding project done by a jurisdiction club. **Committees:** National Forest Products; Wood Promotion. **Formerly:** (1993) International Order of Hoo-Hoo. **Publications:** Hoo-Hoo Log and Tally Magazine, 3/year. **Conventions/Meetings:** annual convention - always September.

Hungarian

18717 ■ American Hungarian Federation (AHF)
c/o Atilla Kocsis
809 Natl. Press Bldg.
Washington, DC 20045
Ph: (202)737-0127
Fax: (202)737-8406
E-mail: info@americanhungarianfederation.org
URL: http://www.americanhungarianfederation.org
Contact: Stephen J. Varga, Pres.
Founded: 1906. **Membership Dues:** individual, $56 (annual) ● patron, $100 (annual) ● freedom fund circle, $195 (annual) ● Col. Kovats circle, $1,956 (annual). **Regional Groups:** 3. **State Groups:** 10. **Local Groups:** 35. **Description:** Americans of Hungarian origin. Seeks to: acquaint newly arrived Hungarians with the ideals of American democracy; familiarize the 2nd and succeeding generations with the history, art, literature, and culture of the nation of which they are descendants and heirs; represent Hungarian American interests. Promotes all actions that guard basic human rights and Western culture. Opposes trends that threaten human freedom and the rights of citizens. Conducts research programs; maintains speakers' bureau; sponsors competitions. **Awards:** Type: recognition. **Committees:** Human Rights; International Relations; Ladies; Public Relations; School; Social Issues; Youth. **Publications:** A.M.Sz Sajtotajekoztato (in English and Hungarian), quarterly ● Directory, annual. **Conventions/Meetings:** biennial meeting.

18718 ■ First Hungarian Literary Society (FHLS)
323 E 79th St.
New York, NY 10021
Ph: (212)288-5002
Fax: (212)772-3175
E-mail: clubonkepzo@clubonkepzo.com
URL: http://www.clubonkepzo.com/FHLS.htm
Contact: Robert Ziegler, Pres.
Founded: 1889. **Members:** 300. **Membership Dues:** individual, $75 (annual) ● patron, $100. **Staff:** 4. **Regional Groups:** 1. **Local Groups:** 6. **Languages:** English, Hungarian. **Description:** Social association for men and women of Hungarian extraction. Conducts charitable programs. **Libraries:** Type: not open to the public. **Holdings:** 1,500. **Formerly:** Hungarian Literary Society. **Conventions/Meetings:** monthly meeting - always 1st Monday.

18719 ■ Hungarian/American Friendship Society (HAFS)
c/o Douglas P. Holmes, Dir.
17327 W Carmen Dr.
Surprise, AZ 85388
Ph: (916)690-4293
E-mail: holmes@dholmes.com
URL: http://www.dholmes.com/hafs.html
Contact: Douglas P. Holmes, Dir.
Founded: 1992. **Staff:** 1. **Nonmembership. Description:** Strives to help people learn how to do their own genealogy in the areas of the former Kingdom of Hungary. **Convention/Meeting:** none. **Computer Services:** Online services. **Publications:** Regi Magyarirszag, quarterly. Newsletter. ISSN: 1085-6307. **Circulation:** 250.

18720 ■ Hungarian Reformed Federation of America (HRFA)
2001 Massachusetts Ave. NW
Washington, DC 20036-1011
Ph: (202)328-2630
Free: (888)KOS-SUTH
Fax: (202)328-7984
E-mail: hrfa@hrfa.org
URL: http://www.hrfa.org
Contact: Jules Gyula Balogh, Pres.
Founded: 1896. **Members:** 18,433. **Staff:** 10. **Budget:** $950,000. **State Groups:** 13. **Local Groups:** 100. **Description:** Fraternal benefit insurance society primarily for Americans of Hungarian descent. Sponsors many fraternal activities; provides student aid funds. Maintains museum and biographical archives. Provides life insurance and other financial services to help secure the conditions of members and their family as well. **Awards:** Type: recognition. **Affiliated With:** National Fraternal Congress of America. **Publications:** Fraternity-Testveriseg (in English and Hungarian), quarterly. Magazine. **Price:** free for members. Alternate Formats: online. **Conventions/Meetings:** quadrennial meeting.

18721 ■ National Federation of American Hungarians (NFAH)
c/o Laszlo Pasztor
196 Hungaria Dr.
Rockwood, PA 15557
Ph: (814)352-7188
Fax: (814)352-8002
E-mail: peter@harkay.com
URL: http://hungarianfed-usa.org
Contact: Laszlo Pasztor, Pres. Emeritus
Founded: 1982. **Members:** 87. **Membership Dues:** minimum fee, $50 (annual). **Staff:** 3. **Regional Groups:** 82. **State Groups:** 3. **Local Groups:** 2. **Languages:** English, Hungarian. **Description:** Americans of Hungarian descent. Seeks to ease the transition of recently-arrived Hungarian immigrants to the U.S. Educates Hungarian Americans regarding Hungarian culture and history. Helps Hungary and Hungarians in the Carpathian Basin to move toward a more democratic society. Supports human rights of all individuals and autonomy of minority communities worldwide. Conducts research and educates public policy experts and officials about issues relevant to Hungary and Hungarians; maintains speakers' bureau. **Awards:** Internship in Washington, D.C. **Frequency:** annual. **Type:** monetary. **Recipient:** for youth 18-26 years old. **Boards:** Board of Directors; Executive Board. **Committees:** Cultural; Human Rights. **Formerly:** National Federation of Hungarian-Americans. **Publications:** Amosz Korcevel (in Hungarian), quarterly. Newsletter ● Autonomy and the New World Order. Book. **Conventions/Meetings:** annual convention.

Indian

18722 ■ Association of Indian Muslims of America (AIM)
PO Box 10654
Silver Spring, MD 20904
E-mail: info@aimamerica.org
URL: http://www.aimamerica.org
Contact: Kaleem Kawaja, Pres.
Founded: 1985. **Members:** 700. **Membership Dues:** regular, $10 (annual). **Staff:** 9. **Regional Groups:** 13. **Description:** Muslim Indians living in the U.S. Provides a forum for discussion and dialogue among Indian Muslims and other Indians living in the U.S., the Indian and U.S. governments, and other Islamic organizations in the U.S. Works to resolve issues and problems unique to Indian Muslims and to improve social interaction among communities. Disseminates information on cultural, economic, educational, and human rights affairs in India, particularly as they affect Muslims. Informs Muslim Indians living in the U.S. of current events in India. Provides humanitarian aid and other forms of support to Muslim Indians through educational assistance and crisis relief funds. Arranges social gatherings on Muslim festivals and Indian national events. Compiles statistics. **Computer Services:** Mailing lists. **Committees:** Education; Publication; Relief. **Formerly:** (1991) Association of Indian Muslims. **Publications:** The AIM, quarterly. Journal. **Circulation:** 800. **Advertising:** accepted. **Conventions/Meetings:** annual conference (exhibits).

18723 ■ Association of Indians in America (AIA)
5415 108 St.
Corona, NY 11368
Ph: (718)271-0453
Fax: (718)271-1906

E-mail: info@aianewyork.org
URL: http://www.aianewyork.org
Contact: Mr. Arish K. Sahani, Pres.
Founded: 1967. **Members:** 5,000. **Membership Dues:** life, $300 ● regular, $30 (annual) ● student, $25 (annual). **Staff:** 55. **State Groups:** 12. **Description:** Immigrants of Asian Indian ancestry living in the U.S. Seeks to continue Indian cultural activities in the U.S. and to encourage full Asian Indian participation as citizens and residents of America. Promotes Indo-U.S. economic relations; furthers facilities for travel and tourism between India and the U.S; fosters Indian studies programs in American academic institutions; has represented Asian Indians at congressional and Senate hearings. Conducts national conferences on timely subjects; sponsors cultural programs. Conducts charitable programs. Holds annual honor banquet. **Awards:** Honor Awards. **Frequency:** annual. **Type:** recognition. **Computer Services:** Mailing lists, of members. **Councils:** Indian Studies; Medical Affairs; Social Scientists; Trade and Economic Affairs; Travel and Tourism; Women; Youth. **Formerly:** (1999) Association of Asian Indians in America. **Publications:** *ANANYA: Book 1997*, bimonthly. Journal. Circulation: 1,000. Advertising: accepted ● *Portrait of India*. Book. **Price:** $79.99/copy. **Conventions/Meetings:** annual meeting.

18724 ■ Friends of India Society International (FISI)
PO Box 73327
Houston, TX 77273-3327
Ph: (281)494-1909
E-mail: fisiusa@yahoo.com
URL: http://www.fisiusa.org
Contact: Gaurang R. Desai, Contact
Founded: 1976. **Members:** 3,000. **Membership Dues:** bronze, $25 (annual) ● silver (5 years term), $100 ● gold (20 years term), $3,000 ● life, $5,000. **Description:** Primarily persons of Indian origin living outside of India. Purposes are to promote social, economic, and political progress within India; to study the short- and long-term problems of Indians living in and outside of India; to function as a people's channel of communication between India and the countries of their residence; to develop internationally a "correct" image of India and India's culture; to work for the cause of human rights, civil liberties, and freedom of expression all over the world; to promote peace and prosperity. Sponsors and supports developmental projects in India. Conducts lectures. **Publications:** *Conference Proceedings*, biennial ● *Satyavani*, monthly. Newspaper ● Booklets ● Newsletter, periodic ● Also publishes other material evaluating events in India. **Conventions/Meetings:** biennial conference ● seminar ● symposium.

18725 ■ Global Organization of People of Indian Origin (GOPIO)
PO Box 1413
Stamford, CT 06904
Ph: (818)708-3885
Fax: (203)322-2233
E-mail: gopio-intl@sbcglobal.net
URL: http://www.gopio.net
Contact: Inder Singh, Pres.
Founded: 1989. **Members:** 1,000. **Membership Dues:** life, $1,000 ● local chapter, $50 (annual). **Description:** Provides educational, research, and charitable programs. Maintains a speakers' bureau. **Computer Services:** Mailing lists. **Publications:** *GOPIO News*, monthly. Newsletter. Circulation: 10,000. Alternate Formats: online. **Conventions/Meetings:** biennial convention.

18726 ■ National Federation of Indian American Associations (NFIA)
319 Summit Hall Rd.
Gaithersburg, MD 20877
Ph: (301)926-3013 (301)935-5321
Fax: (301)926-3378
E-mail: info@nfia.net
URL: http://www.nfia.net
Contact: Dr. Rajen Anand, Pres.
Founded: 1980. **Members:** 200. **Staff:** 1. **Budget:** $100,000. **Regional Groups:** 11. **Description:**

Asian-Indian organizations operating in the U.S. Works to represent and advance the interests of Indians in the U.S. and provide a forum for communication among Indian organizations and Indo-American communities. Coordinates cultural, political, educational, social, economic, and community affairs of Asian Indians residing in North America. Seeks to promote and preserve Indian culture and heritage and foster friendship and understanding between Indians and the people of North America. Works to educate legislators about Indo-American concerns; observes and comments on legislative activities. Develops task forces to deal with issues affecting the Indo-American community. **Awards: Type:** recognition. **Computer Services:** Mailing lists, of Indian organizations in the U.S. and Canada. **Committees:** Improve India-U.S. Relations; Legislative; Political Education. **Formerly:** (1982) National Council of Asian Indian Organizations in North America; (1990) National Federation of Asian Indian Organizations in America. **Publications:** Bulletin, bimonthly. Alternate Formats: online ● Proceedings, biennial. **Conventions/Meetings:** biennial conference (exhibits) ● seminar ● symposium.

18727 ■ Network of Indian Professionals (NetIP)
c/o North America Chapter Development
PO Box 06362
Chicago, IL 60606
Ph: (312)952-0254
E-mail: manasi@netip.org
URL: http://www.netip.org
Contact: Manasi Voruganti, Pres.
Founded: 1990. **Members:** 5,000. **Membership Dues:** individual, $35 (annual). **Description:** Dedicated to professional and cultural development, community service, philanthropy and advancement of South Asian-Americans and their communities. **Committees:** Chapter Development; Community Relations; Corporate Relations; Operations. **Publications:** *Tools to Help Start a New Chapter*. **Price:** $50.00 in U.S.; $55.00 outside U.S. ● Report, quarterly.

Insurance

18728 ■ Alliance of Transylvanian Saxons (ATS)
5393 Pearl Rd.
Cleveland, OH 44129-1597
Ph: (440)842-8442
E-mail: office@atsaxons.com
URL: http://www.atsaxons.com
Contact: David P. Bokesch Sr., Pres.
Founded: 1902. **Members:** 8,892. **Local Groups:** 30. **Languages:** English, German. **Description:** Fraternal benefit life insurance society. Maintains museum. Brings general news about activities of the national and local organizations. **Libraries: Type:** reference. **Holdings:** archival material. **Awards:** Saxon Honor Pin. **Type:** recognition ● **Frequency:** annual. **Type:** scholarship. **Committees:** National; Orphan Fund. **Publications:** *Saxon News Volksblatt*, biweekly ● Annual Report, annual. **Conventions/Meetings:** competition ● annual meeting - always May.

18729 ■ American Foreign Service Protective Association (AFSPA)
1716 N St. NW
Washington, DC 20036-2902
Ph: (202)833-4910
Fax: (202)833-4918
E-mail: paula.jakub@afspa.org
URL: http://www.afspa.org
Contact: John P. Shumate, Exec. VP
Founded: 1929. **Members:** 16,000. **Staff:** 15. **Budget:** $635,000. **Description:** Insurance society for employees of the American Foreign Service. **Additional Websites:** http://www.slfoundation.org. **Publications:** *AFSPA Newsletter*, annual. Alternate Formats: online. **Conventions/Meetings:** annual meeting.

18730 ■ American Fraternal Union (AFU)
PO Box 59
Ely, MN 55731-0059
Ph: (218)365-3143
Free: (800)346-1289
Fax: (218)365-3181
URL: http://www.afu-life.com
Contact: John L. Cheenik, Sec.-Treas.
Founded: 1898. **Members:** 22,846. **Staff:** 14. **Local Groups:** 139. **Description:** Fraternal benefit life insurance society. Persons up to 80 years of age may join, regardless of race, creed, or national background. **Formerly:** (1941) South Slavonic Catholic Union. **Publications:** *New Era*, monthly. **Conventions/Meetings:** quadrennial meeting.

18731 ■ Artisans Order of Mutual Protection (AOMP)
8100 Roosevelt Blvd.
Philadelphia, PA 19152
Free: (800)551-1873
Fax: (215)708-1779
E-mail: glistner@aol.com
URL: http://www.artisansaomp.org
Contact: George J. Listner, Admin.
Founded: 1873. **Members:** 13,806. **Membership Dues:** individual, $8 (annual). **Staff:** 11. **Budget:** $805,500. **Local Groups:** 31. **Description:** Offers adult and juvenile programs and activities, benevolent community activity and competitive life insurance. Promotes friendly interaction among members. **Awards: Type:** scholarship. **Publications:** *The Artisan*, bimonthly. Newsletter. **Conventions/Meetings:** biennial meeting.

18732 ■ Degree of Honor Protective Association (DHPA)
400 Robert St. N, Ste.1600
St. Paul, MN 55101-2029
Ph: (651)228-7600
Free: (800)947-5812
Fax: (651)224-7446
E-mail: jfelling@degreeofhonor.com
URL: http://www.degreeofhonor.com
Contact: Jacqueline A. Felling, CEO/Natl. Pres.
Founded: 1886. **Members:** 38,000. **Staff:** 40. **State Groups:** 23. **Local Groups:** 133. **Description:** Serves as a fraternal benefit life insurance society. Provides children's services; operates charitable and educational programs. **Awards:** Continuing Education Scholarships. **Frequency:** annual. **Type:** scholarship ● Honor U. **Frequency:** annual. **Type:** scholarship. **Recipient:** for promising students ● Julie Snow Scholarship. **Frequency:** annual. **Type:** scholarship ● Teens with a Heart. **Frequency:** annual. **Type:** recognition. **Recipient:** for high school seniors. **Publications:** *Degree of Honor Review*, quarterly. Magazine. Price: included in membership dues. Circulation: 31,000. **Conventions/Meetings:** competition ● quadrennial congress.

18733 ■ Equitable Reserve Association
PO Box 448
Neenah, WI 54957-0448
Free: (800)722-1574
Fax: (920)725-2869
E-mail: generalinfo@equitablereserve.com
URL: http://www.equitablereserve.com
Contact: Melvin L. Rambo, Pres./CEO
Founded: 1897. **Members:** 25,053. **Staff:** 36. **Description:** Provides financial security and peace of mind for individuals and families through quality insurance products and fraternal benefits. **Publications:** *The Guide*, bimonthly. Magazine. Price: free for members ● Annual Report, annual. Alternate Formats: online. **Conventions/Meetings:** quadrennial convention and general assembly.

18734 ■ Federation Life Insurance of America (FLIA)
6011 S 27th St.
Greenfield, WI 53221-4804
Ph: (414)281-6281
Free: (877)690-5827
Fax: (414)281-6405

E-mail: iflia@aol.com
Contact: Constance Pravechek, Sec.-Treas.
Founded: 1913. **Members:** 3,986. **Membership Dues:** $0 (annual). **Staff:** 5. **National Groups:** 10. **Languages:** English, Polish. **Description:** Fraternal benefit life insurance society. Conducts educational and charitable programs; offers children's services. **Awards: Frequency:** annual. **Type:** scholarship. **Recipient:** 5/year membership, accredited college, essay, under age of 25. **Publications:** *The Voice*, quarterly. Newsletter. **Price:** included in membership dues. **Conventions/Meetings:** quadrennial meeting.

18735 ■ Gleaner Life Insurance Society (GLIS)

5200 W U.S. Hwy. 223
PO Box 1894
Adrian, MI 49221-7894
Ph: (517)263-2244
Free: (800)992-1894
Fax: (517)265-7745
E-mail: gleaner@gleanerlife.com
URL: http://www.gleanerlife.com
Contact: Michael J. Wade, Pres./CEO
Founded: 1894. **Members:** 70,000. **Staff:** 50. **Description:** Participates in community projects, hospital visitation work and support, youth organizations, orphan care and education, and other related activities. Participates in Life Office Management education and offers reimbursements to employees who enroll in continuing education courses. Sponsors student loans. **Awards:** Gleaner Life Insurance Society Scholarship Foundation. **Frequency:** annual. **Type:** scholarship. **Recipient:** for an individual who has met membership requirements, has excelled academically, and is involved in community service. **Affiliated With:** National Fraternal Congress of America. **Formerly:** Ancient Order of Gleaners. **Publications:** *Arbor News*, monthly. Newsletter ● *Epistles*, periodic. Newsletter ● *Friday Morning*, biweekly. Newsletter ● *National Gleaner Forum*, quarterly. Magazine. **Conventions/Meetings:** biennial meeting - always in the fall.

18736 ■ Grand Lodge Order of the Sons of Hermann in Texas (OSHT)

c/o Mary Beam, Grand VP/Sec.-Treas.
PO Box 1941
San Antonio, TX 78297-1941
Ph: (210)226-9261
Free: (877)HERMANN
Fax: (210)226-3055
E-mail: lee@texashermannsons.org
URL: http://www.texashermannsons.org
Contact: Mary Beam, Grand VP/Sec.-Treas.
Founded: 1890. **Members:** 79,000. **Staff:** 50. **State Groups:** 154. **Local Groups:** 154. **Description:** Serves as a fraternal benefit life insurance society. **Committees:** Home for the Aged; Law; Youth Activities. **Publications:** *Hermann Sons News*, monthly. Newspaper. **Circulation:** 35,000. **Conventions/Meetings:** quadrennial Grand Lodge Convention.

18737 ■ Honorable Order of the Blue Goose, International (HOBGI)

c/o Terrence M. Maloney, Grand Wielder
12940 Walnut Rd.
Elm Grove, WI 53122
Ph: (414)221-0341
Fax: (262)782-7608
E-mail: terry@bluegoose.org
URL: http://www.bluegoose.org
Contact: Terrence M. Maloney, Grand Wielder
Founded: 1906. **Members:** 10,000. **Staff:** 2. **State Groups:** 65. **Description:** Works as a fraternal organization of property and casualty insurance for people. **Awards: Frequency:** annual. **Type:** recognition. **Recipient:** for winners of educational exams in the U.S. and Canada and various charities. **Publications:** *Grand Nest Bulletin*, annual. **Circulation:** 6,000. **Advertising:** accepted ● *President's Bulletin*, semiannual. **Conventions/Meetings:** annual convention ● annual meeting - August.

18738 ■ Independent Order of Vikings (IOV)

PO Box 5147
Springfield, IL 62705-5147
Free: (877)241-6006
Fax: (217)241-6578
E-mail: member_services@iovikings.org
URL: http://www.iovikings.org
Contact: Arthur W. Harlow Sr., Pres.
Founded: 1896. **Members:** 9,300. **Membership Dues:** national, $12 (annual). **Local Groups:** 29. **Description:** Serves as a fraternal benefit life insurance society. Provides cultural and financial benefits for members. Endeavors to retain the Scandinavian traditions of the past. **Publications:** *Viking Journal: Vikingen*, quarterly. **Price:** available to members only. **ISSN:** 0099-1406. **Circulation:** 6,000. Alternate Formats: online. **Conventions/Meetings:** biennial meeting.

18739 ■ Knights of the Golden Eagle (KGE)

c/o Tim Chubb
412 Brookside Dr.
Perkasie, PA 18944
Ph: (215)345-0929
URL: http://users.erols.com/kgeeaglemiller/knightsofthegoldeneagle.home.html
Contact: Randy Miller, Contact
Founded: 1873. **Members:** 2,300. **Membership Dues:** individual, $12 (annual). **State Groups:** 3. **Local Groups:** 32. **National Groups:** 3. **Description:** Fraternal benefit society for males ages 16-50. Aims are to build character of the highest type; to encourage members in business relations; to assist the unemployed to find employment; to care for orphans and widows; to promote benevolence and practice sympathetic assistance. Maintains health and death fund; donates funds to medical and veterans' associations. Sponsors women's auxiliary Ladies of the Golden Eagle. **Awards:** Lions Eye Bank Delaware Valley - Doylestown Fire Co. **Frequency:** annual. **Type:** scholarship. **Recipient:** for high-school graduates, 18 students in college. **Publications:** Newsletter, semiannual. **Conventions/Meetings:** semiannual Ladies' Banquet - Christmas, April, June ● annual Scholarship Banquet - June ● periodic seminar.

18740 ■ Loyal Christian Benefit Association (LCBA)

PO Box 13005
700 Peach St.
Erie, PA 16514-1305
Ph: (814)453-4331
Free: (800)234-5222
Fax: (814)453-3211
E-mail: lcba@lcba.com
URL: http://www.lcba.com
Contact: Jacqueline Sobania-Robison, Pres./CEO
Founded: 1890. **Members:** 33,000. **Membership Dues:** fraternal benefit, $2 (annual) ● associate, $5 (annual). **Staff:** 35. **Description:** Practicing Christian men, women, and children. Members eligible for added benefits, including scholarships, bereavement, accidental death, prescription discount, newborn and orphan benefits. **Awards: Type:** scholarship ● Vocational Technical Scholarship and College Scholarship. **Frequency:** annual. **Type:** recognition. **Recipient:** for a benefit member of LCBA. **Affiliated With:** National Catholic Office for the Deaf; National Fraternal Congress of America. **Formerly:** (1969) Ladies Catholic Benevolent Association. **Publications:** *Fraternal Leader*, quarterly. Magazine. Alternate Formats: online. **Conventions/Meetings:** quadrennial convention (exhibits).

18741 ■ Luso-American Fraternal Federation (LUSO)

PO Box 2968
Dublin, CA 94568
Ph: (925)828-4884
Free: (877)LAL-LUSO
Fax: (925)828-4554
E-mail: lusoweb@luso-american.org
URL: http://www.luso-american.org
Contact: Manuel A. Minhoto, Exec. VP/CEO
Founded: 1957. **Members:** 14,000. **Staff:** 11. **Budget:** $400,000. **Regional Groups:** 14. **Local Groups:**

122. **Languages:** English, Portuguese. **Description:** Division of Luso-American Life Insurance Society (see separate entry). Sponsors Luso-American Education Foundation (see separate entry). **Awards: Type:** grant. **Recipient:** for study in Portugal/USA ● **Type:** scholarship. **Recipient:** for study in Portugal/USA. **Affiliated With:** Luso-American Life Insurance Society. **Publications:** *The Luso-American*, semiannual. Magazine. Covers council, state, and national activities of members. **Circulation:** 10,800. **Conventions/Meetings:** annual convention, delegates of subordinate councils.

18742 ■ Luso-American Life Insurance Society (LALIS)

PO Box 2968
Dublin, CA 94568
Ph: (925)828-4884
Free: (877)LAL-LUSO
Fax: (925)828-4554
E-mail: lusoweb@luso-american.org
URL: http://www.luso-american.org
Contact: Manuel A. Minhoto, Exec. VP/CEO
Founded: 1957. **Members:** 18,000. **Staff:** 15. **Budget:** $3,447,150. **State Groups:** 8. **Local Groups:** 93. **Languages:** English, Portuguese. **Description:** Promotes Luso-American cultural, social, educational and charitable activities of its members, their families and others. **Libraries: Type:** reference. **Absorbed:** (2002) Portuguese Continental Union of the United States of America. **Formed by Merger of:** (1868) Benevolent Society of California; (1917) Uniao Portuguesa Continental do Estado da California. **Formerly:** (1957) United National Life Insurance Society. **Publications:** *The Luso-American* (in English and Portuguese), semiannual. Magazine. Covers members' activities. **Price:** included in membership dues. **Circulation:** 10,800. **Conventions/Meetings:** biennial convention, delegates of subordinate council - always April.

18743 ■ National Council, Daughters of America (DA)

Address Unknown since 2007
Founded: 1891. **Members:** 3,094. **Membership Dues:** $5 (annual). **Staff:** 5. **State Groups:** 16. **Local Groups:** 3. **National Groups:** 1. **Description:** Fraternal society for women and men. Offers scholastic grants. Supports the American Diabetes Association. **Awards:** Orphan's Fund. **Frequency:** annual. **Type:** monetary. **Recipient:** for children of deceased members ● Scholarship Fund. **Frequency:** annual. **Type:** scholarship. **Recipient:** members and relatives of members, including grandchildren and great-grandchildren. **Computer Services:** database ● mailing lists. **Committees:** National Board of Officers. **Publications:** Newsletter, semiannual. **Price:** free. **Circulation:** 3,094. **Advertising:** not accepted. **Conventions/Meetings:** biennial meeting (exhibits) - always third week of October.

18744 ■ National Fraternal Congress of America (NFCA)

1315 W 22nd St., Ste.400
Oak Brook, IL 60523
Ph: (630)522-6322
Fax: (630)522-6326
E-mail: nfca@nfcanet.org
URL: http://www.nfcanet.org
Contact: Mr. Frederick H. Grubbe, Pres./CEO
Founded: 1886. **Members:** 76. **Staff:** 12. **Budget:** $1,500,000. **State Groups:** 36. **National Groups:** 77. **Description:** Works to unite fraternal benefit societies to address common challenges and to provide and encourage education, training and community outreach at the national and grassroots levels. Represents more than ten million people in 43,000 chapters, making it one of the continent's largest volunteer networks. **Awards:** Fraternalist of the Year. **Frequency:** annual. **Type:** recognition. **Recipient:** to fraternal membership for community service. **Committees:** Law. **Sections:** Actuaries'; Communications; Field Managers'; Fraternal; Human Resources; Investment; Presidents'; Secretaries'; State Fraternal Congresses. **Formerly:** National Fraternal Congress; Associated Fraternities of America. **Publications:**

Fraternal Advantage, monthly. Magazine ● *Join Hands Day Action Guide*, annual. Brochure. **Price:** free. **Circulation:** 45,000. Alternate Formats: online ● *Report of the Annual Meeting*, annual. Proceedings ● *Statistics of Fraternal Benefit Societies*, annual. Report. Contains all statistical information, sales, total members, and more. **Price:** $300.00. **Conventions/Meetings:** annual meeting, association business, motivation, education, social, networking (exhibits).

18745 ■ National Fraternal Society of the Deaf (NFSD)
1118 S 6th St.
Springfield, IL 62703-2406
Ph: (217)789-7429
Fax: (217)789-7489
E-mail: thefrat@nfsd.com
URL: http://www.nfsd.com
Contact: Al Van Nevel, Pres.
Founded: 1901. **Members:** 8,000. **Staff:** 6. **Budget:** $875,000. **Local Groups:** 75. **Description:** Deaf men, women, and children and those involved in the field of deafness. Works to assure that deaf and hard of hearing children receive quality education; aims to protect the right of deaf and hard of hearing citizens. Sponsors a life insurance program. **Libraries: Type:** open to the public. **Holdings:** 1,000. **Subjects:** hearing loss and related topics. **Awards:** All America Football/Basketball. **Frequency:** annual. **Type:** recognition. **Recipient:** for athlete accomplishment ● Frater of the Year. **Frequency:** annual. **Type:** recognition. **Recipient:** to a member of NFSD ● Golden Circle. **Type:** recognition. **Recipient:** to the outstanding members of the society ● Hall of Fame. **Type:** recognition. **Recipient:** to the outstanding members of the society ● Honorary Members. **Type:** recognition. **Recipient:** to individuals who are not eligible for regular insured membership ● **Frequency:** annual. **Type:** scholarship. **Telecommunication Services:** TDD, (217)789-7438. **Affiliated With:** National Fraternal Congress of America. **Formerly:** The Frat. **Publications:** *Commemorative Book*. **Price:** $22.75 plus shipping and handling ● *The Frat*, bimonthly. Magazine. Covers society's activities. Includes listing of new member and obituaries. **Price:** free for members; $8.00 /year for nonmembers. ISSN: 0739-9243. **Circulation:** 5,000. **Advertising:** accepted. **Conventions/Meetings:** quadrennial Governing Body Convention - meeting (exhibits).

18746 ■ Order of United Commercial Travelers of America (UCT)
632 N Park St.
Columbus, OH 43215-8619
Ph: (614)228-3276
Free: (800)848-0123
Fax: (614)228-1898
E-mail: rhunt@uct.org
URL: http://www.uct.org
Contact: Ronald E. Hunt, Exec. VP
Founded: 1888. **Members:** 116,680. **Membership Dues:** general, $12. **Staff:** 80. **Budget:** $9,000,000. **Regional Groups:** 31. **Local Groups:** 461. **Description:** Serves as a fraternal benefit insurance organization. Aids local units for retarded citizens; sponsors youth activities; grants scholarships to teachers of the mentally retarded. Provides benevolent funds to widows and orphans of deceased members, to members who are victims of natural disasters, and to terminally ill cancer patients. Organizes Plant Seeds of Hope, a fundraising campaign to aid retarded citizens. Maintains databases and biographical archives. **Committees:** Cancer; Retarded Citizens; Safety; Youth. **Publications:** *Sample Case*, 3/year. Magazine. Features member news and general interest topics. **Price:** $3.00 for nonmembers. ISSN: 0036-3898. **Circulation:** 120,000. **Advertising:** accepted. Alternate Formats: online. **Conventions/Meetings:** annual Supreme Session - convention - always July.

18747 ■ Police and Firemen's Insurance Association (PFIA)
101 E 116th St.
Carmel, IN 46032
Ph: (317)581-1913
Free: (800)221-7342
Fax: (317)571-5946
URL: http://www.pfia1913.org
Contact: Mark Kemp, Pres.
Founded: 1913. **Members:** 50,000. **Staff:** 32. **State Groups:** 42. **Local Groups:** 573. **Description:** Fraternal benefit insurance society. **Awards: Type:** scholarship. **Publications:** *PFIA Protector*, quarterly. Journal. Features membership activities. **Price:** included in membership dues; $10.00 /year for nonmembers in U.S.; $15.00 /year for nonmembers outside U.S. **Circulation:** 25,000. **Conventions/Meetings:** quadrennial meeting.

18748 ■ Royal Neighbors of America (RNA)
230 16th St.
Rock Island, IL 61201
Ph: (309)788-4561
Free: (800)627-4762
E-mail: contact@royalneighbors.org
URL: http://www.royalneighbors.org
Contact: Ms. Cynthia Tidwell, Pres./CEO
Founded: 1895. **Members:** 200,000. **Staff:** 400. **State Groups:** 42. **Local Groups:** 1,975. **Description:** Serves as fraternal life insurance society founded by women, that offers financial products, fraternal benefits and volunteer opportunities for women, men and children. Offers fraternal benefits to members including Newborn Fraternal benefit, Child Survivor benefit, Fraternal Aid, Disaster Relief program, and College Scholarship program. **Libraries: Type:** reference. **Holdings:** 1,000. **Awards: Type:** scholarship. **Recipient:** for young adult members. **Publications:** *Pacesetter*, quarterly. Newsletter ● *Royal Neighbor*, quarterly. Magazine. **Price:** free for members. ISSN: 0035-905X. **Circulation:** 180,000.

18749 ■ Societe Culinaire Philanthropique (SCP)
305 E 47th St., Ste.11B
New York, NY 10017
Ph: (212)308-0628
Fax: (212)308-0588
E-mail: info@societeculinaire.com
URL: http://www.societeculinaire.com
Contact: Jean-Pierre Stoehr, Pres.
Founded: 1865. **Members:** 450. **Description:** Mutual benefit insurance society for cooks, pastry cooks, butchers, and bakers. Sponsors exhibition and Culinarians' Home Foundation, a home for aged culinarians and their spouses. **Conventions/Meetings:** annual Salon of Culinary Arts - meeting.

18750 ■ SPJST
PO Box 100
Temple, TX 76503
Ph: (254)773-1575
Free: (800)727-7578
Fax: (254)774-7447
E-mail: info@spjst.com
URL: http://www.spjst.com
Contact: Gene McBride, VP
Founded: 1897. **Members:** 44,000. **Staff:** 30. **Budget:** $2,314,000. **State Groups:** 7. **Local Groups:** 112. **Description:** Supports rest home for aged members. Sponsors youth clubs. Maintains museum and a collection of early American and European artifacts from the 18th, 19th, and early 20th centuries. Sponsors charitable activities; conducts educational programs. **Libraries: Type:** reference. **Holdings:** 15,000. **Awards:** Leadership Award. **Frequency:** annual. **Type:** grant. **Recipient:** for young members. **Computer Services:** database. **Formerly:** (2003) Slavonic Benevolent Order of the State of Texas. **Publications:** *Vestnik*, weekly. Newsletter. **Price:** $20.00 for nonmembers. **Conventions/Meetings:** quadrennial meeting.

18751 ■ Supreme Council of the Royal Arcanum (SCRA)
61 Batterymarch St.
Boston, MA 02110-3208
Ph: (617)426-4135
Free: (888)272-2686
Fax: (617)426-2322

E-mail: kenkolek@royalarcanum.com
URL: http://www.royalarcanum.com
Contact: Kenneth J. Kolek, Supreme Sec.
Founded: 1877. **Members:** 18,623. **Staff:** 25. **State Groups:** 21. **Local Groups:** 285. **Description:** Provides numerous fraternal benefits to members. **Awards: Frequency:** annual. **Type:** scholarship. **Recipient:** for members. **Publications:** *125 Commemorative Anniversary Book*. Contains photos, memorabilia and history of Royal Arcanum. ● *Royal Arcanum Bulletin*, quarterly. Provides members with benefits and activities of the society. **Circulation:** 10,000 ● Brochures. **Conventions/Meetings:** biennial conference ● convention.

18752 ■ Travelers Protective Association of America (TPA)
3755 Lindell Blvd.
St. Louis, MO 63108-3476
Ph: (314)371-0533
Fax: (314)371-0537
E-mail: support@tpahq.org
URL: http://www.tpahq.org
Contact: Brian K. Schulte Jr., Exec. Sec.
Founded: 1890. **Members:** 87,000. **Membership Dues:** class A to D, $19-$35 (annual). **Budget:** $1,500,000. **State Groups:** 32. **Local Groups:** 242. **Description:** Serves as a fraternal benefit society for men and women between the ages of 18 and 60. **Awards:** TPA Scholarship Trust for Deaf and Near Deaf. **Frequency:** annual. **Type:** scholarship. **Recipient:** to children and adults suffering deafness or hearing impairment. **Committees:** Community Services; Publicity and Public Relations; Ritual; Safety; Welfare. **Publications:** *TPA Travelers Magazine*, quarterly ● Annual Report, annual ● Bulletin, monthly. **Conventions/Meetings:** annual convention - always June.

18753 ■ U.S. Letter Carriers Mutual Benefit Association (MBA)
100 Indiana Ave. NW, Ste.510
Washington, DC 20001-2144
Ph: (202)638-4318
Free: (800)424-5184
Fax: (202)783-6123
URL: http://www.nalc.org/depart/mba
Contact: Lawrence D. Brown Jr., Chm.
Founded: 1891. **Members:** 312,000. **Local Groups:** 4,656. **Description:** Fraternal benefit life insurance society. **Publications:** Brochures. Contains general descriptions of the basic life insurance, retirement and accident and health insurance plans. Alternate Formats: online. **Conventions/Meetings:** biennial meeting.

18754 ■ Vasa Order of America (VOofA)
c/o Joan Graham, Sec.
5838 San Jose Ave.
Richmond, CA 94804
Ph: (510)526-5512
E-mail: vasajlg@aol.com
URL: http://www.vasaorder.com
Contact: Joan Graham, Sec.
Founded: 1896. **Members:** 25,000. **Staff:** 10. **State Groups:** 19. **Local Groups:** 290. **Languages:** English, Swedish. **Multinational. Description:** A Swedish-American fraternal society offering old-age benefits. Sponsors youth clubs and SCLO. **Libraries: Type:** reference. **Holdings:** archival material, video recordings. **Awards: Type:** scholarship. **Subgroups:** VOA National Archives. **Publications:** *Vasa Star* (in English and Swedish), bimonthly. Magazine. **Price:** included in membership dues. **Circulation:** 12,500. **Advertising:** accepted. **Conventions/Meetings:** quadrennial convention.

18755 ■ William Penn Association (WPA)
709 Brighton Rd.
Pittsburgh, PA 15233-1821
Ph: (412)231-2979
Free: (800)848-7366
Fax: (412)231-8535

E-mail: mail@williampennassociation.org
URL: http://www.williampennassociation.org
Contact: George S Charles Jr., Pres.
Founded: 1886. **Members:** 70,000. **Local Groups:** 6. **National Groups:** 100. **Description:** Serves as a fraternal benefit life insurance society. **Awards: Frequency:** annual. **Type:** scholarship. **Recipient:** for members only. **Absorbed:** (1980) American Hungarian Catholic Society; (1983) Catholic Knights of Saint George. **Formerly:** (1973) William Penn Fraternal Association. **Publications:** *William Penn Life*, monthly. **Price:** free, available to members only. **Circulation:** 20,000. **Conventions/Meetings:** quadrennial convention.

18756 ■ Woman's Life Insurance Society
PO Box 5020
Port Huron, MI 48061-5020
Ph: (810)985-5191
Free: (800)521-9292
Fax: (810)985-6970
URL: http://www.womanslifeins.com
Contact: Janice U. Whipple, Natl. Pres./Chm. of the Board
Founded: 1892. **Members:** 75,000. **Membership Dues:** individual, $50 (annual). **Staff:** 75. **Local Groups:** 365. **Description:** Fraternal benefit life insurance society focusing on the needs of women. Each review or local club engages in local charitable community projects. **Awards:** Member of Distinction Award. **Frequency:** annual. **Type:** recognition. **Recipient:** to the most outstanding member. **Formerly:** (1966) Woman's Benefit Association; (1996) North American Benefit Association. **Publications:** *The Sales Update*, monthly. Magazine. **Circulation:** 500 ● *Woman's Life*, quarterly. Magazine. **Circulation:** 30,000. **Conventions/Meetings:** quadrennial convention.

18757 ■ Workmen's Benefit Fund of the U.S.A. (WBF)
399 Conklin St., Ste.310
Farmingdale, NY 11735-2614
Ph: (516)938-6060
Fax: (516)706-9020
E-mail: info@wbfusa.org
URL: http://www.wbfusa.org
Contact: Charles L. Grossman, CEO
Founded: 1884. **Members:** 10,000. **State Groups:** 15. **Local Groups:** 32. **National Groups:** 2. **Description:** Serves as a fraternal benefit life insurance society. **Awards:** WBF Community Service Scholarship Award. **Frequency:** annual. **Type:** scholarship. **Recipient:** for volunteer service performed by seniors. **Absorbed:** (1971) American Fraternal Insurance Company; (1973) Mutual Benefit and Aid Society. **Publications:** *WBF in Action*, quarterly. Magazine. **Price:** free for members. ISSN: 1061-4444. **Circulation:** 12,000 ● Also publishes WBF Youth In Action. **Conventions/Meetings:** quadrennial conference.

18758 ■ Workmen's Circle (WC)
45 E 33rd St.
New York, NY 10016
Ph: (212)889-6800
Free: (800)922-2558
Fax: (212)532-7518
E-mail: rbk@circle.org
URL: http://www.circle.org
Contact: Robert Kestenbaum, Exec. Off.
Founded: 1900. **Members:** 30,000. **Membership Dues:** individual, $82 (annual) ● couple, $160 (annual). **Staff:** 40. **Budget:** $4,000,000. **Regional Groups:** 7. **State Groups:** 19. **Local Groups:** 171. **Languages:** English, Yiddish. **Description:** Jewish cultural and fraternal benefit life insurance society. Jewish (but not exclusively) men, women, and children. Offers specialized education for children and adults. **Libraries: Type:** reference. **Holdings:** 2,500. **Subjects:** Yiddish and Jewish topics. **Departments:** Adult Resort; Cemetery/Funeral; Children's Summer Camp; Jewish Schools; Medical; Medical Insurance and Health Facilities; Old Age Homes; Social Service. **Divisions:** Camp Kinder Ring; Circle Lodge; Geriatric Centers; Jewish Cultural Life;

Organization; Social and Economic Justice. **Absorbed:** Young Circle League of America. **Publications:** *Kultur Un Lebn* (in English and Yiddish), 3/year. Journal. Provides Yiddish news. **Circulation:** 40,000. **Advertising:** accepted ● *Workmen's Circle Call*, semiannual. Newspaper. Covers association activities. **Circulation:** 30,000. **Advertising:** accepted ● Also publishes Yiddish texts and literary materials. **Conventions/Meetings:** biennial conference (exhibits).

18759 ■ WSA Fraternal Life
11265 Decatur St., Ste.100
Westminster, CO 80234
Ph: (303)451-1494
Free: (800)WSA-LIFE
Fax: (303)451-5112
E-mail: info@wsalife.com
URL: http://www.wsa-life.com
Contact: Randy R. Fuss, Pres./CEO
Founded: 1908. **Members:** 6,000. **State Groups:** 6. **Local Groups:** 35. **Description:** Serves as a fraternal benefit life insurance society. **Formerly:** (1990) Western Slavonic Association. **Publications:** *Fraternal Voice*, monthly. Newsletter. **Conventions/Meetings:** quadrennial meeting.

Intelligence

18760 ■ International High IQ Society
PO Box 3882
New York, NY 10163
E-mail: membership@highiqsociety.org
URL: http://www.highiqsociety.org
Contact: Nathan Heselbauer, Pres./Founder
Founded: 2000. **Membership Dues:** life, $59. **Multinational. Description:** Provides a forum for people who have an IQ in the top five percent of the population. Fosters intellectual thinking and provides social opportunities for members. **Computer Services:** Online services, IQ tests ● online services, puzzles. **Committees:** International Intelligence Testing. **Publications:** *IQ Magazine*, quarterly. Alternate Formats: online.

Iranian

18761 ■ National Iranian American Council (NIAC)
c/o OAI
2801 M. St. NW
Washington, DC 20007
Ph: (202)719-8071 (202)518-6187
Fax: (202)719-8097
E-mail: info@niacouncil.org
URL: http://www.niacouncil.org
Contact: Dr. Trita Parsi, Pres.
Founded: 2002. **Membership Dues:** standard, $40 (annual) ● Capitol Hill Club, $250 (annual) ● Senate Club, $500 (annual) ● Senate Club, $40 (monthly) ● President's Club, $1,000 (annual) ● Council Club, $100 (annual). **Description:** Serves as a catalyst for information sharing and collaboration among Iranian-American organizations. Provides an organized framework for effective networking and civic education for Iranian-Americans. Builds bridges and strong alliances with other communities in a continuing union of friendship and constructive partnership. Educates the American public on Iran's rich cultural heritage and the achievements and contributions of the Iranian American community. **Publications:** *NIAC Congressional Directory.* **Price:** included in membership dues ● Annual Report, annual. Alternate Formats: online ● Newsletter. Alternate Formats: online.

Irish

18762 ■ Ancient Order of Hibernians in America (AOH)
31 Logan St.
Auburn, NY 13021-3925
Ph: (315)252-3895

Fax: (315)252-6996
E-mail: aohpresident@aoh.com
URL: http://www.aoh.com
Contact: Jack Meehan, Pres.
Founded: 1836. **Members:** 191,000. **Budget:** $350,000. **Local Groups:** 736. **Description:** Fraternal benefit insurance society of American Catholics who are Irish by birth or descent. Maintains speakers' bureau; compiles statistics. **Libraries: Type:** reference. **Holdings:** archival material. **Awards:** John F. Kennedy Memorial Medal. **Frequency:** biennial. **Type:** medal. **Publications:** *National Hibernian Digest*, bimonthly. **Conventions/Meetings:** biennial meeting.

18763 ■ Irish Institute (II)
Address Unknown since 2007
Founded: 1950. **Members:** 200. **Membership Dues:** $100. **Description:** United States citizens of Irish birth or extraction. Provides financial support for cultural projects in Ireland and the U.S. **Awards: Frequency:** annual. **Type:** grant. **Formerly:** (1955) Irish Feis Institute. **Conventions/Meetings:** periodic meeting.

18764 ■ Knights of Equity (KOE)
1135 8th Ave.
Freedom, PA 15042
Ph: (412)204-8450
E-mail: supreme@knightsofequity.com
URL: http://www.knightsofequity.com
Contact: Greg Garrison, Contact
Founded: 1895. **Members:** 10,000. **Membership Dues:** regular, $25 (annual). **Staff:** 2. **State Groups:** 3. **Local Groups:** 3. **Description:** Americans who are of Irish ancestry and are practicing Roman Catholics. Seeks to: advance members spiritually, materially, and socially; teach Irish history and culture; help the cause of liberty and freedom for the people of Ireland. Assists orphan homes, homes for the aged, and young men interested in priesthood. Sponsors Celtic courses at universities (for members only). Has purchased trophies for Catholic school athletic activities. Operates speakers' bureau. **Libraries: Type:** reference. **Holdings:** 2,300. **Awards: Frequency:** annual. **Type:** scholarship. **Recipient:** for KOE members and family attending in Detroit University. **Divisions:** Court 5 Buffalo; Court 9 Pittsburgh; Court 6 Detroit; Daughters of Erin. **Publications:** *American-Caitliceah-Gaelic Periodical*, monthly. Newsletter. **Advertising:** accepted ● *Hall of Tara* ● *Knights of Equity Newsletter*, 3/year. **Price:** available to members only ● *Lecturers*, monthly ● *National Minutes of Semiannual Meeting* ● *News Bulletin*, monthly. **Conventions/Meetings:** biennial convention - 2008 Oct. 9-12, Buffalo, NY ● annual convention.

18765 ■ Society of the Friendly Sons of St. Patrick in the City of New York
80 Wall St., Rm. 712
New York, NY 10005
Ph: (212)269-1770
Fax: (212)344-8966
E-mail: sonsstpat@verizon.com
Contact: Raymond C. Teatum, Sec.
Founded: 1784. **Members:** 1,500. **Membership Dues:** individual, $150 (annual). **Staff:** 1. **Description:** Men of Irish descent in the New York City area. Conducts charitable activities. Donations are distributed through other charitable organizations in the New York Metropolitan area, not to individuals. **Libraries: Type:** reference. **Holdings:** books. **Committees:** Charity; Stewards. **Publications:** Yearbook, annual. **Price:** included in membership dues. **Conventions/Meetings:** meeting - 3/year; always January, May, and November, in New York City.

Islam

18766 ■ Council on American-Islamic Relations (CAIR)
453 New Jersey Ave. SE
Washington, DC 20003-4034
Ph: (202)488-8787

Fax: (202)488-0833
E-mail: info@cair.com
URL: http://www.cair-net.org
Contact: Dr. Parvez Ahmed, Chm.
Founded: 1994. **Membership Dues:** general, $35 (annual). **Staff:** 20. **Local Groups:** 20. **Languages:** Arabic, English. **Description:** Promotes positive image of Islam and Muslims in America. **Awards:** Community Achievement Awards. **Frequency:** annual. **Type:** recognition. **Additional Websites:** http://www.cair.com. **Publications:** *Faith In Action*, quarterly. Newsletter ● Handbooks. **Conventions/Meetings:** conference and seminar, with leadership training.

Israel

18767 ■ Americans United for Israel (AUFI)
1002 Hope St.
Stamford, CT 06907
Ph: (209)433-3797
Fax: (209)433-3797
E-mail: info@aufi.org
URL: http://www.aufi.org
Membership Dues: regular, $40 (annual) ● contributing, $100 (annual) ● supporting, $500 (annual) ● sustaining, $1,000 (annual) ● student, senior, $20 (annual). **Description:** Advocates for peace, security and freedom for Israel. Works to support, encourage and defend the United States and Israel in the war against Islam's terror. Participates in the economic, political and media forums where agenda must be heard and endeavors to bring message of peace and security for the United States and Israel to fellow Americans and the world. Urges the leadership of the United States and Israel to recognize and focus on the task at hand: ensuring a life of liberty and security for the two nations. **Publications:** Articles.

Israeli

18768 ■ Israeli Students' Organization in the U.S.A. and Canada
c/o International Student Organization
250 W 49th St., Ste.806
New York, NY 10019
Ph: (212)262-8922
Free: (800)244-1180
Fax: (212)262-8920
E-mail: mailbox@isoa.org
URL: http://www.isoa.org
Contact: Karen Ziv, Exec. Off.
Founded: 1958. **Members:** 3,500. **Local Groups:** 46. **Description:** Israeli citizens who are in the United States or Canada for study and/or training purposes. Gives aid and advise to members in solving their problems during their study or training and upon their return to Israel; sponsors cultural, social, and informative activities in the Israeli spirit and tradition; represents the Israeli student body before Israeli, American, and Canadian authorities and maintains contact with these authorities. Promotes friendship between Israeli students, American Jewish students, other foreign students, American Jewry, and the American public. Maintains a loan fund; provides medical insurance program and discount airfare to Israel. **Publications:** *Igeret*, monthly. Newsletter ● *International Spirit Magazine*, monthly.

Italian

18769 ■ American Committee on Italian Migration (ACIM)
25 Carmine St.
New York, NY 10014
Ph: (212)247-7373
Fax: (212)265-5793
E-mail: acimny@aol.com
URL: http://www.acimimmigra.org
Contact: Rev. Joseph Fugolo CS, Contact
Founded: 1952. **Members:** 8,000. **Budget:** $200,000. **Regional Groups:** 1. **State Groups:** 5.

Languages: English, Italian, Spanish. **Description:** Promotes an understanding and implementation of immigration laws. Offers free assistance to Italian immigrants and others in their problems of resettlement and assimilation into United States society. **Awards:** **Frequency:** recognition. **Type:** recognition. **Recipient:** for service to migrants. **Publications:** *ACIM Newsletter* (in English and Italian), quarterly. **Circulation:** 8,000.

18770 ■ Association of Student and Professional Italian-Americans (ASPI)
115 Charles St., No. 4
New York, NY 10014
Ph: (212)242-3215
E-mail: donotvl@juno.com
Contact: Pasquale D'Onofrio, Pres.
Founded: 1957. **Description:** College graduates or persons with equivalent education; students. Assists Italian-American professionals and Italian exchange students to further there careers and studies; encourages communication among them to create an atmosphere of mutual understanding. Strives to foster responsible leadership within the Italian-American community; promotes interest in Italian culture through educational and social activities. **Programs:** Dances; Dinner Discussions; Guest Speakers; Museum Visits; Picnics; Theatre and Opera Parties. **Conventions/Meetings:** conference - 10/year.

18771 ■ Gruppo Esponenti Italiani (GEI)
PO Box 789
New York, NY 10150
Ph: (212)867-2772
Fax: (212)867-4114
E-mail: geinewyork@aol.com
URL: http://www.gei-ny.com/About%20GEI.htm
Contact: Lucio Caputo, Pres.
Founded: 1974. **Members:** 60. **Membership Dues:** regular, $1,500 (annual). **Staff:** 2. **Budget:** $70,000. **Languages:** English, Italian. **Description:** Senior executives representing major Italian business, communications, industrial, and governmental organizations in the U.S. Fosters cultural and business ties between the U.S. and Italy through nonpartisan educational activities. Provides forum for discussion of major business and governmental issues of concern to Italy and the U.S. Has sponsored a contest for the best article or broadcast by the American media about Italy and contributed toward organization of an Italian school in New York. **Awards:** GEI Award. **Frequency:** annual. **Type:** recognition. **Recipient:** for notable Italians and Americans who have made significant contributions toward greater understanding between Italy and the U.S.

18772 ■ Italian American Cultural Society (IACS)
43843 Romeo Plank Rd.
Clinton Township, MI 48038
Ph: (586)226-1582
Fax: (586)228-1678
E-mail: iacs@iacsonline.net
URL: http://www.iacsonline.net
Contact: Frank J. Palazzolo, Pres.
Founded: 1957. **Members:** 2,500. **Membership Dues:** individual (age 62 and above), $35 (annual) ● individual (age 61 and under), $38 (annual) ● family, $60 (annual) ● patron, $300 (annual) ● benefactor, $500 (annual) ● life, $5,000. **Staff:** 25. **Budget:** $1,250,000. **Description:** Individuals, businesses, and organizations interested in Italian culture and heritage. Seeks to preserve Italian background and recognize Italian-American contributions to the U.S. and the world. Sponsors the Italian Cultural and Community Center, whose activities include: courses and seminars on Italian language, literature, art, and theatre; human relations studies; music, dance, film, art, and drama programs; old world crafts and cooking. Has developed an Italian-American Archive and Library. **Libraries: Type:** open to the public. **Holdings:** archival material, audiovisuals, books, papers, periodicals, photographs. **Awards: Type:** recognition. **Committees:** Athletic; Avanti Network; Fine Arts; Senior Citizen Housing; Senior Citizens. **Affiliated**

With: National Italian American Foundation. **Publications:** *Conference Program*, annual ● *Italian American Cultural Society—Newsletter*, monthly. **Price:** included in membership dues. **Circulation:** 10,000. **Advertising:** accepted ● Monographs. **Conventions/Meetings:** monthly meeting ● annual meeting.

18773 ■ Italian Catholic Federation Central Council (ICF)
675 Hegenberger Rd., Ste.230
Oakland, CA 94621
Ph: (510)633-9058
Free: (888)423-1924
Fax: (510)633-9758
E-mail: info@icf.org
URL: http://icf.org
Contact: Leonard Rossi, Grand Pres.
Founded: 1924. **Members:** 14,000. **Membership Dues:** fraternal/religious, charitable, $30 (annual). **Staff:** 3. **Budget:** $1,500,000. **Local Groups:** 176. **Languages:** English, Italian. **Description:** Catholics of Italian birth or descent. Conducts religious, patriotic, social, cultural, and charitable activities. **Awards:** Family of the Year Award. **Frequency:** annual. **Type:** recognition ● Grand President Award. **Frequency:** annual. **Type:** recognition ● Mother Teresa Award. **Frequency:** annual. **Type:** recognition. **Recipient:** to religious clergy, deacon, or nun for humanitarian service ● Pope John 23 Award. **Frequency:** annual. **Type:** recognition ● Young Adult Leadership Award. **Frequency:** annual. **Type:** recognition. **Recipient:** for outstanding leadership abilities. **Committees:** Heritage; Scholarship; Youth Activities. **Publications:** *Bollettino*, monthly. Newsletter. **Circulation:** 14,000. **Advertising:** accepted. Alternate Formats: online; CD-ROM ● *Ritual Booklet*. Alternate Formats: online. **Conventions/Meetings:** annual convention (exhibits) - always Labor Day weekend.

18774 ■ Italian Charities of America (ICA)
8320 Queens Blvd.
Elmhurst, NY 11373
Ph: (718)478-3100
Fax: (718)478-2665
Contact: Rose Sproviero, Pres.
Founded: 1936. **Members:** 500. **Membership Dues:** $25 (annual). **Staff:** 2. **Languages:** English, Italian. **Description:** Italian charities in America composed of individuals of Italian birth or descent. Renders services in the form of a Christmas party for underprivileged youngsters, leadership training, and youth guidance. Sponsors Senior Center for senior citizens that offers hot meals daily in addition to recreation, craft, drama, dancing, exercise, and Italian language classes. Maintains library of 3000 volumes in the areas of fiction, non-fiction, reference, law, and documentaries. **Libraries: Type:** not open to the public. **Holdings:** 3,000; articles, books, periodicals. **Awards:** Man of the Year. **Frequency:** annual. **Type:** recognition ● Women of the Year. **Frequency:** annual. **Type:** recognition. **Committees:** Aid to Italy; Discrimination; Education; Employment; Grant Application; Immigration and Naturalization; Public Relations; Welfare. **Formerly:** (1951) Italian Charity and Welfare Center. **Publications:** *ICA Report*, monthly. Newsletter. **Price:** free. **Circulation:** 750. **Advertising:** accepted.

18775 ■ Italian Sons and Daughters of America (ISDA)
419 Wood St.
Pittsburgh, PA 15222
Ph: (412)261-3550
E-mail: questions@orderisda.org
URL: http://www.orderisda.org
Contact: Blase W. Manzo, Contact
Members: 5,000. **Local Groups:** 34. **Description:** Fraternal society for Americans of Italian origin and their friends. Provides aid to needy children and senior citizen homes. **Awards:** Leonardo da Vinci Award. **Frequency:** annual. **Type:** recognition ● Man of the Year Award. **Frequency:** annual. **Type:** recognition ● Michaelangelo Award. **Frequency:** annual. **Type:** recognition ● Renaissance Award. **Frequency:** annual. **Type:** recognition ● **Type:** scholarship. **Telecommunication Services:** electronic mail, blase@

ald.net. **Absorbed:** Italo American National Union. **Publications:** Newsletter, monthly. **Conventions/Meetings:** quadrennial meeting.

18776 ■ National Italian American Foundation (NIAF)

1860 19th St. NW
Washington, DC 20009
Ph: (202)387-0600
Fax: (202)387-0800
E-mail: information@niaf.org
URL: http://www.niaf.org
Contact: John Salamone, Exec. Dir./Chief Admin. Off.

Founded: 1975. **Members:** 20,000. **Membership Dues:** student (under age of 24), $25 (annual) ● associate, $45 (annual) ● Young Professional Council (under age of 35), $125 (annual) ● Silver Council, $250 (annual) ● Gold Council, $1,000 (annual) ● Platinum Council, $2,500 (annual). **Staff:** 15. **Budget:** $5,000,000. **Regional Groups:** 11. **State Groups:** 6. **Languages:** English, Italian. **Description:** U.S. citizens of Italian ancestry. Activities include research and education concerning Italian American art, culture, sciences, and social history; lecture series and studies. Acts as liaison with Congress and federal agencies. Compiles statistics; maintains speakers' bureau. Operates student exchange program, scholarships and information referral service. Local groups are known as Affiliates of the National Italian American Foundation. **Libraries:** **Type:** reference. **Holdings:** 2,000; archival material. **Subjects:** Italian American topics. **Awards:** A.P. Giannini Awards. **Type:** recognition ● DiPietro Memorial Awards. **Type:** recognition ● NIAF Achievement Awards. **Frequency:** annual. **Type:** recognition ● NIAF Teacher of the Year Award. **Frequency:** annual. **Type:** recognition. **Recipient:** to an outstanding educator in Italian language and culture. **Boards:** International Advisory. **Committees:** International Relations. **Formerly:** (1978) Italian American Foundation. **Publications:** *The Ambassador*, quarterly. Magazine. **Price:** included in membership dues. **Circulation:** 20,000. **Advertising:** accepted ● *NIAF News*, bimonthly. Newsletter. Features national news and international news related to Italian Americans. **Circulation:** 20,000. **Advertising:** accepted. **Conventions/Meetings:** annual conference and symposium (exhibits) - always October in Washington, DC ● convention.

18777 ■ National Organization of Italian-American Women (NOIAW)

25 W 43rd St., 10th Fl.
New York, NY 10036
Ph: (212)642-2003
Fax: (212)642-2006
E-mail: noiaw@aol.com
URL: http://www.noiaw.org
Contact: Aileen Riotto Sirey PhD, Chair/Founder

Founded: 1980. **Members:** 800. **Membership Dues:** regular, $100 (annual) ● corporate, $500 (annual) ● senior, $50 (annual) ● student, $30 (annual) ● young professional (under 35 years old), $50 (annual) ● benefactor, $1,000 (annual). **Staff:** 2. **Regional Groups:** 4. **State Groups:** 21. **Local Groups:** 2. **National Groups:** 2. **Description:** Women who have at least one parent of Italian heritage. Objectives are to: foster interests and address problems and concerns of Italian-American women; provide network of resources and support for professional, political, and social advancement; increase cultural, educational, and financial opportunities of young people of Italian-American origin; promote awareness and perpetuation of Italian culture and ethnic identity; foster ethnic pride and develop role models for younger Italian-Americans; modify traditional images of women of Italian descent and expand their career choices; help serve the interests of Italian-American communities; provide liaison and promote greater unity with other Italian-American groups and women's ethnic groups. Encourages Italian-American women to monitor and participate in the political process and to serve health and welfare interests of the Italian-American community. Conducts film presentations; sponsors forums, workshops, seminars, cultural events, and

networking meetings; conducts self-help programs. Sponsors Mentor Program for female college students whereby each student is "adopted" by a member who has a career in the student's chosen field. **Awards:** IAF Scholarship Program. **Frequency:** annual. **Type:** scholarship. **Affiliated With:** National Italian American Foundation. **Publications:** Newsletter, quarterly. Contains regional updates and reviews of events. **Conventions/Meetings:** periodic international conference ● annual meeting and luncheon, with award ceremony.

18778 ■ Order Sons of Italy in America (OSIA)

219 E St. NE
Washington, DC 20002
Ph: (202)547-2900
Free: (800)552-OSIA
Fax: (202)546-8168
E-mail: nationaloffice@osia.org
URL: http://www.osia.org
Contact: Philip R. Piccigallo PhD, Exec. Dir.

Founded: 1905. **Members:** 500,000. **Membership Dues:** international, $50 (annual) ● other, $35 (annual). **Staff:** 7. **State Groups:** 29. **Local Groups:** 700. **Description:** Fraternal society for American men and women of Italian descent. Works to keep alive the rich cultural heritage of Italy and the Italian people; has helped to enrich the diversified culture through educational, charitable, social, civic, and philanthropic activities; founded the Commission for Social Justice (see separate entry), the anti-defamation arm of the Italian-American movement, and the Tax-Exempt Sons of Italy Foundation. Maintains Garibaldi-Meucci Museum; compiles statistics. **Awards:** Henry Salvatori Scholarship. **Type:** scholarship. **Recipient:** for senior high school students of Italian descent ● Marconi Award. **Frequency:** biennial. **Type:** recognition ● National Education and Leadership Award. **Frequency:** annual. **Type:** recognition ● National Sports Award. **Frequency:** biennial. **Type:** recognition ● Sons of Italy Italian Language Scholarship. **Type:** scholarship. **Recipient:** for junior/senior undergraduate students. **Affiliated With:** Commission for Social Justice. **Publications:** *Italian America*, quarterly. Magazine. **Price:** $4.95/issue for nonmembers (plus $1.25 for shipping and handling); $15.00 /year for nonmembers in U.S.; $25.00 /year for nonmembers outside U.S.; free for members. **Circulation:** 65,000. **Advertising:** accepted. Alternate Formats: online ● *Italian-American Characters in Television Entertainment* ● *State Newspapers*, monthly ● *Survey of Italian-American Representation.* **Conventions/Meetings:** biennial congress and convention - usually August.

18779 ■ Unico National (UN)

271 US Hwy. 46 W, Ste.A-108
Fairfield, NJ 07004
Ph: (973)808-0035
Free: (800)877-1492
Fax: (973)808-0043
E-mail: mmariniello@unico.org
URL: http://www.unico.org
Contact: Michael Spano, Pres.

Founded: 1922. **Members:** 8,000. **Staff:** 3. **Budget:** $200,000. **Regional Groups:** 3. **State Groups:** 30. **Local Groups:** 150. **Description:** Active members; associate national members are business and professional people of Italian lineage or married to an Italian-American. (Unico is the Italian word for "unique" or "one of a kind".) Sponsors educational, cultural, and civic programs; maintains the Unico Foundation; makes contributions to research in Cooley's Anemia, a blood disease affecting children; conducts seminars; holds literary contest. Supports mental health research and cancer research. **Awards:** Ella Grasso Literary Award. **Frequency:** annual. **Type:** recognition. **Recipient:** for amateur writers of essays and short stories on the Italian-American experience ● Marconi Science Award. **Frequency:** annual. **Type:** medal. **Recipient:** to a U.S. citizen of Italian descent with an outstanding contribution in the field of physical sciences ● Rizzuto Award. **Frequency:** annual. **Type:** scholarship. **Recipient:** to the non-Unican who

has rendered a definite contribution in services or otherwise to UNICO ● Vastola Award. **Frequency:** annual. **Type:** recognition. **Recipient:** to the 10-year member who has rendered exceptional service. **Committees:** Cancer Research; Cooley's Anemia; Literary Contest; Mental Health; National Ethnic Interests; National Scholarships. **Formed by Merger of:** Unico; National Italian Civic League. **Publications:** *ComUnico*, bimonthly. Magazine. **Conventions/Meetings:** annual meeting.

Japanese

18780 ■ Japanese American Citizens League (JACL)

1765 Sutter St.
San Francisco, CA 94115
Ph: (415)921-5225
Fax: (415)931-4671
E-mail: jacl@jacl.org
URL: http://www.jacl.org
Contact: Larry T. Oda, Pres.

Founded: 1929. **Members:** 24,000. **Membership Dues:** individual, $43 (annual) ● couple or family, $75 (annual) ● youth or student, $14 (annual). **Staff:** 12. **Budget:** $1,200,000. **Local Groups:** 112. **Description:** Educational, civil, and human rights organization. Works to defend the civil and human rights of all people, particularly Japanese Americans. Seeks to preserve the cultural and ethnic heritage of Japanese Americans. Resources include library and audiovisual materials. **Awards:** JACL Scholarship Program. **Frequency:** annual. **Type:** scholarship. **Recipient:** for freshman, undergraduate, graduate, law and creative and performing arts students ● **Type:** recognition. **Telecommunication Services:** electronic mail, president@jacl.org. **Committees:** Aging and Retirement; Anti-Asian Violence; Atomic Bomb Survivors; Civil Rights; Employment Discrimination; Ethnic Concerns; Japanese American Research; Leadership Development; Redress; Scholarship; Student Aid; Veterans' Affairs; Women's Concerns Education. **Publications:** *Pacific Citizen*, bimonthly. Newspaper. **Price:** $35.00. **Advertising:** accepted. **Conventions/Meetings:** biennial meeting and convention - always August.

18781 ■ National Association of Japan-America Societies (NAJAS)

1150 Connecticut Ave. NW, Ste.1050
Washington, DC 20036
Ph: (202)429-5545
Fax: (202)429-0027
E-mail: contact@us-japan.org
URL: http://www.us-japan.org
Contact: Samuel M. Shepherd, Pres.

Founded: 1978. **Members:** 40. **Staff:** 2. **Budget:** $350,000. **Description:** A network of Japan-America societies. Works to improve cultural understanding between the people of Japan and the U.S. through corporate, public affairs and educational programs. Activities include cooperative programs forming new societies and common services desired by member organizations. **Formerly:** (1991) Associated Japan-America Societies of the United States. **Publications:** *NAJAS Updates*, monthly. Bulletins. Contains updates sent via e-mail. Alternate Formats: online ● Annual Report, annual. **Conventions/Meetings:** annual meeting.

18782 ■ Nippon Club (NC)

145 W 57th St.
New York, NY 10019
Ph: (212)581-2223
Fax: (212)581-3332
E-mail: info@nipponclub.org
URL: http://www.nipponclub.org

Founded: 1905. **Members:** 2,600. **Staff:** 34. **Languages:** English, Japanese. **Description:** Japanese and other persons who take special interest in Japanese affairs. Maintains club house for social, cultural, and recreational activities of members. Promotes better relations and cultural exchange between Japan and the United States. **Publications:**

The Nippon Club Directory, annual. Contains a list of all of its members, their home addresses and corporate affiliations. ● *Nippon Club News*, monthly. Newsletter. Features the club's activities and events. **Price:** free for members.

Jewelry

18783 ■ Gemological Institute of America: Alumni Association (GIA)
The Robert Mouawad Campus
5345 Armada Dr.
Carlsbad, CA 92008
Ph: (760)603-4135
Free: (800)421-7250
Fax: (760)603-4199
E-mail: alumni@gia.edu
URL: http://www.gia.edu
Contact: Starla Turner GG, Chair
Founded: 1982. **Members:** 5,000. **Membership Dues:** alumnus, $50 (annual) ● VIP, $250 (annual) ● international, $25 (annual). **Staff:** 3. **Multinational. Description:** Works as alumni association for gem and jewelry professionals and students promoting professional growth and advancement. **Telecommunication Services:** electronic mail, teefam@ix. netcom.com. **Publications:** *GIA Alumni Directory*. Alternate Formats: online ● *The Loupe: GIA World News*. **Conventions/Meetings:** seminar.

Jewish

18784 ■ Association of Yugoslav Jews in the U.S.A. (AYJUSA)
Address Unknown since 2007
Founded: 1940. **Members:** 170. **Membership Dues:** individual, $15 (annual) ● family, $24 (annual). **Staff:** 12. **Regional Groups:** 2. **State Groups:** 2. **Local Groups:** 2. **Description:** American Jews originally from the former republic of Yugoslavia. Maintains small library; conducts charitable programs. **Awards:** Generations Award: State of Israel Bonds. **Type:** recognition ● Gilboa Regional Council Award to Association of Yugoslav Jews. **Type:** recognition. **Recipient:** for the construction of dado elazar sport center ● Golden Book of the Jewish National Fund. **Type:** recognition ● The Israel Solidarity Award: Ministry of Finance. **Type:** recognition. **Committees:** Ladies Auxiliary; Relations; Religious. **Projects:** Emergency fund drive for Yugoslavian olim in Israel. **Also Known As:** Udruzenje Jugoslovenskih Jevreja u United States of America. **Publications:** Bulletin (in Czech and English), monthly. **Advertising:** not accepted. **Conventions/Meetings:** annual meeting.

18785 ■ AUFBAU Trust
2121 Broadway
New York, NY 10023
Ph: (212)873-7400
E-mail: editorial@aufbauonline.com
URL: http://www.aufbauonline.com
Founded: 1924. **Members:** 3,500. **Membership Dues:** individual, $60 (annual). **Multinational. Description:** Promotes transatlantic Jewish life.

18786 ■ Bnai Zion Foundation (BZ)
136 E 39th St.
New York, NY 10016
Ph: (212)725-1211
Free: (800)JOIN-399
Fax: (212)684-6327
E-mail: info@bnaizion.com
URL: http://www.bnaizion.com
Contact: Mr. Jack Grunspan, Exec. VP
Founded: 1908. **Members:** 34,000. **Membership Dues:** single or senior individual, $42 (annual) ● family, $56 (annual) ● contributing, $100 (annual) ● supporting, $250 (annual) ● sustaining, $500 (annual) ● high school or college student, $18 (annual) ● life, family, $500 ● life, individual, $400. **Staff:** 28. **Budget:** $1,600,000. **Regional Groups:** 6. **State Groups:** 11. **Local Groups:** 106. **Description:** Fraternal benefit life insurance society of Jewish individu-

als and families. Conducts activities supporting growth and development of Israel and Jewish education. **Libraries: Type:** reference. **Subjects:** Jewish and Israeli issues, Zionist history. **Awards: Type:** scholarship. **Recipient:** for Hebrew scholarship in high school and college. **Committees:** Communications; Cultural; Education; Foundation - Charitable Projects; Fraternal Benefits; Insurance; Israel Bonds; Medical Center in Haifa; Public Relations; Speakers Bureau; Special Children; UJA; Zionist Affairs. **Affiliated With:** American Zionist Movement; World Confederation of United Zionists. **Absorbed:** (1981) Brith Abraham. **Formerly:** (1945) Order of Sons of Zion. **Publications:** *Bnai Zion Voice*, quarterly. Magazine. **Conventions/Meetings:** biennial meeting.

18787 ■ Brith Sholom (BS)
3939 Conshohocken Ave.
Philadelphia, PA 19131
Ph: (215)878-5696
Fax: (215)878-5699
E-mail: jeromeverlin@brithsholom.org
URL: http://www.brithsholom.org
Contact: Jerry Verlin, Pres.
Founded: 1905. **Members:** 6,000. **Staff:** 5. **Budget:** $300,000. **State Groups:** 3. **Local Groups:** 20. **Description:** Jewish fraternal society for men and women 16 years of age and over. Sponsors senior citizens' home in Philadelphia, PA and medical rehabilitation center for Israeli veterans in Haifa, Israel. **Awards: Type:** recognition. **Committees:** Interlodge Sports Activities; Israel Activities; Services to the Armed Forces; Social Actions. **Formerly:** Independent Order of Brith Sholom. **Publications:** *Brith Sholom Presents*, bimonthly. Newsletter. Features current events and membership activities. **Price:** included in membership dues ● *Brith Sholom— President's Report*, annual. Covers the state of the organization. ● *Brith Sholom Resolutions*, annual. Report. Contains political and nonpolitical "white paper positions". **Conventions/Meetings:** annual meeting (exhibits).

18788 ■ Center for Jewish History
15 W 16th St.
New York, NY 10011
Ph: (212)294-8301
E-mail: inquiries@cjh.org
URL: http://www.cjh.org
Contact: Bruce Slovin, Chm.
Description: Committed to preserving the cultural and historical legacy of the Jewish people. **Libraries: Type:** reference. **Holdings:** 500,000; archival material, books, periodicals, photographs. **Subjects:** Jewish history. **Programs:** Samberg Family History. **Publications:** *CJH Newsletter*. **Conventions/Meetings:** Distinguished Jew and Justice Series - lecture.

18789 ■ Central Agency for Jewish Education (CAJE)
12 Millstone Campus Dr.
St. Louis, MO 63146-5576
Ph: (314)432-0020 (314)434-5298
Fax: (314)432-6150
E-mail: jkraus@aol.com
URL: http://www.cajestl.org
Contact: Linda Kraus, Pres.
Founded: 1971. **Description:** Promotes Jewish continuity and improvement of Jewish life through education; seeks to create well-educated individuals knowledgeable about and faithful to the ideals of Judaism. Conducts Camp Kee Tov. **Commissions:** Commission on Afternoon Hebrew School Education; Commission on Conservative Jewish Education; Commission on Reform Jewish Education. **Departments:** Family Education; Teacher Education and School Services. **Programs:** Adult Education; Community Services; Passport to Israel; School Services; Teacher Education.

18790 ■ Foundation for the Advancement of Sephardic Studies and Culture (FASSAC)
c/o Robert Bedford, Exec. VP
34 W 15th St., 3rd Fl.
New York, NY 10011

E-mail: info@sephardicstudies.org
URL: http://www.sephardicstudies.org
Contact: Robert Bedford, Exec. VP
Founded: 1969. **Description:** Committed to preserving and promoting the culture of Sephardic communities of Turkey, Greece, the Balkans, Europe, and the U.S. Emigration, and remembrance of the devastation of the Holocaust. **Councils:** Ladino Preservation. **Publications:** *Last Century of a Sephardic Community: The Jews of Monastir, 1839-1943*. Book. **Price:** $3,495.00 ● *Ottoman Salonica, 1430-1912*. Video. Features the history of the ancient Macedonian city of Salonica and Sephardic Jewish community.

18791 ■ Free Sons of Israel (FSI)
247-25 Jamaica Ave.
Bellerose, NY 11426
Ph: (718)347-1614
Fax: (718)347-1614
E-mail: info@freeson.org
Contact: Steve Kirschner, Deputy Grand Master
Founded: 1849. **Members:** 3,000. **Membership Dues:** $36 (annual). **Staff:** 1. **Regional Groups:** 25. **Description:** Jewish fraternal benefit society. Offers discounted long-term care insurance, blood bank, scholarships, grave availability, IBM Metro Credit Union, free holiday celebrations, member-to-member discounts, etc. Conducts charitable programs on a non-sectarian basis. **Awards:** Hebrew Language Award. **Type:** recognition. **Computer Services:** Mailing lists. **Committees:** Foundation Fund; Scholarship Fund; Social Action. **Formerly:** Independent Order Free Sons of Israel. **Publications:** *The Reporter*, semiannual. Newspaper. **Price:** free. **Circulation:** 3,000. **Advertising:** accepted. **Conventions/Meetings:** triennial convention.

18792 ■ GesherCity
c/o Adam Courtney, Dir.
15 E 26th St., Rm. 916
New York, NY 10010
Ph: (212)786-5108
Fax: (212)481-4174
E-mail: geshercity@geshercity.org
URL: http://www.geshercity.org
Contact: Ben Gordon, Founder/Chm.
Founded: 1998. **Description:** Bridges young adults to the Jewish community by providing access to personal networks and information resources. Offers networked technology, methodologies, brand marketing and best practices to Jewish communities. Aims to establish a global network of "bridges" branded under a common name that can be recognized by Jewish young adults everywhere. **Telecommunication Services:** electronic mail, acourtney@jcca.org.

18793 ■ A Jewish Voice for Peace (JVP)
1611 Telegraph Ave., Ste.806
Oakland, CA 94612
Ph: (510)465-1777
Fax: (510)465-1616
E-mail: info@jewishvoiceforpeace.org
URL: http://www.jewishvoiceforpeace.org
Contact: Mitchell Plitnick, Dir. of Administration and Policy
Founded: 1996. **Description:** Works for peace, democracy, human rights, and respect for international law; supports Israeli and Palestinian security and determination. **Publications:** Newsletter, monthly. Alternate Formats: online ● Annual Report, annual. Alternate Formats: online.

18794 ■ Labor Zionist Alliance (LZA)
c/o Doni Remba, Exec. Dir.
114 W 26th St., Ste.1005
New York, NY 10001-6708
Ph: (212)675-5138 (212)366-1194
Fax: (212)675-7685
E-mail: executive@laborzionist.org
URL: http://www.laborzionist.org
Contact: Kenneth Bob, Pres.
Founded: 1913. **Members:** 5,000. **Membership Dues:** single, $36 (annual) ● couple, $60 (annual) ● sustaining (single/couple), $100 (annual). **Staff:** 3. **Budget:** $100,000. **State Groups:** 22. **Local**

Groups: 250. **Languages:** English, Hebrew, Yiddish. **Description:** Fraternal, educational, and cultural organization. Seeks to strengthen American Jewish life, support Israel, and work for liberal causes and against racial and religious discrimination. Supports a youth movement, Habonim Dror in the United States. Sponsors activities pertaining to Jewish art and culture. Conducts educational, charitable, and cultural programs. **Computer Services:** database. **Committees:** American Affairs; Cultural; Public Affairs; Yiddish; Youth and Aliya; Zionism, Israel and Jewish Affairs. **Affiliated With:** American Zionist Movement. **Formed by Merger of:** (1972) Farbard Labor Zionist Order; Poale Zion - United Labor Zionist Organization of America. **Publications:** *Jewish Frontier*, bimonthly. Journal. **Advertising:** accepted. Alternate Formats: online ● *Yiddisher Kemfer*, bimonthly. **Conventions/Meetings:** biennial convention.

18795 ■ North American Federation of Temple Youth (NFTY)
c/o Union for Reform Judaism
633 3rd Ave., 7th Fl.
New York, NY 10017
Ph: (212)650-4070
Fax: (212)650-4199
E-mail: nfty@urj.org
URL: http://www.nfty.org
Contact: Hope Chernak, Managing Dir.
Members: 500. **Multinational. Description:** Offers the opportunity to explore and live Reform Judaism for young people.

Knights of Pythias

18796 ■ Dramatic Order Knights of Khorassan (DOKK)
110 N Wabash Ave.
Marion, IN 46952-2614
Ph: (765)664-7925
Fax: (765)664-7925
E-mail: mfk46952@mac.com
URL: http://homepage.mac.com/mfk46952/Menu3.html
Contact: Mr. Martin Koehler PIP, Imperial Sec.
Founded: 1895. **Members:** 1,400. **Staff:** 1. **Budget:** $25,000. **Regional Groups:** 50. **Local Groups:** 3. **Description:** Serves as a fraternal order auxiliary of the Supreme Lodge Knights of Pythias. Sponsors humanitarian activities. Offers student loans for the children of members. **Committees:** Humanitarian Activities. **Publications:** *Directory of the Imperial Palace, Dramatic Order Knights of Khorassan*, annual. Contains temple listing. ● *Dokey-Nomad Herald*, 3/year. **Conventions/Meetings:** biennial conference.

18797 ■ Junior Order, Knights of Pythias (JOKP)
c/o Supreme Lodge Knights of Pythias
59 Coddington St., Ste.202
Quincy, MA 02169-4510
Ph: (617)472-8800
E-mail: supremesecretary@pythias.org
URL: http://www.pythias.org/jr-order
Contact: Bobby G. Crowe PSC, Chm.
Founded: 1864. **Members:** 75,000. **Staff:** 4. **State Groups:** 45. **Local Groups:** 841. **Description:** Young men's auxiliary of the Supreme Lodge Knights of Pythias (see separate entry). Promotes the ideals of fraternity, patriotism, health, and character for boys between the ages of 12 and 17. Conducts educational and charitable programs. Participates in community service efforts. **Affiliated With:** Supreme Lodge Knights of Pythias. **Publications:** *Pythian International*, quarterly. Newsletter. **Price:** $5.00/year. ISSN: 0199-0144. **Circulation:** 14,000. **Conventions/Meetings:** biennial meeting.

18798 ■ Supreme Lodge Knights of Pythias (SLKP)
59 Coddington St., Ste.202
Quincy, MA 02169-4510
Ph: (617)472-8800

E-mail: supseckop@earthlink.net
URL: http://www.pythias.org
Contact: Alfred A. Saltzman, Supreme Sec.
Founded: 1864. **Members:** 70,000. **Staff:** 3. **Budget:** $350,000. **Regional Groups:** 6. **State Groups:** 45. **Local Groups:** 775. **Description:** Men seeking to follow the example of the story of Damon and Pythias and encourage brotherly love. **Libraries: Type:** reference. **Holdings:** periodicals. **Subjects:** current news, Pythian International. **Awards:** Poster Contest. **Frequency:** annual. **Type:** monetary. **Computer Services:** Mailing lists, of members. **Committees:** Law; Public Relations. **Affiliated With:** Dramatic Order Knights of Khorassan; Supreme Temple Order Pythian Sisters. **Publications:** *Pythian International*, quarterly. Magazine. Covers the activities of the fraternal order. **Price:** available to members only. ISSN: 0199-0144. **Circulation:** 13,000. Alternate Formats: online. **Conventions/Meetings:** semiannual Supreme Council Meeting ● biennial Supreme Lodge Convention, for officers and representatives from each state - usually 2nd week of August.

18799 ■ Supreme Temple Order Pythian Sisters (STOPS)
PO Box 40713
Portland, OR 97240-0713
E-mail: pythiansisters@pythias.org
URL: http://www.pythias.org/sisters
Contact: Linda Bridges, Supreme Sec.
Founded: 1888. **Members:** 19,000. **State Groups:** 39. **Local Groups:** 647. **Description:** Women's auxiliary of the Supreme Lodge Knights of Pythias (see separate entry). Donates to many projects benefiting blood drives, retarded citizens, and patients suffering from cancer, cystic fibrosis, polio, cerebral palsy, and heart and kidney ailments. **Awards:** Scholarship for Two. **Frequency:** biennial. **Type:** scholarship. **Affiliated With:** Supreme Lodge Knights of Pythias. **Publications:** *Pythian International*, quarterly. Magazine. **Conventions/Meetings:** biennial convention - usually August in even-numbered years.

Korean

18800 ■ Korean American Coalition (KAC)
3727 W 6th St., Ste.515
Los Angeles, CA 90020
Ph: (213)365-5999
Fax: (213)380-7990
E-mail: grace@kacla.org
URL: http://www.kacla.org
Contact: Ms. Grace Yoo, Exec. Dir.
Founded: 1983. **Members:** 70,000. **Membership Dues:** associate, $25 (annual) ● general, $50 (annual). **Staff:** 22. **Budget:** $1,000,000. **Local Groups:** 13. **Languages:** English, Korean. **Description:** Promotes the civic and civil rights interests of the Korean American community through community organizing, education, leadership development, and coalition-building with diverse communities. Represents Korean American concerns and interests to elected officials, private and public agencies, the media, and the general public. Fosters civic awareness and participation among Korean Americans. Develops future leaders in community and civic affairs. Builds multi-ethnic collaboration on shared community concerns. **Libraries: Type:** reference. **Holdings:** 400; archival material, books, clippings, video recordings. **Subjects:** Korean American community related issues and history. **Awards:** KAC Bridge Award. **Frequency:** annual. **Type:** recognition. **Recipient:** for those who are building bridges between ethnic communities or gaps within a single ethnic community ● KAC Distinguished Leadership Award. **Frequency:** annual. **Type:** recognition. **Recipient:** for distinguished leadership in the Korean American community ● Nam Yong Scholarship Award. **Frequency:** annual. **Type:** scholarship. **Recipient:** for three students of higher education based on their display of leadership and service to the community. **Computer Services:** Mailing lists ● online services. **Committees:** Chapter Development; Fundraising; Historian; Leadership Development; Personnel; Program;

Public Affairs; Public Relations; Resource Development. **Publications:** *KAC Monthly*. Newsletter. **Price:** free. **Advertising:** accepted. Alternate Formats: online. **Conventions/Meetings:** monthly Community Forum - meeting - always first Thursday, Los Angeles, CA ● annual conference, leadership development conference for Korean American college students from across the nation ● monthly Wilshire Roundtable - roundtable and luncheon ● monthly Young Leadership Council - meeting.

Kurdish

18801 ■ Kurdish Heritage Foundation of America (KHFA)
345 Park Pl.
Brooklyn, NY 11238
Ph: (718)783-7930
Fax: (718)398-4365
E-mail: kurdishlib@aol.com
URL: http://Kurdishlibrarymuseum.com
Contact: Dr. Vera Beaudin Saeedpour, Dir.
Founded: 1981. **Staff:** 1. **Budget:** $14,000. **Languages:** Arabic, English, Kurdish, Persian, Turkish. **Description:** American scholars, academics. (The Kurds are an ethnic group of 30 million people from the nonpolitical region of Kurdistan, located in the adjoining areas of Syria, Iraq, Iran, Turkey, as well as 6 of the republics of the former Soviet Union.) Aims to maintain the Kurdish Museum, which holds costume, jewelry, weavings, rugs, art, and artifacts, and the Kurdish Library, which holds 2500 volumes, reports, clip files, audio and visual collections, maps and slides. Operates Center for Research. Assists visiting scholars and researchers. Sponsors lectures and exhibitions. **Libraries: Type:** open to the public; reference. **Holdings:** 2,500; articles, audio recordings, books, maps, periodicals, photographs. **Subjects:** Kurds, Middle East, U.S. foreign policy. **Publications:** *International Journal of Kurdish Studies*, semiannual. Contains scholarly articles and research on history, culture, and contemporary affairs. Formerly Kurdish Times. **Price:** included in membership dues; $40.00 /year for nonmembers; $65.00 /year for institutions. ISSN: 1073-6697. **Circulation:** 1,000. **Advertising:** accepted ● *Kurdish Life*, quarterly. Provides an analysis of contemporary events. **Price:** $30.00/year. ISSN: 1861-8457. **Conventions/Meetings:** annual meeting.

Latin American

18802 ■ Committee on US/Latin American Relations (CUSLAR)
316 Anabel Taylor Hall
Cornell Univ.
Ithaca, NY 14853
Ph: (607)255-7293
E-mail: cuslar@cornell.edu
URL: http://www.rso.cornell.edu/cuslar
Contact: Dana Brown, Coor.
Description: Promotes awareness of the culture and politics of Latin American nations and their relationships with the U.S. **Libraries: Type:** reference. **Holdings:** 1,500; books, periodicals, video recordings. **Subjects:** Latin America. **Projects:** Bikes for Chiapas; Cajibio Sister City. **Working Groups:** Central American Free Trade Agreement. **Affiliated With:** Center for Religion, Ethics and Social Policy. **Publications:** *CUSLAR Newsletter*. Alternate Formats: online.

18803 ■ National Latino Peace Officers Association (NLPOA)
PO Box 1717
Las Vegas, NV 89125
Ph: (702)355-8704
Free: (877)657-6200
Fax: (702)388-6082
E-mail: nlpoanv@yahoo.com
URL: http://www.nlpoa.org
Contact: Roy Garivey, Natl. Pres.
Founded: 1972. **Members:** 15,000. **Membership Dues:** individual, associate, $60 (annual). **Lan-**

guages: English, French, Spanish. **Description:** Promotes equality and professionalism in law enforcement. **Awards:** Hispanic Officer of the Year. **Frequency:** annual. **Type:** recognition. **Recipient:** to a Hispanic officer who has enhanced the administration of justice ● Latina of the Year. **Frequency:** annual. **Type:** recognition. **Recipient:** to Latinas with significant contributions to the United States, the association and in their individual communities. **Computer Services:** Mailing lists, of members. **Programs:** After School Martial Arts and Drug Prevention; Anti Graffiti; Hispanic of the Year; Latina of the Year. **Publications:** *El Puente.* Newsletter. Alternate Formats: online.

18804 ■ Tomas Rivera Policy Institute (TRPI)
Univ. of Southern California
School of Policy, Planning, and Development
Ralph and Goldie Lewis Hall
650 Childs Way, Ste.102
Los Angeles, CA 90089-0626
Ph: (213)821-5615
Fax: (213)821-1976
E-mail: info@trpi.org
URL: http://www.trpi.org
Contact: Harry P. Pachon PhD, Pres.
Founded: 1985. **Budget:** $3,000,000. **Description:** Works to assist government and corporate decision-makers to develop and implement policies and programs that improves socioeconomic and educational status of Mexican-origin and Latino population of U.S. **Formerly:** (2004) Thomas Rivera Center. **Publications:** Reports. Contains information about immigration, social political, information technology, education, and health. Alternate Formats: online.

18805 ■ William C. Velasquez Institute (WCVI)
Kelly USA, Bldg. 1670
206 Lombard St., 1st Fl.
San Antonio, TX 78226
Ph: (210)922-3118
Fax: (210)922-7095
E-mail: agonzalez@wcvi.org
URL: http://www.wcvi.org
Contact: Antonio Gonzalez, Pres.
Founded: 1985. **Description:** Conducts research to improve the level of political and economic participation in Latino and other underrepresented communities.

Latvian

18806 ■ American Latvian Association (ALA)
400 Hurley Ave.
Rockville, MD 20850-3121
Ph: (301)340-1914
Fax: (301)340-8732
E-mail: alainfo@alausa.org
URL: http://www.alausa.org
Contact: Raits Eglitis, Exec. Dir.
Founded: 1951. **Members:** 6,200. **Membership Dues:** individual, $30 (annual) ● life, $300 ● life (gold), $800 ● life (amber), $2,000. **Budget:** $556,000. **Regional Groups:** 158. **Languages:** English, Latvian. **Description:** Represents persons of Latvian ancestry or birth. Works to unite Americans of Latvian descent, to strengthen their ethnic heritage, and to acquaint the American public with the Republic of Latvia by making available tapes, records, books, and movies about the Republic of Latvia. Provides assistance to Republic of Latvia. Maintains museum. **Libraries: Type:** reference. **Divisions:** Continuing Education; Cultural Affairs; Education; Public Affairs; Publisher; Sports; Support and Aid to Latvia. **Publications:** *Latvian Dimensions,* quarterly. Magazine. **Price:** $25.00/year; $35.00/2 years. ISSN: 1062-9505. **Circulation:** 5,000. **Advertising:** accepted ● *Latvju Maksla,* annual ● Also publishes textbooks for Latvian weekend schools for a curriculum designed to teach Latvian language, literature, geography, history, and folklore. **Conventions/Meetings:** annual congress - always first weekend of May.

Law Enforcement

18807 ■ Emerald Society of the Federal Law Enforcement Agencies (ESFLEA)
PO Box 16413
Rochester, NY 14616-0413
E-mail: esflea@worldnet.att.net
URL: http://esflea.home.att.net
Contact: Tom Smart, Pres.
Founded: 1995. **Membership Dues:** general, $20 (annual). **Multinational. Description:** Represents federal law enforcement, public safety, military and support personnel of Irish and Gaelic descent. Improves the professionalism of law enforcement agencies. **Awards:** Irishmen of the Year. **Frequency:** annual. **Type:** recognition. **Recipient:** for outstanding contribution to the society ● Law Enforcement Officers of the Year. **Frequency:** annual. **Type:** recognition. **Recipient:** for outstanding law enforcement officers. **Additional Websites:** http://esflea.org.

18808 ■ Fraternal Order of Police, Grand Lodge (FOP)
710 Marriott Dr.
Nashville, TN 37214
Ph: (615)399-0900
Fax: (615)399-0400
E-mail: nationalsecretary@grandlodgefop.org
URL: http://www.grandlodgefop.org
Contact: Leigh Ann Pemberton, Office Mgr.
Founded: 1915. **Members:** 321,000. **Staff:** 13. **State Groups:** 43. **Local Groups:** 1,823. **Description:** Fraternal order of full-time law enforcement officers. Seeks social and economic benefits for members and professional advancement of policemen. Conducts seminars, research, educational, and charitable programs; compiles statistics. Sponsors competitions; maintains speakers' bureau. **Libraries: Type:** reference. **Holdings:** biographical archives. **Awards: Type:** recognition ● Steve Young Memorial Scholarship Program. **Type:** scholarship. **Recipient:** for spouses of fallen law enforcement officers. **Publications:** *Corporate and Tax Affairs of A Lodge* ● *Fair Labor Standards Act Update* ● *FOP Fair Labor Standards Handbook* ● *FOP Journal,* bimonthly. Covers association news and law enforcement topics including federal and state legislation, court decisions, and law enforcement equipment. **Price:** included in membership dues; $16.00 /year for nonmembers; $4.00 each, for nonmembers. **Circulation:** 260,000. **Advertising:** accepted. Alternate Formats: online ● *History 1976* ● *Survey of Salaries and Working Conditions of Police in the U.S.,* annual. Updates service. **Conventions/Meetings:** biennial conference (exhibits).

18809 ■ Law Enforcement Association of Asian Pacifics (LEAAP)
PO Box 11336
Glendale, CA 91226
E-mail: dwong@leaap.org
URL: http://www.leaap.org
Contact: Sgt. Daniel Wong, Pres.
Founded: 1991. **Members:** 6,200. **Membership Dues:** general, $48 (annual). **State Groups:** 1. **Description:** Develops professional standards in the justice system. Strengthens the partnership of law enforcement agencies. Provides social, civic and scholastic functions. Promotes the value of diversity. **Publications:** Newsletter, quarterly. Alternate Formats: online.

18810 ■ Society of Former Special Agents of the Federal Bureau of Investigation (SFSAFBI)
PO Box 1027
Quantico, VA 22134
Ph: (703)640-6469
Free: (800)527-7372
Fax: (703)640-6537
E-mail: socxfbi@socxfbi.org
URL: http://www.socxfbi.org
Contact: Jerry L. Emmons, Chm.
Founded: 1937. **Members:** 8,000. **Membership Dues:** regular, $80 (annual). **Staff:** 7. **Regional Groups:** 7. **Local Groups:** 121. **Description:** Persons who have served at least one year as a special agent of the FBI. Maintains National Executive Placement Committee to help members obtain employment, a foundation to aid needy members and children of deceased members, and a scholarship program. **Awards:** J. Edgar Hoover Memorial Scholarship. **Frequency:** annual. **Type:** monetary. **Recipient:** for colleges and universities that have law enforcement oriented curricula. **Computer Services:** Mailing lists, of members. **Committees:** Chapter; Family Assistance; Historical; Insurance; Investments; Legal. **Publications:** *Grapevine,* monthly. Magazine ● Directory, biennial. **Conventions/Meetings:** annual seminar.

Leadership

18811 ■ National Community for Latino Leadership (NCLL)
1701 K St. NW, Ste.301
Washington, DC 20006
Ph: (202)721-8290 (202)682-4014
Fax: (202)721-8296
E-mail: ncll@latinoleadership.org
URL: http://www.latinoleadership.org
Contact: Alfred Ramirez, Pres.
Founded: 1989. **Description:** Promotes the social, cultural and economic advancement of the Latino community. Aims to develop leaders who are committed to ethical, responsible and accountable actions on behalf of the U.S. Latino population and the broader community. Provides support for Latino leaders through leadership training, technical assistance and resources. **Telecommunication Services:** electronic mail, aramirez@latinoleadership.org.

Lebanese

18812 ■ American Task Force for Lebanon (ATFL)
2213 M St. NW, 3rd Fl.
Washington, DC 20037
Ph: (202)223-9333
Fax: (202)223-1399
URL: http://www.atfl.org
Contact: F. Paul Maloof Esq., Sec./Legal Counsel
Description: Dedicated to heritage of Americans of Lebanese descent; promotes awareness to American public and government on the status of Lebanon.

18813 ■ United Kesrawan Society
Address Unknown since 2007
Founded: 1931. **Description:** Works to united native born persons from Kesrawan District of Lebanon and descendents; promotes loyalty to U.S. government. **Conventions/Meetings:** monthly meeting.

Lithuanian

18814 ■ American Lithuanian Press and Radio Association - Viltis (ALPRA-V)
PO Box 19010
Cleveland, OH 44119-0010
Ph: (216)531-8150
Fax: (216)531-8428
E-mail: dirva@ix.netcom.com
Contact: Mr. Algirdas Matulionis, Pres.
Founded: 1952. **Members:** 850. **Staff:** 3. **Budget:** $120,000. **Languages:** English, Lithuanian. **Description:** Provides information on Lithuanian activities and cultural and social events. **Awards:** Short Story Award. **Frequency:** annual. **Type:** recognition. **Publications:** *Dirva* (in English and Lithuanian), weekly. **Price:** $25.00. **Circulation:** 3,000. **Advertising:** accepted ● Also publishes books in Lithuanian. **Conventions/Meetings:** biennial symposium.

18815 ■ Lithuanian Alliance of America (LAA)
307 W 30th St.
New York, NY 10001
Ph: (212)563-2210

E-mail: labas@megsinet.net
URL: http://www.lithuanianalliance.com
Founded: 1886. **Members:** 3,000. **Staff:** 7. **Local Groups:** 180. **Description:** Serves as a fraternal benefit life insurance society for persons of Lithuanian ancestry and friends. **Libraries: Type:** not open to the public. **Awards: Type:** scholarship. **Committees:** Appeals; Welfare; Youth. **Also Known As:** Susivienijimas Lietuviu Amerikoje. **Publications:** *Tevyne* (in English and Lithuanian), 10/year. Newspaper. Features news and information concerning the Lithuanian community. **Price:** $4.00. **Circulation:** 2,500. Also Cited As: *The Fatherland* ● Also publishes convention workbooks. **Conventions/Meetings:** annual convention ● triennial meeting.

18816 ■ Lithuanian-American Community (LAC)
PO Box 2376
Naperville, IL 60567
Ph: (410)663-0158
Free: (800)625-1170
Fax: (815)327-8881
E-mail: lithuanianusa@yahoo.com
URL: http://javlb.org
Contact: Vytas Maciunas, Pres.
Founded: 1951. **Members:** 1,000,000. **Staff:** 15. **Budget:** $1,000,000. **Regional Groups:** 10. **Local Groups:** 79. **Languages:** English, Lithuanian. **Description:** Individuals of Lithuanian descent united to: support the U.S. Constitution and promote participation in American life; foster and maintain the Lithuanian culture and heritage; promote the development of independent Lithuania. Maintains educational and cultural services and schools teaching Lithuanian language, history, and heritage; these services provide the community with textbooks, periodicals, Lithuanian studies, and general publications. Sponsors and supports National Youth Congresses' folk song and dance festivals, and cultural, educational, and public affairs study seminars and congresses. Maintains speakers' bureau and Lithuanian archives; compiles statistics. **Libraries: Type:** open to the public. **Holdings:** 100,000; articles, books, periodicals. **Awards:** Amber Award. **Frequency:** annual. **Type:** recognition. **Recipient:** for service to organization. **Councils:** Cultural; Economics; Educational; Human Services; Public Affairs; Religious; Social. **Formerly:** (1989) Lithuanian-American Community of the U.S. **Publications:** *Bridges*, 10/year. Magazine. **Price:** $18.00/year. **Circulation:** 2,000. **Advertising:** accepted. Alternate Formats: online ● *Eglute* (in English and Lithuanian), 10/year. Magazine ● *Lituanus*, quarterly. Journal. Covers the arts and sciences. ● *Pensininkas* (in English and Lithuanian), monthly. Magazine ● Also publishes textbooks, monographs, and scientific studies. **Conventions/Meetings:** annual conference (exhibits).

18817 ■ Lithuanian American Council (LAC)
6500 S Pulaski Rd., Ste.200
Chicago, IL 60629
Ph: (773)735-6677
Fax: (773)735-3946
E-mail: altcenter@aol.com
URL: http://www.altcenter.org
Contact: Saulius V. Kuprys Esq., Pres.
Founded: 1915. **Members:** 17. **Membership Dues:** organizational, $100 (annual). **Staff:** 2. **Budget:** $78,000. **Regional Groups:** 15. **State Groups:** 30. **Local Groups:** 186. **National Groups:** 20. **Languages:** English, Lithuanian. **Description:** Federation of Lithuanian-American organizations. Promotes development of independent Lithuania; encourages Lithuanian Americans to promote and support the principles of democracy among Lithuanians. Sponsors speakers' bureau. **Libraries: Type:** not open to the public. **Holdings:** 1,000; archival material. **Subjects:** Lithuania. **Affiliated With:** Joint Baltic American National Committee. **Also Known As:** Amerikos Lietuviu Taryba. **Publications:** *Information Bulletin* (in English and Lithuanian), semimonthly. **Circulation:** 800 ● Also publishes pamphlets and a directory concerning Lithuania. **Conventions/Meetings:** quinquennial congress ● annual convention.

18818 ■ Lithuanian American Roman Catholic Women's Alliance (LCW)
c/o Dale Murray, Pres.
3005 N 124th St.
Brookfield, WI 53005
Ph: (262)786-7359 (630)573-0066
Fax: (262)786-7359
Contact: Dale Murray, Pres.
Founded: 1914. **Members:** 500. **Membership Dues:** women, $10 (annual). **Staff:** 3. **State Groups:** 7. **Local Groups:** 4. **Languages:** Lithuanian. **Description:** Catholic-Lithuanian women or women married to Lithuanians who are interested in their heritage, and in the politics of Lithuania and America. Conducts charitable programs including shipments of books, eyeglasses, and clothing to Lithuania. **Libraries: Type:** reference. **Holdings:** archival material. **Awards:** Outstanding Lithuanian Woman Award. **Frequency:** biennial. **Type:** recognition. **Recipient:** for community service. **Affiliated With:** Lithuanian-American Community; Lithuanian American Council. **Formerly:** (1990) American Lithuanian Roman Catholic Women's Alliance; (1992) Lithuanian Catholic Women. **Publications:** Newsletter (in English and Lithuanian), quarterly. **Price:** $10.00. **Circulation:** 500. **Conventions/Meetings:** biennial meeting, with photos (exhibits); **Avg. Attendance:** 40.

18819 ■ Lithuanian Catholic Alliance (LCA)
c/o Ladies Pennsylvania Slovak Catholic Union
71 S Washington St.
Wilkes-Barre, PA 18701
Ph: (570)823-3513
Free: (888)834-6614
Fax: (570)823-4464
E-mail: lpscu@lpscu.org
URL: http://www.lpscu.org/lca
Contact: Theresa A. Kluchinski, Pres., LPSCU
Founded: 1886. **Members:** 3,069. **Staff:** 4. **State Groups:** 137. **Local Groups:** 7. **Description:** Serves as fraternal benefit life insurance society for male and female members of all faiths. **Formerly:** (1975) Lithuanian Catholic Alliance of America. **Publications:** *Garsas* (in English and Lithuanian), 10/year. **Conventions/Meetings:** triennial meeting.

18820 ■ Lithuanian Catholic Federation Ateitis/USA Section (LCFA)
Address Unknown since 2006
URL: http://www.ateitis.org
Founded: 1910. **Staff:** 1. **Description:** Educational, religious, and cultural organization of Catholic youth. Students and graduates of Lithuanian origin. Founded to defend Christian principles in academic life. Provides guidance to aid members in development of intellectual, moral, and spiritual values and in preparation for civic leadership. Comprised of three autonomous associations: Lithuanian Catholic Youth Association Ateitis for students in fifth through twelfth grades; Ateitis Association of Lithuanian Catholic Alumni for college graduates; Association of Lithuanian Catholic Children for students in first through fourth grades. **Also Known As:** Ateitis (The Future). **Formerly:** American Lithuanian Catholic Federation Ateitis; American Lithuanian Roman Catholic Federation Ateitis. **Publications:** *Ateitis* (in Lithuanian), monthly. **Conventions/Meetings:** quadrennial meeting.

18821 ■ Lithuanian Catholic Press Society (LCPS)
4545 W 63rd St.
Chicago, IL 60629
Ph: (773)585-9500
Fax: (773)585-8284
E-mail: redakcija@draugas.org
URL: http://www.draugas.org
Founded: 1940. **Languages:** English, Lithuanian. **Description:** Represents Lithuanian Catholic press and publishers. **Also Known As:** Draugas. **Publications:** *The Lithuanian Daily Friend-DRAUGAS* (in English and Lithuanian). Newspaper. **Price:** $100.00 in U.S. **Circulation:** 4,500. **Advertising:** accepted.

18822 ■ Lithuanian Roman Catholic Federation of America (LRCFA)
Address Unknown since 2007
Founded: 1906. **Members:** 300,000. **Local Groups:** 140. **Description:** Lithuanian-American Catholic organizations, parishes, religious orders, and publications; agencies and institutions; individuals. Seeks to unite Lithuanian-American Catholics; promotes Catholic action; upholds Lithuanian culture. Operates a camp and retreat center in Michigan; collects archival material about immigration history; is establishing audio- and videocassette library in Lithuanian and English on educational and religious topics. **Publications:** *Lithuanian Daily Draugas* ● *Observer*, monthly ● Bulletin, periodic ● Directory, periodic. **Conventions/Meetings:** biennial conference.

18823 ■ National Lithuanian Society of America (NLSA)
9136 55th Ct.
Oak Lawn, IL 60453
Ph: (708)423-7871
Contact: Peter Buchas, Pres.
Founded: 1949. **Members:** 500. **Local Groups:** 6. **Description:** Americans of Lithuanian descent. Fosters Lithuanian fine arts, handicraft, cultural, and educational activities. Supports the development of independent Lithuania. Maintains speakers' bureau; sponsors lectures. **Awards: Frequency:** annual. **Type:** recognition. **Recipient:** for best Lithuanian novel of the year. **Committees:** America; Worldwide. **Also Known As:** Amerikos Lietuviu Tautine Sajunga. **Publications:** *Bendrarastis Newsletter*, bimonthly. **Advertising:** accepted ● *Dirva*, weekly. Newspaper ● *Naujoji Viltis*, annual ● Books. **Conventions/Meetings:** biennial conference.

18824 ■ United Lithuanian Relief Fund of America (ULRA)
1913 Wallace St.
Philadelphia, PA 19130-3219
Ph: (215)765-2322
Fax: (215)765-0124
E-mail: salrcc@aol.com
URL: http://hometown.aol.com/balfas1/Philadelphia.htm
Contact: Joseph Majauskas, Pres./Dir.
Founded: 1944. **Members:** 2,000. **Staff:** 1. **State Groups:** 14. **Local Groups:** 30. **Description:** Provides aid to Lithuanian refugees in various lands and recovers and rehabilitates stranded and destitute persons of Lithuanian heritage in other countries. Offers educational aid, immigrant and social welfare assistance, and charitable aid to the poor, aged, sick, homeless, and needy. **Conventions/Meetings:** annual board meeting ● triennial meeting and convention.

Lutheran

18825 ■ Lutheran Fraternities of America
PO Box 182033
Shelby Township, MI 48318-2033
Ph: (586)677-2020
Free: (800)765-4428
Fax: (586)677-2050
E-mail: info@gbu.org
URL: http://www.gbu.org/lutheran.htm
Contact: Jennie Kane, Fraternity Coor.
Founded: 1865. **Members:** 7,500. **Description:** Fraternal benefit life insurance society for members of the Lutheran church. Offers financial aid to Lutheran schools, homes, and social ministries and fraternal grants to Lutheran agencies; sponsors other special programs and benefits. Sponsors competitions. **Awards: Type:** scholarship. **Telecommunication Services:** electronic mail, jenny.kane@gbu.org. **Publications:** *Messenger*, semiannual. Newsletter. **Conventions/Meetings:** quadrennial meeting - always November.

18826 ■ Thrivent Financial for Lutherans
4321 N Ballard Rd.
Appleton, WI 54919-0001
Free: (800)847-4836

E-mail: mail@thrivent.com
URL: http://www.thrivent.com
Contact: Mr. Bruce J. Nicholson, Chm./Pres./CEO
Founded: 1902. **Members:** 1,800,000. **Membership Dues:** associate, $10 (annual). **Staff:** 4,137. **Local Groups:** 10,500. **Description:** Fraternal benefit society providing life, disability income, and retirement insurance for Lutherans and their families throughout the U.S. Local branch structure permits development and pursuit of volunteer activities by members, which help others. Provides wellness and educational programs. **Libraries: Type:** reference. **Holdings:** 4,000; books. **Subjects:** business, management, fraternalism, life insurance. **Awards: Type:** grant. **Recipient:** for church-related programs and projects ● **Type:** scholarship. **Committees:** AAL-PAC. **Absorbed:** (2003) Lutheran Brotherhood Foundation. **Publications:** Correspondent, bimonthly. Magazine ● Who's Who, monthly. **Conventions/Meetings:** periodic regional meeting.

18827 ■ United Lutheran Society (ULS)
PO Box 947
Ligonier, PA 15658-0947
Ph: (724)238-9505
Free: (800)235-0857
Fax: (724)238-9506
E-mail: info@ulstoday.org
Contact: Jerry A. Hauser, Sec.-Treas.
Founded: 1893. **Members:** 6,500. **Membership Dues:** individual, $25 (annual). **Staff:** 5. **Local Groups:** 65. **Description:** Serves as a fraternal benefit life insurance society for Lutherans. Conducts educational and charitable programs. **Awards:** Fraternal. **Frequency:** annual. **Type:** recognition. **Recipient:** for adult members ● ULS Scholarship Award. **Frequency:** annual. **Type:** scholarship. **Recipient:** for members. **Formed by Merger of:** (1962) Slovak Evangelical Union; Evangelical Slovak Women's Union. **Publications:** ULS Today, bimonthly. Newsletter. Contains membership activities; includes obituaries. **Price:** free. **Circulation:** 5,000. **Conventions/Meetings:** quadrennial convention.

Macedonian

18828 ■ Macedonian American Friendship Association (MAFA)
57 Jefferson Ave.
Columbus, OH 43215
Ph: (614)668-9656
Fax: (614)457-5926
E-mail: info@macedonianamerican.org
URL: http://www.macedonianamerican.org
Contact: Dr. Vasil Babamov, Pres.
Description: Strengthens the Macedonian-American friendship. Preserves peace in Macedonia by compiling and disseminating information about the situation in Macedonia. Increases public awareness of the problems of the Republic of Macedonia.

18829 ■ Macedonian Patriotic Organization of United States and Canada (MPO)
124 W Wayne St.
Fort Wayne, IN 46802
Ph: (260)422-5900
Fax: (260)422-1348
E-mail: info@macedonian.org
URL: http://www.macedonian.org
Contact: Mr. George Lebamoff, Pres., Central Committee
Founded: 1922. **Membership Dues:** regular, $20 (annual). **Staff:** 6. **Budget:** $150,000. **Regional Groups:** 8. **State Groups:** 20. **Local Groups:** 28. **Languages:** Bulgarian, English, Macedonian. **Multinational. Description:** Conducts educational, cultural, and social activities. Promotes the idea of a free, independent, and democratic Macedonia. Operates speakers' bureau and museum; compiles statistics. **Libraries: Type:** reference. **Holdings:** 4,000; archival material. **Subjects:** Macedonia liberation movement, early immigration. **Awards:** Damian Grueff Society. **Frequency:** annual. **Type:** recognition ● Gotse Delchev Fellowship. **Frequency:** an-

nual. **Type:** fellowship ● Macedonian of Distinction. **Frequency:** annual. **Type:** recognition. **Subgroups:** Macedonian Professional; Macedonian Veterans. **Formerly:** (1952) Union of Macedonian Political Organizations. **Publications:** Macedonian Tribune (in Bulgarian, English, and Macedonian), monthly. Newspaper. **Price:** $35.00/year in U.S.; $50.00/year in Canada; $100.00 outside U.S. via airmail. ISSN: 0024-9009. **Advertising:** accepted. Also Cited As: Makedonska Tribuna ● Page One - Major Events of the 20th Century. Book ● Reflections-A Struggle for Freedom. Booklet ● 75 Years Since Treaty of Bucharest. Booklet. **Conventions/Meetings:** annual convention (exhibits) - always Labor Day weekend ● quarterly meeting ● annual seminar.

Maltese

18830 ■ Maltese-American Benevolent Society (MABS)
Address Unknown since 2007
Founded: 1929. **Members:** 300. **Membership Dues:** individual, $25 (annual). **Staff:** 8. **Budget:** $1,200,000. **Description:** Serves social and patriotic needs of Detroit's Maltese population, estimated to be 66,000 and believed to be the largest in the U.S. Supports children's services. Offers activities for members and their families. **Libraries: Type:** reference. **Holdings:** books, video recordings. **Subjects:** U.S. history, Maltese folklore. **Awards:** Gentleman of the Year Award. **Frequency:** annual. **Type:** recognition. **Recipient:** outstanding service to Maltese community or community in general ● George Zammit Award. **Frequency:** annual. **Type:** recognition. **Recipient:** For outstanding citizenship displayed by an individual of Maltese descent ● Maltese American Scholarship Award. **Frequency:** annual. **Type:** scholarship. **Recipient:** for an outstanding Maltese student. **Committees:** Activities; Benevolent; Educational; Ethnic Studies; Travel; Urban Renewal. **Councils:** Maltese Organizations. **Publications:** Meetings and Conventions, quarterly. Newsletter. **Price:** free. **Circulation:** 180. **Advertising:** not accepted ● Times of Malta, daily. **Conventions/Meetings:** quarterly general assembly ● monthly Ladies Auxiliary - meeting.

Manx

18831 ■ North American Manx Association (NAMA)
c/o Mr. Bradley E. Prendergast, Pres.
6135 N Glenwood Ave., No. 1-W
Chicago, IL 60660
E-mail: beeves@juno.com
URL: http://www.isle-of-man.com/Home/Arts/Humanities/History/Genealogy/NAMA.aspx
Contact: Mr. Bradley E. Prendergast, Pres.
Founded: 1928. **Members:** 700. **Membership Dues:** individual, $15 (annual) ● individual (life), $125-$250 ● family/society, $20 (annual) ● family (life), $200-$325. **Budget:** $5,000. **Regional Groups:** 12. **Multinational. Description:** Individuals with Manx birth, marriage, or descent; Manx men and women and their descendants throughout North America; or anyone interested in the Isle of Man. Formed by independent Manx ethnic self-help and relief associations founded in the United States and Canada throughout the 19th Century by immigrants from the Isle of Man. Works to establish a closer union of all Manx people to stimulate ties with the Isle of Man through the World Manx Association. **Awards:** Heritage Award. **Frequency:** annual. **Type:** recognition. **Recipient:** for outstanding achievement in Manx language, music, arts and crafts by Manx youth. **Publications:** Convention Yearbook, biennial ● Factsheets, periodic ● North American Manx Association—Bulletin, quarterly. Includes listing of new members; also includes obituaries. **Price:** available to members only ● Directory, periodic. **Conventions/Meetings:** biennial convention (exhibits).

Marine Corps

18832 ■ Marine Corps CounterIntelligence Association (MCCIA)
PO Box 1298
Seminole, OK 74818-1298

E-mail: chairman@mccia.org
URL: http://www.mccia.org
Contact: Charlie Teel, Chm.
Founded: 1987. **Members:** 400. **Membership Dues:** general, $35 (annual). **Description:** Fosters fraternal relations among retired, active and former members of the uniformed services. Provides useful services for members and their dependents and survivors. **Awards: Frequency:** annual. **Type:** scholarship. **Recipient:** for impressive achievements of students. **Computer Services:** Online services, e-mail discussion lists. **Programs:** Scholarship. **Publications:** Activity Report, quarterly. Newsletter.

18833 ■ Marine Corps Intelligence Association (MCIA)
PO Box 1028
Quantico, VA 22134-1028
E-mail: mcia@mcia-inc.org
URL: http://mcia-inc.org
Contact: Tony Tang, Pres.
Founded: 1993. **Membership Dues:** regular, $20 (annual) ● associate/auxiliary, $15 (annual) ● corporate, $700 (annual). **Description:** Fosters fraternal relations among regular, reserve, retired and former Marines and members of the uniformed services. Promotes professionalism among the Marine Corps intelligence communities through collective action and its affiliation with other associations. **Awards:** Intelligence Marines of the Year. **Frequency:** annual. **Type:** recognition. **Recipient:** for achievements and contributions to the Marine Corps intelligence field ● Marine Corps Intelligence Association Literary Award. **Frequency:** annual. **Type:** recognition. **Recipient:** for a competitively selected article relating to intelligence. **Publications:** INTSUM Magazine, quarterly. Journal. Contains forum for open discussion of ideas. **Price:** included in membership dues ● Membership Directory, annual. **Price:** included in membership dues.

18834 ■ Marine Corps Interrogator Translator Teams Association (MCITTA)
917 Raughley Hill Rd.
Harrington, DE 19952-3167
E-mail: teamchief@mcitta.org
URL: http://www.mcitta.org
Contact: Harry J. Todd, Team Commander
Founded: 2003. **Description:** Preserves the memory and deeds of Marine interrogators who have fallen in combat. Researches and writes the history of the interrogator translator team. **Telecommunication Services:** electronic mail, 1stsub@mcitta.org ● electronic mail, 2dsub@mcitta.org ● electronic mail, 3dsub@mcitta.org ● electronic mail, px@mcitta.org ● electronic mail, spotreport@mcitta.org. **Publications:** The Spot Report, semiannual. Newsletter. Alternate Formats: online.

Masons

18835 ■ Ancient Egyptian Arabic Order Nobles of the Mystic Shrine (AEAONMS)
2239 Democrat Rd.
Memphis, TN 38132-1802
Ph: (901)395-0150
Fax: (901)395-0115
E-mail: webmaster@aeaonms.org
URL: http://aeaonms.org
Contact: Dr. Ralph Slaughter, Imperial Potentate
Founded: 1893. **Members:** 37,000. **Staff:** 14. **Budget:** $660,000. **State Groups:** 5. **Local Groups:** 1. **National Groups:** 222. **Description:** Serves as fraternal society of 32nd degree Masons. **Awards:** Student Aid Grants. **Frequency:** annual. **Type:** monetary. **Recipient:** for students. **Publications:** The Pyramid, quarterly. Magazine. Alternate Formats: online. **Conventions/Meetings:** annual convention (exhibits) - always August.

18836 ■ Ancient Egyptian Order of Sciots (AEOS)
PO Box 501801
San Diego, CA 92150-1801
Ph: (858)755-0931

Fax: (858)755-0931
E-mail: gparks@san.rr.com
URL: http://www.sciots.org
Contact: William Berman, Contact
Founded: 1905. **Members:** 1,700. **Staff:** 1. **Regional Groups:** 16. **State Groups:** 15. **Description:** Represents Blue Lodge Masons. Renders aid and assistance to underprivileged and undernourished children. Maintains speakers' bureau. **Awards: Type:** recognition. **Computer Services:** Mailing lists, of members. **Committees:** Resolutions; Sciots Foundation (child welfare); Wills and Bequests; Youth Activities. **Publications:** *Ancient Egyptian Order of Sciots Supreme Newsletter*, bimonthly. **Price:** included in membership dues. **Advertising:** accepted. Alternate Formats: online ● *Rituals*, periodic ● *Supreme Pyramid Bulletin*, bimonthly ● *Supreme Pyramid Roster*, annual. **Conventions/Meetings:** competition ● semiannual meeting - always November and first week of May.

18837 ■ Association of Masonic Boards of Relief of the United States and Canada
3 De Saix Blvd.
New Orleans, LA 70119
Ph: (504)949-6347
E-mail: mimi3570@aol.com
Contact: Glen H. Butler, Exec. Sec.
Founded: 1885. **Members:** 15,000. **Staff:** 6. **Regional Groups:** 175. **State Groups:** 40. **Description:** Coordinates and correlates the various forms of Masonic relief throughout the U.S. and Canada; promotes prompt and effective methods of handling cases in interjurisdictional relief; Acts as the agency organizing Masonic relief in times of national disaster when such services are requested by any Grand Lodge or group of Grand Lodges; detects and publishes, in association bulletin, lists of "unworthy Masons and imposters preying upon the Fraternity.". **Formerly:** (2003) Masonic Relief Association of U.S.A. and Canada. **Publications:** *List of Lodges - Masonic*, annual ● *Bulletin*, quarterly. **Circulation:** 15,000. **Conventions/Meetings:** biennial meeting.

18838 ■ Conference of Prince Hall Grand Masters (CPHGM)
PO Box 831020
Tuskegee, AL 36083
Ph: (334)727-5416
Fax: (334)727-7726
Contact: William O. Jones, Pres.
Founded: 1887. **Members:** 500,000. **Regional Groups:** 7. **State Groups:** 46. **Description:** Black fraternal order united to coordinate efforts of member groups in providing leadership in and formulating goals for the black community. Sponsors seminars and workshops to train progressive leaders. Operates charitable program; maintains biographical archives; sponsors competitions. **Awards: Type:** recognition. **Affiliated With:** General Grand Chapter, Order of the Eastern Star. **Publications:** *Conference of Grand Masters*, bimonthly. Newsletter. **Price:** to grand masters only ● *Prince Hall Masonic Directory*, triennial. **Conventions/Meetings:** annual Conference of Grand Masters, Prince Hall Masons (exhibits) - always second weekend in May unless amended.

18839 ■ Daughters of Mokanna (D of M)
126 Hilltop Cir.
Elyria, OH 44035
Ph: (440)365-9536
Fax: (440)365-9536
E-mail: rlusher@aol.com
Contact: Rosemary E. Lusher, Supreme Rodeval Sec.
Founded: 1919. **Members:** 2,500. **Staff:** 3. **Local Groups:** 17. **Description:** Fraternal Masonic order for women relatives of Supreme Council, Mystic Order Veiled Prophets of Enchanted Realm members (see separate entry); current project is the National Humanitarian Project for the Physically Challenged Child and Dentistry for Children with Special Needs. Sponsors competitions for singing groups and drill teams. **Awards: Type:** recognition. **Computer Services:** Online services. **Formerly:** (2004) Supreme Cauldron, Daughters of Mokanna. **Publica-**

tions: *Rosters*, quinquennial ● *Supreme Caldron, Daughters of Mokanna—Proceedings*, annual. **Price:** available to members only. **Conventions/Meetings:** annual meeting - always September.

18840 ■ Daughters of the Nile, Supreme Temple (DNST)
13309 W Meeker Blvd.
Sun City West, AZ 85375-3808
E-mail: information@daughtersofthenile.com
URL: http://www.daughtersofthenile.com
Contact: Alyce S. Thomas, Supreme Queen/Chair
Founded: 1913. **Members:** 49,000. **Staff:** 4. **Local Groups:** 149. **Description:** Represents individuals related to Shriners by birth or by marriage. Assists with philanthropic work of the Shriners' hospitals for children. **Conventions/Meetings:** annual meeting - always June.

18841 ■ Federation of Masons of the World (FMW)
Address Unknown since 2007
Founded: 1958. **Members:** 300,000. **Budget:** $105,000. **Regional Groups:** 38. **State Groups:** 22. **Languages:** Arabic, English, French, Italian, Spanish. **Description:** Masonic jurisdictions in 22 countries. **Awards: Type:** recognition. **Committees:** Charity; Research. **Divisions:** Foreign Countries; International Grand Lodges; State Grand Lodge. **Conventions/Meetings:** biennial meeting (exhibits).

18842 ■ General Grand Chapter, Order of the Eastern Star
1618 New Hampshire Ave. NW
Washington, DC 20009-2549
Ph: (202)667-4737
Free: (800)648-1182
Fax: (202)462-5162
E-mail: easternstar@erols.com
URL: http://www.easternstar.org
Contact: Bonnie Poindexter, Right Worthy Grand Sec.
Founded: 1876. **Members:** 1,000,000. **Staff:** 11. **Multinational. Description:** Master Masons in good standing, and their female relatives. Fraternal order dedicated to social enjoyment, civic interests, and serving the needy. Conducts charitable programs. **Awards: Type:** scholarship. **Recipient:** for students in religious training. **Publications:** *Proceedings of the General Grand Chapter*, periodic. **Conventions/Meetings:** triennial congress.

18843 ■ General Grand Chapter of Royal Arch Masons International
PO Box 489
Danville, KY 40423-0489
Ph: (859)236-0757
Fax: (859)236-6773
E-mail: intlram@yahoo.com
URL: http://yorkrite.com/chapter
Contact: John F. Kirby, Gen. Grand Sec.
Founded: 1797. **Members:** 190,000. **Staff:** 2. **Budget:** $329,000. **Regional Groups:** 3,000. **Description:** Members of symbolic Lodge of Free and Accepted Masons. Functions as a mutual service organization. Offers educational, research, promotional, and administrative aids through its Royal Arch Education Bureau. Promotes and administers philanthropic projects such as the Royal Arch Research Assistance Program, developed to conduct research on central auditory disorders in children. Supports the DeMolay Endowment Fund. Operates statistics and data center. Observes Religious Affirmation Sunday every October. **Libraries: Type:** reference. **Subjects:** Masonic writing. **Awards:** Silver Medal. **Type:** recognition. **Boards:** International Masonic Affairs. **Committees:** Charters and Dispensations; DeMolay Endowment; Foreign Relations; Grievances and Appeals; Jurisprudence; Royal Arch Advancement. **Programs:** General Grand Chapter Membership Identification; Medal Award; Membership Incentive; Ritual; Spiritual Aims. **Publications:** *Directory of Royal Arch Chapters*, every 8-10 years ● *The Royal Arch Advance*, quarterly ● *The Royal Arch Mason Magazine*, quarterly. **Price:** $7.50/year; $11.00/year for foreign countries. ISSN: 0273-6276 ● *Royal Arch Orpheus*.

Book. **Conventions/Meetings:** triennial General Grand Chapter Convocation - meeting.

18844 ■ Heroes of '76
c/o National Sojourners, Inc.
8301 E Boulevard Dr.
Alexandria, VA 22308-1399
Ph: (703)765-5000
Fax: (703)765-8390
E-mail: nationalsoj@juno.com
URL: http://www.nationalsojourners.org
Contact: Maj. Nelson O. Newcombe, Sec.-Treas.
Founded: 1919. **Members:** 10,000. **Staff:** 3. **Regional Groups:** 17. **Local Groups:** 165. **Description:** Fraternal organization. Supports the Collingwood Library and Museum on Americanism located in Mt. Vernon, VA. **Publications:** none. **Libraries: Type:** reference. **Holdings:** 6,000. **Subjects:** early American history. **Affiliated With:** National Sojourners. **Conventions/Meetings:** semiannual meeting - always January and June.

18845 ■ High Twelve International (HI-12)
2029 Washington Ave., Ste.105
Evansville, IN 47714
Ph: (812)422-9770 (812)477-5461
Fax: (812)422-9775
E-mail: high12@high12.org
URL: http://www.high12.org
Contact: James R. Satterthwaite, Pres.
Founded: 1921. **Staff:** 3. **State Groups:** 15. **Local Groups:** 300. **National Groups:** 2. **Multinational. Description:** Master Masons. Seeks to "inculcate the ideals taught in Masonry by uniting in the happy bonds of a fraternal hour." Supports efforts in personal attention to the problems of youth. **Libraries: Type:** reference. **Holdings:** books, periodicals. **Subjects:** masons. **Awards:** High Twelvian of the Year. **Frequency:** annual. **Type:** recognition ● International Founder's Award. **Frequency:** annual. **Type:** recognition. **Recipient:** to men and women with service to masonry or mankind ● Wolcott Foundation Scholarship. **Frequency:** annual. **Type:** scholarship. **Funds:** Clifford W. Jex Memorial Youth; International Endowment. **Publications:** *High Twelvian*, quarterly. Newsletter. **Price:** free. **Advertising:** accepted. **Conventions/Meetings:** annual International Convention (exhibits) - always June.

18846 ■ Imperial Council of the Ancient Arabic Order of the Nobles of the Mystic Shrine for North America
c/o Shriners International Headquarters
2900 Rocky Point Dr.
Tampa, FL 33607-1460
Ph: (813)281-0300
Free: (800)237-5055
Fax: (813)281-7156
E-mail: membership@shrinenet.org
URL: http://www.shrinershq.org
Contact: Nicholas Thomas, Imperial Potentate
Founded: 1872. **Members:** 411,000. **Membership Dues:** individual, $15 (annual). **Staff:** 25. **Budget:** $4,500,000. **Regional Groups:** 19. **Local Groups:** 191. **Description:** Fraternal and charitable organization. Maintains Shriners Hospitals for Children treating orthopedic problems, spinal cord and burn injuries. **Also Known As:** Shriners. **Publications:** *Temple Level 191*. Newsletter. **Conventions/Meetings:** annual Imperial Council Session - meeting (exhibits).

18847 ■ International Order of Job's Daughters, Supreme Guardian Council
c/o Susan M. Goolsby, Exec. Mgr.
233 W 6th St.
Papillion, NE 68046-2210
Ph: (402)592-7987
Fax: (402)592-2177
E-mail: sgc@iojd.org
URL: http://www.iojd.org
Contact: Susan M. Goolsby, Exec. Mgr.
Founded: 1921. **Members:** 24,000. **Regional Groups:** 46. **Languages:** English, Portuguese. **Description:** Girls from 5 countries who are between the ages of 11 and 20 and are related to Master

Masons. Promotes spiritual and character development. Conducts fraternal, patriotic, and educational activities; sponsors philanthropic project annually. **Awards: Frequency:** annual. **Type:** scholarship. **Also Known As:** Job's Daughters; Job's Daughters International; International Center for Job's Daughters. **Publications:** *News Exchange*, quarterly. Newsletter ● Proceedings, annual. **Conventions/Meetings:** annual meeting - always August.

18848 ■ Knights Templar, Grand Encampment, U.S.A.
5909 West Loop S, Ste.495
Bellaire, TX 77401-2402
Ph: (713)349-8700
Fax: (713)349-8710
E-mail: letucker@sbcglobal.net
URL: http://www.knightstemplar.org
Contact: Lawrence E. Tucker, Acting Grand Recorder
Founded: 1816. **Members:** 190,000. **Staff:** 6. **Budget:** $1,400,000. **Regional Groups:** 7. **State Groups:** 50. **Local Groups:** 1,200. **For-Profit. Description:** Represents masonic order. Supports Knights Templar Eye Foundation, which pays for eye treatment, surgery, and hospitalization for the needy. Established the Knights Templar Educational Foundation, which presents loans to deserving students in their last two years of college, or first one to two years of vocational training. **Libraries: Type:** reference. **Holdings:** books, periodicals. **Computer Services:** database. **Publications:** *Building and Sustaining Templar Membership*. Booklet. Alternate Formats: online ● *Knight Templar Magazine*, monthly. Contains news and articles of interest to Masons. Includes highlights from the Masonic family and obituaries. **Price:** $10.00/year in U.S. **Circulation:** 190,000. **Conventions/Meetings:** triennial meeting.

18849 ■ Ladies Oriental Shrine of North America (LOS of NA)
1111 E 54th St., Ste.111
Indianapolis, IN 46220
URL: http://www.midianshrine.org/midian/los.htm
Contact: Shirley McPherson, High Priestess
Founded: 1903. **Members:** 32,000. **Description:** Wives, mothers, sisters, and daughters of members of the Imperial Council of the Ancient Arabic Order Nobles of the Mystic Shrine for North America (see separate entry). Conducts projects to raise funds for the Shriners' Hospitals for Crippled and Burned Children. **Committees:** Hospital. **Affiliated With:** Imperial Council of the Ancient Arabic Order of the Nobles of the Mystic Shrine for North America; Shriners Hospitals for Children. **Publications:** Proceedings, annual. **Conventions/Meetings:** annual Grand Council Session - conference - always May.

18850 ■ Masonic Service Association of North America (MSA)
8120 Fenton St., Ste.203
Silver Spring, MD 20910-4785
Ph: (301)588-4010
Fax: (301)608-3457
E-mail: msana@ix.netcom.com
URL: http://www.msana.com
Contact: Richard E. Fletcher, Exec. Sec.
Founded: 1919. **Members:** 50. **Staff:** 7. **Description:** Agency of Grand Lodges (state) of Masons; educational and welfare organization. Conducts veterans hospital visitation program; provides disaster relief assistance. Maintains library containing proceedings of all American Grand Lodges. **Formerly:** (1998) Masonic Services Association of the United States. **Publications:** *Emessay Notes*, monthly. Newsletter. Alternate Formats: online ● *Focus*, quarterly. Newsletter. Alternate Formats: online ● *Short Talk Bulletin*, monthly ● . **Price:** Also publishes digests, lodge programs, and other material on Freemasonry for speakers, historians, students, and others. **Conventions/Meetings:** annual meeting - always February.

18851 ■ Modern Free and Accepted Masons of the World (MFAMW)
PO Box 1072
Columbus, GA 31902
Ph: (706)322-3326

E-mail: webmaster@modernfree.com
URL: http://www.modernfree.com
Contact: Gregory McCain, Supreme Grand Master
Founded: 1917. **Members:** 18,000. **Membership Dues:** regular, $5 (monthly). **Staff:** 8. **Budget:** $340,000. **State Groups:** 36. **Local Groups:** 432. **Description:** Fellowship organization dedicated to educating members so that its members may become better leaders and citizens. Holds seminars and workshops on topics such as leadership and business skills. Conducts Sunday school classes for children. **Awards:** Jerry B. Baldwin. **Frequency:** annual. **Type:** scholarship. **Publications:** *Searchlight*, monthly. Newspaper. **Price:** $12.00/year. **Conventions/Meetings:** annual Supreme Grand Lodge - convention - always last week in June.

18852 ■ National Federated Craft (NFC)
11 Country Arrow Dr.
Lafayette, IN 47905-8753
Ph: (765)447-7972
E-mail: w.parr@gte.net
Contact: Bill Parr, Sec.-Treas.
Founded: 1929. **Members:** 552. **Membership Dues:** $8 (annual). **Staff:** 5. **Budget:** $7,000. **State Groups:** 1. **Local Groups:** 13. **Description:** Promotes closer association and fellowship among members. Provides assistance to community projects and to youth organizations such as DeMolay International; International Order of Job's Daughters, Supreme Guardian Council; and Supreme Assembly, International Order of Rainbow for Girls. Believes in devotion to God and allegiance to the U.S. and the U.S. Constitution. **Awards: Frequency:** annual. **Type:** recognition. **Computer Services:** database, publishers. **Subgroups:** Craft. **Affiliated With:** DeMolay International; International Order of Job's Daughters, Supreme Guardian Council; Supreme Assembly, International Order of Rainbow for Girls. **Publications:** *National Federated Craft News*, quarterly. Newsletter. **Price:** $3.00 /year for members only. **Conventions/Meetings:** annual convention and meeting.

18853 ■ National League of Masonic Clubs (NLMC)
2244 Locust Ln.
York, PA 17404
E-mail: jschofi863@aol.com
URL: http://hometown.aol.com/JSchofi863/myhomepage/index.qp
Contact: Gordan R. Heath Jr., Sec.-Treas.
Founded: 1905. **Members:** 700. **Staff:** 1. **State Groups:** 7. **Description:** Federation of Masonic clubs. Maintains collection of literature at the George Washington National Masonic Shrine. **Awards:** Achievement Award. **Frequency:** annual. **Type:** recognition. **Recipient:** for members who have done outstanding work for the league ● Distinguished Service Award. **Frequency:** periodic. **Type:** recognition. **Recipient:** for achievement award recipients who have continued to perform outstanding work on behalf of the league ● **Frequency:** annual. **Type:** grant. **Recipient:** for children and/or grandchildren of national league members ● Meritorious Award. **Frequency:** periodic. **Type:** recognition. **Recipient:** for an individual who has made an outstanding contribution in a particular field of endeavor, to the nation, or to mankind; cannot be a member of the national league ● **Frequency:** annual. **Type:** scholarship. **Recipient:** for children and/or grandchildren of national league members. **Publications:** *Information and Reference Manual*, periodic ● *Official Directory of National and State League Officers*, periodic. **Conventions/Meetings:** semiannual board meeting - always February in Pennsylvania, and July in Maryland ● annual board meeting, commemorative memorial services at the crypt of John Paul Jones.

18854 ■ National Sojourners (NS)
8301 E Boulevard Dr.
Alexandria, VA 22308-1316
Ph: (703)765-5000
Fax: (703)765-8390

E-mail: nationalsoj@juno.com
URL: http://www.nationalsojourners.org
Contact: Maj. Nelson O. Newcombe, Sec.-Treas.
Founded: 1918. **Members:** 10,000. **Staff:** 3. **Budget:** $155,000. **Regional Groups:** 17. **Local Groups:** 165. **Description:** Past or present commissioned, warrant and senior non-commissioned officers of the uniformed forces of the U.S. who are Master Masons. Supports the Collingwood Library and Museum on Americanism. **Libraries: Type:** reference; open to the public. **Holdings:** 6,000. **Subjects:** American history. **Awards:** Sojourner Award. **Frequency:** annual. **Type:** recognition. **Recipient:** for outstanding ROTC cadets in the field of Americanism. **Committees:** Americanism; Bridge of Light; Fraternal Relations. **Affiliated With:** Heroes of '76. **Formerly:** (1919) Sojourners Club. **Publications:** *The Sojourner*, quarterly ● *Staff Directory*, annual. **Conventions/Meetings:** annual convention - always June ● annual meeting - always January.

18855 ■ Philalethes Society (PS)
c/o John C. Householder, Jr., Business Mgr.
1670 River Rd.
Beaver, PA 15009
Ph: (724)775-6509
E-mail: psoc@freemasonry.org
URL: http://www.freemasonry.org/psoc
Contact: Nelson King FPS, Ed.
Founded: 1928. **Members:** 4,400. **Membership Dues:** life, $600 ● life; including international airmail, $800 ● regular, $40. **Budget:** $90,000. **Description:** Master Masons who are interested in research and Freemasonry. Recognizes outstanding scholarly research in freemasonry and designates researchers as Fellows. **Awards:** Certificate of Literature. **Frequency:** annual. **Type:** recognition. **Recipient:** to a member who has submitted the results of research into the best article published in the Philalethes magazine ● **Type:** grant. **Recipient:** for writings or film productions that will enhance the image of Freemasonry. **Computer Services:** Mailing lists. **Telecommunication Services:** electronic mail, jchouseholder@freemasonry.org. **Publications:** *Constitution Bylaws*, triennial ● *The Philalethes*, bimonthly. Magazine. **Conventions/Meetings:** annual meeting - always February in Washington, DC ● semiannual meeting.

18856 ■ Red Cross of Constantine - United Grand Imperial Council
c/o Ned E. Dull, Right Illustrious Grand Recorder
PO Box 5716
Springfield, IL 62705-5716
Ph: (217)788-5090
E-mail: info@redcrossconstantine.org
URL: http://redcrossconstantine.org
Contact: Ned E. Dull, Right Illustrious Grand Recorder
Founded: 1872. **Members:** 8,000. **Staff:** 2. **State Groups:** 67. **Local Groups:** 200. **Description:** Aims to commemorate the first elevation of Christianity from the position of a despised and proscribed heresy to that of a legally recognized and honored religion. **Publications:** *Byzantium*, quarterly. Newsletter. Alternate Formats: online. **Conventions/Meetings:** annual general assembly ● annual meeting.

18857 ■ Royal Order of Scotland (ROS)
PO Box 11
Charleroi, PA 15022-0011
Ph: (724)489-0670
Fax: (724)489-0688
E-mail: roos2@verizon.net
URL: http://yorkrite.com/roos
Contact: Sir Edward H. Fowler Jr., Provincial Grand Master
Founded: 1878. **Members:** 8,700. **Membership Dues:** life, $300 ● regular, $35 (annual). **Staff:** 1. **Description:** U.S. Provincial Grand Lodge of fraternal and charitable Masonic order founded in 1314 and "restricted to Masons renowned for service to fellowmen". **Publications:** Proceedings, annual. **Price:** $4.00. **Conventions/Meetings:** annual meeting - 2007 Oct. 13, Fresno, CA.

18858 ■ Supreme Assembly, International Order of Rainbow for Girls (SAIORG)
PO Box 1868
McAlester, OK 74502
Ph: (918)423-1328
Free: (800)843-4674
Fax: (918)423-1329
E-mail: saoffice@tulsaconnect.com
URL: http://www.iorg.org
Contact: Mrs. Marie Renda, Supreme Worthy Advisor
Founded: 1922. **Members:** 1,100,000. **Staff:** 6. **National Groups:** 10. **Description:** Girls' fraternal society composed of active members (unmarried girls from ages 11-20) and majority members (married women or members over 20 years old) in Australia, Brazil, Canada, Germany, Japan, Panama, Philippines, and the United States. **Publications:** none. **Conventions/Meetings:** biennial assembly - 2008 July 26-30, Chicago, IL.

18859 ■ Supreme Council 33rd Degree, Ancient and Accepted Scottish Rite of Freemasonry - Southern Jurisdiction (AASR-SJ)
1733 16th St. NW
Washington, DC 20009-3103
Ph: (202)232-3579
Fax: (202)464-0487
E-mail: cacotto@srmason-sj.org
URL: http://www.scottishrite.org
Contact: Ronald A. Seale, Sovereign Grand Commander
Founded: 1802. **Members:** 425,000. **Staff:** 40. **Regional Groups:** 219. **Description:** Membership composed of Scottish Rite (fourth to 33rd degrees) Masons in all states South of the Ohio River and West of the Mississippi River, all American territorial possessions. Maintains museum. **Libraries:** **Type:** reference. **Holdings:** 175,000; books. **Subjects:** freemasonry, general non-fiction, Robert Burns collection, Lincolniana collection. **Awards:** Grand Cross. **Frequency:** biennial. **Type:** recognition. **Computer Services:** database, information navigator ● online services, masonic collection. **Formerly:** (1993) Supreme Council 33rd Degree, Ancient and Accepted Scottish Rite of Freemasonry - Southern Masonic Jurisdiction. **Publications:** *Amicus Quarterly*. Newsletter. Alternate Formats: online ● *Scottish Rite Journal*, bimonthly. Magazine. Contains masonic and general information of current interest. **Price:** $4.00/year in U.S.; $9.00/3 years; $17.00/year outside U.S. ISSN: 1076-8572. **Circulation:** 425,000. Alternate Formats: online. **Conventions/Meetings:** biennial Supreme Council Session - general assembly - always first Monday of week in odd-numbered years, Washington, DC.

18860 ■ Supreme Council, Ancient Accepted Scottish Rite of Free-Masonry (Northern Masonic Jurisdiction) (AASR-NMJ)
PO Box 519
Lexington, MA 02420-0519
Ph: (781)862-4410
Free: (800)814-1432
Fax: (781)863-1833
E-mail: wwebber@supremecouncil.org
URL: http://www.supremecouncil.org
Contact: Walter E. Webber, Sovereign Grand Commander
Founded: 1813. **Members:** 260,000. **Staff:** 29. **Budget:** $15,000,000. **Regional Groups:** 109. **State Groups:** 15. **Local Groups:** 109. **Description:** Scottish Rite Masons in 15 states East of the Mississippi River and North of the Ohio River. Supports National Heritage Museum and Library, Inc. of National Heritage in Lexington, MA and 32-degree Masonic Learning Center for Children, Inc. and the Abbott Scottish Rite Scholarship Program. Sponsors fellowships in programs related to finding the underlying cause of schizophrenia at 15 universities. **Libraries:** **Type:** reference. **Holdings:** 90,000. **Subjects:** U.S. and Masonic history. **Awards:** Fellowships in Schizophrenia. **Frequency:** annual. **Type:** grant ● Scholarship Awards. **Frequency:** annual. **Type:** scholarship. **Recipient:** for members' children and grandchildren

only. **Publications:** *The Northern Light*, quarterly. Magazine. Provides articles of interest to Masons and their families. **Price:** included in membership dues; $5.00 /year for nonmembers. **Circulation:** 335,000 ● *Supreme Council, Ancient Accepted Scottish Rite of Freemasonry—Annual Proceedings*. **Price:** available to members only. **Conventions/Meetings:** annual meeting (exhibits).

18861 ■ Supreme Council, Mystic Order of Veiled Prophets of the Enchanted Realm (MOVPER)
1696 Brice Rd.
Reynoldsburg, OH 43068
Ph: (614)860-0717
Fax: (614)860-9099
E-mail: humanitarian.foundation@scgrotto.com
URL: http://www.scgrotto.com
Contact: Barbara Izzie, Office Mgr.
Founded: 1890. **Members:** 27,000. **Staff:** 4. **State Groups:** 15. **Local Groups:** 185. **Description:** Fraternal order for Master Masons. Supports Cerebral Palsy research and dentistry for the handicapped. **Awards:** Prophet of the Year. **Frequency:** annual. **Type:** recognition. **Telecommunication Services:** electronic mail, scgrotto@ameritech.net. **Publications:** *The Grotto*, quarterly. **Conventions/Meetings:** annual meeting, with contests - always June.

18862 ■ Supreme Council Order of the Amaranth (SCOA)
PO Box 557579
Chicago, IL 60655-7579
Ph: (708)499-5939
Fax: (708)499-5939
E-mail: ervinej@aol.com
URL: http://www.amaranth.org
Contact: Elsie M. Ervin, Contact
Founded: 1873. **Members:** 38,000. **Staff:** 1. **Budget:** $142,000. **State Groups:** 43. **Local Groups:** 574. **Description:** Fraternal order of men and women of Masonic families. Organized as a fraternal and philanthropic order, affording the privileges of Masonic principles. Contributes to numerous charities and maintains Amaranth Diabetes Foundation to fund research. **Libraries:** **Type:** reference. **Awards:** Amaranth Diabetes Foundation Through ADA. **Frequency:** annual. **Type:** grant. **Recipient:** to a research for cure of diabetes. **Publications:** *Crown and Sword*, quarterly. Newsletter. **Circulation:** 950 ● *Supreme Council Directory*, annual. Contains listings of officers. **Price:** available to members only ● *Transaction of the Supreme Assembly*, annual. Journal. Reports on annual assembly. **Price:** available to members only. **Conventions/Meetings:** annual Supreme Council Assembly - conference.

18863 ■ Tall Cedars of Lebanon of North America (TCLNA)
2609 N Front St.
Harrisburg, PA 17110
Ph: (717)232-5991
Fax: (717)232-5997
E-mail: tclsf@tallcedars.org
URL: http://www.tallcedars.org
Contact: Walter J. Manhart, Supreme Scribe
Founded: 1902. **Members:** 16,000,000. **Staff:** 2. **Regional Groups:** 8. **National Groups:** 100. **Description:** Master Masons in good standing in their Masonic Lodge. Operates Tall Cedar Foundation, which supports muscular dystrophy research. Compiles statistics; maintains Tall Cedar Room in the George Washington Masonic National Memorial, Washington, DC. **Libraries:** **Type:** reference. **Holdings:** 200. **Awards:** Tall Cedar Scholarship. **Frequency:** annual. **Type:** scholarship. **Recipient:** to Masonic youth/child or grandchild of Tall Cedar. **Computer Services:** Mailing lists. **Formerly:** (1972) Tall Cedars of Lebanon of the United States of America. **Publications:** *Board Notes*, bimonthly ● *Cedar Digest*, biennial ● Annual Report, annual ● Proceedings, annual. **Conventions/Meetings:** annual convention - always May or June.

18864 ■ Universal Masonic Brotherhood (UMB)
PO Box 6410
Seffner, FL 33583-6410
Ph: (813)662-3597
Fax: (813)662-3597
E-mail: hmoffice@universalmasonic.com
URL: http://www.universalmasonic.org
Contact: Dr. Frederick McCollough, Grand Commander
Founded: 1960. **Members:** 3,800. **Description:** Fraternal organization promoting harmony and brotherhood. Provides financial and public relations support to charitable organizations. Makes available educational grants and scholarships. **Affiliated With:** National Association for the Advancement of Colored People. **Publications:** *Universal Star*, annual. **Conventions/Meetings:** annual Sovereign Session - meeting, held in conjunction with UMOES - always July ● annual Supreme Convention - meeting, held in conjunction with UMOES - always November.

Middle East

18865 ■ Middle East Information Network
197 Fairmount Ave., Unit 2
Boston, MA 02136
Fax: (617)507-5844
E-mail: info@mideastinfo.com
URL: http://www.mideastinfo.com
Contact: Edward Graham JD, Exec. Dir./Founder
Multinational. Description: Provides accurate and comprehensive information about the Middle East to break down the barriers and stereotypes about Middle Eastern people.

Military

18866 ■ Soldiers' Angels
1792 E Washington Blvd.
Pasadena, CA 91104
Ph: (615)676-0239
E-mail: soldiersangels@gmail.com
URL: http://www.soldiersangels.org
Contact: Don MacKay, CEO
Founded: 2003. **Description:** Provides aid and comfort to the Armed Forces and their families. Aims to ensure that soldiers are loved and supported during and after deployment. **Projects:** Blankets of Hope; Hero Packs; Operation Phone Home; Operation Soldier Helping Children. **Publications:** *Angel Whispers*. Newsletter.

Minorities

18867 ■ Ugbajo Itsekiri USA
PO Box 11465
Washington, DC 20008
E-mail: info@itsekiri.org
URL: http://www.itsekiri.org
Contact: Mr. Hector Ayu, Pres.
Description: Promotes Itsekiri custom, culture and heritage. Fosters social, economic development and political survival of Itsekiri people. Supports Itsekiri people and their values. Strengthens cordiality and unity among Itsekeri sons and daughters. **Computer Services:** Online services, discussion forum.

Morocco

18868 ■ Friends of Morocco (FOM)
PO Box 2579
Washington, DC 20013-2579
Ph: (703)660-9292
E-mail: tresch@att.net
URL: http://www.friendsofmorocco.org
Contact: Mr. Tim Resch, Pres.
Founded: 1988. **Members:** 400. **Membership Dues:** regular (dual), $20 (annual) ● regular (individual), $15 (annual) ● joint (individual), $50 (annual) ● joint

(dual), $65 (annual). **Budget:** $8,000. **Multinational.** **Description:** Represents returned Peace Corps volunteers with experience in Morocco and Moroccans in America. Promotes educational, cultural, charitable, social, literary and scientific exchange between Morocco and the U.S. **Affiliated With:** National Peace Corps Association. **Publications:** Newsletter, quarterly. **Circulation:** 2,500. Alternate Formats: online. **Conventions/Meetings:** annual conference.

Muslim

18869 ■ American Muslim Council (AMC)
1005 W Webster Ave., Ste.3
Chicago, IL 60614
Ph: (773)248-3390
E-mail: info@amcnational.org
URL: http://www.amcnational.org
Contact: Raied N. Abdullah, Pres.
Founded: 1990. **Membership Dues:** regular, $10 (annual). **Description:** Works to increase effective participation of American Muslims in the U.S. political and public policy arenas. **Publications:** Newsletter. **Conventions/Meetings:** annual convention.

Mutual Aid

18870 ■ Artists' Fellowship (AF)
47 5th Ave.
New York, NY 10003
Ph: (646)230-9833
URL: http://www.artistsfellowship.com
Contact: Marc Mellon, Pres.
Founded: 1859. **Members:** 400. **Membership Dues:** active, sustaining, $20 (annual) ● life, $500 ● organization, $250 (annual). **Description:** Established to aid professional fine artists and their families in event of sickness, disability, or bereavement. **Awards:** Benjamin West Clinedinst Memorial Medal. **Frequency:** annual. **Type:** medal. **Recipient:** to an artist for exceptional artistic contribution ● Gari Melchers Memorial Medal. **Frequency:** annual. **Type:** medal. **Recipient:** to an individual who has furthered the interests of the fine arts profession. **Committees:** Relief and Assistance. **Formerly:** (1889) Helpful Society; (1925) Artists Aid Society. **Publications:** Newsletter, semiannual. Alternate Formats: online. **Conventions/Meetings:** annual meeting - usually November or December, New York City.

18871 ■ Federal Employee Education and Assistance Fund (FEEA)
8441 W Bowles Ave., Ste.200
Littleton, CO 80123-9501
Ph: (303)933-7580
Free: (800)323-4140
Fax: (303)933-7587
E-mail: feeahq@aol.com
URL: http://www.feea.org
Contact: Stephen D. Bauer, Exec. Dir.
Founded: 1986. **Members:** 30,000. **Staff:** 8. **Budget:** $1,500,000. **Regional Groups:** 26. **State Groups:** 40. **Local Groups:** 45. **Languages:** English, Spanish. **Description:** Provides educational and emergency financial assistance to civilian federal and postal employees and their families. Conducts charitable and educational programs. Sponsors scholarship program; offers grants and no-interest loans to qualified federal employees experiencing unforeseen personal emergencies. **Awards:** FEEA Scholarship. **Frequency:** annual. **Type:** scholarship. **Recipient:** for qualified federal employees and their dependents. **Affiliated With:** American Federation of Government Employees; Federal Managers Association; National Council of Social Security Management Associations; National Federation of Federal Employees; National Treasury Employees Union; Senior Executives Association. **Publications:** *FEEA Helping Hand*, quarterly. Newsletter. **Circulation:** 140,000. **Advertising:** accepted ● Annual Report, annual ● Brochures. **Conventions/Meetings:** annual meeting ● periodic regional meeting.

18872 ■ Independent United Order of Mechanics - Western Hemisphere (IUOMWH)
Address Unknown since 2007
Founded: 1757. **Description:** Benevolent society. Provides volunteer community services including assistance for the homeless and support of charitable programs. Conducts fundraising activities. **Awards:** **Type:** recognition ● **Type:** scholarship. **Conventions/Meetings:** triennial International Convention - meeting (exhibits).

18873 ■ Riot Relief Fund (RRF)
1125 Park Ave., Ste.6-A
New York, NY 10128
Ph: (212)427-6434
Fax: (212)996-4625
E-mail: trustees@riotrelieffund.org
URL: http://www.riotrelieffund.org
Contact: Peter Megargee Brown, Pres.
Founded: 1863. **Description:** Originally founded to aid families of policemen who were killed during the Civil War draft riots. Is devoted to a strong and dedicated police force for New York City. Provides aid to the surviving spouses of police officers killed in the line of duty; grants scholarships to policemen studying aspects of law enforcement at John Jay College of Criminal Justice. **Awards: Frequency:** annual. **Type:** recognition. **Recipient:** for person who has demonstrated exceptional service to law enforcement. **Publications:** *History of Civil War Draft Riots in New York City.* **Conventions/Meetings:** annual conference - always New York City.

Native American

18874 ■ Alliance of Tribal Tourism Advocates (ATTA)
522 7th St., Ste.210
Rapid City, SD 57701
Ph: (605)341-2378
Fax: (605)341-2280
E-mail: dcook.atta@midconetwork.com
URL: http://www.attatribal.com/attatribal2
Contact: Daphne Richards Cook, Exec. Dir.
Founded: 1993. **Membership Dues:** individual, $25 (annual) ● associate, $50 (annual) ● tribal, $500 (annual). **Description:** Promotes responsible tourism development on reservations and in off-reservation Indian communities. **Committees:** PR/Publicity. **Projects:** Native American Scenic Byway. **Publications:** Newsletter, quarterly. **Price:** included in membership dues. Alternate Formats: online. **Conventions/Meetings:** workshop, tourism workshops and training.

18875 ■ American Indian Philosophy Association (AIPA)
Univ. of New Mexico
Philosophy Dept.
Albuquerque, NM 87131
E-mail: shonnel722@aol.com
URL: http://www.csub.edu/~awaters/aipa/aipa.html
Contact: Anne Waters, Pres.
Membership Dues: unemployed/underemployed/student, $15 (annual) ● graduate student, $20 (annual) ● faculty, $35 (annual). **Description:** Preserves the philosophical achievements of American Indians. Protects the culture of American Indians. Seeks to encourage the thoughtful and careful articulation, study and contemplation of philosophical issues that affect American indigenous people.

18876 ■ Black Indians and Intertribal Native American Association
PO Box 143
Upperstrasburg, PA 17265
Ph: (717)491-1065
Fax: (775)418-6031
E-mail: blackindianz@aol.com
URL: http://blackindians.com
Contact: Chief Jerry Eaglefeather, Contact
Founded: 1992. **Membership Dues:** general, $45 (annual). **Description:** Promotes Black Indians and

inter-tribal Native Americans. **Publications:** Newsletter, monthly. **Price:** free.

18877 ■ Consortia of Administrators for Native American Rehabilitation (CANAR)
105 Jefferson St.
Natchitoches, LA 71457
Ph: (318)354-7400
Fax: (318)354-7300
E-mail: jkelley@clivr.org
URL: http://www.canar.org
Contact: Joseph E. Kelley, Dir.
Membership Dues: consumer, family, student, $20 (annual) ● associate, individual, $75 (annual) ● institution (with less than 5 members), $250 (annual) ● institution (with more than 5 members), $500 (annual). **Description:** Works to advance and improve rehabilitation services for Native Americans. **Telecommunication Services:** electronic mail, cwalker@clivr.org. **Committees:** Bylaws; Human Resources; Legislative; Professional Standards and Research; Special. **Publications:** *CANAR Monograph*, biennial. **Price:** included in membership dues ● Newsletter. **Price:** included in membership dues. Alternate Formats: online.

18878 ■ Heritage Institute
PO Box 860
Clinton, WA 98236-0860
Ph: (360)341-3020
Fax: (360)341-3070
E-mail: customerservice@hol.edu
URL: http://www.hol.edu
Contact: Mike Seymour, Dir.
Description: Provides technical, policy, educational, and financial assistance to American Indian Tribes to pursue sustainable and environmentally sound economic development. **Programs:** InCompass Education; InCompass Energy. **Publications:** *InCompass Energy News.* Newsletter. **Conventions/Meetings:** annual Native American Science Bowl - competition, for students in high schools in Indian communities.

18879 ■ Honor the Earth
2104 Stevens Ave. S
Minneapolis, MN 55404
Ph: (612)879-7529
Fax: (612)813-5612
E-mail: honorearth@earthlink.net
URL: http://www.honorearth.org
Contact: Winona LaDuke, Exec. Dir.
Founded: 1993. **Members:** 200. **Membership Dues:** general (contribution), $35-$100. **Description:** Creates awareness of native environmental issues. Develops financial and political resources for the survival of native communities. Increases the public funding and support for native communities. **Computer Services:** Mailing lists, of members. **Boards:** Advisory. **Publications:** *The Winona LaDuke Reader: A Collection of Essential Writings.* Book. Features issues on Native-Americans and the entire US population. ● Newsletter. Alternate Formats: online ● Brochure. Alternate Formats: online.

18880 ■ Indian Defense League of America (IDLA)
c/o Joseph Rickard, Sr., Pres.
PO Box 305
Niagara Falls, NY 14302
URL: http://idloa.org
Contact: Joseph Rickard Sr., Pres.
Founded: 1926. **Description:** Works to guarantee unrestricted passage on the North American continent for Indian people.

18881 ■ Institute for Tribal Environmental Professionals (ITEP)
PO Box 15004
Flagstaff, AZ 86011
Ph: (928)523-9555 (928)523-0946
Fax: (928)523-1266

E-mail: itep@nau.edu
URL: http://www4.nau.edu/itep
Contact: Mehrdad Khatibi, Interim Dir.
Founded: 1992. **Description:** Works to assist Indian tribes in the management of environmental resources through training and education programs. **Awards:** Student Internships. **Type:** scholarship. **Programs:** American Indian Air Quality Training; Environmental Compliance and Inspection; Environmental Education Outreach; National Tribal Forum Series; Tribal Air Monitoring Support; Tribal Emissions Inventory Software Solution; Tribal Environment Resource Center; Water Resource. **Publications:** *Native Voices*, quarterly. Newsletter. Alternate Formats: online ● Brochures. Alternate Formats: online ● Papers. Alternate Formats: online. **Conventions/Meetings:** workshop.

18882 ■ Lakota Student Alliance (LSA)
PO Box 225
Kyle, SD 57752
Ph: (605)441-9453
E-mail: lakotastudentalliance@yahoo.com
URL: http://www.geocities.com/lakotastudentalliance/index.html
Contact: Robert Quiver Jr., Co-Founder
Founded: 1996. **Members:** 30. **Staff:** 3. **Budget:** $100. **Description:** Advocates, sponsors, and promotes public awareness education among grassroots indigenous people in the struggle toward sovereignty and independence. **Conventions/Meetings:** annual Oglala Commemoration - general assembly.

18883 ■ Midwest Treaty Network (MTN)
21 S Barstow St., Ste.206
Eau Claire, WI 54701
Ph: (715)833-1777 (715)833-8552
Free: (800)445-8615
Fax: (715)833-8552
E-mail: mtn@igc.org
URL: http://www.treatyland.com
Contact: Laura Manthe, Contact
Founded: 1989. **Description:** Represents Native and non-Native groups that work to promote and support Native American sovereignty. **Computer Services:** Mailing lists, email alert list. **Projects:** Wolf Watershed Educational Campaign. **Publications:** Brochure. Alternate Formats: online. **Conventions/Meetings:** periodic conference ● periodic rally.

18884 ■ National Indian Child Welfare Association (NICWA)
5100 SW Macadam Ave., Ste.300
Portland, OR 97239
Ph: (503)222-4044
Fax: (503)222-4007
E-mail: info@nicwa.org
URL: http://www.nicwa.org
Contact: Maruice Lyons, Pres.
Founded: 1983. **Membership Dues:** regular, $25-$49 (annual) ● friend, $50-$99 (annual) ● advocate, $100-$249 (annual) ● protector, $250-$499 (annual) ● benefactor, $500 (annual) ● tribal ICW agency (based on budget), $100-$1,000 (annual) ● organization/institution (standard), $100 (annual). **Staff:** 26. **Description:** Tribes, individuals (Indian and non-Indian), and private organizations concerned with Indian child and family issues. Dedicated to the well being of American Indian children and families. Seeks to promote safe, healthy and culturally strong environments for Indian children; advances the spiritual strength of Indian children; aims to advocate for and assist proper implementation of the Indian Child Welfare Act; promotes effective services to Indian children by child welfare workers; provides technical assistance, education, and leadership. **Libraries:** **Type:** reference. **Holdings:** 3,800; articles, books. **Subjects:** Indian child welfare and family issues, child abuse, neglect information. **Publications:** *NICWA News*, quarterly. Newsletter. **Price:** free ● *Pathways Practice Digest*, bimonthly. Newsletter. Features ICWA practice issues, reports, research papers, and other resources. **Price:** $25.00 for nonmembers. **Conventions/Meetings:** conference, regional conferences ● Protecting Our Children: The

National American Indian Conference on Child Abuse and Neglect ● workshop, with training.

18885 ■ National Indian Justice Center (NIJC)
5250 Aero Dr.
Santa Rosa, CA 95403
Ph: (707)579-5507
Free: (800)966-0662
Fax: (707)579-9019
E-mail: nijc@aol.com
URL: http://www.nijc.indian.com
Contact: Joseph A. Myers, Exec. Dir.
Founded: 1983. **Description:** Works to improve quality of life and administration of justice for Native communities. **Computer Services:** Mailing lists, of members. **Additional Websites:** http://www.nijc.org. **Programs:** Advanced Criminal Law; Alcohol and Substance Abuse; Alternative Methods and Dispute Resolution; Child Abuse and Neglect; Child Sexual Abuse; Civil Law and Procedure in Indian Country; Contracts and Personal Injury; Domestic Violence; Indian Civil Rights Act; Indian Housing Law; Juvenile Justice Systems; Tribal Court Management; Tribal Court Probation; Tribal Government Executives Management Course. **Publications:** *Advanced Crime Law*. Manual. Contains comprehensive examination of the criminal legal process in tribal court systems. **Price:** $75.00 ● *Alcohol & Substance Abuse*. Manual. **Price:** $75.00 ● *Appellate Court Systems*. Manual. Provides information on tribal appellate courts in general. **Price:** $75.00 ● *Bitter Earth: Child Sexual Abuse in Indian Country*. Video. **Price:** $49.00 ● *Child Abuse & Neglect*. Manual. Provides comprehensive presentation of substantive and procedural information necessary to effectively process child abuse and neglect cases. **Price:** $75.00 ● *Child Sexual Abuse*. Manual. **Price:** $75.00 ● *Civil Jurisdiction & Non-Indians*. Manual. Includes video and workbook. **Price:** $75.00 ● *Civil Jurisdiction & Non-Indians*. Video. **Price:** $39.00 ● *Civil Law & Procedure in Indian Country*. Manual. Provides comprehensive information concerning the mechanics and policies of civil procedure in Indian country. **Price:** $75.00 ● *Conflict Resolution: Mediation, Arbitration & Peacemaking*. Manual. Contains alternatives to tribal court resolution of conflicts, which promote conservation of tribal financial resources. **Price:** $75.00 ● *Contracts & Torts/Personal Injury*. Manual. Contains extensive analysis of the two important areas of the law. **Price:** $75.00 ● *Criminal Law & Procedure in Indian Country*. Manual. Provides detailed examination of the responsibilities of law enforcement and tribal court personnel and the legal rights of the accused. **Price:** $75.00 ● *Eliminating Domestic Violence in Indian Country*. Manual. Includes procedural and practical information necessary to effectively address domestic violence issues in Indian country. **Price:** $75.00 ● *Indian Housing Law Quarterly*. Manual. Provides accurate housing information. **Price:** $149.00/year, law firms; $100.00/year, general public; $79.00/year, tribal councils, IHAs, TDHEs, tribal courts; $20.00/year, tribal members ● *The Tribal Court Record*, quarterly. Newsletter. Provides information about issues important to the improvement of tribal court systems. **Price:** $45.00/year; $45.00 one special edition ● *Young Once Indian Forever*. Video. Provides foundation for discussion, interaction and collaboration among the multiple agencies serving tribal child victims of abuse. **Price:** $39.00. **Conventions/Meetings:** periodic conference.

18886 ■ National Society for American Indian Elderly (NSAIE)
200 E Filmore St., No. 151
Phoenix, AZ 85004
Ph: (602)424-0542
E-mail: info@nsaie.org
URL: http://www.nsaie.com
Contact: Steve Wilson, Chm.
Founded: 1987. **Membership Dues:** silver, $25 (annual) ● gold, $50 (annual) ● platinum, $100 (annual) ● patron, $500 (annual). **Description:** Works to assist all Indian elderly service programs, both on-reservation and off, to improve quality of life for American Indian elders. **Awards:** Elder of the Month.

Frequency: monthly. **Type:** recognition. **Recipient:** for members of the tribe ● **Type:** grant. **Recipient:** to tribal members' organizations. **Publications:** *Native Elderly Quarterly*. Newsletter. Alternate Formats: online ● *Wisdom of the Elders*. Book. **Price:** $12.95 plus shipping and handling.

18887 ■ National Tribal Development Association (NTDA)
RR1, Box 694
Box Elder, MT 59521-9722
Ph: (406)395-4095
Fax: (406)395-4096
E-mail: info@ntda.com
Contact: Billianne Morsette, CEO
Founded: 1995. **Description:** Works for the common interest in the development of tribal economies. **Computer Services:** Information services. **Telecommunication Services:** electronic bulletin board.

18888 ■ Native American Business Alliance (NABA)
30700 Telegraph Rd., Ste.1675
Bingham Farms, MI 48025-4566
Ph: (248)988-9344
Fax: (248)988-9348
E-mail: naba@n-a-b-a.org
URL: http://www.native-american-bus.org
Contact: Paul Bresette, Pres.
Membership Dues: general, $125 (annual) ● tribal, $500 (annual) ● corporate, $3,200 (annual). **Description:** Represents Native Americans to the private sector; facilitates business and cultural educational programs. **Computer Services:** database, Native American Business Alliance Directory. **Publications:** *Moccasin Print*, monthly. Newsletter. Alternate Formats: online. **Conventions/Meetings:** annual conference.

18889 ■ Native Elder Health Care Resource Center (NEHCRC)
PO Box 6508, Mailstop F800
Aurora, CO 80045-0508
Ph: (303)724-1483
Fax: (303)724-1474
E-mail: ursula.runningbear@uchsc.edu
URL: http://www.uchsc.edu/ai/nehcrc
Contact: Ursula Running Bear, Contact
Founded: 1994. **Description:** Resource center for older American Indians, Alaska Natives, Native Hawaiians, particularly in culturally competent healthcare. **Publications:** *NEHCRC Bibliography*.

18890 ■ Native Writers' Circle of the Americas (NWCA)
c/o Native American Studies
Univ. of Oklahoma
633 Elm Ave.
216 Ellison Hall
Norman, OK 73019-3119
Ph: (405)325-2312
Fax: (405)325-0842
E-mail: nas@ou.edu
URL: http://www.ou.edu/cas/nas/writers.html
Contact: Clara Sue Kidwell, Dir.
Founded: 1992. **Description:** Dedicated to Native American literature and publishing; maintains by the Native American Studies program at the University of Oklahoma. **Libraries:** **Type:** reference. **Subjects:** works by Native authors. **Awards:** First Book Awards. **Type:** recognition ● First Book Awards: Poetry. **Type:** recognition ● Lifetime Achievement Awards. **Type:** recognition. **Recipient:** for a writer's complete work to date ● Theresa Palmer Memorial Awards. **Type:** recognition. **Recipient:** to an Oklahoma Indian graduating high school senior. **Computer Services:** database, Native American writers' addresses. **Conventions/Meetings:** festival, for Native American writers.

18891 ■ Oyate
2702 Mathews St.
Berkeley, CA 94702
Ph: (510)848-6700
Fax: (510)848-4815

E-mail: oyate@oyate.org
URL: http://www.oyate.org
Contact: Beverly Slapin, Contact
Founded: 1990. **Nonmembership. Description:** Works to see that the lives and histories of Native American people are portrayed honestly. Evaluates texts, resource materials and children's fiction by and about Native people. Distributes children's, young adult, and teacher books and materials, with an emphasis on writing and illustration by Native people. **Publications:** Catalog. Alternate Formats: online ● Books. Contains various Oyate books for sale from $5 to $25. **Conventions/Meetings:** workshop, for teachers.

18892 ■ Red Earth
2100 NE 52nd St.
Oklahoma City, OK 73111
Ph: (405)427-5228
Fax: (405)427-8079
E-mail: cyellowman@redearth.org
URL: http://www.redearth.org
Contact: Connie Hart Yellowman, Exec. Dir.
Membership Dues: individual, elder, $25 (annual) ● family, $45 (annual) ● supporting, $100 (annual). **Description:** Promotes traditions of American Indian history and cultures. **Divisions:** Red Earth Museum. **Conventions/Meetings:** annual festival.

Nepalese

18893 ■ Association of Nepalis in the Americas (ANA)
c/o Anil R. Pathak, Treas.
3609 Ox Ridge Ct.
Fairfax, VA 22033
E-mail: ana@anaonline.org
URL: http://www.anaonline.org
Contact: Krishna Nirola, Pres.
Founded: 1983. **Members:** 125. **Membership Dues:** single, $25 (annual) ● family, $50 (annual) ● life, $500. **Multinational. Description:** Promotes the preservation of Nepali identity and culture in the Americas. Fosters cordial relations among Nepalis and Americans. Demonstrates the effectiveness of the participation of Nepali-Americans in the communities they live in. **Libraries: Type:** reference. **Computer Services:** Mailing lists. **Committees:** Advisory; Cultural; Fundraising; Scholarship. **Publications:** Newsletter. **Conventions/Meetings:** annual convention - every 4th of July.

18894 ■ Nepalese Americas Council (NAC)
3077 N Foxridge Ct.
Ann Arbor, MI 48105
Ph: (734)663-7225
Fax: (734)936-9091
E-mail: adhikary@umich.edu
URL: http://www.nepalcouncil.org
Contact: Dr. Jeetendra Joshi, Pres.
Founded: 1991. **Members:** 25. **Description:** Coordinates and facilitates a partnership among Nepalese and Nepal-related associations in the U.S.A. and Canada for maintaining and fostering Nepalese identity and cultural heritage. Establishes a national coordinating body for Nepalese and Nepal-related associations and societies in the United States and the Americas. Represents and advocates the interests of the Nepalese American communities. Promotes various social, cultural, educational, and economic activities of common interest to Nepalese community in the U.S. and Americas. Fosters friendship and understanding between Nepalese and other people in the Americas. Improves the relationship between the people of Nepal, the United States, and Americas. **Computer Services:** database, member directory. **Special Interest Groups:** Non Resident Nepalis - North American Coordinating Council.

Nigerian

18895 ■ Egbe Omo Yoruba: National Association of Yoruba Descendants in North America
3840 Bladensburg Rd.
Cottage City, MD 20722

Ph: (925)858-2565 (813)309-4850
E-mail: info@yorubanation.org
URL: http://www.yorubanation.org
Contact: Adeola Odusanya, Pres.
Multinational. Description: Promotes the culture, language and tradition of the Yoruba. Seeks to encourage and deliberate on issues paramount to the Yoruba people. Fosters the economic empowerment of the Yoruba. Ensures the advancement of Yoruba traditional institutions. **Computer Services:** Information services, Yoruba resources ● online services, e-mail discussion group. **Committees:** Agriculture and Rural Development; Economic Development; Education; Fundraising; Health; Housing and Urban Development; Internal and Strategic Planning; Political Affairs and Leadership. **Publications:** K' ARO OJI' RE. Newsletter.

18896 ■ Friends of Nigeria (FON)
1203 Cambria Ct.
Iowa City, IA 52246
Ph: (319)351-3375
E-mail: pjhansen@ia.net
URL: http://friendsofnigeria.org
Contact: Peter J. Hansen, Treas./Membership Chm.
Founded: 1996. **Members:** 400. **Membership Dues:** individual, $15 (annual). **Multinational. Description:** Peace Corps volunteers, staff and Nigerians residing in USA. Provides an alumni organization for returned Peace Corps volunteers and staff who served in Nigeria and keep them updated on current events in Nigeria. **Libraries: Type:** open to the public. **Subjects:** Nigeria. **Publications:** Newsletter, quarterly. **Price:** included in membership dues. **Circulation:** 1,450.

Norwegian

18897 ■ Norwegian Club/Det Norske Selskab (NC)
317 E 52nd St.
New York, NY 10022-6302
Ph: (212)877-8953 (212)534-1241
Fax: (212)421-9830
E-mail: rolf_k_stang@hotmail.com
Contact: Rolf Kristian Stang, Pres.
Founded: 1904. **Members:** 150. **Membership Dues:** $40 (annual). **Languages:** Norwegian. **Description:** Promotes cultural ties between America and Norway and encourages use of Norwegian language. **Publications:** none. **Awards:** Erik J. Friis Scholarship. **Type:** scholarship ● **Frequency:** annual. **Type:** scholarship. **Recipient:** for study in Norway. **Conventions/Meetings:** meeting - 8/year ● annual meeting - in May.

18898 ■ Sons of Norway (S/N)
1455 W Lake St.
Minneapolis, MN 55408-2666
Ph: (612)827-3611
Free: (800)945-8851
Fax: (612)827-0658
E-mail: fraternal@sofn.com
URL: http://www.sofn.com
Contact: Ted Fosberg, Pres.
Founded: 1895. **Members:** 69,680. **Membership Dues:** regular, $38 (annual). **Staff:** 43. **Regional Groups:** 8. **State Groups:** 35. **Local Groups:** 400. **Languages:** English, Norwegian. **Multinational. Description:** Fraternal insurance society for persons of Norwegian or other Nordic birth, descent, or affiliation by marriage. Promotes preservation of Norwegian cultural heritage. Provides educational, charitable, and cultural support for programs. Insurance includes life insurance, and insurance, annuities, long-term care, and travel programs. **Libraries: Type:** reference. **Holdings:** 2,000. **Subjects:** Vikings, Norse culture. **Awards: Type:** recognition. **Committees:** Scholarship. **Divisions:** Fraternal Services; General Management; Heritage Programs; Marketing; Policy Issues; Public Relations; Underwriting. **Absorbed:** (1940) Knights of the White Cross; (1950) Daughters of Norway. **Publications:** Convention Report, biennial. **Price:** free, for members only ● Corporate Re-

port, biennial ● Sons of Norway—Directory, annual ● Sons of Norway Viking, monthly. Magazine. Contains articles on Norwegian history, Norwegian-Americans, and current activities of the organization. Includes directory of lodges. **Price:** included in membership dues; $20.00 /year for nonmembers. ISSN: 0038-1462. **Circulation:** 61,000. **Advertising:** accepted. **Conventions/Meetings:** biennial international conference (exhibits).

Odd Fellows

18899 ■ Grand United Order of Odd Fellows (GUOOF)
262 S 12th St.
Philadelphia, PA 19107
Ph: (215)735-8774
Fax: (215)735-2422
Contact: Walcott Pemberton, Grand Sec.
Founded: 1843. **Members:** 108,000. **Regional Groups:** 8. **Description:** Individuals united for social and charitable purposes. Conducts seminars and professional training. Sponsors charitable and educational programs; provides children's services; maintains library. **Publications:** National Directory, biennial ● Bulletin, quarterly. **Conventions/Meetings:** biennial meeting.

18900 ■ Independent Order of Odd Fellows (IOOF)
422 Trade St.
Winston-Salem, NC 27101
Ph: (336)725-5955
Free: (800)235-8358
Fax: (336)722-7317
E-mail: ioofthesgl@bellsouth.net
URL: http://www.ioof.org
Contact: Terry L. Barrett, Sovereign Grand Sec.
Founded: 1819. **Members:** 374,015. **Staff:** 6. **State Groups:** 66. **Local Groups:** 7,678. **National Groups:** 25. **Description:** Fraternal beneficiary society. Maintains research program at Johns Hopkins University, Baltimore, MD; sponsors Education Foundation for financial assistance to students beyond the high school level. Maintains museum. Sponsors educational tour to United Nations and historical landmarks. **Libraries: Type:** reference. **Holdings:** 200; archival material, books. **Subjects:** the order. **Awards:** Outstanding Person Award. **Frequency:** annual. **Type:** recognition. **Recipient:** for humanitarian service of members or nonmembers. **Affiliated With:** International Association of Rebekah Assemblies, IOOF. **Publications:** Independent Order of Odd Fellows—Youth Reporter, quarterly. Newsletter. Contains news for youth members of IOOF. **Price:** $3.00/year. **Circulation:** 500. **Advertising:** accepted ● IOOF News, bimonthly. Newsletter. Includes division reports and obituaries. **Price:** $5.00/year in U.S.; C$6.00/year in Canada; $12.00/year outside U.S. and Canada. **Circulation:** 15,000. **Advertising:** accepted. Alternate Formats: online ● Journal of Proceedings - The Sovereign Grand Lodge, IOOF. **Circulation:** 500 ● Papers. **Conventions/Meetings:** annual convention (exhibits) - always in August.

18901 ■ International Association of Rebekah Assemblies, IOOF (IARA)
422 Trade St.
Winston-Salem, NC 27101
Ph: (336)725-6037
Free: (800)766-1838
Fax: (336)773-1066
E-mail: webmaster@ioof.org
URL: http://www.ioof.org
Contact: Vivian W. Pursell, Sec.
Founded: 1922. **Members:** 66,687. **Staff:** 6. **Description:** Women's auxiliary to the Independent Order of Odd Fellows. Sponsors Educational Foundation that provides loans to members. Participates in Eye Bank and Visual Research. Sponsors youth pilgrimages. **Affiliated With:** Independent Order of Odd Fellows. **Publications:** Fraternal Publication, bimonthly. Journal ● Journal, annual. **Conventions/Meetings:** annual meeting.

18902 ■ Junior Lodge, Independent Order of Odd Fellows (JLIOOF)
c/o Sovereign Grand Lodge Office
422 Trade St.
Winston-Salem, NC 27101
Ph: (336)725-5955
Free: (800)235-8358
Fax: (336)722-7317
E-mail: ioofthesgl@bellsouth.net
URL: http://www.ioof.org
Contact: Terry L. Barrett, Sovereign Grand Sec.
Founded: 1923. **Members:** 457. **Staff:** 6. **State Groups:** 17. **Local Groups:** 37. **Description:** Young men between the ages of 8 and 18. Promotes purity of thought, word, and deed, and high moral standards. Preserves "universal brotherhood by pledging fidelity, honor, and loyalty". **Awards:** Irene Meigs Community Service Award. **Frequency:** annual. **Type:** recognition. **Recipient:** for community service. **Publications:** *Youth Reporter*, quarterly. Newsletter. Contains youth news and features. **Price:** $3.00/year. **Circulation:** 500. **Conventions/Meetings:** annual Youth Day - conference (exhibits).

Orioles

18903 ■ Fraternal Order Orioles (FOO)
716 Maryland Ave. SW
Canton, OH 44710
E-mail: orioleofc@prodigy.net
URL: http://www.fraternalorderorioles.homestead.com
Contact: Carl Nuveman, Pres.
Founded: 1910. **Members:** 10,000. **Staff:** 4. **State Groups:** 2. **Local Groups:** 56. **National Groups:** 65. **Description:** Men's fraternal society with auxiliaries. **Awards:** Fraternal Order of Orioles Scholarship. **Type:** scholarship. **Recipient:** to members or their immediate family members. **Publications:** *Oriole Life*, quarterly. **Conventions/Meetings:** annual Supreme Convention - always first week of August.

Peace

18904 ■ United States Canada Peace Anniversary Association (USCPAA)
PO Box 4564
Blaine, WA 98231-4564
Ph: (360)332-7165
E-mail: info@peacearchpark.org
URL: http://www.peacearchpark.org
Contact: Christina Alexander, Pres.
Founded: 1995. **Membership Dues:** student, $25 (annual) ● individual, $35 (annual) ● family, $50 (annual) ● sponsor, $100 (annual) ● patron, $250 (annual). **Multinational. Description:** Advocates for peace and education to American and Canadian public. Preserves the heritage of peaceful relations between United States and Canada. **Projects:** International Choir Day; International Flag Procession; Peace Arch Interpretive Center; Sculpture Exhibit Expansion.

Polish

18905 ■ Alliance of Poles of America (APA)
6966 Broadway Ave.
Cleveland, OH 44105-1316
Ph: (216)883-3131
E-mail: aop@allianceofpoles.com
Contact: John Borkowski, Natl.Pres.
Founded: 1895. **Members:** 18,000. **Staff:** 5. **Local Groups:** 46. **Languages:** English, Polish. **Description:** Fraternal benefit life insurance society. **Libraries: Type:** open to the public. **Holdings:** 6,000. **Subjects:** Polish history, culture, customs, language. **Awards:** Gold Medal for Meritorious Service. **Frequency:** annual. **Type:** scholarship. **Recipient:** for members. **Publications:** *The Alliancer* (in English and Polish), monthly. Newspaper. **Price:** $10.00/year.

Circulation: 5,000. **Conventions/Meetings:** quadrennial convention.

18906 ■ American Council for Polish Culture (ACPC)
c/o Deborah M. Majka, Pres.
812 Lombard St., Apt. 12
Philadelphia, PA 19147-1308
E-mail: deborah_m_majka@rohmhaas.com
URL: http://www.polishcultureacpc.org
Contact: Deborah M. Majka, Pres.
Founded: 1948. **Members:** 3,200. **Membership Dues:** affiliate club, $5 (annual) ● individual, $10 (annual) ● supporting organization, $200 (annual). **Local Groups:** 35. **Languages:** English, Polish. **Description:** National federation of groups devoted to fostering and preserving Polish ethnic heritage in the U.S. Seeks to: promote understanding and appreciation of Polish culture and creativeness; perpetuate and develop the culture by encouraging higher education and scholarship among people of Polish descent; foster in Americans of Polish origin a consciousness and pride in their heritage; enrich American culture by adding the best from Polish sources of inspiration and accomplishment. Sponsors programs; conducts research; holds educational seminar. Maintains speakers' bureau. **Libraries: Type:** reference. **Holdings:** archival material, artwork, books. **Awards:** Adam Styka. **Frequency:** annual. **Type:** monetary. **Recipient:** to a winner of graphic art competition ● Cultural Achievement Award. **Frequency:** annual. **Type:** recognition. **Recipient:** to a prominent American or Polish American for an outstanding record of achievement in the field of artistic/or cultural endeavors ● Distinguished Service Award. **Frequency:** annual. **Type:** recognition. **Recipient:** for achievement on behalf of Polish American community ● Jozef Hofman. **Frequency:** annual. **Type:** monetary. **Recipient:** for piano accomplishment ● Marcella Kochanska Sembrich. **Frequency:** annual. **Type:** monetary. **Recipient:** for operatic voice achievement ● Pulaski Scholarship. **Frequency:** annual. **Type:** scholarship. **Recipient:** for qualified Polish-American students ● **Type:** scholarship. **Recipient:** for those studying Polish history at Jagiellonian University in Krakow ● Skalny Scholarship. **Frequency:** annual. **Type:** scholarship. **Recipient:** for students pursuing studies at least two years of college or university work at an accredited institution. **Computer Services:** database. **Committees:** ACPC Scholarship; Cultural Exchange; Curriculum for Elementary Schools on Polish Heritage; History; National Registry; Youth Leadership Conference. **Projects:** Jan de Rosen Fund; News Group; Poster Exhibit; Pulaski Film Biography. **Formerly:** (1990) American Council of Polish Cultural Clubs. **Publications:** *American Council for Polish Culture Directory* ● *Polish Heritage*, quarterly. **Price:** $10.00. **Advertising:** accepted. **Conventions/Meetings:** semiannual board meeting - always spring and fall ● competition ● annual meeting and convention - always summer.

18907 ■ American Federation of Polish Jews (AFPJ)
136 E 39th St.
New York, NY 10016
Ph: (212)689-4930
Contact: Jechil M. Dobekirer, VP
Founded: 1960. **Members:** 800. **Membership Dues:** ordinary, $30 (annual). **Regional Groups:** 50. **Languages:** English, Yiddish. **Description:** Seeks to preserve the memory and the history of Polish Jewry through the establishment of an institute to study 1000 years of Jewish Life in Poland at Tel Aviv University in Israel. Participates in negotiations with Polish officials aimed at obtaining compensation for the personal property of Jews and Jewish schools, hospitals, and other public buildings which were confiscated by the Polish government. **Awards: Type:** recognition. **Also Known As:** Federation of Polish Jews in the United States. **Formerly:** World Federation of Polish Jews, American Section. **Publications:** *Bulletin of Activities* (in English and Yiddish), quarterly. **Conventions/Meetings:** annual

conference ● quarterly executive committee meeting ● annual meeting.

18908 ■ Association of the Sons of Poland (ASOP)
333 Hackensack St.
Carlstadt, NJ 07072
Ph: (201)935-2807
Fax: (201)935-2752
E-mail: sonsofpoland@yahoo.com
URL: http://www.angelfire.com/nj/asop/index.html
Contact: Dorothy Kostecka-Wieczerzak, Sec. Gen.
Founded: 1903. **Members:** 5,000. **Staff:** 3. **National Groups:** 35. **Description:** Serves as fraternal benefit life insurance society for men and women and children of Polish ancestry or birth. **Awards:** Scholarship/Achievement Award. **Frequency:** annual. **Type:** scholarship. **Recipient:** for a high school senior who has been a member for a minimum of two years. **Committees:** Scholarship. **Publications:** *Polish American Journal*, monthly. Includes news on current social and religious issues of interest to Polish-Americans and also covers activities of prominent Polish-Americans. **Price:** free, for members only. **Conventions/Meetings:** quadrennial meeting.

18909 ■ Legion of Young Polish Women (LYPW)
Address Unknown since 2007
Founded: 1939. **Members:** 200. **Languages:** English, Polish. **Description:** Women of Polish descent interested in promoting the cultural, social and educational goals of the Polish American community and assisting Poles throughout the world. Provides financial assistance to Polish and American institutions and foundations. Sends medical supplies to Poland and participates in exhibits, competitions, and publications. Since 1945, has sponsored the presentation of debutantes at the annual White and Red Ball. **Conventions/Meetings:** monthly meeting.

18910 ■ National Medical and Dental Association
c/o Dorothy Czarnecki, MD, Exec. Sec.
9412 Acad. Rd.
Philadelphia, PA 19114
E-mail: dotczar2@aol.com
URL: http://www.polishnmda.com
Contact: Dorothy Czarnecki MD, Exec. Sec.
Founded: 1910. **Members:** 400. **Membership Dues:** regular, $40 (annual). **Description:** Polish-American physicians, dentists, and lawyers. Social organization for Polish-American professionals interested in preserving their heritage. **Awards: Frequency:** annual. **Type:** scholarship. **Publications:** *National Medical and Dental Association Bulletin* (in English and Polish), annual. **Circulation:** 1,750. **Advertising:** accepted. **Conventions/Meetings:** annual convention.

18911 ■ Polish American Congress (PAC)
5711 N Milwaukee Ave.
Chicago, IL 60646-6215
Ph: (773)763-9944
Fax: (773)763-7114
E-mail: pacchgo@polamcon.org
URL: http://www.polamcon.org
Contact: Mr. Les Kuczynski Esq., Natl. Exec. Dir.
Founded: 1944. **Members:** 3,000. **Membership Dues:** individual, $20 (annual) ● corporate, $100 (annual) ● corporate patron, $500 (annual) ● corporate sponsor, $1,000 (annual). **Staff:** 5. **State Groups:** 29. **National Groups:** 7. **Languages:** English, Polish. **Description:** Umbrella organization for local and national Polish organizations in the U.S. with more than one million combined members. Promotes improved quality of life for Polish Americans and people in Poland. Assists qualified Polish-Americans in government, business, and other professional fields. Coordinates activities of Polish-American organizations and individuals throughout the U.S; concerns include Polish-American civic, social, cultural, and educational affairs; has established the PAC Charitable Foundation to coordinate extensive medical and humanitarian relief to Poland in cooperation with other relief agencies. Works with the U.S.

State Department regarding Polish and Polish-American matters. Sponsors literary, cultural, and museum projects; conducts research and educational programs. **Libraries: Type:** reference. **Awards:** Freedom Award. **Frequency:** periodic. **Type:** recognition. **Recipient:** to an individual who has exemplified the mission of the Polish American Congress. **Commissions:** Polish Education; Youth. **Committees:** Anti-Bigotry; Cultural Promotion; Domestic Affairs; Heritage Month; Polish Affairs; Polish-Jewish Relations; Refugee and Immigration. **Affiliated With:** Polish Army Veterans Association of America; Polish Beneficial Association; Polish Falcons of America; Polish National Alliance of the United States of North America; Polish Roman Catholic Union of America; Polish Singers Alliance of America; Polish Union of America; Polish Women's Alliance of America; Union of Polish Women in America. **Publications:** *PAC Newsletter*, quarterly ● *Polish American Congress—Newsletter*, periodic. Provides information about Polish-Americans, U.S.-Polish relations, and current affairs in Poland. **Price:** included in membership dues. **Circulation:** 10,000. **Conventions/Meetings:** semiannual general assembly - always June and November.

18912 ■ Polish Arts and Culture Foundation (PACF)
4077 Waterhouse Rd.
Oakland, CA 94602
Ph: (510)599-2244
Fax: (510)531-2721
URL: http://www.polishculturesf.org
Contact: Caria Tomczykowska, Pres.
Founded: 1966. **Members:** 280. **Membership Dues:** basic, $60 (annual) ● senior, student, $50 (annual) ● family, $100 (annual) ● patron, $200 (annual) ● benefactor, $350 (annual) ● corporate, $500 (annual) ● ambassador, $1,200 (annual). **Staff:** 2. **Description:** Promotes Polish historical and culture achievements through exhibits, concerts, and publications. **Computer Services:** Mailing lists. **Publications:** *Forum*, quarterly. Newsletter. **Price:** included in membership dues ● *The Guide to Polonica in the San Francisco Bay Area*. **Conventions/Meetings:** annual Fall Ball - meeting - in November ● annual Gala Polonaise Ball - meeting - in May ● annual meeting - held in January ● annual Swiecone - meeting - held on Saturday before Easter ● annual Swietojanki - meeting - held on last Saturday of June ● annual Wigilja - meeting, a traditional Christmas Dinner - held on second Sunday of December.

18913 ■ Polish Assistance, Inc. (PAI)
15 E 65th St.
New York, NY 10021-6501
Ph: (212)570-5560
Fax: (212)570-5561
E-mail: polishassistance@aol.com
URL: http://www.polishassistance.org
Contact: Bronislaw Chrobok, Chm.
Founded: 1956. **Members:** 700. **Membership Dues:** student, $25 ● supporting, $45 ● donor, $50-$99. **Staff:** 1. **Languages:** English, Polish. **Description:** Renders financial aid and other services to Polish victims of World War II living in the U.S. Sponsors fundraising drives and charity events. Helps finance other organizations. Maintains homes for the aged, disabled, and neglected in the New York City area. **Formerly:** Polish Mutual Assistance. **Publications:** Bulletin, semiannual ● Journal, annual. **Conventions/Meetings:** annual Members Meeting.

18914 ■ Polish Beneficial Association (PBA)
2595 Orthodox
Philadelphia, PA 19137
Ph: (215)535-2626 (215)535-8815
Free: (800)599-2917
Fax: (215)535-0169
E-mail: contactus@polishbeneficial.com
URL: http://www.polishbeneficial.com
Contact: Theodore S. Drejerski, Pres.
Founded: 1900. **Members:** 16,246. **Staff:** 5. **Local Groups:** 105. **Description:** Serves as a fraternal benefit insurance society for persons of Slavic or Polish descent and of the Greek Orthodox or Roman Catholic faith. Engages in patriotic, religious, social, and fraternal activities. **Awards: Type:** scholarship. **Recipient:** for members. **Committees:** Aid and Assistance; Fraternal Activities; School Stipend. **Publications:** *Polish-American Journal*, periodic. **Conventions/Meetings:** quadrennial meeting.

18915 ■ Polish Falcons of America (PFA)
615 Iron City Dr.
Pittsburgh, PA 15205-4397
Ph: (412)922-2244
Free: (800)535-2071
Fax: (412)922-5029
E-mail: info@polishfalcons.org
URL: http://www.polishfalcons.org
Contact: Wallace J. Zielinski, Pres.
Founded: 1887. **Members:** 27,000. **Staff:** 12. **Budget:** $7,000,000. **Regional Groups:** 8. **Local Groups:** 109. **Languages:** English, Polish. **Description:** Serves as fraternal benefit insurance society for persons of Polish or Slavic descent and their spouses or any individual who is judged supportive of the purpose and ethnic heritage of the Polish Falcons of America. Promotes social, educational, and physical fitness activities. Conducts various sporting competitions. Maintains museum. **Libraries: Type:** reference. **Holdings:** 200; archival material. **Subjects:** history of society. **Awards:** Fraternalist of the Year. **Frequency:** annual. **Type:** recognition. **Recipient:** for members who best exemplify the qualities of fraternalism through volunteering ● Gorecki Scholarship. **Frequency:** annual. **Type:** scholarship. **Recipient:** for members who will be undergraduate college or technical school students ● Legion of Honor. **Frequency:** annual. **Type:** recognition ● Service Star Award. **Type:** recognition ● Starzynski Scholarship. **Frequency:** annual. **Type:** scholarship. **Recipient:** for members who will be undergraduate college or technical school students. **Computer Services:** database, membership information and insurance business ● mailing lists, membership notices and publication ● online services. **Publications:** *Polish Falcon* (in English and Polish), monthly. Newspaper. Features press releases and photographs from all lodges. Includes articles and news information concerning significant developments in Europe. **Price:** included in membership dues. **Circulation:** 15,200. Also Cited As: *Sokol Polski*. **Conventions/Meetings:** quarterly board meeting ● quadrennial convention, to review and set policy and to elect officers (exhibits).

18916 ■ Polish National Alliance of the United States of North America (PNA)
6100 N Cicero Ave.
Chicago, IL 60646
Ph: (773)286-0500
Free: (800)621-3723
Fax: (773)286-4836
E-mail: pna@pna-znp.org
URL: http://www.pna-znp.org
Contact: Mr. Frank Spula, Pres.
Founded: 1880. **Members:** 231,000. **Staff:** 100. **Regional Groups:** 17. **State Groups:** 37. **Local Groups:** 750. **Languages:** English, Polish. **Description:** Serves as fraternal benefit life insurance society. Men, women, and children of Polish descent or affiliation and spouses of members. Sponsors fraternal, educational, charitable, and life insurance programs. Conducts Saturday Polish School offering instruction on the Polish language, heritage, and culture. **Awards: Type:** scholarship. **Absorbed:** (1986) Polish Alma Mater of America; (1990) Association of Polish Women in America; (1991) United Polish Women of America. **Publications:** *Zgoda*, semimonthly. **Conventions/Meetings:** quadrennial meeting.

18917 ■ Polish National Union of America (PNUA)
1002 Pittston Ave.
Scranton, PA 18505
Free: (800)724-6352
E-mail: info@pnu.org
URL: http://www.pnu.org
Contact: Mr. Edmund J. Kotula, Pres.
Founded: 1908. **Members:** 30,000. **Staff:** 20. **Budget:** $1,900,000. **Regional Groups:** 12. **Local Groups:** 202. **Description:** Fraternal benefit life insurance society. Maintains Spojnia Manor, a residential health care facility. Provides disaster relief to members. Conducts cultural events. **Awards: Type:** scholarship. **Recipient:** for college. **Telecommunication Services:** electronic mail, sales@pnu.org. **Commissions:** Education and Youth; Fraternal Activities. **Publications:** *Polish Weekly Straz*. Newspaper. **Conventions/Meetings:** competition, in track and field, bowling, basketball, and golf ● quadrennial convention ● annual tour, to Poland.

18918 ■ Polish Nobility Association Foundation (PNAF)
Villa Anneslie
529 Dunkirk Rd.
Baltimore, MD 21212-2014
E-mail: kusza@xtra.co.nz
URL: http://pnaf.us
Contact: Dr. Felix von Leski-Holewinski, Pres.
Founded: 1921. **Members:** 375. **Membership Dues:** student/library/standard bearer, $25 (annual) ● Swordbearer, $50 (annual) ● Cupbearer, $75 (annual) ● Chamberlain, $100 (annual) ● Chancellor, $125 (annual) ● Prince, $150 (annual) ● Castellan, $250 (annual). **Staff:** 2. **Budget:** $4,000. **National Groups:** 57. **Languages:** English, Polish. **Description:** Works to promote the study and appreciation of the history and culture of the Polish Nobility and is a major resource for heraldic name searches, publications and matters related to the Polish nobility. **Libraries: Type:** reference. **Holdings:** 419. **Subjects:** genealogy, history, heraldry. **Awards:** Chivalric-Royal Order of Jagiello. **Type:** recognition ● Chivalric-Royal Order of Piast. **Type:** recognition. **Formerly:** (1997) Polish Nobility Association. **Publications:** *Nobility of the Polish Commonwealth*. Booklet. Includes listing and history of titled and non-titled nobility. **Price:** $13.00. ISSN: 1523-7419 ● *White Eagle*, semiannual. Journal. Contains 12 pages of heraldic, historical, and current happenings. **Price:** included in membership dues; $15.00 for nonmembers, plus shipping and handling. **Circulation:** 500. Also Cited As: *PNAF-Journal*. **Conventions/Meetings:** annual meeting - always summer.

18919 ■ Polish Roman Catholic Union of America (PRCUA)
984 N Milwaukee Ave.
Chicago, IL 60622-4101
Ph: (773)782-2600
Free: (800)772-8632
Fax: (773)278-4595
E-mail: info@prcua.org
URL: http://www.prcua.org
Contact: Wallace M. Ozog, Pres.
Founded: 1873. **Members:** 90,000. **Staff:** 40. **Regional Groups:** 24. **Local Groups:** 571. **Languages:** English, Polish. **Description:** Fraternal benefit insurance society. Sponsors sports and youth activities and children's social and recreation programs. Conducts language school and dance programs. Maintains Polish Museum of America (see separate entry). **Libraries: Type:** open to the public. **Holdings:** 39,848; articles, books, periodicals. **Subjects:** Polish-American history, literature, culture. **Affiliated With:** Polish Museum of America. **Publications:** *Narod Polski* (in English and Polish), bimonthly. Newspaper. **Conventions/Meetings:** quadrennial meeting.

18920 ■ Polish Union of America (PUA)
745 Center Rd.
West Seneca, NY 14224-2108
Ph: (716)677-0220
Free: (800)724-2782
Fax: (716)677-0246
E-mail: punion@ix.netcom.com
URL: http://www.polishunion.com
Contact: James Paul Jozwiak, Natl. Pres.
Founded: 1890. **Members:** 8,000. **Staff:** 7. **Budget:** $500,000. **Local Groups:** 98. **Languages:** English, Polish. **Description:** Fraternal benefit life insurance society. Conducts specialized ethnic cultural, heritage and awareness programs and activities. Provides children's services. Maintains speakers' bureau and

museum. Compiles statistics. **Libraries: Type:** reference. **Holdings:** archival material, artwork, business records. **Subjects:** fraternal and Polish heritage history. **Awards:** Presidential Lifetime Contribution Service Award. **Frequency:** annual. **Type:** scholarship. **Recipient:** for members only ● Service Award. **Frequency:** annual. **Type:** recognition. **Recipient:** for organizational service by Lodge or National Office. **Affiliated With:** National Fraternal Congress of America. **Formerly:** Polska Unia W Ameryce. **Publications:** *Polish Union of America News*, 5/year. Newspaper. **Price:** free for members. **Circulation:** 5,000. **Conventions/Meetings:** quadrennial Grand Convention (exhibits) - always August.

18921 ■ Polish Union of the United States of North America
PO Box 660
Wilkes-Barre, PA 18703-0660
Ph: (570)823-1611
Fax: (570)829-7849
E-mail: polunion@epix.net
URL: http://www.polishunionusa.com
Contact: Ms. Charlotte L. Androckitis, Gen. Sec.
Founded: 1890. **Members:** 11,698. **Local Groups:** 82. **Description:** Serves as a fraternal benefit life insurance society. **Awards:** Fraternalist of the Year. **Frequency:** annual. **Type:** recognition. **Recipient:** for members who exemplify the spirit of fraternalism and volunteerism. **Committees:** Activities; Educational Fund; Progress; Youth. **Affiliated With:** National Fraternal Congress of America. **Publications:** *Fraternal Journal*, monthly. Newspaper. Alternate Formats: online ● *Polish-American Journal*, monthly. **Conventions/Meetings:** quadrennial meeting.

18922 ■ Polish Women's Alliance of America (PWAA)
6643 N Northwest Hwy., 2nd Fl.
Chicago, IL 60631
Ph: (847)384-1200
Free: (888)522-1898
Fax: (847)384-1494
E-mail: pwaa@pwaa.org
URL: http://www.pwaa.org
Contact: Virginia Sikora, Pres.
Founded: 1898. **Members:** 50,000. **Staff:** 30. **State Groups:** 17. **Local Groups:** 600. **Languages:** English, Polish. **Description:** Fraternal benefit life insurance society administered by women. Supports and contributes to charitable and relief foundations in the U.S. and abroad. **Libraries: Type:** reference. **Holdings:** 7,500. **Subjects:** Polish, English, American history and culture. **Telecommunication Services:** electronic mail, padowski@pwaa.org. **Committees:** Civic and Welfare; Cultural and Scholarship; Old Age Assistance; Youth Conference. **Publications:** *Glos Polek* (in English and Polish), monthly. Newspaper. Also Cited As: *The Polish Women's Voice*. **Conventions/Meetings:** quadrennial convention.

18923 ■ Union of Poles in America (UPA)
9999 Granger Rd.
Garfield Heights, OH 44125
Ph: (216)478-0120
Fax: (216)478-0122
E-mail: ralph.bodziony@pna-znp.org
URL: http://www.unionofpoles.com
Contact: Ralph Bodziony, Gen. Sec.
Founded: 1894. **Members:** 10,000. **Staff:** 3. **State Groups:** 42. **Languages:** English, Polish. **Description:** Composed exclusively of members who have freely joined together for their mutual protection and benefit through the instruments of insurance. Provides assistance to its members by offering college scholarships, sports grants, and educational grants. **Awards:** **Frequency:** annual. **Type:** grant. **Recipient:** for sports ● **Type:** scholarship. **Recipient:** for high school and college students. **Publications:** *Kuryer Zjednoczenia*, monthly. Also Cited As: *Courier of the Union*. **Conventions/Meetings:** quadrennial meeting.

18924 ■ Union of Polish Women in America (UPWA)
2636-38 E Allegheny Ave.
Philadelphia, PA 19134-5185
Ph: (215)425-3807
Fax: (215)425-3961
Contact: Sharon Quinn, Sec.
Founded: 1920. **Members:** 9,379. **Staff:** 4. **Regional Groups:** 3. **Local Groups:** 65. **Description:** Fraternal benefit life insurance society of women, men, boys, and girls. Conducts charitable and cultural activities; sponsors folk dances, glee clubs, baton groups, and exhibits. **Awards: Type:** recognition. **Recipient:** for the best essay. **Affiliated With:** National Fraternal Congress of America. **Publications:** *Gwiazda*, weekly. Also Cited As: *Polish Star*. **Conventions/Meetings:** annual District Conference - meeting ● quadrennial meeting.

Portuguese

18925 ■ Portuguese American Leadership Council of the United States (PALCUS)
1316 Pennsylvania Ave. SE, Capitol Hill
Washington, DC 20003
Ph: (202)466-4664
Fax: (202)466-4661
E-mail: palcus@palcus.org
URL: http://www.palcus.org
Contact: Ms. Alda Petitti, Chair
Founded: 1991. **Members:** 314. **Membership Dues:** charter, $500 (annual) ● general, associate, $100 (annual) ● young Portuguese-American, $25 (annual). **Description:** Serves as national advocate and resource for the Portuguese community in the U.S. **Awards:** Scholarships. **Frequency:** annual. **Type:** scholarship. **Recipient:** for Portuguese-American high school students. **Computer Services:** database ● mailing lists. **Programs:** Internships; Judicial/Legal Exchange; Membership Referral; Membership Reward; National Endowment; On-line Mentoring. **Publications:** *LUSUS*, monthly. Newsletter. **Price:** included in membership dues. Alternate Formats: online. **Conventions/Meetings:** conference ● annual meeting.

18926 ■ Portuguese Historical and Cultural Society (PHCS)
PO Box 161990
Sacramento, CA 95816
Ph: (916)392-1048 (916)391-7356
E-mail: info@sacramentophcs.org
URL: http://www.sacramentophcs.com
Contact: Terri White, Pres.
Founded: 1979. **Members:** 380. **Membership Dues:** individual, $12 (annual) ● couple, $20 (annual) ● international, $15 (annual). **Staff:** 20. **Languages:** English, Portuguese. **Description:** Works to promote Portuguese history and culture. **Libraries: Type:** by appointment only. **Holdings:** 100; books. **Subjects:** Portuguese and Portugal. **Awards:** PHCS Scholarship. **Type:** scholarship. **Recipient:** for Portuguese descendants with a grade point of 3 or greater. **Publications:** *O Progresso* (in English and Portuguese), quarterly. Newsletter. Includes historical and genealogical articles. **Price:** included in membership dues. **Circulation:** 450 ● *Portuguese Pioneers of the Sacramento Area*. Book. **Conventions/Meetings:** monthly board meeting.

18927 ■ Portuguese Society Queen St. Isabel
3031 Telegraph Ave.
Oakland, CA 94609
Ph: (510)658-0983 (510)658-0985
Fax: (510)658-6517
Founded: 1898. **Members:** 10,000. **Staff:** 3. **Languages:** Portuguese. **Description:** Sponsors annual charity project. **Libraries: Type:** open to the public. **Holdings:** 100. **Subjects:** fraternal, cultural, and ethnic materials. **Awards: Frequency:** annual. **Type:** scholarship. **Publications:** *Boletim da SPRSI* (in English and Portuguese), quarterly. Magazine. Alternate Formats: diskette ● Newsletter (in English and Portuguese), monthly. **Price:** free. Alternate

Formats: diskette. **Conventions/Meetings:** annual convention and workshop.

Professions

18928 ■ Black Career Women (BCW)
PO Box 19332
Cincinnati, OH 45219-0332
Ph: (513)531-1932
Fax: (513)531-2166
E-mail: linda.parker@uc.edu
URL: http://www.bcw.org
Contact: Linda Bates Parker, Contact
Founded: 1977. **Membership Dues:** regular, $65 (annual). **Description:** African-American professional women. Promotes professional advancement of members; seeks to establish and support "formal Black women's networks". Provides career development resources and educational courses to members; develops information and research on Black women workers; serves as a "supportive forum for the Black woman dealing with the complexities of personal and professional development". **Publications:** Newsletter. **Price:** included in membership dues. Alternate Formats: online. **Conventions/Meetings:** annual Personal Time Off - retreat ● annual seminar and workshop.

18929 ■ National Association of the Professions (NAP)
Hillsboro Executive Center North
350 Fairway Dr., Ste.200
Deerfield Beach, FL 33441-1834
Ph: (954)571-1877
Free: (800)221-2168
Fax: (954)571-8582
E-mail: membership@assnservices.com
URL: http://www.nap-assn.com
Contact: Marisol Dioses, Membership Services Mgr.
Founded: 1968. **Members:** 40,000. **Membership Dues:** individual, $35 (annual) ● individual, $85 (triennial). **Description:** Provides individuals who are active in professions requiring an advanced career with economic benefits and financial services including the following: unsecured loan plans, mortgage loans, group insurance discounts, accounts receivable collections, office supplies, wealth protection, and vision and dental plan. **Publications:** *Association's Forum*, semiannual. Newsletter. **Advertising:** accepted. Alternate Formats: online.

Protestant

18930 ■ Ancient and Illustrious Order Knights of Malta (AIOK of M)
2632 Skylark Rd.
Wilmington, DE 19808-1634
Ph: (302)996-0800
Contact: Harry J. Murvin, Natl.Sec.
Founded: 1842. **Members:** 500. **State Groups:** 2. **Local Groups:** 12. **Description:** Fraternal order of Protestant men. **Libraries: Type:** open to the public. **Holdings:** articles, books. **Subjects:** history of Knights of Malta. **Awards:** Past Commander. **Frequency:** annual. **Type:** recognition. **Recipient:** for leadership ● Past Grand Commander. **Frequency:** annual. **Type:** recognition. **Recipient:** for leadership ● Past Supreme Commander. **Frequency:** annual. **Type:** recognition. **Recipient:** for leadership. **Formerly:** Knights of St. John of Jerusalem, Palestine, Rhodes. **Publications:** *Malta Bulletin*, quarterly. Newsletter. **Conventions/Meetings:** annual meeting - always third week of October.

Puerto Rican

18931 ■ Puerto Rican Studies Association (PRSA)
c/o Latino Studies Program
434 Rockefeller Hall
Cornell Univ.
Ithaca, NY 14853

E-mail: prsa@uiuc.edu
URL: http://www.puertorican-studies.org
Contact: Vilma Santiago-Irizarry, Pres.
Founded: 1992. **Members:** 300. **Membership Dues:** unemployed, emeritus, $10 (biennial) ● student, $10-$20 (biennial) ● regular (based on annual income), $35-$80 (biennial) ● life, $1,000. **Staff:** 3. **Budget:** $12,000. **Description:** Seeks to further Puerto Rican studies. Encourages interaction between individuals and groups from diverse regions, educational institutions, research organizations, community agencies, and individuals engaged in independent scholarly pursuits. **Publications:** *En La Brega*, semiannual. Newsletter. Alternate Formats: online. **Conventions/Meetings:** biennial conference.

Red Men

18932 ■ Degree of Pocahontas, Improved Order of Red Men
4521 Speight Ave.
Waco, TX 76711-1708
Ph: (254)756-1221
Free: (800)923-4287
Fax: (254)756-4828
E-mail: info@redmen.org
URL: http://www.redmen.org
Contact: Donald Routte, Sec.
Founded: 1885. **Members:** 7,154. **Staff:** 3. **State Groups:** 18. **Local Groups:** 145. **Description:** Serves as the ladies auxiliary of the Improved Order of Red Men, a national fraternal organization whose purpose is to inspire a greater love for the United States of America and the principles of American liberty through its members linked together in a common bond of brotherhood and friendship. Helps others through organized local and national charitable efforts directed to Alzheimer's research. **Libraries:** Type: open to the public; reference. **Holdings:** 4,000. **Subjects:** Texas history, Civil War, presidents. **Affiliated With:** Great Council of U.S. Improved Order of Red Men. **Publications:** *History of Improved Order of Red Men*. Book. **Price:** $15.00 ● *Red Men Magazine*, semiannual. **Conventions/Meetings:** biennial congress - always last weekend of September.

18933 ■ Great Council of U.S. Improved Order of Red Men
4521 Speight Ave.
Waco, TX 76711-1708
Ph: (254)756-1221
Free: (800)923-4287
Fax: (254)756-4828
E-mail: info@redmen.org
URL: http://www.redmen.org
Contact: Mr. Brad Buchanan, Sec.
Founded: 1765. **Members:** 14,841. **Staff:** 3. **State Groups:** 19. **Local Groups:** 181. **Description:** Aims to inspire a greater love for the United States of American and the principles of American liberty through its members linked together in a common bond of brotherhood and friendship and to help others through organized local charitable efforts with the national charitable effort directed to Alzheimer's research. Over one million dollars has been given to Alzheimer's research. **Libraries:** Type: reference. **Holdings:** 3,000. **Subjects:** Texas history, Civil War, presidents. **Committees:** Promotional Development. **Affiliated With:** Degree of Pocahontas, Improved Order of Red Men. **Publications:** *Red Men Magazine*, semiannual ● Also published an official history of the order. **Conventions/Meetings:** biennial Great Council Session - meeting - always September.

Refugees

18934 ■ Shelter For Life International (SFL)
502 E New York Ave.
Oshkosh, WI 54901
Ph: (920)426-1207
Free: (888)426-7979
Fax: (920)426-4321
URL: http://www.shelter.org
Contact: Randall Olson, Pres./CEO
Founded: 1979. **Description:** Strives to respond quickly and with compassion to those suffering as a result of conflict or natural disaster. **Formerly:** (2004) Shelter Now International.

Retirees

18935 ■ American Society of Retired Dentists (ASRD)
20283 State Rd. 7
Boca Raton, FL 33498-6901
Ph: (561)395-2773
Free: (800)495-ASRD
Fax: (561)395-2773
Contact: Dr. Harry Mackler, Pres.
Founded: 1981. **Members:** 1,000. **Membership Dues:** $30 (annual). **State Groups:** 12. **Description:** Retired and active dentists. Seeks to aid retired dentists in maintaining financial security; promotes continued social, cultural, and professional activity by retired dentists. Provides members with: opportunities to serve their communities; information on continuing education programs; assistance in maintaining good physical and mental health. Offers retirement and preretirement programs. Conducts charitable program. **Awards:** Type: recognition. **Publications:** *Directory of the American Society of Retired Dentists*, triennial ● *Postgraduate Newsletter*, monthly. **Conventions/Meetings:** annual conference (exhibits) ● luncheon and lecture.

Romanian

18936 ■ American Friends of Romania (AFROM)
PO Box 5884
Bethesda, MD 20824
Ph: (202)966-1922
Fax: (202)966-1922
E-mail: afromdc@yahoo.com
Contact: Peter Nicolae Nicholson, Exec. Dir.
Founded: 1990. **Description:** Fosters the relationship between the U.S. and Romania. Seeks to establish educational exchange programs and internships for Romanian professionals and students to travel to the U.S. to gain the experience needed in the on-going development of the Romanian free market economy. Seeks to foster dialogue between U.S. and Romanian citizens to help resolve common socio-economic problems. Sponsors economic, cultural, artistic, and other events designed to familiarize citizens with each country's heritage. **Convention/Meeting:** none. **Publications:** none. **Awards:** AFROM Romanian Young Visiting Scholar with GWU. **Frequency:** annual. **Type:** scholarship. **Recipient:** double selection: preliminary selection by a Romanian Educational Institution, final selection by GWU or AFROM.

18937 ■ Iuliu Maniu American Romanian Relief Foundation (IMF)
Address Unknown since 2007
Founded: 1952. **Members:** 100. **Membership Dues:** individual, $25 (annual). **Staff:** 3. **Languages:** English, Romanian. **Description:** Supports the care and education of refugee youth of Romanian descent. Aids older refugees who cannot earn a living in exile and helps Romanians with their integration into the American economy. Conducts research and charitable programs; preserves Romanian heritage. **Libraries:** Holdings: articles. **Subjects:** romanian national costumes and artifacts. **Awards:** Frequency: periodic. **Type:** grant. **Recipient:** Romanians in need. **Committees:** Cultural; Ethnography; Immigration and Integration. **Publications:** *Appeal to Members and Friends* (in English and Romanian), annual. Newsletter. Newsletter concerns fundraising. **Circulation:** 800. **Advertising:** not accepted. **Conventions/Meetings:** annual general assembly - always October; **Avg. Attendance:** 100.

18938 ■ Union and League of Romanian Societies (U&L)
7805 Brookpark Rd.
Parma, OH 44129-1111
Ph: (216)351-2094
Fax: (216)351-2094
E-mail: uleague@sbcglobal.net
URL: http://www.romaniansocieties.com
Contact: Daniela Istrate, Pres.
Founded: 1906. **Members:** 745. **Membership Dues:** regular, $25 (annual). **Staff:** 3. **State Groups:** 60. **Languages:** English, Romanian. **Description:** Serves as a cultural fraternal society. **Libraries:** Type: by appointment only. **Holdings:** periodicals. **Awards:** Frequency: annual. **Type:** recognition ● **Frequency:** annual. **Type:** scholarship. **Recipient:** for qualified student members. **Formerly:** (2003) Union and League of Romanian Societies of America. **Publications:** *America Almanac*, annual. **Advertising:** accepted ● *America Romanian News*, monthly. Newspaper. Contains society news, announcements of cultural activities, and news of events in Romania; includes obituaries and meeting notices. **Price:** $18.00 /year for members; $21.00 /year for nonmembers. **Circulation:** 850. **Advertising:** accepted. **Conventions/Meetings:** biennial congress.

Romany

18939 ■ Roma National Congress (RNC)
PO Box 822
Manchaca, TX 78652
Ph: (512)295-4858
E-mail: xulaj@mail.utexas.edu
URL: http://www.romanationalcongress.org
Contact: Rudko Kawczynsi, Contact
Founded: 1979. **Members:** 32. **Languages:** English, French, German, Hungarian, Italian. **Description:** National associations of ethnic minority groups representing 12,000,000 Roma (also known as Romanies or Gypsies). Works to foster unity among members. Promotes human rights and obligations. Advocates protection and preservation of Romani culture and language. Plans to establish museum. Maintains NGO status with the United Nations Children's Fund and the United Nations Economic and Social Council. **Libraries:** Type: open to the public. **Holdings:** 5,000. **Subjects:** Romani culture and language. **Absorbed:** Romani Congress. **Also Known As:** Romano Internacionaino Jekhethanibe. **Publications:** *Buhazi*, quarterly ● *The Geneva Principles* ● *Lacio Drom*, bimonthly ● *Nevipens Romani*, biweekly ● *Romano Nevipen*, monthly ● *Rrom po Drom*, monthly ● *SCHAROTL*, quarterly. Newspaper. Provides information on Swiss nomads. **Conventions/Meetings:** quadrennial World Congress.

Rosicrucian

18940 ■ Rosicrucian Fraternity (RF)
PO Box 220
Quakertown, PA 18951
Ph: (215)536-7048
Free: (800)779-3796
Fax: (215)536-7058
E-mail: bevhall@comcast.net
URL: http://www.soul.org
Contact: Rev.Dr. Gerald E. Poesnecker, Counselor
Founded: 1858. **Staff:** 14. **Regional Groups:** 6. **Languages:** English, Spanish. **Description:** United States descendant of Rosicrucian Fraternity originally founded in Germany in 1614. **Libraries:** Type: reference. **Holdings:** 10,000; books. **Also Known As:** Fraternitas Rosae Crucis. **Conventions/Meetings:** monthly meeting - always in Quakertown, PA.

18941 ■ Rosicrucian Order, AMORC English Grand Lodge (AMORC)
1342 Naglee Ave.
Rosicrucian Park
San Jose, CA 95126-2007
Ph: (408)947-3600
Free: (888)767-2278

Fax: (408)947-3677
URL: http://www.rosicrucian.org
Contact: Julie Scott, Grandmaster/Pres./CEO
Founded: 1915. **Members:** 7,800. **Staff:** 42. **Regional Groups:** 100. **Description:** International philosophical organization. Sponsors the Rosicrucian Egyptian Museum; the Rosicrucian Planetarium; research library; Rosicrucian Peace Garden. **Additional Websites:** http://www.amorc.org. **Also Known As:** Ancient Mystical Order Rosae Crucis. **Formerly:** (1991) Rosicrucian Order. **Publications:** *Rosicrucian Digest* (in Dutch, English, French, German, Japanese, Portuguese, Spanish, and Swedish), quarterly. Magazine. Features updated articles on mysticism, philosophy, arts, and sciences. **Price:** included in membership dues. ISSN: 0035-8339. **Circulation:** 50,000. Alternate Formats: online. **Conventions/Meetings:** biennial meeting.

Russian

18942 ■ Congress of Russian Americans (CRA)
2460 Sutter St.
San Francisco, CA 94115
Ph: (415)928-5841
Fax: (415)928-5831
E-mail: crahq@earthlink.net
URL: http://www.russian-americans.org
Contact: George B. Avisov, Pres.
Founded: 1972. **Members:** 6,500. **Membership Dues:** individual, $40 (annual) ● student and retiree, $15 (annual). **Staff:** 2. **Budget:** $100,000. **State Groups:** 10. **Languages:** English, Russian. **Description:** Americans of Russian descent. Seeks to preserve and promote Russian cultural heritage and to protect the legal, economic, and social interests of Russian-Americans. Operates National Human Rights Committee, which worked for the release of political prisoners in the former Soviet Union. Worked on behalf of Igor Ogurtsov, a dissident who spent 20 years in a Soviet prison and was released in 1987. Distributes aid to individuals and organizations in Russia. Informs Congress; disseminates information. Maintains hall of fame. Operates an office in Washington, DC. **Libraries: Type:** reference. **Holdings:** archival material. **Awards:** The Russian-American Hall of Fame Member. **Frequency:** periodic. **Type:** recognition. **Recipient:** for contribution to U.S. science, arts, social, etc ● **Frequency:** semiannual. **Type:** scholarship. **Committees:** Aid to Needy; Civil Rights; Cultural-Educational; Ethnic Heritage Study; Human Rights; Humanitarian; Publications; Scholarships in Russia. **Publications:** *CRA News* (in English and Russian), quarterly. Newsletter. Bilingual newsletter covering CRA activities. **Price:** included in membership dues. **Circulation:** 8,000 ● *The Russian American*, every 1-2 years. Journal. Summarizes CRA activities in the past year or two; covers Russian-American heritage; bilingual. **Price:** $10.00 plus shipping and handling. **Circulation:** 6,500. **Conventions/Meetings:** triennial conference (exhibits) - usually Memorial Day weekend ● Legislative Convention.

18943 ■ Lemko Association of U.S. and Canada (LA)
c/o Alexander Herenchak, Pres.
PO Box 156
Allentown, NJ 08501
Ph: (609)758-1115
Fax: (609)758-7301
E-mail: herenchak@yahoo.com
URL: http://www.lemko.org/lih/lemkorg.html
Contact: Alexander Herenchak, Pres.
Founded: 1929. **Members:** 800. **Membership Dues:** individual, $10 (annual). **Staff:** 2. **Regional Groups:** 2. **Local Groups:** 10. **Description:** Serves as Carpatho-Russian cultural organization. **Committees:** Festival; Lemko Relief; Talerhof Chapel. **Publications:** *Karpatska Rus* (in English and Russian), biweekly. Newspaper. **Price:** $20.00/year. **Circulation:** 800. **Advertising:** accepted. **Conventions/Meetings:** biennial convention.

18944 ■ Orthodox Society of America (OSA)
29510 Lorain Rd.
North Olmsted, OH 44070-3909
Ph: (440)716-2360
Free: (800)420-1470
Fax: (440)716-1990
E-mail: zubaw@lcba.com
URL: http://www.lcba.com/about/aboutosa.htm
Contact: Wanda Zuba, Contact
Founded: 1915. **Members:** 3,900. **Staff:** 3. **Local Groups:** 29. **Description:** Fraternal benefit life insurance society. **Libraries: Type:** open to the public. **Holdings:** 40. **Awards:** George G. Lichvarik. **Frequency:** annual. **Type:** scholarship. **Recipient:** for students entering college ● Outstanding Young Citizen. **Frequency:** annual. **Type:** grant. **Recipient:** for students entering high school ● Trustee Awards. **Frequency:** annual. **Type:** scholarship. **Recipient:** for students entering an accredited post-graduate or technical school. **Computer Services:** database ● mailing lists ● online services. **Telecommunication Services:** additional toll-free number, (888)230-5222. **Formerly:** (1992) United Russian Orthodox Brotherhood of America. **Publications:** *OSA Messenger*, quarterly. Magazine. **Price:** $3.00. ISSN: 1645-978X. **Circulation:** 2,000. **Conventions/Meetings:** quadrennial meeting (exhibits) - usually October.

18945 ■ Russian Brotherhood Organization of the U.S.A. (RBOUSA)
1733 Spring Garden St.
Philadelphia, PA 19130
Ph: (215)563-2537
Free: (800)726-8721
Fax: (215)563-8106
E-mail: info@rbo.org
URL: http://www.rbo.org
Contact: John Wanko, Pres.
Founded: 1900. **Members:** 7,832. **Staff:** 15. **State Groups:** 5. **Local Groups:** 315. **Description:** Fraternal benefit life insurance society for persons of Russian or Slavic descent. **Awards:** Saints Cyril and Methodius Scholarship. **Frequency:** annual. **Type:** scholarship. **Recipient:** for members. **Publications:** *The Truth*, monthly. Newspaper. Covers news of interest to those of Russian or Slavic descent, with emphasis on the Orthodox church. **Price:** $3.50/year. ISSN: 0041-3690. **Circulation:** 3,600. **Advertising:** accepted. **Conventions/Meetings:** quadrennial conference (exhibits).

18946 ■ Russian Orthodox Catholic Mutual Aid Society of U.S.A. (ROCMAS)
10 Downs Dr.
Wilkes-Barre, PA 18705-3802
Ph: (570)822-8591
Free: (877)4-ROCMAS
Fax: (570)821-7060
E-mail: rocmas@rocmas.org
URL: http://www.rocmas.org
Contact: Bernard Golubiewski, Sec.
Founded: 1895. **Members:** 1,510. **Budget:** $160,000. **Local Groups:** 147. **Description:** Fraternal benefit life insurance society. **Publications:** *Svit*, bimonthly. Also Cited As: *The Light*. **Conventions/Meetings:** quadrennial meeting.

18947 ■ Tolstoy Foundation (TF)
PO Box 578
Valley Cottage, NY 10989
Ph: (845)268-6722
Fax: (845)268-6937
E-mail: info@tolstoyfoundation.org
URL: http://www.tolstoyfoundation.org
Contact: Victoria Wohlsen, Exec. Dir./CEO
Founded: 1939. **Staff:** 50. **Budget:** $3,000,000. **Regional Groups:** 6. **Languages:** English, Russian. **Description:** Focuses on building self-reliance and enhancing opportunities among gifted orphaned and disadvantaged children in Russia and other countries of the former Soviet Union. Preserves the cultural tradition, the heritage and the resources of the Russian Diaspora and operates a nursing home. **Libraries: Type:** reference. **Holdings:** 50,000; books. **Subjects:** Russian language, student manuals. **Divisions:** Libraries; Overseas Operations; Russian

Language School; Supplemental Social Service. **Programs:** Orphan Children. **Affiliated With:** CARE International USA; Interaction/American Council for Voluntary International Action. **Publications:** Newsletter, periodic. **Conventions/Meetings:** annual meeting - usually spring, New York City.

Scandinavian

18948 ■ Augustana Historical Society (AHS)
Augustana Coll.
639 38th St.
Rock Island, IL 61201-2296
Ph: (309)794-7000
Free: (800)798-8100
URL: http://www.augustana.edu/Historical
Contact: Lars Scott, Pres.
Founded: 1930. **Members:** 200. **Membership Dues:** student, $5 (annual) ● single/family, $20 (annual) ● life, $200. **Description:** Conducts research and disseminates material on the history of Augustana College, Augustana Lutheran Church, and the Swedish immigrant founders of these institutions. **Absorbed:** Augustana Swedish Institute. **Publications:** *Augustana Historical Society Publications*, irregular. **Price:** included in membership dues. ISSN: 0897-9758. **Circulation:** 225.

18949 ■ Independent Order of Svithiod (IOS)
5518 W Lawrence Ave.
Chicago, IL 60630
Ph: (773)736-1191
E-mail: info@svithiod.org
URL: http://www.svithiod.org
Contact: Caryn Bean, Pres.
Founded: 1880. **Members:** 1,200. **Staff:** 2. **Local Groups:** 12. **Description:** Fraternal society for men and women of Scandinavian birth or extraction and their spouses. Offers children's services; operates charitable program for members in need. Compiles statistics. Offers scholarships to deserving student members. **Awards: Frequency:** annual. **Type:** recognition ● **Type:** scholarship. **Recipient:** to student members. **Publications:** *Svithiod Journal*, monthly. Newsletter. Covers membership activities. Lists scholarship and award recipients; includes obituaries and statistics. **Price:** included in membership dues. ISSN: 0300-6212. **Circulation:** 1,200. **Conventions/Meetings:** biennial conference.

Scholarship Alumni

18950 ■ Association of American Rhodes Scholars (AARS)
8229 Boone Blvd., Ste.240
Vienna, VA 22182
E-mail: webmaster@americanrhodes.org
URL: http://www.americanrhodes.org
Contact: Stewart Early, Pres.
Founded: 1907. **Members:** 2,100. **Membership Dues:** regular, $50 (annual) ● individual (who has come down from Oxford within the past 5 years), $25 (annual). **Staff:** 1. **Description:** Rhodes scholars living in the U.S., or elected to their scholarships from the U.S. Holds class reunions and regional reunions in the United States and Oxford, England. **Committees:** Aydelotte-Kieffer-Smith Book Fund; Bon Voyage; Development; Investment Management; Reunions and Events. **Publications:** *American Oxonian*, quarterly. Journal. **Price:** $35.00/year ● *The American Rhodes Scholar*, annual. Newsletter.

18951 ■ International Alumni Association of Shri Mahavir Jain Vidyalaya (IAAMJV)
1119 Flanders St.
Garner, NC 27529
Ph: (919)772-8473
Fax: (919)772-8473
E-mail: rameshfofaria@hotmail.com
URL: http://www.iaamjv.org
Contact: Ramesh G. Fofaria, Pres.
Founded: 1991. **Members:** 450. **Multinational. Description:** Promotes the cause of professional educa-

tion in the Jain community. Offers loan scholarship programs aimed at helping Jain students and graduates. Provides social, cultural and religious support to its members. **Awards:** College Education Loan Scholarships. **Frequency:** periodic. **Type:** scholarship. **Recipient:** for U.S. resident students ● Graduate Education Loan Scholarship. **Frequency:** periodic. **Type:** scholarship. **Recipient:** for Indian graduate students in the U.S. ● Undergraduate Education Loan Scholarships in India. **Frequency:** periodic. **Type:** scholarship. **Recipient:** for Indian undergraduate students. **Publications:** Newsletter. Alternate Formats: online.

Scottish

18952 ■ American Scottish Foundation (ASF)
575 Madison Ave., Ste.1006
New York, NY 10022-2511
Ph: (212)605-0338
Fax: (212)605-0222
E-mail: asf@wwbcny.com
URL: http://www.americanscottishfoundation.com
Contact: Alan L. Bain, Pres.
Founded: 1956. **Members:** 3,001. **Membership Dues:** individual, $75 (annual) ● household, $125 (annual) ● donor, $250 (annual) ● sponsor, $500 (annual) ● patron, $750 (annual) ● benefactor, $1,000 (annual) ● senior/student/overseas, $50 (annual). **Budget:** $25,000. **Description:** Americans of Scottish descent and Scots living in the U.S. Aims to build new bonds of friendship and cooperation between the Scottish and American people. Preserves the Scottish heritage. Strengthens the Scottish economy. Brings into one general national association as large a percentage as possible of the more than 22 million Americans of Scottish descent. Raises funds for social charities; established Scotland House in New York City as the cultural, social, hospitality, and information center for Scotland in the U.S. and headquarters for the members of the foundation. Sponsors annual Scottish Ball. **Awards:** Wallace Award. **Frequency:** annual. **Type:** recognition. **Recipient:** for Americans of Scottish descent who have made outstanding contributions to the U.S. **Conventions/Meetings:** periodic meeting ● annual Scottish Studies - meeting and conference.

18953 ■ Association of Scottish Games and Festivals (ASGF)
c/o Roberta M. Goss, Treas.
3000 Walnut Ave.
Altoona, PA 16601-1612
Ph: (814)942-0077
E-mail: robertalhg@aol.com
URL: http://www.asgf.org
Contact: Roberta M. Goss, Treas.
Founded: 1981. **Members:** 90. **Membership Dues:** regular, $125 (annual). **Staff:** 5. **Regional Groups:** 2. **Description:** Groups that conduct Highland Games competitions in the U.S. (Highland Games, which originated in Scotland, are arranged in a manner similar to that of the Olympics; contested events include footraces and caber throwing.) Serves as a forum for the exchange of information among members; seeks to ensure that Highland Games in the U.S. are of high quality. Compiles statistics; also bag pipe band performances and competitions Highland dancing, Scottish clan gatherings, Scottish fair offers imported goods and foods, entertainment. **Computer Services:** database, schedule of Highland Games to be held in the U.S. **Boards:** Executive. **Publications:** Newsletter, quarterly. **Price:** free for members. **Circulation:** 220. **Conventions/Meetings:** annual general assembly (exhibits) - Eastern meeting always December, Alexandria, VA; Western meeting date to be announced.

18954 ■ Council of Scottish Clans and Associations (COSCA)
PO Box 2828
Moultrie, GA 31776-2828
Ph: (229)985-6540
Fax: (229)985-0936

E-mail: secretary@cocsa.net
URL: http://www.cosca.net
Contact: Christie Harrison, Pres.
Founded: 1974. **Members:** 170. **Membership Dues:** organization, $25 (annual). **National Groups:** 170. **Description:** Scottish clan societies and family associations; other Scottish organizations. Acts as referral service for persons seeking information on clan affiliations; aids in the formation of clan societies and family associations. Maintains computerized listings of Scottish clans and family organizations active in the U.S. **Awards:** Ethel MacNeal Harp Scholarship. **Frequency:** annual. **Type:** monetary ● Herbert MacNeal Distinguished Service Award. **Type:** recognition. **Committees:** Charitable; Educational; Fundraising and Development. **Formerly:** (1987) Council of Scottish Clan Associations. **Publications:** The Claymore, quarterly. Newsletter. Contains news pertaining to the Council. **Circulation:** 1,000. Alternate Formats: online. **Conventions/Meetings:** annual meeting, business meeting - Saturday after 4th of July, in Lincoln, NC.

18955 ■ Daughters of Scotia (DOS)
7595 Carter Rd.
Sagamore Hills, OH 44067
Ph: (330)467-6387
Fax: (330)724-9307
E-mail: mlloyd@nauticom.net
URL: http://www.daughtersofscotia.org
Contact: Mrs. Mary Lloyd Klein, Grand Recording Sec.
Founded: 1895. **Members:** 4,000. **Local Groups:** 49. **Description:** Women of Scottish descent or birth. Contributes to arthritis, Alzheimer's, multiple sclerosis, cancer, diabetes, and heart research programs, and various other charities. **Publications:** Scotia News, quarterly. Newsletter. **Conventions/Meetings:** annual convention - 4-days, always third Monday of September.

18956 ■ International Association for Tartan Studies (IATS)
PO Box 138
Skippack, PA 19474
Ph: (610)584-4220
Fax: (610)584-6456
Founded: 1984. **Members:** 200. **Membership Dues:** individual, $25 (annual) ● family, $35 (annual) ● clan or association, $45 (annual) ● corporate or sponsoring, $100 (annual) ● life, $250. **Staff:** 1. **Languages:** English, French, Portuguese, Spanish. **Description:** Scholars, students, and other individuals interested in the preservation and design of tartan and other Scottish traditions. (Tartan is a checkered textile of Scottish origin, whose pattern is used to designate clan affiliation, geographic area, organization or school affiliation or commercial "trademark"). Serves as an information clearinghouse on the use and application of tartan in kilts and other Scottish garments. A member of the Council of Scottish Clans and Associations. Dual membership with the Scottish Tartans Authority, 51 Antholl St., Pitlochry, Scotland. **Libraries: Type:** reference. **Holdings:** 100; artwork, books. **Subjects:** Scottish Tartan or Dress. **Computer Services:** database, computer-generated, full-color pictures of tartans, color printouts. **Affiliated With:** Council of Scottish Clans and Associations. **Also Known As:** Tartan Educational and Cultural Association, Inc. **Publications:** The Tartan Banner, semiannual. Newsletter. Includes articles on research and technical concerns. **Price:** included in membership dues. **Conventions/Meetings:** annual meeting ● periodic seminar, with Tartan and Scottish dress (exhibits) - 3rd Friday of October.

18957 ■ Saint Andrew's Society of the State of New York
150 E 55th St., Ste.3
New York, NY 10022
Ph: (212)223-4248
Fax: (212)223-0748
E-mail: office@standrewsny.org
URL: http://www.standrewsny.org
Contact: Brigid Franklin, Office Mgr.
Founded: 1756. **Members:** 1,100. **Membership Dues:** individual (ages 21-34), $50 (annual) ●

individual (ages 35-64), $75 (annual) ● individual (ages 65 and above), $50 (annual) ● life, $1,350. **Staff:** 1. **Budget:** $140,000. **Description:** Persons of Scottish birth or descent. **Libraries: Type:** reference. **Holdings:** 1,200. **Subjects:** Scotland. **Awards: Frequency:** annual. **Type:** scholarship. **Recipient:** for graduate study ● Scholarships. **Frequency:** annual. **Type:** recognition. **Publications:** The Pibroch, semiannual ● Membership Directory, quinquennial. **Conventions/Meetings:** semiannual meeting - always May and November in New York, NY.

18958 ■ Scottish Heritage U.S.A. (SHUSA)
PO Box 457
Pinehurst, NC 28370
Ph: (910)295-4448
Fax: (910)295-3147
E-mail: shusa@pinehurst.net
URL: http://www.scottishheritageusa.org
Contact: Rev. Douglas F. Kelly, Pres.
Founded: 1965. **Members:** 1,000. **Membership Dues:** senior, $25 (annual). **Staff:** 2. **Description:** Individuals, clan societies, foundations, and corporations. Aims to "recognize and enhance the original bonds of ancestral and national character among the peoples of Scotland and the United States." Works in cooperation with the National Trust for Scotland in a continuing interchange of information, experience, and ideas. Emphasizes on the exchange of people and ideas between Scotland and the U.S. Exchange projects have involved horticulture, conservation, forestry, parks, art, and architecture. **Libraries: Type:** reference. **Holdings:** 200; books. **Subjects:** Scotland, history and travel. **Awards:** Ward Melville Award. **Type:** recognition. **Recipient:** for excellence in volunteer support. **Publications:** Scottish Heritage USA Newsletter, quarterly. **Circulation:** 1,000 ● Pamphlet. **Conventions/Meetings:** semiannual meeting.

Serbian

18959 ■ Serb National Federation (SNF)
One 5th Ave., 7th Fl.
Pittsburgh, PA 15222
Ph: (412)642-7372
Free: (800)538-SERB
Fax: (412)642-1372
E-mail: snf@serbnatlfed.org
URL: http://www.serbnatlfed.org
Contact: Dr. Daniel J. Pyevich, Pres.
Founded: 1901. **Members:** 15,200. **Staff:** 10. **Description:** Serves as a fraternal benefit life insurance society. **Publications:** The American Srbobran, weekly. Newspaper. **Price:** $30.00 for members; $60.00 for nonmembers ● American Srbobran Index 1906-1926 ● Bukvar ● Landmarks in Serbian Culture and History. **Conventions/Meetings:** quadrennial conference.

18960 ■ Serbian National Defense Council of America (SNDC)
5782 N Elston Ave.
Chicago, IL 60646-5546
Ph: (773)775-7772
Fax: (773)775-7779
E-mail: info@snd-us.com
URL: http://www.snd-us.com
Contact: Slavko B. Panovic, Pres.
Founded: 1914. **Description:** Promotes appreciation of Serbian culture and history. Conducts charitable, humanitarian, and religious activities. **Publications:** Sloboda, bimonthly. Newspaper. Alternate Formats: online. Also Cited As: Liberty.

Sicilian

18961 ■ Arba Sicula (AS)
St. John's Univ.
Languages & Literature Dept.
Jamaica, NY 11439
Ph: (718)990-5203
Fax: (718)990-5954

E-mail: cipollag@stjohns.edu
URL: http://www.arbasicula.org
Contact: Prof. Gaetano Cipolla, Pres.
Founded: 1979. **Members:** 2,500. **Membership Dues:** senior, student, $20 (annual) ● regular, foreign, $25 (annual). **Staff:** 5. **State Groups:** 4. **Local Groups:** 2. **Languages:** English, Sicilian. **Multinational. Description:** Persons with an interest in Sicilian culture. Seeks to create a Sicilian ethnic and cultural society for the support and study of the Sicilian language, literature, history, and customs; and to instill and impress social and community consciousness of ethnic heritage. (The name Arba Sicula is translated as "Sicilian Dawn.") Sponsors Sicilian language festivals which include poetry, music, and song. Plans to teach a Sicilian language course in conjunction with St. John's University. Conducts research programs. Sponsors Speaker's Bureau and educational programs. **Libraries: Type:** not open to the public. **Holdings:** 23. **Publications:** *Sicilia Parra*, semiannual. Newsletter. Includes book reviews and poetry. **Price:** included in membership dues. ISSN: 8755-6987. **Circulation:** 2,500. **Advertising:** accepted ● Journal (in English and Sicilian), semiannual. Includes poetry, narratives, language studies, book reviews, art, and history. **Price:** $20.00. ISSN: 0271-0730. **Circulation:** 2,500. **Advertising:** accepted ● Also publishes historical research results, dictionary of translations, grammar, and phrases, and many books on Sicilian culture, history, poetry, language and traditions. **Conventions/Meetings:** annual conference.

Slavic

18962 ■ National Slavic Convention (NSC)
c/o Slavic American National Convention
603 S Ann St.
Baltimore, MD 21221
Ph: (410)276-7676 (410)342-7200
Fax: (410)276-1233
URL: http://www.slavicorganization.com
Contact: Rev. Ivan D. Dornic, Pres.
Founded: 1973. **Members:** 120,000. **Membership Dues:** individual, $10 (annual). **Staff:** 3. **Budget:** $1,000,000. **Regional Groups:** 24. **State Groups:** 24. **Local Groups:** 57. **National Groups:** 5. **Languages:** Croatian, Czech, English, Polish, Russian, Serbian, Slovak, Ukrainian. **Description:** Individuals and organizations of persons of East European, particularly Slavic descent. Seeks to coordinate efforts of various organizations to help individuals with legal, social, economic, educational, and health problems. Conducts specialized education programs. Maintains placement service and charitable program; operates museum. **Libraries: Type:** reference. **Holdings:** 10,000. **Subjects:** Slavic. **Awards:** Slavic OROL. **Frequency:** annual. **Type:** recognition. **Recipient:** for outstanding performance in business, education, arts, and literature. **Councils:** Regional and National. **Formerly:** (1984) Ethnic American Coalition (of Eastern Europeans). **Publications:** *American Slavic Report*, monthly. **Price:** $10.00. **Circulation:** 100,000. **Advertising:** accepted. **Conventions/Meetings:** quadrennial seminar (exhibits) ● triennial Slavic Convention (exhibits).

Slovak

18963 ■ First Catholic Slovak Ladies Association (FCSLA)
24950 Chagrin Blvd.
Beachwood, OH 44122-5634
Ph: (216)464-8015
Free: (800)464-4642
Fax: (216)464-9260
E-mail: info@fcsla.com
URL: http://www.fcsla.com
Contact: Mary Ann S. Johanek, Natl. Pres.
Founded: 1892. **Members:** 76,000. **Staff:** 25. **Regional Groups:** 10. **Local Groups:** 500. **Description:** Serves as a fraternal benefit society selling life insurance and annuities. **Awards: Frequency:** an-

nual. **Type:** scholarship. **Recipient:** for students. **Publications:** *Fraternally Yours*, monthly. Magazine. **Price:** $6.00 /year for nonmembers. **Circulation:** 32,000. **Conventions/Meetings:** quadrennial meeting.

18964 ■ First Catholic Slovak Union of the U.S.A. and Canada (FCSU)
6611 Rockside Rd.
Independence, OH 44131
Ph: (216)642-9406
Free: (800)JED-NOTA
Fax: (216)642-4310
E-mail: fcsu@aol.com
URL: http://www.fcsu.com
Contact: Andrew M. Rajec, Pres.
Founded: 1890. **Members:** 69,000. **Staff:** 15. **Budget:** $50,000. **State Groups:** 18. **Local Groups:** 60. **Description:** Serves as a fraternal benefit life insurance society for Catholic Americans of Slovak descent. Conducts field seminars; sponsors competitions and children's services. Operates museum. **Awards: Type:** recognition. **Also Known As:** Prva Katolicka Slovenska Jednota. **Publications:** *First Catholic Slovak Union*, triennial. Directory ● *Jednota* (in English and Slovak), biweekly. Newspaper. **Price:** included in membership dues; $25.00 for nonmembers in U.S.; $30.00 for nonmembers outside U.S. ● Books. **Conventions/Meetings:** triennial meeting.

18965 ■ National Slovak Society of the United States of America (NSS)
351 Valley Brook Rd.
McMurray, PA 15317-3337
Ph: (724)731-0094
Free: (800)488-1890
Fax: (724)731-0145
E-mail: dblazek@nsslife.org
URL: http://www.nsslife.org
Contact: David G. Blazek FIC, Pres.
Founded: 1890. **Members:** 22,000. **Staff:** 10. **Budget:** $580,000. **Regional Groups:** 15. **Local Groups:** 118. **Languages:** English, Slovak. **Description:** Fraternal benefit life insurance society for men and women of Slovak descent and their families in the United States. Offers aid to orphans, widows, the aged, and disabled persons. Sponsors athletic and cultural programs. Conducts research in cooperation with university and college students. Maintains Slovak hall of fame. **Libraries: Type:** open to the public. **Holdings:** 1,000. **Subjects:** Slovak history, culture, and literature. **Awards:** Peter Vitazoslav Rovnianek Scholarship Fund. **Frequency:** annual. **Type:** scholarship. **Recipient:** for young members who will attend college or trade school ● **Frequency:** annual. **Type:** scholarship. **Recipient:** for senior members who are interested in continuing their intellectual growth. **Publications:** *Kalandar* (in English and Slovak), annual. Yearbook. Almanac. **Price:** $10.00 plus shipping and handling ● *Narodne Noviny* (in English and Slovak), monthly. Newspaper. Price free for members. Also Cited As: *National News* ● *Youth Circle*, quarterly. Magazine. **Conventions/Meetings:** quadrennial convention.

18966 ■ Slovak Catholic Federation (SCF)
c/o Rev. Philip A. Altavilla, Natl. Pres.
408 N Main St.
Taylor, PA 18517-1108
Ph: (570)698-5584 (570)947-1196
Fax: (570)698-8468
E-mail: frfrosty@intiques.com
URL: http://www.slovakcatholicfederation.org
Contact: Rev. Philip A. Altavilla, Natl. Pres.
Founded: 1911. **Members:** 900. **Membership Dues:** individual, $10 (annual) ● church, $50 (annual) ● fraternal branch, $35 (annual). **Staff:** 2. **Budget:** $80,000. **Regional Groups:** 5. **Languages:** English, Slovak. **Description:** Federating and connecting parishes, societies, fraternal organizations, religious communities, and individuals within the U.S. by encouraging pride and knowledge in the Catholic faith tradition and Slovak ethnic heritage. Sponsors pilgrimages. **Libraries: Type:** not open to the public. **Holdings:** articles, books. **Subjects:** Slovakia, listing of all Slovak parishes, clubs, Slovak clergy. **Awards:**

Frequency: quadrennial. **Type:** recognition. **Recipient:** for defense of faith, morals, and advancement of the Slovak people. **Computer Services:** database ● mailing lists. **Formerly:** (1975) Slovak Catholic Federation of America. **Publications:** *Dobry Pastier/ The Good Shepherd* (in English and Slovak), annual. **Circulation:** 900. Also Cited As: *Good Shepherd* ● *The Good Shepherd*, annual. Book. Contains articles by Slovak/Americans or Slovak/Canadians on topics of interest to readers of Slovak heritage. **Price:** free, for members only. **Circulation:** 900. Alternate Formats: CD-ROM ● Also publishes other literature for Americans of Slovak descent and Catholic faith tradition. **Conventions/Meetings:** semiannual conference and board meeting, for representatives of various religious orders, fraternal organizations; to discuss problems, plan pilgrimages - spring and fall ● quadrennial meeting ● seminar, pastoral seminars.

18967 ■ Slovak Catholic Sokol (SCS)
PO Box 899
205 Madison St.
Passaic, NJ 07055
Free: (800)886-7656
Fax: (973)779-8245
E-mail: life@slovakcatholicsokol.org
URL: http://www.slovakcatholicsokol.org
Contact: Steven M. Pogorelec, Supreme Sec.
Founded: 1905. **Members:** 31,000. **Staff:** 11. **Budget:** $4,000,000. **Regional Groups:** 155. **State Groups:** 10. **National Groups:** 19. **Description:** Americans of Slovak or Slav descent. Sponsors gymnastic and athletic activities, including a biennial national track and field meet. Sponsors Junior Slovak Catholic Sokol groups for children. **Libraries: Type:** reference. **Holdings:** 10,000. **Awards:** Slovak Catholic Sokol Scholarship Grant Awards. **Frequency:** annual. **Type:** grant. **Publications:** *Slovak Catholic Falcon* (in English and Slovak), weekly. Newspaper. Contains member news and activities. **Price:** free for members; $30.00 for nonmembers in U.S.; $35.00 for nonmembers outside U.S. ● *Slovak Catholic Sokol Cook Book*. **Conventions/Meetings:** quadrennial meeting.

18968 ■ Slovak League of America (SLA)
205 Madison St.
Passaic, NJ 07055
Ph: (973)472-8993
Fax: (973)669-8483
Contact: Nina W. Holy, Sec.-Treas.
Founded: 1907. **Members:** 5,000. **Membership Dues:** organization, society, individual, $10 (annual) ● life, $200. **Regional Groups:** 3. **Local Groups:** 50. **Languages:** English, Slovak. **Description:** Serves as a cultural and civic federation of Slovak-American organizations representing 500,000 individuals. Supports Slovakia, the oldest Christian nation in Central Europe; promotes a better understanding and appreciation of the Slovak nation, its history, culture, traditions, and desires. Increases mutual appreciation between America and Slovakia in the interests of world peace, freedom, and security. Sponsors scholarship program. **Committees:** Civic; Cultural; Scholarship; Youth. **Publications:** *Slovakia*, annual. **Price:** $10.00. **Circulation:** 1,200. **Conventions/Meetings:** biennial convention, ethnic and cultural ● biennial regional meeting.

18969 ■ SOKOL U.S.A.
PO Box 189
East Orange, NJ 07019-0189
Ph: (973)676-0280
Free: (888)253-0362
Fax: (973)676-3348
E-mail: sokolusahqs@aol.com
URL: http://www.sokolusa.com
Contact: Milan S. Kovac, Supreme Sec.
Founded: 1896. **Members:** 12,000. **Staff:** 5. **Regional Groups:** 13. **Local Groups:** 95. **Languages:** English, Slovak. **Description:** Serves as a fraternal benefit life insurance society. Promotes physical fitness through gymnastic competitions and exhibitions. Maintains camps and halls in several states. **Awards:** Milan Getting Scholarship. **Frequency:** annual. **Type:** scholarship. **Recipient:** for members who are further-

ing their education in a four-year college or university. **Also Known As:** Slovak Gymnastic Union Sokol of the U.S.A. **Publications:** *Sokol Times* (in English and Slovak), monthly, every second Thursday. Provides updated information on current activities and traditions. **Conventions/Meetings:** quadrennial meeting.

Slovenian

18970 ■ American Mutual Life Association (AMLA)
19424 S Waterloo Rd.
Cleveland, OH 44119
Ph: (216)531-1900
Fax: (216)531-8123
E-mail: amla@americanmutual.org
URL: http://www.americanmutual.org
Contact: Albert R. Amigoni, Pres.
Founded: 1910. **Members:** 16,805. **Local Groups:** 45. **Description:** Fraternal benefit life insurance society. Maintains recreation center. **Awards: Type:** scholarship. **Formerly:** (1966) Slovenian Mutual Benefit Association. **Publications:** *Our Voice*, biweekly. Newsletter. **Conventions/Meetings:** quadrennial meeting.

18971 ■ Slovene National Benefit Society (SNPJ)
247 W Allegheny Rd.
Imperial, PA 15126-9774
Ph: (724)695-1100
Free: (800)843-7675
Fax: (724)695-1555
E-mail: snpj@snpj.com
URL: http://www.snpj.com
Contact: Mr. Joseph C. Evanish, Pres.
Founded: 1904. **Members:** 40,000. **Staff:** 30. **Regional Groups:** 14. **Local Groups:** 293. **Description:** Serves as fraternal benefit life insurance society. Maintains scholarship fund, museum, juvenile department, youth circles, and youth and young adult programs. Sponsors sports and team activities. Owns and operates SNPJ Recreation Center and Ethnic Heritage Center in Enon Valley, PA. Bestows membership awards to 50-, 60-, and 70-year members. Conducts sales seminars. Offers Slovene cultural programs. Sponsors competitions; compiles statistics. **Libraries: Type:** reference. **Holdings:** biographical archives. **Awards: Type:** recognition. **Computer Services:** Online services, data service. **Publications:** *Prosveta* (in English and Slovene), weekly. Newspaper. **Price:** included in membership dues. **Circulation:** 22,000. **Advertising:** accepted. Alternate Formats: online ● *Roster of Lodges*, annual ● *Voice of Youth*, monthly. **Conventions/Meetings:** quadrennial convention.

18972 ■ Slovenian Women's Union of America (SWUA)
431 N Chicago St.
Joliet, IL 60432
Ph: (815)727-1926
E-mail: swuhome@swua.org
URL: http://www.swua.org
Contact: Kathleen Ferrante, Pres.
Founded: 1926. **Members:** 5,000. **Membership Dues:** heritage, $20 (annual). **State Groups:** 108. **Local Groups:** 1. **Description:** Consists of Christian women and children of Slovenian ancestry. Conducts research programs. Maintains Slovenian Women's Union Heritage Museum in Joliet, IL. **Libraries: Type:** reference. **Holdings:** archival material. **Awards: Type:** scholarship. **Computer Services:** database. **Committees:** Cultural Heritage; Scholarship. **Formerly:** (2002) Slovenian Women's Union. **Publications:** *Flowers From My Garden*. Book. Contains poems. **Price:** $8.50 ● *From Here to Slovenia*. Book ● *Let's Sing*. Book. Includes different songs. **Price:** $1.00 ● *More Pots and Pans*. Book. Features recipes. **Price:** $15.00 ● *ZARJA - The Dawn*, bimonthly. Magazine. Includes calendar of events, chapter news, and obituaries. **Price:** included in membership dues. ISSN: 0044-1848. **Circulation:** 5,500. **Advertising:**

accepted. **Conventions/Meetings:** quadrennial meeting ● annual State and Regional Conventions.

18973 ■ Society for Slovene Studies (SSS)
259 Kensington Pl.
Syracuse, NY 13210-3307
Ph: (315)472-0538
E-mail: mmilac@syr.edu
URL: http://www.arts.ualberta.ca/~ljubljan/sss.html
Contact: Michael Biggins, Sec.
Founded: 1973. **Members:** 290. **Membership Dues:** regular, $20 (annual) ● joint, $35 (annual) ● student, $5 (annual). **Staff:** 14. **For-Profit. Multinational. Description:** Fosters communication among scholars interested in all aspects of Slovene studies. **Libraries: Type:** open to the public. **Awards:** Graduate Student Prize. **Frequency:** annual. **Type:** monetary. **Recipient:** for a graduate paper in Slovene studies ● Undergraduate Student Prize. **Frequency:** annual. **Type:** monetary. **Recipient:** for an undergraduate paper in Slovene studies. **Publications:** *Slovene Studies*, annual. Journal. **Price:** included in membership dues; $20.00 for nonmembers. ISSN: 0193-1075. **Circulation:** 500 ● Newsletter, semiannual. **Conventions/Meetings:** annual convention, held in conjunction with the American Association for the Advancement of Slavic Studies.

Social Clubs

18974 ■ The Associated Clubs (TAC)
Address Unknown since 2007
Founded: 1936. **Members:** 5,600. **Staff:** 3. **Budget:** $325,000. **Local Groups:** 35. **Description:** Husband and wife social dinner clubs seeking to facilitate an exchange of ideas between local and national leaders in business, public affairs, and the professions, regardless of other club, party, or religious affiliations. Works to keep the public informed on problems of government, business, industry, finance, and the professions through addresses by national leaders. **Computer Services:** database, 9000 speakers. **Affiliated With:** Knife and Fork Club International. **Publications:** *Speakers Guide*, annual. **Advertising:** not accepted. **Conventions/Meetings:** annual meeting - always first weekend in February.

18975 ■ Bald-Headed Men of America (BHMA)
102 Bald Dr.
Morehead City, NC 28557
Ph: (252)726-1855
Fax: (252)726-6061
E-mail: jcapps4102@aol.com
URL: http://members.aol.com/BaldUSA/join.htm
Contact: John T. Capps III, Founder
Founded: 1973. **Members:** 20,000. **Membership Dues:** active, $10 (annual) ● special, $33 (annual). **Staff:** 3. **Budget:** $100,000. **Description:** Bald-headed men who agree with the philosophy "Bald is beautiful." Believes that bald-headed men (whether chrome-dome, balding pate, or bald spot) have extra individual character. Strives to cultivate a sense of pride for all bald-headed men and to eliminate the loss of self-esteem associated with the loss of hair. Promotes National Rub a Bald Head Week; Founder gives speeches and makes television appearances proclaiming "the fun of being bald." Maintains speakers' bureau and charitable programs; compiles statistics. Operates hall of fame. **Publications:** *Chrome Dome*, periodic. Newsletter. Covers conventions and other activities for bald-headed men. **Price:** included in membership dues. **Circulation:** 18,000. **Conventions/Meetings:** annual Bald Power for the Future - convention and support group meeting - always second weekend of September, in Morehead City, NC ● annual competition - 2nd weekend of September.

18976 ■ Chemists' Club
40 W 45th St.
New York, NY 10036
Ph: (212)626-9300
Fax: (212)626-9393

E-mail: info@thechemistsclub.com
URL: http://www.thechemistsclub.com
Contact: John W. Brooks Jr., Pres.
Founded: 1898. **Members:** 1,000. **Membership Dues:** individual, $750 (annual) ● regular, $400 ● retired, academic (must be enrolled in an accredited academic institution), junior (under 35 years of age), $200 ● corporate (includes 10 people), $1,200. **Description:** Professional social club of persons connected with the chemical industry. Gathers and professional disseminates information to individuals involved in the chemistry field. **Libraries: Type:** reference. **Absorbed:** (1989) Mining Club. **Publications:** *The Retort*, semiannual. Newsletter. Covers meeting announcements, upcoming social events, member benefit updates, and industry and trade-related news. Alternate Formats: online. **Conventions/Meetings:** monthly meeting - fall through spring.

18977 ■ DeMolay International
10200 NW Ambassador Dr.
Kansas City, MO 64153
Free: (800)336-6529
Fax: (816)891-9062
E-mail: demolay@demolay.org
URL: http://www.demolay.org
Contact: Jeffrey C. Kitsmiller Sr., Exec. Dir.
Founded: 1919. **Members:** 30,000. **Membership Dues:** life, $50 ● individual, $25 (annual). **Staff:** 9. **Budget:** $1,200,000. **Regional Groups:** 8. **State Groups:** 55. **Local Groups:** 800. **Multinational. Description:** Fraternal organization for young men between the ages of 13 (or 12 years if completed 7th grade) and 21. Seeks to build character and develop leadership abilities in young men. Sponsors social and sporting events; contributes to humanitarian projects and services. Conducts leadership training conferences. Maintains International Supreme Council Order of DeMolay (governing board) and DeMolay Service and Leadership Center (headquarters). **Computer Services:** Mailing lists. **Also Known As:** (1919) Order of DeMolay. **Publications:** *DeMolay Development News*, quarterly. Newsletter. Informs on projects and viability of the association. Alternate Formats: online ● *DeMolay News*, periodic. Newsletter ● *Proceedings of the International Supreme Council Order of DeMolay*, periodic ● Videos. **Price:** $10.00 each. **Conventions/Meetings:** annual DeMolay Convention - meeting - always June.

18978 ■ Girl Friends
5215 Lobello Dr.
Dallas, TX 75229
Ph: (407)425-9880
Fax: (407)425-9972
Contact: M. Jean Butler, Natl.Pres.
Founded: 1927. **Members:** 1,400. **Budget:** $120,000. **National Groups:** 42. **Description:** Black women "who have been friends over the years." Primary aim is to "keep the fires of friendship burning." Conducts charitable projects and contributes annually to a selected charity. **Awards:** The Girl Friends Fund. **Frequency:** annual. **Type:** scholarship. **Recipient:** recognizes high academic achievement and is based on need. **Committees:** Courtesy; National Project; Publicity/Public Relations. **Publications:** *The Chatterbox*, annual. Journal. Contains activities of chapters and its members and family. ● *Chatterletter*, biennial ● *President's Newsletter and Friendship Letter*, annual ● Directory, quinquennial. **Conventions/Meetings:** annual Conclave - meeting - usually May.

18979 ■ Jim Smith Society (JSS)
c/o East Berlin Jim
256 Lake Meade Dr.
East Berlin, PA 17316
Ph: (985)384-0790 (217)259-7458
E-mail: webmaster@jimsmithsociety.com
URL: http://jimsmithsociety.com
Contact: James Smith Jr., Pres.
Founded: 1969. **Members:** 1,800. **Membership Dues:** individual, $15 (annual). **Staff:** 10. **Description:** Social organization for individuals named Jim Smith, including females, with members in U.S., Canada, Australia, New Zealand, Scotland, and

England. Activities include golf tournament, softball games between teams of Jim Smiths. **Publications:** *Jim Smith Society Newsletter*, quarterly. Includes information on members and related events. **Price:** $10.00/year. **Circulation:** 380. **Advertising:** accepted. **Conventions/Meetings:** annual Fun Festival - 3rd weekend in July.

18980 ■ Knife and Fork Club International (KFCI)
Address Unknown since 2007
Founded: 1936. **Members:** 3,600. **Staff:** 3. **Budget:** $150,000. **Local Groups:** 25. **Description:** Social dinner clubs of business and professional men and women. Prominent figures address meetings. Maintains speakers' bureau. **Affiliated With:** The Associated Clubs. **Publications:** *Speakers Guide*, annual. **Conventions/Meetings:** annual board meeting - always first weekend of February.

18981 ■ Lefthanders International (LHI)
Address Unknown since 2007
Founded: 1975. **Members:** 25,000. **Membership Dues:** subscription, $15 (annual). **Staff:** 3. **For-Profit. Description:** Individuals who are lefthanded. Serves the needs and interests of lefthanders worldwide; addresses issues of discrimination and scarcity of products; recognizes lefthanders' accomplishments in areas of sports, entertainment, the arts, and the work world. Offers a complete line of mail order products designed specifically for lefthanders. Coordinates and monitors research; conducts special projects. **Convention/Meeting:** none. **Awards:** Lefthander of the Year Award. **Frequency:** annual. **Type:** recognition. **Recipient:** for those persons in the public eye who have contributed to lefthandedness. **Publications:** *Lefthander Magazine*, bimonthly. For and about southpaws. **Price:** $15.00. **Circulation:** 25,000. **Advertising:** accepted ● *Lefthander's Catalog*.

18982 ■ Lois Link International - USA
c/o Lois Widly, Chair
11155 Meads Ave.
Orange, CA 92869
Fax: (714)639-5065
E-mail: lois@loislink.com
URL: http://www.loislink.com
Contact: Lois Widly, Chair
Founded: 1995. **Members:** 2,700. **Multinational. Description:** Individuals with the name Lois. Promotes appreciation of the name and encourages its continued use. Provides opportunities for members to network and gather. **Libraries: Type:** reference. **Holdings:** archival material, clippings. **Subjects:** people, places, things named Lois. **Formerly:** (1995) Lois International. **Publications:** *Lois Worldwide Directory*. Available to bonafide members only. **Price:** free, for members only ● Newsletter, annual. **Advertising:** accepted. **Conventions/Meetings:** biennial International Tour ● annual Lois Birthday Party, to celebrate all Lois' birthdays ● annual reunion.

18983 ■ The Moles
577 Chestnut Ridge Rd.
Woodcliff Lake, NJ 07677
Ph: (201)930-1923
Fax: (201)930-8501
E-mail: carty.moles@verizon.net
URL: http://themoles.info
Contact: Gerard J. Carty PE, Exec. Dir.
Founded: 1937. **Members:** 750. **Staff:** 3. **Description:** Consists of individuals presently or formerly engaged in tunnel, subway, sewer, foundation, marine, subaqueous, or other heavy construction work. Seeks to exchange construction information, encourage young people to participate in heavy construction, and contribute to raising construction industry standards in engineering and business ethics. **Awards:** Member Award. **Frequency:** annual. **Type:** recognition. **Recipient:** for outstanding achievement in heavy construction ● Non-member Award. **Type:** recognition. **Recipient:** for outstanding achievement in heavy construction. **Committees:** Award; Education; Finance; Membership; Program; Publicity. **Publications:** *Holing Through*, 3/year.

Newsletter. **Circulation:** 850. **Conventions/Meetings:** annual dinner - always the last Wednesday in January ● annual meeting and dinner - always 1st Wednesday in May ● annual Members' Dinner - meeting - always 1st Wednesday in November.

18984 ■ National Conference of State Societies (NCSS)
c/o Reba Morse, Asst. Sec.
8009 Apollo St.
Mason Neck, VA 22079
Ph: (703)339-7099
E-mail: tim_schlack@crapo.senate.gov
URL: http://www.statesocieties.org
Contact: Tim Schlack, Pres.
Founded: 1952. **Members:** 25,000. **Membership Dues:** state society, $50 (annual). **Staff:** 1. **Budget:** $130,000. **State Groups:** 55. **Local Groups:** 1. **Description:** Constituent societies with a total membership of 25,000 delegates from the 50 states and U.S. territories of Guam, American Samoa, and the U.S. Virgin Islands, Commonwealth of Puerto Rico, and the District of Columbia. Works to promote friendly and cooperative relations between state and territorial societies in the Metropolitan Washington, DC, area; fosters, participates in, and encourages educational, cultural, charitable, civic, and patriotic programs. Sponsors Cherry Blossom annual Fashion Show Luncheon, Princesses and Queen, Lantern Lighting Reception, Congressional Reception, Cherry Blossom Cruise, Grand Ball, and other events associated with the National Cherry Blossom Festival held annually the first week in April in the nation's capital. Conducts the newest event which is "Taste of the World", featuring indigenous foods and entertainment from more than 20 embassies. **Awards:** Nancy Moore Thurmond Scholarship. **Frequency:** annual. **Type:** scholarship. **Recipient:** for attributes of Nancy Moore Thurmond. **Computer Services:** Mailing lists, of members. **Committees:** Charity Fund; Cherry Blossom Festival. **Formerly:** (1968) Conference of State Societies. **Publications:** *Cherry Blossom Festival Program*, annual. **Price:** $4.00. **Circulation:** 3,500. **Advertising:** accepted ● *Communicator*, monthly. Newsletter ● *National Cherry Blossom Festival Guide*, annual. **Advertising:** accepted ● *National Conferences of State Societies Directory*, annual. **Advertising:** accepted. **Conventions/Meetings:** monthly board meeting and dinner - 10/year, always in Washington, DC ● annual meeting, sponsoring first annual goodwill tour.

18985 ■ National Federation of Grandmother Clubs of America (NFGCA)
c/o Cure Childhood Cancer
1835 Savoy Dr., Ste.317
Atlanta, GA 30341-1000
Ph: (770)986-0035
Free: (800)443-2873
Fax: (770)986-0038
E-mail: nfcga@earthlink.com
Contact: Barbara Rawlins, Natl. Pres.
Founded: 1938. **Members:** 2,200. **Membership Dues:** individual, $15 (annual). **Staff:** 1. **State Groups:** 15. **Local Groups:** 12. **National Groups:** 80. **For-Profit. Description:** Represents women who have grandchildren or have acquired them through marriage or adoption. Sponsors National Grandmother's Day (second Sunday in October). Raises funds to support research on children's diseases. **Publications:** *Autumn Leaves*, quarterly. Newsletter. Includes memorial list, club highlights, and messages from officers. **Circulation:** 2,400. **Conventions/Meetings:** annual convention - usually October, generally 2nd week.

18986 ■ Overseas Brats (OSB)
PO Box 47112
Wichita, KS 67201
Ph: (316)269-9610
Fax: (316)269-9610
E-mail: joeosbpres@sbcglobal.net
URL: http://www.overseasbrats.com
Contact: Joe Condrill, Pres.
Founded: 1986. **Members:** 2,500. **Staff:** 1. **Description:** U.S. citizens who have lived or attended school

overseas. Serves as a center of information for overseas high school alumni groups. Acts as a forum for members to share thoughts and experiences gained during their travels. Operates placement service. Maintains speakers' bureau. **Libraries: Type:** reference. **Holdings:** photographs. **Awards: Type:** recognition. **Publications:** Magazine, 3/year. Describes life situations of overseas alumni. Includes articles, news briefs, and book reviews. **Price:** included in membership dues. ISSN: 0219-4995. **Circulation:** 2,000. **Advertising:** accepted. **Conventions/Meetings:** annual seminar and workshop, commercial and cultural (exhibits) - always October ● seminar, provides information on organizing overseas alumni groups.

18987 ■ Procrastinators' Club of America (PCA)
PO Box 712
Bryn Athyn, PA 19009
Ph: (215)947-9020
Fax: (215)947-7210
E-mail: procrastinators_club_of_america@yahoo.com
URL: http://geocities.com/procrastinators_club_of_america
Contact: Les Waas, Pres.
Founded: 1956. **Members:** 15,650. **Membership Dues:** life, $21. **Local Groups:** 6. **Multinational. Description:** Individuals who promote the philosophy of relaxation through putting off until later those things that need not be done today. Activities include a Christmas party in June and a Fourth of July picnic in January, plus various unusual and offbeat events that publicize the art of procrastination. Honors "Be Late for Something Day," Sept. 5; celebrates National Procrastination Week (first week in March) late; protested against the War of 1812 in 1966. Maintains speakers' bureau. **Awards:** Procrastinator of the Year Award. **Frequency:** annual. **Type:** recognition. **Recipient:** for special achievement in the art of procrastination ● **Type:** recognition. **Recipient:** for horses that finish last, etc. **Committees:** Annual Predictions; Awards; Finance; Inactivities; Membership; Nomination; Social; Vacillation. **Publications:** *Last Month's Newsletter*, periodic. Contains procrastination articles, club news, essays, and cartoons. **Price:** free for members. **Circulation:** 14,500. **Conventions/Meetings:** periodic meeting.

18988 ■ Redheads International (RI)
Address Unknown since 2006
Founded: 1982. **Members:** 5,000. **Staff:** 3. **Budget:** $30,000. **Regional Groups:** 1. **National Groups:** 5. **For-Profit. Description:** Redheads in 30 countries. United to promote an attractive and positive image of redheads. According to the group, "being a redhead is a special and lucky blessing!" Recognizes famous redheads from history and the arts. Researches redhead history and culture. **Libraries: Type:** reference. **Holdings:** biographical archives. **Subjects:** information pertaining to redheads. **Computer Services:** Mailing lists. **Publications:** *The Redhead Encyclopedia*. Book. Contains information on redhead culture, history, and folklore. **Price:** $19.95 plus $3 shipping. **Advertising:** not accepted. Alternate Formats: online.

18989 ■ Rockette Alumnae Association (RAA)
c/o Jennifer Jiles
365 Cabrini Blvd., No. 3H
New York, NY 10040
Ph: (718)939-0941
E-mail: gdtreimanis@nyc.rr.com
URL: http://rockette2004-ivil.tripod.com/newsletter.html
Contact: Violet Holmes Treimanis, Pres.
Founded: 1955. **Members:** 500. **Description:** Former members of the Radio City Music Hall dance troupe, the Rockettes, united for social and philanthropic causes. Bestows Russell Market Dance Scholarship to dance students in the Dance Division of the Juilliard School of Music. **Publications:** Newsletter, semiannual. **Conventions/Meetings:** meeting - 5/year, always January, March, May,

September, and November in New York, NY ● triennial Spring Charity Ball and Luncheon - meeting.

18990 ■ Rural Culture Society
c/o Andrew J. Smith, MA, Ed./Publisher
PO Box 77
Thiells, NY 10984
Ph: (914)942-5063 (914)942-1326
E-mail: as10984@aol.com
Contact: Andrew J. Smith MA, Ed./Publisher
Founded: 1995. **Members:** 400. **Membership Dues:** subscriber, $25 (annual). **Staff:** 1. **Regional Groups:** 8. **State Groups:** 1. **Local Groups:** 8. **For-Profit. Description:** Individuals interested in rural lifestyles. Seeks to provide a forum for exchange of information. Offers labor exchange and training; provides information on country cooking, folklore and lifestyle tips, provides forum for rural singles to communicate home business, wild food foraging. Acts as lobbyist for rural interest, provides a research library on rural culture, conducts research and compiles data on rural living. **Libraries: Type:** reference; not open to the public. **Holdings:** 3,000; articles, audio recordings, books, clippings, periodicals, video recordings. **Subjects:** history, folklore, nature study, rural crafts and lifestyles, cooking, philosophy of ruralism, music. **Computer Services:** database, network ● mailing lists. **Formerly:** (1996) Rustic Resources; (1999) Rural Cultural Heritage Society. **Publications:** *Rustic Resources*, monthly. Newsletter. Includes information about networking for people with rural interests. **Price:** $25.00/year. **Circulation:** 300. **Advertising:** accepted. **Conventions/Meetings:** annual convention and reunion (exhibits).

18991 ■ Single Gourmet (SG)
211 South St., No. 331
Philadelphia, PA 19147
Ph: (215)732-0260
Fax: (215)733-0912
E-mail: pres@singlegourmetphilly.com
URL: http://www.singlegourmetphilly.com
Contact: Arthur Fischer, Dir.
Founded: 1980. **Local Groups:** 15. **Description:** Serves as social dining club for individuals who have never married or who are divorced, widowed, or separated from their spouse. Aims to offer single men and women the opportunity to meet each other over a good meal. Conducts at least 4 local activities per month, including dinners and meal-oriented trips. **Publications:** Newsletter, monthly.

18992 ■ Sons of the Whiskey Rebellion (SWR)
c/o John H. Norris, Adjutant
PO Box 509
38525 Woodward Ave.
Bloomfield Hills, MI 48304
Ph: (248)646-4300 (248)433-7227
Fax: (248)433-7274
E-mail: jnorris@dickinson.com
Contact: John H. Norris, Adjutant
Founded: 1936. **Members:** 40. **Staff:** 7. **Description:** Persons who have been recommended for and elected to membership. Objectives are the glorification of whiskey and the eradication of taxes. Compiles statistics; conducts research, specialized education, and covert activities. **Libraries: Type:** reference. **Awards: Frequency:** periodic. **Type:** recognition. **Publications:** *Bivouac Notice*, periodic. Newsletter. **Conventions/Meetings:** general assembly and workshop.

18993 ■ Study Circles Resource Center (SCRC)
697 Pomfret St.
PO Box 203
Pomfret, CT 06258
Ph: (860)928-2616
Fax: (860)928-3713
E-mail: scrc@studycircles.org
URL: http://www.studycircles.org
Contact: Amy L. Malick, Communication Dir.
Founded: 1989. **Staff:** 14. **Budget:** $1,500,000. **Description:** Helps communities use study circles-small, democratic, highly participatory discussions-to

involve large numbers of citizens in public dialogue and problem solving on critical social and political issues. **Libraries: Type:** reference. **Holdings:** audiovisuals, books. **Subjects:** discussion programs, citizen participation. **Computer Services:** database, 40,000 organizations and individuals interested in study circles. **Publications:** *Focus on Study Circles*, quarterly. Newsletter. Contains articles on topics such as how to build and sustain study circle programs, and the role of face-to-face public deliberation. **Price:** free. **Circulation:** 10,000. Alternate Formats: online.

18994 ■ Stunts Unlimited (SU)
7551 W Sunset Blvd., Ste.203
Los Angeles, CA 90046-3442
Ph: (323)851-1970
Fax: (323)851-7286
E-mail: info@stuntsunlimited.com
URL: http://www.stuntsunlimited.com
Contact: Scott Waugh, Pres.
Founded: 1970. **Members:** 50. **Description:** Works as a private club of stuntmen, stunt-coordinators, and second-unit directors. **Publications:** none.

Somalia

18995 ■ Somali Family Care Network (SFCN)
2724 Door Ave., Ste.102
Fairfax, VA 22031
Ph: (703)560-0005
Fax: (703)560-9523
E-mail: raqiya@somalifamily.org
URL: http://www.somalifamily.org
Contact: Raqiya Abdalla, Pres.
Description: Works to improve the social and economic opportunities for the Somali community in the US. Serves as the national resource center and referral network for the Somali immigrant community in the United States, as well as for the US refugee and mainstream service providers who interface with the Somali communities in the US. Provides training to strengthen local communities' institution building and leadership development. **Publications:** *Himilo Newsletter*. Alternate Formats: online.

Spanish

18996 ■ World Spanish Congress (WSC)
PO Box 42
Leonia, NJ 07605
Ph: (201)567-7417
Fax: (201)816-9797
E-mail: anthony-f-gonzalez@worldnet.att.net
Contact: Anthony F. Gonzalez, Pres.
Founded: 1980. **Languages:** English, Spanish. **Description:** White Hispanic individuals with Spanish surnames. Seeks to protect civil and religious rights of Spanish-surnamed White Americans throughout the world. Offers children's services and charitable programs. Maintains speakers' bureau, hall of fame, and museum. Compiles statistics. **Libraries: Type:** reference. **Holdings:** archival material. **Publications:** Newspaper, periodic. **Conventions/Meetings:** annual meeting.

Sri Lankan

18997 ■ Association of Sri-Lankans in America (ASIA)
2 E Glen Rd.
Denville, NJ 07834
Ph: (973)627-7855 (973)586-0101
Fax: (973)586-3411
E-mail: jayliyanage@yahoo.com
Contact: Jay P. Liyanage, Chm.
Founded: 1978. **Members:** 2,500. **Regional Groups:** 5. **State Groups:** 5. **Local Groups:** 1. **Description:** Serves as liaison between Americans of Sri-Lankan origin and the U.S. Department of State. Participates in aid programs to Sri-Lanka; promotes Sri-Lankan ethnic values in the U.S. and

seminars on Sri-Lankan issues. Makes travel arrangements for Sri Lankan dignitaries visiting the U.S. Maintains charitable program; conducts research. Provides children's services; compiles statistics; maintains speakers' bureau. **Libraries: Type:** reference. **Holdings:** biographical archives. **Awards:** Patriotism and Humanitarian Awards. **Frequency:** annual. **Type:** recognition. **Recipient:** for humanitarian and patriotic activities done on behalf of SRI Lanicans LSRI LANKA. **Publications:** *Lankian*, annual. **Conventions/Meetings:** biennial meeting and symposium.

Swedish

18998 ■ Swedish Council of America (SCA)
2600 Park Ave.
Minneapolis, MN 55407
Ph: (612)871-0593
Free: (800)981-4SCA
Fax: (612)871-0687
E-mail: swedcoun@swedishcouncil.org
URL: http://www.swedishcouncil.org
Contact: Elise Peters, Exec. Dir.
Founded: 1972. **Membership Dues:** associate affiliate, $50 (annual) ● sustaining affiliate, $250 (annual) ● supporting affiliate, $100 (annual). **Budget:** $175,000. **National Groups:** 300. **Languages:** English, Swedish. **Description:** Swedish-American organizations and individuals united to promote knowledge and understanding of the Swedish heritage in America and to strengthen cultural ties between the U.S. and Sweden. Fosters historical research on Swedish settlement in America and publishes and distributes findings; works to preserve historical and cultural sites, archival materials, and oral histories; encourages schools, colleges, and universities to introduce and expand Swedish studies and the study of modern Sweden; conducts presentations of topics pertaining to American-Swedish affairs. **Libraries: Type:** not open to the public. **Holdings:** articles, books, periodicals. **Subjects:** Swedish immigration, Swedish customs and traditions, Swedish/American history. **Awards:** America's Swede of the Year. **Frequency:** annual. **Type:** recognition ● Glen T. Seaborg Nobel Travel Award. **Frequency:** annual. **Type:** recognition. **Recipient:** to outstanding science or mathematics college student of Swedish descent attending one of five Swedish heritage colleges ● **Type:** grant. **Recipient:** to organizations for projects that relate to or promote Swedish-American culture or understanding ● Great Swedish Heritage Award. **Type:** recognition. **Committees:** Viking Circle. **Publications:** *American-Swedish Handbook*, quadrennial. **Price:** $17.95 plus postage ● *Sweden and America*, quarterly. Magazine ● *Update*. Newsletter. Alternate Formats: online ● Annual Reports, annual. Alternate Formats: online. **Conventions/Meetings:** semiannual board meeting ● semiannual conference.

18999 ■ Swedish Women's Educational Association International (SWEA)
5928 Balfour Ct., Ste.B
Carlsbad, CA 92008
Ph: (760)918-9653
Fax: (760)918-9654
E-mail: office@swea.org
URL: http://www.swea.org
Contact: Sofia Fransson Krall, Admin.
Founded: 1979. **Members:** 8,000. **Staff:** 1. **Budget:** $200,000. **Regional Groups:** 7. **Local Groups:** 77. **National Groups:** 32. **Languages:** English, Swedish. **Multinational. Description:** Women aged 18 and over who are fluent in the Swedish language and interested in preserving and promoting Swedish culture and tradition. **Awards:** $6000 Scholarship for Intercultural Relations. **Frequency:** annual. **Type:** scholarship. **Recipient:** for Swedish students to study abroad ● SWEA $6000 Scholarship in Literature, Language and ARCA Studies. **Frequency:** annual. **Type:** scholarship. **Recipient:** to graduate students for study in Sweden. **Publications:** *SWEA Forum* (in English and Swedish), semiannual. Magazine. **Circulation:** 8,500. **Advertising:** accepted. **Conventions/**

Meetings: annual conference, with representatives from all chapters.

19000 ■ United Swedish Societies (USS)
Address Unknown since 2007
Founded: 1903. **Members:** 4,800. **Languages:** Swedish. **Description:** Federation of 40 Swedish-American organizations. **Awards: Frequency:** periodic. **Type:** scholarship. **Recipient:** swedish ancestry. **Also Known As:** Svenska Central Forbundet. **Conventions/Meetings:** quarterly meeting.

Swiss

19001 ■ American-Swiss Foundation
232 E 66th St.
New York, NY 10021
Ph: (212)754-0130
Fax: (212)754-4512
URL: http://www.americanswiss.org
Contact: Patricia Schramm, Pres.
Founded: 1945. **Members:** 75. **Staff:** 2. **Description:** American and Swiss corporations and individuals interested in maintaining friendship and cultural exchange with Switzerland. Provides a forum for meetings and discussions. Conducts events featuring Swiss and American speakers in New York. **Awards:** Friendship Award. **Type:** recognition. **Recipient:** to an individual who has made significant contribution in furthering friendship between America and Switzerland. **Formerly:** (1946) American Friends of Switzerland; (1972) American Society for Friendship with Switzerland; (1994) American-Swiss Association. **Publications:** *American Swiss Foundation Newsletter,* semiannual. **Conventions/Meetings:** annual Gala Dinner - dinner and lecture ● annual Young Leaders Conference, for individuals ages 28-40, nominated by U.S. Senators - in Switzerland.

19002 ■ North American Swiss Alliance (NASA)
7650 Chippewa Rd., Rm. 214
Brecksville, OH 44141
Ph: (440)526-2257
Fax: (440)526-2257
Contact: Joan J. Spirko, Sec.-Treas.
Founded: 1865. **Members:** 3,000. **Membership Dues:** benevolent member, insurance member, $8 (annual). **Staff:** 1. **Regional Groups:** 20. **Description:** Fraternal benefit life insurance society for persons of Swiss birth or ancestry and friends of Swiss. **Formerly:** (1940) North American Schweizer Bund. **Publications:** *Swiss-American,* quarterly. Newsletter. Tabloid containing news of the alliance and articles of interest to Swiss-Americans; includes obituaries. **Price:** $8.00/year. **Circulation:** 3,000 ● Directory, periodic. **Conventions/Meetings:** quadrennial convention ● meeting.

19003 ■ Swiss Benevolent Society of New York (SBS)
500 5th Ave., Rm. 1800
New York, NY 10110-1804
Ph: (212)246-0655
Fax: (212)246-1366
E-mail: info@swissbenevolentny.com
URL: http://www.swissbenevolentny.com
Contact: Annemarie Gilman, Exec. Dir.
Founded: 1846. **Members:** 600. **Staff:** 4. **Languages:** English, French, German, Italian. **Description:** Social Service - case management in greater New York Area for Swiss community. Maintains Pellegrini, Medicus and Zimmermann Scholarship Funds. **Convention/Meeting:** none. **Committees:** Scholarship; Social Service. **Affiliated With:** Federation of Protestant Welfare Agencies. **Publications:** Annual Report, annual.

Taiwanese

19004 ■ Intercollegiate Taiwanese American Students Association (ITASA)
PO Box 961856
Boston, MA 02196

E-mail: info@itasa.org
URL: http://www.itasa.org
Contact: Jonathan Hwang, Pres.
Founded: 1992. **Members:** 1,000. **Description:** Asian, South Asian, Hong Kong, and Korean students. Promotes Taiwanese American culture, history, performance, activism and friendship. Aims to strengthen the awareness, skills, unity, and leadership of the Taiwanese American community. **Type:** scholarship. **Publications:** *Our Treasury: The Shaping of First-Generation Taiwanese Americans.* Book ● Videos. **Conventions/Meetings:** conference ● retreat.

19005 ■ North America Taiwanese Professors' Association (NATPA)
c/o Dr. Jerry T.J. Chuang, Membership Chm.
9 Manette St.
Gaithersburg, MD 20878
Ph: (301)975-5773
E-mail: sliao@huggins.bsd.uchicago.edu
URL: http://natpa.org
Contact: Shutsung Liao, Exec. Dir.
Founded: 1980. **Members:** 500. **Membership Dues:** regular, $50 (annual) ● retired, $25 (annual). **Budget:** $100,000. **Regional Groups:** 13. **Description:** Professors and senior researchers of Taiwanese origin or descent. Encourages educational exchange and cultural understanding among the Taiwanese and other peoples worldwide. Promotes scientific and professional knowledge. Seeks to further the welfare of Taiwanese communities in North America and Taiwan. Sponsors research and lectures on topics related to Taiwan. **Libraries: Type:** reference. **Holdings:** archival material. **Publications:** Bulletin, semiannual ● Directory, annual ● Newsletter, bimonthly. **Conventions/Meetings:** annual meeting ● symposium.

19006 ■ Society of Taiwanese Americans, Chicago Chapter (SOTA)
c/o Frank Huang
2645 N Forrest Rd.
Arlington Heights, IL 60004
E-mail: sotail@aol.com
URL: http://members.aol.com/sotaIL
Contact: Frank Huang, Contact
Founded: 1993. **Regional Groups:** 8. **Multinational. Description:** Promotes unified community and heritage of Taiwanese Americans for future generations.

19007 ■ Taiwanese American Citizens League (TACL)
3001 Walnut Grove Ave., No. 7
Rosemead, CA 91770
Ph: (626)202-0170
Fax: (626)202-0170
E-mail: tacl@tacl.org
URL: http://www.tacl.org
Contact: Kristy Kao, Pres.
Founded: 1985. **Description:** Aims to advance the quality of life for Taiwanese Americans. **Awards:** Essay Scholarship. **Type:** scholarship ● Journalism Scholarship. **Type:** scholarship. **Programs:** Journalism Internship; Leadership and Identity Development; Summer Internship.

19008 ■ Taiwanese Collegian (TC)
PO Box 1685
Tempe, AZ 85285-1685
E-mail: keng_an@hotmail.com
Contact: Ching-An Yeh, Sec.Gen.
Founded: 1983. **Description:** Represents overseas students from Taiwan. **Awards:** Dr. Ya-yen Lee Memorial Scholarship. **Type:** scholarship. **Computer Services:** Mailing lists. **Projects:** Campus Speech Tours; Diplomacy Training Camp; Embrace 228 Uprising; Environmental Diplomacy; Letters to Educational Testing Services Campaign; TC Summer Camp. **Publications:** *Taiwanese Voices.* Magazine. Alternate Formats: online ● *TC Magazine* (in English, Hakka, and Mandarin Dialects). **Conventions/Meetings:** conference ● Summer and Winter Camps - meeting.

Turkish

19009 ■ American Turkish Society (ATS)
3 Dag Hammarskjold Plz.
305 E 47th St., 2nd Ave., 8th Fl.
New York, NY 10017
Ph: (212)583-7614 (212)583-7683
Fax: (212)583-7615
E-mail: info@americanturkishsociety.org
URL: http://www.americanturkishsociety.org
Contact: Ms. Selen Ucak, Exec. Dir.
Founded: 1949. **Members:** 500. **Membership Dues:** individual, $100 (annual) ● corporate, $500 (annual) ● student, $50 (annual) ● family, $150 (annual). **Staff:** 2. **Budget:** $5,000,000. **Local Groups:** 1. **Languages:** English, French, German, Turkish. **Description:** American and Turkish diplomats, banks, corporations, businessmen, and educators. Promotes economic and commercial relations as well as cultural understanding between the peoples of the United States and Turkey. Serves as information center. Holds a series of lectures and symposia, as well as cultural programs. Sponsors social activities between U.S. and Turkish official and businesspersons. Conducts charitable work including aid for victims of earthquakes and floods. **Libraries: Type:** reference. **Holdings:** 50; articles, periodicals. **Subjects:** Turkish history, culture, economics and finance, Turkish language. **Committees:** Cultural Expansion Initiative; Education; Events. **Programs:** Mehmet Oz Cardiac Fellowship; Teacher Exchange Program; You Can Survive an Earthquake. **Publications:** *ATS Report,* 3/year. Newsletter. Contains information on Turkish politics and the Turkish economy, society events and programs, book reviews, and member profiles. **Price:** free with membership. **Circulation:** 1,500. **Advertising:** accepted ● *You Can Survive an Earthquake* (in English and Turkish). Brochure. Focuses on earthquake preparedness. Alternate Formats: online ● Newsletter, quarterly. **Conventions/Meetings:** biennial Business Luncheon, for the Turkish and American financial community in New York - held in New York, NY ● annual symposium.

19010 ■ Assembly of Turkish American Associations (ATAA)
1526 18th St. NW
Washington, DC 20036
Ph: (202)483-9090
Fax: (202)483-9092
E-mail: assembly@ataa.org
URL: http://www.ataa.org
Contact: Mr. Nurten Ural, Pres.
Founded: 1979. **Members:** 10,050. **Membership Dues:** corporate (minimum), $5,000 (annual) ● Topkapi Club, $2,500 (annual) ● Dolmabahce Club, $1,000 (annual) ● Ciragan Club, $500 (annual) ● advance, $250 (annual) ● family, $100 (annual) ● single, $75 (annual) ● student, $35 (annual). **Staff:** 4. **Budget:** $500,000. **Regional Groups:** 54. **Languages:** English, Turkish. **Description:** Represents associations and individuals who coordinate activities of regional Turkish-American associations for the purpose of presenting an objective view of Turkey and the Turkish-American and Turkish people and enhancing understanding between these people and Americans. Provides educational materials and organizational assistance to Turkish-American community schools and their teachers. Provides speakers to the Turkish-American community and other interested groups concerning issues on the history, culture, and language of Turks. Operates a national leadership training program and teachers' workshop. Sponsors annual Turkish-American Heritage Week and Community forums. **Awards:** Distinguished Service Award. **Type:** recognition ● Turkish American of the Year Award. **Frequency:** annual. **Type:** recognition. **Computer Services:** database ● mailing lists. **Committees:** Central Fundraising; Cultural; Media Watch and Response; Turkish Heritage Week. **Councils:** Business Network; Education. **Publications:** *Armenian Allegations - Myth and Reality.* Handbook. **Price:** $15.00 ● *Occasion Papers Series,* periodic ● *The Turkish Times* (in English and Turkish), biweekly. Newspaper. Covers Turkish-American issues and af-

fairs; includes editorials and business information. **Price:** $30.00/year in U.S.; $150.00/year outside U.S.; $60.00/year bulk, first-class; $75.00/year, first-class in Canada & Mexico. **Circulation:** 30,000. **Advertising:** accepted. **Conventions/Meetings:** annual convention (exhibits) ● symposium.

19011 ■ Federation of Turkish American Associations (FTAA)
821 UN Plz., 2nd Fl.
New York, NY 10017
Ph: (212)682-7688
Fax: (212)687-3026
E-mail: tadfoffice@tadf.org
URL: http://www.tadf.org
Contact: M. Atilla Pak, Pres.

Founded: 1956. **Members:** 40. **Membership Dues:** association, $250 (annual). **Staff:** 4. **Budget:** $320,000. **Languages:** English, Turkish. **Description:** Local organizations (35) of Turkish-Americans in the U.S. Promotes fellowship; works to advance cultural and educational interests; seeks to maintain and preserve knowledge of the cultural heritage of Turkey and the U.S. Maintains Turkish Cultural Center. Observes Children's Day (April 23), Youth and Sports Day (May 19), Turkish Day Parade (3rd Saturday of May), and Ataturks Commemoration Day (Nov. 10). Broadcasts Turkish radio program in New York City. **Libraries: Type:** reference. **Holdings:** 500. **Subjects:** Turkish language, culture, politics. **Computer Services:** Mailing lists, rental of Turkish residential and commercial address. **Formerly:** Federation of Turkish-American Societies. **Publications:** *Gorus* (in English and Turkish), quarterly. Newsletter. Contains articles and community news. **Price:** free. **Circulation:** 10,000. **Advertising:** accepted ● *Vision*, quarterly. Journal. **Price:** free. **Circulation:** 3,000. **Advertising:** accepted. **Conventions/Meetings:** annual Ball - meeting - always anniversary of the founding of the Republic of Turkey (October 29th) ● annual Turkish Week - festival and seminar, includes parade - always May in New York City.

19012 ■ Turkish American Alliance for Fairness (TAAF)
2053 Grant Rd.
PMB No. 550
Los Altos, CA 94024
Ph: (650)562-3565
E-mail: taaf@taaf-org.net
URL: http://www.taaf-org.net

Description: Promotes, advocates and advances issues and viewpoints of importance to Turkish-Americans. Informs Turkish-American individuals in the United States about their rights. Seeks to counter incorrect, biased and prejudiced statements and activities aimed at individuals of Turkish heritage. **Libraries: Type:** lending. **Holdings:** books.

Ukrainian

19013 ■ League of Ukrainian Catholics of America (LUC)
c/o Dr. Michael Labuda, Membership Dir.
14 Prince St.
Plains, PA 18705-1211
E-mail: hilary.kinal@azbar.org
URL: http://ukrainian.faithweb.com
Contact: Hilary Andrew Kinal, Pres.

Founded: 1933. **Members:** 700. **Staff:** 21. **Description:** U.S. citizens of Ukrainian descent who are members of the Eastern Rite of the Roman Catholic Church. Promotes a sense of community among members. Conducts program involving "religious, apostolic, educational, cultural, social, and physical activities". **Committees:** Civic and Educational; Cultural; LUC Beatification; Publicity; Spiritual; Sports. **Formerly:** Ukrainian Catholic Youth League. **Publications:** *ACTION*, periodic. Newsletter. Alternate Formats: online. **Conventions/Meetings:** annual meeting - always October.

19014 ■ Plast, Ukrainian Scouting Organization - U.S.A.
144 2nd Ave.
New York, NY 10003
Ph: (212)475-6960
Fax: (212)533-8991
E-mail: kps@plastusa.org
URL: http://www.plastusa.org
Contact: Ihor Mykyta, Natl. Pres.

Founded: 1911. **Members:** 2,500. **Staff:** 2. **Local Groups:** 19. **Languages:** English, Ukrainian. **Description:** Cub scouts (ages 6-11), boy and girl scouts (ages 11-18), rover scouts (ages 18-31), and senior scouts (over age 31). Has adapted the universal scout principles to the needs and interests of Ukrainian youth to develop their physical, mental, and moral strength and perpetuate Ukrainian traditions, culture, and history. Activities include: weekly troop meetings; annual regional camps for each age group; practical camping and survival skills, leadership training, and character development; training camps for scoutmasters and cubmasters. Maintains a museum in Cleveland, OH. **Libraries: Type:** reference. **Holdings:** archival material. **Publications:** *Hotuys*, bimonthly. Magazine ● *Plastovyj Shliakh*, quarterly ● *Vohon Orlynoyi Rady*, quarterly ● *Yunak*, bimonthly ● *Zhyttia v Plasti*. **Conventions/Meetings:** biennial meeting ● quinquennial World Jamboree - meeting.

19015 ■ Providence Association of Ukrainian Catholics in America (PAUCA)
817 N Franklin St.
Philadelphia, PA 19123
Ph: (215)627-4984 (215)627-2445
Free: (877)857-2284
E-mail: info@provassn.com
URL: http://www.provassn.com

Founded: 1912. **Members:** 15,267. **Budget:** $650,000. **Local Groups:** 211. **Description:** Serves as a fraternal benefit life insurance society. Provides life insurance protection and social, economic and spiritual benefits to its members. Aims: to sustain and spread the religious spirit of the Ukrainian Catholic Church; to assist its members in case of sickness and to support worthy religious and civic causes; to strengthen the faith of Ukrainian Catholics by publishing newspapers, periodicals and books; and to instruct Ukrainians in the history, culture and government of the United States in order to make them good and loyal citizens, conscious of their rights, duties, obligations and privileges. **Awards: Type:** recognition. **Publications:** *America* (in English and Ukrainian), bimonthly. Newspaper. **Circulation:** 3,500. **Advertising:** accepted ● Books ● Pamphlets. **Conventions/Meetings:** annual meeting - always in Philadelphia, PA.

19016 ■ Self Reliance Association of American Ukrainians (SAAU)
108 2nd Ave.
New York, NY 10003-8392
Ph: (212)473-7310
Free: (888)735-3735
Fax: (212)473-3251
E-mail: srnyfcu@aol.com
URL: http://www.selfrelianceny.org/about.htm
Contact: Natalia Duma, Pres.

Founded: 1947. **Members:** 14,900. **Membership Dues:** individual, $5. **Staff:** 2. **Budget:** $34,000. **State Groups:** 21. **Description:** Represents Americans of Ukrainian birth or descent. Aids Ukrainian immigrants. Offers courses in Ukrainian literature and history. Sponsors 16 credit unions. **Libraries: Type:** reference. **Holdings:** 2,291. **Sections:** Senior Citizens. **Conventions/Meetings:** biennial meeting.

19017 ■ Shevchenko Scientific Society (SSS)
63 4th Ave.
New York, NY 10003-5200
Ph: (212)254-5130
Fax: (212)254-5239

E-mail: info@shevchenko.org
URL: http://www.shevchenko.org
Contact: Orest Popovych, Pres.

Founded: 1873. **Members:** 400. **Membership Dues:** scholar, $40 (annual). **Staff:** 2. **Budget:** $150,000. **Regional Groups:** 5. **Languages:** English, Ukrainian. **Description:** Promotes scholarship and education; supports research on Ukraine and Eastern Europe; organizes academic conferences, lectures, and discussion meetings. Provides information to students on institutions of higher learning; makes facilities available for neighborhood educational activities; sponsors concerts and poetry readings for the general public; provides premises for meetings of youth counselors; cooperates with various scholarly institutions and organizations. Conducts research programs. Maintains Speaker's Bureau. Founded in Ukraine in 1873; named after Ukrainian poet, Taras Shevchenko (1814-61). **Libraries: Type:** reference. **Holdings:** 35,000; archival material, books. **Subjects:** Ukraine, Eastern Europe. **Awards: Frequency:** annual. **Type:** grant. **Recipient:** for scholarly contribution ● **Type:** recognition. **Computer Services:** database, library catalog ● mailing lists, members. **Committees:** Bibliographical; Computerization; Grants and Scholarship; Juridical; Liaison; Membership; Publications; Taras Shevchenko; Terminological. **Sections:** Chemical-Biological-Medical; Historical-Philosophical; Mathematical-Physical; Philological; Social Studies; Ukrainian Encyclopedia. **Affiliated With:** American Association for the Advancement of Slavic Studies. **Publications:** Monographs. Provides information on Ukraine and East European studies. ● *Bulletin* (in English and Ukrainian), semiannual. **Price:** free. **Circulation:** 350 ● *Proceedings* ● Also publishes encyclopedias and works of Ukrainian writers. **Conventions/Meetings:** triennial conference, with exhibit of relevant new publications (exhibits).

19018 ■ Ukrainian Fraternal Association (UFA)
371 N 9th Ave.
Scranton, PA 18504-2005
Ph: (570)342-0937
Fax: (570)347-5649
URL: http://members.tripod.com/~ufa_home
Contact: Ivan Oleksyn, Pres.

Founded: 1910. **Members:** 16,000. **Staff:** 12. **Budget:** $1,000,000. **Local Groups:** 150. **National Groups:** 25. **Languages:** English, Ukrainian. **Description:** Fraternal benefit life insurance society. Sponsors youth festivals and children's services. **Libraries: Type:** reference. **Holdings:** archival material. **Awards:** Children's Camp, Sports and Dance School, Scholarship. **Frequency:** annual. **Type:** scholarship. **Formerly:** (1978) Ukrainian Workingmen's Association. **Publications:** *Forum, A Ukrainian Review*, quarterly. Magazine. Covers the artistic, cultural, historic, and religious heritage of Ukrainians; includes information on American and European Ukrainians. **Price:** $20.00/year. **ISSN:** 0015-8399. **Circulation:** 5,000. **Advertising:** accepted ● *Narodna Volya* (in English and Ukrainian), weekly. Newsletter. Includes book reviews, employment opportunities, obituaries, statistics, research reports and news. **Price:** $25.00 /year for nonmembers; $20.00 /year for members. **ISSN:** 0015-8399. **Circulation:** 3,500. **Advertising:** accepted. **Conventions/Meetings:** quadrennial convention ● annual Supreme Counsel - board meeting - always 3rd Monday of June.

19019 ■ Ukrainian Gold Cross (UGC)
Address Unknown since 2007

Founded: 1931. **Members:** 700. **Description:** Women of Ukrainian descent. Assists distressed Ukrainian individuals and families. Sends parcels to Ukrainian families of prisoners of conscience in the USSR. Promotes Ukrainian traditions and arts. Sponsors summer camp for children. **Awards: Frequency:** periodic. **Type:** scholarship. **Departments:** Education; Social Service. **Affiliated With:** General Federation of Women's Clubs. **Publications:** Newsletter (in Ukrainian), semiannual. **Conventions/Meetings:** annual conference.

19020 ■ Ukrainian National Association (UNA)
PO Box 280
Parsippany, NJ 07054
Ph: (973)292-9800
Free: (800)253-9862
Fax: (973)292-0900
E-mail: una@unamember.com
URL: http://www.unamember.com
Contact: Stefan Kaczaraj, Pres.
Founded: 1894. **Members:** 52,926. **Staff:** 70. **Budget:** $10,000,000. **Regional Groups:** 27. **Local Groups:** 250. **Languages:** English, Ukrainian. **Description:** Fraternal benefit life insurance society for persons of Ukrainian and Slavic ancestry and their relatives. Supports cultural activities and sports program; provides aid to students; operates summer resort, children's camps, summer courses in Ukrainian language, history, literature, and art, and a home for senior citizens. **Awards: Frequency:** annual. **Type:** scholarship. **Recipient:** membership, need basis. **Telecommunication Services:** electronic mail, mlysko@unamember.com. **Publications:** *Svoboda* (in Ukrainian), weekly. Newspapers. **Price:** $45.00 /year for members; $55.00 /year for nonmembers. **Circulation:** 7,000. **Advertising:** accepted. Alternate Formats: online ● *Ukraine: A Concise Encyclopedia.* **Price:** $130.00 ● *Ukrainian Weekly.* Newspapers. **Price:** $45.00 /year for members; $55.00 /year for nonmembers. **Advertising:** accepted. Alternate Formats: online. **Conventions/Meetings:** quadrennial meeting (exhibits).

19021 ■ Ukrainian National Women's League of America (UNWLA)
203 2nd Ave.
New York, NY 10003
Ph: (212)533-4646 (212)477-0039
Fax: (212)533-5237
E-mail: unwla@unwla.org
URL: http://www.unwla.org
Contact: Iryna Kurowyckyj, Pres.
Founded: 1925. **Members:** 5,000. **Membership Dues:** regular at large, $50 (annual). **Staff:** 2. **Regional Groups:** 10. **Local Groups:** 119. **Languages:** English, Ukrainian. **For-Profit. Description:** Women of Ukrainian birth or descent living in the United States. Sponsors pre-kindergarten for children ages three to five. Founded the Ukrainian Museum in New York City in 1976. Offers pen pal program for children and adults. **Awards:** Certificate of Merit to members. **Frequency:** annual. **Type:** recognition. **Recipient:** for literary works dealing with Ukrainian history and historical fiction ● UNWL Scholarship. **Type:** scholarship. **Committees:** Archives and Ecology; Arts and Museum; Culture; Education; Public Relations; Scholarship/Student Sponsorship Program; Social Welfare. **Publications:** *Our Life Magazine* (in English and Ukrainian), monthly, except August. Contains articles on Ukrainian culture, history, and personalities; information on organization activities. **Price:** $30.00 /year for nonmembers; $25.00 /year for members; $40.00/year outside U.S.; $3.00/copy. ISSN: 0740-0225. **Circulation:** 3,700 ● Books (in English and Ukrainian). Subjects include children's stories, embroidery, crafts, poetry, and women's issues. **Conventions/Meetings:** triennial meeting, includes art exhibits (exhibits).

19022 ■ United Ukrainian American Relief Committee (UUARC)
1206 Cottman Ave.
Philadelphia, PA 19111
Ph: (215)728-1630
Fax: (215)728-1631
E-mail: uuarc@bellatlantic.net
URL: http://www.uuarc.org
Contact: Larysa Kyj PhD, Pres.
Founded: 1944. **Members:** 130. **Staff:** 4. **Budget:** $200,000. **Multinational. Description:** Federation of 80 state and local relief organizations. Works to aid needy Ukrainians in the United States and abroad. Maintains branches in nine cities in the United States and Europe, and three branches in the Ukraine. **Libraries: Type:** not open to the public. **Holdings:** 2,000. **Publications:** *History of UUARC* (in English

and Ukrainian) ● Newsletters. Alternate Formats: online. **Conventions/Meetings:** triennial convention ● annual meeting - always autumn, in Philadelphia, PA.

19023 ■ The Washington Group (TWG)
PO Box 11248
Washington, DC 20008
Ph: (202)586-7227
Fax: (202)586-3617
E-mail: info@thewashingtongroup.org
URL: http://www.thewashingtongroup.org
Contact: Adrian B. Pidlusky, Pres.
Founded: 1984. **Members:** 450. **Membership Dues:** full, $50 (annual) ● associate, $35 (annual) ● student, $5 (annual). **Staff:** 15. **Budget:** $30,000. **Description:** Ukrainan-American professionals. Sponsors professional, cultural, educational, and social activities; conducts research programs. **Awards:** TWG Fellowship Award. **Type:** fellowship. **Recipient:** for researchers and scholars utilizing Washington, DC area resources. **Committees:** Cultural; Fellowship. **Publications:** *TWG News*, bimonthly. Newsletter. **Price:** free, for members only. **Circulation:** 600. **Advertising:** accepted. **Conventions/Meetings:** monthly board meeting ● annual conference.

Vietnamese

19024 ■ Cambodian Mutual Assistance Association (CMAA)
787 E Broad St.
Columbus, OH 43205
Ph: (614)224-8888
Fax: (614)224-8888
E-mail: cambodianm@yahoo.com
URL: http://www.servintfree.net/cmaa
Contact: Yan Ke, Pres.
Founded: 1984. **Members:** 30. **Budget:** $3,000,000. **Regional Groups:** 2. **State Groups:** 8. **Local Groups:** 1. **Description:** Promotes the advancement of the Cambodian community through job placement assistance and educational programs. **Libraries: Type:** reference. **Awards: Frequency:** annual. **Type:** grant. **Computer Services:** database. **Publications:** *Khmer Lowell*, quarterly. Newsletter. **Price:** free. **Advertising:** accepted. **Conventions/Meetings:** monthly workshop.

19025 ■ National Alliance of Vietnamese American Service Agencies (NAVASA)
1010 Wayne Ave., Ste.310
Silver Spring, MD 20910
Ph: (301)587-2781 (301)587-2782
Fax: (301)587-2783
E-mail: navasa@navasa.org
URL: http://www.navasa.org
Contact: Huy Bui, Exec. Dir.
Founded: 1995. **Membership Dues:** organization (based on budget size), $100-$400 (annual). **Description:** Promotes economic self-sufficiency and active citizenship for Vietnamese-Americans in the US. Assists affiliates in addressing the linguistic, social, economic and civic needs facing community members in their specific localities. Facilitates the transition of Vietnamese refugees and immigrants from dependency to self-sufficiency. Promotes the integration of the Vietnamese American community into American society.

19026 ■ National Association for the Education and Advancement of Cambodian, Laotian, and Vietnamese Americans (NAFEA)
c/o Phouang Sixiengmay-Hamilton
7424 Chinook St. NE
Olympia, WA 98516
Ph: (360)725-6152
E-mail: phamilton@ospi.wednet.edu
URL: http://www.searac.org/nafea.html
Contact: Phouang Sixiengmay-Hamilton, Contact
Founded: 1979. **Members:** 300. **Description:** Seeks to: provide equal educational opportunities for Indochinese-Americans; advance the rights of Indochinese-Americans; acknowledge and publicize contributions of Vietnamese and other Indochinese in

American schools, culture, and society; encourage appreciation of Indochinese cultures, peoples, education, and language. Facilitates the exchange of information and skills among Indochinese professionals and other professionals working with Indochinese-Americans. Works toward legislative needs of Indochinese-Americans in education, health, social services, and welfare. Encourages scholarly excellence and active participation of parents and community members in school and community activities. Conducts networking activities and offers referrals for Indochinese professionals and others working with Indochinese in the fields of education and human services. Operates speakers' bureau. **Awards:** Community Service Award. **Frequency:** annual. **Type:** recognition. **Recipient:** for individuals nominated by local and national organizations, and selected by executive board ● **Type:** scholarship. **Affiliated With:** National Association for Asian and Pacific American Education. **Formerly:** (1989) National Association for Vietnamese American Education. **Publications:** *The Channel.* Newsletter. Alternate Formats: online ● *Channel for Indochinese American Communication*, quarterly. Newsletter. Contains current information on the education and resettlement of Indochinese refugees and their communities. Includes calendar of events. **Circulation:** 3,000 ● *Directory of Indochinese Personnel in Education and Social Services.* **Conventions/Meetings:** annual conference ● workshop.

19027 ■ National Congress of Vietnamese Americans (NCVA)
910 17th St. NW, Ste.314
Washington, DC 20006
Ph: (202)496-1401
Free: (877)592-4140
Fax: (703)719-5764
E-mail: info@ncvaonline.org
URL: http://www.ncvaonline.org
Contact: Hung Quoc Nguyen, Pres./CEO
Founded: 1986. **Description:** Promotes active participation of Vietnamese and Asian Americans in both civic and national matters and in community engagements. Defends human and civil rights secured by law for Vietnamese and Asian Americans. Eliminates prejudices, stereotypes and ignorance against Vietnamese and Asian Americans. Promotes economic development and self sufficiency for Vietnamese and Asian Americans. Fosters youth leadership.

19028 ■ Union of North American Vietnamese Students Association (uNAVSA)
PO Box 433
Westminster, CA 92684
Ph: (504)931-5878
E-mail: minh.nguyen@unavsa.org
URL: http://www.unavsa.org
Contact: Minh Thanh Nguyen, External VP
Founded: 2004. **Multinational. Description:** Aims to network, share common resources, and collaborate with Vietnamese youth organizations across North America. Fosters fundamental leadership and management skills to make individuals and organizations more effective throughout the Vietnamese community. Provides a forum and network to learn from the emerging Vietnamese American and Vietnamese Canadian leaders.

19029 ■ Vietnamese American Council (VAC)
780 S 1st St.
San Jose, CA 95113
Ph: (408)315-8472
E-mail: hvietmy@viet-nam.org
URL: http://www.viet-nam.org
Contact: Mr. Dat T. Nguyen, Exec. Dir.
Founded: 1982. **Description:** Promotes the social, economic and cultural advancement of the Vietnamese American community to the American society. Maintains the Vietnamese cultural heritage. Assists individuals with low income. **Computer Services:** Information services, Vietnam resources. **Programs:** Employment; Inter-Generation; Translation; Tuoi Hac Senior; US Citizenship; Youth Club. **Projects:** Blood Pressure Check-Up; Good Neighbor.

19030 ■ Vietnamese-American Professionals Alliance (VAPA)
PO Box 70804
Sunnyvale, CA 94086
Free: (877)705-6671
Fax: (877)705-6671
E-mail: contact@vapabayarea.org
URL: http://www.vapabayarea.org
Contact: Vy H. Tran, Co-Dir.
Founded: 1993. **Languages:** English, Vietnamese. **Multinational. Description:** Vietnamese American professionals. Supports the community and professionals within the network. **Conventions/Meetings:** monthly meeting - every first Thursday.

19031 ■ Vietnamese Professionals Society (VPS)
5150 Fair Oaks Blvd., Ste.101-128
Carmichael, CA 95608-5758
Ph: (916)484-3519
Fax: (916)484-3519
E-mail: contact@vps.org
URL: http://www.vps.org
Contact: Nguyen Ngoc Danh, Pres.
Founded: 1990. **National Groups:** 10. **Languages:** English, Vietnamese. **Multinational. Description:** Aims to increase the knowledge and understanding of the social and economic conditions in Vietnam, to promote the welfare of the Vietnamese people and through international cooperative effort, to apply science, technology, and humanity to the renovation of Vietnam. Facilitates the exchange of professional information and interaction between Vietnamese and non-Vietnamese professionals, and between groups of Vietnamese of different professions. Provides opportunities for students, professionals, and the public to learn about the current conditions and needs in Vietnam.

Welsh

19032 ■ National Welsh-American Foundation (NWAF)
143 Sunny Hillside Rd.
Benton, PA 17814-7822
Ph: (570)925-6923
Fax: (570)925-6735
E-mail: nwaf@dfnow.com
URL: http://www.wales-usa.org
Contact: Russell Williams, Pres.
Founded: 1980. **Members:** 1,200. **Membership Dues:** individual, $15 (annual) ● family, $20 (annual) ● sustaining, non-profit organization, $50 (annual) ● contributing, commercial organization, $100 (annual) ● patron, $250 (annual). **Staff:** 2. **Description:** Works to promote and preserve Welsh culture and support and recognize Welsh-Americans. Offers scholarships to Welsh-American and Welsh students; provides grants for the restoration of historical sites and museum maintenance; encourages Welsh language study; saves books and artifacts of Welsh heritage for libraries; creates memorials to honor historical events and locations; holds competitions; maintains Speaker's Bureau. **Awards:** Heritage Medallion. **Frequency:** annual. **Type:** recognition. **Recipient:** for service to the Welsh-American community ● NWAF Exchange Scholarship. **Frequency:** annual. **Type:** scholarship. **Recipient:** for a Welsh-American or Welsh student. **Telecommunication Services:** electronic mail, celizwh@intergate.com. **Publications:** *The Eagle and the Dragon*, quarterly. Bulletin ● *Yr Eryr A'r Ddraig*, quarterly. Bulletin. Features the Welsh translation of the Eagle and the Dragon. ● Brochure, biennial. **Conventions/Meetings:** bimonthly executive committee meeting ● annual meeting - in May or October.

19033 ■ St. David's Society of the State of New York (SDS)
Address Unknown since 2007
Founded: 1801. **Members:** 311. **Membership Dues:** individual, $20 (annual) ● $10 (annual). **Staff:** 1. **Languages:** English, Welsh. **Description:** Welsh persons, their descendants, and those connected with them. Collects and preserves information about Wales, its people, and their descendants in the U.S. cultivates knowledge of the history of Wales and of the Welsh language and literature. Aids distressed Welsh persons and their descendants. Supports Welsh language study program and summer schools. **Libraries: Type:** reference. **Holdings:** 500. **Awards:** St. David's Society Scholarship. **Frequency:** annual. **Type:** scholarship. **Recipient:** for students who attend Welsh colleges and to students of Welsh descent. **Committees:** Music and Literature. **Formerly:** Station David's Benevolent Society of the Cities of New York and Brooklyn; (1835) Station David's Benevolent Society; (1841) Station David's Benefit and Benevolent Society of the City of New York. **Conventions/Meetings:** annual meeting - always March 1, St. David's Day, the anniversary of the Patron Saint of Wales, in New York City.

19034 ■ Welsh National Gymanfa Ganu Association (WNGGA)
c/o Dr. John Ellis, Exec. Dir.
PO Box 215
Hartland, MI 48353-0215
Ph: (810)632-7850
Fax: (810)632-7805
E-mail: wngga@comcast.net
URL: http://www.wngga.org
Contact: Dr. John Ellis, Exec. Dir.
Founded: 1929. **Members:** 2,900. **Membership Dues:** individual, $10 (annual) ● life - individual, $150 ● organization, $50 (annual) ● life - over 65, $100. **Staff:** 3. **Budget:** $60,000. **Description:** Strives to promote Welsh religious and cultural heritage and traditions. **Awards:** WNGGA Grant. **Frequency:** annual. **Type:** grant. **Recipient:** to member of Welsh lineage, citizen of U.S. or Canada ● WNGGA Scholarship. **Frequency:** annual. **Type:** scholarship. **Recipient:** to member of Welsh lineage, citizen of U.S. or Canada. **Formerly:** (1971) National Gymanfa GANU Association of U.S. and Canada. **Publications:** *Facts About the WNGGA*, annual. Pamphlet. Describes the organization and member benefits. **Price:** free upon request. **Circulation:** 4,000 ● *Hwyl*, quarterly. Newsletter. Alternate Formats: online ● *Publications and Recordings Price List*, annual. **Price:** free ● *Welsh and English Hymns* (in English and Welsh). Book. Contains hymns. **Price:** $12.00 each; $17.00 enlarged version ● *Welsh Hymns for Non Welsh Singers, Phonetic Edition for 1995 Reformatted Hymnal*. Book. **Price:** $11.00. **Conventions/Meetings:** annual North American Festival of Wales - meeting (exhibits) - always Labor Day weekend.

West Indian

19035 ■ Montserrat Progressive Society of New York (MPSNY)
207 W 137th St.
New York, NY 10030-2425
Ph: (212)283-3346
Fax: (212)368-3165
URL: http://montserrat.search.co.tt
Contact: Ashton Daley, Pres.
Founded: 1914. **Members:** 150. **Description:** Persons from Montserrat, their spouses, and children. Purposes are to: unite people from the West Indian Island of Montserrat; assist in uplifting them socially, morally, and intellectually; promote their general welfare. Raises funds for five scholarships and for assistance to students. Maintains library. **Awards: Type:** recognition. **Recipient:** for meritorious service to the society. **Committees:** Anniversary; Education; Sick; Welfare Program. **Publications:** Newsletter, quarterly. **Conventions/Meetings:** monthly meeting - always second Sunday.

Women

19036 ■ Congressional Club (CC)
2001 New Hampshire Ave. NW
Washington, DC 20009
Ph: (202)332-1155
Fax: (202)797-0698
E-mail: congressionalclub@verizon.net
URL: http://www.thecongressionalclub.com
Founded: 1908. **Members:** 650. **Staff:** 1. **Description:** Women's organization made up of wives of present and former U.S. Representatives, Senators, Cabinet members, Supreme Court Justices, the wives of the President and Vice President of the U.S. and the wife of the Speaker of the House are honorary members. **Committees:** Archives; Community Service; Cookbook; Decorating; Diplomatic; First Lady's Luncheon; Founders Day; House; Museum and Foundation; Press; Year Book. **Publications:** *Cookbook*. **Price:** $48.00 14th Edition, includes shipping and handling; $27.00 13th Edition ● Directory, biennial. **Conventions/Meetings:** weekly luncheon.

19037 ■ General Federation of Women's Clubs (GFWC)
1734 N St. NW
Washington, DC 20036-2990
Ph: (202)347-3168
Free: (800)443-GFWC
Fax: (202)835-0246
E-mail: gfwc@gfwc.org
URL: http://www.gfwc.org
Contact: Ms. Natasha Kalteis, Exec. Dir.
Founded: 1890. **Members:** 150,000. **Membership Dues:** individual, $12 (annual). **Staff:** 20. **Budget:** $2,100,000. **Regional Groups:** 8. **State Groups:** 50. **Local Groups:** 5,000. **Multinational. Description:** International women's volunteer service organization with members from 5,000 clubs. Provides volunteer leadership training and development. Serves state and local clubs in community service programs in the following areas: the arts; conservation; education; home life; public affairs; international affairs. Has established Women's History and Resource Center to promote and document volunteer achievement. **Libraries: Type:** reference; by appointment only; open to the public. **Holdings:** 1,000; archival material, artwork, audio recordings, books, papers, photographs. **Subjects:** women's history, volunteerism. **Awards:** A Year in Pictures. **Frequency:** annual. **Type:** recognition. **Recipient:** for a photo relevant to particular months or seasons ● GFWC Volunteers in Action. **Frequency:** annual. **Type:** monetary. **Recipient:** for a club project photo ● Jane Cunningham Croly/GFWC Print Journalism Award for Excellence. **Frequency:** annual. **Type:** monetary. **Recipient:** for print journalist whose writing best captures the courage, vision and spirit of Mrs. Croly ● The World in Pictures. **Frequency:** annual. **Type:** monetary. **Recipient:** for the best photo. **Programs:** Arts; Conservation; Education; Home Life; International Affairs; President's Special Project: Domestic Violence; Public Affairs. **Publications:** *GFWC Clubwoman Magazine*, bimonthly. Features local, state and national news. **Price:** $6.00/year in U.S. and Canada; $12.00/year outside U.S. and Canada; $11.00/2 years; $16.50/3 years. ISSN: 0745-2209. **Advertising:** accepted ● *Membership Matters*, quarterly. Newsletter. Features membership recruiting and retention techniques, successful membership strategies and membership-specific information. **Conventions/Meetings:** annual convention, brings together leaders and members for educational, networking and training purposes (exhibits) - June. 2008 June 28-July 1, Chicago, IL; 2009 June, Cleveland, OH; 2010 June, Omaha, NE.

19038 ■ IDB Family Association
One Democracy Plz.
6701 Democracy Blvd., Ste.103
Bethesda, MD 20817
Ph: (301)493-6576
Fax: (301)493-6456
E-mail: familya@iadb.org
URL: http://www.iadbfamilyassociation.org
Contact: Patricia Keith, Coor.
Founded: 1965. **Members:** 800. **Staff:** 2. **Languages:** English, Spanish. **Description:** Represents families of bank employees; families of bank officers and of former bank employees are nonvoting members. Aims to promote friendship, cooperation, cultural exchange, and understanding among mem-

bers and their families. Seeks to heighten members' awareness of the opportunities for personal growth in the Washington, DC, area. Facilitates contact and collaboration among all institutions organized with similar aims and interests; cooperates with area institutions in aiding the Washington, DC, Spanish-speaking community. Offers language classes, information seminars, and other educational programs. **Libraries: Type:** reference. **Committees:** Social Assistance; Welcoming. **Divisions:** Communication Division; Education Division; Socio-Cultural Division. **Subcommittees:** Mom and Dads; Reading; Work Group About Domestic Abuse. **Formerly:** Inter-American Development Bank's Wives Association. **Publications:** *Participation* (in English and Spanish), semiannual. Newsletter. Provides information to members, including events and courses. **Price:** free. Alternate Formats: online ● Also publishes information kit, flyers. **Conventions/Meetings:** annual meeting.

19039 ■ United Order True Sisters (UOTS)
Linton Intl. Plz.
660 Linton Blvd., Ste.6
Delray Beach, FL 33444
Ph: (561)265-1557
E-mail: info@uots.org
URL: http://www.uots.org
Contact: Mr. Marion Polonsky, Natl. Pres.
Founded: 1846. **Members:** 2,500. **Membership Dues:** volunteer service, $15-$22 (annual). **Staff:** 1. **State Groups:** 6. **Local Groups:** 18. **Description:** Charitable organization that offers personal service to indigent persons with cancer or AIDS. Sends children with cancer to camp. **Awards: Frequency:** annual. **Type:** grant. **Recipient:** to various individual chapters ● **Frequency:** annual. **Type:** recognition. **Recipient:** to various individual chapters. **Also Known As:** UOTS, Inc. **Publications:** *Are You Aware*, semiannual. Newsletter. Includes current activities and fund raising projects. **Conventions/Meetings:** biennial convention, national, installation of new officers.

19040 ■ Women of Color Resource Center (WCRC)
1611 Telegraph Ave., No. 303
Oakland, CA 94612
Ph: (510)444-2700
Fax: (510)444-2711
E-mail: info@coloredgirls.org
URL: http://www.coloredgirls.org
Contact: Linda Burnham, Exec. Dir.
Founded: 1990. **Membership Dues:** low income, $15 (annual) ● individual, $35 (annual) ● organization, $55 (annual) ● sustainer, $100 (annual). **Multinational. Description:** Works on social justice issues affecting women, including economic inequality, racial discrimination, sexism, and homophobia. **Programs:** Economic Justice and Human Rights. **Projects:** Peace and Solidarity; Popular Education; Sisters of Fire; Women's Human Rights. **Publications:** *National Directory*. **Price:** $22.95 ● *Sister to Sister/S2S*, quarterly. Newsletter. Provides highlights of women-of-color organizing across the U.S. and updates on events and issues. **Price:** $35.00/three issues; $55.00/year for organizations. ISSN: 1090-3887. Alternate Formats: online ● *Women's Education in the Global Economy (WedGE)*. Book. Presents lessons, activities, games and skits for better understanding of the impact of the global economy on women worldwide. **Price:** $24.95.

Woodmen

19041 ■ Modern Woodmen of America (MWA)
PO Box 2005
Rock Island, IL 61204-2005
Ph: (309)786-6481
Free: (800)447-9811
Fax: (309)793-5547
E-mail: memberservice@modern.woodmen.org
URL: http://www.modern-woodmen.org
Contact: Mr. Kenny Massey, Pres.
Founded: 1883. **Members:** 750,000. **Staff:** 425. **Local Groups:** 2,094. **Description:** Serves as fraternal benefit life insurance society. **Libraries: Type:** not open to the public. **Publications:** *The Modern Woodmen*, quarterly. Magazine. Provides a family and financial resource for modern woodmen members. **Conventions/Meetings:** quadrennial convention.

19042 ■ Woodmen Rangers (WR)
c/o Woodmen of the World/Omaha Woodmen Life
  Insurance Society
Woodmen Tower
1700 Farnam St.
Omaha, NE 68102
Free: (800)225-3108
E-mail: wow@woodmen.com
URL: http://www.woodmen.org
Contact: James L. Mounce, Chm./Pres./CEO
Founded: 1903. **Members:** 139,000. **National Groups:** 1,000. **Description:** Serves as youth organization sponsored by Woodmen of the World Life Insurance Society (see separate entry) for boys and girls; active members are 8 to 15 years old participate in programs that enhance leadership training, character, and personal development. Good citizenship and civic responsibility is stressed. Attends summer camp provided by each marketing area. Sponsors local civic and charitable activities. **Affiliated With:** Woodmen of the World/Omaha Woodmen Life Insurance Society. **Formerly:** (1947) Boys of Woodcraft Auxiliary of the Woodmen of the World; (1964) Boys of Woodcraft Sportsmen's Clubs/ Girl of Woodcraft Sportsmen's Clubs; (1983) Rangers and Rangerettes. **Publications:** *Lodge Leader*, quarterly. Magazine ● Manual.

19043 ■ Woodmen of the World/Omaha Woodmen Life Insurance Society (WWLIS)
Woodmen Tower
1700 Farnam St.
Omaha, NE 68102-2002
Free: (800)225-3108
Fax: (402)271-7269
E-mail: wow@woodmen.com
URL: http://www.woodmen.org
Contact: James L. Mounce, Chm./Pres./CEO
Founded: 1890. **Members:** 800,000. **Staff:** 600. **Regional Groups:** 27. **Local Groups:** 2,000. **Description:** Offers insurance protection with member benefits. Product portfolio includes whole life, flexible premium life and term life insurance, cancer insurance, hospital supplement insurance, long term care insurance and annuities. Mutual funds and other investment products are available through a for-profit subsidiary, Woodmen Financial Services, Inc. Woodmen lodges conduct fraternal projects of benefit to people and their communities, including presenting U.S. flags to civic and community organizations, donating equipment to police, fire and rescue units, providing assistance to senior citizens, the physically impaired and orphans, and providing assistance through their disaster relief program with the American Red Cross. "Woodmen" is licensed as Woodmen of the World Life Insurance Society in all states and the District of Columbia, except California, Colorado, Idaho, Montana, Nevada, Oregon, Utah, Washington and Wyoming, where it is licensed as Omaha Woodmen Life Insurance Society. **Libraries: Type:** reference. **Holdings:** 11,000; archival material. **Subjects:** law library. **Awards: Type:** recognition ● **Type:** recognition. **Committees:** Audit; Compensation; Governance; Investment; Judiciary; Legislation; National Fraternal; Rules Governing. **Absorbed:** (1962) United Order of the Golden Cross; (1964) Mutual Benefit Department of the Order of Railroad Telegraphers; (1965) Supreme Forest Woodmen Circle; (1968) New England Order of Protection; (1994) Supreme Camp of the American Woodmen; (2001) Neighbors of Woodcraft. **Publications:** *Chips Magazine*, monthly ● *Lodge Leader*, quarterly. Magazine ● *Shavings*, monthly. Magazine ● *Wfm*, quarterly. Magazine. Contains lodge and member news, product information, and informative articles on health, family living, American history and other topics. **Price:** $3.00/year. **Circulation:** 500,000. Also Cited As: *Woodmen Fraternal Magazine*. **Conventions/Meetings:** biennial Jurisdictional Conventions, meetings of elected delegates from all lodges within a jurisdiction (state or groups of neighboring states) ● quadrennial National Convention.

Adventist

19044 ■ Advent Christian General Conference of America (ACGC)
PO Box 690848
Charlotte, NC 28227
Ph: (704)545-6161
Fax: (704)573-0712
E-mail: execdirect@acgc.us
URL: http://www.adventchristian.org
Contact: Rev. Ronald Thomas, Exec. Dir.
Founded: 1860. **Members:** 28,500. **Staff:** 14. **Budget:** $1,600,000. **Regional Groups:** 5. **State Groups:** 31. **Local Groups:** 306. **National Groups:** 14. **Description:** Serves as an evangelical organization comprising 306 Advent Christian churches in the U.S. and Canada. Seeks to share the Christian faith around the world by encouraging reliance on the Scriptures. Sponsors missions in the U.S., Canada, South Africa, Japan, Ghana, New Zealand, the Philippines, Malaysia, China, Croatia, Honduras, Mexico, India, Liberia, and Nigeria. Supports retirement centers; sponsors workshops and seminars on subjects such as church growth, Christian education, women's ministries, and church music. Operates American Advent Mission Society. Maintains charitable program; compiles statistics. Maintains historical collections at Gordon-Conwell Theological Seminary, South Hamilton, MA and Aurora University, Aurora, IL. **Awards:** Type: recognition. **Affiliated With:** National Association of Evangelicals. **Publications:** *Advent Christian News*, monthly. Newsletter. Alternate Formats: online ● *Advent Christian Witness*, bimonthly. Magazine. **Price:** $15.00 /year for individuals. Alternate Formats: online ● *Insight*, quarterly. Magazine ● *Maranatha Devotions*, quarterly. Book. **Conventions/Meetings:** triennial convention, retirement homes, campgrounds, various ministries (exhibits).

19045 ■ Woman's Home and Foreign Mission Society (WHFMS)
PO Box 23152
Charlotte, NC 28227
Ph: (704)545-6161
Free: (800)676-0694
Fax: (704)753-0712
E-mail: mritchie@acgc.us
Contact: Ms. Mary Ritchie, Admin.Asst.
Founded: 1897. **Members:** 1,381. **Staff:** 2. **Regional Groups:** 5. **State Groups:** 26. **Local Groups:** 103. **Description:** Administered by the Department of Women's Ministries of the Advent Christian Conference. Christian women. Seeks to: unite members for action; encourage spiritual growth; involve women in evangelism and provide them with fellowship, mission education, and service opportunities. Works to provide leadership training and revitalize and increase the ministry potential of local member groups. Provides a means whereby members may share information and ideas. Raises funds to support worldwide Advent Christian ministries and field operations. Supports and encourages growth of children's groups in local ministries. Operates Speaker's Bureau. Holds training seminars and workshops. **Libraries:** Type: reference. **Subjects:** women's issues. **Computer Services:** database, listings of organizational presidents, local spiritual life chairpersons, and local children's group leaders ● mailing lists. **Publications:** *Advent Christian News*, monthly. Newsletter. **Price:** free ● *Advent Christian Witness*, bimonthly. Magazine. **Circulation:** 3,000 ● *Prayer and Praise*, monthly. Bulletin. **Conventions/Meetings:** triennial Advent Christian Women's Conference - meeting (exhibits).

Alternative Medicine

19046 ■ Commission on Religious Counseling and Healing
PO Box 16201
Duluth, MN 55816-1612
Ph: (202)448-2948
Fax: (864)248-4713
E-mail: RBSOCC@juno.com
URL: http://crch.rbsocc.org
Contact: Fr. Timothy Kjera, Moderator
Membership Dues: license fee, $275 (annual). **Regional Groups:** 3. **Multinational. Description:** Represents the theocentric practitioners across the United States and other countries. Provides spiritual, intellectual and physical healing. Protects the rights of practitioners and clients. Offers various therapies. **Computer Services:** database, directory of practitioners.

American Indian

19047 ■ Native American Church of North America of the Cowlitz Indians
Address Unknown since 2007
Founded: 1999. **Members:** 2,000. **Staff:** 6. **Regional Groups:** 2. **State Groups:** 2. **Local Groups:** 2. **Languages:** English, Spanish. **Multinational. Description:** Dedicated to charitable, educational, and scientific human advancement through ministry and immemorial customs of the intertribal confraternity of the Native American Church. Seeks to enable all people in reaching their full potential and to achieve family unit independence for the working poor. **Libraries:** Type: open to the public; by appointment only. **Holdings:** artwork, audiovisuals, books, business records, clippings, periodicals. **Subjects:** Native American Church, Peyote, American Indian Religious Freedom Act, Federal Indian Law, traditional medicine, botany, health, artifacts. **Awards:** Corporate NAC. **Type:** scholarship ● **Type:** grant.

Amish

19048 ■ National Committee for Amish Religious Freedom (NCARF)
15343 Susanna Cir.
Livonia, MI 48154
Ph: (734)464-3908
Fax: (734)427-1419
E-mail: amish@holycrosslivonia.org
URL: http://www.holycrosslivonia.org/amish
Contact: Rev. William C. Lindholm, Chm.
Founded: 1967. **Description:** Professors, clergymen, attorneys, and others interested in "legal defense in behalf of minority groups' religious and educational liberty." Provides legal defense for Amish people, since the committee feels the Amish have religious scruples against defending themselves or seeking court action. Maintains speakers' bureau. **Conventions/Meetings:** conference and seminar.

Anglican

19049 ■ Anglican Association of Biblical Scholars (AABS)
c/o Kevin A. Wilson, Sec.-Treas.
447 Kendall Rd.
Tewksbury, MA 01876
E-mail: secretary@aabs.org
URL: http://www.aabs.org
Contact: Kevin A. Wilson, Sec.-Treas.
Founded: 1991. **Membership Dues:** regular, $20 (annual) ● regular, C$28 (annual) ● associate, $15 (annual) ● associate, C$21 (annual). **Multinational. Description:** Supports biblical scholarship at all levels in the Anglican Communion. Fosters extensive involvement of biblical scholars in the life of Anglican churches. Promotes the development of resources for biblical studies in Anglican theological education. **Awards:** Student Paper Competition. **Frequency:** annual. **Type:** monetary. **Recipient:** for the best paper in biblical exegesis written by a student attending a seminary of the ECUSA. **Telecommunication Services:** electronic mail, kwilson@lcc.lt. **Publications:** Newsletter. Alternate Formats: online ● Papers. Alternate Formats: online.

19050 ■ Anglican Use Association (AUA)
15415 Red Robin Rd.
San Antonio, TX 78255
Ph: (210)695-2944
E-mail: frphillips@aol.com
Founded: 1983. **Description:** Society of Prayer for the Daily Intentions of the Anglican Use within the Catholic Church. **Divisions:** Atonement Academy. **Publications:** *Parish Newsletter*. Alternate Formats: online.

Anglican Catholic

19051 ■ American Friends of the Anglican Centre in Rome
c/o Rev. Norman J. Catir, Jr., Exec. Sec.
31 John St.
Providence, RI 02906
Ph: (401)831-4285
Fax: (401)272-6234

E-mail: director.acr@flashnet.it

Contact: Rev. Norman J. Catir Jr., Exec. Sec.

Founded: 1995. **Staff:** 1. **Description:** Promotes and supports the activities of the Anglican Centre in Rome, Italy. Conducts fundraising campaigns among Episcopalian parishes in the United States.

19052 ■ Anglican Fellowship of Prayer (AFP)
1106 Mansfield Ave.
Indiana, PA 15701
Ph: (724)463-6436 (814)725-4484
E-mail: celinda@fastmail.fm
URL: http://www.afp.org
Contact: Dr. William C. Williams, Pres.

Founded: 1958. **Members:** 12,000. **Staff:** 1. **Budget:** $100,000. **Description:** Conducts educational programs. **Publications:** *Partners in Prayer*, quarterly. Newsletter. **Circulation:** 14,500. Alternate Formats: online. **Conventions/Meetings:** annual conference (exhibits) ● workshop, for prayer and biblical spirituality.

19053 ■ Anglican Order of Archbishop Robert Leighton (AOARL)
Address Unknown since 2007

Founded: 1897. **Staff:** 16. **Budget:** $100,000. **Description:** Organization derives its name from Robert Leighton (1611-84), Archbishop of Glasgow, Scotland. "Christian men of distinction in their field of lifetime endeavor." Selects up to twenty five new members each year. Maintains hall of fame. **Awards:** Document of Honor, The Trench Award. **Frequency:** annual. **Type:** recognition. **Recipient:** Christian men of distinction in their field of lifetime endeavor ● Leighton Order Medal. **Frequency:** annual. **Type:** recognition. **Recipient:** Christian men of distinction in their field of lifetime endeavor. **Boards:** Board of Trustees and Visitors. **Publications:** *The Anglicana Directory*, annual. Lists continuing churches and clergy. **Price:** free online. **Circulation:** 100,000. **Advertising:** accepted. Alternate Formats: online ● *Hillspeak Who's Who*, annual. Directory. **Conventions/Meetings:** annual Leighton Award Ceremony - meeting, held at Archbishop's chapel with ceremonial sword - always November 5. Bay St. Louis, MS - **Avg. Attendance:** 100.

19054 ■ Fellowship of Concerned Churchmen (FCC)
9489 Brown Rd.
Jonesboro, GA 30238
Ph: (770)961-4200
E-mail: whsdws@verizon.net
URL: http://www.netministries.org/see/charmin/cm06091
Contact: Mr. Wallace Spaulding, Pres.

Founded: 1973. **Members:** 300. **Membership Dues:** individual, $40 (annual) ● married couple, $50 (annual). **Staff:** 3. **Description:** Coordinating agent for lay people and clergy concerned with the breakdown of faith and order within the Episcopal Church USA and the Anglican Church worldwide. Encourages Anglican unity by promoting communication and fellowship among Anglican/Episcopal traditionalists dedicated to working for the preservation of historic Anglicanism. Sponsored the Church Congress of St. Louis in 1977 at which time the Affirmation of St. Louis (a document professing doctrinal Anglican principles) was adopted. **Publications:** *Directory of Traditional Anglican and Episcopal Parishes*, biennial. Includes traditional Anglican and Episcopal parishes in the USA, as well as worldwide, providing essential information on each. **Price:** $38.00 for nonmembers; free for members. **Advertising:** accepted ● *Fellowship Teaching Leaflets*. **Conventions/Meetings:** biennial meeting and workshop (exhibits) - odd numbered years.

19055 ■ Society of King Charles the Martyr (SKCM)
PO Box 79212
Waverley, MA 02479-0212
Ph: (781)308-0056

E-mail: wuonola@earthlink.net

Contact: Dr. Mark A. Wuonola, American Rep.

Founded: 1894. **Members:** 380. **Membership Dues:** individual, $10 (annual). **Description:** Individuals with an interest in Charles Stuart (1600-49), King of England (from 1626), who was martyred for defending his faith and was subsequently canonized by the Anglican Church. Seeks recognition of King Charles' sacrifice by the Anglican Communion. Works to celebrate the Feast of Charles Stuart (January 30) and reinstate it in the Kalendar of the Book of Common Prayer. **Publications:** *Church & King*, semiannual. Newsletter. **Price:** included in membership dues ● *SKCM News*, semiannual. Newsletter. Covers membership activities, information on Charles I of England, the Stuarts, and on monarchy; devotion to Charles I; relevant book reviews. **Price:** included in membership dues. ISSN: 1540-045X. **Conventions/Meetings:** annual luncheon, sermon at mass, short business meeting after luncheon.

Animal Welfare

19056 ■ Christians Helping Animals and People
c/o Rev. Frances Arnetta
PO Box 272
Selden, NY 11784
Ph: (631)732-3138
E-mail: gentila2000@yahoo.com
Contact: Rev. Frances Arnetta, Contact

Founded: 1982. **Staff:** 1. **Local Groups:** 1. **Nonmembership. Description:** Committed to Christian ministry, particularly extending ministry to all creatures and those who love them. **Publications:** *Animal Rights: A Biblical View*, ongoing. **Price:** free ● *Coping With the Loss of a Beloved Pet* ● *Questions Christians Should Ask About Animals* ● *Vegetarianism: God's Best for All Concerned*.

Anthroposophical

19057 ■ Anthroposophical Society in America (ASA)
1923 Geddes Ave.
Ann Arbor, MI 48104
Ph: (734)662-9355
Fax: (734)662-1727
E-mail: information@anthroposophy.org
URL: http://www.anthroposophy.org
Contact: Jean Yeager, Admin. Dir.

Founded: 1923. **Members:** 4,000. **Membership Dues:** regular, $120 (annual) ● supporting, $500. **Staff:** 8. **Regional Groups:** 4. **Local Groups:** 75. **Description:** Fosters the life of the soul and the spirit in individuals and society. Promotes the spiritual science of Anthroposophy, which was founded by Austrian philosopher Rudolf Steiner (1861-1925). Conducts educational and research programs. **Libraries:** Type: reference. **Holdings:** 19,000; books, periodicals. **Subjects:** Western thought and spirituality. **Publications:** *Anthroposophy Worldwide*, 10/year. Newspaper. Contains worldwide activities and calendar of events. ● *Directory of Anthroposophical Initiatives*, semiannual. **Price:** $5.00. **Advertising:** accepted. Alternate Formats: online ● *Journal for Anthroposophy*, semiannual. **Price:** $15.00/year. **Advertising:** accepted ● Also publishes booklets on programs offered. **Conventions/Meetings:** periodic conference (exhibits) ● annual general assembly ● workshop.

Armenian

19058 ■ Armenian Church Youth Organization of America (ACYOA)
Eastern Diocese of the Armenian Church of Am.
630 2nd Ave.
New York, NY 10016
Ph: (212)686-0710
Fax: (212)779-3558

E-mail: acyoa@armeniandiocese.org
URL: http://www.acyoa.org
Contact: Greg Andonian, Pres.

Founded: 1946. **Members:** 2,425. **Staff:** 8. **Regional Groups:** 6. **Local Groups:** 35. **Languages:** Armenian, English. **Description:** Young people who are members of the Armenian Church. Conducts religious, educational, cultural, service, social, and recreational programs; sponsors religious conferences, retreats, study, and mission programs. Sponsors service programs in Armenia as part of its Armenia Services Programs; also sponsors leadership seminars. Holds national sports weekend. **Publications:** *Hye Hokin*, quarterly. Newsletter. Alternate Formats: online ● *Membership Handbook*, annual. **Conventions/Meetings:** annual general assembly - always Memorial Day Weekend.

19059 ■ Armenian Missionary Association of America (AMAA)
31 W Century Rd.
Paramus, NJ 07652
Ph: (201)265-2607
Fax: (201)265-6015
E-mail: amaa@amaa.org
URL: http://www.amaa.org
Contact: Mr. Andrew Torigian, Exec. Dir.

Founded: 1918. **Members:** 17,000. **Staff:** 12. **Budget:** $5,000,000. **State Groups:** 2. **Local Groups:** 30. **National Groups:** 4. **Description:** Maintains a range of educational, evangelism, relief, social service, church and child care ministries in 20 countries around the world. Emphasizes full financial disclosure, accountability and careful stewardship of funds. **Libraries:** Type: reference. **Holdings:** 10,000. **Awards:** Type: recognition ● Type: scholarship. **Recipient:** to future pastors and leaders. **Publications:** *AMAA News*, bimonthly. Newsletter. Contains association news. ● *News*, bimonthly ● Annual Report, annual ● Books ● Brochures. **Conventions/Meetings:** competition ● seminar.

Asatru

19060 ■ American Vinland Association (AVA)
537 Jones St.
PMB 2154
San Francisco, CA 94102-2007
E-mail: prudence@freyasfolk.org
URL: http://www.freyasfolk.org

Founded: 1987. **Members:** 300. **Membership Dues:** individual, group/family, $20 (annual). **Staff:** 4. **Budget:** $4,000. **Regional Groups:** 4. **State Groups:** 9. **Local Groups:** 3. **National Groups:** 10. **Description:** Believers dedicated to the promotion and practice of "Elder Troth", a native Heathen folk religion of northern Europe. **Formerly:** Vinland Alliance; (1995) Ring of Troth. **Publications:** *The Yarbok*, annual, published in January. Yearbook. Includes a "yearbook" for members. **Price:** included in membership dues; $10.00 for nonmembers. **Advertising:** accepted ● *Yggdrasil*, quarterly. Journal. Contains articles on gods and goddesses, book reviews, and Troth (the Northern European Tradition). **Price:** included in membership dues. **Circulation:** 300. **Advertising:** accepted. Alternate Formats: online. **Conventions/Meetings:** annual Ravenwood - meeting, outdoor camp out - always in July ● annual Trothmoot - meeting (exhibits) - Labor Day weekend, OH or IN.

19061 ■ Asatru Alliance (AA)
PO Box 961
Payson, AZ 85547
E-mail: eagle@asatru.org
URL: http://www.asatru.org
Contact: Valgard Murray, Spokesperson

Founded: 1972. **Members:** 600. **Local Groups:** 40. **Description:** Practices, promotes, and explores the ancient indigenous religion and culture of the Scandinavian and Germanic peoples. The Norse religion places a high value on human freedom, ancestral heritage, courage, the extended family unit, and harmony with nature. Members celebrate solstices and equinoxes as part of the endless cycle of the years, and set aside other special days to commemorate significant events or to honor deceased members of the clan. While the Norse faith has an afterlife concept, more emphasis is placed on living a full and useful life on earth, exercising freedom and self-reliance and opposing tyranny, bureaucracy, and "global monoculture". **Formerly:** (1977) Viking Brotherhood; (1988) Asatru Free Assembly. **Publications:** *Vor Tru*, quarterly. Magazine. Contains news, current events, and articles on the Asatru community in Vinland. **Price:** $18.00. **Circulation:** 300. **Conventions/Meetings:** annual congress (exhibits).

Ascended Masters

19062 ■ Church Universal and Triumphant (CUT)
PO Box 5000
Gardiner, MT 59030-5000
Ph: (406)848-9500
Free: (800)245-5445
Fax: (800)221-8307
E-mail: tslinfo@tsl.org
URL: http://www.tsl.org
Contact: Ms. Destyne Erickson, Communications Mgr.

Founded: 1958. **Membership Dues:** individual, $10 (monthly). **Staff:** 74. **Languages:** English, French, Portuguese, Russian, Spanish. **Multinational. Description:** Conducts religious services and disseminates the teachings of the Ascended Masters as interpreted by Elizabeth Clare Prophet and Mark L. Prophet. Defines the Ascended Masters as those individuals throughout human history who have reunited with God through the ritual of the ascension. Ascended Masters recognized by the group include Gautama Buddha, Confucius, Kuan Yin, Jesus Christ, Saint Germain, Mother Mary and many more. **Libraries: Type:** open to the public; reference. **Holdings:** 200; archival material, artwork, audio recordings, audiovisuals, books, video recordings. **Subjects:** Jesus' lost years and lost teachings, Mary Magdalene, divine feminine, fallen angels and the origins of evil, human aura, alchemy, reincarnation, karma, twin flames, soul mates, nurturing the soul, the Great White Brotherhood, ascended masters, immortality. **Computer Services:** Information services, CD on demand services via internet, create personalized CDs from large selection of audio files. **Study Groups:** Book. **Subgroups:** The Summit Lighthouse; Summit University; Teaching Centers. **Also Known As:** (1976) The Summit Lighthouse. **Publications:** *Climb the Highest Mountain*. Book ● *Fallen Angels and the Origins of Evil*. Book ● *Forbidden Mysteries of Enoch*, weekly. Book ● *Heart to Heart*, trademarked newsletter to the worldwide community of members, quarterly, 3-4 times /year for members. Contains new products, spiritual teachings, resources, events calendar, and children's materials. **Price:** included in membership dues ● *The Human Aura*. Book ● *The Issa Chronicles - Jesus Lost Years*, five books in series. Book. Features fiction based on documentary research. **Price:** $16.95 ● *Kabbalah*. Book ● *The Lost Teachings of Jesus*, monthly. Book ● *The Lost Years of Jesus*. Book ● *Pearls of Wisdom*, weekly. Newsletter ● *Reincarnation: The Missing Link in Christianity*. Book ● *Saint Germain on Alchemy*. Book ● *Wanting to be Born*. Book ● Audiotapes ● Brochures ● Catalogs ● Videos. **Conventions/Meetings:** quarterly conference - usually Easter, October, New Year's day, and June or July in Park County, MT.

Atheist

19063 ■ American Atheists
PO Box 5733
Parsippany, NJ 07054-6733
Ph: (908)276-7300
Fax: (908)276-7402

E-mail: info@atheists.org
URL: http://www.atheists.org
Contact: Ellen Johnson, Pres.

Founded: 1958. **Members:** 2,300. **Membership Dues:** associate, $15 (annual) ● distinguished citizen and student in U.S., $25 (annual) ● individual, $35 (annual) ● couple/family, $60 (annual) ● wall builder, $150 (annual) ● life, $1,500 ● associate-international, $25 (annual) ● distinguished citizen and student outside U.S., $35 (annual) ● individual outside U.S., $45 (annual) ● couple/family outside U.S., $70 (annual). **Staff:** 4. **Budget:** $250,000. **Description:** Serves as an educational organization dedicated to the absolute separation of state and church. Promotes the philosophy of Atheism and protection of civil rights of Atheists. **Libraries: Type:** reference. **Holdings:** 50,000. **Awards:** American Atheist of the Year Award. **Frequency:** annual. **Type:** recognition. **Additional Websites:** http://www.americanatheist.org. **Publications:** *American Atheist Newsletter*, 10/year. Includes atheist news and thought providing articles on current events and controversies. Discusses religious topics, government and legislative news. **Price:** included in membership dues; $35.00/year for nonmembers. ISSN: 0332-4310. Also Cited As: *Monthly Insider's Newsletter* ● Magazine, quarterly. Alternate Formats: online. **Conventions/Meetings:** annual convention - held Easter weekend ● semiannual regional meeting and conference.

19064 ■ Atheist Alliance, Inc. (AAI)
PO Box 967
Diamond Springs, CA 95619
Free: (866)HERETIC
E-mail: info@atheistalliance.org
URL: http://www.atheistalliance.org
Contact: Bobbie Kirkhart, Pres.

Founded: 1992. **Multinational. Description:** Independent, autonomous atheist societies. Assists isolated and/or disaffected atheists with atheist and free-thought issues of the day; conducts public access television programs. **Libraries: Type:** reference. **Telecommunication Services:** electronic mail, president@atheistalliance.org. **Publications:** *Secular Nation*. **Conventions/Meetings:** annual international conference.

19065 ■ Atheists United (AU)
4773 Hollywood Blvd.
Hollywood, CA 90027-5333
Ph: (323)666-4258
Free: (866)GOD-LESS
E-mail: sbechman@sbcglobal.net
URL: http://www.atheistsunited.org
Contact: Stuart Bechman, Co-Pres.

Founded: 1982. **Members:** 500. **Membership Dues:** regular, $40 (annual) ● family, $45 (annual) ● limited income, $20 (annual) ● platinum, $500 (annual) ● gold, $250 (annual) ● sustaining, $125 (annual) ● life, $1,000. **Local Groups:** 6. **Description:** Promotes complete separation of church and state and public education about atheism. Sponsors lectures and debates. Produces videos. Organizes lobbying activities, media campaigns. Sponsors Speaker's Bureau and charitable programs. **Libraries: Type:** reference. **Holdings:** 240. **Subjects:** atheism, free thought and humanism. **Awards:** AU Awards. **Frequency:** annual. **Type:** recognition. **Recipient:** for members. **Computer Services:** database, membership and subscribers. **Committees:** Events; Outreach. **Publications:** Newsletter, monthly. **Price:** included in membership dues. **Circulation:** 600. Alternate Formats: online ● Also publishes data sheets on religion, history, and atheism. **Conventions/Meetings:** annual Art Fest - festival - November ● annual Awards Banquet ● monthly meeting ● annual Winter Solstice Banquet - meeting.

Athletes

19066 ■ Athletes Abroad for Christ (AAFC)
PO Box 14
New Era, MI 49446
Ph: (231)861-7444

Fax: (231)861-7444
E-mail: christtheking@i2k.com
Contact: Chris Bando, Contact

Multinational. Description: Commits in evangelism and discipleship through clear and faithful proclamation of God's Holy Word. Seeks to minister to athletes throughout the world, including players, coaches/managers, front office, officials, trainers, and groundskeepers interested in learning more about Jesus Christ. Maintains speakers' bureau. **Publications:** *Time for the Truth*, bimonthly. Newsletter.

Baha'i

19067 ■ National Spiritual Assembly of the Baha'is of the U.S. (NSA-US)
1233 Central St.
Evanston, IL 60201
Ph: (847)733-3559
Fax: (847)733-3430
URL: http://www.bahai.us
Contact: Glen Fullmer, Spokesman

Founded: 1927. **Members:** 150,000. **Staff:** 150. **Local Groups:** 7,000. **Description:** National governing body and administrative agency for U.S. adherents of the Baha'i Faith, an independent worldwide religion. (The Baha'i Faith, which follows the writings of Baha'u'llah, teaches the oneness of God, the common foundation of the world's religions, and the oneness of all the races of mankind.) Promotes elimination of all forms of prejudice, economic justice based upon spiritual principles, independent investigation of truth, use of an international auxiliary language, equality of men and women, and a world federal government for the maintenance of a lasting peace. Operates schools and conducts educational programs. Maintains offices in Washington, D.C., and at the United Nations. **Libraries: Type:** reference. **Holdings:** 45,000; articles, books, periodicals. **Subjects:** Bahai Faith. **Formerly:** (1948) National Spiritual Assembly of the Baha'is of the United States and Canada. **Publications:** *The American Baha'i* (in English, Persian, and Spanish), 10/year. Newspaper. **Price:** for members only. ISSN: 1062-1113. **Circulation:** 75,000 ● *World Order*, quarterly. Journal. Covers contemporary life and contemporary religious teachings and philosophy. **Price:** $19.00/year. ISSN: 0043-8804. **Circulation:** 2,000. **Conventions/Meetings:** annual National Bahai Convention, convention of delegates to elect National Spiritual Assembly - usually last weekend of April.

Baptist

19068 ■ ABW Ministries (ABW)
PO Box 851
Valley Forge, PA 19482-0851
Free: (800)ABC-3USA
Fax: (610)768-2275
E-mail: info@abwministries.org
URL: http://www.abwministries.org
Contact: Virginia Holmstrom, Exec. Dir.

Founded: 1951. **Members:** 750,000. **Staff:** 4. **Budget:** $650,000. **Regional Groups:** 31. **Local Groups:** 5,000. **Languages:** English, Spanish. **Description:** Represents women who belong to an American Baptist church. Seeks to undergird the total program of the American Baptist Churches of the U.S.A., through support of missions and church service projects. Conducts studies and acts in matters involving Christian social concern, including local, national, and international affairs; sponsors programs to meet the specific needs of women as well as to integrate them into the life of the church. Trains women in leadership skills. **Formerly:** (1965) National Council of American Baptist Women; (1990) American Baptist Women. **Publications:** *Vital Woman Magazine* (in English and Spanish), 3/year, October, February, June. **Price:** $12.00/year. **Circulation:** 3,000. **Advertising:** accepted. Alternate Formats: online ● Directory, annual ● Also program packet. **Conventions/Meetings:** biennial meeting - always June, odd-numbered years ● annual National Women's Conference - always July, Green Lake, WI.

19069 ■ All-Ukrainian Evangelical Baptist Fellowship (AUEBF)
6751 Riverside Dr.
Berwyn, IL 60402
Ph: (973)539-9393
Fax: (708)788-0999
Contact: Rev. Vladimir Domashovetz, Pres.
Founded: 1949. **Members:** 10,150. **Staff:** 10. **Budget:** $100,000. **State Groups:** 11. **Local Groups:** 63. **Description:** Associations, churches, and church members. Purpose is to coordinate the worldwide ministries of associations of Ukrainian Baptist churches and other church-related organizations and institutions located in countries of the free world. Promotes Baptist ideals and principles by spreading the Gospel of Jesus Christ to Ukrainians in their native language through preaching, publishing, and distributing printed material in the free world and behind the Iron Curtain, broadcasting radio programs, producing musical recordings, and other activities. Provides material aid to relatives of prisoners jailed because of their faith and to other needy believers in the Ukraine. Sends Bibles and other Christian literature to the Ukraine. Sponsors Pastors visiting the Ukraine. Holds special observances and other events. Maintains 10,000 volume library. **Awards:** **Type:** recognition. **Publications:** *Christian Herald* (in English and Ukrainian), quarterly. Magazine. **Price:** $12.00 ● *Messenger of Truth* (in Ukrainian), bimonthly. Journal. Includes book reviews. **Price:** $15.00/year. **Circulation:** 5,000. Alternate Formats: microform ● Also publishes books. **Conventions/Meetings:** quinquennial international conference ● annual Pastor's Conference - meeting - always July. Peterborough, ON, Canada.

19070 ■ American Baptist Historical Society (ABHS)
PO Box 851
Valley Forge, PA 19482-0851
Ph: (610)768-2269 (610)768-2378
Fax: (610)768-2266
URL: http://www.abc-usa.org/abhs
Contact: Dr. Deborah Van Broekhoven, Exec. Dir.
Founded: 1853. **Members:** 735. **Membership Dues:** individual, $25 (annual) ● institution, $35 (annual). **Staff:** 3. **Budget:** $275,000. **Description:** Official depository library of the American Baptist Churches in the U.S.A. and the Baptist World Alliance. Promotes the study of Baptist history and theology; collects Baptist historical documents and printed records. Operates the American Baptist Archives Center at Valley Forge, PA, and the Samuel Colgate-American Baptist Historical Library in Rochester, NY. **Libraries:** **Type:** reference. **Holdings:** 85,000; archival material, books, periodicals. **Subjects:** Baptists. **Awards:** Robert G. Torbet Prize. **Frequency:** annual. **Type:** monetary. **Recipient:** for research essay on Baptist history. **Divisions:** Archives; Library. **Publications:** *American Baptist Quarterly.* Journal. Covers issues of interest to Baptists on historical and contemporary concerns such as Baptist identity, ethnic diversity and church-state issues. **Price:** $40.00/year in U.S.; $52.00/year outside U.S. ISSN: 0015-8992 ● *Primary Source,* quarterly. Newsletter. Contains topics and information for Baptist archivists, historical societies, and researchers of Baptist studies. **Conventions/Meetings:** annual board meeting - usually fall, alternately in Rochester, NY and Valley Forge, PA.

19071 ■ American Baptist Homes and Hospitals Association (ABHHA)
PO Box 851
Valley Forge, PA 19482-0851
Free: (800)ABC-3USA
Fax: (610)768-2453
E-mail: aundreia.alexander@abc-usa.org
URL: http://www.nationalministries.org/caring_ministries/abhha
Contact: Aundreia Alexander, Dir.
Founded: 1930. **Members:** 134. **Staff:** 2. **Description:** Retirement facilities, nursing homes and hospitals, and children's homes and special services.

Provides special programs and educational events for member institutions. Offers consulting network program for member facilities. Compiles statistics. **Libraries:** **Type:** reference. **Holdings:** periodicals. **Awards:** **Frequency:** biennial. **Type:** recognition. **Recipient:** to the Board, staff, and volunteers of member homes. **Formerly:** (1954) Association of Baptist Homes and Hospitals. **Publications:** *Directory of American Baptist Retirement Homes, Hospitals and Nursing Homes, Children's Homes and Special Services,* annual ● *Perspective,* quarterly. Newsletter. **Conventions/Meetings:** regional meeting ● periodic symposium.

19072 ■ Association of Baptists for World Evangelism (ABWE)
PO Box 8585
Harrisburg, PA 17105-8585
Ph: (717)774-7000
Fax: (717)774-1919
E-mail: info@abwe.org
URL: http://www.abwe.org
Contact: Dr. Michael Loftis, Pres.
Founded: 1927. **Members:** 1,377. **Staff:** 65. **Budget:** $35,000,000. **Multinational. Description:** Independent Baptist mission. Establishes churches through evangelism programs. Maintains missions in 61 countries. Conducts evangelistic activities through evangelism, church planting and discipleship. Uses medical personnel, hospitals, clinics and educational institutes to operate student centers near universities. **Libraries:** **Type:** reference. **Holdings:** 2,500. **Awards:** Bomm/Presidential Citation. **Frequency:** annual. **Type:** recognition. **Recipient:** for years of meritorious service. **Computer Services:** Mailing lists, of members. **Formerly:** (1939) Association of Baptists for Evangelism in the Orient. **Publications:** *Access,* 3/year. Bulletin ● *Church Planters Manual.* Offers suggestions for those interested in starting up new congregations. **Price:** $5.00 each ● *Courier,* 3/year ● *Dimensions,* quarterly ● *The Message,* quarterly. Magazine. Informs, instructs and inspires readers to involvement in missions. Alternate Formats: online ● *On Duty in Bangladesh.* Book. Tells the story of the chaos, confusion, agony and intrigue surrounding the bloody birth of Bangladesh. **Price:** $4.00 each ● *President Report,* annual. Annual Report. **Conventions/Meetings:** annual Missionary Candidate - seminar ● annual Missionary Enrichment - conference (exhibits) - always July.

19073 ■ Association of Southern Baptist Campus Ministers (ASBCM)
c/o BCM at Louisiana State University
PO Box 25118
Baton Rouge, LA 70894
Ph: (225)343-0408
Fax: (225)343-0424
E-mail: lsubcm@eatel.net
URL: http://www.lsubcm.org
Contact: Steve Masters, VP
Founded: 1977. **Members:** 150. **Membership Dues:** professional, $35 (annual) ● affiliate, $15 (annual). **Description:** Full-time campus ministers with a graduate degree or five years experience in ministry (125); part-time and volunteer ministers, students, and interested individuals are affiliate members (25). Purposes are to: strengthen the individual's commitment and expertise in the ministry through fellowship and programs; enhance the minister's view of campus and church; promote professional competence among campus ministers; develop and encourage fellowship among members; act as a liaison between campus ministers seeking employment or reassignment and employers seeking campus ministers; share knowledge, personnel, and material resources. Cooperates with seminaries in continuing education. **Awards:** Lifetime Achievement. **Frequency:** annual. **Type:** recognition. **Recipient:** for lifetime achievement in ministry ● Outstanding Contribution to Campus Ministry. **Frequency:** annual. **Type:** recognition. **Recipient:** for outstanding services in ministry. **Committees:** Awards; Continuing Education; Ethics; Healthcare; New Work. **Publications:** *The Campus Minister Journal,* semiannual. **Price:** $7.00/year. **Circulation:** 200 ● *Colleague,* quarterly. Newsletter ●

Membership List, annual. Membership Directory. **Conventions/Meetings:** annual conference (exhibits) - always June.

19074 ■ Association of State Baptist Papers (ASBP)
c/o Alabama Baptist Newspaper
3310 Independence Dr.
Birmingham, AL 35209
Ph: (205)870-4720
Fax: (205)870-8957
URL: http://www.thealabamabaptist.org
Contact: Dr. Bobby S. Terry, Exec. Sec.
Founded: 1926. **Members:** 38. **Staff:** 1. **Budget:** $25,000. **Description:** Publishers of news publications of state conventions affiliated with the Southern Baptist Convention and conventionwide publications. Includes editors, associate and managing editors, business managers, and circulation managers. To provide a forum for the consideration of mutual interests, opportunities for in-service training, and a medium for fellowship. **Formerly:** (2000) Southern Baptist Press Association. **Conventions/Meetings:** annual conference - always February ● semiannual meeting ● seminar ● workshop.

19075 ■ Association of Welcoming and Affirming Baptists (AWAB)
PO Box 259257
Madison, WI 53725
Ph: (608)255-2155
E-mail: mail@wabaptists.org
URL: http://www.wabaptists.org
Contact: Rev. Ken Penning, Exec. Dir.
Founded: 1993. **Members:** 60. **Membership Dues:** church, organization, $100-$10,000 (annual) ● individual (rainbow donor), $50-$4,999 (annual) ● individual (over the rainbow donor), $5,000 (annual) ● household, $85 (annual). **Description:** Supports and affirms the inclusion of gay, lesbian, bisexual, and transgender people within the Baptist community. Strives to end gender discrimination of people based on their sexuality. Collaborates with other religious bodies that support Welcoming Church Programs. **Publications:** *The InSpiriter,* quarterly. Newsletter. Contains information and articles about the association and its members. Features updates from the Baptist community. **Price:** free for members. Alternate Formats: online.

19076 ■ Baptist Bible Fellowship International (BBFI)
PO Box 191
720 E Kearney
Springfield, MO 65801-0191
Ph: (417)862-5001
Fax: (417)865-0794
E-mail: admin@bbfi.org
URL: http://www.bbfi.org
Contact: Gary Grey, Pres.
Founded: 1950. **Members:** 1,500,000. **Description:** Missionaries and churches in 90 countries. Promotes missionary activities. Operates Baptist Bible College and Baptist Bible School of Theology, both in Springfield, Missouri and Baptist Bible College East in Boston, Massachusetts. **Libraries:** **Type:** reference. **Committees:** Church Planting; Education; Missions. **Publications:** *Baptist Bible Tribune and Global Partners,* bimonthly ● *Directory of BBFI Churches and Missionaries,* biennial. Contains list of addresses and phone numbers of Independent Baptist Churches and Pastors. **Price:** $15.00 each ● *Faith Promise Devotional Book.* Booklet. Instructs and challenges families concerning the faith promise plan of mission giving. **Price:** $18.75 each.

19077 ■ Baptist Communicators Association (BCA)
1715K S Rutherford Blvd., No. 295
Murfreesboro, TN 37130
Ph: (615)904-0152
E-mail: bca.office@comcast.net
URL: http://www.baptistcommunicators.org
Contact: Norman Jameson, Pres.
Founded: 1954. **Members:** 350. **Membership Dues:** professional, $75 (annual) ● student, $25 (annual).

Staff: 9. **Description:** Church-related public relations and communications employees of institutions and agencies of the Southern Baptist Convention or state conventions affiliated with the SBC. Serves national agencies of the denomination, state conventions, colleges, hospitals, children's homes, and homes for the aged. Provides research consultation on opinion studies; facilitates exchange of promotional ideas. Offers placement services; maintains biographical archives; compiles statistics. **Awards:** Albert McClellan Award. **Frequency:** annual. **Type:** recognition. **Recipient:** for exceptional achievement in print media and design ● Arthur S. Davenport Award. **Frequency:** annual. **Type:** recognition. **Recipient:** for exceptional achievement in public relations ● Exceptional Achievement Award. **Frequency:** annual. **Type:** recognition. **Recipient:** for excellence in interactive communications ● Fon H. Schofield Award. **Frequency:** annual. **Type:** recognition. **Recipient:** for exceptional achievement in publication photography ● Frank Burkhalter Award. **Frequency:** annual. **Type:** recognition. **Recipient:** for exceptional achievement in news writing ● Leonard Holloway Award. **Frequency:** annual. **Type:** recognition. **Recipient:** for exceptional achievement in feature writing ● M.E. Dodd Award. **Frequency:** annual. **Type:** recognition. **Recipient:** for exceptional achievement in audio-visual communications. **Formerly:** (1998) Baptist Public Relations Association. **Publications:** *BCA News*, bimonthly. Newsletter. Offers practical help to the novice and the seasoned practitioner. ● Membership Directory, annual ● Brochures. Contains information about the organization and its purposes. **Conventions/Meetings:** annual competition ● annual conference - always spring ● annual workshop.

19078 ■ Baptist Joint Committee for Religious Liberty (BJC)
200 Maryland Ave. NE
Washington, DC 20002
Ph: (202)544-4226
Fax: (202)544-2094
E-mail: bjc@bjconline.org
URL: http://www.bjconline.org
Contact: Rev. J. Brent Walker, Exec. Dir.
Founded: 1936. **Members:** 44. **Staff:** 10. **Budget:** $900,000. **Description:** Baptist conventions or conferences (American Baptist Churches in the U.S.A; Baptist General Conference; National Baptist Convention of America; National Baptist Convention, U.S.A. (see separate entry); National Missionary Baptist Convention; Alliance of Baptists, Cooperative Baptist Fellowship, North American Baptist Conference; Progressive National Baptist Convention, Inc; Religious Liberty Council; Seventh Day Baptist General Conference (see separate entry); Baptist state conventions and churches. Provides information and news service to constituents and to the public on church-state relations, human rights, and religious liberty. **Libraries: Type:** reference. **Holdings:** 1,000; archival material, books, periodicals. **Subjects:** religious liberty, first amendment. **Computer Services:** Mailing lists. **Divisions:** Denominational Services; Government Relations; Information Services; Legal and Research Services. **Formerly:** (2005) Baptist Joint Committee on Public Affairs. **Publications:** *Baptist News Service*. Newsletter. News service focusing on coverage of church-state and religious freedom issues in Congress, the Supreme Court, and the White House. **Price:** free ● *Report from the Capital*, 26/year. Newsletter. For Baptist ministers and laypersons advocating church-state separation and religious liberty. Provides church-state news, articles, and opinions. **Price:** $10.00/year; $6.50/year for students. ISSN: 0346-0661. **Circulation:** 10,000 ● Also publishes volumes of conference study papers, staff reports, pamphlets, and briefs. **Conventions/Meetings:** annual meeting - always October, Washington, DC ● biennial National Religious Liberty Conference.

19079 ■ Baptist Mid-Missions (BMM)
7749 Webster Rd.
PO Box 308011
Cleveland, OH 44130-8011
Ph: (440)826-3930

Fax: (440)826-4457
E-mail: info@bmm.org
URL: http://www.bmm.org
Contact: Dr. Gary L. Anderson, Pres.
Founded: 1920. **Members:** 1,100. **Staff:** 42. **Budget:** $26,000,000. **National Groups:** 52. **Description:** Serves as a medium through which independent Baptist churches may cooperate in Baptist missionary activities, direct their missionary funds and refer their young people who are called to missionary service. Supports 558 foreign and 274 active home missionaries. Provides children services. **Libraries: Type:** reference. **Holdings:** 2,000; audio recordings, books, video recordings. **Subjects:** missionary work, countries, religions, cultures. **Awards:** Service Pin Award. **Frequency:** quinquennial. **Type:** recognition. **Recipient:** for years of service (20 years, plus 5 year intervals). **Computer Services:** Information services, client-server network. **Divisions:** Baptist Messianic Ministries; Bibles International; Campus Bible Fellowship; Editorial Bautista Independiente. **Affiliated With:** Fellowship of Missions. **Formerly:** (1953) General Council of Cooperating Baptist Missions. **Publications:** *Burning Wicks*. Book. Covers BMM history from the 1920s to the 1980s. **Price:** $8.95 each ● *Deputation Bulletin*, 3/year ● *Directory and Prayer Calendar*, biennial ● *Harvest Magazine*, 3/year. **Price:** free. **Circulation:** 65,000. Alternate Formats: online ● *It's About Time*, 3/year ● *Practical Guide to Church Planting*. Book ● *The Volunteer*, 3/year ● *Women and Mission Newsletter*, 3/year ● Brochures ● Also publishes missionary biographies and translation of the Bible and the New Testament. **Conventions/Meetings:** annual Candidate Seminar, orientation for new personnel, held in mid-July ● conference - 3/year, always March, July, and November.

19080 ■ Baptist Women in Ministry/Folio (BWIM/FOLIO)
c/o McAfee School of Theology
3001 Mercer Univ. Dr.
Atlanta, GA 30341
E-mail: rtshapard@msn.com
URL: http://www.bwim.info
Contact: Rachel Gunter Shapard, Coor.
Founded: 1983. **Members:** 400. **Membership Dues:** individual, $30 (annual) ● couple/family, $45 (annual). **Staff:** 2. **Budget:** $100,000. **State Groups:** 5. **Description:** Ordained and unordained female Baptist ministers; students of the Baptist ministry; interested individuals. Promotes the image of women as ministers. Fosters support and communication among members. Conducts educational and research programs. **Libraries: Type:** reference. **Holdings:** archival material, archival material, books, clippings, periodicals. **Subjects:** women, ministry, theology, SBC. **Awards:** Addie Davis Award. **Frequency:** annual. **Type:** scholarship. **Recipient:** for outstanding Baptist female theology student in preaching; leadership. **Absorbed:** (1990) Baptist Women in Ministry. **Publications:** *Folio*, quarterly. Newsletter. Includes news and features pertaining to women ministers. **Price:** $15.00/year. ISSN: 0741-1537. **Circulation:** 3,000. Alternate Formats: online. **Conventions/Meetings:** annual meeting (exhibits) - always with CBF in summer.

19081 ■ Baptist World Alliance (BWA)
405 N Washington St.
Falls Church, VA 22046
Ph: (703)790-8980
Fax: (703)893-5160
E-mail: bwa@bwanet.org
URL: http://www.bwanet.org
Contact: Dr. David Coffey, Pres.
Founded: 1905. **Members:** 196. **Membership Dues:** friend in Western Europe and developed world, $50-$100 (annual) ● friend in developing world, $10-$100 (annual) ● friend in North America, $100 (annual) ● ministry partner, $101-$499 (annual) ● ambassador, $500-$999 (annual) ● General Secretary's Circle, $1,000-$4,999 (annual) ● President's Circle, William Carey Church, $5,000 (annual) ● church associate, $250 (annual) ● Global Impact Church, $1,000 (annual) ● organizational association, $5,000 (annual) ●

Adoniram Judson Church, $10,000 (annual). **Staff:** 11. **Budget:** $2,000,000. **Regional Groups:** 6. **National Groups:** 196. **Description:** International Baptist bodies representing more than 42,000,000 individuals. Aims "to exist as an expression of the essential oneness of Baptist people in the Lord Jesus Christ; to impart inspiration to the fellowship; and to provide channels for sharing concerns and skills in witness and ministry." Focuses major activities in the areas of: communications; evangelism and education; world aid; study and research; promotion and development. Conducts relief programs, such as sending aid to distressed peoples and assisting in the rehabilitation of refugees from political and other oppressions. Encourages observation of annual Baptist World Alliance Day on the first Sunday of February. Maintains speakers' bureau and biographical archives; compiles statistics. **Commissions:** Baptist Heritage; Baptist Worship; Baptists Against Racism; Christian Ethics; Church Leadership; Doctrine and Interchurch Cooperation; Human Rights/Justice. **Departments:** Men; Women; Youth. **Divisions:** Baptist World Aid; Communications; Evangelism and Education; Global Impact; Promotion and Development; Study and Research. **Publications:** *The Baptist World*, quarterly. Magazine. **Price:** $20.00. ISSN: 0005-5808. **Circulation:** 12,000. Alternate Formats: microform; online ● *Baptist World Alliance Information Service*, monthly ● *Baptist World Alliance News*, monthly. Newsletter ● *World Congress Reports* ● *World Youth Conference Reports* ● Booklets ● Yearbook. **Conventions/Meetings:** quinquennial Baptist World Congress - meeting (exhibits) - 2010 July 28-Aug. 1, Honolulu, HI ● quinquennial World Youth Conference - meeting - 2008 July 30-Aug. 3, Leipzig, Germany.

19082 ■ Board of International Ministries (BIM)
c/o American Baptist Churches in the U.S.A.
PO Box 851
Valley Forge, PA 19482-0851
Free: (800)222-3872
Fax: (610)768-2088
E-mail: charles.jones@abc-usa.org
URL: http://www.internationalministries.org
Founded: 1814. **Members:** 250. **Staff:** 50. **Budget:** $16,000,000. **Description:** A board of the American Baptist Churches in the U.S.A. Conducts educational, evangelistic, development and medical mission projects in Africa, Asia, the Caribbean, Central America, South America, and Europe. Administers the Boville-Murray Vacation Bible School Fund. **Libraries: Type:** open to the public. **Holdings:** 1,000. **Subjects:** mission work worldwide. **Absorbed:** (1955) Woman's American Baptist Foreign Mission Society; (1991) Vacation Bible Schools. **Also Known As:** American Baptist Foreign Mission Society. **Formerly:** (1845) General Convention of the Baptist Denomination in the United States for Foreign Missions; (1910) American Baptist Missionary Union. **Publications:** *New Life in Spain*. Video. Highlights the efforts of the Spanish Evangelical Baptist Union to reach the Spanish people for Christ. **Price:** $5.00 each ● Brochures ● Newsletters. **Conventions/Meetings:** annual World Mission Conference - always August.

19083 ■ Board of National Ministries (BNM)
c/o American Baptist Churches in the U.S.A.
PO Box 851
Valley Forge, PA 19482-0851
Ph: (610)768-2000
Free: (800)222-3872
Fax: (610)768-2470
E-mail: webmaster@abc-usa.org
URL: http://www.abc-usa.org
Contact: Kate Harvey, Exec. Dir.
Founded: 1832. **Description:** A national program unit of the American Baptist Churches in the U.S.A. **Libraries: Type:** not open to the public. **Subjects:** theology, history of missions. **Absorbed:** Division of Christian Social Concern. **Also Known As:** American Baptist National Ministries. **Formed by Merger of:** American Baptist Home Mission Society; Woman's American Baptist Home Mission Society. **Formerly:**

American Baptist Home Mission Societies. **Conventions/Meetings:** semiannual congress.

19084 ■ Conservative Baptist Association of America

3686 Stagecoach Rd., Ste.F
Longmont, CO 80504-5660
Ph: (720)283-3030
Free: (888)366-3010
Fax: (303)772-5690
E-mail: info@cbamerica.org
URL: http://www.cbamerica.org
Contact: Rev. Stephen LeBar PhD, Exec. Dir.
Founded: 1947. **Members:** 185,000. **Staff:** 3. **Budget:** $650,000. **Regional Groups:** 9. **Description:** Provides leadership, fellowship, counseling services, and specialized support ministries to 1200 member churches in an effort "to advance the cause of Christ through worship, evangelism, instruction, and service throughout the world". Conducts charitable program; offers placement service, chaplaincy endorsement. **Also Known As:** CBAmerica. **Publications:** *Conservative Baptist Association of America—Directory,* annual ● *Front Line,* quarterly. Newsletter ● *Turnings,* bimonthly. Newsletter. **Conventions/Meetings:** annual conference (exhibits).

19085 ■ Continental Baptist Missions (CBM)

11650 Northland Dr.
Rockford, MI 49341-8706
Ph: (616)863-2226
Fax: (616)866-1140
E-mail: cbm@cbmoffice.org
URL: http://www.cbmoffice.org
Contact: Rev. Bill Jenkin III, Pres.
Founded: 1942. **Members:** 200. **Staff:** 13. **Budget:** $1,500,000. **State Groups:** 2. **Languages:** English, Spanish. **Description:** Missionaries. Aims to establish Baptist churches in the U.S. and Canada. **Councils:** CBM Missionary Fellowship. **Affiliated With:** Fellowship of Missions. **Also Known As:** CBM Ministries. **Formerly:** (1982) Hiawatha Baptist Mission. **Publications:** *Contact!,* triennial. Newsletter. **Circulation:** 36,000. Alternate Formats: online. **Conventions/Meetings:** annual conference, meeting of all field personnel and staff for encouragement and instruction - usually July in Ankeny, IA.

19086 ■ Ethics and Religious Liberty Commission of the Southern Baptist Convention (ERLC)

901 Commerce St., Ste.550
Nashville, TN 37203
Ph: (615)244-2495
Fax: (615)242-0065
E-mail: jmartin@erlc.com
URL: http://www.erlc.com
Contact: Dr. Richard D. Land, Pres.
Founded: 1947. **Staff:** 19. **Description:** Serves as an agency of the Southern Baptist Convention representing 42,000 churches and 16,000,000 individuals. Provides a program of moral education, leadership, and action based on biblical principles and contemporary social analysis relating to family life, human relations, economics, daily work, citizenship, war and peace, religious liberty, and other issues. Offers suggestions to churches; works to affect legislation regarding moral and social issues. **Awards:** Distinguished Service Award. **Frequency:** annual. **Type:** recognition ● John Leland Religious Liberty Award. **Frequency:** annual. **Type:** recognition. **Formerly:** (1997) Christian Life Commission of the Southern Baptist Convention. **Conventions/Meetings:** annual seminar, held in conjunction with Southern Baptist Convention ● seminar ● workshop.

19087 ■ General Association of General Baptists (GAGB)

100 Stinson Dr.
Poplar Bluff, MO 63901
Ph: (573)785-7746
E-mail: ron.black@generalbaptist.com
URL: http://www.generalbaptist.com
Contact: Dr. Ron Black, Exec. Dir.
Founded: 1867. **Members:** 75,000. **Local Groups:** 60. **Description:** Individuals interested in encourag-

ing fellowship through cooperative means. (General Baptists encourage acceptance of other denominations in cooperative union work.) Conducts overseas mission work. **Affiliated With:** Baptist World Alliance; National Association of Evangelicals. **Publications:** *General Baptist Messenger,* monthly. **Price:** $12.00 for individual; $10.00 for group. **Advertising:** accepted ● Also publishes leaflets and brochures. **Conventions/Meetings:** annual convention - always July.

19088 ■ General Association of Regular Baptist Churches (GARBC)

1300 N Meacham Rd.
Schaumburg, IL 60173-4806
Ph: (847)843-1600
Free: (888)588-1600
Fax: (847)843-3757
E-mail: garbc@garbc.org
URL: http://www.garbc.org
Contact: Rev. John Greening, Natl. Rep.
Founded: 1932. **Members:** 155,757. **Staff:** 60. **Description:** Baptist church members from 1,415 churches. Perpetuates historic faith and fellowship as delineated in the Bible. Works to advance member churches. **Libraries: Type:** not open to the public. **Holdings:** 2,067; books, periodicals. **Subjects:** theology. **Publications:** *Baptist Bulletin,* monthly. **Price:** $10.00/year. **Circulation:** 24,500 ● *Synergy.* Newsletter. **Price:** free. **Conventions/Meetings:** annual conference (exhibits).

19089 ■ Master's Men of the National Association of Free Will Baptists (MMNAFWB)

PO Box 5002
Antioch, TN 37011-5002
Ph: (615)760-6142
Free: (877)767-8039
E-mail: masters@nafwb.org
URL: http://www.nafwb.org/mm
Contact: Bro. Kenneth Akers, Gen. Dir.
Founded: 1956. **Members:** 2,568. **Membership Dues:** individual, $30 (biennial) ● life, $200 ● church plan, $300 (annual) ● church, $75 (quarterly) ● church, $25 (monthly) ● individual, $20 (annual). **State Groups:** 10. **Local Groups:** 228. **Description:** Consists of men, 17 years of age and older, who are in good standing in their local churches. Aims to enhance individual stewardship. Goals are: to win men and boys to Christ; to under gird the local church program with prayer and voluntary services; to sponsor a men's organization that will provide rewarding Christian fellowship and stimulate soul-winning interests. Sponsors Master's Hands Projects, Layman's Day in October in each local church and Armed Forces Sunday in May. Sponsors Sports Fellowships and Tournaments. **Awards:** Director's Award. **Frequency:** annual. **Type:** recognition. **Recipient:** to Free Will Baptists golfer of the year ● Layman of the Year Award. **Frequency:** annual. **Type:** recognition. **Formerly:** (1976) Master's Men of the Free Will Baptist Church. **Publications:** *Attack: A Magazine for Christian Men,* quarterly. Provides material for group monthly meetings. Covers activities of Free Will Baptist laymen, chapter and state news, and new member information. **Price:** included in membership dues. **Circulation:** 2,500. **Advertising:** accepted ● *Handbook for Master's Men* ● *Master's Men Monthly,* periodic. Newsletter. Covers program studies and fellowship ideas. **Conventions/Meetings:** annual Men's National Conference - convention (exhibits) - usually April.

19090 ■ Mission to the Americas (MTTA)

2530 Washington St.
Denver, CO 80205
Ph: (303)308-1818
Free: (866)447-6018
Fax: (303)295-9090
E-mail: mta@mtta.org
URL: http://www.mtta.org
Contact: Richard Miller, Pres.
Founded: 1950. **Members:** 350. **Staff:** 13. **Languages:** Chinese, English, French, Japanese, Portuguese, Spanish. **Description:** Ministries to the

inner city, campus, and other areas of American life, and establish new churches in North and Central America, the Caribbean, and the American possessions. **Telecommunication Services:** electronic mail, gjeffreys@mtta.org. **Affiliated With:** WorldVenture. **Formerly:** (1998) Conservative Baptist Home Mission Society. **Publications:** *Harvest,* quarterly. Newsletter. Promotes and informs the ministries of the society. **Price:** free. **Circulation:** 25,000. **Conventions/Meetings:** annual conference (exhibits).

19091 ■ National Association of Free Will Baptists (BHMNAFWB)

5233 Mt. View Rd.
Antioch, TN 37013-2306
Ph: (615)731-6812
Free: (877)767-7659
Fax: (615)731-0771
E-mail: mlw@nafwb.org
URL: http://nafwb.net
Contact: Keith Burden, Exec. Sec.
Founded: 1938. **Members:** 102. **Staff:** 10. **Budget:** $2,700,000. **Description:** Free Will Baptist ministers. Promotes evangelistic and church growth activities and the establishment of Free Will Baptist churches in North America. Endorses chaplains for the armed forces. **Formerly:** (2000) Board of Home Missions of the National Association of Free Will Baptists. **Publications:** *Free Will Baptist Year Book,* annual. Yearbook ● *Missiongrams,* bimonthly ● *ONE Magazine,* bimonthly. **Price:** free. **Circulation:** 50,000. Alternate Formats: online. **Conventions/Meetings:** annual meeting - always July.

19092 ■ National Baptist Convention, U.S.A. (NBC USA)

World Center HQ
1700 Baptist World Center Dr.
Nashville, TN 37207
Ph: (615)228-6292
Free: (866)531-3054
Fax: (615)262-3917
E-mail: dtibbs@nationalbaptist.com
URL: http://www.nationalbaptist.com
Contact: Dr. William J. Shaw, Pres.
Founded: 1886. **Members:** 7,500,000. **Staff:** 15. **Regional Groups:** 5. **State Groups:** 69. **National Groups:** 3. **Description:** Seeks to: promote home and foreign missions; encourage and support Christian education; publish and distribute Sunday School and other religious literature. Operates youth camps, student centers, and the American Baptist Theological Seminary. **Awards: Frequency:** annual. **Type:** scholarship. **Boards:** Foreign Mission; Home Mission; Sunday School Publishing; Women's Auxiliary. **Formed by Merger of:** Baptist Foreign Mission Convention; National Baptist Convention; National Baptist Educational Convention. **Publications:** *National Baptist Voice,* quarterly, January, April, July, and October. Journal. **Price:** $5.00/issue. **Advertising:** accepted ● *Record of Annual Sessions.* **Conventions/Meetings:** board meeting ● annual Congress of Christian Education - meeting - always June ● annual convention (exhibits) - always September, on Monday following first Sunday.

19093 ■ Seventh Day Baptist General Conference (SDBGC)

PO Box 1678
Janesville, WI 53547-1678
Ph: (608)752-5055
Fax: (608)752-7711
E-mail: sdbgen@seventhdaybaptist.org
URL: http://www.seventhdaybaptist.org
Contact: Robert F. Appel, Exec. Dir.
Founded: 1802. **Members:** 5,133. **Staff:** 10. **Budget:** $1,066,000. **Description:** Associations and churches. Works to advise or appeal in all matters pertaining to doctrine and discipline, faith, and practice between churches and their respective members. Promotes worship, the spread of the Christian religion, Sabbath observance, Sabbath or Bible schools, and secular and religious education. Provides pensions for ministers of the Gospel and other persons engaged in strictly denominational work. **Libraries: Type:** open to the public. **Subjects:** history, polity, belief. **Tele-**

communication Services: electronic mail, robappel@seventhdaybaptist.org. Boards: Christian Education. Committees: Christian Social Action; Ecumenical Affairs; Faith and Order. Councils: American Sabbath Tract and Communications; Ministry. Funds: Memorial. Affiliated With: Seventh Day Baptist Historical Society; Seventh Day Baptist Missionary Society. Publications: A Choosing People: The History of Seventh Day Baptists. Book. Price: $20.00 ● Sabbath Recorder, monthly. Magazine. Price: free. ISSN: 0036-214X. Alternate Formats: online ● True to the Sabbath, True to Our God. Book. Price: $9.95 ● Pamphlets ● Yearbook. Conventions/Meetings: annual conference - always August.

19094 ■ Seventh Day Baptist Historical Society (SDBHS)
PO Box 1678
Janesville, WI 53547-1678
Ph: (608)752-5055
Fax: (608)752-7711
E-mail: sdbhist@seventhdaybaptist.org
URL: http://www.seventhdaybaptist.org
Contact: Don A. Sanford, Historian

Founded: 1916. Members: 120. Membership Dues: life, $100 ● regular, $10 (annual). Staff: 3. Budget: $48,000. Description: Investigates the history of religious organizations and related subjects, especially those pertaining to Seventh Day Baptists (a group that originated in England and organized in Rhode Island in 1671, which observes Saturday as the Sabbath). Provides reference service for denominational agencies and leaders; compiles statistics. Conducts family research for those with Seventh Day Baptist Roots. Libraries: Type: reference. Holdings: 3,000; archival material, books, business records, clippings, monographs, periodicals. Subjects: Seventh Day Baptist history, Sabbath material, genealogical records. Awards: Gold Headed Cane. Frequency: annual. Type: recognition. Recipient: for significant contribution to Seventh Day Baptist history ● Honorary Membership. Type: recognition. Recipient: for honorary members. Boards: Directors. Affiliated With: Seventh Day Baptist General Conference. Publications: A Choosing People: The History of Seventh Day Baptists. Book. Highlights the comprehensive study of Seventh Day Baptist history. Price: $20.00 ● A Free People in Search of a Free Land. Features the history of migration. Price: $7.50 ● Conscience Taken Captive: A Short History of Seventh Day Baptists. Price: $3.00 ● Entering into Covenant. Features the history of Seventh Day Baptists in Newport. Price: $5.00 ● Greater Than Its Parts. Features the study of Seventh Day Baptist organization and policy. Price: $5.00 ● Pearls from the Past, monthly. Monographs. Included in Sabbath Recorder. ● Annual Report, annual ● Pamphlets. Conventions/Meetings: annual convention, held in conjunction with the Seventh Day Baptist General Conference (exhibits).

19095 ■ Seventh Day Baptist Missionary Society (SDBMS)
119 Main St.
Westerly, RI 02891-2112
Ph: (401)596-4326
Fax: (401)348-9494
E-mail: sdbmissoc@verizon.net
URL: http://www.seventhdaybaptist.org
Contact: G. Kirk Looper, Exec. Dir.

Founded: 1818. Members: 400. Membership Dues: regular, $10 (annual). Staff: 4. Budget: $275,000. Regional Groups: 9. State Groups: 3. Local Groups: 18. National Groups: 90. Description: Members of the Seventh Day Baptist faith. Seeks to spread the Gospel throughout the world and to promote kindred religious and generous works. Engages in evangelism, education, home missions, and church extension for the denomination. Holds area spiritual retreats. Sponsors seminars and training courses for pastoral leaders in Africa, United States, Canada, and the Philippines. Appoints missionary key workers to distribute materials among Sabbath schools and churches to gain missionary interest and support. Compiles statistics. Awards:

Type: recognition. Affiliated With: Baptist World Alliance; Seventh Day Baptist General Conference; Seventh Day Baptist World Federation. Formerly: (1842) Board of Trustees and Directors of Missions. Publications: Missionary Reporter, quarterly. Newsletter. Contains the minutes of board meetings including reports of workers on missionary projects. Price: included in membership dues. Circulation: 400. Alternate Formats: online ● Missions, monthly. Newsletter. Covers Seventh Day Baptist missionary work worldwide. Price: free ● Seventh Day Baptist Yearbook, annual. Price: $17.50 ● Annual Report, annual. Conventions/Meetings: annual Seventh Day Baptist General Conference of USA and Canada, Ltd. - general assembly and seminar, features presentations of different SDB boards and agencies (exhibits).

19096 ■ Seventh Day Baptist World Federation (SDBWF)
4160 County Rd. 1
PO Box 515
Friendship, NY 14739-0515
E-mail: calvin@seventhdaybaptist.org
URL: http://www.seventhdaybaptist.org
Contact: Rev. Joe Samuels, Pres.

Founded: 1964. Members: 17. Description: 7th Day Baptist conferences or conventions representing 20 countries. Encourages fellowship and communication among 7th Day Baptist groups throughout the world. Sponsors exchanges, mutual aid programs, and ecumenical projects. Receives, evaluates, and shares with members statements of need that come to the federation's attention; serves as liaison for individuals offering services or resources. Offers counsel and expertise to members. Bestows recognition to approved 7th Day Baptist movements. Conducts Bible studies; organizes seminars; compiles statistics. Publications: A Dozen Common Excuses. Booklet ● The Sabbath: God's Creation for Our Benefit. Book. Includes discussion questions. Price: $3.00 each (paperback) ● The Sabbath Visitor, weekly. Bulletin. Price: $3.00/year ● SDB World, periodic. Newsletter. Provides information on the federation. Price: free. Circulation: 500. Conventions/Meetings: quinquennial conference.

19097 ■ Southern Baptist Foundation (SBF)
901 Commerce St., Ste.600
Nashville, TN 37203
Ph: (615)254-8823
Free: (800)245-8183
Fax: (615)255-1832
E-mail: sbfdn@sbc.net
URL: http://www.sbfdn.org
Contact: Michael W. Weeks, Pres.

Founded: 1947. Staff: 7. Budget: $957,400. Description: Seeks to motivate and encourage the making of gifts, donations, and benefactions, by deed, will, gift annuity, or otherwise for the advancement, extension and maintenance of the various causes and objects fostered by the Southern Baptist Convention. Telecommunication Services: electronic mail, mweeks@sbc.net. Funds: Balanced; Growth; Income; Total Return Income. Conventions/Meetings: board meeting - usually March, July, and November.

19098 ■ Southern Baptist Historical Library and Archives (SBHLA)
901 Commerce St., Ste.400
Nashville, TN 37203-3630
Ph: (615)244-0344
Fax: (615)782-4821
E-mail: bill@sbhla.org
URL: http://www.sbhla.org
Contact: Bill Sumners, Dir.

Founded: 1951. Members: 6. Staff: 5. Budget: $400,000. Description: Governed by the Council of Seminary Presidents. Assists Baptist churches, associations, conventions, and institutions in recording, preserving, and utilizing historical materials. Aids in procuring and preserving printed and manuscript materials by or about Baptists; operates microfilming program. Sponsors research projects for the convention; provides research services to graduate students

and writers and consulting and advisory services in the development of Baptist historical collections. Denominational archives for the Southern Baptist Convention. Libraries: Type: reference. Holdings: 27,000; artwork, audio recordings, books, films, periodicals, photographs. Subjects: Baptists. Awards: Lynn E. May, Jr. Study Grants. Frequency: annual. Type: monetary. Recipient: for association related research. Formerly: (1998) Historical Commission, Southern Baptist Convention. Publications: Microfilm Catalog of Baptist Historical Materials, periodic. Lists books, periodicals, annuals, church records, archival materials, and theses on microfilm by and about Baptists. Price: free.

19099 ■ Woman's Missionary Union, SBC (WMU)
100 Missionary Ridge
Birmingham, AL 35283-0010
Ph: (205)991-8100
Free: (800)968-7301
Fax: (205)995-4840
E-mail: email@wmu.org
URL: http://www.wmu.com
Contact: Wanda S. Lee, Exec. Dir.

Founded: 1888. Members: 1,000,000. Staff: 120. Budget: $14,000,000. State Groups: 38. Languages: English, Korean, Spanish. Description: Female members of churches that are part of the Southern Baptist Convention. Works to teach, support, and promote individual involvement in missions. Libraries: Type: reference; by appointment only. Holdings: 13,000; archival material, biographical archives, books. Subjects: missions, international studies, doctrine, other religious materials. Awards: Type: scholarship. Recipient: to children of missionaries and for those preparing for mission careers. Publications: Acteens Leader, quarterly. Magazine. Includes planning helps, activity sheets, and content for Acteens meetings. Price: $19.99/year ● Discovery, monthly. Magazine. Features articles of interest to girls in 1st through 4th grade. Price: $14.99/year. ISSN: 0162-198X. Circulation: 122,000 ● GA World, monthly. Magazine. Contains articles of interest to girls in 5th and 6th grades. Price: $14.99/year. ISSN: 1083-3277 ● The MAG, monthly. Magazine. Helps the teenaged girls learn about and be involved in missions in the real world. Price: $17.99/year ● Mission Leader, quarterly. Magazine. Contains latest planning helps for establishing and leading Girls in Action program. Price: $15.99/year. ISSN: 1062-6833. Circulation: 32,700 ● Missions Leader, quarterly. Magazine. Serves as an essential planning tool for all missions leaders in the church. Price: $15.99/year. ISSN: 0162-6825. Circulation: 25,000 ● Missions Mosaic, monthly. Magazine. Features articles of interest to women 18 and up. Price: $18.99/year. ISSN: 1083-3285. Circulation: 219,000 ● Nuestra Tarea (in English and Spanish), quarterly. Magazine. Features Spanish language publication. Price: $18.99/copy ● Share, quarterly. Magazine. Consists of take-home activity leaflets for all Mission Friends. Price: $23.99/year. Circulation: 14,000 ● Start, quarterly. Magazine. Provides teaching plans for each age of Mission Friends. Price: $18.99/year. ISSN: 0162-6841. Circulation: 28,000 ● Yearbook. Conventions/Meetings: annual Inspiration/Business Meeting (exhibits).

19100 ■ Women Nationally Active for Christ (WNAC)
PO Box 5002
Antioch, TN 37011-5002
Free: (877)767-7662
E-mail: info@wnac.org
URL: http://www.nafwb.org/wnac
Contact: Marjorie Workman, Exec. Sec.-Treas.

Founded: 1935. Members: 7,423. Membership Dues: individual, $10 (annual). Staff: 4. Regional Groups: 4. State Groups: 21. Local Groups: 724. National Groups: 5. Description: Provides opportunities for women to fulfill their role in the family, church, and community. Encourages involvement in prayer, study, and action through participation in local groups. Assists young people in making a commitment to Christianity. Contributes to the needs of missions; maintains a missionary provision closet with sheets, towels, and other household items for working missionaries; and participates in mission activities. Encourages the formation of local groups. Provides loans to qualified Christian students attending the Free Will Baptist College in Nashville, TN. Historical materials are currently on loan to the Free Will Baptist College. **Libraries: Type:** reference. **Holdings:** archival material. **Awards: Creative Arts. Frequency:** annual. **Type:** recognition. **Recipient:** for women ● **Frequency:** annual. **Type:** scholarship. **Recipient:** for foreign students. **Formerly:** (1993) Woman's National Auxiliary Convention of Free Will Baptists. **Publications:** *A Manual for Free Will Baptist Women's Organizations.* Manuals ● *First Fruits: Answered Prayer on the Mission Field.* Book. Features a collection of missionary stories. **Price:** $5.00 each ● *Sparks into Flame: A History of WNAC from 1935-1985.* Book. **Price:** $4.00 each ● *Together with God,* bimonthly. Magazine. Includes poetry, bible study, and other articles. **Price:** $12.00/year. ISSN: 0896-0038. **Circulation:** 10,000. **Conventions/Meetings:** annual convention (exhibits) ● annual Creative Arts - competition, creative writing contest (exhibits) - always July ● annual retreat ● seminar ● workshop.

19101 ■ WorldVenture
1501 W Mineral Ave.
Littleton, CO 80120-5612
Ph: (720)283-2000
Free: (800)487-4224
Fax: (720)283-9383
E-mail: info@worldventure.com
URL: http://www.worldventure.com
Contact: Dr. Hans W. Finzel, Pres.

Founded: 1943. **Members:** 600. **Staff:** 50. **Budget:** $23,100,000. **Multinational. Description:** Independent Baptist mission society with 600 evangelical missionaries in 65 countries. **Libraries: Type:** not open to the public. **Holdings:** 3,700; biographical archives, books. **Subjects:** mission. **Divisions:** Advancement/Donor Relations; Church Connections; Finance; International Ministry; Missionary Development; Mobilization. **Affiliated With:** Conservative Baptist Association of America; Evangelical Council for Financial Accountability; Mission to the Americas. **Formerly:** (1996) Conservative Baptist Foreign Mission Society; (2005) CBInternational. **Publications:** *Communique,* quarterly. Newsletter. Covers activities of CBI missionaries. **Price:** free. **Circulation:** 46,000 ● *Impact,* triennial. Magazine. Includes personnel profiles and reports from geographic areas. **Price:** free. ISSN: 0019-2821. **Circulation:** 46,000 ● *Prayer Connection,* monthly ● *Vital Partnerships,* quarterly. Books ● Books ● Films ● Also issues folders, pictures, cards, and other materials about missionary activities. **Conventions/Meetings:** annual conference (exhibits) - held in June or July.

Bible

19102 ■ American Bible Society (ABS)
1865 Broadway
New York, NY 10023-7505
Ph: (212)408-1200
Free: (800)32BIBLE
E-mail: webmaster@americanbible.org
URL: http://www.americanbible.org
Contact: Mr. Paul Irwin, Pres./CEO

Founded: 1816. **Description:** Works to make the Bible readily available to people in the U.S. and around the world. Translates, publishes and distributes the Holy Scriptures. Maintains affiliated offices and agencies throughout the world; its National Church Advisory Council represents more than 100 supporting religious groups. Maintains a collection of rare Bibles and manuscripts, a museum/gallery, and a bookstore. **Libraries: Type:** reference. **Holdings:** 50,000; archival material, monographs, periodicals. **Subjects:** Bible translation, rare Bibles. **Awards:** American Bible Society Award. **Frequency:** annual. **Type:** recognition. **Recipient:** to individual(s) who contribute greatly to the goals of the society ●

American Bible Society Scholarship Award. **Frequency:** annual. **Type:** recognition. **Recipient:** for seminary or college students with high achievement in the study of the Bible. **Projects:** Faith Fund; Good News Fund; Hope Fund. **Sections:** International Relations; Marketing; Office of Development and Communications; Translations and Scripture Resources. **Publications:** *ABS Record,* bimonthly. Magazine. Describes bible society work in USA and around the world. **Circulation:** 450,000 ● *Stewardship Report,* annual. Annual Report ● Also publishes Scriptures in various formats and languages. **Conventions/Meetings:** board meeting - January, May, and September, in New York City.

19103 ■ American Friends of Neot Kedumim (AFNK)
PO Box 236
Howes Cave, NY 12092
Ph: (518)296-8673
E-mail: tikvah4afnk@yahoo.com
URL: http://www.n-k.org.il
Contact: Paula Tobenfeld, Pres.

Founded: 1971. **Membership Dues:** general, $36 (annual). **Staff:** 1. **Description:** Promotes the Biblical Landscape Reserve in Israel. (The reserve is 625 acres of land reclamation that has been turned into a biblical botanical garden illustrating symbols, prayers, and holidays of the Jewish and Christian heritage.) Distributes information about the reserve; raises funds. Conducts charitable and educational programs. **Formerly:** Neot Kedumim. **Publications:** *Neot Kedumim News,* quarterly. Newsletter. **Price:** free. **Circulation:** 4,600. **Conventions/Meetings:** periodic board meeting.

19104 ■ American Scripture Gift Mission (ASGM)
7862 W Irlo Bronson Hwy.
Kissimmee, FL 34747
Ph: (321)284-4593
Free: (877)873-2746
E-mail: asgm@asgm.com
URL: http://www.asgm.com
Contact: Gary Powell, Ministry Mgr.

Founded: 1933. **Staff:** 3. **Budget:** $30,000. **Description:** Publishing ministry serving Christian individuals, churches, and ministries. Engages in the publication, and distribution of scripture booklets and tracts in over 400 languages. **Formerly:** (1993) Scripture Gift Mission/U.S.A.; (1999) SGM International/U.S.A. **Publications:** *Forgiveness Matters.* Booklet. **Price:** free. **Circulation:** 500 ● Also publishes scriptures and portions thereof in more than 400 different languages and dialects.

19105 ■ Associates for Biblical Research (ABR)
PO Box 144
Akron, PA 17501
Ph: (717)859-3443
Free: (800)430-0008
Fax: (717)859-3393
E-mail: office@biblearchaeology.org
URL: http://www.biblearchaeology.org

Founded: 1969. **Members:** 1,200. **Membership Dues:** standard, $35 (annual) ● student, $20 (annual) ● life, $1,000. **Staff:** 4. **Budget:** $150,000. **Description:** Conducts research on biblical archaeology. Sponsors annual tours and excavations in Israel. Offers educational programs and conferences/seminars. **Libraries: Type:** not open to the public. **Holdings:** books, periodicals. **Subjects:** biblical archaeology. **Publications:** *ABR E-Newsletter.* **Price:** free. Alternate Formats: online ● *Bible and Spade,* quarterly. Journal. **Price:** $17.50/year for U.S. subscribers; $27.50/year in Canada and Mexico; $33.50/year for foreign. ISSN: 1079-6959. **Circulation:** 1,000 ● Catalog. Contains books, videos, curriculum materials and other publications of ABR. Alternate Formats: online. **Conventions/Meetings:** annual Biblical Archaeology - seminar and conference, biblical archaeological artifacts (exhibits).

19106 ■ BCM International
309 Colonial Dr.
PO Box 249
Akron, PA 17501-0249
Ph: (717)859-6404
Free: (888)226-4685
Fax: (717)859-6914
E-mail: info@bcmintl.org
URL: http://www.bcmintl.org
Contact: Rev. Martin Windle, Pres.

Founded: 1936. **Members:** 700. **Staff:** 36. **Budget:** $8,000,000. **Languages:** Dutch, English, French, German, Italian, Portuguese, Russian, Spanish, Swahili. **Multinational. Description:** Inter-denominational faith-based global Bible-Centered Ministry dedicated to making disciples of all age groups for the Lord Jesus Christ through evangelism, teaching and training so that churches are established and The Church strengthened. **Awards: Type:** recognition. **Recipient:** for completion of memorization programs. **Departments:** Children's Ministries; Church Ministries; Church Planting; International Ministries; International Training Ministries; Mailbox Bible Club; Protestant Religious Education Services (military); Public School Ministries; Publications/Curriculum; Short-Term Ministries; Urban Ministries. **Divisions:** BCM Africa; BCM Asia; BCM Canada; BCM Caribbean; BCM Europe (Western/Eastern); BCM Latin America; BCM USA. **Programs:** Call-A-Story Phone Ministry; Camping Ministries; Children's Bible Clubs; Compassion Ministries to Disadvantaged; Mentoring Ministry; Street Kids/Orphan Ministry. **Also Known As:** (1985) Bible Centered Ministries. **Formerly:** (1936) Bible Club Movement. **Publications:** *BCM Publications Catalog.* Alternate Formats: online ● *Footsteps of Faith.* Contains Bible teaching and discipleship information aimed at youth individuals. ● *In Step with the Master Teacher Training Course.* Manual. Alternate Formats: CD-ROM ● *International Focus,* biennial. Magazine. Contains updates on BCM ministries around the world. **Price:** free. **Circulation:** 8,000 ● *Steps to Maturity.* Contains Bible teaching and discipleship information aimed at young adults and adults. ● *Tiny Steps of Faith.* Contains Bible teaching and discipleship information aimed at preschool individuals. ● Also publishes catalog of Bible teaching materials. **Conventions/Meetings:** annual conference, with candidate orientation and missionary conferences - always August.

19107 ■ Berean Bible Society (BBS)
PO Box 756
Germantown, WI 53022
Ph: (262)255-4750
Fax: (262)255-4195
E-mail: berean@execpc.com
URL: http://www.bereanbiblesociety.org
Contact: Pastor Paul M. Sadler, Pres.

Founded: 1940. **Staff:** 10. **Multinational. Description:** Promotes religious education and the study of the Bible through dissemination of literature, Bible lectures and conferences, newspaper articles, and tape recordings. **Publications:** *Berean Searchlight,* monthly. Magazine. Serves as a bible study guide. **Price:** free. ISSN: 0005-8890. **Circulation:** 20,000. Alternate Formats: online ● *Exploring the Unsearchable Riches of Christ Videos.* **Price:** $25.00 ● Booklets ● Books ● Audiotapes. **Conventions/Meetings:** annual Berean Bible Fellowship - conference.

19108 ■ Bible League (BL)
PO Box 28000
Chicago, IL 60628
Ph: (708)367-8500
Free: (800)825-4636
Fax: (708)367-8600
E-mail: info@bibleleague.org
URL: http://www.bibleleague.org
Contact: Robert Cole, Pres.

Founded: 1938. **Staff:** 643. **Budget:** $41,000,000. **Multinational. Description:** Exists to bring people around the world into a relationship with Christ and His Church. Provides Bibles and study materials to local churches. Facilitates the spiritual growth of those seeking a relationship with Christ, and helps believers grow in faith. Provides training to people in local churches worldwide who have a vision to reach their nations for Christ. Christians learn to lead Bible studies, to grow existing churches, and to establish new churches in areas where none exist. **Formerly:** (1989) World Home Bible League. **Publications:** *The Bible League Report*, bimonthly. Newsletter. Reports on work progress in foreign countries. **Price:** free. **Circulation:** 100,000.

19109 ■ Bibles for the Blind and Visually Handicapped
3228 E Rosehill Ave.
Terre Haute, IN 47805-1297
Ph: (812)466-4899
Fax: (812)466-0529
E-mail: info@biblesfortheblind.org
URL: http://www.biblesfortheblind.org
Contact: Keith Reedy, Dir.
Description: Works to assist blind and visually impaired individuals to find a Bible in Braille, large print or on cassette.

19110 ■ BLI
PO Box 36720
Colorado Springs, CO 80936-3672
Ph: (614)267-3116
Free: (877)877-7932
Fax: (614)267-7110
E-mail: bli@bli.org
Contact: James R. Falkenberg, Pres.
Founded: 1923. **Staff:** 23. **Description:** Provides foreign language religious literature and funds for producing such literature to missionaries in 170 nations representing more than 400 different mission boards. **Affiliated With:** Evangelical Council for Financial Accountability; Evangelical Fellowship of Mission Agencies; National Association of Evangelicals. **Formerly:** (1967) Bible Mediation League; (2001) Bible Literature International.

19111 ■ Braille Bible Foundation
PO Box 948307
Maitland, FL 32794-8307
Ph: (407)834-3628
Free: (800)766-9080
E-mail: care@careministries.org
Contact: Viola M. Howell, Pres.
Description: Provides the King James Version of the Bible in grade 2 Braille. **Publications:** *Braille Concordance*. Book. Includes three volumes.

19112 ■ Christ Truth Ministries (CTM)
c/o Virginia O'Kane, Exec. Dir.
1233 W 9th Ave.
Upland, CA 91786
Ph: (909)981-2838
E-mail: virginia@christtruthmin.com
URL: http://www.christtruthmin.com/phpnuke/news.php
Contact: Virginia O'Kane, Exec. Dir.
Founded: 1949. **Staff:** 4. **Budget:** $250,000. **Languages:** English, Spanish. **Description:** Distributes Bibles, Bible study materials, and copies of the New Testament and Christian literature to individuals in prison. **Libraries: Type:** open to the public. **Holdings:** 20,000; books, periodicals. **Computer Services:** Mailing lists, of members. **Formerly:** Prisoners Bible Broadcast; (1976) Christ Truth Radio Crusade. **Publications:** *Bible Studies* (in English and Spanish). **Price:** free to inmates. **Circulation:** 400 ● *Sharing Times*, monthly. Newsletter. **Circulation:** 4,000. **Conventions/Meetings:** annual Prison Ministries Conference - meeting (exhibits).

19113 ■ Christian Service Club (CSC)
2110 Enterprise St., SE
Grand Rapids, MI 49508
Ph: (616)455-2490
Fax: (616)455-2490
Contact: Sharon Adema, Exec.Dir.
Founded: 1962. **Members:** 2,869. **Staff:** 2. **Budget:** $39,000. **Regional Groups:** 5. **Description:** Conducts Bible clubs for children. Produces Flannelgraph backgrounds for use as visual aids. **Publications:** *News*, quarterly.

19114 ■ Christians in Government (CIG)
PO Box 71654
Los Angeles, CA 90071
Ph: (213)250-5016 (818)248-8703
E-mail: dfmitch@juno.com
Contact: Daniel Mitchell, Administrator
Founded: 1966. **Staff:** 2. **Regional Groups:** 10. **Local Groups:** 80. **Description:** Encourages the development of Bible study programs and fellowship groups for nonelected, daily government workers. Assists others throughout the U.S. in establishing such groups in accordance with federal law. Conducts indoor and outdoor rallies with speakers and musicians. **Telecommunication Services:** electronic mail, hsmithclef@juno.com ● electronic mail, wmofglencrest@aol.com ● phone referral service. **Formerly:** (1985) Inter-Church Ministries. **Publications:** *Good News.For Those in Public Service*, quarterly. Newsletter. **Circulation:** 500. **Advertising:** accepted. Alternate Formats: online. **Conventions/Meetings:** annual retreat.

19115 ■ Dawn Bible Students Association (DBSA)
199 Railroad Ave.
East Rutherford, NJ 07073
Free: (888)440-DAWN
E-mail: dawnbible@aol.com
URL: http://www.dawnbible.com
Contact: Robert Gorecki, Exec. Dir.
Founded: 1940. **Staff:** 18. **Description:** Represents independent Bible study groups and individuals. Produces radio and television shows; maintains speakers' bureau. **Publications:** *The Dawn*, monthly. Magazine. Alternate Formats: online ● Booklets ● Books ● Also publishes tracts. **Conventions/Meetings:** annual meeting.

19116 ■ Electronic Bible Society (EBS)
PO Box 701356
Dallas, TX 75370
E-mail: ebs@computek.net
URL: http://www.farese.com/ebs.htm
Contact: Jim Bolton, Pres.
Description: Committed to preserving and storing on CD-ROM the historic works of the Christian faith, including the Reformers, the Puritans, biblical encyclopedias, commentaries, Bibles and all public domain works of significance to the Christian. **Computer Services:** Mailing lists.

19117 ■ Institute for Biblical Research (IBR)
c/o Dr. Daniel I. Block, Pres.
Wheaton Coll. Graduate School
501 Coll. Ave.
Wheaton, IL 60187
URL: http://www.ibresearch.org
Contact: Dr. Daniel I. Block, Pres.
Founded: 1973. **Members:** 450. **Membership Dues:** associate, $35 (annual) ● fellow/friend, $55 (annual). **Regional Groups:** 6. **Description:** Individuals actively engaged in Biblical research or ancillary disciplines at a high level of scholarship. Fosters the study of the scriptures within an evangelical Christian context; seeks to establish facilities for the furtherance of Biblical studies and encourages university and college students toward a vocation of Biblical scholarship. Sponsors regional study groups for presentation of papers and discussion. Plans a residential library for Biblical research. **Committees:** Nominating; Worship. **Publications:** *Bulletin for Biblical Research*, semiannual. Journal. Contains scholarly articles and book reviews. **Price:** $12.50 for individuals; $17.50 for institutions. ISSN: 1065-223X. **Circulation:** 1,000. Also Cited As: *BBR* ● Newsletter, annual. Alternate Formats: online. **Conventions/Meetings:** annual conference, with academic addresses and panel discussions.

19118 ■ International Bible Society (IBS)
1820 Jet Stream Dr.
Colorado Springs, CO 80921
Ph: (719)488-9200
Free: (800)524-1588

E-mail: ibsdirectservice@usa.ibs.org
URL: http://www.ibs.org
Contact: Peter Bradley, Pres.
Founded: 1809. **Staff:** 120. **Budget:** $22,600,000. **Description:** A nondenominational mission organization engaged in the translation, publication, and worldwide distribution of Scriptures. Makes available Scriptures translated by Wycliffe Bible Translators and its own translation staff; provides selections of Scriptures complimentary or at low cost for use in evangelism programs by individuals, churches, and organizations. **Libraries: Type:** reference. **Awards:** Golden Word Award. **Frequency:** annual. **Type:** monetary. **Recipient:** for dedication to the word of God. **Additional Websites:** http://www.ibsdirect.com. **Absorbed:** (1992) Living Bibles International. **Formerly:** (1970) New York Bible Society; (1974) New York Bible Society International; (1983) New York City International Bible Society. **Publications:** *New International Version Bible*. Book ● *NIV New Testaments*. Book ● *Scripture Catalog*, annual. Contains listing of scripture products for sale. **Price:** free. **Circulation:** 200,000. **Conventions/Meetings:** annual board meeting.

19119 ■ International Bible Students Association (IBSA)
25 Columbia Heights
Brooklyn, NY 11201-2483
Ph: (718)560-5000
Fax: (718)560-5619
URL: http://www.watchtower.org
Contact: Gene Smalley, Librarian
Founded: 1914. **Description:** Christian Bible students worldwide. Promotes the Christian religion through the dissemination of printed and oral Bible teachings. Organizes Bible studies. **Libraries: Type:** open to the public. **Holdings:** 25,000. **Subjects:** religious and biblical material. **Publications:** *Awake*, semimonthly. Magazine ● *The Watchtower*, semimonthly. Magazine. Specializes in Biblical material, published in 148 languages. **Circulation:** 25,618,000.

19120 ■ International Organization for Septuagint and Cognate Studies (IOSCS)
c/o Eisenbrauns
PO Box 275
Winona Lake, IN 46590-0275
E-mail: bgw1@lehigh.edu
URL: http://ccat.sas.upenn.edu/ioscs
Contact: Ben Wright, Pres.
Founded: 1968. **Members:** 485. **Membership Dues:** student, retired, $15 (annual) ● regular, $23 (annual) ● institution, $27 (annual). **Languages:** English, French, German, Hebrew, Spanish. **Description:** College and university teachers and students; clergy; libraries; membership figure represents participants from 29 countries. Conducts critical study of Jewish Greek Scriptures and related subjects. Holds periodic gatherings for presentation and discussion of research. Sponsors special projects, including new English translation of the Septuagint (NETS). **Awards:** Prize for Outstanding Paper in LXX Studies. **Frequency:** annual. **Type:** monetary. **Recipient:** for outstanding paper in the field of Septuagint studies. **Committees:** Editorial. **Publications:** *BIOSCS*, annual. Bulletin ● *Septuagint and Cognate Studies*. Monograph ● 3-5 Monographs and collections each year in Septuagint and Cognate Studies series. **Conventions/Meetings:** annual meeting ● periodic symposium.

19121 ■ International Society of Bible Collectors (ISBC)
c/o Carl V. Johnson, Pres.
PO Box 26654
Minneapolis, MN 55426
E-mail: 2swedes@usfamily.net
URL: http://www.biblecollectors.org
Contact: Carl V. Johnson, Pres.
Founded: 1964. **Members:** 275. **Membership Dues:** in U.S. and Canada, $25 (annual) ● outside U.S. and Canada, $30 (annual). **Multinational. Description:** Bible collectors, libraries, and Bible societies interested in Bible translation and translators. Promotes Bible collecting, including translations of individual

books of the Bible; seeks to develop a bibliographic listing of new Bible translations and versions, including those with commentaries, where the author has made his own translation of the text. Acts as a clearinghouse for individuals and libraries interested in collecting Bibles and translations. Conducts research on translations. **Libraries: Type:** open to the public; by appointment only. **Subjects:** Bible collections. **Publications:** *Bible Editions and Versions*, quarterly. Journal. Contains book reviews and news of old and current translations and translators. **Price:** included in membership dues; $25.00 for nonmembers in U.S. and Canada; $30.00 for nonmembers outside U.S. and Canada. **Circulation:** 275. **Advertising:** accepted. Also Cited As: *The Bible Collector, Bible Collector's World*. **Conventions/Meetings:** annual meeting, with rare items on display, also rare Bibles for sale and trade, and guest lectures (exhibits) - usually in September, date announced in Journal.

19122 ■ Lutheran Bible Translators (LBT)
PO Box 2050
Aurora, IL 60507-2050
Ph: (630)897-0660
Free: (800)532-4253
Fax: (630)897-3567
E-mail: info@lbt.org
URL: http://lbt.gospelcom.net
Contact: Dr. Marshall Gillam, Exec. Dir.
Founded: 1964. **Members:** 600. **Staff:** 112. **Budget:** $3,700,000. **Description:** Strives to bring God's word to people in their own language. Promotes indigenous leadership and participation in the mission of the organization. Conducts presentations on request. Maintains Speaker's Bureau. **Awards:** Lifetime Achievement Award. **Frequency:** annual. **Type:** recognition. **Recipient:** for leadership and support of organization's mission. **Also Known As:** Messengers of Christ-Lutheran Bible Translators. **Publications:** *Messenger*, quarterly. Newspaper. Provides information on missionaries serving abroad; also covers progress of Bible translation and literacy work. **Price:** free. **Circulation:** 65,000 ● *"Passports" Video Series*. Videos. Contains video series highlighting LBT work around the globe. ● Films. **Conventions/Meetings:** annual meeting.

19123 ■ The Mailbox Club (TMC)
404 Eager Rd.
Valdosta, GA 31602
Ph: (229)244-6812
E-mail: mailorder2@mailboxclub.org
URL: http://www.mailboxclub.org
Contact: John Mark Eager, Dir.
Founded: 1965. **Members:** 6,000. **Staff:** 25. **Budget:** $1,100,000. **National Groups:** 800. **Languages:** English, French, Portuguese, Spanish. **Multinational.** **Description:** Organizations, churches, and individuals seeking to establish and operate Bible correspondence schools. Biblical lessons are sent to people of all ages, graded, and returned by mail. Operates a mail order bookstore. **Convention/Meeting:** none. **Awards:** Certificate of Completion per Course. **Type:** recognition. **Formerly:** Mailbox Club Books. **Publications:** *A Country Called Heaven*. Book ● *Best Friends* ● *Explorers* ● *How to Succeed in Winning Children to Christ* ● *Love and Dating*. Book. **Price:** $12.95 hard cover; $7.95 paperback ● *Love, Dating, and Marriage*. Book. **Price:** $5.95 paperback ● *Love, Dating, and Sex: What Teens Want to Know*. Book.

19124 ■ Neighborhood Bible Studies (NBS)
56 Main St.
Dobbs Ferry, NY 10522
Ph: (914)693-3273
Free: (800)369-0307
Fax: (914)693-4345
E-mail: info@neighborhoodbiblestudy.org
URL: http://www.neighborhoodbiblestudy.org
Contact: Allison Lowrie, Exec. Dir.
Founded: 1960. **Staff:** 20. **National Groups:** 1,280. **Languages:** Arabic, Chinese, English, Finnish, French, German, Indonesian, Italian, Japanese, Laotian, Portuguese, Spanish. **Description:** Encourages and assists churches and individuals in the

formation of adult Bible study groups as a means of sharing the Gospel and teaching spiritual leadership. Advocates an "inductive" approach in Bible study, which entails first presenting the context and meaning of biblical scriptures before relating those scriptures to religious doctrine. Offers consultation services to church leaders; assists in the development of outreach Bible studies in communities, nursing homes, prisons, and drug rehabilitation facilities. Sponsors workshops and leader training seminars. **Libraries: Type:** reference. **Holdings:** 38; books. **Subjects:** the Bible. **Publications:** *How to Start a Neighborhood Bible Study*. Handbook. Contains Bible study discussion guide. **Price:** $5.99/copy; $275.00 complete set ● *Share the Joy Newsletter and Partners*, quarterly.

19125 ■ New Horizon World Center
PO Box 5985
St. Louis, MO 63134
Ph: (314)428-3999
Fax: (314)428-3999
Contact: Robert L. Johnson, Pres.
Founded: 1997. **Staff:** 5. **Nonmembership.** **Description:** Teaches life principles according to Holy Bible; feeds homeless; provides shelter for battered women; provides counseling for couples, singles, career and direction. Offers educational opportunities.

19126 ■ Non-Denominational Bible Prophecy Study Association (NDBPSA)
c/o Dr. Patricia H. Burns, Founder
339 E Laguna Dr.
Tempe, AZ 85282
Ph: (480)967-3066 (480)390-2674
E-mail: bibleprophecy_ndbpsa@yahoo.com
URL: http://netministries.org/see/charmin/CM00407
Contact: Dr. Patricia H. Burns, Founder
Founded: 1983. **Nonmembership. Multinational.** **Description:** Promotes Bible prophecy discussion and fellowship. **Additional Websites:** http://groups.yahoo.com/group/BibleProphecy. **Publications:** *The Book of Revelation Explained*. Serves a self-study aid. **Price:** $20.00 in U.S., plus $3.85 priority mail; $20.00 outside U.S., plus international mailing costs.

19127 ■ Pocket Testament League
PO Box 800
Lititz, PA 17543-7026
Ph: (717)626-8106
Free: (800)636-8785
E-mail: membercare@pocketpower.org
URL: http://www.pocketpower.org
Contact: Thomas Koch, Exec. Dir.
Founded: 1893. **Staff:** 175. **Budget:** $1,300,000. **State Groups:** 2. **National Groups:** 20. **Description:** Worldwide evangelistic ministry with missionaries, associates, and nationals active in evangelism with an emphasis on Scripture distribution, including the U.S.A; proclaiming the gospel of salvation through the Lord Jesus Christ, encouraging Christian growth in established churches, and newly formed assemblies of believers. Provides speakers for churches and Christian organizations. **Divisions:** Operation Campus Ministry. **Publications:** *Worldwide News*, quarterly. Newsletter. Covers the worldwide evangelical activities of the league. **Price:** free. **Circulation:** 15,000. **Conventions/Meetings:** triennial Missions Conference (exhibits).

19128 ■ Society of Biblical Literature (SBL)
Luce Center
825 Houston Mill Rd.
Atlanta, GA 30329
Ph: (404)727-3100 (404)727-3038
Free: (866)727-9955
Fax: (404)727-3101
E-mail: sblexec@sbl-site.org
URL: http://www.sbl-site.org
Contact: Kent Harold Richards, Exec. Dir.
Founded: 1880. **Members:** 8,000. **Membership Dues:** full, $65 ● student, $25 ● associate, $45. **Staff:** 9. **Budget:** $2,000,000. **Regional Groups:** 11. **Description:** Professors and persons interested in biblical studies, ancient world and religious studies.

Seeks to "stimulate the critical investigation of classical biblical literature, together with other related literature, by the exchange of scholarly research both in published form and in public forum". Endeavors to support those disciplines and sub disciplines pertinent to the illumination of the literatures and religions of the ancient Near Eastern and Mediterranean regions, including the study of ancient languages, textual criticism, history, and archaeology. Supports and cooperates with several national and international groups. Conducts research programs; offers placement services. **Awards:** Research Grants. **Frequency:** annual. **Type:** monetary. **Recipient:** to members for excellence of written proposal. **Telecommunication Services:** electronic mail, kent.richards@sbl-site.org. **Affiliated With:** American Academy of Religion; American Council of Learned Societies; American Schools of Oriental Research; International Organization for Septuagint and Cognate Studies; National Association of Professors of Hebrew. **Formerly:** (1964) Society of Biblical Literature and Exegesis. **Publications:** *Academia Biblica*. Book ● *Annual Meeting Seminar Papers and Abstracts*, annual. **Circulation:** 4,000. **Advertising:** accepted ● *Journal of Biblical Literature*, quarterly. Includes scholarly articles, critical notes and book reviews. **Price:** $35.00 for members; $165.00 for nonmembers and institutions. **Circulation:** 9,000. **Advertising:** accepted. Alternate Formats: online ● *Religious Studies News, SBL Edition*, monthly. Includes society news and reports on regional groups. **Circulation:** 15,000. **Advertising:** accepted. Alternate Formats: online ● *Resources for Biblical Studies* ● *Resources for Biblical Study*. Book ● *Review of Biblical Literature*, annual, weekly electronic. Journal. **Price:** $35.00 /year for members; $100.00 /year for nonmembers and institutions. **Circulation:** 9,000. **Advertising:** accepted. Alternate Formats: online ● *Semeia*, quarterly. Journal. **Circulation:** 1,600. **Advertising:** accepted ● *Semeia Studies*. Book ● *Septuagint and Cognate Studies*. Book ● *Society Report*, annual. Contains an overview of the organization. Alternate Formats: online ● *Texts and Translations*. Book ● Catalog. Alternate Formats: online ● Monographs ● Papers. **Conventions/Meetings:** annual international conference, provides forum for international scholars (exhibits) ● annual meeting (exhibits).

19129 ■ Wycliffe Bible Translators (WBT)
PO Box 628200
Orlando, FL 32862-8200
Ph: (407)852-3600
Free: (800)992-5433
Fax: (407)852-3601
E-mail: info_usa@wycliffe.org
URL: http://www.wycliffe.org
Contact: Robert M. Creson, Pres.
Founded: 1934. **Members:** 3,888. **Staff:** 139. **Budget:** $8,623,000. **Regional Groups:** 6. **Description:** Interdenominational, non-sectarian Christian missions organization. Works to assist the Church in making disciples of all nations through Bible translation. Aids national programs seeking to benefit ethnic minority groups in the course of Bible translation work, conducts locally initiated and funded research programs, and assists in educational, agricultural, and medical community development projects. Produces alphabets for heretofore unwritten languages; prepares materials to teach people to read and write their own language; develops and publishes grammar books, dictionaries, and articles based on various aspects of the language; surveys dialects; prepares initial literacy helps; encourages ethnic groups to author authentic indigenous literature and to carry on literacy and bilingual education among their own people. **Publications:** *Ethnologue*. Reference document and list of all languages of the world and their status with regard to Bible translation. ● *I.E.*, 3/year. Magazine ● Also develops and publishes grammar books, dictionaries, and articles based on aspects of indigenous language. **Conventions/Meetings:** triennial Wycliffe USA Delegate Conference.

Blind

19130 ■ Care Ministries
PO Box 1830
Starkville, MS 39760-1830

Ph: (662)323-4999
Free: (800)336-2232
E-mail: care@careministries.org
URL: http://www.careministries.org
Contact: B.J. LeJeune, Dir.
Founded: 1989. **Members:** 1,700. **Staff:** 5. **Budget:** $100,000. **Multinational. Description:** Provides information, spiritual support, and community resources to blind or visually impaired. **Libraries: Type:** reference. **Holdings:** 700; audio recordings. **Subjects:** Christian materials. **Projects:** David. **Publications:** *Evangelical Sunday School Teacher's Edition,* monthly. Audiotape ● *Our Daily Bread,* monthly. Devotional. **Circulation:** 600.

Brethren

19131 ■ Association of Grace Brethren Ministers (AGBM)
c/o Rev. Joel Richards, Pres.
La Loma Grace Brethren Church
1315 La Loma Ave.
Modesto, CA 95354
Ph: (209)523-3738
Fax: (209)523-3774
E-mail: jerichards@sbcglobal.net
URL: http://www.fgbc.org
Contact: Rev. Joel Richards, Pres.
Founded: 1940. **Members:** 550. **Membership Dues:** voluntary, $100 (annual). **Staff:** 1. **Budget:** $40,000. **Description:** Cooperates in and encourages work of the ministry for the Lord Jesus Christ, particularly within the Fellowship of Grace Brethren Churches. **Awards:** Excellence in Ministry. **Frequency:** annual. **Type:** recognition. **Recipient:** to a non-senior pastor for outstanding service for Christ ● Lifetime Achievement Award. **Frequency:** annual. **Type:** recognition. **Recipient:** for 25 years or more of service for Christ with distinction ● Pastor of the Year. **Frequency:** annual. **Type:** recognition. **Recipient:** for faithfulness and excellence in ministry ● Teen Scholarships. **Type:** scholarship. **Computer Services:** Online services, information and coordination. **Additional Websites:** http://www.agbm.org. **Formerly:** (1999) National Fellowship of Grace Brethren Ministries. **Publications:** *Sharpening One Another,* bimonthly. Newsletter. Features information, inspiration and challenge. **Price:** included in membership dues. **Circulation:** 600. **Conventions/Meetings:** annual conference and meeting ● annual Fellowship of Grace Brethren Churches - conference (exhibits).

19132 ■ Brethren Peace Fellowship (BPF)
Box 455
New Windsor, MD 21776
Ph: (410)848-5631 (410)857-4842
E-mail: braune@ccpl.carr.org
Contact: Wilbur Wright, Treas.
Founded: 1967. **Members:** 750. **Regional Groups:** 3. **Description:** Engages in, promotes, and stimulates peace education and action within the Church of the Brethren. Sponsors retreats and nonviolent actions. **Awards:** Brethren Peacemaker of the Year Award. **Frequency:** annual. **Type:** recognition. **Publications:** *Mid-Atlantic BPF Newsletter,* quarterly ● Also publishes peace tracts. **Conventions/Meetings:** annual meeting.

19133 ■ Church of the Brethren General Board Global Mission Partnership
1451 Dundee Ave.
Elgin, IL 60120
Ph: (847)742-5100
Free: (800)323-8039
Fax: (847)742-6103
E-mail: snoffsinger_gb@brethren.org
URL: http://www.brethren.org
Contact: Stanley J. Noffsinger, Gen. Sec.
Founded: 1968. **Staff:** 13. **Budget:** $2,000,000. **Languages:** English, Spanish. **Description:** Serves as mission and service agency of the Church of the Brethren. Participates with other churches and agencies in specific efforts aimed at establishing peace and justice, establishing and strengthening the Christian fellowship for mission and ministry, and improving the conditions of humankind in health, education, and general welfare. Sponsors and conducts individual and community rehabilitation programs; volunteer and salaried programs on six continents; assistance in underdeveloped areas; relief programs in disaster areas; institutional services. **Departments:** Africa Representative; Asia Representative; Church Development; Community Development; Economic Justice; Latin America Representative; New Windsor Service Center; Peace and International Affairs/Europe Representatives; Volunteer Services; Washington Office. **Divisions:** SERRV (Sales Exchange for Refugee Rehabilitation Vocation). **Formed by Merger of:** Foreign Mission Commission; Brethren Service Commission. **Formerly:** (1999) Church of the Brethren General Board World Ministries Commission. **Conventions/Meetings:** annual conference.

Broadcasting

19134 ■ Christian Television Mission (CTM)
PO Box 10242
Springfield, MO 65808-0242
Ph: (417)581-5777
Free: (800)356-2155
Fax: (417)581-5622
URL: http://www.christianlink.com/tv/ctm
Contact: Jack Ward, Field Dir.
Founded: 1956. **Staff:** 3. **Budget:** $180,000. **Description:** Christian resource materials (audio and video), distribute Christian oriented programs to television, cable, and closed circuit broadcasting stations. Presents musical programs to congregations and at conventions. Organizes religious seminars on evangelism, missions, music, fundraising and church growth. **Computer Services:** Information services, Christian resource materials. **Conventions/Meetings:** annual Branson Summit - meeting and seminar, on church growth - usually October.

19135 ■ Communication Commission (NCC/CC)
c/o National Council of Churches U.S.A.
475 Riverside Dr., Ste.880
New York, NY 10015
Ph: (212)870-2048
Fax: (212)870-2030
E-mail: wpattillo@ncccusa.org
URL: http://www.ncccusa.org
Contact: Wesley M. Pattillo, Assoc. Gen. Sec. for Communication
Founded: 1951. **Members:** 15. **Staff:** 6. **Description:** A unit of the National Council of Churches of Christ. Acts on behalf of member denominations and agencies in relating the Christian gospel to the communication media and interpreting the work of the National Council of Churches. Offers news and interpretation services to print and electronic media; produces religious television and radio programs; provides information in communication technologies, media ethics and related fields. **Committees:** Electronic Media Programming; Media Advocacy; News/Media Relations/Worldwide Faith News; Web Managers. **Departments:** Communication. **Formed by Merger of:** Protestant Film Commission; Protestant Radio and Television Commission. **Formerly:** (1975) Broadcasting and Film Commission. **Publications:** *EcuLink,* periodic. Magazine ● Annual Report, annual. Alternate Formats: online ● Also publishes news releases and occasional papers on cable television and emerging technologies. **Conventions/Meetings:** semiannual meeting.

19136 ■ International Christian Media Commission (ICMC)
1601 Windsor Dr.
Kingsburg, CA 93631
URL: http://www.icmc.org
Contact: Dave Adams, International Dir.
Founded: 1986. **Members:** 300. **Staff:** 2. **Budget:** $400,000. **Description:** Provides a network for the discussion and presentation of issues affecting Christians from 125 countries involved in the media. Encourages the sharing of ideas, information, and news with others. Sponsors consultations. **Affiliated With:** World Evangelical Alliance. **Supersedes:** World Evangelical Fellowship Communication Commission. **Publications:** *Media and Message: The Use of Media in Evangelism.* Book ● *The Word in the World* ● Newsletter. **Price:** included in membership dues. **Advertising:** accepted. **Conventions/Meetings:** periodic conference.

19137 ■ National Religious Broadcasters (NRB)
9510 Tech. Dr.
Manassas, VA 20110
Ph: (703)330-7000
Fax: (703)330-7100
E-mail: info@nrb.org
URL: http://www.nrb.org
Contact: Dr. Frank Wright, Pres./CEO
Founded: 1944. **Members:** 1,250. **Membership Dues:** individual, for profit, $320 (annual) ● educational institution, $422 (annual) ● organizational (category A-H), $422-$5,094 (annual) ● organizational (category I-K), $8,488-$13,792 (annual) ● associate retired individual, $98 (annual) ● associate individual, associate faculty individual, $294 (annual) ● associate educational institution, $422 (annual) ● associate company, $582 (annual). **Staff:** 17. **Regional Groups:** 6. **State Groups:** 5. **Description:** Christian communicators. Fosters electronic media access for the Gospel; promotes standards of excellence; integrity and accountability; and provides networking and fellowship opportunities for members. **Libraries: Type:** reference. **Holdings:** archival material, books, clippings, periodicals, photographs. **Subjects:** religious broadcasting industry. **Awards:** Board of Directors' Award. **Frequency:** annual. **Type:** recognition ● Chairman's Award. **Frequency:** annual. **Type:** recognition ● Distinguished Service. **Frequency:** annual. **Type:** recognition ● Milestone. **Frequency:** annual. **Type:** recognition ● Radio Program Producer of the Year. **Frequency:** annual. **Type:** recognition ● Radio Station of the Year. **Frequency:** annual. **Type:** recognition ● Religious Broadcasting Hall of Fame Award. **Frequency:** annual. **Type:** recognition ● Television Program Producer of the Year. **Frequency:** annual. **Type:** recognition. **Committees:** Hispanic NRB; Intercollegiate NRB; Music Licensing. **Departments:** Administrative; Communications; Convention; Finance; Membership. **Publications:** *Directory of Religious Media,* annual. Lists religious radio and television stations, programmers, and suppliers. ISSN: 0731-0331. **Circulation:** 3,000. **Advertising:** accepted. Alternate Formats: CD-ROM ● *Inside NRB,* weekly. Newsletters. Contains news for members. ● *NRB Convention.* Brochure ● *NRB Magazine,* monthly. Contains feature articles on topics in religious broadcasting. **Price:** $24.00/year. ISSN: 0034-4079. **Circulation:** 8,000. **Advertising:** accepted. Alternate Formats: microform. **Conventions/Meetings:** annual conference and convention (exhibits).

Buddhist

19138 ■ American Buddhist Association (ABA)
c/o Bright Dawn Home Spread
W7136 County Rd. U
Plymouth, WI 53073-4538
Ph: (920)528-1364 (773)583-5794
E-mail: brightdawn_1@juno.com
URL: http://www.awakenedone.org
Contact: Richard Brandon, Pres.
Founded: 1955. **Membership Dues:** individual, $60 (annual) ● family, $100 (annual) ● group, $250 (annual). **Description:** Works to study and make known the principles of Buddhism and to encourage the understanding and application of these principles. **Divisions:** Bright Dawn Home Spread; Meditation/Retreat Center. **Publications:** *Heartland Sangha Notes,* quarterly. Newsletter. **Price:** $15.00/year. **Conventions/Meetings:** meeting, services, meetings, workshops, retreats, meditations - 15-18/month.

19139 ■ American Buddhist Movement (ABM)

301 W 45th St.
New York, NY 10036
Ph: (212)489-1075
E-mail: kevin_oneil@verizon.net
URL: http://www.wayofthebudha.com
Contact: Dr. Kevin R. O'Neil, Pres.

Founded: 1980. **Members:** 7,000,000. **Membership Dues:** individual, $35 (annual) ● organization, $500 (annual). **Staff:** 4. **Regional Groups:** 15. **State Groups:** 30. **Local Groups:** 20. **National Groups:** 5. **Multinational. Description:** Buddhist groups and organization, individuals, and meditation center. Aims to support and unify Buddhists in the U.S; encourages the study of Buddhism and the relationship between Buddhism and American culture; foster interreligious cooperation; assist individuals in locating Buddhist groups. Series as a link among American Buddhist groups; disseminates information. Maintains speakers' bureau. Sponsors a prison project to educate prisoners about Buddhism. Supports the American Buddhist Fund. **Libraries: Type:** reference. **Holdings:** 5,000; archival material. **Subjects:** Buddhism, Asian religions. **Awards:** Buddhist Of The Year. **Frequency:** 3/year. **Type:** recognition. **Recipient:** to an individual or group that has accomplished outstanding work for the understanding of Buddhism in the United States ● Human Treasure. **Frequency:** 3/year. **Type:** monetary. **Recipient:** to an individual who has unselfishly worked for peace, human rights and fostered understanding and cooperation between countries and the people on this planet. **Computer Services:** Online services. **Additional Websites:** http://www.buddhismonline.us, http://www.koneil.com. **Programs:** The American Buddhist Church; American Buddhist College. **Study Groups:** Nalanda University. **Subgroups:** United Nations Association of American Buddhists. **Affiliated With:** United Nations. **Publications:** *American Buddhist*, monthly. Magazine. Includes news and current events of the movement and book reviews. **Price:** $15.00 /year for individuals; $20.00 /year for institutions. ISSN: 0747-900X ● *American Buddhist Directory*, monthly. Membership Directory. Includes book reviews and employment opportunities. **Price:** $20.00/year ● *American Buddhist News*, monthly. Newsletter. Covers Buddhist philosophy and literature. Contains annual index, book reviews, and report of Buddhist activities throughout the U.S. **Price:** $15.00 /year for individuals; $20.00 /year for institutions. **Circulation:** 6,000. **Conventions/Meetings:** periodic conference - open to all Buddhist and the general public ● seminar.

19140 ■ American Buddhist Study Center (ABSC)

331 Riverside Dr.
New York, NY 10025
Ph: (212)864-7424
E-mail: hoshinseki@aol.com
URL: http://www.americanbuddhist.org/home4.htm
Contact: Hoshin Seki, Pres.

Founded: 1951. **Members:** 370. **Membership Dues:** regular, $100 (annual) ● benefactor, $500 (annual). **Staff:** 4. **Description:** Represents Buddhists and others interested in Buddhism; activities include a Sunday religious service, monthly book discussion groups, lecture series, classes in Buddhist studies and Japanese cultural events. **Libraries: Type:** reference. **Holdings:** 9,000; books. **Subjects:** Buddhism. **Formerly:** (2000) American Buddhist Academy. **Publications:** *Buddhist Sangha*, monthly. **Conventions/Meetings:** semiannual seminar.

19141 ■ Buddhist Churches of America Federation of Buddhist Women's Associations (BCAFBWA)

c/o Buddhist Churches of America
1710 Octavia St.
San Francisco, CA 94109
Ph: (415)776-5600
Fax: (415)771-6293
E-mail: bcahq@pacbell.net
URL: http://www.buddhistchurchesofamerica.org/home
Contact: Terri Harada, Pres.

Founded: 1952. **Members:** 15,000. **Description:** Women members of Buddhist churches of Jodo Shin- shu faith. Promotes American Buddhism through publications, community service, fundraising, and recreational and educational programs. Makes annual contributions to welfare organizations. **Formerly:** (1989) National Federation of Buddhist Women's Associations. **Conventions/Meetings:** annual meeting.

19142 ■ Buddhist Text Translation Society (BTTS)

c/o International Translation Institute
1777 Murchison Dr.
Burlingame, CA 94010-4504
Ph: (415)332-6221
Fax: (415)332-2376
E-mail: bttsonline@snetworking.com
URL: http://www.bttsonline.org
Contact: Hsuan Hua, Chm.

Founded: 1970. **Members:** 100. **Regional Groups:** 7. **State Groups:** 3. **Local Groups:** 2. **Description:** Represents Buddhist monks and nuns; lay scholars with a minimum of three years of intensive study in Buddhist scriptures, practices, and scriptural languages. Works to translate the Chinese Buddhist Canon into other languages, primarily English; each work is accompanied by an extensive inter-linear commentary to the scripture. Offers a four-year intensive monastic training program and a four-year lay-training program. Maintains speakers' bureau; conducts research programs. Operates library containing the classical Chinese Buddhist Canon, commentaries, and reference works. Maintains the Buddhist Council for Refugee Rescue and Resettlement (see separate entry). **Committees:** Certifying; Editing; Primary Translation; Reviewing. **Publications:** *Buddhist News*, semiannual. Newsletter ● *Vajra Bodhi Sea*, monthly. Journal. **Price:** $4.00/issue; $40.00/year; $100.00 3 years subscription ● Also publishes books on Buddhist meditation, virtuous conduct, poetry, and other subjects. **Conventions/Meetings:** annual conference.

19143 ■ Buddhist Vihara

5017 16th St. NW
Washington, DC 20011
Ph: (202)723-0773
Fax: (202)722-1257
E-mail: mdsiri1@yahoo.com
URL: http://www.buddhistvihara.com
Contact: Ven. Maharagama Dhammasiri, Pres.

Founded: 1966. **Members:** 500. **Membership Dues:** individual, $25 (annual) ● life, $250 ● student, $15 (annual). **Languages:** English, Sinhalese. **Description:** Works to provide a religious and educational center to present Buddhist thought, practice, and culture and, more broadly, to aid cross-cultural communication and understanding - prerequisites for a peaceful world. Formed by the Most Venerable Madihe Pannaseeha, Maha Nayaka Thera, of Sri Lanka, who noted a serious and growing interest in Buddhism in the U.S. after he visited this country in 1964. Offers the perspective of Theravada Buddhism, which it claims is the oldest continuous school of Buddhism that characterizes the cultures of Burma, Laos, Cambodia, Sri Lanka, and Thailand. Conducts Sunday services, operates a bookstore and mail order service, holds discussions, provides lecturers, sponsors classes on Buddhism and meditation for adults and children, and organizes celebrations on days of special Buddhist significance; headquartered in the Washington Buddhist Vihara (Temple), which also houses a shrine room, a meditation room, a garden, and the bookstore. **Libraries: Type:** reference. **Holdings:** 4,000; books. **Subjects:** Buddhism philosophy. **Computer Services:** database ● mailing lists. **Committees:** Book Service; Youth Affairs. **Publications:** *Buddha's Teaching As It Is*. Audiotape ● *Vandana*. Handbook. Contains devotional subjects. ● *Washington Buddhist*, quarterly. Newsletter. **Price:** included in membership dues; $6.00 /year for non-members in U.S. and Canada; $12.00 /year for nonmembers outside U.S. and Canada. **Circulation:** 1,200. **Advertising:** accepted ● Also publishes books about Buddhism. **Conventions/Meetings:** annual general assembly - always December or January, in Washington, DC.

19144 ■ Burma-America Buddhist Association (BABA)

1708 Powder Mill Rd.
Silver Spring, MD 20903
Ph: (301)439-4035
Fax: (301)439-4035
E-mail: sopanyima@aol.com
URL: http://www.ibcdc.org/temples/baba.htm
Contact: Wilson Hurley, Co-Sec.

Founded: 1980. **Members:** 80. **State Groups:** 20. **Local Groups:** 60. **Languages:** Burmese, English, Nepali, Vietnamese. **Description:** Individuals interested in the philosophy and cultural environment of Buddhism. Serves as a religious, educational, and cultural resource center to promote Buddhist (Theravada) thought, beliefs, and practices. Encourages the practice of Insight Meditation (Vipassana), "a discipline to develop mindfulness, to provide an opportunity to find one's self, and see the truth". Promotes the practice of four Buddhist qualities of metta, karuna, mudita, and upekkha to bring about peace for all mankind. Offers meditation sessions, Sunday services, religious counseling services, and educational programs. Conducts cultural activities, bazaars, children's services, and community charity services. Sponsors the Burmese New Year's Day, the Buddha's Enlightenment Day, Buddhist Lent Day, and Robe-Offering Ceremony (Kathina Day). Compiles statistics. **Libraries: Type:** reference. **Holdings:** 1,000. **Subjects:** Buddhism. **Committees:** Ceremonies and Religious Activities; Cultural Affairs and Public Relations. **Affiliated With:** Cambodian Buddhist Society. **Publications:** *Manglarama Journal*, quarterly ● Books. Provides information on Mahasi Sayadaw's meditation. **Conventions/Meetings:** annual conference - always second weekend of April, in Silver Spring, MD ● monthly meeting ● seminar.

19145 ■ Cambridge Buddhist Association (CBA)

75 Sparks St.
Cambridge, MA 02138-2215
Ph: (617)491-8857
Fax: (617)686-3986
URL: http://www.unsui.org
Contact: Dokuro R. Jaeckel, Contact

Founded: 1957. **Staff:** 1. **Languages:** English, Japanese, Spanish. **Description:** A multi-ethnic, nondenominational organization for the promotion of the teachings of Buddha, incorporated by D.T. Suzuki, Shinichi Hisamatsu, Holmes Welch, and John and Elsie Mitchell; conducts regular schedule of zazen, Buddhist services, introductory/refresher workshops on Buddhist practice, children's groups, and retreats at its temple in Cambridge, Massachusetts. Provides facilities for other Buddhist groups in the Boston area, including Sakya Institute, the Community of Interbeing, and the Sri Lanka Association of New England. Does not require formal membership for participation in spiritual activities, but asks that those attending CBA activities for the first time call ahead and speak to a resident monk before coming. **Libraries: Type:** reference. **Holdings:** 2,000. **Publications:** Newsletter, quarterly. **Conventions/Meetings:** retreat ● periodic workshop.

19146 ■ Dharma Realm Buddhist Association (DRBA)

1825 Murchison Dr.
Burlingame, CA 94010-4504
Ph: (415)421-6117
Fax: (415)692-5912
E-mail: paramita@drai.com
URL: http://www.drba.org
Contact: Hsuan Hua, Chm.

Founded: 1959. **Members:** 200,000. **Regional Groups:** 7. **State Groups:** 3. **Local Groups:** 2. **Description:** Promotes Annual Buddhist events at the City of 10,000 Buddhas include: three-week winter meditation session, three-week spring bowing session, three-week summer Sutra recitation session. **Formerly:** (1984) Sino-American Buddhist Association.

19147 ■ First Zen Institute of America (FZIA)
113 E 30th St.
New York, NY 10016
Ph: (212)686-2520
URL: http://www.firstzen.org
Contact: Michael Hotz, Pres.

Founded: 1930. **Members:** 200. **Membership Dues:** associate (foreign), $15 (monthly) ● sustaining, associate, $10 (annual). **Description:** Conducts program of daily meditation in the Rinzai tradition. **Libraries: Type:** reference. **Holdings:** 5,000. **Subjects:** Buddhism, Zen. **Formerly:** (1944) Buddhist Society of America. **Publications:** Zen Notes, quarterly. Journal. Includes lectures and talks by founding Zen Master Sakeian Sasaki. **Price:** $10.00/year in U.S.; $15.00/year outside U.S. ISSN: 0513-9465. **Circulation:** 250. **Conventions/Meetings:** meeting - every Monday and Wednesday.

19148 ■ Foundation for the Preservation of the Mahayana Tradition (FPMT)
1632 SE 11th Ave.
Portland, OR 97214
Ph: (503)808-1588
Fax: (503)808-1589
E-mail: info@fpmt.org
URL: http://www.fpmt.org
Contact: Ven Roger Kunsang, Pres./CEO

Founded: 1975. **Members:** 3,600. **Staff:** 17. **Regional Groups:** 9. **State Groups:** 10. **Local Groups:** 3. **National Groups:** 94. **Description:** Seeks to preserve the study and practice of Buddhist teaching according to Tibetan tradition. Conducts social work and educational programs. **Computer Services:** database. **Telecommunication Services:** electronic mail, fpmt@fpmt.org. **Funds:** Lama Yeshe Sangha; Mani Wheel; Sera Je Food. **Projects:** Ani Liberation Sanctuary; Maitreya; Merit Box; Prajnaparamita Writing. **Publications:** Mandala, periodic. Journal. **Price:** $18.00/year in U.S. and Canada; $30.00/year outside North America; $4.95/issue. **Circulation:** 8,000. **Advertising:** accepted.

19149 ■ Friends of the Western Buddhist Order (FWBO)
c/o Aryaloka Buddhist Centre
14 Heartwood Cir.
Newmarket, NH 03857
Ph: (603)659-5456
URL: http://www.fwbo.org

Founded: 1980. **Members:** 100. **Staff:** 2. **Budget:** $100,000. **Regional Groups:** 4. **National Groups:** 5. **Description:** Members of the Western Buddhist Order (people who have fully committed themselves to following the Buddhist path to enlightenment); Mitras (people who have committed to develop their practice within the organization's context); persons associated with Buddhist activities. Seeks to present Buddhism in a way that is relevant to modern Western culture. Establishes centers where Buddhism is practiced and taught. Offers courses and study groups; provides instruction in meditation and physical disciplines including yoga and T'ai Chi. Sponsors retreat program. Encourages development of Buddhist residential communities for men and women. Develops Right Livelihood businesses that help employees' spiritual development, offer products or services that are beneficial to society, provide a reasonable standard of living for workers, and donate a portion of profits to charitable causes. Raises funds for Buddhist-run social and educational programs in central India and for Tibetans living in Northern India. Maintains speakers' bureau. **Libraries: Type:** open to the public. **Holdings:** 200; books, periodicals. **Subjects:** Buddhism. **Publications:** Dharma Life, quarterly. Magazine. Includes book reviews and advice for committed Western Buddhists. **Price:** $18.00/year. **Advertising:** accepted ● Lotus Realm, quarterly. Magazine. Serves as a guide for women practicing Buddhism. **Price:** $15.00/year ● Mitrata, quarterly. Journal. Explores major themes central to Buddhist teaching and practice. **Price:** $30.00/year ● Books ● Monographs. **Conventions/Meetings:** periodic festival.

19150 ■ Jewel Heart
207 E Washington St.
Ann Arbor, MI 48104
Ph: (734)994-3387
Fax: (734)994-5577
E-mail: programming@jewelheart.org
URL: http://www.jewelheart.org
Contact: Gehlek Rimpoche, Pres./Founder

Founded: 1989. **Membership Dues:** friend, $25-$49 (annual) ● associate, $50-$149 (annual) ● individual, $150-$299 (annual) ● supporting, $300-$599 (annual) ● sustaining, $600-$999 (annual) ● benefactor, $1,000 (annual). **Multinational. Description:** Seeks to serve as a vehicle and witness to the process of personal and cultural transformation. Translates the ancient wisdom of Tibetan Buddhism into contemporary life. Offers a graduated study and practice program based on the teachings of Gehlek Rimpoche. **Telecommunication Services:** electronic mail, gehlek@jewelheart.org.

19151 ■ Kunzang Palyul Choling (KPC)
18400 River Rd.
Poolesville, MD 20837
Ph: (301)349-0440
E-mail: info@tara-md.org
URL: http://www.tara.org
Contact: Jetsunma Ahkon Lhamo, Spiritual Dir.

Founded: 1982. **Members:** 200. **Staff:** 5. **Budget:** $500,000. **Description:** Individuals engaged in the study and practice of Buddhism according to the Nyingmapa tradition of Tibet. Offers teachings and practice sessions in Buddhist philosophy and meditation. Conducts classes and informal talks; sponsors workshops and retreats. Holds 24-hour-a-day vigil of prayer and meditation (unbroken since 1985). Maintains sponsorship program for Tibetan refugee children and youth. Operates gift store and 65-acre wildlife refuge. Maintains 19 stupas (traditional sacred structures); three miles of walking trails and meditation gardens. **Libraries: Type:** open to the public. **Holdings:** 300; books, periodicals, video recordings. **Subjects:** Buddhist philosophy. **Formerly:** World Prayer Center. **Publications:** Publishes brochure, books, booklets, audio and videocassette tapes. **Conventions/Meetings:** weekly meeting, 12-step program.

19152 ■ Mid-America Buddhist Association (MABA)
299 Heger Ln.
Augusta, MO 63332-1445
Ph: (636)482-4037
Fax: (636)482-4037
E-mail: info@maba-usa.org
URL: http://www.maba-usa.org
Contact: Ji Ru, Chm.

Description: Supports monastic order of Buddhist monks and nuns, and its lay followers; promotes understanding of Buddhist teachings.

19153 ■ Soka Gakkai International-United States of America (SGI-USA)
606 Wilshire Blvd.
Santa Monica, CA 90401
Ph: (310)260-8900
Fax: (310)260-8917
E-mail: mail-for-sgi-usa@sgi-usa.org
URL: http://www.sgi-usa.org
Contact: Mr. Daisaku Ikeda, Pres.

Founded: 1963. **Members:** 300,000. **Staff:** 100. **Regional Groups:** 53. **Local Groups:** 2,550. **Languages:** Chinese, English, French, Japanese, Korean, Persian, Spanish, Thai, Vietnamese. **Description:** Promotes peace and individual happiness based on the teachings of the Nichiren school of Mahayana Buddhism. Is affiliated with the worldwide SGI organization. Have monthly discussion and study meetings, as well as numerous social projects like the Earth Charter and United Nations Decade or Creating a Culture of Peace for the Children of the World. **Libraries: Type:** not open to the public; reference. **Holdings:** 3,000; articles, books, periodicals. **Subjects:** Buddhism, peace and disarmament, philosophy, education. **Awards:** Humanitarian Award. **Frequency:** periodic. **Type:** recognition. **Recipient:**

for contributions to peace-building ● Justice Award. **Frequency:** periodic. **Type:** recognition ● Liberty Award. **Frequency:** periodic. **Type:** recognition ● Renaissance Award. **Frequency:** periodic. **Type:** recognition. **Telecommunication Services:** electronic bulletin board, audio streaming of lectures. **Committees:** Youth Peace. **Divisions:** Boys and Girls; Educational Professionals; Fine Artists; GLBT; Health Professionals; Junior and Senior High School; Legal Professionals; Men's; Student; Women's; Young Men's; Young Women's. **Programs:** Victory Over Violence Youth. **Subgroups:** Dance; Language. **Formerly:** (1991) Nichiren Shoshu Soka Gakkai of America. **Publications:** Living Buddhism, monthly. Magazine. Contains Buddhist thought. **Price:** $7.00/month. **Circulation:** 18,000 ● World Tribune (in Chinese, English, Japanese, Korean, Spanish, and Thai), weekly. Newspaper. Includes articles on Buddhism and organizational news. **Price:** $10.00/month. **Alternate Formats:** online ● Also publishes religious and other books. **Conventions/Meetings:** Founding Day Celebration - meeting - always November.

19154 ■ Supreme Master Ching Hai Meditation Association (SMCHMA)
PO Box 730247
San Jose, CA 95173-0247
Ph: (408)998-2342 (408)463-0297
E-mail: info@godsdirectcontact.org
URL: http://www.godsdirectcontact.org
Contact: Edgar Shyuan, Contact

Founded: 1989. **Members:** 10,000. **State Groups:** 12. **Multinational. Description:** Represents individuals of all religious faiths and cultural backgrounds. Works to enable members to elevate their consciousness and develop their inner potential through meditation. Conducts educational programs and lectures. **Publications:** The Key to Immediate Enlightenment. Book ● Questions and Answers. Book ● The Supreme Master Ching Hai News, monthly. Magazine. **Price:** free. **Circulation:** 5,000 ● Audiotapes ● Videos.

19155 ■ Western Young Buddhist League (WYBL)
c/o Buddhist Churches of America
1710 Octavia St.
San Francisco, CA 94109
E-mail: staff@bcayouth.org
URL: http://www.bcayouth.org/YBA%20Groups/ about_wybl.htm
Contact: Lizzie Jones, Pres.

Founded: 1947. **Members:** 1,000. **Local Groups:** 50. **Description:** Young people (ages 18-28) of Jodo Shinshu Buddhist faith. Promotes Buddhism; provides unity and fellowship; conducts charitable and social activities. **Additional Websites:** http://www.geocities.com/da_wybl_conference/WYBL.html. **Publications:** Directory, periodic. **Conventions/Meetings:** annual conference and workshop.

19156 ■ Zen Studies Society (ZSS)
c/o New York Zendo Shobo-Ji
223 E 67th St.
New York, NY 10021-6002
Ph: (212)861-3333
Fax: (212)628-6968
E-mail: office@newyorkzendo.org
URL: http://www.daibosatsu.org
Contact: Eido Tai Shimano Roshi, Abbot

Founded: 1965. **Members:** 300. **Staff:** 16. **Languages:** English, Japanese. **Description:** Provides Zen Buddhist training, practice, and retreats. Maintains Temple (New York Zendo) and Mountain Monastery (Dai Bosatsu Zendo) in New York. **Libraries: Type:** reference. **Holdings:** 2,400. **Subjects:** Zen Buddhism and related topics. **Telecommunication Services:** electronic mail, office@zenstudies.org. **Publications:** Books ● Newsletter, semiannual. Provides information on Zen teachings in America. Includes calendar of events. **Price:** included in membership dues; $5.00 /year for nonmembers. **Circulation:** 6,000. **Alternate Formats:** online.

Catholic

19157 ■ Academy of American Franciscan History (AAFH)
Proj. MUSE
2715 N Charles St.
Baltimore, MD 21218-4319
Ph: (410)516-6989
Fax: (410)516-6968
E-mail: muse@muse.jhu.edu
URL: http://muse.jhu.edu/publishers/aafh
Contact: Jeffrey M. Burns, Dir.
Founded: 1944. **Staff:** 2. **Budget:** $125,000. **Languages:** English, Portuguese, Spanish. **Description:** Aims to promote the study of the influence of religion, in particular of the Franciscan Order, upon the formation of the countries of the Americas. **Libraries: Type:** reference. **Holdings:** 25,000. **Subjects:** Latin American history, especially ecclesiastical. **Awards:** Serra Award of the Americas. **Type:** recognition. **Recipient:** to notable individual for contribution to inter-American understanding and friendship. **Publications:** *A Guide to Nahuatl Manuscripts in United States Repositories.* Book ● *The Americas* (in English and Spanish), quarterly. Journal. **Advertising:** accepted. Alternate Formats: online ● *Hispanic Catholicism in an Age of Transitor.* Monograph ● *Propaganda Fide Series, Vol. 12* ● Also publishes documentary series and biographical series. **Conventions/Meetings:** periodic conference.

19158 ■ ADOREMUS - Society for the Renewal of the Sacred Liturgy
PO Box 300561
St. Louis, MO 63130
Ph: (314)863-8385
Fax: (314)863-5858
E-mail: editor@adoremus.org
URL: http://www.adoremus.org
Contact: Helen Hull Hitchcock, Ed.
Founded: 1995. **Members:** 15,000. **Membership Dues:** basic in U.S., $30 (annual) ● basic outside U.S., $40 (annual) ● patron, $100-$199 (annual) ● sustaining donor, $200-$499 (annual) ● jubilee donor, $500 (annual) ● millennium donor, $1,000 (annual) ● benefactor, $5,000 (annual) ● duc in altum, $10,000 (annual). **Staff:** 3. **Multinational. Description:** Represents Catholic Clergy and individuals. Promotes authentic reform of the Liturgy in accordance with the Second Vatican Council's Constitution on the Liturgy. **Libraries: Type:** not open to the public. **Holdings:** 2,000; books, periodicals. **Subjects:** Catholic theology, scripture, liturgy. **Formerly:** (2003) Society for the Renewal of the Sacred Liturgy. **Publications:** *Adoremus Bulletin,* 10/year. Journal. Covers issues involving Catholic worship, theology, translation, music, art, etc. **Price:** included in membership dues. **ISSN:** 1088-8233. **Circulation:** 15,000. Alternate Formats: online.

19159 ■ Agape: Gospel of Life Disciples
PO Box 192
Franklin, LA 70538
Ph: (337)828-2375
E-mail: agapebooks2002@yahoo.com
Contact: Bernard Bergeron Broussard, Dir.
Founded: 1996. **Members:** 20,000. **Staff:** 5. **State Groups:** 50. **Local Groups:** 2. **Description:** Catholics loyal to the teaching of the Church and in agreement with Pope John Paul. Works to put an end to all violence against life, including abortion, artificial contraception, capital punishment, euthanasia, racism, ethnic cleansing, biological engineering, pornography, addictive drugs, child and spousal abuse, political reform, and war. Provides information; offers mini- and full-length home study courses; conducts research and charitable programs; maintains hall of fame and speaker's bureau. **Libraries: Type:** reference; open to the public. **Holdings:** 5,000; audiovisuals, books, clippings, periodicals. **Subjects:** peace, justice, abortion, racism, poverty, euthanasia, drugs, apologetics, saints, public square, environmental stewardship. **Awards:** Gold Movie Award. **Frequency:** annual. **Type:** monetary. **Recipient:** for a motion picture that embodies the Gospel principles ●

Gold Writing Award. **Frequency:** annual. **Type:** monetary. **Recipient:** for a book, article or essay that champions the Gospel principles ● Ripple of Hope. **Frequency:** annual. **Type:** recognition. **Recipient:** to an individual who works to advance the Gospel principles. **Subgroups:** Star Throwers. **Also Known As:** AGAPE. **Publications:** *Agape,* periodic. Newsletter. **Price:** $10.00/year. **Circulation:** 100,000. **Advertising:** accepted ● *Aquarian Conspiracy,* periodic. Book. **Price:** $10.00/year. **Circulation:** 100,000. **Advertising:** accepted ● *Mary: A Letter Written by the Hand of God.* Book ● *Reveille for Catholics.* Books.

19160 ■ Aid to the Church in Need (ACN-USA)
PO Box 220384
725 Leonard St.
Brooklyn, NY 11222
Free: (800)628-6333
E-mail: info@acnusa.org
URL: http://www.aidtothechurchinneed.org
Contact: Sarkis Boghjalian, Natl. Dir.
Founded: 1947. **Members:** 600,000. **Staff:** 10. **Description:** Catholic organization approved by the Holy See (but open to all Christians). Works through pastoral and social aid to support the Catholic Church wherever persecuted or threatened. Provides support to refugees, religious communities, diocese; prints Bibles for children. **Publications:** *Child's Bible,* bimonthly. Books. Available in 123 languages. ● *I Believe-Catechism.* Books. Available in 18 languages. ● *The Mirror* (in Dutch, English, French, German, Italian, and Spanish), 8/year. Newsletter. Contains information on the progress of sponsored projects and ongoing needs, issues around the world. **Price:** free. Alternate Formats: online.

19161 ■ All Roads Ministry (ARM)
55 Pallen Rd., No. 3
Hopewell Junction, NY 12533
Ph: (845)226-4172
URL: http://www.allroadsministry.com
Contact: Vincent P. Lewis, Co-Founder/Pres.
Founded: 1986. **Staff:** 30. **Multinational. Description:** Serves as Roman Catholic lay association. Works to educate Roman Catholics in evangelism and promotion of Roman Catholic faith; opposes Protestantism. Works to convince "fallen away" or inactive Roman Catholics to return to the Church. Participates in related debates; conducts training sessions. Maintains speakers' bureau. Offers correspondence courses. **Telecommunication Services:** information service, Bible supports for Catholic doctrines. **Also Known As:** Catholic Department of Defense. **Publications:** *Analysis and Explanations,* monthly. Journal. Contains social commentary. **Price:** $30.00/year ● *The ARMament,* monthly. Journal. **Price:** $30.00/year. **Advertising:** accepted ● Books ● Audiotapes ● Also publishes tracts, essays, collections from The ARMament, Catholic Action Handbook, etc.

19162 ■ Ambassadors of Mary (AM)
6003 W Diversey Ave.
Chicago, IL 60639
Ph: (773)622-9542
E-mail: gqlf@eircom.net
URL: http://ambassadorsofmary.com
Contact: Patricia J. Hackett, Pres.
Founded: 1946. **Description:** Religious and laypersons of the Roman Catholic Church worldwide pledged to the apostolic work of winning Catholics "to a more fervent Marian life". Members promote the "interior life of prayer and sacrifice" by adding a prayer or devotion in reparation to the Immaculate Heart of Mary over and above what they were doing previously and by urging other persons to do the same. Sponsors the Pilgrim Virgin movement, in which large replicas of the Statue of Fatima are taken weekly to homes; conducts First Saturday retreats. Maintains distribution center for Marian literature. **Convention/Meeting:** none.

19163 ■ American Benedictine Academy (ABA)
c/o Adel Sautner, OSB, Exec. Sec.
St. Benedict's House
415 S Crow St.
Pierre, SD 57501

Ph: (605)224-0969
E-mail: bennii@dakota2k.net
URL: http://www.osb.org/aba/index.html
Contact: Adel Sautner OSB, Exec. Sec.
Founded: 1948. **Members:** 325. **Membership Dues:** regular, $25 (biennial) ● regular, $20 (annual). **Staff:** 7. **Budget:** $18,000. **Description:** Primarily men and women monastic of the Roman Catholic Order of St. Benedict, plus a growing number of lay oblates of St. Benedict or other persons interested in the Benedictine ethos. Cultivates the Benedictine heritage and dialogue between the heritage and contemporary culture. **Libraries: Type:** not open to the public. **Subjects:** Monastic history. **Awards:** Monastic Studies Grant. **Frequency:** annual. **Type:** grant. **Recipient:** to members. **Sections:** Archives; Information Technology; Monastic Research; Visual Arts. **Publications:** *American Monastic Newsletter,* 3/year, every February, June, and October. Includes information on canon law, notices, bibliography, news of monastic communities, calendar of events, reviews, and commentaries, etc. **Price:** included in membership dues; $5.00 /year for nonmembers. **Circulation:** 500. Alternate Formats: online ● *Pre-Convention Reflection Papers,* biennial. **Price:** $5.00 ● *Proceedings of Biennial Convention.* **Price:** $10.00/issue, plus $2 shipping ● Monographs ● Papers. **Conventions/Meetings:** biennial Junior Essay Competition ● biennial Monastic Culture: The Revitalization of the Mind and the Spirit - convention, visual arts exhibit (exhibits).

19164 ■ American Catholic Union (ACU)
PO Box 2622
Richmond, CA 94802-1622
Ph: (415)232-3323 (502)368-0871
Fax: (502)361-9782
E-mail: orcb1@aol.com
URL: http://www.am-cath.org
Contact: Francis P. Facione PhD, Exec. Dir.
Founded: 1984. **Members:** 250. **Staff:** 2. **Description:** Deacons, priests, bishops, local congregations, denominations, and religious organizations from various independent Catholic jurisdictions. Fosters communication and understanding among independent Catholic jurisdictions; provides a forum for Catholic traditions; represents members' interests before other religious bodies; offers counseling, research, and pastoral training for clergy; fosters and perpetuates traditional Catholic faith, morals, and teachings; sets professional guidelines and standards for clergy. Establishes ministries for the advancement of Catholicism through evangelism, missionary work, education, charity, and healing. Offers educational programs on audio- and videocassettes. Maintains speakers' bureau, biographical archives, and 2500 volume library including doctrinal, liturgical, and pastoral literature regarding the independent Catholic tradition. Conducts charitable programs; compiles statistics. **Publications:** *American Catholic Union Newsletter,* periodic. **Conventions/Meetings:** annual meeting.

19165 ■ American St. Boniface Society
PO Box 1352
Bronx, NY 10466
Ph: (718)994-0989
E-mail: jkerssj@aol.com
Contact: Fr. J. Von Kerssenbrock SJ, Exec. Dir.
Founded: 1920. **Description:** Purpose is to support the Catholic church in eastern European countries through prayer, fundraising, and gift parcels. **Publications:** *Bonifatius Blatt* (in English and German), quarterly. Magazine.

19166 ■ Apostleship of Prayer (AoP)
3211 S Lake Dr., Ste.216
Milwaukee, WI 53235
Ph: (414)486-1152
Fax: (414)486-1159
E-mail: aposprayer@aol.com
URL: http://www.apostlesofprayer.org
Contact: Rev. James M. Kubicki SJ, Natl. Dir.
Founded: 1844. **Members:** 40,000,000. **Staff:** 3. **Regional Groups:** 9. **Local Groups:** 160. **Multinational. Description:** Promotes prayer for the Pope's

monthly intentions and devotion to the Sacred Heart of Jesus. **Publications:** *Pope's Monthly Prayer Intentions* (in English and Spanish), annual ● Also publishes prayer leaflets, prayer cards and catalogs. **Conventions/Meetings:** biennial meeting.

19167 ■ Apostleship of the Sea in the United States of America (AOSUSA)

3211 4th St., NE
Washington, DC 20017-1194
Ph: (202)541-3384
Fax: (202)541-3351
E-mail: aos-usa@usccb.net
URL: http://www.aos-usa.org
Contact: Rev.Fr. John A. Jamnicky, Natl. Dir.
Founded: 1947. **Members:** 747. **Membership Dues:** pastoral/associate/mariner/cruise ship priest/affiliate/student mariner, $60 (annual). **Staff:** 1. **Regional Groups:** 7. **State Groups:** 30. **Local Groups:** 67. **Description:** Roman Catholic Port Chaplains and Cruise Ship Priests. Established for the moral, social, and spiritual welfare of seafarers and those in the maritime industry. Services include hospitality and welcoming programs, and counseling and spiritual services. Conducts annual Chaplain's Training Program and the new "Cruise Ship Priest Program". Maintains charitable programs. **Awards:** Maritime Samaritan Award. **Type:** recognition ● Star of the Sea Award. **Type:** recognition. **Computer Services:** database ● information services. **Telecommunication Services:** electronic bulletin board, yahoo discussion group for members only. **Publications:** *Catholic Maritime Newsletter*, monthly. **Price:** free. **Circulation:** 3,800 ● *Chaplain's Directory*, periodic. **Conventions/Meetings:** annual conference.

19168 ■ Apostolate for Family Consecrations (AFC)

Catholic Familyland
3375 County Rd. 36
Bloomingdale, OH 43910
Ph: (740)765-5500
Free: (800)FOR-MARY
Fax: (740)765-5561
E-mail: info@familyland.org
URL: http://www.familyland.org
Contact: Jerome F. Coniker, Pres.
Founded: 1975. **Members:** 52,000. **Staff:** 55. **Languages:** English, Spanish. **Description:** Individuals interested in bringing the family closer to God. Seeks to transform neighborhoods into God-centered communities. Produces 24-hour, 7-days a week Familyland TV Network with weekly and daily television and radio programs as well as other videotaped and broadcast programs including Be Not Afraid Family Hours, First Saturday, and Sacred Heart Enthronement. Operates bookstore and gift shop. Operates 850-acre Catholic Familyland in Bloomingdale, Ohio. **Libraries: Type:** reference. **Holdings:** 15,000; audio recordings, books, video recordings. **Subjects:** existing AFC programs. **Awards:** Pope John Paul II Family Fidelity Award. **Type:** recognition. **Telecommunication Services:** additional toll-free number, (800)77-FAMILY. **Publications:** *Apostolate's Family Catechism*. Books ● *Catholic Familyland Digest*, bimonthly ● *Marian Multiplier Newsletter*, periodic. **Conventions/Meetings:** Holy Family Fests - festival - weeklong, 4 every summer ● annual Marriage Getaway - meeting ● annual Totus Tuus Family Fest Conference, for children, youth and adults.

19169 ■ Archconfraternity of Christian Mothers (ACM)

220 37th St.
Pittsburgh, PA 15201
Ph: (412)683-2400
Fax: (412)683-7155
E-mail: christianmothers@nauticom.net
URL: http://www.capuchin.com/mothers
Contact: Fr. Lester Knoll OFM, Natl. Dir.
Founded: 1881. **Members:** 3,400. **Description:** Parish confraternities interested in the home-education, character formation, and personality development of children guided primarily by mothers. **Convention/Meeting:** none. **Affiliated With:** National Council of Catholic Women. **Publications:** *The Christian Mother*, quarterly. Bulletin.

19170 ■ Archconfraternity of the Holy Ghost (AHG)

6230 Brush Run Rd.
Bethel Park, PA 15102
Ph: (412)831-0302
Fax: (412)831-0970
E-mail: csspeast@choiceonemail.com
URL: http://www.spiritans.org/comm/arch.html
Contact: Fr. Jeffrey T. Duaime, Dir.
Founded: 1912. **Members:** 4,000. **Membership Dues:** individual, one time, $10 ● family, one time, $20. **Description:** Promotes devotion to the Holy Spirit. **Convention/Meeting:** none.

19171 ■ Association of Catholic T.V. and Radio Syndicators (ACTRS)

Address Unknown since 2006
Founded: 1975. **Members:** 60. **Description:** Major Roman Catholic television and radio program production organizations affiliated with UNDA - U.S.A. Purpose is to address the needs of members in their efforts to promote the Christian gospel via television and radio broadcasting. **Affiliated With:** Catholic Academy for Communication Arts Professionals. **Conventions/Meetings:** semiannual conference - usually Menlo Park, CA; **Avg. Attendance:** 503.

19172 ■ Association for Christian Ethics (ACE)

PO Box 1007
New York, NY 10150
Ph: (718)357-4830
Fax: (718)357-4830
E-mail: info@eth.org
URL: http://www.eth.org
Founded: 1972. **Description:** Serves as an advisory group to the Pope and episcopacy of the Catholic Church.

19173 ■ Association of Hebrew Catholics (AHC)

4120 W Pine Blvd.
St. Louis, MO 63108-2802
E-mail: info@hebrewcatholic.org
URL: http://www.hebrewcatholic.org
Contact: Elias Friedman OCD, Founder
Founded: 1982. **Members:** 800. **Multinational. Description:** Works to establish within the Catholic Church the means by which Catholics of Jewish origin can preserve their identity and heritage. Operates speakers' bureau. Hebrew - English translation services. **Libraries: Type:** open to the public. **Holdings:** articles. **Computer Services:** Online services, discussion forum. **Study Groups:** Prayer. **Publications:** *The Hebrew Catholic*, quarterly. Newsletter. Explores issues, teaches, and provides readership communication. **Price:** $15.00 in U.S. and Canada; $25.00 outside U.S. and Canada. Alternate Formats: online ● Pamphlets, flyers. **Conventions/Meetings:** periodic meeting.

19174 ■ Association of Marian Helpers (AMH)

Eden Hill
Stockbridge, MA 01263
Ph: (413)298-3691
Free: (800)4MARIAN
E-mail: fr.joseph@marian.org
URL: http://www.marian.org/association
Contact: Fr. Seraphim Michalenko MIC, Dir.
Founded: 1945. **Members:** 1,500,000. **Languages:** English, French, Polish, Spanish. **Description:** Promotes "the message of Divine Mercy and devotion to the Immaculate Virgin Mary." Seeks to advance the mission and works of Marian priests and brothers worldwide. Provides prayer and financial assistance to Marian projects and programs worldwide. **Libraries: Type:** reference. **Subjects:** Virgin Mary, Divine Mercy. **Computer Services:** Mailing lists, of members. **Publications:** *Fuente De Miseri Cordia* (in English and Spanish), quarterly. Magazine. **Price:** included in membership dues. **Circulation:** 30,000 ● *Marian Helper*, quarterly. Magazine. Covers spiritual, inspirational and Marian missions. **Price:** included in membership dues. **Circulation:** 6,000 ● *Roze Maryi* (in English and Polish), quarterly. Magazine. **Price:** included in membership dues.

19175 ■ Association of the Miraculous Medal (AMM)

1811 W St. Joseph St.
Perryville, MO 63775-1598
Ph: (573)547-2508
Free: (800)264-6279
Fax: (573)547-1389
E-mail: ammfather@amm.org
URL: http://www.amm.org
Contact: Henry Grodecki C.M., Pres.
Founded: 1918. **Members:** 2,000,000. **Membership Dues:** individual, $0 (annual) ● life, $5. **Staff:** 85. **Budget:** $10,000,000. **Description:** Individuals interested in the miraculous medal fashioned by St. Catherine in Paris, France, in 1830 according to specifications given to her during a vision in which she spoke with the Virgin Mary. Promotes the Catholic faith; seeks to increase interest in the miraculous medal and its mission. Sponsors religious and educational programs; makes available reproductions of the miraculous medal and other objects with religious significance. **Affiliated With:** Alliance of Nonprofit Mailers; Association for Postal Commerce; DMA Nonprofit Federation; National Catholic Development Conference. **Publications:** *Miraculous Medal Bulletin*, 8/year. Newsletter. **Price:** included in membership dues. **Circulation:** 315,000. Alternate Formats: online.

19176 ■ Association for the Rights of Catholics in the Church (ARCC)

3150 Newgate Dr.
Florissant, MO 63033
Ph: (413)477-1080 (215)477-1080
Free: (877)700-2722
Fax: (413)527-5877
E-mail: arcc@arccsites.org
URL: http://arcc-catholic-rights.org
Contact: Leonard Swidler PhD, Pres.
Founded: 1980. **Members:** 600. **Membership Dues:** regular, $25 (annual). **Description:** Catholics and Friends of ARCC (a group of non-Catholic supporters). Purposes are: to bring about substantive structural changes in the Catholic Church; to institutionalize a collegial understanding of the Catholic Church in which decision-making is shared and accountability is realized among all Catholics; to affirm the fundamental rights rooted in the humanity and baptism of all Catholics. Seeks to ensure the rights of all Catholics through the establishment of a Charter of the Rights of Catholics in the Church which advocates: ordination for women and married people; choice of celibacy or marriage for ordained persons; access to information regarding the Church and to the sacraments for those who have remarried. **Additional Websites:** http://arcc-catholic-rights.net. **Telecommunication Services:** electronic mail, dialogue@temple.edu. **Committees:** Advocacy; Charter; Education. **Publications:** *ARCC Light*, bimonthly. Newsletter. Covers association business, consciousness-raising, and opportunities for networking. Includes book reviews. **Price:** included in membership dues. **Circulation:** 1,000. Alternate Formats: online ● *Charter of the Rights of Catholics in the Church: A Catholic Bill of Rights* ● Articles. Alternate Formats: online. **Conventions/Meetings:** annual meeting.

19177 ■ Association of Romanian Catholics of America (ARCA)

Address Unknown since 2007
Founded: 1948. **Members:** 2,500. **Membership Dues:** family, $20 (annual) ● individual, $15 (annual) ● social, $10 (annual). **Staff:** 4. **Budget:** $21,000. **State Groups:** 15. **Languages:** English, Romanian. **For-Profit. Description:** Catholic members of the Romanian Byzantine Rite. Promotes and perpetuates church traditions according to Romanian Byzantine Catholic usage. Serves as a support organization to the Romanian Catholic Diocese of Canton, OH. Maintains collection of archival and documentary

material. Administers financial assistance to ARCA Conference Center, camping programs, and museum. **Libraries: Type:** open to the public. **Holdings:** 20,279. **Subjects:** arts, cultural, religious, nature. **Awards:** ARCA Award. **Type:** recognition ● St. George. **Frequency:** annual. **Type:** recognition. **Recipient:** for outstanding service to the association and the church. **Computer Services:** database. **Divisions:** ARCA-YD National; Fellowship National; Juvenile; Young Adult. **Publications:** *ARCA Center Newsletter*, monthly. **Price:** $5.00/year. **Circulation:** 800. **Advertising:** not accepted. Alternate Formats: CD-ROM. **Conventions/Meetings:** annual conference and meeting ● annual Dance Workshops - conference and workshop - Labor Day weekend.

19178 ■ Assumption Guild (AG)
330 Market St.
Brighton, MA 02135
Ph: (617)783-0400
Fax: (617)783-8030
E-mail: assumptionguild@yahoo.com
URL: http://www.masscardsaa.com
Contact: Fr. John Franck, Contact

Founded: 1955. **Members:** 10,000. **Staff:** 3. **Budget:** $35,000. **Description:** Fundraising organization that financially aids young men who want to become Assumptionist priests; membership in the guild is by contribution. Sponsors the Catholic Mass Association. **Convention/Meeting:** none. **Publications:** none.

19179 ■ Auxiliaries of Our Lady of the Cenacle (AOLC)
513 W Fullerton Pkwy.
Chicago, IL 60614-5999
Ph: (773)528-6404
Fax: (773)549-0554
E-mail: jrennert@cenaclesisters.org
URL: http://www.cenaclesisters.org
Contact: James R. Rennert CFRE, Province Dir. of Development

Founded: 1878. **Members:** 140. **Regional Groups:** 2. **Languages:** English, French. **Description:** Catholic women of all ages and professions interested in a religious, but fully secular life. Vows are received through the Congregation of Our Lady of the Retreat in the Cenacle, and are renewed annually. Members serve God through their own professions, talents, lifestyles, or other apostolic works. Promotes apostolic and personal spiritual growth and development. Activities are usually church-related. **Formerly:** (1960) Aggregation of Congregation of Our Lady of Cenacle. **Publications:** *AC Highlights*, quarterly. Newsletter ● *Feuilles de Liaison des Auxiliaires de Notre Dame Du Cenacle*, bimonthly. Newsletter ● Directory, semiannual. **Conventions/Meetings:** semiannual meeting.

19180 ■ Benedictines for Peace (BFP)
c/o Carol Ann Wassmuth, OSB
465 Keuterville Rd.
Cottonwood, ID 83522-5183
Ph: (208)962-5032
Fax: (208)962-7212
E-mail: st_gertrude_justice@hotmail.com
URL: http://www.mountosb.org/bfp.html
Contact: Carol Ann Wassmuth OSB, Contact

Founded: 1980. **Members:** 3,000. **Description:** Members of the Order of St. Benedict. Promotes a spiritual monastic way of life based on personal and social nonviolence. Supports groups with similar philosophies; cooperates with Pax Christi - U.S.A. Maintains video library. **Convention/Meeting:** none.

19181 ■ Bishop Baraga Association and Archives
c/o Diocese of Marquette
PO Box 1000
Marquette, MI 49855
Ph: (906)225-1141 (906)227-9117
Fax: (906)225-0437

E-mail: edelene@dioceseofmarquette.org
URL: http://www.dioceseofmarquette.org
Contact: Rev. Alexander K. Sample JCL, Exec. Dir.
Founded: 1930. **Members:** 3,000. **Membership Dues:** individual, $10 (annual) ● life, $50. **Staff:** 2. **Description:** Persons interested in promoting the canonization of Bishop Frederic Baraga, first bishop of the Roman Catholic Diocese of Marquette, MI. Maintains archives containing information on the Upper Midwest Region of the United States. **Libraries: Type:** reference. **Holdings:** 800. **Awards:** Baraga Man/Woman of the Year. **Frequency:** annual. **Type:** recognition. **Formerly:** (1998) Bishop Baraga Association. **Publications:** *Baraga Bulletin*, quarterly. **Price:** included in membership dues. ISSN: 1047-5044. **Circulation:** 3,000 ● Also publishes biographies in English and Slovene. **Conventions/Meetings:** annual Bishop Baraga Days - meeting.

19182 ■ Bishops' Committee for Ecumenical and Interreligious Affairs (BCEIA)
3211 4th St. NE
Washington, DC 20017-1194
Ph: (202)541-3000
Fax: (202)541-3183
E-mail: seiamail@usccb.org
URL: http://www.usccb.org/seia
Contact: Rev. James Massa PhD, Exec. Dir.
Founded: 1964. **Members:** 10. **Staff:** 8. **Languages:** English, French, Italian, Spanish. **Description:** Standing committee of the National Conference of Catholic Bishops (see separate entry). Represents bishops who interpret the Decree on Ecumenism of the Second Vatican Council and foster its objectives in the U.S. Sponsors bilateral consultations between Catholic theologians and related experts with partners from several other churches to research ecumenical problems and developments. **Committees:** Anglican-Roman Catholic Consultation; Eastern Orthodox-Roman Catholic Consultation; Lutheran-Roman Catholic Consultation in the United States of America; Oriental Orthodox-Catholic Consultation; Polish National Catholic-Roman Catholic Consultation; Roman Catholic/Presbyterian and Reformed Consultation; Southern Baptist/Roman Catholic Consultation; United Methodist-Roman Catholic Consultation. **Sections:** Secretariat for Catholic-Jewish Relations; Secretariat for Christian Unity; Secretariat for Interreligious Relations. **Formerly:** (1966) Bishops' Commission for Ecumenical Affairs. **Conventions/Meetings:** annual National Workshop for Christian Unity - meeting.

19183 ■ Bishops' Committee on the Liturgy (BCL)
3211 4th St. NE
Washington, DC 20017-1194
Ph: (202)541-3000
Fax: (202)541-3088
E-mail: bcl@usccb.org
URL: http://www.usccb.org/liturgy
Contact: Bishop Donald Trautman, Chm.
Founded: 1958. **Members:** 12. **Staff:** 6. **Budget:** $150,000. **Description:** Bishops from the National Conference of Catholic Bishops (see separate entry) united to form a standing committee of the conference. Aims to deal with matters related specifically to worship in the church; serves as a source of information to the body of bishops as well as the teaching arm in the area of liturgy for the bishops to the American church. **Libraries: Type:** reference. **Holdings:** 1,000; books. **Subjects:** liturgy. **Subcommittees:** Black Liturgy; Hispanic Liturgy and Music; Lectionary; Music. **Formerly:** (1967) Bishops' Committee on the Liturgical Apostolate. **Publications:** *Liturgy Documentary Series*, semiannual ● *Study Test Series*, semiannual ● Newsletter, 10/year. **Price:** $15.00. Alternate Formats: online ● Pamphlets. **Conventions/Meetings:** periodic workshop.

19184 ■ Bishops' Committee on Vocations (BCV)
c/o United States Conferences of Catholic Bishops
3211 4th St. NE
Washington, DC 20017
Ph: (202)541-3033

Fax: (202)541-3222
E-mail: vocations@usccb.org
URL: http://www.usccb.org/vocations/vocation.shtml
Contact: Rev. Edward J. Burns, Exec. Dir.
Founded: 1966. **Members:** 10. **Staff:** 1. **Description:** A committee of the National Conference of Catholic Bishops. Encourages and promotes priesthood and religious vocations; develops policies on how to promote vocations. Conducts research and study programs. Works closely with other vocational organizations. **Affiliated With:** United States Conference of Catholic Bishops. **Conventions/Meetings:** quarterly meeting.

19185 ■ Black and Indian Mission Office
2021 H St. NW
Washington, DC 20006-4207
Ph: (202)331-8542
Fax: (202)331-8544
Contact: Rev.Msgr. Paul A. Lenz, Exec.Dir.
Founded: 1884. **Description:** Coordinates the annual Black and Indian United States Mission Collection in Catholic churches across the United States; these funds go to support priests, nuns, and other religious workers with their programs for evangelization among Black and Native Americans throughout the U.S. **Affiliated With:** Bureau of Catholic Indian Missions; Catholic Negro-American Mission Board.

19186 ■ Blessed Kateri Tekakwitha League (BKTL)
Off. of the Vice-Postulor
136 Shrine Rd.
Martyrs Shrine
Auriesville, NY 12016
Ph: (518)853-3153
Fax: (518)853-3051
E-mail: tekleag@yahoo.com
URL: http://www.leveillee.net/kateri/league.htm
Contact: Fr. Kateri League, Vice Postulator
Founded: 1949. **Members:** 4,000. **Staff:** 1. **Description:** Promotes the knowledge and love of Blessed Kateri Tekakwitha and advocates her canonization. Kateri Tekakwitha (1656-80), also known as Lily of the Mohawks, was an American Indian who was instructed and baptized by Jesuits, lived a life of sanctity, and was made Venerable in 1943 by the Roman Catholic church and blessed by Pope John Paul II on June 22, 1980. Conducts special religious services and programs and makes available cassette tapes, statues, medals, books, chaplets, prints, decals, song records, and other articles honoring Kateri. Distributes novena prayers and prayers for Kateri's canonization; maintains charitable program; operates museum. Plans to conduct research and educational programs. **Libraries: Type:** reference. **Computer Services:** database ● mailing lists. **Telecommunication Services:** information service. **Publications:** *Lily of the Mohawks*, quarterly. Newspaper. **Price:** free. **Circulation:** 3,600 ● Pamphlets ● Also publishes plays and biographies on the life of Kateri; produces and distributes descriptive folder.

19187 ■ Blue Army of Our Lady of Fatima, U.S.A.
674 Mountain View Rd. E
PO Box 976
Washington, NJ 07882
Ph: (908)689-1700 (908)213-2223
E-mail: service@bluearmy.com
URL: http://www.waf.org
Contact: Mr. Michael La Corte, Exec.Dir.
Founded: 1947. **Members:** 250,000. **Staff:** 20. **Regional Groups:** 13. **State Groups:** 52. **Local Groups:** 70. **Multinational. Description:** U.S. branch of the World Apostolate of Fatima. Roman Catholics and others in the U.S. who "acknowledge the spiritual Maternity of Mary over mankind and recognize her as the Mother of God." Seeks world peace and the conversion of the world through fulfillment of the Fatima requests of individual conversion, prayer, penance, and reparation. Marks the anniversaries of Fatima apparitions on the 13th of each month from May to October at the Shrine of the Immaculate Heart of Mary in Washington, NJ. **Also Known As:** World Apostolate of Fatima. **Publica-**

tions: *Hearts Aflame: A Teen Catholic Magazine*, quarterly. Includes letters to the editor column, crossword puzzles, and poems. **Price:** $5.00/year. ISSN: 0893-536X. **Advertising:** accepted ● *Shrine Bulletin*, 3/year. Newsletter. Covers events at the National Blue Army Shrine of the Immaculate Heart of Mary. Also includes calendar of events and hours of services. **Price:** $2.00/year ● *SOUL Magazine*, quarterly. National Catholic magazine with articles on Marian spirituality and Fatima. **Price:** $7.95/year. ISSN: 0038-1756. **Circulation:** 30,000. **Advertising:** accepted ● Also publishes books, audio tapes and other publications on Fatima and Marian spirituality and leaflets on Fatima and Marian spirituality. **Conventions/Meetings:** annual National Rosary Congress - conference, includes speakers and masses.

19188 ■ Brothers and Sisters of Penance of St. Francis (BSP)

c/o Shelley Fahey, Pres.
20939 Quadrant Ave. N
Scandia, MN 55073
Ph: (651)433-2733
E-mail: bspenance@yahoo.com
URL: http://www.bspenance.org
Contact: Shelley Fahey, Pres.

Founded: 1996. **Members:** 200. **Staff:** 5. **Budget:** $3,500. **Local Groups:** 2. **Multinational. Description:** Roman Catholics living in their own homes in a modern adaptation of the original rule of life written for penitents in 1221, which was first rule of the Third Order of St. Francis. **Computer Services:** Mailing lists, for members of group. **Formerly:** (2004) Brothers and Sisters of Penance. **Publications:** Newsletter, monthly. **Circulation:** 200. Alternate Formats: online. **Conventions/Meetings:** annual retreat - 3/year; last weekend of July.

19189 ■ Bureau of Catholic Indian Missions (BCIM)

2021 H St. NW
Washington, DC 20006-4207
Ph: (202)331-8542
Fax: (202)331-8544
Contact: Rev.Msgr. Paul A. Lenz, Exec.Dir.

Founded: 1874. **Description:** Purpose is to conduct religious, charitable, and educational activities at American Indian and Eskimo missions. Maintains speakers' bureau; conducts research programs. **Convention/Meeting:** none. **Publications:** *Bureau of Catholic Indian Missions—Newsletter*, 10/year.

19190 ■ Canon Law Society of America (CLSA)

The Hecker Center, Ste.111
3025 Fourth St., NE
Washington, DC 20017-1102
Ph: (202)832-2350
Fax: (202)832-2331
E-mail: coordinator@clsa.org
URL: http://www.clsa.org
Contact: Rev. Arthur J. Espelage OFM, Exec. Coor.

Founded: 1939. **Members:** 1,550. **Membership Dues:** active/associate, $200 (annual) ● student, $100 (annual). **Staff:** 2. **Description:** Represents catholic priests and religious and laypeople interested in application of church law and ecclesiastical jurisprudence. **Awards:** Role of Law Award. **Frequency:** annual. **Type:** recognition. **Recipient:** for service in canon law, development of canon law. **Committees:** Civil and Canon Law; Clergy Issues; Commentary on Revised Code; Consecrated Life; Lay Ministry; Marriage Research; Minorities; Religious; Rights. **Publications:** *Authentic Interpretation on the 1983 Code* ● *CLSA Advisory Opinions, 1984-1993* ● *Code of Canon Law*. Book. **Price:** $15.00 ● *Code of Canons of the Eastern Churches*. Book ● *Convention Proceedings*, annual ● *Decisions*. Book ● *The Invalid Marriage*. Book. **Price:** $15.00 ● *Law Sections* ● *Marriage Studies*. Book ● Newsletter, quarterly. Alternate Formats: online. **Conventions/Meetings:** annual symposium, on church law - always October.

19191 ■ Canon Law Society of the Orthodox Catholic Church (CLS)

PO Box 16201
Duluth, MN 55816
Ph: (218)624-0207
Fax: (218)733-0349
E-mail: rbsocc@juno.com
URL: http://www.rbsocc.org

Founded: 1986. **Members:** 100. **Membership Dues:** associate, $250 (annual) ● counselor, canon lawyer, $300 (annual). **Staff:** 5. **Budget:** $10,000. **Regional Groups:** 3. **Description:** Canon lawyers, counselors, and other individuals with an interest in canon and divine law. Promotes increased public awareness of canon law; encourages professional advancement of members. Serves as a clearinghouse on canon law; sponsors research and educational programs. **Libraries: Type:** not open to the public. **Holdings:** books, periodicals. **Subjects:** canon and divine law. **Formerly:** (2004) North American Canon Law Society.

19192 ■ Capuchin-Franciscans (Province of Saint Joseph) (CFPSJ)

Capuchin Vocation Off.
301 Church St.
Mount Calvary, WI 53057
Ph: (920)753-7502
Fax: (920)753-7514
E-mail: vocation@capuchinfranciscans.org
URL: http://www.capuchinfranciscans.org
Contact: Daniel Anholzer, Provincial Minister

Founded: 1856. **Members:** 200. **Staff:** 150. **Local Groups:** 33. **Description:** Franciscan fraternity of Catholic priests and brothers dedicated to working among the poor, homeless, elderly, and others who are "suffering from injustices of society." Aims to "empower the powerless" through work in parishes, retreat houses, hospitals, nursing homes, meal programs, high school seminaries, overseas missions, and prisons. **Publications:** *Cap Corps Newsletter* ● *Re-Caps*, bimonthly. **Conventions/Meetings:** triennial meeting.

19193 ■ Catholic Campus Ministry Association (CCMA)

1118 Pendleton St., Ste.300
Cincinnati, OH 45202-8805
Ph: (513)842-0167
Free: (888)714-6631
Fax: (513)842-0171
E-mail: info@ccmanet.org
Contact: Edmund L. Franchi, Exec.Dir.

Founded: 1969. **Members:** 1,000. **Membership Dues:** individual, $110 (annual) ● team plan/diocesan plan, $95 (annual) ● associate, $50 (annual) ● corporate, $125 (annual). **Staff:** 6. **Budget:** $250,000. **Description:** Purposes are: to form a strong and coordinated voice for the church's ministry in higher education; to provide continuing education programs for members; to provide liaison with other individuals and agencies of the church interested in campus ministry and the role of the church in higher education; to advance ecumenical and interfaith understanding and cooperation; to provide guidelines for, and assistance in, developing effective campus ministries. Maintains placement service and speakers' bureau; offers colleague consultation service. **Awards:** Forsyth and Hallinan. **Frequency:** annual. **Type:** recognition ● **Type:** scholarship. **Formerly:** (1969) National Newman Chaplains Association. **Publications:** *Crossroads*, 8/year ● Newsletter ● Directory, annual. **Conventions/Meetings:** annual conference ● biennial meeting (exhibits).

19194 ■ Catholic Church Extension Society of the U.S.A.

150 S Wacker Dr., 20th Fl.
Chicago, IL 60606
Free: (888)473-2484
Fax: (312)236-5276
E-mail: wallj@catholicextension.org
URL: http://www.catholic-extension.org
Contact: Fr. John J. Wall, Pres.

Founded: 1905. **Staff:** 65. **Budget:** $20,700,000. **Description:** Supports missionary work in America. Supports and spreads the Roman Catholic faith across the U.S. and its territories, especially in dioceses where funds are insufficient. Purposes are to raise funds to support priests and religious and lay ministers; build chapel and catechetical centers; provide disaster relief; subsidize various religious education, campus ministry, and evangelization programs in poorer dioceses. Provides seminarian education funding; sponsors religious education programs. **Awards:** Lumen Christi Award. **Frequency:** annual. **Type:** recognition. **Recipient:** for service to the Church in America, especially for exemplary missionary work. **Also Known As:** (1999) Catholic Extension. **Publications:** *Extension Magazine*, monthly. Covers current issues in the developing missions of the Catholic Church in the United States. Includes annual report. **Price:** donation requested. ISSN: 0884-7533. **Circulation:** 100,000. Alternate Formats: online ● Also publishes Catholic parish calendars in English and Spanish.

19195 ■ Catholic Council on Working Life (CCWL)

Address Unknown since 2006
Founded: 1943. **Description:** Laymen and clergy interested in applying Christian social principles to American life, especially urban problems. Promotes study of the moral and ethical dimension of occupational responsibilities, of economic and political policies and practices. Sponsors public forums, study weekends, and service committees organized on occupational lines. Presently inactive. **Libraries: Type:** reference. **Holdings:** 600. **Subjects:** theology, economics, sociology.

19196 ■ Catholic Golden Age (CGA)

PO Box 249
Olyphant, PA 18447
Free: (800)836-5699
E-mail: cgaemail@aol.com
URL: http://www.catholicgoldenage.org
Contact: Rev. Gerald N. Dino, Pres.

Founded: 1974. **Members:** 1,400,000. **Membership Dues:** individual, $12 (annual) ● individual, $28 (triennial). **Staff:** 8. **Local Groups:** 132. **Description:** Catholics 50 years of age and over. Studies and discusses the meaning of a longer life and gerontology, emphasizing religion and spirituality. Provides older persons with motivation to lead self-fulfilling lives. Emphasizes the role of religious faith in the endeavors and activities of older people. Assists the aged in their social, physical, economic, intellectual, and spiritual needs. Sponsors apostolic and charitable work and member-oriented religious worship, stressing participation; also sponsors annual Million Candles celebration by encouraging lighting of candles in homes, offices, and parishes, and uniting in prayer for world peace. Maintains Catholic Golden Age Foundation to sponsor and provide financial assistance to charitable, religious, benevolent, and educational programs designed to enrich the lives of older adults. Offers masses for members, living and deceased; discounts on hotels, motels, rental cars, eyeglasses, merchandise, and prescriptions; group travel rates to places of religious significance; and supplemental insurance at group rates. Participates in local, state, and national forums. Gives discounts on nursing homes and home healthcare. **Programs:** Access to Care; Benefits Vision, Hearing, Dental, and Prescription Drug. **Publications:** *CGA World*, bimonthly. Magazine. Reports on human rights, world peace, and health care and Social Security. Alternate Formats: online. **Conventions/Meetings:** annual conference.

19197 ■ Catholic Institute of the Food Industry (CIFI)

PO Box 296
Bronxville, NY 10708
Ph: (914)697-5206
Fax: (914)697-5212
Contact: Kathy Brauer, Sec.

Founded: 1946. **Members:** 300. **Description:** Practicing Catholics and other Christians associated with the administration or managerial functions of the various branches of the food industry (such as the manufacturing, processing, distribution, purveying, advertising, or selling of foods, beverages, or associated equipment). Conducts charitable program. **Awards:** Man of the Year Award. **Frequency:** annual. **Type:** recognition. **Conventions/Meetings:** quarterly meeting.

19198 ■ Catholic Kolping Society of America (CKSA)

c/o Patricia Farkas, Natl. Admin.
1223 VanHouten Ave.
Clifton, NJ 07013
Ph: (201)712-9550
Free: (877)659-7237
Fax: (201)712-9552
E-mail: patfarkas@optonline.net
URL: http://kolping.org/main.htm
Contact: Patricia Farkas, Natl. Admin.

Founded: 1928. **Members:** 2,300. **Staff:** 1. **Local Groups:** 12. **Description:** Catholic family organization. Seeks to teach members to be "good Christians in the kingdom of God, good workers in their respective trades and professions, good parents in their families, and good citizens in the community of their people". Maintains Kolping Houses as homes providing boarding facilities for men and women, and Kolping Centers. Sponsors local educational and instructional programs; maintains community centers, senior citizens clubs. **Awards:** Distinguished Service Award. **Frequency:** biennial. **Type:** recognition ● Father Krewitt Scholarship. **Frequency:** annual. **Type:** scholarship. **Recipient:** for members. **Affiliated With:** International Kolping Society. **Publications:** *Kolping Banner*, monthly. Newsletter. Covers membership activities; includes obituaries. **Price:** $8.00/year. **Conventions/Meetings:** biennial convention - usually Labor Day weekend ● annual Leadership Seminar.

19199 ■ Catholic League for Religious and Civil Rights (CLRCR)

450 Seventh Ave.
New York, NY 10123
Ph: (212)371-3191
Fax: (212)371-3394
E-mail: cl@catholicleague.org
URL: http://www.catholicleague.org
Contact: Dr. William A. Donohue PhD, Pres.

Founded: 1973. **Members:** 350,000. **Membership Dues:** individual, $30 (annual) ● senior, $20 (annual) ● student, $15 (annual) ● life, $1,000 ● individual foreign, $50 (annual). **Staff:** 15. **Budget:** $3,000,000. **Local Groups:** 14. **Description:** Catholics defending their civil rights. Works to establish the right of Catholic lay and clergy to participate in American society without defamation or discrimination. **Libraries: Type:** reference. **Holdings:** 2,500. **Awards:** Pope John Paul II Religious Freedom Award. **Type:** recognition. **Recipient:** for significant contribution to religious freedom and human rights. **Computer Services:** Mailing lists. **Committees:** Legal Advisory. **Publications:** *Catalyst*, monthly. Journal. Records "Catholic-bashing" and the League's response to it. **Price:** included in membership dues. **Circulation:** 100,000. **Advertising:** accepted. Alternate Formats: online ● *The New Freedom.* Book. **Price:** $19.95 ● *Pius XII and the Holocaust.* Book. **Price:** $9.95 ● *The Politics of the ACLU.* Book. **Price:** $19.95 ● *Report on Anti-Catholicism*, annual. Annual Report. **Price:** $10.00. **Conventions/Meetings:** annual meeting.

19200 ■ Catholic Negro-American Mission Board (CNAMB)

2021 H St. NW
Washington, DC 20006-4207
Ph: (202)331-8542
Fax: (202)331-8544
Contact: Rev.Msgr. Paul A. Lenz, Exec.Dir.

Founded: 1907. **Members:** 7,000. **Description:** Supports Catholic sisters' teaching program among blacks in U.S. **Convention/Meeting:** none. **Formerly:** (1970) Catholic Board for Mission Work Among the Colored People.

19201 ■ Catholic Network of Volunteer Service (CNVS)

6930 Carroll Ave., Ste.506
Takoma Park, MD 20912-4423
Ph: (301)270-0900
Free: (800)543-5046
Fax: (301)270-0901
E-mail: volunteer@cnvs.org
URL: http://www.cnvs.org
Contact: Jim Lindsay, Exec. Dir.

Founded: 1963. **Members:** 235. **Membership Dues:** $550 (annual). **Staff:** 9. **Budget:** $370,000. **Description:** Serves as coordinating center for lay volunteer services; referral service for persons seeking opportunities to serve in U.S. and overseas. Encourages lay people to volunteer their professional skills in faith-based volunteer programs throughout the world. Maintains placement service; offers referral service; compiles statistics. **Awards:** Fr. George Mader Award. **Frequency:** annual. **Type:** recognition. **Recipient:** for commitment to lay volunteer service. **Committees:** Advisory Council. **Formerly:** (1975) International Liaison for Volunteer Service; (1984) International Liaison, U.S. Catholic Coordinating Center for Lay Volunteer Ministries; (1986) International Liaison U.S. Catholic Coordinating Center for Lay Missioners; (1993) International Liaison of Lay Volunteers in Mission (U.S. Catholic Network of Lay Mission Programs). **Publications:** *How Can I Help?*, bimonthly. Newsletter ● *Lay Mission Handbook*, annual, 8 chapters/year ● *The Response*, annual. Directory ● Books. **Conventions/Meetings:** annual conference (exhibits).

19202 ■ Catholic Pamphlet Society of the United States (CPS)

100 Old Maryvale Dr.
Cheektowaga, NY 14225
Ph: (716)833-6617
Fax: (716)833-6617
Contact: Margery Johengen, Bus.Mgr.

Founded: 1938. **Members:** 200. **Staff:** 3. **Description:** Supervisors appointed by pastors to take care of racks displaying religious booklets in Catholic churches. **Publications:** none.

19203 ■ Catholic Traditionalist Movement (CTM)

210 Maple Ave.
Westbury, NY 11590-3117
Ph: (516)333-6470
Fax: (516)333-7535
URL: http://www.latinmass-ctm.org
Contact: Father Gommar A. De Pauw JCD, Founder/Pres.

Founded: 1964. **Description:** American Catholics who support implementation of Vatican Council II (Ecumenical Council) decrees within the framework of traditional Catholic beliefs and practices. A manifesto issued by CTM in March 1965 opposes misinterpretations of some of the liturgical changes promulgated by the Ecumenical Council in Rome, Italy, and made effective in the U.S. in November 1964; it calls for an end to regimented group participation in the mass, a limitation on the use of English in the liturgy, and the recognition of Latin as the liturgical and theological language of the Catholic church. Communicates opinions of laity to the Catholic hierarchy. Coordinating committee conducts theological research; maintains information program; compiles statistics from opinion surveys; and conducts a worldwide broadcast program of traditional Latin mass. **Libraries: Type:** not open to the public; by appointment only. **Holdings:** articles, books, periodicals. **Subjects:** religion, church and state. **Computer Services:** Online services, mass. **Publications:** *Latin Mass: Low & High Gregorian Chant.* Videos ● *Quote Unquote: A Public Information Service of the Catholic Traditionalist Movement*, monthly. Bulletin. Contains recent quotes by famous figures and from newspapers, magazines, and other publications on current religious-related events and developments. **Price:** free. ISSN: 1044-0518 ● *Sounds of Truth and Tradition*, periodic. Newsletter. Covers special developments in the Roman Catholic Church. Includes research reports and statistics.

Price: free. ISSN: 0038-187X ● *Traditional Latin Mass: Low & High* (in English and Latin). Audiotapes. Gregorian Chant. **Price:** $5.00 ● Books.

19204 ■ Catholics Speak Out (CSO)

PO Box 5206
Hyattsville, MD 20782
Ph: (301)699-0042
Fax: (301)864-2182
E-mail: cso@quixote.org
URL: http://www.quixote.org/cso
Contact: Ms. Rea Howarth, Dir.

Founded: 1987. **Members:** 10,500. **Membership Dues:** national, $35 (annual). **Staff:** 1. **Budget:** $120,000. **Languages:** English, French, Spanish. **Description:** Catholics, clergy, and other interested individuals. A project of the Quixote Center. Serves as a network of Catholics seeking to implement change within the Roman Catholic church. Promotes democracy, justice, participation, gender equality, the right to dissent, and financial accountability within the church. Lobbies U.S. bishops and the Vatican; sponsors newspaper ads and opinion surveys on current issues. Conducts educational and research programs; maintains speakers' bureau; compiles statistics. Liaison with International "We Are Church" Movement in seeking Roman Catholic reform. **Publications:** *Agenda for Justice*, periodic. Newsletter. **Circulation:** 5,200. **Advertising:** accepted. Alternate Formats: online ● *The Inclusive New Testament*, periodic. Book. Features a critical feminist interpretation of the New Testament, utilizing up-to-date biblical research. **Price:** $21.25 for members; $25.00 for nonmembers ● *Rome Has Spoken.* Book.

19205 ■ Catholics United for the Faith (CUF)

827 N 4th St.
Steubenville, OH 43952
Ph: (740)283-2484
Free: (800)693-2484
Fax: (740)283-4011
E-mail: info@cuf.org
URL: http://www.cuf.org
Contact: Shannon Hughes, Sec.-Treas.

Founded: 1968. **Members:** 30,000. **Membership Dues:** sustaining, $40 (annual) ● outside U.S., $60 (annual) ● life, $500. **Staff:** 23. **Budget:** $1,200,000. **Local Groups:** 97. **Multinational. Description:** Roman Catholics advocating the support, defense, and advancement of the efforts of the teaching church. Seeks to further among Catholic laity the renewal of the faith called for by Second Vatican Council. Works toward cooperation among bishops, priests, and laymen; is concerned with issues such as catechetics, sex education, pro-life, the liturgy, and spiritual renewal. Has initiated national drives in support of the Pope and his teachings. Deals with issues that conflict with the doctrinal and moral teachings of the church. Testifies before the National Conference of Catholic Bishops; makes written interventions to the Synod of Bishops at Rome, Italy. Maintains speakers' bureau. **Libraries: Type:** reference. **Holdings:** 5,000. **Additional Websites:** http://www.emmausroad.org. **Telecommunication Services:** electronic mail, shughes@cuf.org. **Publications:** *Faith and Life Series.* Books. Contains comprehensive Catholic program. ● *Lay Witness*, bimonthly. Magazine. Informs current events in the Church and the Holy Father's intentions for the month. **Price:** free for members. **Circulation:** 10,000. **Advertising:** accepted ● *St. Theresa: Doctor of the Church* ● Bulletin, monthly ● Pamphlets. **Conventions/Meetings:** annual Springtime of Faith - seminar.

19206 ■ CCVI Incarnate Word Missionaries - Congregation of the Sisters of Charity of the Incarnate Word

4503 Broadway
San Antonio, TX 78209-6297
Ph: (210)828-2224
Fax: (210)828-9741
E-mail: iwg011@ccvisanantonio.org
URL: http://www.ccvisanantonio.org
Contact: Gloria Drews-Vallecillo, Dir.

Founded: 1986. **Members:** 6. **Staff:** 1. **National Groups:** 3. **Languages:** English, Spanish. **Multina-**

tional. Description: Catholic mission working in Mexico, the United States, Guatemala, and Peru. Programs include pastoral work, health care, community work, and religious education. **Subgroups:** Coordinating Group. **Formerly:** (2002) CCVI Volunteers in Mission - Congregation of the Sisters of Charity of the Incarnate Word. **Publications:** *IWM Newsletter* (in English and Spanish), semiannual. **Circulation:** 700. Alternate Formats: online. Also Cited As: *IWM Bulletin.* **Conventions/Meetings:** annual workshop, for new members.

19207 ■ Center for Applied Research in the Apostolate (CARA)
2300 Wisconsin Ave. NW, Ste.400
Washington, DC 20007
Ph: (202)687-8080
Fax: (202)687-8083
E-mail: cara@georgetown.edu
URL: http://cara.georgetown.edu
Contact: Sister Sally Duffy SC, Pres./Exec. Dir.
Founded: 1964. **Staff:** 10. **Description:** Socioscientific research agency that conducts empirical studies that relate to the role of the Catholic Church in the modern world. Aims "to discover, promote, and apply scientific informational resources for practical use to the church's social and religious mission in the modern world." Conducts sociological, financial, and demographic research for church agencies. **Convention/Meeting:** none. **Publications:** *CARA Catholic Ministry Formation Directory,* biennial. Includes mission statements, primary ministries, size of congregations, and statistics. **Price:** $75.00/issue ● *The CARA Report,* quarterly. Newsletter. **Price:** $5.00/issue. ISSN: 1089-5183. Alternate Formats: online.

19208 ■ Central Association of the Miraculous Medal (CAMM)
475 E Chelten Ave.
Philadelphia, PA 19144-5758
Ph: (215)848-1010
Free: (800)523-3674
Fax: (215)848-1014
E-mail: shrine@cammonline.org
URL: http://www.cammonline.org
Contact: Rev. James O. Kiernan CM, Pres.
Founded: 1915. **Members:** 2,527,612. **Languages:** English, Spanish. **Description:** Serves as religious organization promoting devotion to the Blessed Virgin Mary through the Miraculous Medal. (In an apparition in France in 1830, Mary appeared before Catherine Laboure and commissioned her to make the medal of the Immaculate Conception, now known as the Miraculous Medal.) Helps support Vincentian seminarians and infirm priests; assists the poor and needy. **Convention/Meeting:** none. **Funds:** Assisted Living Facility; St. Catherine Infirmary; St. Vincent de Paul; Seminary. **Programs:** Gift Annuity; Planned Giving. **Publications:** *Miraculous Medal Magazine,* quarterly. Covers Catholic topics; includes fiction and poetry. **Price:** included in membership dues. **Circulation:** 210,000.

19209 ■ Central Bureau, Catholic Central Union of America (CBCCUA)
3835 Westminster Pl.
St. Louis, MO 63108-3409
Ph: (314)371-1653
Fax: (314)371-0889
E-mail: centbur@sbcglobal.net
URL: http://www.socialjusticereview.org
Contact: Rev. John H. Miller CSC, Dir.
Founded: 1908. **Members:** 250. **Membership Dues:** elected application, $25 (annual). **Staff:** 3. **Budget:** $85,000. **State Groups:** 3. **Local Groups:** 5. **Description:** Headquarters for the Catholic Central Union of America and National Catholic Women's Union (see separate entries). Promotes Catholic social action, fostered through its periodicals, pamphlets, brochures, and leaflets stressing the Catholic viewpoint in social, economic, religious, intellectual, and political problems affecting contemporary society. Offers mission aid and relief, aid to immigrants, information service, and distribution of Catholic literature to missionaries, institutions, and institutional libraries. Maintains vertical file on 9000 subjects

including biography, politics, and religion. **Libraries: Type:** reference. **Holdings:** 250,000; archival material, audiovisuals, books, business records, periodicals. **Subjects:** religion, sociology, philosophy, history, economics. **Publications:** *Social Justice Review,* bimonthly. Journal. Contains the story of Pope's effort to establish the Kingdom of Christ. **Price:** $20.00/year in U.S.; $23.00/year outside U.S. (plus $7 if airmailed). ISSN: 0037-7767. **Circulation:** 5,350 ● Books ● Pamphlets. **Conventions/Meetings:** annual conference.

19210 ■ The Christophers
12 E 48th St.
New York, NY 10017
Ph: (212)759-4050
Free: (888)298-4050
Fax: (212)838-5073
E-mail: mail@christophers.org
URL: http://www.christophers.org
Contact: Dennis W. Heaney, Pres.
Founded: 1945. **Staff:** 35. **Budget:** $3,000,000. **Languages:** English, Spanish. **Description:** Encourages positive action based on Judao-Christian principles, particularly in education, government, business, and communications. Activities emphasize two basic ideas: "there's nobody like you" and "you can make a difference". Produces the annual, Three Minutes a Day book, calendars, and pamphlets in English and Spanish. Conducts Christopher leadership training courses. Produces radio broadcasts and Christopher Close-up, a syndicated weekly public affairs television program; prepares weekly inspirational newspaper columns. **Convention/Meeting:** none. **Awards:** Christopher Award. **Frequency:** annual. **Type:** recognition. **Recipient:** for adult and children's book, feature length motion pictures, and network television specials that exemplify the highest values of the human spirit ● College Video Contest. **Frequency:** annual. **Type:** monetary ● High School Poster Contest. **Frequency:** annual. **Type:** monetary. **Computer Services:** Online services, publication. **Departments:** Awards; Editorial; Spanish; Television and Radio; Youth. **Publications:** *Christopher News Notes,* 10/year. Pamphlets. Addresses one topic of current personal, family or spiritual concern and gives true life examples of people addressing that issue. **Price:** free. Alternate Formats: online ● *Ecos Christoforos* (in English and Spanish), bimonthly. Newsletter. Addresses one topic of current personal, family or spiritual concern and gives true life examples of people addressing that issue. **Price:** free ● *Three Minutes a Day: The Christophers.* Book. **Price:** $7.00 paperback.

19211 ■ Claretian Volunteers and Lay Missionaries
205 W Monroe St.
Chicago, IL 60606
Ph: (312)236-7782 (312)326-7846
Free: (800)328-6515
Fax: (312)236-7230
E-mail: info@claretians.org
URL: http://www.claretians.org
Contact: John DiMucci, Dir.
Founded: 1983. **Description:** Volunteers who provide assistance to communities in need including areas of Guatemala and Hispanic, African American, and Native American communities in the U.S. **Formerly:** Claretian Volunteers.

19212 ■ Committee on Social Development and World Peace of the United States Catholic Conference
3211 4th St. NE
Washington, DC 20017-1194
Ph: (202)541-3000 (202)541-3181
Fax: (202)541-3339
E-mail: jcarr@usccb.org
URL: http://www.usccb.org/sdwp/index.htm
Contact: John Carr, Sec.
Founded: 1968. **Description:** Staffed by the Department of Social Development and World Peace which maintains an Office of Domestic Social Development (concerned with issues such as the economy, labor, federal budget, and voting rights) and an Office of

International Justice and Peace (concerned with military and political issues as they affect human rights, the arms race, and the global economy). Advises Catholic bishops on issues regarding the Catholic Church's relationship to domestic and foreign policy issues. **Conventions/Meetings:** biennial meeting.

19213 ■ Company of Saint Paul
52 Davis Ave.
White Plains, NY 10605
Ph: (914)946-1019
Contact: Rev. Stuart Sandberg, Pres.
Founded: 1921. **Members:** 143. **Description:** Serves as secular institute of Catholic laypeople and priests. Consecrates their everyday lives to evangelical counsels and apostolic works. **Conventions/Meetings:** monthly meeting.

19214 ■ Conference of Major Superiors of Men (CMSM)
8808 Cameron St.
Silver Spring, MD 20910
Ph: (301)588-4030
Fax: (301)587-4575
E-mail: postmaster@cmsm.org
URL: http://www.cmsm.org
Contact: Fr. Paul Lininger OFM, Exec. Dir.
Founded: 1956. **Description:** Major religious superiors (supervisors) of the Roman Catholic religious orders of men in the U.S. Promotes the welfare of priests, brothers, and candidates in the U.S. Furnishes information and services to members on matters of importance to religious life; provides a forum for an exchange of views of common interest and on the use of personnel and resources for common goals. Serves as a national voice to communicate the views of the major superiors of men on vital and contemporary issues. Supports 4500 missionary priests and brothers in more than 90 countries. Carries out research and educational programs. **Committees:** Priestly Formation; Social Concern. **Also Known As:** Conference of Major Religious Superiors of Men's Institutes of the U.S. **Publications:** *CMSM Assembly Brochure.* Alternate Formats: online ● *CMSM Forum,* quarterly ● *Justice and Peace Alert,* monthly ● Bulletin, monthly. Includes calendar of events; personnel changes; regional reports; annual assembly report. **Price:** included in membership dues ● Directory, annual ● Also publishes books. **Conventions/Meetings:** annual assembly - always August ● annual board meeting.

19215 ■ Confraternity of Penitents (CFP)
520 Oliphant Ln.
Middletown, RI 02842-4600
Ph: (401)849-5421
E-mail: copenitents@yahoo.com
URL: http://www.penitents.org
Contact: Ms. Madeline Pecora Nugent, Minister Gen.
Founded: 1994. **Members:** 100. **Description:** Private Catholic Association of the Faithful whose members live Rule of Life in their own homes. Holds annual retreat, has monthly newsletter, teachings and formation. **Libraries: Type:** open to the public. **Holdings:** articles, artwork, audio recordings, video recordings. **Subjects:** Catholic teachings on faith and penance. **Computer Services:** Online services, Penance Means Conversion email list. **Telecommunication Services:** electronic bulletin board, public forums on Church, humor, saints, St. Francis. **Programs:** Four Year Formation. **Formerly:** (2003) Brothers and Sisters of Penance. **Publications:** *No Greater Love,* monthly. Newsletter. Features articles on penance, conversion, Catholic faith. **Price:** free for members; $16.00 /year for nonmembers ● Handbook. Contains all formation lessons, Rule, Statutes, San Damiano Crucifix reflections, other information on penitential life and the organization. **Price:** $39.95 ● Articles. Alternate Formats: online. **Conventions/Meetings:** annual retreat.

19216 ■ Congregation of the Blessed Sacrament (PEL)
5384 Wilson Mills Rd.
Cleveland, OH 44143-3023
Ph: (440)442-6311 (440)442-7243

Fax: (440)449-3862
E-mail: ssscommunications@blessedsacrament.com
URL: http://www.blessedsacrament.com
Contact: Fr. Tom Smithson, Contact
Founded: 1879. **Members:** 3,050. **Staff:** 3. **Description:** Represents Roman Catholic priests, bishops, and other persons in the ministry. Fosters spiritual ideals of members, through Eucharistic prayer and worship. Aims to deepen the spirituality of those actively involved in the ministry. Functions as a national unit of the PEL existing in the principal countries of Europe. **Computer Services:** Mailing lists. **Formerly:** (1999) Priests Eucharistic League. **Publications:** *Emmanuel*, bimonthly. Magazine. Focuses on Eucharistic spirituality. **Price:** $26.00/year. ISSN: 0013-6719. **Circulation:** 4,250. **Advertising:** accepted.

19217 ■ Congregation of Sisters of Saint Agnes
320 County Rd. K
Fond du Lac, WI 54935-8958
Ph: (920)907-2300 (920)907-2302
Fax: (920)923-3194
E-mail: jquinn@csasisters.org
URL: http://www.csasisters.org
Contact: Sister Joann Sambs CSA, Gen. Superior
Founded: 1858. **Members:** 334. **Local Groups:** 133. **Languages:** English, Spanish. **Description:** Women Religious serving rural and urban communities throughout the U.S., and Latin America. Promotes justice for the economically poor; works to further the role of women in the Catholic Church and society; collaborates with the laity and clergy of other faiths in service programs. Provides staffing at 2 hospitals, a home for the aged, and a coeducational college. Places and supports missionaries in Honduras, and Nicaragua. **Formerly:** (1999) Sisters of the Congregation of Saint Agnes. **Publications:** *Sponsorship Update*. Newsletter. Alternate Formats: online.

19218 ■ CORPUS - National Association for an Inclusive Priesthood (CORPUS)
114 Sunset Dr.
Raynham, MA 02767-1383
Ph: (508)822-6710
Fax: (508)822-6710
E-mail: membersvs@corpus.org
URL: http://www.corpus.org
Contact: Stuart O'Brien, Member Services Dir.
Founded: 1974. **Members:** 3,000. **Membership Dues:** regular, $85 (annual). **Staff:** 4. **Budget:** $60,000. **Regional Groups:** 20. **Description:** Married priests, celibate priests, laity, and religious brothers and sisters. Promotes an "expanded and renewed" priesthood of married and single men and women in the Catholic Church. Maintains speakers' bureau. **Libraries: Type:** open to the public. **Awards:** CORPUS Achievement Award. **Frequency:** annual. **Type:** recognition. **Recipient:** for the reflect values of CORPUS. **Formerly:** (1991) CORPUS - National Association for a Married Priesthood; (1993) CORPUS. **Publications:** *Canonical Reflection on Non-Clerical Priesthood*. Paper ● *CORPUS Reports*, bimonthly. Magazine. **Price:** included in membership dues. **Circulation:** 3,000. **Advertising:** accepted ● *Joined In Christ: A Manual for Wedding Ministry*. Paper ● *Joseph's Son*. Paper ● *Redeeming Humanity*. Paper ● *Sex, Power, and Church Structures*. Paper ● *Shaping the Future Priesthood*. Paper ● *Wake Services*. Paper ● Brochures ● Paper ● Also publishes liturgical source material. **Conventions/Meetings:** annual conference (exhibits).

19219 ■ CUSA: An Apostolate of the Sick and Disabled
176 W 8th St.
Bayonne, NJ 07002-1227
E-mail: ams4@juno.com
URL: http://www.cusan.org
Contact: Anna Marie Sopko, Admin.
Founded: 1947. **Members:** 300. **Membership Dues:** donation, $20 (annual). **Staff:** 2. **National Groups:** 50. **Description:** Disabled and chronically ill persons. Organization is Catholic in leadership, but open to persons of all faiths. Promotes group correspondence

through regular and email and mutual encouragement for spiritual vitalization of illness. Sponsors study clubs for group leaders. **Computer Services:** Online services, juno. **Formerly:** (1986) Catholic Union of the Sick in America; (1998) Catholics United for Spiritual Action. **Publications:** *The Cusan*, semiannual. Magazine. Contains articles on religion and topics of general interest. **Price:** included in membership dues. **Circulation:** 1,200. Alternate Formats: magnetic tape ● *Leaders' Study Club*, annual. Audiotape. Provides lending audiotape library for members.

19220 ■ Edith Stein Guild (ESG)
Address Unknown since 2007
Founded: 1955. **Members:** 900. **Membership Dues:** regular, $20 (annual) ● life, $100. **Staff:** 10. **Description:** Universities and colleges, convents, and interested individuals. Promoted the canonization of Edith Stein (1891-1942), philosopher and Carmelite nun Sister Teresia Benedicta of the Cross, who died in the concentration camp at Auschwitz during World War II. Edith Stein was born to a Jewish family, but converted to Catholicism in 1922. She was beatified on May 1, 1987. Canonization by the Roman Catholic Church in October, 1998. Encourages Judaeo-Christian understanding and fosters among Catholics a better understanding of their Hebrew heritage. Promotes knowledge of the life and writings of Edith Stein; maintains collection of literature on Stein. Promotes relations with Muslims. **Awards:** Edith Stein Award. **Frequency:** periodic. **Type:** recognition. **Recipient:** for writer or other individual making significant contributions to Jewish-Catholic relations. **Boards:** Executive Board. **Publications:** *Catholic Telephone Directory*, annual ● *Edith Stein Guild*, quarterly. Newsletter. **Circulation:** 1,300. **Conventions/Meetings:** annual Day of Recollection - retreat (exhibits) - Easter season ● annual Membership Tea - meeting (exhibits).

19221 ■ Family Rosary (FR)
518 Washington St.
North Easton, MA 02356-1202
Ph: (508)238-4095
Free: (800)299-7729
Fax: (508)238-3953
E-mail: mission@hcfm.org
URL: http://www.familyrosary.org
Contact: Rev. John Phalen CSC, Pres.
Founded: 1942. **Languages:** English, Spanish. **Description:** Seeks to promote the unity and spiritual well-being of families everywhere through family prayer as expressed in the theme: the family that prays together, stays together. Promotes the recitation of the rosary as one of the "best and most efficacious prayers in common that the Christian family is invited to recite and one which the Catholic Church has traditionally proposed to the faithful with particular solicitude and insistence, so that when a family gathering becomes a time of prayer, the rosary will be a frequent and favored manner of prayer." Is a member ministry along with Family Rosary International and the Father Peyton Family Institute headquartered at the same address and Family Theater Productions, located in Hollywood, CA, whose films and movies have been shown throughout the world. **Additional Websites:** http://www.hcfm.org. **Formerly:** (1990) Family Rosary Crusade.

19222 ■ Father Judge Apostolic Center (FJAC)
1292 Long Hill Rd.
Stirling, NJ 07980
Ph: (908)647-7112
Fax: (908)626-0350
E-mail: fjac@fjac.org
URL: http://www.fjac.org
Contact: Fr. Kent Weidie ST, Dir.
Founded: 1976. **Staff:** 10. **Languages:** English, Spanish. **Description:** Seeks "to foster the universal call to holiness of life and to mission and ministries as exercised in the circumstances of people's everyday lives." Strives to nourish faith, especially among the poor, to provide a hospitable and healing environment in which people can discover gifts and

develop skills for ministries, to model and to promote shared ministries, to advance ecumenism by being open to collaboration with members of other religious traditions in the ministries of the Center. Sponsored by the Roman Catholic religious congregation known as the Missionary Servants of the Most Holy Trinity. **Programs:** Assistance to Clergy, Religious, Laity; Divorced and Separated; Prayer, Scripture, Spiritual Reading; Spiritual Growth for Clergy, Religious and Lay. **Formerly:** (1986) Ministries Center for the Laity; (1998) Trinity Ministries Center; (2002) Father Judge Center.

19223 ■ Federation of Diocesan Liturgical Commissions (FDLC)
415 Michigan Ave., Ste.70
Washington, DC 20017
Ph: (202)635-6990
Fax: (202)529-2452
E-mail: nationaloffice@fdlc.org
URL: http://www.fdlc.org
Contact: Joseph M. Skeffington, Assoc. Dir.

Membership Dues: associate, $75 (annual) ● industry, $175 (annual). **Staff:** 50. **Description:** Diocesan liturgical commissions. Promotes increased awareness of diocesan activities, programs, and projects in the United States. Facilitates communication and cooperation among members; serves as a clearinghouse on Catholic liturgy and diocesan activities. **Awards:** Frederick R. McManus Award. **Frequency:** annual. **Type:** recognition. **Recipient:** for significant contribution to pastoral liturgy in the United States ● Tabat Scholarship Fund. **Frequency:** annual. **Type:** scholarship. **Recipient:** for graduate students in liturgical studies. **Telecommunication Services:** electronic mail, joe@fdlc.org. **Projects:** Liturgical Catechesis. **Publications:** *FDLC Directory*, periodic ● *FDLC Newsletter*, bimonthly. Features information about FDLC activities and projects. **Price:** $25.00 /year for nonmembers; included in membership dues. **Advertising:** accepted. Alternate Formats: online ● Books ● Catalog. Alternate Formats: online. **Conventions/Meetings:** annual meeting.

19224 ■ Focolare Movement (FM)
PO Box 496
New York, NY 10021
E-mail: contact_focolare_usa@hotmail.com
URL: http://www.rc.net/focolare
Contact: Chiara Lubich, Founder
Founded: 1943. **Members:** 4,500,000. **Multinational. Description:** International lay movement of more than four million persons whose aim is "to work for the realization of Christ's final prayer for unity" and to spread the Gospel in the world through their own lives. Although most Focolare members are Catholic, it encompasses large numbers of non-Catholics and promotes various ecumenical activities. At its heart are some 4,000 fully dedicated laypeople in 70 countries who live in small communities called Focolare Centers. (Focolare is from the Italian word for hearth.) In the U.S. and Canada, sympathizers of the movement number about 70,000; there are six resident centers in New York City, four in Chicago, IL, one in Boston, MA, two in San Antonio, TX, two in Los Angeles, CA, two in Toronto, ON, Canada, one in Washington, DC, one in Columbus, OH, and one in Dallas, TX. Teenage members in the movement are organized under the name GEN Movement, derived from the term new generation. The international movement has built a large community of 700 people from 45 countries at Loppiano near Florence, Italy. **Awards:** Luminosa Award for Unity. **Frequency:** annual. **Type:** recognition. **Recipient:** for a person or group of persons with significant contribution to the ideal of unity. **Publications:** *Living City*, monthly. Magazine. Contains insights on world issues and dialogue. **Price:** $30.00/year in North America; $60.00/year outside North America. ISSN: 0193-5968. **Circulation:** 7,000. **Advertising:** accepted ● Books (in English, French, German, Italian, Japanese, Korean, Portuguese, and Spanish). Published by New City Press. **Conventions/Meetings:** annual Mariapolis - meeting, family retreat - always summer.

19225 ■ Foundations and Donors Interested in Catholic Activities (FADICA)
1350 Connecticut Ave. NW, Ste.825
Washington, DC 20036
Ph: (202)223-3550
Fax: (202)296-9295
E-mail: info@fadica.org
URL: http://www.fadica.org
Contact: Francis J. Butler, Pres.
Founded: 1976. **Members:** 47. **Membership Dues:** regular, $7,500 (semiannual). **Staff:** 2. **Budget:** $659,775. **Description:** Private grant-giving individuals, agencies, and foundations actively interested in meeting the needs of the Catholic Church. Seeks to enhance members' understanding of major issues and needs in the Catholic Church and to help donors focus their funding programs for maximum assistance to church programs and institutions. Focuses on Catholic schools, involvement of laity, stewardship and finance, and religious vocations. Has sponsored consultations such as How to Run A Catholic Foundation, The Future of Church Funding, The Future of Catholic Higher Education, campus ministry, Catholic Inner City Schools, The Vocations Crisis, Diocesan and Parish finances and Administration. Analyzes the church's needs and activities with church experts; coordinates members' proposals for financial support; strives to increase grantmaking effectiveness. **Libraries:** Type: reference. **Awards:** Carroll Award. **Frequency:** annual. **Type:** recognition. **Recipient:** for outstanding contributions to Catholic causes ● Catholic Leadership Award. **Frequency:** annual. **Type:** recognition. **Publications:** *Catholic Funding Guide*, triennial. Directory. **Conventions/Meetings:** periodic seminar ● symposium - 3/year.

19226 ■ Friends of Old St. Ferdinand (FOSF)
PO Box 222
Florissant, MO 63031
Ph: (314)837-2110 (314)830-0032
Fax: (314)830-0075
URL: http://www.usgennet.org/usa/mo/county/stlouis/oldferdinand.htm
Contact: Scott K. Williams, Contact
Founded: 1958. **Members:** 200. **Membership Dues:** individual, $25 (annual) ● life, $250. **Staff:** 27. **Budget:** $35,000. **Description:** Preserves and protects the buildings, contents, and grounds of the Old St. Ferdinand historic site. Provides information through tours, museum, archives and library. Sponsors presentations to schools and groups on the history of the St. Ferdinand De Florissant Territory and the role played by this place and the people who entered into this place from the 1700s until 1957. **Libraries:** Type: open to the public. **Holdings:** 30; archival material. **Subjects:** regional history. **Committees:** Archives and Library; Display and Acquisition; Endowment Fund for Old St. Ferdinand Shrine; Fundraising; Maintenance and Restoration; Tours/Memorial Plaque. **Publications:** *Christmas Concert Program*, annual. **Advertising:** accepted ● *Feast Day Mass Program*, annual ● *Heart of Oak*. **Price:** $1.00 ● *Old St. Ferdinand Newsletter*, semiannual ● *President's Report*, annual. Newsletter ● *Self-Guide Tour Book*. **Price:** $1.00. **Conventions/Meetings:** monthly board meeting ● monthly Book Fair - meeting - every 2nd Saturday ● annual Christmas Concert - party - every 1st and 2nd Sundays of December ● annual meeting, membership ● annual Old Town Festival - usually 2nd week of October ● annual Re-enactors Encampment from 1800's - festival - first full weekend of April ● weekly Regular Tour, with special tours throughout the year - every Sunday, from April through December ● periodic tour ● annual Valley of the Flowers Festival, family weekend - first full weekend of May.

19227 ■ FutureChurch
17307 Madison Ave.
Lakewood, OH 44107
Ph: (216)228-0869
Fax: (216)228-4872
E-mail: info@futurechurch.org
URL: http://www.futurechurch.org
Founded: 1990. **Membership Dues:** individual, $35 (annual) ● family, $60 (annual) ● fixed income/

student, $20 (annual). **Description:** Parish-based Catholics seeking full participation of all baptized Catholics in the life of the Church. **Publications:** *Focus on FutureChurch*. Newsletter.

19228 ■ Glenmary Research Center (GRC)
1312 5th Ave. N
Nashville, TN 37208
Ph: (615)256-1905 (615)256-1900
Fax: (615)251-1472
E-mail: grc@glenmary.org
URL: http://www.glenmary.org/GRC
Contact: Kenneth Sanchagrin, Dir.
Founded: 1966. **Staff:** 3. **Description:** Sponsored by Glenmary Home Missioners, a society of priests and brothers established in 1939 to provide pastoral ministry in small towns and rural districts of the United States. Seeks to serve the research needs of the Catholic Church in rural America, primarily in evangelization, social ministry, and ecumenism. Compiles data on church membership every ten years. **Telecommunication Services:** electronic mail, ksanchagrin@glenmary.org. **Formerly:** Town and Country Religious Research Center. **Publications:** *Atlas of Religions Change, 1952-90*. Book. Contains maps and analysis of county level census-type data for American religious denominations for the period 1952-1990. **Price:** $55.00 ● *Bare Threads*. Book. Examines the effects of the textile mill work and mill life on the women textile workers and their families in the Deep South. **Price:** $12.00 ● *Black Religion in the Evangelical South*. Book. Examines the development of black religion in the Southern United States. **Price:** $15.00 ● *Churches and Church Membership, 1990*. Book. Contains information on the number of churches, communicants or full members, total adherents and adherents as a percent of total reported adherents. **Price:** $40.00 ● *Geography of Religion in Russia*. Book. Examines the historical evolution of "the religious landscape" in the Russian Empire and the USSR. **Price:** $34.00 ● *It Comes From the People*. Book. Documents the creative survival techniques of small dying community of Ivanhoe, VA. **Price:** $69.95 ● *Major Religious Families by Counties of the United States, 2000*. Features four-color map. **Price:** $17.00 ● *Mission 2009: The Future of the Catholic Church in the South*. Book. Features papers addressed at the 50th anniversary symposium of the Glenmary Home Missioners. **Price:** $13.00 ● *Models of Ministry: An Evaluation in Appalachia*. Book. Examines the four models for ministry (the social service model, provider model, advocacy model and the social change model) in Appalachia. **Price:** $4.00 ● *Moving Beyond Confined Circles*. Book. Features a collection of the writings of William Howard Bishop. **Price:** $12.00 ● *Patterns in Pluralism, 1952-1971*. Book. Seeks to analyze and to aggregate religious trends for the 1952-1971 periods. **Price:** $8.00 ● *Religious Congregations and Membership in the United States 2000*. Includes a 25 x 38 fold-out wall map of Major Religious Families. **Price:** $110.00 ● *Slippin' Away: The Loss of Black-Owned Farms*. Book. Addresses the problem of the loss of black-owned farms. **Price:** $9.00 ● *Small Rural Parish*. Book. Bridges the gap between theology and the actual practice of ministry by suggesting valuable principles applicable to parish ministry. **Price:** $8.00 ● Pamphlets.

19229 ■ Good Tidings (GT)
PO Box 283
Canadensis, PA 18325
Ph: (570)595-2705
E-mail: goodtidings@aol.com
URL: http://www.marriedpriests.org/GoodTidings.htm
Contact: Rev. Cait Finnegan, Contact
Founded: 1983. **Staff:** 2. **Languages:** English, French, Spanish. **Description:** Ministry and support group for women and Catholic priests involved in sexual or romantic relationships or abusive relationships. Provides counseling referrals. **Computer Services:** Mailing lists, support ● online services, counseling services. **Sections:** Good Tidings Counseling Services; Holy Innocents. **Formerly:** (1983) Women and Priests Involved. **Publications:** Newsletter, periodic. **Circulation:** 600.

19230 ■ Grailville
932 O'Bannonville Rd.
Loveland, OH 45140-9740
Ph: (513)683-5750
Fax: (513)683-5752
E-mail: nlt@grail-us.org
URL: http://www.grailville.org
Contact: Bonnie Hendricks, Dir.
Founded: 1940. **Description:** U.S. branch of the International Grail Movement. Christian women's movement working for human liberation through efforts in personal renewal, community development, religious search, education, medical-social agencies, and the arts. Works to develop creative alternatives to present lifestyles and institutions; activities are primarily educational. Conducts programs on topics such as ecology, women's issues, social justice, and spirituality. Maintains offices in Cornwall-on-Hudson, NY, and San Jose, CA. **Additional Websites:** http://www.grail-us.org. **Formerly:** (1999) Grail Movement. **Publications:** Newsletter. Alternate Formats: online. **Conventions/Meetings:** annual conference.

19231 ■ Guild of Catholic Lawyers (GCL)
Address Unknown since 2007
Founded: 1928. **Members:** 400. **Description:** Professional organization of Catholic attorneys. Membership is concentrated in New York metropolitan area. Sponsors religious service and quarterly programs on topical subjects and issues. **Awards:** Charles Carroll Award. **Frequency:** annual. **Type:** recognition. **Committees:** Church-State Relationships; Civil Rights of Individuals; Ethics in Public and Professional Life; Family and Social Justice; Law, Medicine, and Science; Media Rights and Responsibilities. **Conventions/Meetings:** annual Red Mass - meeting - always early fall.

19232 ■ Holy Childhood Association (HCA)
366 5th Ave.
New York, NY 10001
Ph: (212)563-8700
Free: (800)431-2222
Fax: (212)563-8725
E-mail: polly@propfaith.org
URL: http://www.worldmissions-catholicchurch.org
Contact: Msgr. John E. Kozar, Dir.
Founded: 1843. **Members:** 150,000. **Membership Dues:** regular, $1 (annual). **Regional Groups:** 176. **Local Groups:** 1. **Description:** Serves as the official children's mission society of the Catholic Church. Supports pastoral and evangelizing programs for children in more than 110 countries. Furnishes educational programs to schools nationwide and focuses on spreading the Gospel message among the young. **Awards:** Bishop Charles de Forbin Janson Award. **Frequency:** annual. **Type:** recognition ● HCA: Young Catholics in Mission. **Type:** recognition. **Also Known As:** Pontifical Association of the Holy Childhood. **Publications:** *It's Our World*, 3/year. Newsletter ● *Leading the Way*, semiannual. Newsletter ● Also distributes educational material to Catholic schools and U.S. religious education programs. **Conventions/Meetings:** biennial conference.

19233 ■ Holy Cross Foreign Mission Society
c/o Holy Cross Mission Center
PO Box 543
Notre Dame, IN 46556
Ph: (574)631-5477
Fax: (574)631-6813
E-mail: hcmc@nd.edu
URL: http://www.nd.edu/~hcmc/index.htm
Contact: Rev. Thomas W. Smith CSC, Dir.
Founded: 1923. **Staff:** 4. **Description:** Aims to serve and support the social, educational, and religious work of the Holy Cross Fathers, Brothers, and co-workers overseas, especially in Bangladesh, Chile and East Africa. Conducts research programs; compiles statistics. **Libraries:** Type: reference. **Holdings:** 520. **Subjects:** missiology justice and peace, Africa, Asia, Latin and South America. **Publications:** *Holy Cross Mission Center Newsletter*, bimonthly. Contains church news in mission areas. **Circulation:** 500 ● *TRANS-MISSION*, semiannual. Newsletter. **Circulation:** 1,500.

19234 ■ Holy Face Association (HFA)
PO Box 821
Champlain, NY 12919-0821
Ph: (514)747-0357
Fax: (514)747-9147
E-mail: holyface@holyface.org
Contact: Gordon Deery, Dir.
Founded: 1975. **Members:** 20,000. **Staff:** 10. **Languages:** English, French, Spanish. **Description:** Catholic religious order. Promotes adherence to the tenets of Catholicism. Sponsors religious and social service programs. **Computer Services:** database ● mailing lists ● online services. **Programs:** Church; Home; Hospital; Missionary; Prison; School. **Publications:** *Treasure of the Holy Face.* Book. **Conventions/Meetings:** annual Novena - dinner and retreat, spiritual - always Shrove Tuesday and the next 8 days.

19235 ■ Holy Shroud Guild (HSG)
PO Box 993
Canandaigua, NY 14424
Ph: (716)394-2606
Fax: (716)394-9215
E-mail: fcbrink@aol.com
URL: http://users.aol.com/fcbrink/hsg/hsg.htm
Contact: Rev. Frederick C. Brinkmann, Pres.
Founded: 1951. **Description:** Scholars and persons interested in the Shroud of Turin (believed by many to have covered the body of Christ after the Crucifixion). Encourages research and provides information about the Shroud of Turin. **Libraries: Type:** reference. **Holdings:** 1,010. **Subjects:** Shroud of Turin. **Committees:** Scientific Research. **Publications:** Newsletter, quarterly. Covers current scientific investigation and studies of the Shroud of Turin: includes reviews of current literature. **Price:** $12.00/year. Alternate Formats: online ● Books ● Pamphlets ● Also distributes pictures and slides.

19236 ■ Humility of Mary Service (HMS)
c/o Sister's of Humility of Mary
20015 Detroit Rd.
Rocky River, OH 44116
Ph: (440)333-5373
E-mail: info@humilityofmary.org
URL: http://www.humilityofmary.org
Contact: Sister Joanne Gardner HM, Communications Coor.
Founded: 1991. **Members:** 212. **Staff:** 1. **Budget:** $20,000. **Languages:** English, Spanish. **Description:** Volunteers united to bring health care, education, social services, outreach, and pastoral work to the poor and oppressed in the U.S. and the Third World.

19237 ■ Hungarian Catholic Priests' Association in America (HCPAA)
St. Stephen's Church
223 3rd St.
Passaic, NJ 07055
Ph: (973)779-0332
Fax: (973)778-4263
E-mail: istvan07@aol.com
Contact: Rev. Stephen Mustos, Pres.
Founded: 1974. **Members:** 300. **Description:** Priests of Hungarian ancestry and priests of other nationalities who work among Hungarian Catholics in the United States and Canada. Advocates freedom for Hungary and the preservation of national heritage and churches built by Hungarians. Promotes spirituality and contact with the church in Hungary. **Committees:** Canon Law; National Heritage; Spirituality. **Conventions/Meetings:** biennial meeting.

19238 ■ Institute of Apostolic Oblates (IAO)
2125 W Walnut Ave.
Fullerton, CA 92833
Ph: (714)956-1020
Fax: (714)525-8948
E-mail: apostolico@aol.com
URL: http://www.prosanctity.org
Contact: Agnes Rus, Local Moderator
Founded: 1950. **Members:** 300. **Regional Groups:** 4. **State Groups:** 1. **Local Groups:** 1. **National Groups:** 4. **Languages:** English, French, Italian, Malay, Slovene, Spanish. **Description:** Consecrated Roman Catholic laywomen. Promotes "the spread of God's call to holiness through personal contact, prayer, and apostolic activities." Members vow to be forever available to God's message of love and to follow Christ's example of poverty, chastity, and obedience, for the sake of full availability for the apostolate. The three types of Apostolic Oblates include: the Internal Oblate, who serves as a missionary through her community life and is always available to tend to the needs of the institute; the External Oblate, who spreads the message of God's infinite love by developing a spirituality of holiness for her particular career and environment; the Cooperative Oblate, who is married and, therefore, does not take vows and promotes family spirituality. Oblates perpetuate the belief that all Christians must live according to the teachings of Christ. Conducts apostolic programs and spiritual activity. **Libraries: Type:** open to the public. **Holdings:** 4,000. **Subjects:** spirituality, Bible, theology, liturgy, sacraments. **Affiliated With:** Pro Sanctity Movement. **Publications:** *Call to Holiness,* bimonthly ● *Pro Sanctity Newsletter,* periodic ● Also publishes pamphlets. **Conventions/Meetings:** annual conference.

19239 ■ Institute on Religious Life (IRL)
PO Box 410007
Chicago, IL 60641-0007
Ph: (773)267-1195
Fax: (773)267-2044
E-mail: mail@religiouslife.com
URL: http://www.religiouslife.com
Contact: Rev. Thomas G. Doran, Pres.
Founded: 1974. **Members:** 4,000. **Membership Dues:** associate, $20 (annual). **Staff:** 5. **Budget:** $500,000. **Description:** Religious communities or provinces; laity, bishops, priests, and concerned lay individuals. Fosters better understanding and implementation of the teachings of the Magisterium of the Church on religious life, especially by prayer and sacrifice, study and research, education, consultation, publicity, and communication. Conducts conferences, classes and seminars. **Awards:** Pro Fidelitate et Virtute Award. **Frequency:** annual. **Type:** recognition. **Boards:** Advisors; Episcopal Advisory. **Publications:** *Consecrated Life,* annual. Journal. Contains documents, decrees, guidelines, studies, and reports of the Congregation for Religious and Secular Institutes. **Price:** $20.00 in U.S.; $25.00 outside U.S. ● *Religious Life,* bimonthly. Magazine. Provides commentaries and reflections on consecrated life in general and religious life in particular. **Price:** included in membership dues; $20.00 /year for libraries and seminaries; $25.00 outside U.S. ISSN: 0279-0459. **Circulation:** 4,000. **Advertising:** accepted. **Conventions/Meetings:** annual convention - 1st weekend after Easter in Chicago area.

19240 ■ Instituto Nacional Hispano de Liturgia (INHL)
PO Box 18
Washington, DC 20064
Ph: (202)319-6450
Fax: (202)319-6449
E-mail: cua-inhl@cua.edu
URL: http://liturgia.cua.edu
Contact: Rev. Juan J. Sosa, Pres.
Founded: 1979. **Members:** 230. **Membership Dues:** individual, $50 (annual) ● institutional, $150 (annual) ● friend of the institution, $25 (annual). **Staff:** 1. **Regional Groups:** 8. **Languages:** English, Spanish. **Description:** Works to develop liturgical spirituality among Hispanics in the U.S. Conducts lectures and workshops. **Awards:** Founding Members. **Type:** recognition. **Also Known As:** National Institute of Hispanic Liturgy. **Formerly:** (2001) Instituto Nacional de Liturgia Para Hispanos. **Publications:** *Amen* (in English and Spanish), quarterly. Newsletter. **Price:** free ● *Criterios para Las Celebraciones Liturgicas en las Comunidades Hispanas.* Brochure ● *Don y Promesa/Gift and Promise: Customs and Traditions in Hispanic Rites of Marriage* (in English and Spanish). Brochure ● *Liturgia de las Horas.* Brochure ● *Misa, Mesa, Musa: A Collection of Essays on Hispanic Liturgy.* Brochure ● *Religiosidad Popular: Las Imagenes de Jesucristo y la Virgen Maria en America Latina.* Brochure. **Conventions/Meetings:** biennial conference (exhibits).

19241 ■ International Catholic Deaf Association - United States Section (ICDA-US)
7202 Buchanan St.
Landover Hills, MD 20784-2236
Ph: (301)429-0697
Fax: (301)429-0698
E-mail: homeoffice@icda-us.org
URL: http://members.aol.com/Kgkush
Contact: Peter Noyes, Home Office Mgr./Ed.
Founded: 1949. **Members:** 10,000. **Membership Dues:** individual, $12 (annual) ● married, $20 (annual) ● life, $200. **Regional Groups:** 150. **Local Groups:** 130. **National Groups:** 134. **Description:** Deaf persons of the Catholic faith, priests, other religious and laypeople interested in work with the deaf, and parents of deaf children. Maintains special fund for support of missionary priests in their work with the deaf; compiles statistics on adult Catholic deaf and Catholic pupils in state, provincial, and city day schools and classes for the deaf; encourages local groups to arrange monthly communion and Sunday masses with sermons in sign language; promotes sports for the deaf. Works to pass the legislation beneficial to the deaf. Fosters Catholic schools and religious education programs for deaf children; promotes Bible study for deaf adult Catholics and non-Catholics. **Awards:** Chapter of the Year Award. **Frequency:** annual. **Type:** recognition ● Member of the Year Award. **Frequency:** annual. **Type:** recognition ● Memorial Scroll Award. **Frequency:** annual. **Type:** recognition ● Pastoral Worker of the Year Award. **Frequency:** annual. **Type:** recognition. **Additional Websites:** http://www.icda-us.org. **Committees:** Laws; Mission Fund; Public Relations. **Affiliated With:** National Association of the Deaf; National Catholic Office for the Deaf. **Publications:** *Chaplains' News Notes,* bimonthly. Magazine ● *Convention Souvenir Book,* annual ● *The Deaf Catholic,* bimonthly. Newsletter. Covers association and educational and inspirational news on the Catholic faith and pious beliefs. Includes announcements of awards. **Price:** $10.00 /year for nonmembers; included in membership dues. ISSN: 0045-978X ● *ICDA Directory of Chapter Secretaries and Moderators,* annual ● Newsletter, periodic. **Conventions/Meetings:** biennial conference (exhibits) - always July.

19242 ■ International Catholic Stewardship Council (ICSC)
1275 K St. NW, Ste.880
Washington, DC 20005-4077
Ph: (202)289-1093
Fax: (202)682-9018
E-mail: info@catholicstewardship.org
URL: http://www.catholicstewardship.org
Contact: Matthew R. Paratore, Sec. Gen.
Founded: 1962. **Members:** 600. **Membership Dues:** parish, $250-$525 (annual) ● Catholic association, $750 (annual) ● professional firm, $1,000 (annual) ● seminary and school of Theology, religious community, $550 (annual). **Staff:** 3. **Budget:** $350,000. **Regional Groups:** 14. **Description:** Commits to promote the right use of God's gifts of time, talent, and treasure through diocesan and parish leadership. Encourages the adoption of the holistic stewardship concept which stresses that everything is a gift from God, and that gratitude for gifts received is best expressed in right management and ministry to others. Fosters the exchange of ideas and materials among dioceses, parishes, and other church organizations. Maintains Speaker's Bureau and placement service. Compiles statistics. **Awards:** The Archbishop Thomas J. Murphy Award. **Frequency:** annual. **Type:** recognition. **Recipient:** for a parish that best exemplifies stewardship in action ● The Bishop William G. Connare Award. **Frequency:** annual. **Type:** recognition. **Recipient:** for a Diocesan director with long and distinguished service ● Christian Stewardship Award. **Frequency:** annual. **Type:** recognition. **Recipient:** for individuals exemplifying the concept of Christian

stewardship ● Diocesan and Parish Recognition Award. **Frequency:** annual. **Type:** recognition. **Recipient:** for diocese and parish members who promote the theology of stewardship. **Committees:** Annual Conference Program; Board Development and Services; Board Nominations and Elections; Bylaws and Parliamentary Concerns; Diocesan Stewardship and Development Education and Services; Economic Concerns; ICSC Futures in Stewardship Education; Institute and Seminar; Parish Stewardship Education and Services; Religious Life and Stewardship; Seminar on Diocesan Foundation; Stewardship Promotion and Communications; Strategic and Long Range Planning. **Formerly:** (2000) National Catholic Stewardship Council. **Publications:** *Children's Stewardship* (in English and Spanish). Manuals. Presents stewardship as a life to Christ's "little ones". **Price:** $10.00 for members; $15.00 for nonmembers ● *Gladly Will I Spend and be Spent: A Brief History of the National Catholic Council.* Book. **Price:** $15.00 for members; $22.50 for nonmembers ● *Proceedings of Annual Conference* ● *Resource Journal,* semiannual. Contains articles about stewardship and development. **Price:** $10.00 for members; $15.00 for nonmembers ● *Stewardship and Development Guidelines for a Diocesan Office.* Manual. Contains essential information concerning diocesan stewardship and development office. **Price:** $10.00 for members; $15.00 for nonmembers ● *Stewardship: Disciples Respond-A Practical Guide for Pastoral Leaders* (in English and Spanish). Manual. **Price:** $10.00 for members; $15.00 for nonmembers ● *Stewardship Kits For Increased Offertory* ● *Time and Talent* ● *Wills Awareness Seminar Kit* ● Directory, annual ● Newsletter, quarterly ● Also publishes essays. **Conventions/Meetings:** periodic competition ● periodic seminar ● periodic workshop ● annual conference (exhibits) - 2007 Sept. 23-26, Miami, FL; 2008 Oct. 12-15, Chicago, IL; 2009 Sept. 20-23, Dallas, TX; 2010 Sept. 19-22, San Diego, CA.

19243 ■ Jesuit Conference
1616 P St. NW, Ste.300
Washington, DC 20036-1408
Ph: (202)462-0400
Fax: (202)328-9212
E-mail: usjc@jesuit.org
URL: http://www.jesuit.org
Contact: Fr. Thomas H. Smolich SJ, Pres.
Local Groups: 12. **Description:** Serves the Catholic Church by aiding the members of its community to know Christ more fully. Promotes justice and the building of the Kingdom of God here on earth, no matter what the cost. **Formerly:** American Jesuit Missionary Association; (2001) Jesuit Missions. **Publications:** *America,* weekly. Journal. Alternate Formats: online ● *Company.* Magazine. Features articles about the U.S. Jesuits and their ministries. Alternate Formats: online ● *In All Things.* Journal. Alternate Formats: online ● *National Jesuit News,* bimonthly. Newspaper. Alternate Formats: online.

19244 ■ Jesuit Volunteer Corps: Northwest (JVC)
PO Box 3928
Portland, OR 97208-3928
Ph: (503)335-8202
E-mail: jvcnw@jesuitvolunteers.org
URL: http://www.jesuitvolunteers.org
Contact: Jeanne Haster, Exec. Dir.
Founded: 1956. **Members:** 4,500. **Staff:** 6. **Budget:** $450,000. **Regional Groups:** 70. **Description:** Offers men and women an opportunity to work full time for justice and peace. Volunteers are mainly college graduates. Mission is "working with those on the margins of society and structural change in the United States." Challenges volunteers to "integrate Christian faith into their lives by working and living among the marginalized, by living simply and in community with other Jesuit Volunteers." Volunteers are placed for at least one year of service in the states of Oregon, Washington, Montana and Alaska. **Publications:** *Focus,* 3/year. Newsletter. **Circulation:** 6,100.

19245 ■ John La Farge Institute (JFI)
106 W 56th St.
New York, NY 10019-3803
Ph: (212)581-4640
Free: (800)627-9533
Fax: (212)399-3596
E-mail: america@americamagazine.org
URL: http://www.americamagazine.org
Contact: Bro. Francis W. Turnbull SJ, Asst. Ed.
Founded: 1965. **Description:** National center for ecumenical and interracial activity; named in honor of the Jesuit priest John La Farge (1880-1963), former editor of the magazine "America". **Conventions/Meetings:** conference, topics include contemporary problems of interracial, justice, interfaith relations, and other issues with moral dimensions.

19246 ■ Latin Liturgy Association (LLA)
c/o Mr. James F. Pauer, Pres.
PO Box 16517
Rocky River, OH 44116
E-mail: jfpauer@juno.com
URL: http://www.latinliturgy.com
Contact: Mr. James F. Pauer, Pres.
Founded: 1975. **Members:** 1,000. **Membership Dues:** individual in U.S., $15 (annual) ● family, group in U.S., individual outside U.S., $20 (annual) ● life (individual in U.S.), $150 ● life (family, group in U.S., individual outside U.S.), $200 ● family, group outside U.S., $25 (annual) ● life (family, group outside U.S.), $250 ● seminarian in U.S., $5 (annual). **Staff:** 3. **Local Groups:** 12. **Description:** Catholic laity and clergy. Promotes more frequent celebration of the Catholic Mass in Latin. Corresponds with bishops; advertises in Catholic publications; promotes formation of local chapters. Holds national conventions. **Awards:** Domus Dei. **Frequency:** biennial. **Type:** recognition. **Recipient:** for service to the Latin Liturgy. **Publications:** *English Translation of the Rubrics of the 1962 Edition of the Roman Missal.* **Price:** $7.00 ● *Latin Liturgy Association—Latin Mass Directory,* annual. Lists regularly scheduled Latin Masses celebrated in the U.S. and Canada. Includes Masses celebrated according to the old and revised Roman Missals. **Price:** $7.00/copy. **Circulation:** 500. **Advertising:** accepted. Alternate Formats: online ● *Latin Liturgy Newsletter,* quarterly. Reports on the use of Latin in the liturgy of the Roman Catholic Church. Contains book and journal reviews, chapter news, and directory update. **Price:** included in membership dues. **Circulation:** 1,000. **Advertising:** accepted. Alternate Formats: online ● *The Seven Sacraments* (in English and Latin). **Conventions/Meetings:** biennial convention (exhibits).

19247 ■ Lay Carmelite Order of the Blessed Virgin Mary of Mount Carmel
8501 Bailey Rd.
Darien, IL 60561-8417
Ph: (630)969-5050
URL: http://carmelnet.org/toc/toc.htm
Contact: Rev. John Benedict Weber, Dir.
Founded: 1870. **Members:** 10,000. **Membership Dues:** $25 (annual). **Staff:** 7. **Budget:** $300,000. **Regional Groups:** 20. **State Groups:** 27. **Local Groups:** 20. **National Groups:** 275. **Languages:** English, Spanish. **Description:** Secular branch of the Carmelite Order consisting of Catholic men and women, 18 years of age and older, living the Carmelite Rule according to their state in life: married, single, or widowed. Seeks to serve the needs of the church by living the evangelical life according to Carmelite spirituality. Structure consists of separate communities that determine the needs of members. Activities center around regular meetings, study, personal prayer, and the apostolate. Libraries are maintained by each community and by individuals. Retreat programs are organized by the national center. **Awards:** Certificate of Appreciation Award. **Frequency:** biennial. **Type:** recognition. **Recipient:** for those who have given outstanding service to the organization. **Computer Services:** database ● mailing lists. **Committees:** Communities; Lay Carmelites. **Also Known As:** Lay Carmelites; Third Order Carmelites. **Publications:** *Aylesford Carmelite Newsletter,* quarterly. For lay Carmelite members of the Carmelite order and those interested in Carmelite spirituality. **Price:** $10.00/year donation. **Circulation:** 10,000 ● *Introduction to Carmel.* Monograph. **Con-**

ventions/Meetings: biennial Convocations of Lay Carmelites - conference - in even-numbered years ● biennial regional meeting ● seminar, with presentations and religious activities.

19248 ■ Lay Mission-Helpers Association (LMH)
3435 Wilshire Blvd., Ste.1035
Los Angeles, CA 90010-1911
Ph: (213)368-1870
Fax: (213)368-1871
E-mail: info@laymissionhelpers.org
URL: http://www.laymissionhelpers.org
Contact: Janice England, Exec. Dir.
Founded: 1955. **Members:** 700. **Staff:** 4. **Multinational. Description:** Roman Catholic laymen and laywomen serving as missionaries overseas. Objectives are to develop the spiritual life of members and provide assistance in missionary areas. Trains and assigns missionaries to serve in apostolates for a period of three years in areas of Africa, South Pacific, Latin America, and Asia; conducts four-month training course with classes in theology, spirituality, scripture, liturgy, missiology, anthropology, and other subjects; bases assignments on applicants' aptitude and training. Mission activities are in areas such as education, academic instruction at all grade levels, nursing, participation in medical and hospital projects, building and construction, mechanics, bookkeeping, secretarial and clerical work, and other crafts and trades. Provides missionaries with room and board, health care, and money for incidental expenses and necessities. Works in cooperation with Mission Doctors Association. **Convention/Meeting:** none. **Affiliated With:** Mission Doctors Association.

19249 ■ Leadership Conference of Women Religious (LCWR)
8808 Cameron St.
Silver Spring, MD 20910-4113
Ph: (301)588-4955
Fax: (301)587-4575
E-mail: cshinnick@lcwr.org
URL: http://www.lcwr.org
Contact: Carole Shinnick SSND, Exec. Dir.
Founded: 1956. **Members:** 978. **Staff:** 9. **Regional Groups:** 15. **Description:** Exists as a support system and corporate voice for leaders of institutes of women religious (Catholic sisters) in the United States. Aims to promote an understanding of the religious life of Catholic sisters in the United States through its service to religious leaders. Provides regular programs, research, workshops, meetings, and publications to assist members in their development as leaders. **Formerly:** (1971) Conference of Major Religious Superiors of Women's Institutes of the United States of America; (2001) Leadership Conference of Women Religious of the U.S.A. **Publications:** *LCWR Daily Reflection Books,* annual. Contains reflections written by the members of LCWR. ● *LCWR Occasional Papers.* Journal. Offers articles and reflections on topics pertinent to women religious leaders. ● *Mentoring Leadership Manual.* Offers variety of experiences that will accommodate different styles of adult learning. ● *Systems Thinking Handbook.* Reflects the developments in understanding critical thinking and the complex nature of contemporary reality. ● Directory, annual ● Newsletter, monthly. Alternate Formats: online. **Conventions/Meetings:** annual assembly, for the members to vote their officers.

19250 ■ League of St. Dymphna (LOSD)
Natl. Shrine of St. Dymphna
3000 Erie St. S
PO Box 4
Massillon, OH 44648-0004
Ph: (330)833-8478
Fax: (330)833-5193
E-mail: fr_herttna@natlshrinestdymphna.org
URL: http://www.natlshrinestdymphna.org
Contact: Rev. M.M. Herttna, Dir.
Founded: 1938. **Membership Dues:** individual, $2 (annual) ● individual (life), $25 ● family (life), $100. **Description:** Represents Catholics in the U.S. and Canada who offer prayers (novenas) that they may be preserved from nervous disorders and to remem-

ber someone now afflicted. Offers weekly masses for living and deceased members of the league; also offers daily mass and novena prayers. Assists patients in hospitals with therapy; gives aid for eyeglasses, dentures, and clothing. **Publications:** Publishes informational literature.

19251 ■ League of Tarcisians (LT)
c/o National Enthronement Center
PO Box 111
Fairhaven, MA 02719-0111
Ph: (508)999-2680
Fax: (508)993-8233
E-mail: necenter@juno.com
URL: http://www.sscc.org
Contact: Rev. Columban Crotty SSCC, Dir.
Founded: 1917. **Staff:** 2. **Nonmembership. Description:** Catholic group established to organize children as apostles of the Sacred Heart in their homes. **Formerly:** (1969) League of Tarcisians of the Sacred Heart.

19252 ■ Legatus
2640 Golden Gate Pkwy., Ste.118
Naples, FL 34105
Ph: (239)435-3852
Fax: (239)435-3861
E-mail: info@legatus.org
URL: http://www.legatus.org
Contact: Stephen Beal, Exec. Dir.
Founded: 1987. **Staff:** 7. **Local Groups:** 15. **Description:** Represents Roman Catholic CEO's and other corporate executives. Promotes incorporation of ethical teachings of the Roman Catholic Church in the marketplace. Disseminates information; conducts educational programs and retreats. **Telecommunication Services:** electronic mail, pcole@legatus.org. **Publications:** *Legatus Newsletter*, monthly. **Conventions/Meetings:** annual conference ● annual international conference.

19253 ■ Lithuanian Catholic Religious Aid (LCRA)
64-25 Perry Ave.
Maspeth, NY 11378-2411
Ph: (718)326-5202
Fax: (718)326-5206
E-mail: lcra@earthlink.net
URL: http://home.earthlink.net/~lcra
Founded: 1960. **Members:** 141. **Membership Dues:** full, $100 (annual). **Staff:** 2. **Budget:** $250,000. **Languages:** English, Lithuanian. **Description:** Clergy and others desiring to help the Roman Catholic Church in Lithuania. Seeks to inform the public about the church in Lithuania. Collects and distributes material aid for the church and Catholic charities. Conducts meetings; operates speakers' bureau. Compiles statistics. **Libraries: Type:** reference. **Holdings:** archival material. **Subjects:** Lithuanian Catholic Church. **Publications:** *Catholic Lithuania Update*, semiannual. Newsletter. **Circulation:** 12,000 ● *Zinios*, semiannual. Newsletter. **Conventions/Meetings:** annual meeting, for members.

19254 ■ Little Flower Mission League (LFML)
Address Unknown since 2007
Founded: 1957. **Members:** 1,000. **Staff:** 2. **Description:** Individuals with a desire to join and share in the merits of spirituality with the congregation of Brothers of the Holy Eucharist.

19255 ■ Mariannhill Mission Society
23715 Ann Arbor Trail
Dearborn Heights, MI 48127
Ph: (313)561-7140
E-mail: vheier@juno.com
URL: http://www.rc.net/detroit/mariannhill
Contact: Rev. Thomas Heier CMM, Contact
Founded: 1909. **Members:** 14. **Regional Groups:** 1. **Description:** A division of the Congregation of Mariannhill Missionaries. Religious order of priests and brothers. Provides training for missionary candidates; conducts parish work, offers retreats and mission support. **Libraries: Type:** reference. **Holdings:** books, periodicals. **Computer Services:** Mailing lists, of members. **Telecommunication Services:** elec-

tronic mail, leaves-mag@juno.com. **Councils:** Provincial. **Affiliated With:** Mariannhill Mission Society. **Formerly:** U.S. Province of Congregation of Mariannhill Missionaries; (2006) U.S. Region of Congregation of Mariannhill Missionaries. **Publications:** *Leaves*, bimonthly. Magazine. Catholic devotional. **Circulation:** 112,000. **Conventions/Meetings:** biennial meeting ● quarterly Provincial Council Meeting.

19256 ■ Mariological Society of America (MSA)
Marian Lib.
Univ. of Dayton
Dayton, OH 45469-1390
Ph: (937)229-4294
Fax: (937)229-4258
E-mail: cecilia.mushenheim@notes.udayton.edu
URL: http://www.mariologicalsocietyofamerica.us
Contact: Rev. Thomas A. Thompson SM, Exec. Sec.
Founded: 1949. **Members:** 400. **Membership Dues:** seminarian, retiree, $12 (annual) ● associate, $15 (annual) ● professional, $18 (annual) ● supporting, $25 (annual) ● patron, $100 (annual). **Regional Groups:** 1. **Description:** Active members are priests, scholars, and others with theological competence in Marian studies; associate members are those interested in promoting Mariological studies and research. Promotes original research in Marian doctrine and devotion. **Awards:** Cardinal John J. Wright Mariological Award. **Frequency:** periodic. **Type:** recognition. **Recipient:** for outstanding work in the field of Mariology, not necessarily a member of the MSA. **Additional Websites:** http://campus.udayton.edu/mary, http://www.udayton.edu/mary/outdev/msa.html. **Publications:** *Marian Studies: Proceeding of the National Meeting of the Mariological Society of America*, annual. Proceedings. Contains membership list, reprints of papers presented at the meeting, regional reports, and bibliographical survey of Mariological writings. **Price:** included in membership dues; $15.00 /year for individuals; $18.00 /year for institutions in U.S.; $22.00 /year for institutions outside U.S. ISSN: 0464-9680. **Circulation:** 600. **Conventions/Meetings:** annual conference.

19257 ■ Maryheart Crusaders (MC)
22 Button St.
Meriden, CT 06450
Ph: (203)238-9735
Free: (800)879-1957
Fax: (203)235-0059
E-mail: maryheart@msn.com
URL: http://www.maryheartcrusaders.org
Contact: Louise D'Angelo, Pres./Founder
Founded: 1964. **Members:** 2,750. **Staff:** 8. **Description:** Catholic priests, nuns, brothers, deacons, and laypersons who seeks to reunite fallen-away Catholics with the faith. Defends "teachings of the Church, the Pope and Bishops." Members are taught to speak whenever necessary to defend their beliefs or to correct others' misconceptions about the religion. Conducts adult religious education and spiritual growth programs; also provides individual help for those in need of spiritual advice and comfort. Maintains bookstore containing a large selection of Catholic books and religious items including rosaries, medals and chains, and statues; participates in church fairs. **Convention/Meeting:** none. **Publications:** *The Catholic Answer to the Jehovah's Witnesses*. Book. **Price:** $14.50 plus $2.50 postage. **Circulation:** 42,000 ● *Come Climb the Ladder and Rejoice*. Book. **Price:** $12.95 plus shipping and handling ● *Come Home the Door Is Open*. Book. **Price:** $12.00 plus shipping and handling ● *Too Busy for God. Think Again*. Book. **Price:** $5.00 plus shipping and handling ● *The Triumph of the Immaculate Heart of Mary*. Book. **Price:** $20.00 plus shipping and handling ● Pamphlets ● Papers ● Also distributes literature, rosaries, and scapulars.

19258 ■ Maryknoll Fathers and Brothers (MM)
PO Box 308
Maryknoll, NY 10545-0308
Ph: (914)941-7590
Free: (888)627-9566

Fax: (914)944-3613
E-mail: mkweb@maryknoll.org
URL: http://www.maryknoll.org
Contact: John Sivalon, Superior Gen.
Founded: 1911. **Members:** 475. **Multinational. Description:** Priests, brothers, associate priests and seminarians. Purposes: to bring the Gospel of Jesus Christ to poor and oppressed people in 27 foreign countries; assist society to become more aware of human rights and religious freedom issues within those countries; stimulate greater concern for peace in the U.S. and throughout the world; serve as a forum for communicating and disseminating information on topics and issues of justice and peace to members, other individuals, and organizations; establish links with, and collaborate in various programs and activities with churches and secular groups sharing mutual concerns. **Libraries: Type:** reference. **Holdings:** 25,000. **Subjects:** Theology, missiology, church history. **Awards:** Maryknoll Mission Award. **Frequency:** periodic. **Type:** monetary. **Recipient:** for exemplifying Maryknoll values and global vision ● **Type:** recognition. **Additional Websites:** http://society.maryknoll.org. **Telecommunication Services:** electronic mail, lgiordano@maryknoll.org. **Committees:** Maryknoll Office for Global Concerns. **Departments:** Mission Promotion. **Programs:** Justice and Peace; Mission Awareness. **Also Known As:** Maryknoll Priests, Brothers, and Priest and Brother Associates. **Formerly:** (2004) Maryknoll Mission Family. **Publications:** *Justice and Peace Newsnotes*, bimonthly. Newsletter ● *Maryknoll Magazine*, monthly. Features works of Maryknoll missioners overseas. ISSN: 0025-4142. **Circulation:** 425,000. Alternate Formats: online ● *Orbis Books* ● *Revista Maryknoll* (in English and Spanish), monthly. Magazine. Serves as the bilingual Spanish/English counterpart of Maryknoll Magazine. **Circulation:** 75,000. **Conventions/Meetings:** annual meeting, three-week educational program - held in July.

19259 ■ Men of the Sacred Heart (MSH)
Address Unknown since 2007
Founded: 1962. **Members:** 2,500. **Membership Dues:** $6 (annual). **Staff:** 4. **Regional Groups:** 3. **State Groups:** 9. **National Groups:** 1. **Description:** Practicing Catholic men and religious laymen. Promotes enthronement of the Sacred Heart in the family. Conducts charitable programs. **Conventions/Meetings:** triennial meeting.

19260 ■ Militia of the Immaculata Movement
1600 W Park Ave.
Libertyville, IL 60048
Ph: (847)367-7800
Fax: (847)367-7831
E-mail: mi@consecration.com
URL: http://www.consecration.com
Contact: Fr. Patrick Greenough, Pres.
Founded: 1917. **Members:** 5,000,000. **Staff:** 7. **Regional Groups:** 5. **Description:** A worldwide evangelization movement founded by St. Maximilian Kolbe in 1917 that "encourages total consecration to the Blessed Virgin Mary as a means of spiritual renewal for individuals and society. Employs prayer as the main weapon in the spiritual battle with evil. By joining the movement, members become willing instruments of Our Lady, the woman foreshadowed in Genesis 3:15. She leads them to personal sanctification, the conversion of Church opponents and ultimately the Universal reign of The Sacred Heart of Jesus". **Libraries: Type:** open to the public. **Divisions:** First Degree. **Also Known As:** Militia Immaculata. **Formerly:** (1999) Knights of the Immaculata Movement. **Publications:** *Immaculata*, bimonthly. Magazine. **Price:** free for members. **Circulation:** 27,000. **Advertising:** accepted. Alternate Formats: online ● *Marytown Press*, annual. Books ● Also publishes promotional literature. **Conventions/Meetings:** annual Militia Immaculata University - conference.

19261 ■ Missionary Sisters of Our Lady of the Holy Rosary (MSHR)
c/o Sister Helena McNeill
Missionary Sisters of the Holy Rosary
741 Polo Rd.
Bryn Mawr, PA 19010

Ph: (610)520-1976
E-mail: helenamcneill@comcast.net
URL: http://www.mshr.org
Contact: Sister Monica Devine, Congregational Leader

Founded: 1924. **Members:** 387. **Multinational. Description:** Catholic sisters in Africa, Europe, and North and South America. Provides educational, medical, pastoral, and social services. **Publications:** *Information Bulletin*, bimonthly ● *The Second Burial of Bishop Shanahan*. Book ● *Vincula*, bimonthly. Journal. **Conventions/Meetings:** meeting - every 6 years.

19262 ■ Missionary Society of Saint Columban

PO Box 10
St. Columbans, NE 68056
Ph: (402)291-1920
Fax: (402)291-4984
E-mail: mission@columban.org
URL: http://www.columban.org
Contact: Fr. Arturo Aguilar, Region Dir.

Founded: 1918. **Members:** 548. **Languages:** English, Spanish. **Description:** Roman Catholic priests and laypeople working in Chile, Fiji, Japan, Korea, Pakistan, Peru, Philippines, China, Taiwan and North America. Undertakes missionary work for the Roman Catholic Church. **Affiliated With:** Conference of Major Superiors of Men; United States Catholic Mission Association. **Also Known As:** Columban Fathers. **Publications:** *Columban Mission*, 8/year. Magazine. ISSN: 0095-4438. **Circulation:** 110,000 ● *Mission Columbana*, quarterly. Magazine. **Conventions/Meetings:** general assembly.

19263 ■ Missionary Society of Saint Paul the Apostle (MSSPA)

PO Box 31
Lake George, NY 12845
Ph: (518)668-5594
Fax: (518)668-3843
E-mail: lakegeo1@earthlink.net
URL: http://www.paulist.org/spirit/lakegeorge.htm
Contact: Father Kenneth H. McGuire CSP, Dir.

Founded: 1858. **Members:** 198. **Description:** Roman Catholic priests; students preparing for the priesthood. Conducts missionary and ecumenical work in North America and Rome, Italy. **Libraries: Type:** reference. **Holdings:** 30,000. **Subjects:** philosophical and theological works. **Also Known As:** Paulist Fathers. **Publications:** *Register of the Paulist Fathers*, quinquennial. Directory. **Conventions/Meetings:** quadrennial general assembly.

19264 ■ National Association of Diaconate Directors (NADD)

2136 12th St., Ste.105
Rockford, IL 61104
Ph: (815)965-2100
Fax: (815)965-1569
E-mail: naddinfo@nadd.org
URL: http://www.nadd.org
Contact: Deacon Daniel L. Peterson, Vice Chm.

Founded: 1977. **Members:** 300. **Membership Dues:** individual, $375 (annual). **Staff:** 2. **Budget:** $125,000. **Description:** Directors, vicars of deacons, and others responsible for the formation of candidates and the ongoing growth and development of deacons in the various U.S. archdioceses. Promotes communication and information/resource exchange among members. Seeks to develop professional expertise in research, dialogue, formation, and self-evaluation procedures. Proposes effective implementation of solutions to problems of the diaconate, its service, and pastoral needs. Maintains speakers' bureau. Conducts research and educational programs. **Libraries: Type:** reference. **Awards:** NADD Award. **Frequency:** annual. **Type:** recognition ● O'Leary Award. **Type:** recognition ● Philbin Award. **Type:** recognition ● Special Award. **Type:** recognition. **Formerly:** (1995) National Association of Permanent Diaconate Directors. **Publications:** *NADD Info*, quarterly. Newsletter. **Circulation:** 300. **Conventions/Meetings:** annual Directors Institute: Understanding Deacon Spirituality - convention, church and ministry

supplies, books, vestments (exhibits) - 2008 Apr. 20-23, Orlando, FL.

19265 ■ National Association of the Holy Name Society (NAHNS)

c/o Gerard F. Novak
PO Box 12012
Baltimore, MD 21281-2012
Ph: (410)325-1523
Fax: (410)325-1524
E-mail: nahns@juno.com
URL: http://www.holynamesociety.info
Contact: Mr. Joseph Lapointe, Webmaster

Founded: 1969. **Members:** 45. **Membership Dues:** regular, $250 (annual). **Budget:** $75,000. **Regional Groups:** 14. **Description:** Diocesan and archdiocesan unions dedicated to promoting greater respect for the Holy Name of Jesus and other religiously oriented programs of spiritual and corporal works of mercy. Works toward the canonization of Blessed John of Vercelli. Conducts charitable program, seminars, and workshops. Sponsors annual essay contest. Compiles statistics; maintains speakers' bureau. **Libraries: Type:** not open to the public. **Holdings:** archival material, business records. **Awards:** Medallion Circle. **Type:** recognition. **Recipient:** for outstanding service to the organization in parish and community work. **Committees:** Anti-Pornography; Associate Services; Byzantine Liaison; Canadian Unions; Cause for the Canonization of Blessed John of Vercelli; Convention; Diocesan/Archdiocesan Contacts; Evangelization; Father Ron Kneran Youth Essay Contest; Keep Christ in Christmas; Liaison NCCB; Parliamentarian; Prison Ministry; Public Affairs; Public Relations; Respect-Life; Retreats, Religious Activities, and Ecumenism; Social Action; Youth. **Also Known As:** (2006) Confraternity of the Most Holy Name of Jesus. **Publications:** *Holy Name*, bimonthly. Newsletter. **Price:** $10.00/year; $16.00/2 years. Alternate Formats: online ● *Minutes of Board Meetings and Conventions*, annual ● Booklets. **Conventions/Meetings:** annual meeting (exhibits) - always September.

19266 ■ National Association of Priest Pilots (NAPP)

c/o Mel Hemann, Treas.
127 Kaspend Pl.
Cedar Falls, IA 50613-1683
Ph: (319)266-3889
E-mail: info@priestpilots.org
URL: http://www.priestpilots.org
Contact: Rev. Everett Hemann, Pres.

Founded: 1964. **Members:** 135. **Membership Dues:** charter/regular/associate/complimentary, $20 (annual). **Regional Groups:** 3. **Description:** Represents Catholic bishops, priests and deacons who hold, or have held, valid Federal Aviation Agency certificates for flying airplanes; associate members are brothers and seminarians and other friends who hold aviation licenses. Members represent 22 religious orders in 36 states and 12 foreign countries. Encourages use of light aircraft as an efficient, safe, and practical tool in the apostolic work of the priest, especially missionary work. Provides flight and aviation information to missionaries and members. Participates in flight safety clinics; conducts charitable programs. **Also Known As:** Flying Padres. **Publications:** *Directory*, annual ● Newsletter, bimonthly. Alternate Formats: online. **Conventions/Meetings:** annual congress ● seminar, religious and flight.

19267 ■ National Association of State Catholic Conference Directors (NASCCD)

c/o D. Michael McCarron, PhD, Exec. Dir.
PO Box 1677
Tallahassee, FL 32302-1677
Ph: (850)222-3803
Fax: (850)681-9548
E-mail: mccarron@flacathconf.org
URL: http://www.nasccd.org
Contact: D. Michael McCarron PhD, Exec. Dir.

Founded: 1967. **Members:** 40. **Description:** Represents directors and associate directors of state Catholic conference groups. Shares information and deals with problems encountered by the conferences.

State conferences represent the Catholic dioceses in meetings with the media and public. **Conventions/Meetings:** semiannual meeting - always July and December.

19268 ■ National Black Catholic Clergy Caucus (NBCCC)

440 W 36th St.
New York, NY 10018
Ph: (212)868-1847
Fax: (212)563-0787
E-mail: tnbccc@aol.com
URL: http://bcimall.org/nbccc
Contact: A.J. McKnight, Contact

Founded: 1968. **Members:** 650. **Membership Dues:** $100 (annual). **Regional Groups:** 4. **Description:** Represents black priests, brothers, seminarians, and deacons. Purpose is to support the spiritual, theological, educational, and ministerial growth of the black Catholic community within the church. Serves as a vehicle to bring contributions of the black community to the church. Advances the fight against racism within the Catholic Church and society. **Committees:** Liturgy; Theology; Vocations. **Affiliated With:** National Black Sisters' Conference. **Publications:** Directory, annual ● Newsletter, 6-8/year. **Conventions/Meetings:** annual conference.

19269 ■ National Black Catholic Congress (NBCC)

320 Cathedral St.
Baltimore, MD 21201
Ph: (410)547-8496
Fax: (410)752-3958
E-mail: vwashington@nbccongress.org
URL: http://www.nbccongress.org
Contact: Valerie E. Washington, Exec. Dir.

Founded: 1985. **Staff:** 4. **Regional Groups:** 13. **Description:** Represents African American Roman Catholics working in collaboration with National Roman Catholic organizations; works on establishing an agenda for the evangelization of African Americans towards the freedom and growth of African Americans as full participants in Church and society; holds members accountable to their "baptismal commitment to witness and proclaim the Good News of Jesus Christ". **Boards:** Trustees. **Publications:** *A Balm in Gilead: Programs for Parish Implementation*. Book. **Price:** $20.00 ● *African American Catholic Tribune*, quarterly. Newsletter. **Price:** $2.00/year ● *Ambassadors: Speaking for Christ*. Book. **Price:** $10.00 ● *Black Catholic Newsletter*, monthly ● *Rise Up and Rebuild*. Book. **Price:** $20.00. **Conventions/Meetings:** quinquennial congress (exhibits) ● annual Regional Lay Leaders Meeting - workshop, leadership development.

19270 ■ National Black Sisters' Conference (NBSC)

101 Q St. NE
Washington, DC 20002-2166
Ph: (202)529-9250
Fax: (202)529-9370
E-mail: nbsc68@comcast.net
URL: http://nbsc68.tripod.com
Contact: Sister Donna Banfield SBS, Pres.

Founded: 1968. **Members:** 150. **Membership Dues:** full, associate/auxiliary, $100 (annual). **Staff:** 2. **Budget:** $67,000. **Description:** Represents black Catholic religious women and associates. Seeks to foster education, training, and development for black religious women, the larger black community, and society at large. Strives to provide ongoing communication and dialogue focusing on the education and support of African American religious women. **Awards:** Harriet Tubman Award. **Frequency:** annual. **Type:** recognition. **Committees:** Black Women's Project; Education Within the African American Community; Formation. **Publications:** *Joint Black Clergy and Black Sisters* ● *Naming and Claiming Our Resources* ● *Signs of Soul*, quarterly. Newsletter. Reports on activities of the subcommittees, experiences of black women religious with employment opportunities. **Price:** included in membership dues. Alternate Formats: online ● *Tell It Like It Is*. **Conventions/Meetings:** annual Joint Conference, held jointly with NBCSA, NBCCC, and NAACD (exhibits) - always last full week in July.

19271 ■ National Catholic College Admission Association (NCCAA)
20 W Hubbard, 2 E
Chicago, IL 60610
Ph: (312)321-2726
Fax: (312)803-2177
E-mail: national_ccaa@msn.com
URL: http://www.catholiccollegesonline.org
Contact: Mike Konopski, Pres.
Founded: 1959. **Members:** 178. **Membership Dues:** regular, $3,000. **Staff:** 1. **Regional Groups:** 9. **Description:** Represents Catholic colleges and universities. Works to serve students, parents, and counselors in the transition process from high school to college. **Publications:** *The Official Catholic College and University Guidebook*, biennial. Handbook. **Price:** $15.00/copy. **Circulation:** 20,000. Alternate Formats: online.

19272 ■ National Catholic Conference for Total Stewardship (NCCTS)
3408 Waterlily Ct., No. 104
Palm Beach Gardens, FL 33410
Ph: (561)248-9431
E-mail: wood24025@yahoo.com
URL: http://netministries.org/see/charmin/CM00217
Contact: Francis A. Novak, Pres.
Founded: 1980. **Membership Dues:** individual, $25 (annual). **Staff:** 3. **Budget:** $120,000. **Description:** Aims to help people arrive at truth, hope, conversion, and reconciliation. **Libraries: Type:** reference; not open to the public. **Affiliated With:** United States Conference of Catholic Bishops. **Publications:** *The Christian Celebration of Life - Overview*, revised 1996. Video ● *Evolution of Total Stewardship from Stewardship: Tension Between Meaning and Function* ● *Fanning the Flame of Faith*. Audiotape ● *Homily Guides for Preaching Stewardship of Giftedness* ● *Homily Guides for Preaching Stewardship of the Eucharist* ● *Spiritual Formation in Total Stewardship, Guide for Matrix Meetings* ● *Stewards of Evangelization 2000* (in English and Spanish). Video ● Also publishes religious audio tapes "Homily Guides for Bishop, Priests and Deacons and Spiritual Formation Sessions for Laity." Jubilee year; Synod of America; Evangelizing on the Internet. **Conventions/Meetings:** annual board meeting - always November or December, usually in Illinois.

19273 ■ National Catholic Development Conference (NCDC)
86 Front St.
Hempstead, NY 11550-3667
Ph: (516)481-6000
Free: (888)879-6232
Fax: (516)489-9287
E-mail: glehmuth@ncdc.org
URL: http://www.ncdc.org
Contact: Sister Georgette Lehmuth OSF, Pres./CEO
Founded: 1968. **Members:** 450. **Membership Dues:** corporate partner, $1,500 (annual) ● associate (with a gross philanthropic income of less than $500,000), $200-$500 (annual) ● associate (with a gross philanthropic income of $500,000 to $999,999), $800 (annual) ● associate (with a gross philanthropic income of $1 million to $1,999,999), $1,200 (annual) ● associate (with a gross philanthropic income of $2 million and above), $1,700 (annual) ● active (with a gross philanthropic income of less than $100,000 to $1,999,999), $200-$2,000 (annual) ● active (with a gross philanthropic income of $2 million to $5 million and above), $2,400-$4,400 (annual) ● diocesan (depends upon the size of diocese), $500-$1,500 (annual). **Staff:** 9. **Regional Groups:** 4. **Description:** Represents Roman Catholic organizations raising funds for the charitable, welfare, educational, and missionary activities they support; suppliers and consultants are corporate members. Assists members in developing more effective ways to raise money; supports an ethical framework for fundraising activities through Precepts of Stewardship; helps members make the most advantageous use of sound public relations, direct mail, and related social communica-

tions media with their donors and supporters; seeks to increase skills of members and their employees in maintaining effective donor relations. Maintains direct contact with other associations in related fields. **Libraries: Type:** reference. **Awards:** Distinguished Service Award. **Frequency:** annual. **Type:** recognition ● Good Samaritan Award. **Frequency:** annual. **Type:** recognition. **Committees:** Awards; Ethics; Postal; Professional Development; Public Relations. **Programs:** Mentoring. **Affiliated With:** Alliance of Nonprofit Mailers; Independent Sector; National Association for Treasurers of Religious Institutes. **Publications:** *A Guide for Preparing a Statement of Accountability*. Booklet. Provides guidance for the preparation of the organization's Statement of Accountability. ● *Dimensions*, 10/year. Newsletter. **Price:** included in membership dues ● *E-News*, biweekly. Newsletter. Provides insight into current events and happenings in the fundraising world as well as with NCDC. **Price:** free for members. Alternate Formats: online ● *Giving Is An Act of Faith*. Brochure. Features summary of Christian aspects of giving. ● *National Catholic Development Conference and Exposition Resource Guide*, annual. **Circulation:** 1,000. **Advertising:** accepted ● *National Catholic Development Conference—Membership Directory*, annual. Contains a list of new NCDC members. **Price:** included in membership dues. **Conventions/Meetings:** annual conference (exhibits) - always September ● seminar, on fundraising.

19274 ■ National Catholic Office for the Deaf (NCOD)
7202 Buchanan St.
Landover Hills, MD 20784-2236
Ph: (301)577-1684
Fax: (301)577-1684
E-mail: info@ncod.org
URL: http://www.ncod.org
Contact: Arvilla Rank MS, Exec. Dir.
Founded: 1971. **Members:** 325. **Membership Dues:** pastoral, $60 (annual) ● family, $60 (annual) ● student, $25 (annual) ● executive diocese/agency, $225 (annual). **Staff:** 4. **Budget:** $80,000. **Regional Groups:** 7. **Description:** Represents persons or organizations involved in religious work with the persons who are Deaf or Hard of Hearing. Provides information consultation to the Roman Catholic Church's work for persons who are Deaf and Hard of Hearing. Designs and develops programs in religious education for Deaf/Hard of Hearing persons. Develops guidelines/policies in appropriate areas. Conducted the DeSales Project. **Libraries: Type:** reference. **Holdings:** audiovisuals, books, periodicals. **Subjects:** Catholic deaf communities. **Telecommunication Services:** teletype, (301)577-4184. **Affiliated With:** International Catholic Deaf Association - United States Section. **Publications:** *DeSales Project Report on the Spiritual Development of Deaf Persons* ● *My First Eucharist* (in English and Spanish). Video. Features a program for preparing deaf and hard of hearing children for first Holy Communion, includes lesson plans. ● *NCOD Membership Directory*, biennial. **Price:** included in membership dues; $15.00/copy for nonmembers ● *Policy for Working with Sign Language Interpreters in Catholic Religious Settings*, quarterly. Booklet. **Price:** included in membership dues; $15.00 /year for nonmembers in U.S.; $25.00/2 years; $17.00 /year for nonmembers outside U.S. **Advertising:** accepted ● *Principles for Understanding Deaf Ministry & Guidelines for Hiring Pastoral Ministers for the Deaf Community*. Booklet ● *Religious Interpreting Workshop*. Video. Helpful to sign language interpreters in interpreting the Mass. ● *Vision*, quarterly. Magazine. **Price:** included in membership dues; $15.00 /year for nonmembers in U.S.; $25.00/2 years for nonmembers in U.S.; $20.00 /year for nonmembers outside U.S. **Advertising:** accepted. **Conventions/Meetings:** annual Pastoral Week Conference - conference and workshop, focus is on pastoral ministry (exhibits) - in January.

19275 ■ National Catholic Partnership on Disability (NCPD)
415 Michigan Ave. NE, Ste.95
Washington, DC 20017-4501
Ph: (202)529-2933

Fax: (202)529-4678
E-mail: ncpd@ncpd.org
URL: http://www.ncpd.org
Contact: Janice Benton, Exec. Dir.
Founded: 1982. **Membership Dues:** affiliate, $300 (annual). **Staff:** 4. **Description:** Seeks to implement the Pastoral Statement of U.S. Catholic Bishops on Disabled People issued in 1978. Aims to: help individuals with disabilities participate in church activities; aid pastoral workers in their ministry to disabled persons; foster the appointment of diocesan offices of ministry with disabled persons; encourage the acceptance of disabled persons into seminaries and religious communities. Communicates to U.S. Catholic Bishops and national Catholic organizations the needs and concerns of disabled persons. Conducts workshops, retreats, and presentations; develops and disseminates resource materials. **Libraries: Type:** not open to the public. **Holdings:** 2,000; articles, books, periodicals. **Subjects:** disability, access, theology. **Telecommunication Services:** TDD, (202)529-2934. **Formerly:** (2004) National Catholic Office for Persons With Disabilities. **Publications:** *A Loving Justice: The Moral and Legal Responsibilities of the U.S. Catholic Church under the American With Disabilities Act* ● *NCPD E-NEWS*, bimonthly. Newsletter. **Price:** free. Alternate Formats: online ● *Opening Doors: Pastoral Manual* ● Articles. Alternate Formats: online ● Also publishes Opening Doors to People with Disabilities Volume II: The Resource File. **Conventions/Meetings:** conference and regional meeting.

19276 ■ National Catholic Rural Life Conference (NCRLC)
4625 Beaver Ave.
Des Moines, IA 50310-2145
Ph: (515)270-2634
Fax: (515)270-9447
E-mail: ncrlc@aol.com
URL: http://www.ncrlc.com
Contact: Bro. David G. Andrews CSC, Exec. Dir.
Founded: 1923. **Members:** 1,500. **Membership Dues:** individual, $25 (annual) ● parish, $75 (annual) ● organization, $100 (annual). **Staff:** 8. **Local Groups:** 175. **Multinational. Description:** Agency of the Catholic Church engaging in spiritual and educational advocacy efforts in behalf of social justice. Emphasizes on rural America, with a focus on "attaining a just and sustainable food system." Conducts seminars, workshops, and training programs; sponsors educational and advocacy activities in areas such as family farms, food systems, sustainable agriculture, and ecology. Maintains speakers' bureau. **Awards:** St. Isidore and Maria Award. **Frequency:** annual. **Type:** recognition. **Recipient:** to a married couple who exemplifies fidelity to a vocation that combines family integrity, stewardship and faith. **Publications:** *Catholic Rural Life*, biennial. Magazine. **Price:** included in membership dues. ISSN: 1089-6570. Alternate Formats: online ● *Pilgrimage Prayerbook* ● *Prayer in Time of Flood and Storm* ● *Rural Landscapes*, bimonthly. Newsletter. Covers rural and environmental concerns, natural resources, faith issues, the world food situation, poverty, alternative energy, and land ownership. **Price:** included in membership dues. ISSN: 0748-5114. **Circulation:** 3,000 ● *Rural Life Prayers, Blessings, and Liturgies* ● Also publishes other prayer and worship materials from a rural perspective. **Conventions/Meetings:** annual meeting.

19277 ■ National Catholic Women's Union (NCWU)
c/o Social Justice Review
3835 Westminster Pl.
St. Louis, MO 63108-3409
Ph: (314)371-1653
Fax: (314)371-0889
E-mail: centbur@sbcglobal.net
URL: http://www.socialjusticereview.org
Contact: Rev. Edward Krause CSC, Dir.
Founded: 1916. **Members:** 500. **State Groups:** 7. **Local Groups:** 170. **Description:** Represents individual Catholic women and affiliated societies interested in Catholic social action. Sponsors religious

activities, works of charity, mission activities, and maternity guilds. Promotes vocations to the priesthood and the religious life; headquarters, publications office, library, and various programs are maintained by Central Bureau, Catholic Central Union of America (see separate entry). **Sections:** Church Vestments and Altar Linens; Maternity Guilds; Medical Mission Units; Mission and Sewing Circles; Study Clubs. **Conventions/Meetings:** annual conference.

19278 ■ National Christ Child Society (NCCS)
4340 E West Hwy., Ste.202
Bethesda, MD 20814
Ph: (301)718-0220
Free: (800)814-2149
Fax: (301)718-8822
E-mail: office@nationalchristchildsoc.org
URL: http://www.nationalchristchildsoc.org
Contact: Margaret Saffell, Exec. Dir.

Founded: 1887. **Members:** 7,500. **Membership Dues:** national, $7 (annual). **Staff:** 2. **Budget:** $150,000. **Local Groups:** 38. **Description:** Federation of chapters nationwide serving needy children without regard to race or creed. Sponsors settlements, emergency shelters, camps, hospitals, and clinics for medical, dental, baby, pre-and post-natal as well as supplies equipment for institutions and appliances for handicapped children. Prepares layettes for infants and clothing for needy children. Provides facilities for care and treatment of emotionally disturbed children. Conducts volunteer work. Sponsors recreational clubs, activities, parties, and day camps for children (especially the ill or disadvantaged). Provides remedial instruction for children with learning problems; furnishes books, supplies, uniforms, and school transportation for Catholic children. Provides one-on-one mentoring for disadvantaged mothers. **Libraries: Type:** reference. **Holdings:** archival material, audio recordings, books, business records, video recordings. **Awards:** Mary Virginia Merrick Scholars Fund at Catholic University School of Social Work. **Frequency:** annual. **Type:** grant. **Recipient:** for full time graduate students in social work preparing to work with children ● Red Wagon Grant. **Type:** grant. **Recipient:** for chapters to provide a specific project for at-risk children. **Computer Services:** Mailing lists. **Programs:** Challenging Poverty: One Child At A Time. **Publications:** *Challenging Poverty: One Child at a Time.* Manual ● *National Christ Child Brochure* ● *National Christ Child Handbook* ● *National Newsletter*, 3/year. **Conventions/Meetings:** biennial Coming Home - A Capital Celebration - convention - always in Baltimore, MD ● conference, leadership conference.

19279 ■ National Christian Life Community of the United States of America (NCLC)
3601 Lindell Blvd., No. 421
St. Louis, MO 63108-3301
Ph: (314)977-7370
Fax: (314)977-7211
E-mail: pcarter@jpcarter.com
URL: http://www.clc-usa.org
Contact: Dorothy M. Zambrio, Pres.

Founded: 1563. **Members:** 500. **Staff:** 1. **Budget:** $26,000. **Regional Groups:** 55. **State Groups:** 8. **Description:** Represents Roman Catholic adults, parish and interparish groups, and high school and college students. Aims to develop and sustain individuals who commit themselves to service the church and the world in every area of life. Conducts Formation Program and courses for the purpose of introducing and expanding understanding of Christian Life Communities through study and experience. World headquarters is located in Rome, Italy. **Formerly:** (1967) Sodality Movement and Queens Work; (1990) United States National Federation of Christian Life Communities. **Publications:** *Christian Life Communities HARVEST*, quarterly. Newsletter. Contains articles on Christian topics relating to church, community, mission, spirituality, and the teachings of St. Ignatius. **Price:** $24.00/year in U.S.; $28.00/year outside U.S. ISSN: 0739-6422. **Circulation:** 1,000 ● Also publishes informational materials. **Conventions/Meetings:** biennial convention and assembly.

19280 ■ National Committee of Catholic Laymen
215 Lexington Ave., 4th Fl.
New York, NY 10016
Ph: (212)685-6666
Fax: (212)725-9793
Contact: Maria McFadden, Chm.

Founded: 1977. **Membership Dues:** subscription, $35 (annual). **Staff:** 3. **Description:** Supporters are individuals who consider themselves orthodox Catholics and strongly support Pope John Paul II. Represents members' interests in Washington, DC, New York, and Rome, and presents a united voice in the public debate on what the group believes are vital philosophical, social, and legal issues. Disseminates commentary, news, and other information sources regarding developments and changes in the Catholic church, particularly in the U.S. Conducts research. **Computer Services:** Mailing lists. **Publications:** *A Conversation.* Book ● *Catholic Eye*, monthly. Newsletter. Includes reviews of the committee's lobbying efforts and discusses views on philosophical, social, and legal issues. **Price:** $35.00. **Circulation:** 5,000 ● Pamphlets.

19281 ■ National Conference of Diocesan Vocation Directors (NCDVD)
450 Hewett St.
Neillsville, WI 54456
Ph: (715)254-0830
Fax: (715)254-0831
E-mail: office@ncdvd.org
Contact: Mr. Randall Cirner, Exec. Dir.

Founded: 1962. **Members:** 500. **Staff:** 2. **Regional Groups:** 14. **Description:** Supports, educates, provides resources for diocesan vocation directors as they promote all Church vocations, particularly diocesan priesthood. **Awards:** J.S. Paluch Award. **Type:** recognition. **Recipient:** for contributions to vocation ministry. **Affiliated With:** United States Conference of Catholic Bishops. **Publications:** *All For Love*, triennial. Journal. Published for young adults. ● *On the Way to Priesthood.* Journal. Reflection and guide for those discerning priesthood. ● *Vocation Journal*, annual ● Newsletter, quarterly. **Conventions/Meetings:** annual conference and convention (exhibits).

19282 ■ National Council of Bishops, USA (NCOB, USA)
PO Box 1403
Green Cove Springs, FL 32043
Ph: (863)802-4536
Fax: (863)802-4537
E-mail: bishopscouncil@yahoo.com
Contact: Primate Bishop W.A. Andrews DD, Founder

Founded: 2004. **Members:** 12. **Budget:** $10,000. **Regional Groups:** 2. **State Groups:** 2. **Description:** Aims to bring together all bishops across the United States of America. Addresses current issues about the community, state and the country. Seeks to have a speaking voice in the community to local and state governments, and to reestablish order of the church family. **Libraries: Type:** open to the public. **Subjects:** current issues about the community, state and the country, standard of morality within the community. **Awards:** The Humanitarian Award (Act of Benevolence and Quality of Human Life). **Frequency:** annual. **Type:** recognition ● NCOB Award. **Frequency:** annual. **Type:** recognition. **Publications:** Newsletter, quarterly. **Conventions/Meetings:** annual general assembly - every spring ● monthly meeting - every first Thursday.

19283 ■ National Council of Catholic Women (NCCW)
200 N Glebe Rd., Ste.703
Arlington, VA 22203
Ph: (703)224-0990
Free: (800)506-9407
Fax: (703)224-0991
E-mail: nccw01@nccw.org
URL: http://www.nccw.org
Contact: Ellen Bachman, Pres.

Founded: 1920. **Staff:** 10. **Budget:** $600,000. **Local Groups:** 7,000. **Description:** Federation of 6000 national, state, diocesan, interparochial, and parochial organizations of Catholic women. Serves as a forum for Catholic women to share resources, speak on current issues in the church and society, and develop leadership and management skills. Engages in initiating and developing programs in religious, educational, social, and service areas. Members serve on private and public policymaking bodies monitoring a variety of social justice issues. Works to raise funds for foreign relief in conjunction with Catholic Relief Services, Works of Peace, Help-a-Child, and Madonna Plan. **Commissions:** Church; Community Concerns; Family Concerns; International Concerns; Legislation; Organizational Services. **Affiliated With:** United States Conference of Catholic Bishops; Women in Community Service. **Publications:** *Catholic Woman*, bimonthly. Newsletter. **Price:** $15.00/year; $2.50 for current issue; $7.50 for back issue. **Circulation:** 10,500 ● *Leadership Training Video Series.* Videos. **Price:** $20.00 plus shipping and handling ● *Mothers Outreach to Mothers Resource Manual.* Contains a step-by-step guide in implementing a mentoring program for at-risk expectant mothers. ● *NCCW Brochure.* Contains membership information. **Price:** free ● *NCCW Guidance and Resource Manual.* Contains leadership information about planning, building membership, public relations, moderator relationships and commission system. **Price:** $45.00 ● *Women Healing the Wounds.* Brochure. Contains information on what to do when leaving an abusive relationship. ● . **Price:** Also publishes program kits. **Conventions/Meetings:** biennial convention (exhibits).

19284 ■ National Cursillo Movement (NCM)
PO Box 210226
Dallas, TX 75211
Ph: (214)339-6321
Fax: (214)339-6322
E-mail: nationalcursillo.center@verizon.net
URL: http://www.natl-cursillo.org
Contact: Victor Lugo, Natl. Exec. Dir.

Founded: 1957. **Members:** 1,750,000. **Regional Groups:** 12. **State Groups:** 5. **Description:** Represents Catholic Church movement focusing on training and providing assistance for members of the laity in their mission of the Church Evangelization. **Publications:** *National Cursillo Newsletter.* Alternate Formats: online ● *Ultreya Magazine*, bimonthly. **Price:** $10.00/year in U.S.; $12.00/year outside U.S. **Circulation:** 4,000. Alternate Formats: online. **Conventions/Meetings:** annual National Encounter - meeting ● Weekend Course - workshop, 3-day weekend course.

19285 ■ National Enthronement Center
PO Box 111
Fairhaven, MA 02719-0111
Ph: (508)999-2680
Fax: (508)993-8233
E-mail: necenter@juno.com
URL: http://www.sscc.org/pages/x_Enthrone/enthronement_ctr.htm
Contact: Fr. William F. Petrie SSCC, Vocation Dir.

Founded: 1907. **Staff:** 4. **Regional Groups:** 5. **National Groups:** 25. **Description:** Represents Catholic families "recognizing the Sacred Heart as King of the family" by setting up a place of honor or throne in the home to make Christ the king and friend of the home and to make the home a domestic sanctuary wherein Christ can be loved and worshipped. **Affiliated With:** Men of the Sacred Heart. **Formerly:** (1997) Enthronement of the Sacred Heart in the Home. **Publications:** *Heart Exchange.* Newsletter. Contains articles on enthronement, Sacred Heart, and witness. **Price:** free. **Circulation:** 2,000. **Conventions/Meetings:** monthly workshop.

19286 ■ National Evangelization Teams (NET)
110 Crusader Ave. W
West St. Paul, MN 55118-4427
Ph: (651)450-6833
Fax: (651)450-9984

E-mail: ministry@netusa.org
URL: http://www.netusa.org
Contact: Mr. Mark Berchem, Exec. Dir.
Founded: 1981. **Members:** 100. **Membership Dues:** single Catholic aged 18-28, $3,000 (annual). **Staff:** 30. **Languages:** English, Spanish. **Description:** Traveling teams of young adults provide retreat outreach for Catholic youth. Seeks to equip young people for Christian ministry, and to renew their faith through a "clear proclamation of the Gospel." Conducts training sessions on retreat skills, music, and drama. **Also Known As:** NET Ministries, Inc.

19287 ■ National Federation for Catholic Youth Ministry (NFCYM)

415 Michigan Ave. NE, Ste.40
Washington, DC 20017
Ph: (202)636-3825
Fax: (202)526-7544
E-mail: info@nfcym.org
URL: http://www.nfcym.org
Contact: Dr. Robert J. McCarty, Exec. Dir.
Founded: 1982. **Members:** 180. **Staff:** 8. **Budget:** $650,000. **Regional Groups:** 14. **Description:** Represents federation of diocesan youth offices with a combined membership of over two million teenagers. Monitors spiritual, cultural, social, and community services, and physical programs for young people. Locally members sponsor retreats, community service projects, educational workshops, prayer groups, local science fairs, one-act play contests, oratorical contests, writing and photography contests, hobby shows, sports tournaments, and rallies. Holds local and regional conventions and workshops. Maintains small library. **Awards: Type:** recognition. **Computer Services:** Mailing lists. **Committees:** Adult Training and Certification Management; Advocacy Management; Finance Management; Membership Management; Youth Ministry Development. **Sections:** Diocesan; Parish; Regional. **Formerly:** (1951) National Federation of Diocesan Catholic Youth Councils. **Supersedes:** National CYO Federation. **Publications:** *Connections*, quarterly. Newsletter. Contains information about the work of the federation. **Advertising:** accepted ● *Diocesan Youth Directors Directory*, annual. Lists Catholic youth ministry directors throughout the United States. **Price:** included in membership dues ● *NCCGSCF News*, semiannual. Newsletter. **Price:** free for members ● *Utilizing the Youth Ministry Resource Manual.* Alternate Formats: online. **Conventions/Meetings:** annual conference (exhibits).

19288 ■ National Federation of Priests' Councils (NFPC)

333 N Michigan Ave., Ste.1205
Chicago, IL 60601-4002
Ph: (312)442-9700
Free: (888)271-NFPC
Fax: (312)442-9709
E-mail: nfpc@nfpc.org
URL: http://www.nfpc.org
Contact: Rev. Robert J. Silva, Pres.
Founded: 1968. **Members:** 116. **Membership Dues:** Presbyteral Council, $25 (annual). **Staff:** 8. **Budget:** $990,000. **Regional Groups:** 12. **Local Groups:** 116. **Description:** Councils of diocesan priests and priest associations. Provides a national forum for priests on church issues; enables priests' councils to speak with a common voice on issues of national and international importance, in a pastoral-ministerial manner. Seeks to: collaborate in programs of pastoral research and action; implement norms for the renewal of priestly life; provide the means for priests' councils to cooperate with laity, religious, bishops, and others in addressing the needs of the church in the modern world. Facilitates communication among priests' councils. **Awards:** President's Award. **Frequency:** annual. **Type:** recognition. **Recipient:** for a priest who has demonstrated leadership on behalf of priests. **Computer Services:** database ● mailing lists. **Committees:** Ad Hoc Concerns; Administration and Finance; Convention; Programs and Services; Research and Publications; Social Justice Concerns; Strategic Planning. **Publications:** *Touchstone*, quarterly. Newsletter. For priests and their ministries.

Price: included in membership dues; $12.00 /year for nonmembers. **Circulation:** 26,000. **Advertising:** accepted ● Papers, periodic. Features ministry-oriented topics. **Conventions/Meetings:** annual convention (exhibits) - 2008 Apr. 20-24, Orlando, FL - **Avg. Attendance:** 250.

19289 ■ National Institute for the Word of God

487 Michigan Ave. NE
Washington, DC 20017-1518
Ph: (202)529-0001 (202)529-5300
E-mail: wjburke@dhs.edu
URL: http://www.wordofgodinstitute.org
Contact: Fr. John Burke OP, Dir.
Founded: 1972. **Staff:** 5. **Description:** Roman Catholics. Engenders belief in Jesus through preaching centered in Sacred Scripture. Services include: parish Bible missions; conferences on catechetics; lector training; biblical preaching, and Bible sharing. **Formerly:** (1987) Word of God Institute. **Publications:** *GoodNews Letter*, biennial. Newsletter. Contains information on preaching, lecturing, and Bible sharing. **Price:** free. **Circulation:** 2,000 ● Audiotapes ● Books ● Videos. **Conventions/Meetings:** retreat, for priests ● workshop, on liturgy ● workshop, for ordained and lay ministers ● workshop, for lectors ● workshop, on preaching.

19290 ■ National Office for Black Catholics (NOBC)

c/o Archdiocese of Washington Pastoral Center
PO Box 29620
Washington, DC 20017
Ph: (301)853-4579
E-mail: obc@adw.org
URL: http://www.adw.org/cultures/officeblack.asp
Contact: Rev. Msgr. Raymond G. East, Exec. Dir.
Founded: 1970. **Members:** 1,000,000. **Staff:** 9. **Description:** Black priests, sisters, brothers, and laypersons of the Catholic Church. Participating organizations: National Black Sisters' Conference; National Black Catholic Clergy Caucus. Serves as a "foundation for the renewal of the credibility of the church in the black community". Works to coordinate actions designed "to liberate black people and to serve as a unifying strength". Plans to: have specialists and technicians working within the black community to coordinate community organization and development; provide leadership training for youth; attack problems of poverty and deprivation; sensitize blacks to their heritage through historical, cultural, and liturgical experience. Seeks cooperation with groups working toward black liberation. Concerns include: training black and white clergy and religious, Catholic, and non-Catholic laity; influencing decisions involving race and the church; monitoring, in order to prevent, manifestations of racism. Sponsors Pastoral Ministry Institute and Afro-American Culture and Worship Workshop; provides evangelization workshops and leadership training for parish councils and parochial schools. **Libraries: Type:** reference. **Holdings:** 400. **Committees:** Advisory Panel on Culture and Worship; Evangelization. **Departments:** Church Vocations; Culture and Worship; Public Relations. **Publications:** *A Letter to Families.* Book. Alternate Formats: online ● *Catechism of the Catholic Church.* Book. **Price:** $24.95 hardcover; $8.99 paperback. Alternate Formats: online ● *Humane Vitae - On Human Life.* Book. Alternate Formats: online ● *Impact*, bimonthly. Newsletter ● *John Paul II: A Light for the World.* Book. **Price:** $35.00 ● *Journey to the Fullness of Life.* Book. **Price:** $5.95. Alternate Formats: online. **Conventions/Meetings:** biennial meeting.

19291 ■ National Religious Vocation Conference (NRVC)

5401 S Cornell Ave., Ste.105
Chicago, IL 60615-5604
Ph: (773)363-5454
Fax: (773)363-5530
E-mail: nrvc@nrvc.net
URL: http://nrvc.net
Contact: Bro. Paul Bednarczyk CSC, Exec. Dir.
Founded: 1988. **Members:** 1,400. **Membership Dues:** professional, $115 (annual) ● associate, $90

(annual) ● international, $95 (annual) ● group associate, $50 (annual). **Staff:** 4. **Budget:** $635,000. **Regional Groups:** 14. **Description:** Represents vocation directors of religious orders of sisters, brothers, and priests in the United States, Canada, Australia, and New Zealand. Initiates programs at the national level that respond to needs in the area of church vocations; sponsors study programs; provides resource materials; acts as official liaison between member organizations. **Awards:** Harvest Award. **Frequency:** biennial. **Type:** recognition. **Recipient:** for significant contribution by a nonmember of NRVC to vocation ministry in the Catholic Church in the US. **Formed by Merger of:** (1988) National Conference of Religious Vocation Directors; (1988) National Sisters Vocation Conference. **Publications:** *Horizon*, quarterly. Journal. ISSN: 1042-8461. **Circulation:** 2,000 ● *NRVC Membership Directory*, annual. **Price:** available to members only. **Circulation:** 1,200 ● *NRVC News*, monthly. Newsletter. Alternate Formats: online. **Conventions/Meetings:** biennial meeting - always September, on even-numbered years ● workshop, for development of membership.

19292 ■ National Service Committee/Chariscenter USA

PO Box 628
Locust Grove, VA 22508-0628
Free: (800)338-2445
Fax: (540)972-0225
E-mail: chariscenter@nsc-chariscenter.org
URL: http://www.nsc-chariscenter.org
Contact: Walter Matthews, Exec. Dir.
Founded: 1971. **Members:** 10. **Staff:** 6. **Description:** Leaders in the Catholic Charismatic Renewal working "to serve the Lord in renewing the grace of Pentecost in the life and mission of the Church." Facilitates networking among leaders of renewal centers, prayer groups, and national ministries; serves as a resource to the U.S. Bishops and Church leaders; provides guidance and information for individuals, prayer groups, renewal centers, and diocese. **Computer Services:** Mailing lists. **Formerly:** (2002) Charismatic Renewal Services. **Publications:** *Pentecost Today.* Magazine. Alternate Formats: online ● Videos ● Books. **Conventions/Meetings:** Intercession Prayer Summits - conference ● regional meeting ● retreat.

19293 ■ National Shrine of St. Elizabeth Ann Seton (SSC)

333 S Seton Ave.
Emmitsburg, MD 21727
Ph: (301)447-6606
Fax: (301)447-6061
E-mail: office@setonshrine.org
URL: http://www.setonshrine.org
Contact: Karen Harding, Dir.
Founded: 1973. **Staff:** 16. **Description:** Encourages devotion to St. Elizabeth Ann Seton, the first United States born canonized saint. Maintains basilica, museum, and speakers' bureau. **Libraries: Type:** reference. **Awards:** Seton Founder's Award. **Type:** recognition. **Recipient:** for persons exemplifying the values and ideals of St. Elizabeth Ann Seton. **Computer Services:** database. **Formerly:** (2004) Seton Shrine Center. **Publications:** *The Seton Way*, 3/year. Newsletter. **Price:** free. **Circulation:** 9,000. **Conventions/Meetings:** semiannual board meeting.

19294 ■ Night Adoration in the Home (NAH)

c/o National Enthronement Center
PO Box 111
Fairhaven, MA 02719-0111
Ph: (508)999-2680
Fax: (508)993-8233
E-mail: necenter@juno.com
URL: http://www.sscc.org
Contact: Rev. Columban Crotty SSCC, Dir.
Founded: 1927. **Members:** 40,000. **Staff:** 2. **Description:** Spiritual organization of Catholics who spend at least one hour each month in adoration at home (between the hours of 9 p.m. and 6 a.m.) in a spirit of reparation for sins and offenses against God. **Convention/Meeting:** none. **Formerly:** (1969) League of Night Adoration in the Home.

19295 ■ Nocturnal Adoration Society (NAS)
c/o Saint Jean Baptiste Catholic Church
184 E 76th St.
New York, NY 10021
Ph: (212)288-5082
Fax: (212)717-8397
E-mail: sjbrcc@aol.com
URL: http://www.sjbrcc.net/nas.html
Contact: Mr. Paul Monette, Dir.
Founded: 1903. **Members:** 11,431. **Staff:** 2. **Local Groups:** 323. **Description:** Catholic prayer organization whose members gather in church during the nighttime hours once a month. **Convention/Meeting:** none. **Publications:** *NAS Newsletter*, monthly. Contains inspirational information. **Price:** $5.00/year. **Circulation:** 10,100.

19296 ■ North American Association for the Catechumenate (NAAC)
c/o Rev. Bryon Hansen, Newsletter Ed.
5415 SE Powell Blvd.
Portland, OR 97206
Ph: (503)777-1443
E-mail: webcurator@catechumenate.org
URL: http://www.catechumenate.org
Contact: Shirley Griffin, Pres.
Multinational. Description: Provides training and support for churches engaged in the process of baptismal conversion and making Christian disciples. Advocates for and promotes a better understanding of the catechumenal process. Promotes and implements the enculturation and adaptation of the catechumenate. **Telecommunication Services:** electronic mail, stmarks@xprt.net. **Publications:** *NAAC News.* Newsletter. Alternate Formats: online ● Brochure. Alternate Formats: online. **Conventions/ Meetings:** annual meeting.

19297 ■ North American Forum on the Catechumenate (NAFC)
125 Michigan Ave. NE
Washington, DC 20017
Ph: (202)884-9758
Fax: (202)884-9747
E-mail: info@naforum.org
URL: http://www.naforum.org
Contact: James Schellman, Exec. Dir.
Founded: 1982. **Members:** 9,000. **Staff:** 7. **Description:** Parishes, dioceses, priests, directors of religious education, and members of parishes. Seeks to implement the Rite of Christian Initiation of Adults, a document written by Catholic bishops in 1972 detailing how an adult can become a member of the Catholic Church. (Catechumenate is an early church term referring to one who receives instruction in the basic doctrines of Christianity before admission to communicant membership in a church.) Promotes research into issues presented by the catechumenate. Works with the Catholic Church, but independently, to offer instructional services such as: Beginnings Institute, Remembering Church, Beginnings and Beyond, Initiation Ministries, Liturgies of Initiation. Maintains resources on adult initiation and faith development. **Publications:** *Forum Newsletter*, 3/year.

19298 ■ Paulist Memorial Society
Paulist Fathers
3015 4th St. NE
Washington, DC 20017
Ph: (202)269-2500
Free: (800)472-8549
Fax: (202)269-2507
E-mail: development@paulist.org
URL: http://www.paulist.org
Contact: Gail Battle, Exec. Dir.
Founded: 1924. **Members:** 66,000. **Description:** Roman Catholic community of priests whose mission is to promote evangelization, reconciliation, and ecumenism throughout North America. **Affiliated With:** Paulist National Catholic Evangelization Association. **Formerly:** (1998) Paulist League. **Publications:** *Paulist Today*, quarterly. Newsletter. **Price:** free. **Circulation:** 55,000. Alternate Formats: online.

19299 ■ Paulist National Catholic Evangelization Association (PNCEA)
3031 4th St. NE
Washington, DC 20017-1102
Ph: (202)832-5022
Free: (800)237-5515
Fax: (202)269-0209
E-mail: pncea@pncea.org
URL: http://www.pncea.org
Contact: Fr. Kenneth Boyack CSP, Pres.
Founded: 1977. **Members:** 21,000. **Staff:** 20. **Budget:** $2,400,000. **Description:** Represents individuals interested in Catholic evangelization in America. Aims to heighten awareness among active American Catholics regarding non-practicing Catholics and those with no church affiliation. Seeks to develop programs and materials aimed at inactive Catholics and the unchurched to learn about Jesus Christ and the Catholic Church. **Publications:** *Disciples in Mission*, annual. Manual ● *Share the Word*, 7/year. Magazine. Features scripture study based on Sunday readings. **Price:** $17.50/year; $31.50/2 years; $42.00/3 years. ISSN: 0199-5049. **Circulation:** 20,000. **Conventions/Meetings:** annual Disciples in Mission - meeting.

19300 ■ Pious Union of Prayer (PUP)
c/o Sisters of St. Joseph of Peace
PO Box 288
Jersey City, NJ 07303
Ph: (201)798-4141
Contact: Sr. Mary Kuiken CSJP, Editor
Founded: 1898. **Members:** 14,000. **Staff:** 3. **Description:** Catholic spiritual organization under the Sisters of St. Joseph of Peace. "For united prayer and a sharing of the fruits of the apostolate." Maintains residences for working women; supports children and blind persons entrusted to the care of the Sisters. **Computer Services:** Mailing lists. **Publications:** *St. Joseph's Messenger and Advocate of Blind*, 3/yr. Magazine. Contains stories, poems, and inspirational articles for Catholics. **Price:** included in membership dues; $5.00 /year for nonmembers. **Circulation:** 14,000.

19301 ■ Pius X Secular Institute (ISPX)
27 Cove St.
Manchester, NH 03104
Ph: (603)622-4849
E-mail: info@ispx.org
URL: http://www.ispx.org/english.htm
Contact: Fr. Gerald C. LaCroix, Dir.
Founded: 1939. **Members:** 225. **Staff:** 9. **Budget:** C$125,300. **Regional Groups:** 7. **State Groups:** 1. **National Groups:** 5. **Languages:** English, French, Spanish. **Multinational. Description:** Seeks to spread the Gospel, especially among poor and working class individuals. (Secular institutes are societies of Catholic men and women who vow to observe evangelical counsels and to carry out work in the midst of society, bearing witness to the Gospel.) Evangelizes by all possible means. **Councils:** General; Regional. **Conventions/Meetings:** quadrennial general assembly ● periodic retreat.

19302 ■ Pontifical Mission Societies in the United States (PMS)
366 5th Ave., 12th Fl.
New York, NY 10001
Ph: (212)563-8700
Fax: (212)563-8725
E-mail: pmsusa@propfaith.org
URL: http://www.worldmissions-catholicchurch.org
Contact: John E. Kozar, Natl. Dir.
Founded: 1916. **Description:** Seeks to stimulate growth in mission awareness among priests, deacons, men and women religious, candidates to priesthood and religious life, and other persons engaged in pastoral ministry of the Catholic church. **Convention/ Meeting:** none. **Affiliated With:** Holy Childhood Association; Society for the Propagation of the Faith; Society of Saint Peter Apostle. **Formerly:** (1978) Missionary Union of the Clergy in U.S.A.; (1981) Pontifical Missionary Union; (2004) Pontifical Missionary Union of Priests and Religious.

19303 ■ Pro Maria Committee (PMC)
Address Unknown since 2007
Founded: 1952. **Members:** 9,000. **Staff:** 4. **Languages:** English, French. **Description:** Individuals dedicated to the spreading of the devotion to Our Lady of Beauraing, Belgium, and the message and story of her appearances there in 1932-33. Maintains collection of religious articles. **Convention/Meeting:** none. **Divisions:** Marian Union of Beauraing. **Publications:** *Our Lady of Beauraing, 3rd Ed.*. Book. **Advertising:** not accepted.

19304 ■ Pro Sanctity Movement (PSM)
11002 N 204th St.
Elkhorn, NE 68022-3800
Ph: (402)289-2670 (402)553-4418
E-mail: psm@prosanctity.org
URL: http://www.prosanctity.org/gallery.php
Contact: Cathy McDonnell, Dir.
Founded: 1947. **Members:** 3,000. **Membership Dues:** $35 (annual). **Regional Groups:** 3. **State Groups:** 1. **Local Groups:** 1. **National Groups:** 3. **Languages:** English, Italian, Slovene, Spanish. **Multinational. Description:** Represents Catholic laity, priests, and religious groups seeking to develop a closer relationship with Christ by spreading the call to holiness, offering spiritual means to fulfill this call, and gathering people to the Apostolate of Holiness. Promotes days of recollection, weekend retreats, and hours of prayer. Conducts pilgrimages, special events for children, lecture series, and workshops. Maintains collection of books on saints, spirituality, prayer, and theology. **Libraries: Type:** open to the public. **Holdings:** 4,000. **Subjects:** religions, spirituality, prayer, theology, morality. **Computer Services:** database ● mailing lists. **Affiliated With:** Institute of Apostolic Oblates. **Publications:** *Call to Holiness*, bimonthly. Manual.

19305 ■ Raskob Foundation for Catholic Activities
PO Box 4019
Wilmington, DE 19807-0019
Ph: (302)655-4440
Fax: (302)655-3223
URL: http://www.rfca.org
Contact: Frederick J. Perella Jr., Exec. VP
Founded: 1945. **Members:** 106. **Staff:** 10. **Multinational. Description:** Philanthropic foundation composed of Raskob family members. Works to promote religious, charitable, literary, and educational activities. Supports the Roman Catholic Church and related institutions. **Awards:** Responsive Grants. **Frequency:** semiannual. **Type:** grant.

19306 ■ Religious Brothers Conference (RBC)
5420 S Cornell Ave.
Chicago, IL 60615
Ph: (773)483-2306
Fax: (773)493-2356
E-mail: brothersoffice@ameritech.net
URL: http://www.brothersonline.org
Contact: Bro. Stephen Synan, Pres./Exec. Dir.
Founded: 1970. **Members:** 700. **Membership Dues:** regular, associate, $35 (annual). **Staff:** 1. **Description:** Religious brothers, most of whom work and live in the U.S; associate members are priests, sisters, lay, and organizations. Grass roots organization whose goal is to be of service to brothers and their apostolates. Promotes the vocation of religious brotherhood. Provides advocacy for issues of concern to brothers in the church throughout the world. **Awards:** Call to Brotherhood Awards. **Frequency:** annual. **Type:** recognition. **Computer Services:** database, religious brothers. **Affiliated With:** Leadership Conference of Women Religious. **Formerly:** (1997) National Assembly of Religious Brothers; (2002) National Association of Religious Brothers. **Publications:** *Brothers' Voice*, annual. Newsletter. Provides a forum for the opinions and views of religious brothers; also includes book reviews and list of new members. **Price:** included in membership dues. **Circulation:** 2,000 ● *President's Newsletter and Financial Report*, annual. **Circulation:** 2,000 ● *Reflections*, semiannual. Journal. Contains articles on brothers

and religious life. **Price:** included in membership dues. **Circulation:** 2,000. **Conventions/Meetings:** annual convention (exhibits) - always June ● regional meeting ● annual retreat.

19307 ■ Religious Formation Conference (RFC)
8820 Cameron St.
Silver Spring, MD 20910-4152
Ph: (301)588-4938
Fax: (301)585-7649
URL: http://www.relforcon.org
Contact: Janet Mock CSJ, Exec. Dir.
Founded: 1954. **Members:** 1,200. **Membership Dues:** religious institute, $340-$1,035 (annual) ● auxiliary (domestic), $90 (annual) ● auxiliary (international), $100 (annual). **Staff:** 3. **Regional Groups:** 16. **Multinational. Description:** Formation personnel and interested members of religious, secular, or non-canonical communities united to promote the spiritual and professional formation of American Roman Catholic sisters, brothers, priests, and members of secular institutes. Serves as a means for support, education, and information exchange. Encourages and promotes national and regional activities. Disseminates information about formation. Collaborates with other related organizations. **Formerly:** (1976) Sister Formation Conference. **Publications:** *IN-FORMATION*, 5/year. Newsletter ● *Trans-Formation*, 5/year. Bulletin. **Conventions/Meetings:** biennial congress.

19308 ■ Reparation Society of the Immaculate Heart of Mary (RSIHM)
Address Unknown since 2007
Founded: 1946. **Members:** 3,000. **Staff:** 4. **Description:** "Catholics freely promising fulfillment of the Blessed Virgin's request given at Fatima, Portugal, in 1917." Members recite the Rosary daily and practice Christian penance along with special devotions on the First Saturday. Conducts public holy hours on the First Saturday and sponsors daily radio Rosary program. **Publications:** *Fatima Findings*, monthly. Newsletter. Concerned with propagating the message of Our Lady of Fatima and advocating prayer and penance, especially the Rosary devotion. **Price:** $10.00/year inside U.S.; $10.50/year outside U.S. ISSN: 0014-8830. **Circulation:** 1,000. **Advertising:** not accepted ● Also publishes manual, leaflets, and devotional books.

19309 ■ Retreats International (RI)
10 E Pearson St., 3rd Fl.
Chicago, IL 60611
Ph: (312)915-7970
Fax: (312)915-7971
E-mail: retreatsintl@luc.edu
URL: http://www.retreatsintl.org
Contact: Anne M. Luther, Exec. Dir.
Founded: 1977. **Members:** 350. **Membership Dues:** individual, $230 (annual) ● associate, $75 (annual). **Staff:** 5. **Regional Groups:** 22. **Multinational. Description:** Roman Catholic, Protestant, interfaith retreat, renewal and prayer centers and individuals in retreat ministry. Promotes retreat, prayer and renewal ministry. Sponsors Institute for Adult Spiritual Renewal. **Awards:** Oblate Sharing Fund. **Type:** monetary. **Telecommunication Services:** electronic mail, amluther@fbcglobal.net. **Boards:** Council of Area Representatives; Trustees. **Publications:** *The Bridge*, quarterly. Newsletter ● *Directory of Retreat Ministry Centers in U.S. and Canada*, annual. Contains listing of retreat centers, accommodations, and types of programs. **Price:** included in membership dues; $30.00 /year for nonmembers ● Monographs ● Also publishes guideline series and data statistics. **Conventions/Meetings:** board meeting (exhibits) - spring ● meeting, council of area representatives - fall.

19310 ■ Sacred Heart League (SHL)
PO Box 300
Walls, MS 38680-0300
Ph: (601)781-1360
Free: (800)232-9079
Fax: (662)781-3340

E-mail: spiritualdirector@shl.org
URL: http://www.sacredheartleague.org
Contact: Roger Courts, CEO
Founded: 1954. **Members:** 1,300,000. **Staff:** 120. **Description:** Roman Catholics who have special devotion to the Sacred Heart of Jesus. Program services include the Sacred Heart Auto League that promotes prayerful and careful driving and the Apostolate of the Word that publishes, propagates, and distributes devotional literature. Contributions are used for education of candidates to the priesthood; support of the Sacred Heart Southern Missions (including establishment of missions and churches; educational programs for children, especially for the underprivileged; social services for the poor, the sick, and the aged). Conducts charitable program. **Convention/Meeting:** none. **Publications:** *Southern Missioner Newsletter*, quarterly. **Circulation:** 120,000.

19311 ■ St. Ansgar's Scandinavian Catholic League (SASCL)
3 E 28th St.
New York, NY 10016-7408
Ph: (212)876-7719
Fax: (212)620-4687
Contact: Astrid O'Brien, Pres.
Founded: 1910. **Members:** 700. **Membership Dues:** regular, $10 (annual). **Staff:** 5. **Multinational. Description:** Clergy; religious individuals; professional and laypersons. Provides religious, moral, social, and intellectual improvement of its members; aids the Catholic church in Scandinavian countries. Conducts stipend program. Compiles statistics. **Publications:** *St. Ansgar's Bulletin*, annual. Contains news and church information. **Price:** $10.00. **Circulation:** 700 ● Yearbook. **Conventions/Meetings:** quarterly meeting.

19312 ■ St. Jude League (SJL)
205 W Monroe St.
Chicago, IL 60606-5013
Ph: (312)236-7782
Fax: (312)236-8207
E-mail: stjudeleague@claretians.org
URL: http://www.stjudeleague.org
Contact: Fr. Mark Brummel CMF, Dir. of Natl. Shrine of St. Jude
Founded: 1929. **Description:** Represents devotional organization of Roman Catholics, sponsored by the Claretian Fathers and Brothers of the National Shrine of St. Jude, Chicago, IL and devoted to St. Jude Thaddeus, Apostle and "patron of difficult or hopeless cases". **Publications:** *St. Jude Journal*, periodic.

19313 ■ St. Thomas Aquinas Foundation (STAF)
141 E 65th St.
New York, NY 10021-6607
Ph: (212)737-5757
Fax: (212)861-4216
Contact: Rev. Dominic Izzo OP, Pres.
Founded: 1963. **Members:** 10. **Description:** Roman Catholic priests of the Dominican Order. Assists in recruiting personnel and raising funds to complete the authentic (critical) edition of the writings of St. Thomas Aquinas, 13th century philosopher and theologian. Sponsors Leonine Commission. **Conventions/Meetings:** annual meeting.

19314 ■ Saints' Stories
520 Oliphant Ln.
Middletown, RI 02842-4600
Ph: (401)849-5421
URL: http://www.thombs.com/saints
Contact: Madeline Pecora Nugent, Contact
Founded: 1990. **Description:** Distributes 400-word stories of Roman Catholic patron saints for baptismal names.

19315 ■ Secular Institute of Saint Francis de Sales
87 Gerrish Ave. T2
East Haven, CT 06512
Ph: (203)469-3277
Fax: (203)469-2094

E-mail: tkyes03e@aol.com
URL: http://www.secularinstitutes.org/sfs.htm
Contact: Therese C. Keyes, U.S.A. Directress
Founded: 1964. **Members:** 158. **State Groups:** 8. **Languages:** English, German, Portuguese. **Multinational. Description:** A secular institute composed of single, widowed, and divorced Catholic women. Members promote the spirituality of St. Francis de Sales by devoting themselves to evangelical counsels and apostolic work. **Libraries: Type:** reference. **Holdings:** 300; audiovisuals, books, business records, periodicals. **Subjects:** spirituality, religion. **Committees:** Public Relations. **Formerly:** (2001) DeSales Secular Institute. **Publications:** *Rundbrief* (in English and German), quarterly. Newsletter. **Circulation:** 200 ● *Salesian Light*, quarterly. Newsletter. **Circulation:** 150. **Conventions/Meetings:** quadrennial international conference, legislative meeting, general assembly - always in Germany ● quarterly meeting.

19316 ■ Serra International (SI)
70 E Lake St., Ste.1210
Chicago, IL 60601-5938
Ph: (312)419-7411
Free: (800)488-4008
Fax: (312)419-8077
E-mail: serra@serrainternational.org
URL: http://www.serrainternational.org
Contact: John W. Woodward, Exec. Dir.
Founded: 1935. **Members:** 22,000. **Staff:** 9. **Budget:** $700,000. **Regional Groups:** 560. **Multinational. Description:** Catholic men's and women's clubs in 37 countries. Seeks to "foster vocations to the Catholic priesthood and religious life, develop appreciation of the ministerial priesthood and of all religious vocations in the Catholic Church, and to further Catholicism by encouraging its members to fulfill their Christian vocation to service." Conducts surveys and research projects. Holds seminars and leadership training meetings. Maintains speakers' bureau; sponsors competitions. **Publications:** *Club Information Roster*, annual ● *The Serran*, bimonthly. Magazine. **Alternate Formats:** online ● *Vocations Activities Guide*. **Conventions/Meetings:** annual meeting - usually June.

19317 ■ Slovene Franciscan Fathers (SFF)
c/o Slovenian Catholic Mission
PO Box 608
Lemont, IL 60439
Ph: (630)257-2494 (630)257-2068
Fax: (630)257-2359
E-mail: metodofm@sbcglobal.net
URL: http://www.lemont-svs.org
Contact: Rev. Fr. Blaz Chemazar OFM, Contact
Founded: 1912. **Members:** 8. **Description:** Religious brothers and priests of the Order of Friars Minor (OFM) who work in Catholic parishes and apostolates and among Catholics of Slovene birth and descent. **Publications:** *Ave Maria* (in English and Slovene), monthly. Magazine. **Price:** $20.00/year ● Newsletter, periodic.

19318 ■ Society of African Missions (SMA)
23 Bliss Ave.
Tenafly, NJ 07670-3001
Ph: (201)567-0450
Free: (800)318-1209
Fax: (201)541-1280
E-mail: smausa-c@smafathers.org
URL: http://www.smafathers.org
Contact: Rev. Thomas Wright, Provincial Supervisor
Founded: 1856. **Members:** 1,238. **Staff:** 18. **Description:** Roman Catholic missionary priests, brothers, and lay associates from 10 countries in North America and Europe working in Africa. Seeks to establish the Catholic Church throughout the missionary world and to aid in the creation of a native clergy. Helps to fulfill people's needs in clinics, schools, leprosariums, and hospitals. Promotes socio-economic development, peace and justice projects, and agricultural programs. Sponsors educational and charitable programs. Maintains museum of African arts and crafts, mainly from West Africa. **Departments:** African Art Museum; Justice and Peace; Media; Mission Education. **Also Known As:** SMA

Fathers. **Publications:** *Frontline Report*, bimonthly. Newsletter. Highlights the activities of Roman Catholic missionaries. **Price:** included in membership dues. **Circulation:** 30,000. **Conventions/Meetings:** assembly - every 6 years.

19319 ■ Society of the Little Flower (SLF)
1313 Frontage Rd.
Darien, IL 60561-5340
Ph: (630)968-9400
Free: (800)621-2806
Fax: (630)968-9542
E-mail: susan@littleflower.org
URL: http://www.littleflower.org
Contact: Fr. Robert E. Colaresi, Dir.
Founded: 1923. **Members:** 300,000. **Description:** Strives to aid boys studying for the priesthood in Carmelite Seminaries. **Also Known As:** Little Flower Society.

19320 ■ Society of Missionaries of Africa
1624 21st St. NW
Washington, DC 20009-1003
Ph: (202)232-5154
Fax: (202)332-8640
E-mail: info@missionariesofafrica.org
URL: http://www.missionariesofafrica.org
Contact: Fr. John P. Lynch, Exec. Dir.
Founded: 1868. **Members:** 2,300. **Description:** Interracial society of Catholic priests, brothers, and lay associates working in international teams in 22 countries of Africa and in Jerusalem, Israel, Brazil, and Mexico. African dioceses total 98; 82 of these are headed by African bishops. Objectives are to promote the religious and social development of African people by providing U.S. support and personnel for evangelical, educational, social development and social action projects; to promote greater interest and understanding among U.S. people for the problems of human and spiritual development in the new African countries. **Convention/Meeting:** none. **Publications:** *Missionaries of Africa Report*, quarterly. Newsletter. **Price:** $6.00/year. **Circulation:** 60,000.

19321 ■ Society of Our Lady of the Most Holy Trinity (SOLT)
109 W Ave. F
Robstown, TX 78380
Ph: (361)387-2754 (361)387-8090
Fax: (361)387-3818
E-mail: srmarypaul@softhome.net
URL: http://www.solt3.org
Contact: Fr. John McHugh, Contact
Founded: 1958. **Members:** 500. **Budget:** $1,000,000. **Languages:** English, Italian, Russian, Spanish, Tagalog, Thai. **Multinational. Description:** Represents priests, deacons, seminarians, religious sisters, and laity. Forms teams of priests, sisters, and laity to develop ministries in specialized areas. At the request of area bishops, the teams set up ministries in areas such as: providing aid to the Hopi Indians in Arizona; assisting migrant farmers in the U.S; working with homeless children; providing education for teenage delinquents; organizing a drug rehabilitation center in Thailand; working with prisoners. Provides Montessori education. Staffs mission parishes in the Philippines, Mexico, Belize, Guatemala, England, Honduras, Papua New Guinea, Russia, and Haiti. Maintains archives on ministry education. **Publications:** *Communio*, quarterly. Newsletter. **Conventions/Meetings:** annual meeting.

19322 ■ Society for the Propagation of the Faith (SPF)
366 5th Ave.
New York, NY 10001-2211
Ph: (212)563-8700
Free: (800)431-2222
Fax: (212)563-8725
E-mail: pmsusa@propfaith.org
URL: http://www.worldmissions-catholicchurch.org
Contact: Rev. Msgr. John E. Kozar, Natl. Dir.
Founded: 1822. **Regional Groups:** 190. **Description:** Objectives are: to assist the Pope and the bishops of the Catholic church in animating a univer-

sal missionary spirit and in awakening an interest in worldwide mission of the Church among the whole People of God; to educate Catholics about the missionary nature and activity of the Church. Offers mission education programs for youth in high school and religious education programs, as well as for college students, adults, and seminaries; participates in diocesan and national education conferences. Sponsors World Mission Sunday celebrated annually on the next-to-last Sunday of October. **Awards:** Archbishop Edward T. O'Meara Award. **Frequency:** annual. **Type:** recognition. **Recipient:** for journalistic excellence with regard to reporting about the missionary work of the Catholic Church. **Affiliated With:** Holy Childhood Association; Pontifical Mission Societies in the United States; Society of Saint Peter Apostle. **Publications:** *Mission*, quarterly. Magazine. **Circulation:** 1,000,000. **Conventions/Meetings:** annual meeting.

19323 ■ Society of Saint Mary Magdalene
PO Box 28464
St. Petersburg, FL 33709
Ph: (727)548-9173
E-mail: socsmm1@st-mary-magdalene.org
URL: http://www.st-mary-magdalene.org
Founded: 1980. **Members:** 2,469. **Staff:** 3. **Description:** Catholic religious order. Promotes adherence to the tenets of Catholicism. Spreads devotion to St. Mary Magdalene. **Conventions/Meetings:** annual meeting, with Easter Mass - always Easter.

19324 ■ Society of Saint Peter Apostle (SSPA)
366 5th Ave., 12th Fl.
New York, NY 10001-2211
Ph: (212)563-8700
Free: (800)431-2222
Fax: (212)563-8725
E-mail: pmsusa@propfaith.org
URL: http://www.worldmissions-catholicchurch.org
Contact: Rev. Msgr. John E. Kozar, Natl. Dir.
Founded: 1889. **Description:** Invites individuals to aid in the training of candidates for the Catholic priesthood in mission lands and to support the formation of men and women candidates for the religious life in the missions. **Convention/Meeting:** none. **Affiliated With:** Holy Childhood Association; Pontifical Mission Societies in the United States; Society for the Propagation of the Faith. **Formerly:** (1981) Society of St. Peter the Apostle for Native Clergy.

19325 ■ Society of Traditional Roman Catholics (STRC)
PO Box 130
Mead, WA 99021-0130
Fax: (509)489-4060
E-mail: tradition@strc.org
URL: http://www.strc.org
Contact: Larry Martin, Pres.
Founded: 1984. **Members:** 4,540. **National Groups:** 5. **Description:** Works within the Catholic Church for the restoration of the traditional Tridentine rite of the Mass (also known as the Latin Mass). Promotes Catholic values and understanding of Catholic teachings. Compiles statistics regarding support for traditional rites; documents the condition of the church in America; annually reviews results of these efforts with members. Maintains speakers' bureau. **Libraries: Type:** not open to the public. **Holdings:** 2,000; books. **Subjects:** the mass, lives of Saints. **Telecommunication Services:** information service, traditional information, (704)843-0648. **Committees:** Catholic Unity; Hierarchy; Mass; Vatican Liaison. **Affiliated With:** Pax Christi - U.S.A. **Formerly:** (1985) Committee for Catholic Unity. **Publications:** *Catholic Voice*, quarterly. Newsletter. **Circulation:** 5,000 ● *Report to Rome*, annual ● Annual Report, annual ● Currently preparing a prayerbook. **Conventions/Meetings:** annual meeting.

19326 ■ Tekakwitha Conference National Center (TCNC)
PO Box 6768
Great Falls, MT 59406-6768
Ph: (406)727-0147
Free: (800)842-9635

Fax: (406)452-9845
E-mail: tekconf@att.net
URL: http://www.tekconf.org
Contact: Kateri Mitchell, Exec. Dir.
Founded: 1939. **Members:** 1,600. **Membership Dues:** international (ages 18-54), $25 (annual) ● ages 55 and over, $20 (annual) ● archdiocese, organization, $50 (annual) ● Kateri Circle, $25 (annual). **Staff:** 3. **Budget:** $100,000. **State Groups:** 40. **Local Groups:** 128. **Description:** Develops Catholic evangelization in the areas of Native American ministry, catechesis, liturgy, family life, ecumenical cooperation, urban ministry, spirituality, and theology. **Libraries: Type:** reference. **Holdings:** 2,000. **Subjects:** scripture, theology, liturgy, religion, Native Americans. **Committees:** Catechesis; Education; Evangelical Liberation; Family; Liturgy; Ministries; Urban Ministry; Youth Ministry. **Publications:** *Cross and Feathers*, quarterly, every January, March, May and November. Newsletter. Provides information on cultural and spiritual, Kateri Circle, and annual conference. **Price:** included in membership dues. **ISSN:** 1538-1021. **Circulation:** 2,000. **Conventions/Meetings:** annual conference, 4-day conference (exhibits) - July/August.

19327 ■ Third Order of Mary/Marists (TOM)
c/o Fr. Albert Dianni, Dir.
27 Isabella St.
Boston, MA 02116-5216
Ph: (617)426-4448
E-mail: smvocations@aol.com
URL: http://users.aol.com/smvocations/marists.htm
Contact: Fr. Albert Dianni, Dir.
Founded: 1854. **Members:** 5,000. **Membership Dues:** laypeople, $5 (annual). **Description:** Laypeople seeking to deepen their apostolic commitment. Associated with the Marist Fathers (Society of Mary), which was founded in 1816. Fosters the religious and spiritual development of its members according to the spirit of the Marist Fathers. **Computer Services:** database ● mailing lists ● online services. **Publications:** *The Marists*, quarterly. Newsletter. **Price:** $15.00/year. **Circulation:** 5,000.

19328 ■ Thomas More Association (TMA)
Address Unknown since 2007
Founded: 1939. **Description:** Nonprofit publishing house dedicated to the advancement of American Roman Catholic education and culture. Named after Sir Thomas More (1478-1535), Catholic layman who became the first nonclergyman to hold the title of Lord Chancellor of England. **Publications:** *The Critic*, quarterly. Journal. Reports on Catholic arts and culture. **Price:** $20.00/year; $32.00/2 years; $6.00/copy. ISSN: 0011-149X. **Circulation:** 3,000. **Advertising:** not accepted. Alternate Formats: microform ● *Markings*, monthly. Newsletter. Provides reflections on Sunday and holy day liturgical readings written by theologians, priests, and other religious and laypeople. **Price:** $37.95/year. **Circulation:** 3,000. **Advertising:** not accepted ● *Overview*, 11/year. Newsletter. Reports on issues of special interest to Catholics. Topics have included women in the church, black Catholics, and homosexuality. **Price:** free to *Markings* subscribers; $15.95/year for others. **Circulation:** 4,000. **Advertising:** not accepted ● *Thomas More Book Club*, monthly. Newsletter. **Circulation:** 6,000. **Advertising:** not accepted ● Also produces and distributes educational materials on topics related to Catholic thought and doctrine.

19329 ■ Ukrainian Patriarchal World Federation (UPWF)
Address Unknown since 2007
Founded: 1974. **Description:** National societies of Ukrainian Catholics from 8 countries. Seeks organizational autonomy of the Ukrainian Catholic Church and recognition of the Ukrainian Patriarchate by the Holy See of Rome. Works to enrich the religious lives of laymen and engage them in ecumenical dialogue. Coordinates activities of Ukrainian Patriarchal societies. Organizes periodical symposia on theological topics. **Publications:** *The Patriarchate*, monthly. **Conventions/Meetings:** triennial meeting ● annual symposium.

19330 ■ United Catholic Music and Video Association (UCMVA)
PO Box 230
Donnellson, IA 52625
Ph: (319)835-9340
Free: (877)66U-CMVA
Fax: (319)835-9071
E-mail: support@ucmva.com
URL: http://www.ucmva.com
Founded: 2000. **Membership Dues:** patron, $1,000 (annual) ● benefactor, $500 (annual) ● premier, $300 (annual) ● professional, $75 (annual) ● stewardship, $25 (annual). **Description:** Artists, producers, arrangers, retail stores, radio stations, concert promoters, dioceses, and parishes. Supports all forms of Catholic-oriented Christian music and video, including liturgical, praise and worship, contemporary and instrumental compositions. **Awards:** Unity Awards. **Frequency:** annual. **Type:** recognition. **Recipient:** for promising albums, artists, videos, songs, and groups. **Publications:** *UCMVA Award Journal* ● *Unity Newsletter*. **Conventions/Meetings:** annual seminar, for members, music professionals, and those who aspire to a career in the Christian music and video industry.

19331 ■ United Hasroun Men's and St. Laba Ladies Charity Societies
Address Unknown since 2007
Description: Works to uphold Articles of Faith pertaining to Catholic Church, particularly Maronite rites; promotes understanding between people of Hasroun heritage.

19332 ■ United States Association of Consecrated Virgins (USACV)
300 W Ottawa St.
Lansing, MI 48933-1577
Fax: (253)270-5507
E-mail: info@consecratedvirgins.org
URL: http://www.consecratedvirgins.org
Contact: Judith Stegman, Pres.
Description: Fosters communication, solidarity and support among consecrated virgins in the United States of America. Encourages in depth growth in the understanding of consecrated virginity. Promotes understanding of the nature of the vocation of consecrated virginity through educational programs, printed materials and other media. **Telecommunication Services:** electronic mail, president@consecratedvirgins.org. **Publications:** *Consecrated Virginity in Today's Church*. Video ● *The Lamp*. Newsletter. Covers news and articles about consecrated virginity. Includes updates concerning the association and its activities. Alternate Formats: online ● Audiotapes.

19333 ■ United States Catholic Mission Association (USCMA)
3029 4th St. NE
Washington, DC 20017-1102
Ph: (202)832-3112
Fax: (202)832-3688
E-mail: uscma@uscatholicmission.org
URL: http://www.uscatholicmission.org
Contact: Michael Montoya MJ, Exec. Dir.
Founded: 1981. **Members:** 850. **Membership Dues:** individual, $40 (annual). **Staff:** 5. **Description:** Individuals, organizations, and groups promoting global mission in community with others, with primary focus on cross-cultural mission and special emphasis on international justice. Compiles statistics on U.S. missionary personnel overseas. **Libraries: Type:** not open to the public. **Holdings:** books. **Subjects:** cross-cultural studies, missiology, mission trends. **Supersedes:** (1981) United States Catholic Mission Council. **Publications:** *Mission Handbook*, annual. Handbooks. Includes statistics. ● *Mission Update*, quarterly. Newsletter ● Newsletter ● Also publishes brochures. **Conventions/Meetings:** annual conference.

19334 ■ United States Conference of Catholic Bishops (USCCB)
3211 4th St. NE
Washington, DC 20017-1194
Ph: (202)541-3000
Fax: (202)541-3322
E-mail: webcoordinator@usccb.org
URL: http://www.usccb.org
Contact: Msgr. David Malloy, Gen. Sec.
Founded: 1966. **Members:** 371. **Staff:** 350. **Budget:** $50,000,000. **Description:** Canonical body through which the Catholic bishops of the U.S., in the words of the Second Vatican Council decree calling for such an organization, "jointly exercise their pastoral office". **Libraries: Type:** reference; by appointment, only. **Holdings:** 12,000; archival material, books, monographs, periodicals. **Telecommunication Services:** hotline, (800)235-7822. **Formed by Merger of:** (2001) National Conference of Catholic Bishops; (2001) United States Catholic Conference. **Conventions/Meetings:** annual assembly - always November, Washington, DC.

19335 ■ Vernacular Society (VS)
Address Unknown since 2006
Founded: 1946. **Members:** 490. **Membership Dues:** individual, $25 (annual). **Budget:** $1,000. **Description:** Roman Catholic clergy and laity. Supports the use of inclusive language where appropriate in scripture and in the liturgy. Loans tapes on liturgy and vernacular topics for discussion by members; offers books and pamphlets for purchase. Maintains speakers' bureau. **Libraries: Type:** reference. **Holdings:** 422; audiovisuals, books. **Subjects:** Liturgy, scripture, translations. **Publications:** *Vernacular*, occasional. Newsletter. **Circulation:** 450. **Advertising:** not accepted. **Conventions/Meetings:** annual meeting.

19336 ■ Volunteer Missionary Movement - U.S. Office (VMM-USA)
5980 W Loomis Rd.
Greendale, WI 53129-1824
Ph: (414)423-8660
Fax: (414)423-8964
E-mail: vmm@vmmusa.org
URL: http://www.vmmusa.org
Contact: Ms. Sandra McCabe, Exec. Dir.
Founded: 1981. **Members:** 175. **Staff:** 3. **Regional Groups:** 3. **Languages:** English, Spanish. **Description:** Represents Christians possessing a needed skill or profession and willing to work within a local Christian community in a developing country. Recruits, selects, prepares, and sends lay missionaries to serve in Africa, Central America, and the U.S. Seeks to aid the Church in America by serving as a bridge between the church and communities in developing countries. Maintains Speaker's Bureau. **Publications:** *Bridges*, quarterly. Newsletter. **Price:** $15.00/year. **Circulation:** 1,500. **Advertising:** accepted ● *Catholic Directory*, annual ● *Christ in the Margins*. Book ● *Psalms of a Laywoman*, periodic. Book ● *Volunteer Missionary Movement, U.S. Office—Newsletter*, bimonthly. Provides news on overseas and returned missionaries of the organization; also includes regional reports. **Price:** $15.00/year. **Advertising:** accepted. **Conventions/Meetings:** biennial general assembly.

19337 ■ Wanderer Forum Foundation (WFF)
PO Box 542
Hudson, WI 54016-0542
Ph: (651)276-1429
E-mail: wandererforum@juno.com
URL: http://www.wandererforum.org
Contact: Dr. Charles E. Rice, Chm.
Founded: 1965. **Members:** 3,000. **Staff:** 1. **Budget:** $100,000. **Description:** Serves as network of Catholic laity seeking to uphold firmly the teaching authority of the Roman Catholic Church vested in the Pope and those Bishops in union with the Pope. Encourages the study of Church teachings, particularly as found in papal encyclicals, Apostolic Exhortations, and Vatican II documents; defends the family as the basic unit of society and parents as the primary educators of their children. Assists in planning regional "forums" or conferences for spiritual growth; provides documentation on issues within the Catholic Church and society; sponsors seminars; conducts positive action programs; operates speakers' bureau. **Publications:** *Forum Focus*, quarterly. Newsletter.

Contains documentation of issues of concern in Catholic Church. **Price:** $16.00/year. **Circulation:** 3,000. **Conventions/Meetings:** annual National Wanderer Forum - conference, with religious books and articles (exhibits).

19338 ■ We Believe!
1899 Pinehurst Ave.
St. Paul, MN 55116-1336
Ph: (651)698-1857
Fax: (651)699-8360
E-mail: webelieve@webelieve.cc
URL: http://www.webelieve.cc
Contact: Edward Foley, Pres.
Founded: 1994. **Members:** 9,000. **Staff:** 1. **Budget:** $10,000. **Description:** Works to promote liturgical renewal among American Roman Catholics. Conducts educational programs. Maintains Speakers' Bureau. **Computer Services:** Mailing lists, of members. **Publications:** Newsletter, quarterly. **Price:** free. **Circulation:** 9,000. Alternate Formats: online. **Conventions/Meetings:** monthly board meeting.

19339 ■ Women for Faith and Family (WFF)
PO Box 300411
St. Louis, MO 63130-0261
Ph: (314)863-8385
Fax: (314)863-5858
E-mail: info@wf-f.org
URL: http://www.wf-f.org
Contact: Mrs. Helen Hull Hitchcock, Exec. Dir.
Founded: 1984. **Members:** 50,000. **Staff:** 4. **Regional Groups:** 8. **State Groups:** 2. **Description:** Catholic women. Assists orthodox Catholic women in "their effort to provide witness to their faith, both to their families, and to the world". Aids women in understanding the Catholic faith and developing fellowship; provides information on church teachings, documents, family celebration of church year through publications and website, lectures, etc. **Libraries: Type:** reference. **Holdings:** 800. **Subjects:** liturgy, feminism, Catholic doctrine, Catholic reference, human life issues, devotional. **Telecommunication Services:** electronic mail, wf-f@wf-f.org. **Publications:** *Advent/Christmas Family Sourcebook* ● *Lent/Easter Family Sourcebook* ● *Voices*, quarterly. Magazine. **Price:** $1.50. **ISSN:** 1066-8136. **Circulation:** 8,000 ● Brochures. **Conventions/Meetings:** periodic meeting.

19340 ■ Women's Ordination Conference (WOC)
PO Box 2693
Fairfax, VA 22031-0693
Ph: (703)352-1006
Fax: (703)352-5181
E-mail: woc@womensordination.org
URL: http://www.womensordination.org
Contact: Ms. Aisha Taylor, Exec. Dir.
Founded: 1975. **Members:** 2,500. **Membership Dues:** regular, $45 (annual) ● international, $50 (annual) ● student/low income, $25 (annual) ● organization, $100 (annual). **Staff:** 3. **Budget:** $140,000. **Local Groups:** 25. **Description:** Supports women who feel called to the Roman Catholic priesthood. Works to create solidarity among participants and to promote the women's ordination movement. Conducts research programs; compiles statistics, organizes public prayerful protests and holds periodic conferences on women's ordination. Members are women and men committed to creating reform within the Catholic Church. Advocates for the full participation of women in church leadership roles. Believes that "equality will only be achieved through the ordination of women to a renewed priestly ministry in a renewed church". **Libraries: Type:** open to the public; by appointment only. **Holdings:** 500; articles, audio recordings, books, video recordings. **Subjects:** feminist theology, biblical women, general theology, Church history, prayer books, feminist liturgy, saints. **Awards:** Bishop Murphy Scholarships. **Frequency:** annual. **Type:** scholarship. **Recipient:** to women enrolled in theology and ministry programs. **Publications:** *Liberating Liturgies*. Book. Contains a collection of feminist liturgies for those seeking "new ways to express God's importance in their lives", unifying women

through prayer. **Price:** $12.00 ● *NewWomen, New-Church*, quarterly. Newsletter. **Price:** included in membership dues; $1.00/copy; $28.00 /year for libraries in U.S.; $38.00 /year for libraries outside U.S. ISSN: 1043-2221. **Circulation:** 4,000 ● Monographs ● Proceedings ● Also publishes promotional materials. **Conventions/Meetings:** periodic meeting (exhibits) - usually in Washington, DC.

Chaplains

19341 ■ American Catholic Correctional Chaplains Association (ACCCA)
c/o Rev. Thomas R. Houle, Treas.
210 W 31st St.
New York, NY 10001
Ph: (212)564-9070
E-mail: info@catholiccorrectionalchaplains.org
URL: http://www.catholiccorrectionalchaplains.org
Contact: Rev. Thomas R. Houle, Treas.
Founded: 1952. **Members:** 250. **Membership Dues:** professional, $40 (annual) ● volunteer/retiree, $20 (annual). **Description:** Catholic priests, religious individuals, deacons, and laity working full or part time in the correctional field; covering federal, state, county, and city penal and correctional institutions. Works to unify and implement the corrective and rehabilitative efforts of the Catholic Church. Fosters a Catholic approach to the problems in the correctional field, emphasizing the spiritual welfare of inmates. **Awards:** Chaplain of the Year Award. **Frequency:** annual. **Type:** recognition ● Maximillian Kolbe Award. **Type:** recognition. **Formed by Merger of:** American Catholic Prison Chaplains Association. **Publications:** *ACCCA Newsletter*, 3/year. Covers topics regarding Catholic prison ministry. **Price:** included in membership dues. **Advertising:** accepted ● *Manual for a Catholic Chaplain in a Correctional Institution*. **Conventions/Meetings:** annual convention, held in conjunction with American Correctional Association - always August.

19342 ■ American Correctional Chaplains Association (ACCA)
c/o Laurie Etter, Sec.
PO Box 422
East Lyme, CT 06333
Ph: (860)691-6549
E-mail: laurietter@aol.com
URL: http://www.correctionalchaplains.org
Contact: Laurie Etter, Sec.
Founded: 1885. **Members:** 900. **Regional Groups:** 6. **Local Groups:** 51. **Description:** Catholic, Jewish, and Protestant chaplains in federal and state prisons, city and county jails, and juvenile institutions. Provides a forum for exchange of ideas. **Affiliated With:** American Catholic Correctional Chaplains Association. **Publications:** *Correctional Chaplains*, periodic. Directory. **Conventions/Meetings:** annual meeting, held in conjunction with American Correctional Association - always August.

19343 ■ Association of Jewish Chaplains of the Armed Forces (AJCAF)
15 E 26th St., Rm. 1014
New York, NY 10010-1579
Ph: (212)532-4949
Fax: (212)481-4174
E-mail: info@jcca.org
Contact: Rabbi Victor Solomon, Pres.
Members: 800. **Membership Dues:** $10 (annual). **Description:** Present and former Jewish chaplains in the American Armed Forces. **Awards:** Chaplain of the Year. **Frequency:** annual. **Type:** recognition. **Publications:** *Chaplines*. Newsletter. **Conventions/Meetings:** annual meeting.

19344 ■ Association of Professional Chaplains (APC)
1701 E Woodfield Rd., Ste.400
Schaumburg, IL 60173
Ph: (847)240-1014
Fax: (847)240-1015

E-mail: info@professionalchaplains.org
URL: http://www.professionalchaplains.org
Contact: Josephine Schrader, Exec. Dir.
Founded: 1946. **Members:** 3,800. **Staff:** 5. **Budget:** $850,000. **Description:** Ordained clergy or full-time non-ordained ministers serving as chaplains or in a similar capacity, in any setting, who have a B.A., B.D., or M.D. degree and are endorsed as chaplains by their faith group; other persons may hold affiliate membership. Members who are certified chaplains hold status as Board Certified Chaplains of the college. Aims to serve as a means of ecumenical cooperation in chaplaincy matters; to provide a professional identity for chaplains and to interpret their role to other disciplines in the health care field; to provide for the effective communication and sharing of information to promote excellence in pastoral care through high standards and continuing education. Promotes and assists in establishing chaplaincy programs in institutions; conducts research and provides publication of findings by chaplains; publishes literature and papers designed to assist chaplains in their work and to contribute toward the development of a body of literature on pastoral care. Includes services and programs such as: consultation with individuals and institutions; coordination and information on chaplaincy matters; staff studies; liaison with other organizations and agencies. **Libraries: Type:** not open to the public. **Holdings:** books. **Subjects:** pastoral care, ethics. **Awards:** Distinguished Service Award. **Frequency:** annual. **Type:** recognition. **Recipient:** for outstanding contributions in ministry, teaching, or research. **Formerly:** (1968) Chaplains Association of the American Protestant Hospital Association; (1991) College of Chaplains; (1998) College of Chaplains. **Publications:** *APC News*, bimonthly. Newsletter ● *Chaplain as Administrator* ● *Chaplaincy Today*, semiannual. Journal ● *Pastoral Ministry in the AIDS Era*. **Conventions/Meetings:** annual seminar (exhibits).

19345 ■ Christian Chaplain Services (CCS)
PO Box 86307
Los Angeles, CA 90086-0307
Ph: (213)353-9435
Fax: (213)353-9436
Contact: Ron Murray, Business Mgr.
Founded: 1926. **Staff:** 62. **Description:** Chaplains and volunteers who counsel, minister to, and conduct chapel services for prison inmates in order to introduce them to Jesus Christ and accomplish "rehabilitation through regeneration." Operates in California and Mexico. Holds training seminars for correctional chaplains and church pastors on prison visitation and counseling. **Formerly:** (1988) Christian Jail Workers. **Publications:** *Broken Shackles*, semiannual. Newsletter. **Price:** free. **Conventions/Meetings:** annual banquet (exhibits) - held at Hollywood Presbyterian Mears Center; **Avg. Attendance:** 300.

19346 ■ CREDO
PO Box 788160
Twentynine Palms, CA 92278-8160
Ph: (760)830-4989 (760)725-4954
Free: (877)548-5407
Fax: (760)725-4991
E-mail: woodg@29palms.usmc.mil
URL: http://www.29palms.usmc.mil/misc/credo
Contact: Lt. Thomas Smith, Contact
Founded: 1971. **Members:** 2,400. **Staff:** 6. **Description:** Clients are active or retired personnel of the Sea Services (USN, USMC, USCG) and their family members. Provides workshops and retreats that address a variety of problems, including personal conflicts, substance abuse, and parenting difficulties. Seeks to create an atmosphere where maximum personal and spiritual growth can occur in a short time. Promotes continued growth in interpersonal skills. Conducts retreat programs and discussion groups. (CREDO stands for Chaplains Religious Enrichment Development Operation.). **Libraries: Type:** not open to the public. **Computer Services:** Mailing lists, of members. **Publications:** *The Lighthouse*, monthly. Newsletter.

19347 ■ Federation of Fire Chaplains (FFC)
185 County Rd., No. 1602
Clifton, TX 76634
Ph: (254)622-8514
E-mail: chapdir1@aol.com
URL: http://www.firechaplains.org
Contact: Ed Stauffer, Exec. Dir.
Founded: 1978. **Members:** 250. **Membership Dues:** individual, $75 (annual). **Regional Groups:** 6. **Multinational. Description:** Chaplains who work with fire and emergency workers on a paid or volunteer basis. Fosters fellowship among members. Conducts family life seminars; sponsors stress debriefing program for emergency workers, fire chaplains institute for basic and advanced training. **Formerly:** (1992) Fellowship of Fire Chaplains. **Publications:** Newsletter, semiannual. **Conventions/Meetings:** annual seminar.

19348 ■ International Conference of Police Chaplains (ICPC)
PO Box 5590
Destin, FL 32540-5590
Ph: (850)654-9736
Fax: (850)654-9742
E-mail: icpc@icpc.gccoxmail.com
URL: http://www.icpc4cops.org
Contact: Chaplain Rickey Hargrave, Sec.
Founded: 1973. **Members:** 2,700. **Membership Dues:** individual, $125 (annual). **Staff:** 7. **Budget:** $402,100. **Regional Groups:** 21. **Multinational. Description:** Individuals who are or have been law enforcement chaplains (2590); professionals with an interest in chaplaincy. Promotes law enforcement chaplaincy. Provides a forum for the sharing of information. Assists law enforcement agencies in establishing chaplaincy programs. **Libraries: Type:** reference; not open to the public. **Awards:** John A. Price Award for Excellency in Chaplaincy. **Frequency:** annual. **Type:** recognition. **Recipient:** for chaplains doing an outstanding job in their own departments. **Committees:** Continuing Education; Credentials. **Publications:** *Directory of Law Enforcement Chaplains*, periodic. **Price:** included in membership dues ● Journal, quarterly. **Price:** included in membership dues. **Advertising:** accepted ● Handbook. **Conventions/Meetings:** annual seminar, training ● workshop.

19349 ■ JWB Jewish Chaplains Council (JWBJCC)
520 Eighth Ave.
New York, NY 10018
Ph: (212)532-4949
Fax: (212)481-4174
E-mail: info@jcca.org
URL: http://www.jcca.org/jwb
Contact: Rabbi Harold Robinson, Dir.
Founded: 1941. **Members:** 16. **Description:** Representatives from the Central Conference of American Rabbis, the Rabbinical Assembly, and the Rabbinical Council of America (see separate entries). In accordance with U.S. Government regulations, certifies the legitimate ordination of rabbis serving as chaplains in the U.S. Armed Forces and Veterans Administration medical centers. Recruits rabbis to serve as chaplains; provides materials and assistance to rabbinical chaplains and certified Jewish lay leaders. **Formerly:** (1986) Commission on Jewish Chaplaincy. **Publications:** *Chaplines*, quarterly. Newsletter. Alternate Formats: online ● Also publishes pamphlets. **Conventions/Meetings:** annual meeting - always January/February.

19350 ■ Military Chaplains Association of the U.S.A. (MCA)
PO Box 7056
Arlington, VA 22207-7056
Ph: (703)533-5890
Fax: (703)533-5890
E-mail: chaplains@mca-usa.org
URL: http://www.mca-usa.org
Contact: Chaplain Gary Pollitt, Exec. Dir.
Founded: 1925. **Members:** 1,750. **Membership Dues:** regular, associate, $50 (annual). **Staff:** 2. **Budget:** $165,000. **Local Groups:** 20. **Description:** Advocates religious freedom, access, and free exercise

in the Armed Services and Department of Veterans Affairs. Promotes cooperative ministry in order to advance and safeguard the religious rights and needs of all personnel. Represents chaplains of all faiths in the U.S. Army, Navy, and Air Force, Department of Veterans Affairs, and Civil Air Patrol who are on active duty, in the reserves, or retired. Maintains a platform for Joint and inter-agency collaboration and ministry development. Provides information and referral service for inquiries on chaplaincy, chaplains, and religious expression in the Armed Services and Veterans Affairs Department. Participates in The Military Coalition. Promotes the concept and commitment of "chaplaincy" as a calling for life whether in or out of uniform. **Awards:** Chaplain Candidate Scholarship. **Frequency:** annual. **Type:** scholarship. **Recipient:** for chaplain candidates of military services who are enrolled in seminary programs ● Distinguished Service Award. **Frequency:** annual. **Type:** recognition. **Recipient:** to chaplains from the armed services, department of veterans affairs, and civil air patrol ● National Citizenship Award. **Frequency:** annual. **Type:** recognition. **Recipient:** for distinguished leader for their contribution to the welfare of men and women in the armed services, veterans, and their families. **Boards:** Executive Oversight. **Committees:** Nominating; Scholarship. **Formerly:** (1940) Chaplains' Association of U.S. **Publications:** *The Military Chaplain*, bimonthly. Magazine. Includes chapter news, list of new members, and obituaries. **Price:** included in membership dues; $12.00 /year for nonmembers; $30.00/3 years, for libraries. ISSN: 0026-3958. **Circulation:** 1,750. **Advertising:** accepted. **Conventions/Meetings:** annual National Institute - conference and convention (exhibits) - usually April.

19351 ■ National Association of Catholic Chaplains (NACC)
5007 S Howell Ave., Ste.120
Milwaukee, WI 53207-6159
Ph: (414)483-4898
Fax: (414)483-6712
E-mail: info@nacc.org
URL: http://www.nacc.org
Contact: Kathy Eldridge, Dir. of Operations
Founded: 1965. **Members:** 3,400. **Membership Dues:** full, $235-$310 (annual) ● inactive, $95-$150 (annual) ● missionary, $55 (annual) ● emeritus, $45 (annual) ● affiliate, $100 (annual) ● student affiliate, $40 (annual). **Staff:** 9. **Description:** Represents catholic priests, deacons, religious, and laypersons who are chaplains in all types of health care and other institutional facilities throughout the country. Provides clinical pastoral education programs for priests, deacons, religious, and laypersons in accredited centers. Certifies chaplains and supervisors. **Awards:** Distinguished Service Award. **Frequency:** annual. **Type:** recognition. **Recipient:** for individuals making significant contributions to health care chaplaincy ● Outstanding Colleague Award. **Frequency:** annual. **Type:** recognition. **Recipient:** for individuals making significant contributions to health care chaplaincy. **Computer Services:** Mailing lists. **Commissions:** Certification. **Publications:** *Vision*, 10/year. Journal. Outlines certification requirements; contains book reviews, articles on chaplaincy, obituaries, convention highlights, and information on employment. **Price:** included in membership dues; $44.00 /year for nonmembers. ISSN: 1527-2370. **Circulation:** 3,900. Alternate Formats: online. **Conventions/Meetings:** annual convention (exhibits).

19352 ■ National Catholic Conference of Airport Chaplains (NCCAC)
c/o United States Conference of Catholic Bishops
Chicago O'Hare Intl. Airport
PO Box 66353
Chicago, IL 60666
Ph: (773)686-2636 (773)686-2255
E-mail: ordchapel@aol.com
URL: http://www.usccb.org/mrs/pcmr/onmove/airport.
shtml
Founded: 1986. **Members:** 30. **Membership Dues:** pastoral or associate, $25 (annual). **Local Groups:** 19. **Description:** Trains and provides support to Ro-

man Catholics ministering to airport travelers and workers. Encourages communication among airport ministers; seeks to expand airport chaplaincy to all major airports in the U.S. Accredits and certifies individuals for airport chaplaincy. **Affiliated With:** United States Conference of Catholic Bishops. **Publications:** *National Catholic Conference of Airport Chaplains—Newsletter*, bimonthly. **Price:** included in membership dues. **Circulation:** 50 ● Directory, annual. Includes listing of all Catholic airport chapels and chaplaincies in the United States. **Price:** $50.00 for nonmembers ● Proceedings, annual. **Conventions/Meetings:** annual conference and meeting.

19353 ■ Pediatric Chaplains Network (PCN)
c/o Chaplain Karen Black, Sec.-Treas.
Our Children's House at Baylor
3301 Swiss Ave.
Dallas, TX 75204
E-mail: karenbl@baylorhealth.edu
URL: http://www.pediatricchaplains.org
Contact: Chaplain Karen Black, Sec.-Treas.
Founded: 1997. **Membership Dues:** regular, $50 (annual). **Multinational. Description:** Represents pediatric chaplains and others interested in promoting the spiritual care of children and families in healthcare. Sponsors an annual 3-day Chaplains Forum, held in various US cities. Provides an email list-serve for sharing questions and ideas for ministry. **Conventions/Meetings:** annual conference, with presentations on topics of interest and for improving the ministry, held in various cities.

19354 ■ Race Track Chaplaincy of America (RTCA)
PO Box 91640
Los Angeles, CA 90009-1640
Ph: (310)419-1640
Fax: (310)419-1642
E-mail: etorres@racetrackchaplaincy.org
URL: http://www.racetrackchaplaincy.org
Contact: Dr. Enrique Torres, Exec. Dir.
Founded: 1971. **Members:** 100. **Staff:** 50. **Regional Groups:** 7. **State Groups:** 24. **Languages:** English, Spanish. **Description:** Provides religious and social services to persons concerned with horse racing tracks. Sponsors drug and alcohol abuse programs. Holds Bible studies. Conducts charitable program. **Awards: Type:** scholarship. **Publications:** *Insiders Newsletter*, monthly. Covers association activities. **Price:** available to chaplains and board members only. **Advertising:** accepted ● *Winner's Circle*, quarterly. Newsletter. **Price:** free. **Circulation:** 1,300. Alternate Formats: online. **Conventions/Meetings:** annual board meeting (exhibits) - usually January or February ● annual seminar.

Child Welfare

19355 ■ Operation Kid-To-Kid
1820 Jet Stream Dr.
Colorado Springs, CO 80921
Ph: (719)867-2678
E-mail: landerson@usa.ibs.org
URL: http://www.ok2k.org
Contact: LaReau Anderson, Contact
Multinational. Description: Works to create hands-on service projects for children in North America.

Children

19356 ■ International Network of Children's Ministry (INCM)
PO Box 190
Castle Rock, CO 80104
Ph: (303)660-6626
Free: (800)324-4543
Fax: (303)660-6444
URL: http://www.incm.org
Contact: Daryl Bursch, Exec. Dir.
Founded: 1980. **Multinational. Description:** Represents the interests of individuals committed to elevat-

ing ministry to children worldwide. Works to train, encourage, motivate, network and resource Christian leaders who minister to children. **Publications:** *Children's Ministry Newsletter*. **Price:** free. Alternate Formats: online.

Christian

19357 ■ African Peoples' Christian Organization
415 Atlantic Ave.
Brooklyn, NY 11217
Ph: (718)596-1991
Fax: (718)625-3410
Contact: Rev. Herbert Daughtry, Pres.
Founded: 1983. **Members:** 30. **Membership Dues:** individual, $60 (annual). **Staff:** 12. **Regional Groups:** 5. **State Groups:** 5. **Local Groups:** 1. **National Groups:** 5. **Description:** Individuals of African descent who follow the Christian belief system. Promotes human rights and the development and advancement of institutions through affirmation of the African heritage and preservation of traditional Christian beliefs. Seeks to create an African Christian nation. Conducts education and research programs. Operates radio station. **Libraries: Type:** reference. **Holdings:** 100; archival material, audio recordings, books, video recordings. **Subjects:** African culture. **Awards:** Man/Woman of the Year. **Frequency:** annual. **Type:** recognition. **Recipient:** for community service contributions. **Telecommunication Services:** electronic bulletin board. **Divisions:** Borough Chapters; Broadcasts; College; Community Awareness; Enterprises; Lecture Series; Nation Time Rallies; Prison Ministry; Research; Timbuktu Learning Center; Voting Block. **Publications:** *Horizon*, quarterly. Newsletter. **Price:** free. **Circulation:** 2,000. **Conventions/Meetings:** monthly meeting (exhibits).

19358 ■ Alliance for Life Ministries (AFLM)
PO Box 5468
Madison, WI 53705
Ph: (608)833-5569
Fax: (608)833-8278
E-mail: ministry@allianceforlifeministries.org
URL: http://www.alliance4lifemin.org
Contact: Paul Lagan, Pres.
Description: Promotes the sanctity of all human life from a biblical and biological perspective in order to provide a "spiritual awakening" in the nation and the community.

19359 ■ American Council of Christian Churches (ACCC)
PO Box 5455
Bethlehem, PA 18015-0455
Ph: (610)865-3009
Fax: (610)865-3033
E-mail: accc@juno.com
URL: http://www.amcouncilcc.org
Contact: Dr. Ralph G. Colas, Exec. Sec.
Founded: 1941. **Members:** 1,508,771. **State Groups:** 49. **Description:** Comprised of major religious denominations including Bible Presbyterian Churches, Evangelical Methodist Churches, Fellowship of Fundamental Bible Churches, Free Presbyterian Churches of North America, Fundamental Methodist Churches, General Association of Regular Baptist Churches, Independent Baptist Fellowship of North America, Independent Churches Affiliated, and hundreds of independent churches. Promotes fellowship and cooperation among "Bible-believing" churches. (Member churches believe in the "inspiration and inerrancy of Scripture; the triune God; the virgin birth; substitutionary death and resurrection of Christ and His second coming; total depravity of man; salvation by grace through faith; and the necessity of maintaining the purity of the church in doctrine and life"). **Libraries: Type:** reference. **Subjects:** religious research. **Awards:** Contender's Award. **Type:** recognition. **Recipient:** for men who have made outstanding contributions to ACCC's cause ● **Type:** recognition. **Recipient:** for college students/for best paper on a selected subject. **Commissions:** Chaplaincy;

Education; Laymen; Literature; Missions; Radio, Audio and Visual; Relief; Youth. **Publications:** *Fundamental News Service*, bimonthly. Newsletter. Covers major issues facing the church today; provides information on political and social developments that affect Christians. Includes book reviews. **Price:** free. **Circulation:** 15,000 ● Reports. Alternate Formats: online. **Conventions/Meetings:** annual convention (exhibits) - always fall.

19360 ■ American and Foreign Christian Union (AFCU)
475 Riverside Dr., Ste.2050
New York, NY 10015
Ph: (203)797-9447
Fax: (203)790-0670
E-mail: afcupresident@afcubridge.org
URL: http://www.afcubridge.org
Contact: Gregg Foster, Pres.
Founded: 1849. **Members:** 25. **Budget:** $100,000. **Description:** Ministers, businessmen, and women who have had some connection with the American churches in Paris, France and Berlin, Germany. Administers endowment and trust funds for the American church in Paris and the American church in Berlin; maintains the American church in Paris, providing a minister for the church when needed. **Committees:** Berlin; Development; Finance. **Publications:** *Paris Connection*, quarterly. Newsletter. **Circulation:** 800. **Conventions/Meetings:** annual board meeting - spring.

19361 ■ American TFP (ATFP)
PO Box 251
Spring Grove, PA 17362
Free: (888)317-5571
Fax: (717)225-7382
E-mail: tfp@tfp.org
URL: http://www.tfp.org
Contact: Raymond E. Drake, Pres.
Founded: 1973. **Members:** 3,075. **Staff:** 60. **Budget:** $4,500,000. **Regional Groups:** 6. **Description:** Works to enlighten public opinion on the values of the religious and cultural heritage of Christian civilization. Stresses the importance of youth programs and other programs dealing with the family and related sociological issues. Promotes research and the cultural and intellectual development of individuals and institutions through grants and scholarships. Conducts America Needs Fatima Campaign. Sponsors advertisements of public interest and supports cultural exchange program. Conducts research on sociocultural issues. Offers lecture tours; sponsors summer and winter youth programs annually; holds regional seminars. **Libraries: Type:** not open to the public. **Holdings:** 10,000. **Subjects:** history, sociology, philosophy, theology, religion, non-fiction. **Computer Services:** Mailing lists. **Absorbed:** (1992) American Society for the Defense of Tradition, Family and Property. **Formerly:** (1999) Foundation for a Christian Civilization. **Publications:** *Crusade Magazine*, bimonthly. Covers religious topics and activities related to the organization. **Price:** free. **Circulation:** 70,000. Alternate Formats: online ● Books ● Brochures ● Also publishes special studies. **Conventions/Meetings:** annual conference.

19362 ■ American Vision
PO Box 220
Powder Springs, GA 30127
Ph: (770)222-7266
Free: (800)628-9460
Fax: (770)222-7269
E-mail: mail@americanvision.org
URL: http://www.americanvision.org
Contact: Gary DeMar, Pres.
Founded: 1978. **Staff:** 6. **Description:** Works to supply Christians of all denominations the spiritual and educational tools they need to become comprehensive biblical thinkers. **Publications:** *Biblical Worldview*, monthly. Newsletter. **Circulation:** 4,500. Alternate Formats: online ● *To Pledge Allegiance*. Books. Contains history textbook series targeted for junior high and above. ● Articles. Alternate Formats: online.

19363 ■ Association of Christian Therapists (ACT)
6728 Old McLean Village Dr.
McLean, VA 22101
Ph: (703)556-9222
Fax: (703)556-8729
E-mail: actheals@degnon.org
URL: http://www.actheals.org
Contact: Forrest Yanke, Pres.
Description: Health Care professionals and associates in physical, mental and spiritual health care disciplines who are committed to Jesus Christ. Works to create environments in which health care professionals and associates can grow spiritually, experience physical, mental, emotional, relational and spiritual healing, establish mutually and spiritually supportive relationships with other health care professionals and associates. Educates and train. **Publications:** *Inter ACT*, monthly. Newsletter. Contains a variety of educational and spiritual articles and editorials. Alternate Formats: online.

19364 ■ Association of Christians in the Mathematical Sciences (ACMS)
c/o Dr. Robert Brabenec, Exec. Sec.
Dept. of Mathematics
Wheaton Coll.
501 Coll. Ave.
Wheaton, IL 60187
Ph: (630)752-5869
E-mail: robert.l.brabenec@wheaton.edu
URL: http://www.acmsonline.org
Contact: Dr. Robert Brabenec, Exec. Sec.
Founded: 1985. **Members:** 400. **Membership Dues:** regular, $30 (biennial) ● student, retired, $15 (biennial). **Description:** Works to encourage Christians in mathematical sciences to explore relationships with their faith and their discipline. **Publications:** *Bibliography of Christianity and Mathematics* ● *Conference Proceedings*. Contains the proceedings of the first 13 conferences. ● Newsletter. **Conventions/Meetings:** biennial conference - odd-numbered years; usually in May ● annual dinner and lecture, in conjunction with January meetings of AMS and MAA.

19365 ■ Brothers and Sisters in Christ (BASIC)
PO Box 431
Kiln, MS 39556
Ph: (228)255-9251
Fax: (228)255-8927
E-mail: basic@basicministries.com
URL: http://www.basicministries.com
Contact: Henry Pulsifer, Exec. Off.
Founded: 1987. **Staff:** 2. **Multinational. Description:** Christians. Provides ministry training; disseminates information on evangelization. **Publications:** Also publishes gospel tracts and Bible studies.

19366 ■ Center for Christian Studies (CCS)
c/o Fifth Ave. Presbyterian Church
7 W 55th St.
New York, NY 10019
Ph: (212)247-0490
E-mail: rnelson@fapc.org
URL: http://www.christianstudies.org
Contact: Ruth Nelson, Contact
Founded: 1981. **Staff:** 3. **Description:** Works to successfully relate the Christian faith to contemporary life. Defends Christianity against political repression and rhetorical distortions. Provides a base for individuals who have not been drawn to the political and theological extremes. Directs an educational movement focused on secondary and postsecondary schools. Fosters clear thinking on issues that Christians must face in their reflections on the human condition. Provides support for members' work and forum for discussion of ideas and issues shaping the thought and course of contemporary society. Operates Trinity Schools. **Publications:** none.

19367 ■ Center for Organizational and Ministry Development (COMD)
PO Box 49488
Colorado Springs, CO 80949
Ph: (719)590-8808
Fax: (719)590-1818
E-mail: comd@earthlink.net
URL: http://www.comd.org
Contact: Thomas M. Graham PhD, Pres./Founder
Description: Seeks to identify and equip North American and cross-cultural church planters; assist individuals in personal assessment, career development, and ministry enhancement; provides support services to church growth and extension process; assists Christian agencies and groups in organizational development. **Publications:** *Business as Usual in the Missions Enterprise*. Book. **Price:** $13.00 ● *Passing the Baton: Church Planting That Empowers*. Book. **Price:** $17.00 plus shipping and handling ($4.50), California residents add $1.31 sales tax ● *Reconnecting God's Story to Ministry: Crosscultural Storytelling at Home and Abroad*. Book. **Price:** $13.00.

19368 ■ Christian Action Network (CAN)
PO Box 606
Forest, VA 24551-0606
Ph: (434)237-8201
Free: (800)835-5795
E-mail: can@christianaction.org
URL: http://www.christianaction.org
Contact: Martin Mawyer, Pres./Founder
Founded: 1990. **Description:** Promotes pro-family issues and advocates traditional American principles of religious liberty, public virtue and good government.

19369 ■ Christian Business Men's Committee (CBMC)
PO Box 8009
Chattanooga, TN 37414-0009
Ph: (423)698-4444
Free: (800)566-CBMC
Fax: (423)629-4434
E-mail: poneal@cbmc.com
URL: http://www.cbmc.com
Contact: Patrick O'Neal, Exec. Dir./Chief Operating Off.
Founded: 1930. **Members:** 50,000. **Staff:** 75. **Budget:** $5,400,000. **Local Groups:** 650. **Description:** Serves as committees for businessmen of various religious denominations and from different metropolitan areas of the country working together "to present Jesus Christ as Savior and Lord to business and professional men and to develop Christian business and professional men to carry out the great commission." Members and guests meet together for meals, in workplace settings, in homes and in informal gatherings to discuss the realities and principles of biblical truth in the contemporary business world. **Formerly:** (1976) Christian Business Men's Committee International. **Publications:** *CB*, quarterly. Newsletter. Includes information and articles about CBMC ministry, schedule of events and obituaries, publication for members and ministry supporters. **Circulation:** 19,000 ● *Christian Business Men's Committee of U.S.A.—Contact Quarterly*. Magazine. Includes book reviews. **Price:** free for members; $12.95 /year for nonmembers. ISSN: 0890-0442. **Circulation:** 25,000. **Advertising:** accepted. **Conventions/Meetings:** annual Men's Conference (exhibits) - always fall or winter.

19370 ■ Christian Century Foundation (CCF)
104 S Michigan Ave., Ste.700
Chicago, IL 60603-5943
Ph: (312)263-7510
Fax: (312)263-7540
E-mail: main@christiancentury.org
URL: http://www.christiancentury.org
Contact: David Heim, Exec. Dir.
Founded: 1884. **Staff:** 12. **Description:** Represents Board of 20 trustees made up of clergy and laity. Interprets contemporary issues from a Christian perspective. Publishes The Christian Century magazine. **Computer Services:** Mailing lists. **Affiliated With:** Associated Church Press. **Publications:** *The Christian Century*, 26/year. Journal. Contains information on religion in relationship to public affairs, culture, the arts, and moral issues. Includes book reviews. **Price:** $49.00/year; $89.00 for 2 years; $119.00 for 3 years. ISSN: 0009-5281. **Circulation:** 30,000. **Adver-**

tising: accepted. **Alternate Formats:** microform; on-line. **Conventions/Meetings:** annual dinner, one-day event - held in September.

19371 ■ Christian Chiropractors Association (CCA)

2550 Stover, No. B-102
Fort Collins, CO 80525
Ph: (970)482-1404
Free: (800)999-1970
Fax: (970)482-1538
E-mail: carlas@christianchiropractors.org
URL: http://www.christianchiropractors.org
Contact: Carla M. Swihart, Admin.

Founded: 1953. **Members:** 1,250. **Staff:** 4. **Regional Groups:** 6. **Description:** Works to spread the Gospel of Christ throughout the U.S. and abroad. Offers Christian fellowship and works to unify Christian chiropractors around the essentials of the faith, "leaving minor points of doctrine to the conscience of the individual believer." Focuses on world missions; organizing short-term trips and aiding in the placement of Christian chiropractors as missionaries. **Libraries: Type:** reference; not open to the public. **Subjects:** ethics, clinical issues. **Awards:** Chiropractor of the Year Award. **Frequency:** annual. **Type:** recognition. **Recipient:** for a CCA member ● Spouse of the Year Award. **Frequency:** annual. **Type:** recognition. **Recipient:** for the spouse of a CCA member. **Committees:** Home Office; Mission; Nominating. **Publications:** *The Christian Chiropractor Bulletin,* bimonthly. Covers news events. **Circulation:** 1,500 ● *The Christian Chiropractor Journal,* bimonthly ● *Membership Registry,* annual. **Conventions/Meetings:** annual convention.

19372 ■ Christian Communications, Inc. (CCI)

9600 Bellaire Blvd., No. 111
Houston, TX 77036
Ph: (713)778-1155
Free: (800)778-8482
Fax: (713)778-9977
E-mail: cci-usa@cc-us.org
URL: http://www.cc-us.org/usa/default.htm
Contact: Kerry Yung, Contact

Founded: 1981. **Staff:** 4. **Budget:** $150,000. **Description:** Seeks to promote the ministry of God's word through religious publications and cassette tape recordings. **Convention/Meeting:** none. **Libraries: Type:** not open to the public. **Holdings:** 4,000. **Subjects:** religious, research. **Computer Services:** Mailing lists, word processing. **Supersedes:** Defenders of the Christian Faith. **Publications:** *Devotional Letter,* monthly. Newsletter. Contains religious teachings. **Price:** free. ISSN: 0279-1196. **Circulation:** 3,000 ● Also publishes list of books, tracts, and pamphlets available.

19373 ■ Christian Crusade (CC)

Address Unknown since 2006
Founded: 1948. **Members:** 20,000. **Staff:** 4. **Description:** Christian educational ministry whose purposes are "to safeguard and preserve the conservative Christian ideals upon which America was founded; to protect our cherished freedoms, the heritage of every American"; to oppose persons or organizations who endorse socialist or communist philosophies and to expose publicly the infiltration of such influences into American life; as well as to defend the gospel of Jesus Christ. Opposes U.S. participation in the UN, "federal interference in schools, housing and other matters constitutionally belonging to the states," and government competition with private business. Sponsors Good Samaritan Children's Foundation, a worldwide ministry operating and supporting orphanages, schools, leprosy clinics, and ministers in 4 countries. Founded David Livingstone Missionary Foundation. **Libraries: Type:** reference. **Holdings:** 8,000. **Formerly:** Christian Echoes National Ministry. **Publications:** *Christian Crusade Newspaper,* monthly. Covers Christian topics and current events from a conservative perspective. **Price:** $5.00/year. **Circulation:** 15,000. **Advertising:** not accepted ● Books.

19374 ■ Christian Defense League (CDL)

PO Box 9166
Mandeville, LA 70470-9166
Ph: (601)749-8565
Fax: (601)749-8565
E-mail: information@cdlreport.com
URL: http://www.cdlreport.com
Contact: James K. Warner, Ed.

Founded: 1964. **Members:** 15,000. **Staff:** 4. **Regional Groups:** 52. **State Groups:** 52. **Description:** Promotes the preservation of traditional Christian values and the development of Christian public leaders in the U.S. Conducts educational and research programs. Operates speakers' bureau. **Libraries: Type:** reference. **Holdings:** 5,000; archival material. **Publications:** *CDL Report,* monthly. Magazine. **Price:** $35.00/year ● *Christian Vanguard,* monthly. Magazine ● Books. **Conventions/Meetings:** biennial meeting.

19375 ■ Christian Family Renewal (CFR)

c/o Michael Norris
Box 73
Clovis, CA 93613
Ph: (559)347-9324
Contact: Michael Norris, Pres.

Founded: 1970. **Members:** 5,000. **Staff:** 4. **Budget:** $25,000. **Description:** Christians concerned with problems of the modern family. Promotes Christian solutions to problems in business, and education counseling. Sponsors home study programs in Christian counseling and nutrition. **Libraries: Type:** not open to the public. **Computer Services:** Information services, counseling agencies and individuals. **Divisions:** Catholic Fraternity for Restoration. **Publications:** *Jesus And Mary Are Calling You,* annual. Newsletter ● Books ● Pamphlets. Report on pornography, homosexuality, Satanism, and abortion. **Conventions/Meetings:** annual meeting.

19376 ■ Christian Herald Association (CHA)

c/o The Bowery Mission
132 Madison Ave.
New York, NY 10016-7004
Ph: (212)684-2800
Fax: (212)684-3740
E-mail: info@chaonline.org
URL: http://www.chaonline.org
Contact: Edward H. Morgan, Pres.

Founded: 1878. **Staff:** 100. **Description:** Christian organization committed to "preaching the good news of Jesus Christ and obeying Christ's call to help those in need." Operates the Bowery Mission to provide homeless men, substance abusers, and inmates with food, clothing, and the chance to begin a new, Christian life. Operates Kids With A Promise, which introduces disadvantaged urban youth to Christ, and offers them encouragement and counsel through a year-round program that begins with a stay at Mont Lawn youth camp and includes programs of development through tutoring, home and school visits, and group-centered activities at after-school centers guided by trained counselors. **Convention/Meeting:** none.

19377 ■ Christian Holiness Partnership (CHP)

263 Buffalo Rd.
Clinton, TN 37716
Ph: (423)457-5978
Fax: (865)463-7280
URL: http://www.faithandvalues.com/fg_profiles/christian_holiness.asp
Contact: Dr. Marlin Hotle, Exec. Dir.

Founded: 1867. **Members:** 5,000. **Membership Dues:** regular, $35 (annual). **Staff:** 4. **Budget:** $150,000. **For-Profit. Description:** Religious denominations, missionary organizations, and individuals who "accept the inspiration and infallibility" of the Scriptures. Seeks "to promote cooperation among bodies embracing Wesleyan theological distinctiveness". **Awards:** Holiness Exponent. **Frequency:** annual. **Type:** recognition. **Recipient:** for outstanding published works or leadership contributions. **Commissions:** Camp Meeting; Christian Social Action; Evangelism; Higher Education; Missions; Wesleyan

Theological Society; Women's; Youth. **Formerly:** (1999) Christian Holiness Association. **Publications:** *Holiness Digest,* quarterly. Magazine. Serves as a "vehicle for amplification of the message of biblical holiness and is the voice of the CHP to promote its purposes". **Price:** included in membership dues; $10.00 /year for nonmembers. ISSN: 1040-8584. **Circulation:** 12,000. **Advertising:** accepted. Alternate Formats: online ● *News in the CHP World,* periodic. Newsletter ● Also publishes doctrinal position classics. **Conventions/Meetings:** annual International Convention.

19378 ■ Christian Law Association (CLA)

PO Box 4010
Seminole, FL 33775
Ph: (727)399-8300
Fax: (727)398-3907
URL: http://www.christianlaw.org
Contact: Dr. David C. Gibbs Jr., Founder/Pres.

Founded: 1977. **Description:** Provides legal defense, as a ministry to Christians, churches, and ministries in defense of First Amendment rights. Provides updates on how First Amendment rights issues affect the conservative Christian community. Conducts biblical seminars to provide legal education for the layperson and information on how to avoid court cases. **Publications:** *The Legal Alert,* monthly. Newsletter. Contains information concerning legal issues. **Price:** free for members ● *Teacher's Forum,* monthly.

19379 ■ Christian Legal Society (CLS)

8001 Braddock Rd., Ste.300
Springfield, VA 22151-2110
Ph: (703)642-1070
Fax: (703)642-1075
E-mail: clshq@clsnet.org
URL: http://www.clsnet.org
Contact: Samuel B. Casey, Exec. Dir./CEO

Founded: 1961. **Members:** 3,300. **Membership Dues:** attorney, law professor, $175 (annual) ● new attorney, public ministry attorney, campus advisor, $87 (annual) ● law student, $25 (annual) ● judge, judge subscriber, $100 (annual) ● retired attorney, associate, foreign, $50 (annual) ● law student group, $10 (annual). **Staff:** 21. **Budget:** $2,000,000. **Local Groups:** 89. **Description:** Christian attorneys, judges, law professors, law students, paralegals and others committed to proclaiming, loving and serving Jesus Christ in the practice of law; advocates Biblical conflict resolution, religious freedom, and the sanctity of human life. Holds student ministry, conferences, and retreats. **Computer Services:** database ● online services, attorney referrals. **Publications:** *Christian Legal Society—Membership Directory,* annual. Includes members' area of job specialization. **Price:** available to members only ● Books ● Monographs. **Conventions/Meetings:** annual conference (exhibits) - October/November ● meeting.

19380 ■ Christian Military Fellowship (CMF)

PO Box 1207
Englewood, CO 80150-1207
Ph: (303)761-1959
Free: (800)798-7875
Fax: (303)761-4577
E-mail: admin@cmfhq.org
URL: http://www.cmfhq.org
Contact: Bob Flynn, Pres./CEO

Founded: 1977. **Members:** 3,000. **Staff:** 10. **Budget:** $469,000. **Description:** Supports U.S. military personnel and their families, worldwide, with prayer, Bible studies, local fellowships, conferences, referrals, free literature; correspondence, hospitality, and Christian resources. **Formerly:** (1976) Christian Servicemen Fellowship. **Publications:** *Christian Battleplan,* monthly. Serves as a prayer calendar. Alternate Formats: online ● *Christian Report,* quarterly. Newsletter. Alternate Formats: online ● *CMF Directory,* periodic ● Also publishes brochures and educational and devotional literature. **Conventions/Meetings:** periodic conference ● annual convention.

19381 ■ A Christian Ministry in the National Parks (ACMNP)
10 Justin's Way
Freeport, ME 04032
Ph: (207)865-6436
Free: (800)786-3450
Fax: (207)865-6852
E-mail: info@acmnp.com
URL: http://www.acmnp.com
Contact: Dr. Richard P. Camp Jr., Exec. Dir.
Founded: 1946. **Staff:** 6. **Description:** Recommends employment for seminary and college students with private concessionaires operating lodges, inns, restaurants, and stores within national parks; aims to offer students the opportunity to conduct interdenominational worship services and Bible studies for park employees and visitors. **Awards:** Warren Ost Memorial Scholarship. **Frequency:** periodic. **Type:** scholarship. **Recipient:** for seminarians serving on Ministry staff. **Publications:** *Across the Parks*, quarterly. Newsletter. Alternate Formats: online. **Conventions/Meetings:** annual board meeting.

19382 ■ Christian Research (CR)
PO Box 385
Eureka Springs, AR 72632-0385
Ph: (479)253-7185
Fax: (479)253-7185
E-mail: clibrary@ipa.net
URL: http://www.christianresearch.info
Contact: Daniel Gentry, Dir.
Founded: 1958. **Nonmembership. Description:** Works to serve those who do not trust the media or present U.S. public educational system. Seeks useful information concerning the Kingdom of Jesus Christ on this earth. Distributes Christian literature; produces tracts, booklets & books; conducts and encourages Bible research and study. Emphasizes obedience to God and His Word. Opposes Zionism, Communism, personal income taxation, and the United Nations; supports historical revisionism. Acts as a home-schooling resource and arranges speakers. Operates prison ministry. **Libraries: Type:** reference; by appointment only. **Holdings:** 85,000; archival material, audio recordings, books, clippings, periodicals. **Subjects:** Bible study, reference, education, history, health agriculture and survival, law and constitution, economy and theonomy, family matters, Bible archeology, biography, government, earth and natural sciences. **Computer Services:** Information services, data retrieval and searches in subject areas mentioned in listing ● information services, out of print, hard to find. **Formerly:** Pro-American Books. **Publications:** *Children of Light*. Book ● *Cliches of Zoning*. Book ● *Community of Saints*. Book ● *Facts for Action*, quarterly. Newsletter. Covers Christian-Israel news. ● *For the Love (of what passes) For Money*. Book ● *More Light*. Book ● *Satan Dispelled*. Book. **Conventions/Meetings:** seminar.

19383 ■ Christian Research Institute (CRI)
PO Box 8500
Charlotte, NC 28271-8500
Ph: (704)887-8200
Free: (800)228-1563
Fax: (704)887-8299
URL: http://www.equip.org
Contact: Hank Hanegraaff, Pres.
Founded: 1960. **Members:** 5. **Staff:** 50. **Budget:** $10,000,000. **Languages:** English, Portuguese, Russian, Spanish. **Description:** Interdenominational, evangelical, Christian apologetics organization that disseminates information on the cults, the occult, religious movements, ethics, and doctrinal controversies in light of historic, orthodox Christianity. Broadcasts daily, live, call-in radio program, the "Bible Answer Man" which is heard in the U.S. and Canada. "CRI Perspectives" a three-minute radio service announcement on commonly asked apologetic questions is also aired nationwide. **Telecommunication Services:** additional toll-free number, (888)7000-CRI. **Formerly:** (2001) Christian Research Institute International. **Publications:** *Christian Research Journal*, quarterly. Magazine. Specializes in research on the cults, the occult, doctrinal controversies, world religions, and ethics from the perspective of orthodox

Christianity. **Price:** $30.00/year in U.S. and Canada; $60.00/year outside U.S. and Canada; $54.00 per 2-year in U.S. **Circulation:** 40,000. **Advertising:** accepted ● *Christian Research Newsletter*, bimonthly. **Price:** free. **Circulation:** 75,000 ● Articles ● Books.

19384 ■ Christian Restoration Association (CRA)
7133 Central Parke Blvd.
Mason, OH 45040
Ph: (513)229-8000
Free: (877)229-8100
Fax: (513)229-8003
E-mail: thecra@thecra.org
URL: http://www.thecra.org
Contact: H. Lee Mason, Dir.
Founded: 1925. **Staff:** 4. **Description:** Mission agency of the Christian Churches/Churches of Christ. Sponsors evangelistic activities, training programs, and services for local churches and church leaders. Provides adult Bible training by correspondence. **Publications:** *Restoration Herald*, monthly. Magazine. **Price:** $12.00/year; $17.00/year in Canada; $20.00/year in other countries. ISSN: 0034-5830 ● Also publishes teaching tracts. **Conventions/Meetings:** meeting - 3/year.

19385 ■ Christian Seniors Association
139 C St. SE
Washington, DC 20003
Ph: (202)547-4400
Fax: (202)546-6403
E-mail: martin.waugh@christiansenior.org
URL: http://www.christiansenior.org
Contact: Martin E. Waugh DO, Contact
Founded: 2003. **Description:** Religious conservatives over the age of 50 advocating for "all freedoms, rights and liberties granted by God not government". **Publications:** *Faith and Freedom Report* ● *50 Newsletter*.

19386 ■ Citizens for Community Values (CCV)
11175 Reading Rd., Ste.103
Cincinnati, OH 45241-1997
Ph: (513)733-5775
Fax: (513)733-5794
E-mail: info@ccv.org
Contact: Phil Burress, Pres.
Founded: 1983. **Members:** 31,000. **Membership Dues:** individual, family, business, $15 (annual). **Staff:** 6. **Description:** Individuals, families, organizations, businesses and foundations who share CCV's vision. Strives to promote Judeo-Christian moral values and to reduce destructive behaviors contrary to those values through education, active community partnering and empowering individuals at the local and national level. Conducts seminars and training events for citizens, law enforcement personnel, public officials and leaders. **Publications:** *Citizens' Courier*, quarterly. Newsletter.

19387 ■ CLOUT - Christian Lesbians Out
PO Box 5853
Athens, OH 45701
Ph: (740)592-6424
Fax: (740)592-4846
E-mail: clout@seorf.ohiou.edu
URL: http://www.cloutsisters.org
Contact: Rev. Jan Griesinger, Ed.
Founded: 1990. **Multinational. Description:** Acts as a coalition of lesbian Christians. **Publications:** *CLOUTreach*, quarterly. Newsletter. Contains essays by lesbian-feminist theologians, biographies, news and events. Alternate Formats: online.

19388 ■ Community of Celebration
PO Box 309
Aliquippa, PA 15001
Ph: (724)375-1510
Fax: (724)375-1138
E-mail: mail@communityofcelebration.com
URL: http://www.communityofcelebration.com
Founded: 1965. **Members:** 18. **Staff:** 10. **Budget:** $260,000. **Description:** Promotes the gospel of Jesus Christ by living in the community and offering

services to the church and to the world. Committed to seek and serve Christ in all persons. Provides worship leaders for worship events; training in worship leadership; songbooks and recordings. **Libraries: Type:** reference. **Holdings:** 10,000. **Subjects:** religion, music, liturgy, theology, psychology, history, spirituality. **Also Known As:** The Fisherfolk. **Publications:** *Network*, bimonthly. Newsletter. Features news of the life and ministry of members of Celebration, including companions. **Price:** free. **Circulation:** 300 ● *News from Celebration*, semiannual. Newsletter. **Price:** free. **Circulation:** 8,000. **Conventions/Meetings:** annual conference - always June ● periodic retreat.

19389 ■ Concerned Women for America (CWA)
1015 15th St. NW, Ste.1100
Washington, DC 20005-2619
Ph: (202)488-7000
Free: (800)458-8797
Fax: (202)488-0806
E-mail: mail@cwfa.org
URL: http://www.cwfa.org
Contact: Beverly LaHaye, Founder/Chair
Founded: 1979. **Members:** 500,000. **Membership Dues:** $20 (annual). **Staff:** 35. **Description:** Works to protect and promote Biblical values among all citizens - first through prayer, then education, and finally by influencing society. Goal is "for women and like-minded men, from all walks of life, to come together and restore the family to its traditional purpose and thereby allow each member of the family to realize their God-given potential and be more responsible citizens". **Awards:** College Scholarship. **Type:** scholarship. **Recipient:** for high school seniors who plan on attending a conservative Christian college. **Publications:** *Family Voice*, bimonthly. Newsletter. **Price:** $20.00/year. **Conventions/Meetings:** biennial conference.

19390 ■ Cowboys for Christ (CFC)
c/o Ted K. Pressley, Founder/Pres.
PO Box 7557
Fort Worth, TX 76111
Ph: (817)236-0023
E-mail: cfcmail@cowboysforchrist.net
URL: http://www.cowboysforchrist.net
Contact: Ted K. Pressley, Founder/Pres.
Founded: 1970. **Members:** 57,144. **Staff:** 4. **Regional Groups:** 186. **State Groups:** 146. **Local Groups:** 3. **National Groups:** 56. **Multinational. Description:** Interdenominational organization seeking to bring the gospel of Jesus Christ to the livestock industry in 24 countries. Works in conjunction with local churches to provide evangelistic outreach services. Conducts fellowship and worship services at rodeos, livestock shows, and cattle and horse conventions. Organizes Christian booths at rodeos, horse shows, and stock shows. Provides speakers for fairs, horse shows and sales, rodeo and livestock gatherings, and churches of all denominations. Offers Bible Study Program via booklets. Provides counseling services; accepts prayer requests. Establishes a Christian ranch for camping, seminars, and retreats. Airs 30 second broadcast nationwide daily and a one-hour show monthly; also in 24 other countries. **Libraries: Type:** open to the public. **Holdings:** 12,760; articles, books, periodicals. **Subjects:** Christianity in the livestock industry. **Computer Services:** database ● mailing lists. **Committees:** Mountain Ministry. **Publications:** *Christian Ranchman*, monthly. Newspaper. Provides Christian testimonies and news of the ministry. Includes chapter reports and calendar of scheduled chapter meetings. **Price:** free. **Circulation:** 62,996 ● *Rule Book Talk*, monthly. Article. **Price:** free ● Also publishes and distributes bibles, tracts, and other literature on Bible studies. **Conventions/Meetings:** quarterly Camp Meeting - meeting and convention (exhibits) - March, June, September, December.

19391 ■ Disciples Justice Action Network (DJAN)
1040 Harbor Dr.
Annapolis, MD 21403
Ph: (410)212-7964

E-mail: disciplesjustice@comcast.net
URL: http://www.djan.net
Contact: Ken Brooker Langston, Dir.
Founded: 1996. **Members:** 492. **Membership Dues:** individual, $35 (annual) ● small organization, $100 (annual) ● low income, $15 (annual) ● student, $10 (annual). **Description:** Represents the interests of individuals, congregations, and organizations within the Christian Church (Disciples of Christ). Works for greater justice, peace and diversity in churches, communities, and nations. Provides resources for seminarians and other students. **Publications:** *Call to Justice*, quarterly. Newsletter. **Price:** included in membership dues. Alternate Formats: online.

19392 ■ Engineering Ministries International (EMI)
130 E Kiowa St., No. 200
Colorado Springs, CO 80903-1722
Ph: (719)633-2078
Fax: (719)633-2970
E-mail: info@emiusa.org
URL: http://www.emiusa.org
Contact: Glen Woodruff, Pres./CEO
Founded: 1981. **Members:** 3,000. **Membership Dues:** full, $200 (annual) ● sponsor, $1,000 (annual). **Staff:** 55. **Description:** Christian engineering and design professionals. Seeks to "mobilize Christian design professionals to serve the poor in developing countries." Works to "proclaim the Good News of Jesus Christ by empowering people to transform their world through the design and development of hospitals, schools, orphanages, bridges, water supplies, and wastewater facilities". **Publications:** Newsletter, quarterly ● Annual Report, annual. **Conventions/Meetings:** annual conference.

19393 ■ Ex-Masons for Jesus
PO Box 28702
Las Vegas, NV 89126
E-mail: washum@emfj.org
URL: http://www.emfj.org
Contact: Duane Washum, Dir.
Description: Exists for those who have left the Masonic Lodge to follow Jesus Christ. Seeks to "expose the non-Christian nature of the teachings of Freemasonry and to make ourselves available to witness and testify of our firsthand knowledge. Aims to encourage others to renounce Freemasonry and through education, to prevent still others from being seduced into joining". **Publications:** *Ministry to Masons Conference Tape*. Audiotape. **Price:** free in U.S.; $2.00 outside U.S.

19394 ■ Fellowship of Christian Cowboys (FCC)
PO Box 3010
Colorado Springs, CO 80934
Ph: (719)630-7636
E-mail: prayforus@christiancowboys.com
URL: http://www.christiancowboys.com
Founded: 1973. **Description:** Works to present cowboys the challenge, adventure, and commitment of receiving Jesus Christ as Savior and Lord. **Publications:** *The Line Rider*, monthly. **Price:** included in membership dues. **Conventions/Meetings:** Cowboy Church - meeting, church services provided at any venue ● annual Rodeo Bible Camps - meeting - every summer.

19395 ■ Fellowship of Christian Magicians (FCM)
7739 Everest Ct. N
Maple Grove, MN 55311-1815
Ph: (763)494-5655
Fax: (763)494-5650
E-mail: mailcenter@fcm.org
URL: http://www.fcm.org
Contact: Mike Stenberg, Mail Center Sec.
Founded: 1953. **Members:** 2,100. **Membership Dues:** ordinary in U.S., $25 (annual) ● ordinary in Canada, $30 (annual) ● ordinary overseas, $35 (annual). **Staff:** 25. **Budget:** $35,000. **Regional Groups:** 6. **Local Groups:** 45. **National Groups:** 4. **Description:** Christians who illustrate the gospel using magic, ventriloquism, puppets, clowns, chalk, balloons, sto-

rytelling, and other methods. Aims to share ideas and to promote the use of all the arts as a means of teaching the Gospel to professional and amateur members. **Awards:** Heritage Members. **Frequency:** annual. **Type:** recognition. **Recipient:** to member with 25 or more years in organization ● Youth Awards. **Frequency:** annual. **Type:** recognition. **Divisions:** FCM Asian; FCM Europe; FCM German; Malaysian; Scandinavian. **Publications:** *The Christian Conjurer*, bimonthly. Magazine. **Price:** included in membership dues. **Circulation:** 1,500. **Advertising:** accepted. Alternate Formats: diskette; CD-ROM; online ● Directory, semiannual. Features articles on members, events, teaching in all art forms. **Circulation:** 1,600. **Advertising:** accepted. **Conventions/Meetings:** annual International Convention, with more than 150 workshops (exhibits) - always July, 5 days, Monday-Friday.

19396 ■ Fellowship of Christian Peace Officers - U.S.A. (FCPO-USA)
PO Box 3686
Chattanooga, TN 37404-0686
Ph: (423)622-1234
Fax: (423)622-9725
E-mail: grant@fcpo.org
URL: http://www.fcpo.org
Contact: Grant Wolf, Exec. Dir.
Founded: 1971. **Members:** 4,100. **Membership Dues:** individual one-time fee, $20 ● institutional, $50 ● individual renewal, $12 (annual). **Staff:** 3. **Budget:** $150,000. **Local Groups:** 141. **Description:** Full members are sworn law enforcement officers, both active and retired; all other persons are associate members. Dedicated to the goals of evangelism, discipleship and fellowship. Believes a strong husband/wife relationship is vital and involves spouses in many activities. Compiles statistics. **Libraries:** Type: reference. **Holdings:** audio recordings. **Formerly:** (1974) Fellowship of Christian Policemen; (1988) Fellowship of Christian Peace Officers. **Publications:** *The Christian Peace Officer*, quarterly. Newsletter. **Price:** free. **Circulation:** 4,500. Alternate Formats: online. **Conventions/Meetings:** annual conference, weekend spiritual retreat for adults and singles - always fall.

19397 ■ Fellowship of Companies for Christ International (FCCI)
c/o Christ@Work
PO Box 270784
Oklahoma City, OK 73137-0784
Ph: (405)917-1681
Fax: (405)949-0005
E-mail: csr@fcci.org
URL: http://www.fcci.org
Contact: Kent Humphreys, Pres.
Founded: 1980. **Members:** 1,500. **Staff:** 12. **Budget:** $1,200,000. **Regional Groups:** 12. **Local Groups:** 144. **Description:** Chief executive officers of businesses. Trains members to run their businesses in accordance with the teachings of Christ. Encourages Christian business owners and CEOs to operate their businesses and conduct their personal lives according to biblical principles "in pursuit of Christ's eternal objectives". **Publications:** *Fellowship Report*, quarterly. Newsletter. Includes conference reports and book reviews. **Price:** free. **Circulation:** 10,000 ● Audiotapes ● Brochures ● Videos. **Conventions/Meetings:** annual National Conference ● annual Young Executives Conference.

19398 ■ Fellowship of Saint James (FSJ)
PO Box 410788
Chicago, IL 60641
Ph: (773)481-1090
Fax: (773)481-1095
E-mail: fsj@fsj.org
URL: http://www.fsj.org
Contact: James M. Kushiner, Exec. Dir.
Founded: 1970. **Staff:** 7. **Budget:** $900,000. **Non-membership. Description:** Aims to provide opportunities for Protestant, Roman Catholic, and Eastern Orthodox Christians to work and talk together on the basis of shared belief in the fundamental doctrines of the faith as revealed in the Bible and

summarized in the ancient creeds of the church. **Formerly:** (1990) B'Rith Christian Union. **Publications:** *Calendar of the Christian Year*, annual. Includes Biblical illustrations, feasts, and Saints days of the churches of the East and West. **Price:** $12.00 plus $3 shipping and handling ● *Daily Devotional Guide for the Christian Year*, quarterly. Booklet. Contains a schedule of short daily lessons suited to the seasonal, weekly, and holy day themes as found in the Christian year. **Price:** $14.00/year ● *Salvo*, quarterly. Magazine. Contains information about science, contemporary culture, and the significant questions of life. **Price:** $25.99/year. **Circulation:** 2,500. **Advertising:** accepted ● *Touchstone: A Journal of Mere Christianity*, 10/year. Includes news and opinion devoted to a thoughtful appreciation of historic Christian faith. Also includes book reviews and special reports. **Price:** $29.95/year. ISSN: 0897-327X. **Circulation:** 10,000. **Advertising:** accepted. **Conventions/Meetings:** annual Christian Family - seminar and conference.

19399 ■ Full Gospel Business Men's Fellowship International (FGBMFI)
3 Holland
Irvine, CA 92618
Ph: (949)461-0100
Fax: (949)609-0344
E-mail: international@fgbmfi.org
URL: http://www.fgbmfi.org
Contact: Richard Shakarian, Intl. Pres.
Founded: 1953. **Members:** 100,000. **Membership Dues:** individual, $50 (annual) ● individual, $130 (triennial) ● individual, $200 (quinquennial) ● life, $500. **Staff:** 12. **Budget:** $2,000,000. **Local Groups:** 4,000. **Multinational. Description:** Association of local chapters of men "who profess belief in fundamental Christian doctrine, especially the baptism with the Holy Spirit as recorded in Acts 2:4 ('And they were filled with the Holy Ghost and began to speak with other tongues, as the Spirit gave them utterance')." Originally formed by members of Pentecostal churches, the fellowship has come to include increasing numbers of persons from the historic Protestant churches such as Episcopalians, Presbyterians, Baptists, Methodists, and from the Roman Catholic Church. Attempts to make tongue speaking an added dimension of the Christian experience in mainstream churches, rather than splitting off to form new groups. Believes in "the power of God to heal the sick today, as in Bible days." Produces television programs. **Libraries:** Type: reference. **Holdings:** books, software, video recordings. **Publications:** *Voice*, monthly. Magazine. Designed for evangelistic outreach to men. **Price:** $10.00 /year for nonmembers; included in membership dues. ISSN: 0042-8264. **Circulation:** 250,000. **Advertising:** accepted ● *World Chapter Directory*, periodic. **Conventions/Meetings:** annual convention - always July or August ● periodic Regional Conference - meeting.

19400 ■ Global University
1211 S Glenstone Ave.
Springfield, MO 65804-0315
Ph: (417)862-9533
Free: (800)443-1083
Fax: (417)862-0863
E-mail: info@globaluniversity.edu
URL: http://www.globaluniversity.edu
Contact: George M. Flattery EdD, Pres.
Founded: 1967. **Description:** Promotes Christian ministry. Conducts educational programs for individuals wishing to prepare for Christian mission. **Libraries:** Type: reference. **Holdings:** audiovisuals, books, clippings, monographs, periodicals. **Subjects:** education, religion. **Formerly:** (2003) International Correspondence Institute. **Publications:** Publishes foreign language Christian materials and English materials.

19401 ■ Intercessors for America (IFA)
PO Box 915
Purcellville, VA 20134
Ph: (540)751-0980
Fax: (540)751-0984

E-mail: ifa@ifapray.org
URL: http://www.ifapray.org
Contact: Gary Bergel, Pres.
Founded: 1973. **Members:** 50,000. **Staff:** 6. **Budget:** $500,000. **Description:** Christian ministry. Encourages "effective prayer and fasting for the church, the nation, and their leaders". **Publications:** *When You Were Formed in Secret/Abortion in America.* Booklet ● Newsletter, monthly. **Conventions/Meetings:** periodic meeting.

19402 ■ Intercristo
19303 Fremont Ave. N
MS No. 20
Seattle, WA 98133
Fax: (206)546-7375
E-mail: careerhelp@intercristo.com
URL: http://intercristo.searchease.com
Contact: Ron Rutherford, Exec. Dir.
Founded: 1967. **Staff:** 11. **Budget:** $900,000. **Description:** Division of CRISTA Ministries. Provides job exploration and job information service with computerized referrals on current openings with Christian organizations. Has career counseling, which is available through The Birkman Method Assessment Tool. **Computer Services:** database, job openings at non-profit Christian organizations. **Affiliated With:** CRISTA Ministries. **Absorbed:** (1977) Short Terms Abroad. **Also Known As:** International Christian Organization.

19403 ■ International Christian Concern (ICC)
2020 Pennsylvania Ave. NW, No. 941
Washington, DC 20006-1846
Ph: (301)989-1708
Free: (800)422-5441
Fax: (301)989-1709
E-mail: icc@persecution.org
URL: http://www.persecution.org
Contact: Jeff King, Pres.
Founded: 1995. **Multinational. Description:** Works to ensure religious freedom and assists Christians who are victims of persecution worldwide. **Publications:** *CONCERN,* monthly. Newsletter. Contains information about persecuted Christians throughout the world.

19404 ■ International Christian Studies Association (ICSA)
c/o Dr. Oskar Gruenwald, Pres.
1065 Pine Bluff Dr.
Pasadena, CA 91107
Ph: (626)351-0419
E-mail: info@jis3.org
URL: http://www.JIS3.org/abouticsa.htm
Contact: Dr. Oskar Gruenwald, Pres.
Founded: 1983. **Members:** 250. **Languages:** English, French, German. **Multinational. Description:** Scholars, professors, students, professionals, and scientists. Furthers the exploration of knowledge and its integration with Judeo-Christian ethical and spiritual values within an open forum of international, interdisciplinary, and interfaith dialogue. Seeks to expand the understanding of God, man, and the universe. Conducts panels and symposia. **Awards:** David Morsey Award. **Frequency:** annual. **Type:** recognition. **Recipient:** for the best biblical exegesis in JIS ● Oleg Zinam Award. **Frequency:** annual. **Type:** recognition. **Recipient:** for the best essay in JIS. **Publications:** *ICSA Newsletter,* annual. Includes conference news, Institute for Interdisciplinary Research activities, and association news. **Price:** $10.00 for nonmembers; free for members. ISSN: 1051-2772. **Circulation:** 1,000. **Advertising:** accepted ● *JIS Computerized Bibliography, 1989-2006,* annual. Contains study and research guide for college and seminary faculty. **Price:** $25.00/diskette; $30.00/diskette (overseas airmail). ISSN: 1066-8454. Alternate Formats: diskette ● *Journal of Interdisciplinary Studies: An International Journal of Interdisciplinary and Interfaith Dialogue,* annual. Contains topics about totalitarianism, Christian political economy, unity of the arts and sciences, the family, cities in the 21st century. **Price:** $10.00/year for students; $15.00 /year for individuals; $25.00 /year for institutions. ISSN: 0890-0132. **Circulation:** 1,000. **Advertising:**

accepted. **Conventions/Meetings:** quadrennial Science and Religion: The Missing Link - congress (exhibits).

19405 ■ International Convention of Faith Ministries (ICFM)
5500 Woodland Park Blvd.
Arlington, TX 76013
Ph: (817)451-9620
Free: (877)FIT-ICFM
Fax: (817)451-9621
E-mail: questions@icfm.org
URL: http://www.icfm.org
Contact: Dennis Burke, Pres.
Founded: 1979. **Members:** 1,000. **Staff:** 4. **Multinational. Description:** Licensed and ordained ministers. Provides new ministers with assistance in establishing their ministry. Coordinates foreign missions and prison ministries. Brings the Word of Faith on an interdenominational basis to those in the military service. Fosters unity among interdenominational ministries. Supports religious activities of nonprofit religious organizations whose primary objective is to engage in the conduct of religious worship. Disseminates information about the furtherance of the teachings of the Christian faith and tenets. Conducts seminars and ministers workshops. **Committees:** Mission. **Formerly:** (1985) International Convention of Faith, Churches and Ministers. **Publications:** *International Faith Report,* quarterly. Magazine. Contains effective ministry tools and current ICFM news and events. Alternate Formats: online ● Membership Directory, annual. **Conventions/Meetings:** annual convention.

19406 ■ International Cops for Christ (CFC)
PO Box 444
Liverpool, PA 17045
Ph: (717)329-0470
E-mail: mct911@aol.com
URL: http://www.copsforchrist.us
Contact: John McTernan, Contact
Founded: 1974. **Description:** Christian ministry by and for cops. Strives to provide for the spiritual needs of cops through prayer, traveling evangelists, books, booklets, tracts and radio programs. **Publications:** Books ● Booklets.

19407 ■ International Council of Iranian Christians (ICIC)
PO Box 25607
Colorado Springs, CO 80936
Ph: (719)596-0010
Fax: (719)574-1141
E-mail: icic@farsinet.com
URL: http://www.farsinet.com/icic
Founded: 1996. **Multinational. Description:** Promotes the works of evangelism, Christian discipleship and leadership training among Iranians. Deals with issues such as church growth, cooperation across denominations, and the arrival of Iranian Christians in the west.

19408 ■ International Order of the King's Daughters and Sons (IOKDS)
PO Box 1017
Chautauqua, NY 14722-1017
Ph: (716)357-4951
Fax: (716)357-3762
E-mail: iokds5@windstream.net
URL: http://www.iokds.org
Contact: Frances B. Sellew, Pres.
Founded: 1886. **Members:** 10,200. **Membership Dues:** individual, $15 (annual). **Staff:** 2. **Budget:** $100,000. **Multinational. Description:** International, interdenominational, interracial organization for development of spiritual life and stimulation of Christian activities. Local groups operate camps, day care centers, homes for the aged, hospitals, and other service institutions. Sponsors specialized education programs. **Awards: Frequency:** annual. **Type:** scholarship. **Recipient:** for students in the ministry, students in healthcare, and North American Indian students. **Publications:** *Silver Cross,* bimonthly. Magazine. **Price:** $6.00/year. **Circulation:** 2,300. Alternate Formats: online. **Conventions/Meet-**

ings: annual convention - always August, Chautauqua, NY in odd-numbered years and May at various locations in even-numbered years.

19409 ■ International Orthodox Christian Charities (IOCC)
110 West Rd., Ste.360
Baltimore, MD 21204
Ph: (410)243-9820
Free: (877)803-4622
Fax: (410)243-9824
E-mail: relief@iocc.org
URL: http://www.iocc.org
Contact: Bert W. Moyar, Chm.
Founded: 1992. **Multinational. Description:** Works as official humanitarian organization of the Standing Conference of Canonical Orthodox Bishops in the Americas; provides assistance to the poor. **Programs:** Internship; One in Spirit; Tribute. **Projects:** Axios!. **Publications:** *News and Needs,* 3/year. Newsletter. Alternate Formats: online.

19410 ■ Kristana Esperantista Ligo Internacia (KELI)
3578 S Taylor Ave.
Milwaukee, WI 53207-3439
Ph: (414)482-8903
E-mail: espero@milwpc.com
URL: http://www.chez.com/keli
Contact: Jerald Veit, Rep. for U.S.A.
Founded: 1911. **Members:** 500. **Membership Dues:** individual, $25 (annual). **Languages:** English, Esperanto, German, Portuguese. **Multinational. Description:** Christians who speak, read, or write Esperanto. Aims "to create an effective contact among Christians throughout the world and, by means of Esperanto, to make known the Good News of Jesus Christ." Does not teach Esperanto, but works among those who already know the language. Supports fundraising for projects such as E3, whereby medical aid is provided for the blind, mainly in Africa South America, and the Balkans. Supports ecumenism and cooperation among Christians of different denominations and nationalities. **Formerly:** (1998) International Christian Esperanto Association. **Publications:** *Dia Regno: Kristana Esperanto-Gazeto* (in Esperanto), bimonthly. Journal. Covers evangelism, theology, the Bible and the Esperanto language; includes association news, book reviews, and obituaries. **Price:** $16.00/year. ISSN: 0167-9554. Also Cited As: *The Divine Kingdom: Christian Esperanto Magazine* ● *Kristana Esperanto-Jarlibro* (in Esperanto), triennial. Membership Directory. Contains names and addresses of all KELI members, listed according to country. **Price:** available to members only. **Circulation:** 600. Also Cited As: *Christian Esperanto Yearbook* ● Also published a history and a hymnal; individuals and national sections of the association issue newspapers, books, and other Christian materials in Esperanto and national languages. **Conventions/Meetings:** annual Ecumenical Esperanto Congress, includes associational meetings, worship services, excursions.

19411 ■ Mission America Coalition (MAC)
PO Box 13930
Palm Desert, CA 92255
Ph: (760)200-2707
Fax: (760)200-8837
E-mail: info@missionamerica.org
URL: http://www.missionamerica.org
Contact: Dr. Paul A. Cedar, Chm./CEO
Founded: 1993. **Description:** Aims to mobilize Christian leaders and individual Christians to collaborate, emphasizing spiritual unity, evangelism, and revival. **Affiliated With:** Evangelical Council for Financial Accountability. **Publications:** *E-Connections,* monthly. Newsletter. **Price:** free. Alternate Formats: online ● Reports. Alternate Formats: online.

19412 ■ Narramore Christian Foundation (NCF)
250 Colorado Blvd., Ste.200
Arcadia, CA 91007-9877
Ph: (626)821-8400

Fax: (626)821-8409
E-mail: bruce@ncfliving.org
URL: http://www.ncfliving.org
Contact: Dr. Bruce Narramore PhD, Pres.
Founded: 1958. **Budget:** $1,400,000. **Description:**
Aims to help prevent and solve human problems
through the application of scriptural and psychological principles and insights. Seeks to introduce people
to Jesus Christ; Christian growth and maturity; resolution of problems and improving relationships; training
laypeople and Christian leaders. Ministries include:
daily national radio broadcasts; personalized correspondence; publications; production of videotapes;
missionary children. Provides referrals to Christian
counselors; crisis counseling for overseas missionaries. **Publications:** *Psychology for Living*, quarterly.
Magazine. Contains practiced psychology from a
Christian perspective. **Price:** free to supporters of
NCF's non-profit ministries; $20.00 in U.S. and
Canada; $35.00 outside U.S. and Canada. **Circulation:** 9,000. Alternate Formats: online ● Booklets.
Price: free. Alternate Formats: online ● Also publishes 80 booklets on everyday problems.

19413 ■ National Coalition of Men's Ministries (NCMM)
9900 Willows Rd. NE
Redmond, WA 98052
Ph: (425)284-2541
E-mail: office@ncmm.org
URL: http://www.ncmm.org
Contact: Rick Kingham, Pres.
Membership Dues: national (parachurch/servant
ministry or denominational ministry), $300 (annual) ●
affiliate (individual/church/parachurch/servant ministry/denomination), $200 (annual). **Description:** Seeks
to advance men's ministries and to assist in the
discipleship of Christian men. Aims to help spread
the good news of Jesus Christ to all men.

19414 ■ The Navigators (TN)
PO Box 6000
Colorado Springs, CO 80934
Ph: (719)598-1212
Fax: (719)260-0479
E-mail: webmaster@navigators.org
URL: http://www.navigators.org/us/
Contact: Alan Andrews, Dir.
Founded: 1943. **Staff:** 4,000. **Description:** Christian
service organization to "evangelize, establish, and
equip laymen and women and to train workers for
Christ." Staff of individuals representing 64 nationalities serve in 100 countries. Maintains year-round
conference center and summer youth camps. **Publications:** *Discipleship Journal*, bimonthly ● *One to
One Ministry Review and Resources*, quarterly.
Newsletter. Alternate Formats: online ● Also publishes personal Christian growth materials.

19415 ■ Nazarene Compassionate Ministries International (NCM)
6401 The Paseo
Kansas City, MO 64131-1213
Free: (877)626-4145
Fax: (816)333-2948
E-mail: ncm@nazarene.org
URL: http://www.nazcompassion.org
Contact: Rev. Tom Cahill Jr., Exec. Dir.
Description: Works to facilitate the practice of
Christian compassion by responding to pressing human needs and addressing the root cause of problems confronting the poor and the powerless. **Publications:** *NCM Magazine*, quarterly. Newsletter.

19416 ■ Nurses Christian Fellowship (NCF)
PO Box 7895
Madison, WI 53707-7895
Ph: (608)274-9001 (608)443-3722
Fax: (608)274-7882
E-mail: ncf@intervarsity.org
URL: http://ncf.intervarsity.org
Contact: Mary Thompson, Dir.
Founded: 1948. **Staff:** 15. **Description:** Serves as
professional organization and ministry of and for
nurses and nursing students. Provides concern for
the nurse "as a whole person" and advocates quality

care. Seeks to "bring the good news of Jesus Christ
to nursing education and practice." Promotes continuing nurse education through conferences on such
topics as: spiritual care, ethics, suffering, hope, stress
and conflict management. Assesses spiritual needs
and intervene appropriately, and to integrate Christian
faith and contemporary nursing issues. Includes local
activities such as Bible studies, fellowship groups,
conferences, prayer groups, and person-to-person
training for student leaders, advisers, and volunteer
staff. **Publications:** *Journal of Christian Nursing*,
quarterly. Includes articles on spiritual care, ethical
dilemmas, patient experiences, psychology, and
religion. Provides calendar of events, case studies.
Price: $22.95/year. ISSN: 0743-2550. **Circulation:**
10,000. **Advertising:** accepted. Alternate Formats:
microform ● Also publishes Bible study guides,
workshop manuals, and books. **Conventions/Meetings:** annual Called to Cure: Nursing in Today's
World - conference and meeting - always summer, in
central US.

19417 ■ Officers' Christian Fellowship of the U.S.A. (OCF)
3784 S Inca
Englewood, CO 80110-3405
Free: (800)424-1984
E-mail: ocfdenver@ocfusa.org
URL: http://ocf.gospelcom.net
Contact: Robert L. Caslen Jr., Pres.
Founded: 1943. **Members:** 11,000. **Staff:** 45. **Budget:** $2,440,000. **Description:** Officers from all
branches of the U.S. Armed Forces and the Coast
Guard whose commitment to Jesus Christ includes
both concern for and expression within the military.
Aims to: strengthen members to maturity in their
spiritual and secular lives; help members lead men
and women in the military to commit their lives to
Jesus Christ and to grow to spiritual maturity; encourage members in spirit-led prayer, Bible study, and
Christian witness. Helps to organize local Bible study
groups. Owns and operates two retreat centers. **Affiliated With:** Christian Military Fellowship; Evangelical Council for Financial Accountability. **Publications:**
Command, 7/year. Magazine. Features Christian
perspectives on life in the military. **Price:** free for
members; $20.00 /year for nonmembers. **Circulation:** 10,000.

19418 ■ Operation Blessing International (OBI)
977 Centerville Tpke.
Virginia Beach, VA 23463
Ph: (757)226-3401 (757)226-3440
Free: (800)730-2537
Fax: (757)226-3657
E-mail: operation.blessing@ob.org
URL: http://www.ob.org
Contact: Bill Horan, Pres./COO
Founded: 1978. **Description:** Aims to bring hope to
millions through hunger and disaster relief, medical
care, education, and life essentials. Has Hunger
Strike Force which distributes sixty million pounds of
product annually, Bless-A-Child program which offers
meals, clothing, and educational assistance, and
medical team who provides free treatments ranging
from basic to complex that enable people to see,
walk and smile again; and brings relief to victims of
earthquakes, floods, fires, and hurricanes. **Computer
Services:** Mailing lists. **Also Known As:** Operation
Blessing International Relief and Development
Corporation. **Publications:** *Blessings*, monthly.
Magazine. Alternate Formats: online ● Annual
Report, annual. Alternate Formats: online.

19419 ■ Partners Worldwide
2850 Kalamazoo Ave. SE
Grand Rapids, MI 49560-0600
Ph: (616)224-5874
Free: (800)919-7307
Fax: (616)224-0752
E-mail: info@partnersworldwide.org
URL: http://www.partnersworldwide.org
Contact: Doug Seebeck, Exec. Dir.
Founded: 1997. **Multinational. Description:** "Works
for business and professionals who bear witness to

their faith in order to transform communities and nations to reflect the Kingdom of God.". **Formerly:**
(2004) Partners for Christian Development. **Publications:** *Transformations*, quarterly. Newsletter. Alternate Formats: online.

19420 ■ Peace Mission Movement (PMM)
c/o Palace Mission Church Inc.
1622 Spring Mill Rd.
Gladwyne, PA 19035-1021
Ph: (610)525-5598
Fax: (610)525-0634
E-mail: fdipmm@libertynet.org
URL: http://fdipmm.libertynet.org
Contact: Mrs. M.J. Divine, Dir.
Founded: 1933. **Description:** Founded by Rev.
Major J. Divine, better known as Father Divine. (Followers believe that Father Divine fulfills the scriptural
prophecy of the second coming of Christ for the
Christian world and the coming of the Messiah for
the Jewish world.) Represents believers that live
Father Divine's International Modest Code: "No
Smoking. No Drinking. No Obscenity. No Vulgarity.
No Profanity. No Undue Mixing of the Sexes. No
Receiving of Gifts, Presents, Tips or Bribes". Aims to
establish "the kingdom of God on Earth through the
recognition of God's actual presence and by conforming to the teachings of the Sermon on the Mount, the
fundamental laws of the U.S.A., the Constitution and
its amendments, and the Declaration of Independence". **Committees:** Righteous Government Political Action. **Publications:** *The Condescension of God*
● *Enlightenment*, quarterly. Newsletter. Contains
news of Peace Mission's activities. **Price:** free. **Circulation:** 500 ● *Father Divine, His Words of Spirit, Life
and Hope* ● *Father Divine's Sermon Before the Verdict*. **Conventions/Meetings:** weekly meeting, pentecostal (exhibits) - also annual holidays, April 20-30
and September 10-12.

19421 ■ Peace Officers for Christ International (POFCI)
3000 W MacArthur Blvd., Ste.426
Santa Ana, CA 92704-6962
Ph: (714)426-7632
Fax: (714)426-0792
E-mail: info@pofci.org
URL: http://www.pofci.org
Contact: Devin Chase, Pres.
Founded: 1980. **Membership Dues:** individual, $25
(annual). **Regional Groups:** 13. **Languages:** English, Spanish. **Description:** Law enforcement officers and their families. Seeks to "bring officers and
their families to a saving knowledge of our Lord Jesus
Christ." Sponsors conferences, banquets, and home
Bible studies. **Telecommunication Services:** electronic mail, devin@pofci.org ● electronic mail, terry@
pofci.org. **Publications:** *Peacemakers Journal*,
quarterly. Magazine. **Circulation:** 8,000. **Conventions/Meetings:** annual conference ● semiannual
Police Couples - banquet - 2007 Nov. 2-4, Hume,
CA.

19422 ■ Peale Center for Christian Living
c/o Guideposts
39 Seminary Hill Rd.
Carmel, NY 10512
Ph: (971)221-1100
Free: (800)932-2145
E-mail: atyourservice@guideposts.org
URL: http://www.guideposts.com
Contact: Ruth Stafford Peale, Chair/Co-Founder
Founded: 1940. **Members:** 750,000. **Staff:** 40. **Budget:** $14,000,000. **Description:** Prints and distributes
messages books, pamphlets, and magazines. Provides Dial-A-Prayer and radio programming. Operates Positive Thinkers Club and Bible Club to disseminate practical spiritual messages to help
individuals overcome problems of life through the
sharing of faith. **Libraries: Type:** reference. **Holdings:** 1,000; biographical archives. **Subjects:** relevant to positive Christianity. **Formerly:** (1957)
Sermon Publications; (1991) Foundation for Christian
Living. **Publications:** *Bible Club Newsletter*, monthly.
Bible study. ● *PLUS, The Magazine of Positive Think-*

ing, 10/year ● *Positive Thinkers Club Newsletter,* monthly ● Annual Report.

19423 ■ Sojourners
3333 14th St. NW, Ste.200
Washington, DC 20010
Ph: (202)328-8842
Free: (800)714-7474
Fax: (202)328-8757
E-mail: sojourners@sojo.net
URL: http://www.sojo.net
Contact: Jim Wallis, Exec. Dir./Ed.-in-Chief
Founded: 1971. **Members:** 24,000. **Membership Dues:** individual, $30 (annual). **Staff:** 25. **Budget:** $1,400,000. **Description:** Represents Christians for justice and peace offering a voice and vision for social change; offers an alternative perspective on faith, politics, and culture through service programs, publications and events. **Computer Services:** Online services, weekly email magazine. **Publications:** Magazine, bimonthly. **Price:** $30.00/year. ISSN: 0364-2097. **Circulation:** 24,000. **Advertising:** accepted. **Conventions/Meetings:** annual conference ● lecture.

19424 ■ Truckers for Christ
PO Box 1311
Taylorsville, NC 28681
Ph: (828)632-8842
Fax: (828)632-8842
E-mail: prayer@truckersforchrist.org
Contact: Linda Wheat, Sec.
Founded: 1992. **Membership Dues:** donation, $20 (annual). **Description:** Members are truckers, their families, and related transportation employees. Provides fellowship, encouragement and support to drivers and their families. **Publications:** *The Cross-Road News,* quarterly. Newsletter. Contains inspirational articles. **Price:** free. **Circulation:** 2,500. Alternate Formats: online. **Conventions/Meetings:** annual symposium.

19425 ■ World's Christian Endeavor Union (WCEU)
PO Box 326
Liberty Corner, NJ 07938-0326
Ph: (908)604-9440
Fax: (908)604-6190
E-mail: davidgjackson@juno.com
URL: http://www.christianendeavorworld.com
Contact: Rev. David Jackson, Gen. Sec.
Founded: 1895. **Members:** 2,000,000. **Staff:** 3. **Budget:** $34,000. **National Groups:** 70. **Description:** Christian Endeavor societies and unions (interdenominational groups of Christian laymen) in over 75 countries and island groups. Fosters fellowship and unity among members and promotes and reinforces the interests of the Christian Endeavor movement worldwide. Encourages contact with Christians outside of the societies. **Publications:** Newsletter, quarterly. **Conventions/Meetings:** quadrennial convention.

Christian Reformed

19426 ■ Christian Reformed Church - Spanish and World Literature Committee
2850 Kalamazoo Ave. SE
Grand Rapids, MI 49560
Ph: (616)241-1691
Free: (877)279-9994
Fax: (616)224-0803
E-mail: crcna@crcna.org
URL: http://www.crcna.org
Contact: Jerry Dykstra, Exec. Dir.
Founded: 1979. **Members:** 35. **Staff:** 3. **Budget:** $425,000. **Description:** Provides literature in major world languages that strengthens church leadership and assists laypeople in their spiritual growth and faith development. Makes available affordable religious literature with a Biblical Reformed perspective. Operates charitable program. **Libraries: Type:** reference. **Committees:** Arabic; Chinese; French; Korean; Russian; Spanish. **Publications:** Brochure ● Catalog.

Lists Spanish products. ● Bulletin. **Conventions/ Meetings:** quarterly board meeting.

19427 ■ Dynamic Youth Ministries (DYM)
1333 Alger St. SE
PO Box 7259
Grand Rapids, MI 49507
Ph: (616)241-5616
Fax: (616)241-5558
E-mail: gordon@dynamicyouthministries.org
URL: http://calvinistcadets.gospelcom.net/CadetWeb/pages/DYMMinistries.html
Contact: Gordon Dornbush, Office Mgr./Accountant
Founded: 1919. **Members:** 12,000. **Staff:** 10. **Budget:** $3,300,000. **Regional Groups:** 52. **Local Groups:** 700. **Description:** Federation of youth (ages 8 and up), primarily of the Christian Reformed denomination. Promotes the interests and growth of youth organizations in the Christian Reformed and similar Calvinistic churches by providing suitable study and reading material and conducting volunteer service programs, leaders training courses, and rallies. **Libraries: Type:** reference. **Divisions:** Calvinettes aka GEMS; Calvinist Cadet Crops aka Cadets; Young Calvinist Federation aka Youth Unlimited. **Absorbed:** (1955) American Federation of Reformed Young Women Societies. **Formerly:** (1948) American Federation of Reformed Young Men Societies; (1967) Young Calvinist Federation; (1999) United Calvinist Youth. **Publications:** *Crusader.* Magazine ● *Team Magazine,* quarterly. Includes articles on youth issues and pull-out sections with meeting ideas, resource information, and fund-raising tips for youth leaders. **Price:** available to members only ● *Touch.* Magazine. **Conventions/Meetings:** periodic conference ● annual meeting.

19428 ■ World Literature Ministries (WLM)
c/o CRC Publications
2850 Kalamazoo Ave. SE
Grand Rapids, MI 49560
Ph: (616)224-0819 (616)224-0799
Free: (800)426-8355
Fax: (616)224-0834
E-mail: info@crcpublications.org
URL: http://www.crcpublications.org
Contact: Darlene Serrano, Dir.
Founded: 1979. **Staff:** 5. **Budget:** $425,000. **Languages:** English, Korean, Russian, Spanish. **Description:** Provides literature in many languages that strengthens church leadership and assists laypeople in their spiritual growth and faith development. Makes available affordable religious literature with a Biblical Reformed perspective. Operates charitable program. **Additional Websites:** http://www.librosdesafio.org. **Telecommunication Services:** electronic mail, editors@faithaliveresources.org. **Subcommittees:** Korean; Russian; Spanish. **Formerly:** (1993) Christian Reformed Church World Literature Ministries; (1999) CRC World Literature Ministries. **Publications:** Brochures ● Catalog. Lists Spanish products. **Conventions/Meetings:** quarterly board meeting.

Christianity

19429 ■ Advancing Native Missions (ANM)
PO Box 5303
Charlottesville, VA 22905
Ph: (540)456-7111
Fax: (540)456-7222
E-mail: requests@adnamis.org
URL: http://www.adnamis.org
Contact: George A. Ainsworth, Chm.
Multinational. Description: Calls to seek out, evaluate and support native missions groups who have a clear and defined evangelical statement of faith, who are open and transparent in their finances, and who are working among unreached people groups. Helps to take the Gospel of Jesus Christ to the world's remaining unreached people. **Publications:** *Voices,* semiannual. Newsletter.

19430 ■ Promise Keepers (PK)
PO Box 11798
Denver, CO 80211-0798
Ph: (303)964-7600
Free: (800)888-7595
URL: http://www.promisekeepers.org
Contact: Dr. Thomas Fortson, Pres.
Founded: 1990. **Multinational. Description:** Unites men to be passionate followers of Jesus Christ through the effective communication of the 7 Promises. Introduces men to Jesus Christ as their Savior and helps them grow as Christians. **Publications:** *Men of Integrity.* Book. Uses key Bible verses with testimonials on subjects. **Price:** $17.95/issue ● Newsletter. Alternate Formats: online.

Church of God

19431 ■ Women of the Church of God
1201 E 5th St.
Anderson, IN 46018-2328
Ph: (765)648-2102
Fax: (765)608-3094
E-mail: frontdesk@wchog.org
URL: http://www.womenofthechurchofgod.org
Contact: Arnetta Bailey, Exec. Dir.
Founded: 1932. **Members:** 30,000. **Membership Dues:** basic, $6 (annual) ● challenge, $12 (annual) ● life, $100. **Staff:** 3. **Budget:** $2,000,300. **State Groups:** 60. **Local Groups:** 1,700. **Description:** Women affiliated with the Church of God (Anderson, IN). Seeks to creatively and effectively extend the gospel of Jesus Christ, promote spiritual and personal growth, build friendship and interdependence, widen mental horizons and enlarge vision, and encourage the stewardship of all of life. Works to provide leadership and funding for home and overseas missions, ministry to women, and the ministries of the church. **Formerly:** (1975) National Woman's Missionary Society of the Church of God. **Publications:** *Church of God Missions,* bimonthly. **Conventions/Meetings:** annual conference - always June, in Anderson, IN ● quadrennial convention.

Church and State

19432 ■ Americans United for Separation of Church and State (AUSCS)
518 C St. NE
Washington, DC 20002
Ph: (202)466-3234
Fax: (202)466-2587
E-mail: americansunited@au.org
URL: http://www.au.org
Contact: Barry W. Lynn, Exec. Dir.
Founded: 1947. **Members:** 75,000. **Membership Dues:** individual, $25 (annual). **Staff:** 36. **Budget:** $5,700,000. **Local Groups:** 66. **Description:** Educates the American people about the vital role separation of church and state plays in safeguarding religious freedom. Opposes efforts to bridge the gap between church and state by Religious Right groups. Analyzes proposed legislation and advocates for church-state separation in the courts. **Libraries: Type:** not open to the public. **Holdings:** 1,000. **Subjects:** church-state relations. **Awards:** Madison/Jefferson Award. **Frequency:** annual. **Type:** recognition ● Religious Liberty Award. **Type:** recognition. **Formerly:** Protestants and Other Americans United for Separation of Church and State. **Publications:** *America's Legacy of Religious Liberty.* Brochure. Alternate Formats: online ● *Church and State,* 11/year. Magazine. Includes book reviews. **Price:** included in membership dues; $18.00 /year for libraries. ISSN: 0009-6334. **Circulation:** 40,000. Alternate Formats: online ● *Close Encounters with the Religious Right.* Book. Recounts author's experiences tracking Religious Right organizations for over 12 years. **Price:** $18.00 ● *The Most Dangerous Man in America? Pat Robertson and the Rise of the Christian Coalition.* Book. Explains Pat Robertson's theocratic, ultra-conservative political and moral agenda and his plans for the country. **Price:** $14.95 ● *Why the*

Religious Right Is Wrong, 2nd Edition. Book. Contains overview of religious right myths regarding separation of church and state. **Price:** $18.00 ● Pamphlets. **Conventions/Meetings:** triennial conference.

19433 ■ Freedom From Religion Foundation (FFRF)

PO Box 750
Madison, WI 53701
Ph: (608)256-8900 (608)256-5800
Fax: (608)256-1116
E-mail: info@ffrf.org
URL: http://www.ffrf.org
Contact: Annie Laurie Gaylor, Founder/Co-Pres.

Founded: 1978. **Members:** 5,000. **Membership Dues:** individual, $40 (annual) ● household, $50 (annual) ● gung-ho, $75 (annual) ● sustaining, $100 (annual) ● sponsoring, $500 (annual) ● life, $1,000 ● student, $25 (annual) ● subscription, $20 (annual). **Staff:** 5. **Budget:** $500,000. **Regional Groups:** 5. **Description:** Represents "Freethinkers" including atheists, agnostics, rationalists, secularists, and humanists. Promotes the constitutional principle of separation of state and church. Educates the public on matters relating to nontheistic beliefs. Combats fundamentalist thought. Opposes payment of public funds for religious purposes, government favoritism toward religious institutions, illegal activities conducted in the name of religious charities, and the religious campaign against women's rights and against civil rights for homosexuals. Collects information on clergy sexual abuse cases. Operates speakers' bureau; conducts research programs. **Libraries: Type:** not open to the public. **Holdings:** 2,000. **Subjects:** free thought, criticism of religion. **Awards:** Blanche Fearn Memorial Award. **Frequency:** annual. **Type:** scholarship. **Recipient:** for the best student essay contest, one for college students, one for high school seniors ● Freethinker of the Year Award. **Frequency:** annual. **Type:** recognition. **Recipient:** for litigant or court victor in state/church separation lawsuit ● Freethought Heroine Award. **Frequency:** annual. **Type:** recognition. **Recipient:** for a woman freethinker ● Phyllis Stevenson Grams Memorial Award. **Frequency:** annual. **Type:** scholarship. **Publications:** *American Infidel: Robert G. Ingersoll.* Book. **Price:** $25.00/copy ● *The Born Again Skeptic's Guide to the Bible.* Book. **Price:** $20.00/copy ● *Freethought Today,* 10/year. Newspaper. Includes legal cases, features on freethinkers, reports on clergy abuse, philosophical articles, and reports on foundation activities. **Price:** included in membership dues; $20.00 /year for nonmembers. **Circulation:** 5,000. Alternate Formats: online ● *Losing Faith in Faith - From Preacher to Atheist.* Book. **Price:** $25.00/copy ● *One Woman's Fight.* Book. **Price:** $20.00/copy ● *Woe to the Women - The Bible Tells Me So.* Book. **Price:** $20.00/copy ● *Women Without Superstition: "No Gods - No Masters": The Collected Writings of Women Freethinkers of the Nineteenth and Twentieth Centuries.* Book. **Price:** $30.00/copy ● *The World-Famous Atheist Cookbook.* **Price:** $12.00/copy. **Conventions/Meetings:** annual convention, with speakers on freethought and state/church separation - always fall.

19434 ■ National League for the Separation of Church and State (NLSCS)

239 S Juniper St.
Escondido, CA 92025
Ph: (760)489-5211
E-mail: tseditor@aol.com
Contact: Bonnie Lange, Pres.

Founded: 1947. **Members:** 1,000. **Membership Dues:** regular, $20 (annual). **Staff:** 4. **Budget:** $25,000. **Description:** Purposes are: to maintain the separation of church and state; to seek repeal of all laws based upon religious beliefs, particularly those restricting the civil rights of nonbelievers. **Libraries: Type:** not open to the public. **Holdings:** 500; books, clippings, periodicals. **Subjects:** religion, history, politics, economics. **Formerly:** (1965) National Liberal League. **Conventions/Meetings:** annual board meeting - always last Saturday of April, in San Diego, CA.

Churches

19435 ■ Adopt-A-Church International

PO Box 510
Allendale, MI 49401
Ph: (616)892-4260
E-mail: dlem96@adoptachurch.org
URL: http://www.adoptachurch.org
Contact: Daniel L. Lemmen, Founder

Founded: 1991. **Multinational. Description:** Aims to bring together churches and pastors in the United States willing to give spiritual and financial support to churches and families in the West in need of such support. Establishes relationships between churches in the United States and churches in Eastern Europe. Provides support to the hospitals and orphanages of the Eastern European countries in need of equipment and supplies. **Publications:** Newsletter. Alternate Formats: online.

19436 ■ Alban Institute (AI)

2121 Cooperative Way, Ste.100
Herndon, VA 20171
Ph: (703)964-2700
Free: (800)486-1318
Fax: (703)964-0370
E-mail: webmaster@alban.org
URL: http://www.alban.org
Contact: James P. Wind, Pres.

Founded: 1974. **Members:** 8,500. **Membership Dues:** clergy, lay in U.S., $50 (annual) ● retired clergy, seminarian in U.S., $25 (annual) ● clergy, lay outside U.S., $65 (annual) ● retired clergy, seminarian outside U.S., $35 (annual) ● congregation in U.S., $250 (annual) ● congregation outside U.S., $300 (annual) ● institution in U.S., $375 (annual) ● institution outside U.S., $450 (annual). **Staff:** 20. **Budget:** $3,200,000. **Description:** Laity, clergy, executives, and seminary and agency personnel primarily interested in building better congregations. Works to encourage congregations to be vigorous and faithful so that they may equip the people of God to minister within their faith communities and in the world. Assists those who lead or care for congregations; gathers, generates, and shares practical knowledge across denominational lines through action research, consulting and training services, publications, and continuing education. **Publications:** *Congregations,* quarterly. Magazine. Presents "best practices" in congregations. **Price:** $7.00 ● Books. **Conventions/Meetings:** monthly seminar.

19437 ■ American Society for Church Growth (ASCG)

c/o Dr. Alan McMahan
School of Intercultural Stud.
Biola Univ.
13800 Biola Ave.
La Mirada, CA 90639-0001
Ph: (562)944-0351
E-mail: alanmcm@aol.com
URL: http://www.ascg.org
Contact: Eric Baumgartner, Pres.

Founded: 1985. **Members:** 300. **Membership Dues:** individual, $75 (annual) ● student, $25 (annual). **Staff:** 2. **Description:** Serves as a proactive, professional association of global Christian leaders-scholars and practitioners-whose ministry activities are based on the key principles of church growth. Provides a forum for issues pertaining to ministry development, and fellowship. Encourages colleagues in church growth. Compiles statistics and maintains a speaker's bureau. **Awards:** The Donald A. McGavran Award. **Frequency:** annual. **Type:** recognition. **Publications:** *Journal of the American Society of Church Growth,* 3/year. **Price:** $24.00/year. ISSN: 1091-2711. **Circulation:** 400. **Advertising:** accepted. Alternate Formats: online ● Membership Directory. Alternate Formats: online. **Conventions/Meetings:** annual convention (exhibits).

19438 ■ Association of Christian Church Educators (ACCE)

PO Box 1986
Indianapolis, IN 46206-1986
Ph: (317)713-2679
Free: (888)346-2631

Fax: (317)635-4426
E-mail: mail@dhm.disciples.org
URL: http://www.homelandministries.org/Christian-Education/ACCE.htm
Contact: Rev. Arnold C. Nelson Jr., Pres.

Founded: 1947. **Members:** 190. **Membership Dues:** individual, $40 (annual) ● seminary student/retiree, $20 (annual). **Description:** Persons in professional positions in the Christian Church (Disciples of Christ). Supports professional educational ministry and ongoing programs in the ministry. **Awards:** Life Membership. **Frequency:** annual. **Type:** recognition. **Recipient:** for retiring members with 10 years continuous membership. **Formerly:** (1968) National Fellowship of Disciple Directors. **Publications:** *Education Connection,* quarterly. Journal. **Price:** $40.00. **Circulation:** 500. **Conventions/Meetings:** annual conference - always winter.

19439 ■ Association of Unity Churches

PO Box 610
Lee's Summit, MO 64063
Ph: (816)524-7414 (816)524-7750
Fax: (816)525-4020
E-mail: info@mail.unity.org
URL: http://www.unity.org
Contact: Rev. James Trapp, Pres./CEO

Founded: 1966. **Members:** 950. **Staff:** 42. **Regional Groups:** 9. **Description:** Ministers and interested members of Unity Churches and study groups. Serves and supports member ministries by providing human resources, administrative and educational programs, and consultation in accordance with the teachings of the Unity School of Christianity founded by Charles and Myrtle Fillmore. Trains and licenses teachers, ministers, and youth advisors; offers continuing education programs and minister employment service. Holds skills development seminars and workshops; sponsors retreats. Offers media service consultation. Assists with the development of local groups. **Libraries: Type:** reference. **Holdings:** artwork, audiovisuals, books, clippings, monographs, periodicals. **Awards:** The Charles Fillmore Award. **Frequency:** annual. **Type:** recognition ● The Light of God Expressing Award. **Type:** recognition ● The Light of God Expressing Award for the Unity Movement. **Frequency:** annual. **Type:** recognition ● The Myrtle Fillmore Award. **Type:** recognition. **Publications:** *Association of Unity Churches Yearbook,* annual ● *CONTACT,* bimonthly. Magazine ● *Minister's Letter,* bimonthly. Newsletter ● *Policy Manual,* periodic ● Membership Directory, periodic. **Conventions/Meetings:** annual international conference (exhibits).

19440 ■ Disciple Nations Alliance (DNA)

1220 E Washington St.
Phoenix, AZ 85034
Ph: (480)609-7793
Free: (800)248-6427
Fax: (480)951-9035
E-mail: acarson@fhi.net
URL: http://www.disciplenations.org
Contact: Bob Moffitt, Founder

Founded: 1997. **Multinational. Description:** Seeks to help churches practice holistic community ministries. **Conventions/Meetings:** Vision Conferences.

19441 ■ Disciples Ecumenical Consultative Council (DECC)

c/o Council on Christian Unity
130 E Washington St.
PO Box 1986
Indianapolis, IN 46206-1986
Ph: (317)713-2586
Fax: (317)713-2588
E-mail: rozanne@ccu.disciples.org
URL: http://www.disciples.org/ccu/index.html
Contact: Dr. Robert K. Welsh, Pres.

Founded: 1975. **Members:** 13. **Staff:** 1. **National Groups:** 13. **Languages:** English, French, Spanish. **Description:** Churches upholding the Disciples of Christ tradition. Encourages and facilitates member participation in the ecumenical movement and promotes Christian unity. Represents the Disciples of Christ Church at international ecumenical meetings. Facilitates international dialogue with various Protestant, Orthodox, and Roman Catholic churches. **Publications:** *Mid-Stream: an Ecumenical Journal,* quarterly. **Conventions/Meetings:** quinquennial international conference.

19442 ■ IFCA International
PO Box 810
Grandville, MI 49468-0810
Ph: (616)531-1840
Free: (800)347-1840
E-mail: office@ifca.org
URL: http://www.ifca.org
Contact: Rev. Les Lofquist, Exec. Dir.
Founded: 1930. **Members:** 1,200. **Membership Dues:** layman/vocational, $40 (annual). **Staff:** 5. **Regional Groups:** 39. **Description:** Ministers, missionaries, youth leaders, musicians, and ministerial students; churches and organizations. Seeks to offer independent churches the benefits of unity, while allowing them to keep their autonomy. Supports active evangelism; encourages churches to extend their ministry into neighboring communities, the military, and other Christian churches, which the group believes are in harmony with the Word of God. Serves to reinforce members' doctrinal beliefs; provides interchurch fellowship and the sharing of ministers; trains pastors and lay workers. **Computer Services:** database, membership list ● mailing lists, of members. **Commissions:** Military Chaplains. **Committees:** Auditing; Christian Education; Credentials; Institutional Chaplains; Missions; National Youth; Property. **Formerly:** (1998) Independent Fundamental Churches of America. **Publications:** *Church and Ministers Handbook.* **Price:** $20.00. Alternate Formats: online ● *For Such A Time As This - A History of the Independent Fundamental Churches in America.* Book ● *Independent Fundamental Churches of America,* biennial. Directory ● *Voice,* bimonthly. Magazine. **Price:** included in membership dues; $10.00 /year for nonmembers; $18.00/2 years for nonmembers; $26.00/3 years for nonmembers. Alternate Formats: online ● Also publishes educational materials. **Conventions/Meetings:** annual meeting and workshop (exhibits) - last half of June.

19443 ■ International Council of Community Churches (ICCC)
21116 Washington Pkwy.
Frankfort, IL 60423
Ph: (815)464-5690
Fax: (815)464-5692
E-mail: iccc60423@sbcglobal.net
URL: http://www.icccusa.com
Contact: Rev. Michael Livingston, Exec. Dir.
Founded: 1950. **Members:** 135. **Staff:** 3. **Regional Groups:** 3. **State Groups:** 36. **Local Groups:** 180. **National Groups:** 21. **Description:** Promotes the fellowship of community churches, provides an annual meeting for worship, study, fellowship; relates to the larger church through membership in the NCCCUSA and the WCC. Assists congregations in pastoral search process. Provides pension plan and health benefits for members. **Libraries: Type:** reference. **Holdings:** 550. **Subjects:** theology, general ministry. **Awards:** Jordan Scholarship Award. **Type:** scholarship. **Computer Services:** database ● mailing lists. **Commissions:** Clergy Relations; Ecumenical Relations; Faith, Justice and Mission; Laity and Church Relations. **Committees:** Information Services; Jordan Scholarship; New Church and Church Renewal; Staff Affairs. **Formed by Merger of:** Biennial Council of Community Churches; National Council of Community Churches. **Formerly:** International Council of Community Churches; (1969) Council of Community Churches; (1984) National Council of Community Churches. **Publications:** *The Christian Community,* 8/year. Newspaper. **Price:** $12.00/year. **Circulation:** 1,100. **Advertising:** accepted ● *Community Yearbook* ● *The Inclusive Pulpit.* **Conventions/Meetings:** annual conference (exhibits) - usually July. 2008 July 20-24, Los Angeles, CA.

19444 ■ Missionary Church Historical Society
c/o Timothy Erdel
Bethel Coll.
1001 W McKinley Ave.
Mishawaka, IN 46545-5509

Ph: (574)257-2570 (574)259-8511
Fax: (574)257-3499
E-mail: info@bethelcollege.edu
URL: http://www.bethelcollege.edu
Contact: Dr. Steven R. Cramer, Pres.
Founded: 1979. **Members:** 150. **Membership Dues:** individual, institution, $12 (annual). **Staff:** 2. **Description:** Seeks to: gather the materials, documents, pictures, tapes, and artifacts of the Missionary Church and its antecedents; preserve church's historical documents and make them visible for study and display; encourage and sponsor research; publish and encourage the publication of literature dealing with Missionary Church history; and promote interest in the history of the Missionary Church leading to a greater understanding and appreciation of its heritage. Maintains speakers' bureau. **Libraries: Type:** by appointment only. **Holdings:** archival material, books, periodicals. **Subjects:** Anabaptist/Mennonite, Brethren in Christ, Missionary Church denominational materials. **Publications:** *Reflections,* semiannual. Journal. **Price:** included in membership dues. **Circulation:** 400. **Conventions/Meetings:** annual board meeting - always April and September ● semiannual meeting.

19445 ■ National Council of Churches (NCC)
475 Riverside Dr., Ste.880
New York, NY 10115
Ph: (212)870-2227 (212)870-2141
Fax: (212)870-2030
E-mail: news@ncccusa.org
URL: http://www.ncccusa.org
Contact: Rev. Dr. Robert W. Edgar, Gen. Sec.
Founded: 1950. **Description:** Protestant, Anglican, and Orthodox communions. Promotes Christian ecumenical cooperation; works for peace and justice in the U.S; addresses issues ranging from peace, poverty and racism, to the environment, family ministries, and more. Provides educational ministries. Coordinates the production of national network and cable television programming of religious interest. Works to increase the use of the Bible in churches and the marketplace. **Commissions:** Communication; Education and Leadership; Faith and Order; Interfaith Relations; Justice and Advocacy. **Publications:** *New Revised Standard Version of the Bible* ● *Yearbook of American and Canadian Churches,* annual. **Conventions/Meetings:** quarterly board meeting ● annual general assembly.

Churches of Christ—Christian Churches

19446 ■ Disciples of Christ Historical Society (DCHS)
1101 19th Ave. S
Nashville, TN 37212-2109
Ph: (615)327-1444
Fax: (615)327-1445
E-mail: mail@discipleshistory.org
URL: http://www.discipleshistory.org
Contact: Glenn Thomas Carson PhD, Pres.
Founded: 1941. **Members:** 1,450. **Membership Dues:** regular in U.S., $20 (annual). **Staff:** 6. **Budget:** $252,000. **Description:** Works to maintain and further interest in the religious heritage, background, origins, development, and general history of Christian Church (Disciples of Christ), the Christian Churches and Churches of Christ. Maintains museum in Thomas W. Phillips Memorial Building in Nashville, TN, that serves as a research center for writers, historians, and students. Operates speakers' bureau. **Libraries: Type:** reference. **Holdings:** 35,000; archival material. **Awards:** Lockridge Ward Wilson Award. **Frequency:** annual. **Type:** recognition. **Recipient:** for a student seminarian paper pertaining to the history of the Stone-Campbell. **Publications:** *Discipliana,* quarterly. Journal. **Price:** included in membership dues. ISSN: 0732-9881. **Circulation:** 1,500. **Advertising:** accepted. Alternate Formats: microform ● *The Link,* quarterly. Newsletter. **Price:** included in membership dues; $20.00 for nonmembers. **Circulation:** 4,500.

19447 ■ Division of Higher Education, Christian Church-Disciples of Christ
11477 Olde Cabin Rd., Ste.310
St. Louis, MO 63141-7137
Ph: (314)991-3000
Fax: (314)991-2957
E-mail: helm@helmdisciples.org
URL: http://dhedisciples.org
Contact: Dennis Landon, Pres.
Founded: 1894. **Staff:** 5. **Description:** Elected administrative board working to advance the concerns of the Christian Church - Disciples of Christ in higher education and interpret issues in higher education to CCDC leadership. Maintains affiliation with 17 liberal arts colleges and 7 theological seminaries throughout the U.S. **Awards: Type:** grant ● **Type:** recognition ● **Type:** scholarship. **Councils:** Colleges and Universities; Ministries in Higher Education; Theological Education. **Formerly:** (1978) Board of Higher Education. **Publications:** *Articles of Incorporation and Bylaws,* biennial ● *Church/Campus,* quarterly ● Brochures ● Videos. **Conventions/Meetings:** biennial Disciples Seminarians Conference - always alternate year of the general assembly ● biennial general assembly (exhibits).

19448 ■ National Chaplains Association (NCA)
PO Box 635
Groveland, FL 34736
Ph: (352)394-6311 (352)394-7624
E-mail: dvarvel@aol.com
URL: http://www.nca-hq.org
Contact: Doyle E. Varvel, Commander
Founded: 1900. **Description:** Auxiliary of the Calvary Grace Christian Church. Primarily aims to promote the rights of youth and to care for homeless and needy children and adults. Sponsors Junior Chaplain's Corps to provide guidance and recreation for children. Works with law enforcement agencies in the prevention of juvenile delinquency; disseminates information on drug abuse, delinquency, and suicide prevention to public schools. Provides food, clothing, shelter, and financial assistance to the economically disadvantaged; offers assistance to stranded tourists; provides the ill and elderly with transportation to hospitals and clinics; conducts disaster aid programs. Certifies and ordains chaplains. **Awards:** Legion of Honor Award. **Type:** recognition. **Formerly:** (1950) World Youth Council. **Publications:** *The Trail Blazer,* quarterly. Bulletin. **Conventions/Meetings:** annual conference.

19449 ■ United Christian Missionary Society (UCMS)
PO Box 1986
Indianapolis, IN 46206
Ph: (317)635-3100 (317)713-2679
Fax: (317)635-1991
E-mail: jking@dhm.disciples.org
Contact: David A. Vargas, Pres.
Founded: 1919. **Budget:** $1,400,000. **Description:** Serves as an agency of the Christian Church (Disciples of Christ) concerned with the support of missions and ministries of the church at home and abroad. Manages permanent funds and its investments; channels the earnings to two major divisions of the Christian Church (Disciples of Christ): the Division of Homeland Ministries and the Division of Overseas Ministries. **Formed by Merger of:** American Christian Missionary Society; Christian Woman's Board of Missions; The Foreign Christian Missionary Society. **Conventions/Meetings:** annual meeting.

19450 ■ World Convention of Churches of Christ (WCCC)
1279 Brentwood Highlands Dr.
Nashville, TN 37211
Ph: (615)331-1824
Fax: (615)331-1864
E-mail: worldconv@aol.com
URL: http://www.worldconvention.org
Contact: Mr. Jeff L. Weston, Exec. Dir.
Founded: 1930. **Staff:** 3. **Budget:** $150,000. **National Groups:** 176. **Multinational. Description:** Members of the Christian Church (Disciples of Christ)

Christian Churches/Churches of Christ and Churches of Christ (Non-Instrumental); and those practicing other faiths with roots in the Campbell-Stone movement. (The Campbell-Stone movement was an early 19th century movement started by Thomas and Alexander Campbell and Barton W. Stone which created the Christian Church denomination.) Works to proclaim the gospel and promote Christian evangelism, inspiration, and fellowship among member churches. **Awards: Type:** recognition. **Committees:** Endowment Fund Consultative and Investment. **Publications:** *World Christian,* quarterly. Newsletter. **Circulation:** 10,000. **Conventions/Meetings:** quadrennial World Convention (exhibits).

Clergy

19451 ■ American Clergy Leadership Conference (ACLC)
3224 16th St. NW
Washington, DC 20010
Ph: (202)319-3200
Free: (800)291-3793
E-mail: mail@aclc.info
URL: http://www.aclc.info
Contact: Rev. Levy M.B. Daugherty, Exec. Dir.
Membership Dues: regular, $120 (annual). **Description:** Encourages the churches and individuals to promote interfaith unity, church growth, denominational and interfaith unity and cooperation. Works to engage the churches to end racism and societal ills. **Libraries: Type:** reference. **Holdings:** books, reports, video recordings. **Subjects:** Holy Bible, Jewish Bible, Holy Qur'an, philosophy, Christianity, Scripture. **Computer Services:** Information services, words of wisdoms, reflections, speeches ● online services, member e-mail account. **Publications:** *American Clergy.* Magazine. **Price:** $42.00. Alternate Formats: online ● *Lecture Manual Series.* Manuals. Serves as a guide for presenters, a study resource, and a general introduction to IEF perspective. **Price:** $12.95/manual ● Newsletter, monthly.

Congregational Christian

19452 ■ American Congregational Association (ACA)
14 Beacon St., 2nd Fl.
Boston, MA 02108
Ph: (617)523-0604 (617)523-0470
Fax: (617)523-0491
E-mail: mbendroth@14beacon.org
URL: http://www.14beacon.org
Contact: Ms. Margaret Bendroth, Exec. Dir.
Founded: 1853. **Members:** 166. **Staff:** 11. **Budget:** $863,000. **Description:** Maintains Congregational House for religious organizations. Sponsors specialized education and research programs. **Libraries: Type:** lending; reference; open to the public. **Holdings:** 225,000; archival material, books, monographs, periodicals. **Subjects:** colonial history, congregationalism, religion, theology. **Computer Services:** database, archival collections. **Publications:** *Bulletin of the Congregational Library,* 3/year. Includes brief descriptions of all books added to the library in the preceding four months. **Price:** $10.00 donation. ISSN: 0010-5821. **Circulation:** 1,000.

19453 ■ Congregational Christian Historical Society (CCHS)
14 Beacon St.
Boston, MA 02108
Ph: (617)523-0470
Fax: (617)523-0491
E-mail: mbendroth@14beacon.org
URL: http://www.cchsonline.org
Contact: Margaret Bendroth, Exec. Sec./Archivist
Founded: 1952. **Members:** 900. **Membership Dues:** individual, $25 (annual) ● church and other organization, $50 (annual). **Staff:** 2. **Budget:** $21,000. **Description:** Sponsored and supported by various agencies of the Congregational Christian Churches and of the United Church of Christ through its Histori-

cal Council; selected scholars constitute the fellows of the society. Locates and preserves written materials of historical significance to the denomination, promotes anniversary celebrations in the churches, and makes available important documents, church histories, and anniversary programs. Compiles statistics; maintains archives in Congregational Library; sponsors specialized education and research programs. **Libraries: Type:** reference. **Holdings:** 225,000. **Subjects:** congregationalism and religion. **Awards:** Frederick M. Fagley Awards. **Frequency:** annual. **Type:** recognition. **Recipient:** for excellence in church anniversary programs and publications. **Affiliated With:** American Congregational Association. **Publications:** *News from the Congregational Christian Historical Society,* semiannual. Newsletter. **Price:** included in membership dues. ISSN: 0362-1510. **Circulation:** 900 ● Also publishes leaflets and other materials on Congregational history. **Conventions/Meetings:** semiannual meeting.

19454 ■ National Association of Congregational Christian Churches (NACCC)
8473 S Howell Ave.
PO Box 288
Oak Creek, WI 53154-0288
Ph: (414)764-1620
Free: (800)262-1620
Fax: (414)764-0319
E-mail: naccc@naccc.org
URL: http://www.naccc.org
Contact: Ms. Terry Stone, Exec. Dir.
Founded: 1955. **Members:** 435. **Staff:** 9. **Description:** Aims to provide a means whereby Congregational Christian churches may consult and exchange advise on spiritual and temporal matters of common concern; and to encourage the continuance of Christian purposes and practices that have been the historic and accepted characteristics of Congregational Christian churches. Supports the education of ministers through its Congregational Foundation for Theological Studies. Compiles statistics. Operates placement service and mission program. Provides a variety of financial services. Supports youth programming from coast to coast and hosts annual meeting. **Libraries: Type:** reference. **Holdings:** archival material. **Subjects:** congregational history, NACCC history, congregational authors. **Awards:** Citation. **Frequency:** annual. **Type:** recognition. **Recipient:** for meritorious service to Congregationalism. **Committees:** Financial Service; Spiritual Resources; Women, Men and Families; Youth. **Divisions:** Congregational Foundation for Theological Studies; Ministry; Missionary Society; New Church Development. **Also Known As:** NACCC. **Publications:** *The Congregationalist and NACCC News,* 5/year. Magazine. Includes church news and member updates, book reviews, and employment opportunities. ISSN: 0010-5856. **Circulation:** 7,000. **Advertising:** accepted ● *Missions Directory,* periodic. Includes brief descriptions of NACCC approved and supported missions. **Price:** $4.00/issue ● *National Association of Congregational Christian Churches Yearbook,* annual. Provides statistics on operating budget of member churches for the calendar year or the most recent fiscal year; includes member names and addresses. **Price:** $10.00/copy (paper); $5.00 CD. Alternate Formats: CD-ROM. **Conventions/Meetings:** annual meeting, delegates and others (exhibits) ● annual Ministers' Convention - meeting, convocation for ministers (exhibits) - usually in March.

Counseling

19455 ■ American Association of Christian Counselors (AACC)
PO Box 739
Forest, VA 24551
Ph: (434)525-9470
Free: (800)526-8673
Fax: (434)525-9480
E-mail: contactmemberservices@aacc.net
URL: http://aacc.net
Contact: Tim Clinton EdD, Pres.
Members: 50,000. **Membership Dues:** regular, $79 (annual) ● executive, $89 (annual) ● student (with

student chapter), $39 (annual) ● student (no student chapter), $57 (annual). **Multinational. Description:** Represents the interests of individuals committed to assisting Christian counselors. Promotes the profession and the practice of Pastoral Counseling. Aims to equip clinical, pastoral and lay care-givers with Biblical truth and psycho-social insights that minister to hurting persons. Provides pastoral counseling and related educational programs. **Publications:** *Christian Counseling Connection,* quarterly. Newsletter. Focuses on news relevant to Christian counselors. **Price:** included in membership dues ● *Christian Counseling Today,* quarterly. Magazine. Focuses on issues facing today's Christian counselors. **Price:** included in membership dues ● *eNews Monthly.* Newsletter. **Price:** included in membership dues. Alternate Formats: online ● *Marriage and Family: A Christian Journal,* quarterly. Covers timely marriage and family issues. **Price:** included in membership dues ● *Practice Points Newsletter,* quarterly. Contains informative and helpful practice-related articles.

19456 ■ American Association of Pastoral Counselors (AAPC)
9504A Lee Hwy.
Fairfax, VA 22031-2303
Ph: (703)385-6967
Fax: (703)352-7725
E-mail: info@aapc.org
URL: http://www.aapc.org
Contact: Douglas M. Ronsheim, Exec. Dir.
Founded: 1963. **Members:** 3,000. **Membership Dues:** diplomate/fellow, $315 (annual) ● certified pastoral counselor, $254 (annual) ● pastoral counseling educator, pastoral care specialist, regular, and PCT, $146 (annual) ● student, $40 (annual) ● international, $24 (annual). **Staff:** 7. **Budget:** $602,000. **Regional Groups:** 10. **Description:** Pastoral counseling is a form of psychotherapy which uses spiritual resources as well as psychological understanding for healing and growth. Counselors are certified mental health professionals who have had in-depth religious and/or theological training. Represents and sets standards for the profession around the world. Certifies counselors, accredits pastoral counseling centers and approves training programs. "Is a non-sectarian and respects the spiritual commitments and religious traditions of those who needs assistance without imposing counselor beliefs onto the client." Members may join through a process of consultation and review of academic and clinical education. Offers members continuing education opportunities, encourages networks of members for professional support and enrichment, facilitates growth and innovation in the ministry of pastoral counseling and provides both specialized in-service training and supervision in pastoral counseling. **Awards: Type:** recognition. **Recipient:** for research ● **Type:** recognition. **Recipient:** for distinguished contributor. **Publications:** *Currents,* quarterly. Newsletter ● *Journeys,* semiannual. Magazine ● Directory, annual. Alternate Formats: online. **Conventions/Meetings:** annual workshop and conference, plenaries - usually April.

19457 ■ American Board of Examiners in Pastoral Counseling (ABEPC)
c/o Fred Clark, Credentials Committee Chm.
261 Spring St.
Cheshire, CT 06410
Ph: (203)271-3733
Fax: (203)271-3733
E-mail: fredclark51536@aol.com
URL: http://www.corpmgttrust.net
Contact: Fred Clark, Credentials Committee Chm.
Founded: 1921. **Staff:** 4. **Nonmembership. Description:** Offers professional certification examinations to applicants who meet the board's education, internship, and pastoral training requirements. Upon passing the exam, Board Certification is issued to professional Pastoral Counselors in private practices, and to counseling centers, hospitals, chaplaincies, and established educational programs. Annual recertification is required: CEUs, supervision, education, and practice standards must be met; professional, rather than accredited academic training may

suffice for certification. **Convention/Meeting:** none. **Awards: Frequency:** periodic. **Type:** recognition. **Recipient:** for exemplary service and professionalism.

19458 ■ CONTACT USA (CUSA)
PO Box 11078
Trenton, NJ 08620
Ph: (860)464-2144
Fax: (860)464-9432
URL: http://www.contact-usa.org
Contact: Virginia Bainbridge, Exec. Dir.
Founded: 1967. **Staff:** 3. **Budget:** $225,000. **Local Groups:** 60. **Description:** Telephone helpline and crisis intervention centers supported by individuals, corporations, foundations, and churches. Founded to respond to human need by providing confidential/ anonymous assistance on 24 hour access by telephone to trained volunteers. Serves the chronically mentally ill, the lonely, and the depressed. Serves as an accrediting agency for crisis intervention telephone programs. Functions as U.S. national committee of Life Line International (see separate entry). **Committees:** Center Services; Fund Development; Planning Administrative. **Formerly:** (1971) National Council for Telephone Ministries; (1975) CONTACT Teleministry, Inc.; (1989) CONTACT Teleministries U.S.A. **Publications:** *Directory of Centers and Services*, semiannual ● *Preparing to Listen* ● Newsletter, quarterly ● Books ● Handbooks ● Manuals. **Conventions/Meetings:** annual conference (exhibits) - always April or May.

19459 ■ Damien Ministries (DM)
PO Box 10202
Washington, DC 20018-0202
Ph: (202)526-3020
Fax: (202)526-9770
E-mail: info@damienministries.org
URL: http://www.damienministries.org
Contact: James Nickel, Exec. Dir.
Founded: 1987. **Staff:** 10. **Budget:** $600,000. **Languages:** English, Spanish. **Nonmembership. Description:** Nondenominational faith community ministering to people with HIV/AIDS. Operates food bank and transitional home for men and women. Cooperates with religious organizations working with people with AIDS. Sponsors spiritual retreats and visits to hospitals and prisons. Operations currently concentrated in Washington, DC. **Computer Services:** Mailing lists, of members. **Telecommunication Services:** TDD, (202)526-9772. **Publications:** *DamienNews*, quarterly. Newsletter. Alternate Formats: online. **Conventions/Meetings:** bimonthly Ecumenical Retreats - always in Washington, DC, and Chicago, IL.

19460 ■ International Association of Biblical Counselors (IABC)
11500 Sheridan Blvd.
Westminster, CO 80020
Ph: (303)469-4222
Fax: (303)469-1787
E-mail: info@iabc.net
URL: http://www.iabc.net
Contact: Dr. Ed Bulkley, Pres.
Membership Dues: regular, $50 (annual) ● student, $25 (annual). **Multinational. Description:** Represents organizations and individuals who saw the need for basic standards, beliefs and practices in counseling. Promotes Biblical Counseling through seminars, conferences and workshops. Encourages the development of Biblical research and offers a counselor network for the exchange of information and client referral. **Telecommunication Services:** electronic mail, information@iabc.net. **Publications:** *Biblical Counseling International*, periodic. Newsletter. Alternate Formats: online.

19461 ■ Love in Action (LIA)
4780 Yale Rd.
Memphis, TN 38128
Ph: (901)751-2468
Free: (800)201-4129
Fax: (901)751-1922

E-mail: info@loveinaction.org
URL: http://www.loveinaction.org
Contact: Rev. John J. Smid, Exec. Dir.
Founded: 1973. **Members:** 50. **Staff:** 5. **Description:** Seeks to "pursue God's intent for biblical sexuality in His way for His people." Helps individuals through counseling, literature, seminars and speaking engagements, a residential program and support groups. **Libraries: Type:** reference. **Publications:** *Between the Lines*, monthly. Newsletter. **Circulation:** 3,000 ● *Lifelines*, quarterly. Newsletter.

19462 ■ Metanoia Ministries
PO Box 448
Washington, NH 03280
Ph: (603)495-0035
Fax: (603)495-0050
E-mail: info@changeyourmind.net
URL: http://www.changeyourmind.net
Contact: Jim Van Yperen, Founder/Pres.
Founded: 1993. **Members:** 3,500. **Staff:** 2. **Budget:** $120,000. **State Groups:** 15. **Description:** Multidenominational ministry. Provides support to sexually broken people. (Sexual brokenness is defined as bisexual, homosexual, sexually addicted, sexually abused individuals.) Offers group counseling and educational programs. Maintains speaker's bureau for churches, seminars, retreats and conferences. **Libraries: Type:** reference. **Publications:** *Nexus*, monthly. Newsletter. **Price:** free. **Circulation:** 3,600.

19463 ■ Outpost
PO Box 22429
Robbinsdale, MN 55422-0429
Ph: (763)592-4700
Fax: (763)592-4701
E-mail: outpostinfo@outpostministries.org
Contact: Dan Puumala, Exec. Dir.
Founded: 1976. **Staff:** 2. **Budget:** $105,000. **Local Groups:** 3. **Description:** Nondenominational Christian community. Provides assistance to individuals who wish to leave behind their homosexual lifestyle. Offers a support group; maintains speakers' bureau; provides educational programs. **Publications:** *Outpost News*, monthly. Newsletter. **Price:** free. **Circulation:** 1,400. **Conventions/Meetings:** monthly Joshua Fellowship - meeting, description of services/theological perspectives - always first Monday except Labor Day.

19464 ■ Regeneration
PO Box 9830
Baltimore, MD 21284-9830
Ph: (410)661-0284
Fax: (410)882-6312
E-mail: regenbalto@regenerationministries.org
URL: http://www.regenerationministries.org
Contact: Alan P. Medinger, Exec. Dir.
Founded: 1979. **Staff:** 9. **Description:** Provides guidance for men and women who are leaving the homosexual lifestyle. Provides support groups; maintains speakers' bureau; conducts educational programs. **Programs:** New Beginnings. **Publications:** *Regeneration Books Catalog*, annual ● *Regeneration News*, bimonthly. Newsletter. Alternate Formats: online. **Conventions/Meetings:** periodic seminar.

Cults

19465 ■ Cult Awareness Network (CAN)
1680 N Vine St., Ste.415
Los Angeles, CA 90028
Ph: (323)468-0567
Free: (800)556-3055
Fax: (323)468-0562
E-mail: can@cultawarenessnetwork.org
Contact: Nancy O. Meara, Treas.
Founded: 1996. **Members:** 1,000. **Membership Dues:** regular, $100 (annual) ● life, $500. **Staff:** 15. **Budget:** $50,000. **Regional Groups:** 3. **State Groups:** 1. **Local Groups:** 1. **Multinational. Description:** National hotline for factual information about diverse religious groups. Professionals who

provide factual information and answers to religious questions. Provides referral service for information on religions. Promotes "respect for the right of all to believe as they wish". Supports religious freedom. Resolves family difficulties through mediations. **Libraries: Type:** reference. **Holdings:** 350; books, clippings. **Subjects:** religious groups, New Age, alternative religions, spirituality, sociology, philosophy, 1st amendment law, church/state issues. **Awards:** James Madison Religious Freedom Award. **Frequency:** annual. **Type:** monetary. **Recipient:** for significant contribution to religious freedom issues. **Subgroups:** Religious Freedom Advocates. **Affiliated With:** International Association for Religious Freedom. **Formerly:** (1986) Citizens Freedom Foundation. **Publications:** *CAN Update*, quarterly. Newsletter ● *Cult Alert, A Practical Handbook for Saving Families*. **Price:** $14.00/copy ● *The Cult Around the Corner* (in English, French, German, Hungarian, Japanese, and Russian). Book. **Price:** $8.00 plus shipping and handling ● *Tolerance 101: Practical Solutions to Interfaith Family Problems*. Book. **Price:** $14.00/copy. **Conventions/Meetings:** annual conference, interfaith meeting for people to overcome prejudices and ignorance (exhibits) - usually November/March.

19466 ■ Free Minds, Inc. (FMI)
PO Box 3818
Manhattan Beach, CA 90266
Ph: (310)545-7831
E-mail: randy@freeminds.org
URL: http://www.freeminds.org
Contact: Randall Watters, Pres.
Founded: 1992. **Description:** Works to educate the public on the dangers of cults. (According to FM a cult is an organization that uses coercive persuasion to isolate individuals.) **Convention/Meeting:** none. **Libraries: Type:** reference. **Holdings:** books. **Subjects:** psychology and cults. **Additional Websites:** http://www.watchtowernews.org, http://www.exjws. net, http://www.randytv.com. **Formerly:** Bethel Ministries. **Publications:** *Free Minds Journal*, bimonthly. **Circulation:** 3,000. Alternate Formats: online ● Books.

19467 ■ Personal Freedom Outreach (PFO)
PO Box 26062
St. Louis, MO 63136-0062
Ph: (314)921-9800
Fax: (314)921-7390
URL: http://www.pfo.org
Contact: M. Kurt Goedelman, Founder/Exec. Dir.
Founded: 1975. **Staff:** 9. **Description:** Interested Christians. Educates Christians about the "dangers and heretical doctrines" of religious cults. Attempts to reach members of such cults through Christian gospel and seeks to warn them of "unbiblical teachings that may be found within the church itself". **Libraries: Type:** reference. **Holdings:** audiovisuals, books, clippings, periodicals. **Subjects:** Christian apologetics, cults. **Publications:** *The Quarterly Journal*. Newsletter. Features articles, editorials, news updates and book reviews. **Price:** $49.95 CD-ROM; $20.00 in U.S.; $25.00 in Canada; $35.00 outside U.S. and Canada. ISSN: 1083-6853. Alternate Formats: online; CD-ROM ● Audiotape. **Price:** $3.00 plus shipping and handling; $60.00 complete set of conference tapes ● Video. **Price:** $19.95 plus shipping and handling. **Conventions/Meetings:** biennial St. Louis Conference on Biblical Discernment ● annual Witness Now for Jesus Convention - conference (exhibits) - always October, New Ringgold, PA.

19468 ■ Spiritual Counterfeits Project (SCP)
PO Box 4308
Berkeley, CA 94704-0308
Ph: (510)540-0300 (510)540-5767
Fax: (510)540-1107
E-mail: access@scp-inc.org
URL: http://www.scp-inc.org
Contact: Tal Brooke, Pres.
Founded: 1975. **Members:** 18,000. **Membership Dues:** regular, $25 (annual). **Staff:** 7. **Budget:** $450,000. **Description:** A Christian think-tank comprised of individuals from top schools who have spent years on various spiritual paths-(from Sai Baba and

Rajneesh, to TM and the Course in Miracles)-before leaving them. Examines spiritual phenomena and cultural trends such as Cyberspace, Near Death Experiences, Deep Ecology, Gaia, Witchcraft, and UFOs. Maintains extensive files on cults, the occult, and new religious movements. **Libraries: Type:** reference. **Holdings:** 7,000. **Subjects:** apologetics. **Awards:** Evangelical Press Association Award. **Frequency:** annual. **Type:** recognition. **Telecommunication Services:** electronic mail, scp@scp-inc.org. **Publications:** *SCP Journal*, quarterly. Includes research on cults and new religious movements. **Price:** $25.00/year in U.S.; $35.00/year outside U.S. **Circulation:** 5,000 ● *SCP Newsletter*. Includes brief synopsis of journal stories. **Price:** $10.00/year. **Circulation:** 18,000 ● Booklets ● Books ● Catalog.

19469 ■ Watchman Fellowship
PO Box 13340
Arlington, TX 76094-0340
Ph: (817)277-0023
Fax: (817)277-8098
E-mail: pcondra@watchman.org
URL: http://www.watchman.org
Contact: James K. Walker, Pres.
Founded: 1979. **Staff:** 15. **Budget:** $750,000. **State Groups:** 8. **Description:** Provides information and education about cults, the occult, and new religious movements. Offers speakers and educational programs. **Libraries: Type:** open to the public; by appointment only. **Holdings:** archival material, books, clippings, periodicals. **Publications:** *The Watchman Espositor*, bimonthly. Magazine. Alternate Formats: online.

Dance

19470 ■ Sacred Dance Society (SDS)
PO Box 323
Middletown, CA 95461
Ph: (415)971-3573
E-mail: julia@sacreddance.org
URL: http://www.sacreddance.org
Contact: Julia Carter, Co-Chair
Description: Represents the interests of individuals dedicated to the practice of community dance. Practices and believes the religious value of extended community dance rituals. Recognizes and supports other spiritual practices that can help to engender a primary religious or mystical experience. Shares a fundamental belief in the value of creating a safe social environment of peacefulness, loving kindness and mutual respect within the communities.

Daoist

19471 ■ Center for Confucian Science
c/o Dr. Thomas Hosuck Kang, Pres.
1318 Randolph St. NE
Washington, DC 20017
Ph: (202)526-6818
Fax: (202)526-6818
E-mail: tkang@wam.umd.edu
URL: http://www.wam.umd.edu/~tkang/center.html
Contact: Dr. Thomas Hosuck Kang, Pres.
Founded: 1980. **Members:** 100. **Staff:** 2. **Budget:** $10,000. **Regional Groups:** 3. **Languages:** Chinese, English, Japanese, Korean. **Description:** Seeks to spread Confucian teachings throughout the world. Conducts Quiet-Sitting and Confucian Dao meditation. Assists institutions in organizing Confucian societies. Compiles bibliographies and supplies information on Confucianism. **Libraries: Type:** reference; by appointment only. **Holdings:** 500; audiovisuals, books, video recordings. **Subjects:** Confucianism. **Computer Services:** database, bibliography of Confucian studies in Western languages, 1662-present. **Formerly:** (2001) Center for Dao-Confucianism. **Publications:** *A Bibliography on Confucian Studies in Western Languages* (in English, French, German, Italian, Latin, and Russian) ● *Confucian Studies in the West*. Survey. Survey of the spread of Confucianism in the West by Western missionaries

and scholars and its publications in Western languages throughout the world. **Price:** $7.00 ● *Confucius and Confucianism: Questions and Answers*. Book. Catechism for Confucian church, syllabus for classes, reference book for libraries, and general reading for the public. **Price:** $16.00 ● *Why the North Koreans Behave as They Do*. Features information based on Confucian cultural gene theory by analyzing the process of engineering of 25 million human dollies. **Price:** $8.00. **Conventions/Meetings:** annual board meeting.

Divine Science

19472 ■ Divine Science Federation International (DSFI)
8084 Watson Rd., Ste.236
St. Louis, MO 63119
Ph: (314)842-2335
Free: (800)644-9680
Fax: (314)842-2650
E-mail: divscifederation@aol.com
URL: http://divinesciencefederation.org
Contact: Mrs. Pat Mazanec, Sec.
Founded: 1956. **Members:** 1,400. **Staff:** 1. **State Groups:** 16. **National Groups:** 2. **Multinational. Description:** Service organization for members of Divine Science churches and centers and all who are seeking. (The Divine Science message emphasizes the importance of individual freedom in matters of religious belief, stresses that God "is equally present everywhere, is pure Spirit, absolute, changeless, eternal, manifesting in all creation and in every person"; its teachings require autonomy for fellowships and churches.) Seeks to: unite all Divine Science churches, fellowships, and centers; promote Divine Science principles and ideas; present Divine Science teachings to the world as a Christian religion. Sponsors retreats; promotes field trips and seminars. Administers Divine Science/Educational materials. Offers placement service; compiles statistics. **Libraries: Type:** open to the public. **Holdings:** 28,000; books. **Subjects:** healing, omnipresence, biblical studies. **Committees:** Church; Study Group. **Publications:** *At.One.Ment*, bimonthly. Booklet. Contains inspirational articles and daily devotionals. **Price:** $12.00 in U.S.; $14.00 outside U.S. **Circulation:** 200 ● *Divine Science and Healing*. Book. **Price:** $19.95 each ● *Divine Science Its Principle and Practice*. Book. **Price:** $12.95 each ● *In the Light of Healing*. Book. **Price:** $12.95 each ● *Short Lessons in Divine Science*. Book. **Price:** $12.95 each ● *Spirit in Action*, monthly. Newsletter. Includes church, federation, and individual activities, and inspirational material. **Price:** free. **Circulation:** 800 ● *Truth and Health*. Book. **Price:** $16.50 each. **Conventions/Meetings:** biennial conference (exhibits).

19473 ■ Divine Science Ministers Association (DSMA)
8847 Airline Hwy.
Baton Rouge, LA 70815-4004
Ph: (225)924-3780
E-mail: omnip@divinescienceministersassociation.org
URL: http://www.divinescienceministersassociation.org
Contact: Rev. Christine Emmerling, Pres.
Founded: 1984. **Members:** 45. **Membership Dues:** Ordained Divine Science Minister, $35 (annual). **Regional Groups:** 5. **Multinational. Description:** Licensed and ordained Divine Science ministers. Supports and encourages individual ministers to apply and practice the principles of Divine Science in the organization and ministry of individual churches and centers. **Affiliated With:** Divine Science Federation International; International New Thought Alliance. **Formerly:** (2000) Divine Science Ministers Organization. **Conventions/Meetings:** biennial Divine Science Conference, held in conjunction with Divine Science Federation International.

Eastern Orthodox

19474 ■ Fellowship of St. John the Divine
Antiochian Orthodox Christian Archdiocese
PO Box 5238
Englewood, NJ 07631-5238

Ph: (201)871-1355
Fax: (201)871-7954
E-mail: archdiocese@antiochian.org
URL: http://www.antiochian.org/Fellowship
Contact: Joan Farha, Pres.
Founded: 1938. **Members:** 3,500. **Budget:** $300,000. **Regional Groups:** 7. **Local Groups:** 200. **Description:** Orthodox Christian adults. Aims to: cultivate the true spirit and understanding of Eastern Orthodoxy; discipline youth for a fuller participation in the life of the church; perpetuate and disseminate the faith of their forefathers. Promotes and participates in religious lectures, conferences, and retreats; distributes religious material including books to groups, colleges, and universities; sponsors seminarians at various theological schools; cooperates with other Orthodox Christian youth groups and college student fellowships for the common welfare and final union of the church in America. Operates charitable program. Works as the humanitarian arm of the Archdiocese; ministers to various adult-age groups as needed. **Awards:** Adult Fellowship. **Type:** fellowship ● **Type:** recognition ● Senior Fellowship. **Type:** fellowship ● Young Adult Fellowship. **Type:** fellowship. **Committees:** Adult Education and Evangelization; Bible Bowl Contest; Campus Ministry; Christian Education; Creative Arts Contest; Creative Writing Contest; Food for Hungry People; Humanitarian; Library Project; Missionary Activity; Oratorical Contest; Poetry and Photography Festivals; Sacred Music; Social Awareness; Spiritual Involvement. **Formerly:** Syrian Orthodox Youth Organization; (1991) Society of Orthodox Youth Organizations. **Conventions/Meetings:** biennial convention.

19475 ■ Macedonian Orthodox Youth Association of North America (MOYANA)
5083 Onondaga Rd.
Syracuse, NY 13215
Ph: (315)487-1265
Fax: (315)487-1265
E-mail: moyana@moyana.org
URL: http://www.moyana.org
Contact: Metodija A. Koloski, Rep.
Founded: 2001. **Multinational. Description:** Serves to activate and unite the Macedonian Orthodox parish youth for the preservation and promotion of the Orthodox Christian faith. Aims to help the young people of the Diocese enhance their knowledge and appreciation of the Orthodox Christian faith. Promotes cooperation and love among the young people of the Diocese. Addresses the needs of aspiring young adults in the areas of self-identity and spiritual development. Educates all Macedonian Orthodox youth about the true ethnic Macedonian national origin, history, and heritage. **Publications:** Newsletter.

19476 ■ Orthodox People in America
7061 Itaska Dr.
St. Louis, MO 63123
Ph: (314)351-0404
Fax: (314)351-0453
Contact: Rev. Fr. Nick Botonis, Chm.
Founded: 1991. **Members:** 15. **Membership Dues:** regular, $14 (annual). **Staff:** 1. **Budget:** $240. **Languages:** English, Greek. **Description:** Promotes the Eastern Orthodox Christian faith to those who have no knowledge of the Church and its meaning. Provides outreach programs for orphans and the needy. **Publications:** *Angelic Host*. **Price:** $15.00/year ● Pamphlets. **Conventions/Meetings:** annual meeting ● St. Dionysios Theological Seminar.

19477 ■ Orthodox Theological Society in America (OTSA)
50 Goddard Ave.
Brookline, MA 02445-7415
E-mail: jbehr@svots.edu
URL: http://www.otsamerica.org
Contact: Fr. John Behr, Pres.
Founded: 1966. **Members:** 150. **Membership Dues:** individual, $25 (annual). **Description:** Professors of theology; scholars. Aims to serve the Orthodox Church in North America by fostering cooperation among Orthodox theologians; coordinating Orthodox

theological activity in the U.S; providing an opportunity for theological discussions; encouraging research and writing in the field. Organized under the auspices of the Standing Conference of the Canonical Orthodox Bishops in the Americas. **Telecommunication Services:** electronic mail, tonyvrame@mac.com. **Publications:** Report, annual ● Bulletin, periodic ● Membership Directory, periodic. **Conventions/Meetings:** annual conference.

19478 ■ Standing Conference of the Canonical Orthodox Bishops in the Americas (SCOBA)

10 E 79th St.
New York, NY 10021-0106
Ph: (212)570-3593
Fax: (212)774-0202
E-mail: scoba@goarch.org
URL: http://www.scoba.us
Contact: Dionisia Floropoulos, Asst.

Founded: 1960. **Members:** 9. **Staff:** 2. **Description:** Presiding hierarchs of eight Eastern Orthodox ecclesiastical bodies in the Western Hemisphere. Coordinates activities of the Orthodox Church in the Americas. **Commissions:** Campus; Canonical; Christian Education; Communications; Ecumenical Relations; Liturgical; Military and Other Chaplaincies; Missions; Regional Clergy Fellowships; Relief Agency; Study and Planning. **Affiliated With:** Orthodox Theological Society in America. **Publications:** *Guidelines for Orthodox Christians in Ecumenical Relations* ● *The Official Orthodox Directory - 2004.* **Price:** $9.95 perfect bound; $11.95 spiral bound ● *On The Upbeat,* 10/year. Book ● *Orthodox Observer,* 10/year. Book ● *The Word,* 10/year. Book ● *Young Life,* 10/year. Book. **Conventions/Meetings:** semiannual meeting.

Ecumenical

19479 ■ American Forum for Jewish-Christian Cooperation (AFJCC)

c/o Dr. David Z. Ben-Ami, Chm./Founder
1407 Montfort Dr.
Harrisburg, PA 17110
Ph: (717)236-0437
Fax: (717)541-5487
E-mail: display@localnet.com
URL: http://www.va.gov/dmeeo/org/other.htm
Contact: Dr. David Z. Ben-Ami, Chm./Founder

Founded: 1980. **Staff:** 3. **Regional Groups:** 6. **State Groups:** 25. **Local Groups:** 15. **National Groups:** 3. **Languages:** Czech, English, German, Hebrew, Polish, Romanian, Slovak, Yiddish. **Nonmembership. Multinational. Description:** Bishops, clergymen, political leaders, government officials, U.S. ambassadors, ambassadors accredited to Washington, business leaders, ethnic and religious leaders, congress people, and others united to engage in a program of interreligious dialogue and education. Works to combat anti-Semitism and promote pluralism. Fosters understanding between Jews, Christians, Muslims and other faith groups with the aim of achieving national unity and international understanding. Seeks to develop understanding by educating each community in the biblical and moral ground on which they agree, and works to educate society on the value of biblical and ethical principles in the home, business, government, and in social exchange. Works to build better relationships among men and women of all religions, races, and nationalities on civic and social levels. Sponsors programs of speakers, artists, and exhibits on "Celebration of the Faith of America", the celebration of the Judeo-Christian heritage. Attempts to give expression to religious traditions that have influenced American life and to the ideals of equality and fraternity with emphasis on the sacredness of human personality, respect for human rights, and the duty of cooperation for the common welfare. Provides interfaith counseling for couples contemplating marriage. Holds annual Passover Seder with the participation of foreign diplomats accredited to Washington, Inaugural Presidential Interreligious Convocation, interreligious

convocations, religious summit meetings, seminars, and symposium. Assists Ecumenical councils in Hungary, the Czech and Slovak Republics, Austria, Ukraine, Poland, and Germany. Co-sponsors the Leipziger (Germany) Synagogue Choir, composed of non-Jews (Christians) who spend their leisure time presenting Hebraic, Israeli and Yiddish Music to audiences in Europe and the U.S.A. **Libraries: Type:** reference. **Holdings:** 5,000; archival material. **Subjects:** Judaism, Christianity, religious freedom, interfaith relations, Muslim and interfaith studies and affairs. **Awards:** American Statesman Award. **Frequency:** annual. **Type:** recognition. **Recipient:** for a U.S. or European Ambassador ● Religious Freedom Award. **Frequency:** annual. **Type:** recognition. **Recipient:** for a Bishop or statesman. **Publications:** *American Forum,* semiannual. Newsletter. Contains calendar of events; reports and analysis; commentary on Jewish-Christian interfaith relations; ecumenical understanding and cooperation. **Price:** free to contributors and friends. **Advertising:** accepted. **Conventions/Meetings:** annual Passover Seder - meeting.

19480 ■ Center for Christian/Jewish Understanding of Sacred Heart University

c/o Sacred Heart University
5151 Park Ave.
Fairfield, CT 06825-1000
Ph: (203)365-7592
Fax: (203)365-4815
E-mail: daleg@sacredheart.edu
URL: http://www.sacredheart.edu/pages/122_center_for_christian_jewish_understanding.cfm
Contact: Rabbi Joseph H. Ehrenkranz, Exec. Dir.

Founded: 1992. **Members:** 4,000. **Staff:** 4. **Budget:** $500,000. **Description:** Seeks to promote better understanding and interaction between Christians and Jews. **Libraries: Type:** not open to the public. **Holdings:** 6,000. **Subjects:** Catholic, Judaic, Protestant, Muslim religions. **Awards:** Nostra Aetate Award. **Frequency:** annual. **Type:** recognition. **Recipient:** for service to humanity. **Formerly:** (2002) Center for Christian/Jewish Understanding. **Publications:** *CCJU Perspective,* quarterly. Newsletter ● *Our Age (1966).* Book ● *Religion and Violence, Religion and Peace (2000).* Book ● *With My Last Breath, Let Me See Jerusalem (1999).* Book. **Conventions/Meetings:** periodic conference.

19481 ■ Churches Uniting in Christ (CUIC)

475 E Lockwood
Webster Groves, MO 63119-3124
Ph: (314)252-3160
E-mail: prosner@eden.edu
URL: http://www.cuicinfo.org
Contact: Rev. Patrice L. Rosner, Dir.

Founded: 2002. **Staff:** 2. **National Groups:** 11. **Description:** A relationship among nine communions that agree to start living more fully in Christ; members are The African Methodist Episcopal Church, the African Methodist Episcopal Zion Church, the Christian Church (Disciples of Christ), the Christian Methodist Episcopal Church, the Episcopal Church, the International Council of Community Churches, the Presbyterian Church, the United Church of Christ, and the United Methodist Church. Participating as Partners in Faith and Dialogue are the Evangelical Lutheran Church in America and the Moravian Church, North. Two major goals are: "to heed the emphatic call to erase racism by challenging the system of white privilege that has so distorted life in this society and in the churches themselves, and to provide, by the year 2007, a foundation for the mutual recognition and reconciliation of ordained ministry by the members of the organization". **Formerly:** (2003) Consultation on Church Union.

19482 ■ Congress of National Black Churches (CNBC)

Address Unknown since 2007

Founded: 1978. **Members:** 8. **Membership Dues:** denomination, $10,000 (annual). **Staff:** 40. **Budget:** $5,000,000. **Description:** Coalition of eight historically black denominations. Purpose: to promote unity, charity, and fellowship among the member denomina-

tions; to provide the opportunity for the identification and implementation of program efforts that may be achieved more effectively through collective action than by any single denomination. Seeks funding from foundations, corporations, public and government sources, and member denominations. **Awards:** Leadership Award. **Frequency:** annual. **Type:** recognition. **Programs:** Children and Family Development; Economic Development; Leadership Development; National Anti-Drug and Violence Campaign; National Health. **Publications:** *Visions,* quarterly. Newsletter. **Advertising:** not accepted. **Conventions/Meetings:** annual conference; **Avg. Attendance:** 350.

19483 ■ Council on Christian Unity (CCU)

PO Box 1986
Indianapolis, IN 46206-1986
Ph: (317)713-2586
Fax: (317)713-2588
E-mail: rozanne@ccu.disciples.org
URL: http://www.disciples.org/ccu
Contact: Rev. Dr. Robert K. Welsh, Pres.

Founded: 1910. **Staff:** 2. **Budget:** $400,000. **State Groups:** 36. **Nonmembership. Description:** An administrative unit of the Christian Church (Disciples of Christ) reporting to the General Assembly of the Christian Church (Disciples of Christ) and participating in various aspects of the ecumenical movement. **Commissions:** Churches United in Christ; Disciples of Christ-Roman Catholic Dialogue; Disciples - Reformed International Dialogue; Ecumenical Partnership with the United Church of Christ. **Affiliated With:** National Council of Churches of Christ in the U.S.A. **Formerly:** Council on Christian Union; Association for the Promotion of Christian Union. **Publications:** *Called to Unity,* biennial. **Conventions/Meetings:** biennial meeting.

19484 ■ Ecumenical Celebrations (EC)

c/o Church Women United
The Interchurch Center
475 Riverside Dr., Ste.1626A
New York, NY 10115-0002
Ph: (212)870-2347
Free: (800)298-5551
Fax: (212)870-2338
E-mail: cwu@churchwomen.org
URL: http://www.churchwomen.org
Contact: Gail Mengel, Pres.

Founded: 1941. **Members:** 500,000. **Staff:** 13. **Regional Groups:** 8. **State Groups:** 52. **Local Groups:** 1,750. **National Groups:** 10. **Languages:** English, Spanish. **Description:** Serves as a project of Church Women United (see separate entry). Includes participants such as: Protestant, Roman Catholic, Orthodox, and other Christian women. Plans, produces, and promotes World Day of Prayer (first Friday of March), May Fellowship Day (first Friday of May), and World Community Day (first Friday of November). Conducts celebrations including worship, prayer, study, and action. Utilizes resources such as worship services, posters, feature stories, and radio and television advertisements. **Publications:** *The Churchwoman,* quarterly ● *Wellsprings.*

19485 ■ Faith at Work (FAW)

106 E Broad St., Ste.B
Falls Church, VA 22046-4501
Ph: (703)237-3426
Free: (800)245-7378
Fax: (703)237-0157
E-mail: info@faithatwork.com
URL: http://www.faithatwork.com
Contact: Doug Wysockey-Johnson, Exec. Dir.

Founded: 1956. **Members:** 7,200. **Budget:** $350,000. **Regional Groups:** 5. **Description:** Ecumenical network of progressive Christians at the growing edge of the church. Empowers people to explore, discern and act on their many gifts and calls in the complexity of their daily lives for the good of God's world. Provides magazines, resources, events and trainings that give experiences of hearing call, tools for discerning call, and trainings for organizations wanting to provide systems and structures to support call. These efforts are undergirded by the network's cutting edge research and openness to continue learning about the nature and nurture of call. **Working Groups:** Communications; Congregations; Events; Stewardship. **Publications:** Magazine, quarterly. **Circulation:** 7,500. **Conventions/Meetings:** periodic regional meeting.

19486 ■ Fellowship in Prayer (FIP)
291 Witherspoon St.
Princeton, NJ 08542-3227
Ph: (609)924-6863
Fax: (609)924-6910
E-mail: lbaumann@sacredjourney.org
URL: http://www.sacredjourney.org
Contact: Linda D. Baumann, Mgr.
Founded: 1949. **Membership Dues:** domestic, $18 (annual) ● multinational, $26 (annual). **Staff:** 3. **Budget:** $300,000. **Nonmembership. Multinational.** **Description:** Interfaith organization dedicated in encouraging people to deepen their own faith and prayer life. Promotes the practice of prayer and meditation among all religious faiths. Sponsors public lectures, programs, performances, and workshops. **Also Known As:** Sacred Journey. **Publications:** The Gift of Prayer. Book. Treasury of prayers from the world's faith traditions. **Price:** $19.95 ● Sacred Journey: The Journal of Fellowship in Prayer, bimonthly. Contains articles, prayers, poems, and photos by spiritual leaders and lay people of all faiths. **Price:** $18.00 in U.S.; $26.00 outside U.S. ISSN: 1096-5939. **Circulation:** 10,000 ● The Way of Prayer. Booklet. **Price:** $2.00. **Conventions/Meetings:** biennial conference.

19487 ■ Graymoor Ecumenical and Interreligious Institute (GEII)
c/o Mrs. Veronica Sullivan, Business Mgr.
PO Box 300
Garrison, NY 10524-0300
Ph: (845)424-2109 (212)870-2330
Free: (800)338-2620
Fax: (845)424-2163
E-mail: rsullivan@atonementfriars.org
URL: http://www.geii.org
Contact: Mrs. Veronica Sullivan, Business Mgr.
Founded: 1967. **Staff:** 3. **Languages:** English, German, Italian, Spanish. **Multinational. Description:** Works for Christian unity and interreligious dialogue; serves primarily, but not exclusively, the Roman Catholic Church. Operates specialization desks; maintains membership in and collaboration with national and local ecumenical and interreligious organizations and agencies; sponsors annual Week of Prayer for Christian Unity; cooperates with individuals engaged in ecumenical and interreligious work. **Formerly:** Graymoor Ecumenical Institute. **Publications:** Ecumenical Trends, 11/year. Journal. Contains book reviews, editorials, and study resources. **Price:** $20.00/year in U.S.; $22.00/year outside U.S. ISSN: 0360-9073. **Circulation:** 2,400. Alternate Formats: microform ● Graymoor Papers ● Booklets ● Books ● Pamphlets ● Reports ● Also distributes leaflets and posters. **Conventions/Meetings:** seminar ● workshop.

19488 ■ The Interchurch Center (TIC)
475 Riverside Dr.
New York, NY 10115-0002
Ph: (212)870-2200 (212)870-3804
Fax: (212)870-2440
E-mail: tdelduca@interchurch-center.org
URL: http://interchurch-center.library.net
Contact: Sue M. Dennis, Exec. Dir.
Founded: 1948. **Budget:** $10,000,000. **Description:** A center for ecumenical and interfaith cooperation; serves as national headquarters building for a number of religious organizations and their boards and agencies including the National Council of the Churches of Christ in the U.S.A., American Baptist Church, Presbyterian Church (U.S.A.), Reformed Church in America, United Church of Christ, and United Methodist Church. Renovated the New Revised Standard Bible Room. Presents variety of exhibits, programs, worship services, and concerts of cultural, educational, and ecumenical significance. **Libraries: Type:** reference; open to the public; by appointment only. **Holdings:** 13,500; archival material, books, periodicals. **Subjects:** ecumenism, mis-

sions, theology, biblical studies, social issues. **Formerly:** Protestant Center. **Publications:** Tenant Telephone Directory, annual. Provides in-house telephone information. **Price:** $2.00. **Conventions/Meetings:** weekly workshop.

19489 ■ International Association of Ministers Wives and Ministers Widows (IAMWMW)
26 Fowler St.
New Haven, CT 06515
Ph: (203)397-3400 (203)387-7634
Fax: (203)397-1844
E-mail: swkholmes@yahoo.com
URL: http://www.iamwmw.org
Contact: Dr. Janie Charles Holmes, Pres.
Founded: 1941. **Members:** 43,000. **Membership Dues:** life, $100. **Staff:** 20. **Budget:** $250,000. **Regional Groups:** 7. **National Groups:** 11. **Multinational. Description:** Wives and widows of ministers of 103 religious denominations. Seeks to erase barriers existing between religious communions. Sponsors competitions; conducts research; compiles statistics. Maintains museum, hall of fame, and speakers' bureau. **Awards: Type:** recognition. **Committees:** Archives; Endowment; Human Relations; Public Relations; Social Concerns. **Departments:** Education; Student Affairs. **Formerly:** National Association of Ministers' Wives; (1978) National Association of Ministers Wives and Ministers' Widows; (1989) International Radiator Standards Association. **Publications:** Hymnal: On Wings of Song ● The Ministers' Wives Herald, quarterly. Journal. **Price:** included in membership dues. **Circulation:** 2,200. **Advertising:** accepted ● Prayers for All Seasons, annual ● Books. **Conventions/Meetings:** annual conference - always June.

19490 ■ International Prayer Fellowship (IPF)
c/o SEJ Ministry
PO Box 237
Lake Junaluska, NC 28745
Ph: (828)454-6710
Free: (888)525-3586
E-mail: rdowdy@sejumc.org
Contact: Roger Dowdy, Lay Ministry Dir.
Founded: 1966. **Members:** 240. **Staff:** 1. **Description:** Individuals interested in prayer life movements. Promotes prayer on an individual basis and in-group relations. Provides speakers and leaders for conferences or retreats. Offers scholarships. **Publications:** Newsletter, monthly. **Price:** free. **Conventions/Meetings:** annual conference - second week of October.

19491 ■ Koinonia Foundation (KF)
6037 Franconia Rd.
Alexandria, VA 22310
Ph: (703)971-1991
Fax: (703)971-0449
E-mail: info@koinfound.org
URL: http://www.thekoinoniafoundation.org
Contact: Amy C. Lopez, Exec. Dir.
Founded: 1951. **Description:** Serves as ecumenical organization devoted to spiritual education, ecology, and the. arts. Supports efforts to integrate the mind, body, and spirit, and assist in the healing of the planet. Provides grants of $2000 or less for projects that the group feels will further spiritual integration of the planet. **Convention/Meeting:** none. **Awards: Frequency:** annual. **Type:** grant. **Recipient:** for a non-profit organization with the most significant project to fulfill its mission. **Committees:** Proposal Review.

19492 ■ Liturgical Conference (LC)
PO Box 31
Evanston, IL 60204
E-mail: ron.anderson@garrett.edu
URL: http://www.liturgicalconference.org
Contact: E. Byron Anderson, Pres.
Founded: 1940. **Members:** 2,500. **Membership Dues:** regular, $60 (annual). **Multinational. Description:** Ecumenical association of clergy and laypeople interested in the renewal of worship in the Christian churches. **Libraries: Type:** not open to the public. **Subjects:** preaching, worship, ritual. **Computer**

Services: Mailing lists. **Absorbed:** Lutheran Society for Worship, Music and the Arts. **Formerly:** (1943) Benedictine Liturgical Conference. **Publications:** Homily Service (in English and Spanish), monthly. Journal. Contains homily and preaching resource, also used for scripture study. **Price:** $71.00 /year for individuals; $45.00/year for students; $107.00 /year for institutions. ISSN: 0732-1872. **Circulation:** 3,000. Alternate Formats: online ● Liturgy, quarterly. Journal. **Price:** $56.00 /year for individuals; $35.00/ year for students; $87.00 /year for institutions ● Preaching on Death: An Ecumenical Resource. Books ● Landscape of Praise, winner of the 1997 Catholic Press Association Award for liturgy. **Conventions/Meetings:** annual board meeting - every last Saturday of February.

19493 ■ National Association of Diocesan Ecumenical Officers (NADEO)
c/o Rev. Robert B. Flannery, Pres.
St. Francis Xavier Catholic Church
303 S Poplar St.
Carbondale, IL 62901
Ph: (618)457-4556
Fax: (618)457-7368
E-mail: rbflan@globaleyes.net
URL: http://www.nadeo.org
Contact: Rev. Robert B. Flannery, Pres.
Founded: 1972. **Members:** 180. **Membership Dues:** full, $200 (annual) ● associate, $10 (annual). **Description:** Representatives of Roman Catholic dioceses in the U.S. Seeks to stimulate an exchange of ideas, experiences, and evaluations among the ecumenical officers of Roman Catholic archdioceses. Promotes programs that furthers the work of Christian unity and inter-religious cooperation. **Awards:** James Fitzgerald Award. **Frequency:** annual. **Type:** recognition. **Recipient:** for distinguished ecumenical service. **Committees:** Awards; Catholic Jewish Relations; Faiths in the World; Lutheran/Anglican/Roman Catholic; Research and Development. **Publications:** Handbook for Catholic Ecumenical Officers ● NADEO Newsletter, quarterly ● Booklet, annual. **Conventions/Meetings:** annual Catholic Program - conference and seminar, specifically for Catholic participants in the National Workshop for Christian Unity - usually spring ● annual general assembly.

19494 ■ National Association of Ecumenical and Interreligious Staff (NAEIS)
PO Box 7093
Tacoma, WA 98406-0093
Ph: (253)759-0141
Fax: (253)759-9689
E-mail: naeisjan@aol.com
URL: http://www.naeis.org
Contact: Ms. Janet E. Leng, Membership Off.
Founded: 1940. **Members:** 250. **Membership Dues:** associate staff, $75 (annual) ● executive, $125 (annual) ● denominational/interreligious staff, $100 (annual). **Staff:** 1. **Budget:** $50,875. **Regional Groups:** 2. **State Groups:** 24. **Local Groups:** 1,000. **Description:** Executives and other paid staff of ecumenical and interfaith organizations. Develops standards and guidelines for its members; supports publications; arranges for exchange, spiritual enrichment, and professional growth; encourages and assists in recruitment. **Awards:** Award of Excellence. **Frequency:** annual. **Type:** recognition. **Recipient:** to individual, group or organization who provided significant leadership or action in ecumenical and/or interfaith relations, thereby effecting understanding, respect and cooperation with the faith community of their local area. **Computer Services:** database, councils of churches and other ecumenical/interfaith ministries in the U.S. **Formed by Merger of:** (1974) Association of Executive Secretaries; (1974) Employed Council Officers Association. **Formerly:** (1971) Association of Council Secretaries; (1999) National Association of Ecumenical Staff. **Publications:** NAEIS News, semiannual. Newsletter. Contains news of local/regional ecumenical/interreligious organizations around the U.S., calendar of events, and employment opportunity listings. **Price:** $15.00/year. **Circulation:** 1,400.

19495 ■ National Cathedral Association (NCA)
Washington Natl. Cathedral
3101 Wisconsin Ave. NW
Washington, DC 20016-5098
Ph: (202)537-6200 (202)364-6616
Free: (800)622-6304
Fax: (202)364-6600
E-mail: nca@cathedral.org
URL: http://www.cathedral.org/cathedral
Contact: Vanessa Andrews, Dir.
Founded: 1933. **Members:** 14,000. **Membership Dues:** friend, $40 (annual) ● family, $50 (annual) ● contributor, $75 (annual) ● supporter, $125 (annual) ● patron, $250 (annual) ● sustainer, $500 (annual) ● Dean's List, $1,000 (annual). **Staff:** 6. **Regional Groups:** 97. **Description:** National group of persons from many denominations who contribute to support and extend the ministry of the Washington Cathedral (the Cathedral Church of St. Peter and St. Paul in Washington, DC, also known as the National Cathedral), which has no resident congregation. In addition to public worship, the Cathedral hosts ecumenical seminars and conferences and the Cathedral Foundation operates four schools; one of these, a postgraduate institution, the College of Preachers, trains persons from throughout the country. **Publications:** *Cathedral Age*, quarterly. Magazine. **Price:** included in membership dues ● Audiotapes ● Books ● Videos. **Conventions/Meetings:** annual conference (exhibits).

19496 ■ National Conference for Community and Justice (NCCJ)
PO Box 402
Brooklyn, NY 11219-0402
Ph: (718)783-0044 (630)789-6709
Fax: (630)789-6718
E-mail: nationaloffice@nccj.org
URL: http://www.nccj.org
Contact: Alan A. May JD, Interim Pres./CEO
Founded: 1927. **Staff:** 400. **Regional Groups:** 60. **Description:** Represents individuals from all racial, religious, cultural and ethnic groups who, without compromise of conscience or of their distinctive religious differences, work together for better human relations. Works to: promote through education, conflict resolution and advocacy, understanding, and cooperation among all religious, ethnic cultural groups and races; analyze, moderate, and finally eliminate intergroup prejudices that disfigure religious, business, social, and political relations, with a view to the establishment of a social order in which the religious ideals of whole communities and justice shall become the standards of human relationships. Organizes programs on topics including adults, youth, community relations and the administration of justice, equal opportunity in the workplace, community, interfaith relations and with youth and emerging leaders. Conducts training and workshops in human relations. Includes programming initiatives: Voice of Conscience; Diversity Network; National Conversation on Race, Ethnicity and Culture. **Awards:** Humanitarian Awards. **Frequency:** annual. **Type:** recognition. **Formerly:** (1998) National Conference of Christians and Jews. **Publications:** *Calendar of Religious and Ethnic Festivals*, triennial. Lists holy days and ethnic holidays and festivals. ● *NCCJ Annual Report*, annual. Alternate Formats: online ● *NCCJ Newsletter*, semiannual. **Price:** free. Alternate Formats: online ● Brochures ● Also publishes research books and papers. **Conventions/Meetings:** annual board meeting - usually April.

19497 ■ National Council of Churches of Christ in the U.S.A. (NCC)
475 Riverside Dr., Ste.880
New York, NY 10115
Ph: (212)870-2227
Fax: (212)870-2030
E-mail: news@ncccusa.org
URL: http://www.ncccusa.org
Contact: Robert W. Edgar, Gen. Sec.
Founded: 1950. **Members:** 36. **Staff:** 350. **Budget:** $60,000,000. **Description:** Serves as a community of its constituent communions in manifesting one-

ness in Jesus Christ as Divine Lord and Savior and to do together those things which can better be done united than separated. Programs include: providing disaster relief, refugee assistance, and development aid to people throughout the world in cooperation with overseas churches and through Church World Service, the Council's global service and witness ministry, and ministries in education, public policy, justice and unity among Christians and other people of faith. Current emphases include a 10-year mobilization to overcome poverty and efforts toward a more inclusive US ecumenical body. **Also Known As:** National Council of Churches. **Publications:** *EcuLink*, quarterly. Newsletter. Includes developments in Christian education. **Price:** free. **Circulation:** 150,000 ● *Yearbook of American and Canadian Churches*, annual. Provides Compuserve listings plus statistics. **Conventions/Meetings:** annual general assembly and board meeting - usually November.

19498 ■ North American Academy of Ecumenists (NAAE)
c/o Rev. Russell L. Meyer, Membership Sec.-Treas.
5025 Southampton Cir.
Tampa, FL 33647-2031
Ph: (813)910-1532
Fax: (813)435-3239
E-mail: russellm@fbsynod.org
URL: http://www.naae.net
Contact: Rev. Russell L. Meyer, Membership Sec.-Treas.
Founded: 1967. **Members:** 375. **Membership Dues:** regular, $50 (annual) ● student/limited income, $25 (annual). **Multinational. Description:** Individuals engaged in academic teaching related to ecumenism or involved professionally in ecumenical relations and issues. Aims are to: provide professional assistance and support to its members; promote scholarly research for the sake of dialogues between churches; study the adequacy of pertinent educational structures to the needs of an ecumenical age. Conducts research programs. Maintains archives at the Union Theological Seminary in New York City. **Awards:** Annual Student Essay. **Frequency:** annual. **Type:** scholarship. **Recipient:** for the best essay based on theme of upcoming conference ● Student Travel Scholarship to Attend Annual Conference. **Frequency:** annual. **Type:** scholarship. **Recipient:** for travel. **Telecommunication Services:** electronic mail, russellmeyer@att.net. **Formerly:** Ecumenical Association of Professors. **Publications:** *Journal for Ecumenical Studies*. **Price:** included in membership dues ● News of NAAE is included in a section of the *Journal of Ecumenical Studies* and of *Ecumenical Trends*. **Conventions/Meetings:** annual conference, includes tour of local religious sites, in either USA or Canada (exhibits) - normally meets last full weekend in September.

19499 ■ Prayers for Life (PL)
c/o Dr. James F. Nugent, Pres.
Salve Regina Univ.
Ochre Ct.
Newport, RI 02840
Ph: (401)849-5421
E-mail: bspenance@hotmail.com
URL: http://penitents.org/prolifeprayer.html
Contact: Dr. James F. Nugent, Pres.
Founded: 1976. **Members:** 5,000. **Description:** Individuals of any denomination or faith who make a personal commitment to pray daily for human life. Encourages individuals to defend the sanctity of all human life, including the unborn, poor, hungry, ill, emotionally disturbed, and mentally and physically handicapped. Distributes prayer cards and "God is Pro-Life" buttons. **Convention/Meeting:** none. **Publications:** none.

19500 ■ Reformed Ecumenical Council (REC)
2050 Breton Rd. SE, Ste.102
Grand Rapids, MI 49546-5547
Ph: (616)949-2910
Fax: (616)949-2910

E-mail: rec@recweb.org
URL: http://www.recweb.org
Contact: Dr. Richard L. van Houten, Gen. Sec.
Founded: 1946. **Members:** 39. **Staff:** 3. **Budget:** $200,000. **Multinational. Description:** Reformed and Presbyterian churches. Promotes the well-being and integrity of member churches; acts as a network for theological exchange and missionary work. Sponsors studies on ecumenicity, racism and race relations, the social calling of the church, human rights, family and marriage, and secularism. Conducts educational and charitable programs. **Libraries:** Type: reference. Subjects: missions, Ecumenical organizations. **Commissions:** Commission on Human Relations; Mission and Diakonia; Theological Education and Interchange; Youth and Christian Nurture. **Committees:** Executive. **Programs:** Leadership Development Institute; Library and Textbook. **Formerly:** Reformed Ecumenical Synod. **Publications:** *News Exchange*, monthly. Newsletter. **Price:** $10.00. **Circulation:** 2,500. Alternate Formats: online. **Conventions/Meetings:** quadrennial general assembly.

19501 ■ Searching Together Educational Ministries (STEM)
PO Box 377
Taylors Falls, MN 55084
Ph: (651)465-6516
Fax: (651)465-5101
E-mail: jzens@searchingtogether.org
Contact: Jon Zens, Ed.
Founded: 1972. **Membership Dues:** regular, $10 (annual). **Description:** Publishes literature concerning contemporary issues facing the church in light of the Bible. Maintains 5000 volume reference library on theology and church history. Makes available reference list of churches throughout the U.S. **Libraries:** Type: by appointment only. Holdings: 5,000. **Subjects:** theology, church history. **Formerly:** (1982) Baptist Reformation Review. **Publications:** *Searching Together*, quarterly. Journal. Includes book reviews. **Price:** included in membership dues; $10.00 /year for nonmembers. ISSN: 0739-2281. **Circulation:** 3,000. **Advertising:** accepted. Also Cited As: *Baptist Reformation Review* ● Booklets ● Also publishes studies in theology and ethics. **Conventions/Meetings:** annual conference, with speakers, meals and lodging - always 3rd week of July.

19502 ■ Secretariat for Catholic-Jewish Relations (CJR)
3121 Massachusetts Ave. NE, 4th St.
Washington, DC 20017-1194
Ph: (202)541-3000
Fax: (202)541-3183
E-mail: bcl@usccb.org
URL: http://www.usccb.org
Contact: Dr. Eugene J. Fisher, Exec. Sec.
Founded: 1967. **Staff:** 2. **Local Groups:** 250. **Description:** A division of the Bishops' Committee for Ecumenical and Interreligious Affairs (see separate entry) of the Roman Catholic Church. Maintains liaison with Jewish groups in the U.S. and with other Christian bodies that works in the area of Jewish-Christian relations. Acts as a clearinghouse and documentation center for Jewish-Christian activities and special interests; conducts surveys of activities throughout the U.S. Promotes programs such as institutes of Jewish studies for Catholic college professors; disseminates materials on Jewish-Christian relations to diocesan ecumenical groups. Conducts research programs. **Libraries:** Type: reference. Holdings: 500. **Subjects:** Judaic and Jewish-Christian relations. **Additional Websites:** http://www.nccbuscc.org/liturgy/guidelinesjudaism.shtml. **Committees:** Advisory; Religious Education. **Formerly:** Subcommission for Catholic-Jewish Relations. **Conventions/Meetings:** workshop (exhibits) - every 18 months.

19503 ■ Societas Liturgica (SL)
c/o Alan Barthel, Sec.
100 Witherspoon St.
Louisville, KY 40202
Ph: (502)569-5759

Fax: (502)569-8465
E-mail: alnbarthel@aol.com
URL: http://www.societas-liturgica.org
Contact: Alan Barthel, Sec.
Founded: 1967. **Members:** 472. **Membership Dues:** individual, $76 (annual) ● individual, 42 (annual) ● individual, EUR 60 (annual). **Languages:** English, French, German. **Multinational. Description:** Interdenominational organization of religious and laypersons in 45 countries teaching or conducting research in the field of worship. Encourages liturgical study, research, and renewal; seeks to increase understanding of liturgical traditions. **Also Known As:** International Society for Liturgical Study and Renewal. **Publications:** *Studia Liturgica* (in English, French, and German), semiannual. Journal ● Newsletter (in English, French, and German), semiannual. Alternate Formats: online. **Conventions/Meetings:** biennial congress (exhibits).

19504 ■ U.S. Conference for the World Council of Churches (WCC/US)
475 Riverside Dr., Rm. 1371
New York, NY 10115-0031
Ph: (212)870-2533
Free: (888)212-2920
E-mail: dhd@wcc-coe.org
URL: http://usa.wcc-coe.org
Contact: Rev. Deborah DeWinter, Program Exec.
Founded: 1948. **Members:** 28. **Staff:** 3. **Description:** Major Protestant and Orthodox churches in the U.S. Works to interpret the program of the World Council of Churches, an organization of 320 Protestant, Anglican, and Orthodox churches in over 100 countries. **Publications:** *Ecumenical Courier*, quarterly. Newsletter. **Circulation:** 5,000. Alternate Formats: online. **Conventions/Meetings:** annual conference.

Education

19505 ■ Adult Christian Education Foundation (ACEF)
1410 Northport Dr.
Madison, WI 53704-2041
Ph: (608)241-9220
Free: (800)462-2335
Fax: (608)241-9259
E-mail: blest@bethelseries.com
URL: http://www.bethelseries.com
Contact: Betty Mansfield, Dir.
Founded: 1959. **Staff:** 3. **Budget:** $600,000. **Description:** Develops programs of Christian education geared to needs of adults. Sponsors the Bethel Series, a program of biblical study for congregations. **Libraries: Type:** reference. **Subjects:** theological. **Telecommunication Services:** electronic mail, bettym@bethelseries.com.

19506 ■ American Academy of Ministry (AAM)
PO Box 681868
Franklin, TN 37068-1868
Ph: (615)599-9889
Free: (800)288-9673
Fax: (615)599-8985
E-mail: mail@ministry.org
URL: http://www.ministry.org
Contact: Dr. Michael Duduit, Exec. Dir.
Founded: 1993. **Members:** 600. **Membership Dues:** regular, $39 (annual). **Staff:** 1. **Budget:** $5,000. **Description:** Seeks to promote and enhance the practice of ministry among members. Conducts educational programs. **Publications:** Journal, semiannual. **Circulation:** 1,000. **Advertising:** accepted. **Conventions/Meetings:** annual conference - always July.

19507 ■ Association for Clinical Pastoral Education (ACPE)
1549 Clairmont Rd., Ste.103
Decatur, GA 30033-4635
Ph: (404)320-1472
Fax: (404)320-0849

E-mail: acpe@acpe.edu
URL: http://www.acpe.edu
Contact: Rev. Dr. Teresa E. Snorton, Exec. Dir.
Founded: 1967. **Members:** 3,600. **Membership Dues:** student affiliate, retired, $65 (annual) ● individual, $105 (annual) ● clinical, $130 (annual) ● agency, denomination, faith group, seminary, $260 (annual) ● network, $80 (annual). **Staff:** 10. **Budget:** $900,000. **Regional Groups:** 9. **Description:** Certifies clinical pastoral education supervisors and accredits institutions, agencies, and parishes that offers clinical pastoral education to theological students, ordained clergy, members of religious orders, and laypeople. Offers CPE programs as part of theological degree and graduate degree programs, as continuing education for the ministry, as training for chaplaincy and pastoral counseling, and as training for certification as supervisor of clinical pastoral education. **Commissions:** Accreditation; Certification; Professional Ethics; Standards. **Supersedes:** Association of Clinical Pastoral Educators; Council for Clinical Training; Institute of Pastoral Care; Lutheran Council in the U.S.A. **Publications:** *ACPE News*, periodic. Newsletter ● *Directory of Accredited Centers, Member Seminaries, and Certified Supervisors*, annual ● *Standards*, annual. **Conventions/Meetings:** annual conference (exhibits) - 2007 Oct. 24-27, Dallas, TX ● periodic regional meeting.

19508 ■ Association for Religion and Intellectual Life (ARIL)
DBA CrossCurrents
475 Riverside Dr., Ste.1945
New York, NY 10115-0021
Ph: (212)870-2544
Fax: (212)870-2539
E-mail: chashenderson@mindspring.com
URL: http://www.crosscurrents.org
Contact: Charles P. Henderson Jr., Exec. Dir.
Founded: 1930. **Members:** 3,000. **Membership Dues:** individual (with CrossCurrents subscription), $50 (annual). **Staff:** 5. **Budget:** $400,000. **Local Groups:** 27. **Description:** Global network of individuals of faith and intelligence who are committed to connecting the wisdom of the heart and the life of the mind. Brings people together across lines of difference around issues of common concern. **Awards: Type:** fellowship. **Recipient:** for 20 participants of the ARIL Research Colloquium. **Supersedes:** National Institute for Campus Ministries. **Publications:** *Cross Currents*, quarterly. Journal. **Price:** $30.00/year; $10.00/issue; $20.00/year for students and seniors. ISSN: 0011-1953. **Circulation:** 5,000. **Advertising:** accepted. Alternate Formats: microform. **Conventions/Meetings:** annual meeting, large and small groups discussion, prayer, fellowship - usually summer ● annual symposium.

19509 ■ Bishops' Committee on Priestly Formation (BCPF)
c/o United States Conference of Catholic Bishops
3211 4th St. NE
Washington, DC 20017-1194
Ph: (202)541-3033
Fax: (202)541-3222
E-mail: vocations@usccb.org
URL: http://www.usccb.org/vocations/formation.shtml
Contact: Rev. Edward J. Burns, Exec. Dir.
Founded: 1966. **Members:** 8. **Staff:** 1. **Description:** An arm of the United States Conference of Catholic Bishops (see separate entry) concerned with proposing policy to the conference in the area of seminary formation programs. Offers voluntary visitation/evaluation program to U.S. seminaries as requested. Encourages seminaries to seek accreditation. **Affiliated With:** United States Conference of Catholic Bishops. **Publications:** *Program of Priestly Formation.* **Conventions/Meetings:** quarterly meeting.

19510 ■ Campus Ministry Women (CMW)
c/o Rev. Ann Marie Coleman, Sr. Minister
Univ. Church
5655 S Univ. Ave.
Chicago, IL 60637
Ph: (773)363-8142
Fax: (773)363-7086

E-mail: uchurch@universitychurchchicago.org
URL: http://users.rcn.com/uchurch/home.htm
Contact: Rev. Ann Marie Coleman, Sr. Minister
Founded: 1970. **Members:** 250. **Description:** Protestant, Catholic, and Jewish women; interested men are associate members. Serves as a network to empower women to be effective ministers in college and university settings. Provides professional and educational resources to women as they locate and acquire campus ministry positions and develop their skills and careers. Promotes interfaith cooperation; enables women to participate in the development and teaching of a feminist theology reflecting interfaith awareness. Serves as a forum for sharing campus ministry programs and resources. Supports women who are victims of racism, religious bigotry, or discrimination because of their sexual preference; allots money for projects for such women. Advocates hiring and promoting women in religious and campus structures; provides grievance and crisis intervention. **Publications:** Newsletter, periodic ● Newsletter, 5-6/year. **Conventions/Meetings:** annual conference ● regional meeting.

19511 ■ Catholic Academy of Sciences in the United States of America
PO Box 9611
Washington, DC 20016
URL: http://www.catholicacademysciences.org
Contact: Austin David Carroll PhD, Pres.
Founded: 1987. **Members:** 50. **Membership Dues:** academician, corresponding associate, $100 (annual). **Staff:** 2. **Languages:** English, French, German, Italian, Latin, Spanish. **Description:** Scholars with doctorates who are, or have been, academic professors. Seeks to serve God and country through scholarship, and to demonstrate the compatibility of science and religion. Promotes moral and ethical conduct in academia. Maintains a speakers' bureau and museum. Conducts research and offers educational programs. **Libraries: Type:** not open to the public. **Holdings:** 2,000; books, periodicals. **Subjects:** medicine, pure sciences, law philosophy, bioethics, old texts in Spanish, Latin, French, German. **Committees:** Admission; Program; Publication; Research. **Affiliated With:** Pontifical Academy of Sciences. **Publications:** *Bioethics: Rise, Decline, Fall.* Book ● *Directory of Members*, annual. Membership Directory. Includes photographs of academicians. **Circulation:** 2,500 ● *Evolution: Fact, Fiction, Fancy.* Book ● *Proceedings of the Catholic Academy of Sciences*, quinquennial. Book. **Price:** free. **Circulation:** 1,000 ● *Quarterly News Bulletin* ● *Royal Religious Revolutionaries.* Book ● *Stem Cell Research.* Book. Includes a collection of essays. ● *Virtue Found: Virtue Lost.* Book ● *Women, Motherhood and Mary.* Pamphlet ● Monographs, periodic. **Conventions/Meetings:** annual conference, from Jerusalem, sponsored by Holy Land Christian Charities - always third Saturday of October, Washington, DC on campus of Catholic University.

19512 ■ Center for the Ministry of Teaching (CMT)
3737 Seminary Rd.
Alexandria, VA 22304
Ph: (703)461-1885 (703)370-6600
Free: (800)941-0083
Fax: (703)370-6234
E-mail: dlinthicum@vts.edu
URL: http://www.vts.edu/cmt/overview
Contact: Dorothy Linthicum, Coor.
Founded: 1984. **Staff:** 5. **Description:** Serves as part of the Virginia Theological Seminary community. In addition to students and faculty, it serves lay and professional leaders of parishes and churches of all denominations. Aims to improve the quality of Christian education; provide resources and consultant services; and conduct training courses and workshops on topics including teaching in the church, Christian curriculum development, and human growth and development. **Libraries: Type:** reference; lending; open to the public. **Holdings:** 8,500; archival material, books, films, maps, periodicals, video recordings. **Subjects:** religious education, teaching in the church. **Publications:** *Episcopal Teacher*,

quarterly. Newsletter. ISSN: 0895-0830. **Circulation:** 3,800. Alternate Formats: online. **Conventions/Meetings:** annual seminar.

19513 ■ Christian Brothers Conference (CBC)
4351 Garden City Dr., Ste.200
Landover, MD 20785
Ph: (301)459-9410
E-mail: tjohnson@cbconf.org
Contact: Thomas Johnson, Regional Coor.
Founded: 1960. **Members:** 900. **Staff:** 11. **Budget:** $950,000. **Regional Groups:** 7. **Description:** Represents Roman Catholic order of brothers in education. Serves as a forum for the coordination and exchange of information on the support and administration of projects involving U.S. and foreign schools and universities. Conducts youth ministry programs and retreats. Distributes information on vocational and educational activities. **Councils:** Missions Advisory; Regional Education; Regional Vocation/Formation. **Conventions/Meetings:** Supervisory Meeting - 3/year.

19514 ■ Christian Educators Association International (CEAI)
PO Box 45610
Westlake, OH 44145
Ph: (440)250-9566
Free: (888)798-1124
Fax: (440)250-9584
E-mail: info@ceai.org
URL: http://www.ceai.org
Contact: Finn Laursen, Exec. Dir.
Founded: 1953. **Members:** 7,300. **Membership Dues:** educator (based on salary), $89-$139 (annual) ● husband and wife educator, $199 (annual) ● retired educator, $29 (annual) ● associate, $39 (annual) ● college student, $20 (annual) ● active, life, $899 ● retired, life, $379. **Staff:** 15. **Budget:** $650,000. **Regional Groups:** 10. **State Groups:** 5. **Local Groups:** 45. **Description:** Aims to "demonstrate God's love and truth to the educational community and encourage, equip and empower educators serving in public and private school". Resources are available to assist educators of their first amendment rights so they may live out their faith in appropriate, legal ways in their call to education. **Libraries:** Type: reference. **Holdings:** 42. **Awards:** National Christian Educator of the Year. **Frequency:** annual. Type: monetary. **Recipient:** for a member of the CEAI who is an excellent educator, and who inspires students and fellow staff. **Computer Services:** Online services, devotionals for teachers, prayer network, leader contacts. **Affiliated With:** Evangelical Council for Financial Accountability; Evangelical Press Association; National Association of Evangelicals; National Religious Broadcasters. **Formerly:** (1981) National Educators Fellowship; (1984) Christian Educators Association. **Publications:** *CEIA Chapter Handbook.* Alternate Formats: online ● *Great Thoughts*, bimonthly. Contains card deck of famous sayings. ● *Public Schools: Power Prayers.* Booklet ● *Separate But Equal.* Book. **Price:** $13.00 ● *Teachers and Religion in Public Schools.* Book. **Price:** $16.95 ● *Teachers of Vision*, bimonthly. Magazine. **Price:** $20.00 /year for nonmembers. **Circulation:** 8,000. **Advertising:** accepted ● *Teachers' Treasury.* Book. Contains poems about teachers written by teachers. **Price:** $9.00 ● Newsletter, monthly ● Newsletter, quarterly. ISSN: 0882-6609. **Circulation:** 8,000. **Advertising:** accepted. **Conventions/Meetings:** regional meeting.

19515 ■ Christian Educators Fellowship of the United Methodist Church (CEF)
PO Box 24930
Nashville, TN 37202
Free: (866)629-3113
Fax: (615)749-6871
E-mail: cef@umc.org
URL: http://cefumc.org/interior.
asp?ptid=15&mid=5929
Contact: Linda Vogel, Pres.
Founded: 1968. **Members:** 1,100. **Membership Dues:** retired, student, $35 (annual) ● associate,

regular, $75 (annual). **Staff:** 1. **Budget:** $200,000. **Regional Groups:** 5. **State Groups:** 47. **Description:** Church education coordinators and Sunday school teachers. Serves as a forum for exchange of ideas and information among members. Makes available church school curriculum materials. Produces resources to help Christian educators develop in their chosen field. **Publications:** *CEF Christians in Education*, quarterly. Newsletter. Contains information pertinent to Christian educators. **Price:** free for members; $5.00 for nonmembers. **Circulation:** 1,300. **Advertising:** accepted. **Conventions/Meetings:** conference (exhibits).

19516 ■ Ecumenical Theological Seminary (ETS)
2930 Woodward Ave.
Detroit, MI 48201
Ph: (313)831-5200
Fax: (313)831-1353
E-mail: lhannum@etseminary.org
URL: http://www.etseminary.org
Contact: Ms. Lynne Hannum, Contact
Founded: 1980. **Staff:** 9. **Description:** Schools, religious denominations, and other educational agencies. Works to develop and enhance the educational resources that support ministry and community leadership regionally. Offers Doctor of Ministry degree program, Master of Divinity degree programs, and non-degree programs in ministry. Maintains speakers' bureau. **Libraries:** Type: reference. **Holdings:** 25,000; books, periodicals. **Subjects:** biblical studies, theology, church history, pastoral care, ethics. **Absorbed:** (1986) Institute for Advanced Pastoral Studies. **Formerly:** Ecumenical Theological Center. **Publications:** *Catalog of Courses*, annual.

19517 ■ Evangelical Training Association (ETA)
PO Box 327
Wheaton, IL 60189
Ph: (630)384-6920
E-mail: moreinformation@etaworld.org
URL: http://www.etaworld.org
Contact: Yvonne Thigpen, Pres.
Founded: 1930. **Members:** 200. **Membership Dues:** institution, $100 (annual). **Staff:** 15. **Budget:** $750,000. **Languages:** English, Spanish. **Description:** Bible institutes, Bible colleges, and liberal arts colleges and seminaries throughout the world but primarily in the United States and Canada. Fosters a closer cooperation among evangelical Christian institutions. Works to increase interest in the training of church volunteers. Provides curriculum guidance and textbooks. Awards diplomas and certificates. **Formerly:** (1990) Evangelical Teacher Training Association. **Publications:** *Journal of Adult Training*, semiannual. **Price:** free for members; $5.00 for nonmembers. **Circulation:** 2,500 ● *Profile*, quarterly. Newsletter. **Circulation:** 50,000. **Conventions/Meetings:** biennial meeting, held in conjunction with the Accrediting Association of Bible Colleges (exhibits) - always February.

19518 ■ Fellowship of Christian Released Time Ministries (FCRTM)
5722 Lime Ave.
Long Beach, CA 90805
Ph: (562)428-7733
Free: (800)360-7943
E-mail: rtce@io17.com
URL: http://rtce.org
Contact: John Atkinson, Pres.
Founded: 1984. **Members:** 293. **Staff:** 5. **Budget:** $30,000. **Regional Groups:** 3. **Description:** Christians who promote "released time education", the practice of setting aside time during the school day for students to leave their school campus and attend classes of a religious nature. Encourages the training of individuals to teach released time programs, and enlists the help of seminaries and institutions in this effort. Supports related curriculum development. Provides information on the history, legality, and strategy involved in placing released time programs within communities. **Publications:** *Update*, annual. Newsletter. Covers existing and new programs, new

developments in concept and curriculum. **Circulation:** 2,900. **Conventions/Meetings:** conference, state or regional groups meet irregularly.

19519 ■ Hindustan Bible Institute (HBI)
HBI Ministries Intl.
PO Box 584
Forest, VA 24551
Ph: (434)525-5847
Free: (877)424-4634
Fax: (434)525-4727
E-mail: info@hbionline.org
URL: http://www.hbionline.org
Contact: Dr. Paul R. Gupta, Pres./Dir.
Founded: 1950. **Staff:** 21. **For-Profit. Description:** Operates Bible School in Madras and India to train nationals for mission work. Works to create churches in India and elsewhere. Maintains rural medical ministry; operates five orphanages and printing school. Distributes literature; broadcasts evangelical radio programs in six languages in India. **Libraries:** Type: reference. **Holdings:** 25,000; audiovisuals. **Publications:** *Annual Ministry Report*, annual ● *God of the Untouchables.* Book ● *Voice of India*, 2-3/year. Newsletter. Covers student activities, building projects, radio ministry, orphanage, and evangelism. Contains calendar of events and faculty and staff profiles. **Price:** free. **Circulation:** 12,500 ● Newsletter, quarterly. **Conventions/Meetings:** annual Bible Conference - always in India ● Missions Conference - always first week of October, India.

19520 ■ Interdisciplinary Biblical Research Institute (IBRI)
PO Box 423
200 N Main St.
Hatfield, PA 19440-0423
Ph: (215)368-5000
Fax: (215)368-7002
E-mail: webmaster@ibri.org
URL: http://www.ibri.org
Contact: Dr. Robert C. Newman, Dir.
Founded: 1980. **Members:** 150. **Budget:** $18,000. **Local Groups:** 1. **Languages:** English, French, German, Russian. **Description:** Evangelical Christians interested in the relationships between Christianity and academic disciplines, especially science. Seeks to: strengthen the evangelical and academic competence of the Christian Church; defend Christianity against "intellectual attacks" and counter anti-Christian views; prepare Christian scholars for educational work in both Christian and secular institutions. Encourages the development of Christian approaches to academic disciplines, emphasizing biblical exegesis. Fosters research. Offers charitable program; maintains Speaker's Bureau. **Publications:** Audiotapes. Contains lectures on various topics. **Price:** $5.00. Alternate Formats: CD-ROM ● Booklets ● Books. **Conventions/Meetings:** monthly Colloquium Series - seminar.

19521 ■ Japan International Christian University Foundation (JICUF)
475 Riverside Dr., Ste.439
New York, NY 10115-0439
Ph: (212)870-3386
Fax: (212)870-2696
E-mail: info@jicuf.org
URL: http://www.jicuf.org
Contact: David W. Vikner, Pres.
Founded: 1949. **Staff:** 3. **Languages:** English, Japanese. **Description:** Supports International Christian University, a graduate-level institution of 2,800 students, founded in 1949 and located in Mitaka-shi, Tokyo, Japan. **Committees:** Alumni Advisory; Development; Executive; Recruiting Advisory; Trustee. **Publications:** *A New Leaf*, semiannual. Newsletter. Alternate Formats: online. **Conventions/Meetings:** annual board meeting - always spring in New York, NY.

19522 ■ LOGOI
14540 SW 136 St., Ste.200
Miami, FL 33186
Ph: (305)232-5880
Fax: (305)232-3592

E-mail: logoi@logoi.org
URL: http://www.LOGOI.org
Contact: Rev. Les Thompson, Pres./Founder
Founded: 1968. **Staff:** 10. **Budget:** $1,200,000. **Languages:** English, Spanish. **Description:** Promotes religious education for Spanish-speaking adults worldwide. Distances Bible and Seminary training for Spanish pastors worldwide. **Also Known As:** (1980) Facultad Latinoamericana de Estudios Teologicos. **Publications:** *Gracias*, monthly. Newsletter. Contains information for donors and friends. ● *Mission Adventures*. Book. **Price:** $12.95 plus shipping ● Guia Pastoral.

19523 ■ Louis Finkelstein Institute for Religious and Social Studies at the Louis Stein Center (LFIRSS)
c/o Jewish Theological Seminary
3080 Broadway
New York, NY 10027
Ph: (212)678-8000 (212)678-8054
Fax: (212)678-8947
URL: http://www.jtsa.edu/research/finkelstein
Contact: Dr. Alan Mittleman, Dir.
Founded: 1938. **Staff:** 1. **Description:** Established by The Jewish Theological Seminary of America as a graduate school for Catholic, Jewish, and Protestant clergymen and religious leaders. Conducts courses and seminars led by scientists, scholars, theologians, and others to study and explore current social and moral problems and other basic issues confronting clergymen and other leaders. Cooperates with eight theological seminaries in a special series for younger ministers and theological students. Conducts Institute of Ethics for the study of contemporary problems in their moral perspective. Has established extensions in Chicago, IL and Boston, MA. **Formerly:** Institute on Interdenominational Studies; (1986) Institute for Religious and Social Studies. **Publications:** Reprints. Includes papers and materials on religious and social topics.

19524 ■ National Association of Parish Catechetical Directors (NPCD)
c/o National Catholic Educational Association
1077 30th St. NW, Ste.100
Washington, DC 20007-3852
Ph: (202)337-6232
Fax: (202)333-6706
E-mail: nceaadmin@ncea.org
URL: http://www.ncea.org/departments/npcd
Contact: Karen M. Ristau, Pres.
Founded: 1976. **Members:** 1,200. **Membership Dues:** individual, $78 (annual) ● 2-3 members at same parish, $63 (annual) ● 4 or more members at same parish, $48 (annual). **Staff:** 1. **Regional Groups:** 11. **Description:** A subdivision of the National Catholic Educational Association. Directors, coordinators and administrators of religious education/catechesis in Roman Catholic parishes; students considering careers as catechetical leaders; clergy, laity, and others involved in the religious community. Works to act as a representative and advocate for professionals who administer parish catechetical programs; foster cooperation and communication among organizations serving parish catechesis including other NCEA groups and independent associations; promote the spiritual, personal, and professional growth of parish DREs and encourage careers in catechetical ministry. Supports and develops the practice of family catechesis and encourages efforts in adult religious education; urges cooperation among parish leadership, especially parish staff members; promotes competency standards. Provides guidelines for members' contracts, salaries, benefits, and job descriptions. Disseminates information on members' jobs, educational background, salaries, and benefits; reports on parish program activities and surveys. Conducts research. **Awards:** Mustard Seed Award. **Frequency:** annual. **Type:** recognition. **Recipient:** for parental involvement and leadership ● NPCD Emmaus Award for Excellence in Catechesis. **Frequency:** annual. **Type:** recognition. **Recipient:** for contribution to the field of catechesis/religious education ● Religious Educational Excellence Award. **Frequency:** annual. **Type:** recognition. **Recipient:**

for unique programs of excellence. **Committees:** Executive. **Affiliated With:** National Catholic Educational Association. **Formerly:** (1998) National Association of Parish Coordinators/Directors of Religious Education. **Publications:** *Momentum*, quarterly. Journal ● *NPCD News*, quarterly. Newsletter. **Conventions/Meetings:** annual National Convocation - convention, for religious education, held in conjunction with National Catholic Educational Association Convention (exhibits).

19525 ■ National Campus Ministry Association (NCMA)
c/o Bob Turner, Admin. Off.
PO Box 101
Paoli, IN 47454
Ph: (502)314-5445
E-mail: ncma.info@gmail.com
URL: http://www.campusministry.net
Contact: Bob Turner, Admin. Off.
Founded: 1964. **Members:** 365. **Membership Dues:** full-timer, $90 (annual) ● second full-timer at same location, $60 (annual) ● part-timer, $45 (annual) ● sustaining (retired, faculty, board member, former campus minister), $45 (annual) ● student, $30 (annual). **Staff:** 1. **Budget:** $21,950. **Regional Groups:** 5. **Description:** Campus ministers, chaplains, and others involved with churches and universities. Foster the educational development of those ministering in higher education; keeps abreast of both church and university matters; advances ecumenical understanding; and provides a supportive fellowship. Appoints task forces to deal with special interests. Operates speakers' bureau; conducts educational and charitable programs. Sponsors seminars and convocations. **Awards:** Campus Ministry of the Year Award. **Type:** recognition ● G.N.O.M.E. Award. **Frequency:** annual. **Type:** recognition. **Recipient:** for outstanding ministry in higher education ● Rookie of the Year Award. **Type:** recognition. **Formed by Merger of:** (1964) Association of Presbyterian University Pastors and Campus Ministry Association. **Publications:** *Occasional Papers*, semiannual. **Price:** free, for members only. **Circulation:** 600 ● *Realm of Higher Education*, 3/year. Newsletter. **Price:** included in membership dues. **Circulation:** 600. **Conventions/Meetings:** annual conference (exhibits) - always summer.

19526 ■ National Conference for Catechetical Leadership (NCCL)
125 Michigan Ave. NE
Washington, DC 20017
Ph: (202)884-9753
Fax: (202)884-9756
E-mail: kkandefer@nccl.org
URL: http://www.nccl.org
Contact: Leland D. Nagel, Exec. Dir.
Founded: 1905. **Members:** 1,131. **Membership Dues:** individual, $50. **Budget:** $349,000. **Regional Groups:** 35. **Local Groups:** 170. **Description:** Diocesan directors of religious education and their staff; publishers, academics, Diocesan religious education, Associations, and individuals interested in religious education. Fosters communication and unity among members. Addresses the special responsibility to provide lifelong religious education within the Catholic Church; assists members with increasing religious education needs; coordinates religious education and helps to supply needed materials. Aids in formal religious education for children, adults, and handicapped persons. Compiles statistics; provides placement service; operates research programs; conducts charitable program; maintains speakers' bureau. **Libraries: Type:** reference. **Holdings:** archival material. **Awards:** NCLL Catechetical Award. **Frequency:** annual. **Type:** recognition. **Recipient:** for significant contribution in religious education/catechesis. **Computer Services:** database ● mailing lists. **Committees:** Adult Faith Formation. **Programs:** Catechist Formation (Echoes of Faith). **Formerly:** Confraternity of Christian Doctrine; (1966) Continuing Christian Development; (2000) National Conference of Directors of Religious Education; (2002) National Conference for Catechetical Leaders. **Publications:** Directory, annual ● Newsletter, quarterly ● Also publishes

religious education materials. **Conventions/Meetings:** annual conference, for religious education publishers (exhibits).

19527 ■ National Council of Churches, Education and Leadership Ministries Commission (NCC ELMC)
475 Riverside Dr., Ste.880
New York, NY 10115-0500
Ph: (212)870-2141 (212)870-2252
Fax: (212)870-2817
E-mail: news@ncccusa.org
URL: http://www.ncccusa.org
Contact: Dr. Robert W. Edgar, Gen. Sec.
Members: 32. **Staff:** 4. **National Groups:** 14. **Description:** Serves as a place where denominations convene to work together in a wide arena of Christian education, faith formation, leadership development and congregational ministries. Seeks to: provide representatives to the ELMC Program Board; provide financial support to ELMC; recognize the importance of all program ministries and provide personnel and financial support for those specific ministries they choose to work with; share denominational updates, resources and programming with one another; express covenantal community through worship, prayer and personal interaction; respect varied traditions and beliefs and receive them as gifts and personal interaction; share responsibilities for leadership on the Administrative Board; and review the nature of involvement of denominational and church-related agencies in the various committees. **Telecommunication Services:** electronic mail, gpierce@ncccusa.org. **Committees:** Black Congregational Ministries; Continuing Education with Church Educators; Curriculum Research and Theory; Deaf Ministries; Disabilities; Ecumenical Young Adult Ministries Team; Ecumenical Youth Staff Team; Education for Mission; Family Ministry and Human Sexuality; Justice for Children and Their Families; Outdoor Ministries; Pacific Asian American/Canadian Christian Education Ministries; Professional Church Leadership; Public Education and Literacy; Uniform Series. **Task Forces:** Dismantling Racism. **Affiliated With:** National Council of Churches of Christ in the U.S.A. **Formerly:** (1989) National Council of Churches; (1990) Education for Christian Life and Mission; (2003) National Council of Churches, Ministries in Christian Education. **Conventions/Meetings:** annual meeting.

19528 ■ National Organization for Continuing Education of Roman Catholic Clergy (NOCERCC)
333 N Michigan Ave., Ste.1205
Chicago, IL 60601
Ph: (312)781-9450
Fax: (312)442-9709
E-mail: nocercc@nocercc.org
URL: http://www.nocercc.org
Contact: James H. Alphen, Exec. Dir.
Founded: 1973. **Members:** 310. **Staff:** 3. **Regional Groups:** 14. **Multinational. Description:** Represents Roman Catholic dioceses and religious communities in the U.S; institutions or organizations serving clergy or dioceses and religious communities within and outside the U.S. Purposes are: to promote the continuing formation of Roman Catholic clergy in the U.S; to relate to the Committee on Priestly Life and Ministry of the U.S. Conference of Catholic Bishops (see separate entry); to serve directors of continuing education of clergy throughout the U.S. in carrying out their responsibilities in their local situations; to provide a forum for exchange of information, programs, resources, models, and ideas; to provide incentives and assistance for regional cooperation. Conducts training programs for directors. **Awards:** Blessed Pope John XXIII Award. **Frequency:** annual. **Type:** recognition. **Recipient:** to a director of ongoing presbyteral formation whose active participation exemplifies the mission and goals of the organization and whose leadership supports the life and ministry of priests ● President's Distinguished Service Award. **Frequency:** annual. **Type:** recognition. **Recipient:** to an individual who champions the organization's mission and goals in the church. **Affiliated With:** United

States Conference of Catholic Bishops. **Publications:** *Handbook for Directors of Ongoing Formation of Priests* ● *National Organization for Continuing Education of Roman Catholic Clergy—News Notes*, bimonthly. Newsletter. Lists resources in continuing religious education and sample policy statements on continuing education from dioceses and religious orders. **Price:** included in membership dues ● *Priestly Relationships: Freedom Through Boundaries.* Video ● *2005-2006 Sabbatical Programs*, biennial. Catalog. **Price:** $50.00 for members (discounted price). **Conventions/Meetings:** annual convention, plenary sessions, workshops, liturgies, meals, exhibits, other networking opportunities (exhibits) - 2008 Jan. 28-31, AK.

19529 ■ Professional Association of Christian Educators (PACE)
PO Box 140284
Dallas, TX 75214
Ph: (214)841-3566
Free: (800)829-9410
Fax: (214)841-3773
E-mail: mike_lawson@dts.edu
Contact: Michael S. Lawson, Pres.

Founded: 1959. **Members:** 150. **Membership Dues:** full, $75 (annual) ● student/retiree, $50 (annual). **Staff:** 10. **Multinational. Description:** Christian educators and associate ministers. Promotes Christian education. Provides ministry mentoring and provides resources via web site. **Libraries: Type:** reference. **Holdings:** audio recordings, clippings, video recordings. **Computer Services:** database, names and addresses of people and organizations related to Christian education. **Formerly:** (1989) National Association of Directors of Christian Education. **Conventions/Meetings:** periodic regional meeting - as requested by regions.

19530 ■ Religious Education Association: An Association of Professors, Practitioners, and Researchers in Religious Education (REA: APRRE)
1107 Waterfall Ln.
Lakeland, FL 33803
Ph: (863)430-3893
Fax: (863)644-5477
E-mail: reapprre@msn.com
URL: http://www.religiouseducation.net
Contact: Dr. W. Allan Smith, Exec. Sec.

Founded: 1970. **Members:** 460. **Membership Dues:** regular (with income of less than $25,000 up to $65,000 or more), $35 (annual). **Staff:** 2. **Budget:** $30,000. **Multinational. Description:** Represents professors, practitioners, and researchers in religious education in institutions of higher learning, denominational and ecumenical organizations, faith communities, and other agencies. Seeks to foster scholarly inquiry and professional development in the field of religious education and to provide a forum for the interchange of research and experience. Sponsors presentations and discussions for critical response and diverse viewpoints among members. **Awards:** Harper Award. **Frequency:** biennial. **Type:** recognition. **Recipient:** for outstanding work in religious education. **Computer Services:** Mailing lists. **Affiliated With:** Council of Societies for the Study of Religion. **Formerly:** Professors and Research Section of the Division of Christian Education of the National Council of Churches; (2005) Association of Professors and Researchers in Religious Education. **Publications:** *Religious Education*, quarterly. Journal. Contains book reviews. **Circulation:** 3,500. **Advertising:** accepted. **Conventions/Meetings:** annual Culture that Matters: Intercultural Explorations in Religious Education - conference (exhibits) - 2007 Nov. 2-4, Boston, MA.

19531 ■ Society for Values in Higher Education (SVHE)
c/o Portland State University
PO Box 751
Portland, OR 97207-0751
Ph: (503)725-2575
Fax: (503)725-2577

E-mail: society@pdx.edu
URL: http://www.svhe.org
Contact: Marvin A. Kaiser, Exec. Dir.

Founded: 1923. **Members:** 1,375. **Membership Dues:** regular (with annual income of under $50,000 to over $90,000), $80-$135 (annual) ● unemployed, $50 (annual) ● life, $1,000 ● institutional, $500 (annual) ● initial, individual, $75 (biennial). **Staff:** 3. **Budget:** $220,000. **Regional Groups:** 5. **Description:** Individuals with backgrounds in teaching or administration in institutions of higher learning. Aims to advance the concern for values in liberal education. Sponsors projects on teaching, curriculum, and values issues and educational programs. **Libraries: Type:** reference. **Holdings:** 1,400; books. **Subjects:** values and higher education, ethics, humanities. **Awards:** Fellows Lecture Presenter. **Frequency:** annual. **Type:** recognition. **Recipient:** for publications, contributions to the profession and longevity as a fellow. **Computer Services:** database, job search and research assistance, membership directory. **Committees:** Annual Program. **Councils:** Senior Fellows. **Formerly:** (1962) National Council on Religion in Higher Education; (1975) Society for Religion in Higher Education. **Publications:** *Directory of Fellows*, biennial. **Price:** free for members. **Circulation:** 1,400 ● *Society for Values in Higher Education—Newsletter*, quarterly. Contains calendar of events. **Price:** included in membership dues. **Circulation:** 1,400. **Advertising:** accepted. Alternate Formats: online ● *Soundings: An Interdisciplinary Journal*, quarterly. **Price:** $28.00/year. **Circulation:** 2,400. **Advertising:** accepted. **Conventions/Meetings:** annual Fellows Meeting - conference, devoted to scholarly collaborations on 20 topics (exhibits) ● regional meeting - 5/year.

19532 ■ United Ministries in Higher Education (UMHE)
1041 Grandview Ave.
Boulder, CO 80302
Ph: (303)443-3960
E-mail: info@umhe.org
URL: http://www.umhe.org
Contact: Rev. Tamara Boynton, Contact

Founded: 1980. **Members:** 4. **Staff:** 4. **Budget:** $25,000. **Description:** National church agencies of Christian Church (Disciples of Christ), Presbyterian Church (U.S.A.), and United Church of Christ. Provides ministry related to higher education. Program and project areas include AIDS education, identifying models for higher education ministry, church-related colleges, racial/ethnic education, public education, peace education, and science and technology. Conducts research in the areas of cultural pluralism and theological inquiry. **Affiliated With:** National Campus Ministry Association. **Formed by Merger of:** Ministries in Public Education; United Ministries in Higher Education. **Formerly:** Higher Education Ministries Team/United Ministries in Higher Education; (1993) United Ministries in Education. **Publications:** Books ● Monographs ● Also publishes resource listing. **Conventions/Meetings:** annual meeting and board meeting.

Environment

19533 ■ National Religious Partnership for the Environment
49 S Pleasant St., Ste.301
Amherst, MA 01002
Ph: (413)253-1515
Fax: (413)253-1414
E-mail: nrpe@nrpe.org
URL: http://www.nrpe.org
Contact: Paul Gorman, Founder/Exec. Dir.

Founded: 1993. **Description:** Seeks to provide inspiration, moral vision and commitment to social justice for all efforts to protect the natural world and human well-being. Promotes environmental sustainability and justice with religious and moral perspectives.

Episcopal

19534 ■ Anglican Society (AS)
c/o Rev. J. Robert Wright, Pres.
The Gen. Theological Seminary
175 9th Ave.
New York, NY 10011
E-mail: wright@gts.edu
URL: http://www.anglicansociety.org
Contact: Rev. J. Robert Wright, Pres.

Founded: 1932. **Members:** 700. **Description:** Clergy and laity of the Episcopal Church; other interested individuals. Religious study society that promotes the Anglican Catholic faith and practices in accordance with the principles of the Book of Common Prayer. **Formerly:** The Anglican Society in North America. **Publications:** *The Anglican*, quarterly. Magazine. **Price:** $10.00. **Circulation:** 1,500.

19535 ■ Anglicans United (AU)
PO Box 763217
Dallas, TX 75376-3217
Ph: (972)293-7443
Free: (800)553-3645
Fax: (972)293-7559
E-mail: anglicansunited@sbcglobal.net
URL: http://www.anglicansunited.com
Contact: Cherie Wetzel, Contact

Founded: 1987. **Members:** 20,000. **Staff:** 2. **Budget:** $250,000. **Multinational. Description:** Laypeople working to maintain the traditional doctrine of the Episcopal Church. Seeks to influence the structure of the Church to more faithfully reflect the teachings of Jesus Christ. Fosters leadership training and education; facilitates communication among members. **Study Groups:** Joshua Circle of Prayer Warriors. **Also Known As:** Episcopalians United. **Formerly:** (2005) Episcopalians United for Revelation, Renewal, and Reformation. **Publications:** *The Anglican Voice*, 7/year. Newsletter. Latest news from around the Episcopal Church and around the Anglican Communion. **Circulation:** 3,000. Alternate Formats: online.

19536 ■ Assembly of Episcopal Healthcare Chaplains (AEHC)
c/o Jean Scribner, Pres.
Beatrice Community Hosp.
1326 N 10th St.
Beatrice, NE 68310
Ph: (402)223-7372
E-mail: jscribner@bchhc.org
URL: http://www.episcopalchaplain.org
Contact: Jean Scribner, Pres.

Founded: 1951. **Members:** 250. **Membership Dues:** professional, $50 (annual) ● institution, $100 (annual) ● diocese, $150 (annual) ● associate, $25 (annual). **Description:** Institutions, administrators, institutional chaplains, deacons, lay workers, and retired chaplains united to further chaplaincy as an essential expression of the Church's healing ministry by serving as a collegial association for Episcopal ministers in health care and by advocating for specialized ministries in healthcare settings. **Publications:** *Chaplain*, quarterly ● Directory, periodic. **Conventions/Meetings:** annual meeting, held in conjunction with Association of Professional Chaplains.

19537 ■ Associated Parishes for Liturgy and Mission (APLM)
PO Box 10416
Rochester, NY 14610
E-mail: info@associatedparishes.org
URL: http://www.associatedparishes.org
Contact: Leslie Nipps, Sec.

Founded: 1946. **Members:** 1,000. **Membership Dues:** regular, $35 (annual) ● student, retired (minimum), group, $20 (annual) ● sustaining, $50-$100 (annual) ● publisher, $1,500 (annual) ● patron, $100-$500 (annual). **Staff:** 1. **Description:** Purpose is to "proclaim, celebrate, risk, live the Lordship of Jesus Christ and to help people participate in planning, conducting and reflecting upon their corporate worship and its implication for their total life." Specializes in teaching the meaning of liturgy. **Publications:**

Open, 3/year. Journal. Alternate Formats: online ● Brochures. **Price:** $4.00 each, 1-19 copies; $3.00 each, 20-49 copies; $2.50 each, 50 or more copies ● Pamphlets. **Conventions/Meetings:** periodic conference ● annual meeting.

19538 ■ Brotherhood of Saint Andrew (BStA)
PO Box 632
Ambridge, PA 15003
Ph: (724)266-5810
Fax: (724)266-9577
E-mail: brotherhoodofstandrew@verizon.net
URL: http://www.brotherhoodstandrew.org
Contact: Ronald Warfuel, Pres.
Founded: 1883. **Members:** 5,000. **Membership Dues:** regular, $40 (annual) ● junior, $8 (annual) ● life, $600. **Staff:** 3. **Local Groups:** 400. **Description:** Men and boys of the Protestant Episcopal Church. Seeks to "spread Christ's Kingdom among men and youth", to develop lay leadership in the church. Program is based on daily prayer, study, and personal service. Similar groups exist in Canada, British Isles, Ghana, Uganda, West Indies, Philippines, Thailand, and Japan. **Awards:** Legion of Honor. **Frequency:** triennial. **Type:** recognition. **Committees:** Aid to Aged; Associate Field Secretaries; Brotherhood Legion; Evangelism; Outreach; Prison Work; Youth. **Publications:** *St. Andrew's Cross*, quarterly. Newsletter. Includes news from chapters and missionaries throughout the world. Contains book reviews and obituaries. **Price:** included in membership dues. **Circulation:** 6,000. **Conventions/Meetings:** annual meeting, with council meeting ● triennial meeting ● seminar, for evangelistic training.

19539 ■ Church Army (CA)
210 W North Ave.
Pittsburgh, PA 15212-4625
Ph: (412)231-5442
Free: (888)412-5442
Fax: (412)231-5481
E-mail: info@churcharmyusa.org
URL: http://www.churcharmyusa.org
Contact: Capt. Steven G. Brightwell, Dir.
Founded: 1927. **Members:** 47. **Staff:** 4. **Budget:** $250,000. **Regional Groups:** 6. **Description:** Individuals commissioned as evangelists by the presiding bishop of the Episcopal church. Provides recruitment, training, deployment, mutual support, continuing education, and fellowship. **Libraries: Type:** reference. **Holdings:** 5,000; books. **Subjects:** evangelism, purity, church growth, church history, missions, cultural anthropology, revival. **Formerly:** Church Army Society. **Publications:** *Church Army News*, quarterly. Newsletter. **Price:** free. **Circulation:** 4,000 ● *Episcopal Church Directory*, annual. **Conventions/Meetings:** semiannual conference.

19540 ■ Church Pension Fund (CPF)
445 Fifth Ave.
New York, NY 10016
Ph: (212)592-1800
Free: (800)223-6602
Fax: (212)779-3392
E-mail: churchpublishing@cpg.org
URL: http://www.cpg.org
Contact: Monique O'Neill, Admin. Asst.
Founded: 1917. **Members:** 15,000. **Description:** Administers the clergy pension system of the Episcopal church including life, accident, and health benefits; provides pensions and related benefits for the clergy and dependents. **Committees:** Advisory. **Subgroups:** Church Insurance Company. **Publications:** *Click*. Newsletter. Alternate Formats: online ● *The Stewardship of Abundance*. Newsletter. Alternate Formats: online. **Conventions/Meetings:** triennial meeting (exhibits).

19541 ■ Church Periodical Club (CPC)
815 2nd Ave.
New York, NY 10017-4594
Ph: (212)716-6130
Free: (800)334-7626
Fax: (212)867-0395

E-mail: cpc@episcopalchurch.org
URL: http://www.jladefoged.com/cpctest/index.htm
Contact: Pamela Stewart, Admin.
Founded: 1888. **Membership Dues:** regular, $20 (annual) ● life (regular), $250 ● life (parish), $300. **Staff:** 1. **Regional Groups:** 8. **Description:** An affiliated organization of the executive council of the Episcopal church that supports the general church program by providing grants for technical, educational, and religious books and periodicals to missions, hospitals, schools, prisons, clergymen, students, missionaries, and other individuals and institutions both in the U.S. and abroad who cannot obtain them otherwise. Supported by contributions from parish churches and individual donations. Maintains National Books Fund to handle book requests and Miles of Pennies Fund to handle requests for children's books. **Publications:** *CPC Quarterly*. Newsletter. Provides information on club grants, activities, and projects. **Price:** included in membership dues; $3.00 /year for nonmembers. **Circulation:** 2,000 ● Directory, annual. **Conventions/Meetings:** triennial meeting (exhibits).

19542 ■ Concerned Clergy and Laity of the Episcopal Church (CCLEC)
2520 E Piedmont Rd., Ste.F-6
Marietta, GA 30062
E-mail: cclec@aol.com
URL: http://www.episcopalian.org/cclec
Description: Represents Evangelical and Episcopalians. Committed to informing all Episcopalians in order to help the Episcopal Church become faithful to God's Word; aims to spread Christ's love.

19543 ■ Confraternity of the Blessed Sacrament (CBS)
c/o Rev. William Willoughby, III, Gen. Sec.
St. Paul's Church
101 E 56th St.
Savannah, GA 31405
E-mail: frwwiii@aol.com
URL: http://home.sandiego.edu/~baber/CBS
Contact: Rev. William Willoughby III, Gen. Sec.
Founded: 1862. **Members:** 3,500. **Membership Dues:** life, $100. **Local Groups:** 38. **Description:** Serves as Episcopalian devotional society. **Publications:** *A History of the Confraternity of the Blessed Sacrament in the United States*. **Circulation:** 3,500 ● *The Intercession Paper*, quarterly ● *Manual of the Confraternity of the Blessed Sacrament 1950*. Alternate Formats: online. **Conventions/Meetings:** annual conference.

19544 ■ Episcopal Church Building Fund (ECBF)
815 2nd Ave.
New York, NY 10017
Ph: (212)716-6003
Free: (800)334-7626
Fax: (212)867-7626
E-mail: buildchurch@ecbf.org
URL: http://www.ecbf.org
Contact: Rev. Charles N. Fulton III, Pres.
Founded: 1880. **Staff:** 4. **Description:** An agency of the Episcopal church. Aids in planning and financing the building, purchase, improvement, or repair of churches, rectories, and other parochial buildings connected with the Episcopal Church in the United States and Anglican communion. Provides loans and guidance during the planning process. Conducts regional workshops, on-site consultation, and produces resources. **Formerly:** (1973) American Church Building Fund Commission. **Publications:** *The Church For Common Prayer*. Booklet. Provides theological as well as pragmatic insights for developing the space and celebrating the faith as the people of God. **Price:** $5.00 ● *Churches for Common Prayer, Building for the Liturgical Assembly*. Video. **Price:** $29.95 ● *Congregational Builder*, annual. Newsletter. Contains issues related to building projects, space and place, and congregational health. **Price:** free.

19545 ■ Episcopal Communicators (EC)
c/o Jennifer Martin, Membership Coor.
316 Lehman-Outlet Rd.
Dallas, PA 18612

E-mail: lauriewozniak@episcopalwny.org
URL: http://www.episcopalcommunicators.org
Contact: Laurie Wozniak, Pres.
Founded: 1971. **Members:** 205. **Membership Dues:** full, $75 (annual) ● associate, $35 (annual). **Budget:** $5,000. **Description:** Represents persons involved in communications within the Episcopal church. Fosters development of communications expertise within the church; offers fellowship and support; promotes the ministry of communication; provides a forum for discussion of communication issues in the church. **Awards:** Polly Bond Awards. **Frequency:** annual. **Type:** recognition. **Recipient:** for church print, websites and video/audio productions. **Formerly:** (1970) National Diocesan Press. **Publications:** *The Communicator*, periodic. Newsletter. Alternate Formats: online ● *Community in Crisis*. Features a collection of materials from workshops on communicating in the midst of a crisis. ● Survey. Alternate Formats: online. **Conventions/Meetings:** competition ● annual conference and workshop ● workshop.

19546 ■ Episcopal Conference of the Deaf (ECD)
c/o St. Hilda's Episcopal Church
245 W Main St.
Monmouth, OR 97361
Ph: (503)838-6087
E-mail: wmoiser357@earthlink.net
URL: http://www.ecdeaf.com
Contact: Rev. Bill Mosier, Pres.
Founded: 1881. **Members:** 825. **Membership Dues:** regular, $10 (annual). **Budget:** $100,000. **Local Groups:** 60. **Description:** Clergy and laity of the Protestant Episcopal Church who promote church work among the deaf in the United States. Provides public relations and advocacy services. **Awards:** Internship Grants. **Frequency:** semiannual. **Type:** grant. **Recipient:** for ministries located within provinces of ECUSA ● Program Grants. **Frequency:** annual. **Type:** grant. **Recipient:** for ministries located within provinces of ECUSA. **Formerly:** Conference of Church Workers Among the Deaf. **Publications:** *Convention Proceedings*, annual ● *The Deaf Episcopalian*, bimonthly. Newsletter. Includes news on clergy, congregations, and congregation members. **Price:** $10.00 /year for nonmembers; included in membership dues. **Circulation:** 1,200 ● Also publishes hymnal. **Conventions/Meetings:** annual convention (exhibits) - usually July.

19547 ■ Episcopal Evangelical Education Society (EES)
PO Box 20247
Alexandria, VA 22320
Ph: (703)807-1862
E-mail: office@ees1862.org
URL: http://www.ees1862.org
Contact: Day Dodson, Exec. Dir.
Founded: 1862. **Members:** 500. **Membership Dues:** $30 (annual). **Staff:** 2. **Budget:** $145,000. **Description:** Seeks to "communicate the faith by knowledge as well as zeal and to inspire a passion for the Gospel and God's people". **Awards:** Evangelism for the 21st Century. **Frequency:** annual. **Type:** grant. **Recipient:** for project that strengthens the evangelical witness of the Episcopal Church. **Absorbed:** (1961) Episcopal Evangelical Fellowship. **Formerly:** (1997) Evangelical Education Society of the Protestant Episcopal Church.

19548 ■ Episcopal Women's Caucus (EWC)
5665 S Cherokee Bend
New Era, MI 49446-8905
E-mail: elizabeth.downie@ewc-ecusa.org
URL: http://www.ewc-ecusa.org
Contact: Elizabeth Morris Downie, Pres.
Founded: 1971. **Members:** 900. **Membership Dues:** regular, $50 (annual) ● individual, $90 (biennial) ● congregation, organization, $100 (annual) ● library, $50 (annual). **Staff:** 1. **Budget:** $60,000. **Local Groups:** 8. **Description:** Represents lay and ordained men and women concerned with the full ministry of all women and minorities in the church. Provides network of people involved in similar issues. **Computer Services:** database, information to board

and to those starting local chapters, also accounting services ● mailing lists ● online services. **Telecommunication Services:** electronic mail, anne.vandervoort@ewc-ecusa.org. **Publications:** *A Collection of Statements, Papers and Resources on Inclusive Language*, daily. Alternate Formats: online ● *Ruach*, quarterly. Newsletter. **Price:** included in membership dues; $10.00 /year for nonmembers; $50.00 /year for libraries. **Circulation:** 2,400. Alternate Formats: online ● Brochures. Alternate Formats: online ● Pamphlets. Alternate Formats: online. **Conventions/Meetings:** annual conference (exhibits).

19549 ■ Faith Alive (FA)
431 Richmond Pl. NE
Albuquerque, NM 87106
Ph: (505)255-3233
Fax: (505)255-2282
E-mail: faofficenm@aol.com
URL: http://www.faithalive.org
Contact: Thomas G. Riley, Pres.
Founded: 1970. **Members:** 2,500. **Staff:** 3. **Budget:** $152,000. **Description:** Witnessing fellowship within the Episcopal church. Seeks to bring new perspective to vows of baptism and confirmation via weekend programs for adults, teens, and children. **Publications:** *Faith Alive Newsletter*. Alternate Formats: online ● *Good News*, bimonthly. Newsletter. **Price:** free. **Circulation:** 5,700 ● Also distributes preparatory materials for Faith Alive weekends. **Conventions/Meetings:** annual conference, with inspirational speaker, music and Christian fellowship - the weekend after Memorial Day.

19550 ■ Fellowship of Saint Paul (FSSP)
c/o The Society of Saint Paul
St. Paul's Cathedral
2728 Sixth Ave.
San Diego, CA 92103
Ph: (619)298-7261
Fax: (619)298-2689
E-mail: anbssp@earthlink.net
URL: http://www.stpaulcathedral.org/pages/ftc_ssp.htm
Contact: Rev. Canon Andrew Rank, Guardian
Founded: 1958. **Members:** 300. **Description:** Individuals supporting the Society of Saint Paul monastic order through prayer and monetary contributions. Promotes the interests of the Society of Saint Paul and carries the spirit and message of the society beyond the limits of monastic life. **Convention/Meeting:** none. **Publications:** *St. Paul's Printer*, quarterly. Magazine. ISSN: 0038-8815. **Circulation:** 4,000.

19551 ■ Forward in Faith North America
PO Box 210248
Bedford, TX 76095-7248
Free: (800)225-3661
Fax: (817)735-1351
E-mail: fif.northamerica@forwardinfaith.com
URL: http://www.forwardinfaith.com
Contact: Rev. Keith L. Ackerman, Field Dir.
Founded: 1989. **Members:** 18,000. **Membership Dues:** individual, parish, $35 (annual). **Staff:** 3. **Regional Groups:** 4. **State Groups:** 41. **Local Groups:** 182. **Description:** Dioceses, parishes, institutions, and societies of Anglican laity and clergy in North America, Central America, South America and the Caribbean who "embrace the Gospel of Jesus Christ and uphold evangelical faith and order, laboring with zeal for the reform and renewal of the church." Promotes the establishment and implementation of cooperative programs. **Awards:** President's Award for Meritorious Service. **Frequency:** annual. **Type:** recognition. **Recipient:** by presidential nomination. **Computer Services:** database. **Councils:** Forward in Faith. **Formerly:** (2000) Episcopal Synod of America. **Conventions/Meetings:** annual general assembly.

19552 ■ Foundation for Christian Theology (FCT)
c/o The Christian Challenge
1215 Independence Ave. SE
Washington, DC 20003
Ph: (202)547-5409

Fax: (202)543-8704
E-mail: info@challengeonline.org
URL: http://www.challengeonline.org
Contact: Auburn Faber Traycik, Ed./Exec. Dir.
Founded: 1966. **Staff:** 2. **Nonmembership. Multinational. Description:** Purposes are to: defend the faith as the Church has received it; work for the unity of the church under Christ; resist false teaching within the church; restore the Church to its primary mission of preaching and teaching the gospel. **Libraries: Type:** reference. **Holdings:** 43; periodicals. **Subjects:** Anglican/Episcopal and other religious news. **Formed by Merger of:** The Christian Challenge. **Publications:** *The Christian Challenge: The Only Worldwide Voice of Traditional Anglicanism*, 5-6/year. Magazine. Includes news and opinion. **Price:** $24.00/year in U.S.; $27.00/year in Canada; $32.00/year outside U.S. and Canada. ISSN: 0890-6793. **Circulation:** 5,000. **Advertising:** accepted. Alternate Formats: microform; online.

19553 ■ Global Teams
PO Box 490
Forest City, NC 28043
Ph: (828)248-1377
Fax: (828)248-2482
E-mail: inquiries@global-teams.org
URL: http://www.global-teams.org
Contact: Kevin Higgins, Exec. Dir.
Founded: 1982. **Staff:** 5. **Multinational. Description:** An international ministry. Aims to catalyze movements among the unreached that reflect the character of Christ, transform people and cultures, and reproduce more movements. **Telecommunication Services:** electronic mail, membercare@global-teams.org. **Formerly:** (2003) Episcopal World Mission; (2004) EWM Global Teams.

19554 ■ Historical Society of the Episcopal Church (HSEC)
PO Box 2098
Manchaca, TX 78652-2098
Ph: (512)282-3234
Free: (800)553-7745
Fax: (512)280-3902
E-mail: mlofgreen@austin.rr.com
URL: http://www.hsec.us
Contact: May D. Lofgreen, Dir. of Operations
Founded: 1910. **Members:** 1,500. **Membership Dues:** regular, $45 (annual) ● retiree/student, $25 (annual) ● institution, $60 (annual) ● sustaining, $100-$249 (annual) ● patron, $250-$499 (annual) ● benefactor, $500 (annual). **Description:** Promotes historical research on the Episcopal Church. **Awards:** Nelson R. Burr Prize. **Frequency:** annual. **Type:** recognition. **Recipient:** for the best essay on Episcopal Church history by an unpublished author. **Computer Services:** database, Anglican and Episcopal history. **Boards:** International Advisory. **Committees:** Endowment Fund; Historical Society Projects and Grants. **Projects:** African American Episcopal Collection. **Formerly:** (1975) Church Historical Society. **Publications:** *Anglican and Episcopal History*, quarterly. Journal. **Price:** included in membership dues. ISSN: 0896-8039. **Advertising:** accepted. Alternate Formats: online ● *The Historiographer*. Newsletter ● Monographs. **Conventions/Meetings:** biennial conference ● annual meeting and board meeting - usually May or June.

19555 ■ International Order of St. Vincent (IOSV)
126 Coming St.
Charleston, SC 29403
Ph: (843)722-7345
Fax: (843)722-2105
E-mail: director-general@orderstvincent.org
URL: http://orderstvincent.org
Contact: Philip G. Dixon, Dir. Gen.
Founded: 1882. **Members:** 1,000. **Membership Dues:** junior, $7 (annual) ● adult, clergy, supporting, $20 (annual) ● life, $150. **Staff:** 2. **Budget:** $12,000. **Local Groups:** 60. **Multinational. Description:** Anglican (Episcopal) lay ministers and acolytes in the U.S., Canada, South and Central America. Serves as a devotional fellowship for Anglican lay ministers and

other laity living outside of a religious community. Conducts educational, inspirational, and mentorship programs; participates in community service activities. **Libraries: Type:** not open to the public. **Holdings:** 100; books. **Subjects:** liturgy. **Awards: Type:** recognition. **Computer Services:** Online services. **Also Known As:** International Guild of Lay Ministers and Acolytes. **Formerly:** (1915) Guild of St. Vincent; (1999) Order of St. Vincent Society. **Publications:** *The Banner*, annual. Newsletter. **Price:** free. **Circulation:** 2,000. Alternate Formats: online ● Brochure ● Manuals ● Also publishes tracts. **Conventions/Meetings:** periodic seminar ● periodic workshop.

19556 ■ Living Church Foundation (LCF)
816 E Juneau Ave.
PO Box 514036
Milwaukee, WI 53203-3436
Ph: (414)276-5420
Free: (800)211-2771
Fax: (414)276-7483
E-mail: tlc@livingchurch.org
URL: http://www.livingchurch.org
Contact: David A. Kalvelage, Exec. Ed.
Founded: 1878. **Members:** 30. **Staff:** 13. **Budget:** $900,000. **Description:** Clergy and laity. Operates publication and communication within the Episcopal Church and the wider religious community. Conducts research. **Libraries: Type:** reference. **Holdings:** 1,100; archival material. **Formerly:** (1963) Church Literature Foundation. **Publications:** *The Episcopal Musician's Handbook*, annual. Contains helpful guide and resource to church musicians. **Price:** $26.00/copy (regular shipping); $30.50/copy (priority shipping). **Circulation:** 8,000 ● *The Living Church*, weekly. Magazine. Contains insightful articles on newsworthy topics. **Circulation:** 9,000. Alternate Formats: online. **Conventions/Meetings:** annual meeting.

19557 ■ National Guild of Churchmen (NGC)
PO Box 34548
San Diego, CA 92163
Ph: (619)542-8660
Fax: (619)542-8585
E-mail: anbssp@earthlink.net
Contact: Rev. Canon Barnabas Hunt, Pres.
Founded: 1945. **Members:** 3,000. **Description:** Episcopalians organized to maintain, defend, and propagate the doctrine, practice, and teaching of the Anglican Communion as held by the Episcopal Church. **Conventions/Meetings:** none. **Publications:** *St. Paul's Printer*, quarterly. Magazine. ISSN: 0038-8815. **Circulation:** 4,000.

19558 ■ National Network of Episcopal Clergy Associations (NNECA)
c/o Ken Beason
514-14th St.
Paso Robles, CA 93446
Ph: (805)238-0819
E-mail: k_beason@charter.net
URL: http://www.nneca.org
Contact: Ken Beason, Contact
Founded: 1970. **Members:** 1,800. **Membership Dues:** regular, $65 (annual). **Staff:** 1. **Budget:** $75,000. **Regional Groups:** 25. **Description:** Confederation of 25 Episcopal diocesan clergy associations united to foster professional and spiritual development among Episcopal clergy. Advocates for clergy on professional and vocational church issues. Conducts research and educational programs on ministry-related issues, such as evaluation, spiritual health planning, and compensation. Offers consulting services. Maintains speakers' bureau. Conducts research. **Publications:** *Leaven*, 11/year. Journal. **Price:** $25.00 /year for nonmembers; included in membership dues. **Circulation:** 2,200 ● Also publishes research reports. **Conventions/Meetings:** annual meeting.

19559 ■ North American Association for the Diaconate (NAAD)
Executive Off.
815 2nd Ave.
New York, NY 10017

Ph: (646)486-7672
Fax: (253)648-6298
E-mail: naadoffice@aol.com
URL: http://www.diakonoi.org
Contact: Susanne Watson Epting, Exec. Dir.
Founded: 1953. **Members:** 2,200. **Membership Dues:** individual, $50 (annual) ● student, retired deacon, $30 (annual) ● life, $1,000. **Staff:** 5. **Budget:** $69,000. **Description:** Deacons in the Episcopal Church. Supports deacons in the ministry and educates the church in the role of the diaconate. Works with dioceses on training for the diaconate. Attempts to develop support systems with deacons-in-training, model programs, and supporters. Compiles statistics; offers speaker's bureau. **Awards:** St. Stephen Recognition of Diaconal Ministry. **Frequency:** biennial. **Type:** recognition. **Recipient:** recommendation of diocese. **Computer Services:** database, Deacon Director. **Boards:** Governing. **Formerly:** (1974) Central House for Deaconesses; (1985) National Center for the Diaconate. **Publications:** *Deacons in the Episcopal Church.* Booklet. Contains guidelines on selection, formation, ministry and programs. **Price:** $3.00 ● *Diakoneo*, bimonthly. Newsletter. **Price:** included in membership dues. **Circulation:** 1,500. Alternate Formats: online ● *Diakonia-Prophetic Praxis-Agir, 2002.* Book. **Price:** $10.95 ● Books ● Pamphlets ● Reports ● Papers ● Monograph ● Also publishes occasional monographs - 13 in print. **Conventions/Meetings:** biennial conference and meet (exhibits) - usually June, odd years ● annual Deacon Program Directors Conference - usually February or March.

19560 ■ Office of Black Ministries/Episcopal Church Center

c/o Episcopal Church
815 2nd Ave.
New York, NY 10017
Ph: (212)716-6084
Free: (800)334-7626
Fax: (212)867-7652
E-mail: aifill@episcopalchurch.org
URL: http://www.episcopalchurch.org/african_american.htm?menupage=2056
Contact: Rev. Angela S. Ifill, Missioner
Founded: 1973. **Members:** 15. **Staff:** 2. **Description:** Black members of the Episcopal Church representing geographically diverse dioceses, including one diocese outside of the U.S. Works to strengthen the witness of black Episcopalians in the church through programs that include parish and clergy development and international relations. Provides financial assistance and consultations to parishes and church organizations. Compiles statistics. Serves as a commission of the Episcopal Church. **Awards:** Pathways. **Frequency:** annual. **Type:** scholarship. **Recipient:** for students pursuing the ordained ministry in the Episcopal Church ● **Type:** scholarship. **Recipient:** for college students. **Formerly:** Office of Black and Urban Ministries/Episcopal Church Center; (1998) Episcopal Commission for Black Ministries. **Publications:** *Black Ministries in the Episcopal Church.* Film ● *Black Ministries Journal*, biennial. Articles. Includes personal, and theological reflections on various topics and reports. **Price:** $3.00. **Advertising:** accepted ● *Bridges*, quarterly. Newsletter. Alternate Formats: online ● Brochure. Alternate Formats: online. **Conventions/Meetings:** triennial Black Clergy Conference - support group meeting, gathering of black clergy for seminars and workshops ● annual S.O.U.L. Youth Leadership Conference - symposium, gathering of youth and young adults for leadership development.

19561 ■ Order of the Daughters of the King (DOK)

101 Weatherstone Dr., Ste.870
Woodstock, GA 30188
Ph: (770)517-8552
Fax: (770)517-8066
E-mail: dok1885@dok-national.org
URL: http://www.dok-national.org
Contact: Ms. Mary Fletcher, Admin.
Founded: 1885. **Members:** 25,000. **Membership Dues:** senior, $35 (annual) ● junior, $15 (annual).

Staff: 5. **Budget:** $700,000. **Regional Groups:** 9. **Local Groups:** 1,500. **Multinational. Description:** Women and girls in Episcopal, Anglican, Lutheran ECLA and Roman Catholic Churches (and churches in communion with the Episcopal Church or sharing the historic Episcopate) enter the Order by taking vows to pray and serve others for the spread of Christ's Kingdom. They form chapters within local churches for mutual support. Members give to funds for domestic and overseas mission outreach and ministry education. **Awards:** Master's Fund Scholarships. **Frequency:** annual. **Type:** scholarship. **Recipient:** for Episcopal women or members of the order preparing for church work ● Self Denial Fund Grants. **Frequency:** annual. **Type:** grant. **Recipient:** for mission projects, often those carried out by members of the order. **Boards:** Diocesan Assemblies; Province. **Also Known As:** Daughters of the King. **Publications:** *Chapter Manual.* Alternate Formats: online ● *Daughters of the King National Handbook* ● *The Royal Cross*, quarterly. Magazine. **Price:** $5.00/year. Alternate Formats: online ● *Study Guide Leader's Booklet.* Alternate Formats: online ● Brochures. **Price:** free. **Conventions/Meetings:** triennial National Retreat - meeting and retreat (exhibits).

19562 ■ Seamen's Church Institute of New York and New Jersey (SCI)

241 Water St.
New York, NY 10038
Ph: (212)349-9090
Fax: (212)349-8342
E-mail: sci@seamenschurch.org
URL: http://www.seamenschurch.org
Contact: Rev. Dr. Jean R. Smith, Exec. Dir./Pres.
Founded: 1834. **Staff:** 48. **Budget:** $7,000,000. **Description:** Aims to improve the treatment of merchant seafarers entering the Port of New York. Serves as an ecumenical, voluntary agency affiliated with the Episcopal Church, the Institute advocates for the personal, professional and spiritual well being of merchant mariners worldwide. Headquartered in Manhattan, serves every mariner through its three main program divisions: the Center for Maritime Education, Center for Seafarers' Rights, and the Center for Seafarers' Services. Multilingual chaplains visit ninety percent of all vessels entering the port (nearly 3000 vessels). **Awards:** Silver Bell Award. **Frequency:** annual. **Type:** recognition. **Recipient:** for service to maritime industry. **Committees:** Advisory Committees on Maritime Training; Center for Seafarers' Rights; Development; Fine Arts; Investment and Trust Funds; Real Estate; Seafarer Services. **Programs:** Center for Maritime Education. **Affiliated With:** Center for Seafarers' Rights. **Absorbed:** (1975) Church Association for Seamen's Work. **Formerly:** (1906) Seaman's Church Institute of New York. **Supersedes:** Young Men's Auxiliary Education and Missionary Society. **Publications:** *The Lookout*, quarterly. Newsletter. Covers the Merchant Marine and sea-related subjects. Contains book reviews. ISSN: 0024-6425. **Circulation:** 10,000. Alternate Formats: online ● *The Lookout.* Annual Report. **Circulation:** 2,500.

19563 ■ Society of the Companions of the Holy Cross (SCHC)

46 Elm St.
Byfield, MA 01922-2812
Ph: (978)462-6721
Fax: (978)462-1864
E-mail: katenoury@adelynrood.org
URL: http://www.adelynrood.org
Contact: Kate Noury, Contact
Founded: 1894. **Members:** 885. **Membership Dues:** private, $120 (annual). **Staff:** 6. **Budget:** $500,000. **Regional Groups:** 35. **National Groups:** 3. **Description:** Women members of the Episcopal Church united to share common philosophical ideas, intercessory prayer, and fellowship. Promotes social justice, Christian unity, and Christian mission. Sponsors charitable programs. **Libraries: Type:** reference. **Holdings:** 4,500. **Subjects:** religious-spiritual material, women's literature, writings and published material of members. **Also Known As:** (2000) Adelynrood Retreat Center. **Publications:** *Companion Newslet-*

ter, quarterly ● *Corporate Devotions*, published in the summer. **Price:** free for members ● *Intercession Papers*, monthly. **Price:** free for members ● *SCHC Annual Report*, annual. **Price:** free for members. **Conventions/Meetings:** annual conference.

19564 ■ Society for Promoting and Encouraging Arts and Knowledge of the Church (SPEAK)

805 County Rd. 102
Eureka Springs, AR 72632
Ph: (479)253-9701
Free: (800)572-7929
Fax: (479)253-1277
E-mail: speak@speakinc.org
URL: http://www.speakinc.org
Contact: Ret. Rev. E.L. Salmon Jr., Chm.
Founded: 1953. **Staff:** 12. **Budget:** $800,000. **Description:** Aims to promote the arts and knowledge of the Anglican Church. Operates the Episcopal Book Club, which offers quarterly selections to its 3000 members, and the Anglican Bookstore, Operation Pass-Along. Maintains chapel and Howard Lane Foland Library at Hillspeak (three buildings in the Ozarks) where visitors and scholars can stay. **Libraries: Type:** not open to the public. **Holdings:** 12,400. **Subjects:** religion. **Publications:** *The Anglican Digest*, bimonthly. Contains articles on current religious thought written for members of traditional Christian churches. Includes book reviews, and obituaries. **Price:** free, contribution requested. ISSN: 0003-3278. **Circulation:** 115,000. **Advertising:** accepted. **Conventions/Meetings:** annual meeting.

19565 ■ Standing Commission on Church Music (SCCM)

Address Unknown since 2007
Members: 12. **Budget:** $35,000. **Description:** Bishops, priests, and laypersons appointed every three years by the General Convention of the Episcopal Church, primarily to study the role of music in the church, to recommend standards, and to act as a channel of communication. Makes recommendations to the General Convention for improvement and programming based on these studies. Collects hymn texts and tunes toward future hymnal revision. **Formerly:** (1973) Joint Commission on Church Music. **Publications:** *Book of Canticles* ● *Congregational Music for Eucharist* ● *Gradual Psalms* ● *The Hymnal 1982* ● *Hymns III and Songs for Celebration.* **Conventions/Meetings:** semiannual meeting.

19566 ■ Standing Commission on Ecumenical Relations of the Episcopal Church (SCER)

815 2nd Ave.
New York, NY 10017
Ph: (212)716-6220
Free: (800)334-7626
E-mail: ecumenical@episcopalchurch.org
URL: http://www.episcopalchurch.org/ecumenism
Contact: Rev. C. Christopher Epting, Contact
Members: 12. **Staff:** 1. **Budget:** $40,000. **Description:** Bishops, priests, and laity of the Episcopal church who are appointed by the church's presiding bishop and the president of the House of Deputies. Develops policies and strategies regarding relations between the Episcopal church and other religious organizations; executes ecumenical recommendations made by the Episcopal General Convention; nominates representatives for interchurch organizations with which the Episcopal church is affiliated. **Committees:** Anglican-Oriental Orthodox Consultation; Anglican-Orthodox Theological Consultation; Anglican-Roman Catholic Consultation; Consultation on Church Union; Lutheran-Episcopal Coordinating; Methodist-Episcopal Consultation; Working Group with the Polish National Catholic Church. **Publications:** *Handbook for Ecumenism.* **Conventions/Meetings:** semiannual meeting.

Ethics

19567 ■ Center for Applied Christian Ethics (CACE)

Wheaton Coll.
501 Coll. Ave.
Wheaton, IL 60187-5501

Ph: (630)752-5886
Fax: (630)752-5731
E-mail: cace@wheaton.edu
URL: http://www.wheaton.edu/CACE
Contact: Dr. Lindy Scott, Dir.
Founded: 1986. **Description:** Promotes and encourages the formation of moral character and the application of biblical ethics to contemporary moral decisions. **Publications:** *Discernment*, triennial. Newsletter. **Conventions/Meetings:** periodic conference, national and regional ● Exploring Moral Formation: The College Experience - conference.

Evangelical

19568 ■ Center for the Evangelical United Brethren Heritage (EUB)
4501 Denlinger Rd.
Trotwood, OH 45426
Ph: (937)529-2201
Fax: (937)529-2292
E-mail: utscom@united.edu
URL: http://www.united.edu/eubcenter
Contact: Sarah D. Brooks Blair, Dir. of the Library
Founded: 1979. **Members:** 350. **Membership Dues:** regular, $10-$24 (annual) ● supporting, $25-$49 (annual) ● Newcomer-Seybert Associate, $50-$99 (annual) ● Albright-Otterbein, $100-$499 (annual) ● life, $500. **Budget:** $5,000. **Languages:** English, German. **Description:** Individuals interested in the Evangelical United Brethren heritage. Works to preserve the contributions the Evangelical United Brethren Church and its predecessors brought to the United Methodist Church. Conducts educational programs. **Libraries: Type:** lending; open to the public. **Holdings:** 7,000; archival material, audiovisuals, books, monographs, periodicals. **Subjects:** Evangelical United Brethren history. **Awards:** Audrie E. Reber Memorial Award. **Frequency:** annual. **Type:** recognition. **Recipient:** for students enrolled in institutions of higher education. **Publications:** *Telescope-Messenger*, semiannual. Newsletter. **Circulation:** 4,000. **Conventions/Meetings:** periodic conference.

19569 ■ Evangelical Church Alliance (ECA)
205 W Broadway St.
PO Box 9
Bradley, IL 60915
Ph: (815)937-0720
Fax: (815)937-0001
E-mail: info@ecainternational.org
URL: http://www.ecainternational.org
Contact: Rev. Samuel Goebel, Pres./CEO
Founded: 1887. **Members:** 2,285. **Membership Dues:** regular, $125 (annual). **For-Profit. Description:** Associate members are churches and Christian organizations and ministers. Trains and ordains qualified Evangelical ministers. Provides fellowship for Evangelical ministers and those studying to become Evangelical ministers. **Affiliated With:** Evangelical Council for Financial Accountability; National Association of Evangelicals. **Formerly:** (1958) Fundamental Ministerial Association. **Publications:** *The Evangel*, quarterly. Newsletter. **Circulation:** 2,800 ● Membership Directory, annual. **Conventions/Meetings:** annual Recovering the Heart of Ministry - international conference ● annual regional meeting.

19570 ■ Evangelical and Ecumenical Women's Caucus (EEWC)
PO Box 78171
Indianapolis, IN 46278-0171
E-mail: office@eewc.com
URL: http://www.eewc.com
Contact: Alena A. Ruggerio, Contact
Founded: 1974. **Members:** 300. **Membership Dues:** regular, $45 (annual) ● student, low income, $15 (annual). **Staff:** 2. **Regional Groups:** 6. **Local Groups:** 3. **Multinational. Description:** Christian feminists, churches, seminaries, and colleges. Aims to: encourage evangelical women to work for change in their churches and in society; present God's teaching on female-male equality to the whole body of Christ's

church; call men and women to "mutual submission and active discipleship." Believes that the Bible, when properly understood, supports the basic equality of the sexes. **Libraries: Type:** reference. **Holdings:** archival material, articles. **Subjects:** EEWC activities. **Awards:** Conference Scholarship. **Frequency:** biennial. **Type:** scholarship. **Recipient:** for someone who has written a request based on need and has registered for the conference. **Formed by Merger of:** (1991) Evangelical Women's Caucus, International. **Publications:** *Christian Feminism Today*, quarterly. Newsletter. Contains topics of interest addressed to Christian feminists. **Price:** $25.00 /year for nonmembers (individuals); $35.00 /year for nonmembers (institutions); included in membership dues. **Circulation:** 300. Alternate Formats: online. **Conventions/Meetings:** biennial conference (exhibits).

19571 ■ Evangelical Philosophical Society (EPS)
PO Box 1298
La Mirada, CA 90637-1298
Ph: (562)906-4570
Fax: (562)777-4063
E-mail: philchristi@biola.edu
URL: http://www.epsociety.org
Contact: Dr. R. Scott Smith, Sec.-Treas.
Founded: 1974. **Members:** 1,000. **Membership Dues:** full, associate, $30 (annual) ● student, $20 (annual). **Regional Groups:** 2. **Multinational. Description:** Evangelical Christians. Discusses philosophical matters. **Publications:** *Philosophia Christi*, semiannual. Journal. Provides scholarly discussion of philosophy. ISSN: 1529-1634. **Circulation:** 1,400. **Advertising:** accepted. Also Cited As: *Phil Christi*. **Conventions/Meetings:** annual meeting.

19572 ■ Evangelical Theological Society (ETS)
c/o Dr. James A. Borland, Sec.-Treas.
200 Russell Woods Dr.
Lynchburg, VA 24502-3574
Ph: (434)237-5309
Fax: (434)237-5309
E-mail: jaborland@aol.com
URL: http://www.etsjets.org
Contact: Dr. James A. Borland, Sec.-Treas.
Founded: 1949. **Members:** 3,650. **Membership Dues:** full, associate, $30 (annual) ● student, retired, $15 (annual). **Staff:** 2. **Budget:** $280,000. **Regional Groups:** 7. **Description:** Persons with a Th.M. degree or its equivalent (work done in such fields as writing, administration, or teaching) who subscribe to the ETS doctrinal statement: "The Bible alone and the Bible in its entirety is the word of God written and therefore inerrant in the autographs. God is a Trinity; Father, Son, and Holy Spirit, each an uncreated person, one in essence, equal in power and glory". Associate members are evangelicals without the Th.M. degree; student members are those attending schools of college level or above. Membership represents conservative Bible schools and denominations. Fosters conservative biblical scholarship by providing a medium for the oral exchange and written expression of thought and research in the field of the theological disciplines as centered in the Scriptures. **Libraries: Type:** reference. **Holdings:** archival material. **Committees:** Editorial; Program and Arrangements. **Publications:** *ETS Newsletter*. Alternate Formats: online ● *Journal of the Evangelical Theological Society*, quarterly, usually March, June, September, and December. Contains scholarly articles, book reviews, obituaries, and conference reports. **Price:** included in membership dues; $30.00 /year for nonmembers. ISSN: 0360-8808. **Circulation:** 4,300. **Advertising:** accepted. Alternate Formats: microform; online ● Monographs. **Conventions/Meetings:** conference, on defining evangelicalism's boundaries ● annual meeting (exhibits) - 2007 Nov. 14-16, San Diego, CA; 2008 Nov. 19-21, Providence, RI; 2009 Nov. 18-20, Providence, RI.

19573 ■ Media Associates International (MAI)
351 S Main Pl., Ste.230
Carol Stream, IL 60188-2455
Ph: (630)260-9063

Fax: (630)260-9295
E-mail: mailittworld@sbcgolbal.net
URL: http://www.littworld.org
Contact: John D. Maust, Pres.
Founded: 1985. **Staff:** 4. **Budget:** $160,000. **Languages:** English, Spanish. **Description:** Provides consultation for publishers and training for individuals working in print media for Christian missions and agencies in Third World countries. Offers tutorials and consultation in all aspects of print media, including publishing, management, strategic planning, and editorial, graphic design, production, and marketing skills. **Absorbed:** (1987) Evangelical Literature Overseas. **Publications:** *An Asian Palette*. Book ● *An Unfading Vision*. Book. **Price:** $5.95 paperback ● *Getting Your Message Across* (in English, French, and Spanish). Book. **Price:** prices furnished on request ● *How to Write Missionary Letters*. Book. **Price:** $7.45 paperback ● *In Print: How to Plan, Purchase, and Produce Print*. Book ● *Journeys Into Creativity*. Book ● *Llamados a Escribir* (in English and Spanish). Book ● *Servant of Words*. **Price:** $5.95 ● *Trainer Network*, monthly. Newsletter. Provides ideas and resources for Christian print media trainers. **Price:** $8.00 in U.S. Alternate Formats: online ● *Worlds for the World*, quarterly. Newsletter. Covers media training and Christian literature in the Third World. **Price:** free. **Circulation:** 2,000. Alternate Formats: online ● Manuals. Covers the following topics: writing, production, distribution, publishing management, and marketing. ● Also produces audio materials on marketing strategy. **Conventions/Meetings:** biennial Litt World International Print Media Training Conference, print media training (exhibits) ● seminar ● workshop.

19574 ■ National Association of Evangelicals (NAE)
PO Box 23269
Washington, DC 20026
Ph: (202)789-1011
E-mail: info@nae.net
URL: http://www.NAE.net
Contact: L. Roy Taylor, Chm.
Founded: 1942. **Staff:** 10. **Description:** Individuals, denominations, churches, schools, and organizations comprised of approximately 250 organizations representing nearly 45,000 local churches and 30 million people. Commits to the prophetic, and empowering representational ministry of making God known throughout America; members represent a broad range of theological traditions, but all subscribe to the distinctively evangelical NAE Statement of Faith. Member of the World Evangelical Fellowship, a network of 107 such national alliances. **Awards:** Layman of the Year. **Frequency:** annual. **Type:** recognition ● Racial Reconciliation. **Frequency:** annual. **Type:** recognition. **Commissions:** Chaplains; Christian Higher Education; Churchmen; Evangelism; Hispanic; Life Care; Social Action; Women's. **Affiliated With:** Christian Stewardship Association; Evangelical Fellowship of Mission Agencies; National Religious Broadcasters. **Publications:** *The Cascading Flow - Ministry Platform*. Brochure ● *NAE in the New Century*. Audiotapes ● *National Evangelical Directory*, biennial. Contains listings of evangelical organizations, schools, camps, counselors, and media producers. **Price:** included in membership dues; $20.00 for nonmembers. ISSN: 0273-2319. **Circulation:** 15,000. **Advertising:** accepted ● *Washington Insight*, monthly. Newsletter. Reports on federal government affairs of interest to the evangelical leadership. ISSN: 0199-3038. Alternate Formats: online. **Conventions/Meetings:** annual convention (exhibits) - always first week of March ● Initiative Against Sexual Trafficking - conference ● Washington Insight Briefing - conference ● Washington Student Leadership Seminar.

19575 ■ World Evangelical Alliance (WEA)
644 Strander Blvd., No. 154
Seattle, WA 98188
Ph: (202)223-7556 (604)214-8620
Free: (866)823-3073

E-mail: info@worldevangelicalalliance.com
URL: http://www.worldevangelicalalliance.com
Contact: Sylvia Soon, Chief of Staff
Founded: 1951. **Members:** 150,000,000. **Staff:** 10.
Budget: $1,900,000. **Regional Groups:** 7. **National Groups:** 123. **Languages:** English, French, Portuguese, Spanish. **Multinational. Description:** Exists to foster Christian unity and to provide a worldwide identity, voice and platform to Evangelical Christians. "Seeking empowerment by the Holy Spirit, they extend the Kingdom of God by proclamation of the Gospel to all nations and by Christ-centered transformation within society". **Awards:** Religious Liberty Award. **Frequency:** triennial. **Type:** recognition. **Recipient:** for leadership during persecution. **Computer Services:** Online services, press releases, newsletter, prayer requests, organization information, resource, events, and membership. **Commissions:** Information Technology; Leadership Development; Missions; Reconciliation Ministry; Religious Liberty; Theological; Women's Concerns; Youth. **Affiliated With:** International Christian Media Commission. **Formerly:** (2002) World Evangelical Fellowship. **Publications:** *Connections*, 3/year. Journal. **Price:** $54.00/year. **Advertising:** accepted. Alternate Formats: CD-ROM ● *Directory of Evangelical Associations*, biennial. **Advertising:** accepted ● *Evangelical Review of Theology*, quarterly. **Price:** $27.00/year. ISSN: 0144-8153. Alternate Formats: online ● *WEA Religious Liberty Commission Update on Christian Persecution*, bimonthly. Reprint. **Conventions/Meetings:** quadrennial general assembly (exhibits).

19576 ■ World Fellowship of Slavic Evangelical Christians (WFSEC)
PO Box 59
River Grove, IL 60171
Ph: (708)453-7997
E-mail: wfsec@juno.com
Contact: Rev. John M. Sergey, Pres.
Languages: English, Russian. **Description:** No further information was available for this edition. **Conventions/Meetings:** annual meeting.

19577 ■ World Relief
7 E Baltimore St.
Baltimore, MD 21202
Ph: (443)451-1900
Free: (800)535-5433
Fax: (443)451-1975
E-mail: worldrelief@wr.org
URL: http://www.worldrelief.org
Contact: Sammy Mah, Pres./CEO
Founded: 1944. **Staff:** 750. **Budget:** $50,000,000. **Description:** Emergency aid, development assistance, and refugee service of the National Association of Evangelicals. Conducts programs of disaster relief; refugee relief and resettlement; community development programs, including public health, education, and economic assistance. Carries out programs in Asia, Africa, Europe, Latin America, and the U.S. **Awards:** Helping Hands Award. **Frequency:** annual. **Type:** recognition. **Recipient:** for a lifetime of service to the poor. **Divisions:** Executive; International Ministries; Resource Development; Support Ministries; US Ministries. **Affiliated With:** National Association of Evangelicals. **Formerly:** (1965) World Relief Commission of the National Association of Evangelicals; (1967) NAE World Relief Commission; (1979) World Relief Commission. **Publications:** *Touching*, bimonthly. Newsletter. **Price:** free. **Circulation:** 26,000.

Evangelism

19578 ■ Action International Ministries (ACTION)
PO Box 398
Mountlake Terrace, WA 98043-0398
Ph: (425)775-4800
Fax: (425)775-0634

E-mail: info@actionusa.org
URL: http://www.actionintl.org/action
Contact: Candi Arveson, Coor.
Founded: 1974. **Members:** 216. **Staff:** 12. **Budget:** $6,000,000. **Languages:** English, Tagalog. **Multinational. Description:** Christians working with churches and other Christian organizations to evangelize, help individual Christians mature, and minister in the name of Christ, especially to the poor. Attempts to reunite abandoned children with their parents. Conducts research. **Publications:** *ACTION Newsletter*, monthly. Newsletters. **Circulation:** 2,500 ● *Children in Crisis*, 3/year. Newsletters. **Conventions/Meetings:** semiannual Street Children Ministry Seminar, Leadership Dynamic Series, Church Planting Seminars, field conference.

19579 ■ American Tract Society (ATS)
1624 N 1st St.
PO Box 462008
Garland, TX 75046-2008
Ph: (972)276-9408
Free: (800)54-TRACT
Fax: (972)272-9642
E-mail: ats@atstracts.org
URL: http://www.atstracts.org
Contact: Mr. A. Kent Barnard, Exec. VP
Founded: 1825. **Staff:** 25. **Multinational. Description:** An interdenominational, nonsectarian organization that seeks to "diffuse a knowledge of our Lord Jesus Christ as the Redeemer of sinners and to promote the interests of vital godliness and sound morality through the circulation of religious tracts". **Libraries: Type:** reference. **Computer Services:** Mailing lists, includes 6,000 churches and 27,000 individuals. **Divisions:** African-American; Bookstore; Canadian; General Publications; International. **Publications:** Videos. Alternate Formats: online ● Books ● Also publishes religious tracts.

19580 ■ AMF International (AMFI)
PO Box 5470
Lansing, IL 60438-5470
Ph: (708)418-0020
Fax: (708)418-0132
E-mail: amfi@amfi.org
URL: http://www.amfi.org
Contact: Wesley N. Taber, Exec. Dir.
Founded: 1887. **Members:** 10,000. **Staff:** 23. **Budget:** $700,000. **Local Groups:** 5. **Description:** Promotes understanding between Jewish and Christian communities; presents Yeshua (Jesus of Nazareth) as Israel's Messiah; opposes anti-Semitism; encourages support of Israel. **Formerly:** (1953) Chicago Hebrew Mission; (1993) American Messianic Fellowship. **Publications:** *AMF Intercessor*, monthly. Newsletter. Prayer guide. **Price:** free. **Circulation:** 2,700 ● Also publishes tracts and books for Jews and Christians. **Conventions/Meetings:** conference, on the Bible.

19581 ■ Artists in Christian Testimony (ACT)
PO Box 1649
Brentwood, TN 37024-1649
Ph: (615)376-7861
Fax: (615)376-7863
E-mail: info@actinternational.org
URL: http://www.ACTinternational.org
Contact: Rev. Byron L. Spradlin, Pres.
Founded: 1973. **Staff:** 115. **Budget:** $800,000. **Regional Groups:** 2. **State Groups:** 20. **Languages:** English, Japanese, Spanish. **Multinational. Description:** Mission and ministry sending agency for artistic ministers, missionaries and ministries from all disciplines of the arts - who are doing Christian ministry (worship, evangelism, church planting, arts-ministry-leadership development, community impact) domestically or internationally, regionally or locally. Maintains speakers' bureau, facilitates short-term missions projects, regional evangelistic concert projects, prison ministry outreach and arts-ministry training for the local church, Christian organizations and individual Christian artist-ministries. **Libraries: Type:** not open to the public. **Holdings:** 3,000. **Subjects:** worship, arts, music, theology. **Computer Services:** database, worship, music and arts re-

sources for church and ministry. **Departments:** Christian Musicians Fellowship; Drama Presentations; Ministry Training Institute; Music Evangelism Prison Ministry; Visual Arts Ministry; Worship Consulting. **Publications:** *ACT Perspectives*, quarterly. Newsletter. **Price:** free for members. **Circulation:** 5,000. Alternate Formats: online ● *Nashville Christian Musicians Fellowship eNewsletter* ● Also publishes individual missionary prayer letters. **Conventions/Meetings:** annual Arts in Ministry - conference, training conference - in July ● quarterly Building Your Own Music or Arts Ministry to Last a Lifetime - conference and workshop, arts in ministry.

19582 ■ Athletes in Action (AIA)
651 Taylor Dr.
Xenia, OH 45385-7246
Ph: (937)352-1000
E-mail: communications@aia.com
URL: http://www.aia.com
Contact: William Pugh, Pres.
Founded: 1966. **Members:** 400. **Staff:** 365. **Description:** Sports ministry of Campus Crusade for Christ International. Exists to "boldly proclaim the love and trust of Jesus Christ" to those uniquely impacted by sports worldwide by winning, building, and sending athletic influencers. Full-time members work on college campuses and with professional teams. Sponsors competitions, camps and other events. **Awards:** Bart Starr Award. **Frequency:** annual. **Type:** trophy. **Recipient:** to NFL player exemplifying outstanding character and leadership. **Publications:** *Get in the Game*. Newsletter. **Conventions/Meetings:** biennial Campus Crusade for Christ Conference.

19583 ■ Biblical Ministries Worldwide (BMW)
1595 Herrington Rd.
Lawrenceville, GA 30043-5616
Ph: (770)339-3500
Fax: (770)513-1254
E-mail: bmwhq@biblicalministries.org
URL: http://www.biblicalministries.org
Contact: Paul Seger, Gen. Dir.
Founded: 1948. **Members:** 380. **Staff:** 16. **Multinational. Description:** Fundamental missionaries who believe in the centrality of the local church and are committed to establishing and strengthening New Testament churches at the community level. Has "planted the Word of God" through literature distribution, Christian bookstores, door-to-door evangelism, radio music ministries, and the education of local disciples (who then evangelize their neighbors). Works in Europe, South America, Hong Kong, Japan, Canada, South Africa, Australia, Puerto Rico, Cyprus, Palau, and Guam. **Affiliated With:** Fellowship of Missions. **Formed by Merger of:** United Missionary Fellowship; WEF Ministries. **Publications:** *WorldView*, bimonthly. Newsletter. **Price:** free. **Conventions/Meetings:** annual Field Conferences.

19584 ■ Billy Graham Evangelistic Association (BGEA)
1 Billy Graham Pkwy.
Charlotte, NC 28201
Ph: (704)401-2432
Free: (877)247-2426
URL: http://www.billygraham.org
Contact: Franklin Graham, COO
Founded: 1950. **Staff:** 450. **Budget:** $91,000,000. **Multinational. Description:** International evangelical organization. Conducts evangelistic crusades; broadcasts ministries over radio and television. Promotes Bible study. Sponsors schools of evangelism; trains counselors. Named after well-known evangelist Billy Graham. **Convention/Meeting:** none. **Libraries: Type:** reference. **Holdings:** 10,000. **Publications:** *Decision*, monthly. Magazine. Available in Braille.

19585 ■ Bread on the Waters (BOW)
615 N Pleasant Ave.
Lodi, CA 95240
Ph: (209)369-3202

E-mail: bread_on_the_waters@hotmail.com
URL: http://www.breadonthewaters.com
Contact: Kraig Josiah Rice, Pres.
Founded: 1967. **Members:** 3. **Description:** Works as an online Bible teaching ministry of Kraig J. Rice (mainline Christianity doctrine). Is also a literature evangelism ministry. The ministry name comes from a verse in the Bible, "Cast your bread on the waters for you will find it after many days" (Ecclesiastes 11:-1). **Libraries: Type:** reference. **Holdings:** 100; articles. **Subjects:** Bible doctrine, church articles, gospel tracts, none religious writings. **Formerly:** (1984) Maranatha Gospel Bottle Crusade; (1997) Current Evangelism Ministries. **Publications:** *Abortion - An International Evil.* Alternate Formats: online. **Conventions/Meetings:** annual meeting - always May at Cloverdale, CA.

19586 ■ Campus Crusade for Christ International (CCC)

100 Lake Hart Dr.
Orlando, FL 32832
Ph: (407)826-2000 (407)826-2287
Free: (888)278-7233
URL: http://www.ccci.org
Contact: Bill Thomas, Dir.
Founded: 1951. **Members:** 114,000. **Description:** Presents the gospel of Jesus Christ to individuals, groups, and protectorates in 152 countries "to help fulfill the Great Commission of Christ in this generation and to work with other members of the Body of Christ." Activities focus on major discipleship/evangelism related events and include: Bible study groups for students, conferences for students, families, pastors, and laity. Operates over 40 ministries including: Andre Kole; Athletes in Action; Business Executive; Campus (university/college); Christian Embassy; Christian Leadership (faculty); Drama; Family; Here's Life, World (special discipleship/evangelism outreach that has sponsored training by radio in 12 languages and translated the film "Jesus" into 236 languages); Here's Life, America (lay); Here's Life, Black America Now Heritage; Here's Life Christian Resource Centers; Here's Life Inner City; Here's Life Training Centers; Hispanic; International; International Christian Graduate University; International Student; Jesus Film Project; Josh McDowell; Mass Media; Military; Music; Paragon Productions (multimedia); Prayer; Prison; Student Venture (high school). Maintains speakers' bureau; sponsors educational programs. **Publications:** *Departmental Newsletter,* periodic ● *Worldwide Challenge,* bimonthly. Magazine. **Conventions/Meetings:** periodic conference.

19587 ■ CBM Ministries

PO Box 278
Townsend, TN 37882
Ph: (865)448-1200
E-mail: cbmnat@cbmministries.org
URL: http://www.cbmministries.org
Contact: Jerry Traister, Natl. Dir.
Founded: 1935. **Staff:** 80. **Budget:** $380,000. **Regional Groups:** 13. **State Groups:** 9. **Description:** Christians interested in evangelizing children. Trains missionaries to teach children about the gospel. Teaches classes through public schools on a released time basis. Sponsors church retreats for children; maintains 10 summer camps. **Telecommunication Services:** electronic mail, jerry@cbmministries.org. **Formerly:** (1986) Children's Bible Mission, Inc. **Publications:** *Channel,* quarterly. Newsletter. Includes chapter news and calendar of events. **Circulation:** 2,500. **Conventions/Meetings:** annual meeting ● annual Missionaries Conference.

19588 ■ Champions for Life International

PO Box 761101
Dallas, TX 75376-1101
Ph: (972)298-1101
Fax: (972)298-1104
E-mail: info@billglasscfl.org
URL: http://www.billglasscfl.org
Contact: Byron Stuckey, Exec. Dir.
Founded: 1969. **Members:** 55,000. **Staff:** 25. **Budget:** $3,400,000. **Languages:** English, Spanish. **Mul-**

tinational. **Description:** Evangelistic crusade founded by Bill Glass (1935-), former professional football player for the Detroit Lions and the Cleveland Browns. Conducts ecumenical crusades, called "Celebration of Champions", in public places, such as stadiums and sports arenas. Sponsors evangelistic prison ministry involving professional athletes and lay counselors who volunteer for a "Weekend of Champions" or "Day of Champions" which involves training, spiritual enrichment, one-on-one evangelism with prisoners; volunteers pay their own expenses. Through this program, the association aims to help prison inmates "walk with Christ and focus their energies on Him as they grow physically, mentally and spiritually". Conducts youth outreach program "Champions for Today" that uses professional athletes as roles model to communicate to young people in schools, churches, rallies and camps; "Ring of Champions", a mentor program for first-time juvenile offenders. **Awards:** Cross Award. **Type:** recognition. **Recipient:** for volunteers who have attended prison events. **Affiliated With:** Christian Management Association; Christian Stewardship Association; Evangelical Council for Financial Accountability. **Formerly:** (1992) Bill Glass Evangelistic Association; (2002) Bill Glass Ministries. **Publications:** *Goalposts,* quarterly. Magazine. Contains information on all areas of ministry. **Price:** free. **Circulation:** 30,000. Alternate Formats: online. **Conventions/Meetings:** semiannual board meeting.

19589 ■ Child Evangelism Fellowship (CEF)

17482 State Hwy. M
PO Box 348
Warrenton, MO 63383-0348
Ph: (636)456-4321
Free: (800)748-7710
Fax: (636)456-9935
E-mail: custserv@cefonline.com
URL: http://www.cefonline.com
Contact: Reese Kauffman, Pres.
Founded: 1937. **Staff:** 1,650. **Budget:** $12,500,000. **Multinational. Description:** Maintains local chapters throughout U.S., Canada, and 156 countries. Seeks to "take the Gospel of the Lord Jesus Christ to the world's children" by such means as home Bible classes, summer Bible classes, school-related classes, and camps. Promotes and conducts an adult leadership program that includes training schools and teacher training classes. Maintains speakers' bureau. **Formerly:** Child Evangelism Fellowship International. **Publications:** *Praying for the World,* biennial. Directory ● *Teach Kids!,* bimonthly. Articles. **Advertising:** accepted. **Conventions/Meetings:** triennial conference, for CEF worldwide leadership, staff, volunteers (exhibits).

19590 ■ Chosen People Ministries (CPM)

241 E 51st St.
New York, NY 10022
Ph: (212)223-2252
Free: (888)2-YESHUA
E-mail: cpm@chosenpeople.com
URL: http://www.chosenpeople.com
Contact: Dr. Mitch Glaser, Pres.
Founded: 1894. **Staff:** 66. **Description:** Seeks to evangelize Jewish people around the world through evangelistic outreaches, Bible studies, and congregation planting. **Libraries: Type:** reference. **Holdings:** 15,000. **Subjects:** Judeo-Christian history, customs, traditions, theology. **Programs:** Volunteer Involvement. **Formerly:** (1986) American Board of Missions to the Jews. **Publications:** *The Chosen People,* monthly. Newsletter. Alternate Formats: online ● Books ● Videos ● Brochure. Alternate Formats: online ● Articles. Alternate Formats: online.

19591 ■ Christ in Action Ministries (CIA)

PO Box 4200
Manassas, VA 20108
Ph: (703)368-6286
Fax: (703)368-6470
E-mail: denny@christinaction.com
URL: http://www.christinaction.com
Contact: Rev. Denny Nissley, Dir./Co-Founder
Founded: 1982. **Budget:** $245,000. **Languages:** English, Portuguese. **Multinational. Description:**

Aims to spread the gospel of Jesus Christ throughout the U.S. Engages in street preaching and literature distribution at sites across the U.S., particularly at large public gatherings. Works with inner city gangs. Conducts seminars to train evangelists. **Publications:** *Fear No Evil.* Book. **Price:** $10.00 ● Newsletter, monthly ● Also publishes gospel tracts written in "street language.".

19592 ■ Christian Boaters Association (CBA)

112 Marshview Rd.
Savannah, GA 31410
Ph: (912)897-7194
E-mail: info@christianboater.org
URL: http://christianboater.com
Contact: Marlin Simon, Pres.
Founded: 1988. **Members:** 723. **Staff:** 3. **Description:** Christian boaters and other interested individuals. Promotes Christianity and encourages fellowship among boaters. Works with churches, Christian organizations, and "Gospel Vessels" to establish programs and support network. Encourages assistance to fellow boaters and promotes safety; group has established registered nautical "Witness" flag. Compiles statistics. Sponsoring corporation is Christians Afloat. **Awards:** Certificate of Recognition. **Type:** recognition. **Recipient:** for members with outstanding achievement. **Doing business as:** Christians Afloat. **Publications:** *Member Roster,* annual. Directory ● *Shipmate,* quarterly. Newsletter. ISSN: 4044-095X. Alternate Formats: online. **Conventions/Meetings:** annual International Fellowship - convention (exhibits).

19593 ■ Committee on Missionary Evangelism (COME)

PO Box 88085
Grand Rapids, MI 49518
Ph: (616)243-0119 (616)455-8228
E-mail: eldonstevens@juno.com
URL: http://www.comemissions.com
Contact: Dr. Eldon W. Stevens, Pres.
Founded: 1968. **Members:** 30. **Staff:** 2. **Description:** Provides evangelists for impoverished areas in the U.S. or abroad. Promotes "the evangelization of the world through the pulpit ministry of gifted men in local national churches". Seeks to work cooperatively with established missions and missionaries. Conducts evangelists' workshops. **Boards:** Reference. **Projects:** Foreign. **Publications:** *The COME EVANGEL,* quarterly ● *Roster,* periodic. Membership Directory ● Directory, annual. **Conventions/Meetings:** annual conference - always May.

19594 ■ Evangelical Council for Financial Accountability (ECFA)

440 W Jubal Early Dr., Ste.130
Winchester, VA 22601
Ph: (540)535-0103
Free: (800)323-9473
Fax: (540)535-0533
E-mail: info@efca.org
URL: http://www.ecfa.org
Contact: Mr. Ken Behr, Pres.
Founded: 1979. **Members:** 1,179. **Staff:** 10. **Budget:** $1,200,000. **Description:** Works to help evangelical organizations. Shows the giving public that their gifts are being spent and accounted for in a responsible manner. Requires the highest standards of financial accountability and ethics, disclosure to government, donors, and the world. Offers continuing services, consultation, and information to members; interprets its causes before federal and state governments through its Winchester, Virginia office. **Convention/Meeting:** none. **Computer Services:** database. **Committees:** Evangelical Joint Accounting; International; Standards; Standards Advisory. **Publications:** *Accounting and Financial Reporting Guide for Christian Ministries.* Book. **Price:** $20.00 ● *Focus on Accountability,* quarterly. Newsletter. **Price:** included in membership dues ● *Givers Guide.* Brochure. **Price:** free ● *Member List,* annual. Membership Directory. Lists organizations that have been approved as members ● Books.

19595 ■ Evangelical Environmental Network (EEN)
10 E Lancaster Ave.
Wynnewood, PA 19096-3495
Ph: (202)554-1955
Free: (800)650-6600
E-mail: een@creationcare.org
URL: http://www.creationcare.org
Contact: Rev. Jim Ball, Exec. Dir.
Description: Fellowship of believers who seek to share the Gospel with others. **Publications:** *Creation Care*, quarterly. Magazine. **Price:** free. Alternate Formats: online.

19596 ■ Evangelical Press Association (EPA)
PO Box 28129
Crystal, MN 55428
Ph: (763)535-4793
Fax: (763)535-4794
E-mail: director@epassoc.org
URL: http://www.epassoc.org
Contact: Doug Trouten, Exec. Dir.
Founded: 1948. **Members:** 403. **Membership Dues:** associate individual, $70 (annual) ● business affiliate, $250 (annual). **Staff:** 2. **Budget:** $140,000. **Multinational. Description:** Editors and publishers of Christian periodicals. Maintains placement service. **Awards:** Awards of Excellence. **Frequency:** annual. **Type:** recognition ● Higher Goals. **Frequency:** annual. **Type:** recognition ● Joseph Bayly Award. **Frequency:** periodic. **Type:** recognition. **Recipient:** for distinguished service to the field of Christian journalism. **Committees:** Awards; Convention; Ethics; Scholarship. **Special Interest Groups:** Fellowship of Christian Newspapers. **Publications:** *Liaison*, quarterly. Newsletter. **Price:** free to members. **Conventions/Meetings:** annual convention, features workshops, speakers, music, awards, and networking opportunities (exhibits).

19597 ■ Evangelical Social Action Commission (ESAC)
c/o National Association of Evangelicals
PO Box 23269
Washington, DC 20026
Ph: (202)789-1011
E-mail: pr@nae.net
URL: http://www.nae.net
Founded: 1951. **Description:** A commission of the National Association of Evangelicals (see separate entry). Seeks to foster discussion and awareness among Evangelicals of urgent social issues, such as abortion, disarmament, gambling, alcohol abuse, and race relations. Conducts research. **Awards:** Faithful Servant Award. **Frequency:** annual. **Type:** recognition. **Recipient:** for mature individual who has exhibited special ministry in their field of service. **Affiliated With:** National Association of Evangelicals. **Conventions/Meetings:** annual meeting - always first week of March ● workshop.

19598 ■ Evangelism and Home Missions Association (EHMA)
c/o National Association of Evangelicals
PO Box 23269
Washington, DC 20026-3269
Ph: (202)789-1011
E-mail: info@nae.net
URL: http://www.nae.net/index.
cfm?FUSEACTION=nae.mission
Contact: David Melvin, VP/Dir. of Operations
Founded: 1943. **Members:** 47. **Description:** A commission of the National Association of Evangelicals (see separate entry). Individuals representing different denominations (30) and individuals interested in evangelism and mission work (15). Provides resource materials and advisory counsel to members in their efforts to more effectively propagate the gospel of Jesus Christ. Serves as a forum for interaction among evangelical leaders of NAE. Operates speakers' bureau. **Committees:** Church Extension; Evangelism/Church Growth; Special Ministries; Spiritual Life. **Affiliated With:** National Association of Evangelicals. **Formerly:** (1980) Evangelism and Home Mission Commission. **Publications:** *Evangelism and Home Missions Association—Resource Library*, periodic.

Monographs. Presents articles on spiritual life, evangelism, church growth and extension, cross culture ministries, and management. **Conventions/Meetings:** annual workshop and meeting, held in conjunction with NAE.

19599 ■ Fellowship of Christian Airline Personnel (FCAP)
136 Providence Rd.
Fayetteville, GA 30215
Ph: (770)461-9320
E-mail: office@fcap.org
URL: http://www.fcap.org
Contact: Paul M. Curtas, Gen. Dir.
Founded: 1972. **Staff:** 4. **Multinational. Description:** Nondenominational fellowship of airline workers and other interested Christians. Encourages Christian airline personnel to spread the gospel of Jesus Christ as they travel throughout the world. Sponsors FCAP Prayer Fellowship, a worldwide group of men and women who pray for the needs and ministry of the Fellowship. Distributes literature among airline personnel; maintains speakers' bureau. **Publications:** *Howgozit*, quarterly. Newsletter. **Circulation:** 350 ● *Prayer Letter*, monthly ● *Trim Tab*, bimonthly. Magazine ● Brochures. **Conventions/Meetings:** meeting and convention.

19600 ■ Fellowship of Christian Athletes (FCA)
8701 Leeds Rd.
Kansas City, MO 64129
Ph: (816)921-0909
Free: (800)289-0909
Fax: (816)921-8755
E-mail: fca@fca.org
URL: http://www.fca.org
Contact: Les Steckel, Pres./CEO
Founded: 1954. **Staff:** 721. **Budget:** $34,547,350. **Regional Groups:** 17. **State Groups:** 46. **Local Groups:** 6,601. **Description:** Professional and student athletes, present and former; clergy and laypersons. Aims to "present to athletes and coaches and all whom they influence, the challenge and adventure of receiving Jesus Christ as Savior and Lord, serving Him in their relationships and in the fellowship of the church". Sponsors rallies, retreats, summer sports camps, meetings of junior and senior high school and college athletes during the academic year, coaches meetings, athletic clinics, and school assemblies. Maintains National Conference Center in Indiana for retreats and leadership training. **Divisions:** Development; Ministry; Operations; Programs. **Publications:** *Sharing the Victory*, monthly. Magazine. Serves as ministry tool. **Price:** $19.95/year. **Circulation:** 75,000. **Advertising:** accepted ● *Stewardship*, weekly. Newsletter. Represents current tax wise financial issues of the week of the company's funding partners. ● *Team FCA E-News*, weekly. Newsletter. Includes a variety of information from the world of FCA. Alternate Formats: online ● Also distributes literature, video and audiocassettes, and other materials.

19601 ■ First Fruit
14 Corporate Plz.
Newport Beach, CA 92660
Ph: (949)720-3774
Fax: (949)760-5349
E-mail: info@firstfruit.org
URL: http://www.firstfruit.org
Contact: Kimberly Mer, Program Admin.
Description: Works to provide support to Christian ministries with a focus on leadership development, evangelism, and holistic ministry. **Awards:** **Type:** grant.

19602 ■ Friends of Israel Gospel Ministry (FOIGM)
PO Box 908
Bellmawr, NJ 08099
Ph: (856)853-5590
Free: (800)257-7843

E-mail: foi@foigm.org
URL: http://www.foi.org
Contact: William E. Sutter, Exec. Dir.
Founded: 1938. **Nonmembership. Description:** Evangelical Christian ministry originating to help Jewish people escape the Holocaust in Europe. Today the ministry is committed to serving the Biblical mandate to "Pray for the peace of Jerusalem" (Psalm 122:6) and loving people to life in Jesus the Messiah. Seeks to reach Jewish people and Gentiles worldwide in ten countries and four continents through personal contacts, local church education, Bible conferences, tours to Israel, the Institute of Jewish Studies, literature distribution, and a radio ministry. **Additional Websites:** http://sites.silaspartners.com/foi. **Formerly:** (1973) Friends of Israel Missionary and Relief SOC. **Publications:** *Israel My Glory* (in English and Spanish), bimonthly. Magazine. Contains information on biblical teaching and commentary. **Price:** $16.95/year in U.S. and Canada. **Circulation:** 200,000 ● Books ● Brochures ● Also publishes tracts, videos, cassettes, posters, calendars, and cards.

19603 ■ The Gideons International (TGI)
PO Box 140800
Nashville, TN 37214-0800
Ph: (615)564-5000
Fax: (615)564-6000
E-mail: tgi@gideons.org
URL: http://www.gideons.org
Contact: Mr. Jerry Burden, Exec. Dir.
Founded: 1899. **Members:** 250,000. **Staff:** 78. **Regional Groups:** 7. **State Groups:** 44. **Local Groups:** 3,010. **Description:** Christian business and professional men in 180 countries who seek "to win others for the Lord Jesus Christ" by distributing the Bible or portions thereof to individuals, hotels, hospitals, schools, and institutions. **Publications:** *The Gideon*, monthly. Magazine. **Conventions/Meetings:** annual convention.

19604 ■ Hebrew Christian Fellowship (HCF)
PO Box 177
Dresher, PA 19025-0177
Ph: (215)887-3447
E-mail: hcf1033@aol.com
URL: http://www.hcfellowship.org
Contact: Rev. Roger L. Wambold, Dir.
Founded: 1944. **Description:** Churches and individuals working to evangelize Jewish people. Sponsors Jewish outreach programs in churches and colleges. Promotes personal evangelism. Programs are conducted in Israel and the U.S. Sponsors Bible study groups; distributes Bibles and other literature. **Publications:** *Shalom Update*, bimonthly. Newsletter. **Price:** free. **Circulation:** 3,000 ● Brochures. **Conventions/Meetings:** quarterly board meeting.

19605 ■ High School Evangelism Fellowship (Hi-BA)
1 Maple St.
Allendale, NJ 07401
Ph: (201)760-9925
Free: (888)281-4887
Fax: (201)760-9926
E-mail: info@touchtheworld.org
URL: http://www.touchtheworld.org
Contact: Kimberly Wolfe, VP of Student Ministries
Founded: 1944. **Staff:** 38. **Description:** Conducts Bible clubs for high school students in the New York-New Jersey metropolitan areas, Japan, and Russia. Maintains student center in Tokyo, Japan, and a camp 60 miles northeast of Tokyo. Maintains an office and student center in Tambov, Russia 250 miles southeast of Moscow. **Formerly:** (2003) High School Evangelism Fellowship.

19606 ■ International Board of Jewish Missions (IBJM)
PO Box 1386
Hixson, TN 37343
Ph: (423)876-8150
Fax: (423)876-8156

E-mail: amolam@ibjm.org
URL: http://www.ibjm.org
Contact: Dr. Orman L. Norwood, Pres.
Founded: 1949. **Staff:** 15. **Languages:** English, French, German, Hebrew, Portuguese, Russian, Spanish. **Description:** Missionaries working in Argentina, England, France, Israel, Spain, New York, Mexico, Canada, USA, Uruguay, Venezuela, and the Ukraine to establish "Everlasting Nation Fellowships" that will raise the Christian conscience on behalf of the Jews. Utilizes radio facilities to spread the gospel and foster mutual understanding between Jews and Christians. Encourages establishment of New Testament churches near Jewish communities and cooperates with existing churches which deal with the evangelization of Jews. Disseminates information and distributes Old and New Testaments in various languages. Provides assistance to underprivileged Jews who have converted to Christianity, and students preparing for missionary work. Operates Messianic Museum, and year-round museum tours. **Libraries: Type:** reference. **Holdings:** 600; archival material, books, photographs. **Subjects:** Jewish history and religion, Jewish artifacts. **Publications:** *The Everlasting Nation*, bimonthly. Magazine. For pastors, teachers, Christian workers, and supporters. **Price:** $10.00/year. **Circulation:** 18,000 ● *Prayer and Praise*, monthly. **Price:** included in membership dues. **Circulation:** 1,700 ● *Prophecy Edition of the New Testament* ● Booklets ● Books ● Videos. **Conventions/Meetings:** annual Four Day Focus/Candidate School - workshop (exhibits).

19607 ■ International Council of Christian Churches (ICCC)
10977 E 23rd St.
Tulsa, OK 74129
Ph: (918)234-0462
Fax: (918)234-0474
E-mail: ammi7801@aol.com
URL: http://www.iccc.org.sg
Contact: Dr. John Barela, Pres.
Founded: 1948. **Members:** 718. **Membership Dues:** $25 (annual). **Multinational. Description:** Denominations and associations of "Bible-believing churches." Membership closed to groups that are in or represented by the World Council of Churches (see separate entry) or are "standing outside the stream of historic Christianity." Promotes fellowship of fundamental churches and church councils; encourages member bodies to foster a loyal and aggressive revival of Bible Christianity; seeks "to awaken Christians everywhere to the insidious dangers of modernism, and call them to unity of mind and effort against all unbelief and compromise with modernism of every kind." Sponsors training programs and seminars. **Commissions:** Christian Education; Evangelism; Information and Publication; International Affairs; International Christian Youth; Justice and Freedom Missions; New Contacts; Radio; Social and Relief. **Publications:** Also publishes regional papers. **Conventions/Meetings:** periodic congress (exhibits).

19608 ■ International Messianic Jewish Alliance (IMJA)
72-877 Dinah Shore Dr., Ste.103-141
Rancho Mirage, CA 92270
Ph: (760)668-3011 (760)837-0372
Fax: (760)837-0451
E-mail: pliberman@dc.rr.com
URL: http://www.imja.com
Contact: Paul Liberman, Exec. Dir.
Founded: 1925. **Members:** 2,007. **Staff:** 17. **Budget:** $1,000,000. **Regional Groups:** 17. **National Groups:** 17. **Languages:** Dutch, English, French, German, Hebrew, Russian, Spanish. **Description:** Affiliated national alliances. Established for the pastoral care and support for those of Jewish faith who believe in Jesus Christ. Encourages fellowship among Messianic Jews. **Libraries: Type:** open to the public; reference. **Holdings:** 28,000. **Subjects:** theological, biblical, evangelistic, biographical. **Awards: Frequency:** periodic. **Type:** grant ● **Frequency:** periodic. **Type:** scholarship. **Telecommunication Services:** electronic mail, p.liberman@imja.com. **Formerly:** (1992) International Hebrew

Christian Alliance. **Conventions/Meetings:** biennial conference (exhibits).

19609 ■ International Students, Inc. (ISI)
PO Box C
Colorado Springs, CO 80901
Ph: (719)576-2700
Free: (800)474-4147
Fax: (719)576-5363
E-mail: information@isionline.org
URL: http://www.isionline.org
Contact: Doug Shaw, Pres.
Founded: 1953. **Staff:** 190. **Budget:** $1,700,000. **Regional Groups:** 5. **Description:** Nondenominational evangelical Christian organization. Organizes friendship and hospitality programs for international students. Designs programs to meet the students' social needs while providing them with the opportunity to learn about Christianity. Provides leadership training with special emphasis placed on individual social, physical, economic, and spiritual needs. Training is available through such opportunities as area retreats, Bible studies, and conferences. **Additional Websites:** http://www.internationalstudents.org. **Publications:** *Becoming Friends with an International Student*. Booklet ● *The Compact Guide to World Religions*. Book ● *The World at Your Door*. Book. **Conventions/Meetings:** annual National Conference on International Student Ministry, staff and associates training conference - always summer.

19610 ■ Laymen's Home Missionary Movement (LHMM)
1156 St. Matthews Rd.
Chester Springs, PA 19425-2700
Ph: (610)827-7665 (610)827-1586
Fax: (610)827-1615
E-mail: laymens@biblestandard.com
URL: http://biblestandard.com
Contact: Ralph M. Herzig, Exec. Dir.
Founded: 1916. **Members:** 10,000. **Staff:** 10. **National Groups:** 30. **Languages:** Danish, English, French, German, Kannada, Malayalam, Polish, Portuguese, Tamil, Ukrainian. **Multinational. Description:** Interdenominational, nonsectarian movement of Christians united to preach the Gospel and foster Christian behavior; stimulate a greater interest in Bible study; disseminate information and encourage others to spread knowledge of the Bible, particularly as it pertains to the modern world. Provides speakers, ministers for Bible studies, discussions, and funerals. **Libraries: Type:** reference. **Holdings:** 5,500. **Subjects:** secular and religious literature. **Formerly:** The Bible Standard. **Publications:** *The Bible Standard*, bimonthly. Journal. Contains Bible Study and General Christian Articles. **Price:** $12.00. **ISSN:** 1556-8555. **Circulation:** 2,800. Alternate Formats: online. Also Cited As: *Herald of the Epiphany* ● *The Present Truth and Herald of Christ's Epiphany*, bimonthly ● Booklets ● Books ● Magazines ● Also publishes tracts in various languages.

19611 ■ Lederer Messianic Ministries
c/o Messianic Jewish Communications
6120 Day Long Ln.
Clarksville, MD 21029
Ph: (410)531-6644
Free: (800)410-7367
Fax: (410)531-9440
E-mail: website@messianicjewish.net
URL: http://www.messianicjewish.net
Contact: Barry Rubin, Exec. Dir.
Founded: 1920. **Description:** Publishes and distributes Messianic literature with a Jewish perspective. Maintains Judeo-Christian research library. **Formerly:** (1938) Salem Hebrew Lutheran Mission; (1989) Lederer Foundation. **Publications:** *A Way in the Wilderness* ● *Good News According to Matthew* (in English and Yiddish) ● *Jewish New Testament*. Book ● *The Lederer Letter*, monthly. Newsletter. Covers foundation activities, Israel, and Jewish culture and tradition. **Price:** free. **Circulation:** 8,000 ● *The Man with the Book* ● *Messianic Children's Curriculum*. Book ● *Messianic Passover Haggadah* (in English and Spanish). Book. Guides readers through the traditional Passover Seder dinner, step-by-step. **Price:** $4.99/

copy ● *New Testament in Yiddish* ● *The Ox, The Ass, The Oyster* ● *Raisins and Almonds* ● *Would I? Would You?* ● *You Bring the Bagels; I'll Bring the Gospel* (in English and Russian) ● Audiotapes ● Books ● Also releases videos, gift certificates, cassettes, CD's and songbooks.

19612 ■ Life Action Revival Ministries (LAM)
PO Box 31
Buchanan, MI 49107-0031
Ph: (269)697-8600
Free: (800)321-1538
Fax: (269)695-2474
E-mail: info@lifeaction.org
URL: http://www.lifeaction.org
Contact: Byron Paulus, CEO
Founded: 1971. **Staff:** 140. **Description:** Nationwide revival ministry devoted to America's return to living standards communicated through the Bible. Seeks the rebuilding and strengthening of the home and family through various ministries including Life Action Singers (team ministry that tours the U.S. singing about positive alternatives needed among young people and adults). Holds crusades, retreats, seminars, assemblies, and one-night presentations throughout the U.S. and Canada. **Divisions:** Creative Arts; Marketing and PR; Team Outreaches. **Formerly:** (2002) Life Action Ministries. **Publications:** *Heartcry: A Journal on Revival and Spiritual Awakening*, quarterly. Magazine. **Price:** $4.95/copy ● *Revival Report*, 3/year ● *Spirit of Revival*, 1-2/year. Magazine. Addresses topics essential to revival. **Price:** free. **Circulation:** 60,000. Alternate Formats: online ● Brochures. Alternate Formats: online ● Manuals ● Articles. Alternate Formats: online.

19613 ■ Life Outreach International
PO Box 982000
Fort Worth, TX 76182-8000
Ph: (817)267-4211
Free: (800)947-5433
E-mail: feedback@loi.org
URL: http://www.lifetoday.org
Contact: James Robison, Board Chm.
Founded: 1963. **Members:** 53. **Staff:** 140. **Description:** Christian ministry founded by James Robison (1963-). Sponsors daily (Monday-Friday) and weekly (Sunday) Christian television programs in the U.S. and Canada. Outreach support includes international feeding and relief, crusades, seminars and film. **Libraries: Type:** reference. **Subjects:** spiritual resources. **Formerly:** (1991) James Robison Evangelistic Association; (1993) James Robison Life International. **Publications:** Books ● Pamphlets ● Videos. **Conventions/Meetings:** annual conference (exhibits).

19614 ■ Luis Palau Association (LPA)
PO Box 50
Portland, OR 97207
Ph: (503)614-1500
Fax: (503)614-1599
E-mail: info@palau.org
URL: http://www.palau.org
Contact: Mr. David L. Jones, Contact
Founded: 1978. **Staff:** 140. **Budget:** $21,000,000. **Languages:** English, Spanish. **Multinational. Description:** Mission organization founded by Luis Palau (1934-), Argentinean-born evangelist. Conducts evangelistic festivals and outreach programs to bring the word of Christ to the world. Supports service to the church through: Bible teaching; counseling by mail; evangelism training. Conducts daily radio programs (in Spanish and English), and network TV specials. **Subgroups:** Livin It; Next Generation Alliance. **Affiliated With:** Christian Management Association; Evangelical Council for Financial Accountability; Evangelical Press Association; National Association of Evangelicals; National Religious Broadcasters; World Evangelical Alliance. **Formerly:** (1986) Luis Palau Evangelistic Team; (2006) Luis Palau Evangelistic Association. **Publications:** *Proclaim*, bimonthly. Magazine. **Price:** free. **Circulation:** 60,000 ● Books.

19615 ■ Maranatha Volunteers International (MVI)

1600 Sacramento Inn Way, Ste.116
Sacramento, CA 95815
Ph: (916)920-1900
Fax: (916)920-3299
E-mail: information@maranatha.org
URL: http://www.maranatha.org
Contact: John Freeman, Founder
Founded: 1969. **Members:** 35,000. **Languages:** English, Portuguese, Spanish. **Multinational. Description:** Seeks to evangelize the world through construction of churches, schools, orphanages, clinics, hospitals and other needed buildings. **Funds:** Maranatha. **Programs:** $10 Church; Ambassador; 1000 Churches in 1000 Days; Our Children International. **Projects:** Assistance. **Publications:** *Maranatha Guide To Adventure.* Handbook. Alternate Formats: online ● *Maranatha Matters* (in English, Portuguese, and Spanish), periodic. Newsletter. Contains updates of Maranatha happenings. Alternate Formats: online ● *The Volunteer*, quarterly. Magazine. **Price:** free for members ● Videos. **Price:** free ● Brochures. **Price:** free.

19616 ■ Media Fellowship International (MFI)

PO Box 82685
Kenmore, WA 98028
Ph: (425)488-3965
Fax: (425)488-8531
E-mail: mfi@usa.net
URL: http://www.mediafellowship.org
Contact: Pastor Bob Rieth, Founder/Exec. Dir.
Founded: 1987. **Multinational. Description:** Seeks to minister to professionals in the film, radio, print, and television segments of the media and entertainment industry. Offers counseling, referrals, and support groups. Organizes Bible study classes. **Awards:** Media Fellowship International Ambassador Award. **Frequency:** annual. **Type:** fellowship ● **Type:** recognition. **Formerly:** Fellowship of Christians in the Arts, Media and Entertainment. **Publications:** *The Spotlight*, quarterly. Newsletter. **Conventions/Meetings:** semiannual seminar.

19617 ■ Morris Cerullo World Evangelism (MCWE)

PO Box 85277
San Diego, CA 92186-5277
Ph: (858)277-2200
E-mail: morriscerullo@mcwe.com
URL: http://www.mcwe.com
Contact: Dr. Morris Cerullo, Pres.
Founded: 1960. **Members:** 150,000. **Staff:** 135. **Multinational. Description:** Christian missionary organization that functions through ministers and Schools of Ministry in 133 countries. Sponsors Morris Cerullo evangelistic crusades around the world and in major cities of North America. Conducts minister training seminars in various countries, training approximately 50,000 ministers annually. **Libraries: Type:** reference. **Awards: Type:** recognition. **Formerly:** (1987) World Evangelism. **Publications:** *A Call To Prayer For A Nation At War.* Book. **Price:** $5.00 ● *Antichrist Haven: Babylon Made Fellow For The Tribulation.* Book. **Price:** $10.00 ● *Blessed.* Magazine. **Price:** free for members. Alternate Formats: online ● *Christ, Your Healer.* Book. **Price:** $6.00 ● *The End Times.* Newspaper ● *GVA Today*, monthly. Newsletter ● *Victory Miracle Living*, monthly. Features a 48-page teaching lesson. **Conventions/Meetings:** annual conference.

19618 ■ National Apostolate for Inclusion Ministry (NAFIM)

PO Box 218
Riverdale, MD 20738-0218
Ph: (301)699-9500
Free: (800)736-1280
E-mail: info@nafim.org
URL: http://www.nafim.org
Contact: Barbara J. Lampe, Exec. Dir.
Founded: 1968. **Members:** 400. **Membership Dues:** individual, family, $35 (annual) ● sponsor, $100 (annual) ● patron, $200 (annual) ● benefactor, $500 (annual) ● parish/foreign country, $50 (annual). **Staff:**

1. **Budget:** $60,000. **Description:** Chaplains, special educators, religious educators, and professionals in the field of intellectual, cognitive and developmental disabilities; parents and siblings of people with intellectual, cognitive and developmental disabilities; adult and teen volunteers. Promotes full participation of people with intellectual, cognitive and developmental disabilities in the life of the Church. Promotes recognition of the gifts in ministry with people with intellectual, cognitive and developmental disabilities. Focuses on religious education at all stages of life for people with intellectual, cognitive and developmental disabilities. **Awards:** Leadership Award. **Frequency:** annual. **Type:** recognition ● Program Award. **Frequency:** annual. **Type:** recognition ● Service Award. **Frequency:** annual. **Type:** recognition ● Youth Award. **Frequency:** annual. **Type:** recognition. **Committees:** Awards; Public Relations; Resource/Education. **Formerly:** (1978) National Apostolate for the Mentally Retarded; (1993) National Apostolate with Mentally Retarded Persons; (1998) National Apostolate with People with Mental Retardation. **Publications:** *National Apostolate for Inclusion Ministry Messenger*, quarterly. Newsletter. **Price:** included in membership dues ● *National Apostolate for Inclusion Ministry Quarterly Publication.* Magazine. **Price:** included in membership dues. ISSN: 0273-9178. **Circulation:** 800. **Advertising:** accepted. **Conventions/Meetings:** annual conference (exhibits).

19619 ■ Open Air Campaigners, U.S.A. (OAC/USA)

PO Box D
Nazareth, PA 18064
Ph: (610)746-0508
Fax: (610)746-0509
E-mail: usa@oaci.org
URL: http://www.oacusa.org
Contact: Mr. Rex Trent, Chm.
Founded: 1956. **Members:** 50. **Staff:** 22. **Budget:** $700,000. **Description:** Members are staff and committee men who are conservative, evangelical Christians, both pastors and laymen, from various denominations. Engages in outdoor evangelism; presents the claims of Jesus Christ to people who cannot or will not come inside a church building and introduces these people to Bible-believing churches; trains pastors, youth workers, and missionaries in effective methods of open-air work. **Affiliated With:** Association of North American Missions; Evangelical Council for Financial Accountability. **Publications:** *OAC/USA Update*, 1-4/year ● Manuals ● Also prepares illustrated outlines for open-air sermons. **Conventions/Meetings:** annual Open-Air Summer Seminar - always in Lancaster Bible College, Lancaster, PA ● seminar, provides training for Salvation Army, international mission agencies, and Bible colleges.

19620 ■ Pilots for Christ International (PCI)

7869 Meadowgate Dr.
Manassas, VA 20112
Ph: (540)439-0940 (703)791-0448
E-mail: leedearmond@msn.com
URL: http://www.pilotsforchrist.com
Contact: Lee De Armond, Pres.
Founded: 1985. **Members:** 900. **Membership Dues:** first time, $25 ● renewal, $15 (annual). **Regional Groups:** 20. **State Groups:** 4. **Description:** Nondenominational association of pilots and aviation enthusiasts in 16 countries united to foster knowledge of the gospel of Jesus Christ to the aviation community. Distributes Bibles at airports; provides air transportation for nonprofit organizations and persons in need; participates in air shows. Conducts fly-ins. Operates speakers' bureau; provides children's educational programs which includes teen cadets and flying instruction. **Awards:** Christ the King Award. **Frequency:** annual. **Type:** recognition ● Pilot of the Year. **Frequency:** annual. **Type:** recognition. **Publications:** *PCI Newsletter*, bimonthly. **Advertising:** accepted ● *Pilots for Christ Newsletter*, quarterly. **Price:** included in membership dues. **Circulation:** 900. Alternate Formats: online ● Also publishes tracts. **Conventions/Meetings:** annual conference - always third weekend of October.

19621 ■ Pro Athletes Outreach (PAO)

PO Box 1044
Issaquah, WA 98027
Ph: (425)392-6300
Free: (800)733-7306
E-mail: office@pao.org
URL: http://www.pao.org
Contact: Norm Evans, CEO
Founded: 1974. **Staff:** 9. **Description:** Professional athletes from football, baseball, hockey, basketball, tennis, and other sports. Seeks to provide nondenominational, Christian training to professional athletes and their spouses. **Publications:** *Inside Out*, quarterly. Newsletter. Alternate Formats: online ● *The Sports Page*, quarterly. **Price:** free. **Circulation:** 6,000. **Conventions/Meetings:** bimonthly conference and seminar.

19622 ■ Remnant Of Israel (ROI)

PO Box 142633
Irving, TX 75014-2633
Ph: (214)821-0633
Free: (888)352-7153
Fax: (214)821-0633
E-mail: info@remnantofisrael.net
URL: http://www.remnantofisrael.net
Contact: Mr. Mark Drogin, Co-Founder
Founded: 1977. **Members:** 4. **Staff:** 3. **Description:** Seeks to educate Catholics about Jewish people. Promotes better understanding between Catholics and Jews. **Libraries: Type:** reference. **Holdings:** archival material, books, periodicals. **Subjects:** Jewish Catholics, Jewish roots of Catholic faith. **Publications:** *Before the Dawn.* Book ● *Bread From Heaven.* Book ● *Glory of Thy People.* Book ● *Hear, O Israel!*, quarterly. Journal. **Price:** $24.95/year ● *He's a Jew.* Book ● *The Ingrafting.* Book ● *Once a Jew.* Book ● *Queen of the Jews.* Book ● *Richer Than a Millionaire.* Book ● *This Jew.* Book ● Newsletter, annual. **Price:** free. **Circulation:** 14,000.

19623 ■ Revival Fires (Christian Evangelizers Association) (RFCEA)

PO Box 1008
Branson West, MO 65737
Ph: (417)338-2422
Fax: (417)338-6605
E-mail: revivalfr@aol.com
Contact: Cecil Todd, Pres.
Founded: 1964. **Members:** 25,000. **Staff:** 12. **Budget:** $1,000,000. **Languages:** Chinese, English, Indian Dialects, Russian. **Multinational. Description:** Religious congregations. Seeks to spread the gospel worldwide through missionary work. Sponsors television programs and crusades; operates two orphanages, one hospital and out-patient clinic in Kerala State India. **Conventions/Meetings:** monthly Crusade Tours to Russia and China (exhibits).

19624 ■ Saints Alive in Jesus (SAJ)

PO Box 1347
Issaquah, WA 98027
Free: (800)861-9888
E-mail: ed@saintsalive.com
URL: http://www.saintsalive.com
Contact: J. Edward Decker, Founder
Founded: 1979. **Staff:** 8. **Regional Groups:** 7. **State Groups:** 1. **Description:** Former Mormons and other Christians witnessing Jesus Christ to the Mormon people. Aims to "reach as many individual Mormons as possible with the message of true salvation, leading as many as will go to the cross of Calvary." Works to provide evidence that a separation exists between the Christian faith and the Mormon faith. Sponsors seminars; provides counseling, teachers, training aids, and speakers. Provides similar services in the area of Freemasonry and the Lodges. **Libraries: Type:** reference. **Holdings:** 5,000; books. **Computer Services:** database. **Telecommunication Services:** electronic mail, edecker@nwlink.com. **Publications:** *Saints Alive in Jesus Newsletter*, monthly ● Also publishes books, brochures, tracts, and teaching materials; makes available films and videotapes. **Conventions/Meetings:** semiannual meeting.

19625 ■ Skinner Leadership Institute
5875 Solomons Island Rd.
PO Box 190
Tracys Landing, MD 20779
Ph: (301)261-9800
Fax: (301)261-5193
E-mail: bws@skinnerleadership.org
URL: http://www.skinnerleadership.org
Contact: Dr. Barbara Williams Skinner, Pres./Co-Founder
Founded: 1964. **Staff:** 5. **Budget:** $300,000. **Description:** Organized by the late evangelist Tom Skinner to raise a new generation of Christian leaders. Under the leadership of Barbara Williams Skinner, wife of Tom Skinner, conducts spiritual counseling, as well as seminars, on such subjects as leadership and religious education. Works with entertainment, political, and sports leaders, especially African American officials, in "bringing Christ" to their endeavors. Also works with students at Howard University and urban youth at four technology aided learning centers in Washington, DC. Also works on reconciliation between people of diverse races and cultures. **Formerly:** (1997) Tom Skinner Associates. **Publications:** *The News in Black and White*, 3/year. Brochure ● *News in Black and White*, 2-3/year. Newsletter. **Price:** free. **Conventions/Meetings:** annual meeting - always April, in New York City.

19626 ■ WEC International
PO Box 1707
Fort Washington, PA 19034
Ph: (215)646-2322
Free: (888)646-6202
E-mail: trekusa@wectrek.org
URL: http://www.wec-usa.org
Contact: David Hall, Link Dir.
Founded: 1913. **Members:** 1,800. **Staff:** 35. **Budget:** $2,358,500. **Description:** Seeks to evangelize the remaining unevangelized areas of the world and to establish self-sustaining, reproducing churches. **Libraries:** Type: reference. **Holdings:** 1,000; books, periodicals. **Subjects:** missions. **Departments:** Radio Worldwide; Rainbows of Hope (Ministry to children in crisis); WEC Trek (Short-term Teams); Word Worldwide. **Formerly:** Heart of Africa Mission. **Publications:** *WEC.GO*, quarterly. Magazine. Alternate Formats: online ● *Youth*, quarterly. **Conventions/Meetings:** annual USA Staff Conference - always September in Fort Washington, PA.

19627 ■ Word of Life Fellowship (WOL)
PO Box 600
Schroon Lake, NY 12870
Ph: (518)494-6000
Free: (800)331-9673
Fax: (518)494-6306
E-mail: info@wol.org
URL: http://www.wol.org
Contact: Dr. Joe Jordan, Exec. Dir.
Founded: 1940. **Staff:** 309. **Budget:** $30,000,000. **Multinational. Description:** Religious, evangelistic organization particularly interested in "winning young people to Christ and Christian living". Activities include Bible clubs, rallies, and radio programs, Bible institutes, and distribution of literature. Has missionaries in 46 countries. Maintains summer camps throughout the world. Name taken from the Bible, Philippians 2:16: "Holding forth the word of life". **Publications:** *Prayer Letter*, monthly. Newsletter ● Magazine, annual. Contains ministry updates. **Conventions/Meetings:** biennial Missionary Conference - meeting.

19628 ■ Youth Evangelism Association (YEA)
13000 U.S. 41 N
Evansville, IN 47725
Ph: (812)867-2418
Fax: (812)867-8933
E-mail: info@youthevangelism.org
URL: http://www.youthevangelism.org
Contact: Tami Dooms, Pres.
Founded: 1973. **Members:** 17. **Membership Dues:** group exemption affiliate organization, $200 (annual) ● independent organization, $125 (annual) ● local church youth ministry, $50 (annual) ● individual, $25

(annual). **Description:** Youth leaders and ministries. Works to provide youth activities and promote family ministries. Conducts educational and charitable programs. Sponsors competitions; maintains speakers' bureau. **Committees:** Annual Convention; Bible Quizzing; Evangelism Leadership; Teen Talent. **Conventions/Meetings:** annual Evangelism Leadership Conference - convention, with teen talent, bible quizzing ● semiannual Youth Ministry Leadership School - conference.

Evangelization

19629 ■ Missions International
PO Box 93235
Southlake, TX 76092-3235
Ph: (817)410-7706
Free: (888)710-7706
Fax: (817)421-3862
E-mail: info@missionsinternational.org
URL: http://www.missionsinternational.org
Contact: Dr. Bob Mason, Founder/Pres.
Founded: 1997. **Multinational. Description:** Represents individuals dedicated to taking American teams to proclaim the Gospel of Jesus Christ to villages. Aims to establish churches, orphanages, medical clinics and homes among the unreached people of Central and South America, Africa and Southeast Asia. **Publications:** Newsletter, monthly. Alternate Formats: online.

Families

19630 ■ Society of Blessed Gianna Beretta Molla
PO Box 2946
Warminster, PA 18974
Ph: (215)672-3551
E-mail: info@saintgianna.org
URL: http://www.saintgianna.org
Contact: Jim Buffler, Pres.
Founded: 1999. **Multinational. Description:** Promotes holiness in the family and the sanctity of human life by distributing information and holy cards of Blessed Gianna, a young Italian pediatrician who gave her life in 1962 to save her child during a dangerous pregnancy.

Friends

19631 ■ Associated Committee of Friends on Indian Affairs (ACFIA)
c/o Victor White
PO Box 36
Toledo, IA 52342
Ph: (641)484-2329
E-mail: mesquakiefriends@yahoo.com
URL: http://www.acfiaquaker.org
Contact: John Key, Presiding Clerk
Founded: 1869. **Members:** 4,300. **Staff:** 23. **Budget:** $200,000. **Description:** Missionary project of the Religious Society of Friends (Quakers). Works to concentrate in Indian Centers in Alabama, Iowa, and Oklahoma. **Publications:** *Indian Progress*, 3/year. Bulletin. **Circulation:** 1,800. **Conventions/Meetings:** annual conference - usually first weekend in April.

19632 ■ Evangelical Friends International - North American Region (EFI-NAR)
5350 Broadmoor Cir. NW
Canton, OH 44709
Ph: (330)493-1660
Free: (800)334-8863
Fax: (330)493-0852
E-mail: efcer@aol.com
URL: http://www.evangelical-friends.org
Contact: Dr. John P. Williams, Dir.
Founded: 1968. **Staff:** 1. **Budget:** $1,121,619. **Regional Groups:** 6. **National Groups:** 25. **Multinational. Description:** Coalition of Evangelical Friends churches. Conducts worldwide missions, discipling,

and youth activities. **Commissions:** Christian Education; Communication; Leadership; Missions; Youth. **Formerly:** (1968) Association of Evangelical Friends; (1990) Evangelical Friends Alliance; (2003) Evangelical Friends International. **Publications:** *The Friends Voice*, 3/year. Newsletter. Includes news of the evangelical friends movement. **Circulation:** 1,400. **Conventions/Meetings:** annual meeting, coordinating council meeting (exhibits) - always November.

19633 ■ Friends Committee on National Legislation (FCNL)
245 2nd St. NE
Washington, DC 20002-5761
Ph: (202)547-6000
Free: (800)630-1330
Fax: (202)547-6019
E-mail: fcnl@fcnl.org
URL: http://www.fcnl.org
Contact: Joe Volk, Exec. Sec.
Founded: 1943. **Members:** 8,000. **Staff:** 21. **Budget:** $1,300,000. **Description:** Quaker lobby in the public interest. Seeks to bring the concerns, experiences, and testimonies of the Religious Society of Friends to bear on policy decisions. Advocates for social and economic justice committees. Compiles statistics. **Libraries:** Type: reference. **Holdings:** papers. **Subjects:** war and peace, human rights. **Awards:** Edward F. Snyder Award. **Frequency:** annual. **Type:** recognition. **Recipient:** for outstanding member of Congress who has displayed leadership in advancing legislative priorities. **Computer Services:** Mailing lists, weekly legislative alerts, nuclear calendar. **Boards:** Education Fund. **Committees:** General. **Funds:** Education. **Programs:** Intern; Young Adult. **Projects:** Letter Writing. **Publications:** *Action Bulletin*, periodic ● *Indian Report*, quarterly. Newsletter ● *Perspectives*. Reports. Contains information and analysis missing from most news programs and daily papers. Alternate Formats: online ● *Washington Newsletter*, monthly. Contains news and analysis for a selection of domestic and international issues. Alternate Formats: online ● Pamphlets ● Papers. Features topics of concern to friends. ● Annual Report. Alternate Formats: online ● Booklets. Alternate Formats: online ● Brochures. Alternate Formats: online. **Conventions/Meetings:** annual conference - usually 2nd weekend of November.

19634 ■ Friends General Conference (FGC)
1216 Arch St., No. 2B
Philadelphia, PA 19107
Ph: (215)561-1700
Fax: (215)561-0759
E-mail: friends@fgcquaker.org
URL: http://www.fgcquaker.org
Contact: Bruce Birchard, Gen. Sec.
Founded: 1900. **Members:** 32,000. **Staff:** 14. **Budget:** $1,460,000. **Description:** Association of 14 yearly meetings, which include 540 local meetings of the Religious Society of Friends (Quakers). Sponsors retreats and conferences. Offers teacher training for First-day Schools. Operates bookstore; publishes books, booklets, first day school curriculum, and other materials. Sends visitors to many meetings. Lends money for meetinghouse construction and renovation. **Libraries:** Type: reference. **Holdings:** books. **Computer Services:** Online services, bookstore online, upcoming events. **Additional Websites:** http://www.quakerbooks.org. **Committees:** Advancement and Outreach; Christian and Interfaith Relations; Development; Discernment in Long Term; Friends Meetinghouse Fund; Long Range Conference Planning; Ministry and Nurture; Ministry on Racism; Nominating; Publications and Distribution; Religious Education; Traveling Ministries Program; Youth Ministries. **Formerly:** First-Day School General Conference; Friends Union for Philanthropic Labor; Friends Religious Conference; Friends Education Conference. **Publications:** *Blue Book*. Outlines the organization's committee structure and governance policies. Alternate Formats: online ● *Directory for Travelling Friends* ● *FGConnections*. Newsletter. Contains information on the organization's programs and services. Alternate Formats: online ● Books. Alternate Formats: online ● Pamphlets ● Annual

Report, annual. Alternate Formats: online ● Also publishes leaflets and materials for use in First-day schools. Conventions/Meetings: annual Gathering of Friends - conference - always late June or early July.

19635 ■ Friends Historical Association (FHA)
Haverford Coll. Lib.
370 Lancaster Ave.
Haverford, PA 19041-1392
Ph: (610)896-1161
Fax: (610)896-1102
E-mail: fha@haverford.edu
URL: http://www.haverford.edu/library/fha/fha.html
Contact: Joelle Bertolet, Sec.
Founded: 1873. Members: 900. Membership Dues: individual/institution, $15 (annual) ● life, $300 ● perpetual, $1,000 (annual). Staff: 2. Multinational. Description: Persons interested in the study, preservation, and publication of material relating to the history of the Religious Society of Friends (Quakers). Sponsors annual spring excursion to some region associated with the history of Quakerism. Committees: Historical Research; Membership; Nominating; Publications. Divisions: Conference of Quaker Historians and Archivists. Absorbed: (1923) Friends Historical Society of Philadelphia. Publications: Friends in Delaware Valley, 1981. Monograph. Contains information on the Philadelphia Yearly Meeting 1681-1981. Price: $3.00 ● Quaker History, semiannual. Journal. Consists of illuminating articles on Quaker contributions to issues like social justice, education and literature. Includes book and article reviews. Price: included in membership dues; $15.00 /year for nonmembers. ISSN: 0033-5053. Circulation: 900. Alternate Formats: microform. Conventions/Meetings: biennial Conference of Quaker Historians and Archivists ● annual luncheon and meeting, with speaker - always November, in Philadelphia, PA.

19636 ■ Friends United Meeting (FUM)
101 Quaker Hill Dr.
Richmond, IN 47374-1926
Ph: (765)962-7573
Free: (800)537-8838
Fax: (765)966-1293
E-mail: info@fum.org
URL: http://www.fum.org
Contact: Sylvia Graves, Gen. Sec.
Founded: 1902. Members: 245,000. Staff: 18. Budget: $1,839,410. Regional Groups: 27. Local Groups: 1,500. Languages: English, Swahili. Description: Association of 27 Friends yearly meetings cooperate in education, missions, peace, evangelism, and publications. Conducts charitable and educational programs in association with two rural hospitals in Kenya and schools in Ramallah, Palestine. Operates book press and bookstore; holds investments; makes loans. Libraries: Type: reference. Holdings: audio recordings, books, monographs, periodicals, video recordings. Subjects: friends' history, genealogy, missions. Formerly: Five Years Meeting of Friends. Publications: Quaker Life, 10/year. Magazine. Price: $24.00/year in North America; $32.00/ year outside North America; $65.00 for 3 years, in North America. ISSN: 0033-5061. Circulation: 7,500. Advertising: accepted. Conventions/Meetings: triennial congress (exhibits).

19637 ■ Wider Quaker Fellowship (WQF)
1506 Race St.
Philadelphia, PA 19102-1406
Ph: (215)241-7250
Fax: (215)241-7285
E-mail: wqf@fwccamericas.org
URL: http://www.fwccamericas.org/about_us/
   programs/wqf.shtml
Contact: Vicki Hain Poorman, Program Sec.
Founded: 1936. Members: 2,800. Staff: 1. Languages: English, Spanish. Multinational. Description: Represents nonsectarian, spiritual movement of persons and primarily members of other religious denominations, who wish to be in touch with the Religious Society of Friends (Quakers). Maintains fellowship primarily through mailing of literature and correspondence with staff. Includes fellows in 90 countries, although majority live in North America. Affiliated With: Friends World Committee for Consultation. Also Known As: Asociacion de Amigos de los Amigos. Publications: Pamphlets (in English and Spanish), 3/year. Includes selected readings on subjects related to Quakerism or of interest to Quakers. Circulation: 2,800 ● Newsletter, annual. Includes brief stories, excerpt from letters and other items from the Wilder Quacker Fellows. Conventions/Meetings: annual meeting.

Gay/Lesbian

19638 ■ Affirmation/Gay and Lesbian Mormons
PO Box 46022
Los Angeles, CA 90046-0022
Ph: (661)367-2421
E-mail: affirmationlds@earthlink.com
URL: http://www.affirmation.org
Contact: Olin Thomas, Exec. Dir.
Founded: 1977. Members: 400. Membership Dues: individual, $25 (annual) ● student, $15 (annual) ● sustaining, $50 (annual). Regional Groups: 20. Local Groups: 15. Description: Members of the Church of Jesus Christ of Latter Day Saints, commonly referred to as the Mormon Church; friends, relatives, and interested individuals. Works to promote understanding, tolerance, and acceptance of gay men and lesbians as full, equal, and worthy members of the church and society. Maintains that homosexuality and homosexual relationships can be consistent with and supported by the gospel of Jesus Christ. Fosters affirmation, self-acceptance, and self-worth among members. Encourages members' continued spiritual development, and the practice of Christian behavior. Assists members in dealing with personal problems, the church, employers, family, social contacts, and work associates, and in reconciling sexual orientation with traditional Mormon beliefs and other belief systems as they relate to homosexuality. Seeks to educate church members and the public regarding the realities and implications of homosexuality. Provides a forum for dialogue and social interaction among members, church leaders, and peers; seeks to stimulate cultural exposure, emotional stability, and intellectual development among individuals of similar heritage and background. Sponsors lectures, seminars, service projects, and social events. Operates speakers' bureau to provide discussion on topics such as AIDS, education, and outreach. Awards: Paul Mortensen Award. Frequency: annual. Type: recognition. Recipient: for individuals with outstanding leadership and service. Formerly: (1979) Affirmative/Gay Mormons United. Publications: Affinity, monthly. Newsletter. Contains topical articles, personal stories, pen pal listings, and directory. Price: $20.00/year. Circulation: 400 ● Books ● Pamphlets. Alternate Formats: online ● Also publishes local newsletters. Conventions/Meetings: annual conference - usually October.

19639 ■ Affirmation: United Methodists for Lesbian, Gay and Bisexual Concerns (AUMLGBC)
PO Box 1021
Evanston, IL 60204
E-mail: umaffirmation@yahoo.com
URL: http://umaffirm.org
Contact: Vivian R. Waltz, Chair
Founded: 1976. Members: 400. Membership Dues: regular, $25 (annual) ● low income, $10 (annual). Budget: $60,000. Description: Gay/lesbian, bisexual and heterosexual individuals concerned with opening the United Methodist Church to all people. Seeks to affirm the presence of and provide ministry for all individuals in the United Methodist church community regardless of race, class, age, sex, or sexual orientation; enlist the cooperative efforts of other supportive United Methodist groups; act upon opportunities for ecumenical and interfaith action; conduct educational and informational services; keep members informed. Operates justice ministry that works on behalf of discriminated individuals. Sponsors biennial retreat. Affiliated With: Reconciling Ministries Network. Formerly: (1991) Affirmation: United Methodists for Lesbian/Gay Concerns. Publications: Affirmation Newsletter, quarterly. Conventions/Meetings: semiannual meeting - always spring and fall.

19640 ■ American Baptists Concerned (ABC)
PO Box 3183
Walnut Creek, CA 94598
Ph: (925)439-4672
E-mail: info@rainbowbaptists.org
URL: http://www.rainbowbaptists.org
Contact: Chris Boisvert, Communications Coor.
Founded: 1972. Members: 1,000. Membership Dues: regular, $30 (annual). Regional Groups: 2. State Groups: 3. Local Groups: 1. Description: Represents homosexual, bisexual, and heterosexual clergy and laypersons affiliated with the American Baptist Churches/U.S.A. Works to unite gay individuals and their families and friends within the ABCUSA for mutual assistance, support, and education. Seeks to persuade ABCUSA to forthrightly address and deal with the questions and needs of its practicing and nonpracticing gay members. Holds educational workshops; provides speakers. Awards: Randle R. Mixon Award for Christian Service. Frequency: biennial. Type: recognition. Recipient: for outstanding work toward inclusion of sexual minorities within American Baptist Churches. Telecommunication Services: electronic mail, abc@rainbowbaptists.org ● electronic mail, ambaptists@aol.com. Publications: Voice of the Turtle, quarterly. Newsletter. Circulation: 1,100. Conventions/Meetings: annual Rainbow Retreat, with gathering for worship, workshops, and fellowship.

19641 ■ Axios USA
342 E Jericho Tpke., No. 191
Mineola, NY 11501-2111
Ph: (917)513-9368
Fax: (212)989-6211
E-mail: axiosusa@aol.com
URL: http://www.eskimo.com/~nickz/axios.html
Contact: Nicholas P. Zymaris, Pres.
Founded: 1980. Members: 300. Staff: 15. Budget: $1,000. Regional Groups: 9. Description: Gay and lesbian Christians who belong to, have been educated and reared in, or have converted to the Eastern Christian tradition. Seeks to address the issue of human sexuality within Eastern Christianity; affirm that gay men and women can live an active life of prayer and witness; find spiritual strength, stability, and well-being; bridge the gulf between the church community and the gay community through dialogue, prayer, service, and education; provide comfort, help, and support of our brothers and sisters and their families in realizing the joys and responsibilities of God's gift of sexuality; protect against stigmatization, repression, and acts of intolerance; serve others in acts of charity and love as individuals and as a group; study rich and varied heritages and traditions; find a true sense of appreciation for each other and to achieve a spirit of fun and enjoyment in gay and lesbian development. Holds membership meetings, prayer, Vespers, discussions, annual Christmas Party, AIDS Ministry and Network. Conducts research. Maintains speakers' bureau. Offers educational programs. Subgroups: Axios AIDS Ministry and Network. Publications: Axios Newsletter, bimonthly. Contains theological, hagiographics, and other articles of interest to Eastern and Orthodox Christians. Price: $18.00. Circulation: 200. Advertising: accepted. Alternate Formats: online.

19642 ■ Brethren/Mennonite Council for Lesbian, Gay, Bisexual and Transgender Interest (BMC)
PO Box 6300
Minneapolis, MN 55406
Ph: (612)343-2060
Fax: (612)343-2061
E-mail: bmc@bmclgbt.org
URL: http://www.bmclgbt.org
Contact: Carol Wise, Exec. Dir.
Founded: 1976. Staff: 2. Budget: $150,000. Regional Groups: 5. Nonmembership. Description:

Brethren and Mennonite lesbian/gay, bisexual, transgender and nongay men and women, their parents, spouses, relatives, and friends. Offers support to gay people of the Brethren and Mennonite church denominations and fosters dialogue between them and nongay church members. Believes that the traditional attitude of the church toward homosexuals is inconsistent with the Christian ideal. Seeks to disseminate accurate information from biblical studies, social sciences, and theology regarding homosexuality. Maintains speakers' bureau. **Formerly:** Brethren/Mennonite Council for Gay Concerns; (2003) Brethren/Mennonite Council for Lesbian and Gay Concerns. **Publications:** *Connections, Dialogue,* periodic. Newsletter. Includes articles about AIDS, theology and homosexuality, and convention proceedings; also contains calendar of events. **Price:** free ● *NewsNet,* monthly. Newsletter. Alternate Formats: online ● Brochures. **Conventions/Meetings:** periodic meeting ● seminar, covers the topic of human sexuality.

19643 ■ Conference for Catholic Lesbians (CCL)
PO Box 853
Greenport, NY 11944
Ph: (718)680-6107 (212)663-2963
E-mail: catholicwomenl2l@catholicwomenl2l.org
URL: http://cclonline.org
Contact: Karen Doherty, Board Member
Founded: 1982. **Members:** 700. **Membership Dues:** individual, $25 (annual). **Budget:** $25,000. **Local Groups:** 20. **Description:** Women of Catholic heritage and their non-Catholic women friends who recognize the importance of the Catholic tradition in shaping their lives, but who seek to develop and nurture a spiritual life which enhances and affirms their lesbian identity. Provides a forum for exploring spirituality through liturgies and rituals. Promotes Catholic lesbian visibility and community. Advocates women's and lesbian rights and social justice issues in the church and society. Serves as a support network worldwide. Sponsors lectures, retreats, and conferences. **Libraries: Type:** not open to the public. **Awards:** Mary E. Hunt Award. **Frequency:** biennial. **Type:** recognition. **Publications:** *Images,* quarterly. Newsletter. Provides a forum on current Catholic and lesbian issues. **Price:** included in membership dues. **Circulation:** 1,500. **Conventions/Meetings:** semiannual conference and retreat ● biennial National Conference (exhibits).

19644 ■ Courage
c/o St. John the Baptist Church
210 W 31st St.
New York, NY 10001
Ph: (212)268-1010
Fax: (212)268-7150
E-mail: nycourage@aol.com
URL: http://CourageRC.net
Contact: Fr. John F. Harvey OSFS, Dir.
Founded: 1980. **Members:** 2,000. **Staff:** 2. **Regional Groups:** 90. **State Groups:** 7. **Local Groups:** 7. **National Groups:** 73. **Languages:** English, French, Russian, Slovene, Spanish. **Multinational. Description:** Provides spiritual support for men and women with same-sex attractions who desire to live chaste lives in accordance with the teachings of the Roman Catholic Church. **Libraries: Type:** reference. **Subjects:** homosexuality. **Awards: Type:** grant. **Computer Services:** Mailing lists. **Additional Websites:** http://CourageRC.org. **Publications:** *Courage Handbook.* Pamphlet ● *Courage Newsletter,* quarterly. **Circulation:** 1,500 ● *Homosexual Person, New Thinking in Pastoral Care.* Book ● *Pastoral Care and the Homosexual.* Pamphlet ● The truth About Homosexuality, book by Rev. John Harvey. **Conventions/Meetings:** annual conference, with books and tapes (exhibits).

19645 ■ Dignity/USA
PO Box 15373
Washington, DC 20003-0373
Ph: (202)861-0017
Free: (800)877-8797
Fax: (202)543-5511

E-mail: info@dignityusa.org
URL: http://www.dignityusa.org
Contact: Sam Sinnett, Pres.
Founded: 1969. **Members:** 3,000. **Membership Dues:** basic, $45 (annual) ● couple, $84 (annual). **Staff:** 3. **Budget:** $300,000. **Local Groups:** 50. **Description:** Represents bisexuals, gay men, lesbians and transgenders who are members of the Roman Catholic Church; individuals of other religious affiliations; theologians, priests, and nuns. Promotes that gay, lesbian, transgender and bisexual people are members of Christ's mystical body, numbered among the people of God and it is their right, duty, and privilege to live the sacramental life of the church and can express their sexuality in a manner that is consonant with Christ's teachings. Seeks to unite all gay, lesbian, transgender and bisexual Catholics; develop leadership; be an instrument through which Catholics may be heard by the church and society. Works in the areas of spiritual development, education, and social events. Operates National AIDS Project. **Programs:** Angel. **Projects:** Worship and Liturgy. **Also Known As:** Dignity, Inc. **Publications:** *Dignity Dateline,* monthly. Newsletter. **Circulation:** 200 ● *The Dignity/USA Journal,* quarterly. **Price:** included in membership dues. **Circulation:** 2,500. **Advertising:** accepted ● *Theological Pastoral Resources: A Collection of Articles on Homosexuality from a Catholic Perspective.* **Conventions/Meetings:** biennial convention (exhibits).

19646 ■ Evangelicals Concerned (EC)
311 E 72nd St., Ste.1G
New York, NY 10021
E-mail: rblair@ecinc.org
URL: http://www.ecinc.org
Contact: Dr. Ralph Blair, Founder/Pres.
Founded: 1975. **Local Groups:** 20. **Description:** Task force and ministry founded during the national convention of the National Association of Evangelicals (see separate entry), although there is no official affiliation between the two organizations. Evangelical Christians (both homosexual and heterosexual) concerned with "the lack of preparation for dealing realistically with homosexuality in the evangelical community and about the implications of the Gospel in the lives of gay men and lesbians." Consults with leaders of the religious and secular communities; maintains speakers' bureau; makes referrals for counseling; holds Bible studies and worship services. **Publications:** *Evangelicals Concerned—Record,* quarterly. Newsletter. Alternate Formats: online ● *Evangelicals Concerned—Review,* quarterly. Includes literature on religion and homosexuality. ● Also publishes educational materials. **Conventions/Meetings:** semiannual conference - always summer and winter.

19647 ■ Exodus International (EI)
PO Box 540119
Orlando, FL 32854
Ph: (407)599-6872
Free: (888)264-0877
Fax: (407)599-0011
E-mail: conference@exodus.to
URL: http://www.exodus.to
Contact: Alan Chambers, Pres.
Founded: 1976. **Members:** 90. **Membership Dues:** organizational, $100 (annual). **Staff:** 6. **Local Groups:** 105. **Description:** Coalition of Christian ministries and organizations that encourage homosexuals to adopt a heterosexual lifestyle through the "transforming love of Christ and His community." Provides support, resources, and networking for ministries conducting outreach to homosexuals. Operates referral service. **Libraries: Type:** reference. **Holdings:** articles. **Subjects:** church and technology, counseling and ministry, family and friends, homosexuality and society, prevention and recovery. **Computer Services:** Mailing lists. **Publications:** *The Exodus Impact,* monthly. Newsletter. Features stories of men and women who have overcome homosexuality, news of Exodus ministries around the world. **Circulation:** 12,000. Alternate Formats: online ● Audiotape. Features sessions and workshops of Exodus

Annual Conference. **Price:** $7.00. **Conventions/Meetings:** annual conference ● seminar, for training.

19648 ■ Friends for Lesbian, Gay, Bisexual, Transgender, and Queer Concerns (FLGBTQC)
c/o Sue Sierra, Treas.
1314 Wright St.
Ann Arbor, MI 48105
URL: http://flgbtqc.quaker.org
Contact: Andy Doan, Co-Clerk
Founded: 1973. **Members:** 700. **Budget:** $6,000. **Local Groups:** 10. **Multinational. Description:** Gay and lesbian Quakers united to provide support for one another and encourage personal spiritual growth. Seeks to broaden acceptance and understanding by the Quaker faith. Conducts workshops and seminars at various Quaker meetings in America and Canada. **Publications:** *Each of Us Inevitable.* Contains keynote addresses. **Price:** $8.00 ● *Friends for Lesbian and Gay Concerns—Newsletter,* 3/year. **Price:** $15.00 donation. **Circulation:** 1,500 ● *History of Gay Rights Movement in the Religious Society of Friends.* Brochure ● *Inclusive Minutes on Marriage by Religious Society of Friends.* **Conventions/Meetings:** conference, for men - always fall ● conference, for women - always summer ● semiannual meeting - always the weekend closest to George Washington's Birthday and June/July.

19649 ■ Gay, Lesbian and Affirming Disciples Alliance (GLAD)
PO Box 44400
Indianapolis, IN 46244-0400
Ph: (317)634-9297
E-mail: glad@gladalliance.org
URL: http://www.gladalliance.org
Contact: Randy Palmer, Development and Finance Team Leader
Membership Dues: pink triangle, $1,000 (annual) ● rainbow, $500 (annual) ● St. Andrew's Cross, $250 (annual) ● red chalice, $100 (annual) ● couple, $80 (annual) ● individual, $45 (annual) ● low income/student, $15 (annual). **Description:** Works for full dignity and integrity of gay, lesbian, bisexual and affirming individuals within the Christian Church (Disciples of Christ). **Publications:** *Crossbeams,* quarterly. Alternate Formats: online ● *Crosscurrents,* quarterly. **Conventions/Meetings:** annual conference, with Bible study, workshops, worship, singing, discussion.

19650 ■ Integrity
620 Park Ave., No. 311
Rochester, NY 14607-2943
Free: (800)462-9498
E-mail: info@integrityusa.org
URL: http://www.integrityusa.org
Contact: Rev. Susan Russell, Pres.
Founded: 1974. **Members:** 2,500. **Membership Dues:** individual, $35 (annual) ● couple, $60 (annual) ● student, senior citizen, low income, $10 (annual). **Staff:** 1. **Budget:** $130,000. **Regional Groups:** 60. **National Groups:** 3. **Description:** Represents Gay, Lesbian Bisexual and Transgender (GBLT) Justice Ministry in the Episcopal/Anglican Church. Objectives are to: minister to the spiritual needs of GLBT people; work for full participation of GBLT people in church and society; promote the study of human sexuality within a Christian context. Distributes educational materials for clergy and lay persons; offers counseling, AIDS ministries, and worship services. **Awards:** Louie Crew Award. **Frequency:** annual. **Type:** recognition. **Recipient:** for outstanding contributions to integrity. **Publications:** *Integrity—Directory,* annual ● *Integrity Handbook,* biennial ● *The Voice of Integrity,* quarterly. Magazine. Includes church news, book reviews, calendar of events, and chapter news. **Conventions/Meetings:** conference ● annual meeting - except in national church convention years.

19651 ■ Interweave Continental (Unitarian Universalists for Lesbian, Gay, Bisexual and Transgender Concerns)
45 State St., No. 380
Montpelier, VT 05602

E-mail: jjohnstone@uuma.org
URL: http://www.uua.org/interweave
Contact: Rev. Jonalu Johnstone, Pres.
Founded: 1971. **Members:** 150. **Membership Dues:** basic, $35 (annual) ● joint, $50 (annual) ● chapter, $100 (annual) ● sustaining, $75 (annual) ● low income/student/senior, $20 (annual). **Budget:** $15,000. **Regional Groups:** 2. **Local Groups:** 50. **Multinational. Description:** Works to end oppression based on sexual orientation and gender identity. Value and affirm the lives and experience of queer people of faith of all ages, races, ethnicities, income levels, and abilities. Provides and supports leadership, and works in collaboration with other organizations of similar vision, strives to connect and nurture all queer individuals, communities, groups, and their allies. **Libraries: Type:** reference. **Subjects:** sexual orientation and gender identity. **Awards:** Mark Mosher DeWolfe Award. **Frequency:** annual. **Type:** recognition. **Recipient:** for lifelong commitment to making the world better for queer people. **Formerly:** (1993) Unitarian Universalists for Lesbian and Gay Concerns. **Publications:** *InterweaveWorld*, bimonthly. Newsletter. **Price:** included in membership dues. **Circulation:** 650. Alternate Formats: online. **Conventions/Meetings:** annual Convocation - conference, gathering of members and friends to come together to worship, learn, have fun, and be together in community - always in February ● annual Unitarian Universalist General Assembly - always third week in June.

19652 ■ LIFE
PO Box 353
New York, NY 10185
Ph: (212)768-2366 (212)768-2367
E-mail: lifeministry@verizon.net
URL: http://www.life-ministry.com
Contact: Dick DiFiore, Admin. Sec.
Founded: 1983. **Members:** 200. **Staff:** 7. **Budget:** $200,000. **Description:** Nondenominational Christian mission seeking to help people overcome problems of homosexuality. Believes that homosexuality is a "spiritual bondage involving buried emotions, false identity and false concept of God from which people can be set free through an intimate relationship with God through Jesus Christ." Seeks to inform the families of men and women caught in bondage to homosexuality, Church congregations, and the public of what the association believes to be the nature and causes of homosexuality. Believes in loving and fair treatment of homosexual people, but does not support the enactment of laws that endorse or condone homosexual behavior. Provides support groups and speakers; offers counseling services; conducts training. **Also Known As:** Living in Freedom Eternally. **Publications:** *Living in Freedom Eternally - A Christian Ministry to Men and Women Coming out of Homosexuality*. Brochure. **Price:** free ● *Words of LIFE*, quarterly. Newsletter ● Also publishes testimonies and tract; makes available literature and teaching cassettes; first book publication, The Best of Words of Life, A Compendium of 20 Years of Selected Newsletter Articles. **Conventions/Meetings:** Counseling Training Seminar, counselor training.

19653 ■ Lutherans Concerned/North America (LC/NA)
PO Box 4707
St. Paul, MN 55104-0707
Ph: (651)665-0861
Fax: (651)665-0863
E-mail: exec@lcna.org
URL: http://www.lcna.org
Contact: Emily Eastwood, Exec. Dir.
Founded: 1974. **Membership Dues:** individual, $50 (annual) ● household, $75 (annual) ● contributing, $100 (annual) ● sustaining, $250 (annual) ● life - individual, $1,000 ● life - household, $1,500. **Staff:** 2. **Budget:** $80,000. **Regional Groups:** 9. **Local Groups:** 40. **National Groups:** 2. **Description:** Serves as an independent ministry organization supported by member contributions and donations. Members are from all Lutheran backgrounds in the United States and Canada, organized into 40 local chapters. People of all sexual orientation and gender

identities are members. Concerned with three broad areas of focus: Spiritual, Educational and Advocacy. Endorses the federal Employment Non Discrimination legislation. The Reconciling in Christ program of LC encourages Lutheran communities of faith to adopt a public affirmation of welcome to gay, lesbian, bisexual and transgendered people for full participation in the life of the community. **Awards:** Jim Seifkes Justice Maker. **Frequency:** biennial. **Type:** recognition. **Recipient:** for extraordinary contributions of heterosexual persons to the lesbian and gay community. **Committees:** Ecumenical Relations; Endowment Fund; Families Concerned; International Relations; Reconciling in Christ Program; Theology Task Force. **Formerly:** (1950) Lutherans Concerned for Gay People. **Publications:** *The Concord*, quarterly. Newsletter. Contains news, inspirational content, and editorials. **Price:** $20.00/year. ISSN: 0741-9872. **Conventions/Meetings:** biennial assembly and conference (exhibits).

19654 ■ Metropolitan Community Churches (MCC)
PO Box 1374
Abilene, TX 79604
Ph: (310)360-8640
Fax: (325)675-8977
E-mail: info@mcchurch.net
URL: http://www.mcchurch.org
Contact: Dr. Cindi Love, Exec. Dir.
Founded: 1968. **Members:** 43,000. **Staff:** 16. **Budget:** $3,200,000. **Regional Groups:** 17. **Local Groups:** 300. **Description:** Christian group ministering to primarily gay/lesbian communities in 26 countries through worship services and social action. Conducts research and educational programs, participates in ecumenical programs, and sponsors social justice events. **Awards:** Human Rights Award. **Frequency:** biennial. **Type:** recognition. **Computer Services:** database ● mailing lists. **Also Known As:** Metropolitan Community Church. **Formerly:** (2006) Universal Fellowship of Metropolitan Community Churches. **Publications:** *Around The Fellowship*, monthly. Newsletter. Contains general-interest news for gay, lesbian, bisexual, transgender people of faith. **Price:** free. Alternate Formats: online ● *Directory of Congregations and Clergy*, annual. **Price:** free for UFMCC churches and clergy only ● Brochures (in English and Spanish). Features series on the Bible and homosexuality. ● Brochures. Cover AIDS and related topics. **Conventions/Meetings:** biennial conference, general conference; international gathering of gay, lesbian, bisexual, and transgender Christians (exhibits).

19655 ■ More Light Presbyterians for Lesbian, Gay, Bisexual and Transgender Concerns
PMB 246
4737 County Rd. 101
Minnetonka, MN 55345-2634
Ph: (505)820-7082
Fax: (505)820-2540
E-mail: michaeladee@aol.com
URL: http://www.mlp.org
Contact: Michael J. Adee PhD, Field Organizer
Founded: 1974. **Members:** 1,300. **Membership Dues:** student, $25 (annual) ● regular, $50 (annual) ● family, household, $75 (annual). **Staff:** 4. **Budget:** $200,000. **Regional Groups:** 15. **Local Groups:** 20. **Description:** Represents congregations, governing bodies, ministers, elders, deacons, and other members of the Presbyterian church. Seeks to raise the concerns of lesbian, gay, bisexual and transgender people and their parents, families, and friends in the Presbyterian church. Seeks full membership rights, including ordination and marriage for all. **Libraries: Type:** lending. **Holdings:** video recordings. **Awards:** David Sivdt Award. **Frequency:** annual. **Type:** recognition ● Inclusive Church Award. **Frequency:** annual. **Type:** recognition. **Recipient:** for contributions to achieving an inclusive church for lesbian, gay, bisexual, and transgender individuals. **Projects:** Vigil for Justice. **Affiliated With:** National Gay and Lesbian Task Force. **Formerly:** (1999) Presbyterians for Lesbian and Gay Concerns. **Publications:** *More*

Light Update, bimonthly. Newsletter. **Price:** $18.00/year. ISSN: 0889-3985. **Circulation:** 6,000. **Advertising:** accepted. Alternate Formats: online. **Conventions/Meetings:** annual meeting and general assembly, national governing body of Presbyterian Church (exhibits) ● annual More Light Conference.

19656 ■ New Ways Ministry (NWM)
4012 29th St.
Mount Rainier, MD 20712
Ph: (301)277-5674
Fax: (301)864-8954
E-mail: newwaysm@verizon.net
URL: http://mysite.verizon.net/~vze43yrc
Contact: Francis De Bernardo, Exec. Dir.
Founded: 1977. **Members:** 5,000. **Staff:** 4. **Budget:** $250,000. **Description:** Serves as Catholic gay/lesbian ministry group. Aims to provide adequate and accurate information concerning homosexuality and the Roman Catholic church and society; assesses personal and communal attitudes about homosexuality; offers pastoral resources and antidotes to the fears, myths, and prejudices affecting the lives of gay and lesbian persons in the church and society. Promotes theological dialogue; describes and promotes civil rights for homosexual people. Provides consulting services. Conducts specialized education and research programs. Sponsors speakers' bureau. **Libraries: Type:** reference. **Holdings:** 300; archival material, audio recordings, films, video recordings. **Subjects:** homosexuality, religion, gay rights, homophobia, family, parenting. **Awards:** Bridge Building Award. **Frequency:** triennial. **Type:** monetary. **Recipient:** for contribution to reconciliation of church and lesbian/gay community. **Computer Services:** Mailing lists, newsletter, spiritual and educational programs. **Boards:** Advisors. **Publications:** *Bondings*, quarterly. Newspaper. Contains reprinted articles as well as original pieces. Includes book reviews. **Price:** $10.00/year in U.S.; $15.00/year outside U.S. **Circulation:** 4,500 ● *Bridging the Gap: A Theological Debate*. Audiotape ● *Building Bridges: Gay and Lesbian Reality and the Catholic Church*. Book ● *Prayer Journey for Persons with AIDS* ● *Voices of Hope* ● *Womanjourney Weavings*. Newsletter. **Conventions/Meetings:** periodic conference (exhibits) ● retreat, for Catholic parents of gay/lesbian children ● seminar ● symposium ● workshop.

19657 ■ Reconciling Ministries Network (RMN)
3801 N Keeler Ave.
Chicago, IL 60641
Ph: (773)736-5526
Fax: (773)736-5475
E-mail: webspinner@rmnetwork.org
URL: http://www.rmnetwork.org
Contact: Rev. Troy Plummer, Exec. Dir.
Founded: 1984. **Members:** 17,500. **Staff:** 4. **Budget:** $300,000. **Regional Groups:** 5. **Local Groups:** 265. **Description:** United Methodist congregations seeking to affirm the participation of gay and lesbian members in church affairs and to resolve differences and problems between the United Methodist church and homosexuals in the U.S. Provides a network of support and assistance to local congregations wishing to include gay and lesbian persons in their worship and administration. **Formerly:** (2001) Reconciling Congregation Program. **Publications:** *FlashNet*, weekly. Newsletter. Alternate Formats: online ● *How to Become a Reconciling Congregation*. Brochure ● *List of Reconciling Congregations*, periodic ● *Reconciling Congregation Program*. Brochure ● *RMN's General Information Pamphlet*. Includes the mission statement and a description of the activities and affinity groups. Alternate Formats: online. **Conventions/Meetings:** biennial Convocation - meeting.

19658 ■ Seventh Day Adventist Kinship International (SDAKI)
PO Box 49375
Sarasota, FL 34230-6375
Ph: (941)371-7606
Free: (866)732-5677

E-mail: office@sdakinship.org
URL: http://www.sdakinship.org
Contact: Bob Bouchard, Pres.
Founded: 1976. Members: 1,000. Membership Dues: regular, $25 (annual). Regional Groups: 14. Local Groups: 6. Description: Seventh-day Adventist gay men and lesbians and their friends. Works to heighten understanding of homosexuality and related issues. Provides educational materials and speakers; offers AIDS education and support services. Conducts charitable programs. Committees: Editorial. Also Known As: SDA Kinship International. Formed by Merger of: Orion; SDA Kindred. Publications: SDA Kinship Connection, monthly. Newsletter. Includes reports on organization activities, book reviews, and gay/lesbian news briefs. Price: $25.00 /year for members; $40.00 /year for members outside U.S.; included in membership dues ● Brochures. Conventions/Meetings: annual Kampm Acting - meeting ● monthly regional meeting.

19659 ■ United Church of Christ Coalition for Lesbian, Gay, Bisexual and Transgender Concerns
2592 W 14th St.
Cleveland, OH 44113
Ph: (216)861-0799
Free: (800)653-0799
Fax: (216)861-0782
E-mail: office@ucccoalition.org
URL: http://www.ucccoalition.org
Contact: Rev. Ruth Garwood, Natl. Coor.
Founded: 1973. Members: 800. Membership Dues: all, $50. Staff: 4. Budget: $145,000. Regional Groups: 40. Description: Laity and clergy; gay, lesbian, bisexual, transgender and heterosexual members of the United Church of Christ. Provides confidential counseling, support, and referrals; acts as advocate for gay, lesbian, and bisexual concerns within the church and society; encourages communication between individuals and organizations. Wishes to perpetuate the belief that all persons are loved by God and have much to offer regardless of sexual orientation. Programs: Open and Affirming; Youth and Young Adult. Formerly: (1979) United Church of Christ Gay Caucus; (1999) United Church Coalition for Lesbian/Gay Concerns. Publications: ONA Communique, quarterly. Newsletter. Alternate Formats: online ● Waves, 3/year. Newsletter. Price: $15.00. Circulation: 2,200. Alternate Formats: online ● YYA. Newsletter. Conventions/Meetings: annual conference (exhibits).

19660 ■ Unity Fellowship Church Movement (UFCM)
5148 W Jefferson Blvd.
Los Angeles, CA 90016
Ph: (323)938-8322
Free: (866)227-4512
Fax: (323)965-8322
E-mail: motherchurch@ufc-usa.org
URL: http://www.unityfellowshipchurch.org
Contact: Archbishop Carl Bean DM, Founder
Founded: 1985. Members: 3,000. Description: Started as a church for Christian gay, lesbian, bisexual and transgender individuals interested in the teachings of liberation theology from the King James Version of the Bible. Conducts special programs for imprisoned people and youth. Projects: Minority AIDS. Publications: Newsletter, bimonthly. Conventions/Meetings: annual Anniversary Gala Celebration - conference - 2007 Oct. 6, Los Angeles, CA ● annual National Convocation - meeting and workshop - 1st week of October.

19661 ■ World Congress of Gay, Lesbian, Bisexual, and Transgender Jews (WCGLBTJ)
PO Box 23379
Washington, DC 20026-3379
Ph: (202)452-7424 (215)923-2003
Fax: (215)873-0108
E-mail: info@glbtjews.org
URL: http://www.glbtjews.org
Contact: Mr. David Gellman, Pres.
Founded: 1980. Members: 78,000. Staff: 7. Budget: $25,000. Regional Groups: 74. State Groups: 40.

National Groups: 2. Languages: English, French, German, Hebrew, Spanish. Multinational. Description: Gay and lesbian Jewish organizations, synagogues, and social groups. Serves as umbrella organization for Jewish gay and lesbian organizations worldwide. Provides educational outreach to the non-gay community. Operates speakers' bureau. Conducts charitable programs. Libraries: Type: reference. Subjects: Jewish liturgy sensitive to gay and lesbian concerns. Committees: Steering. Publications: Digest, semiannual. Newsletter. Circulation: 25,000. Advertising: accepted. Alternate Formats: online. Conventions/Meetings: biennial international conference (exhibits) ● biennial regional meeting.

Greek Orthodox

19662 ■ Greek Orthodox Ladies Philoptochos Society (GOLPS)
345 E 74th St.
New York, NY 10021-3701
Ph: (212)744-4390
Fax: (212)861-1956
E-mail: philosny@aol.com
URL: http://www.philoptochos.org
Contact: Georgia Skeadas, Pres.
Founded: 1931. Members: 27,000. Membership Dues: regular, $10 (annual). Staff: 6. Budget: $1,500,000. Regional Groups: 9. Local Groups: 475. Languages: English, French, Greek, Spanish. Description: Women 18 years or older of the Greek Orthodox faith. Aim is to preserve the sacredness of the Orthodox family and perpetuate and promote the charitable and philanthropic purposes of the Greek Orthodox Archdiocese of North America. (The word "Philoptochos" is derived from "philo" meaning friend and "ptochos" meaning poor; hence, "friend of the poor.") Seeks to aid individuals in need of assistance. Supports educational institutions. Encourages wider religious activity and participation in the communal aspects of the church, especially among young people. Awards: Certificates of Merit. Frequency: annual. Type: recognition. Recipient: for outstanding service to the Philoptochos Chapter ● Type: scholarship. Recipient: for needy and meritorious students pursuing theological studies for the priesthood. Computer Services: Mailing lists. Committees: Aging; AIDS; Cancer Fund; Cardiac (children's); Children's Medical Fund; Emergency Fund; Hellenic College/Holy Cross Seminary; Homeless; Missions; Patriarchate Fund; St. Basil Academy; St. Photios Shrine; Scholarships; Social Services. Publications: Bylaws and Procedural Manual. Price: $4.00 ● Orthodox Observer (in English and Greek), semimonthly. Newspaper. Price: free for members. Circulation: 200,000 ● Protocol Booklet: A Guide for Special Philoptochos Functions. Price: $5.00 ● Reaching Out. Video. Price: $15.00 ● Voices of Philoptochos. Video. Price: $40.00 ● Reports. Alternate Formats: online. Conventions/Meetings: biennial National Philoptochos - convention, meets concurrently with Greek Orthodox Clergy/Laity Congress ● seminar.

19663 ■ Greek Orthodox Young Adult League (GOYAL)
83 St. Basil Rd.
Garrison, NY 10524
Ph: (646)519-6180
Fax: (646)519-6191
E-mail: youthoffice@goarch.org
URL: http://www.goarch.org
Contact: Rev. Mark A. Leondis, Dir.
Founded: 1951. Members: 35,000. Staff: 3. Regional Groups: 10. Local Groups: 545. Description: Greek Orthodox youth throughout the Americas. Conducts leadership and religious education workshops, athletic tournaments, summer camps, and other activities to assist the church program locally and nationally. Distributes religious films. Formerly: (1982) Greek Orthodox Youth of America. Publications: Young Adult League Manual, annual. Conventions/Meetings: annual conference.

19664 ■ Order of Saint Andrew the Apostle (OSATA)
8 E 79th St.
New York, NY 10021
Ph: (212)570-3550
Fax: (212)774-0214
E-mail: archonant@aol.com
URL: http://www.archons.org
Contact: Athanasia Diamantis, Admin. Asst.
Founded: 1966. Members: 1,000. Staff: 3. Description: Represents Greek Orthodox laymen who have been honored by the Ecumenical Patriarchate of Constantinople with Byzantine titles and offices of church and state. Aims to support the Ecumenical Patriarchate of Constantinople and its philanthropic institutions; assists the Ecumenical Patriarchate in furthering the Ecumenical leadership of the mother church of Constantinople; upholds and defends the historical status of the Ecumenical Patriarchate. Contributes to the support and maintenance of philanthropic and educational institutions in the U.S. Bestows titles annually. Sponsors charities for Greek Orthodox people in Istanbul, Turkey, and children's home and camp. Committees: Human Rights. Councils: Archon National. Formerly: (1980) Knights of Saint Andrew. Publications: The Archon, quarterly. Newsletter. Price: available to members only. Alternate Formats: online ● Banquet Addresses, annual ● Greek Orthodox Archdiocese Yearbook ● In Wisdom Let Us Attend. Video. Provides a history of the Patriarchate. ● Short History of Ecumenical Patriarchate of Constantinople ● Articles, periodic ● Pamphlets ● Annual Reports, annual. Alternate Formats: online. Conventions/Meetings: annual meeting.

19665 ■ Pan American Council for the Preservation of the Hellenic Orthodox Church and the Hellenic Language
5711 W School St.
Chicago, IL 60634
Ph: (773)725-1960
Contact: Nicholas C. Eliopoulos, Sec.
Founded: 1970. Regional Groups: 3. Languages: Greek. Description: Members of the Hellenic Orthodox church. Purpose is to "censure and/or file charges in civil or ecclesiastical courts against archieratical and lesser clergymen when they violate their office, endangering the soundness of the Faith." Seeks to expand the liturgical use of the original Hellenic language of the Gospels and to "trace the validity of a true and vivifying capacitance of charisma in the apostolic succession of ordinators and to identify those devoid of the charisma of the Holy Spirit, being high priests in name only." Compiles statistics; sponsors speakers' bureau and research programs. Committees: Cultural; Historical; Linguistic; Theological. Publications: Pamphlet, quarterly. Conventions/Meetings: annual meeting - always September.

19666 ■ Saint Photios Foundation (SPF)
41 St. George St.
PO Box 1960
St. Augustine, FL 32085
Ph: (904)829-8205
Free: (800)222-6727
Fax: (904)829-8707
E-mail: phillier@stphotios.com
URL: http://www.stphotios.com
Contact: Mrs. Polexeni Maouris Hillier, Assoc. Dir.
Founded: 1981. Members: 7. Staff: 7. Budget: $365,000. Languages: English, Greek. Description: Maintains, preserves, and operates the St. Photios Shrine in St. Augustine, FL, a national institution of the Greek Orthodox Archdiocese of America, that is dedicated to the first colony of Greek people who came to America in 1768. Provides audiovisual presentations and exhibits depicting the life of Greek settlers and the development of the Greek Orthodox church in America. Libraries: Type: open to the public. Holdings: 1,525. Subjects: Orthodox Church, Church history, Old and New Testament, U.S. history, Greece. Awards: St. Photios Award. Frequency: annual. Type: recognition. Recipient: for a member with the most volunteer hours. Computer Services: database ● mailing lists. Boards: Trustees. Committees: Endowment Fund; Long-Range Capital Invest-

ments; Millennium. **Also Known As:** St. Photios Greek Orthodox National Shrine. **Publications:** *Friends*, annual. Newsletter. **Price:** free. **Circulation:** 3,600 ● Also offers variety of cards in both Greek and English. **Conventions/Meetings:** annual meeting and board meeting (exhibits) - always February, St. Augustine, FL.

Health Care

19667 ■ HealthCare Ministries (HCM)
521 W Lynn St.
Springfield, MO 65802
Ph: (417)866-6311
Fax: (417)866-4711
E-mail: fieldprojects@hcmdfm.org
URL: http://www.healthcareministries.org
Contact: Bob McGurty, Dir.
Description: Medical missions arm of the Assemblies of God Foreign Missions. Strives to demonstrate and teach love and compassion in all aspects of the ministry. Conducts seminars, creates short-term medical evangelism teams, and teaches health education.

History

19668 ■ American Society of Church History (ASCH)
c/o Yale Divinity School
409 Prospect St., Rm. S127
New Haven, CT 06511
Ph: (203)432-3158
Fax: (203)432-5356
E-mail: asch@yale.edu
URL: http://www.churchhistory.org
Contact: Kenneth P. Minkema, Exec. Sec.
Founded: 1888. **Members:** 1,400. **Membership Dues:** regular in North America, $50 (annual) ● regular outside North America, $75 (annual) ● retired in North America, $25 (annual) ● retired outside North America, $30 (annual) ● institution in North America, $75 (annual) ● institution outside North America, $100 (annual). **Staff:** 1. **Budget:** $100,000. **Multinational. Description:** Persons interested in studying and researching the history of the Christian church. **Awards:** Schaff, Outler, Brewer, Douglass, Mead. **Frequency:** annual. **Type:** monetary. **Recipient:** for excellence of content. **Computer Services:** Mailing lists. **Committees:** Investment; Nominations and Personnel; Program Policy; Program, Winter Meeting; Research. **Affiliated With:** American Historical Association. **Publications:** *Church History*, quarterly. Journal. **Price:** included in membership dues; $75.00 for nonmembers in U.S.; $100.00 for nonmembers outside U.S. ISSN: 0009-6407. **Circulation:** 3,500. **Advertising:** accepted. **Conventions/Meetings:** semiannual conference - usually April and January.

19669 ■ Conference on Faith and History (CFH)
c/o Paul E. Michelson, Sec.
Dept. of History
Huntington Univ.
Huntington, IN 46750
Ph: (260)359-4242
E-mail: pmichelson@huntington.edu
URL: http://www.huntington.edu/cfh
Contact: Paul E. Michelson, Sec.
Founded: 1967. **Members:** 600. **Membership Dues:** voting, $30 (annual) ● undergraduate student, retired, $20 (annual). **Staff:** 3. **Budget:** $13,000. **Regional Groups:** 1. **Multinational. Description:** Explores the relationship between Christian faith and history. Seeks to learn from scholars outside the Christian tradition. Encourages excellence in the theory and practice of history from the perspective of historic Christianity. **Libraries: Type:** not open to the public. **Holdings:** 1,000; archival material, articles, books. **Subjects:** materials related to purposes of organization. **Affiliated With:** American Historical Association. **Publications:** *Fides et Historia*, semiannual. Journal. **Price:** $20.00/year. ISSN: 1375-2434. **Circu-**

lation: 900. **Advertising:** accepted. **Conventions/Meetings:** biennial meeting - always fall.

Homeless

19670 ■ Homeless Children International (HCI)
PO Box 416
Reidville, SC 29375-0416
E-mail: info@homelesskids.org
URL: http://www.homelesskids.org
Contact: David M. High, Pres.
Multinational. Description: Works to help homeless children worldwide. **Publications:** *Realize*, periodic. Newsletter. Alternate Formats: online.

Homiletics

19671 ■ Academy of Homiletics (AH)
c/o Dr. Jennifer Lord
100 E 27th St.
Austin, TX 78705
E-mail: jharris720@aol.com
URL: http://www.homiletics.org/contact.shtml
Contact: Barbara Lundblad, Pres.
Founded: 1965. **Members:** 390. **Membership Dues:** regular, $50 (annual). **Description:** Represents faculty members in graduate professional schools of theology responsible for teaching courses in homiletics. (Homiletics is the art of delivering homilies or sermons.) Encourages fellowship and exchange of information on developments in scholarship. **Formerly:** (1978) American Academy of Homiletics. **Publications:** *Homiletic*, semiannual. Journal. **Price:** $10.00 /year for individuals in U.S.; $15.00 /year for libraries in U.S. **Conventions/Meetings:** annual conference.

Humanism

19672 ■ American Ethical Union (AEU)
2 W 64th St.
New York, NY 10023-7104
Ph: (212)873-6500
Fax: (212)362-0850
E-mail: aeucontact@aeu.org
URL: http://www.aeu.org
Founded: 1887. **Members:** 4,500. **Staff:** 3. **Description:** Local ethical societies (20) in the United States. National organization of the Ethical Movement, a religious fellowship. **Awards:** Elliott Black Award. **Frequency:** biennial. **Type:** recognition. **Recipient:** for a person who made a significant ethical contribution to society at personal risk and hardship. **Publications:** *Dialogue*, quarterly. Newsletter. **Price:** free, for members only ● *Religious Education Newsletter*, quarterly. Focuses on programs and issues relating to religious education including events calendar, member news, and notices of books and religious education. **Price:** included in membership dues. **Circulation:** 4,500 ● *Washington Report*, 10/year ● Books. Covers ethical culture and religious education curricula. **Conventions/Meetings:** annual general assembly, national business meeting of the AEU attended by society delegates, along with workshops open to the public for a fee.

19673 ■ American Humanist Association (AHA)
1777 T St. NW
Washington, DC 20009-7125
Ph: (202)238-9088
Free: (800)837-3792
Fax: (202)238-9003
E-mail: rspeckhardt@americanhumanist.org
URL: http://www.americanhumanist.org
Contact: Roy Speckhardt, Exec. Dir.
Founded: 1941. **Members:** 6,000. **Membership Dues:** student, $25 (annual) ● initial, $35 (annual) ● Committee of 1000 joint, $100 (annual) ● supporting, $250 (annual) ● President's Circle, $500 (annual) ●

humanist ambassador, $1,000 (annual). **Staff:** 12. **Budget:** $1,075,202. **Regional Groups:** 10. **Local Groups:** 72. **Description:** Persons who are devoted to humanism as a way of life; Humanism presupposes humanity's sole dependence on natural and social resources and acknowledges no supernatural power. (Humanists believe that morality is based on the knowledge that humans are interdependent and, therefore, responsible to one another.) Seeks to spread and promote humanism through discussion groups, educational programs, television, film, radio, and print. Promotes education in ethics as an alternative to religious training for the young; provides counseling services for members and the larger community; certifies humanist counselors, who enjoy the legal status of ordained pastors, priests, and rabbis and maintains speakers' bureau. **Libraries: Type:** reference. **Holdings:** 3,000; archival material, artwork, audiovisuals, books, clippings, periodicals. **Subjects:** humanism, philosophy, sociology. **Awards:** Distinguished Service Award. **Frequency:** annual. **Type:** recognition ● Humanist Arts Award. **Frequency:** annual. **Type:** recognition ● Humanist Heroine Award. **Frequency:** annual. **Type:** recognition ● Humanist of the Year Award. **Frequency:** annual. **Type:** recognition ● Humanist Pioneer Award. **Frequency:** annual. **Type:** recognition. **Committees:** Legal. **Divisions:** Americans for Religious Liberty; Chapter Assembly of the AHA; Humanist Society for Friends and Division of Humanist Counselors and Celebrants; Imagine a World of Wanted Children. **Publications:** *Free Mind*, bimonthly. Newsletter. Includes book reviews, calendar of events, and research updates. **Price:** included in membership dues. **Circulation:** 6,000. **Advertising:** accepted ● *Humanism: Making Bigger Circles*. Film ● *The Humanist*, bimonthly. Magazine. Includes book reviews. **Price:** $12.50 /year for members; $24.95 /year for nonmembers; $5.50/issue. ISSN: 0018-7399. **Circulation:** 18,000. **Advertising:** accepted. Alternate Formats: microform. **Conventions/Meetings:** annual Humanism Oasis in the Desert - conference (exhibits) - usually May.

19674 ■ Council for Secular Humanism (CSH)
PO Box 664
Amherst, NY 14226-0664
Ph: (716)636-7571
Fax: (716)636-1733
E-mail: info@secularhumanism.org
URL: http://www.secularhumanism.org
Contact: David R. Koepsell, Exec. Dir.
Founded: 1980. **Members:** 4,000. **Membership Dues:** individual, $20 (annual) ● family, $34 (annual) ● life, $1,000. **Staff:** 28. **Budget:** $2,500,000. **Local Groups:** 210. **National Groups:** 10. **Multinational. Description:** Fosters interest in and encourages the growth of the traditions of democracy and secular humanism in contemporary society. Inspires and supports publication of journals, articles, monographs, and books that present a democratic secular humanistic point of view. Organizes and supports Secular Organizations for Sobriety; the Academy of Humanism: Campus Freethought Alliance; Robert G. Ingersoll Memorial Committee; Committee for the Scientific Examination of Religion; African-Americans for Humanism; First Amendment Task Force. Conducts lectures. Operates speakers' bureau and charitable program. Maintains museum. **Libraries: Type:** reference. **Holdings:** 42,000; archival material, audiovisuals, books, periodicals. **Subjects:** secular humanism, atheism, skepticism, the paranormal, naturalism. **Awards:** Morris Forkosch Awards. **Frequency:** annual. **Type:** recognition. **Recipient:** for the best humanist book of the year; best article in Free Inquiry, the Council's flagship magazine. **Computer Services:** Online services, selected past articles from Council publications library. **Committees:** Campus Freethought Alliance; Committee for the Scientific Examination of Religion; International Academy of Humanism; Robert Green Ingersoll Memorial. **Formerly:** (1998) Council for Democratic and Secular Humanism. **Publications:** *Free Inquiry*, bimonthly. Journal. Includes book reviews and legislative news; for non-atheists and secular humanists covering

religious philosophy and current events. **Price:** $19.98/year. ISSN: 0272-0701. **Circulation:** 35,000. Alternate Formats: microform ● *Philo,* semiannual. Journal. Contains criticisms of theism and defenses or developments of naturalism. ● *Secular Humanist Bulletin,* quarterly. Newsletter. **Price:** free for members. ISSN: 1063-2611. **Circulation:** 4,800. Alternate Formats: microform ● *Secular Humanist Viewpoints,* semiannual. Pamphlets. Contains information and thought-provoking topics of public interest. **Price:** $1.00/copy; $2.50 6 pamphlets; $4.00 10 pamphlets; $12.00 100 pamphlets. **Conventions/Meetings:** annual conference ● symposium.

19675 ■ International Federation of Secular Humanistic Jews (IFSHJ)
28611 W 12 Mile Rd.
Farmington Hills, MI 48334
Ph: (248)476-9532
Fax: (248)477-9014
E-mail: info@ifshj.org
URL: http://www.ifshj.org
Contact: Myrna Baron, Exec. Dir.
Founded: 1986. **Members:** 15. **Staff:** 5. **National Groups:** 15. **Languages:** English, French, Hebrew, Italian, Russian, Spanish, Yiddish. **Multinational. Description:** National associations of secular humanistic Jews. Advocates secular humanistic Judaism. Conducts cultural, educational, and life cycle programs and celebrations. Sponsors Institute for Secular Humanistic Judaism, which focuses on leadership training and development and training of secular humanistic rabbis to serve communities in the U.S. and abroad. **Awards:** Service Award. **Frequency:** biennial. **Type:** recognition. **Recipient:** for outstanding contribution to the values of secular humanistic Judaism. **Telecommunication Services:** electronic mail, infoeurope@ifshj.org. **Affiliated With:** Congress of Secular Jewish Organizations; Society for Humanistic Judaism; Workmen's Circle. **Formerly:** (1993) International Federation for Secular Humanistic Judaism. **Publications:** *Contemplate,* annual. Book. Contains collection of articles from around the world. ● *Hofesh,* annual. Newsletter. **Conventions/Meetings:** biennial conference.

19676 ■ Washington Ethical Society (WES)
7750 16th St. NW
Washington, DC 20012-1462
Ph: (202)882-6650
Fax: (202)829-1354
E-mail: wes@ethicalsociety.org
URL: http://www.ethicalsociety.org
Contact: Richard A. Nugent, Senior Leader
Founded: 1943. **Members:** 400. **Staff:** 6. **Budget:** $350,000. **Description:** Humanistic religious and educational fellowship. Founded on the view that the development of ethical values is the central and unifying purpose of the religious life. Conducts adult education courses and Sunday school. Offers public affairs programs dealing with current issues that involve ethical principles in action, service programs, seasonal celebrations, and social activities. Provides counseling and referral for members, and ceremonies to celebrate the transitions of life. **Affiliated With:** American Ethical Union. **Publications:** *Creating Ethical Community: Faith in Human Worth.* Monograph. Contains answers to the 50 most frequently asked questions about Ethical Culture. **Price:** $3.00 ● Newsletter, monthly. **Price:** for a donation. Alternate Formats: online. **Conventions/Meetings:** weekly Platform - meeting, explores a particular topic in 1=1 depth, meditation, shared reflection - each Sunday 11:00 AM in Washington, DC.

Hunger

19677 ■ Society of St. Andrew (SoSA)
3383 Sweet Hollow Rd.
Big Island, VA 24526
Ph: (434)299-5956
Free: (800)333-4597
Fax: (434)299-5949

E-mail: sosausa@endhunger.org
URL: http://www.endhunger.org
Contact: Rev. Kenneth C. Horne Jr., Exec. Dir.
Founded: 1979. **Description:** Works to feed the hungry. Sponsors the Loaves and Fishes Club and seasonal programs for spiritual growth and giving, as well as children's programs. **Publications:** *Society of St. Andrew Report,* quarterly. Newsletter. Alternate Formats: online.

Immigration

19678 ■ Catholic Legal Immigration Network (CLINIC)
415 Michigan Ave. NE, Ste.150
Washington, DC 20017
Ph: (202)635-2556
Fax: (202)635-2649
E-mail: national@cliniclegal.org
URL: http://www.cliniclegal.org
Contact: Donald Kerwin, Exec. Dir.
Founded: 1988. **Description:** Provides a full range of legal and non-legal support services to Catholic Charities' and diocesan legal immigration programs; devotes significant resources to the administration of legal services projects that overwhelm local capacity or expertise, or otherwise require national coordination; manages diocesan programs; meets the legal immigration needs of archdioceses, dioceses and congregations through various supporting activities and its own direct representation of the foreign-born religious.

India

19679 ■ Friends of Christ in India (FOCI)
c/o Greenfield Hill Congregational Church
1045 Old Acad. Rd.
Fairfield, CT 06824
Ph: (203)259-5596
E-mail: friendsofchristinindia@yahoo.com
URL: http://www.foci.org
Contact: Dr. David Rowe, Sr. Minister
Founded: 1983. **Description:** Promotes support and relief care to the underprivileged in India. **Publications:** *Consider Jesus* (in English and Telugu). Book. Highlights lessons from the life and ministry of an Indian Evangelist named Azariah. **Price:** $6.00 in U.S. ● Video. Features a sixteen-minute video introduction to the work and history of Friends of Christ in India. **Price:** $6.00 in U.S.

Information Management

19680 ■ Association for the Development of Religious Information Systems (ADRIS)
PO Box 210735
Nashville, TN 37221-0735
Ph: (615)301-8507
E-mail: editor@adris.org
Contact: Mr. Edward Dodds, Ed.
Founded: 1971. **Staff:** 1. **Description:** Aims to promote organizational cooperation, reduce unnecessary program duplication, and share applicable research data and tasks among diverse religious groups and agencies. Works to establish a genuinely symbiotic, interdisciplinary, interdenominational, interfaith and global network of religious information services. Links scientific and academic research interests and resources with the applied needs of denominational, parachurch, and analogous religion-related agencies. **Computer Services:** database, legacy directory ● online services, blog ● online services, organizational communications consulting. **Publications:** *ADRIS Newsletter,* periodic. ISSN: 0300-7022. **Advertising:** accepted. Alternate Formats: online ● *1971 International Directory of Religious Information Systems.*

Interfaith

19681 ■ Interfaith Worker Justice (IWJ)
1020 W Bryn Mawr Ave., 4th Fl.
Chicago, IL 60660
Ph: (773)728-8400
Fax: (773)728-8409
E-mail: info@iwj.org
URL: http://www.iwj.org
Contact: Kim Bobo, Exec. Dir.
Staff: 28. **Description:** People of faith. Organizes the religious community to improve employee wages, benefits, and working conditions, focusing on low-wage workers. Works to reform labor laws. **Telecommunication Services:** electronic mail, bridget@iwj.org. **Formerly:** (2005) National Interfaith Committee for Worker Justice. **Publications:** *Faith Works,* bimonthly. Newsletter. Engages people of faith in discussions about worker justice.

International Affairs

19682 ■ Carnegie Council for Ethics in International Affairs (CCEIA)
Merrill House
170 E 64th St.
New York, NY 10021-7478
Ph: (212)838-4120
Fax: (212)752-2432
E-mail: info@cceia.org
URL: http://www.cceia.org
Contact: Joel H. Rosenthal, Pres.
Founded: 1914. **Members:** 350. **Membership Dues:** contributing fellow, $1,000 (annual) ● academic affiliate, $60 (annual) ● associate, $200 (annual) ● friend, $300 (annual) ● supporter, $500 (annual). **Staff:** 25. **Budget:** $3,000,000. **Description:** Independent, nonpartisan organization dedicated to research and education in the field of ethics and international affairs. Works to promote a greater understanding of the values and conditions that enable peaceful relations among nations. Believes that the moral dimension of international affairs needs to be understood along with political, economic, and security considerations; founded by noted industrialist and philanthropist Andrew Carnegie (1835-1919). **Divisions:** Administration; Asian Programs; Communications; Education and Studies; Ethics and International Affairs; Merrill House Programs. **Roundtables:** Foreign Policy. **Formerly:** (1961) Church Peace Union; (1986) Council on Religion and International Affairs. **Publications:** *Carnegie Council for Ethics in International Affairs Annual Report,* annual ● *Ethics and International Affairs,* semiannual. Journal. Contains global justice, civil society, democratization, international law, intervention, sanctions, and related topics. **Price:** $30.00 /year for individuals in the Americas; EUR 35.00 /year for individuals in Europe; 22.00 /year for individuals rest of the world. ISSN: 0892-6794. **Advertising:** accepted ● *Insider.* Newsletter. **Price:** included in membership dues. Alternate Formats: online ● *Public Philosophy Monographs,* periodic. Contains information to develop a more nuanced understanding of the values underlying public policies in this era of globalization. ● Also publishes collections of lectures and pamphlets on ethics and foreign policy, religion and international affairs, and special studies. **Conventions/Meetings:** semiannual board meeting ● annual meeting.

19683 ■ Commission of the Churches on International Affairs (CCIA)
c/o Rev. Deborah DeWinter, Programme Exec. for the U.S.
475 Riverside Dr., Rm. 1371
New York, NY 10115
Ph: (212)870-3260
Free: (888)212-2920
URL: http://www.wcc-coe.org
Contact: Rev. Deborah DeWinter, Programme Exec. for the U.S.
Founded: 1946. **Members:** 342. **Staff:** 2. **Budget:** $800,000. **Languages:** English, French, German,

Russian, Spanish. **Multinational. Description:** Serves the Anglican, Protestant and Orthodox member churches as a source of information and analysis on global trends, and as a medium of common counsel and action. Maintains consultative relations on behalf of the World Council of Churches with ECSOC, DPI and a wide range of UN Specialized Agencies. **Additional Websites:** http://www.wcc-usa.org. **Publications:** *Background Information Reports*, periodic ● *Quarterly*, periodic. Newsletter ● Report, triennial. **Conventions/Meetings:** annual meeting.

Islamic

19684 ■ American Druze Society (ADS)
2239 Merton Ave.
Los Angeles, CA 90041-1914
Ph: (323)255-1455
Fax: (323)255-9155
E-mail: americandruzesociety@yahoo.com
URL: http://www.druze.com
Contact: Emad Aboulhosn, Pres.
Founded: 1906. **Members:** 27,000. **Membership Dues:** student, $40 (annual) ● husband and wife, $90 (annual) ● individual (not a student), $50 (annual) ● life, $1,000 ● life (husband and wife), $1,500 ● friend of the society, $35 (annual). **Staff:** 3. **Budget:** $100,000. **State Groups:** 14. **Description:** Represents individuals interested in the Druze religion, a branch of Islam whose adherents believe in the brotherhood of mankind among Christians, Jews, and Muslims. Promotes the advancement of the Druze religion; aims to help the needy, helpless, and unfortunate through charitable and humanitarian activities, including disaster relief. Maintains biographical archives; compiles statistics. Conducts classes on the Druze religion and Druze history. **Awards:** President Award. **Frequency:** annual. **Type:** recognition. **Computer Services:** database, membership. **Committees:** Charitable Affairs and Orphan; Council of the Elders; Fine Arts; Religious; Youth. **Funds:** Home; Student Loan. **Formerly:** (1946) Baqura; (1946) ah Adurzia; (1946) Al-Bakorah Adurzia. **Publications:** *Chapter Handbook* ● *Our Heritage*, quarterly. Magazine. Alternate Formats: online ● Yearbook ● Also publishes religious books and pamphlets. **Conventions/Meetings:** Camps - meeting ● lecture ● annual meeting.

19685 ■ Association of Islamic Charitable Projects (AICP)
4431 Walnut St.
Philadelphia, PA 19104
Ph: (215)387-8888
Fax: (215)387-3815
URL: http://www.aicp.org
Contact: Shaykh Husam Qaraqirah, Pres.
Founded: 1990. **Members:** 20,000. **Staff:** 50. **Budget:** $250,000. **Regional Groups:** 15. **State Groups:** 1. **Local Groups:** 1. **Languages:** Arabic, English, French. **Multinational. Description:** Seeks to spread knowledge about Islam. Promotes moderation and refutes those that spread falsehoods about Islam. Offers educational (including grammar school), charitable, and research programs, competitions, and children's services. **Libraries: Type:** reference. **Holdings:** articles, audiovisuals, books. **Subjects:** Islamic jurisprudence. **Computer Services:** Electronic publishing ● mailing lists. **Publications:** Also publishes books and booklets. **Conventions/Meetings:** semiannual DAWRA - seminar and convention.

19686 ■ Council of Masajid of United States (CMUS)
45 Lilac St.
Edison, NJ 08817-4254
Ph: (732)985-3304
Fax: (732)572-0486
E-mail: dawud10@optonline.net
Contact: Dawud Assad, Former Pres.
Founded: 1978. **Members:** 305. **Budget:** $75,000. **Local Groups:** 650. **Languages:** Arabic, English. **Description:** Mosques or clergy who lead prayers at mosques. Promotes better relations and understand-

ing between Muslims and non-Muslims. Administers the Association of Muslim American Lawyers. Sponsors semiannual pilgrimage training session. Operates speakers' bureau. Conducts and participates in interfaith dialogues. **Commissions:** Muslim Educators. **Councils:** Imams; Press and Media. **Departments:** Interreligious. **Affiliated With:** National Conference for Community and Justice; World Conference of Religions for Peace. **Publications:** *Council of Masajid Newsletter*, quarterly ● *Dialog-Interfaith*, 10/year ● *Majallat Al-Masajid*, periodic. Newsletter ● Also publishes circulars and handouts; has published directory. **Conventions/Meetings:** semiannual Hajj and Umrah Conference ● periodic Muslim Family Law Conference ● annual Seerah Conference.

19687 ■ Federation of Islamic Associations in the U.S. and Canada (FIA)
25231 5 Mile Rd.
Redford, MI 48239
Ph: (313)534-3295
Fax: (313)534-1474
E-mail: islamerica@yahoo.com
URL: http://www.islamerica.com
Contact: Nihad Hamed, VP
Founded: 1951. **Members:** 150,000. **Membership Dues:** association, $15 (annual). **Staff:** 7. **Budget:** $150,000. **State Groups:** 35. **Languages:** Arabic, English. **Description:** Religious, political, social, and educational organization that acts as an umbrella for Muslim groups in the U.S. and Canada. Objectives are to: defend the human rights of Muslims and all oppressed people through democratic, political means; promote the spirit, ethics, philosophy, and culture of Muslim heritage; answer questions and correct misconceptions about Islam; promote friendly relations between Muslims and non-Muslims of North America. Conducts charitable program, specialized education, and youth programs; distributes literature to schools, universities, and libraries. Offers placement and computerized services. Sponsors weekly radio program, Muslim Star: Voice of American-Canadian Muslims. **Libraries: Type:** reference. **Holdings:** 2,000; books. **Subjects:** Middle East religion, politics, and arts. **Awards:** **Frequency:** annual. **Type:** scholarship. **Recipient:** for college students. **Committees:** Anti-Defamation; Educational; Political; Religious; Scholarship. **Affiliated With:** United Nations. **Publications:** Books ● Also issues press releases. **Conventions/Meetings:** annual meeting ● seminar, on religious affairs.

19688 ■ Fiqh Council of North America
Address Unknown since 2007
Founded: 1986. **Members:** 10. **Staff:** 2. **Languages:** Arabic. **Description:** Promotes the Islamic way of life to institutions and individuals in North America. Offers legal expertise based on the Qur'an and the Sunnah. Conducts research. **Libraries: Type:** not open to the public; reference. **Holdings:** archival material, audiovisuals, books, clippings, monographs, periodicals. **Subjects:** Islamic law, Qur'anic interpretation. **Formerly:** Islamic Society of North America Fiqh Committee. **Conventions/Meetings:** conference ● semiannual meeting.

19689 ■ Hartford Seminary
77 Sherman St.
Hartford, CT 06105-2260
Ph: (860)509-9500
Fax: (860)509-9509
E-mail: info@hartsem.edu
URL: http://www.hartsem.edu
Contact: Heidi Hadsell, Pres.
Founded: 1834. **Staff:** 50. **Multinational. Description:** Serves as an educational center that seeks increased understanding of Islam and improved relations between Christians and Muslims. Sponsors a national outreach program that provides informational materials and faculty lecturers to churches, colleges and universities, private organizations, and other groups. Conducts research and conferences; operates speakers' bureau; compiles statistics. Offers masters of arts program in religious studies, with a concentration in Christian-Muslim relations. Center is

named for Duncan Black Macdonald (1863-1943), a theologian and Christian missionary interested in Islamic studies. **Libraries: Type:** reference. **Holdings:** 60,000; archival material. **Subjects:** Arabic and Islamic source materials. **Formerly:** (2000) Duncan Black Macdonald Center for the Study of Islam and Christian/Muslim Relations. **Publications:** *The Muslim World*, quarterly. Journal. Includes study of Islam and Christian-Muslim relations in past and present. **Price:** $35.00 /year for institutions; $25.00 /year for individuals; $20.00/year for students. **Circulation:** 1,000. **Advertising:** accepted. **Conventions/Meetings:** periodic meeting.

19690 ■ International Association of Sufism (IAS)
14 Commercial Blvd., Ste.101
Novato, CA 94949
Ph: (415)382-7834
E-mail: ias@ias.org
URL: http://www.ias.org
Contact: Dr. Seyedeh Nahid Angha PhD, Co-Dir.
Founded: 1983. **Membership Dues:** sustaining, $50 (annual) ● associate, $70 (annual) ● friend, $100 (annual) ● benefactor, $500 (annual). **Multinational. Description:** Seeks to promote Sufism goals and principles. Strengthens the unity of scholars, translators, educators and artists in the field of Sufism. Provides a forum for a continuing dialogue between the different schools of Sufism. **Libraries: Type:** reference. **Holdings:** books. **Subjects:** interfaith, interreligious, sufism, Islam, world religions, psychology, history, literature, health, women's spirituality. **Computer Services:** Information services, sufism directory. **Departments:** Sufi Music; Sufi Psychology; Sufi Women; Sufi Youth. **Projects:** Khaneghah; Literacy; Prison; UN Human Rights. **Publications:** *Reflections on Islam and Sufism.* Audiotape. Explains the foundations and principles of Islam and Sufism, and discusses in detail the importance and the practice of purification. **Price:** $50.00 each ● *Reflections on Meditation and Prayer.* Video. Offers clear responses to questions about the nature and practice of meditation and prayer. **Price:** $35.00 each ● *Reflections on Peace.* Audiotape. Addresses the subject of peace. **Price:** $25.00 each ● *Sufism: An Inquiry.* Journal. Serves as a resource for research in self-knowledge. Alternate Formats: online ● *Sufism: The Path of Understanding.* Video. Features an in-depth interview with Shah Nazar Seyed Ali Kianfar and Seyedeh Nahid Angha, that delves into the heart of Sufism and Islam.

19691 ■ Islamic Assembly of North America (IANA)
3588 Plymouth Rd., PMB 270
Ann Arbor, MI 48105
Ph: (734)528-0006
Free: (800)994-IANA
Fax: (734)528-0066
E-mail: iana@iananet.org
URL: http://www.iananet.org
Founded: 1993. **Languages:** Arabic, English, French. **Description:** Representatives of Islamic centers and organizations in the United States and Canada. Seeks to "achieve the final goal of reviving the Islamic nation to its proper state and condition". Coordinates the activities of Islamic organizations; serves as a clearinghouse on Islam; conducts research on current events in Islam; plans to create a media institute to represent the views of Islam in North America. Sponsors theological programs; conducts annual Education Day; operates IANA RadioNet, a live, online broadcasting service. **Publications:** *40 Hadith for Islamic Schools* (in Arabic and English). Book. **Price:** $8.00 each ● *The Friday Prayer - Part 1, 2, and 3* (in Arabic and English). Book. **Price:** $9.00 each ● *The Meaning of the Holy Quran* (in Arabic and English). Book. **Price:** $4.00 each (1 to 27 copies); $70.00 1 box (28 copies) ● *What Did Jesus Really Say?* (in Arabic and English). Book. **Price:** $18.00 each.

19692 ■ Islamic Center of America (ICA)
19500 Ford Rd.
Dearborn, MI 48128
Ph: (313)593-0000

E-mail: info@icofa.com
URL: http://www.icofa.com
Contact: Imam Hassan Al-Qazwini, Resident Scholar
Founded: 1963. **Description:** Provides Muslims a closer following to the Prophet Mohammad's Sunna tradition.

19693 ■ **Islamic Center of New York (ICNY)**
1711 3rd Ave.
New York, NY 10029-7303
Ph: (212)722-5234
Fax: (212)722-5936
Contact: Ziyad Monayair, Dir.
Founded: 1966. **Staff:** 8. **Languages:** Arabic, English. **Description:** Institution to serve the religious and cultural needs of the 800,000-member Muslim community in the metropolitan New York area, to maintain a Mosque for Muslims prayers and to contribute to the well-being of Muslims in America. Serves as a source of information about Islam and its history, civilization, and people. Conducts weekend religious school. Promotes cordial relations between Muslims and non-Muslims. Deals with family problems. Encourages people to abstain from taking drugs and warns them against immorality. Encourages people to be gracious and to help the needy and the orphans, Muslims and non-Muslims alike. **Libraries: Type:** reference. **Holdings:** 8,000. **Publications:** Bulletin, annual. Contains articles about Islam and world culture. **Conventions/Meetings:** conference, includes interfaith dialogues between Muslims, Christians, and Jews from many different countries.

19694 ■ **Islamic Correctional Reunion Association (ICRA)**
PO Box 774
Tinley Park, IL 60477
Ph: (708)429-0093 (708)466-1120
Fax: (708)429-0093
E-mail: mafzalfirdausi@gmail.com
Contact: Mohammad Afzal Firdausi, Pres.
Founded: 1985. **Staff:** 1. **Budget:** $25,000. **Languages:** Arabic, English, Urdu. **Description:** Aims to recruit, organize, and train volunteers from Islamic centers to provide religious services to Muslim inmates in jails and correctional centers. (The group says that Muslim inmates, who make up to 25 percent of the total prison population, receive little guidance and training in the Islamic faith and as a result they form many misconceptions about its teachings.) Conducts educational programs aimed at facilitating authentic knowledge about Islam, individual spiritual growth, and comparative study of religions. Offers Islamic correspondence course, pre-employment education, and vocational training; provides visitation and counseling. Distributes free Islamic, literacy, and vocational literature. **Publications:** God Is One (in Arabic and English), quarterly. Brochures. Covers information on basics of Islam, prophethood, and life after death. **Price:** free. **Conventions/Meetings:** quarterly board meeting.

19695 ■ **Islamic Information Center of America (IICA)**
PO Box 4052
Des Plaines, IL 60016
Ph: (847)541-8141
Fax: (847)824-8436
E-mail: iica1@comcast.net
Contact: Dr. Musa Qutub, Pres.
Founded: 1983. **Staff:** 8. **Budget:** $350,000. **Description:** Provides information about Islam to non-Muslims. Operates speakers' bureau; conducts research. **Libraries: Type:** reference. **Subjects:** Islam. **Publications:** The Invitation, periodic. Articles. Contains articles on the Islamic perspective of contemporary social problems. **Price:** free. **Circulation:** 15,500. **Advertising:** accepted. **Conventions/Meetings:** annual meeting - always January ● seminar and workshop.

19696 ■ **Islamic Mission of America (IMA)**
Address Unknown since 2007
Founded: 1938. **Members:** 1,500. **Membership Dues:** $120 (annual). **Languages:** Arabic, English.

Description: Dedicated to the propagation of the Islamic faith. Prepares students for missionary work. Maintains mosque in Brooklyn, NY and an institute for teaching religion and Arabic. Operates library on all aspects of Islamic education. **Convention/Meeting:** none. **Publications:** The Little Giant, periodic.

19697 ■ **Study of Islam Section**
c/o Omid Safi
Dept. of Philosophy and Religion
Colgate Univ.
13 Oak Dr.
Hamilton, NY 13346
E-mail: osafi@mail.colgate.edu
URL: http://groups.colgate.edu/aarislam
Contact: Omid Safi, Contact
Founded: 1986. **Description:** Promotes the study of current research on Islam and Islamic texts and scriptures. **Conventions/Meetings:** annual meeting.

Jehovah's Witnesses

19698 ■ **Watchtower Bible and Tract Society of New York**
25 Columbia Heights
Brooklyn, NY 11201-2483
Ph: (718)560-5000
Fax: (718)560-5619
URL: http://www.watchtower.org
Contact: Gene Smalley, Contact
Founded: 1909. **Staff:** 5,500. **Description:** Serves as a legal agent for Jehovah's Witnesses, who number 6,000,000 worldwide, with over 1,000,000 members in the U.S. Published in 148 languages including all major ones (Spanish, French, German, etc.). **Libraries: Type:** reference. **Holdings:** 25,000. **Additional Websites:** http://www.jw-media.org. **Publications:** Awake! (in English, French, German, and Spanish), semimonthly. Magazine. Teaching aid on current events and social issues, published in 87 languages. ISSN: 0005-237X. **Circulation:** 22,530,000 ● The Watchtower, semimonthly. Magazine. ISSN: 0043-1087. **Circulation:** 25,618,000 ● Yearbook of Jehovah's Witnesses, annual. **Conventions/Meetings:** annual meeting.

Jewish

19699 ■ **Agudath Israel of America (AIA)**
42 Broadway, 14th Fl.
New York, NY 10004
Ph: (212)797-9000
Fax: (646)254-1600
Contact: Rabbi B. Borchardt, Exec.Dir.
Founded: 1921. **Members:** 100,000. **Staff:** 165. **Local Groups:** 155. **Description:** Members of the Orthodox Jewish faith. To organize Jews for religious, educational, and philanthropic purposes. Maintains legislative and public affairs bureaus and biographical archives; provides placement service, speakers' bureau, research programs, religious and educational programs, and children's services. **Publications:** Coalition, bimonthly. Covers news and current events. **Circulation:** 54,000. **Advertising:** accepted ● The Jewish Observer, monthly, except July and August. Magazine. **Price:** $24.00/year. **Circulation:** 15,000. **Advertising:** accepted. **Conventions/Meetings:** annual convention (exhibits) - always Thanksgiving weekend.

19700 ■ **American Board of Rabbis - Vaad Harabonim of America**
292 5th Ave., 4th Fl.
New York, NY 10001
Ph: (212)714-3598
E-mail: vaadharabbonim@yahoo.com
URL: http://www.angelfire.com/ny2/abor
Contact: Rabbi Mordechai Friedman, Pres.
Membership Dues: regular, $250 (annual). **Languages:** English, Hebrew, Yiddish. **Description:** Serves as an Orthodox Rabbinical organization committed to the dissemination of Authentic Judaism; offers external rabbinical courses toward Semicha/

Certificate of Ordination; provides rabbinical services to the Jewish community. Offers Yeshiva principal placement and pastoral counseling. **Subgroups:** International Lecture Bureau; Scholars in Residence. **Publications:** Torah Letters of Rabbi Friedman. Video. **Price:** $108.00.

19701 ■ **American Conference of Cantors (ACC)**
213 N Morgan St., Ste.1A
Chicago, IL 60607
Ph: (312)491-1034
Fax: (312)491-1087
E-mail: info@accantors.org
URL: http://www.accantors.org
Contact: Cantor Richard Cohn, Pres.
Founded: 1953. **Members:** 450. **Staff:** 3. **Budget:** $450,000. **Regional Groups:** 8. **Description:** Represents cantors who have been invested and commissioned by the Hebrew Union College, School of Sacred Music, New York City and who serve as ministers with Jewish congregations. Conducts educational and charitable programs. Provides placement and pension service for members. **Affiliated With:** Guild of Temple Musicians; Union for Reform Judaism. **Formed by Merger of:** American Conference of Certified Cantors. **Publications:** Cantor's Life Cycle Manual ● Koleinu, monthly. Newsletter. **Price:** for members. **Circulation:** 400 ● Also makes available music pertaining to Jewish liturgy. **Conventions/Meetings:** annual convention, with Judaica and Jewish music (exhibits).

19702 ■ **American Council for Judaism (ACJ)**
c/o Rabbi Howard A. Berman, Exec. Dir.
PO Box 300537
Jamaica Plain Sta.
Boston, MA 02130
Ph: (617)983-1400
Free: (877)326-1400
E-mail: acjhab@aol.com
URL: http://www.acjna.org
Contact: Rabbi Howard A. Berman, Exec. Dir.
Founded: 1943. **Description:** Asserts that Judaism is not a nationality but a religion of universal values; proclaims that Israel is not the homeland of all Jews and that Jews who are not Israelis must live according to their beliefs and not according to Zionist thinking. Seeks greater civic, cultural, and social integration into American life for American Jews; assists American Jews in meeting their obligations in public affairs and religion. **Publications:** Issues of the ACJ, quarterly. Newsletter ● Special Interest Report, bimonthly.

19703 ■ **American Jewish Committee (AJC)**
PO Box 705
New York, NY 10150
Ph: (212)751-4000
Fax: (212)891-1450
E-mail: pr@ajc.org
URL: http://www.ajc.org
Contact: David A. Harris, Exec. Dir.
Founded: 1906. **Members:** 70,000. **Membership Dues:** contributing (minimum), $250 (annual) ● sustaining, $150 (annual) ● regular, $100 (annual) ● under 35 years old, $35 (annual). **Staff:** 335. **Budget:** $20,000,000. **Regional Groups:** 32. **Description:** American citizens from more than 600 communities. Conducts program of education, research, and human relations; combats bigotry; seeks to protect religious and civil rights; supports security for Israel. **Libraries: Type:** reference. **Holdings:** 35,000; archival material, books, clippings, periodicals. **Subjects:** Jewish affairs, history of American Jewish Community. **Awards:** National Human Relations Award. **Frequency:** annual. **Type:** recognition. **Recipient:** for prominent support in community for human relations. **Commissions:** International Relations; Interreligious Affairs; Jewish Communal Affairs; National Affairs. **Committees:** Research. **Divisions:** Project Interchange; Public Relations and Communications. **Programs:** Domestic Policy. **Publications:** American Jewish Committee—Commentary, monthly. Journal. Covers Jewish affairs and contemporary issues; includes book reviews. **Price:** $36.00/

year. ISSN: 0010-2601. **Advertising:** accepted ●
*American Jewish Year Book: A Record of Events and
Trends in American and Worldwide Jewish Life.*
Yearbook. Contains articles relating to trends and
events in Jewish life in the U.S. and abroad. Includes
Hebrew calendars and Jewish demographics. **Price:**
$50.00/year. Alternate Formats: microform ● Articles
● Bibliographies ● Books ● Catalog ● Pamphlets ●
Reprints. **Conventions/Meetings:** annual meeting -
always May.

19704 ■ American Jewish Congress (AJC)

825 Third Ave.
New York, NY 10022
Ph: (212)879-4500
Fax: (212)758-1633
E-mail: chairman@ajcongress.org
URL: http://www.ajcongress.org
Contact: Jack Rosen, Pres.
Founded: 1918. **Members:** 50,000. **Staff:** 100. **Budget:** $6,500,000. **Local Groups:** 300. **Description:**
Represents American Jews opposed to all forms of
racism and committed to the unity, security, dignity,
and creative survival of Jews in Israel, the USSR,
and wherever they may be threatened. Maintains
library. Sponsors the Institute for Jewish-Christian
Relations (see separate entry). **Awards: Type:**
recognition. **Commissions:** International Affairs; Jewish Life and Culture; Law and Social Action; National
Affairs. **Affiliated With:** Conference of Presidents of
Major American Jewish Organizations; Jewish Council for Public Affairs; World Jewish Congress, American Section. **Publications:** *American Jewish Congress—National Report,* 3/year. Newsletter. Covers
congress activities. **Price:** included in membership
dues. **Circulation:** 50,000 ● *Boycott Report: Developments and Trends Affecting the Arab Boycott and
Arab Influence in the USA,* 9/year. Newsletter. **Price:**
included in membership dues; $30.00 /year for
nonmembers. **Circulation:** 5,500 ● *Congress
Monthly.* Magazine. Covers current issues for the
American Jew. Includes book and movie reviews.
Price: $12.50/year. ISSN: 0739-1927. **Circulation:**
30,000. **Advertising:** accepted ● *Judaism: A Quarterly Journal of Jewish Life and Thought.* Covers
religious, moral, historical, and cultural concepts of
Judaism. Includes bibliography, book reviews, and
poetry. **Price:** $6.00/copy for individuals; $10.00/copy
for institutions and libraries; $20.00/year in U.S.; $22.
00/year in Canada. ISSN: 0022-5762. **Circulation:**
30,000. **Conventions/Meetings:** biennial conference.

19705 ■ American Jewish League for Israel (AJLI)

450 7th Ave., Ste.808
New York, NY 10123
Ph: (212)371-1583 (212)279-9413
Fax: (212)279-1456
E-mail: ajlijms@aol.com
URL: http://www.americanjewishleague.org
Contact: Dr. Martin L. Kalmanson, Pres.
Founded: 1957. **Members:** 5,000. **Membership
Dues:** family, individual, $36 (annual) ● life, $300 ●
patron, $100 (annual). **Staff:** 1. **State Groups:** 1. **Local Groups:** 2. **Description:** Zionist organizations
whose objectives are to help rebuild the state of
Israel, strengthen its ties with American Jewry, and
intensify Jewish life in the Diaspora. Sponsors the
University Scholarship Fund, which provides partial
grants towards tuition for US students to spend an
academic year at one of Israel's seven major universities. **Libraries: Type:** not open to the public. **Holdings:** 500. **Subjects:** Jewish, Zionists. **Awards:** Leo
Lipsky Award. **Type:** recognition. **Affiliated With:**
American Zionist Movement; Jewish National Fund;
World Jewish Congress, American Section. **Publications:** *AJLI Newsletter,* quarterly. **Price:** free for
members. **Circulation:** 1,500 ● *News Bulletin of the
American Jewish League for Israel,* quarterly. Includes articles on Israel and Jewish communities.
Price: included in membership dues. **Circulation:**
5,000. Alternate Formats: online. **Conventions/Meetings:** biennial convention.

19706 ■ American Sephardi Federation (ASF)

15 W 16th St.
New York, NY 10011-6301
Ph: (212)294-8350
Fax: (212)294-8348
E-mail: info@americansephardifederation.org
URL: http://www.americansephardifederation.org
Contact: Francesco Spagnolo, Exec. Dir.
Founded: 1973. **Members:** 800. **Membership Dues:**
senior, student, $36 (annual) ● individual, $54 (annual) ● supporting/family/synagogue/institutional,
$100 (annual) ● donor, $270 (annual) ● sponsor,
$500 (annual) ● patron, $1,000 (annual). **Staff:** 5.
Budget: $300,000. **Regional Groups:** 7. **Languages:** English, Farsi, French, Hebrew, Persian,
Spanish, Turkish. **Description:** Represents congregations, organizations, and individual Sephardic
Jews. Works to promote and strengthen Sephardic
identity and awareness. Seeks to educate other Jews
and non-Jews on the Sephardim. Acts as spokesman
to other Jewish organizations; attempts to make Jewish leaders more sensitive to the needs and problems
of the Sephardim in the U.S., Israel, and other
countries. Brings the Sephardic view to Jewish
organizations. Sponsors educational, advocacy, and
leadership development programs. **Libraries: Type:**
reference. **Holdings:** 5,000; archival material,
articles, biographical archives, books, photographs,
video recordings. **Subjects:** Sephardic history,
culture, music, religion, politics. **Awards:** Broome
and Allen Scholarship. **Frequency:** annual. **Type:**
scholarship. **Recipient:** for a graduate and undergraduate student of Sephardic heritage. **Committees:** Steering. **Divisions:** New Leadership; President's Circle; Rabbinical Council of Sephardi Rabbis.
Affiliated With: American Zionist Movement; Conference of Presidents of Major American Jewish Organizations; Jewish Council for Public Affairs; World Jewish Congress, American Section. **Absorbed:** (2002)
Sephardic House. **Publications:** *The Sephardi Report,* quarterly. **Price:** free. **Circulation:** 15,000. **Advertising:** accepted. Alternate Formats: online ● Also
distributes gift certificates, posters and audio/CDs.
Conventions/Meetings: annual convention and
lecture (exhibits).

19707 ■ American Zionist Movement (AZM)

633 3rd Ave.
New York, NY 10017
Ph: (212)318-6100
Fax: (212)935-3578
E-mail: info@azm.org
URL: http://www.azm.org
Contact: Karen J. Rubinstein, Exec. Dir.
Founded: 1939. **Members:** 20. **Membership Dues:**
regular, $50 (annual) ● contributing, $100 (annual) ●
supporting, $250 (annual) ● sustaining, $500 (annual) ● patron, $1,000 (annual). **Staff:** 7. **Budget:**
$750,000. **Regional Groups:** 10. **Description:**
Serves as coalition of 20 member and affiliated
organizations and individuals representing over one
million American Jews. Groups include: American
Jewish League for Israel; Americans for Progressive
Israel; American Sephardi Federation; American Zionist Youth Council; AMIT Women; Association of
Reform Zionists of America; B'nai B'rith; B'nai Zion;
Emunah Women; Hadassah—Women's Zionist Organization of America; Jewish National Fund; Labor
Zionist Alliance; Likud, USA; Religious Zionists of
America; Volunteers for Israel; Zionist Student Movement; Zionist Organization of America. Youth groups
include: BBYO, Betar B'nei Akiva, Habonim-Dror,
Hashomer Hatzair, Masada, NFTY, USY, and Young
Judea. **Divisions:** Adult Zionist Education; Aliyah;
Economic Development; External Relations; Political
Action; Publications; Soviet and Syrian Jewry;
Student and Academic Work; Zionist Youth Movements. **Affiliated With:** NCSJ: Advocates on Behalf
of Jews in Russia, Ukraine, the Baltic States and
Eurasia. **Formerly:** (1948) American Zionist Emergency Council; (1971) American Zionist Council;
(1973) American Zionist Federation. **Publications:**
The Zionist Advocate, quarterly. Newsletter. **Conventions/Meetings:** biennial American Zionist - convention (exhibits).

19708 ■ AMIT

817 Broadway
New York, NY 10003
Ph: (212)477-4720
Free: (800)989-AMIT
Fax: (212)353-2312
E-mail: info@amitchildren.org
URL: http://www.amitchildren.org
Contact: Jan Schechter, Pres.
Founded: 1925. **Members:** 40,000. **Membership
Dues:** individual, $25 (annual). **Staff:** 50. **Regional
Groups:** 9. **State Groups:** 10. **Local Groups:** 225.
Description: Enables Israel's youth to realize their
potential and strengthens Israeli society by educating
and nurturing children from diverse backgrounds
within a framework of academic excellence, religious
values and Zionist ideals. Educates and cares for
Israel's youth, including the most vulnerable. Approaches each child as an individual, maximizing his
or her potential, and enabling students to become
vital and productive members of Israeli society.
Promotes religious tolerance, service to the state and
the recognition that every child is blessed with unique
talents and abilities. Operates more than 60 schools,
youth villages, surrogate family residences and other
programs, constituting Israel's only government-recognized network of religious Jewish education
incorporating academic and technological studies.
Awards: Guardians of the Children Award. **Frequency:** annual. **Type:** recognition. **Recipient:** to
those who have devoted substantial time and effort
to AMIT's children in Israel ● Lifetime Achievement
Award. **Frequency:** annual. **Type:** recognition. **Recipient:** to those who have literally devoted their adult
lifetime to AMIT's cause ● New Leadership Award.
Frequency: annual. **Type:** recognition. **Recipient:** to
young leaders of AMIT who have impacted the
organization. **Departments:** Social Services; Vocational Education; Youth Aliyah and Child Restoration.
Affiliated With: Jewish National Fund. **Formerly:**
(1975) Mizrachi Women's Organization of American;
(1983) American Mizrachi Women. **Publications:**
Magazine, quarterly. Covers articles of Jewish interest. **Price:** included in membership dues. ISSN:
1085-2891. **Circulation:** 40,000. **Advertising:** accepted. Alternate Formats: online ● Also publishes
biography of Bessie Gotsfeld, founder of AMW. **Conventions/Meetings:** biennial convention.

19709 ■ Association of Humanistic Rabbis (AHR)

28611 W 12 Mile Rd.
Farmington Hills, MI 48334
Ph: (248)478-7610
Fax: (248)478-3159
E-mail: rabbimj@shj.org
URL: http://www.shj.org/AHR.htm
Contact: Rabbi Miriam Jerris, VP
Founded: 1967. **Members:** 15. **Regional Groups:**
1. **Description:** Represents Rabbis who support the
philosophy and programs of secular humanistic Judaism. Provides a forum for communication among
humanistic rabbis. Formulates consistent policies on
important issues pertaining to Jewish life. **Affiliated
With:** Society for Humanistic Judaism. **Conventions/
Meetings:** annual meeting - last weekend of October.

19710 ■ Association pour le Retablissement des Institutions et Oeuvres Israelites en France (ARIS)

645 Madison Ave.
New York, NY 10022
Ph: (212)888-8123
Fax: (212)888-8152
E-mail: aeras@stralem.com
Contact: Hirschel B. Abelson, Pres.
Founded: 1943. **Description:** Seeks to aid Jewish
religious and cultural organizations in France. **Conventions/Meetings:** semiannual meeting.

19711 ■ AZRA/World Union for Progressive Judaism North America

633 3rd Ave.
New York, NY 10017-6778
Ph: (212)452-6530
Fax: (212)452-6585

E-mail: wupj@urj.org
URL: http://www.wupj.org/Congregations/
NorthAmerica.aspUnitedStates
Contact: Rabbi Eric Wittstein, VP

Founded: 1926. **Members:** 1,500,000. **Membership Dues:** regular, $36 (annual) ● student, $5 (annual). **Staff:** 6. **Description:** Congregations of Reform, Liberal, and Progressive Jews in 29 countries. Promotes the cause of Progressive Judaism; establishes new congregations and national constituencies; arranges for the training of rabbis and teachers; coordinates activity between constituencies. Represents progressive Jewry at the United Nations and United Nations Educational, Scientific and Cultural Organization. **Awards:** ARZA Roland Gittelsohn Award for Achievement in Zionism. **Frequency:** annual. **Type:** recognition. **Recipient:** to individuals for outstanding service to the people of Israel ● ARZA Roland Gittelsohn Award for Outstanding Unique Zionist Programs. **Frequency:** annual. **Type:** recognition. **Recipient:** to congregations for outstanding unique Zionist programs. **Councils:** Rabbinic. **Affiliated With:** Union for Reform Judaism. **Formerly:** (2000) Association of Reform Zionists of America. **Publications:** *Connections*, weekly. Newsletter. Contains information on newsmakers and current events, the Reform Movement, and missions to Israel. Alternate Formats: online ● *International Conference Reports*, biennial. **Conventions/Meetings:** annual meeting.

19712 ■ Beth Din of America (BDA)
305 7th Ave., 12th Fl.
New York, NY 10001-6008
Ph: (212)807-9042
Fax: (212)807-9183
E-mail: menahel@bethdin.org
URL: http://www.bethdin.org
Contact: Rabbi Jonathan Reiss, Dir.

Founded: 1960. **Staff:** 15. **Description:** Sponsored by Rabbinical Council of America (see separate entry). Beth Din scholars "are exclusively dedicated to the performance of religious activities, settling religious difficulties and clarifying religious problems." Conducts research in Jewish law when pertinent to its cases. Compiles statistics of marriages, divorces, conversions, and adoptions performed properly from the viewpoint of Jewish law. **Convention/Meeting:** none. **Libraries: Type:** reference. **Holdings:** 500. **Subjects:** religion. **Affiliated With:** Rabbinical Council of America. **Publications:** Newsletter.

19713 ■ B'nai B'rith
2020 K St. NW, 7th Fl.
Washington, DC 20006
Ph: (202)857-6600
Free: (888)388-4224
E-mail: website@bnaibrith.org
URL: http://www.bnaibrith.org
Contact: Joel S. Kaplan, Intl. Pres.

Founded: 1947. **Membership Dues:** regular, $85 (annual) ● junior, woman, $42 (annual) ● couple, $127 (annual) ● life (child of the covenant), $250 ● life (individual), $2,500 ● life (couple), $3,750. **Staff:** 10. **Description:** Composed of B'nai B'rith International, the Board of Deputies of British Jews, and the South African Jewish Board of Deputies. Serves in consultative status at the United Nations. **Committees:** Center for Rights and Public Policy; Family Issues. **Departments:** Communications. **Funds:** Donor Development. **Affiliated With:** B'nai B'rith International; United Nations. **Formerly:** (1998) Coordinating Board of Jewish Organizations. **Publications:** *B'nai B'rith Magazine*, quarterly. **Conventions/Meetings:** periodic meeting.

19714 ■ B'nai B'rith International (BBI)
2020 K St. NW, 7th Fl.
Washington, DC 20006
Ph: (202)857-6600
Free: (888)388-4224
Fax: (202)857-2700

E-mail: website@bnaibrith.org
URL: http://bnaibrith.org/index.cfm
Contact: Joel S. Kaplan, Intl. Pres.

Founded: 1843. **Members:** 250,000. **Membership Dues:** regular, $85 (annual) ● junior, woman, $42 (annual) ● couple, $127 (annual) ● life (couple), $3,750 ● life (child of the covenant), $250 ● life (individual), $2,500. **Staff:** 75. **Budget:** $15,000,000. **Regional Groups:** 75. **Local Groups:** 400. **Description:** Jewish men, women, and youth "of good moral character". Offers religious, cultural, civic, and social programs in 51 countries. Maintains speakers' bureau. Conducts programs on important Jewish issues. **Libraries: Type:** reference. **Holdings:** biographical archives. **Commissions:** Anti-Defamation League of B'nai B'rith (see separate entry); B'nai B'rith Hillel Foundations (see separate entry); B'nai B'rith Youth Organizations; Community Volunteer Services; Continuing Jewish Education; Israel; Senior Services. **Committees:** Center for Rights and Public Policy; Family Issues. **Councils:** International. **Departments:** Communications. **Funds:** Donor Development. **Formerly:** Independent Order of B'nai B'rith; (1974) B'nai B'rith. **Publications:** *ADL Bulletin*, monthly ● *B'nai B'rith Magazine*, quarterly ● *B'nai B'rith Today*, bimonthly. Newsletter ● *Business and Professional Directory*, annual. Contains information about the products and services within the regional community. **Advertising:** accepted. Alternate Formats: online. **Conventions/Meetings:** biennial International Convention - meeting (exhibits).

19715 ■ B'nai B'rith Youth Organization (BBYO)
2020 K St. NW, 7th Fl.
Washington, DC 20006
Ph: (202)857-6633
Fax: (202)857-6568
E-mail: mgrossman@bbyo.org
URL: http://www.bbyo.org
Contact: Mr. Matthew Grossman, Exec. Dir.

Founded: 1924. **Members:** 15,000. **Staff:** 100. **Budget:** $7,000,000. **Regional Groups:** 33. **Local Groups:** 950. **For-Profit. Description:** An independent, transdenominational Jewish youth organization for teenagers in the 9th through 12th grades. Offers leadership training programs and travel and educational programs in Israel; has international affiliates in the United States, Canada, Israel, Great Britain, Bulgaria, Australia and New Zealand. **Committees:** Programming; Regional Liaison. **Divisions:** Aleph Zadik Aleph; B'nai B'rith Girls; Teen Connection (Junior High School). **Publications:** *Monday Morning*, biweekly. Newsletter. Contains administrative information and program ideas for staff members. Lists employment opportunities. **Price:** available to members only. **Circulation:** 100.

19716 ■ Bnos Agudath Israel (BAI)
42 Broadway
New York, NY 10004
Ph: (212)797-9000
Fax: (646)254-1600
Contact: Rabbi Boruch Borchardt, Exec. Dir.

Founded: 1922. **Members:** 6,000. **Staff:** 5. **State Groups:** 24. **Local Groups:** 17. **National Groups:** 71. **Description:** Girls' division of Agudath Israel of America. Educates Orthodox Jewish girls about the traditions of their faith and encourages commitment to the Torah in daily living. Activities include community activism and social services. **Publications:** *Kol Bnos*, quarterly. Magazine. **Price:** free for members. **Advertising:** accepted. **Conventions/Meetings:** annual Leadership Convention, leadership training.

19717 ■ Cantors Assembly (CA)
3080 Broadway, Ste.606
New York, NY 10027
Ph: (212)678-8834
Fax: (212)662-8989
E-mail: caoffice@aol.com
URL: http://www.cantors.org
Contact: Steve Stoehr, Pres.

Founded: 1947. **Members:** 475. **Membership Dues:** individual, $700 (annual). **Staff:** 3. **Regional Groups:**

12. **State Groups:** 48. **Description:** Cantors serving in conservative synagogues in the United States, Canada, Israel, South American and European Countries. **Libraries: Type:** reference. **Holdings:** 15; periodicals. **Awards:** Gregor Shelkan Award for Mentoring and Education. **Frequency:** annual. **Type:** recognition. **Recipient:** to a member for great achievement ● Kavod Award. **Frequency:** annual. **Type:** recognition. **Recipient:** for service to Judaism and the Jewish people and the Cantorate ● Max Wohlberg Award for Composition. **Frequency:** annual. **Type:** recognition. **Recipient:** to a member for great achievement ● Moshe Nathanson Award for Conducting. **Frequency:** annual. **Type:** recognition. **Recipient:** to a member for great achievement ● Samuel Rosenbaum Award for Scholarship and Creativity. **Frequency:** annual. **Type:** scholarship. **Recipient:** to a member for great achievement ● Yuval Award. **Frequency:** annual. **Type:** recognition. **Recipient:** for service to organization. **Computer Services:** database ● online services. **Publications:** *Journal of Synagogue Music*, semiannual. **Price:** $15.00. **Circulation:** 675. Alternate Formats: CD-ROM ● Proceedings, annual. **Conventions/Meetings:** semiannual meeting and convention, with vendors of Judaica books, art, music (exhibits) - usually April or May.

19718 ■ Central Conference of American Rabbis (CCAR)
355 Lexington Ave.
New York, NY 10017
Ph: (212)972-3636
Fax: (212)692-0819
E-mail: info@ccarnet.org
URL: http://www.ccarnet.org
Contact: Steven A. Fox, Exec. VP

Founded: 1889. **Members:** 1,700. **Staff:** 13. **Budget:** $1,400,000. **Regional Groups:** 12. **Multinational. Description:** National organization of Reform rabbis. Offers placement service; compiles statistics. Maintains 38 committees. **Libraries: Type:** not open to the public. **Publications:** *CCAR Journal*, quarterly. **Price:** $29.00/year; $14.50/year for students; $7.50/issue. ISSN: 0149-712X. **Advertising:** accepted ● *Gates of Repentance for Young People*, annual. Catalog. Includes liturgies for home and congregational use, guides to Jewish practice and professional books for rabbis and scholars. Alternate Formats: online ● Yearbook ● Also publishes guides and prayer books for Reform Jewish worship and trade volumes on Jewish practice. **Conventions/Meetings:** annual convention (exhibits) - 2008 Mar. 30-Apr. 2, Cincinnati, OH; 2009 Feb. 24-Mar. 1, Jerusalem, Israel.

19719 ■ Central Rabbinical Congress of the U.S.A. and Canada
c/o True Torah Jews Against Zionism
183 Wilson St.
PMB 162
Brooklyn, NY 11211
Ph: (718)384-6765
Fax: (718)486-5574
URL: http://www.jewsagainstzionism.com/rabbinical-
courts/crc/index.cfm

Founded: 1956. **Members:** 250. **Membership Dues:** regular, $18. **Staff:** 5. **Description:** Hasidic rabbis; yeshivas (schools for Talmudic study). Seeks to further Orthodox Judaism and promote strict observance of Kashruth (dietary laws). Opposes Zionism and the existence of Israel as a Jewish state; condemns what the group sees as the general moral corruption of society. Ordains rabbis; conducts marriage ceremonies; maintains rabbinical court of arbitration. Supervises commercial preparation of kosher foods. Organizes public rallies to comment on issues in Judaism. Maintains close liaison with the Jerusalem Chief Rabbinate (Eida Hachreidis). **Divisions:** Kashruth. **Publications:** *Kashrus Directory* (in English and Yiddish), annual. Articles. **Price:** $7.00/copy. **Circulation:** 10,000 ● *Kashruth Directory*, periodic ● Bulletins. **Conventions/Meetings:** periodic meeting.

19720 ■ Chabad Lubavitch
770 Eastern Pkwy.
Brooklyn, NY 11213

Ph: (718)774-4000
Fax: (718)774-2718
E-mail: info@lubavitch.com
URL: http://www.lubavitch.com
Contact: Rabbi Yehuda Krinsky, Exec. Off.

Members: 1,000,000. **Multinational. Description:** Serves as international movement founded for the purpose of proclaiming Judaism and the observance of the Torah worldwide. (The Torah is the body of law and wisdom contained in Jewish scripture and other sacred literature and oral tradition.) Maintains the Kehot Publications Society, through which the group publishes primarily the literature and philosophy of Hasidic teachings. Operates speakers' bureau; offers children's services. Sponsors Central Organization for Jewish Education, Lubavitch Women's Organization, and Machne Israel. **Libraries: Type:** reference. **Holdings:** 125,000. **Also Known As:** Chabad Movement; Lubavitch Movement. **Publications:** Journal, monthly ● Also publishes bibliographies, books, indices, reference materials, and reprints. **Conventions/Meetings:** periodic conference.

19721 ■ CLAL: National Jewish Center for Learning and Leadership
440 Park Ave. S, 4th Fl.
New York, NY 10016-8012
Ph: (212)779-3300
Fax: (212)779-1009
E-mail: info@clal.org
URL: http://www.clal.org
Contact: Donna M. Rosenthal, Exec. Vice-Chair

Founded: 1974. **Staff:** 20. **Description:** Leadership-training institute, think tank and resource center; convenes interdisciplinary seminars to explore the future of Jewish and American life and to encourage civic and spiritual participation; Rabbinic and professional education links modern experience with Jewish wisdom; publications and materials combine Jewish intellectual traditions with cutting-edge scholarship to help transform North American Jewish life. **Publications:** The Book of Jewish Sacred Practices: CLAL's Guide to Everyday and Holiday Rituals and Blessings, weekly. Alternate Formats: online ● CLAL: An Online Journal of Religion, Public Life and Culture, weekly. Alternate Formats: online ● CLAL Update, periodic. Newsletter ● Embracing Life and Facing Death: A Jewish Guide to Palliative Care, annual ● Sacred Days Calendar, annual ● Also publishes works of CLAL faculty. **Conventions/Meetings:** periodic conference.

19722 ■ Commission on Outreach and Synagogue Community
The Union for Reform Judaism
Dept. of Outreach and Synagogue Community
633 3rd Ave.
New York, NY 10017-6778
Ph: (212)650-4230
Fax: (212)650-4239
E-mail: outreach@urj.org
URL: http://urj.org/outreach
Contact: Kathy Kahn, Dir.

Founded: 1978. **Members:** 100. **Staff:** 20. **Languages:** English, Hebrew. **Description:** Sponsored by the Union of American Hebrew Congregations and the Central Conference of American Rabbis. Provides programs for recent converts to Judaism; those considering conversion, interfaith couples, Jewish parents and grandparents of interfaith couples, children of interfaith couples, and those contemplating interfaith marriage; born Jews wishing to reinforce their Jewish identity. Assists temple leadership in developing policies on conversion and intermarriage. **Awards:** Belin Outreach Award. **Type:** grant. **Affiliated With:** Union for Reform Judaism. **Publications:** A Taste of Judaism Program Guide. Books ● Introduction to Judaism ● Jewish Parents of Intermarried Couples ● Reform Jewish Outreach: The Idea Book ● When Love Meets Tradition. Films ● Catalog ● Also publishes educational materials. **Conventions/Meetings:** periodic conference (exhibits) ● periodic retreat ● periodic workshop.

19723 ■ Conference of Presidents of Major American Jewish Organizations (COPMAJO)
633 3rd Ave., 21st Fl.
New York, NY 10017
Ph: (212)318-6111
Fax: (212)644-4135
E-mail: info@conferenceofpresidents.org
URL: http://www.conferenceofpresidents.org
Contact: Malcolm Hoenlein, Exec. Vice Chm.

Founded: 1954. **Members:** 52. **Staff:** 6. **National Groups:** 53. **Description:** Religious, philanthropic, and civic American Jewish organizations. Provides a central coordinating body and primary forum for deliberations and discussions between members on issues of national and international Jewish concern. Promotes cooperative action between members to ensure the security of Jews throughout the world. Originally formed as an informal group of 12 American Jewish organizations.

19724 ■ Congregation Shema Yisrael
PO Box 804
Southfield, MI 48037
Ph: (248)593-5150
E-mail: shema777@aol.com
URL: http://www.shema.com
Contact: Rabbi Loren Jacobs, Founder

Founded: 1986. **Staff:** 2. **Description:** Fosters the belief and growth of the Messianic Jewish movement that believes Jesus Christ is the Messiah. Promotes the group's cause through literature and Bible studies. **Formerly:** (1998) Shema Yisrael. **Publications:** Shema!, monthly. Newsletter. Covers Biblical holidays and Messianic Judaism. **Price:** free. **Conventions/Meetings:** weekly Bible Study - meeting, includes studies of literature - always Saturday morning.

19725 ■ Emunah Women of America (EWA)
7 Penn Plz.
New York, NY 10001
Ph: (212)564-9045
Free: (800)368-6440
E-mail: info@emunah.org
URL: http://www.emunah.org
Contact: Shirley Singer, Exec. VP

Founded: 1948. **Members:** 40,000. **Membership Dues:** individual, $25 (annual) ● life, $250. **Staff:** 15. **Local Groups:** 50. **Multinational. Description:** A network of chapters throughout North America, with affiliated branches in 33 countries throughout the world. Supports and maintains 225 institutions in Israel where over 20,000 needy children are cared for in kindergartens, day care centers, nurseries, girls' homes, vocational training schools, and community colleges. Sponsors tours to Israel. **Formerly:** (1969) Women's Organization of Hapoel Hamizrachi; (1978) Hapoel Hamizrachi Women's Organization. **Publications:** Dinner Journal, annual ● Emunah Magazine, quarterly. Includes current issues and national news. ● Lest We Forget, quarterly. Report. **Conventions/Meetings:** convention - usually May.

19726 ■ Federation of Jewish Men's Clubs (FJMC)
475 Riverside Dr., Ste.832
New York, NY 10115-0022
Ph: (212)749-8100
Free: (800)288-3562
Fax: (212)316-4271
E-mail: international@fjmc.org
URL: http://fjmc.org
Contact: Rabbi Charles E. Simon, Exec. Dir.

Founded: 1929. **Members:** 35,000. **Regional Groups:** 15. **Local Groups:** 300. **Description:** Serves as federation of men's clubs in Conservative Jewish congregations. Co-sponsors Laymen's Institute for adult study courses; sponsors Hebrew Literacy Campaign, Art of Jewish Living Family Education program, and Holocaust Memorial program. Promotes Ramah camps for children. Awards medal to youth showing greatest aptitude for leadership in Jewish life; presents distinguished service award for service to American Jewry; provides program materials and leadership training to local clubs; promotes social action programs and support for local synagogues. Conducts research. **Formerly:**

(1983) National Federation of Jewish Men's Clubs. **Publications:** Torchlight, semiannual ● Also publishes books on Jewish life. **Conventions/Meetings:** biennial international conference (exhibits).

19727 ■ Habonim Dror North America (HDNA)
114 W 26 St., Ste.1004
New York, NY 10001
Ph: (212)255-1796
Fax: (212)929-3459
E-mail: mazkir@habonimdror.org
URL: http://www.habonimdror.org
Contact: Gil Browdy, Gen. Sec.

Founded: 1925. **Members:** 4,000. **Membership Dues:** Maapil/a, $60 (annual) ● Chaver/a, $100 (annual). **Staff:** 7. **Budget:** $1,000,000. **Regional Groups:** 7. **State Groups:** 7. **Local Groups:** 40. **National Groups:** 7. **Languages:** English, Hebrew. **Description:** Jewish young people, ages ten to 25. "To give Jewish boys and girls spiritual, moral, and physical training toward an appreciation of their heritage." Sponsors summer camps for children ages 10 to 17 emphasizing Jewish heritage, Israeli culture, and a kibbutz lifestyle. Offers specialized education and children's services; maintains speakers' bureau and library. Bestows annual Amy-Adina Schulman Fund. **Computer Services:** database ● mailing lists. **Committees:** Va'adat Chashivah (Advisory); Va'adat Chinuch (Education); Va'adat Hastudentim (Student Activities). **Divisions:** Amelim (10-12 years); Bonim (14-18 years); Chotrim (12-14 years); Maapilim (18-25 years). **Affiliated With:** Labor Zionist Alliance; Na'amat U.S.A. **Also Known As:** Habonim Dror Labor Zionist Youth. **Formed by Merger of:** Dror; Ichud Habonim Labor Zionist Youth. **Formerly:** (1983) Ichud Habonim Dror Labor Zionist Youth. **Publications:** Batnua, quarterly. Newsletter. **Price:** free. **Circulation:** 2,000. Alternate Formats: online. **Conventions/Meetings:** quarterly conference ● semiannual congress.

19728 ■ Hadassah, The Women's Zionist Organization of America (HWZOA)
50 W 58th St.
New York, NY 10019
Ph: (212)303-8061
Free: (800)664-5646
Fax: (212)303-4524
E-mail: webmaster@hadassah.org
URL: http://www.hadassah.org
Contact: June Walker, Pres.

Founded: 1912. **Members:** 306,000. **Membership Dues:** regular, $36 (annual) ● life, $360 ● associate, $200 (annual). **Staff:** 263. **Budget:** $95,444,489. **Regional Groups:** 31. **Local Groups:** 1,308. **Description:** Women's, Zionist and Jewish membership organization. Supports healthcare and medical research facilities, educational and youth institutions and park projects in Israel. Promotes health education, Jewish education and research, volunteerism, social action and advocacy in the U.S. **Awards:** Hannah L. Goldberg Study Group Award. **Frequency:** annual. **Type:** recognition. **Recipient:** to the chapter or group with the most outstanding study group ● Henrietta Szold Award. **Frequency:** annual. **Type:** recognition. **Recipient:** for a person who represents the ideals and beliefs of Henrietta Szold, the founder of Hadassah ● National Leadership Award. **Frequency:** annual. **Type:** recognition. **Recipient:** to one woman in each chapter or group who is active in the group's leadership ● Women of Distinction Award. **Frequency:** annual. **Type:** recognition. **Recipient:** to honor outstanding contributions by Jewish Women in different fields. **Divisions:** American Affairs/Domestic Policy; Associates (Men); Community Education; Israel, Zionist and International Affairs; Jewish Family and Adult Education Programs; Network in Israel; Women's Health; Young Judea; Young Women/Young Leaders; Youth Aliyah. **Programs:** Hadassah Read Write Now! Partners Tutoring. **Projects:** Hadassah Funded. **Affiliated With:** Conference of Presidents of Major American Jewish Organizations; Jewish Council for Public Affairs; National Breast Cancer Coalition; NCSJ: Advocates on Behalf of Jews in Russia, Ukraine, the Baltic States and Eurasia; Religious

Coalition for Reproductive Choice; World Confederation of United Zionists. **Formerly:** (1912) Daughters of Zion. **Publications:** *Hadassah Associates Advisor*, semiannual. Newsletter. Disseminates information about Hadassah of interest to male associate members of Hadasah. **Price:** included in membership dues ● *Hadassah International Medical Update*. Newsletter. Disseminates information about the Hadassah medical organization and its activities in over 30 countries. ● *Hadassah Magazine*, monthly. Includes entire spectrum of important issues to Jewish life. ● *Here and There*, quarterly. Newsletter. Features many facets of America's largest women's and Zionist organization. ● *Kol Hamorot/Voice of the Teachers*, semiannual. Newsletter. Contains teachers share ideas, tips, techniques, humor, and teaching experience. **Conventions/Meetings:** annual Hadassah International Congress, with leaders of Hadassah International groups, scientific committees and more than 150 representatives representing 30 countries - always May ● annual Hadassah National Convention (exhibits) - always summer.

19729 ■ Hashomer Hatzair Zionist Youth Movement (HHZYM)
114 W 26th St., No. 1001
New York, NY 10001-0012
Ph: (212)627-2830
Fax: (212)989-9840
E-mail: mail@hashomerhatzair.org
URL: http://www.hashomerhatzair.org
Contact: Rotem Dayan, Office Mgr.
Founded: 1913. **Members:** 2,800. **Staff:** 8. **Regional Groups:** 3. **State Groups:** 1. **Local Groups:** 1. **Multinational. Description:** Represents young people between the ages of ten and 21 who are interested in Zionist ideas and in furthering their knowledge of Israel and Jewish problems, kibbutz and social justice. Operates city youth centers, 2 summer camps, and 2 winter camps. Conducts research and compiles statistics. Maintains educational programs and speakers' bureau. **Computer Services:** database ● mailing lists. **Committees:** Cultural; Educational; Political. **Formed by Merger of:** (1927) Hashomer; (1927) Tzeirai Etr Tzion. **Formerly:** Hashomer Hatzair Zionist Youth Organization; (1992) Hashomer Hatzair Socialist Zionist Youth Movement. **Publications:** *Young Guard*, monthly ● Articles ● Also publishes educational materials. **Conventions/Meetings:** annual meeting ● quarterly meeting.

19730 ■ Hebrew Free Burial Association (HFBA)
224 W 35th St., Rm. 300
New York, NY 10001
Ph: (212)239-1662
Fax: (212)239-1981
E-mail: info@hebrewfreeburial.org
URL: http://www.hebrewfreeburial.org
Contact: Amy Koplow, Exec. Dir.
Founded: 1887. **Staff:** 7. **Budget:** $900,000. **Languages:** English, Hebrew, Russian, Yiddish. **Description:** Provides funeral and burial for people of the Jewish faith who have no family or funds. Supported by contributions. **Convention/Meeting:** none. **Libraries:** Type: reference. **Holdings:** 5; archival material. **Subjects:** burial records. **Computer Services:** database. **Boards:** Directors. **Also Known As:** (2001) Chevra Agudath Achim Chesed Shel Emeth. **Publications:** *Chesed*, 3/year. Newsletter. **Price:** free. **Circulation:** 20,000.

19731 ■ Hillel: The Foundation for Jewish Campus Life
c/o Charles and Lynn Schusterman International
  Center
Arthur and Rochelle Belfer Bldg.
800 8th St. NW
Washington, DC 20001-3724
Ph: (202)449-6500
Fax: (202)449-6461
E-mail: info@hillel.org
URL: http://www.hillel.org
Contact: Avraham Infeld, Pres.
Founded: 1923. **Staff:** 1,000. **Regional Groups:** 10. **Local Groups:** 500. **Description:** Provides cultural,

social, educational, religious enrichment to Jewish college students. Develops campus leadership skills, implements social action programs, and encourages students to explore their Jewish heritage. **Awards:** Elie Wiesel Award for Jewish Arts and Culture. **Type:** recognition ● William Haber Award for Quality Programming for the Jewish Campus Community. **Frequency:** annual. **Type:** recognition. **Publications:** *Hillel Annual Report*, annual ● *Hillel Today*, semiannual. Newsletter. **Conventions/Meetings:** annual Charles Schusterman Leaders Assembly - conference - always August ● periodic Lay Leadership Conference ● annual Professional Staff Conference - always December ● annual Spitzer Forum on Public Policy - conference, student activism - always winter.

19732 ■ Institute for Jewish Medical Ethics
c/o Lisa Kampner Hebrew Academy
645 14th Ave.
San Francisco, CA 94118
Ph: (415)752-7333 (415)752-1777
Fax: (415)752-5851
E-mail: info@hebrewacademy.com
URL: http://www.hebrewacademy.com
Contact: Rabbi Pinchas Lipner, Founder/Dean
Founded: 1982. **Description:** Seeks to identify underlying principles of Jewish law (Halachah) in Biblical, Talmudic, and other works of Jewish scholarship as they relate to medicine. **Conventions/Meetings:** annual conference.

19733 ■ International Federation of Rabbis (IFR)
5600 Wisconsin Ave., No. 1107
Chevy Chase, MD 20815
E-mail: info@intfedrabbis.org
URL: http://www.intfedrabbis.org
Contact: Rabbi Suzanne H. Carter, Pres.
Membership Dues: general, $150 (annual). **Multinational. Description:** Serves as the professional organization of rabbis united by a commitment to Jewish tradition and to facilitate the Jewish spiritual growth and life cycle needs of all. Provides support for members in their professional endeavors and offers continuing education. Encourages professional relationships with rabbis and other rabbinic organizations. Provides a forum for information exchange and interaction among members. **Telecommunication Services:** electronic mail, rebzev@bellsouth.net. **Publications:** Newsletter. **Price:** included in membership dues.

19734 ■ Iranian B'nei Torah Movement (IBTOM)
PO Box 351476
Los Angeles, CA 90035
Ph: (310)652-2115
Fax: (310)652-1901
Contact: Rabbi Yoseph Zargari, Pres.
Founded: 1979. **Budget:** $25,000. **Description:** Ex-Rabbinical students seeking to meet the religious, charitable, and educational needs of Iranian Jews in the United States. Works to enrich their knowledge of Judaism and strengthen feelings of Jewish identity. Sponsors B'nei Torah Sedaka Fund to assist needy Jews, mostly in Israel. **Libraries:** Type: reference. **Subjects:** Farsi publications and materials on Jews, issues affecting Iranian Jews. **Publications:** *Hebrew Persian Calendar*, annual. **Advertising:** accepted ● *Nashriyeh B'nei Torah*, bimonthly. **Price:** free. **Circulation:** 6,000 ● *Nashryehe B'nei Torah* (in Persian), bimonthly. Journal ● Also publishes translations of religious texts and small Jewish prayer books. **Conventions/Meetings:** semiannual conference.

19735 ■ Israel Aliyah Center (IAC)
633 3rd Ave., 21st Fl.
New York, NY 10017-6706
Ph: (212)339-6063
Free: (866)725-4924
Fax: (212)318-6145
E-mail: aliyahny@jazo.org.il
URL: http://www.aliyah.org
Contact: Boaz Herman, Exec. Dir.
Languages: English, Hebrew. **Description:** Seeks to recruit Jewish families and individuals for permanent

settlement in Israel. Promotes the concept of Aliyah (emigration to Israel) throughout the U.S. and Canada. Provides printed material, personal guidance, and other assistance to those contemplating settlement in Israel.

19736 ■ Jewish Chautauqua Society (JCS)
633 3rd Ave.
New York, NY 10017
Ph: (212)650-4100
Free: (800)765-6200
Fax: (212)650-4189
E-mail: jcs@uahc.org
URL: http://www.nftb.org/jcs.html
Contact: Charles Niederman, Chancellor
Founded: 1893. **Members:** 20,000. **Staff:** 10. **Regional Groups:** 13. **Description:** Sponsored by the National Federation of Temple Brotherhoods (see separate entry) comprising 700 men's clubs with 20,000 members in the United States, Canada, and abroad. Conducts a six-phase educational program for better understanding and appreciation of Jews and Judaism by people of all faiths; assigns rabbis to lecture at colleges, private and parochial schools, and seminars; endows resident lectureships on Judaism for college credit; donates Jewish reference books to college libraries. Sponsors institutes for Christian clergy. **Publications:** *Brotherhood Magazine*, 3/year. **Price:** included in membership dues. **Circulation:** 60,000. **Advertising:** accepted ● Annual Report, annual. **Conventions/Meetings:** annual meeting.

19737 ■ Jewish Free Loan Association (JFLA)
6505 Wilshire Blvd., Ste.715
Los Angeles, CA 90048
Ph: (323)761-8830
Fax: (323)761-8841
E-mail: info@jfla.com
URL: http://www.jfla.org
Contact: Mark M. Meltzer, Exec. Dir./CEO
Founded: 1904. **Staff:** 11. **Languages:** English, Farsi, Hebrew, Russian, Spanish. **Description:** Makes loans to low-income individuals and families for emergency and/or constructive purposes, if they are unable to obtain a loan from any other source. **Formed by Merger of:** Hebrew Free Loan; Jewish Loan Fund. **Conventions/Meetings:** annual board meeting.

19738 ■ Jewish Lawyer Guild (JLG)
c/o Bruce N. Lederman, Pres.
Cozen O'Connor
909 3rd Ave., 18th Fl.
New York, NY 10022
Ph: (212)453-3819
E-mail: info@jewishlawyersguild.org
URL: http://www.jewishlawyersguild.org
Contact: Bruce N. Lederman, Pres.
Founded: 1962. **Members:** 750. **Description:** Works to foster among members of the legal profession an interest in Jewish traditions; encourage information exchange; and raise member's esteem for one another. Guild activities include lectures and programs throughout the year that are of interest to the legal and Jewish communities, including an annual program in remembrance of the Holocaust. **Conventions/Meetings:** lecture, by attorneys, judges, scholars, and laypersons on special topics of legal and ethical interest ● monthly meeting.

19739 ■ Jewish National Fund (JNF)
42 E 69th St.
New York, NY 10021
Ph: (212)879-9300
Free: (888)JNF-0099
Fax: (212)570-1673
E-mail: communications@jnf.org
URL: http://www.jnf.org
Contact: Russell F. Robinson, CEO
Founded: 1901. **Staff:** 141. **Regional Groups:** 20. **Description:** Serves as caretaker of the land of Israel, on behalf of its owners Jewish people everywhere. Over the past century, JNF has planted over 240 million trees, built over 180 reservoirs and dams,

developed over 250,000 acres of land, created more than 1,000 parks, provided the infrastructure for 1,000 communities and educated students around the world about Israel and the environment. **Awards:** Shalom Peace Award. **Frequency:** periodic. **Type:** recognition. **Recipient:** to individuals for unprecedented contributions to Israel and peace ● Tree of Life Award. **Frequency:** periodic. **Type:** recognition. **Recipient:** to leaders for accomplishments in industry, government and education. **Absorbed:** (1980) Foundation for the Jewish National Fund. **Also Known As:** Keren Kayemeth Leisrael. **Publications:** B'Yachad, 3/year. Newsletter. **Advertising:** accepted. Alternate Formats: online. **Conventions/Meetings:** dinner, regional, with awards presentations ● annual Leadership Conference - fall.

19740 ■ Jewish Reconstructionist Federation (JRF)
101 Greenwood Ave.
Jenkintown, PA 19046
Ph: (215)885-5601
Fax: (215)885-5603
E-mail: info@jrf.org
URL: http://www.jrf.org
Contact: Mr. Carl Sheingold, Exec. VP
Founded: 1954. **Members:** 50,000. **Budget:** $1,400,000. **National Groups:** 103. **Description:** Federation of synagogues and fellowships committed to the philosophy and program of the Jewish Reconstructionist Movement. Maintains placement service and consulting services. Organize services to affiliates. **Awards: Type:** recognition. **Computer Services:** database. **Commissions:** Education; Inclusion/Disabilities; Israel; Placement; Role of Rabbi. **Committees:** Budget; Strategic Planning. **Absorbed:** (1993) Jewish Reconstructionist Foundation. **Formerly:** Reconstructionist Fellowship of Congregations; (1973) Federation of Reconstructionist Congregations and Fellowships; (1980) Reconstructionist Federation of Congregations and Fellowships; (1997) Federation Reconstructionist Congregations and Havurot. **Publications:** Reconstructionism Today, quarterly. Magazine. **Price:** $12.00/year. **Circulation:** 10,000 ● The Reconstructionist, semiannual. Books. **Circulation:** 1,000 ● Directory, annual ● Pamphlets, annual ● Pamphlets ● Also publishes study guides. **Conventions/Meetings:** biennial convention, about Jewish books and artists (exhibits) - always November.

19741 ■ Jewish Restitution Successor Organization (JRSO)
15 E 26th St., Rm. 906
New York, NY 10010
Ph: (212)696-4944 (646)536-9100
Free: (800)697-6064
Fax: (212)679-2126
E-mail: info@claimscon.org
URL: http://www.claimscon.org
Contact: Saul Kagan, Exec. Sec.
Founded: 1947. **Description:** Discovers, claims, receives, and assists in the recovery of Jewish heirless or unclaimed property; to use or provide for the use of such assets in relief, rehabilitation, and resettlement of surviving victims of Nazi persecution.

19742 ■ Jewish Women International (JWI)
2000 M St. NW, Ste.720
Washington, DC 20036
Ph: (202)857-1300
Free: (800)343-2823
Fax: (202)857-1380
E-mail: lweinstein@jwi.org
URL: http://www.jewishwomen.org
Contact: Loribeth Weinstein, Exec. Dir.
Founded: 1897. **Members:** 75,000. **Membership Dues:** supporting, $36 (annual) ● presidential, $500 (annual). **Staff:** 30. **Local Groups:** 600. **Description:** Strengthens the lives of women, children, and families through education, advocacy and action. Focuses on family violence and the emotional health of children and serves as an agent for change. Community activities include domestic violence awareness, self-esteem projects, interfaith forums, holocaust awareness, hospital humor carts, and other

youth projects. Founded and maintains a residential treatment center for emotionally disturbed children in Jerusalem, Israel. **Awards:** Jewish Women International Perlman Award for Human Advancement. **Frequency:** biennial. **Type:** recognition. **Recipient:** for an individual or group's outstanding contributions to fostering the emotional well-being of children. **Programs:** The Women's Economic Security Fund. **Projects:** The Mother's Day Flower; The Residential Treatment Center in Israel. **Task Forces:** Domestic Abuse Awareness for Women in Need. **Formerly:** (1957) Women's Supreme Council; (1995) B'nai B'rith Women. **Publications:** Embracing Justice: A Resource Guide for Rabbis on Domestic Abuse, periodic. Booklet. Includes sample sermons and text studies. **Price:** $30.00/copy ● Healing and Wholeness: A Resource Guide on Domestic Abuse in the Jewish Community, periodic. Booklet. Contains in depth view of abuse in the Jewish community. **Price:** $21.00/copy ● Jewish Woman, quarterly. Magazine. Includes book reviews and features. **Price:** $18.00/year. ISSN: 0043-759X. **Circulation:** 75,000. **Advertising:** accepted. **Conventions/Meetings:** biennial international conference.

19743 ■ Jews for Morality (JFM)
Gravesend Sta.
PO Box 262
Brooklyn, NY 11223
URL: http://www.jewsformorality.org
Founded: 1979. **Members:** 3,000. **Staff:** 3. **Description:** Aims to preserve "traditional family values, morality, and decency" in America. Opposes pornography, homosexuality, and "indecency in the media.". **Affiliated With:** Jewish Anti-Abortion League. **Conventions/Meetings:** periodic conference.

19744 ■ Kadima
155 5th Ave.
New York, NY 10010-6802
Ph: (212)533-7800
Fax: (212)353-9439
E-mail: youth@uscj.org
URL: http://www.usy.org
Contact: Jules Gutin, Dir.
Founded: 1964. **Members:** 10,000. **Staff:** 350. **Regional Groups:** 17. **Local Groups:** 350. **Description:** Jewish boys and girls in grades five through eight who are members of conservative synagogues. Sponsored by the Department of Youth Activities of the United Synagogue of Conservative Judaism (see separate entry). Aims to involve young people in informal, cultural, educational, recreational, religious, and social activities through their synagogues. Seeks to develop among members a sense of Jewish identity and responsibility to the community. Organizes dances, trips, weekend events, and holiday observances. Sponsors charitable programs. Maintains database, placement service, and library of program aids. **Telecommunication Services:** electronic mail, kadima@uscj.org. **Publications:** Kol Kadima, quarterly. Magazine ● Also publishes numerous materials on education, Jewish holidays, adviser's aid, games, and other activities. **Conventions/Meetings:** seminar ● workshop.

19745 ■ Kolel Chibas Jerusalem (KCJ)
4802-A 12th Ave.
Brooklyn, NY 11219
Ph: (718)633-7112
Free: (866)787-4520
Fax: (718)633-5783
E-mail: pushka@chibasjerusalem.com
URL: http://www.chibasjerusalem.com/id4.htm
Contact: Rabbi Berish Rubin, Exec. Dir.
Founded: 1875. **Staff:** 8. **Budget:** $2,000,000. **State Groups:** 12. **Local Groups:** 3. **Description:** Collects contributions and fixed payments for religious services and memorial prayers; provides charity for over 2 thousand needy families and individuals in Israel. Maintains three free dental clinics in Israel. **Formerly:** (1990) Society of the Devotees of Jerusalem.

19746 ■ League for Yiddish, Inc. (LYI)
45 E 33rd St., No. 203
New York, NY 10016
Ph: (212)889-0380
E-mail: info@leagueforyiddish.org
URL: http://leagueforyiddish.org
Contact: Dr. Sheva Zucker, Exec. Dir.
Founded: 1979. **Members:** 1,000. **Membership Dues:** life, $5,000 ● sustaining, $2,000 (annual) ● patron, $1,000 (annual) ● benefactor, $750 (annual) ● sponsor, $500 (annual) ● donor, $250 (annual) ● friend, $100 (annual) ● institution, $50 (annual) ● individual, $36 (annual) ● student, $18 (annual). **Staff:** 4. **Languages:** English, Yiddish. **Description:** Jewish cultural organization promoting the use of Yiddish as a living language. Sponsors speakers' bureau and research programs; organizes Yiddish language seminars. Maintains Yiddish Language Resource Center, and an extensive collection of Yiddish books for sale. **Libraries: Type:** reference. **Holdings:** 1,500. **Boards:** Editorial; Executive. **Formerly:** (1977) Freeland League. **Publications:** Afn Shvel (in Yiddish), quarterly. Magazine. Covers Yiddish linguistic and literary topics. Contains columns on correct usage and sociolinguistics of Yiddish. **Price:** included in membership dues. ISSN: 0030-7718. **Circulation:** 1,350. Also Cited As: OIFN, SHVEL, OYFN, SHVEL ● English-Yiddish Dictionary of Academic Terminology ● Laytish Mame-Loshn ● Pregnancy, Childbirth, and Early Childhood: An English-Yiddish Dictionary ● Vidervuks: A New Generation of Yiddish Writers ● Yiddish II: an Intermediate and Advanced Textbook ● Videos. **Conventions/Meetings:** semiannual executive committee meeting - January and November.

19747 ■ Lubavitch Youth Organization (LYO)
770 Eastern Pkwy.
Brooklyn, NY 11213
Ph: (718)953-1000
Fax: (718)771-6315
E-mail: lyo770@verizon.net
URL: http://www.saykaddish.com
Contact: Rabbi Shlomo Friedman, Contact
Founded: 1955. **Members:** 100,000. **Staff:** 100. **Description:** Jewish individuals and organizations dedicated to strengthening Jewish identity and commitment. Sponsors youth activities, educational programs, campus activities, chabad houses (retreat homes where Jews can go to rekindle their faith), and mitzvah mobiles (religious caravans meant to provide spiritual uplifting). Operates speakers' bureau and placement service; compiles statistics. **Libraries: Type:** reference. **Holdings:** 25,000. **Awards: Type:** recognition. **Publications:** Wellsprings, bimonthly. Magazine. Includes calendar of events; devoted to the expression of the inner dimension of Torah and the Jewish soul. **Price:** $15.00/year. ISSN: 0887-011X. **Circulation:** 20,000. **Advertising:** accepted. **Conventions/Meetings:** annual convention and conference - always Brooklyn, NY.

19748 ■ Masada/Maccabi Israel Summer Programs
520 8th Ave.
New York, NY 10018
Ph: (212)532-4949
Free: (800)732-1266
Fax: (212)481-4174
E-mail: info@jccmaccabiisrael.org
URL: http://www.jccmaccabix.org
Contact: Naomi Marks, Dir.
Founded: 1961. **Members:** 6,000. **Languages:** English, Hebrew. **Description:** American Jews ages 13-30. Seeks to strengthen members' Jewish identity. **Affiliated With:** Zionist Organization of America. **Publications:** Masada/Maccabi. Newsletter. **Conventions/Meetings:** annual meeting.

19749 ■ MERCAZ USA
155 5th Ave.
New York, NY 10010
Ph: (212)533-7800
Fax: (212)533-2601

E-mail: info@mercazusa.org
URL: http://www.mercazusa.org
Contact: Rabbi Vernon H. Kurtz, Pres.
Membership Dues: family, $54 (annual) ● individual, $36 (annual) ● student, $12 (annual) ● sponsor, $100 (annual) ● donor, $250 (annual) ● benefactor, $500 (annual). **Multinational. Description:** Represents the Conservative Judaism within the World Zionist Organization, the Jewish Agency for Israel, the American Zionist Movement and the Jewish National Fund. Works to increase the impact and influence of Conservative/Masorti Judaism on Israeli society and acts as a force for supporting religious pluralism and securing religious stream funding for the Masorti Movement programs in Israel and throughout the world. **Publications:** *Celebrating the Zionist Dream.* Book. Contains essays commemorating the 100th anniversary of the Zionist Movement. **Price:** included in membership dues ● Newsletter, quarterly. **Price:** free for members. Alternate Formats: online.

19750 ■ Na'amat U.S.A.
350 5th Ave., Ste.4700
New York, NY 10118-4700
Ph: (212)563-5222
Fax: (212)563-5710
E-mail: naamat@naamat.org
URL: http://www.naamat.org
Contact: Alice Howard, Natl. Pres.
Founded: 1925. **Members:** 30,000. **Membership Dues:** individual, $25 (annual) ● life, $250. **Staff:** 25. **Regional Groups:** 4. **State Groups:** 31. **Local Groups:** 500. **National Groups:** 16. **Description:** Cooperates with Na'amat Movement of Working Women and Volunteers to enhance the status of women, children and families in Israel and the United States as a part of a worldwide progressive Jewish women's organization and the Labor Zionist Movement. Through its American Affairs Department, it informs its members on issues of concern and advocates for legislation and social action. **Libraries: Type:** reference. **Holdings:** biographical archives. **Awards:** Golda Meir Human Relations Award. **Frequency:** biennial. **Type:** recognition. **Committees:** American - Zionist Affairs; Audio-Visual Aids; Capital Funds; Israel Tours; Program and Education; Program Fund Raising; Public Relations; Special Gifts. **Task Forces:** Washington. **Formerly:** (1982) Pioneer Women, The Women's Labor Zionist Organization of America; (1985) Pioneer Women/Na'amat, the Women's Labor Zionist Organization of America. **Publications:** *Na'amat Woman* (in English, Hebrew, and Yiddish), quarterly. Magazine. Includes book reviews. **Price:** included in membership dues; $10.00 /year for nonmembers. ISSN: 0888-191X. **Circulation:** 30,000. **Advertising:** accepted ● Also publishes brochures. **Conventions/Meetings:** triennial convention (exhibits).

19751 ■ National Association of Temple Administrators (NATA)
PO Box 936
Ridgefield, WA 98642
Ph: (360)887-0464
Free: (800)966-NATA
Fax: (866)767-3791
E-mail: nataoffice@natanet.org
URL: http://www.rj.org/nata
Contact: Loree Resnik FTA, Pres.
Founded: 1941. **Members:** 450. **Membership Dues:** regular, $255-$1,500 (annual). **Budget:** $150,000. **Regional Groups:** 2. **Local Groups:** 6. **Description:** Full-time administrators of Jewish synagogues affiliated with the Union of American Hebrew Congregations (see separate entry). Conducts educational programs; has established code of standards and ethics. Offers congregational survey service and compiles synagogue research reports and salary reports. Conducts placement service and maintains speakers' bureau. **Libraries: Type:** reference. **Holdings:** archival material. **Awards:** Temple Administration. **Frequency:** annual. **Type:** fellowship. **Recipient:** for Temple Administrators who have met certain standards and complete an examination. **Committees:** Cemeteries; Congregation Surveys; Placement; Research. **Formerly:** (1959) National Association of

Temple Secretaries. **Publications:** Journal, semiannual. **Circulation:** 1,000. **Conventions/Meetings:** annual Convention/Institute of Professional Enrichment - conference and workshop (exhibits).

19752 ■ National Association of Temple Educators (NATE)
633 Third Ave., 7th Fl.
New York, NY 10017-6778
Ph: (212)452-6510
Fax: (212)452-6512
E-mail: nateoff@aol.com
URL: http://rj.org/nate
Contact: Rabbi Stanley T. Schickler RJE, Exec. Dir.
Founded: 1955. **Members:** 950. **Staff:** 2. **Budget:** $350,000. **Languages:** English, Hebrew. **Multinational. Description:** Directors of education in Reform Jewish religious schools, principals, heads of departments, supervisors, educational consultants, students, and authors. Purposes are to: assist in the growth and development of Jewish religious education consistent with the aims of Reform Judaism; stimulate communal interest in Jewish religious education; represent and encourage the profession of temple educator. Conducts surveys on personnel practices, confirmation practices, religious school organization and administration, curricular practices, and other aspects of religious education. Sponsors institutes for principals and educational directors; maintains placement service. **Awards:** Camping Award. **Frequency:** annual. **Type:** recognition ● Curriculum Award. **Frequency:** annual. **Type:** recognition ● Reform Jewish Educator Award. **Frequency:** annual. **Type:** recognition. **Committees:** Consultation and Accreditation; Continuing Education; Curriculum Awards; Educational Research; Family Education; Language Planning; Placement. **Publications:** *NATE News*, quarterly. Newsletter. Alternate Formats: online ● Membership Directory, annual ● Proceedings, annual. **Conventions/Meetings:** annual conference, includes pre-conference Kallah (exhibits).

19753 ■ National Conference of Synagogue Youth (NCSY)
11 Broadway
New York, NY 10004
Ph: (212)613-8233
Fax: (212)613-0633
E-mail: ncsy@ou.org
URL: http://www.ncsy.org
Contact: Rabbi Jack Abramowitz, Dir. of Programs
Founded: 1954. **Members:** 25,000. **Budget:** $10,000,000. **Regional Groups:** 15. **Local Groups:** 465. **Multinational. Description:** Teenage synagogue youth movement of the Union of Orthodox Jewish Congregations of America (see separate entry). Aims to strengthen and deepen the loyalty of Jewish youth to Torah and Mitzvoth, to the Jewish people, and to the orthodox synagogue. Sponsors domestic and overseas summer programs. Operates numerous divisions and services including: Shabbaton weekend retreats, free Teen Torah Centres; public school culture clubs, Drop-In Zones, Latte and Learning programs. **Conventions/Meetings:** annual Yarchei Kallah - convention - late December.

19754 ■ National Council of Jewish Women (NCJW)
53 W 23rd St., 6th Fl.
New York, NY 10010-4204
Ph: (212)645-4048
Free: (800)829-6259
Fax: (212)645-7466
E-mail: action@ncjw.org
URL: http://www.ncjw.org
Contact: Phyllis Snyder, Pres.
Founded: 1893. **Members:** 90,000. **Membership Dues:** regular, $50 (annual) ● life, $350. **State Groups:** 39. **Local Groups:** 200. **Multinational. Description:** Sponsors programs of education, social action, and community service for women, children, and families. Aims to improve the quality of life for individuals of all ages, races, religions, and socioeconomic levels. Advocates measures affecting social welfare, constitutional rights, civil liberties, and equal-

ity for women. Maintains the Research Institute for Innovation in Education at Hebrew University, Jerusalem, Israel. Established Center for the Child in New York to conduct research on issues and actions necessary to shape policies affecting children. Develops community service projects and training materials. **Affiliated With:** Jewish Council for Public Affairs. **Publications:** *NCJW Journal*, 3/year. Magazine. **Circulation:** 50,000 ● Brochures ● Catalog ● Handbooks ● Manuals ● Monographs. **Conventions/Meetings:** triennial Washington Institute - convention (exhibits).

19755 ■ National Council of Young Israel (NCYI)
111 John St., Ste.450
New York, NY 10038
Ph: (212)929-1525
Free: (800)617-NCYI
Fax: (212)727-9526
E-mail: ncyi@youngisrael.org
URL: http://www.youngisrael.org
Contact: Rabbi Pesach Lerner, Exec. VP
Founded: 1912. **Members:** 20,000. **Staff:** 18. **Budget:** $1,200,000. **Regional Groups:** 2. **Description:** Families of traditional Jewish faith in the U.S., Canada, and Israel. Seeks "to perpetuate traditional Judaism; instill a love for Americanism and the principles of democracy; bring Jewish youth back to the synagogue; educate the youth and adults in the heritage and culture of the Jewish people". Benevolent Association in the New York City area; conducts programs nationwide for adults and youths. Sponsors Institute for Jewish Studies, which provides specialized programs in Jewish education. The Institute maintains the Torah Tape Library of cassette tapes on Jewish philosophy, law, the Talmud, and related topics. Sponsors children's services, charitable program, and competitions. Maintains speakers' bureau; compiles statistics. **Awards: Type:** recognition. **Committees:** Admissions; Armed Forces; Education; Employment Bureau; Eretz Israel; Intercollegiate; Public Affairs; Synagogue Standards; Women's League; Youth. **Publications:** *Young Israel Viewpoint*, quarterly. Journal. Includes council news, special features, and Jewish holiday issues. **Price:** included in membership dues; $25.00 /year for nonmembers. ISSN: 0044-0809. **Circulation:** 32,000. **Advertising:** accepted. **Conventions/Meetings:** annual international conference.

19756 ■ National Havurah Committee (NHC)
7135 Germantown Ave., 2nd Fl.
Philadelphia, PA 19119-1842
Ph: (215)248-1335
Fax: (215)248-9760
E-mail: institute@havurah.org
URL: http://www.havurah.org
Contact: Sylvia Woodman, Sec.
Founded: 1979. **Members:** 1,200. **Membership Dues:** individual, $40 (annual) ● family, $80 (annual). **Staff:** 1. **National Groups:** 250. **Languages:** English, Hebrew. **Description:** Aims to provide assistance to individuals who wish to form or have formed a havurah. (A havurah is a small group that comes together to renew its commitment to Judaism. Havurah is Hebrew for fellowship.) Conducts one-week summer study institute with workshops and regional retreats throughout the year. **Formerly:** (1984) National Havurah Coordinating Committee. **Publications:** *Havurah Newsletter*, semiannual. **Advertising:** accepted. Alternate Formats: online ● Directory. Alternate Formats: online. **Conventions/Meetings:** annual Can/Am Retreat, weekend retreat for havurah community ● annual National Havurah Summer Institute - retreat.

19757 ■ North American Federation of Temple Brotherhoods (NFTB)
633 3rd Ave.
New York, NY 10017
Ph: (212)650-4100
Free: (800)765-6200
Fax: (212)650-4189

E-mail: contact@nftb.org
URL: http://www.nftb.org
Contact: Aaron G. Bloom, Pres.
Founded: 1923. **Members:** 30,000. **Staff:** 10. **Regional Groups:** 13. **Local Groups:** 300. **Description:** Aims to enhance the world through the ideal of brotherhood. Involved in education, social action, youth activities, and other programs that contribute to temple and community life. Sponsors Jewish Chautauqua Society (see separate entry), which sponsors accredited college courses and one-day lectures on Judaic topics, provides book grants to educational institutions, produces educational videotapes on interfaith topics, and sponsors interfaith institutes. **Affiliated With:** Jewish Chautauqua Society; Union for Reform Judaism. **Formerly:** (2001) National Federation of Temple Brotherhoods. **Publications:** *ACHIM Magazine*, semiannual. **Circulation:** 30,000. **Advertising:** accepted ● *JCS*, semiannual. Newsletter ● *Presidents' News*, semiannual. Newsletter. **Conventions/Meetings:** biennial meeting.

19758 ■ OK Kosher Certification
391 Troy Ave.
Brooklyn, NY 11213
Ph: (718)756-7500
Fax: (718)756-7503
E-mail: info@ok.org
URL: http://www.ok.org
Contact: Rabbi Don Yoel Levy, Pres.
Founded: 1938. **Languages:** English, French, Hebrew, Italian, Spanish. **Multinational. Description:** International professional association of rabbis who inspect food producing plants and certify food items as kosher. **Telecommunication Services:** electronic mail, ny@ok.org. **Committees:** Advancement of Torah. **Divisions:** O.K. Laboratories. **Formerly:** (1998) Committee for the Furtherance of Torah Observance; (2003) OK Labs - Kosher Certification. **Publications:** *Kosher Spirit*, quarterly. Magazine. **Price:** $2.95/copy. ISSN: 1054-7037. **Circulation:** 91,000. **Advertising:** accepted.

19759 ■ Orthodox Union - Union of Orthodox Jewish Congregations of America (OU)
11 Broadway
New York, NY 10004
Ph: (212)563-4000
Fax: (212)564-9058
E-mail: info@ou.org
URL: http://www.ou.org
Contact: Rabbi Dr. Tzvi Hersh Weinreb, Exec. VP
Founded: 1898. **Members:** 20,850. **Membership Dues:** regular, $54 ● family, $100 ● VIP, $500 ● union associate, $1,000 ● life, $1,800 ● associate, $36. **Staff:** 250. **Regional Groups:** 15. **Description:** Federation of Orthodox Jewish synagogues representing 600,000 members. "For the perpetuation and advancement of traditional Judaism." Serves as national central agency to provide guidance to congregations, youth groups, and individuals; conducts national authoritative Kosher Certification Service, certifying foods through all phases of production as "Kosher" in compliance with Orthodox Jewish dietary laws. Maintains speakers' bureau; offers counseling and assistance in establishing new communities and synagogues; provides children's services; conducts retreats and lecture services. Compiles statistics. Conducts programs for developmentally disabled and deaf individuals. **Awards: Type:** recognition. **Computer Services:** database, synagogue. **Telecommunication Services:** electronic mail, execthw@ou.org ● 24-hour hotline, Kashruth, (212)564-9645. **Committees:** Achdus; Communal Relations; Development; Family Life; Funeral Standards; Institute for Public Affairs; Israel/Aliyah; Israel Center; Kashruth; Limud Torah (Torah study); National Conference of Synagogue Youth (see separate entry); Our Way for the Deaf; Yachad for the Developmentally Disabled; Youth. **Departments:** Kashruth; Youth/NCSY. **Projects:** Mitzvah. **Publications:** *Behind the Union Symbol*, quarterly. Newsletter ● *Jewish Action Magazine*, quarterly ● *Keeping Posted*, quarterly. Magazine ● *Leadership Briefing*, quarterly. Newsletter ● *Luach Limud Torah Diary*, monthly ● *OU Guide to Kosher for Passover Foods*,

annual. Directory ● *Synagogue Trends*, quarterly. Newsletter ● Also publishes catalog of Judaica. **Conventions/Meetings:** biennial meeting (exhibits) - usually November/December.

19760 ■ Ozar Hatorah (OH)
625 Broadway, 11th Fl.
New York, NY 10012
Ph: (212)253-7245
Fax: (212)473-4773
Contact: Henry Shalom, Pres.
Founded: 1944. **Staff:** 500. **Description:** To establish and maintain schools for Jewish youth in Europe and North Africa, providing a combined program of religious and secular education. Operates institutions in Morocco and France, including pre-elementary schools, high schools, boarding schools, teacher training institutes, and vocational schools. Also sponsors adult seminars, evening courses, and summer camps. Operates regional offices in France and Morocco and sponsoring committees in countries outside the United States. In addition, Ozar Hatorah raises funds from individual membership contributions and from allocations of national Jewish organizations or communities for expansion of facilities and development of new schools. **Also Known As:** Society for Jewish Youth Education in the Middle East and North Africa. **Publications:** *Ozar Hatorah*, semiannual. Newsletter.

19761 ■ Rabbinical Alliance of America (RAA)
866 Eastern Pkwy., Apt. 3-E
Brooklyn, NY 11213
Ph: (718)493-5711
Fax: (718)493-5711
Contact: Rabbi Abraham B. Hecht, Pres.
Founded: 1942. **Members:** 500. **Membership Dues:** $50 (annual). **Staff:** 3. **Languages:** English, Hebrew. **Description:** Orthodox rabbis who serve in pulpits and as principals of Jewish day schools and Hebrew schools throughout the world. Supervises Hebrew Schools Program for Adult Studies. Provides placement service aid for indigent Torah scholars; contributes to Jewish charitable causes. Maintains the Rabbinical Court which handles orthodox Jewish divorces, court of arbitration, Dinei Torahs, and family and marriage counselling. **Libraries: Type:** open to the public. **Committees:** Education; Israel; Kashruth; Rabbinical Court of Law. **Publications:** *Perspective*, annual ● *Rabbinic Registry*, biennial ● *Sermon Manual*, biennial ● *Torah Message*, biennial. **Conventions/Meetings:** annual dinner ● monthly meeting, with educational presentations.

19762 ■ Rabbinical Assembly (RA)
3080 Broadway
New York, NY 10027
Ph: (212)280-6000
Fax: (212)749-9166
E-mail: info@rabbinicalassembly.org
URL: http://www.rabassembly.org
Contact: Rabbi Joel H. Meyers, Exec. VP
Founded: 1901. **Members:** 1,600. **Staff:** 10. **Languages:** English, Hebrew. **Multinational. Description:** Seeks to be a creative force shaping the ideology, programs and practices of the Conservative movement; committed to building and strengthening the totality of Jewish life. Publishes learned textbooks, prayerbooks, and works of Jewish interest; administers the work of the Committee on Jewish Law and Standards for the Conservative Movement. Serves the professional and personal needs of members through publications, conferences, and benefit programs; coordinates the Joint Placement Commission of the Conservative movement. **Committees:** Jewish Law and Standards. **Formerly:** Rabbinical Assembly of America. **Publications:** *Bond of Life*. Book. **Price:** $12.00 ● *Conservative Judaism*, annual. Journal. Contains articles which express a serious, critical inquiry of Jewish texts and traditions, legacy and law. **Price:** $28.00 /year for individuals; $50.00 /year for libraries and institutions; $18.00/year for students ● *Conservative Judaism and Jewish Law*. Book ● *Embracing Judaism*. Book. **Price:** $14.00 ● *God in the Teachings of Conservative Judaism*. Book

● *Mahzor for Rosh Hashanah and Yom Kippur*. Book ● *Passover Haggadah*. Book ● *RA Newsletter*, 10/year. **Price:** free for members. **Circulation:** 1,600 ● *Rabbinical Assembly Membership List*, every 12 to 18 months. Membership Directory ● *Selichot Service*. Book ● *Siddur Sim Shalom*. Book. Serves as a prayerbook. ● *Siddur Sim Shalom for Shabbat*. Book. Serves as a prayerbook. ● *Understanding Conservative Judaism*. Book ● *Weekday Prayer Book* ● Proceedings, annual. **Conventions/Meetings:** annual convention (exhibits).

19763 ■ Rabbinical Council of America (RCA)
305 7th Ave., 12th Fl.
New York, NY 10001
Ph: (212)807-7888
Fax: (212)727-8452
E-mail: office@rabbis.org
URL: http://www.rabbis.org
Contact: Rabbi Dale Polakoff, Pres.
Founded: 1935. **Members:** 1,000. **Membership Dues:** full, post semicha student (1st year), $125 (annual) ● retired, $150 (annual) ● regular, $450 (annual). **Staff:** 10. **Budget:** $550,000. **Multinational. Description:** Ordained Orthodox Jewish rabbis. Promotes the widespread study of Torah and the fuller observance of traditional Judaism. Sponsors Yeshivath Hadorom in Rehovoth, Israel and Yeshivat Achuzat Yaakov in Gan Yavne, Israel (schools). **Telecommunication Services:** electronic mail, rabbis@rabbis.org. **Commissions:** Israel; Kashruth. **Committees:** Aging; Bio-Medical Ethics; Campus; Ezra-Russian Affairs; Family and Marriage; Funeral Standards. **Publications:** *Hadorom* (in English and Hebrew), annual ● *Rabbinic Registry*, biennial ● *Record*, quarterly ● *Sermon Manual*, annual ● *Tradition*, quarterly. **Conventions/Meetings:** annual meeting (exhibits) - always May or June.

19764 ■ Reconstructionist Rabbinical Association (RRA)
1299 Church Rd.
Wyncote, PA 19095
Ph: (215)576-5210
Fax: (215)576-8051
E-mail: info@therra.org
URL: http://www.therra.org
Contact: Rabbi Brant Rosen, Pres.
Founded: 1974. **Members:** 200. **Description:** Represents rabbis affiliated with the Reconstructionist movement. **Programs:** Reconstructionist Placement Service. **Publications:** *The Journey of Mourning: A Reconstructionist Guide*. Pamphlet. **Price:** $4.00 individual copy; $3.00 for 5-10 copies; $2.00 for over 10 copies ● *The Rabbi-Congregation Relationship: A Vision for the 21st Century*. Pamphlet. **Price:** $10.00 individual copy; $5.00 for 2-5 copies; $4.00 for 6 or more copies ● *The Reconstructionist*, semiannual. Journal. **Price:** $50.00/2 years; $45.00 for members of JRF affiliates; $12.50 single issue. Alternate Formats: online ● *RRA Rabbi's Manual*. **Conventions/Meetings:** annual convention.

19765 ■ Reform Jewish Appeal (RJA)
c/o Union for Reform Judaism
633 3rd Ave.
New York, NY 10017-6778
Ph: (212)650-4176
Fax: (212)650-4149
E-mail: reformjewishappeal@uahc.org
URL: http://www.urj.org
Contact: Annie Thompson, Dir.
Description: Supplemental fundraising campaign for the Union of American Hebrew Congregations (see separate entry) and Hebrew Union College - Jewish Institute of Religion. **Affiliated With:** Union for Reform Judaism. **Formerly:** Combined Campaign for American Reform Judaism. **Publications:** *Reform Judaism Magazine*, quarterly. **Circulation:** 300,000. **Advertising:** accepted. **Conventions/Meetings:** biennial meeting.

19766 ■ Reform Judaism
2027 Massachusetts Ave. NW
Washington, DC 20036
Ph: (202)387-2800

Fax: (202)667-9070
E-mail: rac@urj.org
URL: http://www.rj.org
Contact: Rabbi David Saperstein, Dir.
Founded: 1953. **Staff:** 4. **Regional Groups:** 14. **Local Groups:** 500. **Description:** A joint commission of the Union of American Hebrew Congregations and the Central Conference of American Rabbis (see separate entries). Encourages the application of prophetic Judaism to everyday life; educates congregations on social justice issues related to domestic and international affairs. Supplies information, program ideas, and reports to the social action committees in most of the 830 Reform synagogues in the U.S. and Canada. **Awards:** Irving J. Fain Award. **Frequency:** biennial. **Type:** recognition. **Recipient:** for local committees. **Additional Websites:** http://www.rac.org. **Affiliated With:** Union for Reform Judaism. **Formerly:** (2000) Commission on Social Action of Reform Judaism. **Publications:** *Chai Impact*, periodic. Newsletter ● *Social Action Manual* ● *Tsedek V'Shalom*, semiannual. Newsletter. **Conventions/Meetings:** general assembly.

19767 ■ Religious Zionist Youth Movement - Bnei Akiva of the United States and Canada (BA)
7 Penn Plz., Ste.205
New York, NY 10001
Ph: (212)465-9536
Fax: (212)465-2155
E-mail: shani@bneiakiva.org
URL: http://www.bneiakiva.org
Contact: Shani Block, Registrar
Founded: 1934. **Members:** 10,000. **Membership Dues:** regular, $36 (annual). **Staff:** 10. **Budget:** $750,000. **Regional Groups:** 15. **Local Groups:** 50. **Languages:** English, Hebrew. **Description:** Religious Zionist youth movement of boys and girls aged ten to 18, with an older group (ages 18-25) serving as the leadership. Promotes Jewish culture and religion with emphasis placed on Israel in modern-day society. Conducts study programs in Israel; operates five regional summer camps; holds annual leadership training seminars in over 20 North American cities. Sponsors the Torah Vaavoda Institute in Beach Lake, PA and Mach Hach Summer Program in Israel. Conducts children's services and charitable program; offers educational programs; operates speakers' bureau. Is a member of the World Organization of Bnei Akiva. **Libraries: Type:** reference. **Holdings:** 1,000. **Subjects:** Zionism, Judaica, Israel. **Absorbed:** Bachad Organization. **Formerly:** Hashomer Hadati, Bnei Akiva; (1993) Bnei Akiva of North America. **Publications:** *Akivon*. Newspaper. For grade-school members of organization of religious Zionist youth. **Price:** included in membership dues. **Circulation:** 3,000 ● *Pinkas l'Madrich*, semiannual. Booklets. Covers Judaic and historical topics. **Price:** free ● *Yedion*, monthly ● *Zraim*, quarterly. Newspaper. Contains opinions on Jewish-related subjects. Includes book reviews and poetry. **Price:** included in membership dues. **Advertising:** accepted ● Also publishes a series of educational, ideological, youth leadership, festival, and camping materials. **Conventions/Meetings:** annual convention (exhibits).

19768 ■ Sephardic Jewish Brotherhood of America (SJBA)
109-09 72nd Rd.
Forest Hills, NY 11375
Ph: (718)685-0080
E-mail: sjbofamerica@aol.com
URL: http://isfsp.org/brotherhood.html
Contact: Mr. Bernard Ouziel, Pres.
Founded: 1915. **Members:** 2,500. **Description:** Sponsors Henry J. Perahia Funds for the Needy Committee. Provides scholarships to members. Offers burial benefits to members. **Committees:** Religious Activities; Scholarship and Education. **Publications:** *Sephardic Brother*, periodic. **Conventions/Meetings:** biennial meeting.

19769 ■ Society for the Advancement of Judaism (SAJ)
15 W 86th St.
New York, NY 10024

Ph: (212)724-7000
E-mail: the.saj@verizon.net
URL: http://www.thesaj.org
Contact: Linda Stern, Chair
Founded: 1922. **Members:** 250. **Staff:** 20. **Description:** A congregation of Jews whose members subscribe to the philosophy of Reconstructionism, which holds that Judaism is not only a religion but a religious civilization, continually evolving. Belongs to the conservative movement, the United Synagogue of Conservative Judaism. Operates elementary and Hebrew high school for grades K-12, as well as adult education programs. **Libraries: Type:** reference. **Holdings:** 2,500. **Affiliated With:** United Synagogue of Conservative Judaism. **Publications:** *SAJ Bulletin*, quarterly. Includes synagogue bulletin. **Advertising:** accepted. **Conventions/Meetings:** annual meeting - always June.

19770 ■ Society for Humanistic Judaism (SHJ)
28611 W 12 Mile Rd.
Farmington Hills, MI 48334
Ph: (248)478-7610
Fax: (248)478-3159
E-mail: info@shj.org
URL: http://www.shj.org
Contact: M. Bonnie Cousens, Exec. Dir.
Founded: 1969. **Members:** 2,500. **Membership Dues:** national, $75 (annual) ● young adult (through age 25), $25 (annual) ● life, $1,800. **Staff:** 5. **Budget:** $300,000. **Local Groups:** 38. **Multinational. Description:** Individuals interested in the ideology of Humanistic Judaism. Purposes are to: promote the philosophy of Humanistic Judaism; encourage communication among Humanistic Jews worldwide and to share their creative work; organize congregations, society chapters, or havurot in communities worldwide; serve the needs of individuals who cannot find in their community a congregation which supports their belief. Maintains speaker's bureau. Publishes resources for humanistic Jews. Assists in leadership training. **Libraries: Type:** reference. **Holdings:** 400. **Subjects:** religion, humanism, Jewish history. **Awards:** Jewish Humanist Leadership Award. **Type:** recognition. **Computer Services:** Mailing lists. **Committees:** Ethical Concerns - Social Responsibility. **Affiliated With:** International Federation of Secular Humanistic Jews. **Publications:** *Guide to Humanistic Judaism*, periodic. Book. Features encyclopedia-like entries on the philosophy and practice of Humanistic Judaism. **Price:** $18.00. Alternate Formats: online ● *High Holidays for Humanists*. Book ● *Humanist Haggadah*, periodic. Book. Contains guidelines for humanistic Jews who want to celebrate Passover with integrity. **Price:** $10.95/copy; $10.00 for audio cassettes. Alternate Formats: online ● *Humanistic Judaism*, quarterly. Journal. Provides a humanistic interpretation on Jewish identity and history; chronicles information on ethics, and humanistic communities. **Price:** $21.00 domestic; $31.00 in Canada and Mexico; $43.00 overseas; $30.00 libraries. ISSN: 0441-4195 ● *Humanorah*, quarterly. Newsletter. **Price:** included in membership dues ● *Judaism Beyond God*, periodic. Book. Contains the four-thousand-year history of the Jewish people. **Price:** $25.00. Alternate Formats: online ● *Judaism in a Secular Age*, periodic. Book. Features the anthology of secular Humanistic Jewish thought. **Price:** $30.00. Alternate Formats: online ● *Literary Genius of the Bible*. Book ● *Meditation Services for Humanistic Judaism*. Book ● Also publishes educational, inspirational, and ceremonial materials. **Conventions/Meetings:** biennial conference - always last weekend of April/1st weekend of May ● periodic workshop.

19771 ■ Struggle to Save Ethiopian Jewry (SSEJ)
2472 Broadway, Ste.316
New York, NY 10025
Free: (866)376-SSEJ
E-mail: info@ssej.org
URL: http://www.studentstruggle.org
Contact: Ellen Wiesel, Honorary Chair
Multinational. Description: Jewish organizations and individuals. Provides food, medical care and other necessities to Jews in Ethiopia. Promotes public awareness.

19772 ■ Union of Orthodox Rabbis of the U.S. and Canada (UORUSC)
235 E Broadway
New York, NY 10002
Ph: (212)964-6337 (212)964-6338
URL: http://www.orthodoxrabbis.org
Contact: Rabbi Hersh M. Ginsberg, Chm.
Founded: 1902. **Members:** 600. **Staff:** 2. **Description:** Orthodox rabbis. Works to foster and promote "Torah true Judaism" in America. **Also Known As:** Agudath Harabonim. **Publications:** Membership Directory. **Conventions/Meetings:** biennial meeting.

19773 ■ Union for Reform Judaism (URJ)
633 3rd Ave.
New York, NY 10017-6778
Ph: (212)650-4000 (212)650-4221
Fax: (212)650-4229
E-mail: urj@urj.org
URL: http://www.urj.org
Contact: Rabbi Eric H. Yoffie, Pres.
Founded: 1873. **Members:** 1,500,000. **Staff:** 450. **Budget:** $20,300,000. **Regional Groups:** 14. **Description:** Central congregational body of Reform Judaism in the Western Hemisphere. Provides religious, educational, cultural, and administrative programs to more than 900 affiliated synagogues. **Awards:** Eisendrath Award. **Frequency:** biennial. **Type:** recognition. **Recipient:** for contributions to the Jewish world ● Reform Judaism Prize for Jewish Fiction. **Frequency:** annual. **Type:** monetary. **Recipient:** for a promising writer of Jewish fiction. **Boards:** Brit Milah Board of Reform Judaism; Transcontinental Music Publications; UAHC Press. **Commissions:** Cantorial Congregational Relations; Cantorial Placement; Educator-Congregational Relations; Jewish Education; Rabbinical - Congregation Relations; Reform Jewish Outreach; Religious Living; Social Action of Reform Judaism; Synagogue Management; Synagogue Music; Worship. **Committees:** Adult Jewish Growth; Camp-Institute; College; Dues Policy Review; Fund for Reform Judaism; Gay and Lesbian Inclusion; HIV/AIDS; Interreligious Affairs; Jewish Family Concerns; Marketing and Communications; New Congregations; New Technologies and Information Systems; Older Adults; Reform Judaism Editorial Board; Small Congregations. **Affiliated With:** American Conference of Cantors; AZRA/World Union for Progressive Judaism North America; Central Conference of American Rabbis; National Association of Temple Administrators; National Association of Temple Educators; North American Federation of Temple Brotherhoods; Women of Reform Judaism, The Federation of Temple Sisterhoods. **Publications:** *Reform Judaism*, quarterly. Magazine. **Price:** included in membership dues; $12.00 /year for nonmembers; $5.00/year for students. ISSN: 0482-0819. **Circulation:** 320,000. **Advertising:** accepted. **Conventions/Meetings:** biennial convention (exhibits) - held in odd numbered years in the fall ● biennial general assembly (exhibits) - held in odd numbered years in the fall.

19774 ■ Union of Sephardic Congregations (USC)
8 W 70th St.
New York, NY 10023
Ph: (212)873-0300
Fax: (212)724-6165
E-mail: office@shearithisrael.org
Contact: Rabbi Marc D. Angel, Pres.
Founded: 1929. **Description:** Affiliated congregations practicing Sephardic (Spanish, Portuguese, or Middle Eastern) Judaism. Publishes and distributes Sephardic prayer books. **Publications:** *Sephardic Prayer Books* ● Publishes Sephardic prayer books (in English and Hebrew).

19775 ■ Union for Traditional Judaism (UTJ)
811 Palisade Ave.
Teaneck, NJ 07666
Ph: (201)801-0707
Fax: (201)801-0449

E-mail: utj-office@utj.org
URL: http://www.utj.org
Contact: Rabbi Ronald D. Price, Exec. VP
Founded: 1983. **Members:** 10,000. **Membership Dues:** individual, $36 (annual) ● family, $50 ● friend, $100 ● sponsor, $250 (annual) ● patron, $500. **Staff:** 10. **Description:** Represents laypeople, educators, Talmudic scholars, cantors, and rabbis who believe in the principles of traditional Judaism; dedicated to the observance of Halakhah (Jewish law) in an open-minded and creative way. Maintains speakers' bureau, and a panel of Halakhic inquiry to answer difficult questions of Jewish law. Conducts educational programs for youth, and sponsors youth conferences. "Taking the MTV Challenge" curriculum, a Jewish response to television values, now in use by more than 300 institutions around the world and across the denominational spectrum. **Libraries: Type:** reference. **Holdings:** 3,000. **Subjects:** Tanakh (Bible), Talmud, Rabbinics, Jewish history, Jewish philosophy. **Computer Services:** Mailing lists ● online services, Kosher Nexus/Hagachelet. **Telecommunication Services:** electronic mail, utj@utj.org. **Publications:** *Cornerstone - Journal*, annual ● *Hagahelet - Newsletter*, quarterly. **Advertising:** accepted ● *Halakhah and the Modern Jew.* Book ● *Kosher Nexus*, quarterly. Newsletter. Contains the latest in the Kosher food industry, reviews, and recipes, all with a sense of humor. **Advertising:** accepted. Alternate Formats: online ● *Tomeikh kaHalakhah*, periodic. Examines issues of Jewish law for the 21st century. **Conventions/Meetings:** annual conference (exhibits).

19776 ■ United Sons of Israel (USI)
Address Unknown since 2007
Description: Entitles members to a burial plot.

19777 ■ United Synagogue of Conservative Judaism (USCJ)
155 5th Ave.
New York, NY 10010-6802
Ph: (212)533-7800
Fax: (212)353-9439
E-mail: info@uscj.org
URL: http://www.uscj.org
Contact: Dr. Raymond B. Goldstein, Pres.
Founded: 1913. **Members:** 1,500,000. **Regional Groups:** 19. **Multinational. Description:** Seeks to advance the cause of Judaism in America and maintain Jewish tradition in its historic continuity. Works to formulate a religious response to pressing social and religious issues such as intermarriage, the environment, child welfare and domestic violence. Commissions address needs in many vital areas—education, youth, substance abuse, Israel, access for the disabled—and work to further religious observance. **Awards:** Solomon Schechter Award. **Frequency:** biennial. **Type:** recognition. **Recipient:** for excellence in synagogue programming. **Telecommunication Services:** TDD, (212)260-7442. **Commissions:** Cantorial Placement; Congregational Insurance; Educator Placement; Jewish Education; Joint Rabbinical Placement; Placement of Synagogue Administrators; Singles; Substance Abuse and Troubled Youth; Youth; Youth Director Placement. **Committees:** Accessibility; Affiliations; Building and Housing; Building Fund; Calendar; College Age Activities; Commitment and Observance; Congregational Standards; Editorial Board; Israel Affairs and Aliyah; Prevention of Intermarriage/Ensuring Jewish Survival; Social Action and Public Policy; Soviet Jewry; United Synagogue Review; Young Leadership. **Departments:** Book Service; Communications; Conferences and Special Events; Development; Education; Finance and Management; Information Services; Israel Affairs; Leadership Development; Operations/Personnel; Programs; Public Affairs; Regional Activities; Services to Congregations; Special Projects; Youth Activities. **Affiliated With:** Cantors Assembly; Federation of Jewish Men's Clubs; Jewish Educators Assembly; Rabbinical Assembly; Solomon Schechter Day School Association; Women's League for Conservative Judaism; World Council of Conservative/Masorti Synagogues. **Formerly:** (1991) United Synagogue of America. **Publications:** *Creating Pil-*

lars, quarterly. Newsletter. Contains information about the Center in Jerusalem. ● *Directory and Resource Guide*, annual. **Advertising:** accepted. Alternate Formats: online ● *ENEWS*, monthly. Newsletter. Alternate Formats: online ● *Etz Hayim Study Companion*, periodic. Book. Contains 41 essays that examine issues relating to the understanding and interpretation of the Bible. **Price:** $22.00/copy ● *Luah 5766*, periodic. Book. Contains information ranging from the laws that pertain to the Torah service to assigning aliyot. **Price:** $14.75/copy ● *The Next Step*, quarterly. Newsletter ● *United Synagogue Review*, semiannual. Magazine. Alternate Formats: online ● Directory, monthly. Alternate Formats: online ● Magazine ● Also publishes and distributes curriculum materials and audiovisual materials, plus holiday materials and other resource materials. **Conventions/Meetings:** biennial convention (exhibits).

19778 ■ United Synagogue Youth (USY)
Rapaport House
155 5th Ave.
New York, NY 10010
Ph: (212)533-7800
Fax: (212)353-9439
E-mail: youth@uscj.org
URL: http://www.usy.org
Contact: Jules A. Gutin, Dir.
Founded: 1951. **Members:** 14,000. **Staff:** 25. **State Groups:** 17. **Local Groups:** 410. **Description:** Jewish youth (ages 13-17) interested in continuing and strengthening their identification with Judaism through study and discussion groups, leadership training, and special interest groups. **Telecommunication Services:** electronic mail, gutin@uscj.org ● TDD, (212)-260-7442. **Publications:** *Achshav!*, quarterly. Magazine. **Circulation:** 14,000 ● *Advisors' Newsletter*, periodic. **Conventions/Meetings:** annual convention (exhibits).

19779 ■ Universal Torah Registry (UTR)
70 W 36th St., Ste.700
New York, NY 10018-8070
Ph: (212)983-4800
Fax: (212)983-4084
E-mail: info@jcrcny.org
URL: http://www.jcrcny.org/html/torah1.html
Contact: Michael S. Miller, Exec. VP/CEO
Founded: 1983. **Description:** Jewish organizations concerned with the theft of valuable sacred scrolls. Aims to provide for the identification and registration of Torahs and other sacred scrolls. Develops methods to deter thefts. Informs the public on safeguarding Torahs. (Torahs comprise the Five Books of Moses, are written by a scribe using a quill, and are worth an average of $25,000.) Provides tools for marking scrolls and a certificate of registry. **Convention/Meeting:** none.

19780 ■ Warsaw Ghetto Resistance Organization (WAGRO)
122 W 30th St., Ste.205
New York, NY 10001
Ph: (212)564-1065
Fax: (212)279-2926
E-mail: max@americangathering.org
Contact: Benjamin Meed, Pres.
Founded: 1962. **Members:** 1,000. **Description:** Former Polish and other European Jews, now American citizens, who survived Nazi persecution in the Warsaw ghetto and other places in Poland. Has established WAGRO Research Foundation, which records survivors' testimonies on wartime experiences. **Publications:** Journal, annual. **Conventions/Meetings:** annual Yom Hashoah Commemoration - meeting, memorial service - always New York City.

19781 ■ Women of Reform Judaism, The Federation of Temple Sisterhoods (WRJ)
633 3rd Ave.
New York, NY 10017
Ph: (212)650-4050
Free: (866)975-5924
Fax: (212)650-4059

E-mail: wrj@urj.org
URL: http://wrj.rj.org
Contact: Shelley Lindauer, Exec. Dir.
Founded: 1913. **Members:** 100,000. **Staff:** 14. **Budget:** $1,000,000. **Regional Groups:** 12. **Local Groups:** 600. **Description:** Women of Reform or liberal Jewish congregations. Works "to intensify Jewish knowledge and to translate religious ideals into practical service to Jewish and humanitarian causes". Activities include: providing services to local affiliates; creating study material for Jewish parents and other adults; encouraging an appreciation of Jewish ceremonials and art; stimulating interest and actively participating in modern Jewish and social problems; working for the blind; supporting Israel and Jewry in the former Soviet Union. Also involved in youth activities, service to the elderly, education on UN affairs, and efforts to improve international understanding. Maintains speakers' bureau. **Awards:** OR AMI Light of My People Award for Special Achievement. **Frequency:** biennial. **Type:** recognition. **Recipient:** for projects of service programs or education of unusual character or significance ● **Type:** scholarship. **Recipient:** for rabbinic student. **Departments:** Leadership Development; Projects; Religious Action; Religious Living. **Affiliated With:** AZRA/World Union for Progressive Judaism North America; JBI International - Jewish Braille Institute of America. **Formerly:** National Federation of Temple Sisterhoods. **Publications:** *Beginning The Journey, Toward a Women's Commentary on Touch.* Features a collection of commentaries by women scholars and clergy. **Price:** $10.00 each ● *Catalog for Sisterhood*, annual ● *Covenant of the Heart.* Book. Contains original prayers, poems and meditations for Sisterhood meetings and individuals. **Price:** $10.00 each ● *Critical Issues, Updates and Alerts*, quarterly ● *Jewish Art Calendar*, annual ● *Notes for Now*, quarterly ● *When Love is Not Enough: Spousal Abuse in Rabbinic and Contemporary Judaism.* Book. **Price:** $15.00 each. **Conventions/Meetings:** biennial general assembly (exhibits).

19782 ■ Women's League for Conservative Judaism (WLCJ)
475 Riverside Dr., Ste.820
New York, NY 10115
Ph: (212)870-1260
Free: (800)628-5083
Fax: (212)870-1261
E-mail: womensleague@wlcj.org
URL: http://www.wlcj.org
Contact: Cory Schneider, Pres.
Founded: 1918. **Members:** 150,000. **Staff:** 19. **Budget:** $800,000. **Regional Groups:** 25. **Local Groups:** 700. **Description:** Composed of Sisterhoods affiliated with the Conservative movement, dedicated to the perpetuation of traditional Judaism and the translation of its ideals into practice. Purposes are: to guide its affiliates in local, national, and international activities, making them aware of their civic responsibilities; to foster Jewish education through study courses, Jewish Family Living Institutes and through the establishment of Synagogue and Sisterhood libraries. Supports Torah Fund - a Campaign for the Jewish Theological Seminary. **Committees:** Adult Education; Bikkur Holim; Books Libraries and Periodicals; Canadian Public Affairs; Community Service; Creative Handcrafts; Disabilities; Elderhostel; Environment; Field Service; Israel Affairs; Jewish Living; Judaica Shop; Keruv; Long Range Planning; Marketing; Membership; Overseas Women's Group; Parliamentary Procedure; Program; Public Relations; Social Action; Torah Fund; Training Services; United Nations; Ways and Means; Youth/School Liaison. **Formerly:** (1947) Women's League of the United Synagogue of America; (1973) National Women's League of the United Synagogue of America. **Publications:** *Ba' Olam*, bimonthly. Newsletter. Provides news and commentary on world affairs. **Price:** $5.00/year ● *Calendar Diary*, annual. Lists Hebrew and English dates and holidays. Includes prayers and readings. **Price:** $6.00. **Circulation:** 18,000 ● *Celebration Series: Rosh Hashanah and Yom Kippur, Hanukkah, Pesah, and Purim.* Booklets. **Price:** $5.00 each ● *Count Your Blessings* ● *Making Your Kitchen*

Kosher: A Step-by-Step Guide. Book ● *Quantity Kosher Cooking I and II* ● *Simhat Bat Kit-Welcoming a Baby Daughter.* **Price:** $7.50 ● *Under the Wings of the Sh'khinah: A Jewish Healing Service* ● *Welcome to the World: A Jewish Baby's Record Book.* **Price:** $15.00 ● *Women's League Outlook*, quarterly. Magazine. For contemporary Jewish families covering programs of social action, health, education, history and culture, and Jewish lifestyles. **Price:** included in membership dues; $12.00 /year for nonmembers; $15.00 overseas. ISSN: 0043-7557. **Circulation:** 85,000. **Advertising:** accepted ● Audiotapes ● Booklets ● Manuals. **Conventions/Meetings:** biennial conference (exhibits) - always fall or winter ● biennial World Affairs Conference - meeting - always fall.

19783 ■ Women's League for Israel (WLI)
Address Unknown since 2007
Founded: 1928. **Members:** 5,000. **Staff:** 6. **Local Groups:** 45. **Description:** Women interested in the redevelopment of Israel and in supporting educational, vocational, and social service programs for residents and newcomers. Maintains homes in Haifa, Jerusalem, Tel Aviv, and Nathanya, Israel and a vocational and rehabilitation center. Built women's dormitory, cafeteria, and student center at Hebrew University in Jerusalem, Israel, and two dormitories for women on Mount Scopus. **Awards:** Freedom Cup Award. **Frequency:** annual. **Type:** recognition. **Formerly:** Women's League for Palestine. **Publications:** *Women's League for Israel—Newsletter*, 3/year. **Price:** free. **Circulation:** 4,500. **Advertising:** not accepted ● Bulletin, quarterly. **Conventions/Meetings:** annual congress ● triennial congress.

19784 ■ World Confederation of United Zionists (WCUZ)
c/o Dor Zion
136 E 39th St.
New York, NY 10016
Ph: (212)725-1211
Fax: (212)684-6327
E-mail: info@dorzion.org
URL: http://www.dorzion.org
Contact: Kalman Sultanik, Exec. Co-Pres.
Founded: 1946. **Members:** 5,000. **Staff:** 2. **National Groups:** 10. **Languages:** English, French, Hebrew, Spanish. **Description:** Is unaffiliated with any Israeli political party, group promotes Zionist education, information, and welfare activities on behalf of Israel. Encourages private and collective agriculture and industry in Israel; strives for an "Israel-centered creative Jewish survival in Diaspora". **Awards:** Louis Lipsky Chair. **Type:** grant. **Formerly:** (1975) World Confederation of General Zionists. **Publications:** *Zionist Information Views* (in English and Spanish), monthly. Newsletter. Reports on membership activities. **Price:** available to members only. **Circulation:** 3,000. **Conventions/Meetings:** quadrennial Zionist Congress - meeting.

19785 ■ World Council of Conservative/Masorti Synagogues (WCS)
3080 Broadway
New York, NY 10027
Ph: (212)678-5319 (212)280-6039
Fax: (212)678-5321
E-mail: worldcouncil@masortiworld.org
URL: http://www.masortiworld.org
Contact: Rabbi Alan H. Silberman, Pres.
Founded: 1956. **Staff:** 2. **Budget:** $250,000. **Languages:** English, French, Spanish. **Description:** Synagogues and organizations that subscribe to the tenets of Conservative Judaism. (Conservative Judaism may be described as a historic movement; it is traditionalist, accepting the scientific method of the study of Judaism in contrast with the more fundamentalist Orthodox branch.) Promotes the growth and development of the Conservative Movement in Israel and throughout the world; supports new congregations and educational institutions. Maintains placement service. **Libraries: Type:** open to the public. **Holdings:** 1,500; books. **Subjects:** conservative Judaism. **Awards: Type:** recognition. **Affiliated With:** Federation of Jewish Men's Clubs; Rabbinical As-

sembly; United Synagogue of Conservative Judaism; Women's League for Conservative Judaism. **Formerly:** (1990) World Council of Synagogues. **Publications:** *Conference Proceedings*, biennial ● *Masorti Olami*, monthly. Newsletter. Includes the newest edition of Masorti Olami News. Alternate Formats: online ● Report, monthly. Includes update of activities, news from Kehillot around the world, upcoming events, holidays and educational resources. **Conventions/Meetings:** biennial convention and general assembly (exhibits).

19786 ■ Young Israel Council of Rabbis (YICR)
c/o National Council of Young Israel
111 John St., Ste.450
New York, NY 10038
Ph: (212)929-1525
Free: (800)617-NCYI
Fax: (212)727-9526
E-mail: ncyi@youngisrael.org
URL: http://www.youngisrael.org
Contact: Shlomo Z. Mostofsky, Natl. Pres.
Founded: 1946. **Members:** 200. **Description:** Rabbis serving 200 Young Israel congregations in the U.S., Canada, and Israel. Encourages study and observance of Judaism and provides spiritual leadership to the Young Israel Movement. Adjudicates issues relating to the Young Israel Synagogues. Maintains speakers' bureau; conducts research and educational programs; provides placement service. Is concerned with welfare of rabbis. **Libraries: Type:** reference. **Awards:** Rabbinic Shofar Award. **Frequency:** annual. **Type:** recognition. **Formerly:** Council of Young Israel Rabbis. **Publications:** *Annual Volume of the Council of Young Israel Rabbis in Israel*, annual. Newsletter ● *The Rabbi's Letter*, quarterly. Newsletter. Contains information designed to enhance the professionalism of practicing congregational rabbis. **Conventions/Meetings:** annual conference (exhibits).

19787 ■ Young Judaea (YJ)
50 W 58th St.
New York, NY 10019
Ph: (212)303-8014
Fax: (212)303-4572
E-mail: info@youngjudaea.org
URL: http://www.youngjudaea.org
Founded: 1909. **Members:** 6,800. **Membership Dues:** regular, $30 (annual). **Staff:** 4,500. **Regional Groups:** 16. **Description:** Serves as an organization for Jewish young people, ages nine through 30, sponsored by Hadassah, The Women's Zionist Organization of America (see separate entry). Develops generations of American Jewish youth rooted in their heritage and dedicated to self-fulfillment as Jews and as Zionists. Provides activities including: leadership training programs, education in Judaism and Zionism, summer camps and year-long study programs in Israel. **Libraries: Type:** reference. **Holdings:** 2,000. **Subjects:** Judaism, Zionism, leadership, Israel, American Jewish community. **Affiliated With:** Hadassah, The Women's Zionist Organization of America. **Formed by Merger of:** Young Judaea; Junior Hadassah. **Formerly:** (2000) Young Judaea/Hashachar. **Publications:** *Daf L'Madrichim*, quarterly ● *Hamagshimin Journal*, 3/year ● *Kol Ha T'nuah*, bimonthly ● *Young Judaean*, bimonthly. **Conventions/Meetings:** annual meeting - always August, Barryville, NY.

19788 ■ Young Men's Division-Zeirei Agudath Israel (YMDZAI)
42 Broadway
New York, NY 10004
Ph: (212)797-9000
Fax: (646)254-1600
Contact: Rabbi Labish Becker, Exec. Off.
Founded: 1926. **Membership Dues:** $10 (annual). **Description:** Encourages young men to remain active in the orthodox Jewish community. Organizes voluntary programs; conducts educational activities including symposia on professions and educational opportunities. **Publications:** *Am Ha Torah*, semian-

nual. Journal. **Price:** $10.00/year. **Conventions/Meetings:** periodic meeting.

19789 ■ Zeirei Agudath Israel (ZAI)
42 Broadway, 14th Fl.
New York, NY 10004
Ph: (212)797-9000
Fax: (646)254-1600
Contact: Rabbi Labisch Becker, Exec. Off.
Founded: 1922. **Members:** 2,000. **Membership Dues:** $18 (annual). **Staff:** 2. **Local Groups:** 25. **Description:** Members are Orthodox Jewish youth who attend or have attended rabbinical seminaries, young ordained rabbis, and professionals or persons attending college. Aims to organize Orthodox Jewish youth into becoming responsible activists on behalf of Jewish causes. Conducts adult education classes. Provides children's services. **Divisions:** Jewish Education; Reshet Shiurei Torah. **Publications:** *Am Hatorah* (in English and Hebrew), semiannual. Journal. Serves as a scholarly research journal. **Price:** $6.00/issue. **Circulation:** 2,500. **Advertising:** accepted ● *DAF Chiluk*, quarterly ● *Haggadah Treasury.* Book ● *ZAI in the News*, annual. Brochure ● Newsletter, monthly. **Conventions/Meetings:** semiannual meeting and symposium ● seminar.

19790 ■ Zionist Organization of America (ZOA)
4 E 34th St.
New York, NY 10016
Ph: (212)481-1500
Fax: (212)481-1515
E-mail: email@zoa.org
URL: http://www.zoa.org
Contact: Morton A. Klein, Pres.
Founded: 1897. **Members:** 100,000. **Membership Dues:** regular, $50 (annual) ● student/senior, $36 (annual) ● sustaining, $100 (annual) ● builder, $180 (annual) ● patron, $250 (annual) ● guardian, $1,000 (annual) ● pillar, $1,800 (annual). **Staff:** 15. **Regional Groups:** 14. **Local Groups:** 40. **Description:** Conducts an educational and informational program for Israel and Jewry. Maintains speaker's bureau, legal aid center, campus programs, and publications. **Libraries: Type:** reference. **Computer Services:** Mailing lists. **Affiliated With:** Conference of Presidents of Major American Jewish Organizations. **Formerly:** (1915) Federation of American Zionists. **Publications:** *ZOA Report*, monthly. Newsletter. **Conventions/Meetings:** periodic banquet ● periodic conference ● periodic lecture ● periodic meeting ● periodic retreat.

Jewish Science

19791 ■ Society of Jewish Science (SJS)
109 E 39th St.
New York, NY 10016
Ph: (212)682-2626
URL: http://www.appliedjudaism.org
Contact: David Goldstein, Exec. Dir.
Founded: 1922. **Members:** 250. **Staff:** 5. **Regional Groups:** 5. **Local Groups:** 1. **Description:** Jewish science applies the teachings of the Jewish faith to daily experience, thereby integrating mental, physical, and spiritual health. Conducts weekly religious services. **Libraries: Type:** reference; by appointment only. **Holdings:** 2,000; audio recordings, books. **Subjects:** Judaica, spirituality. **Study Groups:** Torah Class. **Also Known As:** The Center for Applied Judaism. **Publications:** *How To Live.* Book. **Price:** $15.00 ● *Jewish Science Interpreter*, 8/year. Magazine. **Price:** $15.00/year. ISSN: 0898-7963. **Circulation:** 1,000 ● *Jewish Science Interpreter: A Monthly Message of Health and Happiness Through the Jewish Faith.* Magazine. Includes affirmations and meditations. **Price:** included in membership dues; $15.00 /year for nonmembers. **Circulation:** 1,000 ● *Peace of Mind.* Book. **Price:** $15.00 ● Monographs ● Pamphlets ● Also produces cassettes. **Conventions/Meetings:** Weekly Religious Service/Meditation - meeting - every Sunday at 11:00 A.M.

Krishna Consciousness

19792 ■ International Society for Krishna Consciousness (ISKCON)

c/o New Raman Reti ISKCON of Alachua
PO Box 819
Alachua, FL 32616
Ph: (386)462-2017
E-mail: alachua@pamho.net
URL: http://www.iskcon.com
Contact: Annuttama Dasa, Commissioner

Founded: 1966. **Languages:** Arabic, Chinese, English, French, German, Hindi, Italian, Japanese, Norwegian, Russian, Spanish, Thai. **Multinational. Description:** Individuals interested in Krishna. Nonsectarian cultural, religious, philosophical, and educational movement that represents tradition rooted in ancient India. Dedicated to teaching self-realization and Krishna consciousness through the practice of vegetarianism, bhakti-yoga, and meditation based on the teachings of Srila AC Bhaktivedanta Swami Prabhupada. Maintains multimedia diorama exhibits in Los Angeles, California and Detroit, Michigan. Operates more than 300 centers worldwide. Operates nearly 50 vegetarian restaurants. Conducts research projects; compiles statistics. **Additional Websites:** http://www.afn.org/~iskcon. **Divisions:** Ministry of Communications; Ministry of Education; Ministry of Justice; Ministry of Public Affairs; Television Network. **Publications:** *Back to Godhead*, bimonthly. Magazine ● *ISKCON World Review: Newspaper of the Hare Krishna Movement* (in English and Russian), bimonthly. **Price:** $8.00/year. ISSN: 0748-2280. **Circulation:** 5,000. **Advertising:** accepted. **Conventions/Meetings:** annual international conference (exhibits) - always February/March, Mayapur, India ● periodic regional meeting.

Laity

19793 ■ National Association for Lay Ministry (NALM)

6896 Laurel St. NW
Washington, DC 20012
Ph: (202)291-4100
Fax: (202)291-8550
E-mail: nalm@nalm.org
URL: http://www.nalm.org
Contact: Christopher C. Anderson, Exec. Dir.

Founded: 1981. **Members:** 550. **Membership Dues:** sustaining, $150 (annual) ● contributing, $100 (annual) ● regular, $85 (annual) ● affiliate, limited income, $49 (annual) ● student, $29 (annual) ● organization, $300 (annual) ● affiliated national, local or regional ministerial association, $100-$300 (annual). **Staff:** 1. **Budget:** $60,000. **Regional Groups:** 6. **Description:** Clergy, religious, laypersons, and others dedicated to fostering lay ministries. Supports training and educational programs for lay ministers. Serves as a forum for communication and collaboration; cooperates with other ministry-related organizations. Sponsors and promotes research. Bestows annual tribute. **Awards:** Gaudium et Spes Award. **Frequency:** periodic. **Type:** recognition ● NALM Tribute Award. **Frequency:** annual. **Type:** recognition. **Computer Services:** Mailing lists. **Committees:** Development; Membership; Ministerial Formation; Nominations; Public Relations. **Formerly:** (1984) National Association of Lay Ministry Coordinators. **Publications:** *Chapter Development Manual* ● *The Gospel Call to Collaborative Ministry Planning Guide* ● *Lay Ministry: Newsletter of the National Association for Lay Ministry*, bimonthly ● *Meeting Agendas* ● *Ministry Formation Self-Assessment Instrument* ● Membership Directory, annual. **Conventions/Meetings:** annual conference (exhibits) ● regional meeting.

19794 ■ National Bible Association (NBA)

405 Lexington Ave., 26th Fl.
New York, NY 10174
Ph: (212)907-6427
Fax: (917)368-8005

E-mail: pgiersch@nationalbible.org
URL: http://www.nationalbible.org
Contact: Mr. Peter A. Giersch, Pres.

Founded: 1940. **Members:** 6. **Staff:** 7. **Budget:** $750,000. **Description:** Represents business leaders and individuals with the singular purpose of encouraging everyone to read the Bible; supported by contributions from business leaders and the community at large. Sponsors National Bible Week. Serves as an active proponent for biblical literacy and as an advocate for the appreciation of the historic role of the Bible in life and culture; does not promote any particular version of the Bible, nor any religion or faith view. Works with all interested in the Bible and Bible literacy and promotes the reading of the Hebrew or the Christian Scriptures known as the Bible. **Libraries: Type:** reference. **Holdings:** archival material, books, monographs. **Subjects:** bible translations. **Awards:** Biblical Ethics in Business Life. **Type:** recognition ● Judge Julius Isaacs Lifetime Achievement Award. **Frequency:** annual. **Type:** recognition. **Recipient:** an advocate for the Bible's place in personal and public life ● Witherspoon Chaplains Award. **Type:** recognition. **Additional Websites:** http://www.nationalbible.com, http://www.dailybible.com. **Committees:** Bible Education and Information; Bible Reading; Finance and Development; National Bible Week; Nominating; Public Service Advertising/Media; Recognition. **Councils:** Advisors; Media Advisory; Religious Advisory. **Formerly:** (1986) Laymen's National Bible Committee; (1998) Laymen's National Bible Association. **Publications:** *Daily Bible Reading Guide*. Brochure. **Price:** free ● *Reading the Bible*. Brochures. **Price:** free ● Newsletter, periodic. Reports on National Bible Week; includes association news, book reviews, and obituaries. **Price:** free. **Circulation:** 10,000 ● Monographs ● Pamphlets. **Conventions/Meetings:** annual National Bible Week Luncheon, begins National Bible Week (exhibits) - always prior to Thanksgiving week in New York City.

19795 ■ National Center for the Laity (NCL)

PO Box 291102
Chicago, IL 60629
Fax: (773)776-9036
E-mail: wdroel@cs.com
URL: http://www.catholiclabor.org/NCL.htm
Contact: Bill Droel, Ed.

Founded: 1977. **Members:** 30. **Membership Dues:** $25 (annual). **Budget:** $100,000. **Description:** Promotes interests of laity. Provides speakers' bureau and conducts educational programs. **Libraries: Type:** reference. **Holdings:** archival material, books, monographs. **Subjects:** laity theology. **Awards:** Faith and Work Award. **Frequency:** annual. **Type:** recognition. **Publications:** *Initiatives*, bimonthly. Newsletter. Serves as a digest of faith and work stories. **Price:** $15.00/year. **Circulation:** 6,000. **Conventions/Meetings:** semiannual conference.

Latter Day Saints

19796 ■ Dialogue Foundation (DF)

c/o Dialogue: A Journal of Mormon Thought
PO Box 58423
Salt Lake City, UT 84158
Ph: (801)274-8210
Fax: (801)274-8210
E-mail: dialoguejournal@msn.com
URL: http://www.dialoguejournal.com
Contact: Ms. Lori Levinson, Managing Dir.

Founded: 1966. **Members:** 4,000. **Membership Dues:** subscriber, $37 (annual). **Staff:** 7. **Budget:** $150,000. **Multinational. Description:** Publishes a journal for those interested in Mormon studies on issues of science, social science, history, arts, fiction and poetry. **Libraries: Type:** reference. **Holdings:** 1,000; archival material, books, business records, periodicals, photographs, reports. **Subjects:** Mormon religion related topics, history, science, humanities, fiction, art, poetry. **Awards: Type:** recognition ● Writing Award. **Frequency:** annual. **Type:** monetary. **Recipient:** for quality works of promising young student writers that have been accepted for publication and

best of the year awards in three writing categories. **Computer Services:** Bibliographic search, search engine on website ● electronic publishing, an archive of all journals published from 1966-2006 in full text is available through the website ● online services, ordering of current and back issues, customer service support. **Divisions:** Personal Voices; Poetry; Reviews; Theology. **Affiliated With:** American Theological Library Association; Mormon History Association. **Publications:** *Dialogue: A Journal of Mormon Thought*, quarterly. **Advertising:** accepted ● Also publishes: Lowell L. Bennion: Teacher, Counselor, Humanitarian by Mary Lythgoe Bradford.

19797 ■ Mormon History Association (MHA)

581 S 630 E
Orem, UT 84097
Ph: (801)224-0241 (816)229-7981
Free: (888)642-3678
Fax: (801)224-5684
E-mail: klarry@comcast.net
URL: http://www.mhahome.org
Contact: Larry King, Exec. Dir.

Founded: 1965. **Members:** 1,200. **Membership Dues:** regular, $35 (annual) ● joint with spouse, $45 (annual) ● sustaining, $100 (annual) ● student, $20 (annual) ● patron, $250 (annual) ● donor, $500 (annual) ● institution, $50 (annual). **Staff:** 1. **Budget:** $150,000. **Description:** Professional historians, students, and others interested in the history of Mormonism. Encourages research and writing in field of Mormon history. **Awards:** Ella Larsen Turner-Ella Ruth Turner Bergera Award for Best Biography. **Frequency:** annual. **Type:** monetary. **Recipient:** for the best published biography in the field of Mormon history ● Juanita Brooks Award for Best Graduate Paper. **Frequency:** annual. **Type:** monetary. **Recipient:** to a university or college graduate student for the best paper on Mormon history ● Juanita Brooks Award for Best Undergraduate Paper. **Frequency:** annual. **Type:** monetary. **Recipient:** to a university or college undergraduate student for the best paper on Mormon history ● Leonard J. Arrington Award. **Frequency:** annual. **Type:** recognition. **Recipient:** for meritorious service to Mormon history ● MHA Best Book Award. **Frequency:** annual. **Type:** monetary. **Recipient:** for the best Mormon history publication ● Steven F. Christensen Award for Best Documentary/Bibliography. **Frequency:** annual. **Type:** monetary. **Recipient:** for the best published documentary or bibliography on Mormon history ● T. Edgar Lyon Award for Best Article of the Year. **Frequency:** annual. **Type:** monetary. **Recipient:** for the best published article on Mormon history ● Thomas Rice King Award. **Frequency:** annual. **Type:** monetary. **Recipient:** for the best narrated and researched history, published publicly or privately, of a family deeply involved in the Mormon experience. **Publications:** *Journal of Mormon History*, semiannual. Contains scholarly researches in Mormon history. **Price:** included in membership dues. ISSN: 0094-7342. **Circulation:** 1,200. **Advertising:** accepted ● *Mormon History Association—Newsletter*, quarterly. Contains notices of new books and bibliographies. **Price:** included in membership dues. **Circulation:** 1,200. Alternate Formats: online. **Conventions/Meetings:** annual conference (exhibits) - 2008 May 22-25, Nauvoo, IL; 2009 May 21-24, Sacramento, CA.

19798 ■ Young Women of the Church of Jesus Christ of Latter-Day Saints (YW)

76 N Main
Salt Lake City, UT 84150-6030
Ph: (801)240-2141 (801)240-1000
Free: (800)453-3860
Fax: (801)240-5458
E-mail: youngwomen@ldschurch.org
URL: http://www.lds.org
Contact: Susan W. Tanner, Pres.

Founded: 1869. **Members:** 480,000. **Staff:** 5. **Description:** Girls between the ages of 12 and 18. Seeks to strengthen the spiritual life of young women through Christian values and experiences. Reinforces the values of faith, divine nature, individual worth, knowledge, choice and accountability, good works, and integrity. Works to develop leadership attributes in young women through service in the community. Bestows Young Womanhood Medallion for special achievement. **Formerly:** (1970) Young Women's Mutual Improvement Association.

Leadership

19799 ■ Presidential Prayer Team (PPT)
PO Box 89130
Tucson, AZ 85752-9130
Ph: (520)219-5400
Free: (800)295-1235
Fax: (520)797-7176
E-mail: info@presidentialprayerteam.org
URL: http://www.presidentialprayerteam.org
Contact: Mr. John Lind, Pres./CEO
Founded: 2001. **Description:** Prays daily for the President's administration, cabinet members and other leaders of the nation. **Awards:** American Inspiration Award. **Frequency:** monthly. **Type:** recognition. **Recipient:** for men and women who demonstrate their faith in public life. **Computer Services:** Information services, prayer, church and radio resources ● mailing lists ● online services, poll. **Committees:** Honorary. **Departments:** American Inspiration Award; American Inspiration Radio Program. **Subgroups:** Presidential Prayer Team for Kids.

Lutheran

19800 ■ African American Lutheran Association (AALA)
c/o Rev. Gwendolyn Snell, Corresponding Sec.
11317 Parklawn Dr.
Cleveland, OH 44108
Ph: (216)851-1528
E-mail: gsimani@aol.com
URL: http://www.aala-online.org
Contact: Rev. Gwendolyn Snell, Corresponding Sec.
Membership Dues: student, senior citizen, $15 (annual) ● local, $20 (annual) ● individual, $25 (annual) ● couple, $40 (annual) ● life, $500. **Description:** Aims to strengthen the Christian bonds of the African American community of believers. Unifies and conveys the needs and concerns of African American members of the Evangelical Lutheran Church in America (ELCA). Encourages individuals to become fully involved with the affairs of the church assemblies, synods, regions and congregations. Develops a full sense of partnership between the ELCA and the whole African American community through evangelism, education, stewardship, worship and social ministry.

19801 ■ American Lutheran Publicity Bureau (ALPB)
PO Box 327
Delhi, NY 13753-0327
Ph: (607)746-7511
Fax: (607)746-7511
E-mail: fred@theschumachers.org
URL: http://www.alpb.org
Contact: Pr. Frederick J. Schumacher, Exec. Dir.
Founded: 1914. **Staff:** 3. **Budget:** $100,000. **Description:** Organized by laymen and pastors of the Lutheran church to publicize its teachings, work, and activities in a movement towards Lutheran unity. Helps Lutherans to explain their faith to non-Lutherans and the unchurched and to discuss important issues in church and society. **Libraries: Type:** open to the public. **Subjects:** Lutheran religion. **Computer Services:** Mailing lists, provided to non-profit organizations only. **Publications:** For All the Saints: Prayer Book. **Price:** $35.00 single volume (plus postage); $130.00 4-volume set (postage included) ● Forum Letter, monthly. ISSN: 0046-4732. **Circulation:** 3,300 ● Heaven on Earth: A Lutheran-Orthodox Odyssey. Book. **Price:** $12.50/copy, plus shipping and handling; $10.00 for 5 or more copies, plus shipping and handling ● Lutheran Forum, quarterly. ISSN: 0024-7456. **Circulation:** 3,300. **Advertising:** accepted ● O'Lord, Teach Me to Pray. Book. **Price:** $7.50/copy (plus shipping charge);

$6.75 each, for 10 or more copies (plus shipping charge) ● Pro Ecclesia, quarterly. Journal. **Price:** $28.00/year in U.S.; $30.00 in Canada. **Advertising:** accepted. **Conventions/Meetings:** biennial Inter-Lutheran Forum - meeting.

19802 ■ Concordia Deaconess Conference (CDC)
c/o The Lutheran Church-Missouri Synod
LMCS World Relief and Human Care
1333 S Kirkwood Rd.
St. Louis, MO 63122-7295
Ph: (314)996-1382
Fax: (314)996-1128
URL: http://www.lcms.org/pages/internal.asp-?NavID=9096
Contact: Deaconess Pam Nielsen, Pres.
Founded: 1980. **Members:** 70. **Budget:** $3,000. **Regional Groups:** 4. **Description:** Serves the Lutheran Church-Missouri Synod. Promotes the deaconess ministry; conducts educational programs. Makes available the Deaconess Clara Strehlow Endowment. **Awards:** Paul Zimmerman and Phoebe Award. **Frequency:** quinquennial. **Type:** recognition. **Recipient:** nomination by members. **Publications:** Newsletter, periodic. **Price:** $5.00/year. **Conventions/Meetings:** annual conference.

19803 ■ Concordia Gospel Outreach (CGO)
Box 201
3558 S Jefferson Ave.
St. Louis, MO 63166
Ph: (314)268-1363
Fax: (314)268-1202
E-mail: outreach@cph.org
URL: http://cgo.cph.org
Contact: Annette Frank, Mgr.
Founded: 1958. **Staff:** 2. **Description:** Distributes Bibles and other religious materials to individuals and groups throughout the world and assists others to send useable Gospel resources throughout the world. **Formerly:** (1992) Concordia Tract Mission.

19804 ■ Concordia Historical Institute (CHI)
804 Seminary Pl.
St. Louis, MO 63105-3014
Ph: (314)505-7900 (314)505-7911
Fax: (314)505-7901
E-mail: chi@chi.lcms.org
URL: http://chi.lcms.org
Contact: Dr. Martin R. Noland, Dir.
Founded: 1927. **Members:** 1,000. **Membership Dues:** active, $35 (annual) ● patron, congregational, organizational, $50 (annual) ● friend, $100 (annual) ● sponsor, $500 (annual) ● pacesetter, $1,000 (annual) ● corporate, $200 (annual) ● money-saving (active two years), $65 (annual) ● money-saving (active three years), $95 (annual) ● life, $5,000. **Staff:** 15. **Budget:** $677,500. **State Groups:** 35. **Local Groups:** 3. **Description:** Serves as information bureau and research center on all phases of Lutheranism in America. Locates, collects, and preserves items of historical value for Lutheranism in America. Maintains manuscript collection (2,800,000 items), museum collection (6,000 items), collections of tape and disc recordings, filmstrips, microfilm collection (180,000 feet), slides, photographs, and coin and medal collection. Serves as Department of Archives and History of the Lutheran Church-Missouri Synod. Sponsors research; conducts educational programs. **Libraries: Type:** reference; lending; open to the public. **Holdings:** 58,500; archival material, audiovisuals, books, clippings, monographs, periodicals. **Subjects:** Lutheranism in America. **Awards:** Commendation Award. **Frequency:** annual. **Type:** recognition. **Recipient:** for special contributions to Lutheran Archives/history ● Distinguished Service Award. **Frequency:** annual. **Type:** recognition. **Recipient:** for outstanding contributions to Lutheran history and archives. **Committees:** Awards; Ethnic Archives and History; Historic Sites and Buildings. **Councils:** Director's Advisory; Saxon Lutheran Memorial Advisory. **Formerly:** (1911) Concordia Historical Society. **Publications:** Concordia Historical Institute Quarterly. Journal. Features all aspects of Lutheran history in North America. **Price:** included in membership dues;

$28.00 /year for nonmembers; $7.50/issue for nonmembers. ISSN: 0010-5260. **Circulation:** 1,648. **Advertising:** accepted. Alternate Formats: online ● Historical Footnotes ● Microfilm Index and Bibliography ● Minutes and Reports of the Biennial Conference on Archives and History ● Bulletins. Features various aspects of record archiving and usage. ● Newsletters. **Conventions/Meetings:** biennial Conference on Archives and History - lecture and workshop, for district archivists ● biennial meeting - always fall of odd-numbered years in St. Louis, MO.

19805 ■ Disability Ministries
c/o Evangelical Lutheran Church in America
8765 W Higgins Rd.
Chicago, IL 60631
Ph: (773)380-2700
Free: (800)638-3522
Fax: (773)380-1465
E-mail: info@elca.org
URL: http://www.elca.org/disability
Contact: Lowell Almen, Sec.
Founded: 1988. **Description:** Service organization of the Evangelical Lutheran Church in America. Seeks to: encourage congregations to make their facilities fully accessible to persons with disabilities, and to welcome the participation of the handicapped in all church functions; sensitize children to an understanding of disability and handicap, while meeting the needs of disabled children; help congregations act as a support network for families with a disabled member; promote cooperative efforts between social service agencies and congregations in all areas of program, service, advocacy, and work with and for the handicapped. Maintains resource center concerning ministering to people with handicaps. **Awards:** ELCA Disability Award. **Frequency:** annual. **Type:** monetary. **Recipient:** for an ELCA congregation or committee. **Telecommunication Services:** electronic mail, lcleaver@elca.org ● TDD, (800)442-3522. **Formerly:** Ephphatha Services for the Deaf and Blind; (1985) Ephphatha Services; (1987) Ephphatha Services - Division for Services and Mission in America; (1993) Ministry with Persons with Disabilities. **Publications:** Disability Newsletter, semiannual.

19806 ■ International Lutheran Deaf Association (ILDA)
c/o John Krause, Treas.
9905 Madison St. NE
Blaine, MN 55434
E-mail: jakadk1@msn.com
URL: http://www.lcmsdeaf.org
Contact: John Krause, Treas.
Founded: 1971. **Members:** 500. **Membership Dues:** individual, $20 (biennial). **Staff:** 20. **Regional Groups:** 7. **Description:** Lutherans and others who wish to promote the Christian faith and life of hearing-impaired people worldwide, particularly those in fellowship with The Lutheran Church-Missouri Synod. Works to develop lay leadership; conducts religious activities and service programs. Offers charitable program of overseas mission projects including support for several schools for the deaf. **Awards:** Uriel C. Jones Right Hand Award. **Frequency:** biennial. **Type:** recognition. **Recipient:** to a deaf person with exceptional and meritorious Christian service. **Publications:** The Deaf Lutheran, quarterly. Newsletter. **Price:** $7.50/year. **Circulation:** 850 ● Lutheran Annual, annual. Includes directory. ● Statistical Yearbook of the Lutheran Church-Missouri Synod. **Conventions/Meetings:** biennial competition ● biennial convention - always summer.

19807 ■ International Lutheran Laymen's League (Int'l LLL)
660 Mason Ridge Center
St. Louis, MO 63141
Free: (800)876-9880
E-mail: lh_min@lhm.org
URL: http://www.lhm.org
Contact: Greg E. Lewis, Exec. Dir.
Founded: 1917. **Members:** 150,000. **Staff:** 110. **Budget:** $20,000,000. **Regional Groups:** 15. **State Groups:** 43. **Local Groups:** 1,200. **Description:**

Members of the Lutheran Church-Missouri Synod and Lutheran Church-Canada Communicant interested in lay activities of the church. Sponsors the "Worldwide Lutheran Hour" radio program, "Woman to Woman" radio program, "On Main Street" videos, and television specials. Provides special program materials for affiliated groups; an auxiliary organization of the Lutheran Church-Missouri Synod and Lutheran Church-Canada. **Telecommunication Services:** additional toll-free number, (800)944-3450. **Committees:** Media Services; Resource Development. **Formerly:** (1972) Lutheran Laymen's League. **Publications:** *The Lutheran Layman*, 10/year. Newspaper. Reports on media ministries and membership activities. **Price:** included in membership dues; $5.00 /year for nonmembers. **Circulation:** 160,000. **Conventions/Meetings:** annual meeting.

19808 ■ Lutheran Deaconess Association (LDA)
1304 LaPorte Ave.
Valparaiso, IN 46383
Ph: (219)464-6925
Fax: (219)464-6928
E-mail: deacserv@valpo.edu
URL: http://www.valpo.edu/lda
Contact: Deaconess E. Louise Williams, Exec. Dir.
Founded: 1919. **Members:** 400. **Staff:** 4. **Budget:** $210,000. **Description:** Recruits and educates women for entry into the diaconal ministry. Provides encouragement, support, and services to members of diaconate and laity. Offers placement services; conducts workshops and retreats. **Libraries: Type:** reference. **Awards:** Diakenia en Christo. **Frequency:** annual. **Type:** recognition. **Recipient:** for diaconal service of Lutheran layperson. **Publications:** *Connections*, periodic ● *Diaconalogue*, semiannual ● *LDA Today*, semiannual. Newsletter. Alternate Formats: online. **Conventions/Meetings:** retreat ● workshop.

19809 ■ Lutheran Deaconess Conference (LDC)
1304 LaPorte Ave.
Valparaiso, IN 46383
Ph: (219)464-6925
Fax: (219)464-6928
E-mail: deacserv@valpo.edu
URL: http://www.valpo.edu/lda
Contact: Deaconess E. Louise William, Exec. Dir.
Founded: 1934. **Members:** 180. **Membership Dues:** voluntary, student/graduate of Lutheran Deaconess Association's deaconess education/information program, $60 (annual). **Budget:** $10,000. **Regional Groups:** 18. **Description:** Consecrated deaconesses having completed the educational requirements of the Lutheran Deaconess Association; students in training. Seeks to: develop sisterhood and community among deaconesses; present an opportunity for renewed inspiration and personal and professional growth; encourage women in the church to use their full potential and to shape, promote, and support the total deaconess program. **Publications:** *Address Listing*, annual ● *LDC News*, 8/year. Newsletter. **Conventions/Meetings:** annual conference.

19810 ■ Lutheran Girl Pioneers (LGP)
1611 Caledonia St.
La Crosse, WI 54603
Ph: (608)781-5232
Fax: (608)781-5233
E-mail: lgp@charterinternet.net
URL: http://www.lgp.org
Contact: Judy Hansen, Ed.
Founded: 1955. **Description:** Lutheran girls. Strives to develop leadership in each member and promote service to the Lord and to the world. Supervises constructive recreation preparing Lutheran girls in the way of good citizenship.

19811 ■ Lutheran Historical Conference (LHC)
c/o Marvin A. Huggins, Membership Sec./VP
Concordia Historical Inst.
804 Seminary Pl.
St. Louis, MO 63105

Ph: (314)505-7921
Fax: (314)505-7901
E-mail: luthhist@luthhist.org
URL: http://www.luthhist.org
Contact: Marvin A. Huggins, Membership Sec./VP
Founded: 1962. **Members:** 175. **Membership Dues:** individual/institution, $25 (annual). **Description:** Archivists and librarians from Lutheran churches and institutions; historians of American Lutheranism. Works to coordinate archival, library, research, and photoduplication activities of Lutheran church bodies in the Americas; to provide forum for exchange of ideas and information among members; to disseminate information; and to encourage research and production of scholarly works in the history of Lutheranism in America. Holds biennial meeting with research papers on Lutheran history; publishes papers in Essays and Reports series; publishes newsletter. **Awards:** Distinguished Service Award. **Frequency:** biennial. **Type:** recognition. **Recipient:** for exceptional service in the field of American Lutheran archives and/or history. **Publications:** *American Lutherans Help Shape the World Council of Churches*. Monographs. **Price:** $12.50 ● *Chronicle of Woodville Normal and Academy*. Monographs. **Price:** $12.50 ● *Essays and Reports of Biennial Conference*. Proceedings. Contains conference essays. ● *Fifty Years of Lutheran Convergence: The Canadian Case Study*. Monograph. **Price:** $12.50/copy ● *Historical Guide to Lutheran Church Bodies in North America*. Book. **Price:** $20.00 ● *Letters of Paul Henkel*. Monograph ● *Lutheran Historical Conference Newsletter*, quarterly. Newsletters. Talks about activities of the organization and its members, publications, etc. **Price:** included in membership dues. **Circulation:** 225. Alternate Formats: online. **Conventions/Meetings:** biennial conference - always fall of even numbered years.

19812 ■ Lutheran Human Relations Association (LHRA)
1821 N 16th St.
Milwaukee, WI 53205
Ph: (414)536-0585
Fax: (414)536-0690
E-mail: lhra@lhra.org
URL: http://lhra.org
Contact: Marilyn Miller, Exec. Dir.
Founded: 1953. **Members:** 3,500. **Membership Dues:** individual, $30 (annual) ● family, $40 (annual). **Staff:** 2. **Budget:** $239,000. **Description:** Provides education and skills to address racism and other human oppressions; builds cross-cultural community healing, growth, understanding. **Formerly:** (2003) Lutheran Human Relations Association of America. **Publications:** *Vanguard*, quarterly. Newspaper. Contains articles and information on issues of human relations. **Price:** included in membership dues. ISSN: 0042-2568. **Circulation:** 7,500 ● Also publishes theologically-oriented literature. **Conventions/Meetings:** annual Institute - conference and workshop, on justice issues - usually summer ● workshop, provides training.

19813 ■ Lutheran Men in Mission (LMM)
Evangelical Lutheran Church in Am.
8765 W Higgins Rd.
Chicago, IL 60631
Ph: (773)380-2700
Free: (800)638-3522
Fax: (773)380-2588
E-mail: doug.haugen@elca.org
URL: http://www.elca.org/lmm
Contact: Doug Haugen, Dir.
Founded: 1988. **Members:** 5,000. **Regional Groups:** 65. **Description:** Male members of congregations of the Evangelical Lutheran Church of America. Seeks to involve men in the work of the Church. **Committees:** Child Pornography; Fighting Child Abuse; Self-Help. **Formed by Merger of:** Lutheran Church in America; American Lutheran Church; Association of Evangelical Lutheran Church. **Formerly:** (1969) Brotherhood of the American Lutheran Church; (1983) American Lutheran Church Men; (1988) Association of Lutheran Men. **Publications:**

Men in Mission, quarterly. Newsletter. **Circulation:** 5,000. **Conventions/Meetings:** biennial meeting.

19814 ■ Lutheran Mission Societies (LMS)
c/o Tom Olson
1301 Wilson Ave.
Cloquet, MN 55720
Ph: (218)879-8093
E-mail: pastortomolson@aol.com
Contact: Pastor Tom Olson, Pres.
Founded: 1921. **Members:** 1,000. **Staff:** 4. **Budget:** $60,000. **Local Groups:** 20. **Description:** Conducts mission work and social services in Alaska. Operates a radio station in Naknek, AK. **Formerly:** (1962) Federated Norwegian Lutheran Young People's Societies of America. **Publications:** *The Alaska Update*. Newsletter. Alternate Formats: online ● *Letter*, periodic. **Conventions/Meetings:** annual conference - always August.

19815 ■ Lutheran Services in America (LSA)
c/o Jill Schumann, Pres.
700 Light St.
Baltimore, MD 21230-3850
Ph: (410)230-2702
Free: (800)664-3848
Fax: (410)230-2710
E-mail: jschumann@lutheranservices.org
URL: http://www.lutheranservices.org
Contact: Jill Schumann, Pres.
Description: Alliance of the Evangelical Lutheran Church in America, the Lutheran Church-Missouri Synod and their 300 health and human service organizations. Member organizations provide services to children and families, to older persons and persons with disabilities, including but not limited to adult day care; advocacy; alcohol and substance abuse services, addiction counseling; AIDS ministries; care team ministries; chaplaincy; child day care; children's residential; consultation and development programs for pastors, congregations and community groups; counseling, behavioral health; disaster services; employment services; food, shelter, and/or emergency aid; foster care, adoption; home health care; hospice; housing; life enrichment programs; ombudsman services; prison ministries and refugee resettlement. **Computer Services:** database ● information services. **Publications:** *LSA Today*, quarterly ● Annual Report.

19816 ■ Lutheran Student Movement - U.S.A. (LSM-USA)
8765 W Higgins Rd.
Chicago, IL 60631-4194
Ph: (773)380-2852
Free: (800)638-3522
Fax: (773)380-2750
E-mail: ls.musa@elca.org
URL: http://www.lsm-usa.org
Contact: Nate Kerr, Pres.
Founded: 1969. **Members:** 7,500. **Staff:** 1. **Budget:** $12,700. **Regional Groups:** 12. **Local Groups:** 200. **Description:** College, university, and seminary students from Lutheran and even other denominations in the U.S. Promotes the understanding and advancement of the gospel of Jesus Christ, especially as it relates to today's students. Focuses on the biblical themes of worship, community, and social ministry. Encourages active participation in the life and mission of the Church. Acts as a public voice of Lutheran students to the national Lutheran Church bodies. Participates in the national, regional, and local levels. Sponsors several study/action projects. Maintains resource file. **Libraries: Type:** reference. **Awards:** Hess-Pearson Award. **Frequency:** annual. **Type:** recognition. **Recipient:** for service to organization ● Honorary Lifetime Membership. **Frequency:** annual. **Type:** recognition. **Recipient:** for service to organization. **Telecommunication Services:** electronic mail, apostlemep11@aol.com. **Committees:** International and Multicultural Relations. **Formed by Merger of:** (1969) Lutheran Student Association of America; Gamma Delta. **Publications:** *New Frontiers*, biennial. Newsletter. **Price:** free. **Circulation:** 1,500 ● *Oremus III*. Book ● *Post-Conference Proceedings*, annual ● Also publishes packets for resources on

projects. **Conventions/Meetings:** annual Lutheran Student Movement National Gathering - assembly, for college students from church and secular colleges and universities in the U.S. (exhibits) - end of December-early January (always over New Year's).

19817 ■ Lutheran Volunteer Corps (LVC)
1226 Vermont Ave. NW
Washington, DC 20005
Ph: (202)387-3222
Fax: (202)667-0037
E-mail: director@lutheranvolunteercorps.org
URL: http://www.lutheranvolunteercorps.org
Contact: Rev. Michael Wilker, Exec. Dir.
Founded: 1979. **Staff:** 8. **Budget:** $370. **Description:** Adult volunteers who commit one year to community service. Promotes simplified lifestyle; volunteers live in intentional community. Volunteers provide services in community facilities such as shelters, medical clinics, soup kitchens or provide policy and advocacy work on issues such as affordable housing, hunger issues and the environment. Service is concentrated in urban areas of Baltimore, Maryland; Chicago, Illinois; Milwaukee, Wisconsin; Minneapolis/St. Paul, Minnesota; Washington, DC; Wilmington, Delaware; and Seattle and Tacoma, WA. **Publications:** *Esprit De Corps*, 3/year. Newsletter.

19818 ■ Lutheran Women's Missionary League (LWML)
PO Box 411993
St. Louis, MO 63141-1993
Free: (800)252-5965
Fax: (314)268-1532
E-mail: lwml@lwml.org
URL: http://www.lwml.org
Contact: Norine Stumpf, Office Mgr.
Founded: 1942. **Members:** 200,000. **Staff:** 5. **State Groups:** 40. **Local Groups:** 6,000. **Description:** Women's groups within the congregations of the Lutheran Church-Missouri Synod in the U.S. Works to develop a program of mission education, inspiration, and service for the women of the Lutheran Church-Missouri Synod, and to gather voluntary funds for mission projects. **Committees:** Christian Growth; Member Development; Mission Projects; Mission Service; Program Resources. **Formerly:** (1976) Lutheran Women's Missionary League; (2001) International Lutheran Women's Missionary League. **Publications:** *Convention Manual*, biennial ● *Lutheran Woman's Quarterly*. Magazine. **Price:** $5.00 /year for individuals. Alternate Formats: online ● *LWML Handbook*. **Price:** $7.00. **Conventions/Meetings:** biennial convention.

19819 ■ Lutheran World Relief (LWR)
700 Light St.
Baltimore, MD 21230
Ph: (410)230-2700 (410)230-2800
Free: (800)LWR-LWR2
Fax: (410)230-2882
E-mail: lwr@lwr.org
URL: http://www.lwr.org
Founded: 1945. **Staff:** 45. **Budget:** $48,665,000. **Description:** Works on behalf of the Lutheran churches of the U.S. in overseas programs of community and agricultural development, social service, primary health care, and material aid. Provides aid regardless of race, creed, or political affiliation. Program extends to Asia, Africa, the Middle East, and Latin America. In its overseas program, cooperates with programs of the Lutheran World Federation and national Christian councils, counterpart development, and relief agencies. **Projects:** Chocolate; Coffee; Handcraft. **Affiliated With:** Lutheran World Federation. **Publications:** *Together In Hope*. Book. Recounting LWR's 50 years of relief/development work. ● Annual Report, annual ● Also publishes news updates.

19820 ■ National Lutheran Outdoors Ministry Association (NLOMA)
PO Box 1655
Hillsboro, TX 76645-1655
Free: (877)397-2401
Fax: (254)580-9287

E-mail: nloma@nloma.org
URL: http://www.nloma.org
Contact: Kevin Hall, Pres.
Founded: 1983. **Members:** 120. **Budget:** $40,000. **Description:** Individuals (100) and camps (20) joined to aid in the mission of the Lutheran church and to promote Christian camping and related experience. Provides support for all areas of outdoor ministry. Serves as resource base for camps in the areas of personnel development, site evaluation, program development, and staff recruitment. Conducts seminars and training sessions. Maintains placement service for individuals seeking employment at a member camp. **Formerly:** (1984) Lutheran Outdoors Ministry Association. **Conventions/Meetings:** annual meeting.

19821 ■ Seafarers and International House (SIH)
123 E 15th St.
New York, NY 10003
Ph: (212)677-4800
E-mail: info@sihnyc.org
URL: http://www.sihnyc.org
Contact: Gary A. Grindeland, Exec. Dir.
Founded: 1873. **Staff:** 14. **Budget:** $850,000. **Regional Groups:** 3. **Description:** Offers pastoral care, hospitality, social assistance, advocacy and prayer. Seeks to nurture the human spirit and fosters human dignity. Conducts activities in maritime ports throughout Connecticut, Massachusetts, New Jersey, New York and Rhode Island, as well as in its 84-room hotel open to public. **Libraries: Type:** reference. **Holdings:** 5,000. **Telecommunication Services:** electronic mail, res@sihnyc.org. **Formerly:** Lutheran Seaman's Center; (1965) Seamen's Center; (1985) Seamen and International House. **Publications:** *SIH News*, quarterly. **Price:** free ● Brochure.

19822 ■ Wheat Ridge Ministries
1 Pierce Pl., Ste.250E
Itasca, IL 60143-2634
Ph: (630)766-9066
Free: (800)762-6748
Fax: (630)766-9622
E-mail: wrmail@wheatridge.org
URL: http://www.wheatridge.org
Contact: Richard Herman, Pres.
Founded: 1905. **Members:** 25. **Staff:** 10. **Budget:** $2,000,000. **Description:** Independent Lutheran organization. Provides "seed-money" grants for church-related health and social service projects in nine countries. Raises funds through contributions and by annual distribution of Christmas Seals; current projects include community health and health promotion programs, family counseling and enrichment services, aid for the homeless, projects for the aging, and pastoral care. **Awards: Type:** grant. **Recipient:** for ministries ● Seeds of Hope Awards. **Type:** recognition. **Recipient:** for focus on the mission statement. **Computer Services:** Mailing lists, of members. **Formerly:** (1946) Evangelical Lutheran Sanatorium Association; (1992) Wheat Ridge Foundation. **Publications:** *Annual Project Listing*, annual ● Newsletter, semiannual. **Conventions/Meetings:** semiannual board meeting - usually May and November, in Chicago, IL.

19823 ■ World Mission Prayer League (WMPL)
232 Clifton Ave.
Minneapolis, MN 55403-3497
Ph: (612)871-6843
E-mail: wmpl@wmpl.org
URL: http://www.wmpl.org
Contact: Charles Lindquist, Gen. Dir.
Founded: 1937. **Members:** 5,700. **Staff:** 110. **Budget:** $2,500,000. **Multinational. Description:** Independent Lutheran missionary-sending society. Provides opportunity for lay members, as well as for pastors, to preach the Gospel and labor for its successful propagation among the unevangelized peoples of the earth. **Libraries: Type:** open to the public. **Holdings:** 2,500; books, periodicals, video recordings. **Subjects:** religion, Christian missions, Evangelism. **Absorbed:** American Santal Mission.

Formerly: (1940) South American Mission Prayer League. **Publications:** *Fellow Workers*, quarterly. Magazine. Covers the Mission's efforts at bringing Christianity to the world. Contains Directory of Missionaries. **Price:** $5.00/year; $12.00/3 years; free to contributors. **Circulation:** 9,000 ● *Together In Prayer*, monthly. Newsletter. Alternate Formats: online. **Conventions/Meetings:** annual meeting - always in Minneapolis, MN.

19824 ■ Youth Ministry
c/o Lutheran Church-Missouri Synod
1333 S Kirkwood Rd.
St. Louis, MO 63122-7295
Ph: (314)965-9000
Free: (888)843-5267
Fax: (314)996-1016
E-mail: youth.ministry@lcms.org
URL: http://www.lcms.org
Contact: Rev. Terry K. Dittmer, Dir.
Founded: 1979. **Members:** 100,000. **Staff:** 1. **Regional Groups:** 35. **Local Groups:** 6,200. **Description:** Young adults ranging from junior high age through age 25. Supports youth groups within the Lutheran Church-Missouri Synod and provides young people with the opportunity to carry out their role as Christ's disciples. Fosters fellowship among Lutheran Church-Missouri Synod youth and other youth groups; enables youths to share their faith through evangelistic and mission projects; develops leadership skills; increases dialogue between the church and its young people; encourages the exchange of ideas and resources for improving youth ministry. Offers leadership training and program development for youths on the denominational, district, and congregational levels. Sponsors annual mission project which provides youth with an opportunity to support worldwide mission activity. Maintains Council of District Representatives which identifies issues of concern to youth including leadership, suicide, abortion, and drug and alcohol abuse. Assists local congregations in promoting group Bible study, corporate worship, and mutual caring among youth. **Committees:** Church and Society; Communications and Public Relations; Spiritual Growth and Christian Witness. **Formerly:** (2000) Lutheran Youth Fellowship. **Publications:** *LYF Lines*, 3/year. Newsletter. Updates affiliate youth groups on the organization and resources available to build effective youth groups and programs. Includes calendar of events. **Price:** free for Lutheran church members; $7.00 /year for nonmembers. **Circulation:** 6,500 ● Brochures ● Pamphlet ● Also publishes supplement. **Conventions/Meetings:** annual Leadership Conference ● triennial Youth Gathering - general assembly - usually July or August.

Macedonian

19825 ■ Macedonian Outreach
PO Box 398
Danville, CA 94526-0398
Ph: (925)820-4107
Fax: (925)820-4107
E-mail: macout@acts.org
URL: http://www.macedonianoutreach.com
Contact: Dr. Haig A. Rushdoony, Dir.
Founded: 1992. **Multinational. Description:** Promotes the needs of the Balkans by assisting Christian workers in their work; supplies food, clothing and monetary aid to all in need; brings children with life-threatening medical problems to the U.S. or Europe for treatment. Focuses efforts on the Balkan countries of Albania, Bulgaria, Greece, Romania, and Yugoslavia, including former states such as Bosnia, Croatia, and former Yugoslavian Republic of Macedonia.

Medical

19826 ■ Christian Medical and Dental Associations (CMDA)
PO Box 7500
Bristol, TN 37621

Ph: (423)844-1000
Free: (888)230-2637
Fax: (423)844-1005
E-mail: main@cmda.org
URL: http://www.cmdahome.org
Contact: David Stevens MD, CEO
Founded: 1931. **Members:** 17,500. **Staff:** 75. **Regional Groups:** 6. **Description:** Serves as a voice and ministry for Christian doctors. Aims to "change the heart of healthcare." Promotes positions and addresses policies on health care issues; conducts overseas and domestic medical mission projects; coordinates a network of Christian doctors for fellowship and professional growth; sponsors student ministries in medical and dental schools; distributes educational and inspirational resources; holds marriage and family conferences; provides Third World missionary doctors with continuing education resources; and conducts academic exchange programs overseas. **Awards:** Servant's Award. **Frequency:** annual. **Type:** recognition. **Formerly:** (1988) Christian Medical Society; (1998) Medical Group Missions of the Christian Medical and Dental Society; (2000) Christian Medical and Dental Society; (2000) Global Health Outreach of the Christian Medical and Dental Society. **Publications:** *Christian Doctor's Digest*, 6/year. Magazine. Covers issues on bioethics, medical missions, financial stewardship, marriage and family. **Price:** included in membership dues. **Circulation:** 12,000 ● *Life Support*. Magazine. Alternate Formats: online ● *Member Services & Opportunities*, annual. Brochure ● *News & Views*, weekly. Newsletter. Alternate Formats: online ● *SCAN*. Newsletter. **Price:** free to doctors serving in foreign countries ● *Today's Christian Doctor*, quarterly. Magazine. Contains articles on medical and ethical issues. **Price:** included in membership dues. ISSN: 0009-546X. **Circulation:** 15,000. **Advertising:** accepted ● SCAN is distributed free to doctors serving in foreign countries; public service announcements - CMDS Healthwise (quarterly, CD format). **Conventions/Meetings:** annual convention, with scientific meeting (exhibits) ● annual House of Delegates/National Convention - conference (exhibits) - always June.

19827 ■ Christian Medical Foundation International (CMF)
PO Box 152136
Tampa, FL 33684-2136
Ph: (813)932-3688
E-mail: cmfintl@aol.com
URL: http://www.wwmedical.com/cmf
Contact: William Standish Reed MD, Pres./Founder
Founded: 1962. **Members:** 4,854. **Staff:** 8. **State Groups:** 4. **Description:** Physicians, nurses, clergy, and laity. Seeks to: investigate and promote the Christian spiritual care of those who are ill; educate doctors, nurses, and medical students regarding Christian medical and ethical principles. Maintains speakers' bureau, placement service and biographical archives. Sponsors charitable programs. **Libraries:** Type: reference. **Holdings:** 2,500. **Programs:** Clinical Investigation into Spiritual Healing. **Publications:** *Progress Notes*, bimonthly. **Conventions/Meetings:** annual meeting - always October, in Tampa, FL.

19828 ■ Fellowship of Associates of Medical Evangelism (FAME)
4545 Southeastern Ave.
PO Box 33548
Indianapolis, IN 46203
Ph: (317)358-2480
Free: (800)379-4351
Fax: (317)358-2483
E-mail: medicalmissions@fameworld.org
URL: http://www.fameworld.org
Contact: Rick Wolford, Exec. Dir.
Founded: 1970. **Staff:** 6. **Description:** Builds hospitals and clinics and provides mobile medical units for Christian missionaries outside the U.S; secures and ships medicine and medical supplies. Conducts charitable programs; maintains Speaker's Bureau. **Awards: Type:** scholarship. **Recipient:** for individuals who have been accepted into medical school and are committed to missionary work. **Com-**

puter Services: database ● mailing lists ● online services. **Publications:** *Journal of Medical Missions*, quarterly. Newsletter. Alternate Formats: online.

19829 ■ Health Ministries (HM)
Bd. for Human Care Ministries
1333 S Kirkwood Rd.
St. Louis, MO 63122-7295
Ph: (314)996-1382 (314)996-1375
Free: (800)248-1930
Fax: (314)996-1128
E-mail: healthministries@lcms.org
URL: http://www.lcms.org/pages/internal.asp-?NavID=1889
Contact: Carol Broemmer, Mgr.
Staff: 5. **Budget:** $165,000. **Description:** Consultants to all boards and commissions of the Lutheran Church-Missouri Synod having a relationship to the "healing mission" of the church and health issues of professional church workers. **Telecommunication Services:** electronic mail, carol.broemmer@lcms.org. **Committees:** Inter Lutheran Coordinating Committee Ministerial Health and Wellness. **Formerly:** (1969) Council for Christian Medical Work; (1981) Commission on Health and Healing; (1986) Health and Healing Ministries. **Publications:** *AIDS Alert*. Newsletter ● *Cross and Caduceus*, 3/year. Newsletter. Focuses on health and wellness issues. **Price:** free. **Circulation:** 12,000 ● *Gesundheit*. Newsletter. **Circulation:** 35 ● *Parish Nurse*, quarterly. Newsletter.

19830 ■ Interchurch Medical Assistance (IMA)
500 Main St., Old Main Bldg.
PO Box 429
New Windsor, MD 21776
Ph: (410)635-8720
Free: (877)241-7952
Fax: (410)635-8726
E-mail: communications@interchurch.org
URL: http://www.interchurch.org
Contact: Paul Derstine, Pres.
Founded: 1960. **Members:** 12. **Membership Dues:** organization, $1,000 (annual). **Staff:** 30. **Budget:** $96,000,000. **Multinational. Description:** Provides comprehensive technical and material assistance for overseas health programs of partner churches, faith-based development and relief organizations, and public agencies with similar goals. Focusing on international health issues, assistance is provided to people in need without regard to ethnicity, creed, color, gender, national origin, or religious or political affiliation. **Programs:** IMA Medicine Box; Neglected Disease Partnership; Soroptimist Village Dispensary Kit. **Projects:** Health Development Partnership; HIV/AIDS-Related Partnership; Maternal and Neonatal Health Partnership. **Affiliated With:** Global Health Council. **Publications:** *Interchurch Medical Newsletter*, monthly. **Circulation:** 1,000. Alternate Formats: online ● Annual Report, annual. **Conventions/Meetings:** annual meeting - always last Monday and Tuesday of September in New Windsor, MD.

19831 ■ MAP International (MAP)
PO Box 215000
Brunswick, GA 31521-5000
Ph: (912)265-6010
Free: (800)225-8550
E-mail: map@map.org
URL: http://www.map.org
Contact: Michael J. Nyenhuis, Pres./CEO
Founded: 1954. **Staff:** 100. **Budget:** $111,000,000. **Regional Groups:** 5. **Languages:** English, French, Spanish. **Description:** Promotes the health of people living in the world's poorest communities. Works with partners in the areas of community health development, disease prevention and eradication, relief and rehabilitation and global health advocacy. Promotes access to health services and essential medicines in more than 100 countries each year. **Libraries:** Type: reference. **Holdings:** 3,000; periodicals. **Subjects:** community development, health education. **Awards:** MAP Reader's Digest International Fellowship. **Frequency:** annual. **Type:** fellowship. **Recipient:** to senior medical students. **Departments:** Education

and Information Programs; Medical Supply Program; Resource Development. **Affiliated With:** Evangelical Council for Financial Accountability. **Formerly:** (1976) Medical Assistance Programs. **Publications:** *MAP International Report*, quarterly. Newsletter ● Annual Report.

19832 ■ TECH, Technical Exchange for Christian Healthcare
PO Box 1912
Midland, MI 48641-1912
Ph: (989)837-5515
E-mail: mail@techmd.org
URL: http://www.techmd.org
Contact: Jennie Wood, Exec. Dir.
Founded: 1990. **Membership Dues:** organization, $250 (annual) ● individual, $100 (annual). **Multinational. Description:** Promotes the gospel by helping to improve the efficiency and quality of care provided by medical mission groups and agencies worldwide. **Conventions/Meetings:** conference.

19833 ■ World Medical Mission (WMM)
c/o Samaritan's Purse
PO Box 3000
Boone, NC 28607
Ph: (828)262-1980
Fax: (828)266-1053
E-mail: info@samaritan.org
URL: http://www.samaritan.org
Contact: W. Franklin Graham III, Pres.
Founded: 1977. **Description:** Coordinates medical activities of the evangelical group Samaritan's Purse. Places Christian physicians who serve voluntarily in evangelical mission hospitals overseas and conducts emergency medical relief. Provides assistance in refurbishing and equipping mission hospitals and conducts training sessions. **Publications:** *On Call*, quarterly. Newsletter. Alternate Formats: online ● *The PaceMaker*, quarterly ● *World Medical Mission Newsletter*, bimonthly ● Brochures. **Conventions/Meetings:** annual Prescription for Renewal Conference.

Medical Aid

19834 ■ Medical Missions Response (MMR)
PO Box 57011
Oklahoma City, OK 73157-7011
Free: (866)667-8996
URL: http://www.mmronline.org
Contact: Dr. Rick Donlon, Contact
Multinational. Description: Represents health care workers bound together by their commitment to obey Christ's Great Commission. Endeavors to cross all barriers so that all peoples of the earth may hear the Gospel. Envisions church planting movements among all peoples of the earth. Links volunteer healthcare workers with strategic, short-term, healthcare opportunities around the world. **Publications:** Newsletter.

Mennonite

19835 ■ Mennonite Central Committee (MCC)
21 S 12th St.
PO Box 500
Akron, PA 17501-0500
Ph: (717)859-1151
Free: (888)563-4676
Fax: (717)859-3875
E-mail: mailbox@mcc.org
URL: http://www.mcc.org
Contact: Bruce McCrae, Dir. of Administration and Resources
Founded: 1920. **Members:** 38. **Staff:** 1,350. **Budget:** $63,000,000. **Regional Groups:** 9. **National Groups:** 2. **Multinational. Description:** Relief and service agency of North American Mennonite and Brethren in Christ churches. Administers and participates in programs of agricultural and economic development, education, health, anti-racism, employment development, relief, peace, and disaster service. Serves Africa, Asia, Middle East, Europe,

South, Central, and North America. **Libraries: Type:** reference. **Awards:** Canadian Japanese-Mennonite Scholarship. **Type:** scholarship. **Recipient:** to student enrolled in graduate degree program ● Dwight Moody Wiebe Endowment Fund. **Type:** scholarship. **Recipient:** to former Mennonite Central Committee volunteers enrolled in graduate programs. **Telecommunication Services:** electronic mail, lrg@mcc.org. **Departments:** Administrative Services; Anti-Racism; Communications; Computer Services; Financial Services; Global Family Program; Human Resources; International Programs; Peace and Justice Ministries; Peace Office; Resource Generations Network; Visitor Exchange Program. **Programs:** Affiliated; MCC U.S./MCC Canada; Affiliated; Ten Thousand Villages. **Publications:** A Common Place, bimonthly. Magazine. Introduces MCC's programs and partners. **Price:** free. ISSN: 1083-818X. **Circulation:** 48,000. Alternate Formats: online ● Clusters of Death. Report ● Conciliation Quarterly. Contains information on conflict resolution. **Price:** $12.00/year. **Circulation:** 4,973 ● Damascus Road. Newsletter. Provides anti-racist educational issues. ● MCC Notes, bimonthly. Contains news clips of MCC. **Price:** free for members. **Circulation:** 80,000 ● Peace Office Newsletter, quarterly. Contains analysis of peace issues and conflict situations. **Price:** $10.00/year suggested donation. **Circulation:** 2,039. Alternate Formats: online ● Washington Memo, bimonthly. Contains articles on current U.S. government public policy issues and discussions on peacemaking and justice in domestic and international affairs. **Price:** $10.00/year. **Circulation:** 1,585 ● Women's Concerns Report, bimonthly. Contain reports on women's issues. **Price:** $12.00/year. **Circulation:** 1,324. **Conventions/Meetings:** annual meeting, business of MCC program plans, budget (exhibits) - always June.

19836 ■ Mennonite Church USA Historical Committee
1700 S Main St.
Goshen, IN 46526-4724
Ph: (574)535-7477
Fax: (574)535-7756
E-mail: richp@mennoniteusa.org
URL: http://www.mcusa-archives.org
Contact: Rich Preheim, Interim Dir.
Founded: 1911. **Members:** 400. **Membership Dues:** individual, $25 (annual). **Staff:** 6. **Budget:** $223,000. **Regional Groups:** 9. **Description:** Coordinates the Mennonite Church USA program of historical interpretation and operates two denominational archives. **Libraries: Type:** reference. **Holdings:** archival material. **Subjects:** personal collections and official church records dating back to the 16th century. **Formerly:** (2003) Historical Committee of the Mennonite Church. **Publications:** Mennonite Historical Bulletin, quarterly. **Price:** $25.00/year. ISSN: 0025-9357. **Circulation:** 600. **Conventions/Meetings:** semiannual meeting and workshop.

19837 ■ Mennonite Economic Development Associates (MEDA)
1821 Oregon Pike, Ste.201
Lancaster, PA 17601-6466
Ph: (717)560-6546
Free: (800)665-7026
Fax: (717)560-6549
E-mail: meda@meda.org
URL: http://www.meda.org
Contact: Allan Sauder, Pres.
Founded: 1953. **Members:** 3,100. **Staff:** 230. **Multinational. Description:** Business and professional people of the Mennonite faith who want to express their Christian beliefs through their work, in their community, and through international aid. Goals are to: assist members in discovering ways to apply biblical principles to everyday situations in the marketplace; promote community services; invest human and financial resources abroad to contribute to the creation of business and employment opportunities in less developed countries. Provides developing countries with: consulting and training services in business operation and management fundamentals; seed capital investments; assistance in locating sources of credit; feasibility studies and evaluations;

studies, funds, and advisory services for farmers and farmer associations. Promotes meetings where members can enter into dialogues on issues relating to Christian life in the marketplace such as Christian alternatives to litigation and bankruptcy. Maintains speakers' bureau. **Libraries: Type:** reference. **Holdings:** books, video recordings. **Subjects:** business ethics, economic development. **Absorbed:** (1981) Mennonite Industry and Business Association. **Publications:** The Marketplace, bimonthly. Magazine. **Price:** $20.00/year ● MEDA News, quarterly. Newsletter. Alternate Formats: online ● Year in Review (2004-05): Create A Better World, annual. Annual Report. Alternate Formats: online. **Conventions/Meetings:** annual convention - always November.

19838 ■ Mennonite Education Agency
63846 County Rd. 35, Ste.1
Goshen, IN 46528-9621
Ph: (574)642-3164
Fax: (574)642-4863
E-mail: info@mennoniteeducation.org
URL: http://www.mennoniteeducation.org
Contact: Carlos Romero, Exec. Dir.
Founded: 1905. **Members:** 12. **Staff:** 5. **Description:** Responsible for churchwide educational planning and development and consultation with church high schools, elementary schools, and congregations. Operates three colleges, two seminaries and two universities. **Councils:** Elementary Education; Higher Education; Post-Graduate; Secondary Education. **Formerly:** (2003) Mennonite Board of Education. **Conventions/Meetings:** annual meeting.

19839 ■ Mennonite Voluntary Service (MVS)
PO Box 347
Newton, KS 67114-0347
Ph: (316)283-5100
Free: (866)866-2872
Fax: (316)283-0454
E-mail: service@mennonitemission.net
URL: http://www.mennonitemission.net/Work/Service/
     MVS/default.asp
Founded: 1944. **Members:** 120. **Staff:** 10. **Description:** Volunteers who seek to "follow Jesus Christ in lifestyles of servanthood and simplicity while living in shared households". Works in ministries of healing and hope with the poor and marginalized of the society and with children to elderly in: social services, education, health, housing, legal aid, community development, and environmental. **Publications:** Beyond Ourselves, quarterly. Magazine. Features stories of inspiration related to the mission of Jesus Christ. Alternate Formats: online ● Mission Dei, quarterly. Booklet. Contains a series of biblical and theological essays on the work of mission. Alternate Formats: online ● Opportunity for Service, biennial. Magazine.

19840 ■ Mennonite Women USA
722 Main St.
PO Box 347
Newton, KS 67114-0347
Ph: (316)283-5100
Free: (800)794-5101
Fax: (316)283-0454
E-mail: office@mennonitewomenusa.org
URL: http://www.mennonitewomenusa.org
Contact: Rhoda Keener, Exec. Dir.
Founded: 1997. **Staff:** 4. **Budget:** $195,000. **Regional Groups:** 21. **Local Groups:** 300. **Description:** Ministers to the women of Mennonite Church USA by resourcing women groups and individual women as they nurture their life in Christ, study the Bible, utilize their gifts, hear each other, and engage in mission and service. **Divisions:** Business and Professional Women; Women and Preschool. **Formerly:** (2000) Women's Missionary and Service Commission of the Mennonite Church. **Publications:** Bible Study Guide, annual. Includes Bible study lessons, book list, and seasonal programs. **Price:** $4.00 in U.S.; $5.00 in Canada; $7.00/additional copy. **Circulation:** 3,400 ● Timbrel, bimonthly. Magazine. Features inspirational growth articles and service project opportunities. **Price:** $6.00 in U.S.; $8.00 in

Canada. **Circulation:** 7,000. **Conventions/Meetings:** biennial Mennonite Women Events - assembly (exhibits).

19841 ■ Rosedale Mennonite Missions (RMM)
9920 Rosedale-Milford Center Rd.
Irwin, OH 43029
Ph: (740)857-1366
Fax: (866)883-1367
E-mail: info@rmmoffice.org
URL: http://www.rosedalemennonitemissions.org
Contact: Joe Showalter, Pres.
Founded: 1919. **Members:** 11,000. **Budget:** $2,000,000. **Languages:** English, German, Spanish. **Description:** Establishes churches and conducts evangelical activities worldwide. Operates development and relief projects in Nicaragua, Costa Rica, and Ecuador. Maintains medical clinics; distributes food and clothing; provides agricultural advice and assistance. Limited work in the Middle East. **Awards: Type:** recognition. **Departments:** Service, Evangelism, Nurture and Discipleship Ministries. **Formerly:** (1990) Conservative Mennonite Board of Missions and Charities. **Publications:** Brotherhood Beacon, monthly. Newsletter. **Price:** $17.00. **Circulation:** 4,000. Alternate Formats: online ● Focus, monthly. **Price:** free ● Mosaic, monthly. Bulletin. Contains news, stories and updates from RMM mission locations. Alternate Formats: online ● Pictorial Directory. Alternate Formats: CD-ROM ● Annual Report, annual. Alternate Formats: CD-ROM. **Conventions/Meetings:** quarterly board meeting - usually in Irwin, OH ● annual conference (exhibits).

Messianic Judaism

19842 ■ International Alliance of Messianic Congregations and Synagogues (IAMCS)
PO Box 20006
Sarasota, FL 34276-3006
Ph: (941)923-0193
Free: (866)426-2766
E-mail: info@iamcs.org
URL: http://iamcs.org
Contact: Rabbi Judah Hungerman, Chm.
Founded: 1986. **Members:** 130. **Membership Dues:** Messianic Congregation, $100 (annual). **Multinational. Description:** Messianic Jewish congregations and synagogues. (Messianic Jewish believers following the practices and traditions of Judaism, but believe that Yeshua (Jesus) of Nazareth is the Jewish Messiah.) Promotes the welfare of Messianic synagogues; ordains rabbis. Operates placement service. **Publications:** Spirit of Messiah, quarterly. Magazine. **Price:** free. **Circulation:** 200. Alternate Formats: online. **Conventions/Meetings:** annual Messianic Rabbis Conference (exhibits).

19843 ■ International Federation of Messianic Jews (IFMJ)
PO Box 271708
Tampa, FL 33688
Ph: (813)920-0864
Fax: (813)949-7738
E-mail: hc.emunah@verizon.net
URL: http://www.ifmj.org
Contact: Rabbi George Quinn, Pres.
Founded: 1994. **Membership Dues:** person, $35 ● couple/family, $45. **Languages:** English, Spanish. **Multinational. Description:** Represents the interests of Messianic Sephardic Jews worldwide. Promotes the understanding of Sephardic revival. Works to address issues of concern of the Messianic Sephardic Jews community. Encourages communication among Messianic Jews worldwide. Supports synagogues and congregations around the world. **Publications:** Articles. Alternate Formats: online. **Conventions/Meetings:** annual conference.

19844 ■ Jews for Jesus (JfJ)
60 Haight St.
San Francisco, CA 94102-5802
Ph: (415)864-2600
Fax: (415)552-8325

E-mail: jfj@jewsforjesus.org
URL: http://www.jewsforjesus.org
Contact: David Brickner, Exec. Dir.
Founded: 1973. **Members:** 250,000. **Staff:** 150.
Budget: $13,000,000. **State Groups:** 10. **National Groups:** 10. **Languages:** English, French, German, Hebrew, Russian, Spanish. **Description:** Jewish people who believe that Y'shua (Jesus) is the Messiah and claim their lives have been changed as a result of that belief. Promotes understanding and reconciliation; helps Christians appreciate the Jewish heritage of the church. Provides Jewish evangelism seminars and Messianic music and drama workshops. Sponsors Summer Witnessing Campaign Training Course. Conducts research in Jewish Christian relations and creative communication. Operates speakers' bureau; compiles statistics. **Libraries: Type:** reference. **Holdings:** books, periodicals. **Subjects:** Judaica, theology, missions. **Awards:** Hazel Stone Memorial Scholarship. **Type:** scholarship. **Recipient:** for Bible training to a Jewish woman who believes in Jesus and wants a career in evangelism. **Divisions:** Liberated Wailing Wall; Purple Pomegranate Productions. **Publications:** *Havurah*, quarterly. Newsletter. Includes articles on holiday celebration and maintaining Jewish identity while believing in Christ. Also includes book reviews and calendar of events. **Circulation:** 18,000 ● *Issues: A Messianic Jewish Perspective*, bimonthly. Journal. Includes articles, art, poetry, and book reviews relating to contemporary Messianic Jewish alternatives. ISSN: 0741-0352. **Circulation:** 27,000 ● *Jews for Jesus Briefing Bulletin*, periodic. News release sent to the media. **Price:** free to media. **Circulation:** 800 ● *The Jews for Jesus Newsletter: For the Christian Who Wants to Know More About Jews and Evangelism*, monthly. Includes articles and monthly reports by Jews for Jesus missionaries. ISSN: 0740-5901. **Circulation:** 120,000 ● Articles ● Audiotapes ● Books ● Pamphlets. **Conventions/Meetings:** annual regional meeting.

19845 ■ Messianic Jewish Alliance of America (MJAA)
PO Box 274
Springfield, PA 19064
Free: (800)225-MJAA
Fax: (610)338-0471
E-mail: info@mjaa.org
URL: http://www.mjaa.org
Contact: Joel Chernoff, Gen. Sec.
Founded: 1915. **Members:** 2,500. **Membership Dues:** individual, $25 (annual) ● couple, $40 (annual). **Staff:** 12. **Regional Groups:** 6. **Description:** Represents Jewish believers in (Yeshua) Jesus as the Messiah. Advances the spiritual development and welfare of Messianic Jews; bring about better understanding between Jews and Gentiles and combat anti-Semitism; promote a united witness for the Messiah to the church and synagogue. Operates speakers' bureau. Maintains youth branch, the Young Messianic Jewish Alliance. Conducts charitable programs. **Awards: Type:** fellowship. **Recipient:** for Messianic pastors ● Student Aid. **Frequency:** annual. **Type:** scholarship. **Recipient:** for Messianic Jewish students. **Committees:** International Outreach; International Relations. **Funds:** Russian Emergency Aliyah. **Programs:** Plant a Tree in Israel. **Projects:** Joseph. **Affiliated With:** International Messianic Jewish Alliance. **Formerly:** (1975) Hebrew Christian Alliance of America. **Publications:** *Messianic Jewish Alliance of America—Newsbriefs*, quarterly. Newsletter. Includes calendar of events. **Price:** free. **Circulation:** 3,000 ● *The Messianic Times*. Newspaper. **Price:** included in membership dues ● *MJAA News Brief*, quarterly. Newsletter. **Circulation:** 3,000 ● Papers. Alternate Formats: online. **Conventions/Meetings:** annual Messiah Conference (exhibits) - June/July ● bimonthly regional meeting.

19846 ■ Messianic Jewish Movement International (MJMI)
PO Box 1212
Chandler, AZ 85244-1212
Ph: (480)786-6564
Fax: (480)786-6564

E-mail: office@mjmi.org
URL: http://www.mjmi.org
Contact: Nathan L. Jacobus, Pres.
Founded: 1963. **Members:** 5,300. **Staff:** 6. **Budget:** $240,000. **Regional Groups:** 1. **State Groups:** 1. **Local Groups:** 1. **National Groups:** 2. **Languages:** Dutch, English, German, Hebrew, Russian, Spanish, Yiddish. **Description:** Represents messianic Jews and non-Jews who have found Jesus as "Israel's Messiah and Savior". Seeks to experience their biblical Jewish roots and biblical heritage with Israel. Promotes and teaches Messianic Judaism through television and radio programs and print media. Works to advance Evangelism of Jewish people. Sponsors training seminars. **Libraries: Type:** reference. **Holdings:** books. **Subjects:** Jewish evangelism, Israel, Hebrew, worship, dance. **Publications:** Newsletter, monthly. Alternate Formats: online ● Catalogs.

19847 ■ A Messianic Jewish Perspective (AMJP)
60 Haight St.
San Francisco, CA 94102
Ph: (415)864-2600
Fax: (415)552-8325
E-mail: jfj@jewsforjesus.org
URL: http://www.jewsforjesus.org
Contact: Susan Perlman, Communications Dir.
Founded: 1976. **Languages:** English, Russian. **Multinational. Description:** Jews who do not believe that Jesus Christ is the Messiah but are willing to explore the issue. Represents those with an interest in the Messianic Jewish perspective. Works to investigate the Jewish roots of Christianity; encourages communication among individuals interested in the Jewishness of Christianity Jewish practice (traditions, forms) in light of faith in Christ. Compiles statistics. **Convention/Meeting:** none. **Computer Services:** Online services. **Committees:** Editorial. **Affiliated With:** Jews for Jesus. **Publications:** *Following Y'shua* ● *Future Hope* ● *Issues—A Messianic Jewish Perspective*, bimonthly. Newsletter. Includes book reviews, theological articles, poetry, and "Old World" Jewish folk tale in each issue. **Price:** free. **Circulation:** 60,000 ● *Jesus for Jews*. Book ● *Jewish Doctors Meet the Great Physician* ● *Passover Messianic Haggadah*. Book ● *Services of Testimonies* ● *Testimonies*. Booklets. Alternate Formats: online ● *Witnessing to Jews* ● *The Y'shua Challenge*. Book.

Methodist

19848 ■ Black Methodists for Church Renewal (BMCR)
201 8th Ave. S
PO Box 801
Nashville, TN 37202-0801
Ph: (615)749-6351
Fax: (615)749-6351
E-mail: bmcr@bmcr-umc.org
URL: http://www.bmcr-umc.org
Contact: Bishop Melvin G. Talbert, Exec. Dir.
Founded: 1968. **Members:** 4,000. **Membership Dues:** national (sustaining), $35 (annual) ● student/associate (non-voting), $20 (annual) ● century, $100 (annual) ● life, $500 ● Harry Hosier (life), $1,000. **Staff:** 2. **Budget:** $175,000. **Regional Groups:** 5. **Description:** Black clergy and lay members of the United Methodist church. Serves as platform from which blacks can express concerns to the general church on issues such as: revival and survival of the black church; involvement of blacks within the structure of the church; the conduct of the church as it relates to investment policies and social issues; economic support in the black community; the support of the 11 black colleges. Encourages black Methodists to work for economic and social justice. Works to expose racism in agencies and institutions of the United Methodist church. Seeks improvement of educational opportunities for blacks, the strengthening of black churches, and an increase in the number of black persons in Christian-related vocations. Advocates liberation, peace, justice, and freedom for all people. Supports programs that alleviate suffering in Third World countries. **Publications:** *Board of Directors Directory*, semiannual ● *NOW Newsletter*, quarterly. Includes association and member news. **Price:** included in membership dues. **Circulation:** 5,000. **Conventions/Meetings:** periodic conference ● annual meeting (exhibits).

19849 ■ Fellowship of United Methodists in Music and Worship Arts
PO Box 24787
Nashville, TN 37202-4787
Ph: (615)749-6875
Free: (800)952-8977
Fax: (615)749-6874
E-mail: fummwa@aol.com
URL: http://members.aol.com/fummwa
Contact: David Bone, Admin.
Founded: 1956. **Members:** 2,100. **Membership Dues:** individual, $45 (annual). **Staff:** 1. **Budget:** $100,000. **Regional Groups:** 5. **State Groups:** 50. **Local Groups:** 74. **Description:** Promotes the best in Christian musical culture; trains persons for leadership in parishes. Conducts educational programs. **Awards: Frequency:** annual. **Type:** scholarship. **Recipient:** for college students in music degree programs or special studies in worship. **Computer Services:** Mailing lists, of members. **Formerly:** (1973) National Fellowship of Methodist Musicians; (1979) Fellowship of United Methodist Musicians; (1995) Fellowship of United Methodists in Worship, and Other Arts. **Publications:** *Worship Arts*, bimonthly. Journal. ISSN: 0891-5288. **Circulation:** 2,300. **Advertising:** accepted. **Conventions/Meetings:** biennial National Convocation - convention (exhibits).

19850 ■ Forum for Scriptural Christianity
c/o DBA Good News Magazine
308 E Main
PO Box 150
Wilmore, KY 40390
Ph: (859)858-4661
Free: (800)487-7784
E-mail: info@goodnewsmag.org
URL: http://www.goodnewsmag.org
Contact: James V. Heidinger II, Pres./Publisher
Founded: 1966. **Staff:** 10. **Budget:** $750,000. **State Groups:** 40. **Description:** Acts as forum for evangelical Christianity within the United Methodist Church. Seeks to return Methodism to a more conservative interpretation of Christianity through stressing a five-point program of belief: inspiration of Scripture; virgin birth of Christ; substitutionary atonement of Christ; resurrection of Christ; return of Christ. Believes that the evangelical movement is an important one among the laity and clergy, and should be recognized by the church as such. **Committees:** Continuing Education; Ethnic Minority; Evangelism; Missions; Political Strategy; Renewal Groups; Seminary Life; Women. **Also Known As:** Good News. **Publications:** *Good News*, bimonthly. Magazine. Covers the United Methodist Church and current events in religion. Includes book reviews. **Price:** free to donors; $14.95 /year for nonmembers. ISSN: 0436-1563. **Circulation:** 21,000. **Advertising:** accepted. **Conventions/Meetings:** annual meeting (exhibits) - always July.

19851 ■ General Board of Church and Society of the United Methodist Church (GBCS)
100 Maryland Ave. NE
Washington, DC 20002
Ph: (202)488-5629 (202)488-5600
Fax: (202)488-5619
E-mail: jwinkler@umc-gbcs.org
URL: http://www.umc-gbcs.org
Contact: James E. Winkler, Gen. Sec.
Founded: 1917. **Members:** 63. **Staff:** 36. **Budget:** $2,800,000. **Description:** Conducts programs of research, education, and action in areas including alcohol and drug use and abuse, delinquency and crime, health care, world peace and arms control, immigration, population, civil liberties, race relations, economic justice, hunger, and environment agriculture; about 15,000 local churches maintain commissions engaged in this work. **Awards:** Ethnic Local

Church Grants. **Frequency:** semiannual. **Type:** recognition. **Telecommunication Services:** hotline, legislative hotline, (800)455-2645. **Subgroups:** Ministry of God's Creation; Ministry of God's Human Community; Ministry of Resourcing Congregational Life. **Publications:** *Christian Social Action*, bimonthly. Magazine. **Price:** $15.00/year. **Circulation:** 3,000. **Advertising:** accepted ● Pamphlets ● Also publishes audiovisuals on social issues and the Christian faith. **Conventions/Meetings:** semiannual board meeting and conference ● seminar, covers national and international affairs.

19852 ■ Methodist Federation for Social Action (MFSA)
212 E Capitol St. NE
Washington, DC 20003
Ph: (202)546-8806
Fax: (202)546-6811
E-mail: mfsa@mfsaweb.org
URL: http://www.mfsaweb.org
Contact: Rev. Kathryn J. Johnson, Exec. Dir.
Founded: 1907. **Members:** 5,000. **Membership Dues:** stellar, $500 ● spirited, $200 ● supporting, $150 ● sustaining, $100 ● subscribing, $60. **Staff:** 3. **Budget:** $250,000. **Regional Groups:** 38. **Description:** Independent organization of clergy and laity of the United Methodist Church. Provides witness to the Gospel of Jesus Christ to the world; works on issues of peace, poverty, people's rights and progressive initiatives. Defends human rights and civil liberties as set forth in Biblical tradition and the United Nations Declaration of Human Rights. **Awards:** Ball Award. **Frequency:** annual. **Type:** recognition. **Recipient:** for outstanding and unheralded social witness. **Formerly:** Methodist Federation for Social Service. **Publications:** *Social Questions Bulletin*, bimonthly. Newsletter. Contains analyses of religious, social and political issues. Includes book reviews, research reports, and notices of events. **Price:** included in membership dues; $12.00 /year for nonmembers. ISSN: 0731-0234. **Circulation:** 4,000. **Alternate Formats:** microform. **Conventions/Meetings:** annual conference - 2008 Apr. 22-May 2, Fort Worth, TX.

19853 ■ Mission Society for United Methodists (MSUM)
6234 Crooked Creek Rd.
Norcross, GA 30092-3106
Ph: (770)446-1381
Free: (800)478-8963
Fax: (770)446-3044
E-mail: info@msum.org
URL: http://www.msum.org
Contact: Dr. Philip Granger, Pres./CEO
Founded: 1984. **Staff:** 20. **Multinational. Description:** A voluntary association of United Methodist and other Wesleyan related organizations, pastors, and laity seeking to expand the mission outreach of the Church. Provides missionaries to locations throughout the world where the Gospel has not been heard or heeded; encourages and supports the development of leadership in missions for both the Church and society; challenges all United Methodists with the New Testament imperative to proclaim the Gospel worldwide; establishes and strengthens Christian congregations to help in mission work. Cooperates with Methodists worldwide to achieve these goals. **Committees:** Audit; Field Ministries; Mission Advancement; Missionary Personnel; Nominating; Strategy/Policy. **Affiliated With:** Evangelical Council for Financial Accountability. **Also Known As:** The Mission Society. **Publications:** *Heartbeat*, quarterly. Magazine. **Conventions/Meetings:** semiannual board meeting.

19854 ■ National Federation of Asian-American United Methodists (NFAAUM)
Address Unknown since 2007
Founded: 1975. **Membership Dues:** retired, $20 (annual) ● individual, $30 (annual) ● family, $50 (annual) ● church and agency, $100 (annual). **Staff:** 2. **Regional Groups:** 5. **Description:** Asian-American members of the United Methodist church. Objectives are to: form a national federation of Asian-American caucuses of the 5 jurisdictions of the United Method-

ist church; articulate the concerns, interests, and needs of the Asian-American constituencies in all jurisdictions of the church; advocate the causes of Asian-Americans before appropriate boards and agencies of the church. Coordinates activities of the jurisdictional Asian-American caucuses in relationship with boards and agencies of the church; promotes relevant and meaningful Asian-American ministries at all levels; and encourages full participation of Asian-Americans in all aspects of church life. Constituencies include Chinese, Filipino, Indochinese, Japanese, Korean, Southern Asian, and Taiwanese. Bestows Annual Asian-American Endowment Fund. **Awards:** Endowment Fund. **Frequency:** annual. **Type:** grant. **Publications:** *Asian American News*, quarterly. Newsletter. Includes calendar of events, federation news, resource and job listi ngs, and people in the news. **Price:** included in membership dues. ISSN: 1092-4329. **Circulation:** 2,000. **Advertising:** not accepted ● *Endowment Fund Journal*. Newsletter ● Also publishes National Convocation report books. **Conventions/Meetings:** biennial convention and general assembly (exhibits) ● biennial meeting.

19855 ■ United Methodist Committee on Relief (UMCOR)
475 Riverside Dr., Rm. 330
New York, NY 10115
Ph: (212)870-3552 (212)870-3816
Free: (800)554-8583
E-mail: umcor@gbgm-umc.org
URL: http://gbgm-umc.org/umcor
Contact: Sam W. Dixon, Interim Deputy Gen. Sec.
Founded: 1940. **Staff:** 18. **Budget:** $15,000,000. **Description:** Service organization of the United Methodist church, with a supervising and policy body of 28 persons who represent the national church membership. Guides the denominations in the field of overseas relief, refugee resettlement, and rehabilitation programs to alleviate root causes of hunger. Receives gifts from the church and uses them in 80 countries overseas where the church carries on its program, as well as in the U.S. Channels gifts through Church World Service of the National Council of Churches of Christ in the U.S.A. and through the Commission of Interchurch Aid, Refugee and World Service of the World Council of Churches (see separate entries). **Formerly:** (1968) Methodist Committee for Overseas Relief; (1972) United Methodist Committee on Overseas Relief. **Publications:** *UMCOR Resource Book*, biennial. Serves as a guide to programs and projects. **Price:** $3.00. **Circulation:** 5,000 ● *UMCOR Update*, quarterly. Newsletter. Includes information on current UMCOR projects. **Circulation:** 82,200. **Conventions/Meetings:** semiannual board meeting.

19856 ■ United Methodist Youth Organization
PO Box 340003
Nashville, TN 37203-0003
Ph: (615)340-7184
Free: (877)899-2780
Fax: (615)340-1764
E-mail: youngpeople@gbod.org
URL: http://www.gbod.org/youngpeople
Contact: Ronna Seibert, Exec. Dir.
Founded: 1976. **Members:** 39. **Staff:** 3. **Budget:** $235,000. **Regional Groups:** 68. **Description:** Youth members elected from among representatives of annual conferences (United Methodist regional groupings); adult members are elected from jurisdictional caucuses/conferences or staff representatives of United Methodist boards and agencies with an interest in youth ministry. Initiates and supports special plans and projects at the national level of the church which are of interest to youth; provides for free expression of the conviction of the church's youth on issues vital to them; cooperates with other church agencies in making recommendations regarding the youth ministry of the church; requests suggestions from annual conference youth groups and makes recommendations to general board nominating committees of youth for board membership. Sponsors experimental projects, which have included human relations workshops and legislative affairs programs.

Awards: David W. Self and Richard Smith Scholarship Fund. **Frequency:** annual. **Type:** scholarship. **Recipient:** for members of a United Methodist Church who are graduating high school seniors preparing to enter their first year of college ● Youth Service Fund Grants. **Frequency:** annual. **Type:** grant. **Recipient:** for ministry and youth. **Committees:** Ethnic and Minority Youth Concerns; Project Review; Youth and Social Concerns; Youth Service Fund. **Formerly:** Methodist Council on Youth Ministry; (1976) United Methodist Council on Youth Ministry; (2001) National Youth Ministry Organization. **Publications:** *Book of Resolutions*, biennial. Journal. Contains a summary of actions taken at the Biennial Legislative Assembly. **Price:** $3.00. **Alternate Formats:** online. **Conventions/Meetings:** biennial Convocation and Legislative Assembly - conference, designed to provide youth with a way to allow the church to hear their voice on issues facing the church, the youth themselves, and society as a whole (exhibits).

19857 ■ Women's Division of the General Board of Global Ministries of the United Methodist Church
475 Riverside Dr.
New York, NY 10115
Ph: (212)870-3660
Fax: (212)870-3774
E-mail: umw@gbgm-umc.org
URL: http://gbgm-umc.org/umw
Contact: Jan Love, Chief Exec.
Founded: 1940. **Members:** 1,000,000. **Staff:** 41. **Budget:** $20,000. **Local Groups:** 27,000. **Description:** Women members of the United Methodist Church united to promote spiritual growth and leadership development, and social action among women worldwide. Makes available financial support to ministries and social programs benefiting women, children, and youth in priority areas. **Publications:** *Response*, 11/year. Magazine. Features bible studies, stories of faith, and mission opportunities. **Price:** $18.00/year in U.S.; $24.00/year outside U.S.; $34. 00/2 years in U.S. Alternate Formats: online. **Conventions/Meetings:** quadrennial assembly.

19858 ■ Women's Missionary Council of the Christian Methodist Episcopal Church (WMCCMEC)
c/o Dr. Elnora P. Hamb, Pres.
11321 S Aberdeen St.
Chicago, IL 60643
Ph: (773)264-2273
Fax: (773)264-2274
E-mail: hamb@sbcglobal.net
URL: http://www.cme-church.org/Missionary_Council
Contact: Dr. Elnora P. Hamb, Pres.
Founded: 1918. **Members:** 129,000. **Staff:** 5. **Regional Groups:** 37. **Description:** Women members of the Christian Methodist Episcopal Church. Seeks to: discover and share the mission of the church; promote cooperation, fellowship, and mutual counsel concerning the spiritual life and religious activities of the church; encourage Bible study and assist in spreading the Gospel; research and answer society's needs in order to develop programs and resources that will respond to that need. Conducts educational and charitable programs. **Awards:** Helen B. Cobb Scholarship Grant. **Frequency:** annual. **Type:** scholarship. **Recipient:** for students and pastors in training. **Commissions:** Christian Social Relations; Communications; Education; History. **Divisions:** Service and Outreach; Structure. **Programs:** Aid to Ministers' Widows; The Black Family and Child Advocacy; Christian Social Relations; Ecumenical Relations; Educational Services and Scholarship Aid; Literature and Publications; Marches and Convocations; Missionary Education; Overseas Missions; Personal Stewardship; Projects for Our Colleges; The Relief of Hunger; Spiritual Development; Status of Women. **Affiliated With:** American Bible Society; Bread for the World; Church Women United. **Publications:** *The Missionary Messenger*, monthly. Magazine. **Price:** $15.00/year ● Also publishes handbooks, periodicals, manuals, and missionary education resources. **Con-**

ventions/Meetings: quadrennial assembly ● annual board meeting.

19859 ■ World Federation of Methodist and Uniting Church Women - USA (WFM&UCW)

c/o Mrs. Thelma Johnson
5915 Desmond St.
Cincinnati, OH 45227
Ph: (513)271-7557
URL: http://www.methodistandunitingchurchwomen.org
Contact: Chita Millan, Pres.
Founded: 1939. **Members:** 7,000,000. **Budget:** $65,000. **Regional Groups:** 9. **Local Groups:** 15,000. **National Groups:** 70. **Description:** Methodist women in 70 countries. Promotes peace among nations, the establishment of human rights, and the elimination of discrimination against women in all countries. Fosters spiritual growth; participates in educational and social outreach programs. Exchanges information on religious, social, and economic concerns and issues related to women. Develops counseling and educational programs on such issues as human rights, development, and home-making. Offers leadership training. **Libraries: Type:** reference. **Holdings:** archival material. **Computer Services:** database. **Affiliated With:** World Methodist Council. **Formerly:** World Federation of Methodist Women. **Publications:** *Declaration of Commitment.* Brochure ● *History - A Methodist World Sisterhood.* Book ● *Program Study Material,* annual. Pamphlet ● *Tree of Life,* quarterly. Newsletter. Provides reading material and information to inspire, challenge, educate, and unite members within World Federation. ● *World Federation and United Nations.* Brochure ● *World Federation of Methodist and Uniting Church Women.* Brochures. Contains information in such areas as structure, aims, programmes, consultative status, etc. **Price:** free ● Handbook, quinquennial ● Directory, quinquennial. **Price:** free. **Circulation:** 300. **Conventions/Meetings:** quinquennial World Assembly and Regional Meetings - conference and workshop.

19860 ■ World Methodist Council (WMC)

PO Box 518
Lake Junaluska, NC 28745
Ph: (828)456-9432
Fax: (828)456-9433
E-mail: georgefreeman@charter.net
URL: http://www.worldmethodistcouncil.org
Contact: Dr. George H. Freeman, Gen. Sec.
Founded: 1881. **Members:** 338,844,698. **Staff:** 4. **Budget:** $500,000. **Description:** Fraternal and cooperative association of Methodist, Wesleyan, and other related united churches. Seeks to "draw the branches of the Wesleyan Movement closer together in fellowship and devotion to their mutual heritage and to promote among them evangelistic, educational, historical, and other cooperative movements." Exercises no legislative power over separate denomination members but gives focus and leadership to mutually agreed upon goals and programs. Maintains World Methodist Museum of rare books, records, paintings, sculptures, and other materials pertaining to John Wesley and the beginnings of early Methodism. **Libraries: Type:** open to the public. **Holdings:** 5,000. **Subjects:** religion. **Awards:** World Methodist Peace Award. **Frequency:** periodic. **Type:** recognition. **Recipient:** for heroic service to the cause of peace. **Telecommunication Services:** electronic mail, romawyatt@charter.net. **Committees:** Ecumenics and Dialogue; Education; Evangelism; Family Life; Social and International Affairs; Theological Education; Worship and Liturgy; Youth. **Publications:** *Encyclopedia of World Methodism* ● *Proceedings of World Methodist Conferences* ● *World Methodist Council—Handbook of Information,* quinquennial. Membership Directory. Includes community and membership statistics of World Methodism. **Price:** included in membership dues ● *World Parish: International Organ of the World Methodist Council,* bimonthly. Journal. **Price:** free. ISSN: 0043-8839. **Conventions/Meetings:** quinquennial conference ● annual executive committee meeting - usually September.

19861 ■ World Methodist Historical Society (WMHS)

PO Box 127
Madison, NJ 07940
Ph: (973)408-3189
Fax: (973)408-3909
E-mail: cyrigoyen@gcah.org
URL: http://www.gcah.org/WMHS.htm
Contact: Dr. Charles Yrigoyen Jr., Exec. Sec.
Founded: 1911. **Members:** 200. **Membership Dues:** individual, $5 (annual). **Staff:** 1. **Budget:** $2,000. **Regional Groups:** 4. **Description:** An auxiliary of the World Methodist Council. Oversees the historical activities of world Methodism. Compiles statistics and is currently preparing a union catalog of Methodist manuscript holdings worldwide. **Affiliated With:** World Methodist Council. **Formerly:** International Methodist Historical Union; Methodist Historical Union; (1971) International Methodist Historical Society. **Publications:** *Historical Bulletin,* quarterly. Newsletter. Contains news, notices of meetings and comments about new publication. **Price:** included in membership dues ● Booklets. Covers world Methodist subjects and persons. **Conventions/Meetings:** quinquennial conference.

Ministry

19862 ■ Academy of Parish Clergy (APC)

c/o Dr. Paul J. Binder, Admin. VP
2249 Florinda St.
Sarasota, FL 34231-4414
Ph: (941)922-8633
E-mail: pjbinder2@juno.com
URL: http://www.apclergy.org
Contact: Dr. Paul J. Binder, Admin. VP
Founded: 1968. **Members:** 200. **Membership Dues:** ordinary/fellow, $60 (annual) ● retired, $30 (annual) ● seminary student, $20 (annual) ● life, $800. **Staff:** 11. **Regional Groups:** 6. **Description:** Inter-faith, voluntary, and self-governing association of clergymen and clergywomen who occupy pastoral roles, ordinarily in congregational settings. Works to clarify the vocation and role of parish clergy. Aims to enhance their professional competence by setting standards, imposing self-discipline for effective service, and collectively addressing the needs of their profession. Carry on a continuous study of the emerging forms the ministry is taking in response to the changing needs and challenges of the communities served; confirm the primary role of the ministry found in parish life and to bring about understanding of parish ministry that corresponds to its true character and importance. **Awards:** Book of the Year. **Frequency:** annual. **Type:** recognition. **Recipient:** for the best book that is of benefit to parish ministers ● Parish Pastor of the Year. **Frequency:** annual. **Type:** recognition. **Recipient:** for exceptional performance in parish ministry. **Computer Services:** database. **Publications:** *Academy of Parish Clergy Directory,* annual. **Price:** $5.00 for members ● *Access,* quarterly. Newsletter. Contains news about members and academy meetings. **Price:** included in membership dues. **Circulation:** 200 ● *APC Educational Study Pathways.* Booklet. Issued to new members. Alternate Formats: microform ● *Code of Ethics.* Booklet. Issued to new members. ● *Membership Requirements and Benefits.* Booklet. Issued to new and potential members. **Price:** included in membership dues. **Circulation:** 200 ● *Sharing the Practice,* quarterly. Journal. **Price:** included in membership dues; $25.00 /year for nonmembers; $6.00/copy for nonmembers. ISSN: 0193-8274. **Circulation:** 300. **Advertising:** accepted. Alternate Formats: microform ● *Standard of Competence for Practicing Clergy.* Booklet. Issued to new and potential members. ● *Standards of Competence for Practicing Clergy,* annual. Directory. **Price:** $5.00 for members. **Conventions/Meetings:** annual Convocation - convention (exhibits) ● annual Moving from Membership to Discipleship - conference, with speaker and workshop ● annual symposium.

19863 ■ Association of Full Gospel Women Clergy (AFGWC)

c/o Melanie Conrad, Exec.Dir.
PO Box 2628
Landover Hills, MD 20784
Ph: (301)459-8015
E-mail: info@afgwc.org
Contact: Melanie Conrad, Exec.Dir.
Founded: 1997. **Membership Dues:** $35 (annual). **Staff:** 3. **Description:** Women clergy members. **Publications:** *Women of the Word,* quarterly. Newsletter. **Conventions/Meetings:** annual Women with a Word for the Times - conference.

19864 ■ Aurora Ministries

c/o Aurora Mission
PO Box 1549
Bradenton, FL 34206
Ph: (941)746-2572
Fax: (941)748-2625
E-mail: mission@auroraministries.org
URL: http://www.auroraministries.org
Contact: Rev. Rich Hines, Contact
Description: Seeks to send missionaries to Italy in order to evangelize, disciple, and establish churches.

19865 ■ Christ for the City International (CFCI)

PO Box 241827
Omaha, NE 68124-5827
Ph: (402)592-8332
Free: (888)526-7551
Fax: (402)592-8312
E-mail: info@cfci.org
URL: http://www.cfci.org
Contact: Dr. Duane Anderson, Pres./CEO
Founded: 1995. **Staff:** 10. **Nonmembership. Multinational. Description:** People who share common values, theology, and ministry philosophy. Unites to multiply ministries and send out multinational teams into the least evangelized cities of the world. Evangelizes and unifies the Protestant churches of a city; cares for children at risk as well as training and developing small businesses. **Affiliated With:** Association of Evangelical Relief and Development Organizations; Evangelical Council for Financial Accountability; Evangelical Fellowship of Mission Agencies. **Publications:** *Accelerating International Missions Strategies* ● *Impact.* Newsletter. Alternate Formats: online ● *INSEPA - Urban Ministry Institute Curriculum* (in English and Spanish) ● *Participating Prayer Manual* (in English, Portuguese, and Spanish) ● *Understanding Latin Americans Seminar.* Newsletter ● *Urban Ministry Tool Kit* (in English and Spanish).

19866 ■ Christian Community Development Association (CCDA)

3555 W Ogden Ave.
Chicago, IL 60623
Ph: (773)762-0994
Fax: (773)346-0071
E-mail: info@ccda.org
URL: http://www.ccda.org
Contact: Gordon Murphy, Exec. Dir.
Founded: 1989. **Members:** 500. **Membership Dues:** student, $20 (annual) ● individual, $50 (annual) ● couple, $75 (annual) ● associate, $500 (annual) ● corporate, $5,000 (annual) ● organization, $100-$1,000 (annual). **Description:** Serves as a ministry committed to empowering people in poor communities. Aims to bring together evangelism and social action. Members and their families relocate to live in communities of need, working alongside the community, modeling healthy lifestyles. Works as a clearinghouse. Offers consulting assistance. **Libraries: Type:** open to the public. **Holdings:** papers. **Telecommunication Services:** electronic mail, murphy@ccda.org. **Publications:** *Restorer.* Newsletter. Highlights CCD issues as well as new laws, program ideas, Biblical teaching, and how-to articles. ● Membership Directory. Contains profiles of the members, listed by state and by program. **Conventions/Meetings:** annual conference (exhibits) ● seminar and workshop, for regional and/or local training.

19867 ■ Church Growth Center (CGC)

1230 Hwy. 6
PO Box 145
Corunna, IN 46730
Free: (800)626-8515

E-mail: info@churchdoctor.org
URL: http://www.churchdr.com
Contact: Rev.Dr. Kent R. Hunter, Pres.
Founded: 1976. **Staff:** 4. **Description:** Interdenominational service organization. Works to help churches analyze their congregations, discover their strengths and weaknesses, and provide advice, ideas, and motivation to maintain church growth and vitality. **Publications:** *Global Church Growth: Strategies for Today's Leader,* quarterly. Magazine. **Price:** $23.00/ year. **Circulation:** 1,200. **Advertising:** accepted. **Conventions/Meetings:** workshop and seminar, provides information on mobilizing the laity, church growth and the Christian school, and assimilating new Christians.

19868 ■ Harvest
PO Box 2670
Phoenix, AZ 85002
Ph: (602)258-1083
Fax: (602)258-1318
E-mail: info@harvestfoundation.org
URL: http://www.harvestfoundation.org
Contact: Dr. Robert Moffitt, Pres.
Founded: 1981. **Staff:** 30. **Multinational. Description:** Holistic ministry dedicated to wisdom, stature, favor with God, and favor with man. Promotes the Christian Church around the world to carry out biblical holistic ministry. **Affiliated With:** Food for the Hungry. **Also Known As:** Harvest Foundation.

19869 ■ Institute of Singles Dynamics (ISD)
c/o Don Davidson, Dir./Founder
PO Box 27222
Overland Park, KS 66225-7222
Ph: (816)763-9401
E-mail: don777@swbell.net
URL: http://www.singlesmall.com/isd2.html
Contact: Don Davidson, Dir./Founder
Founded: 1983. **Description:** Provides churches with assistance in developing and improving ministry programs for single adults. Offers consulting services. **Telecommunication Services:** electronic mail, don@singlesmall.com. **Conventions/Meetings:** seminar and workshop.

19870 ■ International Christian Technologists Association (ICTA)
1271 Kelly Johnson Blvd., Ste.240
Colorado Springs, CO 80920
Ph: (719)785-0120
E-mail: gale-listing@icta.net
URL: http://www.icta.net
Contact: Pete Holzmann, Exec. Dir./Founder
Multinational. Description: Provides online source where industry technologists and cross-cultural ministries match expertise to mission information technology needs. Online community for Christian Technologists—resources, stories, discussion and collaboration.

19871 ■ International Network of Prison Ministries (INPM)
Box 227475
Dallas, TX 75222
URL: http://prisonministry.net
Multinational. Description: Promotes crime prevention and rehabilitation through Christian ministry. **Publications:** Newsletter.

19872 ■ Media in Ministry Association (MMA)
c/o Gene Blankenship
2549 Newbolt Dr.
Orlando, FL 32817
Ph: (407)678-0159
Fax: (407)678-0159
E-mail: gene@mediainministry.org
URL: http://www.mediainministry.org
Contact: Gene Blankenship, Contact
Description: Aims to share the Gospel using audio, video, lighting and staging in the community; to share experiences and a faith in Jesus Christ.

19873 ■ Medical Ambassadors International (MAI)
PO Box 576645
Modesto, CA 95357-6645
Ph: (209)524-0600
Free: (888)403-0600
Fax: (209)571-3538
E-mail: info@med-amb.org
URL: http://www.MedicalAmbassadors.org
Contact: Mr. Henri Haber, Dir. of Advancement
Founded: 1980. **Multinational. Description:** Works to minister to the poor of the world, especially children. Trains national health workers and pastors to become trainers of village health evangelists.

19874 ■ Mexican American Cultural Center (MACC)
PO Box 28185
3115 W Ashby Pl.
San Antonio, TX 78228-5104
Ph: (210)732-2156
Fax: (210)732-9072
E-mail: register@maccsa.org
URL: http://www.maccsa.org
Contact: Sis. Maria Elena Gonzalez RSM, Pres.
Founded: 1972. **Members:** 36. **Languages:** English, Spanish. **Description:** Ministers and lay people. Serves as a national pastor education center. Studies Hispanic ministries, especially in the United States and Latin America. Maintains a speaker's bureau. Conducts research and educational programs. **Awards:** Archbishop Patrick Scholarship Trust. **Type:** scholarship. **Publications:** *Vision.* Newsletter. Alternate Formats: online. **Conventions/Meetings:** periodic conference ● periodic seminar.

19875 ■ Mission: Moving Mountains (M:MM)
PO Box 1168
Burnsville, MN 55337-0168
Ph: (952)440-9100
Free: (800)545-7980
Fax: (952)440-9104
E-mail: mmm@movingmountains.org
Contact: Dr. Gary Hipp, CEO
Founded: 1979. **Multinational. Description:** International Christian mission. Spirit-led decision making for community development among the poor. **Publications:** *Celebrate A Feast: A Missionary Cookbook from Africa* ● *Monitor.* Magazine ● Brochure ● Videos.

19876 ■ National Association of Catholic Family Life Ministers (NACFLM)
c/o David Abele, Exec. Dir.
300 Coll. Park
Dayton, OH 45469-2512
Ph: (937)431-5443
Fax: (937)431-5443
E-mail: nacflm@nacflm.org
URL: http://www.nacflm.org
Contact: David Abele, Exec. Dir.
Founded: 1980. **Members:** 400. **Membership Dues:** parish, organization, $100 (annual) ● family/ individual, $30 (annual) ● diocese (1-100,000 population), $150 (annual) ● diocese (100,001-300,000 population), $250 (annual) ● diocese (301,000 or more population), $350 (annual). **Staff:** 2. **Budget:** $250,000. **Regional Groups:** 13. **Languages:** English, Spanish. **Description:** Dioceses and parishes of the Roman Catholic Church and interested individuals. Serves as advocate for families and family ministry in the church and society. Maintains speakers' bureau; conducts educational programs. Member association of the U.S. Catholic Conference of Bishops. **Awards:** NACFLM Award and Recognitions. **Frequency:** annual. **Type:** recognition. **Recipient:** to individuals and/or organizations who have made outstanding contributions to family ministry. **Computer Services:** Mailing lists, of members. **Committees:** Communications; Conference; Education and Formation; Journal; Operations; Resources. **Formerly:** (1989) National Association of Catholic Diocesan Family Life Ministers. **Publications:** *Family Perspectives,* quarterly. Journal. **Price:** $15.00 /year for individuals ● *Foundations,* quarterly. Newsletter. **Price:** $15.00 for individual; $10.00 for parish and

diocesan (multiple) ● *NACFLM Directory,* annual. **Conventions/Meetings:** annual conference ● periodic seminar and workshop.

19877 ■ Samaritan's Purse
PO Box 3000
Boone, NC 28607
Ph: (828)262-1980
Fax: (828)266-1053
E-mail: info@samaritan.org
URL: http://www.samaritanspurse.org
Contact: Franklin Graham, Pres./CEO
Founded: 1970. **Multinational. Description:** Serves as nondenominational evangelical Christian organization committed to spiritual and physical aid to hurting people worldwide; assists victims of war, poverty, natural disasters, disease, and famine with the purpose of sharing God's love through Jesus Christ. Sponsors Operation Christmas Child and World Medical Mission. **Projects:** Children's Heart; Prescription for Hope. **Publications:** *The Call of the Samaritan.* Newsletter. Alternate Formats: online ● *PrayerPoint,* bimonthly. Newsletter. Features stories about projects around the world. ● Annual Report, annual. Alternate Formats: online.

19878 ■ Society for the Increase of the Ministry (SIM)
924 Farmington Ave., No. 100
West Hartford, CT 06107
Ph: (860)233-1732
Fax: (860)233-2644
E-mail: simministry@earthlink.net
URL: http://www.simministry.org
Contact: Rev. John L.C. Mitman, Exec. Dir.
Founded: 1857. **Staff:** 1. **Description:** Works to support candidates preparing for the ordained ministry of the Episcopal Church. **Awards:** **Type:** grant. **Publications:** *The Call,* semiannual. Newsletter. **Conventions/Meetings:** annual meeting.

19879 ■ Wesleyan/Holiness Women Clergy (WHWC Intl.)
c/o Prof. Susie Stanley, Exec. Dir.
Messiah Coll.
1 Coll. Ave.
PO Box 4081
Grantham, PA 17027
Ph: (717)766-2511 (717)691-6021
Fax: (717)691-6040
E-mail: sstanley@messiah.edu
URL: http://www.whwomenclergy.org
Contact: Prof. Susie Stanley, Exec. Dir.
Founded: 1991. **Members:** 200. **Membership Dues:** individual, $25 (annual) ● student, $15. **Staff:** 4. **Budget:** $125,000. **Languages:** Spanish. **Multinational. Description:** Women in ministry or preparing for ministry. Works to equip and encourage divinely called women in professional ministry and professional leadership positions. **Publications:** *Cloud of Witnesses: Portraits of Women Ministries in the Wesleyan/Holiness Movement.* Booklet ● *Come to the Water Conference Newsletter,* 3/year. **Price:** included in membership dues ● *Ezer Conegdo: A Power Like Him, Facing Him as Equal.* Booklet ● *God's Call: From Infilling to Outpouring.* Booklet ● *Inclusive Language Handbook.* Booklet ● *Reclaiming the Wesleyan/Holiness Heritage of Women Clergy: Sermons, a Case Study and Resources.* Booklet ● *Satisfied: Women Hymn Writers of 19th Century Wesleyan/ Holiness Movement.* Booklet ● *Wesleyan Holiness Women Clergy: A Preliminary Bibliography.* **Conventions/Meetings:** biennial Come to the Water - conference (exhibits) - even numbered years.

19880 ■ World Hope International
625 Slaters Ln., Ste.100
Alexandria, VA 22314
Ph: (703)923-9414
Free: (888)466-4673
Fax: (703)923-9418
E-mail: whi@worldhope.net
URL: http://www.worldhope.net
Contact: Jo Anne Lyon, Exec. Dir.
Multinational. Description: Works to mobilize individuals and organizations for the purpose of relief,

economic, and social development. **Affiliated With:** International Longshore and Warehouse Union. **Publications:** *The Waterfront Warrior.* Newsletter.

Mission

19881 ■ Advancing Churches in Missions Commitment (ACMC)

PO Box 5266
Fort Wayne, IN 46895-5266
Ph: (260)492-2262
Free: (877)492-ACMC
Fax: (260)492-9027
E-mail: info@acmc.org
URL: http://www.acmc.org
Contact: Dr. Tom Horn PhD, Exec. VP

Founded: 1974. **Members:** 550. **Membership Dues:** church partner: level 2, $495 (annual) ● church partner: level 1, $295 (annual) ● organizational partner, $350 (annual) ● individual partner, $150 (annual). **Staff:** 15. **Description:** Christian churches, denominations, mission agencies, schools, and interested individuals. Provides assistance to local churches involved in missions and to those beginning their involvement in missions. Objectives are to: increase congregational awareness of current developments in missions worldwide and to encourage their involvement in world evangelization; recognize the enthusiastic involvement of the pastor as an important factor in the church's ministry; assist local churches in establishing and accomplishing their mission goals; expand the number of missions-minded churches in North America. Helps churches maintain a strong and productive relationship with mission agencies. Maintains a resource and document center that provides information to churches. **Formerly:** (1990) Association of Church Missions Committees; (2002) ACMC. **Publications:** *Missions Conference Planner* ● *Missions Policy Handbook* ● *Mobilizer,* quarterly. Magazine ● *Networker,* bimonthly. Newsletter. Provides information on local church missions and mission activities worldwide. Includes calendar of events, new members' listing, and regional news. ● *Sending Out Servants.* Book ● *Directory,* annual. **Price:** available to members only ● Reports. **Conventions/Meetings:** annual conference ● periodic Godsmission Community - conference.

19882 ■ Africa Inland Mission International (AIM)

PO Box 178
Pearl River, NY 10965
Ph: (845)735-4014
Free: (800)254-0010
Fax: (845)735-1814
E-mail: go@aimint.net
URL: http://www.aimint.org/usa
Contact: Dr. Ted Barnett, Dir.

Founded: 1895. **Members:** 742. **Budget:** $16,000,000. **Description:** Missionaries conducting Bible teaching, community development, education, medical work, and evangelization in Angola, Central African Republic, Chad, Islands of the Indian Ocean, Kenya, Lesotho, Madagascar, Mozambique, Namibia, Democratic Republic of Congo, Sudan, Tanzania, Uganda, and urban centers in the United States. Includes activities such as: theological education; radio and television ministries; youth work; technical assistance services; agricultural and community development; relief work; special, industrial, and secondary education. **Libraries: Type:** reference. **Holdings:** 3,200. **Subjects:** Africa. **Affiliated With:** Evangelical Council for Financial Accountability; Interdenominational Foreign Missions Association. **Also Known As:** AIM International. **Formerly:** (1982) Africa Inland Mission. **Publications:** *AIM International,* quarterly. Newsletter. Covers the projects and activities of the mission. Lists employment opportunities. **Price:** free ● *Fuel for Prayer Fires,* monthly. Lists praises and requests for prayer of members. **Price:** free. **Conventions/Meetings:** annual conference ● semiannual meeting.

19883 ■ Agricultural Missions (AM)

475 Riverside Dr., Rm. 725
New York, NY 10115
Ph: (212)870-2553
Fax: (212)870-2959
E-mail: drivera@ag-missions.org
URL: http://www.agriculturalmissions.org
Contact: Joseph D. Keesecker, Exec. Dir.

Founded: 1930. **Members:** 40. **Staff:** 4. **Budget:** $500,000. **Description:** Supports development work in Africa, Asia, Latin America, the Caribbean, and rural U.S. Provides technical assistance and facilitates community-based development through rural organizations; helps plan and support new projects such as sustainable agriculture and appropriate rural technologies; cosponsors international workshops and conferences of rural issues; facilitates a network of contacts among rural people's movements and church-related projects. **Committees:** Education for Future Directions in Rural Missions; Gender and Development. **Programs:** Rural Legal Assistance; Rural Network; Rural Training; Technical Services and Appropriate Technology; Women in Rural Development. **Formerly:** (1933) Agricultural Missions Foundation. **Publications:** *Netline.* Newsletter. **Price:** free. **Circulation:** 600. Alternate Formats: online ● Publishes literature on self help programs and successful methods of working. **Conventions/Meetings:** annual Study Session and Board - meeting.

19884 ■ American Missionary Fellowship (AMF)

PO Box 370
Villanova, PA 19085-0370
Ph: (610)527-4439
Fax: (610)527-4720
E-mail: lkiseley@americanmissionary.org
URL: http://www.americanmissionary.org
Contact: Dr. Lee K. Iseley, Gen. Dir.

Founded: 1817. **Members:** 394. **Staff:** 25. **Budget:** $8,000,000. **Description:** Conducts vacation Bible schools, camp programs, and released time classes. Establishes Sunday schools and churches; sponsors specialized and cross-cultural ministries in urban and rural areas, retirement centers, and among migrant workers. Offers continuing education courses and leadership development and lay training programs using videocassettes. Entirely a missionary association in the U.S. **Committees:** Audit; Development; Investment; Personnel. **Affiliated With:** Evangelical Council for Financial Accountability; Interdenominational Foreign Missions Association. **Formerly:** (1974) American Sunday School Union. **Publications:** *American Missionary Fellowship Directory* ● *American Missionary Fellowship News,* quarterly. Newsletter. Covers missionary activity. ● *Focus and Fellowship,* bimonthly. Bulletin. **Conventions/Meetings:** convention - 5/year ● seminar.

19885 ■ American Society of Missiology (ASM)

c/o Austin Presbyterian Theological Seminary
100 E 27th St.
Austin, TX 78705
Ph: (512)404-4855
Fax: (512)479-0738
E-mail: asm@austinseminary.edu
URL: http://www.asmweb.org
Contact: Arun W. Jones, Sec.-Treas.

Founded: 1972. **Members:** 600. **Membership Dues:** individual, $37 (annual) ● student, $27 (annual) ● retired, $19 (annual). **Staff:** 1. **Budget:** $85,000. **Description:** Persons taking an active scholarly interest in the study of the Christian World Mission. **Committees:** Editorial. **Affiliated With:** Council of Societies for the Study of Religion. **Publications:** *Missiology: An International Review,* quarterly. Journal. Contains research on the history, theology, and methodology of Christian mission; includes book reviews and membership directory. **Price:** $26.00 /year for individuals; $40.00 /year for institutions; $22.00/year for students. ISSN: 0091-8296. **Circulation:** 2,000. **Advertising:** accepted. Alternate Formats: microform; online ● Monographs. **Conventions/Meetings:** annual conference (exhibits).

19886 ■ AMG International

6815 Shallowford Rd.
Chattanooga, TN 37421
Ph: (423)894-6060
Free: (800)251-7206
E-mail: info@amginternational.org
URL: http://www.amginternational.org
Contact: Mr. Paul Jenks, Pres.

Founded: 1942. **Staff:** 60. **Budget:** $6,000,000. **Languages:** English, Greek. **Description:** Worldwide interdenominational faith mission working to spread the gospel around the world. Engages in a program of relief in instituting and supporting orphanages, schools, hospitals, and food and clothing centers; provide relief for individuals and families. Stands for Advancing the Ministries of the Gospel worldwide through newspaper evangelism, relief ministries, children's services, and ministries to local churches. **Libraries: Type:** reference. **Holdings:** 50,000; books. **Subjects:** theology, Christian life. **Also Known As:** Advancing the Ministries of the Gospel. **Formerly:** (1953) American Committee for the Evangelization of the Greeks; (1974) American Mission to Greeks. **Publications:** *AMG News.* Newsletter. **Price:** free. **Circulation:** 20,000 ● *Epiousis Artos* (in Greek), bimonthly. **Price:** $12.00/year. Also Cited As: *Daily Bread* ● *Pulpit Helps,* monthly. Newspaper. **Price:** $15.00/year in U.S.; $20.00/year outside U.S. ● *Voice of the Gospel* (in English and Greek), monthly. **Price:** $20.00/year.

19887 ■ ARISE International Mission

PO Box 1014
College Park, MD 20741
Ph: (410)599-3436 (301)395-2385
E-mail: aim21century@yahoo.com
Contact: Daniel Kim, Pres.

Founded: 1990. **Staff:** 5. **Nonmembership.** **Description:** Christian mission organization engaging in missionary work, literature distribution, theological education, relief aid, and broadcasting and technical assistance. **Libraries: Type:** reference. **Subjects:** mission, theology, history. **Formerly:** (2006) Arise International.

19888 ■ Associate Missionaries of the Assumption (AMA)

11 Old English Rd.
Worcester, MA 01609
Ph: (508)767-1356
Fax: (508)791-2936
E-mail: ama-usa@juno.com
URL: http://www.assumption.us/ama
Contact: Elizabeth Fleming, Co-Dir.

Founded: 1960. **Members:** 200. **Membership Dues:** application fee, $10. **Staff:** 2. **Budget:** $30,000. **Languages:** English, French, Italian, Spanish. **Multinational. Description:** Lay Catholic mission which works to aid individuals in developing and developed countries. Volunteers work in schools, parishes, or social service agencies while living for up to 2 years within a community. Activities include nursing, teaching, evangelization, community development, and work with the mentally disabled. Operates missions in 9 countries including the United States. **Libraries: Type:** reference. **Holdings:** 4,000; books, periodicals. **Subjects:** theology. **Computer Services:** database, mailing services. **Boards:** Advisory. **Publications:** *AMA International,* monthly. Newsletter. Alternate Formats: online. **Conventions/Meetings:** annual conference, orientation week - early June.

19889 ■ Association of North American Missions (ANAM)

PO Box 8667
Longview, TX 75607-8667
Ph: (903)234-2075
E-mail: info@anamissions.org
URL: http://www.anamissions.org
Contact: Dr. Roy Anderson, Exec. Dir.

Founded: 1942. **Members:** 27. **Membership Dues:** independent mission agency, $300 (annual). **Staff:** 2. **Budget:** $60,500. **Regional Groups:** 5. **Description:** Missions of more than five missionaries operating in North America. Aims to make missions more credible and visible; to promote unity and cooperation among members; to collect, organize, and disseminate information relating to missionary work to the public and to act as clearinghouse for members. Offers referral and placement service to qualified missionaries not serving with member missions. Provides information about missions to pastors and schools. Offers workshops and in-depth seminars for mission leaders and missionaries. **Computer Services:** database, membership ● online services, placement service. **Formerly:** (1980) National Home Missions Fellowship. **Publications:** *Association of North American Missions—Notes and Quotes*, bimonthly. Newsletter. Covers activities of member missions. **Price:** included in membership dues ● *Association of North American Missions—Update*, bimonthly. Contains association news and information for mission leaders. **Price:** included in membership dues ● *Journal*, 3/year. Provides information about the needs of missions in North America and the efforts being made to meet them. Lists employment opportunities. **Price:** free ● Also publishes tracts and research project results. **Conventions/Meetings:** annual Executive Forum - convention (exhibits) ● regional meeting.

19890 ■ Association of Professors of Mission (APM)
c/o Dr. Bonnie Sue Lewis, Sec.-Treas.
Univ. of Dubuque Theological Seminary
2000 Univ. Ave.
Dubuque, IA 52001
Ph: (563)589-3648
Fax: (563)589-3110
E-mail: bslewis@dbq.edu
URL: http://www.asmweb.org/apm
Contact: Dr. Bonnie Sue Lewis, Sec.-Treas.
Founded: 1952. **Membership Dues:** active, $15 (annual) ● student, retired, $5 (annual). **Description:** Professors teaching in the field of mission in theological seminaries, divinity schools, other graduate schools of religion, colleges, and universities. Provides opportunity for discussion of problems of research, teaching, and writing in the field of mission, exchange of information on other mutual concerns, and personal fellowship. Conducts lectures. **Conventions/Meetings:** annual conference, held in conjunction with the American Society of Missiology (exhibits) ● seminar.

19891 ■ Avant Ministries
10000 N Oak Trafficway
Kansas City, MO 64155
Ph: (816)734-8500
Free: (800)468-1892
Fax: (816)734-4601
E-mail: info@avmi.org
URL: http://www.avantministries.org
Contact: Dr. Paul Nyquist, Pres./CEO
Founded: 1892. **Members:** 350. **Staff:** 25. **Budget:** $10,000,000. **Description:** Interdenominational Christian organization sending missionaries to do church planning and other related ministries around the world. **Affiliated With:** Evangelical Council for Financial Accountability; Interdenominational Foreign Missions Association. **Formerly:** (2004) Gospel Missionary Union. **Publications:** *The Gospel Message*, quarterly. Newsletter. Covers missionary and GMU news. **Price:** free. ISSN: 0744-5814. **Circulation:** 40,000 ● Also publishes Bible and religious study materials. **Conventions/Meetings:** annual conference - always September, Kansas City, MO.

19892 ■ Bethany International Missions (BIM)
6820 Auto Club Rd., Ste.D
Bloomington, MN 55438
Ph: (952)829-2492
Fax: (952)829-2767
E-mail: bethanys@bethanyinternational.org
URL: http://bethanyinternational.org
Founded: 1963. **Members:** 130. **Staff:** 16. **Budget:** $2,050,000. **Description:** A division of Bethany International, Inc. Christian missionaries worldwide. Supports evangelism by conducting activities such as Bible school and church-planting programs; disseminates literature. Operates programs in the Caribbean, Europe, Central and South America, Asia,

Africa, and Canada. **Affiliated With:** Evangelical Fellowship of Mission Agencies. **Formerly:** (2004) Bethany Fellowship Missions. **Publications:** *Bethany News*, semiannual. Newsletter. Alternate Formats: online.

19893 ■ Bibles For The World (BFTW)
PO Box 49759
Colorado Springs, CO 80949-9759
Free: (888)382-4253
E-mail: info@bftw.org
URL: http://www.biblesfortheworld.org
Contact: Dr. Rochunga Pudaite, Pres.
Founded: 1959. **Staff:** 16. **Budget:** $3,500,000. **National Groups:** 3. **Languages:** Bengali, English, Romanian, Russian, Spanish. **Nonmembership. Description:** Primary goal is to send a copy of the New Testament to all telephone subscribers in the world. Supports educational, evangelization, and religious instruction programs of national missionaries in India. Sponsors Partnership Parents, a program whereby needy children are educated in India through the financial sponsorship of individuals in the U.S. Also sponsors India Children's Choir. **Programs:** Bible Packing Parties; Bibles for Rwanda Campaign; Billion Bible Club. **Formerly:** (1973) Indo-Burma Pioneer Mission; (1976) Partnership Mission. **Publications:** *Beyond the Next Mountain*. Video. Features the story of Rochunga's personal pilgrimage. **Price:** $15.00 ● *India Children's Choir*. Video. Contains concert of the India Children's Choir. **Price:** $15.00 ● *World Report*, quarterly. Newsletter. Provides accounts of BFW's ministry around the world. **Price:** free to donors and supporters and by request. **Circulation:** 35,000. **Conventions/Meetings:** semiannual Short Term Mission Trips - tour.

19894 ■ Brethren in Christ World Missions (BICWM)
PO Box 390
Grantham, PA 17027
Ph: (717)697-2634
Fax: (717)691-6053
E-mail: bicwm@messiah.edu
URL: http://www.bic-church.org/wm
Contact: John Brubaker, Exec. Dir.
Founded: 1898. **Members:** 65. **Staff:** 10. **Budget:** $1,509,000. **Languages:** English, Spanish. **Multinational. Description:** Represents overseas missionaries and Brethren in Christ local congregations in North America. Seeks to foster a fellowship of believers worldwide by offering overseas missionary work and educational and medical activities. Maintains Speaker's Bureau. **Libraries:** Type: reference. **Holdings:** archival material, video recordings. **Computer Services:** Mailing lists. **Programs:** Teens in Missionary Service; Youth Evangelism Service. **Affiliated With:** Evangelical Fellowship of Mission Agencies; National Association of Evangelicals. **Formerly:** (1986) Brethren in Christ Missions. **Publications:** *Partnership Handbook*. Highlights mission projects. Alternate Formats: online ● *Today in Brethren in Christ World Missions*, 10/year. Newsletter. Alternate Formats: online ● *World Christian Intercessors*, monthly. Bulletin ● Brochures ● Pamphlets ● Report, biennial. Alternate Formats: online. **Conventions/Meetings:** semiannual Board for World Missions - board meeting.

19895 ■ Brethren Church Missionary Ministries
524 Coll. Ave.
Ashland, OH 44805
Ph: (419)289-1708
Free: (877)289-1708
Fax: (419)281-0450
E-mail: brethren@brethrenchurch.org
URL: http://www.brethrenchurch.org
Contact: Rev. Ken Hunn, Exec. Dir.
Founded: 1891. **Members:** 13. **Staff:** 4. **Description:** Works to establish new churches in the U.S. and overseas. Conducts training programs for church leadership. **Libraries:** Type: reference. **Holdings:** audio recordings, books, periodicals, video recordings. **Also Known As:** Brethren Missions. **Formerly:** (1999) Brethern Church Missionary Board. **Publica-**

tions: *Brethren Evangelist*, bimonthly. Magazine. **Price:** free. **Circulation:** 7,000. Alternate Formats: online ● Newsletter. **Conventions/Meetings:** annual conference (exhibits) - always July.

19896 ■ Cabrini Mission Corps (CMC)
610 King of Prussia Rd.
Radnor, PA 19087-3623
Ph: (610)971-0821
Fax: (610)971-0396
E-mail: cmcorps@aol.com
URL: http://www.cabrini-missioncorps.org
Contact: Gina Pultorak, Dir.
Founded: 1990. **Members:** 6. **Staff:** 2. **Languages:** English, Spanish. **Description:** Lay mission program of the Missionary Sisters of the Sacred Heart of Jesus. Provides opportunity for laywomen and men to serve others while living simply in the community with the Cabrini Sisters and, sometimes other missioners. Gives themselves for one to two years in ministry sites throughout the U.S. and overseas. Ministry areas include: education, health care, child care, elder care, parish and pastoral ministry, and social services. Commits to a journey of faith in the spirit of St. Francis Xavier Cabrini and strive for personal growth through prayer, ministry and community. **Publications:** *Journeys*, 3/year. Newsletter. **Price:** free.

19897 ■ Call and Response
c/o Mary Lou Doran, Dir.
10636 N 37th Ave.
Phoenix, AZ 85029
URL: http://www.teilhard.com/solidarity/call-response.htm
Contact: Mary Lou Doran, Dir.
Description: Lay Christian missionaries working with orphanages and group homes in Mexico, Guatemala, and the United States. Conducts programs in health care, community work, and education. Disseminates information to raise American awareness of suffering in Guatemala. **Formerly:** Maryknoll Call and Response Program.

19898 ■ CAM International (CAM)
8625 La Prada Dr.
Dallas, TX 75228
Ph: (214)327-8206
Free: (800)366-2264
Fax: (214)327-8201
E-mail: info@caminternational.org
URL: http://www.caminternational.org
Contact: Daniel P. Wicher, Pres.
Founded: 1890. **Members:** 325. **Languages:** English, Spanish. **Description:** Nondenominational evangelistic foreign missionary agency working in Mexico, the 5 republics of Central America, Panama, Spain, and among Hispanics in the United States. **Formerly:** (1976) Central American Mission. **Publications:** *CAM Bulletin*, quadrennial. Newsletter. **Price:** free for members. ISSN: 0195-4334 ● *Touch the World*. Magazine.

19899 ■ Catholic Committee of Appalachia
213 Orchard Run Rd.
Spencer, WV 25276
Ph: (304)927-5798
E-mail: ccappal@citynet.net
URL: http://www.ccappal.org
Contact: Sr. Robbie Pentecost, Exec. Dir.
Founded: 1970. **Members:** 400. **Membership Dues:** $25 (annual). **Staff:** 1. **Budget:** $70,000. **Description:** Catholic clergy, religious, laity, and local organizations and individuals working and interested in the Appalachian region. Advocates local empowerment; engages in church, social, and justice ministries. Works with other Catholic and ecumenical organizations. Offers related workshops. **Awards:** Bishop Walter F. Sullivan Peace and Justice Award. **Frequency:** annual. **Type:** recognition. **Recipient:** person working in Appalachia who exemplifies the commitment to peace and justice modeled by Bishop Sullivan since his installation in 1974. **Telecommunication Services:** electronic mail, rpentecost@chrisapp.org. **Publications:** *At Home in the Web of Life*. Pamphlets ● *PatchQuilt*, quarterly. Newsletter ●

This Land Is Home to Me. Appalachian bishops' pastoral on poverty and powerlessness. ● Pamphlets. **Conventions/Meetings:** annual meeting (exhibits).

19900 ■ Children International
PO Box 219055
Kansas City, MO 64121
Ph: (816)942-2000
Free: (800)888-3089
Fax: (816)942-3714
E-mail: children@children.org
URL: http://www.children.org
Contact: James R. Cook, Pres./CEO
Founded: 1936. **Staff:** 150. **Budget:** $72,000,000. **Languages:** English, Spanish. **Description:** Aims to improve the quality of life of needy children, widows, and other needy individuals. Provides food, clothing, medical care, and education to those in need throughout Latin America, Asia, the Holy Land, and the United States. **Convention/Meeting:** none. **Programs:** Housing; ShareAmerica; Sponsorship. **Projects:** Community. **Formerly:** Holy Land Christian Mission; (1987) Holy Land Christian Mission International. **Publications:** *Journeys*, 3/year, winter, spring, summer. Newsletter. Alternate Formats: online ● Annual Report.

19901 ■ Chinese Christian Mission (CCM)
PO Box 750759
Petaluma, CA 94975
Ph: (707)762-1314
Fax: (707)762-1713
E-mail: ccm@ccmusa.org
URL: http://www.ccmusa.org
Contact: Paul Chan, Gen. Sec.
Founded: 1961. **Staff:** 25. **Budget:** $2,400,000. **Multinational. Description:** Serves as an evangelical faith mission dedicated to reaching Chinese people around the world with the gospel of Jesus Christ. Broadcasts radio programs to foster Christianity in China. Operates placement service providing ministers with churches. Sponsors short-term mission trips to Latin America and East Asia. **Departments:** Audio-Visual; Foreign Missions; I Love China; Literature; Local Evangelism. **Publications:** *Bookroom Catalog* (in Chinese and English), semiannual. Lists books and cassettes available from the Mission. **Price:** free. **Circulation:** 3,000. Alternate Formats: online ● *CCM Annual Report* (in Chinese and English), annual. **Price:** free. **Circulation:** 20,000 ● *CCM Newsletter* (in Chinese and English), bimonthly. Provides update for supporters of the mission. Includes financial report. **Price:** free. **Circulation:** 13,000. Also Cited As: *Thank-You Letter* ● *Challenger*, quarterly. Newspaper. Covers Chinese Christians in North America and China. **Price:** free. ISSN: 1084-2144. **Circulation:** 10,000. Alternate Formats: online ● *Chinese Today* (in Chinese and English), monthly. Newspaper. Contains information on Christian evangelism. ISSN: 1045-6147. **Circulation:** 180,000. Alternate Formats: online ● *Proclaim* (in Chinese and English), bimonthly. Magazine. Promotes worldwide Chinese Christianity. **Price:** free. **Circulation:** 20,000. Alternate Formats: online ● Also publishes books, tracts, charts, posters, and brochures. Makes available slide presentations. **Conventions/Meetings:** Missions Cooperation Conference (exhibits).

19902 ■ Christ for the Nations (CFN)
PO Box 769000
Dallas, TX 75376-9000
Ph: (214)376-1711
Free: (800)933-2364
E-mail: info@cfni.org
URL: http://www.cfni.org
Contact: Dennis Lindsay, Pres./CEO
Founded: 1948. **Staff:** 150. **Description:** A missions organization which seeks to promote the Gospel and Christian endeavors through an international network of interdenominational Bible schools, a Native church building program, literature distribution, assisting orphanages, and relief projects. Hosts conferences and seminars to build the body of Christ, and sponsors mission projects in Israel. **Libraries: Type:** reference. **Holdings:** 45,000. **Subjects:** Biblical. **Formerly:** (1956) Voice of Healing. **Publications:**

Magazine, monthly. Includes information on Christian missions. **Price:** free for members. **Circulation:** 80,000 ● Books ● Yearbook. **Conventions/Meetings:** Christian Teaching Workshops - always in Dallas, TX ● annual Israel Conference ● annual Israel Tour ● annual Mission's Conference ● annual seminar ● annual Women's Conference ● annual Worship Conference.

19903 ■ CHRISTAR
Box 14866
Reading, PA 19612-4866
Ph: (610)375-0300
Free: (800)755-7955
Fax: (610)375-6862
E-mail: info@christar.org
URL: http://www.christar.org
Contact: Dr. Patrick Cate, Pres.
Founded: 1930. **Members:** 395. **Staff:** 42. **Budget:** $10,215,000. **Description:** Nondenominational faith mission emphasizing evangelism, Bible teaching, and church planting. Works in Hong Kong, India, Japan, Middle East, North Africa, Mongolia, Far East, the Philippines, Suriname, Pakistan, Albania, and among Asians living in Germany, England, France, Holland, the Commonwealth of Independent States, and Kenya. Sponsors Christar-North America, which works among Asian immigrants in several U.S. cities. Operates speakers' bureau. **Libraries: Type:** reference. **Holdings:** 2,500; archival material, audiovisuals, books, clippings, monographs, periodicals. **Subjects:** mission, religions of the world, Bible, theology. **Affiliated With:** Evangelical Council for Financial Accountability; Interdenominational Foreign Missions Association. **Absorbed:** (1955) Iran Interior Mission; (1966) Oriental Boat Mission. **Formerly:** (1954) The India Mission; (2001) International Missions. **Publications:** *Christar in View*, quarterly. Magazine. Reports on fields of ministry; missions; general information. **Price:** free. ISSN: 0893-9346. **Circulation:** 22,000 ● *Reaching Asians International*. Book. **Conventions/Meetings:** annual conference, for members only - always June or July, Reading, PA.

19904 ■ Christian Aid Mission
PO Box 9037
Charlottesville, VA 22906
Ph: (434)977-5650
Free: (800)977-5650
E-mail: friends@christianaid.org
URL: http://www.christianaid.org
Contact: Bob Finley, Chm.
Founded: 1953. **Staff:** 50. **Budget:** $8,500,000. **Multinational. Description:** Christian evangelical organization that seeks to "establish witness for the Lord Jesus Christ throughout the world." Locates and investigates independent indigenous missions around the world; provides assistance to such missions. Acts as communication network for U.S. evangelical organizations that wish to assist foreign indigenous missions. Maintains speakers' bureau. **Libraries: Type:** reference. **Holdings:** 2,000; archival material, books, periodicals. **Subjects:** foreign cultures, ethnic groups, theology. **Affiliated With:** Advancing Churches in Missions Commitment; Christian Stewardship Association. **Publications:** *Christian Mission*, quarterly. Magazine. Reports activities of indigenous evangelistic missions in poorer countries. **Price:** free. ISSN: 8750-7765. **Circulation:** 16,000 ● *Missions Insider*. Newsletter. Provides news about indigenous missions around the world. **Price:** free. Alternate Formats: online ● *Prayerline: A Guide to Intercession for Indigenous Missions* (in English and Spanish), monthly. Newsletter. Highlights projects of indigenous evangelistic groups overseas. **Price:** free. **Conventions/Meetings:** semiannual conference.

19905 ■ Christian Literature and Bible Center (CLBC)
PO Box 7130
North Augusta, SC 29861
Ph: (803)279-1981
Fax: (803)279-1270

E-mail: ajlosier@gabn.net
URL: http://www.clbible.org
Contact: Andrew Losier, Contact
Founded: 1952. **Staff:** 2. **Budget:** $25,000. **Local Groups:** 2. **National Groups:** 2. **Description:** Distributes free Christian literature in over 50 languages; conducts Bible correspondence courses using audio-cassette recordings. Supports Faith Bible College and Seminary in Nigeria. Sponsors direct missionary work in Africa and nations worldwide. Conducts research and educational programs and youth camps. Conducts charitable programs. Supplies Bible schools with textbooks written by members. **Libraries: Type:** reference. **Holdings:** 8,000; audio recordings, books, video recordings. **Subjects:** Biblical reference, Bible Doctrine, South Africa, Nigeria. **Publications:** *Amazing Grace*, monthly. Newsletter. **Price:** free. **Circulation:** 1,000. **Conventions/Meetings:** semiannual conference, with a display of biblical textbooks (exhibits) ● annual meeting.

19906 ■ Christian Mission for the Deaf (CMD)
PO Box 28005
Detroit, MI 48228-0005
E-mail: deafwitness@cmdeaf.org
URL: http://www.cmdeaf.org
Contact: Berta Foster, Admin.
Founded: 1956. **Staff:** 3. **Languages:** English, French. **Description:** Evangelical Christian ministry directed toward the deaf in Africa. Operates primary schools, Christian centers, Sunday schools, and camps; has established schools for the deaf in 13 African countries. **Formerly:** (1978) Christian Mission for Deaf Africans. **Publications:** *Deaf Witness*, 3/year. Newsletter. Contains news and prayer requests. **Price:** free. Alternate Formats: online.

19907 ■ Christian Missionary Fellowship (CMF International)
PO Box 501020
Indianapolis, IN 46250-6020
Ph: (317)578-2700
Fax: (317)578-2827
E-mail: missions@cmfi.org
URL: http://www.cmfi.org
Contact: Doug Priest, Exec. Dir.
Founded: 1949. **Members:** 4,589. **Staff:** 26. **Budget:** $7,000,000. **Regional Groups:** 130. **Languages:** English, French, Spanish. **Multinational. Description:** Congregations, auxiliaries, and individual Christians contributing funds to recruit, send, finance, and oversee foreign Christian missionaries. **Libraries: Type:** reference. **Publications:** *Christian Missionary Fellowship—Impact*, semiannual. Newsletter. Covers the fellowship's missions and evangelizing activities. Includes news of members and schedule of activities. **Price:** free. **Circulation:** 6,000. **Conventions/Meetings:** annual meeting (exhibits).

19908 ■ Christian Missions in Many Lands (CMML)
PO Box 13
Spring Lake, NJ 07762-0013
Ph: (732)449-8880
Fax: (732)974-0888
E-mail: cmml@cmmlusa.org
URL: http://www.cmmlusa.org
Contact: Thomas J. Turner, Pres.
Founded: 1921. **Description:** A service organization for brethren assembly missionaries which represents missionaries to the Department of State and before foreign consulates; supplies information to the missionary concerning his proposed field of service and transmission of funds and other services. **Publications:** *Missions*, monthly. Magazine. **Price:** free. Alternate Formats: online.

19909 ■ Christian Pilots Association (CPA)
4100 Newport Pl., Ste.620
Newport Beach, CA 92660
Ph: (949)271-1587 (562)208-2912
Free: (800)917-5656
Fax: (949)271-1595

E-mail: info@christianpilots.org
URL: http://www.christianpilots.org
Contact: Andy Pike, Chm.
Founded: 1972. **Members:** 50. **Membership Dues:** voluntary, $50 (annual). **Staff:** 3. **Budget:** $24,000. **Description:** Volunteer and professional airplane pilots; interested individuals. Aims to mobilize church-oriented pilots in a variety of services in order to carry out the association's motto: "Flying for Jesus and human need." Supports evangelical churches and mission organizations; transports relief supplies, such as food, medical supplies, and clothing to missions throughout the U.S. Other activities include: flying missionaries and preachers to churches; assisting in times of national or international disaster; building orphanages and hospitals; providing doctors and dentists to remote areas. Maintains speakers' bureau; conducts charitable programs, aircraft acquisition, availability, operations, and missions. **Publications:** *CP News*, quarterly. Newsletter. **Price:** free. **Circulation:** 200.

19910 ■ Christians for Peace in El Salvador (CRISPAZ)
2 Lexington St.
East Boston, MA 02128
Ph: (617)567-2900
Fax: (617)249-0769
E-mail: info@crispaz.org
URL: http://www.crispaz.org
Contact: Chris Nauman, Chm.
Founded: 1984. **Staff:** 7. **Budget:** $400,000. **Description:** Interested individuals. Places sponsored volunteers from North America with poor or displaced people in El Salvador in areas designated by Salvadoran church or humanitarian agencies. Works on projects directed by Salvadorans in areas of literacy, health care, pastoral work, education, agriculture, earthquake reconstruction and technology. Operates Communication and Information Network for El Salvador, which provides written information directly from or about El Salvador. **Telecommunication Services:** electronic mail, pazsal@crispaz.org. **Publications:** *Salvanet: The Newsletter of CRISPAZ*, bimonthly. Provides updates about the political, social, cultural, and economic realities in El Salvador. **Advertising:** accepted.

19911 ■ Church of God World Missions (COGWM)
2490 Keith St.
PO Box 8016
Cleveland, TN 37320-8016
Ph: (423)478-7190 (423)478-7155
Free: (800)535-9343
Fax: (423)478-7155
URL: http://www.cogwm.org
Contact: Roland E. Vaughan, Gen. Dir.
Founded: 1910. **Members:** 5,560,671. **Staff:** 74. **National Groups:** 161. **Description:** Department of the Church of God. Promotes the dissemination of the beliefs of individuals of the Church of God to countries outside the United States and Canada. **Awards:** **Type:** recognition. **Publications:** *Save Our World*, quarterly. Magazine. **Price:** free. **Circulation:** 95,000. Alternate Formats: online. **Conventions/Meetings:** biennial general assembly.

19912 ■ Church Planting International (CPI)
PO Box 836
Gainesville, GA 30503-0836
Ph: (770)535-7008
Fax: (770)534-1025
E-mail: cpimission@juno.com
Contact: Dr. G.P. Hutchinson, Exec.Dir.
Multinational. Description: Helps indigenous Churches in the developing countries in Church planting and leadership training.

19913 ■ Crosier Missions (CM)
3510 Vivian Ave. S
Shoreview, MN 55126-3852
Ph: (651)486-7456
Free: (800)407-5875
Fax: (651)287-1130

E-mail: crosier@crosier.org
URL: http://www.crosier.org
Contact: Fr. Stephan Bauer OSC, Dir.
Founded: 1958. **Members:** 15. **Staff:** 1. **Languages:** English, Indonesian. **Description:** Catholic missionaries sponsored by the Crosier Fathers working in Irian Jaya, Indonesia. Provides religious instruction and general education; fosters social development. Maintains museum and speakers' bureau. **Libraries: Type:** reference. **Holdings:** artwork, audiovisuals, books, clippings. **Subjects:** Asmat culture and art. **Additional Websites:** http://www.asmat.org. **Publications:** *Asmat Images*. Book. **Price:** $50.00 ● *Asmat Sketch Book.*

19914 ■ Crossworld
PO Box 306
Bala Cynwyd, PA 19004
Ph: (610)667-7660
Fax: (610)660-9068
E-mail: info@crossworld.org
URL: http://www.crossworld.org
Contact: Bob Simrak, Dir. of Advancement
Founded: 1931. **Members:** 699. **Staff:** 46. **Multinational. Description:** Represents individuals who have a college degree and have completed the candidate orientation program. Seeks to plant Christian churches. Conducts Christian evangelism in 22 countries including Brazil, Haiti, Mexico, Indonesia, and Congo. Encourages "discipleship, which produces spiritual maturity"; provides leadership training to enable converts to organize their own evangelistic activities. Engages in educational, medical, and linguistic programs. **Affiliated With:** Interdenominational Foreign Missions Association. **Absorbed:** (2000) Berean Mission, Inc. **Formerly:** (1980) Unevangelized Fields Missions; (2005) UFM International. **Publications:** *Lifeline*, quarterly. Magazine. **Price:** $5.00/year. **Circulation:** 18,000 ● Also produces and distributes literature. **Conventions/Meetings:** annual meeting.

19915 ■ Domestic/Foreign Missionary Society of the Protestant Episcopal Church (DFMSPECSA)
Episcopal Church Ctr.
815 2nd Ave.
New York, NY 10017
Ph: (212)716-6000
Free: (800)334-7626
Fax: (212)949-8059
E-mail: info@episcopalchurch.org
URL: http://www.episcopalchurch.org
Contact: Rev. Katharine Jefferts Schori, Pres.
Members: 2,300,000. **Staff:** 200. **Description:** Missionaries of the Protestant Episcopal Church. Seeks to expose people in developing regions to Christianity; promotes an improved quality of life for the economically disadvantaged. Coordinates members' activities; sponsors programs to increase the self-sufficiency of people in developing areas.

19916 ■ Dominican Mission Foundation (DMF)
PO Box 15367
San Francisco, CA 94115
Ph: (415)931-2183
Fax: (415)931-1772
E-mail: info@dominicanmission.org
Contact: Fr. Martin de Porres Walsh OP, Dir.
Founded: 1963. **Staff:** 3. **Description:** Roman Catholic individuals promoting the physical, spiritual, intellectual, and social development of all people through missionary work. Maintains one missionary group in Vilnius, Lithuania, 1 missionary group in Guatemala and 2 missionary groups in Mexico (Chiapas and Mexicali), and one missionary group in Tala, Caloocan City, Philippines, which provide scholastic instruction, medical care, and vocational, dietary, and hygienic training programs. **Publications:** *Missionaries in Action*, monthly. Newsletter ● Directory, annual. **Conventions/Meetings:** meeting.

19917 ■ Dominican Volunteers USA
7200 W Div. St.
River Forest, IL 60305-1222
Ph: (708)524-5985 (708)524-5984
Fax: (708)714-9002
E-mail: dvusa@dom.edu
URL: http://dvusa.org
Contact: Donielle Dodde Xu, Marketing and Recruitment Coor.
Founded: 1973. **Description:** Men and women volunteers at least 20 years old who live and work with people in central city, suburban, and rural sites throughout the U.S. for one year. Works to: achieve economic, social, and political justice for all people; provide ways for volunteers to use their skills, abilities, and insight for the service of others; support and foster active spirituality within the Dominican way of life. Offers placement service; maintains speakers' bureau. **Publications:** *Network*, biennial. Newsletter.

19918 ■ EAPE/Campolo Ministries - Evangelical Association for the Promotion of Education (EAPE)
PO Box 7238
St. Davids, PA 19087
Ph: (610)341-1722
Fax: (610)341-4372
E-mail: eape@eastern.edu
URL: http://www.tonycampolo.com
Contact: Dr. Tony Campolo, Contact
Founded: 1971. **Staff:** 4. **Budget:** $800,000. **Description:** Promotes venture philanthropy and service learning; creates, nurtures and supports small, innovative, volunteer-based ministries to at-risk children in the United States, Dominican Republic, Haiti, the United Kingdom, Canada and Africa. Programs include literacy centers, after-school and summer programs, alternative primary and secondary schools, job-creation initiatives and pediatric AIDS hospices. Nurtures and supports the worldwide preaching ministry of Dr. Tony Campolo. **Formerly:** (2001) Evangelical Association for the Promotion of Education. **Publications:** *EAPE News*, bimonthly. Newsletter ● Booklets ● Videos. **Price:** $18.00 each. **Conventions/Meetings:** board meeting.

19919 ■ The Evangelical Alliance Mission (TEAM)
PO Box 969
Wheaton, IL 60189-0969
Ph: (630)653-5300
Free: (800)343-3144
Fax: (630)653-1826
E-mail: info@teamworld.org
URL: http://www.teamworld.org
Contact: Mr. Robert Hodge, Chm.
Founded: 1890. **Members:** 700. **Staff:** 75. **Description:** Missionaries from evangelical Protestant denominations. Carries on evangelism, church planting, and Bible teaching. Conducts radio broadcasts, medical work, distribution of literature, and special campaigns in 40 foreign countries. Supports elementary, secondary and/or higher schools in Chad, Zimbabwe, South Africa, Swaziland, Venezuela, Colombia, Japan, Taiwan, Pakistan, and India. Provides direct assistance to churches to help with missions committees, missions education programs, and missionary conferences. Maintains speakers' bureau. **Libraries: Type:** reference. **Holdings:** 500. **Absorbed:** (2003) Bible Christian Union. **Publications:** *Monthly Prayer Journal*. **Circulation:** 1,500. Alternate Formats: online ● *Prayer Directory*, annual. **Circulation:** 2,000 ● *Vision Report*. Annual Report. Alternate Formats: online. **Conventions/Meetings:** annual meeting - always May or August.

19920 ■ Evangelical Fellowship of Mission Agencies (EFMA)
4201 N Peachtree Rd.
Atlanta, GA 30341
Ph: (770)457-6677
Fax: (770)457-0037

E-mail: efma@efmamissions.org
URL: http://efma.gospelcom.net
Contact: Steve Moore, Pres./CEO
Founded: 1945. **Members:** 100. **Membership Dues:** association (for mission agencies - Christian), $1,200 (annual). **Staff:** 4. **Budget:** $300,000. **Description:** Denominational and nondenominational foreign mission agencies with more than 16,000 missionaries in 130 foreign fields. Provides: united representation before governments; a basis for fellowship; a channel for promoting cooperative effort; information concerning government regulations and international affairs that affects foreign missions and service to missions, churches, and individuals; assistance in securing passports, visas, and other legal documents. Gathers information on world missions. **Committees:** Africa; Asia; Islamics; Latin America; Ministry Education Overseas; Missions Information. **Affiliated With:** National Association of Evangelicals. **Formerly:** (1991) Evangelical Foreign Missions Association. **Publications:** *Member Missions*, semiannual. **Price:** free ● Brochure. **Conventions/Meetings:** annual Fall Mission Executive Retreat - always September ● annual meeting, held in conjunction with the National Association of Evangelicals - always spring.

19921 ■ Evangelical Free Church of America - International Mission (EFCA-IM)
901 E 78th St.
Minneapolis, MN 55420-1334
Ph: (952)853-8453
Fax: (952)853-8474
E-mail: callen@efca.org
URL: http://www.efca.org
Contact: Mr. Daryl Anderson, Assoc. Exec. Dir.
Founded: 1887. **Members:** 9,000. **Staff:** 450. **Budget:** $24,000,000. **Multinational. Description:** Promotes the "proclamation of the gospel" worldwide, the establishment of churches, and Christian compassion ministries. Provides missionary outreach and educational programs. **Formerly:** (2003) Evangelical Free Church Mission. **Publications:** *Beacon*, 8/year. Newsletter. **Price:** $10.00. Alternate Formats: online.

19922 ■ Evangelical Missiological Society (EMS)
PO Box 794
Wheaton, IL 60189
Ph: (630)752-7158
Fax: (630)752-7155
E-mail: ems@wheaton.edu
URL: http://www.missiology.org/EMS
Contact: F. Douglas Pennoyer, Pres.
Founded: 1965. **Members:** 400. **Membership Dues:** student, $15 (annual) ● regular, $30 (annual) ● life, $500. **Staff:** 4. **Regional Groups:** 7. **Description:** Professors of missions in Bible colleges and seminaries, mission organization executives, mission pastors, and missionaries. Unites to improve preparation for and increase understanding of world missions. Organizes regional conferences; compiles statistics. **Publications:** *EMS Occasional Bulletin*, 3/year. Newsletter. **Price:** included in membership dues. Alternate Formats: online ● Also publishes annually, an edited compilation of the best papers presented at regional and national meetings covering a specific theme. Volumes currently available are: Vol. 1 (1994) *Strategy and the Bible*, Vol. 2 (1995) *Christianity and the Religions*, Vol. 3 Spiritual Power and Missions: Raising the Issues, and Vol. 4 Missions and the Social Sciences. Both are included in membership dues and available in bulk. **Conventions/Meetings:** annual National Conference (exhibits) - third week of November, in September every third year.

19923 ■ Evangelism and Missions Information Service (EMIS)
500 Coll. Ave.
Wheaton, IL 60187
Ph: (630)752-7158
Fax: (630)752-7155
E-mail: emis@wheaton.edu
URL: http://bgc.gospelcom.net/emis
Contact: Kenneth Gill, Dir.
Founded: 1964. **Staff:** 5. **Description:** Originally organized as a service arm of the Interdenominational

Foreign Mission Association of North America and the Evangelical Fellowship of Mission Agencies. Provides a channel for exchange of information among persons and organizations interested and involved in the proclamation of the Gospel around the world. Gathers and disseminates missionary and related information; is engaged in the general promotion of all related aspects of Christian service and circulation of this subject matter. **Publications:** *Evangelical Missions Quarterly*. Journal. Includes book reviews. **Price:** $46.95/year (airmail); $36.95/year (print and online versions); $19.95/year (online only); $26.95/year (surface mail). ISSN: 0140-3359. **Circulation:** 6,000. **Advertising:** accepted. Alternate Formats: microform; online. Also Cited As: *EMQ*.

19924 ■ Evangelistic Faith Missions (EFM)
PO Box 609
U.S. Hwy. 50
Bedford, IN 47421
Ph: (812)275-7531
E-mail: efmjsm@juno.com
URL: http://www.efm-missions.org
Contact: Rev. J. Stevan Manley, Pres.
Founded: 1905. **Description:** Sponsors missionary works, including medical, educational, and spiritual services, worldwide. Conducts broadcasts on 42 radio stations in the U.S. and abroad. Provides children's services; compiles statistics. **Awards:** Dale Gowan Scholarship. **Frequency:** annual. **Type:** scholarship ● Mary Gaunce Scholarship. **Frequency:** annual. **Type:** scholarship. **Formerly:** Pentecostal Faith Missions. **Publications:** *Missionary Herald*, monthly. Magazine. Contains missionary reports and spiritual articles. **Price:** $2.00/year. **Circulation:** 25,000. Alternate Formats: online. **Conventions/Meetings:** annual Church Convention.

19925 ■ Evangelize China Fellowship (ECF)
437 S Garfield Ave.
Monterey Park, CA 91754
Ph: (626)288-8828
E-mail: info@ecfusa.org
URL: http://www.ecfusa.org
Contact: Dr. Paul C.C. Szeto, Pres./Gen. Dir.
Founded: 1947. **National Groups:** 18. **Languages:** Chinese, English, German. **Description:** Carries on a program of evangelism, education, and relief work in Hong Kong, Macao, Thailand, Burma, Singapore, Malaysia, Indonesia, Philippines, Vietnam, the United States, and China. Conducts programs in schools, orphanages, and churches. Provides middle and high school English teachers training program. Maintains Chinese Christian Resource Center containing 10,000 volumes in Chinese language. **Libraries: Type:** open to the public. **Holdings:** 10,000; books. **Subjects:** Christianity, church, missions, family, literature. **Awards: Frequency:** annual. **Type:** scholarship. **Recipient:** for Chinese students. **Publications:** *Global Vision*, bimonthly. Magazine. **Price:** free for members. Alternate Formats: online ● *Grace Bridge* (in Chinese and English), quarterly. Magazine. **Price:** free for members ● *Higher Ground*. Video ● *Touching Lives*, quarterly. Newsletter. Reports the news and updates from the sponsorship fields. **Price:** free for members ● Books ● Pamphlets ● Also makes available tapes. **Conventions/Meetings:** annual conference and board meeting ● triennial international conference.

19926 ■ Fellowship International Mission (FIM)
555 S 24th St.
Allentown, PA 18104-6666
Ph: (610)435-9099
Free: (888)FIM-9099
Fax: (610)435-2641
E-mail: info@fimworldwide.org
URL: http://fim.gospelcom.net
Contact: Mr. Dick Albright, Dir. for Administration
Founded: 1950. **Members:** 160. **Staff:** 9. **Budget:** $3,880,000. **Multinational. Description:** Aims to assist churches to fulfill their missionary vision and to help missionaries fulfill their call. Conducts evangelism and other ministries, including church planting. Ministers in 29 countries of the world with concentra-

tions in Africa and Latin America. **Libraries: Type:** reference. **Holdings:** 100. **Subjects:** missions. **Computer Services:** database, financial. **Affiliated With:** Evangelical Council for Financial Accountability; IFCA International; Interdenominational Foreign Missions Association. **Publications:** *The FIM Connection*, quarterly. Newsletter. **Circulation:** 175. Alternate Formats: online. **Conventions/Meetings:** quarterly board meeting, includes orientation for new workers ● annual Candidate Orientation and Training Program - seminar.

19927 ■ Fellowship of Missions (FOM)
c/o Dr. Gerald K. Webber, Pres.
31 Gideon Rd.
Sebring, FL 33870
Ph: (863)382-4301
E-mail: infofom@wadsnet.com
URL: http://www.fellowshipofmissions.org
Contact: Dr. Gerald K. Webber, Pres.
Founded: 1969. **Members:** 27. **Description:** Fundamentalist mission agencies comprising 3,600 missionaries, Encourages and coordinates member efforts to propagate the Gospel. Provides forum for fellowship and exchange among members. Assists in formation of missionary or church fellowships around the world; promotes and supports Bible translations. Acts as accrediting agency for members and serves their interests in governmental matters. Furnishes information concerning the availability of supplies and transportation. Arranges special study groups, linguistics or language institutes, and executive consultation. Maintains files on mission boards; acts as information center for pastors, churches, and prospective missionaries. **Publications:** *Focus on Missions*, 3/year. Newsletter. **Price:** free. **Circulation:** 3,000. Alternate Formats: online ● *FOMenter*, monthly. Newsletter. Addresses needs of mission administrators. **Price:** free. Alternate Formats: online ● Brochure. **Conventions/Meetings:** annual conference - always September ● seminar.

19928 ■ Foundation of Compassionate American Samaritans (FOCAS)
PO Box 428760
Cincinnati, OH 45242
Ph: (513)621-5300
Fax: (513)621-5307
E-mail: focas@focas-us.org
URL: http://www.focas-us.org
Contact: Richard P. Taylor, Exec. Dir.
Founded: 1986. **Staff:** 11. **Budget:** $700,000. **Description:** Seeks to provide for the physical and spiritual needs of the poor. Conducts mission trips; offers children's services and charitable programs. Conducts health projects in Haiti including a USAID child survival project. **Publications:** Newsletter. **Conventions/Meetings:** board meeting - 3/year.

19929 ■ Global Economic Outreach (GEO)
PO Box 12778
Wilmington, NC 28405
E-mail: mail@teamgeo.org
URL: http://www.teamgeo.org
Multinational. Description: Strives to express God's love and glory to people of all nations through employing the poor, establishing healthy communities, engaging volunteers in ministry, and expanding missionary efforts worldwide.

19930 ■ Gospel Literature International (GLINT)
PO Box 4060
Ontario, CA 91761-1003
Ph: (909)481-5222
Free: (800)43-GLINT
Fax: (909)481-5216
E-mail: glintint@aol.com
URL: http://www.glint.org
Contact: Dr. Georgalyn Wilkinson, Pres.
Founded: 1961. **Staff:** 9. **Description:** Missionary service organization. Makes the copyrighted material of Gospel Light Publications, Multnomah Publishers, and other publishers available to overseas publishers. Provides a comprehensive Christian education program for Sunday Schools, Vacation Bible Schools,

and day schools. Publications translated in over 50 languages. Provides technical publishing assistance and limited financial assistance for selected publishing projects. **Computer Services:** Online services, offers foreign language publications to sell on its website. **Projects:** China Leadership Training. **Formerly:** (1972) Gospel Light International. **Conventions/Meetings:** periodic conference.

19931 ■ Gospel Recordings (GR)

41823 Enterprise Cir. N
Temecula, CA 92590-5614
Ph: (951)719-1650
Free: (888)44-GRUSA
Fax: (951)719-1651
E-mail: info1@gospelrecordings.com
URL: http://www.gospelrecordings.com
Contact: Colin Stott, Exec. Dir.
Founded: 1938. **Staff:** 60. **Budget:** $1,600,000. **National Groups:** 40. **Description:** Christian mission with the goal of making Evangelistic messages available in every language through recordings in over 5,500 languages and dialects. **Publications:** *Sounds of Gospel Recordings*, monthly. Newsletter ● Also distributes a listing of recorded languages.

19932 ■ HCJB World Radio

PO Box 39800
Colorado Springs, CO 80949-9800
Ph: (719)590-9800
Fax: (719)590-9801
E-mail: info@hcjb.org
URL: http://www.hcjb.org
Contact: David J. Johnson, Pres.
Founded: 1931. **Staff:** 1,000. **Languages:** English, Spanish. **Description:** Missionary broadcast organization with ministries in more than 100 countries and broadcasts in more than 120 languages and dialects. Also ministers through health care and training. **Additional Websites:** http://beyondthecall.org. **Affiliated With:** Evangelical Council for Financial Accountability; Interdenominational Foreign Missions Association; National Religious Broadcasters. **Formerly:** World Radio Missionary Fellowship. **Publications:** *Amigos*, quarterly. Newsletter. Updates supporters of the fellowship's healthcare ministries. Includes prayer requests. **Price:** free. **Conventions/Meetings:** annual meeting.

19933 ■ Helps International Ministries (HIM)

573 Fairview Rd.
Asheville, NC 28803
Ph: (828)277-3812
Fax: (828)274-7770
E-mail: him@helpsintl.com
URL: http://www.helpsintl.com
Contact: David A. Summey PhD, CEO
Founded: 1976. **Members:** 70. **Budget:** $550,000. **Description:** Serves as service mission composed of skilled missionaries including architects, engineers, builders, CPAs, computer consultants, counselors, teachers etc. qualified by their churches and having church, personal, or retired support. Serves as a helping ministry to supplement the needs of evangelical missionaries and missions in order that they may be more effective in their work. Maintains limited placement service; missionaries (full and part-time) are financially supported by churches and individuals. Makes available a tape presentation of the mission's work. **Computer Services:** Mailing lists. **Committees:** Construction; Organizational; Public Relations. **Affiliated With:** Evangelical Council for Financial Accountability. **Publications:** *HIM Former*, monthly. Newsletter. Reports on the organization's activities. **Circulation:** 850. **Advertising:** accepted ● *Mission Computer Update*, periodic. Newsletter. Reports on latest developments in computer technology for missions. ● *Prayer Calendar*, monthly ● *Staff Directory*, periodic ● Also publishes brochures. **Conventions/Meetings:** annual conference.

19934 ■ IHM Volunteer Program of the Sisters, Servants of the Immaculate Heart of Mary

IHM Center
2300 Adams Ave.
Scranton, PA 18509

Ph: (570)346-5431
E-mail: lunsmk@istersofihm.org
URL: http://ihm.marywood.edu
Contact: Sr. Mary Persico, Pres.
Founded: 1982. **Description:** IHM volunteers united to "serve God's people by actively participating in the mission of the Church; expand their understanding of themselves and the world; live a simple lifestyle in the Christian community; deepen their spirituality through personal and communal prayer and the experience of ministering to others." Conducts educational and charitable programs. **Formerly:** (1992) Lay Associates of the Sisters, Servants of the Immaculate Heart of Mary; (2001) We Care - IHM Volunteer Services of the Sisters, Servants of the Immaculate Heart of Mary. **Publications:** *Journey*, 3/year. Magazine. Focuses on contemporary issues and concerns in the area of ministries, spirituality, religious life, and the Catholic Church. **Price:** free. Alternate Formats: online.

19935 ■ Inter Varsity Christian Fellowship

PO Box 7895
Madison, WI 53707-7895
Ph: (608)274-9001
Fax: (608)274-7882
E-mail: information@intervarsity.org
URL: http://www.intervarsity.org
Contact: Alec D. Hill, Pres./CEO
Founded: 1936. **Description:** Works to make mission an integral part of Christian growth for Inter Varsity students and staff. Provides encouragement and instruction. Offers opportunities for students and college graduates to serve on the missionary field short term (two weeks-two months) or long term (two years). Cooperates with other members worldwide to promote missions and cultural awareness. **Projects:** Global Service; Global Urban Trek; Lingua-Cultural. **Formerly:** (1977) Student Foreign Missions Fellowship; (1981) Student Missions Fellowship; (1990) Student Foreign Missions Fellowship; (2000) Inter Varsity Missions Fellowship. **Publications:** *Student Leadership Journal*, 3/year. **Price:** $12.00/year in U.S.; $16.00/year in Canada and outside U.S.; $20.00 for 10 copies of an issue. Alternate Formats: online. Also Cited As: *SLJ*. **Conventions/Meetings:** annual conference and workshop ● regional meeting ● annual Urbana - convention (exhibits).

19936 ■ Interact Ministries

31000 SE Kelso Rd.
Boring, OR 97009
Ph: (503)668-5571
Free: (800)258-3464
Fax: (503)668-6814
E-mail: info@interactministries.org
URL: http://www.interactministries.org
Contact: Shawn Strannigan, Mobilization Coor.
Founded: 1951. **Members:** 130. **Membership Dues:** regular, $163 (monthly). **Languages:** English, Panjabi, Russian. **Description:** Nondenominational organization of individuals interested in establishing churches and Bible schools among native, Asian, and East Indian immigrant people of North America, especially in Alaska and Canada. Promotes the gospel among indigenous people of Siberia. **Affiliated With:** Interdenominational Foreign Missions Association. **Formerly:** (1951) Alaska Mission; (1988) Arctic Missions. **Publications:** *InterAction*, quarterly. Newsletter. **Price:** free. **Conventions/Meetings:** semiannual conference - always Alaska and Canada.

19937 ■ Interdenominational Foreign Missions Association (IFMA)

PO Box 398
Wheaton, IL 60189-0398
Ph: (630)682-9270
Fax: (630)682-9278
E-mail: info@ifmamissions.org
URL: http://www.ifmamissions.org
Contact: Dr. John Orme, Exec. Dir.
Founded: 1917. **Members:** 109. **Staff:** 4. **Budget:** $193,000. **Multinational. Description:** Foreign missionary societies without denominational affiliation sometimes known as "Independent Faith Missions". Organization accredits its members to the public;

produces literature and information dealing with Protestant missionary endeavor. Member groups sponsor over 13,000 missionaries serving in more than 115 countries. **Committees:** Africa; Asia; Business Administration; China; Development for National Leadership; Europe; Frontier Peoples; Islamics; Jewish Ministries; Latin America; North America; Personnel. **Affiliated With:** Evangelism and Missions Information Service. **Formerly:** (2004) Interdenominational Foreign Mission Association of North America. **Publications:** *Accounting and Financial Reporting Guide for Christian Ministries* ● *Seventy-Five Years of IFMA*. **Conventions/Meetings:** annual Business Meeting ● annual meeting ● semiannual Mission Administration Seminar ● annual workshop.

19938 ■ International Mission Board (IMB)

PO Box 6767
Richmond, VA 23230-0767
Free: (800)999-3113
E-mail: fjeffrey@juno.com
URL: http://www.imb.org
Contact: Larry Riley, Managing Dir.
Founded: 1922. **Members:** 16. **Staff:** 2. **Budget:** $450,000. **Languages:** English, Korean, Spanish. **Description:** Represents pastors and laypeople. Coordinates overseas missions of the Primitive Methodist Church in the U.S.A. Works to spread the gospel of Jesus Christ and to minister to the whole person through medical and church planting educational programs in 8 countries. Bestows periodic award. Conducts educational programs; maintains placement service and speakers' bureau. **Libraries:** Type: reference. **Holdings:** photographs, video recordings. **Formerly:** (1968) Foreign Mission Board. **Publications:** *Gleanings*, monthly ● *Quiche New Testament for Joyabaj*. **Conventions/Meetings:** semiannual meeting - always May and October.

19939 ■ InterServe U.S.A.

PO Box 418
Upper Darby, PA 19082-0418
Free: (800)809-4440
Fax: (610)352-4394
E-mail: ea@ludlow.net
URL: http://www.interserveusa.org/index.php
Contact: Rev. Douglas Van Bronkhorst, Exec. Dir.
Founded: 1964. **Staff:** 10. **Regional Groups:** 4. **Description:** U.S. division of international fellowship maintaining more than 550 workers from Australia, Canada, Great Britain, Holland, India, New Zealand, Hong Kong, Korea, Malaysia, Scotland, Singapore, Switzerland, Ireland, and U.S.A., who work as professionals including doctors, nurses, pharmacists, physiotherapists, evangelists, theologians, teachers, secretaries, agriculturists, and community development engineers in Afghanistan, India, Pakistan, Bangladesh, Nepal, Central Asia, Asia Minor, and the Persian Gulf. International office located in Nicosia, Cyprus. **Absorbed:** (1976) United Fellowship for Christian Service. **Formerly:** (1986) BMMF International/USA. **Publications:** *Go Magazine*, quarterly ● Books ● Brochures. **Conventions/Meetings:** annual conference (exhibits) - always September, in Whiting, NJ.

19940 ■ Lasallian Volunteers

Hecker Ctr., Ste.300
3025 Fourth St. NE
Washington, DC 20017
Ph: (202)529-0047 (267)258-3384
Fax: (202)529-0775
E-mail: dkasievich@cbconf.org
URL: http://www.lasallianvolunteers.org
Contact: David Kasievich, Dir.
Founded: 1988. **Members:** 40. **Staff:** 3. **Description:** Catholic mission working in the United States and overseas. Programs include community work and Christian education. Lay volunteers must be at least 20 years of age and wanting to "respond to Christ's call to serve others". **Publications:** none. **Formerly:** (1992) Christian Brothers Volunteer. **Conventions/Meetings:** semiannual retreat.

19941 ■ Latin America Mission (LAM)

PO Box 527900
Miami, FL 33152-7900
Ph: (305)884-8400
Free: (800)275-8410
Fax: (305)885-8649
E-mail: drbefus@lam.org
URL: http://www.lam.org
Contact: Dr. David R. Befus, Pres.

Founded: 1921. **Members:** 200. **Staff:** 20. **Budget:** $6,534,000. **Languages:** English, Spanish. **Description:** Men and women who, motivated by "their love for the Lord Jesus Christ and in obedience to His commands", encourage, assist, and participate with the Latin church in the task of building the church of Jesus Christ in the Latin world and beyond. **Libraries: Type:** reference. **Holdings:** 500. **Subjects:** missions, religion, theology. **Affiliated With:** Evangelical Council for Financial Accountability; Evangelical Fellowship of Mission Agencies. **Formerly:** (1923) Latin American Evangelistic Campaign. **Publications:** *Community Children*. Book. **Price:** $6.00 ● *Getting With God's Program*. Book ● *The Gospel People*. Book ● *Kingdom Business*. Book ● *Latin America Evangelist*, 3/year. Magazine. **Price:** free ● *Not In Vain*. Book ● *Where There Are No Jobs*. Book. **Price:** $10.00 ● Also makes available audiovisual materials. **Conventions/Meetings:** semiannual board meeting.

19942 ■ Maryknoll Mission Association of the Faithful (MMAF)

Bethany Bldg.
PO Box 307
Maryknoll, NY 10545-0307
Ph: (914)762-6364
Free: (800)818-5276
Fax: (914)762-7301
E-mail: mmaf@mkl-mmaf.org
URL: http://www.maryknoll.org
Contact: Kathy Wright, Admissions Coor.

Founded: 1975. **Members:** 125. **Multinational. Description:** U.S. Catholic men and women active in the church who serve in overseas mission in Africa, Asia and Latin America. Responds to the needs of the poor and oppressed by collaborating with people who are in need. Helps them to recognize their worth and dignity. Encourages them to realize their potential. Ministries include but are not limited to lay and community formation, education, health/AIDS, peace and justice advocacy, pastoral work, ecology, agriculture and parish work. **Affiliated With:** Maryknoll Fathers and Brothers. **Formerly:** MaryKnoll Associate Lay Missioners.

19943 ■ Maryknoll Sisters of Saint Dominic

PO Box 311
Maryknoll, NY 10545-0311
Ph: (914)941-7575
Fax: (914)923-0733
E-mail: inquiry@maryknollaffiliates.org
URL: http://home.maryknoll.org
Contact: Sister Suzanne Moore, Pres.

Founded: 1912. **Members:** 604. **Staff:** 200. **Budget:** $22,570. **Regional Groups:** 26. **Languages:** English, Spanish. **Description:** Catholic women missionaries. Works to "proclaim the Gospel of Jesus Christ" through life witness, pastoral ministry, communication, and community development, education, health, research, and social service programs. Members live and work in twenty-six countries of Africa, Asia, the Central Pacific, Latin America, and the United States. Operates Mission Institute which provides continuing education for missionary and a forum for the discussion of mission trends and critical issues facing mission. Compiles statistics; maintains Heritage exhibit. **Libraries: Type:** reference. **Holdings:** 36,000; archival material, audiovisuals, books, clippings, monographs, periodicals. **Subjects:** theological, spiritual, literature, history, sociological, fiction, foreign languages, biography. **Committees:** Development; Health Services; Hospitality; Information Services; Maryknoll Mission Archives; Office of Global Concerns; Personnel; Treasury. **Publications:** *Congregational Leadership Team Communique*, bimonthly. Newsletter. For congregational use. ● *General Assembly Proceedings*, every 6 years ● *Mary-*

knoll (in English and Spanish), 9/year. Magazine. Contains stories of the organization's efforts to help the poor. Alternate Formats: online. Also Cited As: *Revista Maryknoll* ● *Maryknoll Vocational Newsletter*. Alternate Formats: online ● *Mission Evolving Toward Global Community* ● Membership Directory, annual. **Conventions/Meetings:** general assembly - every 6 years ● periodic World Sections Meeting.

19944 ■ Medical Mission Sisters (MMS)

8400 Pine Rd.
Philadelphia, PA 19111
Ph: (215)742-6100
Fax: (215)342-3948
E-mail: mmsorg@medicalmissionsisters.org
URL: http://www.medicalmissionsisters.org
Contact: Sister Carmelita Perez MMS, Coor.

Founded: 1925. **Members:** 650. **Budget:** $3,500,000. **Regional Groups:** 6. **Multinational. Description:** International women's religious community that combines religious life with practice of full range of health care services. Maintains own health centers and collaborates with governments and other agencies in other facilities in India, Pakistan, Ghana, Uganda, Venezuela, Indonesia, the Philippines, Kenya, Malawi, Ethiopia, Brazil, Peru, U.S., England, Netherlands, Belgium, Germany, Italy, and Mexico. Conducts local training programs for professional, managerial, and grassroots level staffs. **Programs:** Development of Women; Health Care and Education; Low-cost Alternatives; Nutrition Education; Targeted Work for Justice; Wholeness and Wellness. **Publications:** *Medical Mission Sisters News*, semiannual. Newsletter. Features global work and concerns. **Price:** free. **Circulation:** 48,000. **Conventions/Meetings:** annual Central Assembly, leadership meeting of medical mission sisters - always October or November.

19945 ■ Men for Missions International (MFMI)

PO Box A
Greenwood, IN 46142-6599
Ph: (317)881-6752
Fax: (317)865-1076
E-mail: info@mfmi.org
URL: http://www.omsinternational.org
Contact: Kent Eller, Natl. Dir.

Founded: 1954. **Members:** 15,000. **Staff:** 20. **State Groups:** 100. **National Groups:** 4. **Description:** Laymen associated with OMS International, including businessmen, farmers, skilled tradesmen, and others interested in supporting Christian evangelism worldwide. Members adopt projects that provide services to those in need and that match their vocational interests, hobbies, and amount of spare time available. For example, automobile dealers provide cars for missionaries, farmers raise crops or stock for profit to missions, carpenters and construction workers donate time and skills to erect buildings; others raise funds or go to the mission field during their vacations to evangelize. Has built a radio station, medical facilities, school rooms, an evangelism center in Hong Kong, churches worldwide, youth camps in Spain, Brazil, and Ecuador, a seminary in India, and a road accessing primitive areas in Haiti. **Additional Websites:** http://www.mfmi.org. **Telecommunication Services:** electronic mail, mfmi@omsinternational. org. **Departments:** Banquets; Crusades; Farming for Missions; Field Representatives; Projects; Retreats and Professional Services for Missions; Trucking for Missions. **Affiliated With:** OMS International. **Publications:** *Action*, quarterly. Magazine. Contains information on Men For Missions International. **Price:** free. Alternate Formats: online ● *Impacto*. Book ● *Iron Sharpens Iron*. Book. **Price:** $4.95/copy. **Conventions/Meetings:** semiannual United States Cabinet - congress - January.

19946 ■ Mission Advanced Research and Communication Center (MARC)

c/o World Vision International
800 W Chestnut Ave.
Monrovia, CA 91016-3198
Ph: (909)463-2998
Free: (800)777-7752

Fax: (909)463-2999
E-mail: wvresources@worldvision.org
URL: http://www.worldvisionresources.com
Contact: Ms. Jojo Palmer, Mgr. of Operations

Founded: 1966. **Staff:** 10. **Budget:** $900,000. **Description:** A division of World Vision International whose function is "inspiring vision and empowering mission among those who are extending the whole gospel to the whole world." Documents current experience in grass roots holistic Christian development; researches issues and methods arising from the churches' witness in a rapidly urbanizing world; surveys and analyzes trends that influence Christian missions; conducts grass roots training in the use of people-centered strategies for sharing the "good news"; shares information among agencies involved in mission. **Computer Services:** database, Christian ministry information. **Publications:** *World Vision Resources Newsletter*, quarterly. Contains any advancement on current issues. **Price:** free. **Circulation:** 20,000. Alternate Formats: online. Also Cited As: *World Vision Resources Book Catalog* ● Books ● Also publishes summaries.

19947 ■ Mission Aviation Fellowship (MAF)

PO Box 47
Nampa, ID 83653
Ph: (208)498-0800
Free: (800)359-7623
Fax: (208)498-0801
E-mail: maf-us@maf.org
URL: http://www.maf.org
Contact: Kevin Swanson, Pres.

Founded: 1945. **Members:** 176. **Staff:** 306. **Budget:** $31,000,000. **Description:** Serves more than 600 Christian and humanitarian organizations in Africa, Eurasia and Latin America through aviation and electronic communications. Maintains a fleet of nearly 54 aircraft in 23 countries, providing Evangelism and national church support, medical emergency, crisis relief and community development flights. Involves in distance education, leadership development and logistics support. **Projects:** Operation ACCESS!. **Absorbed:** (1962) Missionary Engineering. **Publications:** *Flightwatch*, bimonthly. Newsletter. **Conventions/Meetings:** annual Corporation Meeting - March or September.

19948 ■ Mission Services Association (MSA)

PO Box 13111
Knoxville, TN 37920-0111
Ph: (865)577-9740
Free: (800)655-8524
Fax: (865)573-5950
E-mail: msa@missionservices.org
URL: http://www.missionservices.org
Contact: Reggie Hundley, Exec. Dir.

Founded: 1946. **Staff:** 7. **Budget:** $523,000. **Regional Groups:** 1. **Description:** Promotes the concept of missions and informs the public of trends and events in Christian mission work through distribution of mission publications. Aids in sponsoring mission fairs and faith-promise rallies. **Libraries: Type:** reference. **Holdings:** books. **Subjects:** missionary work. **Publications:** *Horizons*, monthly. Magazine. Contains reports of mission activities worldwide. Includes calendar of events, member news, member profiles, and speakers list. **Price:** $17.00/year; $10.00/additional copy; $75.00/year (5 copies); $125.00/year (10 copies). **Circulation:** 4,000. **Advertising:** accepted. Alternate Formats: online ● *Missionary Directory*, annual. Lists missionaries affiliated with the nondenominational Christian churches and churches of Christ. Includes lists of U.S. homes for youth. **Price:** $17.00/year ● Brochures ● Also publishes brochures. **Conventions/Meetings:** semiannual board meeting.

19949 ■ Mission Training International (MTI)

PO Box 1220
Palmer Lake, CO 80133
Ph: (719)487-0111
Free: (800)896-3710
Fax: (719)487-9350

E-mail: info@mti.org
URL: http://www.mti.org
Contact: Rev. Stephen M. Sweatman PhD, Pres./
CEO

Founded: 1954. **Staff:** 10. **Description:** Works together with the church and mission agencies to train and nurture Christians for effective intercultural service so that the gospel can be clearly and effectively communicated. Offers educational programs and consultations on developing strategies and skills. **Libraries: Type:** reference. **Holdings:** books, periodicals. **Subjects:** missions. **Telecommunication Services:** electronic mail, ssweatman@mti.org. **Affiliated With:** World Evangelical Alliance. **Formerly:** (1996) Missionary Internship. **Publications:** *Program Schedule*, annual. Catalog. Lists educational programs and workshops offered by MTI and a schedule of classes in chronological order. **Conventions/Meetings:** annual Mental Health and Missions - conference - 2007 Nov. 15-18, Angola, IN.

19950 ■ Missionary Church (MC)
PO Box 9127
Fort Wayne, IN 46899-9127
Ph: (260)747-2027
Fax: (260)747-5331
E-mail: mcdenomusa@aol.com
URL: http://www.mcusa.org
Contact: Dr. William Hossler, Pres.

Founded: 1969. **Members:** 34,000. **Staff:** 30. **Budget:** $5,330,000. **Regional Groups:** 14. **State Groups:** 31. **Local Groups:** 400. **National Groups:** 9. **Languages:** Creole, English, Korean, Portuguese, Spanish. **Description:** Conducts denominational work, including church planting in the states. Cooperates with the Evangelical Missionary Church of Canada in conducting overseas activities that include church planting, bible translation, correspondence courses, bible schools and extension seminaries, elementary schools, clinics, youth camps and other programs of evangelism carried out by 122 missionaries, in cooperation with other evangelical mission boards and the national churches in Brazil, Cyprus, Ecuador, Haiti, Dominican Republic, France, Jamaica, Nigeria, Portugal, Russia, Spain, Sierra Leone, Thailand, Indonesia, Guinea, Cuba, Germany, Chad, Venezuela, South Africa, Middle East. Also has established indigenous churches in India and Mexico. Loans missionaries to a number of other mission organizations. **Awards:** 50-Year Gold Watch to Ministers. **Frequency:** biennial. **Type:** recognition ● 40-Year Plaque to Ministers. **Type:** recognition. **Telecommunication Services:** electronic mail, mci@mcusa.org. **Departments:** Church Multiplication; Disciplining Ministries; Overseas Ministries; Services; Stewardship Ministries. **Formed by Merger of:** (1969) United Missionary Church; (1969) Missionary Church Association. **Publications:** *Emphasis on Faith and Living*, bimonthly. Magazine. **Circulation:** 16,000 ● *Priority*, monthly. Designed for church leaders. ● Also publishes in-house directory. **Conventions/Meetings:** biennial General Conference of the Missionary Church (US) (exhibits) - always July.

19951 ■ Missionary Gospel Fellowship (MGF)
PO Box 1535
Turlock, CA 95381
Ph: (209)634-8575
Fax: (209)634-8472
E-mail: mgfhq@mgfhq.org
URL: http://www.mgfhq.org
Contact: Jay Hyatt, Gen. Dir.

Founded: 1939. **Members:** 90. **Staff:** 4. **Languages:** English, Hindi, Spanish, Urdu. **Description:** Christian missionary group. Works to spread the gospel to people in the U.S., Northern Mexico and Canada through missionary programs, designed to reach the stranger (diverse ethnic peoples in North America). **Libraries: Type:** open to the public. **Holdings:** 1,000. **Subjects:** missions, theology, biographies. **Publications:** Bulletin, quarterly. **Price:** free. **Circulation:** 2,500. **Conventions/Meetings:** annual Missionary Conference, to better interaction between missionary senders and missionaries (exhibits).

19952 ■ Missionary Sisters of St. Peter Claver (MSSPC)
c/o Sister M. Aidan
PO Box 401
Chesterfield, MO 63006-0401
Ph: (314)434-8084
URL: http://www.cmswr.org/member_communities/
MSSPC.htm
Contact: Sister M. Aidan, Contact

Founded: 1894. **Description:** Assists missionaries worldwide through fundraising and provision of educational materials and supplies. Disseminates information on missionary activities. **Publications:** *Echo From Africa and Other Continents*, monthly. Magazine. Contains letters from missionaries and supply requests.

19953 ■ Missionary Sisters of the Society of Mary - Marist Missionary Sisters (SMSM)
349 Grove St.
Waltham, MA 02453
E-mail: infomsm@maristmissionarysmsm.org
URL: http://maristmissionarysmsm.org
Contact: Sister Judith Moore, Superior Gen.

Founded: 1845. **Members:** 596. **Languages:** English, French, Spanish. **Description:** Represents women missionaries working primarily in Third World countries. **Libraries: Type:** reference. **Holdings:** video recordings. **Publications:** *Marist Mission Today*, 3/year. Newsletter. **Circulation:** 3,700. **Conventions/Meetings:** annual seminar.

19954 ■ Missionary TECH Team (MTT)
25 FRJ Dr.
Longview, TX 75602-4703
Ph: (903)757-4530
Fax: (903)758-2799
E-mail: administration@techteam.org
URL: http://www.techteam.org
Contact: Birne D. Wiley, Pres.

Founded: 1969. **Members:** 28. **Budget:** $975,000. **Description:** Provides technical support for planning, design, and construction of buildings and facilities for Christian missions and organizations worldwide. Provides technical support in the area of media communication involving video, photography, layout, design, and typesetting. Coordinates activities of volunteers who assist Christian missions. Conducts educational and charitable programs, seminars and workshops; maintains speaker's bureau. Provides children's services. Includes other services such as: architectural design; civil, structural, and environmental engineering; counseling. **Boards:** Advisors; Tech Associates; Trustees. **Affiliated With:** Association of North American Missions; Interdenominational Foreign Missions Association. **Publications:** *TeamWork*, periodic. Newsletter. **Price:** free. **Circulation:** 11,000 ● *TECH Intercessor*, bimonthly. Newsletter. **Price:** free. **Circulation:** 400.

19955 ■ Missionary Vehicle Association (MIVA)
Address Unknown since 2007
Founded: 1971. **Staff:** 4. **Description:** Purpose is to provide means of transportation (including cars, jeeps, trucks, motorcycles, boats, tractors, and bicycles) to Catholic missionaries working in Third World countries. Vehicles are used to reach sick, handicapped, and aged persons in remote areas, deliver food to starving people, transport people needing medical care to hospitals, and preach the Gospel. **Computer Services:** database, donors ● mailing lists. **Also Known As:** MIVA America; (1988) Missionary Vehicle Association of America. **Publications:** *Grant Report*, annual ● *Mission and Ministry Statement*. Booklet ● *MIVA Report*, quarterly. Newsletter. **Circulation:** 8,600. **Advertising:** not accepted ● *Providing the Vital Link* (in English and Spanish). Brochure ● *What is MIVA*. Brochure. **Conventions/Meetings:** semiannual board meeting.

19956 ■ Moody Bible Institute (MBI)
820 N LaSalle Blvd.
Chicago, IL 60610
Ph: (312)329-4000
Free: (800)356-6639

Fax: (800)678-3329
E-mail: pr@moody.edu
URL: http://www.moody.edu
Contact: Dr. Michael J. Easley, Pres.

Founded: 1897. **Staff:** 2. **Description:** Supports the production and distribution of Christian literature worldwide. Assists foreign-based missions in developing printing facilities. Distributes Christian literature to persons in prisons, hospitals, and rescue missions. Sponsors New Believer Library Program, a Christian reading program for prison inmates. **Convention/Meeting:** none. **Formerly:** (1980) Moody Literature Mission; (2000) Moody Literature Ministries.

19957 ■ Mustard Seed Foundation
3330 N Washington Blvd., Ste.100
Arlington, VA 22201
Ph: (703)524-5620
Fax: (703)524-5643
URL: http://www.msfdn.org
Founded: 1954. **Staff:** 206. **Budget:** $1,000,000. **Description:** An international, interdenominational Christian ministry which provides services to aboriginal/tribal peoples of Pacific Rim countries. Service projects include medical clinics, residential homes for children, the handicapped, and the elderly, economic development projects, relief services, and care for unwed mothers. Educational project includes day care, K-12 schools, vocational training, teacher training education, and pastoral training. Evangelism projects include prison ministries, new church development, and support for evangelists and pastors. Discipleship projects include Bible conferences, Sunday school training events, and Church development seminars. **Formerly:** (2003) The Mustard Seed. **Publications:** *Seeds of Hope*, quarterly. Newsletter. **Price:** free. **Circulation:** 6,500. **Conventions/Meetings:** semiannual board meeting.

19958 ■ Nations Ministries (NM)
PO Box 620
Springtown, TX 76082
Ph: (302)729-0835
Fax: (775)367-0527
E-mail: info@allnationsmin.org
URL: http://www.allnationsmin.org
Contact: Riley Donica, Dir.

Founded: 1983. **Staff:** 6. **Description:** Individuals and churches conducting evangelical Christian ministry on American Indian reservations in the U.S. Maintains speakers' bureau. **Awards: Frequency:** periodic. **Type:** recognition. **Publications:** *Indian Nations News*, bimonthly. Newsletter. **Price:** free. **Circulation:** 8,000. **Conventions/Meetings:** annual Rendezvous - conference - last Tuesday, Wednesday and Thursday of April ● periodic Trail Rides - meeting ● annual Youth Camp - meeting - 2nd or 3rd week of June.

19959 ■ Nazarene Missions International (NMI)
6401 The Paseo
Kansas City, MO 64131
Ph: (816)333-7000
Fax: (816)822-8296
E-mail: nmi@nazarene.org
URL: http://www.nazarenemissions.org
Contact: Dr. Daniel D. Ketchum, Gen. Dir.

Founded: 1915. **Members:** 819,383. **Staff:** 9. **Local Groups:** 10,812. **Languages:** English, French, Japanese, Korean, Portuguese, Spanish. **Multinational. Description:** Members of the Church of the Nazarene in 146 countries. Conducts programs for mission education and assists fundraising to carry on the missionary work of the church. Encourages young people to be involved in missions. Compiles statistics. Challenges members to pray for missions. **Libraries: Type:** reference. **Holdings:** archival material, books. **Awards:** Award of Excellence. **Frequency:** annual. **Type:** recognition ● Mission Priority One. **Frequency:** annual. **Type:** recognition. **Recipient:** for a local congregation achieving the four-fold purpose of the NMI. **Committees:** Adult Mission Education; Children's Mission Education; General Mission Education; Youth Mission Education. **Councils:** General NMI. **Affiliated With:** Evangelical Press Association;

Religious Conference Management Association. **Formerly:** (1899) Woman's Missionary Society; (1928) Woman's Foreign Missionary Society; (1952) Nazarene Foreign Missionary Society; (1964) Nazarene World Missionary Society; (2003) Nazarene World Mission Society. **Publications:** *Adult Mission Education Curriculum*, annual. Journal. Contains 12 lessons to teach people about Nazarene missions. **Price:** $22.50 ● *Children's Mission Education Curriculum*. Journal ● *Global Glimpses* (in English, French, Portuguese, and Spanish), quarterly. Newsletter. Contains denominational and interdenominational mission news for local churches. **Price:** free ● *HeartLine*, monthly; Newsletter. **Price:** free ● *International Mission Education Journal* (in English, French, Portuguese, and Spanish), annual. Intended for congregations who do not speak English as their first language. **Price:** free to churches. **Circulation:** 447 ● *Mission Connection*, quarterly. Magazine. Includes information for missionaries, pastors, district leaders, and local leaders of NMI activities. **Price:** free to churches. **Circulation:** 19,500 ● *NMI Handbook and Constitution* ● *Youth Mission Education Curriculum*. Journal ● Brochures. **Conventions/Meetings:** quadrennial convention, aims to conduct the business of the organization and provide inspiration to its membership (exhibits).

19960 ■ New Hope International
PO Box 25490
Colorado Springs, CO 80936
Ph: (719)577-4450
Free: (800)297-9591
Fax: (719)577-4453
E-mail: hank.paulson@newhopeinternational.org
URL: http://www.newhopeinternational.org
Contact: Hank Paulson, Founder/Pres.

Founded: 1971. **Staff:** 95. **Budget:** $1,200,000. **Languages:** Czech, English, Hungarian, Romanian, Russian, Slovak, Ukrainian. **Multinational. Description:** Nondenominational organization seeking to build a moral and spiritual foundation for a new generation in a new Eastern Europe by providing training and literature to the people of that region. Maintains Speaker's Bureau. **Convention/Meeting:** none. **Affiliated With:** Evangelical Council for Financial Accountability; Evangelical Fellowship of Mission Agencies; National Association of Evangelicals. **Also Known As:** New Hope Ministries. **Formerly:** (1998) Eastern European Bible Mission. **Publications:** *Beyond the Wall*. Book. Shows how the Communist philosophy has tried to stamp out religion throughout the Eastern European Communist nations. **Price:** $5.00 ● *Focus*, bimonthly. **Circulation:** 10,000 ● *Global Partnerships*. Book. **Price:** $15.00 ● *Project Letters*, bimonthly. **Circulation:** 10,000.

19961 ■ New Life League International (NLLI)
PO Box 35857
Houston, TX 77235-5857
Ph: (832)242-7750
Fax: (832)242-7751
E-mail: nlch@nlch.net
Contact: David Depew, Pres.

Founded: 1954. **Members:** 201. **Description:** Interdenominational, international missionary society. Ministry in 16 countries includes publication and distribution of religious literature, radio broadcasting, evangelism, church planting, a Bible school, medical missions, and orphanage ministries. **Convention/Meeting:** none. **Formerly:** (2003) New Life League. **Publications:** *New Life News*, quarterly.

19962 ■ New Tribes Mission (NTM)
1000 E 1st St.
Sanford, FL 32771-1441
Ph: (407)323-3430
Free: (866)547-2460
Fax: (407)330-0376
E-mail: ntm@ntm.org
URL: http://www.ntm.org
Contact: Oli Jacobsen, Chm.

Founded: 1942. **Members:** 3,200. **Budget:** $35,000,000. **Multinational. Description:** Ordained and licensed Protestant missionaries and members of the headquarters and missionary training schools staffs. Undertakes evangelical missionary work among indigenous peoples in Latin America, the Far East, and Africa, including teaching of Christian doctrine, Bible translation, research in linguistics, customs and cultures, and literacy programs. Maintains training schools in Wisconsin, Michigan, Pennsylvania, Missouri, Mississippi, Oregon, and Durham, ON, Canada. Prints translated literacy materials, primers, and portions of Scripture in more than 100 languages. Works with over 200 languages in 27 countries. **Libraries: Type:** reference. **Holdings:** 8,000. **Subjects:** theology and missionary. **Publications:** *NTM@Work*, quarterly. Magazine. Features articles on international tribal ministries. **Price:** free. **Circulation:** 40,000 ● *Quarterlies*, quarterly.

19963 ■ New Wineskins Missionary Network (NWMN)
PO Box 278
Ambridge, PA 15003
Ph: (724)266-2810
E-mail: info@newwineskins.org
URL: http://www.newwineskins.org
Contact: Sharon Steinmiller, Dir.

Founded: 1974. **Members:** 4,400. **Staff:** 2. **Budget:** $130,000. **Description:** Episcopalians interested in participation and promotion of world evangelization. Holds mission awareness seminars in Episcopal parishes and dioceses, gives orientations to Episcopal missionaries and cross-cultural workers. Works in conjunction with the Trinity Episcopal School for Ministry to establish Stanway Institute for World Mission and Evangelism and School of World Missions. **Libraries: Type:** reference. **Holdings:** audiovisuals, books, periodicals. **Subjects:** world mission. **Formerly:** (2006) Episcopal Church Missionary Community. **Publications:** *Reach Out*, bimonthly. Newsletter. **Conventions/Meetings:** triennial New Wineskins for Global Mission - conference (exhibits).

19964 ■ North America Indigenous Ministries (NAIM)
PO Box 151
Point Roberts, WA 98281
Ph: (604)946-1227
Fax: (604)946-1465
E-mail: office@naim.ca
URL: http://www.naim.ca
Contact: Bill Tarter, Exec. Dir.

Founded: 1949. **Members:** 14. **Staff:** 80. **Budget:** $6,669,000. **Multinational. Description:** Represents professionals, such as teachers and engineers, who also have some theological training. Aims to establish indigenous Native American churches in urban centers and on reservations. Conducts economic, educational, social, and rehabilitation programs. Offers alcohol treatment and cross-cultural communication seminars. **Affiliated With:** Interdenominational Foreign Missions Association. **Formerly:** North America Indian Mission; (1986) Marine Medical Mission; (2007) North America Indian Ministries. **Publications:** *Intercessor*, bimonthly. Newsletter. Includes prayer requests. **Price:** free. **Circulation:** 250 ● *NAIM News*, semiannual. Newsletter. Contains reporting on new staff, new ministries, and association activities. **Price:** free. **Circulation:** 7,500. **Conventions/Meetings:** annual general assembly.

19965 ■ O.C. International (OCI)
PO Box 36900
Colorado Springs, CO 80936
Ph: (719)592-9292
Free: (800)676-7837
Fax: (719)592-0693
E-mail: oci@oci.org
URL: http://www.onechallenge.org
Contact: Dr. Greg Gripentrog, Pres.

Founded: 1951. **Members:** 325. **Staff:** 44. **Budget:** $10,000,000. **Multinational. Description:** Interdenominational missionary sending organization, specializing in leadership development, research, training and mobilizing church leaders for church growth. Countries of service include, but are not limited to, Brazil, Canada, Guatemala, Mexico, USA, Germany, Greece, Romania, Spain, UK/England, Kenya, Mozambique, South Africa, India, Philippines, Singapore, and Taiwan. **Departments:** Development; Goodwill Ambassadors; International Ministry Team; Personnel; Research; Sports Ambassadors. **Formerly:** (1969) Orient Crusades-Gospel Outreach; (1969) Overseas Crusades; (1980) O.C. Ministries.

19966 ■ OMF International - USA
10 W Dry Creek Cir.
Littleton, CO 80120-4413
Ph: (303)730-4160
Free: (800)422-5330
Fax: (303)730-4165
E-mail: us@omf.org
URL: http://www.us.omf.org
Contact: Neil Thompson, Natl. Dir.

Founded: 1888. **Members:** 1,000. **Regional Groups:** 4. **Description:** Protestant missionaries. American office of international missionary society, which originated in England in 1865 for work in inland China. Church planting, evangelism, training and development work now carried out in most countries of East Asia. Through its publications, the group seeks to mobilize new missionaries and supporters, and educate the public. **Libraries: Type:** reference. **Holdings:** archival material, books. **Telecommunication Services:** additional toll-free number, (800)993-2751. **Councils:** U.S. **Programs:** China; Ethnic Ministries. **Affiliated With:** OMF International - Singapore. **Formerly:** (1951) China Inland Mission; (1965) China Inland Mission Overseas Missionary Fellowship; (1997) Overseas Missionary Fellowship, U.S.A. **Publications:** *East Asia Insight*, 3/year. Newsletter. Helps the American church become aware of and involved with what God is doing among the people of East Asia. **Circulation:** 30,000. Alternate Formats: online ● Also publishes biography and mission studies. **Conventions/Meetings:** annual Regional Prayer Conference.

19967 ■ OMS International
PO Box A
Greenwood, IN 46142
Ph: (317)881-6751
Fax: (317)888-5275
E-mail: info@omsinternational.org
URL: http://www.omsinternational.org
Contact: Sheila Doty, Sec.

Founded: 1901. **Nonmembership. Multinational. Description:** Works as an evangelical, interdenominational faith mission - reaches the nations for Christ through evangelism, theological training and church planting in Asia, Latin America, the Caribbean, Europe and Africa. Joins with those churches in global partnerships to reach the rest of the world. The world headquarters is in the United States; offices are also operated in Australia, Canada, New Zealand, South Africa and the United Kingdom. **Divisions:** Men for Missions International. **Formerly:** (1973) Oriental Missionary Society. **Publications:** *Action*, quarterly. Magazine ● *OMS Outreach*, triennial. Magazine. Alternate Formats: online. **Conventions/Meetings:** periodic regional meeting.

19968 ■ Our Little Brothers and Sisters (OLBS)
PO Box 3134
Alexandria, VA 22302
Ph: (703)836-1233
Free: (888)955-3555
E-mail: olbs@olbsus.org
URL: http://www.nphamigos.org
Contact: Rev. William B. Wasson, Founder

Founded: 1969. **Description:** Maintains orphanages in Haiti, Honduras, Nicaragua, Mexico, El Salvador, Dominican Republic, and Guatea. Provides education, medical services, food, clothing, shelter, and counseling for children. **Additional Websites:** http://www.olbsus.org. **Foreign language name:** Nuestros Pequenos Hermanos.

19969 ■ Paraclete
PO Box 6507
Mesa, AZ 85216-6507
Ph: (480)854-4444
Fax: (480)854-4741

E-mail: info@paraclete.net
URL: http://www.paraclete.net
Contact: Don Parrott, Pres./CEO
Multinational. Description: Assists agencies and churches in their mission to reach the least reached peoples of the world. Helps mission agencies build stronger teams, improve communications and build trust among members. Provides cross-cultural training for North American workers planning for overseas ministry. Empowers teams to better resolve conflict and develop peacemaking skills.

19970 ■ Pilgrim Fellowship (PF)
Address Unknown since 2007
Founded: 1944. **Staff:** 1. **Description:** Forwards funds received to missionaries under its sponsorship. **Convention/Meeting:** none. **Formerly:** (1954) The Pilgrim. **Publications:** *The Pilgrim*, bimonthly. Pamphlet. **Price:** free. **Advertising:** not accepted.

19971 ■ Presbyterian Frontier Fellowship (PFF)
c/o Rev. Bill Young, Exec. Dir.
7132 Portland Ave., Ste.136
Richfield, MN 55423-3264
Ph: (612)869-0062
Free: (800)720-4PFF
Fax: (612)869-1888
E-mail: info@pff.net
URL: http://www.pff.net
Contact: Rev. Bill Young, Exec. Dir.
Founded: 1981. **Staff:** 24. **Budget:** $2,500,000. **Regional Groups:** 7. **Nonmembership. Description:** PFF Presbyterians. PFF seeks to bring Christianity for groups of people worldwide who lack a "viable, evangelizing, culturally indigenous church." Assists the worldwide and national ministries divisions of the Presbyterian Church (USA) through the Presbyterian General Assembly in mobilizing church resources for evangelical, mission, and witness programs. Conducts educational and training programs; maintains speakers' bureau; compiles statistics. **Libraries: Type:** reference. **Holdings:** books, periodicals. **Subjects:** mission. **Awards:** Frontier Mission Project Grants. **Frequency:** semiannual. **Type:** grant. **Telecommunication Services:** electronic mail, byoung@pff.net. **Publications:** *The Frontier and You*, quarterly. Newsletter. **Price:** free. **Circulation:** 4,500. **Conventions/Meetings:** annual Frontier - conference.

19972 ■ Prison Mission Association (PMA)
PO Box 2300
Port Orchard, WA 98366
Ph: (360)876-0918
Fax: (360)876-9579
URL: http://prisonministry.net/pmabcf
Founded: 1955. **Members:** 7. **Staff:** 10. **Budget:** $100,000. **Languages:** English, Spanish. **Description:** Works as a nondenominational ministry-serving prisoners, servicemen, and individuals involved in outreach missions. Aims to provide Biblical teaching for prison inmates and individuals in service and abroad. Provides outreach services by way of Bible study correspondence courses and Bible literature. Students of Bible correspondence courses receive a certificate of accomplishment after each course is completed. Visits and counsels prison inmates. **Libraries: Type:** reference. **Holdings:** books. **Computer Services:** database ● mailing lists. **Divisions:** Bible Correspondence Fellowship. **Publications:** Newsletter (in English and Spanish), quarterly. Covers board meetings and the association's correspondence courses. **Price:** free. **Conventions/Meetings:** quarterly board meeting.

19973 ■ Red Sea Team International
PO Box 2047
Lexington, SC 29071-2047
Ph: (803)358-2330
Fax: (803)358-2330
E-mail: postmaster@rsti.org
URL: http://www.rsti.org
Contact: Herbert Brasher, Natl. Dir.
Founded: 1951. **Members:** 100. **Staff:** 5. **Budget:** $1,100,000. **Languages:** Afar, Arabic, Baluchi, Bambara, English, Farsi, French, Pushtu, Somali, Urdu.

Description: Provides specific countries with agriculturalists, doctors, nurses, and teachers. Attempts to demonstrate Christian love to Muslims. Helps Muslim immigrants in England and Canada locate housing and schools. Sponsors charitable and educational programs. Provides agricultural and medical assistance. **Libraries: Type:** reference; open to the public; lending. **Holdings:** books. **Subjects:** religious, general. **Affiliated With:** Interdenominational Foreign Missions Association. **Formerly:** (1997) Red Sea Mission Team. **Publications:** *Prayer Bulletin*, monthly. Newsletter. Contains prayer requests from and for members. **Price:** free. **Conventions/Meetings:** annual conference and meeting, with business meeting, field reports, and prayer.

19974 ■ Response-Ability (RA)
460 Shadeland Ave.
Drexel Hill, PA 19026
Ph: (610)626-1400
E-mail: ra@ravolunteers.com
URL: http://www.ravolunteers.com
Contact: Elizabeth Eager, Exec.Dir.
Founded: 1991. **Members:** 30. **Staff:** 4. **Regional Groups:** 3. **Description:** Volunteer program sponsored by the Society of the Holy Child Jesus. Places teachers in the U.S. and the Dominican Republic for one year, full time positions. Operates the Teacher Service Program in which participants teach for one year in inner city Catholic schools in Philadelphia, Washington DC, and Los Angeles while earning graduate credits. **Publications:** *RA REACH*. Newsletter.

19975 ■ Romanian Missionary Society (RMS)
1415 Hill Ave.
PO Box 527
Wheaton, IL 60187
Ph: (630)665-6503 (630)665-6512
Fax: (630)665-6538
E-mail: rms@rmsonline.org
URL: http://www.rmsonline.org
Contact: Mr. Stuart Erdenberg, Exec. Dir.
Founded: 1968. **Staff:** 25. **Budget:** $700,000. **Languages:** English, Romanian. **Nonmembership. Multinational. Description:** Exists to facilitate the expansion of God's Kingdom in Romania, through Europe, and onto the uttermost parts of the earth by supporting Christian projects and ministries in Romania, Western Europe, and around the world. These include: preparing teachers, pastors, evangelists and missionaries through student scholarships; propagating the Church through sponsoring pastors and Church building programs; proclaiming the Gospel in Romania through Christian radio; publishing Christian literature and training materials in the Romanian language; providing relief, compassion and witness to orphans and those in need. **Publications:** *Inside Romania*, bimonthly. Newsletter. **Price:** free. **Circulation:** 5,000.

19976 ■ St. Anthony's Guild
4 Jersey St.
East Rutherford, NJ 07073-1012
Ph: (973)778-1915
Fax: (973)777-5687
E-mail: guild@hnp.org
URL: http://www.hnp.org/guild/index.cfm
Contact: Fr. John T. Piccione OFM, Dir.
Founded: 1924. **Members:** 185,000. **Membership Dues:** individual, $10 (annual). **Staff:** 13. **Budget:** $6,000,000. **Description:** Promotes devotion to St. Anthony of Padua (1195-1231), the first Franciscan professor of theology. Supports formation programs and ministries of Franciscan priests and brothers of Holy Name Province. The Guild's Bread for the Poor Fund helps support four Anthony Houses and other works for the poor. Franciscan ministries include soup kitchens, shelters, parishes, schools, and urban ministry centers. **Convention/Meeting:** none. **Computer Services:** Mailing lists, of members. **Telecommunication Services:** electronic mail, hnp@hnp.org. **Publications:** *The Anthonian*, quarterly. Magazine. **Price:** $1.00/issue. ISSN: 1060-0345. **Circulation:** 90,000. Alternate Formats: online.

19977 ■ St. Martin De Porres Guild
141 E 65th St.
New York, NY 10021-6699
Ph: (212)744-2410
Free: (800)850-5228
Fax: (212)737-3875
Contact: Fr. Raymond F. Halligan, Dir.
Founded: 1935. **Members:** 3,500. **Staff:** 4. **Description:** Roman Catholic organization that raises funds for the support of missionary activity by Dominican priests and brothers. The Guild is named in honor of St. Martin de Porres (1579-1639), a Peruvian mulatto Dominican brother who was declared a saint of the Catholic church in 1962. **Formerly:** Blessed Martin Guild.

19978 ■ St. Vincent Pallotti Center for Apostolic Development
415 Michigan Ave. NE
Washington, DC 20017
Ph: (202)529-3330
Free: (877)VOL-LINK
Fax: (202)529-0911
E-mail: pallotti@pallotticenter.org
URL: http://www.pallotticenter.org
Contact: Andrew D. Thompson PhD, Dir.
Founded: 1984. **Regional Groups:** 3. **Languages:** English, Italian, Spanish. **Description:** Promotes a culture of service by supporting an active participation of laity in missionary activities. Serves as a referral service for people interested in participating in faith-based missionary and volunteer programs in the U.S. and overseas. Recruits and supports volunteers for faith-based volunteer programs worldwide; nurtures spiritual formation of volunteers; assists volunteers in reentering the job market upon completion of their mission. Named for St. Vincent Pallotti (1795-1850), who believed that laypeople were no less missionary apostles than clergy or religious. Maintains centers in Washington, DC; Boston, MA; St. Louis, MO; and Oakland, CA. **Libraries: Type:** reference. **Also Known As:** Pallotti Center. **Publications:** *Connections*, annual. Directory. Provides profiles with descriptions and contact information of more than 100 faith-based volunteer programs. **Price:** free. **Circulation:** 30,000. Alternate Formats: online ● *Shared Visions*, quarterly. **Price:** free. Alternate Formats: online ● *Staying Connected*, quarterly. **Price:** free. Alternate Formats: online ● *The What's Next? Notebook*, annual. **Price:** free. Alternate Formats: online.

19979 ■ Salesian Missioners (SLM)
2 Lefevre Ln.
PO Box 30
New Rochelle, NY 10802-0030
Ph: (914)633-8344
Free: (888)608-2327
Fax: (914)633-7404
E-mail: info@salesianmissions.org
URL: http://www.salesianmissions.org
Contact: Marie Carr, Dir.
Founded: 1983. **Members:** 300. **Staff:** 2. **Languages:** English, Spanish. **Description:** Aids disadvantaged youth in Alabama, Bolivia, Philippines, Ecuador, China, Thailand, California, Ohio, New York, Mexico, Papua New Guinea, and Sierra Leone. Provides education, care, counseling, medical services, agricultural and construction assistance. Provides youth services. **Computer Services:** database, word processing Macintosh. **Also Known As:** Salesian Volunteers. **Formerly:** (2000) Salesian Lay Missioners. **Publications:** *SLMS: United in Mission*, periodic. Newsletter. Contains volunteer news. **Conventions/Meetings:** annual Introduction to the Salesian Charism and Work - workshop (exhibits) - always May to June.

19980 ■ Samaritans International
370 E Cedar St.
Mooresville, NC 28115
Ph: (704)663-7951 (704)662-1200

E-mail: info@samaritaninternational.org
URL: http://www.samaritansinternational.org/si/pub_home.cfm
Contact: Stephen Ferguson, Pres.
Founded: 1967. **Staff:** 3. **Description:** An evangelical Christian organization that emphasizes the opportunities for "learning, sharing, and growing" through intercultural experiences. Seeks to: spread the Gospel of Jesus Christ; organize mission teams which undertake special projects in other nations; encourage individuals to participate in a mission project while on vacation. Projects include construction of needed buildings, provision of medical services and health care education, and assistance in community development. Not related to group of the same name also listed in the index. **Formerly:** (1986) Vacation Samaritans; (2001) Samaritans. **Conventions/Meetings:** periodic meeting.

19981 ■ Sharing of Ministries Abroad U.S.A. (SOMA)
5290 Saratoga Ln.
Woodbridge, VA 22193
Ph: (703)878-7667
Fax: (703)878-7015
E-mail: office@somausa.org
URL: http://www.somausa.org
Contact: Mrs. Edwina Thomas, Natl. Dir.
Founded: 1985. **Staff:** 3. **Description:** Missionary organization working to encourage Christian renewal in 36 countries worldwide. Seeks to enable the Anglican Church to "proclaim the Kingdom of God and to minister in the power of the Holy Spirit". In conjunction with local church leaders, missionaries conduct conferences on themes such as discipleship, biblical patterns of leadership, spiritual welfare, ministry to the poor, and social justice. Operates speakers' bureau. **Also Known As:** SOMA U.S.A. **Publications:** *Mission and Prayer Update*, periodic ● *Sharing*, quarterly. Newsletter. Describes current mission activities. Alternate Formats: online.

19982 ■ Side by Side Lay Volunteer Program
5625 Isleta Blvd. SW
Albuquerque, NM 87105
Ph: (505)873-2059 (505)452-9402
Fax: (505)877-2571
E-mail: odmifdcc@aol.com
Contact: Sr. Christina Orejera, Contact
Founded: 1990. **Description:** Offers volunteer lay ministry programs for one year, volunteers must be Christians over 18. Maintains programs in economically deprived areas of New Mexico and Mexico. **Publications:** *Encounter*, quarterly. Newsletter.

19983 ■ Slavic Gospel Association (SGA)
6151 Commonwealth Dr.
Loves Park, IL 61111
Ph: (815)282-8900
Free: (800)242-5350
Fax: (815)282-8901
E-mail: info@sga.org
URL: http://www.sga.org
Contact: Dr. Robert W. Provost, Pres.
Founded: 1934. **Staff:** 46. **Languages:** English, Russian. **Description:** Interdenominational Christian mission agency. In conjunction with national church in the CIS, operates Regional Ministry Centers located in Russia, Ukraine, Belarus, and Kazakhstan to provide, on location and by correspondence, comprehensive Christian training. Sponsors national church planters and assists the church with humanitarian aids. **Libraries: Type:** reference. **Absorbed:** (1989) Eurovision. **Publications:** *InSight*, monthly. Newsletter. Alternate Formats: online ● Translates and distributes Christian books, videotapes, in Russian.

19984 ■ SMA Lay Missionaries
c/o Theresa Hicks, Program Dir.
256 Manor Cir.
Takoma Park, MD 20912
Ph: (301)891-2037
Fax: (301)270-6370

E-mail: smausa-l@smafathers.org
URL: http://www.smafathers.org
Contact: Theresa Hicks, Program Dir.
Description: Catholic, college graduates or have qualifications in their area of expertise, serving in Africa or African-American parishes. Provides a four month formation program, and 3-4 months Language School in country of assignment. Aims to live in faith, helping people to develop skills to help themselves and their communities. Works in the following fields: education, nursing, medical field, agriculture, community development projects, social work and pastoral ministries. **Additional Websites:** http://sma.cua.edu. **Also Known As:** Society of African Missions. **Publications:** *Hear and Dare*, 5/year. Newsletters. Updates on ministries and projects of the SMA Lay Missionaries in Africa and in the U.S. **Circulation:** 1,300. **Conventions/Meetings:** Discernment Weekend - meeting - 3-4/year.

19985 ■ South America Mission (SAM)
5217 S Military Trail
Lake Worth, FL 33463-6019
Ph: (561)965-1833
Fax: (561)439-8950
E-mail: samusa2@southamericamission.org
URL: http://www.southamericamission.org
Contact: William K. Ogden, Exec. Dir./CEO
Founded: 1914. **Members:** 197. **Staff:** 13. **Budget:** $661,000. **Description:** Seeks to evangelize the Indians and inhabitants of South America and to establish self-supporting, self-governing, and self-propagating churches. Works in Brazil, Bolivia, Colombia, Paraguay, and Peru. **Affiliated With:** Advancing Churches in Missions Commitment; Evangelical Council for Financial Accountability; Interdenominational Foreign Missions Association; World Evangelical Alliance. **Formerly:** (1970) South American Indian Mission. **Publications:** *Window on South America*, quarterly. Newsletter. Updates members on mission activity. **Price:** free. **Circulation:** 15,000. **Conventions/Meetings:** annual Leadership Conference.

19986 ■ South American Missionary Society (USA) (SAMS-USA)
PO Box 399
Ambridge, PA 15003
Ph: (724)266-0669
Fax: (724)266-5681
E-mail: info@sams-usa.org
URL: http://www.sams-usa.org
Contact: Stewart Wicker, Pres.
Founded: 1976. **Staff:** 6. **Description:** Participants are Anglican missionaries. Works to recruit, send and support missionaries to be witnesses and make disciples for Jesus Christ in fellowship with the Anglican Church primarily in Latin America. Missionaries share the Gospel, establish churches, train national church leaders, and minister socially through medical clinics and Christian schools. **Publications:** *Missionero*, quarterly.

19987 ■ Spanish World Ministries (SWM)
PO Box 542
Winona Lake, IN 46590
Ph: (574)267-8821
Free: (800)242-8591
Fax: (574)267-3524
E-mail: info@spanishworld.org
URL: http://www.spanishworld.org
Contact: Rev. Cornelius Rivera, Exec. Dir.
Founded: 1959. **Members:** 20. **Staff:** 5. **Budget:** $450,000. **Languages:** English, Spanish. **Multinational. Description:** Aims to propagate the Gospel of Jesus Christ throughout the Spanish-speaking countries of the world. Broadcasts radio ministry; disseminates Gospel and biblical books and pamphlets to Spanish-speaking countries; fosters the creation of churches in Central and South America. Utilizes national missionaries in evangelistic services. **Affiliated With:** IFCA International; National Religious Broadcasters. **Formerly:** (1974) Spanish World Gospel Broadcasting; (2003) Spanish World Gospel Mission. **Publications:** *El Camino* (in English and Spanish), quarterly. Newsletter. **Price:** free. **Circula-**

tion: 5,000. **Conventions/Meetings:** biennial conference, information, planning and strategy of ministry by Spanish World's national associates.

19988 ■ Sports Ambassadors (SA)
Dwight D. Eisenhower Bldg.
110 S Ferall St.
Spokane, WA 99202
Ph: (509)534-0431
Fax: (877)669-6439
E-mail: info@sportsambassadors.org
URL: http://www.sportsambassadors.org
Contact: Mary J. Eisenhower, CEO
Founded: 1952. **Description:** International ministry of OC International (see separate entry), an interdenominational evangelistic missionary organization. Seeks, through sports teams, to "equip Christian athletes with fundamentals for successful Christian growth", and to utilize, through international sports, the unique opportunity for evangelization. College athletes, directors, trainers, and coaches are selected to play on the various sports on the basis of their proven sports ability and "personal commitment to Jesus Christ". Teams annually tour several countries abroad and compete against local and national teams and conduct coaching clinics. Takes part in civic receptions and numerous church and school gatherings. **Publications:** *Prayer Letter*, monthly. Newsletter. Reports on the teams' and ministry's activities. **Price:** free. **Circulation:** 2,000 ● Brochures.

19989 ■ STEER
PO Box 1236
Bismarck, ND 58502
Ph: (701)258-4911
Fax: (701)258-7684
E-mail: steerinc@steerinc.com
URL: http://www.steerinc.com
Contact: Mr. Keith Kost, Exec. Dir.
Founded: 1957. **Members:** 85. **Staff:** 6. **Budget:** $1,000,000. **Multinational. Description:** Evangelical, agricultural and fundraising organization. Seeks to initiate a "global mission awareness". **Publications:** *Prayer Partner Letter*, 3/year. **Price:** free. **Circulation:** 900 ● *STEER Directory*, annual ● *STEER Talk*, 3/year. **Price:** free. **Circulation:** 5,700 ● Annual Report, annual. Alternate Formats: online. **Conventions/Meetings:** annual conference (exhibits).

19990 ■ Teen Missions International (TMI)
885 E Hall Rd.
Merritt Island, FL 32953
Ph: (321)453-0350
Fax: (321)452-7988
E-mail: info@teenmissions.org
URL: http://www.teenmissions.org
Contact: Robert M. Bland, Dir.
Founded: 1970. **Staff:** 183. **Regional Groups:** 1. **National Groups:** 22. **Multinational. Description:** Organizes interdenominational evangelical missionary work projects in areas such as agriculture and community development; programs have operated in 60 countries, including Australia, Brazil, Mongolia, India, Indonesia, Mexico, South Africa, and Zimbabwe. Trains teen and adult missionaries through camps and conferences; operates placement service. Promotes the Christian gospel through the production of films, videos, printed materials, and media presentations. Assists in establishing local teen mission clubs in an effort to encourage evangelical outreach. **Departments:** Bible, Missionary & Work Training Center; Computer Services; Finance; Food Service; International Operations; Literature; Maintenance; Overseas Boot Camps; Print Shop; Promotion/Personnel; Publications. **Divisions:** Shipping/Receiving; U.S. Teams; Video. **Formerly:** (1972) Teen Mission. **Publications:** *Teen Missions Launch Pad*, semiannual. Newspaper. Includes current events, alumni news, and announcements of future activities. **Price:** free. **Circulation:** 65,000. **Advertising:** accepted. Alternate Formats: CD-ROM ● Brochures ● Also makes available films and videotapes. **Conventions/Meetings:** annual conference (exhibits) - always fall.

19991 ■ Trans World Radio (TWR)

PO Box 8700
Cary, NC 27512-8700
Ph: (919)460-3700
Free: (800)456-7897
Fax: (919)460-3702
E-mail: webmaster@twr.org
URL: http://www.twr.org
Contact: Dr. Thomas J. Lowell, Chm.
Founded: 1952. **Staff:** 1,000. **Budget:** $28,000,000. **Description:** Christian missionary organization broadcasting religious, educational, and cultural programs in more than 140 languages from 12 strategic primary stations in Albania, Armenia, Cyprus, Guam, Monaco, Netherlands Antilles, Poland, Russia, Swaziland, Sri Lanka, Uruguay, and Republic of South Africa. Staff includes missionaries who are Bible teachers, technicians, engineers, program production specialists, and other workers. Maintains speakers' bureau. **Projects:** Children's Program; Chinese Ministry Expansion; City Lights; Hannah; Leadership Development in Africa; Memcare by Radio; Oasis of Hope; Radio Bible. **Affiliated With:** Evangelical Council for Financial Accountability; Interdenominational Foreign Missions Association; National Religious Broadcasters. **Formerly:** Voice of Tangier. **Publications:** *Towers to Eternity* (in English and Spanish). Book. **Price:** free ● *TWRadio*, 3/year. Magazine. Reports on overseas missionaries, the results of missionary broadcasts, and introductions to new missionary appointees. **Price:** free. ISSN: 1093-0124. Circulation: 43,500. Alternate Formats: online ● *TWReport*, quarterly. **Price:** free. **Circulation:** 220,000.

19992 ■ Transport for Christ, International (TFC)

1525 River Rd.
Marietta, PA 17547-9403
Ph: (717)426-9977
Fax: (717)426-9980
E-mail: tfcio@transportforchrist.org
URL: http://www.transportforchrist.org
Contact: Scott A. Weidner, Pres.
Founded: 1951. **Staff:** 75. **Budget:** $1,800,000. **Description:** Ministers in the United States, Canada, Russia, and Zambia. Seeks to preach the gospel of Jesus Christ to truckers. Stimulates contact through chaplain services, promotes highway safety by "assisting in the development of spiritual and emotional stability in transport drivers"; cultivates a spirit of goodwill and cooperation within the entire transport industry; extends Christian counsel and friendship to truckers in times of accident, bereavement, or personal and family crisis; establishes chaplaincy programs. Maintains chapels at truckstops, and one mobile chapel that are used at truck shows and rallies and to open new locations. **Formerly:** (1976) Transport for Christ; (1978) New Transport for Christ. **Publications:** *Highway News and Good News*, monthly. Magazine. **Price:** $25.00/donation. **Circulation:** 35,000.

19993 ■ United Indian Missions, International (UIMI)

PO Box 336010
800 8th Ave., Ste.201
Greeley, CO 80633-0601
Ph: (970)330-7788
Fax: (970)392-2559
E-mail: uim@uim.org
URL: http://www.uim.org
Contact: Rev. Warren Cheek, Gen. Dir.
Founded: 1956. **Staff:** 162. **Budget:** $3,750,000. **Languages:** English, Navajo, Spanish. **Multinational. Description:** Establishes indigenous churches among native peoples of North America built on the Scriptures and functioning within their cultural orientation. **Computer Services:** Mailing lists. **Telecommunication Services:** electronic mail, business@ium.org. **Funds:** Native Assistance. **Affiliated With:** Association of North American Missions. **Absorbed:** (1985) Navajo Gospel Crusade. **Also Known As:** UIM International. **Publications:** *Beyond What We Asked*. Book. Features UIM missionaries and their experiences. **Price:** $5.00 includes shipping ● *The*

Hand of the Ancient One. Book. **Price:** $5.00 in U.S.; $7.00 in Canada (includes shipping) ● *Missionary Newsletter*, quarterly ● *UIM Magazine*. **Price:** free ● Video (in English and Spanish), 3/year. Alternate Formats: online ● Brochures (in English and Spanish). Alternate Formats: online ● Also publishes brochures and calendar. **Conventions/Meetings:** periodic Missionary Seminar.

19994 ■ United Sisters of Charity (USC)

PO Box 03305
Highland Park, MI 48203
Ph: (313)862-8918
Fax: (313)891-2950
Contact: Gerald Batie, Dir.
Founded: 1973. **Members:** 20. **Description:** Missionaries conducting charitable activities for the needy. Conducts publicity campaigns; distributes donated items. **Conventions/Meetings:** monthly meeting.

19995 ■ United World Mission (UWM)

9401-B Southern Pine Blvd., Ste.3
Charlotte, NC 28273-5554
Ph: (704)357-3355
Free: (800)825-5896
Fax: (704)357-6389
E-mail: info@uwm.org
URL: http://www.uwm.org
Contact: Rev. John Bernard, Pres./CEO
Founded: 1946. **Members:** 214. **Staff:** 17. **Budget:** $5,700,000. **Languages:** English, Spanish. **Description:** Evangelical mission society organized to participate in world evangelism through saturation church planting. Draws support from independent denominational churches and individuals. Over 150 missionaries and national church leaders work in 30 countries facilitating and training national church pastors serving the following ministries: Bible teaching in Bible schools; Christian day Schools, camps, and correspondence and extension courses; evangelism and church planting in urban and rural areas; literature distribution; medical dispensaries; relief aid. **Additional Websites:** http://ex237.org. **Publications:** *United World Mission News*, quarterly. Newsletter. **Conventions/Meetings:** All Mission Conference.

19996 ■ Ursuline Companions in Mission

c/o Diane Fulgenzi, Coor.
210 Glennon Heights Rd.
Crystal City, MO 63019
Ph: (636)937-6206
Fax: (636)937-7627
E-mail: fulgenzi@osucentral.org
URL: http://www.ursulinecompanions.org
Contact: Diane Fulgenzi, Coor.
Founded: 2000. **Staff:** 1. **Budget:** $33,000. **Regional Groups:** 1. **Languages:** English, Spanish. **Description:** Christian volunteer mission operating in the United States. Programs include crisis intervention, counseling, ministries, education, substance abuse, health care, AIDS ministry, soup kitchens, shelters for the homeless, and migrant worker aid; lay volunteers must have no dependents and be at least 21 years of age for full year; 18 years of age for summer. **Computer Services:** database ● mailing lists. **Formerly:** Companions in Mission. **Publications:** *Companions-Bread for the Journey*, semiannual. Newsletter. **Circulation:** 200. Alternate Formats: online. **Conventions/Meetings:** annual retreat, retreat and orientation.

19997 ■ Voice of China and Asia Missionary Society (VOCA)

PO Box 15
Pasadena, CA 91102
Ph: (626)441-0640
Fax: (626)441-8124
URL: http://www.vocamissionarysociety.org
Contact: Cynthia Stewart, VP of Communications
Founded: 1946. **Staff:** 5. **National Groups:** 4. **Description:** Proclaims the gospel of Christ in the Far East and elsewhere through national workers, literature, evangelism. Sponsors medical clinics and hospitals in Asia and supports medical care units in Korea, Taiwan, and the Philippines. Provides aid to

homes for the needy, handicapped, widowed, and elderly. Sponsors youth camps for the training of future Christian leaders and youth evangelism. Has established schools and churches worldwide. **Supersedes:** China Peniel Missionary Society. **Publications:** *Flashlight*, quarterly. Booklet ● *VOCA Newsletter*, monthly. Alternate Formats: online. **Conventions/Meetings:** periodic conference.

19998 ■ Voice of the Martyrs (VOM)

PO Box 443
Bartlesville, OK 74005
Ph: (918)337-8015
Free: (800)747-0085
Fax: (918)338-0189
E-mail: thevoice@vom-usa.org
URL: http://www.persecution.com
Founded: 1967. **Members:** 150,000. **Staff:** 80. **Budget:** $9,000,000. **Languages:** English, German, Russian, Spanish. **Description:** Seeks to help Christians who are persecuted for their faith in Christ in Communist, Islamic and other restricted nations around the world. Delivers Bibles, Christian literature and material help to those who are persecuted. **Subgroups:** Development Department; Living Sacrifice Books. **Formed by Merger of:** (1967) Jesus to the Communist World; (1967) Jesus to the Iron Curtain. **Formerly:** (1993) Christian Missions to the Communist World. **Publications:** *Link NL*, quarterly. Newsletter. **Price:** free ● *Voice of the Martyrs*, monthly. Newsletter. Provides current and past accounts of the underground church and persecuted Christians in Communist countries. **Price:** free. **Circulation:** 98,000 ● Videos. Contains information on the subject of the persecuted church in Communist/Moslem countries. **Conventions/Meetings:** annual conference - always in April or May.

19999 ■ The Way International (TWI)

PO Box 328
New Knoxville, OH 45871-0328
Ph: (419)753-2523
Fax: (419)753-2903
URL: http://www.theway.org
Contact: Rev. Rosalie F. Rivenbark, Pres.
Founded: 1942. **Staff:** 400. **Languages:** English, French, Spanish. **Description:** Serves as a nondenominational biblical research, teaching, and fellowship ministry. Researches the Scriptures to understand their "inherent and inerrant accuracy regarding Jesus Christ". Seeks to make the knowledge of Jesus Christ and the Scriptures available and teach biblical research truths to others and live the principles of the Word. Offers The Way of Abundance and Power education program, classes, and seminars; also offers The Way Corps, a Christian leadership training course. Maintains The Way Family Ranch—Camp Gunnison, the Leadership, Education, Adventure, Direction Outdoor Academy in Gunnison, CO. Conducts Disciples of the Way Outreach Program, an outreach program. Maintains bookstore. **Formerly:** (1955) Chimes Hour Youth Caravan; (1974) The Way. **Publications:** *The Way Magazine*, bimonthly ● Audiotape ● Brochure. **Conventions/Meetings:** periodic meeting.

20000 ■ World for Christ Crusade (WCC)

1005 Union Valley Rd.
West Milford, NJ 07480
Ph: (973)728-3267 (973)728-5048
Fax: (973)728-3351
E-mail: reustelpstra@aol.com
Contact: Rev. William Stelpstra, Pres.
Founded: 1960. **Description:** Individuals in 4 countries interested in missionary work, worldwide evangelism, social work, or ministering to the underprivileged. Offers worship services; conducts evangelistic crusades. Maintains charitable program which includes providing homes for the elderly, missionaries, and Christian workers. Has organized rehabilitation centers. **Convention/Meeting:** none. **Publications:** *Crusader Magazine*, quarterly ● Newsletter, monthly.

20001 ■ World Gospel Mission (WGM)
PO Box 948
Marion, IN 46952-0948
Ph: (765)664-7331
Fax: (765)671-7230
E-mail: wgm@wgm.org
URL: http://www.wgm.org
Contact: Rev. Hubert Harriman, Pres.

Founded: 1910. **Staff:** 340. **Budget:** $19,000,000. **Multinational. Description:** Interdenominational evangelistic organization conducting mission work in Argentina, Bolivia, West Indies, Haiti, Honduras, India, Japan, Kenya, Mexico, Hungary, Papua New Guinea, Taiwan, Uganda, Paraguay, Tanzania, Ukraine, and the United States. Activities include evangelism, church planting, and theological education. Maintains educational institutions, clinics, hospitals, and agricultural, industrial, and rehabilitation programs. **Divisions:** Administration; Business Ministries (Accounting); Communications Ministries (Information Technology); Communications Ministries (Media Center Services); Communications Ministries (Publishing); Field Ministries; Public Ministries (Adult, Home, Junior, Shut-In, Young People); Public Ministries - Church Ministries - Deputation; Public Ministries (Men With Vision); Public Ministries - World Connection Ministries (high school and college); Resources and Systems (Donor Services); Resources and Systems (Stewardship). **Affiliated With:** Christian Holiness Partnership; Evangelical Council for Financial Accountability. **Publications:** *Call to Prayer*, bimonthly. Magazine. Covers missionary work around the world. Includes prayer calendar and directory. **Circulation:** 32,000. **Conventions/Meetings:** annual International Celebration of Missions - convention - usually held in Marion, IN.

20002 ■ World Impact (WI)
2001 S Vermont Ave.
Los Angeles, CA 90007
Ph: (323)735-1137
Fax: (323)735-2576
E-mail: wiinfo@worldimpact.org
URL: http://www.worldimpact.org
Contact: Dr. Keith Phillips, Pres.

Founded: 1971. **Staff:** 200. **Budget:** $9,000,000. **Description:** Seeks to evangelize disciple and plant churches among U.S. urban poor. Provides job training, housing, food, and clothing to the poor. Operates four elementary and middle schools and four Christian camps. Conducts theological training for inner-city residents who otherwise could not afford it. **Publications:** *World Impact - Bulletin*, monthly. Newsletter. Provides mission update. **Price:** free. **Circulation:** 47,000. Alternate Formats: online.

20003 ■ World Opportunities
1875 Century Park E, Ste.700
Century City, CA 90067
Ph: (323)466-7187
Free: (800)464-7187
Fax: (323)463-8552
E-mail: info@helpthechildren.org
Contact: Dr. Gene Dickey PhD, Pres./CEO

Founded: 1961. **Staff:** 50. **Budget:** $37,000,000. **Description:** Charitable organization that organizes and supports religious and charitable ministries throughout the world through distribution of donated goods. Works to help children worldwide. Acquires large volumes of food clothing, medicines, hygiene items and educational literature, and disperses it through over 200 inner-city distribution centers in the U.S. and in 50 countries overseas. Provides medical supplies and equipment to areas in need. Conducts youth outreach programs. Distributes religious and educational literature. Disseminates information about poverty to the public. **Affiliated With:** Evangelical Council for Financial Accountability; National Religious Broadcasters. **Publications:** Annual Report ● Newsletter, periodic. **Conventions/Meetings:** annual meeting and banquet.

20004 ■ World Salt Foundation (WSF)
6810 Lee St.
Hollywood, FL 33024

Ph: (954)964-2799
URL: http://www.angelfire.com/fl3/worldsalt
Contact: Stephen L. Bening, Chm.

Founded: 1978. **Members:** 1,500. **Description:** Aims to reach the world for Jesus Christ through physical and spiritual guidance. Sends missionaries to U.S. locations and foreign countries including Belize, Brazil, Cameroon, Costa Rica, Guatemala, Hong Kong, Ireland, Mexico, Paraguay, and Puerto Rico. WSF derives its name from the biblical quotation, "Ye are the salt of the earth: but if the salt have lost his savor, wherewith shall it be salted," Matt. 5:13. **Publications:** Annual Report. **Conventions/Meetings:** semiannual conference - always Newnan, GA.

20005 ■ World Team (WT)
1431 Stuckert Rd.
Warrington, PA 18976
Ph: (215)491-4900
Free: (800)967-7109
Fax: (215)491-4910
E-mail: wt-usa@worldteam.org
URL: http://www.worldteam.org
Contact: Leonard K. Maliska Jr., CEO

Founded: 1928. **Members:** 177. **Staff:** 10. **Budget:** $3,600,000. **Languages:** English, French, Portuguese, Spanish. **Multinational. Description:** Interdenominational Christian mission with 425 missionaries serving in 23 areas of the world including Caribbean, South America, Europe, Asia and Africa. Uses a team approach to establish clusters of local national churches through presentation of the Gospel. Fosters national leadership of new churches. Provides ongoing mentoring of established churches to assist them in becoming self-sufficient. Conducts seminars on leadership training and teamwork. **Affiliated With:** Evangelical Council for Financial Accountability; Interdenominational Foreign Missions Association. **Formerly:** (1978) West Indies Mission. **Publications:** *Advance*. Newsletter. Alternate Formats: online ● *Praise and Pray With Us*, monthly ● *World Team Intercessors*, monthly ● *Worldteam Profiles*, quarterly.

20006 ■ World Vision (WV)
PO Box 9716
Federal Way, WA 98063-9716
Ph: (253)815-1000
Free: (888)511-6548
Fax: (253)815-3446
E-mail: info@worldvision.org
URL: http://www.worldvision.org
Contact: Richard Stearns, Pres.

Founded: 1950. **Staff:** 650. **Budget:** $649,000,000. **Languages:** English, Spanish. **Description:** Provides emergency relief and development activities that address the root causes of poverty. Provides children and their communities with access to food, clean water, healthcare, education, and other assistance. Advocates for those made vulnerable by the worldwide AIDS pandemic and for children being oppressed or enslaved; supports training for indigenous leaders. **Divisions:** Human Resources; International Programs; Marketing and Communications; Relational Ministries; Strategic Solutions. **Programs:** The Storehouse; Tools for Transformation; Vision Youth. **Publications:** *World Vision Annual Review*. Annual Report ● *World Vision Magazine*, quarterly. Affirms people responding to God's call to care for the poor by providing information, inspiration, and opportunities for action. **Circulation:** 500,000. Alternate Formats: online ● Handbooks.

20007 ■ World-Wide Missions (WWM)
PO Box 2300
Redlands, CA 92373-0761
Ph: (909)793-2009
Fax: (909)793-6880
E-mail: info@world-widemissions.org
URL: http://www.world-widemissions.org
Contact: Fred M. Johnson, Pres.

Founded: 1950. **Members:** 2,500. **Description:** Pastors, matrons, teachers, superintendents, doctors, nurses, and missionaries. Seeks to evangelize people in Africa, Central and South America, India, Nepal, Korea, New Guinea, and the Southwest Pacific. Works with local churches to set up, staff, and oper-

ate educational centers, medical clinics, and schools. **Convention/Meeting:** none. **Affiliated With:** Evangelical Council for Financial Accountability. **Publications:** Newsletter, monthly ● Annual Report, annual. Alternate Formats: online.

20008 ■ World Witness, Foreign Board of the Associate Reformed Presbyterian Church
1 Cleveland St., Ste.220
Greenville, SC 29601
Ph: (864)233-5226
Fax: (864)233-5326
E-mail: fvandalen@worldwitness.org
URL: http://www.worldwitness.org
Contact: Rev. Frank van Dalen, Exec. Dir./CEO

Founded: 1859. **Members:** 64. **Staff:** 450. **Budget:** $3,200,000. **Languages:** English, Farsi, German, Korean, Punjabi, Russian, Spanish, Turkish, Urdu. **Description:** Missionaries, retired missionaries, and missionary candidates. Works to support missionary work overseas. Sponsors programs in evangelism, education, medical and health care, and relief work. Conducts training programs and seminars. **Formerly:** (2003) Associate Reformed Presbyterian Church, World Witness. **Conventions/Meetings:** annual General Synod - meeting.

20009 ■ Xaverian Missionaries of the United States
12 Helene Ct.
Wayne, NJ 07470
Ph: (973)942-2975
Fax: (973)942-5012
E-mail: askforinfo@xaviermissionaries.org
URL: http://www.XavierMissionaries.org
Contact: Fr. Ivan Marchesin, Provincial Superior

Founded: 1895. **Members:** 900. **Description:** United States branch of the Society of St. Francis Xavier for the Foreign Missions. Religious missionary priests and brothers serving communities in 19 countries. Provides educational services, health care, and social leadership and development programs. **Also Known As:** Xaverian Missionary Fathers; Xaverian Missionaries. **Formerly:** (1998) Xaverian Missioners of the United States. **Publications:** *Xaverian Missions Newsletter*, quarterly. **Circulation:** 40,000. Alternate Formats: online. **Conventions/Meetings:** meeting - every 6 years.

20010 ■ Youth With A Mission (YWAM)
PO Box 7206
Ventura, CA 93006
Ph: (805)642-5327
Fax: (805)642-2588
E-mail: johndawsn@cs.com
URL: http://www.ywam.org
Contact: Mr. John Dawson, Intl. Pres.

Founded: 1960. **Members:** 15,755. **Regional Groups:** 10. **Multinational. Description:** Aims "To Know God and Make Him Known." Comprises of staff members ages range from 16 to 90. Operates training programs, evangelize and do mercy ministries. Operates a 5-month Discipleship Training School (DTS) for all staff; participants minister in their home churches or in other Christian service ministries all over the world upon completion of the DTS. **Publications:** *Go Manual*, annual. Includes addresses, training and service opportunities. ● *The International YWAMer* (in English, French, Portuguese, and Spanish), 3/year. Magazines. Provides information for YWAM staff and friends. **Circulation:** 10,000. **Advertising:** accepted. Alternate Formats: online.

Moravian

20011 ■ Moravian Historical Society (MHS)
214 E Center St.
Nazareth, PA 18064
Ph: (610)759-5070
Fax: (610)759-2461

E-mail: info@moravianhistoricalsociety.org
URL: http://www.moravianhistoricalsociety.org
Contact: Susan M. Dreydoppel, Exec. Dir.
Founded: 1857. **Members:** 507. **Membership Dues:** individual, $50 (annual) ● student, $20 (annual) ● library, institution, additional family, $25 (annual). **Staff:** 2. **Budget:** $196,000. **Description:** Maintains a museum pertaining to Moravian Church history and American colonial life including religious paintings, musical instruments, household equipment, textiles, building materials, and Indian and foreign mission artifacts. Offers educational programs; maintains speaker's bureau. **Libraries: Type:** reference. **Holdings:** 5,000; artwork, audiovisuals, books, clippings, monographs, periodicals. **Subjects:** Moravian history. **Publications:** *The Moravian Historian*, quarterly. Newsletter. Contains society and museum news. Includes calendar of events and information on recent acquisitions. **Price:** included in membership dues. **Circulation:** 500 ● *Transactions of the Moravian Historical Society*, biennial. Journal. Contains scholarly papers on Moravian church history. Also includes minutes of annual meeting. **Price:** included in membership dues. **Circulation:** 500. **Conventions/Meetings:** annual meeting, with vesper - every October in Nazareth, PA.

Mosaism

20012 ■ United Israel World Union (UIWU)
PO Box 561476
Charlotte, NC 28256
E-mail: info@unitedisrael.org
URL: http://www.unitedisrael.org
Contact: James D. Tabor, Ed.
Founded: 1944. **Members:** 1,500. **Staff:** 1. **Budget:** $50,000. **Regional Groups:** 2. **Local Groups:** 25. **Multinational. Description:** Founded by David Horowitz (1903-2002), who devoted his life to the goals and purposes of the organization. Seeks to provide academically oriented historical, Biblical, and archaeological evidence relevant to the identity of the "Ten Lost Tribes" of Israel. Any person, who recognizes and accepts the Hebrew Bible as the basis for his or her daily conduct and supports these goals, may become a member. **Libraries: Type:** reference. **Holdings:** 4,000. **Subjects:** religion, scientific, history, philosophy, archeology. **Awards:** Humanitarian-Brotherhood Award. **Frequency:** annual. **Type:** recognition. **Recipient:** for individuals active in human rights. **Publications:** *United Israel Bulletin*, 3/year. Magazine. Contains biblical and historical research related to Israel and the Lost Tribes. **Price:** free. **Circulation:** 2,500. Alternate Formats: online; diskette. **Conventions/Meetings:** annual meeting and board meeting, with speakers and business meeting - always April, in Charlotte, NC.

Music

20013 ■ Association of Anglican Musicians (AAM)
PO Box 7530
Little Rock, AR 72217
Ph: (828)274-2681
E-mail: cr273@aol.com
URL: http://www.anglicanmusicians.org
Contact: Susan Markley, Communications Officer
Founded: 1966. **Members:** 850. **Membership Dues:** individual, $80 (annual). **Staff:** 1. **Regional Groups:** 10. **Description:** Represents church musicians (laypersons or clergy) serving Episcopal and Anglican churches. Seeks to promote excellence in church music. Fosters a relationship of mutual respect and trust between clergy and musicians actively encouraging and supporting composers and other artists to create works for the church. Maintains communication with and supporting the work of the Standing Commission on Liturgy and Church. Encourages equitable compensation and benefits for professional church musicians. Works closely with seminaries toward the establishment and continuation of courses in music and the allied arts as they relate to worship

and theology. Maintains placement service. **Libraries: Type:** reference. **Holdings:** biographical archives. **Computer Services:** Mailing lists. **Publications:** *A Catalogue of Anthems and Motets for the Sundays of Lectionary Years A, B, and C.* **Price:** $40.00 ● *A History of Music in the Episcopal Church.* **Price:** $30.00 ● *Conflict & Closure: Professional Conduct in Adversity.* **Price:** $10.00 for nonmembers; $5.00 for members ● *Handbook for the Selection, Employment, and Ministry of Church Musicians.* **Price:** $10.00 for members; $15.00 for nonmembers ● *Journal of the AAM*, monthly. **Circulation:** 1,100. **Advertising:** accepted ● Directory, annual. **Conventions/Meetings:** annual conference (exhibits).

20014 ■ Choristers Guild (CG)
2834 W Kingsley Rd.
Garland, TX 75041-2498
Ph: (972)271-1521
Fax: (972)840-3113
E-mail: choristers@choristersguild.org
URL: http://www.choristersguild.org
Contact: Jim Rindelaub, Exec. Dir.
Founded: 1949. **Members:** 5,000. **Membership Dues:** regular, in U.S., $65 (annual) ● regular, in Canada, $90 (annual) ● regular, outside U.S. and Canada, $105 (annual). **Staff:** 9. **Budget:** $1,260,000. **Local Groups:** 70. **Description:** Resource organization for children's church and school choir directors. Aims to: make the children's choir an effective force in the development of Christian character; persuade the church of the value of children's choirs; to enhance musical respect for children's choirs; train adequate leaders; to maintain a central office to which directors may turn for assistance and information. Conducts seminars; provides members with teaching aids including audiovisual aids, videotapes, recordings, and posters. **Awards:** Ruth K. Jacobs Memorial Scholarship. **Frequency:** annual. **Type:** scholarship. **Recipient:** for a Choristers Guild member. **Computer Services:** Mailing lists. **Telecommunication Services:** electronic mail, customerservice@mailcg.com. **Publications:** *Catalog of Resources for Children, Youth, and Handbell Choirs*, annual. Contains listings of music and materials for Church music ministry. Alternate Formats: online ● *The Chorister*, bimonthly. Journal. Contains resources for music ministry; tips for effective rehearsals and performances. Includes chapter news and listings of events. **Price:** included in membership dues. **Circulation:** 6,000. **Advertising:** accepted. **Conventions/Meetings:** annual board meeting - always in Dallas, TX ● periodic seminar, intensive weekend seminars ● periodic workshop, for church musicians (exhibits).

20015 ■ Christian Instrumentalists and Directors Association (CIDA)
c/o Andrew Kamper, Treas.
1401 Ferndale SW
Grand Rapids, MI 49504
URL: http://www.despub.com/CIDA.htm
Contact: Dr. Mark Bailey, Pres.
Founded: 1981. **Members:** 500. **Membership Dues:** director, professional, $20 (annual) ● corporate/business, $40 (annual) ● associate, $7 (annual). **Regional Groups:** 6. **Description:** Christian instrumental musicians. Seeks to encourage its members and provide for their needs. Promotes sacred instrumental music in Christian schools and churches and encourages composers, arrangers, and publishers of such music to develop new works. **Awards:** Director of the Year Award. **Frequency:** annual. **Type:** recognition. **Recipient:** for directors. **Computer Services:** database, sacred list. **Committees:** Publicity; Regional Planning; Sacred Instrumental List. **Absorbed:** (1985) Fellowship of Christian Musicians. **Formerly:** (1993) Christian Instrumental Directors Association. **Publications:** *Listing of Sacred Music Publications*, biennial. Includes instrumental published works for band, orchestra, brass and woodwind ensembles, solos, church orchestras, and instrumental anthems. **Price:** included in membership dues ● Membership Directory, periodic. Includes news of activities and spotlight on members. **Price:** included in membership dues. **Circulation:** 500. **Advertising:** accepted

● Newsletter, 5/year. Covers activities of school, church, and professional groups of interest to Christian musicians, as well as information on events and music reviews. **Price:** included in membership dues. **Advertising:** accepted. **Conventions/Meetings:** biennial Conference on Christian Instrumental Music (exhibits) - always fall.

20016 ■ Church Music Association of America (CMAA)
c/o Dr. Kurt Poterack, Ed.
Christendom Coll.
134 Christendom Dr.
Front Royal, VA 22630
Ph: (540)636-2900
Fax: (540)636-1655
E-mail: editor-at-large@musicasacra.com
URL: http://www.musicasacra.com
Contact: Dr. Kurt Poterack, Ed.
Founded: 1964. **Members:** 1,000. **Membership Dues:** $30 (annual) ● student, $15 (annual). **Description:** Represents organists, choirmasters, choirmembers, and others interested in Roman Catholic liturgical music. Seeks to promulgate the philosophy, techniques, and performance of sacred music in accordance with the directives of the Roman Catholic Church. **Computer Services:** Mailing lists. **Formed by Merger of:** (1964) American Society of Saint Caecilia; Society of Saint Gregory of America. **Publications:** *Sacred Music*, quarterly. Journal. **Price:** included in membership dues; $5.00 each, for nonmembers. ISSN: 0036-2255. **Circulation:** 600. **Advertising:** accepted. **Conventions/Meetings:** annual Liturgical Music and the Restoration of the Sacred - convention - held every June.

20017 ■ Church Music Publishers Association (CMPA)
PO Box 158992
Nashville, TN 37215
Ph: (615)791-0273
Fax: (615)790-8847
URL: http://www.cmpamusic.org
Contact: Phil Perkins, Pres.
Founded: 1925. **Members:** 46. **Description:** Firms publishing music for Christian churches and schools. **Formerly:** Church and Sunday School Music Publishers Association. **Conventions/Meetings:** annual conference - always March or April.

20018 ■ Fellowship of American Baptist Musicians (FABM)
1600 Tall Tree Dr.
Trenton, MI 48183-1860
Ph: (317)635-3552
Fax: (317)635-3554
E-mail: president@fabm.com
URL: http://www.fabm.com
Contact: Bruce Snyder, Pres.
Founded: 1964. **Members:** 500. **Membership Dues:** general, $25 (annual) ● sustaining, $50 (annual) ● patron, $100 (annual) ● life, $500. **Description:** Represents church musicians and others interested in church music including instrumentalists, ministers of music, choir directors, organists, pastors, music committee members, handbell directors and players, and singers. Aims to enrich the spiritual life of church musicians by encouraging, stimulating, and assisting churches in a more effective and significant use of music. Conducts national conference on church music. **Libraries: Type:** reference. **Holdings:** 350. **Subjects:** choral anthems. **Awards:** FABM Scholarships. **Type:** scholarship. **Recipient:** for members (adult and youth). **Computer Services:** Mailing lists. **Publications:** *The Newsletter*, quarterly. Contains general organization information. **Price:** included in membership dues. **Circulation:** 500. **Conventions/Meetings:** annual Conference for Church Musicians - conference and workshop, includes adult, youth and children's choirs, repertoire sessions - always 3rd week in July, in Green Lake, WI.

20019 ■ Guild of Temple Musicians (GTM)
13938A Cedar Rd., No. 115
University Heights, OH 44118-3204

E-mail: shirmidbar@cox.net
URL: http://www.guildoftemplemusicians.org
Contact: Harry Higgins, Pres.
Founded: 1974. **Members:** 300. **Membership Dues:** regular, $65 (annual). **Description:** Individuals involved in Jewish temple music including music directors, organists, choir directors, singers, and teachers. Membership is concentrated in the U.S., Canada, and Israel. Goals are to: preserve Jewish musical tradition through education and awareness of old and new available materials; share ideas and performances through concerts, workshops, and papers; keep members abreast of current developments and trends in the field. Conducts course in conjunction with School of Sacred Music, Hebrew Union College/Jewish Institute of Religion, in New York City, leading to certification. Offers placement service. **Affiliated With:** American Conference of Cantors. **Publications:** *American Organist* ● *Bibliography of Jewish Music Series* ● *Organ List of Jewish Music* ● Newsletter, 3/year. Includes guild news, book reviews, calendar of events, listing of educational and employment opportunities, and musical transcriptions. **Price:** included in membership dues. **Circulation:** 350 ● Directory, semiannual. **Conventions/Meetings:** annual meeting.

20020 ■ Hymn Society in the United States and Canada (HSUSC)

Boston Univ. School of Theology
745 Commonwealth Ave.
Boston, MA 02215-1401
Ph: (617)353-6493
Free: (800)THE-HYMN
Fax: (617)353-7322
E-mail: hymnsoc@bu.edu
URL: http://www.thehymnsociety.org
Contact: Carl P. Daw Jr., Exec. Dir.
Founded: 1922. **Members:** 2,500. **Membership Dues:** student, $40 (annual) ● individual, institutional, $65 (annual) ● retired, $55 (annual) ● donor, $125 (annual) ● patron, $250 (annual). **Staff:** 2. **Budget:** $381,000. **Multinational. Description:** Church musicians, pastors, hymn writers, editors, and others interested in hymnody. Sponsors hymn festivals. Arranges new hymn projects. Holds annual competition for new hymns. **Awards:** Austin Lovelace Scholarship Fund. **Frequency:** annual. **Type:** scholarship. **Recipient:** for attendees of the annual conference ● Fellow of the Hymn Society. **Frequency:** annual. **Type:** recognition. **Recipient:** for distinguished contributions to hymnody. **Projects:** Dictionary of North American Hymnology. **Formerly:** (1990) Hymn Society of America. **Publications:** *The Hymn*, quarterly. Journal. **Price:** included in membership dues. ISSN: 0018-8271. **Circulation:** 2,500. **Advertising:** accepted ● *Papers of the Society*, periodic ● *The Stanza*, semiannual. Newsletter. **Price:** included in membership dues. **Conventions/Meetings:** annual conference (exhibits).

20021 ■ National Christian Choir (NCC)

983 Russell Ave., Ste.A
Gaithersburg, MD 20879-6214
Ph: (301)670-6331
Free: (800)599-4710
Fax: (301)330-7299
E-mail: office@nationalchristianchoir.org
URL: http://nationalchristianchoir.org
Contact: C. Harry Causey, Exec. Dir./Founder
Founded: 1984. **Members:** 200. **Staff:** 4. **Budget:** $526,000. **Description:** Interdenominational Christian choir. Seeks to "glorify God through a unique ministry of music which draws people into a new and deeper relationship with Him." Conducts 10 to 12 concerts per year in the Washington D.C. metropolitan area. Has sung in Orlando, Florida, Los Angeles, California, Colorado Springs, Denver, and Raleigh and has made occasional international tours. Makes recordings for distribution. **Libraries:** Type: reference; not open to the public. **Holdings:** audio recordings, papers. **Subjects:** choral and orchestral music. **Committees:** Finance; Personnel. **Councils:** Choir. **Publications:** Newsletter, quarterly.

20022 ■ National Forum of Greek Orthodox Church Musicians (NFGOCM)

c/o Dr. Vicki Pappas, Natl. Chair
3814 Regents Cir.
Bloomington, IN 47401
Ph: (812)855-8248
Fax: (812)855-9630
E-mail: pappas@indiana.edu
URL: http://www.goarch.org/en/archdiocese/affiliates/nfcm.asp
Contact: Dr. Vicki Pappas, Natl. Chair
Founded: 1976. **Members:** 350. **Budget:** $50,000. **Regional Groups:** 8. **Languages:** English, Greek. **Description:** Works as a ministry of the Greek Orthodox Archdiocese of American, whose purpose is to advance and perpetuate the liturgical musical heritage of the Greek Orthodox Church in America. Seeks to develop liturgical music education programs and materials for children, clergy, choir directors, organists, chanters, choirs, and congregations. Compiles statistics, conducts national surveys. Maintains speakers' bureau. **Awards:** Archbishop's Years of Service Award. **Frequency:** annual. **Type:** recognition. **Recipient:** for those with 25 or more years as a director of a Greek Orthodox Church choir ● Patriarch Athenagoras Distinguished Metropolis Service Medal. **Frequency:** annual. **Type:** medal. **Recipient:** for outstanding liturgical music contributions within one's metropolis ● St. Romanos Medallion for Distinguished National Service. **Frequency:** biennial. **Type:** medal. **Recipient:** for outstanding church music contributions that are national in scope. **Computer Services:** database, addresses ● database, survey data ● mailing lists, church directors, organists, clergy, and parishes. **Committees:** Administration; Assistance to Choirs and Clergy; Byzantine Chant; Church Music Institutes; Public Relations; Publications; Youth Initiative. **Publications:** *Developing a Youth Music Program in Your Parish*. Handbook. **Price:** $15.00/copy ● *Guide to Congregational Singing*. Booklet. **Price:** $10.00/copy ● *Guide to Transcription of Neo-Byzantine Chant*. Handbook. **Price:** $25.00/copy ● *Hymns of the Orthodox Church*. Booklet. Includes instructional audiotape. **Price:** $18.00/copy ● *Journey to Pascha: A Holy Friday Retreat Handbook for Parishes*. **Price:** $10.00. **Circulation:** 700 ● *Liturgical Guidebook*, annual. Handbook. **Circulation:** 700 ● *MUSICA*, periodic. Newsletter. **Circulation:** 1,500 ● *Neumes and Notes E-Newsletter*, quarterly. Newsletters. Alternate Formats: online ● *Repertoire for the Greek Orthodox Church Organist*. Handbook. **Price:** $8.00/copy ● *Senior Voices: Working with Older Adult Singers*. Handbook. **Price:** $15.00 ● *Sharing in Song: A Songbook for Greek Orthodox Gatherings*. **Price:** $10.00 ● *The YouthMusic Connection E-newsletter*, bimonthly. Alternate Formats: online ● Also publishes position statements regarding church music and results of annual surveys. **Conventions/Meetings:** annual meeting - always July. 2008 July 25-30, Washington, DC - **Avg. Attendance:** 40.

20023 ■ Presbyterian Association of Musicians (PAM)

100 Witherspoon St.
Louisville, KY 40202-1396
Ph: (502)569-5288 (502)569-5759
Free: (888)728-7228
Fax: (502)569-8465
E-mail: abarthel@ctr.pcusa.org
URL: http://www.pam.pcusa.org
Contact: Dr. Alan Barthel, Exec. Dir.
Founded: 1970. **Members:** 3,000. **Membership Dues:** institutional, $150 (annual) ● student, $50 (annual) ● senior, $50 (annual) ● sustaining, $125 (annual) ● regular, $80 (annual). **Staff:** 3. **Regional Groups:** 4. **Description:** Represents organists, choir directors, singers, churches, clergy, directors of Christian education, and interested persons of all denominations. Aims to develop the use of music and the arts in the life and worship of individual congregations. Offers assistance in the areas of worship, music, and the arts. Conducts continuing education. Acts as a clearinghouse for job referrals; promotes the professional status of church musicians and recommends salaries and benefits to churches;

certifies church musicians. **Awards:** James Sydnor Memorial Scholarship. **Frequency:** annual. **Type:** scholarship. **Recipient:** to a person from a small or racial ethnic minority church ● Karmen VanDyke Scholarship. **Frequency:** annual. **Type:** scholarship. **Recipient:** to a person from a racial ethnic church ● Raymond H. Ocock Scholarship. **Frequency:** annual. **Type:** scholarship. **Recipient:** for children, youth and adults studying church music ● Will Miller Memorial Scholarship. **Frequency:** annual. **Type:** scholarship. **Recipient:** for youths who are active in the church's music program. **Additional Websites:** http://www.pcusa.org/pam. **Committees:** Archives; Certification; PAM Endorsed Resources; Professional Concerns; Publicity; Referral; Regional Network. **Publications:** *Call To Worship*, quarterly. Journal. **Price:** included in membership dues; $30.00 /year for nonmembers. **Circulation:** 5,000. **Advertising:** accepted ● *Call to Worship: Liturgy, Music, Preaching and the Arts*, quarterly. Journal. **Price:** $30.00 for nonmembers. ISSN: 1534-8318. **Advertising:** accepted ● *Guidelines for Committees Seeking to Employ Church Musicians in Presbyterian Churches* ● *Guidelines for the Employment of Musicians in Presbyterian Churches*. Book ● *PAM Newsletter*, quarterly. **Price:** included in membership dues. **Circulation:** 3,000. **Advertising:** accepted. **Conventions/Meetings:** annual conference, always summer; held in four locations.

20024 ■ Unitarian Universalist Musicians' Network (UUMN)

c/o Donna Fisher, Admin.
2208 Henery Tuckers Ct.
Charlotte, NC 28270
Free: (800)969-8866
E-mail: uumn@uumn.org
URL: http://www.uua.org/uumn
Contact: Donna Fisher, Admin.
Founded: 1982. **Members:** 520. **Membership Dues:** regular, $60 (annual) ● contributing, $100 (annual) ● sustaining, $150 (annual) ● student, over 65, $25 (annual). **Budget:** $30,000. **Regional Groups:** 5. **Description:** Unitarian Universalist directors of music, composers, organists, and volunteer musicians. Offers mutual support and information; encourages professional growth of Unitarian Universalist musicians. Commissions choral and vocal music. **Awards:** Type: recognition. **Computer Services:** Mailing lists. **Publications:** *Guidelines for Unitarian Universalist Musicians* ● *Making Music in Our Churches* ● *UUMN Notes*, 3/year. Newsletter. Includes membership activities. **Price:** included in membership dues. **Circulation:** 1,000. **Advertising:** accepted. **Conventions/Meetings:** annual conference (exhibits) ● workshop.

Muslim

20025 ■ Human Assistance and Development International (HADI)

PO Box 4598
Culver City, CA 90231
E-mail: hadi@hadi.org
URL: http://islamicity.com/hadi/default.htm
Multinational. Description: A Muslim organization "which shall abide by Islamic Law as prescribed in the Qu'ran and Sunnah". Serves as a holding organization of various sub-organizations and associations specializing in certain areas. Provides link to other organizations that have similar objectives; compose of sub-organizations that can be non-profit or profit based depending on legal provisions. Provides planning, management, financial, and information support for its sub-organizations involved in economic, social, educational and scientific development. Sponsors various associations to help in establishing a strong support network for the comprehensive upliftment of the disadvantaged people worldwide. **Divisions:** Computer Information and Research Centers. **Working Groups:** Science and Technology.

20026 ■ Iranian Muslim Association of North America (IMAN)

3376 Motor Ave.
Los Angeles, CA 90034

Ph: (310)202-8181
Fax: (310)202-0878
E-mail: info@iman.org
URL: http://www.iman.org
Contact: Dr. Mohammad Sadegh Namazikhah, Pres./CEO
Membership Dues: regular, $5-$100 (monthly). **Multinational. Description:** Provides an educational environment for the Iranian and Muslim family. Encourages an understanding of the Iranian culture. Promotes cooperation and affiliations within the Iranian and Muslim Community. Provides a forum for sustaining and enhancing the cultural and spiritual identity of people of all races and religions. **Libraries: Type:** open to the public. **Holdings:** audio recordings, books, periodicals, video recordings. **Subjects:** history, mysticism, literature, religion, Islam. **Publications:** Magazine, quarterly. Alternate Formats: online.

20027 ■ Islamic Circle of North America (ICNA)
166-26 89th Ave.
Jamaica, NY 11432
Ph: (718)658-1199
Fax: (718)658-1255
E-mail: info@icna.org
URL: http://www.icna.org
Contact: Dr. Mohammad Yunus, Vice Chm.
Founded: 1971. **Description:** Serves as a non-ethnic, non-sectarian, open to all, independent, North America wide, grass root organization. Aims to seek the pleasure of Allah (SWT) through the struggle of Iqamat-ud-Deen (establishment of the Islamic system of life) as spelled out in the Qu'ran and the Sunnah of Prophet Muhammad.

20028 ■ United American Muslim Association (UAMA)
59-11 8th Ave.
Brooklyn, NY 11220
Ph: (718)438-6919
Fax: (718)438-5187
URL: http://www.fatihcami.org
Founded: 1980. **Languages:** Arabic, English, Turkish. **Description:** Works to assist Muslim people living in the U.S., promotes the spirit of being a Muslim. **Conventions/Meetings:** Summer Camp - meeting, for students.

Mysticism

20029 ■ Astara
10700 Jersey Blvd., Ste.450
Rancho Cucamonga, CA 91730
Ph: (909)948-7412
Free: (800)964-4941
Fax: (909)948-2016
E-mail: mail@astara.org
URL: http://www.astara.org
Contact: Rev. Steven C. Doolittle, VP/Managing Dir./Ed.
Founded: 1951. **Members:** 30,000. **Membership Dues:** one-time fee, $25. **Staff:** 15. **Budget:** $1,000,000. **Description:** Spiritual development provider. Works to publish study material. Produces recordings and instructional tapes in the fields of metaphysics and mysticism. Conducts seminars. Provides material to members from all other religious/new age/metaphysical publishers. **Formerly:** Astara Foundation. **Publications:** *Astara's Book of Life.* **Price:** $3.50 each ● *Astara's Library of Mystical Classics.* Book ● *Voice of Astara,* monthly. Newsletter. Alternate Formats: online ● Books ● Monographs ● Numerous books, audio and video tapes. **Conventions/Meetings:** periodic conference and workshop, new age, self-help, metaphysical.

20030 ■ Cross-Cultural Shamanism Network (CCSN)
PO Box 270
Williams, OR 97544
Ph: (541)846-1313
Fax: (541)846-1204

E-mail: drum@shamansdrum.org
URL: http://www.shamansdrum.org
Contact: Timothy White, Dir./Ed.
Founded: 1985. **Staff:** 2. **Budget:** $120,000. **Description:** Works to educate the public on cross-cultural Shamanism and related traditions. (According to the group Shamanism is the anthropological term for spiritual traditions that utilize trance states for the healing and survival of their communities.) Promotes the study of existing Shamanic cultures. **Publications:** *Shaman's Drum,* quarterly. Journal. **Price:** $20.00 in U.S.; $24.00 outside U.S.; $7.00/back issue; $5.00/back issue (4 or more issues). ISSN: 0887-8897. **Circulation:** 12,000. **Advertising:** accepted.

20031 ■ Earthspirit Community (ESC)
PO Box 723
Williamsburg, MA 01096
Ph: (413)238-4240
Fax: (413)238-7785
E-mail: earthspirit@earthspirit.com
URL: http://www.earthspirit.com
Contact: Deirdre Pulgram Arthen, Dir.
Founded: 1978. **Members:** 1,200. **Membership Dues:** associate, $30 (annual) ● associate (family), $45 (annual) ● supporting, $100 (annual). **Description:** People who believe in the sacredness of nature and harmonize with the seasonal cycles of the earth. Objectives are: to celebrate divinity as found in all life; to educate and inform the public about the group's beliefs; to create a support community with similar associations. Maintains speakers' bureau which presents topics such as nature spirituality, European shamanism, and neo-paganism in America; offers counseling training program, concerts, and social events; sponsors workshops and seminars. **Libraries: Type:** reference. **Holdings:** 5,000. **Subjects:** new age movement, natural healing. **Formerly:** (1983) Athanor Fellowship. **Publications:** *The Earthspirit Community Newsletter,* 8/year. Includes news items, calendar of events, letters, and seasonal articles. **Price:** included in membership dues. **Circulation:** 700 ● *Fireheart,* semiannual. Journal. Includes columns, interviews, and articles about spiritual connection. **Price:** $5.95/copy; $9.00/year. **Circulation:** 3,000. **Advertising:** accepted. **Conventions/Meetings:** quarterly conference.

20032 ■ Foundation for Shamanic Studies (FSS)
PO Box 1939
Mill Valley, CA 94942
Ph: (415)380-8282
E-mail: info@shamanism.org
URL: http://www.shamanism.org
Contact: Michael Harner PhD, Founder/Pres./Dir.
Founded: 1985. **Members:** 3,500. **Membership Dues:** regular, $45 (annual) ● contributing, $70 (annual) ● sponsor, $120 (annual) ● council, $500 (annual). **Staff:** 5. **Languages:** English, French, German, Italian, Japanese, Spanish. **Description:** Works to preserve shamanism through research and training. (Shamanism is an ancient technique used for healing, divination and empowerment by tribal cultures.) Sponsors over 200 workshops and training courses annually. Conducts anthropological research; studies the relationship between shamanism and health. **Libraries: Type:** not open to the public. **Holdings:** 1,800. **Subjects:** anthropology, shamanism, ethnology. **Awards:** Living Treasure of Shamanism. **Type:** recognition. **Publications:** *Shamanism,* semiannual. Journal. Includes articles on topics related to Core Shamanism, and member directory. **Price:** included in membership dues. ISSN: 1042-1513. **Circulation:** 3,500. **Conventions/Meetings:** board meeting.

20033 ■ Peyote Way Church of God
30800 W Klondyke Rd.
Willcox, AZ 85643
Ph: (928)828-3444
Fax: (928)828-3417

E-mail: peyoteway@yahoo.com
URL: http://www.peyoteway.org
Contact: Rabbi Matthew S. Kent, Pres.
Founded: 1977. **Members:** 360. **Membership Dues:** associate, $50 (annual). **Staff:** 2. **Budget:** $25,000. **Description:** Religious sect that uses peyote as a holy sacrament. Believes peyote allows "communicants" to achieve an "awareness of the presence of divinity" and that "growing the holy sacrament peyote is an integral part of peyote worship.". **Libraries: Type:** reference. **Holdings:** 2,000. **Subjects:** children, spiritual, historical, science, education. **Awards:** Certificate of Service. **Frequency:** periodic. **Type:** recognition. **Recipient:** for voluntary services provided to the Church and for community service. **Additional Websites:** http://www.manapottery.com. **Also Known As:** (2005) The Peyote Way Church. **Publications:** Also publishes Word of Wisdom: A Diversity of Interpretation by Thomas Murphy and A Brief History of the Peyote Way Church, Membership Information Brochure, The Spirit Walk Brochure, and Plant the Seed. **Conventions/Meetings:** annual meeting - always September 10, Klondyke, AZ.

20034 ■ Society of Pragmatic Mysticism (SPM)
c/o Leonebel Connaway, Dir.
23501 Vermont Rte. 30
Pawlet, VT 05761
Ph: (802)325-3107
Fax: (802)325-3107
E-mail: connaway@gateway.net
URL: http://www.websyte.com/alan/socpm.htm
Contact: Leonebel Connaway, Dir.
Founded: 1954. **Members:** 20,000. **Staff:** 6. **Budget:** $15,000. **National Groups:** 48. **Description:** Religious organization founded by Mildred Mann (author of numerous books on metaphysical research and interpretation), which teaches that God dwells within each individual and that each person can, with conscious effort and direction of thought, achieve union with the presence of God. Has over 30,000 students throughout the world, reaching them primarily through subscription series and correspondence. **Convention/Meeting:** none. **Libraries: Type:** reference. **Holdings:** 5,000. **Subjects:** metaphysics, spirituality, psychology. **Publications:** Books ● Also publishes Bible and lecture Series, and textbooks.

National Spiritualist

20035 ■ Healers League of the National Spiritualist Association of Churches
c/o Rev. E. Ann Otzelberger, Trustee
PO Box 217
Lily Dale, NY 14752
Ph: (716)595-2000
Fax: (716)595-2020
E-mail: aotzelberger@nsac.org
URL: http://www.nsac.org
Contact: Rev. Lelia Cutler, Pres.
Founded: 1945. **Description:** Accredited and certified healers of the National Spiritualist Association of Churches (see separate entry). Aims to render spiritual healing assistance, through prayers of the individual's choosing, to those who are physically ill or disabled. Sponsors educational seminars; offers instruction in development, interpretation, and technique. Sponsors charitable programs; funds groups providing aid to those in need of financial or physical assistance. Makes recommendations regarding standards and guidelines in compliance with the NSAC. Provides placement service. **Publications:** none. **Conventions/Meetings:** annual meeting - always first full week of October.

20036 ■ Licentiate Ministers and Certified Mediums Society (LMCMS)
c/o Rev. Janet Tisdale, NST, Sec.
9106 W Willow Haven Ct.
Sun City, AZ 85351
Ph: (805)965-4474
Fax: (805)965-4474

E-mail: jtizzy@aol.com
Contact: Rev. Janet Tisdale NST, Sec.
Founded: 1893. **Members:** 507. **Membership Dues:** regular, $10 (annual). **Description:** Lay ministers and certified spiritual mediums. Works to carry out the objectives of the National Spiritualist Association of Churches (see separate entry). Donates money to a program for the benefit of elderly members of the NSAC; makes available scholarships. Contributes monthly articles to "The National Spiritualist Summit.". **Awards:** L.M. and Certified Mediums Society Partial Scholarship. **Frequency:** annual. **Type:** scholarship. **Publications:** Newsletter, periodic. **Conventions/Meetings:** annual meeting, held in conjunction with the NSAC.

20037 ■ Morris Pratt Institute Association (MPI)
11811 Watertown Plank Rd.
Milwaukee, WI 53226-3342
Ph: (414)774-2994
Fax: (414)774-2964
E-mail: info@morrispratt.org
URL: http://www.morrispratt.org
Contact: Morris Pratt, Founder
Founded: 1901. **Members:** 35. **Description:** Represents persons that are interested in supporting and promoting work of the National Spiritualist Association of Churches (see separate entry). Acts as an educational school for the promotion of Spiritualism. **Libraries: Type:** open to the public. **Holdings:** books. **Subjects:** spiritualism and related topics. **Conventions/Meetings:** annual meeting - always May, Milwaukee, WI.

20038 ■ The National Spiritual Alliance (TNSA)
PO Box 88
Lake Pleasant, MA 01347
E-mail: davidjames@deltahousepress.com
URL: http://www.thenationalspiritualallianceinc.org
Contact: David James, Contact
Founded: 1913. **Members:** 200. **Membership Dues:** individual, $10 (annual). **Staff:** 11. **Regional Groups:** 4. **State Groups:** 2. **Local Groups:** 1. **Description:** Serves as Christian fellowship of individuals who believe that "intercommunication between the denizens of different worlds is scientifically established"; churches, camp-meeting associations, state alliances, and Sunday school alliances. Prescribes qualifications of ministers, method of examination, and ceremony by which they are set apart; also prescribes qualifications of associated ministers, licentiates, healers, mediums, missionaries, and other official workers; and issues certificates. Promotes studies of spiritualism. **Libraries: Type:** reference. **Publications:** Newsletter, quarterly. **Advertising:** accepted. **Conventions/Meetings:** annual conference - always July ● semiannual meeting.

20039 ■ National Spiritualist Association of Churches (NSAC)
PO Box 217
Lily Dale, NY 14752
Ph: (716)595-2000
Fax: (716)595-2020
E-mail: lcutler@nsac.org
URL: http://www.nsac.org
Contact: Rev. Lelia Cutler NST, Pres.
Founded: 1893. **Members:** 3,607. **Staff:** 7. **State Groups:** 8. **Local Groups:** 136. **Description:** Represents churches, camps, and societies. Works to teach the science, philosophy and religion of modern spiritualism; to protest against every attempt to compel mankind to worship God in any particular or prescribed manner; to advocate and promote spiritual healing; to protect and encourage the efforts of spiritual teachers and mediums who offer evidence or proof of mankind's "continued intercourse and relationship between the living and the so-called dead." Offers training for certification and ordination, through the Morris Pratt Institute and the college of Spiritual Science. BA, AA, Degree programs offered. Correspondence Courses in Ministry and Religious Studies. Maintains library of books published for and against Spiritualism since 1848. **Libraries: Type:**

open to the public. **Holdings:** 5,000; books, periodicals. **Subjects:** spiritualism, research. **Awards:** NSAC/Stow Memorial. **Frequency:** annual. **Type:** scholarship. **Recipient:** for high school students attending school in Summit, NJ. **Departments:** Education; Endowments; Lyceums; Missionaries; Phenomenal Evidence; Public Relations; Publications. **Publications:** National Spiritualist Summit, monthly. Magazine. Includes directory of ministers, churches, and book list, articles and series on spiritualism and related subjects. **Price:** $24.00 single copy, in U.S.; $75.00 bundle, in U.S.; $33.00 single copy, in Canada; $135.00 bundle, in Canada ● NSAC Yearbook ● President's Report, monthly. Contains information from the NSAC President for the camps, churches and camps. Alternate Formats: online ● Spotlight, 10/year. Magazine. Features articles focusing on the Philosophy of Spiritualism to Religion. **Price:** $10.00 single copy; $40.00 bundle (5) ● Newsletter. Contains the latest breaking news on the global movement of Modern Spiritualism. **Price:** free. Alternate Formats: online. **Conventions/Meetings:** annual congress - in October.

20040 ■ National Spiritualist Teachers Club (NSTC)
c/o Rev. E. Ann Otzelberger, NST, Pres.
4332 Woodlynne Ln.
Orlando, FL 32812
E-mail: nstclub@nsac.org
URL: http://www.nsac.org
Contact: Rev. E. Ann Otzelberger NST, Pres.
Founded: 1927. **Members:** 100. **Description:** Represents members of the National Spiritualist Association of Churches (see separate entry) with a National Spiritualist Teacher's degree. Promotes and provides education and teaching of spiritualism within the NSAC auxiliaries. Serves as a forum for exchanging teaching techniques and ideas. Maintains speakers' bureau. **Awards: Type:** scholarship. **Publications:** National Spiritualist Teachers Newsletter, semiannual. **Conventions/Meetings:** annual meeting - always October ● annual symposium and seminar, on the science, philosophy, and religion of spiritualism.

Neo-American

20041 ■ Neo-American Church, The Original Kleptonian (OKNeoAC)
c/o NeoACT, Inc.
PO Box 3473
Austin, TX 78764
Ph: (512)443-8464
Fax: (512)443-8464
E-mail: inquiries@okneoac.com
URL: http://www.okneoac.com
Contact: Kevin Sanford, Contact
Founded: 1965. **Membership Dues:** individual, $39. **Description:** "Ensures that all members subscribe to the following three principles: (1) Psychedelic substances, such as cannabis and LSD, are religious sacraments since their ingestion encourages Enlightenment, which is the realization that life is a dream and the externality of relations an illusion; (2) Use of psychedelic sacraments is a basic human right and all interference therewith is an assault on this right; (3) Ingestion of the greater sacraments such as LSD and mescaline by those who are unprepared is discouraged. Preparedness is defined as familiarity with the lesser sacraments such as cannabis and nitrous oxide and with solipsist-nihilist epistemological reasoning based on such models as David Hume, Sextus Empiricus and Nagarjuna". **Libraries: Type:** reference. **Holdings:** archival material, artwork, audiovisuals, books, monographs, periodicals. **Awards:** Order of the Toad. **Frequency:** periodic. **Type:** recognition. **Recipient:** for valor ● Sainthood. **Type:** recognition. **Recipient:** for saintliness. **Computer Services:** Online services, publications. **Formerly:** (1965) Neo-American Church. **Publications:** The Boo Hoo Bible. Book. **Price:** $35.00 ● Millbrook: A Narrative of the Early Years of American Psychedelianism. Book. Includes doctrine and early history

of the church with colored photographs. **Price:** $39.00. Alternate Formats: online. **Conventions/Meetings:** annual Board of Toads Congregation - board meeting.

Paganism

20042 ■ Alternative Religions Educational Network (AREN)
c/o William Kilborn, VP/Treas.
PO Box 1893
Trenton, FL 32693
Ph: (321)243-2337
E-mail: aren@aren.org
URL: http://www.aren.org
Contact: Steve Foster, Natl. Pres.
Founded: 1970. **Membership Dues:** regular, in U.S., $15 (annual) ● regular, outside U.S., $30 (annual). **Multinational. Description:** Religious freedom organization. Promotes earth centered religious and spiritual traditions, including witchcraft and paganism. **Libraries: Type:** lending. **Holdings:** books, video recordings. **Computer Services:** database ● mailing lists. **Publications:** ACTION. Newsletter. Alternate Formats: online.

20043 ■ Circle of Earth (CoE)
S Cannon Blvd.
Kannapolis, NC 28083
Ph: (704)784-7317
E-mail: coe@circleofearth.org
URL: http://www.circleofearth.org
Contact: Mike Hill, Pres.
Description: United to bring together Earth based and Pagan religions, currently Celtic Traditionalist, Eclectic Wiccan, Wiccan, Witch (ancient & hereditary), Pagan, Shamanism, Asatru, Druidism. **Publications:** Modern Pagan Newsletter.

20044 ■ Covenant of Unitarian Universalist Pagans (CUUPS)
8190 Beechmont Ave.
Ste.A, PMB 335
Cincinnati, OH 45255-6117
Free: (866)646-3348
E-mail: info@cuups.org
URL: http://www.cuups.org
Contact: Maureen Duffy-Boose, Pres.
Founded: 1997. **Membership Dues:** student/financial hardship, $20 (annual) ● basic active, $35 (annual) ● basic active family, $50 (annual). **Description:** Promotes the practice and understanding of Pagan and Earth-centered spirituality within the Unitarian Universalist Association. Enables networking among Pagan-identified Unitarian Universalists. Promotes interfaith dialogue and encourages the development of theological and liturgical materials. **Telecommunication Services:** electronic mail, president@cuups.org. **Affiliated With:** Unitarian Universalist Association of Congregations. **Publications:** CUUPS News. Newsletter. **Price:** included in membership dues; $18.00 for nonmembers. Alternate Formats: online ● Sacred Cosmos: CUUPS Journal of Liberal Religious Paganism. **Price:** $10.00/issue.

20045 ■ Young AREN
Address Unknown since 2006
Description: Promotes teen pagan and Wiccan spiritual traditions; sister organization of Alternative Religions Educational Network.

Patristics

20046 ■ North American Patristics Society (NAPS)
c/o Clayton N. Jefford, Sec.-Treas.
St. Meinrad School of Theology
200 Hill Dr.
St. Meinrad, IN 47577
Ph: (812)357-6631
Free: (800)548-1784
Fax: (812)357-6964

E-mail: cjefford@saintmeinrad.edu
URL: http://moses.creighton.edu/NAPS
Contact: Clayton N. Jefford, Sec.-Treas.
Founded: 1973. **Members:** 600. **Membership Dues:** regular, $50 (annual) ● student, $26 (annual). **Staff:** 3. **Description:** Represents individuals interested in patristics (the religions of GrecoRoman antiquity, including Byzantium, through the 7th century C.E.). Promotes teachings and research. **Awards:** Society's Award for the Best First Published Article. **Frequency:** annual. **Type:** monetary. **Computer Services:** Mailing lists. **Committees:** Board of Directors; Editorial. **Publications:** *A Decade of Patristic Scholarship, 1970-79* ● *Journal of Early Christian Studies*, quarterly. **Price:** included in membership dues ● *North American Patristics Society—Membership Directory*, biennial. **Price:** included in membership dues ● *North American Patristics Society Monograph Series*, periodic. Monographs ● *Patristics*, semiannual. Newsletter. Contains announcements. **Price:** included in membership dues. **Conventions/Meetings:** annual meeting (exhibits) - at Loyola University in Chicago.

Pensions

20047 ■ Church Benefits Association (CBA)
15000 Commerce Pkwy., Ste.C
Mount Laurel, NJ 08054
Ph: (856)439-0500
Fax: (856)439-0525
E-mail: cba@ahint.com
URL: http://www.churchbenefitsassociation.org
Contact: Deanna Bright, Admin. Asst.
Founded: 1915. **Members:** 50. **Membership Dues:** organization (assets of less than $50 million), $750 (annual) ● organization (assets of $50-100 million), $1,200 (annual) ● organization (assets of $100-200 million), $1,500 (annual) ● organization (assets of $200-300 million), $1,850 (annual) ● organization (assets of $300-500 million), $2,500 (annual) ● organization (assets of $500 million-$10 billion), $3,000-$12,000 (annual). **Staff:** 4. **Description:** Represents administrators of approximately 50 denominational pension funds. Presents papers and facilitates the exchange of ideas on administration of funds. Compiles statistics. **Formerly:** (2004) Church Pensions Conference. **Conventions/Meetings:** annual meeting - usually the week after Thanksgiving.

Pentecostal

20048 ■ Crusaders for Christ (CFC)
585 W Orange Ave.
El Centro, CA 92243
Ph: (760)337-9408
Fax: (760)337-1558
E-mail: admin@crusadersforchrist.org
URL: http://www.crusadersforchrist.org
Contact: Greg Bringle, Pres.
Founded: 1947. **Members:** 5,500. **Staff:** 1. **Budget:** $75,000. **Description:** Children who are members of the Pentecostal Free Will Baptist Church. Conducts social activities with educational and religious instruction included. Operates a summer camp program. Sponsors Annual Youth Week with Bible study and banquet; conducts youth retreats and youth workers training seminars. **Libraries: Type:** reference. **Holdings:** articles, audio recordings, video recordings. **Publications:** *Faith and Practice*. Article ● *Messenger*, monthly. Article. Includes book reviews and Church news. **Price:** $6.20/year. **Circulation:** 3,500 ● *Minutes of the PFWB Church*, biennial. Article ● Newsletter, periodic ● Videos. Alternate Formats: online. **Conventions/Meetings:** biennial Church Conference.

20049 ■ Pentecostal Assemblies of the World (PAW)
3939 N Meadows Dr.
Indianapolis, IN 46205
Ph: (317)547-9541
Free: (866)PAW-4659

Fax: (317)543-0513
E-mail: web_team@pawinc.org
URL: http://www.pawinc.org
Contact: Suff. Bishop A. Glenn Brady, Gen. Sec.
Founded: 1906. **Members:** 1,000,000. **Staff:** 15. **Description:** Seeks to unify religious doctrine and establish new churches. **Awards:** Aida Ford Scholar Award. **Frequency:** annual. **Type:** recognition. **Recipient:** for an apostolic author. **Committees:** International Tape Ministry Convention. **Publications:** *Christian Outlook*, bimonthly. Magazine. **Price:** $24.00/year in U.S.; $40.80 for 2 years in U.S.; $28.00/year outside U.S. **Advertising:** accepted ● *The Late Honorable Bishop David L. Ellis - Contend For The Faith*. Audiotape. **Price:** $4.00 plus shipping and handling ● *The Late Honorable Bishop Francis Smith - The Saga of Isaac*. Audiotape. **Price:** $4.00 plus shipping and handling ● *The Late Honorable Bishop Morris E. Golder - Sin*. Audiotape. **Price:** $4.00 plus shipping and handling ● *The Late Honorable Bishop William Burrell - Seeking Out Leadership*. Audiotape. **Price:** $4.00 plus shipping and handling. **Conventions/Meetings:** annual Summer Convention (exhibits).

20050 ■ Pentecostal Charismatic Churches of North America (PCCNA)
c/o Church of God in Christ
1027 W Tennyson Rd.
Hayward, CA 94544
Ph: (510)783-9377
Fax: (510)783-8673
E-mail: pastorjwm@aol.com
URL: http://www.pccna.org
Contact: Dr. Jerry Macklin, Chm.
Founded: 1994. **Multinational. Description:** Pentecostal/Charismatic evangelical institutions, churches, and groups of churches in North America. Seeks to provide a vehicle of expression and coordination of effort in matters common to all member bodies, including missionary and evangelistic efforts throughout the world. **Publications:** none. **Formerly:** (1995) Pentecostal Fellowship of North America. **Conventions/Meetings:** annual meeting.

20051 ■ Society for Pentecostal Studies (SPS)
PO Box 3802
Cleveland, TN 37320-3802
Ph: (423)614-8577
Fax: (423)614-8555
E-mail: droebuck@leeuniversity.edu
URL: http://www.sps-usa.org
Contact: Dr. David G. Roebuck, Exec. Sec.
Founded: 1970. **Members:** 600. **Membership Dues:** full, $50 (annual) ● associate, $50 (annual) ● student, retired, $25 (annual). **Staff:** 7. **Budget:** $35,000. **Description:** An international organization of scholars, researchers, writers, and church leaders who have an interest in the study of the global Pentecostal and charismatic movements. Provides for discussion of papers dealing with the history, theology, and sociology of Pentecostalism and the charismatic movement. **Awards:** Lifetime Achievement Award. **Frequency:** annual. **Type:** recognition. **Recipient:** for active members with contribution to discipline ● Pneuma Book of the Year Award. **Frequency:** annual. **Type:** recognition. **Recipient:** to a book published within last 2 years. **Computer Services:** Mailing lists. **Publications:** *Pneuma*, semiannual. Journal. Contains theological, historical, and sociological articles. **Price:** $70.00 /year for institutions. ISSN: 0272-0965. **Circulation:** 800. **Advertising:** accepted ● *Society for Pentecostal Studies—Newsletter*, semiannual. Reports on theses and books of interest to the Pentecostal and charismatic movements. **Price:** included in membership dues; $10.00 for nonmembers. **Circulation:** 600. **Conventions/Meetings:** annual conference (exhibits) - usually March.

Poverty

20052 ■ Bright Hope International (BHI)
2060 Stonington Ave.
Hoffman Estates, IL 60195

Ph: (847)519-0012
Fax: (847)519-0024
E-mail: info@brighthope.org
URL: http://www.brighthope.org
Contact: Craig Dyer, Pres.
Founded: 1968. **Description:** Aims to help the poor people obtain the physical resources needed to survive and to improve their quality of life and relationship with God.

Presbyterian

20053 ■ Independent Board for Presbyterian Foreign Missions (IBPFM)
1000 Germantown Pike, Ste.B6
Plymouth Meeting, PA 19462-2482
Ph: (610)279-0952 (610)279-0953
Fax: (610)279-0954
E-mail: info@ibpfm.org
URL: http://www.ibpfm.org
Contact: Rev. Keith H. Coleman, Exec. Dir.
Founded: 1933. **Staff:** 7. **Description:** Serves as an independent, evangelistic organization. Seeks to establish biblical missions in countries outside the U.S. Commits to the Westminster Confession of Faith, and is an approved agency of the Bible Presbyterian Church. Sponsors educational and evangelistic work in 10 countries. Establishes Bible and theological schools, churches, and seminaries. **Affiliated With:** International Council of Christian Churches. **Publications:** *Biblical Missions*, 1-2/year. Magazine. **Price:** free to supporters. ISSN: 0006-0909. **Circulation:** 6,000 ● *Compass*, quarterly. Bulletin. **Circulation:** 6,000. Alternate Formats: online ● Newsletters. **Conventions/Meetings:** semiannual board meeting.

20054 ■ Mission to the World (MTW)
1600 N Brown Rd.
Lawrenceville, GA 30043-8141
Ph: (678)823-0004
Fax: (678)823-0027
E-mail: info@mtw.org
URL: http://www.mtw.org
Contact: Ms. Marty Davis, Communications Dir.
Founded: 1973. **Members:** 850. **Staff:** 85. **Budget:** $42,000,000. **Multinational. Description:** Advances reformed and covenantal church-planting movements through word and deed in strategic areas worldwide. Specific ministry departments include long-term missionaries, short-term (2 week-2-3 year), medical, street child, and university ministry. Works in approximately 65 countries worldwide. **Absorbed:** (1982) World Presbyterian Missions. **Publications:** *Bridges of Grace: Children's Mission Project*. Videos ● *Establishing an Effective Mission Program for Your Church*. Manual. Helps its readers get started. **Price:** free; $4.00 each (donation for more than 1 quantities). Alternate Formats: online ● *Network*, 3/year. Magazine. **Circulation:** 125,000 ● *StreetChild*, quadrennial. Bulletin ● *31 Days of Grace; Supper's Ready; Following God; Faith Promise*. Booklets ● Brochures ● Booklets ● Annual Report, annual.

20055 ■ National Ghost Ranch Foundation (NGRF)
Ghost Ranch Educ. and Retreat Center
HC77, Box 11
Abiquiu, NM 87510
Ph: (505)685-4327 (505)685-4333
Free: (877)804-4678
Fax: (505)685-4519
E-mail: info@ghostranch.org
URL: http://www.ghostranch.org
Contact: Rob Craig, Exec. Dir.
Founded: 1972. **Staff:** 4. **Budget:** $200,000. **Description:** Provides financial and promotional support for Ghost Ranch Education and Retreat Center, owned and supervised by the Presbyterian Church (U.S.A.) and operating in Abiquiu, and Santa Fe, NM. Maintains museums of archeology and paleontology. **Formerly:** (1972) Chimney Rock Foundation. **Publications:** Newsletter, quarterly. Contains articles on activities at Ghost Ranch and Plaza Resolana, fund

raising articles, and program reports. **Price:** free for members; $1.50/copy for nonmembers. **Circulation:** 25,000. **Advertising:** accepted. **Conventions/Meetings:** semiannual board meeting.

20056 ■ Presbyterian Evangelistic Fellowship (PEF)
425 State St.
Bristol, VA 24201
Ph: (276)591-5335
Free: (800)225-5733
Fax: (276)591-5349
E-mail: admin@pefministry.org
URL: http://www.pefministry.org
Contact: Rev. Rick J. Light, Exec. Dir.
Founded: 1958. **Members:** 120. **Staff:** 10. **Budget:** $1,200,000. **Description:** Evangelists involved in worldwide biblical evangelism. Holds revival meetings and open air revivals. Trains evangelists through seminars. Members' ministries include: Evangelistic Preaching Crusades; Children's Evangelism Crusades; Inner-City Evangelism; Multiple Evangelistic Home Studies; Sponsors Smoky Mountain Church Camp in Tennessee; Jewish Evangelism; Evangelism to Alcoholics and Addicts; Evangelism to Elderly, Retired, and Handicaps; Evangelism to Ethnic Group; Evangelism to Homosexuals; Conducts clinics on Prison Ministry, Minority Discipleship, and Church Revival and Reformation. **Affiliated With:** National Association of Evangelicals. **Publications:** *Come. . .Follow*, quarterly. Newsletter ● Newsletter, periodic ● Also publishes pamphlets, monographs, brochures, manuals, and tracts on evangelism and discipleship. **Conventions/Meetings:** periodic Evangelistic Bible Conference ● annual Family Evangelism Conference - always July, in Cullowhee, NC.

20057 ■ Presbyterian Lay Committee (PLC)
PO Box 2210
Lenoir, NC 28645-2210
Ph: (828)758-8716
Free: (800)368-0110
Fax: (828)758-0920
E-mail: laymanletters@layman.org
URL: http://www.layman.org
Contact: Parker T. Williamson, Exec. Ed.
Founded: 1965. **Staff:** 8. **Budget:** $1,500,000. **Description:** Encourages Presbyterian laymen to emphasize the church's mission of spiritual leadership and the teachings of the Bible as the authoritative Word of God. **Publications:** *A Cry of Need and of Joy*. Book. **Price:** $16.95 ● *Great Witch Hunt*. Monograph. **Price:** $5.00 plus shipping and handling ● *I Am With You Always*. Book. Mirrors the truth and beauty of the healing love of God. **Price:** $9.95 plus shipping and handling ● *The Presbyterian Layman*, bimonthly. Newsletter. **Price:** free. **Conventions/Meetings:** annual Faith and Life Conference, for adults and youth - always June, Grove City, PA.

20058 ■ Presbyterian Men (PM)
c/o Floyd M. Gilbert, Pres.
4557 Bob Jones Dr.
Virginia Beach, VA 23462-2462
Ph: (757)467-6435
Free: (800)728-7228
Fax: (757)467-6435
E-mail: contact@presbyterianmen.org
URL: http://presbyterianmen.org
Contact: Floyd M. Gilbert, Pres.
Founded: 1984. **Members:** 4,000. **Membership Dues:** chapter charter, $50 (annual). **Budget:** $80,000. **Regional Groups:** 300. **Description:** Laymen's organization of the Presbyterian Church (U.S.A.). **Awards:** John Calvin Award. **Frequency:** annual. **Type:** recognition ● John Knox Award. **Frequency:** annual. **Type:** recognition ● Mission Man of the Year. **Frequency:** annual. **Type:** recognition. **Computer Services:** database ● mailing lists ● on-line services. **Telecommunication Services:** electronic mail, pmen@ctr.pcusa.org. **Formed by Merger of:** National Council of United Presbyterian Men; Men of the Church Council. **Publications:** *Presbyterian Men in Action*, semiannual. Newsletter. **Circulation:** 4,000. Alternate Formats: online. Also Cited As: *PMIA*. **Conventions/Meetings:** annual board meeting ● an-

nual Gathering - meeting ● annual National Council of Presbyterian Men, Inc. - conference.

20059 ■ Presbyterian-Reformed Ministries International (PRMI)
PO Box 429
Black Mountain, NC 28711-0429
Ph: (828)669-7373
Fax: (828)669-4880
E-mail: prmi@prmi.org
URL: http://www.prmi.org
Contact: Rev. Dr. Zeb Bradford Long, Exec. Dir.
Founded: 1966. **Staff:** 10. **Budget:** $950,000. **National Groups:** 3. **Nonmembership. Multinational. Description:** Aims to ignite the Church in the power of the Holy Spirit through prayer, leadership development, congregational renewal, and mission outreach. Seeks to call the church to prayer and teach the work of prayer, equip clergy and laity for Holy Spirit-empowered ministry, assist congregations in their renewal process and promote the Holy Spirit for the advancement of the Kingdom of God. **Formerly:** (2001) Presbyterian and Reformed Renewal Ministries International. **Publications:** *Moving With the Spirit*, periodic. Newsletter. Contains up-to-date information about PRMI's recent ministry initiatives, upcoming events, teachings and testimonies. **Price:** free. **Circulation:** 14,000. **Conventions/Meetings:** annual Dunamis Fellowship - meeting.

20060 ■ Presbyterian Women (PW)
c/o Ann Ferguson, Coor.
100 Witherspoon St.
Louisville, KY 40202
Free: (888)728-7228
Fax: (502)569-8600
E-mail: ann_ferguson@ctr.pcusa.org
URL: http://www.pcusa.org/pw/index.htm
Contact: Ann Ferguson, Coor.
Founded: 1988. **Members:** 350,000. **Staff:** 18. **Budget:** $5,000,000. **Regional Groups:** 187. **Local Groups:** 10,000. **Languages:** Arabic, English, Korean, Spanish. **Description:** Promotes the Presbyterian church and its teachings. Provides forum for Presbyterian women. Administers to the needs of individuals through missions worldwide; defends the rights of those who are economically and politically powerless; makes political and social commitments to issues involving justice, peace, freedom, and world hunger; examines topics such as apartheid, child abandonment, rape, divorce, and displaced women. Participates in Presbyterian educational ministry and the training of church leaders. Offers economic justice consultations; organizes overseas study seminars and leadership and training events; conducts local, regional, and national workshops. Maintains Speaker's Bureau, biographical archives, and library; offers charitable program; compiles statistics. **Awards:** Women of Faith Award. **Frequency:** annual. **Type:** recognition. **Computer Services:** Mailing lists, selected constituency. **Projects:** Coffee; Energy Stewardship for Congregations; Oikocredit USA; Sweat-Free T. **Affiliated With:** Church Women United. **Formed by Merger of:** (1988) Women of the Church; (1988) United Presbyterian Women. **Publications:** *Etchings of Diversity*. Book ● *Horizons*, bimonthly. Magazine. Includes book reviews, Washington Watch, and information on regional groups and leaders. **Price:** $18.00/year. ISSN: 0010-5163. Alternate Formats: online ● *Justice & Peace Links*, 3/year. Newsletter. **Conventions/Meetings:** triennial meeting and workshop, with plenary sessions, and business meeting (exhibits).

20061 ■ Presbyterians for Renewal
8134 New LaGrange Rd., Ste.227
Louisville, KY 40222-4673
Ph: (502)425-4630
Fax: (502)423-8329
E-mail: pfroffice@pfrenewal.org
URL: http://www.pfrenewal.org
Contact: Paul Detterman, Exec. Dir.
Founded: 1989. **Budget:** $1,500,000. **Regional Groups:** 5. **Description:** Supporters are individuals, congregations, and foundations. Trains church officers. Conducts renewal weekends, officer retreats,

and marriage enrichment programs. Provides placement service; bestows awards; compiles statistics. Operates charitable program and speakers' bureau. **Committees:** Communications; Issues; Pastoral; Renewal; Women; World Missions; Youth. **Programs:** Evangelism Celebration; Fun in the Son (youth); The Great Escape (junior high); Lay Renewal; Son Servants (youth overseas). **Formed by Merger of:** Presbyterians for Biblical Concerns; Covenant Fellowship of Presbyterians. **Publications:** *ReForm*, annual. Journal. **Price:** $5.00 each ● *ReNews*. Newsletter. Alternate Formats: online. **Conventions/Meetings:** semiannual board meeting ● periodic Family Life Conference - meeting ● Leadership Conference ● semiannual Wee Kirk Conference - meeting - always in North Carolina and Oklahoma ● Youth Workers Conference.

Prisoners

20062 ■ Bible Believers Fellowship
PO Box 0065
Baldwin, NY 11510-0065
Ph: (516)739-7746
Fax: (516)739-7748
E-mail: bbfi@prisonministry.org
URL: http://www.prisonministry.org
Contact: Eric Kaestner, Pres./CEO
Founded: 1988. **Description:** Works as a Christian prison ministry, solely evangelical. Provides chaplains with free English and Spanish Christian literature and videos. Also provides free counseling/encouragement. **Computer Services:** Information services, newsletter articles (English/Spanish), testimonies, testimonials, financial accountability, facilities served listing. **Publications:** *Bible Booklets* (in English and Spanish) ● *The Good News Letter*. Newsletter.

Pro-Life

20063 ■ Orthodox Christians for Life (OCLife)
PO Box 805
Melville, NY 11747
Ph: (631)271-4408 (516)271-4408
E-mail: oclifehq@aol.com
URL: http://www.oclife.org
Contact: John Protopapas, Natl. Dir./Co-Founder
Founded: 1986. **Members:** 800. **Membership Dues:** individual, $10 (annual). **Description:** Members of the Eastern Orthodox church. Works to protect the life of all unborn children. Participates in pro-life events. **Publications:** *Rachel's Children*. Newsletter.

20064 ■ Pro Vita Advisors
PO Box 292813
Dayton, OH 45429
Ph: (937)226-1300
Free: (888)438-0800
E-mail: info@provitaadvisors.com
URL: http://www.provitaadvisors.com
Contact: Patricia Pitkus Bainbridge, Co-Founder
Description: People interested in the protection of human life. Dedicated to "exposing and confronting the business aspects of abortion. Offers services that give investors the most up-to-date knowledge of companies involved in the abortion and related industries". **Publications:** *Advisor*, quarterly.

20065 ■ Sisters of Life
St. Frances de Chantal Convent
198 Hollywood Ave.
Bronx, NY 10465
Ph: (718)863-2264
Fax: (718)792-9645
URL: http://www.sistersoflife.org
Contact: John J. O'Connor, Founder
Founded: 1991. **Members:** 43. **Languages:** Chinese, English, French, German, Italian, Spanish, Tagalog. **Description:** Serves as a "contemplative/active religious community dedicated to working towards protecting and advancing a sense of the sacredness of all human life." Participates in pro-life events; offers assistance to women facing unex-

pected pregnancies. **Libraries: Type:** open to the public; reference. **Subjects:** life issues.

Protestant

20066 ■ Bruderhof Communities

Woodcrest Bruderhof
2032 Rte. 213
Rifton, NY 12471
Ph: (845)658-8351
Fax: (845)658-3144
E-mail: rjohnson@bruderhof.com
Contact: Richard Johnson, Contact
Founded: 1920. **Members:** 2,600. **State Groups:** 6. **Description:** A Christian community of men, women, and children living in ten communal settings in the eastern US, England, and Australia, begun by Eberhard & Emmy Arnold in Germany in 1920. Their basis is Christ's Sermon on the Mount, which "calls men and women away from the systems of injustice, violence, fear, and isolation to a new way of peace, love, and brotherhood". **Libraries: Type:** reference. **Formerly:** (1974) Society of Brothers; (1984) Hutterian Society of Brothers; (1999) Hutterian Brethern. **Publications:** *A Plea for Purity*. Book ● *Discipleship*. Book ● *Endangered, Your Child in a Hostile World*. Book ● *God's Revolution*. Book ● *Outcast But Not Forsaken*. Book ● *Six Months to Live*. Book ● *Torches Rekindled*. Book ● Also publishes Seventy times Seven; A Little Child Shall Lead Them; and I Tell You a Mystery. **Conventions/Meetings:** periodic conference.

20067 ■ Federation of Protestant Welfare Agencies (FPWA)

281 Park Ave. S
New York, NY 10010
Ph: (212)777-4800
E-mail: fgoldman@fpwa.org
URL: http://www.fpwa.org
Contact: Fatima Goldman, Exec. Dir./CEO
Founded: 1922. **Members:** 300. **Membership Dues:** agency (with under 1 million budget), $250 (annual) ● agency (with 1 million to 2.49 million budget), $400 (annual) ● agency (with 2.5 million to 4.9 million budget), $600 (annual) ● agency (with over 5 million budget), $900 (annual). **Staff:** 40. **Budget:** $4,000,000. **Description:** Serves as an umbrella organization of approximately 260 affiliated voluntary human service agencies serving over 1.5 million people in the New York metropolitan area. Provides consultative services, educational programs, referral services, and recruitment and screening of volunteers for member agencies and self-help community groups. Assists churches and agencies in securing funds, volunteers, and equipment to improve their emergency feeding programs. Operates Training Institute for social service workers, managers, and board members. Maintains group purchasing service. Funds camping program for disadvantaged children; awards internships for graduate social work studies. Offers Camp Scholarship Program. **Libraries: Type:** not open to the public. **Awards: Frequency:** annual. **Type:** grant. **Recipient:** for member agencies. **Departments:** Development; Policy, Advocacy and Research; Public Affairs. **Programs:** Accreditation; Emergency Cash; HIV/AIDS; Management Assistance; Toy and Gift Drive. **Formerly:** Federation of Institutes Caring for Protestant Children. **Publications:** *FPWA News*, quarterly. Newsletter. Contains federation news. Alternate Formats: online ● Annual Report. **Price:** free by request. Alternate Formats: online ● Also publishes special reports and tracts. **Conventions/Meetings:** annual convention and luncheon (exhibits) - always New York City ● workshop.

Public Relations

20068 ■ Religion Communicators Council (RCC)

475 Riverside Dr., Rm. 1355
New York, NY 10115
Ph: (212)870-2985 (212)870-2402

Fax: (212)870-2171
E-mail: sstruchen@rcn.com
URL: http://www.religioncommunicators.org
Contact: Shirley Whipple Struchen, Exec. Dir.
Founded: 1929. **Members:** 600. **Membership Dues:** professional, $100 (annual) ● associate, $85 (annual) ● student, $25 (annual). **Staff:** 2. **Budget:** $140,000. **Local Groups:** 13. **Description:** Represents persons conducting professional public relations activities, including primary duties in news writing, public information, audiovisuals, radio, television, promotion, marketing, and public relations administration, for any religious communion, organization, or related agency. Aims to provide a network of support for religion communicators; encourage excellence in the communication of religious issues, values, and themes in the public media; provide communications resources for member constituencies; and encourage interfaith dialogue and understanding. **Awards:** DeRose-Hinkhouse Awards. **Frequency:** annual. **Type:** recognition. **Recipient:** for work of members ● Wilbur Award. **Frequency:** annual. **Type:** recognition. **Recipient:** for secular media excellence. **Committees:** Conventions; DeRose-Hinkhouse Awards; Finance/Grants; History; Membership and Chapter; Public Relations; Wilbur Awards. **Formerly:** (1967) National Religious Publicity Council; (2003) Religious Public Relations Council. **Publications:** *How Shall They Hear?*. Handbook. **Price:** $15.00 plus $5 for shipping. **Circulation:** 10,000. Also Cited As: *RPRC Public Relations Handbook* ● *RCC Counselor e-Newsletter*, quarterly. Reports on religious public relations training; also includes council and chapter news. **Price:** free with membership ● *Speaking Faith: The Essential Handbook for Religion Communicators*. Covers issues ranging from establishing a strategic communications plan to crisis communication. ● Directory, annual. Includes information on the council. **Price:** included in membership dues. **Circulation:** 600. Alternate Formats: online. **Conventions/Meetings:** annual convention - usually April.

Pyramidology

20069 ■ Life Understanding Foundation

PO Box 30305
Santa Barbara, CA 93130
Ph: (805)649-5735 (805)649-5721
Fax: (805)649-5735
E-mail: davinajc@aol.com
URL: http://www.dowsing.com/Dowsing/about_luf.htm
Contact: William T. Cox, Pres.
Founded: 1968. **Members:** 8,700. **Languages:** Spanish. **Description:** Dedicated to Humanity's unending search for knowledge, wisdom and understanding. Religious organization based on pyramidology, the study of pyramids, the pyramid form; its mathematics and energy. Believes that the pyramid and its properties can "provide a link to rediscover the ancient sacred sciences." Believes that man did not evolve from the ape, but that his early forefathers were "highly evolved people." Conducts correspondence course; provides spiritual counseling and youth guidance; functions as a pyramid research information clearinghouse. Encourages scriptural study; sponsors lectures, seminars, and workshops. **Convention/Meeting:** none. **Libraries: Type:** reference. **Holdings:** periodicals. **Subjects:** pyramid mysteries, dowsing, self betterment. **Committees:** Research. **Formerly:** (1967) El Cariso Publications. **Publications:** *Ancient Egyptian Technologies*. Monographs ● *Discover Dowsing*. Videos ● *Per Your Records*. Audiotapes ● *Pyramid Guide*, bimonthly. Newsletter ● Books.

Reform

20070 ■ National Reform Association (NRA)

PO Box 8741-WP
Pittsburgh, PA 15221

E-mail: weinwechter@dejazzd.com
URL: http://www.natreformassn.org
Contact: Bill Einwechter, Ed.
Founded: 1864. **Members:** 1,000. **Staff:** 2. **Regional Groups:** 3. **Description:** Interdenominational organization founded for the purpose of maintaining and promoting in American life the Christian principles of civil government. Seeks to combat atheistic ideology. Promotes and encourages election to public office of men and women who will uphold Christian principles in civil government, recognition of the "Lord's Day" as a day of worship and rest, upholding of ideals and standards of the Christian family and the pursuit of national and international peace. Teaches respect for human life. Offers microfilm at Andover-Harvard Theological Library, Cambridge, MA, and University Microfilms International, Ann Arbor, MI. **Publications:** *Christian Statesman*, bimonthly. Journal. Includes book reviews. **Price:** $15.00/year; $12.50/year (renewal). **Circulation:** 1,000. **Advertising:** accepted. Alternate Formats: microform. **Conventions/Meetings:** annual banquet and meeting.

Relief

20071 ■ Association of Evangelical Relief and Development Organizations (AERDO)

3496 Greenwood Dr.
Sierra Vista, AZ 85635
Ph: (520)459-1864
E-mail: dehaanjo@msn.com
URL: http://www.aerdo.net
Contact: John DeHaan, Exec. Dir.
Founded: 1978. **Membership Dues:** associate, $100 (annual) ● agency (based on annual cash income), $300-$500 (annual). **National Groups:** 43. **Description:** Christian agencies and individuals. Provides networking, collaboration and information exchange to support the Church in serving the poor and needy. **Publications:** *AERDO Stars*, monthly. Newsletter. Alternate Formats: online ● *AERDO Update*. Newsletter.

20072 ■ Global MissionAir (GMA)

214 Bel Air Dr.
Yakima, WA 98908-3340
Ph: (509)966-7398
Fax: (509)966-2519
E-mail: website3@globalmissionair.org
URL: http://www.globalmissionair.org
Contact: Duane Anderson, Pres.
Multinational. Description: Aims to propagate faith and carry on humanitarian work, with travel or transportation by aircraft. Transports supplies such as, water, food clothing, medical teams, hospitals and mission teams for distribution to needy people worldwide. Provides service for Christian organizations and groups that reach out to all people and cultures by delivering physical and spiritual help.

20073 ■ World Vision

800 W Chestnut Ave.
Monrovia, CA 91016-3198
Ph: (626)303-8811
Fax: (626)301-7786
E-mail: newsvision@wvi.org
URL: http://www.wvi.org
Founded: 1950. **Multinational. Description:** Provides emergency relief, education, healthcare, economic development and promotion of justice; committed to the well being of all people, especially children.

Religion

20074 ■ Acton Institute for the Study of Religion and Liberty

161 Ottawa NW, Ste.301
Grand Rapids, MI 49503
Ph: (616)454-3080
Fax: (616)454-9454

E-mail: info@acton.org
URL: http://www.acton.org
Contact: Rev. Robert A. Sirico, Pres.
Founded: 1990. **Languages:** English, French, Italian, Polish, Portuguese, Russian, Spanish, Ukrainian. **Multinational. Description:** Promotes a free and virtuous society characterized by individual liberty and sustained by religious principles. **Awards:** Acton Essay Competition. **Frequency:** annual. **Type:** recognition. **Recipient:** to young religious intellectuals ● Calihan Fellowships. **Frequency:** annual. **Type:** fellowship. **Recipient:** to seminarians and graduate students in theology and philosophy ● Homiletics Award. **Frequency:** annual. **Type:** recognition. **Recipient:** to Masters of Divinity and Theology students who prepare sermons targeted toward business people ● Novak Award. **Frequency:** annual. **Type:** monetary. **Recipient:** for new research on the interrelation of religion and economic liberty. **Telecommunication Services:** electronic mail, rsirico@acton.org. **Programs:** Community Outreach; Student Awards and Scholarships; Toward a Free and Virtuous Society. **Publications:** *Acton News and Commentary*, weekly. Newsletter. Alternate Formats: online ● *Acton Notes*, monthly. Newsletter. Features the president's message, news and upcoming events. Alternate Formats: online ● *Christian Social Though Series*. Monographs ● *Environmental Stewardship*, semiannual. Newsletter. Alternate Formats: online ● *Journal of Markets & Morality*, semiannual. **Price:** $25.00 /year for individuals in U.S.; $35.00 /year for individuals outside U.S.; $60.00 /year for institutions in U.S.; $70.00 /year for institutions outside U.S. ● *Liberating Labor: A Christian Economist's Case for Voluntary Unionism*. Monograph ● *Religion & Liberty*, quarterly. Journal. Contains interviews with renowned religious and economic leaders. Alternate Formats: online ● Papers ● Audiotapes. **Conventions/Meetings:** seminar.

20075 ■ Biblical Institute for Social Change (BISC)
c/o Rev. Dr. Cain Hope Felder, Founder/Chm./CEO
Howard Univ. School of Divinity
1400 Shepherd St. NE, Ste.264 and 266
Washington, DC 20017
Ph: (202)269-4311
Fax: (202)269-0051
URL: http://www.biscfelder.org
Contact: Rev. Dr. Cain Hope Felder, Founder/Chm./CEO
Founded: 1990. **Members:** 300. **Membership Dues:** regular, $35 (annual) ● life, $1,000. **Staff:** 4. **Budget:** $135,000. **Description:** Works to increase public understanding of the critical role played by individuals of African descent in biblical history in order to promote self-esteem and social change. Distributes educational materials to African American churches. Encourages scholarship on biblical traditions and their historical relevance to African and African American churches. Maintains speakers' bureau. Distributes the original African Heritage Study Bible. **Publications:** *BISC Quarterly*. Newsletter. Price: free for members; $2.00 for nonmembers. **Advertising:** accepted. **Conventions/Meetings:** annual Convocation - meeting (exhibits) ● seminar and conference ● seminar - 3/year.

20076 ■ Center on Religion and Society (CRS)
c/o Reformed Theological Seminary
2101 Carmel Rd.
Charlotte, NC 28226-6399
Ph: (704)366-5066
Free: (888)621-1521
Fax: (704)366-9295
E-mail: rts.charlotte@rts.edu
URL: http://www.rts.edu
Contact: Mr. Frank Reich, Pres.
Founded: 1984. **Members:** 24. **Membership Dues:** subscription, $24 (annual). **Staff:** 4. **Budget:** $111,000. **Regional Groups:** 1. **Languages:** English, French, German. **Description:** A division of the Howard Center, an interreligious research and educational organization focusing on issues of culture and social change in the contemporary world. Seeks

to address the role of religion in society. Works to present a scholarly interpretation of religion in cultural change. Maintains speakers' bureau. **Libraries: Type:** open to the public. **Holdings:** 200,000. **Publications:** *The Religion and Society Report*, monthly. Newsletter. Includes articles on churches and theology, bioethics, war and peace, and international affairs. **Price:** $24.00/year. ISSN: 0742-6984. **Circulation:** 3,000. **Conventions/Meetings:** periodic The Hippocratic Tradition Today - conference.

20077 ■ Do Right Foundation
991-C Lomas Santa Fe Dr., No. 413
Solana Beach, CA 92075
E-mail: dorightfdn@aol.com
URL: http://www.doright.org
Nonmembership. Description: Strives to help mankind create a more joyful society by promoting learning, innovation, respect for God and His creations, family unity, limited government, private property, free enterprise, and rule of law.

20078 ■ ECKANKAR
PO Box 2000
Chanhassen, MN 55317-2000
Ph: (952)380-2222
Fax: (952)380-2196
URL: http://www.eckankar.org
Contact: Sri Harold Klemp, Spiritual Leader
Founded: 1965. **Membership Dues:** individual, $130 (annual) ● family, $160 (annual). **Languages:** English, French, German, Spanish. **Multinational. Description:** Promotes the religion of Eckankar, or the "Light and Sound of God", teaches how to recognize the Light of God, allows members to decide on social issues for themselves. Have members in more than 100 countries. The religion's spiritual home is the Temple of ECK, in Chanhassen, Minnesota. **Publications:** *A Modern Prophet Answers Your Key Questions about Life*. Book. **Price:** $14.00 ● *Dreams: Your Window to Heaven*. Book. **Price:** $12.00 ● *Exploring Past Lives to Heal the Present*. Book. **Price:** $12.00 ● *How to Find God*. Book. **Price:** $8.95 ● *The Language of Soul*. Book. **Price:** $14.00 ● *The Living Word, Book 1*. **Price:** $14.00 ● *The Living Word, Book 2*. **Price:** $14.00 ● *Love-The Keystone of Life*. Book. **Price:** $14.00 ● *Mystic World*, quarterly. Newsletter. Includes feature articles and Wisdom Notes from Living ECK Master. **Price:** included in membership dues ● *The Spiritual Exercises of ECK*. Book. **Price:** $14.00 ● *Your Road Map to the ECK Teachings: ECKANKAR Study Guide, Volumes 1 and 2*. Book. **Price:** $30.00 ● *Youth Ask a Modern Prophet about Life, Love, and God*. Book. **Price:** $14.00. **Conventions/Meetings:** annual Spiritual Skills Seminar ● annual Worldwide Seminar.

20079 ■ Equal Partners in Faith (EPF)
c/o Washington Office of the UUA
2026 P St. NW
Washington, DC 20036
Ph: (202)296-4673
E-mail: epfinfo@aol.com
URL: http://www.geocities.com/CapitolHill/4497/EqualPartners.html
Contact: Laura Montgomery Rutt, Natl. Organizer
Founded: 1997. **Description:** Religious leaders and people of faith. Provides network support. Promotes equality and diversity.

20080 ■ Federation of Jain Associations in North America (JAINA)
PO Box 700
Getzville, NY 14068
Ph: (716)636-5342
Fax: (716)636-5342
E-mail: jainahq@jaina.org
URL: http://www.jaina.org
Contact: Mr. Kirit C. Daftary, Pres.
Founded: 1981. **Multinational. Description:** Promotes religious and educational activities related to the Jain religion. Develops better understanding of the Jain religion. Assists and promotes humanitarian activities in North America and worldwide. Promotes vegetarianism and nonviolence. Provides and advances academic and cultural exchanges among

Jains. **Libraries: Type:** reference. **Holdings:** 8,000; books. **Awards:** JAINA Adult Recognition Award. **Frequency:** biennial. **Type:** recognition. **Recipient:** for members who have demonstrated large contributions of time and/or personal financial resources for JAINA ● JAINA Ratna Award. **Frequency:** biennial. **Type:** recognition. **Recipient:** for individuals who have contributed significantly in line with the principles of Jainism ● JAINA Youth Recognition Award. **Frequency:** biennial. **Type:** recognition. **Recipient:** for youth members who have outstanding contributions to YJA, YJP or JAINA. **Telecommunication Services:** electronic mail, netrat@att.net. **Publications:** *Jain Digest*, quarterly. Magazine. Contains news and activities of member organizations, community affairs and articles by scholars of Jainism and humanitarian activities. **Circulation:** 10,000 ● *JAINA Spectrum: The Jain Voice of North America*, monthly. Newsletter. Alternate Formats: online.

20081 ■ Focus on the Chinese Family
750 Terrado Plz., No. 123
Covina, CA 91723
Ph: (626)974-5881
Free: (800)232-6459
Fax: (626)974-5396
E-mail: info@focf.org
Contact: Deanna Go, Asst. to the Pres.
Founded: 1995. **Languages:** Chinese, English. **Description:** Promotes biblical family values; provides services, training and resources to Chinese families worldwide; offers caring and referral services. **Publications:** *Ai Jia*, monthly. Magazine. Features issues on marriage, parent-child relationships and spiritual growth. ● Booklets (in Chinese and English). Offers topics on healthy marital relationships, positive parenting skills, and spiritual development. **Conventions/Meetings:** annual retreat, family camps, sports camps, pre-marital classes for engaged couples ● periodic workshop - seasonal.

20082 ■ Independent Catholic Churches International (ICCI)
1035 Indiana St.
Vallejo, CA 94590
Ph: (707)853-0440
E-mail: bishops@independentcatholics.org
Contact: Most Rev. Frederic H. Jones PhD, Presiding Bishop
Founded: 1980. **Members:** 350. **Membership Dues:** clergy, $50 (annual) ● church, ministry, $250 (annual). **Staff:** 9. **Multinational. Description:** Promotes inter-communion and ecclesiastical collaboration, training and support for independent catholic congregations and clergies at all levels. Provides a wide variety of programs and services to the Church and the community at-large. Represents the interests of denominations, churches, ministries, clergies and laity. **Affiliated With:** International Council of Community Churches. **Publications:** *The Independent Catholic*, quarterly. Newsletter. Features congregational ministry success and solutions to share and celebrate fellowship. Alternate Formats: online.

20083 ■ Interfaith Alliance
1331 H St. NW, 11th Fl.
Washington, DC 20005
Ph: (202)639-6370
Free: (800)510-0969
Fax: (202)639-6375
E-mail: info@interfaithalliance.org
URL: http://www.interfaithalliance.org
Contact: Rev. Dr. C. Welton Gaddy, Pres.
Founded: 1994. **Members:** 2,100,000. **Staff:** 15. **Description:** Represents supporters of various faiths. Strives to promote the role of religion as a healing and constructive force in politics and public life. **Telecommunication Services:** electronic mail, tiamemberservices@interfaithalliance.org. **Publications:** *The Light*, quarterly. Newsletter.

20084 ■ International Order of Saint Luke the Physician (OSL)
PO Box 780909
San Antonio, TX 78278-0909
Ph: (210)698-7141
Free: (800)675-9228

Fax: (210)698-7858
E-mail: osl2@satx.rr.com
URL: http://www.orderofstluke.org
Contact: Larry Mitchell, Pres.
Membership Dues: single in U.S., $30 (annual) ● couple in U.S., $35 (annual) ● single in Canada, $41 (annual) ● couple in Canada, $50 (annual). **Multinational. Description:** A Christian healing ministry and fellowship of professional people of all phases of medical work, clergy in the ministry of the Roman, Orthodox, Anglican and Protestant churches, and lay people from all walks of life who believe that the healing ministry of Jesus Christ belongs in the church today. Primary objectives are to: promote the restoration of the apostolic practice of healing as taught and practiced by Jesus Christ, promote the practice of holding healing services in every church, promote a sound pastoral and counseling ministry, develop local chapters to promote healing missions, workshops and prayer groups in their areas, conduct healing missions and teach Christians how to pray for healing, and place healing literature in churches and hospitals. **Computer Services:** Information services ● online services. **Telecommunication Services:** 24-hour hotline, prayerline, (512)280-4543. **Publications:** *Order of St. Luke Handbook for Christian Healing* ● *Sharing, A Journal of Christian Healing*, monthly. **Price:** included in membership dues; $20.00 /year for nonmembers in U.S.; $26.00 /year for nonmembers in Canada; $45.00 /year for nonmembers outside North America. **Conventions/Meetings:** annual conference, with speaker.

20085 ■ Jews for Judaism
c/o Rabbi Bentzion Kravitz, Dir.
PO Box 351235
Los Angeles, CA 90035-1235
Ph: (310)556-3344
Free: (800)477-6631
Fax: (310)556-3304
E-mail: la@jewsforjudaism.org
URL: http://www.jewsforjudaism.org
Contact: Rabbi Bentzion Kravitz, Dir.
Founded: 1985. **Membership Dues:** individual, $36 ● supporter, $54 ● advocate, $100 ● friend, $250 ● sponsor, $500 ● patron, $1,000 ● benefactor, $1,800 ● champion, $2,500. **Multinational. Description:** Provides counseling services, education and outreach programs that enable Jews to rediscover and strengthen their Jewish heritage. **Publications:** *The Jewish Response to Missionaries* (in English, French, German, Hebrew, Portuguese, Russian, and Spanish). Handbook. Alternate Formats: online ● *Lifeline*. Newsletter ● Brochures. Alternate Formats: online.

20086 ■ John Templeton Foundation
300 Conshohocken State Rd., Ste.500
West Conshohocken, PA 19428
Ph: (610)941-2828
Fax: (610)825-1730
E-mail: info@templeton.org
URL: http://www.templeton.org
Contact: Pamela P. Thompson, VP for Communications
Founded: 1987. **Description:** Strives to promote science and religion. Hosts lectures and learning courses. **Awards:** Epiphany Prize. **Frequency:** annual. **Type:** recognition. **Recipient:** to the most inspiring movie and television program ● European Templeton Film Award. **Frequency:** annual. **Type:** recognition. **Recipient:** to films of highest artistic merit ● Martin E.P. Seligman Award. **Type:** recognition. **Recipient:** to a scholar who has completed a PhD dissertation in any area of research ● Templeton European Religion Writer Award. **Type:** recognition. **Recipient:** for an excellent journalist. **Computer Services:** database, research information available on maximsnet. **Publications:** *Milestone*, monthly. Newsletter. Highlights a particular event or achievement from new initiatives, programs in progress, and scientific research findings. Alternate Formats: online ● *Science & Theology News*, monthly. Newspaper. Reports the latest research findings, funding opportunities, discussions about religion, and science and health. Alternate Formats: online.

20087 ■ Living Church of God (LCG)
PO Box 3810
Charlotte, NC 28227-8010
Ph: (704)844-1970
Fax: (704)841-2244
URL: http://www.livingcog.org
Contact: Dr. Roderick C. Meredith, Contact
Multinational. Description: "The Living Church of God is a new organization with an old history. Its leader, Dr. Roderick C. Meredith, was one of the original evangelists ordained by the late Herbert W. Armstrong in December 1952. For almost half a century Dr. Meredith has powerfully proclaimed the truth of God to millions through his hundreds of articles and booklets. He also has broadcast over radio and television to the whole English-speaking world. The Living Church of God is active in North and South America, Europe, Asia, Africa, and Australia. It has scores of ordained ministers and over two hundred congregations". **Publications:** *Beast of Revelation: Myth, Metaphor or Soon-Coming Reality?*. Booklet. **Price:** free. Alternate Formats: online ● *Build a Joyous Marriage*. Booklet. **Price:** free. Alternate Formats: online ● *Do You Believe the True Gospel?*. Booklet. **Price:** free. Alternate Formats: online ● *Fourteen Signs Announcing Christ's Return*. Booklet. **Price:** free. Alternate Formats: online ● *God's Church Through the Ages*. Booklet. **Price:** free. Alternate Formats: online ● *Marriage & Family: Vital Institutions in Crisis*. Magazine. **Price:** free. Alternate Formats: online ● *Overcoming Your Anxieties*. Magazine. **Price:** free. Alternate Formats: online ● *Tomorrow's World*. Magazine ● *The Wages of SIN?*. Magazine. **Price:** free. Alternate Formats: online ● *Who Controls the Weather?*. Magazine. **Price:** free. Alternate Formats: online.

20088 ■ Maclellan Foundation
820 Broad St., Ste.300
Chattanooga, TN 37402
Ph: (423)755-1366
Fax: (423)755-1640
E-mail: info@maclellan.net
URL: http://www.maclellan.net
Contact: Mr. Hugh O. Maclellan Jr., Pres.
Founded: 1945. **Staff:** 10. **Multinational. Description:** "Aims to further the Kingdom of Christ and select local organizations, which foster the spiritual welfare of the community, by providing financial and leadership resources to extend the Kingdom of God to every tribe, nation, and people".

20089 ■ Mentalphysics
PO Box 1000
Joshua Tree, CA 92252
Ph: (760)365-8371 (760)365-3880
Free: (800)394-0508
Fax: (760)228-0626
E-mail: mentalphysics1@aol.com
URL: http://www.mentalphysics.org
Contact: Maria Aquino, CEO
Founded: 1927. **Languages:** English, French, German, Icelandic, Spanish. **Description:** Offers home study courses and meditation instruction. **Formerly:** (2000) Institute of Mental Physics. **Conventions/Meetings:** seminar ● workshop - 2-3/year.

20090 ■ Northern Far East Returned Missionaries Association
PO Box 94342
Las Vegas, NV 89193-4342
Ph: (801)964-2825 (801)782-8233
Fax: (801)964-0551
E-mail: summers@webpipe.net
Contact: George M. McCune, Ed.
Founded: 1966. **Members:** 940. **Staff:** 10. **Multinational. Description:** Returned missionaries of the Northern Far East Mission who served as volunteer representatives in Japan and Korea for the Church of Jesus Christ of Latter-day Saints from 1955 through 1968. The association has no connection with nor is it in any way an official organization of the Church. Objectives are association, friendship, and sharing of information regarding the Church presence and growth in Japan since it officially established a presence in Japan in August 1901. **Publications:** *News-*

letter of the Northern Far East Returned Missionaries Association, annual, February or March. **Conventions/Meetings:** annual reunion, includes Japanese dinner buffet.

20091 ■ Partners for Sacred Places
1700 Sansom St., 10th Fl.
Philadelphia, PA 19103
Ph: (215)567-3234
Fax: (215)567-3235
E-mail: partners@sacredplaces.org
URL: http://www.sacredplaces.org
Contact: Diane Cohen, Founding Co-Dir.
Founded: 1989. **Membership Dues:** Donor's Circle, $125-$250 (annual) ● organization, $100 (annual) ● individual, $35 (annual) ● Cornerstone Society, $500-$5,000 (annual). **Description:** Devoted to the sound use and active community use of America's older religious properties. **Telecommunication Services:** electronic mail, dcohen@sacredplaces.org. **Programs:** Information Clearinghouse. **Publications:** *Advocacy Initiatives* ● *After Sunday*. Video. Features a 25-minute video illustrating the roles of inner-city congregations in their neighborhoods. **Price:** $10.00 for members; $15.00 for nonmembers ● *Open the Doors, See All the People: A Guide to Serving Families in Sacred Places*. Handbook. Contains information for congregational leaders on planning, funding, and managing programs for children and families. **Price:** free ● *Sacred Places at Risk*. Paper. Contains information on how congregations with historic buildings use their properties for community outreach programs. **Price:** $10.00 for members; $15.00 for nonmembers. Alternate Formats: CD-ROM ● *Ten Sacred Places to Save* ● *Why Should We Spend Money on Our Building When There Is So Much Need in the World*. Audiotape. Features a 25-minute audio-CD of reflections from Jewish, mainline and evangelical Protestant, Roman Catholic and Episcopal. **Price:** $5.00 ● *Your Sacred Place Is A Community Asset: A Tool Kit to Attract New Resources and New Partners*. Books. Includes a set of workbooks, case studies, historic timelines, audio and videotapes. **Price:** $95.00 for members; $125.00 for nonmembers. **Conventions/Meetings:** Sacred Trusts Conference.

20092 ■ Society for the Scientific Study of Religion (SSSR)
c/o Arthur E. Farnsley, II, Exec. Off.
Indiana Univ. - Purdue Univ. Indianapolis
Cavanaugh Hall 341
425 Univ. Blvd.
Indianapolis, IN 46202
E-mail: afarnsle@iupui.edu
URL: http://www.sssrweb.org
Contact: Arthur E. Farnsley II, Exec. Off.
Founded: 1949. **Members:** 1,600. **Membership Dues:** regular, $35 (annual) ● student, $15 (annual) ● international, $20 (annual) ● emeritus, $20 (annual). **Staff:** 2. **Budget:** $150,000. **Multinational. Description:** Represents behavioral scientists (anthropologists, sociologists, psychologists, and historians) and others (natural scientists, philosophers, and theologians) involved in teaching, research, and study of religion with scientific methodology and conceptualization. Encourages research, stimulate communication, and facilitate cooperation among individuals and groups engaged in the scientific study of religion with respect to studies, research data, and projects. Serves as informal clearinghouse in the field. Publishes the Journal for the Scientific Study of Religion. **Awards:** Distinguished Article Award. **Frequency:** annual. **Type:** recognition ● Distinguished Book Award. **Frequency:** annual. **Type:** recognition ● Jack Shand Research Awards. **Frequency:** annual. **Type:** monetary. **Recipient:** to individuals conducting scholarly research ● Student Paper Award. **Frequency:** annual. **Type:** recognition. **Recipient:** for an outstanding student paper. **Computer Services:** Mailing lists. **Publications:** *Journal for Scientific Study of Religion*, quarterly. **Price:** $34.00 /year for members; $71.00 /year for institutions. ISSN: 0021-8294. **Circulation:** 2,600. **Advertising:** accepted ● Monograph. **Conventions/Meetings:** annual conference (exhibits).

20093 ■ Spiritual Directors International (SDI)
PO Box 3584
Bellevue, WA 98009-3584
Ph: (425)455-1565
Fax: (425)455-1566
E-mail: office@sdiworld.org
URL: http://www.sdiworld.org
Contact: Liz Budd Ellmann, Exec. Dir.

Founded: 1990. **Members:** 4,700. **Membership Dues:** regular, in U.S., $69 (annual) ● regular, outside U.S., $59 (annual) ● student (send proof of status), $49 (annual). **Regional Groups:** 128. **Multinational. Description:** Supports people interested in and passionate about the ministry of spiritual direction including spiritual directors, chaplains, campus ministers, theology students, faculty, clergy and lay people around the world and across spiritual traditions. Publishes Guidelines for Ethical Conduct, web site forums for members, brochures to educate the public about the value of the ministry of spiritual direction, local and international educational programs promoting contemplative practice. **Computer Services:** Online services, listserv SDITALK. **Publications:** Connections. Newsletter. Presents issues relating to the art of spiritual direction. ● Presence: An International Journal of Spiritual Direction, quarterly. **Price:** included in membership dues. **Circulation:** 6,000. **Advertising:** accepted. **Conventions/Meetings:** annual Conference for Spiritual Leaders ● Pre-Conference Institutes and Workshops ● Symposium for Trainers of Spiritual Directors.

20094 ■ Toward Tradition
PO Box 58
Mercer Island, WA 98040
Ph: (206)236-3046
Free: (800)591-7579
E-mail: myrabbi@towardtradition.org
URL: http://www.towardtradition.org
Contact: Rabbi Daniel Lapin, Pres.

Founded: 1991. **Description:** Works to advance Judeo-Christian values in the United States. Addresses interrelated issues within the structure of family, faith, and fortune. **Publications:** Toward Tradition Newsletter. Alternate Formats: online.

20095 ■ Westar Institute
PO Box 7268
Santa Rosa, CA 95407
Ph: (707)523-1323
Free: (877)523-3545
Fax: (707)523-1350
E-mail: westar@westarinstitute.org
URL: http://www.westarinstitute.org
Contact: Lane C. McGaughy, Chair

Founded: 1986. **Members:** 3,200. **Membership Dues:** associate, $45 (annual) ● professional, $85 (annual). **Description:** Strives for the advancement of religious literacy. Fosters collaborative research in religious studies. Communicates the results of the scholarship of religion to a broad and non-specialist public. Opens up a new kind of conversation about religion through publications, educational programs, and research projects. **Subgroups:** Jesus Seminar; Research Project. **Publications:** Forum, semiannual. Journal. Includes scholarly articles related to the work of Westar Institute seminars. ● Fourth R, bimonthly. Magazine. Addresses a broad range of questions about religion in terms that can be understood by the general reader. **Price:** included in membership dues ● Seminar Papers, semiannual. Consists of the working papers of Westar Institute seminars that form the basis for discussions at the semi-annual meetings. **Price:** $20.00/set. **Conventions/Meetings:** semiannual Jesus Seminar - always spring and fall ● periodic Jesus Seminar on the Road.

20096 ■ Zarathushtrian Assembly
1814 Bayless St.
Anaheim, CA 92802
Ph: (714)520-9577
Fax: (714)520-9620

E-mail: assembly@zoroastrian.org
URL: http://www.zoroastrian.org
Contact: Daruish Irani, Pres.

Founded: 1990. **Staff:** 4. **Languages:** English, Persian. **Description:** Seeks to restore, practice, study, teach, and propagate the message of Zarathushtra as a living and growing religion. Sponsors educational programs, research programs, children's services, and competitions. Maintains speakers' bureau. **Libraries: Type:** by appointment only; reference. **Subjects:** Zarathushtrian studies, Aresta language, Parsi history, Persian literature. **Awards:** Zarathushtrian Assembly. **Frequency:** quarterly. **Type:** scholarship. **Recipient:** for PhD students who are studying at Spenta Graduate School. **Additional Websites:** http://www.zartoshti.org. **Telecommunication Services:** electronic mail, zassembly@aol.com. **Subgroups:** Spenta Graduate School. **Publications:** Message of Zarathushtra. Book. Alternate Formats: online ● Spenta (in English and Persian), quarterly. Journal. **Circulation:** 4,000. **Advertising:** accepted ● Bulletins, bimonthly ● Articles. Alternate Formats: online. **Conventions/Meetings:** monthly board meeting - every first Sunday ● conference.

Religious Administration

20097 ■ Christian Management Association (CMA)
PO Box 4090
San Clemente, CA 92674
Ph: (949)487-0900
Free: (800)727-4CMA
Fax: (949)487-0927
E-mail: cma@cmaonline.org
URL: http://sites.silaspartners.com/cma
Contact: Frank Lofaro, Pres./CEO

Founded: 1976. **Members:** 3,500. **Membership Dues:** premier, $399 (annual) ● gold, $1,000 (annual) ● new, $99 (annual). **Staff:** 11. **Budget:** $1,083,000. **Regional Groups:** 9. **State Groups:** 61. **Description:** Represents CEO's, key leaders and managers who serve Christian organizations and churches. Provides management information, leadership training and strategic networking management through its annual national conference, the Christian Management Institute. Holds bimonthly fellowship meeting for training and information reports. Provides job referral and professional referral service to assist Christian management personnel. **Awards:** Chapter President of the Year Award. **Frequency:** annual. **Type:** recognition. **Recipient:** for the chapter leader showing exemplary skills leading their chapter ● Christian Management Award. **Frequency:** annual. **Type:** recognition. **Recipient:** for individual showing outstanding Christian leadership. **Committees:** Audit; Chapter Development Conference; Legal; Promotional. **Formerly:** (1981) Christian Financial Executives Association; (1990) Christian Ministries Management Association. **Publications:** Christian Management Report, bimonthly. Magazine. Includes book/video reviews and lists new appointments in Christian management. Features columns including tax and business bulletin. **Price:** included in membership dues; $49.00 /year for nonmembers. **Circulation:** 3,500. **Advertising:** accepted. Alternate Formats: online ● Compensation Handbook for Christian Ministries, semiannual. **Conventions/Meetings:** annual convention (exhibits) ● annual The Ministry of Management: A High Calling - conference.

20098 ■ Christian Stewardship Association (CSA)
4700 W Lake Ave.
Glenview, IL 60025
Ph: (847)375-4741
Free: (866)597-1806
Fax: (732)578-6598
E-mail: csa@stewardship.org
URL: http://www.stewardship.org
Contact: Scott Roden, Pres.

Founded: 1963. **Members:** 1,600. **Membership Dues:** individual, $125 (annual) ● organizational (up to 5 people), $395 (annual) ● affiliate, $495 (annual).

Staff: 7. **Budget:** $500,000. **Description:** Works to advance Biblical stewardship and development principles and practices. Works with Christian leaders, fundraisers, educators, laity, and clergy, provides education, research, resources, and networking/partnering. Maintains a speakers' bureau and national training conference. **Libraries: Type:** reference. **Holdings:** 1,000; books, clippings. **Subjects:** stewardship, giving, fundraising-religious. **Affiliated With:** National Association of Evangelicals. **Formerly:** (1990) Christian Stewardship Council. **Publications:** Stewardship Matters, semiannual. Newsletter. Contains articles and resources to help development and stewardship professionals. **Price:** free. **Circulation:** 21,000. **Advertising:** accepted. **Conventions/Meetings:** annual conference (exhibits) - 2008 Jan. 30-Feb. 2, Albuquerque, NM.

20099 ■ National Association of Church Business Administration (NACBA)
100 N Central Expy., Ste.914
Richardson, TX 75080-5326
Ph: (972)699-7555
Free: (800)898-8085
Fax: (972)699-7617
E-mail: info@nacba.net
URL: http://www.nacba.net
Contact: Mr. Simeon May CAE, CEO

Founded: 1956. **Members:** 3,000. **Membership Dues:** active, $150 (annual) ● business, $250 (annual) ● associate, $120 (annual) ● affiliate, $120 (annual) ● student, $35 (annual) ● additional, $100 (annual). **Staff:** 6. **Regional Groups:** 70. **Description:** Represents business administrators and managers employed by local churches or institutions of the Christian church. Aims to train, certify and provide resources for those serving in the field of church administration. Offers placement service; conducts research programs; and compiles statistics. Maintains hall of fame. **Libraries: Type:** reference. **Holdings:** 500; archival material, books. **Subjects:** church management and business. **Awards: Type:** recognition. **Affiliated With:** Christian Management Association. **Formerly:** (1985) National Association of Church Business Administrators. **Publications:** Conference Proceedings, annual ● Electronic Membership and Church Supplier Directory, monthly. Membership Directory. **Price:** included in membership dues. **Advertising:** accepted. Alternate Formats: CD-ROM ● NACBA Gram, monthly. Newsletter. **Price:** included in membership dues. **Circulation:** 3,000. Alternate Formats: online ● NACBA Ledger, quarterly. Magazine. **Price:** included in membership dues. **Circulation:** 3,000. **Advertising:** accepted. **Conventions/Meetings:** annual conference (exhibits).

20100 ■ National Association of Church Personnel Administrators (NACPA)
100 E 8th St.
Cincinnati, OH 45202
Ph: (513)421-3134
Fax: (513)421-3085
E-mail: nacpa@nacpa.org
Contact: Mary Jo Moran PhD, Exec. Dir.

Founded: 1971. **Members:** 1,200. **Membership Dues:** individual, $160 (annual) ● group, $600 (annual). **Staff:** 7. **Budget:** $740,000. **Description:** Personnel administrators of dioceses, religious congregations and parishes. Purposes are: to assist members in their development as church personnel administrators; to identify just personnel procedures and policies; to focus attention on the personnel needs of persons employed by the church in ministerial and other capacities. Functions as human resource consultants. **Awards:** Vision Award. **Frequency:** annual. **Type:** recognition. **Recipient:** for demonstration of vision in supporting just treatment for church workers. **Computer Services:** Mailing lists, consultation services in Human Resources. **Publications:** Newsnotes, bimonthly. Newsletter. **Price:** included in membership dues. **Circulation:** 1,200. Alternate Formats: online ● Membership Directory, annual ● Magazines. **Conventions/Meetings:** annual convention (exhibits) ● workshop, for professional training.

20101 ■ National Association for Treasurers of Religious Institutes (NATRI)
8824 Cameron St.
Silver Spring, MD 20910
Ph: (301)587-7776
Fax: (301)589-2897
E-mail: natri@natri.org
URL: http://www.natri.org
Contact: Barbara Matteson, Exec. Dir.
Founded: 1981. **Members:** 746. **Membership Dues:** regular, associate, $410 (annual). **Staff:** 4. **Budget:** $550,000. **Description:** Religious institutes. Works in collaboration with the Leadership Conference of Women Religious of the United States of America and the Conference of Major Religious Superiors of Men's Institutes of the United States of America. Focuses on fiscal management, legal education, administration, planning, and Christian stewardship. Assists member institutes in fulfilling fiscal responsibilities in order to facilitate their contribution within the community. Sponsors workshops on identification and projection of retirement needs, investment alternatives, money management, and accounting practices. Serves as a resource center for providing information and referrals for members and organizations addressing related issues. **Telecommunication Services:** electronic mail, bmatteson@natri.org. **Affiliated With:** Leadership Conference of Women Religious. **Publications:** *Service Directory*, annual, Lists individuals and firms who provide services to religious institutes. ● Membership Directory, annual ● Newsletter, 5/year. Addresses issues of interest to treasurers; includes annual survey. **Price:** included in membership dues. **Conventions/Meetings:** annual meeting and conference (exhibits) ● annual Orientation to Financial Management - seminar.

20102 ■ North American Association of Synagogue Executives (NAASE)
Rapport House
155 Fifth Ave.
New York, NY 10010
Ph: (646)519-9385
Fax: (631)732-9461
E-mail: office@naase.org
URL: http://www.naase.org
Contact: Harry Hauser, Exec. Dir.
Founded: 1948. **Description:** Serves the professional needs of Jewish executive directors of the Conservative Movement. Enables administrators to serve their congregation effectively. Stimulates interest in professional synagogue administration. Promotes the advancement, growth, value and role of executive directors in the synagogue setting and Jewish communal life. Fosters the advancement of Conservative Judaism. **Committees:** Administrative Resource Center; Amin Tzibur; Archives; Chaver Tribute Program; Contract Library; Internship Development; Mentoring/Buddies Program; Social Action/Community Outreach. **Affiliated With:** United Synagogue of Conservative Judaism. **Publications:** Journal. **Conventions/Meetings:** annual international conference.

20103 ■ United Religions Initiative (URI)
PO Box 29242
San Francisco, CA 94129
Ph: (415)561-2300
Fax: (415)561-2313
E-mail: office@uri.org
URL: http://www.uri.org
Contact: Charles Gibbs, Exec. Dir.
Founded: 2000. **Multinational. Description:** Commits to promote enduring, interfaith cooperation. Seeks to end religiously motivated violence. Creates cultures of peace, justice and healing for the Earth and all living beings. **Publications:** *eUpdate*, bimonthly. Newsletter. Provides news from URI's Cooperation Circles around the world. Alternate Formats: online ● *InterfaithNews.Net*. Newsletter. Provides a repository for interfaith news and stories. Alternate Formats: online. Also Cited As: *INN* ● Annual Report, annual. Includes yearly highlights and summaries of the organization's activities. Alternate Formats: online.

20104 ■ World Council of Religious Leaders (WCRL)
Empire State Bldg.
350 Fifth Ave., Ste.5403
New York, NY 10118
Ph: (212)967-2891
Fax: (212)967-2898
E-mail: hq@wcorl.org
URL: http://www.millenniumpeacesummit.com
Contact: Bawa Jain, Sec. Gen.
Founded: 2002. **Multinational. Description:** Works to bring religious resources to support the work of the United Nations in the quest for peace. Aims to serve as a model and guide for the creation of a community of world religions. Seeks to inspire women and men of all faiths in the pursuit of peace and mutual understanding. Seeks to aid in the development of the inner qualities and external conditions needed for the creation of a more peaceful, just and sustainable world society.

Religious Freedom

20105 ■ American Coalition of Unregistered Churches (ACUC)
PO Box 11
Indianapolis, IN 46206
Ph: (317)783-6753
Fax: (317)781-2775
Contact: Dr. Greg Dixon, Natl.Chm.
Founded: 1983. **Members:** 500. **Description:** Nondenominational unregistered churches seeking to present a "united voice against government encroachment upon our churches and to present a united front to champion religious liberty issues." (Unregistered churches are not incorporated bodies; they believe that "the Lord Jesus Christ is head of the church.") Provides churches with educational materials on constitutional rights and biblical principles; offers information and encouragement to churches experiencing legal conflicts; lobbies for effective legislation. **Libraries: Type:** reference. **Holdings:** 3,000. **Subjects:** American history, constitution, current events in America, and christian faith. **Computer Services:** Mailing lists ● online services. **Publications:** *The Trumpet*, bimonthly. Newspaper.

20106 ■ Christian Freedom International (CFI)
PO Box 535
Front Royal, VA 22630
Ph: (540)636-8907
Free: (800)323-2273
Fax: (540)636-8908
E-mail: info@christianfreedom.org
URL: http://www.christianfreedom.org
Contact: James B. Jacobson, Pres.
Founded: 1983. **Staff:** 5. **Budget:** $850,000. **Description:** Christians seeking to protect the human rights of individuals worldwide to worship and believe in God and to act according to their religious beliefs; concentrates efforts in communist, Islamic, authoritarian, and politically unstable nations. Publicizes information concerning oppression and discrimination suffered by Christians and files written protests against violating governments; encourages supporters to mail written protests. Provides legal counsel for arrested Christians and offers material aid for prisoners and their families. Monitors compliance with international law concerning religious freedom; sends attorneys to visit officials of violating governments. Provides humanitarian aid through support of field hospitals, schools, and orphanages, and the provision of food, clothing, Bibles and other basic life essentials. Holds human rights briefings with members of the U.S. Congress. Maintains speakers' bureau; compiles statistics. **Libraries: Type:** reference. **Holdings:** archival material. **Formerly:** (1987) Christian Response International; (1989) Christian Solidarity, U.S.A.; (1998) Christian Solidarity International, U.S. A.; (2002) Now Christian Freedom International. **Publications:** Magazine, monthly. **Price:** free. **Conventions/Meetings:** annual conference.

20107 ■ Christian Solidarity International (CSI)
870 Hampshire Rd., Ste.T
Westlake Village, CA 91361
Ph: (805)777-7107
Free: (888)676-5700
Fax: (805)777-7508
E-mail: csi@csi-usa.org
URL: http://www.csi-int.org
Contact: Rev. Hans Stuckelberger, Founder/Pres.
Founded: 1977. **Multinational. Description:** Consists of human rights advocates. Seeks to abolish slavery in Sudan, including slave redemption, follow-up care, and advocacy. Focuses on religious liberty, child welfare, and disaster relief.

20108 ■ Society of Saint Stephen
c/o Martha Ann Fox
12805 St. Charles
Little Rock, AR 72211
Ph: (501)954-7916
URL: http://www.phumc.com/StStephen.htm
Contact: Martha Ann Fox, Contact
Founded: 1982. **Members:** 400. **Staff:** 1. **Regional Groups:** 4. **Description:** Ecumenical religious groups; interested Christian and Jewish individuals. Provides support to prisoners and their families, and others who are being imprisoned or persecuted for practicing their religious faith. Encourages the formation of "adoption groups" of persons who "adopt" a particular prisoner and his family. Meets to pray, to write letters to the adopted prisoner, and to fund parcels of material aid. Maintains religious prisoner profiles; presents programs on human rights. Operates speakers' bureau. **Committees:** Interreligious. **Divisions:** Funding Development; Government; Liaison; Membership and Adoption; Travel and Emigration. **Publications:** *Bulletin of the Society of St. Stephen*, quarterly. **Advertising:** accepted ● Brochure. **Conventions/Meetings:** semiannual meeting - always June and December.

Religious Science

20109 ■ Religious Science International (RSI)
PO Box 2152
Spokane, WA 99210-2152
Ph: (509)624-7000
Free: (800)662-1348
Fax: (509)624-9322
E-mail: rsi@rsintl.org
URL: http://www.rsintl.org
Contact: Dr. Candice Becket, Pres.
Founded: 1949. **Members:** 15,000. **Staff:** 9. **Budget:** $2,000,000. **State Groups:** 119. **National Groups:** 15. **Description:** Supports the growth and quality of existing churches and encourages and fosters the pioneering of new works for the purpose of teaching the Science of Mind and the practice of Spiritual Mind Treatment. **Libraries: Type:** open to the public. **Holdings:** audio recordings, books, video recordings. **Subjects:** lectures on the Science of Mind (trademark). **Awards:** Certificates of Appreciation. **Frequency:** annual. **Type:** recognition ● Distinguished Service Award. **Type:** recognition ● Doctor of Divinity. **Type:** recognition ● Doctor of Humanities. **Type:** recognition ● Doctor of Religious Science. **Type:** recognition ● Service Award. **Type:** recognition. **Computer Services:** database ● mailing lists. **Departments:** Credentials; Education; Placement; Practitioners; Youth Education. **Affiliated With:** International New Thought Alliance. **Formerly:** International Association of Religious Science Churches. **Publications:** *Creative Thought*, monthly, to churches only. Magazine. Includes articles, daily prayer affirmations, directory of churches, societies and practitioners. **Price:** $2. 50/copy; $24.95/year. ISSN: 1045-6139. **Circulation:** 10,000 ● Also publishes program materials for young people and classroom materials for churches. **Conventions/Meetings:** annual Asilomar - conference and retreat - usually July ● annual Leadership Conference - February/March.

Religious Studies

20110 ■ Jagannath Organization for Global Awareness (JOGA)
c/o Dr. Naresh C. Das, Chm.
4525 Rutherford Way
Dayton, MD 21036
Ph: (410)531-7445
E-mail: naresh.das@jogaworld.org
URL: http://www.jogaworld.org
Contact: Dr. Naresh C. Das, Chm.
Founded: 2001. **Multinational. Description:** Aims to spread Jagannath culture around the globe. Fosters education, research and promotion of Lord Jagannath's principle of universal brotherhood for peace and prosperity. Improves the educational institutes and education standard in rural areas. **Publications:** *Chirantana,* monthly. Newsletter. Alternate Formats: online ● Reports. Alternate Formats: online.

Religious Understanding

20111 ■ Council for a Parliament of the World's Religions (CPWR)
70 E Lake St., Ste.205
Chicago, IL 60601
Ph: (312)629-2990
Fax: (312)629-2991
E-mail: info@cpwr.org
URL: http://www.cpwr.org
Contact: Rev. Dirk Ficca, Exec. Dir.
Founded: 1988. **Staff:** 10. **Description:** Strives to encourage interreligious dialogue and cooperation in metropolitan Chicago and around the world. Facilitates international parliaments of the world's religions. Promotes interreligious understanding through mutual commitments and creative engagement. **Telecommunication Services:** electronic mail, dirk@cpwr.org. **Programs:** Partners Cities. **Projects:** Creating Community Vision; World in Our Backyard. **Publications:** Audiotapes.

20112 ■ International Fellowship of Christians and Jews (IFCJ)
30 N La Salle St., Ste.2600
Chicago, IL 60602-3356
Ph: (312)641-7200
Free: (800)486-8844
Fax: (312)641-7201
E-mail: info@ifcj.org
URL: http://www.ifcj.org
Contact: Rabbi Yechiel Z. Eckstein, Founder/Pres.
Founded: 1983. **Description:** Promotes understanding and cooperation between Jews and Christians. Builds broad support for Israel. Works to fulfill its vision of reversing the 2000-year history of discord between the Jews and Christians and replace it with a relationship marked by dialogue, understanding, respect and cooperation.

Research

20113 ■ Center for Research in Faith and Moral Development (CRFMD)
Candler Scholarship of Theology
Bishops Hall, Ste.10
Atlanta, GA 30322
Ph: (404)727-2277 (404)634-5698
Fax: (404)727-7399
E-mail: jfowler@emory.edu
Contact: Dr. James W. Fowler, Dir.
Founded: 1980. **Staff:** 1. **Description:** Conducts research utilizing life history techniques to discover how people develop religious beliefs; research is done primarily by students in the theology and personality graduate department at Candler School of Theology at Emory University. **Formerly:** Center for Faith Development. **Publications:** *1993 Manual for Faith Development Research,* periodic. Serves as a research guide for conducting and analyzing Faith Development Interviews. **Price:** $30.00 hard cover only ● *Remembrances of Lawrence Kohlberg* ● Faith

Development Bibliography. **Conventions/Meetings:** periodic conference and seminar.

20114 ■ Chalcedon Foundation (CF)
PO Box 158
Vallecito, CA 95251
Ph: (209)736-4365
Fax: (209)736-0536
E-mail: chaloffi@goldrush.com
URL: http://www.chalcedon.edu
Contact: Mark R. Rushdoony, Pres.
Founded: 1965. **Description:** Bestows grants to scholars who conduct research based on Biblical premises and the application of Biblical faith to life and thought. **Publications:** *Chalcedon e-Letter,* monthly. Newsletter. Alternate Formats: online ● *Chalcedon Report,* monthly. Magazine. Alternate Formats: online. **Conventions/Meetings:** periodic conference.

20115 ■ Church Growth Inc. (CGI)
PO Box 541
Monrovia, CA 91017-0541
Free: (800)844-9286
Fax: (626)305-1286
E-mail: info@churchgrowth.net
URL: http://www.churchgrowth.net
Contact: Dr. Charles Arn EdD, Pres.
Founded: 1973. **Staff:** 16. **Description:** Works to introduce principles of church growth to American churches and to provide them with specific steps for implementing these principles for effective outreach. Sponsors training seminars, workshops, and consultations for churches, districts, and other groups of all denominations worldwide; has formulated a church growth development scale and ten-year growth forecasts of major Protestant denominations in the U.S. **Formerly:** (1993) Institute for American Church Growth. **Publications:** *A Comprehensive Plan for Evangelism* ● *The Contagious Congregation* ● *How to Grow a Church* ● *The Master's Plan.* Video. Church action kit. **Price:** $59.95 ● *Mobilizing Laity for Ministry.* Church action kit. ● *Planting Churches Cross-Culturally.* Book ● *Win Arn Growth Report,* 5/year. Newsletter. Outlines specific principles to help the growth of American churches of all denominations. Reports on all aspects of church outreach. ● Books ● Also publishes advertising flyers; distributes Sunday school and church growth games, posters, films, cassettes, adult study courses, and other materials. **Conventions/Meetings:** periodic conference.

20116 ■ Community for Religious Research and Education (CRRE)
Address Unknown since 2007
Founded: 1973. **Description:** Investigates and promotes publication of "critical thought about religion" and its impact on society. Recent study topics include: religion and labor; rise of the religious right; religion in the Middle East; religious new right; theology and politics; liberation and spirituality. Conducts research. **Libraries: Type:** reference. **Holdings:** archival material.

20117 ■ Institute for Creation Research (ICR)
10946 Woodside Ave.
Santee, CA 92071
Ph: (619)448-0900
Fax: (619)448-3469
E-mail: info@icr.org
URL: http://www.icr.org
Contact: Dr. John D. Morris, Pres.
Founded: 1972. **Staff:** 50. **Budget:** $5,000,000. **Description:** Asserts "the inerrancy of scripture through the abundant evidence in science." Conducts research and education. Operates museum. **Libraries: Type:** reference. **Holdings:** 12,095. **Subjects:** creation and evolutionary science. **Publications:** *Acts and Facts,* monthly. Newsletter. **Price:** free. **Circulation:** 100,000. Alternate Formats: online ● *Days of Praise,* quarterly. **Price:** free. **Circulation:** 250,000. Alternate Formats: online ● Articles. Alternate Formats: online. **Conventions/Meetings:** conference - 15-20/year.

20118 ■ Religious Research Association (RRA)
618 SW 2nd Ave.
Galva, IL 61434-1912
Ph: (309)932-2727
Fax: (309)932-2282
E-mail: bill4329@hotmail.com
URL: http://rra.hartsem.edu
Contact: Dr. William H. Swatos Jr., Exec. Off.
Founded: 1959. **Members:** 500. **Membership Dues:** sustaining, $30 (annual) ● library, $70 (annual) ● student, $14 (annual). **Budget:** $60,000. **Description:** Professional society of church people, educators, social scientists, and others engaged in religious research; associate members are church administrators and students. Seeks to: increase the understanding and assist the implementation of the function of religion in society through the application of the methods and knowledge of the social sciences; promote the availability, circulation, interpretation, and use of religious research materials among religious bodies and other interested groups; cooperate with other professional societies, groups, and individuals interested in the functioning of religion in society; provide an environment for the development of professional awareness, competence, and status on the part of those engaged in research and study of the functioning of religion in society. Does not advocate or lobby for any specific religious group or position. **Awards:** Constant H. Jacquet Research Award. **Frequency:** annual. **Type:** grant. **Recipient:** for applied and basic socioreligious research. **Formerly:** (1951) Religious Research Fellowship. **Publications:** *Context of Religious Research,* semiannual. Newsletter. Contains information on annual meeting, election materials, listings of related organizations' meetings, members' awards and publications. **Price:** included in membership dues. **Circulation:** 500. Alternate Formats: online ● *Review of Religious Research,* quarterly. Journal. Contains a variety of articles, book reviews, and reports on research projects. **Price:** included in membership dues; $70.00 /year for institutions. ISSN: 0034-673X. **Circulation:** 1,000. **Advertising:** accepted ● *20th Anniversary Index to the Review of Religious Research, 1959-1979.* **Conventions/Meetings:** annual conference, held in conjunction with Society for Scientific Study of Religion (exhibits) - always October or November.

Romanian Orthodox

20119 ■ American Romanian Orthodox Youth (AROY)
c/o John E. Lazar, Pres.
18430 W Nine Mile Rd.
Southfield, MI 48075
Ph: (734)646-6420
E-mail: jel@aroy.org
URL: http://www.aroy.org
Contact: John E. Lazar, Pres.
Founded: 1950. **Members:** 2,000. **Staff:** 12. **State Groups:** 16. **Languages:** English, Romanian. **Multinational. Description:** The young people's organization of the Romanian Orthodox Episcopate of America. Promotes the Orthodox Christian faith in America. Sponsors and conducts religious educational summer courses, camps, retreats, sports tournaments, religious publications program, and scholarships. Compiles statistics. **Libraries: Type:** reference. **Holdings:** biographical archives. **Awards:** ARFORA/Martha Gavrila Scholarship for Women. **Frequency:** annual. **Type:** scholarship. **Recipient:** to women in post graduate studies ● ARFORA Undergraduate Scholarship for Women. **Frequency:** annual. **Type:** scholarship. **Recipient:** to selected undergraduate students ● Bujea Memorial Scholarship. **Frequency:** annual. **Type:** scholarship. **Recipient:** to a Canadian student ● Dumitri Golea Goldy-Gemu Scholarship. **Frequency:** annual. **Type:** scholarship. **Recipient:** to undergraduate students ● William R. Stanitz/AROY Scholarship. **Frequency:** annual. **Type:** scholarship. **Recipient:** to active members, high school graduates and college students. **Computer Services:** Mailing lists, of mem-

bers. **Committees:** Chapter Liaison; Fundraising; Historian and Yearbook; Membership; Newsletter; Sports; Website and Public Relations. **Funds:** Romanian Orthodox Episcopate of America Seminarian. **Publications:** *The AROY Newsletter,* bimonthly. Informs, educates, inspires and keeps members and supporters connected with the organization and with one another. **Price:** free. **Advertising:** accepted. Alternate Formats: online. **Conventions/Meetings:** annual conference.

Rosicrucian

20120 ■ Rosicrucian Fellowship
2222 Mission Ave.
Oceanside, CA 92054-2329
Ph: (760)757-6600
Fax: (760)721-3806
E-mail: rosfshp@rosicrucian.org
URL: http://www.rosicrucian.com
Contact: Allen Edwall, Pres.

Founded: 1909. **Staff:** 26. **Languages:** English, French, German, Italian, Portuguese, Spanish. **Multinational. Description:** Students of the Rosicrucian philosophy as presented in The Rosicrucian Cosmo-Conception. The Rosicrucian philosophy "is a logical and sequential teaching concerning the origin, evolution and future development of the world and man, showing both the spiritual and scientific aspects." Purpose of the fellowship is "to make Christianity a living factor in the world. The philosophy, Bible study and spiritual astrology we teach by correspondence courses encourages students to live lives patterned after the precepts taught by Christ Jesus." Conducts two-week school in July and August and one week summer school in Spanish and French. **Libraries: Type:** not open to the public. **Subjects:** esoteric and occult. **Computer Services:** database ● mailing lists ● online services. **Publications:** *Rays From the Rose Cross,* bimonthly. Magazine. Features Christian esoteric subjects, spiritual astrology, healing, western wisdom and bible studies. **Price:** $5.00/issue; $20.00/year in U.S.; $25.00/year outside U.S. ISSN: 0744-432X. **Circulation:** 550 ● Also publishes books and booklets.

Russian Orthodox

20121 ■ Fellowship of Orthodox Christians in America (FOCA)
10 Downs Dr.
Wilkes-Barre, PA 18705
Ph: (570)825-3158 (570)824-0562
Fax: (570)825-0136
E-mail: orthodoxfellowship@yahoo.com
URL: http://www.orthodoxfellowship.org
Contact: Sandra Kapelan, Natl. Admin. Sec.

Founded: 1927. **Members:** 3,000. **Staff:** 1. **Regional Groups:** 13. **Local Groups:** 90. **Description:** Federation of clubs for young men and women of Russian Orthodox faith that are organized for religious, cultural, charitable, social, and athletic purposes. **Awards: Type:** scholarship. **Committees:** Essay Contests; Mission Services; Sales; Scholarship; Seminaries; United Fund Drive. **Departments:** Convention Planning and Operating; Internal/External; Junior; Sports. **Divisions:** Junior; Senior. **Formerly:** (1998) Federated Russian Orthodox Clubs. **Publications:** *Orthodox Christian Journal,* quarterly. Alternate Formats: online ● Directory, annual. **Conventions/Meetings:** annual meeting.

Sabbath

20122 ■ Bible Sabbath Association (BSA)
3316 Alberta Dr.
Gillette, WY 82718
Ph: (307)686-5191
Free: (888)687-5191

E-mail: info@biblesabbath.org
URL: http://www.biblesabbath.org
Contact: Bryan Burrell, Sec.-Treas.

Founded: 1945. **Members:** 168. **Membership Dues:** regular, $25 (annual). **Staff:** 2. **Budget:** $30,000. **Regional Groups:** 2. **Multinational. Description:** Believers in the seventh-day Sabbath, regardless of sect, creed, or denomination. Seeks observance of Saturday as the holy day of the week; opposes enactment of Sunday closing laws or other religious laws by any governmental legislative body. Maintains small library of commentaries and texts on the laws of God and the weekly rest day. **Committees:** Sentinel; Tract and Manuscript Review. **Publications:** *Directory of Sabbath-Observing Groups,* periodic. Includes alphabetical and geographical indexes. **Price:** $15.00/issue. **Advertising:** accepted ● *The Sabbath Sentinel: Serving the Seventh-day Christian Community,* bimonthly. Magazine. Includes personal testimonies, updates on Sunday Blue Laws, legislative news, and new publication information. **Price:** included in membership dues; $15.00 /year for nonmembers. **Circulation:** 1,200. **Advertising:** accepted ● Also publishes tracts and leaflets.

20123 ■ Lord's Day Alliance of the United States (LDA)
PO Box 941745
Atlanta, GA 31145-0745
Ph: (404)693-5530
E-mail: tnorton@ldausa.org
URL: http://www.sundayonline.org
Contact: Timothy A. Norton, Exec. Dir./Ed.

Founded: 1888. **Budget:** $117,000. **Regional Groups:** 4. **Description:** Interdenominational organization united to preserve the Lord's day as a day of rest, worship, Christian service, and family culture. Maintains speakers' bureau. **Libraries: Type:** reference. **Awards:** James P. Wesberry Centennial Award. **Frequency:** annual. **Type:** recognition. **Recipient:** for person making significant contributions to keeping the Lord's Day. **Committees:** Communications; Extension; State and National Affairs. **Publications:** *Sunday,* quarterly. Magazine. **Price:** $5.00/year. **Circulation:** 13,000. **Advertising:** accepted. **Conventions/Meetings:** semiannual board meeting.

20124 ■ Seventh Day Baptist General Conference of the United States and Canada
PO Box 1678
Janesville, WI 53547-1678
Ph: (608)752-5055
Fax: (608)752-7711
E-mail: sbdgen@seventhdaybaptist.org
URL: http://www.seventhdaybaptist.org
Contact: Robert Appel, Exec. Dir.

Founded: 1844. **Members:** 10. **Staff:** 2. **Budget:** $120,000. **Description:** A council of Seventh Day Baptist General Conference. Seeks "to promote observance of Bible Sabbath and to print and distribute literature of Seventh Day Baptist General Conference". **Libraries: Type:** reference. **Holdings:** audio recordings, audiovisuals, films. **Committees:** Electronic Media; Publications; Sabbath Promotion; Sabbath Recorder. **Affiliated With:** Seventh Day Baptist General Conference. **Formerly:** (1986) American Sabbath Tract Society; (2000) American Sabbath Tract and Communication Council. **Publications:** *God's Holy Day (7 Lessons).* Booklets ● *The Helping Hand,* quarterly. Manual. For Bible study. ● *Sabbath Recorder,* monthly. Magazine. ISSN: 0036-214X ● *Seventh Day Baptist Yearbook* ● Books ● Also publishes tracts. **Conventions/Meetings:** annual conference (exhibits).

Science

20125 ■ American Scientific Affiliation (ASA)
PO Box 668
Ipswich, MA 01938
Ph: (978)356-5656
Fax: (978)356-4375

E-mail: asa@asa3.org
URL: http://www.asa3.org
Contact: Dr. Randy Isaac, Exec. Dir.

Founded: 1941. **Members:** 1,800. **Membership Dues:** full, friend, associate, $60 (annual) ● student, student associate, $20 (annual) ● spouse, $10 (annual). **Staff:** 5. **Budget:** $275,000. **Regional Groups:** 8. **Description:** Industrial and academic scientists subscribing to the Christian faith. Seeks to integrate, communicate, and facilitate properly researched science and biblical theology in service to the Church and the science community. Seeks to have theology and science interacting and affecting one another in a positive light. **Computer Services:** database, journal index. **Commissions:** Bioethics; Communications; Creation; Global Resources and Environment; History and Philosophy of Science; Physical Sciences; Science Education; Social Sciences. **Publications:** *American Scientific Affiliation—Newsletter,* bimonthly. Covers membership activities. Includes book reviews and employment opportunities. **Circulation:** included in membership dues. **Circulation:** 2,000. Alternate Formats: online ● *American Scientific Affiliation—Resource,* biennial. Directory. Lists resources in the sciences and their relevance to Christian faith. **Price:** $10.50 plus shipping and handling ● *God Did It, But How?* Robert Fischer 2nd Ed. 1997. Book. Contains articles on issues involving the interaction of science and Christian faith. Contains book reviews and index every three years. **Price:** $30.00 /year for nonmembers; $45.00 /year for institutions. ISSN: 0892-2675. **Circulation:** 3,000. **Advertising:** accepted. Alternate Formats: microform ● *Perspectives On Science and Christian Faith,* quarterly. Journal. **Price:** $35.00 /year for individuals; $55.00 /year for institutions; $20.00/year for students. Alternate Formats: online ● *Teaching Science in a Climate of Controversy.* Booklet. **Price:** $7.00 ● Annual Report, annual. Alternate Formats: online ● Brochure. **Conventions/Meetings:** annual conference and meeting (exhibits) - always July or August.

20126 ■ Creation Health Foundation (CHF)
Address Unknown since 2007
Founded: 1979. **Description:** Individuals who subscribe to the Biblical account of creation and believe that one's view of the world's origin has direct consequences on nutritional and exercise habits and practices. Promotes a creationist approach to the health sciences; feels that belief in the theory of evolution has been "gradually destroying our physical, mental, spiritual, and social health." Encourages optimal nutrition, which the foundation defines as "the spiritual, creationist practice of eating foods as close as possible to the way God created and intended." Holds lectures. Advocates preventive medicine and minimal use of drugs. Disseminates information on topics such as the "harmful effects of homogenized milk and water fluoridation" and the benefits of Vitamin C. Conducts creation-health diagnostic testing clinics and counseling sessions. **Libraries: Type:** reference. **Holdings:** audiovisuals, books, clippings, monographs, periodicals. **Subjects:** Biblical creation and science with special section on health. **Conventions/Meetings:** periodic conference ● seminar.

20127 ■ Creation Research Society (CRS)
PO Box 8263
St. Joseph, MO 64508-8263
Fax: (816)279-2312
E-mail: contact@creationresearch.org
URL: http://www.creationresearch.org
Contact: Dr. Donald B. DeYoung PhD, Pres.

Founded: 1963. **Members:** 1,700. **Membership Dues:** regular, in U.S., $35 ● regular, outside U.S., $43 ● regular, in Canada and Mexico, $53 ● life, $350 ● all other countries, $68. **Description:** Persons with at least a master's degree in some branch of science are voting members; sustaining members are other interested individuals. Members are scientists and laymen who believe that the facts of science support the revealed account of creation in the Bible. Maintains research laboratory in Arizona. Conducts research and disseminates information to the public. **Committees:** Constitution; Editorial; Finance; Internet; Publications; Research. **Publications:** *Creation*

Matters, monthly. Newsletter. Contains articles and news related to scientific creation and evolution. **Price:** included in membership dues. ISSN: 1094-6632. **Circulation:** 1,800. **Advertising:** accepted. Alternate Formats: online ● *Creation Research Society Quarterly*. Journal. Features peer-reviewed scientific articles, scientific notes and book reviews. **Price:** included in membership dues. ISSN: 0092-9166. **Circulation:** 1,800. **Conventions/Meetings:** annual board meeting, closed meeting.

20128 ■ Genesis Institute (GI)
10220 N Nevada, Ste.280
Spokane, WA 99218
Ph: (509)467-7913
Fax: (509)467-0344
E-mail: dave.hutchins@genesisinstitute.org
URL: http://www.genesisinstitute.org
Contact: Dave Hutchins, Co-Founder/Exec. Dir.
Founded: 1984. **Members:** 2,000. **Membership Dues:** donation, $35 (annual). **Staff:** 2. **Budget:** $35,000. **Regional Groups:** 2. **State Groups:** 2. **Local Groups:** 1. **Description:** Individuals seeking to publicize the "value of the Gospel in sciences" and bring "the Bible and science together." Stresses "Creation Evangelism"; believes the universe is less than 6000 years old. Conducts educational and research programs. Offers home schooling services. Maintains museum. **Libraries: Type:** reference. **Holdings:** 1,000. **Subjects:** science, the Bible. **Publications:** *Ark Today*, quarterly. Magazine. Contains religious and scientific educational material. **Price:** included in membership dues. **Circulation:** 6,000 ● *Job and Science Commentary* ● Newsletter ● 52 science projects from book of job. **Conventions/Meetings:** annual conference (exhibits) - always June.

20129 ■ Institute on Religion in an Age of Science (IRAS)
c/o David A. Klotz, Membership Chm.
82 Goose Ln.
Coventry, CT 06238
E-mail: membership@iras.org
URL: http://www.iras.org
Contact: David A. Klotz, Membership Chm.
Founded: 1954. **Members:** 390. **Membership Dues:** student, $40 (annual) ● individual, $70 (annual) ● joint, $80 (annual) ● institutional, $100 (annual). **Budget:** $85,000. **Description:** Represents professionals from the fields of science and religion and interested laypeople. Seeks to provide a channel of communication among the religious and scientific communities and to explore new understanding and possibilities for religion in the light of the sciences. Sponsors annual weeklong conference. **Libraries: Type:** reference. **Holdings:** archival material. **Awards:** Fellow Award. **Frequency:** annual. **Type:** recognition ● Service Award. **Type:** recognition. **Affiliated With:** American Academy of Religion; American Association for the Advancement of Science. **Publications:** *IRAS Newsletter*, semiannual. ISSN: 1048-9525. Alternate Formats: online ● *Zygon, Journal of Religion and Science*, quarterly. **Conventions/Meetings:** annual conference - usually July-August, in Star Island, NH ● periodic meeting.

20130 ■ Reasons to Believe (RTB)
PO Box 5978
Pasadena, CA 91117
Ph: (626)335-1480
Free: (800)482-7836
Fax: (626)852-0178
E-mail: feedback@reasons.org
URL: http://www.reasons.org
Contact: Dr. Hugh Ross, Founder/Pres.
Founded: 1986. **Staff:** 31. **Budget:** $2,500,000. **Regional Groups:** 5. **Description:** Seeks to explain Origins in a Biblically sound and scientifically valid manner, in an effort to remove the doubts of skeptics and strengthen the faith of Christians. Conducts research and educational programs. Operates Speaker's Bureau. **Libraries: Type:** reference. **Telecommunication Services:** hotline, (626)335-5282, 7 days a week, 5-7 pm only, PST ● information service, 'Reasons to Believe' weekly, two hour Webcast from 11 am to 1 pm that discusses science and faith is-

sues, (866)782-7234. **Affiliated With:** American Scientific Affiliation; Campus Crusade for Christ International; Christian Business Men's Committee; Christian Educators Association International; Evangelical Theological Society; Inter Varsity Christian Fellowship; International Students, Inc.; National Association of Evangelicals. **Publications:** *The Ankerberg Debate*. Video ● *Beyond the Cosmos*. Book ● *Connections*, quarterly. Newsletter. Covers science issues and the Bible. **Price:** free. **Circulation:** 50,000. **Advertising:** accepted ● *Creation and Time*. Book ● *Creator and the Cosmos - Third Edition*. Book ● *Fingerprint of God*. Book ● *The Genesis Question - 2nd Edition*. Book ● *Life and Death in Eden*. Audiotapes ● *Lights in the Sky and Little Green Men*. Book ● *Relativity's Revelation*. Videos ● *The rUFO Hypothesis*. Video ● *Solar System Design*. Videos ● *Who Was Adam?*. Video ● Papers ● Also publishes reading lists. **Conventions/Meetings:** annual Who Is the Designer? - conference.

Seventh Day Adventist

20131 ■ Adventist Community Services (ACS)
12501 Old Columbia Pike
Silver Spring, MD 20904-6600
Ph: (301)680-6438
Free: (877)ACS-2702
Fax: (301)680-6125
E-mail: sung.kwon@nad.adventist.org
URL: http://www.communityservices.org
Contact: Sung Kwon, Exec. Dir.
Founded: 1874. **Staff:** 529. **Budget:** $12,000,000. **Regional Groups:** 9. **State Groups:** 50. **Local Groups:** 216. **Description:** Service agency of the Seventh-day Adventist Church. Participates in local, regional, and national disaster relief work. Offers basic social services, health screening, literacy tutoring, and prison ministry. Supports overseas relief work through Adventist Development and Relief Agency, International (see separate entry). Conducts homeless projects and classes in smoking cessation, stress management, nutrition, and family life. Cooperates with existing community agency programs. Holds local seminars and workshops. Services are carried out by 100,000 volunteers in 216 centers and 4600 local churches. Compiles statistics. **Libraries: Type:** reference. **Holdings:** archival material. **Awards: Type:** recognition. **Committees:** Disaster Service; Health Education; Health Screening; Inner City Service; Mentoring/Tutoring. **Formerly:** Health and Welfare Services; (1972) Community Services. **Publications:** *Competent Helping* ● *Disaster Relief Guide* ● *Health Screening Handbook* ● *Ministries of Compassion*. Manual ● *Seventh-Day Adventist Yearbook* ● Newsletter, quarterly ● Brochures. **Conventions/Meetings:** annual meeting (exhibits).

20132 ■ Adventist-Laymen's Services and Industries (ASI)
c/o ASI Ministries
12501 Old Columbia Pike
Silver Spring, MD 20904
Ph: (301)680-6450
Fax: (301)622-5017
E-mail: asi@nad.adventist.org
URL: http://www.asiministries.org
Contact: Debbie Young, Pres.
Founded: 1947. **Members:** 906. **Regional Groups:** 9. **Description:** Represents organizations; services and businesses that are privately owned by Seventh-day Adventist Christians that express commitment to what the group describes as sharing Christ in the marketplace. Seeks to increase integrity and the application of Christian principles of management in the business world. Supports the mission and activities of the Seventh-day Adventist Church. **Libraries: Type:** reference. **Formerly:** Association of Privately Owned Seventh-Day Adventist Services and Industries; (1987) Adventist Self-Supporting Institutions. **Publications:** *ASI Magazine*, quarterly. **Advertising:** accepted. Alternate Formats: online ● *ASI News*, monthly. Newsletter. **Price:** $6.00/year. **Advertising:**

accepted. **Conventions/Meetings:** annual convention (exhibits).

20133 ■ Association of Adventist Forums (AAF)
PO Box 619047
Roseville, CA 95661-9047
Ph: (916)774-1080
Fax: (916)791-4938
E-mail: subscriptions@spectrummagazine.org
URL: http://www.spectrummagazine.org
Contact: Ms. Julie Lorenz, Office Mgr.
Founded: 1968. **Members:** 2,500. **Membership Dues:** individual in U.S. and Canada, $39 (annual) ● individual outside U.S. and Canada, $59 (annual) ● student, $19 (annual). **Staff:** 4. **Local Groups:** 19. **Multinational. Description:** Encourages Seventh-day Adventists to participate, through local chapters, in the discussion of contemporary issues from a Christian viewpoint; fosters Christian intellectual and cultural growth. **Awards: Frequency:** annual. **Type:** recognition. **Councils:** Advisory. **Publications:** *Believing, Behaving, Belonging: Finding New Love for the Church*. Book. **Price:** $14.95 ● *Creation Reconsidered*. Book. **Price:** $10.00 ● *Festival of the Sabbath*. Book ● *Pilgrimage of Hope*. Book ● *Spectrum, the Journal of the Association of Adventist Forums*, quarterly. Magazine. Covers Christian and contemporary issues. Includes book reviews. **Price:** included in membership dues; $39.95 for nonmembers (online access only); $19.95 for student. ISSN: 0890-0264. **Circulation:** 3,000. **Advertising:** accepted. Alternate Formats: online. Also Cited As: *Spectrum Magazine*. **Conventions/Meetings:** annual New Reflections on Brain and Soul - international conference, with speakers.

20134 ■ Christians in Crisis (CIC)
PO Box 293627
Sacramento, CA 95829
Ph: (916)682-0376
E-mail: general@christiansincrisis.net
URL: http://www.christiansincrisis.net
Contact: Pastor Wally Magdangal, Pres./Founder
Founded: 1995. **Nonmembership. Description:** Works towards the protection of religious liberty for all faiths, including non-Christian, but concentrates on Christian believers living under circumstances of religious persecution. Gathers and disseminates information; takes practical action to relieve the material needs of victims of persecution, war, or poverty; distributes Christian literature. Maintains speakers' bureau. **Telecommunication Services:** electronic mail, pastorwally@christiansincrisis.net ● electronic mail, terry@christiansincrisis.net. **Publications:** Newsletter, bimonthly. Includes news of religious persecution. **Price:** free. ISSN: 1044-5846. **Circulation:** 1,700. **Conventions/Meetings:** annual meeting.

Sexuality

20135 ■ Spring of Living Water Ministry
Hope Outreach
PO Box 1067
Enid, OK 73702-1067
Ph: (580)237-4673
Fax: (580)237-7063
E-mail: hrpromo@hopeoutreach.org
URL: http://www.emmanuel-baptist.org/SpringLiving-Water.htm
Contact: Paula Nightengale, Exec. Dir.
Description: Works to encourage homosexual individuals to change their ways. Offers support to family members. Holds weekly group meetings for individuals who have abandoned their homosexual lifestyle. **Additional Websites:** http://www.hope-outreach.org.

Sikh

20136 ■ Council of Khalistan/International Sikh Organization (ISO)
730 24th St. NW, No. 310
Washington, DC 20037

Ph: (202)337-1904
E-mail: khalistan@khalistan.com
URL: http://www.khalistan.com
Contact: Dr. Gurmit Singh Aulakh, Pres.
Founded: 1986. **Membership Dues:** regular, $10. **Staff:** 2. **Budget:** $150,000. **Regional Groups:** 100. **State Groups:** 100. **Local Groups:** 100. **National Groups:** 100. **Languages:** English, Punjabi. **Multinational. Description:** Seeks to promote and educate the public on Sikhism, a divinely-revealed monotheistic religion which supports equality of all mankind, including gender equality. Sikhism was founded around 1500 A.D. and is marked by the rejection of idolatry and the caste system. Promotes international brotherhood and universal justice. Promotes freedom for the Sikh homeland, Khalistan, through education and information. **Publications:** *Freedom in India.* Brochure ● *Why Not Freedom for the Sikh.* Brochure. **Conventions/Meetings:** annual convention.

20137 ■ Sikh Study Circle (SSC)
Irving Sikh Ctr. .
834 N Nursery Rd.
Irving, TX 75061
Ph: (972)579-9646 (972)644-5627
Fax: (972)644-5627
E-mail: sikhstudy@hotmail.com
URL: http://www.sikhstudy.com
Contact: S. Maninber Singh Dhillon, Pres.
Founded: 1971. **Members:** 250. **Membership Dues:** regular, $50 (annual). **Staff:** 1. **Budget:** $100,000. **Description:** Individuals interested in Sikhs and Sikh religious practices. (Sikhs are members of a monotheistic religion founded in India in 1469.) Conducts Sikh religious services; disseminates information about Sikh religion and culture. Sponsors educational and charitable programs; makes available children's services; maintains Gurdwara temple. **Libraries: Type:** reference. **Holdings:** 200. **Publications:** *Southeast Sikh Samachar,* monthly. Newsletter. Publishes programs and financial statements. **Price:** free. **Circulation:** 300. **Advertising:** accepted ● Membership Directory, annual. **Conventions/Meetings:** weekly assembly ● annual Sikh Youth Camp and Cultural Program - meeting.

Social Service

20138 ■ Christian Forum Research Foundation (CFRF)
1111 Fairgrounds Rd.
Grand Rapids, MN 55744
Ph: (218)326-2688
Free: (800)286-5115
E-mail: lpahl@gnn.com
Contact: Sidney Reiners, Dir.
Founded: 1981. **Budget:** $50,000. **Description:** Christian congregations and individuals. Promotes freedom of religion; seeks to improve the quality of life of the underprivileged. Advocates on behalf of religious freedom. Provides humanitarian assistance to victims of poverty, persecution, and natural disaster. **Libraries: Type:** reference. **Holdings:** books, clippings, periodicals. **Subjects:** religious freedom. **Publications:** *Christians in Crisis,* bimonthly. Newsletter. ISSN: 1044-5846. **Circulation:** 1,000. Alternate Formats: online.

20139 ■ Confessing Synod Ministries (CSM)
East Liberty Lutheran Church
5707 Penn Ave.
Pittsburgh, PA 15206-3603
Ph: (412)362-1712
URL: http://www.confessingsynod.com
Contact: Rev. Deborah Byrum, Pastor
Founded: 1982. **Staff:** 1. **Nonmembership. Description:** Six congregations in the Pittsburgh, PA area; interested institutional leaders throughout the U.S. Teaches and practices the prophetic ministry based on scriptural models. (Prophetic means to speak and act out in order to address problems without trying to achieve a consensus.) Instructs pastors and institutional leaders on acting prophetically. Promotes prophetic ministry model in the U.S.

Believes that numerous denominations accommodate big business, politics, and the state instead of challenging the culture and the state and serving the "true Biblical Jesus." Addresses problems such as family addictions/dysfunction, unemployment, and community deterioration. Maintains speakers' bureau, library, and archives; conducts research programs. **Libraries: Type:** reference. **Subjects:** prophetic ministry. **Formerly:** (1986) Denominational Ministry Strategy. **Publications:** *Confessing Synod Paper,* quarterly. Newspaper. Includes articles on family development and sermon tips. **Circulation:** 2,000. **Conventions/Meetings:** annual meeting - always in Pittsburgh, PA.

Social Welfare

20140 ■ Americans Caring for Children Worldwide (ACCW)
PO Box 2300
Redlands, CA 92373
Ph: (909)793-2009
Fax: (909)793-6880
E-mail: info@childrenworldwide.org
URL: http://www.childrenworldwide.org
Contact: Fred M. Johnson, Pres.
Multinational. Description: Ministers to needy people in 33 underdeveloped countries, United States and Canada. Provides spiritual, educational and medical help through its churches, orphanages, schools and clinics.

Spiritual Life

20141 ■ Association of Contemplative Sisters (ACS)
c/o Deborah Gephardt
4125 Woodsly Dr.
Batavia, OH 45103
E-mail: debagep@cinci.rr.com
URL: http://www.geocities.com/contemplatives
Contact: Deborah Gephardt, Pres.
Founded: 1969. **Members:** 350. **Membership Dues:** $25 (annual). **Regional Groups:** 3. **Description:** Sisters in monastic and other religious communities; hermits; consecrated virgins; single lay women; married and widowed women; and women in lay contemplative communities. Strives to help contemporary men and women understand the meaning of life through affirmation of the contemplative dimension of humankind; to encourage contemplative women to unite in the vision of their role; to express the primacy of prayer in a diversity of life-styles; to foster the growth of each person in consciousness and freedom through authentic living-out of contemplative values. **Committees:** Formation; International Contacts; Record Project; Social Justice. **Publications:** *ACS Newsletter,* 3/year. **Price:** $5.00/year. **Circulation:** 400 ● Brochure. **Conventions/Meetings:** biennial assembly ● annual regional meeting.

20142 ■ Pathwork Helpers Association of North America (PHANA)
c/o Ann Norfolk, Membership Sec.
121 W Marylyn Ave.
State College, PA 16801-5928
Ph: (814)278-0474
E-mail: phana@phana.org
URL: http://www.phana.org
Contact: Ann Norfolk, Membership Sec.
Founded: 2002. **Membership Dues:** helper, apprentice helper, $55 (annual). **Multinational. Description:** Promotes both high standards of Pathwork Helpership practice and public recognition and trust in Pathwork Helpership. Increases public visibility and knowledge of Pathwork Helpership. Provides services that assist Pathwork helpers, apprentices, teachers and study group leaders. Promotes communication and cooperation among Pathwork helpers, apprentices, trainees, teachers and group leaders. **Publications:** Annual Report, annual. Alternate Formats: online ● Report. Alternate Formats: online.

20143 ■ Spiritual Life Institute (SLI)
c/o NADA Hermitage
PO Box 219
Crestone, CO 81131
Ph: (719)256-4778
Fax: (719)256-4719
E-mail: nada@fone.net
URL: http://www.spirituallifeinstitute.org
Contact: Fr. William McNamara OCD, Founder
Founded: 1960. **Members:** 20. **Staff:** 1. **Budget:** $400,000. **Multinational. Description:** Ecumenical movement to foster the contemplative spirit through publications and the establishment of contemporary and eremitical contemplative centers based on the primitive Carmelite ideal, under which individuals may go into the desert to pray. Established Holy Hill Hermitage in Skreen, Co. Sligo, Ireland, 1995 to provide European outreach. **Libraries: Type:** reference. **Holdings:** 5,000. **Subjects:** mysticism, spirituality, literature, poetry, world religions. **Awards:** Nova Nada Ecoforestry Award. **Frequency:** annual. **Type:** monetary. **Recipient:** for someone who helps protect the forests in Nova Scotia. **Formerly:** (2003) Spiritual Life Institute of America. **Publications:** *Desert Call,* quarterly. Magazine. Features articles on earthy mysticism, saints and heroes, practical spirituality, and cultural commentary. Includes book reviews. **Price:** $16.00/year. **Circulation:** 3,500 ● *Desert Call: Contemplative Christianity and Vital Culture,* quarterly. Magazine. God's call to intimate depths of every human heart. **Price:** $16.00/year in U.S.; $22.00/year in Canada; $30.00/year outside U.S. and Canada ● *Desert Express,* monthly. **Price:** $7.50/tape ● *Ecstasy and Common Sense.* Book. **Price:** $15.95/copy ● *Theresa of Avila: Mystical Writings.* Book. **Price:** $16.95/copy.

20144 ■ White Mountain Education Association (WMEA)
PO Box 11975
Prescott, AZ 86304
Ph: (928)778-0638
Fax: (928)776-4005
E-mail: staff@wmea-world.org
URL: http://www.wmea-world.org
Contact: Rev. Joleen D. DuBois, Pres.
Founded: 1982. **Members:** 150. **Membership Dues:** general, $25 (annual). **Staff:** 3. **State Groups:** 5. **Languages:** English, Spanish. **Description:** Represents people interested in spiritual growth. Promotes living a creative life of goodness. Publishes books and CD's. **Libraries: Type:** reference. **Holdings:** 3,000. **Subjects:** ageless wisdom, spirituality, religion. **Awards:** Bethany Link Memorial Scholarship. **Frequency:** annual. **Type:** scholarship. **Publications:** *At the Threshold of the New World.* Book. Alternate Formats: online ● *Meditation Monthly International.* Newsletter. **Circulation:** 800. Alternate Formats: online ● *Spiritual Regeneration.* Book. Alternate Formats: online ● *Sunday Talks Vol. 2, Working on Yourself.* Book. Features a collection of lectures by Rev. Joleen DuBois given on Sundays. **Price:** $18.00/copy. **Advertising:** accepted. **Conventions/Meetings:** annual conference.

Spiritual Understanding

20145 ■ Aetherius Society (AS)
6202 Afton Pl.
Los Angeles, CA 90028
Ph: (323)465-9652
Free: (800)800-1354
Fax: (323)465-9652
E-mail: info@aetherius.org
URL: http://www.aetherius.org
Contact: Dr. George King, Founder
Founded: 1955. **Membership Dues:** full, associate, $55 (annual) ● friend, $10 (annual). **State Groups:** 1. **Local Groups:** 4. **Languages:** Dutch, English, French, German. **Description:** Groups in U.S., England, Canada, Australia, Europe, Ghana, Nigeria, and New Zealand. Teaches the wisdom of the masters of other worlds, such as the spirituality of all things in the Universe including the Earth, the Sun,

and the Galaxy. Strives for peace and enlightenment in the world through prayer, self-development, spiritual healing, and teachings. **Libraries: Type:** reference. **Holdings:** audio recordings, films, photographs, video recordings. **Subjects:** religious. **Departments:** Graphic Arts; Health Foods; Lecture Bureau; Motion Picture; Sound; Spiritual Energy Research and Development; Still Photo; Training Group. **Publications:** *Contacts with the Gods from Space*, quarterly. Book. Answers why UFOs are here, what their message is, and how can all cooperate with the God from Space. **Price:** $14.95/copy. **Circulation:** 900 ● *Cosmic Voice*, quarterly. Journal. Gives regular reports on the cosmic activities of the organization. **Price:** $16.00 /year for nonmembers; included in membership dues. ISSN: 1058-4196 ● *The Holy Mountains of the World*. Book. **Price:** $14.95/copy ● *The Nine Freedoms*. Book. Contains teachings from a Cosmic Master; truths never before revealed on Earth. **Price:** $26.95/copy ● *The Twelve Blessings*. Book. Designed as a potent spiritual practice for all serious students in these vitally important days. **Price:** $16.95/copy ● *Visit to the Logos of Earth*. Book. **Price:** $14.95/copy ● *You Are Responsible* ● *You Too Can Heal*. Book. Lifts the veils of secrecy and mystery, which have long clouded this subject. **Price:** $12.95/copy ● Also produces cassettes, videos, books, catalogs, and other printed material. **Conventions/Meetings:** annual meeting (exhibits).

20146 ■ Association for Spirit at Work (ASAW)
36 Sylvan Hills Rd.
East Haven, CT 06513
Ph: (203)467-9084
Fax: (203)467-8809
E-mail: judi@spiritatwork.org
URL: http://www.spiritatwork.com
Contact: Judith A. Neal PhD, Founder/Exec. Dir.
Founded: 1993. **Membership Dues:** change agent, $89 (annual) ● corporate sponsorship, $5,000-$50,000 (annual). **Multinational. Description:** Represents people and organizations who are interested in the study and practice of spirituality in the workplace. Provides community information and education for those who are integrating their work and their spirituality and for those who are called to support societal transformation through organizational development and change. **Awards:** International Spirit at Work Award. **Frequency:** annual. **Type:** recognition. **Recipient:** to highly successful organizations that explicitly nurture spirituality among employees. **Computer Services:** Mailing lists ● online services, chat. **Publications:** *The Spirit at Work Journal* ● Newsletter. **Price:** included in membership dues.

20147 ■ Church of Spiritual Discovery (CSD)
166 W 72nd St.
New York, NY 10023
Ph: (212)724-4081
Fax: (212)799-8797
Contact: Rev. Mary Blake, Dir.
Founded: 1982. **Members:** 70. **Budget:** $25,000. **Description:** A support group that "celebrates the holiness of life and the greatness of creation." Dedicated to spiritual growth, development of human potential, and expansion of consciousness. Seeks individual and collective involvement with the Spirit. Encourages positive commitment to growth, harmony, and balance of mind, body, and spirit. Conducts classes, counseling sessions, and weekly development circle on such topics as meditation for success. **Publications:** Newsletter, periodic. **Conventions/Meetings:** workshop.

20148 ■ Circle Sanctuary
PO Box 9
Barneveld, WI 53507
Ph: (608)924-2216
Fax: (608)924-5961
E-mail: circle@circlesanctuary.org
URL: http://www.circlesanctuary.org
Contact: Selena Fox, Founder
Founded: 1974. **Membership Dues:** sponsor, $50 (annual) ● benefactor, $1,000 (annual) ● subscrib-

ing, $25 (annual). **Multinational. Description:** Ecospirituality resource center serving Wiccan, Pagan, Shamanic, Goddess Spirituality, and other Nature folk worldwide. Sponsors events and does publishing, networking, education, counseling and Nature preservation. **Libraries: Type:** reference. **Holdings:** audio recordings, books, papers, periodicals, video recordings. **Subjects:** Wiccan religion, Paganism, Nature religions. **Formerly:** Circle Sanctuary Network. **Publications:** *Circle Guide to Pagan Groups*, annual. Directory. Contains more than 500 listings of groups, centers, networks, periodicals, stores, and festivals from throughout North America. **Price:** $18.00 in U.S., Canada and Mexico; $21.00 outside U.S., Canada and Mexico ● *CIRCLE Magazine*, quarterly. Journal. Contains news of contacts, resources, gatherings, notices, artwork, invocations, ritual transcripts, and other information from individuals. **Price:** $19.00/year in U.S.; $20.00/year in Canada and Mexico; $34.00/year in Europe; $38.00/year outside North America and Europe. **Advertising:** accepted. **Conventions/Meetings:** annual Beltane Festival - in early May ● monthly Craftway Circle - meeting, study group for women and men ● annual Earth Day - festival, environmental education day - in April ● monthly Full Moon Circle - meeting, ritual group ● monthly Goddess Circle - meeting, study group for women ● annual Green Spirit Festival - in early August ● annual Pagan Spirit Gathering - festival and conference - in late June ● monthly Sanctuary Days - meeting, volunteer work days ● annual Welcome Fall Festival - in early September ● annual Winter Solstice Pageant - competition, multicultural pageant - in mid-December.

20149 ■ Foundation for a Course in Miracles (FACIM)
41397 Buecking Dr.
Temecula, CA 92590-5668
Ph: (951)296-6261
Fax: (951)296-9117
URL: http://www.facim.org
Contact: Kenneth Wapnick PhD, Pres.
Founded: 1983. **Staff:** 12. **Description:** Presents a spiritual philosophy based on *A Course in Miracles*, a set of three books which the group believes has been "channeled from Jesus" and which is based on the premise that in order to remember God and undo feelings of guilt, one must learn how to forgive others. Focuses on the "healing of relationships," which the group perceives as part of the "miracle" of changing perceptions of ourselves and others. **Libraries: Type:** reference. **Holdings:** 500; audiovisuals, books, periodicals. **Subjects:** spirituality, philosophy, psychology, theology. **Publications:** *A Talk Given On A Course in Miracles* (in Danish, Dutch, English, French, German, Portuguese, and Spanish). Book ● *Forgiveness and Jesus*. Book ● *The Lighthouse*, quarterly. Newsletter. **Price:** free. ISSN: 1060-4987. **Circulation:** 10,000. Alternate Formats: online ● *The Metaphysics of Separation and Forgiveness*. Audiotapes. **Conventions/Meetings:** monthly workshop.

20150 ■ Institute for Spiritual and Environmental Awareness (ISEA)
PO Box 310
Bangor, ME 04402-0310
Contact: Sandra J. Baker-Griffith, Exec.Dir.
Founded: 1995. **Members:** 250. **Membership Dues:** minimum fee, $25 (annual) ● maximum fee, $100 (annual). **Multinational. Description:** Seeks to promote "spiritual environmentalism.". **Libraries: Type:** reference. **Holdings:** archival material, articles, artwork, audiovisuals, books, periodicals. **Subjects:** philosophy, environment, Vedas, nature, animal welfare, conservation, ecology, yoga/meditation, vegetarianism, self-sufficient living, healing.

20151 ■ Interfaith Church of Metaphysics (ICOM)
163 Moon Valley Rd.
Windyville, MO 65783
Ph: (417)345-8411
Fax: (417)345-6668

E-mail: som@som.org
URL: http://www.som.org
Contact: Dr. Laurel Clark, Pres.
Founded: 1976. **Members:** 7,500. **Staff:** 20. **Budget:** $35,000. **Regional Groups:** 2. **State Groups:** 9. **Local Groups:** 15. **Description:** Offers truth, inspiration, and guidance to mankind, and a respect for each individual's right to a choice in his approach to understanding and growth that is compatible to his own temperament and background. Sponsors eight-week study courses on such topics as the significance of dreams, karma indenture, self-development, and spiritual discipline. Maintains speakers' bureau. Conducts charitable activities and children's services. Offers ordained minister training program. **Libraries: Type:** reference. **Holdings:** 13,000; archival material, articles, audio recordings, books, periodicals, video recordings. **Subjects:** holy words, scriptures from world religions. **Computer Services:** Mailing lists. **Formerly:** (1994) International Church of Metaphysics. **Publications:** *The Bible Interpreted in Dream Symbols*. Book ● *Discovering the Kingdom of Heaven*. Book ● *Dreams of the Soul - The Yogi Sutras of Patanjali*. Book. **Price:** $9.95 each ● *Karmic Healing*. Book ● *The Most Beautiful Book in the World* ● *Thresholds*, annual. Journal. **Price:** available to members only. ISSN: 1073-7421. **Circulation:** 3,500. **Advertising:** accepted ● *The Universal Language of Mind*. Book. Interprets the Book of Matthew. **Price:** $13.00 in U.S. ● *When All Else Fails*. Book. **Conventions/Meetings:** annual general assembly - always in Windyville, MO.

20152 ■ International Association for Spiritual Consciousness (IASC)
401 W Intl. Airport Rd., No. 17
Anchorage, AK 99518-1168
Ph: (907)344-5533
E-mail: spiritma@iasc-ak.org
URL: http://www.iasc-ak.org
Contact: Debra R. Lachinski PhD, Pres./CEO
Founded: 1996. **Members:** 25. **Staff:** 5. **Budget:** $50,000. **Languages:** English, Sanskrit, Tibetan. **Description:** Seeks to promote holistic health and personal empowerment. **Libraries: Type:** open to the public. **Holdings:** 900. **Subjects:** metaphysical, mystical, spiritual, philosophy, psychology. **Publications:** *The Eternalist*. Newsletter. Contains schedules for classes, meetings and retreats. **Price:** free for members. **Conventions/Meetings:** monthly board meeting.

20153 ■ Makatab Tarighat Oveyssi Shahmaghsoudi (MTO)
PO Box 5827
Washington, DC 20016
Ph: (202)342-0022
Free: (800)820-2180
Fax: (703)430-6530
E-mail: info@mto.org
URL: http://www.mtoshahmaghsoudi.org
Contact: Salaheddin Ali Nader Shah Angha, Contact
Members: 400,000. **Staff:** 400. **Languages:** Arabic, English, Farsi, French, German, Italian, Spanish. **Description:** Individuals who participate in designated religious and educational activities of Makatab Tarighat Oveyssi Shahmaghsoudi. (M.T.O. Shahmaghsoudi maintains that each individual can attain a knowledge of eternal and immutable Truth through a simultaneous process of self-cognition and annihilation of the self in God.) Provides religious instruction; promotes world peace and tranquility on both the interpersonal and international levels. Conducts research on application of Sufism to many areas of study including humanities, science, and art. Provides children's services; operates placement service; conducts charitable program. Maintains museum and archives. Holds public lectures; local chapters hold seminars and symposia. **Libraries: Type:** open to the public. **Holdings:** 100,000. **Subjects:** Sufism, Islam, philosophy, science, literature. **Computer Services:** database ● mailing lists. **Committees:** Art/Music/Culture/Literature; Counseling; Education; Meditation; Physicians; Psychology; Religion; Science; Translation and Editing; Youth. **Also Known As:** School of Islamic Sufism. **Publications:** Also

publishes books, manuals, and technical dictionary. **Conventions/Meetings:** semiannual convention - always February 4 and November 17 ● triennial International Convention.

20154 ■ Mooncircles
c/o Dana Gerhardt, MA
397 Arnos St.
Talent, OR 97540
E-mail: dana@mooncircles.com
URL: http://www.mooncircles.com
Contact: Dana Gerhardt MA, Contact
Founded: 1984. **Members:** 200. **Membership Dues:** in U.S., $12 (annual) ● outside U.S., $16 (annual). **Staff:** 1. **Description:** Devoted to "rituals and attunements honoring the cycles of the waxing and waning moon." A pen pal newsletter for women seeking others of like-mind. **Telecommunication Services:** electronic mail, info@mooncircles.com. **Formerly:** Circles of Exchange.

20155 ■ Muhyiddin Ibn Arabi Society (MIAS)
PO Box 45
Berkeley, CA 94701-0045
Ph: (510)653-2201
E-mail: mias.usa@ibnarabisociety.org
URL: http://www.ibnarabisociety.org
Contact: Angela Culme-Seymour, Pres.
Founded: 1977. **Membership Dues:** individual, $60 (annual) ● fellow, $85 (annual) ● student, $40 (annual). **Description:** Promotes a greater understanding of the writings of Islamic Mystic and Philosopher IBN Arabi (1165-1240) through study, translation and publication. **Libraries: Type:** open to the public. **Holdings:** 500. **Subjects:** IBN Arabi, his school. **Publications:** Journal, semiannual. **Price:** free for members; $18.00 for nonmembers. **Advertising:** accepted ● Proceedings, annual. **Conventions/Meetings:** annual symposium.

20156 ■ Spiritual Frontiers Fellowship International (SFFI)
PO Box 7868
Philadelphia, PA 19101-7868
Ph: (215)222-1991 (215)222-1994
Fax: (215)222-8459
E-mail: admin@spiritualfrontiers.org
Contact: Rev. Dr. Elizabeth W. Fenske PhD, Exec. Dir.
Founded: 1956. **Members:** 1,300. **Membership Dues:** individual/retiree couple, $50 (annual) ● family, $70 (annual) ● retiree, $40 (annual) ● patron, $100-$999 (annual) ● life, $1,000. **Staff:** 1. **Budget:** $100,000. **Local Groups:** 5. **National Groups:** 5. **For-Profit. Description:** Interfaith group of professional and laypersons. Created "to sponsor, explore, and interpret the growing interest in parapsychological phenomena and mystical experience within and outside organized religion as these experiences relate to mystical prayer, spiritual healing, and continuity of consciousness." Sponsors research programs and offers Prayer-Healing Ministry study courses, retreats, conferences, study tours, newsletters, and journals. **Libraries: Type:** reference; lending. **Holdings:** 18,000; periodicals. **Subjects:** parapsychology, religion, metaphysics, consciousness study, topics in the fields of emphasis. **Computer Services:** Online services. **Committees:** Annual Conference; Leadership Training and Group Organization; Research; Retreats and Seminars; Study Groups. **Affiliated With:** Academy of Spirituality and Paranormal Studies, Inc. **Publications:** *SFFI Newsletter*, semiannual. **Price:** included in membership dues. **Circulation:** 1,100 ● *Spiritual Frontiers Fellowship Thirtieth Anniversary Booklet Series*. Booklets ● *Spiritual Frontiers Journal*, semiannual ● *Spiritual Insights for Daily Living*. Book. **Conventions/Meetings:** annual conference and retreat ● annual conference ● periodic seminar ● periodic tour.

20157 ■ Spiritual Unity of Nations (SUN)
PO Box 9553
Wyoming, MI 49509
Ph: (616)531-1339
Free: (800)704-2324
Fax: (616)531-2294

E-mail: unityofnations@aol.com
URL: http://www.spiritualunityofnations.org
Description: Seeks "unity, harmony, and love among all persons, peoples, and nations". Accepts all religions and philosophies as valid and recognizes each individual's right to "express his or her concept of the Creative Force of the Universe". Encourages individuals to work within their own religious affiliation without dogma. Promotes comparative study of religions and metaphysical seminars, lectures, and conferences. **Publications:** *Revelation for Our Time*. Book. **Price:** $20.00 ● *Sun Up Newsletter*, quarterly. Alternate Formats: online.

20158 ■ Tayu Center (TC)
PO Box 11554
Santa Rosa, CA 95406
Ph: (707)829-9579
E-mail: tayu@sonic.net
URL: http://www.sonic.net/tayu
Contact: Stuart Goodnick, Contact
Founded: 1976. **Description:** A Fourth Way spiritual school founded by Tayu teacher Robert Daniel Ennis. (The Tayu practice is a form of meditation, called Self Observation, that focuses awareness on the workings of the human organism and "opens the way to full and continuous access to the true mind.") Conducts study and work groups, public talks, and residential training programs. Operates a retail bookstore and teashop in Sebastopol, CA. **Formerly:** (1980) Tayu Institute; (1986) Tayu Fellowship. **Publications:** *The Way Fourth*, quarterly. Newsletter. Includes membership news, interviews, poetry, and calendar of events. **Price:** $13.00/year ● *The Way of Tayu*. Booklet ● Audiotapes.

20159 ■ Temple of Man (TM)
c/o George Herms
1437 Cabrillo Ave.
Venice, CA 90291
Ph: (310)276-4768
Contact: George Herms, Dir.
Founded: 1960. **Members:** 411. **Staff:** 2. **Regional Groups:** 2. **Local Groups:** 13. **Description:** Interdenominational association of artists, poets, and professionals who seek to further the spiritual unification of men and women through creative expression. Presents the artistic works of members and nonmembers. Dedicated to the concept that religion *should enable us to liberate ourselves from meaningless dogmas and superstitions and live as free spirits*, and that religion through art should be a unifying element. Believes that *Art is Love is God*, and *The Temple of Man is Within You*. Maintains art collection and poetry library. **Libraries: Type:** reference. **Holdings:** 1,200; artwork, books, clippings, periodicals. **Subjects:** poetry, spiritual writings. **Computer Services:** database, INFO BAZA. **Committees:** Archive of the Origins of California Modern Art (1940s through 1960s). **Publications:** *Black Ace Book*, periodic. Journal. Contains anthology of poetry, and writing, and letters; and photographs. **Price:** $25.00/copy ● *Information Newsletter*, annual ● Books. Contains poetry. ● Catalogs. Contains art. **Conventions/Meetings:** annual Shrine Event - general assembly, art, recent publications, photographs (exhibits) - held in the fall. Los Angeles, CA - **Avg. Attendance:** 50.

20160 ■ Temple of Understanding (TOU)
211 E 43rd St., Ste.1600
New York, NY 10017
Ph: (212)573-9224
Fax: (212)573-9225
E-mail: info@templeofunderstanding.org
URL: http://www.templeofunderstanding.org
Contact: Alison Van Dyk, Chair/Exec. Dir.
Founded: 1960. **Membership Dues:** student, monastic, $15 (annual) ● general, $60 (annual) ● contributing, $100 (annual) ● supporting, $250 (annual) ● sustaining, $750 (annual). **Description:** Develops national and international programs promoting religious understanding among all faiths. **Awards:** Juliet Hollister. **Frequency:** annual. **Type:** recognition. **Recipient:** for promising religious leader, synagogue, church and mosque.

20161 ■ Thanks-Giving Square
PO Box 131770
Dallas, TX 75313-1770
Ph: (214)969-1977
Free: (888)305-1205
Fax: (214)754-0152
E-mail: tgs@thanksgiving.org
URL: http://www.thanksgiving.org
Contact: Tatiana Androsov, Exec. Dir./Pres.
Founded: 1964. **Staff:** 7. **Languages:** English, French, German, Italian, Russian, Spanish. **Multinational. Description:** Celebrates and promotes the value and spirit of thanksgiving for both sacred and secular cultures throughout the world. Maintains chapel, hall, and museum at Thanks-Giving Square in Dallas; conducts group tours; sponsors educational programs, research, and seminars. Funded by the Thanks-Giving Foundation. **Libraries: Type:** reference. **Councils:** Interfaith. **Formerly:** (2003) Center for World Thanksgiving. **Publications:** Brochures ● Newsletter, periodic. **Conventions/Meetings:** periodic Convocation of World Thanksgiving - meeting ● annual National Day of Prayer Interfaith Breakfast - meeting ● annual Thanksgiving Dinner - dinner and seminar.

20162 ■ Truth Missionaries Chapter of Positive Accord (TMC+A)
PO Box 42772
Evergreen Park, IL 60805-0772
Ph: (773)342-0159
Contact: Archbishop Val Matthews, Pres.
Founded: 1970. **Members:** 275. **Regional Groups:** 3. **Description:** Individuals interested in the concept "God includes Goddess", as the group believes the Bible elucidates. The organization endorses the following statement, "Jesus was not God until She initiated him after She resurrected him. She also enabled Jesus' conception; Jesus is savior, humanly, She is co-savior, divinely." Believes in the creed "Try to avoid hypocrisy and Try to treat others as you would find at least tolerable, if so treated by them." Conducts educational, charitable, and research programs. **Libraries: Type:** reference. **Holdings:** books, clippings, periodicals. **Publications:** *God's Real Goddess & Supplemental Topics*. Book ● *TMCA Further in Touch Newsletter*, periodic. **Circulation:** 300. **Conventions/Meetings:** weekly meeting.

20163 ■ Universal Pantheist Society (UPS)
PO Box 3499
Visalia, CA 93278
E-mail: ups@pantheist.net
URL: http://www.pantheist.net/society
Contact: Harold W. Wood Jr., Dir.
Founded: 1975. **Membership Dues:** low income/student/retired, $8 (annual) ● regular, $15 (annual) ● contributing, $20 (annual) ● sustaining, $25 (annual) ● supporting, $50 (annual) ● donor, $100 (annual) ● benefactor, $500 (annual) ● patron, $1,000 (annual). **Description:** Individuals who "identify God with nature rather than an anthropomorphic being," and who see the improvement of their relationship with the natural world as their fundamental religious responsibility. In Universal Pantheism, subscription to any particular creed or belief is replaced by a system of reverent behavior toward the earth. Conducts research, charitable, and educational programs. **Libraries: Type:** reference. **Holdings:** archival material. **Awards:** Spinoza Award. **Frequency:** annual. **Type:** recognition. **Recipient:** for individuals who have made significant contributions to the establishment of a Pantheist world view. **Publications:** *God and Belief: The Pantheist Alternative* ● *Pantheism and Earth Keeping*. **Price:** free ● *Pantheist Vision*, quarterly. Newsletter. **Price:** $15.00/year, for e-mail; $25.00/year, for ground mail. ISSN: 0742-5368 ● *The Pantheist World View*.

20164 ■ Urantia Foundation
533 Diversey Pkwy.
Chicago, IL 60614
Ph: (773)525-3319
Free: (888)URA-NTIA
Fax: (773)525-7739

E-mail: urantia@urantia.org
URL: http://www.urantia.org
Contact: Jay Peregrine, Gen. Mgr./Exec. Dir.
Founded: 1950. **Staff:** 11. **Languages:** English, Finnish, French, Korean, Russian, Spanish. **Multinational. Description:** An educational foundation created to promote, improve, and expand the comprehension and understanding: of cosmology and the relation of the planet to the universe; "the genesis and destiny of man and his relation to God" and the teachings of Jesus Christ. Encourages a realization and appreciation of the "Fatherhood of God and the Brotherhood of Man" in order to increase and enhance the comfort, happiness, and well-being of man. **Publications:** *The Urantia Book* (in English, Finnish, French, Korean, Russian, and Spanish). Alternate Formats: online ● *Urantia Book - Audio Version.* Audiotape ● *Urantia Book - CD ROM Version* (in English, Finnish, and French). Alternate Formats: CD-ROM ● *Urantia Book Concordance* ● *Urantian News,* semiannual. Newsletter. Alternate Formats: online ● Brochures ● Also publishes study aids and various brochures.

20165 ■ Wainwright House (WH)
260 Stuyvesant Ave.
Rye, NY 10580-3115
Ph: (914)967-6080
Fax: (914)967-6114
E-mail: registrar@wainwright.org
URL: http://www.wainwright.org
Contact: Mark Austin, Co-Chm./Pres.
Founded: 1951. **Members:** 500. **Membership Dues:** belong, $75 (annual) ● associate, $150 (annual) ● trustee, $500 (annual) ● grand patron, $1,000 (annual). **Staff:** 10. **Budget:** $800,000. **Description:** Provides a stimulating environment with dedicated leadership for people in search of intellectual, physical, and spiritual growth. Offers residential, nonresidential, public, and nonprofit conferences, seminars, and workshops in such areas as health, psychology, ethics, global issues, spiritual development, and the arts. Maintains bookstore, retreat facility, and meditation room. **Libraries: Type:** reference. **Holdings:** 2,000. **Computer Services:** Mailing lists, of members. **Affiliated With:** Friendship Ambassadors Foundation; YMCA of the USA. **Formerly:** Laymen's Movement for a Christian World; (1983) Wainwright House Center for Development of Human Potential. **Publications:** Newsletter, 3/year. Updates activities at the center. **Circulation:** 800. Alternate Formats: online ● Also publishes fliers and brochures.

Subud

20166 ■ Subud United States of America
14019 NE 8th St., Ste.A
Bellevue, WA 98007
Ph: (425)643-1904
Fax: (425)643-2725
E-mail: subudusa@subudusa.org
URL: http://www.subudusa.org
Contact: Melinda Wallis, Office Mgr.
Founded: 1961. **Members:** 2,500. **Staff:** 3. **Regional Groups:** 7. **Local Groups:** 90. **Description:** Individuals who wish to worship God through the Subud exercise of latihan. (Developed in 1933 by an Indonesian, Mohammed Subuh, latihan is described by the group as "true worship of God through our surrender to His Will," and that it "arises spontaneously from within after contact with the power of God has been received by transmission through a person in whom the power already has been established." According to the group, Subud is not in itself a religion, nor is it a teaching.) Conducts charitable program; compiles statistics. **Libraries: Type:** reference. **Holdings:** archival material. **Computer Services:** database, membership. **Affiliated With:** Subud International Cultural Association - U.S.A.; Subud Youth Association. **Formerly:** Subud North America. **Publications:** *The Inner Life,* periodic. Magazine. Alternate Formats: online ● *Loving Your Fellow Man.* Book. **Price:** $11.00 ● *The Meaning of Subud.* Book. **Price:** $10.20 ● *Songs and Prayers of*

Bapak. Book. **Price:** $8.20 ● *Subud USA Life,* bimonthly ● *Subud USA News,* bimonthly. Newsletter. **Price:** free for members. **Advertising:** accepted. Alternate Formats: online ● Books ● Directory, annual. **Conventions/Meetings:** annual National Congress, business meeting for members and families ● quadrennial World Congress.

Tattooing

20167 ■ Christian Tattoo Association (CTA)
115 W Mulberry St.
Kokomo, IN 46901
Ph: (765)461-3081
E-mail: jayme@xtat.org
URL: http://www.xtat.org
Contact: Jayme Whitaker, Pres.
Multinational. Description: Aims to bring together Christians who are interested in tattoos and the art of tattooing. Promotes the art of tattooing particularly within the Christian community. Brings a relevant Christian voice to the tattoo industry and subculture. Provides a resource and a response to Christians and churches regarding tattoos and tattooing. **Conventions/Meetings:** convention ● workshop and meeting.

Theology

20168 ■ Chatlos Foundation
PO Box 915048
Longwood, FL 32791-5048
Ph: (407)862-5077
E-mail: info@chatlos.org
URL: http://www.chatlos.org
Founded: 1953. **Multinational. Description:** Funds non-profit organizations that provide services to bible colleges/seminaries, religious causes, medical concerns, liberal arts colleges, and social concerns. **Awards: Frequency:** quarterly. **Type:** grant. **Publications:** *Guidelines for Giving.* Brochure.

Theosophical

20169 ■ Theosophical Book Association for the Blind (TBAB)
54 Krotona Hill
Ojai, CA 93023
Ph: (805)614-4977
Fax: (805)646-2121
E-mail: tbab@compuserve.com
URL: http://abacus-es.com/tbab
Contact: Dennis Gottschalk, Dir.
Founded: 1910. **Staff:** 4. **Description:** Publishes, prints, and disseminates Braille and audio-recorded literary materials on theosophy, metaphysics, esoteric philosophy, occultism, meditation, healing, consciousness exploration, and spiritual awareness and perception. Conducts charitable program. **Convention/Meeting:** none. **Libraries: Type:** reference. **Holdings:** 1,700. **Publications:** *The Braille Star Theosophist,* semiannual. **Price:** free. ISSN: 0006-8918. **Circulation:** 5,000.

20170 ■ Theosophical Society in America (TSA)
PO Box 270
Wheaton, IL 60189-0270
Ph: (630)668-1571
Free: (800)669-9425
Fax: (630)668-4976
E-mail: olcott@theosophical.org
URL: http://www.theosophical.org
Contact: Betty Bland, Pres.
Founded: 1886. **Members:** 5,540. **Membership Dues:** basic, $45 (annual) ● student, $24 (annual) ● life, $1,100. **Staff:** 48. **Budget:** $3,000,000. **Local Groups:** 130. **Description:** Forms a nucleus of the universal brotherhood of humanity without distinction of race, creed, sex, caste or color; encourages the comparative study of religion, philosophy, and sci-

ence; investigates unexplained laws of nature and the powers latent in humanity. Holds educational programs and study courses; presents films. Operates Quest Book Shops. **Libraries: Type:** reference. **Holdings:** 20,000; archival material, audiovisuals, books, periodicals. **Subjects:** theosophy, religion, philosophy. **Telecommunication Services:** electronic mail, olcott@theosmail.net. **Departments:** Archives; Bookkeeping; Education; Fieldwork; Information; Membership; National Lodge; Olcott Institute; Public Programs; Quest Book Shop; Quest Books; Quest Magazine; Theosophical Book Gift Institute; Theosophical Publishing House. **Also Known As:** Quest Books; Theosophical Publishing House. **Publications:** *The Messenger,* monthly. Books ● *The Messenger,* bimonthly. Newsletter. Contains membership information. **Price:** included in membership dues; $15.97 for nonmembers. ISSN: 0003-1402. **Circulation:** 4,500 ● *The Quest,* bimonthly. Magazine. Provides articles, book reviews, letters to the editor, and association news. **Price:** included in membership dues; $20.94 /year for nonmembers in U.S.; $31.74 /year for nonmembers outside U.S. and Canada; $27.78 /year for nonmembers in Canada. **Circulation:** 4,500. Alternate Formats: online. **Conventions/Meetings:** annual Social Action as Spiritual Practice - conference - 2007 Nov. 9-11, Atlanta, GA.

20171 ■ United Lodge of Theosophists (ULT)
245 W 33rd St.
Los Angeles, CA 90007
Ph: (213)748-7244
Fax: (213)748-0634
E-mail: inquiry@theosophycompany.org
URL: http://www.theosophycompany.org
Founded: 1909. **Staff:** 9. **State Groups:** 5. **National Groups:** 9. **Languages:** Danish, English, French, Italian, Spanish, Swedish. **Multinational. Description:** School of Theosophy. Works to disseminate the Fundamental Principles of the Philosophy of Theosophy, and the exemplification in practice of those principles. **Libraries: Type:** reference; lending. **Holdings:** 5,000; books. **Subjects:** history, philosophy, religion. **Additional Websites:** http://www.ULT.org, http://www.ult-la.org. **Publications:** *Theosophy,* quarterly. Magazine. Contains information on the theosophical movement. **Price:** $20.00/year. ISSN: 0040-5906. **Circulation:** 800 ● Books ● Magazines ● Also publishes publications list. **Conventions/Meetings:** weekly lecture.

Tithing

20172 ■ Tithing Foundation
c/o Book Center
1100 E 55th St.
Chicago, IL 60615
Ph: (773)256-0681
Fax: (773)256-0688
E-mail: info@tithingfoundation.org
URL: http://www.tithingfoundation.org
Contact: Rev. Robert J. Furreboe, Exec. Dir.
Founded: 1916. **Members:** 15. **Staff:** 2. **Budget:** $50,000. **Description:** Maintains speakers' bureau. Furnishes materials on tithing. **Libraries: Type:** not open to the public. **Holdings:** 50; books. **Subjects:** tithing and stewardship. **Formerly:** (1938) The Layman Tithing Company; (1997) Layman Tithing Foundation. **Publications:** *A Tither's Meditation on the Psalms.* Book. **Price:** $11.00 ● *Tithing Digest,* periodic. Catalog. Includes lists of books, booklets, mailing and bulletin inserts, tapes, videos, buttons and caps available from the organization. **Price:** free. **Circulation:** 10,000 ● Also publishes and distributes literature on tithing. **Conventions/Meetings:** annual board meeting, display of books and pamphlet (exhibits) - April/May.

Trucking

20173 ■ Association of Christian Truckers (ACT)
PO Box 187
Brownstown, IL 62418

Ph: (618)427-3737
Fax: (618)427-3677
E-mail: actangel@frontiernet.net
URL: http://www.associationofchristiantruckers.org/index.shtml
Contact: Kris Tackitt, Chaplain
Founded: 1976. **Description:** Aims to bring Christian trucking professionals together and advance the cause of Christ on the nation's highways. **Publications:** *Wheels Alive*, 8/year. Magazine. **Circulation:** 45,000. **Conventions/Meetings:** One Hour Prayer Service - meeting ● weekly Trucker's Wives and Children Prayer Service - meeting - every Sunday, 1-2 pm.

20174 ■ HMI Ministries
PO Box 8451
Grand Rapids, MI 49518-8451
Ph: (616)455-5760
Free: (800)452-0951
Fax: (616)455-5761
E-mail: info@hmiministries.org
URL: http://www.hmiministries.org
Contact: Raleigh Huls, Founder
Founded: 1974. **Description:** Works "to spread the Word of God to the nation's truck drivers and thereby help lead them to accept Jesus Christ as Lord and Savior". **Publications:** *Homeward Bound*, quarterly. Newsletter. **Price:** free. Alternate Formats: online ● Brochure.

Ultimatism

20175 ■ Ultimatist Religious Bodies on Earth (URBOE)
PO Box 1098
Erie, PA 16512-1098
Fax: (814)454-6029
E-mail: urboe@aol.com
Contact: Ron Hill, VP
Founded: 1983. **Description:** Organizations and individuals who study, practice, promote, and teach Ultimatism, a religious teaching and way of life that helps spiritual persons fully develop intellectually, emotionally and spiritually. Strives to represent to the public Ultimatists' convictions on moral, spiritual, political, economic, social, denominational, and ecumenical matters. Develops and maintains religious, educational, and charitable work; charters churches and fellowship groups; ordains ministers. Provides courses and personal religious counseling; conducts seminars and religious services. Maintains 4000 volume library on religion, philosophy, psychology, and history; compiles organizational and doctrinal information on religious bodies. **Libraries: Type:** reference. **Holdings:** 4,000; artwork, books, periodicals. **Subjects:** spirituality, vegetarianism, meditation, religion, philosophy, theology, pacifism, conscientious objection. **Computer Services:** database ● mailing lists ● online services. **Absorbed:** Ultimatist Life Society. **Publications:** *Ultimatist News*, monthly. Newsletter ● *What Ultimatism Teaches*, monthly ● Also publishes books and correspondence lists. **Conventions/Meetings:** annual meeting.

Unitarian Universalist

20176 ■ Liberal Religious Educators Association (LREDA)
PO Box 691254
San Antonio, TX 78269
Ph: (210)641-7247
E-mail: lreda@uua.org
URL: http://www.uua.org/lreda
Contact: Susan Archer, Pres.
Founded: 1949. **Members:** 550. **Membership Dues:** active voting, $140 ● supportive, $75 ● student, new member, $45 ● institution/organization, $55. **Budget:** $98,000. **Regional Groups:** 12. **Description:** Represents Unitarian-Universalists and other trained persons who are professional religious education directors or ministers of education. Seeks to improve professional standards and practice and enhance the liberal religious education of children and adults through continuing education of its members. Compiles statistics on professional practices and salaries. Provides group health and medical insurance. **Libraries: Type:** reference. **Holdings:** books. **Telecommunication Services:** electronic mail, aekhadr@msn.com. **Committees:** Fahs Lecture; LREDA Integrity Team; Mentoring; Nominating; Representative to UUA Campus Ministry Advisory; Representative to UUA Renaissance Program Advisory; 21st Century. **Funds:** Representative to UUA Annual Program. **Formerly:** (1954) Unitarian Educational Directors Association; (1981) Liberal Religious Education Directors Association. **Publications:** *Liberal Religious Education Journal*, periodic ● *LREDA Newsletter*, periodic. Alternate Formats: online ● *Sabbatical Leave Handbook for Professional Religious Educators and Congregations*. Alternate Formats: online ● Pamphlets. Interprets functions of religious educators. **Conventions/Meetings:** annual conference - usually October ● annual meeting - held each June at Denomination's General Assembly.

20177 ■ Unitarian Universalist Christian Fellowship (UUCF)
PO Box 6702
Tulsa, OK 74156
Ph: (918)691-3223
E-mail: uucfoffice@aol.com
URL: http://www.uuchristian.org
Contact: Rev. Ron Robinson, Exec. Dir.
Founded: 1944. **Members:** 1,100. **Membership Dues:** individual, $50 (annual) ● student, $15 (annual). **Staff:** 1. **Budget:** $65,000. **Local Groups:** 10. **Description:** Unitarian Universalist Christian chapters and individuals. Purposes are: to uphold and promote liberal Christianity within the Unitarian Universalist Association; to service Christian Unitarian Universalists according to their expressed religious needs; to promote the historic Unitarian and Universalist witness and conscience within the Church Universal. Holds seminars, workshops, retreats, and convocations. **Libraries: Type:** reference. **Holdings:** archival material. **Awards:** Clayton Bowen Prize in Biblical Scholarship. **Frequency:** annual. **Type:** monetary. **Formerly:** (1946) Unitarian Christian Advance; (1947) Unitarian Christian Committee; (1969) Unitarian Christian Fellowship. **Publications:** *Good News*, bimonthly. Newsletter. Contains membership activities news. **Price:** included in membership dues. ISSN: 0890-4375. **Circulation:** 1,100 ● *Unitarian Universalist Christian*, annual. Journal. Contains articles on theology, liturgy, church history, and related concerns. Includes book reviews. **Price:** included in membership dues; $30.00 /year for nonmembers. ISSN: 0362-0492. **Circulation:** 1,200. **Advertising:** accepted. Alternate Formats: microform ● Books ● Monographs ● Pamphlets. **Conventions/Meetings:** annual meeting.

20178 ■ Unitarian Universalist Historical Society (UUHS)
PO Box 38
Duxbury, MA 02331-0038
Ph: (781)934-2781
E-mail: revebs@aol.com
URL: http://www.uua.org/uuhs
Contact: Rev. Gordon Gibson, Pres.
Founded: 1978. **Members:** 400. **Membership Dues:** individual, $25 (annual) ● household, $40 (annual) ● student, $15 (annual). **Staff:** 1. **Budget:** $20,000. **Description:** Persons interested in the history of liberal religion. Sponsors educational and research projects and publications. Assists with maintenance of archives library at Harvard Divinity School, a repository for documents relating to both Unitarian and Universalist history. **Libraries: Type:** reference; not open to the public. **Awards: Frequency:** periodic. **Type:** recognition. **Recipient:** for historical research in history of liberal religion. **Affiliated With:** American Historical Association. **Formed by Merger of:** (1978) Universalist Historical Society; Unitarian Historical Society. **Publications:** *Journal of Unitarian Universalist History*, periodic. Contains scholarly articles. **Price:** included in membership dues; $15.00 others. **Circulation:** 500 ● *UUHS News*, periodic. Newsletter. **Con-**

ventions/Meetings: annual meeting, held in conjunction with Unitarian Universalist General Assembly.

20179 ■ Unitarian Universalist Ministers Association (UUMA)
25 Beacon St.
Boston, MA 02108
Ph: (617)848-0498
Fax: (617)848-0973
E-mail: administrator@uuma.org
URL: http://www.uuma.org
Contact: Ken Sawyer, Pres.
Founded: 1961. **Members:** 1,400. **Membership Dues:** regular/associate in U.S. and Canada, $225 (annual) ● candidate in U.S. and Canada, $35 (annual). **Staff:** 1. **Regional Groups:** 23. **Multinational. Description:** Promotes the interests of ministers of the Unitarian Universalist church. **Telecommunication Services:** electronic mail, publications@uuma.org. **Affiliated With:** Unitarian Universalist Association of Congregations. **Publications:** *Handbook on Sabbatical Leaves for Ministers and Congregations*. **Price:** $10.00 each ● *Unitarian Universalism*, annual. Journal. Contains papers on liberal religions themes in U.S. ministries. ● Newsletter, quarterly. Alternate Formats: online ● Videos. **Price:** $20.00 each. **Conventions/Meetings:** annual Ministry Days - meeting - always June.

20180 ■ Unitarian Universalist Service Committee (UUSC)
130 Prospect St.
Cambridge, MA 02139-1845
Ph: (617)868-6600
Free: (800)388-3920
Fax: (617)868-7102
E-mail: programs@uusc.org
URL: http://www.uusc.org
Contact: Dr. Charlie Clements, Pres./CEO
Founded: 1963. **Members:** 20,000. **Membership Dues:** student/youth, $10-$75 (annual) ● senior, $20-$100 (annual) ● general, $40-$250 (annual) ● dual student/youth, $20-$500 (annual) ● dual senior, $40-$1,000 (annual) ● dual general, $75-$2,500 (annual). **Staff:** 40. **Budget:** $4,200,000. **Languages:** Creole, English, French, Spanish. **Description:** International human rights organization. Advances human rights through a potent combination of advocacy, education and grassroots partnership. Focuses on civil and political rights, indigenous rights and women's rights. **Awards:** Banner Award. **Frequency:** annual. **Type:** recognition. **Recipient:** for members ● James Luther Adams Award. **Type:** recognition ● Social Action Leadership Award. **Frequency:** annual. **Type:** recognition. **Recipient:** for volunteer work on human rights issues ● Vision of Justice Sermon Award. **Type:** recognition. **Recipient:** for a sermon that exemplifies UUSC's commitment to justice issues worldwide. **Programs:** Grassroots Organizing; Human Rights; US Volunteer Workcamps; Welfare and Human Rights Monitoring Project; Women's Rights. **Formed by Merger of:** (1963) Unitarian Service Committee; Universalist Service Committee. **Publications:** *Searching for Everardo*. Book. **Price:** $25.00 hardcover ● *Service Committee News*, 3/year. Newsletter. Alternate Formats: online ● *Welfare & Human Rights Monitoring Report* ● *Witness to War*. Book. **Price:** $25.00 hardcover; $10.00 paperback. **Conventions/Meetings:** annual meeting and general assembly, held in conjunction with Unitarian Universalist Association of Boston (exhibits).

20181 ■ Unitarian Universalist Women's Federation (UUWF)
25 Beacon St.
Boston, MA 02108
Ph: (617)948-4692
Fax: (617)742-2402
E-mail: uuwf@uua.org
URL: http://www.uuwf.org
Contact: Nancy W. Van Dyke, Pres.
Founded: 1963. **Members:** 5,000. **Membership Dues:** student/senior, $15 ● regular, $45 ● group, $15 (annual). **Staff:** 6. **Budget:** $400,000. **Local Groups:** 200. **Description:** Federation of women's groups and individual members in local Unitarian

Universalist Churches in the U.S. and Canada. Works for human rights for all, especially rights of women. Promotes: Supreme Court decision in favor of abortion; quality in childcare centers; concern for the family; action on clergy sexual misconduct; prevention of violence against women; work for and with the aging; work in area of women and religion. Sponsors volunteer representatives in Washington, DC. Operates speakers' bureau. Provides training in non-hierarchical leadership. Offers programs and curriculum on women's spirituality and multi-cultural issues. **Awards:** Ministry to Women Award. **Frequency:** annual. **Type:** recognition. **Recipient:** to an individual or group that has ministered to women in an outstanding manner. **Committees:** Margaret Fuller Award for Religious Feminisms Panel; UUWF Grants Panel. **Programs:** Margaret Fuller Award. **Projects:** Margaret Fuller Conversation. **Formed by Merger of:** Alliance of Unitarian Women; Association of Universalist Women. **Publications:** *The Communicator*, 5/year. Newsletter. Focuses on women's issues. **Circulation:** 800. Alternate Formats: online ● Books ● Pamphlets ● Also publishes studies, discussions, curricula and other materials. **Conventions/Meetings:** biennial convention and conference ● meeting ● retreat.

20182 ■ Young Religious Unitarian Universalists (YRUU)

25 Beacon St.
Boston, MA 02108
Ph: (617)948-4350
Fax: (617)367-4798
E-mail: yruu@uua.org
URL: http://www.uua.org/yruu
Contact: Jesse Jaeger, Youth Programs Dir.

Founded: 1981. **Nonmembership. Description:** Local youth groups grouped by districts. Aims to establish youth empowerment, religious and social questioning, cooperation between youth and adult, worship, learning, fellowship, and social action. Offers youth leadership and empowerment training and lends support to various conferences. **Publications:** *Synapse*, semiannual. Magazine. **Price:** free. **Circulation:** 15,000. **Advertising:** accepted. **Conventions/Meetings:** annual Youth Council Meeting, reviews previous mandates and develops new initiative for the coming year.

United Church of Christ

20183 ■ Biblical Witness Fellowship (BWF)

PO Box 102
182 High St.
Candia, NH 03034-0102
Free: (800)494-9172
Fax: (603)483-1035
E-mail: areformer@aol.com
URL: http://www.biblicalwitness.org
Contact: Rev. David Runnion-Bareford, Exec. Dir.

Founded: 1984. **Description:** Clergy and laity of the United Church of Christ interested in the renewal of the church. Provides a ground for witness and renewal at the local level through congregational support and programming; seeks to provide the means of reform beyond the local level. Works to: reverse membership decline; regain lost congregations; expand missionary work; help people organize to witness to the church the concerns of the faith; gain the right of congregations shaping policies of the church; restore the church's historic faith. Opposes the Synod's: inclusive language in church policy; pro-choice stance on abortion; affirmation of theological pluralism; advocacy of non-biblical views in human sexuality; the setting aside of historic affirmation of the primacy of biblical authority. Provides assistance for congregations seeking evangelical pastors. Operates charitable program. **Supersedes:** United Church People for Biblical Witness. **Publications:** *Faithful & Loving Journal*, periodic. Newsletter ● *Issues in Sexual Ethics*. Book ● *The Witness*, periodic. Newsletter. **Conventions/Meetings:** biennial meeting ● seminar.

20184 ■ Evangelical and Reformed Historical Society (ERHS)

555 W James St.
Lancaster, PA 17603
Ph: (717)290-8734 (717)290-8711
Fax: (717)735-8157
E-mail: erhs@lancasterseminary.edu
URL: http://www.erhs.info
Contact: Dianne Russell, Contact

Founded: 1863. **Members:** 300. **Membership Dues:** individual, $25 (annual) ● institution, $50 (annual) ● sponsor, $100 (annual) ● life, $250. **Staff:** 2. **Budget:** $35,000. **Description:** Seeks to stimulate interest in the heritage of the Reformed Church in the United States, the Evangelical Synod of North America, and the Evangelical and Reformed Church. Collects and preserves historical materials of the church and makes it available to all who are interested. Maintains official archival repositories in the Philip Schaff Library, Lancaster Theological Seminary, Lancaster, PA and in the Eden Theological Seminary Library, Webster Groves, MO. **Libraries: Type:** open to the public. **Holdings:** 7,040; archival material, biographical archives, books. **Subjects:** church history, theology, genealogy. **Formerly:** Historical Society of the Reformed Church in the United States; (1965) Historical Society of the Evangelical and Reformed Church; (1989) Evangelical and Reformed Historical Society, United Church of Christ; (1992) Evangelical and Reformed Historical Society and Archives of the United Church of Christ; (1998) Evangelical and Reformed Historical Society, United Church of Christ. **Publications:** *Evangelical and Reformed Historical Society—News*, semiannual. Newsletter. Provides book reviews, calendar of events, and research updates. **Price:** included in membership dues. **Circulation:** 1,000. **Conventions/Meetings:** annual meeting - always fall.

20185 ■ United Church of Christ Justice and Witness Ministries

c/o United Church of Christ
700 Prospect Ave.
Cleveland, OH 44115-1110
Ph: (216)736-3704
Fax: (216)736-3703
E-mail: fordjond@ucc.org
URL: http://www.ucc.org/justice/index.html
Contact: Rev. Diane Ford Jones, Minister

Founded: 1967. **Members:** 350. **Staff:** 38. **Regional Groups:** 6. **Local Groups:** 4. **Description:** Represents ministers of United Church of Christ who work to maximize the impact of African American and other people of color constituencies within the UCC. **Formerly:** United Church of Christ Ministers for Racial and Social Justice; (2001) Commission for Racial Justice; (2001) United Church of Christ Commission for Racial Justice. **Publications:** *Witness for Justice*, weekly. Newsletter. **Price:** $50.00/year. **Conventions/Meetings:** annual meeting - usually June.

Ushers

20186 ■ National United Church Ushers Association of America (NUCUAA)

PO Box 363863
North Las Vegas, NV 89036-7863
Ph: (206)240-1174
E-mail: cemccraneyjr@aol.com
URL: http://www.nationalchurchushers.org
Contact: Charles E. McCraney Jr., Pres.

Founded: 1919. **Members:** 35,000. **Membership Dues:** individual, $3 (annual). **Staff:** 30. **Budget:** $200,000. **Regional Groups:** 4. **State Groups:** 30. **Local Groups:** 154. **Description:** Active church ushers. Conducts ushering education and public relations. Maintains ushering school. Grants scholarship to junior ushers. Sponsors piano, oratorical, essay, and vocal solo competitions; maintains placement service, charitable program, children's services, and speakers' bureau. **Awards:** Usher of the Year Award. **Frequency:** annual. **Type:** recognition. **Recipient:** outstanding service throughout the year. **Computer Services:** database ● mailing lists. **Committees:**

Alumni; Art Craft; Doorkeeper; Education; Health Unit; Historical; Historical Society; LeRoy Johnson Building Fund; Malcom Taylor Music U.S. Department of; Memorial; Outreach; Past National Officers; President's Council; Public Relations; R.E. Harshaw Education Foundation; School of Ushering; Training and Development; Wm. H. Davis Honor Club. **Departments:** Junior and Young People's; Young Adult. **Formerly:** (1980) National United Church Ushers Association. **Publications:** *Convention Journal*, annual ● *National Doorkeeper*, quarterly ● Directory, annual. **Conventions/Meetings:** annual meeting, small vendors - last full week of July.

Vedanta

20187 ■ Ramakrishna - Vivekananda Center (RVC)

17 E 94th St.
New York, NY 10128
Ph: (212)534-9445
Fax: (212)828-1618
E-mail: rvcnewyork@worldnet.att.net
URL: http://www.ramakrishna.org
Contact: Swami Adiswarananda, Minister

Founded: 1933. **Description:** Works as a religious organization that serves as a self-sustaining and accredited unit of the Ramakrishna Order of India. Provides teachings that are based on the system of Vedanta, which combines the religion and philosophy of the Hindus as explained by Sri Ramakrishna (1836-86) and Swami Vivekananda (1863-1902). Holds spiritual services; conducts Sunday services and weekly classes. **Convention/Meeting:** none. **Libraries: Type:** reference. **Holdings:** books, photographs. **Subjects:** Indian and Western thought and culture. **Publications:** *Hinduism: It's Meaning for the Liberation of the Spirit*. Book ● *Man in Search of Immortality: Testimonials from the Hindu Scriptures*. Book ● *Monthly Announcement*. **Price:** free ● *Raja-Yoga* ● *Self-Knowledge* ● *The Upanishads* ● *Vivekananda: A Biography* ● *Vivekananda: The Yogas and Other Works*. Book ● *Vivekananda, World Teacher*. Book. **Price:** $21.99 ● Books.

Vegetarianism

20188 ■ Christian Vegetarian Association

PO Box 201791
Cleveland, OH 44120
Ph: (216)283-6702
Free: (866)202-9170
Fax: (216)283-6702
E-mail: cva@christianveg.com
URL: http://www.all-creatures.org/cva
Contact: Dr. Stephen R. Kaufman MD, Chm.

Founded: 1999. **Members:** 3,200. **Membership Dues:** sustainer, $25 (annual). **Staff:** 2. **Budget:** $40,000. **Languages:** English, French, Spanish. **Multinational. Description:** Promotes vegetarianism as good, responsible Christian stewardship because it protects God's earth, prevents cruelty to God's animals, helps relieve world hunger, and is good for health. **Libraries: Type:** reference; not open to the public; by appointment only. **Holdings:** articles, books, clippings, monographs. **Subjects:** Christianity and vegetarianism. **Publications:** *Honoring God's Creation*. Book. Alternate Formats: CD-ROM.

Waldensian

20189 ■ American Waldensian Society (AWS)

PO Box 398
Valdese, NC 28690
Ph: (336)716-4745
Free: (866)825-3373
E-mail: info@waldensian.org
URL: http://www.waldensian.org
Contact: Rev. Francis J. Rivers Meza, Pres.

Founded: 1906. **Staff:** 1. **Languages:** English, Italian, Spanish. **Description:** Promotes mission solidarity among U.S. church constituencies and Waldensian-Methodist churches in Italy and Latin America. Waldensians claim to be the earliest continuing Protestant group in the world dating back to 1173. **Libraries: Type:** reference. **Telecommunication Services:** electronic mail, frivers@wfubmc.edu. **Formerly:** American Waldensian Aid Society. **Publications:** *Into the Light*, semiannual. Newsletter. Reports on Waldensian ministry overseas. **Price:** free. ISSN: 1092-5708.

Wiccan

20190 ■ Church and School of Wicca
PO Box 297
Hinton, WV 25951-0297
Ph: (304)466-2613
Free: (800)407-6660
Fax: (304)466-1518
E-mail: school@citynet.net
URL: http://www.wicca.org
Contact: Gavin Frost PhD, Founder
Founded: 1967. **Members:** 2,000. **Membership Dues:** student registration, $10 (annual) ● active student, $20 (monthly) ● church, $100 (annual). **Staff:** 3. **Regional Groups:** 20. **Local Groups:** 5. **Multinational. Description:** Disseminates information to the public concerning Witchcraft as a religion. Conducts research and educational programs; compiles statistics; maintains speakers' bureau. **Libraries: Type:** reference. **Holdings:** 30; books. **Subjects:** the occult. **Awards: Type:** scholarship. **Recipient:** for prisoners without funds. **Publications:** *Survival*, bimonthly. Magazine. **Price:** $15.00/year. **Circulation:** 4,000. **Conventions/Meetings:** semiannual Beltane Bash or Samhain Seminar - conference, seminar style, lecture format - April, October ● annual Pagan Pride Day - festival - always September, in Greenbrier State Forest, WV.

20191 ■ The Witches' Voice (TWV)
c/o Wren Walker, Co-Founder
PO Box 4924
Clearwater, FL 33758-4924
E-mail: wren@witchvox.com
URL: http://www.witchvox.com
Contact: Wren Walker, Co-Founder
Founded: 1995. **Description:** Focuses on the understanding of witches and witchcraft.

Women

20192 ■ African-American Women's Clergy Association (AWCA)
Address Unknown since 2007
Founded: 1969. **Members:** 167. **Local Groups:** 20. **Description:** Lay and ordained women clergy. Seeks to promote and encourage the clergy as a profession for women. Operates shelter for homeless and battered women in Washington, DC. **Awards: Type:** scholarship. **Recipient:** for women interested in the clergy ● Social Activist of the Year Award. **Frequency:** annual. **Type:** recognition. **Formerly:** (1992) American Women's Clergy Association. **Conventions/Meetings:** annual meeting.

20193 ■ Aglow International (AI)
PO Box 1749
Edmonds, WA 98020-1749
Ph: (425)775-7282
Free: (800)755-2456
Fax: (425)778-9615
E-mail: aglow@aglow.org
URL: http://www.aglow.org
Contact: Laurie Lischke, Exec. Dir.
Founded: 1967. **Members:** 17,000. **Staff:** 30. **Budget:** $2,800,000. **Regional Groups:** 12. **State Groups:** 145. **Local Groups:** 4,000. **National Groups:** 164. **Languages:** English, French, Spanish. **Multinational. Description:** Aims to "lead women to Jesus Christ and provide opportunities for Christian women to grow in their faith and minister to others". Works to restore and mobilize women around the world. Promotes gender reconciliation in the Body of Christ as God designed and amplifies awareness of global concerns from a Biblical perspective. **Computer Services:** database. **Subgroups:** Bible Studies; Prayer; Support. **Formerly:** (1995) Women's Aglow Fellowship International. **Publications:** *Connection* (in English and Spanish), quarterly. Newsletter. **Price:** free to covenant partners. **Circulation:** 35,000. Alternate Formats: online. Also Cited As: *Fast Access-Connection* ● *Fashioned for Intimacy*. Book. **Price:** $12.00 plus shipping and handling ● *The Journey of a Woman*. Book. Features author's true to life story. **Price:** $12.00 plus shipping and handling ● *Receive All God Has to Give*. Booklet. **Price:** $1.00 plus shipping and handling ● *Where Hearts are Shared Cookbook*. Contains simple recipes and tips for entertainment. **Price:** $18.99 plus shipping and handling. **Conventions/Meetings:** biennial Aglow Conference - always even-numbered years ● biennial international conference - always odd-numbered years.

20194 ■ Black Women in Church and Society (BWCS)
700 Martin Luther King Jr. Dr. SW
Atlanta, GA 30314
Ph: (404)527-5713
Fax: (404)527-5715
E-mail: jharrell@itc.edu
URL: http://www.itc.edu/pages/wsp/WSPBWCS.htm
Contact: Dr. Jacquelyn Grant PhD, Dir./Founder
Founded: 1981. **Staff:** 5. **Nonmembership. Description:** Women in ministry, both ordained and laity. Seeks to provide structured activities and support systems for black women whose goals include participating in leadership roles in church and society, a platform for communication between laywomen and clergywomen. Conducts research into questions and issues pivotal to black women in church and society. Compiles statistics. Maintains a research/resource center and a library with subject matter pertaining to liberation, especially black theology, feminism, and womanist movements. **Computer Services:** Mailing lists. **Programs:** Black Women in Ministry Internship; Ford Fellows in Community Service Ministry Internship; Womanist Scholars. **Conventions/Meetings:** Dialogue - meeting ● semiannual seminar.

20195 ■ Church Women United (CWU)
475 Riverside Dr., Ste.1626a
New York, NY 10115
Ph: (212)870-2347
Free: (800)298-5551
Fax: (212)870-2338
E-mail: cwu@churchwomen.org
URL: http://www.churchwomen.org
Contact: Gail Mengel, Natl. Pres.
Founded: 1941. **Members:** 500,000. **Staff:** 14. **Budget:** $1,300,000. **Regional Groups:** 8. **State Groups:** 52. **Local Groups:** 1,400. **Languages:** English, Spanish. **Description:** Represents ecumenical movement uniting Protestant, Roman Catholic, Orthodox, and other Christian church women into one Christian community. Supports peace, human rights, justice, and the empowerment of women. Works to strengthen the presence of ecumenical women in both the national and global arenas through offices in Washington, DC and the United Nations. Activities include Intercontinental Grants for Mission, Citizen Action, Poverty of Women, and ecumenical and international relations. Sponsors World Day of Prayer (first Friday in March), May Fellowship Day (first Friday in May), and World Community Day (first Friday in November). **Awards:** Intercontinental Grants and Loans. **Frequency:** annual. **Type:** grant. **Recipient:** to projects for women. **Telecommunication Services:** electronic mail, pburkhardt@churchwomen.org. **Committees:** Action/Global Concerns; Ecumenical Leadership Development. **Funds:** Sister Endowment Fund for the Future Campaign. **Formerly:** (1950) United Council of Church Women; (1966) Department of United Church Women of the National Council of Churches; (1969) Church Women United in the U.S.A. **Publications:** *Churchwoman*, quarterly. Magazine. Programmatic resources and news for CWU leaders. **Price:** $10.00/year. ISSN: 0009-6598. **Circulation:** 6,000. **Advertising:** accepted ● *Churchwoman News and Updates*, bimonthly. Newsletter. **Price:** $15.00/year in U.S.; $20.00/year outside U.S. Alternate Formats: online. **Conventions/Meetings:** periodic conference.

20196 ■ International Association of Women Ministers (IAWM)
c/o Rev. Carol S. Brown, Treas.
579 Main St.
Stroudsburg, PA 18360
Ph: (570)421-7751
Fax: (570)421-7718
E-mail: csbrown550@hotmail.com
URL: http://geocities.com/womenministers
Contact: Rev. Carol S. Brown, Treas.
Founded: 1919. **Members:** 400. **Membership Dues:** $5-$40 (annual). **Regional Groups:** 9. **State Groups:** 1. **Local Groups:** 1. **National Groups:** 7. **Multinational. Description:** Women in 20 countries who are licensed, ordained, or otherwise authorized by any evangelical denomination to preach or who are preparing for the ministry. Promotes equal ecclesiastical rights for women and encourages young women to take up ministerial work. Conducts research on the ecclesiastical status of women. **Additional Websites:** http://www.womenministers.org. **Telecommunication Services:** electronic mail, iawmpage@aol.com. **Publications:** *Woman's Pulpit*, quarterly. Newsletter. Covers developments affecting the role of women in organized religion. **Price:** included in membership dues; $15.00 /year for libraries. ISSN: 0043-7397. **Circulation:** 450. **Conventions/Meetings:** annual general assembly.

20197 ■ International Disciples Women's Ministries (IDWM)
PO Box 1986
Indianapolis, IN 46206
Ph: (317)713-2679 (317)713-2663
Free: (888)346-2631
Fax: (317)635-4426
E-mail: odw@dhm.disciples.org
URL: http://www.discipleswomen.org
Contact: Adonna Bowman, Sec.-Treas.
Founded: 1949. **Members:** 80,000. **Staff:** 3. **Budget:** $200,000. **Regional Groups:** 35. **Local Groups:** 2,354. **Multinational. Description:** Women who are members of the Christian Church (Disciples of Christ) and others who accept the purpose of the DWM. Administered by The Office of Disciples Women, Division of Homeland Ministries, of the Christian Church (Disciples of Christ) in the U.S. and Canada. "Provides opportunities for spiritual growth, enrichment, education, and creative ministries to enable women to develop a sense of personal responsibility for the whole mission of the Church of Jesus Christ", through a program of study, worship, and service and through preparation of women for fuller participation in the total church life. Provides materials to local groups for programs on topics such as stewardship of life, Christian social relations, local church concerns, and the world mission of the church. **Programs:** Cabinet and Executive; Developing; Leader Development; Organizational Resources; Social Action Involvement; Status of Women. **Formerly:** (2006) International Christian Women's Fellowship. **Publications:** *Called, Gifted and Sent*, annual. Manual. Serves as a leadership and programming manual for disciples women. ● *World CWF Newsletter*, semiannual ● Brochures ● Yearbook, annual. **Conventions/Meetings:** quadrennial assembly.

20198 ■ MOMS in Touch International (MITI)
PO Box 1120
Poway, CA 92074-1120
Ph: (858)486-4065
Free: (800)949-MOMS
Fax: (858)486-5132
E-mail: info@momsintouch.org
URL: http://www.momsintouch.org
Contact: Fern Nichols, Pres./Founder
Founded: 1984. **Staff:** 17. **Regional Groups:** 32,000. **Multinational. Description:** Encourages mothers and others to meet and to pray for children and schools; to be a positive influence; to support

public and private schools; and to pray that schools may be guided by biblical values and high moral standards. **Publications:** *Heart to Heart from MOMS in Touch*, 3/year. Newsletter. **Circulation:** 48,000. Alternate Formats: online ● *Leadership Newsletter*. Alternate Formats: online ● Booklet (in Arabic, Chinese, English, French, German, Italian, Portuguese, Romanian, Russian, Spanish, Swahili, and Swedish). **Price:** $5.00 ● Brochure. **Conventions/Meetings:** conference, covers the topic of leadership ● annual retreat.

20199 ■ National Council of Churches - Women in Ministry Group
Address Unknown since 2007
Founded: 1973. **Members:** 12. **Staff:** 1. **Budget:** $20,000. **Description:** National denominational staff who represent the interests of women in leadership positions within a church. Works to eliminate discrimination, sexual harassment, and other employment-related offenses against women working in the church. Acts as a forum for discussion among staffs who provide denominational services to female clergy. Promotes programs to bring women seminarians together ecumenically. Conducts research programs. Compiles statistics. **Publications:** none. **Subgroups:** Women in Ministry. **Formerly:** National Council of Churches Commission on Women in Ministry. **Conventions/Meetings:** semiannual Women's Interseminary Conference.

20200 ■ Re-Formed Congregation of the Goddess - International (RCG-I)
PO Box 6677
Madison, WI 53716
Ph: (608)226-9998
E-mail: rcgi@rcgi.org
URL: http://www.rcgi.org
Contact: Jade River, Contact
Founded: 1982. **Members:** 2,010. **Staff:** 3. **Description:** Women who have signed an Affirmation of Women's Spirituality and define themselves as being on a positive path of spiritual growth. Acts as a network for the exchange of information and ideas; provides support for women with similar interests. **Also Known As:** (2002) Of a Like Mind. **Publications:** *Of A Like Mind*, quarterly. Newspaper. Covers wellness, astrology, tarot, psychic development, dreams, herbs, ethics, politics, the Craft, herstory, etc. Includes book reviews. **Price:** $5.00/sample copy. **Circulation:** 10,000. **Advertising:** accepted. **Conventions/Meetings:** annual Hallows Gathering - conference ● annual Priestess Gathering - conference, for women involved in goddess spirituality (exhibits).

20201 ■ Women Church Convergence (WCC)
c/o Bridget Mary Meehan
5856 Glen Forest Dr.
Falls Church, VA 22041
Ph: (703)671-1972 (703)283-2929
Fax: (703)379-2487
E-mail: sofiabmm@aol.com
URL: http://www.women-churchconvergence.org
Contact: Bridget Mary Meehan, Contact
Founded: 1977. **Members:** 2,000. **Description:** National Catholic organizations concerned with the empowerment of women in society and the church. Seeks to create a political base that will bring a "gospel perspective" to issues of racism, classism, and sexism in the institutional church. Works to make women aware of the Catholic Church's stance on these issues. **Libraries: Type:** reference. **Holdings:** archival material, articles. **Telecommunication Services:** electronic mail, kimhealth@earthlink.net. **Committees:** Oral History; Pentecost Liturgy. **Formerly:** (1988) Women in the Church Coalition. **Conventions/Meetings:** quadrennial conference ● semiannual meeting.

20202 ■ Women In Conscious Creative Action (WICCA)
PO Box 5296
Eugene, OR 97405
Ph: (541)485-3654
Fax: (541)485-3654

E-mail: normahp@iglide.net
URL: http://www.wiccawomen.com
Contact: Rev. Norma Joyce, Priestess
Founded: 1983. **Membership Dues:** regular, $13 (monthly). **Staff:** 3. **Regional Groups:** 2. **Description:** Seeks to promote the creative spiritual powers of women. Conducts educational programs; maintains speakers' bureau. **Awards:** Staff Carrier. **Frequency:** annual. **Type:** recognition. **Formerly:** Women In Constant Creative Action. **Publications:** *On Wings*, bimonthly. Newsletter. **Price:** $15.00/year. **Conventions/Meetings:** annual Celebration Gathering - meeting.

20203 ■ Women's Alliance for Theology, Ethics and Ritual (WATER)
8121 Georgia Ave., Ste.310
Silver Spring, MD 20910
Ph: (301)589-2509
Fax: (301)589-3150
E-mail: water@hers.com
URL: http://www.hers.com/water
Contact: Ms. Mary E. Hunt PhD, Co-Dir.
Founded: 1983. **Members:** 2,000. **Membership Dues:** $40 (annual). **Staff:** 3. **Languages:** English, Spanish. **Description:** Participants include ministers, members of religious communities, and individuals seeking spiritual renewal from a feminist and liberation perspective. Promotes religious education inclusive of women's experiences and viewpoints of spirituality. Offers programs, projects and publications related to feminist issues in religion. Also offers special liturgies and rituals and counseling. Sponsors study groups. Provides consulting services. **Libraries: Type:** by appointment only; lending; open to the public. **Holdings:** 5,000. **Subjects:** feminist issues in religion. **Computer Services:** Mailing lists. **Additional Websites:** http://www.his.com/water. **Publications:** *Return Blessings* ● *Waterwheel*, quarterly. Newsletter. ISSN: 0898-6606 ● *Women and the Gospel Traditions—Feminist Celebrations* ● *Women Crossing Worlds*, periodic. Directory ● *Women of Fire—A Pentecost Event* ● *Women's Rites* ● Audiotapes. **Conventions/Meetings:** periodic conference.

20204 ■ Women's Missionary Society, AME Church (WMS)
1134 11th St. NW
Washington, DC 20001
Ph: (202)371-8886
Fax: (202)371-8820
E-mail: webmaster@wms-amec.org
URL: http://www.wms-amec.org
Contact: Mrs. Jamesina M. Evans, Intl. Pres.
Founded: 1944. **Members:** 800,000. **Staff:** 3. **National Groups:** 20. **Multinational. Description:** Women members of the African Methodist Episcopal Church. Seeks to help each woman and youth grow in the knowledge and experience of God through his son Jesus Christ. Seeks fellowship with women in other lands. Provides opportunities and resources to meet the changing needs and concerns of women and youth through intensive training, recruitment, and Christian witnessing. Sponsors administrative retreats, health institutes, health initiatives focusing on Breast Cancer, Prostate Cancer, etc., AIDS, etc., Sojourner Project, international exchanges, missionaries, leadership training programs, and educational programs for religious leaders. Operates women's information bureau; compiles statistics. Organizes charitable activities; offers children's services. **Libraries: Type:** reference. **Holdings:** archival material, photographs. **Subjects:** history, constitutions and bylaws. **Awards:** The President's Award. **Frequency:** annual. **Type:** recognition. **Divisions:** Young People's and Children. **Affiliated With:** Bread for the World; Children's Defense Fund; Church Women United; National Association for the Advancement of Colored People; United Nations. **Formed by Merger of:** Women's Parent Mite Missionary Society; Women's Home and Foreign Missionary Society. **Publications:** *Inspirational Preparatory Workbook* ● *Missionary Magazine*, 9/year ● *President's Newsletter (Missionary Alert)*, quarterly ● *Women's Missionary Society Handbook* ● *Young People's Division Newsletter*, quarterly ● Pamphlets

● Also publishes resources guides and study books. **Conventions/Meetings:** competition ● quadrennial convention (exhibits).

20205 ■ Women's Spirituality Forum (WSF)
PO Box 11363
Oakland, CA 94611
Ph: (510)444-7724 (510)893-3097
Fax: (510)444-7724
Contact: Zsuzsanna Budapest, Pres./Chief Exec.
Founded: 1971. **Membership Dues:** regular, $13 (annual). **Staff:** 3. **Description:** Seeks to bring women's spirituality into the mainstream and feminist awareness. Promotes "the female side of one's concept of god, natural laws, and the empowerment of women". Conducts classes and workshops. Performs rites of passage, blessings, memorials, and other community services. Provides telephone inquiries and referrals. **Computer Services:** Mailing lists. **Formerly:** (1989) Susan B. Anthony Women's Spirituality Education Forum. **Conventions/Meetings:** annual Goddess 3K - festival, with art, music, workshops, rituals (exhibits).

20206 ■ World Day of Prayer International Committee (WDPIC)
475 Riverside Dr., Rm. 729
New York, NY 10115
Ph: (212)870-3049
Fax: (212)864-8648
E-mail: wdpic@worlddayofprayer.net
URL: http://www.worlddayofprayer.net
Contact: Eileen King, Exec. Dir.
Founded: 1967. **Staff:** 2. **Regional Groups:** 100. **Description:** Christian women united to observe a common day of prayer conducted on the first Friday in March. Through World Day of Prayer, women "affirm their faith in Jesus Christ; share their hopes and fears, their joys and sorrows, their opportunities and needs". Encourages women to "become aware of the whole world and no longer live in isolation; to share the faith experience of Christians in other countries and cultures; to take up the burdens of other people and pray with and for them; to become aware of their talents and use them in the service of society". Affirms "that prayer and action are inseparable and that both have an imponderable influence in the world". **Formerly:** (2002) International Committee for World Day of Prayer. **Publications:** *World Day of Prayer Journal*, annual. Contains reports on World Day of Prayer services. **Price:** $4.00. **Conventions/Meetings:** quadrennial meeting.

Writers

20207 ■ Jerry B. Jenkins Christian Writers Guild
5525 N Union Blvd., Ste.200
Colorado Springs, CO 80918
Ph: (719)495-5177
Free: (866)495-5177
Fax: (719)495-5181
E-mail: contactus@christianwritersguild.com
URL: http://www.christianwritersguild.com
Contact: Ms. Kerma Murray, Operations Dir.
Founded: 1965. **Members:** 1,800. **Membership Dues:** regular, $149 (annual). **Staff:** 50. **For-Profit. Multinational. Description:** Exists to train, equip and support writers who desire to promote a Biblically based, Christian worldview through their writing. **Formerly:** (2001) Christian Writers Guild. **Conventions/Meetings:** annual Writing for the Soul Conference, open to the public.

Yoga

20208 ■ 3HO Foundation
6 Narayan Ct.
Espanola, NM 87532
Ph: (505)367-1326
Free: (888)346-2420
Fax: (505)753-1999

E-mail: yogainfo@3ho.org
URL: http://www.3ho.org
Contact: Yogi Bhajan, Founder
Founded: 1969. **Members:** 265,000. **Description:** Represents students and teachers of Kundalini Yoga, which includes all types of Yoga, who practice the "Healthy, Happy, Holy way of life" as taught by Yogi Bhajan. Provides nursery school education as well as sponsors teacher training courses. Provides lectures and demonstrations of the Kundalini Yoga technique; teaches gourmet vegetarian cooking. Has certified government-funded drug rehabilitation center in Tucson, AZ. Operates Kundalini Research Institute to investigate all aspects of the drug rehabilitative and other beneficial aspects of Kundalini Yoga. Also offers legal services and operates free food kitchens. Maintains women's division, Grace of God Movement for the Women of the World (see separate entry). **Publications:** *Beads of Truth*, quarterly. Magazine ● *Experience of Consciousness* ● *Guru Nanak, Guru for the Aquarian Age* ● *Keeping Up Connections*, quarterly. Includes Yoga technology, excerpts of lectures by Yogi Bhajan and recipes. ● *Peace Lagoon* ● *Teachings of Yogi Bhajan*. **Conventions/Meetings:** annual Training Camp - meeting, for women - always summer, Espanola, NM ● semiannual Yoga Conference - always June or July, Espanola, NM, and December, Orlando, FL.

20209 ■ Agni Yoga Society (AYS)
319 W 107th St.
New York, NY 10025-2799
Ph: (212)864-7752
Fax: (212)864-7704
E-mail: info@agniyoga.org
URL: http://www.agniyoga.org
Contact: Edgar Lansbury, Pres.
Founded: 1946. **Members:** 600. **Membership Dues:** associate, $25 (annual) ● contributing, $50 (annual) ● patron, $100 (annual). **Staff:** 5. **Budget:** $50,000. **Description:** "Promotes study and research in Eastern philosophy and comparative religion." Encourages study of esoteric literature and Eastern sources; associated with the Nicholas Roerich Museum. **Convention/Meeting:** none. **Telecommunication Services:** electronic mail, director@agniyoga.org.

20210 ■ Ananda Marga (AM)
97-38 42nd Ave., 1F
Corona, NY 11368
Ph: (718)898-1603
Fax: (718)898-1604
E-mail: info@anandamarga.org
URL: http://www.anandamarga.org
Contact: Ramananda Avadhuta, Pres.
Founded: 1955. **Members:** 450. **Regional Groups:** 16. **State Groups:** 50. **Local Groups:** 100. **Multinational. Description:** Serves as a "global socio-spiritual movement which teaches that it is the duty of every individual to use all of his or her potential for the all-around advancement of one's self and the society as a whole." Provides free instruction in meditation and yoga practices. Service projects have included extensive disaster relief locally and globally in cooperation with the American Red Cross (see separate entry) and other agencies; community food and nutrition projects; prison projects; group homes for teenagers and women ex-offenders; ecological community development; co-ops and schools. Provides traveling missionaries and teachers of meditation and related spiritual practices. Sponsors speakers' bureau. **Libraries: Type:** reference. **Holdings:** 2,500. **Subjects:** spirituality, humanities, arts, sciences. **Departments:** Disaster Relief; Education; Medical; Permanent Relief; Prevention of Cruelty to Animals and Plants; Renaissance Artists and Writers Association; Renaissance Universal; Social Security; Women's Welfare. **Formerly:** (1974) Ananda Marga Yoga Society. **Publications:** *Ananda Marga Review*, quarterly ● *Baba's Grace: A Guide for Human Conduct* ● *The Circle of God* ● *Discourses on Tantra*, *Namah Shiva Shantaya* ● *Namami Krsna Sundaram* ● *New Renaissance*, quarterly. Magazine. **Price:** $15.00/year. Alternate Formats: online ● *New Renaissance News*. Newsletter. Alternate Formats: online ●

Proutist Economics: The Liberation of Intellect and Neo-Humanism ● *The Spiritual Philosophy of Shrii Shrii Anandamurti: A Commentary* ● *What's Wrong With Eating Meat* ● *Yoga for Health: Yoguic Treatments and Natural Remedies*. **Conventions/Meetings:** semiannual meeting - always July and December, Willow Springs, MO.

20211 ■ Eureka Society (ES)
PO Box 3117
Montrose, CO 81402-3117
E-mail: info@eurekasociety.com
URL: http://www.eurekasociety.com
Contact: Bruce K. Avenell, Dir./Founder
Founded: 1969. **Members:** 95. **Membership Dues:** regular, $45 (monthly). **Staff:** 4. **State Groups:** 7. **Description:** Represents individuals seeking spiritual growth through a self-directed, nondevotional meditation program. Promotes Elan Vital system of meditation, which involves some advanced but little-known yoga exercises; Elan Vital does not espouse any one philosophy, but seeks the "truth and beauty of all religions." Develops audiovisual aids for introductory talks and as instructional materials for students; prepares members for public speaking; conducts children's services, group holiday gatherings, and other social events; holds weekly group meditation meetings. Is currently adapting program for telecommunications access. **Telecommunication Services:** electronic mail, bka@eurekasociety.com. **Publications:** *A Reason for Being*. Booklet. **Price:** $6.95 ● *Dragon Master* ● *Effects of the Environment on Your Spiritual Structure*. Booklet ● *Elan Vital Communicator*, bimonthly ● *Escape to Immortality*. Book. **Price:** $19.95. Alternate Formats: CD-ROM ● *Sexual Magic: The Energy Potential of Intimate Relationship*. Booklet. **Price:** $6.95 ● *Silver Sun*, quarterly. Newsletter ● *Spectrums and Dimensions*, monthly. Newsletter. Alternate Formats: online. **Conventions/Meetings:** annual retreat - always Mt. Shasta, CA.

20212 ■ Self-Realization Fellowship (SRF)
3880 San Rafael Ave., Dept. 9W
Los Angeles, CA 90065-3298
Ph: (323)225-2471
Fax: (323)225-5088
URL: http://www.yogananda-srf.org
Contact: Sri Daya Mata, Pres.
Founded: 1920. **Description:** Persons interested in scientific practice of yoga "to attain direct personal experience of God." Maintains temples and centers throughout the world; trains SRF teachers in monastic order; supplies 3 1/2 year series of lessons to members; operates day and residential grade schools, high schools, colleges, free medical dispensary, and hospital in India. **Publications:** *Center Bulletin*, quarterly ● *Jahresheft*, annual ● *Self-Realization Fellowship Lessons*, biweekly ● *Self-Realization Magazine*, quarterly ● Also publishes books and recordings. **Conventions/Meetings:** annual meeting - usually Los Angeles, CA.

20213 ■ Sri Aurobindo Association (SAA)
PO Box 163237
Sacramento, CA 95816
Ph: (209)339-3710
Fax: (209)339-3715
E-mail: saa@collaboration.org
URL: http://www.collaboration.org
Contact: David Hutchinson, Pres.
Founded: 1976. **Members:** 200. **Budget:** $6,000. **Description:** Aims to further the work and projects related to the spiritual vision of a transformed humanity as espoused by Sri Aurobindo. Sri Aurobindo (1872-1950) was an English-educated political activist and author whose spiritual experiences changed his life. With the help of Mira Richard (1878-1973), known as Mother, Aurobindo taught integral yoga, which includes traditional forms of yoga and the psychology of the internal psychic self. **Formerly:** (1987) Matagiri Sri Aurobindo Center. **Publications:** *Collaboration*, 3/year. Journal. Contains articles and essays related to integral yoga. **Price:** $20.00/year in U.S.; $32.00/year outside U.S.; $40.00/year for

patron. ISSN: 0164-1522. **Circulation:** 320. Alternate Formats: online. **Conventions/Meetings:** annual conference.

20214 ■ Yoga Research Foundation (YRF)
569 SW 102 Ave.
Miami, FL 33143
Ph: (305)666-2006
E-mail: orderyoga@bellsouth.net
URL: http://www.yrf.org
Contact: Swami Jyotirmayananda, Founder
Founded: 1969. **Membership Dues:** regular, $20 (annual). **Description:** Serves as an international movement in "elevating the consciousness, alleviating suffering and enriching the lives of all humanity" through Integral Yoga. (Integral Yoga, a modern method for integrating the personality, combines the practices of the four major yogas: Raja Yoga, the Yoga of Meditation; Bhakti Yoga, the Yoga of Devotion; Karma Yoga, the Yoga of Action; Jnana Yoga, the Yoga of Wisdom.) The foundation believes that Integral Yoga can provide "a basis for upgrading the cultural growth of humanity while bringing about a worldwide level of social and religious harmony". Conducts regular classes in teaching of yoga, vedanta, and Indian philosophy. Sponsors children's yoga classes and daily lectures. Offers work-study program. **Libraries: Type:** reference. **Holdings:** audio recordings, books. **Subjects:** yoga. **Formerly:** International Yoga Society. **Publications:** *International Yoga Guide*, monthly. Magazine. **Price:** $15.00/year. **Circulation:** 1,000 ● Articles. Alternate Formats: online ● Publishes over 30 books.

Youth

20215 ■ American Youth Foundation (AYF)
8706 Manchester Rd., Ste.102
St. Louis, MO 63134
Ph: (314)963-1321 (603)539-6607
Fax: (314)963-9243
E-mail: kelly.ethington@ayf.com
URL: http://www.ayf.com
Contact: Anna Kay Vorsteg, Dir. of Development and Alumni Relations
Founded: 1925. **Staff:** 38. **Budget:** $5,000,000. **Description:** Develops leadership in youth and the adults and institutions that serve young people by helping them achieve their personal best, live balanced lives, and serve others. Maintains Miniwanca in Shelby, MI, and Merrowvista Education Center in Tuftonboro, NH. Programs include Leadership Compact, high school program and residential camping. Inspires people to discover and develop their personal best, to seek balance in mental, physical, social and spiritual living and to make a positive difference in their communities and in the wider world. **Awards:** I Dare You Leadership Award. **Frequency:** annual. **Type:** recognition. **Recipient:** for high school junior who has demonstrated leadership potential, balanced living, and personal integrity ● I Dare You Scholarship. **Frequency:** annual. **Type:** scholarship. **Recipient:** for a youth who has demonstrated great servant leadership. **Committees:** Merrowvista Advisory. **Councils:** Miniwanca Advisory. **Affiliated With:** Association for Experiential Education; National Association of Secondary School Principals. **Publications:** *The Founder Fire*, 3/year. Newsletter. Provides information for alumni, donors, and volunteers. **Circulation:** 25,000. Alternate Formats: online ● Publications describing programs. **Conventions/Meetings:** Leadership Conference - 3 in the summer.

20216 ■ Awana Clubs International
1 E Bode Rd.
Streamwood, IL 60107-6658
Ph: (630)213-2000
Free: (866)292-6227
Fax: (877)292-6232
E-mail: customerservicehelp@awana.org
URL: http://www.awana.org
Contact: Jack D. Edgar, Pres./CEO
Founded: 1950. **Members:** 1,000,000. **Membership Dues:** registration, $95 (annual). **Staff:** 250. **Re-**

gional Groups: 10,972. State Groups: 50. Multinational. Description: Serves as youth ministry committed to "reaching boys and girls with the gospel of Christ and training them to serve Him". Awards: Citation Award. Frequency: annual. Type: recognition. Recipient: for outstanding achievement ● Meritorious Trophy. Frequency: annual. Type: recognition. Recipient: for outstanding achievement ● Timothy Trophy. Frequency: annual. Type: recognition. Recipient: for outstanding achievement. Programs: Cubbies; Evangelism; JV; Sparks; T0mp;T; Training; 24-7. Formerly: Awana Youth Association. Publications: Awana Family Connection, monthly. Newsletter. Price: free. Alternate Formats: online ● Parent Pause, monthly. Newsletter. Features parenting tips and family centered activities. Price: free. Alternate Formats: online ● Annual Report, annual.

20217 ■ CSB Ministries (CSB)
PO Box 150
Wheaton, IL 60189
Ph: (630)424-1330
Free: (800)815-5573
Fax: (630)424-1318
E-mail: office@csbministries.org
URL: http://www.csbministries.org
Contact: Mr. Joe Coughlin, Founder
Founded: 1937. Membership Dues: organization, $100 (annual). Staff: 16. Local Groups: 350. Description: Works with local evangelical, protestant churches through two distinct divisions: Christian Service Brigade and Girls Alive! Provides Christ-centered weekday programs whose aim is to "win boys and girls to Christ, guide them in personal study of the Word of God, and train them in Christian living". Gears to meet the needs of youth for physical, mental, social, spiritual and leadership development through such activities as weekly meetings, devotions and achievement; both programs are action-oriented and make God's word the basis for development; a father-son program for first and second grade boys helps prepare them for the give and take of group activity while giving fathers an opportunity to spend meaningful and constructive time with them. Provides standards, curriculum and assistance to local church leaders. Sponsors leadership and training classes conducted by its field staff. Conducts 13 summer camps. Computer Services: database, membership ● mailing lists. Programs: Battalion; Girls Alive; Stockade; Tadpoles; Tree Climbers. Formerly: (2002) Christian Service Brigade. Publications: Also publishes other educational materials for leaders. Conventions/Meetings: weekly meeting, Battalion (boys grades 7-12), Brigade Air (grades 9-12), Stockade (boys grades 3-6), Girls Alive (girls, grades 1-6), Tree Climbers (boys grades 1-2), Tadpoles (pre-school).

20218 ■ National Network of Youth Ministries (NNYM)
12335 World Trade Dr., Ste.16
San Diego, CA 92128
Ph: (858)451-1111 (510)583-0430
Fax: (858)451-6900
URL: http://youthworkers.net
Contact: Doug Tegner, Exec. Dir.
Founded: 1981. Description: Promotes spiritual growth through youth ministry. Councils: Ministry. Publications: Network Magazine, quarterly. Alternate Formats: online ● Take5, monthly. Newsletter. Alternate Formats: online ● Youth Ministry Yellow Pages, annual. Directory. Alternate Formats: online.

20219 ■ Pioneer Clubs (PC)
PO Box 788
Wheaton, IL 60189-0788
Ph: (630)293-1600
Free: (800)694-2582
Fax: (630)293-3053
E-mail: info@pioneerclubs.org
URL: http://www.pioneerclubs.org
Contact: Mr. J. Duane Cheek, Marketing Mgr.
Founded: 1939. Members: 125,000. Staff: 37. Local Groups: 2,500. Multinational. Description: Works as a church-sponsored midweek club program for boys and girls age two through grade 12, is the program of choice for more than 2,500 churches across the country. Each week this Christ-centered program integrates spiritual and personal development; emphasizes evangelism and discipleship; and gives children opportunities to learn new skills, make friends, have fun and develop Christian values that affect every area of their lives. The organization is headquartered in Wheaton, IL, and has served churches across North America with effective and educationally sound programs. Awards: Virginia C. Patterson Continuing Education Fund. Frequency: annual. Type: scholarship. Recipient: to a high school graduate who demonstrates both participation and leadership experience in a local pioneer clubs program, as well as service in local church, school, and community. Divisions: Camp Cherith. Also Known As: Pioneer Girls, Pioneer Boys. Formerly: (1941) Girls' Guild; (1980) Pioneer Girls. Publications: InContact, 3/year. Newsletter. Gives news about the club's activities and fundraising progress. ● Kids Count! Children's Ministry eNewsletter, 10/year, every month except December and July. Provides timely tips and tools for those working in the children's ministry field. Available in electronic format only. Alternate Formats: online ● Pioneer Clubs Leadership eNewsletter, monthly. Newsletters. Provides timely tips and tools for Pioneer Clubs leaders. Available in electronic format only. Alternate Formats: online ● Pioneer Clubs Ministry Resources Catalog, annual. Describes and pictures club curriculum, leader resource books, club promotion resources, and gear and accessories. Alternate Formats: online ● Annual Report, annual.

20220 ■ Teen Challenge International (TC)
PO Box 1015
Springfield, MO 65801
Ph: (417)862-6969
Fax: (417)862-8209
E-mail: tcusa@teenchallengeusa.com
URL: http://www.teenchallengeusa.com
Contact: Mike Hodges, Pres.
Founded: 1958. Members: 2,500. Staff: 6. Budget: $800,000. Regional Groups: 8. State Groups: 43. Description: Aims to evangelize persons experiencing problems that significantly affect their lives. Seeks to guide young people in Christianity so that they can apply biblical principles to vocations and family, church, and social relationships, and restore their social, spiritual, and physical well-being. Program participants undergo five phases of rehabilitation: confrontational evangelism through street meetings, prison services, substance abuse prevention programs, and other assistance-oriented activities; crisis intervention and referral; induction, involving 10-12 weeks of Bible study and character development; residential program, involving 8-12 months of Christian instruction and academic and vocational improvement; re-entry, during which the local center provides assistance such as temporary housing, personal and family counseling, and help in securing employment. Maintains speakers' bureau. Local centers offer telephone and drop-in counseling. Participants and members make radio and television appearances. Associated with the Division of Home Missions within the General Council of the Assemblies of God. Divisions: Home Missions. Formerly: National Teen Challenge; (1998) Teen Challenge National; (2003) Teen Challenge International, USA; (2003) Teen Challenge World Wide Network. Publications: The Cross and the Switchblade. Video. Features the portrayal of David Wilkerson's courageous mission and Nicky Cruz's dramatic conversion. Price: $15.00/copy. ● Directory of Teen Challenge Centers, semiannual. Price: free for members ● Praise and Thanksgiving. Brochure ● Reaching the Lost. Brochure. Conventions/Meetings: annual conference.

20221 ■ Young Life (YL)
PO Box 520
Colorado Springs, CO 80901
Ph: (719)381-1800
Fax: (719)381-1755
E-mail: mat@sc.younglife.org
URL: http://www.younglife.org
Contact: Denny Rydberg, Pres.
Founded: 1941. Staff: 3,171. Budget: $204,457,847. Regional Groups: 54. Local Groups: 932. Multinational. Description: Introduces adolescents to Jesus Christ and helps them grow in their faith. Committed to making an impact on kids' lives and preparing them for the future, builds positive relationships with young people in order to share the good news of God's love. Is active in all 50 states and more than 50 foreign countries, reaching an estimated one million teenagers annually. More than 75,000 kids spend a weekend during the school year or a week in the summer at one of Young Life's 21 camping properties in operation in the United States and Canada. Publications: Inside Young Life, bimonthly. Newsletter. Informs, equips and encourages staff. Sent to all Young Life staff. Circulation: 3,200 ● Relationships, 3/year, every fall, winter and spring. Magazine. Goes out to all current donors and to all Young Life staff. Includes inspiring stories and updates from around the mission. Circulation: 200,000 ● Young Life Informer, semimonthly. Newsletter. Contains important mission announcements. Circulation: 15,000. Alternate Formats: online ● Annual Report, annual, every March. Conventions/Meetings: quadrennial conference, for all staff.

20222 ■ Youth for Christ/U.S.A. (YFC/USA)
PO Box 4478
Englewood, CO 80155
Ph: (303)843-9000
Fax: (303)843-9002
E-mail: info@yfc.net
URL: http://community.gospelcom.net/Brix/yfcusa/public
Contact: Daniel S. Wolgemuth, Pres.
Founded: 1944. Staff: 1,861. Budget: $57,000,000. Regional Groups: 8. Local Groups: 215. Description: Fights juvenile delinquency through counseling and Youth Guidance programs for youth penal institutions. Carries on projects in various countries through Youth for Christ International. Maintains placement service. Programs for staff are: area refreshers; college training; intern training; and summer training. Programs for youth are: camps; Campus Life Clubs; counseling; short-term missions and work projects overseas; and Youth Guidance work with troubled teenagers. Sponsors "Lighten Up!" radio. Subgroups: Campus Life; Campus Life/Middle School; City Life; Project Serve; Teen Parents; 3 Story Evangelism (TM); World Outreach; Youth Guidance. Affiliated With: Evangelical Council for Financial Accountability; Evangelical Fellowship of Mission Agencies; National Religious Broadcasters. Publications: Life's Growing Adventure. Booklet. Helps its readers develop their relationship with Jesus. Price: $20.00/copy ● Annual Report, annual. Price: free. Circulation: 1,000. Conventions/Meetings: annual convention, for staff and board (exhibits) - always January or February.

Aerospace

20223 ■ Airlift/Tanker Association (A/TA)
9312 Convento Terr.
Fairfax, VA 22031-3809
Ph: (703)385-2802
Fax: (703)385-2803
E-mail: ata@atalink.org
URL: http://www.atalink.org
Contact: Bud Traynor, Contact
Founded: 1975. **Members:** 6,700. **Membership Dues:** regular, $40 (annual) ● life, $500. **Multinational. Description:** Active duty and retired USAF, U.S. Army Airborne, airlines, Civil Reserve Air Fleet, Reserve, and Air National Guard personnel; members of the aerospace industry. Perpetuates the comradeship and brotherhood of all airlift and tanker refueling, both military and civilian; provides a forum for membership; furthers the airlift/tanker mission. Seeks to enhance the future of aviation. Maintains Airlifters Hall of Fame and honors outstanding airmen. **Awards:** General P.K. Carlton Award for Valor. **Frequency:** annual. **Type:** recognition. **Recipient:** to outstanding airlift or tanker aircrew or aircrew member for valor ● General Robert "Dutch" Huyser Award. **Frequency:** annual. **Type:** recognition. **Recipient:** for an outstanding pilot, navigator, flight engineer, loadmaster, and boom operator who sustained excellence in airmanship. **Formerly:** (1992) Airlift Association. **Publications:** *The Airlift/Tanker (A/TQ)*, quarterly. Magazine. **Price:** $30.00/year. **Circulation:** 8,000. **Advertising:** accepted. **Conventions/Meetings:** annual Airlift/Tanker Convention and Symposium - congress, exhibitors and attendees could participate in the airlift and tanker community's premier event (exhibits) ● annual meeting and symposium, for members.

20224 ■ American Fighter Aces Association (AFAA)
9404 E Marginal Way S
Seattle, WA 98108-4907
Ph: (206)768-7155
Fax: (206)764-5707
E-mail: afaa@museumofflight.org
Contact: Harold Rubin, Exec. Admin.
Founded: 1960. **Members:** 1,000. **Membership Dues:** individual, $35 (annual). **Staff:** 1. **Budget:** $120,000. **Regional Groups:** 3. **Description:** United States civilian or military personnel who served honorably as fighter pilots in World War I, World War II, Korea, or Vietnam and who destroyed at least 5 enemy aircraft in the air. Seeks to "serve our country in peace as we did in war", support continued development of progressive aerospace weapons systems to defend the U.S., and encourage young people to enter the aerospace field. **Libraries: Type:** reference; open to the public. **Holdings:** 150; archival material, biographical archives, books, clippings, periodicals. **Subjects:** military aviation history, American fighter aces. **Awards:** Airmanship Award. **Frequency:** annual. **Type:** recognition. **Recipient:** for students at the Air Force Academy ● David Mc-

Campbell Award. **Type:** recognition ● Francis S. Gakreski. **Frequency:** annual. **Type:** recognition. **Recipient:** for outstanding young fighter pilots in the Air Force, Navy, and Marine Corps ● Joseph J. Foss Award. **Type:** recognition. **Publications:** *American Fighter Aces and Friends Bulletin*, quarterly. Magazine. Includes book reviews and obituaries, news of the aces, and feature articles about aces. **Price:** included in membership dues. **Circulation:** 1,700. **Advertising:** accepted ● *Roster*, annual. Membership Directory. **Conventions/Meetings:** annual reunion (exhibits).

20225 ■ Daedalian Foundation (DF)
PO Box 249
Universal City, TX 78148-0249
Ph: (210)945-2113 (210)945-2111
Fax: (210)945-2112
E-mail: icarus@daedalians.org
URL: http://www.daedalians.org
Contact: Col. John H. Hanna, Sec.
Founded: 1959. **Members:** 16,000. **Membership Dues:** regular, $16 (annual). **Staff:** 2. **Budget:** $275,000. **Local Groups:** 80. **Description:** Encourages study in aeronautic and astronautic fields. Financed by donations from members of the Order of Daedalians. **Libraries: Type:** not open to the public. **Holdings:** 800; books. **Awards:** Daedalian Foundation Descendants Scholarship Program. **Frequency:** annual. **Type:** scholarship. **Recipient:** for descendants of Daedalian members ● **Frequency:** annual. **Type:** recognition. **Recipient:** for distinguished performance in military activities and promotion of safety in flight. **Telecommunication Services:** electronic mail, icarus@texas.net. **Affiliated With:** Order of Daedalians. **Publications:** *Daedalian Roll Call*, periodic. Directory ● *Daedalus Flyer*, quarterly. Magazine. Contains information about the Order of Daedalians and its foundation. **Circulation:** 16,000. Alternate Formats: online. **Conventions/Meetings:** annual convention.

20226 ■ Order of Daedalians
PO Box 249
Universal City, TX 78148-0249
Ph: (210)945-2111
Fax: (210)945-2112
E-mail: daedalus@daedalians.org
URL: http://www.daedalians.org
Contact: Lt. Col. Dale Shaw, Sec.
Founded: 1934. **Members:** 16,000. **Membership Dues:** named/hereditary, $25 (annual) ● life (30 and under age group), $635 ● life (31-35 age group), $615 ● life (36-40 age group), $580 ● life (41-45 age group), $535 ● life (46-50 age group), $490 ● life (51-55 age group), $440 ● life (56-60 age group), $385 ● life (61-65 age group), $335 ● life (66-70 age group), $280 ● life (71-75 age group), $230 ● life (76 and over age group), $185. **Staff:** 5. **Budget:** $300,000. **Local Groups:** 85. **Description:** Military pilots of heavier-than-air powered aircraft who were commissioned as officers in the U.S. military services before November 12, 1918; descendants and designates of such pilots. Active duty, retired, or scheduled

to draw title retired pay via reserve/guard duty. **Libraries: Type:** reference. **Holdings:** 500; books, papers, periodicals. **Subjects:** early aviation history in the U.S. **Awards:** Admiral James S. Russel Naval Navigation Flight Safety Award. **Frequency:** annual. **Type:** recognition. **Recipient:** for the most effective flight safety accident prevention program ● Brigadier General Carl I. Hutton Memorial Award. **Frequency:** annual. **Type:** recognition. **Recipient:** for outstanding professionalism ● Daedalian JROTC Achievement Award. **Frequency:** annual. **Type:** recognition. **Recipient:** to outstanding cadets ● Daedalian Weapons System Award. **Frequency:** annual. **Type:** recognition. **Recipient:** for major contributions to the development of an outstanding weapon system ● Lieutenant General Harold L. George Civilian Airmanship Award. **Frequency:** annual. **Type:** recognition. **Recipient:** for the demonstration of heroism above and beyond normal operational requirements ● Lieutenant Generals Millard F. and Hubert R. Harmon Award. **Frequency:** annual. **Type:** recognition. **Recipient:** for the outstanding cadet in the USAF Academy ● Major General Benjamin D. Foulois Memorial Award. **Frequency:** annual. **Type:** recognition. **Recipient:** for the best flying safety record ● Major General Eugene L. Eubank Services Award. **Frequency:** annual. **Type:** recognition. **Recipient:** for the best overall small base MWR program in the USAF. **Affiliated With:** Daedalian Foundation. **Publications:** *Daedalus Flyer*, quarterly. Magazine. **Price:** included in membership dues. ISSN: 1083-2831. **Circulation:** 16,000. Alternate Formats: online ● *Official Flight Manual*. Alternate Formats: online ● *Quarterly Flight Activity Report*. Alternate Formats: online. **Conventions/Meetings:** annual meeting, membership meeting and awards presentations.

20227 ■ Tuskegee Airmen, Inc. (TAI)
PO Box 9166
Arlington, VA 22219-1166
Ph: (703)286-7653
E-mail: rdavis@tuskegeeairmen.org
URL: http://tuskegeeairmen.org
Contact: Russell C. Davis, Pres.
Founded: 1972. **Members:** 1,684. **Budget:** $65,000. **Regional Groups:** 3. **Local Groups:** 40. **Description:** Majority of members are black men and women involved in aviation in the military services, service academies, and ROTC units; former airmen who flew in a segregated U.S. Army Air Corps. Seeks to maintain a relationship among those who fought and served in World War II overseas and at home. Strives to motivate minority students in the proper curriculum for opportunities in high tech society. Provides information about the contributions black Americans have made to aviation history. Maintains speakers' bureau. Operates museum at Historic Fort Wayne in Detroit, MI. **Libraries: Type:** reference. **Holdings:** archival material. **Awards: Type:** recognition ● **Type:** scholarship. **Recipient:** to students interested in aviation or aerospace careers. **Formerly:** Do Do Club. **Publications:** *The Lonely Eagles*. Book ● *Tuskegee Airmen, Inc., Membership Roster*, annual. Membership Directory ● Newsletters. Alternate Formats: on-

line ● Also publishes a historical biography of members. **Conventions/Meetings:** annual conference (exhibits) - always August.

Air Force

20228 ■ 17th Bomb Group Reunion Association (17th BGRA)
c/o Ted Baker, Mgr.
453 Hamilton Ave.
Almont, MI 48003-8620
Ph: (810)798-8758
Fax: (810)798-8754
E-mail: tabaker26@msn.com
URL: http://www.geocities.com/bombgroup17
Contact: Ted Baker, Mgr.
Founded: 1978. **Members:** 2,800. **Staff:** 4. **Description:** U.S. Air Force and Air Corps veterans who served in the 17th Bomb Group during World War II and in the 17th Bomb Wing from the Korean War to the present. Seeks to keep members informed of activities. Provides historical information on the 17th Bomb Group. **Libraries: Type:** reference. **Holdings:** archival material, photographs. **Publications:** *Roster of the 17th Bomb Group Reunion Association,* every 3-4 years. Membership Directory ● *The 17th Sortie,* bimonthly. Reports on association activities; includes historical articles and reminiscences of members. **Conventions/Meetings:** annual reunion - always fall.

20229 ■ 43rd Bomb Group Association
PO Box 360
Snyder, TX 79550-0360
Ph: (602)840-7101
E-mail: jimcher@adelphia.net
URL: http://www.kensmen.com
Contact: Jim Cherkauer, Pres.
Founded: 1981. **Members:** 900. **Membership Dues:** individual, $15 (annual) ● life, $100. **Staff:** 3. **National Groups:** 800. **Description:** Veterans and present members of the 43rd Bomb Group and 43rd Bombardment Wing - SW PAC-5th AF. Seeks to preserve friendships made during members' military service. Maintains memorials in Colorado Springs, CO, Mareeba, QLD, Australia, Wright Patterson Air Force Museum in Dayton, OH, and Langley Air Force Base, VA. Operates museum. **Computer Services:** Mailing lists, of members ● online services, publications. **Publications:** *43rd Bomb Group Association Roster,* triennial. Membership Directory. Arranged alphabetically and by squadron and state. **Price:** included in membership dues. **Circulation:** 800. Alternate Formats: online ● *43rd Bomb Group Newsletter,* quarterly. **Price:** included in membership dues. **Circulation:** 800. Alternate Formats: online ● Also publishes group history. **Conventions/Meetings:** annual reunion and meeting (exhibits).

20230 ■ 369th Fighter Squadron Association, 359th Fighter Group
511 Crest Haven Dr.
Pittsburgh, PA 15239
Ph: (412)793-7619
URL: http://www.359fg.org
Contact: Anthony Chardella, Chm.
Founded: 1973. **Members:** 469. **Membership Dues:** $12 (annual). **Staff:** 9. **Description:** World War II veterans of the 359th Fighter Group and associated units. Works toward the installation of memorials to the 359th in the U.S. and England. Bestows annual scholarship. Maintains museum; conducts educational and charitable programs. Maintains a library open to members only. **Libraries: Type:** not open to the public. **Holdings:** books. **Subjects:** World War II to present. **Affiliated With:** P-51 Mustang Pilots Association. **Publications:** *Flight Patterns,* quarterly. Newsletter. **Price:** free to members. **Circulation:** 600 ● *Roster,* periodic ● *The 359th in World War II.* **Conventions/Meetings:** annual reunion.

20231 ■ 381st Bomb Group Memorial Association (381 BGMA)
c/o Joseph K. Waddell, Jr., Sec.-Treas.
PO Box 6064
Madison, WI 53716-0064

Ph: (608)222-4591
URL: http://www.381st.org
Contact: Joseph K. Waddell Jr., Sec.-Treas.
Founded: 1976. **Members:** 1,200. **Membership Dues:** individual, $10 (annual) ● life (based upon age at time of application), $40-$120. **Staff:** 1. **Description:** Individuals who erected a memorial at an English military base. Maintains contacts with former WWII unit members. Raises funds to establish a scholarship fund for descendants of Ridgewell Airdrome organizations. **Awards:** Gen. Joseph Nazzaro Scholarship. **Frequency:** annual. **Type:** scholarship. **Recipient:** for descendants of veteran members scholastic. **Committees:** Memorial; Scholarship. **Affiliated With:** Eighth Air Force Historical Society. **Publications:** *Directory 381st BGMA,* annual. Membership Directory. Lists current members and deceased former members. **Price:** free for members. **Circulation:** 1,050 ● *The 381st Flyer,* semiannual. Newsletter. **Price:** free for members. **Conventions/Meetings:** annual reunion.

20232 ■ 401st Bombardment Group (Heavy) Association
PO Box 15356
Savannah, GA 31416
Ph: (912)598-0276
E-mail: membership@401bg.com
URL: http://www.401bg.com
Contact: George H. Menzel, Exec. VP
Founded: 1973. **Members:** 1,453. **Membership Dues:** regular, $10 (annual). **Staff:** 1. **Multinational. Description:** Officers and enlisted men who served in the 401st Bombardment Group of the Eighth (U.S.) Air Force, which was based in England during World War II. Conducts research programs; compiles statistics. Offers membership to family and friends of these veterans. **Computer Services:** database ● mailing lists. **Publications:** *Poop From Group,* quarterly. Newsletter. Includes news about POWs, obituaries, and reunion information. **Price:** included in membership dues. **Circulation:** 1,453. **Conventions/Meetings:** biennial reunion, artifacts, photos, models (exhibits).

20233 ■ 461st Bombardment Group Association
c/o Hughes Glantzberg, Webmaster/Ed.
PO Box 926
Gunnison, CO 81230
Ph: (970)209-2788
E-mail: webmaster@461st.org
URL: http://www.461st.org
Contact: Hughes Glantzberg, Webmaster/Ed.
Membership Dues: life, $25 ● associate, child, $10 (annual). **Description:** Perpetuates the history of the 461st Bombardment Group (H), 15th Air Force, and the memory of those who gave their lives in the defense of America. **Publications:** *Liberaider,* semiannual. Newsletter. Alternate Formats: online. **Conventions/Meetings:** annual reunion.

20234 ■ 494th Bombardment Group (H) Association 7th Air Force
3160 E Main St., No. 103
Mesa, AZ 85213-9519
Ph: (480)924-6801
E-mail: charleywilcox@494thbombgroup.com
URL: http://kelleys_kobras.home.att.net/494wing/wing.htm
Contact: Charley F. Wilcox, Chm.
Founded: 1977. **Members:** 636. **Membership Dues:** individual, $10 (annual) ● life, $75. **Description:** Veterans of the U.S. Army Air Forces who served in the 494th Bombardment Group (H) during its tour in the Pacific Theater in 1944-45. Seeks to preserve a spirit of camaraderie among members. Conducts research programs. **Additional Websites:** http://www.494thbombgroup.com. **Also Known As:** Kelley's Kobras. **Publications:** *494th Bombardment Group Association,* semiannual. Newsletter. **Circulation:** 950 ● *Kelley's Kobras,* semiannual. Newsletter. **Circulation:** 950 ● *Roster of Members,* biennial. Membership Directory. **Conventions/Meetings:** annual reunion.

20235 ■ Air Force Navigators Observer Association (AFNOA)
c/o Clem Smith, Treas.
1095 Harriet
Canyon Lake, TX 78133-5244
E-mail: clem@gvtc.com
URL: http://www.afnoa.org
Contact: Clem Smith, Treas.
Founded: 1985. **Members:** 3,000. **Membership Dues:** regular, $15 (annual) ● life (under age 55), $200 ● life (age 55-60), $175 ● life (age 61-65), $150 ● life (age 66-70), $100 ● life (70 years old and above), $75 ● life (80 years old and above), $45. **Budget:** $15,000. **Description:** Individuals who trained in or taught navigation at any U.S. Air Force Base; interested Air Force navigators and observers. Seeks to locate and reunite the estimated 80,000 men who passed through any Air Force Base from 1940 to the present. Perpetuates the memory of navigators and navigating lore. Promotes renewed friendship among members. **Awards:** Outstanding Navigator Award. **Type:** trophy. **Recipient:** to the graduates of navigator class at Randolph AFB. **Computer Services:** Mailing lists, of members. **Formerly:** Ellington Navigators Observers Association. **Publications:** *DR Ahead,* quarterly. Newsletter. Includes anecdotes and reunion data. **Price:** included in membership dues. **Circulation:** 3,000. **Conventions/Meetings:** biennial reunion (exhibits) - always odd-numbered years.

20236 ■ Air Forces Escape and Evasion Society (AFEES)
c/o Clayton C. David
19 Oak Ridge Pond
Hannibal, MO 63401-6539
Ph: (573)221-0441
E-mail: davidafe@adams.net
URL: http://www.rafinfo.org.uk/rafescape/afees-usa.htm
Contact: Clayton C. David, Contact
Founded: 1964. **Members:** 800. **Membership Dues:** regular, $20 (annual) ● life, $100. **Staff:** 10. **Description:** Former members of the U.S. Air Force who, having been shot down in enemy territory during World War II, evaded capture or escaped from capture to return to Allied control. Fosters international goodwill and acts as a clearinghouse for information about escape and evasion networks and members of underground organizations. Honors foreign nationals who assisted members. Encourages reunions in Europe, Canada, and the U.S. between members and their helpers. **Libraries: Type:** reference. **Holdings:** archival material. **Publications:** *Communications,* quarterly. Journal. Includes membership news and book reviews. **Price:** included in membership dues. **Circulation:** 1,500 ● Newsletter, semiannual. **Conventions/Meetings:** annual reunion and conference.

20237 ■ Airman Memorial Foundation (AMF)
5211 Auth Rd.
Suitland, MD 20746
Ph: (301)899-3500
Free: (800)638-0594
Fax: (301)899-8136
E-mail: staff@afsahq.org
URL: http://www.amf.org
Contact: Mr. Richard M. Dean, CEO/Chm.
Founded: 1983. **Staff:** 4. **Budget:** $300,000. **Description:** Represents the professional and personal interests of 135,000 Air Force, Air Force Reserve Command and Air National Guard active duty, retired and veteran enlisted members and their families. **Libraries: Type:** open to the public. **Holdings:** archival material, articles, clippings, maps, monographs, photographs. **Awards: Frequency:** annual. **Type:** scholarship. **Recipient:** to air force dependents, ranging from $1000 to $3000 ● **Frequency:** biennial. **Type:** scholarship. **Recipient:** to deserving air force dependents, ranging from $1000 to $3000. **Computer Services:** database, AMF/Ca$he Collegiate Financial Info Data Base Service, lists 150000 grants from 4200 resources at no cost to requester through Base Support Centers. **Affiliated With:** Air

Force Sergeants Association. **Conventions/Meetings:** AFSA International Annual Convention (exhibits).

20238 ■ Association of Air Force Missileers (AAFM)
PO Box 5693
Breckenridge, CO 80424
Ph: (970)453-0500
Fax: (970)453-0500
E-mail: aafm@afmissileers.org
URL: http://www.afmissileers.org
Contact: Col. Charles G. Simpson, Exec. Dir.

Founded: 1993. **Members:** 3,000. **Membership Dues:** missileer, sponsor, $20 (annual) ● $50 (triennial) ● life, $300 ● student, active duty enlisted, $14 (triennial) ● student, active duty enlisted, $5 (annual). **Budget:** $45,000. **Description:** Current and former U.S. Air Force officers and enlisted members and interested individuals. Seeks to preserve the heritage of the USAF missile force. Encourages contact among members; keeps missileers informed; facilitates unit reunions, recognizes outstanding missileers. **Libraries: Type:** not open to the public. **Holdings:** 500; articles, books, photographs. **Subjects:** missiles. **Awards:** AF Space Command Enlisted Recognition. **Frequency:** annual. **Type:** grant. **Recipient:** to AFSPL's outstanding enlisted men and women ● Colonel Edward D. Payne Award for ICBM Maintenance. **Type:** recognition ● General Samuel C. Phillips Award for ICBM Operations. **Frequency:** annual. **Type:** recognition ● Missile Heritage Fund. **Frequency:** annual. **Type:** grant. **Recipient:** to museums with missile related displays. **Computer Services:** Online services, museum. **Publications:** *AAFM Newsletter*, quarterly. **Price:** included in membership dues. **Circulation:** 2,700. Alternate Formats: online ● Membership Directory, triennial. **Price:** included in membership dues. **Circulation:** 2,100. **Advertising:** accepted. Alternate Formats: CD-ROM; online. **Conventions/Meetings:** biennial meeting (exhibits) - even-numbered years.

20239 ■ Mosquito Association
c/o John Dichard, Treas.
2202 County Rd. 331
Nacogdoches, TX 75961
E-mail: srooney@lanset.com
URL: http://www.mosquitokorea.org
Contact: John Dichard, Treas.

Founded: 1955. **Members:** 900. **Membership Dues:** individual, $25 (annual). **Staff:** 10. **Budget:** $5,000. **Regional Groups:** 5. **Local Groups:** 3. **Description:** U.S. Air Force veterans and UN observers who served with the 6147th Tactical Control Group from 1950-56. Fosters continued fellowship among those who served with the unit during the Korean War. Maintains museum and archives of war souvenirs, artifacts, memorabilia, and an historical account of the unit during active duty. Compiles statistics. **Libraries: Type:** not open to the public. **Holdings:** 40. **Subjects:** Korean War. **Awards:** Ed Damico Memorial Award. **Frequency:** annual. **Type:** recognition ● Mosquito Award. **Frequency:** annual. **Type:** recognition. **Computer Services:** database, membership, press release addresses. **Formerly:** (1985) Mosquito Historical Foundation. **Publications:** *Mosquito Directory*, annual. Alphabetically, by state, deceased, MIA-KIA-POW, photos. **Price:** $15.00. **Circulation:** 350 ● *Mosquito News*, quarterly. **Price:** free for members. **Circulation:** 600 ● *Mosquitoes in Korea*. Book. **Price:** $15.00 ● *Radio Jeeps in the Korean War*. Book. **Price:** $25.00 ● *Terry and the Pirates Funny Book*. **Price:** $15.00. **Conventions/Meetings:** annual Mosquito Reunion, with photo albums, personal histories, and MIA-KIA-POW albums (exhibits).

20240 ■ Second Bombardment Association (SBA)
c/o Richard K. Radtke, Pres.
60 Villa Heights Ct.
Algoma, WI 54201-1463
Ph: (920)487-3343

E-mail: ektdar@greenbaynet.com
URL: http://www.members.cox.net/dfcarlock/Home.htm
Contact: Richard K. Radtke, Pres.
Founded: 1985. **Members:** 1,200. **Membership Dues:** individual, $25 (biennial) ● life, $100. **Description:** Persons who served in the Second Bomb Group or the Second Bombardment Wing; widows of members of these groups; interested individuals. Promotes camaraderie and seeks to perpetuate the history of the Second Bombardment Wing; works to advance public awareness of the heritage of the Second Bomb Wing and Group; fosters good public relations among citizens of the U.S. and the U.S. Armed Forces. Visits U.S. Air Force installations and receives briefings on developments in matters regarding national defense; constructed a Second Bombardment Wing memorial at Wright Air Force Base in 1991. **Awards:** Second Bombardment Association Scholarship. **Frequency:** annual. **Type:** scholarship. **Recipient:** for children of active-duty wing members. **Telecommunication Services:** electronic mail, dfcarlock@cox.net. **Publications:** *Defenders of Liberty*. Book. Contains history of men and their aircraft 1918-1993. Includes detailed accounts of combat missions during World War II. **Price:** $54.75 for nonmembers, plus shipping and handling ● *Second Bombardment Association Newsletter*, semiannual. Includes list of new members. **Price:** free. **Circulation:** 1,200. **Advertising:** accepted ● Also publishes an organizational history. "Defenders of Liberty"-Publication completed, ready to go into 2nd printing. **Conventions/Meetings:** biennial reunion (exhibits) - always fall, odd numbered years.

20241 ■ Society of Air Force Physician Assistants (SAFPA)
PO Box 340838
San Antonio, TX 78234-0838
E-mail: info@safpa.org
URL: http://www.safpa.org
Contact: Pamela Lucas, Pres.
Membership Dues: fellow, affiliate, $35 (annual) ● fellow, $150 (quinquennial). **Description:** Promotes quality, cost-effective, and accessible healthcare; promotes profession of Air Force physician assistant. **Telecommunication Services:** electronic mail, safpa_dal_01@safpa.org ● electronic mail, president@safpa.org. **Publications:** *SAFPA Towner-Shaeffer Report*. **Conventions/Meetings:** annual conference.

American Legion

20242 ■ American Legion (AL)
c/o Public Relations Division
PO Box 1055
Indianapolis, IN 46206
Ph: (317)630-1200 (317)630-1253
Free: (800)433-3318
Fax: (317)630-1368
E-mail: natlcmdr@legion.org
URL: http://www.legion.org
Contact: Mr. Paul Morin, Natl. Commander
Founded: 1919. **Members:** 2,657,623. **Membership Dues:** wartime military veteran, $20 (annual). **Staff:** 260. **Regional Groups:** 5. **State Groups:** 50. **Local Groups:** 14,500. **Description:** Consists of honorably discharged wartime veterans of the U.S. armed forces. Provides a unified voice for veterans .in Washington, DC. Offers free assistance with Veterans Administration claims and benefits. Sponsors American Legion baseball competition, national high school oratorical contest, and children's services; cosponsors National Education Week. Maintains museum. **Libraries: Type:** reference. **Holdings:** 10,000. **Subjects:** military history. **Awards:** American Legion Air Force Academy Award. **Frequency:** annual. **Type:** recognition. **Recipient:** to the cadet of the graduating class of the air force academy who demonstrates the highest proficiency in all academic subjects ● American Legion Baseball Graduate of the Year Award. **Frequency:** annual. **Type:** recognition. **Recipient:** to major league baseball player who played

American legion baseball as a teenager and best exemplifies the principles and purposes of the program in sportsmanship, citizenship, general good conduct, integrity and playing ability ● The American Legion Coast Guard Academy Award. **Frequency:** annual. **Type:** recognition. **Recipient:** to the cadet of the graduating class of the United States coast guard academy who is considered to have personally excelled in athletics ● American Legion Fourth Estate Award. **Frequency:** annual. **Type:** recognition. **Recipient:** for an outstanding achievement in the field of journalism ● The American Legion Merchant Marine Academy Award. **Frequency:** annual. **Type:** recognition. **Recipient:** to the graduating midshipman of the merchant marine academy, enrolled in the pre-commissioning seminar course, and selected by the academy faculty ● The American Legion Military Academy Award. **Frequency:** annual. **Type:** recognition. **Recipient:** to the cadet of the graduating class at the United States military academy with the highest standing in chemistry ● The American Legion Naval Academy Award. **Frequency:** annual. **Type:** recognition. **Recipient:** to the graduating midshipman of the United States naval academy who stands highest in those English, history and government courses taken to complete a foreign affairs major ● Distinguished Public Service Award. **Frequency:** annual. **Type:** recognition. **Recipient:** to one or more persons of the United States congress ● Distinguished Service Medal. **Frequency:** annual. **Type:** medal. **Recipient:** for outstanding service to the nation and to the programs of the American legion ● Employer of the Year Award for Hiring Veterans. **Frequency:** annual. **Type:** recognition. **Recipient:** to an employer for its outstanding achievement in the employment and retraining of veterans ● National Commanders Public Relations Award. **Frequency:** annual. **Type:** recognition. **Recipient:** to an outstanding individual and/or organization for distinguished public service in the field of communications ● National Law Enforcement Officer Of the Year Award. **Frequency:** annual. **Type:** recognition. **Recipient:** to the outstanding law enforcement officer whose accomplishments have contributed to the preservation of law and order as well as the American way of life. **Commissions:** American Legion Magazine; Americanism; Children and Youth; Economic; Foreign Relations; Internal Affairs; Legislative; National Convention; National Security; Public Relations; Veterans Affairs and Rehabilitation. **Affiliated With:** American Legion Auxiliary; Sons of the American Legion. **Publications:** *American Legion Magazine*, monthly. Dedicated to American war veterans and their families. **Price:** included in membership dues; $12.00 /year for nonmembers. **Circulation:** 3,100,000. **Advertising:** accepted ● *Digest of National Convention*, annual. Proceedings. **Circulation:** 300 ● *Dispatch*, monthly. Newspaper. Contains organizational news and activities. **Price:** $15.00/year. **Circulation:** 20,000. **Advertising:** accepted ● *National Executive Committee*, 3/year. Proceedings. Contains proceedings of the spring convention, and fall national executive committee meetings ● *Need-A-Lift?*, annual. Directory. Lists educational scholarships, grants, and financial assistance available to children of veterans. **Price:** $2.00. **Conventions/Meetings:** annual convention, exhibit hall for registered attendees; election of national officers; establishes mandates of organization (exhibits).

20243 ■ Forty and Eight
777 N Meridian St., Rm. 204
Indianapolis, IN 46204
Ph: (317)634-1804
Fax: (317)632-9365
E-mail: voiturenationale@msn.com
URL: http://fortyandeight.org
Contact: Steven Stocks, Sec.
Founded: 1920. **Members:** 68,000. **Staff:** 9. **Local Groups:** 1,050. **Description:** Fraternal organization of veterans who are also members of the American Legion. Contributes aid to underprivileged children. **Awards:** Charles W. Ardery, Jr. Award. **Frequency:** annual. **Type:** recognition. **Recipient:** to the Grande Voiture which performed the greatest service to La Societe Child Welfare ● N. Carl Nielson Award. **Fre-**

quency: annual. **Type:** recognition. **Recipient:** to the Grande Voiture which performed the greatest service to La Societe Child Welfare ● **Type:** scholarship. **Recipient:** for nurses in training. **Telecommunication Services:** electronic mail, srstocks@aol.com. **Programs:** Americanism; Box Car; Carville Star; Child Welfare; George B. Boland Trust Fund; Nurses Training; POW/MIA; Youth Sports. **Publications:** *Forty and Eighter*, monthly. Newspaper. Alternate Formats: online ● *Petite Communique*. Report. Alternate Formats: online. **Conventions/Meetings:** annual meeting.

20244 ■ National American Legion Press Association (NALPA)

PO Box 1055
Indianapolis, IN 46206
E-mail: geonalpa@mindspring.com
URL: http://www.nalpa.legion.org
Contact: George W. Hooten, Exec. Dir.
Founded: 1923. **Members:** 1,900. **Membership Dues:** regular, $10 (annual). **Staff:** 3. **State Groups:** 34. **Local Groups:** 900. **Description:** Represents editors and staff writers of 800 local, district, county, and state American Legion (see separate entry) publications; persons responsible for the news services of the Legion on state and national levels. Exchanges ideas and information to improve the Legion press. Assists in organization of new publications in this field; holds annual contest for best papers in four divisions and for best original editorial. **Formerly:** American Legion Press Association. **Publications:** *NALPA Newsletter*, quarterly. **Price:** $6.00 /year for members; $15.00 /year for nonmembers. Alternate Formats: online. **Conventions/Meetings:** annual meeting, held in conjunction with AL - always August.

American Revolution

20245 ■ Black Revolutionary War Patriots Foundation (BRWPF)

729 15th St. NW, Ste.500
Washington, DC 20005
Ph: (202)452-1776
Free: (800)888-9811
Fax: (202)728-0770
E-mail: blackpatriots@blackpatriots.org
Contact: Rhonda Roberson Esq., Pres.
Founded: 1985. **Staff:** 5. **State Groups:** 2. **Local Groups:** 1. **Description:** Strives to establish a memorial, develop awareness and educate Americans about the efforts of the 5,000 participants of African heritage during the Revolutionary War. **Committees:** History; Site and Design. **Affiliated With:** American Society of Association Executives; Independent Sector. **Also Known As:** The Patriots Foundation; (2001) Black Patriots Foundation. **Conventions/Meetings:** periodic meeting.

20246 ■ Daughters of the Cincinnati (DC)

122 E 58th St.
New York, NY 10022
Ph: (212)319-6915
URL: http://fdncenter.org/grantmaker/cincinnati
Founded: 1894. **Members:** 550. **Description:** Women descendants of the officers of George Washington's Continental Army or Navy. **Awards:** **Type:** scholarship. **Recipient:** for high school seniors who are daughters of commissioned officers of the armed services. **Publications:** Yearbook. **Conventions/Meetings:** annual meeting - always January, New York City.

20247 ■ Descendants of the Signers of the Declaration of Independence (DSDI)

c/o Thomas G. Heyward, Pres. Gen.
PO Box 353
Bluffton, SC 29910-0353
E-mail: president@dsdi1776.com
URL: http://dsdi1776.com
Contact: Thomas G. Heyward, Pres. Gen.
Founded: 1907. **Members:** 950. **Membership Dues:** $45 (annual). **State Groups:** 13. **Description:** Lineal

descendants of a signer of the Declaration of Independence; includes seniors (adults over 18 years of age) and juniors. Places tablets at birthplaces, homes, and graves of signers; contributes toward restoration and preservation of Independence Hall and other historic monuments. Offers financial support for genealogical research on signers. Presents annual post-secondary scholarships to active members. Maintains genealogical archives. Sponsors "Sounds of Liberty" programs. **Awards:** DSDI Merit Scholarship. **Frequency:** annual. **Type:** scholarship. **Recipient:** for DSDI members ● DSDI Patriot Award. **Type:** recognition. **Recipient:** to the society for unselfish devotion that inspires the patriot ancestors in their quest for freedom. **Committees:** Scholarship. **Publications:** *The Genealogical Register of the Descendants of the Signers of the Declaration.* Book. Consists of volume I-VII, covering 10 states. **Price:** $59.50 additional 4 dollars handling fee ● *Spirit of '76*, 3/year. Newsletter. Contains society updates, minutes, etc. **Circulation:** 1,200 ● Membership Directory, periodic. **Conventions/Meetings:** congress - 3/year ● annual meeting, held within 13 colonies - fall and spring ● meeting, held within 13 colonies - 3/year ● meeting - 3/year.

20248 ■ General Society, Sons of the Revolution (SR)

201 W Lexington Ave., Ste.1776
Independence, MO 64050-3718
Ph: (816)254-1776
Free: (800)593-1776
Fax: (816)254-1783
E-mail: gssr1776@sbcglobal.net
URL: http://www.sr1776.org
Contact: Paul F. Davis, Gen. Pres.
Founded: 1876. **Members:** 5,800. **Staff:** 1. **Budget:** $100,000. **State Groups:** 30. **Local Groups:** 17. **Description:** Descendants, on either parent's side, of veterans of the American forces who served in the Revolution of 1776, or of American officials whose activities made them liable to charges of treason under British law. Activities include: sponsoring essay contests; erecting and preserving historic plaques; holding commemorative gatherings; marking Revolutionary soldiers' graves. **Libraries: Type:** reference. **Holdings:** 50. **Subjects:** genealogy, history. **Awards:** Modern Patriot Award. **Frequency:** triennial. **Type:** recognition. **Publications:** *Drumbeat*, semiannual. Newsletter. Alternate Formats: online ● *Sons of the Revolution: A History, 1975-2001.* Book. Contains separate history of every State Society. **Price:** $30.00 plus shipping and handling ● Proceedings, triennial. **Conventions/Meetings:** annual general assembly and board meeting ● triennial meeting.

20249 ■ Hereditary Order of Descendants of the Loyalists and Patriots of the American Revolution (HODL&PAR)

c/o James Raywalt, Registrar Gen.
300 N Hill Rd.
Sutton, WV 26601
Ph: (304)765-0321
Fax: (304)765-0322
E-mail: jraywalt@aol.com
Contact: James Raywalt, Registrar Gen.
Founded: 1972. **Members:** 300. **Membership Dues:** full, $15 (annual) ● associate, $10 (annual) ● full - life, $300 ● associate - life, $200 ● initiation fee - full, $50 ● initiation fee - associate, $40. **Staff:** 12. **Regional Groups:** 2. **Local Groups:** 4. **Description:** Persons having both a loyalist and a patriot ancestor; associate members are those having only a patriot or a loyalist ancestor. Works to replace lost or destroyed historical records of members, many of which were burned during the Revolutionary War period; records lineage of members, but does not trace lineage for the public. Visits graves on Memorial Day; commemorates the Fourth of July. Maintains speakers' bureau. **Libraries: Type:** not open to the public. **Holdings:** 50; articles, books, periodicals. **Subjects:** Revolutionary War loyalist information. **Awards: Frequency:** annual. **Type:** grant. **Committees:** Medals and Awards. **Publications:** *Crown and Eagle*, semiannual. Newsletter. Includes items on both loyalist and patriotic ancestry, obituaries, and lists of new

members. **Price:** included in membership dues. **Circulation:** 300 ● *History and Membership Roster, 1973-1983.* Membership Directory ● *Yearbook and Membership Roster, 1993.* **Conventions/Meetings:** annual meeting and dinner - always April, Washington, DC ● annual meeting and dinner - always October, Washington, DC.

20250 ■ National Society of the Children of the American Revolution (NSCAR)

1776 D St. NW, Rm. 224
Washington, DC 20006-5303
Ph: (202)638-3153
Fax: (202)737-3162
E-mail: hq@nscar.org
URL: http://www.nscar.org
Founded: 1895. **Members:** 10,000. **Membership Dues:** regular, $8 (annual). **Staff:** 5. **State Groups:** 41. **Local Groups:** 600. **Description:** Lineal descendants of patriots of the American Revolution from birth to 22 years of age. Supports several mountain schools in the South. Maintains museum of authentic pre-19th century objects. **Computer Services:** On-line services. **Committees:** American Indian; Conservation; Government Studies; Mountain Schools; National Heritage; Publicity. **Affiliated With:** National Society, Daughters of the American Revolution. **Publications:** *CAR Magazine*, quarterly. Newsletter. Provides information for members and lecturers. **Price:** $8.00/year. **Circulation:** 5,000. **Advertising:** accepted. **Conventions/Meetings:** annual convention, project displays (exhibits) - always April, Washington, DC.

20251 ■ National Society, Daughters of the American Revolution (DAR)

1776 D St. NW
Washington, DC 20006-5303
Ph: (202)628-1776 (202)628-4780
Fax: (202)879-3252
E-mail: prospectivemembers@dar.org
URL: http://www.dar.org
Contact: Presley Merritt Wagoner, Pres. Gen.
Founded: 1890. **Members:** 170,000. **Membership Dues:** basic, $25 (annual) ● life, $40. **Staff:** 130. **Budget:** $14,000,000. **State Groups:** 54. **Local Groups:** 3,000. **Description:** Women descendants of Revolutionary War patriots. Conducts historical, educational, and patriotic activities. Maintains DAR Library of Genealogical Material; DAR Museum of Decorative Arts; and Americana Collection of pre-1830 documents; organizes Junior American Citizens Clubs for schoolchildren; maintains two schools in the South and supports others; founded National Society of the Children of the American Revolution (see separate entry); initiated September 17-23 annually, Constitution Week. **Libraries: Type:** reference. **Holdings:** 180,000. **Subjects:** genealogy, U.S. history. **Awards:** American History Scholarship Award. **Frequency:** annual. **Type:** scholarship ● **Type:** recognition. **Recipient:** for school-age children displaying good citizenship ● ROTC Medal. **Type:** recognition. **Recipient:** for graduating ROTC cadets of outstanding ability and achievement ● **Type:** scholarship. **Recipient:** for occupational therapy and nursing students. **Committees:** American Heritage; American History Month; American Indians; Americanism and DAR Manual for Citizenship; Children of the American Revolution; Congressional; Conservation; Constitution Week; DAR Good Citizens; DAR Museum; DAR Service for Veteran-Patients; Ethics; Flag of the United States of America; Friends of the Library; Genealogical Records; Honor Roll; Insignia; Junior American Citizens; Junior Membership; Lineage Research; Motion Picture, Radio, and Television; Museum Docents; National Defense Committee of the Daughters of the American Revolution; Public Relations; Units Overseas. **Affiliated With:** National Society of the Children of the American Revolution. **Publications:** *American Spirit*, bimonthly. Magazine. Covers association activities; includes information on genealogy, the American Revolutionary period, and current national defense issues. **Price:** $18.00/year. ISSN: 0011-7013. **Circulation:** 40,000. **Advertising:** accepted. Also Cited As: *DAR Magazine* ● *DAR Newsletter*, monthly ● *Directory of Committees*, an-

nual ● *Manual for Citizenship* ● *Patriot Index* ● Proceedings, annual. **Conventions/Meetings:** annual Continental Congress - early July, Washington, DC ● annual meeting - first or second week of July - Washington, DC.

20252 ■ National Society, Sons of the American Revolution (NSSAR)
1000 S 4th St.
Louisville, KY 40203
Ph: (502)589-1776
Fax: (502)589-1671
E-mail: whiten@prodigy.net
URL: http://www.sar.org
Contact: Nathan A. White Jr., Pres. Gen.
Founded: 1889. **Members:** 26,000. **Membership Dues:** regular, $25 (annual) ● life (age 40 and below, decreases $12.50/year thereafter), $750. **Staff:** 13. **Budget:** $500,000. **State Groups:** 54. **Local Groups:** 460. **Description:** Represents the descendants of men and women who served the patriot cause in the Revolutionary War. Sponsors competitions; operates museum. **Libraries: Type:** open to the public. **Holdings:** 27,000. **Subjects:** George Washington, genealogy, history. **Awards: Type:** recognition. **Committees:** Americanism; Historical Oration Contest; Patriotic Action; Registration; Revolutionary War Graves. **Publications:** *SAR Magazine*, quarterly. Contains news about patriotic, historical and educational activities at the national, state and local chapter levels. **Conventions/Meetings:** annual congress.

20253 ■ Society of the Cincinnati (SC)
2118 Massachusetts Ave. NW
Washington, DC 20008-2810
Ph: (202)785-2040 (202)785-0729
Fax: (202)785-0729
URL: http://www.thesocietyofthecincinnati.addr.com
Contact: Mrs. Sandra Prucher, Exec. Dir.
Founded: 1783. **Members:** 3,500. **Staff:** 15. **Local Groups:** 14. **Description:** Male descendants of officers commissioned in the Continental Army and Navy in the American Revolution who gave the required length of service, of certain officers in the French Army and Navy, and of other foreign officers (only 1 person may represent an officer). State societies (13) represent the original colonies. Also exists in France. Maintains Anderson House in Washington, DC. Bestows Triennial Society of the Cincinnati Prize to an author of a distinguished work on any aspect of American history from the Revolution through the end of the Washington presidency. Was named after Lucius Quinctius Cincinnatus, a hero of the fifth century B.C. who saved Rome from threatened hostile invasions and returned to his farm without thought of personal reward. The city of Cincinnati, OH was named in honor of the society by the first governor of the Northwest Territory, Major General Arthur St. Clair, an original member of the society. **Libraries: Type:** reference. **Holdings:** 30,000; archival material. **Subjects:** the American Revolution, the art of war, the decorative arts. **Publications:** *Cincinnati Fourteen*, semiannual. Newsletter ● *George Rogers Clark Lectures on the Revolutionary War and Early National History*. Book. **Conventions/Meetings:** triennial congress.

20254 ■ Society of the Descendants of Washington's Army at Valley Forge
c/o Dr. Rynell S. Novak, Commander-in-Chief
624 W Univ. Dr., No. 241
Denton, TX 76201-1889
Ph: (940)387-3092
Fax: (940)387-3092
E-mail: rsnovak@juno.com
URL: http://www.valleyforgesociety.org
Contact: Dr. Rynell S. Novak, Commander-in-Chief
Founded: 1976. **Members:** 1,100. **Membership Dues:** individual, $20 (annual) ● junior (under 18 years of age), $5. **Staff:** 13. **State Groups:** 8. **Description:** Descendants of officers and men serving in the Continental Army under the command of General George Washington at Valley Forge from Dec. 19, 1777 through June 19, 1778. Compiles rolls of all the soldiers at Valley Forge to preserve their

names and honor for posterity and to discover, compile, preserve, and publish the incidents of the encampment. Compiles statistics. **Libraries: Type:** reference. **Holdings:** archival material, artwork, business records, clippings. **Subjects:** society history. **Awards:** Student Award in Early American History. **Frequency:** annual. **Type:** recognition. **Recipient:** for juniors in high school. **Also Known As:** DVF; (2005) Washington's Army at Valley Forge. **Publications:** *The Encampment Newsletter*, quarterly. Includes historical announcement on the Valley Forge encampment and announcements of awards of the annual meeting, called an Encampment. **Price:** included in membership dues. **Circulation:** 1,125 ● *Membership Roster*, periodic. Directory. Includes short history and bylaws. ● *Not By Bread Alone*. Contains history of some of the units and commanding offices at the V.F. Encampment - 1777-1778. **Conventions/Meetings:** annual Encampment - conference and convention, plus historic tours and social events - always in Valley Forge, PA.

Armed Forces

20255 ■ 29th Infantry Division Association
c/o William C. McCleaf
PO Box 74
Blue Ridge Summit, PA 17214-0074
Ph: (717)794-2530
E-mail: twoniner@adelphia.net
URL: http://www.29thdivisionassociation.org
Contact: John E. Wilcox Jr., Natl. Exec. Dir.
Founded: 1920. **Membership Dues:** regular, $10 (annual). **Description:** Aims to perpetuate the spirit of the 29th Division in the World Wars. **Affiliated With:** World Health Organization. **Publications:** *Beyond the Beachhead*. Book. **Price:** $15.00 plus shipping and handling of $3.95 ● *The Clay Pidgeons of St. Lo*. Book. **Price:** $15.00 plus shipping and handling of $3.95 ● *Eye Witness at Omaha Beach*. Book. **Price:** $15.00 plus shipping and handling of $3.95 ● *Midnight of the Soul*. Book. **Price:** $12.00 plus shipping and handling of $3.95 ● *115th Infantry in WWII*. Book. **Price:** $25.00 plus shipping and handling of $3.95 ● *29, Let's Go! 29th Division History*. Book. **Price:** $29.00 plus shipping and handling of $3.95.

20256 ■ 33rd Infantry Division Association
PO Box 13618
Mill Creek, WA 98082-1618
Ph: (425)741-3549
Fax: (425)745-1127
E-mail: goldencr@ismi.net
URL: http://www.ismi.net/goldencross
Contact: Lt. Col. Glen Toalson, Contact
Founded: 1985. **Description:** Aims to perpetuate the spirit of the 33rd Infantry Division. **Telecommunication Services:** electronic mail, billendicott@seanet.com. **Publications:** Newsletter, quarterly. **Price:** $15.00. **Conventions/Meetings:** reunion.

20257 ■ 35th Division Association
PO Box 5004
Topeka, KS 66605
E-mail: josephfurtak@sbcglobal.net
URL: http://expage.com/page/35thinfdiv
Contact: William H. Sachs, Contact
Description: Promotes the history of the 35th Infantry Division. **Publications:** *Santa Fe Express*, bimonthly. Newspaper. **Price:** $9.00/year.

20258 ■ Soldiers for the Truth
PO Box 54365
Irvine, CA 92619-4365
E-mail: info@sftt.org
URL: http://www.sftt.org
Contact: Eilhys England Hackworth, Chm./CEO
Membership Dues: supporter, $30. **Description:** Represents the voices of service people, veterans and retirees. Informs the public, the Congress and the media on the needs of the Armed Forces. Ensures the efficient and effective service of military institutions by providing readiness, leadership, equip-

ment and training. **Computer Services:** Mailing lists, of members ● online services, forums. **Publications:** *DefenseWatch*. Magazine. Alternate Formats: online.

Army

20259 ■ 11th Airborne Division Association
4218 N Cris Hollow Rd.
Fayetteville, AR 72704-7435
Ph: (479)442-2222
Free: (800)537-4022
E-mail: dickhoyt@aol.com
URL: http://members.aol.com/dickhoyt/index.html
Contact: Anthony V. Biebel, Sec.
Founded: 1973. **Members:** 4,900. **Membership Dues:** associate, regular, $15 (annual) ● life, $150 ● Angelette, $5 (annual). **Staff:** 32. **Budget:** $25,000. **Regional Groups:** 15. **National Groups:** 113. **Description:** Comprises of veterans who served in the 11th Airborne Division beginning with its activation in 1943. Serves as fraternal association of former paratroopers and glidermen. Maintains hall of fame and museum; compiles statistics. **Libraries: Type:** reference. **Holdings:** archival material. **Awards: Type:** recognition. **Committees:** Memorial Statue. **Also Known As:** The Angels. **Publications:** *Voice of the Angels*, quarterly. Newspaper. **Price:** included in membership dues. **Circulation:** 5,500. **Advertising:** accepted. Alternate Formats: CD-ROM. **Conventions/Meetings:** biennial convention (exhibits).

20260 ■ 13th Airborne Division Association
c/o Robert deLisle, Treas.
PO Box 1332
Tualatin, OR 97062-1332
Ph: (913)722-1143 (503)692-3658
E-mail: bob13thabn@aol.com
Contact: Robert deLisle, Treas.
Founded: 1981. **Members:** 1,100. **Description:** Former members of the 13th Airborne Division and subordinate units. At end of the war, the division consisted of the 326th Glider Infantry 517th Parachute Infantry, 515th Parachute Infantry Regiments, supporting artillery and special troops. Perpetuates the common bond and memories of all airborne soldiers and promotes the airborne concept in current U.S. Army forces. Works with other airborne veterans organizations. Compiles statistics; supports museum. **Awards: Type:** recognition. **Publications:** *Thirteener*, quarterly. Newsletter. Contains membership activities. Includes information on new members and obituaries. **Price:** included in membership dues. **Circulation:** 1,100. **Advertising:** accepted ● Article, monthly. Included in *Static Line* newspaper. **Conventions/Meetings:** annual reunion.

20261 ■ 24th Infantry Division Association
c/o Billy Johnson, Ed.
2416 Kimberly Dr.
Fayetteville, NC 28306
Ph: (910)424-3840
E-mail: bj24sf45@aol.com
URL: http://home.att.net/~victory24
Contact: Gene E. Spicer, Pres.
Founded: 1945. **Members:** 3,000. **Membership Dues:** individual, $15 (annual) ● life, $150. **Staff:** 8. **Budget:** $25,000. **Regional Groups:** 1. **Description:** Veterans who served or now serving in the 24th Division of the U.S. Army and all attached units. Maintains museum and hall of fame. Compiles statistics. **Libraries: Type:** reference. **Holdings:** 200; archival material, books, video recordings. **Subjects:** World War II, Korean War, Gulf War. **Awards:** Verbeck. **Frequency:** annual. **Type:** scholarship. **Recipient:** for individual from the immediate family of an association member, a grandchild or a legally adopted person. **Publications:** *Division History*, 5/year. Magazine ● *Taro Leaf*, quarterly. Newsletter. Includes historical information about World War II and the Korean War, book reviews, and obituaries. Help in locating buddies, kin, etc. **Price:** included in membership dues. **Circulation:** 3,000. **Conventions/Meetings:** annual reunion.

20262 ■ 25th Infantry Division Association
PO Box 7
Flourtown, PA 19031-0007
E-mail: tropicltn@aol.com
URL: http://www.25thida.com
Contact: Morgan J. Sincock, Exec. Dir.
Founded: 1949. **Members:** 4,500. **Membership Dues:** individual, $15 (annual) ● life, $150 ● auxiliary, $7 (annual) ● life - auxiliary, $75. **Staff:** 2. **Regional Groups:** 10. **Description:** Veterans and current members of the 25th Infantry Division, U.S. Army. Seeks to unite division members to uphold the spirit of the division and promote the standards and ideals of the army. Provides the opportunity to renew friendships formed during combat. Maintains museum and speakers' bureau. **Awards:** Educational Memorial Scholarship. **Frequency:** annual. **Type:** scholarship. **Recipient:** to grandchild of member ● Murray Scholarship. **Frequency:** annual. **Type:** scholarship. **Committees:** Archives; Historian; Scholarship. **Also Known As:** Tropic Lightning Association. **Publications:** *Tropic Lightning Flashes*, quarterly. Magazine. **Price:** free for members. **Circulation:** 5,000. **Advertising:** accepted. **Conventions/Meetings:** annual meeting (exhibits).

20263 ■ 32nd Infantry Division Veterans Association
c/o Pamela McVeigh, Sec.
1715 Nelson Ave. SE
Grand Rapids, MI 49507-2148
Ph: (616)452-6311
E-mail: p.mcveigh@comcast.net
URL: http://www.32nd-division.org
Contact: Frank M. Kopling, Pres.
Founded: 1919. **Members:** 7,000. **Membership Dues:** life, $50. **Staff:** 8. **Regional Groups:** 7. **Local Groups:** 40. **National Groups:** 27. **Description:** U.S. Army veterans who served in the 32nd Red Arrow Infantry Division, which saw action in Europe in World War I, the Pacific Theater in World War II, and during the Berlin Crisis of 1960. **Telecommunication Services:** electronic mail, fmkopling@milwpc.com. **Publications:** *32nd Division News*, quarterly. Newsletter. **Conventions/Meetings:** annual meeting (exhibits) - always August 27-31.

20264 ■ 43rd Infantry Division Veterans Association
c/o Howard F. Brown, Sec.-Treas.
150 Lakedell Dr.
East Greenwich, RI 02818-4716
Ph: (401)884-7052
Fax: (401)884-7052
E-mail: brownhowieb@aol.com
URL: http://www.geocities.com/Pentagon/Quarters/9543
Contact: Sylvio Ciummo, Commander
Founded: 1945. **Members:** 1,400. **Membership Dues:** regular, $10 (annual) ● life, $50-$75. **Staff:** 1. **Regional Groups:** 3. **State Groups:** 3. **Description:** Veterans aid organization whose membership is comprised of veterans of the 43rd Infantry Division who served in World War II and the Korean War. Maintains museum. Offers educational programs. **Awards:** Certificate of Appreciation and Distinguished Service Award. **Type:** scholarship. **Recipient:** to members and progeny only. **Formerly:** (1989) 43rd Infantry Division Association. **Publications:** *B Co-Med Newsletter*, bimonthly ● *43d Bulletin*, quarterly. Covers activities of local chapters and individual members. Includes new member information and obituaries. **Price:** included in membership dues ● *RI Chapter Newsletter*, quarterly ● *Sunbelt Chapter Newsletter*, quarterly. **Conventions/Meetings:** annual reunion, promotion of related books and materials (exhibits).

20265 ■ 63rd Infantry Division Association
c/o Donna LaCosse, Natl. Sec.-Treas.
PO Box 86
Morocco, IN 47963
Ph: (219)285-2861

E-mail: joyclint@comcast.net
URL: http://www.63rdinfdiv.com
Contact: Donna LaCosse, Natl. Sec.-Treas.
Founded: 1949. **Membership Dues:** regular, $15 (annual). **Description:** Aims to perpetuate the spirit of the 63rd Infantry Division. **Publications:** *Blood and Fire*, 3/year. Newsletter ● *63rd Infantry Division Newsletter*. Alternate Formats: online.

20266 ■ 95th Infantry Division Association
PO Box 376
Willow Springs, IL 60480
E-mail: bob@woodfamilies.com
URL: http://www.woodfamilies.com/95th/95th.html
Contact: Mel Esarey, Pres.
Membership Dues: regular, $15 (annual). **Description:** Commits to perpetuate the spirit of the 95th Infantry Division. **Publications:** *The Bravest of the Brave*. Article. Alternate Formats: online ● *Calendar*. **Price:** included in membership dues ● *The Journal*. Magazine. Alternate Formats: online ● Journal, 3/year. **Price:** included in membership dues. **Conventions/Meetings:** monthly executive committee meeting - 3rd Tuesday ● annual reunion.

20267 ■ 96th Infantry Division Association
PO Box 581254
Salt Lake City, UT 84158
E-mail: dizzydon@aol.com
URL: http://www.96th-infantry-division.com/index.htm
Contact: Tom Roby, Pres.
Description: Dedicated to the 96th Infantry Division (the "Deadeye" division), U.S. Army, World War II; their wives, children and friends. **Conventions/Meetings:** reunion.

20268 ■ 100th Infantry Division Association
c/o Patti Bonn
PO Box 629
Bedford, PA 15522
Ph: (814)632-8308
E-mail: aegis@bedford.net
URL: http://www.100thww2.org
Contact: Patti Bonn, Contact
Membership Dues: regular, $25 (annual). **Description:** Dedicated to the 100th Infantry Division. **Publications:** Newsletter, 3/year. **Price:** included in membership dues. **Conventions/Meetings:** annual convention - September.

20269 ■ 101st Airborne Division Association
c/o Mr. Sam Bass, Exec. Sec.-Treas.
PO Box 929
Fort Campbell, KY 42223-0929
Ph: (931)431-1099
Fax: (931)431-0195
E-mail: 101stairbornedivisionassociation@comcast.net
URL: http://www.screamingeagle.org
Contact: Mr. Sam Bass, Exec. Sec.-Treas.
Founded: 1945. **Members:** 9,500. **Membership Dues:** regular, $25 (annual) ● $101 (quinquennial). **Staff:** 4. **Budget:** $140,000. **Regional Groups:** 33. **Description:** Preserves the comradeship established in the service and disseminates information. Membership is open to individuals who served in the 101st Airborne Division and its attached units and their families and direct descendents. Conducts charitable activities and offers scholarships to members and their dependents. **Awards:** Chappie Hall Scholarship. **Frequency:** annual. **Type:** scholarship. **Recipient:** to members and relatives of current or deceased members of the association based on academic standing, community activities and need. **Committees:** Advisory; Awards; Constitution and By-Laws; Don F. Pratt Memorial; Memorial; Reunion; Screaming Eagle Support Fund. **Publications:** *The Screaming Eagle*, quarterly. Magazine. Provides information on memorials, events, and activities of the association. Includes obituaries and quinquennial directory. **Price:** included in membership dues; included in life memberships. **Circulation:** 8,000. **Advertising:** accepted. Alternate Formats: online; diskette; CD-ROM ● Books. **Conventions/Meetings:** annual reunion (exhibits) - usually August.

20270 ■ 104th Infantry Division National Timberwolf Association
c/o Glen E. Lytle, Sec.-Treas.
4002 Jasmine Dr.
Wichita, KS 67226
Ph: (316)636-5334
Fax: (316)636-9644
E-mail: info@104infdiv.org
URL: http://www.104infdiv.org
Contact: Glen E. Lytle, Sec.-Treas.
Membership Dues: regular, $10 (annual). **Description:** Represents World War II veterans of the 104th Infantry Division of the U.S. Army. **Publications:** *Timberwolf Howl*, semiannual, January and June. **Price:** included in membership dues. **Conventions/Meetings:** annual reunion.

20271 ■ 164th Infantry Association of the United States
Address Unknown since 2007
Founded: 1946. **Members:** 580. **Membership Dues:** $10 (annual). **Description:** Individuals with honorable service in or with any 164th Infantry Unit from 1883 to 1955. Seeks to perpetuate the friendships developed during members' military service and to foster devotion and loyalty to God, state, and nation. **Publications:** *An Account of the 164th Infantry Regiment on Guadalcanal*, quarterly. Newsletter. **Price:** included in membership dues. **Circulation:** 580. **Advertising:** not accepted ● *The History of the 164th Infantry Unit* ● *Infantry News*, quarterly. **Conventions/Meetings:** annual reunion.

20272 ■ 187th Airborne Regimental Combat Team Association (RAKKASANS)
4015 Royal Arch Ct.
Concord, CA 94519-1225
Ph: (510)686-0813
E-mail: rakkasan@fuse.net
URL: http://www.geocities.com/Pentagon/9187
Contact: Jim Hoeh, Pres.
Founded: 1981. **Members:** 2,800. **Budget:** $75,000. **Regional Groups:** 14. **State Groups:** 7. **Description:** Represents the honorably discharged veterans who served with the 187th Airborne Regimental Combat Team on or after Feb. 21, 1943; current active duty personnel with the regiment. Seeks to: preserve the history of the regiment; assist active duty personnel; honor late members of the regiment. Supports establishment of a Korean War Memorial in Washington, DC, and erection of a memorial in Arlington National Cemetery honoring the 187th Airborne Regimental Combat Team. Operates museum. Is compiling a history of the Regiment based on members' experiences in World War II, Korea, and Vietnam. **Libraries:** **Type:** reference. **Holdings:** 500. **Awards:** **Type:** recognition. **Publications:** *Rakkasan Shimbun*, quarterly. Magazine. Covers regimental activities and history. Includes notices of planned events and obituaries. **Price:** included in membership dues. **Circulation:** 2,800. **Advertising:** accepted ● Membership Directory, annual. **Conventions/Meetings:** competition ● annual reunion (exhibits).

20273 ■ 749th Tank Battalion Association Friends
PO Box 187
Elyria, OH 44036-0187
Ph: (440)366-7001 (440)322-4617
Contact: Col. George A. Baker, Planner
Founded: 1945. **Members:** 450. **Membership Dues:** $10 (annual). **Regional Groups:** 3. **State Groups:** 3. **Description:** Active and retired members and friends of the 749th tank battalion who served from 1943-1946; widows of deceased members. Seeks to maintain camaraderie among combat service veterans. Operates museum; offers member services and aid. **Formerly:** (2000) 749th Bn Assn. **Publications:** *749 Newsletter*, quarterly. Bulletin. **Conventions/Meetings:** semiannual reunion.

20274 ■ American Airborne Association (AAA)
10301 McKinstry Mill Rd.
New Windsor, MD 21776-7903
Free: (888)567-2927

Fax: (410)775-7760
E-mail: eagle187@hughes.net
URL: http://www.americanairborneassn.org
Contact: Ret. Col. W.E. Weber, Pres.
Founded: 1996. **Members:** 2,000. **Membership Dues:** regular, $20 (annual) ● associate, $35 (annual). **Staff:** 3. **Budget:** $15,000. **Regional Groups:** 8. **State Groups:** 50. **Local Groups:** 12. **Description:** Represents members of U.S. Airborne. **Publications:** *Airborne Quarterly.* Magazine. **Price:** $20.00 in U.S.; $25.00 in Canada, Mexico; $35.00 other foreign nations.

20275 ■ DUSTOFF Association (DA)
PO Box 8091
San Antonio, TX 78208
E-mail: info@dustoff.org
URL: http://www.dustoff.org
Contact: Timothy Burke, Pres.
Founded: 1980. **Members:** 1,300. **Membership Dues:** officer/civilian, $15 (annual) ● enlisted, $7 (annual) ● life (officer/civilian), $100. **Staff:** 9. **Description:** Officers and enlisted personnel, aviation crew members, and physicians and nurses who were engaged in or supported Army aeromedical evacuation programs. Seeks to maintain relationships formed during aeromedical evacuation service. Works to promote aeromedical evacuation; keeps members informed of developments in the field. Maintains medical and aviation museums. (DUSTOFF now stands for Dedicated Unhesitating Service To Our Fighting Forces; it was originally the call sign of the first aeromedical helicopter evacuation unit in Vietnam, and the name caught on as the informal call sign of every subsequent evacuation unit.) **Awards:** Crewmember of the Year. **Frequency:** annual. **Type:** recognition ● Hall of Fame. **Frequency:** annual. **Type:** recognition ● Rescue of the Year. **Frequency:** annual. **Type:** recognition. **Publications:** *DUSTOF-Fer,* semiannual, June, November. Newsletter. Alternate Formats: online. **Conventions/Meetings:** annual reunion (exhibits) - usually February, in San Antonio, TX.

20276 ■ Fourth Armored Division Association (FADA)
c/o Richard C. Schenker, Sec.
760 Crestview Dr.
Sharpsville, PA 16150-8332
E-mail: rick@theschenkers.com
URL: http://webplaza.pt.lu/~gries
Contact: Richard C. Schenker, Sec.
Founded: 1946. **Members:** 1,050. **Membership Dues:** individual, $15 (annual) ● life, $100. **Description:** Veterans who served at any time in the U.S. Army's Fourth Armored Division or its attached units. (The Fourth was deactivated in 1946 after seeing action in Europe during World War II.) Seeks to promote camaraderie and friendship among members; donates funds to Veteran's Administration Hospitals and Museums. **Libraries: Type:** not open to the public. **Awards:** Past President's Award. **Frequency:** annual. **Type:** recognition. **Recipient:** for outstanding association's performance. **Publications:** *Rolling Together,* quarterly. Newsletter. **Price:** free for members. **Circulation:** 1,050. **Conventions/Meetings:** annual reunion.

20277 ■ Headquarters 310th Command Association
PO Box 203
Vienna, VA 22183-0203
Ph: (540)297-5511
Fax: (540)297-5500
E-mail: cwcessna@earthlink.net
Contact: Stephen O. Richey Jr., Pres.
Founded: 1987. **Members:** 1,500. **Membership Dues:** individual, $15 (annual) ● life, $150. **Description:** Former members of the HQ, 310th Logistical Command, the HQ, 310th Field Army Support Command, the HQ, 310th Theater Support Command, the HQ, 310th Theater Army Area Command and the HQ, 9th Theater Support Command. Promotes a spirit of camaraderie among members. Maintains comprehensive files of operational orders, letters, memos, photographs, and other correspondence of the 310th

and 9th. Compiles statistics available for member use. **Libraries: Type:** reference. **Holdings:** 13; archival material, photographs. **Subjects:** HQ, 310th and 9th activities. **Awards: Frequency:** annual. **Type:** recognition. **Recipient:** for a member who travels the greatest distance to attend the annual meeting. **Computer Services:** database ● mailing lists. **Publications:** *HQ 310th Command Association Newsletter,* semiannual. Includes member death notices, and past and upcoming events of the Association. **Price:** free. **Circulation:** 1,500. **Advertising:** accepted. **Conventions/Meetings:** annual reunion and luncheon, photographs, orders, letters, and memos (exhibits) - usually second Saturday in April, Washington, DC area.

20278 ■ National 4th Infantry (Ivy) Division Association
c/o Gregory A. Rollinger, Exec. Dir.
8891 Aviary Path
Inver Grove Heights, MN 55077
Ph: (651)994-0556
Free: (651)845-4040
Fax: (651)994-0576
E-mail: 4idaexecdirector@comcast.net
URL: http://www.4thinfantry.org
Contact: Gregory A. Rollinger, Exec. Dir.
Founded: 1917. **Members:** 4,000. **Membership Dues:** active/associate/memorial, $15 (annual). **Regional Groups:** 28. **National Groups:** 5. **Description:** Represents veterans who served with the U.S. Army 4th Infantry Division since World War I. Objectives are to: honor and perpetuate the memory and achievements of the officers and men who distinguished themselves by their services and sacrifices while with the 4th Infantry; unite and promote fellowship among their descendants; assist in the relief and education of their children; promote national defense; encourage historical research pertaining to the World Wars; acquire and preserve members' service records, documents, and relics. Marks scenes of activities of the 4th Infantry Division; celebrates anniversaries of prominent events of wars; fosters patriotism. Provides scholarships for members and their families. **Awards:** 4th Infantry Division Association Scholarship. **Frequency:** annual. **Type:** scholarship. **Recipient:** for members or members' relatives ● Ralph E. Lingert Service Award. **Frequency:** annual. **Type:** recognition. **Recipient:** for a member who has shown devotion to duty and steadfast loyal dedication to the association. **Committees:** Auditing; Finance; Membership; Memorial; Nominating; Resolutions; Reunion Advisory; Scholarship; Welfare. **Publications:** *Ivy Leaves,* quarterly. Magazine. Contains articles that are of interest to all 4th Infantry Division veterans. **Price:** included in membership dues. **Circulation:** 4,700. **Conventions/Meetings:** annual reunion, memorabilia, vendors (exhibits) - always July or August.

20279 ■ National Association of the Sixth Infantry Division
W6839 Washington Ave.
Elkhorn, WI 53121-2817
Ph: (262)742-2108
Fax: (262)742-3670
E-mail: admin@6thinfantry.com
URL: http://www.6thinfantry.com
Contact: Robert Beutlich, Sec.-Treas.
Founded: 1937. **Members:** 900. **Membership Dues:** individual, $20 (triennial) ● individual, $15 (biennial) ● individual, $10 (annual). **Staff:** 1. **Regional Groups:** 1. **State Groups:** 1. **Local Groups:** 1. **Description:** Represents honorably discharged soldiers of units of the Sixth Infantry Division of the U.S. Army who served as officers or enlisted men during World War I, World War II, or the Korean War. Seeks to foster and perpetuate what the group considers true Americanism and to uphold the U.S. Constitution. Works to continue and strengthen comradeship among members and to preserve the memories, traditions, and incidents of their service experiences. **Libraries: Type:** open to the public. **Subjects:** military (Alaska site). **Computer Services:** Online services. **Formerly:** (1943) National Association of the Sixth Infantry Division; (1972) National As-

sociation of the Sixth Infantry/Motorized Division; (1987) National Association of the Sixth Infantry Division; (1989) National Association of the Sixth Infantry/Motorized Division. **Publications:** *Sightseer,* 3/year. Newsletter. Contains correspondence from members and veterans' information and experiences. **Price:** included in membership dues. **Circulation:** 900 ● Membership Directory. Alternate Formats: online. **Conventions/Meetings:** annual Sixth Infantry Division - convention.

20280 ■ Signal Corps Regimental Association (SCRA)
PO Box 7740
Fort Gordon, GA 30905-0740
Ph: (706)364-1755
Fax: (706)364-1756
E-mail: manager@signalcorps.org
URL: http://www.signalcorps.org
Contact: Mr. Bryan Tuschen, Mgr.
Membership Dues: individual, $18 (annual) ● individual, $45 (triennial) ● life, $200. **Description:** Works to preserve the proud heritage of the U.S. Army Signal Corps Regiment, and Signal units throughout the world. **Awards:** Brevet Colonel. **Frequency:** annual. **Type:** recognition. **Recipient:** for a member of the association ● Order of Mercury. **Frequency:** annual. **Type:** recognition. **Recipient:** for a member of the association ● Wahatchee. **Frequency:** annual. **Type:** recognition. **Recipient:** for a member of the association.

20281 ■ Society of the First Infantry Division
1933 Morris Rd.
Blue Bell, PA 19422-1422
Ph: (215)661-1969
Free: (888)324-4733
Fax: (215)661-1934
E-mail: soc1id@aol.com
URL: http://www.bigreddone.org
Contact: Jennifer Sanford, Admin.
Founded: 1919. **Description:** Dedicated to the 1st Infantry Division (The Big Red One) of the U.S. Army. **Conventions/Meetings:** Vietnam Tours ● World War II Battlefield Tours.

20282 ■ U.S. Army Ranger Association (USARA)
PO Box 52126
Fort Benning, GA 31995-2126
Ph: (703)830-2484 (706)565-8199
Fax: (703)830-2484
E-mail: lincgerman@aol.com
URL: http://www.ranger.org
Contact: Linc German, Pres.
Founded: 1973. **Members:** 1,000. **Membership Dues:** ranger, $35 (annual) ● life (ranger), $250 ● life (at least 63 years of age), $200 ● ranger, $105 (3/year) ● ranger, $175 (5/year). **Regional Groups:** 5. **State Groups:** 53. **Local Groups:** 106. **National Groups:** 4. **Multinational. Description:** Represents graduates of the U.S. Army Ranger School, Fort Benning, GA, Ranger Unit who fought in all conflicts and Wars since World War II, as well as Rangers currently on active duty around the world, and those who served as Advisors to International Ranger organizations and assigned to Vietnam era Long Range Reconnaissance Patrol (LRRP/LRP) Companies. Aims to preserve the heritage of the U.S. Army Rangers and their performance in training and leadership. Functions as an umbrella organization fostering communication between various ranger alumni units. Compiles statistics; conducts educational and charitable programs in support of the Ranger Community. **Awards:** Ranger Leadership Awards. **Frequency:** periodic. **Type:** recognition. **Recipient:** for rangers of all units and eras. **Computer Services:** database ● mailing lists. **Divisions:** Southern, Northern, Central, Western and International Regions. **Publications:** *The Ranger Register,* quarterly. Magazine. **Price:** $10.00/copy; $14.00 international mailing edition. **Circulation:** 1,000. **Advertising:** accepted. Alternate Formats: CD-ROM; online. **Conventions/Meetings:** annual Best Ranger - competition - always in Fort Benning, GA ● Ranger Annual Picnic, normally scheduled to coincide with the change of command

of the ranger regiment or the ranger training brigade (exhibits) - always in the Columbus/Fort Benning, GA area ● annual Ranger Muster - convention and conference, the major annual event; a multi day affair normally at a site of military, historical or entertainment significance; camaraderie prevails (exhibits) - rotates between the four divisions or regions.

20283 ■ Women's Army Corps Veterans Association (WACVA)
PO Box 5577
Fort McClellan, AL 36205-0577
Ph: (256)820-6824
E-mail: info@armywomen.org
URL: http://www.armywomen.org
Contact: Ann Tyler, Pres.
Founded: 1946. **Members:** 4,098. **Membership Dues:** individual, $20 (annual). **Staff:** 8. **Budget:** $30,000. **Regional Groups:** 62. **Description:** Veterans of the United States Women's Army Corps and Women's Army Auxiliary Corps, women soldiers and officers of the line who are on a tour of active duty with, or have been honorably discharged from, the United States Army, and women who have served honorably or are serving in the United States Reserve or Army National Guard. Seeks "to be of service to all veterans and the communities in which we live and promote justice, tolerance, peace and goodwill". Conducts hospital and community service programs. Supports the U.S. Army Women's Museum at Ft. Lee, VA. Has assisted in the establishment of Women's Army Corps Veterans Redwood Memorial Grove in Big Basin Redwoods State Park, CA. Conducts charitable projects and educational programs. **Awards:** Pallas Athene Award. **Type:** recognition. **Recipient:** to four outstanding ROTC cadets ● Women's Army Corps Veteran's Association Scholarship. **Frequency:** annual. **Type:** scholarship. **Recipient:** to student who was related to a woman that is serving or has served in the U.S. army. **Committees:** Community Projects; Hospital. **Publications:** *The Channel*, bimonthly. Newsletter. Covers membership activities; includes directory listing national and chapter officers. **Price:** included in membership dues. **Circulation:** 4,300 ● *The Yearbook.* Directory. **Conventions/Meetings:** annual meeting and convention - always August.

Awards

20284 ■ America's Foundation (AF)
PO Box 2016
Learned, MS 39154-2016
Ph: (601)885-2288
E-mail: spiritofamerica@hotmail.com
URL: http://www.angelfire.com/ms/champsite
Contact: Vince Thornton, Sec.
Founded: 1969. **Membership Dues:** regular, $20 (annual). **Description:** Honors top high school athletes, citizens, and leaders. Nominations are submitted by fans, players, and coaches from public and private schools. Recipients must display talent in any field of sports, leadership, or citizenship activities. Winners are proclaimed honorary citizens by various cities, welcomed by the Mississippi state legislature, and honored at the annual Banquet of Champions at which the Gold, Silver, and Bronze Spirit of America medals are presented. Spirit of America Day is proclaimed by the governor of Mississippi and by local municipalities in tribute to honorees. Maintains charitable program. **Awards:** The Spirit of America Award. **Frequency:** annual. **Type:** medal. **Recipient:** for athletic, leadership and citizenship excellence. **Computer Services:** Online services, archives. **Boards:** Awards. **Committees:** Scouting; Spirit of America Alumni. **Publications:** *The Spirit of America Day*, annual. Booklet. **Price:** $2.00. **Circulation:** 500. **Conventions/Meetings:** annual Banquet of Champions (exhibits) - always first Monday of March in Jackson, MS.

20285 ■ Congressional Medal of Honor Society (CMHS)
40 Patriots Point Rd.
Mount Pleasant, SC 29464
Ph: (843)884-8862
Fax: (843)884-1471
E-mail: medalhq@earthlink.net
URL: http://www.cmohs.org
Contact: Victoria Leslie, Dir. of Operations
Founded: 1958. **Members:** 149. **Staff:** 2. **Regional Groups:** 6. **Description:** Has established a fund to pay a stipend to widows upon the death of Congressional Medal of Honor recipients and education assistance to children of recipients. Purposes are: to form a bond of friendship and comradeship among all holders of the Congressional Medal of Honor; to protect, uphold and preserve the dignity and honor of the medal at all times and on all occasions; to foster and perpetuate Americanism. **Libraries: Type:** open to the public. **Holdings:** 2,000; biographical archives, books. **Subjects:** military. **Awards:** Patriots Award. **Frequency:** annual. **Type:** recognition. **Recipient:** for an outstanding American ● **Type:** scholarship. **Recipient:** for relatives of CMH men. **Publications:** *CMHS Newsletter*, quarterly. Bulletin. **Price:** free, for members only. **Advertising:** accepted. **Conventions/Meetings:** annual convention, with general meeting (exhibits).

20286 ■ Horatio Alger Association of Distinguished Americans (HAADA)
99 Canal Center Plz.
Alexandria, VA 22314
Ph: (703)684-9444
Fax: (703)684-9445
E-mail: association@horatioalger.com
URL: http://www.horatioalger.com
Contact: Terrence J. Giroux, Exec. Dir.
Founded: 1947. **Members:** 300. **Staff:** 6. **Budget:** $3,500,000. **Description:** Named for Horatio Alger (1832-99), American Unitarian clergyman and author of children's books, who is best known for his fictional accounts of heroes who progress from modest beginnings to outstanding achievement. Objectives are to recognize modern-day individuals whose own initiative and efforts led to significant achievement; promote appreciation of the contribution business makes to the economic stability and quality of life for all Americans; serve as a channel of communication between business and education; promote the free enterprise system to the youth of America. **Libraries: Type:** reference. **Holdings:** books. **Awards:** Horatio Alger Awards. **Frequency:** annual. **Type:** recognition. **Recipient:** for modern day individuals whose initiative and efforts led to significant success ● **Frequency:** annual. **Type:** scholarship. **Recipient:** for eligible seniors whose schools host a Youth Seminar. **Formerly:** (1981) Horatio Alger Awards Committee. **Publications:** *Charting the Course: The Next 50 Years*, annual. Annual Report. **Circulation:** 2,500 ● *The Forum*, semiannual. Newsletter. Includes news of members, and scholarship news. ● *Only in America A Legacy in Achievement*. Brochure ● *Only In America Opportunity Still Knocks*, annual. Video. **Price:** $35.00. **Circulation:** 3,000 ● Also publishes an informational packet for schools. **Conventions/Meetings:** annual Horatio Alger Awards Activities - dinner, includes awards ceremony ● Horatio Alger Youth Seminars, in secondary schools.

20287 ■ Ladies Auxiliary, Military Order of the Purple Heart, United States of America (LAMOPH)
5413-B Backlick Rd.
Springfield, VA 22151-3960
Ph: (703)642-5360
Fax: (703)642-2054
E-mail: info@purpleheart.org
Contact: Judith Spaulding, Pres.
Founded: 1932. **Members:** 5,000. **Membership Dues:** regular, $20 (annual). ● associate, $10 (annual) ● life, $50-$125. **Staff:** 4. **Budget:** $150,000. **Regional Groups:** 6. **State Groups:** 23. **Local Groups:** 210. **Description:** Female blood lineal descendants and adopted female descendants of veterans who have been wounded in combat and awarded the Purple Heart. Activities include: hospital work; child welfare and rehabilitation projects. **Libraries: Type:** reference. **Holdings:** periodicals. **Subjects:** purple heart. **Awards: Frequency:** annual. **Type:** recognition. **Recipient:** for hospital work,

membership, community service, and service to Auxiliary ● **Frequency:** annual. **Type:** scholarship. **Computer Services:** Mailing lists, magazine. **Committees:** Americanism; Chapel of Four Chaplains; Civil Defense; Community Service; Freedom's Foundation; HVWP; VAVS. **Publications:** *Directory of Departments and Units*, annual ● *The Purple Heart Magazine*, bimonthly. **Conventions/Meetings:** annual conference and meeting (exhibits) - usually August 8-12.

20288 ■ Legion of Valor of the United States of America (LVUSA)
c/o Philip J. Conran, Natl. Adj.
4706 Calle Reina
Santa Barbara, CA 93110-2018
Ph: (805)692-2244
E-mail: pconran@cox.net
URL: http://www.legionofvalor.com
Contact: Philip J. Conran, Natl. Adj.
Founded: 1890. **Members:** 800. **Membership Dues:** regular, $20 (annual) ● life, $150. **Staff:** 1. **Regional Groups:** 5. **Description:** Nation's senior organization of veterans; membership open to all recipients of the Medal of Honor, the Distinguished Service Cross, the Navy Cross, or the Air Force Cross. Maintains museum of archived military citations. **Awards:** Bronze Cross for Achievement. **Frequency:** annual. **Type:** recognition. **Recipient:** for outstanding ROTC cadets ● Silver Cross for Valor. **Frequency:** annual. **Type:** recognition. **Recipient:** for acts of heroism involving the saving of life. **Computer Services:** database ● mailing lists. **Formerly:** (1933) Medal of Honor Legion; (1961) Army and Navy Legion of Valor of the United States. **Publications:** *General Orders*, bimonthly. Newsletter. **Price:** included in membership dues; $20.00 /year for nonmembers. Alternate Formats: online. **Conventions/Meetings:** annual conference - summer ● annual convention.

20289 ■ Military Order of the Purple Heart of the United States of America (MOPH)
5413-B Backlick Rd.
Springfield, VA 22151-3915
Ph: (703)642-5360 (703)354-2140
Free: (888)668-1656
Fax: (703)642-1841
E-mail: bbacon@purpleheart.org
URL: http://www.purpleheart.org
Contact: William S. Bacon, Natl. Adj.
Founded: 1932. **Members:** 37,000. **Membership Dues:** individual, $20 (annual) ● life (under 60 years of age to over 70 years of age), $75-$125 ● life (with 100&percent; service connected disability), $75. **Staff:** 95. **Budget:** $5,000,000. **Regional Groups:** 6. **State Groups:** 45. **Local Groups:** 485. **Description:** Persons awarded the Purple Heart Medal for wounds received in action while members of the Armed Forces of the U.S. Conducts service and welfare work on behalf of disabled and needy servicemen and veterans and their dependents. **Awards:** George Washington Medallion of Merit. **Frequency:** annual. **Type:** recognition. **Committees:** Americanism; Legislative; VAVS; Welfare. **Publications:** *The Purple Heart Magazine*, bimonthly. **Price:** $12.00/year. ISSN: 0279-0653. **Circulation:** 40,000. Alternate Formats: online. **Conventions/Meetings:** annual convention (exhibits) - always August.

20290 ■ National Women's Hall of Fame (NWHF)
PO Box 335
Seneca Falls, NY 13148
Ph: (315)568-8060
Fax: (315)568-2976
E-mail: greatwomen@greatwomen.org
URL: http://www.greatwomen.org
Contact: Billie Luisi-Potts, Exec. Dir.
Founded: 1969. **Members:** 3,000. **Membership Dues:** individual, $25 (annual) ● senior, student, $15 (annual) ● hall patron, $500 (annual) ● hall friend, $250 (annual) ● hall sponsor, $100 (annual) ● family, $50 (annual). **Staff:** 5. **Budget:** $250,000. **Description:** Aims "to honor in perpetuity those women citizens of the United States whose contributions to the arts, athletics, business, education, government,

the humanities, philanthropy, and science, have been of greatest value for the development of their country." Maintains hall of fame; inductees selected by independent panel of judges; offers special exhibits. Sponsors annual essay and new media contest. Conducts special activities with school age groups. Maintains speakers' bureau; offers educational programs. **Libraries: Type:** reference. **Holdings:** 3,000; archival material, books. **Subjects:** American women's history and biography. **Awards:** President's Award. **Type:** recognition. **Formerly:** (1979) Women's Hall of Fame. **Publications:** Newsletter, quarterly. **Conventions/Meetings:** annual Honors Induction Ceremony - meeting (exhibits) - usually in Seneca Falls, NY.

Bay of Pigs

20291 ■ Bay of Pigs Veterans Association (BPVA)
1821 SW 9th St.
Miami, FL 33135
Ph: (305)649-4719
Fax: (305)649-9769
E-mail: bgd2506@bellsouth.net
URL: http://www.brigada2506.com
Contact: Felix I. Rodriguez, Pres.
Founded: 1963. **Members:** 1,500. **Membership Dues:** regular, $60 (annual). **Staff:** 3. **State Groups:** 11. **Local Groups:** 1. **Description:** Cuban exiles, members of the 2506 Brigade, who invaded Cuba on Apr. 17, 1961 and were defeated by Fidel Castro's forces at Cochinos Bay (Bay of Pigs). Promotes "the liberation of Cuba." Disseminates information about the "Communist take-over in Cuba and its real threat for America." Maintains hall of fame; compiles statistics. **Libraries: Type:** reference. **Holdings:** 5,000. **Subjects:** Cuban history, military history. **Also Known As:** Asociacion de Combatientes de la Brigada de Asalto 2506. **Publications:** Giron (in Spanish), quarterly. Journal. Contains information related to Cuban community and Bay of Pigs veterans. **Price:** free. **Circulation:** 5,000. **Advertising:** accepted. **Conventions/Meetings:** biennial general assembly - in February ● monthly Reunion.

Cadets

20292 ■ American Cadet Alliance (ACA)
PO Box 144
Sea Girt, NJ 08750-0144
Ph: (732)840-4500
Fax: (732)458-1075
E-mail: crtornow@militarycadets.org
URL: http://www.militarycadets.org
Contact: Col. Charles R. Tornow, Natl. Commander
Founded: 1909. **Members:** 2,500. **Membership Dues:** cadet, instructor, $40 (annual) ● adult non-commissioned officer, midshipman/officer candidate, $50 (annual) ● commissioned officer, patron, $60 (annual) ● active duty armed forces personnel, $35 (annual). **Regional Groups:** 6. **State Groups:** 12. **Local Groups:** 45. **Description:** Military-oriented youth program for boys and girls ages 12-18 interested in the Armed Forces. Provides members with the opportunity to gain first-hand experience in the traditions and career opportunities associated with the country's Armed Forces. Conducts programs such as specialized instruction in military history, customs and courtesies, leadership and personal development, as well as two-week summer training programs emphasizing high-adventure activities such as orienteering, map, compass and land navigation, mountain climbing and rappelling, marksmanship, and scuba diving. Consists of the U.S. Naval Cadet Corps, Marine Cadet Corps and Army Cadet Corps. **Computer Services:** database, via modem server. **Additional Websites:** http://www.acacadets.org, http://www.AdventureBeginsHere.org, http://www.Military-AdventureCamp.org. **Boards:** Awards; Directors; Governors; Military Advisors; Promotion; Trustees. **Affiliated With:** Association of the United States Army; National Rifle Association of America. **For-**

merly: (1909) Colonel Cody's Boy Scouts; (1911) American Naval and Marine Scouts; (1927) New York Junior Naval Militia; (1933) Junior Naval Reserve of America; (1938) American Nautical Cadets; (1956) American Nautical Alliance. **Publications:** Anchor, quarterly. Bulletin. **Price:** included in membership dues. **Advertising:** accepted. Alternate Formats: online ● General Information Brochure ● Recruiting Brochure ● Review Journal, annual ● Sponsorship Brochure ● Training Manual. **Conventions/Meetings:** annual Executive Leadership Conference - executive committee meeting, strategic planning meeting - always October.

Californian

20293 ■ Los Californianos (LC)
PO Box 600522
San Diego, CA 92160-0522
Ph: (858)538-3027 (619)582-3664
E-mail: latejedora@loscalifornianos.org
URL: http://www.loscalifornianos.org
Contact: Ms. Benita H. Gray, Dir.
Founded: 1969. **Members:** 725. **Membership Dues:** ordinary, provisional, historian, corresponding, $20 (annual) ● individual (over 65 years of age), $16 (annual) ● junior, $7 (annual) ● life (65 years or older), $200 ● life (under 65 years of age), $400. **Budget:** $20,000. **State Groups:** 1. **Description:** Represents the interests of descendants of the Hispanics who arrived in Alta (upper) California prior to Feb. 2, 1848; libraries, historical organizations, and schools are historical or corresponding members. Seeks to preserve the heritage of the early Hispanic Spanish Californians in Alta California. Provides authentic interpretation of Alta California's history via oral, written, pictorial, or other methods. Conducts research of genealogical, civil, religious, military, and cultural activities in Alta California and promotes preservation of this heritage. Sponsors historic and cultural speakers/tours/entertainment at meetings. Provides genealogical resources at meetings for members and the public. **Libraries: Type:** reference; open to the public. **Holdings:** 300; articles, books, periodicals. **Subjects:** mission records of California, family genealogies. **Committees:** Archives; Genealogy; Heritage Preservation; Landgrants; Publications. **Publications:** Antepasados, semiannual. Monograph. Contains translations and transcriptions of historic Spanish documents. ● Noticias Para Los Californianos, quarterly. **Conventions/Meetings:** quarterly meeting, includes access to genealogical library, board & general meetings, tours, speakers, hospitality, dinner, and brunch - always January, April, July, and October, in California ● workshop, on genealogy.

Canada

20294 ■ French/Canadian/Metis Genealogical Society
c/o Minnesota Genealogical Society
5768 Olson Memorial Hwy.
Golden Valley, MN 55422-5014
E-mail: robin.panlener@state.mn.us
URL: http://www.mngs.org
Contact: Robin PanLener, Pres.
Founded: 1969. **Members:** 816. **Membership Dues:** individual in U.S., $20 (annual) ● individual in U.S., $38 (biennial) ● regular, in Canada, $25 (annual) ● regular, in Canada, $48 (biennial) ● regular, outside U.S. and Canada, $25 (annual). **Languages:** English, French. **Multinational. Description:** People interested in French, Canadian and Metis genealogy. Aims to promote interest and scholarly research internationally in family history. Sponsors four workshops per year and publishes several publications. **Libraries: Type:** open to the public. **Holdings:** 618. **Subjects:** French, Canadian, Metis history and genealogy. **Telecommunication Services:** information service, library information service; Wednesday 9am-3pm central time (763)595-9347. **Committees:** Acquisitions & Cataloguing; External Communications; Fundraising; Journal; Membership; Newsletter;

Research; Volunteers. **Affiliated With:** Minnesota Genealogical Society. **Formerly:** (2002) Northwest Territory, Canadian and French Heritage Center. **Publications:** Canadian-American Journal of History & Genealogy for Canadian, French & Metis Study, semiannual. Contain study and research of groups. **Price:** included in membership dues. **Circulation:** 816. **Conventions/Meetings:** semiannual meeting.

Civil Rights and Liberties

20295 ■ Heritage Preservation Association (HPA)
PO Box 356
Mansfield, GA 30055
Ph: (404)435-5184
E-mail: hpahq@yahoo.com
URL: http://www.hpa.org
Contact: P. Charles Lunsford, Pres.
Founded: 1993. **Membership Dues:** individual, $40 (annual). **Description:** Works to fight political correctness and cultural bigotry in the South.

Civil War

20296 ■ Armies of Tennessee, CSA and U.S.A.
PO Box 91
Rosedale, IN 47874
Ph: (765)548-2594
Fax: (765)548-0177
E-mail: genmickeywalker@aol.com
Contact: Mickey M. Walker, Commanding Gen.
Founded: 1958. **Members:** 300. **Membership Dues:** $20 (annual). **Staff:** 9. **Regional Groups:** 15. **Local Groups:** 40. **Description:** Affiliation of "military" units in the style of the original Confederate Army and Navy seeking "to perpetuate the memory of the men who served in grey" during the Civil War. Organized in three departments: Confederate State Militia; Confederate Legion; Confederate Navy, Marines, and Cadets. Conducts educational programs and research on ideals, arms accoutrements, battles, military leaders, logistics, and tactics of the Civil War; promotes respect and adherence to Southern ideals. Conscripts and trains persons of good character throughout the Free World for service with the reactivated commands and historic units of the Confederacy; participates in battle reenactments and related military and memorial events. **Awards: Frequency:** periodic. **Type:** recognition. **Sections:** Cadets; Confederate States Militia; Marines; Medical; Navy; Nurses. **Formerly:** (1977) Confederate High Command, International; (1978) Confederate States Volunteers; (1986) Army of Tennessee, CSA. **Publications:** Battle Call, monthly. Newsletter. Includes historical articles relating to the Civil War, news of battle reenactments and related military and memorial events, and membership news. **Price:** included in membership dues. **Circulation:** 350. **Conventions/Meetings:** competition ● annual meeting (exhibits).

20297 ■ Auxiliary to Sons of Union Veterans of the Civil War (ASUVCW)
2449 Center Ave.
Alliance, OH 44601-4531
Ph: (330)823-6919
E-mail: president@asuvcw.org
URL: http://www.asuvcw.org
Contact: Beatrice Greenwalt, Historian
Founded: 1883. **Members:** 3,412. **Membership Dues:** Civil War descendent, $10 (annual). **Staff:** 3. **Regional Groups:** 2. **Local Groups:** 508. **Description:** Women relatives of descendants of Union veterans of the Civil War. Promotes patriotism; presents American flags; supports veterans' hospitals. **Libraries: Type:** not open to the public. **Awards: Type:** scholarship. **Committees:** Local Auxiliary; National Auxiliary; State Auxiliary. **Affiliated With:** Sons of Union Veterans of the Civil War. **Publications:** The Banner, quarterly. **Circulation:** 4,204. **Conventions/Meetings:** monthly Local Meeting ● annual National Meeting ● annual State Meeting.

20298 ■ Children of the Confederacy (CofC)

c/o Mrs. Harold J. Trammel, 3rd VP Gen.
UDC Bus. Off.
328 N Blvd.
Richmond, VA 23220-4009
Ph: (804)355-1636
Fax: (804)353-1396
E-mail: hqudc@rcn.com
URL: http://www.hqudc.org/CofC
Contact: Ms. Mary Katherine Miller, Pres.
Founded: 1954. **Members:** 2,200. **State Groups:** 23. **Local Groups:** 195. **Description:** Boys and girls from infancy to age 18 who are lineal or collateral descendants of men and women who served honorably in the Army, Navy, or Civil Service of the Confederate States of America or gave Material Aid to the Cause; children who are lineal or collateral descendants of members of the United Daughters of the Confederacy (see separate entry) whose papers are acceptable by the present requirements for membership. Sponsors educational, patriotic, memorial, historical, and benevolent activities. Conducts programs on the "true history" of the South, the War Between the States, and the Confederate forces; observes Confederate memorial days. Holds essay contests. Seeks letters, diaries, scrapbooks, reminiscences, and relics for state archives. **Awards: Type:** scholarship. **Recipient:** to students with 3.5 GPA, some require membership in organization. **Committees:** Confederate Memorial Stamp; Credentials; Education; Handbook; History; Insignias; Memorial Building; Monuments and Markers; New Business; Patriotic Service; Publicity. **Affiliated With:** United Daughters of the Confederacy. **Publications:** *The Courier,* quarterly. Newsletter ● *General Convention Minutes,* annual. Handbook. **Conventions/Meetings:** annual conference and convention - usually in July.

20299 ■ Daughters of Union Veterans of the Civil War, 1861-1865 (DUVCW)

503 S Walnut St.
Springfield, IL 62704-1932
Ph: (217)544-0616
E-mail: duvcw@sbcglobal.net
URL: http://www.duvcw.org
Contact: Ms. Cynthia Van Antwerp, Registrar
Founded: 1885. **Members:** 4,000. **Staff:** 1. **State Groups:** 18. **Local Groups:** 110. **Description:** Lineal descendants of Union veterans of the U.S. Civil War. Objectives are to perpetuate the memories of veterans of the U.S. Civil War, their loyalty to the Union, and their sacrifices for its preservation. Seeks to: keep alive the history of those who participated in the struggle for the maintenance of free government; aid the descendants of Union veterans of the Civil War; assist those who are worthy and needy; cooperate in movements relating to veterans, civic, and welfare projects; inculcate a love of country and patriotism; promote equal rights and universal liberty; honor Union veterans of the Civil War by placing flowers on graves on Memorial Day. Conducts genealogical projects. Supports and maintains public museum in Springfield, IL. Conducts volunteer work in veterans' hospitals. Supports local historical societies. Takes part in patriotic ceremonial programs and holiday observances. Conducts specialized education programs. **Libraries: Type:** reference. **Holdings:** archival material. **Subjects:** heritage records. **Awards: Frequency:** annual. **Type:** recognition. **Recipient:** to one cadet at each of four military academies ● **Frequency:** annual. **Type:** scholarship. **Recipient:** for students. **Committees:** Heritage; Legislative; Youth. **Formerly:** (1925) National Alliance Daughters of Veterans. **Publications:** *General Orders,* quarterly. **Circulation:** 4,000 ● *Roster of National Members,* annual. Membership Directory ● Some of the different Tents or Departments and committees have published books on their ancestors, Statues, Memorials across the United States pertaining to the GAR. **Conventions/Meetings:** annual convention - usually in August ● annual State Department Conventions - usually April through July.

20300 ■ Hood's Texas Brigade Association (HTBA)

PO Box 619
Hillsluis, TX 76645

Ph: (254)582-2555
Fax: (254)582-7591
E-mail: m.hartzog@mail.utexas.edu
URL: http://www.htba1872.org
Contact: Dr. John Versluis, Dir.
Founded: 1966. **Members:** 1,000. **Membership Dues:** individual, $10 (annual). **Description:** Direct and collateral descendants of members of Hood's Texas Brigade of the Civil War. The Brigade fought with Robert E. Lee for 4 years. Maintains Confederate Research Center and Museum. **Libraries: Type:** reference. **Holdings:** 8,000; articles, books, periodicals. **Subjects:** Civil War, Hood's Texas Brigade. **Telecommunication Services:** electronic mail, jversluis@hillcollege.edu. **Publications:** *Valor,* annual. Newsletter. Contains association news. **Alternate Formats:** online. **Conventions/Meetings:** biennial reunion - always in Hillsboro, TX.

20301 ■ Ladies of the Grand Army of the Republic (LGAR)

c/o Janice M. Corfman, PNP, Treas.
9057 State Rte. 83
Holmesville, OH 44633
Ph: (330)279-4393
Fax: (330)279-2458
E-mail: jmclgar@aol.com
URL: http://www.rootsweb.com/~nlgar/home.html
Contact: Lynne Bury, Pres.
Description: Works to perpetuate the memory of the Grand Army of the Republic and of the men who saved the Union in 1861 to 1865. Assists in the preservation and availability for research the documents and records pertaining to the Grand Army of the Republic and its members. Honors those who have patriotically served the country in any way. Teaches patriotism and the duties of citizenship, the history of the country, and the love and honor of the American flag. Opposes any movement that would weaken loyalty to, or make for the destruction of the Constitutional Union. Sustains the American principles of representative government and of equal rights and impartial justice for all Americans. Membership is open to female descendants of Union Veterans of the Civil War.

20302 ■ Military Order of the Loyal Legion of the United States (MOLLUS)

1805 Pine St.
Philadelphia, PA 19103
Ph: (517)694-9394
Fax: (517)694-0817
E-mail: pcinc@prodigy.net
URL: http://suvcw.org/mollus/molid.htm
Contact: Mr. Keith Harrison, Junior Vice Commander-in-Chief
Founded: 1865. **Members:** 1,000. **State Groups:** 17. **Description:** Male descendants of honorably discharged commissioned officers serving in the Union forces during the Civil War and descendants of the brothers or sisters of such officers. **Awards:** Loyal Legion Award Medal. **Type:** medal ● ROTC Awards. **Type:** recognition. **Publications:** *Loyal Legion Historical Journal,* quarterly. Covers membership news and activities; includes historical articles on the Civil War. **Price:** included in membership dues; $10.00 /year for nonmembers. **Circulation:** 1,000. **Conventions/Meetings:** annual convention and congress, meeting of Commander-in-Chief to conduct national business of the Order.

20303 ■ Military Order of the Stars and Bars (MOSB)

PO Box 100
Daphne, AL 36526
Ph: (251)626-0151
Free: (877)790-6672
E-mail: mosbhq@aol.com
URL: http://www.mosbihq.org
Contact: Dr. C. Anthony Hodges, Lt. Commander Gen.
Founded: 1938. **Members:** 2,015. **Membership Dues:** individual, $25 (annual) ● life, $100-$300. **Staff:** 5. **Budget:** $150,000. **State Groups:** 19. **Local Groups:** 121. **Description:** Represents members of Sons of Confederate Veterans (see separate entry)

whose ancestors served as commissioned Confederate officers or elected or appointed officials of the executive or legislative branch of the Confederate civil government during the Civil War. **Libraries: Type:** reference; not open to the public. **Holdings:** 350; archival material. **Subjects:** Confederate veterans, unit histories. **Awards:** Douglas S. Freeman Literary Award. **Frequency:** annual. **Type:** monetary. **Recipient:** for best book on the Confederacy. **Committees:** Genealogy; Handbook; Headquarters Operation; Resolution; Rules and Credentials; Time and Place. **Councils:** General Executive; Southern Attorneys. **Affiliated With:** Sons of Confederate Veterans. **Formerly:** (1978) Order of the Stars and Bars. **Publications:** *Officers Call,* quarterly. Newsletter. **Price:** $3.00/issue. **Advertising:** accepted. **Alternate Formats:** online. **Conventions/Meetings:** annual reunion (exhibits) - usually August.

20304 ■ Sons of Confederate Veterans (SCV)

c/o Ben C. Sewell, III, Exec. Dir.
PO Box 59
Columbia, TN 38402-0059
Ph: (931)380-1844 (931)388-9303
Free: (800)380-1896
Fax: (931)381-6712
E-mail: exedir@scv.org
URL: http://www.scv.org
Contact: Ben C. Sewell III, Exec. Dir.
Founded: 1896. **Members:** 33,000. **Membership Dues:** individual, $20 (annual). **Staff:** 9. **Budget:** $1,100,000. **Regional Groups:** 3. **State Groups:** 36. **Local Groups:** 820. **Description:** Lineal and collateral descendants of Confederate Civil War veterans. Engages in historical and benevolent activities. **Libraries: Type:** reference. **Holdings:** 500; archival material. **Subjects:** Confederate veterans, unit histories. **Awards:** Brooks Medical Research Fund. **Frequency:** annual. **Type:** monetary. **Recipient:** to medical school graduates who descended from Confederate military veterans and perform medical research ● Stand Watie Scholarship. **Frequency:** annual. **Type:** scholarship. **Councils:** General Executive. **Affiliated With:** Military Order of the Stars and Bars. **Also Known As:** United Confederate Veterans. **Publications:** *Confederate Veteran,* bimonthly. Magazine. **Price:** $26.00/year. **Circulation:** 37,000. **Advertising:** accepted. **Conventions/Meetings:** annual convention and reunion (exhibits) - usually August.

20305 ■ Sons of Union Veterans of the Civil War (SUVCW)

c/o Lee F. Walters, Exec. Dir.
PO Box 1865
Harrisburg, PA 17105-1865
Ph: (717)232-7000
E-mail: execdir@suvcw.org
URL: http://suvcw.org
Contact: Lee F. Walters, Exec. Dir.
Founded: 1881. **Members:** 7,500. **Membership Dues:** regular (from Jan 1 - June 30), $41 (semiannual) ● regular (from July 1 - December 31), $25 (semiannual). **Staff:** 1. **State Groups:** 26. **Local Groups:** 230. **Description:** Male descendants of veterans of the Union Army, Navy, or Marine Corps of the Civil War. Activities include observance of national holidays, especially Memorial Day. Marks graves of Civil War veterans; supervises care and upkeep of Civil War memorials; encourages proper teaching of American history in schools. Does not maintain information records of Civil War veterans or service records of discharge. Operates charitable program and offers children's services. **Awards:** SUVCW Commander-in-Chief's Scholarship. **Frequency:** annual. **Type:** scholarship. **Computer Services:** Online services, general and membership inquiries. **Committees:** Americanism and Education; Constitution and Regulations; Grave Registration; History; Legislative; Lincoln Tomb Observance; Membership; Military Affairs; Program and Policy. **Affiliated With:** Auxiliary to Sons of Union Veterans of the Civil War; Daughters of Union Veterans of the Civil War, 1861-1865. **Formerly:** (1925) Sons of Veterans, USA. **Publications:** *The Banner,* quarterly. Journal. Includes historical articles on the Civil War period and Grand Army of

the Republic. **Price:** $12.00/year. **Circulation:** 7,500. **Conventions/Meetings:** annual National Encampment - conference (exhibits) - usually 2nd week of August.

20306 ■ United Daughters of the Confederacy (UDC)

UDC Bus. Off.
328 N Blvd.
Richmond, VA 23220-4009
Ph: (804)355-1636
Fax: (804)353-1396
E-mail: hqudc@rcn.com
URL: http://www.hqudc.org
Contact: Mrs. Janice K. Langford, Pres. Gen.

Founded: 1894. **Members:** 20,000. **Staff:** 7. **State Groups:** 33. **Local Groups:** 1,000. **National Groups:** 728. **Description:** Women no less than 16 years of age who are lineal or collateral blood descendants of men and women who served honorably in the Army, Navy, or Civil Service of the Confederate States of America, or gave Material Aid to the Cause. The objectives of the organization are historical, educational, benevolent, memorial, and patriotic. **Libraries: Type:** reference; by appointment only. **Holdings:** 2,500. **Subjects:** Civil War years (1861-1865). **Awards:** Mrs. Simon Baruch University Award. **Frequency:** biennial. **Type:** monetary. **Committees:** Benevolent; Children of the Confederacy; Education; History; Memorial; Patriotic; Southern Literature; Southern Poets. **Publications:** *Annual General Minutes*, annual. Handbook ● *United Daughters of the Confederacy Magazine*, 11/year. **Price:** $15.00/year. **Circulation:** 9,500. **Advertising:** accepted. **Conventions/Meetings:** annual conference and convention - always November.

Coast Guard

20307 ■ Coast Guard Auxiliary Association (CGAUXA)

9449 Watson Indus. Park
St. Louis, MO 63126
Ph: (314)962-8828
Fax: (314)962-6804
E-mail: executivedirector@cgauxa.org
URL: http://nws.cgaux.org
Contact: Martin L. Phillips, Exec. Dir.

Founded: 1960. **Members:** 36,000. **Membership Dues:** supporter level associate, $25 (annual) ● sustainer level associate, $50 (annual) ● lifesaver level associate, $100 (annual) ● navigator level associate, $500 (annual) ● commander's circle level associate/corporate, $1,000 (annual) ● captain's circle level associate/corporate, $2,500 (annual) ● commodore's circle level associate/corporate, $5,000 (annual) ● admiral's circle level associate/corporate, $10,000 (annual) ● president's circle level associate/corporate, $25,000 (annual). **Staff:** 5. **Budget:** $996,000. **Description:** Supports the voluntary efforts of the U.S. Coast Guard Auxiliary. Provides business services for the volunteer organization; comprised of all members of the U.S. Coast Guard Auxiliary as well as associate members who provide monetary contributions to support the various auxiliary programs. Volunteers perform various duties in support of the U.S. Coast Guard including recreational boating safety through public education classes, vessel safety checks, public outreach and public affairs programs; marine and environmental protection; operational and administrative support missions with the U.S. Coast Guard; homeland security missions, including maritime domain awareness education and observations reporting. **Libraries: Type:** reference. **Holdings:** articles, books, periodicals, photographs. **Subjects:** auxiliary and recreational boating. **Additional Websites:** http://www.cgauxa.org. **Publications:** *The Beacon*, quarterly. Newsletter ● *Educational Books/Materials for Boating Safety Courses* ● *The Navigator*, quarterly. Magazine ● Manuals. For internal guidance of the auxiliary. **Conventions/Meetings:** annual convention (exhibits).

20308 ■ United States Coast Guard Chief Petty Officers Association (USCG CPOA)

5520-G Hempstead Way
Springfield, VA 22151-4009
Ph: (703)941-0395
Fax: (703)941-0397
E-mail: cgcpoa@aol.com
URL: http://uscgcpoa.org
Contact: Tom R. Scaramastro, Exec. Dir.

Founded: 1969. **Members:** 12,000. **Membership Dues:** individual, $24 (annual) ● life (ages 35 and below), $450 ● life (ages 36 to 50), $400 ● life (ages 51 or over), $350. **Staff:** 2. **Budget:** $200,000. **State Groups:** 59. **Description:** U.S. Coast Guard Chief Petty Officers and USCG Enlisted (EG and below) who are active, retired, or reserve. Aims to: promote the welfare of Coast Guard enlisted personnel and their dependents; promote social and recreational activities on the local level; foster cooperation with all local civic groups; aid in the interest of handicapped or hospitalized children and other people in need; foster patriotism and a belief in the democratic form of government. Assists in the recruitment of U.S. Coast Guard. **Awards: Type:** recognition. **Recipient:** to individuals and chapters for achievement, citizenship, and civic participation ● **Type:** scholarship. **Committees:** College Assistance Fund. **Publications:** *The Chief*, quarterly. Magazine. **Price:** included in membership dues; $11.00 for nonmembers ● *National News*, quarterly. Newsletter. **Conventions/Meetings:** annual meeting - always August.

Colonial

20309 ■ Colonial Order of the Acorn (COA)

20 MacKenzie Glen
Greenwich, CT 06830
Ph: (203)661-3993
Fax: (203)661-3992
Contact: John Badman III, Chancellor

Founded: 1894. **Members:** 185. **Membership Dues:** $5 (annual). **Description:** Male descendants or residents of the North American colonies, which became the 13 original states. Members are primarily from NY, NJ, CT, PA, though 60&percent; of its members came from other parts of the U.S. Acorn signifies the members of the 13 colonies who were the "Acorns from which grew the Tall Oak of the U.S." Cherishes and perpetuates American traditions and associations; promotes patriotism and loyalty to American national institutions; encourages social intercourse among the descendants of the nation's founders; stimulates vigilance and united action in the preservation and promotion of political theories and principles of America's forefathers without regard to political party divisions or ecclesiastical denominations. Collects and preserves records of colonial incidents; encourages preparation and study of historical and patriotic papers and history. **Publications:** Yearbook, every 12-14 years. **Conventions/Meetings:** semiannual meeting and dinner - always November and May.

20310 ■ Descendants of Founders of New Jersey (DFNJ)

816 Grove St.
Point Pleasant Beach, NJ 08742
E-mail: eogden@njfounders.org
URL: http://www.njfounders.org
Contact: Evelyn Ogden, Registrar

Founded: 1982. **Members:** 250. **Membership Dues:** basic, $12 (annual) ● life, $150. **Description:** Individuals aged 18 and over who can prove descent from a founder of the state of New Jersey. Defines founders as people who, prior to April 17, 1702, either settled or financed settlement in what is now New Jersey. Promotes fellowship among members; seeks to identify new founders and their descendants. **Libraries: Type:** reference. **Awards: Frequency:** annual. **Type:** recognition. **Computer Services:** Online services, genealogical information about founders of new jersey ● online services, membership forms. **Publications:** *Founders of New Jersey: Brief Biographies by Descendants*. Book. Contains a comprehen-

sive index to names found in the biographical entries. **Price:** $20.00 ● Bibliographies ● Brochure. **Conventions/Meetings:** semiannual meeting - always May and November, in New Jersey.

20311 ■ Flagon and Trencher - Descendants of Colonial Tavern Keepers (F&T)

c/o James Raywalt, Pres./Registrar
300 N Hill Rd.
Sutton, WV 26601-1206
E-mail: jraywalt@aol.com
URL: http://www.flagonandtrencher.org
Contact: James Raywalt, Pres./Registrar

Founded: 1962. **Members:** 1,000. **Membership Dues:** life, $75 ● supplemental fee, $25. **Staff:** 3. **Description:** Descendants of persons operating a tavern, inn, or other type of hostelry on, or prior to, July 4, 1776. Collects and disseminates information on taverns and their keepers, customs, recipes, menus, and other pertinent data; develops a collection of genealogic records of tavern-keeping ancestors. **Formerly:** (1999) Flagon and Trencher. **Publications:** *Colonial Tavernkeepers*, periodic. Journal. Presents a collection of sketches of members' ancestors. **Price:** $5.00/issue ● Directory, periodic. **Conventions/Meetings:** annual meeting and luncheon - always June at a pre-1776 Inn.

20312 ■ General Society of Colonial Wars (GSCW)

c/o Langsdale Library
Univ. of Baltimore
1420 Maryland Ave.
Baltimore, MD 21201
E-mail: gscw@ubalt.edu
URL: http://www.gscw.org

Founded: 1892. **Members:** 4,250. **State Groups:** 31. **Description:** Male descendants of men who rendered military or civil service to the colonies between 1607 (settlement of Jamestown, VA) and 1775 (battle of Lexington). Conducts research and educational programs. **Libraries: Type:** not open to the public. **Holdings:** 5,000. **Subjects:** colonial era history, proceedings of Society of Colonial Wars. **Awards:** Samuel Victor Constant Award. **Type:** recognition ● **Frequency:** annual. **Type:** scholarship ● Student Essay Contest. **Frequency:** annual. **Type:** grant. **Recipient:** for essay on Colonial Era. **Computer Services:** database ● mailing lists. **Publications:** *The Gazette*, quarterly. Newsletter. **Price:** free for members. **Circulation:** 4,250 ● *General Society of Colonial Wars Yearbook*, annual ● Various publications by the 31 State Societies relating to the Colonial Era 1607-1775. **Conventions/Meetings:** annual congress.

20313 ■ Hereditary Order of the First Families of Massachusetts (FF-MA)

300 N Hill Rd.
Sutton, WV 26601-1206
Ph: (304)765-0321
Fax: (304)765-0322
E-mail: jraywalt@aol.com
Contact: James Raywalt, Genealogist Gen.

Founded: 1985. **Members:** 516. **Staff:** 5. **State Groups:** 48. **Description:** Lineal descendants of individuals who settled in the Massachusetts Bay Colony before 1650. Commemorates anniversaries and events of the early Massachusetts Bay period. Seeks to correct what the group feels are misconceptions regarding the events leading to the founding of Massachusetts Bay Colony, its early history, and the Puritans who established the colony. Serves as a forum for the exchange of information among members; disseminates information on the contributions of the Puritans in the development of America. **Publications:** Directory, biennial. List of Members. **Price:** free ● Pamphlets.

20314 ■ Holland Society of New York (HSNY)

122 E 58th St.
New York, NY 10022
Ph: (212)758-1675
Fax: (212)758-2232

E-mail: hollsoc@aol.com
URL: http://www.hollandsociety.org
Contact: Rev. Louis O. Springsteen, Sec.
Founded: 1885. **Members:** 1,000. **Membership Dues:** regular (age 30 and over), $60 (annual) ● regular (age 18-29), $20 (annual) ● life (age 0-75 and over), $250-$750. **Staff:** 5. **Budget:** $170,000. **Regional Groups:** 25. **Description:** Descendants in the direct male line of settlers in the Dutch Colonies in North America prior to 1675. Collects and preserves data on the early history of the Dutch Colonies and the genealogy of descendants of early settlers. Has translated baptismal, marriage, and death records of early Dutch churches. Conducts research and historical publications programs. **Libraries: Type:** not open to the public. **Holdings:** 15,000; books, clippings, photographs. **Subjects:** New Netherlands. **Publications:** *De Halve Maen: Magazine of the Dutch Colonial Period in America*, quarterly. Includes society news and obituaries. **Price:** included in membership dues; $28.50 /year for nonmembers in U.S.; $32.50 /year for nonmembers outside U.S. ● Directory, annual ● Newsletter, quarterly. Includes society activities and announcements of family Association meetings. **Conventions/Meetings:** annual assembly, memorial church service ● annual banquet.

20315 ■ Jacques Timothe Boucher Sieur de Montbrun Heritage Society (JTBSMHS)
c/o Peggy Binkley, Treas.
4009 Ivy Dr.
Nashville, TN 37216
E-mail: timothydemonbreun@comcast.net
URL: http://www.genealogy.com/users/d/e/m/ Timothy-Demonbreun
Contact: Peggy Binkley, Treas.
Founded: 1975. **Members:** 550. **Membership Dues:** active and associate, $15 (annual). **Regional Groups:** 3. **Description:** Descendants of French pioneer and nobleman Pierre Boucher (1622-1717) and his great-grandson Timothe de Montbrun (1747-1826), early French-Canadian governor of Illinois Territory and settler of Nashville, TN; associate members are nondescendants. Aims to promote the study of North American French colonial history as it relates to de Montbrun and his ancestors. (The de Montbrun family has been historically noted as the first European family that occupied the site of Nashville, TN). **Libraries: Type:** not open to the public. **Holdings:** 200; biographical archives, books. **Subjects:** history, biographies, genealogy. **Computer Services:** database, history and data on Boucher, de Montbrun and allied families. **Committees:** Cemetery Preservation; Monument; Research and Publications. **Also Known As:** Timothy Demonbreun Society. **Publications:** *The Timothy Demontbrun Heritage Society*, quarterly. Journal. Contains articles, announcements pictures, poems, and genealogic data. **Price:** free, for members only. **Circulation:** 450 ● Also publishes biographical monographs and reprints. **Conventions/Meetings:** annual Timothy Demonbreun Day - conference (exhibits) - on varying dates in Nashville, TN ● annual Timothy Demonbreun Society Rendezvous - meeting and lecture, reprints, memorabilia, fund-raising items (exhibits).

20316 ■ Jamestowne Society (JS)
PO Box 17426
Richmond, VA 23226
Ph: (804)673-6006
URL: http://www.jamestowne.org
Contact: Kelly Carson Johnson, Exec. Dir.
Founded: 1936. **Members:** 5,500. **Membership Dues:** life, $300. **Staff:** 1. **Regional Groups:** 23. **State Groups:** 23. **Description:** Represents lineal descendants of early settlers of Jamestown, VA. **Awards:** Jamestowne Society Fellowship. **Frequency:** annual. **Type:** fellowship. **Publications:** *Jamestowne Society Newsletter*, semiannual ● *Qualifying Ancestor List*. Directory. Lists all qualifying ancestors to join the society. **Price:** $15.00 ● *Roster of Members 1995*. Membership Directory. **Price:** $20.00. **Conventions/Meetings:** semiannual meeting and luncheon - always second Saturday in May and November.

20317 ■ National Society of the Colonial Dames of America (NSCDA)
2715 Que St. NW
Washington, DC 20007
Ph: (202)337-2288
Fax: (202)337-0348
E-mail: info@dumbartonhouse.org
URL: http://www.nscda.org
Contact: Mr. Bill Birdseye, Dir.
Founded: 1891. **Members:** 15,500. **State Groups:** 44. **Description:** Consists of women whose direct ancestors held positions of leadership in the Thirteen Colonies in the period before July 5, 1776. **Additional Websites:** http://www.dumbartonhouse.org. **Conventions/Meetings:** biennial meeting.

20318 ■ National Society Colonial Dames XVII Century
1300 New Hampshire Ave. NW
Washington, DC 20036-1595
Ph: (202)293-1700
E-mail: registrar@colonialdames17c.net
URL: http://www.colonialdames17c.net
Contact: Mrs. Richard E. Hemmingway, Pres. Gen.
Founded: 1915. **Members:** 14,000. **Staff:** 3. **State Groups:** 47. **Local Groups:** 398. **Description:** American women who are lineal descendants of persons who lived and served prior to 1701 in one of the Original Colonies in the geographical area of the present United States of America. Aids in preservation of records and historical sites and fosters interest in historical colonial research. Maintains a museum collection. **Libraries: Type:** open to the public. **Holdings:** archival material, papers. **Subjects:** lineage, birth, cemetery records, county histories. **Awards:** General Scholarship. **Frequency:** annual. **Type:** scholarship ● Pocahontas Scholarship. **Frequency:** annual. **Type:** scholarship. **Committees:** Colonial Heritage Research and Records; Flag Custodian; Grave Markers; Heraldry and Coats of Arms; Marking and Preservation of Historic Sites; Museum; Music; National Defense; NSCDXVIIC General Scholarship; Pocahontas Projects; Veterans Service. **Publications:** *Seventeenth Century Review*, quarterly. Magazine. **Conventions/Meetings:** annual conference (exhibits) - always April, Washington, DC.

20319 ■ National Society Colonial Daughters of the 17th Century
c/o Mrs. Donald Zimmerman
PO Box 200
Harvel, IL 62538
Ph: (217)526-4530
Fax: (217)526-3725
E-mail: zimfarm@consolidated.net
Contact: Mrs. Donald Zimmerman, Contact
Founded: 1896. **Description:** Women lineally descended from ancestors who rendered service to the American colonies from 1607 to 1699. Membership is by invitation only. Preserves the memory of the founders of the nation; commemorates historical incidents of the colonial period; collects and preserves colonial relics and documents; and erects tablets at places of historical interest relating to that period. **Publications:** *Lineage Books*. Contains chapter listings, membership roster, and ancestor index.

20320 ■ National Society, Daughters of the American Colonists (DAC)
2205 Massachusetts Ave. NW
Washington, DC 20008
Ph: (202)667-3076
Fax: (202)667-0571
E-mail: nsdac@excite.com
URL: http://www.nsdac.org
Contact: Ms. Georgia Holder, Natl. Pres.
Founded: 1921. **Members:** 7,000. **State Groups:** 51. **Local Groups:** 332. **Description:** Women descended from men and women who gave civil or military service to the Colonies prior to the Revolutionary War. **Libraries: Type:** reference. **Awards: Type:** scholarship. **Committees:** Award to U.S. Army, Navy, Coast Guard, Air Force, and Merchant Marine Academy Honor Cadets; Colonial and Genealogical Records; Colonial Heritage; Flag and Banner Service; Memorials and Marking Historical Spots; Microfilm;

National Defense; Patriotic Education; Veterans Services. **Publications:** *Colonial Courier*, 3/year ● Directory, annual ● Handbook. **Conventions/Meetings:** annual general assembly - always April in Washington, DC.

20321 ■ National Society of Descendants of Lords of the Maryland Manors (NSDLMM)
Address Unknown since 2007
Founded: 1938. **Members:** 107. **Membership Dues:** lineal, $20 (annual). **Description:** Descendants of the First Baron of Baltimore or of colonists granted a manor by the Lord Proprietor of the Province of Maryland. Works to identify and mark locations of manors established in the colonial era. Seeks to stimulate patriotism, understanding of American history, and devotion to the ideals of liberty as expressed in the Declaration of Independence, the U.S. Constitution, and the Bill of Rights. Encourages interest in literature, history, art, and science. Sponsors annual pilgrimage to and erection of memorials at early manorial sites in Maryland. **Libraries: Type:** reference. **Holdings:** 4. **Subjects:** scrapbooks. **Awards: Type:** recognition. **Committees:** History of the Society; Memorial Marking. **Publications:** *Annual Report by the President* ● *Register, The National Society of Descendants of Lords of the Maryland Manors*, biennial. **Conventions/Meetings:** annual meeting.

20322 ■ National Society, Sons of the American Colonists
c/o Arthur Louis Finnell, Natl. Registrar
3917 Heritage Hills Dr., No. 104
Minneapolis, MN 55437-2633
Ph: (952)831-3607
E-mail: drg@execpc.com
URL: http://my.execpc.com/~drg/wisac.html
Contact: Arthur Louis Finnell, Natl. Registrar
Founded: 1956. **Members:** 300. **Membership Dues:** life, $25. **State Groups:** 6. **Description:** Fosters interest in historical and genealogical research of the colonial era. Assists in the preservation of colonial records and historic sites. **Publications:** *The Colonial Son*, semiannual. Newsletter. **Circulation:** 300 ● Also publishes Roster of Colonial Ancestors and Members; National Society Sons of the American Colonists 1997. **Conventions/Meetings:** annual General Court - banquet - always April in Washington, DC.

20323 ■ National Society Women Descendants of the Ancient and Honorable Artillery Company (DAH)
c/o Mrs. Daniel P. Moroney, Pres. Gen.
49 Carriage Hill Dr.
Windham, ME 04062-4927
Ph: (207)893-0175
E-mail: barbara@cobbemail.com
URL: http://my.execpc.com/~drg/wiwdah.html
Contact: Mrs. Daniel P. Moroney, Pres. Gen.
Founded: 1927. **Members:** 1,400. **State Groups:** 27. **Description:** Women of lineal descent from members of the Ancient and Honorable Artillery Company (1637-1774), or from the clergy who preached on the Drumhead Election Day (1638-1774) or of the General Court (Boston) of 1638. Compiles genealogical data. **Awards: Type:** scholarship. **Recipient:** to those who excel in history in Hillside School for Boys; to women studying the Preservation of Historical Architecture. **Publications:** *Genealogical Data of the Members of the Ancient and Honorable Artillery Company of Massachusetts* ● *History and Lineage Books I-VII, X* ● Yearbook. **Conventions/Meetings:** annual Rendezvous - congress - always Washington, DC.

20324 ■ Order of Americans of Armorial Ancestry (OAAA)
PO Box 453
Abingdon, MD 21009-0453
Ph: (410)515-1824

E-mail: ahallgren@yahoo.com
Contact: Mr. George William Hallgren Sr., Gen. Pres.
Founded: 1903. **Members:** 600. **Membership Dues:**
life, $200. **Description:** Descendants of immigrants
who were settlers in one of the 48 contiguous states
of the U.S. or descendants of those who had a proved
right to bear coat of armor in their original countries.
Promotes genealogical, biographical, and historical
research on the ancestry of American families of
armorial descent, and prints the research results.
Invites people for membership. **Publications:** *The
Armorial Herald*, semiannual. Newsletter. **Price:** available to members only. **Conventions/Meetings:** annual meeting - always April in Washington, DC.

20325 ■ Order of Descendants of the Ancient and Honorable Artillery Company
300 N Hill Rd.
Sutton, WV 26601
Ph: (304)765-0321
Fax: (304)765-0322
E-mail: jraywalt@aol.com
Contact: James Raywalt, Genealogist Gen.
Founded: 1988. **Members:** 150. **Membership Dues:**
life, $250 ● regular, $25 (annual). **Staff:** 5. **Description:** Men or women with descent from a member of
the Ancient and Honorable Artillery Company of Massachusetts between 1637-1774, and direct descendants of the siblings of those members. **Conven-
tions/Meetings:** semiannual meeting - April in
Washington, DC and October in Massachusetts.

20326 ■ Order of Descendants of Colonial Physicians and Chirurgiens (ODCPC)
5204 Kenwood Ave.
Chevy Chase, MD 20815-6604
Ph: (301)654-7233
Contact: John M. Pogue MD, Pres.Gen.
Founded: 1974. **Members:** 300. **Membership Dues:**
life, $150. **Description:** Direct descendants of physi-
cians, chirurgiens (archaic for surgeons), licensed
midwives, and other accredited healers who practiced
medicine during the U.S. colonial period, 1607-1783.
Objectives are to: identify and honor medical people
of colonial days; "promote love of America"; encourage fellowship among descendants. Collects and
preserves books on genealogical and biographical
history and documentation; maintains fund and
bestows medical scholarships and Honorary Memberships; compiles statistics. Has lectures at Annual
Meetings. **Awards:** Medical Scholarship. **Frequency:**
triennial. **Type:** scholarship. **Publications:** Membership Directory, triennial. **Conventions/Meetings:** annual meeting, includes lectures - always April.
Washington, DC - **Avg. Attendance:** 45.

20327 ■ Order of First Families of Connecticut 1631-1662
300 N Hill Rd.
Sutton, WV 26601
Ph: (304)765-0321
Fax: (304)765-0322
E-mail: jraywalt@aol.com
Contact: James Raywalt, Genealogist Gen.
Founded: 2004. **Membership Dues:** life, $250 ●
regular, $25 (annual). **Staff:** 5. **Description:** Descen-
dants of individuals who settled in any of the Con-
necticut settlements prior to 1662. **Conventions/
Meetings:** semiannual meeting - always April in
Washington, DC and October in Connecticut.

20328 ■ Order of First Families of Rhode Island and Providence Plantations (OFFR&PP)
300 N Hill Rd.
Sutton, WV 26601
Ph: (304)765-0321
Fax: (304)765-0322
E-mail: jraywalt@aol.com
Contact: James Raywalt, Registrar Gen.
Founded: 1991. **Members:** 200. **Membership Dues:**
life, $200 ● regular, $20 (annual). **Staff:** 8. **Descrip-
tion:** Collection and preservation of historical and
genealogical records of the founding families of
Rhode Island. **Publications:** *The Lively Experiment*,

semiannual. Magazine. **Conventions/Meetings:**
semiannual meeting, fall meeting is a business meeting - always April in Washington, DC and October in
Rhode Island.

20329 ■ Order of the Founders and Patriots of America (OFPA)
c/o National Society, Daughters of Founders and
Patriots of America
The Woodward Bldg.
733 15th St. NW, No. 915
Washington, DC 20005-2112
E-mail: info@founderspatriots.org
URL: http://www.founderspatriots.org
Contact: Alden Atwood, Governor Gen.
Founded: 1896. **Members:** 1,200. **State Groups:**
22. **Description:** Men who are lineal descendants, in
the male line of either parent, of an ancestor who
settled in any of the colonies now included in the
U.S. prior to May 13, 1657, and whose intermediate
ancestors in the same line served the patriot cause
during the American Revolution. Promotes discovery,
collection, and preservation of records, documents,
manuscripts, monuments, and history relating to the
first colonists, and their ancestors and descendants.
Maintains lineage papers of members. **Awards:** Frequency: annual. **Type:** recognition. **Recipient:** for
outstanding college or university ROTC units in each
of four U.S. Army ROTC regions ● **Frequency:** annual. **Type:** recognition. **Recipient:** for outstanding
Army National Guard and Air National Guard units.
Publications: *Bulletin*, semiannual. Magazine ●
Founders of Early American Families 1607-1657 ●
Register of Ancestors, quinquennial. **Conventions/
Meetings:** annual General Court - meeting - always
May 13.

20330 ■ Pilgrim Edward Doty Society (PEDS)
c/o Mary Lee Merrill, Membership Chair
52 Cushing Rd.
PO Box 45
Warren, ME 04864
E-mail: membership-24@edward-doty.org
URL: http://www.edward-doty.org
Contact: Mr. Benjamin Doten, Governor
Founded: 1982. **Members:** 900. **Membership Dues:**
life, $150 ● junior, regular, $10 (annual). **Budget:**
$8,000. **Description:** Individuals descended from or
interested in the history and lineage of Edward Doty,
a signer of the Mayflower Compact and a passenger
on the Mayflower, which landed at what is now Plymouth, MA on December 21, 1620. Promotes the
memory of Edward Doty through educational programs, the establishment of a memorial fund, and
the dissemination of literature on the lives of Doty
and other descendents of the Plymouth settlement.
Sponsors research and charitable programs. **Computer Services:** database, child lines ● electronic
publishing, list of members. **Publications:** *Child
Lines of Edward* ● *Doty-Doten Book* ● Membership
Directory, semiannual. **Price:** included in membership dues ● Newsletter, 3/year. **Price:** included in
membership dues. **Circulation:** 900. **Conventions/
Meetings:** triennial dinner - always September or
October.

20331 ■ Piscataqua Pioneers (PP)
Address Unknown since 2006
Founded: 1905. **Members:** 700. **Membership Dues:**
life, $100 ● $10 (annual). **Description:** Maine and
New Hampshire direct descendants of those who
settled prior to July 1776 in the Piscataqua Valley,
location of the first settlement in New Hampshire.
Works to secure and preserve the records of the Pis-
cataqua Valley pioneers and their descendants. **Li-
braries:** Type: reference. **Holdings:** 1,200; books.
Subjects: genealogical and historical material
complete set original membership applications with
some references attached. **Publications:** *Pioneers,
Register of Members and Ancestors*, every 10 years.
Quinquennial updates. ● *Piscataqua Pioneers*. Book.
Selected biographies of early settlers in Northern
New England. ● *Piscataua Pioneers 1623 - 1775*,
quinquennial. Register of members and ancestors
July 1996. **Price:** $45.00 plus $6 S&H ● Newsletter,
annual ● Plans to publish newsletter. **Conventions/

Meetings: annual meeting and luncheon - always
last Saturday in July.

20332 ■ Plymouth Historical Society (PHS)
155 S Main St.
Plymouth, MI 48170-1635
Ph: (734)455-8940
Fax: (734)455-7797
E-mail: secretary@plymouthhistory.org
URL: http://www.plymouthhistory.org
Contact: Sanford Burr, Pres.
Founded: 1990. **Members:** 200. **Membership Dues:**
student (under age 18), $10 (annual) ● individual,
$25 (annual) ● family, $40 (annual) ● sustaining, $75
(annual) ● corporate, patron, $150 (annual) ● Lincoln
Club, $300 (annual) ● corporate patron, $250 (annual) ● corporate Lincoln Club, $500 (annual). **Staff:**
5. **Description:** Direct lineal descendants from an
individual who settled in the Plymouth Colony before
1692. **Conventions/Meetings:** semiannual meeting -
always April in Washington, DC and October in Massachusetts.

20333 ■ Society of the Ark and the Dove (SAD)
PO Box 16374
Baltimore, MD 21201
E-mail: membership@thearkandthedove.com
URL: http://www.thearkandthedove.com
Contact: Worthington Peter Pearre, Sec.
Founded: 1910. **Members:** 212. **Membership Dues:**
regular, $50 ● life, $350. **Description:** Represents
direct descendants of Sir George Calvert (Baron of
Baltimore); persons with ancestors who came in
1633, under the command of Governor Leonard Cal-
vert, in the ships The Ark or The Dove to settle the
Province of Maryland. **Publications:** *Chronicles*,
semiannual. Newsletter. **Conventions/Meetings:**
semiannual assembly - always spring and fall.

20334 ■ Society of Daughters of Holland Dames (SDHD)
c/o Barbara Brinkley, Dir. Gen.
PO Box 82
Jay, NY 12941-0082
Ph: (518)946-2501
E-mail: info@hollanddames.org
URL: http://www.hollanddames.org
Contact: Barbara Brinkley, Dir. Gen.
Founded: 1895. **Members:** 150. **Membership Dues:**
junior, $50 (annual) ● individual, $75 (annual) ● life,
$2,250. **Description:** Female descendants of settlers
of New Netherlands prior to 1674. Promotes the
principles of Dutch ancestors; collects genealogical
and historical documents relating to the Dutch in
America. **Telecommunication Services:** electronic
mail, babrinkley@cs.com.

20335 ■ Society of the Descendants of the Colonial Clergy (SDCC)
17 Lowell Mason Rd.
Medfield, MA 02052-1709
E-mail: alebarba@mymailstation.com
URL: http://www.colonialclergy.org
Contact: Mr. Alexander Joshua Smith Jr., Contact
Founded: 1933. **Members:** 1,200. **Membership
Dues:** life, $175 ● ordinary, $45 (annual). **Descrip-
tion:** Lineal descendants of clergymen regularly
ordained, installed, or settled over any Christian
Church in the thirteen colonies prior to July 4, 1776.
Aims "to cherish the memory of the lives and works
of the colonial clergy in America; to collect and
preserve documents, histories, biographical sketches,
and memorials pertaining to the colonial clergy of
America and the parishes they served.". **Publica-
tions:** *Colonial Clergy*, semiannual. Newsletter.
Price: included in membership dues. **Conventions/
Meetings:** annual meeting - usually first Saturday of
November in Massachusetts.

20336 ■ Sons of Colonial New England National Society
300 N Hill Rd.
Sutton, WV 26601
Ph: (304)765-0321

Fax: (304)765-0322
E-mail: registrar@nsscne.org
URL: http://www.nsscne.org
Contact: James K. Raywalt, Registrar Gen.
Founded: 1985. **Members:** 325. **Membership Dues:** regular, $25 (annual) ● life, $250. **Staff:** 10. **Description:** Collection and preservation of historical and genealogical records of pre-revolution New England. Celebrates colonial New England heritage. **Awards: Frequency:** annual. **Type:** grant. **Recipient:** for New England historical societies. **Publications:** *The Pine Tree Colonial*, semiannual. Newsletter. **Price:** included in membership dues. **Conventions/Meetings:** annual meeting.

Disabled Veterans

20337 ■ Blinded American Veterans Foundation (BAVF)
PO Box 65900
Washington, DC 20035-5900
Ph: (202)462-4430
Fax: (301)622-3330
E-mail: email@bavf.org
URL: http://www.bavf.org
Contact: Sgt. John Fales Jr., Pres.
Founded: 1985. **Budget:** $75,000. **Nonmembership. Description:** Assists blinded and sensory-disabled veterans in attaining their full potential through research, rehabilitation, and re-employment. Offers employment networking and rehabilitation and resource counseling; provides funding for rehabilitation centers. Operates speakers' bureau and placement service; compiles statistics. Conducts research, educational, and charitable programs. **Awards: Type:** recognition. **Telecommunication Services:** electronic mail, sgtshaft@bavf.org. **Publications:** *Raising Cane*, quarterly. Newspaper. Covers veteran legislation and programs; large-print. **Price:** free. **Circulation:** 10,000. **Conventions/Meetings:** annual Flag Week Picnic, includes congressional reception - always near June 14 (Flag Day), in Washington, DC.

20338 ■ Disabled American Veterans (DAV)
PO Box 14301
Cincinnati, OH 45250-0301
Ph: (859)441-7300
Free: (877)426-2838
Fax: (859)442-2090
E-mail: feedback@davmail.org
URL: http://www.dav.org
Contact: Arthur H. Wilson, CEO
Founded: 1920. **Members:** 1,200,000. **Membership Dues:** individual, $40 (annual) ● life (below 40 years old), $250 ● life (ages between 41 and 60), $230 ● life (ages between 61 and 70), $180 ● life (over 70 years old), $140. **Staff:** 631. **Budget:** $146,000,000. **State Groups:** 52. **Local Groups:** 1,940. **Description:** Veterans with service-connected disabilities. Major activity is service to disabled veterans and their families. Employs approximately 260 National Service Officers in Department of Veterans Affairs (VA) offices in 50 states and Puerto Rico to act as free-of-charge attorneys-in-fact, counseling and processing veterans' claims for compensation and benefits. Provides services in areas including disaster relief, employment, legislation, advocacy, and transportation. **Awards:** Disabled Veteran of the Year. **Frequency:** annual. **Type:** recognition ● Employment of Disabled Veterans. **Frequency:** annual. **Type:** recognition. **Committees:** Credentials; Employment; Hospital and Voluntary Services; Nomination of National Officers; Reports. **Affiliated With:** Disabled American Veterans Auxiliary; National Order of Trench Rats. **Publications:** *DAV Magazine*, bi-monthly. Covers issues affecting disabled veterans and their families; includes association, department, chapter, and member news. **Price:** included in membership dues; $15.00 /year for nonmembers. ISSN: 0885-6400. **Circulation:** 1,100,000. Alternate Formats: online. **Conventions/Meetings:** annual convention - always summer. 2008 Aug. 9-12, Las Vegas, NV ● annual Mid-Winter Conference - 2008 Mar. 2-5, Arlington, VA.

20339 ■ Disabled American Veterans Auxiliary (DAVA)
PO Box 14301
Cincinnati, OH 45250-0301
URL: http://www.dav.org
Contact: James W. Jackson, Chm.
Founded: 1922. **Members:** 200,000. **Membership Dues:** life, 71-79 years old, $140 ● life, 61-70 years old, $180 ● life, 41-60 years old, $230 ● life, 40 or younger, $250. **Staff:** 10. **Regional Groups:** 21. **State Groups:** 50. **Local Groups:** 1,920. **Description:** Women relatives of service-connected disabled veterans, and women eligible in their own right to membership in the Disabled American Veterans (see separate entry). Aids the parent organization (DAV) and serves veterans and their dependents. Programs include: volunteer hospital work, Americanism, community service, child welfare, and legislative activities. Sponsors educational loan fund for children of DAV members. Provides services and support (financial aid) to DAVA widows. **Publications:** *DAV and Auxiliary Magazine*, bimonthly. **Price:** free for members. Alternate Formats: online ● Annual Report, annual. Alternate Formats: online. **Conventions/Meetings:** annual meeting.

20340 ■ Gay, Lesbian, Bisexual, and Transgendered Disabled Veterans of America (GLBTDVA)
c/o Sgt. Sharon F. Daugherty, II
3124 Scranton St.
Aurora, CO 80011
E-mail: disabled_vets@geocities.com
URL: http://www.geocities.com/pentagon/1151/enter.html
Contact: Sgt. Sharon F. Daugherty II, Contact
Founded: 1996. **Staff:** 3. **Description:** Works to assure that gay, lesbian, bisexual, and transgendered disabled veterans receive equal benefits and services, are not discriminated against and are treated with respect by VA service providers. Acts as an advisor to the Secretary of Veteran Affairs regarding issues affecting gay and lesbian veterans; recruits Field Representatives to be spokespersons; conducts fundraising activities; disseminates information to the public. **Formerly:** Lesbian Disabled Veterans of America.

20341 ■ National Order of Trench Rats (NOTR)
PO Box 1068
Kingston, PA 18704-0068
Ph: (570)714-2554
Fax: (570)714-1429
E-mail: notrir70@aol.com
URL: http://notrimperial.com/index.html
Contact: Paul C. Bailey, Contact
Founded: 1924. **Members:** 7,500. **Staff:** 3. **Regional Groups:** 21. **State Groups:** 36. **Local Groups:** 210. **Description:** Fraternal organization of male members of the Disabled American Veterans (see separate entry). Membership is by invitation. Promotes the fellowship of ex-servicemen "for the further benefit of the disabled man and to provide a fun and philanthropic order for the Disabled American Veterans." Contributes funds to assist in DAV legislative program and hospital work; takes part in charitable and civic activities. Provides titles for officers such as Golden Rodent, Silver Rodent, Blue Rodent, Bubonic Plague, Black Plague, Hole-y Rat, and Iron Claw. Is a recognized auxiliary of DAV. **Awards: Type:** recognition. **Telecommunication Services:** electronic mail, notr70@notrimperial.com. **Committees:** Rehabilitation. **Publications:** Bulletin, 5/year. **Conventions/Meetings:** annual meeting.

20342 ■ Operation Appreciation (OA)
c/o Non-Commissioned Officers Association of the U.S.A.
10635 1H 35 N
San Antonio, TX 78233
Ph: (703)549-0311
Free: (800)662-2620
Fax: (703)549-0245

E-mail: rschneiden@ncoadc.org
URL: http://www.ncoausa.org
Contact: Gene Overstreet, Pres./CEO
Founded: 1985. **Staff:** 6. **Budget:** $900,000. **Description:** Participants include veterans and citizens concerned with showing appreciation to disabled veterans. Helps hospitalized disabled veterans by raising funds by encouraging the public to send cards to boost their morale. Supports the veteran members of the two armed forces retirement homes (United States Soldier and Airman home in Washington D.C. and the Navel Home in Gulfport, MS). Assists lobbyists' efforts to increase disabled veterans' benefits. **Publications:** none. **Convention/Meeting:** none. **Telecommunication Services:** electronic mail, veterans@ncoadc.org. **Programs:** America's Children for America's Heroes; Intern; State Legislative; Veterans Outreach; Voter Registration. **Affiliated With:** Non Commissioned Officers Association of the United States of America; Operation Appreciation. **Also Known As:** National Defense Foundation.

20343 ■ Paralyzed Veterans of America (PVA)
801 18th St. NW
Washington, DC 20006-3517
Ph: (202)872-1300
Free: (800)424-8200
Fax: (202)785-4452
E-mail: info@pva.org
URL: http://www.pva.org
Contact: Mr. Louis Irvin, Exec. Dir.
Founded: 1947. **Members:** 19,000. **Regional Groups:** 32. **Description:** Veterans who have incurred an injury or disease affecting the spinal cord and causing paralysis. Through national service program, assists veterans, dependents, and survivors in obtaining Department of Veterans Affairs benefits due them; works for federal benefits of various kinds. Sponsors wheelchair sporting events. Promotes legislation to create accessibility to establishments and facilities for individuals with a disability. Sponsors research, rehabilitation, and educational programs. Founded the Spinal Cord Research Foundation to fund spinal cord research projects and fellowships. Also founded the Education and Training Foundation to provide grants to improve the knowledge, abilities, and skills of health professionals, spinal cord impaired patients, and their loved ones. **Departments:** Communication; Government Relations; Veterans Benefit. **Publications:** *Paraplegia News*, monthly. Magazine. Reports on organization efforts to ensure better care for persons with spinal cord injuries and diseases. Contains chapter and veteran news. **Price:** $23.00/year in U.S.; $39.00/2 years in U.S.; $32.00/year outside U.S.; $57.00/2 years outside U.S. ISSN: 0031-1766. **Circulation:** 80,000. **Advertising:** accepted ● *Sports-n-Spokes*, bimonthly. Magazine. Features articles on wheelchair sporting activities. Includes calendar of events and new product reviews. **Price:** $21.00/year in U.S.; $38.00/2 years in U.S.; $27.00/year outside U.S.; $50.00/2 years outside U.S. ISSN: 0161-6706. **Advertising:** accepted ● Booklets. **Conventions/Meetings:** annual meeting.

Dog

20344 ■ United States War Dogs Association (USWDA)
1313 Mt. Holly Rd.
Burlington, NJ 08016
Ph: (609)747-9340 (609)234-4539
E-mail: canines@uswardogs.org
URL: http://uswardogs.org
Contact: Ronald L. Aiello, Pres.
Founded: 2000. **Membership Dues:** active, $20 (annual) ● supporting/veteran, $30 (annual) ● life, $250. **Description:** Promotes the history of military service dogs. Establishes permanent war dog memorials. Educates the general public on the invaluable service of war dogs to United States. Supports service dogs' organizations through fundraising. **Computer Services:** Information services, war dogs resources ● mailing lists, of members ● online services, message forum and chat room. **Publications:** Newsletter.

Family Name Societies

20345 ■ A.D. Johnson Family Association (ADJFA)

c/o John S. Walker, Family Historian/Pres.
930 W Long Ave.
Du Bois, PA 15801-3512
Ph: (814)371-5149
Fax: (814)371-5149
E-mail: adjohnsonfamily@comcast.net
Contact: John S. Walker, Family Historian/Pres.

Founded: 1981. **Members:** 100. **Staff:** 1. **Regional Groups:** 2. **State Groups:** 2. **Local Groups:** 1. **Languages:** English, French, German. **Description:** Individuals related to the families of A.D. Johnson, Sarah Dillon Johnson, Dennison Johnson, Wealthy Johnson Hoover, and Edward and Esther Wheaton Johnson of Branford, CT, and Edward Johnson of Canterbury, England, founder of Woburn, MA. Conducts genealogical research on Johnson and related families; conducts educational programs. Provides care and replacement of family member gravestones. No collect calls or Sunday/Holiday calls are accepted. **Libraries: Type:** reference. **Holdings:** 1,000. **Subjects:** records on more than 2,500 Johnson related surnames; Clearfield, Bradford and Huntingdon Counties, Pennsylvania; Branford, Connecticut, and Woburn, Massachusetts; as well as Canterbury, England. **Computer Services:** Mailing lists, family research. **Conventions/Meetings:** annual reunion, features family genealogy and photographs (exhibits) - always mid-July in Raystown Dam, Huntingdon County, PA.

20346 ■ Adam Hawkes Family Association (AHFA)

c/o Cynthia Hawkes Meehan, Pres.
65 Center St.
Danvers, MA 01923
E-mail: mmais@sbcglobal.net
URL: http://freepages.family.rootsweb.com/~ahfa
Contact: Cynthia Hawkes Meehan, Pres.

Founded: 1876. **Members:** 250. **Membership Dues:** lineal descendant, $6 (annual) ● lineal descendant and spouse, $10 (annual) ● junior, $2 (annual) ● subscribing, $6 (annual). **Description:** Lineal descendants of Adam Hawkes (1605-1672) of Saugus, MA, and of John and Matthew Hawkes, who arrived in America before 1635; spouses of lineal descendants. Unrelated persons interested in the Hawkes/Hawks family line may join as subscribing (nonvoting) members. Seeks to publish Hawkes family genealogies and histories. Answers queries regarding the Hawkes/Hawks family line free of charge if accompanied by a self-addressed, stamped envelope. **Libraries: Type:** reference. **Subjects:** Hawkes/Hawks family genealogy. **Awards:** Hazen Wheeler Memorial Scholarship. **Frequency:** annual. **Type:** grant. **Recipient:** for member in good standing, at least one year enrolled and full time in an accredited college or university ● **Frequency:** annual. **Type:** scholarship. **Telecommunication Services:** electronic mail, samflint77@aol.com. **Publications:** *Hawkes Happenings*, semiannual. Newsletter. **Price:** free for members; $6.00 to subscribers. ISSN: 1067-9766. **Circulation:** 200 ● *Hawkes/Hawks In the 1920 Census, Soundex*. Contains information on the New England, Pacific/Rocky Mountain, South Central, South East, Mid-Atlantic, and North Central areas. **Price:** $7.50 per area ● *Hawkes Talks 1969-1989*. Bulletin. **Price:** $10.00 ● *Our Hawkes/Hawks Inventors, Their Inventions & Their Families*. **Price:** $8.00. **Conventions/Meetings:** annual reunion (exhibits) - always last Saturday of July in an area relevant to Hawkes/Hawles family history.

20347 ■ Adam Wise Family Association (AWFA)

29801 Highview Cir.
San Juan Capistrano, CA 92675
Ph: (949)661-4808
Fax: (949)661-2265
E-mail: rhrh3@cox.net
Contact: Rachel Hayward, Founder

Membership Dues: ordinary, $10 (annual). **Description:** Individuals with an interest in the history and genealogy of the descendants of Adam Wise. Promotes study of wise family history and genealogy. Facilitates exchange of information among members; gathers and disseminates information on the Wise family. **Publications:** *Adam Wise Family (Ancestors and Descendants of Johann Adam Weiss 1724-1781)*. Book. **Price:** $40.00.

20348 ■ Adams Family Association (AFA)

Address Unknown since 2006
Founded: 1979. **Staff:** 20. **National Groups:** 1. **Description:** Descendants of Jesse Allen Adams (1791-1866) and Elizabeth Bryant (1792-1832); other interested individuals. Facilitates communication among members of the Adams family. Gathers and disseminates genealogical and historical information pertaining to the Adams and related families. Conducts educational programs. **Libraries: Type:** reference. **Holdings:** biographical archives. **Subjects:** family history, adams family cook book. **Awards:** Adams Family Association Scholarship. **Frequency:** annual. **Type:** scholarship. **Recipient:** for first-year college freshman or family members by birth or marriage. **Committees:** Reunion; Scholarship. **Publications:** *Adams Family Chronicle*, semiannual. Newsletter. Contains family news, announcements and events. **Price:** $5.00. ISSN: 8755-5026. **Circulation:** 80. **Advertising:** not accepted. Alternate Formats: online ● *Adams Family Cook Book* ● *The History of the Adams Family*. Book ● Monographs ● Also publishes reunion program. **Conventions/Meetings:** annual Adams Family Reunion, quilts, books, artifacts - always 2nd weekend in October, Eufaula, AL, Lakepoint Resort.

20349 ■ Addington Association (AA)

12407 Millstream Dr.
Bowie, MD 20715
E-mail: association@addingtonassociation.org
URL: http://addingtonassociation.org
Contact: Jerry Sue Bowersox, Sec.-Treas.

Founded: 1988. **Members:** 100. **Membership Dues:** regular, $5 (annual). **Staff:** 2. **Budget:** $1,600. **Description:** Individuals interested in the genealogy and family history of people with the surname Addington. Promotes genealogical and historical study and interest. Conducts research and educational programs. **Libraries: Type:** reference. **Holdings:** 3; archival material, books, clippings, periodicals. **Subjects:** Addington family history and genealogy. **Publications:** Newsletter, 3/year, published in June, October, and February. Contains current news and yearly reunion information. **Price:** included in membership dues. **Circulation:** 100 ● Directory, annual. **Conventions/Meetings:** annual reunion, family trees, historical pictures and documents (exhibits) - always in late July.

20350 ■ Agnew Association of America (AAA)

Address Unknown since 2006
Founded: 1984. **Members:** 165. **Budget:** $2,500. **Description:** Individuals and descendants of Scotch-Irish heritage with the surname Agnew. Promotes the study of and interest in members' lineage. **Libraries: Type:** reference. **Holdings:** archival material, books. **Subjects:** Agnew family genealogy. **Publications:** *Agnewsletter*, quarterly. Covers membership activities; includes member profiles, new member listing, and list of upcoming events. **Price:** available to members only. **Conventions/Meetings:** biennial meeting.

20351 ■ Alden Kindred of America (AKA)

PO Box 2754
Duxbury, MA 02331-2754
Ph: (781)934-9092
Fax: (781)934-9149
E-mail: info@alden.org
URL: http://www.alden.org
Contact: Linda Osborne, Pres.

Founded: 1901. **Members:** 1,500. **Membership Dues:** junior, active, associate, $75 (annual) ● family (museum), $50 (annual) ● individual (museum), $25 (annual) ● business (museum), family, $100 (annual) ● life, $500-$1,000. **Staff:** 2. **Budget:** $60,000. **Description:** Descendants of John Alden and Priscilla Mullins Alden. Promotes interest in Alden family history and genealogy. Conducts educational programs; maintains Alden House Museum and Alden Barn. **Awards:** Donnell B. Young Scholarship. **Frequency:** annual. **Type:** scholarship. **Recipient:** for graduating high school senior member of AKA. **Publications:** Newsletter, semiannual. **Conventions/Meetings:** annual reunion (exhibits) - always first Saturday of August.

20352 ■ Alderson Cousins

c/o James A. Cross, Newsletter Ed.
Box 2245
El Cajon, CA 92021
E-mail: jimacross@cts.com
URL: http://www.fridley.net/alderson.htm
Contact: James A. Cross, Newsletter Ed.

Founded: 1989. **Members:** 50. **Membership Dues:** general, $8 (annual). **Description:** Individuals with the surname Alderson and its variants; others with an interest in the Alderson family. Promotes study of, and interest in, Alderson family history and genealogy. Serves as a clearinghouse on the Alderson family; provides assistance to Alderson family historians and genealogists. **Libraries: Type:** reference. **Holdings:** archival material. **Subjects:** Alderson family birth and death records and wills, land, cemetery, military pensions. **Computer Services:** database, Alderson family genealogies, vital records, census ● online services, genealogy website. **Publications:** *Alderson Roots and Branches*, quarterly. Newsletter. **Circulation:** 100. Alternate Formats: online.

20353 ■ Alford American Family Association (AAFA)

PO Box 1297
Florissant, MO 63031
Ph: (314)831-8648
E-mail: aafa@alfordassociation.org
URL: http://www.alfordassociation.org
Contact: Max R. Alford, Pres.

Founded: 1987. **Members:** 1,100. **Membership Dues:** regular, in U.S., $25 (annual) ● regular, outside U.S., $35 (annual). **Staff:** 15. **Budget:** $25,000. **Description:** Works to collect, record, and preserve biographical data on Alfords (and other spelling variations) and their ancestors. Disseminates educational information on Alford family history. Fosters communication among members. Aims to educate members and young Alford descendants on history and the family, as it relates to U.S. history. **Libraries: Type:** not open to the public; reference; lending. **Holdings:** archival material, books, clippings, monographs, periodicals. **Subjects:** history of the Alford family. **Awards: Frequency:** periodic. **Type:** recognition. **Computer Services:** database. **Publications:** *AAFA Action*, quarterly. Journal. Contains articles by members, news stories, member lineages, etc. **Price:** included in membership dues. ISSN: 1082-3212. **Circulation:** 550 ● *AAFA Online*, monthly. Newsletter. Contains information about AAFA. Alternate Formats: online ● Brochure. **Conventions/Meetings:** annual meeting and reunion - always 2nd weekend of October.

20354 ■ Allison Family Association

c/o Sandra Allison
10095 County Rd. 5120
Rolla, MO 65401-9717
Ph: (573)341-3549
Fax: (573)364-5310
E-mail: als@gte.net
URL: http://www.allisonclan.net
Contact: Sandra Allison, Contact

Founded: 1969. **Members:** 12,532. **Regional Groups:** 1,513. **State Groups:** 3,280. **Local Groups:** 964. **Description:** Individuals with the surname Allison; interested members of other family lines. Conducts genealogical research; sponsors history seminars. Provides indexing service; operates Speaker's Bureau; compiles statistics. **Libraries: Type:** reference. **Holdings:** 428; biographical archives. **Subjects:** genealogical. **Computer Services:** database. **Publications:** *Allison Family Line.* Booklets ● *Allison Family Lines,* bimonthly. Newsletter ● *Allison Journal,* annual. Alternate Formats: CD-ROM; online; magnetic tape ● *Allison Line Abstracting,* monthly ● *Allison Lines,* semiannual. Directory ● *Allison News Bulletin,* bimonthly. **Conventions/Meetings:** annual meeting (exhibits).

20355 ■ Allton, Alton, Aulton Family Association
c/o Cecil C. Alton
15510 Laurel Ridge Rd.
Dumfries, VA 22026-1019
Ph: (703)670-4842
E-mail: cecil.alton@comcast.net
URL: http://home.comcast.net/~cecil.alton
Contact: Cecil C. Alton, Contact
Founded: 1992. **Members:** 110. **Membership Dues:** regular, $12 (annual) ● contributing, $15 (annual) ● sustaining, $20 (annual). **Staff:** 1. **Budget:** $2,000. **Description:** Individuals interested in the family history and genealogy of people with the surname Alton and its variant spellings. Promotes genealogical study. Conducts research to uncover overseas ancestral links for individuals with the surname Alton, (includes Altom, Altum and Altham). **Additional Websites:** http://groups.aol.com/aaaafn. **Publications:** *Alton-Allton-Aulton Newsletter,* quarterly. **Price:** free. **Conventions/Meetings:** annual reunion.

20356 ■ American Clan Gregor Society
c/o Lois Ann Garlitz, Registrar
238 West 1220 N
American Fork, UT 84003
E-mail: gregor@webcom.com
URL: http://acgs.thecapitalscot.com
Contact: Lois Ann Garlitz, Registrar
Founded: 1909. **Members:** 600. **Membership Dues:** individual, $25 (annual). **State Groups:** 30. **Description:** Traces historical and genealogical material relating to the MacGregor clan. Sponsors competitions; offers educational, charitable, and research programs. **Libraries: Type:** reference; by appointment only. **Holdings:** 1,000; archival material, articles, books, clippings, periodicals. **Subjects:** historical and genealogical material relating to the McGregor clan. **Awards:** Edward May Magruder. **Frequency:** annual. **Type:** scholarship. **Recipient:** for a student enrolled in the school of medicine at University of Virginia. **Computer Services:** Mailing lists, of members. **Publications:** *Society Yearbook,* annual. **Price:** $10.00. **Circulation:** 700. **Conventions/Meetings:** annual MacGregor's Gathering - meeting (exhibits).

20357 ■ Andlauer Family Association
3929 Milton Dr.
Independence, MO 64055-4043
Ph: (816)373-5309
E-mail: groversar@aol.com
Contact: Robert L. Grover, Pres.
Founded: 1963. **Members:** 100. **Description:** Exchanges information among family members. **Publications:** none. **Convention/Meeting:** none.

20358 ■ Anneke Jans and Everardus Bogardus Descendants Association (AJEBDA)
c/o Mr. William Brower Bogardus, Founder
1121 Linhof Rd.
Wilmington, OH 45177-2917
Ph: (937)382-3803
E-mail: gosthunt@nycap.rr.com
URL: http://freepages.genealogy.rootsweb.com/~ghosthunter/Anneke/page0.htm
Contact: Mr. William Brower Bogardus, Founder
Founded: 1978. **Members:** 1,000. **Staff:** 2. **Description:** Descendants of Anneke Jans and Everardus Bogardus. Promotes interest in family history and genealogy. Conducts genealogical research. Plans to trace the descendants of Adam Brouwer of Brooklyn to the seventh generation, and Jan Brouwer of Flatlands for several generations also. **Libraries: Type:** by appointment only. **Holdings:** 1,500; articles, artwork, books, clippings, maps, periodicals. **Subjects:** Colonial families, New York and New Jersey history, genealogy. **Publications:** *Anneke JANS-BOGARDUS and Adam BROUWER Research Aid Bibliography.* Book. **Price:** $13.00 includes postage ● *Dear Cousin,* periodic. Newsletter ● *Dear Cousin: A Charted Genealogy of the Descendants of Anneke Jans Bogardus (1605-1663) to the 5th Generation.* Book. **Price:** $30.00 in U.S. and Canada (includes postage); $33.00 outside U.S. and Canada (includes postage) ● *Directory of Genealogical and Historical Articles Published in - de Halve Maen From 1923 to 1991.* **Price:** $8.00.

20359 ■ Ansley Family Association (AFA)
c/o Judy Candler, Chair
782 Wisham Rd.
Thomson, GA 30824
E-mail: c_jcandler@bellsouth.net
URL: http://www.ansley-family-assn.org
Contact: Judy Candler, Chair
Founded: 1978. **Members:** 200. **Membership Dues:** family, $10 (annual). **Staff:** 10. **Regional Groups:** 5. **Local Groups:** 10. **Multinational. Description:** Individuals with the surname Ansley or its variants and others related to the Ansley family through marriage or adoption. Promotes interest in Ansley family genealogy. Supports and assists Ansley genealogists. **Libraries: Type:** not open to the public; lending. **Holdings:** 20; archival material, audio recordings, books, clippings, video recordings. **Subjects:** Ansley family genealogy. **Computer Services:** database, Brother's Keeper Genealogy ● mailing lists ● online services. **Publications:** *Ansley Family Directory,* biennial. Contains a directory of known cousins. **Price:** $10.00/copy ● *Ansley Reunion,* semiannual. Newsletter. Contains family news, history and genealogy. **Price:** included in membership dues. **Circulation:** 350. **Conventions/Meetings:** annual reunion, with historical and genealogical information (exhibits).

20360 ■ Archer Association
PO Box 6233
McLean, VA 22106
Ph: (703)264-1372
E-mail: garcher@wdn.com
URL: http://www.archercousins.com/ArcherAssn
Contact: George W. Archer, Pres.
Founded: 1982. **Members:** 100. **Description:** Represents genealogists and family historians. Collects, preserves, and disseminates information on persons in the U.S. and Canada with the surname Archer and its variants. Offers research service. **Publications:** Books ● Also publishes indexes.

20361 ■ Association of Blauvelt Descendants (ABD)
3367 W 113th Ave.
Westminster, CO 80031-7179
Ph: (303)438-7267
Fax: (303)404-9099
E-mail: secretary@blauvelt.org
URL: http://www.blauvelt.org
Contact: Doris A. Blauvelt, Membership Sec.
Founded: 1926. **Members:** 700. **Membership Dues:** adult, $15 (annual) ● associate, $10 (annual) ● junior, $5 (annual) ● family, $35 (annual) ● life, $750 ● associate life, $250. **Staff:** 20. **Multinational. Description:** Descendants of Gerrit Hendricksen, Dutch settler and farmworker of Manhattan Island, NY. (Hendricksen's children and their descendants used the surname Blauvelt.) Promotes public interest in the genealogy, history, and ancestry of Dutch settlers in New York City. Seeks to perpetuate family traditions and collect genealogical information. Conducts research and disseminates findings. **Libraries: Type:** reference. **Holdings:** archival material, books, periodicals. **Subjects:** genealogy, generations 1-7. **Awards:** ABD Scholarship. **Frequency:** annual. **Type:** scholarship ● Association of Blauvelt Descendants. **Frequency:** annual. **Type:** scholarship. **Recipient:** for a high school student applying for college ● Raymond and Carolyn Blauvelt. **Frequency:** annual. **Type:** scholarship. **Recipient:** for a high school student applying for college ● Starr and Dorothy Schofield Blauvelt. **Frequency:** annual. **Type:** scholarship. **Recipient:** for a high school student applying for college. **Publications:** *Blauvelt Family Genealogy, Revised Ed. Vol. I, Generations 1-6.* Book. **Price:** $35.00/copy ● *Blauvelt Family Genealogy, Revised Ed. Vol. II, Generation 7.* Book. **Price:** $40.00/copy ● *Blauvelt News,* 3/year. Newsletter. **Price:** included in membership dues; $12.00 /year for nonmembers. **Circulation:** 500. **Conventions/Meetings:** annual reunion and meeting - September.

20362 ■ Aurand - Aurant - Aurandt Family Association
Address Unknown since 2007
Founded: 1988. **Members:** 175. **Membership Dues:** ordinary, $10 (triennial). **Budget:** $1,000. **National Groups:** 1. **Description:** Individuals with the surname Aurand or its variants; others with an interest in Aurand family genealogy. Promotes study of, and interest in, Aurand family genealogy and history. Provides support and assistance to Aurand family genealogists. **Libraries: Type:** reference. **Holdings:** 3; archival material. **Subjects:** Aurand family genealogy. **Computer Services:** Mailing lists. **Publications:** Newsletter, 3/year. **Conventions/Meetings:** annual board meeting ● triennial reunion.

20363 ■ Austin Families Genealogical Society (AFGS)
23 Allen Farm Ln.
Concord, MA 01742-2202
Ph: (978)369-8591
E-mail: queries@austins.org
URL: http://www.austins.org
Contact: Dr. Michael Edward Austin, Pres./Ed.
Founded: 1979. **Members:** 618. **Membership Dues:** individual, $12 (annual). **Staff:** 7. **Multinational. Description:** Represents Austin Family researchers. Exchanges Austin information. Specializes in Austin histories and genealogies. Conducts research programs. Publishes Austin-related queries. Sponsors International Austin Conventions and new Austin-Austen Research Center. **Libraries: Type:** reference. **Subjects:** Austin histories, genealogies. **Awards:** AFGS Austin Genealogical Research Award. **Frequency:** annual. **Type:** recognition. **Recipient:** for most significant contribution towards publishing Austin genealogical research. **Formerly:** (2005) Austins of America Genealogical Society. **Publications:** *Austin Families Register,* 3/year. Newsletter. **Circulation:** 800 ● *Austins of America - Volume 1.* Book. Contains index of 18,000 people and 4,000 places. **Price:** $75.00 plus $6 postage and handling ● *Austins of America - Volume 3.* Book. **Price:** $75.00 plus shipping and handling ($6) ● *Austins of America - Volume 2.* Book. **Price:** $75.00 plus shipping and handling ($6). **Conventions/Meetings:** annual international conference (exhibits).

20364 ■ Baker Family International
c/o Crystal Jensen, Genealogist
326 Panhorst
Staunton, IL 62088-1829
URL: http://members.tripod.com/~Crystal_J/Baker.html
Contact: Crystal Jensen, Genealogist
Founded: 1987. **Members:** 277. **Membership Dues:** regular, $15 (annual). **Staff:** 20. **Budget:** $4,500. **Description:** Seeks to preserve research on all branches of the Baker family. Fosters exchange among researchers working on the Baker family. Collaborates with genealogical libraries. **Convention/Meeting:** none. **Libraries: Type:** reference. **Holdings:** archival material, books, clippings. **Subjects:** Baker family groups in the U.S. and Europe. **Publications:** *Baker Family News International,* annual. Newsletter. ISSN: 0893-5831. **Circulation:** 227. Alternate Formats: microform.

20365 ■ Ballew Family Association of America
c/o Paul Ballew, Treas.
4227 Sandy Br. Dr.
Buford, GA 30519
Ph: (816)454-4218 (205)680-4711

E-mail: paulballew@bellsouth.net
URL: http://www.ballewassn.org
Contact: William Wayne Ballew, Pres.
Founded: 1980. **Members:** 455. **Membership Dues:** general, $10 (annual). **Staff:** 4. **Regional Groups:** 6. **State Groups:** 1. **Local Groups:** 1. **Description:** Descendants of the Ballew family; interested others. Conducts genealogical research; studies the history of families related to the Ballew name. **Libraries: Type:** reference. **Holdings:** books, business records, clippings, periodicals. **Subjects:** genealogy. **Publications:** *ANCESTORS, Ancient Ancestors and Their Descendants.* Book. **Price:** $99.00 for members; $110.00 for nonmembers ● *The Ballew Family Journal,* annual. **Conventions/Meetings:** annual International Ballew Reunion and Seminar - reunion and seminar.

20366 ■ Barney Family Historical Association (BFHA)

7503 Ridgebrook Dr.
Springfield, VA 22153
E-mail: bfha@aol.com
URL: http://www.barneyfamily.org
Contact: William C. Barney, Pres./Ed.
Founded: 1979. **Members:** 425. **Membership Dues:** individual, $10 (annual) ● individual, $15 (biennial) ● individual, $20 (triennial). **Description:** Collects information on the Barney family history. **Convention/Meeting:** none. **Libraries: Type:** reference. **Holdings:** archival material, books, clippings, monographs, periodicals. **Subjects:** Barney family history. **Publications:** *Barney Family News,* quarterly. Newsletter. **Price:** included in membership dues; $10.00 /year for nonmembers. ISSN: 1045-344X. **Circulation:** 425 ● *Genealogy of the Barney Family in America.* Book. **Price:** $59.00.

20367 ■ Bater Surname Organization (BSO)

Address Unknown since 2007
Founded: 1894. **Members:** 150. **Description:** Works to record and publish descendants of the Bater surname and its variants, Batter and Batt. **Libraries: Type:** open to the public. **Holdings:** 100; books. **Computer Services:** Mailing lists. **Telecommunication Services:** phone referral service. **Publications:** *Bater Book,* periodic. Newsletter. **Price:** $55.00. **Advertising:** not accepted. **Conventions/Meetings:** annual reunion - in Michigan.

20368 ■ Beall Family Association (BFA)

30 SE Gilham
Portland, OR 97215-1366
URL: http://www.geocities.com/Athens/5568/beall-stuff.html
Contact: William R. Beall, Ed.
Founded: 1991. **Members:** 140. **Membership Dues:** regular, $12 (annual). **Description:** Individuals interested in researching the surname Beall and its variants, Beale, Beal, Beals, Bale, and Bell. Works to consolidate, update, and correct information relating to the Beall families. **Libraries: Type:** reference. **Holdings:** articles, books, clippings, periodicals. **Subjects:** Beall family history. **Publications:** *Beall Genealogical News,* semiannual. Newsletter. Contains family history, genealogy, and biography. **Price:** included in membership dues. **Circulation:** 160. **Conventions/Meetings:** periodic reunion.

20369 ■ Bell Family Association of the United States

c/o Alta Jean Ginn, Membership Coor.
12147 Holly Knoll Cir.
Great Falls, VA 22066
Ph: (703)430-6745
Fax: (703)444-4597
E-mail: aginn@cox.net
URL: http://www.clanbell.org/usa
Contact: Alta Jean Ginn, Membership Coor.
Founded: 1985. **Members:** 445. **Membership Dues:** individual, $20 (annual) ● couple, $25 (annual). **Description:** Scottish descendants and friends of Family/Clan Bell. Studies Bell family and Scottish genealogy and history. Shares family stories and information. Offers the Association Genealogy program. **Libraries: Type:** open to the public. **Subjects:** Bell

history. **Awards: Type:** recognition. **Computer Services:** database of 500,000 names ● mailing lists. **Publications:** *NABELICH,* quarterly. Newsletter. Contains history, news, and a query section. **Price:** included in membership dues. **Circulation:** 500. **Conventions/Meetings:** periodic Gathering of Bells - convention (exhibits) - usually held in conjunction with Scottish Clans; various times of the year.

20370 ■ Bigelow Society

PO Box 807
Springfield, OR 97477
Ph: (541)741-6969
E-mail: bigsoctreas@aol.com
URL: http://bigelowsociety.com
Contact: John C. Bigelow, Treas.
Founded: 1976. **Members:** 450. **Multinational. Description:** Members of the Bigelow family. Studies the Bigelow family and allied names. Conducts genealogical research. **Libraries: Type:** reference. **Holdings:** 2; books. **Subjects:** family genealogy. **Computer Services:** Mailing lists, of members. **Publications:** *Forge: The Bigelow Family Genealogy,* quarterly. Newsletter. **Price:** $20.00/year. **Circulation:** 500. **Conventions/Meetings:** annual reunion and meeting, with entertainment, meals, barbecues, music (exhibits) - usually summer.

20371 ■ Blackburn Family Association (BFA)

608 S 16th St.
Philadelphia, PA 19146
Ph: (215)893-9343
E-mail: khowley@aol.com
URL: http://www.blackburn-tree.org
Contact: Kevin R. Howley, Sec.-Treas.
Founded: 1985. **Members:** 420. **Membership Dues:** regular, $12 (annual). **Description:** Families and individuals, especially descendants of John Blackburn (born in County Armagh, Ireland in the 17th century), interested in studying and preserving the Blackburn heritage. Supports historic preservation and research projects including restoration of Quaker cemeteries. Erects monuments in memory of early U.S. settlers. Provides genealogical and historical information to libraries. **Computer Services:** database, genealogical ● mailing lists. **Publications:** *Blackburn Annual Report,* annual. **Price:** free. **Circulation:** 6,000. **Advertising:** accepted ● *Blackburn Beginnings,* quarterly. **Price:** $12.50/year. **Circulation:** 420. **Conventions/Meetings:** biennial Blackburn Family Reunion (exhibits).

20372 ■ Blair Society for Genealogical Research (BSGR)

c/o Bryce D. Blair, Pres.
726 Falling Oaks Dr.
Medina, OH 44256-2778
E-mail: brydblair1@zoominternet.net
URL: http://www.blairsociety.org
Contact: Bryce D. Blair, Pres.
Founded: 1983. **Members:** 350. **Membership Dues:** active, in U.S., $18 (annual) ● contributing, $30 (annual) ● regular, in Canada, Mexico, $23 (annual) ● regular, outside U.S. and Canada, $28 (annual) ● patron, $500 (annual) ● life, $250. **Multinational. Description:** Individuals with the surname Blair and its variants; others with an interest in Blair family genealogy. Promotes interest in, and study of, Blair family genealogy; seeks to preserve family records and artifacts. Conducts educational programs; assists Blair family genealogists. **Libraries: Type:** reference; lending; not open to the public. **Holdings:** books, clippings. **Subjects:** Blair family genealogy. **Computer Services:** database, BSGR ancestral ● mailing lists. **Telecommunication Services:** electronic bulletin board, blair-society-L list. **Publications:** *Blair Family Magazine,* quarterly. Newsletter. Features Blair family genealogical research data. **Price:** included in membership dues ● Brochure ● Annual Report, annual. Alternate Formats: online ● Books. **Conventions/Meetings:** biennial convention.

20373 ■ Blencowe Families Association (BFA)

c/o Helen Blincoe Simpson
550 N Darlington St.
Rosemead, CA 91770-4312

Ph: (626)280-2506
E-mail: simpsonhb@earthlink.net
URL: http://www.blencowefamilies.com
Contact: Helen Bimcoe Simpson, Sec.
Founded: 1985. **Members:** 150. **Membership Dues:** individual, $8 (annual). **Staff:** 4. **Budget:** $1,500. **Multinational. Description:** Individuals with the surname Blencowe or its variant spellings: Blencow, Blencowe, Blenko, Blinco, Blincow, and Blincoe; others with an interest in family history and genealogy. Promotes study of Blencowe family history and genealogy. Facilitates exchange of information among members. **Computer Services:** database ● online services. **Publications:** *The Blencowe Families.* Book. Features a history of Blencowes since 1472. **Price:** $30.00 in North America ● *Blencowe Families Association Newsletter,* quarterly. Contains historical articles and queries. **Price:** included in membership dues. **Circulation:** 200. Alternate Formats: online. **Conventions/Meetings:** biennial reunion, family gathering.

20374 ■ Bloss-Pyles-Ross-Sellards Family

4031 Grand Ave.
Deland, FL 32720
Ph: (386)985-0909
E-mail: sellardsfamily@cfl.rr.com
Contact: Harry L. Sellards Jr., Contact
Founded: 1975. **Description:** Promotes genealogical research and study. Gathers and disseminates genealogical and historical information; conducts research. **Libraries: Type:** not open to the public. **Holdings:** books, clippings, periodicals. **Subjects:** history, genealogy. **Publications:** Booklets.

20375 ■ Blunden Family History Association

12041 Royce Waterford Cir.
Tampa, FL 33626
Ph: (813)792-2562
Fax: (813)792-8031
E-mail: america4b@msn.com
Contact: Mrs. America M. Carlson, Contact
Founded: 1984. **Description:** Individuals with an interest in the history and genealogy of the Blunden family. Promotes research and study of Blunden family genealogy. Conducts research and educational programs; provides assistance to Blunden family genealogists. **Formerly:** Blondin.

20376 ■ B'Man Family Association

c/o Chris Beeman, Founder
3416 Mayhurst Dr.
Indian Trail, NC 28079
Ph: (704)882-5676
E-mail: bman@bman.com
URL: http://www.bman.com
Contact: Chris Beeman, Founder
Founded: 1977. **Members:** 50. **Membership Dues:** individual, $10 (annual). **Staff:** 1. **Description:** Individuals with any form of the B'Man surname. Fosters communication and exchange among members. Accepts queries from non-members free of charge. **Convention/Meeting:** none. **Libraries: Type:** not open to the public. **Holdings:** 24; books. **Subjects:** B'Man surname. **Publications:** *B'Man Family Newsletter,* semiannual. **Price:** included in membership dues ● Descendants of Thomas Beeman of Kent, Connecticut by Clarence E. Beeman and Gwen B. Bjorkman.

20377 ■ Boggess Family Association

2811 Hwy. 59 S, No. 400
Livingston, TX 77351
Ph: (281)799-1444
E-mail: bitsybarr@hotmail.com
Contact: Ms. Bitsy Barr, Pres.
Founded: 1988. **Members:** 100. **Membership Dues:** family, $23 (annual). **Description:** Members of the Boggess and related families. Seeks to unite Boggess family members. Conducts genealogical research and distributes information. **Libraries: Type:** reference. **Publications:** *Boggess Family Newsletter,* semiannual. Contains photo album, newspaper articles, generation charts, English research results, and queries. **Price:** $15.00/year. **Circulation:** 100.

Conventions/Meetings: annual reunion, genealogy study group - usually July.

20378 ■ Bolling Family Association (BFA)

PO Box 591
Vienna, VA 22183-0591
Ph: (703)281-7489
Fax: (703)281-1052
E-mail: ciddad@aol.com
URL: http://www.bolling.net
Contact: Stewart Bentley, Pres.

Founded: 1991. **Members:** 500. **Membership Dues:** $20 (annual). **Budget:** $10,000. **Multinational. Description:** Descendants of the Bolling/Bowling/Bowlin/Bolen immigrants to the American continent. Promotes the maintenance of family ties and the preservation of family records. Conducts research programs; compiles statistics; operates the Bolling Foundation to preserve historic sites and holds biennial family reunions to promote fellowship and genealogical research and information exchange. **Libraries: Type:** not open to the public; lending. **Holdings:** archival material, articles, biographical archives, business records, papers, photographs. **Subjects:** genealogical records, historical site data, master data base containing over 70,000 records of individuals with Bolling sounding names. **Computer Services:** database, genealogical records of more than 70,000 individuals and DNA test results on samples submitted by members, bibliography of books of family interest. **Publications:** *Bolling Family Newsletter*, quarterly. Contains news about the association, historical reports, and a member inter-communication column. **Conventions/Meetings:** annual board meeting ● biennial Bolling Family Association Reunion, a three-day event including two receptions, a banquet, one full day of tours of family related sites, a business meeting, genealogical seminar, and displays (exhibits) - odd-numbered years. 2007 Oct. 4-7, Williamsburg, VA.

20379 ■ Bondurant Family Association (BFA)

c/o Jack Bondurant, Treas.
5112 Mt. Vernon Memorial Hwy.
Alexandria, VA 22309
E-mail: jbondur999@aol.com
URL: http://www.bondurant-family.org
Contact: Jack Bondurant, Treas.

Founded: 1987. **Members:** 250. **Membership Dues:** individual/family, $20 (annual). **Description:** Conducts research on ancestors and descendants of Jean-Pierre Bondurant (1677-1734), who was born in France and died in Virginia. **Publications:** *Bondurant Family Association Newsletter*, quarterly. Contains research on ancestors and descendants of J.P. Bondurant. **Price:** $10.00/year. **Circulation:** 230. **Conventions/Meetings:** annual convention, family memorabilia only.

20380 ■ Boone Society

40 Church Ct.
Sumter, SC 29150-4257
E-mail: info@boonesociety.com
URL: http://www.boonesociety.org
Contact: Rochelle Evans Cochran, Pres.

Founded: 1996. **Members:** 500. **Membership Dues:** individual, $20 (annual) ● family, $25 (annual) ● life, $200 ● explorer, $50 (annual). **Multinational. Description:** Works to identify and preserve Boone sites, artifacts and history. Provides reference services for Boone researchers and genealogists; acts as clearinghouse for bibliographic works; conducts education and research programs; compiles statistics; maintains Speaker's Bureau. **Computer Services:** database, Boone family genealogy data ● mailing lists. **Committees:** Genealogy; Historical Research; Newsletter; Reunions; Sarah's Circle; Site Preservation. **Publications:** *Compass*, quarterly. Newsletter. **Price:** $6.00 single issue for nonmembers; $115.00 entire archive for nonmembers; free for members. **Circulation:** 500. **Advertising:** accepted ● *Daniel Boone and the Defeat at Blue Licks*. Book. **Price:** $16.95 single copy ● Brochure ● Directory. **Price:** $10.00 single copy. **Conventions/Meetings:** biennial reunion and lecture, with historic site tours (exhibits) - always even years.

20381 ■ Boyt/e - Boyet/t/e Association

c/o Wendy Bebout Elliott, Pres.
1060 Magnolia Ave.
Placentia, CA 92870-4423
Ph: (714)993-1168
Fax: (714)993-1167
E-mail: welliott@fullterton.edu
Contact: Wendy Bebout Elliott, Pres.

Founded: 1981. **Members:** 30. **Membership Dues:** general, $25 (annual). **Staff:** 1. **Description:** Individuals with the surnames Boyt or Boyet or their variant spellings; others with an interest in the families' history and genealogy. Promotes interest in family history and genealogy. Serves as a clearinghouse on the Boyt and Boyet families. **Libraries: Type:** by appointment only; reference. **Holdings:** 10,000; books, periodicals. **Subjects:** Boyt, Boyet, Boyett, Boyette and Boyte family history and genealogy. **Computer Services:** database. **Publications:** *Boyt/e - Boyet/t/e Newsletter*, quarterly. No longer being published but old editions are still available. **Alternate Formats:** online.

20382 ■ Brainard-Brainerd-Braynard Family Association

Address Unknown since 2007

Founded: 1988. **Members:** 250. **Membership Dues:** ordinary, $15 (annual). **Staff:** 1. **Budget:** $3,500. **National Groups:** 1. **Description:** Individuals with the surname Brainard and its variants; others with an interest in Brainard family history and genealogy. Promotes study of Brainard family genealogy. Facilitates communication and good fellowship among members; conducts genealogical research; provides support and assistance to Brainard family genealogists. **Libraries: Type:** open to the public. **Holdings:** 10. **Publications:** *Newsletter of the Daniel Brainerd Society*, quarterly. **Price:** $15.00. **Circulation:** 250. **Advertising:** accepted.

20383 ■ Brancheau-Branchaud Family Association

c/o Douglas J. Miller, Pres.
22023 W Sunrise View Pl.
Santa Clarita, CA 91390
Ph: (661)296-8740
E-mail: djmill@earthlink.net
URL: http://www.fchsc.org/branchereau.html
Contact: Douglas J. Miller, Pres.

Founded: 1984. **Members:** 150. **Local Groups:** 1. **Description:** Individuals with the surname Brancheau and its variants; others with an interest in the Brancheau family. Promotes study of, and interest in, Brancheau family history and genealogy. Conducts genealogical research; provides assistance to Brancheau family genealogists. **Computer Services:** database, Brancheau family genealogy.

20384 ■ Brantley Association of America

4750 Oakleigh Manor Dr.
Powder Springs, GA 30127
Ph: (770)428-4402
E-mail: brantleyassoc@bellsouth.net
URL: http://www.brantleyassociation.com
Contact: John Kenneth Brantley, Pres.

Founded: 1987. **Members:** 607. **Membership Dues:** family, $16. **Staff:** 4. **Budget:** $5,000. **For-Profit. Description:** Conducts genealogical research on the Brantly and Brantley surname. Seeks to connect the various Brantley lines to the common ancestor, Edward Brantley, who immigrated to the state of Virginia in 1638. **Libraries: Type:** reference; not open to the public; by appointment only. **Holdings:** 18; books. **Subjects:** census (including U.S. census (Brantley) 1790-1840), histories, marriages, county record abstractions. **Awards:** Light Span Academic Excellence Award. **Type:** recognition ● R.J. Taylor Foundation. **Type:** recognition. **Publications:** *Edward Brantley - His Life - His Progeny*. Video. Documents the voyage of Edward Brantley to America. Includes aerial and ground footage of Brantley lands. **Price:** $19.50/copy ● *Hancock County, Georgia Court of Ordinary Minutes 1817-1837* ● *Hancock County, Georgia Court of Ordinary Minutes 1799-1817* ● *The Records of the Church at Williams Creek*. **Price:** $23.50 plus shipping and handling ● *U.S. Brantley*

Census Records 1790-1840. **Price:** $9.50 ● Report, semiannual. **Price:** $7.50 for members.

20385 ■ Britenburg Surname Organization (BSO)

c/o Warren D. Steffey
6750 E Main St., No. 106
Mesa, AZ 85205-9049
Ph: (480)833-2165 (480)396-9779
Fax: (480)396-9778
Contact: Warren D. Steffey, Pres.

Founded: 1975. **Description:** Individuals with the surname Britenburg or its variant spellings; others with an interest in the Britenburg family. Promotes study of Britenburg family history and genealogy. Facilitates communication and good fellowship among members; assists Britenburg family genealogists. Also included are the following surnames: Herl, Pocock, Steffey, and Stout.

20386 ■ Brough/Wilson/Willson Family Organization

Address Unknown since 2007

Founded: 1978. **Members:** 4. **Staff:** 1. **Description:** Conducts genealogical research. **Libraries: Type:** not open to the public. **Holdings:** 1. **Subjects:** family history. **Formerly:** (2002) Brough/Nielsen/Wilson/Willson Family Organization.

20387 ■ Bunker Family Association of America (BFA)

c/o Jo Ann Snyder, Treas.
PO Box 1907
Milton, WA 98354-1907
Ph: (856)589-6140
E-mail: gilbunker@snip.net
URL: http://www.bunkerfamilyassn.org
Contact: Mr. Gil Bunker, Pres.

Founded: 1913. **Members:** 500. **Membership Dues:** individual in U.S., $20 (annual) ● individual in Canada, $25 (annual) ● individual outside U.S. and Canada, $30 (annual) ● life, $300-$500. **Staff:** 12. **Budget:** $4,000. **Multinational. Description:** Collects, preserves, and publishes Bunker (variants are Bunkers, Buenker, Beunker, Buncker, and Verboncouer) surname genealogical and general information. The Bunker Surname DNA Project was launched in 2002. **Libraries: Type:** not open to the public. **Holdings:** articles, books, clippings. **Subjects:** Bunkers. **Awards:** Annabelle Moore Scholarship. **Frequency:** annual. **Type:** scholarship. **Recipient:** for a member or member sibling and graduating high school senior. **Computer Services:** database ● mailing lists, not available to the public. **Affiliated With:** Federation of Genealogical Societies. **Publications:** *Bunker Banner*, quarterly, published in February, May, August and November. Newsletter. **Price:** included in membership dues. **Circulation:** 500 ● *Bunker Banner 1971-1995*. Newsletters. Contains reprint of 25 years of newsletters. **Price:** $55.00 plus $3 for postage and handling ● *Bunker Family History 1984*. Contains a history of Bunkers, including wills, stories, poems, famous and infamous Bunkers, and more. **Price:** $15.00 paperback (plus $1.50 for postage and handling) ● *Bunker Genealogy, 1942*. Reprint. Contains information on Bunkers from Charlestown, Nantucket, Delaware, and Maryland. **Price:** $55.85 plus $3 for postage and handling ● *Bunker Genealogy, 1971-1983*. Reprint. Originally published in eight consecutive, loose-leaf installments, Dover branch update. **Price:** $40.78 plus $2 for postage and handling ● *Bunker Genealogy, 1965*. Reprint. Includes Charlestown, Nantucket and unconnected branches. **Price:** $34.00 plus $2 for postage and handling ● *Bunker Genealogy, 1961*. Reprint. Includes entries to the 12th Dover Branch generation compiled for over 5 decades. **Price:** $36.25 plus $2 for postage and handling ● *Bunker Genealogy, 1931*. Reprint. Includes research from James 1 to 11th generation with census records from Maine. **Price:** $27.60 plus $2 for postage and handling. **Conventions/Meetings:** annual convention - always mid-June.

20388 ■ Burleson Family Association (BFA)
5810 Make Peace Ln.
Corpus Christi, TX 78414
E-mail: jdwalsh3@austin.rr.com
URL: http://www.bfa4.homestead.com/bfa.html
Contact: James D. Walsh, Pres.
Founded: 1981. **Members:** 950. **Membership Dues:** regular, $15 (annual) ● contributing, $37 (annual) ● sustaining, $75 (annual). **Description:** Members of the Burleson family and interested others. Facilitates tracing the Burleson lineage. Works to preserve Burleson family history. **Libraries: Type:** reference; not open to the public; by appointment only. **Holdings:** archival material, books, clippings. **Publications:** *Burleson Family Bulletin*, quarterly. ISSN: 0730-1405. **Circulation:** 500. **Conventions/Meetings:** annual reunion.

20389 ■ Cahill Cooperative Ancestors
2050 Cedar Johnson Rd.
West Branch, IA 52358
Ph: (319)643-2829
E-mail: cahill_ancestors@prodigy.net
URL: http://pages.prodigy.net/cahill_ancestors
Contact: Jim Cahill, Partner
Founded: 1987. **Members:** 600. **Staff:** 1. **Description:** Helps search for unknown relatives by free organization and comparison of family histories. Website assists registry of a family's earliest known generations. Also, has generic Cahill background and file of newsletters 1987-2000. **Computer Services:** database, 600 family histories, free comparison and reports. **Formerly:** (1990) Cahill Immigrant Information Exchange; (2003) Cahill Cooperative.

20390 ■ Caton Family Association (CFA)
c/o Barbara Caton
212 W Sunset Pl.
Farmington, NM 87401
Ph: (505)327-9501
E-mail: bmc@gobrainstorm.net
Contact: Barbara Caton, Contact
Founded: 1988. **Members:** 50. **Membership Dues:** individual, $10 (annual). **Staff:** 1. **Description:** Individuals with the surname Caton, other members of the Caton family, and other interested individuals. Promotes study of, and interest in, the family of Thomas Caton and his descendants in Virginia, Missouri, Oklahoma, and New Mexico. Serves as a clearinghouse on Caton family history and genealogy; provides assistance to family historians and genealogists. **Conventions/Meetings:** biennial reunion - 3rd weekend in July.

20391 ■ Champe Surname Organization
Address Unknown since 2007
Description: Conducts genealogy and family history research. Family names covered include Bodine, Bogart, Van Sant, Tueller, Kunz, Millspaugh, Bergen, Lubbertson, Rogers, Shepherd, and Walker. **Libraries: Type:** open to the public.

20392 ■ Chapman Family Association (CFA)
c/o Robert L. Sonfield, Jr., Exec. Dir.
770 S Post Oak Ln., Ste.435
Houston, TX 77056-1913
Ph: (713)877-8333
Fax: (713)877-1547
E-mail: cfa@chapmanfamilies.org
URL: http://www.chapmanfamilies.org
Contact: Robert L. Sonfield Jr., Exec. Dir.
Founded: 1994. **Members:** 259. **Membership Dues:** active, $26 (annual). **Staff:** 10. **Description:** Works on the collection, preservation, and dissemination of the genealogy and history of the Chapman Family. **Libraries: Type:** reference. **Holdings:** 60. **Subjects:** Chapman family. **Affiliated With:** National Knitwear and Sportswear Association. **Formerly:** New England Knitted Outerwear Manufacturers Association; (1981) New England Knitted Outerwear Association.

20393 ■ Chartier Family Association (CFA)
13095 SW Glenn Ct.
Beaverton, OR 97008-5664
Ph: (503)646-8186
Fax: (503)646-8186
E-mail: vlchartier@ieee.org
Contact: Vernon L. Chartier, Chm.
Founded: 1982. **Members:** 200. **Regional Groups:** 3. **State Groups:** 3. **Languages:** English, French. **Description:** Individuals who have purchased or subscribe to Chartier family publications. Conducts genealogical research on the Chartier family in Europe and North America. Local groups hold semiannual and triennial meetings. **Publications:** *Actualites Historiques Chartier* (in English and French), semiannual. Newsletter. Actualites Historiques Chartier. **Price:** $20.00 ● *Chartiers in North America*. Book.

20394 ■ Clan Campbell Society, North America (CCS(NA))
3704 Kantrel Pl.
Valrico, FL 33594-6920
Ph: (813)685-4638
E-mail: vicepresident@ccsna.org
URL: http://www.ccsna.org
Contact: Robert St. John Jr., VP
Founded: 1974. **Members:** 2,500. **Regional Groups:** 13. **State Groups:** 50. **National Groups:** 4. **Multinational. Description:** Individuals interested in Scottish heritage, especially the history and genealogy of the Campbell family. Seeks to educate its members and the public about the Clan Campbell, Scotland, and the Scottish people. Conducts charitable activities; sponsors competitions. Promotes and conducts genealogical research. Compiles statistics; maintains genealogical archives and library. **Libraries: Type:** not open to the public. **Holdings:** 600. **Subjects:** Scotland and Campbell history and genealogy. **Formerly:** (2003) Clan Campbell Society. **Publications:** *Video Lecture on Clan Campbell History* ● Journal, quarterly. Includes calendar of events, essays, and information searches. **Price:** included in membership dues; $6.25 each, for nonmembers. ISSN: 0731-955X. **Circulation:** 4,000. **Conventions/Meetings:** annual convention, for general membership.

20395 ■ Clan Carmichael U.S.A. (CCUSA)
c/o Kathy Gambill, Membership Chair
3298 S Beddow St.
Terre Haute, IN 47802
E-mail: contact@carmichael.org
URL: http://www.carmichael.co.uk
Contact: Kathy Gambill, Membership Chair
Founded: 1993. **Members:** 350. **Membership Dues:** regular, in U.S., $20 (annual) ● regular, outside U.S., $28 (annual). **Description:** Individuals with the surname Carmichael or its variants; others with an interest in the Carmichael clan. Promotes interest in, and study of, Carmichael clan history and genealogy. Promotes good fellowship among members; conducts educational programs; provides assistance to Carmichael clan historians and genealogists; participates in charitable activities. **Awards:** Clan Carmichael USA Scholarship. **Frequency:** annual. **Type:** scholarship. **Recipient:** for students interested in Scottish history and culture. **Additional Websites:** http://www.carmichael.org. **Publications:** *Eagle Gate*, quarterly. Newsletter. **Conventions/Meetings:** annual board meeting - summer ● annual meeting.

20396 ■ Clan Chisholm Society - United States Branch
PO Box 1091
Keene, NH 03431
Ph: (603)357-5003
E-mail: questions@clanchisholmsociety.org
URL: http://www.clanchisholmsociety.org
Contact: Mrs. Val Chisholm Perry, Pres.
Founded: 1950. **Members:** 250. **Membership Dues:** regular, $15 (annual) ● associate, $10 (annual) ● junior (under 18 years), $5 (annual). **National Groups:** 6. **Description:** Clan Chisholm is an ancient Highland Clan dating back to at least 1249; clan lands extended through the fertile valley of Strathglass, Invernesshire, Scotland. Binds together those whose ancestors had wandered afar. **Libraries: Type:** not open to the public. **Holdings:** articles, books, clippings. **Telecommunication Services:** electronic mail, jperry6@ne.rr.com. **Affiliated With:** Council of Scottish Clans and Associations. **Formerly:** (1998) Clan Chisholm in America. **Publications:** *Clan Chisholm Journal*, annual. **Circulation:** 600 ● *The Clanship*, biennial. Newsletter. **Circulation:** 350. **Conventions/Meetings:** biennial board meeting and regional meeting, genealogy (exhibits) ● quinquennial International Gathering of Chisholms - reunion.

20397 ■ Clan Colquhoun Society of North America
2984 Mike Dr.
Marietta, GA 30064
E-mail: sijepuis@bellsouth.net
URL: http://www.geocities.com/clancolquhoun_na/home.html
Contact: Jim Kilpatrick, Pres.
Founded: 1981. **Members:** 410. **Membership Dues:** individual, $35 (annual). **Description:** Individuals with the surname Colquhoun or Calhoun and their variant spellings. Seeks to identify clan members; promotes genealogical research. Facilitates communication and good fellowship among members; participates in Highland Games; provides assistance to Colquhoun family genealogists. **Libraries: Type:** reference. **Holdings:** archival material, monographs. **Subjects:** Colquhoun family history, genealogy. **Awards:** GRAD II Piper Stone Mountain Games. **Frequency:** annual. **Type:** recognition. **Computer Services:** Online services, publication. **Publications:** *The Highlander*, bimonthly. Newsletter. **Price:** $10.00 for nonmembers; included in membership dues ● *Society Newsletter*, quarterly. **Price:** included in membership dues. Alternate Formats: online. **Conventions/Meetings:** annual meeting.

20398 ■ Clan Cunningham Society of America (CCSA)
4575 W 111th Ave.
Westminster, CO 80031-2025
Ph: (303)460-8736
Fax: (303)439-7847
E-mail: query@clancunningham.us
URL: http://www.clancunningham.us
Contact: Larry A. Augsbury, High Commissioner
Founded: 1984. **Members:** 727. **Membership Dues:** individual, family, $25 (annual) ● individual, family, $49 (biennial) ● individual, family, $70 (triennial) ● life (age under 30), $600 ● life (age 30-39), $500 ● life (age 40-49), $400 ● life (age 50-59), $300 ● life (age over 60), $200. **Staff:** 6. **Budget:** $3,734. **Regional Groups:** 3. **For-Profit. Description:** Serves as charitable and educational organization. Promotes the Scottish culture of which Clan Cunningham played a significant part. Seeks to educate society in the role Scots have played and the contributions Scots have made, including Cunninghams, to the development of civilization. **Awards:** Clansman of the Year Award. **Frequency:** annual. **Type:** recognition. **Recipient:** to the member whose efforts have the greatest impact on the furtherance of the discovery, preservation and dissemination of Scottish, Celtic and clan Cunningham heritage ● Clanswoman of the Year Award. **Frequency:** annual. **Type:** recognition. **Recipient:** to the member whose efforts have the greatest impact on the furtherance of the discovery, preservation and dissemination of Scottish, Celtic and clan Cunningham heritage. **Computer Services:** database, genealogical ● online services, membership dues' credit card payment service. **Additional Websites:** http://www.geocities.com/clancunninghamusa. **Committees:** By-laws; Election; Web Site Development. **Publications:** *The Cunningham Communique*, quarterly. Newsletter. Includes articles, history, genealogy, and recipes. **Price:** free for members. **Conventions/Meetings:** International Gathering - meeting - at least every 3 years.

20399 ■ Clan Currie Society
PO Box 541
Summit, NJ 07902-0541
Ph: (908)273-3509
Fax: (908)273-4342
E-mail: clancurrie@mail.com
URL: http://www.clancurrie.com
Contact: Robert Currie, Pres.
Founded: 1991. **Members:** 3,000. **Budget:** $50,000. **Multinational. Description:** Originally formed in

1959 as a family name society for individuals of Scottish/Irish descent who have the surname Currie, Curry, Currey, Corey, MacCurrie, MacCurry, MacCorey, or MacMhuirich. In addition, to preserving and promoting the history and accomplishments of the worldwide clan Currie; members utilize the society's Website as a genealogical research tool to trace family roots around the world. More recently, the society has become a leading force in promoting the history and culture of Scotland and its influence on the world at large, through a number of outreach programs, including award-winning documentary films, concerts, traveling exhibitions, and special events, Burns Night celebrations, and public speaking engagements. Since 2000, the society has played a leading role in the observance of National Tartan Day; produces the Annual Tartan Day Observances at the Ellis Island Immigration Museum in cooperation with the National Park Service. **Libraries: Type:** reference. **Holdings:** 30; archival material, audiovisuals, business records, films, video recordings. **Subjects:** Scottish history, Celtic poetry, traveling exhibitions. **Computer Services:** database, genealogical. **Publications:** *Clan News*, monthly. Newsletters. Features society news from around the world. **Circulation:** 3,000. Alternate Formats: online ● *Clansfolk Profiles*. Newsletters. Features profiles of notable members of the worldwide Clan Currie. **Conventions/Meetings:** annual Gathering of the Clan - meeting, cultural Scottish games (exhibits).

20400 ■ Clan Davidson Society

c/o Elaine Davidson, Sec.-Treas.
235 Fairmont Dr.
North Wilkesboro, NC 28659
E-mail: mdavid8928@aol.com
URL: http://clandavidsonusa.com
Contact: Michael Davidson, Pres.
Founded: 1981. **Members:** 525. **Membership Dues:** single, family, $20 (annual) ● life, $300. **Staff:** 7. **Regional Groups:** 15. **Description:** Seeks to assist Davidsons with a common heritage and background to associate themselves together. **Libraries: Type:** open to the public. **Holdings:** archival material, articles, books, clippings. **Telecommunication Services:** electronic mail, clankitty@aol.com. **Publications:** *The Sporran*, biennial. Newsletter. **Circulation:** 450. **Conventions/Meetings:** annual board meeting and meeting, general meeting of membership plus election of officers - 3rd weekend of October in Stone Mountain, GA.

20401 ■ Clan Douglas Society of North America (CDSNA)

c/o John Douglas, Sec.
116 Wake Forest Dr.
Warner Robins, GA 31093
E-mail: jdarbyd@juno.com
URL: http://www.clandouglassociety.org
Contact: John Douglas, Sec.
Membership Dues: regular, in U.S., $20 (annual) ● regular, in Canada, C$30 (annual) ● regular, in U.S., $55 (triennial) ● regular, in Canada, C$80 (triennial) ● life, in U.S., $200-$300 ● life, in Canada, C$300-C$445. **Description:** People who are descendants of or bear the name of Douglas. Works to foster and promote understanding and good fellowship among descendants and to study and learn about their heritage. Sells apparel. **Awards: Frequency:** annual. **Type:** scholarship. **Recipient:** for individuals who have dedicated to continue their education in the field of Scottish art. **Computer Services:** database. **Publications:** *Dubh Ghlase*, quarterly. Newsletter. Features articles about family history and activities across the nation.

20402 ■ Clan Drummond Society of North America

c/o Charles McRobbie
6 Bernard Ln.
Methuen, MA 01844
Ph: (978)682-0130
E-mail: perth4637@aol.com
URL: http://www.angelfire.com/al/metaphysicsgalore/Drummond.html
Contact: Charles McRobbie, Contact
Founded: 1985. **Members:** 120. **Membership Dues:** general, $20 (annual). **Staff:** 3. **Description:** People

who bear the name or are descendents of Drummonds. Works to promote the general interest of the clan and to cultivate the spirit of kinship and fellowship. Sponsors festivals and hosts on-line database. **Publications:** Newsletter, quarterly. **Price:** included in membership dues.

20403 ■ Clan Forrester Society (CFS)

1034 Blue Heron Dr.
Commerce, GA 30529
Ph: (706)335-7688
E-mail: benforrester@forresterfamily.org
URL: http://forresterfamily.org
Contact: Ben Forrester, Pres.
Founded: 1963. **Members:** 150. **Membership Dues:** individual, $10 (annual) ● family, $15 (annual). **Description:** Descendants of the Forrester, Forester, Forrister, and Foster family. **Computer Services:** Mailing lists. **Formerly:** (1986) Forrester Genealogical Association. **Publications:** *Corstorphine Journal*, quarterly. Newsletter.

20404 ■ Clan Graham Society (CGS)

c/o Norris Graham, Membership VP
PO Box 70
Yucca, AZ 86438
Ph: (520)855-2415
E-mail: richard_graham@mindspring.com
URL: http://www.clan-graham-society.org
Contact: Richard Graham, Pres.
Founded: 1975. **Members:** 2,000. **Membership Dues:** regular, family, $25 (annual). **Description:** Members of the Clan Graham. Promotes the "general interests of the clan;" seeks to "cultivate the spirit of kinship, fellowship, and social intercourse among the Clan members throughout the United States and Canada." Serves as a clearinghouse on Clan Graham history and genealogy, and on Scottish history and culture. Sponsors social and educational activities. **Libraries: Type:** lending; reference. **Holdings:** books. **Subjects:** Clan Graham history and genealogy. **Awards:** Distinguished Service. **Frequency:** periodic. **Type:** recognition. **Publications:** *Clan Graham News*, quarterly. **Conventions/Meetings:** annual meeting.

20405 ■ Clan Guthrie USA

c/o Carrie Guthrie-Whitlow, Treas.
PO Box 121
Port Orchard, WA 98366
E-mail: clanguthrieinfo@aol.com
URL: http://www.clanguthrie.org
Contact: Harry Guthrie, Pres.
Founded: 1982. **Membership Dues:** individual/family, $20 (annual) ● life, $250. **Description:** People who bear the name or are descendents of Guthries. Works to offer Guthries a chance to communicate and learn more about their heritage. Participates in festivals, sponsors a tent at several Highland games, offers catalog sales and publishes newsletters. **Publications:** *Clan Guthrie News*, quarterly. Newsletter. Features articles about Guthrie and updates on the development in genealogy.

20406 ■ Clan Hamilton Society

PO Box 1245
Summerville, SC 29484-1245
E-mail: treasurer@clanhamilton.org
URL: http://www.clanhamilton.org
Contact: Philip G. Dixon, Sec.
Founded: 1975. **Members:** 1,500. **Membership Dues:** regular, associate, family, $20 (annual) ● junior, $6 (annual) ● life (ages 40), $350 ● life (ages 40-49), $300 ● life (ages 50-59), $250 ● life (ages 60 plus), $200. **Staff:** 5. **Multinational. Description:** Represents people who bear the name or are descendents of Hamilton. Seeks to gain connection recognition and communication with other Hamiltons throughout the world. Publishes newsletters and informational materials, sponsors games and festivals. **Publications:** *An Darach*, quarterly. Newsletter. **Price:** included in membership dues.

20407 ■ Clan Hunter Association USA

512 S Washington St., Ste.307
Royal Oak, MI 48067
E-mail: marty.hunter@gmail.com
URL: http://www.hunterclanusa.org
Contact: Martha Hunter, Membership Off./Treas.
Founded: 1995. **Members:** 650. **Membership Dues:** $25 (annual). **Budget:** $7,800. **Description:** People who are descendents of a Scot bearing the name of Hunter. Strives to preserve and encourage all Scottish heritage and traditions. Sponsors and participates in Scottish Highland games and festivals. **Awards: Type:** scholarship. **Publications:** *Hunters' Horn*, quarterly. Newsletter. **Price:** free for members. **Circulation:** 650. **Conventions/Meetings:** annual meeting.

20408 ■ Clan Irwin Association (CIA)

c/o Guy C. Irvin, Chm.
226 1750th Ave.
Mount Pulaski, IL 62548-6635
Ph: (217)792-5226
E-mail: guyirvin@frontiernet.net
URL: http://www.clanirwin.org
Contact: Guy C. Irvin, Chm.
Founded: 1976. **Members:** 1,100. **Membership Dues:** ordinary, $20 (annual) ● ordinary, $50 (triennial) ● ordinary - life, $400 ● senior - life (55 years or over), $250. **Regional Groups:** 10. **Description:** Members of the Irwin family. Promotes interest in family history and genealogy and Scottish history and culture. Seeks to identify and unite members of the Irwin clan. Serves as a clearinghouse on the Irwin family and its history. Participates in Highland Games and other Scottish cultural activities; sponsors tours of Scotland; makes available Irwin clan memorabilia. **Publications:** Booklet, quarterly.

20409 ■ Clan Johnston(e) in America

c/o Dr. Stephen A. Johnston, Pres.
215 SE Maynard Rd.
Cary, NC 27511
Ph: (919)380-7707
E-mail: sajscot@aol.com
URL: http://clanjohnston.org
Contact: Dr. Stephen A. Johnston, Pres.
Founded: 1976. **Members:** 500. **Membership Dues:** individual, $20 (annual) ● family, $25 (annual) ● junior, $10 (annual). **Budget:** $7,630. **Multinational. Description:** Descendants of the Johnstone, Johnston, or Johnson families who emigrated to the U.S. from Scotland. Collects, preserves, and disseminates information on the families; promotes interest in genealogical research. Awards scholarships and grants. Conducts charitable programs; participates in Scottish highland games and other festivals. Maintains biography and library. **Committees:** Genealogical; Membership; Nominating. **Formerly:** (1998) Johnston(e) Clan in America. **Publications:** *Spur and Phoenix*, quarterly. Newsletter. **Price:** free for members. Alternate Formats: online. **Conventions/Meetings:** annual meeting - always September or October.

20410 ■ Clan Keith Society

c/o Sandra K. Glasscock, Natl. Sec.
1809 N Sandal
Mesa, AZ 85205-3559
E-mail: secretary@clankeithusa.org
URL: http://www.clankeithusa.org
Contact: Sandra K. Glasscock, Natl. Sec.
Description: People who are descendents of a Scot bearing the name of Keith. Strives to preserve and encourage all Scottish heritage and traditions. Sponsors and participates in Scottish Highland games and festivals. Bestows scholarships. **Awards: Type:** scholarship. **Publications:** Newsletter.

20411 ■ Clan Leslie Society International (CLSI)

PO Box 845
Jackson, NJ 08527
E-mail: lkseich@optonline.net
URL: http://www.clanlesliesociety.org
Contact: Robert E. Leslie, Commissioner
Founded: 1978. **Members:** 600. **Membership Dues:** associate, lineal, $21 (annual) ● inceptor (under 18

years old), $7. **Staff:** 10. **Budget:** $6,000. **Regional Groups:** 8. **Multinational. Description:** Descendants of Scotland's Clan Leslie. Seeks to identify and gather members of the Leslie Clan worldwide. Gathers and disseminates information on the Clan Leslie and its diaspora, and on Scottish history and culture. Sponsors social, cultural, and educational activities. **Libraries: Type:** by appointment only; reference. **Holdings:** archival material, periodicals. **Subjects:** Clan Leslie history and genealogy, related clan genealogies. **Awards: Frequency:** periodic. **Type:** scholarship. **Recipient:** for students researching Clan Leslie history or genealogy. **Formerly:** (2003) Clan Leslie Society. **Publications:** *Grip Fast*, quarterly. Newsletter. **Price:** available to members only. **Circulation:** 500 ● Monographs, periodic ● Journal, annual. **Conventions/Meetings:** biennial convention, in conjunction with Highland Games.

20412 ■ Clan MacDuff Society of America

c/o Kim Duprest, Membership Chm.
526 E Charleston Ave.
Phoenix, AZ 85022
Ph: (602)866-2570
E-mail: kimduprest@qwest.net
URL: http://www.clanmacduff.org
Contact: Kim Duprest, Membership Chm.

Founded: 1974. **Members:** 1,000. **Membership Dues:** individual, $15 (annual) ● family, $20 (annual). **Regional Groups:** 9. **Description:** Descendants of the MacDuff clan. Promotes interest in the history and genealogy of the MacDuff clan; encourages communication and good fellowship among members. Participates in cultural and educational programs pertaining to Scotland and Scottish history; facilitates genealogical study. **Awards:** Convener of the Year. **Frequency:** annual. **Type:** recognition ● Meritorious Service Award. **Type:** recognition. **Recipient:** for members who have served the clan for many years. **Publications:** *Mac Dhubhaich*, quarterly. Newsletter. **Conventions/Meetings:** annual meeting - usually in June or July.

20413 ■ Clan MacIntyre Association

c/o Alan B. MacIntyre, VP of Membership
900 Stagecoach Rd.
Chapel Hill, NC 27514-3924
E-mail: macintyre@macintyreclan.org
URL: http://www.macintyreclan.org
Contact: Alan B. MacIntyre, VP of Membership

Founded: 1978. **Members:** 426. **Membership Dues:** regular, $20 (annual) ● regular, $35 (biennial) ● patron, $40 (annual) ● patron, $75 (biennial) ● life, $350. **National Groups:** 223. **Description:** People who are descendents of a Scot bearing the name of MacIntyre. Strives to preserve and encourage all Scottish heritage and traditions. Sponsors and participates in Scottish Highland games and festivals, publishes newsletter. **Libraries: Type:** reference. **Holdings:** 20. **Subjects:** genealogy. **Publications:** *Clan MacIntyre: A Journey to the Past*. Book. ISSN: 0194-2123. **Circulation:** 450 ● *Per ARDUA*, quarterly. Newsletter. **Price:** included in membership dues.

20414 ■ Clan MacIntyre Society

650 N Sprague Ave.
Tacoma, WA 98403-1013
E-mail: ascot2aw@hotmail.com
URL: http://www.clanmacintyresociety.org
Contact: Alan Wright, VP of Membership/Treas.

Membership Dues: regular, $30 (annual). **Description:** People who are descendents of a Scot bearing the name of MacIntyre. Strives to preserve and encourage all Scottish heritage and traditions. Sponsors and participates in Scottish Highland games and festivals. **Awards: Type:** scholarship. **Publications:** Newsletter, quarterly. **Price:** included in membership dues.

20415 ■ Clan MacKay Society (CMS)

c/o David R. McKay, Pres.
5461 Poplar Dr.
Monroe, MI 48161
Ph: (734)457-1772

E-mail: mckay@gatecom.com
URL: http://www.clanmackayusa.org
Contact: David R. McKay, Pres.

Membership Dues: individual, $20 (annual) ● family, $25 (annual). **Description:** Individuals with the surname McKay and its variant spellings. Promotes appreciation of Scottish history and culture; facilitates communication among members of the McKay clan. Participates in Scottish cultural activities; sponsors social and recreational programs; serves as a clearinghouse on the McKay clan and its history and genealogy.

20416 ■ Clan MacKenzie Society in the Americas

PO Box 300337
Waterford, MI 48330
E-mail: membership@clanmackenzie.com
URL: http://www.clanmackenzie.com
Contact: Howard Mackenzie-Wright, Sec.

Founded: 1974. **Members:** 1,000. **Membership Dues:** regular, $20 (annual). **Budget:** $15,000. **Regional Groups:** 10. **Description:** Fosters fellowship among members. Offers charitable and educational programs. **Awards:** Scottish Harp Awards. **Frequency:** annual. **Type:** scholarship. **Recipient:** for a member or relative of members. **Publications:** *Tulach Ard*, quarterly. Newsletter. **Circulation:** 1,000.

20417 ■ Clan Mackintosh of North America

c/o Carl R. McIntosh, Pres.
133 Steeplechase N
Columbia, SC 29209
Ph: (803)647-7573
E-mail: carlrmack@hotmail.com
URL: http://www.cmna.org
Contact: Carl R. McIntosh, Pres.

Founded: 1981. **Membership Dues:** individual, $10 (annual) ● family, $15 (annual). **Multinational. Description:** People who are descendants of a Scot bearing the name of Mackintosh. Strives to preserve and encourage all Scottish heritage and traditions, particularly those of Clan Mackintosh. Sponsors and participates in annual meetings, Scottish Highland games and festivals, disseminates information and clan data. **Publications:** *Mists of Moigh*. Newsletter. **Price:** included in membership dues. Alternate Formats: online.

20418 ■ Clan MacLennan Association, U.S.A.

c/o Winton D. MacLennan, Pres.
1032 Lockridge Ln.
Ashland City, TN 37015
E-mail: thescotsmanus@yahoo.com
URL: http://www.clan.maclennan.com/usa
Contact: Marilyn Baumeister, Recording Sec.

Founded: 1971. **Members:** 367. **Membership Dues:** individual, $15 (annual). **Regional Groups:** 5. **National Groups:** 7. **Description:** Family association for persons of MacLennan descent and associated septs. Conducts research, educational, and charitable programs. Collects statistics; sponsors competitions; maintains speakers' bureau. **Libraries: Type:** reference; open to the public; by appointment only. **Holdings:** archival material. **Subjects:** genealogy. **Awards: Frequency:** annual. **Type:** trophy. **Recipient:** for excellence judged at games. **Computer Services:** database, available at Stone Mountain Games. **Committees:** Finance; Membership; Program. **Councils:** Executive. **Publications:** *The Clan Piper*, quarterly. Newsletter. Includes clan news, meeting announcements, and activities. **Price:** included in membership dues. **Circulation:** 400. **Advertising:** accepted. Alternate Formats: online. **Conventions/Meetings:** annual executive committee meeting, includes special meetings (exhibits).

20419 ■ Clan Macneil Association of America

c/o Ms. Rhonwn Darby McNeill, Membership VP
PO Box 230693
Montgomery, AL 36123-0693
Ph: (334)834-0612

E-mail: rdmatmgm@aol.com
URL: http://www.clanmacneilusa.net
Contact: C. MacNeill Baker Jr., Pres.

Founded: 1921. **Members:** 1,200. **Membership Dues:** regular, $25 (annual) ● foreign, $30 (annual) ● life, $1,000. **Description:** Individuals with the surname Macneil, O'Neill, McNeil, Mcneill, Neal, MacNeally, MacNealedge, MacKneale, and other variations. Promotes interest in the heritage of the descendants of the Macneil Clan. Maintains active genealogical desk. **Telecommunication Services:** electronic mail, neill46@aol.com. **Publications:** *BARRA*. Book. Contains maps, drawings, and illustrations. **Price:** $5.00 ● *The Galley*. Newsletter. **Price:** included in membership dues. **Circulation:** 1,250. **Conventions/Meetings:** annual meeting - always second week of July, in Linville, NC ● periodic meeting.

20420 ■ Clan Macpherson Association

c/o William MacPherson, Chm.
2728 Fairview Ave. E, No. 303
Seattle, WA 98102
URL: http://www.clan-macpherson.org
Contact: William MacPherson, Chm.

Founded: 1947. **Membership Dues:** regular/spouse, associate and junior regular, $25 (annual) ● spouse life, $35 ● life (junior, associate), $350. **Multinational. Description:** People who are descendents of a Scot bearing the name of Macpherson. Dedicated to developing interest in the clan and to promote its welfare. Sponsors and participates in Scottish Highland games and festivals. **Publications:** *Creag Dhubh*, annual, every spring. Journal. **Price:** included in membership dues ● *The Urlar*, quarterly. Journal. **Price:** free. **Conventions/Meetings:** annual meeting.

20421 ■ Clan MacRae Society of North America (CMSNA)

306 Surrey Rd.
Savannah, GA 31410-4407
E-mail: mccrea@comcast.net
URL: http://www.macrae.org
Contact: Lorraine McCrea, Contact

Membership Dues: student, $15 (annual) ● individual, family, $25 (annual) ● patron, $100 (annual) ● life (aged 62 and older), $300 ● life (aged 61 and below), $500. **Description:** Individuals with the surname MacRae and its variant spellings. Promotes interest in the history and genealogy of the MacRae clan, and in the history and culture of Scotland. Gathers and disseminates information on Scottish culture and MacRae family genealogy; sponsors social activities; assists in the maintenance of Eilean Donan Castle in Scotland; participates in traditional Scottish activities. **Publications:** *Eilean Donan Castle*. Book ● *History of the Clan MacRae*. Book ● *Sgurr Uaran*, monthly. Newsletter.

20422 ■ Clan Maitland Society of North America (CMSNA)

c/o Rosemary Maitland Thom, Sec.
7016 Carrondale Way
Las Vegas, NV 89128-3339
E-mail: rthomnvprdcan@aol.com
URL: http://www.clanmaitland.org.uk
Contact: Mr. G. Larry Holdridge Sr., Pres.

Founded: 1980. **Members:** 185. **Membership Dues:** individual, $25 (annual) ● family, $30 (annual). **Regional Groups:** 1. **National Groups:** 3. **Description:** Represents families and individuals who are descendants or relatives of the Maitland and Lauderdale surnames Mautalent/Matalon. **Libraries: Type:** not open to the public. **Subjects:** genealogy of families, history of the family and its principal members. **Publications:** *Maitland Matters*, quarterly. Newsletter. Includes annual yearbook. **Price:** free for members; $25.00 for nonmembers. **Conventions/Meetings:** annual meeting - always in the fall.

20423 ■ Clan Matheson Society (CMS)

c/o Malcolm Matheson, III, Chief Lieutenant
PO Box 307
The Plains, VA 20198
Fax: (540)687-5569

E-mail: clanmathsn@aol.com
URL: http://www.clanmatheson.org
Contact: Malcolm Matheson III, Chief Lieutenant
Members: 265. **Membership Dues:** individual, $13 (annual). **Description:** Members of the Matheson family. Promotes study of family history and genealogy; encourages interest in Scottish culture. Gathers and disseminates information about the Matheson clan and its history; participates in Highland Games and other Scottish cultural activities; assists clan historians and genealogists. **Libraries:** Type: reference. **Holdings:** archival material. **Subjects:** Matheson clan history and genealogy.

20424 ■ Clan Maxwell Society of the USA
246 DeLee Dr.
Kingsport, TN 37663
E-mail: webmaster@clanmaxwellusa.com
URL: http://www.clanmaxwellusa.com
Contact: Catherine Long, Sec.
Founded: 1964. **Members:** 450. **Membership Dues:** regular, $15 (annual). **Description:** People who are descendents of a Scot bearing the name of Maxwell or related families. Aims to link Maxwells with each other and with their Scottish roots. Sponsors and participates in annual meetings, Scottish Highland games and Scottish festivals. **Publications:** *House of Maxwell*. Newsletter. **Price:** included in membership dues.

20425 ■ Clan McLaren Association of North America (CMANA)
Address Unknown since 2007
Founded: 1983. **Members:** 325. **Membership Dues:** woodbadge, $10 (annual) ● individual, $25 (annual) ● life, $250. **Description:** Members of the McLaren family. Promotes interest in McLaren family history and genealogy; encourages appreciation of Scottish history and culture. Supports historians and genealogists; participates in Highland Games and other Scottish cultural events. **Libraries:** Type: reference. **Holdings:** archival material, business records. **Subjects:** McLaren family history and genealogy.

20426 ■ Clan Menzies Society, North American Branch (CMSNAB)
c/o Dr. David A. Mathewes, Commissioner
323 Rough Water Point
Canton, NC 28716-8196
Ph: (828)648-4255
E-mail: mathewes@charter.net
URL: http://www.menzies.org
Contact: Dr. David A. Mathewes, Commissioner
Founded: 1984. **Members:** 210. **Membership Dues:** regular, $36 (annual) ● regular - life, $160 ● joint - life, $240 ● youth (under 18), $10 (annual). **National Groups:** 2. **Description:** Members of the Menzies family. Promotes interest in Menzies clan history and genealogy, and in Scottish history and culture. Supports maintenance of the Menzies Castle in Scotland; participates in Highland Games and other Scottish cultural activities; assists Menzies clan historians and genealogists. **Libraries:** Type: by appointment only; reference. **Holdings:** archival material, books, clippings. **Subjects:** Menzies clan history, genealogy. **Publications:** *The Red and White*, quarterly. Newsletter. **Price:** included in membership dues. **Circulation:** 290. Alternate Formats: online. **Conventions/Meetings:** annual meeting.

20427 ■ Clan Moffat Society
c/o Sgt. Richard S. Badger
201 Pleasant St. SW
Vienna, VA 22180
Ph: (703)938-9133 (703)242-8887
E-mail: skendhu@aol.com
URL: http://www.clanmoffat.org
Contact: Sgt. Richard S. Badger, Contact
Membership Dues: regular, $20 (annual) ● youth/student (age 18-25), $12 (annual) ● Canadian, $24 (annual) ● Canadian youth/student (age 18-25), $14 (annual) ● life, $350 ● patron, $500 (annual). **Description:** People who are direct lineal descendents of a Scot bearing the name of Moffat over 18 years of age; dedicated to genealogical and historical research into the Scottish Clan Moffat. Sponsors and

participates in annual meetings, Scottish Highland games and Scottish festivals. Publishes newsletter. **Computer Services:** database, genealogy. **Publications:** *Moffatana*, 3-4 times/year. Newsletter. Contains information about membership; includes news from the Society.

20428 ■ Clan Moncreiffe Society of North America (CMSNA)
c/o Mike W. Moncrief, Membership Chm.
1405 Plaza St. SE
Decatur, AL 35603
E-mail: mikemoncrief@bellsouth.net
URL: http://www.moncreiffe.org
Contact: Mike W. Moncrief, Membership Chm.
Founded: 1998. **Membership Dues:** individual, family, associate, $25 (annual). **Multinational. Description:** Promotes knowledge and pride in the Scottish heritage. Establishes and promotes the Scottish arts of piping, drumming, field athletics, country and highland dancing, and history. Assists members with their genealogical research. Facilitates communication and cooperation among members. **Publications:** Newsletter. Informs members of current, past, and planned events of the society.

20429 ■ Clan Montgomery Society International (CMSI)
c/o Rowan Perkins, Treas.
701 Fiske Ln.
Newark, DE 19711-3133
E-mail: treasurer@clanmontgomery.org
URL: http://www.clanmontgomery.org
Contact: Rowan Perkins, Treas.
Founded: 1981. **Members:** 1,500. **Membership Dues:** individual in U.S., $20 (annual) ● individual outside U.S., $25 (annual) ● life, in U.S., $250 ● life, outside U.S., $300. **Regional Groups:** 18. **Multinational. Description:** People who are descendants of or bear the name of Montgomery. Dedicated to the history, genealogy, research and promotion of the surname Montgomery. Attends Scottish Highland games and Scottish festivals. **Formerly:** (2003) Clan Montgomery International. **Publications:** Newsletter, quarterly. **Price:** included in membership dues. **Circulation:** 900. **Conventions/Meetings:** annual meeting.

20430 ■ Clan Munro Association
176 Neptune Rd.
Orange Park, FL 32073-3231
Ph: (904)272-2931
E-mail: dorismall@aol.com
URL: http://www.clanmunrousa.org
Contact: Doris Munro Small, Acting Membership Sec.
Founded: 1968. **Members:** 725. **Membership Dues:** family (including children under age of eighteen), $30 (annual). **Staff:** 15. **Description:** People who are descendents of a Scot bearing the name of Munro. Strives to preserve and encourage all Scottish heritage and traditions. Sponsors and participates in Scottish Highland games and festivals, publishes newsletter, sponsors scholarships. **Awards:** Type: scholarship. **Publications:** *Eagle*, annual. Newsletter ● *Munro Eagle*, annual. Magazine. **Conventions/Meetings:** annual meeting.

20431 ■ Clan Napier in North America (CNNA)
c/o Brig. Gen. John H. Napier, III, Lieutenant to the Chief
Kilmahew, Rte. 2
Box 614
Ramer, AL 36069-9254
E-mail: mjnapier@cottagesoft.com
URL: http://www.napier.ac.uk/depts/clan_napier/home.html
Contact: Brig. Gen. John H. Napier III, Lieutenant to the Chief
Founded: 1985. **Members:** 300. **Membership Dues:** active, $15 (annual) ● life, $100 ● family, $25 (annual). **Budget:** $1,200. **Description:** Napiers by birth, descent, or adoption living on the North American continent. (Variant surnames include Napper, Nap-pier, Nipper, and, according to some sources, Leper,

Raper, and Rapier.) Promotes pride and camaraderie among all Napiers. Helps Napier descendants establish their ancestral lineage. Conducts genealogical research on Napier families in North America, especially known descendants of Patrick Napier in America prior to and their antecedents in Great Britain. Promotes continuing recognition of the Napier clan through articles and advertisements in Scottish-American publications. Places historical markers and conducts tours. **Libraries:** Type: reference. **Holdings:** 175; archival material, books, clippings, periodicals. **Subjects:** Scottish and Napier history. **Computer Services:** database, genealogical data on known descendants of Patrick Napier prior to 1850 ● mailing lists. **Affiliated With:** Council of Scottish Clans and Associations; Scottish Heritage U.S.A. **Publications:** *Sans Tache*, annual. Newsletter. Features clan activities, news for and about members, genealogical data, and notice of books and articles about, by, and for Napiers. **Circulation:** 300 ● Brochure ● Membership Directory. **Conventions/Meetings:** annual Wapenschaw - meeting - always 2nd Saturday in July; in conjunction with Grandfather Mountain Highland Games, Linville, NC.

20432 ■ Clan Pollock
300 Hillwood Blvd.
Nashville, TN 37205-1308
Ph: (615)356-2016
E-mail: apollockis@comcast.net
URL: http://www.clanpollock.com
Contact: A.D. Pollock Jr., Pres.
Founded: 1979. **Members:** 520. **Membership Dues:** regular and associate, $15 (annual). **State Groups:** 14. **Description:** Families sharing common surnames and Scottish ancestry. Fosters the study of Scottish heritage with emphasis on the Pollock clan. **Computer Services:** database, genealogical. **Publications:** *The Pollag*, quarterly. Newsletter. **Price:** included in membership dues. **Circulation:** 575. Alternate Formats: online. **Conventions/Meetings:** annual meeting (exhibits).

20433 ■ Clan Ramsey Association of North America
c/o David F. Ramsey, Membership Chm./Treas.
434 Skinner Blvd., Ste.105
Dunedin, FL 34698
Ph: (727)734-7020
Fax: (775)871-3812
E-mail: davidf.ramsey@verizon.net
URL: http://www.clanramsay.org
Contact: David F. Ramsey, Membership Chm./Treas.
Founded: 1977. **Members:** 420. **Membership Dues:** individual, $25 (annual). **Budget:** $2,000. **Regional Groups:** 2. **State Groups:** 15. **Description:** Participates at the Highland Games throughout U.S. and Canada. Provides educational programs. **Computer Services:** database ● mailing lists. **Publications:** *Ramsey Report*, quarterly. Newsletter. **Price:** $25.00. **Circulation:** 420. **Advertising:** accepted. **Conventions/Meetings:** annual Grandfather Mountain Highland Games - regional meeting (exhibits) - held in July in Grandfather Mountain, NC.

20434 ■ Clan Rose Society of America (CRSA)
c/o Dorothy Blount, Sec.-Treas.
5530 Truman Mountain Rd.
Gainesville, GA 30506-3842
E-mail: info@clanrose.org
URL: http://www.clanrose.org
Contact: Elizabeth Rose, Chief
Founded: 1970. **Members:** 235. **Membership Dues:** regular, $20 (annual) ● sustaining, $30 (annual) ● life, $250. **Budget:** $3,000. **Description:** North American descendants of the Scottish Rose family. Works to preserve the family heritage and Tradition of Kilravock in North America and to unite the American descendants of the Scottish Roses. Supports cultural projects in Scotland and North America; maintains the Clan Rose Archives at the Virginia Historical Society. **Libraries:** Type: open to the public. **Publications:** Newsletter, quarterly. **Conventions/Meetings:** annual reunion - second weekend of July.

20435 ■ Clan Ross Association of the United States
c/o W. Hugh Ross, Pres.
1004 N Bowen Rd.
Arlington, TX 76012
Free: (800)880-2476
Fax: (817)795-2566
E-mail: pres.hugh.ross@rossclan.org
URL: http://www.ClanRossAssociation.org
Contact: W. Hugh Ross, Pres.
Founded: 1976. **Members:** 850. **Membership Dues:** individual/family, $25 (annual) ● life, $375. **Staff:** 10. **Budget:** $16,000. **Regional Groups:** 7. **State Groups:** 50. **Description:** Persons of Ross ancestry or family names connected with Ross. Supports a museum. **Libraries: Type:** reference. **Holdings:** books. **Subjects:** clan history, some genealogy. **Awards:** Clan Ross Scholarship. **Frequency:** annual. **Type:** scholarship. **Recipient:** for studying Scottish music, dance or subjects. **Subgroups:** Clan Ross Foundation. **Publications:** Clan Ross News, quarterly. Newsletter. Contains clan information and items of special interest. **Price:** included in membership dues. **Circulation:** 850. **Conventions/Meetings:** annual board meeting, held in conjunction with Scottish games (exhibits).

20436 ■ Clan Scott Society
c/o Mr. David M. Scott, Membership Sec.
PO Box 13021
Austin, TX 78711-3021
E-mail: info@clanscottsociety.org
URL: http://www.clanscottsociety.org
Contact: Mr. David M. Scott, Membership Sec.
Founded: 1971. **Members:** 600. **Membership Dues:** regular, associate, $30 (annual) ● life, $100-$700. **Description:** Represents the interests of individuals bearing the surname Scott, or one of the following associated families (septs), however spelled: Buccleuch, Harden, Balwearie, Geddes, Laidlaw, Langlands, Napier or a name originating from Roxburghshire or the Middle March of the Borders of Scotland or be directly connected by descent or marriage to such a name. Fosters cultural, historical, and genealogical studies. Sponsors and participates in Scottish festivals and Highland games in the United States. **Libraries: Type:** reference; by appointment only. **Holdings:** archival material, biographical archives, clippings, photographs, reports. **Subjects:** genealogical reference materials. **Awards: Frequency:** periodic. **Type:** scholarship. **Recipient:** for education in Scottish performing arts. **Computer Services:** Information services, cultural and genealogical information, clan news and updates via email. **Committees:** Genealogy. **Affiliated With:** Caledonian Foundation USA; Council of Scottish Clans and Associations; National Genealogical Society. **Formerly:** Clan Scott, U.S.A.; Clan Scott Society of the Americas. **Publications:** Stag and Thistle, quarterly. Newsletter. Features articles related to culture, history and genealogy. **Price:** included in membership dues. **Circulation:** 600. Alternate Formats: online. **Conventions/Meetings:** annual meeting, business meeting for society-location rotates to various sites and gatherings in North America (exhibits).

20437 ■ Clan Shaw Society
c/o Mr. Meredith L. Shaw, Pres.
3031 Appomattox Ave., No. 102
Olney, MD 20832-1498
E-mail: randiward@aol.com
URL: http://www.cplx.net/shaw
Contact: Mr. Meredith L. Shaw, Pres.
Founded: 1983. **Members:** 1,000. **Membership Dues:** individual, $15 (annual) ● family, $20 (annual) ● sustaining, $25 (annual). **Regional Groups:** 25. **Description:** Represents persons bearing the surname Shaw and/or descendants of a Shaw or one of the septs of the clan, including relationships by marriage. (Clan Shaw is based principally on the Scottish Clan Shaw heritage, but welcomes all Shaws regardless of believed national origin.) Seeks to provide opportunities for communication between and socializing among members, to further genealogical research on the Shaw lineage, and to bring credit to Clan Shaw and the family name. Conducts research

and educational programs; sponsors competitions; maintains museum. **Libraries: Type:** reference; not open to the public; by appointment only. **Holdings:** archival material, books, clippings. **Subjects:** persons bearing the Shaw name, or the names of any of the 13 septs of the clan; clan history, lands, historic sites, accomplishments. **Awards:** Clansman of the Year. **Frequency:** annual. **Type:** recognition. **Recipient:** for officers or members who make significant contributions to the clan over several years ● Order of the Dagger. **Frequency:** annual. **Type:** recognition. **Recipient:** for officers or members who make significant contributions to the clan over several years. **Affiliated With:** Council of Scottish Clans and Associations; International Association for Tartan Studies. **Publications:** An Biodag (The Dagger), quarterly. Newsletter. Includes news and pictures of Shaw activities, schedule of upcoming events, genealogical information, membership lists, and articles on notable Shaws. **Price:** included in membership dues. **Circulation:** 1,000 ● Also publishes a history of the clan. **Conventions/Meetings:** annual convention and regional meeting.

20438 ■ Clan Sinclair Association U.S.A. (CSAUSA)
c/o Mel Sinclair, Pres.
224 Bransfield Rd.
Greenville, SC 29615
Ph: (864)268-3550
E-mail: mel@clansinclairsc.org
URL: http://www.clansinclairusa.org
Contact: Mel Sinclair, Pres.
Founded: 1978. **Members:** 600. **Membership Dues:** regular, $20 (annual) ● sponsor, $35 (annual). **Description:** Families and individuals who are descendants of or related to the Sinclair family. Encourages a closer relationship among members through the continuation of traditions. Offers assistance in genealogical research; disseminates educational information. **Libraries: Type:** reference. **Holdings:** archival material. **Subjects:** Sinclair family genealogy and history. **Awards: Type:** scholarship. **Computer Services:** Online services, discussion forums. **Telecommunication Services:** electronic mail, wginn@cox.net. **Divisions:** Sinclair Trust. **Publications:** Sinclair Families in America. Book ● Sinclair Heritage Cookbook ● Yours Aye, quarterly. Newsletter. **Conventions/Meetings:** annual meeting.

20439 ■ Clan Sutherland Society of North America
c/o George W. Sutherland, VP
9301 Harris Glen Dr.
Charlotte, NC 28269
E-mail: mrbillm5@carolina.rr.com
URL: http://www.clansutherland.org
Contact: George W. Sutherland, VP
Founded: 1976. **Members:** 300. **Membership Dues:** individual, $18 (annual) ● family, $25 (annual) ● junior (under 18), $5 (annual) ● overseas, $20 (annual) ● life (individual), $270 ● life (family), $375. **Staff:** 4. **Budget:** $5,000. **Description:** Persons of Sutherland lineage (variant spellings accepted) and of the Septs, Cheyne, Duffus, Federith, Gray, Keith, Mowat, and Oliphant ancestries. Seeks to foster a spirit of kinship by providing a focal point for expression of clan sentiment and encouraging communication between members. Promotes friendship and loyalty among members. Seeks to promote public knowledge of and interest in the history and traditions of the Sutherland name. Encourages deeper understanding of the cultural background of the clan by publishing scholarly articles on the historical and social aspects of the Sutherland name. Attempts to establish family connections between members. Maintains genealogical records. **Libraries: Type:** reference; not open to the public; by appointment only. **Holdings:** archival material, books, clippings, monographs. **Subjects:** Sutherland family history, family trees. **Awards: Frequency:** annual. **Type:** scholarship. **Computer Services:** database, genealogical records. **Affiliated With:** Council of Scottish Clans and Associations. **Publications:** The Dunrobin Piper, monthly. Newsletter. **Price:** free for members. **Conventions/Meetings:** annual meeting.

20440 ■ Clan Young
c/o Mr. Charles A. Pickering, Treas.
84 Columbus Ave.
West Bridgewater, MA 02379
E-mail: capickering@comcast.net
URL: http://www.clanyoung.info
Contact: Mr. Charles A. Pickering, Treas.
Founded: 1983. **Members:** 1,000. **Membership Dues:** regular, in U.S., $15 (annual). **Description:** Seeks to cultivate a spirit of kinship among those of the name Young, their descendants and members of Clan Septs; to give opportunities to learn more of the proud heritage of the Clan and of Scotland; to provide interesting and accurate information on the Clan's history; to collect and preserve historical, literary and generalized records and relics of Clan Young and Scotland; to encourage the giving of aid and hospitality to members of the Clan; to honor the Scottish heritage and inspire members and descendants the pride and spirit of their Scottish ancestors. **Libraries: Type:** reference. **Holdings:** 50. **Subjects:** Young genealogy. **Computer Services:** Information services, Clan Young resources ● online services, discussion forum. **Also Known As:** (2001) Young Surname Organization. **Formerly:** (2004) Born Young; (2004) Clan Young Society. **Publications:** Clan Young Times, quarterly. Newsletter. Features genealogical research of Young and Jung families. **Price:** included in membership dues. ISSN: 0885-1247. **Circulation:** 200. **Advertising:** accepted ● Also publishes biographical sketches. **Conventions/Meetings:** annual meeting.

20441 ■ Cloud Family Association (CFA)
c/o Linda Boose, Sec.-Treas.
508 Crestwood Dr.
Eastland, TX 76448
E-mail: lboose@classicnet.net
URL: http://homepages.rootsweb.com/~cloud
Contact: Linda Boose, Sec.-Treas.
Founded: 1978. **Members:** 150. **Membership Dues:** individual, $25 (annual). **Description:** Individuals interested in researching the Cloud surname. Acts as a clearinghouse for Cloud family history and genealogy. **Libraries: Type:** reference; by appointment only. **Holdings:** archival material, books, clippings. **Subjects:** Cloud family. **Computer Services:** database. **Additional Websites:** http://mykindred.com/cloud. **Publications:** Cloud Family Journal, quarterly. ISSN: 0883-0940. **Circulation:** 200. Alternate Formats: CD-ROM. **Conventions/Meetings:** annual Genealogy Research and Discussion - reunion - always in July.

20442 ■ Coatney/Courtney Family Association (CCFA)
c/o Carol Kosanke Peterson, AG
499 N Trellis Ct.
Newport News, VA 23608
Ph: (757)369-0511
E-mail: kosanke@cox.net
Contact: Carol Kosanke Peterson AG, Contact
Founded: 1984. **Staff:** 1. **Description:** Individuals interested in the history and genealogy of people with the surname Coatney and its variant spellings. Promotes increased interest in, and study of, family history and genealogy. Provides support and assistance to family historians and genealogists; facilitates exchange of information among members. **Publications:** Coatney/Courtney Exchange. Alternate Formats: CD-ROM.

20443 ■ Cogswell Family Association (CFA)
c/o Mrs. Claire G. Cogswell-Daigle, Sec.
21 Old Belchertown Rd.
Ware, MA 01082
Ph: (863)471-2735
E-mail: secr@cogswell.org
URL: http://www.cogswell.org
Contact: Mrs. Claire G. Cogswell-Daigle, Sec.
Founded: 1989. **Members:** 406. **Membership Dues:** individual, $20 (annual) ● family, $30 (annual) ● life, $1,000. **Budget:** $8,000. **Description:** Individuals with an interest in the family history and genealogy of people with the surname Cogswell and its variant spellings. Promotes historical and genealogical interest and study. Gathers and disseminates information

on the Cogswell family and its history. Publishes Cogswell Genealogical Book, 1620 to date of Cogswells in America. **Awards:** Scholarship to Cogswell College. **Frequency:** annual. **Type:** scholarship ● Scholarship to School for Deaf. **Frequency:** annual. **Type:** scholarship. **Publications:** Cogswell Courier, 3/year. Newsletter. **Price:** included in membership dues. **Circulation:** 406 ● Descendants of John Cogswell. Book. **Price:** $55.00 for members, plus shipping and handling; $65.00 for nonmembers, plus shipping and handling. **Conventions/Meetings:** annual reunion, in different parks throughout the United States and Canada.

20444 ■ Corbin Research (CR)
Address Unknown since 2007
Founded: 1972. **Budget:** $5,000. **Description:** Records information on persons with the surname Corbin in their family tree. Conducts genealogical research. Compiles statistics. **Libraries: Type:** reference. **Holdings:** 100. **Computer Services:** database. **Publications:** Corbin Records. **Advertising:** not accepted ● Directory, periodic. Lists approximately 50,000 names. **Conventions/Meetings:** periodic reunion.

20445 ■ Corson/Colson Family History Association (CCFHA)
c/o Iverne Corson Rinehart
2300 Cedarfield Pkwy., No. 476
Richmond, VA 23233
Ph: (804)747-8180
E-mail: grandmar21@excite.com
URL: http://homepages.rootsweb.com/~ccfha
Contact: Iverne Corson Rinehart, Contact
Founded: 1987. **Members:** 150. **Membership Dues:** voting, $14 (annual). **Budget:** $2,160. **Regional Groups:** 12. **Description:** Descendants or individuals interested in Corson or Colson ancestry. Collects and shares information on the origins and descent of individuals with the surname Corson and its variants. Works to maintain communication among descendants. Compiles statistics. **Libraries: Type:** reference. **Holdings:** 12. **Subjects:** history and genealogy of the periods being studied. **Committees:** Communications. **Publications:** CCFHA Directory, biennial. Contains listings of members and subscribers. **Price:** included in membership dues. **Circulation:** 185 ● Corson Cousins, quarterly. Newsletter. **Price:** $10.00 /year for nonmembers; included in membership dues. **Circulation:** 185. **Advertising:** accepted.

20446 ■ Covert Family Association (CFA)
c/o Diane Covert Siddons, Ed.
303 W Violet St.
Tampa, FL 33603
Ph: (813)238-3816
Contact: Diane Covert Siddons, Ed.
Founded: 1987. **Members:** 40. **Membership Dues:** general, $5 (annual). **Staff:** 1. **Description:** Promotes genealogical research into the Covert surname and the history of the Coverts and related families. Collects and distributes data and assists researchers. Compares family group sheets and attempts to connect families and researchers. (The Covert Family Association was active in the late 1800s and early 1900s, became inactive due to lack of interest, and was revived in 1987). **Libraries: Type:** reference. **Holdings:** 150; archival material. **Subjects:** genealogical materials. **Publications:** The Covert Activities. Book. Contains family group sheet for all CFA members. **Price:** $20.00 plus $3 for postage ● Covert Activities Newsletter, quarterly. Includes genealogical articles, historic and current events. **Price:** included in membership dues. **Circulation:** 40 ● The First Five Years. Contains Covert Activities Newsletters and indexes for 1987-1991. **Price:** $12.00 plus $3 for postage ● The Second Five Years. Contains Correct Activities Newsletters & Indexes for 1992-1997. **Price:** $12.00 plus $3 for postage.

20447 ■ Coward Family Organization
Address Unknown since 2007
Founded: 1891. **Nonmembership. Description:** Members of the Coward, Cowart, or Cowherd families; interested others. Promotes the history and genealogy of the families. **Publications:** Coward Family Newsletter, semiannual. **Circulation:** 300. **Advertising:** accepted. **Conventions/Meetings:** annual reunion, with charts, pictures (exhibits) - Jackson County, NC - **Avg. Attendance:** 50.

20448 ■ Crandall Family Association (CFA)
PO Box 1472
Westerly, RI 02891
E-mail: thecrandalls@riconnect.com
URL: http://www.cfa.net/cfa/contents.html
Contact: Cassandra E. Crandall, Treas.
Founded: 1986. **Members:** 215. **Membership Dues:** individual, associate, $15 (annual) ● family, $20 (annual) ● life, $150. **Staff:** 10. **Description:** Descendants and friends of Elder John Crandall of Rhode Island. **Publications:** Crandall Corner, 3/year. Newsletter.

20449 ■ Crispell Family Association (CFA)
PO Box 35
Tafton, PA 18464-0035
E-mail: genealogist@crispell.org
Contact: Sharon S. Robinson, Pres.
Founded: 1969. **Members:** 85. **Membership Dues:** individual, $25 (annual) ● household, $40 (annual). **Staff:** 6. **Description:** Preserves Huguenot Heritage in New Poltz, NY. Maintains genealogy of Antoine Crispell. Compiles statistics. **Libraries: Type:** reference. **Holdings:** 5. **Subjects:** New York history, genealogy. **Computer Services:** database, descendants of Antoine Crispell. **Publications:** The Crispell Chronicles, 3/year. Newsletter. Contains information on association and members. **Price:** included in membership dues. **Circulation:** 150 ● The Crispell Family in America Volumes I-V, annual. Contains family genealogy. **Conventions/Meetings:** annual meeting - always first Saturday of August in Ulster Co., NY.

20450 ■ Crowl Name Association (CNA)
c/o A. Crowell
1600 Brentworth Way
Reno, NV 89521
E-mail: toronto@eohio.net
URL: http://www.crowlconnections.org
Contact: Gail Komar, Chm.
Founded: 1984. **Members:** 105. **Membership Dues:** library, $6 (annual) ● individual, $15 (annual) ● individual, $27 (biennial). **Description:** Individuals and institutions with an interest in the family history and genealogy of people with the surname Crowl, and its variant spellings (Crowell, Croll, Crull, Kroll, Krall, Grauel, Graul, Croel, Kroel, and Krawl). Promotes genealogical and historical research and study. Conducts educational programs. **Projects:** Crowl DNA. **Publications:** Crowl Connections, quarterly. Newsletter. Contains names and all its variant spellings. **Price:** included in membership dues. **Circulation:** 105. **Alternate Formats:** online.

20451 ■ Curtis/Curtiss Society
c/o Jennifer L. Seney, Membership Sec.
25605 Apple Blossom Ln.
Wesley Chapel, FL 33544
E-mail: jld6959@aol.com
URL: http://www.curtis-curtiss.com
Contact: Jennifer L. Seney, Membership Sec.
Founded: 1939. **Members:** 575. **Membership Dues:** minor (under 21), $5 (annual) ● single, $15 (annual) ● couple, $20 (annual) ● life, $200. **Description:** Individuals with an interest in the family history of people with the surname Curtis/Curtiss/Curtice and its variant spellings. Promotes interest in genealogy. Conducts research. **Libraries: Type:** reference. **Holdings:** 50; archival material, articles, artwork, books, clippings, monographs. **Subjects:** Curtis family history. **Formerly:** (1999) John and Elizabeth Curtis/Curtiss Society. **Publications:** Curtis/s Chronicle, quarterly. Newsletter. **Price:** included in membership dues. **Alternate Formats:** online. **Conventions/Meetings:** annual meeting and reunion, family materials, written, photos (exhibits) - second Saturday of October.

20452 ■ Dameron Family Association
c/o John P. Dameron, Membership Dir./Treas.
1932 Orphanage Rd.
Danville, VA 24540
E-mail: dameron@chatmosscable.com
URL: http://ddfa.org
Contact: Kathy Near, Advisor
Founded: 1981. **Members:** 200. **Membership Dues:** basic, $15 (annual) ● sustaining, $25 (annual) ● patron, $50 (annual). **Description:** Represents individuals with the surname Dameron or Damron. Collects and disseminates genealogical information on family descendants. **Publications:** Dameron/Damron Newsletter, semiannual. **Price:** included in membership dues. **Conventions/Meetings:** annual reunion.

20453 ■ Dannenmueller-Hoefler Family Association
1039 State Rd. W
Warrenton, MO 63383
Ph: (636)456-4610
E-mail: dorjour@socket.net
Contact: Dorey Schrick, Contact
Founded: 1985. **Members:** 50. **Description:** Members of the Dannenmueller-Hoefler family and other interested individuals. Promotes study of Dannenmueller-Hoefler family history and genealogy. Serves as a clearinghouse on the Dannenmueller-Hoefler family and its history; assists family historians and genealogists. **Publications:** Newsletter.

20454 ■ Daubenspeck-Doverspike Family Exchange
Address Unknown since 2007
Founded: 1980. **Members:** 80. **Description:** Individuals involved in genealogical research on the Daubenspeck and Doverspike families. Works to assist genealogical research on this family. Promotes cooperation among family members and researchers. Provides computerized information on the above families. **Publications:** none. **Convention/Meeting:** none. **Computer Services:** database, genealogical information on the Daubenspeck and Doverspike families.

20455 ■ Denison Society (DS)
PO Box 42
Mystic, CT 06355-0042
Ph: (860)536-9248
Fax: (860)536-9248
E-mail: info@denisonsociety.org
URL: http://www.denisonsociety.org
Contact: Wayne Denison, Sec.
Founded: 1930. **Members:** 1,200. **Membership Dues:** active junior, $20 (annual) ● active adult descendent, spouse, $30 (annual) ● life, $500 ● active family, $40 (annual). **Staff:** 1. **Budget:** $55,000. **Description:** Descendants of Captain George Denison, who settled in what is now Stonington, CT in 1654. Promotes interest in Denison family history and genealogy, and the history of colonial America. Serves as a clearinghouse on the Denison family and its history. Maintains Pequotsepos Manor, built by the Denison family in 1717, and Old Denison Cemetery. **Libraries: Type:** by appointment only. **Holdings:** archival material, clippings. **Subjects:** Denison family history and genealogy. **Publications:** Denison Family Genealogy. Book. **Price:** $60.00/copy ● Denison Newsletter, periodic. **Conventions/Meetings:** annual Denison Day - reunion and meeting - always first Saturday in August.

20456 ■ Descendants of Daniel Cole Society
Address Unknown since 2007
Founded: 1987. **Members:** 48. **Membership Dues:** regular, $10 (annual). **Description:** Descendants of Daniel Cole.

20457 ■ Dick Family Association (DFA)
Address Unknown since 2007
Founded: 1987. **Members:** 118. **Description:** Libraries; genealogists and researchers interested in surnames containing the word Dick. Facilitates exchange of information among members; compiles

genealogical records using census, birth, marriage, and death data obtained from primary sources. **Publications:** *Dick Etc. Newsletter*, quarterly.

20458 ■ Doane Family Association of America (DFA)
c/o Mrs. Eunice Brabec, Membership Chair
461 Dellbrook Ave.
South San Francisco, CA 94080
E-mail: kkblair31@aol.com
URL: http://www.doanefamilyassociation.org
Contact: Ms. Katherine K. Blair, Historian
Founded: 1911. **Members:** 3,000. **Membership Dues:** individual, $15 (biennial) ● family, $25 (biennial) ● life, $50. **Regional Groups:** 10. **State Groups:** 9. **Description:** Descendants of Deacon John Doane (1590-1685), who emigrated from England to Plymouth, MA in 1629. Seeks to "create interest in the history and welfare of Deacon John Doane." Serves as a clearinghouse on the Doane family and its history and genealogy; sponsors social and educational activities. **Libraries: Type:** not open to the public. **Holdings:** 2; archival material, books, clippings. **Subjects:** Doane family history, genealogy. **Awards: Frequency:** annual. **Type:** scholarship. **Publications:** *Doane Family Book 1.* **Price:** $23.00 ● *Doane Family Book 2*, annual. **Price:** $33.00 ● *Southwestern Ontario Doans.* **Price:** $33.00 ● Newsletter, semiannual ● Proceedings, biennial. Features information after the reunion. **Conventions/Meetings:** biennial reunion - always even-numbered years.

20459 ■ Dobie Clan of North America (DCNA)
Address Unknown since 2007
Founded: 1987. **Members:** 250. **Membership Dues:** ordinary, $10 (annual). **National Groups:** 3. **Description:** Members of the Dobie family. Promotes interest in Dobie family history and genealogy and Scottish history and culture. Facilitates communication among members; gathers and disseminates information on the Dobie clan; sponsors social, cultural, and educational programs. **Libraries: Type:** not open to the public. **Holdings:** archival material. **Subjects:** Dobie family history and genealogy; Scottish history and culture. **Awards: Frequency:** annual. **Type:** scholarship. **Recipient:** for children of clan members. **Publications:** *The Dobie Connection*, periodic. Newsletter. Contains information about family activities and vital statistics. **Price:** $5.00. **Circulation:** 150. **Advertising:** not accepted. **Conventions/Meetings:** annual convention - third weekend in August ● biennial convention - alternates annually between Canada and US ● biennial Genealogy - conference, showcases archives/past and present history (exhibits).

20460 ■ Dodge Family Association (DFA)
10105 W 17th Pl.
Lakewood, CO 80215
Ph: (303)237-4947
E-mail: barbdodge@dodgefamily.org
URL: http://www.dodgefamily.org
Contact: Norman E. Dodge, Pres.
Founded: 1971. **Members:** 800. **Membership Dues:** regular, $20 (annual) ● life (under age 65), $325 ● life (age 65 and older), $200. **Description:** Members of the Dodge family. Promotes goodwill and fellowship among members; promotes family genealogical and historical research. Serves as a clearinghouse on Dodge family history and genealogy; sponsors social and educational activities. **Libraries: Type:** reference; lending; not open to the public. **Holdings:** archival material, articles, books. **Subjects:** Dodge family history and genealogy. **Computer Services:** Mailing lists. **Projects:** DNA. **Publications:** *Dodge Family Journal*, bimonthly. Newsletter. Alternate Formats: online ● *The National Statesman*, monthly. Newsletter. **Price:** included in membership dues ● Bulletin. Alternate Formats: online. **Conventions/Meetings:** annual reunion - every third Saturday of January.

20461 ■ DuBois Family Association (DBFA)
c/o Terry L. DuBois, Pres.
76715 McLeod Rd.
Myakka City, FL 34251

E-mail: dbfa@juno.com
URL: http://www.dbfa.org
Contact: Terry L. DuBois, Pres.
Founded: 1966. **Membership Dues:** individual, $20 (annual) ● individual, $50 (triennial) ● household (2 adults), $30 (annual) ● household (2 adults), $50 (biennial) ● family (2 adults, 3 children), $60 (annual) ● contributor, $50 (annual) ● donor, $100 (annual) ● patron, $500 (annual). **Description:** Aims to preserve and purchase the DuBois Fort, the homestead of a grandson of Louis DuBois, a patentee of New Paltz, New York, and the Huguenot heritage. **Computer Services:** Mailing lists. **Publications:** *DuBois Family News*, semiannual. Newsletter. Alternate Formats: online ● *Genealogy of the DuBois Family.* Features twenty volumes of DuBois family history. **Price:** $11.00 each (volumes 1-13 on separate discs); $80.00 entire 13 volumes on CD; $16.00/unbounded printout of volumes 1-13; $10.00/hardcopy of selected volumes. Alternate Formats: CD-ROM. **Conventions/Meetings:** annual reunion - 3rd week of October.

20462 ■ Duncan Surname Association (DSA)
8080 N Illinois St.
Indianapolis, IN 46260-2939
E-mail: cduncan22@comcast.net
URL: http://www.dsa.duncanroots.com
Contact: Terry Duncan, Ed.
Founded: 1989. **Members:** 625. **Membership Dues:** life, $15. **Staff:** 3. **Description:** Individuals sharing research on the Duncan surname. Wishes to identify all Duncans in the United States prior to 1850 and tie the family histories together. Travels to Salt Lake City to obtain additional information for the database each year. Offers existing data to members free of charge. **Convention/Meeting:** none. **Libraries: Type:** reference. **Subjects:** genealogy, Duncan family history. **Computer Services:** database ● mailing lists ● record retrieval services. **Also Known As:** DSA. **Publications:** *Duncan Association*, quarterly. Newsletter. **Price:** $3.00 back issues. Alternate Formats: online.

20463 ■ Dunlop - Dunlap Family Society (DDS)
c/o Mr. Peter Dunlop, Pres.
PO Box 652
East Aurora, NY 14052
Ph: (716)655-2521
E-mail: papdunlop@hotmail.com
URL: http://www.clandunlop.org
Contact: Mr. Peter Dunlop, Pres.
Founded: 1980. **Members:** 200. **Membership Dues:** family, $25 (annual). **Description:** Individuals with the surname Dunlop and its variant spellings; other members of the Dunlop family. Promotes interest in Scottish history and culture and the Dunlop family and its history. Conducts family historical and genealogical research; sponsors social activities. **Publications:** *Merito*, quarterly. Newsletter. Alternate Formats: online. **Conventions/Meetings:** annual Grandfather Mountain Highland Games - meeting - in Linville, NC.

20464 ■ Dunnavant/Donavant Family Association
3929 S Milton Dr.
Independence, MO 64055-4043
Ph: (816)373-5309
E-mail: groversar@aol.com
Contact: Robert L. Grover, Pres.
Founded: 1963. **Members:** 200. **Description:** Persons with the surname Dunnavant or Donavant. Seeks to share family and genealogical information among members. **Publications:** none. **Convention/Meeting:** none.

20465 ■ Duty's in America (DA)
Address Unknown since 2007
Founded: 1978. **Staff:** 2. **National Groups:** 1. **Languages:** English, Spanish. **Description:** Members of the Duty and related families. Promotes study of Duty and related family histories and genealogies. Serves as a clearinghouse on the Duty family; assists family historians and genealogists; sponsors educational and social activities. **Libraries: Type:** by appointment only; reference. **Holdings:** 15; archival mate-

rial, books, clippings, monographs. **Subjects:** Duty and related family histories, wills, censuses 1790-1930, duty plus, land deeds, cemeteries, Bibles.

20466 ■ Easterling Family Genealogical Society (EFGS)
1124 Pearl Valley Rd.
Wesson, MS 39191-9361
E-mail: lmmeast@earthlink.net
URL: http://www.easterling.org
Contact: Letson E. Easterling Sr., Pres.
Founded: 1985. **Members:** 500. **Membership Dues:** regular, $15 (annual) ● life, $150. **Description:** Lateral and collateral members and relatives of the Easterling family. Compiles and preserves the history and artifacts of the family; conducts genealogical and historical research and prepares genealogies for members. Assists members in locating historical records of their descendants. **Libraries: Type:** reference. **Awards: Type:** recognition. **Publications:** *Easterling Family Genealogical Society Newsletter*, quarterly. **Price:** available to members only ● *Family History*. Book. **Conventions/Meetings:** annual reunion - always Saturday and Sunday preceding Labor Day in Laurel, MS.

20467 ■ Eddy Family Association (EFA)
c/o Elaine Darrah, Treas.
322-A Trescony St.
Santa Cruz, CA 95060-4753
E-mail: president@eddyfamily.com
URL: http://www.eddyfamily.com
Contact: John Paul Eddy, Pres.
Founded: 1920. **Members:** 800. **Membership Dues:** individual, $15 (annual) ● couple, $25 (annual) ● family, $30 (annual) ● individual, life, $200. **Staff:** 6. **Description:** Represents individuals descended from, or interested in, John and Samuel Eddy, pioneer settlers of Massachusetts who came from England in 1630 on the ship Handmaid. Works to preserve family history. Locates and records information about ancestors and descendants. Compiles statistics. Contributes to St. Dunstan's Church, in England, where William Eddy was vicar 1587-1616. Maintains 1600s Eddy Burying Ground, Swansea, MA. **Libraries: Type:** reference. **Holdings:** archival material, books, clippings, periodicals. **Subjects:** historical. **Awards:** Appreciation for Volunteerism Award. **Frequency:** annual. **Type:** recognition. **Recipient:** for type and length of service. **Committees:** Executive Committee-at-Large. **Publications:** *Eddy Family Mailing*, semiannual. Newsletter. **Price:** included in membership dues. **Circulation:** 900 ● *Eddys in America and Supplements 1940, 1950, 1968, 1980*. Book. **Price:** $30.00 ● *EFA Bulletin*, annual. **Conventions/Meetings:** annual Eddy Family/Eddy Homestead Reunion, joint membership meeting - always second Saturday of August, in Middleboro, MA.

20468 ■ Elder Brewster Society
c/o Gregory E. Thompson, Historian/Membership Chm.
PO Box 355
Branford, CT 06405
E-mail: gthomp5749@aol.com
URL: http://mysite.verizon.net/brewstersociety
Contact: Gregory E. Thompson, Historian/Membership Chm.
Founded: 1978. **Members:** 500. **Membership Dues:** individual in U.S., $12 (triennial) ● individual outside U.S., $15 (triennial). **Description:** Descendants of William Brewster who have had their Brewster lineage approved by the Historian of the Brewster Society. Honors the memory of Elder William Brewster; encourages camaraderie among Brewster cousins; collects, preserves, and shares lineage data relating to descendants; assists non-members in Brewster lineages; encourages and assists with membership in the society of Mayflower Descendants. **Libraries: Type:** by appointment only; reference. **Holdings:** archival material, biographical archives. **Computer Services:** database, of Brewster descendants which is available for reference by members of the society. **Publications:** *Elder Brewster Press*, semiannual. Newsletter. **Circulation:** 500. **Conven-

tions/Meetings: triennial meeting, coincides with the Mayflower Society Triennial - always in September.

20469 ■ Eller Family Association (EFA)
c/o Thomas J. Eller, Pres.
1311 Masters Dr.
Woodland Park, CO 80863
E-mail: thomas.eller@eller.org
URL: http://www.eller.org
Contact: Thomas J. Eller, Pres.

Founded: 1987. **Members:** 300. **Membership Dues:** regular, $25 (annual) ● life, $250. **Budget:** $3,000. **State Groups:** 4. **Description:** Researches, compiles, and publishes Eller genealogy and family history. Restores and maintains cemeteries and other sites of meaning to the Eller families. Promotes local family reunions. **Libraries: Type:** lending; reference; open to the public. **Holdings:** 14; audiovisuals, books, clippings, periodicals. **Subjects:** Eller genealogy and family history. **Awards:** J.W. Hook Memorial Award. **Frequency:** biennial. **Type:** recognition. **Recipient:** for notable research and service. **Computer Services:** database, clearing house for genealogical data ● mailing lists. **Publications:** Eller Chronicles, quarterly. Journal. **Price:** $15.00/year. **Circulation:** 300. Alternate Formats: online ● Eller Genealogies. Reprints. **Conventions/Meetings:** biennial Eller Family Conference (exhibits) - always July ● international conference and meeting.

20470 ■ Elliot Clan Society USA
c/o Evelyn M. Elliott, Treas.
2146 Deer Trail
Suwanee, GA 30024
E-mail: dublincolleen@earthlink.net
URL: http://www.elliotclan.com
Contact: Robert Bruce Elliott, Pres.

Founded: 1977. **Membership Dues:** single, $15 (annual) ● family, $20 (annual). **Multinational. Description:** People who bear the name or are descendents of Elliots. Works to promote the general interest of the clan and to cultivate the spirit of kinship and fellowship. Sponsors festivals and hosts on-line database.

20471 ■ Elswick Family Association
Address Unknown since 2007
Founded: 1970. **Members:** 250. **National Groups:** 1. **Description:** Descendants of John Elswick I (d. 1759). Promotes fellowship among family members and assembles, preserves, and publishes family records. Conducts educational and research programs, and compiles statistics. **Libraries: Type:** reference; not open to the public. **Holdings:** archival material, books, clippings, monographs. **Subjects:** Elswick family history and genealogy. **Awards:** Reunion Awards. **Frequency:** annual. **Type:** recognition. **Recipient:** by category. **Committees:** Reunion Planning. **Publications:** Newsletter, periodic. Family news. **Price:** for members only. **Advertising:** not accepted. Also Cited As: printed. **Conventions/Meetings:** annual Elswick Family Reunion, family records and heirlooms (exhibits) - always second Sunday in August, Breaks Interstate Park, VA.

20472 ■ Enders Family Association
c/o David Enders, Pres.
56 Marie Dr.
Halifax, PA 17032
Ph: (717)362-8959
E-mail: endersabst@comcast.net
URL: http://www.endersfamily.org
Contact: David Enders, Pres.

Founded: 1912. **Members:** 1,000. **Membership Dues:** life, $10. **Multinational. Description:** Descendants and spouses of Phillip Christian and Anna Apolonia Degan Enders. Provides family history, genealogy, and member certificate. Hosts family reunions. **Publications:** Captain Enders Legion (2001). Book. Features the Enders family in the Civil War. ● The Enders Connection, semiannual. Newsletter. Contains information about the association and its members. **Price:** free. **Circulation:** 550. Alternate Formats: online ● Enders Family Genealogy (1990) Vol. 2. Book. Features updates of Enders Family Genealogy Vol. 1. **Price:** $20.00 single copy ● Enders Family

Genealogy (1960) Vol. 1, semiannual. Book. Features history of the Enders family from 1740-1959 in America. **Price:** free. **Circulation:** 550. Alternate Formats: online ● Enders Family Genealogy Vol. 3. Book. **Price:** $75.00 single copy. **Conventions/Meetings:** annual reunion - every 2nd Saturday of August.

20473 ■ Eskridge Family Association (EFA)
c/o Fran Markowski, Treas.
1931 Medallion Ct.
Forest Hill, MD 21050-2761
E-mail: frandk412@yahoo.com
URL: http://www.eskridgefamilyassociation.org
Contact: Hildreth Segar Bottom, Pres.

Founded: 1937. **Members:** 703. **Membership Dues:** regular, $15 (annual). **Description:** Descendants of Colonel George Eskridge and others interested in genealogy, historical preservation, and ecological conservation, especially the Chesapeake Bay and its tributaries. Conducts research; maintains genealogical records. Works for the preservation of historic buildings. Operates museum. **Libraries: Type:** reference. **Holdings:** biographical archives. **Computer Services:** database, membership roster. **Publications:** Eskridge Family Association News, semiannual. Newsletter. **Price:** included in membership dues. Alternate Formats: online. **Conventions/Meetings:** annual meeting - usually October.

20474 ■ Etchingham Family Tree (EFT)
Address Unknown since 2007
Founded: 1980. **Members:** 30. **Membership Dues:** individual, $50 (annual). **Description:** Persons researching the surname Etchingham. Collects and disseminates genealogical information. **Libraries: Type:** reference. **Holdings:** 30; articles, books. **Subjects:** genealogy. **Computer Services:** database, family history. **Publications:** Roster, annual. Newsletter. **Advertising:** not accepted. **Conventions/Meetings:** periodic conference and workshop (exhibits).

20475 ■ Fagan Family Association
Address Unknown since 2007
Founded: 1967. **Members:** 300. **Description:** Persons researching the surnames Fagan, Fagin, Fagon, and Feagin. Collects and disseminates genealogical information. **Libraries: Type:** reference. **Subjects:** genealogical records. **Publications:** Descendants of Patrick Fagan-Genealogy. **Conventions/Meetings:** periodic reunion.

20476 ■ Felton Family Association (FFA)
PO Box 253
West Boylston, MA 01583
E-mail: secretary@feltonfamily.org
URL: http://www.feltonfamily.org
Contact: Cora Felton Anderson, Historian

Founded: 1988. **Members:** 240. **Membership Dues:** single, $15 (annual) ● family, $20 (annual) ● life (family), $250 ● life (single), $125. **Description:** Members of the Felton family. Facilitates communication and good fellowship among members. Gathers and disseminates information on Felton family history and genealogy; sponsors educational and social activities. Plans to maintain archive. **Libraries: Type:** open to the public. **Holdings:** 5. **Subjects:** 1700s to current. **Publications:** Felton Family Newsletter, quarterly. Contains news of family activities. **Price:** included in membership dues. **Circulation:** 200. **Conventions/Meetings:** reunion.

20477 ■ Flippin Family Association
12206 Brisbane Ave.
Dallas, TX 75234-6528
Ph: (972)241-2739
Fax: (972)620-1416
E-mail: lemstar@juno.com
Contact: Nova A. Lemons, Ed./Founder

Description: Persons researching the surnames Flippin, Flippen, Flipping and their families. Collects information and identifies ancestors.

20478 ■ Forby Family Historical Society (FFHS)
5521 Colorow Dr.
Morrison, CO 80465
Ph: (303)697-2721
E-mail: forbygw@aol.com
Contact: George W. Forby, Exec. Off.

Founded: 1987. **Description:** Persons with the surnames Forby and its variant spelling Forbey. Collects and disseminates genealogical and historical information. **Computer Services:** database. **Conventions/Meetings:** triennial reunion - June or July.

20479 ■ Fretz Family Association (FFA)
572 Kohlers Hill Rd.
Lenhartsville, PA 19534
Ph: (610)756-6697
E-mail: info@fretzassociation.org
Contact: Keith Fretz, Pres.

Founded: 1888. **Members:** 300. **Membership Dues:** regular, $7 (annual). **Description:** Descendants of John and Christian Fretz. Seeks to preserve family history. **Publications:** Fretz Family History. Book. Features the genealogy and history of Fretz Family Association; available in 4 volumes. **Price:** $30.00 each ● FretzLetter, quarterly. Newsletter. Includes births, deaths, genealogy information, and interesting family facts. **Price:** $5.00/year. **Circulation:** 300. **Conventions/Meetings:** quarterly board meeting ● annual reunion - always second Saturday in August.

20480 ■ Friend Family Association of America (FFAA)
PO Box 96
Friendsville, MD 21531
Ph: (301)746-4220 (301)746-4690
E-mail: president@friendfamilyassociation.com
URL: http://www.friendfamilyassociation.org
Contact: Ivory Steinard, Pres.

Founded: 1976. **Members:** 400. **Membership Dues:** regular, $25 (annual) ● life (60 or older), $150 ● life (under 60), $250 ● initiation, $23. **Staff:** 1. **Budget:** $6,000. **Description:** Works to promote historical and genealogical research. Collects, records, and preserves historical and genealogical data; disseminates historical and genealogical data through educational programs and social activities; maintains a National Heritage Museum, speaker's bureau and library. **Libraries: Type:** reference; open to the public. **Holdings:** 1,000; archival material, articles, audiovisuals, books, clippings, periodicals. **Subjects:** history, genealogy, native American. **Computer Services:** database, genealogy. **Publications:** Friendship News, quarterly. Newsletter. **Circulation:** 600 ● Books ● Pamphlets. **Conventions/Meetings:** biennial seminar (exhibits) - even numbered years.

20481 ■ Frisbie - Frisbee Family Association of America
c/o Mary Frisbie, Sec.-Treas.
45982 180th Ave.
Lake Mills, IA 50450-7498
Ph: (641)568-3234
E-mail: dfrisbie@wctatel.net
Contact: Mary Frisbie, Sec.-Treas.

Founded: 1950. **Members:** 300. **Description:** Descendants of Edward Frisbie (1621-1690). Answers inquiries. **Libraries: Type:** reference. **Subjects:** 14 generations of the Frisbie/Frisbee family. **Publications:** Frisbie Genealogy. Book ● Bulletin, quarterly. Features news of births, deaths, marriages, and accomplishments of current and past family members. **Price:** included in membership dues. **Circulation:** 300.

20482 ■ Fullam Family Organization (FFO)
Address Unknown since 2007
Founded: 1986. **Members:** 94. **Staff:** 1. **National Groups:** 1. **Description:** Descendants of Philip Fullam and Ellen Kennedy. **Conventions/Meetings:** quinquennial picnic, photos, genealogies (exhibits).

20483 ■ Fuller Society
c/o John Hoffman
42 Sugar Maple Ln.
Tinton Falls, NJ 07724-2716
E-mail: pjs5686exp@aol.com
Contact: Ruth Thrash, Treas.
Founded: 1992. **Members:** 575. **Membership Dues:** regular, $10 (annual) ● life, $150. **Staff:** 7. **Description:** Descendants of the Mayflower Pilgrims Dr. Samuel Fuller and Edward Fuller. Promotes genealogical research and social gatherings of descendants of Samuel and Edward Fuller. **Libraries: Type:** reference. **Holdings:** archival material, books, periodicals. **Subjects:** history, genealogy. **Awards:** Bridget Lee Fuller Scholarship. **Frequency:** annual. **Type:** scholarship. **Recipient:** for descendant of the Mayflower Pilgrims. **Publications:** *Fuller Society Newsletter*, 3/year. Contains genealogical and historical information. **Price:** $2.00/copy for nonmembers. ISSN: 1077-6583. **Circulation:** 500. **Conventions/Meetings:** annual meeting (exhibits).

20484 ■ Fuqua(y) Family Association
5805 Scottsville Rd.
Bowling Green, KY 42104
Ph: (270)781-3982
Contact: Dorothy Graves, Pres.
Founded: 1987. **Members:** 100. **Membership Dues:** family, $10 (annual) ● retired (over 65), $5. **Description:** Individuals with the surname Fuqua or Fuquay and variations such as Feuquay and Faqua. Collects, researches, and disseminates genealogical data on the Fuqua(y) family name. Compiles statistics. **Libraries: Type:** reference. **Holdings:** archival material, books, clippings. **Subjects:** genealogical, historical, vols: 15 biographical data on Fuqua(y) name. **Computer Services:** database, Roots IV. **Publications:** *Fuqua(y) Family Association Newsletter*, quarterly. **Price:** included in membership dues. **Circulation:** 106. **Conventions/Meetings:** annual Fuqua(y) Family Reunion (exhibits).

20485 ■ Gafford Family Association of America
PO Box 1416
Oxford, MS 38655
Ph: (662)234-7602
Fax: (662)513-3298
E-mail: ga_gafford@bellsouth.net
Contact: Gerald Gafford, CEO
Founded: 1994. **Members:** 98. **Membership Dues:** full, $15 (annual). **State Groups:** 50. **Description:** Seeks to unite individuals with the Gafford (or related) surname, including variations. Exchanges and preserves research, photos, and records. Gathers cemetery records, and conducts historical research of the Gafford name. Conducts educational and research programs. Provides children's services. Maintains hall of fame. Collect photos-records, life histories, restores head stones in cemeteries. **Libraries: Type:** not open to the public; reference. **Holdings:** archival material, articles, books, clippings, periodicals. **Computer Services:** database ● electronic publishing ● mailing lists. **Formerly:** (1999) Gafford Family of America Association. **Publications:** *The Gafford Newsletter*, quarterly. **Price:** $15.00/year. **Conventions/Meetings:** annual reunion (exhibits).

20486 ■ Gaylord Family Organization
c/o Barry C. Wood
1910 S Church St.
Lodi, CA 95240
Ph: (209)366-2773
E-mail: bcwood2162@sbcglobal.net
URL: http://freepages.genealogy.rootsweb.com/
~gaylord
Contact: Barry C. Wood, Contact
Founded: 1978. **Members:** 200. **Description:** Conducts genealogical research on descendants of William Gaylord (1590-1673) in the United States. Acts as a clearinghouse for genealogical information. **Publications:** none. **Convention/Meeting:** none. **Computer Services:** database ● mailing lists.

20487 ■ George McCleave Family Organization (GMFO)
114 E Main St.
Oaktown, IN 47561
Ph: (812)882-9371
Contact: Richard Carl Rodgers II, Contact
Founded: 1982. **Members:** 726. **Staff:** 2. **Description:** Descendants of George McCleave, was married in Wilmington, New Castle Co., Delaware in 1746, Resided in London Britain Twp., Chester Co., Pennsylvania about 1751, and is believed to have been born in Ireland about 1725. Promotes study of McCleave and related family history and genealogy; facilitates communication among members. Serves as a clearinghouse on McCleave family history and genealogy; provides assistance to family historians and genealogists; sponsors social activities. **Libraries: Type:** not open to the public. **Holdings:** archival material, artwork, books, business records, periodicals, video recordings. **Subjects:** McCleave family history and genealogy.

20488 ■ Germroth Family Association International
Address Unknown since 2007
Founded: 1980. **Members:** 2,036. **Membership Dues:** general, $20 (annual). **Staff:** 2. **National Groups:** 1. **Languages:** Dutch, German. **Description:** Persons interested in German genealogy particularly the history of the Germroth surname and all its various spellings. Collects German genealogical records and records of the Germroth family name. Works to document the Germroth family name and decendents of the Germroth family name living in the U.S., Canada, and the German-speaking nations of Europe. Works to advance German-American studies, to promote German-American understanding, and to study German-Americana. **Libraries: Type:** not open to the public. **Holdings:** 2,000. **Subjects:** German history, politics, and genealogy. **Computer Services:** database, German surnames. **Publications:** *Beyond the Cold War: American Foreign Policy and the German Question*. **Price:** $19.95 ● Papers. Covers German genealogy, German AMericana, and Germroth family line.

20489 ■ Geshkewich Surname Organization (GSO)
Address Unknown since 2007
Founded: 1985. **State Groups:** 1. **Description:** Individuals with the surname Geshkewich and its variant spellings; other members of the Geshkewich family. Promotes study of Geshkewich family history and genealogy. Serves as a clearinghouse on the Geshkewich family and its history; conducts research and assists family historians and genealogists. **Libraries: Type:** reference. **Holdings:** books, clippings, periodicals. **Subjects:** Geshkewich family history and genealogy. **Publications:** *Geshkewich Family News*, annual. Newsletter.

20490 ■ Gideon Family Association (GFA)
160 W Dunedin Rd.
Columbus, OH 43214
Ph: (614)263-4232
E-mail: mgideon@columbus.rr.com
Contact: Mark R. Gideon, Sec.
Founded: 1987. **Description:** Individuals interested in researching the surname Gideon. Collects and disseminates biographical, genealogical, and historical information. **Convention/Meeting:** none. **Publications:** Plans to publish monthly newsletter.

20491 ■ Gilstrap Family Association (GFA)
c/o Marcus D. Gilstrap
1921 N Harrison
San Angelo, TX 76901-1335
Ph: (915)949-0792 (325)949-0792
E-mail: marcusg2@cox.net
URL: http://familytreemaker.genealogy.com/users/g/i/
l/Marcus-D-Gilstrap
Contact: Marcus D. Gilstrap, Contact
Founded: 1991. **Staff:** 2. **Description:** Members of the Gilstrap family. Promotes study of Gilstrap family history and genealogy. Serves as a clearinghouse on the Gilstrap family and its history; supports and as-

sists family history and genealogy. **Libraries: Type:** reference. **Holdings:** archival material, clippings, periodicals. **Subjects:** Gilstrap family history, genealogy.

20492 ■ Goff/Gough Family Association
c/o Allen S. Goff, Pres.
2125 Davis Rd.
Waynesboro, VA 22980
Ph: (540)942-3188
E-mail: 2goff@ntelos.net
URL: http://www.goff-gough.com
Contact: Allen S. Goff, Pres.
Founded: 1982. **Members:** 209. **Membership Dues:** regular, $18 (annual) ● sustaining, $25 (annual) ● initial, $15. **Description:** Persons with the surnames Goff or Gough; descendants of a Goff/Gough family; anyone who endorses the purposes of the association. Seeks to stimulate an interest in the history of the Goff/Gough families and their descendants, especially those living in the United States. Maintains a web page to assist members with genealogical research. Promotes projects that will further the research of the Goff/Gough families and their descendants. Encourages communications among members conducting genealogical research. **Libraries: Type:** reference; not open to the public. **Holdings:** archival material, articles, books, clippings, periodicals. **Subjects:** Goff/Gough family, genealogical information. **Awards:** Certificate of Recognition. **Type:** recognition. **Recipient:** for members who have made significant contributions to the association. **Computer Services:** database, Goff/Gough records, 1850 Census Goff/Gough, newsletter indices. **Publications:** *Goffs/Goughs: Ancestors and Descendants*, quarterly. Newsletter. **Price:** included in membership dues. **Circulation:** 250. **Conventions/Meetings:** biennial general assembly and workshop.

20493 ■ Goodenow Family Association (GFA)
163 Landham Rd.
Sudbury, MA 01776-3156
E-mail: treasurer@goodenowfamily.org
URL: http://www.goodenowfamily.org
Contact: Kathy Truesdell, Corresponding Sec.
Founded: 1988. **Members:** 200. **Membership Dues:** family, $20 (annual) ● life, $200. **Description:** Collects information on descendents of persons with the surnames Goodenow, Goodenough, Goodnow, and Goodno; seeks to locate members of those families. Conducts research programs. **Libraries: Type:** reference. **Holdings:** archival material. **Computer Services:** database, genealogical. **Publications:** *Goodenows' Ghosts*, quarterly. Newsletter. Includes genealogical information, feature articles, and queries. **Price:** included in membership dues. **Circulation:** 225. Also Cited As: *Ghosts* ● *Goodenows Who Originated in Sudbury, MA 1638 A.D.*. Book. **Price:** $53.50 in U.S. **Conventions/Meetings:** biennial reunion, family history (exhibits).

20494 ■ Goodwin Family Organization (GFO)
39 Lost Trail Rd.
Roswell, NM 88201-9509
Ph: (505)625-0961
E-mail: hgoodwin@sbcglobal.net
URL: http://www.geocities.com/heartland/farm/2995/
daniel.htm
Contact: Alice B. Sharp, Pres.
Founded: 1978. **Members:** 10. **Membership Dues:** individual, $18 (annual). **Staff:** 2. **Description:** Promotes genealogical research. Facilitates contact between relatives. **Libraries: Type:** reference. **Holdings:** 150. **Subjects:** family history. **Publications:** *Goodwin News*, semiannual. Newsletter. **Price:** $15.00 included in membership dues. ISSN: 0892-1423. **Circulation:** 200. **Advertising:** accepted. **Conventions/Meetings:** annual reunion (exhibits).

20495 ■ Graves Family Association (GFA)
20 Binney Cir.
Wrentham, MA 02093
Ph: (508)384-8084

E-mail: ken.graves@gravesfa.org
URL: http://www.gravesfa.org
Contact: Kenneth V. Graves, Pres.
Founded: 1976. **Members:** 600. **Membership Dues:** regular, $20 (annual) ● sustaining, $40 (annual) ● regular, outside U.S. and Canada, $30 (annual) ● life, $600. **Staff:** 2. **Multinational. Description:** Descendants of a Graves, Greaves, or Grave family worldwide; anyone interested in the family name. Works to collect, preserve, and publish all information on the Graves, Greaves, or Grave family name. Provides research programs, reunions, and trips to ancestral sites. **Libraries: Type:** reference; open to the public; by appointment only. **Holdings:** archival material, books, monographs, periodicals. **Computer Services:** database ● electronic publishing ● record retrieval services. **Publications:** *Graves Family Bulletin*, bimonthly. Newsletter. **Price:** included in membership dues for individuals; $20.00 /year for libraries and other institutions. ISSN: 0146-0269. **Circulation:** 750. Alternate Formats: online ● Membership Directory. **Price:** included in membership dues ● Books. Contains information about Graves/Greaves family. **Conventions/Meetings:** biennial conference and regional meeting ● periodic reunion.

20496 ■ Grawunder and Graffunder Connection
13108 Penn Ave.
Burnsville, MN 55337
Ph: (952)890-3240
E-mail: ggconnection@isd.net
Contact: Gladys Grovender, Co-Ed.
Founded: 1987. **Membership Dues:** per volume, $5. **Staff:** 3. **Description:** Conducts genealogical research on the surnames Grawunder and Graffunder and on variations of spellings of these surnames. Maintains speakers' bureau. **Libraries: Type:** reference. **Holdings:** archival material, books, clippings, periodicals. **Subjects:** Prussian, Posen and Pomeranian history, information on the surnames Grawunder and Graffunder. **Formerly:** Grawunder Connection. **Publications:** Newsletter, quarterly. **Price:** $5.00/year.

20497 ■ Griesemer Family Association (GFA)
PO Box 814
Lompoc, CA 93438-0814
Ph: (805)736-9637
E-mail: thistle.gfa@verizon.net
Contact: Albert C. Hardy Jr., VP/Ed./Asst. Historian
Founded: 1927. **Members:** 544. **Description:** Griesemer family members. Seeks to "perpetuate the family name in all its 42 spellings." Facilitates communication and good fellowship among members; gathers and disseminates information on Griesemer family history and genealogy. **Publications:** *Thistle*, semiannual. Newsletter. **Price:** $3.00. **Conventions/Meetings:** annual reunion - always last Sunday in August.

20498 ■ Grinnell Family Association
c/o Mr. F. Hugh Grinnell, Pres.
10290 N Alder Spring Dr.
Oro Valley, AZ 85737
Ph: (520)797-3055
E-mail: grinnell797@hotmail.com
URL: http://www.grinnellfamily.org
Contact: Mr. F. Hugh Grinnell, Pres.
Founded: 1980. **Members:** 200. **Membership Dues:** individual, $15 (annual). **Description:** Descendants of Matthew Grinnell, who emigrated to America circa 1635. Works to continue research on the Grinnell name and share this information with other interested parties. Provides research programs. **Libraries: Type:** by appointment only. **Holdings:** archival material, artwork, books, clippings, monographs, periodicals. **Subjects:** Grinnell family genealogy. **Computer Services:** Online services, genealogical queries. **Publications:** *Genealogy*, approximately every ten years. Book. Contains a genealogy of the Grinnell family. **Price:** $60.00 ● *Grinnell Family Association of America Official Newsletter*, semiannual. **Circulation:** 350. **Conventions/Meetings:** reunion, for members and others who are related to the Grinnell

family - twice every five years; meets at Seekonk, MA, site of the first Grinnell reunion.

20499 ■ Groberg - Holbrook Genealogical Organization (GHGO)
1605 S Woodruff
Idaho Falls, ID 83404
Ph: (208)522-3185 (208)522-3571
Fax: (208)522-3060
E-mail: mmpowell9@msn.com
URL: http://www.dvgroberg.com
Contact: Joseph Groberg, Contact
Founded: 1985. **Members:** 50. **Membership Dues:** individual, $25 (annual). **Staff:** 2. **Description:** Members of the Groberg and Holbrook families; other interested individuals. Seeks to strengthen family ties and foster and encourage family genealogical research. Serves as a clearinghouse on the Groberg and Holbrook families and their histories; assists family historians and genealogists. **Libraries: Type:** not open to the public; reference. **Holdings:** archival material, audio recordings, books. **Subjects:** Groberg and Holbrook family histories and genealogies. **Telecommunication Services:** electronic mail, tom@govirtuoso.com. **Publications:** *Our Family Links*, quarterly. Newsletter.

20500 ■ Grover Family Organization
3929 Milton Dr.
Independence, MO 64055-4043
Ph: (816)373-5309
E-mail: groversar@aol.com
Contact: Robert L. Grover, Pres.
Founded: 1961. **Members:** 2,000. **Description:** Persons with the surname Grover. Seeks to share family and genealogical information among members. **Publications:** none. **Convention/Meeting:** none.

20501 ■ Hallam Association
c/o Henrietta Nichols
300 Greenglade Ave.
Worthington, OH 43085-2223
Ph: (614)888-1236
E-mail: henriettan@aol.com
Contact: Henrietta Nichols, Contact
Founded: 1995. **Description:** Traces all branches of the Hallam family from early England to the present day. **Status Note:** (2006) Defunct.

20502 ■ Hamilton National Genealogical Society (HNGS)
116 W Vine St.
Vicksburg, MI 49097
E-mail: membership@hamiltongensociety.org
URL: http://www.hamiltongensociety.org
Contact: Russell David Hamilton, Sec.
Founded: 1978. **Members:** 425. **Membership Dues:** in U.S., $25 (annual) ● in Canada and Mexico, $39 (annual) ● outside U.S., $53 (annual) ● life, $300. **Staff:** 2. **Description:** Persons interested in genealogical research and preservation of records. Works to collect information on the surname Hamilton and its variations, including Hamelton, Hambleton, Hambelton, and Hambleton. **Libraries: Type:** reference. **Holdings:** archival material, books. **Subjects:** Hamilton records. **Computer Services:** database, family records. **Publications:** *The Connector*, quarterly. Newsletter. **Price:** included in membership dues. ISSN: 1051-9300. **Circulation:** 450.

20503 ■ Hans/Henry Segrist Family Organization (HSFO)
145 New Haven Dr.
Urbana, OH 43078
Ph: (937)653-6500
E-mail: secrist@ctcn.net
Contact: Arlene J. Secrist, Contact
Founded: 1987. **Members:** 25. **Staff:** 3. **Description:** Individuals with the surname Segrist and its variant spellings. Seeks to locate and unite family members. Conducts genealogical and historical research and disseminates findings; sponsors social activities.

20504 ■ Harden - Hardin - Harding Family Association (HHHFA)
2500 Winningham Rd.
Crewe, VA 23930
Ph: (434)645-8595
E-mail: oranhj@meckcom.net
Contact: James Oran Harding, Contact
Founded: 1983. **Members:** 1,423. **Membership Dues:** regular, $20 (annual) ● sustaining, $25 (annual). **Staff:** 7. **Budget:** $10,000. **Regional Groups:** 50. **State Groups:** 45. **Local Groups:** 100. **Description:** Individuals with the surname Harden and its variant spellings; other members of the Harden family. Promotes study of family history and genealogy. Serves as a clearinghouse on the Harden family and its history; conducts research; assists family historians and genealogists. **Libraries: Type:** by appointment only; reference. **Holdings:** archival material, articles, audio recordings, books, periodicals, video recordings. **Subjects:** Harden family history and genealogy. **Awards:** Member of the Year. **Frequency:** annual. **Type:** recognition. **Computer Services:** database, membership list and genealogies. **Publications:** Newsletter, quarterly. **Conventions/Meetings:** annual reunion.

20505 ■ Harrison Family Association (HFA)
Address Unknown since 2007
Founded: 1994. **Description:** Descendants of William Henry Harrison, who was born in North Carolina in 1834. Promotes study of Harrison family history and genealogy. Provides support and assistance to Harrison family historians and genealogists; facilitates communication among Harrison family members. **Libraries: Type:** reference. **Holdings:** archival material, books, clippings, monographs. **Subjects:** Harrison family history and genealogy. **Publications:** Newsletter, annual. **Conventions/Meetings:** annual reunion.

20506 ■ Hartshorn Family Association (HFA)
1204 4th St. Dr. SE
Conover, NC 28613
Ph: (828)464-4981
Fax: (828)464-0025
E-mail: derickh@charter.net
URL: http://homepages.rootsweb.com/~hartshrn
Contact: Derick S. Hartshorn, Pres.
Founded: 1983. **Members:** 505. **Membership Dues:** associate, $15 (annual). **Staff:** 2. **Budget:** $12,250. **Regional Groups:** 5. **Multinational. Description:** Researches the surnames Hartshorn, Hartshorne, Hartson, and related family lines. Collects and disseminates genealogical information. **Libraries: Type:** by appointment only. **Holdings:** 1,517; books, periodicals. **Subjects:** genealogy, history. **Computer Services:** database, 211,000 names ● information services, member research. **Publications:** *Hartshorn/e Migration to America*, quarterly. Hartshorn family settlements. **Price:** included in membership dues. **Circulation:** 311. Alternate Formats: online ● *The Hartshorn Family in America*, annual. Book. Contains about Hartshorn surnames. **Price:** $59.00 ● *Hartshorn Hotline*, quarterly. Newsletter. Includes membership listing. **Price:** $12.00/year ● *The Hartshorns of Monmouth County, New Jersey* ● *The Hartshorns of Ohio* ● *The Hartshorns of Pittsburg, Kansas*. **Conventions/Meetings:** annual Hartshorn Reunion - England, 10 days in the English Midlands ● annual Hartshorn Reunion - New England (exhibits).

20507 ■ Hasbrouck Family Association (HFA)
PO Box 176
New Paltz, NY 12561
Ph: (845)255-3223
Fax: (845)255-0624
E-mail: info@hasbrouckfamily.org
URL: http://www.hasbrouckfamily.org
Contact: Robert W. Hasbrouck Jr., Pres.
Founded: 1957. **Members:** 500. **Membership Dues:** regular, $20 (annual) ● life (under age 65), $350 ● life (over 65 years of age), $200. **Description:** Committed to the preservation of the Hasbrouck family history and the Huguenot heritage. **Publications:**

Hasbrouck Family Association Journal. Newsletter. Alternate Formats: online.

20508 ■ Hathaway Family Association (HFA)
2231 Riverside Ave.
Somerset, MA 02726-4104
E-mail: wsh@hathawayfunerals.com
URL: http://www.geocities.com/leannewiese
Contact: William S. Hathaway Jr., Pres.
Founded: 1911. **Members:** 411. **Membership Dues:** ordinary, $15 (annual). **Description:** Members of the Hathaway family. Seeks to identify and unite family members; promotes study of Hathaway family history and genealogy. Serves as a clearinghouse on the Hathaway family and its history; sponsors social activities. **Publications:** *Hathaways of America.* Book. **Price:** $53.00 ● *Hathaways 1200-1980.* Book. **Price:** $25.00 plus shipping and handling ● Newsletter, quarterly. **Price:** $10.00. **Conventions/Meetings:** annual meeting - always June.

20509 ■ Haviland Family Organization (HFO)
19662 Westover Ave.
Rocky River, OH 44116-4037
Ph: (440)331-6444
E-mail: budhaviland@aol.com
Contact: Bud Haviland, Contact
Founded: 1985. **Description:** Members of the Haviland family. Encourages study of Haviland family history and genealogy. Conducts research and serves as a clearinghouse on Haviland family history and genealogy; assists family historians and genealogists.

20510 ■ Hawkins Association
PO Box 2392
Setauket, NY 11733
E-mail: olyre@flash.net
URL: http://www.hawkinsgenealogy.org
Contact: William Randall Hulse, Pres.
Founded: 1935. **Members:** 150. **Membership Dues:** individual, family, $10 (annual). **Description:** Descendants of Robert and Mary of Massachusetts, Zachariah Hawkins of New York, and Joseph Hawkins of Connecticut. Conducts genealogical research.

20511 ■ Haymore Family Organization
437 Pimlico Dr.
St. George, UT 84790
Ph: (435)656-4485
E-mail: r-mcoleman@juno.com
Contact: Ronald Coleman, Contact
Founded: 1970. **Members:** 800. **Regional Groups:** 2. **Description:** Conducts research on the Haymore family. Works to maintain Haymore homes and cemeteries. Conducts research and charitable programs; compiles statistics. Maintains museum; has published 2 books. **Libraries: Type:** reference; by appointment only. **Holdings:** archival material, books, clippings, monographs, periodicals. **Computer Services:** database ● mailing lists. **Telecommunication Services:** electronic bulletin board. **Formerly:** (1996) Hamor, Hamour. **Publications:** *Haymore Heritage.* Books.

20512 ■ Hazelbaker Families
PO Box 450154
Grove, OK 74345-0154
Ph: (918)786-2360
Contact: Imogene Sawvell Davis, Exec. Off.
Founded: 1976. **Description:** Persons with the surname Hazelbaker and their relatives. Collects family and historical data. **Libraries: Type:** open to the public. **Holdings:** 2,000. **Subjects:** genealogy.

20513 ■ Heald Family Association (HFA)
250 Robinson Rd.
Cave Junction, OR 97523-9719
Ph: (541)592-3203
Contact: Jack Heald, Pres.
Founded: 1967. **Members:** 500. **Staff:** 1. **Description:** Heald family members and other interested individuals. Promotes study of Heald family history and genealogy. Gathers and disseminates information on the Heald family and its history; plans to publish book. **Libraries: Type:** reference. **Holdings:**

archival material, audio recordings, books, monographs, periodicals, video recordings. **Subjects:** Heald family history and genealogy.

20514 ■ Heiney Family Tree (HFT)
Address Unknown since 2007
Founded: 1980. **Members:** 150. **Membership Dues:** individual, $50 (annual). **Description:** Persons interested in researching the surnames Heiney and Heiny. Collects and disseminates genealogical data. **Libraries: Type:** open to the public. **Holdings:** 70; books, periodicals. **Subjects:** genealogy. **Computer Services:** database, family history. **Publications:** *Roster,* annual. Newsletter. **Advertising:** not accepted. **Conventions/Meetings:** annual conference and workshop (exhibits) - always August, Denver, CO.

20515 ■ Henlein/Heinlein Family Association
c/o Enid I. Beihold, Founder
11502 Grace Terr.
Indianapolis, IN 46236
Ph: (317)823-2376
E-mail: ebeihold@comcast.net
Contact: Enid I. Beihold, Founder
Founded: 1985. **Description:** Persons researching the surname Heinline and its variant spellings. Promotes genealogical research and seeks to preserve family history. Produces indices. Compiles statistics. **Formerly:** (1990) Heinline Clearinghouse. **Publications:** *The Chanticleer,* quarterly. Newsletter. Includes pedigree charts. **Price:** $15.00/year. **Advertising:** accepted.

20516 ■ Higdon Family Association (HFA)
112 Blossom Ln.
Clinton, TN 37716
URL: http://www.higdonfamily.org
Contact: Janice J. Higdon, Pres.
Founded: 1975. **Members:** 160. **Membership Dues:** regular, $30 (annual). **Description:** Individuals with the surname of Higdon. Promotes communication among members of the Higdon family. Provides historical and genealogical information. Conducts educational activities. **Publications:** *Colonial Higdons and Some of Their Descendants.* Book. **Price:** $28.95 ● *Descendants of Joseph Huffman Higdon and Margaret Matilda Berry Higdon.* Book. **Price:** $28.95 ● *Higdon Family Association Newsletter,* bimonthly. Contains research information, notes on family happenings, and HFA Annual Meeting updates. **Price:** included in membership dues. ISSN: 0739-3199. **Conventions/Meetings:** annual meeting.

20517 ■ Hinman Family Association (HFA)
c/o Joan Hinman, Sec.-Treas.
46 Main St.
Stamford, NY 12167
E-mail: thinman@hinmanfamily.com
URL: http://www.hinmanfamily.com
Contact: James E. Burnes III, Pres.
Founded: 1974. **Members:** 200. **Membership Dues:** regular, $15 (annual). **Description:** Promotes genealogical research on the Hinman family. **Computer Services:** database, family lineages. **Publications:** *Hinman Heritage,* quarterly. Newsletter. ISSN: 0885-2367. **Circulation:** 200. **Conventions/Meetings:** biennial reunion - even-numbered years.

20518 ■ Hoefler Family Association (HFA)
1039 Hwy. W
Warrenton, MO 63383
Ph: (636)456-4610
E-mail: dorjour@socket.net
Contact: Dorey Schrick, Contact
Founded: 1992. **Members:** 60. **Membership Dues:** individual, $2 (annual). **Description:** Members of the Hoefler family and other interested individuals. Promotes study of Hoefler family history and genealogy. Serves as a clearinghouse on the Hoefler family and its history; assists family historians and genealogists. **Libraries: Type:** reference. **Holdings:** archival material, articles, books, clippings. **Subjects:** Hoefler family history and genealogy. **Publications:** *Hoefler Herald-USA,* annual. Newsletter. **Price:** included in membership dues.

20519 ■ Holloway - Ralston Family Association (HRFA)
7650 Fairview Rd.
Tillamook, OR 97141
Ph: (503)842-6036
Fax: (503)842-6036
E-mail: orella@wcn.net
Contact: Orella Chadwick, Contact
Founded: 1953. **Members:** 60. **Description:** Members of the Ralston and Holloway families. Seeks to identify and unite Ralston and Holloway family members; promotes interest in family history and genealogy. Gathers and disseminates information on the Holloway and Ralston families and their histories; sponsors social activities. **Libraries: Type:** reference. **Holdings:** 2; artwork, business records, clippings, periodicals. **Subjects:** Holloway and Ralston family histories and genealogies. **Publications:** *Holloway-Ralston Family Favorites.* Book ● *Holloways.* Book ● *Ralstons.* Book. **Conventions/Meetings:** annual Holloway Ralston - reunion, albums, scrapbooks, card playing, cribbage tournaments - usually June around Father's Day.

20520 ■ Honaker Family Association
PO Box 3636
Alexandria, VA 22302-0636
Ph: (703)751-7321
Fax: (703)751-7321
Contact: Thomas G. Hanlin, VP
Founded: 1989. **Members:** 300. **Membership Dues:** personal, family, $15 (annual). **Staff:** 1. **Description:** Known descendants of Swiss-German emigrant Hans Jacob Honaker. **Libraries: Type:** not open to the public. **Holdings:** 200; books. **Subjects:** genealogical and family reference. **Publications:** *Honaker Family Newsletter,* quarterly. **Price:** included in membership dues. ISSN: 1529-692X. **Circulation:** 300. **Conventions/Meetings:** annual reunion (exhibits) - always second Saturday of August.

20521 ■ House of Boyd Society (HBS)
c/o Lauren M. Boyd, Pres.
6 Sylvia Cir.
Novato, CA 94947-2025
E-mail: president@clanboyd.org
URL: http://www.clanboyd.org
Contact: Lauren M. Boyd, Pres.
Founded: 1988. **Members:** 400. **Membership Dues:** individual in U.S., $15 (annual) ● couple in U.S., $20 (annual) ● life (individual in U.S.), $150 ● individual outside U.S., $18 (annual) ● couple outside U.S., $23 (annual) ● life (individual outside U.S.), $180. **Multinational. Description:** Studies the history of the Boyd's of Scotland and Ireland; promotes the exchange of genealogical information; increases the appreciation of the unique values of Scottish and Celtic culture; and participates in Scottish and Celtic Festivals and other educational programs. **Libraries: Type:** reference. **Subjects:** Scottish heritage, heraldry, genealogy. **Awards:** House of Boyd Scholarship. **Frequency:** annual. **Type:** scholarship. **Recipient:** to members or children of members persuing studies that preserve our Scottish heritage dance, music, history, language or other related field. **Computer Services:** Record retrieval services, genealogy file. **Telecommunication Services:** electronic mail, boyd-l@rootsweb.com. **Also Known As:** Clan Boyd. **Publications:** *The Dean Road,* quarterly. Newsletter. **Price:** included in membership dues. ISSN: 1087-223X. **Circulation:** 500. **Advertising:** accepted. **Conventions/Meetings:** annual General Meeting and Gathering of the Clan, general meeting of the corporation and gathering of the clan and families, held at a different venue each year.

20522 ■ Hoyt Family Association (HFA)
360 Watson Rd.
Paducah, KY 42003-8978
E-mail: hoyt-haight@listserv.northwest.com
URL: http://www.geocities.com/heartland/plains/8432/hoyt5.htm
Contact: Roy F. Olson Jr., Founder/Ed.
Founded: 1983. **Members:** 100. **Membership Dues:** individual, $20 (annual). **Description:** Individuals with the surname Hoyt or its variant spellings. Seeks to

identify and unite Hoyt family descendants. Serves as a clearinghouse on Hoyt family history and genealogy; provides assistance to genealogical researchers; sponsors social and educational activities. **Libraries: Type:** by appointment only; reference. **Holdings:** 300; archival material, articles, artwork, books, clippings, periodicals. **Subjects:** Hoyt family history and genealogy. **Publications:** *Hoyt's Issue*, semiannual. Magazine. **Price:** included in membership dues. **Advertising:** accepted. **Conventions/Meetings:** annual reunion.

20523 ■ The Hubbell Family Historical Society (THFHS)
5601 Brisbane Dr.
Chapel Hill, NC 27514
E-mail: membership@hubbell.org
URL: http://www.hubbell.org
Contact: Mary Ann Hubbell, Membership Chair
Founded: 1981. **Members:** 500. **Membership Dues:** individual/couple, $15 (annual) ● contributing, $50 (annual) ● proud, $200 (annual) ● participating, $100 (annual) ● society/library, $10 (annual). **Multinational. Description:** Gathers information and artifacts on the history of the Hubbell family. **Libraries: Type:** open to the public. **Holdings:** 500; articles, artwork, books, papers. **Subjects:** history of Hubbell family. **Awards:** Hubbell Hall of Fame. **Frequency:** annual. **Type:** recognition. **Recipient:** for service and accomplishments to the association ● Hubbell Scholarship. **Frequency:** annual. **Type:** monetary. **Recipient:** to descendants of Richard Hubbell. **Computer Services:** Mailing lists. **Publications:** *Family Notes*, semiannual, every spring and fall. Newsletter. Features news of the society and current news and information. **Price:** included in membership dues ● Newsletter, annual. Contains a genealogical journal of the Hubbell family. **Price:** included in membership dues. **Circulation:** 500. **Conventions/Meetings:** biennial reunion (exhibits).

20524 ■ Hudson Family Association (HFA)
c/o Patricia G. Semple, Membership Sec.-Treas.
2600 Cobre Valle Ln.
Plano, TX 75023
Ph: (469)241-1161
Fax: (972)398-1038
E-mail: pespas@aol.com
URL: http://www.hudsonfamilyassociation.org
Contact: Patricia G. Semple, Membership Sec.-Treas.
Founded: 1973. **Members:** 350. **Membership Dues:** individual, $20 (annual) ● household, $25 (annual) ● contributing, $30 (annual) ● patron, $50 (biennial). **Budget:** $12,000. **Description:** Individuals and families interested in the history of the Hudson family and variant spellings of the name, including Hutson, Hudsons, Hoedsons, and Hodsons. Gathers information on ancestors who were early settlers in America. Continues to conduct new research and organize material into workbooks. Maintains 260 workbooks of Hudson data. **Libraries: Type:** reference; not open to the public; by appointment only. **Holdings:** archival material. **Subjects:** Hudson family history, genealogy. **Awards:** Outstanding Member. **Frequency:** annual. **Type:** recognition. **Computer Services:** database, Master Index ● record retrieval services, 108,000 members' lines. **Publications:** *Hudson Family Association Bulletin*, quarterly. Includes articles of interest to Hudson researchers. **Price:** included in membership dues. ISSN: 0363-8847. **Circulation:** 460. Alternate Formats: CD-ROM. **Conventions/Meetings:** annual convention, lectures, database searches, business meeting, banquet, installation of officers - every last weekend of July.

20525 ■ Huebotter Family Organization
2634 Assoc. Rd., Apt. A110
Fullerton, CA 92835
Ph: (714)990-5946
Contact: Nancy M. Huebotter, Pres.
Founded: 1984. **Members:** 150. **Description:** Collects, preserves, and maintains Huebotter family genealogical and historical information. **Computer Services:** database, genealogical information. **Publications:** *Huebotter Happenings*, annual. Newsletter.

20526 ■ Innes Clan Society (ICS)
c/o Ms. Carole Innes, Membership Chair
129 Ravenna Dr.
Long Beach, CA 90803
E-mail: meinnes@sbcglobal.net
URL: http://www.clan-innes.org
Contact: Stephen Innes, Pres.
Founded: 1984. **Members:** 290. **Membership Dues:** family, $20 (annual) ● sustaining, $40 (annual). **Multinational. Description:** Descendants of or individuals related to the Innes clan; individuals interested in Scottish heritage. Seeks to strengthen relations within the Innes clan and encourage Scottish kinship. Conducts research; and collects literary, historical, and genealogical records, documents, and relics relating to Clan Innes and Scottish cultural heritage. Maintains genealogical archives. **Libraries: Type:** open to the public. **Subjects:** genealogical information on various Innes families. **Publications:** *Broken Inheritance - The History of Clan Innes in the North-East of Scotland*. Booklet ● *The Bullrush*, quarterly. Newsletter. Contains information on membership and Scottish ancestry. Includes calendar of events. ● Membership Directory, periodic. **Conventions/Meetings:** annual meeting.

20527 ■ International Association of Clan MacInnes
c/o Randy McInnis, Chm., Scholarship Committee
1413 Autumn Ridge Ln.
Fort Mill, SC 29708
E-mail: norm@macinnes.org
URL: http://www.clanmacinnes.org
Contact: Norman MacInnis, Pres.
Founded: 1970. **Members:** 500. **Membership Dues:** individual (in U.S.), $25 (annual) ● life (in U.S.), $500 ● individual (in Australia), $A 50 (annual) ● life (in Australia), $A 1,000 ● individual (in Canada), C$32 (annual) ● life (in Canada), C$650 ● individual (in UK/Scotland), 17 (annual) ● life (in UK/Scotland), 340. **Regional Groups:** 7. **Description:** Members of the Clan MacInnes family. Promotes interest in clan history and genealogy, and in Scottish history, music, dance, and culture. Conducts MacInnes Clan historical and genealogical research; participates in Highland Games and other Scottish cultural activities; supports maintenance of Clan MacInnes historical sites in Scotland. **Awards: Frequency:** annual. **Type:** scholarship. **Recipient:** for students in Scottish arts. **Additional Websites:** http://www.macinnes.org. **Formerly:** (2001) Clan MacInnes Society. **Publications:** *The Thistle and the Bee*, 3/year. Newsletter. **Conventions/Meetings:** annual meeting.

20528 ■ International Association of the Skubinna Family
16 3rd St. NE
Washington, DC 20002-7312
Ph: (202)546-0126
E-mail: mskubinna@hotmail.com
Contact: Dr. Martin Skubinna PhD, Pres.
Founded: 1990. **Members:** 200. **Staff:** 1. **Budget:** $15,000. **Regional Groups:** 4. **Local Groups:** 3. **Languages:** English, German, Lithuanian, Polish. **For-Profit. Description:** Conducts genealogical research on the Skubinna family. Sponsors charitable programs. **Libraries: Type:** reference; not open to the public. **Holdings:** 30. **Subjects:** Skubinna family genealogy, East Prussian history, Michigan, Iowa, and North Dakota histories. **Computer Services:** database, history, genealogy ● electronic publishing, monthly Internet newsletter. **Publications:** *History of the Skubinna Family*. Book. **Price:** $60.00. Alternate Formats: microform. Also Cited As: *University Microfilm International LD01277* ● *Skubinna Family Newsletter*. **Price:** free. **Circulation:** 100. Alternate Formats: online ● *Skubinna Family Reunion 1992*.

20529 ■ International Molyneux Family Association (IMFA)
PO Box 10306
Bainbridge Island, WA 98110
Ph: (206)842-0565
Fax: (206)842-6636

E-mail: mxworld_us@mindspring.com
URL: http://homepages.rootsweb.com/~imfa/home.html
Contact: Marie Mullenneix Spearman, Pres.
Founded: 1986. **Members:** 300. **Membership Dues:** individual in U.S., $14 (annual) ● individual in Canada, $16 (annual). **Multinational. Description:** Members of the Molyneux family. Encourages family historical and genealogical research; facilitates communication among members. Serves as a clearinghouse on the Molyneux family, including Molineux, Molyneaux, Mullenix, Mullinix, Mullinax, Mulno, Mulnix, Mullinicks, Mollineaux and any other variation; provides support and assistance to family historians and genealogists. **Libraries: Type:** not open to the public. **Holdings:** 25; archival material, articles, books, clippings, periodicals. **Subjects:** Molyneux family history and genealogies. **Publications:** *MXWorld*, quarterly. Newsletter. **Price:** $3.00 each; $12.00/year. ISSN: 1530-4132. **Circulation:** 300.

20530 ■ Isaac Garrison Family Association (IGFA)
5567 Ecton Rd.
Winchester, KY 40391
Ph: (859)842-3028
E-mail: edwanna@meginc.com
Contact: Edwanna Garrison Chenault, Exec. Sec.
Founded: 1960. **Members:** 500. **Membership Dues:** $5 (annual). **Description:** Descendants of Isaac Garrison. **Libraries: Type:** open to the public. **Computer Services:** Mailing lists. **Publications:** *The Family of Isaac Garrison*. Book. Contains family history information; currently out of print. **Circulation:** 500 ● *The Garrison Gazette*, semiannual. Newsletter. **Conventions/Meetings:** biennial Garrisons Family Reunion, family displays (exhibits) - July ● periodic reunion, regional.

20531 ■ Jacob Hochstetler Family Association (JHFA)
1102 S 13th St.
Goshen, IN 46526
Ph: (574)533-7819
E-mail: dhoch@maplenet.net
URL: http://www.hostetler.net
Contact: Daniel E. Hochstetler, VP
Founded: 1988. **Members:** 700. **Membership Dues:** individual or family, $10 (annual). **Description:** Descendants of the Swiss German Jacob Hochstetler, who emigrated from Europe to North America in 1738. Promotes appreciation of the heritage shared by Hochstetler family members. Sponsors family historical and genealogical research; conducts social and educational activities. **Libraries: Type:** not open to the public; by appointment only; reference. **Holdings:** 350. **Subjects:** Hochstetler family history and genealogy. **Publications:** *H/H/H Family Newsletter*, quarterly. Features 10 pages of family history, genealogy and activities. **Price:** included in membership dues. ISSN: 1045-7623. **Circulation:** 750. **Conventions/Meetings:** quinquennial Nationwide Gathering of Descendants of Jacob Hochstetler - reunion and seminar, non-commercial, family-related (exhibits).

20532 ■ James Happy Family Organization (JHFO)
Address Unknown since 2007
Description: Descendants of James Happy, who married Mary Burgin in Delaware in 1775 and died in Kentucky in 1814. Seeks to unite members; promotes interest in the Happy family and its history. Serves as a clearinghouse on Happy family history and genealogy. **Libraries: Type:** by appointment only. **Holdings:** archival material, books. **Subjects:** Happy family history and genealogy.

20533 ■ James Leonard Williams Family Organization (JLWFO)
114 E Main St.
Oaktown, IN 47561
Ph: (812)882-9371
Contact: Richard Carl Rodgers II, Contact
Founded: 1982. **Members:** 379. **Staff:** 2. **Description:** Descendants of James Leonard Williams, born

in Ohio, about 1823, owned a plow and wagon factory in PerryCo., Indiana, and related families including the Bicknell family of Rhode Island. Promotes study of Williams family history and genealogy. Gathers and disseminates information on the Williams family; provides support and assistance to historians and genealogists. **Libraries: Type:** reference; by appointment only; not open to the public. **Holdings:** archival material, artwork, audio recordings, books, periodicals, video recordings. **Subjects:** Williams family history and genealogy. **Computer Services:** database.

20534 ■ James Redman Miller Family Organization (JRMFO)
114 E Main St.
Oaktown, IN 47561
Ph: (812)882-9371
Contact: Richard Carl Rodgers II, Contact
Founded: 1982. **Members:** 1,648. **Staff:** 2. **Description:** Descendants of James Redman Miller, who was born near the end of the 18th century in Lincoln County, KY, other individuals with an interest in the Miller family and its history. Promotes study of Miller family history and genealogy. Gathers and disseminates information on the Miller family and its history; provides assistance to family historians and genealogists. **Libraries: Type:** reference; by appointment only; not open to the public. **Holdings:** archival material, artwork, books, clippings, periodicals. **Subjects:** Miller family history and genealogy. **Computer Services:** database.

20535 ■ Johann Frederick Mouser Family Organization (JFMFO)
114 E Main St.
Oaktown, IN 47561
Ph: (812)882-9371
Contact: Richard Carl Rodgers II, Contact
Founded: 1984. **Members:** 722. **Staff:** 2. **Description:** Descendants of Johann Frederick Mouser, who was born in Germany in 1740 and died in North Carolina in 1799. Promotes and facilitates Mouser family historical and genealogical research. Serves as a clearinghouse on Mouser family history and genealogy; sponsors social activities. **Libraries: Type:** by appointment only; not open to the public; reference. **Holdings:** archival material, books, clippings. **Subjects:** Mouser family history and genealogy. **Computer Services:** database, Mouser family genealogy.

20536 ■ John Bosher Family Organization
Address Unknown since 2007
Founded: 1959. **Description:** Seeks to exchange information on the Bosher family and others connected to the family, which came from England and Scotland in the 17th century, including Stewart, Doss, Napier, Rudd, Rutledge, Meador, Lowry, Wood, Anderson, Williams, Nelson, Wheeler, McCune, Gunn, Holland, Byrd, Waller, and Edwards.

20537 ■ John Carver Family Organization
c/o Jay G. Burrup, Genealogist
6602 W King Valley Rd.
West Valley City, UT 84128-4217
Ph: (801)250-9017
E-mail: burrupfam@aol.com
Contact: Jay G. Burrup, Genealogist
Description: Descendants of John Carver (1822-1912) and his wives. (Carver was born in Herefordshire, England, immigrated to the United States in 1850, and died in Plain City, UT.) Promotes study of family history and genealogy; encourages communication among Carvers' descendants. Provides assistance to Carver family historians and genealogists. **Publications:** *Carver Crier*, periodic. Newsletter. **Circulation:** 300. **Conventions/Meetings:** periodic reunion.

20538 ■ John Clough Genealogical Society (JCGS)
c/o John R. Clough, Treas.
PO Box 242
Harwich, MA 02645
E-mail: seapop@netzero.net
URL: http://ourworld.cs.com/cloughgenl
Contact: John R. Clough, Treas.
Founded: 1939. **Members:** 300. **Membership Dues:** individual, $12 (annual). **Description:** Strives to provide genealogical information to all members. **Libraries: Type:** reference; not open to the public. **Holdings:** 3; archival material, audiovisuals, books, clippings, monographs. **Subjects:** descendants of John Clough of Salisbury, MA. **Computer Services:** database, Clough descendants. **Subgroups:** Clough-Genealogy-L. **Publications:** *Descendants of John Clough of Salisbury, MA.* Book. Contains data for descendants through generations. **Price:** $30.00 ● *JCGS Bulletin*, 2-4/year. Contains articles pertaining to Clough history, DNA, trips, experiences, etc. **Price:** included in membership dues. **Circulation:** 300 ● *The Story of John Clough of Salisbury, Massachusetts.* Book. Contains a compilation of reference works. **Price:** $12.50. **Conventions/Meetings:** annual board meeting - summer.

20539 ■ John Libby Family Association (JLFA)
c/o Patricia Libbey Davis, Sec.
195 Deacon Haynes Rd.
Concord, MA 01742-4711
Ph: (978)369-6250
E-mail: pittypatd@aol.com
URL: http://www.libbyfamily.org
Contact: Rick Libbey, Pres.
Founded: 1904. **Members:** 900. **Membership Dues:** ordinary, $15 (annual) ● life, $150. **Budget:** $4,000. **Regional Groups:** 1. **Description:** Members of the Libby family. Promotes interest in Libby family history and genealogy. Participates in the maintenance of the Parish House of the First Congregational Church in Scarborough, ME; gathers and disseminates information on the Libby family and its history. **Libraries: Type:** reference; open to the public. **Holdings:** books, clippings, monographs. **Subjects:** Libby family history and genealogy. **Computer Services:** On-line services, forum. **Committees:** Genealogical. **Publications:** *Libby Family in America 1882 - 1982, Vol II.* Book ● *Libby Family in America 1602 - 1881.* Book ● *The Libby Family 1882-1982.* Book ● Newsletter, semiannual. **Conventions/Meetings:** annual reunion and meeting - usually 4th Saturday in September.

20540 ■ John More Association (JMA)
c/o Judith Erikson, Treas.
188 Bay Shore Dr.
Plymouth, MA 02360
E-mail: cindy@rahman.com
URL: http://johnmore.com
Contact: Patricia Hile Yewcic, Pres.
Founded: 1890. **Members:** 14,000. **Membership Dues:** head of household, $15 (annual) ● life (age 59 and below), $250 ● life (age 60-79), $200. **Budget:** $2,500. **Description:** Direct descendants and spouses of Betty Taylor More (1738-1823), and John More (1745-1840). Works to preserve genealogical records of the More family and perpetuate the family ties. Conducts educational and research programs; compiles statistics; maintains museum. **Publications:** *Historical Journal of the More Family*, semiannual. Contains 13,000 descendants indexed by surname, genealogical number, and zipcode. **Price:** $8.00/year ● *The John and Betty Stories.* Book. Contains stories about the lives of John and Betty More during Pioneer times. **Price:** $15.00 for More descendants; $18.00 for others ● Directory, quinquennial. Lists family descendants. **Conventions/Meetings:** quinquennial reunion (exhibits).

20541 ■ John Morgan Evans of Merthyr Tydil (JMEMT)
Address Unknown since 2007
Founded: 1940. **Members:** 200. **Staff:** 2. **State Groups:** 1. **Local Groups:** 1. **National Groups:** 1. **Description:** Descendants of John Morgan Evans who lived in MerthyrTydil county borough in southern Wales. Compiles genealogical information. **Computer Services:** database. **Publications:** *Project Genesis: A Record of the Evans Family*, annual.

20542 ■ John Thomas Martin Family Organization (JTMFO)
Address Unknown since 2007
Founded: 1983. **Staff:** 3. **Regional Groups:** 2. **State Groups:** 1. **Local Groups:** 1. **Description:** Descendants of John Thomas Martin (1795-1860) and related families. Promotes interest in Martin family history and genealogy; facilitates communication among Martin family members. Serves as a clearinghouse on family history and genealogy; sponsors social activities. Central and western North Carolina. **Publications:** *The Martin Family.* Book. Available from Broad River Genealogical Society, Inc., PO Box 2261, Shelby, NC 28151-2261. **Price:** $15.00 postage paid. **Conventions/Meetings:** annual reunion - always third Saturday of August. Lincoln, NC.

20543 ■ Joseph Cox and Mary Rue Family Association (JCMRFA)
Address Unknown since 2007
Founded: 1986. **Description:** Descendants of Joseph Cox and Mary Rue. Conducts genealogical research in an effort to locate as many descendants as possible. **Publications:** *Cox Clan Newsletter*, semiannual. Includes information on current genealogical research. **Conventions/Meetings:** periodic reunion.

20544 ■ Joseph Goodbrake Montgomery Family Organization
5750 Carr Factory Rd.
Benton, WI 53803
Ph: (608)759-2755
E-mail: glynneim@mhtc.net
Contact: Glen Montgomery, Chm.
Founded: 1980. **Members:** 155. **Staff:** 2. **Budget:** $150. **Description:** Descendants or relatives by marriage of Joseph Montgomery. Serves as a social and genealogical organization; collects statistics. **Libraries: Type:** reference; not open to the public; by appointment only. **Holdings:** books, clippings, periodicals, photographs. **Publications:** *Family Reunion Montgomery*, annual. Bulletin. **Circulation:** 55. **Conventions/Meetings:** annual picnic and meeting - always second weekend in July.

20545 ■ Judkins Family Association (JFA)
c/o Kathi Judkins Abendroth
1538 NW 60th St.
Seattle, WA 98107-2328
E-mail: ksunset33@comcast.net
URL: http://www.geocities.com/Heartland/Oaks/1781
Contact: Kathi Judkins Abendroth, Contact
Founded: 1985. **Members:** 115. **Description:** Descendants of Job, Samuel, Obediah, and Thomas Judkins; other interested individuals. Seeks to unite members of the Judkins family. Gathers and disseminates genealogical and historical information on the Judkins family. Assists in genealogical research. **Libraries: Type:** reference. **Holdings:** 100; archival material. **Subjects:** Judkins in America. **Conventions/Meetings:** biennial reunion (exhibits).

20546 ■ Junkins Family Association (JFA)
c/o Kathy Junkins
9 Springside Ct.
Yardley, PA 19067
Ph: (215)428-9491
E-mail: kathy@kjunkins.com
URL: http://www.kjunkins.com
Contact: Alan D. Junkins, Pres./Founder
Founded: 1984. **Members:** 120. **Membership Dues:** individual, $10 (annual) ● family, $15 (annual) ● contributing, $35 (annual) ● sustaining, $70 (annual). **Description:** Descendants of Robert Junkins (1621-1699) and interested individuals. Promotes and preserves the history and genealogical records of the surname Junkins. Conducts genealogical research. Maintains and restores Junkins burial grounds; operates museum. **Libraries: Type:** reference. **Holdings:** 25; archival material, artwork, audio recordings, books, clippings, video recordings. **Subjects:** Scotland, Maine, Ohio, Kansas. **Computer Services:** Mailing lists, genealogy. **Committees:** Burial Ground; Memorial. **Publications:** *Junkins Family Association Newsletter*, semiannual. **Price:** included in member-

ship dues. **Circulation:** 250. **Conventions/Meetings:** biennial reunion (exhibits).

20547 ■ Kelsey Kindred of America (KKA)

c/o Mrs. Suzanne Kelsey Hall, Membership Sec.
244 Mountain Rd.
North Granby, CT 06060
Ph: (860)653-8233
Fax: (860)632-0724
URL: http://www.thekelseykindred.org
Contact: Mrs. Suzanne Kelsey Hall, Membership Sec.

Founded: 1928. **Members:** 900. **Membership Dues:** active, $10 (annual). **Description:** Descendants of William Kelsey, an early Puritan settler. Seeks to locate all descendants; promotes friendship and fellowship among members. Perpetuates the memory of Kelsey ancestors. Facilitates genealogical research for known descendants. **Libraries: Type:** reference. **Holdings:** 7. **Subjects:** William Kelsey family history. **Awards:** The Robert Gaber Award. **Frequency:** annual. **Type:** scholarship. **Recipient:** for essay on genealogy. **Computer Services:** Online services, general discussion. **Publications:** *Kelsey Family News Bulletin*, semiannual. Newsletter. Covers family news and association activities. **Price:** included in membership dues. **Circulation:** 900. Alternate Formats: online ● *Kelsey Genealogy Volumes*, periodic. Features series of documented lineages. **Conventions/Meetings:** annual reunion.

20548 ■ Kerr Family Association of North America (KFA)

c/o Mr. Joe F. Kerr, Jr.
7980 Ridgewood Rd.
Goodlettsville, TN 37072-9461
E-mail: membership@kerrfamilyassociation.com
URL: http://www.kerrfamilyassociation.com
Contact: Mr. Joe F. Kerr Jr., Contact

Founded: 1979. **Members:** 400. **Membership Dues:** individual, $15 (annual) ● family, $20 (annual). **Multinational. Description:** Individuals and families interested in the history of the Kerr family history. Explores the history of the Kerr family surname back to the 12th century. Conducts research on Kerr ancestors, including those with name variations such as Ker, Keir, Karr, Carr, Carre, de Ker, and de Karis. **Computer Services:** Mailing lists, of members. **Publications:** *Border Line*, quarterly. Newsletter. **Circulation:** 450. **Conventions/Meetings:** annual meeting.

20549 ■ Kershner Family Association (KFA)

101 Potters Way
Lexington, SC 29073
E-mail: bbrown45822@peoplepc.com
Contact: Mr. William Brown, Contact

Founded: 1978. **Members:** 100. **Regional Groups:** 1. **Description:** Represents members of the Kershner family. Promotes study of Kershner family history and genealogy. Serves as a clearinghouse on the Kershner family and its history; supports and assists family historians and genealogists.

20550 ■ Kilts Family Association (KFA)

c/o Herman W. Witthoft, Sr.
141 Hudson Ave.
Chatham, NY 12037
Ph: (518)392-4544
E-mail: hw15@juno.com
URL: http://www.geocities.com/kiltsfamily/TOC.htm
Contact: Herman W. Witthoft Sr., Contact

Founded: 1931. **Members:** 775. **Budget:** $1,000. **Description:** Individuals with the surname Kilts and its variant spellings. Promotes communication among members of the Kilts family. Serves as a clearinghouse on family history and genealogy; sponsors social activities.

20551 ■ Kjaerulf Family Association (KFA)

c/o Cap Kjaerulf
358 S Bentley Ave.
Los Angeles, CA 90049-3219
Ph: (310)472-9206

E-mail: capkierulff@msn.com
URL: http://www.kiermeet.com
Contact: Cap Kjaerulf, Contact

Founded: 1982. **Members:** 100. **Description:** Members of the Kjaerulf family. Promotes communication among members; seeks to increase interest in Kjaerulf family history and genealogy. Sponsors social and educational activities. **Publications:** *KFA Newsletter*, semiannual. **Price:** $10.00/two years. **Circulation:** 200 ● *Twentieth Century Kjaerulfs*. Book. Lists members of the Kjaerulf family. **Price:** $49.00/copy. **Conventions/Meetings:** quadrennial reunion.

20552 ■ Kump Family Association (KFA)

7783 S 4950 W
West Jordan, UT 84084-5516
E-mail: webmaster@kump.org
URL: http://www.kump.org

Founded: 2004. **Members:** 25. **Regional Groups:** 1. **Multinational. Description:** Individuals with the surnames Kump, Kumpf, and their variants; others with an interest in Kump family genealogy. Promotes interest in, and study of, Kump family genealogy. Facilitates communication and good fellowship among members; provides assistance to Kump family genealogists; conducts research programs. **Libraries: Type:** by appointment only. **Holdings:** archival material. **Subjects:** Kump family genealogy. **Also Known As:** (2006) Kump Family Organization.

20553 ■ Lasher Family Association (LFA)

PO Box 1194
Kingston, NY 12402
Ph: (845)339-5279
E-mail: lashers@localnet.com
URL: http://www.angelfire.com/folk/lasher_family_web
Contact: June Crispell, Sec.

Founded: 1937. **Members:** 200. **Membership Dues:** individual, $3 (annual). **Staff:** 5. **Description:** Individuals with the surname Lasher or its variant spellings. Promotes increased interest in family history and genealogy; seeks to identify and bring together members of the Lasher and related families. Gathers and disseminates information on the Lasher family; sponsors social activities. **Libraries: Type:** not open to the public. **Subjects:** genealogy. **Computer Services:** Mailing lists, of members ● online services, discussion group. **Publications:** *Lasher Letter*, semiannual. Newsletter. **Price:** included in membership dues. **Conventions/Meetings:** annual meeting - always first Sunday of August.

20554 ■ Lillard Family Association (LFA)

Address Unknown since 2007
Founded: 1979. **Members:** 23,000. **Staff:** 1. **Budget:** $3,500. **Description:** Members of the Lillard and related families. Promotes study of Lillard family history and genealogy; seeks to identify and unite Lillard family members. Gathers and disseminates information on the Lillard family and its history; assists family historians and genealogists; sponsor social activities. **Libraries: Type:** reference. **Holdings:** 25; archival material, articles, books, clippings, periodicals. **Subjects:** Lillard family history and genealogy, census year books. **Publications:** *Lillard Family Newsletter*, annual. **Price:** Free. **Circulation:** 3,900. **Advertising:** not accepted. **Conventions/Meetings:** annual meeting - 2nd weekend in June; **Avg. Attendance:** 300.

20555 ■ Littlefield Family Newsletter

PO Box 912
Ogunquit, ME 03907-0912
Ph: (207)646-0436
E-mail: lfn@maine.rr.com
URL: http://www.littlefieldhistory.com
Contact: Peter Woodbury, Ed.

Founded: 1991. **Staff:** 2. **Nonmembership. Description:** Compiles and disseminates information on the surname Littlefield. **Libraries: Type:** reference. **Holdings:** 14. **Subjects:** manuscripts, genealogical records. **Formerly:** (1995) Littlefield Clearinghouse and Information Exchange. **Publications:** Journal, quarterly. **Price:** $12.50/year. **Circulation:** 300 ● Back issues of newsletter are available.

20556 ■ Litzenberger-Litzenberg Association

c/o Homer L. Litzenberg, III, Pres.
3233 Simberlan Dr.
San Jose, CA 95148-3128
Ph: (408)270-7227
E-mail: litzassoc@litzenberg.org
URL: http://www.litzenberg.org
Contact: Homer L. Litzenberg III, Pres.

Founded: 1991. **Members:** 97. **Staff:** 10. **Budget:** $8,000. **Regional Groups:** 2. **Languages:** English, French, German, Russian. **Description:** Descendants of people who used any surname recognized as derived from the German words Lutzel Burg, such as Lutzelburger, Litzenberger, Litsenberg, Litsinberger, Litchenburg, etc. Promotes genealogical research. Conducts social activities. **Libraries: Type:** not open to the public. **Holdings:** 10. **Computer Services:** Mailing lists. **Publications:** *Litzenberger and Litzenberg: Origins of the Names and the Families* (in English and German). Book. Contains biographies and indexes. **Price:** $75.00. **Circulation:** 500 ● *Litzenberger-Litzenberg Newsletter*, quarterly. **Price:** $15.00/year. **Circulation:** 80. **Conventions/Meetings:** annual reunion, family gathering (exhibits).

20557 ■ Locke Surname Organization (LSO)

7650 Fairview Rd.
Tillamook, OR 97141-9714
Ph: (503)842-6036
Fax: (503)842-6036
E-mail: orella@wcn.net
Contact: Orella Chadwick, Contact

Founded: 1978. **Members:** 60. **Membership Dues:** individual, $15 (quarterly). **Description:** Individuals with the surname Locke and other Locke family members. Promotes genealogical research on the Locke family. Serves as a clearinghouse on the Locke family and its history; conducts research; assists family historians and genealogists. **Libraries: Type:** not open to the public; reference. **Holdings:** artwork, books, business records, clippings, periodicals. **Subjects:** Locke family history and genealogy. **Publications:** *Exchange*, quarterly. Newsletter. **Price:** included in membership dues.

20558 ■ Lorin Elias Bassett Family Organization (LEBFO)

c/o Irvin Gene Bassett, Pres.
1055 E Hillcrest Dr.
Springville, UT 84663
Ph: (801)489-6298
E-mail: ibassett@itsnet.com
Contact: Irvin Gene Bassett, Pres.

Founded: 1976. **Members:** 70. **Membership Dues:** individual, $12 (annual). **Description:** Descendants of Loren Elias Bassett, who was born 1809 in Granby, Hartford, Connecticut son of Elias Bassett and Lucy nee Gillett. Seeks to locate all descendants of Elias Bassett; encourages good fellowship among members. Conducts genealogical research. **Publications:** *Report of Bassett Research*, annual. Newsletter. **Conventions/Meetings:** annual reunion.

20559 ■ Lucky Mee Family Association (LMFA)

Address Unknown since 2007

Founded: 1977. **Members:** 173. **Membership Dues:** general, $12 (annual) ● life, $100. **Staff:** 5. **National Groups:** 1. **Description:** Individuals with the Mee surname and related families. Maintains genealogical archives and library. Conducts research; compiles statistics; bestows awards. **Libraries: Type:** reference. **Subjects:** Mee families and allied families. **Awards:** Lifetime Certification, Appreciation Certificate. **Frequency:** annual. **Type:** recognition. **Computer Services:** database. **Telecommunication Services:** electronic mail, joemee@dzn.com. **Publications:** *Lucky Mee Family Association*, quarterly. Newsletter. **Price:** included in membership dues; $3.00/for nonmembers. **Advertising:** not accepted ● *2002 Yearbook*. **Price:** $3.00 postage paid. **Circulation:** 200. **Conventions/Meetings:** annual conference and reunion (exhibits) - Denver, CO.

20560 ■ Luther Family Association (LFA)
2027 Spyglass Ct.
Lakeland, FL 33810-6737
Ph: (863)815-2505
E-mail: luthergen@juno.com
Contact: George A. Luther, Exec. Sec./Genealogist
Founded: 1936. **Members:** 1,011. **Membership Dues:** contributing, $10 (annual). **Staff:** 10. **Regional Groups:** 4. **Description:** Descendants of John Luther (1595-1645), an English ship's captain who emigrated to Massachusetts between 1630 and 1635 and was killed by Indians while on a trading venture near Delaware Bay in 1645. Seeks to preserve the history and genealogy of the family of Captain John Luther. Encourages and coordinates regional and national family reunions. Conducts genealogical research programs; maintains museum. **Libraries:** Type: reference. **Holdings:** books. **Subjects:** genealogy of the Luther family and related families. **Computer Services:** database ● mailing lists. **Publications:** *The Luther Family Newsletter*, quarterly. Contains results of genealogical research, obituaries and birth notices, family and association news. **Price:** included in membership dues. ISSN: 0896-4602. **Circulation:** 500 ● *The Luther Genealogy*. Book. **Conventions/Meetings:** quinquennial reunion, family memorabilia (exhibits).

20561 ■ Lybarger Memorial Association (LMA)
PO Box 611
Delaware, OH 43015-0611
Ph: (419)774-9830
E-mail: lybarger@midohio.net
Contact: Lee H. Lybarger, Ed.
Founded: 1985. **Members:** 400. **Membership Dues:** family, $10 (annual). **Description:** Individuals with the surname Lybarger and its variant spellings; other members of the Lybarger family. Promotes interest in Lybarger family history and genealogy; facilitates communication and cooperation among members. Owns and maintains the Lybarger Lutheran Church in Madley, PA and other historic properties associated with Lybarger family history; provides support and assistance to family historians and genealogists; sponsors social activities. **Awards:** Distinguished Service Award. **Frequency:** annual. **Type:** recognition. **Recipient:** for those who have supported and/or furthered the objectives of LMA. **Publications:** *The Lybarger Descendants*. Book. **Price:** $38.00 for members; $42.00 for nonmembers ● *Lybarger Linkages*, semiannual. Newsletter. **Price:** free. ISSN: 0887-9354. **Circulation:** 1,000. **Conventions/Meetings:** annual reunion.

20562 ■ MacCartney Clan Society (MCS)
Address Unknown since 2007
Founded: 1970. **Members:** 150. **Staff:** 2. **Description:** Individuals interested in the history and genealogy of the MacCartney name and its variants. Maintains hall of fame. **Libraries:** Type: reference. **Holdings:** archival material. **Publications:** *McCartney Newsletter*, quarterly. **Price:** $6.00. **Circulation:** 100. **Advertising:** not accepted.

20563 ■ MacFaddien Family Society
c/o Norman J. McFaddien, Sr.
5297 Black River Rd., Gn D1
Sardinia, SC 29143
Ph: (803)473-2643
E-mail: njmcfsr@ftc-i.net
Contact: Norman J. McFaddien Sr., Contact
Founded: 1936. **Members:** 200. **Membership Dues:** family, $10 (annual) ● life, $150. **Staff:** 4. **Budget:** $500. **Regional Groups:** 2. **State Groups:** 1. **Local Groups:** 1. **Description:** Strives to inform members of genealogical connections. Provides educational, charitable, and research programs; compiles statistics; maintains a museum and genealogical library. **Libraries:** Type: reference; open to the public. **Holdings:** 150; archival material, books, business records, clippings. **Subjects:** McFaddin, McFoyden, McFaden, MacPhaidin and related families as Willerspoons, Roses, Williams, Burgesses, Cousars, Harvins, Dickeys, Plowders, Nelsons, Montgomeries, Epps, DuBose, and DuPonts. **Computer Services:**

database, descendant and genealogical charts and family tree maker ● mailing lists, family members ● record retrieval services. **Committees:** Homecoming. **Publications:** *MacFaddien News*, semiannual. Newsletter. Features family news. **Price:** included in membership dues. **Circulation:** 225. **Conventions/Meetings:** annual Homecoming - reunion, homecoming, artifacts and books (exhibits) - always May.

20564 ■ MacLellan Clan in America
c/o Ms. Nancy Sears, Treas.
PO Box 397
Simpsonville, KY 40067-0397
Ph: (502)722-5067
E-mail: nancy.sears@louisville.edu
Contact: Ms. Nancy Sears, Treas.
Founded: 1980. **Members:** 450. **Regional Groups:** 9. **Description:** Represents MacLellans and their families. Brings together members of the MacLellan family. Provides news on what MacLellans are doing around the world. Aids members in their genealogy research. **Libraries:** Type: reference. **Subjects:** genealogy, family histories, Scottish history. **Awards:** Scottish Studies. **Type:** scholarship. **Computer Services:** database, genealogy index of various spellings of MacLellan. **Publications:** *Think On*, quarterly. Newsletter. **Price:** included in membership dues. ISSN: 1066-601X. **Circulation:** 900. **Conventions/Meetings:** annual board meeting, with membership meeting.

20565 ■ MacThomas North America
210 Belford Ave.
Huntington, WV 25701
E-mail: macthomasnaboard@macthomasnorthamerica.com
URL: http://macthomasnorthamerica.com
Founded: 2003. **Members:** 70. **Membership Dues:** individual, $15 (annual) ● friend of MacThomas, $10 (annual) ● family, $25 (annual). **Staff:** 5. **State Groups:** 6. **Multinational. Description:** An independent, incorporated association of descendants of the greater, international MacThomas family, including the Clan of MacThomas. Retains ancestral connections to Scotland but places higher priority on "those that migrated to these shores and thrived". Current information, updated weekly, on website. **Libraries:** Type: reference; open to the public. **Subjects:** MacThomas and associated Sept names. **Awards:** **Frequency:** annual. **Type:** recognition. **Recipient:** for a member sponsoring the annual gathering. **Committees:** Ancestral Research; Finance and Fundraising; Publicity; Recruiting and Membership; Social Events; Termed. **Affiliated With:** Council of Scottish Clans and Associations. **Formerly:** (2003) Clan MacThomas. **Publications:** Newsletter (in English and Gaelic), quarterly. **Conventions/Meetings:** annual The MacThomas Clan Gathering - meeting.

20566 ■ Magny Families Association (MFA)
5 Fieldstone Ct.
Newburgh, NY 12550
Ph: (845)565-3638
E-mail: kbschoony@aol.com
URL: http://www.hometown.aol.com/kbschoony/myhomepage/index.html
Contact: Kenneth B. Schoonmaker, Historian
Founded: 1979. **Members:** 130. **Membership Dues:** individual, $15 (annual). **Multinational. Description:** Individuals interested in the history and genealogy of families with the surname Magny or its variant spellings of Manee, Maney, Manney, Manny, Many. Seeks to identify and unite family members, promotes accurate genealogical research. Gathers and disseminates information on Magny family history and genealogy. **Affiliated With:** Huguenot Historical Society. **Also Known As:** (2000) Manee, Maney, Manney, Manny, Many. **Publications:** *Magny Families Association Newsletter*, semiannual. **Price:** included in membership dues. **Conventions/Meetings:** biennial reunion.

20567 ■ Marley Family Association
c/o Michael D. Frost, PhD, Archivist
8910 W 62nd Terr.
Merriam, KS 66202

Ph: (913)362-4600
Free: (800)292-2273
Fax: (913)362-4627
E-mail: eriworld@aol.com
URL: http://www.marleyfamily.org
Contact: Michael D. Frost PhD, Archivist
Founded: 1990. **Members:** 150. **Membership Dues:** individual, $20 (annual). **Staff:** 3. **Description:** Genealogical organization. **Libraries:** Type: reference; not open to the public; by appointment only. **Holdings:** 500; archival material, articles, books, clippings. **Subjects:** Marley surname, including variant spellings. **Computer Services:** database ● mailing lists. **Publications:** *Marley Family Association Newsletter*, 3/year. Hardcopy current editions. First ten years available on CD-ROM. **Price:** included in membership dues. **Circulation:** 200. **Conventions/Meetings:** annual conference and board meeting, includes business meeting (exhibits) - always August.

20568 ■ Maxfield Family Organization (MFO)
250 S 100th E
Hyrum, UT 84319
Ph: (435)245-6984
E-mail: pierson01@msn.com
Contact: Dianne Pierson, Coor.
Founded: 1978. **Members:** 14. **Staff:** 1. **Description:** Individuals with the surname Maxfield or its variant spellings; other members of the Maxfield family. Promotes study of family history and genealogy. Serves as a clearinghouse on the Maxfield family and its history; provides assistance to family historians and genealogists. **Libraries:** Type: reference. **Holdings:** archival material, articles, clippings. **Subjects:** Maxfield family history and genealogy.

20569 ■ Maybee Society (MaySoc)
10809 16th Ave. SE, No. 218
Everett, WA 98208
Ph: (425)385-8377
E-mail: maybee3@verizon.net
URL: http://freepages.genealogy.rootsweb.com/~maysoc/index.html
Contact: Barbara Maybee Carter, Exec. Sec.
Founded: 1986. **Members:** 331. **Membership Dues:** individual, $15 (annual) ● e-mail, $8 (annual). **Staff:** 5. **Budget:** $2,500. **Multinational. Description:** Members of the Maybee family and interested genealogists. Seeks to find the background history and genealogy of all the branches of the Mabee - Mabey - Mabie - Maeby - Mabille - Maby - Maybee - Maybie family, and making this material available for all members of the family, and to preserve the research that has been carried on by many dedicated researchers and students. Serves as a clearinghouse on the Maybee family and its history; assists family historians and genealogists. **Libraries:** Type: reference. **Holdings:** 2,000; artwork, audio recordings, books, clippings, periodicals, video recordings. **Subjects:** Maybee family history and genealogy. **Computer Services:** database, historical records of Maybees and related lines. **Telecommunication Services:** electronic mail, maysoc@comcast.net. **Publications:** *Maybee Communicator*, quarterly. Newsletter. **Price:** included in membership dues. Alternate Formats: online. **Conventions/Meetings:** annual reunion - summer at Mabee House in Rotterdam, New York.

20570 ■ Mazur Surname Organization (MSO)
Address Unknown since 2007
Description: Individuals with the surname Mazur and its variant spellings; other Mazur family members. Promotes interest in family history and genealogy. Serves as a resource for family historians and genealogists; conducts research; sponsors social activities. **Libraries:** Type: not open to the public; reference. **Holdings:** books, clippings, periodicals. **Subjects:** Mazur family history and genealogy.

20571 ■ McAdams Historical Society
14018 Davana Terr.
Sherman Oaks, CA 91423
Ph: (818)789-1086

E-mail: mcadams@jps.net
URL: http://www.mcadamshistory.com
Contact: R. Michael McAdams, Dir.
Founded: 1982. **Members:** 500. **Membership Dues:** individual, $15 (annual). **Description:** Family members and individuals interested in the MacAdam, McAdam, McAdams, and McCaddams allied families. Preserves the history of the MacAdam family. Collects and shares family information. **Libraries: Type:** reference. **Holdings:** archival material, books, clippings, periodicals. **Subjects:** MacAdam, McAdam, McAdams, McCaddams, other allied families. **Computer Services:** database. **Publications:** *McAdams Family Newsletter*, bimonthly. **Circulation:** 500 ● *Sons of Adam.* Book. **Price:** $37.50.

20572 ■ McCune Family Association (MFA)
Address Unknown since 2007
Founded: 1972. **Members:** 600. **Membership Dues:** individual, $15 (annual). **Regional Groups:** 9. **Description:** Descendants of Matthew McCune, who was born on the Isle of Man in 1811 and died in Utah in 1889. Promotes study of Matthew McCune's descendants, ancestors and descendants and ancestors of his spouses and siblings through fostering closer association, coordination of genealogical research and preservation of histories, family heirlooms and artifacts, photographs, videos, oral histories, negatives, audio tapes, and other related documents. **Libraries: Type:** reference. **Holdings:** archival material, articles, artwork, books, business records, video recordings. **Subjects:** McCune family history and genealogy. **Also Known As:** Matthew McCune Family Association; McKeown Family Association; McEwan Family Association; McCoon Family Association. **Publications:** *Matthew McCune Family History, Vol. 1AB & Vol. 2AB.* Book. 1AB Covers Matthew McCune, his extant diaries and spouses. 2AB covers the children and spouses of his first wife, Sarah Elizabeth Caroline Scott. ● *McCune Family Association Newsletter*, annual. **Price:** $20.00 donation. **Circulation:** 650. **Conventions/Meetings:** annual reunion (exhibits); **Avg. Attendance:** 100.

20573 ■ McCurdy Family Association (SMFA)
Address Unknown since 2007
Founded: 1992. **Membership Dues:** ordinary, $7 (annual) ● ordinary, C$9 (annual). **Budget:** $400. **Description:** Primarily descendants of Samuel McCurdy. Promotes interest in, and study of, McCurdy family history and genealogy and the history of Surry, NH. Facilitates communication among members; provides assistance to family historians and genealogists; compiles and maintains records of McCurdy family members. **Conventions/Meetings:** biennial reunion.

20574 ■ McGregor Family Association (MFA)
8517 E Krail St.
Scottsdale, AZ 85250
Ph: (480)483-5970
E-mail: larryexpl@aol.com
Contact: Larry L. McGregor, Treas.
Description: McGregor family members. Promotes study of McGregor family history and genealogy; facilitates communication and good fellowship among members. Serves as a clearinghouse on the McGregor family and it history; sponsors research, educational, and social activities.

20575 ■ Meader Family Association (MFA)
158 Ashdown Rd.
Ballston Lake, NY 12019
Ph: (518)399-5013
URL: http://www.themeaderfamily.org
Contact: Glenn S. Meader Jr., Pres.
Founded: 1974. **Membership Dues:** voting, $10 (annual). **Description:** Members of the Meader family and other interested individuals. Promotes study of Meader family history and genealogy. Facilitates communication among members; sponsors research; assists family historians and genealogists. Has dedicated a monument at the Meader Garrison Site in Dover, NH. **Libraries: Type:** by appointment only; reference. **Holdings:** archival material, articles, books, clippings. **Subjects:** Meader family history

and genealogy. **Publications:** *Ancestry and Descendants of Jonathon Griffen 1757-1837.* Book ● *John Meader of Piscataqua.* Book. Consists of four volumes. ● Newsletter, annual. **Conventions/Meetings:** annual meeting.

20576 ■ Merier-Gourley-Roark Family Organization (MGRFO)
Gourley Hill
80 Ivy & N Bowen's Mill Rd.
Broxton, GA 31519
Ph: (912)384-1033
E-mail: gourleyhill@hotmail.com
Contact: Mrs. Winifred Merier Gourley, Family Genealogist
Description: Members of the Merier, Gourley, and Roark families. Promotes interest in family history and genealogy. Facilitates communication and good fellowship among members; gathers and disseminates historical and genealogical information; sponsors social activities.

20577 ■ Miles Merwin Association (MMA)
PO Box 35771
Dallas, TX 75235
Ph: (214)750-1934
E-mail: mma@merwin.org
URL: http://merwin.org
Contact: Lee Merwin, Ed.
Founded: 1957. **Members:** 500. **Membership Dues:** individual, $12 (annual) ● sustaining, $50 (annual). **Description:** Descendants of Miles Merwin (1623-97). Promotes study of Merwin family history and genealogy. Gathers and disseminates historical and genealogical information on the Merwin family. **Telecommunication Services:** electronic mail, milestones@merwin.org. **Publications:** *The Merwin Family in North America.* Book. Features immigrants will of 1697 (first ten generations) published in 1978. Subsequent generations are printed in Volumes II, III and IV. **Price:** $35.00 ● *Milestones*, 3/year. Newsletter. **Conventions/Meetings:** annual reunion - June to July.

20578 ■ Milliron - Millison - Muhleisen Family Exchange
Address Unknown since 2007
Founded: 1980. **Members:** 70. **Description:** Works to assist genealogical research on this family. Promotes the cooperation among family members and researchers. **Publications:** none. **Convention/Meeting:** none. **Computer Services:** database, genealogical information.

20579 ■ Moody Family Association (MFA)
Address Unknown since 2007
Founded: 1994. **Description:** Descendants of Jonas Lunis Moody, who was born in North Carolina in 1874. Promotes study of Moody family history and genealogy. Gathers and disseminates information on Moody family genealogy; facilitates communication among Moody family members. **Libraries: Type:** reference. **Holdings:** archival material, articles, books, clippings, monographs. **Subjects:** Moody family history and genealogy.

20580 ■ Mumpower Family Association (MFA)
Address Unknown since 2007
Founded: 1978. **Members:** 400. **Description:** Clearinghouse for genealogical information on the Mumpower family. Records information on the Mumpower, Mumbauer, Mumbower families. **Libraries: Type:** reference. **Subjects:** Mumpower genealogy. **Publications:** *Isaac Booher Mumpower.* Contains the history of the Booher Mumpower side of the family. **Price:** $20.00 free shipping ● *Liberty Church 1840.* Directory. Lists all people who have attended the Liberty Church for the past 60 years. **Price:** $20.00 free shipping ● *Mumpower.* Newsletter. **Advertising:** not accepted ● *Mumpower Directory.*

20581 ■ Murray Clan Society North America
c/o Charles D. Murray, Pres.
112 Ruth Ln.
La Vergne, TN 37086

E-mail: corkymurray@hotmail.com
URL: http://clanmurray.org/default.html
Contact: Charles D. Murray, Pres.
Founded: 1969. **Members:** 350. **Membership Dues:** individual, family, $15 (annual) ● life, $300. **Description:** Descendants of the Scottish Murray clan and its septs. Conducts genealogical research; facilitates contact among members. **Telecommunication Services:** electronic mail, membership@clanmurray.org. **Publications:** *Aitionn*, quarterly. Newsletter. **Price:** included in membership dues.

20582 ■ National Aldrich Family Association
c/o Ms. Patricia Hand, Treas.
847 S Main St.
Bellingham, MA 02019
E-mail: neaton@wesleyan.edu
URL: http://www.geocities.com/SouthBeach/Marina/2343
Contact: Nancy L. Eaton, Pres.
Founded: 1963. **Members:** 75. **Membership Dues:** family, $5 (annual). **Staff:** 5. **Description:** Possible, probable, and proven descendants of George Aldrich (1605-83), a pioneer settler of Mendon, MA in 1663. Encourages genealogical research, particularly concerning the Aldrich family and related surnames including Bartlett, Capron, Dunbar, Evans, Hayward, Osborne, Pray, Puffer, Randall, Shaw, Thayer, and White. Gathers and disseminates information. **Additional Websites:** http://freepages.genealogy.rootsweb.com/~aldrichnaa. **Formerly:** (2003) National Aldrich Association. **Publications:** *National Aldrich Association*, semiannual. Newsletter. Includes meeting minutes, photographs, and questions from members. **Price:** included in membership dues. **Circulation:** 100. **Conventions/Meetings:** annual reunion.

20583 ■ National Association of Lively Families (NALF)
c/o Russell Lively, Treas.
172 Fireside Ln.
Ringgold, GA 30736
Ph: (706)291-2307
E-mail: ben@livelyfamilies.com
URL: http://www.livelyfamily.com
Contact: John Lively, Pres.
Founded: 1937. **Members:** 255. **Membership Dues:** individual/family, $15 (annual). **Description:** Individuals with the surname Lively or its variant spellings. Promotes interest in Lively family history and genealogy; facilitates communication and good fellowship among members. Gathers and disseminates information on the Lively family and its history; assists family historians and genealogists. **Publications:** *Livelys of America 1690-1968.* Book. **Price:** $45.00/copy ● *Livin' Lively*, quarterly. Newsletter. **Conventions/Meetings:** annual reunion - always first weekend in August.

20584 ■ National Association of the Van Valkenburg Family (NAVVF)
PO Box 313
Carson City, NV 89702
E-mail: members@navvf.org
URL: http://www.navvf.org
Contact: L.V. Lammert, Pres.
Founded: 1970. **Members:** 800. **Membership Dues:** regular, $8 (annual). **Description:** Descendants of Lambert Van Valkenburg. Preserves and advances the Van Valkenburg family heritage. Fosters the ideals of honor, integrity, independence, and loyalty. Assembles and publishes the Van Valkenburg genealogy; serves as a central repository for family records and artifacts. Sponsors social events. **Publications:** *NAVVF News Notes*, quarterly. **Price:** included in membership dues ● *The Van Valkenburg Family in America.* **Conventions/Meetings:** annual reunion - 1st week of August.

20585 ■ National Grigsby Family Society (NGFS)
4418 Kiowa St.
Pasadena, TX 77504-3544
Ph: (281)998-8594

E-mail: administrator@grigsby.org
URL: http://www.grigsby.org
Contact: Mrs. Judy C. Doughty, Admin.
Founded: 1981. **Members:** 380. **Membership Dues:** sustaining, $15 (annual) ● contributing, $25 (annual) ● sponsor, $50 (annual). **Budget:** $6,000. **Regional Groups:** 1. **Description:** Descendents of John and Jane Prosser Grigsby and others with the surname Grigsby; libraries and genealogical and historical societies. Promotes communication and friendship among members. Conducts genealogical research. **Libraries: Type:** reference. **Holdings:** biographical archives. **Subjects:** Grigsby and allied family histories and genealogies. **Telecommunication Services:** electronic mail, jdoughty@ev1.net. **Publications:** *Grigsby Family Memorabilia, Vols. I and II; NGFS Newsletters 1981-1995.* Books ● *National Grigsby Family Society Directory,* annual ● *NGFS Newsletter,* quarterly. Includes genealogical research findings and information regarding association activities. **Price:** included in membership dues. **Circulation:** 500. **Conventions/Meetings:** annual board meeting - always in October ● triennial reunion.

20586 ■ Neal Dougan-Theodorus Scowden Family Organization
165 4th St.
Aultman, PA 15713-9605
Ph: (724)726-5653
E-mail: rfdo@yourinter.net
Contact: Richard F. Dougan, Historian
Founded: 1983. **Members:** 200. **Staff:** 2. **Regional Groups:** 2. **Local Groups:** 2. **Description:** Members of the Dougan and Scowden families. Conducts research and provides family history to all branches of the families. Corresponds informally with members of the families. **Publications:** none. **Libraries: Type:** reference; open to the public; by appointment only. **Holdings:** archival material, audiovisuals, books, clippings. **Subjects:** family genealogy, American history, Western Pennsylvania. **Computer Services:** database, Family Tree Maker ● mailing lists. **Conventions/Meetings:** regional meeting ● seminar, genealogy ● trade show.

20587 ■ Nesbitt-Nisbet Society: A Worldwide Clan Society
c/o Mr. Tom Nesbitt, Sec.
210 W Beaver St.
Zelienople, PA 16063
E-mail: tomnesbitt@zoominternet.net
URL: http://www.ibydeit.com
Contact: Mr. Tom Nesbitt, Sec.
Founded: 1981. **Members:** 400. **Membership Dues:** general, $25 (annual). **Multinational.** **Description:** Members of the Nesbitt or Nisbet clan. Shares genealogical information and family history. Conducts research. **Libraries: Type:** reference; not open to the public. **Holdings:** 25; archival material, books, monographs, periodicals. **Subjects:** Nesbitt and Nisbet family history, clan history for Saleto members. **Projects:** NN Society DNA Testing. **Publications:** *Nesbitt-Nisbet Society Newsletter,* quarterly. **Circulation:** 400 ● 25 Books and publications on Nesbitt-Nisbet family history - for sale to members only. **Conventions/Meetings:** periodic Highland Games Participation - regional meeting ● annual Official Clan Gathering - reunion (exhibits).

20588 ■ Nims Family Association (NFA)
PO Box 99
Deerfield, MA 01342-0099
E-mail: nimsfamily@nimsfamily.com
URL: http://www.nimsfamily.com
Contact: Ronald Graham, Pres.
Founded: 1979. **Members:** 459. **Membership Dues:** family or individual, $10 (annual). **Description:** Individuals with the surname Nims. **Conventions/Meetings:** biennial reunion - even numbered years, in October.

20589 ■ Nixon Family Association (NFA)
5817 144th St. E
Puyallup, WA 98375-5221
Ph: (253)537-8288

E-mail: janetgb@worldnet.att.net
Contact: Janet Nixon Baccus, Pres.
Founded: 1980. **For-Profit. Description:** Collects and disseminates information on the surnames Nixon and Baccus. Offers assistance in adoption searches. Operates genealogy classes. Maintains speakers' bureau. **Libraries: Type:** reference. **Holdings:** 1,200; books, clippings. **Subjects:** genealogical and historical material.

20590 ■ Norvell Family Organization (NFO)
Address Unknown since 2007
Founded: 1980. **Members:** 150. **Staff:** 5. **Regional Groups:** 4. **State Groups:** 2. **Description:** Persons researching the surnames Norvell, Norval, Norvil, Norville, and Nowell. Collects and disseminates information; maintains biographical archives and library. **Libraries: Type:** open to the public. **Subjects:** surnames. **Computer Services:** database, maintains surname database. **Publications:** *Norvell News Nuggets,* periodic. Newsletter. Covers census information, queries, court records, and marriages pertaining to Norvell, etc. surnames. **Price:** free. **Advertising:** not accepted. **Conventions/Meetings:** annual reunion (exhibits) - always last Sunday in September, Forest City, NC; August in OH; reunion annually in Texas ● annual reunion - each June.

20591 ■ Oblinger/Oplinger Family Association (OOFA)
c/o Richard H. Oplinger, Pres.
1535 Morning Star Dr.
Allentown, PA 18106-8760
Ph: (610)336-9330
E-mail: roplinger@fast.net
Contact: Richard H. Oplinger, Pres.
Founded: 1914. **Members:** 400. **Description:** Preserves the family history associated with the Oblinger, Uplinger, Oplinger, and derivative names. Conducts research. **Publications:** *History of Uplinger-Oplinger Family.* Journal. **Conventions/Meetings:** annual reunion (exhibits).

20592 ■ O'Hare Family Association (OFA)
7472 Whistlestop Way
Roseville, CA 95747
Ph: (916)791-0405
E-mail: dewald@prenticenet.com
Contact: Joe Dewald, Contact
Description: O'Hare family members and other interested individuals. Promotes study of O'Hare family history and genealogy. Conducts research on the O'Hare family's formation in County Down, Ireland; provides assistance to family historians and genealogists.

20593 ■ Ouderkerk Family Genealogical Association (OFGA)
700 Atlanta Country Club Dr.
Marietta, GA 30067
E-mail: info@ouderkirk.com
URL: http://www.ouderkirk.com
Contact: H. John Ouderkirk, Pres./Ed.
Founded: 1981. **Members:** 450. **Membership Dues:** individual, $5 (annual). **Staff:** 2. **Description:** Persons of Ouderkerk, Ouderkirk, Odekirk, and Oderkirk descent. Conducts genealogical research. **Computer Services:** database, family geology. **Publications:** *Ouderkerk Family Genealogy Volume II.* Book. **Price:** $45.00 ● *Ouderkerk Family Saga.* Book. Includes articles and pictures that cover many personal and family events. **Price:** $40.00 ● *Quderkerk Family Newsletter,* quarterly. **Price:** included in membership dues. **Circulation:** 600. **Conventions/Meetings:** annual reunion.

20594 ■ Owen Family Association (OFA)
PO Box 692
Westtown, PA 19395-0692
Ph: (610)399-0146
E-mail: arnieowen@comcast.net
URL: http://www.geocities.com/Heartland/Ridge/1402
Contact: Arnold C. Owen, Pres.
Founded: 1985. **Members:** 315. **Membership Dues:** individual, $10 (annual). **Description:** Individuals interested in researching the Owen surname. **Com-**

puter **Services:** Online services, Owen information exchange. **Publications:** *Owen Family News,* quarterly. Newsletter. **Conventions/Meetings:** biennial conference - October of odd numbered years.

20595 ■ Owsley Family Historical Society
916 N Ridge Dr.
Columbus, GA 31904
Ph: (706)324-7237
E-mail: rbodine996@aol.com
Contact: Ronny O. Bodine, Pres.
Founded: 1978. **Members:** 268. **Staff:** 11. **Budget:** $7,000. **Description:** Seeks to collect, preserve, and disseminate knowledge and information of a genealogical, historical, and biographic nature of the Owsley family, including Ousley and Housley family members. Promotes interest in accurate research in the fields of genealogy, history, and biography. Compiles and updates an Owsley Family Registry. Encourages the preservation of historic buildings and monuments. Locates and marks sites involved in the Owsley family history. **Libraries: Type:** open to the public. **Subjects:** Owsley history, genealogy. **Computer Services:** database. **Publications:** *Lineages of Members,* biennial. Book. Features lineages of all society members showing Owsley descent. **Price:** $8.00. **Circulation:** 100 ● *Newsletter Subject Index Sept. 1978 - Dec. 1999* ● *Owsley Family Historical Society Newsletter,* quarterly. Contains society news, original historical and genealogical research relating to the Owsley family and related families. **Price:** included in membership dues. **ISSN:** 1089-9308. **Circulation:** 250.

20596 ■ Paisley Family Society
c/o Martha Pasley Milam Brown, USA Commissioner
2205 Pine Knoll Cir.
Conyers, GA 30013
E-mail: mbrown2205@aol.com
Contact: Duncan W. Paisley, Chieftain
Founded: 1988. **Members:** 800. **Membership Dues:** individual, $30 (annual). **Regional Groups:** 6. **Description:** Nonsectarian, nonpolitical family association for anyone with the surnames Paisley, Pasley, Pasly, or other variants most commonly originating in Southwest Scotland and Ireland. Aims to promotes a spirit of kinship among members and stimulate interest in the surname Paisley and its variants by conducting genealogical and historical research programs. **Libraries: Type:** reference; open to the public. **Holdings:** 50. **Subjects:** genealogy. **Computer Services:** database ● mailing lists ● record retrieval services. **Councils:** Australia; Canadian; New Zealand; Scottish; USA. **Publications:** *The Journal of the Paisley Family Society,* annual. **Price:** included in membership dues. **Advertising:** accepted. **Conventions/Meetings:** monthly board meeting (exhibits) ● annual meeting - always May in Moffat, Scotland ● quarterly regional meeting ● triennial reunion - always held in Scotland.

20597 ■ Parke Society
10942 Firecreek Dr.
Houston, TX 77043-2732
E-mail: 70741.2122@compuserve.com
URL: http://www.parke.org
Contact: Fr. Michael Parks, Exec. Dir./Historian
Founded: 1963. **Members:** 600. **Membership Dues:** individual, $25 (annual) ● life, $250 ● initial, $15. **Budget:** $20,000. **Description:** Persons interested in Parke ancestry. Includes immigrants and their descendants of Parke surname variations, whose origin was in the British Isles. Emphasizes research of Park(e)(s) genealogy. Serves as a clearinghouse of biographical and historical records. Offers some assistance with research; conducts research in local cemeteries; prepares biographical sketches of interesting ancestors. **Libraries: Type:** lending; not open to the public; by appointment only. **Holdings:** 1,000; archival material, books. **Subjects:** Parke family history and genealogy. **Computer Services:** database, all individuals with Park, Parke, Parkes, or Parks surname linked to the British Isles. **Publications:** *Newsletter of the Parke Society,* 3/year. Covers society and Park/e/s genealogical research news. **Price:** included in membership dues. **ISSN:** 0148-

3994. **Circulation:** 1,000. Alternate Formats: microform. **Conventions/Meetings:** annual Convocation - meeting and symposium, includes business meeting and research assistance (exhibits) - usually held during last full weekend of September.

20598 ■ Pellien/Jaeger/Loretan/Steiner/Ross Society (PJLSRS)
10435 W Concordia Ave.
Milwaukee, WI 53222
Ph: (414)259-1315 (414)771-8803
Fax: (414)771-8827
E-mail: pellien@execpc.com
Contact: Paul L. Pellien, Contact
Founded: 1987. **Members:** 300. **Staff:** 2. **Budget:** $300. **Regional Groups:** 2. **Local Groups:** 4. **Description:** Individuals with an interest in the Pellien, Jaeger, Loretan, Steiner, and Ross families. Seeks to facilitate study of family history and genealogy. Function as a clearinghouse on the histories and genealogies of families comprising the Pellien line; provides information and assistance to family historians and genealogists. **Libraries: Type:** reference. **Subjects:** Pellien and related family histories and genealogies. **Computer Services:** database, Pellien and related family genealogies. **Publications:** *Buffalo Roots News*, annual. Newsletter. **Circulation:** 300.

20599 ■ Pierre Chastain Family Association (PCFA)
c/o Susan Slape-Hoysagk, Membership Chair/Ed.
92012 Hagen Dr.
Astoria, OR 97103
E-mail: chestnut_tree@gmx.net
URL: http://www.pierrechastain.com
Contact: William F. Fenn, Pres.
Founded: 1975. **Members:** 400. **Membership Dues:** family, $15 (annual) ● life, $150. **Description:** Individuals and families interested in the Chastain family history. Dedicates to the preservation of Chastain records and information. Includes families with the surnames of Chastain, Chasteen, Chastaine, Shasteen, Shastine, Chasten, Castine, and Shastid as descendants of Dr. Pierre Chastain, a French Huguenot who migrated to America in 1700. Shares Chastain genealogy and family history. Supervises and directs the compilation of genealogical records. Provides historian and librarian services. Offers pedigree charts and family group sheets. **Libraries: Type:** not open to the public; reference. **Holdings:** books, periodicals. **Subjects:** genealogy. **Computer Services:** database ● mailing lists ● record retrieval services. **Publications:** *Chestnut Tree*, quarterly. Journal. Covers Chastain genealogy and family history. **Price:** included in membership dues; $4.00/issue for nonmembers. **Circulation:** 400 ● *PCFA Membership Directory*, annual. Contains names, addresses, phone numbers, and lineages for members of the Pierre Chastain Family Association. **Price:** $6.00 available to members only. **Conventions/Meetings:** annual reunion and board meeting.

20600 ■ Platt Family Association (PFA)
c/o Janet M. DeFonce, Sec.
26 Harvest Hill Dr.
Trumbull, CT 06611
Ph: (203)268-2430 (203)878-6094
E-mail: r.platt@snet.net
URL: http://freepages.genealogy.rootsweb.com/~plattfamilyassn/pfahome.html
Contact: Richard N. Platt Jr., Pres.
Founded: 1982. **Members:** 150. **Membership Dues:** individual, $10 (annual) ● family, $15 (annual). **Description:** Members of the Platt family. Promotes interest in family history and genealogy; identifies and unites Platt family members. Conducts research and provides assistance to family historians and genealogists; sponsors social activities. **Publications:** *Platt Family Newsletter*, quarterly. Contains family news and genealogy. **Price:** $10.00/year. **Circulation:** 200. **Conventions/Meetings:** annual reunion and meeting, genealogy - 2nd Saturday of July.

20601 ■ Pontius Family Association (PFA)
c/o B.J. Bongo, Treas.
21810 Fairmont Blvd.
Shaker Heights, OH 44118-4816
E-mail: bjbongo@msn.com
URL: http://pontiusfamilyassociation.org
Contact: B.J. Bongo, Treas.
Founded: 1968. **Members:** 390. **Membership Dues:** regular, $7 (annual) ● regular, $14 (biennial) ● regular, $20 (triennial) ● life (under 65 years old), $100 ● life (65-70 years old), $75 ● life (above 70 years old), $50. **Description:** Individuals with the surnames Pontius, Pontious, Punches, Pontzius, Poncy, and Pountious; descendants of individuals with these surnames. Gathers and disseminates information on the Pontius family and its activities; fosters genealogical research. Maintains Pontius family registry. **Telecommunication Services:** TDD, (800)421-1220. **Publications:** *Bridge Builder*, periodic. Magazine. **Price:** included in membership dues. ISSN: 0743-8958 ● Newsletter, 3/year. **Conventions/Meetings:** annual meeting.

20602 ■ Prall Family Association (PFA)
c/o Richard D. Prall, Historian/Ed.
14104 Piedras Rd. NE
Albuquerque, NM 87123
Ph: (505)299-8386
E-mail: questions@prallfamily.name
URL: http://www.prallfamily.name
Contact: Richard D. Prall, Historian/Ed.
Founded: 1986. **Members:** 140. **Membership Dues:** individual, $12 (annual). **Description:** Individuals interested in the history and genealogy of the Prall and related families. Promotes historical and genealogical research and study. Seeks to identify and unite Prall family members. Gathers and disseminates information on the Prall and related families. **Telecommunication Services:** electronic mail, louiser@prallfamily.name ● electronic mail, terryp@prallfamily.name ● electronic mail, webmaster@prallfamily.name. **Publications:** *Prall Newsletter*, quarterly. Contains history of the Prall, allied families, and current family news. **Price:** included in membership dues. ISSN: 1061-3641. **Circulation:** 200. **Conventions/Meetings:** quadrennial reunion.

20603 ■ Premm Family Association (PFA)
7472 Whistlestop Way
Roseville, CA 95747
Ph: (916)791-0405
E-mail: dewald@prenticenet.com
Contact: Joe Dewald, Contact
Description: Individuals with the surname Premm and other Premm family members. Promotes Premm family genealogical research. Gathers and disseminates information on Premm family history and genealogy; sponsors research and educational programs. **Computer Services:** database, Premm family history and genealogy.

20604 ■ Purcell Family of America
2962 Moreland Ave.
Oceanside, NY 11572
Ph: (516)764-7068 (631)777-2223
Fax: (516)764-1585
E-mail: jfpurcell@hotmail.com
URL: http://www.snowgoosegallery.com/pfa.htm
Contact: Joe Frank Purcell, VP/Sec.
Founded: 1972. **Members:** 200. **Membership Dues:** individual, $25 (annual). **Staff:** 3. **Description:** Serves as genealogy association sharing news of Purcell, Pursell, Pursley, Purcel or Parsel family. **Publications:** *Purcell Family of America Journal*, quarterly. Contains 56 pages plus annual index. **Price:** included in membership dues; $5.00/copy for nonmembers. **Conventions/Meetings:** triennial reunion, with tabletop presentation of family genealogical information (exhibits).

20605 ■ Rader Association
2633 Gilbert Way
Rancho Cordova, CA 95670-3513
Ph: (916)366-6833

E-mail: jim@rader.org
URL: http://www.rader.org
Founded: 1991. **Description:** Represents persons researching on the surnames Rader, Rotter, Roder, and Raeder. **Libraries: Type:** by appointment only. **Computer Services:** database. **Publications:** Newsletter. ISSN: 1069-0905.

20606 ■ Ralph Shepard Family Organization (RSFO)
1672 Forests Ct. NE
Atlanta, GA 30341
Ph: (770)457-6644
E-mail: shepardjoe@msn.com
Contact: Joseph E. Shepard, Contact
Description: Descendants of Ralph Shepard, who arrived in North America in 1635. Promotes communication and exchange of information among Shepard family historians and genealogists. Serves as a clearinghouse on Shepard family genealogy; authenticates family historical and genealogical research. **Libraries: Type:** reference. **Holdings:** archival material, articles, books, business records, clippings, periodicals. **Subjects:** Shepard family history and genealogy.

20607 ■ Reed-Reid Clearinghouse
207 Auburn Dr.
Dalton, GA 30720
Ph: (706)278-1504
Contact: Joseph W. Reid, Contact
Founded: 1980. **Description:** Provides family history information for those with the surname Reid, Reed, and the names Carter, Bagley, Daniel, Pryor, Gardner, Glawson, Wilson, Bailey, Brown, Suggs, Bynum, Flye. Serves as a clearinghouse for genealogical data. All records are kept at the James Earl Carter Library at Georgia Southwestern College.

20608 ■ Reynolds Family Association (RFA)
c/o Marilyn J. Newton, Registrar
2240 130th St.
Winterset, IA 50273-8479
E-mail: marenewt@aol.com
URL: http://www.reynoldsfamily.org
Contact: Marilyn J. Newton, Registrar
Founded: 1892. **Members:** 500. **Membership Dues:** individual, $10 (annual) ● life, $100. **Description:** Individuals interested in the history and genealogy of Reynolds families who settled in colonial America and Canada. Collects and maintains a permanent record of Reynolds family history; also studies variant spellings of the surname. Assists in genealogical research for members. Works to establish acquaintance and continued communication among Reynolds families; fosters recognition of a common ancestry. Maintains archives. **Computer Services:** database. **Publications:** *Reynolds Family Association Centennial Collection*. Book. Includes archival genealogical material corrected and updated. **Price:** $65.00 ● *Reynolds Recollections*, bimonthly. Newsletter. Includes genealogical information and association updates. **Price:** included in membership dues. **Conventions/Meetings:** annual reunion and meeting.

20609 ■ Rich Family Association (RFA)
PO Box 142
Wellfleet, MA 02667
Ph: (508)432-2883
E-mail: drdickrich@aol.com
URL: http://www.richfamilyassociation.org
Contact: George Lewis III, Treas.
Founded: 1872. **Members:** 400. **Membership Dues:** regular, $20 (annual) ● life, $150. **Description:** Persons descended from the Rich family. Assists members in tracing their ancestry. **Libraries: Type:** reference. **Holdings:** archival material. **Awards:** Rich Family Association Scholarship. **Frequency:** annual. **Type:** scholarship. **Recipient:** to any student whose family is a member in good standing of RFA and who is now or will be attending an institution of higher learning. **Publications:** *Kinfolk*, quarterly. Newsletter. Includes genealogical records and queries, family history, and reports of deaths, births, and marriages. **Price:** $20.00/year. ISSN: 0556-9796. **Circulation:**

700. **Conventions/Meetings:** annual reunion, with genealogical data (exhibits).

20610 ■ Rickey Family Association (RFA)
235 15th St. NE
Salem, OR 97301-4228
Ph: (503)363-4389
E-mail: rickeyroot@aol.com
Contact: Stanton M. Rickey, Pres.
Founded: 1989. **Members:** 1,100. **Membership Dues:** active, $15 (annual). **Staff:** 2. **Description:** Descendants of the Rickey surname. Works to preserve the Rickey family heritage. Clearinghouse for exchange of family history; conducts research and educational programs; compiles statistics. Database of 25,000 Rickey descendants. **Libraries: Type:** not open to the public; by appointment only. **Holdings:** archival material, articles, books, clippings, monographs. **Subjects:** genealogy, family history. **Awards: Type:** recognition. **Computer Services:** database, Rickey and associated spousal surnames ● mailing lists ● record retrieval services. **Publications:** *Rickey Roots & Revels*, quarterly. Newsletter. **Price:** $15.00. ISSN: 1058-0263. **Circulation:** 1,250. **Conventions/Meetings:** annual Rickey Revel XIII - reunion.

20611 ■ Risley Family Association (RFA)
PO Box 552
Clarkson, NY 14430
Ph: (716)637-6419
E-mail: roygcgrfa@aol.com
URL: http://members.aol.com/risleyfa/index.html
Contact: Roy D. Goold, Pres.
Founded: 1889. **Members:** 750. **Membership Dues:** initial, $10 (annual) ● regular, $6 (annual). **Description:** Families whose members are descendants of Richard Risley, Sr., and members of the Wrisley, Rizley, and Riseley families in America. Makes available to members genealogical, historical, and biographical data about the Risley family in the U.S. and England. **Awards:** Certificate of Appreciation, Honorary Risley. **Frequency:** annual. **Type:** recognition. **Additional Websites:** http://www.risleyfamily.org. **Telecommunication Services:** electronic mail, johncase3@aol.com. **Boards:** Managers. **Formerly:** (1917) Descendents of Richard Risley. **Publications:** *Cemetery Records* ● *Descendants of Richard Risley in America* ● *Descendants of Richard Risley, 21 Vols.*, annual. Booklet. Includes reunion programs, articles about the family. **Price:** available for members only. ISSN: 1048-8901 ● *Genealogy 5 Vols.*, periodic. Booklet. **Price:** available to members only ● *Risley Record*, quarterly. Newsletter. Contains articles on Risley family history, genealogy, and biography. **Price:** $2.00/issue. ISSN: 1050-7922. **Circulation:** 770 ● *Risleys on Risleys*. **Conventions/Meetings:** annual Risley/Wrisley/Rizley/Riseley Family Reunion, genealogical exhibits (exhibits) - always second weekend in August.

20612 ■ Robert Bruce Bradley Family Organization
5750 Carr Factory Rd.
Benton, WI 53803
Ph: (608)759-2755
E-mail: glynneim@mhtc.net
Contact: Lynne Bradley Montgomery, Chair
Founded: 1990. **Members:** 60. **Staff:** 2. **Description:** Promotes family name; descendants or relatives by marriage of Robert Bradley. **Libraries: Type:** reference. **Holdings:** 1; articles, books, clippings, photographs. **Subjects:** genealogy.

20613 ■ Rockafellow Family Association (RFA)
1425 Watersmeet Lake Rd.
Eagle River, WI 54521-8316
Ph: (715)477-1425
E-mail: maxrock@newnorth.net
Contact: Max E. Rockafellow, Family Historian
Founded: 1990. **Members:** 160. **Membership Dues:** individual, $20 (3/year). **Staff:** 2. **Description:** Members of the Rockafellow family. Seeks to identify and unite Rockafellow family members. Serves as a clearinghouse on Rockafellow family history and

genealogy; sponsors social activities. **Libraries: Type:** by appointment only. **Holdings:** 27; archival material, articles, books, clippings, periodicals. **Subjects:** Rockafellow Family history, genealogy, photos. **Computer Services:** database, family database-group sheets, listings. **Publications:** *Rockafellow Genealogy*, on demand. Contains listings. **Price:** $25.00 includes postage. **Conventions/Meetings:** annual reunion, genealogy, family photos, annual group picture, food, games, bond fire - July/August.

20614 ■ Ronald Lee Shankland Family Organization (RSFO)
2048 Forest Park Dr.
Jackson, MI 49201
Ph: (517)783-6742 (941)923-0968
E-mail: ronald.l.shankland@prodigy.net
Contact: Ron Shankland, Contact
Founded: 1990. **Description:** Members of the Shankland/Shanklin family. Seeks to identify and unite Shankland family members; encourages interest in family history and genealogy. Serves as a clearinghouse on the Shankland family and its history; provides assistance to family historians and genealogists; sponsors social activities. **Formerly:** (1999) Robert Shankland Family Organization.

20615 ■ Rose Family Association (RFA)
1474 Montelegre Dr.
San Jose, CA 95120-4831
Ph: (408)268-2137
Fax: (408)268-2165
E-mail: christine4rose@cs.com
URL: http://ourworld-top.cs.com/christine4rose/index.htm
Contact: Christine Rose, Contact
Founded: 1966. **Members:** 700. **Membership Dues:** subscribing, $20 (annual) ● contributing, $22 (annual) ● sustaining, $26 (annual). **Description:** Members of the Rose family and other interested individuals. Promotes study of Rose family history and genealogy. Serves as a clearinghouse on the Rose family and its history; assists family historians and genealogists. **Additional Websites:** http://www.Christine4Rose.com. **Publications:** *Rose Family Bulletin*, quarterly ● Newsletter, quarterly.

20616 ■ Runkle Family Association (RFA)
PO Box 14
Ringoes, NJ 08551
E-mail: patmast@aol.com
URL: http://homepages.rootsweb.com/~runkle
Contact: Patricia Masterson, Pres.
Founded: 1990. **Members:** 35. **Membership Dues:** individual, family, $20 (annual). **Description:** Individuals with the surname Runkle or its variant spellings. Promotes study of Runkle family history and genealogy. Facilitates communication and good fellowship among Runkle family descendants; provides assistance to family historians and genealogists; maintains historic Runkle Cemetery. **Publications:** Newsletter, semiannual. **Alternate Formats:** online. **Conventions/Meetings:** annual reunion.

20617 ■ Saleeby-Saliba Family Association
PO Box 87094
Highland Sta.
Fayetteville, NC 28304
E-mail: crs1920@aol.com
URL: http://www.saleeby-saliba.org
Contact: Eli Leonard Saleeby, Pres.
Description: Represents members of the Saleeby-Saliba family. **Publications:** *Salleeby-Saliba Family Book* (in Arabic and English). **Price:** $100.00 Arabic version; $55.00 English version. **Conventions/Meetings:** annual meeting.

20618 ■ Sapp Family Association
712 NW 95th Terr.
Gainesville, FL 32607
Ph: (352)332-2065
E-mail: sapps@aol.com
URL: http://www.members.aol.com/sapps/Archive
Contact: Mitchell E. Sapp, Contact
Founded: 1988. **Members:** 130. **Membership Dues:** regular, $20 (annual). **Budget:** $2,000. **Description:**

Individuals interested in researching the surname Sapp and its variant spellings, such as Zapp and Zapft. Conducts educational and research programs; compiles statistics. **Libraries: Type:** reference; open to the public; by appointment only. **Holdings:** 200; articles, books, clippings. **Telecommunication Services:** electronic mail, sapp@gru.net. **Publications:** *Sapp Family Newsletter*, quarterly. **Price:** $20.00/year. **Circulation:** 150.

20619 ■ Schaarschmidt Family Association and Data Bank (SFADB)
PO Box 75
Moran, WY 83013
Ph: (307)543-2420
Fax: (307)543-2420
E-mail: geobuff@aol.com
Contact: John Sharsmith, Contact
Founded: 1980. **Description:** Promotes study of, and interest in, the Schaarschmidt family. Collects, maintains, and disseminates genealogical and historical information pertaining to the Schaarschmidt family. **Libraries: Type:** reference. **Holdings:** archival material. **Subjects:** Schaarschmidt family history and genealogy.

20620 ■ Schreckengost Family Exchange
Address Unknown since 2007
Founded: 1980. **Members:** 77. **Description:** Provides assistance for genealogical research on the Schreckengost family (all spellings). Promotes cooperation among family members and researchers. Maintains computerized database on the family. **Publications:** none. **Convention/Meeting:** none. **Computer Services:** database, genealogical information on the Schreckengost family.

20621 ■ Scruggs Family Association (SFA)
c/o Patricia Scruggs Trolinger, Sec.
61300 E 110 Rd.
Miami, OK 74354-4726
Ph: (918)542-5772
E-mail: ottawahillpt@neok.com
URL: http://www.geocities.com/Scruggs_family
Contact: Patricia Scruggs Trolinger, Sec.
Founded: 1981. **Members:** 150. **Membership Dues:** regular, $25 (annual). **Description:** Individuals with the surname of Scruggs or its variants and allied lines, and others interested in genealogy. Seeks to gather information on the history and genealogy of the Scruggs family and allied lines. **Publications:** *Searching for Scruggs*, semiannual. **Conventions/Meetings:** biennial reunion.

20622 ■ Sears Family Association (SFA)
c/o L. Ray Sears, III, Ed.
2028 Amber Rd.
Oklahoma City, OK 73170
Ph: (405)703-0779
E-mail: lrsears@cox.net
URL: http://www.searsr.com
Contact: L. Ray Sears III, Ed.
Founded: 1976. **Members:** 220. **Membership Dues:** individual, $10 (annual). **Staff:** 10. **Description:** Descendants of Richard Sears, who landed at Plymouth, MA in 1632. Promotes genealogical research. **Libraries: Type:** reference. **Holdings:** archival material, books, clippings, periodicals. **Subjects:** Sears family and Cape Cod. **Computer Services:** database, listing 40,000 descendants of Sears. **Publications:** *Sears Family Association Newsletter*, semiannual. **Price:** $10.00/issue. **Circulation:** 220 ● *Sears Genealogy*. **Alternate Formats:** CD-ROM ● *Sears Genealogy Catalogue*. Covers 8,000 descendants of Richard Sears, Yarmouth, Plymouth colony. **Price:** $25.00. **Alternate Formats:** CD-ROM.

20623 ■ Seeley Genealogical Society (SGS)
PO Box 337
Abilene, KS 67410-0337
E-mail: queries@seeley-society.net
URL: http://www.seeley-society.net
Contact: James R. Seeley, Pres.
Founded: 1965. **Members:** 395. **Membership Dues:** voting, $8 (annual) ● life, $100 ● voting, $15 (biennial) ● voting, $21 (triennial) ● voting, $30 (quinquen-

nial). **Description:** Descendants of the Seeley family and its variants (Seely, Seelye, Seela, Sealey, Cilley, Seale, Ceely, Seily, etc.); individuals interested in genealogy, history, or biography. Seeks to maintain and provide genealogical information on all Seeley ancestors. Encourages study of family history; promotes exchange of information. **Libraries: Type:** reference. **Subjects:** genealogical data, Seeley family. **Telecommunication Services:** electronic mail, membership@seeley-society.net. **Publications:** *Descendant of Robert Seeley (1602-1667) and Obadiah Seely (1614-1657) Generations One Through Five.* Book. **Price:** $17.00 each ● *Seeley Genealogy Society Newsletter,* quarterly. **Price:** $2.00. Alternate Formats: online ● *The Seventh Generation Families Descendant Robert Seeley (1602-1667) and Obadiah Seely (1614-1657).* Book. **Price:** $25.00 each ● *SGS CD Rev: 15 July 2004.* Contains the publications, other Seeley compilations and Seeley research reports, all in MS Word. Alternate Formats: CD-ROM. **Conventions/Meetings:** biennial reunion and meeting (exhibits).

20624 ■ Shafer Family Association (SFA)
141 Hudson Ave.
Chatham, NY 12037
Ph: (518)392-4544
E-mail: hw15@juno.com
Founded: 1990. **Members:** 150. **State Groups:** 1. **Description:** Individuals with the surname Shafer or its variant spellings. Promotes communication and good fellowship among members; seeks to advance study of family history and genealogy. Works to identify family members; sponsors social activities.

20625 ■ Shanks Family Association (SFA)
Address Unknown since 2007
Founded: 1980. **Members:** 15. **Description:** Doctors, attorneys, teachers, laborers, and housewives. Conducts genealogical research on the Shank family throughout the United States to establish the family line. Works to determine the origin of the name. **Telecommunication Services:** electronic mail, ticktoc@execpc.com. **Publications:** Newsletter, quarterly.

20626 ■ Shirley Family Association (SA)
c/o Betty Shirley, Pres.
10256 Glencoe Dr.
Cupertino, CA 95014
E-mail: bettyshirley@comcast.net
URL: http://www.shirleyassociation.com
Contact: Betty Shirley, Pres.
Founded: 1978. **Members:** 400. **Membership Dues:** regular, $20 (annual). **Description:** Individuals interested in preserving the history of the Shirley family. Seeks to unite Shirley descendants; provides research assistance to members; makes available census records. **Computer Services:** database, research data archives. **Projects:** DNA Testing. **Publications:** *Shirley News,* quarterly. Newsletter. **Price:** included in membership dues. **Conventions/Meetings:** annual meeting.

20627 ■ Skinner Surname Organization (SSO)
c/o Gregg Legutki
PO Box 2594
Rancho Cucamonga, CA 91729
E-mail: gregg@skinnerkinsmen.org
URL: http://www.skinnerkinsmen.org
Contact: Gregg Legutki, Contact
Founded: 1984. **Members:** 300. **Membership Dues:** individual, $16 (annual). **Staff:** 3. **Description:** Individuals with the surname Skinner; other Skinner family members and interested individuals. Promotes interest in Skinner family history and genealogy. Facilitates communication among Skinner family members; supports and assists Skinner family historians and genealogists. **Libraries: Type:** reference; not open to the public. **Holdings:** archival material, articles, books, periodicals. **Subjects:** Skinner family history and genealogy. **Computer Services:** Mailing lists. **Publications:** *Skinner Kinsmen*

Update, quarterly. Newsletter. ISSN: 0985-0202. **Circulation:** 125. **Advertising:** accepted. Also Cited As: *SKU.*

20628 ■ Smith-Hedrick Family Association
1164 Heber Springs Rd. S
Heber Springs, AR 72543-8464
Ph: (501)362-2180
E-mail: drwsmith@cox.net
Contact: Wayne Smith MD, Newsletter Ed.
Founded: 1964. **Members:** 200. **Staff:** 3. **Budget:** $900. **Description:** Persons interested in the surname Smith or Hedrick. Researches, publishes, and preserves the surnames Smith and Hedrick. **Libraries: Type:** reference. **Holdings:** 275; archival material, books, clippings, periodicals. **Subjects:** history of Smiths and Hedricks, Southern history, northeast Arkansas history, New England States. **Computer Services:** database ● mailing lists. **Publications:** *Smith-Hedrick Newsletter,* bimonthly. Announces births, deaths, promotions, retirements, sketches, brags, and assorted miscellaneous news, and family group sheets. **Price:** free. **Circulation:** 150. Alternate Formats: online. **Conventions/Meetings:** annual Smith-Hendrick Reunion, family charts, pictures, scrapbook (exhibits).

20629 ■ Snodgrass Clan Society (SCS)
8221 Stonewall Dr.
Vienna, VA 22180-6947
Ph: (703)560-6631
E-mail: paulsnodgrass@cox.net
URL: http://www.snodgrass-clan.com
Contact: Paul D. Snodgrass, Ed.
Founded: 1977. **Members:** 160. **Membership Dues:** ordinary, $15 (annual). **Description:** Individuals interested in Snodgrass family history and genealogy. Promotes genealogical research; facilitates communication and cooperation among members. Serves as a clearinghouse on Snodgrass family history and genealogy; assists genealogical researchers. **Libraries: Type:** reference; lending. **Holdings:** archival material. **Subjects:** Snodgrass family history, genealogy. **Publications:** *The Mace,* semiannual, April and October. Journal.

20630 ■ Society of the Hawley Family
PO Box 964
Southeastern, PA 19399-0964
E-mail: president@hawleysociety.org
URL: http://www.hawleysociety.org
Contact: Linda D. Hawley, Pres.
Founded: 1923. **Members:** 200. **Membership Dues:** individual, $10 (annual) ● family, $25 (annual). **State Groups:** 1. **Local Groups:** 1. **Description:** Persons researching the surname Hawley. Seeks to trace Hawley's to earliest person in each family line; publicizes achievements of ancestors. Promotes family fellowship and discovery of relatives. Compiles genealogical information (in the process of being computerized). **Libraries: Type:** reference. **Holdings:** 100. **Also Known As:** Hawley Society. **Publications:** *Hawley Bulletin,* semiannual. **Price:** included in membership dues ● Membership Directory, quinquennial ● Pamphlets. **Conventions/Meetings:** annual reunion - usually October.

20631 ■ Society of Mareen Duvall Descendants
c/o Barrett L. McKown, Registrar
3580 S River Terr.
Edgewater, MD 21037
Ph: (410)798-4531
Fax: (410)798-4883
E-mail: bmckown@aacpl.net
URL: http://www.duvallsociety.org
Contact: Barrett L. McKown, Registrar
Founded: 1927. **Members:** 624. **Membership Dues:** regular, sustaining, associate, $15 (annual) ● life, $200. **Budget:** $4,000. **Description:** Direct descendants of Mareen Duvall, a planter and merchant who emigrated from France to Maryland in 1655. Unites individuals and families who are offspring of Duvall's 12 children. Studies Duvall history and preserves and restores Duvall relics. **Libraries: Type:** reference. **Holdings:** 25; archival material, books, clippings.

Subjects: Duvall family, early history. **Publications:** *Excavations at Mareen Duvall's Middle Plantation of South River Hundred.* Book. **Price:** $40.00 ● *Mareen Duvall of Middle Plantation.* Book. **Price:** $50.00 post paid ● Newsletter, semiannual. Alternate Formats: online ● Brochure. **Conventions/Meetings:** board meeting - 3/year; every 4th Saturday, in January, April, and July ● annual meeting - always October, in Maryland.

20632 ■ Society of Stukely Westcott Descendants of America
c/o Lewis O. Westcott, Registrar
8121 Beverly Dr.
Prairie Village, KS 66208
E-mail: betw@prodigy.net
URL: http://www.westcottsociety.com
Contact: Lewis O. Westcott, Registrar
Founded: 1934. **Membership Dues:** regular, $10 (annual). **Description:** Descendants of Stukeley Westcott. Seeks to identify and unite family members. Gathers and disseminates information on Westcott/Wescott family history and genealogy; sponsors social activities. **Publications:** *Westcott Family Quarterly,* QRT. Newsletter. **Conventions/Meetings:** biennial reunion.

20633 ■ Southern Bean Association (SBA)
c/o Dianna B. Hokanson, Ed.
4010 Longherridge Dr.
Pearland, TX 77581
Ph: (281)482-0304
Fax: (281)482-5121
E-mail: dianna@pearland.com
URL: http://www.southernbeanassociation.org
Contact: Dianna B. Hokanson, Ed.
Founded: 1972. **Members:** 200. **Membership Dues:** individual, $15 (annual). **Description:** Persons with the surname Bean/Been/Beene/Bain, or who have the name in their background, and who have a connection in the South. **Libraries: Type:** lending; not open to the public. **Holdings:** archival material, books, periodicals. **Subjects:** family histories, state and county histories, census, Revolutionary War. **Publications:** *Beanstalk,* quarterly. Newsletter. **Conventions/Meetings:** annual convention and board meeting - always 3rd week of June.

20634 ■ Sparks Family Association (SFA)
c/o James A. Hopper
27909 83rd Dr. NW
Stanwood, WA 98292-9513
E-mail: nancy@sparksfamilyassn.org
URL: http://www.sparksfamilyassn.org
Contact: James A. Hopper, Contact
Founded: 1953. **Members:** 900. **Membership Dues:** active, $10 (annual). **Budget:** $20,000. **Description:** Members of the Sparks and related families and other individuals with an interest in genealogy. Seeks to identify and preserve historical artifacts and genealogical information pertaining to the Sparks family. Conducts research; provides assistance to Sparks family historians and genealogists. **Telecommunication Services:** electronic mail, jahopper@sparksfamilyassn.org. **Publications:** *Sparks Quarterly.* Newsletter. **Price:** included in membership dues.

20635 ■ Spurlock Family Association (SFA)
c/o Bill Spurlock
5950 Western Hills Dr.
Norcross, GA 30071
E-mail: bill@spurlockfamily.org
URL: http://www.spurlockfamily.org
Contact: Bill Spurlock, Contact
Founded: 1988. **Members:** 85. **Description:** Individuals with the surname Spurlock or a variant. Preserves family history; acts as a clearinghouse for genealogical information. Compiles statistics. **Libraries: Type:** reference. **Holdings:** archival material, audio recordings, books, papers. **Subjects:** Spurlock genealogy. **Awards: Type:** recognition. **Computer Services:** database, census. **Telecommunication Services:** electronic mail, nstramler@aol.com. **Formed by Merger of:** (1990) Spurlock/Scurlock Family; Allied Lines. **Publications:** *Spurlock Family Bulletin,* monthly. Alternate Formats: online ● *Spur-*

lock Family Newsletter, semiannual. Contains genealogical and historical information. **Advertising:** accepted. Alternate Formats: CD-ROM; diskette; online.

20636 ■ **Steere Family Association (SFA)**
82 Waltham St., No. 8
Boston, MA 02118
E-mail: randy535@aol.com
URL: http://www.steerefamily.com
Contact: Randall Steere, Pres.
Founded: 1930. **Members:** 1,000. **Budget:** $5,000. **Description:** Members of the Steere family. Facilitates communication and good fellowship among members; promotes interest in family history and genealogy. Conducts research and educational programs; sponsors social activities; maintains historic cemeteries. **Libraries: Type:** not open to the public. **Holdings:** archival material, biographical archives, books, clippings, photographs. **Subjects:** Steere family history and genealogy. **Publications:** Newsletter, periodic ● Books. **Conventions/Meetings:** annual reunion - always summer, in Rhode Island.

20637 ■ **Stires Family Association**
Address Unknown since 2007
Founded: 1977. **Members:** 45. **Membership Dues:** $10 (annual). **Staff:** 10. **Description:** Promotes the history of the surname Stires and its variants (Styers, Stiers, Stire, Steyr, Steer, Steyer, Steiermark, Stoehr, Steirs, Steers, Steier, Steeres, Styer, Stehr, and Stohr). Conducts educational programs. **Libraries: Type:** reference. **Holdings:** archival material, books, clippings, monographs, periodicals. **Subjects:** Stires family history. **Publications:** *Stires Family Newsletter*, monthly. Focus on Stires research. **Price:** $10. 00/year. **Circulation:** 45. **Advertising:** accepted. **Conventions/Meetings:** Jost Stier to America from Germany 1710-2010 Reunion - summer 2010, New Jersey.

20638 ■ **Stovall Family Association (SFA)**
c/o Thomas Stovall, Journal Ed.
3345 Tibey Ct.
Dubuque, IA 52002
Ph: (563)557-9227
E-mail: linstov@aol.com
URL: http://www.geocities.com/tommy_stovall/sfa
Contact: Linda M. Stovall, Pres.
Founded: 1989. **Members:** 550. **Membership Dues:** family, $15 (annual). **Staff:** 1. **Budget:** $8,500. **Regional Groups:** 3. **State Groups:** 2. **Local Groups:** 3. **Description:** Individuals with the Stovall/Stoval/ Stoveall surname. Promotes interest in Stovall family history and heritage. Conducts genealogical research; provides research assistance. Conducts educational programs. **Libraries: Type:** reference. **Holdings:** 20; archival material, books, periodicals. **Subjects:** Stovall genealogy. **Awards:** Honorary Member. **Frequency:** triennial. **Type:** recognition. **Recipient:** for service. **Computer Services:** database, free Stovall database search. **Telecommunication Services:** electronic mail, tomstov@aol.com. **Also Known As:** (2000) Stoval, Stoveal, Stoball. **Publications:** *Stovall Journal*, quarterly. **Price:** $15.00. **Circulation:** 550. **Conventions/Meetings:** triennial reunion, family trees, Bibles, heirlooms, crafts (exhibits) ● triennial reunion (exhibits).

20639 ■ **Streeter Family Association (SFA)**
c/o Ms. Erma Hosmer
PO Box 1071
Ceres, CA 95307
E-mail: weebah@hotmail.com
URL: http://freepages.genealogy.rootsweb.com/
~streeter/sfa
Contact: Ms. Erma Hosmer, Contact
Founded: 1984. **Membership Dues:** general, $18 (annual) ● life, $300. **Multinational. Description:** Individuals and families with the surname Streeter or Streator; friends of Streeter families and interested others. Compiles and disseminates genealogical information to Streeters in the U.S. and Canada. Maintains biographical archives. **Computer Services:** Mailing lists. **Projects:** Streeter Surname DNA. **Publications:** *Milford B. Streeter Genealogy*.

Reprint ● *Streeter National Newsletter*, semiannual. **Price:** included in membership dues. ISSN: 0887-1841. **Circulation:** 325. **Conventions/Meetings:** annual reunion and board meeting.

20640 ■ **Strong Family Association of America (SFAA)**
c/o Anita J. Brown, Corresponding Sec.
PO Box 546
Kendallville, IN 46755-0546
E-mail: membership@strongfamilyofamerica.org
Contact: Anita J. Brown, Corresponding Sec.
Founded: 1975. **Members:** 550. **Membership Dues:** individual, $15 (annual) ● family, $20 (annual) ● individual - life, $200 ● family - life, $250. **Multinational. Description:** Individuals with the surname Strong or a variant. Promotes unity among family members and awareness of family heritage. Collects and preserves artifacts and information related to the family. Conducts research and educational programs; compiles statistics. **Libraries: Type:** reference; lending. **Holdings:** archival material. **Awards: Type:** recognition. **Computer Services:** database. **Programs:** Update. **Publications:** *History of the Strong Family*. Book. **Price:** $60.00 plus shipping and handling ● *SFAA Directory*, annual ● *SFAA Newsletter*, quarterly ● *Strong Family Update*. Updates the history of the Descendants of Elder John Strong, originally published in 1871, volumes I to V. ● Books. **Conventions/Meetings:** annual Family Gathering - reunion - always 2nd weekend of August. 2008 Aug. 8-10, Eureka Springs, AR - **Avg. Attendance:** 100.

20641 ■ **Studebaker Family National Association (SFNA)**
6555 S State Rte. 202
Tipp City, OH 45371-9444
Ph: (937)667-7013
E-mail: sfna@highstream.net
URL: http://www.studebakerfamily.org
Contact: Ms. Carol Erisman, Office Mgr.
Founded: 1964. **Members:** 2,060. **Membership Dues:** individual, $20 (annual) ● life, $400. **Staff:** 2. **Description:** Promotes the genealogy and family history of the Studebaker family. Offers research statistics; maintains a museum. **Libraries: Type:** reference. **Holdings:** archival material, books. **Computer Services:** database ● electronic publishing ● mailing lists. **Publications:** *Studebaker Family*, quarterly. Newsletter. **Circulation:** 2,060. **Conventions/Meetings:** annual board meeting ● quinquennial reunion.

20642 ■ **Sumner Family Association (SFA)**
7540 Rolling River Pkwy.
Nashville, TN 37221-3322
Ph: (615)646-9946
E-mail: charles.sumner@juno.com
URL: http://homepages.rootsweb.com/~lcompton/
sumner/SFA
Contact: Mr. Charles Hanson Sumner, Dir.
Founded: 1982. **Members:** 350. **Membership Dues:** individual, family, $5 (biennial). **Multinational. Description:** Individuals with the surname Sumner and its variants, and their families. Works to locate and maintain communication with Sumners around the world. Provides genealogies; maintains computerized records. **Publications:** *Sumner Search*, periodic. Newsletter. **Price:** included in membership dues. **Circulation:** 350. Alternate Formats: CD-ROM; diskette.

20643 ■ **Tackett Family Association (TFA)**
c/o Jim W. Tackitt, Pres.
260 Bella Vista Way
Rio Vista, CA 94571
E-mail: jim@tackettfamilies.com
URL: http://www.tackettfamilies.com
Contact: Jim W. Tackitt, Pres.
Founded: 1963. **Members:** 1,400. **Description:** Descendants of Lewis Tacquett and those with related surnames. Collects, preserves, and disseminates genealogical information related to Tackett families in America. **Computer Services:** database. **Formerly:** (1989) American Pioneers. **Publications:** *Tackett Family Journal*, quarterly. ISSN: 1052-7753. **Circulation:** 400. Also Cited As: *American Pioneers: Tackett-*

Tacket-Tackitt Families in America. **Conventions/Meetings:** annual Tackett Reunion (exhibits) - always second Sunday in July, Virgie, KY.

20644 ■ **Taft Family Association (TFA)**
c/o Berneta M. DeVries, Sec.-Treas.
PO Box 406
Mendon, MA 01756
E-mail: pallen@crocker.com
URL: http://freepages.genealogy.rootsweb.com/~taft
Contact: Patricia Allen, Pres.
Founded: 1955. **Members:** 400. **Membership Dues:** family, $8 (annual). **Description:** Descendants of Robert and Sarah Taft, who immigrated to the United States in 1675. Promotes study of Taft family history and genealogy. Gathers and disseminates information on the Taft family and its history; serves as a forum for the exchange of information among family historians and genealogists; sponsors research and social programs. **Libraries: Type:** lending; not open to the public. **Holdings:** articles, books, clippings, monographs. **Subjects:** Taft family history, genealogy. **Publications:** *Taft Tree Talk*, semiannual. Newsletter. **Price:** included in membership dues ● Book. **Conventions/Meetings:** annual reunion - usually fourth Saturday in June.

20645 ■ **Templin Family Association**
c/o Marvin T. Templin, Pres./Genealogist
107 County Rd. 60
Athens, TN 37303-6656
E-mail: mttemplin@aol.com
URL: http://templin.rootsweb.com/tempassoc.htm
Contact: Marvin T. Templin, Genealogist
Founded: 1972. **Members:** 220. **Membership Dues:** individual, family, $6 (biennial). **Description:** Conducts genealogical research on Templin family ancestors using family Bible records; census, tax, marriage, birth, and death records in official files of city, county, and state bureaus; written histories, biographies, land files, and archives from various states, foreign countries, genealogical societies, and patriotic associations, including the Daughters of the American Revolution and the Sons of the American Revolution. Also researches family lines of members related by marriage. **Telecommunication Services:** electronic mail, harry.templin1@verizon.net. **Publications:** *Templins of Indiana, of Tennessee, and of Ohio*. Book. Contains Templin family genealogies. **Conventions/Meetings:** biennial reunion - always even years in summer.

20646 ■ **Tevebaugh - Teverbaugh Surname Organization (TTSO)**
Address Unknown since 2007
Founded: 1990. **Staff:** 2. **Description:** Individuals with the surname Tevebaugh and Teverbaugh and their variant spellings; other members of the Tevebaugh family. Seeks to identify and unite Tevebaugh family members; promotes interest in family history and genealogy. Serves as a clearinghouse on the Tevebaugh family and its history; sponsors genealogical research.

20647 ■ **Thomas Minor Society (TMS)**
c/o O. Geral Wilde, Sec.
815 N 300 W
Provo, UT 84604
Ph: (801)377-8294
E-mail: secretary@tmsociety.org
URL: http://www.tmsociety.org
Contact: O. Geral Wilde, Sec.
Founded: 1979. **Members:** 500. **Membership Dues:** descendant, spouse, dependent children, $15 (annual). **Staff:** 1. **Budget:** $6,000. **Regional Groups:** 2. **State Groups:** 1. **Description:** Descendants of Thomas Minor. Seeks to identify and unite members of the Minor family; promotes interest in family history and genealogy. Conducts historical and genealogical research and disseminates results; sponsors social and educational activities. **Libraries: Type:** not open to the public. **Holdings:** 7; articles, books, clippings. **Subjects:** Minor family history and genealogy. **Computer Services:** Information services, descendants of Thomas Minor. **Formerly:** (2005) Thomas Minor Family Society. **Publications:** *The Minor Dia-*

ries. Book. **Price:** $35.00 each (plus $2.50 shipping and handling). **Circulation:** 600. **Conventions/Meetings:** annual reunion.

20648 ■ Tripp Family Association (TFA)

Address Unknown since 2007
Founded: 1996. **Description:** Individuals with the surname Tripp and other Tripp family members. Promotes interest in Tripp family history and genealogy. Serves as a clearinghouse on the Tripp family and its history; assists family historians and genealogists.

20649 ■ Turnbull Clan Association (TCA)

c/o Wally R. Turnbull, Pres.
5216 Tahoe Dr.
Durham, NC 27713
Ph: (919)361-5041 (919)824-5100
Fax: (775)254-6739
E-mail: president@turnbullclan.com
URL: http://www.turnbullclan.com
Contact: Wally R. Turnbull, Pres.
Founded: 1978. **Members:** 300. **Membership Dues:** primary, $20 ● spouse/student, $10. **Staff:** 4. **Budget:** $6,000. **Multinational**. **Description:** Serves as an international Scottish heritage association of the Turnbull clan and septs. Promotes cultural heritage and clan family history. **Formerly:** (2004) Turnbull Clan Association of North America. **Publications:** *Bullseye*, monthly. Newsletter. **Price:** $20.00/year. Alternate Formats: online. **Conventions/Meetings:** annual meeting.

20650 ■ Urbain Baudreau Graveline Genealogical Association (UBGGA)

PO Box 905
Palmer, MA 01069
Ph: (413)283-8378
Free: (800)887-2878
Fax: (413)283-2556
E-mail: info@ubgga.com
URL: http://www.ubgga.com
Contact: Thomas W. Gravelin, Pres.
Founded: 1978. **Members:** 308. **Membership Dues:** regular, $20 (annual) ● sponsor, $25 (annual) ● benefactor, $100 (annual). **Languages:** English, French. **Description:** Works to collect genealogical and historical information. Conducts educational and charitable programs; compiles statistics. **Libraries: Type:** not open to the public. **Holdings:** 1,400; periodicals. **Subjects:** genealogy history. **Computer Services:** Mailing lists, of members. **Publications:** *The Descendants* (in English and French), semiannual. Newsletter. Provides genealogical research and historical information. **Price:** included in membership dues. ISSN: 0894-1831. **Circulation:** 308. **Conventions/Meetings:** biennial convention - odd-numbered years.

20651 ■ Van Voorhees Association (VVA)

c/o Mr. Albert T. Van Voorhies
9 Purdy Ave.
East Northport, NY 11731-4501
E-mail: president@vanvoorhees.org
URL: http://www.vanvoorhees.org
Contact: Mr. Albert T. Van Voorhies, Contact
Founded: 1932. **Members:** 950. **Membership Dues:** junior, $2 (annual) ● regular, $10 (annual) ● sustaining, $15 (annual) ● contributing, $30 (annual) ● life, $200. **Staff:** 4. **Regional Groups:** 2. **Local Groups:** 1. **Description:** Members of the Van Voorhees family. Promotes communication and good fellowship among members. Assists family historians and genealogists; sponsors social activities. **Libraries: Type:** reference. **Holdings:** archival material, articles, books, clippings, periodicals. **Subjects:** Van Voorhees family history and genealogy. **Publications:** *Through a Dutch Door.* Book. Includes 17th century origins. ● *The Van Voorhees Family in America.* Book. Includes information about the first six generations. ● *Van Voorhees Newsbrief*, 3/year. Newsletter. **Price:** included in membership dues. **Circulation:** 950. **Conventions/Meetings:** annual reunion, displays of various family materials - always first Saturday in October.

20652 ■ Vawter - Vauter - Vaughter(s) Family Association (VVV)

c/o J.W. Vawter, Pres.
11298 N US Hwy. 59
Nacogdoches, TX 75965
Ph: (936)560-5254
Fax: (936)569-8626
E-mail: patricia@vawterfamily.org
URL: http://vawterfamily.org
Contact: J.W. Vawter, Pres.
Founded: 1977. **Members:** 300. **Membership Dues:** individual, $10 (annual). **Description:** Individuals with the surname Vawter and its variant spellings; other members of the Vawter and related families. Promotes the study of Vawter family history and genealogy; facilitates communication among Vawter family members. Gathers and disseminates family historical and genealogical information. **Publications:** Newsletter, quarterly. Alternate Formats: online. **Conventions/Meetings:** annual reunion, archives of the association collections and research of members (exhibits) - 3rd weekend of July.

20653 ■ Veitch Historical Society (VHS)

c/o Patricia A. McConnell, VP, Membership
134 Rhonda Dr.
Universal City, TX 78148-3420
Ph: (210)659-6813
E-mail: jmcconn529@aol.com
URL: http://veitchhistoricalsociety.org
Contact: Patricia A. McConnell, VP, Membership
Founded: 1976. **Members:** 400. **Membership Dues:** individual, family, $15 (annual). **Regional Groups:** 19. **Description:** Individuals with the surname Veitch and its variant spellings; other members of the Veitch family. Promotes study of Veitch family history and genealogy; identifies and preserves historic properties and landmarks figuring in Veitch family history. Conducts Veitch family historical and genealogical research; disseminates information on the Veitch family; maintains historic properties and landmarks. **Awards:** Veitch Historical Society Scholarship. **Frequency:** annual. **Type:** monetary. **Recipient:** for descendants of Veitch, Veach, Veatch, and Veech. **Publications:** *Veitch Chronicle*, triennial. Newsletter. Contains Veitch news, history, and genealogy. **Price:** included in membership dues ● *We Veitches, Veatches, Veaches, Veeches, An Historical Treasury of the Descendants of James Veitch, the Sheriffe*. Book. Three volume set. **Price:** $75.00. **Conventions/Meetings:** annual convention and workshop, includes meetings, sightseeing, and visiting.

20654 ■ Waltermire Family Association (WFA)

141 Hudson Ave.
Chatham, NY 12037
Ph: (518)392-4544
E-mail: hw15@juno.com
Contact: Doris E. Witthoft, Pres.
Founded: 1992. **Members:** 225. **Staff:** 1. **Budget:** $500. **Regional Groups:** 1. **State Groups:** 1. **Local Groups:** 1. **Description:** Individuals with the surname Waltermire and its variant spellings. Facilitates communication among members of the Waltermire family. Conducts social activities. **Publications:** *Waltmire Family News*, biennial. Newsletter. **Circulation:** 225. **Conventions/Meetings:** conference.

20655 ■ Wardner Family Historical Association

c/o Jon Wardner, Chm.
2921 Overridge Dr.
Ann Arbor, MI 48104
Ph: (734)973-8039
E-mail: wardner35@msn.com
Contact: Jon Wardner, Chm.
Founded: 1976. **Members:** 90. **Membership Dues:** individual, $15 (annual) ● life, $150. **Staff:** 5. **Description:** Individuals interested in the Wardner family history. Shares family data, photos, and genealogical information. **Libraries: Type:** reference. **Holdings:** archival material, photographs. **Subjects:** family Bibles, Wardner family history. **Computer Services:** database. **Publications:** *Wardners in America*, periodic. Book. Contains information on

family history and genealogy. **Price:** $39.00 includes shipping ● *Words on Wardners*, semiannual. Newsletter. **Circulation:** 550. **Conventions/Meetings:** quadrennial reunion.

20656 ■ Wefel Family Association (WFA)

555 Freeman Rd., Ste.91
Central Point, OR 97502
Ph: (541)664-3622
E-mail: ralphmwefel@cs.com
Contact: Ralph M. Wefel, Chm.
Founded: 1990. **Members:** 200. **Staff:** 1. **Regional Groups:** 1. **Multinational**. **Description:** Individuals with the surname Wefel and its variant spellings; other Wefel family members. Seeks to identify and unite members of the Wefel family. Conducts and promotes family historical and genealogical research; sponsors social activities. **Publications:** *Wefel Across the USA*, annual. Newsletter. Contains news of Wefel family worldwide. **Circulation:** 200.

20657 ■ Wells Family Research Association

PO Box 5427
Kent, WA 98064-5427
E-mail: orinwells@wells.org
URL: http://www.rootsweb.com/~wellsfam/wfrahome.html
Contact: Orin R. Wells, Pres.
Founded: 1988. **Members:** 500. **Membership Dues:** regular, in North America, $12 (annual) ● regular (in Australia and New Zealand), $A 16 (annual) ● regular (in UK and other European countries), EUR 8 (annual). **Staff:** 2. **National Groups:** 3. **Multinational**. **Description:** Open to anyone interested in genealogical research on Wells surname. Seeks to share research information and computerize Wells' information shared through the newsletter, website, and between members and nonmembers. Current project is an international DNA analysis study. **Libraries: Type:** reference. **Holdings:** 50; archival material, books, clippings. **Subjects:** Wells' family information. **Computer Services:** database, matching researchers and family lines. **Publications:** *Wells Chronicles*, quarterly. Journal. Contains Wells genealogical information. **Price:** included in membership dues. **Circulation:** 550. **Conventions/Meetings:** periodic board meeting.

20658 ■ Wert Family History Association (WFHA)

PO Box 240
Port Royal, PA 17082-0240
Ph: (717)527-4399 (717)527-2622
Fax: (717)527-4398
E-mail: jwert@mdi-wert.com
URL: http://www.mdi-wert.com
Contact: Dr. Jonathan M. Wert Jr., Pres.
Founded: 1990. **Members:** 400. **Staff:** 2. **Description:** Individuals with the surname Wert and its variant spellings (Wirt, Wirth, Wertz, etc.); others with an interest in Wert family history and genealogy. Promotes Wert family historical and genealogical scholarship. Serves as a clearinghouse on the Wert family; assists historians and genealogists. **Libraries: Type:** reference. **Holdings:** archival material, articles, books, clippings. **Subjects:** Wert family history and genealogy. **Computer Services:** database, individuals with the surname Wert and its variant spellings. **Publications:** *Wert Family Newsletter*, annual. Alternate Formats: online ● *Wert History*. Book.

20659 ■ Wilkerson/Wilkinson Clearinghouse (WWC)

Address Unknown since 2007
Description: Individuals with the surname Wilkerson or Wilkinson and its variants. Gathers information on the history and genealogy of the Wilkerson/Wilkinson family.

20660 ■ William Burrup Family Organization

c/o Jay G. Burrup, Genealogist
6602 W King Valley Rd.
West Valley City, UT 84128-4217
Ph: (801)250-9017

E-mail: burrupfam@aol.com
Contact: Jay G. Burrup, Genealogist
Members: 500. **Membership Dues:** descendant, $10 (annual). **Description:** Persons interested in the genealogy of the William and Hannah Maria Byington Burrup family, who settled in Utah and Southeastern Idaho. **Computer Services:** Mailing lists. **Publications:** *Burrup Family Newsletter*, periodic. **Circulation:** 150 ● Book: Faith with Every Footstep: A history of William Burrup and Hannah Maria Byington. **Conventions/Meetings:** periodic reunion.

20661 ■ William Geddes Family Organization (WGFO)
c/o Jay G. Burrup, Genealogist
6602 W King Valley Rd.
West Valley City, UT 84128-4217
Ph: (801)250-9017
E-mail: burrupfam@aol.com
Contact: Jay G. Burrup, Genealogist
Members: 500. **Description:** Descendants of William Geddes (1832-1899) and his wives. Geddes immigrated from Scotland in 1854 and settled in Utah and Southeastern Idaho. Seeks to centralize and coordinate Geddes family historical and genealogical research in Scotland and Ireland. Serves as a clearinghouse on the Geddes family and its history; sponsors social activities. **Publications:** *Geddes Gazette*, annual. Newsletter. **Circulation:** 350. **Conventions/Meetings:** periodic reunion.

20662 ■ William Jacob Heckman Family Organization (WJHFO)
200 Los Robles Way
Woodland, CA 95695
Ph: (530)666-5493
Fax: (530)753-7376
E-mail: wlmarble52@hotmail.com
Contact: William Marble, Contact
Founded: 1988. **Members:** 30. **Budget:** $1,000. **Description:** Descendants of William Jacob Heckmann. Promotes and facilitates historical and genealogical research pertaining to the Heckmann and related families. Gathers and disseminates information on the Heckman and related families; assists family historians and genealogists. **Libraries: Type:** not open to the public.

20663 ■ William Kindel Family Organization (WKFO)
111 Shelley Ct.
Folsom, CA 95630
Fax: (916)985-3179
Contact: Fred Kindel, Contact
Founded: 1985. **Staff:** 1. **Description:** Promotes study of the genealogy of William Kindel (17811865) and his wife Elizabeth Webb (1783-1865). Conducts research; serves as a clearinghouse on Kindel and Webb family history and genealogy. **Libraries: Type:** reference. **Holdings:** books, clippings, periodicals. **Subjects:** Kindel and Webb family history and genealogy. **Computer Services:** database, 11,100 Kindels and connections.

20664 ■ Wingfield Family Society
90 Woodstone
Buffalo Grove, IL 60089
E-mail: rwingfi594@aol.com
URL: http://www.wingfield.org
Contact: Billy Wingfield, Pres.
Founded: 1987. **Members:** 900. **Membership Dues:** household, $25 (annual). **Multinational. Description:** Individuals with the surname Wingfield and their relatives or interested persons. **Computer Services:** database, The Master Genealogist. **Telecommunication Services:** electronic mail, vance@wingfield.org. **Publications:** *Monuments of the Ancient Saxon Family of Wingfield*, quarterly. Newsletter. Contains 10 pages of historical and general Wingfield information. **Price:** included in membership dues. ISSN: 1084-5887. **Circulation:** 1,000 ● *Some Records of a Wingfield Family*. Book. **Price:** $35.00 ● *Virginia's True Founder-Edward-Maria Wingfield* ● *Wingfield Arrival Immigration List*, triennial. **Price:** included in membership dues. Alternate Formats: online ● *Wingfield Family Society Newsletter*, quarterly. **Price:** $4.

00/copy ● Wingfield: It's Church, Castle and College. **Conventions/Meetings:** annual reunion and meeting, personalized items from the Wingfield store, and general historical information (exhibits) - usually May.

20665 ■ Woenne/Wonne/Winne Family Association
12800 Briar Forest Dr., Ste.83
Houston, TX 77077-2206
Ph: (281)531-1956
E-mail: bmist@juno.com
Contact: Bernice Mistrot, Sec.
Founded: 1979. **Members:** 75. **Languages:** English, German. **Description:** Persons with the surname Woenne, Wonne or Winne. Records and preserves family history and genealogical records. Compiles statistics. **Libraries: Type:** reference. **Holdings:** archival material. **Publications:** *The Woenne Book*. Booklet. Features the history of Woenne family in Germany and U.S. **Price:** $20.00.

20666 ■ Wolfensberger Family Association (WFA)
c/o David E. Wolfenbarger, Treas.
768 Chain Ridge Rd.
St. Louis, MO 63122
Ph: (314)961-5032
E-mail: bobwolfenbarger@worldnet.att.net
URL: http://www.wolfensberger.org
Contact: W. Frank Wolfenbarger, Pres.
Founded: 1994. **Members:** 400. **Membership Dues:** regular, in U.S., $10 (annual) ● regular, outside U.S., $15 (annual). **Budget:** $4,000. **Languages:** English, German. **Description:** Descendants of Knight Balderbert (1233-1259), who may have participated in the Third Crusade and founded Castle Wolfsburg near Bauma, Switzerland. Promotes interest in the history and genealogy of the Wolfsberger family. Provides support and assistance to family historians and genealogists; facilitates communication among individuals with the surname Wolfensberger and its variant spellings. **Libraries: Type:** reference; not open to the public. **Holdings:** articles. **Subjects:** Wolfensberger family history and genealogy. **Awards:** Award of Merit. **Frequency:** annual. **Type:** recognition. **Recipient:** to an individual who provided outstanding service to the Wolfensberger family. **Publications:** *Wolfensberger Family Association Newsletter*, quarterly. **Circulation:** 500. **Conventions/Meetings:** periodic board meeting and conference.

20667 ■ Young Surname Organization (YSO)
Address Unknown since 2007
Founded: 1985. **Members:** 200. **Membership Dues:** individual, $15 (annual). **Staff:** 1. **Description:** Individuals with the surname Young or Jung and other members of the Young and related families. Promotes study of Young family history and genealogy. Functions as a resource for family historians and genealogists; facilitates communication and good fellowship among Young family members. **Libraries: Type:** reference. **Holdings:** archival material, articles, books, clippings. **Subjects:** Young family history and genealogy. **Also Known As:** (2000) Born Young Newsletter. **Publications:** *Born Young Newsletter*, quarterly. Accepts queries related to genealogy research; publishes historical articles related to persons with young surname (and variant spellings). **Price:** included in membership dues; $15.00 nonmember. ISSN: 0885-1247. **Circulation:** 200. **Advertising:** not accepted.

20668 ■ Zang Family Organization
c/o Gary P. Zang, CPIM, Chm.
15186 Kelly St.
Spring Lake, MI 49456
E-mail: gzang@juno.com
Contact: Gary P. Zang CPIM, Chm.
Founded: 1978. **Description:** Persons with the surname Zang. Promotes and researches the history of the surname Zang. Assists others in genealogical research. **Publications:** none. **Convention/Meeting:** none. **Libraries: Type:** reference. **Holdings:** archival material.

20669 ■ Zartman Association of America (ZAA)
c/o I. William Zartman, Pres.
713 Quaint Acres
Silver Spring, MD 20904
Ph: (301)622-5151
Fax: (301)622-5151
E-mail: zartman@jhu.edu
Contact: I. William Zartman, Pres.
Founded: 1908. **Members:** 1,400. **Regional Groups:** 4. **Description:** Families of American descendents of Alexander and Anna Zartman. Perpetuates the cultural heritage of and promotes contact among members. **Also Known As:** Zortman Association. **Publications:** *The New Zartman Family Book, 1610-1985*. **Price:** $40.00 ● *The Zartman Family History, 1692-1942* ● *The Zartman Family History, 1692-1907* ● *Zartman News*. Newsletter. **Conventions/Meetings:** annual Zartman Family International Reunion (Z-FAIR) - always second Sunday of August, in Brickerville, PA.

Flag

20670 ■ National Flag Day Foundation (NFDF)
c/o The Flag of the United States of America
418 S Broadway
Baltimore, MD 21231
Ph: (410)433-0943
Free: (410)563-FLAG
E-mail: linda@flagday.org
URL: http://www.flagday.org
Contact: Richard M. Patterson, Pres.
Founded: 1982. **Members:** 300. **Staff:** 1. **Budget:** $130,000. **Regional Groups:** 1. **State Groups:** 50. **Description:** Encourages patriotism by promoting National Flag Day, which is observed annually on June 14 and includes the Annual National Pause for the Pledge of Allegiance, a program inviting people throughout America to simultaneously recite the Pledge of Allegiance. Conducts public education programs on the history and origins of the flag and major events in American history. Maintains speakers' bureau. **Libraries: Type:** reference. **Holdings:** audio recordings, books, clippings, video recordings. **Subjects:** American history. **Awards:** Koerber Patriotism Award. **Frequency:** annual. **Type:** recognition. **Recipient:** for extraordinary services and support of patriotic programs of education for national unity. **Additional Websites:** http://www.usflag.org. **Programs:** Living American Flag; Pause for the Pledge of Allegiance. **Projects:** Star-Spangled Banner 50-State Living American Flag. **Supersedes:** U.S. Flag Association; Honor America. **Publications:** *General Educational Resource Handbook*. Includes classroom and teacher materials on the Star-Spangled Banner Flag and historic events. Alternate Formats: online ● Newsletter, semiannual. **Price:** free.

20671 ■ Star-Spangled Banner Flag House Association (SSBFH)
844 E Pratt St.
Baltimore, MD 21202
Ph: (410)837-1793
Fax: (410)837-1812
E-mail: info@flaghouse.org
URL: http://www.flaghouse.org
Contact: Sally Johnston, Exec. Dir.
Founded: 1927. **Members:** 550. **Membership Dues:** family, $35 (annual) ● individual, $25 (annual) ● patron, $50 (annual) ● banner, $100 (annual). **Staff:** 7. **Budget:** $256,000. **Languages:** English, Italian. **Description:** Maintains as a national historic landmark the 1793 house where Mary Pickersgill made the flag that flew over Fort McHenry in 1814 and inspired Francis Scott Key to write the words of the national anthem. Maintains a collection of early American art. Operates adjacent 1812 Museum and museum shop and provides guided tours. Conducts research. Opened a 12,600 square foot museum. **Libraries: Type:** reference. **Holdings:** 500; archival material, books. **Subjects:** 1812 era. **Publications:** *AMERICANA* ● *The Art of the Flag House* ● *The*

Flag House Story ● Francis Scott Key: Poet and Patriot ● The Star, quarterly. Newsletter ● The Star Spangled Banner Flaghouse, Hands-on History. Brochures ● Pamphlets ● Also distributes information packets and teachers' guide material. **Conventions/Meetings:** Flag Symposium ● annual meeting - always April/May, Baltimore, MD ● Society of the War of 1812 Conference.

Genealogy

20672 ■ Acadian Cultural Society (ACS)
PO Box 2304
Fitchburg, MA 01420-0015
E-mail: info@acadiancultural.org
URL: http://acadiancultural.org
Contact: Bruce W. Caissie, Pres.
Founded: 1985. **Members:** 800. **Membership Dues:** individual, $20 (annual) ● family, $30 (annual). **Budget:** $6,000. **Description:** Works to preserve and promote Acadian heritage among people of Acadian descent. Provides a forum for the exchange of Acadian information; conducts educational and research programs. **Libraries: Type:** reference; open to the public. **Holdings:** books, clippings, periodicals. **Subjects:** Acadian history, genealogy, culture. **Publications:** Le Reveil Acadien, quarterly. Journal. Contains articles of Acadian genealogical, historical, or cultural interest. ISSN: 0738-0488. Also Cited As: The Acadian Awakening. **Conventions/Meetings:** annual meeting - always October in Massachusetts.

20673 ■ American Biographical Institute Research Association (ABIRA)
c/o American Biographical Institute
PO Box 31226
Raleigh, NC 27622
Ph: (919)781-8710
Fax: (919)781-8712
E-mail: research@abiworldwide.com
URL: http://www.abiworldwide.com/ABIResearch.htm
Contact: C.L. White, Managing Dir.
Founded: 1979. **Members:** 2,000. **Membership Dues:** individual, $195 (annual) ● life, $875. **Staff:** 18. **For-Profit. Description:** Professional men and women who are listed in "Who's Who" publications united to share contacts, ideas, and talents. Fosters correspondence and organizes tours. Conducts educational programs. **Libraries: Type:** reference. **Holdings:** archival material. **Awards: Type:** recognition. **Computer Services:** database, labels, diskette ● mailing lists. **Publications:** Digest, annual. Magazine. ISSN: 0196-0652. **Circulation:** 2,000. **Advertising:** accepted ● Newsletter, quarterly. **Circulation:** 2,000. **Conventions/Meetings:** annual International World Forum - conference (exhibits).

20674 ■ American-Canadian Genealogical Society (ACGS)
PO Box 6478
Manchester, NH 03108-6478
Ph: (603)622-1554
E-mail: acgs@acgs.org
URL: http://www.acgs.org
Contact: Gerard Savard, Pres.
Founded: 1973. **Members:** 2,200. **Membership Dues:** individual in U.S., $30 (annual) ● individual in Canada, $38 (annual) ● life (in U.S.), $450 ● life (in Canada), $570 ● institution outside U.S. and Canada, $50 (annual). **State Groups:** 1. **Languages:** English, French. **Multinational. Description:** Genealogists interested in ancestries of French-Canadian origin. Serves as resource center for the collection, preservation, and dissemination of American-Canadian and Franco-American genealogical information. Acquires and purchases repertories, genealogies, notarial records, indexes, histories, biographies, journals, census records, and other pertinent data. Encourages the gathering of personal and public data such as is found in Bibles, newspapers, directories, histories, and photographs. Promotes the gathering of civil and church records for publication and/or genealogical research. Encourages individual members to research their family lineage and contribute a

copy of their findings. Conducts genealogical conferences and workshops; sponsors speakers' bureau. **Libraries: Type:** open to the public. **Holdings:** 8,000. **Subjects:** family genealogy, history, marriage records. **Computer Services:** database, library holdings ● database, 3 million scanned images of original Canadian church records. **Committees:** Computer; Editorial; Library; Research Service; Workshops. **Absorbed:** (1985) Acadian Genealogical and Historical Association of New Hampshire; (1997) Acadian Genealogical and Historical Association. **Publications:** American Canadian Genealogist, quarterly. Journal. Includes book reviews, research updates and statistics. **Price:** $25.00/year. ISSN: 1076-3902. **Circulation:** 2,000. **Advertising:** accepted. **Conventions/Meetings:** annual conference and lecture (exhibits) - always fourth Friday weekend in September ● annual workshop (exhibits) - always fourth Friday weekend in April.

20675 ■ American College of Heraldry (ACH)
1836 Ashley River Rd., Ste.396
Charleston, SC 29407-4781
Fax: (904)216-7403
E-mail: info@americancollegeofheraldry.org
URL: http://www.americancollegeofheraldry.org
Contact: David Robert Wooten, Exec. Dir.
Founded: 1972. **Members:** 2,012. **Membership Dues:** individual, $39 (annual). **Description:** Persons having coats of arms or who are interested in heraldry. Includes activities such as: registration of coats of arms officially recognized by foreign office of arms; registration of coats of arms borne in the absence of official recognition; design and registration of new coats of arms for members having no heraldic arms; registration of genealogical lineages. **Libraries: Type:** not open to the public. **Holdings:** 700; articles, books, periodicals. **Subjects:** heraldry, chivalry, flags. **Awards:** Distinguished Fellow. **Frequency:** periodic. **Type:** recognition. **Recipient:** for major contributions to the art and science of heraldry ● Fellow. **Type:** recognition. **Publications:** The Armiger's News, quarterly. Journal. Presents costs of arms and biographies of armigers borne in America. Includes heraldic news, book reviews, and obituaries. **Price:** free for members; $10.00 /year for libraries ● The Heraldic Register of America Volumes 1-10, periodic ● Introduction to the American College of Heraldry. Pamphlet. **Conventions/Meetings:** annual board meeting.

20676 ■ American Family Records Association (AFRA)
PO Box 15505
Kansas City, MO 64106
Contact: Janice Schultz, Pres.
Founded: 1978. **Members:** 215. **Membership Dues:** individual, $22 (annual). **Description:** Institutes and individuals including genealogists, historians, and adoptologists seeking to improve education and availability of information in the fields of family history, genealogy, local history, and adoptive relationships. Conducts training programs to teach research and recording techniques of family history and genealogical data. Maintains a genealogy circulating collection. **Libraries: Type:** reference. **Holdings:** 6,000; books. **Subjects:** genealogy. **Computer Services:** database, members' pedigree tables ● online services, ancestors. **Publications:** Family Records Today, semiannual. Journal. Contains genealogical and family history records, adult adoptee-birth parent articles, legislative updates, book reviews, and calendar of events. **Price:** included in membership dues. ISSN: 0736-1858. **Advertising:** accepted ● Brochure ● Catalog ● Also publishes pedigree chart book and conference papers. **Conventions/Meetings:** annual conference (exhibits) - always July, 3rd weekend, Kansas City, MO metro area.

20677 ■ American-French Genealogical Society (AFGS)
78 Earle St.
PO Box 830
Woonsocket, RI 02895-0870
Ph: (401)765-6141
Fax: (401)765-6141

E-mail: misskoko@aol.com
URL: http://www.afgs.org
Contact: Janice Burkhart, Pres./Librarian
Founded: 1978. **Members:** 2,000. **Membership Dues:** individual in U.S., family in U.S., $32 (annual) ● individual outside U.S., family outside U.S., $40 (annual) ● institutional in U.S., $27 (annual) ● institutional outside U.S., $30 (annual) ● life, in U.S., $384 ● life, outside U.S., $480. **Languages:** English, French. **Description:** Seeks to study and preserve Franco-American heritage and French-Canadian culture in the U.S. by assisting members in researching their ancestors and the events that shaped their lives. Offers research services. Conducts educational programs. **Libraries: Type:** reference; open to the public; lending. **Holdings:** 10,000; archival material, biographical archives, periodicals. **Subjects:** family histories and genealogies, vital statistics. **Awards:** Hall of Fame. **Frequency:** annual. **Type:** recognition. **Recipient:** for individuals of French-Canadian ancestry ● Special Achievement. **Frequency:** annual. **Type:** recognition. **Computer Services:** Mailing lists, of members. **Committees:** Cemetery Project of RI; Cultural Affairs; Publications; Research. **Publications:** AFGnewS, bimonthly. Newsletter. Alternate Formats: online; diskette ● Beginning Franco-American Genealogy. Handbook ● Je Me Souviens, semiannual. Journal. **Advertising:** accepted ● La Cuisine de la Grandmere Volumes I and II. Features French-Canadian cookbooks. ● Also publishes marriage and birth record books from New England and death record books. Dictionnaire National des Canadiens Francais Blue Drouin Series (men), Orange Drouin Series (women) and red series-3 volumes. **Conventions/Meetings:** monthly board meeting ● annual meeting - always October ● weekly meeting.

20678 ■ American Society of Genealogists (ASG)
PO Box 1515
Derry, NH 03038-1515
URL: http://www.fasg.org
Contact: Marsha Hoffman Rising, Pres.
Founded: 1940. **Members:** 50. **Multinational. Description:** Specialists in genealogy and heraldry chosen on the basis of their published work in these fields; membership limited to 50 fellows. Promotes scientific methods of genealogical research through publication of articles in genealogical and historical periodicals and through instructorships at genealogical institutes, seminars, and conferences. **Libraries: Type:** not open to the public. **Awards:** ASG Scholar Award. **Frequency:** annual. **Type:** scholarship. **Recipient:** for genealogists, genealogical librarians and researchers ● Jacobus Award. **Frequency:** annual. **Type:** recognition. **Recipient:** for the best book in the field of genealogy. **Publications:** The Genealogist, quarterly. Journal. **Price:** $25.00/year in U.S.; $45.00 for two years; $33.00/year outside U.S.; $60.00 for two years foreign subscription. ISSN: 0197-1468. **Circulation:** 800. **Conventions/Meetings:** annual meeting.

20679 ■ Ark-La-Tex Genealogical Association (ALTGA)
PO Box 4463
Shreveport, LA 71134-0463
E-mail: jjohnson747@cox.net
URL: http://www.rootsweb.com/~laaltga
Contact: Ray Owens, Pres.
Founded: 1955. **Members:** 215. **Membership Dues:** individual, $20 (annual) ● additional family, $25 (annual). **Description:** Genealogists whose interests lie in the South, especially in the states of Arkansas, Louisiana, and Texas. Collects, preserves, and makes available genealogical materials, documents, and records. Encourages interest in genealogy and sponsors educational programs for its development. Promotes and publicizes the city of Shreveport, LA as a major genealogical research center research center for those interested in records of the entire state of Louisiana, as well as the Arkansas and Texas areas. Cooperates with and assists all other genealogical-historical societies and libraries to advance the study of genealogy. Supports and contributes to the Genealogy Room of the Shreve

Memorial Library in Shreveport, LA. **Libraries: Type:** open to the public. **Holdings:** 36. **Computer Services:** Mailing lists, of members. **Publications:** *The Genie,* quarterly. Journal. **Conventions/Meetings:** annual workshop - every 2nd Saturday of August.

20680 ■ Association of the German Nobility in North America (DAGNA)
1101 W 2nd St.
Benicia, CA 94510
Ph: (707)745-1605
E-mail: gvonstud@aol.com
Contact: Gilbert Von Studnitz, Pres.
Founded: 1980. **Members:** 56. **Staff:** 2. **Languages:** English, German. **Description:** Individuals belonging to noble families in German-speaking areas and who now reside in North America. Seeks to unify and further the cultural ties of individuals belonging to the historical German nobility. Sponsors genealogical studies; compiles statistics on the number of German nobles in North America. **Libraries: Type:** reference. **Holdings:** 685. **Subjects:** genealogy, monarchism, heraldry. **Divisions:** Briefadel (Newer Noble Houses); Uradel (Ancient Noble Houses). **Publications:** *Das Eiserne Buch des Deutschen Adels,* annual. Directory. Lists members under two categories: Uradel (ancient nobility) and Briefadel (new nobility). **Price:** available to members only. **Circulation:** 100 ● *Deutscher Adelsbote,* quarterly. Includes family histories, obituaries, and statistics. **Price:** included in membership dues. **Circulation:** 500. **Advertising:** accepted. Also Cited As: *Der Adelsbote; Deutsche Adelige Hier* ● *Karlrobert Kreiten Cultural Review,* quarterly. Journal. Provides information on concert pianist Karlrobert Kreiten. Includes news of art show openings and music reviews. **Circulation:** 1,000. **Advertising:** accepted. **Conventions/Meetings:** annual conference ● seminar.

20681 ■ Association Houde International
c/o John Houde
Box 82
Glencoe, IL 60022
E-mail: johnh@goglencoe.com
Contact: John Houde, Contact
Founded: 1990. **Languages:** English, French. **Description:** Serves as a clearinghouse for information on the lineage of the Houde family and related family names. Conducts genealogical research programs. Coordinates installation of information plaques on public buildings in France and Quebec. **Libraries: Type:** reference. **Holdings:** archival material. **Publications:** *French Migration to North America/l'Emigration Francaise en l'Ameriquedu Nord* (in English and French). Book. **Price:** $20.00 in U.S.; $23.00 in Canada; EUR 115.00 in France. **Conventions/Meetings:** periodic meeting.

20682 ■ Augustan Society (AS)
PO Box 75
Daggett, CA 92327-0075
Ph: (760)254-9223
Fax: (760)254-1953
E-mail: rcleve@msn.com
URL: http://www.augustansociety.org
Contact: Dr. Robert L. Cleve, Chm.
Founded: 1957. **Members:** 500. **Membership Dues:** regular, $48 (annual). **Staff:** 2. **Budget:** $120,000. **Multinational. Description:** Persons interested in the fields of genealogy, heraldry, monarchy, and chivalry; members of chivalric orders; herald artists; authors. Maintains research service for genealogy and heraldry. Chronicles the usage of coat armor in the Americas and researches, files, and reports on genealogies. Informs members about histories and happenings of chivalric orders, nobility, royalty, and monarchy. Prepares exhibits and materials on medals and decorations. **Libraries: Type:** reference. **Holdings:** 100,000. **Subjects:** heraldry, genealogy, mythology, shamanism, history, royalty and nobility, chivalry, Native Americans, Celts and Druids. **Awards:** Fellowship. **Frequency:** annual. **Type:** recognition. **Recipient:** for best assistance to the society. **Committees:** Chivalry; Heraldry; Monarchy. **Publications:** *The Augustan.* Journal. **Price:** $16.00 for members; $24.00 for nonmembers. **Circulation:**

2,000. **Advertising:** accepted ● *Roll of Arms.* **Conventions/Meetings:** annual meeting.

20683 ■ Bishop Hill Heritage Association (BHHA)
PO Box 92
Bishop Hill, IL 61419-0092
Ph: (309)927-3899
E-mail: bhha@winco.net
URL: http://www.bishophill.com
Contact: Mike Wendel, Contact
Founded: 1962. **Members:** 350. **Membership Dues:** general, $25 (annual). **Staff:** 5. **Budget:** $200,000. **Description:** Seeks to preserve Bishop Hill as a living community and restore and maintain historical properties. Provides educational and research programs; offers children services; maintains museum. **Libraries: Type:** by appointment only. **Holdings:** archival material, articles, audiovisuals, books, business records, clippings. **Subjects:** Bishop Hill Colony, 1846-1861. **Publications:** *Bishop Hill Heritage Association News Bulletin,* quarterly. **Conventions/Meetings:** quarterly board meeting.

20684 ■ Board for Certification of Genealogists (BCG)
PO Box 14291
Washington, DC 20044
E-mail: office@bcgcertification.org
URL: http://www.bcgcertification.org
Contact: Connie Lenzen CG, Pres.
Founded: 1964. **Members:** 350. **Staff:** 1. **Description:** Works to formulate and administer standards of professional genealogical research. Grants certification in classifications of Certified Genealogists, Certified Genealogical Lecturers, and Certified Genealogical Instructors. Maintains free online roster of persons who have been certified. Investigates and offers resolutions for complaints against the work of certificants. **Publications:** *BCG Application Guide.* Book. Provides requirements and procedures for certification. **Price:** $10.00 plus shipping and handling ● *BCG Genealogical Standards Manual.* Book. Clarifies, codifies, and organizes standards generally accepted in the field. **Price:** $20.00 plus shipping and handling ● *Onboard,* 3/year, January, May, September. Newsletter. Includes information about board activities and certification procedures. **Price:** $15.00. **Circulation:** 1,000.

20685 ■ Clan Fergusson Society of North America (CFSNA)
15079 Wagonwheel
Sisters, OR 97759
E-mail: j.fergie@centurytel.net
URL: http://www.cfsna.org
Contact: John F. Ferguson, Pres.
Founded: 1972. **Membership Dues:** regular, associate, $25 (annual) ● new (includes one time $5 initiation fee), $30 (annual) ● life (age 60 and over), $300 ● life (under age 60), $500. **Multinational. Description:** Descendants of the Scottish Fergusson clan bearing the surname Ferguson, Fergie, Fergus, Ferries, Forgie, Keddie, Kiddie, Macadie, MacFergus, MacKeddie, MacKerras, and MacKersey. Conducts genealogical research; facilitates contact among members. **Publications:** *The Bee Line,* quarterly. Newsletter. Features news, excerpts, and information of interest to Fergusons, and all Scots who care about their heritage. **Price:** included in membership dues.

20686 ■ Continental European Family History Association (CEFHA)
c/o John Movius, Pres./Webmaster
PO Box 2660
Salt Lake City, UT 84110-2660
Ph: (801)288-1501
E-mail: cew@xmission.com
URL: http://cefha.org
Contact: John Movius, Pres./Webmaster
Founded: 2001. **Members:** 120. **Membership Dues:** individual, small group, $25 (annual) ● large group (over 500 members), $50 (annual) ● medium group (over 250 members), $35 (annual). **Staff:** 4. **National Groups:** 35. **Languages:** Czech, Dutch, English,

Finnish, French, German, Latvian, Lithuanian, Polish, Romanian, Russian, Slovak. **Description:** Genealogists and genealogical societies specializing in continental European family history. Covers all of the old German, Austro-Hungarian and Russian Empires, the Balkans, all of Scandinavia, plus Armenia, Azerbaijan, Georgia, and Turkey. Collects and disseminates information on conducting family history. Offers research assistance to members. Provides speakers for FHC Seminars, genealogy society meeting and conferences. **Libraries: Type:** reference. **Holdings:** archival material. **Subjects:** Central and East European genealogy and family history. **Awards: Frequency:** annual. **Type:** recognition. **Recipient:** for contribution to genealogy. **Computer Services:** database ● online services. **Absorbed:** (1992) East European Family History Association. **Formerly:** (2003) Federation of East European Family History Societies. **Publications:** *FEEFHS Journal,* annual. **Price:** included in membership dues. **Circulation:** 500. **Conventions/Meetings:** annual International Convention - regional meeting and convention (exhibits).

20687 ■ Czechoslovak Genealogical Society International (CGSI)
PO Box 16225
St. Paul, MN 55116
Ph: (763)595-7799
E-mail: info@cgsi.org
URL: http://www.cgsi.org
Contact: Eugene Aksamit, Pres.
Founded: 1988. **Members:** 4,000. **Membership Dues:** individual, $25 (annual) ● family, $30 (annual) ● sponsor, $45 (annual) ● individual, $45 (biennial) ● family, $55 (biennial) ● sponsor, $85 (biennial). **Budget:** $100,000. **Description:** Individuals of Bohemian, Moravian, Silesian, Carpatho-Rusyn, Slovakian, German, or Jewish descent. Promotes research and interest in Czechoslovakian culture and genealogy. Provides a forum for information exchange; collects and disseminates research materials. **Libraries: Type:** reference. **Holdings:** 1,850; audiovisuals, books, clippings, maps, periodicals. **Subjects:** history, genealogy, Czech and Slovak language and culture. **Computer Services:** Online services, research message board. **Formerly:** (1991) Czechoslovak Genealogical Society. **Publications:** *Czechoslovak Surname Index,* annual. Booklet. Contains seven volumes. **Price:** $5.00 ● *Nase Rodina,* quarterly. Newsletter. Includes research articles, book reviews, announcements of meetings and events, and research queries. **Price:** included in membership dues; $20.00 for nonmembers. ISSN: 1045-8190. **Circulation:** 4,300. **Advertising:** accepted ● *Rocenka,* biennial. Yearbook. ISSN: 1030-5532 ● Videos. Features genealogical workshops. **Conventions/Meetings:** biennial Genealogical/Cultural Conference (exhibits) ● quarterly general assembly.

20688 ■ Daughters of the Republic of Texas (DRT)
510 E Anderson Ln.
Austin, TX 78752
Ph: (512)339-1997
Fax: (512)339-1998
E-mail: drt_busoffice@sbcglobal.net
URL: http://www.drt-inc.org
Contact: Nelma Toney Wilkinson, Gen. Pres.
Founded: 1891. **Members:** 6,470. **Membership Dues:** individual, $20 (annual). **Staff:** 4. **Local Groups:** 106. **Description:** Women over age 16 who are lineal descendants of men or women who lived in Texas during the time of the Republic. Members are custodians of the Alamo, San Antonio, TX, the French Legation, Austin, TX, and the Republic of Texas Museum, Austin, TX. Operates museum of early Texas history artifacts. **Libraries: Type:** reference; open to the public; by appointment only. **Holdings:** archival material, books, clippings. **Subjects:** Texas history. **Publications:** *Daughters Reflections,* semiannual. Newsletter. **Price:** available to members only. **Conventions/Meetings:** annual meeting - always second week of May.

20689 ■ Dominican Institute of Genealogy (DIG)

Address Unknown since 2006

Founded: 1983. **Members:** 28. **Budget:** DP 120,000. **Languages:** Spanish. **Description:** Historians, academics, and genealogy researchers. Encourages the study and practice of genealogy in the Dominican Republic. Identifies the ancestors of Dominican families and constructs family trees. Compiles statistics. **Libraries: Type:** reference. **Holdings:** archival material. **Conventions/Meetings:** annual conference ● triennial general assembly.

20690 ■ Family and Church History Department of the Church of Jesus Christ of Latter-Day Saints

c/o Family History Library
35 NW Temple St.
Salt Lake City, UT 84150-3400
Ph: (801)240-2584
Free: (866)406-1830
Fax: (801)240-1794
E-mail: fhl@ldsfs.net
URL: http://www.familysearch.org
Contact: Richard E. Turley Jr., Managing Dir.

Founded: 1894. **Staff:** 700. **Description:** A department of the Church of Jesus Christ of Latter-day Saints Promotes local and family history (genealogical) research; microfilms and preserves genealogical data, genealogical researchers. Maintains 3,000 family history centers in 64 countries. **Convention/Meeting:** none. **Libraries: Type:** reference. **Holdings:** 2,300,000; archival material, biographical archives, books, periodicals. **Subjects:** oral history interviews, family group records, genealogy, local and family histories, civil and church records. **Computer Services:** database, FamilySearch: Ancestral File and Pedigree Resource File (1880 U.S., 1881 British, 1851 British, 1881 Canadian Censuses), on CD-ROM & Internet ● database, FamilySearch: International Genealogical Index, on CD-ROM & Internet ● database, FamilySearch: Library Catalog, on CD-ROM & Internet ● database, FamilySearch: Social Security Death Index, on CD-ROM & Internet. **Divisions:** Acquisitions; Member Needs; Product Engineering; Records and Information Systems; Research Support Services. **Formerly:** (1944) Genealogical Society of Utah; (1975) Genealogical Society of the Church of Jesus Christ of Latter-day Saints; (2000) Family History Department of the Church of Jesus Christ of Latter-day Saints. **Publications:** *Introduction to Family History.* Manual. Emphasizes doctrines related to family history and includes many quotations from general authorities. **Price:** $4.50 each ● *News of the Family History Library*, quarterly. Newsletter. ISSN: 1052-8644. **Circulation:** 2,100 ● *Research Outlines*, periodic ● *Together Forever*. Video. Offers powerful truths that can make someone's marriage rewarding and a more meaningful family relationship. **Price:** free.

20691 ■ Federation of Genealogical Societies (FGS)

PO Box 200940
Austin, TX 78720-0940
Ph: (512)336-2731
Free: (888)FGS-1500
Fax: (512)336-2732
E-mail: fgs-office@fgs.org
URL: http://www.fgs.org
Contact: Wendy Bebout Elliott PhD, Pres.

Founded: 1975. **Members:** 584. **Membership Dues:** associate, $25 (annual). **Description:** Genealogical societies, genealogical libraries, historical societies, family associations, and other organizations dealing with genealogy and family history. Aims to: stimulate the activities of state and local organizations interested in genealogy and family history; collect, preserve, and disseminate information with reference to genealogical and historical data; promote careful documentation and scholarly genealogical writing and publication; avoid duplication of effort; promote interest in genealogy and family history. Supports state organizations' efforts to promote legislation to open and protect the integrity of birth, death, and marriage records. Provides educational programs to further

genealogical knowledge. Acts as collection agent for National Archives Gift Fund. **Awards: Type:** recognition. **Publications:** *A Guide for the Organization and Management of Genealogical Societies* ● *FGS Forum*, quarterly. Reports on genealogical activities; provides information on records preservation and state and federal legislation affecting genealogical research. **Price:** included in membership dues. **Circulation:** 5,000. **Advertising:** accepted. **Conventions/Meetings:** annual conference and seminar (exhibits).

20692 ■ Genealogical Institute (GI)

c/o Arlene H. Eakle, PhD, Founder/Pres.
875 N 300 E
Tremonton, UT 84337-1010
Free: (800)377-6058
Fax: (435)257-8622
E-mail: arlene@arleneeakle.com
URL: http://arleneeakle.com
Contact: Arlene H. Eakle PhD, Founder/Pres.

Founded: 1972. **Membership Dues:** regular, $97 (annual). **Staff:** 5. **Description:** Publisher and distributor of genealogical how-to-do-it materials. Conducts training activities and client research. Operates speakers' bureau. **Libraries: Type:** open to the public; reference. **Holdings:** 20,000; archival material, audio recordings, books, maps, periodicals, photographs. **Subjects:** family history, genealogy. **Formerly:** (1972) Genealogy Copy Service. **Publications:** *Do Your Family Tree.* Videos ● *Immigration Digest*, periodic. Journal. Contains information about genealogical research resources. Includes maps, bibliographies, and book reviews. **Price:** $13.50/issue, plus shipping and handling. **Circulation:** 500. **Advertising:** accepted ● *Research News*, periodic. Provides notices of new sources available for genealogical research. Includes indexes and reviews of newly published guides and sourcebooks. **Price:** $3.00/issue, plus shipping and handling ● *Booklets* ● *Books* ● Also publishes work forms and outlines; makes available audiotapes, source outlines and charts, and teaching aids. **Conventions/Meetings:** annual Genealogy Symposium - workshop.

20693 ■ Genealogical Society of Flemish Americans (GSFA)

18740 13 Mile Rd.
Roseville, MI 48066
Ph: (810)776-9579
E-mail: marroets@yahoo.com
URL: http://www.rootsweb.com/~gsfa
Contact: Margaret Roets, Corresponding Sec.

Founded: 1976. **Members:** 225. **Membership Dues:** family in U.S. and Canada, $15 (annual) ● outside U.S. and Canada, $17 (annual). **Budget:** $2,500. **Multinational. Description:** People of Flemish or Dutch ancestry residing in the U.S., Canada, or Belgium. Seeks to promote interest in and preserve Belgian culture and history. Assists in genealogical research; assists members with translations. Sponsors programs for the genealogical and historical societies. Conducts oral history and educational programs, including lacemaking and a demonstration of Christmas customs. **Libraries: Type:** reference. **Holdings:** 200; archival material, artwork. **Subjects:** history, art, geography of Belgium. **Telecommunication Services:** electronic mail, lvandamm@ismi.net. **Committees:** Acquisitions; Books and Periodicals. **Publications:** *Flemish American Heritage*, semiannual. Magazine. **Price:** included in membership dues; $5.00 postpaid for libraries. **Circulation:** 250 ● *GSFA Newsletter*, semiannual. Contains genealogical information and personal notes on members. **Price:** included in membership dues ● *Translation of Vital Records from Flemish, French, and Latin* ● *What's Behind My Flemish Name* ● Also makes genealogical charts available. Book of 5 genealogical charts of numbers. **Conventions/Meetings:** monthly meeting - except June, July, December.

20694 ■ German Genealogical Society of America (GGSA)

c/o Southern California Genealogical Society
417 Irving Dr.
Burbank, CA 91504-2408
Ph: (818)843-7247

Fax: (818)843-7262
E-mail: scgs@earthlink.net
URL: http://www.scgsgenealogy.com

Founded: 1986. **Members:** 300. **Membership Dues:** associate, $8 (annual) ● individual in U.S., $22 (annual) ● individual outside U.S., $30 (annual) ● contributing, $30 (annual) ● supporting, $50 (annual). **Staff:** 12. **Description:** Individuals and libraries interested in German genealogy. Encourages and assists individuals in the study of German genealogy and the history of the German-speaking areas of Europe. Provides translation and research services and access to foreign telephone directories, family files, and surname index. Aims to acquire and maintain one of the largest collection of German genealogical research material in the United States. **Libraries: Type:** reference. **Holdings:** 2,700; archival material, books, clippings, maps, periodicals. **Subjects:** German genealogical references. **Additional Websites:** http://feefhs.org/ggsa/frg-ggsa.html. **Conventions/Meetings:** meeting - 4-5/year.

20695 ■ German Research Association (GRA)

PO Box 711600
San Diego, CA 92171-1600
E-mail: membership@gragen.org
URL: http://www.gragen.org
Contact: Kitty Taylor, Pres.

Founded: 1977. **Members:** 500. **Membership Dues:** individual, family, $18 (annual). **Budget:** $10,000. **Description:** Helps and shares with members genealogical research in Germanic lands and U.S. Provides repository of books, microfilms, and related source materials at the San Diego Family History Center. Provides programs and seminars, with speakers on various Germanic research topics, and workshops (members helping members with specific research problems). Provides limited assistance by mail to members; quarterly publication abstracts German-language periodicals and other relevant newsletters, provides articles, and publishes lineage register and queries. Long-term project to extract passenger lists for 1850-1855, not included in "Germans to America" (published in newsletter). **Libraries: Type:** reference. **Holdings:** 500; books, periodicals. **Subjects:** Germanic genealogical research. **Publications:** *The German Connection*, quarterly. Journal. Contains current information on foreign research methods and materials, as well as Germanic customs, history, and cultural heritage. **Price:** $18.00. ISSN: 8755-1756. **Circulation:** 600. **Conventions/Meetings:** monthly workshop, includes presentations - first Saturday, except July and holiday weekends.

20696 ■ Immigrant Genealogical Society (IGS)

PO Box 7369
Burbank, CA 91510-7369
Ph: (818)848-3122
Fax: (818)716-6300
E-mail: lural@juno.com
URL: http://www.immigrantgensoc.org
Contact: Ron Grider, Pres.

Founded: 1982. **Members:** 700. **Membership Dues:** regular, $25 (annual) ● family, $30 (annual) ● contributing, $35 (annual) ● foreign, $40 (annual). **Description:** Individuals interested in genealogy. Works to trace foreign ancestors, particularly from German-speaking areas of Europe. Provides Research services that includes: searches of German genealogical bibliographies, telephone directories, and *Familienkundliche Nachrichten*, a German genealogical publication for research queries; mail order inquiries of German maps and researchers. **Libraries: Type:** reference. **Holdings:** audio recordings, books, maps, periodicals, software. **Subjects:** genealogy and local history; German immigrant sources (including passenger lists), New England, Pennsylvania, NY, NJ; large collection of German language genealogical sources, Switzerland, Mecklenburg. **Committees:** German Genealogical Research Group. **Special Interest Groups:** Pommern. **Also Known As:** Immigrant Library. **Publications:** *German-American Genealogy*, semiannual. Journal. Contains articles, queries, maps, and FANA listings.

Price: included in membership dues. **Circulation:** 700 ● *Immigrant Genealogical Society Newsletter*, monthly. **Circulation:** 700 ● *Pommern S.I.G. Newsletter (Die Pommerschen Leute)*, quarterly. **Conventions/Meetings:** monthly meeting, includes genealogical speakers - usually first Friday ● monthly workshop - usually second Sunday.

20697 ■ International Association of Jewish Genealogical Societies (IAJGS)
c/o Anne Feder Lee, Pres.
7207 Kuahono St.
Honolulu, HI 96825
Ph: (808)395-0115
E-mail: president@iajgs.org
URL: http://www.iajgs.org
Contact: Anne Feder Lee, Pres.
Founded: 1987. **Members:** 75. **Multinational.** **Description:** Acts as an umbrella organization for Jewish genealogical societies worldwide representing 10,000 individuals. Coordinates efforts to advance the work of its members. **Awards:** Lifetime Achievement Award. **Frequency:** annual. **Type:** recognition ● Outstanding Contribution to Jewish Genealogy. **Frequency:** annual. **Type:** recognition. **Recipient:** for contributions via internet, print or electronic product ● Outstanding Programming or Project. **Frequency:** annual. **Type:** recognition. **Recipient:** for a program or project that advances the objectives of Jewish genealogy ● Outstanding Publication by a Member Organization of IAJGS. **Frequency:** annual. **Type:** recognition. **Formerly:** (1998) Association of Jewish Genealogical Societies. **Conventions/Meetings:** annual International Conference on Jewish Genealogy - meeting and seminar, with research trips (exhibits) - usually June or July.

20698 ■ International Society for British Genealogy and Family History (ISBGFH)
PO Box 350459
Westminster, CO 80035-0459
Ph: (303)422-9371
E-mail: admin@isbgfh.org
URL: http://www.isbgfh.org
Contact: Gordon Gray, Pres.
Founded: 1979. **Members:** 500. **Membership Dues:** single in North America, $20 (annual) ● family, $25 (annual) ● life, single, $300 ● life, family, $375 ● single outside North America, $25 (annual). **Multinational.** **Description:** Professional and amateur genealogists with an interest in the genealogy and family history of persons of British descent. **Awards:** Writing Contest. **Frequency:** annual. **Type:** recognition. **Publications:** *International Society for British Genealogy and Family History—Newsletter*, quarterly. Includes articles, book reviews and suggested reading list for beginning genealogical researchers. **Price:** included in membership dues. ISSN: 0736-8054. **Circulation:** 800 ● Also publishes research findings; makes available list of suggested texts for experienced researchers. **Conventions/Meetings:** annual workshop, with research in the family history library.

20699 ■ Irish Genealogical Foundation (IGF)
PO Box 7575
Kansas City, MO 64116
Fax: (816)454-2410
E-mail: mike@irishroots.com
URL: http://www.irishroots.com
Contact: Michael O'Laughlin, Contact
Founded: 1978. **Members:** 7,000. **Membership Dues:** basic online only (Irish Roots Cafe), $29 (periodic) ● regular (with 6 issues of Journal of Irish Families), $59 (annual) ● gold (includes online and hardcopy journal, extra free choice, with 12 issues of Journal of Irish Families), $114 (annual). **Staff:** 1. **Multinational.** **Description:** Genealogists, historians, rare book collectors, and Irish-American enthusiasts. Promotes Irish cultural preservation. Seeks to assist researchers in Irish family history and genealogy. Offers audiocassette programs. Operates speakers' bureau. **Libraries:** **Type:** reference. **Holdings:** 3,000. **Subjects:** history, family research, biography. **Computer Services:** database, Irish surname spelling, family history, periodical index ● mailing lists, of buyers. **Also Known As:** Irish Family Journal. **Publica-**

tions: *Beginners Guide to Irish Family Research.* Book. **Price:** $12.95 ● *The Book of Irish Families, Great and Small.* **Price:** $32.95 ● *Complete Book for Tracing Your Irish Ancestors.* **Price:** $26.00 ● *Complete Book of Irish Family Names.* **Price:** $15.00 ● *Families of Co. Clare.* Book. **Price:** $34.00 ● *Families of Co. Cork.* Book. **Price:** $34.00 ● *Families of Co. Dublin.* Book. **Price:** $34.00 ● *Families of Co. Galway.* Book. **Price:** $34.00 ● *Families of Co. Limerick.* Book. **Price:** $34.00 ● *Gaelic Titles and Forms of Address.* Book. **Price:** $19.95 ● *The Irish Book of Arms.* Book. **Price:** $75.00 ● *Irish Names and Surnames.* Book. **Price:** $39.95 ● *Keating's History of Ireland.* Book. Includes three volumes. **Price:** $125.00 ● *King James Irish Army List.* Book. **Price:** $125.00 ● *Master Book of Irish Placenames.* **Price:** $24.00 ● *Master Book of Irish Surnames.* **Price:** $24.00 ● *O'Lochlainn's Personal Journal of Irish Families*, monthly. Contains family and surname research articles and listings and book reviews. **Price:** included in membership dues; $119.00 for nonmembers. **Circulation:** 15,000. **Advertising:** accepted. Also Cited As: *Irish Family Journal* ● *Poetry and Song of Old Ireland.* Book. **Price:** $45.00 ● *Social History of Ancient Ireland.* Book. **Price:** $145.00 ● *Tribes and Customs of Hy Fiachrach.* Book. **Price:** $129.00. **Conventions/Meetings:** periodic Genealogy Seminar ● annual Irish Family Reunion - meeting (exhibits) - usually May or September in Ireland ● periodic Irish Family Seminar.

20700 ■ Irish Genealogical Society International (IGSI)
5768 Olson Memorial Hwy.
Golden Valley, MN 55422
E-mail: questions@irishgenealogical.org
URL: http://www.irishgenealogical.org
Contact: Virginia McDermott, Contact
Founded: 1976. **Members:** 25. **Membership Dues:** regular, in U.S., $25 (annual) ● regular, outside U.S., $30 (annual). **Description:** A division of the Institute of Family History and Genealogy (see separate entry). Genealogists united to promote and encourage the study of Irish genealogy and other types of Irish studies. Holds seminars and lectures. Maintains 150 volume library and biographical archives. **Committees:** Genealogy; Heraldry. **Supersedes:** Irish Family History Society. **Publications:** *Irish Genealogy*, periodic ● *Manual for Irish Genealogy* ● *The Septs*, quarterly. Journal. **Price:** included in membership dues. **Conventions/Meetings:** monthly meeting - always second Monday, Pawtucket, RI.

20701 ■ Italian Genealogical Group (IGG)
PO Box 626
Bethpage, NY 11714-0626
E-mail: info@italiangen.org
URL: http://www.italiangen.org
Contact: Angela LaGiglia, Pres.
Founded: 1993. **Members:** 616. **Membership Dues:** individual in U.S., $22 (annual) ● individual outside U.S., family, $27 (annual). **Description:** Individuals of Italian descent. Promotes study of Italian family history and genealogy. Serves as a clearinghouse on Italian history, culture, and genealogy; sponsors educational and social programs. **Libraries:** **Type:** not open to the public; reference. **Holdings:** 170; books, periodicals. **Subjects:** Italian history, culture, genealogy. **Computer Services:** database, Italian surnames. **Publications:** *Italian Genealogical Newsletter*, monthly. Contains timely articles of interest to members. **Advertising:** accepted. Alternate Formats: online. **Conventions/Meetings:** monthly meeting - September to June.

20702 ■ Jewish Genealogical Society (JGS)
PO Box 286398
New York, NY 10128-0004
Ph: (212)294-8326
E-mail: info@jgsny.org
URL: http://www.jgsny.org
Contact: Alex E. Friedlander, Pres.
Founded: 1977. **Members:** 839. **Membership Dues:** regular, $36 (annual) ● out of town, outside U.S., $36 (annual) ● family, $45 (annual) ● sustaining, $60 (annual) ● supporting, $100 (annual) ● patron, $250

(annual). **Description:** Aims to nurture, assist and promote Jewish genealogical research through innovative programs, seminars and workshops; disseminate information through a quarterly journal, web site, and publications; and support archival programs and repositories. Although the group does not conduct research for individuals, it does offer advice, assistance, and sources to members searching for genealogical information. **Libraries:** **Type:** reference; open to the public. **Holdings:** books. **Computer Services:** database, Brooklyn naturalization. **Publications:** *DOROT*, quarterly. Journal. **Price:** included in membership dues. **Circulation:** 1,175. **Advertising:** accepted ● *Genealogical Resources in New York.* Book. Serves as a guide to genealogical resources in libraries, archives, and government agencies in New York. **Price:** $42.50 for members; $49.95 for nonmembers. Alternate Formats: online ● *Syllabus - 19th International Conference on Jewish Genealogy, 1999*, periodic ● Reports. **Price:** $3.00 ● Brochure. Alternate Formats: online. **Conventions/Meetings:** annual Basics and Beyond - seminar - always March ● periodic International Conference on Jewish Genealogy ● monthly lecture, program - September through June.

20703 ■ Johannes Schwalm Historical Association (JSHA)
PO Box 127
Scotland, PA 17254-0127
E-mail: halschwalm@prodigy.net
URL: http://www.jsha.org
Contact: Hal Schwalm, Webmaster
Founded: 1979. **Members:** 425. **Membership Dues:** individual, $25 (annual). **Description:** Individuals and associations. Promotes and performs research regarding Hessians who remained in America and their descendants. (Hessians were German auxiliaries to the British Crown in North America during the American Revolution.) Publishes, preserves, and disseminates information on Hessian art, culture, heritage, history, genealogy, and the economic, religious, and social practices of Americans whose ancestors came to the U.S. as Hessians during the Revolutionary War. Maintains biographical archives and depository. **Libraries:** **Type:** reference. **Holdings:** archival material, books, clippings, monographs. **Subjects:** Hessian soldiers and their descendants. **Computer Services:** database ● mailing lists. **Committees:** Editorial. **Publications:** *The Hessians - The Journal of the Johannes Schwalm Historical Association.* **Conventions/Meetings:** annual meeting (exhibits) - always the weekend following July 4.

20704 ■ Knowles/Knoles/Noles Family Association (KKNFA)
c/o Robert B. Noles, Historian
133 Acadian Ln.
Mandeville, LA 70471
Ph: (985)845-4688
Fax: (985)845-4688
E-mail: rbnoles@bellsouth.net
URL: http://www.kknfa.org
Contact: Robert B. Noles, Historian
Founded: 1983. **Members:** 100. **Membership Dues:** individual (and spouse), $20 (annual) ● library, $45 (annual) ● business, $60 (annual) ● student, $5 (annual). **Budget:** $2,000. **Description:** Genealogical association open to descendants of all Knowles ancestors (all spellings of Knowles) and associated lines. Holds membership and research meetings at various locations around the country on even numbered years. Sponsors Knowles (all spellings of Knowles) genealogical research. **Libraries:** **Type:** not open to the public. **Holdings:** articles, books, business records, clippings, periodicals. **Subjects:** genealogies for all Knowles ancestors. **Awards:** Knowles Kousin. **Type:** recognition. **Recipient:** to research contributor ● **Type:** recognition. **Computer Services:** database, genealogy of Knowles/Knoles/Noles lines. **Publications:** *Knowles Ancestral Times*, quarterly. Newsletter. Contains information bulletins. **Price:** included in membership dues. **Circulation:** 80. **Advertising:** accepted. Alternate Formats: online. Also Cited As: *KAT* ● Newsletter, quarterly. Contains news information on the association. **Price:**

$15.00 for members. **Conventions/Meetings:** biennial Knowles Genealogies - reunion.

20705 ■ Lancaster Mennonite Historical Society (LMHS)
2215 Millstream Rd.
Lancaster, PA 17602-1499
Ph: (717)393-9745
Fax: (717)393-8751
E-mail: lmhs@lmhs.org
URL: http://www.lmhs.org
Contact: Beth E. Graybill, Dir.
Founded: 1958. **Members:** 2,800. **Membership Dues:** individual, $30 (annual) ● family, $45 (annual) ● sustaining, $100 (annual) ● supporting, $250 (annual) ● benefactor, $500 (annual) ● patron, $1,000 (annual). **Staff:** 8. **Budget:** $500,000. **Languages:** English, German. **Multinational. Description:** Individuals interested in the historical background, religious thought and expression, culture, and genealogy of Mennonite- and Amish-related groups originating in Pennsylvania. Sponsors field trips and exhibits. Maintains speakers' bureau, library, archives, and museum. Conducts historical and genealogical seminars, research publications, and children's programs. Compiles statistics. **Libraries: Type:** open to the public. **Holdings:** 29,000; archival material, books, maps, periodicals, photographs, video recordings. **Subjects:** church history, family history, theology, local history, cemetery plots. **Awards:** Community Historians Award. **Frequency:** annual. **Type:** monetary. **Recipient:** for high school level projects in local school. **Computer Services:** database. **Boards:** Hans Herr House. **Publications:** *Mennonite Sources and Documents Series.* Books ● *Mirror*, bimonthly. Newsletter. **Price:** $5.00/year. ISSN: 0738-7237. **Circulation:** 9,500 ● *Pennsylvania Mennonite Heritage*, quarterly. Journal. **Price:** $25.00/year. ISSN: 0148-4036. **Circulation:** 3,100 ● Books. **Conventions/Meetings:** periodic competition ● annual conference (exhibits) ● annual Genealogy Conference (exhibits) ● periodic lecture ● periodic seminar.

20706 ■ Morse Society (MS)
3 Poplar Rd.
Beacon, NY 12508
E-mail: president@morsesociety.org
URL: http://www.morsesociety.org
Contact: Dr. Stafford-Ames Morse, Pres.
Founded: 1892. **Members:** 778. **Membership Dues:** regular, in U.S., $20 (annual) ● regular, in Canada, $22 (annual) ● overseas, $25 (annual). **Staff:** 11. **Budget:** $20,000. **Description:** Membership fee by age. Individuals with an interest in the history and genealogy of the Morse and Moss families in North America. Promotes accurate historical and genealogical research. Conducts research; gathers and preserves records pertaining to Morse and Morss family history and genealogy; provides assistance to family historians and genealogists; sells Morse family memorabilia. **Libraries: Type:** reference. **Holdings:** 75; archival material, books. **Subjects:** Morse and Moss family history and genealogy. **Computer Services:** database, Morse, Moss family history and genealogy. **Publications:** *Morse Newsletter*, quarterly. Contains 24 pages of information. **Price:** included in membership dues. **Circulation:** 800. Alternate Formats: online. **Conventions/Meetings:** biennial reunion - even numbered years, always in October in Massachusetts or other eastern locations.

20707 ■ Mountain Press Research Center
PO Box 400
Signal Mountain, TN 37377-0400
Ph: (423)886-6369
Free: (800)856-4713
Fax: (423)886-5312
E-mail: jimd@mountainpress.com
URL: http://www.mountainpress.com
Contact: James L. Douthat, Owner
Founded: 1980. **Staff:** 2. **For-Profit. Description:** Works as a genealogical and historical research center. Promotes genealogical and historical research in the mid-Atlantic and Southeastern regions of the U.S. Provides research materials and information. Conducts training events. Arranges displays of

genealogical and historical materials. **Libraries: Type:** reference. **Holdings:** 12,000. **Subjects:** genealogy and history. **Computer Services:** Mailing lists, of addresses and areas of interest. **Publications:** *Southern Genealogical Index*, quarterly ● *Tennessee Genealogy and History*, 3/year. **Price:** $20.00/year. **Circulation:** 500 ● Books. **Conventions/Meetings:** workshop.

20708 ■ National Genealogical Society (NGS)
3108 Columbia Pike, Ste.300
Arlington, VA 22204-4304
Ph: (703)525-0050
Free: (800)473-0060
Fax: (703)525-0052
E-mail: ngs@ngsgenealogy.org
URL: http://www.ngsgenealogy.org
Contact: Janet A. Alpert, Pres.
Founded: 1903. **Members:** 18,000. **Membership Dues:** organization/society, senior, $50 (annual) ● individual, $55 (annual) ● family, $70 (annual) ● contributing, $100 (annual) ● sustaining, $250 (annual) ● patron, $500 (annual) ● benefactor, $1,000 (annual) ● senior - family, $65 (annual) ● life, $2,500. **Staff:** 12. **Budget:** $1,500,000. **Description:** Individuals, families, societies and organizations. Promotes genealogical research and education; stimulates and fosters preservation and publication of records of genealogical interest including national, state, county, township, city, town, church, cemetery, Bible, and family records. **Libraries: Type:** reference; lending. **Holdings:** 30,000; books, periodicals. **Subjects:** genealogy, local history, source material, family history. **Awards:** Award of Distinction. **Frequency:** annual. **Type:** recognition. **Recipient:** for outstanding individual ● Award of Merit. **Frequency:** annual. **Type:** recognition. **Recipient:** for individuals, nonprofit genealogical or historical organization ● Distinguished Service Award. **Frequency:** annual. **Type:** recognition. **Recipient:** for a member of NGS ● Family History Writing Award. **Frequency:** annual. **Type:** recognition ● Filby Award for Librarianship. **Frequency:** annual. **Type:** recognition ● Honorary Member. **Frequency:** annual. **Type:** recognition. **Recipient:** for an individual or institution ● Rubincam Youth Award. **Frequency:** annual. **Type:** recognition. **Committees:** Family Health and Heredity; Genealogical Standards; Records Preservation and Access; Youth Resources. **Publications:** *National Genealogical Society—Newsletter*, bimonthly. Provides information on current events in genealogy and news of the society. **Price:** included in membership dues. **Circulation:** 17,500. **Advertising:** accepted ● *National Genealogical Society Quarterly.* Journal. Contains documented genealogies and articles. **Price:** included in membership dues. **Circulation:** 17,500. **Advertising:** accepted ● *UPfront with NGS*, semimonthly. Newsletter. Contains events calendar, press releases and NGS announcements. Alternate Formats: online. **Conventions/Meetings:** annual Conference in the States, exhibitors represent societies, software companies, booksellers (exhibits).

20709 ■ National Society Descendants of Early Quakers (NSDEQ)
PO Box 453
Abingdon, MD 21009-0453
Ph: (301)262-1019
Fax: (301)262-5037
E-mail: mlwinton@terraworld.net
URL: http://www.terraworld.net/mlwinton
Contact: Mrs. Frederic J. Licht, Natl. Overseer
Founded: 1980. **Members:** 265. **Membership Dues:** life, $100 ● junior, $20 ● regular, $35. **Staff:** 9. **State Groups:** 1. **Description:** Represents lineal and collateral descendants of early members of the Religious Society of Friends, commonly known as Quakers. Promotes appreciation for and preservation of historical and genealogical information regarding Quakers. Sponsors educational programs; maintains library and biographical archives. **Publications:** *Plain Language*, annual. Magazine. Includes directory. **Price:** included in membership dues. **Conventions/Meetings:** annual meeting - always April, in Washington, DC.

20710 ■ New England Historic Genealogical Society (NEHGS)
101 Newbury St.
Boston, MA 02116
Ph: (617)536-5740
Free: (888)296-3447
Fax: (617)536-7307
E-mail: info@nehgs.org
URL: http://www.newenglandancestors.org
Contact: Mr. D. Brenton Simons, Pres./CEO
Founded: 1845. **Members:** 21,000. **Membership Dues:** research, $75 (annual) ● family, $90 (annual) ● student, $35 (annual) ● associate, $250-$499 (annual) ● patron (minimum), $1,500 (annual) ● life (minimum), $3,000 ● life benefactor (minimum), $6,000 ● friend of society, $125-$249 (annual) ● sustaining, $250-$499 (annual). **Staff:** 50. **Budget:** $5,000,000. **Description:** Collects and preserves materials relating to family history and local history, mainly pertaining to the six New England states, New York state, Quebec, Atlantic Canada, Ireland and England, but also has material available for every region in the U.S. Conducts lectures, tours, and other programs on local and national levels, and maintains an extensive online database of searchable names and data. **Libraries: Type:** reference; open to the public. **Holdings:** 300,000; archival material, books, papers. **Subjects:** genealogy, local history. **Awards:** Coddington Award of Merit. **Frequency:** periodic. **Type:** recognition. **Recipient:** for genealogical excellence. **Computer Services:** database, genealogical databases available to members. **Telecommunication Services:** electronic mail, nehgs@nehgs.org. **Publications:** *New England Ancestors*, 5/year. Magazine. **Circulation:** 21,000. **Advertising:** accepted. Alternate Formats: online ● *The New England Historical and Genealogical Register*, quarterly. Journal. Contains articles, announcements, and genealogical queries. **Circulation:** 21,000. **Advertising:** accepted. Alternate Formats: online ● Also publishes genealogical records, indexes to source materials, and family genealogies. **Conventions/Meetings:** annual Come Home to New England - seminar, allowing members unable to visit the society on a regular basis to partake in staffed lectures and research their ancestry ● periodic seminar and workshop.

20711 ■ New York Genealogical and Biographical Society (NYG&B)
122 E 58th St.
New York, NY 10022-1939
Ph: (212)755-8532
Fax: (212)754-4218
E-mail: publications@nygbs.org
URL: http://www.newyorkfamilyhistory.org
Contact: William P. Johns, Exec. Dir.
Founded: 1869. **Members:** 3,100. **Membership Dues:** outside New York City, $50 (annual) ● inside New York City, $60 (annual). **Staff:** 12. **Budget:** $1,100,000. **Description:** Collects, preserves, and makes available to the public, information relating to genealogy, biography, and history, especially of the state of New York. **Libraries: Type:** open to the public. **Holdings:** 130,000; books, films, papers, periodicals. **Subjects:** genealogy and local history of New York and Eastern U.S. **Awards:** NYG&BS Book Award. **Frequency:** annual. **Type:** recognition. **Recipient:** for the best compiled N.Y. genealogy. **Publications:** *The New York Genealogical and Biographical Record*, quarterly. Magazine. Contains genealogy articles, records, and information pertaining to New York City and State family history. Includes annual report and book reviews. **Price:** included in membership dues; $30.00 /year for nonmembers. ISSN: 0028-7237. **Circulation:** 3,200. **Advertising:** accepted. Alternate Formats: microform ● *NYG&B Newsletter*, quarterly ● Also publishes source records from New York; offers list of publications. **Conventions/Meetings:** monthly lecture.

20712 ■ Ohio Genealogical Society (OGS)
713 S Main St.
Mansfield, OH 44907-1644
Ph: (419)756-7294
Fax: (419)756-8681

E-mail: ogs@ogs.org
URL: http://www.ogs.org
Contact: Thomas Stephen Neel, Library Dir.
Founded: 1959. **Members:** 6,550. **Membership Dues:** single, $32 (annual) ● joint, $37 (annual) ● family, $42 (annual) ● student, $25 (annual) ● life (single), $600 ● life (joint), $900. **Staff:** 3. **Budget:** $357,925. **Regional Groups:** 3. **State Groups:** 2. **Local Groups:** 96. **For-Profit. Description:** Genealogists, historians, libraries, and other interested individuals from throughout the U.S. Promotes genealogical research and the preservation of historical records in Ohio. Facilitates the exchange of ideas and information. Sponsors educational programs on family lineage in Ohio. Maintains speakers' bureau. **Libraries: Type:** reference. **Holdings:** 25,000; periodicals. **Subjects:** genealogy, Ohio history. **Awards:** Ohio Book Award. **Frequency:** annual. **Type:** recognition. **Computer Services:** database, on web site. **Divisions:** Cemetery; Education; Library; Publicity. **Publications:** *Chapter Directory*, periodic. Includes Ohio genealogical books being sold by local chapters. **Price:** $10.00. **Circulation:** 500. **Advertising:** accepted ● *First Families of Ohio Roster* ● *Ohio Cemeteries* ● *Ohio Civil War Genealogy Journal*, quarterly. Magazine. Contains information on family history and documentation on Ohio's Civil War soldiers. **Price:** $20.00. **Circulation:** 1,000. **Advertising:** accepted ● *Ohio Genealogical Society Quarterly*. Magazine. Features condensed family histories, church, cemetery, and court records, newspaper abstracts, Bible records and book notices. **Price:** included in membership dues. **Circulation:** 6,550. **Advertising:** accepted ● *Ohio Genealogy News*, bimonthly. Magazine. Includes calendar of events, chapter announcements, library acquisitions, queries, and membership information. **Price:** included in membership dues. **Circulation:** 6,550. **Advertising:** accepted ● *Ohio Records and Pioneer Families*, quarterly. Contains cemetery and family records, court abstracts, and genealogical articles. **Price:** $20.00. **Circulation:** 1,400. **Conventions/Meetings:** annual Chapter Management Seminar - competition, training for chapter officers ● annual conference (exhibits).

20713 ■ Orangeburgh German Swiss Genealogical Society (OGSGS)

PO Box 974
Orangeburg, SC 29116-0974
E-mail: joejones@joejones.com
URL: http://www.rootsweb.com/~scogsgs
Contact: Josephine F. Shuler, Pres./Exec. Sec.
Founded: 1981. **Members:** 400. **Membership Dues:** individual, $18 (annual) ● family, $24 (annual). **Description:** Descendents of Settlers of Orangeburg, SC from 1735-1800; others interested in Orangeburg genealogy and history. Collects, preserves, and disseminates information on the early settlers of Orangeburg; provides information about research sources; promotes fellowship among members. **Libraries: Type:** reference. **Holdings:** 125. **Subjects:** family histories. **Committees:** Local Arrangements; Publications. **Publications:** *OGSGS Membership File*, quarterly. Newsletter ● *Orangeburgh German-Swiss Newsletter*, quarterly. Includes book reviews, information requests, president's report, cemetery records, and other genealogical data. ● Also publishes lineage charts. **Conventions/Meetings:** annual Oktoberfest - meeting (exhibits) ● annual seminar and meeting (exhibits).

20714 ■ Orphan Train Heritage Society of America (OTHSA)

PO Box 322
Concordia, KS 66901
Ph: (785)243-4471
E-mail: othsa@msn.com
URL: http://www.orphantrainriders.com
Contact: Stephanie Haiar, Curator
Founded: 1986. **Members:** 350. **Membership Dues:** orphan trail rider, $10 (annual) ● spouse of orphan trail rider, $15 (annual) ● life (orphan trail rider), $100 ● nonrider, $25 (annual) ● joint (nonrider), $35 (annual) ● life (individual), $250 ● life (joint), $350. **Staff:** 1. **Budget:** $35,000. **State Groups:** 12. **Descrip-**tion: Orphan train riders and their descendants, genealogists, and others interested in the orphan trains. (Orphan trains were used by the New York Children's Aid Society and other charitable institutions from 1854 to the early 1930's to relocate inner-city orphans to sparsely-populated rural areas where they were more likely to find adoptive homes.) Seeks to gather and disseminate information concerning orphan train riders and their biological families. Conducts genealogical research. Maintains Orphan Train Riders Research Center, a museum with archive of newspapers, census records, oral histories, letters, and photographs pertaining to the orphan trains. Makes available educational packets. Operates speakers' bureau; compiles statistics. **Libraries: Type:** reference; by appointment only. **Holdings:** 210. **Subjects:** social work, foster care, New York census data, orphan train history, New York Children's Aid Society, New York Foundling Hospital, genealogy, orphan train riders. **Awards:** Charles Loring Brace Award. **Frequency:** annual. **Type:** recognition. **Recipient:** for the best person(s) who worked towards preserving the history of Orphan Train Rides placed out by the Children's Aid Society ● Sister Irene Award. **Frequency:** annual. **Type:** recognition. **Recipient:** for person or persons' best preserving the history of Orphan Train Rides placed out by the New York Foundling Hospital. **Computer Services:** database, train riders. **Additional Websites:** http://www.orphantraindepot.com. **Telecommunication Services:** electronic mail, bbranches@quietfire.com. **Committees:** Public Relations; Research. **Publications:** *Crossroads*, quarterly. Newsletter. Includes research reports, and personal stories. **Price:** included in membership dues; $25.00 /year for nonmembers. ISSN: 1044-5544. **Circulation:** 2,500 ● *Orphan Train Riders: Their Own Stories Vols. 1-4.* Book. **Conventions/Meetings:** annual reunion and workshop, special programs featuring orphan train rider stories, exhibits, and programs, as well as local activities and fun food (exhibits).

20715 ■ Palatines to America: Researching German-Speaking Ancestry (Pal-Am)

611 E Weber Rd.
Columbus, OH 43211-1097
Ph: (614)267-4700
E-mail: info@palam.org
URL: http://www.palam.org
Contact: Odell Miller, Pres.
Founded: 1975. **Members:** 3,290. **Membership Dues:** individual, $35 (annual) ● family, $40 (annual) ● life, $875. **Staff:** 2. **State Groups:** 8. **Description:** Genealogists, researchers and other individuals interested in the migration of German-speaking people from Europe to America. Promotes interest in and study of German immigration; facilitates information exchange on the social and historical backgrounds of German-speaking immigrants. Maintains immigrant ancestor register and ancestor charts. **Libraries: Type:** reference. **Holdings:** 5,000; books, periodicals. **Subjects:** Germanic genealogy, German history, European history. **Awards:** Citation. **Type:** recognition ● Harvey Harsh. **Frequency:** annual. **Type:** recognition. **Computer Services:** Information services, web catalog. **Affiliated With:** Federation of Genealogical Societies. **Publications:** *Palatine Immigrant*, quarterly. Magazine. Contains articles on the life and times of immigrants; includes instructional articles and other genealogical research information. ISSN: 0884-5735 ● *Palatine Patter*, quarterly. Newsletter. Contains information on national and regional activities. **Conventions/Meetings:** annual conference - always June.

20716 ■ Polish Genealogical Society of America (PGSA)

984 N Milwaukee Ave.
Chicago, IL 60622
E-mail: pgsamerica@aol.com
URL: http://www.pgsa.org
Contact: Edmund Iwanski, Pres.
Founded: 1978. **Members:** 2,000. **Membership Dues:** regular, in U.S., $20 (annual) ● regular, in Canada, $25 (annual) ● regular, outside U.S. and Canada, $35 (annual). **Budget:** $70,000. **Lan-**guages: English, German, Latin, Polish, Russian. **Description:** Family tree hobbyists involved in researching ancestors from Poland (including Lithuanians and Jews and Russians) and all areas formerly associated with Poland. Promotes Polish genealogical study and establishes communication among researchers. Informs members of new sources of information. **Libraries: Type:** open to the public. **Holdings:** 1,000; books. **Subjects:** Polish history, atlases, genealogy, language, customs, etc. **Awards:** Wigilia Medal. **Frequency:** annual. **Type:** medal. **Recipient:** for contributions to Polish genealogy. **Affiliated With:** Polish Museum of America. **Formerly:** (1993) Polish Genealogical Society. **Publications:** *Dictionary of Surnames in Current Use in Poland at the Beginning of the 21st Century.* **Price:** $25.00/copy. Alternate Formats: CD-ROM; online ● *First names of the Polish Commonwealth: Origins and Meanings.* Book. Includes names of Czech, German, Greek, Hebrew, Hungarian, Latin, Russian, Ukrainian, Lithuanian and Yiddish origin. **Price:** $20.00/copy ● *Geographic Dictionary of the Kingdom of Poland.* Alternate Formats: CD-ROM ● *The Latin Church in the Polish Commonwealth in 1772.* Book. **Price:** $17.00/copy ● *Polish Parish Records of the Roman Catholic Church; Their Use and Understanding in Genealogical Research.* Book. Discusses baptismal, marriage, and death records. **Price:** $12.00/copy ● *Polish Surnames Origins & Meanings.* Book. **Price:** $25.00 each; for paperback copy ● *Rodziny*, quarterly. Journal. Presents a broad range of timely material and emphasizes well-researched articles. ● *Roman Catholic Parishes in the Polish People's Republic in 1984.* Book. Helps in locating parishes in modern Poland. **Price:** $20.00/copy ● Also publishes article reprints. **Conventions/Meetings:** annual meeting, presentations/discussion (exhibits) - fall ● quarterly meeting.

20717 ■ Presidential Families of America (PFA)

c/o Rev. Barry Christopher Howard, Pres.
10939 W 59th Pl.
Arvada, CO 80004-4732
E-mail: bch@hereditary.us
URL: http://www.presidentialfamilies.org
Contact: Rev. Barry Christopher Howard, Pres.
Founded: 1995. **Members:** 125. **Membership Dues:** life (under 40), $250 ● life (age 40-49), $200 ● life (age 50-59), $150 ● life (over 60), $100 ● regular, $20 (annual) ● auxiliary, $10 (annual) ● supplemental, $60 (annual). **Staff:** 5. **Budget:** $5,000. **Description:** Persons who share direct or collateral kinship with any American president. Encourages research regarding family histories of presidents of the United States of America. Assembles and preserves presidential genealogical information. Requires self addressed stamped envelope for direct response. Inquiries must include pedigree chart clarifying kinship with a president. Does not conduct research for individuals. **Libraries: Type:** not open to the public. **Holdings:** 36; archival material, articles, artwork, books, clippings, periodicals. **Subjects:** families of American presidents. **Awards:** P.F.A. Scholarships. **Frequency:** periodic. **Type:** scholarship. **Recipient:** for outstanding research ● P.F.A Awards. **Frequency:** periodic. **Type:** recognition. **Recipient:** for outstanding support. **Councils:** Executive. **Publications:** *Presidential Families Gazette*, 3/year. Newsletter. Contains society news and presidential kinship information. **Price:** included in membership dues ● Also publishes rosters and genealogies. **Conventions/Meetings:** triennial assembly.

20718 ■ Pursuing Our Italian Names Together (POINT)

Box 14966
Las Vegas, NV 89114-4966
E-mail: pointereditor@aol.com
URL: http://www.point-pointers.net
Contact: Thomas Edward Militello MD, Ed.
Founded: 1987. **Members:** 5,000. **Membership Dues:** individual, $30 (annual) ● outside U.S., $50 (annual). **Local Groups:** 28. **Description:** Individuals of Italian descent. Promotes genealogical and historical research into Italian ancestry. **Special Inter-**

est Groups: POINTers In Person. Affiliated With: Federation of Genealogical Societies. Also Known As: (1987) POINT; (1987) POINTers. Publications: *POINTers-The American Journal of Italian Geneal-ogy*, quarterly. Price: included in membership dues. ISSN: 1065-9749. Circulation: 2,000. Advertising: accepted. Conventions/Meetings: biennial National Conference - convention (exhibits).

20719 ■ Rainier Society

Chateaux L'Aiglon
31 rue Royale, Ste.E
Kettering, OH 45429-1474
Ph: (937)299-9896
E-mail: therainierfamily@yahoo.com
Contact: Lawrence Kent PhD, Founder/Pres.
Founded: 1993. Description: Dedicated to genea-logical research seeking to identify all of the family Rainier, a "quest undertaken in the spirit of the 18th century navigator, Peter Rainier, for whom Mount Rainier was named in 1792 by his fellow navigator, the explorer George Vancouver". Libraries: Type: not open to the public. Holdings: 200; archival mate-rial, biographical archives, books, periodicals. Sub-jects: genealogical and historical. Affiliated With: Presidential Families of America.

20720 ■ Ron Bremer Seminars

HC 65, Box 425
Fredonia, AZ 86022
Ph: (928)875-8397
E-mail: ronbremer@juno.com
Contact: Ronald Allan Bremer, Dir.
Founded: 1985. Members: 150. Membership Dues: life, $100. Staff: 3. Languages: English, French, German, Spanish. For-Profit. Multinational. De-scription: Provides help in conducting genealogical research. Libraries: Type: reference. Holdings: 2,000. Subjects: genealogy, family history. Awards: Vincent L. Jones. Frequency: annual. Type: recogni-tion. Recipient: for proficiency. Subgroups: Alumni. Formerly: (2001) Progenitor Genealogical Society; (2002) Genealogy Research Institute; (2007) Ron Bremer Institute. Publications: *Roots Digest*, peri-odic. Newsletter. Features jurisdictional research information and news. Price: included in member-ship dues. Alternate Formats: online.

20721 ■ Russian Nobility Association in America (RNAA)

971 1st Ave.
New York, NY 10022
Ph: (212)755-7528
E-mail: rna@russiannobility.org
URL: http://www.russiannobility.org
Contact: Dr. Cyril E. Geacintov, Pres.
Founded: 1938. Members: 90. Budget: $30,000. Description: Persons listed in nobility archives of the former Russian Imperial Senate. Compiles immigra-tion records of former Russian nobles in America. Provides assistance to the needy. Publications: none. Libraries: Type: reference. Holdings: 2,000; biographical archives. Subjects: history and geneal-ogy. Absorbed: (1969) Russian Historical and Genealogical Society in America. Conventions/Meetings: annual meeting.

20722 ■ Saint Nicholas Society of the City of New York (SNSCNY)

c/o Jill Spiller, Exec. Dir.
122 E 58th St.
New York, NY 10022-1909
Ph: (212)753-7175
Fax: (212)980-0769
URL: http://www.saintnicholassociety.org
Contact: Jill Spiller, Exec. Dir.
Founded: 1835. Members: 400. Membership Dues: regular, $125 (annual). Staff: 1. Description: Mem-bership by invitation restricted to male descendants of persons living in New York State prior to 1785. Preserves the historical heritage of New York City to sustain its future. Convention/Meeting: none. Awards: St. Nicholas Society of Medal of Merit. Frequency: annual. Type: recognition. Recipient: for outstanding ability and service ● Washington Irv-ing Medal. Frequency: annual. Type: recognition.

Recipient: for literary excellence. Publications: *The Weathercock*, semiannual ● Membership Directory, biennial. Contains names, addresses, titles, and ancestors.

20723 ■ Scotch-Irish Foundation (SIF)

PO Box 181
Bryn Mawr, PA 19010
Ph: (610)527-1818
Fax: (610)527-1818
URL: http://www.scotch-irishcentral.org/Scotch-Irish%20Foundation.html
Contact: John W. McPherson, Pres.
Founded: 1949. Members: 230. Membership Dues: life, $10. Description: Individuals with maternal or paternal Scotch-Irish ancestry. Compiles biographical archives and library containing books, documents, and historical materials relating to the Scotch-Irish people in Scotland and Ireland and their immigration to the U.S. Libraries: Type: reference. Holdings: 700. Computer Services: Online services, library catalogued into the Online Computer Library Center. Affiliated With: Scotch-Irish Society of the United States of America. Publications: *Library and Ar-chives of the Scotch-Irish Foundation*, periodic. Catalog. Provides list of library acquisitions.

20724 ■ Scotch-Irish Society of the United States of America (SIS)

PO Box 181
Bryn Mawr, PA 19010
URL: http://www.rootsweb.com/~sisusa
Contact: Richard K. McMaster PhD, Pres.
Founded: 1890. Members: 350. Membership Dues: individual, $20 (annual) ● life (under 60 years old), $500 ● life (60-70 years old), $400 ● life (over 70 years old), $300. Description: Individuals of Scotch-Irish descent through one or both parents. Works "to broaden, deepen, and enlarge the principles from which our nation has drawn the sustaining power for its development by recalling past achievements, remembrances, and associations." Encourages com-munication among Ireland, Scotland, and the U.S. to promote better understanding of the Scotch-Irish heritage. Collects books relating to Scotch-Irish his-tory from the date of the original Ulster Plantation under James I of England, and the transportation of the planters and their descendants to the American colonies; also collects family registrations and histories including letters, journals, and other docu-ments. Sponsors the Scotch-Irish Foundation. Librar-ies: Type: reference. Holdings: 350; archival mate-rial. Affiliated With: Scotch-Irish Foundation. Formerly: (1961) Pennsylvania Scotch-Irish Society. Publications: *Activity Report*, quarterly ● Brochure. Explains the history of the group. Conventions/Meetings: annual meeting and luncheon - always December in PA.

20725 ■ Society of Richmond County Descendants (SRCD)

PO Box 848
Rockingham, NC 28380
Ph: (910)997-6641
E-mail: descendants@richmondcodescendants.org
URL: http://www.richmondcodescendants.org
Contact: Joe M. McLaurin, Pres.
Founded: 1988. Members: 500. Description: Rep-resents descendants of one or more persons who lived in or are living in Richmond County, NC; interested individuals. Works to collect and preserve historical and genealogical information on Richmond County and its people. Supports the Richmond County Historical Collection. Convention/Meeting: none. Publications: *Richmond County Record*, quarterly. Journal.

20726 ■ Spencer Historical and Genealogical Society (SHGS)

c/o Marion G. Spencer, Pres.
3214 Wintergreen Terr.
Grapevine, TX 76051

E-mail: jandsspencer@earthlink.net
URL: http://www.shgs.org
Contact: Marion G. Spencer, Pres.
Founded: 1978. Members: 600. Staff: 9. Multina-tional. Description: Historians, genealogists, and other individuals with an interest in the Spencer fam-ily. Promotes accurate and permanent recording of family history, vital statistics, and individual ac-complishments of direct family descendants and oth-ers related to or otherwise associated with the numer-ous Spencer lines. Facilitates exchange of informa-tion among members; serves as a clearinghouse for Spencer family history and genealogy. Libraries: Type: reference. Holdings: archival material, books. Subjects: Spencer family history and genealogy. For-merly: Spencer Family Association. Publications: *le Despencer*, quarterly. Journal. Conventions/Meet-ings: biennial meeting - in even-numbered years, usually September.

20727 ■ Vesterheim Genealogical Center and Naeseth Library

415 W Main St.
Madison, WI 53703
Ph: (608)255-2224
Fax: (608)255-6842
E-mail: vesterheimgen2@mcleodusa.net
URL: http://www.vesterheim.org/genealogy
Contact: Blaine Hedberg, Chair of Genealogical Research
Founded: 1975. Members: 1,800. Membership Dues: individual, $30 (annual) ● senior (individual, 65 years old or over), $30 (annual) ● international (residing outside U.S.), $35 (annual). Staff: 4. Bud-get: $150,000. Description: Members of the Norwe-gian American Genealogical Center interested in learning about their heritage. Promotes the study of Norwegian heritage and ethnic background; provides for searches of library and archival collections; serves as clearinghouse for inquiries. Assembles transcripts of cemetery, census, and church records with in-dexes; offers suggestions to researchers. Conducts workshops and tours. Libraries: Type: reference; by appointment only; lending. Holdings: 5,100. Sub-jects: Norwegian genealogy, Norwegian-American genealogy. Formerly: Vesterheim Genealogical Center. Publications: *Norwegian Tracks*, triennial. Newsletter. Includes articles on Norwegian and Norwegian-American local history, transcriptions, book lists, new items in collection, and upcoming events. Price: included in membership dues. Circula-tion: 1,800.

20728 ■ Welsh-American Genealogical Society (WAGS)

60 Norton Ave.
Poultney, VT 05764-1029
E-mail: wagsjan@sover.net
URL: http://www.rootsweb.com/~vtwags
Contact: Dr. Arturo L. Roberts, Pres./Exec. Dir.
Founded: 1990. Members: 800. Membership Dues: regular in U.S., $10 (annual) ● regular in Canada, $11 (annual) ● regular in UK, $14 (annual). Staff: 5. Languages: English, Welsh. Description: Promotes Welsh heritage, family history, and aids Welsh researchers. Libraries: Type: reference; open to the public; by appointment only. Holdings: 200; archival material, articles, audiovisuals, books, clippings, periodicals. Subjects: Welsh genealogy, history and culture. Computer Services: Online services, publication. Publications: Newsletter (in English and Welsh), quarterly. Price: $2.00 each; included in membership dues. ISSN: 1520-8249. Circulation: 500.

20729 ■ World Chamberlain Genealogical Society (WCGS)

c/o Welton C. Chamberlain, Corresponding Sec.
PO Box 246
Pinckney, MI 48169-0246
E-mail: corrsec@chamberlain-society.org
URL: http://www.chamberlain-society.org
Contact: Welton C. Chamberlain, Corresponding Sec.
Founded: 1996. Members: 297. Membership Dues: regular, $25 (annual) ● life, $400. Description:

People of the family name Chamberlain and its variant spellings. Encourages genealogical research on the Chamberlain surname. Seeks to build a comprehensive data base that can be utilized to explore the origins and details of the various lines of the name. **Libraries: Type:** open to the public. **Holdings:** archival material, articles, books, clippings, papers. **Subjects:** Chamberlain genealogy. **Committees:** Standing Committee on Ancestry. **Publications:** *The Chamberlain Key,* quarterly. Newsletter. Includes genealogy and results of research. **Price:** included in membership dues; $5.00/back issue. **Conventions/Meetings:** quarterly board meeting ● annual meeting, for members.

20730 ■ World Jewish Genealogy Organization (WJGO)
PO Box 420
Brooklyn, NY 11219
Ph: (718)435-4400
Fax: (718)633-7050
Contact: Rabbi Naftali Halberstam, Pres.
Founded: 1980. **Members:** 295. **Staff:** 5. **Description:** Researchers and scholars of Jewish genealogy. Encourages research and publication of Jewish biographies, bibliographies, and genealogies. **Convention/Meeting:** none. **Libraries: Type:** reference. **Holdings:** 10,000; biographical archives. **Subjects:** genealogy. **Computer Services:** database, sources necessary for compiling family histories and genealogies. **Also Known As:** Yochsin Institute. **Publications:** *Encyclopedia of Jewish Genealogy.* Contains 1,500 volumes. ● Publishes dictionaries of Jewish first and last names, cities, and countries, translated into Hebrew and in Spellings; plans to publish *Encyclopedia of Jewish Genealogy.*

20731 ■ York County Genealogical Society (YCGS)
Address Unknown since 2007
Founded: 1985. **Members:** 150. **Membership Dues:** organization and library, $10 (annual) ● regular and family, $15 (annual). **Staff:** 3. **Budget:** $2,000. **Regional Groups:** 1. **Local Groups:** 1. **Local. Description:** Conducts limited research and makes available genealogical source data pertaining to York County, ME. Assists others in family genealogy research. (Limited Assistance). **Libraries: Type:** reference. **Holdings:** 175; books, periodicals. **Subjects:** genealogy, local history. **Publications:** *York County Genealogical Society Journal,* quarterly. Includes genealogical records such as births, deaths, and diary excerpts. **Price:** included in membership dues. **Circulation:** 150. **Advertising:** not accepted.

Historic Preservation

20732 ■ Abraham Lincoln National Cemetery Support Committee
c/o George E. Sangmeister
28 Kansas St.
Frankfort, IL 60423-1477
Ph: (815)469-2176
Fax: (815)469-0295
Contact: George E. Sangmeister, Chm.
Founded: 1968. **Members:** 40. **Description:** Facilitates the establishment of the Abraham Lincoln National Cemetery in Illinois and the provision of continuing support and participation in events commemorating all U.S. military veterans. **Affiliated With:** Makassed Philanthropic Islamic Association.

Huguenot

20733 ■ Huguenot Historical Society (HHS)
18 Broadhead Ave.
New Paltz, NY 12561-1403
Ph: (845)255-1660
Fax: (845)255-0376
E-mail: info@huguenotstreet.org
URL: http://huguenotstreet.org
Contact: Mr. Eric Roth, Interim Dir.
Founded: 1894. **Members:** 3,300. **Membership Dues:** individual, $35 (annual). **Staff:** 31. **Budget:**

$810,000. **Regional Groups:** 10. **Description:** Persons interested in the preservation of Huguenot history. Restores and maintains the stone houses and buildings of Huguenot St., now a National Landmark Historic District, at New Paltz, NY; the site now includes seven house museums, an additional farm complex, a 100-acre wildlife sanctuary, and a rebuilt 18th century French church. Conducts interpretive tours, children's services, specialized education, and research programs. **Libraries: Type:** reference; by appointment only; open to the public. **Holdings:** 6,000; archival material, books. **Subjects:** Huguenot history, genealogy, local culture. **Awards:** Huguenot Historical Society Scholarships. **Frequency:** annual. **Type:** scholarship. **Subcommittees:** Bevier-Elting; Crispell; Deyo; Freer-Low; Gerow; LeFevre; Magny; Schoonmaker; Terwillinger. **Also Known As:** (2006) Historic Huguenot Street. **Publications:** *On Huguenot Street,* semiannual. Newsletter. **Price:** free. **Circulation:** 3,000. **Conventions/Meetings:** annual meeting - always second Saturday of June ● seminar.

20734 ■ Huguenot Society of the Founders of Manakin in the Colony of Virginia (HSFMCV)
c/o Dr. Ann Woodlief, Natl. Librarian
Natl. HQ
981 Huguenot Trail
Midlothian, VA 23113
Ph: (804)794-5702
E-mail: manakintown@yahoo.com
URL: http://huguenot-manakin.org
Contact: Dr. Ann Woodlief, Natl. Librarian
Founded: 1922. **Members:** 1,485. **Membership Dues:** regular, $25. **State Groups:** 11. **Description:** Descendants of the Huguenots who founded Manakin, VA, in 1700, and other Huguenot residents of Virginia prior to 1786. (Huguenots were 16thand 17th-century French Protestants persecuted for their faith; many fled to other countries, including the American colonies.) Seeks to promote interest in and to erect memorials commemorating Manakin's Huguenot settlers. Encourages preparation of papers and essays on Manakin Huguenots and the Huguenot movement in general. Sponsors competitions. **Libraries: Type:** open to the public; reference. **Holdings:** 750; archival material, books, clippings, periodicals. **Subjects:** genealogical and historical documents on Manakin and all Virginia Huguenot settlers. **Awards: Frequency:** annual. **Type:** scholarship. **Recipient:** for an undergraduate student. **Publications:** *The Huguenot,* biennial. Magazine. Includes reports on the administration of the society. **Price:** included in membership dues ● Bulletin, semiannual. **Conventions/Meetings:** annual assembly ● semiannual State Branch Meeting.

20735 ■ National Huguenot Society (NHS)
9033 Lyndale Ave. S, Ste.108
Bloomington, MN 55420-3535
Ph: (952)885-9776
E-mail: awards@huguenot.netnation.com
URL: http://huguenot.netnation.com
Contact: Grace V. Rice, Archives Chair
Founded: 1951. **Members:** 5,000. **Staff:** 1. **State Groups:** 48. **Description:** Individuals of Protestant faith over 18 years old and lineally descended from the Huguenots who, because of religious persecution in France, emigrated to America after the promulgation of the Edict of Toleration in 1787. Commemorates the events of Huguenot history. Collects and preserves historical data and relics of Huguenot life, manners, and customs. Sponsors patriotic, educational, charitable, and religious projects. **Supersedes:** (1933) Federation of Huguenot Societies. **Publications:** *Cross of Languedoc,* semiannual. Newsletter. **Circulation:** 3,800 ● *Register of Qualified Huguenot Ancestors of the National Huguenot Society, 4th Edition, 1995 and updates 1996-2003.* **Conventions/Meetings:** annual congress - always Washington, DC.

Intelligence

20736 ■ National Counter Intelligence Corps Association (NCICA)
c/o Jerry Malme, Chm.
6198 Morris Rd.
Geneseo, NY 14454

Ph: (585)243-0819
E-mail: malmeju@aol.com
URL: http://ncica.org/home.html
Contact: Jerry Malme, Chm.
Founded: 1946. **Members:** 750. **Membership Dues:** life, $200 ● individual, $15 (annual) ● individual, $25 (biennial). **Staff:** 4. **Budget:** $12,000. **Regional Groups:** 8. **Local Groups:** 10. **Description:** Represents former special agents of the U.S. Army, Air Force, Navy, and Marine Counter Intelligence Corps and military intelligence. **Libraries: Type:** not open to the public. **Subjects:** intelligence. **Awards:** President/Convention Coordinator Annual Plaque. **Frequency:** annual. **Type:** recognition. **Boards:** Governors. **Publications:** *Golden Sphinx,* quarterly. Newsletter. Contains information on membership activities. **Price:** included in membership dues. **Circulation:** 800. **Conventions/Meetings:** annual convention and reunion.

Israel

20737 ■ American Veterans of Israel (AVI)
136 E 39th St.
New York, NY 10016-0914
Ph: (352)392-6525
E-mail: rlowenstein@jou.ufl.edu
URL: http://www.israelvets.com
Contact: Paul Kaye, Pres.
Founded: 1949. **Members:** 500. **Description:** Men and women, both Jewish and Gentile, who were actively engaged in illegal immigration, underground movements, and Israel Defense Forces that led to the creation of the State of Israel. Volunteers from Western Europe, South Africa, and North America were given the designation "Machal", a Hebrew word meaning "volunteers from abroad". Machal groups still exist in Canada, England, Israel, United States, and South Africa. Seeks to remind world of the part the members played in creating Israel and to memorialize those Americans and Canadians who gave their lives. Participates with other Jewish groups on issues affecting Jews. Provides speakers to organizations and schools; sponsors charitable programs. **Publications:** Newsletter, quarterly. **Price:** free. **Conventions/Meetings:** biennial meeting ● annual Memorial Service - meeting - always in West Point, NY.

20738 ■ Friends of Israel Disabled Veterans (FIDV)
1133 Broadway, Ste.232
New York, NY 10010
Ph: (212)689-3220
Fax: (212)253-4143
E-mail: info@fidv.org
URL: http://www.fidv.org
Contact: Karen Berger, Natl. Campaign Exec.
Founded: 1987. **Staff:** 4. **Local Groups:** 1. **National Groups:** 2. **Multinational. Description:** Organizes fundraising and educational activities on behalf of the 48,000 disabled Israeli veterans and the institutions that provide services to them and their families. These institutions are known as the Beit Halochem sports, rehabilitation and social centers, located in Tel Aviv, Jerusalem, and Haifa and the Beit Kay Convalescent Center also located in Israel. **Programs:** Activities for Children; Combined Treatments; Cultural and Creative Activities; Family-Oriented Programming; Hydrotherapy; The Physical Therapy; Rehabilitative Therapy; Research and Medicine. **Formerly:** (2000) Friends of Israel Disabled War Veterans (Beit Halochem). **Publications:** *To live again.* Videos ● Newsletter, 3/year. News of local events and stories of disabled vets. **Price:** free. **Circulation:** 30,000 ● Brochures. **Conventions/Meetings:** annual Victims of Terror Benefit - meeting.

Korean War

20739 ■ 2nd Infantry Division (2id), Korean War Veterans Alliance
c/o Ralph Hockley, Sec.
10027 Pine Forest Rd.
Houston, TX 77042-1531

Ph: (713)334-0271
Fax: (713)334-0272
E-mail: rmh-2id-kwva@earthlink.net
URL: http://www.2id.org
Contact: Ralph Hockley, Sec.
Founded: 1990. **Members:** 3,000. **Membership Dues:** regular, associate, $5 (annual) ● life, $40. **Staff:** 1. **Languages:** English, French. **Multinational. Description:** Works to unite old units and veterans from the 2nd Infantry Division (2id) of Korean War Veterans. **Computer Services:** database ● mailing lists. **Publications:** *2nd Infantry Division Korean War Vets Alliance Bulletin,* quarterly. **Conventions/Meetings:** annual reunion.

20740 ■ Association of 40th Infantry Division Korean War Veterans
c/o Sid Sultzbaugh, Sec.
2029 G St.
Lorain, OH 44052
E-mail: deehawk@kellnet.com
URL: http://www.kellnet.com/veterans/aba.htm
Contact: Sid Sultzbaugh, Sec.
Founded: 1992. **Membership Dues:** active, $10 (annual). **Description:** Promotes the 40th Infantry Division of Korean War Veterans. Active (voting) membership is limited to those who served with the division anytime from June 25, 1950 until the division left Korea. **Publications:** *Roster of Members.* Membership Directory ● Newsletter, semiannual, every June and December.

20741 ■ Chosin Few (CF)
238 Cornwall Cir.
Chalfont, PA 18914-2318
Ph: (215)822-9093
Fax: (215)822-1137
E-mail: chosinfewhq@aol.com
URL: http://home.hawaii.rr.com/chosin
Contact: Don H. Gee, Business Mgr.
Founded: 1983. **Members:** 4,200. **Membership Dues:** associate, $15 (annual) ● regular, $35 (annual). **Staff:** 2. **Local Groups:** 50. **Multinational. Description:** U.S., Republic of Korea, Australian, and British veterans who participated in the fighting around Chosin Reservoir in November and December, 1950. (The battles around the Chosin Reservoir represented the surprise response of the Chinese army to the Allied invasion of North Korea.) Promotes continued fellowship among Allied veterans of the Chosin battles. Works to recover the remains of Americans listed as missing-in-action in the Korean War and account for Americans thought to be held as prisoners-of-war in North Korea. Works for the recognition of cold injury benefits by the Department of Veterans Affairs on behalf of all Korean War veterans suffering latent effects of cold injury incurred during their service in Korea. **Committees:** Cold Injury; MIA/POW; Reunion. **Publications:** *Chosin Few Membership Directory,* biennial ● *News Digest,* quarterly. Newsletters. Contains information on the organization's activities and its members. **Circulation:** 5,000. **Conventions/Meetings:** biennial reunion.

20742 ■ Korean War Veterans Association (KWVA)
163 Deerbrook Trail
Pineville, LA 71360
Ph: (703)842-7429
E-mail: info@kwva.org
URL: http://www.kwva.org
Contact: Bill Hutton, Sec.
Founded: 1985. **Members:** 15,500. **Membership Dues:** regular, $20 (annual) ● life - regular, $150 ● associate, $12 (annual). **Budget:** $246,000. **State Groups:** 12. **Local Groups:** 150. **National Groups:** 160. **Description:** Korean War veterans; families of those listed as killed, missing-in-action, or prisoner-of-war; individuals who served at least 90 days in Korea. Supports what the association considers the "founding ideals" of the U.S; promotes the pride and dignity of veterans; works toward developing recognition of those who lost their lives in Korea; fosters camaraderie and communication among members; perpetuates the memory of the war in which they

fought. Works to develop Korean War Memorial Library Museum. **Awards:** College Educational Award. **Frequency:** annual. **Type:** monetary. **Computer Services:** Mailing lists. **Councils:** Executive. **Publications:** *The Graybeards,* bimonthly. Newsletter. **Circulation:** 15,500. **Advertising:** accepted. Alternate Formats: CD-ROM; online ● *Membership Roster,* annual. Directory. **Price:** available to members only. **Conventions/Meetings:** annual Business Meeting and Reunion - held in July ● Executive Council - board meeting - 3/year.

Marine Corps

20743 ■ 1st Marine Division Association (FMDA)
410 Pier View Way
Oceanside, CA 92054
Ph: (760)967-8561
Free: (877)967-8561
Fax: (760)967-8567
E-mail: oldbreed@sbcglobal.net
URL: http://www.1stmarinedivisionassociation.org
Contact: Col. Len Hayes, Exec. Dir.
Founded: 1947. **Members:** 15,000. **Membership Dues:** veteran, $30 (annual) ● life, $300 ● senior, $150 (annual). **Staff:** 3. **Regional Groups:** 52. **Description:** Veterans who have served in the 1st Marine Division; personnel who served with attached or supporting units. Provides an opportunity for members to re-establish and/or maintain contact with their fellow servicemen. **Awards:** Elsie Sadowsky Citizenship Award. **Frequency:** annual. **Type:** monetary. **Recipient:** for a high school junior or senior who is academically outstanding and a significant contributor to their community ● **Type:** scholarship. **Recipient:** for dependents of deceased or permanently 100&percent; disabled veterans who qualify for membership. **Publications:** *Old Breed News,* bimonthly. Magazine. Includes information that facilitates camaraderie and about local chapter activities and reunions. **Price:** free for members ● *Reunion Journal* ● Directory. **Conventions/Meetings:** annual reunion.

20744 ■ Devil Pups (DP)
2815 Townsgate Rd., No. 325
Westlake Village, CA 91361-3097
Ph: (805)497-9810
Fax: (805)557-4966
E-mail: info@devilpups.com
URL: http://www.devilpups.com
Contact: R.H. Lindsay, Pres.
Founded: 1954. **Members:** 30. **Staff:** 4. **Budget:** $145,000. **Description:** Youth project sponsored by former U.S. Marine Corps Reservists. Promotes moral and physical responsibility in youth and seeks to teach "self-control, self-respect, self-responsibility" and "respect for our flag and pride in our country". Boys and Girls between the ages of 14 and 17 camp for ten days during the summer at Camp Pendleton, CA, to observe Marine activities and to have the opportunity to associate with Marine leaders. Activities concentrated in California only.

20745 ■ Loyal Escorts of the Green Garter (LEGGS)
c/o Jeanne Cantrell, Treas.
11 Brown St.
Irving, TX 75061
E-mail: donaldconnon@hotmail.com
URL: http://www.jocokyroots.com/WMALoyalEscorts.htm
Contact: Jeanne Cantrell, Treas.
Founded: 1972. **Members:** 578. **Membership Dues:** regular, $25 (biennial) ● life (30 years old and under), $375 ● life (31-45 years of age), $145 ● life (46-60 years of age), $125 ● life (61-70 years of age), $100 ● life (71-80 years of age), $75 ● life (80 years of age and older), $50. **Description:** An ancillary of the Women's Marine Association that is composed of husbands and relatives of WMA members. Provides support for the WMA. **Publications:** none. **Conventions/Meetings:** biennial meeting.

20746 ■ Marine Corps Cryptologic Association (MCCA)
4486 Sandalwood St.
Napa, CA 94558-1766
Free: (877)856-9562
E-mail: jay4486@sbcglobal.net
URL: http://www.mccaonline.org
Contact: Bill Haney, Pres.
Founded: 1989. **Members:** 460. **Membership Dues:** general, $15 (annual). **Description:** Encourages social camaraderie between current and former cryptologic marines. Preserves the history of marine corps cryptology. **Publications:** Newsletter, quarterly.

20747 ■ Marine Corps League Auxiliary (MCLA)
8626 Lee Hwy., Ste.207
Fairfax, VA 22031
Ph: (703)207-0626
Fax: (703)207-0264
E-mail: kwashaba@comcast.net
URL: http://www.nationalmcla.org
Contact: Karen Washabaugh, Natl. Pres.
Founded: 1937. **Members:** 3,300. **State Groups:** 51. **National Groups:** 400. **Description:** Mothers, stepmothers, grandmothers, wives, sisters, daughters, stepdaughters, granddaughters or widows of men honorably discharged or now serving in the U.S. Marine Corps; women who have been honorably discharged or who currently serve in the U.S. Marine Corps or Marine Corps Reserves. **Committees:** Americanism; Budget; Bylaw and Administrative Procedure; Child Welfare; Girl Scout; History; Memorial Fund; National President Project; Rehabilitation; Scholarship; Uniform. **Affiliated With:** Military Order of the Devil Dog Fleas. **Publications:** *The Marine's Magazine,* quarterly. **Conventions/Meetings:** annual meeting.

20748 ■ Marine Corps Mustang Association (MCMA)
Bunker 127
Mountain City, GA 30562
Free: (866)937-6262
Fax: (866)939-6262
E-mail: mustangbusmgr@windstream.net
URL: http://www.marinecorpsmustang.org
Contact: Roger V. Speeg, Business Mgr.
Founded: 1985. **Members:** 1,600. **Membership Dues:** individual (for the first year; $35 each year thereafter), $40 ● individual (extended), $90 (triennial) ● individual (extended), $120 (quinquennial). **Staff:** 3. **Budget:** $125,000. **Regional Groups:** 1. **National Groups:** 5. **Description:** Present and former Marine officers of U.S. Marine Corps or Marine Corps Reserve who were promoted from enlisted to the officer ranks. Promotes camaraderie between members and dedication to the traditions of the Marine Corps. Provides a forum for social interaction. Compiles historical records of Mustangs and their achievements. Provides financial aid to Marines and others in need. **Libraries:** Type: reference. **Holdings:** biographical archives. **Awards:** Mustang Spirit Award. **Frequency:** annual. **Type:** recognition. **Recipient:** for a graduate of Marine Warrant Officers' Basic Class. **Publications:** *Mestengo,* quarterly. Newsletter. **Price:** $2.50/copy. **Circulation:** 2,000. Alternate Formats: online ● Membership Directory, annual. **Advertising:** accepted. **Conventions/Meetings:** annual Mustang Muster - reunion.

20749 ■ Marine Embassy Guard Association (MEGA)
c/o Tony Lopez, Sec.
70 Stringari Ln.
Belfry, MT 59008
Ph: (406)664-3130
E-mail: tlopez@embassymarine.org
URL: http://www.embassymarine.org
Contact: Virgil M. Johnson, Chm.
Founded: 1996. **Members:** 300. **Membership Dues:** regular, $25 (annual) ● life (70 years old and above), $75 ● life (61 to 69 years old), $100 ● life (51 to 60 years old), $150 ● life (41 to 50 years old), $200 ● life (40 years old and below), $250. **Description:** Encourages Marines to volunteer in the Marine

Security Guard Program. Renders aid to Marines and other individuals who are in need. Promotes camaraderie and esprit de corps. **Computer Services:** database, BN Honor Grads ● database, MSG poems ● information services, MSG detachments. **Telecommunication Services:** electronic mail, vjohnson@eticomm.net. **Publications:** *MEGA Newsletter.*

20750 ■ Military Order of the Devil Dog Fleas (MODDF)
10620 N McGee St.
Kansas City, MO 64155
Ph: (816)734-5579
URL: http://kennel-modd.org/fleas.htm
Contact: Lois Box, Exec. Sec.
Founded: 1939. **Members:** 400. **Staff:** 2. **Description:** Persons who belong to the Marine Corps League. **Affiliated With:** Marine Corps League Auxiliary. **Conventions/Meetings:** annual meeting and convention, with Marine Corps League.

20751 ■ Second Marine Division Association (SMDA)
PO Box 8180
Camp Lejeune, NC 28547
Ph: (910)451-3167
Fax: (910)451-3167
E-mail: peter.grimes@usmc.mil
URL: http://www.2marine.com
Contact: Peter Grimes, Exec. Dir.
Founded: 1949. **Members:** 6,500. **Membership Dues:** regular, associate, $20 (annual) ● life, $150 ● active duty, $10 (annual). **Staff:** 2. **Regional Groups:** 5. **State Groups:** 14. **Description:** Anyone who has served in the Second Marine Division, Fleet Marine Force. Provides scholarships to students who are dependents of members or former members of the Second Marine Division. Operates charitable program. **Libraries: Type:** reference; by appointment only; not open to the public. **Awards:** Follow Me Award. **Frequency:** annual. **Type:** recognition. **Recipient:** for marksmanship ● John Henry Balch Award. **Frequency:** annual. **Type:** recognition. **Recipient:** for outstanding performance ● Lt.Gen. Julian C. Smith Award. **Frequency:** annual. **Type:** recognition. **Recipient:** for leadership ● MGen. Clayton B. Vogel Award. **Frequency:** annual. **Type:** recognition. **Recipient:** for leadership ● Tarawa Award. **Frequency:** annual. **Type:** recognition. **Recipient:** for leadership. **Publications:** *Follow Me,* quarterly. Newsletter. Contains information for members of current association events, military news, and chapter activities. **Circulation:** 6,500. **Advertising:** accepted ● *Second Marine Division Association Directory,* quinquennial. **Conventions/Meetings:** annual Division Birthday Celebration - assembly ● annual reunion.

20752 ■ Women Marines Association (WMA)
PO Box 8405
Falls Church, VA 22041-8405
Free: (888)525-1943
E-mail: wma@womenmarines.org
URL: http://www.womenmarines.org
Contact: Paula Sarlls, Pres.
Founded: 1960. **Members:** 3,500. **Membership Dues:** regular, $15 (annual) ● life, $120-$220. **Staff:** 15. **Budget:** $60,000. **Local Groups:** 78. **Description:** Women in the U.S. Marine Corps or the U.S. Marine Reserve, or those who have been honorably discharged; those honorably separated or retired from the U.S. Marine Corps. Perpetuates comradeship among members and promotes the welfare of all women of the Marine Corps; encourages responsible civic leadership and citizenship; fosters patriotism in American youth through education; provides entertainment, care, and assistance to hospitalized veterans. Maintains charitable program. Member of Navy-Marine Corps Council; Marine Corps Council. **Awards:** MCJROTC Award. **Frequency:** annual. **Type:** recognition. **Recipient:** to outstanding Marine Corps Junior ROTC cadets in high schools across the United States ● Molly Marine Award. **Frequency:** monthly. **Type:** recognition. **Recipient:** to women graduates of the Recruit Training program ● National Service award. **Type:** recognition. **Recipient:** for

outstanding service to WMA ● **Type:** scholarship. **Recipient:** to qualified applicants sponsored by WMA members. **Committees:** Matching Funds; MCJROTC; Scholarship; VAVS. **Programs:** Auxiliary; Veterans Affairs Volunteer Service. **Publications:** *WMA 'Nouncements,* quarterly. Newsletter. Includes information on membership, conventions, chapters, and current leadership of the association and the Marine Corps. **Price:** included in membership dues. **Circulation:** 3,500. **Advertising:** accepted ● *Women Marines Association—Membership Directory,* biennial. Includes application forms. **Price:** available to members only. **Circulation:** 3,500. **Conventions/Meetings:** biennial competition - even-numbered years ● biennial convention.

Mexican War

20753 ■ Descendants of Mexican War Veterans (DMWV)
PO Box 830482
Richardson, TX 75083-0482
E-mail: mjweditor@corridor.net
URL: http://www.dmwv.org
Contact: Jerry Bullock, Ed.
Founded: 1989. **Members:** 550. **Membership Dues:** full, associate, $30 (annual). **Regional Groups:** 1. **Description:** Descendants of Mexican War veterans; individuals interested in the Mexican War. Seeks to honor U.S. Veterans of the War With Mexico (1846-1848). Works to erect monuments in honor of the veterans of the Mexican War. Assists members with limited genealogical research. Helps preserve the Palo Alto Battlefield in south Texas. Transcribes the name of every U.S. veteran of the Mexican War from a variety of printed and microfilmed sources. Erected a 35 foot flagpole at site of original Fort Brown in May, 1996 as a memorial to the defenders of the fort during the siege of 1846. Erected memorial to Alexander Kenaday, founder of National Association of Veterans of the Mexican War, 1997. Initiated placement of Texas Historical Commission markers at Camp Belknap on the Rio Grande (1996) and Brazos IS. Military Depot (1997). **Libraries: Type:** reference. **Holdings:** 200; archival material, artwork, books, clippings, periodicals, video recordings. **Subjects:** Mexican War (1846-1848). **Publications:** *Alabama Volunteers in the Mexican War: A History and Annotated Roster.* Book. **Price:** $28.00 for nonmembers; $25.50 for members ● *American Eagle,* quarterly. Newsletter. **Price:** $20.00 /year for nonmembers. ISSN: 1049-9008. **Circulation:** 150 ● *The Eutaw Rangers in the War with Mexico.* Book. **Price:** $28.00 for nonmembers; $25.50 for members ● *Mexican War Journal,* quarterly. **Price:** $30.00 /year for nonmembers. ISSN: 1062-5615. **Circulation:** 150 ● *U.S. Veterans of the War with Mexico: A Guide to Genealogical Research.* Book. **Price:** $13.00 for members, plus shipping and handling of $3; $15.50 for nonmembers, plus shipping and handling of $3. **Conventions/Meetings:** annual meeting - always September.

Military

20754 ■ American Retirees Association (ARA)
2009 N 14th St., Ste.300
Arlington, VA 22201
Ph: (703)527-3065
Fax: (703)528-4229
E-mail: contactara@aol.com
URL: http://www.americanretireesassociation.org
Contact: Frank W. Ault, Exec. Dir.
Founded: 1984. **Members:** 1,500. **Membership Dues:** general, $25 (annual). **Staff:** 4. **Description:** Active, reserve, and retired members of the uniformed military services of the United States. Seeks to address what the group feels are inequities in the Uniformed Services Former Spouses' Protection Act (USFSPA). Provides advisory services to military retirees and second families adversely affected by these laws; lobbies for amendments to the USFSPA. **Publications:** *Divorce and the Military II.* Book.

Price: $25.00. **Circulation:** 15,000 ● Newsletter, bimonthly. **Price:** $25.00. **Circulation:** 1,500. **Conventions/Meetings:** meeting, for the executive committee.

20755 ■ Escort Carrier Sailors and Airmen Association (ECSAA)
c/o Henry A. Pyzdrowski, Sr., Pres.
3916 Merriam Rd.
Minnetonka, MN 55305-5045
Ph: (952)935-5454
Fax: (952)935-5454
E-mail: pyzzaz@earthlink.net
URL: http://www.escortcarriers.com
Contact: Henry A. Pyzdrowski Sr., Pres.
Founded: 1991. **Members:** 2,400. **Membership Dues:** individual, $20 (annual) ● individual, $35 (biennial) ● individual, $50 (triennial) ● life (under age 70), $135 ● life (70-74 years of age), $100 ● life (age 75 and over), $75. **Description:** Promotes knowledge and interest in the vital role played by escort carriers during World War II and the Korean War. **Boards:** Governors. **Publications:** *The Piper,* bimonthly. Newspaper. **Conventions/Meetings:** annual convention.

20756 ■ Society of the 3rd Infantry Division
c/o Raymond C. Anderson, Sec.-Treas.
10 Paddington Ct.
Hockessin, DE 19707-9766
Ph: (302)239-1525
E-mail: march5@aol.com
URL: http://www.warfoto.com/3div.htm
Contact: Raymond C. Anderson, Sec.-Treas.
Founded: 1919. **Members:** 3,500. **Membership Dues:** individual in U.S., active duty soldier, $10 (annual) ● individual outside U.S., $30 (annual) ● life, $75-$340. **Staff:** 12. **Budget:** $26,000. **Regional Groups:** 3. **Local Groups:** 25. **Description:** Past and present members of the 3rd Infantry Division of the U.S. Army and attached and supporting units; families of veterans of the division. Fosters and strengthens associations and friendships formed during service with the Third Infantry Division. Honors the Third Infantry Division War Dead and perpetuates their memory. Encourages and achieves the mutual benefit and support resulting from a close and cooperative alliance between the Society and the Third Infantry Division, U.S. Army. Supports the government of the United States. Assists in the maintenance of monuments dedicated to the Third Infantry Division. Organizes and conducts wreath laying and memorial ceremonies. **Libraries: Type:** reference. **Holdings:** archival material. **Subjects:** military history. **Awards:** NCO of the Year. **Frequency:** annual. **Type:** recognition ● Service and Audie Murphy Achievement Award. **Frequency:** annual. **Type:** recognition. **Recipient:** for service and dedication to the society and nation ● Soldier of the Year Award. **Frequency:** annual. **Type:** recognition. **Computer Services:** Mailing lists, membership, roster, newsletter. **Committees:** Audit; Awards; Constitution/By-Laws; Membership; Nominations; Public Relations. **Publications:** *National Roster,* triennial. Magazine. Contains lists of name, address, unit, rank and period of service. **Price:** included in membership dues. **Circulation:** 3,500. Alternate Formats: magnetic tape ● *Watch on the Rhine,* bimonthly. **Conventions/Meetings:** annual reunion, memorabilia (exhibits) - usually fall.

20757 ■ Society of the Fifth Division
c/o Jeff Tuttle, Sec.
1711 Corsica Dr.
Yuba City, CA 95993-1638
Ph: (530)755-4405
E-mail: secretary@societyofthefifthdivision.com
URL: http://www.societyofthefifthdivision.com
Contact: Phil Maniscalco, Interim Natl. Pres.
Founded: 1919. **Membership Dues:** regular, associate, $15 (annual) ● life, $50-$150. **Description:** Works to perpetuate and memorialize the valiant acts and patriotic deeds of the Fifth Division. **Computer Services:** Online services, list of members. **Publications:** *Red Diamond,* quarterly. Magazine. Includes member listing. **Conventions/Meetings:** reunion.

Military Families

20758 ■ American Gold Star Mothers (AGSM)
2128 Leroy Pl. NW
Washington, DC 20008
Ph: (202)265-0991
Fax: (202)265-6963
E-mail: goldstarmoms@yahoo.com
URL: http://www.goldstarmoms.com
Contact: Betty J. Pulliam, Natl. Pres.
Founded: 1928. **Members:** 1,100. **Membership Dues:** regular, $10 (annual). **Staff:** 1. **State Groups:** 29. **Local Groups:** 150. **Description:** Represents mothers whose sons or daughters have made the supreme sacrifice while in any branch of the Military or Naval Service of the United States of America, or died as a result of such service. **Libraries: Type:** not open to the public. **Awards:** James Parks in Conjunction with Department of Veterans Affairs. **Type:** recognition. **Committees:** Veterans Administration Voluntary Service. **Publications:** *Gold Star Mother*, bimonthly. Newsletter. **Conventions/Meetings:** annual meeting - always June/July.

20759 ■ American Legion Auxiliary (ALA)
777 N Meridian St., 3rd Fl.
Indianapolis, IN 46204-1420
Ph: (317)955-3845
Fax: (317)955-3884
E-mail: alahq@legion-aux.org
URL: http://www.legion-aux.org
Contact: Ms. Lucia Anderson, Public Relations Mgr.
Founded: 1919. **Members:** 1,000,000. **Staff:** 24. **Budget:** $5,000,000. **State Groups:** 51. **Local Groups:** 10,500. **Description:** Mothers, wives, sisters, daughters, grandmothers, granddaughters, and great granddaughters of members of the American Legion or of men and women who were in the U.S. Armed Forces during World War I or II, the Korean War, the Vietnam War, Grenada/Lebanon, Panama, or Persian Gulf and lost their lives in war service or died after honorable discharge; women who served in the armed forces during these periods of hostility. **Committees:** Americanism; Children and Youth; Community Service; Education; Girls State; Legislative; National Security; Poppy; Veterans Affairs and Rehabilitation. **Publications:** *National News*, bimonthly. Magazine. **Price:** $7.00/year. **Circulation:** 820,000. **Advertising:** accepted. **Conventions/Meetings:** competition ● annual convention (exhibits) - usually August or September.

20760 ■ American War Mothers (AWM)
5415 Connecticut Ave. NW; Ste.L30
Washington, DC 20015
Ph: (202)362-0090
Fax: (202)362-2395
URL: http://www.va.gov/vso/index.
cfm?template=viewreport&Org_ID=29
Contact: Millie P. Baker, Natl. Corresponding Sec.
Founded: 1917. **Members:** 1,000. **Staff:** 2. **Budget:** $49,000. **State Groups:** 19. **Local Groups:** 80. **Description:** Natural mothers of veterans, servicemen, and servicewomen. Holds Veterans' Day services at the U.S. Capitol and Mothers' Day services at Arlington Cemetery. Conducts volunteer services in VA hospitals. **Awards:** Award of Appreciation. **Frequency:** biennial. **Type:** recognition. **Committees:** Americanism; Hospitalization; Legislative; Memorials. **Publications:** *American War Mothers Newsletter*, quarterly. **Conventions/Meetings:** biennial convention - always odd-numbered years. 2007 Sept., Washington, DC.

20761 ■ Ancient and Honorable Artillery Company of Massachusetts (A&HAC)
Armory Faneuil Hall, 4th Fl.
Boston, MA 02109
Ph: (617)227-1638
Fax: (617)227-7221
E-mail: ahac.curator@verizon.net
URL: http://www.ahacsite.org
Contact: Lt. John F. McCauley, Museum Curator
Founded: 1636. **Members:** 1,000. **Staff:** 2. **State Groups:** 1. **Description:** Descendants of persons who served in Massachusetts artillery company during 1638-1738; interested others. Sponsors annual trip abroad. Conducts social activities and ceremonial services. Maintains museum. **Libraries: Type:** reference. **Holdings:** 10,000; archival material, artwork, books, business records, clippings, periodicals. **Subjects:** 18th, 19th, and 20th century military information. **Awards:** ROTC Award. **Frequency:** annual. **Type:** recognition. **Recipient:** to colleges in Massachusetts. **Also Known As:** Ancients. **Publications:** *Drumhead*, periodic. Newsletter. **Circulation:** 1,000. **Conventions/Meetings:** annual June Day - banquet, with elections and parade in Boston - always in June.

20762 ■ Army Distaff Foundation/Knollwood (ADF)
6200 Oregon Ave. NW
Washington, DC 20015
Ph: (202)541-0149
Free: (800)541-4255
Fax: (202)364-2856
E-mail: marketing@armydistaff.org
URL: http://www.armydistaff.org
Contact: Mrs. Kristina Vest, Marketing and Admissions Dir.
Founded: 1959. **Members:** 2,500. **Membership Dues:** foundation, $60 (annual). **Staff:** 12. **Budget:** $5,682,000. **Description:** Provides retirement housing and health care services to active and retired military officers, and their female relatives. Operates Knollwood, a military retirement community with independent apartments, assisted living and nursing care. **Awards:** Eisenhower Distinguished Citizen Award. **Frequency:** annual. **Type:** recognition. **Recipient:** for exceptional support of uniformed services and their families. **Also Known As:** Knollwood. **Publications:** *Army Distaff Foundation—Annual Report*. **Price:** free ● *Bugle Call*, semiannual. Newsletter. Covers foundation activities and projects of interest to members. **Price:** included in membership dues. ISSN: 0899-9694. **Circulation:** 2,500. **Conventions/Meetings:** annual meeting - always 3rd Wednesday or Thursday of April in Washington, DC.

20763 ■ Blue Star Mothers of America (BSM)
c/o Karen Stevens, Pres.
PO Box 471
Hazel Green, AL 35750
E-mail: president@bluestarmothers.org
URL: http://www.bluestarmothers.org
Contact: Karen Stevens, Pres.
Founded: 1942. **Members:** 2,200. **Membership Dues:** regular, $10 (annual). **State Groups:** 6. **Local Groups:** 166. **Description:** Mothers of current or past military service personnel. Works to assist veterans and their families; attempt to better the lives of servicemen abroad, participate in numerous community service and beautification projects; and promote patriotic sentiment. Studies and supports legislation concerning the welfare of veterans and national security. Collects money for the Chaplains Emergency Fund which provides for the needs of indigent, hospitalized veterans. Sponsors child welfare programs and supports national civil defense projects. Maintains archives. **Awards:** Educational Assistance. **Frequency:** annual. **Type:** monetary. **Publications:** *Blue Star Mother Yearbook*, annual. **Price:** $7.00. **Advertising:** accepted. **Conventions/Meetings:** annual conference - always October.

20764 ■ Catholic War Veterans Auxiliary of the U.S.A. (CWVA)
441 N Lee St.
Alexandria, VA 22314-2301
Ph: (703)549-3622
Fax: (703)684-5196
E-mail: cwvwebmaster@juno.com
URL: http://www.cwv.org/laux/laux.htm
Contact: Concetta Provenza, Natl. Pres.
Founded: 1949. **Members:** 6,000. **Staff:** 5. **State Groups:** 15. **Local Groups:** 275. **Description:** Represents mothers, widows, sisters, daughters, granddaughters, and nieces of living and deceased members of the Catholic War Veterans of the U.S.A. **Committees:** Americanism; Catholic Action; Civics; Education; Legislation; VAVS; Welfare; Youth Activities. **Formerly:** (1990) Catholic War Veterans of the U.S.A. Auxiliary. **Conventions/Meetings:** annual meeting, held in conjunction with the CWV.

20765 ■ Gold Star Wives of America (GSW)
PO Box 361986
Birmingham, AL 35236
Free: (888)751-6350
E-mail: info@goldstarwives.org
URL: http://www.goldstarwives.org
Contact: Joan Young, Pres.
Founded: 1945. **Members:** 13,000. **Membership Dues:** regular, basic, $25 (annual) ● life (based on age), $200-$500. **Budget:** $62,000. **Regional Groups:** 8. **Local Groups:** 53. **Description:** Widows of servicemen who died while on active duty or from service-connected disabilities. Promotes patriotism. Conducts volunteer work in veteran and civilian hospitals. Testifies before congressional committees on behalf of service widows. Notifies widows and their children of changes in VA benefits. **Computer Services:** Mailing lists, of members. **Committees:** Community Service; Education; Fundraising; Hospital Service; Legislation. **Formerly:** American Widows of World War II; (1948) Gold Star Wives of World War II. **Publications:** *Gold Star Wives Newsletter*, quarterly. Includes the volunteer activities of the association and legislation report. **Price:** available to members only. **Conventions/Meetings:** annual convention and general assembly.

20766 ■ Jewish War Veterans of the U.S.A. - National Ladies Auxiliary (JWVA)
1811 R St. NW
Washington, DC 20009-1603
Ph: (202)265-6280
Fax: (202)634-5662
E-mail: jwv@jwv.org
URL: http://www.jwv.org
Contact: Charlene Ehrlich, Pres.
Founded: 1928. **Members:** 15,000. **Staff:** 4. **Budget:** $100,000. **Regional Groups:** 300. **State Groups:** 14. **Local Groups:** 2. **National Groups:** 300. **Description:** Sisters, wives, mothers, daughters, widows, and lineal descendants of Jewish veterans of wars of the United States. Sends gifts to servicemen overseas; conducts youth programs; provides service to hospitalized veterans. Has furnished a surgical wing at Chaim Sheba Medical Center in Israel and has contributed equipment to an amniotic laboratory there. Provides children's services; conducts charitable programs. **Awards:** Humanity Award. **Frequency:** annual. **Type:** recognition. **Recipient:** for military academies ● **Type:** scholarship. **Recipient:** for financial needs and scholastic achievement. **Computer Services:** database. **Committees:** Action and Jewish Affairs; Aid to Israel; Americanism; Child Welfare; Community Relations; Consumer Affairs; Hospital; Leadership; Legislation; MIA/POW Red Ribbon Campaign; Scholarship; Servicemen's Service; United Nations; Veterans Administration Volunteer Service; Veterans Service. **Affiliated With:** Jewish War Veterans of the U.S.A. **Publications:** Bulletin, quarterly. **Price:** included in membership dues. **Advertising:** accepted. **Conventions/Meetings:** annual convention ● annual executive committee meeting.

20767 ■ National Association of Military Widows (NAMW)
4023 25th Rd. N
Arlington, VA 22207
Ph: (703)527-4565
Fax: (703)527-3881
E-mail: shirleydalton@home.com
URL: http://www1.va.gov/vso/index.cfm
Contact: Jean Arthurs, Pres.
Founded: 1978. **Members:** 7,000. **Membership Dues:** military widow, $12 (annual). **Description:** Widows of careermen and reservists in all branches of the uniformed services whose husbands died either during active service or following disability or nondisability retirement. Seeks equitable legislation and survivor benefit programs, and monitors all legislation and programs affecting military widows in Congress, the Department of Defense, and Veterans

Administration. **Convention/Meeting:** none. **Publications:** *National Association of Military Widows—Newsletter*, quarterly. Contains information on issues affecting military widows. **Price:** included in membership dues. **Circulation:** 7,000.

20768 ■ National Military Family Association (NMFA)
2500 N Van Dorn St., Ste.102
Alexandria, VA 22302-1601
Ph: (703)931-6632
Free: (800)260-0218
Fax: (703)931-4600
E-mail: families@nmfa.org
URL: http://www.nmfa.org
Contact: Mr. Eduardo Gadsden USMC, Chief Operating Off.
Founded: 1969. **Members:** 30,000. **Membership Dues:** military family, patron, affinity, $20 (annual) ● military family, patron, affinity, $50 (triennial) ● life (military family, patron), $300 ● junior military, $15 (annual) ● military affiliate, $100-$500. **Staff:** 20. **Description:** Military personnel and spouses; active duty and retired; Reserve and National Guard of the Army, Navy, Air Force, Marine Corps, Coast Guard, U.S. Public Health Service, and the National Oceanic and Atmospheric Administration. Serves as an advocate for military families through involvement in policies affecting them. Seeks to educate military members and their families of their benefits and rights and to study issues affecting military families. Conducts workshops to inform members of rights, benefits, and proposed legislation. **Awards:** Margaret Vinson Hallgren Award. **Frequency:** annual. **Type:** recognition. **Recipient:** for lifetime contribution to the organization by a headquarters volunteer ● NMFA Award. **Frequency:** annual. **Type:** recognition ● Novella Gibson Whitehead Award. **Frequency:** annual. **Type:** recognition. **Recipient:** for lifetime contribution to the organization by a local representative volunteer ● Very Important Patriot Award. **Frequency:** annual. **Type:** recognition. **Recipient:** for outstanding volunteer service to the military community. **Committees:** Financial Development; Government Relations; Marketing and Membership; Public Relations; Volunteer and Representative Services. **Formerly:** (1984) National Military Wives Association. **Publications:** *The Voice*, monthly. Newsletter. Provides news and analysis of issues affecting service families such as health care, housing, relocation, spouse employment, and child care. **Price:** included in membership dues. ISSN: 1075-0975. **Circulation:** 30,000 ● Also publishes fact sheets on quality of life issues. **Conventions/Meetings:** annual Military Families: Money and Mobility - luncheon, includes presentation of awards.

20769 ■ Navy Wifeline Association (NWA)
Washington Navy Yard, Bldg. 120
Washington, DC 20374
Ph: (202)433-2332
URL: http://www.thach.navy.mil/Welcome_aboard/navy_wifeline_association.htm
Founded: 1965. **Description:** Spouses of both officers and enlisted personnel in the Navy, Marine Corps, and Coast Guard. Serves as a clearinghouse for information and provides resource assistance in an effort to better educate members on the importance of their spouses' careers. Provides information on many aspects of military lifestyle. Fosters a sense of belonging among families of naval personnel to help them meet the challenges of a military lifestyle and combat the problems encountered due to family separation and constantly changing environments. **Computer Services:** Mailing lists, Navy Family Lifeline. **Publications:** *Bride's Kits*. Brochures ● *Financial and Personal Affairs* ● *Guidelines for Launching Clubs and Support Groups* ● *Guidelines for Spouses of Senior Enlisted Leaders* ● *Guidelines for the Spouses of Commanding Officers and Executive Officers* ● *Navy Family Lifeline*, quarterly. Magazine. Includes articles about and for navy families worldwide. **Price:** free ● *Navy Wifeline*, quarterly. Newsletter ● *Ombudsman Journal*, quarterly. Magazine. Includes articles of interest and information for ombudsmen worldwide. **Price:** free ● *Overseaman-

ship* ● *Sea Legs* ● *Social Customs and Traditions of the Naval Services*. Brochures ● Booklets. **Price:** free ● Pamphlets. **Conventions/Meetings:** seminar.

20770 ■ Society of Military Widows (SMW)
c/o Dee Ruelas, Treas.
2486 N Camino Valle Verde
Tucson, AZ 85715
Free: (800)842-3451
E-mail: benefits@militarywidows.org
URL: http://www.militarywidows.org
Contact: Patricia D. Shecter, Pres.
Founded: 1968. **Members:** 4,900. **Membership Dues:** $12 (annual). **Local Groups:** 30. **Description:** Widows of deceased career or active duty military personnel; affiliate members are persons who support the society's goals. Seeks to obtain equity for military widows under the Survivor Benefit Plan and to educate the public concerning the problems and needs of military widows. Monitors federal legislation affecting military widows; provides members with fact sheets on changes in survivor benefits. Has introduced bills before Congress and testified before congressional committees. Conducts surveys. Maintains the ROTH (Reach Out To Help) program by local chapter, a support system for the newly widowed, and sponsor social and educational activities. **Publications:** none. **Libraries: Type:** open to the public. **Holdings:** photographs. **Awards: Type:** recognition. **Affiliated With:** National Association for Uniformed Services. **Conventions/Meetings:** annual conference.

20771 ■ Sons of the American Legion (SAL)
PO Box 1055
Indianapolis, IN 46206
Ph: (317)630-1200
Fax: (317)630-1413
E-mail: sal@legion.org
URL: http://www.sal.legion.org
Contact: Brian O'Hearne, Natl. Adjutant
Founded: 1932. **Members:** 312,000. **Regional Groups:** 5. **State Groups:** 53. **Local Groups:** 5,500. **Description:** Male descendants, stepsons, and adopted sons of members of the American Legion or of deceased veterans of wartime military service who were eligible for Legion membership. Supports the principles of the AL and conducts patriotic activities. Operates charitable program. **Telecommunication Services:** electronic mail, salnatladj@aol.com. **Commissions:** Americanism; Children and Youth; Internal Affairs. **Committees:** Child Welfare; Community Service; Member Training and Development. **Affiliated With:** American Legion. **Publications:** *National Update*, quarterly. Newsletter. Alternate Formats: online ● *Sons of the American Legion Administrative Manual*. Alternate Formats: online ● *Squadron Handbook* ● Directory, annual ● Brochures ● Handbook. Alternate Formats: online. **Conventions/Meetings:** annual meeting - usually September.

20772 ■ Veteran Corps of Artillery, State of New York, Constituting the Military Society of the War of 1812 (VCA)
7th Regiment Armory
643 Park Ave.
New York, NY 10021
Ph: (212)249-3919
Fax: (212)249-3919
E-mail: info@vca1790.org
URL: http://www.vca1790.org
Contact: BG David J. Ramsay, Commandant
Founded: 1790. **Members:** 325. **Description:** Hereditary society of descendants of any defender of the country in the American Revolution and the War of 1812 who served honorably in the armies and navies of the U.S. Nonhereditary members may qualify for membership in the Artillery Service Detachment (active members who appear regularly for drill and pistol practice in the armory and take part in parades and historical celebrations) provided they are eligible under State of New York law. Honorary membership is given to officers of flag rank, governors, and the U.S. president. Participates in military and official ceremonies. Maintains museum. **Libraries: Type:** reference. **Holdings:** archival material,

books. **Subjects:** military history. **Awards:** Marksmanship. **Frequency:** annual. **Type:** recognition. **Recipient:** for proficiency in small arms. **Computer Services:** database. **Committees:** Armory; Discipline; Membership; Uniform. **Formed by Merger of:** (1848) Veterans Corps of Artillery, State of New York; Military Society War of 1812. **Publications:** *Red Book*, biennial. Directory ● *Veterans Corps of Artillery, State of New York, Constituting the Military Society of the War of 1812: Roster and General Information*, periodic. Directory. **Price:** included in membership dues. **Conventions/Meetings:** annual dinner - always January in New York City ● annual meeting.

20773 ■ World War II War Brides (WWIIWBA)
c/o Ms. Erin Craig, VP
PO Box 1812
El Centro, CA 92244
Ph: (760)352-4191
E-mail: classicalmuse@sbcglobal.net
Contact: Ms. Erin Craig, VP
Founded: 1996. **Members:** 347. **Membership Dues:** all, $10 (annual). **Budget:** $3,000. **Languages:** Czech, Danish, Dutch, English, French, German, Italian, Luxembourgish, Romanian, Slovak, Welsh. **Description:** Aims to join together foreign born wives and husbands of U.S. military personnel who married during the WWII era and who have the common bond of coming to a different country to live, accepting a new culture and contributing their many talents to the U.S. Welcomes women and men from foreign countries who have married U.S. military personnel since WWII and certain members of their families. Demonstrates that people, once enemies, can forget the past and join together in harmony to create a better understanding among different cultures joining together as one. Supports each other with physical and emotional assistance through difficult times and share times of joy and happiness. **Publications:** *War Brides Courier*, bimonthly. Newsletter. Contains reunion information, letters from members. **Price:** included in membership dues. **Circulation:** 293. **Conventions/Meetings:** annual convention.

Military History

20774 ■ Navy and Marine Living History Association (NMLHA)
c/o Rick Horn, Treas.
2523 Ambling Cir.
Crofton, MD 21114
E-mail: rick_horn@urscorp.com
URL: http://www.navyandmarine.org
Contact: Rick Horn, Treas.
Description: Promotes an awareness of America's nautical history. Supports living history member units who portray the sailors and marines who played a role in the formation of the country in the period 1750-1900. Provides a forum for the exchange of information between member groups as well as a resource of original research and historical documentation for members. **Publications:** *On Deck!*. Magazine. Contains articles about the history of the navy, as well as related features. Alternate Formats: online.

Military Police

20775 ■ CID Agents Association (CIDAA)
1896 Carlisle Rd.
Traverse City, MI 49686-9156
Ph: (231)932-2388
E-mail: cidaa@coslink.net
URL: http://www.cidaa.net
Contact: Charlene Oestman-Thibeau, Membership Chair
Founded: 1945. **Members:** 1,350. **Membership Dues:** general, $20 (annual). **Staff:** 20. **Local Groups:** 6. **Description:** Seeks to advance the unification of CID (Criminal Investigation Division) agents, past and present. Promotes an atmosphere of friendship and goodwill among members as well as the name of the CIDAA (Criminal Investigation

Division Agents Association) and the army CID. Supports the Army Criminal Investigation Division (CID). **Libraries: Type:** not open to the public. **Holdings:** archival material. **Subjects:** Army Criminal Investigation Division (CID), Criminal Investigation Division Agents Association (CIDAA). **Awards:** CID Hall of Fame. **Frequency:** annual. **Type:** monetary ● CID Soldier of the Year. **Frequency:** annual. **Type:** monetary. **Computer Services:** database, directory of members. **Publications:** *Year 2005 Gold Book.* **Price:** included in membership dues ● Newsletter, quarterly. **Price:** included in membership dues. **Circulation:** 1,547. **Conventions/Meetings:** annual board meeting ● annual meeting, for members, with elections - September, October or November.

20776 ■ Military Police Regimental Association (MPRA)
PO Box 2182
Fort Leonard Wood, MO 65473
Ph: (573)329-5317
E-mail: mpra@webound.com
URL: http://mpra.freehosting.net/home.htm
Contact: Merle D. Jones, Pres.
Founded: 1988. **Members:** 1,500. **Membership Dues:** active, $12 (annual) ● active, $22 (biennial) ● active, $30 (triennial). **Staff:** 1. **Local Groups:** 23. **Description:** Active duty, reserve, or retired members of the Military Police Corps Regiment; other military personnel and interested civilians. Works to preserve the history of the Military Police Corps; promotes solidarity among members and fosters literary, educational, and artistic endeavors. Seeks to improve the Military Police Regimental Military Grove. Provides member locator service. Supports the Military Police Corps Regimental Museum. **Telecommunication Services:** electronic mail, jonesm@wood.army.mil. **Committees:** Memorial Grove; Museum. **Supersedes:** Military Police Association. **Publications:** *MPRA Newsletter,* quarterly. **Price:** free for members. **Advertising:** accepted. **Conventions/Meetings:** annual meeting - always September, in Fort McClellan, AL.

20777 ■ Retired Military Police Association (RMPA)
c/o Mack H. Mullins, Exec. Dir.
PO Box 25542
Fayetteville, NC 28314
Ph: (910)867-4292
E-mail: rmpamack@aol.com
URL: http://www.rmpa.20m.com
Contact: Mack H. Mullins, Exec. Dir.
Founded: 1994. **Members:** 850. **Membership Dues:** regular, $15 (annual). **Description:** Retired military police personnel. Works with active duty military police and civilian police during catastrophes. Conducts periodic conferences and special events. Performs volunteer work and charitable services. Aims to build a youth retreat in McDowell County, WV, in order to work with youth drug problems. **Publications:** Newsletter, 3/year. **Price:** free. **Circulation:** 650. **Conventions/Meetings:** annual conference.

Navy

20778 ■ American Battleship Association (ABA)
PO Box 711247
San Diego, CA 92171
Ph: (858)271-6106
E-mail: mardav63@aol.com
Contact: Margaret J. Graham, Sec.-Treas.
Founded: 1963. **Members:** 1,172. **Membership Dues:** $5 (annual). **Staff:** 2. **Description:** Social organization of officers and enlisted men currently or previously in the armed forces who served aboard a U.S. Navy battleship. Engages in the swapping of sea stories and memorializing of battleships and those who manned them. **Publications:** *American Battleship Association—Master Roster,* annual. Membership Directory. **Price:** included in membership dues. **Advertising:** accepted ● *Ole Salt's Digest,*

semiannual. Newsletter. **Price:** included in membership dues. **Advertising:** accepted. **Conventions/Meetings:** annual reunion, photos and books (exhibits).

20779 ■ Fleet Reserve Association (FRA)
125 N West St.
Alexandria, VA 22314-2709
Ph: (703)683-1400
Free: (800)FRA-1924
Fax: (703)549-6610
E-mail: news-fra@fra.org
URL: http://www.fra.org
Contact: Joseph L. Barnes, Natl. Exec. Sec.
Founded: 1924. **Members:** 149,000. **Membership Dues:** U.S. Navy, Marine Corps, Coast Guard, $20 (annual). **Staff:** 21. **Budget:** $4,000,000. **Regional Groups:** 9. **State Groups:** 304. **Description:** Active duty enlisted personnel in the U.S. Navy, Marine Corps, Coast Guard, Fleet Reserves of the Navy, and Fleet Marine Corps and Coast Guard; retired members of these services. **Libraries: Type:** reference. **Awards: Frequency:** annual. **Type:** scholarship. **Recipient:** to promising students. **Telecommunication Services:** electronic mail, fra@fra.org. **Publications:** *Naval Affairs Magazine,* monthly. **Price:** $7.00. ISSN: 0028-2409. **Circulation:** 160,000. **Advertising:** accepted ● *On Watch,* bimonthly. Newspaper. **Price:** free for members. ISSN: 1047-1731. **Circulation:** 160,000. **Conventions/Meetings:** annual convention, vendor displays (exhibits).

20780 ■ Force Recon Association (FRA)
PO Box 783
Angels Camp, CA 95222
Ph: (209)607-6961
E-mail: commchief@forcerecon.com
URL: http://www.forcerecon.com
Contact: Dick Sasser, Exec. Dir.
Founded: 1980. **Members:** 1,900. **Membership Dues:** regular, associate, $40 (annual). **Budget:** $40,000. **Description:** U.S. Marine Corps or Navy officers and enlisted personnel who served with a Force Recon Company from 1957 to present, or in an Amphibious Reconnaissance unit between 1943 and 1957; Air Force, Army, Marine Corps, and Navy personnel who have made a significant contribution to Force Recon operations; military personnel or civilians who have aided Force Recon or Amphibious Reconnaissance units. (Force Recon and Amphibious Reconnaissance units are special operations intelligence-gathering units that take place on shore, under covert conditions.) Provides a forum for members to remain in contact with one another. Compiles statistics; conducts charitable program; sponsors competitions. **Awards:** Recon Team Leader of the Year Award. **Type:** recognition ● **Frequency:** annual. **Type:** scholarship. **Committees:** Legislative; Memorial Scholarship. **Publications:** *Sitrep,* quarterly. Newsletter. **Price:** free, for members only. **Advertising:** accepted ● Newsletter, quarterly ● Report, quarterly. **Conventions/Meetings:** annual reunion - always August/September.

20781 ■ National Association of Fleet Tug Sailors (NAFTS)
19416 Mohawk Rd.
Bend, OR 97702-8908
Ph: (541)410-0297
Free: (866)652-2038
E-mail: snipe@nafts.com
URL: http://www.nafts.com
Contact: Tom Thomas, Contact
Founded: 1990. **Members:** 225. **Membership Dues:** general, $25 (annual). **Staff:** 25. **Description:** Former and current members of the U.S. Navy and U.S. Coast Guard who served on tug type and salvage type military ships. Acquires and preserves ATF and ARS ships as memorials. **Libraries: Type:** not open to the public. **Holdings:** 15. **Subjects:** tugboat experiences. **Publications:** *The Towline,* quarterly. Magazine. Contains information on the association and its members. **Price:** $25.00/copy. **Circulation:** 1,600. **Advertising:** accepted. **Conventions/Meetings:** annual reunion (exhibits).

20782 ■ National Chief Petty Officers' Association (NCPOA)
c/o William A. Williams, Membership Dir.
106 Waring Welfare Rd.
Boerne, TX 78006-7925
Ph: (830)537-4899
E-mail: mkluttz2@carolina.rr.com
URL: http://www.goatlocker.org/ncpoa
Contact: M. Glenn Kluttz, Pres.
Founded: 1988. **Members:** 2,600. **Membership Dues:** individual, $15 (annual) ● life (ages 25-29), $335 ● life (ages 30-34), $307 ● life (ages 35-39), $280 ● life (ages 40-44), $252 ● life (ages 45-49), $225 ● life (ages 50-54), $197 ● life (ages 55-59), $170 ● life (ages 60-64), $142 ● life (ages 65-69), $115 ● life (ages 70-74), $87 ● life (ages 75 and up), $60. **Staff:** 6. **State Groups:** 6. **Description:** Active duty, retired, and veteran chief petty officers in the U.S. Navy, Coast Guard, and Reserves. Seeks to publicize the accomplishments of members, and to increase awareness of the duties and responsibilities of chief petty officers. Facilitates camaraderie and good fellowship among members. Encourages advancement of the Navy and Coast Guard through research and education. **Awards:** Bart Longo Scholarship Program. **Frequency:** annual. **Type:** monetary. **Funds:** Scholarship. **Publications:** *The Chiefs,* quarterly. Newspaper. **Price:** included in membership dues. **Circulation:** 2,600. **Advertising:** accepted ● *NetChiefs Online Newsletter,* daily. Alternate Formats: online. **Conventions/Meetings:** annual convention - always October.

20783 ■ Naval Order of the United States (NOUS)
PO Box 2714
Merrifield, VA 22116-2714
Ph: (703)323-0929 (904)221-0923
Fax: (904)221-0923
E-mail: navalorder@cox.net
URL: http://www.navalorder.org
Contact: Capt. Carter Conlin, Commander Gen.
Founded: 1890. **Members:** 1,850. **Membership Dues:** regular, associate, $40 (annual) ● life, $500. **Budget:** $45,000. **Local Groups:** 24. **Description:** Persons who have served as officers or enlisted members of the U.S. Navy, Marine Corps, Coast Guard, USPHS, USMM or NOAA and their descendants over 18 years of age; and its allies. Naval authors and Naval historians are eligible for associate membership. Seeks to transmit to posterity the names and memories of the great naval commanders, their companion officers, and their subordinates in the wars of the United States. Encourages research and publication of literature pertaining to naval history and science. Establishes libraries to preserve all documents, rolls, books, portraits, and relics relating to the Navy and its heroes of all times. Conducts naval history research. Promotes, preserves, celebrates and enjoys Naval history and heritage. **Libraries: Type:** reference. **Holdings:** archival material. **Subjects:** naval history and heritage, Naval Order of US records. **Awards:** Admiral of the Navy George Dewey Award. **Frequency:** annual. **Type:** recognition. **Recipient:** to a distinguished American for service to the Naval services and their history and heritage in a civilian capacity ● Distinguished Sea Service Officer. **Frequency:** annual. **Type:** recognition. **Recipient:** for distinguished Sea Service career, flag or general officer ● Midshipmen of U.S. Naval Academy Writing Contest. **Type:** recognition ● Outstanding Coast Guard Academy Junior Officer Instructor. **Type:** recognition ● Outstanding Graduate Naval Flight Officer. **Type:** recognition. **Computer Services:** database ● mailing lists, of members. **Formed by Merger of:** (1893) Naval Commandery of America; (1893) Naval Legion of the United States. **Publications:** *Centennial Register of Companions 1890-1990* ● *General Commandery Newsletter,* quarterly ● *Naval History.* Magazine. Contains information published by the US Naval Institute. **Price:** included in membership dues. **Conventions/Meetings:** annual congress.

20784 ■ Navy Mail Service Veterans Association (NMSVA)
2768 State Rte. 29
Dolgeville, NY 13329

Ph: (315)429-8645
E-mail: rjorry1@cny.rr.com
Contact: Robert Jorry, Treas.
Founded: 1972. **Members:** 225. **Membership Dues:** individual, $5 (annual). **Staff:** 4. **Description:** Veterans who served in the Navy mail service, including fleet record and fleet post offices, armed guard mail units, and Coast Guard and Marine Corps postal units; widows and widowers of Navy mail service veterans. Promotes camaraderie among members. Collaborates with the National Postal Museum in Washington, DC to display artifacts and present the history of the Navy mail service. **Awards:** Perfect Attendance. **Type:** recognition. **Computer Services:** Mailing lists. **Publications:** Newsletter, semiannual. **Circulation:** 225. **Conventions/Meetings:** annual reunion - September or October.

20785 ■ Navy Seabee Veterans of America (Navy S.V.A.)
c/o Mel Ramige, Natl. Sec.
555 Fairview Ave.
Creve Coeur, IL 61610-3237
Ph: (309)699-7344
Free: (800)SEA-BEE5
Fax: (309)699-1201
E-mail: navysvasecy@worldnet.att.net
URL: http://www.nsva.org
Contact: Mel Ramige, Natl. Sec.
Founded: 1948. **Members:** 5,854. **Membership Dues:** regular, $20 (annual) ● life (up to 40 years old), $180 ● life (40-69 years old), $155 ● life (70-up), $130. **Staff:** 4. **State Groups:** 11. **Local Groups:** 116. **Description:** Veterans of the Naval Construction Forces and the Navy Civil Engineer Corps. Promotes and strengthens comradeship between members and preserve service-created friendships; fosters and maintains interest in SEABEE activities and assists others associated with SEABEE organizations; assists in rehabilitation and welfare of veterans who served in military forces of the U.S. in time of war and peace. **Awards:** Seabee Memorial Scholarship Association (SMSA). **Frequency:** annual. **Type:** scholarship. **Recipient:** to child or grandchild of Seabee. **Computer Services:** Information services, connecting Seabees with other Seabees. **Formerly:** (1983) Seabee Veterans of America. **Publications:** Can Do, quarterly. Magazine. **Price:** included in membership dues. **Circulation:** 5,800. **Advertising:** accepted. **Conventions/Meetings:** annual convention and reunion.

20786 ■ Patrol Craft Sailors Association (PCSA)
c/o Jim Heywood
7005 Bridge Rd.
Cincinnati, OH 45230
Ph: (315)487-2623 (513)233-2775
E-mail: buckypcsa@juno.com
URL: http://www.ww2pcsa.org
Contact: Duane D. Walters, Pres.
Founded: 1987. **Members:** 2,000. **Membership Dues:** regular, $15 (annual) ● associate, $10 (annual). **Staff:** 13. **Budget:** $32,640. **Regional Groups:** 6. **State Groups:** 2. **Local Groups:** 1. **Description:** World War II, Korea and active duty U.S. Navy officers and enlisted serving, or having served, on patrol coastal ships and craft. Seeks to maintain fellowship and communication among members. Offers educational programs; maintains biographical archives. Maintains a collection of resource information for writers and others interested in Naval history and tracing former shipmates; collection is housed in a museum in Bay City, MI. **Libraries:** Type: open to the public. **Holdings:** 6,000. **Subjects:** WWII, Korea, patrol craft sailors. **Awards:** Department of Defense - 50th Anniversary W.W. II Commemorative Community. **Type:** recognition. **Recipient:** for planned/conducted commemorative programs 1991-1995. **Computer Services:** database ● mailing lists ● online services. **Publications:** PCSA Newsletter, quarterly. Includes subchaser news and updates, photos, and book reviews. **Price:** included in membership dues. **Circulation:** 2,000. **Conventions/Meetings:** annual reunion, archive museum (exhibits).

20787 ■ Salisbury Sound Association (SSA)
c/o Capt. Marian Bruce, Sec.
813 Branding Iron St. SE
Albuquerque, NM 87123
Ph: (505)293-3841
E-mail: brubru@comcast.net
Contact: Capt. Marian Bruce, Sec.
Founded: 1983. **Members:** 825. **Membership Dues:** $15 (annual). **Description:** Men who served aboard the seaplane tender USS Salisbury Sound (AV-13) from 1945-67. Seeks to promote a positive attitude for defense of the United States and help members in need. **Libraries:** Type: reference. **Holdings:** archival material. **Publications:** Newsletter, quarterly. Includes calendar of events. **Conventions/Meetings:** annual reunion.

20788 ■ Tin Can Sailors - The National Association of Destroyer Veterans (TCS)
PO Box 100
Somerset, MA 02726
Ph: (508)677-0515
Free: (800)223-5535
Fax: (508)676-9740
E-mail: terrymiller@destroyers.org
URL: http://www.destroyers.org
Contact: Terry Miller, Exec. Dir.
Founded: 1976. **Members:** 24,000. **Membership Dues:** $25 (annual). **Staff:** 10. **Description:** Destroyer veterans. Promotes camaraderie among destroyermen. Assists reunion groups. **Libraries:** Type: reference. **Holdings:** 2,000; archival material, audiovisuals. **Subjects:** U.S. Navy destroyers. **Awards:** Type: grant. **Recipient:** to support destroyers serving as museum/memorial ships ● Thomas J. Peltin Destroyer Museum Grant Program. **Frequency:** annual. **Type:** grant. **Recipient:** for US Navy destroyers in museum status in the United States to be used for restoration projects and maintenance. **Committees:** Bull Session; Museum Accession. **Programs:** Historic Destroyers in Museum Status Grant. **Publications:** The Tin Can Sailor, quarterly. Newspaper. Includes articles on Navy Destroyer Service. **Price:** included in membership dues. **Circulation:** 26,000. **Conventions/Meetings:** Regional Bullsession - meeting - usually 22/year ● annual reunion (exhibits).

20789 ■ United States Navy Memorial Foundation (USNMF)
701 Pennsylvania Ave. NW, Ste.123
Washington, DC 20004
Ph: (202)737-2300
Free: (800)821-8892
Fax: (202)737-2308
E-mail: ahoy@lonesailor.org
URL: http://www.lonesailor.org
Contact: Rear Admiral (Ret) Richard A. Buchanan, Pres./CEO
Founded: 1977. **Members:** 70,000. **Staff:** 30. **Budget:** $5,000,000. **Description:** Seeks to preserve America's naval heritage through creation and operation of the United States Navy Memorial in Washington, DC. Also operates a 2400 square foot Naval Heritage Center adjacent to the memorial, a Ship's Store, naval historical exhibits, and The Navy Memorial Log. **Libraries:** Type: open to the public. **Holdings:** 600; photographs. **Subjects:** naval history. **Awards:** Lone Sailor Award. **Frequency:** annual. **Type:** recognition. **Recipient:** to Navy veterans who have distinguished themselves in civilian life through public service and national leadership ● Naval Heritage Award. **Frequency:** annual. **Type:** recognition. **Recipient:** to individuals who have not served in the sea services, but who have contributed to America's naval and maritime heritage. **Computer Services:** database, navy Memorial Log listing over 250,000 sea services veterans. **Publications:** The Lone Sailor, quarterly. Newsletter. Holds events at navy memorial. **Price:** included in membership dues. **Circulation:** 150,000 ● Also publishes brochures and guides.

20790 ■ U.S. Navy TACAMO Survivors
c/o Michael A. Vos, Exec. Dir.
5144 Waterloo Rd.
Burlington, KY 41005
Ph: (606)586-6016
Fax: (606)586-0528
E-mail: mvos@tacamo.org
URL: http://www.tacamo.org
Contact: Michael A. Vos, Exec. Dir.
Description: Seeks to maintain a fraternal community for the sailors of the TACAMO. **Awards:** Type: scholarship. **Recipient:** for members' children/grandchildren. **Publications:** Newsletter, semiannual.

20791 ■ USS (BB-42) Idaho Association
PO Box 711247
San Diego, CA 92171
Ph: (858)271-6106
E-mail: mardav63@aol.com
URL: http://www.ussidaho.com
Contact: Margaret J. Graham, Exec. Sec.
Founded: 1957. **Members:** 420. **Membership Dues:** $10 (annual). **Staff:** 2. **Description:** Officers and enlisted men who served in the battleship USS Idaho from 1919-47. Promotes fellowship among members. **Publications:** Big Spud, semiannual. Newsletter. Includes stories from shipmates. **Price:** available to members only. **Circulation:** 500. **Advertising:** accepted. **Conventions/Meetings:** annual reunion, photos, books, and ship model (exhibits).

20792 ■ USS Chilton Association
c/o H. Edward Ritterhoff, Sec.-Treas.
1000 SW 6th St.
Lee's Summit, MO 64081-2616
Ph: (816)358-8624
E-mail: hrit@aol.com
URL: http://usschilton.tripod.com
Contact: H. Edward Ritterhoff, Sec.-Treas.
Founded: 1997. **Members:** 525. **Membership Dues:** veteran, $5 (annual). **Staff:** 8. **Budget:** $2,000. **Description:** Military veterans (Navy, Marine, and Army) who served aboard USS Chilton APA-38 (later LPA-38) between 1943 and 1972. **Publications:** USS Chilton Newsletter, quarterly. **Circulation:** 525. **Conventions/Meetings:** annual convention and reunion, picture albums, history, artifacts, mementos (exhibits).

20793 ■ USS Intrepid Association of Former Crew Members (USSIAFCM)
Intrepid Sq.
86 N River Pier
New York, NY 10036-1012
Ph: (631)261-1568
Free: (800)343-CVII
E-mail: norm@wa3key.com
URL: http://ussintrepid.com/intrepid.html
Contact: Richard A. Torggler, Membership Chm.
Founded: 1985. **Members:** 1,400. **Membership Dues:** regular, $25 (annual). **Staff:** 15. **State Groups:** 32. **Description:** U.S. Navy veterans who served on the aircraft carrier Intrepid. (The Intrepid was launched in 1943 and took part in World War II, and the Vietnam War. It is now a national historic landmark and floating museum harbored outside New York City.) Maintains exhibits on board the Intrepid and a memorial to people who died while serving on the Intrepid. **Libraries:** Type: reference. **Holdings:** archival material, artwork, books, clippings. **Awards:** **Frequency:** annual. **Type:** scholarship. **Recipient:** for families of crew members. **Publications:** The Ketcher, monthly. Newsletter. **Price:** included in membership dues. **Advertising:** accepted. **Conventions/Meetings:** monthly board meeting - 3rd Saturday on board USS Intrepid ● annual reunion - always in New York City.

20794 ■ USS Leyte CV32 Association
c/o William A. Crawford
170 NW Silver Glen
Lake City, FL 32055-4899
Ph: (904)737-4673

E-mail: crawdaddy@crawford.net
URL: http://www.ussleytecv32.com
Contact: Clarkson B. Farnsworth, Pres.

Founded: 1987. **Members:** 1,500. **Membership Dues:** individual, $10 (annual). **Staff:** 8. **Description:** Individuals who served aboard ship company or air group of the aircraft carrier USS Leyte (CV-32 CVA 32-CVS-32) during 1946-1959. Promotes fellowship among members. **Publications:** *Leyte News*, quarterly. Newsletter. Informs members of past and upcoming reunions. **Circulation:** 1,500. **Conventions/Meetings:** annual reunion, ship and air group memorabilia (exhibits).

20795 ■ USS Liberty Veterans Association (USSLVA)

c/o Moe Shafer, Treas.
Blazer Associates, Inc.
4994 Lower Roswell Rd., Ste.33
Marietta, GA 30068
E-mail: jimandjoe@ussliberty.com
URL: http://www.ussliberty.org
Contact: Moe Shafer, Treas.

Founded: 1982. **Members:** 800. **Membership Dues:** associate, $20 (annual). **Staff:** 6. **Regional Groups:** 5. **National Groups:** 600. **Description:** Survivors of the 1967 Israeli attack of the electronic surveillance ship, USS Liberty, other crewmen, family members, and supporters worldwide. Seeks to publicize and educate the public about the attack and to honor the shipmates who died in the attack. Assists authors, television and movie producers, and other researchers in locating documents regarding the USS Liberty. Maintains speakers' bureau; operates library. Sponsors annual essay and scholarship contest. **Publications:** *Liberty News*, quarterly. Newsletter. Provides a forum for the exchange of information about the attack on the USS Liberty and the "subsequent cover-up". Includes meeting announcements. **Price:** $15.00/year for members; $20.00/year for associate members. **Circulation:** 600. Also Cited As: *USS Liberty News*. **Conventions/Meetings:** triennial convention (exhibits).

20796 ■ USS LSM-LSMR Association

c/o Larry Glaser
237 Duquesne Blvd.
New Kensington, PA 15068
E-mail: labetco@acninc.net
Contact: Larry Glaser, Contact

Founded: 1989. **Members:** 3,100. **Membership Dues:** individual, $15 (annual) ● life (over 65 years old), $150. **Staff:** 8. **Regional Groups:** 8. **State Groups:** 5. **Description:** Crew members who served on one of the 494 LSMs (landing ship mediums) or 60 LSMRs (landing ship medium rockets). Gathers together to share memories and stories. Organizes side trips, tours, banquet, and dances for members. **Also Known As:** LSM National Association. **Formerly:** (1995) National LSM Association. **Publications:** *Alligator Alley*, quarterly. Newsletter. **Price:** included in membership dues. ISSN: 1097-0983. **Circulation:** 3,200 ● *LSM-LSMR History Vol. I and Vol. II*. Books. **Conventions/Meetings:** annual reunion and meeting (exhibits).

20797 ■ USS Nevada Association (BB-36/SSBN-733)

Address Unknown since 2007

Founded: 1953. **Members:** 444. **Membership Dues:** $10 (annual). **Staff:** 30. **National Groups:** 1. **Description:** Individuals currently serving or who served aboard the battleship USS Nevada. Serves as a social organization. Sponsors charitable program; maintains small collection of historical items from the USS Nevada. **Libraries: Type:** open to the public; reference. **Subjects:** BB-36 and SSBN-733. **Awards:** Sailors of the Year on SSBN-733. **Frequency:** annual. **Type:** recognition. **Recipient:** as determined by C.O. **Committees:** Social Planning Activities. **Publications:** *Annual Roster*. **Advertising:** not accepted ● *Scuttlebutt*. Newsletter. **Conventions/Meetings:** annual reunion (exhibits).

20798 ■ USS Nimitz (CVN-68) Association

c/o Raymond D. Bigelow
5021 S 25th St.
Milwaukee, WI 53221
E-mail: waldoj@cox.net
URL: http://ussnimitzassociation.org
Contact: Waldo Brunner, Pres.

Founded: 1997. **Members:** 550. **Membership Dues:** regular (plus $15 initiation fee), $20 (annual). **Staff:** 4. **Description:** Represents shipmen of the USS Nimitz (CVN-68). **Awards: Frequency:** annual. **Type:** scholarship. **Computer Services:** database, membership. **Publications:** Newsletter, quarterly. **Circulation:** 600. **Conventions/Meetings:** annual reunion.

20799 ■ USS Pyro AE-1 and AE-24 Association

c/o Jared S. Cameron, Pres.
3808 Brighton Ct.
Alexandria, VA 22305-1571
Ph: (703)837-1977
E-mail: jaredcameron@comcast.net
URL: http://www.usspyro.com
Contact: Jared S. Cameron, Pres.

Founded: 1983. **Members:** 215. **Membership Dues:** individual, $20 (annual) ● life (based on age), $25-$250. **Description:** Individuals who served on the USS Pyro AE-1 or AE-24 and their families. Seeks to perpetuate the memory of deceased naval veterans; promotes continued camaraderie among members. Conducts social and educational programs; raises funds for veterans' organizations. **Libraries: Type:** not open to the public. **Holdings:** archival material, articles, business records. **Subjects:** USS Pyro, veterans' issues. **Publications:** *USS Pyro Scuttlebutt*, quarterly. Newsletter. **Price:** free. **Conventions/Meetings:** annual reunion.

20800 ■ USS Wisconsin Association

c/o Dom Menta
HC 1 Box 1021
Tannersville, PA 18372
Ph: (570)620-1446
E-mail: dombb64@ptd.net
URL: http://www.usswisconsin.org
Contact: William Henson, Pres.

Founded: 1988. **Members:** 1,400. **Membership Dues:** regular, associate, $15 (annual). **Description:** Represents individuals who served on the U.S.S. Wisconsin in WW II, Korea, and the Gulf War. Seeks to encourage and maintain contact between former crewmembers. **Libraries: Type:** open to the public. **Holdings:** archival material, photographs. **Subjects:** history of the U.S.S. Wisconsin. **Publications:** *Badger*, quarterly. Newsletter. **Price:** included in membership dues. **Circulation:** 1,500. **Conventions/Meetings:** biennial reunion - even numbered years in September.

20801 ■ Veteran's Association of the USS Iowa (IOWAVETS)

2916 NW Bucklin Hill Rd., No. 169
Silverdale, WA 98383
Ph: (360)692-6032
Fax: (360)824-9032
E-mail: kjoggpr@aol.com
URL: http://www.ussiowa.org
Contact: Gerald E. Gneckow, Pres.

Founded: 1978. **Members:** 3,775. **Membership Dues:** family, battleship enthusiast, $15 (annual). **Description:** U.S. Navy veterans and Marines who served on the battleship USS Iowa. (The USS Iowa was launched in 1942 and served in World War II, the Korean War, and the 80s. It is no longer in service.) Encourages contact between former crewmembers. Sponsors USS Iowa Preservation Fund. Seeks to preserve the ship as a museum; will include plaques, artifacts, photographs, and other memorabilia. **Libraries: Type:** reference. **Holdings:** archival material, photographs. **Publications:** *Roster*, semiannual. Newsletter. **Price:** included in membership dues ● *USS Iowa Veterans Association Newsletter*, quarterly. Includes membership activities. **Price:** included in membership dues. **Conventions/Meetings:** annual reunion.

20802 ■ WAVES National (WN)

c/o Gloria Galati, Exec. Sec.
16547 S Red Rock Dr.
Strongsville, OH 44136
Ph: (440)655-0100
E-mail: sharonsnw1124@aol.com
URL: http://www.womenofthewaves.com
Contact: Ms. Sharon Woods, Pres.

Founded: 1979. **Members:** 4,008. **Membership Dues:** regular, $15 (annual). **Staff:** 22. **Budget:** $70,000. **Regional Groups:** 12. **State Groups:** 35. **Local Groups:** 135. **Description:** Women who have served on active duty in the U.S. Navy and can show proof of service and an honorable discharge; women who are currently on active duty or who have retired from or served in the U.S. Navy, Naval Reserve, Navy Nurse Corps, Women Marines, or Coast Guard. Encourages principles of patriotism and loyalty to God, country, and family among former WAVES (Women Accepted for Volunteer Emergency Service) who have served since World War II, and other women who have served in the Sea Services. Provides a network of support and assistance and an opportunity for locating, communicating, and associating with former SEA Service women; serves as a medium of exchange between its local units. Keeps members informed about veterans benefits and policy changes. **Libraries: Type:** reference. **Subjects:** WWII, Korea, Vietnam. **Formerly:** (1986) Waves National Corporation. **Publications:** *White Caps*, bimonthly. Newsletter. **Price:** included in membership dues. **Circulation:** 6,500. **Alternate Formats:** online. **Conventions/Meetings:** biennial convention, memorabilia (exhibits) ● biennial regional meeting.

Officers

20803 ■ Military Officers Association of America (MOAA)

201 N Washington St.
Alexandria, VA 22314-2520
Ph: (703)549-2311
Free: (800)234-6622
Fax: (703)838-8173
E-mail: msc@moaa.org
URL: http://www.moaa.org
Contact: VAdm. USN (Ret.) Norbert R. Ryan Jr., Pres.

Founded: 1929. **Members:** 370,000. **Membership Dues:** regular, $24 (annual). **Staff:** 96. **Budget:** $12,000,000. **State Groups:** 36. **Local Groups:** 420. **Description:** Active duty, retired, National Guard, Reserve, former commissioned officers, warrant officers of the following uniformed services and their surviving spouse: Army, Marine Corps, Navy, Air Force, Coast Guard, Public Health Service, NOAA. Supports strong national defense and represents and assists members, their dependents and survivors with active duty and retirement issues and benefits. Sponsors educational assistance program, survivor assistance, and travel, insurance, and career transition services. **Libraries: Type:** lending; reference; not open to the public. **Holdings:** books, periodicals. **Awards:** Educational Assistance. **Frequency:** annual. **Type:** grant. **Recipient:** for unmarried undergraduate students under the age of 24 who are dependent children of active, reserve, and retired uniformed service personnel ● **Type:** monetary. **Recipient:** for unmarried undergraduate students under the age of 24 who are dependent children of active, reserve, and retired uniformed service personnel. **Computer Services:** Electronic publishing, legislative update ● online services, career center - job placement assistance, resume database, job listings ● online services, financial education center - estate planning, college funding, investment allocation and tax help. **Committees:** Chapters; Educational Assistance; Finance; Government Relations; Health Care; Insurance; Investment; Member Services; Membership; Publications. **Formerly:** (2003) The Retired Officers Association. **Publications:** *Help Your Surviving Spouse - Now!*, annual. Booklet ● *Marketing Yourself for a Second Career*. Booklet ● *The Military Officer*, monthly. Journal. Reports on national defense, military history, retirement planning, second-career opportunities, and legislation affecting uniformed service retirees. **Price:** included in membership dues; $20.00 /year for nonmembers. **ISSN:** 0034-6160. **Circulation:** 400,000. **Advertising:** accepted. Alternate Formats: microform ● *National Guard/Reserve Retirement Benefits.* Booklet ● *Planning for a Military Retirement.* Booklet ● *SBP Made Easy.* Booklet ● *Today's Officer,* quarterly. Journal. Provides news service for second career officers and those still serving in uniform. Features news, entertainment, polls, discussion forums. **Price:** included in membership dues; $12.00/year for those not eligible for membership; $24.00 overseas; $3.00/copy. **Circulation:** 100,000. **Advertising:** accepted. Alternate Formats: online; microform. **Conventions/Meetings:** annual meeting.

20804 ■ Military Order of Foreign Wars of the United States (MOFW)
c/o Col. Duane H. Bartrem, Commander Gen.
5985 Austin Way
Grand Ledge, MI 48837
Ph: (517)627-9072
E-mail: dhbartrem@aol.com
URL: http://www.foxfall.com/mofw.htm
Contact: Col. Duane H. Bartrem, Commander Gen.
Founded: 1894. **Members:** 1,346. **Staff:** 14. **Budget:** $10,000. **State Groups:** 13. **Description:** Represents former and present commissioned officers who served in or during a U.S. war with a foreign power and their direct descendants. **Awards:** MOFW Awards to USMA, USNA, USAFA, USCGA, and USMMA. **Frequency:** annual. **Type:** recognition. **Recipient:** for outstanding graduates of U.S. service academies. **Publications:** *MOFW Newsletter,* semi-annual. **Circulation:** 1,260. **Conventions/Meetings:** biennial convention, business/social.

20805 ■ National Order of Battlefield Commissions (NOBC)
c/o Robert C. Evans, Natl. Commander
2506 King St.
Alexandria, VA 22301
Ph: (703)838-5548
E-mail: rcevans@mmm.com
URL: http://www.battlefieldcommissions.org
Contact: Robert C. Evans, Natl. Commander
Founded: 1979. **Members:** 890. **Membership Dues:** individual, $15 (annual) ● life, $100. **State Groups:** 6. **Description:** Individual members of the U.S. Armed Forces, both active and retired, who received their commission as officers due to leadership abilities demonstrated in combat. Fosters spirit of camaraderie and shared experience among members. **Awards:** Commendors Trophy. **Frequency:** annual. **Type:** trophy. **Recipient:** for service to organization. **Publications:** *Mustang News,* quarterly. Newsletter. **Circulation:** 1,500. **Advertising:** accepted. **Conventions/Meetings:** annual convention.

20806 ■ Sea Service Leadership Association (SSLA)
PO Box 100356
Arlington, VA 22210
Ph: (703)732-1976
E-mail: wopaman@aol.com
URL: http://www.sealeader.org
Contact: Lt. Dawn Frank USN, Pres.
Founded: 1978. **Members:** 125. **Membership Dues:** regular (voting), $20-$40 (annual) ● affiliate (non-voting), $15-$30 (annual). **Description:** Serves as a professional forum for leaders in the U.S. Navy, Marines, and Coast Guard. Supports the continuing professional development of members; seeks to increase female participation in the sea services. Serves as a clearinghouse on the sea services; provides a forum for the discussion of affecting individuals with military careers; provides career planning and other educational materials; facilitates networking among members. **Awards:** Joy Bright Hancock Award for Leadership. **Frequency:** annual. **Type:** recognition. **Recipient:** for leadership. **Formerly:** (2006) Women Officers Professional Association. **Conventions/Meetings:** annual Professional Develop Symposium (exhibits) - in June.

Patriotism

20807 ■ American Patriots Association (APA)
c/o Terry Lynch, Pres./Founder
PO Box 241035
Montgomery, AL 36124-1035
E-mail: terrylynch@aol.com
URL: http://www.byteland.org/apa
Contact: Terry Lynch, Pres./Founder
Membership Dues: student patriot, $10 ● citizen patriot, $20 ● soldier patriot, $50 ● officer patriot, $100 ● corporate patriot, $250 ● sponsoring patriot, $500 ● life, $1,000 ● benefactor patriot, $5,000. **Description:** Promotes, supports, defends and works to insure freedom, liberty and patriotism in the United States of America. Advocates for nonviolence, civil rights and liberty for people of all races, religions and national origin. **Publications:** Newsletter.

20808 ■ Centennial Legion of Historic Military Commands (CLHMC)
c/o Capt. Richard Lynch
46 Highland Ave.
Jaffrey, NH 03452
Ph: (603)532-6415
E-mail: cavalrycpt@hailstorm.org
URL: http://www.centenniallegion.com
Contact: Col. Howard J. Leonard, Contact
Founded: 1876. **Members:** 1,500. **Membership Dues:** regular, $60 (annual). **Staff:** 15. **Regional Groups:** 3. **State Groups:** 13. **National Groups:** 13. **Description:** Active National Guard and State Guard units and military veterans associations. Purposes are to: perpetuate the military organizations of the original 13 states that served and protected the U.S. in the early days of its history before, during, and after the Revolutionary War; unite military commands still existing (or their successors), keep their traditions alive, and preserve the records of their military achievements; foster patriotism and respect for the flag and the Constitution; honor all citizens who have served or are presently serving in the armed forces; aid in upholding the national institutions of the U.S. in their integrity. Offers educational programs; conducts shooting competition. **Libraries: Type:** not open to the public. **Subjects:** military, history. **Awards: Type:** recognition. **Conventions/Meetings:** annual Commanders' Meeting - always November ● annual Directors' Meeting.

20809 ■ National Pledge of Allegiance Foundation (NPAF)
15285 West Morningtree Dr.
Surprise, AZ 85374
E-mail: sawyertom007@aol.com
Contact: Kevin M. Newman, Exec.Dir.
Founded: 1989. **Description:** Participants include individuals interested in promoting world peace and citizenship through the understanding and appreciation of the Pledge of Allegiance of the United States of America and its ideals. Offers children's services and charitable and educational programs. Maintains Contemporary American Patriot Club, speakers' bureau, and a hall of fame. Conducts research. **Convention/Meeting:** none. **Libraries: Type:** reference. **Holdings:** archival material. **Publications:** Disseminates cassette tapes with patriotic messages from prominent Americans.

20810 ■ Patriotic Order Sons of America (POSA)
3368 Memphis St.
Philadelphia, PA 19134-4510
Ph: (215)634-2546
Fax: (215)634-3705
E-mail: posofa.info@verizon.net
URL: http://www.posofa.org
Contact: Nancy L. Kernaghan, Admin. Assist.
Founded: 1847. **Members:** 1,400. **Staff:** 3. **Budget:** $20,000. **Regional Groups:** 30. **National Groups:** 3. **Description:** Civilian patriotic fraternal order of American-born men "who place fealty to country above every other consideration." Seeks to: enhance appreciation of the heritage of freedom; establish a feeling of devotion to country, its institutions, the

Constitution, and respect for the flag; support and defend the public schools; oppose foreign interference in state and national affairs and all "subversive movements" against the constitutional government and the powers of law and order; work for "adequate restriction" of immigration and advocate a firm program and legislation for the national defense and the nation's security. Studies legislative trends, sponsors citizens' rallies through Valley Forge Sons of America Headquarters and the national research, patriotic education, and service center of the order; these bodies sponsor a council of honor to annually determine recipients of award certificates, medals of honor, scholarships, and other awards for individuals and groups to be recognized by the center. Local groups present flags to public schools and churches, mark historical places, and bestow five awards for distinguished service to the country; has assisted in preservation of Washington's Headquarters at Valley Forge, PA, the Betsy Ross Flag House in Philadelphia, PA, and the Cruiser Olympia. **Libraries: Type:** by appointment only. **Holdings:** 2,000. **Awards:** Excellence in Educational Endeavor. **Frequency:** annual. **Type:** recognition. **Recipient:** for an American citizen ● Junior American. **Frequency:** annual. **Type:** recognition. **Recipient:** for an American junior citizen ● Outstanding Civic Leadership. **Frequency:** annual. **Type:** recognition. **Recipient:** for an American citizen ● Praiseworthy Literary Expression. **Frequency:** annual. **Type:** recognition. **Recipient:** for an American citizen. **Committees:** Civic Service; Educational; Honors and Awards; Patriotic; Personnel; Program Service. **Publications:** *Camp News,* bimonthly. Journal. Features organizational items and proclamations. **Price:** $5.00. **Circulation:** 500. **Conventions/Meetings:** annual conference.

Pennsylvania Dutch

20811 ■ Pennsylvania German Society (PGS)
PO Box 244
Kutztown, PA 19530
Ph: (484)646-4227
Fax: (484)646-4228
E-mail: pgs@kutztown.edu
URL: http://www.pgs.org
Contact: David L. Valuska PhD, Pres.
Founded: 1891. **Members:** 1,100. **Membership Dues:** life (in U.S. and Canada), $1,000 ● benefactor (in U.S. and Canada), $500 (annual) ● sponsor (in U.S. and Canada), $250 (annual) ● sustaining (in U.S. and Canada), $100 (annual) ● couple and institution (in U.S. and Canada), $60 (annual) ● patron (in U.S. and Canada), $55 (annual) ● associate (in U.S. and Canada), $25 (annual) ● patron and institution (outside U.S. and Canada), $90 (annual). **Staff:** 2. **Budget:** $150,000. **Multinational. Description:** Descendants of German, Swiss, and Alsatian pioneers who settled in Pennsylvania and other states; others interested in collecting and preserving landmarks and records of the culture, language, and history of the Pennsylvania Germans (sometimes referred to as Pennsylvania Dutch). Maintains collection of publications. Conducts workshops for educators. **Libraries: Type:** reference. **Holdings:** 32; archival material. **Subjects:** Pennsylvania German. **Awards: Frequency:** annual. **Type:** recognition. **Absorbed:** (1966) Pennsylvania German Folklore Society. **Publications:** *Annual Volumes,* annual. Book. Focuses on various aspects of the Pennsylvania German culture. **Circulation:** 1,100 ● *Der Reggeboge: The Rainbow,* periodic. Journal. Includes articles and book reviews. **Price:** included in membership dues. **Circulation:** 1,100 ● *Dialect Publication Series.* **Price:** $12.00 for members; $15.00 for nonmembers ● *Sources and Document Series.* Books. **Price:** $12.00 for members (volumes 4 to 13); $15.00 for nonmembers (volumes 4 to 13); $16.00 for members (volume 14); $20.00 for nonmembers (volume 14) ● Booklets ● Also distributes postcards. **Conventions/Meetings:** annual conference (exhibits).

20812 ■ Society of the Descendants of the Schwenkfeldian Exiles (SDSE)
105 Seminary St.
Pennsburg, PA 18073-1898

Ph: (215)679-3103
Fax: (215)679-8175
E-mail: info@schwenkfelder.com
URL: http://www.centralschwenkfelder.com/exile
Contact: Sara B. Borr, Membership Sec.
Founded: 1920. **Members:** 475. **Membership Dues:** descendant, associate, $15 (annual) ● life, $300. **Description:** Individuals interested in preserving: the teachings of Casper Schwenckfeld von Ossig (1489?-1561), German nobleman, and leader of the Protestant Reformation in Silesia, who became a religious fugitive; the history of the Schwenkfeldian religious exiles and their descendants. (The Schwenkfelders were forced to leave Silesia and many emigrated to Pennsylvania during the 1730s.) Maintains museum. Compiles genealogical data on exile descendants. **Libraries: Type:** reference. **Holdings:** 40,000. **Boards:** Officers and Board of Governors. **Also Known As:** Schwenkfeldian Exile Society. **Publications:** Newsletter, semiannual ● Booklets ● Also publishes historical articles. **Conventions/Meetings:** annual meeting - always October in Pennsburg, PA.

Philanthropy

20813 ■ Military, Veterans and Patriotic Service Organizations of America (MVPSOA)
21 Tamal Vista Blvd.
Corte Madera Plz., Ste.209
Corte Madera, CA 94925
Free: (800)626-6526
Fax: (415)924-1379
E-mail: info@mvpsoa.org
URL: http://www.mvpsoa.org
Contact: Carri Harte, Contact
Description: Represents pre-screens national and international military, veterans, and patriotic service organizations for potential giving. **Publications:** Newsletter, quarterly ● Annual Report, annual. Alternate Formats: online ● Report, annual.

Philippines

20814 ■ Military Order of the Carabao (MOC)
c/o The Army and Navy Club
901 17th St. NW
Farragut Sq.
Washington, DC 20006-2503
URL: http://www.carabao.org
Contact: Ltg. Marvin L. McNickle USAF, First Vice Commander
Founded: 1900. **Members:** 1,510. **Membership Dues:** individual, $75 (annual). **Description:** Commissioned officers of the U.S. armed services who have served in or adjacent to the Philippines during peace or war. **Conventions/Meetings:** annual dinner.

Pilgrims

20815 ■ General Society of Mayflower Descendants (GSMD)
PO Box 3297
Plymouth, MA 02361-3297
Ph: (508)746-3188
Fax: (508)746-2488
E-mail: gsmd.libr@verizon.net
URL: http://www.themayflowersociety.com
Contact: Edward D. Sullivan, Governor Gen.
Founded: 1897. **Members:** 27,000. **Staff:** 8. **Local Groups:** 52. **Multinational. Description:** Descendants of passengers of the Mayflower, the vessel that transported the Pilgrims from England to Plymouth, MA in 1620. Conducts research into descendants of the Mayflower Pilgrims. **Libraries: Type:** reference. **Holdings:** 6,000; books, films, periodicals. **Subjects:** history and genealogy. **Also Known As:** Mayflower Society. **Publications:** Building the Mayflower II. Video. Traces the fascinating project from initial design through shipbuilding and launch, to its triumphant sail across the Atlantic. **Price:** $10.00

each ● Mayflower Families Through Five Generations. Books. Features individual Pilgrim family lineages. ● The Mayflower Pilgrims. Video. **Price:** $18.00 each; $20.00 for DVD copy ● Mayflower Quarterly. Magazine. Contains latest news of the Society, including photographs of events and members involved in activities. **Price:** $15.00 /year for nonmembers; included in membership dues. **Circulation:** 28,000. **Conventions/Meetings:** triennial Mayflower Society Congress - meeting - always September, Plymouth, MA ● annual Report and Conference.

20816 ■ Governor William Bradford Compact (GWBC)
c/o Mrs. L.W. Pogue, Historian
5204 Kenwood Ave.
Chevy Chase, MD 20815-6604
URL: http://members.aol.com/calebj/society_bradford.html
Contact: Mrs. L.W. Pogue, Historian
Founded: 1946. **Members:** 500. **Membership Dues:** lineal descendant of Gov. William Bradford of Plimoth Colony, Massachusetts, $8 (annual). **Description:** Descendants of William Bradford (1590-1657), who came to America on the Mayflower in 1620 and served as governor of the Plymouth Colony for 33 years. Seeks to honor the memory of Governor Bradford. Promotes communication among members; establishes a record of accomplishments of the governor's descendants. Contributes to maintenance of repositories and memorials including Pilgrim Hall and the Bradford statue in Plymouth, MA; has donated historical artifacts to the Smithsonian Institution. Provides children's services; maintains speakers' bureau; compiles statistics; conducts educational and research programs. **Libraries: Type:** reference. **Holdings:** archival material, artwork, audiovisuals, books, clippings, periodicals. **Subjects:** Mayflower, Pilgrim history, Plymouth Colony. **Awards:** Merit Certificate. **Frequency:** annual. **Type:** recognition. **Recipient:** for merit. **Computer Services:** Mailing lists. **Formerly:** Bradford Family Compact. **Publications:** Bradford Journal, semiannual. Reports upon the accomplishments of the Society and recounts achievements of outstanding members along with their Vignettes. **Price:** free, for members only. ISSN: 1531-4383. **Circulation:** 570. Also Cited As: Bradford Journal, Descendants of Governor William Bradford of Plymouth Colony ● Directory of Descendants of Governor William Bradford 1945-1986 ● Pilgrim Scroll ● Brochures ● Bulletin, periodic ● Also publishes bookmarks and bookplates. **Conventions/Meetings:** periodic competition ● annual general assembly (exhibits) - in Plymouth and Kingston, Massachusetts ● annual luncheon - always spring in Washington DC Metro Area.

20817 ■ Pilgrim Society (PS)
Pilgrim Hall Museum
75 Court St.
Plymouth, MA 02360
Ph: (508)746-1620
Fax: (508)747-4228
E-mail: pegbaker@pilgrimhall.org
URL: http://www.pilgrimhall.org
Contact: Peggy MacLachlan Baker, Dir.
Founded: 1820. **Members:** 700. **Membership Dues:** individual, $35 (annual) ● family, dual, $45 (annual) ● senior, student, $25 (annual) ● sustaining, $100 (annual) ● supporting, $250 (annual) ● patron, $500 (annual) ● individual life, $1,000 ● family, dual life, $1,500. **Staff:** 10. **Budget:** $350,000. **Description:** Seeks to collect, preserve, and display artifacts and written and photographic records relating to the Pilgrims, the Plymouth Colony, and the Town of Plymouth; encourages research in these areas; maintains Pilgrim Hall. Operates museum. Conducts research and educational programs. **Libraries: Type:** reference. **Holdings:** 10,000; archival material. **Subjects:** Pilgrims, Plymouth. **Departments:** Administrative; Archives and Library; Collections. **Publications:** Annual Report, annual. **Conventions/Meetings:** annual meeting - always December 21, in Plymouth, MA.

20818 ■ Pilgrims of the United States
122 E 58th St., 2nd Fl.
New York, NY 10022-1909
Ph: (212)753-7178
Fax: (212)980-0769
E-mail: pilgrims@bestweb.net
Contact: Ms. Jill Spiller, Exec.Sec.
Founded: 1903. **Members:** 700. **Membership Dues:** $150 (annual). **Staff:** 1. **Description:** An association of men and women in alliance with The Pilgrims of Great Britain, that seeks to foster brotherhood between Americans, the British and other English-speaking peoples. In addressing current, national and international issues, it emphasizes enduring historic, cultural, economic and social bonds among nations. **Publications:** List of Members and Proceedings of the Annual Meeting, annual. **Price:** free for members. **Circulation:** 700.

Pioneers

20819 ■ Alaska Yukon Pioneers (AYP)
Address Unknown since 2007
Founded: 1923. **Members:** 1,400. **Staff:** 1. **Local Groups:** 1. **Description:** Social organizations in the Pacific Northwest of former Alaskans and Yukoners. Perpetuates ideals and traditions of early Alaska Yukon pioneers. **Awards: Type:** scholarship. **Recipient:** for the University of Alaska, Fairbanks. **Computer Services:** Mailing lists. **Publications:** Alaska Yukon Pioneers Newsletter, monthly ● Alaska Yukon Pioneers Roster, biennial. **Conventions/Meetings:** annual reunion, held in conjunction with the International Sourdough Reunion.

20820 ■ International Society Daughters of Utah Pioneers (ISDUP)
300 N Main St.
Salt Lake City, UT 84103-1699
Ph: (801)532-6479
Fax: (801)532-4436
E-mail: info@dupinternational.org
URL: http://www.dupinternational.org
Contact: Mary A. Johnson, Pres.
Founded: 1901. **Members:** 24,000. **Membership Dues:** Utah Pioneer Heritage, $10 (annual). **Staff:** 34. **Budget:** $350,000. **Regional Groups:** 186. **State Groups:** 100. **Local Groups:** 1,000. **National Groups:** 600. **Description:** Descendants of Utah pioneers. Publishes the histories of Utah pioneers; places historical markers; preserves pioneer documents, relics, and craftsmanship. Maintains Pioneer Memorial Museum and Carriage House in Salt Lake City. **Libraries: Type:** reference. **Awards:** Royalty Pageant. **Type:** scholarship. **Computer Services:** database, membership and artifacts. **Committees:** Documents Preservation; History; Marker; Museum Artifacts; Relics. **Formerly:** (1993) National Society Daughters of Utah Pioneers. **Publications:** Chronicles of Courage. Books ● Historical Brochure, 9/year ● Legacy, quarterly. Newsletter ● Pioneer Pathways, annual. Book. **Price:** $16.00 ● Pamphlets. Contains information on historical pioneers. **Conventions/Meetings:** annual convention - always last Friday of September or first Friday of October, Salt Lake City, UT ● annual seminar - always first Saturday of June.

20821 ■ National Society - First Families of Minnesota (NSFFM)
Address Unknown since 2007
Founded: 1991. **Members:** 100. **Membership Dues:** individual, $5 (annual). **Description:** Descendants of families who settled in Minnesota prior to its achieving statehood in 1858. Promotes interest and study of Minnesota's early settlement by Europeans. Serves as a clearinghouse on Minnesota history and the history and genealogy of Minnesota pioneer families. **Libraries: Type:** reference. **Holdings:** archival material. **Subjects:** Minnesota pioneer families, state history.

20822 ■ National Society of the Sons of Utah Pioneers (NSSUP)
3301 E 2920 S
Salt Lake City, UT 84109
Ph: (801)484-4441
Free: (888)827-2746
Fax: (801)484-2067
E-mail: sup@networld.com
URL: http://www.sonsofutahpioneers.org
Contact: Mr. Jay Smith, Pres.
Founded: 1933. **Members:** 2,700. **Membership Dues:** individual, $30 (annual) ● life, $150. **Staff:** 5. **Regional Groups:** 11. **State Groups:** 21. **Local Groups:** 15. **Description:** Men ages 18 or older who are interested in preserving the history and names of the pioneers who settled the West. Sponsors historical treks, promotes pageants, and conducts other historical activities. Participates in Pioneer Village, Farmington, UT, in museums of life in the pioneer West. Conducts research. Maintains Pioneer Historical Gallery. **Libraries:** Type: reference. **Holdings:** 1,000; articles, books, periodicals. **Subjects:** genealogy, pioneer history. **Awards:** Type: scholarship. **Recipient:** for youth exhibiting "pioneer" qualities ● Tomorrow's Pioneer Award. **Frequency:** annual. **Type:** recognition. **Recipient:** for modern pioneers. **Committees:** Trails and Landmarks (National Historical Committee). **Formerly:** (1955) Sons of Utah Pioneers. **Publications:** *PIONEER*, quarterly. Magazine. Provides historical information on pioneers and society news. Includes obituaries. **Price:** included in membership dues; $15.00 /year for nonmembers. **Circulation:** 7,500. **Advertising:** accepted ● Also publishes contest stories for historical archives. **Conventions/Meetings:** annual convention, with encampment.

20823 ■ Society of California Pioneers (SCP)
300 4th St.
San Francisco, CA 94107-1272
Ph: (415)957-1849
Fax: (415)957-9858
E-mail: info@californiapioneers.org
URL: http://www.californiapioneers.org
Contact: Peter J. Flagg, Exec. Dir.
Founded: 1850. **Members:** 3,000. **Membership Dues:** bay area, $125 (annual) ● non-bay area, $65 (annual) ● age 21-30, $35 (annual) ● life, $2,500. **Staff:** 7. **Description:** Direct descendants of pioneers who arrived in California prior to 1850. Sponsors cultural and historical programs. Maintains museum and art gallery of California history and heritage. **Libraries:** Type: reference; by appointment only. **Holdings:** 15,000; archival material, biographical archives, books, maps, periodicals. **Subjects:** California history and heritage. **Publications:** *The Pioneer*, annual. Journal. **Conventions/Meetings:** Exhibitions - meeting, related to California art, history, culture (exhibits).

20824 ■ Society of Indiana Pioneers (SIP)
140 N Senate Ave.
Indianapolis, IN 46204-2207
Ph: (317)233-6588
E-mail: jreveritt@aol.com
URL: http://www.indianapioneers.com
Contact: Ms. Jamia Jacobsen, Pres.
Founded: 1916. **Members:** 950. **Membership Dues:** regular, associate, $20 (annual) ● junior (17 years or younger), $10 (annual) ● life, $500. **Staff:** 1. **Description:** Individuals having at least one ancestor who was a resident of Indiana during the pioneer period, lasting from 1825-1850. Seeks to honor the memory of Indiana pioneers and their work, which opened Indiana to settlement. Works with other historical agencies to disseminate information on the history of Indiana, its leaders, and its residents. Sponsors trips for members within Indiana or to adjoining states. **Awards: Frequency:** annual. **Type:** recognition. **Recipient:** for an outstanding member of the Indiana Junior Historical Society. **Publications:** *Yearbook of the Society of Indiana Pioneers*, annual. **Price:** $5.00 ● Book. **Conventions/Meetings:** annual meeting and dinner - always November, Indianapolis, IN.

20825 ■ Sons and Daughters of Oregon Pioneers (SDOP)
PO Box 6685
Portland, OR 97228
E-mail: mpmiller@eoni.com
URL: http://www.webtrail.com/sdop
Contact: Mr. Merle Miller, Contact
Founded: 1901. **Members:** 1,200. **Membership Dues:** adult, $10 (annual) ● junior, $3 (annual). **Description:** Lineal descendants of pioneers who arrived in the Oregon country prior to Feb. 14, 1859, the day Oregon became a state. Aims to pursue social and literary activities. Preserves historic sites. Strives to perpetuate the memory of Oregon pioneers. Conducts annual membership meeting; statehood banquet; annual picnic; and other social and history related events. **Awards:** Miss Pioneer Oregon Scholarship. **Frequency:** annual. **Type:** scholarship. **Recipient:** for pioneer descendant; appreciate pioneer heritage; and exhibit poise. **Computer Services:** Mailing lists. **Boards:** Directors. **Publications:** *SDOP News*, 5/year. Newsletter. Contains eight pages of news, calendar of events and historical articles. **Circulation:** 1,100 ● "Reflections of Oregon Pioneer Families," book of 130 stories, pub. 1994. **Conventions/Meetings:** annual meeting - always in June.

20826 ■ Sons and Daughters of Pioneer Rivermen (SDPR)
c/o Mrs. J.W. Rutter, Sec.
126 Seneca Dr.
Marietta, OH 45750
Ph: (740)373-7829
URL: http://s-and-d.hspsi.org
Contact: Mrs. J.W. Rutter, Sec.
Founded: 1939. **Members:** 1,100. **Membership Dues:** full, $15 (annual) ● spouse, child under 18, $1 (annual). **Staff:** 2. **Regional Groups:** 3. **Description:** Sponsors permanent exhibits in the River Museum, Marietta, OH. Provides material for the Inland Rivers Library, Cincinnati, OH. Not a reference for family genealogy research. **Libraries:** Type: open to the public. **Subjects:** U.S. inland waterways history. **Awards:** J Mack Gamble Fund. **Frequency:** annual. **Type:** monetary. **Publications:** *S&D Reflector*, quarterly. Magazines. **Price:** $5.00/copy. ISSN: 1087-9803. **Circulation:** 1,100. **Conventions/Meetings:** annual meeting (exhibits) - always September, third weekend, in Marietta, OH.

Polish

20827 ■ Polish Army Veterans Association of America (PAVA)
119 E 15th St., Ste.1
New York, NY 10003
Ph: (212)358-0306
Fax: (212)982-2755
Contact: Eugene Witt, Gen.Adj.
Founded: 1921. **Members:** 7,000. **Staff:** 2. **State Groups:** 12. **Local Groups:** 125. **Description:** Veterans of World Wars I and II who served with the Polish Armed Forces. Furnishes aid to disabled veterans who receive no compensation from any other source, through the sale of flowers on annual Cornflower Day. **Publications:** *Veteran*, monthly. **Conventions/Meetings:** triennial meeting.

20828 ■ Polish Legion of American Veterans, U.S.A., Ladies Auxiliary (PLAVA)
Address Unknown since 2007
Founded: 1921. **Members:** 10,000. **State Groups:** 16. **Local Groups:** 87. **Description:** Women related to veterans of Polish descent who have served in the U.S. armed forces. Presents annual scholarships to graduating high school seniors. Conducts charitable and social service programs; assists hospitalized exservicemen; aids widows and orphans. **Committees:** Americanism-Essay Programs; Scholarship; Women's Forum on National Security; Youth. **Publications:** *News*, quarterly ● Journal, periodic. **Conventions/Meetings:** biennial meeting.

Politics

20829 ■ Hereditary Order of the Families of the Presidents and First Ladies of America (HOFPFLA)
300 N Hill Rd.
Sutton, WV 26601-1206
Ph: (304)765-0321
Fax: (304)765-0322
E-mail: president@presidentsandfirstladies.org
URL: http://www.presidentsandfirstladies.org
Contact: James Raywalt, Pres.
Founded: 2003. **Membership Dues:** basic, $20 (annual) ● life, $200. **Staff:** 10. **Description:** Collection and preservation of historical and genealogical records of the families of Presidents and First Ladies of America. Must show common ancestry with President and First Lady of what is now known as the U.S. Also includes United States in Congress Assembled under the Articles of Confederation, the Continental Congress of the USA, the Continental Congress of the United Colonies of America, the Confederate States of America, and the Republics of California, West Florida, and Texas. **Publications:** *Executive Papers*, annual. Magazine. **Conventions/Meetings:** annual First Ladies Tea - meeting - always April in Washington, DC ● annual White House Dinner - meeting - always September.

Prisoners of War

20830 ■ American Ex-Prisoners of War (AXPOW)
3201 E Pioneer Pkwy., No. 40
Arlington, TX 76010-5396
Ph: (817)649-2979
Fax: (817)649-0109
E-mail: hq@axpow.org
URL: http://www.axpow.org
Contact: Robert Fletcher, Commander
Founded: 1942. **Members:** 27,000. **Membership Dues:** individual, $40 (annual) ● couple, $50 (annual). **Staff:** 7. **Budget:** $750,000. **Regional Groups:** 8. **State Groups:** 40. **Local Groups:** 300. **Description:** Former military prisoners of war and civilian internees. Seeks to: acquaint the public with the needs, problems, and handicaps associated with prisoners of war; promote research in the fields connected with injuries, diseases, and syndromes stemming from imprisonment; advocate and foster complete and effective reconditioning programs for ex-prisoners of war; foster patriotism and civic loyalty; encourage fraternal and historical activities. Conducts lobbying activities in Washington, DC to assist ex-POWs. Programs include: Veterans Administration Volunteer Service, a volunteer service in local VA medical centers; National Service Officers, which aids former POWs in filing claims with the VA and assists widows in filing claims; MedSearch, which compiles and distributes medical findings regarding ex-POWs to medical facilities, government agencies, and others. Maintains MedSearch files; local groups maintain museums. **Libraries:** Type: reference. **Holdings:** archival material. **Awards:** Barbed Wire Award. **Frequency:** annual. **Type:** recognition. **Recipient:** for a member of congress. **Committees:** Legislative; MedSearch; National Service Officers; VAVS. **Formerly:** (2000) Bataan Relief Organization. **Publications:** *Ex-POW Bulletin*, 11/year. Magazine. Provides news of comrades and events. Includes book reviews, chapter news, legislative reports, etc. **Price:** included in membership dues; $20.00 /year for nonmembers in U.S.; $30.00 /year for nonmembers outside U.S. ISSN: 0161-7451. **Circulation:** 22,000. **Advertising:** accepted ● *Medical Research Bulletin*, periodic. **Conventions/Meetings:** annual general assembly and workshop (exhibits) - fall.

20831 ■ National Alliance of Families For the Return of America's Missing Servicemen
PO Box 40327
Bellevue, WA 98015-0327
Ph: (425)881-1499

Fax: (425)881-1499
E-mail: dolores@nationalalliance.org
URL: http://www.nationalalliance.org
Contact: Dolores Alfond, Chair
Founded: 1990. **Description:** Works for the return of America's missing servicemen and live Prisoners of War (POWs). Facilitates the accurate accounting of the missing, the recovery and scientific identification of remains or reasonable explanation as to why return, recovery and or accounting is impossible to Prisoners of War (POWs). **Computer Services:** Mailing lists, of members. **Publications:** *Bits 'N' Pieces.* Newsletter.

20832 ■ P.O.W. Network
PO Box 68
Skidmore, MO 64487-0068
Ph: (660)928-3304
Fax: (660)928-3303
E-mail: info@pownetwork.org
URL: http://www.pownetwork.org
Contact: Charles Schantag, Contact
Founded: 1989. **Budget:** $20,000. **Description:** Distributes information on those still missing or held prisoner of war. Verifies "phony" Vietnam ex-POW's. Maintains biographies on returnees and those still POW/MIA. Operates archive of historical documentation. **Libraries: Type:** not open to the public. **Holdings:** archival material, books, papers, periodicals, photographs, reports. **Computer Services:** database, prisoner of war info.

20833 ■ Rolling Thunder
PO Box 216
Neshanic Station, NJ 08853
Ph: (908)369-5439
Fax: (908)369-2072
E-mail: rtnj1@worldnet.att.net
URL: http://www.rollingthunder1.com
Contact: Artie Muller, Exec. Dir.
Founded: 1987. **Membership Dues:** general, $30 (annual). **Description:** Works to publicize the POW-MIA issue. Educates the public about the many American POWs that had been left behind after all past wars. Protects future veterans from being left behind. **Computer Services:** Online services, chatroom ● online services, discussion forum. **Committees:** Education; Gold Star Mothers; Security; Sunshine. **Publications:** *Rolling Thunder Times.* Newsletter. **Conventions/Meetings:** monthly board meeting - 3rd Sunday ● monthly meeting - 3rd Sunday.

Spanish American War

20834 ■ Independence Seaport Museum (ISM)
Penn's Landing
211 S Columbus Blvd., Walnut St.
Philadelphia, PA 19106
Ph: (215)925-5439 (215)413-8628
Fax: (215)925-6713
E-mail: seaport@phillyseaport.org
URL: http://www.phillyseaport.org
Contact: Michele Blazer, Contact
Founded: 1958. **Members:** 1,200. **Membership Dues:** individual, $35 (annual) ● family, household, $45 (annual) ● family plus, $75 (annual) ● navigator, $150 (annual) ● first mate, $300 (annual) ● harbor pilot, $500 (annual). **Staff:** 50. **Description:** Maintains the Cruiser Olympia, last survivor of the Spanish-American War fleets. (The cruiser was Admiral Dewey's flagship at the Battle of Manila Bay, 1898, and brought back the Unknown Soldier from World War I, 1922.) Also maintains the Becuna, a World War II submarine. Offers interactive galleries, a wooden boat building shop, library and education center. Conducts special activities for children and adults throughout the year. **Libraries: Type:** by appointment only. **Holdings:** 25,000; books, maps, papers, periodicals, photographs. **Subjects:** maritime history, photo journals, passengers' list. **Awards: Type:** recognition ● **Frequency:** monthly. **Type:** recognition. **Committees:** Curators; Historical;

Research; Restoration. **Divisions:** Sea Cadets; Sea Explorer Units. **Formerly:** (1997) Cruiser Olympia Association. **Publications:** *Bounding Billows,* quarterly.

20835 ■ National Fort Daughters of '98, Auxiliary United Spanish War Veterans
c/o Mrs. Berna Mae Reinwald, Natl. Sec./
Quartermaster
32028 Mt. Vernon
Rockwood, MI 48173-9650
Ph: (313)379-4996
E-mail: johnnyreb6@aol.com
URL: http://www.geocities.com/sonsofspanwar/
Daughtersof98.html
Contact: Mrs. Berna Mae Reinwald, Natl. Sec./
Quartermaster
Founded: 1934. **Members:** 250. **Membership Dues:** regular, $2 (annual). **Staff:** 18. **State Groups:** 2. **Local Groups:** 10. **Description:** Daughters, daughters-in-law, and other female descendants and legal relatives of veterans of the Spanish American War. Aims to unite the descendants of Spanish American War Veterans and perpetuate the memory of these veterans. Donates clothing and funds to homes for needy children. Donates money and school supplies for homeless veterans, families, and children in depressed areas. **Awards:** Clara Barton Nursing Scholarship Award. **Frequency:** annual. **Type:** scholarship. **Recipient:** to a nursing or medical student. **Programs:** Americanism; Child Welfare. **Affiliated With:** Sons of Spanish American War Veterans. **Publications:** Bulletin, periodic. Includes directory and obituaries. ● Proceedings, annual. **Conventions/Meetings:** annual meeting.

20836 ■ Sons of Spanish American War Veterans (SSAWV)
c/o Rev. Henry L. Reinewald, PNP, Natl. Sec.
32028 Mt. Vernon
Rockwood, MI 48173-9650
Ph: (734)379-4996
URL: http://www.geocities.com/sonsofspanwar
Contact: Rev. Henry L. Reinewald PNP, Natl. Sec.
Founded: 1927. **Members:** 200. **Membership Dues:** regular, $3 (annual). **Staff:** 3. **State Groups:** 3. **Local Groups:** 4. **Description:** Natural and adopted sons, sons-in-law, nephews, grandsons, and grandsons-in-law of veterans who served in the war with Spain, the Philippine Insurrection, and the China Relief Expedition. Conducts annual Hiker Memorial Services in Washington, DC, during April. Operates museum; sponsors charitable program. **Libraries: Type:** open to the public. **Committees:** Cruiser USS Olympia; Greetings. **Affiliated With:** National Fort Daughters of '98, Auxiliary United Spanish War Veterans. **Publications:** *Sons of Spanish American War Veterans—Convention Minutes,* annual. Report. Includes obituaries. **Price:** included in membership dues. **Circulation:** 200 ● *Two General Orders,* annual. Report. **Conventions/Meetings:** annual convention, held in conjunction with Daughters of '98 Auxiliary USWV and Auxiliary United Spanish War Veterans.

Spanish Civil War

20837 ■ Veterans of the Abraham Lincoln Brigade (VALB)
799 Broadway, Rm. 227
New York, NY 10003
Ph: (212)674-5552
URL: http://www.alba-valb.org
Contact: Peter N. Carroll, Contact
Founded: 1939. **Members:** 260. **Membership Dues:** associate, $30 (annual). **Regional Groups:** 4. **Description:** American volunteers who fought in the Spanish Civil War. Believes in Abraham Lincoln's philosophy that a "government of the people, by the people, for the people, shall not perish from the earth." Works to expand the growth of democracy in Spain and to continue to financially support former Spanish Civil War prisoners. Maintains archives and speakers' bureau; conducts charitable programs.

Publications: *Heart of Spain* ● *The Volunteer,* quarterly. Newsletter. Alternate Formats: online. Also Cited As: *Volunteer for Liberty.*

Special Forces

20838 ■ Special Forces Association (SFA)
PO Box 41436
Fayetteville, NC 28309-1436
Ph: (910)485-5433
Fax: (910)485-1041
E-mail: sfahq@sfahq.org
URL: http://www.sfahq.org
Contact: James C. Dean, Exec. Sec.
Founded: 1964. **Members:** 18,049. **Membership Dues:** associate, general, decader, $25 (annual) ● life, $300. **Staff:** 4. **Budget:** $115,000. **Local Groups:** 81. **Description:** Active and retired military men who are now, or who have been, assigned or attached to any U.S. Army Special Forces unit or units. Perpetuates the Special Forces traditions and honors Special Forces troop members who have died. (Members of the Special Forces, particularly those who were in Vietnam, are popularly known as the "Green Berets", after their distinctive headgear.). **Awards:** Educational Grant. **Frequency:** annual. **Type:** grant. **Recipient:** to members and their children ● **Type:** recognition. **Recipient:** to graduates of the Special Warfare School. **Formerly:** (1964) United States Army Special Forces Decade Club; (1968) United States Army Special Forces Decade Association. **Publications:** *The Drop,* quarterly. Magazine. Includes listing of new members, obituaries, chapter news, and feature articles on special operations. **Price:** included in membership dues. **Circulation:** 8,000. **Advertising:** accepted. **Conventions/Meetings:** annual meeting, for members (exhibits) - always June or July.

Travel

20839 ■ Special Military Active Retired Travel Club (SMART)
600 Univ. Off. Blvd., Ste.1A
Pensacola, FL 32504
Ph: (850)478-1986
Free: (800)354-7681
E-mail: rvsmarttrvl@cs.com
URL: http://www.smartrving.net
Contact: Celina Worman, Exec. Mgr.
Founded: 1982. **Members:** 3,000. **Membership Dues:** regular, $35 (annual) ● associate, $20 (annual) ● Canadian and SEATO/NATO, $40 (annual) ● family, $55 (annual). **Staff:** 2. **Regional Groups:** 8. **Multinational. Description:** Retired and active duty personnel from the five uniformed services, including the ready Reserve and National Guard of the U.S; active and retired members from the public health service and the National Oceanic Atmospheric Association, Medal of Honor Awardees, former POW's, 100&percent; service connected veterans, and surviving spouses of persons eligible for membership. Provides comradeship and recreational activities for those interested in RV lifestyle; assists military installations with improvement and expansion of their campgrounds (FAMCAMPS and Travel Camps); provides travel and camping information specifically related to persons with a military background. Offers caravans. **Publications:** *Membership Roster.* Directory. Provides a listing of members who offer assistance to other traveling members having emergency situations in their area. ● *Traveler,* quarterly. Magazine. Contains information on national and chapter activities. Alternate Formats: online. **Conventions/Meetings:** annual National Muster - seminar and workshop, both regional and local chapters; with activities, entertainment, and fellowship.

Veterans

20840 ■ 78th Division Veterans Association
c/o Herman A. Gonzales
104 Oak Glen Rd.
Pittsburgh, PA 15237

Ph: (412)364-1609
Fax: (412)369-7829
E-mail: red78div@bellatlantic.net
URL: http://www.78thdivision.org
Contact: Gabriel Augustine, Pres.
Founded: 1919. **Members:** 3,326. **Membership Dues:** general, $15 (annual) ● life, $100. **Staff:** 9. **Description:** Veterans of the 78th Division. Seeks to preserve the contacts and traditions of the Lightning Division. **Awards:** Jonah E. Kelley Award. **Frequency:** annual. **Type:** monetary. **Recipient:** for graduating senior from Keyser High School, Keyser, WV. **Publications:** *The Flash,* quarterly. Magazine. Contains information and pictures relating to experiences during World War II, and members' correspondence. **Price:** included in membership dues. **Circulation:** 3,400. **Conventions/Meetings:** biennial convention.

20841 ■ 82nd Airborne Division Association
PO Box 9308
Fayetteville, NC 28311-9308
Ph: (910)822-4534
Fax: (910)822-2537
E-mail: abn82dassn@aol.com
URL: http://fayettevilleonline.com/airborne82dassn
Contact: Robert F. Anderson, Sec.
Founded: 1944. **Members:** 28,000. **Membership Dues:** individual, $15 (annual) ● life (under 50 years old), $150 ● life (over 50 years old), $100. **Staff:** 2. **Budget:** $350,000. **State Groups:** 96. **Local Groups:** 11. **Description:** Veterans throughout the United States and overseas and active members of the 82nd Airborne Division stationed at Ft. Bragg, NC. Works to develop the common bond existing between all men and women who served with the 82nd Airborne Division and other airborne units. Assists and serves on matters concerning veterans' benefits. Maintains museum containing history of achievements of the 82nd Airborne Division. Supports an educational fund for children of members. **Libraries: Type:** reference. **Holdings:** archival material. **Awards: Type:** recognition. **Publications:** *82nd Airborne Division Association—Bulletin,* monthly. Newsletter. **Circulation:** 300 ● *Paraglide,* quarterly. Magazine. Includes chapter news and obituaries. **Price:** included in membership dues. ISSN: 0420-280. **Circulation:** 27,000. **Advertising:** accepted. **Conventions/Meetings:** annual All American Week - meeting - always May (week before Memorial Day weekend) ● annual convention - always August.

20842 ■ 90th Division Association
c/o James Reid, Exec. Sec.-Treas.
17 Lake Shore Dr.
Willowbrook, IL 60527-2221
Ph: (630)789-0204
Fax: (630)789-0499
E-mail: reids@90thdivisionassociation.org
URL: http://www.90thdivisionassoc.org
Contact: Ret. Col. Leon Crenshaw, Pres.
Membership Dues: regular, in U.S., $20 (annual) ● international, $30 (annual). **Description:** Supports and represents current and former members of the 90th Infantry Division, its World War II attached units (537 Anti-Aircraft Artillery (AW) Battalion, 712 Tank Battalion, 607 Tank Destroyer Battalion, 773 Tank Destroyer Battalion), as well as The 90th Army Reserve Command, The 90th Regional Support Command, and the 90th Regional Readiness Command. **Publications:** *A History of the 90th Division in World War II.* Book. **Price:** $30.00 in U.S. ● $40.00 outside U.S. Alternate Formats: online. **Conventions/Meetings:** annual reunion.

20843 ■ 369th Veterans' Association (TVA)
PO Box 91
New York, NY 10037-0091
Ph: (212)281-3308
Fax: (212)281-6308
E-mail: natlvets@earthlink.net
URL: http://www.home.earthlink.net/~natlvets/id3.html
Contact: Nathaniel James, Pres.
Founded: 1953. **Members:** 2,500. **Membership Dues:** regular, $25 (annual) ● life, $150. **Staff:** 10.

Budget: $30,000. **Regional Groups:** 6. **State Groups:** 11. **Local Groups:** 10. **National Groups:** 10. **Description:** Represents veterans of World War I, World War II, the Korean Conflict, the Vietnam War, Desert Shield/Storm, Operations Iraqi and Enduring Freedom. Seeks to support all patriotic endeavors of the U.S., and to assist members and their families through charitable programs and community activities. Donates funds, equipment, and other supplies to children's camps, needy families, religious institutions, Veterans Administration Hospitals, and community and senior citizen centers. Provides children's services, including sponsoring Little League baseball teams and a basketball team and a tutorial program. Sponsors the rehabilitation of apartment buildings in New York City, and a four million dollar housing development for senior citizens and the handicapped. Conducts seminars and counseling sessions to assist unemployed veterans, and offers study classes to adults for preparation in Civil Service examinations. Sponsors the annual Dr. Martin Luther King, Jr. Memorial Parade in New York City. **Libraries: Type:** reference. **Awards: Type:** recognition. **Recipient:** for elementary school children at graduation ● **Type:** scholarship. **Recipient:** for children of members. **Computer Services:** Online services, support to member veterans. **Programs:** Black History. **Publications:** *369th News Bulletin,* quarterly. **Conventions/Meetings:** annual conference.

20844 ■ African American Post Traumatic Stress Disorder Association (AAPTSDA)
12208 Pacific Hwy. SW, Ste.1
Lakewood, WA 98499
Ph: (206)220-4505 (253)589-0766
Free: (866)322-0766
Fax: (253)589-0769
E-mail: aapslee@vba.va.gov
URL: http://www.aaptsdassn.com
Contact: Sidney Lee, Pres.
Founded: 1999. **Membership Dues:** individual, $30 (annual) ● associate, $15 (annual) ● life, $200. **Description:** Helps family members, physicians, public officials and society understand and identify the symptoms of Post Traumatic Stress Disorder (PTSD). Provides safe homes and shelters to veterans and their families. Educates the veterans and their dependents of their benefits from services they provided. **Computer Services:** Information services, PTSD (Post Traumatic Stress Disorder) resources. **Publications:** Newsletter.

20845 ■ Air Commando Association (ACA)
PO Box 7
Mary Esther, FL 32569
Ph: (850)581-0099
Fax: (850)581-8988
E-mail: aircomando1@earthlink.net
URL: http://www.specialoperations.net
Contact: Felix Sambogna, Pres.
Founded: 1967. **Members:** 2,400. **Membership Dues:** regular, associate, $20 (annual) ● life, $150. **Description:** Active and retired U.S. military personnel who have taken part in special operations; widows of special operations veterans. Brings members together for social activities. Sponsors humanitarian projects; has provided medical supplies and services to refugees in Central America. **Publications:** Newsletter, quarterly. **Conventions/Meetings:** annual reunion and general assembly (exhibits) - always October, Columbus Day weekend.

20846 ■ Air Weather Association (AWA)
1697 Capri Way
Charlottesville, VA 22911-3534
Ph: (434)296-2832 (434)296-9966
E-mail: airweaassn@aol.com
URL: http://www.airweaassn.org
Contact: James Kevin Lavin, Chm.
Founded: 1987. **Members:** 4,900. **Membership Dues:** life, $9. **Budget:** $12,000. **Description:** Men and women who have served, or currently serving, in the U.S. Army Air Corps/Air Weather units including Weather Reconnaissance and Weather Training units; widows and widowers of veterans of the U.S. Air Force Weather Services, USAFR and ANG

weather personnel are also encouraged to become members. Promotes camaraderie among members of weather units and fosters the goals of modern meteorological support to the U.S. Air Force and Army. **Awards:** Outstanding Airmen of the Year Award. **Frequency:** annual. **Type:** recognition. **Recipient:** for Airmen chosen by the US Air Force. **Publications:** *Air Weather Association Newsletter,* annual. Contains current news and historical articles. **Price:** included in membership dues. **Circulation:** 4,900. **Advertising:** accepted ● *Roster of Members,* annual. Membership Directory. **Conventions/Meetings:** biennial reunion (exhibits) - always even-numbered years.

20847 ■ Air Weather Reconnaissance Association (AWRA)
c/o Joseph Tabaco, Membership Chm.
59 3rd St.
Ronkonkoma, NY 11779-5366
Free: (800)697-5072
E-mail: awra038@aol.com
URL: http://www.awra.us
Contact: Ralph Ruyle, Sec.-Treas.
Founded: 1992. **Members:** 500. **Membership Dues:** individual, $5 (annual) ● life, $30. **Description:** Former members of air weather reconnaissance units. Promotes camaraderie among members. Sponsors social and recreational activities for members and their families. **Computer Services:** database, membership. **Publications:** Newsletter, annual. **Conventions/Meetings:** annual reunion.

20848 ■ American GI Forum of United States
2870 N Speer Blvd., Ste.103
Denver, CO 80211
Ph: (303)458-1700 (303)964-0701
Free: (866)244-3628
Fax: (303)458-1634
E-mail: agifnat@agifnat.ipmail.att.net
URL: http://www.agif.us
Contact: Laura Flores, Treas.
Founded: 1948. **Members:** 250,000. **Membership Dues:** veteran, women, youth, $25 (annual). **Staff:** 3. **Regional Groups:** 10. **State Groups:** 32. **Local Groups:** 650. **Languages:** English, Spanish. **Description:** Represents veterans of the Armed Forces of the U.S., primarily of Mexican origin, and their families. Aims to "foster and perpetuate the principles of American democracy based on religious and political freedom for the individual and equal opportunity for all." Includes special: Business Development Center provides assistance in starting or expanding businesses; Hispanic Education Foundation raises funds for scholarships, grants, and research in education relating to the Hispanic; National Veterans Outreach Program; SER-JOBS for Progress. Works to advance members in the mass media field, and in political representation. Maintains museum. **Libraries: Type:** open to the public. **Holdings:** biographical archives. **Awards: Frequency:** annual. **Type:** recognition. **Recipient:** for members and outstanding Hispanics. **Committees:** Civil Rights; Educational Foundation; Housing; Prisoner of War; Scholarship; Veterans Affairs. **Also Known As:** GI Forum. **Publications:** *Forumeer's,* monthly. Newsletter. **Circulation:** 100,000. **Advertising:** accepted ● *History of American GI Forum,* quarterly. Newsletter. Available in two volumes. **Price:** free. **Circulation:** 200,000. **Advertising:** accepted ● *Information Bulletin,* monthly. **Conventions/Meetings:** annual National Convention (exhibits) ● annual State Convention (exhibits).

20849 ■ American Gulf War Veterans Association (AGWVA)
PO Box 85
Versailles, MO 65084
Ph: (573)378-6049
Free: (800)231-7631
Fax: (573)378-5998
E-mail: webmaster@gulfwarvets.com
URL: http://www.gulfwarvets.com/index.html
Contact: Joyce Riley von Kleist RN, Spokesperson
Description: Works to assist Gulf War service members and families to obtain treatment for symptoms collectively known as the "Gulf War Illness".

20850 ■ American Military Retirees Association (AMRA)
5436 Peru St., Ste.1
Plattsburgh, NY 12901
Ph: (518)563-9479
Free: (800)424-2969
Fax: (518)324-5204
E-mail: info@amra1973.org
URL: http://www.amra1973.org
Contact: Mr. Bernard Matt Dillon, Natl. Pres.
Founded: 1973. **Members:** 27,000. **Membership Dues:** regular, $18 (annual) ● regular, $49 (triennial) ● life (age 70 and over), $80 ● life (age 56-69), $105 ● life (age 46-55), $155 ● life (age 45 and under), $200. **Staff:** 4. **Budget:** $30,000. **State Groups:** 57. **Local Groups:** 2. **National Groups:** 8. **Multinational. Description:** Persons honorably retired for length of service or disability from all branches and grades of the armed forces and their widows or widowers; persons still on active duty. Aims to: maintain "COLA" Program; authorization for all military retirees regardless of age; maintain adequate care at military/VA medical facilities. Works to support or oppose Legislation in the best interests of members and to protect the earned privileges and benefits of military retirees. Testifies before Congress on Legislation affecting members. Sponsors Letter-writing campaigns. Offers supplemental health insurance program. Member of National Military & Veterans Alliance. **Libraries: Type:** reference. **Holdings:** video recordings. **Awards:** Sergeant Major Douglas R. Drum Scholarship. **Frequency:** annual. **Type:** scholarship. **Computer Services:** database. **Publications:** *AMRA eNews*, periodic. Articles. Alternate Formats: online ● *AMRA News*, bimonthly. Newsletter. Keeps members informed of AMRA activities and current legislation. **Price:** included in membership dues. **Circulation:** 6,000. **Conventions/Meetings:** annual board meeting.

20851 ■ American Veterans Alliance (AVA)
818 Concord St. NE
Salem, OR 97301
Ph: (503)391-2981
Free: (800)249-9741
E-mail: ava@veterans.org
URL: http://vets.com
Contact: Chuck Napier, Exec. Dir.
Founded: 1996. **Members:** 14,000. **Membership Dues:** full, $10 (annual) ● life (under 65), $150 ● life (65 and over), $50 ● associate, $7 (annual) ● associate, life, $112 ● allied, $12 (annual) ● allied, life, $187. **Description:** Members are American veterans, family and friends. Mission is to support veterans' benefits and rights. Assists veterans in obtaining benefits due them from various government agencies. Promotes maintaining and expanding veteran benefits, and influencing legislation to reorganize the Veterans Administration into "a more effective and less bureaucratic organization dedicated to assisting veterans and their families in time of need". Promotes the patriotic, benevolent and fraternal aims of the association in bringing veterans and their families together as an effective and influential organization. Promotes the veterans cause, bringing a sense of patriotism to all Americans and bringing together all veterans in a more benevolent manner towards all. Open to all who meet AVA criteria, regardless of race, color, sex, creed, national origin and sexual orientation. AVA is a member at large organization with each member working on his or her own collectively with other members in their own local area to promote ideals and goals of the organization. Local posts can be formed, but membership in a local post is not mandatory. Provides a national registry and storage for veterans documents and certificates, as well as direct assistance in obtaining veteran documentation. **Publications:** *The United Veteran*, quarterly. Newsletter. Email. Alternate Formats: online. **Conventions/Meetings:** periodic meeting, held online.

20852 ■ American Veterans Association - National Headquarters (AVA)
c/o Nancy Jennejahn
PO Box 191
Hamlin, NY 14464-0191

Ph: (585)964-8112
Contact: Nancy Jennejahn, Contact
Founded: 1990. **Members:** 100. **Membership Dues:** veteran with honorable discharge, $17 (annual) ● $15 (annual). **Staff:** 6. **Local Groups:** 1. **Description:** American veterans. Conducts civic and community service programs. Fosters communication among members. **Awards: Frequency:** annual. **Type:** recognition. **Publications:** *AVA*, monthly. Newsletter. **Price:** free to members. **Conventions/Meetings:** monthly meeting.

20853 ■ American Veterans That Enlisted Underage (AVTEU)
Address Unknown since 2006
Founded: 1991. **Members:** 1,200. **Membership Dues:** $15 (annual). **Description:** Current personnel and veterans of the U.S. Military who are or were under the age of 17 during any time of their service periods. Fosters sharing of experiences among members. **Formerly:** (2001) Veterans of Underage Military Service. **Publications:** *America's Youngest Warriors*. Book. **Price:** $25.00 ● *The Underage Veteran*, bimonthly. Newsletter. **Conventions/Meetings:** annual convention ● meeting.

20854 ■ AMVETS - American Veterans
4647 Forbes Blvd.
Lanham, MD 20706-4380
Ph: (301)459-6181
Free: (800)810-7148
Fax: (301)459-7924
E-mail: vworts@amvets.org
URL: http://www.amvets.org
Contact: Joseph T. Kolano, Pres.
Founded: 1944. **Members:** 190,000. **Membership Dues:** individual, $25 (annual) ● life, $150. **Staff:** 25. **Regional Groups:** 6. **State Groups:** 40. **Local Groups:** 1,400. **Description:** Works to promote world peace, preserve the American way of life and help veterans to help themselves; membership is open to anyone who is currently serving, or who has honorably served in the Armed Forces of the United States-to include the National Guard and Reserves-at anytime after September 15, 1940. Follows all veterans legislation on Capitol Hill and plays a key role in its enactment. Provides assistance to veterans with claims through a network of service offices through the United States. **Awards:** Silver Helmet Award. **Frequency:** annual. **Type:** recognition. **Committees:** Americanism; Armed Services; Auxiliary Liaison; Brotherhood; Building; Civil Service and Employment; Community Service; Compulsive Diseases; Constitution and Bylaws; Credentials; Finance; Grievance; Homeless Veterans; Honors and Awards; Hospital and Service; Junior AMVETS; Membership; National Defense and Foreign Relations; National Executive; National Highway; National Programs; Personnel; POW/MIA; Programs; Resolutions; Scholarship; Sons of AMVETS; Uniform and Insignia; VAVS; Vietnam Veterans; Women Veterans. **Formerly:** AMVETS (American Veterans of World War II, Korea and Vietnam). **Publications:** *American Veteran*, quarterly. Magazine. **Price:** included in membership dues; $10.00 /year for nonmembers in U.S.; $11.00 /year for nonmembers outside U.S. ISSN: 0027-853X. **Circulation:** 180,000. **Advertising:** accepted. **Conventions/Meetings:** annual convention and seminar, includes business sessions to determine future leadership and organizational policy (exhibits) - always August ● semiannual National Executive Committee - meeting - April and December.

20855 ■ Army and Navy Union, U.S.A. (ANU)
c/o Mr. Milton D. Reed, Natl. Adjutant Gen.
2002 Tallmadge Rd.
Kent, OH 44240
Ph: (330)673-9373
Fax: (330)673-8371
E-mail: anu@armynavy.net
URL: http://www.armynavy.net
Contact: Mr. Milton D. Reed, Natl. Adjutant Gen.
Founded: 1886. **Members:** 12,330. **Membership Dues:** life (age over 81), $1 ● life (age 70-80), $50 ● life (age 61-70), $100 ● life (age 46-60), $150 ● life (age 31-45), $200 ● life (age through 30), $250.

Regional Groups: 7. **State Groups:** 12. **Local Groups:** 153. **Description:** Servicemen and veterans of the armed forces during peace or war. Participates in veterans service work of all types. Provides children's services. Maintains nine county councils and 11 departments. **Awards: Frequency:** annual. **Type:** recognition. **Recipient:** for West Point Military Academy, Annapolis Naval Academy, and Air Force Academy. **Committees:** Americanism; Education; Senior Citizens; VAVS. **Publications:** *Army and Navy Union, U.S.A.—Newsletter*, quarterly ● *General Orders*, quarterly ● *History of the Army and Navy Union*. **Conventions/Meetings:** annual conference - always August.

20856 ■ Beirut Veterans of America (BVA)
c/o Debra Reisert
8219 Sara Ln.
Georgetown, IN 47122
E-mail: debra72@yahoo.com
URL: http://www.beirutveterans.org
Contact: Randy Gaddo, Pres.
Founded: 1992. **Membership Dues:** general, $15 (annual) ● life (member under 56 years of age), $150 ● life (member over 56 years of age), $100. **Description:** Represents military members who served in Lebanon from June 1958 to March 1984. Aims to keep the memories alive for comrades who "paid the supreme sacrifice" in supporting America's quest for peace in Lebanon.

20857 ■ Berlin Veterans Association
244 E Hamel Rd.
Huachuca City, AZ 85616-8140
Ph: (520)456-1910
Fax: (520)456-1910
E-mail: berlinvets@cs.com
URL: http://ourworld.cs.com/_ht_a/arose1doz/berlin-vets
Contact: Les Rosenbaum, Pres.
Founded: 1996. **Members:** 700. **Membership Dues:** regular, $20 (annual) ● reserve active, $10 (annual) ● associate, $14 (annual). **Staff:** 6. **Languages:** English, German. **Description:** Works for fraternization of individuals stationed in Berlin between 1945-1994. **Libraries: Type:** reference. **Holdings:** 2; books, photographs. **Subjects:** Berlin documents, Berlin photos (1930-2002). **Awards:** Honorary Membership Award. **Frequency:** annual. **Type:** recognition ● Life Membership Award. **Frequency:** annual. **Type:** recognition. **Formerly:** Berlin U.S. Military Veterans Association. **Publications:** Newsletter, quarterly. **Price:** free. **Circulation:** 700. **Conventions/Meetings:** annual meeting.

20858 ■ Black Veterans for Social Justice (BVSJ)
665 Willoughby Ave.
Brooklyn, NY 11206
Ph: (718)852-6004
Fax: (718)852-4805
E-mail: admin@bvsj.org
URL: http://www.bvsj.org
Contact: Job Mashariki, Pres./CEO
Founded: 1979. **Description:** Represents black veterans of the military services. Aids black veterans in obtaining information concerning their rights, ways to upgrade a less-than-honorable discharge, and Veterans Administration benefits due them and their families. Seeks to prohibit discrimination against black veterans. Provides educational programs. Facilitates veterans' sharing of skills acquired while in service; services include counseling and community workshops on veteran issues and a program to provide services to veterans in local prisons. Assists veterans who have suffered from the effects of Agent Orange, an herbicide containing dioxin, used as a defoliant in Vietnam until 1969. Provides children's services; Conducts programs; offers placement service; maintains speakers' bureau. **Formerly:** (1992) Black Veterans. **Publications:** Newsletter. Alternate Formats: online. **Conventions/Meetings:** annual meeting.

20859 ■ Catholic War Veterans of the U.S.A. (CWV)
441 N Lee St.
Alexandria, VA 22314
Ph: (703)549-3622
Fax: (703)684-5196
E-mail: cwvlmt@aol.com
URL: http://www.cwv.org
Contact: Jose M. Garcia, Natl. Commander
Founded: 1935. **Members:** 25,000. **Membership Dues:** regular, $20 (annual). **Staff:** 3. **Description:** Represents American veterans of the Catholic faith. Conducts charitable programs for the welfare and rehabilitation of veterans and their dependents. **Awards:** Celtic Cross. **Frequency:** annual. **Type:** recognition. **Recipient:** for outstanding achievement in promoting devotion to God, country, and home ● Father Washington Medal. **Frequency:** annual. **Type:** medal. **Recipient:** for a Catholic man or woman, heroism or outstanding civic endeavors ● Honor et Veritas. **Frequency:** annual. **Type:** recognition. **Recipient:** for an outstanding American. **Publications:** Catholic War Veteran, quarterly. Magazine. **Circulation:** 25,000. **Advertising:** accepted. **Conventions/Meetings:** annual meeting and convention - always August.

20860 ■ Center for Veterans Issues (CVI)
3312 W Wells St.
PO Box 080168
Milwaukee, WI 53208
Ph: (414)345-3917 (414)342-4284
Free: (888)393-4878
Fax: (414)342-1073
E-mail: info@cvivet.org
URL: http://www.cvivet.org
Contact: Robert A. Cocroft, CEO
Founded: 1989. **Staff:** 40. **Budget:** $2,000,000. **State Groups:** 1. **Local Groups:** 1. **Nonmembership. Description:** Provides administration and management for veterans' organizations.

20861 ■ Center for Women Veterans (CWV)
c/o Department of Veteran Affairs-Central Office
810 Vermont Ave. NW
Washington, DC 20420
Ph: (202)273-6193
Fax: (202)273-7092
E-mail: 00w@va.gov
URL: http://www1.va.gov/womenvet
Contact: Irene Trowell-Harris RN, Dir.
Description: Strives to assure that women veterans receive benefits and services on a par with male veterans, that they encounter no discrimination, and are treated with respect and dignity. **Committees:** Advisory Committee on Women Veterans.

20862 ■ Circle of Friends for American Veterans
210 E Broad St., Ste.202
Falls Church, VA 22046
Ph: (703)237-8980
Free: (800)528-5385
Fax: (703)237-8976
E-mail: info@vetsvision.org
URL: http://vetsvision.org
Contact: Brian Hampton, Pres.
Founded: 1993. **Description:** Advocates on behalf of homeless American veterans. **Publications:** Veterans' Vision, monthly. Newsletter. Features the experience and dedication of national veterans' advocates on the economic, political, social and international issues. **Conventions/Meetings:** monthly Networking/Policy Receptions - meeting.

20863 ■ Coalition to Salute America's Heroes (CSAH)
100 Broadway
Ossining, NY 10562
Ph: (914)432-5400
Free: (888)447-2588
Fax: (914)923-3898

E-mail: info@saluteheroes.org
URL: http://www.saluteheroes.org
Contact: Ray Clifford, Exec. Dir.
Founded: 2004. **Description:** Provides a way to help severely wounded and disabled Operation Enduring Freedom and Operation Iraqi Freedom veterans and their families rebuild their lives. Raises funds for the benefit of service-members and their families. Initiates programs targeted to the specific needs of wounded and injured veterans. **Publications:** Road to Recovery. Newsletter. Alternate Formats: online.

20864 ■ Coast Guard Combat Veterans Association (CGCVA)
PO Box 544
Westfield Center, OH 44251
Ph: (330)887-5539
Fax: (330)887-5639
E-mail: uscgw64@neo.rr.com
URL: http://www.coastguardcombatvets.com
Contact: Gil M. Benoit, Pres.
Founded: 1985. **Members:** 1,700. **Membership Dues:** regular, $25 (biennial). **Staff:** 4. **Budget:** $25,000. **Description:** Coast Guard combat veterans and their families. Promotes the U.S. Coast Guard. Conducts charitable programs. Maintains records of Coast Guard Combat Veterans Association. **Libraries: Type:** lending; reference; not open to the public. **Holdings:** archival material, artwork, clippings, monographs. **Subjects:** coast guard, personnel, ships, aviation. **Awards:** Outstanding CG Person. **Frequency:** annual. **Type:** recognition. **Recipient:** for officer or enlisted; high degree of risk; active duty: regular or reserve, awarded CG medals ● **Frequency:** annual. **Type:** scholarship. **Recipient:** for a relative of sponsor member (son, daughter, grandson or granddaughter); second year student of Jr. College or third year student of a four year college. **Boards:** Trustees. **Formerly:** (1985) S.E. Asia Vets (SEA Vets). **Publications:** Quarterdeck Log, quarterly. Newsletter. Contains general info articles of past and present activities. **Price:** available to members only. **Circulation:** 1,700. **Conventions/Meetings:** biennial reunion and convention, memorabilia (exhibits).

20865 ■ Cold War Veterans Association (CWVA)
PO Box 13042
Overland Park, KS 66282-3042
E-mail: comments@coldwarveterans.com
URL: http://www.coldwarveterans.com
Membership Dues: Platinum Club, $100 (annual) ● Gold Club, $99 (annual) ● Silver Club, $49 (annual) ● Dues-Paying Club, $15 (annual). **Description:** Supports honorably discharged veterans and active-duty personnel who served at any time during the Cold War period, September 2, 1945 to December 26, 1991. (Reservists and National Guardsmen who engaged in basic training, advanced training, and/or annual training during this period are eligible). **Awards:** Fox Fall Cold War Medal. **Type:** recognition. **Publications:** Cold War History Calendar ● Cold War Times, bimonthly. Magazine. Alternate Formats: online. **Conventions/Meetings:** Cold War Victory Day - meeting.

20866 ■ Cuban American Veterans Association (CAVA)
PO Box 140305
Coral Gables, FL 33114-0305
Ph: (305)534-0372
E-mail: webmaster@veteranscava.org
Contact: Rafael G. Crespo, Pres.
Description: Represents and supports Cuban American veterans. **Conventions/Meetings:** annual banquet, with awards ceremony.

20867 ■ Friends and Buddies of the Hour Glass Association (FBHGA)
c/o Ms. Mary Jean Wise
3001 Richmond Ave.
Mattoon, IL 61938-2349

Ph: (217)234-6534
URL: http://www.vets.com/alumni/army/infantry.txt
Contact: Ms. Mary Jean Wise, Contact
Founded: 1990. **Members:** 123. **Membership Dues:** veteran, $20 (biennial). **Staff:** 2. **Description:** Veterans of all units of the 7th Infantry Division, as well as the Navy, Marines, Coastguard, Air Force, and the Army who served during World War II and the Korean War, and in Vietnam, Honduras, Grenada, Panama, and Saudi Arabia; active duty personnel in any service. Fosters and maintains friendships and contacts between members of the units of all armed forces. **Publications:** The Hour Glass Times, annual. Newsletter. **Price:** included in membership dues. **Circulation:** 123. **Advertising:** accepted ● Yearbook, periodic. **Conventions/Meetings:** biennial reunion and banquet.

20868 ■ Grosse Pointe War Memorial Association (GPWMA)
32 Lake Shore Dr.
Grosse Pointe Farms, MI 48236
Ph: (313)881-7511
Fax: (313)884-6638
E-mail: mweber@warmemorial.org
URL: http://www.warmemorial.org
Contact: Mark R. Weber PhD, Pres.
Founded: 1949. **Members:** 2,900. **Staff:** 125. **Budget:** $4,000,000. **Description:** Works to honor individuals who have served in the armed forces and provide educational, cultural, civic and patriotic activities for citizens. Maintains a war memorial museum. Offers continuing educational courses and lectures in the areas of art, dance, and health. Conducts charitable activities. Provides children's and family programs. **Projects:** Veterans Legacy. **Publications:** All Pointes Bulletin, quarterly ● Program of Events, annual. Catalog ● Brochure. **Conventions/Meetings:** monthly board meeting.

20869 ■ Hispanic American Veterans Association (HAVA)
Address Unknown since 2007
Founded: 1978. **Description:** Represents Hispanic American veterans; dedicated to welfare of veterans.

20870 ■ Homes for Our Troops (HFOT)
1 Taunton Green
Taunton, MA 02780
Ph: (508)823-3300
Free: (866)787-6677
Fax: (508)823-5411
E-mail: info@homesforourtroops.org
URL: http://homesforourtroops.org
Contact: John S. Gonsalves, Founder/Pres.
Founded: 2004. **Description:** Assists disabled and seriously injured veterans and their immediate families. Builds and remodels handicap accessible homes for severely wounded veterans. **Publications:** Newsletter. Alternate Formats: online.

20871 ■ International Association of Airborne Veterans (IAAV)
Address Unknown since 2007
Founded: 1981. **Description:** Paratroopers and ex-paratroopers worldwide. Fosters goodwill among members; conducts jump tours. **Publications:** Paradventure, quarterly. Newsletter. **Conventions/Meetings:** meeting - 3/year.

20872 ■ Iraq War Veterans Organization (IWVO)
PO Box 571
Yucaipa, CA 92399
E-mail: info@iraqwarveterans.org
URL: http://www.iraqwarveterans.org
Contact: Russell K. Terry, Founder/CEO/Webmaster
Multinational. Description: Promotes the social welfare of the community. Assists disabled and needy war veterans and members of the U.S. Armed Forces and their dependents, and the widows and orphans of deceased veterans. Provides entertainment, care and assistance to hospitalized veterans or members

of the U.S. Armed Forces. Provides insurance benefits for its members or dependents of its members.

20873 ■ Jewish War Veterans of the U.S.A. (JWV)
1811 R St. NW
Washington, DC 20009
Ph: (202)265-6280
Fax: (202)234-5662
E-mail: jwv@jwv.org
URL: http://www.jwv.org
Contact: Herb Rosenbleeth, Exec. Dir.
Founded: 1896. **Members:** 100,000. **Staff:** 39. **State Groups:** 23. **Local Groups:** 400. **Description:** American veterans of Jewish faith who served in the wars of the U.S. Works to perpetuate Americanism, fight anti-Semitism, combat bigotry, preserve the memories and records of patriotic American Jews, maintain National Service Offices throughout the country and provide a voice on Capitol Hill for veterans' legislation and issues of concern to the American Jewish community. Maintains National Museum of American Jewish Military History; conducts specialized education programs. **Committees:** Action; Awards; Boy Scout; Housing; Insurance; Soviet Jewry. **Publications:** The Jewish Veteran, bimonthly. Magazine. Includes news and articles and issues of concern to veterans and Jews. **Price:** $10.00/year. ISSN: 0047-2018. **Circulation:** 100,000. **Advertising:** accepted ● Jews in American Wars ● The JWV Story. **Conventions/Meetings:** annual convention (exhibits).

20874 ■ Ladies Auxiliary to the Veterans of Foreign Wars of the United States (LAVFWUS)
406 W 34th St., 10th Fl.
Kansas City, MO 64111
Ph: (816)561-8655
Free: (866)299-1286
Fax: (816)931-4753
E-mail: info@ladiesauxvfw.com
URL: http://www.ladiesauxvfw.org/eWeb/StartPage.aspx
Contact: Linda K. Meader, Natl. Pres.
Founded: 1914. **Members:** 634,404. **Membership Dues:** life (age through 20), $220 ● life (age 21-25), $210 ● life (age 26-30), $200 ● life (age 31-35), $190 ● life (age 36-40), $185 ● life (age 41-45), $175 ● life (age 46-50), $170 ● life (age over 46), $50-$160. **Staff:** 28. **State Groups:** 51. **Local Groups:** 6,336. **Description:** Wives, widows, mothers, stepmothers, grandmothers, daughters, foster daughters, stepdaughters, granddaughters, sisters, half sisters, stepsisters, and foster sisters of persons eligible for membership in the VFW. Conducts 11 community service and patriotic programs. **Awards: Frequency:** annual. **Type:** fellowship. **Recipient:** for cancer research; postdoctoral only ● Humanitarian Awards. **Frequency:** annual. **Type:** recognition. **Recipient:** for outstanding service to mankind ● Outstanding Young Volunteers of the Year Awards. **Frequency:** annual. **Type:** monetary. **Recipient:** for volunteers between the age of 12 and 15 ● Young American Creative Patriotic Art Scholarships. **Frequency:** annual. **Type:** scholarship. **Recipient:** for students. **Programs:** Americanism; Buddy Poppy; Cancer Aid and Research; Community Service; Hospital and VAVS; Junior Girls Units; Legislative; Rehabilitation; VFW National Home for Children; VFW-PAC; Youth Activities. **Publications:** Demeter. Manual. Contains approved parliamentary law and procedure for auxiliary meetings. **Price:** $20.00/copy ● Ladies Auxiliary VFW Magazine, bimonthly. Alternate Formats: online ● Podium Edition. Book. Contains combined edition of Bylaws, booklet of instructions and rituals. **Price:** $7.00/copy. **Conventions/Meetings:** annual convention (exhibits) - usually August ● annual Mid-Year Conference - usually March.

20875 ■ National Association for Black Veterans (NABVETS)
PO Box 11432
Milwaukee, WI 53211
Free: (877)622-8387

Fax: (414)342-1073
E-mail: membership@nabvets.com
URL: http://www.nabvets.com
Contact: Robert A. Cocroft, Chm.
Founded: 1970. **Members:** 25,000. **Membership Dues:** active, $25 (annual) ● life, silver, $250 ● life, gold, $500 ● life, diamond, $1,000. **Budget:** $350,000. **Local Groups:** 13. **Description:** Black and other minority veterans, primarily those who fought in Vietnam. Represents the interests of minority veterans before the Veterans Administration. Operates Metropolitan Veterans Service to obtain honorable discharges for minority and low-income veterans who in the organization's opinion unjustly received a less than honorable discharge. Defends incarcerated veterans through its Readjustment Counseling Program; operates job creation program; offers services to geriatric and homeless veterans. Conducts workshops to acquaint lawyers and clinicians with problems associated with Post Traumatic Stress Disorder. Sponsors geriatric seminar and training program. Operates library of military regulations; compiles statistics; maintains speakers' bureau. **Computer Services:** Mailing lists, of members. **Formerly:** (1970) Interested Veterans of the Central City. **Publications:** Eclipse, quarterly. Magazine. **Circulation:** 20,000. **Conventions/Meetings:** annual conference.

20876 ■ National Association of County Veterans Service Officers (NACVSO)
c/o Jim Golgart, Treas.
LeSueur County Veteran Services
88 S Park Ave.
Le Center, MN 56057-1600
Ph: (507)357-2251
E-mail: aknowles@sampsonnc.com
URL: http://www.nacvso.org
Contact: Ann G. Knowles, Pres.
Founded: 1989. **Membership Dues:** individual, $30-$45 (annual). **Description:** Promotes the rights of veterans and their dependents through education, communication, and technology. Assists in the development and promotion of states veterans' programs. **Committees:** Budget and Finance; Education; Legislative; Membership. **Conventions/Meetings:** annual conference - 2008 June, Charleston, SC; 2009 June, San Diego, CA.

20877 ■ National Coalition for Homeless Veterans (NCHV)
333 1/2 Pennsylvania Ave. SE
Washington, DC 20003-1148
Free: (800)VET-HELP
Fax: (202)546-2063
E-mail: nchv@nchv.org
URL: http://www.nchv.org
Contact: Cheryl Beversdorf, Pres./CEO
Founded: 1990. **Members:** 250. **Membership Dues:** organization with under $500,000 budget, $300 (annual) ● organization with over $500,000 budget, $500 (annual). **Staff:** 6. **Budget:** $1,000,000. **Description:** Seeks to end homelessness among veterans by shaping public policy, promoting collaboration, and building the capacity of service providers. Offers educational and charitable programs, statistics, and a speakers' bureau. **Computer Services:** database ● mailing lists. **Telecommunication Services:** electronic mail, nchv1@nchv.org. **Publications:** Newsletter, bimonthly ● Brochure, periodic. **Conventions/Meetings:** annual conference and board meeting.

20878 ■ National Gulf War Resource Center (NGWRC)
3027 Walnut St.
Kansas City, MO 64108
Ph: (816)531-7183
Free: (866)531-7183
E-mail: pdavidson@ngwrc.org
URL: http://www.ngwrc.org
Contact: Paul Davidson, Exec. Dir.
Founded: 1995. **Membership Dues:** individual, $25 (annual). **Multinational. Description:** Supports veterans and others with illnesses related to the Gulf War.

20879 ■ National Museum of American Jewish Military History (JWV-NMI)
1811 R St. NW
Washington, DC 20009
Ph: (202)265-6280 (202)265-6281
Fax: (202)462-3192
E-mail: nmajmh@nmajmh.org
URL: http://www.nmajmh.org
Contact: Mr. Jack Berman, Pres.
Founded: 1958. **Members:** 35,000. **Membership Dues:** single, $25 (annual) ● family, $36 (annual) ● friend, $50 (annual). **Staff:** 5. **Budget:** $4,000,000. **Description:** Organization and corporations united to preserve the records of Jews who served in the U.S. armed forces and educate the public about their contributions to America's freedom. Collects and displays objects, memorabilia, medals, and honors won by Jewish men and women in the military; publicizes the history of Jewish participation in U.S. armed forces. Gathers and exhibits archival materials; conducts research, museum tours, and public events. Maintains list of Jewish war dead; operates museum. Compiles statistics. **Libraries: Type:** reference. **Holdings:** 5,000; archival material. **Subjects:** military. **Awards:** Col. "Mickey" Marcus Humanitarian Award. **Frequency:** annual. **Type:** recognition. **Recipient:** for service and leadership ● Uriah P. Levy Award. **Type:** recognition. **Computer Services:** database ● mailing lists ● online services. **Committees:** Executive; Exhibits. **Affiliated With:** Jewish War Veterans of the U.S.A.; Jewish War Veterans of the U.S.A. - National Ladies Auxiliary. **Formerly:** Jewish War Veterans, U.S.A. National Memorial; (1958) National Shrine to the Jewish War Dead. **Publications:** Museum News, quarterly. Newsletter. Includes popular history and museum events. **Price:** included in membership dues. **Circulation:** 45,000. **Advertising:** accepted. Alternate Formats: online. Also Cited As: The Veteran ● Also publishes exhibition catalogs. **Conventions/Meetings:** annual convention (exhibits).

20880 ■ National Native American Veterans Association (NNAVA)
PO Box 761475
San Antonio, TX 78245
E-mail: info@nnava.org
URL: http://www.nnava.org
Contact: James Cates, Chm.
Membership Dues: general, $25 (annual) ● life, $150. **Description:** Educates and assists Native American veterans. Aims to assist the families of Native American veterans to obtain veteran rights, entitlements and benefits.

20881 ■ National Veterans Legal Services Program (NVLSP)
PO Box 65762
Washington, DC 20035
Ph: (202)265-8305
Fax: (202)328-0063
E-mail: info@nvlsp.org
URL: http://www.nvlsp.org
Contact: Barton F. Stichman, Co-Dir.
Description: Aims to ensure that the nation honors the pact made with veterans. Has been instrumental in the passage of landmark veterans rights legislation; also recruits, trains and assists thousands of volunteer lawyers and veterans advocates. **Publications:** The Veterans Advocate, quarterly. Journal ● Veterans Benefits Manual. Contains insight and analysis from a team of experts.

20882 ■ National Veterans Organization of America (NVOA)
PO Box 2510
Victoria, TX 77902-2510
Ph: (210)200-8756
Contact: Douglas McArthur, Service Off.
Founded: 1982. **Members:** 5,000. **Regional Groups:** 6. **Description:** Represents veterans. Disseminates information on behalf of all veterans. Strives to help the military eliminate inefficiency and overspending and obtain better benefits for veterans and their families. Provides Agent Orange assistance and an advocate to assist veterans applying for

benefits. Plans to: conduct nonpartisan lobbying; establish a speakers' bureau; establish a library and a committee to visit military installations and evaluate conditions. **Awards: Type:** recognition ● **Type:** scholarship. **Formerly:** (2001) National Veterans Association. **Publications:** Newsletter ● Reports.

20883 ■ Non Commissioned Officers Association (NCOA)

10635 IH 35 N
San Antonio, TX 78233
Ph: (703)549-0311
Free: (800)662-2620
Fax: (703)549-0245
E-mail: goverstr@ncoausa.org
URL: http://www.ncoausa.org
Contact: Gene Overstreet, Pres./CEO
Founded: 1960. **Members:** 80,000. **Membership Dues:** regular, $30 (annual) ● apprentice, auxiliary, $20 (annual) ● life - regular (depends on age), $150-$400 ● life - auxiliary (depends on age), $60-$250. **Staff:** 14. **Budget:** $5,000,000. **State Groups:** 38. **Local Groups:** 120. **Description:** Noncommissioned and petty officers of the United States military serving in grades E1 through E9 from all five branches of the U.S. Armed Forces; includes active duty and retired personnel, members of the Reserve and National Guard components, and personnel who held the rank of NCO/PO at the time of separation from active duty under honorable conditions. Works for patriotic, fraternal, social and benevolent purposes. Offers veterans job assistance, legislative representation, and grants. Conducts charitable program. **Awards:** Bettsy Ross Educational Grants. **Frequency:** quarterly. **Type:** grant. **Recipient:** to members of the NCOA International Auxiliary ● NCOA Scholarships. **Frequency:** annual. **Type:** scholarship. **Recipient:** to spouses and children of NCOA members. **Also Known As:** NCO Association. **Publications:** *Today's NCOA Journal*, bimonthly. Provides news concerning active duty and retired military personnel. Also includes membership news and calendar of events. **Price:** included in membership dues. **Circulation:** 80,000. **Advertising:** accepted. **Conventions/Meetings:** annual meeting and convention (exhibits).

20884 ■ Operation Truth

770 Broadway, 2nd Fl.
New York, NY 10003
Ph: (212)982-9699
Fax: (212)982-8645
E-mail: info@optruth.org
URL: http://www.optruth.org
Contact: Paul Rieckhoff, Exec. Dir./Founder
Founded: 2004. **Members:** 300. **Description:** Aims to connect the American public with the troops who are serving or had served in Iraq and Afghanistan. Empowers citizens to tangibly support the troops before, during and after deployment. **Computer Services:** database, photo and video gallery ● database, veterans' profiles ● information services, conflict background ● information services, resources for veterans.

20885 ■ Red River Valley Fighter Pilots Association (RRVFPA)

PO Box 1553
Front Royal, VA 22630-0033
Ph: (540)636-9798
Fax: (540)636-9776
E-mail: rrvariverrats@aol.com
URL: http://www.river-rats.org
Contact: John L. Hope, Exec. Dir.
Founded: 1969. **Members:** 3,600. **Staff:** 1. **Budget:** $180,000. **National Groups:** 70. **Description:** Unites aerial combat veterans avowing patriotism and defense of the U.S. Constitution as its guiding principle. **Awards: Frequency:** annual. **Type:** scholarship. **Programs:** River Rat Scholarship; Scholarship Assistance; Scholarship Grant. **Also Known As:** River Rats. **Publications:** *Mig Sweep*, quarterly. Magazine. **Price:** free for members Only. **Conventions/Meetings:** annual reunion.

20886 ■ Regular American Veterans (RAV)

1309 Harrison Ln.
Austin, TX 78742-2871
Ph: (512)386-8387
Free: (800)981-8387
Fax: (512)385-1181
E-mail: rav@onr.com
URL: http://www.regularamericanveterans.com
Contact: John Hearon, Natl. Commander
Founded: 1879. **Members:** 1,011. **Membership Dues:** individual, $10 (annual) ● life, $125. **Staff:** 2. **Budget:** $98,000. **Regional Groups:** 9. **State Groups:** 52. **Local Groups:** 10. **Description:** Honorably discharged veterans who have served in peace or war. Members of the National Guard and Armed Forces Reserve. Honorably discharged veterans of allied nations. **Awards:** JR ROTC Medal. **Frequency:** annual. **Type:** scholarship. **Recipient:** to high school seniors, deserving members of high school ROTC regardless of grade. **Also Known As:** (1948) Regular and Disabled Service Association. **Publications:** *The American War Veteran*, annual. Magazine. **Price:** free. **Advertising:** accepted ● *The Voice - The American War Veteran*, quarterly. Journal. **Conventions/Meetings:** annual convention - always October ● semiannual National Council of Administration - meeting.

20887 ■ Regular Veterans Association (RVA)

5200 Wilkinson Blvd.
Charlotte, NC 28208-5450
Ph: (704)394-6105
Fax: (704)391-9998
Contact: Archie L. Hargett, Natl.Cmdr.
Founded: 1934. **Members:** 35,511. **Membership Dues:** military, $5 (annual) ● veteran, $125 ● life, $125 ● national, $15 (annual). **Staff:** 2. **Budget:** $64,000. **Regional Groups:** 9. **Local Groups:** 475. **Description:** Active, retired, disabled, and honorably discharged members of the Armed Forces of the United States who served in peace or war. Provides assistance to veterans, widows, and family members in obtaining government benefits. Sponsors service programs through the Veterans Administration; conducts welfare programs to assist disabled and needy veterans. Established National Rehabilitation and Service Foundation to assist veterans and military personnel with service program administration, benefits, travel, insurance, and fundraising. Maintains hospital programs. Participates in veterans rehabilitation and employment programs and in programs on patriotic holidays such as Memorial Day, Veterans Day, Fourth of July, Pearl Harbor Day, and Armed Forces Day. A subgroup, Military Order of the Mosquito, serves as a social branch of the RVA, working in VA and community hospitals on a volunteer basis. The Order of the Golden Eagle, an honor group within the RVA, offer service to veterans, and work for veterans rehabilitation and for legislative goals for veterans' benefits. Plans to establish a toll-free number. **Awards:** Golden Eagle Award. **Type:** recognition. **Recipient:** to persons who demonstrate Americanism ● Medal of Valor. **Frequency:** annual. **Type:** medal. **Recipient:** bestowed to military units for service in Granada and Lebanon ● Order of the Compassionate Heart Knighthood Award. **Frequency:** annual. **Type:** medal. **Recipient:** bestowed in three degrees to individuals who provide service to combat wounded and disabled veterans ● **Type:** recognition. **Recipient:** for outstanding policeman and fireman who demonstrate heroism ● **Type:** scholarship. **Recipient:** for children of veterans on a local basis. **Computer Services:** Mailing lists, membership. **Committees:** Americanism; Armed Forces; Defense; Employment; National Awards; National Defense; National Employment; National Security; National Veterans Political Action; Patriotism; Public Relations; Rehabilitation; Service Officers; Veterans' Benefits. **Departments:** Ladies Auxiliary; Philippines. **Formed by Merger of:** U.S. Maimed Soldiers League; Regular and Disabled Service Association. **Formerly:** (1950) Regular Veterans Association; (1999) Regular Veterans Association of the United States. **Publications:** *The Voice*, quarterly. Contains information on association activities and veterans/military personnel benefits. **Price:** included

in membership dues. **Advertising:** accepted. **Conventions/Meetings:** annual National Council of Administration - meeting - always in December ● annual National Muster - meeting - always August ● regional meeting.

20888 ■ The Retired Enlisted Association (TREA)

1111 S Abilene Ct.
Aurora, CO 80012
Ph: (303)752-0660
Free: (800)338-9337
Fax: (303)752-0835
E-mail: editor@trea.org
URL: http://www.trea.org
Founded: 1963. **Members:** 100,000. **Staff:** 15. **Budget:** $2,500,000. **Local Groups:** 48. **Description:** Retirees who have served in the military as enlisted persons; medically retired persons or enlisted persons who have been on active duty for at least 10 years. Associate members are widows/widowers of retired enlisted persons. Supports the rights and benefits of retired enlisted persons and their families. Lobbies at national, state, and local levels for: issues concerning retired enlisted persons; keeping commissaries open; protecting unemployment compensation, Veterans Administration disability compensation, and cost-of-living allowances; encouraging the addition of national cemeteries; keeping medical facilities open. Sponsors cultural and social activities for members through local chapters. Conducts seminars and sponsors travel and insurance programs. **Awards:** Ben Pearson Award. **Frequency:** annual. **Type:** recognition. **Recipient:** for outstanding service by a TREA member ● Marjorie Holt Award. **Frequency:** annual. **Type:** recognition. **Recipient:** for outstanding service to veterans ● TREA National Scholarship. **Frequency:** annual. **Type:** scholarship. **Recipient:** for children/grandchildren/great grandchildren of TREA members and TREA auxiliary members. **Telecommunication Services:** additional toll-free number, (888)882-0835. **Committees:** Athletic; Bylaws and Standing Rules; Chapter Start-Up and Assistance; Convention; Credentials; Finance; Five-Year Plan; Legislative Affairs; Membership; Nominations; Public Relations; Scholarship. **Publications:** *The Retired Enlisted Association—The Voice*, bimonthly. Magazine. Updates members on the current status of military and VA benefits. Includes association information and legislative updates. **Price:** included in membership dues. **Circulation:** 85,000. **Advertising:** accepted. Alternate Formats: online ● *The Voice e-Mag*, bimonthly. Newsletters. **Advertising:** accepted. **Conventions/Meetings:** annual seminar (exhibits) - usually September.

20889 ■ Second Bomb Wing Association (SBWA)

Address Unknown since 2007
Founded: 1986. **Members:** 300. **Membership Dues:** individual, $20 (annual). **Staff:** 4. **Budget:** $25,000. **Description:** U.S. Armed Forces veterans who served with the 2nd Bomb Wing at Tucson, AZ, or Savannah, GA, during the period of 1947 to 1963. Associate members are widows of former members. Promotes fellowship among members. Supports the 8th AF Museum at Barksdale Air Force Base, LA. **Publications:** *Biographical Roster*, biennial. Directory ● Newsletter, semiannual. **Conventions/Meetings:** biennial meeting.

20890 ■ Supreme Pup Tent, Military Order of the Cootie (MOC)

604 Braddock Ave.
Turtle Creek, PA 15145-2068
Ph: (412)824-2240
Free: (877)688-6206
Fax: (412)824-1850
E-mail: headquarters@lotcs.org
URL: http://www.lotcs.org
Contact: Jack Roberts, Supreme Quartermaster
Founded: 1920. **Members:** 37,800. **Membership Dues:** regular, $20 (annual). **Staff:** 4. **Budget:** $500,000. **Regional Groups:** 16. **State Groups:** 46. **Local Groups:** 1,015. **Description:** Honor degree members of the Veterans of Foreign Wars of the

U.S.A. serving the VFW. Members visit and entertain hospitalized veterans and support the VFW National Home for Children in Eaton Rapids, MI. Conducts seminars. **Awards:** Christi Braun Scholarship. **Frequency:** annual. **Type:** scholarship. **Recipient:** for children residing at the VFW National Home for Children ● **Type:** recognition. **Committees:** Hospital Commission; Scholarship and Athletics. **Divisions:** Grand Councils; Grand Districts/Areas; Grand Pup Tents; Supreme Council; Supreme Pup Tent. **Affiliated With:** Veterans of Foreign Wars of the United States. **Publications:** Cootie Courier Newspaper, quarterly. **Price:** $10.00/year. **Circulation:** 30,000. **Advertising:** accepted ● Grand and Pup Tent Publications, monthly ● Program Book, annual ● Roster, annual. Membership Directory ● Bulletin, periodic. **Conventions/Meetings:** annual Supreme Scratch - meeting, military items, souvenirs, badges, pins - always third week in August.

20891 ■ Swift Boat Veterans for Truth
c/o Weymouth D. Symmes, Treas.
PO Box 26184
Alexandria, VA 22313
E-mail: latch@swiftvets.com
URL: http://www.swiftvets.com
Contact: Weymouth D. Symmes, Treas.
Description: Represents former military officers and enlisted men who served in Vietnam on U.S. Navy "Swift Boats" or in affiliated commands. **Publications:** Newsletter. Alternate Formats: online.

20892 ■ Transgender American Veterans Association (TAVA)
PO Box 4513
Akron, OH 44310
E-mail: president@tavausa.org
URL: http://www.tavausa.org
Contact: Monica F. Helms, Pres.
Membership Dues: basic, $35 (annual) ● advanced, $50 (annual) ● gold, $100 (annual) ● diamond, $250 (annual) ● life, $500. **Description:** Addresses concerns for fair and equal treatment of transgender veterans and active duty service members. **Programs:** Operation: Invisible Ribbon.

20893 ■ Ukrainian American Veterans (UAV)
PO Box 172
Holmdel, NJ 07733-0172
Ph: (732)888-0494
E-mail: uav.nc@att.net
URL: http://www.uavets.org
Contact: Anna Krawczuk, Natl. Commander
Founded: 1946. **Members:** 1,100. **Local Groups:** 30. **Description:** Men and women of Ukrainian descent or extraction who served in the U.S. Armed Forces. Unites American veterans of Ukrainian descent; perpetuates the memory of other Ukrainian veterans; sustains the constitution, government, and laws of the U.S; and promotes a spirit of peace and goodwill. Sponsors patriotic observances on holidays such as Memorial Day and the Fourth of July. Provides veterans affairs programs; cooperates with local community groups through local posts. Maintains documentation and research foundation. Maintains ladies auxiliary. Operates speakers' bureau; sponsors charitable program; compiles statistics. **Libraries:** Type: reference. **Awards:** Type: recognition. **Recipient:** for educational, artistic, or cultural achievements. **Formerly:** Ukrainian American War Veterans. **Publications:** Ukrainian American Veterans Tribune, quarterly. Newsletter. Contains national and local post news. Includes calendar of events. **Circulation:** 1,100. **Advertising:** accepted ● Also publishes annual convention journal. **Conventions/Meetings:** annual meeting (exhibits).

20894 ■ U.S. Naval Cryptologic Veterans Association (NCVA)
PO Box 16009
Pensacola, FL 32507-6009
Ph: (850)455-6026 (850)492-7856
Free: (800)872-6282

E-mail: executivedirector@usncva.org
URL: http://www.usncva.org
Contact: Robert H. Anderson III, Exec. Dir.
Founded: 1978. **Members:** 3,454. **Membership Dues:** regular, associate, social, $20 (annual) ● family, $30 (annual). **Description:** Provides fraternal, social, and recreational activities for naval cryptologic veterans. Advocates for strong and adequate U.S. Armed Forces to maintain security interests. Strengthens the security capabilities of the cryptologic agencies of the Department of Defense. Preserves the history of cryptology. **Computer Services:** Online services, discussion. **Publications:** Cryptolog, quarterly. Newspaper. **Price:** included in membership dues. **Conventions/Meetings:** annual reunion, social gathering that ends on a Saturday evening with a dinner or dance - fall, usually around the last week of August or during September.

20895 ■ U.S.S. LCI National Association
101 Rice Bent Way, No. 6
Columbia, SC 29229
Ph: (803)865-5665
Fax: (803)865-5654
E-mail: maxeyusn@aol.com
URL: http://www.usslci.com
Contact: Robert McLain, Sec.
Founded: 1990. **Members:** 5,200. **Membership Dues:** life, $100 ● general, $25 (annual). **Staff:** 12. **State Groups:** 49. **Description:** Men who served on the LCI (landing craft infantry) ships that were part of the flotilla operations commissioned by the U.S. Navy from 1942-1944. Includes the rocket, gun, and mortar LCI ships. Unites former shipmates for fellowship. Searches for LCI veterans. Hopes to secure a ship and establish a memorial. **Libraries:** Type: open to the public. **Holdings:** 10; books. **Subjects:** LCI history. **Awards:** US Navy Memorial - D-Day Museum. **Frequency:** annual. **Type:** monetary. **Computer Services:** database ● mailing lists ● online services. **Also Known As:** Landing Craft Infantry National Association. **Publications:** LCI History Book. Books. **Price:** included in membership dues. **Circulation:** 3,200 ● LCI History Book Vol. I and II. Books ● LCI Newsletter-ELSIE ITEM, quarterly. **Conventions/Meetings:** annual reunion (exhibits) - always in April or May.

20896 ■ USS Wainwright Veterans Association
c/o Mr. Ed Cookenham, Pres.
3654 Appling Lake Dr.
Memphis, TN 38133
Ph: (901)388-3049
E-mail: edward.cookenham@stjude.org
URL: http://www.usswainwright.org
Contact: Mr. Ed Cookenham, Pres.
Membership Dues: individual, $15 (annual) ● life, $200. **Description:** Promotes fellowship and camaraderie among men that served aboard all USS Wainwright warships from pre-commissioning through decommissioning. **Computer Services:** Information services, ships resources ● online services, discussion forum. **Committees:** Reunion; Ship Naming; Ships History; Ships Store. **Publications:** Newsletter. Alternate Formats: online.

20897 ■ Veterans for Common Sense (VCS)
1025 Vermont Ave. NW 7th Fl.
Washington, DC 20003
Ph: (202)483-9222
Fax: (202)483-9312
E-mail: vfa@vi.org
URL: http://www.veteransforcommonsense.org
Contact: Bobby Muller, Pres.
Founded: 2002. **Members:** 12,000. **Description:** Believes that war veterans must play a key role in public debate over national issues, particularly national security. **Computer Services:** Mailing lists. **Publications:** Annual Report, annual. Alternate Formats: online.

20898 ■ Veterans of Foreign Wars of the United States (VFW)
406 W 34th St.
Kansas City, MO 64111
Ph: (816)756-3390

Fax: (816)968-1199
E-mail: info@vfw.org
URL: http://www.vfw.org
Founded: 1899. **Members:** 1,900,000. **Membership Dues:** $20 (annual). **Staff:** 220. **Budget:** $73,000,000. **State Groups:** 54. **Local Groups:** 8,500. **Description:** Overseas veterans of the Spanish American War, World Wars I and II, the Korean and Vietnam wars, the Persian Gulf War, Grenada, Panama, and Lebanon in which an overseas campaign medal was received. Seeks to: insure the national security through maximum military strength; speed the rehabilitation of the nation's disabled and needy veterans; assist the widows, orphans, and dependents of disabled and needy veterans; promote Americanism through education in patriotism and constructive service to the communities. Sponsors charitable programs; maintains museum. **Programs:** Buddy Poppy; Citizenship Education and Community Services; Legislative Service; Military Assistance; National Security and Foreign Affairs; Veterans Service; Youth Development, Scholarship and Recognition. **Affiliated With:** Ladies Auxiliary to the Veterans of Foreign Wars of the United States. **Formed by Merger of:** American Veterans of Foreign Service; Army of the Philippines. **Publications:** VFW Magazine, monthly. Includes member news, benefits update, and legislative report. **Price:** included in membership dues; $15.00 /year for nonmembers in U.S.; $20.00 /year for nonmembers outside U.S. ISSN: 0161-8598. **Advertising:** accepted. **Conventions/Meetings:** annual convention (exhibits).

20899 ■ Vietnam Veteran Wives (VVW)
PO Box 396
Republic, WA 99166
Ph: (509)775-8893
E-mail: danna@vietnamveteranwives.com
URL: http://www.vietnamveteranwives.com
Contact: Danna Hughes, Pres.
Founded: 1996. **Description:** Advances the research and distribution of information about Post-Traumatic Stress Disorder (PTSD), Agent Orange and Gulf War diseases. Provides special education and tutoring for the children of Vietnam veterans. **Computer Services:** Mailing lists, of members. **Publications:** Newspaper ● Magazine ● Brochure.

20900 ■ Women Veterans of America (WVA)
c/o Colleen Mussolino, Natl. Commander
PO Box 72
Bushkill, PA 18324
Ph: (570)588-4674
Fax: (570)588-1165
E-mail: collvet@ptd.net
URL: http://www.womenveteransofamerica.com
Contact: Colleen Mussolino, Natl. Commander
Founded: 1990. **Membership Dues:** individual, $15 (annual) ● life, $100-$150. **Description:** Advocates for women veteran's rights, issues, and benefits. Provides information and support to women veterans and women currently serving the military. Assists women in obtaining veteran benefits.

20901 ■ Women's Overseas Service League (WOSL)
PO Box 7124
Washington, DC 20044-7124
E-mail: carolhabgood@sbcglobal.net
URL: http://www.wosl.org
Contact: Bob Patrick, Contact
Founded: 1921. **Members:** 800. **Membership Dues:** regular, $20 (annual). **Staff:** 4. **Regional Groups:** 5. **Local Groups:** 30. **Description:** Women who served overseas with the armed services, American Red Cross, Special Services, or with any agency approved by the U.S. government to work with the armed forces during World Wars I and II, Korean conflict, Vietnam, Persian Gulf, or aftermath; women of the U.S. Armed Forces or her allies. Carries on patriotic activities, services to disabled veterans, and aid to members in need. **Awards:** Freedom Foundation Youth Awards. **Frequency:** annual. **Type:** monetary ● **Type:** scholarship. **Recipient:** to women. **Committees:** International Relations; Patriotic; Public Relations; Scholarship; Service; UN Representative.

Publications: *Carry On*, quarterly. Magazine. **Conventions/Meetings:** annual meeting.

Veterans of Foreign Wars

20902 ■ Iraq and Afghanistan Veterans of America (IAVA)
770 Broadway, 2nd Fl.
New York, NY 10003
Ph: (212)982-9699
Fax: (212)982-8645
E-mail: info@optruth.org
URL: http://www.iava.org
Contact: Paul Rieckhoff, Exec. Dir./Founder
Founded: 2004. **Description:** Seeks to empower Iraq and Afghanistan troops and veterans to use their credibility and experiences to speak the truth about the realities of war, its implications on the health of the U.S. military, and effects on the national security. Ensures that the enactment of policies provide proper training and benefits to these troops and veterans. Supports its members in their patriotic endeavors. **Publications:** Newsletter, monthly. Covers news and current issues concerning the association and its members. Alternate Formats: online.

Vietnam Veterans

20903 ■ Tan Son Nhut Association (TSNA)
PO Box 236
Penryn, PA 17564-0236
E-mail: tansonnhut@aol.com
URL: http://www.tsna.org
Contact: Robert Gales, Pres.
Founded: 1995. **Membership Dues:** life, $180 ● regular, $20 (annual) ● regular, $80 (quinquennial). **Description:** Perpetuates the history of Tan Son Nhut Air Base, Republic of Vietnam. Recognizes and honors those who served at or were affiliated with Tan Son Nhut Air Base. Conducts benevolent, cultural, educational and social programs. **Publications:** *Revetments*, bimonthly. Newsletter. Alternate Formats: online.

20904 ■ Vietnam Dog Handler Association (VDHA)
c/o Robert L. Palochik, Treas.
8203 Parting Clouds Ct.
Las Vegas, NV 89117-7614
E-mail: partingclouds@juno.com
URL: http://www.vdhaonline.org
Contact: Robert L. Palochik, Treas.
Founded: 1993. **Members:** 2,000. **Description:** Seeks to reunite veteran war dog handlers and honor the memory of their war dog partners. Educates the public on what dogs have done to save American lives on the battlefields of foreign Wars. Contributes to war dog memorial projects throughout the country. **Publications:** *DOGMAN*, SAN. Newsletter. Contains stories, articles and remembrances written by members of the VDHA. **Price:** free. Alternate Formats: online.

Vietnam War

20905 ■ 11th Armored Cavalry's Veterans of Vietnam and Cambodia (11th ACVVC)
PO Box 1948
Plainview, TX 79073-1948
E-mail: armor11acr@aol.com
URL: http://www.11thcavnam.com
Contact: Ollie Pickral, Treas.
Founded: 1984. **Members:** 6,000. **Membership Dues:** individual, $15 (annual) ● life, $100. **Staff:** 15. **Budget:** $50,000. **Regional Groups:** 50. **Description:** Individuals who served with or were affiliated with the 11th Armored Cavalry Regiment in Vietnam and Cambodia from August 1966 to March 1972; wives, parents, and children of those troopers killed in action. Promotes members' physical, mental, and social development. Fosters communication and

exchange among members. Locates and reunites former comrades who served together in Vietnam and Cambodia. **Libraries:** Type: reference. **Holdings:** 1; books. **Subjects:** Blackhorse Regiment in Vietnam. **Awards:** Blackhorse Scholarship. **Frequency:** annual. Type: scholarship. **Recipient:** for the children of 11th ACR troopers killed, wounded, or disabled while serving with the Regiment ● Blackhorse Trooper of the Year Award. Type: recognition ● Jack Quilter Award. **Frequency:** annual. **Type:** recognition. **Recipient:** for member of the 11th ACVVC. **Computer Services:** Mailing lists, of members. **Publications:** *Thunder Run*, quarterly. Bulletin. Contains articles, announcements, death notices, and biographies of members. **Price:** included in membership dues. **Circulation:** 6,000. **Conventions/Meetings:** annual reunion (exhibits) - 1st week of August.

20906 ■ 77th Artillery Association
PO Box 141
Boonville, MO 65233-0141
Ph: (660)882-5390
Free: (866)884-77FA
Fax: (660)882-8204
E-mail: doc@77fa.org
URL: http://www.77fa.org
Contact: Doc Bosma, Dir.
Founded: 1987. **Members:** 1,872. **Membership Dues:** basic, $20 (annual) ● life, $150. **Budget:** $10,000. **Regional Groups:** 3. **Description:** Individuals who served with the 77th artillery regiment. Seeks to keep alive the camaraderie felt by members during their military service. Conducts research and historical programs. Operates Speaker's Bureau. **Libraries:** Type: reference. **Holdings:** biographical archives, reports, video recordings. **Subjects:** Vietnam artillery operations. **Computer Services:** database, 77th artillery veterans ● record retrieval services, buddy search. **Subgroups:** 4/77th Artillery Veterans; 1/77th Artillery Veterans; 77th Artillery Korea Veterans; 6/77th Artillery Veterans; 2/77th Artillery Veterans. **Affiliated With:** 25th Infantry Division Association; 101st Airborne Division Association; National 4th Infantry (Ivy) Division Association. **Formerly:** 1/77 Artillery Veterans Association; (1988) 1/77th Artillery Vietnam Veterans Association. **Publications:** *En Garde Review*, quarterly. Newsletter. Covers association news and activities. **Price:** $20.00/year. **Circulation:** 1,040. **Advertising:** accepted ● *Reunion Book and Roster*, biennial. **Conventions/Meetings:** semi-annual conference and reunion (exhibits) ● biennial 77th Artillery Reunion - general assembly, a gathering of the current and past soldiers of the various battalions of the 77th field artillery regiment (exhibits).

20907 ■ America's Victory Force (AVF)
Address Unknown since 2007
Founded: 1966. **Description:** Vietnam War veterans who promote an anti-Communist, pro-American philosophy. Serves as a fraternal organization for patriotic Vietnam War veterans. Sponsors educational program in military defense. Offers charitable program; maintains speakers' bureau.

20908 ■ Associates of Vietnam Veterans of America (AVVA)
8605 Cameron St., Ste.400
Silver Spring, MD 20910-3718
Ph: (301)585-4000
Free: (800)882-1316
Fax: (301)585-0519
E-mail: haber2@atlanticbb.net
URL: http://www.avva.org
Contact: Mary Miller, Pres.
Founded: 1999. **Membership Dues:** regular, $20 (annual) ● regular, $50 (triennial) ● life (age 49 and under), $250 ● life (age 50-55), $225 ● life (age 56-60), $200 ● life (age 61-65), $175 ● life (age 66 and over), $150. **Description:** Promotes and represents Vietnam veterans, their families, and communities. **Awards:** Better Chance Scholarship. Type: scholarship. **Recipient:** to students who are financially in need of money ● Bronze Medallion. Type: medal ● Fellowship Award. **Frequency:** annual. Type: recognition ● Humanitarian Award. **Type:** recognition.

Committees: By-Laws; Disciplinary; Long Range Planning; Paper Safe; Policy and Procedure Manual; Public Relations; Scholarship; State Structure. **Affiliated With:** Vietnam Veterans of America. **Conventions/Meetings:** biennial meeting.

20909 ■ Gamewardens of Vietnam Association (GVA)
c/o John W. Woody, Pres.
PO Box 701786
San Antonio, TX 78270
Free: (866)220-7477
E-mail: laurence.bissonnette@worldnet.att.net
URL: http://www.tf116.org
Contact: John W. Woody, Pres.
Founded: 1968. **Members:** 950. **Membership Dues:** life (plus), $225 ● life, $200 ● associate, $15 (annual). **Regional Groups:** 3. **Description:** Veterans of the U.S. Navy River Patrol Force, Task Force 116, Operation Gamewarden, Brown Water Navy, or in support thereof, who served in Vietnam during the years 1966-71. Seeks to preserve the memory of Operation Gamewarden and to maintain the friendships formed by those serving in the task force. Honors the memories of veterans killed in Vietnam. Promotes projects to assist members and their families. **Libraries:** Type: reference. **Holdings:** 300; books. **Subjects:** Vietnam, U.S. Navy's role in the Vietnam conflict. **Awards:** Gamewarden Scholarship. **Frequency:** 3/year. Type: scholarship. **Recipient:** for children or grandchildren/descendants of River Patrol Force veterans, TASK FORCE 116, and any U.S. Military Unit which served in support of Operation Gamewarden. **Publications:** *The Brown Water Log*, quarterly. Newsletter. **Conventions/Meetings:** biennial reunion.

20910 ■ Mobile Riverine Force Association (MRFA)
c/o Albert B. Moore, Pres.
106 Belleview Dr. NE
Conover, NC 28613
Ph: (828)464-7228
E-mail: mrfa@charter.net
URL: http://www.mrfa.org
Contact: Albert B. Moore, Pres.
Membership Dues: regular, $15 (annual) ● regular, $40 (triennial). **Description:** Works to honor the Army and Navy men who served in the Mekong Delta, Vietnam. **Publications:** *River Currents*, quarterly. Newsletter. Alternate Formats: online. **Conventions/Meetings:** annual reunion.

20911 ■ National War Dog Memorial Fund
c/o Connecticut River
Community Bank
1190 Silas Deane Hwy.
Wethersfield, CT 06109
E-mail: john.burnam@rcn.com
URL: http://www.nationalwardogsmonument.org
Contact: John C. Burnam, Exec. Dir.
Founded: 1993. **Members:** 2,000. **Membership Dues:** associate, $20 (annual) ● life, $250. **Description:** Represents veteran war dog handlers who served during the Vietnam War, as well as dog loving supporters of all ages and genders. **Telecommunication Services:** electronic mail, vdhadogman@mac.com. **Publications:** *Dogman*, bimonthly. Newsletter. Contains articles and photos. Alternate Formats: online.

20912 ■ PBR Forces Veterans Association (PBR-FVA)
732 Amer. Inn Rd.
Villa Ridge, MO 63089-2214
Ph: (636)451-5688 (636)742-9742
Fax: (636)451-5688
E-mail: info@pbr-fva.org
URL: http://www.pbr-fva.org
Contact: Robert L. Creel, Membership Chm.
Founded: 1998. **Membership Dues:** life, $175 ● associate, $300 (annual). **Description:** Represents former Task Force 116 (T.F. 116) Sailors and members of the Army 458th Transportation Co. and others of the Brown Water Navy, united for fraternity and historical accuracy concerning the Vietnam War.

Awards: James E. Williams Scholarship Fund. **Frequency:** annual. **Type:** scholarship.

20913 ■ Veterans of the Vietnam War (VVnW)
805 S Township Blvd.
Pittston, PA 18640-3327
Ph: (570)603-9740
Free: (800)843-8626
Fax: (570)603-9741
E-mail: wnwnatl@epix.net
URL: http://www.vvnw.org
Contact: Peter J. Forbes, Natl. Commander
Founded: 1978. **Members:** 15,000. **Membership Dues:** veteran and concerned citizen, $25 (annual) ● life, $200. **Staff:** 3. **Description:** Veterans and non-veterans united to aid veterans of all eras; POW/MIAs, United Veterans Beacon House Projects (Homeless Program). Maintains collection of literature on such subjects as Agent Orange, post-traumatic stress syndrome, employment, and incarcerated veterans. Maintains speakers' bureau; compiles statistics. **Libraries:** Type: reference. **Holdings:** 300. **Awards:** Veteran of the Year Award. **Frequency:** annual. **Type:** recognition ● Volunteer of the Year Award. **Type:** recognition. **Computer Services:** Information services, veterans information ● mailing lists, POW/MIA listings. **Committees:** Agent Orange Victims International; Employment; Health Care; Incarcerated Veterans; Job Training and Apprenticeship Program; National Vietnam Veterans Coalition; Post-Traumatic Stress Disorder Studies; POW/MIAs; United Veterans Beacon House Project (Homeless Program). **Publications:** *The Veteran Leader*, quarterly. Newsletter. Includes information on VA benefits. **Price:** $50.00/year. **Advertising:** accepted. **Conventions/Meetings:** annual convention (exhibits).

20914 ■ Vietnam Combat Veterans (VCV)
PO Box 715
White Pine, MI 49971
Ph: (906)885-5599
E-mail: johndv8@aol.com
URL: http://www.themovingwall.org
Contact: John Devitt, Chm./Founder
Founded: 1980. **Members:** 375. **Budget:** $57,000. **Description:** Works to make the public aware of American airmen and soldiers who are POW/MIAs in Southeast Asia; seeks the return of live POW/MIAs to the U.S; sponsors a traveling display of a half-scale model of the Vietnam Veterans Memorial Wall. Conducts research into governmental programs that affect veterans. Sponsors seminars and public announcements on the POW/MIA issue. **Boards:** Veterans Service. **Committees:** Archives; Art; Library; Museum; Network.

20915 ■ Vietnam Helicopter Pilots Association (VHPA)
5530 Birdcage St., Ste.105
Citrus Heights, CA 95610-7698
Free: (800)505-VHPA
Fax: (916)966-8743
E-mail: hq@vhpa.org
URL: http://www.vhpa.org
Contact: Tom Payne, Sec.-Treas.
Founded: 1983. **Members:** 11,900. **Membership Dues:** general, $36 (annual) ● life, $450. **Regional Groups:** 18. **Description:** All who flew helicopters in Vietnam during the Vietnam conflict (1961-75). Seeks to perpetuate spirit of camaraderie among members. Maintains reference library of books, periodicals, business records, and archival materials related to U.S. Army flight school, Vietnam helicopter units, and current flying. Compiles statistics. **Computer Services:** database. **Publications:** *Annual Reunion Photo Book*, annual ● *Historical Reference Directory, Vol. I*, periodic. **Price:** $10.00 includes postage and handling ● *Historical Reference Directory, Vol. II*, periodic. **Price:** $15.00 includes postage and handling ● Membership Directory, annual. **Price:** $20.00 available to members only ● Newsletter, bimonthly. **Price:** included in membership dues; $36.00 /year for nonmembers. **Circulation:** 7,000. **Advertising:** accepted ● Also publishes a calendar. **Conventions/Meetings:** annual meeting, held in conjunction with

Helicopter Association International (exhibits) ● annual reunion - always 4th of July weekend.

20916 ■ Vietnam Veterans Memorial Fund (VVMF)
1023 15th St. NW, 2nd Fl.
Washington, DC 20005
Ph: (202)393-0090
Fax: (202)393-0029
E-mail: vvmf@vvmf.org
URL: http://www.vvmf.org
Contact: Jan C. Scruggs, Pres./Founder
Founded: 1979. **Staff:** 11. **Description:** Preserves the legacy of the Vietnam Veterans Memorial to educate and promote healing from the effects of the Vietnam War. **Committees:** Design and Construction; Public Relations; Sculpture Design.

20917 ■ Vietnam Women's Memorial Foundation (VWMF)
1735 Connecticut Ave. NW, 3rd Fl.
Washington, DC 20009
Free: (866)822-8963
E-mail: vwmfdc@aol.com
URL: http://www.vietnamwomensmemorial.org
Contact: Diane Carlson Evans, Pres./Founder
Founded: 1984. **Budget:** $20,000. **Description:** Works to identify and document women who served during the Vietnam War; placed the Vietnam Women's Memorial in Washington, DC, on November 11, 1993, to honor their service. Educates the public regarding the contributions of women during the Vietnam War; maintains Speaker's Bureau. **Formerly:** (2002) Vietnam Women's Memorial Project. **Publications:** *Celebration of Patriotism and Courage*, annual. Report. **Price:** $5.00.

War of 1812

20918 ■ General Society of the War of 1812
c/o Mr. Timothy C. Harris, VP Gen.
6184 Stinson Blvd. NE
Fridley, MN 55432-5835
E-mail: gsw1812@netscape.net
URL: http://www.societyofthewarof1812.org
Contact: Timothy C. Harris, VP Gen.
Founded: 1814. **Members:** 1,600. **State Groups:** 23. **Description:** Male descendants of veterans of the War of 1812. "Perpetuates the memory and victories of the War of 1812; encourages research and publication of historical data; and cherishes, maintains, and extends the institution of American freedom and fosters true patriotism and love of country.". **Awards:** ROTC - 1812 Ribbon. **Frequency:** annual. **Type:** recognition. **Recipient:** for outstanding college ROTC senior. **Absorbed:** Society of the War of 1812 in Connecticut; (1894) New England Association of Soldiers of the War of 1812. **Formed by Merger of:** (1892) Association of Descendants of Defenders of Baltimore; (1892) Society of the War of 1812 in Pennsylvania. **Publications:** *War Cry of 1812*, periodic. Newsletter. **Circulation:** 1,600 ● Yearbook, triennial ● Also publishes registers. **Conventions/Meetings:** triennial convention.

20919 ■ National Society, United States Daughters of 1812
1461 Rhode Island Ave. NW
Washington, DC 20005-5402
Ph: (202)745-1812
URL: http://www.usdaughters1812.org
Contact: Charlotte Young Slinkard, Natl. Pres.
Founded: 1892. **Members:** 3,800. **Membership Dues:** national, state, chapter, $18 (annual). **Budget:** $60,000. **State Groups:** 38. **Local Groups:** 144. **Description:** Women descendants of those who rendered civil, military, or naval service during the years 1784-1815. Promotes patriotism and seeks to increase knowledge of American history by preserving documents and relics, marking historic spots, recording family histories and traditions, and celebrating patriotic anniversaries. Maintains museum; compiles statistics. **Libraries:** Type: reference. **Holdings:** 4,000; archival material, books. **Subjects:** 1812

historical period, genealogy. **Awards:** Limited State Daughters of 1812. **Frequency:** annual. **Type:** recognition. **Recipient:** for two outstanding midshipmen graduates of the U.S. Naval Academy ● **Frequency:** annual. **Type:** recognition. **Recipient:** for an outstanding graduate of West Point. **Computer Services:** Mailing lists. **Committees:** American Merchant Marine Library; Flora Adams Darling Daughters; Insignia; Lineage and Historical Records; Location of 1812 Graves; Mountain Schools; National Defense; School of the Ozarks; Star Spangled Banner Flag House; Veterans' Rehabilitation. **Publications:** *1812 Ancestors Index, Vol. II 1970-1992, Vol. III 1992-2003* ● Newsletter, semiannual. Includes news of national and state societies and chapters. **Advertising:** accepted. **Conventions/Meetings:** annual Associate Council - conference (exhibits) - always April, Washington, DC.

War Resistance

20920 ■ Iraq Veterans Against the War (IVAW)
PO Box 8296
Philadelphia, PA 19101
Ph: (215)241-7123
Fax: (215)241-7177
E-mail: ivaw@ivaw.org
URL: http://www.ivaw.org
Contact: Michael Hoffman, Co-Founder
Founded: 2004. **Membership Dues:** unemployed, active duty, $1 (annual) ● student, low income, $5 (annual) ● general, $10 (annual). **Description:** Represents group of veterans from "Operation Enduring Freedom" and "Operation Iraqi Freedom", committed to ending the war in Iraq by "immediate withdrawal of all occupying forces". Believes "that the governments that sponsored these wars are indebted to the men and women which were forced to fight them and must give their soldiers, Marines, sailors and airmen the benefits that are owed to them upon their return home". **Publications:** Newsletter. Alternate Formats: online.

Widowhood

20921 ■ Veterans' Widows International Network (VWIN)
c/o Edmee J. Hills, Natl. Chair
3657E S Laredo St.
Aurora, CO 80013
Ph: (303)693-4745 (303)756-8920
E-mail: vetsurvivors@aol.com
URL: http://www.vetsurvivors.com
Contact: Edmee J. Hills, Natl. Chair
Founded: 1995. **Membership Dues:** regular, $15 (annual). **Multinational. Description:** Represents the interests of veterans' widows, reaching out to other veterans' survivors across the United States and overseas. Works to inform survivors of benefits and privileges for which they might quality. Directs survivors to where they will receive best attention and keeps them abreast of new legislative changes. Gives survivors a sense of community with other veterans' survivors. **Telecommunication Services:** electronic mail, vwin95@aol.com. **Publications:** Newsletter. Alternate Formats: online.

Witches

20922 ■ Associated Daughters of Early American Witches (ADEAW)
c/o Mrs. Marlene Wilkinson, Gen. Pres.
6876 Richard Wilson Dr.
Millington, TN 38053-3934
E-mail: adeaw@yahoo.com
URL: http://www.adeaw.us
Contact: Mrs. Marlene Wilkinson, Gen. Pres.
Founded: 1987. **Membership Dues:** life, $50 ● individual, $25 (annual). **Description:** Women aged 16 and older who can prove descent from an ancestor who was accused or convicted of the practice of

witchcraft in New England prior to 31 December 1699. Seeks to identify and preserve the "names of those accused of witchery in that portion of Colonial America now known as the United States of America". Conducts historical and genealogical research; participates in charitable programs; sponsors social activities. **Conventions/Meetings:** annual general assembly - always April.

World War I

20923 ■ National Ladies Auxiliary to Veterans of World War I of the U.S.A.
767 SW 4th St., Rm. 101
Forest Lake, MN 55025-1547
Ph: (651)775-2180
Contact: Opal Petersen, Natl. Sec.-Treas.
Founded: 1953. **Members:** 6,000. **Staff:** 1. **Regional Groups:** 3. **State Groups:** 23. **Local Groups:** 200. **Description:** Female relatives of Veterans of World War I of U.S.A. (see separate entry). Conducts patriotic, historical, and educational programs. **Committees:** Americanism; Hospital-Community Services; Legislative; Publicity; Veterans Administration Voluntary Services. **Publications:** *Ladies Auxiliary Veterans of WWI*, quarterly. Newsletter. **Price:** $5.00/year. **Advertising:** accepted. **Conventions/Meetings:** annual convention.

20924 ■ Veterans of World War I of U.S.A. (VWWI)
c/o Ms. Muriel Sue Kerr, CEO/Exec. Dir./Natl. Adjutant
PO Box 8027
Alexandria, VA 22306-8027
Ph: (703)405-7047
E-mail: muriel971@aol.com
URL: http://www1.va.gov/vso/index. cfm?template=viewreport&Org_ID=104
Contact: Ms. Muriel Sue Kerr, CEO/Exec. Dir./Natl. Adjutant
Founded: 1949. **Members:** 13. **Description:** Fraternal organization to represent Veterans of the First World War. Membership is limited to only those who served Honorably during that period of the fighting War known as World War One. Organized to lobby for pensions and benefits for World War I veterans and their surviving spouses. Continue to participate in Veterans Day, General Pershing Graveside ceremonies, and Memorial Day events at Arlington National Cemetery. Average age of membership is 106 years young. The National Ladies Auxiliary to the Veterans of World War 1 hold the annual national conventions, while this organization (VWW1) has one volunteer (Muriel Sue Parkhurst Kerr) who will continue until the last man or woman seeks to uphold the memory of those who served in World War I and to speak for those unable to speak for themselves. **Libraries: Type:** not open to the public. **Conventions/Meetings:** annual Veterans of World War I and its Ladies Auxiliary National Convention.

World War II

20925 ■ 4th Marine Division Association WWII (FMDA)
337 Redwood Rd.
Venice, FL 34293-1124
E-mail: usmcgman@aol.com
URL: http://fightingfourth.com
Contact: John Stone, Exec. Sec./Ed.
Founded: 1947. **Members:** 2,767. **Membership Dues:** regular, $20 (annual) ● life, $75. **Staff:** 1. **Description:** Veterans of the 4th Marine Division who served in World War II. Holds memorial services for those killed during WWII; has erected memorial monuments on Iwo Jima, Saipan, Tinian, Kwajalein, and Maui, Hawaii and in many individual state and national cemeteries in honor of Marines killed while serving the association. **Libraries: Type:** reference. **Holdings:** archival material. **Awards: Frequency:** periodic. **Type:** recognition. **Committees:** Maui Memorial Park; Monuments and Memorials; Scholar-

ship. **Publications:** *4th Marine Division Newsletter*, quarterly. **Conventions/Meetings:** annual reunion.

20926 ■ 6th Bomb Group Association
c/o Harry H. George, Historian/Board Member
1170 Gulf Blvd., Apt. 703
Clearwater, FL 33767-2781
Ph: (727)517-2577
E-mail: famdad@aol.com
Contact: Harry H. George, Historian/Board Member
Founded: 1984. **Members:** 700. **Membership Dues:** individual, family, $15 (annual). **Staff:** 12. **Description:** World War II Air Force veterans who served with the 6th Bomb Group (B-29s), on Tinian, Mariana Islands; widows of these servicemen; and others pending application and approval of the board. Acts as the central registry for 6th Bomb Group veterans; promotes and preserves fellowship among members; and preserves history of 6th Bomb Group during World War II. **Libraries: Type:** reference. **Holdings:** audiovisuals. **Subjects:** memorabilia, including WWII records. **Awards:** Memorial Plaques. **Frequency:** periodic. **Type:** recognition. **Recipient:** for installation at Air Force Bases and locations in USA. **Computer Services:** database ● mailing lists, notice of reunions. **Publications:** *6th Bomb Group Newsletter*, semiannual. Provides review of activities and future plans; lists Officers. **Price:** included in membership dues. **Circulation:** 700. **Advertising:** accepted. **Conventions/Meetings:** annual reunion, with photo slides, books, video tapes (exhibits) - fall.

20927 ■ 17th Airborne Division Association
PO Box 4793
Dowling Park, FL 32064-1508
Ph: (386)658-1292
Fax: (386)658-1292
E-mail: ejsiergiej@alltel.net
Contact: Edward J. Siergiej, Sec.-Treas.
Founded: 1954. **Members:** 3,542. **Membership Dues:** regular, honorary, $15 (annual). **Description:** Veterans of the 17th Airborne Division of World War II. Perpetuates the spirit of comradeship of those who served with the division. Leads pilgrimages to Europe; holds reunions with British, Polish, French, German, Belgian, and Russian World War II veterans. Maintains Church Restoration Fund, West Point Scholarship, and scholarship awards to schools in Bastogne and Houfalize, Belgium. **Libraries: Type:** reference. **Subjects:** historical records of the Division in World War II. **Awards:** West Point Scholarship. **Type:** scholarship. **Computer Services:** database ● mailing lists. **Committees:** Dissolution; Memorial; War Room. **Publications:** *Thunder From Heaven*, semiannual. Newsletter. Includes calendar of events, member profiles, obituaries, reunion reports, scholarship reports, and want ad page for information on members. **Price:** included in membership dues. **Circulation:** 3,542. **Advertising:** accepted. **Conventions/Meetings:** annual reunion and banquet, golf tournament, memorial service, war room exhibit (exhibits).

20928 ■ 22nd Bomb Group Association
c/o Don Hatch
PO Box 5281
Huntsville, AL 35814
Ph: (256)837-8456
Fax: (256)895-9375
Contact: Don Hatch, Pres.
Founded: 1950. **Members:** 654. **Membership Dues:** $25 (annual). **Staff:** 7. **Description:** Consists of World War II veterans and following generations. **Libraries: Type:** not open to the public. **Holdings:** 200. **Subjects:** Air Corps, Air Force Groups in the SW Pacific from 1942-1945, Space Program from 1957-1997. **Publications:** *22nd Bomb Group Association Newsletter*, quarterly. Includes pertinent information and news in full color. **Price:** included in membership dues. **Circulation:** 750. **Conventions/Meetings:** annual reunion, with memorabilia, World War II literature, and photographs.

20929 ■ 27th Troop Carrier Squadron Foundation
c/o Office of the Secretary
15003 SE 46th St.
Bellevue, WA 98006

Ph: (425)641-9427
Fax: (425)641-9427
E-mail: gruberbob@seanet.com
Contact: Robert B. Gruber, Sec.
Founded: 1987. **Members:** 275. **Membership Dues:** associate or relative of squadron veteran, $10 (annual) ● squadron veteran, $15 (annual). **Staff:** 5. **Description:** Veterans who served in the 27th Troop Carrier Squadron and their next of kin. (The 27th Troop Carrier Squadron was active from January 19, 1942 to December 27, 1945, and served in Burma and China during World War II.) Works to record the history of the China-Burma-India Theater; promotes camaraderie among members. Provides assistance to communities wishing to establish Air Force memorials; gathers memorabilia related to the 27th Troop Carrier Squadron and military operations in Southeast Asia during World War II. Conducts research; participates in charitable programs; maintains speakers' bureau; compiles statistics. **Libraries: Type:** reference. **Holdings:** archival material, audio recordings, papers, photographs, video recordings. **Subjects:** 27th Troop Carrier Squadron, Tenth Air Force, 14th Air Force. **Publications:** *Archival Reports and Tales*, 10/year. Newsletter ● *Secretarial Report*, periodic. **Conventions/Meetings:** annual convention ● periodic regional meeting.

20930 ■ 70th Infantry Division Association
c/o Ms. Diane Kessler, Sec.
73 Providence Hill Rd.
Atkinson, NH 03811
Ph: (603)362-9737
E-mail: fgrzejka@aol.com
URL: http://www.trailblazersww2.org
Contact: Andy McMahon, Pres.
Founded: 1962. **Members:** 1,600. **Membership Dues:** regular, associate, $20 (annual) ● life, $100. **Staff:** 11. **Budget:** $50,000. **Regional Groups:** 4. **Description:** Veterans of the 70th Infantry Division who served during World War II and were known as the Trailblazers. Promotes the interests of the 70th Infantry Division; seeks to perpetuate the memory of the division. Establishes contact with individuals who fought with the 70th Infantry Division. Compiles statistics. **Libraries: Type:** reference. **Holdings:** archival material. **Awards:** Outstanding Trailblazer Award. **Frequency:** biennial. **Type:** recognition. **Recipient:** for service. **Publications:** *Association Roster*, biennial. Directory. **Circulation:** 2,000 ● *Reunion Activity*, biennial ● *Trailblazer*, quarterly. Magazine. **Price:** included in membership dues. **Conventions/Meetings:** biennial congress and reunion, with division, army and WWII memorabilia (exhibits) - usually late summer.

20931 ■ 84th Infantry Division, Railsplitter Society
c/o Forrest T. Lothrop, Exec. Sec.-Treas.
PO Box 827
Sioux Falls, SD 57101-0827
Ph: (605)334-8787
E-mail: liladay@aol.com
Contact: Forrest T. Lothrop, Exec. Sec.-Treas.
Founded: 1945. **Members:** 2,000. **Membership Dues:** veteran (World War II), $15 (annual) ● life, $60. **Staff:** 3. **State Groups:** 6. **Description:** Men who served in the 84th Infantry Division during World War II. Seeks to develop and maintain fellowship among those who served together. Organizes reunions. **Awards:** Bolling Cross. **Frequency:** annual. **Type:** recognition. **Recipient:** chosen by the president ● Order of the Eagle. **Frequency:** annual. **Type:** recognition. **Recipient:** chosen by the president ● Railsplitter of the Year. **Frequency:** annual. **Type:** recognition. **Recipient:** members vote in secret ballot for the man they feel is most deserving. **Publications:** *The Railsplitter*, 3/year. Newsletter. **Price:** included in membership dues. **Circulation:** 2,300. **Conventions/Meetings:** annual reunion.

20932 ■ 86th Chemical Mortar Battalion Association
c/o CSM George L. Murray, Adj.
818 W 62nd St.
Anniston, AL 36206

Ph: (256)820-4415
E-mail: betmat@earthlink.net
URL: http://www.4point2.org/86cmb.htm
Contact: CSM George L. Murray, Adj.
Founded: 1960. **Members:** 160. **Staff:** 1. **Description:** Veterans who served in the 86th Chemical Mortar Battalion in World War II. Promotes the history of the battalion; fosters communication among members. Compiles statistics. **Awards:** Achievement Award and Scholarship. **Frequency:** annual. **Type:** scholarship. **Recipient:** for a graduating senior from high school. **Committees:** Achievement Awards; Legal; Reunion; Sunshine; Tour. **Publications:** *History of the 86th Chemical Mortar Battalion*, 3/year. Newsletter ● *The Lobster*, 3/year. Bulletin. Includes roster of members. **Conventions/Meetings:** annual reunion.

20933 ■ 94th Infantry Division Association
c/o Harry Helms, Sec.-Treas.
609 Dogwood Dr.
Downingtown, PA 19335
Ph: (610)363-7826
E-mail: secretary@94thinfdiv.com
URL: http://www.94thinfdiv.com
Contact: Harry Helms, Sec.-Treas.
Founded: 1950. **Members:** 2,100. **Membership Dues:** basic, $10 (annual) ● life, $50. **Staff:** 3. **Budget:** $15,000. **Regional Groups:** 14. **Description:** Veterans who served with the 94th Infantry Division or its attached units between Sept. 15, 1942 and May 8, 1945. Seeks to preserve and reestablish the friendships made while in service in the 94th Infantry Division during World War II and to commemorate comrades who died in the war. **Awards:** Soldier of the Year with 94th Reserve Unit, Devens, MA. **Frequency:** annual. **Type:** recognition. **Telecommunication Services:** electronic mail, webmaster@94thinfdiv.com. **Publications:** *The Attack*, 3/year. Magazine. **Price:** included in membership dues. **Circulation:** 2,100. **Conventions/Meetings:** annual reunion.

20934 ■ 99th Infantry Division Association (NIDA)
PO Box 99
Marion, KS 66861
E-mail: donna@99div.com
URL: http://www.99div.com
Contact: Donna Bernhardt, Contact
Founded: 1950. **Members:** 3,123. **Membership Dues:** individual, $10 (annual). **Staff:** 2. **Budget:** $30,000. **Description:** U.S. Army veterans who served in the 99th Infantry Division, which fought in Europe during World War II. Fosters communication among members. **Libraries:** Type: reference. **Holdings:** archival material. **Publications:** *Checkerboard*, bimonthly. Newspaper. **Price:** included in membership dues. **Circulation:** 3,500. Alternate Formats: online. **Conventions/Meetings:** annual reunion and convention (exhibits).

20935 ■ 106th Infantry Division Association
c/o John Kline
11 Harold Dr.
Burnsville, MN 55337
Ph: (952)890-3155
Fax: (952)426-1131
E-mail: jpk@mm.com
URL: http://www.mm.com/user/jpk
Contact: John Kline, Contact
Founded: 1945. **Members:** 1,625. **Membership Dues:** individual, $10 (annual) ● life, $75. **Staff:** 5. **Regional Groups:** 20. **State Groups:** 28. **Multinational. Description:** Veterans who served in the 106th Infantry Division in World War II in the European theater or who were attached; also interested associates. **Libraries:** Type: reference. **Holdings:** 32; books, periodicals. **Subjects:** military. **Awards:** Order of the Golden Lion. **Frequency:** periodic. **Type:** recognition. **Recipient:** for members' outstanding service. **Also Known As:** Golden Lions. **Publications:** *The Cub*, quarterly. Magazine. Reports on membership activities. **Price:** included in membership dues ● *Membership Roster*, periodic. Membership Directory. **Conventions/Meetings:** annual

regional meeting and dinner, in commemoration of the annual anniversary of the Battle of the Bulge - usually December ● annual reunion - usually September.

20936 ■ 147th Engineers Veterans Association
439 Greenlow Rd.
Baltimore, MD 21228
Ph: (410)747-0291
Contact: Col. George A. Itzel, Chm.
Founded: 1945. **Members:** 200. **Membership Dues:** private/unit veteran, $20 (annual). **Staff:** 3. **Local Groups:** 3. **National Groups:** 4. **Description:** World War II Army veterans who served in the 147th Engineers and fought in the June 6, 1944 invasion of Omaha Beach in Normandy, France. Promotes camaraderie among members. Maintains monument at Omaha Beach. **Libraries:** Type: not open to the public. **Holdings:** 10; books. **Subjects:** Normandy. **Computer Services:** Mailing lists. **Committees:** Executive. **Publications:** *147th Veterans Association Newsletter*, quarterly. **Conventions/Meetings:** annual reunion and conference.

20937 ■ 303rd Bomb Group (H) Association
c/o William H. Cox, Pres.
441 Sandstone Dr.
Vacaville, CA 95688-4225
Ph: (707)448-0571
E-mail: pilotrb36@aol.com
URL: http://www.303rdbga.com
Contact: William H. Cox, Pres.
Founded: 1975. **Members:** 1,964. **Membership Dues:** regular (associate), $25 (annual) ● life (family), $100 ● life (associate), $150. **Description:** Individuals who were members of, or attached to, the 303rd Bomb Group at its training bases, or its operating base in Molesworth, England during World War II. Interested persons, as well as widows and other relatives of Group members, are also eligible to join. Perpetuates the training and combat history of the 303rd, and the memory of lost comrades. Offers social, educational, patriotic, and recreational activities. Sponsors special events. **Libraries:** Type: open to the public. **Holdings:** 150; books. **Subjects:** aviation history, 303rd BG activities. **Awards:** Distinguished Service Award. **Type:** recognition. **Recipient:** for service in the 303rd Bomb Group during World War II. **Computer Services:** Mailing lists, of members. **Telecommunication Services:** electronic mail, edmiller@pldi.net. **Affiliated With:** Eighth Air Force Historical Society. **Also Known As:** Hell's Angels Bomb Group. **Formerly:** (2000) Three Hundred Third BGA Membership. **Publications:** *Hell's Angels Newsletter*, quarterly. Features wartime and present day photos and stories. **Price:** included in membership dues. **Circulation:** 1,964 ● *303rd Bomb Group "Hell's Angel's" Directory*, biennial. Membership Directory. **Conventions/Meetings:** annual reunion and board meeting, with photographs, mission records, uniforms, equipment (exhibits).

20938 ■ 325th Glider Infantry Association
c/o Jesse Oxendine, Chm.
1812 Woodberry Rd.
Charlotte, NC 28212
Ph: (704)537-4912
E-mail: joxendine6@carolina.rr.com
URL: http://www.325glider.com
Contact: Jesse Oxendine, Chm.
Founded: 1980. **Members:** 200. **Membership Dues:** widow, $10 (annual) ● associate, $20 (annual). **Description:** Veterans of the 325th Glider Infantry Regiment, World War II, 82nd Airborne Division. Promotes and preserves the history of the World War II glider soldier. Conducts research on the history of the 325th Glider Infantry. **Computer Services:** Mailing lists. **Committees:** Golf Outing; Hospitality Room. **Publications:** *Glider Tow Line*, quarterly. Newsletter. Alternate Formats: online. **Conventions/Meetings:** annual reunion (exhibits).

20939 ■ 397th Bomb Group Association
PO Box 1786
Rockville, MD 20849-1786
Ph: (301)460-4488

Fax: (301)460-2075
E-mail: nevinprice@erols.com
Contact: Nevin F. Price, Sec.-Treas.
Founded: 1967. **Members:** 1,100. **Description:** Former members of the 397th Bomb Group and their immediate families. (A B-26 Marauder bomber group, the 397th was active in England, France, Belgium, Germany, and the Netherlands during World War II.) Keeps members in touch and promotes camaraderie. Consists of the 596th, 597th, 598th, and 599th bomb squadrons. **Awards:** Type: recognition. **Computer Services:** database, listing of individuals who served with the group ● mailing lists. **Affiliated With:** B-26 Marauder Historical Society. **Publications:** *The Party Line*, periodic. Newsletter. **Circulation:** 1,100. **Conventions/Meetings:** biennial reunion.

20940 ■ 452nd Bomb Wing/Group Association
901 Poling Dr.
Columbus, OH 43224-1936
Ph: (614)267-9083 (614)447-8519
Free: (800)452-9099
E-mail: hanknorth@core.com
URL: http://www.geocities.com/bombgroup17/452h2.html
Contact: Hank North, Sec.
Founded: 1975. **Members:** 1,150. **Membership Dues:** individual, $10 (annual). **Staff:** 4. **Description:** U.S. Army Air Corps veterans who served in the 452nd Bomb Group during World War II. Promotes camaraderie among members. **Libraries:** Type: reference. **Holdings:** archival material. **Computer Services:** Mailing lists. **Publications:** *Poop from the Group*, quarterly. Newsletter. Contains letters from members, including Europeans. **Price:** included in membership dues. **Circulation:** 1,300. **Conventions/Meetings:** annual reunion.

20941 ■ 483rd Bombardment Group (H) Association (FBGHA)
c/o Sandee West Maeda, Sec.
1050 E 5th Ave.
Escondido, CA 92025
Ph: (480)832-3567
E-mail: lvlt2u@msn.com
URL: http://www.483rd.com
Contact: Stanton Rickey, Pres.
Founded: 1979. **Members:** 1,400. **Membership Dues:** regular, $15 (annual). **Description:** Former members of the 483rd Bomb Group (H). Preserves the history of their squadrons and groups that fought in World War II. Makes available squadron caps, scarves, cap pins, and group insignia decals. Provides scholarship funds. **Libraries:** Type: reference. **Holdings:** archival material, books, photographs. **Awards:** Type: recognition. **Committees:** Clipped Wings. **Publications:** *Unit Newsletter*, quarterly ● *Unit Roster*, annual. **Conventions/Meetings:** annual reunion.

20942 ■ 504th Parachute Infantry Regiment Association (FPIA)
c/o Ross M. Goddard, Pres.
600 W Ponce De Leon Ave.
Decatur, GA 30030-2953
Ph: (404)378-0407
E-mail: info@504pirassociation.org
URL: http://www.504pirassociation.org
Contact: Ross M. Goddard, Pres.
Founded: 1942. **Members:** 500. **Membership Dues:** regular, $10 (annual) ● life (must be a life member of 82nd Association), $75 ● active duty, $5 (annual) ● life, active duty (must be a life member of 82nd Association), $50. **Staff:** 4. **Description:** A loosely-formed organization of paratroopers who served with the 504th Regiment Combat Team, 376th Parachute Field Artillery, and 307th Engineers. Contributes to the support of a museum in Nijmegen, Netherlands and related World War II projects. **Committees:** 504 RCT Dinner Reunion; Historical. **Also Known As:** Devils in Baggy Pants. **Publications:** *Devils in Baggy Pants*, quarterly. Newsletter. **Price:** included in membership dues ● *504 Register*. **Conventions/Meetings:** annual conference ● annual reunion and

dinner, held in conjunction with 82nd Airborne Division Association (exhibits).

20943 ■ 508th Parachute Infantry Regiment Association

c/o Kenneth Merritt
1517 Atwick Dr.
Fayetteville, NC 28304-3901
Ph: (910)425-5818
E-mail: kmerritt2@nc.rr.com
URL: http://www.508pir.org
Contact: O.B. Hill, Founder/Chm.
Founded: 1975. **Members:** 1,150. **Budget:** $25,000. **Description:** Veterans of the 508th Parachute Infantry Regiment who served from 1942 to 1945. (During the period the regiment was attached to the 82nd Airborne Division as a regimental combat team.) Arranges reunions to renew and continue wartime friendships. Has completed friendship projects such as parks, monuments, and museums in England, France, and the Netherlands; has dedicated a grove of trees and a plaque in Arlington National Cemetery. Sponsors trips to wartime battle sites. Conducts slide presentations. Maintains museum. **Awards:** O.B. Hill Award. **Frequency:** annual. **Type:** recognition. **Publications:** *508 Newsletter*, quarterly. **Price:** free. **Circulation:** 1,500 ● *Membership Roster*, annual. Membership Directory ● Also contributes monthly article to *Static Line*. **Conventions/Meetings:** annual reunion (exhibits).

20944 ■ 509th Parachute Infantry Association

PO Box 860
Huntsville, AL 35804
E-mail: bls509@bellsouth.net
Contact: Barry Simpson, Contact
Founded: 1970. **Members:** 800. **Description:** Veterans of the original 509th Parachute Infantry. Seeks to preserve the comradeship and traditions of the unit. Maintains battalion records. Compiles statistics; operates museum. **Libraries: Type:** reference. **Holdings:** archival material. **Publications:** *Static Line*, monthly ● *Your 509th Connection*, quarterly. Newsletter. **Price:** included in membership dues. **Conventions/Meetings:** annual meeting.

20945 ■ 517th Parachute Regimental Combat Team Association (517 PRCT)

c/o Mr. Gene Frice, Pres.
1420 NE Sharkey
Bend, OR 97701
E-mail: webmaster@517prct.org
URL: http://www.517prct.org
Contact: Mr. Gene Frice, Pres.
Founded: 1945. **Members:** 1,440. **Staff:** 1. **Description:** Individuals who served honorably with the 517th Parachute Regimental Combat Team during World War II. (The combat team consists of the 517th Parachute Infantry Regiment, the 460th Parachute Field Artillery Battalion, and the 596th Parachute Combat Engineer Company.) Seeks to: preserve and patriotically revere the memory of the men who served in the combat team; perpetuate "Airborne Spirit" as a heritage for future generations; support and enhance the fame and glory of the combat team; maintain and strengthen the bonds of comradeship among members. Gathers and disseminates information about the men of the 517th; provides for local and national reunions. **Publications:** *The Thunderbolt*, quarterly. Newsletter. **Circulation:** 1,575 ● Also publishes a unit history. **Conventions/Meetings:** biennial reunion ● tour, battlefields in Belgium, France, Italy, and Germany.

20946 ■ 526th Armored Infantry Battalion Association

PO Box 456
Yolo, CA 95697
Ph: (530)662-8160
E-mail: 526aib@sbcglobal.net
URL: http://www.526th.org
Contact: Sherrie Morrison, Sec.-Treas.
Founded: 1976. **Members:** 620. **Membership Dues:** individual, $30 (annual) ● exchange, $30 (annual). **Staff:** 2. **Languages:** English, French, German. **Description:** Veterans who served in the 526th armored

infantry during WWII. Promotes camradeship among the surviving members and their families and friends. Informs members of social events and disseminates historical information on 526th infantry battalion. Conducts research programs; maintains speakers' bureau. **Libraries: Type:** reference. **Holdings:** 51; archival material, audio recordings, books, clippings, periodicals, video recordings. **Subjects:** historical facts pertaining to the association. **Computer Services:** database, (available for members only). **Publications:** *The Pekan* (in English and French), quarterly. Newsletter. **Price:** included in membership dues. **Circulation:** 710. Alternate Formats: online ● Directory, quarterly. Alternate Formats: CD-ROM. **Conventions/Meetings:** annual reunion.

20947 ■ 704th Tank Destroyer Battalion Association

Address Unknown since 2007
Founded: 1977. **Members:** 60. **Membership Dues:** open, $10 (annual) ● life, $50. **Staff:** 5. **Description:** World War II veterans from the 704th Tank Destroyer Battalion, Fourth Armored Division. Has dedicated memorials in Arracourt, France and displays at Bastogne Historical Center, Belgium and Armor Circle, Fort Knox, KY. Sponsors displays at Clervaux, Luxembourg, Diekirch, Belgium; and Arlon, Belgium. **Libraries: Type:** reference. **Holdings:** 5. **Subjects:** Combat History, 704th Tank Destroyer Battalion, book Men of the 704 - published in 1998. **Awards: Frequency:** annual. **Type:** scholarship. **Recipient:** for an honored deceased or renowned member. **Computer Services:** Mailing lists, roster. **Publications:** *Five Star Review*, quarterly. Newsletter. Includes items pertaining to World War II and particularly to the Fourth Armored Division and 704th Tank Destroyer Battalion. **Price:** included in membership dues; $1.50 for nonmembers. **Circulation:** 60. **Advertising:** not accepted. **Conventions/Meetings:** annual convention, includes history of the Fourth Armored Division and the 704th Tank Destroyer Battalion (exhibits) ● biennial reunion.

20948 ■ 829th Signal Service Association

700 Ocean Ave., Unit 426
Spring Lake, NJ 07762
Ph: (201)385-2246
Contact: Nino Caridi, Pres.
Founded: 1950. **Members:** 225. **Membership Dues:** voluntary (spouse is free), $15 (annual). **Staff:** 8. **Regional Groups:** 6. **Description:** World War II Army veterans who belonged to the 829th, 6662nd, and 3195th signal service companies and served in North Africa and Europe. Promotes fellowship and nostalgia. **Also Known As:** 829-6662-3195th Association. **Publications:** *The Association News*, semiannual. Newspaper ● *Roster*, annual. Membership Directory ● *Signal Service Newsletter*, semiannual. **Conventions/Meetings:** reunion (exhibits) - every 18 months.

20949 ■ Americal Division Veterans Association (ADVA)

c/o Mr. Roger Gilmore, Natl. Adjutant
PO Box 830662
Richardson, TX 75080
E-mail: gilmoraces@aol.com
URL: http://www.americal.org
Contact: Mr. Roger Gilmore, Natl. Adjutant
Founded: 1945. **Members:** 3,400. **Membership Dues:** regular, $15 (annual) ● life (75 years old and older), $75 ● life (under age 75), $165. **Staff:** 3. **Budget:** $28,500. **Regional Groups:** 9. **Description:** World War II and Vietnam veterans. Strengthens and preserves camaraderie among members through fraternal, historic, patriotic, and social activities. Operates museum. **Awards:** American Division Scholarship Foundation. **Frequency:** annual. **Type:** scholarship. **Recipient:** for children and grandchildren of Americal Division veterans. **Publications:** *Americal Newsletter*, quarterly. Covers the activities of those who have served with the Americal Division. Includes listing of new and deceased members. **Price:** included in membership dues. **Circulation:** 3,500 ● *Under the Southern Cross (WWII)*. **Conventions/**

Meetings: annual reunion (exhibits) - always 2nd or 3rd week in June.

20950 ■ American Defenders of Bataan and Corregidor (ADBC)

c/o Joseph L. Alexander
9407 Fern Glen
San Antonio, TX 78240
Ph: (210)690-0837
E-mail: frphillips@sprintmail.com
URL: http://harrisonheritage.com/adbc
Contact: Rev. Robert W. Phillips, Natl. Chm.
Founded: 1946. **Members:** 2,647. **Membership Dues:** life, $25. **Staff:** 7. **Regional Groups:** 5. **State Groups:** 10. **Local Groups:** 10. **Description:** World War II veterans of the armed forces who served in defense of Wake Island, Guam, northern China, the Dutch East Indies, Asian Flood, and the Philippine Islands from December 1941 to May 1942 (95&percent; were taken prisoner by the Japanese). Conducts fraternal and patriotic activities; promotes civic programs to commemorate Bataan Day (April 9). Compiles medical information on physical disabilities resulting from 42 months of starvation, while subjected to harsh treatment and tropical diseases. **Publications:** *QUAN Magazine*, 5/year. **Price:** $25.00/year. **Circulation:** 5,000. **Conventions/Meetings:** board meeting ● annual convention.

20951 ■ American Merchant Marine Veterans (AMMV)

PO Box 151205
Cape Coral, FL 33915-1205
Ph: (239)549-1010
Fax: (239)549-1990
E-mail: ammvnatl@aol.com
URL: http://www.usmm.org
Contact: Barbara Reher, Natl. Admin.
Founded: 1983. **Members:** 4,000. **Membership Dues:** individual, $25 (annual). **Staff:** 3. **Budget:** $48,000. **Regional Groups:** 12. **Local Groups:** 70. **Description:** U.S. Merchant Marine veterans and seamen serving in allied Merchant Marine fleets during World War II. Seeks to promote comradeship among members. Perpetuates the memory of deceased Merchant Mariners and provides assistance to their widows. Fosters recognition of the "services and sacrifices" of merchant seamen. Advocates preserving American freedom by encouraging loyalty to the Constitution and U.S. laws. Promotes the maintenance of what the group feels is a strong, well-trained Merchant Marine force as "a potent arm of defense and offense as it has already been proven to be." Maintains speakers' bureau (some chapters only); compiles statistics. **Libraries: Type:** not open to the public. **Holdings:** books, periodicals. **Subjects:** maritime: current and historical. **Awards:** Honorary. **Frequency:** periodic. **Type:** recognition. **Recipient:** for outstanding service to Merchant Marine veterans and the U.S. Flag Merchant Marine. **Computer Services:** Mailing lists. **Publications:** *American Merchant Marine Newsletter*, quarterly. Magazine. **Price:** $12.00/year. **Circulation:** 5,000 ● *Gulfstream Log*, bimonthly. Newsletter. **Price:** free. **Circulation:** 400 ● Also produces newsletters from other chapters. **Conventions/Meetings:** annual convention, with small scale posters, photos, banners (exhibits) - May or June.

20952 ■ American Rosie the Riveter Association (ARRA)

c/o Dr. Frances T. Carter, Founding Pres./Natl. Exec. Dir.
3470 Loch Ridge Dr.
Birmingham, AL 35216-4475
Ph: (205)822-4106
Fax: (205)822-4106
E-mail: fran.carter@juno.com
URL: http://www.rootsweb.com/~usarra
Contact: Dr. Frances T. Carter, Founding Pres./Natl. Exec. Dir.
Founded: 1998. **Members:** 2,075. **Membership Dues:** active volunteer, $10 (annual). **Staff:** 1. **Local Groups:** 11. **Multinational. Description:** Women whose work was designed to contribute to the war effort and their female descendants. Members recog-

nize and preserve the history and legacy of working women, including volunteer women, during World War II. Promotes cooperation and fellowship among such members and their descendants. Furthers the advancement of patriotic ideals and loyalty to the United States of America. **Libraries: Type:** reference. **Holdings:** books. **Publications:** *Recruitment Tool.* Brochure ● *Rosie's Mail Call,* quarterly. Newsletter. **Price:** free, for members only. **Circulation:** 1,658. Alternate Formats: online. **Conventions/Meetings:** annual convention - every 2nd or 3rd weekend of June.

20953 ■ Association of Invalids and Veterans of World War II from the Former USSR and Other European Countries
Address Unknown since 2006
Founded: 1977. **Members:** 422. **Membership Dues:** $1 (monthly). **Staff:** 15. **Budget:** $6,000. **State Groups:** 2. **Local Groups:** 12. **National Groups:** 1. **Languages:** English, Russian. **Description:** Veterans from World War II from the former USSR. Defends the spiritual and material interests of World War II veterans. Activities include: distribution of free food, organization of trips throughout the U.S. **Libraries: Type:** open to the public. **Holdings:** 250; books. **Publications:** *Unforgettable, Unforgettable Second Issue, We are 25* (in Russian). Book. Includes remembrances of World War II, history of Association from 1977-2002. **Price:** $5.00. **Advertising:** not accepted. **Conventions/Meetings:** annual Day of Victory - meeting ● annual meeting - November, after 2 years election of President and members of committee. Philadelphia, PA ● New Year Celebration of Jubilee.

20954 ■ B-26 Marauder Historical Society (MHS)
3900 E Timerod
Tucson, AZ 85711
E-mail: admin@b-26mhs.org
URL: http://www.b-26mhs.org
Contact: Mr. Philip Gutt, Exec. Dir.
Founded: 1988. **Members:** 4,600. **Membership Dues:** basic, $35 (annual). **Staff:** 10. **Regional Groups:** 5. **Multinational. Description:** Individuals who built, flew in, or provided ground crew support to Martin B-26 Marauder aircraft during World War II; other persons interested in the Marauder. (The B-26 Marauder, built by the Glenn L. Martin Company from 1940 to 1945, was a twin-engine, medium-load and -altitude airplane used as a tactical bomber in Europe and North Africa, the Aleutian Islands, and the Pacific region during World War II.) Seeks to preserve the memory of the Marauder, "and assure its rightful place in history." Works to: establish contact with all B-26 units and others associated with the B-26, including Ferrying Groups/Squadrons and former or current employees of the Glenn L. Martin Company; WASPs, RAF, FFAF, SAAF, USN, USMC; survey aviation museums and similar places to determine their needs regarding items relating to the B-26, and to select pictorial and model displays to be provided to these museums and other appropriate institutions. Conducts fundraising efforts. Publishes a calendar and list of all B-26 unit reunions. **Libraries: Type:** not open to the public. **Holdings:** articles, books, periodicals. **Subjects:** aviation, military technical manuals. **Computer Services:** database, 40 B-26 unit contacts ● database, 44000 names of found, deceased, or lost persons. **Publications:** *The Marauder Thunder,* quarterly. Newsletter. **Price:** included in membership dues. **Circulation:** 5,500. Alternate Formats: online. **Conventions/Meetings:** periodic general assembly and workshop.

20955 ■ Battle of Ormoc Bay Association
c/o Mr. William M. Dallam, Sec.-Treas.
117 Tuscarora St.
Harrisburg, PA 17104
URL: http://www.ormocbattle.com/veteran.htm
Contact: Mr. William M. Dallam, Sec.-Treas.
Founded: 1984. **Members:** 325. **Membership Dues:** regular, $15 (annual). **Staff:** 2. **Budget:** $3,000. **Description:** Comprised of individuals who served aboard naval ships that took part in the Battle of Or-

moc Bay, Leyte Philippine Islands in December 1944; crew members of associated ships from World War II, the Korean War, Vietnam, or peacetime Navy; families of above members. **Libraries: Type:** open to the public. **Holdings:** 300. **Subjects:** battle of Ormoc Bay. **Publications:** *The Poop Sheet,* quarterly. Newsletter. Features member news, reunion news, and articles. **Price:** included in membership dues. **Conventions/Meetings:** annual reunion - always fall.

20956 ■ China-Burma-India Hump Pilot Association (CBI-HPA)
3509 Huntington Dr.
Amarillo, TX 79109-4043
Ph: (806)352-4449
Fax: (806)352-7024
E-mail: jv28800@aol.com
URL: http://www.cbihpa.org
Contact: Jay Vinyard, Pres.
Founded: 1945. **Members:** 3,000. **Membership Dues:** regular, $25 (annual) ● life, $75. **Staff:** 2. **Description:** Represents air crew veterans who fought in the China-Burma-India Theater of World War II. Maintains museum. **Libraries: Type:** reference. **Holdings:** 4; archival material. **Subjects:** World War II. **Awards: Type:** recognition. **Publications:** *China-Airlift-The Hump.* Book. Contains three volumes. ● *Roster,* periodic. Directory ● Newsletter, 3/year. **Conventions/Meetings:** annual reunion, includes social affair (exhibits).

20957 ■ Eighth Air Force Historical Society (8AFHS)
c/o Mamie Kent, Mgr.
PO Box 956
Pooler, GA 31322
Ph: (912)748-8884
E-mail: membershipmanager@8thafhs.org
URL: http://www.8thafhs.org
Contact: Mamie Kent, Mgr.
Founded: 1975. **Members:** 20,000. **Membership Dues:** individual, $25 (annual). **Staff:** 3. **Budget:** $100,000. **State Groups:** 47. **Description:** Helps veterans contact their units, and former World War II veterans. Provides for the collections, restoration, preservation, and display of the Eighth Air Force memorabilia. Promotes educational activities relative to the history of the Eighth Air Force. Aims to build an oral history database. The foundation includes museum exhibits, a print collection, a document collection, a bibliographic project, and a biographical project. **Awards: Type:** recognition. **Publications:** *The 8th AF News,* quarterly. Newsletter. Contains war stories and other items of interest to members. Includes book reviews, chapter news, obituaries, and letters from members. **Price:** included in membership dues. **Circulation:** 20,000. **Advertising:** accepted ● *Honoring the American Past.* Booklet. Provides an overview of the Eighth Air Force and the role it played in World War II. **Price:** $25.00. **Conventions/Meetings:** annual reunion (exhibits) ● reunion ● tour.

20958 ■ First Special Service Force Association (FSSFA)
262 Pine Knob Cir.
Moneta, VA 24121-2609
Ph: (540)297-8304
Fax: (540)297-1136
E-mail: storfssf@infionline.net
Contact: William Woon, VP
Founded: 1947. **Members:** 900. **Membership Dues:** active, $20 (annual) ● associate, $20 (annual) ● life, $135 ● class A associate, $20 (annual). **Staff:** 3. **Budget:** $30,000. **Regional Groups:** 4. **State Groups:** 7. **Multinational. Description:** Fellowship organization of veterans of World War II First Special Service Force and their families. Maintains monument in Helena, MT, which is supported by the First Service Special Force Memorial Trust, a separate Montana trust. **Libraries: Type:** reference. **Holdings:** 120; archival material, books, clippings, monographs, periodicals. **Subjects:** FSSF in World War II. **Awards:** Eugene V. McCormick Award. **Frequency:** annual. **Type:** recognition ● Frederick Award for Outstanding Soldier. **Frequency:** annual. **Type:** recognition. **Recipient:** for individuals selected by

their respective commands, U.S. Army Special Forces Command. **Committees:** By Laws; Nominating; Publications; Time and Place. **Also Known As:** Devil's Brigade; Black Devils. **Status Note:** (2006) Defunct. **Publications:** *The Spearhead,* semimonthly, February, March, June, July, October, and November. Newsletter. **Price:** free, for members only. **Circulation:** 1,100. **Conventions/Meetings:** annual reunion.

20959 ■ Flying Tigers of the 14th Air Force Association
4801 Courthouse St., Ste.220
PO Box 934236
Williamsburg, VA 23188
Ph: (757)229-4631 (757)973-0277
Fax: (757)229-8912
Contact: Robert Lee, Pres.
Founded: 1948. **Members:** 3,000. **Membership Dues:** individual, $15 (annual). **Staff:** 10. **Budget:** $42,000. **State Groups:** 20. **Local Groups:** 5. **Description:** Veterans of service in China during World War II, known as the Flying Tigers. Members served with the American Volunteer Group, the China Air Task Force, and/or the 14th Air Force between December 20, 1941 and December 15, 1945. General Claire Lee Chennault (1890-1958) served as commander of the flying Tigers, whose insignia was a flying tiger with an Air Force star. Holds a memorial service each May at Arlington National Cemetery, Washington, DC. **Publications:** *Flying Tigers of the 14th Air Force Association—Directory of Members,* annual. Membership Directory. **Price:** included in membership dues. ISSN: 1521-8708. **Circulation:** 3,000 ● *Jing Bao Journal,* quarterly. Contains war stories and other articles of interest to members. Includes information on new members and lists deaths. **Conventions/Meetings:** annual reunion - always in May.

20960 ■ International B-24 Liberator Club (IBLC)
1672 Main St., Ste.E
PMB-124
Ramona, CA 92065-5257
Ph: (760)788-3624
Free: (866)788-3624
Fax: (760)789-8911
E-mail: info@bomberlegends.com
URL: http://www.bomberlegends.com
Contact: Robert E. McGuire, Founder
Founded: 1968. **Members:** 3,500. **Membership Dues:** regular, $20 (annual). **Staff:** 2. **Budget:** $45,000. **For-Profit. Description:** Crewmembers of Liberator and Privateer airplanes used during World War II; ground crews and support personnel of groups and squadrons; production personnel, historians, writers, modelers, World War II aviation enthusiasts, and relatives of crewmen. Seeks to: promote the role of the Liberator and Privateer airplanes in World War II; recognize achievements involving the airplanes and its crewmen; encourage the preservation of articles, photographs, and documents concerning the history of the Liberator and Privateer airplanes. Offers assistance to writers and researchers. Sponsors exhibits and establishes museum displays. Compiles data on missing-in-action and killed-in-action crewmen and makes information available to their survivors. Maintains speakers' bureau. **Libraries: Type:** reference. **Holdings:** 350; books, photographs. **Subjects:** Liberator and Privateer airplanes. **Also Known As:** Liberator Club. **Publications:** *Bomber Legends Magazine,* quarterly. **Circulation:** 5,000. **Advertising:** accepted. **Conventions/Meetings:** periodic meeting.

20961 ■ Merrill's Marauders Association (MMA)
c/o Philip Piazza, Pres.
13033 Azalea Dr.
Seneca, SC 29678-4508
E-mail: historian@marauder.org
URL: http://www.marauder.org
Contact: Philip Piazza, Pres.
Founded: 1947. **Members:** 1,000. **Description:** Men who served in Merrill's Marauders during World War II. (The Marauders were composed of soldiers who

volunteered for a "dangerous and hazardous mission" and subsequently fought behind Japanese lines in Burma.) To perpetuate the traditions and heritage of this unusual combat unit. Maintains liaison with present-day ranger training programs and units. In 1969, the name "Merrill's Marauders" was reactivated by the Army for the 75th Ranger Regiment. Maintains hall of fame at Ft. Benning, GA; plans to construct ranger memorial at Ft. Benning with a single arch memorial commemorating all rangers and a pavilion with individual memorial stone sculptures for each ranger group. Presents silver compasses to the top graduates of ranger class annually. **Publications:** *Burman News*, quarterly. Newsletter ● *Directory*, annual. **Conventions/Meetings:** annual reunion (exhibits) - always September.

20962 ■ Navajo Code Talkers Association (NCTA)

PO Box 1182
Window Rock, AZ 86515
Ph: (520)871-5468
E-mail: info@presencesantafe.com
URL: http://www.lapahie.com/NCTA.cfm
Contact: Dr. Samuel Billison, Pres.
Founded: 1971. **Members:** 40. **Membership Dues:** regular, $10 (annual). **State Groups:** 1. **Local Groups:** 1. **Languages:** English, Navajo, Spanish. **Description:** Navajos who served as communicators or "code talkers" in the Marine Corps during World War II. These men formulated a code using the intricate Navajo language, earning them the reputation of providing the "only foolproof, unbreakable code in the history of warfare". Promotes the welfare of the Indian veteran; recommends scholarships to descendants of Navajo code talkers. Assists in programs for schools, colleges and universities, and other organizations. Makes available children's services. Operates speakers' bureau for schools K-12 and universities, church organizations, service organizations, women's organizations and other national organizations and overseas military camps. **Libraries: Type:** reference. **Holdings:** audio recordings, video recordings. **Subjects:** taped interviews of code talkers. **Awards: Type:** scholarship. **Recipient:** for children or grandchildren of code talkers. **Committees:** Scholarship. **Affiliated With:** American Legion; Marine Corps League; Veterans of Foreign Wars of the United States. **Publications:** *Navajo Code Talkers*. Brochure ● *We Talked Navajo*, periodic. Journal. Contains information on six Marine Division Combats, list of officers of NCTA and association activities. ● Also publishes cards and pamphlets. **Conventions/Meetings:** monthly Business Meeting, includes WWII mementos and awards, books on code talkers, posters (exhibits) - usually 1st or 2nd Saturday.

20963 ■ P-47 Thunderbolt Pilots Association

PO Box 1266
Ridgewood, NJ 07451-1266
E-mail: p47webmaster@comcast.net
URL: http://www.p47pilots.com
Contact: John Rutherford, Natl. Sec.
Founded: 1961. **Members:** 1,800. **Membership Dues:** regular, $15 (annual) ● life, $100. **Regional Groups:** 7. **Description:** World War II pilots who have flown the P-47 airplane, prior to 1956. Facilitates communication among members. Has dedicated memorial, located at the U.S. Air Force Museum and the U.S. Air Force Academy, to WWII pilots, ground support personnel, manufacturers and designers. **Publications:** *Jug Letter*, quarterly. Newsletter. **Price:** included in membership dues ● *Membership Directory*, triennial ● Books ● Videos. **Conventions/Meetings:** annual reunion (exhibits).

20964 ■ P-51 Mustang Pilots Association

1040 SE 58th Ave.
Hillsboro, OR 97123-6326
Ph: (503)591-9312
Fax: (503)591-8712
Contact: Maj. Edwin Slaughter USAF, Pres.
Founded: 1980. **Members:** 1,050. **Membership Dues:** individual, $20 (annual) ● life, $100. **Staff:** 5. **Regional Groups:** 15. **Languages:** English, French, German. **Description:** Pilots who flew P-51 Mustang

airplanes during World War II or the Korean War; interested individuals. Seeks to unite members through the sponsorship of various events and activities. Donated plaques to the Shipol Museum in the Netherlands, the U.S. Air Force Academy in Colorado Springs, CO, a museum in France, and a new museum in Oregon. Conducts charitable program, regional events and activities, and research programs. **Libraries: Type:** reference. **Holdings:** books, business records, periodicals. **Awards: Type:** recognition. **Publications:** *National Directory—P-51 Mustang Pilots Association* (in English, French, and German), quadrennial. Includes list of new members. **Advertising:** accepted ● *P-51 Mustang Book* ● *P-51 Mustang Pilots Newsletter*, quarterly. **Conventions/Meetings:** annual reunion (exhibits) ● periodic Warbird Air Show.

20965 ■ Pearl Harbor Survivors Association (PHSA)

PO Box 1816
Carlsbad, CA 92018-1816
Ph: (760)727-9027 (760)419-5878
Fax: (760)727-9087
E-mail: jimarine@roadrunner.com
URL: http://www.pearlharborremembered.net
Contact: James L. Evans, Natl. Sec.
Founded: 1958. **Members:** 7,400. **Membership Dues:** regular, $10 (annual). **Staff:** 4. **Regional Groups:** 8. **State Groups:** 47. **Local Groups:** 150. **Description:** Members of the U.S. Armed Forces stationed on the island of Oahu or offshore within a three-mile limit during the Japanese attack on Pearl Harbor, December 7, 1941. Commemorates that "day of infamy" and to honor the memory of those killed in the attack. Seeks to obtain proclamations from governors and mayors declaring December 7th as "Pearl Harbor Remembrance Day." Conducts educational programs to foster patriotism and show the value of American freedom. Presents bronze grave markers to widows of members. **Publications:** *Pearl Harbor-Gram*, quarterly. Magazine. **Price:** $6.00/year. **Circulation:** 12,362. **Advertising:** accepted. **Conventions/Meetings:** biennial convention, for Pearl Harbor survivors from throughout the country - always held in Hawaii ● biennial general assembly (exhibits) - always December.

20966 ■ Pilot Class 43-D Association

c/o Francis J. Dutko
316 Florida Ave.
Gulf Breeze, FL 32561
Ph: (850)932-3467
Fax: (850)932-3467
E-mail: duke43d@hotmail.com
URL: http://home.att.net/~af-retired/43-D.html
Contact: Francis J. Dutko, Contact
Founded: 1984. **Members:** 1,050. **Membership Dues:** full, $10 (annual). **Staff:** 11. **Budget:** $5,000. **Local Groups:** 1. **Description:** Former military pilots who graduated from World War II pilot class 43-D in April 1943, regardless of graduation field or training command. (Widows of former members receive life memberships without payment of dues.) Dedicated to celebrating comradeship among members who prefer to be called "Delta Eagles". **Libraries: Type:** reference. **Holdings:** archival material, books. **Subjects:** 43-D history. **Also Known As:** Delta Eagles. **Publications:** *43-Delta Eagle*, 3/year, March, July, December. Newsletter. Features articles on World War II aviation history, news about reunions, and updates on activities of members. **Price:** included in membership dues. **Circulation:** 350. **Conventions/Meetings:** annual Gathering of Delta Eagles - reunion, memorabilia, pictures, yearbooks from training (exhibits).

20967 ■ Polar Bear Association of World War II

448 Princeton Dr.
Costa Mesa, CA 92626-6129
Contact: Joseph S. Keller, Sec.
Founded: 1956. **Members:** 400. **Membership Dues:** regular, $20 (biennial). **Regional Groups:** 8. **Description:** Veterans of World War II who served with the 339th Infantry or associated arms in the Italian Campaign. **Also Known As:** 339th Infantry Regi-

ment; 85th Infantry Division. **Publications:** *Membership Roster*, 3/year. Newsletter. **Price:** included in membership dues. **Circulation:** 425 ● *The Polar Bear*, 3/year. Newsletter ● Also publishes booklets. **Conventions/Meetings:** biennial reunion - fall.

20968 ■ PT Boats, Inc. (PTBI)

PO Box 38070
Germantown, TN 38183-0070
Ph: (901)755-8440
Fax: (901)751-0522
E-mail: ptboats@ptboats.org
URL: http://www.ptboats.org
Contact: Alyce N. Guthrie, Exec. VP
Founded: 1946. **Members:** 9,300. **Membership Dues:** non-PT veteran, $25 (annual). **Staff:** 4. **Budget:** $405,000. **Description:** Individuals who served in P.T. boats or support groups in World War II (8000) and those interested in P.T. boats (model builders and others) (500). Purposes are: to preserve P.T. boats for posterity; to compile history of all squadrons, tenders, and bases; to maintain two P.T. boats in original condition; to display memorabilia. Maintains museum. **Libraries: Type:** reference. **Holdings:** 200; archival material. **Subjects:** PT boats of WWII, torpedoes, Packard engines. **Awards: Frequency:** annual. **Type:** recognition. **Also Known As:** PT Boats All Hands; PT Boats, Bases and Tenders; (2000) WWII PT Boats, Tenders and Bases. **Publications:** *All Hands*, semiannual. Magazine. **Price:** included in membership dues. **Circulation:** 9,000. **Advertising:** accepted ● *At Close Quarters*. Book. Contains paperback reprint of 1962 book about PT boats. **Price:** $38.00/copy ● *Early Elco PT Boats*. Book. Features history of 1970 and 1977 Elcos. Includes photographs and drawings. **Price:** $15.00/copy ● *Knights of the Sea*. Book ● *The Life and Times of a Country Doctor*. Book. Contains life story of the late Frederick Ludwig. **Price:** $15.00/copy ● *U.S. Mosquito Fleet*. Book. Includes photographs, line drawings and illustrations. **Price:** $16.00/copy ● Videos. **Conventions/Meetings:** annual WWII PT Boats, Bases and Tenders Reunion, exhibits limited to historical items (exhibits).

20969 ■ Second Air Division Association (2ADA)

Address Unknown since 2007
Founded: 1947. **Members:** 6,500. **Membership Dues:** individual, $20 (annual). **Description:** Those who served in the headquarters, 14 B-24 Liberator bomber groups, and the five fighter groups of the Second Air Division of the 8th Air Force stationed in England during World War II. Maintains the 2AD Memorial Room in the Norwich Central Library, Norwich, England, as a living memorial to the 6697 members of the division who died in World War II; the room contains American books, periodicals, and audiovisual equipment to be used by local schools. Promotes fellowship among members. **Publications:** *Second Air Division Association—Journal*, quarterly. Covers the activities and recollections of members. Includes articles on WW2 Air Forces and on Britain and historical data. **Circulation:** 8,000. **Advertising:** not accepted. **Conventions/Meetings:** annual convention.

20970 ■ SHAEF and ETOUSA Veterans Association

c/o Alan Reeves, Natl. Commander
2301 Broadway
San Francisco, CA 94115
Ph: (415)921-8322
Fax: (415)921-8322
E-mail: afreeves@webtv.net
URL: http://www.shaef.org
Contact: Alan Reeves, Natl. Commander
Founded: 1985. **Members:** 750. **Membership Dues:** regular, $15 (annual). **Staff:** 3. **Description:** World War II veterans assigned to Supreme Headquarters, Allied Expeditionary Forces and European Theater of Operations, US Army Headquarters and attached units. Seeks to reunite veterans who served at the above commands; testimony to commander General Eisenhower. **Computer Services:** database, membership roster ● database, reunion attendees. **For-**

merly: (1992) SHAEF Veterans Association. **Publications:** *Membership Roster*, annual. **Membership Directory** ● *SHAEF Communique*, quarterly. Newsletter. Contains membership news, obituaries, and book reviews. **Price:** included in membership dues. **Circulation:** 350. **Conventions/Meetings:** annual reunion - in October.

20971 ■ Sino-American Cooperative Organization (SACO)
c/o Willie Baker
2810 Highlands Blvd.
Spring Valley, CA 91977
E-mail: del1@delsjourney.com
URL: http://www.delsjourney.com/saco/saco.htm
Contact: Willie Baker, Contact
Founded: 1948. **Members:** 900. **Membership Dues:** regular/associate, $25 (annual). **Description:** U.S. Navy veterans who were based in Mainland China between 1942 and 1945; family members. Continues wartime friendships; works to maintain Taiwan's independence. Sponsors charitable programs. **Libraries: Type:** not open to the public. **Holdings:** 20; books, periodicals. **Subjects:** mentoring naval group China or SACO. **Awards:** SACO Ring, for President. **Frequency:** annual. **Type:** recognition. **Recipient:** to the presiding president. **Publications:** *Convention Letter*, annual ● *SACO Directory and By-Laws* ● *SACO News*, annual. Newsletter. Contains information on naval events. **Price:** included in membership dues. **Conventions/Meetings:** annual reunion.

20972 ■ Sixth Marine Division Association
c/o Florence Doman, Membership Mgr.
704 Cooper Ct.
Arlington, TX 76011-5550
E-mail: gyrene629@aol.com
URL: http://www.sixthmarinedivision.com
Contact: Bill Pierce, PR Chm.
Founded: 1970. **Members:** 4,230. **Membership Dues:** individual, $65 (annual) ● life, $1,834. **Budget:** $50,000. **Description:** World War II veterans of the Sixth Marine Division (Okinawa) and the First Provisional Marine Brigade (Guam). Seeks to preserve the history and traditions of the Sixth Marine Division and the U.S. Marine Corps. Promotes patriotism, democracy and camaraderie among members. Maintains charitable programs. **Awards:** Plaque of Appreciation. **Frequency:** annual. **Type:** recognition ● **Type:** scholarship. **Subgroups:** Sons and Daughters Chapter. **Publications:** *First Provisional Marine Brigade History Book Progress Report*, annual ● *The Striking Sixth*, quarterly. Newsletter. Alternate Formats: online ● Directory, quadrennial ● Membership Directory. Alternate Formats: online. **Conventions/Meetings:** semiannual reunion.

20973 ■ Topographic Engineers of World War II
PO Box 995
Olathe, KS 66051
Ph: (913)764-3886
Contact: Ed Redinger, Exec.Sec.
Founded: 1946. **Members:** 548. **Description:** Social organization of persons who served as topographic engineers in the U.S. Army during World War II. **Publications:** *Topo Topics*, quarterly. Newsletter. Provides membership activities information. **Price:** available to members only. **Circulation:** 450. **Conventions/Meetings:** annual meeting - always fall.

20974 ■ U.S. Merchant Marine Veterans of World War II (USMMVWWII)
SS Lane Victory, WWII Cruises
455 WWII Cargo Ship
Berth 94
PO Box 629
San Pedro, CA 90733-0629
Ph: (310)519-9545
Fax: (310)519-0265
E-mail: sslanevictory@juno.com
URL: http://www.lanevictory.org
Contact: Clint Johnson, Pres.
Founded: 1985. **Members:** 8,000. **Membership Dues:** associate, $28 (annual) ● individual, $36 (annual) ● life, $500 ● sponsor, $1,000 (annual) ●

patron, $5,000 (annual) ● plank owner, $10,000 (annual). **Staff:** 1. **State Groups:** 12. **Description:** Persons who served aboard American flag vessels from September 1939 through December 1946; persons who performed honorary service for the U.S. Merchant Marine during World War II. Maintains World War II Victory ship S.S. Lane Victory as a memorial and museum of the Merchant Marine in World War II. Works for the issuance of a U.S. postage stamp commemorating World War II merchant seamen and other privateers and seamen who served the U.S. after 1765. Maintains museum. Conducts research and educational programs. Offers children's services. Compiles statistics. **Libraries: Type:** reference. **Holdings:** archival material. **Supersedes:** Brotherhood of Merchant Seamen and Privateers. **Publications:** *Anchor Light*, monthly. Newsletter. Includes research and chapter reports. **Price:** included in membership dues. **Circulation:** 10,000. **Advertising:** accepted ● *The Last Victory*. Book. **Conventions/Meetings:** monthly meeting - always 2nd Monday in San Pedro, CA.

20975 ■ U.S. Navy Salvage Divers Reunited
Address Unknown since 2007
Founded: 1983. **Members:** 525. **Description:** Salvage and deep sea divers who served in U.S. Navy. Aims to locate and unite divers nationwide. Collects Navy Salvage memorabilia. Maintains museum and archives. Compiles statistics. **Libraries: Type:** reference. **Holdings:** 250; audiovisuals, books, business records, clippings, periodicals, video recordings. **Subjects:** diving and salvage. **Awards:** Appreciation for Services. **Frequency:** annual. **Type:** recognition. **Computer Services:** Membership list ● database ● mailing lists. **Publications:** *Descending Line II*, quarterly. Newsletter. Provides news on membership activities, history of group, and upcoming reunions. **Price:** free. **Circulation:** 550. **Advertising:** not accepted. **Conventions/Meetings:** annual reunion (exhibits); **Avg. Attendance:** 150.

20976 ■ United States Submarine Veterans of World War II
c/o United States Submarine Veterans Inc.
PO Box 3870
Silverdale, WA 98383-3870
Ph: (360)337-2978
E-mail: office@ussvi.org
URL: http://www.ussubvetsofworldwarii.org
Contact: H.T. Vande Kerkhoff, Sec.-Treas.
Founded: 1956. **Members:** 15,000. **Membership Dues:** regular, $10 (annual). **Regional Groups:** 7. **State Groups:** 50. **Local Groups:** 74. **Description:** Persons who served aboard U.S. Navy submarines during World War II. Perpetuates the memory of individuals who gave their lives in submarine warfare. Maintains national memorials at New London, CT and Pearl Harbor, HI; also maintains various state memorials. **Awards: Frequency:** annual. **Type:** scholarship. **Recipient:** for sons and daughters of submarine veterans. **Publications:** *Polaris*, bi-monthly. **Price:** included in membership dues. **Circulation:** 9,000. **Advertising:** accepted. **Conventions/Meetings:** annual convention.

20977 ■ USS North Carolina Battleship Association
c/o Harold A. Smith, Pres.
11 Charles Cir.
Scarborough, ME 04074-9735
Ph: (207)883-5062 (910)251-5797
Fax: (910)251-5807
E-mail: ncbb55@battleshipnc.com
URL: http://www.battleshipnc.com
Contact: Harold A. Smith, Pres.
Founded: 1964. **Members:** 750. **Membership Dues:** former crewman, $10 (annual) ● life, $100. **Description:** U.S. Navy veterans that served on board the USS North Carolina during World War II. Fosters communication among members. (During the war members served in the North Atlantic, Guadalcanal, the Solomon Islands, and Japan. The USS North Carolina is now decommissioned and stationed at Wilmington, NC.). **Libraries: Type:** reference. **Holdings:** archival material, photographs. **Computer**

Services: Record retrieval services, mailing list of members, personnel deck logs and individual service data. **Special Interest Groups:** Associate Membership. **Also Known As:** Showboat. **Publications:** *Tarheel*, semiannual. Newsletter. **Circulation:** 800. **Conventions/Meetings:** annual reunion - April.

20978 ■ Veterans of the Battle of the Bulge (VBOB)
PO Box 101418
Arlington, VA 22210-4418
Ph: (703)528-4058
E-mail: johnbowen@battleofthebulge.org
URL: http://www.battleofthebulge.org
Contact: Stanley Wojtusik, Pres.
Founded: 1981. **Members:** 14,000. **Membership Dues:** individual, $15 (annual) ● life (age 70 and under), $125 ● life (over 70 years old), $75. **Budget:** $100,000. **State Groups:** 46. **Description:** World War II veterans who were awarded the Ardennes Campaign (Battle of the Bulge) battle star; other veterans, family members of eligible veterans; interested others. Objectives are to: foster international peace and goodwill; promote friendship; perpetuate the memory of sacrifices involved; preserve historical data and sites. Sponsors visit the battle area, attend reunions, and memorial services. Maintains museum in Ft. Meade, MD. Encourages the issuance of a commemorative postage stamp. **Libraries: Type:** reference. **Holdings:** photographs. **Publications:** *Bulge Bugle*, quarterly. Journal. Includes first person accounts as well as other facts and stories about the Battle of the Bulge. **Price:** included in membership dues. **Conventions/Meetings:** annual conference (exhibits).

20979 ■ Women Airforce Service Pilots WWII (WASPWWII)
Texas Woman's Univ.
TWU Libraries
PO Box 425528
Denton, TX 76204-5528
Ph: (940)898-3701 (940)898-3752
Fax: (940)898-3764
E-mail: womansc@mail.twu.edu
URL: http://www.twu.edu/wasp
Contact: Dawn Letson, Archivist
Founded: 1946. **Members:** 850. **Membership Dues:** regular, $25 (annual) ● life, $200. **Staff:** 7. **Regional Groups:** 3. **Description:** Women who graduated from or trained as civilian pilots in the U.S. Army Air Force between 1942 and 1944; military pilots of the Women Auxiliary Ferrying Squadron which merges with the Women's Flying Training Detachment to become the Women Airforce Service Pilots. Offers friendship and assistance to female pilots who flew together from training bases in Houston or Sweetwater, TX, and army air bases throughout the U.S. Provides information to students conducting research on the history of the association. Assists local groups in organizing exhibits in schools and museums. Has Woman's Collection at Texas Woman's University, which is the official archive for the WAFS/WASP. **Libraries: Type:** reference. **Holdings:** 42,000; archival material, clippings. **Subjects:** women pilots, World War II, women's history. **Awards:** Falcon Foundation Scholarship. **Frequency:** annual. **Type:** scholarship. **Recipient:** for Air Force Academy. **Additional Websites:** http://www.wasp-wwii.org. **Telecommunication Services:** electronic mail, dletson@twu.edu. **Formerly:** (1980) Order of Fifinella. **Publications:** *WASP News*, quarterly. Newsletter. **Price:** free. **Circulation:** 800 ● *WASP Roster*, biennial. Membership Directory ● Brochure ● Newsletter, semiannual. **Conventions/Meetings:** biennial reunion.

World Wars

20980 ■ 1st Fighter Association
c/o Bob Correia, VP
3 Midway Dr.
Warwick, RI 02886-8114
Ph: (401)737-3268

E-mail: robtcorr@aol.com
URL: http://www.1stfighter.org
Contact: Bob Correia, VP
Founded: 1976. **Members:** 400. **Membership Dues:** regular (includes newsletter, announcements and reunions), $20 (annual). **Budget:** $2,000. **Description:** Individuals who served in the U.S. 1st Fighter Group, 1st Pursuit Group, 1st Tactical Fighter Wing, or subordinate squadrons that participated in World Wars I and II; active members of these units; spouses of deceased members are honorary members. Seeks to perpetuate the bonds of friendship formed by members while in the service; has erected a memorial at the Air Force Museum, Dayton, Ohio to fighters who lost their lives in battle. **Additional Websites:** http://www.1stfighter.com/default.html. **Formerly:** (1994) 1st Fighter Group Association. **Publications:** *First Fighter News*, periodic. Newsletter. **Price:** included in membership dues. **Advertising:** accepted. Alternate Formats: online ● *Membership Roster*, periodic. **Conventions/Meetings:** biennial reunion (exhibits).

20981 ■ 30th Infantry Division Association (TIDA)

c/o Frank W. Towers, Pres./Historian
2915 W SR, No. 235
Brooker, FL 32622-5167
Ph: (352)485-1173
Fax: (352)485-2763
E-mail: towersfw@windstream.net
URL: http://30thinfantry.org
Contact: Frank W. Towers, Pres./Historian
Founded: 1946. **Members:** 1,500. **Membership Dues:** veteran, $10 (annual) ● associate, $15 (annual) ● life, $75. **Staff:** 1. **Regional Groups:** 8. **State Groups:** 4. **Description:** Members of the 30th Infantry Division and attached units who served in World Wars I and II united to perpetuate friendships formed during combat. Bestows annual Old Hickory Award. **Awards:** Old Hickory Award. **Frequency:** annual. **Type:** recognition. **Publications:** *30th Division News*, quarterly. Newsletter. Features general news of interest on activities. **Price:** included in membership dues. **Circulation:** 1,500. **Conventions/Meetings:** annual reunion.

20982 ■ Federation of French War Veterans (FFWV)

18 E 41st St., No. 401
New York, NY 10017-6222
Ph: (212)213-0812 (646)872-1111
Fax: (718)591-3551
E-mail: bruceboeglin@hotmail.com
URL: http://www.frenchwarveterans.com
Contact: Bruce Boeglin, Pres.
Founded: 1919. **Members:** 150. **Membership Dues:** combat veteran, $30 (annual). **Staff:** 3. **Languages:** English, French. **Description:** Veterans of the World Wars and other conflicts who are of French origin or descent. Operates hall of fame. **Libraries: Type:** reference. **Holdings:** 150. **Subjects:** world wars. **Awards:** Diplome d'Honneur. **Frequency:** periodic. **Type:** recognition. **Recipient:** for members and benefactors ● 50th Anniversary of Liberation of France Medal. **Type:** medal. **Recipient:** for qualified U.S. Vets of WWII. **Computer Services:** Mailing lists. **Publications:** *Les Voix de la Federation* (in English and French), 3/year. **Price:** free to members. **Advertising:** accepted ● Directory (in English and French), periodic. **Conventions/Meetings:** annual general assembly - usually last Sunday in April.

20983 ■ Military Order of the World Wars (MOWW)

435 N Lee St.
Alexandria, VA 22314
Ph: (703)683-4911
Free: (877)320-3774
Fax: (703)683-4501
E-mail: moww@comcast.net
URL: http://www.militaryorder.net
Contact: Brig. Gen. Roger C. Bultman, Chief-of-Staff
Founded: 1919. **Members:** 10,000. **Membership Dues:** regular/hereditary/former, $40 (annual) ● hereditary perpetual (21 years old and above), regular perpetual, $350 ● memorial perpetual, $200. **Staff:** 4. **Budget:** $650,000. **Regional Groups:** 15. **State Groups:** 39. **Local Groups:** 160. **Description:** Commissioned officers and warrant officers who served in the active or reserve components of any of the uniformed services. Promotes patriotic education in schools. Supports Junior and Senior ROTC programs and Boy Scouts and Girl Scouts of America. **Libraries: Type:** reference. **Awards:** Commander-in-Chief. **Frequency:** annual. **Type:** recognition. **Recipient:** for individuals ● Distinguished Service. **Frequency:** annual. **Type:** recognition. **Recipient:** for an American citizen who has made a contribution to National Defense ● Gold Patrick Henry Medallion. **Frequency:** annual. **Type:** recognition. **Recipient:** for individuals ● Outstanding Order of the World Wars. **Frequency:** annual. **Type:** recognition. **Recipient:** for individuals ● Outstanding Service. **Frequency:** annual. **Type:** recognition. **Recipient:** for individuals ● **Frequency:** annual. **Type:** recognition. **Recipient:** for ROTC cadets. **Computer Services:** database ● mailing lists. **Committees:** Distinguished Service Award; Law and Order; Leadership; Memorials; National Security; ROTC. **Programs:** Patriotic Education. **Formerly:** (1921) American Officers of the Great War. **Publications:** *History of the MOWW: The First Fifty Years* ● *MOWW - Decade of the 80s* ● *MOWW - Decade of the 70s* ● *National Roster of Officials*, annual ● *Officer Review*, 10/year. Magazine.

Price: $15.00/year. ISSN: 0736-7317. **Circulation:** 12,000. **Advertising:** accepted. **Conventions/Meetings:** annual meeting, mid-winter general staff meeting - usually late July or early August.

20984 ■ Order of Lafayette (OL)

c/o Bruce A. Laue, Pres. Gen.
243 W 70th St., Apt. 6f
New York, NY 10023-4321
E-mail: orderoflafayette@hotmail.com
URL: http://www.phoenixmasonry.org/masonicmuseum/fraternalism/order_of_lafayette.htm
Contact: Bruce A. Laue, Pres. Gen.
Founded: 1958. **Members:** 200. **Membership Dues:** original member, hereditary member, $35 (annual). **Description:** Officers who served in France during World Wars I and II and civilians who honor France. Seeks to strengthen the traditional friendship of U.S. with France. **Awards:** Freedom Award. **Frequency:** annual. **Type:** recognition. **Recipient:** for distinguished leadership in combating communism and totalitarianism. **Conventions/Meetings:** Freedom Award Dinner.

20985 ■ Rainbow Division Veterans Memorial Foundation (RDVMF)

c/o Mrs. Suellen McDaniel, Natl. Membership Off.
1400 Knolls Dr.
Newton, NC 28658-9452
Ph: (828)464-1466
E-mail: millennium@rainbowvets.org
URL: http://www.rainbowvets.org
Contact: Mrs. Suellen McDaniel, Natl. Membership Off.
Founded: 1919. **Members:** 3,000. **Membership Dues:** Rainbow Division veteran, extended family, veteran, active duty 42nd Division Army National Guard, $10 (annual). **Staff:** 3. **State Groups:** 38. **Local Groups:** 10. **Description:** Represents veterans who served in the 42nd Rainbow Division during World War I or World War II, extended family members, and veterans and active duty personnel 42nd division U.S. Army National Guard. Perpetuates the memory of comrades who have died; fosters patriotism and loyalty. Maintains national Rainbow monuments, organizes wreath-laying ceremonies and supports Rainbow museums and archives. **Libraries: Type:** reference. **Subjects:** history of World War I and World War II. **Awards:** John D. Carr Award. **Frequency:** annual. **Type:** recognition. **Formerly:** (2003) National Association Rainbow Division Veterans. **Publications:** *Rainbow Reveille*, 5/year. Newsletter. **Price:** included in membership dues. **Circulation:** 3,000. **Conventions/Meetings:** annual meeting, for memorial foundation trustees and general membership meetings - in July.

Advertising

20986 ■ Antique Advertising Association of America (AAAA)
PO Box 76
Petersburg, IL 62675
E-mail: twgeneral@comcast.net
URL: http://www.pastimes.org
Contact: Michael Hunt, Contact
Membership Dues: regular, in U.S., $35 (annual) ● regular, in Canada, $45 (annual) ● regular, outside U.S. and Canada, $55 (annual). **Multinational. Description:** Represents collectors of popular and antique advertising. **Telecommunication Services:** electronic mail, aaaanewsletter@mac.com. **Publications:** *PastTimes*, bimonthly. Newsletter. **Price:** included in membership dues; $2.00/back issue. Alternate Formats: CD-ROM. **Conventions/Meetings:** annual convention.

Aerospace

20987 ■ Academy of Model Aeronautics (AMA)
5161 E Memorial Dr.
Muncie, IN 47302
Ph: (765)287-1256
Free: (800)435-9262
Fax: (765)289-4248
E-mail: jcherry@modelaircraft.org
URL: http://www.modelaircraft.org
Contact: Jim Cherry, Exec. Dir.
Founded: 1936. **Members:** 170,000. **Membership Dues:** open, $58 (annual) ● extra - family, $30 (annual) ● youth (below 19), $15 (annual). **Staff:** 49. **Budget:** $8,200,000. **Description:** Persons interested in model aircraft; membership includes model airplane flyer's sporting license, which permits participation in officially sanctioned competitions and official recognition of national and world records when established. Serves as an autonomous division of the National Aeronautic Association of the U.S.A. (see separate entry) and represents the International Aeronautical Federation. Maintains hall of fame, and model aircraft museum. Compiles statistics. **Libraries: Type:** reference. **Holdings:** biographical archives. **Subjects:** aviation. **Awards:** AMA/Charles Hampton Grant Scholarships. **Frequency:** annual. **Type:** scholarship. **Recipient:** to high school seniors who will be pursuing a continuing academic program at an accredited college or university ● Flying Site Development/Improvement Grant. **Frequency:** annual. **Type:** grant. **Recipient:** for assistance on a project. **Committees:** Business Opportunity; Contest Boards; Contest Coordinators; Finance; Information Systems; Radio Control Frequencies; Safety; Sound. **Affiliated With:** National Aeronautic Association. **Publications:** *Model Aircraft Competition Regulations*, biennial ● *Model Aviation*, monthly. Alternate Formats: online ● *National Newsletter*, bimonthly. Compiles headquarters' news articles, tips, cartoons

and humor gathered across the country. **Conventions/Meetings:** annual meeting, held in conjunction with National Aeromodeling Championships (exhibits).

20988 ■ Aeronautica and Air Label Collectors Club (AAL)
c/o Basil S. Burrell, Sec.-Treas.
PO Box 1239
Elgin, IL 60121-1239
Fax: (847)468-0840
E-mail: bsburrell@hotmail.com
URL: http://www.americanairmailsociety.org
Contact: Basil S. Burrell, Sec.-Treas.
Founded: 1941. **Members:** 250. **Membership Dues:** regular, in U.S., $20 (annual) ● regular, outside U.S., $25 (annual). **Description:** Collectors of aeronautica, air labels, postcards, and timetables. Provides research material on the history of the world's airlines. **Libraries: Type:** not open to the public. **Holdings:** 1,000. **Awards: Type:** recognition. **Affiliated With:** American Air Mail Society. **Publications:** *Aeronautica and Air Label Collector*, quarterly. Newsletter. Features published as part of Jack Knight Air Log. **Advertising:** accepted ● *Air Transport Catalog of the World*. **Conventions/Meetings:** annual conference.

20989 ■ Aeronca Lovers Club (ALC)
Address Unknown since 2007
Founded: 1982. **Members:** 300. **Staff:** 2. **Description:** Owners and pilots of the Aeronca airplane; interested others. Provides technical and parts information on maintenance and restoration of the Aeronca airplane. (The Aeronca was last produced in 1953; approximately 10,000 Aeroncas remain in operation.) **Convention/Meeting:** none. **Publications:** *Aeronca Lovers Club Newsletter*, quarterly.

20990 ■ Aerostar Owners Association (AOA)
2608 W Kenosha St., No. 704
Broken Arrow, OK 74012
Ph: (918)258-2346
E-mail: info@aerostar-owners.com
URL: http://www.aerostar-owners.com
Contact: Ken Bacon, Exec. Dir.
Founded: 1971. **Members:** 400. **Membership Dues:** individual, $175 (annual). **Description:** Owners of Aerostar aircraft; other interested individuals. (Aerostar airplanes are twin-engine, executive class craft.) Promotes flying and maintenance of Aerostar airplanes. Conducts social activities; facilitates exchange of information. **Publications:** *Aerostar Log*, quarterly. Magazine. **Advertising:** accepted. **Conventions/Meetings:** annual meeting - in fall.

20991 ■ Air Mail Pioneers (AMP)
c/o Ms. Nancy Allison Wright, Pres.
PMB 504 C5
26910 92nd Ave. NW
Stanwood, WA 98292-5437
Ph: (360)387-2009
Fax: (360)387-3089

E-mail: nancy.brucewright@verizon.net
URL: http://www.airmailpioneers.org
Contact: Ms. Nancy Allison Wright, Pres.
Founded: 1943. **Members:** 125. **Staff:** 1. **Budget:** $1,000. **Description:** Former employees of the U.S. Post Office Department, Air Mail Service, between May 15, 1918 and August 31, 1927. Seeks to aid in recording the history of the Air Mail Service and preserving the mementos of that group. Donates historical material to the Smithsonian Institution in Washington, DC, and other museums. **Convention/Meeting:** none. **Computer Services:** Online services, publication. **Publications:** *Air Mail Pioneer's Newsletter*, 2-3/year. Includes news of members and Air Mail Service history. Alternate Formats: online.

20992 ■ American Aviation Historical Society (AAHS)
2333 Otis St.
Santa Ana, CA 92704-3846
Ph: (714)549-4818
E-mail: pres@aahs-online.org
URL: http://www.aahs-online.org
Contact: Robert Brockmeier, Pres.
Founded: 1956. **Members:** 4,332. **Membership Dues:** regular, in U.S., $39 (annual) ● regular, in Canada and Mexico, $44 (annual) ● in other country, $57 (annual). **Staff:** 1. **Regional Groups:** 15. **Description:** Represents individuals interested in aircraft and research in aviation history; aviation and aerospace museums; libraries with aviation research sections. Works to document important personnel and events in aviation history; provides referral assistance to authors. Maintains Willis L. Nye Memorial Fund, which provides annual award for best researched and documented article. **Libraries: Type:** reference. **Holdings:** 21,000; archival material, audiovisuals, books, photographs. **Subjects:** aircraft and aircraft markings, aviation history, military unit histories. **Awards: Type:** grant ● **Frequency:** annual. **Type:** recognition. **Recipient:** for best researched and documented article ● **Type:** scholarship. **Publications:** *Catalog - Negative Lending Library*, periodic ● *Index*, decennial. Journal ● *Museum and Display Aircraft of the United States* ● Journal, quarterly ● Monographs ● Newsletter, quarterly. **Conventions/Meetings:** annual meeting.

20993 ■ American Bonanza Society (ABS)
PO Box 12888
Wichita, KS 67277
Ph: (316)945-1700
Fax: (316)945-1710
E-mail: bonanza7@bonanza.org
URL: http://www.bonanza.org
Contact: Nancy F. Johnson, Exec. Dir.
Founded: 1967. **Members:** 10,300. **Membership Dues:** regular, in North America, $55 (annual) ● regular, outside North America, $93 (annual) ● life, $1,000. **Staff:** 6. **Budget:** $1,200,000. **Regional Groups:** 7. **Multinational. Description:** People interested in exchanging information and ideas concerning the flying, maintenance, and modification of Beechcraft Bonanza, Baron, and Travel Air models.

Promotes flying safety. Sponsors service clinics through Air Safety Foundation. **Libraries: Type:** not open to the public. **Holdings:** 1,000; books, periodicals. **Subjects:** general aviation, specific to type models. **Awards:** Airplane of the Month. **Frequency:** monthly. **Type:** recognition. **Recipient:** for aircrafts owned by members. **Subgroups:** ABS Air Safety Foundation. **Publications:** *ABS Magazine*, monthly. Contains information on maintenance, piloting techniques, aircraft restoration, aviation events and aircraft insurance. **Advertising:** accepted ● *ABS Membership Directory*, annual. **Price:** free, for members only. **Advertising:** accepted ● Video. **Price:** $84.00. **Conventions/Meetings:** annual convention, seminars of interest to bonanza, baron, travel air, debonair owners and operators; with trade show (exhibits) - usually September or October ● meeting.

20994 ■ American Navion Society (ANS)
PMB 335
16420 SE McGillivray, Ste.103
Vancouver, WA 98683-3461
Ph: (360)833-9921 (623)975-4052
Fax: (623)975-4062
E-mail: flynavion@yahoo.com
URL: http://www.navionsociety.org
Contact: Gary Rankin, Pres.

Founded: 1960. **Members:** 1,000. **Membership Dues:** regular, in U.S., $50 (annual) ● regular, in Canada, $54 (annual) ● other country, $64 (annual). **Staff:** 2. **For-Profit. Description:** Owners of a light aircraft known as the Navion. Provides technical and modification data, maintenance assistance, membership club, social activities. Sets handicaps for Navions in various air activities; (Navion is a contraction of North American Aviation, the company which designed and built about 1100 of these aircraft immediately following World War II. Production was discontinued during the Korean War.) Sells airframe parts. **Libraries: Type:** reference. **Holdings:** 300. **Subjects:** technical phases of aviation. **Awards:** Navioneer of the Year. **Frequency:** annual. **Type:** recognition. **Recipient:** for involvement with clubs activities. **Publications:** *Aircraft Manuals for Navions* ● *Membership Roster*, triennial. Membership Directory ● *Navioneer*, bimonthly. Magazine. Contains information on parts and social activities. **Price:** included in membership dues. **Circulation:** 1,000. **Advertising:** accepted ● Newsletter, periodic. **Advertising:** accepted ● Also publishes guide to purchase of used Navion aircraft and technical publications. **Conventions/Meetings:** annual competition and convention (exhibits) - usually 1st or 2nd week in July ● annual National Fly-In Convention - usually July.

20995 ■ American Yankee Association (AYA)
PO Box 1531
Cameron Park, CA 95682-1531
Ph: (530)676-4292
Fax: (530)676-3949
E-mail: sec@aya.org
URL: http://grumman.net/aya
Contact: Nigel Thomas, Pres.

Founded: 1976. **Members:** 2,000. **Membership Dues:** regular, in U.S. and Canada, $30 (annual) ● regular, outside U.S. and Canada, $10 (annual). **Staff:** 2. **Budget:** $65,000. **Regional Groups:** 16. **Multinational. Description:** Enthusiasts, owners, and pilots of Grumman, Gulfstream, and American light aircraft. Promotes safety and the sharing of operating and maintenance information. Fosters fellowship among members. Conducts seminars. Compiles statistics; sponsors competitions. **Awards:** Lauren Larsen Award. **Frequency:** annual. **Type:** recognition. **Recipient:** for an individual who has been of most help to the association in the prior year. **Computer Services:** database, membership list. **Publications:** *American Star*, bimonthly. Newsletter. **Price:** $2.50 for members only. **Circulation:** 2,000. **Advertising:** accepted ● *Membership Roster*, annual. Membership Directory. **Conventions/Meetings:** annual convention ● Fly-In - meeting.

20996 ■ Antique Airplane Association (AAA)
22001 Bluegrass Rd.
Ottumwa, IA 52501-8569
Ph: (641)938-2773
Fax: (641)938-2093
E-mail: antiqueairfield@sirisonline.com
Contact: Robert L. Taylor, Pres.

Founded: 1953. **Members:** 6,500. **Membership Dues:** full, $36 (annual) ● associate, $24 (annual) ● life, $500. **Staff:** 7. **Regional Groups:** 23. **Description:** Persons interested in restoring, preserving, and flying antique and classic aircraft built before World War II. Majority of members are employed in aviation industry. Holds annual local and regional meets called "fly-ins." Maintains Air Power Museum. Collectively, members own approximately 3000 airplanes, some built prior to 1910. **Libraries: Type:** reference. **Awards: Frequency:** annual. **Type:** recognition. **Recipient:** membership votes. **Publications:** *Antique Airplane Digest*, semiannual ● *Antique Airplane News*, semiannual ● *APM Bulletin*, semiannual. **Advertising:** accepted. **Conventions/Meetings:** annual meeting (exhibits) - always Labor Day weekend.

20997 ■ Bellanca-Champion Club
PO Box 100
Coxsackie, NY 12051
Ph: (518)731-6800
E-mail: robert@bellanca-championclub.com
URL: http://www.bellanca-championclub.com
Contact: Robert Szego, Pres.

Founded: 1986. **Members:** 1,600. **Membership Dues:** full, $35 (annual) ● outside U.S., $41 (annual). **Staff:** 3. **Budget:** $110,000. **Multinational. Description:** Dedicated to the Bellanca Cruisair, Cruisemaster, Viking, American Champion Citabria, Decathlon, Scout, Champion and AviaBellanca Skyrocket lines of aircraft, their furtherance, history, preservation and maintenance. The Bellanca-Champion Club welcomes all owners, pilots and enthusiasts. **Libraries: Type:** reference. **Holdings:** 1,400; archival material, artwork, books. **Subjects:** aircraft built by Bellanca, Champion, American Champion, Aeronca, AviaBellanca. **Awards:** Best Airplane. **Type:** recognition. **Computer Services:** database, all technical details on Bellanca, Champion, and related type airplanes. **Committees:** East Coast Fly-In; West Coast Fly-In. **Affiliated With:** Aircraft Owners and Pilots Association; Experimental Aircraft Association; National Space Society. **Publications:** *B-C Contact!*, quarterly. Newsletter. Contains technical information on Bellanca and Champion aircraft manufactured between 1920-2003; includes statistics, research information, etc. **Price:** included in membership dues; $7.50/issue for nonmembers. ISSN: 0899-6954. **Circulation:** 1,600. **Advertising:** accepted. Alternate Formats: online ● *Complete Guide to Wood Wing Bellancas, Vols. 1, 2, and 3*. Books ● *Cruisair Plane Reports* ● *Cruisemaster Plane Report*. Manuals ● *Decathlon - Citabria, Champion Plane Reports* ● *Viking Plane Reports* ● Also publishes Parts, Service and Operating Manuals and Supplements for Champion and Bellanca airplanes, and other special parts and service manual supplements. **Conventions/Meetings:** annual Bellanca-Champion Club East Coast Fly-In - meeting, with dinner and Sunday brunch (exhibits) ● annual Bellanca-Champion Club West Coast Fly-In - meeting, with dinner on Saturday (exhibits) ● annual EAA Airventure - meeting ● annual Sun N' Fun - meeting (exhibits).

20998 ■ Bird Airplane Club (BAC)
c/o Jeannie Hill
PO Box 328
Harvard, IL 60033-0328
Ph: (815)943-7205
E-mail: dinghao@owc.net
Contact: Dick Hill, Contact

Founded: 1967. **Members:** 150. **Description:** Owners of Bird airplanes; former producers of the aircraft; individuals engaged in restoring or researching the Bird airplane, which was built by the Bird Aircraft Company from 1928 to 1933. Promotes restoration and use of Bird aircraft. Disseminates historical and maintenance information; maintains spare parts referral service. Participates in flying activities nationwide.

Libraries: Type: reference. **Holdings:** 3,000; archival material, books, periodicals. **Subjects:** aviation. **Affiliated With:** Antique Airplane Association; Experimental Aircraft Association. **Publications:** *Birds I View*, periodic. Newsletter ● *History of the Bird Airplane*. Book ● *History of the Tank Aero Engines*. **Conventions/Meetings:** semiannual Bird Club - meeting (exhibits).

20999 ■ Cardinal Club (CC)
PO Box 6806
Santa Maria, CA 93456
Ph: (805)922-1146
Fax: (316)721-6065
E-mail: info@cardinalclub.com
URL: http://www.cardinalclub.com
Contact: Nancy Osterhout, Dir.

Founded: 1981. **Members:** 3,000. **Membership Dues:** individual, $32 (annual). **Staff:** 2. **Budget:** $60,000. **For-Profit. Description:** Owners of Cessna Cardinal series aircraft; other interested individuals. Disseminates information on maintenance of Cessna 177 series airplanes, which are no longer in production, and on spare parts availability. **Libraries: Type:** reference. **Holdings:** 100. **Subjects:** Cessna cardinals. **Publications:** *Cardinal Club Newsletter*, bimonthly. Journal. **Price:** included in membership dues. **Circulation:** 1,200. **Advertising:** accepted ● *Index of Topics*, semiannual. Booklet. **Conventions/Meetings:** annual convention (exhibits).

21000 ■ Central States Association (CSA)
9283 Lindbergh Blvd.
Olmsted Falls, OH 44138-2407
Ph: (440)826-3055
E-mail: jschuber@juno.com
URL: http://www.canardzone.com/csa
Contact: Terry Schubert, Exec. Off.

Founded: 1984. **Members:** 900. **Membership Dues:** regular, $25 (annual). **Staff:** 1. **Multinational. Description:** Pilots, builders, and owners of Rutan and canard type aircraft. Publishes a periodical that provides for the exchange of information on the plane's maintenance, modification, and preservation. Compiles statistics. **Publications:** *Central States*, quarterly. Newsletter. **Price:** $20.00/year. **Advertising:** accepted. **Conventions/Meetings:** semiannual meeting - always spring and fall.

21001 ■ Cessna Owner Organization (COO)
PO Box 5000
Iola, WI 54945
Free: (888)692-3776
E-mail: help@cessnaowner.org
URL: http://www.cessnaowner.org
Contact: Randy Augustinak, Dir.

Founded: 1975. **Members:** 8,000. **Membership Dues:** in U.S., $48 (annual) ● in U.S., $89 (biennial) ● in U.S., $119 (triennial) ● foreign, $63 (annual) ● foreign, $119 (biennial) ● foreign, $164 (triennial). **For-Profit. Description:** Represents owners, pilots and enthusiasts of Cessna airplanes. Provides technical information and assistance to members. **Libraries: Type:** reference. **Computer Services:** database. **Affiliated With:** Piper Owner Society. **Formed by Merger of:** Cessna Skylane Society; Cessna Skyhawk Association; Cessna Centurion Society. **Publications:** *Aircraft Modifications and Avionics for Piper and Cessna Airplanes*, annual. Book. Covers modifications and avionics for Piper and Cessna aircraft. Includes a list of parts suppliers. **Price:** $5.00. **Advertising:** accepted ● *The Cessna Owner*, monthly. Magazine. Contains articles on Cessna aircraft maintenance, legal issues in aviation, insurance, and restoration; includes book reviews. **Price:** included in membership dues. **Circulation:** 5,500. **Advertising:** accepted. Alternate Formats: online ● *The Standard Catalog of Cessna Single Engine Aircraft*. Book. Covers every Cessna single-engine (non-military) aircraft made between 1911 and 1992. Includes photos, historical information, and specifications. **Conventions/Meetings:** annual Cessna Fly-in - convention.

21002 ■ Cessna Pilots Association (CPA)
3940 Mitchell Rd.
Santa Maria, CA 93455
Ph: (805)934-0493

Fax: (805)934-0547
E-mail: info@cessna.org
URL: http://www.cessna.org
Contact: John M. Frank Jr., Dir.
Founded: 1984. **Members:** 14,000. **Membership Dues:** in North America, $45 (annual) ● outside North America, $55 (annual). **Staff:** 10. **Description:** Individuals who own, fly, or have an interest in Cessna aircraft. Provides technical support service for owners of Cessna planes; disseminates information regarding proper repair and maintenance procedures; advises members on specific repair problems. Operates an educational and technical facility in Santa Maria, CA, that offers weekend classes on Cessna aircraft. **Libraries: Type:** reference. **Subjects:** service letters, bulletins, manuals, indexes, salvage yards. **Computer Services:** Online services, members' forum. **Publications:** *Cessna Pilots Association Magazine*, monthly. Contains technical information on Cessna aircraft. **Price:** included in membership dues. ISSN: 0888-1898. **Circulation:** 14,000. **Advertising:** accepted. Alternate Formats: online ● *E-ATIS*, weekly. Newsletter. Features timely information on Cessna aircraft. **Circulation:** 8,800. Alternate Formats: online. **Conventions/Meetings:** annual convention (exhibits).

21003 ■ Cherokee Pilots' Association (CPA)
PO Box 1996
Lutz, FL 33549
Ph: (813)242-7814
Free: (800)292-6003
E-mail: terry@piperowner.com
URL: http://piperowner.com
Contact: Terry Lee Rogers, Exec. Sec.
Founded: 1980. **Members:** 4,600. **Membership Dues:** individual, $36 (annual) ● in Canada, Mexico, $38 (annual) ● other country, $46 (annual). **Staff:** 1. **Budget:** $100,000. **For-Profit. Description:** Owners and operators of PA-28 and PA-32 Cherokee airplanes manufactured by Piper Aircraft Company. Aims to encourage safety in flying. Provides information on aircraft operation and maintenance; facilitates the exchange of experiences among members. **Publications:** *Piper Owners' Magazine*, monthly. **Circulation:** 4,900. **Conventions/Meetings:** annual conference.

21004 ■ Commemorative Air Force (CAF)
PO Box 62000
Midland, TX 79711-2000
Ph: (432)563-1000
Fax: (432)563-8046
E-mail: publicrelations@cafhq.org
URL: http://www.commemorativeairforce.org
Contact: Robert R. Rice, Pres.
Founded: 1957. **Members:** 9,000. **Membership Dues:** associate, $45 (annual) ● wing, squadron or detachment, $25-$50 (annual) ● colonel, $160 (annual) ● life, $1,960. **Staff:** 24. **Budget:** $2,000,000. **Regional Groups:** 75. **Description:** Persons interested in preserving, in flying condition, military aircraft that played important roles in World War II; and perpetuating in the minds and hearts of all Americans the spirit and memory of the accomplishments of those planes and the people who built, maintained, and flew them. Demonstrates the planes which participated by the members in over 300 events per year in the U.S. Maintains American Combat Airman Hall of Fame and Conventional Museum as well as hangaring aircraft for public display. Maintains over 70,000 military aviation artifacts and memorabilia from the war years 1939-1945. **Libraries: Type:** reference. **Holdings:** 23,000. **Awards: Type:** recognition. **Divisions:** Controller; Development; Maintenance; Membership; Museum; Operations; Public Relations. **Formerly:** (2003) Confederate Air Force. **Publications:** *The Co-Pilot Communique*, quarterly. Newsletter. Contains information produced by the CAF's American Airpower Heritage Museum. **Circulation:** 10,000 ● *CONTRAILS*, monthly. Newsletter. Includes information and news about the CAF. **Price:** included in membership dues. **Circulation:** 10,000 ● *The DISPATCH: American Airpower 1939-1945 - A Proud Heritage*, quarterly. Magazine. Includes features about CAF airplanes. **Price:** included in mem-

bership dues; $45.00/year for associate members. **Circulation:** 10,000. **Advertising:** accepted. **Conventions/Meetings:** annual AIRSHO - show (exhibits).

21005 ■ Continental Luscombe Association (CLA)
c/o Patti Sani, Sec.-Treas.
10251 E Central Ave.
Del Rey, CA 93616-9711
Ph: (559)888-2745
E-mail: cla-jim-patti@pacbell.net
URL: http://www.luscombe-cla.org
Contact: Jim Sani, Pres.
Founded: 1975. **Members:** 275. **Membership Dues:** regular, in U.S., $20 (annual) ● regular, in Canada, $27 (annual) ● foreign, $35 (annual). **Staff:** 4. **Budget:** $5,000. **Description:** Owners and admirers of aircraft manufactured by the Luscombe Airplane Corporation. Promotes maintenance and preservation of Luscombe airplanes. Serves as a clearinghouse on small aircraft and their maintenance; facilitates exchange of information among members. **Awards: Frequency:** annual. **Type:** recognition. **Recipient:** for members displaying outstanding flying skills. **Computer Services:** database ● electronic publishing ● mailing lists. **Publications:** *Luscombe Courant*, bimonthly. Newsletter. **Price:** included in membership dues. **Circulation:** 275. **Advertising:** accepted. **Conventions/Meetings:** annual Fly-In - meeting ● annual Gathering of Luscombes - convention and party - always May, in Columbia, CA. 2008 May 16-18, Columbia, CA; 2009 May 15-17, Columbia, CA; 2010 May 21-23, Columbia, CA.

21006 ■ Corben Club (CC)
c/o Vintage Aircraft Association
PO Box 127
Blakesburg, IA 52536
Ph: (641)938-2773
Fax: (641)938-2093
E-mail: antiqueairfield@sirisonline.com
URL: http://www.vintageaircraft.org/type/Corben.html
Contact: Robert L. Taylor, Pres.
Founded: 1985. **Members:** 125. **Description:** Owners, pilots, and enthusiasts of Corben aircraft. Acts as a source of information on the flying, maintenance, and restoration of Corben airplanes. Encourages the exchange of information among members. **Awards:** Best Corben. **Type:** trophy. **Recipient:** judged by attendees-ballot. **Publications:** *Corben Courier*, periodic. **Conventions/Meetings:** annual Fly-In - meeting - always Labor Day weekend.

21007 ■ EAA Ultralight Association (EAAUA)
EAA Aviation Ctr.
PO Box 3086
Oshkosh, WI 54903-3086
Ph: (920)426-6527
E-mail: membership@eaa.org
URL: http://www.eaa.org/ultralights
Contact: Carla Larsh, Chair
Founded: 1980. **Members:** 6,150. **Description:** A division of the Experimental Aircraft Association (see separate entry). Licensed pilots and ultralight enthusiasts. Informs members of federal aviation regulations, the latest trends in safe ultralight flying, light homebuilts and kit planes, and how-to information for basic aircraft design and construction. Works closely with Congress and the Federal Aviation Administration on matters concerning ultralight flying and general recreational flying; monitors federal regulations and advises members. Sponsors chapter fly-ins. **Awards:** EAA Ultralight Hall of Fame Award. **Frequency:** annual. **Type:** recognition. **Recipient:** for individuals or groups who have made extraordinary contributions. **Telecommunication Services:** electronic mail, ultralights@eaa.org. **Publications:** *EAA Sport Pilot*, monthly. Magazine. **Conventions/Meetings:** annual meeting - always July/August in Oshkosh, WI.

21008 ■ EAA Vintage Aircraft Association (VAA)
EAA Aviation Center
PO Box 3086
Oshkosh, WI 54903-3086

Ph: (920)426-4800 (920)426-4825
Free: (800)843-3612
Fax: (414)426-6865
E-mail: vintageaircraft@eaa.org
URL: http://www.vintageaircraft.org
Contact: Henry G. Frautschy, Exec. Dir.
Founded: 1971. **Members:** 9,300. **Membership Dues:** individual, $36 (annual). **Staff:** 2. **Local Groups:** 22. **Description:** A division of the Experimental Aircraft Association (see separate entry). Individuals interested in preserving and restoring Antique, Classic, and Contemporary aircraft. (Antique aircraft include airplanes made by the original manufacturer on or before August 31, 1945; Classic aircraft are those constructed by the original manufacturer between September 1, 1945 and Dec. 31, 1955; Contemporary aircraft are those constructed by the original manufacturer between January 1, 1956 and December 31, 1967.) Conducts meetings, displays, and specialized educational programs relating to aviation with emphasis on restoration, construction, repair, maintenance, and care of antique and classic aircraft and engines. Seeks to improve safety and educational aspects of classic and antique aviation. **Libraries: Type:** open to the public. **Formerly:** (1999) EAA Antique/Classic Division. **Publications:** *Vintage Airplane*, monthly. Magazine. Includes calendar of events, information on new members, and listing of clubs, technical and feature articles on aircraft restoration and history. **Price:** included in membership dues. ISSN: 0091-6943. **Circulation:** 10,000. **Advertising:** accepted ● Pamphlets. **Advertising:** accepted. **Conventions/Meetings:** annual EAA Air-Venture - convention, held in conjunction with EAA Convention and Sport Aviation Exhibition (exhibits) - always held in Oshkosh, WI.

21009 ■ EAA Warbirds of America (WB)
EAA Aviation Center
PO Box 3086
Oshkosh, WI 54903-3086
Ph: (920)426-4874 (920)426-4800
Fax: (920)426-6865
E-mail: warbirds@eaa.org
URL: http://www.warbirds-eaa.org
Contact: Bill Fischer, Exec. Dir.
Founded: 1965. **Members:** 7,000. **Membership Dues:** individual, $45 (annual) ● basic, $55 (annual) ● regular, in U.S. and Canada (Warbirds and EAA), $85 (annual). **Staff:** 2. **Regional Groups:** 23. **Description:** Members of the Experimental Aircraft Association (see separate entry) who operate, own, or are interested in historic military aircraft including World War II fighters, bombers, trainers, and liaison aircraft as well as piston-engined and jet aircraft of the Korean and Vietnam eras. Promotes and encourages the preservation, maintenance, and flying of military aircraft. Sponsors fly-in competitions. **Awards:** EAA Warbirds of America Hall of Fame. **Frequency:** annual. **Type:** recognition. **Recipient:** for individuals who have furthered the cause of the organization. **Affiliated With:** Experimental Aircraft Association. **Publications:** *Warbirds*, 8/year. Magazine. Provides information on members, ex-military aircraft and historical articles. **Price:** included in membership dues. ISSN: 0744-6624. **Circulation:** 7,100. **Advertising:** accepted ● *Warbirds Newsletter*, quarterly. **Conventions/Meetings:** annual Air-Venture - convention (exhibits) - always July/August, Oshkosh, WI, in conjunction with EAA ● annual Sun 'n Fun Fly-In - meeting - always April, Lakeland, FL.

21010 ■ Ercoupe Owners Club (EOC)
PO Box 7117
Ocean Isle Beach, NC 28469-1117
Ph: (919)471-9492 (910)575-2758
Fax: (919)477-2194
E-mail: coupeclub@aol.com
URL: http://www.ercoupe.org
Contact: Skip Carden, Exec. Dir.
Founded: 1970. **Members:** 1,500. **Membership Dues:** in U.S., $30 (annual) ● outside U.S., $35 (annual). **Regional Groups:** 13. **Description:** Individuals with an interest in the Ercoupe airplane. Works to provide technical and safety information on the Ercoupe. Assists owners in solving problems related to

the plane. **Libraries: Type:** reference. **Publications:** *Coupe Capers*, monthly. Newsletter. Alternate Formats: online. **Conventions/Meetings:** annual meeting (exhibits) ● periodic regional meeting.

21011 ■ F-4 Phantom II Society
3053 Rancho Vista Blvd., Ste.H-102
Palmdale, CA 93551
E-mail: f4phantomsociety@bellsouth.net
URL: http://www.f4phantom.com
Contact: Steve Billings, VP, Administration
Founded: 1984. **Members:** 850. **Membership Dues:** regular, $40 (annual) ● life, $200-$250. **Staff:** 3. **Multinational. Description:** Promotes the study and preservation of the McDonnell Douglas F-4 Phantom II jet fighter plane. **Libraries: Type:** reference. **Publications:** *Smoke Trails*, quarterly. Journal. Includes stories of aircraft and crews and book reviews. **Price:** included in membership dues; $10.00/back issue for nonmembers. **Circulation:** 850. **Advertising:** accepted. **Conventions/Meetings:** annual PhanCon - meeting and tour, of F-4 operations (exhibits).

21012 ■ Fairchild Club (FCHLD)
7645 Echo Point Rd.
Cannon Falls, MN 55009
Ph: (507)263-2414
E-mail: fchld@cvtel.net
URL: http://www.fairchildclub.com
Contact: John Berendt, Pres.
Founded: 1963. **Members:** 400. **Membership Dues:** general, $20 (annual). **Description:** Represents individuals interested in aircraft manufactured by the Fairchild Company. Promotes preservation, restoration, and use of Fairchild aircraft. Facilitates communication among members. **Awards:** Best Fairchild. **Frequency:** annual. **Type:** recognition. **Computer Services:** Mailing lists, of members. **Affiliated With:** Antique Airplane Association. **Publications:** *Fairchild Flyer*, quarterly. Newsletter. **Conventions/Meetings:** annual meeting - always Labor Day weekend.

21013 ■ First Flight Society (FFS)
PO Box 1903
Kitty Hawk, NC 27949
Ph: (252)441-1903
Fax: (252)441-1903
E-mail: dec17@firstflight.org
URL: http://www.FirstFlight.org
Contact: Ms. Pat Morrison, Office Admin.
Founded: 1927. **Members:** 500. **Membership Dues:** individual, $35 (annual) ● individual (life), $350 ● family, $50 (annual). **Staff:** 1. **Description:** Individuals interested in commemorating the first flight of the Wright brothers and the birthplace of the airplane. Works to foster public awareness of and interest in the origin, history, and future of flight. Preserves, protects, and maintains the site of the Wright brothers' first successful flight. Maintains First Flight Shrine (hall of fame) to honor aviation pioneers; supports the construction, operation, and maintenance of facilities and structures that depict the physical conditions and record the flight achievements at the original site. **Formerly:** (1966) Kill Devil Hills Memorial Association. **Publications:** *Wright Flyer*, periodic. Newsletter. **Price:** included in membership dues; $1.00 for nonmembers. **Circulation:** 500. Alternate Formats: online ● Brochures. **Conventions/Meetings:** Wright Brothers Annual Commemoration - luncheon, celebration (exhibits) - always December 17, in Kill Devil Hill.

21014 ■ Flying Apache Association (FAA)
Address Unknown since 2007
Founded: 1978. **Members:** 150. **Membership Dues:** $25 (annual). **Multinational. Description:** Owners of Apache airplanes and other persons interested in restoring and preserving the Apache aircraft, a small twin-engine plane manufactured in the 1950s and '60s. Disseminates information on Apache parts and equipment. Conducts educational forums on aircraft maintenance and safety. Operates charitable programs. **Awards: Type:** recognition. **Publications:** *Flying Apache Membership Directory*, annual ● Bul-

letin, periodic ● Newsletter, bimonthly. **Conventions/Meetings:** competition ● annual Fly-In - meeting ● seminar.

21015 ■ Funk Aircraft Owners Association (FAOA)
c/o Thad Shelnutt, Treas.
2836 California Ave.
Carmichael, CA 95608
Ph: (916)971-3452
E-mail: pilotthad@aol.com
URL: http://www.funkflyers.org/FAOA/faoamain.htm
Contact: Thad Shelnutt, Treas.
Founded: 1978. **Members:** 187. **Membership Dues:** regular, $12 (annual). **Description:** Owners and former owners of Funk aircraft; interested individuals. Promotes the continued flying of Funk aircraft. Assists members in locating parts. Occasionally holds slide show presentation on the history of the aircraft. **Awards: Type:** recognition. **Publications:** *Funk Flyer*, 10/year. Newsletter. **Price:** included in membership dues. **Conventions/Meetings:** competition ● annual reunion (exhibits) - always Coffeyville, KS.

21016 ■ Helicopter Club of America (HCA)
Address Unknown since 2007
Founded: 1978. **Members:** 200. **Membership Dues:** $20 (annual). **Budget:** $100,000. **Description:** Individuals interested in promoting the sport of helicopter flying on a national and international basis. Maintains speakers' bureau. U.S. representative of the International Aeronautical Federation (see separate entry, *International Organizations*), a division of the National Aeronautic Association of the U.S.A. (see separate entry), and sponsors all helicopter competitions and other events in the U.S. on their behalf. **Convention/Meeting:** none. **Awards: Type:** recognition. **Publications:** Newsletter, quarterly.

21017 ■ International B and B Fly-Inn Club (IBBFIC)
c/o Bill Maasberg
PO Box 1956
Columbia, CA 95310
Ph: (209)532-2350 (209)532-4122
Contact: Bill Maasberg, Pres.
Founded: 1984. **Members:** 1,500. **Membership Dues:** recreational, $20 (annual) ● renewal, $15 (annual). **Staff:** 2. **Description:** Commercial and private airplane pilots. Operates lodging program whereby members can fly to one another's home cities, be met at the airport, and stay in the home of another member. (B & B in the group's title refers to bed and breakfast accommodation.) **Convention/Meeting:** none. **Publications:** Directory, annual. **Price:** included in membership dues. **Circulation:** 1,500. **Advertising:** accepted ● Newsletter, quarterly. **Price:** included in membership dues.

21018 ■ International Bird Dog Association (IBDA)
c/o Suzanne Cobb, Membership Dir.
1845 Port Stanhope Pl.
Newport Beach, CA 92660
E-mail: suz4l19@aol.com
URL: http://www.ibdaweb.com
Contact: Suzanne Cobb, Membership Dir.
Founded: 1985. **Members:** 500. **Membership Dues:** individual in U.S., $30 (annual) ● individual in Canada, $35 (annual) ● individual outside U.S. and Canada, $45 (annual). **Multinational. Description:** Aviation enthusiasts interested in the Cessna L-19/O-1 aircraft, also known as the Bird Dog. (The Bird Dog was manufactured between 1950 and 1960, and was flown in combat in Korea and Vietnam.) Works to maintain remaining aircraft and preserve the L-19 heritage; seeks to unite L-19 pilots and crews. Plans to establish museum. **Libraries: Type:** reference. **Holdings:** 50; artwork, audiovisuals, books, business records, clippings, periodicals. **Subjects:** L-19, other liaison. **Awards:** Aircraft Restoration Awards. **Frequency:** annual. **Type:** recognition. **Publications:** *Membership Roster*, periodic. Membership Directory ● *Observer*, quarterly. Newsletter. **Price:** included in membership dues. **Circulation:** 600. **Conventions/Meetings:** annual Fly-In - meeting, with L-19 and

other liaison aircraft (exhibits) - always 3rd week of July in Keokuk, Iowa.

21019 ■ International Cessna 120/140 Association
PO Box 830092
Richardson, TX 75083-0092
Ph: (405)391-6773
E-mail: my140@mcloudteleco.com
URL: http://www.cessna120-140.org
Contact: Dick Acker, Sec.-Treas.
Founded: 1976. **Members:** 1,400. **Membership Dues:** regular, $25 (annual) ● overseas, $35 (annual). **State Groups:** 50. **Multinational. Description:** Pilots, owners, and enthusiasts of Cessna 120/140 aircraft. Stimulates the preservation and upkeep of the Cessna 120/140, a classic aircraft. **Libraries: Type:** open to the public; reference. **Holdings:** 1; archival material, articles, photographs, reports. **Subjects:** service letters, advertisements, service methods/modifications. **Awards: Type:** recognition ● Various Best Aircraft. **Frequency:** annual. **Type:** recognition. **Recipient:** for hard work and innovation. **Formerly:** (1980) Cessna 120/140 Association. **Publications:** *Membership List*, periodic. Membership Directory. **Advertising:** accepted. **Conventions/Meetings:** annual Fly-In - meeting (exhibits).

21020 ■ The International Cessna 170 Association (TIC170A)
22 Vista View Ln.
Cody, WY 82414-9606
Ph: (307)587-6397
Fax: (307)587-4297
E-mail: headquarters@cessna170.org
URL: http://www.cessna170.org
Contact: Ms. Jan Billeb, Exec. Sec.
Founded: 1969. **Members:** 1,550. **Membership Dues:** individual, $45 (annual). **Staff:** 1. **Description:** Owners and enthusiasts of Cessna 170 aircraft united to preserve and promote the classic airplane. Provides information on services, parts, and flying techniques. Conducts forums on insurance, safety, and general aviation information. **Awards: Frequency:** annual. **Type:** recognition. **Publications:** *Flypaper*, monthly. Newsletter. Contains calendar and member want ads. **Circulation:** 1,550 ● *The 170 Book*. Includes an updated history of the International Cessna 170 Association. **Price:** $20.00/copy ● *The 170 News*, quarterly. Magazine. **Price:** included in membership dues. **Advertising:** accepted ● Membership Directory, biennial. **Conventions/Meetings:** competition ● annual convention and seminar - always summer ● periodic Regional Fly-ins - meeting.

21021 ■ International Council of Air Shows (ICAS)
751 Miller Dr. SE, Ste.F4
Leesburg, VA 20175
Ph: (703)779-8510
Fax: (703)779-8511
E-mail: icas@airshows.org
URL: http://www.icashq.org
Contact: Bruce Wilson, Pres./CEO
Founded: 1968. **Members:** 980. **Membership Dues:** organization, $295 (annual). **Staff:** 5. **Budget:** $1,025,000. **Regional Groups:** 5. **Multinational. Description:** Air show sponsors, performers, and producers; military demonstration teams; Department of Defense, Federal Aviation Administration, and transport Canada officials. Associate members are insurance companies or agents, public relations agencies, concessionaires, printers, and others whose businesses benefit from air shows. Offers advice on air show planning, continuity, programming, management duties, fundraising, cost controls, and concession income. Provides for exchange of ideas on sponsorships, release preparation, and community relations programs. **Awards: Type:** recognition. **Recipient:** for excellence, showmanship, and military base/community relations. **Publications:** *Air Shows*, quarterly. Magazine. Provides substantive editorial and commentary specifically designed to help in running air show business better. ● *ICAS Air Show Industry Guide*, annual. Membership Directory.

Provides links to who and where peers, vendors and prospective customers in the air show industry and how to get in touch with them. **Advertising:** accepted ● *ICAS Air Show Manual.* Includes a checklist for air show operations planning guide. **Conventions/Meetings:** annual meeting and seminar (exhibits) - always first weekend in December ● annual seminar and conference.

21022 ■ International Pietenpol Association (IPA)
PO Box 127
Blakesburg, IA 52536
Ph: (641)938-2773
Fax: (641)938-2093
E-mail: antiqueairfield@sirisonline.com
URL: http://www.vintageaircraft.org/type/Pietenpol.html
Contact: Robert L. Taylor, Pres.

Founded: 1965. **Members:** 600. **Membership Dues:** individual, $15 (annual). **Description:** Owners and aficionados of the Pietenpol airplane, a 50-year-old design for a homebuilt craft that utilizes an automobile engine. Aims to stimulate, educate, and assist those interested in the history, building, and flying of the Pietenpol. Holds seminars on design and construction. **Libraries: Type:** reference. **Holdings:** archival material. **Subjects:** Pietenpols built and flown during the past 50 years. **Affiliated With:** Antique Airplane Association. **Publications:** *International Pietenpol News,* quarterly. Newsletter. **Conventions/Meetings:** annual Fly-In - meeting - always Labor Day weekend, Blakesburg, IA.

21023 ■ International Wheelchair Aviators (IWA)
PO Box 2799
Big Bear City, CA 92314
Ph: (909)585-9663
Fax: (909)585-7156
E-mail: iwaviators@aol.com
URL: http://wheelchairaviators.org
Contact: Mike Smith, Pres.

Founded: 1972. **Members:** 230. **Membership Dues:** general, $20 (annual). **Description:** Paraplegics from the U.S., Canada, and Europe who fly airplanes; interested individuals. Educates the public about the ability of the disabled to fly planes and provides fellowship for paraplegic pilots. Disseminates information about flying to the disabled. **Formerly:** California Wheelchair Aviators. **Publications:** *IWA Newsletter,* bimonthly. **Price:** included in membership dues. **Advertising:** accepted. Alternate Formats: CD-ROM ● *Membership Roster,* bimonthly. Newsletter. **Price:** included in membership dues. **Advertising:** accepted. **Conventions/Meetings:** monthly Fly-In - meeting, informal get-together.

21024 ■ Interstate Club (IC)
c/o Brent Taylor
PO Box 127
Blakesburg, IA 52536
Ph: (641)938-2773
Fax: (641)938-2093
E-mail: antiqueairfield@sirisonline.com
URL: http://www.vintageaircraft.org/type/Interstate.html
Contact: Brent Taylor, Contact

Members: 120. **Description:** A specialty club of the Antique Airplane Association. Individuals who own or restore Interstate Cadet aircraft. (The Interstate Cadet is a light, two-seat, propeller-driven airplane that is often used as a bush plane.) Promotes restoring and flying of Interstate Cadet aircraft. Maintains museum. Compiles statistics. **Libraries: Type:** reference. **Holdings:** archival material. **Awards:** Best Interstate. **Frequency:** annual. **Type:** recognition. **Recipient:** voted by ballot. **Affiliated With:** Antique Airplane Association. **Publications:** *Interstate Intercom,* 3/year. Newsletter. **Conventions/Meetings:** annual Fly-In - meeting - in conjunction with AAA ● annual meeting - always Labor Day weekend.

21025 ■ League of World War I Aviation Historians
16820 25th Ave. N
Plymouth, MN 55447
E-mail: membership@overthefront.com
URL: http://www.overthefront.com
Contact: Richard L. Bennett, Pres./Chm.

Founded: 1986. **Members:** 1,400. **Membership Dues:** regular, $60 (annual). **Staff:** 20. **Regional Groups:** 1. **State Groups:** 3. **Description:** Historians and enthusiasts of aviation history. Promotes the investigation and preservation of the history of air war during 1914-1918. Conducts research programs; compiles statistics. **Awards:** Mike Carr Award. **Frequency:** annual. **Type:** recognition. **Recipient:** for the league benefactor ● Thornton B. Hooper Award for Excellence in Aviation History. **Frequency:** annual. **Type:** recognition. **Recipient:** for editorial excellence. **Also Known As:** Over the Front. **Publications:** *The First Team: Thornton D. Hooper and America's First Bombers.* Book ● *Over the Front,* quarterly. Journal. Includes illustrations, maps, aircraft profiles, book reviews, and articles by aviation historians. **Price:** $37.00/year (4th class delivery); $48.00/year (1st class delivery). ISSN: 0888-272X. **Circulation:** 2,000. **Advertising:** accepted. Alternate Formats: online; CD-ROM. **Conventions/Meetings:** biennial Over The Front Seminar - meeting, with educational seminar and guest speakers on WWI aviation subjects (exhibits) - even numbered years.

21026 ■ Lighter-Than-Air Society (LTA)
526 S Main St., Ste.232
Akron, OH 44311
Ph: (330)535-5827 (330)535-0100
Fax: (330)668-1105
E-mail: suggest@blimpinfo.com
URL: http://www.blimpinfo.com
Contact: Joseph C. Huber Jr., Chm.

Founded: 1952. **Members:** 1,000. **Membership Dues:** active, in U.S. and Canada, $25 (annual) ● active, outside U.S. and Canada, $35 (annual) ● benefactor, in U.S. and Canada, $100 (annual) ● life (age 70 and above), $225 ● life (age 55-70), $325 ● life (up to age 55), $425. **Multinational. Description:** Persons interested in the history and development of the lighter-than-air field of aviation (balloons and airships). Works to further knowledge of the history, science, and techniques of buoyant flight. Aims to establish museum in Akron. **Libraries: Type:** reference. **Holdings:** 1,200; archival material, books, clippings, photographs. **Subjects:** LTA history and technology. **Awards:** Achievement Award. **Frequency:** annual. **Type:** recognition. **Recipient:** for contributions in lighter-than-air aviation and achievement in the field of buoyant flight. **Committees:** Museum Project: Akron Airship Historical Center. **Formerly:** (1970) Wingfoot Lighter-Than-Air Society. **Publications:** *Buoyant Flight,* bimonthly. Newsletter. Contains general interest on LTA history, technology and advanced development. **Price:** included in membership dues. ISSN: 0361-5065. **Circulation:** 900. **Advertising:** accepted. Also Cited As: *Bulletin of The LTA Society.* **Conventions/Meetings:** annual banquet, historic artifacts displayed (exhibits) - usually second Saturday in October, Akron, OH ● meeting and lecture, thematic programs, audio-visual - 7/year, always second Thursday in January, February, March, April, May, September, and November.

21027 ■ Luscombe Endowment (LE)
2487 S Gilbert Rd., Ste.106
PMB 113
Gilbert, AZ 85296
Ph: (480)650-0883 (484)762-6711
Fax: (480)988-1094
E-mail: mr.luscombe@luscombesilvaire.info
URL: http://www.luscombe.org
Contact: Doug Combs, Contact

Founded: 2000. **Members:** 1,200. **Membership Dues:** first class, $25 (annual) ● 3rd class, $20 (annual) ● users of service, $30 (annual). **Staff:** 2. **Budget:** $19,000. **Description:** Owners and pilots of the antique Luscombe airplane, which was produced from 1934 to 1959; interested individuals. Seeks to recount experiences and exchange information about the plane and its maintenance. **Libraries: Type:** reference. **Holdings:** 20. **Awards:** Plaques and Letters for Workmanship. **Type:** recognition. **Recipient:** for outstanding aircraft, restoration efforts and historical contributions related to the luscombe aircraft. **Computer Services:** Record retrieval services, historical aircraft information. **Additional Websites:** http://www.luscombesilvaire.info. **Telecommunication Services:** electronic bulletin board, group maintenance discussions and questions forum. **Affiliated With:** Antique Airplane Association; Continental Luscombe Association; Experimental Aircraft Association. **Formerly:** (2004) Luscombe Association. **Publications:** *Luscombe Association News,* bimonthly. Newsletter. **Circulation:** 1,200. **Advertising:** accepted ● *Luscombe's Golden Age.* Book. Includes detailed accounts and descriptive 3-view scale drawings of each Luscombe model. **Price:** $26.00 original (with signature); $25.00 plain (without signature) ● Reprints, on demand. Features various reprints of manuals and handbooks. ● Catalogs. **Conventions/Meetings:** annual convention (exhibits).

21028 ■ Monocoupe Club (MC)
1218 Kingstowne Pl.
St. Charles, MO 63304
E-mail: monocoupe@sbcglobal.net
URL: http://www.monocoupe.com
Contact: Bob Coolbaugh, Ed.

Founded: 1967. **Members:** 248. **Membership Dues:** in U.S., $15 (annual) ● outside U.S., $20 (annual). **Staff:** 2. **Budget:** $3,500. **Description:** Individuals dedicated to the history, preservation, and restoration of Monocoupe aircraft. Acts as clearinghouse for sales and parts information on Monocoupes. Sponsors competitions and educational programs. Maintains speakers' bureau. **Libraries: Type:** reference. **Holdings:** archival material. **Subjects:** Monocoupe Airplane and Engine Company. **Awards:** Clayton Folkerts Design Excellence Award. **Frequency:** annual. **Type:** recognition. **Computer Services:** Mailing lists. **Affiliated With:** Antique Airplane Association; Experimental Aircraft Association. **Publications:** *Monocoupe Flyer,* monthly. Newsletter. Includes articles on Monocoupe racing history, and restoration projects and techniques. **Price:** $15.00/year. **Circulation:** 220. **Advertising:** accepted ● Directory, annual. **Advertising:** accepted ● Manuals ● Reprints. **Conventions/Meetings:** biennial Fly-In and Reunion - meeting, aircraft parts, seminars on restoration, flight demonstrations (exhibits).

21029 ■ National 210 Owners Association
PO Box 1065
La Canada Flintridge, CA 91011
Ph: (818)952-6212
Fax: (818)952-6212
E-mail: avmas98@aol.com
Contact: Hazel W. Kelly, Treas.

Founded: 1976. **Members:** 2,500. **Membership Dues:** full, $30 (annual). **Staff:** 10. **Budget:** $240,000. **Regional Groups:** 8. **State Groups:** 50. **Local Groups:** 1. **Description:** Pilots and owners of the Cessna 210, a single-engine, six-seat airplane that is no longer manufactured. Seeks to preserve and promote the Cessna 210; provides information on maintenance, flying techniques, and safety. Arranges tours and trips. Sponsors local Civil Air Patrol (CAP) squadrons as well as CAP charter Senior Units No. 04210. The mission of 04210 is emergency and medical transport using the Cessna 210 airplane. Operates AVMAS - American Veterans Medical Airlift Service under agreement with VA hospital in the USA. On request of VA hospital AVMAS airlifts patients to hospitals for medical care. **Libraries: Type:** reference. **Holdings:** artwork. **Subjects:** maintenance, equipment, safety, training, adventures of Cessna 210 airplanes. **Awards:** Audie Murphy Award. **Frequency:** monthly. **Type:** recognition. **Divisions:** American Veterans Medical Airlift Service. **Publications:** *National 210 Airletter,* quarterly. Newsletter. Features an analysis of accidents involving Cessna aircraft and information on safety inspection procedures, accident prevention, and maintenance. **Price:** $30.00/year. **Circulation:** 6,000. **Advertising:** accepted. Alternate Formats: online. **Conventions/**

Meetings: semiannual Cessna Jamboree - meeting ● annual Veterans Salute - meeting and symposium, includes fly-ins (exhibits).

21030 ■ National Aeronca Association (NAA)
304 Adda St.
Roberts, IL 60962-8049
E-mail: nationalaeroncassociation@yahoo.com
URL: http://www.aeroncapilots.com
Contact: Jim Thompson, Pres.
Founded: 1988. **Members:** 1,400. **Membership Dues:** in U.S., $25 (annual) ● in Canada, $35 (annual) ● other country, $45 (annual). **Regional Groups:** 1. **Description:** Owners and enthusiasts of Aeronca aircraft. Seeks to facilitate information exchange on the restoration and preservation of Aeronca planes. Sponsors annual forum; plans to maintain museum. **Absorbed:** (1988) Aeronca Club. **Publications:** *National Aeronca Association Magazine*, quarterly. **Price:** included in membership dues. **Advertising:** accepted. **Conventions/Meetings:** biennial meeting (exhibits) - always held during even numbered years.

21031 ■ National Biplane Association (NBA)
PO Box 470350
Tulsa, OK 74147-0350
Ph: (918)665-0755
Fax: (918)665-0039
URL: http://www.nationalbiplaneassn.org
Contact: Charles W. Harris, Expo Chm.
Founded: 1987. **Membership Dues:** single, $25 (annual) ● family, $40 (annual) ● foreign, $10 (annual). **Description:** Promotes history, development, and preservation of biplane aircraft. **Libraries: Type:** reference. **Subjects:** biplane aircraft. **Awards:** Chairman's Award. **Frequency:** annual. **Type:** recognition. **Recipient:** for biplanes ● Grand Champion. **Frequency:** annual. **Type:** recognition. **Recipient:** for biplanes ● Reserve Grand Champion. **Frequency:** annual. **Type:** recognition. **Recipient:** for biplanes ● Robert P. Moore Memorial Award. **Frequency:** annual. **Type:** recognition. **Recipient:** for biplanes. **Divisions:** National Biplane Center. **Sections:** Biplane Museum. **Publications:** *Biplane News*, quarterly. Newsletter. **Price:** included in membership dues. **Conventions/Meetings:** annual National Convention and Exposition, Biplane Expo, with awards - 1st weekend of June, in Frank Phillips Field.

21032 ■ National Intercollegiate Flying Association (NIFA)
PO Box 15081
Monroe, LA 71207
Ph: (318)325-6156
Fax: (318)325-6156
E-mail: nifahq@hotmail.com
URL: http://www.nifa.us
Contact: Gary Hemphill, Exec. Dir.
Founded: 1948. **Members:** 2,000. **Membership Dues:** general, $300 (annual). **Budget:** $32,000. **Regional Groups:** 11. **Local Groups:** 80. **Description:** College and university students interested in flying light airplanes. Conducts regional and national competitions. **Committees:** Judges; Legal; Planning; Rules. **Formerly:** National Intercollegiate Flying Club. **Publications:** *Bluebook - NIFA Judges Training Manual* ● *Contact*, bimonthly. Newsletter ● *Redbook - Rules for Intercollegiate Flight Competitions*. **Conventions/Meetings:** annual meeting and competition (exhibits).

21033 ■ National Stinson Club (NSC)
c/o International Stinson Club
PO Box 3311
San Jose, CA 95157-3311
Ph: (408)272-8120
URL: http://www.stinsonclub.org
Contact: George Allemand, Chm.
Founded: 1972. **Members:** 80. **Membership Dues:** inside U.S., $20 (quarterly) ● outside U.S., $25 (quarterly). **Staff:** 1. **Budget:** $1,000. **Regional Groups:** 3. **Description:** Enthusiasts and restorers of aircraft made by Stinson Aircraft Corporation during the 1920s, '30s, and '40s. (Stinson aircraft are of tube and fabric construction and usually have radial

engines; later models were equipped with flat 4 and 6 cylinder engines.) Compiles information to help members locate, retrieve, and restore the aircraft. Displays the restorations at fly-ins across the U.S. **Libraries: Type:** open to the public. **Awards:** Best Stinson Trophy. **Frequency:** annual. **Type:** trophy. **Recipient:** for quality of restoration. **Affiliated With:** Antique Airplane Association; Experimental Aircraft Association. **Publications:** *Stinson Plane Talk*, bimonthly. Newsletter. **Circulation:** 100. **Conventions/Meetings:** periodic Regional Fly-Ins - seminar (exhibits).

21034 ■ National World War II Glider Pilots Association (NWWIIGPA)
21 Phyllis Rd.
Freehold, NJ 07728
Ph: (732)462-1838
E-mail: ww2gp@aol.com
URL: http://www.ww2gp.org
Contact: George I. Theis, Natl. Treas.
Founded: 1971. **Members:** 1,200. **Membership Dues:** associate, $12 (annual). **Budget:** $14,000. **Regional Groups:** 14. **State Groups:** 50. **Description:** World War II glider pilots. Restores and/or rebuilds World War II combat CG 4A (Waco) gliders and other gliders or aircraft to flying condition for display. Collects and preserves items of historical significance and memorabilia pertinent to the Glider Pilot Program of the World War II Army Air Forces. Attempts to develop and preserve a complete history of the World War II Glider Pilot Program. Raises funds to provide facilities for the display of restored gliders and aircraft associated with the Glider Pilot Program. Maintains library, Glider Pilots Museum, and Silent Wings Museum in Lubbock, TX. **Awards:** Bickett Ellington Award. **Frequency:** annual. **Type:** recognition ● Most Outstanding Wing Commander Award. **Type:** recognition. **Computer Services:** database ● mailing lists. **Telecommunication Services:** electronic mail, tip14@juno.com. **Committees:** Help Fund. **Publications:** *Roster*, annual. Journal ● *Silent Wings*, quarterly. Newsletter. **Conventions/Meetings:** annual reunion - in October.

21035 ■ OX5 Aviation Pioneers
PO Box 7974
Pittsburgh, PA 15216-7974
Ph: (412)341-5650
E-mail: ox5nationalhqs@hotmail.com
URL: http://www.ox5pioneers.org
Contact: Jim Ricklefs, Pres.
Founded: 1955. **Members:** 4,000. **Membership Dues:** pioneer, historian, $20 (annual). **Staff:** 2. **State Groups:** 32. **Local Groups:** 1. **Description:** Represents men and women who, prior to December 31, 1940: soloed or flew aircraft powered by OX5 engines; owned OX5-powered aircraft; actively and directly participated in the design, construction, maintenance, or operation of OX5-powered aircraft; worked as mechanics in the repair, overhauling, or maintenance of OX5 engines. Maintains hall of fame. **Awards: Type:** recognition. **Formerly:** (1973) OX5 Club of America. **Publications:** *OX5 News*, periodic. **Conventions/Meetings:** annual reunion.

21036 ■ Piper Owner Society (POS)
PO Box 5000
Iola, WI 54945
Ph: (715)445-5000
Free: (866)697-4737
Fax: (715)445-4053
E-mail: ddkowalski@piperowner.org
URL: http://www.piperowner.org
Contact: David Kowalski, Publisher
Founded: 1985. **Members:** 5,500. **Membership Dues:** in U.S., $48 (annual) ● outside U.S., $63 (annual). **Staff:** 12. **Description:** Represents owners, pilots, and enthusiasts of Piper planes. Provides technical information and assistance to members. **Libraries: Type:** reference. **Affiliated With:** Cessna Owner Organization. **Publications:** *Aircraft Modifications and Avionics for Piper and Cessna Aircraft*, annual. Book. Covers modifications and avionics for Piper and Cessna aircraft. Includes list of parts suppliers. **Price:** $19.95. **Advertising:** accepted ● *PIP-*

ERS, monthly. Magazine. Includes articles on Piper aircraft maintenance, legal issues in aviation, insurance, and restoration; includes book reviews. **Price:** included in membership dues. **Circulation:** 3,500. **Advertising:** accepted ● *The Standard Catalog of Piper Single Engine Aircraft*. Book. Covers every Piper single-engine aircraft produced between 1930 and 1990. Includes photos, historical features, and specifications for each model. ● *Standard Catalog of Piper Twin Engine Aircraft*. Book. Covers every Piper twin-engine airplane produced from 1954-1993. Includes photos, historical features, and specifications for each model. **Price:** $29.95. **Conventions/Meetings:** annual meeting (exhibits).

21037 ■ Popular Rotorcraft Association (PRA)
PO Box 68
Mentone, IN 46539-0068
Ph: (574)353-7227
Fax: (574)353-7021
E-mail: prahq@pra.org
URL: http://www.pra.org
Contact: Rusty Nance, Pres.
Founded: 1962. **Members:** 4,000. **Membership Dues:** regular, in U.S., $35 (annual). **State Groups:** 61. **Local Groups:** 70. **Description:** Individuals who build and fly privately owned noncommercial rotorcraft (autogiros, helicopters and other rotorcraft). Aids members in problems of licensing, certifying, building, flying, safety, engineering, maintenance, and pilot training. Represents members before the Federal Aviation Administration. Sponsors seminars and educational programs, and contests; makes available scholarships. Maintains small library of technical magazines and back issues of magazines on rotorcraft design and engineering. Operates museum. **Awards: Type:** recognition. **Publications:** *Rotorcraft*, 8/year. Magazine. Promotes the building, flying, and safety of rotorcraft. **Price:** free, for members only. **ISSN:** 0032-4620. **Circulation:** 4,000. **Advertising:** accepted. **Conventions/Meetings:** annual International Convention (exhibits) - usually late July.

21038 ■ Porterfield Airplane Club (PAC)
91 Hickory Loop
Ocala, FL 34472-4122
Ph: (352)687-4859
Contact: Chuck Lebrecht, Exec.Dir.
Founded: 1962. **Members:** 65. **Membership Dues:** individual, $5 (annual). **Description:** Owners, pilots, and enthusiasts of aircraft manufactured by the American Eagle and Porterfield companies. Works to facilitate communication and information exchange among members in the areas of flying, restoring, and maintaining their airplanes. **Convention/Meeting:** none. **Awards:** Best Restoration Porterfield Produced Aircraft. **Frequency:** annual. **Type:** recognition. **Affiliated With:** Antique Airplane Association; Experimental Aircraft Association. **Publications:** *Porterfield Airplane Club*, quarterly. Newsletter.

21039 ■ Precision Aerobatics Model Pilots Association (PAMPA)
158 Flying Cloud Isle
Foster City, CA 94404
Ph: (650)345-0130
Fax: (650)578-8454
E-mail: shareen_fancher@control-line.org
URL: http://www.control-line.org
Contact: Shareen Fancher, Treas.
Founded: 1973. **Members:** 2,000. **Membership Dues:** regular, in U.S. (periodical mail), $35 (annual) ● regular, in Canada and Mexico (airmail), other nation (surface mail), $40 (annual) ● regular, in U.S. (first class mail), $50 (annual) ● other nation (air mail), $65 (annual) ● regular, in U.S. (family), $5 (annual). **Staff:** 16. **Budget:** $50,000. **Description:** Stunt model airplane pilots and control line precision aerobatics enthusiasts. Represents competing and noncompeting stunt flyers around the world; seeks to maintain a means of communication among control line stunt flyers; votes on issues affecting control line stunts. Conducts competitions; compiles statistics; maintains hall of fame and museum; conducts research programs. **Libraries: Type:** reference.

Holdings: archival material, audio recordings, books, clippings, periodicals, video recordings. **Subjects:** control line aerobatic model aircraft. **Awards:** PAMPA Hall of Fame to Extraordinary Modelers. **Frequency:** biennial. **Type:** recognition. **Recipient:** for individuals who have made significant contributions to the hobby/sport of control line aerobatics. **Affiliated With:** Academy of Model Aeronautics. **Publications:** *Everything You've Always Wanted Know About Stunt*, periodic. Brochure. Describes control line precision aerobatics, PAMPA, and AMA. **Price:** free ● *Old Time Stunt Construction Drawings*. Book ● *Pioneers of Control Line Flying*. Book ● *Stunt News*, bimonthly. Magazine. **Price:** included in membership dues. **Circulation:** 2,000. **Advertising:** accepted. **Conventions/Meetings:** annual meeting, in conjunction with the AMA Nationals (exhibits) - usually July.

21040 ■ Rearwin Club (RC)
c/o Eric Rearwin
PO Box 70044
Richmond, CA 94807
Ph: (510)724-2500
Contact: Eric Rearwin, Contact
Founded: 1980. **Members:** 140. **Membership Dues:** regular, $15. **Description:** Owners, pilots, and enthusiasts of Rearwin aircraft. Serves as an information clearinghouse on the flying, maintenance, and restoration of Rearwin airplanes. Offers advice and technical assistance to members. Participates in flying activities. **Awards:** Rearwin Family Awards. **Frequency:** annual. **Type:** monetary. **Publications:** *Rearwin Register*, quarterly. **Conventions/Meetings:** annual meeting - always Labor Day weekend ● periodic meeting.

21041 ■ Short Wing Piper Club (SWPC)
309 Main St.
PO Box 166
Halstead, KS 67056
Ph: (316)835-3650 (316)835-3307
E-mail: membership@shortwing.org
URL: http://www.shortwing.org
Contact: Mr. Cliff VanVleet, Pres.
Founded: 1979. **Members:** 2,800. **Membership Dues:** regular, in U.S. and Canada, $30 (annual) ● regular, outside U.S. and Canada, $40 (annual). **Staff:** 4. **Budget:** $60,000. **Regional Groups:** 42. **For-Profit. Description:** Owners, pilots, and enthusiasts of Piper aircraft including the Vagabond, Clipper, Pacer, Tri-Pacer, and Colt models, which were manufactured between 1947 and 1963. Works to promote the preservation, operation, and maintenance of Short Wing Piper aircraft; assist members in locating new or used parts; provide tips on modifying aircraft for a safer and smoother ride; make flying more economical. **Libraries: Type:** not open to the public; lending. **Holdings:** books, periodicals, video recordings. **Subjects:** aircraft maintenance, flying, history, tools. **Awards:** Grand Champion. **Frequency:** annual. ● **Type:** recognition. **Funds:** Short Wing Piper Education Foundation. **Formerly:** (1984) Tri-Pacer Owners Club. **Publications:** *Short Wing Piper News*, bimonthly. Newsletter. Includes maintenance reports, new product information, and chapter news. **Price:** $30.00/year. **Circulation:** 3,500. **Advertising:** accepted. **Conventions/Meetings:** annual meeting and seminar (exhibits) - always summer ● annual seminar, on aircraft and flying techniques (exhibits).

21042 ■ Silver Wings Fraternity (SWF)
PO Box 44208
Cincinnati, OH 45244
Ph: (513)732-5852
Free: (800)554-1437
Fax: (513)732-5853
E-mail: cardinal5@msn.com
URL: http://www.silverwings.org
Contact: Don Fairbanks, Sec./Ed.
Founded: 1958. **Members:** 2,500. **Membership Dues:** individual, $15 (annual) ● husband and wife, $20 (annual) ● regular, outside U.S., $30 (annual) ● life (individual), $200. **Regional Groups:** 16. **Description:** Individuals who made a solo flight in a powered aircraft at least 25 years before application

for membership. Encourages and promotes interest in and the advancement of Aviation, including through organized youth challenge programs. **Awards:** Bernie Geier Distinguished Service Award. **Type:** recognition ● Carl Fromhagen Leadership Award. **Frequency:** annual. **Type:** recognition. **Recipient:** for outstanding member in the field of aviation ● Elrey B. Jeppesen Youth Challenge Award. **Type:** recognition ● Evelyn Bryan Johnson Aviation Award. **Type:** recognition ● Kathy Charles Newsletter Award. **Type:** recognition ● Russ Brinkley Innovation Award. **Type:** recognition. **Boards:** Directors. **Publications:** *Slipstream*, bimonthly. Newsletter. Contains news of organization and members. **Price:** included in membership dues. **Circulation:** 2,500. **Conventions/Meetings:** annual convention and board meeting - always October ● annual Sun and Fun Fly-In - meeting and board meeting - always April, Lakeland, FL.

21043 ■ Society of Antique Modelers (SAM)
c/o Mike Myers, Pres./Legal Counsel
911 Kilmary Dr.
Glendale, CA 91207-1105
Ph: (818)241-9154
E-mail: mikemyersgln@charter.net
URL: http://www.antiquemodeler.org
Contact: Mike Myers, Pres./Legal Counsel
Founded: 1964. **Members:** 2,700. **Membership Dues:** regular, in U.S., $25 (annual) ● regular, outside U.S., $40 (annual). **Regional Groups:** 4. **State Groups:** 50. **Local Groups:** 116. **National Groups:** 6. **Description:** Persons interested in the restoration and flying of the old-time gas and rubber-powered model airplanes manufactured from 1935 to 1942. **Libraries: Type:** not open to the public. **Holdings:** periodicals. **Subjects:** modeling, 1930's to 1950's. **Affiliated With:** Academy of Model Aeronautics. **Publications:** *SAM Speaks*, bimonthly. Newsletter. **Price:** included in membership dues. **Circulation:** 3,000. **Advertising:** accepted. **Conventions/Meetings:** annual Champs - meeting and competition (exhibits) - every fall.

21044 ■ Staggerwing Club (SC)
c/o Jane Hoff
10741 S 25th E
Idaho Falls, ID 83406
E-mail: mdp@staggerwing.co.uk
Contact: Jane Hoff, Contact
Founded: 1971. **Members:** 500. **Membership Dues:** ordinary, $25 (annual) ● overseas, 30 (annual). **Multinational. Description:** Owners and admirers of Beechcraft 17 aircraft. Promotes preservation and maintenance of Beechcraft 17s. Serves as a clearinghouse on Beechcraft 17s and their maintenance. Sponsors competitions; maintains speakers' bureau; operates museum; compiles statistics. **Libraries: Type:** lending; reference; not open to the public. **Holdings:** 1,000; articles, artwork, books, clippings, periodicals. **Subjects:** Beechcraft 17 history, operation, and maintenance. **Computer Services:** database ● mailing lists. **Publications:** *Staggerwing News*, quarterly. Newsletter. **Price:** included in membership dues ● Directory, periodic. **Conventions/Meetings:** annual Staggerwing Fly In - convention.

21045 ■ Stampe Club International (SCI)
2940 Falcon Way
Midlothian, TX 76065
Ph: (214)723-1504
E-mail: andymcluskie@compuserve.com
URL: http://ourworld.compuserve.com/homepages/andymcluskie
Contact: Don Peterson, Exec. Off.
Founded: 1985. **Members:** 90. **Membership Dues:** $25 (annual). **Staff:** 1. **Budget:** $1,000. **Description:** Individuals owning or interested in the Stampe aircraft. (The Stampe, produced from 1930 through 1950, is a Belgian-manufactured biplane with an open cockpit). Promotes the Stampe biplane; shares experiences, stories, and technical information among those who own or fly the Stampe. Compiles statistics; sponsors competitions. **Libraries: Type:** not open to the public. **Holdings:** articles, books, periodicals. **Subjects:** Stampe. **Telecommunication**

Services: electronic mail, stamper@aol.com. **Publications:** *The Stampe Collector*, quarterly. Newsletter. **Price:** $25.00/year. **Circulation:** 65. **Advertising:** accepted. Alternate Formats: diskette. **Conventions/Meetings:** annual Fly-In - meeting.

21046 ■ Stearman Restorers Association (SRA)
Chino Airport
7000 Merrill Ave., Box 90
Chino, CA 91710-8800
E-mail: twowings@theofficenet.com
URL: http://www.stearman.net
Contact: Larry Johnson, Sec.
Founded: 1966. **Members:** 1,467. **Membership Dues:** regular, in U.S., $35 (annual) ● regular, in Canada and Mexico, $40 (annual) ● regular, outside North America, $45 (annual). **Staff:** 5. **Description:** Individuals with an interest in Stearman aircraft. (Stearman planes were manufactured in the 1930s and 1940s.) Promotes preservation and flying of Stearman airplanes. Operates in cooperation with the Antique Airplane Association and the Experimental Aircraft Association, which do not have Stearman divisions of their own. **Affiliated With:** Antique Airplane Association; Experimental Aircraft Association. **Publications:** *The Stearman Flying Wire*, quarterly. Newsletter. **Price:** included in membership dues. **Circulation:** 1,500. **Advertising:** accepted. **Conventions/Meetings:** annual meeting - always September, in Galesburg, IL.

21047 ■ Swift Museum Foundation (SMF)
PO Box 644
McMinn County Airport, Hangar 4
Athens, TN 37371-0644
Ph: (423)745-9547 (423)774-9696
Fax: (423)745-9869
E-mail: swiftlychs@aol.com
URL: http://www.globetemcoswift.com
Contact: Denis Arbeau, Contact
Founded: 1968. **Members:** 700. **Membership Dues:** family, $45 (annual) ● life, $1,000 ● individual, $35 (annual). **Staff:** 2. **Regional Groups:** 7. **State Groups:** 2. **Description:** Owners and individuals dedicated to the appreciation, restoration, and preservation of the Globe/Temco Swift aircraft. Conducts forums; sponsors research programs. Supplies replacement parts to owners. Maintains museum of certificates, engineering drawings, jigs, and tooling. Conducts specialized education; compiles statistics. **Libraries: Type:** reference. **Holdings:** archival material, books, photographs. **Awards: Type:** recognition. **Formerly:** (1980) International Swift Association. **Publications:** *Member Roster*, monthly. Newsletter. **Circulation:** 700 ● Newsletter, monthly. **Advertising:** accepted. **Conventions/Meetings:** annual Fly-In - convention ● annual Swift National - competition (exhibits).

21048 ■ Travel Air Club (TAC)
PO Box 127
Blakesburg, IA 52536
Ph: (641)938-2773
Fax: (641)938-2093
E-mail: antiqueairfield@sirisonline.com
Contact: R.L. Taylor, Contact
Founded: 1983. **Members:** 140. **Description:** Individuals with an interest in Travel Air aircraft. (Travel Air airplanes were manufactured in the 1930s.) Helps members locate, restore, and fly Travel Air airplanes. **Awards:** Best Travel Air. **Frequency:** annual. **Type:** recognition. **Recipient:** voted by the members. **Affiliated With:** Antique Airplane Association. **Publications:** *Travel Air Tails*, periodic. **Conventions/Meetings:** annual Fly-In - meeting - always Labor Day weekend.

21049 ■ Twin Bonanza Association (TBA)
19684 Lakeshore Dr.
Three Rivers, MI 49093
Ph: (269)279-2540
Fax: (269)279-2540

E-mail: forward@twinbonanza.com
URL: http://www.twinbonanza.com
Contact: Richard I. Ward, Dir.
Founded: 1986. **Members:** 155. **Membership Dues:** regular, in U.S. and Canada, $35 (annual) ● international, $45 (annual). **Staff:** 2. **Description:** Dedicated to preserving the historical meaning of the Twin Civilian Model 50 series and Military I23/U8 series Twin Bonanza, as well as networking with individuals interested in Beechcraft Twin Bonanza aircraft. Promotes the preservation of aircraft, which were manufactured between 1950 and 1962. **Libraries:** **Type:** reference. **Holdings:** archival material, books, clippings, periodicals. **Computer Services:** database, aircraft owners and aircraft registration. **Publications:** *Beechcraft-Twin Bonanza-Craft of the Masters,* quarterly. Book. **Price:** $24.95 plus shipping and handling ($4.50) ● *Twin Bonanza Association Newsletter,* quarterly. **Price:** included in membership dues. **Conventions/Meetings:** annual conference - always September or October.

21050 ■ Twirly Birds (TB)
c/o Jim Hamilton, Pres.
7140 Rolling Acres Trail
Fair Oaks Ranch, TX 78015-4021
Ph: (830)755-4566
E-mail: jchamtx@wmconnect.com
URL: http://www.twirlybirds.org
Contact: Jim Hamilton, Pres.
Founded: 1949. **Members:** 250. **Membership Dues:** individual, $10 (annual). **Multinational. Description:** Represents pioneering pilots of helicopters and other vertical takeoff aircraft. Individuals who have soloed a helicopter or other vertical takeoff aircraft in sustained flight prior to VJ Day are classified as founder members; individuals who soloed helicopters over 20 years ago are classified as general members. Facilitates exchange of experience and opinions on the progress of the helicopter and other vertical takeoff aircraft. Maintains files on helicopter history. **Awards: Type:** recognition. **Publications:** *Twirly Bird Newsletter,* semiannual. **Conventions/Meetings:** semiannual meeting, held in conjunction with the American Helicopter Society and Helicopter Association International.

21051 ■ United Flying Octogenarians (UFO)
PO Box 11114
Montgomery, AL 36111-0114
Ph: (334)832-2413
E-mail: pilotherb@yahoo.com
URL: http://www.unitedflyingoctogenarians.org
Contact: Herbert K. Sloane, Sec.-Treas.
Founded: 1982. **Members:** 405. **Membership Dues:** qualified pilot, $12 (annual). **Multinational. Description:** Social organization for pilots who have commanded an aircraft in flight after reaching age 80. **Computer Services:** Mailing lists, of members. **Publications:** *UFO News,* semimonthly. Newsletter. **Price:** available to members only. **Conventions/Meetings:** annual convention, held in conjunction with Aircraft Owners and Pilots Association or EAA Fly-In (Oshkosh).

21052 ■ United States Ultralight Association (USUA)
104 Carlisle St.
Gettysburg, PA 17325
Ph: (717)339-0200
Fax: (717)339-0063
E-mail: usua@usua.org
URL: http://www.usua.org
Contact: Mr. Dale Hooper, Exec. VP
Founded: 1985. **Members:** 6,000. **Membership Dues:** individual, $30 (annual). **Staff:** 3. **Budget:** $460,000. **Regional Groups:** 12. **Local Groups:** 110. **Description:** Ultralight aviation enthusiasts. Promotes the sport of ultralight and microlight aviation. (Ultralights and microlights are very light, slow planes used for recreational flight.) Represents members' interests on federal, state, and local levels; keeps members abreast of ultralight advancement. Conducts educational programs. Compiles statistics. **Libraries: Type:** reference. **Holdings:** audiovisuals. **Awards:** Colibri Diploma. **Frequency:** annual. **Type:**

recognition. **Recipient:** to an individual who has made an outstanding contribution to the development of microlight flying by his/her action, work, achievements, initiative or devotion ● John Moody Award. **Frequency:** annual. **Type:** recognition. **Recipient:** to an individual, group or organization who has made significant contributions or advancements of enduring value in the sport of ultralight aviation ● USUA Club of the Year. **Frequency:** annual. **Type:** recognition. **Recipient:** for overall excellence in programs and activities for beginners and novices ● USUA Regional Representative of the Year Award. **Frequency:** annual. **Type:** recognition. **Recipient:** to outstanding regional representative ● Worthington Cup. **Frequency:** annual. **Type:** recognition. **Recipient:** for the longest open distance flight of over 200 statute miles in a part 103 powered ultralight. **Committees:** Safety and Training. **Programs:** Airmen and Vehicle Registration; National Ultralight Training; 3rd Party Liability Insurance; Ultralight Instructor. **Publications:** *Air and Space.* Magazine ● *Kitplanes.* Magazine. **Price:** $20.00 ● *Ultraflight.* Magazine. **Price:** $24.95 ● *Ultralight Flying!,* monthly. Magazine. **Price:** $35.00. **Advertising:** accepted. **Conventions/Meetings:** periodic competition ● annual meeting, with presentations and awards ceremonies (exhibits) - usually February.

21053 ■ Whirly-Girls - International Women Helicopter Pilots
c/o Teen Corey
PO Box 265
Pinehurst, TX 77362
E-mail: tcoreywg@aol.com
URL: http://www.whirlygirls.org
Contact: Teen Corey, Contact
Founded: 1955. **Members:** 1,374. **Membership Dues:** initial, $75 (annual) ● regular, $35 (annual). **Staff:** 1. **Multinational. Description:** Women helicopter pilots. Stimulates interest among women in rotary-wing aircraft. **Awards: Type:** scholarship. **Recipient:** to a woman for helicopter flight training; plus 5 awards for advanced helicopter training. **Publications:** *Collective Pitch,* quarterly. Newsletter. **Circulation:** 1,000 ● *Membership List,* periodic. Membership Directory. **Conventions/Meetings:** annual banquet, includes awards ● annual conference, held in conjunction with Helicopter Association International (exhibits).

21054 ■ World Airline Historical Society (WAHS)
PO Box 489
Ocoee, FL 34761
Fax: (407)522-9352
E-mail: president@wahsonline.com
URL: http://www.wahsonline.com
Contact: Duane Young, Pres.
Founded: 1975. **Members:** 800. **Membership Dues:** bulkreate, in U.S., $30 (annual) ● surface mail, outside U.S. and Canada, $45 (annual) ● first class, in U.S., $40 (annual) ● air mail, outside U.S. and Canada, $35 (annual). **Staff:** 12. **Budget:** $18,000. **Regional Groups:** 1. **Description:** Individuals interested in collecting various items of airline memorabilia, including airplane models, airline schedules, postcards, posters, photos, and publications from airlines. Promotes the study of airlines and airliners and the preservation of airline memorabilia. Maintains small library of books and magazines. **Computer Services:** Mailing lists. **Formerly:** (1985) World Airline Hobby Club. **Publications:** *Captain's Log,* quarterly. Magazine. **Price:** $20.00/year. **Circulation:** 1,400. **Advertising:** accepted ● *Membership Roster,* annual. Membership Directory. **Conventions/Meetings:** annual Airliner's International - convention, with flea market type vendor area (exhibits).

21055 ■ World Beechcraft Society (WBS)
c/o American Printing & Publishing
8609 S 212th St.
Kent, WA 98031
Ph: (310)577-0527
Free: (866)732-3927
Fax: (301)577-1920

E-mail: wbs@worldbeechcraft.com
URL: http://www.worldbeechcraft.com
Contact: Steve Oxman, Pres.
Membership Dues: individual, $60 (annual). **Multinational. Description:** Provides a network for owners and operators of Beechcraft to share information about their planes. **Publications:** Magazine, bimonthly. Features articles from members sharing information about their airplanes and flying experiences, both locally and around the world. **Advertising:** accepted ● Newsletter, periodic. Features personal experience. **Conventions/Meetings:** semiannual meeting, major fly-ins ● periodic regional meeting.

21056 ■ World War I Aeroplanes (WWI AERO)
15 Crescent Rd.
Poughkeepsie, NY 12601
Ph: (845)473-3679
URL: http://www.aviation-history.com/ww1aero.htm
Contact: Leonard E. Opdycke, Publisher
Founded: 1961. **Members:** 2,400. **Membership Dues:** regular in U.S., $42 (annual) ● regular outside U.S., $47 (annual). **Staff:** 3. **Budget:** $145,000. **Multinational. Description:** Individuals, museums, libraries, and universities in 10 countries. Provides documentation, research, and information to restorers, builders, modelers, and historians of pre-World War I, World War I, and between-wars airplanes. **Convention/Meeting:** none. **Libraries: Type:** reference. **Holdings:** 500. **Subjects:** early aviation. **Publications:** *Skyways: The Journal of Airplane 1920-1940,* quarterly. Includes original technical drawings, photographs, book reviews, and comments. **Price:** included in membership dues; $42.00 /year for nonmembers in U.S.; $47.00 /year for nonmembers outside U.S. ISSN: 1051-6956. **Circulation:** 1,200. **Advertising:** accepted ● *WWI Aero: The Journal of Early Aeroplane,* quarterly. Provides technical information on airplanes built between 1900-1919; includes original technical drawings, photographs, book reviews, and comments. **Price:** included in membership dues; $42.00 /year for nonmembers in U.S.; $47.00 /year for nonmembers outside U.S. ISSN: 0736-198X. **Circulation:** 1,300. **Advertising:** accepted ● Catalog. **Price:** $12.00.

Alcoholic Beverages

21057 ■ International Bird Beer Label Association (IBBLA)
PO Box 2551
Homer, AK 99603
E-mail: birdbeers@ibbla.com
URL: http://www.ibbla.com
Founded: 1993. **Multinational. Description:** Fosters a worldwide appreciation of birds and brew. **Formerly:** (2000) American Bird Beer Label Association.

Amateur Radio

21058 ■ ACB Radio Amateurs (ACBRA)
c/o Mike Duke, Pres.
4911 Old Canton Rd., Apt. 239
Jackson, MS 39211
Ph: (601)432-6293
Fax: (601)982-6746
E-mail: k5xu@concentric.net
URL: http://www.acb.org/resources/sports.html
Contact: Mike Duke, Pres.
Members: 50. **Description:** Blind and visually impaired individuals interested in ham radio operation. Provides call sign directories, manual exchange programs, and new operator assistance. **Affiliated With:** American Council of the Blind. **Publications:** Newsletter, periodic. Alternate Formats: magnetic tape. **Conventions/Meetings:** annual convention (exhibits).

21059 ■ American CB Radio Association (ACBRA)
Address Unknown since 2007
Founded: 1976. **Staff:** 2. **Description:** CB radio enthusiasts. Encourages proper and courteous use

of CB airways. **Publications:** Handbook, periodic. Includes discount lodging and car rental directory.

21060 ■ American Radio Relay League (ARRL)
225 Main St.
Newington, CT 06111-1494
Ph: (860)594-0200
Free: (888)277-5289
Fax: (860)594-0259
E-mail: hq@arrl.org
URL: http://www.arrl.org
Contact: Joel Harrison, Pres.

Founded: 1914. **Members:** 171,000. **Membership Dues:** regular, in U.S., $39 (annual) ● senior, $36 (annual) ● regular, in Canada, $49 (annual) ● regular, outside U.S. and Canada, $62 (annual) ● blind/family, $8 (annual). **Staff:** 115. **Budget:** $13,200,000. **Regional Groups:** 15. **State Groups:** 70. **Local Groups:** 1,900. **Description:** Licensed amateur radio operators in the U.S. and others interested in amateur radio communication and experimentation. Operates a nationwide message handling network, the National Traffic System, with members serving as official relay stations, observers, emergency coordinators, and bulletin stations. Maintains Museum of Amateur Radio; sponsors contests. Operates an experimental equipment laboratory. Serves as secretariat for International Amateur Radio Union (see separate entry). **Awards: Type:** recognition. **Recipient:** for operating proficiency. **Publications:** QST, monthly. Magazine. **Advertising:** accepted. Alternate Formats: CD-ROM ● Radio Amateur's Handbook, annual. Includes book, CD ROM and Bonus "1926 Handbook" reproduction. **Price:** $54.95 hardcover/ $39.95 softcover ● Also publishes special booklets for beginners and others on antennae and mobile and radio fundamentals. **Conventions/Meetings:** annual meeting (exhibits).

21061 ■ American Shortwave Listeners Club (ASWLC)
16182 Ballad Ln.
Huntington Beach, CA 92649-2272
Ph: (714)846-1685
E-mail: aswlc@yahoogroups.com
URL: http://groups.yahoo.com/group/ASWLC
Contact: Stewart MacKenzie, Gen. Mgr.

Founded: 1959. **Members:** 500. **Membership Dues:** individual, $10 (annual). **Staff:** 4. **Budget:** $12,000. **Regional Groups:** 1. **Local Groups:** 1. **Description:** Hobbyists interested in listening to shortwave radio broadcasts, or "DXing." Seeks to advance the DXing hobby on a worldwide basis and promote contacts between DXers. Holds contests for members; tracks "clandestine" radio stations and fights radio jamming; compiles statistics on broadcasting and listening equipment. Conducts research programs. **Libraries: Type:** reference. **Holdings:** 39; biographical archives. **Subjects:** shortwave radio. **Telecommunication Services:** electronic mail, wdx6aa@earthlink.net. **Conventions/Meetings:** monthly Shortwave Radio Listening - meeting, open to general public (exhibits) - first Saturday.

21062 ■ ARRL Foundation (ARRLF)
225 Main St.
Newington, CT 06111
Ph: (860)594-0397 (860)594-0200
Fax: (860)594-0259
E-mail: foundation@arrl.org
URL: http://www.arrl.org/arrlf
Contact: Mary M. Hobart, Sec.

Founded: 1973. **Nonmembership. Description:** Seeks to study and contribute to the development of amateur radio programs and other innovative programs related to the purposes of the American Radio Relay League (see separate entry). Conducts fundraising programs for development of amateur radio projects and for scholarships. **Committees:** Grant; Scholarship. **Affiliated With:** American Radio Relay League.

21063 ■ Association of Clandestine Radio Enthusiasts (ACE)
PO Box 1
Belfast, NY 14711-0001
E-mail: acehdq@localnet.com
URL: http://www.frn.net/ace
Contact: John T. Arthur, Exec. Mgr.

Founded: 1980. **Members:** 560. **Membership Dues:** individual, in U.S., $22 (annual) ● regular, in U.S., Canada, and Mexico, $27 (annual) ● other country, $40 (annual). **Staff:** 5. **Multinational. Description:** Individuals interested in clandestine and pirate radio communications. **Libraries: Type:** reference. **Holdings:** 1,895; articles, books, periodicals. **Subjects:** pirate, clandestine and illegal communications. **Awards:** DX Certificates. **Type:** recognition. **Recipient:** for stations qsl'd. **Publications:** The Monthly ACE. Newsletter. Provides extensive coverage of Pirate Radio activity. **Price:** $22.00. **Circulation:** 459. **Advertising:** accepted. Alternate Formats: online. **Conventions/Meetings:** annual WinterFest - meeting (exhibits) - always March.

21064 ■ Association of North American Radio Clubs (ANARC)
c/o Dr. Harold Cones, Chm.
2 Whit Ct.
Newport News, VA 23606
E-mail: hcones@cnu.edu
URL: http://www.anarc.org
Contact: Dr. Harold Cones, Chm.

Founded: 1964. **Members:** 18. **Membership Dues:** $8 (annual). **Staff:** 8. **Budget:** $1,000. **Description:** National and regional radio clubs with headquarters in North America. Promotes interchange of ideas and information among members. Advances public interest in radio recreation; acts as liaison between listeners and equipment manufacturers. **Awards:** International DXer of the Year. **Frequency:** annual. **Type:** recognition. **Recipient:** for outstanding contributions to the hobby ● North American Shortwave DXer of the Year. **Frequency:** annual. **Type:** recognition. **Recipient:** to a person for his/her outstanding contribution to the hobby. **Telecommunication Services:** electronic bulletin board, (913)345-1978. **Committees:** Awards; Contests; Governmental Affairs; Preserve Radio Verifications; 7240 Net; Update; World Wide Web. **Publications:** ANARC Club List, periodic. Membership Directory. **Price:** $1.00. **Circulation:** 150 ● ANARC Guide to U.S. Monitoring Laws. Journal. Features a review of monitoring laws in each state. **Price:** $7.50. **Circulation:** 150. **Conventions/Meetings:** annual Winter Shortwave Listeners Festival - convention (exhibits) - 3rd Friday and Saturday of March.

21065 ■ Collins Collectors Association (CCA)
PO Box 354
Phoenix, MD 21131
E-mail: floyd@hi-rescom.com
URL: http://www.collinsradio.org
Contact: Floyd Soo, Pres.

Membership Dues: regular, $20 (annual) ● overseas, $25 (annual). **Description:** Promotes the use and care of Collins amateur radio equipment. Preserves the history and lore of Collins radio equipment. Provides an information archive for Collins radio equipment. **Publications:** The Signal, quarterly. Newsletter. Alternate Formats: online.

21066 ■ Friends of Radio for Peace International (FRFPI)
PO Box 3165
Newberg, OR 97132
E-mail: info@rfpi.org
URL: http://www.rfpi.org
Contact: Debra L. Latham, CEO

Founded: 1980. **Members:** 1,000. **Membership Dues:** individual, $40 (annual) ● family, organization, $50 (annual) ● life, $1,000. **Staff:** 15. **Budget:** $200,000. **Languages:** English, French, German, Spanish. **Description:** Promotes and supports Radio For Peace International, a short-wave radio station dedicated to peace, which broadcasts worldwide as well as on the Internet. Conducts educational programs. Broadcasts new courses each quarter that

includes topics such as peace, environment, human rights, social justice, and marginalized peoples. **Libraries: Type:** reference; not open to the public. **Holdings:** 5,000. **Subjects:** media, communication. **Awards:** Distinguished World Citizen Award. **Frequency:** annual. **Type:** recognition. **Recipient:** for extraordinary public service ● World Citizen Humanitarian. **Frequency:** annual. **Type:** recognition. **Formerly:** Earth Communications. **Publications:** Vista (in English, German, and Spanish), quarterly. Newsletter. Includes program announcements, progress reports, and schedule of broadcasts. **Price:** included in membership dues. **Circulation:** 1,000. **Advertising:** accepted. Alternate Formats: CD-ROM; magnetic tape. **Conventions/Meetings:** annual International Advisory - meeting (exhibits) - always January.

21067 ■ International Amateur Radio Union (IARU)
PO Box 310905
Newington, CT 06131-0905
Ph: (860)594-0200
Fax: (860)594-0259
E-mail: iaru@iaru.org
URL: http://www.iaru.org
Contact: David Sumner, Sec.

Founded: 1925. **Members:** 159. **Regional Groups:** 3. **Description:** Federation of national amateur radio societies. Purpose is to represent the interests of radio amateurs, encourage effective agreements among national amateur radio societies, enhance and promote amateur radio, and further international goodwill. **Affiliated With:** American Radio Relay League. **Publications:** Calendar, semiannual. Newsletter. **Circulation:** 250. **Conventions/Meetings:** periodic meeting ● annual regional meeting.

21068 ■ International Handicappers' Net (IHN)
300 Luman Rd., No. 40
Phoenix, OR 97535
Ph: (541)535-6797
E-mail: calburt@charter.net
URL: http://webpages.charter.net/calburt
Contact: Calvin J. Burt, Pres./Mgr.

Founded: 1958. **Members:** 4,000. **Staff:** 8. **Description:** Licensed radio amateurs who have a disability or handicap of some kind. Promotes international fellowship by radio communication among handicapped and nonhandicapped licensed radio amateurs. Seeks to assist and enable handicapped and disabled persons to enter the worldwide fraternity of amateur radio operators. Makes referrals for specialized equipment, devices, and modification to meet specific needs. Operates radio network on 14287 MHz at 1600 to 1800 UTC (1500 to 1700 UTC during daylight savings time), Monday through Friday. **Convention/Meeting:** none. **Also Known As:** (1984) International Order of Handicapped Radio Amateurs. **Publications:** Brochure.

21069 ■ International Radio Club of America (IRCA)
PO Box 60241
Lafayette, LA 70596
E-mail: ircamember@ircaonline.org
URL: http://www.ircaonline.org
Contact: Philip Bytheway, Ed.-in-Chief

Founded: 1964. **Members:** 200. **Membership Dues:** SDXM/DXM in U.S., $30 (annual) ● DXM in Canada, $36 (annual) ● DXM and SDXM in U.S., $35 (annual) ● DXM and SDXM in Canada, $41 (annual). **Staff:** 11. **Description:** For radio enthusiasts interested in listening for distant radio stations on the standard AM broadcast band. Members are known as BCB DXers (for broadcast band radio listeners) and collect "QSLs" (or verifications of reception). Provides members with tips on radio listening, answers to questions on the radio industry, and information from the Federal Communications Commission. **Libraries: Type:** reference. **Awards:** Ric Heald Award. **Frequency:** annual. **Type:** recognition. **Recipient:** for outstanding contribution for a single year ● Ted Vasilopoulos Award. **Frequency:** annual. **Type:** recognition. **Recipient:** for substantial contribution to the hobby. **Committees:** Countries List. **Affili-**

ated With: Association of North American Radio Clubs. **Publications:** *Countries List*, annual. Directory. Lists countries that have MW stations. ● *DX Monitor*, 30/year. Newsletter. Contains members' logs, articles on radio stations, receiver reviews, technical articles, and DX tips. **Price:** included in membership dues; $30.00 /year for nonmembers. ISSN: 0899-9732. **Circulation:** 100. Alternate Formats: online ● *IRCA Almanac*, periodic ● *IRCA Membership List*, annual. Membership Directory ● *Mexican Log*, annual. Booklet. Lists AM stations in Mexico. **Price:** $10.00 in U.S. and Canada. **Circulation:** 100 ● *Slogans List*. **Price:** $5.00 for members; $6.00 for nonmembers; $5.50 overseas ● *TIS List* ● Also publishes abbreviations list and technical manual. **Conventions/Meetings:** annual convention, gathering of some members hosted by a member (exhibits) ● annual DX Contest - competition.

21070 ■ Lambda Amateur Radio Club (LARC)
PO Box 21669
Cleveland, OH 44121-0669
E-mail: larc@lambdaarc.com
URL: http://www.lambdaarc.com
Contact: Mr. Doug Braun, Pres.
Founded: 1975. **Members:** 40. **Membership Dues:** individual, $20 (annual). **Staff:** 5. **Budget:** $1,000. **Description:** Gay, lesbian, bisexual, and transgender amateur radio operators, short wave radio listeners, and others interested in radio, electronics, and computers; anyone supportive of sexual minorities. Acts as a forum for the exchange of information among gay men and lesbians interested in ham radios. Offers support; fosters sense of community among members. Promotes the Amateur Radio Service. Conducts "on the air meetings" several times a week. Aids members in obtaining their Amateur Radio Licenses. Offers "DXPeditions," trips to exotic locations for amateur radio operations. Sponsors charitable programs. Conducts speakers' bureau; offers educational programs. **Libraries: Type:** reference. **Subjects:** amateur radio. **Awards: Frequency:** annual. **Type:** recognition. **Publications:** *Lambda Net News*, monthly. Newsletter. **Price:** included in membership dues. **Circulation:** 70. **Advertising:** accepted. **Conventions/Meetings:** annual Dayton Hamvention - competition (exhibits) - usually in May ● regional meeting.

21071 ■ Longwave Club of America (LWCA)
45 Wildflower Rd.
Levittown, PA 19057
Ph: (215)945-0543
E-mail: weoliver@comcast.net
URL: http://www.lwca.org
Contact: John Davis, Contact
Founded: 1974. **Members:** 530. **Membership Dues:** regular, in U.S. and Canada, $21 (annual) ● regular, outside U.S. and Canada, $26 (annual). **Description:** Amateur radio enthusiasts and others interested in reception and transmission of radio signals below 540 KHz, the longwave part of the radio spectrum. Seeks to: explore possibilities and techniques in longwave transmissions; encourage DXing; promote activity on the 1750 meter band. **Convention/Meeting:** none. **Libraries: Type:** reference. **Holdings:** archival material. **Subjects:** newsletters. **Affiliated With:** Association of North American Radio Clubs. **Publications:** *Beacon Guide*, periodic ● *Beacon Guide Updaters*, 3/year ● *Lowdown*, monthly. Newsletter. Provides information on transmissions and experimental work in longwave radio; covers work on the 1750 Meter band. **Price:** included in membership dues. **Circulation:** 550 ● *Lowdown Index*, annual.

21072 ■ North American Shortwave Association (NASWA)
45 Wildflower Rd.
Levittown, PA 19057
Ph: (215)945-0543 (610)678-0937
Fax: (610)921-6256
E-mail: rdangelo3@aol.com
URL: http://www.naswa.net
Contact: Richard A. D'Angelo, Exec. Dir.
Founded: 1961. **Members:** 2,000. **Membership Dues:** regular (in U.S., Canada, and Mexico), $29 ●

regular (in Central/South America and Europe), $36 ● regular (in Asia, Africa and Pacific), $40. **Description:** Comprised of radio hobbyists and professional monitors and individuals interested in the hobby of shortwave broadcast monitoring and/or program listening. Provides a means for exchanging information, news and ideas. **Committees:** Awards Program; Country List. **Affiliated With:** Association of North American Radio Clubs. **Publications:** *The Journal*, monthly. Covers international broadcast transmissions on shortwave radio. Contains frequencies and descriptions of program content. **Price:** included in membership dues. ISSN: 0160-1989. **Circulation:** 1,600. **Conventions/Meetings:** annual Winter Shortwave Listeners Festival - convention, with seminars and forums about shortwave radio monitoring.

21073 ■ Old Old Timers Club (OOTC)
c/o Milbert Wells, Exec. Sec.
3191 Darvany Dr.
Dallas, TX 75220-1611
Ph: (214)352-4743
E-mail: maw5jnk@sbcglobal.net
URL: http://www.ootc.us
Contact: Milbert Wells, Exec. Sec.
Founded: 1947. **Members:** 4,301. **Membership Dues:** individual, $10 (annual) ● life (age 85-89), $75 ● life (age 80-84), $100 ● life (age 75-79), $125 ● life (below age 75), $150. **Staff:** 14. **Budget:** $11,000. **Regional Groups:** 11. **State Groups:** 6. **Local Groups:** 7. **Multinational. Description:** Men and women active in amateur, military, or commercial radio communication forty or more years ago. Seeks to provide contact between members through radio communication and publications. Maintains biographical archives of members. The Old Old Timers Club is distinct from The Old Timers' Club (see separate entry). **Libraries: Type:** not open to the public. **Holdings:** 1. **Subjects:** actuaries and biographical info of members. **Awards:** Year Awards. **Type:** recognition. **Recipient:** for those celebrating 50 years, 60 years, and 70 years. **Publications:** *OOTC Roster*, triennial. Membership Directory. Contains call sign, listing of first calls referenced to last calls, all members living or dead listed, constitution/bylaws and officers/directors. **Price:** $20.00. Alternate Formats: CD-ROM ● *Spark Gap Times*, quarterly. Contains news, membership biographies and articles. **Price:** $10.00/year. **Circulation:** 1,000. **Conventions/Meetings:** annual conference.

21074 ■ Quarter Century Wireless Association (QCWA)
c/o Chuck Walbridge, Gen. Mgr.
PO Box 3247
Framingham, MA 01705-3247
Ph: (508)405-1930
Fax: (508)405-1965
E-mail: qcwagm@rcn.com
URL: http://www.qcwa.org
Contact: Chuck Walbridge, Gen. Mgr.
Founded: 1947. **Members:** 10,000. **Membership Dues:** individual, $20 (annual) ● individual, $35 (biennial) ● individual, $50 (triennial) ● life, $300. **Staff:** 2. **Local Groups:** 187. **Description:** Amateur radio (wireless) operators throughout the world who were licensed for operation at least 25 years ago. Encourages friendship and cooperation among members; to promote interest in amateur radio communications and in the advancement of electronics; to use the knowledge and experience of members for the benefit of all radio amateurs. Compiles statistics. Resources include hall of fame. **Libraries: Type:** reference. **Holdings:** 500; archival material, books, periodicals. **Subjects:** history of communications, including rosters of clubs and associations from 1910 to the present. **Awards:** Hall of Fame Award. **Type:** recognition. **Recipient:** for QCWA member who made an outstanding contribution to amateur radio ● Silent Key Scholarship Award. **Frequency:** annual. **Type:** scholarship. **Recipient:** for students who are radio amateurs. **Computer Services:** Mailing lists, of members. **Committees:** Scholarship. **Publications:** *Hotline Report*, quarterly. **Advertising:** accepted ● *Membership Roster*, annual. Membership Directory. **Price:** $10.00. Alternate Formats: CD-ROM ● *News*,

quarterly. Newsletter ● *QCWA Journal*, quarterly. **Price:** $5.00/year. **Conventions/Meetings:** semiannual board meeting - always fall ● annual conference ● annual convention.

21075 ■ Worldwide Television-FM DX Association (WTFDA)
PO Box 501
Somersville, CT 06072
E-mail: mbugaj@snet.net
URL: http://www.anarc.org/wtfda
Contact: Tim McVey, Contact
Founded: 1968. **Members:** 270. **Membership Dues:** in U.S., $24 (annual) ● in Canada, $26 (annual) ● full-time student, $15 (annual). **Description:** Individuals from various countries interested in watching/listening to distant television and radio programs (VHF, UHF, and FM radio only). DX is a radio term meaning distance. **Computer Services:** Mailing lists. **Affiliated With:** Association of North American Radio Clubs. **Formerly:** (1967) Worldwide Monitors Radio Club. **Publications:** *VHF-UHF Digest*, monthly. Bulletin. Contains member reports of abnormal VHF and UHF signal propagation; also contains FM and TV station changes, technical data, and equipment reviews. **Price:** included in membership dues. **Circulation:** 300. **Advertising:** accepted. Alternate Formats: online ● *WTFDA TV Station Guide*. Provides a complete listing of North American television stations. **Conventions/Meetings:** annual convention.

Amusement Parks

21076 ■ National Amusement Park Historical Association (NAPHA)
PO Box 871
Lombard, IL 60148-0871
E-mail: admin@napha.org
URL: http://www.napha.org
Contact: James Futrell, Historian
Founded: 1978. **Members:** 1,100. **Membership Dues:** household, corporate, $40 (annual) ● institution, $35 (annual) ● household, corporate outside North America (with one copy of all publications), $55 (annual) ● institution outside North America, $45 (annual) ● household, corporate outside North America (with two copies of all publications), $80 (annual). **Staff:** 15. **Description:** Persons interested in the preservation and history of past and present amusement parks. Promotes the enjoyment of amusement parks; acquires and documents information concerning amusement parks; preserves and displays memorabilia from amusement parks. Presents audiovisual shows to the public, civic groups, and libraries. **Awards:** Life Membership Award. **Frequency:** annual. **Type:** recognition. **Recipient:** for leadership in and commitment to preserving the heritage and tradition of the amusement park industry. **Publications:** *NAPHA News*, bimonthly. Journal. **Price:** included in membership dues. **Circulation:** 500 ● *NAPHA Newsflash*, monthly. Newsletter. Contains news on today's amusement parks. **Price:** included in membership dues. **Circulation:** 500. **Conventions/Meetings:** convention - 3/year ● meeting - 5/year.

Animal Breeding

21077 ■ American Miniature Llama Association (AMLA)
PO Box 8
Kalispell, MT 59903
Ph: (406)755-3438
E-mail: amla@lamaregistry.com
URL: http://www.miniaturellamas.com
Contact: Julie Chapman, Pres.
Founded: 1999. **Membership Dues:** general, $25 (annual). **Description:** Provides information and opportunities to owners, breeders and individuals interested in miniature llamas. Aims to raise healthy llamas with good breeding conformation. **Computer Services:** database, llama records ● information services, miniature llama standard and classifications.

Animals

21078 ■ Alpaca Llama Show Association (ALSA)

c/o Cheryl Ryberg, Sec.
607 California Ave.
Pittsburgh, PA 15202
Ph: (412)761-0211
Fax: (412)761-0212
E-mail: alsa@nauticom.net
URL: http://www.alsashow.org
Contact: Cheryl Ryberg, Sec.

Membership Dues: adult, $45 (annual) ● life, $500 ● youth (18 years or younger), $25 (annual). **Description:** Promotes and sanctions Llama and Alpaca shows. **Computer Services:** Online services, membership directory. **Publications:** Directory, annual. Lists shows and articles relating to showing and grooming Llamas and Alpacas.

21079 ■ American Gerbil Society (AGS)

18893 Lawrence 2100
Mount Vernon, MO 65712
E-mail: donna.anastasi@agsgerbils.org
URL: http://www.agsgerbils.org
Contact: Donna Anastasi, Pres.

Founded: 1999. **Membership Dues:** individual, $10 (annual) ● family, $17 (annual) ● junior, $5 (annual). **Languages:** English, Portuguese, Spanish. **Multinational. Description:** Represents the interests of breeders, owners and gerbil enthusiasts. Promotes the humane treatment of gerbils and other rodents. Supports and educates its members concerning proper breeding and caring for gerbils. Compiles and maintains a breeder listing, gerbil registration records and show records. Creates and maintains an Internet resource to facilitate membership, gerbil registration and owner education. **Telecommunication Services:** electronic mail, mountash@mfx.net. **Publications:** *Gerbil Tales*, quarterly. Newsletter. **Price:** included in membership dues. Alternate Formats: online ● Brochure. **Price:** free. Alternate Formats: online.

21080 ■ American Working Dog Federation (AWDF)

c/o Al Govednik, Pres.
4282 Illinois Hwy. 17
Alpha, IL 61413
Ph: (309)334-3403
E-mail: algovfh@yahoo.com
URL: http://www.awdf.net
Contact: Al Govednik, Pres.

Founded: 1989. **Description:** Develops awareness of the need to provide a broader base to represent the working dog throughout the world. Preserves and protects the heritage of the various working breeds in America. Seeks to have American working titles recorded and recognized worldwide. Aims to become affiliated with the Federation Cynologique Internationale (FCI).

21081 ■ American Working Malinois Association (AWMA)

c/o Cele Danner, Membership Chair
8146 Old State Rd.
Mattoon, IL 61938
Ph: (217)234-2999
E-mail: cele61920@yahoo.com
URL: http://www.workingmalinois.com
Contact: Anne Camper, Pres.

Membership Dues: individual, $30 (annual) ● family, $50 (annual). **Description:** Preserves and promotes the Belgian Malinois breed. Promotes IPO and Schutzhund training for the working dog. Furthers the development and maintenance of the Belgian Malinois as a working dog. Supports the use of working dogs for search and rescue work, police work, guide dog work and in other ways for which working dogs are utilized. **Telecommunication Services:** electronic mail, anne_c@erc.montana.edu. **Publications:** *AWMA Magazine*, quarterly. Alternate Formats: online.

21082 ■ Federation for the American Staffordshire Terrier (FAST)

c/o Leri Hanson
619 W 35th St.
Long Beach, CA 90806
Ph: (562)427-2259
E-mail: msalpha2u@aol.com
URL: http://www.fast.4t.com
Contact: Calise A. Shoemaker, Pres.

Membership Dues: club, $50 ● individual in North America, $25 ● individual outside North America, $40 ● family in North America, $30 ● family outside North America, $45. **Description:** Preserves and promotes the American Staffordshire Terrier as a working dog. Educates the members and the general public about the proper maintenance of the breed.

21083 ■ International Lama Registry (ILR)

PO Box 8
Kalispell, MT 59903
Ph: (406)755-3438
Fax: (406)755-3439
E-mail: ilr@lamaregistry.com
URL: http://www.llamaregistry.com
Contact: Kathi McKinney, Pres.

Membership Dues: regular, associate, $45 (annual) ● youth associate, $10 (annual). **Description:** Promotes registration of llamas, guanacos, and crossbreds (llama-alpacas, llama-guanacos, etc.). The group takes the spelling 'Lama' instead of 'Llama' because the genus name for three of the four South American camelids is Lama and the registry covers more camelids than just the llama (but does not accept camels, for which there is a separate registry). **Publications:** *ILReport*, monthly. Newsletter. **Price:** included in membership dues. **Advertising:** accepted. Alternate Formats: online.

21084 ■ North American Saddle Mule Association (NASMA)

c/o Leslie Packard, Exec.Sec.
445 Lane Rd.
Chester, NH 03036
Ph: (603)490-9530
Fax: (603)483-2669
E-mail: lpackard@email.msn.com
URL: http://www.nasma.net
Contact: Leslie Packard, Exec.Sec.

Founded: 1994. **Members:** 740. **Membership Dues:** individual, $20 (annual) ● life, $250 ● individual, $120 (10/year) ● youth, $10 (annual). **Description:** Represents and promotes saddle mules as exceptional show, trail and pleasure animals, and promotes the saddle mule industry. **Awards:** Lifetime Achievement Award. **Type:** recognition ● Youth scholarships. **Frequency:** annual. **Type:** scholarship. **Publications:** *Mules and More*, monthly. Magazine. **Price:** $24.00/year. **Advertising:** accepted ● *Saddle Mule News*.

21085 ■ Southwestern Donkey and Mule Society (SDMS)

c/o Lou Ann Guthrie, Sec.
7973 FM 1126
Barry, TX 75102
Ph: (903)695-2395
E-mail: ccqh1@airmail.net
URL: http://www.swdonkeymulesociety.com
Contact: Rori Travis, Pres.

Founded: 1973. **Membership Dues:** individual, family, $15 (annual). **Description:** Promotes and represents the interest of donkey and mule owners in Southern and Western United States. **Awards:** High Point Donkey. **Type:** recognition ● High Point Mule. **Type:** recognition ● High Point of the Year. **Frequency:** annual. **Type:** recognition ● High Point Sub-Junior. **Type:** recognition ● High Point Youth. **Type:** recognition ● Southwestern Donkey and Mule Society Scholarship. **Type:** scholarship. **Committees:** Hearing; Show. **Programs:** Scholarship. **Publications:** *Mule News and Donkey Tales*, quarterly. Newsletter. **Price:** included in membership dues. **Conventions/Meetings:** annual banquet, with White Elephant Auction ● annual meeting ● show.

Antiques

21086 ■ Abingdon Pottery Club (APC)

c/o Linda Thomas
1544 180th St.
Galesburg, IL 61401
Ph: (309)462-2951
E-mail: atkins@abingdon.net
URL: http://www.abingdon.net/~aacc/content/pottery.html
Contact: Linda Thomas, Contact

Founded: 1977. **Members:** 230. **Membership Dues:** single, $8 (annual) ● joint, $10 (annual). **Description:** Promotes collection of and historical interest in Abingdon pottery. **Publications:** *Abingdon Pottery Club—Newsletter*, quarterly. **Price:** included in membership dues. **Circulation:** 300 ● Catalogs. Contains Abingdon pottery. **Conventions/Meetings:** seminar ● annual show and banquet.

21087 ■ American Historical Print Collectors Society (AHPCS)

94 Marine St.
Farmingdale, NY 11735-5605
E-mail: currierives2000@yahoo.com
URL: http://www.ahpcs.org

Founded: 1975. **Members:** 565. **Membership Dues:** regular, $35 (annual) ● contributing, overseas, $50 (annual) ● patron, $75 (annual) ● benefactor, $100 (annual) ● life, $1,000. **Budget:** $35,000. **Description:** Collectors of original American historical prints, including aquatints, mezzotints, etchings, copper and steel engravings, and lithographs and woodcuts; dealers in prints; museum print curators; art historians; others interested in early American graphic art. Seeks to foster the collection, preservation, study, and exhibition of original prints produced from the 17th through the 19th centuries in America. Conducts limited research in order to identify, locate, and authenticate old prints. Sponsors traveling print exhibitions. **Libraries:** Type: open to the public. **Awards:** Ewell L. Newman Award. **Frequency:** annual. **Type:** monetary. **Recipient:** for a book or books using historical American prints to present an important subject also, $500 award ● **Frequency:** annual. **Type:** fellowship. **Computer Services:** Mailing lists, self-sticking labels. **Publications:** *American Historical Print Collectors Society—Newsletter*, quarterly. Announces museum exhibitions of historical American prints and lists auction prices of prints. Includes calendar of events. **Price:** included in membership dues. ISSN: 0277-7061. **Circulation:** 565. **Advertising:** accepted ● *An Audubon Concordance-Migration through the Plate Numbers*. Monographs ● *Currier and Ives-The New Best 50*. Monographs ● *Imprint*, semiannual. Journal. Includes guides to major print collections and book reviews; scholarly articles. **Price:** included in membership dues. ISSN: 0277-7061. **Circulation:** 565 ● *Robert Braun: Identifying Audubon Bird Prints, Originals, States, Editions, Restrikes, and Facsimiles and Reproductions*. Monographs ● Membership Directory, annual. Contains alphabetical and geographic lists. ● Bibliographies. **Conventions/Meetings:** annual meeting, 3 days of lectures and exhibits (exhibits) ● seminar and workshop, on printmaking and the care, conservation, and restoration of antique prints.

21088 ■ Antique Stove Association (ASA)

2321 E Pioneer
Duluth, MN 55804
E-mail: moleye1@yahoo.com
URL: http://www.antiquestoveassociation.org
Contact: Norman Howe, Contact

Founded: 1984. **Members:** 650. **Membership Dues:** regular, commercial restorer/dealer, $25 (annual). **Staff:** 2. **Budget:** $6,000. **Description:** Antique stove restorers, dealers, collectors, and interested individuals. Promotes communication among those interested in antique stoves. **Libraries:** Type: reference. **Holdings:** 2,020; books, periodicals. **Subjects:** stove history. **Committees:** Parts Identification. **Publications:** *The Antique Stove Association—Membership Roster*, biennial. Membership Directory. **Price:** included in membership dues. **Circulation:** 650 ● *The Antique*

Stove Association—Yearbook, annual. Covers a different type of antique stove each year; includes quarterly supplement. **Price:** $30.00. **Circulation:** 650 ● *Stove Parts Needed*, quarterly. Newsletter. Contains articles on stove restoration technology, trends in demand and supply, obsolete parts sources, and inventories in need of owners. **Price:** included in membership dues. **Circulation:** 650. **Advertising:** accepted. **Conventions/Meetings:** annual convention (exhibits).

21089 ■ Antique Stove Information Clearinghouse (ASIC)
421 N Main St.
Monticello, IN 47960-1932
Ph: (574)583-6465
Contact: Clifford Boram, Sec.
Founded: 1982. **Languages:** English, French. **For-Profit. Description:** Not an association. Assists antique stove owners in need of stove parts; brings buyers and sellers together. Offers restoration consultation services. Locates, sells, and reprints catalogs. **Libraries: Type:** by appointment only. **Holdings:** 2,000; articles, books, periodicals. **Subjects:** stoves, pre-1935. **Publications:** *How to Get Parts Cast for Your Antique Stove*. Booklet. **Price:** $5.00 including postage ● *What Is My Antique Stove Worth?*. Article.

21090 ■ Antique Telescope Society (ATS)
c/o Dr. Walter H. Breyer, Sec.
1878 Robinson Rd.
Dahlonega, GA 30533
E-mail: whbreyer@alltel.net
URL: http://webari.com/oldscope
Contact: Dr. Walter H. Breyer, Sec.
Members: 200. **Membership Dues:** regular or astronomy club, $40 (annual) ● extended, $72 (biennial) ● student, $25 (annual) ● associate (2nd family member), $10 (annual) ● nonprofit (library, museum, etc.), $30 (annual) ● contributing, $100 (annual) ● sustaining, $250 (annual) ● benefactor, $500 (annual). **Multinational. Description:** Works for the preservation, collection and learning about antique telescopes, historic observatories and related equipment and materials. **Computer Services:** Online services, email discussion group. **Publications:** *Journal of the Antique Telescope Society*, quarterly. **Price:** included in membership dues. **Conventions/Meetings:** annual convention - every fall.

21091 ■ Blue/White Pottery Club (BWPC)
PO Box 460517
Aurora, CO 80015
Ph: (303)690-8649
E-mail: bwstoneware@aol.com
URL: http://www.blueandwhitepottery.org
Contact: Doug Holmes, Sec.
Founded: 1981. **Members:** 550. **Membership Dues:** individual, $15 (annual) ● additional household, $5 (annual) ● additional household under age 12, $1 (annual). **Description:** Collectors of blue/white pottery, and antique stoneware. Conducts educational programs. **Libraries: Type:** reference. **Holdings:** periodicals. **Subjects:** blue and white stoneware. **Publications:** *Blue/White Pottery Newsletter*, quarterly. **Price:** included in membership dues. **Circulation:** 500. **Conventions/Meetings:** annual convention (exhibits) - always second weekend in June.

21092 ■ Chicago Map Society (CMS)
c/o Newberry Library
60 W Walton St.
Chicago, IL 60610
Ph: (312)255-3689 (312)255-3600
E-mail: spadaforad@newberry.org
URL: http://www.newberry.org/smith/cms/cms.html
Contact: David Spadafora, Pres./Librarian
Founded: 1976. **Members:** 180. **Membership Dues:** general, $25 (annual) ● contributing, $50 (annual) ● sustaining, $100 (annual). **Description:** Represents teachers, collectors, librarians, dealers, and interested individuals. Supports and encourages the study and preservation of maps and related materials. **Conventions/Meetings:** monthly lecture, includes social gathering.

21093 ■ Conestoga Society (CS)
16725 Collinson
Eastpointe, MI 48021
Contact: C. Noire, Exec. Officer
Founded: 1964. **Members:** 100. **Staff:** 1. **Description:** Persons interested in the history and preservation of the Conestoga wagon.

21094 ■ Foundation for the Study of the Arts and Crafts Movement at Roycroft (FSA/CM)
46 Walnut St.
East Aurora, NY 14052
Ph: (716)652-3333 (716)655-0571
Fax: (716)655-0562
E-mail: info@roycroftshops.com
URL: http://www.roycroft.org
Contact: Kitty Turgeon, Exec. Dir.
Founded: 1989. **Members:** 650. **Membership Dues:** individual, $25 (annual). **Staff:** 3. **Budget:** $55,000. **Description:** Represents individuals interested in getting information about and collecting mission, prairie, and other arts and crafts pieces from the arts and crafts era (1895-1930). Studies the works of William Morris, Elbert Hubbard and Roycrofters, furniture designer Gustav Stickley, and architects Frank Lloyd Wright and Greene & Greene. Encourages the collecting of antiques from the Craftsman era and the Roycroft shops. Operates speakers' bureau. Sponsors educational programs. Group is currently expanding with Elderhostel and higher visibility. **Libraries: Type:** reference. **Holdings:** 100; archival material, books. **Subjects:** arts and crafts, furniture, philosophy, lifestyle; written works or published by Roycrofters and E. Hubbard. **Awards:** Mary Roelofs Stott Fund. **Frequency:** semiannual. **Type:** monetary. **Recipient:** for student or individual involved in writing or music. **Councils:** Mary Roelofs Stott Roycroft Fund. **Publications:** *Annual Issue*, annual. Annual Report. **Price:** included in membership dues ● *Craftsman Homeowner*. Newsletter. Features scholarly articles on the lifestyles and works of the arts and crafts era. **Price:** $7.00/issue; $25.00/year. **Circulation:** 1,000. **Advertising:** accepted. **Conventions/Meetings:** annual Arts and Crafts - California Symposium - conference (exhibits) ● annual meeting.

21095 ■ Magic Lantern Society of the United States and Canada (ML SOCIETY)
c/o Richard Moore, Sec.-Treas.
259 Fitch Hill Rd.
Guilford, CT 06437-1028
Ph: (360)830-5209
E-mail: dmooremls@aol.com
URL: http://www.magiclanternsociety.org
Contact: Sharon Koch, Pres.
Founded: 1977. **Members:** 150. **Membership Dues:** general, $25 (annual). **Regional Groups:** 2. **Description:** Magic lantern collectors and enthusiasts. Promotes the exchange of information among persons interested in magic lanterns (lantern slide projectors dating back to the 17th century) and other kinetic "vintage" type optical toys; collects and tabulate information on magic lantern manufacturers, slide makers, and lantern slide artists; cooperates with libraries in the establishment of an inventory of all slide collections. Maintains speakers' bureau. Sponsors educational and entertainment programs for schools, colleges, historical societies, service clubs, and retirement communities. **Publications:** *Magic Lantern Gazette*, quarterly. Bulletin ● *Membership Book*, annual ● Also publishes occasional reprints and information sheets. **Conventions/Meetings:** biennial convention - usually held in June or July.

21096 ■ The Questers (TQ)
210 S Quince St.
Philadelphia, PA 19107-5534
Ph: (215)923-5183
URL: http://www.questers1944.org
Contact: Janet Holly, Natl. Pres.
Founded: 1944. **Members:** 13,750. **Membership Dues:** general, $15 (annual). **State Groups:** 19. **Local Groups:** 850. **Description:** Promotes the study and appreciation of antiques and objects of art and their historical backgrounds; aids in the restoration and preservation of historical places. Has donated several antique pieces to the White House and has contributed financially to historic houses, villages, and foundations. Sponsors annual scholarship at Columbia University for graduate studies in the field of architectural restoration. Maintains library of 1000 volumes on history, people, and artifacts. **Awards:** Founder's Award. **Frequency:** annual. **Type:** recognition. **Recipient:** for research conferred on Questers by fellow members. **Publications:** *National Quester Directory*, annual ● *The Quester Quarterly*. Newsletter. **Conventions/Meetings:** annual convention - always May.

Appliances

21097 ■ Antique Fan Collectors Association (AFCA)
c/o Dick Boswell, Treas.
2245 Harrison Ave.
Lincoln, NE 68502
E-mail: president@fancollectors.org
URL: http://www.fancollectors.org
Contact: Geoff Dunaway, Pres.
Founded: 1980. **Members:** 500. **Membership Dues:** junior (under 18, in North America), $25 (annual) ● foreign (outside North America), $70 (annual) ● regular, in North America, $50 (annual). **Staff:** 1. **Description:** Individuals interested in antique mechanical and electrical fans. **Awards:** Michael G. Breedlove Brass Fan Award. **Frequency:** annual. **Type:** recognition. **Recipient:** to a member who has served well beyond the call of duty to support the organization in a variety of ways. **Formerly:** (2001) American Fan Collectors Association. **Publications:** *The Fan Collector*, bimonthly. Newsletter. Includes stories about fans, manufacturers and collectors along with "how-to" articles on fan restoration. **Price:** included in membership dues. **Circulation:** 500. **Advertising:** accepted. **Conventions/Meetings:** annual Fan Fair - convention, with technical and historical seminars and an awards banquet - usually July.

21098 ■ Hoover Historical Center (HHC)
Walsh Univ.
1875 E Maple St.
North Canton, OH 44720-3331
Ph: (330)499-0287 (330)499-9200
Fax: (330)494-4725
E-mail: ahaines@walsh.edu
URL: http://www.walsh.edu/hooverhistoricalcent.htm
Contact: Mrs. Ann Haines, Operations Coor.
Founded: 1978. **Members:** 110. **Staff:** 10. **Multinational. Description:** Promotes the history and heritage of the Hoover family and the Hoover vacuum cleaner company and the evolution of the vacuum cleaner. Maintains historical home of Hoover family with Victorian decor and herb gardens. **Libraries: Type:** reference. **Holdings:** 200; books, periodicals. **Subjects:** Victorian customs, architecture, clothing, vacuum cleaner history, company history, preservation, Ohio politics, agriculture, WWII, herbs and herb gardening. **Awards:** Helen Hoover Rose Award. **Frequency:** annual. **Type:** recognition. **Recipient:** to a volunteer who serves the center consistently and in several areas ● Volunteer of the Year Award. **Frequency:** annual. **Type:** recognition. **Recipient:** for most hours donated. **Subgroups:** Docent; General Volunteer; Herb Society; Hoover Sweepers. **Publications:** *Center News*, quarterly. Newsletter. Contains history column, program descriptions, director's message; reports from the Herb Society President; Sports Page (1860s baseball club), etc. **Price:** free to volunteers. **Circulation:** 150 ● Brochures, periodic. **Price:** free. **Conventions/Meetings:** annual Christmas on Hoover Farm - festival (exhibits) - always first Sunday of December. 2007 Dec. 2, North Canton, OH ● annual Herb Garden Tours - for 1 day, always July ● annual Tales in Thyme - festival, with outdoor storytelling - each Monday in August ● annual Vintage Baseball - competition, with Hoover sweepers play baseball with 1860s rules and vintage attire - May-September.

21099 ■ The Old Appliance Club (TOAC)
PO Box 65
Ventura, CA 93002
Ph: (805)643-3532
E-mail: toac@sbcglobal.net
URL: http://www.antiquestoves.com/toac
Contact: Jack Santoro, Founder
Founded: 1994. **Members:** 6,000. **Membership Dues:** individual in U.S., $39 (quarterly). **Staff:** 4. **For-Profit. Description:** Persons interested in all classic American old home appliances from the 1900s to the 1960s. Gathers and disseminates information on classic home appliance service providers, dealers, and parts. **Libraries: Type:** not open to the public. **Holdings:** 500; archival material, articles, artwork, books, clippings, periodicals. **Subjects:** old mechanical and electrical home appliances, all varieties, makes and models. **Publications:** *The Old Road Home*, quarterly. Newsletter. **Price:** included in membership dues. **Circulation:** 6,000. **Advertising:** accepted. Alternate Formats: online ● Also publishes Classic Range Do-It-Yourself Restoration Series.

Arms

21100 ■ Armor and Arms Club (AAC)
c/o Dean K. Boorman, Pres.
Dean Boorman & Associates
40 Edgemont Rd.
Montclair, NJ 07042-2305
Ph: (973)744-8838
Fax: (973)746-4814
E-mail: dboorman@comcast.net
Contact: Dean K. Boorman, Pres.
Founded: 1921. **Members:** 115. **Membership Dues:** by invitation, $50 (annual). **Budget:** $5,000. **Description:** Brings together persons interested in ancient arms, armor and antique arms. **Awards: Frequency:** semiannual. **Type:** grant. **Recipient:** for museums and visiting scholars. **Publications:** Newsletter, 5/year. **Conventions/Meetings:** dinner - 4-5/year.

21101 ■ Japanese Sword Society of the United States (JSS/US)
PO Box 513
Albuquerque, NM 87103-0513
E-mail: barry@hennick.ca
URL: http://www.jssus.org
Contact: Barry Hennick, Ombudsman
Founded: 1960. **Members:** 1,000. **Membership Dues:** regular in U.S. and Canada, $40 (annual) ● regular outside U.S. and Canada, $60 (annual). **Description:** Collectors of Japanese samurai swords and related objects united to discuss and illustrate the study, preservation, and history of samurai blades, their furnishings, and related arts. Encourages research and publication of articles pertaining to this field; supports translation program to make available to members articles appearing originally in languages other than English. **Libraries: Type:** reference. **Holdings:** 150; books, video recordings. **Subjects:** swords, fittings, armour. **Publications:** *Art and the Sword*, annual. Bulletin ● Newsletter, bimonthly ● Newsletter, bimonthly. **Advertising:** accepted.

21102 ■ Miniature Arms Collectors/Makers Society (MACMS)
c/o William Adrian, Pres.
2502 Fresno Ln.
Plainfield, IL 60544
Ph: (815)254-8692
E-mail: mas-memship@msn.com
URL: http://www.miniaturearms.com
Contact: William Adrian, Pres.
Founded: 1973. **Members:** 200. **Membership Dues:** regular, in U.S., $30 (annual) ● regular, outside U.S., $35 (annual). **Staff:** 6. **Multinational. Description:** Professionals, craftsmen, and other individuals interested in collecting or making all types of miniature arms. Seeks to establish high ethical standards in the making and collecting of miniature arms; promotes the knowledge of miniature arms and their historical importance; studies and preserves fine miniature arms for posterity. Disseminates informa-

tion about miniature arms. **Libraries: Type:** open to the public. **Holdings:** photographs. **Awards: Type:** recognition. **Committees:** Competition. **Affiliated With:** National Rifle Association of America. **Also Known As:** Miniature Arms Society. **Publications:** *The Art of Miniature Firearms*, periodic. Book. Includes some of the finest collector's items in existence and exquisite replicas of accessories. **Price:** $100.00/copy, plus shipping and handling; $50.00 for miniature print, plus shipping and handling ● *Miniature Arms*, quarterly. Journal. Includes biographies and how-to articles. **Price:** free, for members only. **Circulation:** 300. **Advertising:** accepted. **Conventions/Meetings:** annual Houston Gun Show (exhibits) - always April/May ● annual meeting (exhibits) - always April or May.

21103 ■ National Automatic Pistol Collectors Association (NAPCA)
PO Box 15738
St. Louis, MO 63163
Ph: (314)638-6505
E-mail: info@napca.net
URL: http://napca.net
Contact: Tom Knox, Pres.
Founded: 1968. **Members:** 850. **Membership Dues:** regular, in U.S. and Mexico, $50 (annual) ● regular, in Canada, $55 (annual) ● international, $65 (annual). **Staff:** 3. **Description:** Collectors of semiautomatic pistols. Provides forum for exchange of information about the hobby. Members conduct research on an individual basis. **Libraries: Type:** reference. **Holdings:** 300. **Subjects:** firearms. **Awards: Type:** recognition. **Formerly:** Auto Mag or Automatic Magazine. **Publications:** *Auto Mag*, monthly. Magazine. **Price:** included in membership dues ● Directory, annual. **Conventions/Meetings:** annual meeting.

21104 ■ Winchester Arms Collectors Association (WACA)
PO Box 367
Silsbee, TX 77656
Ph: (409)385-5768
Fax: (409)385-5726
E-mail: david.bichrest@winchestercollector.org
URL: http://www.winchestercollector.org
Contact: David P. Bichrest, Exec. Sec.
Founded: 1977. **Members:** 1,800. **Membership Dues:** regular, in U.S., $40 (annual) ● regular, in Canada, $50 (annual) ● in other country, $60 (annual) ● life, $750. **Staff:** 1. **Budget:** $100,000. **Description:** Individuals interested in Winchester arms and accessories produced during the life of the Winchester Repeating Arms Company. Sponsors research. Promotes firearm ownership. Conducts specialized education; compiles statistics. Conducts three meetings per year. **Libraries: Type:** not open to the public. **Holdings:** 40. **Subjects:** arms history, American history, frontiers. **Awards:** WACA Bronze Award. **Frequency:** annual. **Type:** recognition. **Recipient:** for outstanding educational displays. **Computer Services:** Online services, answer questions on Winchester arms history. **Affiliated With:** National Rifle Association of America. **Publications:** *The Winchester Collector*, quarterly. Journal. Contains information on Winchester and American history. **Price:** included in membership dues. **Circulation:** 2,000. **Advertising:** accepted ● *Winchester Reloading Tools and Implements*. Handbook ● Membership Directory. **Price:** available to members only. **Conventions/Meetings:** periodic board meeting, in conjunction with the collector shows (exhibits) ● annual Cody Gun Show - conference and show (exhibits) ● annual Eastern Show (exhibits) ● annual Western Show (exhibits) - in Reno, NV.

Art

21105 ■ North American Quilling Guild (NAQG)
c/o Tina Reed, Membership Chair
515 State St.
Salina, KS 67401

E-mail: info@naqg.org
URL: http://www.naqg.org
Contact: Patricia Caputo, Pres.
Founded: 2000. **Membership Dues:** in U.S., $25 (annual) ● in Canada, $30 (annual) ● Mexico and abroad, $35 (annual). **Multinational. Description:** Represents enthusiastic and dedicated quillers worldwide. Promotes the art of quilling and ensures that it is passed on to future generations. Provides support and assistance to help quillers discover and perfect their quilling technique, and share information, patterns, and tips. **Telecommunication Services:** electronic mail, president@naqg.org. **Publications:** *Quill America*, quarterly. Newsletter. **Price:** included in membership dues. Also Cited As: *QA*.

Artifacts

21106 ■ Authentic Artifact Collectors Association (AACA)
c/o Cliff Jackson, Pres.
323 Hamme Mill Rd.
Warrenton, NC 27589
E-mail: president@theaaca.com
URL: http://www.theaaca.com
Contact: Cliff Jackson, Pres.
Founded: 1998. **Members:** 2,658. **Description:** Promotes the collection of legally procured, authentic ancient artifacts. Helps new collectors recognize real and fake artifacts. Upholds the rules of conduct pertaining to the collection and the sale of ancient relics. **Publications:** Newsletter, quarterly. Alternate Formats: online.

Artists

21107 ■ Sandicast Collectors Guild
3300 W Castor St.
Santa Ana, CA 92704-3908
Ph: (714)424-0111
Free: (800)233-0070
Fax: (714)424-0054
E-mail: sales@jillsonroberts.com
URL: http://www.sandicast.com
Founded: 1990. **Membership Dues:** regular, in North America (includes gift sculpture), $25 (annual) ● regular, outside North America (includes gift sculpture), $30 (annual). **Description:** Represents collectors of sculpted animal work by Sandra Brue for the Sandicast Collection. **Publications:** *Paw Press Guild Newsletter*. **Price:** included in membership dues ● Catalog. **Price:** included in membership dues.

21108 ■ Thomas Kinkade Collectors' Society
c/o Members Service Department
900 Lightpost Way
Morgan Hill, CA 95037
Free: (800)366-3733
Fax: (408)201-5232
E-mail: collectors_society@kinkade.com
URL: http://www.thomaskinkade.com
Membership Dues: regular, $65 (annual). **Description:** Collectors of works of art by the artist, Thomas Kinkade. **Publications:** *The Beacon*, quarterly. Newsletter. Contains information about Thom, his family, travel and events. Features product information, fun contests, and photos.

Arts

21109 ■ Quimper Club International
c/o Susan Cox, Sec.
6715 Desco Dr.
Dallas, TX 75225
E-mail: contact@quimperclub.org
URL: http://www.quimperclub.org
Contact: Susan Cox, Sec.
Founded: 1999. **Membership Dues:** regular, $40 (annual) ● regular, $100 (triennial). **Multinational. Description:** Aims to educate and inform its mem-

bers about Quimper faience and other French faience. Promotes appreciation and encourages collection of Quimper faience. Fosters fellowship and interaction among members. **Telecommunication Services:** electronic mail, secretary@quimperclub. org. **Publications:** *QClub Update*, monthly. Newsletter. **Price:** included in membership dues. Alternate Formats: online ● Journal, semiannual. Features reference and information articles about Quimper pottery. **Price:** included in membership dues. **Advertising:** accepted ● Membership Directory.

Arts and Crafts

21110 ■ Studio Art Quilt Associates (SAQA)
PO Box 572
Storrs, CT 06268-0572
Ph: (860)487-4199
E-mail: msielman@sbcglobal.net
URL: http://www.saqa.com
Contact: Martha Sielman, Exec. Dir.
Founded: 1989. **Members:** 750. **Membership Dues:** active, in U.S., $40 (annual) ● professional artist in U.S., $105 (annual) ● active, outside U.S., $50 (annual) ● professional artist outside U.S., $115 (annual) ● sponsor, $100 (annual) ● patron, corporate, $500 (annual) ● angel, platinum, $5,000 (annual) ● gold, $1,000 (annual). **Staff:** 1. **Budget:** $70,000. **Regional Groups:** 17. **Multinational. Description:** Serves artists working in the art quilt medium. Seeks to establish art quilts as contemporary fine art; documents the historical significance of the art quilt movement; educates the public; serves as a forum for the professional development of quilt artists; acts as a resource for curators, dealers, consultants, teachers and collectors. Maintains speakers' bureau. **Awards:** Cream Award. **Frequency:** annual. **Type:** monetary. **Recipient:** to a deserving rookie. **Publications:** *SAQA Journal* ● Newsletter, 3/year. Addresses the professional needs of artists working in the art quilt medium. **Price:** included in membership dues. **Circulation:** 1,000. **Advertising:** accepted ● Bulletin. Alternate Formats: online. **Conventions/Meetings:** The Business of Fiber Art - conference (exhibits) ● symposium.

Astrology

21111 ■ Council of Vedic Astrology (CVA)
4601 W Lovers Ln.
Dallas, TX 75209
Ph: (214)352-2488
E-mail: members@councilvedicastrology.org
URL: http://www.councilvedicastrology.org
Contact: Dennis Flaherty, Pres.
Founded: 1993. **Membership Dues:** student initial registration, $50 ● professional initial registration, $95 ● supporting, $500 (annual) ● life, $1,008. **Description:** Seeks to understand and promote the art and practice of Vedic astrology. Provides access and communication within the growing community of Vedic astrologers. **Formerly:** (2003) American Council of Vedic Astrology. **Publications:** Journal, semiannual. **Price:** included in membership dues ● Membership Directory. **Price:** included in membership dues. **Conventions/Meetings:** annual conference ● annual symposium and lecture.

Astronomy

21112 ■ Amateur Astronomers, Inc. (AAI)
PO Box 111
Garwood, NJ 07027-0111
Ph: (908)276-2730
E-mail: clayton2@netzero.net
URL: http://www.asterism.org
Contact: Dr. Lew Thomas, Corresponding Sec.
Founded: 1949. **Members:** 320. **Membership Dues:** initial, $3 (annual) ● regular, $21 (annual) ● sustaining, $31 (annual) ● sponsor, $46 (annual) ● family, $5 (annual). **Staff:** 25. **Budget:** $5,000. **Description:**

Individuals united to further knowledge of astronomy and to popularize astronomy with the public. Has designed, built, and installed an observatory-quality 10-inch refractor telescope and a 24-inch Cassegrain reflector telescope. Conducts monthly lecture and weekly open house at Sperry Observatory; sponsors eclipse and astrophotographic field trips, star parties, and research and educational programs; offers scholarship. Maintains speakers' bureau. **Libraries: Type:** not open to the public. **Holdings:** 1,000. **Subjects:** astronomy, optics, science. **Awards:** E.T. Pearson Scholarship. **Frequency:** annual. **Type:** scholarship. **Recipient:** for an astronomy major. **Computer Services:** Mailing lists. **Telecommunication Services:** electronic bulletin board, (732)709-0569 ● hotline, events update line, (732)276-STAR. **Committees:** Computer; Eclipse Expeditions; Education; Instrument Qualification; Observation; Research; Technical. **Publications:** *The Asterism*, 9/year. Newsletter. **Price:** included in membership dues. **Circulation:** 600 ● *Sperry Observations: Journal of Amateur Astronomers*, annual. **Conventions/Meetings:** monthly General Membership Meeting - general assembly - September through May, on the 3rd Friday.

21113 ■ Association of Lunar and Planetary Observers (ALPO)
c/o Matthew L. Will, Sec.-Treas.
PO Box 13456
Springfield, IL 62791-3456
E-mail: will008@attglobal.net
URL: http://www.lpl.arizona.edu/alpo
Contact: Julius L. Benton Jr., Exec. Dir.
Founded: 1947. **Members:** 650. **Membership Dues:** sustaining, $60 (annual) ● sponsor, $120 (annual). **Multinational. Description:** Promotes among amateur astronomers lunar and planetary astronomy via telescopic observation. **Awards:** Walter Haas Observing Award. **Frequency:** annual. **Type:** recognition. **Recipient:** for observational skill. **Computer Services:** Information services, website contains latest observational data and guidance for performing observations. **Programs:** Lunar and Planetary Training. **Sections:** Comets; Computing; Eclipses; Instruments; Jupiter; Lunar; Mars; Mercury; Mercury/Venus Transits; Meteorites; Meteors; Minor Planets; Publications; Remote Planets; Saturn; Solar; Venus; Youth. **Affiliated With:** Astronomical League. **Publications:** *ALPO Section Directory*, annual. Membership Directory. **Price:** $5.00. Alternate Formats: CD-ROM ● *Journal of the Association of Lunar and Planetary Observers*, quarterly. Includes book reviews, section reports, announcements, and news of future solar system events to be observed. **Price:** included in membership dues. ISSN: 0039-2502. **Circulation:** 650. **Advertising:** accepted. **Conventions/Meetings:** annual conference (exhibits).

Automobile

21114 ■ 71 429 Mustang Registry
c/o Mr. Marvin Scothorn, Dir.
6250 Germantown Pike
Dayton, OH 45418-1634
E-mail: mescothorn@earthlink.net
URL: http://429mustangcougarinfo.50megs.com/71_429_mustang_registry.htm
Contact: Mr. Marvin Scothorn, Dir.
Founded: 1981. **Members:** 235. **Description:** Owners and admirers of 1971 Ford Mustang automobiles. Promotes restoration and preservation of these cars. **Libraries: Type:** reference. **Subjects:** information on accurate restoration of 71 429 mustangs. **Computer Services:** database ● mailing lists.

21115 ■ 1937-1938 Buick Club
PO Box 21000
Oakland, CA 94620
E-mail: torquetube3738@yahoo.com
URL: http://clubs.hemmings.com/frameset. cfm?club=1937-1938buick
Contact: Mark Jordan, Ed.
Founded: 1980. **Members:** 600. **Membership Dues:** regular in U.S. and elsewhere, $40 (annual) ● regular

in Canada, $35 (annual). **Staff:** 2. **Budget:** $14,000. **Multinational. Description:** Owners of Buick automobiles manufactured in 1937-38. Promotes restoration and preservation of 1937-38 Buicks. Conducts social activities; provides technical assistance to members. **Publications:** *Torque Tube*, bimonthly. Magazine. Features information, tips and stories about cars. **Circulation:** 560. **Advertising:** accepted. **Conventions/Meetings:** annual East and West Coast Meets - meeting - always summer.

21116 ■ 1948-50 Packard Convertible Roster
84 Hoy Ave.
Fords, NJ 08863
Ph: (732)738-7859
Fax: (732)738-7625
E-mail: stellacapp@earthlink.net
Contact: Stella Pyrtek-Blond, Ed.
Founded: 1990. **Staff:** 2. **Description:** Owners of 1948-50 Packard convertible automobiles; interested others. Promotes preservation and enjoyment of the automobiles. **Convention/Meeting:** none. **Affiliated With:** Packard Club. **Publications:** *Roster of 1948-50 Packard Convertibles*, annual. Newsletter. **Price:** $5.00/issue.

21117 ■ 1953-54 Buick Skylark Club
c/o Joanne DePeppo, Treas.
51 Statesville Quarry Rd.
Lafayette, NJ 07848
Fax: (973)300-0022
E-mail: buick5354@aol.com
URL: http://members.aol.com/buick5354
Contact: Joanne DePeppo, Treas.
Founded: 1978. **Members:** 200. **Membership Dues:** single, $15 (annual) ● family, $20 (annual). **Description:** Owners and admirers of Buick Skylark automobiles built in 1953 and 1954. Promotes preservation and maintenance of classic Buicks. Serves as a clearinghouse on 1953 and 1954 Buick Skylarks; facilitates communication and good fellowship among members. **Publications:** Newsletter, quarterly. **Conventions/Meetings:** annual meet.

21118 ■ 1956 Studebaker Golden Hawk Owners Register
31654 Wekiva River Rd.
Sorrento, FL 32776-9233
E-mail: fjagh56@earthlink.net
URL: http://www.1956goldenhawk.com
Contact: Frank Ambrogio, Contact
Founded: 1989. **Members:** 260. **Staff:** 1. **Description:** Owners of 1956 Studebaker Golden Hawks. **Formerly:** (1999) 56 Studebaker Golden Hawk Owners Register. **Publications:** *56J Only*, 3/year. Newsletter. **Price:** free. **Circulation:** 295. Alternate Formats: online. **Conventions/Meetings:** annual National Studebaker Meeting - general assembly.

21119 ■ 1958 Cadillac Owners Association
c/o David Becker, Dir
PO Box 850029
Braintree, MA 02185
Ph: (781)843-4485
E-mail: sdn58@aol.com
URL: http://www.1958cadillac.com
Contact: David Becker, Dir.
Founded: 1991. **Members:** 690. **Membership Dues:** life, $22. **Staff:** 2. **Multinational. Description:** Owners and admirers of 1958 Cadillac automobiles. Promotes preservation and restoration of 1958 Cadillacs. Facilitates communication among members; gathers and disseminates information on 1958 Cadillacs. **Libraries: Type:** by appointment only; reference. **Holdings:** archival material, articles, books, business records, clippings, periodicals. **Subjects:** 1958 Cadillacs. **Telecommunication Services:** electronic mail, coa1958@aol.com. **Formerly:** (1991) 1958 Cadillac Owners Association of New England. **Publications:** *Newsletter of Motordom's Masterpiece*, bimonthly. **Price:** included in membership dues. **Advertising:** accepted ● Membership Directory, annual. **Advertising:** accepted. **Conventions/Meetings:** semiannual Cadillac Day - show - always 3rd Sunday of May and first Sunday after the 4th of July.

21120 ■ 1965-66 Full Size Chevrolet Club
c/o Harold J. Foos, Pres.
15615 State Rd. 23
Granger, IN 46530
E-mail: paul.c@attglobal.net
URL: http://clubs.hemmings.com/6566fscc
Contact: Harold J. Foos, Pres.
Founded: 1983. **Members:** 2,120. **Membership Dues:** regular, $18 (annual) ● foreign, $23 (annual). **Staff:** 7. **Description:** Represents owners and enthusiasts interested in the preservation and restoration of Chevrolet 1965-66 Caprice, Impala SS, Impala, Bel Air, and Biscayne automobiles. Holds local and regional swap meets. **Libraries:** Type: reference. **Holdings:** 15; archival material. **Subjects:** 1965 and 1966 full size Chevrolets. **Computer Services:** Mailing lists. **Committees:** Steering. **Publications:** *Cross Flags*, bimonthly. Newsletter. **Advertising:** accepted ● *1965-66 Full-Size Chevrolet Club—Newsletter*, bimonthly. Provides technical information on available parts for Chevrolet automobiles built during 1965-66. Includes classified ads for parts. **Price:** included in membership dues. **Circulation:** 1,581. **Advertising:** accepted ● *1965-66 Full Size Chevrolet Club—Roster*, periodic ● Directory, bimonthly. **Conventions/Meetings:** annual International Meet - banquet, with cars, parts, vendors (exhibits) - summer ● annual meet ● show - 3/year.

21121 ■ 1970 Dart Swinger 340s Registry
PO Box 9
Wethersfield, CT 06129-0009
Ph: (860)257-8434
E-mail: dartsclub@snet.net
URL: http://clubs.hemmings.com/frameset.
    cfm?club=1970DART
Contact: Joel Cooper, Contact
Founded: 1986. **Members:** 200. **Staff:** 1. **Budget:** $500. **Description:** Owners of 1970 Dodge Dart "Swinger 340" automobiles. Works to locate and authenticate all 13,785 1970 Dodge Dart Swinger 340s known to have been produced. **Libraries:** Type: reference. **Holdings:** 20; books, clippings. **Subjects:** Dodges. **Publications:** *Scat Chat*, quarterly. Newsletter. Lists car shows and swap meets across the U.S. and Canada. **Price:** $10.00 donation. **Circulation:** 300. **Advertising:** accepted. Alternate Formats: online. **Conventions/Meetings:** annual Chrysler Convention - convention and show, with one show - always weekend before Labor Day.

21122 ■ 1971 GTO and Judge Convertible Registry
14906 Ferness Ln.
Channelview, TX 77530
Ph: (281)452-0855
E-mail: gcgtos@aol.com
URL: http://www.gulfcoastgtos.com
Contact: Eric L. Stevens, Contact
Founded: 1989. **Members:** 50. **Staff:** 1. **Description:** Represents owners of 1971 GTO or Judge Convertibles. Collects vehicle registry information to locate, verify, and record data on the number of these vehicles still existing. **Libraries:** Type: reference; not open to the public. **Holdings:** books, periodicals. **Computer Services:** database, of colors, engines and transmissions. **Affiliated With:** GTO Association of America.

21123 ■ 1995 Corvette Pace Car Registry
c/o T. Noel Osborn, Dir.
11825 IH-10 W, Ste.213
San Antonio, TX 78230-1040
Ph: (210)641-7733
Fax: (210)641-9654
E-mail: thewave@texas.net
URL: http://www.idavette.net/clubs/95registry.htm
Contact: T. Noel Osborn, Dir.
Founded: 1995. **Members:** 180. **Budget:** $1,000. **Description:** Participates in national Corvette events. Compiles history and track of 1995 pace cars for eventual inclusion in archives of National Corvette Museum. **Publications:** *Pacesetter*, quarterly. Newsletter. Features review of events and issues around the '95 Corvette Pace cars. **Price:** free. **Circulation:** 180. **Advertising:** accepted.

21124 ■ 66,67,68 High Country Special Mustang Registry
6874 Benton Ct.
Arvada, CO 80003-4244
Ph: (303)424-3866
E-mail: hicountrybob@comcast.net
Contact: Bob Teets, Founder
Founded: 1982. **Description:** Owners and enthusiasts of High Country Special Mustang automobiles, model years 1966, '67, and '68. Collects and decodes descriptive information contained in vehicle information numbers. Compiles statistics. Assists enthusiasts, owners and potential owners. **Convention/Meeting:** none. **Publications:** none. **Libraries:** Type: reference. **Formerly:** (1993) 66,67,68 High Country Special.

21125 ■ Abarth Register, U.S.A. (ARUSA)
c/o Gerald Rothman
54 School St., Ste.102
Westbury, NY 11590-4469
Ph: (516)876-8754
Contact: Gerald Rothman, Dir.
Founded: 1973. **Members:** 250. **Membership Dues:** individual, in U.S., $35 (annual) ● individual, outside U.S., $40 (annual). **Staff:** 3. **Languages:** English, French, German, Italian. **Description:** Owners of Abarth and Cisitalia automobiles, vintage Italian race cars manufactured from 1949 to 1971. Established to restore, preserve, and enjoy the Abarth and Cisitalia marque. Members gather 3-4 times a year in the U.S. and Europe to participate in races with their Abarths and Cisitalias. Maintains hall of fame. **Libraries:** Type: reference. **Holdings:** archival material. **Subjects:** Abarth and Cisitalia races and history from 1949-present. **Awards:** Golden Scorpion Award for Outstanding Service. **Frequency:** annual. **Type:** recognition. **Recipient:** for achievement in service. **Publications:** *The Stinger*, quarterly. Membership Directory. **Circulation:** 250. **Advertising:** accepted. **Conventions/Meetings:** annual Concorso Italiano - meeting, with sport clothing and vintage cars (exhibits) - always August, Quail Lodge, Carmel Valley, CA ● Mille Miglia - always May, Brescia, Italy ● annual Monterey Historic Auto Race - competition (exhibits) - always August. Monterey, CA.

21126 ■ Airflow Club of America (ACA)
c/o John Librenjak, Pres.
3595 McKinley St.
Riverside, CA 92506
Ph: (951)788-4678
Fax: (951)788-4087
E-mail: librenjak@sbcglobal.net
URL: http://www.airflowclub.com
Contact: John Librenjak, Pres.
Founded: 1962. **Members:** 600. **Membership Dues:** active, $28 (annual) ● joint, $30 (annual) ● regular, outside North America, $35 (annual). **Staff:** 6. **Regional Groups:** 3. **Description:** Owners and fanciers of Chrysler and DeSoto airflow automobiles and Dodge airflow trucks (1934-37). Focuses on the restoration and preservation of these automobiles and their related history and lore. **Libraries:** Type: not open to the public. **Publications:** *Airflow Directory*, annual ● *Airflow Newsletter*, monthly. **Conventions/Meetings:** annual meeting.

21127 ■ Alfa Romeo Association (ARA)
PO Box 1458
Alameda, CA 94501
E-mail: vice-president@alfaromeoassociation.org
URL: http://www.alfaromeoassociation.org
Contact: Stan Deller, VP
Membership Dues: regular, $30 (annual) ● associate, $35 (annual). **Description:** Promotes the ownership, maintenance, preservation, operation and enjoyment of vehicles produced by Alfa Romeo. **Publications:** *Overheard Cams*, monthly. Magazine. **Price:** included in membership dues. **Circulation:** 600. **Advertising:** accepted. **Conventions/Meetings:** monthly meeting - every 1st Wednesday except January and December.

21128 ■ Alfa Romeo Owners Club (AROC)
PO Box 12340
Kansas City, MO 64116-0340
Ph: (816)459-7462
Free: (877)399-2762
E-mail: admin@aroc-usa.org
URL: http://www.aroc-usa.org
Contact: Jolene Justus, Admin.
Founded: 1958. **Members:** 4,800. **Membership Dues:** individual, family, $60 (annual). **Staff:** 1. **Regional Groups:** 47. **Description:** Owners and enthusiasts of Alfa Romeo automobiles. Promotes knowledge of the history and tradition of the Alfa Romeo marque; provides technical information for efficient and safe operation of Alfas. Chapters organize socials and amateur driving events and conduct technical seminars and driver's schools to teach safe and skillful driving on the highway and in competitions. **Libraries:** Type: reference. **Subjects:** technical manuals. **Publications:** *Alfa Owner*, monthly. Magazine. Contains club news, upcoming events and chapter happenings. **Price:** included in membership dues. **Circulation:** 5,000. **Advertising:** accepted ● Manuals. **Conventions/Meetings:** annual meeting.

21129 ■ Allante Appreciation Group (AAG)
Address Unknown since 2006
URL: http://66.34.30.72/
Founded: 1994. **Members:** 1,800. **Membership Dues:** $40 (annual). **Description:** Owners or interested fans organizing to enhance the appreciation of the Cadillac Allante automobile. Provides services, lending library, support groups and sponsors Local and National meets. **Libraries:** Type: lending. **Subjects:** Cadillac Allante cars. **Telecommunication Services:** electronic mail, marsteller.j.a.@wcsmail.com. **Publications:** *Allante World*, 8/year. Newsletter. Contains tech information, hints, tips, and personal interest stories. **Price:** included in membership dues. **Conventions/Meetings:** periodic meeting, local and national meets.

21130 ■ AMC Pacer Club (AMCPC)
c/o Frank E. Wrenick, Pres./Founder
2628 Queenston Rd.
Cleveland Heights, OH 44118-4320
URL: http://www.amcpacer.com
Contact: Frank E. Wrenick, Pres./Founder
Founded: 1993. **Members:** 250. **Membership Dues:** standard, $12 (annual). **Description:** Persons interested in the Pacer automobiles manufactured by American Motors Corporation from 1975-1980. Promotes and encourages the preservation, restoration, and collection of Pacers as well as the collection and preservation of all forms of information and printed material relating to them. **Publications:** *Pacer News*, quarterly. Newsletter. **Circulation:** 250. **Conventions/Meetings:** annual convention and meet.

21131 ■ AMC Rambler Club (AMCRC)
c/o Brian Yacino, Pres.
6 Murolo Rd.
North Grosvenordale, CT 06255-1814
Ph: (860)923-0485
E-mail: brian.yacino@amcrc.com
URL: http://www.amcrc.com
Contact: Brian Yacino, Pres.
Founded: 1980. **Members:** 1,300. **Membership Dues:** regular, in U.S., $24 (annual) ● regular, in Canada, $26 (annual) ● overseas, $33 (annual). **State Groups:** 19. **Local Groups:** 10. **Multinational. Description:** Individuals interested in 1958-1969 American Motors Corporation automobiles. Encourages and promotes the preservation, restoration, and collection of these automobiles, as well as the collection and preservation of all forms of information and printed material relating to them. Provides a parts locator service and technical and mechanical assistance services. **Libraries:** Type: reference. **Holdings:** books, papers. **Awards:** Type: recognition. **Publications:** *Ad Release*, monthly. Brochure. **Price:** $8.00/year in U.S.; $9.00/year in Canada; $10.00/year overseas ● *AMC Rambler Club—Roster and Parts Guide*, annual. **Price:** included in membership dues. **Circulation:** 1,300 ● *Club Store Handbook* ● *1958-1969 Production Handbook* ● *The Rambler*

Reader, quarterly. Newsletter. Contains general and technical information on AMC Rambler automobiles. **Price:** included in membership dues. **Circulation:** 1,300. **Conventions/Meetings:** Local Meets ● annual National/International Meet.

21132 ■ American Austin/Bantam Club (AABC)

c/o Marilyn Sanson, Treas.
724 Maple Dr.
Kirkville, NY 13082
Ph: (315)656-7568
E-mail: echancellor@kyonline.net
URL: http://clubs.hemmings.com/clubsites/americanaustinbantam
Contact: Elmer Chancellor, Pres.
Founded: 1962. **Members:** 750. **Membership Dues:** regular, in U.S., $20 (annual) ● regular, outside U.S., $25 (annual). **Description:** Owners and enthusiasts of American Austin and American Bantam cars, trucks, jeeps, and trailers built in Butler, PA from 1930 to 1936. Aims to promote preservation and restoration of American Austin (1930-36) and American Bantam (1938-41) vehicles. Offers free classified advertisement service to members; conducts car show competitions. **Awards:** Roy Evans Trophy. **Frequency:** annual. **Type:** trophy. **Publications:** *American Austin/Bantam Club News*, bimonthly. Newsletter. Includes restorations, classified, events, and personal stories. **Price:** included in membership dues. **Advertising:** accepted ● *American Bantam Owner's Manual* ● *Membership and Vehicle Roster*, annual. Membership Directory. **Conventions/Meetings:** annual meet and show (exhibits).

21133 ■ American Bugatti Club (ABC)

600 Lakeview Terr.
Glen Ellyn, IL 60137
Ph: (630)380-5480 (773)380-5480
E-mail: quiltbug57@sbcglobal.net
URL: http://www.AmericanBugattiClub.org
Contact: Paul Simms, Sec.
Founded: 1960. **Members:** 450. **Membership Dues:** regular, $75 (annual) ● junior (under 30 years old), $30 (annual). **Description:** Promotes the preservation and appreciation of the work of Ettore Bugatti (1881-1947), provides network for owners of Bugatti motor cars and other enthusiasts. Maintains a Registrar of Bugattis in North America. **Publications:** *Membership List*, quinquennial. Membership Directory ● *Pur Sang*, quarterly. Journal. Includes information on member activities, technical and research information, and calendar of events. **Price:** included in membership dues; $75.00/year. **Circulation:** 500. **Advertising:** accepted. **Conventions/Meetings:** periodic rally.

21134 ■ American Camaro Association (ACA)

5786 Buckeye Rd.
Macungie, PA 18062
Ph: (610)966-2492
E-mail: karlz28@earthlink.net
URL: http://clubs.hemmings.com/frameset.cfm?club=americancamaro
Contact: Karl Scheffy, Co-Founder/Pres.
Founded: 1992. **Membership Dues:** regular, $20 (annual). **Description:** Aims to unite Camaro clubs across the nation to post functions and events, exchange information, assist local club editors, and lobby for causes. **Additional Websites:** http://www.americancamaro.org. **Publications:** *Camaro Review*. Newsletter. **Price:** included in membership dues. Alternate Formats: online.

21135 ■ American Chevelle Enthusiasts Society (ACES)

2576 Memorial Blvd., No. 167
Springfield, TN 37172
Ph: (615)643-2237
URL: http://www.chevelles.com/aces/intro.htm
Contact: Chuck Hanson, Pres.
Membership Dues: regular, $40 (annual) ● Canadian, $50 (annual) ● foreign, $70 (annual). **Description:** Works exclusively to preserve and maintain classic 1964-72 Chevelles, Malibus, and El Caminos. **Publications:** *Chevelle World*, bimonthly. Magazine.

Features member's Chevelles car. **Price:** included in membership dues. **Advertising:** accepted.

21136 ■ American Jeepster Club (AJC)

c/o Jim Serr, Pres.
PO Box 653
Lincoln, CA 95648
Ph: (916)645-8761
E-mail: ajc-acct@psyber.com
URL: http://www.off-road.com/jeepster
Contact: Jim Serr, Pres.
Founded: 1988. **Description:** Works to assist American owners of 1966-1973 Jeepsters. Supports members and increases the number of events so as to encourage greater participation on the promotion and preservation of Jeepsters. **Telecommunication Services:** electronic mail, jeepsterjim@psyber.com. **Publications:** Newsletter, quarterly. Contains list of Jeepster owners, vehicle information, parts information, and stock fix-it tips from fellow members. **Price:** $5.00/back issue.

21137 ■ American Lancia Club (ALC)

c/o Neil Pering, Membership Sec.
27744 Via Ventana
Los Altos Hills, CA 94022
Ph: (650)941-7497 (650)424-6835
Fax: (650)493-2689
E-mail: nc-es.pering@prodigy.net
URL: http://americanlanciaclub.org
Contact: Steve Person, Pres.
Founded: 1956. **Members:** 800. **Membership Dues:** regular, in U.S., $35 (annual) ● regular, in Canada or Mexico, $40 (annual) ● all other countries, $45 (annual). **Regional Groups:** 2. **Description:** Represents owners and enthusiasts of Lancia automobiles. Disseminates information on the Lancia automobile including technical tips and advertisements. Works to preserve and display one of the most distinguished and innovative marques in the history of the automobile. **Libraries: Type:** reference. **Holdings:** biographical archives. **Awards: Type:** recognition. **Publications:** *Lancia Enthusiast*, monthly. Newsletter. **Advertising:** accepted ● *Lanciana*, quarterly ● Directory, biennial. **Conventions/Meetings:** semiannual reunion - always in Eastern United States and U.S. West Coast.

21138 ■ American MGB Association (AMGBA)

PO Box 11401
Chicago, IL 60611
Ph: (773)878-5055
Free: (800)723-MGMG
Fax: (773)769-3240
E-mail: info@mgclub.org
URL: http://www.mgclub.org
Contact: Frank J. Ochal, Pres.
Founded: 1975. **Members:** 3,000. **Membership Dues:** regular, in U.S., $35 (annual) ● regular, outside U.S., $45 (annual). **Staff:** 10. **Budget:** $100,000. **Regional Groups:** 12. **State Groups:** 50. **Local Groups:** 38. **Description:** MGB car owners and enthusiasts. Aims to assist owners in the upkeep and maintenance of their cars. Has Local groups that sponsor technical sessions, rallies, and picnics. Provides information on MG Marque history. Compiles statistics on chassis numbers, engine numbers, and other information on cars. **Libraries: Type:** reference. **Holdings:** periodicals. **Subjects:** automobiles. **Awards: Type:** recognition. **Publications:** *The Octagon*, bimonthly. Newsletter. Includes calendar of events and parts availability information. **Price:** included in membership dues. **Circulation:** 4,500. **Advertising:** accepted. **Conventions/Meetings:** annual meeting (exhibits).

21139 ■ American MGC Register (AMGCR)

2809 Copter Rd.
Pensacola, FL 32514
Ph: (850)478-3171
Fax: (850)475-5335

E-mail: amgcr@juno.com
URL: http://www.mgcars.org.uk/amgcr
Contact: Keith Sanders, Chm.
Founded: 1980. **Members:** 700. **Membership Dues:** regular, in U.S. and Canada, $20 (annual) ● regular, outside U.S. and Canada, $25 (annual). **Staff:** 1. **Budget:** $8,000. **State Groups:** 4. **Description:** Owners and enthusiasts of the MGC automobile. Focuses on the preservation and use of the car. Assists members in restoring and locating parts. Makes available regalia, including patches, pins, and buckles. Sponsors competitions; compiles statistics. **Awards: Type:** recognition. **Publications:** *The Best of "C" Notes*. Book. **Price:** $24.95 ● *'C' Notes*, quarterly. Newsletter. **Price:** included in membership dues. **Circulation:** 400. **Advertising:** accepted ● Membership Directory, annual ● Also publishes reprints of workshop manuals and parts lists. **Conventions/Meetings:** annual meet (exhibits) - always August or September.

21140 ■ American Motors Owners Association (AMO)

c/o Don P. Loper
1615 Purvis Ave.
Janesville, WI 53548
Ph: (608)752-8247
E-mail: nashnut@ticon.net
URL: http://www.amonational.com
Contact: Darryl A. Salisbury, Pres.
Founded: 1974. **Members:** 1,900. **Membership Dues:** individual in U.S., $35 (annual) ● individual in Canada and Mexico, $40 (annual) ● overseas, $45 (annual) ● vendor, business, $100 (annual). **Staff:** 1. **Budget:** $45,000. **Regional Groups:** 30. **Description:** Owners and enthusiasts of AMC vehicles built from 1958-1988. Aims to aid and encourage ownership, use, and enjoyment of AMC vehicles; to encourage preservation and restoration of these vehicles; and to increase communications and fellowship among owners. **Libraries: Type:** reference. **Awards: Type:** recognition. **Publications:** *American Motoring Magazine*, bimonthly. **Circulation:** 1,900 ● *Classified American*, 10/year. Contains advertisements only. **Advertising:** accepted ● *Concours Rulebook* ● *Membership Roster*, triennial. Membership Directory. **Conventions/Meetings:** annual International Convention - meet and show, with car show/swap meet (exhibits) - always July or August.

21141 ■ Antique Auto Racing Association (AARA)

c/o Paul O'Malley, Sec.-Treas.
PO Box 181
Capon Bridge, WV 26711
Ph: (304)856-2042
URL: http://www.antiqueautoracing.com
Contact: Dale Mathews, Pres.
Founded: 1973. **Members:** 150. **Description:** Persons interested in the history of auto racing and in preserving, restoring, and driving antique race cars as well as collecting memorabilia related to antique race cars. **Committees:** Technical. **Publications:** *AARA Driver*, monthly. Newsletter. **Price:** included in membership dues. **Advertising:** accepted. **Conventions/Meetings:** Race Meet ● show (exhibits) - 4-5/year.

21142 ■ Antique Automobile Club of America (AACA)

PO Box 417
Hershey, PA 17033
Ph: (717)534-1910
Fax: (717)534-9101
E-mail: general@aaca.org
URL: http://www.aaca.org
Contact: Steven L. Moskowitz, Exec. Dir.
Founded: 1935. **Members:** 65,000. **Membership Dues:** general (includes spouse if applicable), $30 (annual) ● student, $12 (annual) ● junior, $10 (annual) ● life, $600. **Regional Groups:** 400. **Description:** Collectors, hobbyists, and others interested in the preservation, maintenance, and restoration of automobiles and in automotive history. Encourages historical research. Sponsors Glidden Tour. **Libraries: Type:** open to the public. **Holdings:** 100,000;

books, periodicals. **Subjects:** automobiles, commercial vehicles, motorcycles, fire apparatus. **Awards: Type:** recognition. **Publications:** *Antique Automobile*, bimonthly. Magazine. ISSN: 0003-5831. **Circulation:** 40,000. **Advertising:** accepted ● *The Rummage Box*, quarterly. **Conventions/Meetings:** regional meeting and meet - 9/year ● annual trade show (exhibits) - always February, Philadelphia, PA.

21143 ■ Antique Studebaker Club (ASC)
PO Box 1715
Maple Grove, MN 55311-6715
Ph: (763)420-7829
Fax: (763)420-7849
E-mail: registration@cornerstonereg.com
URL: http://www.theantiquestudebakerclub.com
Contact: Mark R. Wheeler, Membership Sec.

Founded: 1971. **Members:** 1,500. **Membership Dues:** regular delivery in U.S., $25 (annual) ● foreign, $42 (annual) ● first class delivery in U.S., $33 (annual). **Multinational. Description:** Private collectors and restorers. Promotes the collection, restoration, and preservation of antique Studebaker vehicles produced before World War II. **Awards:** Albert Erskine Award. **Frequency:** annual. **Type:** recognition. **Recipient:** for the best article about Studebakers restoration. **Committees:** Car Information. **Publications:** *Antique Studebaker Review*, bimonthly. Magazine. Contains information and restoration articles about Pre-war Studebakers. **Advertising:** accepted ● *Roster of Members*, annual. **Conventions/Meetings:** annual International Meet - convention, with car show (exhibits) - June or July.

21144 ■ Aston Martin Owners Club (AMOC)
c/o Susan Laskey, Sec.
645 5th Ave., Ste.900
New York, NY 10022
Ph: (212)830-6160
Fax: (212)265-4350
E-mail: secretary@amoc-na.org
URL: http://www.amoc-na.org/web/index.php
Contact: Susan Laskey, Sec.

Members: 4,000. **Membership Dues:** individual, $163 (annual) ● family, $173 (annual). **Description:** Acts as club for enthusiasts of Aston Martin model vehicles. **Telecommunication Services:** electronic mail, slaskey@freeman-co.com. **Publications:** *AM*. Magazine. **Price:** included in membership dues ● *AMOC Quarterly*. Newsletter. **Conventions/Meetings:** annual meeting.

21145 ■ Auburn-Cord-Duesenberg Club (ACD)
c/o Barbara Pietracatella, Membership Sec.
536 McClean Ave.
Staten Island, NY 10305-3644
Ph: (718)981-0549
E-mail: auburncars@aol.com
URL: http://www.acdclub.org
Contact: Barbara Pietracatella, Membership Sec.

Founded: 1952. **Members:** 2,000. **Membership Dues:** individual in U.S. and Canada, $45 (annual) ● joint in U.S. and Canada, $50 (annual) ● individual (foreign), $70 (annual) ● joint (foreign), $75 (annual) ● life, in U.S., $700 ● life, in Canada, $800 ● life (foreign), $1,400. **Staff:** 10. **Description:** Persons interested in preserving Auburn, Cord, and Duesenberg automobiles. Collects historical material pertaining to ACD automobiles and associated companies; maintains library of books, pamphlets, articles, and photographs. Sponsors competitions. **Awards:** Man/Woman of the Year. **Frequency:** annual. **Type:** recognition. **Publications:** Directory, 10/year. **Price:** included in membership dues. **Advertising:** accepted ● Newsletter, 10/year. **Price:** included in membership dues. **Conventions/Meetings:** annual International Reunion - always Labor Day weekend, in Auburn, IN ● periodic Mini-meets - meeting.

21146 ■ Austin Bantam Society (ABS)
1589 N Grand Oaks Ave.
Pasadena, CA 91104
Ph: (626)791-2617

Fax: (626)798-5746
URL: http://www.sandiegowow.com/pbac
Contact: Norman T. Booth, Membership Chm.
Founded: 1969. **Members:** 320. **Membership Dues:** regular, in U.S., $20 (annual) ● regular, outside U.S., $25 (annual). **Multinational. Description:** Individuals interested in the preservation and restoration of the American Austin and Bantam automobiles. Focuses on pre-World War II British Austin "7s" and cars using genuine Austin and Bantam parts. **Awards: Type:** recognition. **Computer Services:** Mailing lists. **Additional Websites:** http://clubs.hemmings.com/frameset.cfm?club=pbac. **Formerly:** (2006) Pacific Bantam Austin Club. **Publications:** *Rooster Tails*, bimonthly. Includes club news and maintenance advice. **Price:** included in membership dues. **Circulation:** 320 ● Newsletter, periodic. **Conventions/Meetings:** quarterly meeting ● annual meeting, trophy meet and mini-tour ● seminar, instructs members on methods of properly restoring car parts and complete restoration ● annual Trophy Meet - competition.

21147 ■ Austin-Healey Club of America (AHCA)
c/o Mr. Mike Schneider, Membership Dir.
110 N Rastetter
Louisville, KY 40206
Free: (888)5-HEALEY
Fax: (502)893-5410
E-mail: membership@healeyclub.org
URL: http://www.healeyclub.org
Contact: Mr. Mike Schneider, Membership Dir.

Founded: 1961. **Members:** 3,700. **Membership Dues:** individual, $40 (annual). **Regional Groups:** 45. **Description:** Owners or aficionados of Austin-Healey or Austin-Healey Sprite automobiles. Aims to preserve the Austin-Healey and to maintain the highest standards of the marque by sharing technical and mechanical information within the club and with other Austin-Healey clubs worldwide. Functions as a social group for Austin-Healey owners; promotes courtesy and safety on the roads. Conducts programs on restoration and maintenance of the marque; sponsors a judging school. Holds technical sessions, driving events, and competitions. Compiles list of car serial numbers. **Libraries: Type:** reference. **Awards: Type:** recognition. **Publications:** *Healey Marque*, monthly. Magazine. Features technical articles, international and area club news, and events and stories related to the Austin-Healey automobile. **Price:** $40.00/year; $56.00/year overseas surface; $76.00/year overseas air. ISSN: 1523-6463. **Circulation:** 3,800. **Advertising:** accepted ● *Membership Book*, annual. **Price:** included in membership dues. **Circulation:** 3,800. **Advertising:** accepted ● Manuals. Provides information on parts. **Conventions/Meetings:** annual Conclave - meeting.

21148 ■ Austin-Healey Club USA (AHCUSA)
8002 NE Hwy. 99, Ste.B
PMB 424
Vancouver, WA 98665-8813
Ph: (661)328-0953
E-mail: phila@healey.org
URL: http://www.healey.org/index.shtml
Contact: Phillip Anderson, Membership Dir.

Founded: 1961. **Members:** 3,000. **Membership Dues:** regular, in North America, $35 (annual) ● regular, outside North America, $60 (annual). **Description:** Promotes interest in the history, maintenance, restoration and enjoyment of all Austin-Healey vehicles. **Libraries: Type:** reference. **Holdings:** articles. **Awards:** President's Award. **Frequency:** annual. **Type:** recognition. **Recipient:** for individuals with outstanding service to the club. **Publications:** *Austin-Healey Calendar*. **Price:** $5.00 for nonmembers; included in membership dues ● *Austin-Healey Magazine*. **Price:** included in membership dues. **Advertising:** accepted ● *Austin-Healey Resource Book*, annual. **Price:** included in membership dues.

21149 ■ Austin-Healey Sports and Touring Club (AHSTC)
309 E Broad St.
Quakertown, PA 18951-1703
Ph: (215)536-6912

E-mail: info@austin-healey-stc.org
URL: http://www.austin-healey-stc.org
Contact: Rick Brodeur, Membership Coor.
Founded: 1976. **Members:** 400. **Membership Dues:** in U.S., $30 (annual). **Regional Groups:** 6. **Description:** Austin-Healey automobile owners and enthusiasts. Provides social activities, technical information, and vehicle maintenance assistance. Maintains library of repair and technical manuals, historical information, data on cars, and serial numbers. **Awards:** George Null-AHSTC Clubperson of the Year. **Frequency:** annual. **Type:** recognition. **Recipient:** for active club participant who exhibits qualities of the late George Null. **Publications:** *Flash*, monthly. Newsletter. Includes technical information and regional news. ISSN: 0889-9282. **Circulation:** 500. **Advertising:** accepted ● *Membership Listing*, annual. Membership Directory. **Conventions/Meetings:** annual Encounter - convention.

21150 ■ Automobile License Plate Collectors Association (ALPCA)
508 Coastal Dr.
Virginia Beach, VA 23451
E-mail: secretary@alpca.org
URL: http://alpca.org
Contact: Michael Liscio, Sec.-Treas.

Founded: 1954. **Members:** 3,300. **Membership Dues:** regular, in U.S., $29 (annual). **Staff:** 2. **Regional Groups:** 15. **Description:** Persons interested in collecting license plates or related data. Compiles statistics and disseminates information about current and expired license plates, systems of registration, and laws. **Publications:** *The ALPCA Register*, bimonthly. Magazine. **Circulation:** 3,300. **Conventions/Meetings:** annual international conference (exhibits) - always midsummer.

21151 ■ Automobile Objects d'Art Club (AODC)
252 N 7th St.
Allentown, PA 18102
Ph: (610)432-3355
Fax: (610)820-9368
E-mail: oldtoy@aol.com
Contact: David K. Bausch, Pres.

Founded: 1984. **Members:** 24. **Membership Dues:** individual, $25 (semiannual). **Staff:** 1. **Budget:** $25,000. **Local Groups:** 1. **Description:** Individuals interested in objects d'art of early automobiles, such as prints, paintings, and bronzes. Seeks to preserve the history of early motoring. Conducts expositions at art museums; gives lectures and slide presentations. Maintains speakers' bureau and museum; conducts research, educational, and charitable programs. **Libraries: Type:** not open to the public. **Holdings:** 275. **Subjects:** auto history. **Publications:** *Automobilia*, monthly. Newsletter. **Price:** included in membership dues. **Advertising:** accepted. **Conventions/Meetings:** annual meeting ● semiannual workshop (exhibits).

21152 ■ Avanti Owners Association International (AOAI)
c/o Cornerstone Registration
PO Box 1743
Maple Grove, MN 55311-6743
Ph: (763)420-7829
Fax: (763)420-7849
E-mail: mikebaker@aoai.org
URL: http://www.aoai.org
Contact: Mike Baker, Pres.

Founded: 1965. **Members:** 2,000. **Membership Dues:** regular, in U.S., $25 (annual) ● regular, outside U.S., $31 (annual). **Local Groups:** 16. **Multinational. Description:** Owners of Avanti and Avanti II automobiles. Provides members with historical and technical data about the Avanti. **Absorbed:** (1986) Avanti Club of America. **Publications:** *Avanti*, quarterly. Magazine. Contains current information on the Avanti automobile, including articles on repair and parts. **Price:** $25.00/year. **Circulation:** 2,000. **Advertising:** accepted ● *Avanti Owners Association International—Membership Roster*, annual. Membership Directory. Contains listing of current, active members by country and state. **Conventions/Meetings:** annual International Meet - meeting.

21153 ■ Berkeley Exchange (BE)
46 Elm St.
North Andover, MA 01845
Ph: (978)687-3421
Contact: Nat Stevens, Exec. Officer
Founded: 1980. **Members:** 300. **Description:** Owners and enthusiasts of the Berkeley, a British sports car manufactured in Great Britain from 1956 to 1961. The exchange is dedicated to the preservation and restoration of the Berkeley automobile and serves as a network for the exchange of information. Participates in car meets. **Publications:** *Berkeley Exchange,* bimonthly. Newsletter. **Price:** $20.00/year. **Advertising:** accepted. **Conventions/Meetings:** annual meeting.

21154 ■ BMW Car Club of America (BMW CCA)
640 S Main St., Ste.201
Greenville, SC 29601
Ph: (864)250-0022
Fax: (864)250-0038
E-mail: wynne_smith@bmwcca.org
URL: http://www.bmwcca.org
Contact: Wynne Smith, Exec. Dir.
Founded: 1969. **Members:** 49,000. **Membership Dues:** general, $40 (annual). **Staff:** 5. **Local Groups:** 59. **Description:** Owners of BMW (Bavarian Motor Works) automobiles and other interested persons. Promotes interest in BMW automobiles through technical, social, and driving events; encourages the exchange of information among members; club is independent of any commercial interests. Conducts charitable programs. **Libraries: Type:** reference. **Special Interest Groups:** Coupe; Little Cars; Vintage/Classic. **Publications:** *Friends of BMW,* semiannual. Directory. Contains list of volunteers offering assistance to fellow members on the road. **Price:** free to those included in listing; $5.00/copy for other members. **Advertising:** accepted ● *Roundel Magazine,* monthly. Includes product reviews, technical articles, maintenance tips, and articles about classic "Bimmers" to BMWs in racing. **Price:** included in membership dues. **Advertising:** accepted ● Also publishes chapter newsletters. **Conventions/Meetings:** annual Oktoberfest - meeting (exhibits).

21155 ■ BMW CS Registry
c/o Art Wegweiser
5341 Gibson Hill Rd.
Edinboro, PA 16412
Ph: (814)734-5107
E-mail: art@bmwcsregistry.org
URL: http://www.bmwcsregistry.org
Contact: Art Wegweiser, Contact
Founded: 1981. **Membership Dues:** regular, in U.S., $25 (annual) ● regular, outside U.S., $35 (annual). **Description:** Represents special interest group of BMW aficionados of the CS Coupe. **Formerly:** The CS Register. **Publications:** Newsletter, bimonthly. Includes history and promotion of the BMW E9. **Price:** included in membership dues.

21156 ■ BMW Vintage Car Club of America (BMWVCCA)
PO Box S
San Rafael, CA 94913
Ph: (415)897-0220 (415)479-4378
E-mail: tom@bmwvintage.org
URL: http://www.bmwvintage.org
Contact: Thomas V. Graham, Pres.
Founded: 1976. **Members:** 175. **Membership Dues:** $15 (annual). **Description:** Owners and admirers of pre-war, Veritas, 501, and V-8 models of BMW automobiles. Promotes the restoration and preservation of these cars. Facilitates information exchange among members; helps members locate parts. **Convention/Meeting:** none. **Absorbed:** (1986) BMW 507 Register. **Publications:** *BMW Klassiker,* quarterly. Bulletin. Includes classified ads for car parts. **Price:** included in membership dues. **Circulation:** 170. **Advertising:** accepted. Alternate Formats: online ● *BMW Vintage/Classic Register,* annual. Directory.

Lists members and their models of BMWs. **Price:** included in membership dues. **Circulation:** 175.

21157 ■ Borgward Owners' Club (BOC)
77 New Hampshire Ave.
Bay Shore, NY 11706
Ph: (516)273-0458
Fax: (516)666-5446
E-mail: leftyny@aol.com
URL: http://clubs.hemmings.com/frameset.
    cfm?club=borgward
Contact: Dyck Livant, Exec. Off.
Founded: 1974. **Members:** 100. **Membership Dues:** $25 (annual). **Staff:** 1. **Description:** Owners and enthusiasts of Borgward, Goliath, and Lloyd vehicles. Provides members with information about repairs and availability of parts at discount prices. **Publications:** Membership Directory, periodic. **Advertising:** accepted ● Newsletter, quarterly ● Also publishes list of vehicle owners by state. **Conventions/Meetings:** periodic meeting (exhibits).

21158 ■ Boss 302 Registry
c/o Randy Ream
1817 Janet Ave.
Lebanon, PA 17042-1845
Ph: (717)274-5280
E-mail: jfinley2@dhol.org
URL: http://www.boss302.com
Contact: Randy Ream, Contact
Founded: 1981. **Members:** 900. **Membership Dues:** $10 (annual). **Description:** Works to locate all factory Ford Mustang Boss 302's. Compiles statistics; conducts research programs. **Convention/Meeting:** none. **Computer Services:** database, VIN numbers. **Publications:** Newsletter, periodic. **Price:** $10.00/year; $1.50 each (back issue). **Circulation:** 900.

21159 ■ Boss 429 Owners Directory
PO Box 8035
Spokane, WA 99203
Ph: (509)448-0252
E-mail: stephen@bossperformance.com
URL: http://www.bossperformance.com
Contact: Steve Strange, Exec. Off.
Founded: 1974. **Description:** Owners of 1969-1970 Ford Boss 429 Mustangs; other interested individuals. Facilitates exchange of information among members; operates restoration and parts services. Maintains Boss 429 Registry to preserve and record vehicle information. **Libraries: Type:** reference. **Holdings:** archival material, photographs. **Subgroups:** BOSS 429 Registry. **Publications:** *Boss 429 Mustang World Registry.* Books. Provides information on Ford Boss 429 engines and cars. **Price:** $15.00 ● *Boss Performance,* periodic. Newsletter.

21160 ■ Brabham Register
c/o John Hafkenshiel, Founder
1611 Alvina Ave.
Sacramento, CA 95822
Ph: (916)454-1115
Fax: (916)453-0843
URL: http://www.nvo.com/brabhams/registercontact
Contact: John Hafkenshiel, Founder
Founded: 1979. **Members:** 121. **Membership Dues:** individual, $10 (annual) ● one-time fee, $50. **Staff:** 1. **For-Profit. Multinational. Description:** Owners of Brabham racing cars. Promotes the restoration and preservation of Brabham racing cars. Disseminates information on the vehicle to Brabham owners. Offers information on locations to obtain parts for the Brabham. **Convention/Meeting:** none. **Libraries: Type:** reference. **Holdings:** archival material, periodicals. **Subjects:** Brabham racing cars. **Formerly:** (2003) Brabham Owners Register. **Publications:** *Brabham Register Newsletter,* semiannual. Includes technical reports and lists of members. **Price:** included in membership dues. **Circulation:** 120.

21161 ■ Bricklin International Owners Club (BIOC)
664 Hickory Hill Ct.
Streetsboro, OH 44241
Ph: (330)474-1153

Fax: (435)203-1274
E-mail: membership@bricklin.org
URL: http://www.bricklin.org
Contact: Mr. George J. Malaska, Membership Dir.
Founded: 1976. **Members:** 400. **Membership Dues:** individual, in U.S., $40 (annual) ● international, $50 (annual). **Regional Groups:** 13. **Description:** Local car clubs and individuals united for meets, rallies, and technical assistance in the preservation of the out-of-production Bricklin automobile. Compiles statistics. **Awards: Type:** recognition. **Computer Services:** database, members only. **Committees:** Bricklinalia. **Formerly:** Bricklin International; NEA Bricklin Club. **Publications:** *Brickline,* quarterly. Magazine. Provides host of invaluable information relating to parts, service, technical data and appearance tips. **Circulation:** 500. **Advertising:** accepted ● Directory, annual. **Conventions/Meetings:** annual B.I.G. (Bricklins in Gathering) - competition. (exhibits) - usually 3rd week of July ● meet - 3/year ● seminar.

21162 ■ Buick Club of America (BCA)
PO Box 360775
Columbus, OH 43236-0775
Ph: (614)472-3939
Fax: (614)472-3222
E-mail: buickcluboffice@aol.com
URL: http://www.buickclub.org
Contact: Mike Book, Office Mgr.
Founded: 1966. **Members:** 9,700. **Membership Dues:** general, $35 (annual). **Staff:** 2. **Regional Groups:** 6. **Local Groups:** 70. **Description:** Promotes the development, publication, and interchange of technical, historical, and other information among members who are interested in Buick automobiles; also promotes fellowship among members. Encourages the maintenance, restoration, and preservation of all models produced by the Buick Motor Division of General Motors. **Awards:** Buick National Driven Award. **Frequency:** annual. **Type:** recognition. **Recipient:** for local, regional, and national car shows ● Senior Award. **Type:** recognition. **Recipient:** for Buick achieving the highest standards. **Computer Services:** database, membership ● mailing lists. **Publications:** *Buick Bugle,* monthly. Includes restoration and maintenance advice. **Price:** included in membership dues. **Circulation:** 9,700. **Advertising:** accepted ● Membership Directory, biennial ● Also publishes technical and historical information about Buick automobiles. **Conventions/Meetings:** competition ● annual Display Conference (exhibits).

21163 ■ Buick GS Club of America (GSCA)
625 Pine Point Cir.
Valdosta, GA 31602
Ph: (229)244-0577
E-mail: buick455@juno.com
URL: http://www.buickgsca.com
Founded: 1982. **Members:** 5,100. **Membership Dues:** in U.S. and Canada, $35 (annual) ● outside U.S. and Canada, $45 (annual). **Staff:** 4. **Budget:** $150,000. **Regional Groups:** 8. **State Groups:** 14. **For-Profit. Description:** Owners and enthusiasts of the Buick Gran Sport automobile, manufactured from 1965 to 1973, and the Buick Grand National, manufactured in 1986 and 1987. Promotes the collectibility of the high-performance Buick muscle cars. Assists in the upkeep and maintenance of GS and GN automobiles. Provides parts sources and technical information. **Libraries: Type:** reference. **Awards: Type:** recognition. **Computer Services:** Mailing lists, of members. **Telecommunication Services:** electronic mail, webmaster@buickgsca.com. **Publications:** *GS National Directory,* annual ● *GS X-tra,* bimonthly. Magazine. **Price:** free, for members only. **Circulation:** 5,000. **Advertising:** accepted. Alternate Formats: CD-ROM. **Conventions/Meetings:** annual Buick GS Nationals - competition, drag racing (exhibits) ● annual show (exhibits) - always first weekend of May in Bowling Green, KY.

21164 ■ Cadillac Drivers Club (CDC)
c/o Wray Tibbs, Pres.
5825 Vista Ave.
Sacramento, CA 95824-1428

Ph: (916)421-3193
Contact: Wray Tibbs, Pres.
Founded: 1971. **Members:** 130. **Membership Dues:** $25 (annual). **Staff:** 7. **Description:** Drivers of Cadillac and LaSalle automobiles. Promotes Cadillac ownership and maintenance and preservation of classic Cadillacs. Serves as a clearinghouse on Cadillacs and their maintenance; conducts educational programs; sponsors competitions; participates in charitable activities; maintains speakers' bureau; compiles statistics. **Libraries: Type:** reference; not open to the public. **Holdings:** 100; archival material, books, clippings, periodicals. **Subjects:** Cadillac restoration, automotive mechanics. **Awards:** Most-Improved Cars. **Frequency:** annual. **Type:** recognition ● Public Service. **Frequency:** annual. **Type:** recognition. **Computer Services:** Online services. **Publications:** *Leland Letters,* bimonthly. Newsletter. Offers repair tips and historical reviews. **Price:** included in membership dues. **Circulation:** 100. **Advertising:** accepted. **Conventions/Meetings:** annual Apple Hill Tour - October ● annual Father's Day Picnic ● annual Renewal Pot Luck - board meeting - always third Sunday in January.

21165 ■ Cadillac-LaSalle Club (CLC)
PO Box 360835
Columbus, OH 43236-0835
Ph: (614)478-4622
Fax: (614)472-3222
E-mail: clcoffice@cadillaclasalleclub.org
URL: http://www.cadillaclasalleclub.org
Contact: Glenn L. Brown, Pres.
Founded: 1958. **Members:** 7,500. **Membership Dues:** in U.S., $50 (annual) ● in Canada and Mexico, $55 (annual) ● other countries, $65 (annual) ● life - domestic, $750 ● life - foreign, $1,000. **Regional Groups:** 45. **Description:** Persons interested in Cadillac or LaSalle automobiles. Seeks to preserve, restore, and enjoy Cadillac and LaSalle cars of all models. **Awards:** Henry M. Leland Award. **Frequency:** annual. **Type:** recognition. **Recipient:** for an outstanding club member who has performed acts of great merit ● LaSalle Discovery Award. **Frequency:** annual. **Type:** trophy. **Recipient:** for individuals who have promoted the LaSalle automobile ● Newsletter Excellence Award. **Frequency:** annual. **Type:** recognition. **Recipient:** for outstanding newsletter editors ● Norm Uhlir Regional Activity Award. **Frequency:** annual. **Type:** recognition. **Recipient:** for regions that demonstrated outstanding overall activity ● Self-Starter Author of the Year Award. **Frequency:** annual. **Type:** recognition. **Recipient:** for outstanding contributions to the CLC publication. **Absorbed:** Brougham Owners Association. **Publications:** *The Self Starter,* 11/year. Magazine. **Price:** included in membership dues. **Circulation:** 7,500. **Advertising:** accepted ● Directory, annual. Lists members by state and by car. **Advertising:** accepted. **Conventions/Meetings:** annual Grand National - meeting, features meeting culminating in judged car show (exhibits) - summer.

21166 ■ California Association of Tiger-Owners (CAT)
18771 Paseo Picasso
Irvine, CA 92603
Ph: (949)854-2561 (562)906-4457
Fax: (323)912-1961
E-mail: rick@catmbr.org
URL: http://www.catmbr.org
Contact: Rick Mueller, Treas.
Founded: 1969. **Members:** 700. **Membership Dues:** single in U.S., $30 (annual) ● single in Canada, couple in U.S., $32 (annual) ● single outside U.S. and Canada, $40 (annual). **Multinational. Description:** National organization of enthusiasts of Sunbeam Tiger and Alpine automobiles. Provides information about the Sunbeam marque and manufactures supply parts for members. Conducts social functions. Sponsors research programs and specialized education. Compiles statistics. **Libraries: Type:** open to the public. **Holdings:** periodicals. **Subjects:** Sunbeam Tiger, Alpine automobiles. **Awards:** Lord Rootes. **Frequency:** annual. **Type:** recognition. **Committees:** Parts Development; Social. **Publications:**

Roster, annual. Membership Directory. Contains a listing of members. **Price:** free. **Advertising:** accepted ● *Shopnotes Anthology,* annual ● *Tiger Tales,* monthly. Newsletter. Includes schedule of events, technical information, and classified ads from members. **Circulation:** 700. **Advertising:** accepted. **Conventions/Meetings:** monthly meeting ● periodic Tigers United - competition.

21167 ■ Capri Club North America (CCNA)
PO Box 701
Johnstown, OH 43031
E-mail: capri@capriclub.com
URL: http://www.capriclub.com
Contact: Marc Morgan, Club Exec.
Founded: 1997. **Membership Dues:** regular in North America, $15 (annual) ● regular outside North America, $25 (annual). **Multinational. Description:** Represents Ford Capri enthusiasts throughout North America. Preserves the 1969-1987 Ford Capri of Europe. Provides a clearinghouse for Capri owners in the U.S., Canada, Mexico, Caribbean and elsewhere. Facilitates communication and cooperation among members. **Publications:** Newsletter ● Reports. Alternate Formats: online.

21168 ■ Challenger T/A Registry (CTACC)
PO Box 9632
Ketchikan, AK 99901-4632
Ph: (907)225-2709
E-mail: sixpak340@att.net
URL: http://www.challengertaregistry.com
Contact: Barry Washington, Contact
Members: 460. **Staff:** 1. **Multinational. Description:** Dedicated to owners of Dodge Challenger T/A automobiles. **Formerly:** (2004) Challenger T/A Car Club. **Publications:** *Challenger T/A Registry Newsletter,* semiannual, during winter and summer. **Price:** $12.00/year in Canada; $22.00 two years in Canada; $10.00/year in U.S.; $18.00 two years in U.S. **Circulation:** 300. **Advertising:** accepted.

21169 ■ Checker Car Club of America (CCCA)
c/o Roy M. Dickinson, Ed.
10530 W Alabama Ave.
Sun City, AZ 85351-3544
Ph: (623)974-4987
Fax: (623)974-4987
E-mail: info@checkercarclub.org
URL: http://www.checkertaxistand.com/the_checker_car_club_of_america
Contact: Joe Fay, Pres.
Founded: 1982. **Members:** 900. **Membership Dues:** in North America, $20 (annual) ● outside U.S., $25 (annual). **Description:** Individuals interested in Checker automobiles. Promotes the preservation, enjoyment, and exchange of information on Checker automobiles, produced by the Checker Motors Corporation from 1922 to 1982 and traditionally used as taxicabs. Plans to hold national meets. **Computer Services:** Mailing lists. **Publications:** *The Checkerboard News,* quarterly. Newsletter. Contains articles, stories and pictures of Checker cars. **Price:** included in membership dues. **Circulation:** 800. **Advertising:** accepted ● Directory, annual. **Conventions/Meetings:** annual Awkscht Fest - festival (exhibits) - always first Sunday of August in Macungie, PA ● annual California Chapter Meet and Show - every last Sunday of July in Arcadia, CA ● biennial Car Show - always last Saturday of June in Hickory Corners, MI.

21170 ■ Chevrolet Nomad Association (CNA)
PO Box 265
Davenport, NE 68335
Ph: (740)967-1955
E-mail: cna.club@gmail.com
URL: http://www.chevynomadclub.com
Contact: Shelby Roberts, Sec.
Founded: 1989. **Members:** 1,300. **Membership Dues:** in U.S., $30 (annual) ● in Canada, $35 (annual) ● outside U.S. and Canada, $40 (annual). **Staff:** 2. **Regional Groups:** 3. **Description:** Individuals interested in Chevrolet Nomad automobiles manufactured from 1955-57. Works to preserve and show Nomads. **Publications:** *Nomad Post,* 10/year. Maga-

zine. Contains articles about the Nomads, coming events, classified section and information on the annual convention. **Price:** included in membership dues. **Advertising:** accepted. **Conventions/Meetings:** annual meet (exhibits) - mid-July ● annual meeting.

21171 ■ Chevy and Geo Club
PO Box 11238
Chicago, IL 60611
Ph: (773)769-6262
E-mail: info@chevyclub.com
URL: http://www.chevyclub.com/cc.htm
Contact: Robert Thomas, Pres.
Founded: 1984. **Members:** 750. **Membership Dues:** general in U.S., $25 (annual) ● e-member, $15 (annual) ● general outside U.S., $35 (annual). **Budget:** $10,000. **Description:** Owners and admirers of Chevy and Geo automobiles. Promotes Chevy and Geo ownership. Gathers and disseminates information on Chevys and Geos and their care and maintenance. **Formerly:** (1998) Geo Club; (1999) Geo and Chevy Club. **Publications:** *World.* Magazine. **Circulation:** 750. **Advertising:** accepted.

21172 ■ Chevy GMC International Truck Club (CGITC)
PO Box 7411
Midland, TX 79708-7411
E-mail: cgitc@chevygmcclub.com
URL: http://www.chevygmcclub.com
Contact: Joshua Brady, Pres.
Membership Dues: in U.S., $32 (annual) ● in U.S., $55 (biennial) ● outside U.S., $37 (annual) ● family, $5 (annual). **Description:** Dedicated to the preservation and restoration of 1911-1987 Chevy and GMC trucks. **Formerly:** (2004) National Chevy/GMC Truck Association. **Publications:** *Pickups 'n Panels in Print.* Magazine.

21173 ■ Christian Motorsports Ministries (CMM)
PO Box 129
Mansfield, PA 16933
Ph: (570)549-2282
Free: (888)548-2282
E-mail: cpo7@loving-hearts.org
URL: http://www.christianmotorsports.com
Contact: Roland Osborne, Chm.
Founded: 1996. **Members:** 5,000. **Membership Dues:** general, $20 (annual). **Staff:** 7. **Budget:** $250,000. **Multinational. Description:** High energy motorsports interest flavored from the Christian perspective. **Computer Services:** Mailing lists. **Formerly:** (1979) CPPA; (1980) Chrysler Power. **Publications:** *Christian Motorsports Illustrated,* quarterly. Magazine. Includes news and information about motorsports personalities from a spiritual perspective. **Price:** included in membership dues. **Circulation:** 11,000. **Advertising:** accepted ● *CMI News,* monthly. Newsletter. **Price:** included in membership dues. **Advertising:** accepted. **Conventions/Meetings:** annual meet.

21174 ■ Chrysler 300 Club International
4900 Jonesville Rd.
Jonesville, MI 49250
Ph: (517)849-2783
Fax: (517)849-7445
E-mail: crossram@optonline.net
URL: http://www.chrysler300club.com
Contact: Eleanor Riehl, Exec. Sec.
Founded: 1968. **Members:** 1,000. **Membership Dues:** individual, $20 (annual). **Description:** Individuals interested in the preservation of 1955-1965 and 1970 Hurst letter-series 300 automobiles built by Chrysler Corporation. Conducts national and local meets; compiles statistics. Maintains complete up-to-date list of letter Series 300s and owners; also maintains authentication service. Includes projects such as: reproduction parts, N.O.S. parts locating, and copies of factory specifications. **Libraries: Type:** reference. **Committees:** Concours Standards. **Formerly:** Chrysler 300 Club. **Publications:** *Chrysler 300 Club International—Membership Directory,* annual. Features geographically arranged listings.

Price: included in membership dues. **Circulation:** 1,000 ● *Chrysler 300 Club News*, quarterly. Newsletter. Includes calendar of events, classified ads listing cars and parts, minutes of meetings, information on new members, and technical data. **Price:** included in membership dues. **Circulation:** 1,000. **Advertising:** accepted ● *News-Flite*, quarterly. Newsletter. Includes calendar of events and classified ads listing cars and parts. **Price:** included in membership dues. **Circulation:** 1,000. **Advertising:** accepted. **Conventions/Meetings:** semiannual Car Show - spring and fall.

21175 ■ Chrysler Town and Country Owners Registry (CTCOR)

c/o John Slusar
10240 W Natl. Ave.
West Allis, WI 53227-2029
Ph: (414)384-1843
Fax: (414)384-1843
E-mail: tandcregistry@cs.com
URL: http://clubs.hemmings.com/tandcregistry
Contact: John Slusar, Contact

Founded: 1973. **Members:** 430. **Membership Dues:** regular, $35 (annual). **Staff:** 4. **Multinational. Description:** Aims to restore and promote the Chrysler Town and Country automobile of 1941-1950, the Chrysler Royal Station Wagon of 1949-1950, and the Chrysler Le Baron Town and Country Convertible of 1983-1986. **Libraries: Type:** reference. **Holdings:** archival material. **Subjects:** Chrysler Town and Country automobiles, Royal Station Wagon, and Le Baron convertible. **Awards:** Award for Excellence. **Frequency:** annual. **Type:** recognition. **Computer Services:** Mailing lists. **Additional Websites:** http://local.aaca.com/tcor. **Affiliated With:** National Woodie Club; WPC Club. **Publications:** *The Registry*, annual. Directory. Contains directory of owners and roster. **Circulation:** 430 ● *Timber Tales*, quarterly. Newsletter. **Price:** $35.00/year. **Circulation:** 430. **Conventions/Meetings:** periodic Grand National Show, held in conjunction with other Chrysler clubs (exhibits).

21176 ■ Citroen Quarterly Car Club (CQCC)

PO Box 130030
Boston, MA 02113-0001
Ph: (617)742-6604
E-mail: citroenquarterly@comcast.net
URL: http://home.comcast.net/~citroenquarterly
Contact: Michael Cox, Exec. Off./Ed.

Founded: 1982. **Members:** 1,000. **Description:** Promotes the preservation of Citroen automobiles. **Publications:** *Citroen Quarterly*. Journal. Includes technical maintenance articles and classifieds. **Price:** $20.00/year in North America; $25.00/year overseas; $18.00/year in U.S.; $25.00/year in Canada. **Circulation:** 1,000. **Advertising:** accepted ● *Citroen Quarterly Archives*. Journal. **Price:** $5.00/issue in North America; $7.00/issue outside North America. **Alternate Formats:** online. **Conventions/Meetings:** annual Citroen Quarterly Rendezvous - meeting (exhibits).

21177 ■ Classic Car Club of America (CCCA)

1645 Des Plaines River Rd., Ste.7A
Des Plaines, IL 60018-2206
Ph: (847)390-0443
Fax: (847)390-7118
E-mail: classiccarclub@aol.com
URL: http://www.classiccarclub.org
Contact: Jon Lee, Pres.

Founded: 1951. **Members:** 5,000. **Membership Dues:** active in U.S. and Canada and Mexico, $45 (annual) ● regular, outside U.S., $57 (annual) ● associate, $7 (annual). **Regional Groups:** 26. **Multinational. Description:** Hobbyists who collect and restore luxury automobiles built between 1925 and 1948. Annually presents 9 trophies. Maintains library on automotive history; operates museum. **Committees:** Awards; CARavan; Technical Services. **Publications:** *The Classic Car*, quarterly. Magazine. **Price:** available to members only ● Bulletin, 8/year ● Directory, annual. **Conventions/Meetings:** annual conference (exhibits) - always January.

21178 ■ Classic Chevy International (CCI)

5140 S Washington Ave.
Titusville, FL 32780
Ph: (321)269-9680
Free: (800)284-4096
Fax: (321)383-2059
E-mail: info@classicchevy.com
URL: http://www.classicchevy.com
Contact: Michael Wilson, Exec. Off.

Founded: 1974. **Members:** 30,000. **Membership Dues:** in U.S., $39 (annual) ● outside U.S., $54 (annual). **Staff:** 30. **State Groups:** 250. **Description:** Promotes the preservation and restoration of 1955, 1956, and 1957 Chevrolets. Compiles statistics. Supplies variety of reproduction parts for restoration. **Awards: Type:** recognition. **Telecommunication Services:** additional toll-free number, (800)456-1957 ● additional toll-free number, (800)285-7461. **Formerly:** (2004) Classic Chevy Club International. **Publications:** *Classic Chevy World*, monthly. Magazine. Devotes solely to full-size Classic Chevy's 1955-72. ● *How to Restore Your 57 Chevy* ● *Judging/Restoration Guidelines*. Book ● Also publishes shop manuals and factory assembly manuals. **Conventions/Meetings:** periodic competition ● annual convention.

21179 ■ Classic Jaguar Association (CJA)

c/o Dick Strever
524 Elk Valley Rd.
Crescent City, CA 95531
Fax: (707)464-9594
E-mail: strever@email.com
URL: http://www.classicjaguar.org
Contact: Don Becker, Pres.

Founded: 1961. **Members:** 500. **Membership Dues:** individual, $40 (annual). **Staff:** 1. **Description:** International organization of owners or enthusiasts of prewar SS cars and post-war models of Jaguar; also accepts membership of later model Jaguar owners. Has members and officers in 16 countries. Promotes ownership and operation of these automobiles. Conducts technical and historical research. Maintains spare parts coordination worldwide. Gives technical assistance to members and will provide consultation or proofreading service to persons writing about the vehicles. Holds regional concours d'elegance shows, social events, and driving activities. **Libraries: Type:** reference. **Holdings:** 200; articles, books. **Subjects:** technical articles related to services, parts, and owner's manuals for S.S. and Jaguar cars. **Additional Websites:** http://www.classicjaguar.net. **Affiliated With:** Jaguar Clubs of North America. **Publications:** *News and Technical Bulletin*, bimonthly. Contains technical articles on association new cars and parts for sale. **Circulation:** 500. **Advertising:** accepted ● Also offers technical reprint service and publishes SS-1, SS-2, SS Jag, XK-120, XK-140, XK-150 Mark IV and V Registers. **Conventions/Meetings:** semiannual Spring & Fall Swap Meet - meeting, includes swap meet (exhibits) - spring and fall.

21180 ■ Classic Thunderbird Club International (CTCI)

1308 E 29th St.
Signal Hill, CA 90755-1842
Ph: (562)426-2709
Free: (800)488-2709
Fax: (562)426-7023
E-mail: ctcioffice@ctci.org
URL: http://www.ctci.org
Contact: Dave Van Winkle, Pres.

Founded: 1961. **Members:** 8,800. **Membership Dues:** car club, $32 (annual). **Staff:** 2. **State Groups:** 120. **Local Groups:** 114. **Description:** Owners of 1955, 1956, and 1957 Ford Thunderbird cars. Encourages the upkeep and preservation of "classic" Thunderbird automobiles. Maintains library consisting mainly of Ford Motor Co. sales literature, repair manuals, and parts books related to the 1955-1957 Fords and Thunderbirds. Sponsors competitions at local, regional, and national levels. **Publications:** *The Early Bird*, bimonthly. Magazine. Contains relaxed articles, newsletters and items for sale to members. **Price:** included in membership dues. **Circulation:** 7,000. **Advertising:** accepted ● *Membership Roster*, semiannual. Membership Directory ●

Restoration Details Manual ● Also publishes shop manuals and automatic transmission manuals. **Conventions/Meetings:** biennial regional meeting and meet - always odd-numbered years ● biennial Regionals and International Conventions & Car Show - meeting and meet (exhibits) - always even-numbered years.

21181 ■ Club Elite North America (CE)

c/o Michael Ostrov, Sec.
6238 Ralston Ave.
Richmond, CA 94805-1519
Ph: (510)232-7764
Fax: (510)232-7764
E-mail: mikeostrov@webtv.net
Contact: Michael Ostrov, Sec.

Founded: 1970. **Members:** 225. **Membership Dues:** individual, $20 (annual). **Description:** Owners of the 1959-63 Lotus Elite automobile or early Lotus sports racing models. Aids owners in the maintenance of their cars. **Convention/Meeting:** none. **Publications:** *Club Elite Newsletter*, 3/year. **Price:** included in membership dues. **Circulation:** 300. **Advertising:** accepted ● *Club Elite Register*, annual ● Also publishes technical articles, interchangeable parts lists, for sale and wanted lists, and maintenance articles.

21182 ■ Cobra Owners Club of America (COCOA)

672 N Ranchroad Dr.
Orange, CA 92869
Ph: (714)546-5670 (714)970-8991
E-mail: cocoaoc@cocoaoc.org
URL: http://www.cocoaoc.org
Contact: Bob Stockwell, Pres.

Founded: 1963. **Members:** 200. **Regional Groups:** 4. **Description:** Individuals owning automobiles manufactured by Shelby-American, Inc. (Mustang GT-350 or GT-500, Cobra 289, Cobra 427, and Ford GT-40 MK-1, MK-2, or MK-4). Works to advocate on the appreciation, preservation, and restoration of the marque. Conducts social activities and technical and racing programs. **Convention/Meeting:** none. **Libraries: Type:** reference. **Awards: Type:** recognition. **Recipient:** for racing.

21183 ■ Contemporary Historical Vehicle Association (CHVA)

PO Box 493398
Redding, CA 96049-3398
E-mail: raymoan100-carstuff@yahoo.com
URL: http://clubs.hemmings.com/frameset.cfm?club=chva
Contact: Mary Jean Flory, Contact

Founded: 1967. **Members:** 1,300. **Membership Dues:** regular in U.S., $25 (annual) ● regular outside U.S., $35 (annual) ● life, $300 ● junior, $5 (annual). **Budget:** $29,000. **Regional Groups:** 22. **Description:** Dedicated to the preservation, restoration, and acclamation of all road vehicles at least 20 years old. Supports legislation protecting these vehicles and their collectors, conducts research on their history, and seeks accuracy in their restoration; trains in competition judges; sponsors technical information service for members and CHVAid (help for members in distress while traveling in their antique automobiles). Holds two national competition car shows, several regional car shows, and tours across the country each year. **Awards:** Writing Awards. **Frequency:** annual. **Type:** recognition. **Recipient:** for writing. **Publications:** *Action Era Vehicle*, 5/year. **Price:** $4.00/copy. ISSN: 0044-6092. **Circulation:** 1,500. **Advertising:** accepted ● *CHVA Membership Roster*, every 2-3 years. Membership Directory. **Conventions/Meetings:** annual board meeting, with cars, picture albums, regional displays (exhibits) - between May and August.

21184 ■ Corrado Club of America (CCA)

PO Box 29
Bala Cynwyd, PA 19004-0029
E-mail: ccainfo@corrado-club.com
URL: http://www.corrado-club.com
Contact: Jeff Storey, Pres.

Founded: 1995. **Multinational. Description:** Promotes appreciation and preservation of the Volkswagen Corrado. Aims to bring together all Corrado owners and enthusiasts from all over North America through exchange of information. Conducts motor sports activities. **Publications:** *Spoilers Up*, quarterly. Newsletter.

21185 ■ Corvair Society of America (CORSA)
PO Box 607
Lemont, IL 60439-0607
Ph: (630)257-6530
Fax: (630)257-5540
E-mail: corvair@corvair.org
URL: http://www.corvair.org
Contact: Harry Jensen, Exec. Sec.
Founded: 1969. **Members:** 5,500. **Membership Dues:** domestic, $38 (annual). **Staff:** 2. **Budget:** $200,000. **Local Groups:** 133. **Multinational. Description:** Enthusiasts of the Corvair automobile united for technical assistance and parts availability. Holds national and local meets. **Awards:** Frank Winchell Memorial Corvair Scholarship. **Frequency:** annual. **Type:** scholarship. **Committees:** Competitions; Concours; Museum; Parts and Repairs; Technical. **Publications:** *CORSA Communique*, monthly. Magazine. Includes calendar of events, news, feature articles, and technical information about the Corvair. **Price:** included in membership dues. ISSN: 0164-7873. **Circulation:** 5,300. **Advertising:** accepted. Alternate Formats: online ● *Membership Roster*, annual. Membership Directory. **Conventions/Meetings:** annual meeting (exhibits) - always June/July.

21186 ■ Corvette Club of America (CCA)
PO Box 9879
Bowling Green, KY 42102-9879
Free: (866)482-1191
E-mail: info@corvetteclubofamerica.com
URL: http://www.corvetteclubofamerica.com
Contact: Garnett S. Rogers, Pres./Dir.
Founded: 1989. **Members:** 7,400. **Membership Dues:** individual, $50 (annual) ● family, $80 (annual). **Staff:** 3. **Budget:** $50,000. **For-Profit. Description:** Promotes restoration, reconstruction, and education about Chevrolet Corvette automobiles. Sponsors racing events. Conducts educational and charitable programs and children's services. Maintains Speaker's Bureau. **Publications:** *Corvette Capers*, quarterly. Newsletter. Includes 32 information pages. **Price:** free, for members only. **Circulation:** 7,400. **Advertising:** accepted. Alternate Formats: online. **Conventions/Meetings:** convention (exhibits).

21187 ■ Crosley Automobile Club (CAC)
307 Schaeffer Rd.
Blandon, PA 19510
E-mail: cac@crosley.net
URL: http://www.ggw.org/cac
Founded: 1969. **Members:** 1,100. **Membership Dues:** individual in U.S., $20 (annual) ● individual outside U.S., $25 (annual). **Regional Groups:** 11. **Description:** Individuals interested in the Crosley automobile. Conducts national yearly meets. Assists members in locating and selling parts and cars and in restoration. **Libraries: Type:** reference. **Publications:** *Membership Roster*, biennial ● *Quarterly* ● Booklets. **Conventions/Meetings:** annual Crosley Nationals - meeting, show and flea market at Fulton County Fairgrounds, Wauseon, Ohio (exhibits) - always second Saturday of July.

21188 ■ Crown Victoria Association (CVA)
PO Box 6
Bryan, OH 43506-9141
Ph: (419)636-2475
Fax: (419)636-8449
E-mail: fordpart@bright.net
URL: http://clubs.hemmings.com/clubsites/crownvictoria
Contact: Toby Gorny, Pres./Founder
Founded: 1978. **Members:** 2,025. **Membership Dues:** regular, in U.S. and Canada, $39 (annual) ● overseas, $59 (annual). **Description:** Individuals with an interest in Ford automobiles manufactured during the 1954-1956 era. Seeks to disseminate general information on these cars and inform members of available automobiles and parts. **Publications:** Fo-

MoCo Times, monthly. Newsletter. **Price:** included in membership dues. **Advertising:** accepted. **Conventions/Meetings:** annual convention (exhibits).

21189 ■ Cyclone Montego Torino Registry (CMTR)
19 Glyn Dr.
Newark, DE 19713-4016
Ph: (302)737-4252
E-mail: robscyclone@aol.com
URL: http://clubs.hemmings.com/cyclonemontego-torinoregistry
Contact: Robert Day, Contact
Founded: 1992. **Members:** 150. **Membership Dues:** regular, in U.S., $7 (annual) ● regular, in Canada, $8 (annual) ● regular, outside U.S. and Canada, $10 (annual). **Staff:** 5. **Description:** Owners and admirers of Cyclone, Torino, and Montego automobiles manufactured between 1964-76, and 1968-79 Rancheros, 1970-71 Torino Cobras, 1970 1/2 Falcons, and 77-79 LTD II's and Cougars. Promotes collection, preservation, and restoration of classic Ford and Mercury cars. **Libraries: Type:** reference. **Holdings:** archival material, artwork, clippings. **Subjects:** Ford and Mercury midsize automobiles manufactured from 1964-79. **Computer Services:** database, decode VIN numbers, decode when and where car was built as well as how the options fit in with other known cars. **Telecommunication Services:** electronic mail, robert.day@atk.com. **Formerly:** (1985) Cyclone Torino Montego Registry. **Publications:** *Registry Update*, 3/year. Newsletter. **Price:** $6.00 in U.S.; $7.00 in Canada; $8.00 outside U.S. and Canada. **Circulation:** 160. **Advertising:** accepted. **Conventions/Meetings:** periodic Winner Ford Show.

21190 ■ DARTS Club (D.A.R.T.S.)
PO Box 9
Wethersfield, CT 06129-0009
Ph: (860)257-8434
E-mail: dartsclub@snet.net
URL: http://clubs.hemmings.com/frameset.cfm?club=dartsclub
Contact: Joel Cooper, Ed./Founder
Founded: 1986. **Members:** 200. **Staff:** 1. **Budget:** $2,500. **Description:** Promotes the preservation, restoration, and enjoyment of Dodge Dart automobiles. **Libraries: Type:** not open to the public. **Holdings:** 25; books. **Subjects:** Dodge cars and trucks. **Computer Services:** database ● mailing lists. **Also Known As:** Dart Automotive Refurbishing Technical Services. **Publications:** *Scat Chat*, quarterly. Newsletter. **Price:** $2.50. **Circulation:** 250. **Advertising:** accepted. Alternate Formats: online. **Conventions/Meetings:** annual Chrysler Convention - convention and show, car show for charity - always week before Labor Day.

21191 ■ Davis Registry
6487 Munger Rd.
Ypsilanti, MI 48197-9014
Ph: (734)434-5581
E-mail: kfnut@umich.edu
URL: http://www.suarezweb.org/davis
Contact: Mr. Thomas Taylor, Dir./Ed.
Founded: 1993. **Members:** 33. **Staff:** 3. **Multinational. Description:** Serves as a worldwide clearinghouse for information regarding the history, technical background, upkeep, restoration, preservation, current prices, and any other aspect of the three-wheeled Davis automobiles and military vehicles built by the Davis Motorcar Company from 1947 to 1949. **Publications:** Bulletin, quarterly. Contains an informal interchange of information among a geographically widespread group of persons who own, or have interest in, the Davis. **Price:** $2.00 standard; $4.00 with color or index. **Circulation:** 33 ● Videos. Alternate Formats: online.

21192 ■ DeLorean Owners Association (DOA)
c/o Tony Hilger, Magazine Dir.
7 Hydrangea St.
Ladera Ranch, CA 92694
Ph: (818)576-9932

E-mail: info@deloreanowners.org
URL: http://deloreanowners.org
Contact: Bob Giedeman, Pres.
Founded: 1983. **Members:** 5,000. **Membership Dues:** regular in U.S., $72 (annual) ● regular outside U.S., $87 (annual). **Description:** Aims to provide opportunity to meet and communicate information about the DeLorean marque. **Libraries: Type:** reference. **Holdings:** 80. **Publications:** *DW*, quarterly. Magazine. Contains technical information, event listings, products, history and exclusive feature stories. **Price:** included in membership dues. **Advertising:** accepted. **Conventions/Meetings:** DeLorean Expo - meeting (exhibits).

21193 ■ DeSoto Club of America (DCA)
403 S Thorton
Richmond, MO 64085
Ph: (816)470-3048
URL: http://clubs.hemmings.com/frameset.cfm?club=desotomo
Contact: Walter O'Kelly, Pres.
Founded: 1969. **Members:** 600. **Membership Dues:** regular, in Canada, $15 (annual) ● regular, outside U.S., $25 (annual). **Description:** Individuals interested in DeSoto automobiles. Seeks to preserve and advance future restoration of the DeSoto; promotes participation in events of DeSotos for public appreciation and gratification. Sponsors meets and flea markets. **Publications:** *Club Member and Car Roster*, annual ● *DeSoto Days*, annual. Newsletter. Covers the preservation and restoration of DeSoto automobiles. Includes listings of items wanted and for sale, and new member information. **Price:** included in membership dues. **Circulation:** 700. **Advertising:** accepted. **Conventions/Meetings:** tour.

21194 ■ DKW Club of America
c/o Robert Paul, Membership Sec.
4406 Bridle Rd.
Bartlesville, OK 74006
Ph: (918)333-5182
E-mail: alcoc628s@yahoo.com
URL: http://www.dkwclub.org
Contact: Robert Paul, Membership Sec.
Founded: 1989. **Members:** 150. **Membership Dues:** in U.S., $17 (annual) ● outside U.S., $23 (annual). **Staff:** 4. **Budget:** $2,000. **Description:** Owners and admirers of DKW automobiles. Promotes preservation and restoration of DKWs. Serves as a clearinghouse on DKW automobiles; assists members with maintenance and restoration issues and in acquiring spare parts. Produces DKW regalia. **Publications:** *Blue Cloud*, quarterly. Newsletter. Includes annual membership roster. **Price:** $5.00 plus shipping and handling. **Circulation:** 150. **Advertising:** accepted. **Conventions/Meetings:** semiannual regional meeting.

21195 ■ Dodge Brothers Club (DBC)
c/o Barry Cogan
PO Box 292
Eastpointe, MI 48021-0292
Ph: (313)884-4327
E-mail: info@dodgebrothersclub.org
URL: http://www.dodgebrothersclub.org
Contact: Gerry Egland, Pres.
Founded: 1983. **Members:** 1,200. **Membership Dues:** individual in U.S., $20 (annual) ● individual outside North America, $26 (annual). **Regional Groups:** 1. **Description:** Owners and others interested in the preservation and enjoyment of Dodge Brothers motor vehicles of model year 1938 and earlier. Serves as an information exchange. **Telecommunication Services:** electronic mail, membership@dodgebrothersclub.org. **Publications:** *Dodge Brothers Club—News*, bimonthly. Newsletter. **Price:** included in membership dues; $20.00 /year for nonmembers in U.S.; $26.00 /year for nonmembers outside U.S. ISSN: 1060-0817. **Circulation:** 1,100. **Advertising:** accepted. **Conventions/Meetings:** annual meeting.

21196 ■ Early Ford V-8 Club of America

PO Box 2222
Livermore, CA 94551-2222
Free: (866)427-7583
URL: http://www.e-collector.org/framework/early-fordv8.php
Contact: Carol Rasmussen, Contact
Founded: 1963. **Members:** 9,400. **Membership Dues:** regular, in U.S., $35 (annual) ● joint, in U.S., $38 (annual) ● regular, in Canada, $43 (annual) ● joint, in Canada, $46 (annual) ● regular in Pacific Rim and Europe, $50 (annual) ● joint in Pacific Rim and Europe, $53 (annual) ● regular in Mexico and South America, $52 (annual) ● joint in Mexico and South America, $55 (annual). **Staff:** 4. **Regional Groups:** 154. **Multinational. Description:** Persons interested in restoration of the early Ford V-8 automobile. **Publications:** *Roster of Members*, annual. Membership Directory ● *V-8 Times*, bimonthly. Magazine. **Conventions/Meetings:** annual meeting.

21197 ■ Eastern Museum of Motor Racing (EMMR)

PO Box 688
Mechanicsburg, PA 17055
Ph: (717)528-8279
E-mail: jlh3@erols.com
URL: http://www.emmr.org
Contact: Deb Wright, Contact
Founded: 1975. **Members:** 1,100. **Membership Dues:** person and spouse, $20 (annual) ● life, $200. **Description:** Individuals interested in the history of American auto racing and the preservation of auto racing artifacts. Operates museum that features restored vintage cars and other memorabilia. Restores racetrack for exhibition racing of vintage cars. Sponsors research projects; conducts educational programs. Maintains hall of fame. **Libraries: Type:** reference. **Holdings:** archival material, artwork, books, clippings, periodicals, photographs. **Subjects:** tracks, autos, drivers, owners. **Computer Services:** Online services, message board. **Formerly:** (1989) Williams Grove Old Timers. **Publications:** Brochure ● Newsletter, bimonthly. **Conventions/Meetings:** annual Auto Show - meeting and convention - third weekend of August ● monthly board meeting - always 1st Tuesday ● annual festival - third weekend of June.

21198 ■ Eastern Packard Club

PO Box 1259
Stratford, CT 06615
Ph: (203)374-7757
URL: http://clubs.hemmings.com/frameset.
    cfm?club=easternpackard
Contact: Ron Eastwood, Pres.
Founded: 1964. **Members:** 400. **Membership Dues:** individual, spouse, foreign, $25 (annual). **Description:** Enthusiasts and owners of Packard automobiles. Promotes the preservation and restoration of the Packard. Provides activities for the exchange of information on the history of the Packard automobile. Encourages participation in automobile shows and parades. **Awards:** Crawford Award. **Frequency:** annual. **Type:** recognition. **Recipient:** for best restoration of a Packard automobile. **Publications:** *Eastern Packard Club News Bulletin*, bimonthly. Features 20-page publication and Packard photo (8x10). **Price:** included in membership dues. **Circulation:** 470. **Advertising:** accepted ● Directory, annual. **Conventions/Meetings:** competition ● annual Packard Car Show - meeting and show (exhibits) - always third Sunday of October.

21199 ■ Edsel Club

19296 Tuckaway Ct.
Fort Myers, FL 33903-1244
Ph: (941)731-8027 (239)731-8027
Fax: (941)731-8027
E-mail: edselworld@earthlink.net
URL: http://www.edselworld.com
Contact: Robert Mayer, Chm.
Founded: 1997. **Members:** 300. **Membership Dues:** regular in U.S. and Canada, $25 (annual) ● regular outside U.S. and Canada, $30 (annual). **Staff:** 18. **Budget:** $6,000. **Regional Groups:** 4. **State Groups:** 10. **Description:** Owners and others interested in the preservation and restoration of the Edsel automobile. The Edsel, produced by the Ford Motor Company for the model years 1958-1960. **Libraries: Type:** reference. **Holdings:** 45. **Subjects:** Edsel production, parts, manuals. **Awards:** Edsel Anniversary Trophy. **Frequency:** annual. **Type:** trophy. **Recipient:** for outstanding person doing service for the Edsel, highest point car in silver class ● Ford Motor Company Trophy. **Frequency:** annual. **Type:** trophy. **Recipient:** to highest point car in gold class ● Founders Trophy. **Frequency:** annual. **Type:** recognition. **Recipient:** to highest point car in bronze class. **Publications:** *Annual Edsel Calendar*, annual. **Price:** $5.00/copy ● *Edsel World*, semiannual. Magazine. **Price:** included in membership dues. **Circulation:** 300. **Advertising:** accepted ● *The Roundup*, quarterly. Newsletter. **Conventions/Meetings:** annual Grand National Event - show - usually spring.

21200 ■ Edsel Owner's Club (EOC)

c/o Kathye M. Higdem
9211 Portland Ave. S
Minneapolis, MN 55420-3839
Ph: (952)884-3091
E-mail: eoc@edsel.com
URL: http://www.edsel.com/eoc/club.htm
Contact: Kathye M. Higdem, Contact
Founded: 1969. **Membership Dues:** regular, in U.S., $35 (annual) ● regular, in Canada, $40 (annual) ● regular, outside U.S. and Canada, $45 (annual) ● associate, $15 (annual). **Multinational. Description:** Dedicated to the preservation, maintenance and promotion of the Edsel automobile. **Publications:** *The Big E*, 5/year. Magazine. Includes annual full color Edsel calendar issue. **Price:** included in membership dues ● *The Greenline*, 8/year. Newsletter. **Price:** included in membership dues. **Conventions/Meetings:** annual convention.

21201 ■ Elgin Motorcar Owners Registry

2226 E Apache Ln.
Vincennes, IN 47591
Ph: (812)888-4172
Fax: (812)888-5471
E-mail: jwolf@vinu.edu
URL: http://beaver.vinu.edu/Eowners.HTM
Contact: Mr. Jay Wolf, Contact
Founded: 1996. **Members:** 6. **Multinational. Description:** Aims to track down and keep track of all cars made by the Elgin Motorcar Company.

21202 ■ Erskine Registry (ER)

1144 Dockside Dr.
Lutz, FL 33559
Ph: (813)948-1822
Fax: (813)948-8353
E-mail: searaydave@prodigy.com
URL: http://members.tripod.com/~erskine_registry/
    erskine.html
Contact: Dave Oliver, Contact
Founded: 1968. **Members:** 200. **Staff:** 1. **Description:** Owners of Erskine cars, built by Studebaker from 1927 to 1930. Exchanges ideas and parts. Compiles statistics. **Affiliated With:** Antique Studebaker Club; Studebaker Driver's Club.

21203 ■ Fairlane Club of America (FCA)

340 Clicktown Rd.
Church Hill, TN 37642
Ph: (423)245-6678
Fax: (423)245-2456
E-mail: fca@fairlaneclubofamerica.com
URL: http://www.fairlaneclubofamerica.com
Contact: Bob Mannel, Contact
Founded: 1981. **Members:** 3,400. **Membership Dues:** regular, in U.S., $35 (annual) ● regular, in Canada, $47 (annual) ● overseas, $64 (annual). **Staff:** 2. **Description:** Persons dedicated to the enjoyment, restoration and preservation of Fairlane/Torino automobiles, manufactured by the Ford Motor Company from 1962 to 1976 (including 1962/63 Meteors, 1966/67 Comets and 1968/76 Mercury Intermediates). Assists members in the enjoyment and preservation of their vehicles through articles on the automobiles, technical information, restoration ideas, and by offering opportunities to gather together and to exchange information between members. **Publications:** *Fairlaner*, bimonthly. Magazine. Contains 48 pages. **Price:** included in membership dues. **Circulation:** 3,400. **Conventions/Meetings:** annual National Meet - show, car show.

21204 ■ Falcon Club of America (FCA)

PO Box 113
Jacksonville, AR 72078-0113
Ph: (501)982-9721
E-mail: fca@falconclub.com
URL: http://www.falconclub.com
Contact: Chuck Beason, Pres.
Founded: 1979. **Members:** 3,500. **Membership Dues:** regular, in U.S., $25 (annual) ● regular, outside U.S., $30 (annual). **Staff:** 27. **Regional Groups:** 7. **National Groups:** 40. **Description:** Owners of the Ford Falcon automobile devoted to its preservation and restoration. Provides a medium of exchange for ideas, technical information, and parts availability. **Libraries: Type:** reference. **Subjects:** auto manuals. **Awards: Type:** recognition. **Publications:** *Falcon News*, monthly. Newsletter. **Advertising:** accepted ● Membership Directory, annual. **Conventions/Meetings:** annual meet (exhibits) - always third weekend of July ● show.

21205 ■ Ferrari Club of America (FCA)

PO Box 720597
Atlanta, GA 30358
Free: (800)328-0444
Fax: (800)328-0444
E-mail: info@ferrariclubofamerica.org
URL: http://www.ferrariclubofamerica.org
Contact: Paul Gilpatrick, Chm.
Founded: 1962. **Members:** 3,500. **Membership Dues:** regular, $135 (annual). **Budget:** $120,000. **Regional Groups:** 14. **State Groups:** 1. **Description:** Individuals and firms having an interest in Ferrari automobiles. Aims are: to inspire ownership, operation, restoration, and preservation of Ferrari automobiles; to serve members as a source of information regarding Ferrari history and technical data; to organize meets and exhibits; to assist members in locating Ferrari automobiles and parts. **Libraries: Type:** reference. **Holdings:** archival material. **Awards: Type:** recognition. **Publications:** *News Bulletin*, monthly. Features articles, regional event calendars, classified ads and racing reports. ● *Prancing Horse*, quarterly. Magazine. **Alternate Formats:** online ● Bulletin, monthly. **Conventions/Meetings:** competition ● annual meet (exhibits) ● seminar.

21206 ■ Ferrari Owners Club (FOC)

18000 Studebakers Rd., Ste.700
Cerritos, CA 90703
Ph: (562)467-6957
Fax: (562)467-6954
E-mail: national@ferrariownersclub.org
URL: http://www.ferrariownersclub.org
Contact: Gary Opp, Membership Chm./Dir.
Founded: 1961. **Members:** 900. **Membership Dues:** regular, in U.S., Canada, and Mexico, $125 (annual) ● other country, $150 (annual). **Staff:** 1. **Regional Groups:** 6. **Description:** Represents Ferrari owners and enthusiasts. Promotes and seeks to further the enjoyment of the Ferrari automobile. Sponsors special events. **Awards: Type:** recognition. **Publications:** *FOC Directory and Yearbook*, annual ● Newsletter, monthly. **Conventions/Meetings:** competition ● monthly rally and tour, includes time trials ● annual West Coast Ferrari Literature and Model Meet (exhibits).

21207 ■ Fiero Owners Club of America (FOCOA)

1598 S Anaheim Blvd., Unit B
Anaheim, CA 92805-6230
Ph: (714)917-2007
Fax: (714)917-2161
E-mail: fierophilhuff@fieroowners.com
URL: http://clubs.hemmings.com/frameset.
    cfm?club=fieroowners
Contact: Phil Huff, Dir.
Founded: 1983. **Members:** 5,500. **Membership Dues:** in U.S., $34 (annual) ● outside U.S., $45 (an-

nual). **Staff:** 3. **Description:** Pontiac Fiero automobile owners interested in learning more about the Fiero, produced by Pontiac between 1984 and 1988. Provides a network for the sharing of knowledge and information through publications, rallies, conventions, and local chapters. Maintains museum-archive and hall of fame. Compiles statistics; conducts research programs. **Awards: Type:** recognition. **Publications:** *Fiero Owner*, quarterly. Magazine. Includes updates and modification information. **Price:** $5.00. **Advertising:** accepted. **Conventions/Meetings:** annual Fiero Festival (exhibits).

21208 ■ FoMoCo Owners Club
Address Unknown since 2007
Founded: 1985. **Members:** 250. **Membership Dues:** $20 (annual). **Staff:** 10. **Regional Groups:** 2. **Description:** Individuals dedicated to the exhibition, preservation, and restoration of Edsel, Ford, Lincoln, and Mercury automobiles. Conducts charitable activities; sponsors educational programs. **Publications:** *FOMOCO Owners Club Newsletter*, monthly. **Advertising:** not accepted. **Conventions/Meetings:** annual meeting (exhibits).

21209 ■ Ford Galaxie Club of America (FGCoA)
PO Box 429
Valley Springs, AR 72682-0429
Ph: (870)743-9757
E-mail: director@galaxieclub.com
URL: http://www.galaxieclub.com
Contact: Mark Reynolds, Dir.
Founded: 1983. **Members:** 2,500. **Membership Dues:** regular, in U.S. and Canada, $35 (annual) ● overseas, $52 (annual) ● regular, in U.S. and Canada (life), $550 ● overseas (life), $750. **Staff:** 3. **Regional Groups:** 10. **Description:** Owners and admirers of the Galaxie automobile, built by the Ford Motor Company between the years 1959 and 1974. Promotes the restoration, preservation, and enjoyment of Galaxies; seeks to unite Galaxie owners. **Libraries: Type:** not open to the public. **Holdings:** 19; periodicals. **Subjects:** Galaxies '59 through '74. **Computer Services:** database. **Publications:** *Galaxie Gazette*, bimonthly. Magazine. **Circulation:** 2,500. **Advertising:** accepted. **Conventions/Meetings:** annual Northeast Meet; Northwest Meet; Southeast Meet - meeting (exhibits).

21210 ■ GM Futurliner
4521 Majestic Vue
Zeeland, MI 49464
Ph: (616)875-3058
E-mail: donscar@i2k.com
URL: http://www.futurliner.com
Contact: Don M. Mayton, Proj. Dir.
Founded: 1998. **Members:** 300. **Staff:** 50. **Budget:** $25,000. **Multinational. Description:** Project of the National Automotive and Truck Museum of the United States. Works to promote and restore the GM Futurliner; only twelve were known to have been built. **Affiliated With:** National Automotive and Truck Museum of United States. **Publications:** *Futurliner News*. Newsletter. Alternate Formats: online ● Video. **Price:** $25.00 plus shipping and handling ● Reports. Alternate Formats: online.

21211 ■ Goodguys Rod and Custom Association
PO Box 9132
Pleasanton, CA 94566
Ph: (925)838-9876
Fax: (925)820-8241
E-mail: info@good-guys.com
URL: http://www.good-guys.com
Contact: Marc Meadors, Sr. VP
Founded: 1983. **Members:** 70,000. **Membership Dues:** regular, in U.S., $30 (annual) ● regular, outside U.S., $45 (annual). **Staff:** 40. **Description:** Promotes and produces automotive events, focused on vintage vehicles, which are fun for the entire family. **Publications:** *Goodguys Yearbook*, annual. Contains coverage of the previous auto season. **Price:** $5.00 ● *The Goodtimes Gazette*, monthly. Magazine. Contains articles and information on

events, hot rod heroes, companies, cars and their owners, and classified ads. **Price:** included in membership dues. **Advertising:** accepted. **Conventions/Meetings:** meeting ● meeting ● periodic show, street machines, various Rod and Custom events.

21212 ■ Graham Owners Club International (GOCI)
c/o Gloria Reid, Treas.
3240 Shawn Way
Hayward, CA 94541
Ph: (510)886-7599
Fax: (510)733-5081
E-mail: grreid@sbcglobal.net
URL: http://www.graham-paige.com
Contact: Gloria Reid, Treas.
Founded: 1971. **Members:** 600. **Membership Dues:** regular, in U.S., $23 (annual) ● regular, outside U.S., $27 (annual). **Regional Groups:** 3. **Description:** Owners of Graham, Graham Paige, Graham Brothers antique automobiles and trucks, and others interested in the Graham-Paige marque. Paige and Jewett automobiles and Graham-Bradley tractors are welcome also. Compiles statistics. **Awards: Type:** recognition. **Publications:** *Membership Roster*, annual. Membership Directory ● *The Supercharger*, quarterly. Magazine. Contains selected Graham stories, technology, articles, and car parts ads. **Price:** included in membership dues. **Conventions/Meetings:** annual meeting - always June.

21213 ■ GTO Association of America (GTOAA)
PO Box 455
Timnath, CO 80547-0455
Ph: (970)221-0754
E-mail: president@gtoaa.org
URL: http://www.gtoaa.org
Contact: Bob Alexander, Pres.
Founded: 1979. **Members:** 4,000. **Membership Dues:** regular, in U.S., $30 (annual) ● regular, in Canada, $33 (annual) ● regular, outside U.S. and Canada, $40 (annual) ● associate in the same family, $5 (annual). **Staff:** 7. **State Groups:** 50. **Description:** Persons owning or interested in Pontiac GTO and GT-37 automobiles produced between 1964 and 1974. Promotes the preservation and restoration of GTO automobiles. Appoints technical advisors to assist members with repair and restoration of their cars. Sponsors swap meet and competitions at which members' cars are judged. Compiles statistics on GTO production. **Libraries: Type:** not open to the public. **Holdings:** books, papers, periodicals. **Computer Services:** Mailing lists. **Publications:** *The Legend*, monthly. Magazine. Contains articles on restoration and technical information. **Advertising:** accepted. **Conventions/Meetings:** annual meet and show (exhibits).

21214 ■ Gull Wing Group International (GWGI)
776 Cessna Ave.
Chico, CA 95928-9571
Ph: (530)345-6701
Fax: (530)891-5038
E-mail: contact@gullwinggroup.org
URL: http://www.gullwinggroup.org
Contact: Gary Estep, Business Office Mgr.
Founded: 1961. **Members:** 600. **Membership Dues:** regular, in North America and Canada, $90 (annual) ● regular, outside North America and Canada, $110 (annual). **Staff:** 1. **Regional Groups:** 6. **Description:** Owners of either a Mercedes-Benz 300SL Gullwing Coupe or Mercedes-Benz 300SL Roadster; associate members need not own a car. Seeks to maintain and preserve, to the highest standards, the type 300SL Mercedes-Benz automobile, manufactured from 1954 through 1963. Holds technical instruction sessions. **Committees:** Technical Review. **Formerly:** (1983) Gullwing Group. **Publications:** *Technical Tips Manual* ● *300 Star Letter*, monthly. Magazine ● Directory, annual ● Also publishes a book and registry of cars. **Conventions/Meetings:** annual conference (exhibits).

21215 ■ Haynes-Apperson Owners Club (HAOC)
Address Unknown since 2007
Founded: 1951. **Members:** 125. **Description:** Owners of Haynes-Apperson, Haynes, and Apperson automobiles. Objectives are to provide information to owners and to keep a record of all Haynes and Apperson cars still in existence. Gives lectures; compiles statistics. Maintains museum and 100 volume library including catalogs, papers, and biographical archives. **Publications:** none. **Conventions/Meetings:** annual conference - always first Sunday in July, Kokomo, IN.

21216 ■ Heartland Vintage Thunderbird Club of America (HVTCA)
Address Unknown since 2007
Membership Dues: in U.S., $25 (annual) ● outside U.S., $35 (annual). **Description:** Car club for 1958-1971 Ford Thunderbird owners and enthusiasts. **Publications:** Newsletter, monthly. Specialized Thunderbird parts info, technical articles, monthly reports from chapter clubs, free advertising and classified picture ads for members. **Price:** included in membership dues. **Conventions/Meetings:** semiannual International Thunderbird Show - usually May and August.

21217 ■ Henry Nyberg Society
17822 Chicago Ave.
Lansing, IL 60438
Ph: (708)474-3416
Fax: (708)474-3416
E-mail: nyberg1soc@aol.com
URL: http://clubs.hemmings.com/nyberg
Contact: Bob Youngberg, Contact
Founded: 1990. **Members:** 40. **Description:** Individuals interested in auto manufacturer Henry Nyberg and the vehicles he designed and produced between 1903 and 1913. Promotes research, education, and scientific activities associated with the design, production, preservation, and acquisition of the Nyberg automobile, truck, fire apparatus, race car, and motorcycle. Collects information, photographs, artifacts, advertisements, and items related to Nyberg vehicles for public display in museums; disseminates information to the public. **Convention/Meeting:** none. **Publications:** *Nyberg Update*, periodic. Newsletter.

21218 ■ H.H. Franklin Club (HHFC)
Cazenovia Coll.
Cazenovia, NY 13035
E-mail: fbhantak@aol.com
URL: http://www.franklincar.org
Contact: Mark Sullivan, Pres.
Founded: 1951. **Members:** 850. **Membership Dues:** regular, in U.S., $30 (annual) ● regular, outside U.S., $40 (annual). **Local Groups:** 4. **Description:** Works to collect and publish the history of the Franklin and other air-cooled automobiles of the period. Encourages preservation of such cars and related material. Maintains library of club owned materials relating to Franklin Automobiles and the H-H Franklin Manufacturing Company. **Libraries: Type:** not open to the public. **Telecommunication Services:** electronic mail, dderusha@rochester.rr.com. **Committees:** Librarian; Technical. **Publications:** *Air Cooled News*, 3/year. Magazine. **Price:** included in membership dues ● *Franklin Service Station*, quarterly. Newsletter. **Advertising:** accepted ● *Registry of Franklin Car Owners*, biennial ● *Roster of Members*, biennial. Membership Directory. **Conventions/Meetings:** annual Franklin Trek - meeting, automobiles (exhibits) - always third week of August in Cazenovia, NY ● Regional Meet.

21219 ■ Historic Motor Sports Association (HMSA)
2029 Verdugo Blvd., No. 1010
Montrose, CA 91020
Ph: (818)249-3515
Fax: (818)249-4917
E-mail: hmsa@hmsausa.com
URL: http://www.hmsausa.com
Contact: Cris Vandagriff, Pres.
Founded: 1979. **Members:** 1,000. **Membership Dues:** full, $200 (annual). **Staff:** 4. **Description:** Indi-

viduals interested in auto racing history. Conducts races each June in Sonoma, CA, and August in Monterey, CA. **Publications:** Newsletter.

21220 ■ Horseless Carriage Club of America (HCCA)

40637 Hwy. 41
Oakhurst, CA 93644
Ph: (559)658-8800
Free: (888)832-2374
Fax: (559)683-0598
E-mail: office@hcca.org
URL: http://www.hcca.org
Contact: Michael Bruce Rimmer, Pres.
Founded: 1937. **Members:** 5,100. **Membership Dues:** domestic, $45 (annual) ● foreign, $55 (annual) ● life (domestic), $1,250 ● life (foreign), $1,500. **Regional Groups:** 88. **Local Groups:** 100. **Description:** Hobbyists who are interested in the preservation, accessories, archives, and romantic lore of old cars. Sponsors four annual tours and three swap meets for larger cars and for one- and two-cylinder cars. **Libraries:** Type: reference. **Holdings:** archival material. **Awards: Frequency:** annual. **Type:** recognition. **Recipient:** for best regional group publications and car restorations. **Publications:** *Horseless Carriage Gazette*, bimonthly. Magazine. **Price:** included in membership dues. ISSN: 0018-5213. **Circulation:** 5,000. **Advertising:** accepted ● *Membership Roster*, triennial. Membership Directory. **Conventions/Meetings:** annual conference.

21221 ■ Hudson-Essex-Terraplane Club (HET Club)

PO Box 8412
Wichita, KS 67208-0412
Ph: (316)744-1363
E-mail: charlottesargent@cox.net
URL: http://www.hudsonclub.org
Contact: Charlotte Sargent, Membership Chair
Founded: 1959. **Members:** 3,600. **Budget:** $45,000. **Regional Groups:** 4. **Local Groups:** 45. **Description:** Persons from 21 countries interested in preserving and restoring automobiles built by the Hudson Motor Car Company from 1909 to 1957, including the Hudson, Essex, Terraplane, Dover, Jet, Railton, Brough Superior, and any of the custom body styles built during the classic era from 1925 to 1936. **Libraries:** Type: reference. **Holdings:** books, periodicals, photographs. **Subjects:** shop repair. **Publications:** *Club Roster*, every 2-3 years. Membership Directory ● *White Triangle News*, bimonthly. Newsletter. **Price:** $20.00/year. ISSN: 0164-5145. **Circulation:** 3,600. **Conventions/Meetings:** annual meeting.

21222 ■ Hudson Essex Terraplane Historical Society

c/o Ms. Sue Figert Meyer, Pres.
342 Mass Ave., No. 500
Indianapolis, IN 46204
Ph: (317)257-1175 (317)860-2903
Fax: (317)263-2550
E-mail: sue@rubin-levin.net
URL: http://www.hudsonclub.org/hethist/hethisthome.htm
Contact: Ms. Sue Figert Meyer, Pres.
Founded: 1990. **Membership Dues:** life, $1,000 ● contributing, $100 (annual) ● associate, $25 (annual). **Description:** Members organize for charitable, educational and scientific purposes. Discovers, collects and memorializes the history and products produced by the Hudson Motor Car Company from 1909 to 1954. Aims to collect cars, pictures, books, drawings, and establish a museum.

21223 ■ Hurst/Olds Club of America (H/OCA)

3626 Meadowview Ct.
Decatur, IL 62526
E-mail: hocadirector@sbcglobal.net
URL: http://www.hurstolds.com
Contact: Calvin Badgley, Dir.
Founded: 1983. **Members:** 600. **Membership Dues:** regular, $25 (annual). **Description:** Hurst/Olds enthusiasts. Seeks to perpetuate interest in and promote preservation of Hurst/Olds automobiles, which have been produced since 1968 by the Olds-

mobile Division of the General Motors Corporation. Maintains Hurst/Olds registry. Holds car shows annually across the U.S. **Libraries:** Type: reference. **Holdings:** archival material, artwork, books, clippings. **Subjects:** Hurst/Olds autos. **Awards: Frequency:** 10/year. **Type:** recognition. **Publications:** *Thunder and Lightning*, bimonthly. Newsletter. **Advertising:** accepted. **Conventions/Meetings:** annual meeting and meet.

21224 ■ Inliners International

c/o Jean Weigt, Membership Chair
14 E Main St.
Winters, CA 95694
Ph: (530)795-0224
E-mail: weigts@sbcglobal.net
URL: http://www.inliners.org
Contact: Jean Weigt, Membership Chair
Founded: 1981. **Members:** 1,400. **Membership Dues:** in U.S., $28 (annual) ● in Canada, overseas, $38 (annual). **Regional Groups:** 10. **Description:** Admirers, collectors, racers and mechanics of inline engines. Acts as a forum for the exchange of information on inline engines. **Convention/Meeting:** none. **Publications:** *12 Port News*, 6/year. Newsletter. **Price:** included in membership dues. **Circulation:** 1,500. **Advertising:** accepted.

21225 ■ International 190SL Group

c/o Shirley Freese, Membership Mgr.
258 E Paul Revere Dr.
Chesterton, IN 46304-9370
Ph: (219)926-3216 (716)385-2338
E-mail: dafreese01@aol.com
URL: http://www.190slgroup.com
Contact: Tom Hamilton, Pres.
Founded: 1983. **Members:** 850. **Membership Dues:** regular, in U.S., $35 (annual) ● regular, in Canada, $40 (annual) ● international, $45 (annual). **Staff:** 3. **Local Groups:** 7. **Multinational. Description:** Represents owners and enthusiasts of the Mercedes-Benz 190SL, a car manufactured from 1955 to 1963. Dispenses information to members on restoration, repair, and maintenance. **Awards:** National Best of Show. **Frequency:** annual. **Type:** recognition. **Recipient:** for restoration and repair efforts. **Computer Services:** Mailing lists, available to club members, non solicitation only. **Formerly:** International 190SL Lone Group, Inc. **Publications:** *190SL Group Newsletter*, monthly. **Price:** included in membership dues. **Circulation:** 550. **Advertising:** accepted ● Membership Directory, annual. **Conventions/Meetings:** annual Car Show - show and meet (exhibits).

21226 ■ International Amphicar Owners Club (IAOC)

202 E Nebraska Ave.
Berthoud, CO 80513
E-mail: amphipoda@yahoo.com
URL: http://www.amphicar.com
Contact: John Bevins, Pres./Webmaster
Membership Dues: regular, $30 (annual). **Multinational. Description:** Encourages the preservation, ownership and operation of the amphibious vehicle known as the Amphicar. Aims to promote links with other Amphicar groups. Provides a central point of contact for the press and any other media organization. **Publications:** Newsletter. **Alternate Formats:** online.

21227 ■ International Camaro Club (ICC)

2001 Pittston Ave., Dept. HOL
Scranton, PA 18505
Ph: (570)585-4082
E-mail: vfitom@aol.com
URL: http://clubs.hemmings.com/frameset.cfm?club=icccamaroregistry
Contact: D.M. Crispino, VP
Founded: 1984. **Members:** 3,000. **Membership Dues:** regular, in U.S., $20 (annual) ● regular, in Canada, $25 (annual) ● regular, outside U.S. and Canada, $35 (annual). **Description:** Chevrolet Camaro enthusiasts and local Camaro clubs. Provides a forum for the exchange of information and parts. Sponsors shows and rallies. Operates Trim Tag ID Project, which compiles codes for trim tags that ap-

pear on the Camaro; these codes are used to aid in restorations and purchasing of cars. Maintains a pace car registry. Maintains a Yenko SYC Registry. **Libraries:** Type: reference. **Awards:** Member of the Year Award. **Frequency:** annual. **Type:** recognition ● **Type:** recognition. **Publications:** *In the Fast Lane*, bimonthly. Newsletter. Provides technical data, calendar of events, regional news, and classified ads listing cars and parts. **Price:** included in membership dues; $2.00 for nonmembers. **Circulation:** 2,500. **Advertising:** accepted. **Conventions/Meetings:** semiannual Camaro Street Nationals East - show, pace car seminars (exhibits).

21228 ■ International Edsel Club (IEC)

2541 Colony Ave.
Lindenhurst, IL 60046
E-mail: kyedsel@bellsouth.net
URL: http://www.internationaledsel.com
Contact: Jack Whipple, Pres.
Founded: 1969. **Members:** 1,025. **Membership Dues:** joint, $20 (annual) ● individual, $25 (annual) ● international, $30 (annual). **Staff:** 5. **Regional Groups:** 2. **State Groups:** 20. **National Groups:** 20. **Description:** Individuals in 11 countries interested in the preservation, restoration, and collection of Ford Edsel automobiles. Distributes information. **Publications:** *Edseletter*, monthly. Newsletter. Contains association news, statistics, calendar of events, and listings of award recipients, parts wanted, and cars for sale. **Price:** included in membership dues. **Advertising:** accepted. **Alternate Formats:** online ● Membership Directory, annual. **Conventions/Meetings:** annual rally - last weekend of July.

21229 ■ International King Midget Car Club (IKMCC)

c/o Paula Jasper, Sec.
2425 Ervin Ln.
Stockport, OH 43787
Ph: (740)559-3983
E-mail: secretary@kingmidgetcarclub.org
URL: http://www.kingmidgetcarclub.org
Contact: Paula Jasper, Sec.
Founded: 1992. **Members:** 200. **Membership Dues:** regular, $15 (annual). **Multinational. Description:** Represents enthusiasts and owners of King Midget vehicles. Supplies parts support and information for King Midget vehicles from 1986-1995. **Telecommunication Services:** electronic mail, membership@kingmidgetcarclub.org. **Publications:** Newsletter. **Price:** included in membership dues.

21230 ■ International Mercury Owners Association (IMOA)

6445 W Grand Ave.
Chicago, IL 60707-3410
Ph: (773)622-6445
Fax: (773)622-3602
E-mail: info@mercuryclub.com
URL: http://www.mercuryclub.com
Contact: Jerry Robbin, Pres.
Founded: 1991. **Members:** 1,400. **Membership Dues:** regular, in U.S. and Canada, $35 (annual) ● regular, outside U.S. and Canada, $40 (annual). **Regional Groups:** 11. **Description:** Owners of, and individuals interested in, Mercury automobiles. Offers owners and collectors assistance in locating parts, sharing information, and buying/selling cars. Sponsors national car shows. **Publications:** *Quicksilver*, quarterly. Newsletter. Includes photos, stories, tech articles and classifieds. **Price:** included in membership dues. **Advertising:** accepted. **Conventions/Meetings:** periodic International Car Show - meeting, car show/swap meet (exhibits).

21231 ■ International Mustang Bullitt Owners Club (IMBOC)

PO Box 376
Springboro, OH 45066
E-mail: membership@imboc.com
URL: http://www.imboc.com
Contact: Greg Autry, Coor.
Membership Dues: supporting, $37 (annual). **Multinational. Description:** Promotes and preserves the Ford Mustang Bullitt car. Serves as an information

and communication source for Ford Mustang Bullitt owners. Facilitates cooperation and communication among members.

21232 ■ International Society for Vehicle Preservation (ISVP)

PO Box 50046
Tucson, AZ 85703-1046
Ph: (520)622-2201
Fax: (520)792-8501
E-mail: isvp@dakotacom.net
URL: http://www.aztexcorp.com/root/isvp.html
Contact: Walter R. Haessner, Exec. Dir.
Founded: 1983. **Members:** 1,500. **Membership Dues:** associate, $18 (annual) ● national club associate, $88 (annual) ● local club associate, $35 (annual) ● endowing associate, $150 (annual) ● life, associate, $750. **Description:** Car clubs; automobile restorers and preservationists; automotive engineers and historians; interested others. Seeks to collect and preserve information related to the origin and development of self-propelled vehicles. Promotes preservation of self-propelled vehicles, literature, artifacts, and related products. Sanctions and conducts world class concours d'elegances, educational seminars, and awards program. **Libraries:** Type: reference. **Holdings:** 1,000. **Subjects:** transportation history and how-to. **Awards:** IAMA Award. **Frequency:** annual. **Type:** trophy. **Recipient:** for excellence in automotive media. **Publications:** *The Cameron Story - History of the Cameron Car.* Books ● *Restoration Magazine,* semiannual. **Price:** $3.00/copy ● *Restoration News Bulletin,* bimonthly. **Price:** included in membership dues; $1.00/copy for nonmembers. ISSN: 0736-5934. Alternate Formats: online ● Films. **Conventions/Meetings:** annual International Automotive Media Conference - conference and seminar, includes hosted luncheons and dinners, awards ● lecture ● workshop.

21233 ■ International Thunderbird Club (ITC)

c/o Kitty Mummert, Treas.
20 Northview Dr.
Hanover, PA 17331-4521
Ph: (717)632-2818
E-mail: normkitty@blazenet.net
URL: http://www.intl-tbirdclub.com
Contact: Kitty Mummert, Treas.
Founded: 1993. **Members:** 1,200. **Membership Dues:** regular, in U.S. and Canada, $26 (annual) ● other country, $35 (annual). **Staff:** 25. **Budget:** $35,000. **Regional Groups:** 7. **State Groups:** 2. **Local Groups:** 15. **National Groups:** 11. **Description:** Seeks to encourage the use and preservation of classic and antique Thunderbirds. Researches and disseminates information; conducts educational programs; holds competitions. **Libraries:** Type: reference. **Holdings:** articles, artwork, clippings. **Subjects:** Thunderbirds from 1955 to present. **Awards:** President's Award. **Frequency:** annual. **Type:** recognition. **Computer Services:** database ● mailing lists ● online services. **Publications:** *Thunderbird Script,* bimonthly. Newsletter. **Circulation:** 1,200. **Advertising:** accepted. **Conventions/Meetings:** annual International Convention (exhibits) ● regional meeting.

21234 ■ Iso and Bizzarrini Owners Club (IBOC)

2025 Drake Dr.
Oakland, CA 94611
Ph: (510)339-8347
Fax: (510)339-8347
URL: http://home.tiscali.nl/isorivolta/isoclubs.htm
Contact: Jack Freethy, Pres.
Founded: 1981. **Members:** 190. **Membership Dues:** in U.S. and Canada, $45 (annual) ● outside North America, $55 (annual). **Regional Groups:** 4. **Multinational. Description:** Owners and enthusiasts of the high-speed automobiles Iso (manufactured from 1963 to 1974) and Bizzarrini (manufactured from 1966 to 1971) automobiles, including the Bizzarrini GT America, Bizzarrini GT 1900, Iso Fidia, Iso Grifo, Iso Lele, and Iso Rivolta. Encourages the preservation and restoration of the automobiles; promotes appreciation of the marques. Bestows awards; maintains

biographical archives; compiles statistics. **Awards:** Annual Meeting Best Of Show Founders Award. **Frequency:** annual. **Type:** trophy. **Recipient:** service to club. **Publications:** *Bresso Express,* bimonthly. Newsletter. **Advertising:** accepted ● *Griffon,* quarterly. Magazine ● Membership Directory, annual. **Conventions/Meetings:** annual Monterey Historical Race Weekend - meeting - always August, Monterey, CA.

21235 ■ Italian Car Registry (ICAR)

Address Unknown since 2007
Founded: 1980. **Members:** 2,000. **Languages:** Italian, Spanish. **Description:** Individuals, museums, and organizations owning or interested in preserving unusual Italian automobiles. Records histories of Italian cars; brings together owners of similar types of low-production Italian cars. Conducts research; collects and distributes information. **Convention/Meeting:** none. **Libraries:** Type: reference. **Formerly:** Registry of Italian Oddities. **Publications:** *The Italian Car Registry,* semiannual. Directory. Contains listings of Italian cars by maker, type, and chassis number. **Advertising:** not accepted.

21236 ■ Jaguar Clubs of North America (JCNA)

c/o Nelson Rath, Admin. Mgr./Treas.
234 Buckland Trace
Louisville, KY 40245
Ph: (502)244-1672
Free: (888)258-2524
E-mail: nrath@jcna.com
URL: http://www.jcna.com
Contact: Nelson Rath, Admin. Mgr./Treas.
Founded: 1954. **Members:** 6,500. **Regional Groups:** 59. **Description:** Jaguar clubs in U.S., Canada, and Mexico representing a combined membership of 6500. Works to: foster and encourage a spirit of mutual interest and assistance for Jaguar automobile enthusiasts; promote public interest in motoring and motor sports; develop road safety; encourage an improved understanding of traffic laws; promote social and motoring events. Conducts individual vehicle history search services. **Libraries:** Type: reference. **Holdings:** archival material. **Subjects:** technical information. **Awards:** Andrew Whyte Award. **Frequency:** annual. **Type:** recognition. **Recipient:** for service to national organization ● Frederic S. Horner Sportsmanship Award. **Type:** recognition. **Publications:** *Jaguar Journal,* bimonthly. **Price:** $22.00 /year for nonmembers in U.S. and Canada; $40.00 /year for nonmembers outside U.S. and Canada; free for members. ISSN: 0743-3913. **Circulation:** 6,500. **Advertising:** accepted. **Conventions/Meetings:** biennial Car Show - meet (exhibits) ● annual conference and seminar - always March ● Driver and Navigator Championships - rally ● annual National Concours d'Elegance Car Show - competition and show ● Slalom Championships - competition.

21237 ■ Jewett Owners Club (JOC)

Address Unknown since 2007
Founded: 1982. **Members:** 9. **Description:** Owners of Jewett automobiles manufactured by the Paige Company from 1922 to 1927. Assists members in locating Jewett automobiles and parts. Maintains registry; distributes technical information. **Convention/Meeting:** none.

21238 ■ Jordan Register (JR)

2099 Pheasant Dr.
Yuba City, CA 95993
Ph: (530)673-7382
E-mail: worledge@succeed.net
URL: http://www.carhopp.net/jordan.htm
Contact: Art Worledge, Contact
Founded: 1980. **Members:** 85. **Membership Dues:** individual, $20 (annual). **Staff:** 1. **Budget:** $750. **Description:** Owners and enthusiasts of Jordan automobiles, manufactured in Cleveland, OH from 1916 to 1931. Seeks to expand information about the Jordan automobile and the life of Edward S. "Ned" Jordan (1882-1958), the company founder. Holds informal gatherings at flea markets and local and national auto

shows. Compiles statistics. **Publications:** *The Arrowhead,* quarterly. Journal. Provides recently uncovered literature and parts sources. **Price:** included in membership dues. **Circulation:** 150. **Advertising:** accepted ● Newsletter, quarterly. **Price:** included in membership dues. **Circulation:** 100. **Conventions/Meetings:** biennial convention (exhibits).

21239 ■ The Judge GTO International (TJGTOI)

114 Prince George Dr.
Hampton, VA 23669
Ph: (757)838-2059
E-mail: thejudge@pcdocs.net
URL: http://www.thejudgeschambers.net
Contact: Robert McKenzie, Pres.
Founded: 1982. **Members:** 750. **Membership Dues:** individual, $25 (annual). **Multinational. Description:** Owners and admirers of 1969-71 Pontiac GTO Judge automobiles. Seeks to preserve the GTO Judge. Offers parts service; aids in restoration; provides advice; encourages collection of memorabilia; compiles statistics; sponsors annual convention in Virginia Beach, VA. Aids others seeking to purchase a GTO Judge and free information and personal advice. **Libraries:** Type: reference; not open to the public. **Holdings:** 150; archival material. **Computer Services:** Mailing lists. **Publications:** *The Judge GTO,* quarterly. Newsletter. **Advertising:** accepted.

21240 ■ Kaiser-Darrin Owners Roster

734 Antram Rd.
Somerset, PA 15501-8856
Ph: (814)445-6135 (814)443-6468
Fax: (814)443-9452
E-mail: daveandjodell@cs.com
URL: http://clubs.hemmings.com/kaiserdarrinroster
Contact: David C. Antram, Exec. Off.
Members: 400. **Staff:** 2. **Description:** Persons who own or are interested in preserving and restoring the Kaiser-Darrin, a limited production, two-seater, fiberglass bodied sportscar built by the Kaiser-Willys Corporation; only 435 Kaiser-Darrins were produced during its brief 1954 model year production run. Seeks to promote communication between owners for restoration help, maintenance advice, sources for parts, and support of parts remanufacturing projects. Conducts educational programs. **Libraries:** Type: reference. **Subjects:** company history, cars of the 1940's-50's. **Affiliated With:** Kaiser-Frazer Owners Club International. **Publications:** *Kaiser Darrin Owners' Roster Update,* semiannual. Newsletter. **Circulation:** 400. **Conventions/Meetings:** annual competition and convention, cars/literature (exhibits) ● annual convention and workshop (exhibits).

21241 ■ Kaiser-Frazer Owners Club International (KFOCI)

PO Box 182
Kimberly, WI 54136
E-mail: kaiserfrazerlibrary@yahoo.com
URL: http://www.kfclub.com
Contact: Jack Mueller, Historian
Founded: 1959. **Members:** 1,450. **Membership Dues:** associate, spouse, $5 (annual) ● regular, in U.S., $30 (annual) ● regular, in Canada, $35 (annual) ● overseas, $50 (annual) ● life, $500 ● life (associate, spouse), $60. **Description:** Persons who own or are interested in preserving and restoring Kaiser, Frazer, Henry-J, Allstate, and postwar Willys automobiles. Aids in problems of car maintenance, locating parts, and acquiring or trading cars. Maintains library of literature on Kaiser-Frazer automobiles. **Telecommunication Services:** electronic mail, neubie@torchlake.com. **Formerly:** Kaiser-Frazer Owners Clubs of America. **Publications:** *Kaiser-Frazer Magazine,* quarterly ● *Membership Book,* periodic ● Bulletin, monthly. **Advertising:** accepted ● Also publishes specifications and paint codes of every model K-F car. **Conventions/Meetings:** annual meeting.

21242 ■ Karmann Ghia Club of North America (KGCNA)

4200 Park Blvd., No. 151
Oakland, CA 94602
Ph: (510)567-9957

Fax: (510)567-9975
E-mail: richard@karmannghia.org
URL: http://www.karmannghia.org
Contact: Richard Troy, Founder/Pres.
Founded: 1994. **Membership Dues:** in U.S., $25 (annual) ● outside U.S., $40 (annual). **Multinational. Description:** Represents Karmann Ghia enthusiasts worldwide. Serves the needs of the Karmann Ghia community. Preserves and promotes the Karmann-Ghia Volkswagen. **Publications:** *Karmann Chronicles*. Newsletter. **Price:** included in membership dues; $6.00 for nonmembers. Alternate Formats: online.

21243 ■ Kissel Kar Klub
c/o Wisconsin Automotive Museum
147 N Rural St.
Hartford, WI 53027
Ph: (262)673-7999
Fax: (262)673-7999
E-mail: kisselkarklub@wisconsinautomuseum.com
URL: http://www.wisconsinautomuseum.com
Contact: Dale W. Anderson, Exec. Dir.
Founded: 1957. **Members:** 198. **Staff:** 1. **Multinational. Description:** Owners of automobiles manufactured by the Kissel Motor Car Co. of Hartford, WI (1906-1931); former Kissel officers and employees. Works to: protect the Kissel name; maintain a list of surviving Kissel-built motor cars; authenticate the model years of members' cars; assemble pertinent history and assist historians, librarians, and authors with accurate information; aid owners in restoring cars and obtaining parts; help prospective owners locate Kissel cars. Maintains library of magazine articles, copies of company records, and correspondence with company officers. **Libraries: Type:** reference. **Holdings:** 900. **Subjects:** Kissel. **Publications:** *The Kisselgraph*, annual. Newsletter ● Directory, periodic. **Conventions/Meetings:** annual Kissel Homecoming - general assembly - always August in Hartford, WI.

21244 ■ Kustom Kemps of America (KKOA)
26 Main St.
Cassville, MO 65625-9400
Ph: (417)847-2940
Fax: (417)847-3647
E-mail: kustomkemps@mo-net.com
URL: http://www.kustomkempsofamerica.com
Contact: Jerry E. Titus, Pres.
Founded: 1980. **Members:** 11,000. **Membership Dues:** individual, $33 (annual) ● life, $350. **Budget:** $100,000. **Description:** Enthusiasts of custom cars and trucks from 1935 to 1964. (Kemp is slang from the late 1950s indicating a customized car or truck.) Seeks to restore and manufacture custom cars of the hot-rodding industry. Operates Late Model Smoothie Division for nonstock cars and trucks produced from 1965 to the present. Maintains hall of fame. **Libraries: Type:** open to the public. **Awards: Type:** recognition. **Publications:** *KKOA - the Trendsetter*, bimonthly. Magazine. **Advertising:** accepted. **Conventions/Meetings:** annual Outdoor Car Show (exhibits) ● bimonthly regional meeting.

21245 ■ Lamborghini Club America (LCA)
PO Box 649
Orinda, CA 94563
Ph: (925)253-9399 (925)254-2107
Fax: (925)253-9397
E-mail: heady@eudoramail.com
URL: http://www.lamborghiniclub.com
Contact: James Heady, Pres./Publisher
Founded: 1978. **Members:** 1,500. **Membership Dues:** regular, in U.S. and Canada, $65 (annual) ● regular, outside U.S. and Canada, $90 (annual). **Multinational. Description:** Lamborghini automobile owners and enthusiasts. Provides assistance in locating parts and reputable service facilities. Disseminates information; sponsors social gatherings. **Formerly:** (1989) Nuova Lamborghini Club. **Publications:** *Lamborghini Club Magazine*, quarterly. Contains technical articles, want ads, and calendar of events. **Price:** $15.00. **Circulation:** 1,500. **Advertising:** accepted. **Conventions/Meetings:** quarterly meeting (exhibits).

21246 ■ Late Great Chevrolet Association (LGCA)
5140 S Washington Ave.
Titusville, FL 32780
Free: (800)683-1961
Fax: (321)383-2059
E-mail: info@lategreatchevy.com
URL: http://www.lategreatchevy.com
Contact: Danny B. Howell, Pres.
Founded: 1980. **Members:** 16,000. **Membership Dues:** individual, $40 (annual). **Staff:** 18. **State Groups:** 56. **Description:** Seeks to preserve and restore 1958-1964 Chevrolets. Sponsors competitions; supplies a variety of reproduction parts for restoration. **Awards: Type:** recognition. **Publications:** *Late Great Chevys*, monthly. **Conventions/Meetings:** annual meeting.

21247 ■ Les Amis de Panhard and Deutsch Bonnet (LADP&DB-USA)
7992 Oak Creek Dr.
Reno, NV 89511-1065
Ph: (775)853-8452
E-mail: panhardusa@aol.com
URL: http://www.panhardusa.org
Contact: John A. Peterson, Ed.
Founded: 1960. **Members:** 85. **Membership Dues:** regular, $15 (annual). **Staff:** 1. **Languages:** English, French. **Description:** Owners and fans of DB and Panhard automobiles, which are of French manufacture. The DB is named after Charles Deutsch and Rene Bonnet, who built fiberglass coupes and roadsters, using Panhard running gear and power train, from about 1957 to 1963. **Libraries: Type:** open to the public. **Holdings:** 20. **Subjects:** Panhard 1954-67, D-B 1953-61. **Formerly:** (1990) DB - Panhard Registry. **Publications:** *Club Name*, quarterly. Newsletter. **Price:** included in membership dues. **Circulation:** 80. **Advertising:** accepted. **Conventions/Meetings:** annual meeting, engine display (exhibits).

21248 ■ Lincoln and Continental Owners Club (LCOC)
PO Box 1715
Maple Grove, MN 55311-6715
Ph: (763)420-7829
Free: (866)427-7583
Fax: (763)420-7849
E-mail: lcoc@cornerstonereg.com
URL: http://www.lcoc.org
Founded: 1953. **Members:** 5,000. **Membership Dues:** national, $36 (annual) ● regional, $20-$40 (annual) ● overseas, $54 (annual). **Staff:** 5. **Budget:** $145,000. **Regional Groups:** 26. **Description:** Persons interested in preserving and restoring Lincolns and Continentals. Provides information on location and exchange of replacement parts and restoration service. **Awards: Frequency:** annual. **Type:** recognition. **Recipient:** for best cars at car shows. **Formerly:** (1988) Lincoln Continental Owners Club. **Publications:** *Authenticity Manuals*. **Price:** $65.00 for members; $90.00 for nonmembers ● *Continental Comments*, bimonthly. Magazine. **Price:** included in membership dues. **Advertising:** accepted ● *Continental Comments Directory Issue*, annual. **Conventions/Meetings:** annual competition.

21249 ■ Lincoln Owners' Club (LOC)
c/o Reuben Taylor, Membership Chm.
699 Revere Rd.
Glen Ellyn, IL 60137
Ph: (630)469-1447
E-mail: bilpuch@yahoo.com
URL: http://www.lincolnownersclub.com
Contact: H. Gene Nau, Pres.
Founded: 1958. **Members:** 1,102. **Description:** Persons interested in preserving and restoring Lincoln cars produced from 1920-1940, ending with the K Series cars and not including the Zephyr or Continental. **Publications:** *Fork and Blade*, semiannual. Magazine. Features articles and photos on Lincoln motorcars, contains coverage of association's activities and Lincoln Motor Company history. ● *Lincoln Owners' Club Newsletter*, bimonthly. Contains timely news, classified ads, recommended suppliers and a

calendar of events. **Advertising:** accepted. **Conventions/Meetings:** annual meeting - always October in Hershey, PA.

21250 ■ Lincoln Zephyr Owner's Club (LZOC)
c/o Shirley Hopkins, Membership Dir.
PO Box 733
Loleta, CA 95551-0733
Ph: (707)768-1938
Fax: (707)768-1938
E-mail: lincolnzephyr@cox.net
URL: http://www.lzoc.org
Contact: Shirley Hopkins, Membership Dir.
Founded: 1967. **Members:** 1,200. **Membership Dues:** U.S. bulk rate mail, $35 (annual) ● U.S. first class mail/Canada and Mexico airmail, $43 (annual) ● all, $53 (annual). **Regional Groups:** 3. **Multinational. Description:** Persons who own, or are interested in, the Lincoln-Zephyr automobile circa 1936-48. Promotes the preservation, restoration, and exhibition of this automobile class, including all cars that were based on the Zephyr mechanical elements. **Libraries: Type:** reference. **Holdings:** archival material, articles, periodicals. **Publications:** *Club Directory*, annual. **Circulation:** 1,200. **Advertising:** accepted ● *Way of the Zephyr*, bimonthly. **Conventions/Meetings:** Gathering of the Faithful - show, with car show, get together with other people who like Lincoln Zephyrs and continentals, hold seminars, swap parts, and go on a tour (exhibits) - 3/year ● annual Swap Meet.

21251 ■ London Vintage Taxi Association - American Section (LVTA)
PO Box 445
Windham, NH 03087-0445
Ph: (603)893-8919 (603)893-5550
Fax: (603)893-6388
E-mail: lvtauk@binternet.com
URL: http://www.lvta.co.uk
Contact: John Freeston, Sec.
Founded: 1984. **Members:** 125. **Membership Dues:** regular, $48 (annual). **Description:** Owners and enthusiasts of retired taxicabs of London. Seeks to promote the restoration and preservation of vintage London taxis. Facilitates the exchange of technical information. Maintains historical records and restoration parts and data. **Libraries: Type:** reference. **Holdings:** archival material, biographical archives. **Subjects:** vintage London taxis. **Publications:** *American Section Notes*, monthly. Newsletter. Includes reports, membership information, and technical tips. ● *London Newsletter*.

21252 ■ Lotus, Ltd.
PO Box L
College Park, MD 20741
Ph: (301)982-4054
Fax: (301)982-4054
E-mail: hq@lotuscarclub.org
URL: http://www.lotuscarclub.org
Contact: Cora A. Gregorie, Corresponding Sec.
Founded: 1973. **Members:** 1,400. **Membership Dues:** regular, in U.S., $35 (annual) ● regular, outside U.S., $40 (annual). **Staff:** 1. **Budget:** $50,000. **Local Groups:** 13. **Description:** Owners and enthusiasts of Lotus automobiles (ownership not required for membership). Aims to provide and exchange information on Lotus cars. **Formerly:** (1998) Lotus. **Publications:** *Lotus ReMarque*, monthly. Newsletter. Includes Lotus' news, calendar of events, technical, and feature articles. **Price:** included in membership dues. **Circulation:** 1,400. **Advertising:** accepted ● *Membership Roster*, annual. Membership Directory ● Reprints. **Conventions/Meetings:** annual Lotus Owners Gathering - meeting and conference (exhibits).

21253 ■ LOVEfords
c/o John Rotella, Pres./Founder
2484 W Genesee Tpke.
Camillus, NY 13031-9610
Ph: (315)672-5548

E-mail: info@lovefords.org
URL: http://www.lovefords.org
Contact: John Rotella, Pres./Founder
Founded: 2000. **Members:** 400. **Staff:** 3. **Multinational. Description:** Ford, Mercury, Edsel, and Lincoln owners (and fans) exchange information, pictures, and memorabilia. **Libraries: Type:** open to the public. **Holdings:** 200. **Subjects:** Ford, Mercury, Edsel, Lincoln. **Computer Services:** Online services, Pop3 email accounts. **Telecommunication Services:** electronic mail, director@lovefords.org.

21254 ■ Marlin Auto Club
c/o Stan Kelly, Treas.
3195 Woodmont Dr.
San Jose, CA 95118
Ph: (408)269-7788 (812)256-2069
E-mail: j1959w@aol.com
URL: http://marlinautoclub.com
Contact: Kevin Wright, Pres.
Founded: 2000. **Members:** 180. **Membership Dues:** regular, in U.S., $20 (annual) ● regular, in Canada, $26 (annual) ● regular, outside U.S. and Canada, $30 (annual). **Staff:** 4. **Regional Groups:** 19. **State Groups:** 43. **Local Groups:** 19. **Description:** Strives to restore and preserve the 1965-1967 Marlin Automobile; only 17,419 were produced. Ownership not required to join. **Telecommunication Services:** electronic mail, marlin4@aol.com. **Publications:** *Fish Tales*, quarterly. Newsletter. **Circulation:** 225. **Conventions/Meetings:** annual Marlin National Meets - show (exhibits).

21255 ■ Marmon Club (MC)
c/o Marge Iaccino, Sec.
No. 4 Country Rte. 22
Hudson, NY 12534-9521
Ph: (518)828-5581
E-mail: wearever@tvconline.net
URL: http://www.marmonclub.com
Contact: Marge Iaccino, Sec.
Founded: 1970. **Members:** 250. **Membership Dues:** regular, in U.S. and Canada, $24 (annual) ● regular, outside U.S. and Canada, $29 (annual). **Multinational. Description:** Represents individuals who have interest in the history, preservation, driving, and restoration of Marmon and Roosevelt automobiles built in the years of 1902-1933. **Publications:** *Marmon Club Directory*, annual. Membership Directory. Lists all members' names, addresses, phone numbers, and their Marmon and Roosevelt automobiles. **Price:** included in membership dues. **Circulation:** 400. **Advertising:** accepted ● *The Marmon News*, bimonthly. Newsletter. **Price:** included in membership dues. **Conventions/Meetings:** annual Mighty Marmon Muster - general assembly.

21256 ■ The Maserati Club (TMC)
325 Walden Ave.
Harriman, TN 37748
Ph: (865)882-9230
E-mail: sec@themaseraticlub.com
URL: http://www.themaseraticlub.com
Contact: Seymour G. Pond, Chm.
Founded: 1986. **Members:** 700. **Membership Dues:** individual or corporate in U.S., $65 (annual) ● individual or corporate outside U.S., $90 (annual) ● patron in U.S., $165 (annual) ● patron outside U.S., $200 (annual). **Staff:** 35. **Regional Groups:** 11. **National Groups:** 5. **Languages:** English, Italian, Japanese. **Multinational. Description:** Owners and admirers of Maserati automobiles. Promotes ownership, restoration, and maintenance of Maseratis. Gathers and disseminates information; facilitates exchange of information among members. **Libraries: Type:** not open to the public. **Holdings:** 43; periodicals. **Subjects:** Maserati automobiles. **Awards:** Concours. **Frequency:** annual. **Type:** recognition. **Computer Services:** Online services, educational. **Absorbed:** (2002) Maserati Owners Club of North America. **Formerly:** (1997) Maserati Club of America. **Publications:** *Il Tridente*, biennial. Magazine. Features the finest Maserati publication in the world today. **Price:** $65.00/year. **Circulation:** 800. **Advertising:** accepted. Alternate Formats: online. **Conven-**

tions/Meetings: monthly board meeting - always last Wednesday ● meet.

21257 ■ Maserati Information Exchange (MIE)
1620 Indus. Dr. SW, Ste.F
Auburn, WA 98001-6555
Ph: (253)833-2598
Fax: (253)735-0946
E-mail: mci@maseratinet.com
URL: http://www.maseratinet.com
Contact: Gary Farmer, Contact
Founded: 1976. **Members:** 3,000. **For-Profit. Description:** Owners and enthusiasts of Maserati sports automobiles, manufactured in Italy from 1926 to the present. Provides members with information and technical assistance and conducts meets. Maintains $10 million inventory of new and used parts. Publishes quarterly magazine (80 pages) for membership. **Also Known As:** MIE Corp. **Publications:** *Viale Ciro Menotti*, quarterly. Magazine. **Advertising:** accepted. **Conventions/Meetings:** annual meet - usually August.

21258 ■ Maverick/Comet Club International (MCCI)
421 E State St.
Albany, IN 47320
E-mail: mavtricks@yahoo.com
URL: http://www.maverickcometclub.org
Contact: Shawn Simpson, Pres.
Founded: 1993. **Members:** 350. **Membership Dues:** regular, $20 (annual). **Multinational. Description:** Represents enthusiasts and owners of 1970-1977 Ford Mavericks and Mercury Comets. Preserves and promotes the 1970-1977 Ford Mavericks and Mercury Comets. Facilitates communication and cooperation among members. **Telecommunication Services:** electronic mail, rpbidlack@juno.com. **Publications:** *Shorthorns*, bimonthly. Newsletter. **Price:** included in membership dues. **Conventions/Meetings:** annual Round-Up Nationals - show.

21259 ■ Mazda Club (MC)
PO Box 11238
Chicago, IL 60611
Ph: (773)769-6262
Fax: (773)769-3240
E-mail: info@mazdaclub.com
URL: http://www.mazdaclub.com
Contact: Robert Thomas, Pres.
Founded: 1988. **Members:** 1,250. **Membership Dues:** regular, in U.S., $25 (annual) ● regular, outside U.S., $35 (annual). **Description:** Admirers of Mazda automobiles. Promotes Mazda ownership. Gathers and disseminates information on Mazdas and their care and maintenance. **Telecommunication Services:** electronic mail, rob@mazdaclub.com. **Publications:** *Only Way*, quarterly. Magazine. **Circulation:** 1,250.

21260 ■ Mercedes-Benz Club of America (MBCA)
1907 Lelaray St.
Colorado Springs, CO 80909-2872
Ph: (719)633-6427
Free: (800)637-2360
Fax: (719)633-9283
E-mail: david@mbca.org
URL: http://www.mbca.org
Contact: David Cummings, Exec. Dir.
Founded: 1956. **Members:** 30,000. **Membership Dues:** domestic, $45 (annual) ● international, $55 (annual) ● second section, $15 (annual). **Staff:** 6. **Budget:** $1,000,000. **Regional Groups:** 11. **Local Groups:** 90. **Description:** Owners and others interested in Mercedes-Benz cars. Sponsors national events and local section rallies, concours d'elegance, and gymkhanas. Provides technical information on maintenance and parts. Conducts educational and research programs; sponsors charitable activities. **Awards: Type:** recognition. **Committees:** Budget; Elections; Leadership; National Events; Newsletter; Raffle; Star; Technical; Vintage. **Publications:** *Star*, bimonthly. Magazine. **Circulation:** 30,000. **Advertising:** accepted ● Also publishes local newsletters from assigned section. **Conventions/Meetings:** semian-

nual Business Meeting - November and May ● annual convention (exhibits).

21261 ■ Mercedes-Benz M-100 Owner's Group
910 Suellen Dr.
Reading, PA 19605
Ph: (610)921-0462
Fax: (610)921-3318
E-mail: hammel6626@aol.com
URL: http://www.m-100.cc
Contact: Stu Hammel, Pres.
Founded: 1989. **Members:** 325. **Membership Dues:** regular, in U.S., $80 (annual) ● regular, outside U.S., $95 (annual). **Multinational. Description:** Owners and enthusiasts of the special models of Mercedes-Benz with "M-100" V-8 engines. Aims to share knowledge of the history and maintenance of the cars and to expand recognition of the cars. Offers educational and research programs, competitions, statistics, and a speaker's bureau. **Libraries: Type:** reference; not open to the public. **Holdings:** archival material, articles, artwork, books, periodicals. **Publications:** *Lode Star*, quarterly. Newsletter. **Price:** included in membership dues. **Circulation:** 500. **Advertising:** accepted. **Conventions/Meetings:** annual convention and board meeting - moves around in Phoenix, Colorado Springs, or New York.

21262 ■ Metropolitan Owners Club of North America (MOCNA)
c/o Betty Jacobson, Treas.
2308 Co. Hwy. V
Sun Prairie, WI 53590
E-mail: mbjaco@fastbytes.com
URL: http://www.mocna.org
Contact: Betty Jacobson, Treas.
Founded: 1975. **Members:** 2,000. **Membership Dues:** individual in U.S. and Canada, $20 (annual) ● individual outside U.S. and Canada, $29 (annual) ● life, in U.S. and Canada, $266 ● life, outside U.S. and Canada, $366. **Regional Groups:** 25. **Description:** Seeks to preserve the Metropolitan automobile produced by Austin Motor Co., Ltd. of Birmingham, England for American Motors, Inc. between 1954 and 1961. Disseminates information concerning restoration and maintenance of the Metropolitan. **Libraries: Type:** reference. **Holdings:** periodicals. **Subjects:** metropolitan automobiles. **Publications:** *Cumulative Index to Maintenance Items in the Met Gazette*, monthly. Magazine. **Advertising:** accepted ● *Membership Roster*, annual. Membership Directory ● *The Met Gazette*, monthly. Newsletter. **Circulation:** 2,000. **Advertising:** accepted ● *Parts-Interchange Manual*. **Conventions/Meetings:** biennial meeting.

21263 ■ MG Drivers Club of North America
18 George's Pl.
Clinton, NJ 08809-1334
Ph: (908)713-6251
Fax: (908)713-6251
E-mail: mgdriversclub@hotmail.com
URL: http://www.mgdriversclub.com
Contact: Richard F. Miller, Managing Dir.
Founded: 1997. **Members:** 600. **Membership Dues:** full, $20 (annual). **Multinational. Description:** Promotes the MG Marque automobile. **Awards:** Cecil Kimber Enthusiasts Award. **Frequency:** annual. **Type:** trophy. **Recipient:** for significant contribution to the MG Marque. **Publications:** *The Log Book*, quarterly. Newsletter. **Price:** included in membership dues. **Circulation:** 650. **Advertising:** accepted. **Conventions/Meetings:** annual The Drive-In - convention.

21264 ■ Microcar and Minicar Club (MMC)
PO Box 43137
Upper Montclair, NJ 07043-0137
E-mail: info@microcarworld.org
URL: http://microcarworld.org
Contact: Ernest Freestone, Ed.
Founded: 1991. **Members:** 900. **Membership Dues:** regular, in U.S., $25 (annual) ● overseas, $35 (annual). **Description:** Enthusiasts of mini- and microcars, which the groups define as being eleven feet long or less, with engine displacement of less than

1,000 cubic centimeters. Promotes interest in mini- and microcars and related vehicles. Gathers and disseminates parts and repair and maintenance information; makes available free classified advertisements to members; distributes memorabilia. **Publications:** *Microcar and Minicar Club Membership Application.* Brochure ● *Minutia,* quarterly. Magazine. **Circulation:** 900. **Advertising:** accepted. **Conventions/Meetings:** periodic meet.

21265 ■ Mid-Century Mercury Car Club (MCMCC)

c/o Rusty Bethley
1816 E Elmwood Dr.
Lindenhurst, IL 60046
Ph: (847)356-2555
E-mail: cruzinmer@aol.com
URL: http://clubs.hemmings.com/frameset.
  cfm?club=midcenturymercury
Contact: Carl H. Walter, Ed.
Founded: 1977. **Members:** 200. **Membership Dues:** regular, in U.S. and Canada, $15 (annual) ● regular, outside U.S. and Canada, $21 (annual). **Description:** Individuals united to promote the appreciation and preservation of the 1949-51 Mercury car, stock or custom. **Libraries: Type:** not open to the public. **Holdings:** 100; articles, books. **Subjects:** 1949-1951 Ford and Mercury products. **Awards: Type:** recognition. **Publications:** *Wings of Mercury,* annual. Membership Directory. **Price:** included in membership dues. **Circulation:** 300. **Advertising:** accepted. **Conventions/Meetings:** annual Car Show - Sunday before Memorial Day ● annual meeting (exhibits) - usually Memorial Weekend.

21266 ■ Midstates Jeepster Association (MJA)

c/o Barb Conrad, Sec.-Treas.
7721 Howick Rd.
Celina, OH 45822
E-mail: danwright3@comcast.net
URL: http://mjaweb.org
Contact: Barb Conrad, Sec.-Treas.
Founded: 1966. **Members:** 400. **Membership Dues:** basic, $25 (annual). **Description:** Seeks to promote the restoration and preservation of "America's last production touring car," the Willys-Overland Jeepster produced in Toledo, OH from 1948 to 1951. Provides members with factory production schedules, serial numbers, original paint data, wiring diagrams, maintenance and restoration information, and other Jeepster data. **Publications:** *Midstates Jeepster Association—Newsletter,* monthly. **Conventions/Meetings:** semiannual meet, non-competitive - always spring and fall.

21267 ■ Midwest Sunbeam Registry (MSR)

20700 Huntington Way
Prior Lake, MN 55372-9725
Ph: (952)440-6300
E-mail: wbjennings@integraonline.com
Contact: William B. Jennings, Board Chm.
Founded: 1981. **Members:** 120. **Description:** Represents collectors and enthusiasts of Sunbeam Alpine and Tiger sports cars throughout the U.S. who preserve and restore Sunbeam Alpine and Tiger sports cars manufactured in England. Promotes good fellowship among members through car-related activities. Conducts technical training sessions. Compiles statistics. **Libraries: Type:** reference. **Holdings:** artwork, books, periodicals. **Subjects:** British sports cars. **Publications:** *Midwest Sunbeam Registry—Membership Roster,* annual. Membership Directory ● *Sunbeam Sentinel,* monthly. Newsletter.

21268 ■ Milestone Car Society (MCS)

626 N Park Ave.
Indianapolis, IN 46204
Ph: (317)636-9900
E-mail: dinodriver@ori.net
URL: http://www.milestonecarsociety.org
Contact: Dr. Malcolm E. Boone DDS, Dir.
Founded: 1971. **Members:** 600. **Membership Dues:** individual, $25 (annual) ● patron, $50 (annual) ● life, $300. **Budget:** $4,000. **Regional Groups:** 5. **State Groups:** 4. **Description:** Multi-marque automobile

society established for the enjoyment of selected, nominated milestone era (1945-72) foreign and domestic cars. **Libraries: Type:** reference; open to the public. **Holdings:** 33; articles, periodicals. **Subjects:** automotive. **Publications:** *Mile Post,* quarterly. Newsletter. Covers nominations and automotive articles. **Price:** included in membership dues. **Advertising:** accepted ● *Roster of Members and Cars,* biennial. Membership Directory. **Conventions/Meetings:** annual meeting (exhibits) - usually last weekend of July.

21269 ■ Mini Car Club, U.S.A. (MCC)

172 Park St.
Montclair, NJ 07042
Ph: (973)746-8165
Fax: (973)746-8165
E-mail: bkwaloff@aol.com
Contact: Boris Kwaloff, Managing Dir.
Founded: 1966. **Members:** 79. **Description:** Owners of tiny automobiles, including the B.M.C. Mini, Austin 850, Austin Cooper, Morris 850, and Morris Cooper. **Publications:** *Mini Motoring,* quarterly ● Newsletter, monthly. **Conventions/Meetings:** annual meeting.

21270 ■ Model A Ford Cabriolet Club (MAFCC)

PO Box 1487
Conroe, TX 77305
Ph: (936)441-8209
E-mail: asgrandle@earthlink.net
URL: http://clubs.hemmings.com/clubsites/modelaca-
  briolet
Contact: Larry Machacek, Coor.
Founded: 1980. **Members:** 400. **Membership Dues;** regular, in U.S., Canada, Mexico, $12 (annual) ● regular, outside U.S. and Canada, $14 (annual). **Description:** A special interest group of the Model A Ford Club of America and a Special Body Style Interest Region of the Model "A" Restorers Club. Owners and enthusiasts of the Cabriolet dedicated to its restoration and preservation. (Cabriolets are a rare body style of the Model A Ford manufactured from 1929 through 1931.) Works for the collection and dissemination of information and parts. Compiles statistics; encourages gatherings at antique car shows; does not require ownership of a Cabriolet. **Divisions:** 1931 68-C Cabriolet; 1930-31 68-B Cabriolet; 1929 68-A Cabriolet. **Formerly:** (1984) Model A 68-B Cabriolet Club. **Publications:** *Cabrioletter,* quarterly. Newsletter. Contains technical articles, classified ads, and club announcements. **Price:** free for members ● *Index,* annual ● *Membership Roster,* biennial. Membership Directory. **Conventions/Meetings:** annual meeting, held in conjunction with the Antique Automotive Club of America's Eastern Division National Fall Show - usually second weekend of October in Hershey, PA.

21271 ■ Model A Ford Club of America (MAFCA)

250 S Cypress
La Habra, CA 90631-5515
Ph: (562)697-2712 (562)697-2737
Fax: (562)690-7452
E-mail: info@mafca.com
URL: http://www.mafca.com
Contact: Sandra Aguirre, Office Mgr.
Founded: 1955. **Members:** 15,500. **Membership Dues:** regular, in U.S., $30 (annual) ● regular, outside U.S., $34 (annual). **Staff:** 5. **Regional Groups:** 5. **National Groups:** 308. **Description:** Represents persons interested in restoring and preserving Model A Ford cars (1928-31). **Libraries: Type:** reference. **Formerly:** (1957) Model A Restorers Club of Southern California. **Publications:** *The Restorer,* bimonthly. Magazine. Contains information about club activities and restoration processes. **Price:** included in membership dues. ISSN: 0482-4040. **Circulation:** 15,500. **Advertising:** accepted. **Conventions/Meetings:** biennial meeting.

21272 ■ Model A Ford Foundation

PO Box 95151
Nonantum, MA 02495-0151

E-mail: fordsong@msn.com
URL: http://www.Maffi.org
Contact: George Tynan, Pres.
Founded: 1986. **Members:** 700. **Membership Dues:** family/associate, $25 (annual) ● life, $350 ● bronze, $100 (annual) ● silver, $250 (annual) ● gold, $500 (annual). **Budget:** $50,000. **Description:** Promotes the preservation of the Model A Ford and its era (1928-1931). Conducts charitable, educational, and research programs; maintains speakers' bureau and museum. **Libraries: Type:** reference. **Holdings:** 1,000; archival material, artwork, books, periodicals. **Subjects:** America 1928-1931. **Publications:** *A Preserver,* quarterly. Newsletter. **Circulation:** 700. **Conventions/Meetings:** annual meeting.

21273 ■ Model "A" Restorers Club (MARC)

6721 Merriman Rd.
Garden City, MI 48135
Ph: (734)427-9050
Fax: (734)427-9054
E-mail: talk@modelaford.org
URL: http://www.modelaford.org
Contact: Rick Sturim, Pres.
Founded: 1952. **Members:** 9,900. **Membership Dues:** regular, in U.S., $35 (annual) ● regular, in Canada and international, $40 (annual) ● regular, in U.S. and Canada (airmail), $46 (annual) ● international (airmail), $53 (annual). **Staff:** 3. **Regional Groups:** 169. **Description:** Represents automotive enthusiasts interested in preserving Model A Ford cars and trucks and related literature and accessories. (The Model A was produced between 1928 and 1931). Compiles statistics. **Libraries: Type:** reference. **Subjects:** historical information on the Model A Ford. **Awards:** Ken Brady. **Frequency:** annual. **Type:** recognition. **Recipient:** for a member who has made the most significant contribution to the club ● **Type:** recognition. **Committees:** Driving Awards; Fashion Standards; Insurance; Judging Standards; Technical; Touring Class; Youth. **Publications:** *Judging Standards and Restoration Guidelines.* Book. **Price:** $30.00 ● *Model A News,* bimonthly. Magazine ● Booklet. Provides information on judging and fashion standards. **Conventions/Meetings:** competition ● annual meet.

21274 ■ Model "T" Ford Club of America (MTFCA)

PO Box 126
Centerville, IN 47330-0126
Ph: (765)855-5248
Fax: (765)855-3428
E-mail: admin@mtfca.com
URL: http://www.mtfca.com
Contact: Jay G. Klehfoth, Exec. Dir.
Founded: 1965. **Members:** 8,500. **Membership Dues:** regular, in U.S., $29 (annual) ● regular, in Canada, $35 (annual) ● regular, outside U.S. and Canada, $36 (annual). **Staff:** 2. **Local Groups:** 125. **Description:** Individuals interested in the history, restoration and operation of the Model T Ford. Maintains collection of catalogs, photos, and pamphlets. Compiles statistics. **Libraries: Type:** reference. **Awards:** Walter Rosenthal Trophy. **Frequency:** annual. **Type:** trophy. **Recipient:** for the member contributing the most to the hobby. **Publications:** *The Model T Ford-The Car That Changed the World.* Book. **Price:** $39.95 ● *The Model T Ford - The Care That Changed the World.* Book ● *The Vintage Ford,* bimonthly. Magazine. Provides information on Ford cars built in 1908 to 1927. **Price:** included in membership dues. ISSN: 0042-6350. **Circulation:** 9,000. **Advertising:** accepted ● Manuals. Covers restoration of electrical system, transmission, carburetor, Rucks-tell axle, engine, speedometers, and front and rear axles. **Price:** $6.00 each ● Videos. Contains restoration information. **Conventions/Meetings:** annual dinner and tour, includes awards - always first quarter ● tour.

21275 ■ Model "T" Ford Club International (MTFCI)

PO Box 276236
Boca Raton, FL 33427-6236
Ph: (561)750-7170

E-mail: hgustav@aol.com
URL: http://www.modelt.org
Contact: Howard Gustavson, Exec. Dir.
Founded: 1952. **Members:** 4,300. **Membership Dues:** regular in U.S., $30 (annual) ● regular outside U.S., $35 (annual). **Budget:** $125,000. **National Groups:** 110. **Multinational. Description:** Hobbyists interested in the preservation and restoration of antique Model T Ford automobiles. Sponsors restoration, photography, and safety slogan contests. Local groups conduct activities including tours, restoration contest, parades, and parts exchanges. **Publications:** *Model T Ford Service Bulletins.* Contains 114 bulletins - 944 pages assembled with cover and index. **Price:** $45.00 plus shipping and handling; $5.00 each, in U.S.; $14.00 each, in Canada; $8.00 each, outside U.S. and Canada ● *Model T Times,* bimonthly. Magazine. **Price:** included in membership dues. ISSN: 0891-6187. **Conventions/Meetings:** annual meeting ● annual tour.

21276 ■ Mopar Scat Pack Club
Address Unknown since 2007
Founded: 1980. **Members:** 500. **Membership Dues:** general, $25 (annual). **Staff:** 5. **Budget:** $10,000. **Regional Groups:** 6. **Description:** Individuals dedicated to the preservation and restoration of Chrysler high-performance cars. Collects and shares information and statistics on parts, technical matters, and car history. Sponsors shows, swap meets, and races. Offers members discounts on parts and services, restoration tips, and technical seminars at sponsored events. Compiles lists of Chrysler high-performance car production figures and parts needed for sale nationwide. Maintains historical collection of parts books, dealer brochures, and pictures, (The word scat in the name refers to the common American slang for fast movement.). **Libraries: Type:** reference. **Holdings:** articles, books. **Subjects:** mopar performance, restoration. **Awards: Type:** recognition. **Committees:** National Convention; Show. **Publications:** *Mighty Mopars,* bimonthly. Newsletter. Covers association activities, automobile shows, and other news. **Price:** $2.00. **Circulation:** 500. **Advertising:** accepted ● *MOPAR Restoration Guide,* annual. Lists dealers and vendors of Mopar automobile parts, accessories, and restoration supplies in the United States and Canada. **Price:** included in membership dues; $2.50/year for nonmembers. **Circulation:** 500. **Advertising:** accepted ● *MOPAR Scat Pack—Club Roster,* annual. **Circulation:** 500. **Advertising:** not accepted. **Conventions/Meetings:** annual Mopar Nationals - convention, car show, drag race, swap meet (exhibits).

21277 ■ Morgan 3/4 Group
c/o Dean Meyer, Membership Dir.
233 Mountain Rd.
Ridgefield, CT 06877
Ph: (203)438-7374
Fax: (203)438-0080
E-mail: dean@ndma.com
URL: http://www.morgan34.org
Contact: Dean Meyer, Membership Dir.
Founded: 1960. **Members:** 300. **Membership Dues:** regular, $35 (annual). **Staff:** 10. **Regional Groups:** 4. **Description:** Represents owners and enthusiasts of Morgan automobiles, which enthusiasts call "the last of the real sports cars." Conducts technical sessions, tours and rallies, concours, social events; compiles statistics on members' car types and models. **Awards:** Harry Carter Esprit du Vent. **Type:** recognition. **Formerly:** (1976) Morgan Owners Group. **Publications:** *Membership Roster,* annual. Membership Directory ● *The Morganeer,* 8/year. Newsletter. **Advertising:** accepted ● Also publishes technical articles. **Conventions/Meetings:** annual Autumn Mog - meeting, with multiple driving, showing, social events - September or October, location central to New England.

21278 ■ Morgan Car Club (MCC)
616 Gist Ave.
Silver Spring, MD 20910
Ph: (301)585-0121

E-mail: edh@morgandc.com
URL: http://www.morgandc.com
Contact: Ed Herman, Pres.
Founded: 1959. **Members:** 350. **Description:** Morgan car owners, past owners, parts suppliers, and other interested parties. Promotes interest in the Morgan automobile; encourages fellowship among Morgan owners, drivers, and enthusiasts. Compiles statistics; maintains placement service. **Libraries: Type:** reference. **Awards: Type:** recognition. **Affiliated With:** Morgan Sports Car Club. **Publications:** *CARpentry, the Collected Technical Tips for the Rough Rider.* Book ● *MOG Review,* annual. Magazine ● *Morgan Car Club—Roster of Members,* annual. Directory ● *Rough Rider,* monthly. Newsletter. **Conventions/Meetings:** annual Morgan Owners Gathering - meeting (exhibits).

21279 ■ Morgan Plus Four Club (MPFC)
5073 Melbourne Dr.
Cypress, CA 90630
Ph: (714)828-3127 (310)214-5517
Free: (877)MOG-PLUS
E-mail: gerry.willburn@bigfoot.com
URL: http://www.mog.org
Contact: Gerry Willburn, Membership Chm.
Founded: 1955. **Members:** 300. **Membership Dues:** regular, $40 (annual). **Description:** Owners of Morgan cars. Enjoys and promotes the Morgan car. **Publications:** *Morgan Plus Four Club—Format,* monthly. Newsletter. Provides information on Morgan automobile maintenance and club activities. Includes calendar of events, meeting minutes, and list of Morgans for sale. **Price:** included in membership dues; $30.00 /year for members. **Circulation:** 350. **Advertising:** accepted ● *Roster.* **Conventions/Meetings:** monthly meeting.

21280 ■ Morgan Three-Wheeler Club - USA Group
c/o Chris Towner
56 Brick Hill Rd.
Orleans, MA 02653-2711
Ph: (508)255-6432 (508)255-9393
Fax: (508)255-9393
E-mail: mtwc@btopenworld.com
Contact: Chris Towner, Contact
Founded: 1945. **Members:** 850. **Description:** Owners and enthusiasts of Morgan three-wheeled automobiles, made in England from 1910 to 1952. Promotes the preservation of Morgan three-wheelers. Offers technical advice. **Libraries: Type:** reference. **Holdings:** articles, artwork, books, periodicals. **Subjects:** three wheelers. **Awards:** Enthusiasts Award. **Frequency:** annual. **Type:** recognition. **Affiliated With:** Morgan Three-Wheeler Club. **Publications:** *The Bulletin,* monthly. Features group reports, tech articles, and history. **Price:** included in membership dues. **Circulation:** 850. **Advertising:** accepted. **Conventions/Meetings:** annual meeting, dinner/dance, awards, general meeting, spares fair, appointments.

21281 ■ Morris Minor Registry (MMR)
c/o Tony Burgess, Exec. Off.
318 Hampton Park
Westerville, OH 43081-5723
Ph: (614)899-2394
Fax: (614)899-2493
E-mail: minornews@aol.com
URL: http://hometown.aol.com/morrisminr/default.
    html
Contact: Tony Burgess, Exec. Off.
Founded: 1974. **Members:** 700. **Membership Dues:** full, $20 (annual) ● overseas, $30 (annual). **Staff:** 2. **Regional Groups:** 33. **Description:** Owners of Morris Minor automobiles and interested individuals united for mutual assistance in finding parts for and repairing the cars. Compiles statistics on the Morris Minor automobiles still on the road in the U.S. and Canada. **Convention/Meeting:** none. **Libraries: Type:** reference. **Publications:** *Minor News,* bimonthly. Newsletter. Features excerpts from the press and classified ads for automobile parts and literature wanted or for sale. **Price:** included in membership dues. **Circulation:** 700. **Advertising:** accepted.

21282 ■ Muntz Jet Registry
21303 NE 151st St.
Woodinville, WA 98077-7612
Ph: (425)788-6587
Fax: (425)844-2331
E-mail: bvmunsen@aol.com
Contact: Victor Munsen, Exec. Officer
Founded: 1983. **Staff:** 1. **Description:** Conducts research and disseminates information concerning the history, current ownership, restoration, and needed and available parts for Muntz jet automobiles, which were produced from 1951-53. Compiles statistics. **Libraries: Type:** reference. **Holdings:** archival material. **Formerly:** (2001) Muntz Registry. **Publications:** Journal, biennial. Contains articles on the history of the Muntz jet automobile. **Circulation:** 200. **Conventions/Meetings:** biennial convention, for Muntz jet owners and enthusiasts.

21283 ■ Mustang Club of America (MCA)
4051 Barrancas Ave.
PMB 102
Pensacola, FL 32507
Ph: (850)438-0626
Fax: (850)438-0626
E-mail: mcaofficemanager@cox.net
URL: http://www.mustang.org
Contact: Arley Whitsell, Pres.
Founded: 1976. **Members:** 9,400. **Membership Dues:** regular, in U.S., $30 (annual) ● regular, in Canada, $40 (annual) ● other countries, $65 (annual) ● regular, in U.S., $120 (5/year). **Staff:** 2. **Regional Groups:** 162. **Description:** Owners and enthusiasts of Ford Mustang automobiles produced since 1964. Aims to preserve and maintain Ford Mustang cars and to serve as an accurate technical source of information concerning these automobiles. Offers restoration advice. Sponsors national and grand national shows. Operates charitable program. **Awards:** The Mustang Hall of Fame. **Type:** recognition. **Recipient:** for individuals whose contributions and activities to Ford Mustang will serve as an inspiration and example to the club ● **Type:** recognition. **Computer Services:** Mailing lists. **Publications:** *Judging Rule Book,* annual ● *Mustang Times,* monthly. Magazine. **Circulation:** 9,400. **Advertising:** accepted. **Conventions/Meetings:** quinquennial Mustang Anniversary Celebration - show, car show and open track at Nashville Superspeedway ● Swap Meet (exhibits) - 3-4/year.

21284 ■ Mustang II Network
115 McDonald Dr.
Houghton Lake, MI 48629
Ph: (313)475-4231
E-mail: stangii@mustangii.com
URL: http://www.mustangii.net
Contact: Timothy M. Grahl, Contact
Multinational. Description: Serves as the official registry for 1974-1978 Mustang II's. Works to promote the Mustang II.

21285 ■ Mustang Owners Club International (MOCI)
Address Unknown since 2007
Founded: 1975. **Members:** 650. **Membership Dues:** in U.S., $15 (annual) ● outside U.S., $18 (annual). **Description:** Owners and enthusiasts with an interest in the preservation and promotion of Ford Mustangs produced since 1965. **Libraries: Type:** reference. **Holdings:** 500; books, periodicals. **Formerly:** (1983) Mustang Owners Club. **Publications:** *Pony Express,* bimonthly. Newsletter. **Advertising:** accepted. **Conventions/Meetings:** annual meeting ● regional meeting ● seminar ● show.

21286 ■ Nash Car Club of America (NCCA)
c/o Jim Bracewell, Membership Chm.
1N274 Prarie Ave.
Glen Ellyn, IL 60137
Ph: (630)469-5848
E-mail: bracewell@nashcarclub.org
URL: http://www.nashcarclub.org
Contact: Jim Bracewell, Membership Chm.
Founded: 1970. **Members:** 1,800. **Membership Dues:** regular, in U.S., $30 (annual) ● international,

$48 (annual) ● regular, in Canada, $33 (annual) ● life in U.S., $570 ● life in Canada, $590 ● life (international), $950. **Staff:** 23. **Regional Groups:** 21. **Description:** Persons interested in Nash cars and their history. Works to aid and promote the preservation and restoration of Nash and related vehicles. Maintains listing of reproduced parts and library research service. Provides advisors for nearly all models and years. Conducts restoration workshops. Holds tours and picnics. **Libraries: Type:** reference. **Awards:** Robert Aaron Award. **Frequency:** annual. **Type:** recognition. **Recipient:** for outstanding club work ● Thomas B. Jeffery Award. **Frequency:** annual. **Type:** recognition. **Recipient:** for outstanding club work. **Computer Services:** database. **Publications:** *Marketplace*, bimonthly. Newsletter. Contains ads for Nash automobile parts and literature wanted or for sale. **Price:** included in membership dues. **Circulation:** 2,000. **Advertising:** accepted ● *Nash Times*, bimonthly. Magazine. Provides technical information, restoration tips, and regional and other news. Includes calendar of events and new member information. **Price:** included in membership dues. **Circulation:** 2,000. **Advertising:** accepted ● *Roster*, annual. Membership Directory. Contains list of all members and their cars. **Price:** included in membership dues. **Circulation:** 2,000 ● Handbook. **Price:** included in membership dues. **Conventions/Meetings:** annual Grand NASHional - meeting (exhibits) ● semiannual NASHionals - regional meeting.

21287 ■ National Antique Oldsmobile Club (NAOC)

4 Lindworth Dr.
St. Louis, MO 63124-1454
E-mail: naoc@mindspring.com
URL: http://www.antiqueolds.org
Contact: Fred H. Deusch, Sec.
Founded: 1981. **Members:** 2,000. **Membership Dues:** regular, in U.S. (third class mail) $30 (annual) ● regular, in U.S. (first class mail) $38 (annual) ● regular, in Canada and Mexico, $40 (annual) ● foreign, $50 (annual). **Description:** Represents persons interested in Oldsmobile cars produced prior to 1966. Seeks to preserve Oldsmobile autos and encourage restoration of the cars. Promotes participation in events concerning Oldsmobiles. **Publications:** *Runabouts to Rockets*, monthly. Newsletter. Contains articles about Olds from 1897-1966. **Circulation:** 1,800. **Conventions/Meetings:** annual meeting, flea market, parade, car show, business meeting and awards banquet (exhibits) - always summer.

21288 ■ National Chevelle Owners Association (NCOA)

Address Unknown since 2006
Founded: 1982. **Members:** 7,000. **Membership Dues:** individual in U.S., $30 (annual) ● in Canada, $40 (annual). **Staff:** 3. **State Groups:** 27. **For-Profit. Description:** Individuals dedicated to the preservation of stock, modified, and custom 1964-1987 Chevelles and El Caminos. Offers technical and factory information and listings of parts available to members. **Publications:** *The Chevelle Report*, monthly. Magazine. Contains technical articles, factory information, and car photos. **Price:** $3.00/copy. **Circulation:** 7,000. **Advertising:** accepted. **Conventions/Meetings:** annual Chevelle and El Camino Showdown - show and seminar (exhibits); **Avg. Attendance:** 500.

21289 ■ National Chevy Association (NCA)

947 Arcade St.
St. Paul, MN 55106-3850
Ph: (651)778-9522
Free: (800)785-5354
Fax: (651)778-9686
E-mail: info@nationalchevyassoc.com
URL: http://www.nationalchevyassoc.com
Contact: Paul Nimis, Co-Founder
Founded: 1985. **Membership Dues:** regular, in U.S., $25 (annual) ● regular, in Canada, $45 (annual) ● foreign, $65 (annual). **Description:** Promotes the 1953 and 1954 Chevrolet automobiles. **Publications:** *Partsline*, monthly. Newsletter. Contains technical advice, classified ads and letters from fellow association members.

21290 ■ National Corvette Owners Association (NCOA)

900 S Washington St., Ste.G-13
Falls Church, VA 22046
Ph: (703)533-7222
Fax: (703)533-1153
E-mail: headquarters@ncoa-vettes.com
URL: http://www.ncoa-vettes.com
Contact: Donna Sandoval, Membership Mgr.
Founded: 1975. **Members:** 20,000. **Membership Dues:** individual, $39 (annual). **Staff:** 5. **For-Profit. Description:** Corvette owners and enthusiasts united to encourage and increase the enjoyment and popularity of Corvette automobiles. Provides members with benefits such as interior discounts, and auto supply discounts. Maintains reference book collection. **Convention/Meeting:** none. **Libraries: Type:** reference. **Publications:** *For Vetts Only*, 11/year. Newsletter. Includes calendar of events. **Price:** included in membership dues. **Circulation:** 17,000. **Advertising:** accepted.

21291 ■ National Corvette Restorers Society (NCRS)

6291 Day Rd.
Cincinnati, OH 45252-1334
Ph: (513)385-8526 (513)385-6367
Fax: (513)385-8554
E-mail: ncrscincy@aol.com
URL: http://www.ncrs.org
Contact: Vito Cimilluca, Pres.
Founded: 1974. **Members:** 16,000. **Membership Dues:** regular, in U.S., $35 (annual) ● regular, in Canada, $42 (annual) ● regular, outside U.S. and Canada, $60 (annual). **Staff:** 6. **Regional Groups:** 38. **Description:** Works for the purpose of preservation, restoration, and enjoyment of Corvettes produced from 1953 through 1989 and of all related material. Encourages and publishes studies and research pertaining to their development and history. Conducts research projects and technical sessions. Compiles statistics. **Awards:** NCRS Duntov Mark of Excellence. **Frequency:** annual. **Type:** recognition. **Recipient:** for individuals who restore and preserve 1953-1974 Corvettes ● NCRS McLellan Mark of Excellence Award. **Frequency:** annual. **Type:** recognition. **Recipient:** for individuals who restore and preserve 1953-1974 Corvettes. **Computer Services:** database ● online services. **Telecommunication Services:** electronic mail, info@ncrs.org. **Publications:** *Corvette Restorer*, quarterly. Magazine. **Price:** included in membership dues. ISSN: 0747-2048. **Circulation:** 15,000. Alternate Formats: CD-ROM ● *Driveline*, bimonthly. Newsletter. **Price:** included in membership dues. **Circulation:** 15,000. **Advertising:** accepted. **Conventions/Meetings:** competition ● annual convention ● annual meeting.

21292 ■ National Council of Corvette Clubs (NCCC)

c/o Rhonda Higgins
907 Oakcrest Dr.
Champaign, IL 61821-4167
Free: (800)245-8388
E-mail: info@corvettesnccc.org
URL: http://www.corvettesnccc.org
Contact: Roger Mitchell, Pres.
Founded: 1959. **Members:** 17,500. **Membership Dues:** individual, $35 (annual) ● spouse/companion, dependent (16-21 years old), $10 (annual) ● life, $335. **Budget:** $150,000. **Regional Groups:** 16. **Local Groups:** 308. **Description:** Federation of clubs of owners of Corvette automobiles. Raffles a new Corvette each year with proceeds benefitting the National Kidney Foundation. Compiles statistics. Sanctions a full calendar of events. **Awards:** Duntov Performance Award. **Frequency:** annual. **Type:** recognition. **Recipient:** for outstanding performance in achieving purposes and ideals of the NCCC ● Educational Scholarships. **Frequency:** annual. **Type:** scholarship. **Recipient:** for members and their children. **Committees:** Awards; Convention Steering. **Programs:** Charity and Grants; Competition; Scholarship. **Publications:** *Blue Bars*, quarterly. Magazine. Includes organization activities, technical information, and articles. **Price:** included in membership dues.

Circulation: 9,500. **Advertising:** accepted ● *NCCC Sanctioned Competition Manual*. **Price:** $7.00 plus shipping and handling ● Handbook, quadrennial. **Conventions/Meetings:** competition, for amateurs ● annual convention (exhibits).

21293 ■ National DeSoto Club (NDC)

c/o Barrett Taft, Membership Sec.
1323 W Beach Rd.
Oak Harbor, WA 98277
Ph: (360)720-2465
E-mail: penguin008@comcast.net
URL: http://www.desoto.org
Contact: Barrett Taft, Membership Sec.
Founded: 1986. **Members:** 1,600. **Membership Dues:** standard, $22 (annual) ● optional, Mexico and Canada, outside U.S. (air mail) $30 (annual). **Staff:** 8. **Budget:** $50,000. **Local Groups:** 10. **Description:** Owners and enthusiasts of the DeSoto car, manufactured 1928-61 by the Chrysler Corporation; companies selling or servicing antique automobiles. Encourages the preservation and restoration of the DeSoto. Assists members in locating complete vehicles and automobile parts. Maintains collection of sales literature and technical information on the DeSoto. **Libraries: Type:** not open to the public. **Subjects:** DeSoto automobile. **Awards:** Hernando DeSoto Award. **Frequency:** annual. **Type:** recognition. **Computer Services:** database, DeSoto automobile roster ● database, membership roster ● database, salvage yard directory ● online services. **Programs:** International Member Assistance. **Formerly:** Buckeye DeSoto Club. **Publications:** *DeSoto Adventures*, bimonthly. Magazine. **Price:** $18.00/year for members. **Circulation:** 1,900. **Advertising:** accepted. **Conventions/Meetings:** annual Convention and Car Show (exhibits) - usually July or August.

21294 ■ National Firebird and T/A Club (NFTAC)

PO Box 11238
Chicago, IL 60611
Ph: (773)769-6262
Fax: (773)769-3240
E-mail: info@firebirdtaclub.com
URL: http://www.firebirdtaclub.com
Contact: Robert Thomas, Pres.
Founded: 1984. **Members:** 2,000. **Membership Dues:** individual, $35 (annual) ● regular, outside U.S., $45 (annual). **Staff:** 2. **Local Groups:** 25. **Description:** Owners of Firebird automobiles, produced since 1967 by the Pontiac division of the General Motors Corporation. Promotes the magic of Firebird. Disseminates technical and historical information on the Firebird; acts as a Firebird registry. Conducts technical sessions; sponsors competitions. **Awards: Type:** recognition. **Computer Services:** Mailing lists, of members. **Formerly:** (1999) National Firebird Club. **Publications:** *The Eagle*, quarterly. Newsletter. Includes calendar of events and membership list updates. **Price:** included in membership dues. **Circulation:** 2,000. **Advertising:** accepted. Alternate Formats: online. **Conventions/Meetings:** annual meeting.

21295 ■ National Impala Association (NIA)

PO Box 968
2928 4th Ave.
Spearfish, SD 57783-0968
Ph: (605)642-5864
Fax: (605)642-5868
E-mail: info@nationalimpala.com
URL: http://www.nationalimpala.com
Contact: Dennis L. Naasz, Pres./Ed.
Founded: 1980. **Members:** 2,600. **Staff:** 2. **Regional Groups:** 9. **Description:** Owners of full-size automobiles manufactured by Chevrolet from 1958-1970. Provides technical advisory staff and parts inventory for individuals wishing to restore full-size Chevys. **Publications:** *Impala News*, bimonthly. Magazine. Includes car features and technical articles. **Price:** $35.00/year. ISSN: 0273-5894. **Advertising:** accepted. **Conventions/Meetings:** annual International Convention (exhibits).

21296 ■ National Indy 500 Collectors Club
1920 Patton Dr.
Speedway, IN 46224
E-mail: ni500cc@ni500cc.com
URL: http://www.ni500cc.com
Contact: Mr. John Darlington, Pres.
Founded: 1985. **Members:** 350. **Membership Dues:** individual in U.S. and Canada, $10 (annual) ● individual outside U.S., $15 (annual). **Multinational.** **Description:** Individuals interested in auto racing and history of the Indianapolis motor speedway. Promotes and operates programs to preserve the history of the Indianapolis speedway. Conducts research programs. **Publications:** *The Short Chute,* quarterly. Newsletter. Contains club notes and member spotlights, for sale/wanted ads. **Price:** included in membership dues. **Circulation:** 350. **Advertising:** accepted. Alternate Formats: online. **Conventions/Meetings:** annual First Turn Gang - general assembly (exhibits) - every last Sunday of May.

21297 ■ National Monte Carlo Owners Association (NMCOA)
204 Shelby Dr.
Greensburg, PA 15601-4974
E-mail: administrator@montecarloclub.com
URL: http://www.montecarloclub.com
Contact: Larry Ashcraft, Founder
Founded: 1985. **Members:** 3,000. **Membership Dues:** regular, in U.S., $35 (annual) ● regular, in Canada, $40 (annual) ● foreign, $45 (annual) ● regular, in U.S., $68 (biennial) ● regular, in Canada, $78 (biennial) ● foreign, $85 (biennial). **Description:** Owners of all types of Monte Carlo automobiles, produced by the Chevrolet division of General Motors Corporation. Compiles statistics. **Libraries: Type:** reference. **Holdings:** archival material. **Awards: Type:** recognition. **Publications:** *The Class of Monte Carlo,* bimonthly. Magazine. **Conventions/Meetings:** annual meeting ● annual Monte Nationals - convention.

21298 ■ National Nostalgic Nova (NNN)
PO Box 2344
York, PA 17405
Ph: (717)252-4192 (717)252-2383
Fax: (717)252-1666
E-mail: sales@nnnova.com
URL: http://www.nnnova.com
Contact: Wayne Bushey, Founder
Founded: 1982. **Members:** 5,500. **Membership Dues:** third class, $30 (annual) ● first class, air mail, $40 (annual) ● overseas, $50 (annual). **Regional Groups:** 11. **Description:** Individuals interested in the Chevrolet Nova and Chevy II. Promotes interest in the preservation, restoration, and history of the 1962-79 Chevy Nova. Provides for fellowship, distributes information, and makes parts available. **Awards: Type:** recognition. **Publications:** *Nova Times,* monthly. Magazine. **Circulation:** 5,500. **Advertising:** accepted. **Conventions/Meetings:** annual Nova Meets - convention.

21299 ■ National Old Timers Auto Racing Club (NOTARC)
c/o Pete Poodiack, Exec. Dir.
4 Rita Dr.
Bethel, CT 06801-3025
Ph: (203)791-8536
E-mail: ppoodiack@aol.com
URL: http://clubs.hemmings.com/frameset.
   cfm?club=nationaloldtimersarc
Contact: Pete Poodiack, Exec. Dir.
Founded: 1977. **Members:** 350. **Membership Dues:** ordinary, $15 (annual). **Description:** Former race car drivers, owners, builders, members of the race media, and interested others. Promotes the preservation of auto racing history. Maintains National Auto Racing Hall of Fame and Museum. **Libraries: Type:** reference. **Holdings:** 40; photographs. **Subjects:** binders of vintage. **Publications:** *From the Cockpit,* bimonthly. Bulletin. **Price:** included in membership dues. **Circulation:** 350. **Advertising:** accepted. **Conventions/Meetings:** annual Hall of Fame Induction - banquet - always late October.

21300 ■ National Street Rod Association (NSRA)
4030 Park Ave.
Memphis, TN 38111
Ph: (901)452-4030
URL: http://www.nsra-usa.com
Contact: Gilbert L. Bugg Jr., VP
Founded: 1970. **Members:** 54,000. **Membership Dues:** regular, $28 (annual) ● life, $650 ● regular, $55 (biennial). **Staff:** 10. **Description:** Street rod builders and enthusiasts. Conducts automotive events; attempts to influence state and federal legislation that is auto-oriented. (Street rods are modified antique cars using new automotive parts. They are designed for street use as family cars, however, and not for drag racing.) Annual events include: Street Rod Nationals; Street Rod Nationals North; Street Rod Nationals West; Street Rod Nationals East; Street Rod Nationals South; Mid-American Street Rod Nationals; Golden State Street Rod Nationals; Rocky Mountain Street Rod Nationals; Southeast Street Rod Nationals; Southwest Street Rod Nationals. **Publications:** *StreetScene,* monthly. Magazine. **Circulation:** 54,000. **Advertising:** accepted. **Conventions/Meetings:** annual meeting.

21301 ■ National Woodie Club (NWC)
c/o John Lee, Ed.
PO Box 6134
Lincoln, NE 68506
Ph: (402)488-0990
E-mail: johnlee@neb.rr.com
URL: http://nationalwoodieclub.com
Contact: John Lee, Ed.
Founded: 1974. **Members:** 3,200. **Membership Dues:** regular, in U.S., $35 (annual) ● regular, in U.S. (1st class mail), $45 (annual) ● regular, in Canada, $48 (annual) ● regular, outside U.S. and Canada, $60 (annual). **Staff:** 1. **Budget:** $70,000. **Regional Groups:** 10. **Description:** Owners, restorers, and aficionados of wood-bodied cars. Seeks to: promote interest in the beauty, usefulness, and uniqueness of wood-bodied cars; unite owners of these cars to exchange information and compare building techniques; preserve history of these vehicles. **Libraries: Type:** reference. **Holdings:** 500. **Subjects:** woodie car history, rebuilding techniques, reference photos. **Awards:** NWC Book Scholarships. **Frequency:** annual. **Type:** monetary. **Recipient:** for high school seniors going to college. **Publications:** *Membership Roster,* annual. Directory. **Price:** free for members. ISSN: 0149-1636. **Circulation:** 3,000. **Advertising:** accepted ● *National Woodie Club 30th Anniversary Book.* Provides in-depth, retro, and folkloric look of wood and metal autos. ● *Woodie Times,* monthly. Magazine. **Price:** included in membership dues. **Advertising:** accepted.

21302 ■ New England M.G. "T" Register Limited (NEMG"T"RL)
PO Box 1957
Cary, NC 27512-1957
Ph: (704)544-1253
E-mail: csearles@rochester.rr.com
URL: http://www.nemgt.org
Contact: Charlie Searles, Chm.
Founded: 1964. **Members:** 8,500. **Membership Dues:** regular, $40 (annual). **Budget:** $100,000. **Local Groups:** 35. **Description:** People who own vintage M.G. automobiles. Unites to maintain, preserve, and enjoy vintage M.G. cars. **Libraries: Type:** reference. **Holdings:** 41. **Subjects:** cars, owners, technical. **Awards:** Kudson-Churchill Scholarship Trust. **Frequency:** annual. **Type:** scholarship. **Recipient:** for qualified candidates seeking higher education in journalism or automotive technology. **Computer Services:** database, registered M.G. vehicles. **Also Known As:** The Register. **Publications:** *Cecil Kimber Centenary Book.* Contains rare articles and photos about Cecil Kimber. **Price:** $30.00 for members; $35.00 for nonmembers ● *M.G. TD Restoration Manual.* Book. Contains wood framing, panel replacement, trimming, wiring, and engine works. **Price:** $45.00 plus shipping and handling ● *The Sacred Octagon,* bimonthly. Magazine. Contains articles about the organization's events, chapters, and techni-

cal information. **Price:** included in membership dues; $35.00 /year for nonmembers. **Circulation:** 9,000. **Advertising:** accepted. Alternate Formats: online ● *T Type Restoration Handbook.* **Price:** $30.00 for members; $35.00 for nonmembers. **Conventions/Meetings:** annual GOF Mk-75 - meeting, mid-year gathering (exhibits).

21303 ■ Nineteen Thirty-Two Buick Registry (NTTBR)
3000 Warren Rd.
Indiana, PA 15701
Ph: (412)463-3372
Fax: (412)463-8604
E-mail: buick32@adelphia.net
Contact: McClellan G. Blair, Registrar
Founded: 1974. **Members:** 1,654. **Staff:** 1. **For-Profit. Description:** Owners of 1925-1935 Buick automobiles. Collects and disseminates information; reproduces needed parts by sharing tooling expenses. Sponsors lectures; compiles statistics. **Libraries: Type:** reference. **Holdings:** 5,000; artwork, books, periodicals. **Subjects:** Buick 1904-1985. **Computer Services:** database, membership and parts list. **Publications:** Monograph, periodic. **Circulation:** 2,000 ● Newsletter, periodic ● Newsletter. **Price:** free. **Circulation:** 1,800. **Conventions/Meetings:** annual Boom to Bust Buick Bash - convention, autos of participants (exhibits).

21304 ■ Nissan Infiniti Car Owners Club (NICO)
237 Fernwood Blvd., Ste.111
Fern Park, FL 32730-2116
Ph: (602)828-8908
E-mail: greg@nicoclub.com
URL: http://www.nicoclub.com
Contact: Greg Childs, CEO
Members: 34,000. **Staff:** 35. **Description:** Provides up-to-date information on the Nissan/Infiniti product line; discussion forums based upon make and model; access to after market manufacturer's showroom displaying the latest in hightech performance parts; racing coverage from grassroots import drag racing to Infiniti IRL and Nissan endurance world-cup racing. **Publications:** Newsletter, bimonthly.

21305 ■ North American Auto Union Register
Address Unknown since 2007
Founded: 1984. **Description:** Provides history, parts, sources, and information on Auto Union and DKW automobiles. (DKW cars were manufactured in Germany from 1930 to 1965; the car is the forerunner of the present day Audi.) **Publications:** none. **Convention/Meeting:** none.

21306 ■ North American English and European Ford Registry (NAEFR)
PO Box 11415
Olympia, WA 98508
Ph: (360)754-9585
E-mail: ifhp@aol.com
URL: http://clubs.hemmings.com/NAEFR
Contact: Michael MacSems, Contact
Founded: 1991. **Members:** 200. **Membership Dues:** active, $18 (annual). **Staff:** 1. **Budget:** $2,500. **For-Profit. Description:** Owners and enthusiasts of English and German Ford automobiles. (English Fords are automobiles manufactured or sold in the U.K; models include the Anglia, Prefect, Consul, Cortina, Thames, Escort, Popular, Corsair, Capri, Zephyr, and Zodiac.) Promotes enjoyment of European Ford automobiles through cooperation, information sharing, and mutual encouragement. Provides parts exchange and source information. **Convention/Meeting:** none. **Libraries: Type:** reference. **Holdings:** 40; books, clippings, periodicals. **Subjects:** English and European Ford automobiles. **Publications:** *English Ford Lines and Taurus Crest,* bimonthly. Newsletter. Includes letters, stories, nostalgia, and tips on English and European Fords; also includes free classified ad section. **Price:** included in membership dues. **Circulation:** 200. **Advertising:** accepted.

21307 ■ North American Mini Moke Registry (NAMMR)
c/o Sherry Chandler, Ed.
1779 Kickapoo St.
South Lake Tahoe, CA 96150
Ph: (530)577-7895
E-mail: mokeregistry@twobearsden.com
URL: http://clubs.hemmings.com/mokeregistry
Contact: Sherry Chandler, Ed.
Founded: 1982. **Members:** 95. **Membership Dues:** $18 (annual). **Description:** Individuals who own or are interested in the Austin Mini Moke, an English automobile designed by Sir Alec Issigonis and first produced in 1964. Works to facilitate communication among members. **Convention/Meeting:** none. **Publications:** *Moke Chronicles*, quarterly. Newsletter.

21308 ■ NSU Enthusiasts U.S.A.
2909 Utah Pl.
Alton, IL 62002
Ph: (618)462-9195
E-mail: stuchlik2@aol.com
Contact: Terry Stuchlik, Pres.
Founded: 1971. **Members:** 117. **Membership Dues:** $15 (annual). **Description:** Owners and enthusiasts of NSU automobiles. NSU is an acronym for Neckarsulm, the German city where the automobiles were manufactured. Promotes the preservation of NSU cars; provides information on such cars including the availability of parts and other reference materials; promotes social activities among members. Conducts interchange of technical material. Maintains library of repair manuals. **Formerly:** (1973) NSU/U.S.A. Enthusiasts' Club. **Publications:** *Membership List*, annual ● *Neckarsulm News*, quarterly. **Price:** included in membership dues. **Advertising:** accepted. **Conventions/Meetings:** annual meeting - usually September.

21309 ■ Oakland-Pontiac Enthusiast Organization (OPEO)
3520 Warringham Dr.
Waterford, MI 48329-1380
Ph: (248)623-7573
Fax: (248)623-6180
Contact: Daniel L. Hosler, Pres.
Founded: 1971. **Members:** 250. **Membership Dues:** $10 (annual). **Regional Groups:** 1. **National Groups:** 250. **Description:** Owners and enthusiasts dedicated to the preservation and restoration of Oakland and Pontiac automobiles over ten years old. **Libraries: Type:** reference. **Holdings:** 1,000; books, clippings. **Subjects:** Pontiac and Oakland automobiles. **Computer Services:** database, membership. **Publications:** *Membership Roster*, annual. Directory. **Advertising:** accepted ● *Warrior*, monthly. Newsletter. **Price:** $10.00/year. **Circulation:** 300. **Advertising:** accepted. **Conventions/Meetings:** monthly meeting ● annual show - always third Sunday in July. Waterford, MI.

21310 ■ Oldsmobile Club of America (OCA)
PO Box 80318
Lansing, MI 48908
Ph: (517)663-1811
Fax: (517)663-1820
E-mail: oca@oldsclub.org
Founded: 1971. **Members:** 6,500. **Membership Dues:** 3rd class, $30 (annual) ● 1st class, $40 (annual). **Local Groups:** 46. **Description:** Owners and enthusiasts of Oldsmobile cars made from 1897 to the present. Promotes mutual assistance in keeping cars on the road and in locating parts and service. Encourages research into the old car hobby field. **Awards: Type:** recognition. **Recipient:** for competition in restoration and preservation. **Publications:** *Journey With Olds*, monthly. Magazine. **Circulation:** 6,500. **Advertising:** accepted ● ASM. **Conventions/Meetings:** annual general assembly, with car show - summer.

21311 ■ Online Imperial Club
c/o Elijah Scott
40 Signal Hill Ct.
Rock Spring, GA 30739

E-mail: webmaster@imperialclub.com
URL: http://www.imperialclub.com
Contact: Elijah Scott, Contact
Description: Online club for the promotion and appreciation of Chrysler Imperial and Chrysler New Yorker Brougham automobiles.

21312 ■ Opel Association of North America (OANA)
630 Watch Hill Rd.
Midlothian, VA 23113
Ph: (804)379-9737
E-mail: cdg@goindesign.com
URL: http://clubs.hemmings.com/frameset.cfm?club=oana
Contact: Charles D. Goin, Founder
Founded: 1995. **Members:** 200. **Membership Dues:** full, $30 (annual) ● life, $50. **Staff:** 3. **Budget:** $4,000. **Regional Groups:** 11. **Description:** Owners and admirers of Opel automobiles, which were available in the United States from 1960-75. Promotes collection, preservation, and maintenance of classic Opels. Facilitates communication and good fellowship among members; sponsors competitions. **Libraries: Type:** reference; by appointment only. **Holdings:** archival material. **Subjects:** Opel automobiles. **Awards:** Best Car. **Frequency:** annual. **Type:** recognition. **Publications:** *Opel Exchange*, bimonthly. Newsletter. **Advertising:** accepted. Alternate Formats: online. **Conventions/Meetings:** board meeting - 2-3/year ● annual National Meet - show ● periodic regional meeting.

21313 ■ Opel Motorsports Club (OMC)
c/o Dick Counsil, Treas.
3824 Franklin St.
La Crescenta, CA 91214
E-mail: joinomc@opelclub.com
URL: http://www.opelclub.com
Contact: Dick Counsil, Treas.
Founded: 1980. **Members:** 250. **Membership Dues:** regular, $45 (annual). **Staff:** 9. **Regional Groups:** 10. **Multinational. Description:** Owners and enthusiasts of Opel automobiles. (Opel automobiles have been manufactured in Russelsheim, Federal Republic of Germany since 1899.) Promotes the Opel automobile, friendships among members, sportsmanship, and competence in vehicle maintenance and operation. Facilitates information exchange, especially technical information regarding service and parts. **Libraries: Type:** reference. **Holdings:** 250; articles, periodicals. **Subjects:** Opel automobiles. **Formerly:** Opel Motorsports Club AG. **Publications:** *The Blitz*, monthly. Newsletter. Contains club business, tech tips, classified ads, and display ads. **Price:** included in membership dues. **Circulation:** 250. **Advertising:** accepted ● *Roster of Members*, annual. Membership Directory ● *Roster of Parts Sources*, annual. **Conventions/Meetings:** monthly meeting - usually 2nd Saturday, in Los Angeles, CA ● annual picnic - usually the second weekend of August.

21314 ■ Organization of Bricklin Owners (OBO)
PO Box 24775
Rochester, NY 14624-0775
Ph: (585)247-1575
E-mail: orgbricklinowners@aol.com
Contact: Joseph F. DeLorenzo, Founder/Pres.
Founded: 1975. **Members:** 711. **Membership Dues:** initial, $25 ● renewal, $10 (biennial). **Staff:** 2. **Description:** Owners of Bricklin SV-1 motorcars united for assistance in the maintenance and preservation of their cars. Provides members with technical, accessory, and service and parts information available upon request. **Publications:** *OBO News Update*, periodic. Newsletter ● Manuals. **Conventions/Meetings:** annual rally, includes concours and swap meet.

21315 ■ Pacific Northwest Region of the Lincoln and Continental Owners Club (PNWR/LCOC)
c/o Chris Gray
21707 W Lost Lake Rd.
Snohomish, WA 98290
URL: http://www.lincoln-club.org
Contact: Chris Gray, Contact
Founded: 1954. **Members:** 100. **Membership Dues:** regional, $15 (annual) ● national, $36 (annual). **Staff:**

1. **Languages:** English, French. **Multinational. Description:** Owners of Lincoln and Continental automobiles; other interested individuals. Promotes preservation of vintage Lincolns and Continentals; facilitates camaraderie among members. Conducts research, educational, and social activities; sponsors charitable programs; maintains speakers' bureau. Maintains an archive of historical and technical data regarding Lincoln and Continental motorcars and the Lincoln Motor Company, Ford Motor Company - Lincoln Mercury Division. **Libraries: Type:** by appointment only; reference. **Holdings:** 3,000; archival material, artwork, books, clippings, periodicals, video recordings. **Subjects:** Lincoln and Continental automobiles. **Awards:** Clara Bryant Ford Award - Lincoln. **Frequency:** annual. **Type:** recognition ● Della Forker Chrysler Award - Imperial. **Frequency:** annual. **Type:** recognition ● Directors' Citation. **Frequency:** periodic. **Type:** recognition. **Recipient:** for an individual promoting interest in the history of Lincoln and Continental automobiles ● Edsel Bryant Ford Award - Continental. **Frequency:** annual. **Type:** recognition ● Edsel Bryant Ford Award - Lincoln. **Frequency:** annual. **Type:** recognition ● Eleanor Bryant Ford Award. **Frequency:** annual. **Type:** recognition ● Ellen Hull Leland Award - Cadillac. **Frequency:** annual. **Type:** recognition ● Henry M. Leland Award - Cadillac. **Frequency:** annual. **Type:** recognition ● Hermann C. Brunn Award - Custom Coach. **Frequency:** annual. **Type:** recognition ● Walter P. Chrysler Award - Imperial. **Frequency:** annual. **Type:** recognition. **Subgroups:** North American Land Yacht Regatta. **Publications:** *Continental Connector*. Newsletter. Contains timely information about meets and events in the area - Lincoln meets and other car-related events. **Price:** included in membership dues ● *Continental Connoisseur*, bimonthly. Magazine. Includes 12-pages of Lincoln-Continental related material, club activities and other historical automotive information. **Price:** free for members. **Advertising:** accepted. **Conventions/Meetings:** quarterly board meeting ● annual meeting (exhibits) ● annual North American Land Yacht Regatta - tour.

21316 ■ Packard Automobile Classics (PAC)
PO Box 360806
Columbus, OH 43236-0806
Ph: (614)478-4946
Free: (800)478-0012
Fax: (614)472-3222
E-mail: pacnatoffice@aol.com
URL: http://www.packardclub.org
Contact: Mike Rigsby, Membership VP
Founded: 1953. **Members:** 4,500. **Membership Dues:** regular in, U.S., $40 (annual) ● regular in Canada, $45 (annual) ● regular in Mexico, $55 (annual) ● overseas, $95 (annual) ● life, $1,000. **Staff:** 3. **Regional Groups:** 50. **Description:** Individuals interested in preserving and restoring Packard automobiles, which were produced between 1899 and 1958. Sponsors annual summer national tour. **Libraries: Type:** reference. **Holdings:** archival material, audio recordings, films. **Awards:** Alice H. Ramsey Award. **Frequency:** annual. **Type:** trophy. **Recipient:** for the best female fashion ● Alvan Macauley Award. **Frequency:** annual. **Type:** recognition. **Recipient:** for the pre-war best of show Packard ● Best Unrestored Award. **Frequency:** annual. **Type:** recognition. **Recipient:** to a Packard with intrinsic value and historical significance ● Bill Snodgrass Award. **Frequency:** annual. **Type:** recognition. **Recipient:** to the region's winner of news bulletin for the previous calendar year ● Bradley Skinner Award. **Frequency:** annual. **Type:** recognition. **Recipient:** to the best 1915-1923 Twin Six Packard attending a National Meet ● Founders Award. **Frequency:** annual. **Type:** recognition. **Recipient:** to the owner of the best preserved pre-1929 Packard ● George L. Weiss Award. **Frequency:** annual. **Type:** recognition. **Recipient:** for exceptional perseverance, dedication and effort in preserving the Packard automobile ● Henry B. Joy Award. **Frequency:** annual. **Type:** trophy. **Recipient:** for the best male fashion ● James J. Nance Award. **Frequency:** annual. **Type:** recognition. **Recipient:** for the post-war best of show Packard ● Lil Ferreira Award. **Frequency:** annual. **Type:** recogni-

tion. **Recipient:** for a committee person with outstanding contributions on a regional level ● Tom Fetch Award. **Frequency:** annual. **Type:** recognition. **Recipient:** to the person who has driven the longest distance in a PAC National Meet ● Wayne Merriman Award. **Frequency:** annual. **Type:** recognition. **Recipient:** to the owner of the best conditioned Packard. **Computer Services:** Online services. **Committees:** Emeritus; Judging; Legislative Info Task Force; Long Range Planning; Nominating; Packard Roster Keepers; Special Awards; Technical. **Publications:** *Cormorant News Bulletin*, monthly. Newsletter. **Price:** included in membership dues. ISSN: 0045-8554. **Circulation:** 4,500. **Advertising:** accepted. Alternate Formats: online ● *Packard Automobile Classics—Directory*, annual. **Price:** available to members only. **Advertising:** accepted ● *The Packard Cormorant*, quarterly. Magazine. Contains articles on the history of the Packard Company. **Price:** included in membership dues. ISSN: 0362-9368. Alternate Formats: online. **Conventions/Meetings:** annual competition and meet (exhibits) ● seminar.

21317 ■ Packard Club (PAC)

PO Box 360806
Columbus, OH 43236-0806
Ph: (614)478-4946
Free: (800)478-0012
Fax: (614)472-3222
E-mail: pacnatoffice@aol.com
URL: http://www.packardclub.org
Contact: Mike Rigsby, VP for Membership

Founded: 1953. **Members:** 5,000. **Membership Dues:** regular, in U.S., $40 (annual) ● regular, in Canada, $45 (annual) ● Mexico (airmail), overseas (surface), $55 (annual) ● overseas (airmail) $95 (annual) ● life, in U.S., $1,000 ● patron contribution (optional), $10 (annual). **Regional Groups:** 51. **Multinational. Description:** Works to preserve originality in the products and history of The Packard Motor Car Company. **Libraries: Type:** reference. **Holdings:** articles, audio recordings, books, video recordings. **Awards:** Alvan Macauley Award. **Frequency:** annual. **Type:** recognition. **Recipient:** for the Pre-War Best of Show ● Best Unrestored Award. **Frequency:** annual. **Type:** recognition. **Recipient:** for encouraging preservation of unmolested Packards being allowed to age gracefully ● Bill Snodgrass Award. **Frequency:** annual. **Type:** recognition. **Recipient:** to the region whose News Bulletin was chosen as winner for the previous calendar year ● Bradley Skinner Award. **Frequency:** annual. **Type:** recognition. **Recipient:** for best 1915-23 Twin Six at the National Meet ● The Founders Award. **Frequency:** annual. **Type:** recognition. **Recipient:** to the owner of the best preserved pre-1929 Packard ● James J. Nance Award. **Frequency:** annual. **Type:** recognition. **Recipient:** for the Post-War Best of Show ● Lil Ferreira Award. **Frequency:** annual. **Type:** recognition. **Recipient:** for outstanding contribution of a committee person, on a regional level, working on a National Meet Planning Committee ● Tom Fetch Award. **Frequency:** annual. **Type:** recognition. **Recipient:** to a person who drove the longest distance to the PAC National Meet in a Packard ● Vintage Fashion Award. **Frequency:** annual. **Type:** recognition. **Recipient:** for the most accurate period male (Henry B. Joy Award) and female (Alice H. Ramsey Award) fashions ● Wayne Merriman Award. **Frequency:** annual. **Type:** recognition. **Recipient:** to the owner of the Packard judged best brought back to life by an individual or individuals. **Publications:** *The Cormorant Magazine*, quarterly. Contains news for Packard owners and enthusiasts. **Price:** $8.00/back issue ● *The Cormorant News Bulletin*, monthly. Newsletter. Contains meet news, technical help, photo showcase, classified ads, automotive watch, upcoming events, and commercial providers of parts. **Advertising:** accepted. **Conventions/Meetings:** annual meet.

21318 ■ Packard V-8 Roster, '55-'56

84 Hoy Ave.
Fords, NJ 08863
Ph: (732)738-7859
Fax: (732)738-7625

E-mail: stuartrblond@earthlink.net
Contact: Stuart Blond, Ed.

Founded: 1983. **Description:** Serves as clearinghouse of information on 1955-56 Packard and Clipper automobiles. Compiles statistics. **Libraries: Type:** reference. **Publications:** *Roster of 1955-56 Packards and Clippers*, annual. **Price:** $5.00/issue.

21319 ■ Packards International Motor Car Club (PIMCC)

302 French St.
Santa Ana, CA 92701
Ph: (714)541-8431
Fax: (714)836-4014
E-mail: markbeythoun@e-ventcentral.com
URL: http://www.packardsinternational.com
Contact: Don Hull, Pres.

Founded: 1963. **Members:** 2,500. **Membership Dues:** regular, in U.S., $45 (annual) ● regular, in Canada and Mexico, $50 (annual) ● regular, outside U.S., Canada and Mexico, $65 (annual). **Staff:** 1. **State Groups:** 9. **Description:** Packard owners and enthusiasts dedicated to the driving enjoyment and preservation of Packard automobiles. Sponsors driving tours. **Libraries: Type:** reference. **Holdings:** books, clippings, periodicals. **Publications:** *News Counselor*, quarterly. Newsletter. **Circulation:** 2,500. **Advertising:** accepted ● *Packards International Magazine*, quarterly. **Price:** $30.00 /year for nonmembers; $10.00 for back issues; included in membership dues ● Manuals. All years of the Packard automobile available. **Conventions/Meetings:** annual National Driving Tour - meeting.

21320 ■ Pantera International (PI)

330 Central Ave., No. 25
Fillmore, CA 93015
Ph: (805)524-5248
Fax: (805)378-7100
E-mail: george@panteracars.com
URL: http://www.panteracars.com
Contact: George Pence, Pres.

Founded: 1973. **Members:** 500. **Membership Dues:** regular, in U.S., $75 (annual) ● regular, outside U.S., $85 (annual). **Staff:** 3. **Description:** Represents owners of the de Tomaso Pantera automobile and interested individuals united to share technical information on the car. **Additional Websites:** http://www.pantera.net. **Publications:** *Pantera International—News*, quarterly. Magazine. Includes engineer's explications, new member listings, and how-to articles. **Price:** included in membership dues. **Circulation:** 500. **Advertising:** accepted.

21321 ■ Pantera Owners Club of America (POCA)

6092 Trinette Ave.
Garden Grove, CA 92845
Ph: (714)897-6964
Fax: (714)892-5990
E-mail: jpoca2@hotmail.com
URL: http://www.panteraclub.com
Contact: Judith McCartney, Membership Chair

Founded: 1973. **Membership Dues:** regular, in U.S., $75 (annual) ● foreign, $90 (annual). **Description:** Promotes the history, maintenance, restoration, and preservation of DeTomaso automobiles. **Publications:** *Profiles*, quarterly. Magazine. **Price:** included in membership dues; $6.00/back issue ● Newsletter, monthly. **Price:** included in membership dues; $2.00/ back issue ● Brochure. Alternate Formats: online ● Articles. **Price:** $5.00 ● Manuals ● Bulletins. **Conventions/Meetings:** annual convention ● monthly meeting.

21322 ■ Pierce-Arrow Society (PAS)

PO Box 16022
Oakland, CA 94610-6022
E-mail: info@pierce-arrow.org
URL: http://www.pierce-arrow.org
Contact: Ralph McKittrick, Pres.

Founded: 1957. **Members:** 1,100. **Membership Dues:** regular, in U.S., $30 (annual) ● 1st class, $45 (annual) ● regular, outside U.S. and Canada, $60 (annual). **Regional Groups:** 6. **Multinational. Description:** Owners and enthusiasts interested in Pierce-Arrow

automobiles. Provides technical answering service and restoration assistance. **Libraries: Type:** not open to the public. **Awards:** Bernard J. Weis Trophy. **Frequency:** annual. **Type:** trophy. **Recipient:** for the owner of the most authentically restored Pierce-Arrow ● Henry E. & Pauline S. Becker Trophy. **Frequency:** annual. **Type:** recognition. **Recipient:** to a member who drives his Pierce-Arrow the farthest distance ● R. Vale Faro Trophy. **Frequency:** annual. **Type:** trophy. **Recipient:** to the most original Pierce-Arrow displayed at the Annual Meeting. **Telecommunication Services:** electronic mail, membership@pierce-arrow.org. **Publications:** *The Arrow*, quarterly. Journal. Features historical articles, photos, and information on the Pierce-Arrow automobile. **Price:** included in membership dues; $5.00/copy for nonmembers. **Circulation:** 1,100 ● *Emporium*, 8/year. Newsletter. Features trading news. **Price:** included in membership dues. **Circulation:** 1,100. **Advertising:** accepted ● *The Parts and Service Directory*, periodic. Lists sources for reproduction or suitable replacement parts as well as specialized services needed for Pierce-Arrow restoration and maintenance. Alternate Formats: online ● *Pierce-Arrow Service Bulletin*, bimonthly. Newsletter. Features restoration information, reprints of factory technical bulletin, and answers to member questions. **Price:** included in membership dues; $1.00/copy for nonmembers ● *Pierce-Arrow Society—Index of Technical Information*, annual. **Price:** included in membership dues; $2.00/copy for nonmembers. **Circulation:** 1,100 ● *Pierce-Arrow Society Products Catalog*, periodic. Includes announcements of products of interest to Pierce-Arrow enthusiasts. ● *Pierce-Arrow Society—Roster of Members and Register of Vehicles*, annual. Membership Directory. Lists members alphabetically and geographically; lists vehicles chronologically by serial number. **Price:** included in membership dues; $5.00 for nonmembers. **Circulation:** 1,100. **Conventions/Meetings:** annual general assembly - 2008 June 24-29, Lexington, KY.

21323 ■ Pioneer Automobile Touring Club (PATC)

c/o Dick Longcoy
2060 Bethel Rd.
Lansdale, PA 19446-5920
Ph: (610)584-4294
Contact: Dick Longcoy, Contact

Founded: 1968. **Members:** 250. **Description:** Owners of automobiles manufactured in or before 1915. Promotes touring of vintage automobiles. **Publications:** none. **Conventions/Meetings:** annual Spring Tours - meeting ● annual Touring Meeting.

21324 ■ Plymouth Barracuda/Cuda Owners Club (PB/COC)

c/o Ann M. Curman, Sec.
36 Woodland Rd.
East Greenwich, RI 02818-3430
URL: http://www.pbcoc.org
Contact: Jay M. Fisher, Founder/Dir.

Founded: 1978. **Members:** 800. **Membership Dues:** regular, in U.S. and Canada, $22 (annual) ● regular, outside U.S. and Canada, $25 (annual). **Staff:** 6. **Description:** Owners and others interested in the preservation and restoration of 1964-74 Plymouth Barracuda automobiles. **Libraries: Type:** reference. **Holdings:** books. **Publications:** *Club Roster*, annual. Membership Directory ● *Plymouth Barracuda/ Cuda Bulletin*, bimonthly. **Price:** included in membership dues. **Conventions/Meetings:** annual meeting and show - summer/fall, Northeast U.S.

21325 ■ Plymouth Owners Club (POC)

PO Box 416
Cavalier, ND 58220-0416
Ph: (701)549-3746
Fax: (701)549-3744
E-mail: mark@turbinecar.com
URL: http://www.plymouthbulletin.com
Contact: Robert S. Kerico, Pres.

Founded: 1957. **Members:** 3,800. **Membership Dues:** regular, in U.S. and Canada and outside North America, $28 (annual) ● airmail outside North America, $45 (annual). **Regional Groups:** 21. **De-**

scription: Persons interested in the collection, preservation, and use of 1928-1978 Plymouth cars, 1937-1941 trucks, and Fargo commercial vehicles; Plymouth Division of Chrysler Corporation is an honorary member. Promotes authentic restoration and exhibition of early models; provides technical assistance and exchange of information. Sponsors competitions with judging in 12 classes. Provides technical advice and copy service of out-of-print Plymouth materials. Maintains roster of all 1928-1978 Plymouth cars and trucks and Fargo commercial vehicles. **Libraries: Type:** reference. **Holdings:** video recordings. **Subjects:** Plymouth. **Awards:** Chrysler Cup. **Frequency:** annual. **Type:** recognition ● Editor's Award. **Frequency:** annual. **Type:** recognition ● Mayflower Award. **Frequency:** annual. **Type:** recognition. **Computer Services:** Mailing lists, membership roster. **Formerly:** (1965) Plymouth Four Cylinder Owners Club; (1990) Plymouth Four and Six Cylinder Owners Club. **Publications:** *Membership - Cars*, annual. Lists cars and parts owned by members. **Advertising:** accepted ● *Plymouth Bulletin*, bimonthly. **Price:** included in membership dues; $2.00 sample copy; $3.00 back issues. ISSN: 0032-1737. **Advertising:** accepted. Alternate Formats: online. **Conventions/Meetings:** Plymouth Grand National - meet - 3/year.

21326 ■ Police Car Owners of America (PCOOA)
172 County Rd. 136
Eureka Springs, AR 72631-9138
Ph: (479)253-2364
Fax: (479)253-2382
E-mail: pcooa@policecarowners.com
URL: http://www.policecarowners.com
Contact: Sgt. James Post, Founder
Founded: 1991. **Members:** 1,000. **Membership Dues:** regular, in U.S., $25 (annual) ● regular, in Canada, $30 (annual) ● regular, outside U.S. and Canada, $35 (annual) ● regular, in U.S., $47 (biennial) ● regular, in Canada, $57 (biennial) ● regular, outside U.S. and Canada, $67 (biennial) ● life, $250. **Multinational. Description:** Owners of restored police vehicles and retired cruisers dedicated exclusively to the collection of police car models. **Publications:** Newsletter. **Price:** $2.00/back issue ● Articles. Alternate Formats: online. **Conventions/Meetings:** annual convention - usually summer.

21327 ■ Pontiac-Oakland Club International (POCI)
PO Box 539
Victor, NY 14564
Ph: (401)769-8451
Free: (877)368-3454
Fax: (585)924-2756
E-mail: pociworldhq@aol.com
URL: http://www.poci.org
Contact: Robert Desrochers, Pres.
Founded: 1972. **Members:** 10,500. **Membership Dues:** active in U.S., $31 (annual) ● active in Canada, $33 (annual) ● active outside U.S. and Canada, $42 (annual) ● associate, $24 (annual). **Budget:** $150,000. **Local Groups:** 60. **Description:** Persons interested in the history, restoration, and preservation of Pontiac and Oakland automobiles. Assists owners of Pontiac and Oakland automobiles with the restoration of their vehicles. Maintains staff of volunteer technical advisers. Conducts research pertaining to original specifications and production history. Provides computerized services. **Libraries: Type:** reference. **Awards:** Trophy. **Frequency:** annual. **Type:** recognition. **Publications:** *Membership Roster*, annual. Membership Directory. Lists all POCI members and types of cars. **Price:** free. **Advertising:** accepted ● *Smoke Signals*, monthly. Magazine. **Price:** free for members. **Circulation:** 10,500. **Conventions/Meetings:** annual competition and convention, car show and parts swap (exhibits).

21328 ■ Porsche Club of America (PCA)
PO Box 1347
Springfield, VA 22151-0347
Ph: (703)321-2111
Fax: (703)321-2110

E-mail: admin@pca.org
URL: http://www.pca.org
Contact: Prescott Kelly, Pres.
Founded: 1954. **Members:** 51,000. **Membership Dues:** individual, $42 (annual). **Staff:** 5. **Regional Groups:** 140. **Description:** Represents persons owning Porsche automobiles. **Committees:** Activities; Parade Advisory; Policy; Public Relations; Technical. **Publications:** *Porsche Panorama*, monthly. Magazine. Includes technical section. **Price:** included in membership dues. ISSN: 0147-3565. **Advertising:** accepted. **Conventions/Meetings:** annual Porsche Parade - meeting - usually July or August.

21329 ■ Professional Car Society (PCS)
c/o Gregg D. Merksamer, Publicity Chm.
29 Old Oak Rd.
Warwick, NY 10990-3142
Ph: (845)986-6857
Fax: (845)986-6858
E-mail: merks62@warwick.net
URL: http://www.professionalcar.org
Contact: Gregg D. Merksamer, Publicity Chm.
Founded: 1976. **Members:** 1,200. **Membership Dues:** regular, in North America, $24 (annual) ● regular, outside North America, $28 (annual) ● life, $500. **Regional Groups:** 25. **Description:** Automobile collectors interested in vintage funeral, rescue, livery, and related professional vehicles. Seeks to preserve and enhance appreciation of vintage professional vehicles. **Libraries: Type:** reference. **Subjects:** photos and sales literature detailing the history of individual funeral coach, ambulance and limousine builders. **Committees:** Chapter Relations; Club Store; Publications; Publicity; Research and Archives; Technical Advice. **Publications:** *The Professional Car*, quarterly. Magazine. **Price:** $6.00 each. **Circulation:** 1,200 ● *Roster*, biennial. **Conventions/Meetings:** annual meeting (exhibits).

21330 ■ Renault Owners Club of North America (ROCONA)
c/o Ray Dietz, New Member Sec.
1250 Lanier Rd.
Martinsville, VA 24112-5212
Ph: (619)561-6687
E-mail: membership@renaulttownersclub.org
URL: http://www.renaulttownersclub.org
Contact: Jacques Lynn, Membership Sec.
Founded: 1991. **Members:** 315. **Membership Dues:** online - in U.S., international, $15 (annual) ● postal - in U.S., Mexico and Canada, $20 (annual) ● postal - outside U.S., Mexico and Canada, $30 (annual). **Multinational. Description:** Represents the interests of Renault owners and enthusiasts in North America. Encourages preservation and restoration of these vehicles. Facilitates communications and fellowship among owners. **Telecommunication Services:** electronic mail, ranfdietz@hotmail.com. **Publications:** *Renault News*, quarterly. Newsletter. Covers all the major Renault events in North America. **Price:** included in membership dues. Alternate Formats: online.

21331 ■ REO Club of America
c/o Marilyn Cooper, Sec.
1323 W Maple Ave.
Enid, OK 73703-4512
Ph: (651)457-6968
E-mail: reoclub@yahoo.com
URL: http://clubs.hemmings.com/reo
Contact: Marilyn Cooper, Sec.
Founded: 1973. **Membership Dues:** regular, in U.S., Canada, and Mexico, $18 (annual) ● international, $27 (annual) ● life, $500. **Regional Groups:** 6. **Multinational. Description:** Persons interested in REO automobiles and trucks. (REO cars were manufactured by the Ranson E. Olds Factory in Lansing, MI from 1905 to 1936; trucks were manufactured at the same plant until 1976.) Serves as a forum for exchange of ideas, information, and parts for owners and admirers of early REO trucks and cars; to help members restore and preserve their vehicles. Maintains staff of technical advisers. **Libraries: Type:** reference. **Holdings:** archival material. **Subjects:** REO technical manuals. **Awards:** Fran Silky Award.

Frequency: annual. **Type:** recognition. **Recipient:** various ● Ray Wood Award. **Frequency:** annual. **Type:** recognition. **Recipient:** various. **Additional Websites:** http://www.reoclub.org. **Publications:** *REO ECHO*, bimonthly. Newsletter. Contains items of interest to club members, including but not limited to: history of various vehicles, want ads, chapter info, convention news. **Price:** included in membership dues. **Advertising:** accepted ● Directory, biennial. Provides a list of members, including vehicles owned. **Conventions/Meetings:** annual convention - usually July.

21332 ■ Rickenbacker Automobile Club of America (RACA)
Address Unknown since 2007
URL: http://www.dreamwater.org/rickenbacker/
Founded: 1969. **Members:** 55. **Membership Dues:** $15 (annual). **Staff:** 3. **National Groups:** 1. **Description:** People interested in the preservation of the Rickenbacker car. Seeks to preserve and promote the Rickenbacker car for all posterity and to serve members' interests to this end. Sponsors social gatherings. Acts as clearinghouse for exchange of information. Presently active. **Formerly:** (2004) Rickenbacker Car Club of America. **Publications:** *Hat in the Ring News*, semiannual. Newsletter. Contains club news and technical information. **Price:** $2.00. **Circulation:** 70. **Advertising:** accepted. **Conventions/Meetings:** meet.

21333 ■ Riviera Owners Association (ROA)
PO Box 37
Beatrice, NE 68310
Ph: (402)651-8735
Fax: (402)228-0518
E-mail: roa@rivowners.org
URL: http://www.rivowners.org
Contact: Sean Cahill, Contact
Founded: 1984. **Members:** 3,200. **Membership Dues:** regular in U.S., $30 (annual) ● regular outside U.S., $35 (annual). **Regional Groups:** 21. **Description:** Owners of Buick Riviera automobiles, which have been manufactured from 1963 to the present. Promotes ownership and preservation of Rivieras. Serves as a clearinghouse on Rivieras and their restoration and maintenance; facilitates communication among members. **Libraries: Type:** reference; not open to the public. **Holdings:** 16; articles, artwork, clippings. **Subjects:** Buick Riviera automobiles. **Publications:** *The Riview*, bimonthly. Magazine. **Price:** included in membership dues. ISSN: 1047-2193. **Circulation:** 3,100. **Advertising:** accepted. Alternate Formats: online. **Conventions/Meetings:** annual meeting.

21334 ■ Road Race Lincoln Register (RRLR)
640 Homestead Ave.
Metairie, LA 70005
Ph: (504)831-4335
E-mail: bigeasy3@msn.com
URL: http://clubs.hemmings.com/clubsites/road-racelincoln/index.cfm
Contact: Bill Culver, Ed.
Founded: 1972. **Members:** 325. **Membership Dues:** in U.S., $30 (annual) ● outside U.S., $35 (annual). **Multinational. Description:** Persons interested in Lincoln automobiles built from 1949 to 1957. Promotes restoration and preservation of these vehicles and provides members with information on restoration and parts availability. Maintains historical files of production information; disseminates historical information on the production and performance application of these vehicles. **Libraries: Type:** reference. **Holdings:** archival material, periodicals. **Subjects:** technical and marketing information relative to Road Race Lincolns; service bulletins. **Absorbed:** (1981) Fifty-Six Fifty-Seven Lincoln Registry. **Publications:** *Viva Carrera!*, quarterly. Newsletter. Includes technical articles, photos, information on restoration. **Price:** included in membership dues. **Circulation:** 350. **Advertising:** accepted. **Conventions/Meetings:** annual Eastern Meet - convention (exhibits) - September/October ● annual Midwest Meet - convention (exhibits) - always late July.

21335 ■ Rolls-Royce Owners' Club (RROC)
191 Hempt Rd.
Mechanicsburg, PA 17050
Ph: (717)697-4671
Free: (800)879-7762
Fax: (717)697-7820
E-mail: rrochq@rroc.org
URL: http://www.rroc.org
Contact: Timothy E. Younes, Exec. Dir.
Founded: 1951. **Members:** 9,200. **Membership Dues:** regular, $60 (annual) ● junior, $15 (annual). **Staff:** 5. **Budget:** $1,000,000. **Regional Groups:** 25. **Local Groups:** 24. **Description:** Persons interested in preserving and restoring automobiles produced by Rolls-Royce Ltd., Rolls-Royce Motors, Ltd., Rolls-Royce of America, and Bentley Motors (1931) Ltd. Exchanges technical, historical, and general information. Reprints owners' manuals and technical materials. **Committees:** Activities; Information Technology; Judging; Merchandise; Post War; Pre-War. **Publications:** *Directory and Register*, biennial ● *The Flying Lady*, bimonthly. Magazine. Contains technical and historical information. **Price:** included in membership dues. **Advertising:** accepted. Alternate Formats: online ● *Manual for Judges*. Alternate Formats: online. **Conventions/Meetings:** annual meet - 2008 June 22-28, Williamsburg, VA; 2009 June, New Orleans, LA ● annual meeting.

21336 ■ Rometsch Registry
2510 N Larchmont Ave.
Santa Ana, CA 92706
Fax: (714)542-5217
E-mail: autokomp@hotmail.com
URL: http://www.rometschregistry.org
Contact: Oystein Asphjell, Contact
Founded: 1978. **Members:** 50. **Budget:** $10,000. **Description:** Owners of Rometsch automobiles. Works to account for all remaining automobiles built by Rometsch of Berlin, Germany. **Conventions/Meetings:** quadrennial meeting - always Bad Camberg, Germany.

21337 ■ Rover Saloon Touring Club of America (RSTCA)
c/o Glen Wilson
733 S Providence Rd.
Wallingford, PA 19086
Ph: (484)443-5000
E-mail: glenwilson@rstca.com
URL: http://www.rstca.com
Contact: Glen Wilson, Contact
Founded: 1997. **Description:** Works to locate classic Rover automobiles in the U.S., provide contact, technical support, and information exchange.

21338 ■ S2000 Club of America (S2KCA)
7808 Hardwick Ct.
Plano, TX 75025
Ph: (972)527-8169
E-mail: info@s2kca.com
URL: http://www.s2kca.com
Contact: David Grooters, Pres.
Founded: 2001. **Membership Dues:** general, $35 (annual). **Description:** Represents the interests of Honda S2000 owners and enthusiasts. Fosters a sense of community among members through communication on a regional and national scale. Hosts online forums and sponsors a wide range of activities throughout the country. **Telecommunication Services:** electronic mail, monkeymaker1@comcast.net. **Publications:** Newsletter. Contains updates on club happenings, S2000 related tips, event reports and interviews. **Price:** included in membership dues.

21339 ■ Saab Club of North America (SCNA)
30 Puritan Dr.
Port Chester, NY 10573
E-mail: nines@earthlink.net
URL: http://www.saabclub.com
Contact: Ian Glenday, Pres.
Founded: 1971. **Members:** 2,500. **Membership Dues:** regular, in U.S., $40 (annual) ● regular, outside U.S., $45 (annual). **Staff:** 2. **Budget:** $100,000. **Local Groups:** 31. **For-Profit. Description:** Represents owners and enthusiasts of Swedish-

manufactured Saab automobiles. Helps members exchange information on the care and maintenance of all Saab models. **Formerly:** Chicago Saab Club; Saab Clubs of America; Saab Clubs of North America. **Publications:** *NINES*, bimonthly. Magazine. Contains technical do-it-yourself articles, news and history related to Saab automobiles. **Price:** $40.00 included in membership dues. ISSN: 1530-0730. **Circulation:** 2,500. **Advertising:** accepted. **Conventions/Meetings:** annual National Saab Owners Convention, includes technical sessions (exhibits).

21340 ■ Sabra Automobile Connection
Address Unknown since 2007
Founded: 1985. **Members:** 59. **Staff:** 1. **Description:** Promotes the interest and history of rare Sabra automobiles which were manufactured in 1962 and 1963 by Reliant Corp. in England and by Autocars Ltd. in Israel. Compiles serial numbers of existing Sabra vehicles; disseminates information. Maintains ownership lists. **Libraries:** Type: not open to the public; reference. **Holdings:** artwork, books, periodicals. **Formerly:** (2002) Sabra Connection. **Publications:** *Sabra Automobile Connection*, periodic. Contains history and updates on the Sabra automobile. **Price:** free. **Advertising:** accepted.

21341 ■ Saxon Owners Registry (SOR)
c/o Walter H. Prichard, Jr., Ed.
5250 NW Highland Way
Corvallis, OR 97330
Ph: (541)752-6231
E-mail: prichard@proaxis.com
Contact: Walter H. Prichard Jr., Ed.
Founded: 1975. **Members:** 100. **Staff:** 1. **Budget:** $200. **Description:** Persons interested in acquiring, restoring, and preserving Saxon automobiles. Attempts to determine how many of the 90,000 Saxons that were manufactured are still in existence. Helps those restoring Saxons to locate parts and information. **Libraries:** Type: not open to the public. **Subjects:** original factory sales literature, owners' manuals, list of parts wanted or for sale. **Publications:** *Saxon Times*, semiannual. Newsletter. Includes roster of owners. **Price:** free. **Conventions/Meetings:** annual meeting (exhibits) - always second Saturday in April, Portland, OR.

21342 ■ Shelby American Automobile Club (SAAC)
PO Box 788
Sharon, CT 06069
Fax: (860)364-0769
E-mail: saac@saac.com
URL: http://www.saac.com
Contact: Kenneth Eber, Dir.
Founded: 1975. **Members:** 5,850. **Membership Dues:** regular, in U.S. and Canada, $47 (annual) ● regular, outside U.S. and Canada, $50-$60 (annual). **Staff:** 3. **Regional Groups:** 50. **For-Profit. Description:** Represents owners and enthusiasts of Shelby G.T. 350 and G.T. 500, Cobra, Tiger, and Ford G.T. automobiles. Dedicated to the history, preservation, care, and enjoyment of the sports cars manufactured between 1962 and 1970 by Shelby American, Inc. Services include parts and technical assistance information and insurance assistance at reasonable prices. **Libraries:** Type: reference. **Holdings:** archival material, artwork, books, clippings, periodicals, photographs. **Subjects:** Shelby American Automobiles. **Telecommunication Services:** electronic mail, hq@saac.com. **Absorbed:** Cobra Club. **Publications:** *The Shelby American*. Magazine. **Price:** included in membership dues. **Advertising:** accepted ● *The Shelby American Guide*. Book ● *Shelby American World Registry*, every 10 years. Book. Provides complete information on every car Shelby built. **Price:** $125.00. **Circulation:** 5,000 ● *Shelby Buyers Guide*. Book ● *Snake Bite Bulletin*, bimonthly. Newsletter. Includes calendar of events. **Price:** included in membership dues. **Advertising:** accepted. **Conventions/Meetings:** annual convention and seminar, with historical displays, car shows, on-track driving, vintage races (exhibits) - usually July or August.

21343 ■ Silver Ghost Association (SGA)
c/o Jim Bannon, Membership Dir.
1115 Western Blvd.
Arlington, TX 76013
Ph: (817)861-6605
Fax: (817)861-1029
E-mail: sga.membership@silverghost.org
URL: http://www.silverghost.com
Contact: Jim Bannon, Membership Dir.
Membership Dues: spouse, $15 (annual) ● individual, $55 (annual). **Description:** Promotes participation of Silver Ghost cars in meets, tours; provides operation, repairs, and service information. **Publications:** *Membership Listing*, annual, usually August. Membership Directory ● *Silver Ghost Tourer*, quarterly. Contains technical articles and general information on Ghosts. ● *Tech Bible 1998*. Contains compendium of Silver Ghost technical material. **Price:** $150.00 in U.S. and Canada. **Conventions/Meetings:** annual Mid-Winter Fling - meeting - January or February ● Technical Sessions - meeting, for members only ● Wholly Ghost Tours.

21344 ■ Slant 6 Club of America
Box 4414
Salem, OR 97302
Ph: (503)581-2230
Contact: Jackson A. Poehler, Mgr.
Founded: 1980. **Members:** 2,000. **Membership Dues:** individual, $25 (annual). **Budget:** $40,000. **Regional Groups:** 24. **Description:** Collectors and restorers of Slant 6 vehicles, most notably mid-1960s Darts and Valiants, but includes all Slant 6 powered cars and trucks (Slant 6 vehicles are cars manufactured from 1960 to 1983 and trucks manufactured from 1961 to 1987 by the Chrysler Corporation. Slant 6 is a six cylinder engine that is slanted at a 30 degree angle). Promotes the maintenance, restoration, and preservation of Slant 6 powered vehicles. **Libraries:** Type: reference. **Formerly:** (1985) Dart/Valiant Slant 6 Club of America. **Publications:** *Slant 6 News*, quarterly. Magazine. Includes technical articles and information on chapter meets. **Price:** included in membership dues. **Circulation:** 2,100. **Advertising:** accepted. **Conventions/Meetings:** periodic regional meeting ● periodic show, for judging ● periodic tour and picnic.

21345 ■ Society of Automotive Historians (SAH)
1102 Long Cove Rd.
Gales Ferry, CT 06335-1812
Ph: (860)464-6466
Fax: (860)464-2614
E-mail: bobewing35@hotmail.com
URL: http://www.autohistory.org
Contact: Michael Berger, Pres.
Founded: 1969. **Members:** 1,000. **Membership Dues:** individual, organization, $40 (annual). **Regional Groups:** 6. **Local Groups:** 6. **Multinational. Description:** Writers, researchers, librarians, students, educators, hobbyists, publishers, industry figures, museums, and other individuals. Aims to the preserve and record the history of the automobile, the industry, its people, its attendant industries, and supporting structures. Conducts research. Includes activities such as: rescuing and placing historical material in publicly accessible libraries and archives. **Awards:** Carl Benz Award. **Frequency:** annual. **Type:** recognition. **Recipient:** for best article on automotive history subjects ● E.P. Ingersoll Award. **Frequency:** annual. **Type:** recognition. **Recipient:** for best presentation of automotive history in other print media ● Friend of Automotive History Award. **Frequency:** annual. **Type:** recognition. **Recipient:** to an individual who has made a contribution to automotive history ● James J. Bradley Memorial Award. **Frequency:** annual. **Type:** recognition. **Recipient:** for outstanding work relating to the preservation of auto literature and artifacts ● Nicholas Joseph Cugnot Award. **Frequency:** annual. **Type:** recognition. **Recipient:** for best book about automotive history (separate awards for books in English and languages other than English) ● Richard and Grace Brigham Award. **Frequency:** annual. **Type:** recognition. **Recipient:** for best overall treatment of automo-

tive history ● Student Paper Award. **Frequency:** annual. **Type:** recognition. **Recipient:** for best research paper by college/university student on topic of auto history. **Subgroups:** Henry M. LeLand; Indiana Hoosier Heritage; Pioneer; Southern California; United Kingdom; Wisconsin. **Affiliated With:** American Historical Association. **Publications:** *Automotive History Review*, semiannual. Magazine. Contains in-depth articles on automotive history. **Price:** free for members. ISSN: 1056-2729. **Circulation:** 1,000 ● *SAH Journal*, bimonthly. Newsletters. Contains news of the organization, short feature articles. **Price:** free for members. ISSN: 1057-1973. **Circulation:** 1,000. **Advertising:** accepted ● Membership Directory, biennial. **Conventions/Meetings:** annual dinner, in conjunction with the fall Antique Automobile Club of America car show and flea market in Hershey, PA - always October ● annual European Meeting - early February, Paris, France ● biennial History Conferences, co-sponsored by National Association of Automobile Museums.

21346 ■ Solid Axle Corvette Club (SACC)
PO Box 2288
North Highlands, CA 95660-8288
Ph: (916)991-7040
Fax: (916)991-7044
E-mail: sacc@bigfoot.com
URL: http://www.solidaxle.org
Contact: Noland Adams, Pres.
Founded: 1994. **Members:** 1,000. **Membership Dues:** individual/business in U.S., $30 (annual) ● individual/business in Canada, $40 (annual) ● individual/business outside U.S. and Canada, $50 (annual). **Regional Groups:** 4. **Multinational. Description:** Those who enjoy 1953 through 1962 Corvettes. Promotes the sharing of solid axle technical information among members. **Publications:** *On Solid Ground*, quarterly. Magazine. **Advertising:** accepted. **Conventions/Meetings:** annual convention and regional meeting (exhibits).

21347 ■ Sports Car Club of America (SCCA)
PO Box 19400
Topeka, KS 66619-0400
Ph: (785)357-7222
Free: (800)770-2055
Fax: (785)232-7228
E-mail: membership@scca.com
URL: http://www.scca.org
Contact: Mr. Jim Julow, Pres./CEO
Founded: 1944. **Members:** 60,000. **Membership Dues:** regular, $45 (annual) ● military, $35 (annual) ● spouse, $20 (annual) ● family, $95 (annual) ● individual, $60 (annual). **Staff:** 47. **Budget:** $9,000,000. **Regional Groups:** 110. **Description:** Competition sports car owners and enthusiasts. Sanctions professional FIA international events and amateur national and regional races. Sanctions World Challenge and Trans-Am Tour series; also conducts race driver schools, rallies (professional European-style and precision driving tests over a given route at an exact speed), gymkhanas (intricate driving maneuvers in a cleared area), and concours d'elegance (rating cars by a correlation of age, condition, and equipment of the vehicle). Issues competition driver licenses. Establishes safety regulations for competitions. Conducts educational and charitable programs. **Awards: Type:** recognition. **Computer Services:** Electronic publishing ● mailing lists. **Telecommunication Services:** electronic mail, president@scca.com. **Committees:** Competition Board; Planning; Pro Rally Board; Professional Competition Board; Road Rally Board; Solo Advisory; Solo Events; Solo Safety. **Publications:** *Sports Car*, monthly. Magazine. Includes race results. **Price:** $2.95. ISSN: 0300-6387. **Circulation:** 50,000. **Advertising:** accepted. Alternate Formats: online ● Directory, annual. Lists racing officials. **Price:** $2.00/issue. **Conventions/Meetings:** annual conference and seminar (exhibits) - always February.

21348 ■ Squire SS-100 Registry
c/o Arthur R. Stahl
11826 S 51st St.
Phoenix, AZ 85044-2313

Ph: (480)893-9451
E-mail: squirepal@aol.com
URL: http://www.squiress-100.org
Contact: Arthur R. Stahl, Contact
Founded: 1987. **Members:** 50. **Membership Dues:** individual, $40 (annual). **Staff:** 2. **Regional Groups:** 2. **Description:** Owners and enthusiasts of Squire SS-100 automobiles. Traces ownership and maintains records of ownership of the Squire SS-100. **Libraries: Type:** reference. **Holdings:** archival material, books, clippings, monographs, periodicals. **Computer Services:** database ● mailing lists. **Formerly:** Squire SS-100 Club. **Publications:** *Maintenance and Repair Manual*, periodic ● *Membership Newsletter*, bi-monthly. **Price:** included in membership dues ● *Roster of Owners*, periodic. Directory. **Price:** included in membership dues. **Circulation:** 50. **Conventions/Meetings:** semiannual meeting ● periodic regional meeting and workshop.

21349 ■ Steam Automobile Club of America (SACA)
c/o Tom Kimmel, Pres.
PO Box 8
Berrien Springs, MI 49103
Ph: (269)471-7408 (978)486-9695
E-mail: sacapres@steamautomobile.com
URL: http://www.steamautomobile.com
Contact: Tom Kimmel, Pres.
Founded: 1958. **Members:** 600. **Membership Dues:** regular, $25 (annual) ● foreign, $35 (annual). **Staff:** 3. **Regional Groups:** 5. **Local Groups:** 4. **Description:** Represents persons interested in restoration of antique steam cars, preservation of steam car history, and the design, development, and production of a modern steam car. **Publications:** *Steam Automobile Bulletin*, quarterly. Newsletter. Contains articles, technical information, classified ads, and chapter news. **Price:** included in membership dues. **Circulation:** 600. **Advertising:** accepted. **Conventions/Meetings:** annual general assembly ● annual meet, with speakers.

21350 ■ Studebaker Driver's Club (SDC)
PO Box 1715
Maple Grove, MN 55311-6715
Ph: (763)420-7829
Fax: (763)420-7849
E-mail: registration@cornerstonereg.com
URL: http://www.studebakerdriversclub.com
Contact: Jan Lockmon, Sec.
Founded: 1962. **Members:** 13,000. **Membership Dues:** adult (with periodical class mail), $27 (annual) ● adult (with first class mail), $60 (annual) ● student/young adult, $19 (annual) ● foreign (with surface mail), $44 (annual) ● foreign (with air mail), $121 (annual). **Budget:** $300,000. **Regional Groups:** 50. **Description:** Owners of Studebaker automobiles and trucks. Attempts to aid in the restoration of, procure parts for, and reproduce old instruction manuals of the Studebaker car. Supports Studebaker Vehicle Museum in South Bend, IN. Compiles statistics. **Libraries: Type:** reference. **Holdings:** 2,500. **Subjects:** Studebaker, Rockne, Erskine, Packard automobiles. **Awards:** Minnie Barnes Award. **Frequency:** annual. **Type:** recognition. **Recipient:** for region that leads in helping the sick, disabled, or underprivileged. **Computer Services:** Mailing lists, of members only. **Absorbed:** (1974) Studebaker Owners Club. **Publications:** *Membership Roster*, annual. Membership Directory. **Price:** $16.00. Alternate Formats: CD-ROM ● *Parts and Service Directory*, periodic ● *Turning Wheels*, monthly. Magazine. Contains articles about Studebaker cars, trucks, and people. **Price:** included in membership dues. ISSN: 1052-3251. **Circulation:** 13,000. Alternate Formats: online ● Regional groups also publish newsletters. **Conventions/Meetings:** annual convention and show (exhibits) ● biennial convention and meet (exhibits) - usually Australia or New Zealand, Easter time ● annual meet.

21351 ■ Stutz Club
PO Box 86
Greenford, OH 44422
Ph: (330)730-9498
Fax: (330)730-9498

E-mail: stutzclub@mpbarry.com
URL: http://www.stutzclub.org
Contact: Michael P. Barry, VP of Membership
Founded: 1987. **Members:** 380. **Membership Dues:** active, $40 (annual). **Budget:** $9,000. **Description:** Stutz automobile owners and enthusiasts. Promotes fellowship and the maintenance and preservation of Stutz automobiles. Works to preserve Stutz literature, memorabilia, and technical information. Conducts exhibitions of Stutz automobiles for charitable organizations and research programs. Compiles statistics. **Libraries: Type:** reference. **Subjects:** Stutz history. **Awards:** Peter Helck Stutz Memorial Trophy. **Frequency:** annual. **Type:** trophy. **Recipient:** for significant contributions and support of the Stutz Club with dedication over the years. **Computer Services:** database, membership and Stutz vehicles owned ● information services, Stutz resources ● on-line services, forum. **Committees:** Technical. **Publications:** *Directory of Members and Vehicles*, periodic. **Circulation:** 400 ● *The Splendid Stutz*. Book. **Price:** $69.95 plus shipping and handling ● *Stutz News*, quarterly. Newsletter. Includes historical and technical information, classifieds, and stories submitted by members. **Price:** available to members only. **Circulation:** 375. **Advertising:** accepted. **Conventions/Meetings:** annual Grand Stutz Meet, social, Stutz car show, membership meeting (exhibits).

21352 ■ Subaru 360 Drivers' Club
2341 S Circle X Pl.
Tucson, AZ 85713
Ph: (520)290-6492
E-mail: subaru360nut@aol.com
URL: http://www.subaru360club.org
Contact: Ed Parsil, Sec.-Treas./Ed.
Founded: 1980. **Members:** 400. **Membership Dues:** $6 (annual). **Budget:** $1,700. **Description:** Represents past, present, or potential owners and drivers of 1968 to 1970 two-cylinder Subaru 360 automobiles. Aims to keep these vehicles functional. Provides information on parts availability and maintenance procedures. Forms united effort to keep parts available and licensing rights unrestricted for vehicles. Offers help in documenting value of Subaru 360s for insurance purposes. **Publications:** *Roster*, annual. **Circulation:** 375 ● Newsletter, quarterly. **Price:** included in membership dues. **Circulation:** 400. **Conventions/Meetings:** annual Southwest Unique Little Car Show (exhibits).

21353 ■ Sunbeam Rapier Registry (SRR)
c/o James Mazour, Founder
3212 Orchard Cir.
West Des Moines, IA 50266
Ph: (515)226-9475
E-mail: jmazour@aol.com
URL: http://clubs.hemmings.com/sunbeam
Contact: James Mazour, Founder
Founded: 1992. **Members:** 30. **Membership Dues:** individual in U.S., $16 (annual) ● individual in Canada, $19 (annual) ● overseas, $20 (annual). **Description:** Owners and admirers of the Sunbeam Rapier automobile, manufactured in England from 1956 to 1967. Promotes restoration and preservation of Sunbeam Rapiers. Maintains registry of Sunbeam Rapiers; facilitates exchange of information among members. **Computer Services:** database, registry of Sunbeam Rapier automobiles in North America. **Formerly:** (2003) Sunbeam Rapier Registry of North America. **Publications:** *Rapier News*, quarterly. Newsletter. **Advertising:** accepted ● A registry listing all known Sunbeam Rapier cars and their owners is published every five years.

21354 ■ Tigers East/Alpines East (TE/AE)
PO Box 1260
Kulpsville, PA 19443-1260
Ph: (610)913-7872
E-mail: teae@aol.com
URL: http://www.teae.org
Contact: Anthony DiBattista, Pres.
Founded: 1975. **Members:** 650. **Membership Dues:** single in U.S., $33 (annual) ● single outside U.S., $36 (annual) ● single in U.S., $60 (biennial) ● single outside U.S., $66 (biennial). **Regional Groups:** 11.

Multinational. **Description:** Promotes the restoration and preservation of the Sunbeam automobiles. **Libraries: Type:** reference. **Holdings:** photographs. **Awards:** Lord Rootes Trophy. **Frequency:** annual. **Type:** trophy. **Computer Services:** database. **Publications:** *Rootes Review*, monthly. Newsletter. Contains membership news and social calendar. **Price:** included in membership dues. **Circulation:** 650. **Advertising:** accepted. Alternate Formats: diskette ● *Tigers East/Alpines East Roster*, annual. Directory. **Conventions/Meetings:** annual convention (exhibits) - second weekend in October.

21355 ■ Topolino Register of North America (TRNA)
3301 Shetland Rd.
Beavercreek, OH 45434
Ph: (937)426-0098
E-mail: mike7353@aol.com
Contact: Michael M. Self, Registrar
Founded: 1969. **Members:** 54. **Description:** Owners and others interested in Fiat Topolino automobiles and their derivatives. Serves as a central exchange for information, technical advice, and parts sources for owners of Fiat Topolino automobiles, and related vehicles including the Simca Cinq, Siata Amica, and Nardi-Crosley. Attempts to locate all remaining Topolinos in North America by serial numbers. Conventions/Meetings: none. **Libraries: Type:** reference. **Holdings:** books. **Subjects:** technical restoration data.

21356 ■ Toyota Owner's and Restorer's Club (TORC)
2849 Long Beach Blvd.
Long Beach, CA 90806
Ph: (760)753-8022
Fax: (760)753-8058
E-mail: events@toyotaclub.org
URL: http://www.toyotaclub.org
Contact: Stuart Resor, Founder
Founded: 1995. **Membership Dues:** regular, in U.S., $25 (annual) ● regular, outside U.S., $35 (annual). **Description:** Represents Toyota automobile enthusiasts. Provides networking with other club members; discounts at participating Toyota dealerships; once a year club meet world wide; and an answer man to solve technical questions. **Telecommunication Services:** electronic mail, resorarchitect@cox.net. **Publications:** Newsletter, bimonthly. **Price:** included in membership dues. **Conventions/Meetings:** annual All Toyotafest - specialty show (exhibits).

21357 ■ TR8 Car Club of America (TR8CCA)
c/o Joe Worsley, Membership Coor./Treas.
1591 Peoples Creek Rd.
Advance, NC 27006-7451
Ph: (336)998-6501
E-mail: e.krakowski@prodigy.net
URL: http://www.team.net/TR8/tr8cca
Contact: Joe Worsley, Membership Coor./Treas.
Founded: 1983. **Members:** 400. **Membership Dues:** in U.S. and Canada, $15 (annual) ● outside U.S. and Canada, $20 (annual). **Description:** Individuals who enjoy the TR8 automobile, which was manufactured from 1978 to 1982, and was the last model produced by British Leyland's Triumph division. Provides technical and parts location information to members. **Convention/Meeting:** none. **Telecommunication Services:** electronic mail, jworsley@yadtel.net. **Publications:** Membership Directory, annual ● Newsletter, quarterly.

21358 ■ Triumph Register of America (TRA)
c/o John Warfield, Pres.
934 Coachway
Annapolis, MD 21401
Ph: (410)974-6707
E-mail: firsttr2@aol.com
URL: http://www.triumphregister.com
Contact: John Warfield, Pres.
Founded: 1974. **Members:** 1,100. **Membership Dues:** regular, $25 (annual). **Staff:** 10. **Local Groups:** 20. **Description:** Represents owners and enthusiasts of Triumph sports cars of the TR-2/3 series, manufactured between 1953 and 1962. Aids

owners in the preservation, maintenance, and enjoyment of their classic sports cars. Conducts technical workshops and rallies through local centers. Provides advertisement and information on new and second-hand spare parts. **Telecommunication Services:** electronic mail, jeff@integrateinc.com. **Committees:** Chief Judge; Factory Build Records; National Meet; Technical Video; TR Mart. **Publications:** *TRA National Newsletter*, quarterly. **Price:** included in membership dues. **Circulation:** 1,100. **Advertising:** accepted. Alternate Formats: online. **Conventions/Meetings:** annual meeting, sports car club meeting - usually 4th weekend of June.

21359 ■ Tucker Automobile Club of America (TACA)
9509 Hinton Dr.
Santee, CA 92071-2760
Ph: (619)596-3028
E-mail: info@tuckerclub.org
URL: http://www.tuckerclub.org/index.php
Contact: Mr. Jay A. Follis, Dir.
Founded: 1973. **Members:** 500. **Membership Dues:** regular, in U.S. and Canada, $30 (annual) ● regular, outside U.S. and Canada, $50 (annual). **Description:** Persons interested in the Tucker automobile, which was manufactured in 1948 by the Tucker Corporation, Chicago, IL. Established Tucker Historical Collection and Library (HCL) at the Gilmore Car Museum in Hickory Corners, Michigan. **Libraries: Type:** open to the public; by appointment only. **Holdings:** archival material, articles, audio recordings, books, business records, photographs. **Awards:** Preston and Vera Tucker Memorial Scholarship. **Frequency:** annual. **Type:** recognition. **Recipient:** for students ● William J. Cammack Memorial Scholarship. **Frequency:** annual. **Type:** recognition. **Recipient:** for students. **Publications:** *Tucker Topics*, monthly. Newsletter. **Price:** included in membership dues. ISSN: 1540-6954. **Advertising:** accepted ● *Tucker Tribune*, monthly. Newsletter. Email newsletter. **Price:** free. **Circulation:** 1,100. Alternate Formats: online.

21360 ■ TVR Car Club North America (TVRCCNA)
c/o Marshall Moore, Pres.
3559 Overbrook Dr.
Roanoke, VA 24018
Ph: (540)772-0952
E-mail: tvrccna@cox.net
URL: http://www.tvrccna.org
Contact: Marshall Moore, Pres.
Founded: 1973. **Members:** 500. **Membership Dues:** regular, $35-$40 (annual) ● overseas, $45-$50 (annual). **Staff:** 6. **Regional Groups:** 8. **Multinational. Description:** Represents owners and enthusiasts of TVR automobiles. (The TVR sports car is totally handcrafted by TVR Engineering, Ltd., of England.) Works to preserve and maintain the TVR marque. Offers spare parts service for members. **Libraries: Type:** reference. **Holdings:** 90; artwork, audiovisuals, books, clippings, periodicals, photographs. **Subjects:** factory records, production topics. **Awards:** Trevor Award. **Frequency:** annual. **Type:** recognition. **Recipient:** for best combination of member and car. **Computer Services:** database, chassis registry ● database, factory records ● mailing lists, chassis registry ● mailing lists, factory records. **Subgroups:** Canadian Region; New England Region; North Central Region; Northeast Region; Pacific N.W. Region; Southeast Region; Southwest Region; UK Region; Western Region. **Also Known As:** TVR Car Club. **Formerly:** (1989) TVR Car Club of England, U.S. Area. **Publications:** *TVR Times*, bimonthly. Newsletter. Contains part sources listings, article reviews, technical tips, and schedule of upcoming events. **Price:** included in membership dues. **Circulation:** 600. **Advertising:** accepted. Alternate Formats: diskette; online. **Conventions/Meetings:** annual Out of the Woodwork - competition and convention - Columbus Day weekend.

21361 ■ United Council of Corvette Clubs (UCCC)
1861 Springfield
Flint, MI 48503

Ph: (412)444-5555
Free: (866)457-2582
E-mail: lewisbecoats@hotmail.com
URL: http://www.unitedcouncil.com
Contact: Lewis J. Becoats, Pres.
Founded: 1985. **Members:** 300. **Membership Dues:** member-at-large, $35. **Budget:** $30,000. **Regional Groups:** 17. **Description:** Chevrolet Corvette enthusiasts. Promotes appreciation of Corvette automobiles. Conducts educational programs; sponsors competitions; undertakes charitable activities. **Libraries: Type:** not open to the public. **Holdings:** archival material, articles, business records. **Subjects:** Corvettes, spare parts. **Awards:** UCCC Awards. **Frequency:** annual. **Type:** scholarship. **Recipient:** for members and supporters. **Publications:** *Corvette Chronicle*, quarterly. Newsletter. **Circulation:** 300. **Advertising:** accepted. Alternate Formats: CD-ROM ● *UCCC Directory*, annual. **Circulation:** 300 ● Brochure, quarterly. **Circulation:** 300. **Advertising:** accepted. Alternate Formats: CD-ROM. **Conventions/Meetings:** annual board meeting (exhibits) - usually in July ● annual convention (exhibits) ● periodic regional meeting (exhibits).

21362 ■ United Ford Owners (UFO)
PO Box 32419
Columbus, OH 43232
Ph: (614)265-9095 (740)927-2854
E-mail: figs1@earthlink.net
URL: http://www.unitedfordowners.com
Contact: Rena Figley, Sec.
Founded: 1985. **Members:** 300. **Membership Dues:** regular, $15 (annual). **Description:** Owners of vehicles manufactured by the Ford Motor Company and interested individuals. Promotes interests of members. Maintains library of books, periodicals, and videos on automotive-related subjects. **Publications:** Newsletter, monthly. **Price:** included in membership dues. **Circulation:** 300. Alternate Formats: online. **Conventions/Meetings:** annual Fall Super Swap - meet (exhibits) - always Thanksgiving weekend, Columbus, OH.

21363 ■ United Four-Wheel Drive Associations (UFWDA)
14525 SW Milikan Way 22622
Beaverton, OR 97005-2343
Ph: (920)667-4940 (416)447-1246
Free: (800)448-3932
Fax: (619)390-1705
E-mail: info@ufwda.org
URL: http://www.ufwda.org
Contact: Wayne Groom, Pres.
Founded: 1976. **Members:** 30,000. **Budget:** $149,000. **Regional Groups:** 30. **Multinational. Description:** Advisory and individual members' clubs. Aims to work with land problems and establish better communication between four-wheelers and the government. Operates charitable program benefiting the March of Dimes Birth Defects Foundation. Compiles statistics. **Affiliated With:** March of Dimes Birth Defects Foundation. **Publications:** *United's VOICE*, quarterly. Newspaper. Includes updates of activities of regional associations. **Price:** included in membership dues. **Circulation:** 25,000. **Advertising:** accepted. Alternate Formats: CD-ROM; online. **Conventions/Meetings:** annual conference (exhibits) - summer ● annual Delegate Meeting - convention.

21364 ■ United Mopar Club
313 N Stewart Rd.
Liberty, MO 64068
Ph: (816)781-0095
Fax: (816)781-3520
Contact: Mark D. Miller, Pres.
Founded: 1975. **For-Profit. Description:** Individuals who own Chrysler automobiles. Makes available spare parts. **Formerly:** Mopar Trans-Am Association.

21365 ■ United Street Machine Association (USMA)
430 N Batchewana
Clawson, MI 48017
Ph: (248)280-0342

E-mail: usmainc@hotmail.com
URL: http://www.usmacarshows.com
Contact: Ralph A. Haney, Pres.
Founded: 1979. **Members:** 1,200. **Membership Dues:** initial, $30. **Description:** Individuals interested in owning and showing muscle cars, street rods, customs, 4 by 4's, and trucks. Conducts charitable programs. **Awards: Type:** recognition. **Recipient:** for best in class. **Publications:** Newsletter, every 45 days. **Price:** free for members. **Circulation:** 1,200. **Advertising:** accepted. **Conventions/Meetings:** biennial National Car Show (exhibits).

21366 ■ Veteran Motor Car Club of America (VMCCA)

c/o Mike Welsh, Sec.
7501 Manchester Ave.
Kansas City, MO 64138
Ph: (816)298-6412 (979)826-3111
Free: (800)428-7327
Fax: (602)978-1106
E-mail: vsecretary@vmcca.org
URL: http://www.vmcca.org
Contact: Jamie Crandall, Pres.
Founded: 1938. **Members:** 5,800. **Membership Dues:** active in U.S., $37 (annual) ● foreign, $45 (annual). **Regional Groups:** 17. **Local Groups:** 67. **Description:** Represents collectors and others interested in antique automobiles and related items. **Awards:** Bronze. **Type:** recognition. **Recipient:** for outstanding vehicles owned by members ● Gold. **Type:** recognition. **Recipient:** for outstanding vehicles owned by members ● Silver. **Type:** recognition. **Recipient:** for outstanding vehicles owned by members. **Affiliated With:** National Auto Racing Historical Society. **Publications:** *The Bulb Horn*, bimonthly. Magazine. **Advertising:** accepted. **Conventions/Meetings:** annual meeting - usually January or February ● Revival AAA Glidden Tour.

21367 ■ Vintage Chevrolet Club of America (VCCA)

1751 E Rte. 66
Glendora, CA 91740-3813
Ph: (626)963-2438
E-mail: editor@vcca.org
URL: http://www.vcca.org
Contact: Shirley Whitesell, Membership Sec.
Founded: 1961. **Members:** 8,800. **Membership Dues:** regular, in U.S., $30 (annual) ● regular, in U.S. (joint), $35 (annual) ● regular, in Canada and international, $40 (annual) ● life, in Canada and international, $1,000 ● life, in U.S. (joint), $100. **Regional Groups:** 66. **Local Groups:** 5. **Languages:** English, French, Italian, Spanish. **Description:** Represents persons interested in restoration and preservation of vintage Chevrolet automobiles. Currently recognizes all Chevrolet-built vehicles at least 15 years old. Sponsors meets and car shows. Provides insurance and technical sponsorship for all approved functions. **Publications:** *Generator and Distributor*, monthly. Magazine. **Price:** included in membership dues. **Circulation:** 7,900. **Advertising:** accepted. **Conventions/Meetings:** annual Installation Banquet.

21368 ■ Vintage Sports Car Club of America (VSCCA)

c/o Anthony S. Carroll, Sec.
170 Wetherill Rd.
Garden City, NY 11530
Ph: (413)584-4210
E-mail: edwardh@gullwingsearch.com
URL: http://www.vscca.org
Contact: John J. Schieffelin, Pres.
Founded: 1958. **Members:** 900. **Description:** Vintage sports car owners and enthusiasts. Encourages acquisition, preservation, restoration, and operation of sports and racing cars built before World War II, and rare and unusual sports cars built between 1944 and 1959. Sponsors competitive events and exhibitions; serves as a source of technical information. **Publications:** *Vintage Sports Car*, quarterly. Journal. Features vintage car information. **Circulation:** 950. **Advertising:** accepted. **Conventions/Meetings:** annual meeting.

21369 ■ Vintage Thunderbird Club International (VTCI)

c/o Marilyn Paliani, Exec. Sec.
1304 Greenwood
Schertz, TX 78154-2808
Ph: (210)566-2118
E-mail: lpaliani@satx.rr.com
URL: http://www.vintagethunderbirdclub.org/welcome.htm
Contact: Mr. Lou Paliani, Pres.
Founded: 1968. **Members:** 2,500. **Membership Dues:** regular, in U.S. and Canada, $35 (annual) ● regular, outside U.S. and Canada, $55 (annual). **State Groups:** 42. **Local Groups:** 50. **Description:** Owners of 1955 to today's Ford Thunderbird automobiles. Encourages restoration and maintenance of the cars, exchanges pertinent information, and participates in group events of a car oriented nature. Provides technical assistance. **Libraries: Type:** reference. **Holdings:** archival material, books, periodicals, photographs. **Awards: Type:** recognition. **Recipient:** for the best show car and/or winners of events at meets. **Committees:** Judges Training. **Formerly:** (1989) Vintage Thunderbird Club of America. **Publications:** *Membership Roster*, annual. Membership Directory. **Price:** included in membership dues. **Circulation:** 2,500. **Advertising:** accepted ● *Thunderbird Scoop*, bimonthly. Magazine. Contains maintenance instructions, spare parts information, and regional and local chapter news. ● Also publishes original factory specifications and concours rules. **Conventions/Meetings:** annual competition ● annual convention - always August or September. 2008 Aug. 5-10, Colorado Springs, CO ● meet ● regional meeting - 5/year.

21370 ■ Vintage Triumph Register (VTR)

PO Box 655
Howell, MI 48844
E-mail: vbbrannon@bellsouth.net
URL: http://www.vtr.org
Contact: Vernon Brannon, Pres.
Founded: 1974. **Members:** 3,000. **Membership Dues:** regular, in U.S., $30 (annual) ● regular, in Canada and Mexico, $35 (annual) ● anywhere else, $40 (annual). **Budget:** $70,000. **Regional Groups:** 73. **Local Groups:** 50. **Description:** Represents persons interested in preserving and enjoying Triumph automobiles. Provides advice and assistance for the maintenance, restoration, and preservation of the marque. Investigates parts and literature sources and makes them available to members. Conducts research into the history of the marque. **Libraries: Type:** reference. **Awards: Frequency:** annual. **Type:** recognition. **Recipient:** for the best restored and most original automobiles by model. **Computer Services:** Mailing lists, Auto-X Triumphs, serves as a discussion group/forum. **Departments:** Autocross; The English Channel; TVT Back Issues; The Vintage Triumph. **Programs:** Traveler Assistance. **Absorbed:** (1981) Triumph Sports Owners Association. **Publications:** *Vintage Triumph*, quarterly. Magazine. Includes historical and technical information. Contains calendar of events, advertisements, cars and parts for sale. **Price:** included in membership dues. **ISSN:** 0147-9695. **Circulation:** 3,000. **Advertising:** accepted ● Brochure. **Alternate Formats:** online. **Conventions/Meetings:** annual competition and convention (exhibits) ● annual convention (exhibits).

21371 ■ Vintage Volkswagen Club of America (VVWCA)

c/o Peter Cook, Pres.
99 Pine Ln.
Westwood, MA 02090-1220
Ph: (781)329-6921
E-mail: bsvwoc@aol.com
URL: http://www.vvwca.com
Contact: Peter Cook, Pres.
Founded: 1976. **Members:** 800. **Membership Dues:** regular, in U.S., $24 (annual) ● regular, in Canada and Mexico, $45 (annual) ● overseas, $55 (annual) ● decal, $1 (annual). **Staff:** 5. **State Groups:** 50. **Description:** Represents owners and enthusiasts of Volkswagen-based automobiles which are air-cooled. Promotes the acquisition, preservation, and restora-

tion of the vintage cars. Facilitates exchange of technical and mechanical information and information concerning the location of original parts and old literature. Works to establish beneficial relationships with Volkswagen factories and dealers. **Committees:** Nominating. **Publications:** *Vintage Voice*, bimonthly. **Price:** included in membership dues. **Circulation:** 1,000. **Advertising:** accepted. **Alternate Formats:** online.

21372 ■ Volkswagen Club of America (VWCA)

PO Box 154
North Aurora, IL 60542
Ph: (630)896-2803
E-mail: vwclub@vwclub.org
URL: http://www.vwclub.org
Contact: Tom Janiszewski, VP
Founded: 1955. **Members:** 2,500. **Membership Dues:** individual, $26 (annual) ● regular, outside U.S., $32 (annual). **Description:** Represents owners and enthusiasts of Volkswagen and Audi automobiles. Disseminates information on maintenance and restoration of Volkswagen vehicles. Local clubs hold rallies, parties, and other automotive and social events. **Awards:** Rallye Cup. **Frequency:** annual. **Type:** recognition. **Recipient:** based on monitored performance ● Wolfsburg Trophy. **Frequency:** annual. **Type:** recognition. **Recipient:** based on monitored performance ● Woodbury Dunn Safety Award. **Frequency:** annual. **Type:** recognition. **Recipient:** based on monitored performance. **Publications:** *The VW Autoist*, bimonthly. Magazine. Includes car service tips and news from Europe. **Price:** included in membership dues. **Circulation:** 2,500. **Advertising:** accepted ● Newsletter. **Conventions/Meetings:** Maifest - festival - always spring ● annual National Convention (exhibits) - always summer ● Oktoberfest - festival - always fall.

21373 ■ Volvo Club of America (VCOA)

Box 16
Afton, NY 13730
Ph: (607)639-2279
Fax: (607)639-2280
E-mail: lee@vcoa.org
URL: http://www.vcoa.org
Contact: Lee Cordner, Pres.
Founded: 1982. **Members:** 4,000. **Membership Dues:** regular, $35 (annual). **State Groups:** 23. **Description:** Owners and enthusiasts of Volvo automobiles produced from the 1930s to the present. Promotes ownership of Volvos and communication among Volvo owners. Provides technical information and assistance. Encourages safe driving and the use of safety devices such as seat belts. Sponsors regional and national activities. **Publications:** *Rolling*, bimonthly. Magazine. **Price:** included in membership dues; $30.00 for nonmembers in U.S. **Circulation:** 4,500. **Advertising:** accepted. **Conventions/Meetings:** annual banquet and meet (exhibits) ● rally ● workshop.

21374 ■ Wills Sainte Claire Museum

2408 Wills St.
Marysville, MI 48040
Ph: (810)987-2854
E-mail: willsmuseum@sbcglobal.net
URL: http://www.willsautomuseum.com
Contact: Terry Ernest, Dir.
Founded: 1955. **Members:** 145. **Membership Dues:** regular, $25 (annual). **Staff:** 3. **Budget:** $12,000. **Description:** Owners of Wills Sainte Claire automobiles (about 82 cars accounted for), former owners, and interested individuals. Supplies members with information and parts needed in restoring cars. Museum features seven WSC autos on display, open monthly, 2nd Sunday. **Libraries: Type:** reference. **Holdings:** articles, books, periodicals. **Subjects:** Wills Sainte Claire automobiles. **Awards:** Spirit of C.H. Wills Award. **Frequency:** annual. **Type:** recognition. **Also Known As:** Wills Club. **Formerly:** (2003) Wills Sainte Claire Owners Club. **Publications:** *Gray Goose News*, quarterly. Newsletter. **Price:** free to paid museum members. **Circulation:** 150. **Advertising:** accepted ● *The Wills Club Registry*, annual ●

Also publishes reprints of owners manuals and shop manuals. **Conventions/Meetings:** annual Wills Auto Reunion - meeting.

21375 ■ Willys Overland Jeepster Club (WOJC)
255 Thompsonville Rd.
McMurray, PA 15317
E-mail: jeepsternews@comcast.net
URL: http://www.jeepsterclub.com
Contact: Jim Sommer, Communications Dir./Ed.
Founded: 1966. **Members:** 438. **Membership Dues:** initial fee, $23 (annual) ● renewal fee, $20 (annual). **Description:** Promotes interest in the Willys Overland Jeepster Phaeton, "the last touring car phaeton body style built in the U.S." According to WOJC statistics, only 19,131 such vehicles were made between 1948 and 1951. **Telecommunication Services:** electronic mail, jeepsternews@adelphia.net. **Publications:** *Club Roster*, annual. Membership Directory ● *Jeepster News*, monthly. Newsletter. **Price:** $20.00/year. **Circulation:** 518. **Conventions/Meetings:** annual Founders Day Meet - meeting and meet - usually in fall ● meet - usually in spring.

21376 ■ Willys-Overland-Knight Registry (WOKR)
c/o Duane A. Perrin, Registrar
1749 Chain Bridge Rd.
McLean, VA 22102-2934
E-mail: elp90@aol.com
URL: http://www.wokr.org
Contact: Duane A. Perrin, Registrar
Founded: 1960. **Members:** 1,300. **Membership Dues:** active in U.S., $27 (annual) ● joint in U.S., $31 (annual) ● patron, $5 (annual) ● active in Canada, $29 (annual) ● joint in Canada, active outside U.S. and Canada, $33 (annual) ● joint outside U.S. and Canada, $37 (annual). **Regional Groups:** 12. **Multinational. Description:** Persons interested in the restoration and maintenance of the Knight sleeve-valve engine and pre-World War II Willys-Overland automobiles. Provides historical and technical information and reproduces some hard-to-find parts. **Libraries: Type:** reference. **Holdings:** 500,000. **Subjects:** historical and technical automobile drawings. **Formerly:** (1968) National Registry of Willys - Knight Automobiles. **Publications:** *Knight-Overland Starter*, quarterly. Magazine. Contains club news and historical articles. **Price:** included in membership dues. **Circulation:** 1,300 ● *Roster of Members*, biennial. Membership Directory ● *WOKR News*, monthly. Newsletter. **Conventions/Meetings:** annual International Meet - convention - usually late July.

21377 ■ Winged Warriors/National B-Body Owners Association (WW/NBOA)
216 12th St.
Boone, IA 50036-2019
Ph: (515)432-3001
E-mail: hemi@willinet.net
URL: http://wwnboa.org
Contact: Sue George, Pres.
Founded: 1975. **Members:** 600. **Membership Dues:** in U.S., $30 (annual) ● outside U.S., $40 (annual). **Staff:** 8. **Description:** Auto enthusiasts. Seeks to account for each produced 1962 to 1974 Bigblock Plymouth and Dodge B-Body, 1969 Charger Daytona, and 1970 Superbird automobiles. Assembles historical information on the vehicles; promotes local and regional meets; aids members in restoring their cars. **Libraries: Type:** reference. **Holdings:** 200; periodicals. **Awards: Type:** recognition. **Computer Services:** database, contains serial numbers of automobiles ● database, membership list. **Publications:** *Winged Warrior/B-Body Review*, monthly. Newsletter. Contains restoration and technical info, reprints of old literature and features on members' cars; also includes VIN number research, and advertising. **Price:** included in membership dues. **Advertising:** accepted. Also Cited As: *Winged Warrior*. **Conventions/Meetings:** annual competition, cars and restoration parts displays (exhibits).

21378 ■ Worldwide Camaro Club
c/o Eckler's Camaro
5140 S Washington Ave.
Titusville, FL 32780-7318
Free: (800)283-0691
Fax: (321)383-2059
E-mail: info@ecklerscamaro.net
URL: http://www.worldwidecamaro.com
Contact: Thomas Striklin, Brand Mgr.
Founded: 1984. **Members:** 15,000. **Membership Dues:** regular, in U.S., $19-$39 (annual) ● regular, outside U.S., $34-$132 (annual). **Staff:** 4. **State Groups:** 52. **Description:** Owners and enthusiasts interested in Camaro automobiles built between 1967 and 1994. Works with technicians and car dealers on writing educational and technical information concerning the Camaro. Holds swap meets, car shows, and other programs including trim tag code research and cruise-ins. Provides discount cards on parts and services from advertisers. Compiles statistics. Plans to create museum. **Libraries: Type:** reference. **Holdings:** 1,500; books, periodicals. **Subjects:** automobiles, mechanics, dealers. **Awards: Type:** recognition. **Computer Services:** Mailing lists, of members. **Formerly:** (2000) United States Camaro Club; (2006) Worldwide Camaro Association. **Publications:** *Camaro Enthusiast*, bimonthly. Magazine. **Price:** included in membership dues. **Circulation:** 15,000. **Advertising:** accepted. **Conventions/Meetings:** annual show and convention (exhibits) - usually July or August.

21379 ■ WPC Club (WPCC)
PO Box 3504
Kalamazoo, MI 49003-3504
Ph: (269)375-5535
Fax: (269)375-5535
E-mail: ijsmale@chryslerclub.org
URL: http://www.chryslerclub.org
Contact: Richard Bowman, Pres./Ed.
Founded: 1962. **Members:** 5,000. **Membership Dues:** in U.S. and Canada, Mexico, $35 (annual) ● outside U.S., $37 (annual). **Budget:** $140,000. **Regional Groups:** 29. **Description:** Individuals dedicated to the preservation, restoration, and enjoyment of Chrysler product cars. Conducts social activities; houses library. **Awards:** Chrysler Cup. **Frequency:** annual. **Type:** recognition ● Chuck and Lois Jensen Award. **Type:** recognition ● Dr. David G. Briant. **Type:** recognition ● President's Cup. **Frequency:** annual. **Type:** recognition. **Publications:** *WPC News*, monthly. Magazine. Covers the history and vehicles of the Chrysler Corporation. **Price:** included in membership dues. **Advertising:** accepted ● Magazine. **Advertising:** accepted. **Conventions/Meetings:** International Winter Photo Meet ● annual meeting - mid-July.

21380 ■ Z Car Club Association (ZCCA)
6 Jason Dr.
Londonderry, NH 03053
Ph: (603)425-2270
Fax: (603)218-6149
E-mail: director@zcca.org
URL: http://www.zcca.org
Contact: Paul W. Gasparola, Exec. Dir.
Founded: 1990. **Members:** 3,500. **Membership Dues:** active club, $2 (annual). **Staff:** 4. **Local Groups:** 35. **Description:** Serves as a grassroot organization promoting the Nissan Z Car. **Libraries: Type:** open to the public. **Holdings:** 1. **Telecommunication Services:** electronic mail, mdgoddard@up.com. **Conventions/Meetings:** annual convention (exhibits).

21381 ■ Zimmerman Registry (ZR)
2081 Madelaine Ct.
Los Altos, CA 94024
Ph: (650)967-2908
Contact: C. A. Zimmerman, Founder
Founded: 1990. **Members:** 35. **Staff:** 2. **Local Groups:** 1. **Languages:** English, German. **Multinational. Description:** Promotes the preservation of Zimmerman automobiles, which were produced in Auburn, IN from 1907-1915. Provides restoration information. Compiles statistics. **Publications:** none.

Convention/Meeting: none. **Libraries: Type:** reference. **Holdings:** 10. **Subjects:** Zimmerman and other air cooled vehicles.

Banks

21382 ■ Mechanical Bank Collectors of America (MBCA)
PO Box 13323
Pittsburgh, PA 15242
E-mail: info@mbca.com
URL: http://www.mechanicalbanks.org
Contact: Ray Haradin, Sec.
Founded: 1955. **Members:** 450. **Membership Dues:** regular, $45 (annual). **Description:** Represents antique enthusiasts interested in furthering knowledge about antique mechanical banks. **Formerly:** Mechanical Bank Collectors of Rhode Island. **Publications:** *The Banker*, 3/year. Newsletter. Contains periodical based on the collecting of mechanical banks. **Price:** available to members only. **Circulation:** 450. **Advertising:** accepted ● *Mechanical Banker*, 3/year. Journal. **Conventions/Meetings:** annual convention - always last week of September.

21383 ■ Still Bank Collectors Club of America (SBCCA)
c/o Mr. Elliotte Harold, Membership Chm.
440 Homestead Ave.
Metairie, LA 70005
Ph: (504)833-2715
Fax: (504)833-9050
E-mail: contact@stillbankclub.com
URL: http://www.stillbankclub.com
Contact: Mr. Elliotte Harold, Membership Chm.
Founded: 1966. **Members:** 550. **Membership Dues:** in U.S., $35 (annual) ● outside U.S., $45 (annual). **Description:** Organizations, companies, and individuals. Encourages the collection of antique and contemporary still banks and assists members in building their collections. (Toy banks that have no mechanical parts and do not move are called still banks). **Libraries: Type:** reference. **Holdings:** periodicals. **Subjects:** all still bank types. **Publications:** *Penny Bank Post*, 3/year. Journal. Features articles on banks by experts. **Price:** included in membership dues. **Circulation:** 525 ● *SBCCA Handbook*. Includes a membership directory. **Conventions/Meetings:** annual convention and banquet, with room shopping, educational programs, and auctions (exhibits) - always first or second weekend of June.

Beer

21384 ■ American Breweriana Association (ABA)
PO Box 595767
Fort Gratiot, MI 48059
Ph: (810)385-7101
Fax: (810)385-7121
E-mail: jseelow142@comcast.net
URL: http://www.americanbreweriana.org
Contact: Mr. John Seelow, Exec. Dir.
Founded: 1982. **Members:** 3,000. **Membership Dues:** regular, $25 (annual). **Staff:** 3. **Budget:** $90,000. **Regional Groups:** 3. **Description:** Promotes the interest of collectors of brewery advertising and antiques, brewery historians, breweries, beer distributors and retailers, industrial workers, and beer workers. Promotes increased public knowledge of brewing history. Serves collectors and historians. Preserves the memories and artifacts of historic breweries in the U.S. Aims to restore the former brewery at Potosi, WI, into a National Brewery Museum. Provides an exchange service allowing collectors of beer labels, coasters, crown caps, openers, and printed material to exchange duplicates with other members. Assists members with research regarding brewery history and the industry. **Libraries: Type:** reference. **Holdings:** 350. **Subjects:** brewery happenings, history, collecting. **Awards:** Excellence in Literature. **Frequency:** annual. **Type:** recognition. **Recipient:** for significant contributions in

writing on brewery history ● Historical Preservation. **Type:** recognition. **Study Groups:** Chicagoland Breweriana Society; Columbine Chapter; Mississippi Valley Chapter; Port of Potosi Chapter. **Publications:** *American Breweriana Journal*, bimonthly. Contains book reviews and news features on beer, brewing, and collectibles. **Price:** included in membership dues. ISSN: 0748-8343. Circulation: 3,000. **Advertising:** accepted ● *Directory of the American Breweriana Association*, annual. **Price:** included in membership dues. **Circulation:** 3,000. **Conventions/Meetings:** annual convention, with business and educational sessions, area tours, public brewery advertising show, banquet, and social events (exhibits) - always in the third week of June.

21385 ■ Brewmeisters Anonymous (BA)
20634 W Narramore Rd.
Buckeye, AZ 85326
Ph: (623)386-0656 (623)561-1931
E-mail: brewmeisters@brewarizona.org
URL: http://www.brewarizona.org
Contact: Mike Grant, Pres.
Founded: 1985. **Members:** 62. **Membership Dues:** family, $25 (annual). **Description:** Promotes the appreciation of beer and improvement of the quality and methods of home brewing. **Libraries: Type:** reference. **Holdings:** photographs. **Publications:** Newsletter. Alternate Formats: online. **Conventions/Meetings:** monthly conference and workshop (exhibits).

21386 ■ Eastern Coast Breweriana Association (ECBA)
c/o Larry Handy, VP
PO Box 1541
North Wales, PA 19454
Ph: (215)412-2344
E-mail: ohhugo1@aol.com
URL: http://www.eastcoastbrew.com
Contact: Larry Handy, VP
Founded: 1970. **Members:** 500. **Membership Dues:** single, $25 (annual) ● family, $30 (annual). **Description:** Represents collectors of beer and brewery advertising items. Works to unite individuals interested in collecting breweriana. Preserves the history of the brewing industry for posterity. **Libraries: Type:** lending. **Holdings:** 425. **Subjects:** brewery history, beer, brewing. **Awards:** Golden Pen. **Frequency:** annual. **Type:** recognition. **Recipient:** for original written articles ● Hall of Foam. **Frequency:** annual. **Type:** recognition. **Publications:** *American Breweries II*. Book. **Price:** $25.00 ● *ECBA Roster*, annual. Membership Directory ● *The KEG*, quarterly. Newsletter. **Conventions/Meetings:** annual convention (exhibits) - 3rd week of July ● periodic regional meeting.

Bicycle

21387 ■ Bikes Belong Coalition (BBC)
PO Box 2359
Boulder, CO 80306
Ph: (303)449-4893
Fax: (303)442-2936
E-mail: mail@bikesbelong.org
URL: http://bikesbelong.org
Contact: Tim Blumenthal, Exec. Dir.
Membership Dues: retailer (based on annual revenue), $100-$500 (annual). **Staff:** 8. **Description:** Promotes bicycling as a safe, convenient and healthy activity for people of all ages. Supports groups that promote bicycling. **Computer Services:** Mailing lists. **Telecommunication Services:** electronic mail, tim@bikesbelong.org.

Bird

21388 ■ African Love Bird Society (ALBS)
PO Box 142
San Marcos, CA 92079-0142

E-mail: shobrd@comcast.net
URL: http://www.africanlovebirdsociety.com
Contact: Barbara Theeke, Chair
Founded: 1976. **Members:** 600. **Membership Dues:** individual in U.S., $25 (annual) ● dual in U.S., $30 (annual) ● individual outside U.S., $40 (annual) ● dual outside U.S., $45 (annual). **Multinational. Description:** Serves as an International organization of aviculturists dedicated to the improvement and standardization of all species of Agapornis (African love birds) and their mutations. **Libraries: Type:** reference. **Holdings:** 100; books. **Subjects:** birds. **Awards: Type:** recognition. **Recipient:** for in-house work. **Publications:** *Agapornis World*, bimonthly. Journal. **Price:** included in membership dues ● *Agapornis World Roster*, annual.

21389 ■ African Parrot Society (APS)
301 E Garfield St.
Clarinda, IA 51632
E-mail: aps@wingscc.com
URL: http://www.wingscc.com/aps
Contact: Randy Karg, Publisher
Founded: 1990. **Members:** 700. **Membership Dues:** regular, in U.S., $15 (annual) ● regular, outside U.S., $25 (annual). **Staff:** 10. **Description:** Owners and admirers of African parrots. Promotes responsible pet ownership; seeks to increase interest in, and appreciation of, African parrots. Conducts research and educational programs. **Libraries: Type:** open to the public. **Holdings:** 27; periodicals. **Subjects:** African parrots. **Computer Services:** database, list of back issues ● mailing lists ● online services, information on African parrots. **Additional Websites:** http://www.wingscentral.org/aps. **Telecommunication Services:** electronic bulletin board, discussion groups. **Affiliated With:** American Federation of Aviculture. **Publications:** *ARK*, quarterly. Newsletter. Contains information about African parrots. Alternate Formats: online ● Surveys. Alternate Formats: online. **Conventions/Meetings:** annual conference, photos and membership information; in conjunction with the American Federation of Aviculture.

21390 ■ American Association of Spanish Timbrado Breeders (AASTB)
6831 El Banquero Pl.
San Diego, CA 92119
Ph: (619)582-9698
E-mail: canariesandmore@cox.net
URL: http://members.cox.net/timbrados
Contact: David J. Benites, Founder/Pres.
Founded: 1998. **Membership Dues:** general, $25 (annual). **Description:** Seeks to promote and expand the hobby of keeping, breeding, appreciating and exhibiting the Spanish Timbrado. Protects the Spanish Timbrado canaries and encourages the preservation of the quality of their song. Provides a center of information and advice on all matters pertaining to Spanish Timbrado canaries.

21391 ■ American Bird Conservation Association
Address Unknown since 2007
Founded: 1991. **Members:** 350. **Membership Dues:** $15 (annual). **Staff:** 6. **Budget:** $4,000. **Description:** Members actively improve conservation and the environment, promote and provide housing and habitat for native birds, with special emphasis on purple martins and bluebirds. **Libraries: Type:** open to the public. **Awards: Frequency:** annual. **Type:** recognition. **Recipient:** for holding the annual convention in home residence. **Affiliated With:** North American Bluebird Society. **Publications:** *A.B.C.A. Yearend Report*, annual, every spring. Newsletter. Contains comments, letters to the editor, member records, membership lists and addresses. **Price:** included in membership dues. **Circulation:** 350. **Advertising:** accepted. **Conventions/Meetings:** annual Memorial Day Bird Convention, with nationally known speakers - on Memorial Day ● annual seminar - always February in Mt. Hope, OH.

21392 ■ American Budgerigar Society (ABS)
c/o Dinah Moore, Sec.
521 Westview St.
Lenoir, NC 28645

Ph: (828)754-2480
E-mail: secretary@abs1.org
URL: http://www.abs1.org
Contact: Louise Loepke, Pres.
Founded: 1941. **Members:** 1,800. **Membership Dues:** regular, $30 (annual) ● dual, outside U.S., $40 (annual) ● junior, $15 (annual). **Budget:** $30,000. **Regional Groups:** 13. **Description:** Parakeet fanciers including breeders, owners, exhibitors, and. Sponsors and furnishes patronage for competitive exhibitions; maintains standard of perfection, judges' panel, registration division, and traceable bands. Maintains educational and research programs. Compiles show statistics. Furnishes breeding and dietary information to members. **Libraries: Type:** not open to the public. **Holdings:** 300; articles, books, periodicals. **Subjects:** genetics, disease, breeding, feeding. **Awards:** Exhibitor of the Year. **Frequency:** annual. **Type:** recognition. **Recipient:** to top breeders of each division. **Committees:** Education; Hall of Fame. **Divisions:** Judges Panel; Products. **Publications:** *American Budgerigar Society—Bulletin*, monthly. Magazine. Covers breeding, feeding, and exhibiting parakeets. Includes show reports and calendar of events. **Price:** included in membership dues. **Advertising:** accepted. **Conventions/Meetings:** annual All American - competition ● annual convention and board meeting (exhibits).

21393 ■ American Canary Fanciers Association (ACFA)
c/o Ned Setabouha, Pres.
16124 S Hoover St.
Gardena, CA 90247
Ph: (310)323-0217
E-mail: nedseta@sbcgobal.net
URL: http://www.acfa-canaryclub.com
Contact: Ned Setabouha, Pres.
Founded: 1980. **Membership Dues:** general, $20 (annual). **Description:** Promotes, encourages and develops the proper breeding and care of all canaries through scientific research and education of the members and the general public. **Publications:** Newsletter, monthly. **Price:** for members.

21394 ■ American Cockatiel Society (ACS)
11152 Blackwood Dr.
New Port Richey, FL 34654
Free: (888)221-1161
E-mail: acspresident@tiels.com
URL: http://www.acstiels.com
Contact: Gerald Oldberg, Pres.
Founded: 1977. **Members:** 2,000. **Membership Dues:** single in U.S., $20 (annual) ● dual in U.S., $25 (annual) ● single outside U.S., $35 (annual) ● dual outside U.S., $40 (annual) ● single in Canada and Mexico, $28 (annual) ● dual in Canada and Mexico, $33 (annual). **Staff:** 33. **Regional Groups:** 7. **State Groups:** 33. **Multinational. Description:** Represents bird breeders and fanciers interested in the care and breeding of cockatiels. Conducts specialized education for breeders and establishes standards for judging cockatiels on the show bench. Sponsors competitions. Conducts research and audiovisual programs; maintains speakers' bureau; sponsors seminars; compiles statistics. **Publications:** *American Cockatiel Society Magazine*, quarterly. **Advertising:** accepted ● Bulletin, quarterly. Addresses the care, breeding, exhibiting of cockatiels and additional information on pet care and genetics. **Advertising:** accepted. **Conventions/Meetings:** annual Cockatiel Show (exhibits).

21395 ■ American Dove Association (ADA)
7037 Haynes Rd.
Georgetown, IN 47122
Ph: (812)923-3483 (615)444-3683
E-mail: secretary@doveline.com
URL: http://www.doveline.com
Contact: George Schutt, Pres.
Founded: 1970. **Members:** 500. **Membership Dues:** regular, $20 (annual) ● outside U.S., $30 (annual) ● senior citizen, $16 (annual) ● junior (age 17 below), $10 (annual) ● family, $21 (annual). **Description:** Represents dove enthusiasts. Sponsors competitions. **Awards: Type:** recognition. **Committees:** Elec-

tion; Show; Standards. **Formerly:** (1959) Great Lakes Dove Association. **Publications:** *Doveline*, bimonthly. Newsletter. Contains articles on the appreciation and care of doves. Includes book reviews, calendar of events, and research news. **Price:** included in membership dues. **Circulation:** 500. **Advertising:** accepted ● *Membership List and Breeders Directory*, annual ● *Ringneck Doves - Their Care and Enjoyment*. Book. **Conventions/Meetings:** annual meeting - always October, in Louisville, KY.

21396 ■ American Federation of Aviculture (AFA)

PO Box 7312
North Kansas City, MO 64116
Ph: (816)421-2473
Fax: (816)421-3214
E-mail: afaoffice@aol.com
URL: http://www.afabirds.org
Contact: Dr. Benny J. Gallaway PhD, Pres.

Founded: 1974. **Members:** 9,000. **Membership Dues:** individual, $40 (annual) ● family, $45 (annual) ● supporting, $75 (annual) ● commercial, $125 (annual). **Staff:** 2. **Budget:** $350,000. **State Groups:** 50. **Local Groups:** 200. **National Groups:** 20. **Description:** Represents hobbyist groups of aviculturists; commercial enterprises dealing in bird supplies and individuals. Promotes and encourages aviculture as a means of conserving bird life through captive breeding programs. Informs the public of the need for this type of conservation work. Encourages scientific research; work directly with endangered species of bird wildlife. Monitors legislation affecting aviculture. Prepares movie and slide programs concerning successful breeding programs and suggesting ways of establishing new programs. Maintains more than 15 committees. Compiles statistics. **Libraries: Type:** not open to the public. **Awards:** Avy Awards. **Frequency:** annual. **Type:** recognition. **Recipient:** for service. **Publications:** *Annual Convention Proceedings*, annual. **Advertising:** accepted ● *Fast Ad*, monthly. Newsletter. **Price:** included in membership dues. **Circulation:** 9,000. **Advertising:** accepted ● *Watchbird*, bimonthly. Journal ● *Watchbird Index*, annual. **Conventions/Meetings:** annual convention (exhibits) - always August ● seminar, for aviculturists, veterinarians and the public.

21397 ■ American Singers Club (ASC)

c/o Ron Moy, Sec.-Treas.
1141 Norwood Ave.
Oakland, CA 94610-1837
Ph: (510)524-4077
E-mail: asctreasurer@yahoo.com
URL: http://www2.upatsix.com/asc
Contact: Ron Moy, Sec.-Treas.

Founded: 1934. **Members:** 400. **Membership Dues:** single, in U.S., $20 (annual) ● single, outside U.S., $22 (annual) ● dual, $25 (annual). **State Groups:** 19. **Local Groups:** 5. **Description:** Promotes the raising and showing of canaries bred and judged for beautiful song. **Awards: Type:** recognition. **Recipient:** for regional and national shows. **Publications:** *Breeding Methods*, periodic ● Membership Directory, annual ● Newsletter, quarterly ● Also publishes constitution and by-laws. **Conventions/Meetings:** periodic competition.

21398 ■ American Waterslager Society (AWS)

c/o Tom Trujillo, Pres.
556 S Cactus Wren St.
Gilbert, AZ 85296
Ph: (480)892-5464
E-mail: thomas.trujillo@elpaso.com
URL: http://www.waterslagers.com
Contact: Tom Trujillo, Pres.

Founded: 1991. **Members:** 120. **Membership Dues:** general, $25 (annual). **Multinational. Description:** Represents individuals who share the common interests and enjoyment in hearing the world-renowned song of the Belgian Waterslager. Promotes, preserves and protects the Belgian Waterslager Song Canary. **Publications:** Newsletter, quarterly. **Price:** for members.

21399 ■ Bird Clubs of America (BCA)

c/o Georgi Higel, Dir.
PO Box 1433
Waldorf, MD 20604-1433
Ph: (301)843-3683
E-mail: ggsgoffins@netzero.net
URL: http://www.birdclubsofamerica.org
Contact: Georgi Higel, Dir.

Founded: 1992. **Staff:** 4. **State Groups:** 1. **Local Groups:** 50. **National Groups:** 4. **Description:** Concerned species breeders working together to achieve avicultural excellence. **Libraries: Type:** reference. **Holdings:** 200. **Subjects:** birds, management, breeder, pet, and legislative materials. **Awards:** Outstanding Service to Aviculture. **Frequency:** annual. **Type:** recognition. **Telecommunication Services:** electronic mail, cvmga@aol.com. **Affiliated With:** African Parrot Society; Amazona Society; International Parrotlet Society; Tanygnathus Society. **Publications:** *AVI-Support Directories*, monthly. Directory. Contains species support pages, management series, association updates. **Circulation:** 60. Alternate Formats: online ● Also publishes avi-reference pages, pet information pages, species support pages government and birds guides, breeder information guides, and club member guide. **Conventions/Meetings:** National Amazona Convention (exhibits).

21400 ■ Central States Roller Canary Breeders Association (CSRCBA)

c/o Robert W. Wild, Sec.-Treas.
305 Grosvenor St.
Bolingbrook, IL 60440-1043
E-mail: r.wild@comcast.net
Contact: Robert W. Wild, Sec.-Treas.

Founded: 1937. **Members:** 100. **Membership Dues:** affiliate, $15 (annual) ● independent, $30 (annual). **Local Groups:** 4. **Description:** Breeders of roller canaries united to promote their hobby. **Awards: Frequency:** annual. **Type:** recognition. **Recipient:** for breeder achievement. **Publications:** *Vocal Roll*, quarterly. Newsletter. Includes show reports, progress reports, and show schedules. **Price:** included in membership dues. **Conventions/Meetings:** annual competition ● annual show.

21401 ■ COM-U.S.A.

c/o Bob Garguillo, Pres.
Bob's Auto Radiator Ser.
400 Bloomfield Ave.
Bloomfield, NJ 07003
Ph: (973)429-9353
Fax: (973)748-8508
E-mail: chats@upatsix.com
URL: http://www3.upatsix.com/com-usa/index.html
Contact: Bob Garguillo, Pres.

Founded: 1972. **Members:** 200. **Membership Dues:** individual, $20 (annual). **Description:** Promotes and educates bird fanciers in the art of genetic cage-bird breeding. Seeks to ensure the survival and propagation of all avian species, with special emphasis on endangered species, such as the Venezuelan Black Hooded Red Siskin. Conducts monthly educational meetings to teach the art of identifying, classifying, pairing, and breeding all kinds of cage birds with particular attention to color-breeding. (Group's name is the acronym for Confederation Ornithologie Mondiale). **Formerly:** (1981) Greater North American Color-Bred Judge Association; (1985) Greater North American Aviculturist and Cage Bird Judges Association. **Publications:** Bulletin, monthly. **Conventions/Meetings:** annual Cage Bird Exhibition - meeting (exhibits) - always second week of November, Dunellen, NJ.

21402 ■ Exotic Bird Society of America

9724 5th Ave.
Orlando, FL 32824-8423
Ph: (407)855-3367
E-mail: charles@ebsoa.org
URL: http://ebsoa.org
Contact: Charles J. Tillman, Pres.

Membership Dues: single, $10 (annual) ● couple, $15 (annual) ● family, $20 (annual) ● group, $30 (annual). **Description:** Advances and encourages the knowledge, protection, care and propagation of

exotic birds. Promotes the exchange of knowledge and information about exotic birds in the United States. **Computer Services:** Mailing lists. **Publications:** *Birdbrain Express*. Newsletter. **Price:** for members.

21403 ■ International Association of Avian Trainers and Educators (IAATE)

350 St. Andrews Fairway
Memphis, TN 38111
Ph: (901)685-9122
Fax: (901)685-7233
E-mail: secretary@iaate.org
URL: http://www.iaate.org
Contact: Kate Friedman, Sec.

Founded: 1993. **Members:** 340. **Membership Dues:** professional, $50 (annual) ● active, associate, $40 (annual) ● student, $25 (annual). **Description:** Professionals in the field of avian science who manage, train, and present education programs with native and exotic birds. **Awards:** Behavior of the Year Award. **Frequency:** annual. **Type:** recognition. **Recipient:** for the best bird behavior incorporated into a show ● Conservation Award. **Frequency:** annual. **Type:** monetary. **Recipient:** for members' effort to promote conservation ● Husbandry Behavior of the Year Award. **Frequency:** annual. **Type:** recognition ● Interpretive Behavior of the Year Award. **Frequency:** annual. **Type:** recognition. **Recipient:** for best paper that uniquely describes anything relating to birds. **Committees:** Avian Care and Management; Conference. **Publications:** *IAATE Flyer*, quarterly. Newsletter. Includes information on animal training and management, especially birds. **Price:** included in membership dues. **Circulation:** 340. **Conventions/Meetings:** annual conference and workshop.

21404 ■ International Conure Association (ICA)

c/o Brent Andrus, Treas.
PO Box 70123
Las Vegas, NV 89170
E-mail: ica@conure.org
URL: http://www.conure.org
Contact: Cheryl Burns, Pres.

Founded: 1997. **Membership Dues:** individual, $20 (annual) ● family, $30 (annual) ● junior, $15 (annual). **Multinational. Description:** Aims to study conures in captivity and in the wild. Disseminates information on the proper caring, breeding, feeding of conures in the home and aviary. Assists persons in locating the perfect pet or breeder, by way of advertisements and by maintaining a database of members and what they are breeding, selling or looking to buy. Promotes the breeding of less common conures. **Telecommunication Services:** electronic mail, cheryl@conure.org ● electronic mail, conurelady@msn.com ● electronic mail, brent@conure.org. **Projects:** ICA Yellow-Eared Conure. **Publications:** Journal, quarterly.

21405 ■ International Gloster Breeders Association (IGBA)

c/o Candace Pezzuti, Sec.-Treas.
3844 Lindell Rd.
Las Vegas, NV 89103
Ph: (702)876-8949
E-mail: thebirdbreeder@aol.com
URL: http://www.igbaglostersusa.com
Contact: Carol Casper, Pres.

Founded: 1972. **Membership Dues:** single, $20 (annual) ● dual, $25 (annual). **Description:** Promotes the Gloster Fancy Canary. **Awards:** Best Gloster Consort. **Frequency:** annual. **Type:** recognition ● Best Gloster Corona. **Frequency:** annual. **Type:** recognition. **Affiliated With:** National Cage Bird Show. **Publications:** *GlosterGems*, quarterly. Newsletter. **Price:** included in membership dues. **Conventions/Meetings:** specialty show.

21406 ■ International Parrotlet Society (IPS)

PO Box 2428
Santa Cruz, CA 95063-2428
Ph: (831)688-5560

E-mail: ips@internationalparrotletsociety.org

URL: http://www.internationalparrotletsociety.org

Contact: Sandee L. Molenda, Sec.

Founded: 1992. **Members:** 500. **Membership Dues:** individual, $25 (annual) ● family, international, $30 (annual). **Budget:** $15,000. **Multinational. Description:** Owners, breeders, and admirers of parrotlets. Promotes interest in parrotlets and seeks to insure breeding conducive to species improvement. Sponsors parrotlet breeding cooperatives. Conducts research and educational programs like Parrotlet Placement Program; sponsors competitions; maintains speakers' bureau; compiles statistics. **Awards:** Best Parrotlet and Best Parrotlet in Show Awards. **Frequency:** annual. **Type:** recognition. **Computer Services:** database ● mailing lists ● online services. **Committees:** Rescue. **Affiliated With:** American Federation of Aviculture; Bird Clubs of America; International Aviculturists Society; Society of Parrot Breeders and Exhibitors. **Publications:** Journal, bimonthly. Features photograph of a different species or mutation of parrotlet. **Advertising:** accepted. **Conventions/Meetings:** semiannual board meeting and conference, in conjunction with major agricultural events ● annual Great American Bird Show, with awards (exhibits) ● annual National Cage Bird Show, with awards (exhibits).

21407 ■ National Cage Bird Show (NCBS)

c/o Dorothy Eggers, 2nd VP

4910 Anthony Ln.

Pasadena, TX 77505

Ph: (281)487-1321

E-mail: deggers@houston.rr.com

URL: http://www.ncbs.org

Contact: Dorothy Eggers, 2nd VP

Founded: 1947. **Members:** 400. **Description:** Cage bird fanciers. Promotes and coordinates national cage bird shows and exhibitions. Sponsors competitions. **Awards: Type:** recognition. **Publications:** Bulletin, 3/year. **Conventions/Meetings:** annual meeting.

21408 ■ National Cockatiel Society (NCS)

c/o Wendy LaBanca, Membership Sec.

140 Almy St.

Warwick, RI 02886-3604

Ph: (401)732-0693

E-mail: membership@cockatiels.org

URL: http://www.cockatiels.org

Contact: Wendy LaBanca, Membership Sec.

Founded: 1983. **Membership Dues:** single, $20 (annual) ● dual, $25 (annual). **Description:** Educates members on the proper care, handling, maintenance, and breeding of cockatiels. Supports avian research. Encourages selective breeding and developing color mutations through the study of genetics. Supports closed banding and record keeping. **Computer Services:** database, members and band numbers for NCS use only. **Publications:** National Cockatiel Society Journal, bimonthly. Newsletter. **Advertising:** accepted. **Conventions/Meetings:** annual board meeting, in conjunction with National Cage Bird Show (exhibits).

21409 ■ National Color-Bred Association (NCA)

c/o Henry Vela, Treas.

109 Neece Dr.

Irving, TX 75060

E-mail: henryvela30@hotmail.com

URL: http://www.nationalcolorbred.org

Contact: Tony Farrugia, Pres.

Founded: 1978. **Members:** 300. **Membership Dues:** single, dual, $25 (annual). **For-Profit. Description:** Individuals interested in color-bred canaries and in exhibiting birds at local and national shows. Aims to promote color breeding of canaries. Sponsors competitions. **Awards:** Breeder of the Year Award. **Frequency:** annual. **Type:** recognition ● Rosettes to Affiliated Local Clubs. **Type:** recognition. **Affiliated With:** National Cage Bird Show. **Publications:** National Color-Bred Association Newsletter, quarterly ● Also publishes reprints of articles by British color

breeders. **Conventions/Meetings:** annual National Cage Bird Show - meeting - always third weekend of November.

21410 ■ National Finch and Softbill Society (NFSS)

c/o Ms. Rebecca Mikel, Exec. Sec.

13779 US 12 E

Union, MI 49130

Ph: (269)641-7209

E-mail: spkennel@aol.com

URL: http://www.nfss.org

Contact: Sally Huntington, Pres.

Founded: 1983. **Members:** 1,240. **Description:** Aviculturists, bird enthusiasts, and individuals interested in preserving and propagating avian fauna. Promotes the preservation of finches and other softbilled birds. (Softbilled birds are characterized by their diet of fruits and insects.) Keeps members informed of news involving bird-related legislation and fosters exchange of information among members. Works to establish exhibition standards for finch species. Provides banding program to ensure the recording of breeding information and a healthy gene pool. Sponsors Championship Exhibitor Program. Maintains judges panel. Compiles statistics. Operates speakers' bureau. **Libraries: Type:** reference. **Holdings:** books, business records, clippings, monographs, periodicals. **Subjects:** finches, softbilled birds. **Awards: Type:** recognition. **Committees:** Standards. **Programs:** FinchSave. **Formerly:** (1987) National Finch Society. **Publications:** Handbook of the NFS, biennial ● National Finch and Softbill Society Journal, bimonthly. **Conventions/Meetings:** competition ● show, held in conjunction with the National Cage Bird Show (exhibits).

21411 ■ National Institute of Red Orange Canaries and All Other Cage Birds (NIROC)

1304 Fern Dr.

Mount Prospect, IL 60056

Ph: (847)437-4738 (847)437-5704

Fax: (847)437-8375

Contact: Nancy Serchuk, Pres.

Founded: 1930. **Members:** 200. **Membership Dues:** $17 (annual). **Description:** Cage bird breeders and fanciers. Instructs in proper care and breeding of cage birds. Established judging standards for color bred canaries. **Awards: Frequency:** annual. **Type:** recognition. **Publications:** Annual Show Catalog-Bulletin, bimonthly. **Advertising:** accepted ● Bulletin, monthly. **Conventions/Meetings:** annual meeting (exhibits) - always November. Chicago, IL ● monthly meeting ● semiannual show.

21412 ■ National Pigeon Association (NPA)

c/o Pat Avery, Co-Sec.-Treas.

PO Box 439

Newalla, OK 74857-0439

Ph: (405)386-6884

E-mail: james4bird@aol.com

URL: http://www.npausa.com

Contact: Pat Avery, Co-Sec.-Treas.

Founded: 1920. **Members:** 2,000. **Membership Dues:** junior, $5 (annual) ● adult, $20 (annual) ● family, $25 (annual). **Staff:** 2. **Budget:** $90,000. **Regional Groups:** 8. **State Groups:** 77. **Description:** Owners, breeders, trainers, and admirers of pigeons. Promotes responsible bird ownership; encourages keeping of pigeons as a hobby. Conducts research and educational programs; maintains hall of fame. **Libraries: Type:** reference. **Holdings:** 7; books, periodicals. **Subjects:** pigeons. **Awards:** NPA Hall of Fame. **Frequency:** annual. **Type:** recognition. **Recipient:** for individuals who have exhibited pigeons for ten years or more ● NPA Master Breeder. **Frequency:** annual. **Type:** recognition. **Recipient:** for individuals who have breed pigeons of outstanding quality. **Computer Services:** database, web pages. **Publications:** Encyclopedia of Pigeon Standards, quarterly. Book. Contains reviews, events and educational articles. **Price:** $39.95 for members; $49.95 for nonmembers. **Circulation:** 2,900. **Advertising:** accepted. Alternate Formats: CD-ROM ● NPA Quarterly Review. Newsletter. **Price:** $4.50 each. **Circulation:** 2,200. **Advertising:** accepted. Alternate

Formats: CD-ROM ● Pigeons of the 21st Century in North America. Book. **Price:** $36.45 softbound; $66.45 hardbound ● Reports. **Price:** $10.00 includes shipping and handling ● Brochure. Alternate Formats: online. **Conventions/Meetings:** annual Grand National Convention and Show - convention and show (exhibits).

21413 ■ North American Cockatiel Society (NACS)

c/o Renee Martin, Band/Membership Chair

PO Box 143

Bethel, CT 06801-0143

E-mail: nacscindy@comcast.net

URL: http://www.cockatiel.org

Contact: Cynthia Kiesewetter, Pres.

Founded: 1997. **Membership Dues:** household, $14 (annual) ● regular, in Canada or Mexico, $20 (annual) ● overseas, $26 (annual). **Multinational. Description:** Works to educate pet cockatiel owners and breeders of North America. **Computer Services:** database, breeder list ● information services, pet cockatiel resources ● mailing lists ● online services, chat board (Tiel Town). **Publications:** Newsletter, quarterly.

21414 ■ North American Parrot Society (NAPS)

c/o Gary Morgan, Pres./Chm.

15341 Kingston St.

Brighton, CO 80602-7439

Ph: (303)659-9544

E-mail: burdmn@aol.com

URL: http://www.northamericanparrotsociety.com

Contact: Gary Morgan, Pres./Chm.

Founded: 1995. **Membership Dues:** regular, in U.S., $25 (annual) ● regular, outside U.S., $35 (annual) ● regular, in U.S., $70 (triennial). **Description:** Promotes the showing and breeding of parrots. **Affiliated With:** Bird Clubs of America. **Publications:** NAPS Journal. **Conventions/Meetings:** meeting.

21415 ■ Pionus Breeders Association (PBA)

c/o Larry Ring, Chm.

PO Box 150

Pilot Hill, CA 95664

Ph: (530)885-7868

E-mail: ringlaw@inreach.com

URL: http://www.pionusbreedersassociation.com

Contact: Larry Ring, Chm.

Founded: 1980. **Membership Dues:** general, in U.S., $12 (annual) ● general, in Canada, C$15 (annual) ● overseas, $20 (annual). **Multinational. Description:** Promotes the exchange of avicultural and scientific knowledge regarding the husbandry, reproduction and biology of parrots of the genus Pionus. Promotes the conservation of wild Pionus by supporting and assisting in the protection of habitat critical to the long-term survival of these birds. **Computer Services:** Information services, Pionus parrots resources. **Publications:** Newsletter, quarterly. Contains tips for breeding Pionus.

21416 ■ Society of Parrot Breeders and Exhibitors (SPBE)

c/o Dr. Al Decoteau, CEO

PO Box 546

Hollis, NH 03049

Ph: (603)672-4568

E-mail: spbe1@aol.com

URL: http://www.spbe.org

Contact: Dr. Al Decoteau, CEO

Founded: 1986. **Members:** 4,000. **Membership Dues:** individual in U.S., $25 (annual) ● individual in U.S., $65 (triennial) ● individual outside U.S., $45 (annual). **Staff:** 40. **Regional Groups:** 90. **Languages:** English, Spanish. **Description:** Aviculturists; parrot breeders and exhibitors. Seeks to prevent parrot extinction. Provides assistance to breeders. Works to prevent the hybridization of parrots. Maintains show standards and classifications; makes available sanctioned panel of judges. Is involved in conservation; conducts research and educational programs. Maintains Speaker's Bureau, hall of fame and Parrot Preservation Project. **Awards:** Carolina Parakeet Award. **Frequency:** biennial. **Type:** recognition. **Recipient:** for outstanding service to parrots and the SPBE ● **Type:** recognition. **Recipient:** for breeders of difficult to breed species. **Computer Services:** Online services. **Projects:** Breeding Academy; Parrot Preservation. **Publications:** *Journal of the Society of Parrot Breeders and Exhibitors,* quarterly. **Price:** included in membership dues. **Circulation:** 3,500. **Advertising:** accepted. **Conventions/Meetings:** annual Great American Bird Show - meeting, with bird and specialty shows (exhibits) ● meeting and show.

21417 ■ Stafford Canary Club of America (SCCA)

c/o Don Platz
3090 Sparr Blvd.
Glendale, CA 91208
URL: http://www.staffords-usa.com
Contact: Don Platz, Contact
Founded: 1993. **Membership Dues:** individual, $20 (annual) ● junior breeder, $5 (annual) ● family, $30 (annual). **Multinational. Description:** Represents individuals interested in breeding and propagation of the Stafford. Promotes exchange of knowledge regarding the Stafford Canary and friendship among members. **Publications:** *SCCA Newsletter,* quarterly. **Price:** included in membership dues. **Conventions/Meetings:** annual board meeting - weekend in October.

21418 ■ Toledo Bird Association, Zebra Finch Club of America (TBAZFCA)

Address Unknown since 2007
Founded: 1968. **Members:** 65. **Membership Dues:** individual and family, $15 (annual). **Staff:** 11. **Regional Groups:** 35. **State Groups:** 15. **Local Groups:** 15. **Description:** Bird breeders and hobbyists. Educates the bird fancier in the best method of raising, training, and breeding cage birds, including zebra finches. **Awards:** Gold Medalian. **Frequency:** annual. **Type:** recognition. **Publications:** Bulletin, monthly. **Conventions/Meetings:** annual show - always last Saturday in September.

21419 ■ United Gloster Breeders (UGB)

c/o Barbara Rosario, Sec.-Treas.
715 Avocado Ct.
Del Mar, CA 92014-3911
E-mail: b.rosario@juno.com
URL: http://www.glosters-usa.com
Contact: Barbara Rosario, Sec.-Treas.
Membership Dues: single, $20 (annual) ● dual, $25 (annual). **Multinational. Description:** Advances the study, breeding, exhibiting, running and maintenance of the purebred Gloster Fancy Canary around the world. Provides an educational and progressive environment to assist interested novices and seasoned experts in the improvement of all Glosters in an atmosphere of friendship and camaraderie.

21420 ■ U.S. Association of Roller Canary Culturists (USARCC)

533 Beach Ave.
Bronx, NY 10473
Ph: (718)328-9343
Contact: Raul Thomas, Pres.
Founded: 1940. **Members:** 75. **Description:** Aims to improve and promote the culture and song of the roller song canary; issue and register leg bands. Offers specialized education. **Awards: Type:** recognition. **Conventions/Meetings:** annual Roller Song Contest - competition (exhibits).

Blues

21421 ■ International Blues Society

PO Box 82053
Los Angeles, CA 90037
Ph: (661)267-0495
Fax: (661)267-0495
Contact: Tina Mayfield, Exec.Dir.
Founded: 1988. **Members:** 125. **Membership Dues:** individual, $15 (annual). **Staff:** 5. **Budget:** $2,000. **Description:** Strives to promote understanding of the

blues and its heritage. Promotes a variety of blues shows throughout the year. Sponsors gospel and jazz shows using local artists. **Libraries: Type:** not open to the public. **Holdings:** archival material, business records. **Subjects:** blues artists. **Awards:** Percy Mayfield Award. **Frequency:** annual. **Type:** scholarship. **Recipient:** for promoters, club owners, students. **Publications:** Newsletter, bimonthly. **Circulation:** 150. **Advertising:** accepted. **Conventions/Meetings:** monthly meeting.

Boating

21422 ■ Annapolis Naval Sailing Association (ANSA)

58 Bennion Rd.
Annapolis, MD 21402-5054
Ph: (703)644-4912
E-mail: membership@ansa.org
URL: http://www.ansa.org
Contact: Joanna Nicol, Membership Chair
Membership Dues: regular, $45 (annual) ● family, $55 (annual) ● enlisted individual, $30 (annual) ● geographically separated, $25 (annual). **Description:** Aims to promote fleet readiness and personal professionalism and strengthen naval ties to the national marine heritage through small craft training programs; facilitates safe sailing and competitive boating among members; assists the Naval Station, Annapolis, in furthering boating and sailing as part of the Station's Morale, Welfare, and Recreation program, and to stimulate acquisition of craft suitable for purposes of the association; establish and maintain contacts and liaison between members and other yachting organizations, both civilian and military.

21423 ■ Antique and Classic Boat Society (ACBS)

422 James St.
Clayton, NY 13624
Ph: (315)686-2628
Fax: (315)686-2680
E-mail: hqs@acbs.org
URL: http://www.acbs.org
Contact: Kathy Snyder, Contact
Founded: 1975. **Members:** 5,200. **Membership Dues:** junior, $15 (annual) ● regular, $35 (annual) ● associate, $100 (annual) ● life, $750. **Staff:** 1. **Budget:** $100,000. **Regional Groups:** 40. **Description:** Represents individuals interested in antique and classic boating. Serves as an information clearinghouse and fosters the exchange of information and ideas. Works to establish and monitor protocol as it relates to antique and classic boating. Holds annual seminar on judging and classification; sponsors competitions and social functions; compiles statistics. **Awards: Type:** recognition. **Committees:** Gold Cup; Judging. **Publications:** *Rudder,* quarterly. Magazine. ISSN: 1089-5300. **Advertising:** accepted ● Directory, annual. Alternate Formats: online. **Conventions/Meetings:** annual meeting ● quarterly meeting.

21424 ■ Center for Wooden Boats (CWB)

1010 Valley St.
Seattle, WA 98109-4468
Ph: (206)382-2628
Fax: (206)382-2699
E-mail: cwb@cwb.org
URL: http://www.cwb.org
Contact: Dick Wagner, Founding Dir.
Founded: 1978. **Members:** 3,000. **Membership Dues:** student, senior, $15 (annual) ● individual, $35 (annual) ● household, $50 (annual) ● contributing, $100 (annual) ● benefactor, $250 (annual) ● sustaining, $500 (annual). **Staff:** 9. **Budget:** $600,000. **Description:** Maritime historians, craftspeople, sailors, and others with an interest in preserving traditional wooden watercraft. Provides experience in maritime skills such as basic woodworking, restoring or building traditional boats, and boat handling and sailing. Offers introductory instruction in boat building and master classes for experts. Sponsors traditional maritime skills instruction for "high risk" teenagers (those who currently are not capable of functioning in

main stream society due to emotional and physical traumatic experiences). Operates "living museum" of maritime exhibits, special displays, and demonstrations. Maintains speakers' bureau. **Libraries: Type:** lending; reference; open to the public. **Holdings:** 2,000; books, monographs, periodicals. **Subjects:** maritime. **Awards:** Ed Monk Scholarship. **Frequency:** annual. **Type:** scholarship. **Recipient:** to professional boat builders ● Volunteer of the Year. **Frequency:** annual. **Type:** recognition. **Recipient:** for a volunteer who exhibits dedication, enthusiasm, leadership, and commitment to the goals of the organization. **Computer Services:** database ● mailing lists. **Publications:** *Boatbuilders' Directory,* triennial ● *Coast Salish Canoes* ● *Davis Boats* ● *Poulsbo Boat* ● *Sawdust,* bimonthly. Newsletter. Includes association news and calendar of events. ● *Shavings,* bimonthly. Newsletter. Includes articles on traditional boat design, construction, and use. ISSN: 0734-0680. **Advertising:** accepted. **Conventions/Meetings:** annual Lake Union Wooden Boat Festival (exhibits) - first Friday-Sunday in July ● quarterly Regatta - meeting ● workshop, on maritime skills and children's boat models - about 50/year.

21425 ■ Chris Craft Antique Boat Club (CCABC)

112 14th St. SE
Cedar Rapids, IA 52403
Ph: (319)364-1519
E-mail: bbasler@chris-craft.org
URL: http://www.chris-craft.org
Contact: Wilson W. Wright, Exec. Dir.
Founded: 1973. **Members:** 2,900. **Membership Dues:** individual, $35 (annual). **Staff:** 3. **Description:** Individuals who own vintage Chris-Craft boats or are interested in restoring or maintaining vintage motorboats. (Chris-Craft boats have been manufactured since the early 1900s, and the company played a leading role in the early development of gasoline-powered pleasure boats. Chris-Craft boats are distinguished by their varnished wooden hulls of Philippine mahogany.) Aids members in finding spare parts; furnishes maintenance and management information; maintains archive documenting hull numbers manufactured by the Chris-Craft company from 1922-70. Facilitates communication among members; co-sponsors antique boat show and jamborees. Maintains speakers' bureau. Compiles statistics. Offers group insurance program. **Convention/Meeting:** none. **Libraries: Type:** reference. **Holdings:** 200. **Subjects:** vintage boats. **Awards:** Best Chris Craft. **Frequency:** annual. **Type:** recognition. **Recipient:** for any boat show with more than seventy five boats on display, selected locally. **Computer Services:** database, for members only ● mailing lists, not available to public ● online services, discussion group. **Committees:** Cobra Council; Commander Division; Sailboat Division; Sea Skiff Section. **Formerly:** Antique Boat Club. **Publications:** *Brass Bell,* quarterly. Journal. Contains analyses on specific Chris Craft boats; includes member profiles, listing of boats for sale, and calendar of events. **Price:** free for members; $25.00 /year for nonmembers. ISSN: 1527-75X. **Circulation:** 3,000. **Advertising:** accepted. Alternate Formats: online ● Also reproduces owner's, parts, and instruction manuals and showroom catalogs of most 1928-1970 designs. Album and tapes of Chris Crafts.

21426 ■ Classic Yacht Association (CYA)

5267 Shilshole Ave. NW, Ste.107
Seattle, WA 98107
Ph: (206)937-6211
E-mail: pnwcommodore@classicyacht.org
URL: http://www.classicyacht.org
Contact: John Murphey, Vice Commodore
Founded: 1971. **Members:** 500. **Regional Groups:** 5. **Description:** Owners of power-driven pleasure boats built before December 1942. Promotes and encourages an interest in the preservation, restoration, and maintenance of this type of craft. Sponsors 50 yachting events in California, Pacific Northwest, and Alaska. **Telecommunication Services:** electronic mail, georgeh@classicyacht.org. **Publications:** *Classic Yacht Association Membership Roster,* an-

nual. Membership Directory ● *Classic Yachting*, quarterly. Newsletter. **Conventions/Meetings:** annual meeting.

21427 ■ Electric Boat Association of the Americas (EBAA)
PO Box 2155
Beaufort, NC 28516
Fax: (252)729-1640
E-mail: ebaa@ec.rr.com
Founded: 1992. **Members:** 500. **Membership Dues:** individual, $35 (annual). **Staff:** 2. **Budget:** $25,000. **National Groups:** 1. **Description:** Promotes electric-powered boating. Sponsors electric boat races and exhibitions. **Telecommunication Services:** electronic mail, keithgovals@infoave.net. **Formerly:** Electric Boat Association of America. **Publications:** *Electric Boat Journal*, quarterly. Newsletter. **Price:** included in membership dues. ISSN: 1073-158X. **Circulation:** 1,000. **Advertising:** accepted. **Conventions/Meetings:** annual convention (exhibits).

21428 ■ Gar Wood Society (GWS)
c/o The Antique Boat Museum
750 Mary St.
Clayton, NY 13624
Ph: (315)686-4104
Fax: (315)686-2775
URL: http://www.garwood.com
Contact: Anthony S. Mollica Jr., Pres.
Founded: 1979. **Members:** 400. **Membership Dues:** domestic, $15 (annual) ● regular outside North America, $20 (annual). **Budget:** $5,000. **Multinational. Description:** Classic and antique motor boat enthusiasts, Gar Wood boat owners, marine historians and museums, boating publications, and boat builders. Encourages the preservation and active use of Gar Wood boats and stimulates a public awareness of the value and craftsmanship involved in their production. Maintains Gar Wood sales literature, historic photographs, and boating magazines from the Gar Wood era. Gives videotape presentations; compiles statistics. **Libraries: Type:** by appointment only. **Holdings:** 3,000; articles, biographical archives, photographs. **Subjects:** specifications, prices, productions, correspondence, dealer network. **Awards:** Gar Wood of the Year Award. **Frequency:** annual. **Type:** recognition. **Recipient:** for accuracy and quality of restoration. **Computer Services:** Mailing lists. **Additional Websites:** http://www.abm.org. **Committees:** Technical Research. **Publications:** *The American Wooden Runabout*. Book. **Price:** $15.00. **Circulation:** 24,000 ● *Gar Wood Boats: Classics of a Golden Era* (in English and French). Book. Contains reference information on history of Gar Wood Boats. **Price:** $30.00. ISSN: 0760-3060. **Circulation:** 24,000 ● *Gar Wood News*, quarterly. Newsletter. Includes meeting reports and lists boats and accessories wanted and for sale. ● *Gar Wood Owner's Directory*, biennial ● *Member Service Bulletin*, periodic. **Conventions/Meetings:** annual meeting, held in conjunction with Antique and Classic Boat Society (exhibits) - always early fall.

21429 ■ Gulf Yachting Association (GYA)
c/o Janet Miller-Schmidt, Sec.-Treas.
2777 Lakeshore Dr.
Mandeville, LA 70448
Ph: (985)624-8152
E-mail: janetmiller-schmidt@msn.com
URL: http://www.gya.org
Contact: Janet Miller-Schmidt, Sec.-Treas.
Founded: 1901. **Members:** 38. **Membership Dues:** individual, $15 (annual) ● associate, $20 (annual). **Description:** Yacht racing enthusiasts. Strives to promote yacht racing. Hosts sanctioned yachting events. **Publications:** *Perpetual Trophies of the Gulf Yachting Association*. Book. Alternate Formats: online.

21430 ■ International Hydrofoil Society (IHS)
PO Box 51
Cabin John, MD 20818
E-mail: president@foils.org
URL: http://www.foils.org
Contact: John Meyer, Pres.
Founded: 1970. **Members:** 250. **Membership Dues:** regular, $20 (annual) ● student, $10 (annual) ●

sustaining, $250 (annual). **Budget:** $4,000. **Description:** Serves the needs of technical and non-technical members who design, build, operate, or simply are interested in hydrofoil ships, boats, and models. Maintains a hall of fame. **Libraries: Type:** by appointment only. **Holdings:** archival material, artwork, books, clippings, monographs, periodicals. **Subjects:** military and commercial hydrofoil design, testing, operations. **Awards:** The IHS Award. **Frequency:** periodic. **Type:** recognition. **Computer Services:** Online services. **Publications:** *Advanced Marine Vehicle*, annual. Alternate Formats: CD-ROM ● Newsletter, quarterly. Covers all aspects of hydrofoils. **Price:** free for members and authors. **Circulation:** 300. Alternate Formats: online. **Conventions/Meetings:** monthly board meeting and regional meeting.

21431 ■ National Women's Sailing Association (NWSA)
70A Pleasant St.
Marblehead, MA 01945
Free: (866)631-6972
Fax: (781)631-2889
E-mail: wsf@womensailing.org
URL: http://www.womensailing.org
Contact: Valli Cook, Pres.
Founded: 1993. **Members:** 500. **Membership Dues:** individual, $45 (annual) ● student, $25 (annual) ● household (two persons residing at same address), $80 (annual) ● associate, $100 (annual) ● silver patron, $250 (annual) ● gold patron, $500 (annual) ● platinum, $1,000 (annual). **Staff:** 2. **Description:** Works to enhance the lives of women and girls through education and access to the sport of sailing. **Formerly:** (2004) Women's Sailing Foundation. **Publications:** *Women's Sailing Resource*, biennial. Booklet. **Price:** $4.00/copy. **Conventions/Meetings:** annual Pacific Sail Expo - show and seminar, includes on-water clinics - in April ● annual Sail Boat Show - show and seminar - in October ● annual Sail Expo - meeting and seminar - in January.

21432 ■ Nautical Research Guild (NRG)
31 Water St., Ste.7
Cuba, NY 14727
Ph: (585)968-8111
Fax: (585)968-8111
E-mail: nrghomeoffice@thenrg.org
URL: http://www.naut-res-guild.org
Contact: Ms. Valerie Slocum, Office Mgr.
Founded: 1948. **Members:** 1,700. **Membership Dues:** regular, $35 (annual). **Budget:** $70,000. **Multinational. Description:** Ship model builders, artists, and historians; nautical museums and libraries. Collects and disseminates nautical information including: illustrations and plans of ships, boats, and craft of all kinds; techniques for modeling ships; rigging instructions; maritime history. **Awards:** Howard I. Chapelle Award. **Frequency:** quinquennial. **Type:** monetary. **Recipient:** for outstanding research leading to a historically accurate ship model. **Publications:** *Nautical Research Journal*, quarterly. Contains articles on ship model building, nautical research, and marine art; includes book and product reviews. **Price:** $35.00/year in U.S.; $40.00/year in Canada; $43.00/year in Mexico and overseas. ISSN: 0738-7245. **Circulation:** 1,700. **Advertising:** accepted. Alternate Formats: microform ● *Ship Modeler's Shop Notes*. Papers ● Handbook. **Conventions/Meetings:** annual conference (exhibits) - 2007 Sept., Manitowoc, WI; 2008 Oct., Baltimore, MD; 2009 Oct., Astoria, OR.

21433 ■ North American Steam Boat Association (NASBA)
c/o Earle Jones, Ed.
1876 Lakeland Dr.
Finksburg, MD 21048
Ph: (410)549-3446
E-mail: esjones@adelphia.net
URL: http://www.pcez.com/~artemis/NASAhome.htm
Contact: Earle Jones, Ed.
Membership Dues: regular, in U.S., $23 (annual) ● regular, in Canada, $26 (annual) ● in UK and Europe, $30 (annual) ● other country, $35 (annual). **Multinational. Description:** Promotes the steamboating

hobby. Provides a correspondence link among hobby steamboaters. **Publications:** *The Smokestack*, bimonthly. Magazine.

21434 ■ Northwest Schooner Society (NWSS)
PO Box 9504
Seattle, WA 98109
Free: (800)551-NWSS
E-mail: info@nwschooner.org
URL: http://www.nwschooner.org
Founded: 1994. **Description:** Sponsors voyages of up to a week long on historic ships; provides opportunity for teens and adults to experience American history. Organizes environmental cruises on the schooner Zodiac and schooner Lavengro. **Telecommunication Services:** electronic mail, captkarl@nwschooner.org.

21435 ■ Pacific Dragon Boat Association (PDBA)
c/o Doug Schryver, Treas.
7176 SE Johnson St.
Hillsboro, OR 97123
E-mail: schryver.doug@cnf.com
URL: http://www.pdbausa.org
Contact: Doug Schryver, Treas.
Founded: 1999. **Membership Dues:** full, $300 (annual) ● associate, $100 (annual) ● individual associate, $50 (annual). **Description:** Fosters amateur national and international dragon boat competition, representing California, Hawaii, Oregon, Washington, Alaska, and Nevada. **Telecommunication Services:** electronic mail, les.hopper@latitude33.com ● electronic mail, kimwasabi@comcast.net ● electronic mail, swahlberg@juno.com ● electronic mail, president@pdbausa.org ● electronic mail, vicepresident@pdbausa.org. **Conventions/Meetings:** annual Regional Championship Race - competition.

21436 ■ Richardson Boat Owners Association (RBOA)
c/o Chamber of Commerce
15 Webster St.
North Tonawanda, NY 14120
E-mail: president@richardsonboats.com
URL: http://www.richardsonboats.com
Contact: Catherine McLeod, Pres.
Founded: 1973. **Members:** 120. **Membership Dues:** regular, $30 (annual). **Regional Groups:** 4. **Description:** Owners of Richardson boats. Promotes the preservation of Richardson boats and public education about the preservation of antique boats. Maintains library of Richardson sales promotions. Conducts research programs; compiles statistics. **Awards: Type:** recognition. **Committees:** Awards; Rendezvous. **Publications:** *Cruisabout*, quarterly. Newsletter. Contains technical information, letters from members, meeting notices, and items of interest. **Price:** free for members. **Circulation:** 135. **Advertising:** accepted ● Membership Directory, annual. **Conventions/Meetings:** quarterly meeting - usually spring & fall ● annual Rendezvous - general assembly and meeting - always summer.

21437 ■ Traditional Small Craft Association (TSCA)
PO Box 350
Mystic, CT 06355
E-mail: emevans@calmail.berkeley.edu
URL: http://www.tsca.net
Contact: Elizabeth Evans, Pres.
Founded: 1975. **Members:** 800. **Membership Dues:** individual, family, $20 (annual) ● individual sponsor, $50 (annual) ● patron, $100 (annual). **Local Groups:** 1. **National Groups:** 24. **Description:** Individuals who own or are interested in traditional small craft; boat builders and maritime museums. Seeks to preserve the history, building skills, and use of traditional small craft (boats for rowing and sailing that originated before the internal combustion engine). Holds on-the-water workshops and meets. Monitors legislation affecting recreational boats and boating. **Awards:** John Gardner Fund. **Frequency:** annual. **Type:** grant. **Recipient:** for community based groups and anyone with demonstrated interest in and knowledge of traditional small craft. **Councils:** Execu-

tive. **Publications:** *The Ash Breeze*, quarterly. Journal. **Price:** included in membership dues; $4.00 for nonmembers. **Circulation:** 900. **Advertising:** accepted. **Conventions/Meetings:** annual John Gardner Small Craft Work - meeting - always first or second weekend of June, Mystic, CT.

21438 ■ **Wooden Canoe Heritage Association (WCHA)**
PO Box 117
Tamworth, NH 03886
Ph: (610)705-0436
E-mail: bcconrad@alltel.net
Contact: Bill Conrad, Pres.
Founded: 1979. **Members:** 2,100. **Membership Dues:** individual in U.S., $25 (annual) ● individual in Canada, $30 (annual). **Regional Groups:** 8. **Description:** Individuals, museums, libraries, and boat and canoe builders dedicated to the preservation, restoration, study, construction, use, and appreciation of North American wooden and birchbark canoes. Seeks to stem the destruction of historic examples of wooden and bark canoes and to research and perpetuate the theories and craftsmanship that went into their construction. Disseminates information on restoration techniques and materials; conducts demonstrations and displays; maintains referral service. Collects information about current and historic canoe builders and their craft; compiles statistics. **Computer Services:** database, wooden canoe owners. **Publications:** *Builders' Directory*, semiannual. Membership Directory. **Price:** $2.00/copy, for members; $3.00/copy, for nonmembers ● *Wooden Canoe*, bimonthly. Magazine. Includes classified ads. **Price:** $3.75/issue for nonmembers; included in membership dues. ISSN: 0198-991X. **Circulation:** 2,100. **Advertising:** accepted ● Books, semiannual. Includes reprints of old canoe catalogs. ● Catalogs ● Reprints. **Conventions/Meetings:** annual assembly (exhibits) - 3-4 days at the end of July ● lecture ● workshop.

Bottles

21439 ■ **Federation of Historical Bottle Collectors (FOHBC)**
c/o June Lowry, Business Mgr.
401 Johnston Ct.
Raymore, MO 64083
Ph: (816)318-0160
E-mail: osubuckeyes71@aol.com
URL: http://www.fohbc.com
Contact: June Lowry, Business Mgr.
Founded: 1969. **Members:** 1,200. **Membership Dues:** in U.S., $30 (annual) ● in Canada, $35 (annual) ● outside U.S. and Canada, $45 (annual). **Regional Groups:** 4. **State Groups:** 1. **Local Groups:** 110. **Description:** Antique bottle collectors clubs (110) and interested individuals (800). Seeks to educate and inform the public on antique bottle collecting. Encourages the writing of research and true stories related to bottles. Maintains speakers' bureau and hall of fame. Distributes list of photographic slide programs; maintains calendar of club show dates. **Awards:** Type: recognition. **Recipient:** for the best educational display of bottles by individuals or clubs. **Committees:** Competition Chairmen. **Publications:** *Bottles and Extras*, bimonthly. Magazine. Contains articles, show calendar and advertising. **Price:** free, for members only. **Circulation:** 1,000. **Advertising:** accepted ● *Directory of Members at Large and Member Clubs*, annual. **Conventions/Meetings:** annual conference (exhibits).

21440 ■ **International Association of Jim Beam Bottle and Specialties Clubs (IAJBBSC)**
2965 Waubesa Ave.
Madison, WI 53711-5964
Ph: (608)663-9661
Fax: (608)663-9664
E-mail: jimbeamclubs@aol.com
URL: http://www.jimbeamclubs.com
Contact: Cecil Gillingham, Pres.
Founded: 1971. **Members:** 4,000. **Membership Dues:** individual in U.S. and Canada, $25 (annual) ●

individual outside U.S. and Canada, $30 (annual). **Staff:** 1. **Regional Groups:** 12. **Local Groups:** 118. **Description:** Individuals interested in studying, stimulating, and encouraging interest in Jim Beam bottle collecting; individual affiliates must be affiliated through the association's local club. Furthers the hobby of Jim Beam bottle collecting. Sponsors charity projects. **Formerly:** (1971) National Association of Jim Beam Bottle and Specialties Clubs. **Publications:** *Beam Around the World*, monthly. Newsletter. **Conventions/Meetings:** annual International Convention - congress (exhibits).

21441 ■ **International Chinese Snuff Bottle Society (ICSBS)**
2601 N Charles St.
Baltimore, MD 21218
Ph: (410)467-9400
Fax: (410)243-3451
E-mail: icsbs@snuffbottle.org
URL: http://www.snuffbottle.org
Contact: John G. Ford, Pres.
Founded: 1968. **Members:** 525. **Membership Dues:** regular, $125 (annual) ● dealer, patron, $500 (annual) ● sponsor, $250 (annual) ● benefactor, $1,000 (annual). **Staff:** 3. **Regional Groups:** 5. **Multinational. Description:** Collectors, dealers, and museums in 29 countries interested in snuff bottles. The bottles, which were made only in China toward the beginning of the Ch'ing Dynasty (middle 17th century), are generally 2 to 4 inches in height and have been rendered in many kinds of materials; may be inlaid, enameled, carved, painted, or otherwise finished. Promotes scholarship regarding the nature and sources of snuff bottles. Organizes exhibitions and museum visits. **Libraries:** Type: not open to the public. **Holdings:** 120. **Formerly:** (1975) Chinese Snuff Bottle Society. **Publications:** *The International Chinese Snuff Bottle Society*, annual. Directory ● *Journal of the Chinese Snuff Bottle Society*, 3/year. **Price:** included in membership dues. **Circulation:** 525. **Advertising:** accepted. **Conventions/Meetings:** annual convention (exhibits) - usually October ● seminar.

Bridge

21442 ■ **American Bridge Association (ABA)**
2828 Lakewood Ave. SW
Atlanta, GA 30315
Ph: (404)768-5517
Fax: (404)767-1871
E-mail: ababridge@bellsouth.net
URL: http://www.ababridge.org
Contact: Leola Rucker, Sec.
Founded: 1932. **Members:** 4,224. **Membership Dues:** individual, $25 (annual) ● student, $10 (annual). **Staff:** 4. **Regional Groups:** 202. **State Groups:** 189. **Local Groups:** 7. **National Groups:** 8. **Description:** Represents individuals, primarily blacks, interested in the game of bridge. Encourages the playing of duplicate bridge. Sponsors annual tournaments as benefits for charitable organizations. **Publications:** Bulletin, quarterly. **Price:** $1.25/copy. ISSN: 0164-319X. **Conventions/Meetings:** semiannual competition - always spring and summer.

21443 ■ **American Bridge Teachers' Association (ABTA)**
1254 26th Ave.
San Francisco, CA 94122-1505
Ph: (415)566-4592
E-mail: bridgelady@earthlink.net
URL: http://www.abtahome.com
Contact: Deborah Murphy, Sec.
Founded: 1957. **Members:** 500. **Membership Dues:** individual, $35 (annual). **Staff:** 6. **Regional Groups:** 12. **State Groups:** 52. **Description:** Bridge teachers, bridge club directors, and bridge writers. Seeks to improve professional standards. **Awards:** Book of the Year. **Frequency:** annual. **Type:** recognition. **Recipient:** for the best bridge writer of the year ● Honorary Member. **Type:** recognition. **Recipient:** for service to bridge teachers or the game of bridge ●

Software of the Year. **Frequency:** annual. **Type:** recognition. **Recipient:** for best bridge software. **Publications:** Magazine, quarterly. **Price:** $4.00 for members, plus shipping and handling; $6.00 for nonmembers, plus shipping and handling. **Circulation:** 1,000. **Advertising:** accepted. **Conventions/Meetings:** annual conference, immediately preceding the summer nationals of the American Contract Bridge League (exhibits) ● seminar, three days, for those who wish to achieve teacher status.

21444 ■ **American Contract Bridge League (ACBL)**
2990 Airways Blvd.
Memphis, TN 38116-3847
Ph: (901)332-5586
Free: (800)467-1623
Fax: (901)398-7754
E-mail: service@acbl.org
URL: http://www.acbl.org
Contact: Mr. Jay Baum, CEO
Founded: 1937. **Members:** 167,000. **Membership Dues:** regular, $35 (annual) ● life master service, $32 ● household, $64 (annual) ● junior, $14 (annual) ● patron, $250 (annual) ● household patron, $350 (annual). **Staff:** 350. **Budget:** $16,000,000. **Regional Groups:** 25. **Local Groups:** 3,300. **Description:** Contract bridge players (in Canada, U.S., Mexico, Bermuda, and Puerto Rico) who take part in club, local, regional, and North American tournaments. Establishes, interprets, and enforces rules and regulations governing the game of contract bridge. Maintains record of masterpoints awarded to individuals at tournaments and club games. Sponsors Charity Foundation, annually awarding $250,000 to various charitable organizations, and Educational Foundation, that provides information on contract bridge to new and young players across North America. Compiles statistics. **Libraries:** Type: reference. **Holdings:** 3,500; archival material, books. **Subjects:** contract bridge and related games. **Awards:** $500 Youth Flight. **Frequency:** annual. **Type:** scholarship. **Recipient:** to each member of pair with highest score in September ACBL-wide Instant Matchpoint Game ● $1000 King of Bridge. **Frequency:** annual. **Type:** scholarship. **Recipient:** to a graduating high school senior with best record at bridge ● Homer Shoop $5000 Preteen 10-year Maturity Bond Certificate. **Frequency:** annual. **Type:** scholarship. **Recipient:** to ACBL member, 12 years old or younger, with best achievement at bridge. **Computer Services:** database, masterpoint accounts ● database, membership records. **Telecommunication Services:** additional toll-free number, (800)264-2743, sales department. **Formerly:** U.S. Bridge Association; (1929) American Auction Bridge League; (1934) American Bridge League. **Publications:** *ACBL Bridge Series: Club, Diamond, Heart and Spade Student Texts and Teacher Manuals* (in English, French, and Japanese). Consists of a progression of five courses, each focusing on a different aspect of the game. **Price:** $15.00 ● *The Bridge Bulletin*, monthly. Magazine. Includes information for players at all levels. **Price:** included in membership dues. **Advertising:** accepted ● *The Bridge Teacher*, 3/year. Manual ● *Club Manager's Newsletter*, 3/year ● *Encyclopedia of Bridge*, every 8 years. Book ● *The Grapevine*, 3/year. Newsletter ● Handbook, annual. Includes details of the rules and regulations and policies and procedures of the ACBL. Alternate Formats: online. **Conventions/Meetings:** Championship Tournaments - competition (exhibits) - 3/year, always spring, summer, and fall ● periodic Regional and Sectional Tournaments - competition.

Bus

21445 ■ **Graham Brothers Truck and Bus Club (GBTBC)**
9894 Fairtree Dr.
Strongsville, OH 44149
Ph: (440)238-4956
Contact: Edwin L. Brinkman, Founder
Founded: 1967. **Members:** 200. **Description:** Owners of Graham Brothers trucks and buses which were

manufactured from 1921 to 1929 by the Graham Bros. Co. in Detroit, MI and Evansville, IN and Stockton, CA. The vehicles were sold through Dodge dealers; the buses were used as school buses and parlor coaches. Maintains owners roster; shares information concerning these models.

21446 ■ International Bus Collectors Club (IBC)

Address Unknown since 2007

Founded: 1976. **Members:** 979. **Description:** Motor bus owners and operators and individuals interested in the motor bus industry. Objective is to preserve the history of the North American motor bus industry. Conducts educational program; constructs models; sponsors events, such as Bus Bash for which the club organizes a bus gathering to show the public the benefits of buses. Displays historic coach and provides listing of historic coaches to be used in movies and films. **Libraries: Type:** reference. **Holdings:** books, photographs. **Awards: Type:** recognition. **Publications:** *International Bus Collector Journal*, 3/year ● Books ● Newsletter, 3-6/year ● Videos ● Also publishes photo sets. **Conventions/Meetings:** semiannual Bus Bash - meeting (exhibits) - always Memorial Day weekend and Labor Day weekend.

21447 ■ Motor Bus Society (MBS)

PO Box 261
Paramus, NJ 07653-0261
E-mail: membership@motorbussociety.com
URL: http://www.motorbussociety.org
Contact: Richard Phillippi, Treas.

Founded: 1948. **Members:** 1,200. **Membership Dues:** individual in U.S., $35 (annual) ● individual in Canada, $40 (annual) ● individual outside U.S. and Canada, $45 (annual). **Multinational. Description:** Bus industry professionals, hobbyists and others interested in the history of bus lines, terminals, and equipment. Sponsors motor coach tours of bus properties. **Libraries: Type:** reference. **Holdings:** 90,500; books, photographs. **Subjects:** motor buses, bus operations, 1900-present. **Formerly:** (1954) National Motor Bus Association. **Publications:** *Motor Coach Age*, quarterly. Magazine. Features in-depth history of a transit operation and includes historical photographs and researched rosters. **Price:** included in membership dues; $6.00 for nonmembers. **Circulation:** 1,200. **Advertising:** accepted. **Conventions/Meetings:** semiannual convention - always spring and fall.

Carousels

21448 ■ National Carousel Association (NCA)

c/o Barbara May, Exec. Sec.
PO Box 19039
Baltimore, MD 21284-9039
E-mail: nca_carousel@yahoo.com
URL: http://www.nca-usa.org
Contact: Barbara May, Exec. Sec.

Founded: 1973. **Members:** 1,600. **Membership Dues:** individual, $47 (annual) ● contributing, $100 (annual) ● sustaining, $500-$1,000 (annual). **Budget:** $50,000. **Description:** Promotes conservation, appreciation, knowledge, and enjoyment of the art of the classic wooden carousel and especially the preservation of complete wooden carousels. Conducts research. **Libraries: Type:** reference. **Holdings:** archival material, articles, photographs. **Subjects:** wooden carousels. **Awards:** National Historic Carousel Award. **Frequency:** annual. **Type:** recognition. **Recipient:** to carousel owners who have preserved their carousels ● **Type:** recognition. **Recipient:** to members for outstanding preservation efforts. **Committees:** Census; Fund Raising; Information and Technical Assistance; Legal Counsel; Preservation and Conservation; Public Relations. **Formerly:** (1975) National Carousel Roundtable. **Publications:** *Census of Wooden Carousels*, biennial. **Advertising:** accepted ● *Merry-Go-Roundup*, quarterly ● *NCA News*, periodic. Newsletter. **Conventions/Meetings:** annual conference and lecture

(exhibits) ● annual Technical Assistance Conference - seminar, on wood carving, restoration, and painting.

Cat

21449 ■ Abyssinian Cat Club of America (ACCA)

c/o Harford Gillaspie, Sec./Scorer
23700 Stagecoach Rd.
Volcano, CA 95689
Ph: (209)296-7390
E-mail: dexterus@volcano.net
URL: http://www.abyworld.com/acca
Contact: Harford Gillaspie, Sec./Scorer

Membership Dues: first class mail/associate in U.S., $32 (annual) ● first class mail/associate in U.S., $62 (biennial) ● surface, in Canada and Mexico, $30 (annual) ● surface, in Canada and Mexico, $58 (biennial) ● air mail, in Canada and Mexico, $39 (annual) ● air mail, in Canada and Mexico, $76 (biennial) ● air mail, Japan, $45 (annual) ● air mail, Japan, $88 (biennial) ● air mail, other foreign, $40 (annual). **Multinational. Description:** Promotes informed breeding and ownership of Abyssinian cats. **Publications:** Newsletter, quarterly. Contains articles, show reports, and photos. **Price:** included in membership dues. **Advertising:** accepted.

21450 ■ American Association of Cat Enthusiasts (AACE)

PO Box 213
Pine Brook, NJ 07058
Ph: (973)335-6717
Fax: (973)334-5834
E-mail: registrar@aaceinc.org
URL: http://www.aaceinc.org
Contact: Ken K. Taylor, Pres.

Founded: 1993. **Members:** 300. **Membership Dues:** in U.S. and Canada, $25 (annual) ● family, $35 (annual) ● life, $250. **Staff:** 1. **Regional Groups:** 4. **State Groups:** 6. **Local Groups:** 12. **Description:** Individuals interested in cats and their welfare. Acts as an animal welfare association and cat registry. Licenses cat show judges and offers training programs for aspiring cat judges. Works to educate the public and veterinarians, especially on unusual breeds. Sanctions cat shows, sponsors educational programs, donates money to research projects pertaining to feline disease. Maintains Speaker's Bureau. **Libraries: Type:** reference; not open to the public; by appointment only. **Subjects:** cats. **Awards:** Annual Awards. **Frequency:** annual. **Type:** recognition. **Recipient:** for highest scoring cats, kittens, alters and household pets. **Computer Services:** database, pedigree records, show records ● electronic publishing ● mailing lists ● record retrieval services. **Committees:** Disciplinary; Investigative; Protest. **Publications:** *The Enthusiast*, quarterly. Newsletter. **Price:** free. **Advertising:** accepted ● *The Enthusiasts*, quarterly. Brochures. Contains variety of cat-related topics. **Price:** free. **Advertising:** accepted ● *Yearbook of Awards*, annual. **Conventions/Meetings:** semiannual board meeting.

21451 ■ American Cat Association (ACA)

c/o Susie Page
8101 Katherine Ave.
Panorama City, CA 91402
Ph: (818)781-5656
Contact: Susie Page, Corporate Sec.

Founded: 1897. **Staff:** 1. **Description:** Cat register. Objectives are to: promote and protect the welfare of cats and cat owners; maintain a stud book registry of cats.

21452 ■ American Cat Fanciers Association (ACFA)

PO Box 1949
Nixa, MO 65714-1949
Ph: (417)725-1530
Fax: (417)725-1533

E-mail: acfa@aol.com
URL: http://www.acfacats.com
Contact: Connie Vandre, Exec. Dir.

Founded: 1955. **Members:** 800. **Membership Dues:** regular, in U.S., $50 (annual) ● family, $15 (annual) ● junior, $5 (annual) ● regular, U.S. and Canada, $60 (annual) ● regular, in Canada, $40 (annual). **Staff:** 3. **Regional Groups:** 80. **Multinational. Description:** Breeders and exhibitors of purebred cats; individuals interested in educating the public regarding the health and welfare of domesticated cats. Maintains studbook registry and licenses cat shows and cat judges. Registers pedigreed cats. Sponsors charitable program; compiles statistics. Breed sections recognized include Abyssinian, American Curl Longhair, American Curl Shorthair, American Shorthair, American Wirehair, American Bobtail shorthair, American Bobtail longhair, Balinese, Bengal, Birman, Bombay, British Shorthair, Burmese, Chartreux, Cornish Rex, Cymric, Devon Rex, Egyptian Mau, Exotic Shorthair, Havana Brown, Highland Fold, Himalayan, Japanese Bobtail shorthair, Japanese Bobtail Longhair, Korat, Longhair Exotic, Maine Coon Cat, Manx, Norweign Forest, Ocicat, Oriental Longhair, Oriental Shorthair, Persian, Ragamuffin, Ragdoll, Russian Blue, Scottish Fold, Selkirk Rex Shorthair, Selkirk Rex Longhair, Siberian, Turkish Van, Siamese, Singapura, Snowshoe, Somali, Sphynx Tonkinese, Turkish Angora. Records domestic household pets. **Libraries: Type:** not open to the public. **Awards:** Inter-American. **Frequency:** annual. **Type:** recognition. **Recipient:** for final winners in the show ● Legacy of Achievement. **Frequency:** annual. **Type:** recognition. **Recipient:** to cats who have excelled in the show ring during several seasons of their show career ● Legacy of Excellence. **Frequency:** annual. **Type:** recognition. **Recipient:** to cats who have excelled in the production of ACFA Grand Champion offspring ● Regional Inter-American. **Type:** recognition. **Recipient:** for final winners in the show or season. **Committees:** Genetics; Historian; International Division; Jurisprudence; New Breed Mentorship; Public Relations. **Councils:** Judges. **Funds:** Fund Raising. **Publications:** *ACFA Bulletin*, bimonthly. Newsletter. Contains news, views, and show calendars. **Price:** available to members only. **Circulation:** 1,300. **Advertising:** accepted. Alternate Formats: online ● *AFCA Parade of Royalty*, annual. Yearbook. Includes awards list and photographs. **Advertising:** accepted ● *Breed Standards of Perfection*. Book ● *Clerking Manual* ● *Robinson's Genetics for Cat Breeders and Veterinarians*, periodic. Book. Features fully revised edition to re-establish Genetics for Cat Breeders as the text of choice in the field of feline genetics. **Price:** $73.95/copy ● *Show and Registration Rules*. Handbook ● Articles, periodic. Includes history of past ACFA presidents, junior ACFA and special issues about cats. **Conventions/Meetings:** semiannual board meeting, show held during August meeting (exhibits) - always February and August.

21453 ■ Calico Cat Registry International

PO Box 944
Morongo Valley, CA 92256
Ph: (760)363-6511
Contact: Judith Lindley, Pres./Founder

Founded: 1978. **Membership Dues:** general, $2. **Staff:** 1. **Multinational. Description:** Seeks to achieve recognition of tricolor and tortoiseshell cats by color alone, rather than by bone structure and body form. Compiles statistics. Registry for tortoiseshell, tortie and white and calico cats by specific color and patterns. **Libraries: Type:** reference. **Holdings:** clippings. **Subjects:** tortoiseshell, calico cats. **Publications:** *Calicos and Kin*. Handbook. **Price:** $20.00/copy ● *Handbook of Calico Cat Registry*. **Price:** $7.50/copy.

21454 ■ Cat Fanciers' Association (CFA)

PO Box 1005
Manasquan, NJ 08736-0805
Ph: (732)528-9797
Fax: (732)528-7391

E-mail: cfa@cfa.org
URL: http://www.cfa.org
Contact: Pam DelaBar, Pres.
Founded: 1906. **Members:** 664. **Membership Dues:** cat club, $90 (annual). **Staff:** 25. **Budget:** $2,250,000. **Regional Groups:** 9. **National Groups:** 664. **Description:** Federation of all-breed and specialty cat clubs. Promotes the welfare of cats, register pedigrees, and license shows held under association rules. **Libraries: Type:** open to the public. **Holdings:** books, periodicals. **Subjects:** cats. **Awards:** National Award Winner. **Frequency:** annual. **Type:** recognition. **Recipient:** for cats, their owners, and breeders based on achievement in competition over a year-long period. **Publications:** *Cat Fanciers' Almanac,* bimonthly. Magazine. **Price:** $29.00/year; $7.00/ issue. ISSN: 8750-898X. **Circulation:** 6,000. **Advertising:** accepted ● *CFA Complete Cat Book.* Provides both breeders and pet owners with an easy, authoritative, and engaging reference book on their pet. **Price:** $29.95 plus shipping and handling ● *CFA Yearbook,* annual. **Price:** $30.00 plus shipping and handling ● *Show Rules.* Booklet. **Price:** $5.00 ● *Show Standards Booklet.* **Price:** $7.00. **Conventions/Meetings:** annual meeting (exhibits) - always June.

21455 ■ Cat Fanciers' Federation (CFF)

PO Box 661
Gratis, OH 45330
Ph: (937)787-9009
Fax: (937)787-4290
E-mail: cff@siscom.net
URL: http://www.cffinc.org
Contact: Stan Buchanan, Pres.
Founded: 1919. **Members:** 100. **Membership Dues:** individual, $45 (annual). **Description:** Federation of local clubs of persons who own, breed, and exhibit cats and who are interested in the general welfare of cats. Maintains records on the ancestry of cats; encourages the holding of shows; trains judges; creates and promulgates rules and standards for judging cats, holding shows, and recording ancestry. Local clubs hold annual cat shows under federation rules, usually for the benefit of humane organizations. **Awards:** Parade of Perfection Award. **Frequency:** annual. **Type:** recognition. **Recipient:** for highest scoring cats in all CFF shows. **Committees:** Rules. **Councils:** Judges. **Publications:** *CFF Newsletter,* quarterly. **Price:** $15.00/year. **Advertising:** accepted ● *CFF Yearbook,* annual. **Advertising:** accepted ● *Show Rules and Standards.* **Conventions/Meetings:** semiannual meeting - always March and September.

21456 ■ Cornish Rex Society

c/o Phyllis Jacobowitz, Ed.
57 Pires Dr.
Oakdale, CT 06370
E-mail: csco@bellsouth.net
URL: http://www.flickoff.com/crs.htm
Contact: Phyllis Jacobowitz, Ed.
Founded: 1976. **Members:** 90. **Membership Dues:** first family in U.S. and Canada, $10 (annual) ● first family outside U.S. and Canada, $13 (annual) ● two family in U.S. and Canada, $15 (annual). **Staff:** 6. **Description:** Breeders and owners of Cornish Rex cats; other interested individuals. Promotes interest in and advancement of the Cornish Rex breed. Conducts educational, research, and humane programs. Compiles statistics. **Convention/Meeting:** none. **Awards:** Best Cornish Rex Award. **Frequency:** annual. **Type:** recognition. **Recipient:** for top cats, kittens, and alters. **Publications:** *The Wave Link,* bimonthly. Newsletter. Contains articles on the breed, pedigree information, and letters from members. **Price:** included in membership dues. **Circulation:** 90. **Advertising:** accepted.

21457 ■ Feral Cat Friends (FCF)

8255 White Oak Rd.
Garner, NC 27529
Ph: (919)662-5365 (919)906-9710
Fax: (919)772-2212
E-mail: info@feralcatfriends.org
URL: http://www.feralcatfriends.org
Description: Feral cat owners and fanciers. Works to manage overpopulation. Places adoptable cats.

21458 ■ Friends of Feral Felines (FFF)

PO Box 473385
Charlotte, NC 28247
Ph: (704)348-1578
E-mail: fffcharlotte@yahoo.com
URL: http://www.friendsofferalfelines.org
Founded: 1998. **Description:** Provides humane management of feral cats through a trap, sterilize, vaccinate, and release program. Promotes public awareness through education and information about feral cats. **Computer Services:** Information services, about feral cats. **Publications:** *Cat's Tale,* quarterly. Newsletters. Features information about local efforts of the organization and local feral cats in the Greater Charlotte, NC area. **Alternate Formats:** online. **Conventions/Meetings:** bimonthly meeting, discusses feral cat issues, current group activities, volunteer opportunities, and fundraisers; open to the public (exhibits) - every 1st Tuesday of even-numbered month (February, April, June, August, October, and December).

21459 ■ Happy Household Pet Cat Club (HHPCC)

c/o Dorothy Lewis, Treas.
14508 Chester Ave.
Saratoga, CA 95070
E-mail: treasurer@hhpcc.org
URL: http://hhpcc.org
Contact: Dorothy Lewis, Treas.
Founded: 1968. **Members:** 700. **Membership Dues:** one or two people at the same address, $20 (annual) ● additional family, $1 (annual). **Multinational. Description:** Promotes the welfare of all cats, neuter/ spay programs; works to upgrade status of household pet cat in general, especially in show environment. **Publications:** *HHPCC Happenings,* bimonthly. Newsletter. **Alternate Formats:** online.

21460 ■ The International Cat Association (TICA)

PO Box 2684
Harlingen, TX 78551
Ph: (956)428-8046
Fax: (956)428-8047
E-mail: membership@ticaeo.com
URL: http://www.tica.org
Contact: Ms. Leslie Bowers, Business Mgr.
Founded: 1979. **Members:** 3,500. **Membership Dues:** regular, $25 (annual). **Staff:** 10. **Description:** Persons interested in educating the public on the general welfare of the cat and its value as a pet. Maintains registration records and ancestry information; conducts judging schools and genetic seminars; operates charitable program; compiles statistics. Sponsors cat shows and other competitions. **Libraries: Type:** open to the public. **Holdings:** 98. **Subjects:** cats. **Awards:** Cats of the Year. **Frequency:** annual. **Type:** recognition. **Recipient:** for individual cats; based on show research. **Additional Websites:** http://www.ticaeo.com. **Committees:** Genetics. **Publications:** *By-Laws,* annual. **Price:** $7.00 ● *Registration Rules* ● *Show Rules* ● *Standards* ● *TICA TREND,* bimonthly. Newsletter. **Price:** $2.50 each. **Circulation:** 300. **Advertising:** accepted ● *TICA Yearbook,* annual. **Conventions/Meetings:** semiannual board meeting ● annual convention, with awards banquet and cat show (exhibits).

21461 ■ International Sphynx Society (ISS)

c/o Patricia Hawk, Sec.-Treas.
320 E Beresford Ave.
Deland, FL 32724
Ph: (386)822-9569
E-mail: phawk@cfl.rr.com
URL: http://www.internationalsphynxsociety.com
Contact: Robert Sterling, Pres.
Membership Dues: associate, $10 (annual) ● regular voting, $20 (annual) ● junior, $5 (annual). **Description:** Promotes the sphinx cat breed. **Publications:** Newsletter. **Price:** included in membership dues, plus shipping and handling. **Conventions/ Meetings:** annual meeting.

21462 ■ National Birman Fanciers (NBF)

c/o Stephanie Wilson, Sec.
415 Debbi Ct.
Hanover, PA 17331
E-mail: bircat@earthlink.net
URL: http://www.vcnet.com/valkat/nbf/nbf1.html
Contact: Sharon Lann, Pres.
Founded: 1980. **Members:** 280. **Membership Dues:** regular (single), $20 ● regular (family), $25 ● associate, $15. **Regional Groups:** 7. **Description:** Owners and exhibitors of the Birman cat, a blue-eyed, long-hair breed with white paws and a coat that does not mat. Promotes the exchange of information regarding the history and progress of the breed; encourages ownership, development, and exhibition of the breed; gathers and disseminates information about feline health research; emphasizes careful breeding and the ethical sale of kittens. Scores and ranks the best Birmans in the country; sponsors annual NBF Cat Show and competitions. **Affiliated With:** Cat Fanciers' Association. **Publications:** *NBF News,* quarterly. Newsletter. Includes annual membership directory. **Price:** $15.00. **Circulation:** 280. **Advertising:** accepted ● *NBF Show Catalog,* annual. **Price:** $3.00. **Advertising:** accepted. **Conventions/Meetings:** annual Business Conference (exhibits).

21463 ■ Norwegian Forest Cat Breed Council

c/o Cat Fanciers' Association
PO Box 1005
Manasquan, NJ 08736-0805
E-mail: dawn@skogeier.com
URL: http://www.nfcbc.org
Contact: Dawn M. Shiley, Sec.
Founded: 1985. **Members:** 12. **Membership Dues:** individual, $5 (annual). **Description:** Breeders and owners of Norwegian Forest Cats. Works to promote healthy and beautiful cats. **Awards:** Paddy Trophy. **Frequency:** semiannual. **Type:** recognition. **Recipient:** for top show cat of the breed. **Conventions/ Meetings:** biennial meeting.

21464 ■ Rex Breeders United

c/o Diane Straka, Sec.
446 Itasca Ct. NW
Rochester, MN 55901
E-mail: rexbreedersunited@juno.com
Contact: Diane Straka, Sec.
Founded: 1969. **Members:** 60. **Membership Dues:** regular, $12 (annual). **Budget:** $1,000. **Description:** Promotes the health and welfare of cats in general, and specifically, the Cornish Rex cat; encourages the exhibition of the Cornish Rex cat and provides recognition of outstanding Cornish Rex cats; and promotes public awareness, interest, and increased knowledge of the Cornish Rex breed. **Convention/ Meeting:** none. **Awards: Frequency:** annual. **Type:** recognition. **Recipient:** for outstanding Cornish Rex cats. **Publications:** *The Forum,* quarterly. Newsletter. ISSN: 0896-3988. **Circulation:** 60. **Advertising:** accepted.

21465 ■ Sacred Cat of Burma Fanciers (SCBF)

c/o Jane Bridenstein, Sec.
945 Peachcrest Ct. NE
Grand Rapids, MI 49505-6434
Ph: (616)459-5269
E-mail: janebirmist@sbcglobal.net
URL: http://www.scbf.com
Contact: Jane Bridenstein, Sec.
Founded: 1972. **Members:** 300. **Membership Dues:** single, $20 (annual) ● family (not more than 2 voting members), $25 (annual) ● associate, $15 (annual). **Description:** Breeders and owners of Burma cats; individuals who are interested in the general welfare of cats. Purposes are to: encourage breeding standards of the Burma cat set by the Cat Fanciers' Association; educate breeders and exhibitors on these standards; promote interest and knowledge of breeding through education and educational literature. **Publications:** Newsletter, quarterly. Includes articles about nutrition, breeding, showing, grooming, general health topics and fun stories about living with Birman. **Conventions/Meetings:** annual show (exhibits) - always fourth week of August.

21466 ■ Selkirk Rex Breed Club (SRBC)
c/o Debi Kallmeyer
PO Box 213
Aromas, CA 95004-0213
E-mail: woolibaar@selkirkrexcats.org
URL: http://www.selkirkrexcats.org
Contact: Debi Kallmeyer, Contact
Founded: 1993. **Members:** 25. **Membership Dues:** breeder, $15 (annual) ● dual (breeders at same address), $20 (annual). **Staff:** 1. **Description:** Promotes the breeding and exhibition of Selkirk Rex, a new cat breed, in CFA. Sponsors competitions and educational programs. **Convention/Meeting:** none. **Libraries: Type:** reference; not open to the public. **Holdings:** archival material, articles, artwork, clippings, periodicals. **Subjects:** Selkirk Rex. **Computer Services:** Mailing lists, pedigrees, history. **Publications:** *Woolgathering*, quarterly. Newsletter. Features grooming tips, showing tips, health tips and other information of interest to Selkirk Rex breeders. **Price:** included in membership dues. **Advertising:** accepted. Alternate Formats: online.

21467 ■ Somali Cat Club of America (SCCA)
5027 Armstrong
Wichita, KS 67204
E-mail: pandacats@aol.com
URL: http://www.ladybear.com/Somalis
Contact: Maureen Rosenbaum, Pres.
Founded: 1972. **Members:** 100. **Membership Dues:** individual, $15 (annual) ● family, $25 (annual). **Staff:** 20. **Regional Groups:** 14. **Description:** Works to promote the Somali breed of cats. Sponsors educational programs. **Awards: Frequency:** annual. **Type:** recognition. **Recipient:** for cats receiving most points in competition during year. **Computer Services:** Mailing lists, list of breeders. **Telecommunication Services:** phone referral service, list of breeders. **Publications:** Newsletter, quarterly. **Circulation:** 100. **Advertising:** accepted. **Conventions/Meetings:** annual meeting and competition.

21468 ■ Somali International Cat Club
c/o George Hilton, Treas.
2210 21st St.
Lake Charles, LA 70601
E-mail: somali@prodigy.net
Contact: Monique Belton, Pres.
Founded: 1994. **Members:** 60. **Membership Dues:** individual, $16 (annual) ● family, $26 (annual) ● regular, outside U.S., $30 (annual). **Description:** Individuals interested in the Somali cat. Seeks the health advancement of the Somali breed. Offers club scoring. Conducts educational programs; maintains speakers' bureau and hall of fame. **Libraries: Type:** reference. **Holdings:** periodicals. **Subjects:** Somali cats around the world. **Awards: Type:** recognition. **Publications:** Newsletter, semimonthly. **Price:** included in membership dues. **Circulation:** 60. **Advertising:** accepted. **Conventions/Meetings:** annual meeting.

21469 ■ Traditional Cat Association (TCA)
c/o Diana Fineran, Sec.-Treas./Founder
PO Box 178
Heisson, WA 98622-0178
E-mail: info@traditionalcats.com
URL: http://www.traditionalcats.com
Contact: Diana Fineran, Sec.-Treas./Founder
Founded: 1987. **Members:** 2,000. **Membership Dues:** individual, $15 (annual) ● junior, $10 (annual). **Staff:** 12. **Regional Groups:** 14. **State Groups:** 50. **Local Groups:** 10. **National Groups:** 20. **Description:** Breeders and fanciers of traditional cats. Promotes, preserves, protects, and perpetuates the traditional cat. Operates kitten referral services. Conducts educational, charitable, and research programs. Sponsors competitions and shows; compiles statistics. Maintains registry, placement services, hall of fame, and museum. **Libraries: Type:** reference. **Holdings:** 150; archival material. **Subjects:** cats. **Awards:** National Champion Awards. **Frequency:** annual. **Type:** recognition. **Recipient:** for judging at shows. **Additional Websites:** http://www.siamesecats.org. **Formerly:** (1987) Traditional Siamese Breeders and Fanciers Association. **Publi-**

cations: *TCA Newsletter*, monthly. Includes suggestions on how to care for cats, for-sale listings, and information on member activities. **Price:** $1.25/month. **Advertising:** accepted. Alternate Formats: CD-ROM; online; magnetic tape. **Conventions/Meetings:** annual meeting.

21470 ■ Traditional and Classic Cat International (TCCI)
c/o Randi Briggs, Sec.
7615 Clyde Way
Smartville, CA 95977
E-mail: tccat@tccat.org
URL: http://www.tccat.org
Contact: Randi Briggs, Sec.
Founded: 1987. **Membership Dues:** general, $15 (annual). **Multinational. Description:** Promotes and protects the traditional and classic cats. Works to ensure the continuation of a gene pool supporting health, longevity and the traditional physical characteristics of the cat breeds admitted to the Association. Brings back and maintains the "Old Style" look of each breed. Gives support to and preserves those types of cats once recognized as champions. **Computer Services:** Mailing lists, of members. **Programs:** Cattery Inspection; Youth. **Publications:** *TCCI Newsletter*, monthly. **Price:** included in membership dues. **Advertising:** accepted.

21471 ■ United Burmese Cat Fanciers (UBCF)
4116 Pine Cone Terr.
North Port, FL 34286
Ph: (941)426-4691
Contact: Mrs. Robert Bolling, Sec.
Founded: 1960. **Members:** 300. **Membership Dues:** regular, $8 (annual). **Staff:** 11. **Regional Groups:** 11. **Description:** Owners, breeders and enthusiasts of Burmese cats. Works to improve the quality of Burmese cats. Conducts educational and research programs. **Libraries: Type:** reference. **Holdings:** archival material, periodicals. **Subjects:** Burmese cats. **Publications:** *United Burmese Cat Fanciers Newsletter*, quarterly. **Circulation:** 300. **Advertising:** accepted. **Conventions/Meetings:** periodic board meeting.

21472 ■ United Cat Federation (UCF)
c/o Georgann Chambers, Recorder
5510 Ptolemy Way
Mira Loma, CA 91752
Ph: (951)685-3252
E-mail: georgann@ragdoll.com
Contact: Georgann Chambers, Recorder
Founded: 1946. **Members:** 200. **Description:** Federation of cat clubs. Registers cats and kittens; promotes interests of breeders and exhibitors of cats; encourages improvement of the breeds of cats; promulgates rules for the management of cat shows; fosters the improvement of the welfare of cats in general. **Awards: Frequency:** annual. **Type:** recognition. **Recipient:** for the highest scoring cat of each breed and division. **Publications:** *UCF—Forts*, bimonthly. Newsletter. **Conventions/Meetings:** annual meeting - always July.

21473 ■ United Silver Fanciers (USF)
c/o Vicki Blandford, Sec./Membership Chair
1535 Northwold Dr.
Atlanta, GA 30350
Ph: (770)671-1121
E-mail: peerage@bellsouth.net
URL: http://www.unitedsilverfanciers.com
Contact: Vicki Blandford, Sec./Membership Chair
Founded: 1972. **Members:** 400. **Membership Dues:** individual, $45 (annual). **Multinational. Description:** Enthusiasts and breeders of Silver and Golden Persian and exotic short hair cats. Seeks to stimulate interest in the Silver Persian cat, which is distinguished by green eyes and long white hairs tipped with black. **Convention/Meeting:** none. **Affiliated With:** Cat Fanciers' Association. **Publications:** Newsletter, quarterly. Features cats and cat-related articles. **Price:** $40.00 in U.S.; $70.00 outside U.S. **Circulation:** 400.

Ceramics

21474 ■ Belleek Collectors' International Society (BCS)
PO Box 1498
Great Falls, VA 22066
Ph: (703)272-6270
Free: (800)BEL-LEEK
Fax: (703)272-6271
E-mail: info@belleek.com
URL: http://www.belleek.ie
Contact: Angela H. Moore, Contact
Founded: 1979. **Members:** 8,000. **Membership Dues:** individual, $43 (annual). **Staff:** 3. **Regional Groups:** 30. **Multinational. Description:** Collectors and persons interested in purchasing limited editions of pottery produced by Belleek Ireland, Inc. Maintains Belleek Collector's Hall of Fame and Belleek Museum. Conducts educational programs; conducts tours of the Belleek Pottery in Ireland. Sponsors international conventions. **Awards:** Belleek Hall of Fame. **Frequency:** annual. **Type:** recognition. **Recipient:** for members with outstanding contribution to the BCIS. **Computer Services:** Mailing lists, labels. **Formerly:** (1998) Belleek Collectors' Society. **Publications:** *The Belleek Collector*, 3/year. Magazine. **Conventions/Meetings:** biennial convention (exhibits) ● biennial tour.

21475 ■ CAS Collectors
2000 Wisconsin Ave. N
Golden Valley, MN 55427
E-mail: cascollect@aol.com
URL: http://www.cascollectors.com
Contact: Hank Kuhlmann, Pres.
Founded: 1994. **Members:** 250. **Membership Dues:** general, $25 (annual). **Description:** Collectors and admirers of ceramics produced by the Ceramics Arts Studio (CAS) of Madison, WI. Promotes increased awareness of the CAS and its products. Serves as a clearinghouse on CAS ceramics and activities; facilitates sale and trading of CAS products. Conducts educational programs; compiles statistics. **Libraries: Type:** reference; not open to the public. **Holdings:** articles, books. **Subjects:** Ceramics Arts Studio. **Additional Websites:** http://www.ceramicartsstudio.com. **Formerly:** (2004) Ceramic Arts Studio Collectors Association. **Publications:** *CAS Collectors Quarterly*. Newsletter. Contains information about Ceramic Arts Studio and CAS Collectors. **Price:** included in membership dues. **Advertising:** accepted ● Membership Directory. **Price:** included in membership dues. **Conventions/Meetings:** annual Collectors Convention - held in August.

21476 ■ Haviland Collectors International Foundation (HCIF)
PO Box 271383
Fort Collins, CO 80527
E-mail: haviland@aeroinc.net
URL: http://www.havilandcollectors.com
Contact: Paul Ohland, Corresponding Sec.
Founded: 1990. **Members:** 500. **Membership Dues:** individual, $40 (annual). **Description:** Owners and admirers of Haviland China objects. Promotes "the study of porcelain and pottery produced by the Haviland family in France and America". Facilitates communication and cooperation among members; serves as a clearinghouse on Haviland China; promotes China exhibits. **Awards: Frequency:** periodic. **Type:** scholarship. **Publications:** *Celebrating 150 Years of Haviland China, 1842-1992*. Book. **Price:** $19.95/copy, plus $2.50 postage ● *Charles Field Haviland: China Identification Guide*. Book. **Price:** $10.00 ● *Dining with Flowers: Haviland Porcelain from 1860 to 1910*. Book. **Price:** $15.00 plus $3.50 postage ● *Haviland Quarterly*. Newsletter. Contains informative articles. Alternate Formats: CD-ROM ● *Porcelain Theodore Haviland*. Book. Contains pictures of factory operations and workers. **Price:** $10.00. **Conventions/Meetings:** annual conference (exhibits) - 2008 June 12-15, Hartford, CT.

21477 ■ International Association of Duncan Certified Ceramic Teachers (IADCCT)
c/o Larry Knight, Pres.
1463 Sabra Rd.
Toledo, OH 43612
Ph: (419)476-7489
Fax: (419)476-7489
E-mail: info@iadcct.com
URL: http://www.iadcct.com
Contact: Larry Knight, Pres.
Founded: 1972. **Members:** 500. **Membership Dues:** individual, $25 (annual) ● couple, $40 (annual) ● youth (under 18 with parent member), $15 (annual). **Local Groups:** 17. **Multinational. Description:** Ceramics teachers interested in promoting ceramics as a hobby. Conducts educational courses. **Awards:** Cleo Curtis Award. **Frequency:** annual. **Type:** recognition. **Recipient:** for members. **Publications:** *International Association of Duncan Certified Ceramic Teachers Newsletter*, quarterly. Alternate Formats: online. **Conventions/Meetings:** periodic regional meeting ● seminar.

21478 ■ International Nippon Collectors Club (INCC)
c/o Dick Bittner
8 Geoley Ct.
Thurmont, MD 21788
E-mail: info@nipponcollectorsclub.com
URL: http://www.nipponcollectorsclub.com
Contact: Jennifer Cavedo, Contact
Founded: 1979. **Members:** 400. **Membership Dues:** in U.S. and Canada, $30 (annual) ● outside U.S. and Canada, $50 (annual). **Staff:** 10. **Regional Groups:** 11. **Multinational. Description:** Collectors of Nippon porcelain from 4 countries. (Nippon porcelain is hand-painted chinaware that was manufactured in Japan between 1891 and 1921, and is generally marked with the word Nippon, which is Japanese for Japan. It is distinctive from other porcelain in that its decorative glaze is placed on the clay body before the piece is fired.) Provides information on artifacts and collecting. Operates speakers' bureau. **Computer Services:** database ● mailing lists. **Publications:** *INCC Newsletter and Journal*, bimonthly. Contains color photographs of beautiful Nippon items, educational articles, profiles of fellow members and historical information on Nippon porcelain. **Price:** included in membership dues ● Membership Directory, annual. **Price:** included in membership dues ● Newsletter, bimonthly. Contains information on Chapter Club activities, auction results and many other informative articles. **Conventions/Meetings:** annual convention (exhibits).

21479 ■ Lladro Society (LS)
c/o Lladro Museum
43 W 57th St.
New York, NY 10019
Ph: (212)838-9356
Free: (800)785-3490
Fax: (212)758-1928
E-mail: newyork-museum@us.lladro.com
URL: http://www.lladro.com
Contact: Alain Viot, CEO/Managing Dir.
Founded: 1985. **Membership Dues:** new, $50 ● renewal, $35 (annual). **Staff:** 10. **Languages:** Dutch, English, French, Italian, Japanese, Spanish. **For-Profit. Description:** Collectors of Lladro porcelain figurines and decorative. Provides members with information on Lladro porcelains, including special interest stories, store locations, and road show exhibits. Maintains Lladro Museum and Gallery in New York City and Beverly Hills, CA. **Publications:** *Expressions* (in English and Spanish), quarterly. Magazine. Contains information on the production and availability of Lladro sculpture. **Price:** included in membership dues. **Advertising:** accepted.

21480 ■ Majolica International Society
1275 1st Ave.
PMB 103
New York, NY 10021
E-mail: secretary@majolicasociety.com
URL: http://www.majolicasociety.com
Contact: Gabrielle Ehrenthal, Pres.
Founded: 1989. **Members:** 450. **Membership Dues:** in U.S., $50 (annual) ● outside U.S., $65 (annual). **Regional Groups:** 4. **National Groups:** 5. **For-Profit. Description:** Promotes the study and appreciation of Victorian majolica and its historic and cultural relationship to ceramics. (Majolica is a type of 19th century pottery made with a brilliant lead glaze.) Provides a forum for the exchange of information among members and other groups interested in ceramic art. Sponsors educational programs. Conducts speakers' bureau. **Computer Services:** Mailing lists, of members. **Publications:** *Majolica International Society Newsletter: Majolica Matters*, quarterly. **Price:** free, for members only. **Circulation:** 450. **Advertising:** accepted. **Conventions/Meetings:** annual convention ● annual meeting and lecture, includes sale of majolica (exhibits).

21481 ■ M.I. Hummel Club (MIHC)
Goebel Plz.
PO Box 11
Pennington, NJ 08534-0011
Free: (800)666-2582
E-mail: memsrv@mihummel.com
URL: http://club.mihummel.com
Contact: Carrie Kulak, Club Mgr.
Founded: 1977. **Members:** 215,000. **Membership Dues:** individual, $50 (annual). **Staff:** 125. **Local Groups:** 110. **Description:** Collectors of M.I. Hummel figurines. Provides information about M.I. Hummel figurines and other products made by W. Goebel Porzellanfabrik in Germany; membership includes a free figurine and exclusive offers. **Formerly:** (1989) Goebel Collectors' Club. **Publications:** *Insights*, quarterly. Magazine. **Conventions/Meetings:** annual convention.

21482 ■ Old Sleepy Eye Collectors' Club of America (OSECCA)
1405 10th Ave. SE
Rochester, MN 55904-5369
Ph: (507)254-3024
E-mail: ose@oldsleepyeyecollectors.org
URL: http://www.oldsleepyeyecollectors.org
Contact: Dick Shoesmith, Pres.
Founded: 1976. **Members:** 1,050. **Membership Dues:** individual, $10 (annual). **Description:** Individuals interested in Old Sleepy Eye pottery and mill items. Old Sleepy Eye is a logotype of an Indian head profile that has been imprinted on various stoneware, pottery, and advertising items since the late 19th century. Fosters interest in and knowledge of Old Sleepy Eye. **Publications:** *Club Roster*, annual. Membership Directory ● Directory, annual. Included in newsletter. **Price:** free, for members only ● Newsletter, quarterly. **Price:** available to members only. **Advertising:** accepted. **Conventions/Meetings:** annual convention, auction, business meeting, room hopping and commemorative (exhibits) - late July or early August ● annual meeting and seminar (exhibits).

21483 ■ Phoenix Bird Collectors of America
1107 Deerfield Ln.
Marshall, MI 49068
Ph: (269)781-9791
E-mail: koates120@earthlink.net
Contact: Joan Collett Oates, Contact
Founded: 1976. **Members:** 75. **Membership Dues:** ordinary, $15 (annual). **Staff:** 1. **Description:** Collectors and admirers of Phoenix Bird chinaware. Promotes collection and preservation of Phoenix Bird products. Facilitates communication and cooperation among members; serves as a clearinghouse on Phoenix Bird China. **Libraries:** Type: open to the public. **Holdings:** 5. **Publications:** *Phoenix Bird Chinaware*. Book. **Price:** $15.00/copy for Book IV; $17.95/copy for Book V ● *Phoenix Bird Discoveries*, semiannual. Newsletter. **Price:** included in membership dues; $12.00 for nonmembers. **Conventions/Meetings:** periodic convention.

21484 ■ Society of Tobacco Jar Collectors (STJC)
1705 Chanticleer Dr.
Cherry Hill, NJ 08003
Ph: (856)489-8363
Fax: (856)489-8364
E-mail: agurst@aol.com
URL: http://www.tobaccojarsociety.com
Founded: 1992. **Members:** 200. **Membership Dues:** regular in U.S., $35 (annual) ● regular outside U.S., $40 (annual). **Description:** Collectors and admirers of antique tobacco jars. Promotes study and appreciation of tobacco jars and their manufacture, design, artistic merit, and history. Conducts educational programs; serves as a clearinghouse on antique tobacco jars. **Publications:** *Tobacco Jar Quarterly*. Newsletter. **Price:** included in membership dues. **Advertising:** accepted. Alternate Formats: CD-ROM; online ● *What Are Tobacco Jars?*. Brochure. **Conventions/Meetings:** annual convention - usually fall.

21485 ■ Tea Leaf Club International (TLCI)
960 Bryden Rd.
Columbus, OH 43205
Ph: (614)258-5258
Fax: (614)258-6663
E-mail: tealeafclubintl@cs.com
URL: http://www.tealeafclub.com
Contact: Mr. Dale Abrams, Dir.
Founded: 1980. **Members:** 700. **Membership Dues:** individual, $30 (annual) ● joint (in the same address), $30 (annual). **Regional Groups:** 11. **Description:** Collectors of Tea Leaf ironstone China and its variants. Works to research Tea Leaf ironstone China and to instruct and inform interested collectors. Holds auctions and conducts workshops and seminars for the exchange of information and display of rare and unusual pieces. **Libraries:** Type: reference. **Holdings:** 14; archival material, business records. **Subjects:** Tea Leaf ironstone China. **Awards:** Exceptional Service Award. **Frequency:** annual. **Type:** recognition. **Funds:** Tea Leaf Education Fund. **Publications:** *Tea Leaf Readings*, 5/year. Newsletter. **Price:** included in membership dues. **Conventions/Meetings:** annual meeting - always September.

21486 ■ Transferware Collectors Club (TCC)
734 Torreya Ct.
Palo Alto, CA 94303
E-mail: merlinbl@pacbell.net
URL: http://www.transcollectorsclub.org
Contact: David Hoexler, Pres.
Membership Dues: regular, in North America, $30 (annual) ● regular, outside North America, $40 (annual). **Description:** Serves as a forum for sharing of interests and information by collectors, dealers, scholars, and admirers of English transferware. **Publications:** *TCC Newsletter*, quarterly. Bulletin. Features articles concerning transferware, including new discoveries, visits to significant collections, and book reviews. **Conventions/Meetings:** annual meeting and lecture.

21487 ■ Wedgwood International Seminar (WIS)
c/o Mr. Michael R. Mitchell, Treas.
PO Box 674
Ontario, CA 91762-8674
E-mail: k.mcleod@utoronto.ca
URL: http://www.w-i-s.org
Contact: Mr. Michael R. Mitchell, Treas.
Founded: 1956. **Members:** 500. **Membership Dues:** couple, $50 (annual) ● single, $35 (annual) ● student, $20 (annual). **Description:** Serves Wedgwood collectors specializing in 18th-20th century Wedgwood ceramics and individuals interested in other English ceramics. (Wedgwood is fine earthenware, pearlware, stoneware, or bone china body created by English potter Josiah Wedgwood, 1730-95; Jasperware is a hard stoneware body typically tinted light or dark blue, although it may be yellow, black, red, terra-cotta, green or cream-colored, and bears small detailed classical figures in cameo relief applied in white). **Committees:** Scholarship. **Publications:** *WIS Proceedings*, annual. Book. Contains

transcripts of lectures delivered at the annual seminar. **Price:** included in membership dues; $25.00 for nonmembers. **Conventions/Meetings:** annual seminar (exhibits).

21488 ■ White Ironstone China Association (WICA)

c/o Diane Dorman
PO Box 855
Fairport, NY 14450-0855
E-mail: dieringer1@aol.com
URL: http://www.whiteironstonechina.com
Contact: Diane Dorman, Contact

Founded: 1994. **Members:** 600. **Membership Dues:** individual, joint (at same address), $30 (annual). **Budget:** $15,000. **Regional Groups:** 9. **State Groups:** 9. **Description:** Comprised of owners, collectors, and admirers of white ironstone china, which was first manufactured by Charles James Mason in Staffordshire, England in 1813. Promotes collection, preservation, and restoration of white ironstone china pieces. Serves as a clearinghouse on white ironstone china and its collection; facilitates exchange of information among members; conducts educational programs. **Committees:** Audit; Education. **Publications:** *White Ironstone Notes*, quarterly. Newsletter. **Price:** included in membership dues. **Advertising:** accepted ● Membership Directory, annual. **Price:** included in membership dues. **Conventions/Meetings:** periodic board meeting (exhibits) ● annual convention, with speakers, exhibitions, auction, sale, show and tell, tour, and other activities (exhibits) - first weekend of May ● periodic regional meeting.

Chess

21489 ■ All Service Postal Chess Club (ASPCC)

c/o Mr. Steven Ledford, Sr., Dir.
2 Skiff St., No. 303
Hamden, CT 06514
Ph: (203)287-0349
E-mail: steven.ledford@gmail.com
URL: http://hometown.aol.com/aspchask/Index.html
Contact: Mr. Steven Ledford Sr., Dir.

Founded: 1957. **Members:** 219. **Membership Dues:** regular, $15 (annual) ● regular, outside U.S. and other foreign, $25 (annual) ● regular, in Canada and Mexico, $18 (annual). **Staff:** 20. **Budget:** $2,500. **Description:** Individuals, civilian and military, united to promote postal chess activity in the U.S. Armed Services. Holds annual club championship, Hawver Cup Championship, and other chess tournaments. Participates in team matches with foreign clubs. Sponsors educational programs and e-mail tournaments. **Convention/Meeting:** none. **Computer Services:** Mailing lists. **Formerly:** (1987) USO-All Service Postal Chess Club. **Publications:** *King's Korner*, bimonthly. Newsletter. Includes new members listing, tournament news, and club ratings. **Price:** included in membership dues; $2.00/issue for nonmembers. **Circulation:** 225. **Advertising:** accepted ● Also publishes information sheet and rules.

21490 ■ American Chess Association (ACA)

3612 N Silver Sand Ct.
North Las Vegas, NV 89032-7688
E-mail: amchess@lvcm.com
URL: http://www.geocities.com/radale/aca/index.htm
Contact: Stan Vaughan, Dir.

Founded: 1857. **Members:** 85,000. **Membership Dues:** life, $1. **Staff:** 13. **State Groups:** 50. **Local Groups:** 2,000. **Description:** National governing body for chess in the U.S. Promotes chess play at all levels. Represents the U.S. within the World Chess Federation; maintains chess rankings; sponsors tournaments. **Libraries:** Type: not open to the public. **Holdings:** 10,000; books. **Subjects:** chess. **Awards:** U.S. Chess Championship. **Frequency:** annual. **Type:** recognition. **Recipient:** to national tournament winner. **Computer Services:** database, chess rankings. **Publications:** *American Chess Monthly*. Maga-

zine. **Price:** $20.00/year. **Conventions/Meetings:** annual convention.

21491 ■ American Postal Chess Tournaments (APCT)

PO Box 147
Western Springs, IL 60558-0147
Ph: (630)268-8287
E-mail: apct@aol.com
URL: http://correspondencechess.com/apct
Contact: James Warren, Ed.

Founded: 1967. **Members:** 500. **Membership Dues:** 1st class, $24 (annual). **Staff:** 2. **For-Profit. Description:** Conducts a variety of postal chess tournaments. Offers charitable program; compiles statistics. **Convention/Meeting:** none. **Libraries:** Type: reference. **Holdings:** archival material. **Awards:** Best Postal Chess Magazine. **Frequency:** annual. **Type:** recognition. **Recipient:** for magazine content and presentation. **Computer Services:** Online services, e-mail chess tournaments. **Publications:** *APCT News Bulletin*, bimonthly. Covers postal chess and e-mail chess. **Price:** $5.00/issue; $24.00/year. **Circulation:** 500. **Advertising:** accepted.

21492 ■ Chess Collectors International (CCI)

c/o Floyd Sarisohn, Membership Chm.
PO Box 166
Commack, NY 11725
Ph: (631)543-7667 (631)543-1330
Fax: (516)543-7901
E-mail: lichess@aol.com
URL: http://www.chesscollectors.com
Contact: Floyd Sarisohn, Membership Chm.

Founded: 1984. **Members:** 1,500. **Membership Dues:** regular, $50 (annual). **Description:** Collectors of chess sets and related items, members in 32 countries. Seeks to study and promote the art and history of chess sets and artifacts. Conducts research and disseminates information on chess art and history. Plans to award scholarships and prizes. Holds displays at libraries and museums. **Publications:** *Chess Collector*, 3/year. Newsletter. **Price:** available to members only. **Circulation:** 1,500. **Advertising:** accepted. **Conventions/Meetings:** biennial congress and seminar (exhibits) - usually May ● periodic meeting.

21493 ■ Chess in the Schools

520 8th Ave., 2nd Fl.
New York, NY 10018
Ph: (212)643-0225
Fax: (212)564-3083
E-mail: info@chessintheschools.org
URL: http://www.chessintheschools.org
Contact: Marley J. Kaplan, Pres./CEO

Founded: 1955. **Description:** Works to stimulate and enhance children's learning skills by teaching chess to kindergarten through 8th grade children in New York City public schools. **Awards:** Albert Brilliancy Prizes. **Frequency:** annual. **Type:** recognition. **Recipient:** for specific games ● Lerner Prize. **Frequency:** annual. **Type:** recognition. **Recipient:** for volunteers. **Formerly:** (1997) American Chess Foundation. **Publications:** *64 Squares*, 3/year. Newsletter. **Conventions/Meetings:** quarterly board meeting.

21494 ■ Correspondence Chess League of America (CCLA)

15 Crossbrook Pl.
Livingston, NJ 07039-3710
E-mail: herbhickman@comcast.net
URL: http://www.chessbymail.com
Contact: Mr. Herbert Hickman, Pres.

Founded: 1897. **Members:** 600. **Membership Dues:** individual, $25 (annual). **Description:** Persons interested in playing chess by mail. Members are rated according to playing strength. Sponsors Correspondence Chess Championship, Class Championship, Team Championship, and other tournaments. **Convention/Meeting:** none. **Awards:** Type: medal ● Type: monetary ● Type: recognition ● Type: trophy. **Publications:** *Chess Correspondent*, bimonthly. Magazine. Includes updates, progress reports, articles, annotated games, league ratings,

and tournaments results. **Price:** included in membership dues; $16.00/year for nonmembers in U.S.; $18.00/year for nonmembers outside U.S.; $7.50/year for libraries and institutions. ISSN: 0009-3327. **Circulation:** 1,000. **Advertising:** accepted.

21495 ■ United States Braille Chess Association (USBCA)

c/o Jay Leventhal, Sec.
111-20 76th Rd., Apt. 5L
Forest Hills, NY 11375-6451
Ph: (718)275-2209
E-mail: jleventhal@nyc.rr.com
URL: http://www.crisscrosstech.com/usbca
Contact: Jay Leventhal, Sec.

Founded: 1972. **Members:** 40. **Membership Dues:** regular, $15 (biennial). **Description:** Blind or legally blind chess players. Aims to encourage and popularize chess playing among the blind in the U.S. and abroad. Sponsors correspondence chess games, tournaments, and chess Olympic teams; has cosponsored, with the Lions Club (see separate entry), the U.S. Braille Chess Championship. **Computer Services:** Information services, library of chess materials ● mailing lists, of blind and visually impaired chess players. **Affiliated With:** Chess in the Schools. **Publications:** *Challenger*, biennial. Magazine. Contains results, scores and analyses of chess games. Includes general chess news, instructional articles on chess, and sources of chess books. **Price:** $12.00/year for members; $20.00 for 2 years, for members.

21496 ■ United States Chess Federation (USCF)

PO Box 3967
Crossville, TN 38557
Ph: (931)787-1234
Free: (800)903-8723
Fax: (931)787-1200
E-mail: feedback@uschess.org
URL: http://www.uschess.org
Contact: Mr. Bill Hall, Exec. Dir.

Founded: 1939. **Members:** 85,000. **Membership Dues:** adult, $41 (annual) ● senior, $36 (annual) ● youth, $19 (annual) ● scholastic, $17 (annual) ● young adult, $25 (annual) ● family (plan no. 1), $64 (annual) ● family (plan no. 2), $35 (annual). **Staff:** 39. **Budget:** $6,000,000. **State Groups:** 49. **Local Groups:** 2,369. **Description:** Governing body of United States chess players unit of the World Chess Federation. Conducts various scholastic tournaments and all championship events, including National Open, U.S. Championship, U.S. Junior, U.S. Open, and U.S. Women's. Sends teams abroad to compete in international events and maintains rating system for every U.S. Chess tournament. Works with affiliated groups to promote chess in schools, communities, the Armed Forces, and other organizations. Recommends and sells chess equipment and books. Charitable program. **Libraries:** Type: reference. **Holdings:** 12,000. **Subjects:** chess and related subjects. **Computer Services:** Mailing lists, of members. **Publications:** *Chess Life*, monthly. Magazine. Includes book reviews and chess analyses. **Price:** included in membership dues; $40.00/year for nonmembers. ISSN: 0197-260X. **Circulation:** 65,000. **Advertising:** accepted. Alternate Formats: microform. Also Cited As: *Chess Life and Review* ● *School Mates*, quarterly. Magazine. Includes profiles and chess analyses for juvenile chess players. **Price:** included in membership dues. ISSN: 1040-7707. **Circulation:** 30,000. **Advertising:** accepted ● *USCF Rating List*, bimonthly. Booklet. **Price:** included in membership dues. **Circulation:** 2,200.

Climbing

21497 ■ American Canyoneering Association (ACA)

PO Box 1208
Cedar City, UT 84721-1208

Ph: (435)590-8889
URL: http://www.canyoneering.net
Contact: Rich Carlson, Contact
Founded: 1999. **Membership Dues:** supporting, $15 (annual). **Description:** Promotes safety, responsibility and ethics in American canyoneering. Fosters constructive communication with the international canyoneering community. **Computer Services:** Information services, canyoneering resources ● online services, forum. **Publications:** Newsletter.

21498 ■ American Safe Climbing Association (ASCA)

PO Box 1814
Bishop, CA 93515
Ph: (650)843-1473
E-mail: greg@safeclimbing.org
URL: http://www.safeclimbing.org
Contact: Greg Barnes, Dir.
Founded: 1998. **Membership Dues:** supporter, $25 ● contributor, $50 ● advocate, $150 ● mentor, $1,000. **Description:** Seeks to replace unsafe anchors and reduce the visual and environmental impacts of climbing. Educates the public about climbing safety. **Computer Services:** Information services, bolting resources ● information services, climbing resources ● information services, safety resources.

Clowns

21499 ■ Clowns of America, International (COAI)

PO Box C
Richeyville, PA 15358-0532
Ph: (724)938-8765
Free: (888)522-5696
E-mail: coaibusinessmgr@aol.com
URL: http://www.coai.org
Contact: Shirley Long, Business Mgr.
Founded: 1968. **Members:** 6,500. **Membership Dues:** individual in U.S., senior outside U.S., $30 (annual) ● individual outside U.S., $35 (annual) ● senior in U.S., junior Joey, $25 (annual) ● life, $500. **Budget:** $90,000. **Local Groups:** 200. **Description:** Professional and amateur clowns, magicians, puppeteers, jugglers, and others who present a humorous program for the circus, radio, television, stage, and screen; friends of clowns and persons interested in clowning as a profession or hobby. Includes activities such as: training sessions, and entertaining in parades and shows. Provides entertainment for charitable organizations and events. Promotes first week of August as National Clown Week. **Libraries:** **Type:** reference. **Holdings:** 7; audio recordings, books, video recordings. **Subjects:** clown instruction in basic makeup, skit preparation, face painting. **Awards:** Best of the Press Award. **Frequency:** annual. **Type:** recognition. **Recipient:** for the best newsletter produced by a COIA alley in good standing ● Charlie Award. **Frequency:** annual. **Type:** trophy. **Recipient:** for the clown alley which best documents and celebrates International Clown Week ● Clown of the Year. **Frequency:** annual. **Type:** recognition. **Recipient:** to member who has outstanding qualities as a clown. **Computer Services:** Mailing lists. **Formerly:** (1984) Clowns of America. **Supersedes:** Clown Club of America. **Publications:** *The New Calliope* (in English and Spanish), bimonthly. Magazine. **Price:** included in membership dues. **Circulation:** 6,000. **Advertising:** accepted. **Conventions/Meetings:** annual competition and convention ● annual conference (exhibits).

21500 ■ International Shrine Clown Association (ISCA)

PO Box 102
Marine, IL 62061-0102
Ph: (618)887-4544
E-mail: hound4@apci.net
URL: http://www.shrineclowns.com
Contact: Bob Bassett, Sec.
Membership Dues: regular, $16 (annual). **Multinational. Description:** Promotes fun and entertainment for any occasion. Exchanges ideas, practices and

methods of operations for the betterment of all shrine clown units or clubs. Promotes acquaintance, friendship and fellowship among members. Supports the philanthropy of shrinedom through the Sneaker Fund. **Publications:** *Clown Alley*, bimonthly. Magazine. **Price:** included in membership dues; $16.00 /year for nonmembers. **Advertising:** accepted.

21501 ■ World Clown Association (WCA)

c/o Pat Lay Wilson, Admin.
PO Box 77236
Corona, CA 92877-0107
Free: (800)336-7922
Fax: (951)272-3979
E-mail: patlaywils@aol.com
URL: http://www.worldclownassociation.com
Contact: Phyllis Sheffield, Pres.
Founded: 1983. **Membership Dues:** regular, $27 (annual) ● retiree, junior, $21 (annual) ● family, $15 (annual) ● international, $33 (annual) ● life, $500. **Regional Groups:** 10. **Multinational. Description:** Focuses on educating members and fellow clowns in clown arts, particularly in areas of makeup, wardrobe, and variety skills of clowns. Encourages the spread of the art of clowning around the world. **Awards:** Alley of the Year. **Frequency:** annual. **Type:** recognition. **Recipient:** for a member Alley that sets the standards for other Alleys around the world ● Bo Dino Scholarships. **Frequency:** annual. **Type:** scholarship. **Recipient:** for members who attend clown education programs. **Computer Services:** Online services, kids coloring pages; eye games. **Committees:** Alley; Audits; Bo Dino Scholarship; Bylaws/Handbook; Convention; Elections; Insurance; Publications. **Publications:** *Alley*, quarterly. Newsletter. Alternate Formats: online ● *Clowning Around*, 8/year. Magazine. Alternate Formats: online ● Handbook. Alternate Formats: online.

Coins

21502 ■ National Token Collectors Association (NTCA)

c/o Clark Rohmer, Sec.
PO Box 281
Ormond Beach, FL 32175
URL: http://users.pullman.com/fjstevens/tokens/ntca.html
Contact: Clark Rohmer, Sec.
Membership Dues: regular, in U.S., $30 (annual) ● regular, in Canada, $40 (annual) ● regular, outside U.S. and Canada, $45 (annual). **Description:** Promotes the hobby of collecting merchant trade tokens. Disseminates information about tokens. Cultivates friendly relations among collectors, dealers, students and scholars. **Publications:** *Talkin' Tokens*, monthly. Newsletter. Includes articles about tokens, listings of tokens for sale and token shows. **Price:** for members.

Collectors

21503 ■ 52 Plus Joker

c/o Clarence Peterson, Sec.-Treas.
12290 W 18th Dr.
Lakewood, CO 80215
E-mail: denverpete@comcast.net
URL: http://www.52plusjoker.org
Contact: Clarence Peterson, Sec.-Treas.
Founded: 1985. **Members:** 500. **Membership Dues:** in U.S. and Canada, $20 (annual) ● outside U.S. and Canada, $30 (annual). **Description:** Collectors of antique or unusual playing cards and related material. Promotes antique card collecting; acts as a clearinghouse for the exchange of information on cards and deck collecting. Sponsors educational programs and auctions. **Libraries:** **Type:** reference. **Also Known As:** American Antique Playing Card Collector's Club. **Publications:** *Clear the Decks*, quarterly. Newsletter. Contains information on club activities and playing cards. **Price:** included in membership dues. **Circulation:** 500. **Advertising:** accepted. **Conventions/Meetings:** annual convention, includes auctions and educational sessions (exhibits).

21504 ■ Advertising Cup and Mug Collectors of America (ACMCA)

c/o Janie Turtle
Box 5706
Coralville, IA 52241
E-mail: e-mail@turlesministry.com
URL: http://www.turtlesministry.com
Contact: Janie Turtle, Contact
Founded: 1987. **Members:** 20. **Membership Dues:** $10 (annual). **Staff:** 1. **Budget:** $100. **Local Groups:** 1. **Description:** Collectors of advertising cups, mugs, and other drinking vessels. Promotes the collection of advertisement-bearing drinking vessels as a hobby. Facilitates communication and exchange of information among members; gathers and disseminates information on rare, collectible, and historic cups and mugs. Maintains speakers' bureau. **Libraries:** **Type:** reference. **Holdings:** articles, artwork, clippings. **Subjects:** collectible drinking vessels. **Computer Services:** database. **Publications:** *Cup Letter*, periodic. Newsletter. Updates on cup collecting and interviews with members. **Price:** $2.00 per issue. **Circulation:** 25. **Advertising:** accepted ● Also publishes I Love Christmas! for Christmas Enthusiasts; On the Fridge for Magnet Collectors Yard Sale! For Yard and Garage Sale Fans Nail-News & Information Letter for Editors.

21505 ■ Alice in Wonderland Collectors Network

2765 Shellingham Dr.
Lisle, IL 60532
Ph: (630)637-8530
E-mail: collectalice@comcast.net
URL: http://collectalice.home.comcast.net
Contact: Joel Birenbaum, Contact
Founded: 1985. **Members:** 50. **Description:** Provides a vehicle for collectors to help each other find Alice in Wonderland and Lewis Carroll items and exchange information on this subject. Supplies lists of items available for sale or trade by members. Disseminates information on new collectibles entering the market. **Convention/Meeting:** none. **Computer Services:** database, Alice in Wonderland books in all languages.

21506 ■ American Bell Association International (ABAII)

7210 Bellbrook Dr.
San Antonio, TX 78227-1002
E-mail: coordinator@americanbell.org
URL: http://www.americanbell.org
Founded: 1940. **Members:** 1,500. **Membership Dues:** single, $35 (annual). **Regional Groups:** 51. **Multinational. Description:** Bell collectors, enthusiasts, ringers, antique dealers, and bell dealers. Maintains historical files; makes available scholarships in bell studies. **Publications:** *Bell Tower*, bimonthly. Magazine. **Price:** included in membership dues. **Advertising:** accepted ● Directory, every 3-4 years. **Conventions/Meetings:** annual international conference (exhibits) - always last week in June.

21507 ■ American Collectors of Infant Feeders (ACIF)

c/o Shirley Hickman, Corresponding Sec.
18 Fountain Lake Ln.
Buffalo, MO 65622
E-mail: hickman@centurytel.net
URL: http://www.acif.org
Contact: Shirley Hickman, Corresponding Sec.
Founded: 1973. **Members:** 220. **Membership Dues:** individual, $30 (annual). **Multinational. Description:** Studies the history of infant feeding devices from early pottery feeding vessels through glass nursers of the 1950s to plastic nursers of the 1980s. Includes glass, tin, pewter, porcelain, and silver bottles, pap boats, medicine spoons, and other related feeding items. **Publications:** *A Guide to American Nursing Bottles*. Book. **Price:** $30.00 for members; $35.00 for nonmembers ● *Keeping Abreast*, quarterly. Newsletter. **Price:** included in membership dues. **Conventions/Meetings:** annual convention.

21508 ■ American Fish Decoy Association (AFDA)
624 Merritt St.
PO Box 250
Fife Lake, MI 49633
Ph: (231)879-3912
Contact: John E. Shoffner, Dir.
Founded: 1990. **Members:** 170. **Membership Dues:** $25 (annual). **For-Profit. Description:** Collectors and enthusiasts of fish decoys and lures. Promotes the hobbies of fish decoy collecting and fishing. Disseminates historical and current information on fishing decoys. **Libraries: Type:** reference. **Holdings:** artwork. **Publications:** *American Fish Decoy Forum*, quarterly. Newsletter. **Price:** included in membership dues. **Circulation:** 170. **Conventions/Meetings:** semiannual Fish Decoy Show - meeting, features fish decoys and sporting collectibles (exhibits) - always April and October.

21509 ■ American Hatpin Society
c/o Cathy Miller, VP
2505 Indian Creek Rd.
Diamond Bar, CA 91765-3307
E-mail: info@americanhatpinsociety.com
URL: http://americanhatpinsociety.com
Contact: Jodi Lenocker, Pres.
Founded: 1989. **Members:** 245. **Membership Dues:** ordinary, $40 (annual). **Staff:** 7. **Local Groups:** 1. **Multinational. Description:** Collectors of hatpins. Promotes collection, preservation, and restoration of hatpins and related fashion accessories. Serves as a clearinghouse on hatpins and their history; facilitates exchange of information among members; conducts educational programs. **Computer Services:** Mailing lists, of members. **Publications:** Newsletter, quarterly. **Price:** included in membership dues. **Conventions/Meetings:** quarterly regional meeting - always second Saturday of January, April, July, and October.

21510 ■ American Lock Collectors Association (ALCA)
8576 Barbara Dr.
Mentor, OH 44060
Ph: (440)257-2346
E-mail: admin@alca-online.org
Contact: Robert W. Dix, Pres.
Founded: 1970. **Members:** 375. **Membership Dues:** regular, in U.S., $18 (annual) ● regular, in Canada, $22 (annual) ● regular, outside U.S. and Canada, $30 (annual). **Staff:** 3. **Description:** Represents collectors of old locks, handcuffs, keys, and safes. **Publications:** *Journal of Lock Collecting*, bimonthly. Includes calendar of events. **Price:** $16.00/year in U.S.; $20.00/year in Canada; $30.00/year outside U.S. and Canada. **Advertising:** accepted. Alternate Formats: CD-ROM. **Conventions/Meetings:** annual show, with padlock displays, locks bought, sold, and traded (exhibits).

21511 ■ American Matchcover Collecting Club
PO Box 18481
Asheville, NC 28814-0481
Ph: (828)254-4487
Fax: (828)254-4487
E-mail: bill@matchcovers.com
URL: http://www.matchcovers.com
Contact: Bill Retskin, Ed.
Founded: 1986. **Members:** 250. **Membership Dues:** regular, $10 (quarterly). **Staff:** 2. **Description:** Collectors of matchcovers, matchboxes, ephemera, specialty items, and labels. Promotes matchcover collecting to preserve the history of the hobby and the match industry. Compiles statistics. **Libraries: Type:** reference. **Holdings:** archival material, artwork. **Awards:** Best Older Matchcover Display. **Frequency:** 3/year. **Type:** recognition. **Recipient:** for owner of a Matchcover's outstanding condition, age, uniqueness and scarcity. **Computer Services:** database, for members only ● mailing lists, for members only. **Formerly:** American Matchcover Collecting Club; (1992) Front Striker Bulletin. **Publications:** *The Front Striker Bulletin*, quarterly. ISSN: 1041-1852. **Advertising:** accepted. Alternate Formats: online ●

The Matchcover Collector's Price Guide, 2nd Ed.. Book. **Price:** $25.20. **Advertising:** accepted.

21512 ■ American Pencil Collectors Society (APCS)
c/o Andrew L. Westberg, Pres.
916 Wall St.
North Mankato, MN 56003
Ph: (507)344-0643
E-mail: president@pencilcollector.org
URL: http://www.pencilcollector.org
Contact: Andrew L. Westberg, Pres.
Founded: 1958. **Members:** 280. **Membership Dues:** individual, $10 (annual). **Description:** Hobbyists interested in collecting writing instruments of all kinds. **Computer Services:** database, of active members; used to generate mailing labels, track payment of dues. **Publications:** *The Pencil Collector*, bimonthly. **Advertising:** accepted ● Membership Directory, biennial. Lists of active members by member number and by state of residence. **Price:** free to active members. **Conventions/Meetings:** biennial convention, displays of writing instruments; buying, selling, and trading; election of officers, usually an auction (exhibits).

21513 ■ American Society of Bookplate Collectors and Designers (ASBC&D)
PO Box 380340
Cambridge, MA 02238-0340
Ph: (781)393-9970
Free: (800)608-3828
Fax: (781)393-9972
E-mail: exlibrisusa@hotmail.com
URL: http://www.bookplate.org
Contact: James P. Keenan, Dir.
Founded: 1922. **Members:** 250. **Membership Dues:** individual, $85 (annual). **Multinational. Description:** Collectors and designers of bookplates, including etchers, metal and wood engravers, and wood and linoleum cutters; membership is limited; "many of the world's finest contemporary book illustrators are featured in the ASBC&D publications." Collaborates with public and private libraries in sponsoring exhibitions of bookplates. Makes periodic additions to collection of bookplate books and prints that the society presented to the Library of Congress in 1923. **Publications:** *Contemporary World Ex Libris*, periodic. Catalog. Contains 500 illustrations for travelling exhibition. **Price:** $12.00 ● *Ex Libris Chronicle: The International Collector*, quarterly. Newsletter. Includes membership list. **Price:** $50.00/year. **Circulation:** 400. **Advertising:** accepted ● Yearbook, annual. Limited edition. **Price:** $50.00. **Conventions/Meetings:** biennial International Ex Libris Congress - meeting, world conference of more than 50 nations (exhibits) - usually first week in September or last week of August.

21514 ■ American Spoon Collectors (ASC)
PO Box 243
Rhinecliff, NY 12574
Ph: (845)876-0303
Fax: (845)876-2037
E-mail: campania@hvc.rr.com
URL: http://www.campanian.org/americanspoon.html
Contact: Robert M. Wilhelm, Ed.
Founded: 1974. **Members:** 500. **Membership Dues:** regular, $20 (annual). **Staff:** 2. **Regional Groups:** 4. **Multinational. Description:** Represents collectors of antique and modern souvenir spoons who share their interest through meetings on local, regional, national, and international levels. **Libraries: Type:** reference. **Holdings:** 10; articles, books. **Subjects:** souvenir spoons, souvenir spoon collecting. **Awards: Type:** recognition. **Formed by Merger of:** (1980) Southern California Souvenir Spoon Collectors Society; Souvenir Spoon Collectors of America. **Publications:** *Spooners Forum*, monthly. Newsletter. Contains editorials, historical, art, patent articles, and computer column. **Price:** $20.00/year in U.S.; $28.00/year in Canada; $40.00/year for airmail outside U.S. and Canada; $3.00 each. **Circulation:** 500. **Conventions/Meetings:** competition ● annual conference (exhibits).

21515 ■ Anheuser-Busch Collectors Club
c/o Steinland Gifts and Collectibles
14 N 679 Rte. 25, Ste.A
East Dundee, IL 60118
Ph: (847)428-3150 (847)428-3154
Free: (800)498-3215
Fax: (847)428-3170
E-mail: steinland@aol.com
URL: http://www.steinland.com/collectors_club.htm
Membership Dues: regular, $40 (annual). **Description:** Represents collectors of Anheuser-Busch collectibles. **Publications:** *First Draft*. Magazine. **Price:** included in membership dues ● *Official Club Binder*. Magazine. Contains facts about steins and Anheuser-Busch. **Price:** included in membership dues.

21516 ■ Antique and Art Glass Salt Shaker Collectors Society (AAGSSCS)
c/o Maralyn Ridgway, Membership Chair
116 Lisa Ct.
Weirton, WV 26062-9661
E-mail: caroleandbob@cbantiques.com
URL: http://www.antiquesaltshakers.com
Contact: Brian Calkins, VP
Founded: 1983. **Members:** 220. **Membership Dues:** single, two-member family, $20 (annual). **Description:** Collectors of Victorian and art salt shakers. Encourages communication among members and provides for the exchange of information. **Formerly:** (1987) Salt Shaker Collectors Club. **Publications:** *The Pioneer*, quarterly. Newsletter. Covers association and industry news. **Price:** included in membership dues. **Advertising:** accepted. Also Cited As: *Salt Shaker Collectors Newsletter* ● *Roster of Members*, annual. Membership Directory. **Conventions/Meetings:** annual conference (exhibits) - always last full weekend of July.

21517 ■ Antique Barbed Wire Society (ABWS)
4423 Loveland Dr.
Kearney, NE 68845
E-mail: gman204b@charter.net
URL: http://www.antiquebarbedwiresociety.com
Membership Dues: domestic, $20 (annual) ● international, $30 (annual). **Multinational. Description:** Promotes the hobby of collecting, preserving, exhibiting and interpreting the historical heritage of barbed wire and other related items. Establishes a means of worldwide compilation and storage of permanent records, files, pictures, patent data and all associated information for future referencing through the Internet and advanced technology. **Computer Services:** Information services, barbed wire resources. **Publications:** *The Barbed Wire Collector*, bimonthly. Magazine. Informs interested individuals about the many aspects of barbed wires and related items. **Price:** $4.00 each. **Advertising:** accepted.

21518 ■ Antique Comb Collectors Club International (ACCCI)
73 Manassas Pl.
Laurel Springs, NJ 08021-2822
E-mail: comber@iserv.net
URL: http://www.geocities.com/Heartland/Pointe/5350
Contact: Darcy Ysseldyke, Treas.
Founded: 1993. **Members:** 110. **Membership Dues:** family/group, $27 (annual). **Staff:** 9. **Budget:** $1,500. **Languages:** English, French. **For-Profit. Multinational. Description:** Freelance collectors who wear, sell, study, and display antique and ancient decorations for the hair. Seeks to conduct research and share information about antique ornamental head accessories and to unite people with similar interests. Gathers oral and written histories from collectors; studies the manufacturing techniques, preservation of materials, styles, dating cultures, and care of these ornaments. Maintains speakers' bureau. Presents programs upon request. **Formerly:** (1998) Antique Comb Collectors Club. **Publications:** *Antique Comb Collector*, bimonthly. Newsletter. Contains historical, care, display, conservation, patent, and marketing information, research reports, and member profiles. **Price:** included in membership dues; $2.25 with S.A. S.E. for sample. ISSN: 0892-7162. **Advertising:** ac-

cepted ● *Dating Made Easy.* Handbook ● *Hair Combs.* Brochure. **Conventions/Meetings:** biennial conference and convention (exhibits) - usually spring.

21519 ■ Antique Doorknob Collectors of America (ADCA)

PO Box 31
Chatham, NJ 07928-0031
Ph: (973)635-6338
E-mail: antiquedoorknobs@comcast.net
URL: http://www.antiquedoorknobs.org
Contact: Rich Kennedy, Sec.
Founded: 1981. **Members:** 300. **Membership Dues:** regular, in U.S., $25 (annual) ● regular, in Canada, Mexico, Caribbean, $27 (annual) ● international, $32 (annual). **Staff:** 2. **Description:** Promotes the study and preservation of ornamental hardware. **Libraries: Type:** reference. **Holdings:** 300; archival material, books, periodicals. **Subjects:** hardware. **Telecommunication Services:** electronic mail, bwk@discoverys.net. **Affiliated With:** Lock Museum of America. **Publications:** *The Doorknob Collector,* bimonthly. Newsletter. Contains historical articles and calendar of events. **Price:** $25.00 /year for nonmembers; included in membership dues. **Circulation:** 300. **Advertising:** accepted. **Conventions/Meetings:** annual convention and workshop, includes auctions (exhibits) ● annual meeting and seminar (exhibits).

21520 ■ Association of Coffee Mill Enthusiasts (ACME)

c/o Robert P. Palmer, Treas.
PO Box 86
Olivet, MI 49076-0086
E-mail: rpalmer@ia4u.net
URL: http://www.millmania.com/index.html
Contact: Robert P. Palmer, Treas.
Founded: 1994. **Members:** 275. **Membership Dues:** regular, in U.S., $40 (annual) ● regular, outside U.S. and Canada, $50 (annual). **Staff:** 4. **Budget:** $10,000. **Languages:** English, French. **Description:** Collectors and admirers of antique coffee mills. Promotes and facilitates collection of coffee mills. Gathers and disseminates information about coffee mills, their provenance, and value. Serves as a forum for exchange of information among members. Conducts research programs. **Publications:** *Grinder Finder,* quarterly. Newsletter. Features a publication discussing coffee mills and their history. **Price:** included in membership dues; $2.50/copy of back issues. **Circulation:** 275. **Advertising:** accepted. **Conventions/Meetings:** annual convention.

21521 ■ Association of Collecting Clubs (ACC)

18222 Flower Hill Way, No. 299
Gaithersburg, MD 20879
Ph: (301)926-8663
E-mail: info@collectors.org
URL: http://collectors.org/acc/about_acc.asp
Contact: Larry L. Krug, Pres.
Founded: 2002. **Membership Dues:** club, $25 (annual). **Description:** Offers support and represents collectors. **Publications:** Newsletter. Features news about collecting clubs and their activities, collecting issues and coverage of projects and events. Alternate Formats: online.

21522 ■ Bead Society of Los Angeles (BS)

PO Box 241874
Los Angeles, CA 90024-9674
E-mail: info@beadsocietyla.org
URL: http://www.beadsocietyla.org
Contact: Adel Boehm-Mabe, Pres.
Founded: 1975. **Members:** 250. **Membership Dues:** regular, $40 (annual) ● two at same address, $60 (annual). **Staff:** 8. **Budget:** $17,000. **Description:** Bead collectors and others interested in old, new, ethnic, and contemporary beads and jewelry. Aims to study and disseminate information on beads. Sponsors research programs; conducts study groups. **Awards: Frequency:** annual. **Type:** grant. **Recipient:** for research. **Committees:** Bazaar; Newsletter. **Formerly:** (2000) The Bead Society. **Publications:** *Bead Society Newsletter,* quarterly. Includes membership activities information and articles on beads and

related subjects. **Price:** included in membership dues. **Circulation:** 300. **Conventions/Meetings:** semiannual Bead Society Bazaar - meeting (exhibits) - usually April and October ● monthly lecture ● semiannual workshop.

21523 ■ Betty Boop International Collectible Club (BBICC)

534 N Montebello Blvd.
Montebello, CA 90640
Ph: (323)728-2728
Fax: (323)722-1313
E-mail: bettyboopcollectorsclub@msn.com
Contact: Denise Hagopian, Contact
Founded: 1997. **Members:** 2,700. **Membership Dues:** in U.S., $25 (annual) ● outside U.S., $50 (annual) ● manufacturer, $200 (annual). **Staff:** 5. **Budget:** $20,000. **Regional Groups:** 2. **Local Groups:** 1. **Languages:** English, Spanish. **Description:** Collectors and manufacturers of collectible items related to Betty Boop, a cartoon character originated in the 1920s. Promotes appreciation of Betty Boop cartoons; seeks to facilitate the trade in Betty Boop collectibles. Conducts research to establish secondary market values of Betty Boop collectibles; documents creation and production of new Betty Boop artwork and collectibles; conducts social activities. **Libraries: Type:** by appointment only; not open to the public. **Holdings:** 2,000; archival material, articles, artwork, audio recordings, books, video recordings. **Subjects:** Betty Boop. **Awards:** Baby Betty Boop Look-A-Like Contest. **Frequency:** annual. **Type:** recognition. **Recipient:** for newborns to children age 5; biggest eyes, best looks, original costume. **Telecommunication Services:** electronic mail, bettyboopfestival@msn.com. **Publications:** *Betty Boop News,* quarterly. Newsletter. **Price:** $25.00/yr. **Circulation:** 300. **Advertising:** accepted. Alternate Formats: CD-ROM. **Conventions/Meetings:** annual Antique Swap Meet, includes 1930s and vintage Betty Boop - usually July ● annual Betty Boop Collector's Festival, with booths, baby contest, tattoo contest, display antique items, collector's club social (exhibits) - always third weekend in July ● annual Holiday Meeting and Demonstration - last Sunday in November ● Meeting and Champagne Brunch - lecture - always mid-March.

21524 ■ Beyond the Pond.International Frog Collectors Club

PO Box 201413
Bloomington, MN 55420
E-mail: lmfroglady@mn.rr.com
URL: http://frogcollectors.com
Contact: Linda Maher, Ed.
Founded: 1985. **Members:** 200. **Membership Dues:** individual, $20 (annual) ● foreign individual, $25 (annual). **Staff:** 3. **Description:** Collectors of objects depicting frogs, such as figurines, toys, and jewelry. Serves as a forum for contact among collectors worldwide; encourages collecting. Spreads the word of frog related events. **Awards:** Featured Collector Award. **Frequency:** quarterly. **Type:** recognition. **Formerly:** (2002) Frog Pond - Frog Collectors Club. **Publications:** *Beyond the Pond. . .,* quarterly. Newsletter. Includes articles on different species of frogs and toads and collecting frog and toad-related items. **Price:** $20.00 in U.S.; $25.00 outside U.S.; $5.00 for sample issue. **Circulation:** 400. **Advertising:** accepted. **Conventions/Meetings:** annual convention, gathering of frog collectors for fellowship and entertainment, education.

21525 ■ Big Little Book Collector's Club (BLBC)

PO Box 1242
Danville, CA 94526
Ph: (925)837-2086
E-mail: larry@biglittlebooks.com
URL: http://www.biglittlebooks.com
Contact: Lawrence F. Lowery, Pres.
Founded: 1982. **Members:** 1,300. **Membership Dues:** individual in U.S., $15 (annual) ● individual in Canada, $18 (annual) ● individual outside U.S. and Canada, $21 (annual). **Staff:** 2. **Description:** Collectors, dealers, and enthusiasts of the Big Little Books

series. Provides a communication network to bring together collectors and dealers of Big Little Books. **Libraries: Type:** not open to the public. **Holdings:** periodicals. **Formerly:** (2003) Big Little Book Collector's Club of America. **Publications:** *Big Little Times,* bimonthly. Newsletter. **Price:** included in membership dues; $3.00 for nonmembers in U.S.; $4.00 for nonmembers in Canada; $5.00 for nonmembers outside U.S. and Canada. **Circulation:** 900. **Advertising:** accepted ● *Collector's Guide to Big Little and Similar Books.* **Price:** $12.95 ● *The Golden Age of Big Little Books - 1932-1938.* Contains complete history and listing. **Price:** $150.00. **Conventions/Meetings:** annual meeting, toys and paper collectibles (exhibits) - always 3rd weekend of July in San Jose, CA ● annual meeting - always October.

21526 ■ Brewery Collectibles Club of America (BCCA)

747 Merus Ct.
Fenton, MO 63026-2092
Ph: (636)343-6486
Fax: (636)343-6436
E-mail: bcca@bcca.com
URL: http://www.bcca.com
Contact: Mike England, Pres.
Founded: 1970. **Members:** 4,000. **Membership Dues:** regular, $30 (annual). **Staff:** 2. **National Groups:** 110. **Languages:** English, French, Italian, Japanese, Portuguese, Spanish. **Description:** Represents individuals of all ages and interests who collect beer cans and related items. Maintains hall of fame. **Libraries: Type:** reference. **Holdings:** 200. **Awards:** Can of the Year. **Frequency:** annual. **Type:** recognition. **Recipient:** for the best designed beer can currently on the market produced in the U.S. and abroad. **Formerly:** (2005) Beer Can Collectors of America. **Publications:** *American Beer Cans 1975-1988.* Book ● *News Report,* bimonthly. **Advertising:** accepted ● *Roster of Members,* annual. Membership Directory ● Catalog. Includes all known beer cans (U.S. and foreign). **Conventions/Meetings:** annual CANvention - meeting - always September.

21527 ■ Brewster Kaleidoscope Society (BKS)

PO Box 95
Damascus, MD 20872
Ph: (706)348-6950
Fax: (706)348-6951
E-mail: admin@brewstersociety.com
URL: http://www.brewstersociety.com
Contact: Sherry Moser, Dir.
Founded: 1986. **Members:** 700. **Membership Dues:** individual, $45 (annual) ● regular, outside U.S., $50 (annual). **Staff:** 4. **For-Profit. Description:** Designers, collectors, and sellers of kaleidoscopes. Promotes interest in kaleidoscopes and fosters interaction among members. Maintains private museum. **Awards:** Brewster Award for Creative Ingenuity. **Frequency:** periodic. **Type:** recognition. **Recipient:** for creative ingenuity ● People's Choice Awards. **Frequency:** annual. **Type:** recognition. **Recipient:** for the 3 top favorites. **Publications:** *Brewster News Scope,* quarterly. Newsletter. Includes calendar of events, new designs and information on antique kaleidoscopes. **Price:** included in membership dues. **Circulation:** 500. **Advertising:** accepted. Alternate Formats: online. **Conventions/Meetings:** annual convention (exhibits).

21528 ■ Butter Pat Patter Association

c/o Mary Dessoie, Founder
265 Eagle Bend Dr.
Bigfork, MT 59911-6235
URL: http://www.antiqueweb.com/articles/butter-pats4.html
Contact: Mary Dessoie, Founder
Founded: 1997. **Description:** Promotes butter pat miniature plate fine china, used to hold individual portions of butter. **Publications:** *The Patter,* monthly. Newsletter. **Advertising:** accepted.

21529 ■ Cabbage Patch Kids Collectors Club

c/o BabyLand General Hospital
PO Box 714
Cleveland, GA 30528

Ph: (706)865-2171
Fax: (706)219-3148
E-mail: sales@cabbagepatchkids.com
URL: http://www.cabbagepatchkids.com/pages/collectors_club/collectors_club.html
Founded: 1978. **Description:** Represents collectors of Cabbage Patch Kids dolls, created by Xavier Roberts. **Publications:** *BabyLand In General.* Newsletter. **Price:** included in membership dues.

21530 ■ Call and Whistle Collectors Association (CWCA)
c/o James C. Fitch
2839 E 26th Pl.
Tulsa, OK 74114
Ph: (918)747-3202
E-mail: jchesterf@aol.com
URL: http://members.aol.com/jchesterf
Contact: James C. Fitch, Contact

Founded: 1996. **Members:** 55. **Membership Dues:** regular, in U.S., $20 (annual) ● regular, outside U.S. and Canada, $25 (annual). **Description:** Collectors of antique bird calls and whistles. Promotes collection, preservation, and restoration of antique calls and whistles. Facilitates communication among members; serves as a clearinghouse on antique bird calls and whistles. **Publications:** *Whistle Notes*, quarterly. Newsletter. **Advertising:** accepted. **Conventions/Meetings:** annual convention.

21531 ■ Callmakers and Collectors Association of America
c/o William R. Bailey, Membership Chm.
137 Kingswood Dr.
Clarksville, TN 37043
Ph: (931)647-0902 (813)310-8875
E-mail: jameshbjr@aol.com
URL: http://ccaacalls.org
Contact: James Bennett, Pres.

Founded: 1987. **Members:** 500. **Membership Dues:** regular, $25 (annual). **Description:** Promotes interest in and exchange information about the American folk art of calling, both games and duck and goose calls. **Publications:** Newsletter, quarterly. **Advertising:** accepted. **Conventions/Meetings:** meeting ● quarterly Swap Meets.

21532 ■ Canadian Corkscrew Collectors Club (CCCC)
c/o Milt Becker
One Madison St., 5B
East Rutherford, NJ 07073
Ph: (973)773-9224
E-mail: ccccdues@aol.com
URL: http://www.corkscrewnet.com/CCCC.htm
Contact: Milt Becker, Contact

Founded: 1981. **Membership Dues:** general, $30 (annual). **Multinational. Description:** Represents the interests of corkscrew collectors. Promotes the hobby of corkscrew collection. **Publications:** *Quarterly Worme.* Newsletter. **Price:** included in membership dues ● Membership Directory.

21533 ■ Candy Container Collectors of America
c/o Jim Olean, Membership Chm./Treas.
115 MacBeth Dr.
Lower Burrell, PA 15068-2628
E-mail: lost_in_candyland2004@yahoo.com
URL: http://www.candycontainer.org
Contact: Jim Olean, Membership Chm./Treas.

Founded: 1984. **Members:** 400. **Membership Dues:** family, $25 (annual). **Multinational. Description:** Represents collectors of old glass candy container toys. **Publications:** *The Candy Gram*, quarterly. Newsletter. Contains articles and letters from members and includes a section for buying and selling candy containers. **Price:** included in membership dues. Alternate Formats: online. **Conventions/Meetings:** annual convention - usually last week of June.

21534 ■ Carriage Association of America (CAA)
3625 Amick Way
Lexington, KY 40509
Ph: (859)231-0971 (856)935-1616
Fax: (859)231-0973
E-mail: info@caaonline.com
URL: http://www.caaonline.com
Contact: Jerry Rider, Pres.

Founded: 1960. **Members:** 3,500. **Membership Dues:** regular, $55 (annual) ● regular, $100 (biennial) ● regular, $145 (triennial) ● life, $750. **Staff:** 2. **Budget:** $200,000. **Regional Groups:** 12. **Description:** Collectors, restorers, historians, and users of horse-drawn vehicles. Sponsors clinic on driving, harnessing, and restoration. **Libraries: Type:** reference. **Holdings:** 1,500; books, periodicals. **Subjects:** carriages, driving, restoration, horses. **Computer Services:** database ● mailing lists. **Publications:** *Carriage Journal*, quarterly. **Advertising:** accepted ● *Membership Roster*, annual. Membership Directory ● *The New Hub*, monthly. Newsletter. **Advertising:** accepted. **Conventions/Meetings:** annual conference, with auction (exhibits).

21535 ■ Cash Registers Collectors Club of America (CRCCA)
PO Box 20534
Dayton, OH 45420-0534
URL: http://members.aol.com/ergofred/ncr/info/club.htm

Membership Dues: regular, $20 (annual). **Description:** Fosters an interest in preservation and collecting of antique cash registers. **Publications:** *Bronze Idol*, quarterly. Newsletter. **Price:** included in membership dues. **Conventions/Meetings:** semiannual meeting.

21536 ■ Casino Chip and Gaming Token Collectors Club (CC&GTCC)
c/o Ralph Myers, Membership Off.
PO Box 35769
Las Vegas, NV 89133-5769
Free: (877)4CC-GTCC
E-mail: membership@ccgtcc.com
URL: http://www.ccgtcc.com
Contact: Ralph Myers, Membership Off.

Founded: 1988. **Members:** 2,500. **Membership Dues:** individual, $30 (annual) ● associate, $5 (annual) ● outside U.S., $55 (annual). **Staff:** 6. **Budget:** $100,000. **Local Groups:** 1. **Description:** Member club of the American Numismatic Association. Collectors of casino gaming chips and tokens. Coordinates the exchange of information regarding gaming chips and tokens and the casinos where they are used. Conducts educational programs and competitions. **Libraries: Type:** not open to the public. **Holdings:** 100; articles, books, video recordings. **Subjects:** casino collectibles. **Awards:** Best Article. **Frequency:** annual. **Type:** recognition. **Recipient:** for best magazine article selected by editor of quarterly publication ● Chip of the Year. **Frequency:** annual. **Type:** recognition ● Convention Chip Design Contest. **Frequency:** annual. **Type:** monetary. **Recipient:** for individual selected by committee ● Convention Design Contest. **Frequency:** annual. **Type:** monetary ● Token of the Year. **Frequency:** annual. **Type:** recognition ● Top Recruiter. **Frequency:** annual. **Type:** recognition. **Recipient:** for individual who has recruited the most number of new club members. **Computer Services:** Mailing lists, of members. **Committees:** Auction; Convention Medal/Chip Design Contest; Election; Hall of Fame; Standards and Grading. **Publications:** *Casino Chips and Gaming Tokens News*, quarterly. Magazine. Reports casino openings and closings and chip, token, auction and collectibles show information; contains classified. **Price:** included in membership dues. **Circulation:** 2,000. **Advertising:** accepted. Also Cited As: *CCTN* ● *Club Directory*, periodic. Membership Directory ● Auctions catalog in conjunction with the annual Las Vegas Conventions. **Conventions/Meetings:** annual Casino Collectibles Show and Convention - convention and show (exhibits).

21537 ■ Cat Collectors (CC)
PO Box 2738
Parker, CO 80134
Ph: (303)805-5884
E-mail: catcollectors@earthlink.net
URL: http://www.catcollectors.com
Contact: Marilyn Dipboye, Pres.

Founded: 1982. **Members:** 1,000. **Membership Dues:** regular, in U.S., $20 (annual) ● regular, in Canada, $27 (annual) ● regular, outside U.S. and Canada, $36 (annual). **For-Profit. Description:** Individuals who collect cat memorabilia. Seeks to inform members of markets for contemporary and antique cat collectible items; to keep informed of museum cat collections and exhibits; to learn about authors and artists who specialize in cats; to facilitate the purchase, trade, and selling of cat items; and to review cat books. Conducts programs to assist humane organizations and programs. Researches collectible items and provides appraisals to the public for a fee and to members free of charge. Sponsors raffles and auctions for charity. **Publications:** *Cat Collectors Catalogue*, bimonthly. Includes notices of new and antique cat items for sale. **Price:** included in membership dues. **Circulation:** 1,000. **Conventions/Meetings:** annual convention, speakers, vendors room, raffles, buy-sell-swap, flea market and booksale (exhibits) - always 3rd weekend in June ● annual meeting.

21538 ■ Cavanagh's Coca-Cola Collectors' Society (CCCS)
11455 Lakefield Dr., Ste.400
Duluth, GA 30097
Ph: (678)366-2800
Fax: (678)366-2801
E-mail: ccccs@cavanaghgrp.com

Membership Dues: individual in U.S., $10 (annual) ● individual outside U.S., $15 (annual). **Description:** Sanctioned by the Coca-Cola Company, represents collectors of Cavanagh Coca-Cola collectibles.

21539 ■ Chicago Playing Card Collectors (CPCC)
1319 E Sanborn
Palatine, IL 60067
Ph: (770)992-7478
Fax: (847)966-1044
E-mail: altxcc@aol.com
URL: http://www.cpccinc.org
Contact: Betsy Behrendt, Contact

Founded: 1950. **Members:** 600. **Membership Dues:** adult, $25 (annual) ● junior, $14 (annual) ● senior, $21 (annual). **Description:** Persons interested in the collecting and study of playing cards. Members participate in card trading, discussions, exhibits, films, and other activities covering the history, lore, manufacture, and use of playing cards. Conducts lectures, exhibits, and question-and-answer sessions for libraries, schools, television and radio, and other educational organizations. **Libraries: Type:** reference. **Holdings:** 4. **Subjects:** history of playing cards. **Publications:** *Playing Card Mail Auctions*, quarterly ● *Reference Guides and Classification Listings*, semiannual ● Bulletin, quarterly. **Price:** included in membership dues ● Membership Directory, annual ● Prepares monthly article on playing cards for *Hobbies Magazine* and has published a 500-year history of playing cards. **Conventions/Meetings:** annual meeting (exhibits).

21540 ■ Christmas Seal and Charity Stamp Society (CS&CSS)
c/o Florence H. Wright, Sec.-Treas.
PO Box 18615
Rochester, NY 14618-0615
E-mail: fwright2@rochester.rr.com
URL: http://cscss.home.att.net
Contact: Florence H. Wright, Sec.-Treas.

Founded: 1931. **Members:** 350. **Membership Dues:** regular, in U.S., $15 (annual) ● regular, in Canada and Mexico, $17 (annual) ● regular, outside U.S., Canada and Mexico, $27 (annual). **Multinational. Description:** Collectors of charity seals. Research organizations worldwide that have issued charity or fundraising seals and publishes the information so that collectors can properly identify the seals in their collections. Conducts occasional lectures, slide-shows, and auctions. **Awards: Type:** recognition. **Recipient:** for exhibits. **Affiliated With:** American Philatelic Society. **Publications:** *Green's Catalog of the TB Seals of the World*, quinquennial. **Price:** $13.00 U.S. National; $8.00 local accessories; $24.00 foreign. Alternate Formats: CD-ROM ● *Mosbaugh's Red Cross Seals of the World Catalog* ● *Mosbaugh's U.S. All Fund Seal Catalog*, periodic ● *Seal News*, quarterly. Newsletter. Contains articles, resource pages, foreign seal report, U.S. seal report, auction, and more. **Price:** included in membership dues. **Advertising:** accepted ● Reprints. **Conventions/Meetings:** periodic meeting, Christmas and charity seals.

21541 ■ Cigarette Pack Collectors Association (CPCA)

c/o Richard Elliot
86 Plymouth Grove Dr.
Kennebunk, ME 04043
E-mail: cigpack@aol.com
URL: http://members.aol.com/cigpack/index.html
Contact: Richard Elliot, Contact

Founded: 1976. **Members:** 250. **Membership Dues:** regular, $10 (annual). **Staff:** 1. **Description:** Collectors of cigarette packs, tins, and advertising materials. Emphasizes on obsolete U.S. brands but international wrappers are also collected. Promotes interest in the preservation of obsolete cigarette packs. Encourages active trading among collectors and exchanges information on the history of the cigarette industry. **Publications:** *Brandstand*, quarterly. Newsletter ● Directory, annual. **Conventions/Meetings:** biennial convention, with members' display collections (exhibits).

21542 ■ Citrus Label Society

c/o Noel Gilbert, Sec.-Treas.
131 Miramonte Dr.
Fullerton, CA 92835
E-mail: trspellman@prodigy.net
URL: http://www.citruslabelsociety.com
Contact: Noel Gilbert, Sec.-Treas.

Founded: 1976. **Members:** 242. **Membership Dues:** regular, associate and spouse, $20 (annual) ● associate, organization, $16 (annual) ● contributing, $30 (annual) ● regular and spouse, $24 (annual) ● contributing and spouse, $34 (annual). **Description:** Members are collectors of citrus crate labels. Promotes the collection, sharing, and preservation of citrus crate labels and the history of the citrus fruit industry and it holds exhibitions of citrus labels, pictures, and paraphernalia. Conducts educational programs. **Libraries: Type:** reference. **Holdings:** archival material. **Subjects:** production, processing, and marketing in the citrus industry. **Formed by Merger of:** (1976) Pacific Antique Label Society; Tri-County Citrus Label Collectors. **Publications:** *The Citrus Peal*, quarterly. Newsletter. **Price:** included in membership dues. **Conventions/Meetings:** monthly meeting, label displays (exhibits) - January, April, July, October in Sherman Oaks; February, May, August, November in Orange.

21543 ■ Cloisonne Collectors Club (CCC)

Box 96
Rockport, MA 01966
Ph: (978)546-6930
Contact: Kay Whitcomb, Pres.

Founded: 1974. **Members:** 100. **Description:** Collectors of cloisonne items. (Cloisonne is the method of applying wires and glass enamel to metal and firing it in a kiln, producing a colorful glass finish.) Disseminates information on the art and history of cloisonne enameling, including profiles of enamellers. Educates the public on the process and prices of cloisonne items at public auctions. Keeps members informed of exhibits and other related events. Maintains library and archive. **Committees:** North American Committee of Enamel Creators. **Publications:** *The Cloison*, quarterly. Newsletter. **Price:** $15.00/year. **Conventions/Meetings:** quarterly meeting.

21544 ■ Coin Operated Collectors Association (COCA)

c/o Dan Davids
15200 Mansel Ave.
Lawndale, CA 90260
E-mail: djdavids@earthlink.net
URL: http://www.coinopclub.org
Contact: Dan Davids, Contact

Membership Dues: regular, in U.S., $33 (annual) ● regular, in Canada, $35 (annual) ● overseas, $50 (annual). **Multinational. Description:** Stimulates knowledge of and interest in the collection of vintage coin-operated machines. Promotes understanding and appreciation of the positive effects of the coin-operated machines. **Computer Services:** Online services, discussion forum. **Publications:** *COCA Times*, 3/year. Magazine. Contains articles related to the collecting of pre-1950 coin operated machines. **Price:** included in membership dues; $15.00 plus shipping and handling.

21545 ■ Colonial Coverlet Guild of America (CCGA)

c/o Laurie Coolidge
536 Arizona Ave.
Glenwood, IL 60425
E-mail: bjdoig@ameritech.net
URL: http://coverletguild.org
Contact: Laurie Coolidge, Contact

Founded: 1923. **Members:** 110. **Membership Dues:** single, $20 (annual) ● family, $25 (annual). **Local Groups:** 1. **Description:** Owners of early American handwoven coverlets. Promotes the preservation and registration of early American handwoven coverlets; increases awareness of these art pieces. Researches the history of coverlets since 1820. Maintains museum collection of 107 coverlets at DuPage County Historical Museum. **Libraries: Type:** reference. **Holdings:** archival material, books. **Subjects:** early American handwoven textiles. **Publications:** Newsletter, quarterly. Contains current information on finds and prices and historical material on weavers and coverlets. **Price:** included in membership dues. **Conventions/Meetings:** annual Discovery Day - meeting, with coverlets and collection at DuPage County Historical Museum (exhibits) - always last Saturday in April.

21546 ■ Conchologists of America (COA)

c/o Doris Underwood, Membership Dir.
698 Sheridan Woods Dr.
West Melbourne, FL 32904-3302
E-mail: thomas@rt66.com
URL: http://www.conchologistsofamerica.org
Contact: Doris Underwood, Membership Dir.

Founded: 1972. **Members:** 1,300. **Membership Dues:** regular, in U.S., $25 (annual) ● regular, in Canada and Mexico, $30 (annual) ● other country, $40 (annual). **Description:** Professional and amateur shell collectors interested in mollusks. Supports conservation and strives to protect the natural habitats of mollusks. Encourages harvesting of shells and shellfish without endangering wild populations. **Libraries: Type:** reference. **Holdings:** articles. **Awards: Frequency:** annual. **Type:** grant. **Recipient:** for graduates and post-graduates in the field of malacology. **Publications:** *American Conchologist*, quarterly. Journal. Includes scientific and popular articles on mollusks, book reviews, travel articles, convention news and updates, trophy winners, and profiles. **Price:** included in membership dues. ISSN: 1072-2440. **Circulation:** 1,650. **Advertising:** accepted. Also Cited As: *Conchologists of America Bulletin* ● *1992-1993 Index Supplement*. **Price:** $2.50 ● *Organization History*. **Price:** $2.00 ● *Publication Index 1973-1996*. **Price:** $5.00 ● Membership Directory, annual. **Price:** available to members only ● Monographs, periodic. **Conventions/Meetings:** annual meeting and symposium (exhibits) - always summer ● annual Shell Auction - convention, to benefit grants program and publication ● Shell Sales Bourse - convention.

21547 ■ Cookie Cutter Collectors Club (CCCC)

PO Box 245
Cannon Falls, MN 55009

E-mail: asmjem@frontiernet.net
URL: http://www.cookiecuttercollectorsclub.com
Contact: Joyce Moorhouse, Sec.-Treas.

Founded: 1972. **Members:** 750. **Membership Dues:** individual, $20 (annual) ● couple, $30 (annual). **Description:** Collectors, tinsmiths, and individuals in the antique and flea market business interested in the collection of cookie cutters and other cookie shaping tools, such as molds and rollers. Researches, records, and shares information on cookie shaping devices and certain workable recipes for special cookie cutters. Collects cutter-related materials. Discusses recipes and other uses of cutters. Keeps abreast of new cutter sources and special offers. Presents programs to other groups. Maintains Cookie Cutter Museum in Joplin, Missouri. **Computer Services:** Information services, about the club. **Formerly:** (1976) Cookie Cutter Club. **Publications:** *Cookie Crumbs*, quarterly. Newsletter. **Conventions/Meetings:** biennial convention (exhibits).

21548 ■ Corn Items Collectors Association (CIC)

c/o Robert S. Chamberlain
9288 Poland Rd.
Warrensburg, IL 62573
Ph: (217)674-3334 (217)454-6413
Fax: (217)674-3334
E-mail: lain@frontiernet.net
Contact: Robert S. Chamberlain, Sec.-Treas.

Founded: 1985. **Members:** 250. **Membership Dues:** individual, $20 (annual). **For-Profit. Description:** Persons interested in corn item collecting. Promotes corn item collecting; encourages displays of collections. Holds flea markets. **Libraries: Type:** reference. **Holdings:** books, clippings, periodicals. **Subjects:** corn item collecting. **Awards: Frequency:** periodic. **Type:** recognition. **Recipient:** for best corn items display. **Publications:** *The Bang Board*, quarterly. Newsletter. **Circulation:** 250. **Advertising:** accepted ● Membership Directory, annual. Contains names, phone numbers, and items collected. **Conventions/Meetings:** Show and Tell - meeting - 3/year.

21549 ■ Cow Observers Worldwide (COW)

240 Wahl Ave.
Evans City, PA 16033
E-mail: moosletter@cow.net
URL: http://www.cow.net
Contact: Jason Scott, Founder

Founded: 1993. **Members:** 350. **Membership Dues:** regular, in U.S., $10 (annual) ● regular, in Canada, $12 (annual) ● regular, outside U.S. and Canada, $17 (annual). **Staff:** 2. **Budget:** $1,800. **Description:** Cow lovers, animal lovers, and farmers. Promotes the collection of cow items; encourages members to exchange information; provides a social forum. Maintains collection of cow antiques, art, and collectibles. **Libraries: Type:** reference. **Holdings:** artwork, books, clippings, periodicals. **Subjects:** cows, cow art, dairy industry. **Publications:** *Cow-Buying Guide*, biennial. Directory. Lists names, addresses, and phone numbers of individuals and organizations buying or selling cow-related merchandise. **Price:** $3.50 for members; $5.00 for nonmembers. **Circulation:** 300. **Advertising:** accepted ● *The MOOsletter*, quarterly. Newsletter. Includes fiction and poetry on cows, articles on cows and cow collectibles. **Price:** included in membership dues. ISSN: 1087-6294. **Circulation:** 500. **Advertising:** accepted.

21550 ■ Cracker Jack Collectors Association (CJCA)

c/o Deb Gunnerson, Membership Chair
3225 Edward St. NE
St. Anthony, MN 55418
E-mail: raegun@comcast.net
URL: http://www.tias.com/mags/cjca
Contact: Stewart Callner, Pres.

Founded: 1993. **Members:** 200. **Membership Dues:** individual in U.S., $20 (annual) ● family in U.S., $24 (annual) ● individual in Canada, $25 (annual). **Description:** Collectors of Cracker Jack prizes and related items. Promotes collection and preservation of Cracker Jack memorabilia. Gathers and disseminates information on Cracker Jack collectibles and their availability; facilitates exchange of information and promotes good fellowship among members. **Publications:** *Prize Insider*, 10/year. Newsletter. **Price:** included in membership dues. **Advertising:** accepted ● Membership Directory. **Conventions/Meetings:** annual board meeting ● annual convention.

21551 ■ Crowncap Collectors Society International (CCSI)
c/o Ron Powell, Pres.
13222 Blueberry Hill Ln.
Valley Center, CA 92082-5405
Ph: (760)749-8736
E-mail: askccsi@aol.com
URL: http://www.bottlecapclub.org
Contact: Ron Powell, Pres.
Founded: 1986. **Members:** 200. **Membership Dues:** individual in U.S., $15 (annual) ● individual in U.S., $20 (annual) ● in Canada and Mexico, $16 (annual). **Description:** Collectors of crown closure bottle caps found on soda and beer bottles. (The crown closure bottle cap was invented by William Painter and usually carries a design representing the soda or beer manufacturer on its surface.) Promotes preservation of the crown bottle cap and interest in the history of the brewing and bottling industry. **Libraries: Type:** open to the public. **Holdings:** 33. **Subjects:** crown closures. **Publications:** *Annual Roster*. Newsletter. **Price:** included in membership dues ● *CrownCappers' Exchange*, 3/year. Newsletter. Contains roster updates and informative articles relating to the hobby. **Price:** free for members; $4.00/copy for nonmembers. **Advertising:** accepted. **Conventions/Meetings:** annual Crownvention - convention - March or April.

21552 ■ Cupid Collectors Club (CCC)
c/o Ted Lussem, Treas.
2919 John Patterson Rd.
Des Moines, IA 50317
E-mail: ingles12@mchsi.com
URL: http://www.cupidcollectorsclub.com
Contact: Glen Tull, Pres.
Founded: 1996. **Members:** 90. **Membership Dues:** individual, $20 (annual). **Description:** Collectors and admirers of Cupid prints produced in the late nineteenth and early twentieth centuries. Promotes collection of Cupid prints and seeks to raise awareness of these prints and their provenance. Conducts research and educational programs; serves as a clearinghouse on Cupid prints. **Publications:** *Cupid Awake, Cupid Asleep and a Whole Lot More.*, annual. Book. Contains history and examples of cupid prints, postcards, etc. **Price:** $65.00 for members ● *Cupid Capers*, quarterly. Newsletter. **Conventions/Meetings:** annual convention (exhibits).

21553 ■ Currier and Ives Dinnerware Collectors
c/o Edward Michniewicz, Treas.
7022 Shaker Rd.
Loudon, NH 03307-1130
Ph: (603)783-4023
E-mail: aupperlee@bhc.edu
URL: http://www.royalchinaclub.com
Contact: Edward Michniewicz, Treas.
Founded: 1996. **Members:** 375. **Membership Dues:** individual, $15 (annual) ● life, $150. **Description:** Promotes collecting of Currier and Ives dinnerware, as well as any dinnerware made by Royal. **Publications:** Newsletter, quarterly. **Price:** included in membership dues. **Conventions/Meetings:** annual meeting, includes business meeting, show and tell, buy/sell/trade/, lunch/dinner (exhibits).

21554 ■ Czech Collector's Association (CCA)
c/o Patti Ferguson, Dir. of Membership
9 Mockingbird Ln.
Shawnee, OK 74804
E-mail: info@antelopeantiques.com
URL: http://www.czechcollectors.org
Contact: Sandra MacMillan, Pres.
Founded: 1995. **Members:** 300. **Membership Dues:** individual, $35 (annual) ● platinum sponsor, $500 ● couple (same address), institutional, $50 (annual).

Description: Promotes the collection of Czechoslovakian arts and antiques. **Libraries: Type:** reference. **Holdings:** articles, books. **Subjects:** Czechoslovakian, Austrian and Bohemian arts and antiques. **Publications:** Newsletter, semiannual. **Conventions/Meetings:** annual convention and seminar - 2008 June, Nashville, TN; 2009 June, Burlington, VT.

21555 ■ Dedham Pottery Collectors Society (DPCS)
c/o Jim Kaufman
248 Highland St.
Dedham, MA 02026-5833
Free: (800)283-8070
E-mail: dpcurator@aol.com
URL: http://www.dedhampottery.com
Contact: Jim Kaufman, Contact
Founded: 1993. **Members:** 200. **Membership Dues:** subscriber, $21 (annual). **Staff:** 1. **For-Profit.** **Description:** Individuals with an interest in Dedham pottery. Promotes the study and collection of Dedham pottery. Gathers and disseminates information on the Dedham Pottery Company and the Chelsea Ceramic Art Works and their products. **Publications:** Newsletter, quarterly. Provides information on history and collection of Dedham and Chelsea Ceramic pottery. **Price:** $5.00/issue. **Circulation:** 200.

21556 ■ Diecast Exchange Club (DEC)
Address Unknown since 2007
Founded: 1983. **Members:** 2,005. **Membership Dues:** in U.S., $20 ● in Canada, $25 ● outside North America, $32. **Description:** Individuals interested in collecting and exchanging small diecast vehicles. Seeks to furnish members with information on the production of such toys, swap meets, and old and rare vehicles. Sponsors charitable program. **Publications:** Newsletter, monthly. **Conventions/Meetings:** annual meeting.

21557 ■ Disabled Veterans Keychain Tag and Chauffeur's Badge Collectors Newsletter
c/o Dr. Edward H. Miles, Ed.
888 8th Ave.
New York, NY 10019
Ph: (212)765-2660
Fax: (212)765-2714
E-mail: emiles33@aol.com
Contact: Dr. Edward H. Miles, Ed.
Founded: 1984. **Members:** 125. **Membership Dues:** collector, $10. **Description:** Collectors and dealers of miniature license plate key chains, chauffeur badges, and gum cards picturing license plates. Helps members exchange information on key chain origin, availability, value, trading, buying, and selling. Many of the key chains were made from 1942-75 by Disabled American Veterans (see separate entry). **Formerly:** Key Chain Collectors Club; (1987) Key Chain Tag and Mini License Plate Collectors Club; (2001) License Plate Key Chain and Mini License Plate Collectors Club. **Publications:** *Key Chain News*, bimonthly. Newsletter. **Conventions/Meetings:** annual meeting (exhibits).

21558 ■ Divco Club of America (DCoA)
PO Box 1142
Kingston, WA 98346-1142
E-mail: editor@divco.org
URL: http://www.divco.org
Contact: Les Bagley, Ed.
Founded: 1991. **Membership Dues:** individual, $24 (annual) ● family, $26 (annual) ● business, $36 (annual). **Multinational. Description:** Seeks to preserve the history of Divco delivery trucks, characterized by multi-stop trucks bringing goods and services to customer doors. **Libraries: Type:** reference. **Holdings:** books. **Subjects:** Divco trucks, multi-delivery trucks. **Publications:** *Divco News*, bimonthly. Newsletter. Contains articles about Divco and multi-stop history, restoration, operation and collectibles. **Price:** included in membership dues. **Advertising:** accepted.

21559 ■ Dreamsicles Club
c/o Cast Art Industries
1693 Rimpau Ave.
Corona, CA 92881-3202
Ph: (909)371-3025
Free: (800)437-5818
Fax: (909)371-0674
E-mail: info@dreamsiclesclub.com
URL: http://www.toysplus.com/dreamsicles/db/club-detail.htm
Contact: James Farrell, Contact
Founded: 1993. **Members:** 110,000. **Description:** Promotes the hobby of collecting Dreamsicles figurines. **Publications:** *Clubhouse Magazine.* Includes photos, news and inside information about figurines. ● *Dreamsicle Journal.*

21560 ■ Early American Pattern Glass Society (EAPGS)
c/o Fred Phelps, Membership Chm.
PO Box 266
Colesburg, IA 52035-0266
E-mail: fredlmia@msn.com
URL: http://www.eapgs.org
Contact: Fred Phelps, Membership Chm.
Founded: 1994. **Members:** 700. **Membership Dues:** individual, $20 (annual) ● family, $25 (annual). **Multinational. Description:** Fosters and encourages the collection, appreciation, study and documentation of early American pattern glassware, primarily from 1850-1915. **Programs:** Pattern Profiles. **Publications:** *News Journal*, quarterly. Newsletter. Contains articles, glass-related articles, reprints, upcoming sales and events. **Price:** included in membership dues ● Membership Directory. **Price:** included in membership dues. **Conventions/Meetings:** annual meeting, with speakers, auction ● periodic seminar.

21561 ■ Early Typewriter Collectors Association (ETC)
c/o Rich Cincotta
PO Box 286
Southborough, MA 01772
E-mail: etcetera@writeme.com
URL: http://typewriter.rydia.net/etcetera.htm
Contact: Rich Cincotta, Contact
Founded: 1987. **Members:** 300. **Membership Dues:** regular, in U.S., Canada and Mexico, $20 (annual) ● regular, outside U.S., Canada and Mexico, $25 (annual). **Languages:** English, German. **Description:** Individuals dedicated to the collection and preservation of antique typewriters and their accessories including mechanical calculators, check protectors, ribbon tins and other office items. Seeks to encourage communication among members and to strengthen friendships through the exchange of ideas. **Publications:** *ETCetera* (in English and German), quarterly. Magazine. Includes book reviews and research and regional meeting reports. **Price:** included in membership dues; $25.00 for nonmembers in North America; $30.00 for nonmembers outside North America. ISSN: 1062-9645. **Circulation:** 300. **Advertising:** accepted ● *ETCetera*, quarterly. Newsletter. Features interviews with fellow collectors, articles on interesting machines, classifieds and many more subjects including other office machinery. **Price:** $30.00 in North America; $35.00 elsewhere ● *Roster of Members*, annual. Membership Directory.

21562 ■ Egg Cup Collectors' Corner
c/o Dr. Joan M. George
67 Stevens Ave.
Old Bridge, NJ 08857
E-mail: drjgeorge@nac.net
URL: http://www.angelfire.com/fl/eggcups
Contact: Dr. Joan M. George, Contact
Founded: 1986. **Members:** 275. **Membership Dues:** $20 (annual). **Multinational. Description:** Represents international collectors of egg cups who share information, as well as buy, sell, and trade egg cups of all types. Conducts educational programs. **Publications:** Newsletter, quarterly. **Advertising:** accepted.

21563 ■ EKJ (Emmett Kelly Jr.) Collectors' Society
c/o Flambro Imports
1530 Ellsworth Indus. Dr.
Atlanta, GA 30318-3752
Ph: (404)352-1381
Free: (800)352-6276
Fax: (404)352-2150
E-mail: info@area51collectibles.com
URL: http://www.area51collectibles.com/emkeljrcolso.
html
Description: Dedicated to collecting Emmett Kelly Jr. figurines, musicals, miniatures and more. **Additional Websites:** http://www.flambro.com. **Telecommunication Services:** additional toll-free number, (800)355-2582. **Publications:** EKJ Catalog ● Newsletter, quarterly.

21564 ■ Emmett's Elite
c/o Flambro Imports
1530 Ellsworth Indus. Dr.
Atlanta, GA 30318-3752
Ph: (404)352-1381
Free: (800)352-6276
Fax: (404)352-2150
E-mail: flambro@flambro.com
URL: http://www.flambro.com
Description: Focuses on the collection of Emmett Kelly Jr. figurines, musicals, miniatures and more. **Telecommunication Services:** additional toll-free number, (800)777-4802. **Publications:** EKJ Catalog ● Newsletter, quarterly.

21565 ■ Fairy Lamp Club
c/o James L. Sapp
PO Box 438
Pine, CO 80470-0438
E-mail: jimsapp7@msn.com
URL: http://www.fairy-lamp.com
Contact: James L. Sapp, Contact
Founded: 1996. **Members:** 160. **Membership Dues:** regular, in U.S., $20 (annual) ● regular, outside U.S., $25 (annual). **Multinational. Description:** Dedicated to research of information related to Victorian and contemporary fairy lamps. **Additional Websites:** http://www.fairylampclub.com. **Publications:** Fairy Lamp, quarterly, February, May, August, November. Newsletter. Focuses on Victorian era lamps. **Price:** included in membership dues ● Membership Directory.

21566 ■ Family Circle of PenDelfin
c/o Susan Beard
230 Spring St. NW, Ste.1238
Atlanta, GA 30303
Free: (800)872-4876
URL: http://www.pendelfin.biz/pendelfin/collectorscorner/information/family_circle.htm
Contact: Susan Beard, Contact
Description: For collectors of PenDelfin products.
Additional Websites: http://www.pendelfin.co.uk.

21567 ■ Fan Association of North America (FANA)
c/o Ms. Linda S. Rousseau, Public Relations Chair
90 Prescott Rd.
Brentwood, NH 03833
Ph: (603)772-4534
E-mail: lindarou@rcn.com
URL: http://www.fanassociation.org
Contact: Ms. Linda S. Rousseau, Public Relations Chair
Founded: 1982. **Members:** 230. **Membership Dues:** individual in U.S., $50 (annual) ● individual outside U.S., $60 (annual). **Regional Groups:** 4. **Multinational. Description:** Individuals united to promote, collect, and conserve folding fans and rigid handscreens. Promotes appreciation of fans. Supports fan research. Advises members on collecting and conserving fans. Encourages fan exhibitions in museums. Facilitates exchange of knowledge and ideas among members. **Libraries: Type:** reference; lending; not open to the public. **Holdings:** 140; articles, books, clippings, periodicals, photographs, video recordings. **Subjects:** handheld fans. **Awards:** FANA Grants. **Frequency:** annual. **Type:** monetary. **Recipient:** to

organizations, entities or individuals who have appropriate projects regarding education, research, publication, exhibition or conservation related to fans. **Computer Services:** Electronic publishing, semiannual journals, for printing in full color. **Committees:** Grant; Museum; Public Relations. **Formerly:** (1982) East Bay Fan Guild. **Publications:** FANA Forum, quarterly. Newsletter. **Circulation:** 250. **Advertising:** accepted. Alternate Formats: online ● FANA Journal, semiannual. Magazine. Contains fan-related information and photos. **Price:** included in membership dues. **Circulation:** 250. **Advertising:** accepted. **Conventions/Meetings:** annual Assemblage - meeting and symposium, with lectures, sale, auction (exhibits) - usually spring.

21568 ■ Fiesta Collectors Club
PO Box 471
Valley City, OH 44280
URL: http://www.chinaspecialties.com/for_fiesta_collectors.htm
Membership Dues: individual, $12 (annual). **Description:** Represents collectors of Fiesta dinnerware. **Publications:** Newsletter, quarterly, March, June, September, and December. **Advertising:** accepted.

21569 ■ Figural Bottle Opener Collectors Club (FBOC)
c/o Charles Reynolds, Pres.
2836 Monroe St.
Falls Church, VA 22042
Ph: (703)533-1322
E-mail: johnf129@aol.com
URL: http://members.aol.com/johnf129/history.htm
Contact: Charles Reynolds, Pres.
Founded: 1978. **Members:** 150. **Membership Dues:** regular, $20 (annual). **Description:** Collectors of three-dimensional, free-standing figural bottle openers. Conducts research into the origin and manufacture of figural bottle openers. Identifies and codes openers. **Publications:** Figural Bottle Openers Identification Guide, quarterly. Newsletter ● The Opener, quarterly. Newsletter ● Directory, annual. Contains membership information updated quarterly. **Conventions/Meetings:** annual meeting - always May or June.

21570 ■ Figures Collectors Club
c/o Colleen Lewis
11174 Hunts Corners Rd.
Clarence, NY 14031-2035
Ph: (716)741-8399
Fax: (716)759-7462
E-mail: bripvc@toyline.com
Contact: Colleen Lewis, Contact
Founded: 1995. **Membership Dues:** ordinary, $24 (annual). **Description:** Collectors of cartoon and character plastic figures and related objects. Promotes collection of cartoon items; facilitates exchange of information among members. Serves as a clearinghouse on cartoon figure collectibles; maintains PVC collectible catalogue; informs members of new cartoon and character figures collectible figure releases. Plans to publish reference guide. **Formerly:** (2000) PVC Collectors Club. **Publications:** Newsletter, quarterly. Contains news of new cartoon and character figures. **Advertising:** accepted. Alternate Formats: online.

21571 ■ Flow Blue International Collectors Club (FBICC)
c/o Jim Swan, Membership Chm.
PO Box 442464
Lawrence, KS 66044
URL: http://www.flowblue.com
Contact: Jim Swan, Membership Chm.
Founded: 1986. **Members:** 1,300. **Membership Dues:** individual in U.S., $39 (annual) ● individual outside U.S., $49 (annual). **Regional Groups:** 6. **Multinational. Description:** Collectors and other individuals interested in flow blue, mulberry, or related antique china. Seeks to stimulate and maintain interest in the collection of such china. Promotes the exchange of information among members. Encourages educational endeavors in the study of antique

china; sponsors cooperative efforts with museums. **Committees:** Education. **Publications:** Blueberry Notes, bimonthly. Newsletter. **Advertising:** accepted ● Flow Blue Readings. Articles. Includes samples of the work generated by members. **Conventions/Meetings:** annual meeting and convention (exhibits).

21572 ■ Frankoma Family Collectors Association
c/o Ms. Donna Frank, Sec.
1300 Luker Ln.
Sapulpa, OK 74066-6024
Ph: (918)224-6610
E-mail: ffca4donna@aol.com
URL: http://www.frankoma.org
Contact: Ms. Donna Frank, Sec.
Founded: 1994. **Membership Dues:** family, $35 (annual). **Description:** Represents collectors dedicated to the appreciation, preservation, and promotion of Frankoma Pottery. **Telecommunication Services:** electronic mail, ffca4deb@aol.com. **Publications:** Pot & Puma, quarterly. Journal. **Price:** $5.00 ● Prairie Green Sheet, quarterly ● Articles. **Conventions/Meetings:** annual Family Reunion - convention - every September.

21573 ■ Gartlan USA's Collectors' League
560 Stokes Rd., Ste.23 - No. 397
Medford, NJ 08055-2905
Ph: (609)953-0606
Fax: (609)953-0938
E-mail: info@gartlanusa.com
URL: http://www.gartlanusa.com/club.html
Contact: R.H. Gartlan, Pres.
Founded: 1989. **Membership Dues:** individual, $35 (annual) ● renewal, $25 (annual). **Description:** Works to collect limited-edition entertainment and sports collectibles. **Publications:** Collectors Illustrated, quarterly. Newsletter. **Price:** free for members.

21574 ■ German Gun Collectors' Association (GGCA)
PO Box 385
Meriden, NH 03770
Ph: (603)469-3438
Fax: (603)469-3800
E-mail: jaeger@valley.net
URL: http://www.germanguns.com
Contact: Dietrich Apel, Founder
Founded: 1998. **Membership Dues:** regular, in U.S., $36 (annual) ● regular, outside U.S. and Canada, $50 (annual) ● small business, $100 (annual) ● corporate, $250 (annual) ● regular, in Canada, $39 (annual). **Multinational. Description:** Preserves the history of German hunting and sporting guns and their makers. Collects and shares information on German guns and the heritage of the German hunting tradition. **Computer Services:** database, member directory ● database, trade directory. **Publications:** The Gunmaker, quarterly. Journal. **Price:** included in membership dues. Also Cited As: Der Waffenschmied.

21575 ■ Global Lottery Collectors Society (GLCS)
c/o George Beilke
1532 E 59th Pl.
Tulsa, OK 74105-8008
E-mail: secretary@lotterycollectors.com
URL: http://www.lotterycollectors.com
Contact: Mr. Stephen Tuday, Pres.
Founded: 1987. **Members:** 225. **Membership Dues:** regular, in U.S., $15 (annual) ● regular, outside North America, $27 (annual). **Budget:** $6,000. **Description:** Individuals interested in collecting instant and non-instant tickets and items related to lotteries worldwide. Exchanges information, tickets and hobby materials. **Formerly:** (2003) Lottery Collectors Society. **Publications:** The Lotologist Monthly. Newsletter. Includes information on new instant ticket issues and lottery practices. **Price:** included in membership dues. **Circulation:** 250. **Advertising:** accepted. **Conventions/Meetings:** annual convention (exhibits).

21576 ■ Glove Collector (GCC)

14057 Rolling Hills Ln.
Dallas, TX 75240-3807
Ph: (972)699-1808
E-mail: glovecollector@tx.rr.com
URL: http://www.glovecollector.com
Contact: Joe Phillips, Contact
Founded: 1990. **Members:** 75. **Membership Dues:** regular, $29. **Staff:** 1. **For-Profit. Description:** Collectors of vintage and old time baseball gloves. Provides information on collecting vintage baseball gloves. Conducts research programs. **Libraries: Type:** reference. **Holdings:** clippings, periodicals. **Publications:** *Autograph Player Baseball Glove Finder.* Book. **Price:** $12.95 ● *Glove Catalog Source Book* ● *Vintage Baseball Glove Pocket Guide.* Book. **Price:** $8.95 ● *Vintage Baseball Glove Source Book.* **Price:** $34.95 ● Newsletter, bimonthly. **Price:** $18. 95. **Circulation:** 500. **Advertising:** accepted.

21577 ■ Golf Collectors Society (GCS)

PO Box 3103
Ponte Vedra Beach, FL 32004-3103
Ph: (904)400-3400
Fax: (904)683-2189
E-mail: kbednarski@golfcollectors.com
URL: http://www.golfcollectors.com
Contact: Karen Bednarski, Exec. Dir.
Founded: 1970. **Members:** 1,500. **Membership Dues:** regular, $50 (annual). **Regional Groups:** 10. **Multinational. Description:** Golf enthusiasts who collect the artifacts of the game. Encourages meetings and correspondence among collectors of "golfiana"; acts as clearinghouse of news and information. Hosts regional trade shows and hickory tournaments, as well as an annual meeting and trade show. **Awards:** Founders Award. **Frequency:** annual. **Type:** recognition. **Recipient:** for those who have made a significant contribution to the well being of the GCS in particular and/or to golf collecting in general. **Computer Services:** database. **Publications:** *The Bulletin,* quarterly. Newsletter. Covers membership activities; includes book reviews and reports on golf historical research and newly discovered golf artifacts. **Circulation:** 1,500. **Advertising:** accepted ● *Webzine,* monthly. Newsletters. **Advertising:** accepted. Alternate Formats: online ● Membership Directory, annual. **Price:** available to members only. **Circulation:** 1,500. **Conventions/Meetings:** regional meeting - 10/year ● annual trade show and meeting (exhibits).

21578 ■ Great Britain Collectors Club (GBCC)

c/o Parker A. Bailey, Jr., Sec.-Treas.
2341 SW 86th Terr.
Davie, FL 33324-5358
E-mail: pbaileyjr@comcast.net
URL: http://www.gbstamps.com/gbcc
Contact: Tim Burgess, Pres.
Founded: 1979. **Members:** 435. **Membership Dues:** in North America, $25 (annual) ● outside North America, $35 (annual). **Staff:** 1. **Multinational. Description:** Collectors interested in postage stamps of Great Britain. Provides members with information about these stamps and other philatelic material of England. **Formerly:** (1989) Great Britain Correspondence Club. **Publications:** *The Chronicle,* quarterly. Journal. Includes membership directory. **Price:** included in membership dues; $3.00 each, for nonmembers. **ISSN:** 0887-6819. **Circulation:** 450. **Advertising:** accepted ● *Handbook of British Philately for the Intermediate Collector,* periodic. **Price:** $8.00 each. **Conventions/Meetings:** annual meeting.

21579 ■ Hammered Aluminum Collectors Association (HACA)

PO Box 1346
Weatherford, TX 76086
Ph: (817)594-4680
E-mail: alumnumist@sbcglobal.net
Contact: Dannie A. Woodard, Publisher/Ed.
Founded: 1986. **Members:** 350. **Membership Dues:** $20 (annual). **Staff:** 1. **Description:** Collectors of hammered aluminum. Promotes interest in hammered aluminum collectibles. Helps collectors locate special items; conducts research and educational programs. **Convention/Meeting:** none. **Libraries: Type:** reference. **Holdings:** books, periodicals. **Subjects:** hammered aluminum collectibles. **Publications:** *The Aluminist,* bimonthly. Newsletter. **Price:** $20.00/year. **Advertising:** accepted ● *Hammered Aluminum - Hand Wrought Collectibles - Book II.* **Price:** $24.95 plus shipping and handling. **Advertising:** accepted ● Yearbook.

21580 ■ Harbour Lights Collectors Society

PO Box 459
West Kennebunk, ME 04094-0459
Free: (800)365-1219
Fax: (888)579-1911
E-mail: harbourlights@harbourlights.com
URL: http://www.harbourlights.com/society
Contact: Kim Andrews, CEO
Membership Dues: regular, in U.S., $39 (annual) ● regular, in U.S., $58 (biennial) ● regular, in U.S., $86 (triennial) ● regular, in Canada and Mexico, $49 (annual) ● regular, in Canada and Mexico, $73 (biennial) ● regular, in Canada and Mexico, $101 (triennial) ● regular, outside U.S., Canada and Mexico, $64 (annual) ● regular, outside U.S., Canada and Mexico, $83 (biennial) ● regular, outside U.S., Canada and Mexico, $111 (triennial). **Description:** Serves as light house collectors' society. **Publications:** *Lighthouse Legacy,* quarterly. Newsletter. Contains information about society, products news, events, and appearances, lighthouse lore, collectors' corner and more. **Price:** $5.00 first class mail, in U.S. only.

21581 ■ Heather's Teddy Bear Organization

c/o Arlene Marie Wood, CEO/Pres.
16 Oakdale Rd.
Terryville, CT 06786
Ph: (860)585-1735
Contact: Arlene Marie Wood, CEO/Pres.
Founded: 1995. **Members:** 9,000. **Staff:** 4. **Description:** Aims to promote, purchase, and distribute "healthy" new "Teddy Bears for Tears" to children in acute, traumatic medical emergencies. **Libraries: Type:** by appointment only. **Holdings:** 300; clippings. **Subjects:** marketing, nonprofit, business, groups. **Awards:** Winter Wood Poetry Award. **Frequency:** annual. **Type:** monetary. **Recipient:** for poetry guidelines, judges. **Publications:** *Heather's Teddy Bear Organization Newsletter,* annual. Includes membership list. **Advertising:** accepted. **Conventions/Meetings:** periodic board meeting (exhibits).

21582 ■ Homer Laughlin China Collectors Association (HLCCA)

PO Box 721
North Platte, NE 69103-0721
Fax: (308)534-7015
E-mail: info@hlcca.org
URL: http://www.hlcca.org
Contact: Sandra Bond, Pres.
Founded: 1998. **Membership Dues:** individual, $25 (annual) ● couple, $40 (annual). **Multinational. Description:** Represents the interests of collectors, antiques dealers and historians who share a common interest in dinnerware and other pottery products that were produced by the Homer Laughlin China Company. Provides an educational forum for all those who are interested in the important contribution of HLC to the American culture. **Publications:** *The Dish,* quarterly. Magazine. Contains information on topics relevant to anyone interested in HLC. **Price:** included in membership dues.

21583 ■ Horn and Whistle Enthusiasts Group (HWEG)

c/o Mr. Eric C. Larson, Publisher/Webmaster
2 Abell Ave.
Ipswich, MA 01938
E-mail: hornwhistlepub@aol.com
URL: http://www.hornandwhistle.net
Contact: Mr. Eric C. Larson, Publisher/Webmaster
Founded: 1982. **Members:** 240. **Staff:** 5. **Description:** Dedicated to the preservation of horns and whistles. Disseminates information regarding horns and whistles used in industrial, maritime, railroad, signaling and warning applications. **Formerly:** Air Horn and Steam Whistle Enthusiasts. **Publications:** *Horn and Whistle,* quarterly. Newsletter. Contains articles, photographs, news items, catalogs, data sheets, stories, and other features on horns and whistles. **Price:** $18.00/year in U.S. and Canada; $25.00/year outside U.S. and Canada. **Circulation:** 240. **Advertising:** accepted.

21584 ■ Howdy Doody Memorabilia Collectors Club (HDMCC)

c/o Jeff Judson, Founder/Newsletter Ed.
8 Hunt Ct.
Flemington, NJ 08822
Ph: (908)782-1159
E-mail: jtjudson@earthlink.net
Contact: Jeff Judson, Founder/Newsletter Ed.
Founded: 1978. **Members:** 300. **Membership Dues:** individual, $24 (annual). **Staff:** 4. **Description:** Fans of The Howdy Doody Show, the popular kids' television show which ran from 1947 to 1960. Keeps the spirit and the history of Doodyville. Fosters communication among collectors. **Also Known As:** Doodyville Historical Society. **Publications:** *Howdy Doody Times,* monthly. Newsletter. **Price:** included in membership dues. **Circulation:** 300. **Advertising:** accepted. **Conventions/Meetings:** annual Doodyville Historical Society Convention - meeting (exhibits).

21585 ■ Hull Pottery Association

c/o Nancy Ankeney, Membership Chair
4201 Brentwood Dr.
Columbia, MO 65203
Ph: (573)445-6583
E-mail: rosebud@kiva.net
URL: http://www.hullpotteryassociation.org
Contact: Nancy Ankeney, Membership Chair
Membership Dues: individual, $10 (annual) ● couple, $15 (annual). **Description:** Seeks to preserve the heritage of Hull Pottery.

21586 ■ Hummel Collectors Club (HCC)

1261 Univ. Dr.
Yardley, PA 19067-2857
Ph: (215)493-6204 (215)493-6705
Free: (888)548-6635
Fax: (215)321-7367
E-mail: customerservice@hummels.com
URL: http://www.hummels.com
Contact: Dorothy Dous, Pres.
Founded: 1975. **Members:** 10,000. **Membership Dues:** regular, in U.S., $35 (annual) ● regular, in Canada and Europe, $40 (annual) ● other, $45 (annual). **Staff:** 7. **For-Profit. Description:** Dealers and collectors interested in Hummel figurines, plates, bells, lamps, music boxes, and other items based on the drawings by a German nun, Sister Maria Innocentia Hummel. Seeks to familiarize collectors with trademarks, mold variations, and rare pieces, and to discover and document one-of-a-kind rarities. Compiles list of production by trademark. Conducts monthly mail auction, minimum of 3,000 pieces. Conducts bi-monthly public auctions in Yardley, PA. Minimum of 300 pieces. **Awards:** MI Hummel Figurine. **Frequency:** quarterly. **Type:** recognition. **Recipient:** for club member drawn by computer. **Formerly:** International Goebel Collectors Club. **Publications:** *Monthly Auction Results* ● Newsletter, quarterly. Offers information, surveys, questions and answers, and buy/sell/trade sections. **Price:** $35.00/year. **Advertising:** accepted. Alternate Formats: online.

21587 ■ Ice Screamers (IS)

c/o Judy Snyder
PO Box 465
Warrington, PA 18976
Ph: (215)343-2676
E-mail: info@icescreamers.com
URL: http://www.icescreamers.com
Contact: Judy Snyder, Contact
Founded: 1982. **Members:** 550. **Membership Dues:** regular, in U.S., $20 (annual) ● regular, outside U.S., $30 (annual). **Description:** Ice cream and soda fountain enthusiasts; individuals interested in the history of the industry; collectors of ice cream and soda

fountain memorabilia. Encourages communication and information exchange among members. **Publications:** Newsletter, quarterly. Contains articles about soda fountain and ice cream collectibles. **Price:** $20.00 for members. **Circulation:** 550. **Advertising:** accepted. **Conventions/Meetings:** annual convention, ice cream collectibles (exhibits) - late June.

21588 ■ Interlac
c/o Kevin McConnell
6 Stoney Bridge Rd.
Rockaway, NJ 07866
E-mail: mranziety@yahoo.com
URL: http://members.aol.com/interlac
Contact: Kevin McConnell, Contact
Founded: 1976. **Members:** 50. **Membership Dues:** waitlister, $10. **Description:** Membership is limited to 50 individuals interested in promoting and preserving the Legion of Super-Heroes comic series, other comics, science fiction, and pop culture. Seeks to promote friendship and communication among members through a bimonthly mailing to which each member must contribute. Should an individual fail to offer contribution, membership is forfeited and is open to the next person on the waiting list. Maintains hall of fame. **Libraries: Type:** reference. **Holdings:** 20,000; archival material. **Awards: Type:** recognition. **Formerly:** (1976) Legion Amateur Publishing Alliance (LEAPA); (1977) Legion Fan Club. **Publications:** *Interlac Bulletin*, bimonthly ● *Interlac Directory*, semiannual ● *Legion Concordance*. **Conventions/Meetings:** annual meeting ● bimonthly meeting.

21589 ■ International Association of R.S. Prussia Collectors
c/o Leslie Schultz
PO Box 185
Lost Nation, IA 52254
E-mail: lschultz@netins.net
URL: http://www.rsprussia.com
Contact: Leslie Schultz, Contact
Founded: 1985. **Membership Dues:** family, in U.S., $30 (annual). **Multinational. Description:** Educates collectors and the general public about R.S. Prussia and related porcelain. Offers opportunities to share information, authenticate pieces and provide fellowship among collectors of R.S. Prussia porcelain. **Computer Services:** Information services, R.S. Prussia resources ● online services, forum. **Publications:** Newsletter, quarterly. **Price:** included in membership dues ● Brochure. Alternate Formats: online.

21590 ■ International Association of Silver Art Collectors (IASAC)
Box 28415
Seattle, WA 98118
E-mail: iasacnancy@comcast.net
Contact: Nancy Yee, Sec.-Treas.
Founded: 1985. **Members:** 200. **Membership Dues:** new member, $20 (annual) ● renewal, $15 (annual) ● new member outside U.S., $30 (annual) ● renewal outside U.S., $20 (annual). **Description:** Collectors and enthusiasts of silver art bars and rounds. Promotes fellowship and enjoyment of the hobby. Provides information; conducts competitions. Makes available commemorative silver art bars and rounds. **Libraries: Type:** reference. **Holdings:** archival material, books, business records, clippings. **Subjects:** silver art bars and rounds. **Awards:** Duane Spellman Award for Distinguished Service. **Frequency:** annual. **Type:** recognition. **Affiliated With:** American Numismatic Association. **Formerly:** (1985) International Association of Silver Bar Collectors. **Publications:** *The Silver Bugle*, bimonthly. Newsletter. **Advertising:** accepted. **Conventions/Meetings:** annual meeting, with an exhibit of IASAC coins and medals from 1985 to date (exhibits).

21591 ■ International Autograph Collectors Club and Dealers Alliance (IACC-DA)
PO Box 848486
Hollywood, FL 33084
E-mail: registration@iada-cc.com
URL: http://www.iada-cc.com
Contact: Stephen Koschal, Exec. Dir.
Founded: 1997. **Membership Dues:** dealer, $195 (annual) ● collector, $29 (annual). **Multinational.**

Description: Promotes the art of autograph and memorabilia collecting. Aims to unite autograph collectors and dealers. Provides collector members and collectors information about acquiring and purchasing autographs from respected dealers in the industry. **Publications:** Directory, annual. Contains profiles of dealer members. Alternate Formats: online.

21592 ■ International Bond and Share Society (IBSS)
PO Box 430
Hackensack, NJ 07602-0430
Ph: (201)489-2440
Fax: (201)592-0282
E-mail: ibss@scripophily.org
URL: http://www.scripophily.org
Contact: Richard T. Gregg, Pres.
Founded: 1978. **Members:** 1,000. **Membership Dues:** individual, $25 (annual) ● individual outside U.S., 12 (annual). **Description:** Collectors of antique certificates of stocks and bonds. Encourages and supports efforts in collecting obsolete certificates and financial historical documents. **Formerly:** Bond and Share Society. **Publications:** *Scripophily*, quarterly. Magazine. **Price:** included in membership dues. **Advertising:** accepted ● Directory, annual. **Conventions/Meetings:** periodic meeting (exhibits).

21593 ■ International Bossons Collectors Society (IBCS)
8316 Woodlake Pl.
Tampa, FL 33615-1728
Ph: (813)885-2038
E-mail: normanderocher@verizon.net
URL: http://www.bossons.org
Contact: Norm Derocher, Pres./Exec. Dir.
Founded: 1981. **Members:** 400. **Membership Dues:** individual, $45 (annual). **State Groups:** 1. **Multinational. Description:** Works to collect Bossons artware. **Publications:** *Bossons Briefs*, quarterly. Newsletter. **Conventions/Meetings:** annual meeting.

21594 ■ International Brick Collectors' Association (IBCA)
c/o Peggy French, Managing Ed.
1743 Lindenhall Dr.
Loveland, OH 45140-2144
Ph: (316)831-9713
E-mail: brickcollector@gmail.com
URL: http://www.tlgwindpower.com/tweety/brick_map.htm
Contact: Jim Graves, Librarian
Founded: 1983. **Members:** 1,000. **Membership Dues:** regular, $15 (annual). **Description:** Individuals interested in the collection, history, manufacture, and technological aspects of bricks. Works to foster communication and trade among members. **Libraries: Type:** not open to the public. **Holdings:** 3,500. **Subjects:** brick manufacturing. **Computer Services:** database, brick brands and manufacturing listing. **Telecommunication Services:** electronic mail, pfrench001@cinci.rr.com. **Publications:** *Journal of the IBCA*, 3/year. Contains articles on bricks and brick collecting. **Price:** $2.00. **Conventions/Meetings:** semiannual Traders' Meeting (exhibits).

21595 ■ International Coleman Collectors Club (ICCC)
c/o Charleen Becker, Treas.
1822 E Fernwood
Wichita, KS 67216
E-mail: cmc70mdc73@mn.rr.com
URL: http://www.colemancollectorsclub.com
Contact: Don Colston, Pres.
Members: 300. **Membership Dues:** single, $25 (annual) ● family, international (single or family), $30 (annual). **Multinational. Description:** Represents collectors of Coleman lanterns, lamps, irons, stoves, hollow wire fixtures, and all products of the Coleman Company. **Publications:** *Business Directory*. Contains paid advertisements from individuals and companies who offer parts and/or services for the Coleman enthusiast. **Advertising:** accepted. Alternate Formats: online ● *Club and Website Directory*. Alternate Formats: online ● *The Coleman eLight*, 3/year, January, May, September. Newsletter. Fea-

tures technical, historical, reference and humor. **Price:** included in membership dues. **Advertising:** accepted. Alternate Formats: online ● *The Coleman Lite*, bimonthly. Newsletter. **Conventions/Meetings:** annual convention - usually 3rd weekend in June.

21596 ■ International Collector's Club of Hatpins and Hatpin Holders (ICCH&HH)
Address Unknown since 2007
Founded: 1977. **Members:** 500. **Description:** Individuals who collect hatpins and hatpin holders. Maintains speakers' bureau, library, and biographical and photo archives. **Publications:** *Collector's Encyclopedia of Hatpins and Hatpin Holders* ● *Hatpins and Hatpin Holders: An Illustrated Value Guide* ● *Pictorial Journal of Hatpins and Hatpin Holders*, annual ● *Points*, 10/year. Newsletter. **Conventions/Meetings:** annual meeting (exhibits).

21597 ■ International Collectors Guild
c/o Penny Hayes
PO Box 487
Artesia, CA 90701-0487
Ph: (714)521-1612
Contact: Penny Hayes, Pres.
Founded: 1971. **Members:** 100. **Membership Dues:** $15 (annual). **Local Groups:** 1. **Description:** Collectors of fine collectibles. Works to acquaint people with the hobby of collecting fine collectibles and plates through speakers and displays. **Publications:** *Platter Patter*, monthly. Newsletter. **Price:** free with membership. **Advertising:** accepted. **Conventions/Meetings:** monthly meeting (exhibits) - always second Sunday of each month. Bellflower, CA.

21598 ■ International Correspondence of Corkscrew Addicts (ICCA)
c/o Dr. Bert Giulian
649 Johns Dr.
Camp Hill, PA 17011
Ph: (717)737-5828
E-mail: corkscrew@bullworks.net
URL: http://www.bullworks.net/virtual/icca/icca.htm
Contact: Dr. Bert Giulian, Contact
Founded: 1974. **Members:** 50. **Membership Dues:** individual, $100 (annual). **Description:** Represents collectors of corkscrews. **Conventions/Meetings:** annual meeting.

21599 ■ International Match Safe Association (IMSA)
PO Box 791
Malaga, NJ 08328
Ph: (856)694-4167
E-mail: mrvesta1@aol.com
URL: http://www.matchsafe.org
Contact: Ken Koelling, Membership Chm.
Founded: 1998. **Membership Dues:** general, $50 (annual) ● general, $200 (quinquennial). **Multinational. Description:** Represents the interests of individuals who collect and preserve match safes. Promotes the preservation, education and study of match safes. **Publications:** Newsletter, quarterly. Contains articles, price trends, reproduction information and classified ads. **Price:** included in membership dues ● Membership Directory, annual. **Price:** free for members.

21600 ■ International Perfume Bottle Association (IPBA)
c/o Shari Maxson Hopper, Membership Sec.
PO Box 1299
Paradise, CA 95967
E-mail: paradise@sunset.net
URL: http://www.perfumebottles.org
Contact: Connie Linne, Pres.
Founded: 1988. **Members:** 1,500. **Membership Dues:** regular, in U.S., $45 (annual) ● regular, in Canada, $50 (annual) ● regular, outside U.S., $55 (annual). **Regional Groups:** 6. **Multinational. Description:** Collectors of perfume and scent bottles and related items. Conducts educational programs. **Libraries: Type:** not open to the public. **Holdings:** 75. **Subjects:** perfume bottle collecting. **Formerly:** International Perfume and Scent Bottle Collectors As-

sociation; (1988) Perfume and Scent Bottle Collectors. **Publications:** *Perfume Bottle Quarterly*. Newsletter. **Price:** included in membership dues; $7.50 for nonmembers. **Circulation:** 1,300. **Advertising:** accepted. Alternate Formats: CD-ROM; online. **Conventions/Meetings:** annual convention, with seminars and workshops (exhibits).

21601 ■ International Railroad and Transportation Postcard Collectors Club
Address Unknown since 2007
Founded: 1979. **Members:** 1,000. **Membership Dues:** in U.S., $20 (annual) ● foreign, $25 (annual). **Staff:** 1. **National Groups:** 1. **Description:** Individuals in all countries interested in the collection of transportation postcards. Conducts research on the distribution of cards by different publishers to educate the collector on the number of postcards available. Compiles statistics and checklist. Latest checklist covered bridges, now compiling checklist on lighthouses from around the world. **Libraries: Type:** reference. **Subjects:** transportation postcards. **Publications:** *Membership Roster*, annual. Directory. **Advertising:** accepted ● *Transport World*, quarterly. Contains checklist of postcards. **Price:** included in membership dues. **Advertising:** accepted. **Conventions/Meetings:** competition.

21602 ■ International Sand Collectors Society (ISCS)
PO Box 117
North Haven, CT 06473-0117
Ph: (203)239-5488
Fax: (203)239-5488
E-mail: iscs@juno.com
URL: http://www.sandcollectors.org
Contact: Nicholas D'Errico, Dir.
Founded: 1969. **Members:** 200. **Membership Dues:** individual in U.S., $12 (annual) ● individual outside U.S., $15 (annual). **National Groups:** 14. **Multinational. Description:** Individuals who collect sand for pleasure and study. Purpose is to promote the collection, classification, and retention of sand samples from commercial, historic, recreational, and notable geographic sites. **Awards:** Rex R. Elliott Award. **Frequency:** annual. **Type:** recognition. **Divisions:** Biogenic Sands; Educators; Gemology; Geography; Geology; Historical mortars; Industrial Silica; Microscopy; Mineralogy; Ocean Beaches; Photographs; Planetary geology; Psychometry; Sand castles; Sand painting; Sedimentary. **Publications:** *The Sand Paper*, quarterly. Newsletter. Includes information on storage and classification systems. **Price:** included in membership dues. **Conventions/Meetings:** semiannual meeting ● periodic Sand Swops and Socializing - regional meeting (exhibits).

21603 ■ International Scouting Collectors Association (ISCA)
c/o Craig Leighty, Pres.
1012 Bartlett Rd.
Pleasanton, CA 94566
E-mail: craig.leighty@gene.ge.com
URL: http://www.scouttrader.org
Contact: Craig Leighty, Pres.
Founded: 1970. **Members:** 1,000. **Membership Dues:** youth in North America, $10 (annual) ● adult in North America, $25 (annual) ● adult outside North America, $40 (annual) ● life, $350. **Description:** Collectors of Scouting memorabilia. Promotes interest in the history of Scouting through the collection and trading of related memorabilia. Facilitates communication and trading among members. Sponsors memorabilia shows, called "trade-o-rees" around the country. Provides information on trade-by-mail opportunities. Conducts educational programs. **Awards:** Distinguished Service Award. **Frequency:** annual. **Type:** recognition. **Recipient:** for individuals who have contributed significantly to the hobby of scouting memorabilia and to scouting ● George Boxer Memorial. **Frequency:** annual. **Type:** recognition. **Recipient:** for outstanding scouter/collector making noteworthy contribution to hobby. **Computer Services:** Mailing lists. **Committees:** Advisory; Distinguished Service Award; Ethics; Nominations. **Formerly:** Western Traders Association; (2001) American

Scouting Traders Association. **Publications:** *American Scouting Traders Association Report*, quarterly. Newsletter. Contains news and reports on ASTA functions, trade-o-rees, Scouting memorabilia and its history, new patches issued, and a complete roster of members. **Price:** included in membership dues; $5.00 for back issues plus postage. ISSN: 1079-6576. **Circulation:** 1,000. **Advertising:** accepted. Also Cited As: *American STAR* ● Journal, quarterly. **Price:** included in membership dues. **Conventions/Meetings:** periodic Trade-O-Rees - meeting, traders and collectors of Boy Scout memorabilia (exhibits).

21604 ■ International Society of Animal License Collectors (ISALC)
928 SR 2206
Clinton, KY 42031
Ph: (270)653-6060
Fax: (270)653-3030
E-mail: tagman2@earthlink.net
Contact: Dr. William J. Bone, Sec.-Treas./Ed.
Founded: 1976. **Members:** 123. **Membership Dues:** in U.S., $10 (annual) ● outside U.S., $15 (annual). **Multinational. Description:** Persons interested in collecting animal license tags and certificates and related materials. Compiles statistics and disseminates information about dog licensing laws, license issuance by jurisdiction, and systems of registration. Holds competitions to find oldest dog tag from each state or country. Compiles statistics of oldest-known dog tags issued by each town, city, country, or state agency. Research program has been broadened to include a special survey of all known dog tags issued prior to 1900 and all dog tags issued on military installations & a listing of all foreign countries that have issued tags. **Awards:** Owney Award. **Frequency:** periodic. **Type:** recognition. **Recipient:** for contributions to the hobby. **Publications:** *Membership Roster*, annual. Membership Directory. **Advertising:** accepted ● *Paw Prints*, quarterly. Newsletter. **Conventions/Meetings:** annual conference (exhibits) ● regional meeting.

21605 ■ International Society of Antique Scale Collectors (ISASC)
3616 Noakes St.
Los Angeles, CA 90023
Ph: (323)263-6878
Fax: (323)263-3147
E-mail: peg@sympatico.ca
URL: http://www.isasc.org
Contact: Peter Laycock, Pres.
Founded: 1976. **Members:** 550. **Membership Dues:** active, $65 (annual) ● associate, $65 (annual). **Budget:** $80,000. **National Groups:** 2. **Description:** Represents museums, institutions, and individuals who collect antique scales and weights. Fosters communication among collectors in 16 countries and to add to the body of existing knowledge of scales and weights. Acts as a medium for exchange and dissemination of information. **Libraries: Type:** not open to the public. **Holdings:** books, periodicals. **Subjects:** scales, weights, metrology, history. **Computer Services:** Mailing lists. **Publications:** *Bibliography of Weighing Instruments* ● *Equilibrium*, quarterly. Journal. Contains historical illustrated material and information on scales and weights. ISSN: 0893-2883. Also Cited As: *EQM* ● *President's Newsletter*, quarterly ● Articles ● Books ● Catalogs ● Membership Directory, annual ● Pamphlets. **Conventions/Meetings:** annual convention and seminar, special events and auction - mid May.

21606 ■ International Swizzle Stick Collectors Association (ISSCA)
c/o Ray P. Hoare, Co-Chm.
PO Box 1117
Bellingham, WA 98227-1117
Ph: (604)936-7636
E-mail: veray.issca@shaw.ca
URL: http://www.swizzlesticks-issca.com
Contact: Ray P. Hoare, Co-Chm.
Founded: 1985. **Members:** 110. **Membership Dues:** individual, $30 (annual) ● spouse, $10 (annual) ● in Canada, $35 (annual) ● international resident, $40 (annual). **Staff:** 3. **Description:** Swizzle stick collec-

tors. Promotes interest in the hobby and its history, and cooperation and communication among hobbyists. Provides information on swizzle stick collecting. **Libraries: Type:** reference. **Holdings:** 18; business records, clippings. **Subjects:** swizzle stick collecting. **Computer Services:** Electronic publishing, Help Wanted Guide ● electronic publishing, Stick Locator. **Publications:** *Swizzle Stick News*, monthly. Newsletter. Includes articles by and about members of ISSCA, editor's notes, and a help wanted section where members can exchange information. **Price:** included in membership dues. **Circulation:** 110. **Advertising:** accepted. **Conventions/Meetings:** biennial conference, opportunity for collectors to gain and exchange knowledge and trade swizzle sticks in quantity (exhibits).

21607 ■ International Willow Collectors (IWC)
c/o Edie Cronk, Membership Chm.
2408 46th St.
Des Moines, IA 50310
E-mail: info@willowcollectors.org
URL: http://www.willowcollectors.org
Contact: Dean Swearingen, Treas.
Founded: 1986. **Members:** 290. **Membership Dues:** individual in U.S., $30 (annual) ● family, $40 (annual) ● individual outside U.S., $35 (annual). **Regional Groups:** 4. **State Groups:** 4. **Local Groups:** 4. **Multinational. Description:** Persons who collect Willow-pattern china and other Willow items. Promotes the study and enjoyment of Willow. Facilitates communication among members. **Libraries: Type:** reference. **Holdings:** archival material, artwork, books, business records, clippings, periodicals. **Subjects:** ceramics, willow memorabilia. **Publications:** *The Willow Review*, quarterly. Newsletter. **Price:** $23.00/year. **Circulation:** 1,000. **Advertising:** accepted. **Conventions/Meetings:** annual convention, with auction, show and sale (exhibits).

21608 ■ Just for Openers (JFO)
PO Box 64
Chapel Hill, NC 27514
E-mail: jfo@mindspring.com
URL: http://www.just-for-openers.org
Contact: John Stanley, Ed.
Founded: 1979. **Members:** 275. **Membership Dues:** individual, $20 (annual). **Staff:** 1. **Budget:** $3,500. **Description:** Represents collectors of bottle openers and corkscrews. **Publications:** *American Breweries II*. Book. Offers 18,000 entries for nearly 8,000 known American brewing firms, tracing names, addresses, and dates of operation. **Price:** $20.00 plus shipping and handling ● *Just for Openers Newsletter*, quarterly. **Price:** $20.00/year. **Advertising:** accepted ● *2005 Handbook of United States Beer Advertising Openers and Corkscrews*. Includes information of all known beer advertising openers for each type. **Price:** $20.00 in U.S. **Conventions/Meetings:** annual conference (exhibits).

21609 ■ Kate Greenaway Society
c/o Deltiologists of America
PO Box 8
Norwood, PA 19074
E-mail: postcardclassics@juno.com
URL: http://www.deltiologists-america.com
Contact: James Lewis Lowe, Dir.
Founded: 1970. **Description:** Represents collectors of Kate Greenaway books, souvenirs, buttons and other items. Seeks at renewing interests of collecting memorabilia from the late writer-artist. **Affiliated With:** Deltiologists of America.

21610 ■ Krystonia Collector's Club
125 W Ellsworth
Ann Arbor, MI 48108
Ph: (734)332-8773
URL: http://www.krystonia.net
Contact: Martha Nichols, Dir.
Founded: 1989. **Members:** 22,000. **Membership Dues:** club, $30 (annual). **Staff:** 5. **Description:** Individuals interested in collecting Krystonia role-playing game figurines, a fantasy line consisting of dragons and wizards made of porcelain. **Publications:** *Chronicles of Krystonia*. Book ● *Krystonia III*. Book ●

Krystonian Adventures. Book ● *Phargol Horn*, quarterly. Newsletter. **Price:** included in membership dues ● *Wonderous Webb*. Book.

21611 ■ Little Elegance Memories of Yesterday

Address Unknown since 2007

Founded: 1991. **Members:** 20,000. **Membership Dues:** $22 (annual). **Staff:** 3. **Local Groups:** 10. **For-Profit. Description:** Producer of porcelain bisque figurines. **Formerly:** (2000) Memories of Yesterday Collectors Society. **Publications:** *Sharing Memories*, quarterly. Newsletter. **Price:** included in membership. **Circulation:** 35,000. **Advertising:** not accepted. **Conventions/Meetings:** annual Society Social - general assembly; **Avg. Attendance:** 350.

21612 ■ M. T. Bottle Collectors Association (MTBCA)

PO Box 1581
Deland, FL 32721
Ph: (386)734-3651 (386)789-5255
Fax: (386)789-4667
Contact: C.W. Marks, VP

Founded: 1970. **Members:** 82. **Membership Dues:** individual, family, $10 (annual). **Description:** Individuals with an interest in antique bottles. Promotes collection of M.T. bottles. Conducts educational programs. **Affiliated With:** Federation of Historical Bottle Collectors. **Publications:** *Diggers Dispatch*, monthly. Newsletter. Contains information on glass, artifacts, historical events. **Price:** free. **Circulation:** 85. **Advertising:** accepted ● Annual club membership roster. **Conventions/Meetings:** annual Bottle and Insulator Show - trade show, educational antique glass exhibits (exhibits).

21613 ■ Manuscript Society (MS)

1960 E Fairmont Dr.
Tempe, AZ 85282-2844
E-mail: manuscrip@cox.net
URL: http://www.manuscript.org
Contact: Edward C. Oetting, Exec. Dir.

Founded: 1948. **Members:** 1,800. **Membership Dues:** personal, in North America, $60 (annual) ● personal, outside North America, $75 (annual) ● contributing, $100 (annual) ● sustaining, $250 (annual) ● benefactor, $500 (annual) ● patron, $1,000 (annual). **Staff:** 3. **Description:** Collectors, dealers, librarians, curators, writers, and historians interested in autographs and original related material such as manuscripts, letters, and documents. **Awards:** Richie Maass Research Grant. **Frequency:** annual. **Type:** grant. **Publications:** *Autograph Collector's Checklist*. Book. **Price:** $17.20 ● *History in Your Hands*. Book ● *Manuscripts*, quarterly. Journal. **Price:** included in membership dues; $7.00 for nonmembers ● *Manuscripts: The First Twenty Years*. Book ● *News*, quarterly. Newsletter. **Price:** included in membership dues ● Membership Directory, periodic. **Conventions/Meetings:** annual convention - always May.

21614 ■ Matchbox U.S.A. (MBUSA)

62 Saw Mill Rd.
Durham, CT 06422
Ph: (860)349-1655
E-mail: mtchboxusa@aol.com
URL: http://www.charliemackonline.com
Contact: Charles Mack, Ed./Sole Proprietor

Founded: 1977. **Members:** 1,000. **Membership Dues:** standard class in U.S., $35 (annual) ● airmail outside U.S., $46 (annual) ● 1st class in U.S., $43 (annual). **Description:** Collectors and enthusiasts of matchbox cars. Promotes the enjoyment of collecting matchbox cars. Provides exchange of new product information. Operates museum of more than 28,000 matchbox toys. **Libraries: Type:** reference. **Holdings:** archival material, books, clippings, periodicals. **Subjects:** matchbox toys. **Publications:** Magazine, monthly. **Price:** $32.00 for 3rd Class; $39.00 for 1st Class; $42.00 outside U.S. **Circulation:** 1,000. **Advertising:** accepted ● Bulletin. **Conventions/Meetings:** annual Matchbox, Diecast Toy and Racing Collectibles Show - meeting, toy show (exhibits).

21615 ■ McDonald's Collectors Club

1153 S Lee St.
PO Box 200
Des Plaines, IL 60016-0200
E-mail: questions@mcdclub.com
URL: http://www.mcdclub.com
Contact: William Thomas, Pres.

Founded: 1990. **Members:** 400. **Membership Dues:** individual, $25 (annual) ● family, $30 (annual) ● individual outside U.S., $30 (annual) ● family outside U.S., $35 (annual) ● junior, $25 (annual). **Regional Groups:** 6. **Multinational. Description:** Individuals interested in McDonald's Restaurant memorabilia. Promotes the collection, trade, and enjoyment of McDonald's collectibles, including Happy Meal toys, boxes, and store displays; McDonald character dolls, toys, glasses, and papergoods; crew buttons and lapel pins; trayliners; and early advertising. Donates money to Ronald McDonald Children's House Charities. **Publications:** Newsletter, quarterly. **Price:** included in membership dues. **Circulation:** 400. **Advertising:** accepted. **Conventions/Meetings:** annual convention and meet (exhibits).

21616 ■ Midwest Decoy Collectors Association (MDCA)

6 E Scott St., No. 3
Chicago, IL 60610-2321
Ph: (312)337-7957 (847)842-8847
Fax: (312)337-9679
E-mail: hcdesch@rcn.com
URL: http://www.midwestdecoy.org
Contact: Herb Desch, Pres.

Founded: 1966. **Members:** 1,000. **Membership Dues:** regular, $15 (annual). **Description:** Decoy collectors. Finds and preserves old decoys; identifies decoy carvers. Provides forum for buying and selling decoys among members. Conducts programs by individual members. **Libraries: Type:** reference; open to the public. **Telecommunication Services:** electronic mail, mdc@midwestdecoy.org. **Publications:** Membership Directory, annual. Lists all members and their collection interests. **Price:** included in membership dues. **Circulation:** 1,000. **Conventions/Meetings:** annual National Antique Decoy and Sporting Collectibles - lecture (exhibits) - always last full weekend in April ● annual show - 2008 Apr. 25-26, St. Charles, IL; 2009 Apr. 24-25, St. Charles, IL.

21617 ■ Miniature Piano Enthusiast Club (MPEC)

633 Pennsylvania Ave.
Hagerstown, MD 21740
E-mail: mpec2000@hotmail.com
URL: http://www.angelfire.com/music2/miniaturepi-anoclub
Contact: Janice E. Kelsh, Founder

Founded: 1990. **Members:** 60. **Membership Dues:** regular, $15 (annual). **Staff:** 1. **Multinational. Description:** Manufacturers and collectors of miniature pianos. Promotes interest in miniature pianos; facilitates exchange of information. Conducts research on the history of miniature pianos; encourages continuing education. Sponsors exhibit. Plans to establish museum. **Libraries: Type:** reference. **Subjects:** greeting cards, postcards depicting miniature pianos. **Awards:** Miniature Piano Enthusiast Club Award. **Frequency:** quinquennial. **Type:** recognition. **Publications:** *Musically Yours!*, quarterly. Newsletter. Includes information on new and antique pianos and facts about composers. **Price:** $15.00/year. **Circulation:** 60. **Advertising:** accepted. **Conventions/Meetings:** annual convention (exhibits).

21618 ■ National Association of Avon Collectors (NAAC)

PO Box 7006
Kansas City, MO 64113
URL: http://findavon.com/localcollectorclubs.html
Contact: Connie Clark, Pres.

Founded: 1971. **Members:** 90. **Membership Dues:** organization, $25 (annual). **Staff:** 4. **Description:** Member clubs representing approximately 10,000 collectors of merchandise manufactured by Avon Products, Inc. Seeks to promote and encourage Avon

collecting. Supplies members with accurate and timely information about the hobby. Provides direct communication with all members and with Avon Products, Inc. Fosters harmonious relations between members and promote their best interests. Supports Avon bottle shows throughout the U.S. and Canada. **Awards:** annual. **Type:** recognition. **Formerly:** (1982) National Association of Avon Clubs. **Publications:** *Avon Times*, monthly. Newsletter. Includes show calendar. **Price:** $24.00/year. **Advertising:** accepted ● *Bud Hastin's Avon and CPC Collectables Encyclopedia 16th Edition/2000*. Book. **Price:** $29.95 each. **Conventions/Meetings:** annual convention, dealers for buying and selling (exhibits).

21619 ■ National Association of Breweriana Advertising (NABA)

PO Box 64
Chapel Hill, NC 27514
E-mail: naba@mindspring.com
URL: http://www.nababrew.org
Contact: Mary White, Dir.

Founded: 1972. **Members:** 1,000. **Membership Dues:** regular, in U.S., $25 (annual) ● regular, in Canada, $30 (annual) ● overseas, $40 (annual). **Description:** Collectors of brewery advertising such as signs, trays, labels, coasters, mirrors, and tap knobs; show promoters, dealers, and individuals involved in the brewery industry. Encourages the collection, preservation, and study of American breweriana. Conducts research on brewery histories. **Libraries: Type:** reference. **Additional Websites:** http://www.nababrew.com. **Publications:** *Breweriana Collector*, quarterly. Journal. Covers the history of brewing and beer advertising. Includes book reviews, calendar of events, and new member information. **Price:** included in membership dues. **Circulation:** 1,000. **Advertising:** accepted ● Membership Directory, annual. **Conventions/Meetings:** annual meeting, includes auction - first weekend of August.

21620 ■ National Association of Collectors (NAC)

18222 Flower Hill Way, No. 299
Gaithersburg, MD 20879
Ph: (301)926-8663
Fax: (301)926-7648
E-mail: nac@collectors.org
URL: http://collectors.org
Contact: Larry L. Krug, Pres.

Founded: 2002. **Membership Dues:** individual, $5 (annual) ● group (up to 10), $25 (annual). **Description:** Seeks to identify and address concerns common to all collectors: appraisals, security, conservation, restoration, displaying collections, collection management, dispersal and estate planning, research, etc. **Projects:** Reproductions.

21621 ■ National Association of Milk Bottle Collectors (NAMBC)

c/o The Milkroute (T.M.R.)
18 Pond Pl.
Cos Cob, CT 06807
E-mail: milkroute@yahoo.com
URL: http://www.milkroute.org
Contact: Mr. David Whitehead, Pres.

Founded: 1980. **Members:** 1,800. **Membership Dues:** individual in U.S., $20 (annual) ● individual in Canada, $22 (annual) ● overseas resident, $25 (annual). **Staff:** 2. **Description:** Milk bottle enthusiasts. Gathers and disseminates information relating to the collection and research of milk bottles; studies and documents the history of the fluid milk industry. Supports the National Bottle Museum. Maintains Speaker's Bureau. **Awards:** Dannheim Emerging Leader Award. **Frequency:** annual. **Type:** monetary. **Publications:** *The Milk Route*, monthly. Newsletter. Contains a wide variety of articles, dairy histories, illustrations, members' classified ads, mystery bottles and show calendar. **Price:** included in membership dues ● *Milk Route Member Directory*, annual. **Price:** included in membership dues. **Advertising:** accepted. **Conventions/Meetings:** annual meeting (exhibits) - always first weekend of June, Hershey, PA.

21622 ■ National Association of Miniature Enthusiasts (NAME)
PO Box 69
Carmel, IN 46082-0069
Ph: (317)571-8094
Free: (800)571-6263
Fax: (317)571-8105
E-mail: name@miniatures.org
URL: http://www.miniatures.org
Contact: John Purcell, Exec. VP/Chief Operating Off.
Founded: 1972. **Members:** 7,000. **Membership Dues:** regular, in U.S., $35 (annual) ● additional family, $14 (annual) ● regular, outside U.S., $37 (annual) ● youth, $17 (annual). **Staff:** 3. **Budget:** $383,000. **Regional Groups:** 16. **Local Groups:** 400. **Description:** Works to stimulate and enhance interest in the construction and collection of miniatures as historical and creative art forms. Provides instruction and training to those interested in miniature building and collecting through publications, workshops, permanent and temporary exhibitions, programs, conferences and conventions. Recognizes outstanding achievement in the creation and promotion of miniatures as an art form. Stimulates the exchange of information through the support of regional groups. Maintains a collection and museum devoted to the art and history of miniatures. **Libraries:** Type: reference. **Holdings:** 300; articles, books, periodicals. **Subjects:** miniatures. **Awards:** Academy of Honors. **Frequency:** annual. **Type:** recognition ● Founder's Award. **Frequency:** annual. **Type:** recognition ● President's Membership Grant. **Frequency:** annual. **Type:** grant. **Publications:** *Miniature Gazette*, bimonthly. Magazine. Contains historical, educational and feature articles. Regional information is shared and work projects are included. **Price:** included in membership dues. **Circulation:** 10,000. **Advertising:** accepted ● *Regional Newsletters*. **Conventions/Meetings:** conference and workshop, held locally, regionally and nationally; known as house parties (exhibits) ● annual meeting and symposium (exhibits) - always July or August.

21623 ■ National Autumn Leaf Collectors Club (NALCC)
PO Box 7929
Moreno Valley, CA 92552-7929
Ph: (951)653-6308
Fax: (951)653-5537
E-mail: bescom@nalcc.org
URL: http://nalcc.org
Contact: Paul Simpkins, Pres.
Founded: 1978. **Members:** 3,700. **Membership Dues:** full, $25 (annual). **Description:** Represents collectors of Autumn Leaf pattern dinnerware and accessories distributed through The Jewel Tea Company. **Computer Services:** Information services, club news, national convention and show dates. **Publications:** Newsletter, bimonthly, beginning in January each year. **Price:** free for members. **Conventions/Meetings:** annual meeting.

21624 ■ National Button Society (NBS)
c/o Lois Pool, Sec.
2733 Juno Pl.
Akron, OH 44333-4137
URL: http://www.iwantbuttons.com/NBS/index.htm
Contact: Lois Pool, Sec.
Founded: 1938. **Members:** 4,400. **Membership Dues:** adult, $20 (annual) ● junior age 8-17, $2 (annual) ● dual, $30 (annual). **State Groups:** 45. **Description:** Collectors and dealers of antique and modern buttons, members of the button trade, manufacturers, libraries, and museums. **Libraries:** Type: reference. **Holdings:** 61; archival material. **Subjects:** button manufacturing, button collecting. **Awards:** Type: recognition. **Additional Websites:** http://www.buttonsintime.com/nbs.htm. **Committees:** Public Relations; Recording Modern Sets. **Sections:** Junior; Shut-In. **Publications:** *National Button Bulletin*, 5/year. Includes annual *Membership Directory and Roster of State Officers and Local Clubs.* **Price:** included in membership dues. ISSN: 0027-884X. **Circulation:** 4,500. **Advertising:** accepted ● Book ● Booklets ● Also publishes material on various types of antique and modern button. **Conventions/Meet-**

ings: annual National Button Show (exhibits) - second week of August.

21625 ■ National Cap and Patch Association (CAP)
Address Unknown since 2007
Founded: 1983. **Members:** 30. **Membership Dues:** $17 (annual). **For-Profit. Description:** Cap collectors. Seeks to trade or sell baseball style caps with logos advertising different companies or events. **Libraries:** Type: open to the public. **Publications:** *Cap Member Directory*, annual. **Price:** included in membership dues ● Newsletter, quarterly.

21626 ■ National Elephant Collectors Society (NECS)
Address Unknown since 2007
Founded: 1981. **Members:** 1,000. **Staff:** 2. **Description:** Collectors of elephant memorabilia interested in contributing to and promoting the preservation of the elephant. Provides information on the origin, habitat, care, and folklore of the elephant. Aids members in expanding collections through correspondence with other collectors. Works with organizations to prevent the extinction of the elephant. Offers classes to school children in all collecting. Maintains small museum. **Libraries:** Type: not open to the public. **Holdings:** 400. **Subjects:** elephants. **Publications:** *Jumbo Jargon*, quarterly. Newsletter. **Price:** included in membership dues. **Advertising:** accepted.

21627 ■ National Fishing Lure Collectors Club (NFLCC)
c/o Colby Sorrells, Sec.-Treas.
PO Box 509
Mansfield, TX 76063
Ph: (817)473-6748
E-mail: texasbassbugger@yahoo.com
URL: http://www.nflcc.com
Contact: Colby Sorrells, Sec.-Treas.
Founded: 1976. **Members:** 5,000. **Membership Dues:** regular, in U.S., $25 (annual) ● regular, in Canada, $50 (annual) ● regular, outside U.S., $75 (annual). **Budget:** $200,000. **Regional Groups:** 10. **Description:** Collectors of all aspects of fishing tackle including lures, rods, reels, motors, tackle accessories, and paper. Promotes the historical documentation of fishing tackle makers of the past and assists members with their appraisal and identification efforts. **Libraries:** Type: reference. **Holdings:** archival material, artwork, books, clippings, monographs, periodicals. **Subjects:** fishing tackle makers and their biographies. **Publications:** *Gazette*, quarterly. Newsletter. Includes swap meet calendar, club news, historic articles on tackle makers, classified advertisements and tips to collectors. **Price:** included in membership dues ● *Membership List*, annual. Membership Directory ● Magazine, semiannual. Includes information on tackle companies, tips and ideas, special feature stories, photographs, and drawings. **Alternate Formats:** online. **Conventions/Meetings:** regional meeting, with old fishing equipment (exhibits) - 20-25/year ● Regional Swap Meets - regional meeting.

21628 ■ National Graniteware Society (NGS)
PO Box 9248
Cedar Rapids, IA 52409-9248
Ph: (616)361-8697
E-mail: 4alisonbrown@comcast.net
URL: http://www.graniteware.org
Contact: Alison Brown, Pres.
Founded: 1986. **Members:** 600. **Membership Dues:** individual, $25 (annual). **Regional Groups:** 6. **State Groups:** 6. **Description:** Promotes the preservation and collection of graniteware. Offers assistance to individuals or groups interested in forming a graniteware collectors' state chapter. (The name graniteware is derived either from the items' speckled appearance, resembling granite, or from the term Granite Iron Ware, a product of the St. Louis Stamping Co., one of the first manufacturers to obtain a patent. Graniteware was produced in many colors as well as in speckled, spattered, shaded, marbled, mottled, swirled, and veined designs). **Formerly:** (1986) American Graniteware Association. **Publica-**

tions: *Membership Roster*, annual. Membership Directory ● *National Graniteware Newsletter*, quarterly. **Conventions/Meetings:** annual meeting (exhibits) - always fourth Friday in July.

21629 ■ National Marble Club of America (NMCA)
Address Unknown since 2007
Founded: 1983. **Members:** 1,011. **Membership Dues:** individual, $12 (annual). **Staff:** 2. **Description:** Collectors of marbles; enthusiasts of the game of marbles. Promotes the hobby of marble collecting. Seeks to "bring back" and preserve the game of marbles. Teaches children how to play marbles. Sponsors competitions and marble playing demonstrations. **Libraries:** Type: reference. **Holdings:** 46; artwork, books, clippings, periodicals. **Subjects:** marble collecting and playing—-History of Marbles. **Awards:** Good Sportsmanship Award. **Frequency:** annual. **Type:** trophy. **Recipient:** for marble tournament winner. **Publications:** *History, Manufacture, Collecting and Playing*. **Advertising:** accepted ● Newsletter, quarterly. **Price:** included in membership dues; available to members only. **Circulation:** 981. **Advertising:** accepted. **Conventions/Meetings:** annual National Marble Tournament of America - competition (exhibits) - always June ● annual Township Championship - competition - every April.

21630 ■ National Pop Can Collectors (NPCC)
c/o Lance Meade, Membership Dir.
335 Dellwood St. S
Cambridge, MN 55008
E-mail: sodacans@sherbtel.net
URL: http://www.canogram.com
Contact: Lance Meade, Membership Dir.
Founded: 1976. **Members:** 100. **Membership Dues:** in U.S., $25 (annual) ● outside U.S., $30 (annual). **Staff:** 3. **Regional Groups:** 5. **Description:** Collectors of soda cans; other interested individuals. Works to promote the collection of soda cans and associated items, including advertisements, bottles, openers, trays, and caps. **Computer Services:** Mailing lists, membership roster. **Publications:** *Can-O-Gram*, bimonthly. Newsletter. Features updates and articles. **Price:** included in membership dues. **Circulation:** 200. **Advertising:** accepted. **Conventions/Meetings:** annual EXTRAVA-CAN-ZA - meet, with trade sessions.

21631 ■ National Shaving Mug Collectors Association (NSMCA)
c/o Dick Leidlein, VP
3443 Boston Twp Line Rd.
Richmond, IN 47374
Ph: (765)935-7736
E-mail: dleidlein@parallax.ws
URL: http://www.nsmca.net
Contact: Dick Leidlein, VP
Founded: 1980. **Members:** 500. **Membership Dues:** couple, household, $35 (annual). **Description:** Collectors of shaving mugs and other shaving equipment. Promotes collection of shaving paraphernalia as a hobby. Facilitates communication and trading among members; gathers and disseminates information on shaving mugs and related equipment. **Libraries:** Type: not open to the public. **Holdings:** archival material, articles, clippings, periodicals. **Subjects:** shaving mugs, shaving paraphernalia. **Publications:** Newsletter, quarterly. **Price:** included in membership dues ● Directory, annual ● Brochure. **Conventions/Meetings:** semiannual convention - always in spring and fall.

21632 ■ National Shelley China Club (NSCC)
591 W 67th Ave.
Anchorage, AK 99518-1555
Ph: (907)562-2124
Fax: (907)562-0473
URL: http://www.nationalshelleychinaclub.com
Contact: Kay Hinderliter, Pres.
Founded: 1990. **Members:** 600. **Membership Dues:** individual, $35 (annual) ● family, $50 (annual). **Multinational. Description:** Represents collectors of Shelley Pottery and Shelley Fine Bone China. **Publications:** *Shelley*, periodic. Newsletter. Contains

informative articles about Shelley and Wileman, regional meetings, sales, and events. **Price:** included in membership dues. **Conventions/Meetings:** annual conference.

21633 ■ National Society of Arkansas Pottery Collectors (NSAPC)
2006 Beckenham Cove
Little Rock, AR 72212
URL: http://home.flash.net/~gemoore/nsapc.htm
Description: Represents collectors of Arkansas pottery. **Publications:** Newsletter, quarterly. **Price:** $20.00/year.

21634 ■ National Toothpick Holder Collectors' Society (NTHCS)
PO Box 852
Archer City, TX 76351
E-mail: information@nthcs.org
URL: http://www.nthcs.org
Contact: Ms. Christine Groves, Contact
Founded: 1973. **Members:** 700. **Membership Dues:** individual in U.S., $20 (annual) ● multiple household, $25 (annual) ● individual outside U.S., $23 (annual) ● multiple household outside U.S., $28 (annual). **Description:** Represents collectors of antique toothpick holders. Aims to share information and knowledge about toothpick holders. Invites recognized authorities and researchers of glass and antiques to speak at meetings. Has sponsored annual limited editions of toothpick holders. **Libraries: Type:** reference. **Holdings:** video recordings. **Subjects:** glass, collecting, toothpick holders. **Awards: Type:** recognition. **Recipient:** for convention displays. **Telecommunication Services:** electronic mail, tpinfo@glass-works.com ● electronic mail, membership@nthcs.org. **Formerly:** (1976) Toothpick Holder Collectors' Society. **Publications:** Toothpick Bulletin, 10/year. Newsletters. Contains information on identification of patterns, reproductions, and trading and selling. Includes research reports. **Price:** included in membership dues ● Membership Directory, annual. **Price:** free, for members only. **Conventions/Meetings:** annual conference (exhibits) - usually the second full weekend of August.

21635 ■ National Valentine Collectors' Association (NVCA)
c/o Nancy Rosin, VP
PO Box 1404
Santa Ana, CA 92702
E-mail: nancyrosin@aol.com
URL: http://telebody.com/valentines/languageoflove-ephsoc.html
Contact: Nancy Rosin, VP
Founded: 1977. **Members:** 400. **Membership Dues:** individual, $16 (annual). **Description:** Private collectors, museum curators, and others interested in learning about the history and value of antique valentines. Promotes the exchange of information about valentine collecting; keeps in contact with museums around the country to obtain pictures for newsletter articles. Holds quarterly auction. Maintains large collection of news clippings, articles, and valentines; holds book with valentine rarity and values. Local programs include displays and slide shows. Operates speakers' bureau. **Libraries: Type:** not open to the public. **Holdings:** artwork, books. **Subjects:** valentines. **Publications:** Primer & Price guide. **Price:** $14.95 plus $2.50 for postage ● Booklets, quarterly. **Advertising:** accepted ● Bulletin, quarterly. ISSN: 1044-8896. **Advertising:** accepted ● Membership Directory, annual. **Conventions/Meetings:** semiannual conference (exhibits).

21636 ■ New Mexico Barbed Wire Collectors Association (NMBWCA)
PO Box 102
Stanley, NM 87056
Ph: (505)832-4339
Fax: (505)832-2552
Contact: Dan Sowle, Pres.
Founded: 1972. **Members:** 150. **Membership Dues:** individual, $10 (annual). **Staff:** 6. **State Groups:** 1. **Description:** Collectors and admirers of "primitives," particularly barbed wire and related items. Seeks to

sustain and expand participation in the collection of such items. Facilitates communication and cooperation among members; participates in charitable programs; maintains museum and hall of fame; makes available children's services; sponsors competitions. **Libraries: Type:** reference. **Holdings:** archival material, articles, artwork, books, clippings, periodicals. **Subjects:** collection of primitives. **Publications:** Wire, Barb and Nail, bimonthly. Newsletter. **Price:** included in membership dues. **Circulation:** 200. **Advertising:** accepted. **Conventions/Meetings:** annual Barb Wire and Collectors Show - conference and board meeting (exhibits) - always third weekend in July.

21637 ■ Newspaper Collectors Society of America (NCSA)
c/o Rick Brown
6031 Winterset Dr.
Lansing, MI 48911-4860
Ph: (517)887-1255
E-mail: help@historybuff.com
URL: http://www.historybuff.com
Contact: Rick Brown, Contact
Founded: 1984. **Description:** Individuals, museums, libraries, and historical societies that collect newspapers. Promotes the hobby of newspaper collecting; disseminates information about the history of journalism and printing; encourages fellowship among members. Offers referral service for buying and selling of antique newspapers via website. Maintains online newspaper archive. **Formerly:** (1997) History Buffs Home Page.

21638 ■ North American Society of Pipe Collectors (NASPC)
PO Box 9642
Columbus, OH 43209-0642
E-mail: john@naspc.org
URL: http://www.naspc.org
Contact: John Tolle, Pres.
Founded: 1994. **Members:** 808. **Membership Dues:** regular, in U.S., $14 (annual) ● regular, in Canada, $17 (annual). **Multinational. Description:** Promotes pipe smoking and collecting, information sharing, knowledge of tobaccos and fellowship with other pipe smokers. **Publications:** Newsletter, quarterly. **Price:** included in membership dues. **Conventions/Meetings:** annual trade show - 2008 Aug. 21, Columbus, OH; 2009 Aug. 28, Columbus, OH; 2010 Aug. 29, Columbus, OH.

21639 ■ North American Torquay Society (NATS)
136007 Maxson Ct.
Spotsylvania, VA 22553
E-mail: president@torquayus.org
URL: http://www.torquayus.org
Contact: Shelby Scherr, Pres.
Founded: 1989. **Members:** 425. **Membership Dues:** individual, $25 (annual) ● joint, $30 (annual) ● regular, outside U.S. and Canada, $35 (annual). **Budget:** $10,000. **Regional Groups:** 6. **Multinational. Description:** Collectors, dealers, and individuals interested in Torquay potteries. Promotes the study and enjoyment of Torquay pottery. (Torquay is a generic term used by collectors and dealers when referring to the South Devon potteries in England.) Disseminates information; conducts research; exchanges ideas. **Libraries: Type:** reference. **Holdings:** artwork, books, business records, clippings, periodicals. **Subjects:** South Devon pottery, Torquay pottery. **Awards:** Outstanding Member Award. **Frequency:** periodic. **Type:** recognition. **Publications:** Membership Roster, periodic. Directory. **Advertising:** accepted ● The Torquay Collector, quarterly. Magazine. Provides a forum for members to share their collections and viewpoints. **Price:** free for members; $5.00 for nonmembers. **Circulation:** 425. **Advertising:** accepted. **Conventions/Meetings:** annual conference, slide and oral presentations and sales (exhibits).

21640 ■ North American Trap Collector Association (NATCA)
PO Box 94
Galloway, OH 43119
Ph: (614)878-6011

Fax: (614)878-7621
E-mail: trappersworld@rrohio.com
URL: http://www.usedtraps.com/natca
Contact: Tom Parr, Ed.
Founded: 1985. **Members:** 1,350. **Membership Dues:** individual in U.S. and Canada, $25 (annual) ● individual outside U.S. and Canada, $35 (annual) ● life, $350 ● life (over age 60), $250. **Staff:** 1. **Regional Groups:** 7. **Description:** Individuals interested in collecting trapping artifacts. Researches the history of the early fur trade; supports current fur trade activities; collects and exchanges information about traps and related items. **Libraries: Type:** reference. **Holdings:** 116; archival material, articles, business records. **Subjects:** mouse traps and bear traps. **Publications:** TRAPS, bimonthly. Newsletter. Contains stories and articles by members, old trap ads, photographs, calendar of events and swap meets, and classified ads. **Price:** included in membership dues. **Circulation:** 1,350. Also Cited As: Trading, Researching, and Preserving Steeltraps. **Conventions/Meetings:** annual meeting, swap meet (exhibits) - always March in Sidney, OH ● annual meeting, swap meet - always WA ● annual meeting, swap meet - always Glenwood, IA ● annual meeting, swap meet - always Buhl, AL.

21641 ■ Northeastern Spoon Collectors Guild (NSCG)
PO Box 12072
Albany, NY 12212
E-mail: bownor@aol.com
URL: http://www.souvenirspoons.com/nscg
Contact: Anne Marek, Pres.
Founded: 1987. **Members:** 150. **Membership Dues:** initial, $15. **Description:** Spoon collectors. Promotes the enjoyment of spoon-collecting hobby. **Publications:** The Cauldron, quarterly. Newsletter. **Price:** included in membership dues. **Advertising:** accepted ● Northeastern Spoon Collectors Guild Roster of Fellow Spooners, annual. Directory. **Price:** included in membership dues. **Conventions/Meetings:** semiannual regional meeting.

21642 ■ Novelty Salt and Pepper Shakers Club
PO Box 416
Gladstone, OR 97027-0416
E-mail: dmac925@yahoo.com
URL: http://www.saltandpepperclub.com
Contact: Louise Davis, Membership Coor.
Founded: 1987. **Members:** 1,200. **Membership Dues:** primary, $30 (annual) ● associate, $5 (annual) ● junior, $10 (annual). **Staff:** 1. **Local Groups:** 23. **Description:** Collectors of salt and pepper shakers. Serves as a forum for the exchange of information for members. Sponsors competitions. **Telecommunication Services:** electronic bulletin board. **Publications:** Novelty Salt and Pepper Shakers Club Newsletter, quarterly. **Price:** included in membership dues. **Circulation:** 1,100. **Advertising:** accepted. **Conventions/Meetings:** annual convention, theme related (exhibits) - always July ● annual convention, with contests, speakers, buying/selling and auctions (exhibits).

21643 ■ Occupied Japan Club (OJC)
c/o Florence Archambault, Sec./Ed.
29 Freeborn St.
Newport, RI 02840-1821
Ph: (401)846-9024
E-mail: florence@aiconnect.com
URL: http://www.ojclub.com
Contact: Florence Archambault, Sec./Ed.
Founded: 1979. **Members:** 300. **Membership Dues:** regular, $20 (annual). **Description:** Individual collectors of items manufactured in Japan during the U.S. occupation (1945-52) and stamped "Made in Occupied Japan." Aims to exchange information. Increases individual collections through trading and buying. **Also Known As:** O.J. Club. **Publications:** The Upside Down World of an O.J. Collector, bimonthly. Newsletter. **Price:** included in membership dues. **Circulation:** 300. **Advertising:** accepted. **Conventions/Meetings:** periodic meeting (exhibits).

21644 ■ Old Reel Collectors Association (ORCA)
c/o Roger Schulz, Sec.-Treas.
160 Shoreline Walk
Alpharetta, GA 30022
E-mail: sroger748@aol.com
URL: http://www.orcaonline.org
Contact: Roger Schulz, Sec.-Treas.
Founded: 1990. **Membership Dues:** regular, in U.S., $30 (annual) ● regular, in Canada, $35 (annual) ● regular, outside U.S. and Canada, $40 (annual). **Multinational. Description:** Encourages the collection and preservation of old fishing reels. Provides education through the collection and distribution of historical and technical data on fishing reels, their development and their inventors and manufacturers from the earliest times through the present day. **Computer Services:** Online services, message board. **Publications:** *The Reel News*, bimonthly. Newsletter ● Brochure.

21645 ■ On the Lighter Side, International Lighter Collectors (OTLS)
PO Box 1733
Quitman, TX 75783-2733
Ph: (903)763-2795
Fax: (903)763-4953
E-mail: info@otls.com
URL: http://www.otls.com
Contact: Judith Sanders, Chair
Founded: 1983. **Members:** 900. **Membership Dues:** in U.S. and Canada, $42 (annual) ● overseas, $47 (annual). **Staff:** 8. **Multinational. Description:** Individuals interested in the history of lighters and lighter manufacturers. Facilitates the exchange of information and lighter trading among members. Conducts research programs. **Libraries: Type:** reference. **Publications:** *On the Lighter Side*, bimonthly. Newsletter. **Circulation:** 1,000. **Advertising:** accepted. **Conventions/Meetings:** annual convention (exhibits).

21646 ■ Oughtred Society
c/o Clark McCoy, Membership Sec.
PO Box 69
Pleasanton, CA 94566
E-mail: oughtredsociety@comcast.net
URL: http://www.oughtred.org
Contact: Clark McCoy, Membership Sec.
Founded: 1991. **Members:** 370. **Membership Dues:** regular, in U.S., $35 (annual) ● regular, outside U.S., $40 (annual). **Description:** Encourages the study and collection of the history of slide rules; promotes numeracy. **Libraries: Type:** not open to the public. **Holdings:** 300. **Subjects:** slide rules, calculators, jettons, planimeters. **Publications:** *Journal of the Oughtred Society*, semiannual. **Price:** included in membership dues; $12.50 back issues. ISSN: 1061-6292. **Circulation:** 350. **Advertising:** accepted ● Various works related to slide rules; two so far, others under consideration. **Conventions/Meetings:** meeting and conference (exhibits) - 3/year.

21647 ■ Paperweight Collectors' Association (PCA)
PO Box 4153
Emerald Isle, NC 28594
Ph: (336)869-2769
Fax: (336)869-8974
E-mail: info@paperweight.org
URL: http://www.paperweight.org
Contact: James Lefever, Pres.
Founded: 1953. **Members:** 1,100. **Membership Dues:** personal/household in U.S., $60 (annual) ● personal/household outside U.S., $80 (annual) ● personal/household in U.S., $110 (biennial) ● personal/household outside U.S., $150 (biennial). **Staff:** 1. **Budget:** $50,000. **Regional Groups:** 18. **Description:** Individual collectors, museums, art galleries, artist/makers, and dealers. Provides information to members and others on the history, origin, quality, genuineness, and availability of paperweights. Stimulates interest in the production and collection of high-quality paperweights. **Committees:** Education; Publications. **Publications:** *Annual Bulletin of the Paperweight Collectors Association, Inc.*, annual. Contains articles about antique paperweights and contemporary artists. **Price:** $35.00. ISSN: 1077-4548. **Circulation:** 2,000. **Advertising:** accepted ● *PCA Newsletter*, quarterly. Includes informational articles, updates and calendar of events. **Price:** included in membership dues. **Circulation:** 1,000. **Conventions/Meetings:** biennial convention and workshop, artists' and dealers' displays of paperweights (exhibits) - always odd-numbered years.

21648 ■ Partisan Prohibition Historical Society (PPHS)
PO Box 2635
Denver, CO 80201
Ph: (303)237-4947
E-mail: earldodge@dodgeoffice.net
URL: http://www.prohibitionists.org
Contact: Earl F. Dodge, Dir.
Founded: 1963. **Members:** 800. **Membership Dues:** booster club, $20 (annual). **Staff:** 2. **Description:** Individuals interested in preserving the historical aspects of the Prohibition movement. (Prohibition refers to the period in the U.S. when the manufacture and sale of alcoholic beverages was federally restricted by the 18th Amendment. Ratified in 1919, the amendment was repealed in 1933 by the 21st Amendment.) Collects temperance and prohibition era memorabilia such as campaign buttons, books, old magazines, and pictures. Operates speakers' bureau. **Libraries: Type:** reference. **Holdings:** 500; books. **Subjects:** prohibition movement. **Awards: Frequency:** annual. **Type:** recognition. **Recipient:** for individuals and groups who have contributed toward the preservation of the tradition of the prohibition party, a political party formed in 1869 that fostered the institution of prohibition. **Affiliated With:** Prohibition National Committee. **Publications:** *National Statesman*, 10/year. Newsletter. **Conventions/Meetings:** biennial meeting - usually June.

21649 ■ Peanut Pals (PP)
c/o Lyle Augustine, Jr.
32 E Diaz Ave.
Nesquehoning, PA 18240
E-mail: info@peanutpals.org
URL: http://www.peanutpals.org
Contact: Tony Scola, Pres.
Founded: 1978. **Members:** 640. **Membership Dues:** primary, $20 (annual) ● associate, $10 (annual). **Budget:** $12,000. **Regional Groups:** 3. **Description:** Individuals with a common interest in the study and collection of Planters Peanuts memorabilia. Exchanges information about the history of the Planters Peanut Company and the multitude of items marketed by or associated with the company for the past 90 years. Focuses on interesting people connected with Planters and biographical sketches of members giving accounts of their years in collecting Planters memorabilia. **Libraries: Type:** reference. **Holdings:** 23; papers. **Subjects:** company history, collectibles, collectors. **Publications:** *Peanut Pals Directory*, annual. **Price:** included in membership dues. **Circulation:** 640 ● *Peanut Papers*, bimonthly. Newsletter. **Price:** included in membership dues. **Circulation:** 640. **Advertising:** accepted. **Conventions/Meetings:** annual meeting and convention, national (exhibits).

21650 ■ Pen Collectors of America (PCA)
PO Box 174
Garden Prairie, IL 61038-0174
Ph: (319)372-3730
Fax: (319)372-0882
E-mail: info@pencollectors.com
URL: http://www.pencollectors.com
Contact: Roger E. Wooten, Treas.
Founded: 1991. **Members:** 2,000. **Membership Dues:** regular, in U.S., $40 (annual) ● regular, in U.S., $105 (triennial) ● regular, outside U.S., $60 (annual) ● regular, outside U.S., $150 (triennial). **Description:** Seeks to foster and maintain the integrity of pen collecting. Promotes the use of fountain pens. Encourages effective education, communication and understanding among all collectors. Strives to define pen collecting as an international hobby. **Libraries: Type:** reference. **Subjects:** vintage pens. **Projects:** PENS for KIDS. **Publications:** *PENnant*, 3/year. Journal.

21651 ■ Pepsi-Cola Collectors Club (PCCC)
PO Box 817
Claremont, CA 91711
Ph: (909)946-6026
Fax: (909)946-4786
URL: http://www.pepsigifts.com/pcccinfo.html
Contact: Bob Stoddard, Contact
Founded: 1983. **Membership Dues:** primary, $18 (annual) ● associate, $2 (annual) ● primary (overseas), $30 (annual). **Description:** Collectors and enthusiasts of Pepsi memorabilia. Promotes the collecting of Pepsi items. **Publications:** Newsletter, bimonthly. **Price:** included in membership dues. **Advertising:** accepted. **Conventions/Meetings:** annual Pepsi Fest - festival.

21652 ■ Pewter Collectors Club of America (PCCA)
504 W Lafayette St.
West Chester, PA 19380-2210
Ph: (860)673-6637
E-mail: simplepewter@bluefrog.com
URL: http://members.aol.com/pewterpcca
Contact: Louise Graver, Membership Chair
Founded: 1934. **Members:** 550. **Membership Dues:** individual/family, $60 (annual). **Regional Groups:** 4. **Description:** Collectors of pewter objects; dealers, museums, pewter restorers, and libraries. Promotes discussion and development of information on the styles, markings, and early manufacture of pewter objects, especially antique pewter made in the colonial and early federal periods in the U.S., as well as the United Kingdom (England, Ireland, Scotland, Wales) and continental Europe. Sponsors displays of pewter objects. Supports pewter-related programs sponsored by museums and historical societies. **Libraries: Type:** reference. **Holdings:** 100; archival material, books, monographs. **Subjects:** pewter and related subjects. **Awards: Frequency:** annual. **Type:** grant. **Recipient:** for research. **Committees:** Authenticity; Grants-in-Aid; Library; Membership; Programs; Publications; Publicity. **Publications:** Bulletin, semiannual. Includes research reports. **Price:** available to members only ● Catalogs ● Membership Directory, biennial ● Newsletter, semiannual. Includes book reviews, exhibit news, review of national meetings, announcements of regional meetings, and auction news. **Price:** available to members only. **Conventions/Meetings:** semiannual meeting (exhibits) - always April/May and October ● semiannual regional meeting - New England, the mid-Atlantic, midwestern, and western areas of the U.S.

21653 ■ Pickard Collectors Club
300 E Grove St.
Bloomington, IL 61701
Ph: (309)828-5533
Fax: (309)829-2266
E-mail: info@pickardchinacollectors.org
URL: http://www.pickardchinacollectors.org
Contact: Walter Koenig, Pres.
Founded: 1991. **Members:** 250. **Membership Dues:** single, $30 (annual) ● family, $40 (annual). **Description:** Collectors of Pickard hand painted porcelain. Seeks to expand appreciation of hand painted porcelain. Conducts research on artists who worked at the Pickard factory in Illinois. **Awards:** Joy Luke Founders Award. **Frequency:** annual. **Type:** recognition. **Recipient:** for research and/or recognition for service. **Publications:** Membership Directory, quarterly. **Advertising:** accepted ● Newsletter, quarterly. **Alternate Formats:** online. **Conventions/Meetings:** annual convention (exhibits) - always May ● annual meeting.

21654 ■ Promotional Glass Collectors Association (PGCA)
c/o Marilyn Johnston, Treas.
528 Oakley
Central Point, OR 97502
Ph: (541)664-1503

E-mail: board@pgcaglassclub.com
URL: http://www.pgcaglassclub.com
Contact: Fred Stepanian, Pres.
Members: 425. **Membership Dues:** general, $15 (annual). **Description:** Represents collectors of cartoon characters, advertising and sports drinking glasses and related memorabilia and collectibles. **Computer Services:** database, glass collection ● online services, message board.

21655 ■ Red Wing Collectors Society (RWCS)
2000 W Main St., Ste.300
Red Wing, MN 55066-1993
Ph: (651)388-4004 (651)385-7716
Free: (800)977-7927
Fax: (651)388-4042
E-mail: rwcsmem@redwing.net
URL: http://www.redwingcollectors.org
Contact: Sue Jones Tagliapietra, Interim Pres.
Founded: 1977. **Members:** 5,000. **Membership Dues:** primary, $25 (annual) ● associate, $10 (annual). **State Groups:** 8. **Description:** Dedicated to the preservation of Red Wing and American pottery. Represents individuals who collect Red Wing stoneware and pottery; offers bi-monthly newsletter, website, and annual national convention that includes educational seminars, auction and show and sale. **Telecommunication Services:** electronic mail, rwcsi@redwing.net. **Committees:** Auction; Commemorative; Display; Education; Housing. **Publications:** Red Wing Collectors Newsletter, bimonthly. **Price:** included in membership dues. **Conventions/Meetings:** annual convention, offers education seminars for both adults and kids, display and events, show & sale, auction, picnic, and banquet (exhibits) - every July in Red Wing, MN.

21656 ■ Road Map Collectors Association (RMCA)
PO Box 158
Channelview, TX 77530-0158
E-mail: rhorwitz@roadmaps.org
URL: http://www.roadmaps.org
Contact: Richard Horwitz, Pres.
Founded: 1994. **Members:** 300. **Membership Dues:** individual in U.S., $15 (annual) ● individual in Canada, $16 (annual) ● individual (international), $20 (annual). **Staff:** 3. **Multinational. Description:** Collectors of road maps. Promotes collection and preservation of road maps. Facilitates communication and trading among members; serves as a clearinghouse on road maps and their collection. **Computer Services:** database ● mailing lists ● online services. **Formerly:** (2000) Road Map Collectors of America. **Publications:** The Legend, quarterly. Newsletter. Contains historical information about maps and club news. **Price:** included in membership dues. **Circulation:** 400. **Advertising:** accepted. **Conventions/Meetings:** annual Map Expo - convention - always in September.

21657 ■ Rose Bowl Collectors (RBC)
PO Box 244
Danielsville, PA 18038-0244
Ph: (610)760-8134
E-mail: bankie@concentric.net
URL: http://www.arsh.com/art-glass/collect/bankie
Contact: Johanna S. Billings, Founder
Founded: 1994. **Members:** 100. **Membership Dues:** individual, $20 (annual). **Staff:** 1. **Description:** Represents collectors of rose bowls. Promotes collection, preservation, and restoration of rose bowls. Facilitates exchange of information among members; conducts educational programs. **Publications:** Newsletter, quarterly. **Price:** $25.00 /year for nonmembers; included in membership dues. **Advertising:** accepted.

21658 ■ Safety Razor Collectors Guild (SRCG)
Address Unknown since 2007
Founded: 1985. **Multinational. Description:** Promotes the collection and preservation of safety razors, safety razor blades, and other related items. Provides recognition and registration of individual collectors, collector organizations, and commercial

dealers. Establishes rating and ethical standards. Conducts educational programs. Offers historical information. **Publications:** none.

21659 ■ Society of Inkwell Collectors (SOIC)
PO Box 324
Mossville, IL 61552-0324
Ph: (309)579-3040
E-mail: inkwellsociety@aol.com
URL: http://www.soic.com
Contact: Charles L. Van Tine, Exec. Dir.
Founded: 1981. **Members:** 500. **Membership Dues:** individual in U.S., $35 (annual) ● individual outside U.S., $40 (annual). **Staff:** 11. **For-Profit. Multinational. Description:** Collectors of inkwells, pens, and accessories. Educational organization that encourages research and facilitates the exchange of information concerning history, identification, and market prices of inkwells. Provides selling and trading area for members; offers professional appraisal referrals. **Libraries: Type:** reference. **Holdings:** 75; audiovisuals, books, clippings, periodicals. **Subjects:** inkwells, bottles and pens, history of writing, repair and cleaning techniques. **Committees:** Library. **Publications:** Inkwells and Accessories: A Collector's Guide to Useful Resources (Vol. I). **Advertising:** accepted ● McGraw Book of Antique Inkwells (Vol. I) ● The Stained Finger, quarterly. Newsletter. Includes section on items wanted. **Price:** included in membership dues. **Advertising:** accepted. **Conventions/Meetings:** biennial convention and show (exhibits).

21660 ■ Souvenir Building Collectors Society (SBCS)
c/o Bob Kneisel, Treas.
1278 Mar Vista Ave.
Pasadena, CA 91104-2951
E-mail: laragoeke@yahoo.com
Contact: Bob Kneisel, Treas.
Founded: 1994. **Members:** 325. **Membership Dues:** individual, in U.S., $25 (annual) ● regular, in Canada and international (add $5 for airmail postage), $25 (annual). **Multinational. Description:** Seeks to inform, entertain and educate collectors of souvenir buildings and monuments throughout the world. **Publications:** Souvenir Building Collector, quarterly. Newsletter. Includes illustrations. ISSN: 1092-4353. **Circulation:** 350. **Advertising:** accepted. **Alternate Formats:** online. **Conventions/Meetings:** annual convention.

21661 ■ Spark Plug Collectors of America (SPCOA)
PO Box 2229
Ann Arbor, MI 48106
Ph: (734)646-7735
E-mail: spcoa1@global.net
Contact: W.H. Bond, Founder/Dir.
Founded: 1975. **Members:** 300. **Membership Dues:** in U.S., $25 (annual) ● outside U.S., $30 (annual). **Staff:** 5. **Description:** Individuals interested in collecting antique ignition devices, primarily spark plugs, of which over 5000 brands have been built since 1890. **Libraries: Type:** reference. **Holdings:** clippings, photographs. **Publications:** The Ignitor, quarterly. Journal. **Advertising:** accepted. **Conventions/Meetings:** semiannual meeting - always August, Portland, IN and October, Hershey, PA.

21662 ■ Stangl Fulper Collectors Club (SFCC)
PO Box 538
Flemington, NJ 08822
E-mail: sherylmeissner@stanglfulper.com
Contact: Sheryl Meissner, VP/Events Coor.
Membership Dues: initial, $25 (annual). **Description:** Promotes history and collecting of Stangl and Fulper potteries. **Publications:** Newsletter, quarterly. **Conventions/Meetings:** annual Auction - meeting - every June ● monthly meeting - every last Wednesday ● annual Pottery Show - every October.

21663 ■ Statue of Liberty Club (SLC)
c/o Dick Izsak, Treas.
3665 Orchard Way
Powell, OH 43065

Ph: (216)831-2646
Fax: (216)831-0497
E-mail: info@statueoflibertyclub.com
URL: http://www.statueoflibertyclub.com
Contact: Dick Izsak, Treas.
Founded: 1991. **Members:** 250. **Membership Dues:** individual, $20 (annual). **Staff:** 4. **Regional Groups:** 2. **Description:** Provides a network for collectors of Statue of Liberty memorabilia. Encourages the exchange of information on values and history of specific items. Donates monetary gifts to the Statue of Liberty museum and art gallery. Maintains speakers' bureau and museum. **Libraries: Type:** not open to the public. **Holdings:** archival material, artwork, audiovisuals, books, clippings, periodicals. **Subjects:** history, advertising. **Publications:** Statue of Liberty Collectors' Club Newsletter, 3/year. Contains articles and information about Statue of Liberty collectibles. Contains classified section. **Price:** included in membership dues. **Circulation:** 400. **Advertising:** accepted. **Conventions/Meetings:** biennial meeting, conducts lectures and visits to the Statue of Liberty (exhibits).

21664 ■ Steiff Club
PO Box 460
Raynham Center, MA 02768-0460
Ph: (508)828-2377
Free: (800)830-0429
Fax: (508)821-4477
URL: http://www.steiffusa.com/club/homeclub.aspx
Members: 55,000. **Membership Dues:** individual (other states), $55 (annual) ● individual (in NY), $57 (annual) ● individual (in MA), $57 (annual) ● individual (in NV), $58 (annual). **Description:** Works to collect Steiff teddy bears. **Computer Services:** Information services, Exchange Market, Reader's Service. **Publications:** Steiff Club Magazine, quarterly. **Price:** included in membership dues.

21665 ■ Stein Collectors International (SCI)
PO Box 222076
Newhall, CA 91322
E-mail: layers@wa-net.com
URL: http://www.steincollectors.org
Contact: Steven Steigerwald, Exec. Dir.
Founded: 1965. **Members:** 1,700. **Membership Dues:** regular, in U.S., $35 (annual) ● regular, in Canada and Mexico, $40 (annual) ● other country, $45 (annual). **Regional Groups:** 30. **Multinational. Description:** Collectors and individuals in 10 countries interested in steins and other drinking vessels. (Steins are covered drinking mugs, usually used for beer. Most steins originate in Germany, where they have been made for nearly 5 centuries. Materials used have included copper, glass, ivory, pewter, porcelain, pottery, silver, and stoneware.) Fosters the collection and study of antique and modern beer steins. Operates clearinghouse for anonymous communication among members. Maintains museum/library. **Libraries: Type:** open to the public; by appointment only. **Holdings:** 400; articles, books, periodicals, video recordings. **Subjects:** beer steins and their manufacturers. **Awards:** Jack Heimann Service Award. **Frequency:** annual. **Type:** recognition ● Jack Lowenstein Editor's Award. **Frequency:** annual. **Type:** recognition ● Master Steinologist Award. **Frequency:** annual. **Type:** recognition. **Publications:** Prosit, quarterly. Magazine. Contains information on steins, stein festivals, chapter & convention news, and index. Also features stein exchange. **Price:** included in membership dues. **Circulation:** 1,700. **Advertising:** accepted ● Membership Directory, periodic. **Conventions/Meetings:** annual convention (exhibits).

21666 ■ Texas Date Nail Collectors Association (TDNCA)
c/o Jerry Waits, Sec.
501 W Horton
Brenham, TX 77833
Ph: (979)830-1495
E-mail: csebesta@alpha1.net
URL: http://www.NailerNews.com
Contact: Jerry Waits, Sec.
Founded: 1970. **Members:** 250. **Membership Dues:** regular, $20 (annual). **Staff:** 3. **Description:** Persons

interested in collecting date nails; date nails are driven into railroad ties and utility structures mainly to identify the date on which they were installed. Provides a medium for members to sell and trade nails. Offers information on the history of their use by railroads, treatment companies, and utility companies; membership is welcome worldwide, but the focus is primarily on North American date nails. **Libraries: Type:** open to the public. **Holdings:** photographs. **Publications:** *Date Nails and Railroad Tie Preservation.* Book. **Price:** $28.00 ● *Nailer News*, quarterly. Newsletter. **Price:** free for members ● *Railroad Date Nails: Collecting for Fun.* Pamphlet. Features a brief and illustrated guide to the hobby. **Price:** $6.00. **Conventions/Meetings:** monthly meeting ● semiannual trade show - always March in Texas, and August, rotating around the U.S.

21667 ■ Thimble Collectors International (TCI)
1039 Hill Rd., No. 121
Pickerington, OH 43147
E-mail: tci@thimblecollectors.com
URL: http://www.thimblecollectors.com
Contact: Peggy Green, Pres.
Founded: 1978. **Members:** 750. **Membership Dues:** regular, in U.S., $25 (annual) ● regular, outside U.S., $30 (annual). **Regional Groups:** 43. **Multinational. Description:** Provides information to members about thimble collecting. Promotes research and scholarship, and publishes specialized booklets on thimbles and related needlework tools. Encourages friendship and service among members who have formed or belong to regional thimble groups. **Libraries: Type:** reference; lending; not open to the public. **Holdings:** archival material, articles, audiovisuals, books, papers, photographs. **Subjects:** thimbles: sterling, gold, brass, aluminum, porcelain, wood, metal, antique, whimsicle; sewing collectibles. **Committees:** Education. **Publications:** *American Belleek Porcelain Thimbles.* **Advertising:** accepted ● *British Commemorative and Souvenir Thimble* ● *Introduction to Sewing Trade Cards* ● *Membership List*, biennial. Membership Directory ● *Thimble Collectors International Bulletin*, quarterly. **Price:** included in membership dues. **Circulation:** 700. **Advertising:** accepted ● *Threadwinders.* **Conventions/Meetings:** biennial conference, with presentations, sales mall, auction (exhibits) - even-numbered years; in August.

21668 ■ Thimble Guild
Address Unknown since 2007
Founded: 1970. **Description:** Individuals interested in learning about thimbles. Promotes research and study on the history of thimbles. **Libraries: Type:** not open to the public. **Holdings:** books, clippings, periodicals. **Subjects:** thimbles, sewing tools. **Publications:** *Thimble Guild*, quarterly. Newsletter. **Advertising:** not accepted.

21669 ■ Trade Card Collectors Association
Box 284
Marlton, NJ 08053
E-mail: trdcardguy@aol.com
URL: http://www.tradecardcollectors.com
Contact: Dave Cheadle, Contact
Founded: 1994. **Members:** 500. **Membership Dues:** individual, $35 (annual). **Description:** Collectors of 19th century advertising cards. Unites, informs, and entertains fellow collectors. Annual summer convention with collection exhibits & dealers bourse. **Publications:** *Advertising Trade Quarterly.* Magazine. **Price:** included in membership dues; $8.00 for nonmembers ● *An Introductory Guide to Collecting Advertising Trade Cards.* Booklet. **Price:** $3.00 postpaid ● *Victorian Trade Cards Historical Reference and Value Guide.* **Price:** $20.00 for members; $23.00 for nonmembers. **Conventions/Meetings:** annual convention (exhibits).

21670 ■ UHL Collectors Society
c/o Amy Busler, Sec.-Treas.
398 S Star
Santa Claus, IN 47579
Ph: (812)544-2987 (812)544-2069

E-mail: sae102568@aol.com
URL: http://www.uhlcollectors.org
Contact: Amy Busler, Sec.-Treas.
Founded: 1985. **Members:** 11. **Membership Dues:** family, $15 (annual). **Description:** Represents collectors of UHL pottery/stoneware. **Conventions/Meetings:** annual convention - last weekend of June.

21671 ■ Universal Autograph Collectors Club (UACC)
c/o Michael Hecht, Pres.
1489 W Cypress Ave.
San Dimas, CA 91773
E-mail: michael.f.hecht@smithbarney.com
URL: http://www.uacc.org
Contact: Michael Hecht, Pres.
Founded: 1965. **Members:** 1,400. **Membership Dues:** regular, in U.S., $30 (annual) ● regular, in Canada and Mexico, $35 (annual) ● in UK and Europe, 27 (annual) ● other foreign, $50 (annual) ● life, $1,000. **Budget:** $40,000. **Regional Groups:** 11. **Description:** Autograph and book collectors, dealers, and persons interested in the art of autograph collecting (philography). Encourages the study of acquiring, accumulating, and displaying autographs, signed philatelic covers, letters, manuscripts, documents, signed photos, speeches, baseballs, and other material. Provides members with research and study information, trading sessions, auction information, and other services. **Awards:** UACC Literary Awards. **Frequency:** annual. **Type:** monetary. **Recipient:** for 3 best articles published in the Pen and Quill. **Computer Services:** Mailing lists, of members. **Committees:** Ethics. **Publications:** *Pen and Quill*, bimonthly. Books. Includes articles, addresses, and advertisements. **Price:** $2.00 each. **Circulation:** 1,400. **Advertising:** accepted ● Monographs. **Conventions/Meetings:** annual board meeting ● show, for autographs.

21672 ■ Vaseline Glass Collectors, Inc. (VGCI)
14560 Schleisman
Corona, CA 92880
E-mail: vaselineglass@vaselineglass.org
URL: http://www.vaselineglass.org
Contact: Tom Foozer, Pres.
Founded: 1998. **Membership Dues:** single, $25 (annual) ● additional (spouse/significant), $5 (annual) ● junior (below 18 years old), $10 (annual) ● corporate, foreign, $35 (annual). **Multinational. Description:** Seeks to educate and unify Vaseline Glass collectors. Provides useful information for collectors and other individuals interested in Vaseline Glass. **Computer Services:** database, pictures of vaseline glass ● information services, Vaseline Glass resources. **Publications:** *Glowing Report*, semiannual. Newsletter.

21673 ■ Vintage Fashion/Costume Jewelry Club (VFCJ)
PO Box 265
Glen Oaks, NY 11004
Ph: (718)939-3095
Fax: (718)939-7988
E-mail: vfcj@aol.com
URL: http://www.lizjewel.com/vf
Contact: Lucille Tempesta, Owner/Publisher
Founded: 1991. **Membership Dues:** regular, in U.S. and Canada, $25 (annual) ● regular, outside U.S. and Canada, $30 (annual). **Multinational. Description:** Individuals who share an interest in vintage costume jewelry. Serves as information center and facilitates knowledge pertaining to vintage costume jewelry. **Publications:** *Vintage Fashion and Costume Jewelry*, quarterly. Newsletter. Contains articles covering aspects of collecting vintage costume jewelry such as restoration, repair, and helpful hints. **Price:** $20.00/year in U.S. and Canada; $25.00/year outside U.S. and Canada; $5.00/copy. **Conventions/Meetings:** biennial convention (exhibits).

21674 ■ Walt Disney Collectors Society (WDCS)
PO Box 6220
Burbank, CA 91510-6220
Free: (800)932-5749

E-mail: info@getandcollect.nl
URL: http://home.disney.go.com/guestservices/faqs
Founded: 1933. **Members:** 123. **Membership Dues:** individual (includes free gift sculpture), $50 (annual). **Multinational. Description:** Celebrates Walt Disney Classics Collection of sculptures. **Additional Websites:** http://disney.com, http://www.getandcollect.nl/WDCC6.htm. **Publications:** *Newsflash*, quarterly. Newsletter. **Price:** included in membership dues. Alternate Formats: online ● *Sketches*, quarterly. Magazine. Offers previews of Walt Disney Classics Collection releases and events.

21675 ■ Whisky Pitcher Collectors Association of America (WPCAA)
22862 Bluejay Ave.
Mattawan, MI 49071
Ph: (269)668-4169
E-mail: djcrowe@iserv.net
URL: http://www.pubjug.com
Contact: Deborah Crowe, Contact
Founded: 1992. **Membership Dues:** regular, in U.S., $18 (annual) ● regular, in Canada and Mexico, $21 (annual) ● overseas, $24 (annual). **Multinational. Description:** Furthers public knowledge of whisky pitcher (Pub Jug) collecting. Serves as a forum for collectors. Promotes communication and fellowship among collectors. **Publications:** *Black and White*, bimonthly. Newsletter. **Price:** included in membership dues; $20.00 for nonmembers with additional fee for colored version.

21676 ■ Wooton Desk Owners Society (WDOS)
9-20 166th St.
Whitestone, NY 11357
Ph: (718)767-9758
Free: (800)879-8631
Fax: (718)767-8172
E-mail: er4books@aol.com
Contact: Eileen Dubrow, Sec.
Founded: 1975. **Members:** 150. **Membership Dues:** one-time fee, $39. **Description:** Private collectors, museums, historic researchers, and dealers. Acts as information exchange. Maintains placement service; compiles statistics; conducts research programs. **Libraries: Type:** reference. **Holdings:** archival material, books, clippings. **Publications:** *Wooton Desk Catalogue.* Reprint ● Newsletter ● Exhibition catalogues.

21677 ■ World Chapter of Disneyana Enthusiasts
PO Box 470116
Celebration, FL 34747-0116
Ph: (407)275-2756
E-mail: info@magicalmountain.net
URL: http://www.magicalmountain.net/worldchapter/worldchapter.asp
Contact: Linda Rose, VP
Founded: 1986. **Members:** 1,200. **Membership Dues:** general, $17 (annual). **Staff:** 15. **Regional Groups:** 44. **Description:** Collectors and enthusiasts interested in Disney memorabilia, history, and lore. Promotes communication and fellowship among disneyana collectors and enthusiasts. Participates with local charities and volunteer organizations. Conducts educational programs. **Libraries: Type:** open to the public. **Subjects:** Disneyana. **Awards:** Chapter Member of the Year. **Frequency:** annual. **Type:** recognition. **Computer Services:** Online services, CompuServe - Florida Forum 72000, 2255. **Publications:** *Mouse Tales and Review*, quarterly. Newsletter. Contains articles, photos, and news of Walt Disney World and the World Chapter. **Price:** included in membership dues; $15.00 for nonmembers in U.S.; $20.00 for nonmembers outside U.S. **Circulation:** 700. **Advertising:** accepted. Alternate Formats: online. **Conventions/Meetings:** biennial World Chapter Disneyana Convention (exhibits) - always in Anaheim, CA ● quarterly World Chapter Meeting (exhibits) - always in Orlando, FL.

21678 ■ World's Fair Collectors Society (WFCS)
PO Box 20806
Sarasota, FL 34276-3806
Ph: (941)923-2590
E-mail: wfcs@aol.com
URL: http://members.aol.com/Bbqprod/wfcs.html
Contact: Michael R. Pender, Pres.
Founded: 1968. **Members:** 500. **Membership Dues:** regular in U.S. (first class), $13 (annual) ● regular in Canada, $15 (annual) ● regular outside U.S. and Canada, $20 (annual). **Staff:** 2. **Budget:** $8,000. **Multinational. Description:** Individuals in 8 countries interested in preserving the history of world expositions by collecting and researching World's Fair memorabilia. Provides for the exchange of ideas and World's Fair items. **Libraries: Type:** reference. **Holdings:** 1,000; books, maps, periodicals, photographs. **Affiliated With:** American Topical Association. **Publications:** *Fair News*, 3/year. Magazine. **Price:** $13.00/year first class mail; $15.00/year in Canada; $25.00/year outside North America. ISSN: 1043-3740. **Circulation:** 200. **Advertising:** accepted ● *Fair News Researcher's Guide* ● Directory, periodic. **Conventions/Meetings:** periodic meeting (exhibits).

21679 ■ Zeiss Historical Society of America (ZHSA)
73 Winsor Pl.
Glen Ridge, NJ 07028
E-mail: john.t.scott@verizon.net
URL: http://www.zeisshistorica.org
Contact: John Scott, Treas./Ed.
Founded: 1846. **Members:** 485. **Membership Dues:** regular in U.S., $40 (annual) ● regular outside U.S., $50 (annual). **Staff:** 5. **Multinational. Description:** Collectors of cameras, microscopes, telescopes, and other optical equipment; former employees of the Zeiss company; people in the camera industry; historians. Dedicated to the study and exchange of information regarding the history of the Carl Zeiss Optical Company and its affiliates. (Zeiss, 1816-88, was a German manufacturer of optical instruments who founded an optical factory in Jena in 1846.) Holds discussions; compiles statistics. **Libraries: Type:** reference. **Holdings:** archival material. **Subjects:** Zeiss. **Telecommunication Services:** electronic mail, lngubas@zeisshistorica.org. **Publications:** *Journal of the Zeiss Historical Society*, semiannual. **Price:** included in membership dues ● *Zeiss related Annual Dividend*, annual. Catalog. Features rare items for reproduction. **Price:** included in membership dues. **Conventions/Meetings:** annual conference (exhibits).

Comics

21680 ■ Friends of Lulu
83 Russell St., Ste.3R
Brooklyn, NY 11222
E-mail: info@friends-lulu.org
URL: http://www.friends-lulu.org
Contact: Shannon Crane, Pres.
Membership Dues: adult, $30 (annual) ● student, $20 (annual) ● junior (under 18 years old), $10 (annual). **Description:** Promotes female readership and participation in the comic book industry. **Awards:** Kim Yale Award for Best New Talent. **Frequency:** annual. **Type:** recognition. **Recipient:** for individuals who are within two years of their first professionally published work ● Lulu of the Year. **Frequency:** annual. **Type:** recognition. **Recipient:** for the creator, book, or other entity whose work best exemplifies Friends of Lulu's mission statement ● Volunteer of the Year Award. **Frequency:** annual. **Type:** recognition. **Recipient:** for individuals who have volunteered time and effort to advance Lulu's goals ● Women Cartoonists Hall of Fame. **Frequency:** annual. **Type:** recognition. **Recipient:** for individuals who have published work whether self-published, company-published, or net-published. **Publications:** *How To Get Girls (Into Your Store)*. Handbook. Alternate Formats: online ● *Storytime*. Book. **Price:** $9.95.

Contests

21681 ■ Miss America Organization
Two Miss Am. Way, Ste.1000
Atlantic City, NJ 08401
Ph: (609)345-7571
Fax: (609)345-6079
E-mail: info@missamerica.org
URL: http://www.missamerica.org
Contact: Art McMaster, Acting Pres./CEO
Founded: 1921. **State Groups:** 51. **Description:** Works to provide personal and professional opportunities for young American women and promote their voice in culture, politics and the community. Holds the Miss America competition; conducts achievement programs; provides scholarships for young women; maintains Speaker's Bureau. **Libraries: Type:** by appointment only. **Subjects:** Miss America history. **Awards: Type:** scholarship. **Publications:** *Program Book* ● Newsletter. Alternate Formats: online. **Conventions/Meetings:** annual convention ● annual Miss America - competition.

Correspondence

21682 ■ Friends' Health Connection (FHC)
PO Box 114
New Brunswick, NJ 08903
Ph: (732)418-1811
Free: (800)483-7436
Fax: (732)249-9897
E-mail: info@friendshealthconnection.org
URL: http://www.friendshealthconnection.org
Contact: Roxanne Black, Exec. Dir.
Founded: 1988. **Members:** 5,000. **Membership Dues:** voluntary (initiation), $30 ● regular, $15 (annual). **Staff:** 8. **Description:** Provides emotional support for individuals who suffer from or have overcome a common disease, illness, handicap, or injuries from an accident. Matches persons on a one-to-one basis according to age, health problem, and interests. Connects caregivers; this service is intended for mutual support and is not for romantic purposes. **Computer Services:** Online services, registrations and information. **Formerly:** (1995) Long Distance Love. **Publications:** *Health Connection*, annual. Newsletter. **Price:** included in membership dues. **Advertising:** accepted ● Newsletters. **Conventions/Meetings:** Wellness Lecture Series.

21683 ■ Golden Threads
PO Box 1688
Demorest, GA 30535-1688
Ph: (706)776-3959
E-mail: goldenthreads@earthlink.net
URL: http://www.home.earthlink.net/~goldengurl
Contact: Mary C. Davidson, Ed.
Founded: 1985. **Members:** 100. **Membership Dues:** individual, $55 (semiannual). **Multinational. Description:** Promotes correspondence between lesbian women via letters, telephone, tapes and email. **Awards:** GLAAD Golden Threads. **Type:** recognition ● S.A.G.E. Lifetime Achievement Award 1998. **Type:** recognition. **Publications:** Newsletter, quarterly. Includes book, tape, video reviews, list of resources, poetry, lands and places, events, health, and progress reports regarding equal rights. **Price:** $53.00 for 2 issues. **Circulation:** 200. **Advertising:** accepted. **Conventions/Meetings:** annual Celebrations - meeting - always last weekend of June, Provincetown, MA ● annual Silver Threads - meeting - January, Florida.

21684 ■ International Pen Friends (IPF)
c/o Lorrin Lee, Rep.
500 Univ. Ave., No. 2415
Honolulu, HI 96826
Ph: (808)949-5000
Free: (888)378-6634
E-mail: lorrin@lorrinlee.com
URL: http://www.pen-pals.net/ipf
Contact: Lorrin Lee, Rep.
Founded: 1967. **Members:** 300,000. **Membership Dues:** regular, $18-$28. **Languages:** English,

French, German, Portuguese, Spanish. **Multinational. Description:** Individuals who wish to correspond with people from different nations or cultures; correspondents are matched by age, sex, and language. Participants live in 192 countries and include speakers of 5 languages (English, German, Spanish, French, and Portuguese). Provides programs for school classes and youth groups, students ages 8-17 years, all ages and seniors; not open to prisoners. **Publications:** *Penpal Bulletin*. **Price:** free ● *People and Places*, quarterly. Magazine. Features pen-pal stories by members. **Price:** $30.00/year; $10.00/issue. **Advertising:** accepted.

21685 ■ National Postal Arts Association (NPAA)
Address Unknown since 2007
Founded: 1986. **Members:** 10,000. **State Groups:** 50. **Description:** Artists utilizing correspondence to encourage mail art. Sponsors exhibitions. Compiles statistics. Maintains hall of fame, speakers' bureau, and museum. **Libraries: Type:** reference. **Holdings:** archival material. **Awards: Type:** recognition. **Affiliated With:** International Artists Network. **Publications:** *Directory of Mail Art Publications*. **Conventions/Meetings:** periodic conference.

21686 ■ New Dawn (ND)
PO Box 11462
Takoma Park, MD 20913
E-mail: beddy888@hotmail.com
URL: http://thenewdawn.freeyellow.com
Contact: Maryalls Bedford, Contact
Founded: 1980. **Members:** 4,853. **Membership Dues:** regular, $18 (quarterly) ● regular, $30 (semiannual) ● regular, $48 (annual). **Staff:** 1. **Budget:** $10,000. **For-Profit. Description:** Lesbians interested in corresponding with other gay women. Functions as an exchange service through which members identify individuals with whom they wish to correspond. **Convention/Meeting:** none. **Publications:** Magazine, quarterly. Contains letters, art, photos and resources. **Price:** included in membership dues; $5.00/issue for nonmembers. **Circulation:** 5,000. **Advertising:** accepted.

21687 ■ Prison Pen Pals (PPP)
PO Box 120074
Fort Lauderdale, FL 33312
E-mail: joy@perry.net
URL: http://prisonministry.net/ftcpm
Contact: Mrs. Joy Perry, Contact
Founded: 1975. **Nonmembership. Multinational. Description:** Persons who agree to write to prisoners. Encourages prisoners to aspire to healthy, normal lives by keeping them in touch with the outside world and showing them that someone cares. Supplies list of prisoners nationwide who want pen pals. **Also Known As:** Freedom Through Christ Prison Ministry.

21688 ■ Single Booklovers
PO Box 1658
Andalusia, PA 19020
Ph: (215)638-9966
Free: (800)717-5011
E-mail: info@singlebooklovers.com
URL: http://www.singlebooklovers.com
Contact: Katherine Borish, Co-Dir.
Founded: 1970. **Members:** 1,400. **Membership Dues:** individual, $27 (annual). **For-Profit. Description:** Single, divorced, and widowed individuals who wish to meet or correspond with those who share similar reading and cultural interests. **Publications:** Newsletter, monthly. Includes sketches of members, short stories, poetry, and articles. **Price:** included in membership dues. **Conventions/Meetings:** periodic dinner.

21689 ■ Singles in Agriculture (SIA)
118 E Front Ave.
Stockton, IL 61085
Ph: (815)947-3559
Fax: (815)947-3559

E-mail: sianationaloffice@singlesinag.org
URL: http://www.singlesinag.org
Contact: Carollynn Fink, Pres.
Founded: 1986. **Members:** 1,300. **Membership Dues:** basic/associate (per couple), $40 (annual) ● regular, $45 (annual). **State Groups:** 12. **Description:** Single persons at least 18 years of age who have agricultural background or are currently working in a job related to agriculture. Works to enrich the lives of members through a friendship correspondence program. Promotes and conducts educational, recreational, and social activities. **Telecommunication Services:** electronic mail, singlesinag@blkhawk. net. **Publications:** *Over the Back Fence*, quarterly. Newsletter. **Price:** $28.00/year. **Circulation:** 1,300 ● Membership Directory, quarterly. **Price:** $35.00/year. **Circulation:** 1,000. **Conventions/Meetings:** annual Anniversary Event - meeting - always June ● annual Campout - meeting - always August ● annual convention - always February or March.

21690 ■ Student Letter Exchange (SLE)
211 Broadway, Ste.201
Lynbrook, NY 11563
Ph: (516)887-8628
Fax: (516)887-8631
E-mail: custserv@pen-pal.com
URL: http://www.pen-pal.com
Contact: Wayne Dankert, Pres.
Founded: 1936. **Description:** Seeks to build international goodwill through pen pal correspondence between young people (ages 8 to 19) in the U.S. and 100 other countries. **Publications:** Brochure. **Price:** free with stamped self-addressed envelope.

21691 ■ Unmarried-Catholics Correspondence Club (UCCC)
Address Unknown since 2007
Founded: 1980. **Members:** 1,000. **Membership Dues:** $38 (annual). **Description:** Catholics who are 18 years of age or older. Seeks to "unite unmarried Catholics in friendship." **Convention/Meeting:** none. **Publications:** Newsletter, periodic ● Also publishes update lists and roster.

21692 ■ Wishing Well (WW)
PO Box 178440
San Diego, CA 92177-8440
Ph: (858)695-3139
Fax: (858)695-3139
E-mail: laddiewww@aol.com
URL: http://www.wishingwellwomen.com
Contact: Lynn Frank, Ed.
Founded: 1974. **Members:** 500. **Membership Dues:** level A, $25 (bimonthly) ● level B, $40 (quarterly) ● level C, $60 (annual) ● level D, $80 (biennial). **Staff:** 2. **For-Profit. Multinational. Description:** Network of lesbians interested in writing to other women. Serves as a confidential exchange through which members identify other individuals with whom they wish to correspond and meet in person. **Libraries: Type:** open to the public. **Publications:** *The Wishing Well*, bimonthly. Newsletter. Includes descriptions of members, resources, and classified ads, poetry, book/music reviews, and letters/notes from members. **Price:** included in membership dues; $5.00/sample copy. ISSN: 1525-3902. **Circulation:** 3,000. **Advertising:** accepted. Alternate Formats: online. Also Cited As: *Laddies Ventures*. **Conventions/Meetings:** bimonthly meeting - usually San Diego County, CA.

21693 ■ Worldwide Friendship International (WWFI)
PO Box 562
Randallstown, MD 21133
Ph: (410)922-2795
E-mail: wwfi@us.net
URL: http://ladiesdigest.com
Contact: Elton Smith, Pres.
Founded: 1986. **Members:** 7,671. **Staff:** 2. **Budget:** $6,000. **Languages:** Chinese, English, French, Italian, Japanese, Portuguese, Spanish. **For-Profit. Description:** Seeks to bridge the gap between people of all nations through correspondence, and to assist those who wish to have pen friends at home and abroad. Participants range in age from 10 to 73 years

and represent 127 countries. **Convention/Meeting:** none. **Computer Services:** database, Pen Pals.

Crafts

21694 ■ American Needlepoint Guild (ANG)
2810 Crossroads Dr., Ste.3800
Madison, WI 53718
Ph: (608)443-2476
Fax: (608)443-2474
E-mail: membership@needlepoint.org
URL: http://www.needlepoint.org
Contact: Susan H. Davis, Pres.
Founded: 1972. **Members:** 10,500. **Membership Dues:** regular, in U.S., $33 (annual) ● regular, in Canada and Mexico, $45 (annual) ● international, $53 (annual) ● life - patron (international), $1,000. **Staff:** 8. **Budget:** $290,000. **Local Groups:** 168. **Multinational. Description:** Males and females of all ages who enjoy needlepoint. Seeks to provide educational and cultural development through participation in and encouragement of interest in the art and history of needlepoint. Sponsors amateur and professional needlework exhibits; offers correspondence courses and teacher and judging certification programs; sponsors annual seminar. **Computer Services:** Information services ● mailing lists. **Telecommunication Services:** electronic mail, faq@ needlepoint.org. **Committees:** Chapter Program; Educational Correspondence Courses; Judging Certification Program; Master Teacher Program; Visual Materials Library. **Publications:** *Needle Pointers*, bimonthly. Magazine. Contains articles, charted designs, book reviews, guild information, news of chapter activities, and calendar of events. **Price:** included in membership dues. **Circulation:** 10,300. **Advertising:** accepted ● Newsletter, bimonthly. Contains information about ANG's programs and activities. Alternate Formats: online. **Conventions/Meetings:** annual seminar, features needlework exhibit and classes in needlepoint (exhibits) - 2008 Sept. 5-12, Indian Wells, CA; 2009 Aug. 28-Sept. 4, New Orleans, LA.

21695 ■ American Quilter's Society (AQS)
PO Box 3290
Paducah, KY 42002-3290
Ph: (270)898-7903
Free: (800)626-5420
Fax: (270)898-1173
E-mail: kelly@aqsquilt.com
URL: http://www.americanquilter.com
Contact: Meredith Schroeder, Co-Founder/Pres.
Founded: 1984. **Members:** 70,000. **Membership Dues:** regular, $19 (annual). **Staff:** 12. **For-Profit. Description:** Quilters, quilt shops, and quilt guilds. Promotes quilters and quilting; encourages improvement in quilting skills. **Awards: Frequency:** periodic. **Type:** recognition. **Committees:** Appraisal. **Publications:** *American Quilter*, quarterly. Magazine. **Price:** $18.00. ISSN: 8756-6591. **Circulation:** 70,000. **Advertising:** accepted. Alternate Formats: diskette ● *AQS Update*, bimonthly ● *Show Quilts*, annual. Catalog. **Price:** $18.00 regular ● Books. **Conventions/Meetings:** competition ● annual Spring Show - conference and seminar - always in Paducah, KY.

21696 ■ American Sewing Guild (ASG)
9660 Hillcroft, Ste.510
Houston, TX 77096
Ph: (713)729-3000
Free: (877)ICANSEW
Fax: (713)721-9230
E-mail: info@asg.org
URL: http://www.asg.org
Contact: Margo Martin, Exec. Dir.
Founded: 1978. **Members:** 20,000. **Membership Dues:** first year, $35 (annual) ● subsequent, $30 (annual). **Staff:** 6. **Budget:** $600,000. **Local Groups:** 130. **Description:** Home sewers and people interested in sewing. Provides current sewing information and advice through lectures, demonstrations, classes, seminars, and fashion shows. Seeks to improve communication between home sewers and sewing indus-

try. Encourages the development of neighborhood workshop groups. **Awards:** Community Service Volunteer of the Year. **Frequency:** annual. **Type:** recognition. **Recipient:** for a member with outstanding service and dedication to the community service projects ● Member of the Year. **Frequency:** annual. **Type:** recognition. **Recipient:** for a member with outstanding service, accomplishment, and support to the organization. **Publications:** *Notions*, quarterly. Magazine. Contains sewing articles. **Price:** free for members. **Circulation:** 19,000. **Advertising:** accepted. **Conventions/Meetings:** annual convention (exhibits) - always August.

21697 ■ The Applique Society (TAS)
PO Box 89
Sequim, WA 98382-0089
Free: (800)597-9827
Fax: (800)597-9827
E-mail: tas@theappliquesociety.org
URL: http://www.theappliquesociety.org
Contact: Jaydee Price, Pres.
Founded: 1996. **Members:** 3,000. **Membership Dues:** regular, in U.S., $20 (annual) ● regular, in Canada, $25 (annual) ● regular, outside U.S. and Canada, $30 (annual). **Local Groups:** 106. **Multinational. Description:** Provides a network for ideas, teachers, tools, shops, fabrics, and applique groups. **Publications:** *The Applique Society Newsletter*, bimonthly. Alternate Formats: online. **Conventions/Meetings:** annual Quilt Show - meeting, with appliqued quilts and garments.

21698 ■ Contemporary Quilt Art Association (CQA)
PO Box 95685
Seattle, WA 98145-2685
E-mail: ledmond@comcast.net
URL: http://www.contemporaryquiltart.com
Contact: Lorraine Edmond, Membership Chair
Founded: 1986. **Members:** 106. **Membership Dues:** resident of Washington state, $50 (annual) ● sponsoring, corporate, $100 (annual). **Description:** Strives to educate the public and promote public interest in the contemporary quilt. Encourages public and private collecting of the contemporary quilt and supports quilt artists. **Publications:** *Fine Art Quilts: Work by Artists of the Contemporary QuiltArt Association*. Book ● Newsletter, monthly. **Conventions/Meetings:** monthly meeting, open to the public - every second Saturday.

21699 ■ Craft Yarn Council of America (CYCA)
PO Box 9
Gastonia, NC 28053
Ph: (704)824-7838
Fax: (704)824-0630
E-mail: info@craftyarncouncil.com
URL: http://www.craftyarncouncil.com
Contact: Mary Colucci, Exec. Dir.
Founded: 1981. **Members:** 9. **Staff:** 3. **Description:** Companies that produce craft yarn. Operates Certified Instructors Program; Knitting and Crocheting Program, through which the council organizes classes to train teachers. **Publications:** none. **Convention/Meeting:** none. **Affiliated With:** American Yarn Spinners Association.

21700 ■ Crochet Association International (CAI)
Address Unknown since 2007
Founded: 1976. **Members:** 15,000. **Description:** Crocheters, craft store owners and distributors, yarn and cord dealers and manufacturers, and craft magazine and book publishers. Goals are to gather, distribute, and promote creation of useful heirlooms and to assist those interested in the art of crocheting. Provides educational opportunities through workshops, fairs, and seminars. Maintains speakers' bureau and consulting services. **Libraries: Type:** not open to the public. **Holdings:** 3,200. **Subjects:** crochet. **Publications:** *Crochet Via The Double End Hook* ● *Elmore Method of Crochet*. Booklet ● *Tunisian Crochet In Color and Patterns* ● *Vol 2: More Elmore*. **Conventions/Meetings:** annual meeting.

21701 ■ Embroiderers' Guild of America (EGA)

335 W Broadway, Ste.100
Louisville, KY 40202
Ph: (502)589-6956
Fax: (502)584-7900
E-mail: egahq@egausa.org
URL: http://www.egausa.org
Contact: Karen L. Wojahn, Pres.

Founded: 1958. **Members:** 19,000. **Membership Dues:** individual, $24 (annual). **Staff:** 4. **Regional Groups:** 13. **Local Groups:** 353. **Description:** People interested in the art of needlework. Aims to set and maintain high standards of design, color, and workmanship in all kinds of embroidery. Sponsors exhibitions; offers examinations for teaching certification; serves as an information source for needlework in the U.S. Conducts classes and correspondence on all types of needlework. Presents certificate for successful completion of Master Craftsman Programs. **Libraries: Type:** reference; lending. **Holdings:** 5,000; books, video recordings. **Subjects:** all phases of needlework. **Awards:** Educators' Award of Excellence. **Frequency:** annual. **Type:** recognition. **Recipient:** for EGA members to recognize an individual educator ● Gold Thread Award. **Frequency:** annual. **Type:** recognition. **Recipient:** for outstanding individuals ● Research Fellowship. **Frequency:** annual. **Type:** grant. **Recipient:** for research in embroidery and textile arts. **Formerly:** Embroiderers' Guild of London, American Branch. **Publications:** *Needle Arts*, quarterly. Magazine. **Price:** included in membership dues. **Circulation:** 19,000. **Advertising:** accepted. **Conventions/Meetings:** annual lecture and seminar (exhibits) ● annual meeting and seminar ● annual National/Regional Seminars - competition (exhibits).

21702 ■ Enamelist Society (ES)

6105 Bay Hill Cir.
Jamesville, NY 13078
E-mail: webmaster@enamelistsociety.org
URL: http://www.enamelistsociety.org
Contact: Averill Shepps, Pres.

Founded: 1987. **Members:** 600. **Membership Dues:** individual/family, $35 (annual) ● supporting, $80 (annual) ● sustaining, $125 (annual) ● student, $20 (annual) ● sponsor, $250 (annual). **Description:** Craftspeople and artisans who create enamel artwork. Promotes enameling and disseminates information on its artistic and technical aspects. (Enamel is a thin film of glass fired onto metal objects to create a smooth finish.) Operates speakers' bureau; maintains museum. **Libraries: Type:** reference. **Holdings:** 300. **Awards:** The Creative Arts Award. **Frequency:** biennial. **Type:** recognition. **Recipient:** for a living enamelist who shows creativity, has the technique and presentation throughout his/her career ● Lifetime Achievement Award. **Frequency:** biennial. **Type:** recognition. **Recipient:** for a living enamelist who shows development of techniques, innovation in design, fine craftsmanship, and who shares his/her knowledge to others ● Woodrow W. Carpenter Award. **Frequency:** biennial. **Type:** recognition. **Recipient:** for contributions to the art of enameling. **Publications:** *Enamelist Society Newsletter*, quarterly. **Price:** included in membership dues. **Advertising:** accepted. **Conventions/Meetings:** biennial competition, juried enamel exhibition (exhibits) ● biennial conference and workshop (exhibits).

21703 ■ Guild of American Papercutters (GAP)

PO Box 512
Godley, TX 76044
E-mail: gapmembership@meserole.net
URL: http://www.papercutters.org
Contact: Shannon Reinbold-Gee, Pres.

Founded: 1988. **Members:** 500. **Membership Dues:** individual in North America, family in North America, $36 (annual) ● individual outside North America, family outside U.S., $46 (annual). **Description:** Unites fellow papercutters to share ideas, display artwork, and increase public appreciation and awareness of this art form. Offers demonstrations and exhibits. **Publications:** *First Cut*, quarterly. Magazine. **Price:**

included in membership dues. **Circulation:** 500. **Advertising:** accepted. **Conventions/Meetings:** Collection - meeting - 3/year ● biennial conference and workshop (exhibits).

21704 ■ Handweavers Guild of America (HGA)

1255 Buford Hwy., Ste.211
Suwanee, GA 30024
Ph: (678)730-0010
Fax: (678)730-0836
E-mail: hga@weavespindye.org
URL: http://www.weavespindye.org
Contact: Sandra Bowles, Exec. Dir./Ed.-in-Chief

Founded: 1969. **Members:** 9,000. **Membership Dues:** individual, $35 (annual) ● family, guild affiliate, $45 (annual) ● student, $20 (annual) ● guild affiliate, $90 (biennial) ● individual, $68 (biennial). **Staff:** 7. **Regional Groups:** 120. **Description:** Individuals, weaving arts guilds, educational institutions, teachers, suppliers, and libraries. Seeks to promote participation and interest in handcrafted textiles; encourage the development of places to work, sell, exhibit, and teach; bring about cooperation among agencies and individuals interested in the textile arts, fiber arts and related fields. **Libraries: Type:** not open to the public. **Holdings:** 3,000; articles, books, periodicals. **Subjects:** fiber arts. **Awards:** Certificates of Excellence. **Frequency:** biennial. **Type:** recognition. **Recipient:** for handspinning and handweaving ● HGA and Dendel Scholarship. **Frequency:** annual. **Type:** scholarship. **Recipient:** for further education of students in the fiber fields. **Computer Services:** Mailing lists, of members. **Committees:** Education; Scholarships; Slide Library; Small Expressions Exhibits; Textile Library. **Publications:** *Shuttle Spindle and Dyepot*, quarterly. Journal. Includes book reviews, calendar of events, guild news, weaving updates, artist profiles, and news; featured articles are: fiber art and artists. **Price:** included in membership dues. ISSN: 0049-0423. **Circulation:** 10,000. **Advertising:** accepted. **Conventions/Meetings:** biennial Convergence - convention and workshop, with seminars, "make-it-take it" studio classes (exhibits) - 2008 June 22-28, Tampa, FL.

21705 ■ International Guild of Miniature Artisans (IGMA)

PO Box 629
Freedom, CA 95019-0629
Ph: (831)724-7974
Free: (800)711-IGMA
Fax: (831)724-8605
E-mail: info@igma.org
URL: http://www.igma.org
Contact: Carol Hardy, Guild Admin.

Founded: 1979. **Members:** 1,500. **Membership Dues:** individual, $40 (annual) ● family, $15 (annual) ● outside U.S., $45 (annual). **Staff:** 3. **Description:** Individuals interested in promoting miniatures as an art form. Seeks to increase awareness and appreciation of high quality workmanship and the unique skills and requirements of the miniaturist through public education; recognize and honor qualified artisans; encourage the development of new artisans; establish a standard of consistent, professional, and fair conduct by artisans and dealers. Promotes the placement of miniatures in museum and gallery exhibits and collections. Serves as an avenue of communication through which the needs of the artisan, collector, and dealer can be expressed and served. Conducts annual Guild School. Grants Fellow and Artisan status to members who have achieved excellence in their field. **Awards:** Crystal Award. **Frequency:** annual. **Type:** recognition. **Recipient:** for outstanding contributions to miniatures ● The Don Buttfield Award. **Frequency:** annual. **Type:** recognition ● Guild School Scholarship. **Frequency:** annual. **Type:** scholarship. **Recipient:** for Guild School students. **Telecommunication Services:** electronic mail, igmashow@aol.com. **Committees:** Advertising; Artisan and Fellow Selection; Bylaws; Contributions/Fund Raising; Crystal Award and Don Buttfield Award; Education; Elements of Style; Ethics; Finance; Long Range Planning; Nominating. **Publications:** *The Cube*, periodic. Newsletter. **Price:** free ● Annual

Report, annual. Alternate Formats: online. **Conventions/Meetings:** annual Colonial Williamsburg Guild Study Program - workshop - 4 days every January ● annual The Guild School - meeting - one week every June in Castine, Maine ● annual The Guild Show - meeting and show, with sale, auction and classes (exhibits) - usually April, in New York, NY ● workshop.

21706 ■ International Machine Quilters Association (IMQA)

PO Box 419
Higginsville, MO 64037
Ph: (660)584-8171
Fax: (660)584-3841
E-mail: admin@imqa.org
URL: http://www.imqa.org
Contact: Frederick Hill, Pres.

Membership Dues: regular and associate, $25 (annual) ● corporate, $125 (annual). **Multinational. Description:** Seeks to promote quilting as an industry, a hobby, and an art form. Advances the use of technology as an essential tool in modern quilting. Increases the prestige, artistry, creativity, professionalism and recognition of quilts. **Awards:** IMQA Grants. **Frequency:** annual. **Type:** grant. **Recipient:** for longarm or shortarm quilters. **Telecommunication Services:** electronic mail, membership@imqa.org. **Publications:** *On Track!*, quarterly. Magazine. Contains informative articles, resources, ideas, and industry trends. **Price:** included in membership dues. **Conventions/Meetings:** annual show - 2008 May 14-17, Overland Park, KS.

21707 ■ International Old Lacers, Inc. (IOLI)

c/o Laurie J. Hughes, Membership Chair
1151 Shenandoah Dr.
Sunnyvale, CA 94087-2221
E-mail: ljh@gis.net
URL: http://www.internationaloldlacers.org
Contact: Lee Daly, Pres.

Founded: 1953. **Members:** 1,500. **Membership Dues:** regular, in U.S., Canada and Mexico, $30 (annual) ● in Africa and Pacific, $41 (annual) ● in Europe, $38 (annual) ● in South America, $33 (annual) ● additional family member, $10 (annual). **Budget:** $50,000. **Regional Groups:** 10. **State Groups:** 78. **Local Groups:** 200. **Multinational. Description:** Lacemakers and collectors with an international membership. Promotes all aspects of lace by studying, demonstrating, entering exhibitions and competitions. Assists local groups selecting teachers for their seminars, planning meetings and activities. **Libraries: Type:** not open to the public. **Holdings:** 596; books, video recordings. **Subjects:** lace related. **Awards:** Lace Contest. **Frequency:** annual. **Type:** recognition. **Recipient:** for lace design and proficiency. **Telecommunication Services:** electronic mail, daly@garden.net. **Formerly:** (1971) National Old Lacers. **Publications:** *The International Old Lacers Bulletin*, quarterly. Journal. Includes information on local workshops and lace days, book reviews, and work advice. **Price:** included in membership dues. **Circulation:** 1,500. **Advertising:** accepted. Also Cited As: *National Old Lacers Bulletin* ● *IOLI Directory*, annual. **Conventions/Meetings:** annual convention (exhibits) - always August or September. 2008 July 26-Aug. 3, Crystal Lake, IL - **Avg. Attendance:** 350.

21708 ■ International Quilt Association (IQA)

7660 Woodway, Ste.550
Houston, TX 77063
Ph: (713)781-6864
Fax: (713)781-8182
E-mail: iqa@quilts.com
URL: http://www.quilts.org
Contact: Charlotte Warr Andersen, Pres.

Founded: 1979. **Membership Dues:** general, $22 (annual) ● general, in Canada and Mexico, $35 (annual) ● international, $38 (annual). **Multinational. Description:** Works for the preservation of the art of quilting. Increases the prestige, artistry, creativity, professionalism and recognition of quilts. Fosters the appreciation of quilts and quilting as an art form throughout the world. **Publications:** *Quilts: A World* *of Beauty*, quarterly. Journal. Features quilts from the Judged Show and news about members.

21709 ■ International Wildlife Carving Association

c/o Byrn Watson, Pres.
194 Summerside Dr.
Centralia, WA 98531
Ph: (360)736-1082
E-mail: jobyrn@comcast.net
URL: http://iwfca.com
Contact: Bob L. Sutton, Chm.
Founded: 1988. **Members:** 900. **Membership Dues:** club, $250 (annual) ● sponsor, $100 (annual) ● competitor, $10 (annual) ● competitor, $40 (quinquennial) ● life, $500. **Staff:** 15. **Budget:** $10,000. **National Groups:** 12. **Description:** Wildlife carvers. IWCA is an association that sets the rules and helps the IWCA member shows. **Awards:** International Hunting Decoy Championship. **Frequency:** annual. **Type:** monetary. **Recipient:** for judged competitions ● Novice and Intermediate Carver of the Year. **Frequency:** annual. **Type:** monetary. **Recipient:** for judged competitions ● Youth Instructor Grants. **Frequency:** annual. **Type:** grant. **Recipient:** for the youth. **Subgroups:** The Back Bay Wildfowl Guild, Inc.; The Currituck Wildlife Guild; East Carolina Wildlife Arts Guild; The North American Wildfowl Carving Championship; Ocean City Wildfowl Art Show; Ohio Decoy Collectors and Carvers Association; Pacific Flyway Decoy Association; Pacific Southwest Wildlife Arts; World Fish Carving Championship. **Publications:** Newsletter, quarterly. Contains news update for members. **Price:** for members. **Circulation:** 900. **Conventions/Meetings:** annual workshop, at affiliated shows.

21710 ■ The Knitting Guild Association (TKGA)

1100-H Brandywine Blvd.
PO Box 3388
Zanesville, OH 43701-7303
Ph: (740)452-4541
Free: (800)274-6034
Fax: (740)452-2552
E-mail: tkga@tkga.com
URL: http://www.tkga.com
Contact: Debby Johnston, Program Coor.
Founded: 1984. **Members:** 12,000. **Membership Dues:** individual in U.S., $27 (annual) ● individual in Canada and Mexico, $34 (annual) ● individual outside U.S., Canada and Mexico, $42 (annual) ● retail in U.S., $50 (annual) ● retail in Canada and Mexico, $57 (annual) ● retail outside U.S., Canada and Mexico, $65 (annual). **Staff:** 10. **Budget:** $600,000. **National Groups:** 200. **Description:** Represents shop owners and individuals interested in knitting. Provides education and a means of communication to those wishing to improve the quality of workmanship and creativity of their knitting projects. **Awards:** Design Competition. **Frequency:** annual. **Type:** recognition. **Recipient:** for first 3 places for each category. **Committees:** Education; Publication. **Special Interest Groups:** Master Hand Knitting; Master Machine Knitting. **Formerly:** (2004) The Knitting Guild of America. **Publications:** *Cast On*, quarterly. Magazine. Contains articles on improving knitting skills, and latest designs and techniques for hand and machine knitters; includes book reviews. **Price:** included in membership dues. **Circulation:** 35,000. **Advertising:** accepted. Alternate Formats: CD-ROM ● *Convention Brochure*, annual ● *Seminar Brochure*, quarterly. **Conventions/Meetings:** conference and seminar (exhibits) ● annual convention (exhibits).

21711 ■ National Academy of Needlearts (NAN)

c/o Carlene Harwick
E 9526 E Munising Ave.
Munising, MI 49862
Ph: (906)387-5162
E-mail: charwick@charter.net
URL: http://www.needleart.org
Contact: Carlene Harwick, Contact
Founded: 1985. **Members:** 200. **Membership Dues:** associate, friend of NAN, $25 (annual) ● graduate,

$35 (annual) ● life, $500. **Multinational. Description:** Individuals with a needle arts teacher's certificate; associate members are individuals enrolled in Certification Program. Certifies teachers of the needle arts; sponsors correspondence courses and a two-year honors research program. Has developed a needle arts judging certification program. **Awards:** Lifetime Achievement Award. **Type:** recognition. **Recipient:** for a needle artist who upholds the highest ideals of the academy ● **Frequency:** annual. **Type:** scholarship. **Recipient:** for individuals seeking additional levels of needle arts certification. **Computer Services:** Mailing lists, of members. **Committees:** Education. **Supersedes:** National Textile Resource and Research Center. **Publications:** *Academy Nanthology*, quarterly. Newsletter. **Circulation:** 250 ● *Assembly Brochure*, annual ● *Educational Brochure*, annual. **Conventions/Meetings:** annual Assembly for Embroiderers - meeting and seminar (exhibits) - usually March.

21712 ■ National Association of Wheat Weavers (NAWW)

c/o Dianne Gardner, Treas.
RR1 Box 123
Formoso, KS 66942
E-mail: wheatwhiz@aol.com
URL: http://www.geocities.com/heartland/plains/4565
Contact: Dianne Gardner, Treas.
Founded: 1987. **Members:** 285. **Membership Dues:** in U.S., $25 (annual) ● outside U.S., $30 (annual). **Multinational. Description:** Wheat weavers, straw artists, patrons, and interested others. Seeks to preserve and promote wheat weaving (also known as corn doll making) and other forms of straw art. Sponsors demonstration classes for conventions, schools, and 4-H gatherings. Conducts open classes at Conventions Senior Centers-Extension groups, and Mission Society Circles or groups. Demonstrations at Kansas State Fair, schools and museums. **Libraries: Type:** open to the public. **Subjects:** wheat. **Additional Websites:** http://www.geocities.com/naww-strawart. **Publications:** *Gleanings*, periodic. Newsletter. **Price:** included in membership dues. **Advertising:** accepted ● Brochure. **Advertising:** accepted. **Conventions/Meetings:** annual meeting and trade show, open to public, with classes and demonstrations (exhibits) - usually April.

21713 ■ National Guild of Decoupeurs (NGD)

1017 Pucker St.
Stowe, VT 05672
Ph: (802)253-3903
E-mail: mdpeer@aol.com
URL: http://www.decoupage.org
Contact: Marion D. Peer, Contact
Founded: 1971. **Members:** 300. **Membership Dues:** electronic, $40 (annual) ● regular, in U.S. and Canada, $50 (annual) ● overseas - individual, $60 (annual). **Staff:** 1. **Regional Groups:** 5. **Description:** Seeks to: distinguish decoupage as an art in itself; identify authentic decoupage; maintain high quality in the art. Offers generalized and specialized educational programs including correspondence course. **Libraries: Type:** reference. **Subjects:** Digest I, Digest II, elements at design for decoupeurs. **Awards: Type:** recognition. **Recipient:** for achievement in laymember, journeyman, and master craftsman status. **Committees:** Standards and Judging; Visual Aids. **Publications:** *Dialogue*, quarterly. Newsletter. **Advertising:** accepted ● *Digest I* ● *Digest II* ● Videos ● Yearbook. Includes directory. **Conventions/Meetings:** annual National Convention and Decoupage Exhibition - conference (exhibits) - usually April or May.

21714 ■ National Pig Carvers Association (NPCA)

Address Unknown since 2007
Founded: 1980. **Members:** 100. **Staff:** 2. **Description:** Carvers of small wooden pigs; interested individuals. Provides interaction between individuals interested in the woodcarving craft. **Awards:** Member of the Year. **Frequency:** annual. **Type:** recognition. **Publications:** *Pigcarvers News*, monthly. Newsletter. Reports on organization and member activities. **Price:**

free. **Circulation:** 100. **Advertising:** not accepted. **Conventions/Meetings:** annual conference.

21715 ■ National Quilting Association (NQA)

PO Box 12190
Columbus, OH 43212-0190
Ph: (614)488-8520
Fax: (614)488-8521
E-mail: nqaquilts@sbcglobal.net
URL: http://www.nqaquilts.org
Contact: Marcia Knopp, Sec.
Founded: 1970. **Members:** 4,000. **Membership Dues:** individual, $20 (annual). **Staff:** 2. **Regional Groups:** 300. **Description:** Persons interested in quilts or quilting. Works to further understanding of quilts or quilting and to compile information about quilts, past and present. Holds annual quilt show. Offers teacher and judge certification programs, master quilter program, grants, and educational services. **Awards: Frequency:** annual. **Type:** grant. **Recipient:** for quilt-related activities ● **Type:** recognition. **Committees:** Education; Grant; Judges' Certification; Masters Guild; Teachers' Certification. **Publications:** *Quilting Quarterly*. Magazine. **Price:** included in membership dues. **Circulation:** 6,000. **Advertising:** accepted. **Conventions/Meetings:** annual competition and show, quilt show, vendor mall, and quilting classes (exhibits) ● annual Quilt Show (exhibits).

21716 ■ National Wood Carvers Association (NWCA)

PO Box 43218
Cincinnati, OH 45243
Ph: (513)561-0627
E-mail: nwca@chipchats.org
URL: http://www.chipchats.org
Contact: Edward F. Gallenstein, Pres./Ed.
Founded: 1953. **Members:** 20,000. **Membership Dues:** regular, in U.S., $14 (annual) ● regular, outside U.S., $16 (annual). **Staff:** 4. **Multinational. Description:** Amateur and professional woodcarvers and whittlers; suppliers of tools and products for the hobby; writers and publishers of books and magazines about carving. Provides members with information about carving, including project ideas and patterns, names of books and booklets, material, wood and tool suppliers, and methods of finishing and mounting carvings. **Awards: Type:** scholarship. **Publications:** *Chip Chats*, bimonthly. Magazine. **Price:** included in membership dues. ISSN: 0577-9294. **Circulation:** 45,000. **Conventions/Meetings:** annual meeting.

21717 ■ Northwest Regional Spinners' Association (NwRSA)

c/o Kris Heidner, Membership Chair
3300 166th Pl. SW
Lynnwood, WA 98037
Ph: (425)741-2774
E-mail: aklinect@hotmail.com
URL: http://www.nwrsa.org
Contact: Ann Klinect, Pres.
Founded: 1983. **Members:** 600. **Membership Dues:** individual, associate, $25 (annual) ● family, $30 (annual). **State Groups:** 4. **Description:** Promotes and encourages awareness and skills in the art and craft of handspinning in the community at large. Provides a communication network for those who engage in the art and craft of handspinning. Encourages the formation of other regional associations throughout the country. Conducts workshop tours with instructors of national and international acclaim. **Libraries: Type:** reference. **Holdings:** 600; books, periodicals, video recordings. **Subjects:** spinning, weaving, dyeing, fiber arts. **Awards:** Lee Lewis Study Grant. **Frequency:** annual. **Type:** grant. **Recipient:** for members and associates to expand the knowledge of the craft of hand spinning through research and study ● NwRSA Outreach Grant Fund. **Frequency:** annual. **Type:** grant. **Recipient:** to the most outstanding member. **Committees:** Audit; Conference; Grants; Library; Media; Newsletter; Publicity; Website. **Publications:** *Loose Threads*, 10/year. Newsletter. Contains news, events, dyeing information, and book reviews. **Price:** included in membership dues. **Advertising:** accepted ● Brochure. **Conventions/Meet-**

ings: annual conference and workshop, includes sales tables, competition, and fellowship (exhibits).

21718 ■ Quilters Hall of Fame
PO Box 681
Marion, IN 46952
Ph: (765)664-9333
Fax: (765)664-9333
E-mail: quiltershalloffame@sbcglobal.net
URL: http://www.quiltershalloffame.org
Contact: Hazel Carter, Pres.
Founded: 1979. **Members:** 425. **Membership Dues:** individual, $30 (annual) ● associate, $50 (annual) ● donor, $75 (annual) ● sponsor, guild, $100 (annual) ● patron, $250 (annual) ● benefactor, $500 (annual) ● president's circle and corporate, $1,000 (annual) ● individual (65 years and older), $20 (annual) ● student, $20 (annual). **Staff:** 1. **Budget:** $51,700. **Local Groups:** 1. **Description:** Promotes quilting as an art form and seeks to preserve the history of quilting. Maintains Quilters Hall of Fame to honor quilters who have made outstanding contributions to the art form; moved into the Marie Webster's home in Marion, IN, July 2004. **Libraries: Type:** open to the public. **Holdings:** 150; articles. **Subjects:** quilts, quilt blocks, patterns. **Awards:** Honoree of the Quilters Hall of Fame. **Frequency:** annual. **Type:** recognition. **Recipient:** for outstanding contributions to Quilting. **Formerly:** (1979) Continental Quilting Congress. **Publications:** *The Quilters Hall of Fame Newsletter*, semiannual. Contains organization activities, honoree news, and educational articles. **Price:** free for members. **Circulation:** 1,500 ● Quilt Celebration Catalog - annual. **Conventions/Meetings:** annual Celebration - lecture and workshop, with quilt shows, auction, Marie Webster house tours, classes, demonstrations (exhibits).

21719 ■ Smocking Arts Guild of America (SAGA)
PO Box 2846
Grapevine, TX 76099
Free: (800)520-3101
E-mail: president@smocking.org
URL: http://www.smocking.org
Contact: Ms. Kate Westlake, Pres.
Founded: 1979. **Members:** 2,500. **Membership Dues:** individual in U.S., $30 (annual) ● individual outside U.S., $35 (annual) ● business, $100 (annual) ● student, $15 (annual). **Staff:** 1. **Budget:** $250,000. **Regional Groups:** 5. **Local Groups:** 120. **Multinational. Description:** Needleart enthusiasts, designers, instructors, business owners, and others interested in smocking, embroidery, fine hand sewing, and/or fine machine sewing. Works to preserve and foster the art of smocking and related needlework through education communication and quality workmanship. Conducts artisan program in four areas of study including smocking, embroidery and heirloom stitching. Offers correspondence courses. **Awards: Frequency:** annual. **Type:** recognition. **Recipient:** for judged entries at Design Show. **Computer Services:** database, proprietary membership list. **Committees:** Standard. **Publications:** *SAGANEWS*, quarterly. Newsletter. Includes patterns and national and chapter activities. **Price:** included in membership dues. **Circulation:** 3,500. **Advertising:** accepted. **Conventions/Meetings:** seminar and regional meeting - always spring, 2-4/year ● annual workshop and convention (exhibits).

21720 ■ Society of Decorative Painters (SDP)
393 N McLean Blvd.
Wichita, KS 67203-5968
Ph: (316)269-9300
Fax: (316)269-9191
E-mail: sdp@decorativepainters.org
URL: http://www.decorativepainters.org
Contact: Cristy Keeton, Office Coor.
Founded: 1972. **Members:** 28,000. **Membership Dues:** individual, $35 (annual) ● business, $65 (annual). **Staff:** 13. **Budget:** $2,500,000. **Local Groups:** 300. **Languages:** English, Japanese, Spanish. **Description:** Individuals interested in tole and decorative painting; decorative painting supplies retailers, distributors, and wholesalers. Aims to further interest

in the field. Increases the quality of teaching and painting. Promotes an awareness of quality in the field as well as education in the decorative painting field; collects past and present decorative painting art forms. **Awards:** Certified Decorative Artist. **Frequency:** annual. **Type:** recognition. **Recipient:** for individuals passing the program ● Master Decorative Artist. **Frequency:** annual. **Type:** recognition. **Recipient:** for individuals passing the program. **Affiliated With:** Craft and Hobby Association. **Formerly:** (1999) National Society of Tole and Decorative Painters. **Publications:** *The Decorative Painter*, bimonthly. Magazine. **Price:** available to members only. **Advertising:** accepted ● Books, annual. Design books (pattern, description and instructions). **Conventions/Meetings:** annual convention and trade show, includes over 400 booths (exhibits).

21721 ■ Victorian Hairwork Society (VHS)
c/o Leila Cohoon
1333 S Noland Rd.
Independence, MO 64055
Ph: (816)833-2955
E-mail: lcohoon@aol.com
URL: http://www.hairworksociety.org
Contact: Leila Cohoon, Contact
Founded: 1997. **Members:** 120. **Membership Dues:** individual, $35 (annual). **Staff:** 2. **Description:** Admirers of Victorian hairwork crafts, including hair jewelry and hair flowers. Seeks to preserve the craft tradition of Victorian hairwork. Facilitates exchange of information among members; serves as a clearinghouse on Victorian hairwork. **Computer Services:** Mailing lists. **Publications:** *Parlor Chat*, periodic. Newsletter. Contains information on the association. **Alternate Formats:** online. **Conventions/Meetings:** annual HairBall - convention.

21722 ■ World Organization of China Painters (WOCP)
2641 NW 10th St.
Oklahoma City, OK 73107-5400
Ph: (405)521-1234
Fax: (405)521-1265
E-mail: wocporg@theshop.net
URL: http://www.theshop.net/wocporg
Contact: Pat Dickerson, Exec. Dir.
Founded: 1967. **Members:** 8,000. **Membership Dues:** in U.S., $34 (annual) ● outside U.S., $39 (annual) ● club in U.S., $27 (annual) ● club outside U.S., $30 (annual). **Staff:** 3. **Regional Groups:** 6. **Local Groups:** 316. **National Groups:** 3. **Description:** Teachers, dealers, and other individuals involved or having an interest in porcelain China painting. Promotes and teaches the art of porcelain painting. Conducts research and educational programs. Sponsors China painting classes and hand-painted China exhibits. Maintains museum. **Libraries: Type:** reference. **Subjects:** porcelain and porcelain artists. **Publications:** *China Painter*, bimonthly. Magazine. Contains information relating to China painting and lessons. **Price:** included in membership dues. ISSN: 0889-8195. **Circulation:** 8,000. **Advertising:** accepted. **Conventions/Meetings:** biennial meeting, educational meeting ● biennial Porcelain Inspirations - convention, hand painted China and supplies (exhibits).

Cryptography

21723 ■ American Cryptogram Association (ACA)
3300 Darby Rd., Ste.7114
Haverford, PA 19041
E-mail: treasurer@cryptogram.org
URL: http://www.cryptogram.org
Contact: Felicia F. Gonzalez, Treas.
Founded: 1932. **Members:** 600. **Membership Dues:** regular, in North America, $18 (annual) ● regular, outside U.S., $22 (annual). **Description:** Hobbyists interested in cryptography and cryptanalysis (translating cipher or code messages into plain language). Compiles statistics. **Libraries: Type:** reference. **Holdings:** archival material. **Awards:** Greg Mellen Memo-

rial Cryptology Scholarship. **Frequency:** annual. **Type:** scholarship. **Recipient:** for the study of cryptology in the undergraduate curricula ● Undergraduate Paper Competition in Cryptology. **Frequency:** annual. **Type:** recognition. **Recipient:** for the study of cryptology in the undergraduate curricula. **Publications:** *ACA and You*. Manual ● *ACA Directory*, annual ● *The Cryptogram*, bimonthly. Journal. **Price:** included in membership dues. ISSN: 0045-9151 ● *Novice Notes* ● *Three Ways to Solve Cryptograms*. **Conventions/Meetings:** annual meeting.

Dog

21724 ■ Afghan Hound Club of America (AHCA)
c/o Donna Amos, Corresponding Sec.
10457 W Liberty Ct.
Beach Park, IL 60099
Ph: (847)599-3505
E-mail: k.d.amos@comcast.net
URL: http://clubs.akc.org/ahca
Contact: Donna Amos, Corresponding Sec.
Founded: 1937. **Members:** 410. **Membership Dues:** individual, $20 (annual). **Regional Groups:** 37. **Description:** Breeders and owners of purebred Afghan hounds. Compiles statistics; conducts educational programs. **Libraries: Type:** reference. **Holdings:** archival material. **Subjects:** breed information. **Awards: Frequency:** annual. **Type:** recognition. **Computer Services:** Online services, information and referral services. **Affiliated With:** American Kennel Club. **Publications:** *Afghan Hound Review*, bimonthly. Magazine. **Price:** $36.00. **Advertising:** accepted ● *Afghan Hounds in America* ● *Exhibitors Catalog*, annual ● *Introduction to the Afghan Hound* ● *Topknot News*, 3/year. Newsletter. **Price:** $15.00 /year for nonmembers in U.S.; $25.00 /year for nonmembers outside U.S.; included in membership dues. **Circulation:** 400 ● Also makes available films and slide shows. **Conventions/Meetings:** annual seminar, for judges (exhibits) ● annual specialty show and meeting (exhibits).

21725 ■ Airedale Terrier Club of America (ATCA)
c/o Shirley VanOver, Sec.
1897 S Tulane Rd.
Hernando, MS 38632
Ph: (662)429-3815
E-mail: sviredale@aol.com
URL: http://www.airedale.org
Contact: Virginia M. Latham Smith, Pres.
Founded: 1900. **Members:** 950. **Membership Dues:** full (plus $5 initial fee outside U.S.), $25 (annual). **Description:** Owners, breeders, and exhibitors of purebred Airedale terriers. Aims to: encourage and promote the breeding of purebred Airedale terriers; define the ideal type of Airedale terrier and to urge the adoption of this type; protect and advance the interests of the Airedale terrier by supporting specialty shows, exhibitions, and matches. Presents trophies. Fosters fellowship and good sportsmanship among dog lovers. **Affiliated With:** American Kennel Club. **Publications:** *American Airedale*, quarterly. Newsletter. **Price:** $18.00 /year for nonmembers. ISSN: 1059-4477 ● *Membership List*, annual. Membership Directory. **Conventions/Meetings:** annual meet - always first Friday of October, in Philadelphia, PA.

21726 ■ Akita Club of America (ACA)
9337 B Katy Fwy., No. 150
Houston, TX 77024
Ph: (908)879-4404
E-mail: vicepres@akitaclub.org
URL: http://www.akitaclub.org
Contact: Nancy Amburgey, Pres.
Founded: 1960. **Members:** 600. **Membership Dues:** family, $40 (annual) ● individual, $30 (annual). **Regional Groups:** 6. **Description:** Owners, breeders, and dog show and obedience exhibitors; individuals interested in the betterment of the Akita breed. Conducts research in breeding and whelping Akita dogs; cooperates with leading veterinary schools;

has compiled a concise Akita history including translations of ancient Japanese articles on the origin of the breed. Disseminates information. **Committees:** Akita Breed Standard Review; Breeders Education; Judges and Education; National Dog Show; Obedience Training; Public Education. **Affiliated With:** American Kennel Club. **Formerly:** Akita Kennel Club of America. **Publications:** *Listing of Akita Breeders and Akita Dog*, quarterly. Magazine. **Circulation:** 600 ● Manual ● Monographs. Contains information on good breeding practices. ● Newsletter, monthly ● Also publishes guides, puppy checklist, and stud book register. **Conventions/Meetings:** annual meeting and show (exhibits) ● annual National Specialty Show (exhibits).

21727 ■ Alaskan Malamute Club of America (AMCA)
c/o Leneia R. Rogowski, Corresponding Sec.
640 E 50 N
Hyrum, UT 84319
Ph: (435)245-3634
E-mail: info@alaskanmalamute.org
URL: http://www.alaskanmalamute.org
Contact: Leneia R. Rogowski, Corresponding Sec.
Founded: 1952. **Members:** 1,100. **Membership Dues:** adult, $40 (annual) ● additional adult in the same household, junior, $5 (annual) ● affiliate club, $60 (annual) ● non-affiliate club, $10 (annual). **Budget:** $32,000. **Regional Groups:** 10. **Description:** Breeders and owners of purebred Alaskan Malamute dogs. Conducts educational programs and supports studies on the problem of dwarfism in the breed. Compiles statistics on dogs winning awards. **Awards: Frequency:** annual. **Type:** recognition. **Recipient:** to show and working dogs. **Committees:** Genetic; Master Plan; Show Awards; Working Dog Certification. **Affiliated With:** American Kennel Club. **Publications:** *AMCA Newsletter*, monthly. Provides information to breeders. **Price:** included in membership dues; $42.00 /year for nonmembers; $4.00/back issue for nonmembers. **Circulation:** 1,100. **Advertising:** accepted. **Conventions/Meetings:** annual meeting ● show.

21728 ■ All American Premier Breeds Administration (AAPBA)
2001 Delameter Rd.
Castle Rock, WA 98611
Ph: (360)274-4209
Free: (888)937-7487
E-mail: aapba@aapba.com
URL: http://www.aapba.com
Contact: John C. Booker, Pres.
Founded: 1997. **Description:** Represents the interests of dog breeders, owners and enthusiasts. Educates the public on the responsibilities of pet ownership. Promotes and conducts dog sports and dog showing competitions.

21729 ■ Amateur Field Trial Clubs of America (AFTCA)
1300 Tripp Rd.
Somerville, TN 38068
Ph: (901)465-1556
Fax: (901)465-0427
E-mail: aftca@aol.com
URL: http://www.fielddog.com/aftca
Contact: Mrs. Linda Hunt, Sec.-Treas.
Founded: 1924. **Members:** 450. **Membership Dues:** club, $75 (annual). **Staff:** 2. **Description:** Local field trial clubs of nonprofessional owners/handlers of dogs used in hunting upland game birds such as quail, pheasant, and partridge. Promotes conservation and improves bird dogs for hunting and pleasure. Regulates, controls, and conducts field trials on upland game birds. Sanctions trials held by local clubs. Sponsors national amateur championships in the following divisions: Chicken; Grouse; Pheasant; Pheasant Shooting Dog; Quail; Shooting Dog; Woodcock. Compiles statistics. **Additional Websites:** http://www.aftca.org. **Conventions/Meetings:** annual Field Trial - meeting.

21730 ■ American Association of Black Russian Terriers (AABRT)
c/o Karen Magill, Treas.
341 Laurel Dr.
Danville, CA 94526
Ph: (925)820-1636
Fax: (925)837-9241
E-mail: lrc460@aol.com
URL: http://www.aabrt.com
Contact: Leanne Chase, Pres.
Membership Dues: individual, $25 (annual) ● household, $35 (annual) ● junior, $12 (annual). **Description:** Provides a forum for owners and individuals interested in Black Russian Terriers. Informs breeders and owners on the proper care of Black Russian Terriers. **Computer Services:** Information services, Black Russian Terriers resources ● online services, message board. **Telecommunication Services:** electronic mail, kcmagill@pacbell.net. **Publications:** *The Sentinel*. Newsletter. Alternate Formats: online.

21731 ■ American Belgian Malinois Club (ABMC)
21710 Cove Point Farm Rd.
Tilghman, MD 21671
Ph: (410)886-2232
E-mail: covepoint@earthlink.net
URL: http://www.american-belgian-malinois-club.org
Contact: Jim Moses, VP
Founded: 1990. **Members:** 280. **Membership Dues:** individual, $35 (annual) ● family, $55 (annual) ● junior, $10 (annual). **Budget:** $6,000. **Multinational**. **Description:** Owners, breeders and enthusiasts of the Belgian Malinois. Promotes and protects the interests of the breed through good sportsmanship. Supports AKC-sanctioned matches and shows; conducts educational programs; compiles statistics; offers breeder list and referral. **Libraries: Type:** lending. **Holdings:** archival material, audiovisuals, books, clippings, periodicals, photographs. **Subjects:** Belgian dogs. **Awards:** AKC Titles. **Frequency:** periodic. **Type:** recognition. **Recipient:** completes an AKC title. **Committees:** Membership; Rescue. **Publications:** *The Malinois Performer*, bimonthly. Newsletter. **Price:** $20.00 /year for nonmembers; included in membership dues. **Advertising:** accepted. **Conventions/Meetings:** bimonthly board meeting, reports and issues brought to the board ● annual convention ● annual National Specialty - show - usually in spring.

21732 ■ American Bloodhound Club (ABC)
c/o Jan Rothwell
193 Captain Clark Hwy.
Wilton, NH 03086-5727
E-mail: olbay101@aol.com
URL: http://www.bloodhounds.org
Contact: Cindy Andrews, Pres.
Founded: 1953. **Members:** 700. **Membership Dues:** individual, family in U.S., $40 (annual) ● junior in U.S., $20 (annual). **Regional Groups:** 6. **Description:** Represents owners, breeders, and exhibitors of purebred bloodhounds. **Telecommunication Services:** electronic mail, secncreek@aol.com. **Affiliated With:** American Kennel Club. **Publications:** *Bloodhound Bulletin*, quarterly. **Price:** $25.00 /year for members; $80.00 /year for nonmembers ● *Roster*, annual ● Newsletter, periodic. **Price:** included in membership dues. **Advertising:** accepted ● Also publishes bloodhound handbook. **Conventions/ Meetings:** annual meeting.

21733 ■ American Bouvier des Flandres Club (ABDFC)
c/o David Raper, Treas.
1718 Trinity Rd.
Raleigh, NC 27607-4920
E-mail: david_raper@worldnet.att.net
URL: http://www.bouvier.org
Contact: David Raper, Treas.
Founded: 1963. **Members:** 450. **Membership Dues:** regular, $30 (annual) ● junior, $15 (annual). **Description:** Owners and breeders of Bouvier des Flandres dogs, which are large, powerfully built, wiry-haired working dogs native to Belgium. Conducts sanctioned matches, specialty shows, seminars, and workshops.

Compiles statistics concerning Bouvier rankings. Maintains library. **Libraries: Type:** not open to the public. **Holdings:** periodicals. **Subjects:** bouvier des flandres. **Awards:** Versatility. **Type:** recognition. **Programs:** Futurity; Register of Merit; Versatility. **Affiliated With:** American Kennel Club. **Publications:** *Dirty Beards*, quarterly. Magazine. Contains information about sponsored events, OFA registry, and PennHIP. **Price:** $50.00/year. **Circulation:** 450. **Advertising:** accepted ● *Membership-Breeders Directory*, annual ● *Secretary's Bulletin*, periodic ● Also publishes brochures. **Conventions/Meetings:** annual meeting (exhibits) - always October.

21734 ■ American Boxer Club (ABC)
c/o Barbara E. Wagner, Sec.
6310 Edward Dr.
Clinton, MD 20735-4135
Ph: (301)868-2364
Fax: (301)877-0278
E-mail: jtc76@aol.com
URL: http://americanboxerclub.org
Contact: Barbara E. Wagner, Sec.
Founded: 1935. **Members:** 1,500. **Budget:** $25,000. **Description:** Breeders and owners of purebred boxers; includes 600 individuals and 54 member clubs. **Affiliated With:** American Kennel Club. **Conventions/Meetings:** semiannual meeting - always spring and fall.

21735 ■ American Brittany Club (ABC)
c/o Mary Jo Trimble, Sec.
10370 Fleming Rd.
Carterville, IL 62918
Ph: (618)985-2336
Fax: (618)985-5103
E-mail: trimnatchbritts@midamer.net
URL: http://clubs.akc.org/brit
Contact: Mary Jo Trimble, Sec.
Founded: 1928. **Members:** 2,900. **Membership Dues:** full, $30 (annual) ● associate, $3 (annual). **Staff:** 1. **Regional Groups:** 87. **Description:** Owners, breeders, and exhibitors of purebred Brittany dogs united to discourage the breed from becoming split into groups of "field dogs" and "bench dogs" and to strive to keep it forever a "dual dog." **Awards:** Hall of Fame For Dogs and People, Life Memberships. **Type:** recognition. **Recipient:** for significant contributions to the sport of field trialing. **Committees:** Field Trial Regulations; Futurity; Legal; National Trials. **Affiliated With:** American Kennel Club. **Formerly:** Brittany Spaniel Club of America. **Publications:** *American Brittany*, monthly. Magazine. **Price:** included in membership dues; $30.00 /year for nonmembers. **Advertising:** accepted ● *The Book of the American Brittany* ● *Official Book of the Brittany*. **Conventions/ Meetings:** annual meeting (exhibits) - always November, Booneville, AR ● annual Summer Specialty - specialty show.

21736 ■ American Brussels Griffon Association (ABGA)
c/o Linda Vance, Sec.
PO Box 11
Shirley, IL 61772-0011
Ph: (309)828-4311
E-mail: fistfaces@aol.com
URL: http://www.brussels-griffon.info
Contact: Linda Vance, Sec.
Founded: 1945. **Members:** 175. **Membership Dues:** regular (single, associate domestic), $35 (annual) ● regular (couple), $40 (annual) ● junior, $10 (annual) ● associate foreign, $50 (annual). **Description:** Breeders, owners, and exhibitors of the Brussels Griffon, a toy dog of Belgian origin. Participates in all-breed shows throughout the country. Conducts educational programs and competitions. **Committees:** Breed Standard; Charitable Giving Analysis; Health; Specialty Investigation. **Publications:** *ABGA Quarterly*, 3/year. Newsletter. **Conventions/Meetings:** annual specialty show.

21737 ■ American Bullmastiff Association (ABA)
c/o Walker Weeks, Membership Chm.
2425 Therese St.
Jefferson City, MO 65101

Ph: (573)635-0088
E-mail: dwalkerw@yahoo.com
URL: http://clubs.akc.org/aba
Contact: Walker Weeks, Membership Chm.
Members: 600. **Membership Dues:** couple, $45 (annual) ● individual, $35 (annual) ● junior, senior, $20 (annual). **Regional Groups:** 14. **Description:** Breeders, exhibitors, and fanciers of purebred Bullmastiff dogs united for the welfare, betterment, preservation, and protection of the breed. Conducts referral and information service. Maintains Rescue Committee that helps to find homes for Bullmastiffs found in dog pounds and shelters. **Libraries: Type:** reference. **Holdings:** archival material. **Awards:** Health and Research Committee Grant. **Type:** grant ● **Type:** recognition. **Committees:** Health/Research; Rescue. **Publications:** Bulletin, 3/year. **Price:** $12.00. **Advertising:** accepted ● Handbook ● Newsletter, bimonthly. **Conventions/Meetings:** periodic meeting, specialty show (exhibits) ● annual specialty show.

21738 ■ American Canine Education Foundation (ACEF)

c/o Lt. Wallace H. Pede, CEO
7200 Tanager St.
Springfield, VA 22150
Ph: (703)451-5656
Fax: (703)451-5979
E-mail: acef04@yahoo.com
URL: http://www.scja.org
Contact: Lt. Wallace H. Pede, CEO
Founded: 1985. **Members:** 550. **Staff:** 3. **Description:** Patrons include dog show judges, breeders, exhibitors etc. Conducts programs and courses for judges and prospective judges. Has established a Judges Institute at Indiana University of Pennsylvania and holds annual institutes throughout the country. Patronship is by donation. **Additional Websites:** http://skyhidogs.com/pages/ACEF.htm. **Affiliated With:** Senior Conformation Judges Association. **Formerly:** (2002) Senior Conformation Judges Association Education Fund; (2005) American Canine Education Fund. **Conventions/Meetings:** annual Judges Institute - seminar.

21739 ■ American Cavalier King Charles Spaniel Club (ACKCSC)

6000 High Bluff Ct.
Raleigh, NC 27612
E-mail: lkdunham@mindspring.com
URL: http://www.ackcsc.org
Contact: Lu Dunham, Corresponding Sec.
Membership Dues: regular, $30 (annual) ● associate, $30 (annual) ● overseas, $35 (annual). **Description:** Works for the promotion and protection of the Cavalier King Charles Spaniel breed of dogs and represents its interests in the AKC. **Programs:** Founding Partners. **Publications:** Annual Report, annual. **Price:** $13.00 1997-1998 Ed., plus shipping and handling ($3); $20.00 1999-2000 Ed., plus shipping and handling ($3) ● Catalog, annual. **Price:** $20.00. **Alternate Formats:** online. **Conventions/Meetings:** National Specialty - show.

21740 ■ American Chesapeake Club (ACC)

PO Box 58082
Salt Lake City, UT 84158
E-mail: president@amchessieclub.org
URL: http://www.amchessieclub.org
Contact: Melissa Schumann, Pres.
Founded: 1918. **Members:** 1,322. **Membership Dues:** household, $45 (annual) ● individual, $30 (annual) ● junior, $20 (annual). **Description:** Owners, breeders, and exhibitors of purebred Chesapeake Bay retrievers (state dog of Maryland), "the only American-bred sporting dog". Aims to foster and encourage the breeding of the Chesapeake; to conserve game through the increased use of Chesapeakes in upland game and waterfowl shooting; to improve the breed; to disseminate information concerning the breed; to improve breed standards. Supports annual entry shows, Specialty Show, Specialty Field Trial, and All-Breed Field Trial, as well as other recreational events. **Libraries: Type:** reference. **Holdings:** articles, books. **Affiliated With:** American Kennel Club. **Publications:** ACC Bulletin,

bimonthly ● Breed Book. **Price:** $24.00 ● Training Manual ● Membership Directory, annual. **Conventions/Meetings:** annual Hunt Test - meeting, with field trial ● annual Specialty Dog Show and Obedience Trial - meeting, follows A.K.C. regulations ● annual Specialty Field Trial - meeting.

21741 ■ American Dobermann Association (ADA)

PO Box 2231
Snohomish, WA 98291-2231
Ph: (425)397-7630
Fax: (425)397-8747
E-mail: americandobermann@verizon.net
URL: http://www.zorzifamily.com/dobermann
Contact: Roberto Zorzi, Contact
Membership Dues: single, $60 (annual) ● family, $90 (annual) ● youth, $30 (annual) ● single (foreign), $80 (annual) ● family (foreign), $120 (annual). **Description:** Seeks to promote and preserve the Dobermann breed as protection, and as a family companion and working dog. Enhances the Dobermann breed by educating the general public, promoting responsible breeding, and sponsoring sport events. Protects and advances the interests of the Dobermann. **Publications:** Dobermann Friend, quarterly. Magazine. **Advertising:** accepted.

21742 ■ American Dog Breeders Association (ADBA)

c/o Kate Greenwood, Pres.
PO Box 1771
Salt Lake City, UT 84110
Ph: (801)936-7513
Fax: (801)936-4229
E-mail: bstofshw@adba.cc
URL: http://www.adba.cc
Contact: Kate Greenwood, Pres.
Founded: 1909. **Staff:** 15. **For-Profit. Description:** Processes genealogy information on the American Pit Bull Terrier. **Awards:** ADBA Leaders of the Future Scholarship. **Frequency:** annual. **Type:** scholarship. **Recipient:** for existing students, or for students who are entering their first year at a university, college or trade school. **Publications:** American Pit Bull Terrier Gazette, quarterly. Magazine. Contains show information and articles on American Pit Bull Terriers. **Price:** $30.00 in U.S. and Canada; $50.00 overseas. **Circulation:** 6,000. **Advertising:** accepted. **Conventions/Meetings:** annual meeting - usually February, March.

21743 ■ American Dog Show Judges (ADSJ)

c/o Carl G. Leipmann, Sec.
9144 W Mt. Morris Rd.
Flushing, MI 48433
Ph: (810)639-7075
Fax: (810)639-7075
E-mail: cen06886@centurytel.net
URL: http://www.adsj.org
Contact: Carl G. Leipmann, Sec.
Membership Dues: single, $35 (annual) ● joint (same household), $60 (annual). **Description:** Promotes the welfare and education of AKC-approved Dog Show Judges in America. Furthers the advancement of purebred dogs. **Libraries: Type:** lending. **Holdings:** video recordings. **Subjects:** AKC breed. **Publications:** The Voice, 3/year. Newsletter. Contains ADSJ news, viewpoints on current issues and other related topics. **Price:** included in membership dues.

21744 ■ American Eskimo Dog Club of America (AEDCA)

c/o Lynn McClure, Pres.
3242 S 187th St.
Seatac, WA 98188
Ph: (206)242-9944
E-mail: anglhrt@earthlink.net
URL: http://mywebpages.comcast.net/jamarsch/aedca
Contact: Lynn McClure, Pres.
Membership Dues: single, $25 (annual) ● joint, $40 (annual). **Description:** Seeks to promote and encourage quality in the breeding of purebred American Eskimo Dogs. Protects and advances the interests of the breed. Encourages sportsmanlike competition at

dog shows and obedience trials. **Publications:** AEDCA Review. Newsletter. **Conventions/Meetings:** annual meeting, in conjunction with the Club's National Specialty Show - always in March or May.

21745 ■ American Fox Terrier Club (AFTC)

c/o Mrs. Anne E. Smith
6838 Lake Shore Rd.
Derby, NY 14047
Ph: (717)292-5259
E-mail: jeeplovers@verizon.net
URL: http://www.aftc.org
Contact: Jo Hubbs, Pres.
Founded: 1885. **Members:** 650. **Membership Dues:** single in U.S. (plus 10 initiation fee), $30 (annual) ● married couple in U.S. (plus 20 initiation fee), $40 (annual) ● single in Canada and Mexico (plus 10 initiation fee), $35 (annual) ● married couple in Canada and Mexico (plus 20 initiation fee), $45 (annual) ● single outside U.S. (plus 10 initiation fee), $50 (annual) ● married couple outside U.S. (plus 20 initiation fee), $65 (annual). **Regional Groups:** 1. **Multinational. Description:** Owners, breeders, and exhibitors of purebred fox terriers (both smooth and wire coat). Operates placement service; compiles statistics. **Libraries: Type:** reference. **Holdings:** archival material. **Awards:** Champion Meersbrook Bristles Challenge Cup. **Frequency:** annual. **Type:** recognition. **Recipient:** for the Best Wire Fox Terrier, dog or bitch, at each of the three shows during the year which the Grand Challenge Cup shall be offered ● Champion Sabine Result Trophy. **Frequency:** annual. **Type:** trophy. **Recipient:** for the best Smooth Fox Terrier, dog or bitch, at each of the three shows during the year which the Board of Governors shall consider most desirable. **Committees:** Competition. **Affiliated With:** American Kennel Club. **Publications:** Directory, annual ● Newsletter, bimonthly. **Conventions/Meetings:** competition ● annual meeting - always in Philadelphia, PA.

21746 ■ American Kennel Club (AKC)

260 Madison Ave.
New York, NY 10016
Ph: (212)696-8200
Fax: (212)696-8299
E-mail: info@akc.org
URL: http://www.akc.org
Contact: Ronald H. Menaker, Chm.
Founded: 1884. **Members:** 567. **Staff:** 403. **Local Groups:** 4,500. **National Groups:** 150. **Description:** All-breed, specialty breed, obedience, and field trial dog clubs. Maintains stud book registry and pedigree records; approves standards for judging breeds eligible for registration; adopts and enforces rules governing shows, obedience trials, hunting tests, and field trials. Supervises a public and children's education program promoting responsible dog ownership. Provides free information to the public. Offers judging education; compiles statistics. **Libraries: Type:** reference. **Holdings:** 18,000; audiovisuals, books, periodicals. **Subjects:** dog. **Awards:** Awards for Canine Excellence. **Frequency:** annual. **Type:** recognition. **Recipient:** for outstanding dogs that have performed some exemplary act, whether large or seemingly small that has significantly benefited a community or individual ● Breeder of the year Award. **Frequency:** annual. **Type:** recognition. **Recipient:** for breeders who have dedicated their lives to improving the health, temperament and quality of purebred dogs ● Lifetime Achievement Awards. **Frequency:** annual. **Type:** recognition. **Recipient:** for individuals who have made outstanding contributions to the sport of purebred dogs on a national level ● **Type:** scholarship. **Recipient:** for students enrolled in veterinary school within the U.S. who are studying in canine area and undergraduates active in sport of purebred dogs. **Computer Services:** Mailing lists. **Telecommunication Services:** phone referral service, breeder information and referral service, (900)407-7877. **Departments:** Agility; Canine Good Citizen; Club Education/Booth Services; Club Relations; Companion Animal Recovery; Conference and Travel; Customer Service; DNA Operations and Educational Services. **Publications:** AKC Awards, monthly. Magazine. **Price:** $89.00/year in U.S.; $109.00/year

in Canada; $114.00/year outside U.S. and Canada. ISSN: 0888-627X. **Circulation:** 14,000 ● *AKC Dog Care and Training.* Book ● *AKC Family Dog,* bimonthly. Magazine. **Price:** $9.95/year ● *Complete Dog Book,* every 2-3 years ● *Puppies,* annual. Magazine ● *Pure-Bred Dogs - American Kennel Gazette,* monthly. Magazine. **Price:** $24.95/year; $31.95/year (with AKC events calendar). ISSN: 0033-4561. **Circulation:** 55,000. **Advertising:** accepted. Alternate Formats: microform. Also Cited As: *AKC Gazette* ● *The Stud Book Register,* monthly. **Conventions/Meetings:** competition ● quarterly congress.

21747 ■ American Lhasa Apso Club (ALAC)
c/o Joyce Johanson, Membership Chair
126 Kurlene Dr.
Macomb, IL 61455
Ph: (309)837-1665
E-mail: jk-johanson@wiu.edu
URL: http://www.lhasaapso.org
Contact: Leslie Baumann, Pres.
Founded: 1959. **Members:** 500. **Membership Dues:** individual, $35 (annual). **Description:** Promotes and encourages high ethical standards for breeding and exhibiting the Lhasa Apso and encourages a cooperative effort for the betterment of the breed. Holds one specialty show and one futurity show per year. Offers educational programs for members and judges. **Awards: Type:** recognition. **Affiliated With:** American Kennel Club. **Publications:** *Lhasa Bulletin,* quarterly. Magazine. **Price:** included in membership dues. **Conventions/Meetings:** annual National Specialty Dog Show - meeting (exhibits).

21748 ■ American Maltese Association (AMA)
c/o Richard Glenn, Pres.
10175 Reese Rd.
Clarkston, MI 48348
E-mail: juliep@swfla.rr.com
URL: http://www.americanmaltese.org
Contact: Richard Glenn, Pres.
Founded: 1960. **Members:** 400. **Membership Dues:** individual, $25 (annual). **Regional Groups:** 3. **Description:** Owners, breeders, and exhibitors of Maltese dogs. Conducts educational programs. Participates in charitable program. Compiles statistics on the Maltese breed. **Awards:** Top Breeders. **Frequency:** annual. **Type:** recognition. **Recipient:** to a member ● Top Winning Maltese Dog. **Frequency:** annual. **Type:** recognition. **Affiliated With:** American Kennel Club. **Publications:** *Maltese R/X,* annual. Newsletter. **Price:** $25.00 for 2 years in U.S.; $30.00 for 2 years in Canada; $50.00 for 2 years outside U.S. and Canada ● *Directory,* annual ● Also publishes information on puppy care. **Conventions/Meetings:** competition ● annual meeting, in conjunction with The Westminster Dog Show (exhibits) - always February, in New York City.

21749 ■ American Manchester Terrier Club (AMTC)
c/o Paula Hradkowsky, 1st VP
2274 Broomstick Ln.
Green Lane, PA 18054
Ph: (215)679-4607
E-mail: seav@pcpartner.net
URL: http://clubs.akc.org/mtca
Contact: Paula Hradkowsky, 1st VP
Founded: 1958. **Members:** 240. **Membership Dues:** junior, $10 (annual) ● individual, $25 (annual) ● family, $30 (annual). **Regional Groups:** 8. **Local Groups:** 3. **Description:** Owners, breeders, and exhibitors of purebred Manchester terriers. Conducts matches, shows, and obedience trials; promotes the breeding of toy and standard purebred Manchester terriers; encourages the acceptance of the American Kennel Club (see separate entry) breed standard of excellence. Compiles statistics; maintains hall of fame; conducts educational programs. **Libraries: Type:** reference; lending; not open to the public. **Holdings:** archival material, artwork, audiovisuals, clippings, periodicals. **Subjects:** Manchester terriers. **Awards:** Good Sportsmanship Award. **Frequency:** annual. **Type:** recognition ● Hall of Fame. **Frequency:** annual. **Type:** recognition ● Register of Merit. **Frequency:** annual. **Type:** recognition. **Tele-**

communication Services: electronic mail, rashal@yahoo.com. **Committees:** Archives; Breed Brochure; Breed Standard Revision; Breeder Referral; By-Laws and Constitution; Education; Ethics; Hall of Fame; Health; Judges Selection; Newsletter; Obedience; Rescue; Standing Rules; Sunshine. **Affiliated With:** American Kennel Club. **Formerly:** (1958) American Toy Manchester Terrier Club. **Publications:** *AMTC Newsletter,* quarterly. Includes committee reports, board actions, statistics, health news, and show announcements. **Price:** included in membership dues; $20.00 /year for nonmembers. **Circulation:** 200. **Advertising:** accepted ● *Breed Brochure* ● *Education Guide* ● *Membership List,* annual. **Conventions/Meetings:** annual meeting and show (exhibits).

21750 ■ American Miniature Schnauzer Club (AMSC)
105 Fite's Creek Rd.
Mount Holly, NC 28120-1149
Ph: (704)827-6544 (704)687-3556
E-mail: secretary@amsc.us
URL: http://amsc.us
Contact: Ms. Terrie Houck, Sec.
Founded: 1933. **Members:** 620. **Membership Dues:** individual, $20 (annual). **Local Groups:** 21. **Description:** Represents owners, breeders, and exhibitors of purebred miniature schnauzer dogs. **Affiliated With:** American Kennel Club. **Publications:** *AMSCOPE,* monthly. Newsletter. **Price:** included in membership dues ● Booklets. Provides information on raising, care, grooming, and showing of miniature schnauzers. **Conventions/Meetings:** annual meeting - always first Saturday in October, Philadelphia, PA ● specialty show.

21751 ■ American Pointer Club (APC)
c/o Susan Bleckley, Recording Sec.
327 Lugonia St.
Newport Beach, CA 92663
Ph: (949)515-4454
E-mail: recordingsecretary@americanpointerclub.org
URL: http://www.americanpointerclub.org
Contact: Susan Bleckley, Recording Sec.
Founded: 1938. **Members:** 211. **Membership Dues:** single, $35 (annual) ● family, $50 (annual) ● junior, $15 (annual) ● additional adult, $20 (annual). **Description:** Breeders and owners of purebred pointers. Awards several trophies annually in competition, shows, and field trials. Maintains hall of fame; compiles statistics. **Affiliated With:** American Kennel Club. **Publications:** *APC Breeders Directory,* annual ● *Pointer Points,* bimonthly. Magazine ● Membership Directory, annual ● Yearbook. **Conventions/Meetings:** annual specialty show.

21752 ■ American Pomeranian Club (APC)
c/o Cindy Boulware, Pres.
6450 Rolling Heights Cir.
Kaufman, TX 75142
Ph: (972)962-3872
Fax: (972)962-3872
E-mail: contact@americanpomeranianclub.org
URL: http://americanpomeranianclub.org
Contact: Cindy Boulware, Pres.
Founded: 1887. **Members:** 450. **Membership Dues:** individual, in U.S., $30 (annual) ● individual, outside U.S., $35 (annual) ● junior, in U.S. (must be under 18 years old), $10 (annual) ● household, in U.S., $45 (annual) ● household, outside U.S., $50 (annual). **Staff:** 12. **Regional Groups:** 25. **Description:** Breeders and owners of purebred Pomeranians. Compiles statistics; offers children's services; participates in charitable program. Conducts educational programs. **Awards:** Top Breeder, Top Exhibitor, Special Humanitarian. **Frequency:** annual. **Type:** recognition. **Committees:** AKC Video; Judges Education; Standard. **Affiliated With:** American Kennel Club. **Publications:** *APC Information Booklet.* **Price:** $2.00 plus postage ● *APC Roster,* annual. Directory ● *Pomeranian Review,* bimonthly. Magazine. Contains articles of interest to Pomeranian owners. **Price:** $10.00/issue; $45.00 /year for individuals (first class mail); $37.00 /year for individuals (second class mail). **Circulation:** 650. **Advertising:** accepted. **Conventions/**

Meetings: competition ● annual meeting (exhibits) ● annual specialty show.

21753 ■ American Rottweiler Club (ARC)
c/o Pam Grant, Pres.
43 Huntsman Dr.
Plano, IL 60545
Ph: (630)552-8740
E-mail: quailrdg@comcast.net
URL: http://www.amrottclub.org
Contact: Pam Grant, Pres.
Founded: 1974. **Members:** 1,600. **Membership Dues:** individual, family ($15 for each additional household member), $30 (annual). **Regional Groups:** 9. **Local Groups:** 36. **Description:** Individuals interested in the protection and promotion of the Rottweiler dog. Conducts educational programs; compiles statistics. **Awards:** Friend of the Rottweiler. **Frequency:** annual. **Type:** recognition ● Gaines Award. **Frequency:** annual. **Type:** recognition ● Production Award. **Frequency:** annual. **Type:** recognition ● Top ARCITE. **Frequency:** annual. **Type:** recognition ● Top Ten Award. **Frequency:** annual. **Type:** recognition. **Committees:** AKC Slide Show; Illustrated Standards; Judges Education; Judging Selection; Production. **Affiliated With:** American Kennel Club. **Supersedes:** Rottweiler Club of America. **Publications:** *ARK Newsletter,* quarterly. Includes articles on health issues and listings of clubs and upcoming shows. **Price:** $30.00/year. **Circulation:** 1,700. **Advertising:** accepted ● *Rottweiler Pictorial* ● Membership Directory, periodic ● Also publishes *Your New Rottweiler Puppy* and *Rottweiler Ownership Illustrated Standard.* **Conventions/Meetings:** annual meeting - always Memorial Day weekend.

21754 ■ American Sealyham Terrier Club (ASTC)
c/o Sharon Yard, Pres.
14111 Rehoboth Church Rd.
Lovettsville, VA 20180-3217
Ph: (540)882-3492
E-mail: shenandoa@erols.com
URL: http://clubs.akc.org/sealy
Contact: Sharon Yard, Pres.
Founded: 1913. **Members:** 350. **Membership Dues:** family, in U.S. and Canada, $30 (annual) ● individual, in U.S. and Canada, $20 (annual) ● associate, outside U.S. and Canada, $15 (annual) ● junior, $5 (annual). **Regional Groups:** 1. **Description:** Owners, breeders, and exhibitors of purebred Sealyham terriers. Encourages exhibition and working trials. Sponsors competitions. **Awards: Type:** recognition. **Affiliated With:** American Kennel Club. **Publications:** *Official Book of the Sealyham Terrier.* **Price:** $40.00 ● *Sealy Barks,* bimonthly. Newsletter. **Conventions/Meetings:** annual meeting - always October, in Pennsylvania.

21755 ■ American Shetland Sheepdog Association (ASSA)
c/o Mrs. Beverly B. Muhlenhaupt, Corresponding Sec.
7274 S Chase Way
Littleton, CO 80128-4945
Ph: (303)979-8998
E-mail: traceerville@earthlink.net
URL: http://www.assa.org
Contact: Mrs. Beverly B. Muhlenhaupt, Corresponding Sec.
Founded: 1929. **Members:** 1,000. **Membership Dues:** individual, associate, regular (outside U.S.), $25 (annual). **Regional Groups:** 70. **Description:** Experienced Sheltie fanciers devoted to the betterment of the Shetland Sheepdog breed. Establishes breeding standards. Seeks to safeguard the breed against unwarranted changes in order to prevent overpopulation of the breed, the propagation of genetic disorders, and attendant community relations problems caused by abandoned animals. **Libraries: Type:** lending; not open to the public. **Holdings:** audiovisuals. **Awards:** Junior Showman Scholarship. **Frequency:** annual. **Type:** scholarship. **Recipient:** to high school seniors/undergraduate college students who are organization members or members' children

● Spoon Award. **Frequency:** annual. **Type:** recognition. **Recipient:** for members who have completed an advance performance title or AKC conformation championship on a Sheltie. **Committees:** National Show. **Programs:** Regional Mentoring. **Affiliated With:** American Kennel Club; National Animal Interest Alliance. **Publications:** *ASSA National Procedure Manual.* Alternate Formats: online ● *Bulletin Board,* quarterly. Newsletter. **Price:** free for members. **Circulation:** 1,000. **Advertising:** accepted ● *Fun With Shelties Coloring Book.* **Price:** $5.00 ● *The Shetland Sheepdog.* Pamphlet. **Price:** $1.25 plus shipping and handling ● Handbooks. Includes a review of the year's specialty shows, champions, and advanced obedience titlists. **Price:** $15.00 handbook 12-13; $20.00 handbook 14; $25.00 handbook 16-20; $30.00 handbook 21-22. **Conventions/Meetings:** semiannual board meeting ● annual meeting ● annual National Specialty Dog Show - 2008 Apr. 12-20, Greeley, CO.

21756 ■ American Shih Tzu Club (ASTC)
279 Sun Valley Ct.
Ripon, CA 95366
E-mail: aakotze@earthlink.net
URL: http://www.shihtzu.org
Contact: Alyce A. Kotze, Corresponding Sec.

Founded: 1964. **Members:** 450. **Membership Dues:** regular, junior (under 18, no vote), special (plus $25 initiation fee), $40 (annual). **Local Groups:** 16. **Description:** Owners and breeders of Shih Tzu dogs, a small, long-haired breed of Tibetan-Chinese origin. Sponsors competition at annual specialties and research on health issues. Provides breed information, breeder referral, rescue assistance; compiles statistics. **Awards:** Type: recognition ● Register of Merit (ROM). **Frequency:** annual. **Type:** recognition. **Recipient:** to a member owned Shih Tzu who have produced champions (6 for dogs; 4 for bitches). **Committees:** Awards; Breed Referral; Health Research Education; Judges Education; National Specialty Shows; Rescue/Welfare; World Shih Tzu Liaison. **Affiliated With:** American Kennel Club; American Kennel Club. **Supersedes:** Shih Tzu Club of America. **Publications:** *Historical Record,* biennial. Book. Contains listings of the Shih Tzu with agility, conformation or obedience titles each year. **Price:** $5.00 postage per volume in U.S.; $10.00 postage per volume outside U.S.; $15.00 per volume (minimum) ● *Shih Tzu Bulletin,* quarterly. Magazine. Provides information to members about Club business. Also includes articles of breed and general sport interest. **Price:** included in membership dues; $45.00 for nonmembers in U.S.; $60.00 for nonmembers outside U.S. **Conventions/Meetings:** annual Specialty Show (exhibits).

21757 ■ American Sighthound Field Association (ASFA)
c/o Marilyn Standerford, Pres.
15054 Dayton St.
Omaha, NE 68137
Ph: (402)895-6426
E-mail: president@asfa.org
URL: http://asfa.org
Contact: Marilyn Standerford, Pres.

Founded: 1972. **Members:** 121. **Regional Groups:** 10. **Description:** Represents sighthound enthusiasts. **Awards:** Field Champion. **Type:** recognition ● Lure Courser of Merit. **Type:** recognition. **Publications:** *ASFA Rulebook.* Alternate Formats: online ● *Field Advisory News,* bimonthly. Journal. Covers activities of lure-coursing sighthounds; includes listing of titles, clubs, judges, rules, and trial schedules and results. **Price:** $30.00/year. **Circulation:** 700. **Advertising:** accepted. **Conventions/Meetings:** annual Convention of Delegates.

21758 ■ American Spaniel Club (ASC)
c/o Kathleen L. Patterson, Sec.
PO Box 4194
Frankfort, KY 40604-4194
Ph: (502)352-4290
Fax: (502)352-4291
E-mail: asc.secretary@gmail.com
URL: http://www.asc-cockerspaniel.org
Contact: Kathleen L. Patterson, Sec.

Founded: 1881. **Members:** 1,350. **Membership Dues:** married couple, $55 (annual) ● club, $35 (annual) ● individual (over 18), $30 (annual) ● individual (under 18), $15 (annual). **Staff:** 1. **Regional Groups:** 5. **State Groups:** 60. **Local Groups:** 51. **Description:** Breeders and owners of purebred Cocker Spaniels and other flushing spaniel breeds in the United States and throughout the world. Sponsors health registry of Cocker Spaniels who have passed tests of genetic soundness for various diseases. Provides judges' education. **Awards:** **Frequency:** annual. **Type:** recognition. **Recipient:** for junior handlers under age 18 ● Versatility Award. **Frequency:** annual. **Type:** recognition. **Recipient:** for members with breed-obedience-fieldwork-dogs. **Committees:** Health-Education and Research; Health Registry; Rescue. **Affiliated With:** American Kennel Club. **Publications:** *A Study of the Cocker Spaniel.* Booklet. **Price:** $12.00 in U.S.; $10.00 at shows; $14.00 outside U.S. ● *Health Registry.* Alternate Formats: online ● Annual Report, annual ● Bulletin, 3-4/year. **Price:** available to members only. Alternate Formats: online. **Conventions/Meetings:** annual Flushing Spaniel Show, for Flushing spaniel breeds (exhibits) ● annual National Cocker Spaniel Show, for cocker spaniels with educational and medical seminars (exhibits).

21759 ■ American Toy Fox Terrier Club (ATFTC)
c/o Dr. Richard Lichty, Pres.
7522 Barrs Lake Rd.
Duluth, MN 55803-9738
Ph: (218)525-3449
E-mail: rlichty@umdced.com
URL: http://www.atftc.com
Contact: Dr. Richard Lichty, Pres.

Membership Dues: single, $20 (annual) ● family, $25 (annual) ● junior, $10 (annual). **Description:** Encourages and promotes quality in the breeding of purebred Toy Fox Terriers. Promotes the health and well being of Toy Fox Terriers. Provides information and services to members about health issues and breeding of Toy Fox Terriers. **Computer Services:** Information services, Toy Fox Terrier resources. **Conventions/Meetings:** annual show.

21760 ■ American Water Spaniel Club (AWSC)
c/o Linda Ford, Pres.
4919 Conejo Rd.
Fallbrook, CA 92028-9390
Ph: (760)723-1706
E-mail: fordcaws@tfb.com
URL: http://www.americanwaterspanielclub.org
Contact: Linda Ford, Pres.

Founded: 1985. **Members:** 250. **Membership Dues:** single associate, $28 (annual) ● associate household, $36 (annual) ● full (single), $35 (annual) ● full (household), $45 (annual). **Budget:** $20,000. **Multinational. Description:** Owners, breeders, and admirers of water spaniels. Promotes quality breeding and acceptance of breed standards as approved by the American Kennel Club. Represents the interests of breeders; provides shelter and care to abandoned and abused water spaniels; conducts educational programs; sponsors competitions; compiles statistics. **Libraries:** Type: reference. **Holdings:** archival material, articles, audio recordings, books, periodicals, video recordings. **Subjects:** American water spaniels. **Awards:** Brockman Award. **Frequency:** annual. **Type:** recognition. **Recipient:** for top American water spaniel at American Kennel Club Show. **Publications:** *Breed Pictorial,* annual. Newsletter. **Advertising:** accepted ● *Review,* quarterly. Newsletter. **Advertising:** accepted. **Conventions/Meetings:** bimonthly board meeting ● annual National Specialty Show (exhibits) - always August.

21761 ■ American Whippet Club (AWC)
c/o Carolyn Mountan, Membership Chair
1092 Schultz Ln.
Latrobe, PA 15650
Ph: (719)594-9974
E-mail: mountan@westol.com
URL: http://www.americanwhippetClub.net
Contact: Carolyn Mountan, Membership Chair

Founded: 1930. **Members:** 510. **Membership Dues:** individual, $25 (annual). **Description:** Represents breeders and owners of purebred Whippet dogs. **Libraries:** Type: reference. **Holdings:** archival material. **Awards:** Register of Merit. **Type:** recognition. **Recipient:** for producing shares and dams ● Registrar of Merit Excellent. **Frequency:** annual. **Type:** recognition. **Recipient:** for top producing sires and dams ● Versatility Award. **Frequency:** annual. **Type:** recognition. **Recipient:** for accomplishments in multiple venues. **Committees:** Educational; Genetic Defect; Show. **Publications:** *Whippet News,* monthly. Newsletter. Features show and race calendars and show results. Contains statistics and *Whippet News Annual,* a magazine. **Price:** included in membership dues; $30.00 /year for nonmembers. **Circulation:** 500. **Advertising:** accepted. **Conventions/Meetings:** annual National Specialty Show - competition (exhibits) - always April ● seminar.

21762 ■ American White Shepherd Association (AWSA)
c/o Melanie Fuellgraf, Membership Chair
316 N Trail
Butler, PA 16002
E-mail: valleydogs2000@yahoo.com
URL: http://www.awsaclub.com
Contact: Jean Reeves, Pres.

Founded: 1995. **Membership Dues:** individual, $15 (annual) ● family, $25 (annual). **Description:** Protects, promotes and advances the interests of purebred White Shepherds. Preserves their natural working and herding instincts through research and sound genetic breeding practices. Seeks to promote global recognition and acceptance of the White Shepherd as a distinct breed. **Publications:** *AWSA Times,* bimonthly. Newsletter. Alternate Formats: online.

21763 ■ American Working Collie Association (AWCA)
c/o Kristin Thober
347 Linebrook Rd.
Ipswich, MA 01938
E-mail: jccollie@worldnet.att.net
URL: http://www.awca.net
Contact: Judy Cummings, Sec.

Membership Dues: individual, $20 (annual) ● individual in Canada, $22 (annual) ● individual - international, $30 (annual) ● junior, $11 (annual) ● junior in Canada, $13 (annual) ● junior - international, $17 (annual) ● joint in Canada, $27 (annual) ● joint - international, $35 (annual). **Description:** Promotes the working ability of the Collie. Provides programs and activities that show the versatility of the Collie. **Publications:** *Collie Connection,* quarterly. Newsletter. **Price:** included in membership dues. **Advertising:** accepted.

21764 ■ Arizona Canine Academy
Address Unknown since 2007

Founded: 1999. **Members:** 100. **Staff:** 6. **Description:** Dog trainers and obedience instructors; dog writers and behaviorists; other professionals in the field. Works to develop the best dog training possible by assisting members with training, instruction, and behavior problems. Welcomes beginners in the dog training field. Offers an eight week on starting your own dog training business. **Publications:** none. **Telecommunication Services:** TDD, through Paws With a Cause, (502)378-6715. **Formerly:** (2000) Trainers Network. **Conventions/Meetings:** periodic seminar, for trainers/instructors.

21765 ■ Association for People with Dogs Named Marty (APDNM)
c/o Marty Sheets, Exec. Dir.
22201 King Rd.
Woodhaven, MI 48183

E-mail: kpbhill@aol.com
Contact: Marty Sheets, Exec. Dir.

Founded: 1997. **Members:** 500. **Staff:** 6. **Description:** Represents people with dogs named Marty. Promotes the use of the name "Marty" for a dog's name. **Publications:** *Marty Watch*. Newsletter.

21766 ■ Australian Cattle Dog Club of America (ACDCA)
c/o Tracy L. Johnson, Sec.
7221 Sandy Plains Ave.
Las Vegas, NV 89131
Ph: (702)395-2080
E-mail: secretary@acdca.org
URL: http://www.acdca.org
Contact: Joyce Rowland, Pres.

Founded: 1967. **Members:** 350. **Membership Dues:** single, $35 (annual) ● family, $45 (annual) ● junior, $15 (annual). **Regional Groups:** 6. **Description:** Individuals interested in promoting the Australian cattle dog breed and perfecting its natural qualities. (The Australian cattle dog is an intelligent, prick-eared dog with a short, dense, straight coat generally found on farms and ranches and used for herding cattle and other animals.) Strives to protect the breed and encourage sportsmanlike competition at dog shows, working trials, and obedience trials. Sponsors herding, obedience, and conformation competitions; compiles statistics. Offers seminars on judging; conducts research and disseminates information on topics relating to canine health. **Libraries: Type:** reference. **Subjects:** Australian cattle dog breed standards, specialty show results. **Awards: Type:** recognition. **Committees:** Awards; Education; Historian; International; Obedience; Protection and Safeguard of the Breed; Publicity; Register of Merit; Rescue; Standard; Working. **Publications:** *Breeder's Directory*, annual ● *Membership List*, annual. Membership Directory ● Newsletter, quarterly. **Conventions/Meetings:** annual National Specialty - conference and show - between September 15 and October 15.

21767 ■ Australian Shepherd Club of America (ASCA)
6091 E State Hwy. 21
Bryan, TX 77808-9652
Ph: (979)778-1082
Fax: (979)778-1898
E-mail: manager@asca.org
URL: http://www.asca.org
Contact: Patrick MacRoberts, Pres.

Founded: 1957. **Members:** 6,500. **Membership Dues:** full (single) $40 (annual) ● full (dual), $55 (annual) ● life, $300 ● service (1 person), $8. **Staff:** 5. **Budget:** $400,000. **Regional Groups:** 81. **Description:** Promotes the breeding of purebred Australian shepherds. Provides education on ethical breeding practices and encourages quality competitions. Maintains breed standards. Operates the Aussies Rescue and Placement Helpline, which finds good homes for orphaned Australian shepherds. Offers placement service; sponsors competitions. Maintains hall of fame. **Libraries: Type:** reference; not open to the public. **Holdings:** archival material, artwork, audiovisuals, books, business records, clippings. **Subjects:** Australian shepherd historical files. **Awards:** Conformation Title. **Type:** recognition ● Obedience Title and Tracking Title. **Type:** recognition ● Working and Agility Title. **Type:** recognition. **Recipient:** for qualifying scores. **Computer Services:** database, registry, title certification, pedigree information, and membership. **Committees:** Agility; Conformation; Obedience; Stockdog. **Programs:** Agility; Conformation; Junior Showmanship; Obedience; Stockdog; Tracking. **Publications:** *Aussie Times*, bimonthly. Magazine. Provides reports from officers, yearly program standings; reports from affiliate clubs, and articles and stories on Aussies. **Price:** free for members. **Circulation:** 6,500. **Advertising:** accepted ● *Secretary's Report*, monthly ● *Shows and Trials*. Newsletter. **Price:** $25.00/year. **Conventions/Meetings:** annual National Specialty Meeting (exhibits).

21768 ■ Australian Terrier Club of America (ATCA)
c/o Mike Liga, Corresponding Sec.
3114 W El Caminto
Phoenix, AZ 85051-6018
E-mail: info@australianterrier.org
URL: http://www.australianterrier.org
Contact: Mike Liga, Corresponding Sec.

Founded: 1958. **Members:** 200. **Membership Dues:** regular (plus $5 initiation fee), $25 (annual) ● junior (plus $5 initiation fee), $8 (annual). **Regional Groups:** 5. **Description:** Breeders and fanciers of purebred Australian terriers. Maintains records for the breed; sponsors specialty shows and participates in all-breed shows. Conducts educational activities and competitions. **Libraries: Type:** reference. **Holdings:** artwork, audiovisuals, books, business records, clippings, periodicals. **Subjects:** Australian terrier dogs. **Awards: Frequency:** annual. **Type:** recognition. **Publications:** *Talkabout*, quarterly. Newsletter. **Price:** $15.00 in U.S.; $20.00 outside U.S. **Circulation:** 275. **Advertising:** accepted. **Conventions/Meetings:** annual Specialty Dog Show - meeting.

21769 ■ Authentic Hovawarts of North America (AHNA)
PO Box 527
Redwood Valley, CA 95470
Ph: (925)458-1252
E-mail: a1hovawarts@aol.com
URL: http://www.hovawarts.org
Contact: Barbara Baker, Pres.

Membership Dues: individual, $35 ● joint, $55. **Multinational. Description:** Works to preserve the health, temperament and conformation of the original German working dog. Ensures that hovawarts in North America are authentic representatives of the established international dog fancy. Focuses on the needs of hovawarts before the needs of breeders and owners. **Publications:** Newsletter.

21770 ■ Basenji Club of America (BCOA)
c/o Anne L. Graves, Sec.
5102 Darnell
Houston, TX 77096
E-mail: info@basenjiclubofamerica.info
URL: http://www.basenji.org
Contact: Anne L. Graves, Sec.

Founded: 1942. **Members:** 890. **Membership Dues:** individual, associate, $15 (annual) ● family, $25 (annual) ● junior (in conjunction with adult), $2 (annual) ● junior (alone), $7 (annual). **Local Groups:** 20. **Description:** Owners, breeders, and exhibitors of purebred Basenji dogs. Operates placement service, educational, and rescue programs. **Libraries: Type:** reference. **Awards:** Diane Coleman Award. **Frequency:** annual. **Type:** recognition. **Recipient:** for top group winning basenji ● Junior Handling Award. **Frequency:** annual. **Type:** recognition ● Reveille Re-Up Award. **Frequency:** annual. **Type:** recognition. **Recipient:** for champion producing stud (top). **Committees:** Breed Standard; Coursing and Racing; Events; Field Trials; Health and Research; Historian; Junior Showmanship; Obedience; Tallier. **Affiliated With:** American Kennel Club. **Publications:** *Basenji Bulletin*, quarterly. Features club news. **Price:** included in membership dues. **Advertising:** accepted. Alternate Formats: CD-ROM ● *BCOA Bulletin Board*, 8/year. Contains board business and voting results, AKC notices. ● *Membership Roster*, annual. Membership Directory. **Conventions/Meetings:** annual Dog Show - meeting, in conjunction with Annual Speciality Dog Show.

21771 ■ Basset Hound Club of America (BHCA)
c/o Gwen McCullagh, Corresponding Sec.
1743 Rte. 206
Skillman, NJ 08558-1914
Ph: (908)359-1372
Fax: (908)450-1170
E-mail: gwenm10100@aol.com
URL: http://www.basset-bhca.org
Contact: Richard Nance, Pres.

Founded: 1935. **Members:** 995. **Membership Dues:** individual, family, $38 (annual). **Local Groups:** 34.

Description: Breeders and owners of purebred basset hounds. Sponsors specialty shows, field trials, obedience trials, and annual tracking test. **Awards: Type:** recognition. **Committees:** Awards; Education; Field Trial Advisory; Obedience and Tracking; Register of Merit; Show. **Affiliated With:** American Kennel Club. **Publications:** *Basset Hound*, annual. Yearbook ● *Field Training with a Basset Hound* ● *Membership List*, annual. Membership Directory ● *Tally-Ho*, bimonthly ● *Tracking with a Basset Hound*. **Conventions/Meetings:** annual meeting.

21772 ■ Bearded Collie Club of America (BCCA)
c/o Carol Sirrine, Corresponding Sec.
5652 Clinton Ave. S
Minneapolis, MN 55419
Ph: (612)866-9014
E-mail: cas4beardies@earthlink.net
URL: http://beardie.net/bcca
Contact: Carol Sirrine, Corresponding Sec.

Founded: 1969. **Members:** 950. **Regional Groups:** 15. **Description:** Represents exhibitors, breeders, and dog owners. Provides education and information on breed betterment. Compiles statistics. **Libraries: Type:** reference. **Awards: Type:** recognition. **Publications:** *Beardie Bulletin*, quarterly. **Price:** $12.00 for members. **Advertising:** accepted ● Newsletter, monthly ● Brochures. **Conventions/Meetings:** annual competition (exhibits) ● annual Specialty Show - meeting (exhibits).

21773 ■ Belgian Sheepdog Club of America (BSCA)
c/o Claire M. Trethewey, Corresponding Sec.
2373 NW 185th Ave., No. 163
Hillsboro, OR 97124-7076
E-mail: clairedelune@alfirin.net
URL: http://www.bsca.info
Contact: Claire M. Trethewey, Corresponding Sec.

Founded: 1958. **Members:** 500. **Membership Dues:** individual ($55 initiation fee), $50 (annual) ● family ($85 initiation fee), $75 (annual) ● junior, $35 (annual) ● life, $25. **Regional Groups:** 4. **Description:** Breeders, owners, and exhibitors of purebred Belgian sheepdogs. Compiles statistics; conducts specialized education programs. **Awards: Type:** recognition. **Affiliated With:** American Kennel Club. **Publications:** *Breeder's Directory*, annual. Alternate Formats: online ● *National Belgian Newsletter*, bimonthly. **Conventions/Meetings:** annual competition ● annual meeting and symposium.

21774 ■ Bernese Mountain Dog Club of America (BMDCA)
c/o Stephanie Sotiros, Membership Chair
3109 Leahey
Stevens Point, WI 54481
E-mail: admin@bmdca.org
URL: http://www.bmdca.org
Contact: Stephanie Sotiros, Membership Chair

Founded: 1968. **Members:** 1,200. **Membership Dues:** regular (in U.S.), $30 (annual) ● regular (in Canada and Mexico), $45 (annual) ● foreign and overseas, $55 (annual) ● regular (second adult in the same household), junior, senior, $12 (annual) ● junior (with adult), $6 (annual). **Description:** Owners, breeders, and admirers of Bernese mountain dogs (large draft dogs, native to Switzerland, used for farming, guarding, herding, or pulling milk carts). Aims to encourage and promote the breeding of purebred Bernese mountain dogs and strives for perfection in their natural qualities. Encourages sportsmanlike competition at dog shows. Conducts sanctioned matches, specialty shows, and obedience trials. Promotes junior competition. Helps to place dogs needing new homes. Contributes to public education on the breed; compiles statistics. **Committees:** Agility; Awards; Berner-Garde; Bylaws; Club Historian; Draft; Education; Futurity; Health; Herding; International Alliances; Judges Education; Junior Advisor; Legislative Affairs; Obedience; Public Relations; Publications; Records; Rescue; Specialty Coordinator; Ways and Means; Website. **Councils:** Regional Club. **Publications:** *The Alpenhorn*, semimonthly. Newsletter. **Price:** $35.00/year in U.S.; $50.00/year in Canada and Mexico; $65.00/year outside U.S., Canada and Mexico ● Yearbook, annual. Contains information on member dogs who have had special accomplishments in past year. **Price:** $45.00. **Circulation:** 500. **Conventions/Meetings:** annual National Specialty Breed Show - specialty show, AKC sanctioned dog events, 400 entries.

21775 ■ Bichon Frise Club of America (BFCA)
c/o Cyndie Adams, Corresponding Sec.
1039 Windsor St.
Reading, PA 19604-2334
Ph: (610)374-7293
E-mail: membership@bichon.org
URL: http://www.bichon.org
Contact: Cyndie Adams, Corresponding Sec.
Founded: 1964. **Members:** 350. **Membership Dues:** open, $25 (annual). **Regional Groups:** 13. **State Groups:** 18. **Local Groups:** 13. **Description:** Breeders, owners, and others interested in the purebred Bichon Frise, a small sturdy dog of Mediterranean descent having a thick wavy white coat. Advances and protects the Bichon Frise breed. Promotes dog shows, obedience trials, and good sportsmanship. Studies Bichon Frise health problems. Sponsors educational and research programs. **Libraries: Type:** open to the public. **Holdings:** books. **Subjects:** history, general info. **Awards:** Breeder of Top Ten Winning Bichon Frises, Owner of Top Ten Winning Bichon Frises. **Frequency:** annual. **Type:** recognition. **Recipient:** for top 10 champions bred by members and top 10 champions owned by members ● Register of Merit. **Frequency:** annual. **Type:** recognition. **Recipient:** for the sire and dam of a recognized number of champions. **Computer Services:** Information services, mail out. **Telecommunication Services:** phone referral service, (336)945-9788. **Committees:** Awards; Educational; Health Research; Judges Research; Register of Merit; Rescue of Bichon Frises. **Affiliated With:** American Kennel Club. **Publications:** *Breeders Directory*, periodic ● *Illustrated Discussion for the Bichon Frise Standard*. Book. **Price:** $10.00 ● *Your Bichon Frise*, periodic. Book. **Price:** $6.00 ● Bulletin, quarterly. Provides reports from officers, committees, regional clubs, and veterinarians. Includes information on shows. **Price:** included in membership dues. **Conventions/Meetings:** annual meeting and seminar (exhibits) ● annual National Meeting and Specialty Show - competition, sales booths commercial, art, jewelry, dog items (exhibits) ● National Specialty Show.

21776 ■ Bluetick Breeders of America (BBOA)
c/o Marty Waddell, Membership Chm.
1089 Jackson Ave.
Tipton, IA 52772
Ph: (563)886-6855
E-mail: mwaddell@netins.net
URL: http://www.bluetickbreedersofamerica.com
Contact: Marty Waddell, Membership Sec.
Founded: 1959. **Members:** 1,000. **Membership Dues:** single, $20 (annual) ● family, $25 (annual). **Regional Groups:** 7. **Description:** Breeders of the Bluetick coonhound, a hunting dog known for its scenting ability, treeing instinct, and strong voice. (A series of small black spots, or ticks, on the dog's body appear almost blue and account for the animal's name.) Sponsors competitions. **Awards: Type:** recognition. **Committees:** Zone Nomination. **Affiliated With:** United Kennel Club. **Publications:** *Breed Book*, annual. **Price:** included in membership dues. **Advertising:** accepted. **Conventions/Meetings:** annual meeting.

21777 ■ Border Terrier Club of America (BTCA)
PO Box 641044
Beverly Hills, FL 34464
Ph: (802)253-9450
E-mail: borderterrieredu@aol.com
URL: http://clubs.akc.org/btca
Contact: Jean Clark, Interim Gen. Education Coor.
Founded: 1949. **Members:** 800. **Membership Dues:** junior, $5 (annual) ● single, $25 (annual) ● house-

hold, $35 (annual). **Regional Groups:** 5. **Description:** Owners and breeders of Border terriers. Purposes are to: bring the natural qualities of the Border terrier to perfection; encourage the organization of independent, local Border terrier specialty clubs; urge members and breeders to accept the standard of the breed as approved by the American Kennel Club as the only standard of excellence by which Border terriers may be judged; conduct sanctioned matches. Compiles records of litters that enable the club to refer prospective buyers to breeders in their area. Sponsors research programs. **Awards:** Certificates of Merit. **Frequency:** annual. **Type:** recognition. **Recipient:** for sires and dames producing the greatest number of champions ● Challenge Trophies. **Frequency:** annual. **Type:** recognition ● Eddie Award. **Frequency:** annual. **Type:** recognition. **Recipient:** for a member doing obedience with a Border Terrier. **Committees:** Awards. **Publications:** *Border Terrier in Brief*. Booklet ● *The Borderline*, quarterly. Newsletter. **Price:** $30.00 /year for nonmembers in U.S.; $40.00 /year for nonmembers outside U.S. **Advertising:** accepted ● Yearbook, annual. **Conventions/Meetings:** annual specialty show, dog-related vendors (exhibits).

21778 ■ Borzoi Club of America (BCOA)
c/o Karen Mays, Sec.
3336 Bagley Passage
Duluth, GA 30097-3789
Ph: (908)647-3027
E-mail: bcoa@borzoiclubofamerica.org
URL: http://www.borzoiclubofamerica.org
Contact: Karen Mays, Sec.
Founded: 1903. **Members:** 579. **Membership Dues:** single, $35 (annual) ● junior (under age 18 without family membership), $10 (annual) ● household, foreign, $40 (annual). **Regional Groups:** 17. **Description:** Owners, breeders, and exhibitors of purebred Borzoi dogs, a sighthound hunter of both small and large games. Conducts obedience trials coursing and conformation events. Provides information on the breed and on locating breeders. Maintains archives, including past specialty winners. Compiles statistics. **Awards:** Type: recognition. **Recipient:** for obedience, lure coursing, and top conformation. **Committees:** Conformation; Coursing; Ethics; Fudges Education; Judging; Obedience; Rescue; Specialty; Utility. **Affiliated With:** American Kennel Club. **Formerly:** (1936) Russian Wolfhound Club of America. **Publications:** *The Borzoi*. Book ● *Borzoi Connection*, quarterly. Magazine. **Price:** $30.00 for members; $40.00 for nonmembers. **Advertising:** accepted ● *Coursing with Borzoi*. Pamphlet ● *Guidelines for Breeders of Borzoi*. Pamphlet ● *Showing the Borzoi in Conformation*. Pamphlet ● *So You Want a Borzoi*. Pamphlet ● *Visualization of the Borzoi Standard*. Booklet ● Yearbook, annual. Includes directory. **Conventions/Meetings:** annual National Specialty - seminar and meeting ● annual specialty show (exhibits).

21779 ■ Boston Terrier Club of America (BTCA)
c/o Joyce Fletcher, Corresponding Sec.
3878 Banks Rd.
Cincinnati, OH 45245-2602
Ph: (513)943-9432
Fax: (513)943-9425
E-mail: candcbostons@cinci.rr.com
URL: http://bostonterrierclubofamerica.org
Contact: Joyce Fletcher, Corresponding Sec.
Founded: 1891. **Members:** 425. **Membership Dues:** regular, $30 (annual). **Description:** Owners, breeders, and exhibitors of purebred Boston Terriers. **Affiliated With:** Boston Terrier Club of America. **Publications:** *Coast to Coast*, 5/year. Newsletter. **Price:** available to members only. **Conventions/Meetings:** annual National Specialty Show - workshop and meeting, with conformation and obedience shows (exhibits).

21780 ■ Bull Terrier Club of America (BTCA)
c/o Naomi Waynee, Exec. Sec.
1122 E Carol Ave.
Phoenix, AZ 85020-2611

Ph: (602)943-6027
E-mail: nwaynee@cox.net
URL: http://www.btca.com
Contact: Dr. Dale R. Schuur, Pres.
Founded: 1897. **Members:** 742. **Membership Dues:** single, $75 (annual) ● couple, $80 (annual) ● single (in other country), $95 (annual) ● couple (in other country), $100 (annual) ● spouse of current member, $25 (annual). **Description:** Breeders and owners of purebred bull terriers. Sponsors annual competitions. Conducts specialized education programs; maintains buyer-breeder information service. Operates speakers' bureau and placement service; compiles statistics. **Awards: Type:** recognition. **Affiliated With:** American Kennel Club. **Publications:** *Barks*, quarterly. Newsletter. **Price:** $45.00 in U.S., Canada and Mexico (1st class postage); $55.00 for overseas (airmail). **Advertising:** accepted ● *Record*, annual. **Advertising:** accepted. **Conventions/Meetings:** annual meeting.

21781 ■ Cairn Terrier Club of America (CTCA)
37667 Timber Dr.
Elizabeth, CO 80107
Ph: (303)646-9657
Fax: (303)646-0261
E-mail: brodiea@msn.com
URL: http://www.cairnterrier.org
Contact: Ann Brodie, Corresponding Sec.
Founded: 1917. **Members:** 450. **State Groups:** 1. **Description:** A member of the American Kennel Club (see separate entry). Represents owners, breeders, and exhibitors of purebred Cairn terriers. Holds annual puppy sweepstakes. **Awards: Type:** recognition. **Publications:** *Cairn Terrier Yearbook*, annual ● *Grooming the Cairn Terrier* ● Catalogs. **Conventions/Meetings:** annual meeting - always October in Lansdale, PA ● annual specialty show.

21782 ■ Canaan Dog Club of America (CDCA)
c/o Ms. Tracey Kopea, Sec.
1175 Iroquois Run
Macedonia, OH 44056
E-mail: canaandog@bigplanet.com
URL: http://cdca.org
Contact: Ms. Tracey Kopea, Sec.
Founded: 1965. **Members:** 150. **Membership Dues:** single in U.S., $20 (annual) ● household in U.S., single outside U.S., $25 (annual) ● household outside U.S., $30 (annual). **Staff:** 9. **Regional Groups:** 2. **Description:** Promotes breeding of purebred Canaan dogs. Provides a breeder referral service and a Canaan Dog information package. **Publications:** *The Canaan Kibitzer*, quarterly. Newsletter. **Price:** $18.00 for nonmembers. **Circulation:** 175. **Advertising:** accepted. **Conventions/Meetings:** annual National Specialty Show - show and meeting.

21783 ■ Cardigan Welsh Corgi Club of America (CWCCA)
c/o Tricia Olson, Pres.
7446 Park Pl.
Boulder, CO 80301-3959
Ph: (303)530-7107
E-mail: olynmawr@4dv.net
URL: http://www.cardigancorgis.com
Contact: Michele Neubauer-Pinkett, Corresponding Sec.
Founded: 1936. **Members:** 650. **Membership Dues:** single, $30 (annual) ● household, $40 (annual) ● junior, associate, $25 (annual). **Staff:** 12. **Budget:** $35,000. **Regional Groups:** 5. **Local Groups:** 10. **Description:** Breeders and owners of purebred Cardigan Welsh Corgis. Compiles statistics. Conducts educational programs. Promotes responsible breeding dog ownership. **Libraries: Type:** reference. **Holdings:** archival material. **Awards:** Good Sportsmanship Award. **Frequency:** annual. **Type:** recognition ● Service Award. **Type:** recognition. **Affiliated With:** American Kennel Club. **Publications:** *Cardigan Handbook*, biennial. Illustrated history for Welsh Corgis. ● *The Cardigan News Bulletin*, 3/year. **Circulation:** 650. **Advertising:** accepted ● *Cardigan News-*

letter, bimonthly. **Conventions/Meetings:** competition ● annual specialty show.

21784 ■ Cavalier King Charles Spaniel Club of America (CKCSC)

PO Box 330
Conway, NH 03818
Ph: (603)447-5218
Fax: (603)447-5419
E-mail: teubank@excoresources.com
URL: http://www.ckcsc.org
Contact: Ted Eubank, Pres.
Founded: 1954. **Members:** 2,600. **Membership Dues:** regular, associate, $45 (annual) ● foreign, $55 (annual). **Staff:** 3. **Budget:** $275,000. **Regional Groups:** 4. **Description:** Breeders and owners of the Cavalier King Charles spaniel, a breed of toy spaniel that has four recognized colors: the Blenheim, chestnut and white; the Tricolor, black, white, and tan; the Black and Tan; the Ruby. Serves as a registering body for Cavalier King Charles spaniels. **Committees:** Breeder Affairs; By-Laws; Education; Legal Advisory; Performance Events; Rescue; Show Rules. **Publications:** *Cavalier King Charles Spaniel Yearbook*, annual ● Bulletin, quarterly. **Conventions/Meetings:** annual meeting.

21785 ■ Chihuahua Club of America (CCA)

c/o Bruce Shirky, Pres.
11489 S Foster Rd.
San Antonio, TX 78218
E-mail: bshirky@texas.net
URL: http://www.chihuahuaclubofamerica.com
Contact: Bruce Shirky, Pres.
Founded: 1923. **Members:** 500. **Membership Dues:** individual, $25 (annual) ● club, $35 (annual). **State Groups:** 47. **Description:** Owners and breeders of Chihuahua dogs. **Libraries: Type:** reference. **Holdings:** archival material, audiovisuals. **Awards:** Best Breed. **Frequency:** annual. **Type:** recognition ● Dog World. **Frequency:** annual. **Type:** recognition ● Good Sportsmanship. **Frequency:** annual. **Type:** recognition ● Top Producer. **Frequency:** annual. **Type:** recognition. **Affiliated With:** American Kennel Club. **Publications:** *Chi-Chatter Newsletter*, bimonthly ● *Chihuahua Club of American Handbook*. Includes articles, pictures, and pedigrees. **Advertising:** accepted ● *Membership Roster*, annual. Membership Directory. **Conventions/Meetings:** competition ● annual show and meeting - always October, Chicago, IL.

21786 ■ Chinese Shar-Pei Club of America (CSPCA)

c/o Jo Ann T. Redditt, Sec.
3510 Washington Ct.
Alexandria, VA 22302
Ph: (217)498-6850 (703)671-0645
Fax: (928)222-5938
E-mail: orientpubl@aol.com
URL: http://www.cspca.com
Contact: Karen Kleinhans, Pres.
Founded: 1974. **Members:** 10,500. **Membership Dues:** individual, $45 (annual) ● family, associate in Canada, $50 (annual) ● associate, outside U.S. and Canada, $60 (annual) ● junior, $40 (annual) ● associate in U.S., $35 (annual). **Regional Groups:** 12. **Description:** Represents individuals interested in the preservation and improvement of the Chinese Shar-Pei dog. Seeks to educate the public on the characteristics and appearances of the Chinese Shar-Pei breed. Establishes standards for the breed. **Libraries: Type:** not open to the public. **Holdings:** books. **Subjects:** studs and breeders. **Awards:** William Morrison Award. **Frequency:** annual. **Type:** recognition. **Recipient:** for top stud, top brood bitch and best breeder of all time. **Publications:** *The Barker*, bimonthly. Magazine. Contains information about breeds. **Price:** included in membership dues. **Advertising:** accepted. **Conventions/Meetings:** annual meeting (exhibits) - always May ● show.

21787 ■ Chow Chow Club, Inc. (CCCI)

c/o Dr. Joyce A. Dandridge, Corresponding Sec.
8132 Eastern Ave. NW
Washington, DC 20012-1312

Ph: (202)726-9155
E-mail: secretary@chowclub.org
URL: http://www.chowclub.org
Contact: Cody Milligan, Pres.
Founded: 1906. **Members:** 640. **Membership Dues:** individual, $25. **Regional Groups:** 22. **Description:** Represents owners, breeders, and exhibitors of Chow Chow dogs. Compiles statistics. **Affiliated With:** American Kennel Club. **Publications:** *Chow Life*, quarterly ● Bulletin, quarterly. **Conventions/Meetings:** competition ● specialty show.

21788 ■ Clumber Spaniel Club of America (CSCA)

c/o Vonda Poole, Membership Sec.
874 Orchard Terrace Dr.
New Wilmington, PA 16142-4222
E-mail: vonjapoole@aol.com
URL: http://www.clumbers.org
Contact: Marianne Stone, Sec.
Founded: 1972. **Members:** 475. **Membership Dues:** single, $45 ● household, $50 ● non-voting junior, $12. **Description:** Individuals interested in promoting the breeding and perfection of natural qualities of the Clumber Spaniel. Sponsors competitions and shows. **Committees:** Hunting Tests; Obedience; Tracking Tests. **Affiliated With:** American Kennel Club. **Publications:** *The Bulletin*, bimonthly. **Price:** included in membership dues; $35.00 for nonmembers. **Advertising:** accepted ● Also publishes brochure. **Conventions/Meetings:** annual meeting.

21789 ■ Collie Club of America (CCA)

c/o Sally Futh, Dir.-at-Large
47 Kielwasser Rd.
Washington, CT 06794-1119
Ph: (860)868-2863
E-mail: ccasec@tctelco.net
URL: http://www.collieclubofamerica.org
Contact: Sally Futh, Dir.-at-Large
Founded: 1886. **Members:** 2,300. **Membership Dues:** single (in U.S., Canada and Mexico), $35 (annual) ● joint (in U.S., Canada and Mexico), $40 (annual) ● single (in other country), $50 (annual) ● joint (in other country), $65 (annual). **Budget:** $80,000. **Local Groups:** 70. **Description:** Owners, breeders, and exhibitors of purebred Collie dogs. Conducts educational, charitable, and research programs. Compiles statistics. **Libraries: Type:** reference. **Holdings:** archival material. **Awards:** Breeder of the Year (Rough). **Frequency:** annual. **Type:** recognition. **Recipient:** for breeding champions ● Breeder of the Year (Smooth). **Frequency:** annual. **Type:** recognition. **Recipient:** for breeding champions. **Computer Services:** Online services, referral. **Committees:** Breed Improvement; Education; Health Education; Herding; Judge's Education; Obedience, Working Collie. **Affiliated With:** American Kennel Club. **Publications:** *American Collie Champions*. Book. Includes pictures of recently titled champions. **Price:** $45.00. **Circulation:** 2,000 ● *Collie Breeder's Handbook* ● *Collie Club of America Bulletin*, bimonthly. Contains information on kennel management, health, and history of the breed. **Price:** included in membership dues. **Circulation:** 2,300. **Advertising:** accepted ● *Collie Club of America Year Book*, annual. Yearbook. **Advertising:** accepted ● *Herding With Your Collie*. Booklets ● *Training Your Collie in Obedience*. Booklet ● Books ● Also publishes calendar. **Conventions/Meetings:** annual competition (exhibits) ● annual National Specialty Show (exhibits).

21790 ■ Colonial Rottweiler Club (CRC)

c/o Anthony DiCicco, Pres.
10 Oceanview Rd.
Lynbrook, NY 11563
Ph: (516)593-6392
E-mail: tonyshoes@aol.com
URL: http://www.colonialrottclub.org
Contact: Anthony DiCicco, Pres.
Founded: 1956. **Members:** 300. **Membership Dues:** individual, associate, $30 (annual) ● family, $35 (annual) ● junior, $18 (annual). **Description:** Breed club for owners or breeders of Rottweilers. **Awards:** Volunteer of the Year. **Frequency:** annual. **Type:** recognition. **Committees:** Achievement Awards;

ADOA Delegate; Archivist; Medallions; Newsletter; Press Coordinator; Website. **Publications:** Newsletter, bimonthly. **Advertising:** accepted. **Conventions/Meetings:** annual Specialty Conformation and Obedience - competition.

21791 ■ CorgiAid

c/o Joyce Trittipo, Treas.
4038 Cherokee Dr.
Madison, WI 53711
Fax: (208)693-8342
E-mail: yourfriends@corgiaid.org
URL: http://www.corgiaid.org
Contact: Vicki Neff, Pres.
Description: Represents animal lovers. Rescue team for Welsh Corgis and corgi mixes. Extends aid for the benefit of animal welfare.

21792 ■ Curly-Coated Retriever Club of America (CCRCA)

c/o David Ferguson, Treas.
90 N Gunflint Lake Rd.
Grand Marais, MN 55604
Ph: (218)388-0300
E-mail: ferguson@boreal.org
URL: http://www.ccrca.org
Contact: Kathie Johnston, Pres.
Founded: 1979. **Members:** 200. **Regional Groups:** 5. **Description:** Owners, breeders, and fanciers of curly-coated retriever dogs. Seeks to promote, protect, and improve the curly-coated retriever as characteristically suited for field, show, and obedience. Disseminates information; conducts specialty events to encourage interest in the breed. Compiles statistics. **Libraries: Type:** reference. **Holdings:** archival material. **Awards: Type:** recognition. **Committees:** Archives; -Field; Health; Hips and Eyes; Judges Education; Public Education; Rescue; Show Plans; Shows and Trophies. **Publications:** *Curly Commentator*, bimonthly. Newsletter. **Price:** $25.00. **Circulation:** 200 ● Also publishes breeders' list of available puppies and dogs. **Conventions/Meetings:** annual specialty show and competition (exhibits).

21793 ■ Dachshund Club of America (DCA)

c/o Andra O'Connell, Sec.
1793 Berme Rd.
Kerhonkson, NY 12446-3128
Ph: (409)755-6569
E-mail: candachs@aol.com
URL: http://www.dachshund-dca.org
Contact: Carl Holder, Pres.
Founded: 1895. **Members:** 1,800. **Membership Dues:** household, $70 (annual) ● single in Canada, $64 (annual) ● household in Canada, $84 (annual) ● foreign single, $86 (annual) ● foreign household, $106 (annual) ● individual (caveat: sponsorship required), $50 (annual). **Local Groups:** 50. **Description:** Enthusiasts of purebred dachshunds. Sponsors specialty and match shows, field trials, obedience trials, tracking trials, educational seminar, and lectures. Maintains biographical archives and library of stud books, show catalogs, and pedigree references. Compiles statistics. **Awards: Type:** recognition. **Committees:** Health. **Funds:** Health and Welfare Trust. **Affiliated With:** American Kennel Club. **Publications:** Newsletter, quarterly. **Conventions/Meetings:** annual meeting.

21794 ■ Dalmatian Club of America (DCA)

c/o Mary Widder, Membership Chair
864 Ettin Ave.
Simi Valley, CA 93065
Ph: (805)583-5914
E-mail: widderm@sbcglobal.net
URL: http://www.thedca.org
Contact: Mary Widder, Membership Chair
Founded: 1905. **Members:** 1,200. **Membership Dues:** regular, in U.S., $40 (annual) ● regular, in Canada and Mexico, $50 (annual) ● regular, outside U.S., Canada and Mexico, $60 (annual). **Staff:** 9. **Regional Groups:** 30. **Description:** Owners, breeders, and exhibitors of purebred Dalmatians. Conducts specialized education and research programs; compiles statistics. Maintains biographical archives. **Libraries: Type:** open to the public. **Holdings:** 100;

books, video recordings. **Subjects:** Dalmatians. **Awards: Type:** recognition. **Recipient:** for performance. **Committees:** Club Historian; Education; Research; Specialty Steering; Spotter; Trophies. **Affiliated With:** American Kennel Club. **Publications:** *Dalmatian Standard.* Magazine. **Advertising:** accepted ● *The Official Book of the Dalmatian.* Contains information about the Dalmatian breed. ● *The Spotter,* quarterly. Magazine. **Advertising:** accepted ● Also publishes membership list. **Conventions/Meetings:** annual Specialty Show and Obedience Trial (exhibits).

21795 ■ Dandie Dinmont Terrier Club of America (DDTCA)
c/o Gail B. Isner, Sec.
151 Junaluska Dr.
Woodstock, GA 30188-3135
E-mail: tamtop@earthlink.net
URL: http://clubs.akc.org/ddtca
Contact: Norma J. Ryan, Pres.
Founded: 1932. **Members:** 300. **Regional Groups:** 5. **Description:** Breeders and owners of purebred Dandie Dinmont terriers. Promotes and advances the breeding of pure-bred Dandie Dinmont Terriers and does all possible to bring their natural qualities to perfection. **Affiliated With:** American Kennel Club. **Publications:** *Mustard and Pepper,* quarterly. **Advertising:** accepted. **Conventions/Meetings:** annual Dog Show.

21796 ■ Desert German Shorthaired Pointer Club (DGSPC)
c/o Susan Clemons, Sec.
PO Box 3958
Chino Valley, AZ 86323
Ph: (602)938-5096 (928)636-7938
E-mail: myvizslas@aol.com
URL: http://www.dgspc.org
Contact: Kenneth E. Hart, Pres.
Membership Dues: single, $20 (annual) ● family, $25 (annual). **Description:** Encourages and promotes the ethical breeding and use of German Shorthaired Pointers through education, activities and philosophy. Conducts specialty shows, trials and hunting tests under the rules of the American Kennel Club. Promotes a congenial and friendly atmosphere among members of other pointing dog clubs. **Telecommunication Services:** electronic mail, snomel@earthlink.net. **Publications:** *Shorthair Fanfare.* Newsletter. **Alternate Formats:** online.

21797 ■ Doberman Pinscher Club of America (DPCA)
c/o Lesley Reeves-Hunt, Membership Sec.
6400 Tripp Rd.
China, MI 48054
Ph: (810)326-3792
E-mail: dpcamembersecy@aol.com
URL: http://www.dpca.org
Contact: Lesley Reeves-Hunt, Membership Sec.
Founded: 1929. **Members:** 2,200. **Membership Dues:** domestic, $30 (annual) ● foreign, $40 (annual). **Regional Groups:** 62. **Description:** Breeders and owners of purebred Doberman Pinschers. Objectives are to: preserve and protect the breed; urge members to accept the standard of the breed as approved by the American Kennel Club (see separate entry); encourage sportsmanlike competition. Sponsors rescue, temperament testing, shows, obedience trials, and tracking tests. Conducts and supports research; offers specialized education programs; compiles statistics. **Libraries: Type:** reference. **Holdings:** archival material, films, video recordings. **Subjects:** interviews with knowledgeable fanciers. **Awards:** Lifetime Achievement. **Frequency:** annual. **Type:** recognition. **Recipient:** for service. **Computer Services:** Mailing lists, of members. **Telecommunication Services:** information service, Doberman breeder referral service, general information. **Committees:** Albino; Breeders Education; Educational Materials; Exhibitors Education; Judges Education; Public Education; Register of Merit; Rescue. **Publications:** *The Beginners Doberman Pinscher.* Booklet. **Price:** $3.50 each ● *Educational Materials Series.* Monographs. **Price:** $4.00/set, for members;

$6.00/set, for nonmembers; $42.00 complete series, for members; $57.00 complete series, for nonmembers ● *Illustrated Standard.* Booklet. **Price:** $5.00 each ● *The Pipeline,* 2-3/year ● *Yearbook and Directory of Breeders.* **Price:** $4.00 each. **Conventions/Meetings:** annual meeting (exhibits) - first full week of October.

21798 ■ English Cocker Spaniel Club of America (ECSCA)
c/o Mrs. Kate D. Romanski, Corresponding Sec.
PO Box 252
Hales Corners, WI 53130
Ph: (414)529-9714
E-mail: kmoore@kabree.com
URL: http://www.ecsca.org
Contact: Mrs. Kathleen Moore, Pres.
Founded: 1936. **Members:** 730. **Membership Dues:** individual, $30 (annual) ● junior, $10 (annual) ● specialty club, $50 (annual). **Regional Groups:** 11. **Description:** Breeders, owners, exhibitors, and fanciers of purebred English cocker spaniels. Sponsors specialty shows, obedience trials, field trials, hunting and tracking tests, agility trials, and working tests. Compiles statistics on top winning English cocker spaniels in bench obedience, field, and agility events annually. Maintains national breed rescue operation. **Awards: Frequency:** annual. **Type:** trophy. **Recipient:** for accomplishments attained by member-owned English Cockers. **Committees:** Bench Show; Field/Working; Health Education; Judge Education; Publicity/Information; Rescue; Statistics; Trophy. **Publications:** *ECSCA Review,* quarterly. Magazine. Contains breed information, articles of interest, and sponsors ads of members. **Price:** $20.00 /year for members; $40.00 /year for nonmembers. **Circulation:** 500 ● *The English Cocker Spaniel Handbook.* **Price:** $12.00 ● *The English Cocker Spaniel 1986-1999.* Book. Includes two volumes that cover history of breed to end of 20th century. **Price:** $40.00 plus shipping and handling ($5) ● *The English Cocker Spaniel, 1936-1986.* Book. Includes two volumes that cover the history of the breed. **Price:** $40.00 plus shipping and handling ($5) ● *Yearbook,* annual. **Price:** $20.00. **Conventions/Meetings:** annual meeting and specialty show.

21799 ■ English Setter Association of America (ESAA)
17842 W Club Vista Dr.
Surprise, AZ 85374-2907
Ph: (623)556-4712
E-mail: settereng@aol.com
URL: http://www.esaa.com
Contact: Dawn S. Ronyak, Sec.
Founded: 1936. **Members:** 1,000. **Description:** Owners, breeders, and exhibitors of purebred English setters. **Affiliated With:** American Kennel Club. **Publications:** Booklet, annual ● Newsletter, periodic. **Conventions/Meetings:** annual Judges Workshop at National Specialty Show - meeting and workshop, vendor booths (exhibits).

21800 ■ English Shepherd Club (ESC)
c/o Mary Peaslee, Pres.
551 Mayotte Rd.
East Fairfield, VT 05448-9799
E-mail: marypeaslee@comcast.net
URL: http://www.englishshepherd.org
Contact: Mary Peaslee, Pres.
Founded: 1954. **Members:** 300. **Membership Dues:** regular, $25 (annual). **Description:** Persons interested in the English Shepherd breed. Works to support, promote, and maintain the English Shepherd as an all-purpose working and family dog. (Descended from the shepherd dogs of the British Isles, the English Shepherd is considered a versatile and adaptive dog able to drive and heel livestock. Standing at an average of 21 inches and weighing about 50 pounds, the shepherd is characterized by a glossy straight or wavy coat, with color patterns variously including black, tan, sable, and white.) Encourages the breeding of purebred English Shepherds and works to foster the shepherd's natural working instincts and other qualities. Aids members in training and working dogs; helps in the purchase and place-

ment of English Shepherds. Works in coordination with National English Shepherd Rescue. **Libraries: Type:** reference. **Holdings:** books, periodicals, video recordings. **Subjects:** training herd dogs. **Affiliated With:** United Kennel Club. **Formerly:** (1954) English Shepherd Club of American. **Publications:** *Breeders Directory,* monthly. Includes directory of breeders. **Price:** $5.00 ● *Membership List,* periodic. Membership Directory ● *Shepherd's Call,* bimonthly. **Price:** included in membership dues. **Circulation:** 275. **Advertising:** accepted ● Brochures ● Also publishes training instructions. **Conventions/Meetings:** periodic meeting, clinics. ●

21801 ■ English Springer Spaniel Field Trial Association (ESSFTA)
c/o Aime Weniger, Membership Sec.
24452 Overlake Dr.
Lake Forest, CA 92630
Ph: (949)581-7510
E-mail: mail@essfta.org
URL: http://www.essfta.org
Contact: Dean Reinke, Pres.
Founded: 1924. **Members:** 900. **Membership Dues:** individual, $35 (annual) ● family, $45 (annual) ● junior, $10 (annual). **Description:** Aims to promote quality purebred English Springer Spaniels. Coordinates field and show activities for springer spaniels in the U.S. Sponsors National Amateur Field Trial and National Specialty Show. **Committees:** Agility; Field; Genetic/Health; Hunting; Judges Education; National Amateur; National Specialty; Obedience; Rescue; Show; Tracking; Working. **Affiliated With:** American Kennel Club. **Publications:** *The Conduct and Judging of Spaniel Field Trials.* Booklet. Contains explanation on the rules of judging field trials. **Price:** $3.50 plus shipping and handling ● *The English Springer Spaniel in North America.* Book. Highlights the history of the breed from its introduction to North America. **Price:** $12.00 plus shipping and handling ● *Field Trial Management.* Booklet. Outlines procedures in conducting field trials for Spaniels. **Price:** $3.50 plus shipping and handling ● *The Spaniel Manual.* Contains information in purchasing an English Springer Spaniel. **Price:** $2.00 plus postage. **Conventions/Meetings:** annual meeting - always last weekend of February.

21802 ■ English Toy Spaniel Club of America (ETSCA)
c/o Marjorie Garritson
PO Box 1722
Carlsbad, CA 92018
Ph: (760)433-2450
Fax: (760)433-4905
E-mail: chasen@engtoy.com
URL: http://www.etsca.org
Contact: Bruce Van Deman, Pres.
Members: 60. **Description:** Owners and admirers of purebred English toy spaniels organized to preserve and promote the English toy spaniel breed. Bestows ribbons and trophies at annual specialty show; sponsors annual seminar which includes a program by leading breeders and American Kennel Club (see separate entry) judges. Assists in matching puppies with new owners. Sponsors competitions; compiles statistics; maintains library. **Committees:** Breed Standard; Historical; Publicity; Trophies. **Publications:** *Membership List,* annual. Membership Directory ● *Show Catalog,* annual. **Advertising:** accepted ● Newsletter, quarterly ● Bulletin, quarterly ● Also publishes breed column in the *AKC Gazette.* **Conventions/Meetings:** annual specialty show (exhibits).

21803 ■ Epagneul Breton USA
288 Clayton St., Ste.204
Denver, CO 80206
E-mail: info@ceb-usa.org
URL: http://www.ceb-usa.org
Multinational. Description: Promotes cooperation, education and understanding among breeders and owners of the Epagneul Breton. Encourages the testing of all dogs, especially those that are considered to be of breeding quality. Organizes and offers assistance in field and conformational events. Supports breeders who choose breeding stock using the

results of such events in conjunction with the utilization of health and genetic screening procedures now available. **Telecommunication Services:** electronic mail, committee@ceb-usa.org.

21804 ■ Field Spaniel Society of America (FSSA)
351 E Kerley Corners Rd.
Tivoli, NY 12583
Ph: (845)756-2595
E-mail: maxinereed@webjogger.net
Contact: Ms. Maxine Reed, Sec.
Founded: 1972. **Members:** 275. **Membership Dues:** regular, $25-$35 (annual). **Regional Groups:** 2. **Description:** Owners and admirers of field spaniels. Promotes responsible breeding and pet ownership; seeks to increase public awareness and appreciation of field spaniels. Maintains breed registry; conducts educational and public relations activities. **Libraries: Type:** not open to the public. **Holdings:** archival material, audiovisuals, books, periodicals, photographs, video recordings. **Affiliated With:** American Kennel Club. **Publications:** *Field Spaniel Fancier*, quarterly. Newsletter. **Price:** included in membership dues. **Advertising:** accepted. Alternate Formats: online; CD-ROM.

21805 ■ Finnish Spitz Club of America (FSCA)
c/o Jeanne Pacheco, Membership Chair
40 Taft Ave.
North Dartmouth, MA 02747-2304
Ph: (508)999-4788
E-mail: jpngp@aol.com
URL: http://www.finnishspitzclub.org
Contact: Jeanne Pacheco, Membership Chair
Founded: 1975. **Membership Dues:** regular, foreign, $30 (annual) ● associate, junior, $12 (annual). **Description:** Works to encourage and promote the breeding of purebred Finnish Spitz. **Committees:** Audit; Awards; Breed Directory/Club Info; Cards and Flowers.

21806 ■ Flat-Coated Retriever Society of America (FCRSA)
c/o Joan Dever, Membership Sec.
13208 Mandarin Rd.
Jacksonville, FL 32223-1746
Ph: (904)268-0325
E-mail: devrfcr@aol.com
URL: http://www.fcrsainc.org
Contact: Dave Bunde, Pres.
Founded: 1960. **Members:** 700. **Membership Dues:** family, $30 (annual). **Budget:** $40,000. **Regional Groups:** 7. **Description:** Promotes quality breeding of purebred flat-coated retrievers. Sponsors obedience trial and other field and show events. Maintains hall of fame; compiles statistics; conducts educational programs. **Libraries: Type:** reference. **Holdings:** archival material. **Awards: Type:** recognition. **Publications:** *FCRSA Newsletter*, quarterly. **Price:** $5.00. **Circulation:** 700. **Advertising:** accepted ● Brochure. **Conventions/Meetings:** competition ● annual meeting and specialty show (exhibits) ● seminar, for judge of shows.

21807 ■ Fox Terrier Network (FTN)
c/o Pam Bishop, VP
31415 Hawthorne St.
Menifee, CA 92584
Ph: (951)672-2008
Free: (888)FOX-TERR
E-mail: info@foxterrier.com
URL: http://www.foxterrier.com
Contact: Rosalind Barsch, Pres.
Founded: 1996. **Members:** 150. **Membership Dues:** single, $20 (annual) ● married, $25 (annual) ● regular outside U.S., $30 (annual). **Multinational. Description:** Promotes care and understanding of wire and smooth fox terrier breeds. **Publications:** *All Things Fox Terrier*, bimonthly. Newsletter. Contains information on smooth and wire fox terriers. **Price:** included in membership dues; $3.00 for nonmembers.

21808 ■ French Bull Dog Club of America (FBDCA)
c/o Pat Kosinar
2108 Inverness Dr.
Lawrence, KS 66047-1959
E-mail: mail@frenchbulldogclub.org
URL: http://www.frenchbulldogclub.org
Contact: Jan Grebe, Pres.
Founded: 1897. **Members:** 430. **Membership Dues:** general, $25 (annual). **Regional Groups:** 4. **Description:** Represents breeders and owners of purebred French bulldogs. **Affiliated With:** American Kennel Club. **Publications:** *Frenchie Forum*, quarterly. Newsletter. **Price:** included in membership dues. **Circulation:** 450. **Conventions/Meetings:** annual National Specialty - meeting - always fall.

21809 ■ German Shepherd Dog Club of America (GSDCA)
c/o Gail Hardcastle
49 Lakeview Rd.
White Salmon, WA 98672
Ph: (509)493-2114
E-mail: ghardcastle@starband.net
URL: http://www.gsdca.org
Contact: Lew Bunch, Pres.
Founded: 1923. **Members:** 5,400. **Membership Dues:** individual in U.S., $66 (annual) ● family in U.S., $100 (annual) ● individual outside U.S., $90 (annual) ● family outside U.S., $124 (annual). **Regional Groups:** 114. **Description:** Represents individuals with an interest in German Shepherds. **Awards:** Hero Dog. **Frequency:** annual. **Type:** recognition. **Committees:** Breeders Code; Education; Foreign Liaison; Futurities; Hero Dogs; Hip Dysplasia; Obedience; Publicity; Register of Merit; Search and Rescue; Title Pins; Veterinary Liaison; Videocassette Library. **Affiliated With:** American Kennel Club. **Absorbed:** (1949) German Shepherd Dog Club of New England. **Publications:** *Blue Book* ● *German Shepherd Dog Review*, monthly. Magazine. **Price:** $55.00/year. **Circulation:** 4,000. **Advertising:** accepted ● *Roster*, annual. **Conventions/Meetings:** annual meeting (exhibits) - always fall.

21810 ■ German Shepherd Dog Club of America - Working Dog Association (GSDCA-WDA)
c/o Joy Schultz, Recorder/Admin.
1699 N Jungle Den Rd., No. 45
Astor, FL 32102
Ph: (386)749-4574
Fax: (386)749-4244
E-mail: wda@verizon.net
URL: http://www.gsdca-wda.org
Contact: Ken Downing, Pres.
Founded: 1982. **Membership Dues:** individual, $66 (annual) ● individual (overseas), $90 (annual) ● family, $100 (annual) ● family (overseas), $124 (annual). **Description:** Works for the welfare of the German Shepherd dog. Provides enthusiasts with a framework for activities in the US patterned after those available to the German Shepherd dog community. Provides clubs with qualified trial and conformation judges for sanctioned events. **Telecommunication Services:** electronic mail, joy@usa2net.net. **Programs:** GSDCA-WDA K-9; GSDCA-WDA Trial Helper; Junior. **Affiliated With:** German Shepherd Dog Club of America.

21811 ■ German Shorthaired Pointer Club of America (GSPCA)
c/o Charlie Blackbourn, Pres.
200 Goede Rd.
Edgerton, WI 53534
Ph: (608)884-4342
E-mail: cebourn@jvlnet.com
URL: http://www.gspca.org
Contact: Charlie Blackbourn, Pres.
Founded: 1939. **Members:** 2,000. **Membership Dues:** individual, $37 (annual) ● family, $42 (annual) ● foreign individual, $50 (annual) ● foreign family, $55 (annual) ● individual junior, $10 (annual). **Local Groups:** 65. **Description:** Breeders and owners of purebred German shorthaired pointers. Sponsors National Amateur Championship Stake, National

Championship Stake, National Championship Gun Dog Stake, National Specialty Show, National Field Futurity, National Show Futurity, and Puppy Sweepstakes. Maintains hall of fame; compiles statistics. **Libraries: Type:** not open to the public. **Holdings:** artwork, books, periodicals. **Subjects:** history of the breed. **Awards:** Dog-of-the-Year Award. **Frequency:** annual. **Type:** recognition. **Affiliated With:** American Kennel Club. **Publications:** *Shorthair Journal*, monthly. Magazine. Provides field trial results, information on shows, and list of breeders. **Price:** included in membership dues. **Circulation:** 2,500. **Advertising:** accepted ● Yearbook, annual. **Conventions/Meetings:** annual conference and meeting (exhibits) - always Memorial Day weekend.

21812 ■ German Wirehaired Pointer Club of America (GWPCA)
c/o Sue Mueller, Treas.
W12203 870th Ave.
River Falls, WI 54022
E-mail: st.croix.wirehairs@pressenter.com
URL: http://www.gwpca.com
Contact: Mark Sargent, Pres.
Founded: 1959. **Members:** 278. **Membership Dues:** single, $30 (annual) ● family, $35 (annual). **State Groups:** 15. **Description:** Owners and fanciers of German wirehaired pointers. Promotes the breeding of German wirehaired pointers; encourages sportsmanlike competition in dog shows, field trials, and obedience trials. Conducts national amateur championship stakes. Compiles statistics. **Awards:** Carl Schnell Memorial Trophy. **Frequency:** annual. **Type:** recognition ● Field and Show Award. **Type:** recognition. **Publications:** *GWPCA Wire News*, quarterly. Journal. Includes statistics, articles, board news, and calendar of events. **Price:** $4.00/copy. **Advertising:** accepted ● Newsletter, quarterly ● Yearbook, annual. **Conventions/Meetings:** annual meeting - always October.

21813 ■ Giant Schnauzer Club of America (GSCA)
c/o Tami Stoller, Sec.
5301 Finney Rd.
Salida, CA 95368
Ph: (209)545-3231
E-mail: tami@gsca.info
URL: http://www.giantschnauzerclubofamerica.com
Contact: Cindy Kennard, Pres.
Founded: 1962. **Members:** 400. **Membership Dues:** single, $40 (annual) ● dual, $50 (annual). **Regional Groups:** 4. **Description:** Pet owners and beginner and professional breeders and handlers. Works to: improve and preserve the character and form of the giant schnauzer breed; advance interest in this breed, and conduct dog shows, obedience trials, and sanctioned matches. Makes donations to universities for research. Maintains home placement service for animals who have been abandoned or taken to a welfare facility. Compiles statistics. **Libraries: Type:** reference. **Subjects:** animals, breeders. **Awards: Type:** recognition. **Additional Websites:** http://gsca. info. **Committees:** Adoption and Rescue; Archives; Awards and Trophies; Breed and Obedience; Carting; Congratulatory; Education; Health and Hereditary Disease; Information Center; Performance Events; Puppy Fund; Temperament Testing. **Affiliated With:** American Kennel Club. **Publications:** *Giant Schnauzer Source Book*. Yearbook. Contains photographs, pedigrees and information about Giant Schnauzers. ● *Giant Steps*, bimonthly. Magazine. Includes news, events and information about the club. **Price:** included in membership dues. **Advertising:** accepted ● *What You Should Know About the Giant Schnauzer*. Book. Contains information from experienced Giant Schnauzer owners, breeders and handlers. **Price:** $10.00 for members; $15.00 for nonmembers ● Also publishes leaflets and newsletters. **Conventions/Meetings:** annual show and conference.

21814 ■ Golden Retriever Club of America (GRCA)
c/o Jolene Carey, Admin. Asst.
PO Box 20434
Oklahoma City, OK 73156

Ph: (850)877-4817
E-mail: careyjolen@aol.com
URL: http://www.grca.org
Contact: Christine Miele, Pres.
Founded: 1938. **Members:** 4,500. **Membership Dues:** single in U.S., $65 (annual) ● family in U.S., $70 (annual) ● single in Canada and Mexico, $115 (annual) ● family in Canada and Mexico, $120 (annual) ● single (all other countries), $215 (annual) ● family (all other countries), $220 (annual). **Budget:** $400,000. **Local Groups:** 53. **Multinational.** Description: Owners and breeders of purebred golden retriever dogs. Conducts annual national field and obedience trials, dog show, and tracking tests. Compiles statistics; maintains hall of fame; offers information service. Donates to canine research programs. **Libraries: Type:** reference. **Holdings:** archival material. **Committees:** Educational Programs; Health and Genetics; National Rescue; Public Education; Puppy Referral; Statistics. **Affiliated With:** American Kennel Club. **Publications:** *Golden Retriever News*, bimonthly. Magazine. **Price:** included in membership dues. **Circulation:** 4,000. **Advertising:** accepted ● *Golden Retriever Yearbook*, annual ● Also publishes Acquiring a Golden Retriever, Introduction to the Golden retriever and "Color Me Golden" a children's coloring book. **Conventions/Meetings:** annual National Specialty - meeting, dog show, obedience and field trials, agility trial, awards banquet (exhibits) - always September or October.

21815 ■ Gordon Setter Club of America (GSCA)
c/o Mary Ann Leonard, Corresponding Sec.
698 Cheesman Rd.
St. Louis, MI 48880
Ph: (989)681-2516
Fax: (989)681-2386
E-mail: mal1@cmsinter.net
URL: http://www.gsca.org
Contact: Mary Ann Leonard, Corresponding Sec.
Founded: 1924. **Members:** 1,100. **Membership Dues:** junior, $16 (annual) ● single (includes enrollment), $41 (annual) ● family (includes enrollment), $51 (annual). **Regional Groups:** 12. **Local Groups:** 14. **Description:** Owners and breeders of purebred Gordon setters. Holds specialty shows and field trials and hunting tests. Supports canine research programs. Offers breed study program for members and judges of the American Kennel Club. **Libraries: Type:** not open to the public; by appointment only. **Holdings:** articles, books, photographs. **Subjects:** history of breed. **Awards: Frequency:** annual. **Type:** recognition. **Committees:** Breed Study; CCA-Genetics; Rescue. **Publications:** *The Gordon Setter Club Pictorial*, annual. Directory ● *Review*, quinquennial ● Newsletter, monthly. **Conventions/Meetings:** semiannual meeting (exhibits).

21816 ■ Great Dane Club of America (GDCA)
c/o Mrs. Linda Ridder, Pres.
2933 Archer Ln.
Springfield, OH 45503-1284
E-mail: lindaridder@sbcglobal.net
URL: http://www.gdca.org
Contact: Mrs. Linda Ridder, Pres.
Founded: 1889. **Members:** 2,000. **Description:** Breeders and owners of purebred Great Danes. Maintains breeders referral and liaison with 50 other clubs in the U.S. Sponsors specialty shows and educational programs. **Libraries: Type:** reference. **Committees:** Breed Code/Color Research; Judges; Standard. **Affiliated With:** American Kennel Club. **Publications:** *Illustrated Standard of the Great Dane* ● Yearbook, biennial ● Booklets ● Bulletin, bimonthly ● Pamphlets ● Also makes available slides and videotapes. **Conventions/Meetings:** annual specialty show (exhibits).

21817 ■ Great Pyrenees Club of America (GPCA)
c/o Valerie Seeley, Sec.
242 Woodland Dr.
Lincroft, NJ 07738-1332
Ph: (732)530-9288

E-mail: pyrlesspyrs@aol.com
URL: http://clubs.akc.org/gpca
Contact: Jean Cave-Pero, Pres.
Founded: 1934. **Members:** 800. **Membership Dues:** first applicant (includes $10 initiation fee), $40 (annual) ● second family (includes $10 initiation fee), $25 (annual). **Regional Groups:** 85. **Local Groups:** 25. **Description:** Represents breeders and owners of purebred Great Pyrenees dogs. Operates hall of fame. **Publications:** *GPCA Membership List*, annual. Membership Directory ● *Titleholders Book*, annual ● Bulletin, bimonthly. **Conventions/Meetings:** annual meeting, with dog show and seminar - usually April.

21818 ■ Greyhound Club of America (GCA)
c/o Helen Hamilton
1543 Oslo Ct.
Livermore, CA 94550
Ph: (972)475-5843
E-mail: vims@sbcglobal.net
URL: http://www.greyhoundclubofamerica.org
Contact: Bill Hempel, Pres.
Founded: 1907. **Members:** 155. **Membership Dues:** individual, $30 (annual). **Description:** Owners, breeders, and exhibitors of purebred AKC registered greyhounds. Sponsors dog shows. Provides information about the breed. Compiles statistics; conducts educational programs. **Libraries: Type:** reference. **Committees:** Rescue. **Affiliated With:** American Kennel Club. **Publications:** *Greyhounds in America*. Book ● Newsletter, quarterly. Contains news, facts, stories, and other items about the club. **Price:** included in membership dues; $35.00 /year for nonmembers; $45.00/year for overseas nonmembers. **Circulation:** 200. **Advertising:** accepted. **Conventions/Meetings:** semiannual meeting ● semiannual show.

21819 ■ Hunting Retriever Club (HRC)
c/o Mark Lanier, Pres.
20836 Plank Rd.
Zachary, LA 70791
Ph: (225)279-0174
E-mail: president@h-r-c.org
URL: http://www.ukcdogs.com
Contact: Mark Lanier, Pres.
Founded: 1984. **Members:** 5,000. **Membership Dues:** single, in U.S., $25 (annual) ● single, outside U.S., $30 (annual) ● family, in U.S., $30 (annual) ● family, outside U.S., $35 (annual). **Staff:** 38. **National Groups:** 110. **Description:** Duck and bird hunters and upland game hunters interested in retrievers. Works to train and test hunting retrievers; to maintain the inherent working qualities of hunting dogs in their natural environment; and to use humane, thoughtful, and proven dog training techniques. Offers children's services and educational programs. **Libraries: Type:** reference. **Holdings:** 21; archival material, books, clippings, periodicals. **Subjects:** hunting retrievers, working dogs. **Awards:** Grand Hunting Retriever Champion. **Type:** recognition ● Hunting Retriever Champion. **Type:** recognition. **Recipient:** for dogs that have passed the testing program, training sessions, clinics, hunting tests, and national hunts. **Computer Services:** Online services. **Additional Websites:** http://www.huntingretrieverclub.org. **Affiliated With:** United Kennel Club. **Publications:** *Hunting Retriever Magazine*, bimonthly. **Price:** included in membership dues; $25.00 for nonmembers in U.S.; $30.00 for nonmembers outside U.S. ISSN: 8750-6629. **Circulation:** 5,500. **Advertising:** accepted. **Conventions/Meetings:** annual meeting - always June.

21820 ■ International Borzoi Council (IBC)
c/o Shen Smith, International Conference Coor.
PO Box 175
Elk Rapids, MI 49629
Ph: (231)264-6665
Fax: (231)264-6667
E-mail: sbs@bokhara.com
URL: http://www.internationalborzoiconference.org
Contact: Shen Smith, International Conference Coor.
Founded: 1986. **Members:** 200. **Membership Dues:** regular, $30. **Description:** Represents serious breeders and fanciers of the Borzoi. (The Borzoi, also

known as the Russian wolfhound, is a large, long-haired dog from the greyhound family which originated in Russia and was used for pursuing wolves). **Committees:** Archives/History; Coursing; Standard Interpretation. **Publications:** Newsletter, periodic. **Conventions/Meetings:** triennial conference ● periodic seminar.

21821 ■ International French Brittany Club of America (IFBC)
PO Box 104
Pettibone, ND 58475-0104
E-mail: fbrittdog@yahoo.com
URL: http://www.frenchbrittany4u.org
Contact: Rita Stalcup, Pres.
Membership Dues: regular, $10 (annual) ● life, $30. **Multinational. Description:** Protects and advances the Epagneul Breton breed. Educates the public about the nature of the breed and the responsibilities of ownership. Facilitates communication and fellowship among members.

21822 ■ International Kennel Club of Chicago (IKC)
6222 W North Ave.
Chicago, IL 60639
Ph: (773)237-5100
Fax: (773)237-5126
E-mail: ikc-olsen@sbcglobal.net
URL: http://www.ikcdogshow.com
Contact: Ms. Dori Auslander, Sec.
Founded: 1938. **Budget:** $500,000. **Description:** Issues premium lists and catalogs of shows. Manages dog shows and a pet expo held annually for consumers. **Committees:** Agility Liaison; Benching; Building Management; Catalog Advertising; Junior Dog Judging; Media Relations; Obedience and Rally; Show. **Conventions/Meetings:** annual All-Breed Dog Show (exhibits) - always Chicago, IL.

21823 ■ International Kennel Society
c/o Brad Trom
PO Box 757
Blooming Prairie, MN 55917-0757
Ph: (507)583-7718
Fax: (507)583-7718
E-mail: stockbury@mailstation.com
Contact: Brad Trom, Registrar
Founded: 1994. **Members:** 550. **Membership Dues:** individual, $12 (annual). **Multinational. Description:** Individuals with an interest in rare dog breeds. Seeks to promote, protect, and preserve uncommon and unusual dog breeds. Maintains breed registries and serves as a clearinghouse on rare dog breeds; sponsors competitions. **Libraries: Type:** by appointment only. **Holdings:** archival material, artwork, audio recordings, books, periodicals, video recordings. **Subjects:** dogs. **Formerly:** (2005) International Rare Breed Dog Club.

21824 ■ Irish Setter Club of America (ISCA)
c/o Mr. Robert A. Robinson, Pres.
1826 Palmcroft Way NE
Phoenix, AZ 85007-1740
Ph: (602)253-6260
Fax: (530)872-2170
E-mail: brobinson4@cox.net
URL: http://www.irishsetterclub.org
Contact: Ms. Jeanette Holmes, Recording Sec.
Founded: 1891. **Members:** 1,520. **Membership Dues:** individual, $45 (annual) ● family, $55 (annual) ● senior, junior, $30 (annual). **Staff:** 19. **Regional Groups:** 4. **Local Groups:** 49. **Description:** Breeders and owners of purebred Irish setters. Contributes support to canine research projects. Conducts charitable and educational programs. Compiles statistics. **Libraries: Type:** reference. **Awards: Type:** recognition. **Committees:** Health; Rescue. **Affiliated With:** American Kennel Club. **Publications:** *Breeders' Directory*, annual. **Advertising:** accepted ● *Memo to Members*, bimonthly. Includes information on show winners. **Price:** included in membership dues. **Circulation:** 1,470. **Advertising:** accepted ● *Pictorial*, quinquennial. **Conventions/Meetings:** competition ● annual specialty show, includes field trial, agility, obedience.

21825 ■ Irish Terrier Club of America (ITCA)
c/o Gale Cummings, Corresponding Sec.
37 Clapp St.
Norton, MA 02766-2709
Ph: (508)285-9655
E-mail: terrier.itca@verizon.net
URL: http://www.itca.info
Contact: Gale Cummings, Corresponding Sec.
Founded: 1897. **Members:** 470. **Membership Dues:** individual, $30 (annual). **Regional Groups:** 4. **Local Groups:** 4. **Description:** Represents Irish terrier owners, breeders, and show exhibitors. Encourages and promotes the breeding of purebred Irish terriers. Protects and advances the interests of the breed. Encourages sportsmanlike competition at dog shows, field trials and obedience trials. Conducts sanctioned matches and specialty shows under AKC rules. **Libraries: Type:** open to the public. **Holdings:** 5; archival material, artwork, biographical archives, books, photographs, video recordings. **Subjects:** Irish terrier breed: 1948, 1970, 1983, 1997; photo collection. **Awards:** Edward O'Keefe Memorial Trophy. **Frequency:** annual. **Type:** trophy. **Recipient:** to owner of the dog or bitch defeating the greatest number of Irish terriers by virtue of winning best of breed ● Jeremiah O'Callaghan Trophy. **Frequency:** annual. **Type:** trophy. **Recipient:** to owner winning the greatest number of points at all AKC shows ● John Best Memorial Breeder Trophy. **Frequency:** annual. **Type:** trophy. **Recipient:** to the breeder of the best of breed Irish terrier at the ITCA national specialty held in conjunction with Montgomery County Kennel Club ● Martha Hall Memorial Trophy. **Type:** trophy. **Recipient:** to the dog or bitch winning bred-by exhibitor class the greatest number of times during the trophy year ● Micheal Gately Memorial Trophy. **Frequency:** annual. **Type:** trophy. **Recipient:** to the owner of the dog or bitch accumulating the greatest number of O' Callaghan trophy points during the year, regardless of ownership, by virtue of winning best of breed ● Rudolf Jensen Memorial Trophy. **Frequency:** annual. **Type:** trophy. **Recipient:** to the owner of the dog or bitch defeating the greatest number of Irish terriers by virtue of winning the best of breed the greatest number of times ● Suzanne Griffiths Obedience Trophy. **Frequency:** annual. **Type:** trophy ● Thomas H. Mullins Memorial Trophy. **Frequency:** annual. **Type:** trophy. **Recipient:** to the owner of the dog or bitch accumulating the greatest number of inter-breed points by virtue of being placed in the terrier group or best in show. **Affiliated With:** American Kennel Club. **Publications:** *Irish Terrier Breed Book* ● *Irish Terrier Puppy Pamphlet.* Pamphlets ● *ITCA Breed Book,* annual. Provides information on breeds. **Price:** $25.00. **Circulation:** 1,500 ● Newsletter, quarterly. **Conventions/Meetings:** annual meeting - always October, in Philadelphia, PA.

21826 ■ Irish Water Spaniel Club of America (IWSCA)
c/o Kim Kezer
86 High St.
Amesbury, MA 01913
E-mail: dedeselph@aol.com
URL: http://clubs.akc.org/iwsc
Contact: Dede Selph, VP
Founded: 1937. **Members:** 250. **Multinational. Description:** Owners, breeders, and exhibitors of purebred Irish water spaniels. Promotes the breed in obedience work, field and water trials, and conformation shows. **Affiliated With:** American Kennel Club. **Publications:** Newsletter, monthly. **Conventions/Meetings:** regional meeting and show ● annual specialty show.

21827 ■ Irish Wolfhound Club of America (IWCA)
c/o Judy Simon, Sec.
7155 Co. Rd. 26
Maple Plain, MN 55359
Ph: (763)479-1638
E-mail: stoneybrookjudy@aol.com
URL: http://www.iwclubofamerica.org
Contact: Beverly Little, Pres.
Founded: 1926. **Members:** 1,600. **Membership Dues:** individual, $20 (annual). **Regional Groups:** 7.

Description: Seeks to encourage and promote the breeding of purebred Irish Wolfhounds and to do all possible to bring their natural qualities to the attention of the public. Urges members and breeders to accept the standard of the breed as approved by The American Kennel Club. **Affiliated With:** American Kennel Club. **Publications:** *Harp and Hound,* semiannual. Magazine. Includes photographs, news stories, articles and specialty results. **Price:** included in membership dues ● Also publishes books, periodicals, audiovisual material, art, and archival material on the history and care of Irish Wolfhounds and Irish Wolfhound pedigrees. **Conventions/Meetings:** annual specialty show and meeting, national specialty show - always spring.

21828 ■ Italian Greyhound Club of America (IGCA)
c/o Lynette Coyner, VP
10061 S Deer Creek Rd.
Littleton, CO 80127-9514
Ph: (303)697-7527
E-mail: charislgs@aol.com
URL: http://www.italiangreyhound.org
Contact: Jack Downing, Pres.
Founded: 1954. **Members:** 190. **Membership Dues:** initial (includes application fee), $30 (annual) ● regular, $20 (annual). **Description:** Breeders and owners of purebred Italian greyhounds. Conducts educational programs. Sponsors competitions. Maintains placement service and hall of fame. **Awards: Frequency:** annual. **Type:** recognition. **Committees:** Health; Rescue; Slide Presentation; Specialty. **Affiliated With:** American Kennel Club. **Conventions/Meetings:** annual meeting.

21829 ■ Jack Russell Terrier Club of America (JRTCA)
PO Box 4527
Lutherville, MD 21094-4527
Ph: (410)561-3655
Fax: (410)560-2563
E-mail: jrtca@worldnet.att.net
URL: http://www.terrier.com
Contact: Glen Churchfield, Chm.
Founded: 1976. **Members:** 8,500. **Membership Dues:** single adult, $45 (annual) ● family, $50 (annual) ● family youth, $15 (annual) ● youth, $25 (annual). **Staff:** 5. **State Groups:** 16. **Description:** Owners and admirers of Jack Russell terriers. Promotes education on the breed; maintains registration. Sponsors trials. Operates rescue program for displaced dogs. Conducts research and educational programs; compiles statistics. **Libraries: Type:** reference. **Awards: Type:** recognition. **Telecommunication Services:** electronic mail, gchurchf@columbus.rr.com. **Committees:** Breeders; Disciplinary; Judges; Nominating; Representatives; Trial. **Publications:** *JRTCA Directory of Breeders,* annual. **Price:** $10.00. **Advertising:** accepted ● *Stud Book,* periodic ● *True Grit,* bimonthly. Magazine. **Price:** included in membership dues. **Circulation:** 5,000. **Advertising:** accepted.

21830 ■ Japanese Chin Club of America (JCCA)
c/o Trish Swagerty, Treas.
PO Box 90056
Houston, TX 77290
E-mail: ajackson@japanesechinonline.org
URL: http://www.japanesechinonline.org
Contact: Ann Jackson, Pres.
Founded: 1920. **Members:** 350. **Membership Dues:** household, $40 (annual) ● individual, $30 (annual) ● junior, $10 (annual) ● foreign household, $58 (annual) ● foreign individual, $48 (annual). **Staff:** 9. **Regional Groups:** 1. **Description:** Represents breeders and owners of purebred Japanese Chins. Compiles statistics. **Awards:** Catherine Cross - Best of Breed. **Frequency:** semiannual. **Type:** recognition. **Committees:** AKC Delegate; AKC Gazette Columnist; Awards; Breeder Referral and Rescue; By-Laws; Ethics; Health; Historian. **Affiliated With:** American Kennel Club. **Formerly:** (1977) Japanese Spaniel Club of America. **Publications:** *Chin Chit Chat,* bimonthly. Magazine. **Price:** included in mem-

bership dues; $20.00 /year for nonmembers in U.S.; $40.00 /year for nonmembers outside U.S. **Circulation:** 360. **Advertising:** accepted. Alternate Formats: CD-ROM; diskette ● Membership Directory, annual. **Conventions/Meetings:** semiannual show and meeting (exhibits) ● semiannual specialty show.

21831 ■ Keeshond Club of America (KCA)
c/o Carolyn Schaldecker, Corresponding Sec.
1571 Twin Valley Dr. NE
Solon, IA 52333
E-mail: imagine@southslope.net
URL: http://www.keeshond.org
Contact: Holly Wisner, Pres.
Founded: 1935. **Members:** 431. **Membership Dues:** individual, $20 (annual) ● family, $25 (annual) ● junior, $10 (annual). **Local Groups:** 21. **Description:** Owners, breeders, and exhibitors of Keeshonds. Offers specialized education on owning and protecting dogs. Conducts charitable program and provides placement service. Operates hall of fame; maintains registers of merit. **Awards:** Top Obedience. **Frequency:** annual. **Type:** recognition ● Top Show Best of Show. **Frequency:** annual. **Type:** recognition ● Top Show Dog. **Frequency:** annual. **Type:** recognition. **Affiliated With:** American Kennel Club. **Publications:** *Secretaries Report,* quarterly. **Conventions/Meetings:** annual specialty show.

21832 ■ Komondor Club of America (KCA)
c/o Steve Persons, Pres.
9280 NE Baseline Dr.
Runnells, IA 50237
Ph: (515)967-5324
E-mail: personsip@aol.com
URL: http://clubs.akc.org/kca
Contact: Steve Persons, Pres.
Founded: 1967. **Members:** 250. **Membership Dues:** family, $40 (annual) ● individual, $30 (annual). **Staff:** 11. **Regional Groups:** 5. **Description:** Owners and fanciers of Komondorok (rare Hungarian guard dogs). Objectives are to: educate the public about the breed; encourage intelligent breeding programs; preserve the integrity of the breed. Provides new homes for homeless Komondorok. Compiles statistics; conducts educational programs. **Awards: Type:** recognition. **Computer Services:** database, breed information. **Telecommunication Services:** electronic mail, komsinva@lynchburg.net. **Committees:** Education; Specialty Show; Welfare. **Affiliated With:** American Kennel Club. **Publications:** *Komondor Komments,* quarterly. Magazine. **Price:** $30.00 /year for nonmembers in U.S.; $35.00 /year for nonmembers outside U.S.; included in membership dues. **Advertising:** accepted. **Conventions/Meetings:** annual America Specialty Show ● annual meeting.

21833 ■ Kuvasz Club of America (KCA)
c/o Richard Rosenthal, Treas.
6050 Peachtree Pkwy., Ste.240-216
Norcross, GA 30092
E-mail: treasurer@kuvasz.com
URL: http://www.kuvasz.com
Contact: Michele Hill, Sec.
Founded: 1966. **Members:** 200. **Membership Dues:** single, $45 (annual) ● couple, $50 (annual). **Staff:** 9. **Description:** Owners, breeders, and exhibitors of the Hungarian Kuvasz (a large, all-white, agile guard dog); interested individuals. Seeks to encourage and promote the breeding of purebred Kuvasz dogs and to protect the breed. Sponsors educational programs and competitions. **Awards: Frequency:** annual. **Type:** recognition. **Committees:** Adoption/Rescue. **Affiliated With:** American Kennel Club. **Publications:** *Kuvasz Quarterly.* Newsletter. **Price:** included in membership dues; $45.00 /year for nonmembers. **Advertising:** accepted ● Brochure. **Conventions/Meetings:** annual meeting.

21834 ■ Ladies Kennel Association of America (LKA of A)
c/o Ms. Tracey E. Monahan, Chair
190 Merrits Rd.
Farmingdale, NY 11735

Ph: (516)777-1512
URL: http://infodog.com/clubs/2001161902.htm
Contact: Ms. Tracey E. Monahan, Chair
Founded: 1901. **Members:** 14. **Description:** Holds annual all-breed dog show and encourages the intelligent breeding of purebred dogs. **Convention/Meeting:** none. **Affiliated With:** American Kennel Club.

21835 ■ Mastiff Club of America (MCOA)
c/o Jodi LaBombard, Membership Sec.
30 Blue Heron Dr.
Rochester, NY 14624
Ph: (585)594-5354
E-mail: brimstonemastiffs@yahoo.com
URL: http://mastiff.org
Contact: Jodi LaBombard, Membership Sec.
Founded: 1929. **Members:** 834. **Membership Dues:** regular, in U.S., $35 (annual) ● regular, in Canada, $38 (annual) ● rest of the world, $45 (annual). **Budget:** $35,000. **Multinational. Description:** Owners and breeders of purebred Mastiff dogs. Maintains hall of fame and placement service for unwanted Mastiffs. Compiles statistics. **Awards:** Best of Breed. **Frequency:** annual. **Type:** recognition ● Best of Opposite Sex. **Frequency:** annual. **Type:** recognition. **Committees:** Breeder Referral; Code of Ethics; Judge's Education; Rescue. **Affiliated With:** American Kennel Club. **Publications:** MCOA Bulletin ● MCOA Journal, quarterly. **Price:** $21.00/year in U.S.; $28.00/year in Canada; $37.00/year for other countries; $38.00/year in Australia, New Zealand, and Japan ● MCOA Membership Directory, annual. **Conventions/Meetings:** annual Dog Show and Competition - show and competition (exhibits) ● annual specialty show.

21836 ■ Miniature Bull Terrier Club of America (MBTCA)
c/o Kathy Flaugh, Membership Chair
9224 Kinlock Dr.
Indianapolis, IN 46256-2242
Ph: (317)849-0929
E-mail: flaughmbts@comcast.net
URL: http://www.minibull.org
Contact: Giselle Simonds, Pres.
Founded: 1966. **Members:** 130. **Membership Dues:** individual, $25 (annual) ● couple, $30 (annual) ● foreign, $35 (annual). **Regional Groups:** 1. **Description:** Owners of registered miniature bull terriers. Promotes the breeding of miniature bull terriers. Holds competitions. Offers placement service. **Awards:** **Type:** recognition. **Recipient:** for obedience training of terriers, high scoring working terriers, champions, and producers of champions. **Publications:** A Little Bull., bimonthly ● The Miniature, periodic. **Conventions/Meetings:** monthly meeting ● annual specialty show.

21837 ■ Miniature Pinscher Club of America (MPCA)
c/o Christine Filler, Sec.
35038 N 10th St.
Desert Hills, AZ 85086
Ph: (602)717-7909
E-mail: mpcasecretary@minpin.org
URL: http://www.minpin.org
Contact: Mrs. Sandee White, Pres.
Founded: 1929. **Members:** 551. **Membership Dues:** individual, $45 (annual) ● family, $60 (annual) ● other, $65 (annual). **Local Groups:** 9. **Description:** Breeders and owners of purebred miniature pinschers registered with the American Kennel Club (see separate entry). Conducts charitable and educational programs; operates hall of fame. **Awards:** **Type:** recognition. **Publications:** The Pinscher Patter, quarterly. **Price:** included in membership dues. **Conventions/Meetings:** annual specialty show.

21838 ■ National Amateur Retriever Club (NARC)
c/o Retriever Field Trial News
4379 S Howell Ave., Ste.17
Milwaukee, WI 53207-5053
Ph: (414)481-2760
Fax: (414)481-2743

E-mail: retrievernews@mindspring.com
URL: http://www.working-retriever.com/narc
Contact: Wayne Bleazard, Pres.
Founded: 1956. **Members:** 130. **Membership Dues:** club, $50 (annual). **Staff:** 1. **Budget:** $25,000. **Description:** Represents field trial clubs of amateurs who run registered retrievers in AKC licensed field trials, a series of tests in which the dogs retrieve birds and establish qualifications for entry into the national competition. The national championship determines a national amateur retriever champion each year. **Awards:** National Amateur Field Champion. **Frequency:** annual. **Type:** recognition. **Recipient:** for successful completion of 10 competitive series, ranked number 1 as determined by three judges. **Publications:** National Amateur Championship Stake. Catalog. Features list of dogs running in National Competition. **Price:** $5.00. **Advertising:** accepted. **Conventions/Meetings:** annual National Amateur Championship Competition - June.

21839 ■ National American Eskimo Dog Association (NAEDA)
c/o Sally Bedow, Treas.
1978 School Rd.
Port Lavaca, TX 77979
Ph: (361)552-9083
E-mail: besota@earthlink.net
URL: http://www.eskie.com/naeda
Contact: Sally Bedow, Treas.
Founded: 1969. **Members:** 525. **Membership Dues:** individual, $15 (annual) ● senior, $7 (annual) ● junior, $2 (annual). **Local Groups:** 25. **Description:** Individuals interested in American Eskimo dogs. Seeks to better the breed; conducts conformation and obedience shows. **Affiliated With:** United Kennel Club. **Publications:** INAEDA Newsletter, quarterly. Contains association news, breed information, and information on upcoming shows. **Price:** included in membership dues. **Conventions/Meetings:** semiannual meeting - always Memorial Day weekend and third weekend of October.

21840 ■ National American Pit Bull Terrier Association (NAPBTA)
c/o Michael Snyder, Pres.
239 SW 118th St.
Seattle, WA 98146
Ph: (206)244-5055
E-mail: napbtapresident@comcast.net
URL: http://www.napbta.com
Contact: Michael Snyder, Pres.
Founded: 1980. **Members:** 150. **Membership Dues:** individual, $20 (annual) ● family (any two adults living in the same household), $30 (annual) ● club, $45 (annual). **State Groups:** 18. **Description:** Owners and fanciers of the United Kennel Club registered American pit bull terriers. (American Pit bull terriers are short-haired dogs that are a cross breed between a bulldog and a terrier.) Fights breed specific legislation. Promotes a positive image of the United Kennel Club registered American pit bull terrier. Holds national breed show yearly and other shows throughout the year at the discretion of the association. **Awards:** National GRCH. **Frequency:** annual. **Type:** recognition. **Affiliated With:** United Kennel Club. **Publications:** Bloodlines, monthly. Magazine. Includes UKC dog magazine. **Price:** $24.00/year. **Advertising:** accepted ● Bulletin, bimonthly. **Conventions/Meetings:** annual National Show - meeting and competition, with dog show consisting of conformation, obedience, weight pull and sometimes agility conformation competitions; open only to UKC registered American Pit Bull Terriers; obedience and agility open to any UKC registered dog.

21841 ■ National Association of Dog Obedience Instructors (NADOI)
PMB 369
729 Grapevine Hwy.
Hurst, TX 76054-2085
E-mail: corrsec2@nadoi.org
URL: http://www.nadoi.org
Contact: Jane Clark, Pres.
Founded: 1964. **Members:** 600. **Membership Dues:** individual, family, $45 (annual). **Staff:** 30. **Description:** Dog obedience instructors who have met certain standards as established by the association. Promotes improved dog obedience instruction. Endorses instructors; serves as a network for communication among members. Maintains speakers' bureau. **Publications:** FORWARD, quarterly. Magazine. **Price:** $6.00/year. **Advertising:** accepted ● NADOI "Good Puppy" Handbook ● NADOI News, bimonthly. Newsletter. **Conventions/Meetings:** annual Conference and Membership Meeting - meeting and workshop - always spring.

21842 ■ National Association of Louisiana Catahoulas (NALC)
PO Box 1041
Denham Springs, LA 70727-1041
Ph: (225)665-6082
Contact: Mrs. J. S. Eaves, Pres.
Founded: 1977. **Description:** Owners of Louisiana Catahoulas in the United States and Canada. (The Louisiana Catahoula is the state dog of Louisiana.) Sponsors working cow trials, bayings, dog shows, and obedience trials. Maintains registration office. **Publications:** The Catahoula Collection. Book ● Directory, periodic. Lists certified breeders. ● Newsletter, quarterly. **Conventions/Meetings:** show - 10/year.

21843 ■ National Beagle Club of America (NBCA)
c/o Dr. Emily Southgate, Sec.
PO Box 642
Middleburg, VA 20118
URL: http://clubs.akc.org/NBC
Contact: William E. Bobbitt Jr., Pres.
Founded: 1887. **Members:** 500. **Membership Dues:** individual, $30 (annual) ● couple, $60 (annual). **Description:** Breeders and others interested in beagles. Works to improve the beagle as a field and show dog; encourages beagling, including holding of field trials and registering of packs of beagles. **Affiliated With:** American Kennel Club. **Conventions/Meetings:** annual meeting - always second Friday of November, in Aldie, VA.

21844 ■ National Bird Dog Challenge Association (NBDCA)
32 County Rd., 30 SW
Montrose, MN 55363
Free: (866)909-THTV
E-mail: tournamenthunter@frontiernet.net
URL: http://www.nbdca.com
Contact: Dan Sojka, Contact
Founded: 1995. **Members:** 5,200. **Membership Dues:** single, $35 (annual) ● family, $45 (annual) ● life (per dog), $395. **Description:** Brings together men, women, and children who share a mutual interest for bird dogs, upland game bird hunting, and the preservation of the sport. Fosters camaraderie among its members and fellow competitors. Sponsors the Bird Dog Challenge (BDC) tournament.

21845 ■ National Cesky Terrier Club of America (NCTCA)
c/o Sharon Lesniak, Pres.
5275 Crestway Dr.
Bay City, MI 48706
Ph: (989)686-2044
E-mail: brigadoonsl@chartermi.net
URL: http://www.cesky.org
Contact: Sharon Lesniak, Pres.
Membership Dues: single in U.S., $15 (annual) ● dual in U.S., single outside U.S., $20 (annual) ● dual outside U.S., $25 (annual). **Description:** Represents the interests of Cesky Terrier breeders, owners and enthusiasts. Protects and advances the Cesky Terrier breed. Promotes ethical and quality breeding of the Cesky Terrier in the United States. Provides rescue services to Cesky Terriers in need. **Telecommunication Services:** electronic mail, lh1988@verizon.net. **Publications:** Newsletter. **Price:** included in membership dues.

21846 ■ National Entlebucher Mountain Dog Association (NEMDA)
c/o DeeAnn Devey, Membership Chair
11957 S Noelle Rd.
Sandy, UT 84092
E-mail: president@nemda.org
URL: http://www.nemda.org
Contact: Jan Vincent, Pres./Events Chair
Founded: 1998. **Members:** 200. **Membership Dues:** regular, in U.S., $30 (annual) ● regular, in Canada, $40 (annual) ● associate in U.S., $15 (annual) ● associate in Canada, $20 (annual). **Multinational. Description:** Protects and advances the Entlebucher Mountain Dog breed. Educates the public about the nature of the breed and the responsibilities of ownership. Encourages and promotes medical research concerning genetic defects which may afflict the Entlebucher. **Awards:** Guthrie Award. **Frequency:** periodic. **Type:** recognition. **Recipient:** for registered dogs which have earned titles in three separate categories from national dog performance organizations. **Publications:** *Entlebook*, quarterly. Newsletter. Features training articles, book reviews, national events and articles regarding health issues of the breed. **Price:** included in membership dues.

21847 ■ National Greyhound Association (NGA)
PO Box 543
Abilene, KS 67410
Ph: (785)263-4660
Fax: (785)263-4689
E-mail: nga@ngagreyhounds.com
URL: http://www.ngagreyhounds.com
Contact: Gary Guccione, Sec.-Treas.
Founded: 1906. **Members:** 2,900. **Membership Dues:** full, $70 (annual) ● associate, $50 (annual). **Staff:** 15. **Description:** Registry of greyhound dogs. Focuses on the improvement and development of the greyhound breed and the advancement and promotion of the greyhound racing industry. **Libraries: Type:** reference. **Holdings:** 200. **Awards:** Greyhound Hall of Fame. **Frequency:** annual. **Type:** scholarship. **Recipient:** for individuals ● **Type:** recognition. **Publications:** *The Greyhound Review*, monthly. Magazine. Contains news and information on Greyhound racing. **Price:** $30.00/year; $3.00/copy. **Circulation:** 4,000. **Advertising:** accepted ● *Greyhound Stud Book*, annual. **Price:** $25.00. **Conventions/Meetings:** competition ● semiannual meeting - always late April and mid-October, Abilene, KS.

21848 ■ National Labrador Retriever Club (NLRC)
c/o Leigh Green, Membership Chair
1408 Bel Air Blvd.
Sanford, FL 32771-4616
E-mail: nlrcmembership@bellsouth.net
URL: http://labradorretrievers.org
Contact: Sue Willumsen, Pres.
Founded: 1934. **Members:** 755. **Membership Dues:** full, $30 (annual) ● associate, $20 (annual). **Staff:** 10. **Description:** Breeders and owners of purebred Labrador retrievers. Maintains hall of fame and museum. Conducts specialized education programs; compiles statistics. **Libraries: Type:** open to the public. **Holdings:** 200; books, periodicals. **Awards:** Hall of Fame. **Frequency:** annual. **Type:** recognition. **Recipient:** for dogs and people. **Affiliated With:** American Kennel Club. **Formerly:** (2005) Labrador Retriever Club. **Publications:** *The Labrador Connection*, bimonthly. Newsletter. **Advertising:** accepted. **Conventions/Meetings:** annual convention (exhibits).

21849 ■ National Shiba Club of America (NSCA)
c/o Sue Thomas
1210 W Indian Hills Dr., No. 24
St. George, UT 84770-6376
E-mail: info@shibas.org
URL: http://www.shibas.org
Contact: Jacey Holden, Pres.
Founded: 1992. **Membership Dues:** single, $25 (annual) ● family, $35 (annual). **Description:** Promotes the Shiba Inu dog; dedicated to breeders abiding by

a strict code of ethics. Provides breeder referrals and Registry of Merit. **Telecommunication Services:** electronic mail, membership@shibas.org. **Publications:** *Shiba-E-News*, quarterly. Newsletter. **Price:** included in membership dues. Alternate Formats: online ● Brochure. **Conventions/Meetings:** specialty show.

21850 ■ National Toy Fox Terrier Association (NTFTA)
c/o Patricia Johnson, Pres.
51215 Sand Song Ave.
Johnson Valley, CA 92285-2961
Ph: (760)364-3130
Fax: (760)364-9256
E-mail: patrickstoyfox@aol.com
URL: http://www.nationaltoyfoxterrier.org
Contact: Patricia Johnson, Pres.
Founded: 1949. **Members:** 357. **Membership Dues:** single, $25 (annual) ● family, $30 (annual) ● junior, $10 (annual). **Staff:** 6. **State Groups:** 20. **Description:** Breeders, owners, and enthusiasts of toy fox terriers. Promotes the toy fox terrier and encourages adherence to standards for the breed as set by the United Kennel Club (see separate entry). (The smallest breed of fox terrier, toy fox terriers are predominantly white with black and tan markings, weigh under seven pounds, have a shoulder height of 11 inches and under, and are known for their intelligence.) Sponsors competitions. **Awards:** Dam of the Year Award. **Frequency:** annual. **Type:** recognition. **Recipient:** to the owner of the dam whose descendants have received the most championship titles in the previous year ● Gaines Good Sportsmanship Award. **Type:** recognition ● Membership Award. **Type:** recognition ● Sire of the Year Award. **Frequency:** annual. **Type:** recognition. **Recipient:** to the owner of the sire whose descendants have received the most championship titles in the previous year. **Computer Services:** Mailing lists, of members. **Committees:** Sunshine. **Publications:** *Breeders Directory*, periodic ● *National History Book*. **Conventions/Meetings:** annual meeting - always third weekend of August ● annual show and board meeting - always spring.

21851 ■ Newfoundland Club of America (NCA)
PO Box 2614
Cheyenne, WY 82003-2614
Ph: (716)683-1578
E-mail: info@newfdogclub.org
URL: http://www.newfdogclub.org
Contact: Roger Frey, Pres.
Founded: 1930. **Members:** 1,321. **Budget:** $95,000. **Regional Groups:** 25. **Description:** Owners and breeders of purebred Newfoundland dogs. Conducts regional specialties and water trials. Operates national and regional rescue service for displaced Newfoundland dogs. **Awards: Type:** recognition. **Telecommunication Services:** electronic mail, jolly-roger.jollyroger@verizon.net. **Affiliated With:** American Kennel Club. **Publications:** *NCA Membership List*, annual. Membership Directory ● *Newf Tide*, quarterly. Magazine. **Price:** included in membership dues; $55.00 for nonmembers in U.S.; $70.00 for nonmembers outside U.S. (bulk mail); $110.00 for nonmembers outside U.S. (airmail) ● *The Newfoundland and You* ● *Water Trial Training Manual*. **Conventions/Meetings:** annual National Specialty Show (exhibits) - always April or May ● periodic regional meeting and competition, specialties and water trials.

21852 ■ North American Deutsch Kurzhaar Club (NADKC)
c/o Rich Dobey, Treas.
1017 S Fourth Ave.
Libertyville, IL 60048
E-mail: info@nadkc.org
URL: http://www.nadkc.org
Contact: Rich Dobey, Treas.
Founded: 1993. **Membership Dues:** international, $20 (annual) ● family, $25 (annual) ● regular, $50 (annual) ● life, $500. **Multinational. Description:** Represents Deutsch Kurzhaar enthusiasts. Promotes and improves the Deutsch Kurzhaar (German Short-

hair) in accordance with the principles originated by the Deutsch Kurzhaar Verband (DKV). Supports the efforts of other versatile hunting dog breeding and testing organizations. Facilitates communication and fellowship among members. **Publications:** Newsletter. **Price:** included in membership dues.

21853 ■ North American Jack Russell Terrier Association (NAJRTA)
c/o Nan Owen, Treas.
415 Walker Hollow Dr.
Monterey, TN 38574
Ph: (931)839-7462
E-mail: fono@frontiernet.net
Contact: Liz McKinney, Pres.
Founded: 2000. **Membership Dues:** individual, $15 (annual) ● family, $20 (annual). **Multinational. Description:** Encourages and promotes the breeding of better and finer purebred Jack Russell Terriers as recognized by the United Kennel Club, Inc. (UKC). Promotes the breed and increases its popularity in a responsible manner. Educates interested fanciers as to the merits and versatility of this breed. Encourages ethical and knowledgeable breeding practices. Promotes good sportsmanship in the training and exhibition of dogs. **Telecommunication Services:** electronic mail, jkrusel@swva.net. **Publications:** Yearbook. Showcases the previous year's activities in the club's history. ● Newsletter ● Articles. Alternate Formats: online.

21854 ■ North American Kai Association (NAKA)
3410 Galbraith Line Rd.
Yale, MI 48097
E-mail: naka@kai-ken.org
URL: http://www.kai-ken.org
Contact: Marsha Short, Pres.
Description: Promotes the responsible ownership and breeding of the Kai. Informs and educates the public about the breed. Preserves the natural characteristic of the breed by encouraging members to participate in canine activities including but not limited to agility, companion, conformation and obedience. **Telecommunication Services:** electronic mail, marsha@kai-ken.org.

21855 ■ North American Llewellin Breeders Association (NALBA)
3413 Forrester Ln.
Waco, TX 76708
Ph: (254)752-1526
E-mail: info@nalba.org
URL: http://www.nalba.org
Contact: Chuck Wilson, Pres.
Membership Dues: regular, $100 (annual) ● associate, $50 (annual). **Multinational. Description:** Perpetuates and extends the purity and values of the Llewellin Setter bloodline. Restores and perpetuates wild Upland Game Birds on the North American Continent. Promotes, conducts and fosters research, education, training and publication in ornithological sciences, to make studies with reference to the enhancement of knowledge concerning Upland Game Birds of the North American Continent. **Telecommunication Services:** electronic mail, chuck@whiterockllewellins.com.

21856 ■ North American Ring Association (NARA)
c/o Jennifer Sunga, Treas.
PO Box 175
Ryde, CA 95680-0175
Ph: (707)746-8584
Fax: (707)745-0825
E-mail: jensunga@peoplepc.com
URL: http://www.ringsport.org
Contact: Jennifer Sunga, Treas.
Founded: 1989. **Members:** 230. **Membership Dues:** full, $75 (annual). **Budget:** $4,000. **Multinational. Description:** Works to promote the French ring sport in the United States. Oversees matches and assists members to win titles for their dogs. **Awards:** Domestic Training Award. **Frequency:** annual. **Type:** recognition. **Recipient:** for the highest scoring dog trained in the U.S. ● Lobo Award. **Frequency:** annual. **Type:**

recognition. **Recipient:** for the highest scoring German Shepherd. **Publications:** *North American Ring Associations' Rulebook.* Alternate Formats: online ● *Ring Sport News,* bimonthly. Newsletter. **Price:** included in membership dues; $35.00 /year for nonmembers. **Conventions/Meetings:** quarterly board meeting.

21857 ■ North American Sheep Dog Society (NASDS)

Address Unknown since 2007

Founded: 1941. **Members:** 1,100. **Staff:** 1. **State Groups:** 51. **Description:** Enthusiasts and breeders of Border collie sheepdogs. Purpose is to promote the breed and to register all Border collies. Maintains stud books on Border collies bred and raised in Canada and the U.S. Sponsors Supreme Champion trials. **Publications:** *Breeders List,* annual.

21858 ■ North American Teckel Club (NATC)

c/o Carrie Hamilton, Sec.
9621 Bachelor Rd.
Kutztown, PA 19530
E-mail: natc.board@teckelclub.org
URL: http://www.teckelclub.org
Contact: Carrie Hamilton, Sec.

Founded: 1999. **Members:** 45. **Membership Dues:** individual ($25 per additional member of the household), $50 (annual). **Multinational. Description:** Maintains the physical and mental hunting aptitudes of the dachshund breed. Preserves the dachshund's hunting heritage. Promotes its usefulness in the field and supports the breeding of dachshunds with sound bodies and stable temperaments. Develops and conducts field tests designed to evaluate the hunting qualities of dachshunds. Encourages sportsmanlike behavior in all activities involving dachshunds. **Telecommunication Services:** electronic mail, hamiltce@juno.com. **Publications:** *Teckel Talk,* bimonthly. Newsletter. **Price:** included in membership dues. Alternate Formats: online ● Report. Alternate Formats: online.

21859 ■ North American Working Bouvier Association (NAWBA)

426 3rd Ave.
West Haven, CT 06516
Ph: (203)241-6574
E-mail: nadaevans@comcast.net
URL: http://www.nawba.net
Contact: David Evans, Pres.

Description: Preserves, promotes and advances the Bouvier des Flandres as a protective heritage working breed. Establishes programs to verify the mental and physical attributes suiting the dog to his work. Promotes and encourages training and use of the Bouvier for work consistent with the heritage and of the breed, including protection work, obedience, tracking and herding. **Publications:** Journal, quarterly. Features collection of articles, pictures and commentaries.

21860 ■ Norwegian Elkhound Association of America (NEAA)

c/o Karen Elvin, Corresponding Sec.
14465 St. Croix Trail N
Marine on St. Croix, MN 55047
Ph: (860)774-3174
E-mail: neaainfo@mac.com
URL: http://www.neaa.net
Contact: Ginger Leeuwenburg, Coor.

Founded: 1935. **Members:** 500. **Membership Dues:** individual, $25 (annual) ● combined, $35 (annual). **Budget:** $40,000. **Regional Groups:** 12. **Local Groups:** 2. **Description:** Owners, breeders, and exhibitors of Norwegian Elkhounds. Supports other dog shows throughout the year. Conducts regional education seminars and operates special committees. Sponsors competitions. **Libraries: Type:** not open to the public. **Holdings:** articles, books, periodicals, video recordings. **Awards:** Ed Schlesinger Outstanding Service Award. **Frequency:** annual. **Type:** recognition. **Recipient:** for the most outstanding person(s) ● Susan D. Phillips Top Awards. **Frequency:** annual. **Type:** recognition. **Recipient:** for the most outstanding person(s), associa-

tion(s), and/or corporation(s) ● Wells and Catherine Peck Award. **Frequency:** biennial. **Type:** recognition. **Recipient:** for the most outstanding person(s). **Affiliated With:** American Kennel Club. **Publications:** *NEAA Cookbook.* **Price:** $5.00 ● *NEAA Yearbook,* biennial. Features top producers, prestige winners, and other Elkhounds worthy of mention. ● *Norwegian Elkhound News,* bimonthly. Newsletter. **Advertising:** accepted ● Also publishes descriptive booklet, pamphlet, and breeder's guide. **Conventions/Meetings:** annual meeting (exhibits) ● biennial specialty show.

21861 ■ Norwich and Norfolk Terrier Club (NNTC)

c/o Carol Jordan, Membership Chair
604 Old Fritztown Rd.
Reading, PA 19607-1016
Ph: (610)775-0792
E-mail: norweim@aol.com
URL: http://www.norwichandnorfolkterrier.org
Contact: Barbara Miller, Pres.

Founded: 1947. **Members:** 350. **Membership Dues:** dual, $35 (annual) ● regular, $25 (annual). **Budget:** $10,000. **Regional Groups:** 4. **Description:** Member of the American Kennel Club (see separate entry). Represents owners, breeders, and exhibitors of purebred Norwich and Norfolk terriers. Holds match and specialty shows. **Awards:** Agility Award. **Frequency:** annual. **Type:** trophy. **Recipient:** to members ● Cleanrun Award. **Frequency:** annual. **Type:** trophy. **Recipient:** to members ● Conformation Award. **Frequency:** annual. **Type:** trophy. **Recipient:** to members ● High Rising Trophy - Norwich Bitch. **Frequency:** annual. **Type:** trophy. **Recipient:** to members ● John Paul Jones - Norwich Dog. **Frequency:** annual. **Type:** trophy. **Recipient:** to members ● Maplehurst Trophy - Norfolk Bitch. **Frequency:** annual. **Type:** trophy. **Recipient:** to members ● Neversink Trophy. **Frequency:** annual. **Type:** trophy. **Recipient:** to a Norwich and Norfolk Terrier ● Obedience Award. **Frequency:** annual. **Type:** trophy. **Recipient:** to members ● Partee Trophy - Norfolk Dog. **Frequency:** annual. **Type:** trophy. **Recipient:** to members ● Register of Merit. **Frequency:** annual. **Type:** recognition. **Recipient:** to a sire or dam ● River Bend Cup - Norwich and Norfolk. **Frequency:** annual. **Type:** trophy. **Recipient:** to members ● Versatility Award. **Frequency:** annual. **Type:** trophy. **Recipient:** to members. **Computer Services:** database, pedigree. **Committees:** Breeders Guide and Study Registry; Members Education; Notions; Publications; Rescue; Standards; Trophies. **Programs:** Rescue and Rehoming. **Formerly:** (1979) Norwich Terrier Club. **Publications:** *The Norwich and Norfolk News,* semiannual. Newsletter. Includes kennel and stud listings. **Price:** included in membership dues; $15.00 for nonmembers in U.S.; $20.00 for nonmembers outside U.S. **Circulation:** 780 ● Membership Directory, annual ● Article. Alternate Formats: online. **Conventions/Meetings:** annual meeting, sale of breed related notions/veterinary studies, coincides with Montgomery County KC show in Ambler, PA (exhibits) - October, in Bensalem, PA.

21862 ■ Old English Sheepdog Club of America (OESCA)

c/o Colleen Allen Grady, Pres.
3643 N Pearl St.
Tacoma, WA 98407
Ph: (253)262-1797
E-mail: cagradyoes@aol.com
URL: http://www.oldenglishsheepdogclubofamerica.org
Contact: Colleen Allen Grady, Pres.

Founded: 1905. **Members:** 1,585. **Membership Dues:** individual, $45 (annual) ● household, $50 (annual) ● junior, $20 (annual). **Staff:** 12. **Regional Groups:** 5. **Description:** Represents breeders, owners, and exhibitors of purebred Old English sheepdogs. Offers specialized education program in proper care and breeding. **Affiliated With:** American Kennel Club. **Publications:** *Old English Times,* bimonthly ● Membership Directory, annual ● Yearbook, biennial. **Conventions/Meetings:** annual specialty show.

21863 ■ Otterhound Club of America (OHCA)

c/o Margaret Neubauer, Sec.
2185 Seeman St. SW
East Sparta, OH 44626-9727
Ph: (330)484-4845
E-mail: otterhound@sbcglobal.net
URL: http://clubs.akc.org/ohca
Contact: Margaret Neubauer, Sec.

Founded: 1960. **Members:** 140. **Membership Dues:** individual, $25 (annual) ● couple, $35 (annual). **Description:** Breeders, owners, and fanciers of the Otterhound, a British dog first bred in the 13th century and brought to North America in the 1950s. Seeks to serve as a network on Otterhound breeding, care, and history. Maintains archives; sponsors competitions. **Computer Services:** database, Otterhound. **Committees:** Nominating; Rescue. **Affiliated With:** American Kennel Club. **Publications:** *The Voice,* bimonthly. Newsletter. **Price:** included in membership dues ● Yearbook, biennial. **Conventions/Meetings:** annual specialty show.

21864 ■ Papillon Club of America (PCA)

c/o Darlene Atkinson, Pres.
8017 Glen Alta Way
Citrus Heights, CA 95610-0512
E-mail: secretary@papillonclub.org
URL: http://www.papillonclub.org
Contact: Paula Botwinick, Recording Sec.

Founded: 1930. **Members:** 525. **Membership Dues:** regular, $35 (annual) ● junior, $10 (annual). **Staff:** 9. **Local Groups:** 5. **Description:** Owners, breeders, and exhibitors of purebred Papillon dogs (an old spaniel breed formerly known as Continental Spaniel). Maintains hall of fame; compiles statistics. **Committees:** Breed Award; Educational; Junior Showmanship; Obedience Awards; Specialty Awards; Specialty Show. **Publications:** *Breed Handbook* ● *Common Medical Disorders of the Papillon.* Book. Contains eighteen common medical conditions of Papillon. **Price:** $22.50 plus shipping and handling ● *Pap Talk,* monthly. Newsletter ● *Pap Talk Scrapbook* ● *Papillon Primer* ● *Roster,* annual ● Membership Directory, annual. **Conventions/Meetings:** annual specialty show (exhibits).

21865 ■ Parson Russell Terrier Association of America (PRTAA)

c/o Marcia Walsh, Pres.
839 Canada Rd.
Woodside, CA 94062
Ph: (650)851-4044
E-mail: marcialen@comcast.net
URL: http://www.prtaa.org
Contact: Marcia Walsh, Pres.

Founded: 1985. **Membership Dues:** single, $25 ● household, $40. **Description:** Promotes breeding, working and continuance of the pure bred Parson Russell terrier. Recognizes the breed as the Jack Russell Terrier in 1997 (the name was officially changed in 2003 to the Parson Russell Terrier, in keeping with its UK origin). **Formerly:** (2003) Jack Russell Terrier Association of America.

21866 ■ Pekingese Club of America (PCA)

c/o T. Diane Renihan, Sec.
9161 159th Ct. N
Jupiter, FL 33478-6313
Ph: (561)743-0888
Fax: (561)743-0303
E-mail: kuanyinjade@aol.com
URL: http://www.geocities.com/pekes.geo
Contact: James Jaeger, Pres.

Founded: 1909. **Members:** 379. **Membership Dues:** individual, $25 (annual) ● overseas, $30 (annual). **Description:** Represents owners, breeders, and exhibitors of purebred Pekingese dogs. **Affiliated With:** American Kennel Club. **Publications:** *Lion Dog News,* quarterly. Bulletin. **Price:** free for members. **Advertising:** accepted. **Conventions/Meetings:** periodic show.

21867 ■ Pembroke Welsh Corgi Club of America (PWCCA)

c/o Anne H. Bowes, Corresponding Sec.
PO Box 2141
Duxbury, MA 02331-2141
Ph: (781)934-0110
Fax: (781)934-6597
E-mail: secretary@pembrokecorgi.org
URL: http://www.pembrokecorgi.org
Contact: Anne H. Bowes, Corresponding Sec.
Founded: 1936. **Members:** 500. **Staff:** 5. **Regional Groups:** 15. **Description:** Represents owners and breeders of purebred Pembroke Welsh Corgi dogs. **Affiliated With:** American Kennel Club. **Publications:** *Illustrated Standard* ● Handbook, annual ● Newsletter, quarterly. Contains photo advertisements from members of the PWCCA, articles, specialty critiques, etc. **Conventions/Meetings:** annual show (exhibits) - always September.

21868 ■ Peruvian Inca Orchid Dog Club of America (PIOCA)

c/o Jean Schroeder, AKC Liaison
17502 S 750 W
Wanatah, IN 46390
Ph: (219)733-9480
E-mail: jean@willabe.com
URL: http://www.peruvianincaorchid.com
Contact: Jean Schroeder, AKC Liaison
Founded: 1985. **Members:** 30. **Membership Dues:** single/family in U.S., $20 (annual) ● single/family outside U.S., $25 (annual). **Staff:** 6. **Description:** Breeders, exhibitors, and owners of Peruvian Inca Orchid dogs (also known as Perro Sin Pello del Peru). Provides information records of conformation and field events; conducts breed rescue; maintains breeders listings, holds dog shows (Breed specific). **Libraries:** Type: open to the public. **Holdings:** books. **Subjects:** history of the breed, standards of breed, conformation, health. **Awards:** Confirmation and Field Obedience Championship. **Frequency:** annual. **Type:** recognition. **Recipient:** for the champion under AKC rules and regulations. **Computer Services:** database, breed referral ● mailing lists. **Affiliated With:** American Kennel Club. **Publications:** *Moonflower Moments*, annual. Newsletter. Contains information of interest to members and dog show judges. **Price:** free for members. **Circulation:** 50. **Advertising:** accepted. Alternate Formats: online. **Conventions/Meetings:** annual board meeting - always May ● annual specialty show, dog show.

21869 ■ Poodle Club of America (PCA)

c/o Ms. Peggy McDill, Corresponding Sec.
24922 Las Marias Ln.
Mission Viejo, CA 92691-5119
Ph: (949)378-6701
E-mail: poodleclubsecy@aol.com
URL: http://www.poodleclubofamerica.org
Contact: Mrs. Doris Cozart, Pres.
Founded: 1931. **Members:** 286. **Regional Groups:** 49. **Description:** Owners, breeders, exhibitors, and judges of purebred poodles. Works to: encourage and promote owning, breeding, and training of purebred poodles and formation of local poodle specialty clubs; urge acceptance of American Kennel Club (see separate entry) standards as sole criteria; protect and advance interests of the breed; conduct sanctioned and licensed specialty shows and obedience trials under regulations of the AKC. Maintains Poodle Club of America Foundation. **Committees:** Agility; Breed Standard; Genetic Anomalies; Obedience; Poodles in America; WC/WCX. **Affiliated With:** American Kennel Club. **Publications:** *Illustrated Study of the Poodle Breed Standard* ● *Poodle Papers*, quarterly. Newsletter. Seven volumes. **Price:** free, for members only. Alternate Formats: online ● *Poodles in America*. Book. Seven volumes. **Conventions/Meetings:** semiannual specialty show (exhibits).

21870 ■ Portuguese Water Dog Club of America (PWDCA)

c/o Pat Qvigstad, Membership Chair
111 Foxtail Cir.
Golden, CO 80403
Ph: (303)582-5009
Fax: (303)582-0925
E-mail: foxtailsh2os@msn.com
URL: http://www.pwdca.org
Contact: Karen Arends, Pres.
Founded: 1972. **Members:** 1,200. **Membership Dues:** associate and active, $55 (annual) ● foreign, $80 (annual). **Regional Groups:** 10. **State Groups:** 47. **Description:** Individuals interested in the history and preservation of Portuguese Water Dogs; owners of such dogs. There are fewer than 4,500 Portuguese Water Dogs left in the world and 4,000 of these are in the U.S. Purposes are to: encourage the selective breeding of purebred Portuguese Water Dogs and to do all that is possible to bring their natural qualities to perfection; protect and advance the interests of the breed. Attempts to locate Portuguese Water Dogs anywhere in the world; registered by the American Kennel Club (see separate entry). Sponsors workshops; conducts research to compile history and medical information of the breed; compiles statistics. **Awards:** Type: recognition. **Committees:** Education; Health; Historian; Rescue and Relocation; Show; Water Trials/Working Dog. **Publications:** *The Courier*, bimonthly. Magazine. Includes book reviews, event schedules, health and training articles, game commentaries, and regional reports. **Price:** included in membership dues. **Circulation:** 1,000. **Conventions/Meetings:** annual meeting and specialty show.

21871 ■ Professional Handlers Association (PHA)

17017 Norbrook Dr.
Olney, MD 20832-2623
Ph: (301)924-0089
Fax: (301)924-0089
E-mail: manager@phadoghandlers.com
URL: http://www.phadoghandlers.com
Contact: Kathleen Bowser, Exec. VP
Founded: 1926. **Members:** 231. **Description:** Seeks to promote the interests of individuals who show purebred dogs at dog shows as a profession. Enhances the stature of professional dog handling. Provides information on purebred dogs to interested persons. Sponsors seminars and lectures. **Conventions/Meetings:** annual show.

21872 ■ Pug Dog Club of America (PDCA)

c/o Donna Manha, Sec.
449 Maar Ave.
Fremont, CA 94536
E-mail: pugsrus2@comcast.net
URL: http://www.pugs.org
Contact: Michael Anderson, Pres.
Founded: 1931. **Members:** 500. **Membership Dues:** individual, $20 (annual). **Regional Groups:** 12. **Description:** Represents owners, breeders, and exhibitors of purebred Pug dogs. **Committees:** Advertising; Annual Awards; Education; Good Sportsmanship; Show; Trophy. **Affiliated With:** American Kennel Club. **Publications:** *A Celebration of the Pug 1885-1985* ● *History of the Pug Dog Club of America* ● Membership Roster, annual. Membership Directory ● *PDCA Bulletin*, quarterly ● *Pug Talk Magazine*, bimonthly. **Conventions/Meetings:** annual board meeting and show.

21873 ■ Puli Club of America (PCA)

c/o Michael Rohe, Corresponding Sec.
5032 Winton Ridge Ln.
Cincinnati, OH 45232
Ph: (513)541-6819
E-mail: cordonblue1@msn.com
URL: http://www.puliclub.org
Contact: Michael Rohe, Corresponding Sec.
Founded: 1951. **Members:** 390. **Membership Dues:** individual, associate, junior, $25 (annual) ● household, $35 (annual). **Regional Groups:** 5. **Description:** Works to promote the breeding of purebred Puli dogs and "to perfect their natural qualities." Urges members to accept the standard of the breed approved by the American Kennel Club (see separate entry) as the only standard of excellence by which Puli shall be judged. Conducts sanctioned matches, specialty shows, and obedience trials under the rules of AKC. **Committees:** Health Education; Judges

Education. **Publications:** *Book of Title Holders*, annual ● *Breeders Directory*, periodic ● *Puli News*, bimonthly. Newsletter. **Price:** included in membership dues; $18.00 for nonmembers ● Also publishes grooming and breed pamphlets. **Conventions/Meetings:** annual meeting.

21874 ■ Pyrenean Mastiff Club of America (PMCA)

4083 W Ave. L, No. 107
Quartz Hill, CA 93536
Ph: (661)724-0268
Fax: (815)301-2908
E-mail: pyreneanmastiff@hughes.net
URL: http://www.pyreneanmastiff.org
Founded: 1996. **Membership Dues:** new, $65 ● renewal, $55 (annual). **Description:** Preserves and encourages the ethical breeding of the Pyrenean Mastiff in accordance with the current F.C.I. Standard. Encourages and assists in the organization of specialties and shows in representation of the Pyrenean Mastiff breed. Maintains a breeding regulations program to ensure the protection and longevity of the Pyrenean Mastiff breed. **Computer Services:** Information services, facts about Pyrenean Mastiff. **Publications:** *Unknown Spanish Giant*, triennial. Newsletter. **Price:** for members. Alternate Formats: online.

21875 ■ Rhodesian Ridgeback Club of the U.S. (RRCUS)

c/o Ross Jones, Corresponding Sec.
2008 Dorothy St. NE
Albuquerque, NM 87112
Ph: (505)296-3611
E-mail: rossbod@abq-nm.com
URL: http://www.rrcus.org
Contact: Ross Jones, Corresponding Sec.
Founded: 1957. **Members:** 800. **Membership Dues:** single, $50 (annual) ● family, $75 (annual) ● associate (single, nonvoting), $45 (annual). **Regional Groups:** 12. **Description:** Individuals interested in the Rhodesian Ridgeback dog. Works to promote the breed. Provides members with continuing educational programs and information about the breed. Maintains special adoption service to rescue Rhodesian Ridgebacks. **Libraries:** Type: reference. **Awards:** Frequency: annual. **Type:** recognition. **Affiliated With:** American Kennel Club. **Publications:** *Annual of Champions*, annual. Magazine. Contains information on new AKC champions of record and title holders. **Price:** included in membership dues. **Circulation:** 800. **Advertising:** accepted ● *Breeders Directory*, annual ● *The Ridgeback*, bimonthly. Magazine. Includes training tips, member news, regional reports, and statistics. **Price:** available to members only. **Advertising:** accepted ● Also publishes code of ethics and standards; elaboration of the standard; history and training materials. **Conventions/Meetings:** annual National Specialty Show - competition, includes judging in conformation, obedience, lure coursing, and other field events.

21876 ■ Saint Bernard Club of America (SBCA)

c/o Joan Zielinski, Corresponding Sec.
29625 144th Ave. SE
Kent, WA 98042
Ph: (253)631-1352
E-mail: joan@stoans.com
URL: http://www.saintbernardclub.org
Contact: Howard Dees, Pres.
Founded: 1888. **Members:** 900. **Membership Dues:** individual, $45 (annual) ● family, $50 (annual) ● individual outside U.S., $40 (annual). ● family, outside U.S., $50 (annual). **Local Groups:** 23. **Description:** Owners and breeders of purebred St. Bernard dogs. Conducts specialized education and research programs; maintains placement service; compiles statistics. Sponsors charitable projects. **Libraries:** Type: reference. **Holdings:** 500; video recordings. **Subjects:** dog shows, seminars, historic, present, etc. relating to St. Bernards. **Awards:** Brood Bitch, Stud Dog. **Frequency:** annual. **Type:** recognition. **Recipient:** for greatest number of champion puppies produced in a given year ● Outstanding Breeder. **Frequency:** annual. **Type:** recognition. **Recipient:**

for conformation and obedience titles ● Stud Dog. **Frequency:** annual. **Type:** recognition. **Recipient:** for greatest number of champion puppies produced in a given year. **Computer Services:** Mailing lists, of members. **Committees:** Education; Research; Ways and Means; Working Dog and Illustrated Standard. **Affiliated With:** American Kennel Club. **Publications:** *Fact and Fiction and The Illustrated Standard.* Pamphlet ● *Owner Responsibility.* Pamphlet ● *The Saint Fancier,* bimonthly. Magazine. Contains articles and includes local club reports and minutes. **Price:** included in membership dues. **Advertising:** accepted ● *SBCA National Catalog,* periodic. Includes ads and show entries. **Circulation:** 500. **Advertising:** accepted ● *The Young St. Bernard.* Pamphlet ● Magazine, annual. Contains photos of dogs that received AKS conformation and obedience titles, health articles, action of Board of Directors. ● Membership Directory, annual. **Conventions/Meetings:** annual National Specialty Show (exhibits).

21877 ■ Saluki Club of America (SCOA)
c/o Lois-Ann Snyder, Recording Sec.
1203 N Coolidge Rd.
Oconomowoc, WI 53066
Ph: (920)474-4765
E-mail: secretary@salukiclub.org
URL: http://www.salukiclub.org
Contact: Diana Farmer, Pres.
Founded: 1927. **Members:** 180. **Multinational. De-scription:** Owners, breeders, and exhibitors of purebred Saluki dogs (formerly known as gazelle hounds and Persian greyhounds). Sponsors research programs on disease and genetic problems in the Saluki; conducts specialized education programs for breeders, judges, and owners. **Libraries: Type:** reference. **Holdings:** archival material, artwork, books. **Awards:** Humane Award. **Frequency:** annual. **Type:** recognition. **Recipient:** for charitable donation of prize money ● **Frequency:** annual. **Type:** recognition. **Committees:** Club Liaison; Desert-Bred; Res-cue. **Affiliated With:** American Kennel Club; American Sighthound Field Association. **Publications:** *SCOA Yearbook,* periodic ● Newsletter, quarterly. Reports on club activities and meetings. Includes articles about research and medicine. **Price:** included in membership dues. **Circulation:** 150. **Conventions/Meetings:** competition ● annual specialty show and symposium - always June, Lexington, KY.

21878 ■ Samoyed Club of America (SCA)
c/o Beverly Delaney, Membership Chair
49 Fred Short Rd.
Saugerties, NY 12477
Ph: (845)246-7509
Fax: (845)247-0188
E-mail: ala-kasam@hvc.rr.com
URL: http://www.samoyed.org
Contact: Beverly Delaney, Membership Chair
Founded: 1923. **Members:** 1,600. **Membership Dues:** individual, $25 (annual) ● family, $35 (annual). **Staff:** 15. **Budget:** $80,000. **Local Groups:** 27. **De-scription:** Fanciers of the Samoyed breed of dogs. Purposes are to: further the breeding of purebred Samoyeds and to work to bring their natural qualities to perfection; encourage organization of independent local Samoyed clubs in those localities where there are sufficient fanciers of the breed to meet the requirements of the American Kennel Club (see separate entry); urge members and breeders to ac-cept the standard of the breed as approved by the AKC as the only standard of excellence by which Samoyeds shall be judged; protect and advance the interests of the breed and to encourage sportsman-like competition at dog shows and obedience trials; conduct sanctioned matches, and herding and obedi-ence trials under the rules of the AKC. Makes avail-able educational service to the public. Maintains statistics of breed accomplishments. Offers referral service for individuals desiring to own Samoyeds. **Libraries: Type:** not open to the public. **Holdings:** archival material, articles, books. **Subjects:** Samoyeds. **Awards:** Broad Bitch. **Frequency:** an-nual. **Type:** recognition ● Obedience. **Frequency:** annual. **Type:** recognition ● **Frequency:** annual. **Type:** recognition ● Stud Dog. **Frequency:** annual.

Type: recognition ● Top Conformation. **Frequency:** annual. **Type:** recognition. **Publications:** *Illustrated Breed Standard.* Pamphlet. **Price:** $3.50 ● *Member-ship List,* annual. Membership Directory ● *The SCA Bulletin,* quarterly. Newsletter. Contains articles, SCA club news, independent club news and breed adver-tising. **Price:** $35.00 for members; $20.00/issue for nonmembers. **Advertising:** accepted ● *Selecting and Purchasing Your Samoyed and Living With Your Samoyed.* Booklet ● Also publishes bimonthly column in *AKC Gazette.* **Conventions/Meetings:** annual National Specialty - specialty show (exhibits) - usu-ally September or October.

21879 ■ Schipperke Club of America (SCA)
c/o Michelle Lane, Membership Chair
38540 26th St. E
Palmdale, CA 93550
Ph: (661)273-1590
E-mail: klane5862@aol.com
URL: http://www.schipperkeclub-usa.org
Contact: LeeAnn Stusnick, Pres.
Founded: 1929. **Members:** 270. **Membership Dues:** individual, $25 (annual) ● household, $45 (annual) ● junior, $12 (annual). **Regional Groups:** 7. **Descrip-tion:** Persons interested in the Schipperke dog breed. Encourages the propagation of purebred Schip-perkes. Compiles statistics; sponsors competitions and research programs. **Awards: Type:** recognition. **Affiliated With:** American Kennel Club. **Publica-tions:** Bulletin, quarterly. **Price:** $40.00 in U.S. and Canada; $55.00 in Europe; $60.00 in Australia ● Membership Directory, annual. **Conventions/Meet-ings:** annual specialty show ● annual symposium.

21880 ■ Scottish Deerhound Club of America (SDCA)
c/o Mary Varda, Membership Sec.
38 Cambridge Rd.
Madison, WI 53704
E-mail: tannochbrae1@hughes.net
URL: http://www.deerhound.org
Contact: Janet Porter, Pres.
Founded: 1960. **Members:** 364. **Membership Dues:** single, $45 (annual) ● family, $55 (annual). **Regional Groups:** 5. **Description:** Represents Scottish deer-hound owners and breeders. Promotes the quality of the breed and educate members. Compiles statistics. **Awards: Type:** recognition. **Publications:** *The Clay-more,* bimonthly. Newsletter. Includes health informa-tion, listings of new title holders, and announcements of new litters. **Price:** $35.00/year. **Circulation:** 500. **Advertising:** accepted. **Conventions/Meetings:** an-nual specialty show and seminar.

21881 ■ Scottish Terrier Club of America (STCA)
c/o Ms. Connie Smith, Corresponding Sec.
9103 Lanshire Dr.
Dallas, TX 75238
Ph: (214)341-4655
E-mail: lanshire@flash.net
URL: http://clubs.akc.org/stca
Contact: Jim Orsborn, Chm.
Founded: 1900. **Members:** 1,600. **Membership Dues:** family, $70 (annual) ● individual, $60 (annual) ● junior, $45 (annual). **Regional Groups:** 22. **De-scription:** Represents breeders and owners of purebred Scottish Terriers. Conducts specialized education and research programs; compiles statistics; sponsors competitions. **Awards: Type:** recognition. **Computer Services:** database, genetic health ● database, ScottiePhile health articles. **Committees:** Advertising; Agility; Annual Awards; Annual Awards Tally and Title; Computer Technology; Earthdog; Judge Education; Scottish Terrier Information Ex-change. **Affiliated With:** American Kennel Club. **Pub-lications:** *Amplification and Clarification of the Scot-tish Terrier Standard* ● *Bagpiper,* quarterly. **Price:** included in membership dues; $40.00 /year for nonmembers. **Advertising:** accepted. Alternate Formats: online ● *Grooming Manual.* **Price:** $8.00 plus shipping and handling ● Handbook, quinquen-nial. **Price:** $32.50 plus shipping and handling. **Con-ventions/Meetings:** semiannual specialty show.

21882 ■ Senior Conformation Judges Association (SCJA)
c/o Lt. Col. Wallace H. Pede, CEO
7200 Tanager St.
Springfield, VA 22150
Ph: (703)451-5656
Fax: (703)451-5979
E-mail: scja@cox.net
URL: http://www.scja.org
Contact: Lt. Col. Wallace H. Pede, CEO
Founded: 1983. **Members:** 1,200. **Membership Dues:** individual, $30 (annual) ● couple, $40 (an-nual). **Staff:** 3. **Description:** Dog show judges knowledgeable in determining how well an animal conforms to its breed's standards. Emphasizes and assists with the education of judges, prospective judges, and dog breeders. Represents judges' posi-tions and acts on their behalf with all national Kennel Clubs with regard to rules, regulations, and policies. Recognizes and records the contribution of senior dog show judges to the dog fancy. **Awards: Type:** recognition. **Affiliated With:** American Canine Educa-tion Foundation. **Publications:** *SCJA Sound Judg-ment,* quarterly. Newsletter. **Conventions/Meetings:** seminar ● symposium.

21883 ■ Siberian Husky Club of America (SHCA)
c/o Julia Rylander, Corresponding Sec.
PO Box 319
Lake Stevens, WA 98258
E-mail: shcainfo@msn.com
URL: http://www.shca.org
Contact: Gerry Dalakian, Pres.
Founded: 1938. **Members:** 535. **Membership Dues:** individual, $25 (annual) ● couple, $50 (annual). **Re-gional Groups:** 42. **Description:** Exhibitors, owners and breeders of Siberian husky dogs, a medium-sized working dog with body proportions and form reflecting a balance of power, speed, and endurance, with well furred body, ears, and brush tail curved over the back; the breed is probably best known as a sled dog and is often used in competitive racing. Compiles breed records, responsible for writing the breed standard, ethical breeding codes, public information, National Specialty shows. Gives funds to research laboratories. **Awards:** Margaret Grant Service Award. **Frequency:** annual. **Type:** recognition. **Recipient:** for service for the betterment of the Siberian Husky. **Committees:** Area Clubs; Breeder Referral; Constitu-tion; Gazette Columnist; Genetics; Historian; Judges Education; Legislative; Membership; National Special-ties; Obedience; Public Education; Rescue; Specialty Advisory; Ways and Means; Working Sled Dog. **Af-filiated With:** American Kennel Club. **Publications:** *A Partnership for Life - Learning to Understand your Siberian Husky* ● *SCHA Information Booklet* ● *SHCA Newsletter,* 5/year. Magazine ● *SHCA Referral Direc-tory,* annual ● *Your Siberian Husky - It's Hips and Eyes* ● Directory, annual. Includes record champions, pictures, specialty results, and membership list. **Ad-vertising:** accepted. **Conventions/Meetings:** annual National Specialty Dog Show - specialty show and meeting, dog show, obedience trial, agility trial (exhibits).

21884 ■ Silky Terrier Club of America (STCA)
c/o Rita Rich
7730 Hudson Oaks Dr.
Houston, TX 77095
E-mail: silkyrescue@yahoo.com
URL: http://www.silkyterrierclubofamerica.org
Contact: Diane Angeli, Sec.
Founded: 1955. **Members:** 425. **Description:** Own-ers, exhibitors, and breeders of silky terriers, a toy breed originating in Australia; a mature dog weighs eight to ten pounds, is about nine inches high, and has long hair of a bluish tone. Encourages adher-ence to code of ethics and formation of area clubs for the breed; offers promotional materials and presents trophies at specialty shows. Offers children's services. **Committees:** Education; Health. **Affiliated With:** American Kennel Club. **Publications:** *Breeders List,* annual ● Newsletter, monthly ● Yearbook, annual. **Conventions/Meetings:** annual specialty show.

21885 ■ Skye Terrier Club of America (STCA)
c/o Lynne Kuczynski Veazie, Sec.
1215 Pennsylvania Ave.
Emmaus, PA 18049-3515
Ph: (610)965-8619
E-mail: stcasec@hotmail.com
URL: http://clubs.akc.org/skye
Contact: Lynne Kuczynski Veazie, Sec.
Founded: 1938. **Members:** 180. **Regional Groups:** 2. **Description:** Breeders and owners of purebred Skye terriers. Operates speakers' bureau and charitable program. Compiles statistics. **Libraries: Type:** reference. **Holdings:** archival material, business records. **Subjects:** Skye terriers. **Awards: Type:** recognition. **Committees:** Archives; Education; Judge Selection; Show; Standard. **Affiliated With:** American Kennel Club. **Publications:** *The Bulletin*, quarterly. Newsletter. Covers club activities and specialty show results; contains statistics and research reports. **Price:** included in membership dues; $20.00 for nonmembers; $30.00 for nonmembers outside U.S. **Circulation:** 300. **Advertising:** accepted ● *The Skye Terrier Handbook* ● Membership Directory, annual ● Videos. **Conventions/Meetings:** annual seminar and competition - October ● annual specialty show.

21886 ■ Spinone Club of America (SCOA)
PO Box 307
Warsaw, VA 22572
Ph: (804)333-0309
E-mail: spinone@spinone.com
URL: http://www.spinone.com
Contact: James Channon, Pres.
Founded: 1987. **Membership Dues:** single in U.S., $35 (annual) ● single outside U.S., family in U.S., $40 (annual) ● family outside U.S., $45 (annual). **Description:** Promotes the Spinone Italiano dog breed. Provides rescue assistance, litter registry. **Publications:** Newsletter.

21887 ■ Staffordshire Terrier Club of America (STCA)
c/o Lynne Clements, Sec.
PO Box 184
Molalla, OR 97038
Ph: (503)829-4832
E-mail: stcasecretary@amstaff.org
URL: http://www.amstaff.org
Contact: Carla Restivo, Pres.
Founded: 1936. **Members:** 400. **Membership Dues:** single, $35 (annual) ● family, $45 (annual) ● junior, $10 (annual). **Regional Groups:** 7. **Description:** Owners and breeders of purebred American Staffordshire terrier dogs. Conducts specialized education programs; sponsors competitions. **Awards: Type:** recognition. **Committees:** Archives; Awards; Obedience and Working Dogs; Yearbook. **Affiliated With:** American Kennel Club. **Publications:** *Breeders' Directory*, annual ● Magazine, quarterly. Contains news, events, and information about the club. **Price:** included in membership dues; $40.00 for nonmembers, in U.S.; $53.00 for nonmembers, in Canada and Mexico; $61.00 in other countries ● Yearbook. **Conventions/Meetings:** annual specialty show.

21888 ■ Standard Schnauzer Club of America (SSCA)
c/o Judy Houskeeper, Publications Mgr.
7907 S 44th West Ave.
Tulsa, OK 74132-3466
Ph: (918)446-6761
Fax: (918)224-6866
E-mail: vp1@standardschnauzer.org
URL: http://www.standardschnauzer.org
Contact: Judy Houskeeper, Publications Mgr.
Founded: 1925. **Members:** 725. **Membership Dues:** individual/family, $40-$45 (annual). **Regional Groups:** 8. **State Groups:** 8. **Local Groups:** 8. **Multinational. Description:** Represents owners, breeders, and exhibitors of standard schnauzer dogs. Sponsors shows. **Libraries: Type:** not open to the public. **Holdings:** books. **Subjects:** literature on Schnauzers. **Awards: Type:** Agility Dog of the Year. **Frequency:** annual. **Type:** recognition. **Recipient:** to a dog with the highest number of wins ● Best of Op-

posite Obedience. **Frequency:** annual. **Type:** recognition. **Recipient:** to a dog with the highest number of wins ● Brood Bitch of the Year. **Frequency:** annual. **Type:** recognition. **Recipient:** to a dog with the highest number of wins ● Dog of the Year. **Frequency:** annual. **Type:** recognition. **Recipient:** to a dog with the highest number of wins ● Junior Handler of the Year. **Frequency:** annual. **Type:** recognition ● Stud Dog of the Year. **Frequency:** annual. **Type:** recognition. **Recipient:** to a dog with the highest number of wins. **Computer Services:** database ● mailing lists ● online services. **Committees:** Awards; Breed Standard; Education; Health; Judge's Selection; Obedience and Performance; Publications; Specialty. **Affiliated With:** American Kennel Club. **Publications:** *Grooming Guide and Illustrated Standard*. Newsletter. Alternate Formats: CD-ROM ● *Pepper 'n' Salt*, 3/year. Magazine. Accepts advertising from members only. **Advertising:** accepted. Also Cited As: *PNS* ● *The Standard Schnauzer in America*. Book. **Conventions/Meetings:** annual specialty show.

21889 ■ Tibetan Spaniel Club of America (TSCA)
c/o Connie Buckland, Membership Chair
608 N Wintergarden Rd.
Bowling Green, OH 43402
Ph: (419)352-1176
E-mail: info@tsca.ws
URL: http://tsca.ws
Contact: Connie Buckland, Membership Chair
Description: Encourages and promotes the selective breeding of purebred Tibetan Spaniels. Protects and advances the interests of the breed. Encourages sportsman-like competition at dog shows and obedience trials. Promotes the education of the breeders, fanciers and the general public concerning the welfare and preservation of the breed as a means of sustaining the quality of the breed. **Telecommunication Services:** electronic mail, westview@bghost.net. **Committees:** Archives; Health and Education; Judges Education; Rescue; Show Records; Ways and Means. **Publications:** *TSCA Newsletter*, quarterly. **Price:** $35.00 for nonmembers; $45.00 foreign.

21890 ■ Tibetan Terrier Club of America (TTCA)
c/o Robert Kreis, Pres.
PO Box 6243
Denver, CO 80206
E-mail: rescue@ttca-online.org
URL: http://www.ttca-online.org
Contact: Robert Kreis, Pres.
Founded: 1957. **Members:** 350. **Membership Dues:** associate in U.S., regular in U.S., $30 (annual) ● junior in U.S., $20 (annual) ● household in U.S., foreign, $45 (annual). **Description:** Owners and admirers of Tibetan Terrier dogs. **Telecommunication Services:** electronic mail, jackiefaust@comcast.net. **Publications:** Journal, annual ● Newsletter, monthly ● Yearbook, annual. **Conventions/Meetings:** annual meeting ● show.

21891 ■ Treeing Walker Breeders and Fanciers Association (TWBFA)
c/o Larry Hawke, Sec.
520 B County Rd. 2575
Loudonville, OH 44842
Ph: (419)994-4563
URL: http://treeingwalkerbreeders.com
Contact: Larry Hawke, Sec.
Founded: 1964. **Members:** 2,500. **Membership Dues:** regular, $20 (annual). **Staff:** 25. **Budget:** $25,000. **Description:** Night hunters, hobbyists, breeders, dog fanciers, and bench show persons interested in the Treeing Walker coonhound breed. Maintains hall of fame and museum; compiles statistics; conducts charitable programs. **Awards:** Ladies Appreciation Award. **Type:** recognition ● Lavern Miller Memorial Award. **Type:** recognition ● Lifetime Membership Award. **Type:** recognition ● Outstanding Male and Female Member. **Type:** recognition. **Computer Services:** database, point standings ● mailing lists. **Committees:** Bench Show Rules; Ethics; Night Hunt Rules; Treeing Walker Sectional

Events. **Affiliated With:** United Kennel Club. **Publications:** Directory, annual ● Handbook, annual ● Newsletter, annual. **Conventions/Meetings:** annual conference and board meeting (exhibits) ● semiannual show, field trial and night hunt (exhibits) - spring and winter.

21892 ■ United Doberman Club (UDC)
c/o Julianne Ferado, Membership Sec.
PO Box 58455
Renton, WA 98058-1455
Ph: (425)226-4810 (217)424-8984
E-mail: udcdoberman@shaw.ca
URL: http://www.uniteddobermanclub.com
Contact: Anne Rammelsberg, Recording Sec.
Founded: 1990. **Membership Dues:** individual in U.S., Canada and Mexico, $50 (annual) ● family in U.S., Canada and Mexico/individual (international), $65 (annual) ● junior, $30 (annual) ● family (international), $80 (annual). **Multinational. Description:** Preserves and protects the Doberman and its heritage as a Working Dog. Advances the interests of the breed by educating members and the general public about working ability, conformation, temperament, health, breeding, training and maintenance of the total Doberman. Offers activities, programs and educational opportunities to individuals dedicated to preserve and protect the Doberman breed. **Awards:** Versatility Companion Award. **Frequency:** annual. **Type:** recognition. **Recipient:** to recognize the trainability and versatility of the Doberman Pinscher ● Versatility Companion Excellent Award. **Frequency:** annual. **Type:** recognition. **Recipient:** to acknowledge and honor the Doberman who approaches excellence. **Telecommunication Services:** electronic mail, arammelsberg@mail.millikin.edu. **Publications:** *UDC Focus*, quarterly. Magazine. Provides information on the current activities of the association. **Price:** included in membership dues. **Advertising:** accepted. **Conventions/Meetings:** annual specialty show - every spring.

21893 ■ United Kennel Club (UKC)
100 E Kilgore Rd.
Kalamazoo, MI 49002-5584
Ph: (269)343-9020
Fax: (269)343-7037
E-mail: cstickley@ukcdogs.com
URL: http://www.ukcdogs.com
Contact: Wayne R. Cavanaugh, Pres.
Founded: 1898. **Staff:** 48. **Description:** Registry for purebred dogs. Maintains records and pedigrees and establishes rules for events. Promotes improvement of dog breeds; sponsors events to test merit and quality of individual dogs. Awards championships for outstanding dogs. Conducts seminars for show judges, masters of hounds, and for training and handling of dogs. Compiles statistics. Maintains computerized services. **Libraries: Type:** reference. **Holdings:** 4,700. **Committees:** Masters of Hounds for World Championship; Purina Awards; Rules. **Departments:** Champions; Field Operations; Litters; Registration. **Affiliated With:** Hunting Retriever Club; Treeing Walker Breeders and Fanciers Association. **Publications:** *Bloodlines*, monthly. Magazine. Features breed articles, book reviews and profiles of fascinating people in the world of dogs. **Price:** $6.00 for sample issues; $24.00/year. **Circulation:** 5,000. **Advertising:** accepted ● *Coonhound Bloodlines*, monthly. Magazine. Features articles by the nation's top trainers. **Price:** $25.00/year; $4.50 for sample issues. **Circulation:** 18,000. **Advertising:** accepted ● *Hunting Retriever Magazine*, bimonthly. Features articles by respected and well-known writers as well as first hand contributions by U.K.C./HRC members and clubs. **Price:** $25.00 /year for individuals; $30.00/year for family. **Circulation:** 4,000. **Advertising:** accepted.

21894 ■ United Schutzhund Clubs of America (USA)
3810 Paule Ave.
St. Louis, MO 63125-1718
Ph: (314)638-9686
Fax: (314)683-0609

E-mail: usaoffice@germanshepherddog.com
URL: http://www.germanshepherddog.com
Contact: Kelly J. Hope, Office Mgr.
Members: 5,000. **Membership Dues:** single, $60 (annual) ● family (2 persons at the same address), $90 (annual) ● youth (age 21 and under), $12 (annual) ● single (foreign), $75 (annual) ● family (foreign), $112 (annual). **Staff:** 4. **Budget:** $382,600. **Regional Groups:** 11. **Local Groups:** 261. **Description:** Owners, breeders, and handlers of German Shepherd Dogs. Schutzhund means "protection dog", and refers to a sport that develops and evaluates traits, such as tracking and obedience, that make dogs more useful and better companions to their owners. Supports the use of these dogs for search and rescue work, police work, customs and border patrol work, and guide dog work. Promotes breed surveys, maintains a breed registry for German Shepherds, and conducts an annual National Schutzhund III Championship. **Libraries: Type:** lending; not open to the public. **Publications:** *Schutzhund USA*, bimonthly. Magazine. **Price:** included in membership dues. ISSN: 0194-5033. **Circulation:** 5,000. **Advertising:** accepted ● *USA Newsletter*. Contains information on the association. Alternate Formats: online. **Conventions/Meetings:** semiannual congress.

21895 ■ United States Border Collie Club (USBCC)
c/o Laura Carson, Treas.
1712 Hertford St.
Greensboro, NC 27403
E-mail: info@bordercollie.org
URL: http://www.bordercollie.org
Contact: Eileen Stein, Pres.
Founded: 1975. **Members:** 500. **Membership Dues:** in U.S., $15 (annual) ● in Canada, $18 (annual) ● outside U.S. and Canada, $24 (annual) ● life (in U.S.), $120 ● life (in Canada), $180 ● life (outside U.S. and Canada), $240. **Description:** Owners, breeders, exhibitors, and others interested in border collie dogs. Seeks to promote the welfare of the breed and to preserve the border collie as a working stock dog, with emphasis on the dog's natural ability to handle sheep; advocates careful breeding and alerts breeders to possible genetic defects, such as hip dysplasia, progressive retinal atrophy, and collie eye anomaly. Discourages attempts to define border collies by their physical appearance alone. Encourages good sportsmanship; sponsors sheep dog trials. Operates placement service for homeless border collies. Sponsors semiannual training clinic for sheep dog handlers. **Publications:** Newsletter, quarterly. **Advertising:** accepted ● Books. **Advertising:** accepted ● Brochures ● Manuals.

21896 ■ United States Boxer Association
c/o Joyce Mosa, Sec.
RD No. 2, Box 70
Valley Grove, WV 26060
Ph: (989)469-3236
E-mail: timdog@centurytel.net
URL: http://users.adelphia.net/~jon4jan
Contact: Tim Clothier, Treas.
Founded: 1992. **Membership Dues:** single, $29 (annual) ● family, $39 (annual). **Description:** Preserves, protects and promotes the working dog heritage of the Boxer breed in the United States. Promotes and encourages the training and use of the Boxer for work that is consistent with the breed, including tracking, obedience and protection work.

21897 ■ United States Kerry Blue Terrier Club (USKBTC)
c/o Bob Nazak, Membership Chm.
842 Oak Grove Dr.
Mineral, VA 23117
Ph: (540)894-9331
E-mail: bobnazak@aol.com
URL: http://www.uskbtc.org
Contact: Tom Rogers, Pres.
Founded: 1926. **Members:** 385. **Membership Dues:** single (active), $30 (annual) ● single (associate), $35 (annual) ● joint (active), $40 (annual) ● joint (associate), $45 (annual) ● junior, $2 (annual). **Description:**

Breeders and owners dedicated to the well-being, breeding, and exhibiting of purebred Kerry Blue terriers. Conducts specialized education and research programs; maintains placement service; sponsors competitions. Offers breeders list and educational materials. **Libraries: Type:** by appointment only; not open to the public. **Holdings:** articles. **Awards: Type:** recognition. **Affiliated With:** American Kennel Club. **Publications:** *Kerry Blue Terrier Handbook*, every 6-8 years. **Price:** $10.00 plus shipping and handling ● *Kerry Blueprints*, quarterly. Magazine ● Also publishes information pamphlet, ear setting pamphlet, and grooming chart. **Conventions/Meetings:** annual meeting - always in Ambler, PA.

21898 ■ United States Lakeland Terrier Club (USLTC)
c/o Harold Tatro, Treas.
10301 Brangus Dr.
Crowley, TX 76036
Ph: (817)297-2398
E-mail: jmckissick@msn.com
URL: http://www.uslakelandterrier.org
Contact: Pat Rock, Pres.
Founded: 1954. **Members:** 220. **Description:** Owners and breeders of Lakeland terriers. Conducts specialty shows. Maintains placement service; conducts educational programs. **Awards: Type:** recognition. **Affiliated With:** American Kennel Club. **Publications:** *Lakelander*, monthly ● Also publishes brochure. **Conventions/Meetings:** annual dinner.

21899 ■ United States Neapolitan Mastiff Club (USNMC)
1910 Hwy. 293 N
Princeton, KY 42445
Ph: (270)365-2527
Fax: (270)365-2527
E-mail: pegnoca@aol.com
URL: http://www.neapolitan.org
Contact: Peggy Wolfe, Pres.
Founded: 1990. **Membership Dues:** US individual associate, full, subscription, $35 (annual) ● US family, full, subscription, $50 (annual) ● international associate, international subscription, $45 (annual). **Description:** Protects and advances the Neapolitan Mastiff dog breed. Promotes and encourages quality in breeding of Neapolitan Mastiffs. Supports and sponsors shows to provide the opportunity for fans to see the dogs and for Neapolitan Mastiff owners to showcase their own dogs. **Awards:** Breeder Hall of Fame. **Frequency:** periodic. **Type:** recognition. **Recipient:** for member breeder who has bred 15 or more dogs or bitches which have earned their championships under any owners ● Exhibitor Hall of Fame. **Frequency:** periodic. **Type:** recognition. **Recipient:** for member owner who has exhibited and earned championships on 10 or more dogs owned by them when the championship was awarded ● Road Warrier of the Year. **Frequency:** annual. **Type:** recognition. **Recipient:** to the owner of the dog that has logged the most appearances at AKC shows. **Telecommunication Services:** electronic mail, president@neapolitan.org. **Publications:** *Neogram*, quarterly. Magazine.

21900 ■ United States Rottweiler Club (USRC)
c/o Liz Crawley, Membership Off.
6060 Keller Dr.
Sun Prairie, WI 53590
Fax: (608)466-4263
E-mail: president@usrconline.org
URL: http://www.usrconline.org
Contact: Andreas Mueller, Pres.
Membership Dues: single, $55 (annual) ● foreign single, $67 (annual) ● family, $60 (annual) ● foreign family, $72 (annual). **Multinational. Description:** Promotes and protects the Rottweiler breed. Conducts Schutzhund Trials. Offers the Breed Suitability Test (BST) at all Full Member Club Shows. **Awards:** Bronze Merit Award. **Frequency:** periodic. **Type:** recognition. **Recipient:** for member dogs that have been awarded a V rating at a USRC Sanctioned Show ● Gold Merit Award. **Frequency:** periodic. **Type:** recognition. **Recipient:** for member dogs that have obtained a level of excellence in the conforma-

tion ring, on the working field and have met strict breeding requirements ● Silver Merit Award. **Frequency:** periodic. **Type:** recognition. **Recipient:** for member dogs that have been awarded a V rating at a USRC Sanctioned Show and a Schutzhund or IPO title ● Sports Medal. **Frequency:** periodic. **Type:** recognition. **Recipient:** for a member who is in good standing with the organization. **Telecommunication Services:** electronic mail, execbrd@usrconline.org ● electronic mail, inquiry@usrconline.org. **Publications:** *USRC Magazine*. **Price:** $15.00/copy. **Advertising:** accepted.

21901 ■ Vizsla Club of America (VCA)
c/o Barbara Snyder, Pres.
1317 Fourth Ave.
Schenectady, NY 12303-1619
Ph: (518)377-4979
E-mail: bajosvizs@aol.com
URL: http://clubs.akc.org/vizsla
Contact: Barbara Snyder, Pres.
Founded: 1952. **Members:** 850. **Membership Dues:** associate (single), $30 (annual) ● associate (household), $35 (annual) ● junior (10-18 years old), $20 (annual) ● voting (single), $40 (annual) ● voting (household), $45 (annual). **Regional Groups:** 28. **Description:** Owners of Vizsla pointer-retriever dogs, which are native to Hungary. Encourages high standards in breeding for hunting ability and conformation; promotes interest in training the Vizsla for field trials, as gundogs, in obedience, for bench shows, and as companions; supports research and education to reduce or eliminate undesirable or detrimental congenital traits in the breed; sponsors trial and specialty show. Maintains files on the history of the Vizsla breed; maintains hall of fame. **Awards:** VCA Medallion. **Type:** medal ● Versatility Certificate. **Type:** recognition. **Affiliated With:** American Kennel Club. **Publications:** *Is the Vizsla the Right Breed for You?* ● *Presenting the Vizsla*. Brochure ● *Vizsla News*, bimonthly ● Membership Directory, annual. **Conventions/Meetings:** annual show and workshop, includes field trial, specialty & obedience show, and judges workshops (exhibits) - always October/ November.

21902 ■ Weimaraner Club of America (WCA)
c/o Ellen Dodge, Exec. Sec.
PO Box 489
Wakefield, RI 02880-0489
Ph: (401)782-3725
E-mail: wcadodge@netsense.net
URL: http://www.weimclubamerica.org
Contact: Ellen Dodge, Exec. Sec
Founded: 1946. **Members:** 3,000. **Membership Dues:** individual, $35 (annual) ● family, $40 (annual) ● junior, $15 (annual). **Staff:** 3. **Local Groups:** 37. **Description:** Owners, breeders, and exhibitors of purebred Weimaraner dogs. **Awards: Type:** recognition. **Committees:** Agility; Breed Register of Merit; Breeders Education; Field Advisory; Hall of Fame; Health Coordinator; Judges Education; Junior Program; National Show; Obedience; Ratings/Hunting; Standards; Tracking. **Affiliated With:** American Kennel Club. **Publications:** *The Complete W.C.A Handbook*. Alternate Formats: online ● *The Weimaraner Magazine*, monthly. **Price:** included in membership dues; $35.00 /year for nonmembers. ISSN: 0162-315X. **Circulation:** 2,100. **Advertising:** accepted. **Conventions/Meetings:** annual National Championships Field Trial - show (exhibits) - always first week of December, Ardmore, OK ● annual National Specialty and Membership Meeting - specialty show (exhibits).

21903 ■ Welsh Springer Spaniel Club of America (WSSCA)
c/o Carla Vooris, Corresponding Sec.
783 Ellington Farm Rd.
Manson, NC 27553
Ph: (252)456-3645
E-mail: mysticacres783@aol.com
URL: http://www.wssca.com
Contact: Carla Vooris, Corresponding Sec.
Founded: 1961. **Members:** 200. **Membership Dues:** family (plus $10 for each additional family), $40 (an-

nual) ● in U.S. and Canada (single, non-voting), $30 (annual) ● outside U.S. (single, non-voting), $50 (annual). **Description:** Individuals who own or are interested in Welsh Springer Spaniels. Promotes the breed. Maintains breed rescue service and hall of fame. Compiles statistics. **Libraries: Type:** reference. **Holdings:** archival material. **Awards:** Cicero Gus Cup. **Frequency:** annual. **Type:** recognition. **Recipient:** for animal obedience ● Deckard Cup. **Frequency:** annual. **Type:** recognition. **Recipient:** for the top Welsh Springer Spaniel ● Founder's Cup. **Frequency:** annual. **Type:** recognition. **Recipient:** to the Welsh Springer Spaniel that has defeated the most Welsh Springer Spaniels in conformation in a year ● Olympian Cup. **Frequency:** annual. **Type:** recognition. **Recipient:** for the top Welsh Springer Spaniel bitch ● Wildfire Award. **Type:** recognition. **Recipient:** for top owner-handler (amateur). **Publications:** *The Starter Barks*, quarterly. Newsletter. Informational advertising relating to Welsh Springer Spaniels. **Price:** included in membership dues. **Advertising:** accepted. **Conventions/Meetings:** competition ● annual National Specialty - meeting.

21904 ■ West Highland White Terrier Club of America (WHWTCA)

c/o Nancy Staab, Corresponding Sec.
824 Hudson St.
St. Albans, WV 25177
Ph: (304)727-2510
E-mail: correspondingsecretary@westieclubamerica.com
URL: http://www.westieclubamerica.com
Contact: Nancy Staab, Corresponding Sec.

Founded: 1909. **Members:** 825. **Membership Dues:** active, junior, $25 (annual). **Description:** Represents owners, breeders, and exhibitors of purebred West Highland White Terriers. Aims to encourage and promote quality in the breeding of purebred West Highland White Terriers and to do all possible to bring their natural qualities to perfection; to encourage the organization of independent local West Highland White Terrier Specialty Clubs in those localities where there are sufficient fanciers of the breed to meet the requirements of The American Kennel Club; to urge members and breeders to accept the standard of the breed as approved by The American Kennel Club as the only standard of excellence by which West Highland White Terriers shall be judged; to do all in its power to protect and advance the interest of the breed. **Awards:** Registry of Merit (ROM). **Frequency:** annual. **Type:** recognition. **Recipient:** to a member's male Westie who has sired 10 AKC champions of record or female Westie who has produced 5 AKC champions of record. **Affiliated With:** American Kennel Club. **Publications:** *Westie Imprint*, quarterly. Magazine. **Advertising:** accepted. **Conventions/Meetings:** annual meeting.

21905 ■ Westminster Kennel Club (WKC)

149 Madison Ave., Ste.402
New York, NY 10016-6713
Ph: (212)213-3165 (212)213-3212
Fax: (212)213-3270
E-mail: write@wkcpr.org
URL: http://www.westminsterkennelclub.org
Contact: Peter R. Van Brunt, Pres.

Founded: 1877. **Members:** 50. **Staff:** 1. **Description:** Sponsors annual dog show with 141 breeds and varieties. Presents group and best of breed trophies, medals, and prizes. **Awards: Frequency:** annual. **Type:** recognition. **Recipient:** for best dog in show. **Committees:** Dog Show. **Publications:** *Official Guidebook*, annual ● Catalog, annual. Contains names and details of dogs entered in show. **Conventions/Meetings:** annual show - always February, in New York City.

21906 ■ White German Shepherd Dog Club of America (WGSDCA)

c/o Tracie Karsjens, National Show and Trial Coor./Ed./Webmaster
22761 Claire Ct.
Rogers, MN 55374

E-mail: tim@atlaskennels.com
URL: http://www.wgsdca.com
Contact: Timothy Karsjens, Pres.

Founded: 1997. **Membership Dues:** full in U.S., $20 (annual) ● family in U.S., $25 (annual) ● junior in U.S., $5 (annual) ● full in Canada, $29 (annual) ● family in Canada, $34 (annual) ● junior in Canada, $14 (annual). **Multinational. Description:** Protects and advances the white-coated German Shepherd Dog breed. Encourages and educates all members and the general public as to the nature, purpose, care and breeding of quality purebred White German Shepherd dogs. Encourages sportsmanlike competition at dog shows, obedience trials, tracking tests and any other working or service tests. **Telecommunication Services:** electronic mail, webmaster@wgsdca.org. **Publications:** Newsletter. **Price:** included in membership dues.

21907 ■ Working Pit Bull Terrier Club of America (WPBTCA)

c/o Aja Harris, Sec.
2608 Kentucky Ave.
Baltimore, MD 21213
E-mail: president@wpbtca.com
URL: http://www.wpbtca.com
Contact: Ron Marshall, Pres.

Founded: 2003. **Membership Dues:** single in U.S., $30 (annual) ● single outside U.S., $35 (annual) ● family in U.S., $40 (annual) ● family outside U.S., $45 (annual) ● life, $250. **Description:** Preserves, promotes and protects the American Pit Bull Terrier (APBT) as a working dog. Supports other organizations promoting working dogs. Educates the public about the breed's temperament, working ability, health, training, conformation and the need to preserve the breed. Conducts events that promote the American Pit Bull Terrier as a working breed.

21908 ■ Working Riesenschnauzer Federation (WRSF)

c/o Martha Galuszka, Membership Dir.
324 Oakwood Ave.
West Hartford, CT 06110
Ph: (860)233-2286
E-mail: mjgaluszka@aol.com
URL: http://www.workingriesenschnauzer.com
Contact: William Webber, Pres.

Founded: 1991. **Membership Dues:** regular, $30 (annual) ● junior, $10 (annual). **Multinational. Description:** Presents and protects the Giant Schnauzer and its heritage as a working dog. Educates members about the working ability, conformation, temperament, health, breeding, training and maintenance of the Giant Schnauzer. Conducts competitions designed to test the working capacities of the Giant Schnauzer. Seeks to establish a permanent marking system to authenticate the identity, veterinary evaluations and earned titles of individual dogs. **Publications:** *Schnauzer Browser*, quarterly. Newsletter. Alternate Formats: online.

21909 ■ World Bulldog Alliance (WBA)

c/o Ray Giacobbe, Pres.
1700 Ridgewood Ave., Ste.D
Holly Hill, FL 32117
Ph: (386)437-4762
E-mail: wbaregistry@aol.com
URL: http://www.worldbulldoggealliance.com
Contact: Ray Giacobbe, Pres.

Founded: 2000. **Multinational. Description:** Works for the improvement and promotion of the modern day bulldog. Unites the breeders and owners of modern day bulldog. Sets standard and creates a registration database and meeting place for information, education and discussion.

21910 ■ World Wide Kennel Club (WWKC)

PO Box 62
Mount Vernon, NY 10552
Ph: (914)771-5219 (914)654-8574
Fax: (914)654-0364

E-mail: wwkc1com@aol.com
URL: http://www.worldwidekennel.qpg.com
Contact: Roseanne Nuzzolo, Pres.

Founded: 1961. **Members:** 35,000. **Membership Dues:** single dog, $25 ● litter, $40. **Staff:** 22. **Languages:** English, French, German, Italian, Spanish. **Multinational. Description:** People interested in exhibiting, running, registering, purchasing, or selling purebred dogs. Dedicated to the protection and advancement of these dogs. Works to adopt and enforce uniform rules and regulations and encourage breed improvement and adherence to breed standards. Discourages in-breeding. Provides registry service. **Publications:** *Dog Fancy*, monthly. Magazine. **Advertising:** accepted ● *Dog World Magazine*, monthly. **Advertising:** accepted. **Conventions/Meetings:** quarterly Dog Shows - competition, with obedience trials ● quarterly seminar.

21911 ■ WTCARES

c/o Lyn Hollis, Committee Chair
164 N Forrest Ave.
Camden, TN 38320-1217
Ph: (731)584-6530
E-mail: hollishaven@aol.com
URL: http://www.wtcares.org
Contact: Lyn Hollis, Committee Chair

Founded: 1984. **Members:** 300. **Staff:** 22. **Description:** A program of the Welsh Terrier Club of America (see separate entry). Provides assistance to Welsh terriers who are without owners, homes, or kennels. Participates both in the rescue and the placement of Welsh Terriers who need new homes. **Formerly:** (2001) Welsh Terrier Club of America Rescue Service. **Publications:** *WT Cares the Rescue Service of the Welsh Terrier Club of America*. Brochure. Contains information on how to apply to the rescue and placement program. Includes list of members. Mailed on request. **Conventions/Meetings:** annual meeting - always first weekend of October, Horsham, PA.

21912 ■ Yorkshire Terrier Club of America (YTCA)

c/o Shirley Patterson, Sec.
PO Box 265
St. Peters, PA 19470-0265
E-mail: ytca_vp@ytca.org
URL: http://www.ytca.org
Contact: Janet Jackson, Pres.

Founded: 1951. **Members:** 540. **Membership Dues:** general, $20 (annual). **Budget:** $25,000. **Regional Groups:** 17. **Local Groups:** 18. **Description:** Breeders and owners of purebred Yorkshire terriers. Provides referral service. **Awards:** Merit Award for Breeders and Yorkshire Terrier. **Frequency:** annual. **Type:** recognition. **Affiliated With:** American Kennel Club. **Publications:** *Illustrated Standard for Yorkshire Terriers*. Booklet. Describes breed standard. **Price:** $10.00 ● *Yorkie Express*, quarterly ● *Yorkshire Terrier Heritage*. **Conventions/Meetings:** annual meeting, with specialty show for Yorkshire terriers (exhibits).

Dolls

21913 ■ Amy's Doll Lover's Club

399 Winfield Rd.
Rochester, NY 14622
Ph: (585)266-4956
E-mail: amysmail@localnet.com
URL: http://webspawner.com/users/amysdolls/index.html
Contact: Amy Reed, Founder

Founded: 1996. **Members:** 10. **Membership Dues:** ordinary, $25 (annual). **Description:** Collectors of Barbie dolls and accessories. Promotes interest and participation in the collection of Barbie memorabilia; encourages study of the history of the Barbie doll. Facilitates communication and good fellowship among members; participates in charitable and fundraising activities. **Formerly:** (1999) Barbie Lovers Club. **Publications:** Newsletter, monthly. **Conventions/Meetings:** monthly meeting - always second Sunday.

21914 ■ Annalee Club
c/o Annalee Mobilitee Dolls, Inc.
PO Box 708
Meredith, NH 03253
Ph: (603)279-3333
Free: (800)433-6557
Fax: (603)279-6659
E-mail: customerservice@annalee.com
URL: http://www.annalee.com
Membership Dues: regular, $32 (annual). **Description:** Devoted to collecting Annalee Dolls. **Formerly:** (2003) Annalee Doll Society. **Publications:** *The Collector*. Magazine. **Price:** included in membership dues. **Conventions/Meetings:** annual Summer Social - meeting - held in Meredith, New Hampshire.

21915 ■ Chatty Cathy Collectors Club (CCCC)
PO Box 4426
Seminole, FL 33775
E-mail: chattynme@aol.com
URL: http://www.ttinet.com/chattycathy
Contact: Melissa Gilkey Mince, Ed.
Founded: 1989. **Members:** 250. **Membership Dues:** regular in U.S., $32 (annual) ● regular in Canada, $35 (annual) ● regular outside North America, $38 (annual). **Staff:** 1. **Description:** Collectors of Chatty Cathy dolls and memorabilia. Promotes collection and preservation of Chatty Cathy dolls and accessories. Facilitates communication and trading among members; serves as a clearinghouse on Chatty Cathy dolls and associated memorabilia. **Computer Services:** Online services. **Publications:** *Chatty News*, quarterly. Newsletter. **Price:** included in membership dues. **Conventions/Meetings:** annual luncheon.

21916 ■ Doll Artisan Guild (DAG)
118 Commerce Rd.
PO Box 1113
Oneonta, NY 13820-5113
Ph: (607)432-4977
Fax: (607)432-2042
E-mail: info@dollartisanguild.org
URL: http://dollartisanguild.org
Contact: Karin Goulian, Exec. Dir.
Founded: 1977. **Members:** 12,000. **Membership Dues:** individual in U.S., $39 (annual) ● individual outside U.S., $54 (annual). **Staff:** 1. **Multinational.** **Description:** Serves individuals interested in authentic reproductions of antique porcelain dolls, modern dolls, and creation of original porcelain dolls. Educates members about the art of dollmaking; conducts seminars on the reproduction of dolls. Offers manufacturers' discounts on supplies. Gives advice to members through The Doll Center in Oneonta, NY. Holds lectures, seminars, workshops, events, competitions, conventions, and festivals worldwide. **Awards:** Aurora. **Frequency:** periodic. **Type:** recognition. **Recipient:** for individuals who display fine examples of dollmaking ● Eva's Choice. **Frequency:** periodic. **Type:** recognition. **Recipient:** for individuals who display fine examples of dollmaking ● Magge. **Frequency:** periodic. **Type:** recognition. **Recipient:** for individuals who display fine examples of dollmaking ● Millie. **Frequency:** periodic. **Type:** recognition. **Recipient:** for individuals who display fine examples of dollmaking ● Rolf Ericson's Award for Outstanding Doll Sculpture. **Frequency:** periodic. **Type:** recognition. **Recipient:** for individuals who display fine examples of dollmaking. **Computer Services:** Mailing lists, 8000 U.S. names. **Publications:** *DOLLS Beautiful*, quarterly. Magazine. Provides news for porcelain dollmakers. **Price:** included in membership dues. **Advertising:** accepted. **Conventions/Meetings:** annual convention, with workshops, salesroom, banquet, award and graduation ceremonies (exhibits) ● biennial International Convention - meeting, with an exhibit of competition dolls (exhibits).

21917 ■ Ginny Doll Club
PO Box 338
Oakdale, CA 95361
Ph: (209)848-0300
Free: (877)848-0300
Fax: (209)848-4423

E-mail: info@voguedolls.com
URL: http://www.voguedolls.com
Description: Dedicated to collecting Ginny Dolls. **Telecommunication Services:** electronic mail, sales@voguedolls.com ● electronic mail, service@voguedolls.com. **Publications:** *The Ginny Journal*, quarterly.

21918 ■ International Doll Makers Association (IDMA)
c/o Judy Kroeger, Pres.
1110 Jungle Dr.
Duncanville, TX 75116
Ph: (972)298-5662 (972)345-0805
E-mail: srlovell@swbell.net
URL: http://www.idmadolls.com
Contact: Judy Kroeger, Pres.
Founded: 1972. **Members:** 350. **Membership Dues:** individual in U.S. and Canada, $30 (monthly) ● individual outside U.S. and Canada, $40 (annual). **Staff:** 10. **Budget:** $50,000. **Regional Groups:** 20. **Description:** Dollmakers. Works as an educational organization in the area of dollmaking. Encourages members to display their artwork. Conducts programs on sculpting, china painting, costuming, and other media. Conducts charitable programs. **Awards:** Doll Competition. **Frequency:** annual. **Type:** recognition. **Formerly:** (1976) International Doll Makers Association; (1985) International Doll Makers Association - Internationals. **Publications:** *Broadcaster*, quarterly. Magazine. Provides association news. **Price:** available to members only. **Circulation:** 400. **Advertising:** accepted. Alternate Formats: online. **Conventions/Meetings:** annual Carousel of Dolls - competition and workshop, with salesroom ● annual meeting (exhibits) - always June/July ● seminar, with lectures ● workshop.

21919 ■ International Foundation of Doll Makers (IFDM)
PO Box 120187
Clermont, FL 34712
Ph: (352)394-1404
Free: (866)370-8017
Fax: (352)394-1270
E-mail: info@ifdm.org
Founded: 1986. **Members:** 4,000. **Staff:** 4. **Multinational.** **Description:** Professional and nonprofessional doll makers; sculptors, dressmakers, and wig makers; doll collectors and enthusiasts. Objective is to advance doll making through sharing of techniques. Sponsors competition; bestows Golden Bell Award. Holds workshops. **Publications:** *Doll Makers Workshop*, bimonthly. Magazine. **Conventions/Meetings:** annual meeting.

21920 ■ International Rose O'Neill Club Foundation (IROCF)
PO Box 668
Branson, MO 65616
E-mail: wisteriahs@excite.com
URL: http://www.irocf.org
Contact: Ed Clark, Pres.
Founded: 1967. **Members:** 1,000. **Membership Dues:** individual $20 (annual) ● family, $25 (annual). **Multinational.** **Description:** Individuals interested in preserving the works and memory of Rose O'Neill, and in furthering the cultural arts. Rose O'Neill was an artist, writer, and illustrator who created the Kewpie doll in 1909. (Kewpie dolls are plump, cupid-like baby dolls that were first popular prior to World War I.) Maintains speakers' bureau; conducts research on Rose O'Neill and her work; compiles statistics. Sponsors internal contests. **Awards:** **Frequency:** annual. **Type:** scholarship. **Recipient:** for students planning to major in an area of arts (ex. graphic art, fine art and performing art, art education). **Formerly:** (1975) National Rose O'Neill Club; (2006) International Rose O'Neill Club. **Publications:** *Kewpiesta Kourier*, quarterly. Newsletter. **Conventions/Meetings:** annual Kewpiesta - conference (exhibits) - always April, Branson, MO.

21921 ■ Lawton Collector's Guild
c/o The Lawton Doll Co.
548 N 1st St.
Turlock, CA 95380
Ph: (209)632-3655
Fax: (209)632-6788
E-mail: customerservice@lawtondolls.com
URL: http://www.lawtondolls.com/html/guilddolls.html
Founded: 1989. **Membership Dues:** individual, $50 (annual). **Description:** Provides Lawton doll enthusiasts information about the dolls, the artist and the company. **Publications:** *The Lawton Collectors Guild Quarterly*. Bulletin. **Price:** included in membership dues.

21922 ■ Lizzie High Society
220 N Main St.
Sellersville, PA 18960
Ph: (215)453-8200
Free: (800)763-6557
E-mail: lizzie1@bellatlantic.net
URL: http://www.lizziehigh.com
Membership Dues: new (comes with binder), $30 ● individual, $22 (annual). **Description:** Devoted to collecting Lizzie High wooden dolls. **Publications:** Newsletter.

21923 ■ National Antique Doll Dealers Association (NADDA)
PO Box 462
Natick, MA 01760-0005
Ph: (508)545-1424
E-mail: nasdoll@comcast.net
URL: http://www.nadda.org
Contact: Constance Blain, Pres.
Founded: 1986. **Multinational.** **Description:** Promotes integrity and honesty in the doll collecting world. Advances the study of the historical significance, maintenance, restoration and classification of antique dolls. **Computer Services:** database, member directory ● mailing lists. **Publications:** Newsletter.

21924 ■ National Institute of American Doll Artists (NIADA)
c/o Diana Rew, Treas.
8320 Maplewood St.
Lenexa, KS 66215
Ph: (913)894-2382
Fax: (913)888-5167
E-mail: rewbird@aol.com
URL: http://www.niada.org
Contact: Antonette Cely, Pres.
Founded: 1963. **Members:** 153. **Membership Dues:** artist, $100 (annual) ● patron, $50 (annual) ● individual, $25 (annual). **Description:** Represents professional doll artists and patrons interested in the recognition of original dolls. Encourages national recognition of fine, creative, original dolls. Members' dolls are individually made and recognized as fine art; they are exhibited in many museums and galleries and are included in museum collections. Artists produce limited edition, one-of-a-kind, and commercial designs. **Libraries:** Type: reference. **Holdings:** archival material. **Committees:** Standards. **Publications:** *The Art of the Doll*. Book. Contains colored photographs. **Price:** $15.00 ● *Artists Directory*, biennial ● Newsletter, quarterly. **Conventions/Meetings:** annual conference (exhibits) - each summer.

21925 ■ Original Doll Artists Council of America (ODACA)
c/o Myra Sherrod, 2nd VP
1251 Garden Circle Dr., 2C-C
St. Louis, MO 63125
Ph: (314)894-1489
E-mail: robin@odaca.org
URL: http://www.odaca.org
Contact: Robin Foley, Pres.
Founded: 1976. **Members:** 80. **Membership Dues:** artist, $35 (annual) ● auxiliary, $15 (annual). **Description:** Artists who create original dolls. Promotes original doll artists and their work; educates collectors about the art of dollmaking. Seeks to achieve and maintain a high quality of dollmaking. Sponsors

Aux-ODACA, a nonartist support group for member artists. **Awards:** Joan Ross Sweetheart Award. **Frequency:** annual. **Type:** recognition. **Recipient:** to a member (artist or aux) for their outstanding effort in support and service. **Publications:** *Expressions*, quarterly. Newsletter. Contains information on the association and its members. **Price:** included in membership dues ● Membership Directory, annual. **Conventions/Meetings:** annual luncheon, doll sale of artist member work only (exhibits).

21926 ■ Original Paper Doll Artists Guild (OPDAG)
PO Box 14
Kingfield, ME 04947
Ph: (207)265-2500
Fax: (207)265-2500
E-mail: info@opdag.com
URL: http://www.opdag.com
Contact: Jenny Taliadoros, Publisher
Founded: 1984. **Members:** 350. **Membership Dues:** regular, in U.S., $27 (annual) ● regular, in Canada and Mexico, $33 (annual) ● overseas, $40 (annual). **Staff:** 5. **Description:** For paper doll artists and enthusiasts. Promotes the art and hobby of creating and collecting paper dolls. **Convention/Meeting:** none. **Libraries:** Type: reference. **Holdings:** audio recordings, books, video recordings. **Subjects:** paper dolls, art instruction, business and marketing. **Awards:** Lifetime Achievement Award in Paper Doll Art. **Frequency:** periodic. **Type:** recognition. **Recipient:** for an individual in industry for 20 years who promotes, teaches, and produces paper doll art. **Publications:** *Paper Doll Studio*, quarterly. Magazine. Showcases paper doll art, featured artists, networking, convention reports, drawing tips and how-to's. **Price:** included in membership dues. **Circulation:** 400.

21927 ■ Strawberry Shortcake Chat Group
c/o Jennifer Bowles, Ed.
138 E Main Cross
Greenville, KY 42345
Ph: (270)338-4318
Fax: (270)338-6856
E-mail: jenniferbowles@bellsouth.net
URL: http://www.strawberrybonkers.com
Contact: Jennifer Bowles, Ed.
Founded: 1996. **Members:** 30. **Staff:** 1. **Description:** Owners and admirers of Strawberry Shortcake dolls. Promotes collection and preservation of Strawberry Shortcake dolls. Facilitates communication among members; serves as a clearinghouse on Strawberry Shortcake dolls. **Formerly:** (2006) Strawberry Shortcake Doll Club.

21928 ■ United Federation of Doll Clubs (UFDC)
10900 N Pomona Ave.
Kansas City, MO 64153
Ph: (816)891-7040
Fax: (816)891-8360
E-mail: info@ufdc.org
URL: http://www.ufdc.org
Contact: Ms. Teresa Faller, Admin.
Founded: 1949. **Members:** 16,000. **Membership Dues:** individual, $32 (annual). **Staff:** 3. **Budget:** $1,500,000. **Regional Groups:** 17. **Local Groups:** 825. **Description:** Represents doll collectors, museums, and libraries. Promotes educational and charitable work. **Libraries:** Type: reference; open to the public. **Awards:** Awards of Excellence. **Frequency:** annual. **Type:** recognition. **Recipient:** for meritorious service ● Ralph W. Griffith Award. **Frequency:** annual. **Type:** recognition. **Recipient:** for outstanding dealer-member. **Computer Services:** database. **Formerly:** National Doll and Toy Collectors. **Publications:** *Doll News*, quarterly. Magazine. **Price:** $14.00/year. ISSN: 0191-460X. **Circulation:** 16,000. **Advertising:** accepted. **Conventions/Meetings:** annual convention (exhibits).

Electricity

21929 ■ National Insulator Association (NIA)
c/o Donald Briel, Membership Dir.
PO Box 188
Providence, UT 84332
E-mail: don.briel@comcast.net
URL: http://www.nia.org
Contact: Donald Briel, Membership Dir.
Founded: 1973. **Members:** 1,000. **Membership Dues:** regular, family, club, $12 (annual) ● junior, $5 (annual). **Description:** Members include collectors or any person interested in communication and electrical insulators, as well as other artifacts connected with insulators, such as telephone, telegraph, power transmission, railroads, and lightning protection devices. **Publications:** *Crown Jewels of the Wire*, annual. Directory ● *Drip Points*, quarterly. Newsletter. **Conventions/Meetings:** annual meeting and convention, with show.

Engines

21930 ■ Early Day Gas Engine and Tractor Association (EDGE&TA)
c/o Larry Voris, Pres./Dir.
2340 S Luster Ave.
Springfield, MO 65804
Ph: (417)882-7195
Fax: (417)882-7195
E-mail: lgvoris@sbcglobal.net
URL: http://www.edgeta.org
Contact: Larry Voris, Pres./Dir.
Founded: 1957. **Members:** 8,000. **Membership Dues:** regular, $4 (annual). **Regional Groups:** 110. **Description:** Promotes interest in collecting, restoring, preserving, exhibiting gasoline and oil engines, gas/diesel and steam tractors, power driven farm machinery, and other equipment of historical value. **Committees:** Hall of Fame; Magazine Articles; National/Regional Show; Safety; Steam. **Publications:** Newsletter. Alternate Formats: online.

Ephemera

21931 ■ Ephemera Society of America (EPHSOC)
PO Box 95
Cazenovia, NY 13035-0095
Ph: (315)655-9139
Fax: (315)655-9139
E-mail: info@ephemerasociety.org
URL: http://ephemerasociety.org
Contact: Susanne Johnson, Admin. Dir.
Founded: 1980. **Members:** 1,000. **Membership Dues:** regular, in U.S., $40 (annual) ● regular, in Canada, $45 (annual) ● international, $55 (annual). **Staff:** 1. **Multinational. Description:** Institutions, museums, libraries, schools and individuals interested in, or concerned with, the collection, preservation, study, and educational use of printed and handwritten ephemera. Defines ephemera as the minor transient documents of everyday life; collections include such items as tickets, letterheads, labels, timetables, trade cards, bills of lading, magazines, newspapers, greeting cards, catalogs, and menus. Promotes communication among members; makes available sources of information on the collection and conservation of ephemera. Sponsors sales and exchange sessions, and ephemera fairs. **Awards:** Maurice Rickards Award. **Type:** recognition. **Publications:** *Ephemera Journal*, every 2-3 years. **Price:** included in membership dues ● *Ephemera News*, quarterly. Magazine. **Price:** included in membership dues. ISSN: 0734-3337. **Advertising:** accepted ● Membership Directory, annual. **Advertising:** accepted ● Monographs. **Price:** $15.00. **Conventions/Meetings:** annual Ephemera Fair/Conference, with paper show and members' forums (exhibits) - always in March ● meeting (exhibits).

21932 ■ National Association of Paper and Advertising Collectors (NAPAC)
1425 W Main St.
PO Box 500
Mount Joy, PA 17552
Ph: (717)653-1833
Free: (800)800-1833
Fax: (717)653-6165
E-mail: dmsater@engleonline.com
Contact: Denise M. Sater, Ed.
Founded: 1979. **Members:** 3,000. **Membership Dues:** 3rd class, $15 (monthly) ● 1st class, $30 (monthly) ● air mail Canada, $35 (monthly) ● air mail outside North America, $40 (monthly). **For-Profit. Description:** Publishing company. **Libraries:** Type: reference. **Holdings:** 2,000. **Publications:** *Paper & Advertising Collector*. Papers. **Circulation:** 5,000. **Advertising:** accepted.

Fan Clubs

21933 ■ Little Mouse Club (LMC)
c/o David Jordan
603 Brandt Ave.
New Cumberland, PA 17070
Ph: (717)774-1778
E-mail: littlemouseclub@yahoo.com
URL: http://www.geocities.com/Heartland/Ranch/3220/main.html
Contact: David Jordan, Contact
Founded: 1999. **Members:** 100. **Membership Dues:** family, individual, $25 (annual). **Staff:** 2. **Budget:** $3,000. **Multinational. Description:** Individuals interested in mice as pets or show animals. Promotes the enjoyment of mice. Conducts educational programs and holds shows. Promotes breeding of fancy show mice. **Libraries:** Type: not open to the public. **Holdings:** 50; books, periodicals. **Subjects:** mice. **Awards:** Best In Show, Best American Mouse, Best English Mouse, Best Pet Mouse. **Frequency:** semiannual. **Type:** recognition. **Recipient:** based on published internationally recognized standards ● Most Valuable Member. **Frequency:** annual. **Type:** recognition. **Computer Services:** Electronic publishing, "The Loop" electronic newsletter, consulting service for breeders, members may email with problems. **Additional Websites:** http://www.arborwin.com/lmc. **Committees:** Website. **Affiliated With:** American Fancy Rat and Mouse Association. **Publications:** *How to Care for 40 Cages in 15 Minutes a Day*, Ethics. Pamphlets. **Price:** included in membership dues. Alternate Formats: online ● *LMC Packet*, bimonthly. Pamphlets. Contains various information on mouse care and breeding. **Price:** $25.00/year. **Circulation:** 103 ● *LMC Packet*, bimonthly. Papers. Includes calendar of events, technical articles, show reports, and animal care and management articles; medicine droppers, other small items and toys. **Price:** included in membership dues. **Circulation:** 100. Alternate Formats: online ● *LMC Standards Book*. **Price:** included in membership dues ● *Mouse Genetics*. Handbook. **Price:** $5.00 ● *Poster*. Features 42 different Fancy Breeds of Mice and genetics information. **Price:** $10.00. **Conventions/Meetings:** periodic Mouse Swap and Ice Cream Social - conference, with rare mice, equipment, and cages (exhibits) ● periodic Standards Show (exhibits) - always May (Memorial Day Sunday) & October (Columbus Day Sunday), Harrisburg, PA.

Fencing

21934 ■ U.S. Academy of European Fencing
350 Fifth Ave., Ste.3304
New York, NY 10118
Ph: (212)971-1331
Contact: Robert Grieser, Exec.Dir.
Founded: 1993. **Members:** 55. **Staff:** 12. **Budget:** $75,000. **Languages:** English, French, Hungarian, Italian. **Description:** Dedicated to advancing the study of the fencing arts. Camps, clinics, classroom study and special programs geared toward children and teens. Engaged in foreign exchange programs. Conducts research in areas of the fencing arts including those related to theater and film.

Ferret

21935 ■ American Ferret Association (AFA)
PMB 255
626-C Admiral Dr.
Annapolis, MD 21401
Free: (888)FERRET-1

Fax: (801)927-9818
E-mail: afa@ferret.org
URL: http://www.ferret.org
Contact: Penny Hendrix, Pres.

Founded: 1991. **Members:** 2,000. **Membership Dues:** individual, $30 (annual) ● veterinarian, $50 (annual) ● corporation, $100 (annual) ● foreign, $40 (annual). **Budget:** $50,000. **Description:** Promotes the domestic ferret as a companion animal. Works with legislators and associations to increase public awareness of the ferret. Participates in pet fairs and conferences. **Libraries:** Type: reference. **Holdings:** articles. **Subjects:** ferrets, related medical. **Publications:** *AFA Ferret Shelter Guidelines.* **Price:** $7.00 plus shipping and handling ● *American Ferret Report,* quarterly. Newsletter. **Price:** included in membership dues. **Circulation:** 800. **Advertising:** accepted ● *Exhibitor Handbook* ● *Ferrets 101.* Brochure. Contains general ferret care and information. ● *What is a Ferret?.* Brochure. **Conventions/Meetings:** biennial show and competition (exhibits) ● annual Small Mammal Veterinary Conference - meeting (exhibits) ● Veterinary Symposium.

21936 ■ Ferret Fanciers Club (FFC)

Address Unknown since 2007

Founded: 1983. **Members:** 3,000. **Membership Dues:** individual, $20 (annual) ● outside U.S., $30 (annual). **Staff:** 2. **Budget:** $100,000. **Description:** Veterinarians and ferret owners. (Ferrets are domesticated European polecats that are used in hunting rodents.) Seeks to promote the health and preservation of ferrets. Fosters information exchange among ferret owners, breeders, and fanciers. Works to promote state legalization of ferrets as household pets. Encourages high standards in breeding practices. Promotes the registration of ferrets and ferret shows. Disseminates medical information on ferrets to healthcare professionals, teaching and research institutions, and animal centers. Makes available to the public information on ferret care, nutrition, breeding, and medical requirements. Conducts competitions and develops judging standards. Sponsors Ferret Blood Donor Program, a national program to provide ferret blood donors in medical emergencies. Sponsors market research; operates speakers' bureau and charitable program. **Libraries:** Type: not open to the public. **Holdings:** 5; books. **Subjects:** Ferrets. **Awards:** Type: recognition. **Computer Services:** Mailing lists. **Telecommunication Services:** phone referral service, 24-hour hotline to assist owners with medical emergencies and in locating lost ferrets. **Committees:** Black-Footed Ferret Preservation; Health; Judging Standards; Legalization. **Publications:** *Ferret Medical Directory.* **Advertising:** accepted ● *Ferret Owners Manual* ● *Ferret Yearbook* ● *Hotels Motels and Campgrounds Accepting Small Pets.* Directory. Lists motels, hotels, and campgrounds that accept small pets. ● *International Ferret Review,* quarterly. **Price:** $20.00 in U.S.; $30.00 outside U.S. **Advertising:** accepted ● *Step-By-Step Book About Ferrets* ● *Veterinary Directory,* periodic. **Conventions/Meetings:** annual conference and workshop (exhibits); **Avg. Attendance:** 300.

Film

21937 ■ Golden Raspberry Award Foundation (GRAF)

PO Box 835
Artesia, CA 90702-0835
E-mail: headberry@razzies.com
URL: http://www.razzies.com
Contact: John Wilson, Hd.

Founded: 1980. **Members:** 655. **Membership Dues:** individual in California, $25 (annual) ● individual outside California, $25 (annual) ● friend of the GRAF, $50 (annual) ● RAZZberry Inner Sanctum, $75 (annual) ● Berry important, $100 (annual) ● supporting patron, $250 (annual) ● life, $500 ● basic renewal, $20 (annual). **Description:** Individuals with an interest in film and the Academy Awards. Promotes appreciation of the worst in world cinema. Selects films and actors for awards recognizing what the group

feels are the "worst cinematic performances" each year. Facilitates communication and good fellowship among members. **Libraries:** Type: not open to the public. **Holdings:** 400; books, clippings, video recordings. **Subjects:** film. **Awards:** Worst Actor. **Frequency:** annual. **Type:** recognition ● Worst Actress. **Frequency:** annual. **Type:** recognition ● Worst Picture. **Frequency:** annual. **Type:** recognition. **Also Known As:** Razzie Awards. **Publications:** *Razzie Reporter,* 3/year. Newsletter. **Price:** included in membership dues. **Circulation:** 475. Alternate Formats: online. **Conventions/Meetings:** annual RAZZIE Awards Show - always in conjunction with the Oscar Awards show.

Fire Fighting

21938 ■ Fire Mark Circle of the Americas (FMCA)

c/o Dave Oldham, Sec.
1113 Grant Ct.
Taylorville, IL 62568-9351
Ph: (217)824-5308
Fax: (217)824-5727
E-mail: information@firemarkcircle.org
URL: http://www.firemarkcircle.org
Contact: Dave Oldham, Sec.

Founded: 1972. **Members:** 300. **Membership Dues:** individual, $30 (annual). **Description:** Persons in the insurance industry, fire fighters, museum directors, and others. Aims to bring together persons interested in the origin and history of fire insurance companies, their fire marks, fire brigades and fire fighting equipment, firemen's badges, medals and tokens, old insurance company signs, and all that pertains to the history of fire insurance. Exchanges and records information and preserves the relics of the early days of fire insurance. Compiles statistics; holds auctions. **Libraries:** Type: reference. **Holdings:** biographical archives. **Awards:** Max Klein Award. **Frequency:** annual. **Type:** recognition. **Recipient:** to individual signing most new members ● Morton Werner Award. **Type:** recognition. **Recipient:** for outstanding contributions and support to FMCA. **Committees:** Archives; Auction; Convention; Counterfeit; Future Convention Sites; Market Value; Membership; Nominating; Old Signs; Publication; Publicity. **Publications:** *Fire Mark Circle of the Americas—Journal,* annual. Contains articles on the history of fire fighting equipment and fire insurance items. **Price:** included in membership dues ● *Fire Mark Circle of the Americas—Membership Directory and By-Laws,* annual. Lists members and their collecting interests; arranged alphabetically and geographically. **Price:** included in membership dues. **Circulation:** 500 ● *Footprints of Assurance* ● *Insurance Auto Tags* ● *The Signevierist,* quarterly. Newsletter. Offers member collectors' information. **Price:** included in membership dues. Alternate Formats: online ● *Signs of Insurance.* Book. Contains illustrated history of insurance company signs and their origins. **Conventions/Meetings:** annual convention - usually third weekend of September.

21939 ■ International Fire Buff Associates (IFBA)

c/o Mr. William M. Mokros, Exec. VP
11017 N Redwood Tree Ct.
Mequon, WI 53092
Fax: (262)236-0095
E-mail: executiveoffice@ifba.org
URL: http://www.ifba.org
Contact: Mr. William M. Mokros, Exec. VP

Founded: 1953. **Members:** 5,000. **Regional Groups:** 11. **Description:** Persons interested in the fire service, fire fighters and allied emergency services, for the purpose of promoting the welfare of fire fighters and allied emergency service workers and their departments. Acts as a citizens' public relations group for fire departments and other related agencies. Local groups aid fire fighters at the scene of emergencies and other events by providing support services. Establishes and operates museums of interest to the fire service, historical compilations for

local departments, fire activity communications and charitable activities to support local and national fire service endeavors. **Awards:** Fire Buff of the Year. **Frequency:** annual. **Type:** recognition. **Computer Services:** Electronic publishing. **Publications:** *Code for Fire Buffing* ● *Turn Out,* semiannual. Magazine. Contains compilation of activities in news article or story formats. **Conventions/Meetings:** annual convention.

21940 ■ National Historical Fire Foundation (NHFF)

c/o Hall of Flame Museum
6101 E Van Buren St.
Phoenix, AZ 85008
Ph: (602)275-3473
Fax: (602)275-0896
E-mail: webmaster@hallofflame.org
URL: http://www.hallofflame.org
Contact: Dr. Peter M. Molloy, Exec. Dir.

Founded: 1961. **Description:** Operates Hall of Flame Museum of antique fire fighting vehicles, equipment, documents, and publications. Maintains 8000 item library of books, newspaper clippings, manuscripts, and statistics on fire fighting. Sponsors research and services for children. **Libraries:** Type: not open to the public. **Holdings:** 8,000. **Subjects:** history on fire fighting in U.S.

21941 ■ Society for the Preservation and Appreciation of Antique Motor Fire Apparatus in America (SPAAMFAA)

PO Box 2005
Syracuse, NY 13220-2005
Ph: (734)632-0350
Fax: (734)632-0967
E-mail: corsec@spaamfaa.org
URL: http://www.spaamfaa.org
Contact: Mr. George A. Valrance, Corresponding Sec.

Founded: 1958. **Members:** 3,600. **Membership Dues:** individual, $25 (annual) ● organization, family, $30 (annual). **Regional Groups:** 56. **Description:** Individuals interested in old fire fighting methods and apparatus, or who own or wish to own antique (defined as at least 25 years old) fire fighting apparatus. Chartered by the New York State Education Department as a nonprofit, educational, and historical society dedicated to fire service history and to preserving, restoring, and operating antique fire service apparatus. Conducts research; provides maintenance information and historical data. Sponsors Antique Apparatus Shows and Musters (competitive exhibitions). Participates in local Fire Prevention Week activities and cooperates in public relations efforts of units of the fire service. **Libraries:** Type: reference. **Holdings:** archival material, audiovisuals, books, clippings, periodicals. **Publications:** *Enjine! Enjine!,* quarterly. Magazine. **Price:** included in membership dues. **Circulation:** 3,000. **Advertising:** accepted ● *The Silver Trumpet,* quarterly. Newsletter ● *SPAAMFAA Roster of Members and Apparatus Owned,* annual. Membership Directory. **Conventions/Meetings:** annual meeting.

Firearms

21942 ■ Antique Reloading Tool Collector's Association (ARTCA)

c/o Tom Quigley
PO Box 1567
Castle Rock, WA 98611
E-mail: merwinhulbertco@aol.com
URL: http://www.antiquereloadingtools.org
Contact: Tom Quigley, Contact

Membership Dues: general, $35 (annual). **Description:** Works to preserve and study antique reloading tools. Provides a forum for individuals interested in collecting and trading old loading/reloading tools. **Libraries:** Type: reference. **Holdings:** archival material. **Computer Services:** Online services, message board.

21943 ■ Association of Ohio Longrifle Collectors (AOLRC)

c/o Dan Smith, Sec.
23003 State Rte. 339
Beverly, OH 45715
Ph: (740)984-4896
E-mail: jclip2@yahoo.com
URL: http://www.aolrc.org
Contact: Dan Smith, Sec.
Founded: 1975. **Members:** 280. **Membership Dues:** individual, $15 (annual). **Staff:** 10. **State Groups:** 1. **Description:** Gun collectors interested in the Ohio-made muzzle-loading longrifle. Promotes the study and preservation of muzzle-loading rifles. Sponsors exhibit. Conducts educational programs. **Libraries: Type:** reference. **Holdings:** 5; biographical archives. **Subjects:** early Ohio gunsmiths. **Computer Services:** Mailing lists, of members. **Affiliated With:** National Muzzle Loading Rifle Association; National Rifle Association of America. **Publications:** *AOLRC Newsletter*, semiannual. Includes biographical sketches of the makers of Ohio rifles. **Price:** included in membership dues. **Circulation:** 285. **Conventions/Meetings:** annual convention and workshop, longrifles and feature gunsmith (exhibits) - usually 1st weekend of April in Marietta, OH.

21944 ■ Browning Collectors Association (BCA)

711 Scott St.
Covington, KY 41011
E-mail: cw@browningcollectors.com
URL: http://www.browningcollectors.com
Contact: Charles P. Wagner, Sec.
Founded: 1979. **Members:** 850. **Membership Dues:** regular, in U.S., $30 (annual) ● regular, outside U.S., $35 (annual) ● life, $400. **Multinational. Description:** Collectors, dealers, and other individuals interested in Browning firearms. Promotes interest in the historical background of Browning arms. Provides a forum for exchange of information on collectible arms. Conducts research on the history of individual Browning arms. **Publications:** Newsletter, bimonthly. Features question and answer section and classified section for Browning items. **Advertising:** accepted. **Conventions/Meetings:** annual meeting, includes Browning display - usually in Tulsa, OK.

21945 ■ Glock Collectors Association (GCA)

PO Box 1063
Maryland Heights, MO 63043
Ph: (314)878-2061
Fax: (314)878-2061
E-mail: casteck@prodigy.net
URL: http://www.glockcollectors.com
Founded: 1995. **Membership Dues:** general, $25 (annual) ● life, $250 ● general, $100 (quinquennial). **Description:** Promotes the collection, research and preservation of Glock firearms, products and related collectibles for posterity. **Computer Services:** Mailing lists, of members ● online services, bulletin board. **Affiliated With:** National Rifle Association of America. **Publications:** Newsletter.

21946 ■ High Standard Collectors' Association (HSCA)

PO Box 1578
Decatur, IL 62525
E-mail: wsbagpb@charter.net
URL: http://www.highstandard.org
Contact: William Bryant, Pres.
Founded: 1991. **Membership Dues:** regular, $20 (annual) ● life, $500. **Description:** Establishes collaboration among individuals interested in collection, possession, and use of firearms. Promotes the collection and study of High Standard firearms. **Computer Services:** database, lists of members and areas of expertise ● online services, information exchange. **Publications:** Newsletter, 3/year. Contains articles and classified ads.

21947 ■ L.C. Smith Collectors Association

c/o Frank Finch, Exec. Dir./Corresponding Sec.
1322 Bay Ave.
Mantoloking, NJ 08738
E-mail: frankfinch@msn.com
URL: http://www.lcsmith.org
Contact: Frank Finch, Exec. Dir./Corresponding Sec.
Founded: 2003. **Membership Dues:** basic, $25 (annual) ● life, $300. **Description:** Educates members and the public about all aspects of the L.C. Smith shotgun, its history and production. Promotes a positive and responsible use of firearms to members and the public. Encourages the creation of the L.C. Smith museum. **Computer Services:** Information services, L.C. Smith guns resources ● online services, forum. **Publications:** *L.C. Smith Speaks For Itself*, annual. Newsletter. **Price:** free for members. **Advertising:** accepted. Alternate Formats: online.

21948 ■ National Mossberg Collectors Association (NMCA)

PO Box 487
Festus, MO 63028
Ph: (636)937-6401
E-mail: vic@havlinsales.com
URL: http://www.mossbergcollectors.org
Contact: Victor Havlin, Pres.
Founded: 1988. **Members:** 1,067. **Membership Dues:** regular, in U.S. and Canada, $12 (annual) ● international, $25 (annual). **Budget:** $4,000. **Multinational. Description:** Individuals interested in preserving and displaying O.F. Mossberg firearms, optics, and accessories dating from 1919 to the present. Participates in National Rifle Association of America shows and regional arms shows. Conducts research. **Libraries: Type:** reference. **Awards: Type:** recognition. **Affiliated With:** National Rifle Association of America. **Publications:** *More Gun for the Money*. Book. **Price:** $30.00 softcover; $45.00 hardcover ● *NMCA News*, quarterly. Newsletter. Features articles and technical data on Mossberg firearms. **Price:** $10.00/year; $3.95/copy. **Circulation:** 1,000. **Advertising:** accepted.

21949 ■ Thompson Collectors Association (TCA)

PO Box 1675
Ellicott City, MD 21041-1675
E-mail: tca1934@comcast.net
URL: http://home.comcast.net/~tca1934
Contact: Carol Troy, Pres.
Founded: 1990. **Members:** 300. **Membership Dues:** regular, $30 (annual). **Multinational. Description:** Promotes interest in the study, collection, possession, preservation and use of Thompson Submachine guns and accessories. Encourages safe handling and proper care of firearms. Fosters good sportsmanship among its members. **Affiliated With:** National Rifle Association of America. **Publications:** Articles. Alternate Formats: online ● Newsletter, quarterly.

21950 ■ Weatherby Collectors Association (WCA)

PO Box 478
Pacific, MO 63069
Ph: (636)271-3336
E-mail: wcasecretary@aol.com
URL: http://www.weatherbycollectors.com
Contact: David Duffy, Exec. Dir.
Membership Dues: regular, $30 (annual). **Multinational. Description:** Promotes interest in the collection of Weatherby arms. Provides a forum for the interchange of information on collectible Weatherby arms. Encourages members to practice responsible ownership and proper use of firearms. **Publications:** Newsletter, bimonthly. **Price:** included in membership dues.

Fish

21951 ■ American Cichlid Association (ACA)

c/o Claudia Dickinson, Ambassador-at-Large
PO Box 5078
Montauk, NY 11954
Ph: (631)668-5125
E-mail: ivyrose@optonline.net
URL: http://www.cichlid.org
Contact: Claudia Dickinson, Ambassador-at-Large
Membership Dues: regular, in U.S., $25 (annual) ● regular, in U.S., $50 (biennial) ● regular, in U.S., $70 (triennial) ● life (in U.S.), $375 ● regular, in Canada and Mexico, $35 (annual) ● regular, in Canada and Mexico, $70 (biennial) ● regular, in Canada and Mexico, $105 (triennial) ● life (in Canada and Mexico), $420 ● other (with Buntbarsche Bulletin only), $30 (annual) ● other (with Buntbarsche Bulletin only), $60 (biennial) ● other (with Buntbarsche Bulletin only), $90 (triennial) ● other (with BB and TP), $45 (annual) ● other (with BB and TP), $90 (biennial) ● other (with BB and TP), $135 (triennial). **Description:** Aquarium association specializing in the perch-like fishes of the family called Cichlidae (Cichlids). Maintains a speaker's bureau. **Awards:** Mike Sheridan Tankbuster Award. **Frequency:** annual. **Type:** recognition. **Recipient:** for individuals chosen at all-cichlid show during the annual convention. **Committees:** Nomenclature. **Publications:** *Buntbarsche Bulletin*, bimonthly. Contains articles about cichlids. **Advertising:** accepted ● *Trading Post*, bimonthly. Newsletter. Contains information on where members can buy, sell or trade various species of cichlids. **Advertising:** accepted. **Conventions/Meetings:** annual convention.

21952 ■ American Killifish Association (AKA)

c/o Steve Sump
10518 Briarwood Ct.
Elyria, OH 44035
E-mail: spoggy@comcast.net
URL: http://www.aka.org
Contact: Peter Tirbak, Chm.
Founded: 1961. **Members:** 950. **Membership Dues:** regular, in U.S., $26 (annual) ● regular, in Canada and Mexico, $35 (annual) ● regular, outside North America (airmail), $48 (annual). **Staff:** 12. **Budget:** $35,000. **Regional Groups:** 24. **Local Groups:** 22. **Description:** Aims to propagate and study the killifish (Cyprinodontidae) family. **Libraries: Type:** not open to the public. **Holdings:** periodicals. **Subjects:** scientific, general hobbyist information on the killifish. **Publications:** *A World of Killies - Volumes 1-3* ● *Business Newsletter*, monthly. Contains business and service reports. **Price:** included in membership dues. **Circulation:** 1,200. **Also Cited As:** *BNL* ● *Index*, annual ● *Journal of the American Killifish Association*, bimonthly. **Advertising:** accepted ● *Roster*, biennial. Directory. **Conventions/Meetings:** annual National Convention, workshops, fish show, banquet (exhibits) - always Memorial Day weekend.

21953 ■ American Livebearer Association (ALA)

5 Zerbe St.
Cressona, PA 17929-1513
Ph: (570)385-0573
Fax: (570)385-2781
E-mail: tjb100@psualum.com
URL: http://www.livebearers.org
Contact: Timothy J. Brady, Membership Chm.
Founded: 1971. **Members:** 450. **Membership Dues:** regular, in U.S., $20 (annual) ● regular, outside North America, $27 (annual) ● regular, in Canada, $22 (annual). **Staff:** 10. **Multinational. Description:** Aims to gather, organize, and disseminate the knowledge of livebearers, to promote fellowship among members, and to further the conservation of species and their natural habitat. Promotes interest in and study of this fish; encourages selective breeding to improve recognized species and subspecies. Conducts research and educational programs. **Libraries: Type:** open to the public. **Holdings:** 182. **Awards:** Merit Breeder Award. **Type:** recognition. **Recipient:** for members who breed and raise twelve or more individual species ● Vern Parish. **Frequency:** annual. **Type:** scholarship. **Recipient:** for graduate students. **Publications:** *Livebearer Trader*, bimonthly, even months. Contains listing of livebearer stock. ● *Livebearers*, bimonthly, odd months. Journal. **Conventions/Meetings:** annual convention, a 3-day event with seminars, fish show, banquet, auction,

roundtables, sales and vendors (exhibits) - usually in April or May ● Fish Shows ● seminar.

21954 ■ Apistogramma Study Group (ASG)

PO Box 504
Elkhorn, WI 53121
E-mail: info@apisto.com
URL: http://www.apisto.com
Contact: Daryl Szyska, Contact
Founded: 1980. **Members:** 300. **Membership Dues:** regular, in U.S., $18 (annual) ● regular, in Canada and international, $20 (annual). **Staff:** 10. **Multinational. Description:** Breeders and admirers of apistogramma (a family of fish comprising all South American and West African Dwarf Cichlids). Promotes increased interest in these fish; supports selective breeding programs. **Publications:** The Apisto-Gramm, quarterly. Journal. Contains up-to-date information on Apistogramma and related dwarf cichlid. **Price:** included in membership dues; $6.95 for nonmembers (in U.S. and Canada); $7.95 for nonmembers (international). **Advertising:** accepted.

21955 ■ Associated Koi Clubs of America (AKCA)

PO Box 3345
Orange, CA 92857-0345
Ph: (714)731-5610
E-mail: judgedahl@hotmail.com
URL: http://www.akca.org
Contact: Joan Finnegan, Chair
Founded: 1980. **Members:** 7,755. **Membership Dues:** club, $100 (annual). **Staff:** 2. **Regional Groups:** 21. **Local Groups:** 104. **Multinational. Description:** Clubs comprising owners and enthusiasts of koi. (Koi is an ornamental variety of the Japanese carp, related to the goldfish, which is said to be capable of being held, petted, and trained to do tricks.) Provides educational services and materials. Advises new or potential owners on such subjects as pond construction, filter design, medical problems, and results of koi shows. **Awards:** Koi Fish of the Year. **Frequency:** annual. **Type:** recognition ● Koi Person of the Year. **Frequency:** annual. **Type:** recognition. **Additional Websites:** http://www.koiusa.com. **Publications:** Basic KOI Ponds, Filters & Water. Books. Volumes I and II. **Price:** $25.00 ● Judging & Buying KOI. Book. **Price:** $25.00 ● KOI. Book. **Price:** $35.00. **Advertising:** accepted. **Conventions/Meetings:** monthly board meeting - 2nd Friday, Orange, CA ● annual convention (exhibits) - last weekend in June.

21956 ■ Breeder's Registry

5541 Columbia Dr. N
Fresno, CA 93727
E-mail: tlang@aquariusaquarium.org
URL: http://www.breedersregistry.org
Contact: Tom Lang, Pres./CEO
Founded: 1993. **Membership Dues:** benefactor (minimum), $100 (annual) ● sponsor, $75 (annual) ● contributor, $50 (annual) ● individual, $25 (annual). **Description:** Promotes information exchange about breeding and rearing marine fishes and invertebrates, particularly those kept or cultured in closed system aquaria. **Computer Services:** database, CLOWNFISH. **Publications:** Reports. Contains information on specific breeding efforts.

21957 ■ Goldfish Society of America (GFSA)

PO Box 551373
Fort Lauderdale, FL 33355
Ph: (954)423-0663
E-mail: info@goldfishsociety.org
URL: http://www.goldfishsociety.org
Contact: Terry Cusick, Chm.
Founded: 1972. **Members:** 1,000. **Membership Dues:** individual in U.S., $25 (annual) ● individual in Canada and Mexico, $30 (annual). **Staff:** 15. **Regional Groups:** 5. **Multinational. Description:** Club of goldfish breeders, collectors and enthusiasts. Caters to both beginners and advanced hobbyists. **Committees:** Advertising and Marketing; Article Submission; Breeder Registry; Internet; Membership; Shows and Judging. **Publications:** Goldfish Report, bimonthly. Magazine. **Price:** $25.00/year. **Circula-**

tion: 1,000. **Advertising:** accepted. Alternate Formats: online ● Also publishes beginners' guides. **Conventions/Meetings:** periodic competition.

21958 ■ Hawaiian International Billfish Tournament (HIBT)

PO Box 4800
Kailua-Kona, HI 96745
Ph: (808)329-6155
Fax: (808)329-1148
E-mail: hibt@hawaii50.net
URL: http://www.hibtfishing.com
Contact: Sherry Vann, Contact
Founded: 1958. **Members:** 1,000. **Description:** Sportfishing enthusiasts; fishing tournament participants; individuals interested in billfish conservation. Promotes highest ideals of sportsmanship in billfishing tournaments; supports conservation programs and principles that work to preserve marine game fish. **Telecommunication Services:** electronic mail, fishvann@hawaii.rr.com. **Affiliated With:** International Game Fish Association; Pacific Ocean Research Foundation. **Formerly:** (2000) Hawaiian International Billfish Association. **Publications:** Billfisher, quarterly. Newsletter ● Official Tournament Program Book, annual ● Also publishes news releases. **Conventions/Meetings:** semiannual Fishing Tournaments - competition.

21959 ■ International Betta Congress (IBC)

c/o Steve Van Camp, Membership Chm./Sec.
923 Wadsworth St.
Syracuse, NY 13208
Ph: (315)454-4792
E-mail: bettacongress@yahoo.com
URL: http://www.ibcbettas.org
Contact: Steve Van Camp, Membership Chm./Sec.
Founded: 1965. **Members:** 600. **Membership Dues:** individual in North America (mail), $35 (annual) ● family in North America (mail), $37 (annual) ● individual outside North America (mail), $40 (annual) ● family outside North America (mail), $42 (annual) ● life, $500 ● junior, $19 (annual). **Budget:** $25,000. **Multinational. Description:** Tropical fish hobbyists whose interest is with the Betta genus. Aims are to: organize Betta fanciers throughout the world; establish and conduct training courses for the certification of judges; define and establish standards for judging Bettas. Sponsors research and investigation of the Betta genus; encourages exchange of information; offers technical assistance in the breeding and raising of Bettas. Maintains Species Maintenance Program. Organizes competitions, shows, workshops, and seminars; compiles statistics, operates technical assistance library on the breeding, raising, and showing of Bettas. **Libraries: Type:** reference. **Holdings:** articles, audiovisuals, reports. **Subjects:** freshwater tropical fish, Betta genus, Betta splendens. **Committees:** Awards and Nominations; Judging Board; Programs; Research and Grants; Species Maintenance; Technical Assistance. **Publications:** FLARE, bimonthly. Magazine. Covers research in breeding and showing of Bettas at IBC sanctioned Betta shows. Includes annual membership list, show calendar, and show results. **Price:** included in membership dues; $2.00/copy for nonmembers. **Circulation:** 600. **Advertising:** accepted ● Membership Handbook. **Conventions/Meetings:** annual convention (exhibits) - always third weekend of June.

21960 ■ International Fancy Guppy Association (IFGA)

c/o Mr. Alan Opdyke, Pres.
PO Box 1183
Snellville, GA 30078
Ph: (770)979-3878
E-mail: redguppy@fancyguppy.com
URL: http://www.ifga.org
Contact: Mr. Alan Opdyke, Pres.
Founded: 1965. **Members:** 22. **Membership Dues:** regular, $25 (annual). **Multinational. Description:** Represents guppy clubs and interested individuals in 3 countries. Promotes understanding and interest in the fancy guppy through exhibitions and discussions. Provides aid for member groups' exhibitions. Establishes and updates standards for shows and judging.

Maintains hall of fame. **Awards:** Master Breeder. **Frequency:** periodic. **Type:** recognition. **Recipient:** for highest level of breeding and competition. **Supersedes:** American Guppy Association. **Publications:** Official Rules and Judging Standards ● Newsletter, 11/year. Features show rules and results, articles and more. **Price:** $25.00/year. **Circulation:** 300. **Advertising:** accepted. **Conventions/Meetings:** Sanctioned Guppy Exhibits/Competition (exhibits) - April-November, as scheduled.

21961 ■ International Women Fly Fishers (IWFF)

141 Wiggins Ct.
Pleasant Hill, CA 94523
Ph: (925)934-2461
E-mail: info@intlwomenflyfishers.org
URL: http://www.intlwomenflyfishers.org
Contact: Nancy Zakon, Pres.
Founded: 1996. **Members:** 300. **Membership Dues:** individual in U.S., $25 (annual) ● individual outside U.S., $30 (annual) ● women (18 and under), $15 (annual). **Multinational. Description:** Women fly fishers. Promotes and educates women in the sport of fly fishing. Provides newsletters. Hosts annual events. **Publications:** Newsletter, quarterly. **Conventions/Meetings:** annual festival, with guest speakers, hands-on sessions to improve skills in casting, fishing techniques, fly tying and knot tying (exhibits) - fall.

21962 ■ North American Fish Breeders Guild (NAFBG)

c/o D.L. Sponenberg
RR 2, Box 67-L
Orangeville, PA 17859
Ph: (717)683-6126
E-mail: nafbg-mem@rocketmail.com
URL: http://www.characin.com/carey/reviews/societies/nafbg.html
Contact: D.L. Sponenberg, Contact
Description: Breeders of tropical fish, aquarium owners, and other interested individuals and organizations. Promotes high standards of practice and ethics in the breeding and sale of aquarium fish; makes members aware of laws and regulations regarding the sale of fish; works to increase public interest in keeping fish as pets.

21963 ■ Pacific Coast Cichlid Association (PCCA)

PO Box 28145
San Jose, CA 95159-8145
E-mail: ellenbej@pacbell.net
URL: http://www.cichlidworld.com
Contact: Mr. Jim Ellenberger, Membership Chm.
Founded: 1980. **Members:** 135. **Membership Dues:** single, $20 (annual) ● single, $35 (biennial) ● family, $25 (annual) ● family, $45 (biennial) ● foreign, $40 (annual) ● electronic-publication emailed, $15 (annual) ● electronic-publication emailed, $25 (biennial). **Description:** Promotes the breed of cichlid fish. **Publications:** Cichlid Blues, bimonthly, odd months. Newsletters. **Price:** $1.00 for nonmembers; included in membership dues ● Cichlidae Communique, bimonthly, even months. Journal. **Price:** included in membership dues. **Conventions/Meetings:** monthly meeting, with speaker, raffle, and auction - every second Saturday.

21964 ■ Rainbowfish Study Group of North America (RSG)

c/o Cary Hostrawser, Show Sanctioning Coor.
12920 Zachary Cir. N
Dayton, MN 55327
Ph: (612)422-9446
E-mail: kristopher.kortright@twcable.com
URL: http://rainbowfishes.com
Contact: Cary Hostrawser, Show Sanctioning Coor.
Membership Dues: regular, in North America, $10 (annual) ● regular, outside North America, $15 (annual). **Multinational. Description:** Represents breeders and admirers of rainbowfish (rainbowfish are small, brilliantly colored members of the wrasse and parrotfish families, and are indigenous to tropical seas). Promotes increased interest in these fish; sup-

ports selective breeding programs. **Publications:** *Rainbow Times*. Newsletter. Contains breeding and maintenance reports, listing of fish and eggs for sale, and other articles of interest.

21965 ■ Rocky Mountain Cichlid Association (RMCA)

c/o Sam Chin, Treas.
2309 Oswego St.
Aurora, CO 80010
Ph: (303)364-7983
E-mail: anpacman1@aol.com
URL: http://www.rmcichlid.org
Contact: Sam Chin, Treas.

Founded: 1973. **Membership Dues:** regular, $15 (annual). **Description:** Promotes the cichlid breed of fish. **Committees:** Bowl Show; Greeter; Grow-out; Hospitality; Programs; Publications. **Publications:** *The Cichlidafile*, monthly. Newsletter. Alternate Formats: online. **Conventions/Meetings:** monthly meeting - usually 2nd Sunday of September through June.

Fishing

21966 ■ American Crappie Association (ACA)

125 Ruth Ave.
Benton, KY 42025
Ph: (270)395-4204
Fax: (270)395-4381
E-mail: office@crappieusa.com
URL: http://www.crappieusa.com
Contact: Darrell VanVactor, Pres.

Membership Dues: individual, $20 (annual) ● individual, $55 (triennial) ● life - individual, $250 ● spouse, youth, $10 (annual). **Description:** Promotes crappie fishing. Seeks to influence national manufacturers to produce more and better crappie fishing products. Links crappie anglers with destination lakes, resorts, guides and other anglers through the ACA referral service. **Libraries: Type:** reference. **Holdings:** articles. **Subjects:** angler profiles, fishing techniques, fishing, crappie fishing. **Computer Services:** Online services, message board. **Also Known As:** (2005) Crappie USA. **Publications:** *Crappie Journal*. Alternate Formats: online ● *Crappie 2000*. Newsletter. Alternate Formats: online.

21967 ■ International Association of Fly Fishing Veterinarians (IAFFV)

c/o Walter E. Weirich, PhD, Sec.-Treas.
7957 W Juniper Shadows Way
Tucson, AZ 85743
Ph: (715)325-2628 (520)572-1488
E-mail: dsesi@aol.com
URL: http://www.iaffv.org
Contact: Don Sawyer, Pres.

Membership Dues: individual, $35 (annual) ● couple, $45 (annual). **Multinational. Description:** Provides high quality veterinary continuing education, while enjoying pristine fishing destinations.

21968 ■ International Bonefishing Society (IBS)

205A Plaza Dr.
Greenville, NC 27858
Ph: (252)353-4440
Free: (866)427-4636
Fax: (252)353-4941
E-mail: staff@intlbonefishingsociety.com
URL: http://www.intlbonefishingsociety.com

Membership Dues: general, $35 (annual). **Multinational. Description:** Represents the interests of individuals who share a passion for bonefishing and related types of fishing. Gathers and disseminates accurate and reliable data about bonefishing and related types of fishing to members. Enhances the pleasure and passion of the sport by forming a collegial network that facilitates communication, socialization and recreation. **Computer Services:** database, bonefishing destination ● online services, bulletin board. **Publications:** *IBS Newsletter*, quarterly. Contains current events, personal and collegial

information and current travel issues. ● Catalog. Alternate Formats: online.

21969 ■ International Fellowship of Fishing Rotarians (IFFR)

c/o Greg Foster
7600 NE 137 Pl.
Citra, FL 32113
Ph: (352)236-4504
E-mail: fishrotary@mindspring.com
URL: http://www.iffr.homestead.com
Contact: J. William Rewalt, Pres.

Membership Dues: individual, $30 (biennial). **Multinational. Description:** Promotes friendship between Rotarians who enjoy recreational fishing. Promotes interaction between the members of the Fellowship and the youth of their respective communities so that young men and women may learn about the Rotary International, sport fishing, the environment and the proper management of fishing resources. **Telecommunication Services:** electronic mail, jrewalt@candw.ky. **Publications:** *The Mullet Wrapper*, quarterly. Newsletter. **Price:** included in membership dues. Alternate Formats: online.

21970 ■ National Teen Anglers (NTA)

1177 Bayshore Dr., No. 207
Fort Pierce, FL 34949
Ph: (772)519-0482
E-mail: alb@teenanglers.org
URL: http://www.teenanglers.org
Contact: Capt. Al Bernetti, Pres.

Description: Represents the interests of individuals dedicated to educating young adults interested in learning more about angling. Provides an opportunity for all teens to participate in a no-fee program that will teach them the art of fishing, conservation and essential details of boating with emphasis on safety. Strives to help members seek and acquire the knowledge, skills and attitudes necessary to be successful in life. Helps steer teens away from involvement with drugs and crime. **Computer Services:** Online services, classroom ● online services, message board. **Publications:** Newsletter. Alternate Formats: online.

Flowers

21971 ■ American Brugmansia and Datura Society (ABADS)

51431 State Hwy. 14
Chariton, IA 50049
E-mail: info@abads.org
URL: http://www.americanbrugmansia-daturasociety.org
Contact: Patricia Hartman Reynolds, Pres.

Founded: 2002. **Membership Dues:** individual, $15 (annual) ● business, $25 (annual). **Multinational. Description:** Works to bring together both professional and amateur collectors, home gardeners, growers and hybridizers worldwide, whose common bond is their love for Brugmansia and Datura. Promotes the cultivation of Brugmansia and Datura hybrids. Maintains a Brugmansia seed bank. Provides an online forum for members and non-members. **Telecommunication Services:** electronic mail, patricia@abads.org. **Publications:** *The Trumpeter*, semiannual. Newsletter.

Games

21972 ■ American Autoduel Association (AADA)

c/o Steve Jackson Games
PO Box 18957
Austin, TX 78760
Ph: (512)447-7866
Fax: (512)447-1144
E-mail: info@sjgames.com
URL: http://www.sjgames.com
Contact: Steve Jackson, Pres./Ed.-in-Chief

Founded: 1983. **Members:** 1,000. **For-Profit. Description:** Represents individuals interested in play-

ing and promoting the game Car Wars. Sponsors tournaments. **Telecommunication Services:** electronic bulletin board, contains tournament announcements ● electronic mail, sj@sjgames.com. **Publications:** *Autoduel Quarterly*. Magazine. **Conventions/Meetings:** annual Car Wars World Championship Tournament - meeting.

21973 ■ American Checker Federation (ACF)

c/o Jonathan Chappell, Treas.
3721 Falcon Crest Dr., Apt. 201
Louisville, KY 40219
E-mail: alanmillhone@usacheckers.com
URL: http://usacheckers.com
Contact: Alan Millhone, Pres.

Founded: 1948. **Members:** 1,000. **Membership Dues:** regular, $25 (annual) ● life, $1,000 ● associate, junior, $10 (annual). **Staff:** 1. **Regional Groups:** 10. **State Groups:** 40. **Local Groups:** 100. **National Groups:** 75. **Description:** Master and expert checker players and supporters of the game in the U.S., Canada, and other countries. Promotes checkers on a national and international scale as a dignified intellectual pastime. Stages world title match in odd-numbered years (cooperating with English Draughts Association); promotes district tournaments; encourages competition by mail, including matches between players in the U.S. and Great Britain. Maintains museum/hall of fame in Petal, MS. Sponsors a youth program for players 7-21 years of age. **Libraries: Type:** open to the public; by appointment only. **Holdings:** 150; books. **Subjects:** checkers. **Awards:** Hall of Fame. **Frequency:** annual. **Type:** recognition. **Computer Services:** database, membership roster ● mailing lists, labels. **Formed by Merger of:** (1948) American Checker Association; (1948) National Checker Association. **Publications:** *ACF Bulletin*, bimonthly. Newsletter. Records official actions; reports news of checkers including results of official tournaments and affiliated tournaments. **Price:** $25.00/year. ISSN: 1045-8034. **Circulation:** 1,000 ● *Checker Power*. Book. Contains 32 pages of problem solving for beginners. **Price:** $8.40/copy in U.S.; $14.40/copy outside U.S. ● *Play Checkers With Me*. Book. Features the story about a six years old dinosaur that likes to play checkers. **Price:** $10.00/copy in U.S.; $14.00/copy outside U.S. ● *Tournament Manual*. Contains method for teaching checkers to kids. **Price:** $4.95/copy. **Conventions/Meetings:** biennial The National GAYP - convention - always in odd years ● biennial United States Open Tournament - convention - always even-numbered years.

21974 ■ American Crossword Federation (ACF)

PO Box 69
Massapequa Park, NY 11762
Ph: (516)795-8823
E-mail: crosswordpuzzles@aol.com
Contact: Stanley Newman, Pres.

Founded: 1983. **Members:** 6,000. **For-Profit. Description:** Crossword enthusiasts promoting the game of crossword puzzle-solving as a means of education and entertainment. Creates custom-made crossword puzzles for businesses; syndicates crosswords to newspapers, magazines, and websites; sponsors puzzle-solving competitions and an annual Crossword-theme Cruise. Maintains speakers' bureau. **Convention/Meeting:** none. **Publications:** *Tough Cryptics*, bimonthly. Contains cryptic crosswords, contests, and book reviews. **Price:** $30.00/year. **Circulation:** 2,000 ● Also publishes crossword books.

21975 ■ American Go Association (AGA)

PO Box 397
New York, NY 10113-0397
Ph: (917)817-7080
E-mail: aga@usgo.org
URL: http://www.usgo.org
Contact: Michael Lash, Pres.

Founded: 1933. **Members:** 2,250. **Membership Dues:** full (in U.S.), $30 (annual) ● full (international), $35 (annual) ● youth, $10 (annual) ● limited, $15 (annual) ● sustainer, $50 (annual) ● individual sponsor, $100 (annual) ● institutional sponsor, $500 (annual) ● life, $1,000. **Staff:** 10. **Budget:** $80,000. **Regional Groups:** 3. **Local Groups:** 150. **Description:** Promotes the ancient Asian board game of "Go" in the US. (Invented in China in approximately 2000 B.C., Go has a simple rule structure, great subtlety, and many levels of play.) Maintains a numerical rating system. Conducts specialized education program; operates Speaker's Bureau. **Libraries: Type:** reference. **Holdings:** 20. **Subjects:** game of Go. **Awards: Type:** recognition. **Computer Services:** Information services, rating service. **Publications:** *American Go Association - E-Journal,* biweekly. Contains upcoming events, reporting on Go events and game reviews. Circulation: 8,000. Alternate Formats: online ● *American Go Journal - Yearbook,* annual, updated weekly online. **Price:** $30.00. **ISSN:** 0148-0243. **Circulation:** 2,250. **Advertising:** accepted. Alternate Formats: online ● *Club List,* annual ● *Go Teacher's Information Packet* ● *Inside the AGA Rating System* ● *Resource List* ● *Tournament Guide* ● *The Way to Go* ● Also makes available tutorial shareware computer program. **Conventions/Meetings:** annual competition, local and regional (exhibits) - August ● annual U.S. Go Congress - always August.

21976 ■ Association of Game and Puzzle Collectors (AGPC)
PMB 321
197M Boston Post Rd. W
Marlborough, MA 01752
E-mail: agca@agca.com
URL: http://www.agpc.org
Contact: Martha Folsom, Pres.

Founded: 1985. **Members:** 400. **Membership Dues:** individual, $35 (annual). **Budget:** $15,000. **Description:** Individuals (400) and institutions (25) interested in the study, preservation, and collection of American games, including board and card games, puzzles, marbles, and related play things. Encourages publication of information pertaining to games and game companies. Answers inquires, but does not supply appraisals. S.A.S.E. requested. **Libraries: Type:** reference. **Holdings:** archival material. **Subjects:** game instructions, catalogs, game company histories, puzzles, puzzle history. **Formerly:** (2001) American Game Collectors Association. **Publications:** *Game Researchers' Notes,* 3/year. Newsletter. **Price:** included in membership dues. **Circulation:** 450. **Advertising:** accepted ● *Game Times,* 3/year. Includes articles about games, calendar of events, book reviews, classified ads that are related to games. **Price:** included in membership dues. **Circulation:** 450. **Advertising:** accepted ● Membership Directory, annual. **Conventions/Meetings:** annual convention and meeting (exhibits) - usually fall.

21977 ■ Boardgame Players Association (BPA)
1541 Redfield Rd.
Bel Air, MD 21015
E-mail: doncon99@toad.net
URL: http://www.boardgamers.org
Contact: Ken Guttermuth, Chm.

Founded: 1998. **Membership Dues:** associate, $10 (annual) ● family (per person), $50-$60 (annual) ● sustaining, charter, $60-$80 (annual) ● tribune, $100 (annual) ● sponsor, $500 (annual) ● exhibitor, $200-$300 (annual) ● vendor, $450-$600 (annual). **Multinational. Description:** Supports the shared interests of board game players. Fosters camaraderie and sportsmanship among board game players and enthusiasts. Serves as a portal for boardgamers to enjoy their favorite games. **Awards:** Caesar Award. **Frequency:** annual. **Type:** recognition. **Recipient:** to the player who earned the most laurels over the course of the BPA year ● GM of the Year. **Frequency:** annual. **Type:** recognition. **Recipient:** to an individual who sacrificed his/her time in coordinating all activities and events of the association ● Hobby Service Award. **Frequency:** annual. **Type:** recognition. **Recipient:** to a member who has shown dedication in supporting the boardgaming hobby ● WBC Sportsmanship Award. **Frequency:** annual. **Type:** recognition. **Recipient:** to the player who has shown appropriate conduct and attitude during competitions.

Publications: Newsletter, monthly. Alternate Formats: online. **Conventions/Meetings:** annual World Boardgaming Championships - convention, with tournaments - 2008 Aug. 5-10, Lancaster, PA; 2009 Aug. 4-9, Lancaster, PA; 2010 Aug. 3-8, Lancaster, PA.

21978 ■ Committee for the Advancement of Role-Playing Games (CAR-PGa)
1127 Cedar
Bonham, TX 75418
Ph: (903)583-9296
E-mail: waltonwj@aol.com
URL: http://members.aol.com/waltonwj/carpga.htm
Contact: Paul Cardwell Jr., Chm.

Founded: 1987. **Members:** 50. **Staff:** 1. **Budget:** $350. **Description:** Individuals interested in role-playing games. (Role-playing games are improvised, open-ended stories in which the referee or game master sets the scene and players describe the actions of individual characters. Play depends on imagination and group interaction within elaborate rule systems. Questions are resolved within set probabilities by random number generation, usually accomplished with various types of dice.) Advocates the role-playing game hobby and defends gamers from slander, libel, and illegal action. Promotes the recreational and educational benefits of role-playing games and their use in psychological and sociological treatment. Maintains information service for players, game publishers and retailers, and the media. Operates speaker's bureau; conducts research. **Libraries: Type:** reference. **Holdings:** archival material, books, clippings, monographs, periodicals. **Subjects:** backmasking, false memory syndrome, satanic panic episodes, livestock mutilations, collective delusions held by individuals against role-playing games, role playing game, rule design, playing techniques, ethics. **Additional Websites:** http://www.theescapist.com/carpga.htm. **Publications:** *CAR-PGa Newsletter,* monthly. Includes lists of archival material acquired, commentary, house-organ material, reports on projects, new products and convention calendar. **Price:** $12.00/year in North America; $13.50/year outside North America. **ISSN:** 1071-7129. **Circulation:** 45 ● *Role-Playing and the Gifted Student.* Paper. Features an update of Gifted Education International paper. ● *RPG as an Academic Subject.* Survey ● *Setting the Record Straight.* Booklets. Includes a point by point examination of anti-game publications. ● *Trophy List Refuted.* Booklets ● *Women's Gamers' Survey* ● Membership Directory, semiannual. **Price:** available to members only ● Also publishes bibliography of peer-reviewed studies, appellate court decisions, and other scholarly works.

21979 ■ Committee for the Game (CG)
1460 SW A Ave.
Corvallis, OR 97333-4219
Ph: (541)753-6236
E-mail: caploc@peak.org
Contact: Dunbar Aitkens, Exec. Officer

Founded: 1976. **For-Profit. Description:** Sponsors glass plate game playing annually. **Conventions/Meetings:** annual meeting.

21980 ■ Domino Players Association of America
Address Unknown since 2007

Founded: 1992. **Members:** 2,650. **Membership Dues:** individual, $15 (annual) ● student, $15 (annual). **Staff:** 6. **Budget:** $24,000. **Regional Groups:** 10. **State Groups:** 35. **Local Groups:** 4. **Description:** Domino enthusiasts who promote the game of dominoes as a means of enjoyment and education in arithmetic and mathematics. Conducts and compiles research on history of dominoes. Sponsors tournaments for elementary schools, high schools, colleges, and professionals. **Libraries: Type:** reference. **Holdings:** clippings. **Subjects:** dominoes. **Awards: Frequency:** periodic. **Type:** recognition. **Computer Services:** database ● mailing lists. **Publications:** *Domino World,* semiannual. Newsletter. Provides information on domino products, events, and current happenings in the domino world. **Conventions/Meetings:** monthly tour.

21981 ■ International Backgammon Association (IBA)
1300 Citrus Isle
Fort Lauderdale, FL 33315-1324
Ph: (954)527-4033
E-mail: susanlboydusa@netzero.net
Contact: Susan L. Boyd, Sec.-Treas.

Founded: 1974. **Members:** 3,500. **Membership Dues:** individual, $10 (annual). **Staff:** 2. **For-Profit. Description:** Backgammon enthusiasts; backgammon clubs and club directors. Promotes the game of backgammon. Provides tips on game strategy and keeps members informed of tournaments held worldwide. Operates charitable program. **Publications:** *Backgammon Tournament Notices,* annual, 1-2/year. Brochures. **Conventions/Meetings:** annual World Championship - competition - always July, Monaco, France.

21982 ■ International Fantasy Gaming Society (IFGS)
PO Box 3577
Boulder, CO 80307
Ph: (303)443-1012
E-mail: clerk@ifgs.org
URL: http://www.ifgs.org
Contact: Nicole Corbin Lawson, Pres.

Founded: 1981. **Members:** 400. **Membership Dues:** regular, $10 (annual) ● foreign, $20 (annual) ● associate, junior, $2 (annual). **Staff:** 1. **Budget:** $30,000. **Local Groups:** 15. **Description:** Individuals interested in live-action fantasy role-playing. Works to organize role-playing games using fantasy scenarios. **Computer Services:** Information services, game scoring system ● mailing lists. **Telecommunication Services:** electronic mail, board@ifgs.org. **Publications:** *The Chainmail,* bimonthly. Newsletter. **Circulation:** 400 ● *IFGS Fantasy Rulebook* ● Also publishes rulebooks on espionage and fantasy gaming and game design handbook.

21983 ■ National Mah Jongg League (NMJL)
250 W 57th St.
New York, NY 10107
Ph: (212)246-3052
Fax: (212)246-4117
URL: http://www.nationalmahjongleague.org
Contact: Ruth Unger, Pres.

Founded: 1937. **Members:** 215,000. **Membership Dues:** individual (standard size card), $6 (annual) ● individual (large print card), $7 (annual). **State Groups:** 1. **Description:** Promotes the game of Mah Jongg. **Publications:** *Mah Jongg Made Easy With Tiles and Cards.* **Price:** $8.95 ● *Newsbulletin,* annual ● *Official Standard Rules,* annual. **Price:** $6.00 standard size; $7.00 large print size. **Conventions/Meetings:** annual competition.

21984 ■ National Puzzlers' League (NPL)
c/o Joseph J. Adamski
2507 Almar St.
Jenison, MI 49428
E-mail: treasurer@puzzlers.org
URL: http://www.puzzlers.org
Contact: Craig Hamilton, Ed.

Founded: 1883. **Members:** 490. **Membership Dues:** regular, $18 (annual) ● foreign, $25 (annual). **Staff:** 6. **Multinational. Description:** Hobbyists interested in word puzzles. **Study Groups:** Graffiti on the Sphinx. **Publications:** *The Enigma,* monthly. Journal. Contains verse puzzles, cryptograms, forms, and cryptic crossword puzzles. **Price:** $18.00/year; $25.00/year for overseas or large type edition. **Circulation:** 400 ● *NPL Directory,* annual. **Price:** included in membership dues. **Circulation:** 400. **Conventions/Meetings:** annual convention - always July.

21985 ■ National Scrabble Association (NSA)
PO Box 700
403 Front St.
Greenport, NY 11944
Ph: (631)477-0033
Fax: (631)477-0294

E-mail: info@scrabble-assoc.com
URL: http://www.scrabble-assoc.com
Contact: John D. Williams Jr., Exec. Dir.
Founded: 1978. **Members:** 10,000. **Membership Dues:** individual, in U.S., $20 (annual) ● regular, in Canada, $22 (annual) ● regular, outside U.S. and Canada, $27 (annual). **Staff:** 6. **Budget:** $600,000. **Local Groups:** 200. **Description:** Scrabble players. Sanctions, organizes, and publicizes Scrabble crossword game tournaments in the U.S. and Canada. Supervises compilation of the *Official Scrabble Players Dictionary*, which is the word authority of the NSA. Licenses Scrabble players clubs throughout the U.S. and Canada. **Libraries: Type:** not open to the public. **Holdings:** 300. **Subjects:** words, games, dictionaries, clubs, hobbies. **Awards:** Director of the Year. **Frequency:** annual. **Type:** recognition. **Boards:** Advisory. **Committees:** Dictionary; Rules. **Also Known As:** Scrabble Players. **Formerly:** (1990) Scrabble Crossword Game Players. **Publications:** *Scrabble News*, 8/year. Newsletter. **Price:** included in membership dues; $18.00 /year for nonmembers. **Advertising:** accepted. **Conventions/Meetings:** biennial National Scrabble Championship - meeting ● biennial World Scrabble Championship - meeting.

21986 ■ North American Tiddlywinks Association (NATwA)
c/o Rick Tucker
PO Box 1701
Falls Church, VA 22041-0701
Ph: (703)671-7098 (703)983-6731
E-mail: ricktucker@tiddlywinks.org
URL: http://tiddlywinks.org
Contact: Rick Tucker, Contact
Founded: 1966. **Members:** 100. **Description:** Tournament tiddlywinks players. Promotes the growth of the game; provides a framework for all levels of competition; ensures the availability of regulation sets and mats; recruits new players. Sponsors formal and informal matches, including national pairs and singles matches and individual pairs. Maintains tiddlywinks archives. Maintains "Closet of Fame" containing equipment and clothing used by famous players. **Libraries: Type:** by appointment only. **Holdings:** 6,000; archival material, articles, books, periodicals, photographs, video recordings. **Subjects:** tiddlywinks tournament records, games and sets (old and new), ephemera, historical photos and materials, event photos and materials. **Computer Services:** Bibliographic search, on website ● database, of tiddlywinks publishers; old and new ● mailing lists, for members. **Telecommunication Services:** electronic bulletin board, for members only. **Publications:** *Newswink*, semiannual. Newsletter. ISSN: 1063-2336. **Alternate Formats:** online ● *Rules of Tournament Tiddlywinks* ● Also publishes songbooks. **Conventions/Meetings:** reunion - every ten years.

21987 ■ Puzzle Buffs International (PBI)
41 Park Dr.
Port Clinton, OH 43452
Ph: (419)734-2600
Fax: (419)734-2868
E-mail: info@puzzlebuffs.com
URL: http://www.puzzlebuffs.com
Founded: 1979. **Members:** 60,000. **Membership Dues:** life, $24. **Staff:** 10. **For-Profit. Description:** Individuals who share an interest in word puzzles and word games. Seeks to showcase the puzzle-solving skills of members and to inform the public about the mental exercise and enjoyment of puzzling. Provides complimentary puzzles to patients at Veteran's Administration hospitals, nursing homes, and other institutions. Conducts charitable and educational programs; compiles statistics. Maintains museum and speakers' bureau. **Libraries: Type:** open to the public. **Subjects:** history, origin, and development of word puzzles. **Awards: Type:** recognition. **Formerly:** Scrambl-Gram. **Publications:** *Bigfoot Crosswords*, quarterly. Magazine ● *Color Cross*, quarterly. Magazine ● *GIANTS - The World's Largest Crosswords*, 10/year. Magazine. Includes Christian crosswords, TV puzzles, and puzzles for kids. **Price:** $2.75 plus shipping and handling. **Advertising:** ac-

cepted ● *Puzzle Buffs Newsletter*, quarterly. **Conventions/Meetings:** competition ● semiannual meeting.

21988 ■ Role Playing Game Association Network (RPGA)
PO Box 707
Renton, WA 98057-0707
Free: (800)324-6496
Fax: (425)687-8287
E-mail: rpgahq@wizards.com
URL: http://www.wizards.com/default.asp?x=rpga
Contact: Robert Wiese, Coor.
Founded: 1980. **Members:** 8,000. **Membership Dues:** individual and family, plus $10 for each additional family member, $20 (annual). **Staff:** 4. **Local Groups:** 125. **Multinational. Description:** Role-playing and fantasy game players, clubs, and retailers. (Role-playing and fantasy games are improvised, open-ended stories in which the referee or game-master sets the scene and players describe the actions of individual characters. Play depends on imagination and group interaction within elaborate rule systems.) Maintains branches in Australia and England. Promotes the fantasy and role-playing game hobby and encourages continued improvement of games. Seeks to facilitate communication between players. Holds competitions; bestows awards. Maintains library and hall of fame. **Computer Services:** Online services, message boards, internet. **Programs:** Game Master. **Publications:** *Polyhedron Magazine*, bimonthly. Includes gaming articles, classified ads and convention listing. **Price:** included in membership dues. **Circulation:** 8,000. **Advertising:** accepted. **Conventions/Meetings:** annual Winter Fantasy Gaming Conference - meeting (exhibits) - always 2nd weekend of February, Milwaukee, WI.

21989 ■ Strategy Gaming Society (SGS)
c/o Prof. George Phillies, Treas.
87-6 Park Ave.
Worcester, MA 01605
Ph: (508)831-5334 (508)754-1859
E-mail: phillies@4liberty.com
URL: http://www.gametableonline.com/StrategyGamingSociety.htm
Contact: Prof. George Phillies, Treas.
Founded: 1973. **Members:** 200. **Membership Dues:** individual in U.S., $15 (annual) ● individual in Canada and Mexico, $18 (annual) ● individual in other countries, $30 (annual). **Staff:** 12. **Budget:** $3,000. **Local Groups:** 10. **Description:** Private hobbyists; game conventions, gaming clubs, and hobby stores. Promotes the hobby of amateur strategy gaming. (Strategy gaming involves the use of strategy to resolve simulations of conflict or war, often within a science fiction, fantasy, political, or historical scenario; such games may be played through roleplaying or on a computer or gameboard.) Disseminates information about the gaming community. Provides matching and ratings services. **Libraries: Type:** reference. **Holdings:** biographical archives. **Committees:** Board-gaming; Computer Games; Diplomatic Games; Miniatures; Non-War Gaming/Family Games; Role-gaming; Science Fiction Games. **Formed by Merger of:** American Wargaming Association; National Wargaming Alliance. **Publications:** *Jeff Pimper's All the World's Wargames*, quinquennial. Lists published board games. **Price:** $4.00/volume (available in 4 volumes) ● *SGS Guide to Running Conventions* ● *Strategist*, monthly. Magazine ● *Wargamer's Encyclopedia Dictionary*. **Conventions/Meetings:** periodic competition.

21990 ■ U.S. Carrom Association (USCA)
PO Box 411
Wanaque, NJ 07465
Ph: (973)801-9032 (973)610-9795
E-mail: usca@uscarrom.org
URL: http://www.carrom.org
Contact: Hasmukh Patel, Pres.
Founded: 1990. **Membership Dues:** basic ($15 after July 1st), $25 (annual) ● life, $400. **Staff:** 1. **Description:** Seeks to organize and network carrom players and tournaments. Sponsors competitions. **Additional**

Websites: http://www.uscarrom.org. **Telecommunication Services:** electronic mail, president@carrom.org.

21991 ■ United States Othello Association (USOA)
7 Peter Cooper Rd., Ste.10G
New York, NY 10010
Ph: (212)475-8911
E-mail: peddler@usothello.com
URL: http://www.usothello.com
Contact: David Parsons, Pres.
Founded: 1979. **Members:** 100. **Membership Dues:** regular, $8 (annual). **Staff:** 1. **Description:** Persons dedicated to the advancement of the game of Othello (a game played with 64 black and white discs, popular a century ago in England under the name Reversi). Conducts, sponsors, or sanctions tournaments and maintains a national rating system for active players. Aids members in learning game strategy and in improving their playing skills. **Awards:** U.S. National Othello Champion. **Frequency:** annual. **Type:** recognition. **Publications:** *Othello: Brief and Basic*. Manual. **Price:** $5.00 for members; $6.00 for nonmembers ● *Othello Quarterly*. Journal. Contains reports of tournaments, game analyses, instructional material, and tournament announcements. **Price:** included in membership dues; $12.00 for nonmembers outside U.S. **Circulation:** 250.

Gaming

21992 ■ North American Confederation of the Red Dragon (NACORD)
c/o Tim Steed
8155 Carmelita Ct.
Avon, IN 46123
E-mail: members@conf-federation.us
URL: http://www.conf-federation.us
Contact: Tim Steed, Contact
Membership Dues: regular, $10 (annual). **Multinational. Description:** Aims to unite North American Rag'Narok players in partnership with Rackham. Supervises the yearly national championship of Confrontation and other Rackham games. Promotes gaming and artistic efforts within the framework of war games using fantasy figurines, painting and model making. Supports the creation of clubs and coordinates action with affiliated associations. **Telecommunication Services:** electronic mail, secretary@nacord.com. **Publications:** *Aarklash Observer*, quarterly. Newsletter. **Price:** included in membership dues.

Gardening

21993 ■ African Violet Society of America (AVSA)
2375 North St.
Beaumont, TX 77702
Ph: (409)839-4725
Free: (800)770-AVSA
Fax: (409)839-4329
E-mail: avsa@earthlink.net
URL: http://www.avsa.org
Contact: Jenny Daugereau, Office Mgr.
Founded: 1946. **Members:** 9,000. **Membership Dues:** individual, in U.S., $25 (annual) ● individual, outside U.S., $27 (annual) ● associate, in U.S., $10 (annual) ● associate, outside U.S., $11 (annual) ● commercial, in U.S., $37 (annual) ● commercial, outside U.S., $38 (annual) ● life, in U.S., $600 ● life, outside U.S., $750. **Staff:** 3. **National Groups:** 414. **Description:** Amateur and commercial African violet growers interested in the propagation and culture of African violets. Sponsors competitions. Offers grants to universities and individuals researching African violets. Maintains hall of fame. Offers workshops and judging schools. **Libraries: Type:** reference. **Holdings:** video recordings. **Subjects:** pest control, propagation, cultures, new introductions. **Awards:** Bronze Medal. **Type:** medal. **Recipient:** for individuals who have excelled at horticultural achievement.

Publications: *African Violet Magazine*, bimonthly. Provides growing information for professional and amateur growers. Includes calendar of events, list of available library materials, and obituaries. **Price:** included in membership dues; $3.75/copy for nonmembers. ISSN: 0002-0265. **Circulation:** 9,000. **Advertising:** accepted. Alternate Formats: online ● *African Violet Master Variety List*, periodic. Directory. Lists registered varieties and species of the African violet from the inception of registration February 25, 1949. Reprinted when needed. **Price:** $24.00/copy ● *Handbook for African Violet Growers, Exhibitors, and Judges.* **Conventions/Meetings:** annual convention, with show (exhibits).

21994 ■ All-America Gladiolus Selections (AAGS)
c/o Samuel N. Fisher
11734 Rd. 33 1/2
Madera, CA 93638-8465
Ph: (559)645-5329
Fax: (559)645-1300
E-mail: kfgladus@madnet.net
Contact: Samuel N. Fisher, Exec.Sec.
Founded: 1953. **Members:** 15. **Staff:** 1. **Budget:** $2,000. **Description:** Amateur and commercial growers of gladiolus. Rates gladiolus seedlings submitted for test by gladiolus hybridizers; conducts research programs to determine the value and quality of the gladiolus. Compiles statistics. **Awards:** All-America. **Type:** recognition. **Recipient:** for high-quality seedlings (approximately five percent). **Affiliated With:** North American Gladiolus Council. **Conventions/Meetings:** annual Trial Gardens - competition.

21995 ■ American Begonia Society (ABS)
PO Box 471651
San Francisco, CA 94147-1651
Ph: (918)333-1587
E-mail: membership@begonias.org
URL: http://www.begonias.org
Contact: Donna Marsheck, Membership Sec.
Founded: 1932. **Members:** 2,000. **Membership Dues:** family (U.S., Mexico, and Canada), $25 (annual) ● family (foreign), $45 (annual). **Staff:** 17. **Budget:** $40,000. **Regional Groups:** 3. **Local Groups:** 41. **Description:** Plant growers, hobbyists, shade plant specialists, and growers of exotic plants interested in growing begonias and other shade plants. Encourages the introduction and development of new types of these plants; works to standardize the nomenclature of begonias; gathers and disseminates information regarding type, propagation, and culture of begonias and companion plants. Conducts research programs. Sponsors competitions; conducts judges' training program. Maintains speakers' bureau. **Libraries: Type:** reference. **Holdings:** 100. **Subjects:** begonias, other shade plants. **Awards:** Introduction Award. **Frequency:** annual. **Type:** recognition ● Original Literary Material Award. **Frequency:** annual. **Type:** recognition ● Outstanding Begonia Hybrid Award. **Frequency:** annual. **Type:** recognition ● **Type:** scholarship ● Service Award. **Frequency:** annual. **Type:** recognition. **Committees:** International Registration Authority for Begonia Cultivators. **Departments:** Branch Relations; History; Judging; Nomenclature; Public Relations; Research; Round Robin; Seed Fund; Slide Library. **Formerly:** (1934) California Begonia Society. **Publications:** *Begonia Culture Bulletin*, bimonthly. ISSN: 0096-8684. **Circulation:** 1,500. **Advertising:** accepted ● *The Begonian*, bimonthly. Magazine. **Advertising:** accepted ● *Point Scoring System for Judging Begonia* ● *Suggested Guide to Classification of Begonia for Show Purposes.* **Conventions/Meetings:** annual meeting (exhibits).

21996 ■ American Bonsai Society (ABS)
PO Box 351604
Toledo, OH 43635-1604
E-mail: gduncanabs@buckeye-express.com
URL: http://www.absbonsai.org
Contact: Gloria Duncan, Exec. Sec.
Founded: 1967. **Membership Dues:** individual, $40 (annual) ● family, $50 (annual) ● supporting, $75 (annual) ● sustaining, $150 (annual) ● sponsor, $250

(annual) ● life, $1,000. **Staff:** 1. **Description:** Individuals, clubs, and organizations united to promote interest in and knowledge of bonsai, described by the society as part horticulture, part art-pruning, shaping, and container-growing to produce beautiful, dwarfed, three-dimensional forms suggesting natural trees or landscapes. Seeks to further education in the art. Conducts lecture-demonstrations and a bazaar. **Awards:** Ben Oki Award. **Frequency:** annual. **Type:** grant. **Recipient:** for service to the bonsai society. **Funds:** Educational Memorial. **Publications:** *Bonsai, Journal of the American Bonsai Society*, quarterly. Covers various aspects of the Bonsai art form including styling, pots, and trees. Includes book reviews. **Price:** included in membership dues. **Advertising:** accepted ● Brochures. **Conventions/Meetings:** annual meeting and board meeting ● symposium ● workshop.

21997 ■ American Boxwood Society (ABS)
PO Box 85
Boyce, VA 22620-0085
E-mail: info@boxwoodsociety.org
URL: http://www.boxwoodsociety.org
Contact: Mr. Henry F. Fierson Jr., Pres.
Founded: 1961. **Members:** 400. **Membership Dues:** individual, $35 (annual) ● family, $50 (annual) ● contributing, $75 (annual) ● sustaining, $100 (annual) ● life, $500. **Description:** Represents persons interested in the care, growth, and propagation of boxwood. Promotes the use of boxwood in landscaping and evaluates varieties with greater resistance to weather and other conditions. Sponsors and partially funds research tasks on the genus Buxus. **Telecommunication Services:** electronic mail, graywolfcaw@comcast.net. **Publications:** *Boxwood An Illustrated Encyclopedia*. Book. **Price:** $110.00 plus shipping and handling ($10 1st class, $5 book rate) ● *The Boxwood Bulletin*, quarterly. **Price:** included in membership dues. ISSN: 0006-8535. **Circulation:** 400 ● *Boxwood Handbook.* **Price:** $15.00 plus postage ($3.00) ● *Buyer's Guide for Boxwood.* Book. **Price:** $8.00. **Conventions/Meetings:** annual conference and workshop (exhibits) - usually second Wednesday of May.

21998 ■ American Camellia Society (ACS)
Massee Lane Gardens
100 Massee Ln.
Fort Valley, GA 31030
Ph: (478)967-2358
Fax: (478)967-2083
E-mail: ask@camellias-acs.com
URL: http://www.camellias-acs.org
Contact: Ann Walton, Exec. Dir.
Founded: 1945. **Members:** 4,700. **Membership Dues:** single, $50 (annual) ● joint, $55 (annual) ● sustaining, $50 (annual) ● patron, $125 (annual) ● life single, $500 ● life joint, $550 ● life single outside U.S., $560 ● life joint outside U.S., $620. **Staff:** 7. **Budget:** $100,000. **Description:** Hobbyists, academicians, and nurserymen interested in camellia culture. Promotes interest in the genus Camellia and scientific research in its culture; standardizes its varietal names and certify new varieties. Conducts grafting and air-layering demonstrations. **Libraries: Type:** reference. **Holdings:** 1,500; books. **Subjects:** horticulture. **Awards:** Fellow Award. **Type:** recognition. **Committees:** Exhibitions and Awards; Horticulture; Research; Varietal Registration. **Publications:** *American Camellia Yearbook*, annual ● *Camellia Culture for Beginners.* Booklet ● *Camellia Journal*, quarterly. **Conventions/Meetings:** competition ● semiannual meeting.

21999 ■ American Community Gardening Association (ACGA)
c/o Franklin Park Conservatory
1777 E Broad St.
Columbus, OH 43203
Free: (877)275-2242
E-mail: plantlot@aol.com
URL: http://www.communitygarden.org
Contact: Gerard Lordahl, Pres.
Founded: 1979. **Members:** 150,000. **Membership Dues:** basic, $25 (annual) ● professional, $50 (an-

nual) ● organization, $100 (annual) ● library, $75 (annual) ● sustaining, $500 (annual) ● sponsor/corporate, $1,000 (annual) ● senior, youth, student, $10-$25 (annual). **Budget:** $100,000. **For-Profit. Description:** Community gardening groups and supporting businesses organized to promote community gardening and greening in urban, suburban and rural communities. Supports a network of community garden program organizers. Maintains information clearinghouse and speakers' bureau; promotes resource exchange. Provides information and technical assistance network; conducts educational programs. Operates computerized community garden electronic bulletin board and database. **Awards:** ACGA Certificates of Recognition. **Frequency:** annual. **Type:** recognition. **Computer Services:** Mailing lists, of members. **Committees:** Communications; Education; Fiscal Management; Membership; Nominations; Programs; Public Relations. **Publications:** *Community Gardener*, 3/year. Newsletter. Contains national community gardening events, articles, and research. **Price:** included in membership dues ● *National Community Garden Survey 1996.* Monograph. Alternate Formats: online ● Video. **Price:** $40.00 for members; $45.00 for nonmembers. **Conventions/Meetings:** annual conference (exhibits) - usually last week of September ● annual convention and regional meeting - mid-February.

22000 ■ American Daffodil Society (ADS)
PO Box 522
Hawkinsville, GA 31036
Ph: (614)451-4747
Fax: (614)451-2177
E-mail: jager@cstel.net
URL: http://daffodilusa.org
Contact: Rod Armstrong Jr., Pres.
Founded: 1954. **Members:** 1,300. **Membership Dues:** individual, $20 (annual) ● $50 (triennial) ● household, $25 (annual) ● junior, $5 (annual). **Staff:** 1. **Budget:** $30,000. **Regional Groups:** 8. **Multinational. Description:** Amateur and professional growers of daffodils. Conducts educational programs by slide rental. **Libraries: Type:** lending; reference; not open to the public. **Holdings:** books, periodicals. **Subjects:** daffodils. **Awards:** Gold Medal. **Frequency:** annual. **Type:** medal. **Recipient:** for the improvement of Daffodil ● Silver Medal. **Frequency:** annual. **Type:** medal. **Recipient:** for service. **Committees:** Awards; Breeding and Selection; Miniatures; Research; Schools; Species Conservation. **Publications:** *Daffodil Data Bank*, annual. Illustrated, on CD-ROM, with approximately 4100 photos plus all information in data bank. **Price:** $36.00; $150.00 for CD-ROM. Alternate Formats: CD-ROM ● *Daffodil Journal*, quarterly. Provides information on daffodils and culture. **Price:** included in membership dues. ISSN: 0011-5290. **Circulation:** 1,300. **Advertising:** accepted ● *Daffodils to Show and Grow*, every 3-4 years. Directory. Highlights cultivars likely to be found in gardens, shows, and commerce. **Price:** $8.00 ● *Miniature Daffodil Identification in Color.* **Price:** $20.00 color photos. **Conventions/Meetings:** annual convention, with daffodil show (exhibits).

22001 ■ American Fuchsia Society (AFS)
c/o Judy Salome
6979 Clark Rd.
Paradise, CA 95969
Ph: (530)876-8517
E-mail: ejsalome@aol.com
URL: http://www.americanfuchsiasociety.org
Contact: Ms. Judy Bligh, Pres.
Founded: 1929. **Members:** 900. **Membership Dues:** individual, $19 (annual). **Staff:** 2. **Regional Groups:** 23. **Description:** Amateur gardeners, professional gardeners, and nurserymen. Promotes the culture and registration of fuchsias, their hybridizing, and exhibition in fairs. Collects and publishes information on the propagation and culture of fuchsias; offers workshops on culture techniques and subjects of special interest. Sponsors branch garden shows and competitions. Holds annual Fuchsia Judging School. **Libraries: Type:** reference. **Holdings:** 200. **Subjects:** culture, history, genus fuchsia. **Awards:** Achievement Award. **Type:** recognition. **Recipient:**

for outstanding service performed by a member in the field of service and/or fuchsia culture ● Longevity Award. **Type:** recognition ● Photography Awards. **Frequency:** annual. **Type:** recognition. **Frequency:** for accomplishments in photography. **Publications:** *American Fuchsia Society Bulletin*, bimonthly. Includes annual introductions of new varieties and annual International Edition. **Price:** included in membership dues. ISSN: 0194-3456. **Circulation:** 700. **Advertising:** accepted ● *Fuchsia Judging Manual*. **Conventions/Meetings:** biennial convention, fuchsia societies of West Coast rotate responsibility (exhibits) - held August or September of even years.

22002 ■ American Gourd Society (AGS)
PO Box 2186
Kokomo, IN 46904-2186
E-mail: rehmje@valkyrie.net
URL: http://americangourdsociety.org
Contact: Bob James, Pres.
Founded: 1970. **Members:** 4,000. **Membership Dues:** regular, in U.S., $15 (annual) ● regular, outside U.S., $22 (annual). **Staff:** 3. **Budget:** $60,000. **Regional Groups:** 17. **State Groups:** 14. **Local Groups:** 75. **Description:** Promotes gourdcraft and the raising and use of gourds for both decorative and practical purposes. Disseminates information on culture, harvesting, curing, uses of gourds for gourdcraft, and members' experiences with gourds. **Committees:** Executive. **Supersedes:** (1937) Gourd Society of America. **Publications:** *American Gourd Society—Bulletin*, quarterly. **Price:** $5.00/copy, plus shipping and handling. **Advertising:** accepted ● *The Gourd*, quarterly. Newsletter. Covers culture and crafting of gourds and uses for gourds. Contains information on gourd shows and displays, and sources of seeds and dry gourds. **Price:** included in membership dues. ISSN: 0888-5672. **Advertising:** accepted ● *Gourd Craft*. Book ● *The Gourd Journal*. Book. **Price:** $6.00. **Conventions/Meetings:** annual show, held in each state chapter (Florida, Indiana, Missouri, California, Illinois, Tennessee, Kentucky, Alabama, Texas, and North Carolina) - always first full weekend of October.

22003 ■ American Hemerocallis Society (AHS)
c/o Kevin P. Walek, Pres.
9122 John Way
Fairfax Station, VA 22039-3042
Ph: (703)798-5501
E-mail: president@daylilies.org
URL: http://www.daylilies.org
Contact: Kevin P. Walek, Pres.
Founded: 1946. **Members:** 8,500. **Membership Dues:** individual, $25 (annual) ● dual, $30 (annual) ● life, $750. **Staff:** 4. **Budget:** $200,000. **Regional Groups:** 15. **Local Groups:** 180. **Description:** Amateur and commercial growers of the genus Hemerocallis (daylily). Provides registration service for assignment and recording of cultivar names and color slide service. Conducts research on culture and improvement of the genus. Maintains biographical archives; compiles statistics. **Libraries:** **Type:** not open to the public. **Subjects:** daylilies. **Awards:** **Frequency:** annual. **Type:** recognition. **Recipient:** for individuals who have showed outstanding work in breeding improved varieties of Hemerocallis. **Committees:** Accredited Shows; Awards and Honors; Display Gardens; Exhibition; Judges Clinics; Popularity Poll; Publications; Publicity; Scientific; Slides and Video; Special Services. **Publications:** *Checklist of Registered Cultivars*, annual. Lists registrations. ● *Daylily Journal*, quarterly. Lists awards, honors and popularity poll results. **Price:** included in membership dues. **Circulation:** 10,000. **Advertising:** accepted. Also Cited As: *The Hemerocallis Journal* ● *Daylily Judges Handbook*, periodic ● *Illustrated Guide to Growing Daylilies*. Handbook. Contains information on growing, landscaping, and classifying daylilies. **Price:** $8.00 ● *Membership Roster*, biennial. Membership Directory ● *Regional Newsletter*, 2-4/year ● Also publishes checklist of all newly named clones (over 35,000) and specialty booklets. **Conventions/Meetings:** annual convention and meeting ● Flower Show.

22004 ■ American Hibiscus Society (AHS)
PO Box 1580
Venice, FL 34284-1580
Ph: (941)484-6459
E-mail: hibiscusfiend@mchsi.com
URL: http://www.americanhibiscus.org
Contact: Sam Anders, Pres.
Founded: 1950. **Members:** 2,000. **Membership Dues:** individual, $25-$35 (annual). **Local Groups:** 20. **Multinational. Description:** Amateur and commercial growers of hibiscus. Works to encourage and promote the development and improvement of the hibiscus. Names and registers new and known varieties. Conducts research, specialized education, and charitable programs; offers hibiscus gardener's service. **Awards:** Hibiscus of the Year Award. **Frequency:** annual. **Type:** recognition. **Computer Services:** database, Nomenclature. **Committees:** Nomenclature; Seed Bank; Seedling Evaluation; Slide Bank. **Publications:** *Hibiscus Handbook*. **Price:** $13.00 ● *Hibiscus Illustrated*. Catalog. **Price:** $10.00 ● *The Seed Pod*, quarterly. Newsletter. Contains articles for Hibiscus growers. Includes reports on Hibiscus shows, calendar of events, chapter shows dates, and obituaries. **Price:** included in membership dues. ISSN: 0745-3590. **Circulation:** 2,000. **Advertising:** accepted. **Conventions/Meetings:** annual convention, for members - usually third weekend of June.

22005 ■ American Horticultural Society (AHS)
7931 E Boulevard Dr.
Alexandria, VA 22308-1300
Ph: (703)768-5700
Free: (800)777-7931
Fax: (703)768-8700
E-mail: dhundley@ahs.org
URL: http://www.ahs.org
Contact: Deane Hundley, Pres.
Founded: 1922. **Members:** 35,000. **Membership Dues:** general, $35 (annual). **Staff:** 18. **Budget:** $2,500,000. **Description:** Represents amateur and professional gardeners. Aims to educate and inspire people of all ages to become successful and environmentally responsible gardeners by advancing the art and science of horticulture. Operates free seed exchange and gardeners' information service for members. Offers internships and children's services. **Libraries:** **Type:** reference. **Holdings:** 2,000. **Subjects:** gardening, horticulture. **Awards:** Great American Gardeners Awards. **Frequency:** annual. **Type:** recognition. **Recipient:** for outstanding achievements, excellence, and innovation in the art and science of horticulture. **Committees:** Awards and Citations; Communications; Development; Education; Membership. **Publications:** *AHS A-Z Encyclopedia of Garden Plants*. Book. **Price:** $80.00 for nonmembers; $50.00 for members ● *AHS Encyclopedia of Plants and Flowers*. Book. **Price:** $60.00 for nonmembers; $36.00 for members ● *AHS Great Plant Guide*. Book. **Price:** $30.00 for nonmembers; $18.00 for members ● *The American Gardener*, bimonthly. Magazine. Includes profiles of individual plant groups, and information about garden design, prominent horticulturists, plant research and hunting. **Price:** included in membership dues. ISSN: 1087-9978. **Circulation:** 35,000. **Advertising:** accepted ● Annual Report, annual. Alternate Formats: online. ● Also publishes other major reference books. **Conventions/Meetings:** annual Great American Gardeners - conference ● annual National Children and Youth Gardening Symposium, with K-12 educators and landscape designers promoting techniques, venues and ideas for developing gardening in the schools, communities and back yards (exhibits).

22006 ■ American Hosta Society (AHS)
c/o Sandie Markland, Membership Sec.
8702 Pinnacle Rock Ct.
Lorton, VA 22079-3029
Ph: (703)690-3021
E-mail: ahsmembershipsecretary@earthlink.net
URL: http://www.hosta.org
Contact: Mary Schwartzbauer, Pres.
Founded: 1968. **Members:** 3,422. **Membership Dues:** individual (in U.S.), $25 (annual) ● family (in U.S.), $29 (annual) ● individual (in Canada), $39 (annual) ● family (in Canada), $43 (annual) ● individual (in Europe), $51 (annual) ● family (in Europe), $55 (annual) ● individual (in Asia, Japan, Australia, New Zealand), $59 (annual) ● family (in Asia, Japan, Australia, New Zealand), $62 (annual) ● life (in U.S.), $500 ● life (in Canada), $780 ● life (in Europe), $1,020 ● life (in Asia, Japan, Australia, New Zealand), $1,180. **Staff:** 6. **Budget:** $151,206. **Regional Groups:** 8. **State Groups:** 50. **Local Groups:** 47. **Description:** Individuals and organizations interested in growing hostas (a plant also known as the plantainlily). Promotes knowledge concerning plants and registers new plants. Maintains speakers' bureau, slide file, and collections at Minnesota Landscape Arboretum and other arboretums. Conducts research. **Libraries:** **Type:** reference. **Holdings:** 34; archival material. **Subjects:** hostas, gardens. **Awards:** Alex J. Summers Distinguished Merit Award. **Frequency:** annual. **Type:** recognition. **Recipient:** for a named Hosta ● Big Bucks Award. **Type:** recognition. **Recipient:** for leaves (Hosta) ● Cut Leaf Show Awards. **Frequency:** annual. **Type:** recognition ● Tour Garden Awards. **Type:** recognition. **Computer Services:** Mailing lists, of members. **Committees:** Auction of Plants; Audit and Finance; Awards and Honors; Bylaws and Standing Rules; Classification Checklist; Convention; Display Garden; Exhibition; Exhibitions/Leaf Show; Garden Plant design; Historian; Membership/Expulsion; Memorials; Miscellaneous Plant sales; New and Current Publications; Newsletter Coordination; Nomenclature; Ombudsman; Parliamentarian; Popularity Poll; Protocol and Procedures; Publicity; Registrar; Round Robins; E-mail; Scientific Meeting; Slide Programs; Special Service. **Affiliated With:** British Hosta and Hemerocallis Society. **Publications:** *American Hosta Society E-Yearbook and Membership Directory*, annual ● *Journal of American Hosta Society*, 3/year. Covers society news and the growing of hosta plants. Includes membership list and hosta registry. **Price:** included in membership dues. **Circulation:** 3,422. **Advertising:** accepted. **Conventions/Meetings:** annual competition and tour, garden bus tours (exhibits) ● annual convention.

22007 ■ American Hydrangea Society (AHS)
PO Box 986
Grayson, GA 30017
E-mail: pgryan@acninc.net
URL: http://www.americanhydrangeasociety.org
Contact: Genia Ryan, Pres.
Founded: 1994. **Members:** 560. **Membership Dues:** individual, $20 (annual) ● household, $25 (annual). **Description:** Represents growers and other individuals with an interest in the genus Hydrangea. Promotes the study of the cultivation of Hydrangea and related plant species. Conducts educational programs and serves as a clearinghouse on Hydrangea. Hosts members only garden tour each June. **Computer Services:** Information services, about the society. **Publications:** *AHS Newsletter*, quarterly. **Conventions/Meetings:** meeting - 3/year - January, April, and October.

22008 ■ American Iris Society (AIS)
c/o Tom Gormley, Membership Sec.
PO Box 28
Cedar Hill, MO 63016-0028
Ph: (636)274-6149
Fax: (636)274-6149
E-mail: aismemsec@earthlink.net
URL: http://www.irises.org
Contact: Tom Gormley, Membership Sec.
Founded: 1920. **Members:** 7,500. **Membership Dues:** single (in U.S., Canada and Mexico), $25 (annual) ● dual (in U.S., Canada and Mexico), single (overseas), $30 (annual) ● single - life, $450 ● dual - life, $545 ● dual (overseas), $35 (annual) ● youth, $5 (annual). **Regional Groups:** 24. **Local Groups:** 170. **Multinational. Description:** Represents horticulturists, commercial dealers, organizations, and amateurs interested in the genus Iris. Collects and publishes data concerning the breeding, classification, cultivation, exhibition, and history of Irises. Acts as international registration authority for the genus

Iris. Trains and accredits judges and accredits Iris shows. Supplies test garden and public planting services; supports research, education, and conservation of the Iris. Conducts seminars and operates speakers' bureau. Maintains historical archives open by appointment to students, researchers, and hybridizers. Sponsors competitions. **Libraries: Type:** not open to the public. **Awards:** Distinguished Service Medal. **Frequency:** annual. **Type:** medal. **Recipient:** for outstanding service ● Dykes Memorial. **Frequency:** annual. **Type:** medal. **Recipient:** for highest percentage of votes received from accredited judges ● Hybridizers Medal. **Frequency:** annual. **Type:** medal. **Recipient:** to hybridizers' outstanding work with Iris. **Committees:** Awards; Exhibitions; Historical; Judges and Judges Training; Slides; Test Gardens; Youth. **Programs:** Round Robin. **Publications:** *Basic Iris Culture.* Pamphlet. Presents a how-to reference on irises. **Price:** $1.25 ● *Bulletin of the American Iris Society,* quarterly. Journal. **Price:** free for members. ISSN: 0747-4172. **Circulation:** 6,500. **Advertising:** accepted ● *Judges Handbook* ● *Registrations and Introductions,* annual ● *Ten-Year Checklist (1990-1999)* ● *The World of Irises.* Serves as a basic reference on Irises and Iris growing. **Price:** $27.00. ISSN: 0747-4172 ● *Membership Directory,* periodic. **Conventions/Meetings:** annual board meeting - 2007 Nov. 2-4, Raleigh, NC; 2008 Oct. 31-Nov. 2, Tulsa, OK ● annual convention - 2008 Apr. 14-19, Austin, TX; 2009 May 11-16, Kansas City, MO.

22009 ■ American Ivy Society (AIS)
PO Box 2123
Naples, FL 34106-2123
Ph: (845)688-5318
Fax: (845)688-5318
E-mail: info@ivy.org
URL: http://www.ivy.org
Contact: Suzanne Pierot, Pres.
Founded: 1973. **Members:** 400. **Membership Dues:** general, $20 (annual) ● commercial, $50 (annual) ● institution, $30 (annual) ● family, $25 (annual). **Regional Groups:** 2. **Description:** Represents horticulturists, botanists, nurserymen, garden experts, and home gardeners interested in the cultivation and propagation of ivy and topiary. Aims to bring order to the naming of various cultivars of Hedera (ivy). Acts as the international registrar for the genus Hedera. Provides information and identification service; maintains research center in Dayton, OH, regional ivy standard reference collection at Lewis Ginteo Botanical Garden, Richmond, VA, and display collection at American Horticultural Society Headquarters in Alexandria, VA. Operates speakers' bureau. **Publications:** *Between the Vines,* 3/year. Newsletter. ISSN: 1051-8959 ● *Care of Ivies* ● *Characteristics, Culture, and Uses of Winter-hardy Hedera Species and Cultivars* ● *Index to Ivy Journal Photographs and Concise Descriptions 1980-1984* ● *Index to Ivy Photographs and Concise Descriptions 1985-1994* ● *Ivy Bibliography* ● *Ivy Journal,* annual. Contains history, terminology and photographs of ivies, articles on ivy culture and unusual varieties, and information of membership activities. **Price:** included in membership dues; $30.00 /year for institutions. ISSN: 0882-4142. **Circulation:** 400. Also Cited As: *Ivy Bulletin 1975-1981* ● *Preliminary Checklist of Cultivated Hedera* ● *Standards of Judging Ivies* ● *Untersuchungen zur Entstehung und Stabilitat der Panaschuerungen bei Hedera.* **Conventions/Meetings:** annual convention.

22010 ■ American Pentemon Society (APS)
c/o Dwayne Dickerson, Membership Sec.
600 S Cherry St., Ste.127
Denver, CO 80246
E-mail: parsont@peak.org
URL: http://www.penstemon.org
Contact: Dwayne Dickerson, Membership Sec.
Founded: 1946. **Members:** 500. **Membership Dues:** regular, in U.S. and Canada, $10 (annual) ● overseas, $15 (annual). **Description:** Home gardeners, professional nurserymen, and hybridizers interested in the genus Penstemon (wildflowers, also known as beard tongues) and new hybrids. Conducts seed exchange to distribute desirable species and new

hybrid strains to members. Compiles botanical studies and keys to identification. Operates 14 correspondence circles (round robins) in which members share experiences and discuss all phases of penstemon culture. **Committees:** Preservation; Round Robins; Seed Exchange. **Publications:** *American Penstemon Society—Bulletin,* semiannual. Provides technical advice and information on members' gardens. Includes manual for beginners. **Price:** included in membership dues. **Advertising:** accepted ● *List and Description of Named Cultivars in the Genus Penstemon* ● *Manual for Beginners with Penstemons.* Pamphlet ● *Penstemon Field Identifiers* ● *Penstemon Nomenclature* ● Also publishes botanical studies, technical booklets on parts of the genus, and identification charts. **Conventions/Meetings:** annual conference.

22011 ■ American Peony Society (APS)
c/o Claudia Schroer, Membership Sec.
713 White Oak Ln.
Kansas City, MO 64116-4607
Fax: (816)459-7430
E-mail: cjschroer@kc.rr.com
URL: http://www.americanpeonysociety.org
Contact: Claudia Schroer, Membership Sec.
Founded: 1903. **Membership Dues:** individual, $20 (annual). **Description:** Avocational growers of peonies. Registers new varieties. Serves as an International Registrar of Peonies. **Publications:** *American Peony Society Bulletin,* quarterly ● *Peony Handbook.* **Price:** $5.00. **Conventions/Meetings:** annual conference and seminar (exhibits).

22012 ■ American Primrose Society (APS)
c/o Julia Haldorson, Treas.
PO Box 210913
Auke Bay, AK 99821
E-mail: treasurer@americanprimrosesociety.org
URL: http://www.americanprimrosesociety.org
Contact: Julia Haldorson, Treas.
Founded: 1940. **Members:** 700. **Membership Dues:** individual, $25 (annual) ● individual, $70 (triennial) ● individual overseas, $32 (annual). **Staff:** 10. **State Groups:** 6. **Local Groups:** 2. **Multinational. Description:** Represents gardeners. Aims to popularize primulas and to establish standardized nomenclature of species and hybrids and standard rules of judging. Sponsors annual seed exchange. Conducts schools for judging of primrose plants. Maintains speakers' bureau. **Libraries: Type:** reference. **Holdings:** 60; audiovisuals, books, monographs. **Subjects:** Primulas. **Awards: Type:** recognition. **Publications:** *Primrose,* quarterly. Journal. Contains articles on the propagation and culture of plants of the genus Primula. Includes abstracts, chapter news, membership list, and show reports. **Price:** included in membership dues; $25.00/year in U.S. and Canada; $32.00/year outside U.S. and Canada. ISSN: 0162-6671. **Circulation:** 700. **Advertising:** accepted. **Conventions/Meetings:** annual banquet (exhibits) ● competition ● annual National Primrose Show - always spring.

22013 ■ American Rhododendron Society (ARS)
PO Box 525
Niagara Falls, NY 14304
Ph: (416)424-1942
E-mail: lauragrant@arsoffice.org
URL: http://www.rhododendron.org
Contact: Laura Grant, Exec. Dir.
Founded: 1945. **Members:** 5,000. **Membership Dues:** individual, $35 (annual) ● family, $40 (annual) ● commercial, corporate, $90 (annual) ● sustaining, $50 (annual) ● sponsoring, $100 (annual) ● life individual, $1,000. **Staff:** 2. **Budget:** $170,000. **State Groups:** 72. **Multinational. Description:** Amateur and professional growers of rhododendrons and azaleas. Promotes and develops interest in the growing and culture of rhododendrons and azaleas through information dissemination. Registers names of new hybrids for North America only. Offers specialized education program; compiles statistics; registers names of new clonal selections. Maintains Rhododendron Research Foundation and seed exchange

for members interested in propagation. **Libraries: Type:** not open to the public. **Subjects:** rhododendron, azalea. **Awards:** Gold, Silver, Bronze. **Frequency:** annual. **Type:** recognition. **Recipient:** for volunteerism. **Computer Services:** database. **Committees:** Honors-Awards; Research; Seed Exchange. **Publications:** *American Rhododendron Society— Journal,* quarterly. Contains information on the growth and care of the flowering plant rhododendron, including soil pH levels, landscape design, and planting. **Price:** included in membership dues. ISSN: 0745-7839. **Advertising:** accepted. Alternate Formats: online ● *The Fundamentals of Rhododendron and Azalea Culture.* Booklet ● *Rhododendron and Azalea Care Guide.* Brochures ● Handbook, periodic. **Conventions/Meetings:** annual competition (exhibits) ● annual conference - usually April or May.

22014 ■ American Rose Society (ARS)
8877 Jefferson Paige Rd.
PO Box 30000
Shreveport, LA 71119
Ph: (318)938-5402
Fax: (318)938-5402
E-mail: ars@ars-hq.org
URL: http://www.ars.org
Contact: Michael Craft, Exec. Dir.
Founded: 1892. **Members:** 23,000. **Membership Dues:** individual, $37 (annual) ● senior, $34 (annual) ● individual, $100 (triennial) ● senior joint (age 65 and above), $122 (triennial) ● senior joint, $47 (annual) ● senior (age 65 and above), $92 (triennial) ● corporate, $250 (annual) ● life, $1,000 ● regular, outside U.S., $47 (annual) ● Canadian, $42 (annual) ● life, senior (age 65 and above), $500 ● joint, $50 (annual). **Staff:** 22. **Budget:** $1,500,000. **Local Groups:** 358. **Description:** Amateur gardeners, commercial growers, related dealers, and local rose societies and garden clubs. Establishes rules and sponsors national and district rose shows; conducts school for and accredits rose show judges; sponsors research on rose growing problems; conducts a rose name registration system; provides rose growing/culture referrals. **Libraries: Type:** reference. **Holdings:** 3,000; books, periodicals. **Subjects:** rose growing and gardening. **Awards:** Award of Excellence. **Frequency:** annual. **Type:** recognition. **Recipient:** for a miniature rose novelty, bud form, flower form, color opening, color finishing, substance, habit, quantity of blooms, vigor, foliage, disease/insect resistance. **Computer Services:** Mailing lists, of members. **Committees:** National Miniature Rose Test Program; Old Garden Rose; Program Service; Public Gardens; Rose Registration. **Programs:** National Trial Grounds. **Absorbed:** (1989) American Rose Foundation. **Publications:** *American Rose Annual,* annual. Magazine. Covers all aspects of rose growing in extended format of magazine. **Price:** $10.00. ISSN: 0003-0899. **Circulation:** 23,000. **Advertising:** accepted ● *Handbook for Selecting Roses,* annual ● *Modern Roses,* approximately every 5 years ● Bulletins. Covers exhibiting, miniature roses, rose arrangements and old garden roses. **Conventions/Meetings:** semiannual convention, educational/rose show (exhibits) - always spring and fall ● show.

22015 ■ Aril Society International (ASI)
c/o Donald Eaves, Gen. Sec.
1102 County Rd. 192
Carbon, TX 76435
E-mail: sjordan@unm.edu
URL: http://www.arilsociety.org
Contact: Patricia Toolan, Pres.
Founded: 1956. **Members:** 300. **Membership Dues:** single, $10 (annual) ● single, $28 (triennial) ● family, $13 (annual). **Staff:** 24. **Description:** Persons interested in the preservation of native species of aril and aril hybrid irises and crossing these with other bearded irises to create "a more gardenable plant." Disseminates information concerning rare arils and methods of growing them. Offers programs to educate gardeners and judges. Conducts research into records of botanists who discovered the rare arils. Supports an annual plant sale of aril and arilbred cultivars. **Libraries: Type:** reference. **Holdings:** 37; audiovisuals. **Subjects:** botany, iris. **Awards:** Clar-

ence G. White Medal. **Frequency:** annual. **Type:** medal. **Recipient:** to IRIS voted best in class by majority of the judges ● William Mohr Medal. **Frequency:** annual. **Type:** medal. **Recipient:** to IRIS voted best in class by majority of the judges. **Committees:** Display Gardens; Plant Sale; Scientific. **Also Known As:** The Aril Society. **Publications:** *Aril Society International—Newsletter*, triennial. **Price:** included in membership dues. **Circulation:** 300. **Advertising:** accepted ● *Aril Society International—Yearbook*, annual. Contains articles on growing Arils and Arilbreds, information on membership activities, and an annual report. **Price:** included in membership dues; $11.00/copy for nonmembers. **Circulation:** 350. **Advertising:** accepted ● *Comprehensive Membership/Cultural.* Booklets. **Conventions/Meetings:** annual meeting, for selling plants ● annual meeting, with board meetings held by mail (exhibits).

22016 ■ Azalea Society of America (ASA)
c/o John Brown, Sec.
1000 Moody Bridge Rd.
Cleveland, SC 29635-9789
Ph: (864)836-6898
E-mail: jbrown51@bellsouth.net
URL: http://www.azaleas.org
Contact: John Brown, Sec.
Founded: 1977. **Members:** 815. **Membership Dues:** regular, $25 (annual) ● contributing, $50 (annual) ● sustaining, $100 (annual) ● endowment, $200 (annual) ● life, $500. **Local Groups:** 7. **Description:** Collectors and hybridizers interested in improving and sharing their experiences on techniques of hybridization, propagation, and culture of azaleas. Aids in standardizing the identification of azaleas and the registration of new hybrids. Sponsors educational seminars and lectures as well as cutting auctions, plant sales, and other activities. Sponsors competitions. **Awards:** Distinguished Service Award. **Frequency:** annual. **Type:** recognition ● F.P. Lee Commendation. **Frequency:** annual. **Type:** recognition. **Computer Services:** Mailing lists. **Publications:** *The Azalean*, quarterly. Journal. **Price:** included in membership dues. **Circulation:** 820. **Advertising:** accepted ● *Roster*, semiannual ● *Bulletin*, periodic. **Conventions/Meetings:** annual meeting.

22017 ■ Bonsai Clubs International (BCI)
PO Box 8445
Metairie, LA 70011-8445
Ph: (504)832-8071
Fax: (504)834-2298
E-mail: bcibizness@aol.com
URL: http://www.bonsai-bci.com
Contact: Donna Banting, Managing Ed.
Founded: 1958. **Members:** 2,500. **Membership Dues:** individual, club, federation, $36 (annual) ● youth under 18 years of age, $20 (annual) ● silver, $100 (annual) ● gold, $500 (annual) ● platinum, $1,200 (annual) ● life, $1,200. **Staff:** 1. **Budget:** $105,000. **Regional Groups:** 17. **National Groups:** 344. **Multinational. Description:** Represents the interests of individuals and clubs interested in practicing bonsai (the art of growing miniature trees in containers). Assists bonsai clubs and educates the public through publications, programs, activities, ideas, and educational exhibitions. **Awards:** Ben Oki International Design Award. **Frequency:** annual. **Type:** monetary. **Recipient:** for nonprofessional members ● Ismail Saleh Award. **Frequency:** annual. **Type:** monetary. **Recipient:** to member ● Lertre Award. **Frequency:** annual. **Type:** monetary. **Recipient:** to member ● Pedro Morales Latin American Design Award. **Frequency:** annual. **Type:** monetary. **Recipient:** for nonprofessional members. **Telecommunication Services:** electronic mail, bcieditor@aol.com ● electronic mail, ic.su@msa.hinet.net. **Committees:** Cultural; Educational. **Formerly:** (1967) Bonsai Clubs Association. **Publications:** *Bonsai Magazine*, bimonthly. Serves as the official publication. **Price:** $9.00/issue. ISSN: 1068-6193. **Circulation:** 3,000. **Advertising:** accepted. Alternate Formats: CD-ROM; online ● *How to Start and Maintain a Bonsai Club* ● *The International Bonsai Teachers Register* ● *Program Ideas.* Includes a list of activity

programs. **Conventions/Meetings:** annual convention, with demonstrations, tours (exhibits).

22018 ■ Bromeliad Society International (BSI)
c/o Joyce Brehm, Pres.
5088 Dawne St.
San Diego, CA 92117-1352
E-mail: membership@bsi.org
URL: http://www.bsi.org
Contact: Joyce Brehm, Pres.
Founded: 1950. **Members:** 1,610. **Membership Dues:** individual (in U.S.), $30 (annual) ● dual (in U.S.), $35 (annual) ● society/institution (in U.S.), $30 (annual) ● commercial (in U.S.), $60 (annual) ● fellowship (in U.S.), $45 (annual) ● life (in U.S.), $800 ● individual, society/institution (international), $40 (annual) ● dual (international), $45 (annual) ● commercial (international), $70 (annual) ● fellowship (international), $55 (annual) ● life (international), $800. **Staff:** 2. **Budget:** $80,000. **Local Groups:** 90. **Description:** Represents persons interested in the growing and propagation of the bromeliad family of plants (herblike plants that include the pineapple, Spanish moss, and ornamentals). Encourages exhibitions of bromeliads and sponsors they're planting in botanical gardens and public parks. Sponsors internships at Bromeliad Identification Center. **Awards: Type:** scholarship. **Computer Services:** database, bromeliad identification and hybrid registration ● mailing lists. **Committees:** Bromeliad Identification; Conservation; Hybrid Registration; Judging Accreditation and Handbook; Slides. **Formerly:** (2003) Bromeliad Society. **Publications:** *Bromeliad Society Journal*, bimonthly. Provides information on the bromeliad family of plants for both hobby growers and scientific researchers. Includes index. **Price:** included in membership dues. ISSN: 0090-8738. **Circulation:** 1,600. **Advertising:** accepted ● *Colorful Bromeliads.* Book ● *Hybrid Checklist* ● *Index to Journal Articles*, annual ● *Roster of BSI Members*, biennial. Membership Directory. **Price:** included in membership dues. **Circulation:** 1,600. **Advertising:** accepted ● Also publishes glossary and cultural handbook. **Conventions/Meetings:** biennial World Conference.

22019 ■ Cactus and Succulent Society of America (CSSA)
c/o Clifford Meng, Treas.
PO Box 2615
Pahrump, NV 89041-2615
Ph: (775)751-1320
Fax: (775)751-1357
E-mail: cssa@viawestdu.net
URL: http://www.cssainc.org
Contact: Clifford Meng, Treas.
Founded: 1929. **Members:** 3,000. **Membership Dues:** domestic, $45 (annual) ● regular, outside U.S. (Allen air drop), $50 (annual) ● regular, outside U.S. (via airmail), $90 (annual) ● spouse/partner, $10 (annual) ● life, $750. **Local Groups:** 81. **Description:** Botanists, nurserymen, and hobbyists interested in cactus, other succulents, and desert plants. Works to: unite persons with a common hobby; help members grow and enjoy unusual plants; aid in the conservation of such flora. Disseminates information on the culture and naming of cacti and other succulents. Operates speakers' bureau; conducts research and educational programs. **Libraries: Type:** reference. **Holdings:** archival material, books, monographs, periodicals. **Subjects:** cactus, succulents. **Awards:** Fellow Award. **Frequency:** annual. **Type:** scholarship ● Special Service Award. **Type:** scholarship. **Publications:** *Cactus and Succulent Journal*, bimonthly. **Price:** $35.00 /year for nonmembers; included in membership dues. **Circulation:** 3,000. **Advertising:** accepted ● *Haseltonia*, annual. Yearbook. **Price:** $32.00. **Circulation:** 2,000 ● *To the Point*, bimonthly. Newsletter. **Conventions/Meetings:** biennial convention (exhibits) - usually June, July or August ● annual Show and Sale - competition, features competitive show plants (exhibits).

22020 ■ Combined North American Cottage Garden Society and North American Dianthus Society (NACGS/NADS)
Address Unknown since 2007
Founded: 1991. **Members:** 200. **Membership Dues:** individuals in U.S., $15 (annual) ● individuals in

Canada and Mexico, $18 (annual) ● outside North America, $20 (annual) ● lifetime, $240. **Staff:** 1. **Budget:** $2,000. **Multinational. Description:** Individuals with an interest in the plant genus Dianthus, which includes carnations and sweet williams. Promotes professional and recreational cultivation of Dianthus. Serves as a clearinghouse on the genus; provides support and assistance to growers and arboreta; makes available seed distribution service. Sponsors competitions; maintains speakers' bureau. **Awards:** Golden Bill. **Frequency:** annual. **Type:** recognition. **Recipient:** outstanding Dianthus cultivar. **Formerly:** (1999) American Dianthus Society; (2003) North American Dianthis Society. **Publications:** *Gilliflower Times*, quarterly. Newsletter. Devoted to the culture and history of the genus Dianthus, including pinks, carnations, sweet williams, sweet johns, and their relatives and cultivars. ISSN: 1074-0074. **Circulation:** 200. **Advertising:** accepted. **Conventions/Meetings:** biennial board meeting.

22021 ■ Cymbidium Society of America (CSA)
c/o Jose Rodriguez, Membership Sec.
172 River Run Cir.
Sacramento, CA 95833
Ph: (916)927-1810
E-mail: jose.j.rodriguez@spk01.usace.army.mil
URL: http://cymbidium.org
Contact: Jose Rodriguez, Membership Sec.
Founded: 1946. **Members:** 1,000. **Membership Dues:** active, $30 (annual). **Staff:** 25. **State Groups:** 8. **Local Groups:** 8. **Multinational. Description:** Avocational and commercial growers of cymbidium and other outdoor-grown orchids. Seeks to stimulate and extend the appreciation of cymbidiums, paphiopedilums, and other cool-growing orchids. Strives to develop, acquire, and disseminate information concerning these beautiful and enchanting orchids. **Awards:** Gold, Silver, and Bronze Medals. **Type:** recognition. **Recipient:** for flower quality. **Committees:** Awards; Cymbidium Congress. **Publications:** *CSA Journal*, bimonthly. **Price:** included in membership dues. ISSN: 1541-5341. **Circulation:** 1,000. **Advertising:** accepted ● Membership Directory, periodic. Contains basic information, names and addresses of members. **Conventions/Meetings:** annual Cymbidium Congress - congress and meeting, in conjunction with the Santa Barbara International Orchid Show - usually mid-March in Santa Barbara, CA.

22022 ■ Dwarf Iris Society of America (DISA)
c/o Hugh Thurman, Pres.
521 Kickapoo Trail
Frankfort, KY 40601-1716
E-mail: dwarfiris.soc@www4.net
URL: http://dir.gardenweb.com/directory/dis
Contact: Hugh Thurman, Pres.
Founded: 1950. **Members:** 200. **Description:** Growers, hybridizers, and fanciers of dwarf-bearded irises. Seeks to popularize and create improved varieties of the dwarf-bearded iris. Maintains a collection of portfolios; locates historic varieties. A section of the American Iris Society (see separate entry). **Libraries: Type:** reference. **Holdings:** audiovisuals. **Affiliated With:** American Iris Society. **Publications:** *Dwarf Iris Society Newsletter*, quarterly. Covers membership activities; includes varietal comments and obituaries. **Price:** included in membership dues. **Conventions/Meetings:** annual conference ● annual meeting and symposium.

22023 ■ Epiphyllum Society of America (ESA)
PO Box 1395
Monrovia, CA 91017-1395
E-mail: info@epiphyllumsociety.org
URL: http://www.epiphyllumsociety.org
Contact: Mrs. Patricia Ballard, Membership Sec.
Founded: 1940. **Members:** 350. **Membership Dues:** regular, in U.S., $17 (annual) ● regular, in Canada and Mexico, $20 (annual) ● in other country, $25 (annual). **Regional Groups:** 4. **National Groups:** 5. **Description:** Epiphyllum fanciers and commercial dealers. Collects, studies, and grows the epiphyl-

lums, both the true species and the hybrids and the closely allied species of cacti. As official International Registration Authority (IRA), the society compiles directory of correct names and detailed descriptions of the hybrids together with their synonyms and publishes an international registry. **Libraries: Type:** reference. **Awards: Type:** recognition. **Publications:** *The Directory of Species and Hybrids*, annual. Includes addenda to editions reissued every six years. **Price:** $19.00 for members in U.S. (direct mail); $32.00 for nonmembers in U.S. (direct mail); $22.00 for members in Canada and Mexico (direct mail); $35.00 for nonmembers in Canada and Mexico (direct mail). **Circulation:** 450 ● *Epiphyllum Bulletin*, quarterly. **Price:** available to members only. **Advertising:** accepted. **Conventions/Meetings:** annual Cut Flower Show and Plant Sale - always May ● monthly meeting - except January.

22024 ■ Garden Club of America (GCA)
14 E 60th St., 3rd Fl.
New York, NY 10022-7147
Ph: (212)753-8287
Fax: (212)753-0134
E-mail: info@gcamerica.org
URL: http://www.gcamerica.org
Contact: Millie Roman, Exec. Admin.
Founded: 1913. **Members:** 17,000. **Staff:** 7. **Budget:** $1,500,000. **Local Groups:** 195. **Description:** Amateur gardeners. Seeks to stimulate the knowledge and love of gardening among amateurs, aid in the protection of native plants and birds, and encourage civic planting. **Libraries: Type:** reference. **Holdings:** 4,000. **Awards:** GCA Award in Coastal Wetland Studies. **Frequency:** annual. **Type:** grant. **Recipient:** to graduate students pursuing advanced degrees in coastal wetlands science ● GCA Awards for Summer Environmental Studies. **Frequency:** annual. **Type:** monetary. **Recipient:** for college students to pursue study following their freshman, sophomore, or junior year ● GCA Awards in Tropical Biology. **Frequency:** annual. **Type:** grant. **Recipient:** to PhD candidates; selects two per year ● GCA Fellowship in Ecological Restoration. **Frequency:** annual. **Type:** fellowship. **Recipient:** to graduate students pursuing an advanced degree ● GCA Interchange Fellowship and Martin McLaren Scholarship. **Type:** fellowship. **Recipient:** to college graduates who have earned a BS or BA degree ● GCA Summer Scholarship in Field Botany. **Frequency:** annual. **Type:** scholarship. **Recipient:** to college undergraduates following their freshman year and graduate students up to the Masters degree. **Publications:** Bulletin, bimonthly. **Conventions/Meetings:** annual meeting.

22025 ■ Garden Writers Association (GWA)
10210 Leatherleaf Ct.
Manassas, VA 20111
Ph: (703)257-1032
Fax: (703)257-0213
E-mail: info@gardenwriters.org
URL: http://www.gwaa.org
Contact: Robert LaGasse, Exec. Dir.
Founded: 1948. **Members:** 1,800. **Membership Dues:** active, associate, $85 (annual) ● student, $25 (annual) ● allied (White, Green), $275-$500 (annual) ● allied (Red, Yellow, Blue), $1,000-$5,000 (annual). **Staff:** 2. **Budget:** $200,000. **Description:** Professional newspaper and periodical garden writers; garden photographers; radio and television broadcasters; book authors in horticultural and allied fields and other various garden communicators. Maintains Talent Directory Service, which refers requests from editors to qualified writers and photographers. Conducts tours. **Awards:** Quill and Trowel Communications Award. **Frequency:** annual. **Type:** recognition. **Computer Services:** Online services, speakers' bureau, bookstore. **Programs:** Plant A Row for the Hungry. **Subgroups:** Garden Writers Foundation. **Formerly:** (2003) Garden Writers Association of America. **Publications:** *Garden Trends*, monthly. Newsletter. **Price:** $99.00 for members; $150.00 for nonmembers. **Alternate Formats:** online ● *Garden Writers Association of America—Membership Directory*, annual. Includes calendar of events. **Circulation:** 1,800. **Advertising:** accepted ● *GWAA News-*

letter, bimonthly. Includes calendar of events and listing of new books. **Price:** included in membership dues; $80.00 /year for institutions. **Advertising:** accepted ● *Quill and Trowel Newsletter*, bimonthly. Includes news on writers' rights and intellectual property protections. **Advertising:** accepted. Alternate Formats: online. **Conventions/Meetings:** symposium - 3/year ● annual symposium, educational seminar with local garden tours (exhibits) ● trade show.

22026 ■ The Gardeners of America (TGOA)
PO Box 241
Johnston, IA 50131-6245
Ph: (515)278-0295
Fax: (515)278-6245
E-mail: tgoasecy@dwx.com
URL: http://www.tgoa-mgca.org
Contact: Dale Davies, Pres.
Founded: 1932. **Members:** 5,400. **Membership Dues:** individual, $25-$35 (annual) ● 2 person at same address, $30 (annual). **Staff:** 2. **Regional Groups:** 14. **National Groups:** 79. **Description:** Professional and home gardeners. Sponsors local beautification programs and flower and vegetable judging school. Offers consultation services on horticulture. Provides judging training. Sponsors gardening programs for youth and the elderly, including Gardening From The Heart, a program for the disadvantaged. Sponsors annual Giant Sunflower and Big Pumpkin Contests for youth 16-years-old and younger. **Libraries: Type:** reference. **Holdings:** 2,000; audiovisuals. **Subjects:** plants, flowers, landscaping. **Awards: Type:** recognition. **Recipient:** for individuals who have demonstrated outstanding work in horticulture in a spirit of service ● **Frequency:** annual. **Type:** recognition. **Recipient:** for winners of annual photo contest ● **Type:** recognition. **Recipient:** for contributors of outstanding articles printed in club or gardening literature ● **Type:** recognition. **Recipient:** for participants in garden shows ● **Frequency:** annual. **Type:** scholarship. **Recipient:** for college scholars. **Committees:** Awards; Book Review; Building and Grounds; Calendar; Environmental Issues; Gardening from the Heart; National Beautification; Newclubs; Newsletters; Photography; Publicity/Membership; Website; Youth Educational Gardening. **Formerly:** (1992) Men's Garden Clubs of America. **Publications:** *Gardener*, bimonthly. Magazine. Includes award winning plants, book lists, calendar of events, member profiles, and new products. **Price:** included in membership dues; $20.00 /year for nonmembers. ISSN: 0016-464X. **Circulation:** 4,800. **Advertising:** accepted ● Directory, annual. **Conventions/Meetings:** annual convention - usually summer.

22027 ■ Gesneriad Hybridizers Association (GHA)
1122 E Pike St.
Seattle, WA 98122-3916
E-mail: ombudsman@gesneriadsociety.org
URL: http://www.aggs.org
Contact: Susan Grose, Ombudsman
Founded: 1977. **Members:** 300. **Membership Dues:** in U.S., $25 (annual) ● outside U.S., $30 (annual). **Description:** Commercial and amateur hybridizers of plants and those interested in the Gesneriaceae plant family. Facilitates the exchange of information regarding gesneriad hybridization and its results. Compiles statistics. **Awards:** Best New Introduction. **Type:** recognition. **Recipient:** for the individual presenting the best new hybrid. **Publications:** *CrossWords*, 3/year. Newsletter. Provides information, research results, and suggestions on gesneriad hybridization. Contains association news and calendar of events. **Price:** included in membership dues. **Circulation:** 300. **Conventions/Meetings:** annual convention (exhibits) - always July.

22028 ■ Gesneriad Society
c/o Bob Clark, Membership Chm.
1122 E Pike St.
PMB 637
Seattle, WA 98122-3916

E-mail: ombudsman@gesneriadsociety.org
URL: http://www.aggs.org
Contact: Bob Clark, Membership Chm.
Founded: 1950. **Members:** 2,000. **Membership Dues:** individual in U.S., $25 (annual) ● family in U.S., $26 (annual) ● sustaining in U.S., $35 (annual) ● research in U.S., $50 (annual) ● life (in U.S.), $375 ● individual outside U.S., $30 (annual) ● family outside U.S., $31 (annual) ● sustaining outside U.S., $40 (annual) ● research outside U.S., $55 (annual) ● life (outside U.S.), $450. **Budget:** $30,000. **Regional Groups:** 40. **Multinational. Description:** Represents amateur and semi-professional gardeners who grow gloxinias or related plants indoors in a window garden, under fluorescent lights, or in home greenhouses. Provides information on new and known gesneriads. Funds research on gesneriads and related topics; seeks to educate the public about gesneriads and their culture. Distributes rare and unusual gesneriads through seed fund. Facilitates the exchange of information by circulating "round robins" in which members write about their plants. Maintains lending library of books and slide programs on gardening. **Libraries: Type:** not open to the public. **Holdings:** books, periodicals. **Subjects:** gesneriads. **Awards: Frequency:** annual. **Type:** recognition. **Computer Services:** Mailing lists. **Committees:** Archives; Awards; Awards of Appreciation; Botanical Review; Conventions; Endowment Fund; Gesneriad Register; Historian; Insurance; International Register; Judging; Library and Education; Parliamentarian; Photography Properties; Publicity Membership Promotion; Research Fund; Round Robins; Seed Fund; Shows and Judging; Standing Rules. **Subgroups:** Gesneriad Hybridizers Association (see separate entry). **Formerly:** American Gloxina Society; (2006) American Gloxinia and Gesneriad Society. **Publications:** *Appraisal*, 3/year. Newsletter. For judges. **Advertising:** accepted ● *Crosswords*. Newsletter. For hybridizers. **Price:** $8.00/year ● *Gesneriad Register* ● *The Gloxinian*, quarterly. Journal. **Price:** $20.00/year. **Advertising:** accepted ● *Handbook on Shows and Judging* ● Booklets. **Conventions/Meetings:** monthly competition (exhibits) ● annual conference (exhibits) ● annual Flower Show (exhibits).

22029 ■ Heritage Rose Foundation (HRF)
PO Box 831414
Richardson, TX 75083
E-mail: steprose@mac.com
URL: http://www.heritagerosefoundation.org
Contact: Stephen Scanniello, Pres.
Founded: 1986. **Members:** 600. **Membership Dues:** organization (in U.S., Canada and Mexico), $35 (annual) ● organization (in other countries), $40 (annual) ● individual/family (in U.S.), $25 (annual) ● individual/family (in Canada and Mexico), $27 (annual) ● individual/family (in other countries), $30 (annual) ● senior/family, student (in U.S.), $20 (annual) ● senior/family, student (in Canada and Mexico), $22 (annual) ● senior/family, student (in other countries), $25 (annual). **Staff:** 1. **Description:** Individuals interested in old-fashioned roses. Collects, preserves, studies, and promotes old-fashioned roses. Locates commercial sources of specific old-fashioned roses and identifies "mystery" roses; provides information on growing roses from cuttings and photographing them to facilitate identification. Conducts educational programs. **Publications:** *California's Rose Heritage*. Journal. **Price:** $25.00 book rate shipping; $30.00 priority shipping; $16.00 wholesale ● *Heritage Rose Foundation News*, quarterly. Newsletter. **Price:** $2.00 for back issues. ISSN: 1084-0907. **Circulation:** 600. **Conventions/Meetings:** annual conference.

22030 ■ Heritage Roses Group (HRG)
c/o Beverly Dobson, Sec.
916 Union St., No. 302
Alameda, CA 94501
E-mail: heritageroses@gmail.com
URL: http://www.heritagerosesgroup.org
Contact: Beverly Dobson, Sec.
Founded: 1975. **Members:** 1,000. **Membership Dues:** regular, $12 (annual) ● overseas, $26 (annual). **Regional Groups:** 6. **Description:** Persons

who grow or who are interested in old varieties of roses. Aids members in searching for hard-to-locate rose varieties; facilitates exchanges of cuttings and suggests sources for old varieties. Provides round-robin letter service for those interested in particular types of old roses. Conducts research. **Convention/Meeting:** none. **Publications:** *The Rose Letter*, quarterly. Newsletter. Contains articles written by members about rose-related subjects. **Price:** included in membership dues. **Circulation:** 1,000.

22031 ■ Hobby Greenhouse Association (HGA)
8 Glen Terr.
Bedford, MA 01730-2048
Ph: (781)275-0377
E-mail: jhale24@worldnet.att.net
URL: http://www.hobbygreenhouse.org
Contact: Janice L. Hale, Publications Dir.
Founded: 1976. **Members:** 1,200. **Membership Dues:** individual in U.S., $28 (annual) ● individual in Canada and Mexico, $30 (annual) ● individual outside North America, $31 (annual). **Staff:** 1. **Budget:** $30,000. **Regional Groups:** 3. **Multinational. Description:** Greenhouse owners and those who grow plants indoors with lights; windowsill and porch gardeners. Promotes the hobby of greenhouse and indoor gardening. Provides information on plants and diseases, propagation of seeds, insect control, and greenhouse building and maintenance. **Libraries: Type:** not open to the public. **Holdings:** 186; books, video recordings. **Subjects:** indoor gardening, residential greenhouses, house plants, outdoor gardening. **Computer Services:** Bibliographic search. **Committees:** Bookshop; E-mail Correspondence; Horticultural Advisory; Resources; Round-Robin Letters; Seed Bank. **Publications:** *Directory of Manufacturers of Residential Greenhouses and Distributors of Imported Greenhouses*, annual. Contains annotated list of over 50 manufactures. **Price:** $2.50 ● *HGA News*, quarterly. Newsletter. Includes association and membership news. **Price:** included in membership dues. **Circulation:** 1,300 ● *Hobby Greenhouse*, quarterly. Magazine. Includes articles, book reviews, new product news, and an annual index. **Price:** included in membership dues. **Circulation:** 1,400. **Advertising:** accepted. **Conventions/Meetings:** biennial convention, includes field trip to botanical garden ● annual meeting.

22032 ■ Indoor Gardening Society of America (IGSA)
c/o Jacqueline Hodes
763 Ave. A
New York, NY 10009
Ph: (212)242-6785
E-mail: info@indoorgarden.org
URL: http://indoorgarden.org
Contact: Jacqueline Hodes, Contact
Founded: 1965. **Members:** 1,500. **Membership Dues:** regular, $20 (annual) ● corresponding, $10 (annual). **Local Groups:** 20. **Description:** Indoor and outdoor amateur gardeners, nurseries, and interested professionals. Organized to practice, promote, and spread the knowledge of horticulture by means of artificial light and other forms of indoor gardening. Sponsors local lectures, demonstrations, and courses in indoor light gardening. Contributes light units to hospitals and schools and offers training on unit maintenance. Members participate in the society's round robins. **Committees:** Community Services; Education; Round Robins; Seed Exchange. **Formerly:** (1985) Indoor Light Gardening Society of America.

22033 ■ International Aroid Society (IAS)
c/o Dan Levin, Pres.
255 King Ave.
Piedmont, CA 94610
Ph: (510)547-5052
E-mail: levin@pixar.com
URL: http://www.aroid.org
Contact: Dan Levin, Pres.
Founded: 1977. **Members:** 500. **Membership Dues:** individual in U.S., $25 (annual) ● individual outside U.S., $30 (annual) ● library, $35 (annual). **Multina-**

tional. **Description:** Individuals interested in the plant family Araceae, commonly known as aroids, of which the best known members are philodendrons and anthuriums. Sponsors educational programs at seminars and collecting trips to foreign countries. Plans to establish aroid herbarium. **Libraries: Type:** reference. **Subjects:** aroids. **Awards:** Monroe Birdsey. **Type:** recognition. **Committees:** Education and Plant Identification; Plant Introduction. **Publications:** *Aroideana*, annual. Journal. **Price:** included in membership dues. ISSN: 0197-0321. **Circulation:** 550. **Advertising:** accepted ● *The Genera of Araceae*. Book. **Price:** $135.00 in U.S.; $147.00 outside U.S. (surface mail); $157.00 outside U.S. (air mail) ● *Plants of the Arum Family*. Book. **Price:** $35.00/copy in U.S.; $42.00/copy outside U.S. (surface mail); $44.00/copy outside U.S. (air mail) ● *Books* ● *Newsletter*, quarterly. **Price:** free for members. **Alternate Formats:** online. **Conventions/Meetings:** annual meeting and show (exhibits) - always September ● bimonthly meeting.

22034 ■ International Carnivorous Plant Society (ICPS)
1564-A Fitzgerald Dr.
Pinole, CA 94564-2229
E-mail: carl@carnivorousplants.org
URL: http://www.carnivorousplants.org
Contact: Carl Mazur, Pres.
Founded: 1979. **Members:** 1,200. **Membership Dues:** individual, $25 (annual). **Regional Groups:** 5. **Multinational. Description:** Provides educational and informational exchanges, supports horticultural and scientific studies, encourages cultivation and appreciation, and aids in propagation and dissemination of carnivorous plants. Initiates and supports conservation strategies for threatened carnivores. Maintains a seed bank for members. **Publications:** *Carnivorous Plant Newsletter*, quarterly. Includes color and black-and-white photographs. Contains reviews of current literature, seed bank, and listings of carnivorous plant sources. **Price:** $25.00/year. ISSN: 0190-9215. **Circulation:** 1,200. **Advertising:** accepted. **Conventions/Meetings:** annual international conference.

22035 ■ International Lilac Society (ILS)
c/o William F. Tschumi
3 Paradise Ct.
Cohoes, NY 12047-1422
Ph: (440)946-4400 (440)602-3855
Fax: (440)602-3857
E-mail: dgressley@holdenarb.org
URL: http://lilacs.freeservers.com
Contact: David P. Gressley, Sec.
Founded: 1971. **Members:** 400. **Membership Dues:** individual or family, in U.S., $20 (annual) ● sustaining, in U.S., $30 (annual) ● commercial and institutional, in U.S., $50 (annual) ● individual or family, in Europe, 15 (annual) ● sustaining, in Europe, 20 (annual) ● commercial or institutional, in Europe, 25 (annual) ● life, in U.S., $500 ● life, in Europe, 175. **Regional Groups:** 11. **Description:** Individuals, nonprofit organizations, and commercial nurserymen from North America, Europe and Asia in the Syringa genus. Disseminates information on lilacs; promotes the use of lilacs in public and private landscaping; stimulates interest in growing new and better lilacs. Provides for seed and scion exchange among members; assists members who have problems in growing lilacs. Assists nurserymen with cultivating desirable species and cultivars. **Libraries: Type:** reference. **Holdings:** 30. **Subjects:** lilacs. **Awards:** Arch McKean Award. **Frequency:** annual. **Type:** recognition ● Award of Merit. **Type:** recognition ● Honor and Achievement Award. **Frequency:** annual. **Type:** recognition ● President's Award. **Type:** recognition. **Committees:** Convention; Educational; Honors, History, Legal; Lilacs. **Publications:** *Edward A. Upton Scrapbooks of Lilac Information (Vol. 1-4)*. **Price:** $22.50 for nonmembers; $18.50 for members ● *International Register of Cultivar Names in the Genus Syringa*, periodic. Book. Contains updates to the Register. **Price:** $25.00/copy for nonmembers; C$17.50/copy for members. **Alternate Formats:** CD-ROM ● *Lilac Study*. Bulletin. Contains line drawings of lilac flowers, foliage and stem detail as well as

descriptions of form and color. **Price:** $10.00 ● *Lilacs: Proceedings of Annual Convention*. Includes fiscal reports, obituaries, and research reports. **Price:** included in membership dues. **Circulation:** 450. **Advertising:** accepted ● *New Lilac Culture*. Bulletin ● *Quarterly Journal of the International Lilac Society*. Includes address changes, association news, and new member listing. **Price:** $5.00/issue. ISSN: 1046-9761 ● Produces CD-ROM of Lilac Cultures. **Conventions/Meetings:** annual meeting and convention, with lectures, garden tours, lilac auctions, award banquets (exhibits).

22036 ■ International Oleander Society (IOS)
PO Box 3431
Galveston, TX 77552-0431
Ph: (409)762-9334
Fax: (409)762-7278
E-mail: fhead@msn.com
URL: http://www.oleander.org
Contact: Elizabeth S. Head, Exec. VP
Founded: 1967. **Members:** 200. **Membership Dues:** double, $15 (annual) ● contributing, $20 (annual) ● life, $150 ● individual, $10 (annual). **Description:** Horticulturists, hybridizers, business and professional individuals, and gardeners in 14 countries. Encourages and promotes the development of oleanders (Nerium). Offers advice on propagation, ideal planting conditions, and common oleander diseases. Sponsor research project. Loans books and a set of 80 slides of oleanders grown at Galveston, Texas. Sends cuttings and seeds of oleanders upon request from April to September, charging only small fee along with postage and handling. **Libraries: Type:** not open to the public. **Awards: Frequency:** periodic. **Type:** recognition. **Recipient:** for hybridization of outstanding variety. **Formerly:** (1984) National Oleander Society. **Publications:** *The Intrepid Gardner's Guide to Oleanders*. Video ● *Nerium News*, quarterly. Newsletter. Contains society news and new member listings. **Price:** included in membership dues. ISSN: 1096-5726. **Circulation:** 200 ● *Oleanders: Guide to Culture and Selected Varieties on Galveston Island*. Book ● *Welcome to the Wonderful World of Oleanders*. Brochure. **Conventions/Meetings:** annual A Bloomin' Event Oleander Festival (exhibits) - always May in Galveston, TX ● annual meeting - always October in Galveston, TX.

22037 ■ International Waterlily and Water Gardening Society (IWGS)
6828 26th St. W
Bradenton, FL 34207
Ph: (941)756-0880
Fax: (941)756-0880
E-mail: info@iwgs.org
URL: http://www.iwgs.org
Contact: Paula Biles, Exec. Dir.
Founded: 1984. **Members:** 500. **Membership Dues:** individual, $30 (annual). **Staff:** 1. **Budget:** $100,000. **Multinational. Description:** Represents the interests of waterlily enthusiasts, aquatic nursery operators, growers, affiliate societies, and botanical garden organizations. Fosters the furtherance of all aspects of water gardens and their associated plants. Supports and promotes education, research, and conservation in these areas. Acts as a registrar for Nymphaea and Nelumbo, Hall of Fame, New Waterlily Competition and Aquatic Plant Selections. **Libraries: Type:** reference. **Holdings:** 1,000; archival material, articles, books, clippings, papers, periodicals. **Subjects:** waterlilies, aquatic plants, water gardening. **Awards:** Best New Waterlilies. **Frequency:** annual. **Type:** recognition. **Recipient:** for the best new hybrids in several different categories ● Hall of Fame Award. **Frequency:** annual. **Type:** recognition ● Research. **Frequency:** annual. **Type:** grant. **Recipient:** for research in all aspects of aquatic plants. **Computer Services:** Mailing lists ● online services, membership tracking. **Committees:** Victoria Conservancy. **Subcommittees:** Nelumbo and Nymphaea Registrations. **Formerly:** (1988) Water Lily Society; (1999) International Water Lily Society. **Publications:** *Society Membership List*, periodic. Membership Directory ● *Water Garden Journal*, quarterly. Contains articles, letters, and question and answer section.

Price: included in membership dues. **Circulation:** 500. **Conventions/Meetings:** annual meeting, with seminars, tours, banquet - always July or August.

22038 ■ Median Iris Society (MIS)
c/o Ann Henson, Sec.
6401 Cedar Rd.
Iuka, IL 62849-2815
Ph: (618)822-6584
E-mail: erni@midwest.net
URL: http://www.medianiris.com
Contact: Perry Dyer, Pres.

Founded: 1955. **Members:** 500. **Description:** Autonomous section of American Iris Society (see separate entry). Gardeners interested in medium-sized irises. Promotes hybridizing and showing. Compiles statistics. **Libraries: Type:** reference. **Awards: Type:** recognition. **Computer Services:** Mailing lists. **Committees:** Display Gardens; Exhibitions; Research; Round Robins; Symposium. **Publications:** *Check List of Median Iris Registrations*, annual ● *Medianite*, quarterly. **Conventions/Meetings:** annual meeting, held in conjunction with AIS.

22039 ■ National Chrysanthemum Society (NCS)
10107 Homar Pond Dr.
Fairfax Station, VA 22039-1650
Ph: (703)978-7981
E-mail: galen.goss@mums.org
URL: http://www.mums.org
Contact: Mr. Galen L. Goss, Exec. Dir.

Founded: 1944. **Members:** 800. **Membership Dues:** general, $20 (annual). **Staff:** 1. **Local Groups:** 35. **Description:** Amateur growers of chrysanthemums. **Committees:** Awards; Design Developments; International Relations; Judges Schools and Credentials; Show. **Publications:** *The Chrysanthemum*, quarterly. Journal. Provides articles and reports on chrysanthemum culture, growing, and arranging. Includes association news and chapter news. **Price:** included in membership dues. ISSN: 0090-5771. **Circulation:** 800. **Advertising:** accepted ● Magazines. **Conventions/Meetings:** annual show and meeting - usually October or November.

22040 ■ National Fuchsia Society (NFS)
Address Unknown since 2007
Founded: 1941. **Members:** 105. **Membership Dues:** $15 (annual). **Local Groups:** 3. **Description:** Persons interested in the culture of fuchsias and other shade plants. Compiles statistics. Maintains speakers' list. **Libraries: Type:** reference. **Holdings:** films. **Publications:** *A to Z on Fuchsias*. Book. **Advertising:** accepted ● *Fuchsia Fan*, bimonthly. **Advertising:** accepted. **Conventions/Meetings:** competition ● annual Fuchsia and Shade Plant Show and Sale - meeting - always June.

22041 ■ National Garden Clubs
4401 Magnolia Ave.
St. Louis, MO 63110
Ph: (314)776-7574
Fax: (314)776-5108
E-mail: headquarters@gardenclub.org
URL: http://www.gardenclub.org
Contact: Kitty Larkin, Pres.

Founded: 1929. **Members:** 310,047. **Staff:** 11. **Regional Groups:** 8. **State Groups:** 51. **Local Groups:** 11,008. **Description:** Federation of garden clubs. Seeks to protect and conserve natural resources through teacher-training environmental education workshops; encourages the improvement of roadsides and parks; assists in establishing botanical gardens and horticultural centers. Conducts Landscape Design Schools. Grants scholarships in horticultural education, conservation, and landscape design. **Libraries: Type:** reference. **Holdings:** 2,000. **Formerly:** (2001) National Council of State Garden Clubs. **Publications:** *National Gardener*, quarterly. Magazine. **Price:** $6.50/year in U.S.; $15.00/year outside U.S. ● Catalog. Alternate Formats: online. **Conventions/Meetings:** annual meeting (exhibits).

22042 ■ National Gardening Association (NGA)
1100 Dorset St.
South Burlington, VT 05403
Ph: (802)863-5251
Free: (800)538-7476
Fax: (802)864-6889
E-mail: mikem@garden.org
URL: http://www.garden.org
Contact: Michael Metallo, Pres.

Founded: 1973. **Members:** 280,000. **Membership Dues:** regular, $25 (annual). **Staff:** 22. **Budget:** $3,000,000. **Description:** Serves as a clearinghouse for home, community and educational gardening information. Conduct programs providing technical assistance, materials, and grants to children's gardens nationwide. Sponsor events forums and programs to raise the awareness for the benefits of gardening. Constituents include home gardeners, community garden groups, nursing and rehabilitation homes, schools, youth clubs, camps, educators and parents. Aims to promote home, school and community gardening as a means to renew and sustain the essential connection between people, plants and the environment. Promotes environmental responsibility, advance multi-disciplinary learning and scientific literacy, and create partnerships that restore and enhance communities. **Libraries: Type:** reference. **Holdings:** 1,000. **Subjects:** gardening, pest control, weed. **Awards:** Dutch Bulb Awards. **Frequency:** annual. **Type:** recognition ● Healthy Sprouts Award. **Frequency:** annual. **Type:** recognition. **Recipient:** for schools and community groups teaching plant-based programs ● Youth Garden Grant. **Frequency:** annual. **Type:** grant. **Recipient:** for education, sustainability and community support. **Computer Services:** database, searchable plant-based information ● electronic publishing, newsletter, curriculum, articles ● online services, membership list. **Additional Websites:** http://www.kidsgardening.com, http://www.nationalgardenmonth.org. **Departments:** Education. **Funds:** Gardens for All. **Programs:** Adopt a School Garden; Grant Award. **Formerly:** (1977) Gardens for All; (1985) Gardens For All, the National Association for Gardening. **Publications:** *Environmental Survey*, triennial. Contains statistical survey data on environmental attitudes and information. **Price:** $495.00 ● *Gardening with Kids*, 3/year. Catalog. Contains plant-based curriculum and educational materials. **Circulation:** 300,000 ● *Growing Ideas*, quarterly. Newsletter. For teachers and individuals using indoor gardening with children. **Price:** $9.00/year. **Circulation:** 20,000 ● *Growing Ventures*, printed as needed. Book. Features stories of actual classroom, school-wide and community business projects. Includes guidelines, activities and worksheets. **Price:** $16.95. **Circulation:** 10,000 ● *Math in the Garden*, printed as needed. Book. Uses a mathematical lens to take children on an educational filled exploration of the garden. **Price:** $29.95. **Circulation:** 20,000 ● *National Gardening Survey*, annual. Includes a market research study of the consumer market for lawn and garden products, statistics and trends. **Price:** $120.00/copy for nonprofit organizations; $495.00/copy for nonmembers ● *What Gardeners Think*, triennial. Survey. Contains surveyed data on gardeners attitudes and opinions. **Price:** $495.00.

22043 ■ National Junior Horticultural Association (NJHA)
c/o Carole S. Carney, Exec. Sec.
15 Railroad Ave.
Homer City, PA 15748-1378
Ph: (724)479-9112
Fax: (724)479-3254
E-mail: carole@njha.org
URL: http://www.njha.org
Contact: Carole S. Carney, Exec. Sec.

Founded: 1935. **Members:** 12,500. **Staff:** 1. **State Groups:** 45. **Description:** Conducts educational programs for young people interested in horticulture. Maintains separate divisions for junior members (14 and under) and senior members (15-22). Sponsors projects and contests in production and marketing, demonstration, horticulture, achievement and leadership, gardening, experimental horticulture, environmental beautification, and public speaking. Supports programs through funds contributed by individuals and business and horticultural groups. **Awards: Type:** monetary ● **Type:** recognition ● Scottish Gardening Scholarship. **Type:** scholarship. **Recipient:** for persons 17-20 who wish to participate in a one year horticultural study and work experience program in Scotland ● **Type:** trophy. **Projects:** Achievement and Leadership; Demonstration Contests; Digital Imagery; Environmental Awareness; Horticulture Connections; Horticulture Contest; State Spirit Contest; Young America Horticulture. **Formerly:** National Junior Vegetable Growers Association. **Publications:** *Going and Growing*, 2-3/year. Newsletter. **Price:** free. **Circulation:** 3,700. **Advertising:** accepted. Alternate Formats: online ● *Horticulture Contest Study Manual*. Alternate Formats: online ● *Youth Coordinator Manual*. **Conventions/Meetings:** annual convention - always November.

22044 ■ National Pond Society (NPS)
Address Unknown since 2006
Founded: 1989. **Members:** 10,000. **Staff:** 2. **Description:** Individuals with an interest in garden and other decorative ponds. Promotes pond keeping as a hobby. Serves as a clearinghouse on pond keeping and related matters; facilitates exchange of information among members; conducts pond tours. **Publications:** Magazine, periodic. **Conventions/Meetings:** annual show.

22045 ■ North American Fruit Explorers (NAFEX)
1716 Apples Rd.
Chapin, IL 62628-4048
Ph: (217)245-7589
E-mail: vorbeck@csj.net
URL: http://www.nafex.org
Contact: Jill Vorbeck, Contact

Founded: 1967. **Members:** 3,000. **Membership Dues:** regular, in U.S., $13 (annual) ● regular, in Canada, $17 (annual) ● overseas, $20 (annual). **Budget:** $25,000. **Description:** Hobbyist fruit growers and breeders. Aims to educate individuals and disseminates information concerning fruit growing and the best varieties for the various climates of North America. Attempts to discover outstanding clonal varieties and test in various areas displays grafting and other propagation techniques at annual meetings. **Libraries: Type:** reference. **Holdings:** 250; audiovisuals, books, periodicals, video recordings. **Subjects:** horticulture, agriculture. **Awards:** Milo Gibson. **Frequency:** annual. **Type:** recognition. **Recipient:** for outstanding work in the field of pomology. **Committees:** Fruit Testing. **Publications:** *Pomona*, quarterly. Magazine. Contains members' accounts of their fruit growing experiences plus reports on particular fruits and/or special areas of culture. **Price:** included in membership dues. **Conventions/Meetings:** annual meeting and lecture.

22046 ■ North American Gladiolus Council (NAGC)
14625 E C Ave.
Augusta, MI 49012-9652
Ph: (269)237-3581
Fax: (269)237-3581
E-mail: rgmglads@gwi.net
URL: http://gladworld.org
Contact: Ms. Diana Langshaw, Pres.

Founded: 1945. **Members:** 500. **Membership Dues:** individual in U.S. and Canada, $20 (annual) ● individual outside U.S. and Canada, $25 (annual) ● commercial grower, $30 (annual). **Staff:** 15. **Budget:** $2,000. **Regional Groups:** 4. **National Groups:** 3. **Description:** Commercial and amateur growers and hybridizers of gladiolus; affiliated gladiolus societies and garden clubs. Coordinates efforts to: improve and popularize the gladiolus; develop and promote international classification of the gladiolus; foster and promote research on improving the gladiolus and the control of insect damage; collect and disseminate cultural information; recognize valuable contributions to the gladiolus industry. Maintains speakers' bureau, hall of fame, and several trial gardens. **Libraries:**

Type: reference. **Holdings:** books, films, periodicals. **Subjects:** gladiolus culture. **Awards:** Achievement Award. **Frequency:** annual. **Type:** recognition ● Gold Medal Awards. **Frequency:** annual. **Type:** medal. **Recipient:** for outstanding work with gladiolus. **Telecommunication Services:** phone referral service, membership service, (207)495-2244. **Committees:** Arrangers Club; Bulb Auction; Bulletin Ethics; Classification; Film Library; Judging Standards and Accreditation; Newcomers; Parentage and Registration; Promotion; Research; Show Reports; Winning Variety Compilation. **Divisions:** Commercial Growers. **Publications:** *Bulb Buyer's Guide*, periodic. Directory. Lists gladiolus bulb growers. **Price:** free. **Advertising:** accepted ● *Gladiograms*, semiannual. Newsletter. Provides research articles and nontechnical information on gladiolus culture and disease control. **Price:** available to members only ● *How to Grow Glorious Gladiolus* ● *North American Gladiolus Council—Bulletin*, quarterly. Covers gladiolus culture including articles on arrangement, hybridization, insect damage and control, disease, and classification. **Price:** included in membership dues. ISSN: 1526-9361. **Circulation:** 600. **Advertising:** accepted. **Conventions/ Meetings:** annual convention - always 3rd week of January.

22047 ■ North American Heather Society (NAHS)

c/o Mario A. Abreu, Pres.
PO Box 673
Albion, CA 95410-0673
Ph: (707)937-3155
Fax: (707)964-3114
E-mail: abreu@mcn.org
URL: http://www.northamericanheathersoc.org
Contact: Mario A. Abreu, Pres.
Founded: 1977. **Members:** 400. **Membership Dues:** household, $15 (annual) ● household, $28 (biennial). **Staff:** 12. **Regional Groups:** 6. **Description:** Heather-growing gardeners, individuals in the nursery profession, and horticultural experts in the U.S. and Canada. Seeks to promote a greater interest in heathers; to further knowledge of these plants; to furnish a forum for those individuals interested in discussing the use and problems of heathers. Conducts heather trials to test different cultivars of heathers under different climatic conditions to prove their "garden worthiness." Establishes, maintains, and supports heather displays and trial gardens throughout the U.S. and Canada. Maintains speakers' bureau. **Libraries: Type:** reference. **Holdings:** books, periodicals. **Affiliated With:** Heather Society. **Formerly:** (1984) Pacific Northwest Heather Society. **Publications:** *Hardy Heather Species*. Book ● *Heather News*, quarterly. Journal. Contains information on heathers and on members and chapter activities. **Price:** $12.00/year. ISSN: 1041-6838. **Circulation:** 500. **Advertising:** accepted ● Membership Directory, annual ● Brochures. **Conventions/Meetings:** annual conference (exhibits).

22048 ■ North American Lily Society (NALS)

c/o Linda Smith, Pres.
1419 Anglers Rd.
Beaufort, MO 63013-1712
E-mail: lkscrosk@yhti.com
URL: http://www.lilies.org
Contact: Linda Smith, Pres.
Founded: 1947. **Members:** 1,500. **Membership Dues:** junior in U.S., $10 (annual) ● junior outside U.S. and Canada, $25 (annual) ● individual in U.S., $20 (annual) ● individual outside U.S. and Canada, $35 (annual) ● sustaining outside Canada, $100 (annual) ● individual outside Canada (life), $350 ● household (life)/fellow outside Canada (life), $500 ● patron outside Canada (life), $1,000 ● junior in Canada, $15 (annual) ● individual in Canada, $25 (annual) ● sustaining in Canada, $120 (annual) ● individual in Canada (life), $450. **Regional Groups:** 22. **Multinational. Description:** Hobbyists, growers, university researchers, and dealers interested in lily culture and breeding. Conducts judging schools and lily research. **Libraries: Type:** reference. **Holdings:** 200. **Awards: Type:** recognition. **Recipient:** for the best lily; 24 awards available in various divisions.

Committees: Awards and Standards; Judges' Training and Accreditation; Lily Popularity Poll; Regional Affiliation; Research; Round Robins; Seed Exchange; Slides. **Publications:** *Let's Grow Lilies*. Book. Features illustrations of lily culture. **Price:** $7.00/copy ● *Lily Disease Handbook*. Helps the home gardener recognize, understand and control lily diseases. **Price:** $3.00 in U.S.; $4.50 in Canada ● *Lily Judging Handbook*. **Price:** $7.50 in U.S.; $12.00 in Canada ● Bulletin, quarterly. Provides membership activity information. **Price:** included in membership dues. **Circulation:** 1,500. **Advertising:** accepted ● Yearbook. **Price:** included in membership dues. **Circulation:** 1,500. **Conventions/Meetings:** annual meeting (exhibits) - always June or July with International Lily Show.

22049 ■ North American Rock Garden Society (NARGS)

c/o Jacques Mommens, Exec. Sec.
PO Box 67
Millwood, NY 10546
Ph: (914)762-2948
E-mail: nargs@advinc.com
URL: http://www.nargs.org
Contact: Jacques Mommens, Exec. Sec.
Founded: 1934. **Members:** 4,500. **Membership Dues:** individual, in U.S. and Canada, $30 (annual) ● individual, outside U.S. and Canada, $35 (annual) ● life (60 years old and below), $600 ● life (over 60 years old), $540. **Regional Groups:** 33. **Multinational. Description:** Persons interested in cultivation of alpine and saxatile plants. Membership includes gardeners from 32 countries. Goals are to increase knowledge of rock garden plants, their value, habits, and geographical distribution and to promote good design and construction of rock gardens. Maintains seed exchange and color slide collection. Operates mail order bookstore; holds lectures. **Libraries: Type:** reference. **Formerly:** (1994) American Rock Garden Society. **Publications:** *Rock Garden Quarterly*. Bulletin. Contains articles from around the world on alpines and other wildflowers, plant exploration, and construction and design of rock gardens. **Price:** included in membership dues; $7.00/copy. ISSN: 1081-0765. **Circulation:** 4,600. **Advertising:** accepted ● *Seed List*, annual ● Membership Directory, biennial. **Conventions/Meetings:** conference - 3/year; always January, February, late spring ● workshop.

22050 ■ Pacific Orchid Society of Hawaii (POS)

PO Box 1091
Honolulu, HI 96808
E-mail: brunsoni001@hawaii.rr.com
URL: http://www.geocities.com/RainForest/Vines/ 7097
Founded: 1946. **Members:** 150. **Local Groups:** 1. **Description:** Represents individuals interested in orchid culture. Sponsors lectures and orchid displays in Honolulu, HI. Maintains small library. **Affiliated With:** American Orchid Society. **Publications:** *Beginners Handbook for Orchid Growing in Hawaii*, periodic ● *Na Okika O Hawaii: Hawaii Orchid Journal*, periodic. **Conventions/Meetings:** bimonthly meeting - every third Monday of even-numbered months except in December.

22051 ■ Plumeria Society of America (PSA)

PO Box 22791
Houston, TX 77227-2791
Ph: (713)946-9175
E-mail: estafford@pdq.net
URL: http://www.theplumeriasociety.org
Contact: Eulas Stafford, Pres.
Founded: 1979. **Members:** 150. **Membership Dues:** regular, $20 (annual) ● associate, $15 (annual). **Description:** Individuals who grow plumerias and local nurserymen who specialize in plumerias (a genus of tropical American shrubs or trees which is also known as Frangipani, the flower of the red jasmine). Seeks to learn more about plumerias and their care, cultivation, and propagation; and to develop cultivars (varieties). Seeks to educate the public on plumerias; maintains international registration authority for

plumeria cultivars. Provides research grants. Sponsors seminars, slide shows, and lectures. **Libraries: Type:** open to the public. **Holdings:** audiovisuals, books. **Subjects:** plumeria cultivars. **Committees:** Newsletter; Program; Publicity; Registration; Research; Social. **Publications:** *Plumeria Potpourri*, 5/year. Newsletter. **Price:** included in membership dues ● *Registration of Plumeria Cultivars*, periodic. **Conventions/Meetings:** periodic conference and seminar ● biennial Flower Show and/or Plant Sale - meeting ● quarterly meeting - always second Tuesday of March, May, July, and October, in Houston, TX.

22052 ■ Reblooming Iris Society (RIS)

c/o Barbara Aitken, Pres.
608 NW 119th St.
Vancouver, WA 98685
Ph: (360)573-4472
E-mail: aitken@flowerfantasy.net
URL: http://www.rebloomingiris.com
Contact: Barbara Aitken, Pres.
Founded: 1967. **Members:** 450. **Membership Dues:** single, $7 (annual) ● single, $18 (triennial) ● single (life), $120 ● dual, $8 (annual) ● dual, $21 (triennial) ● dual (life), $150. **Description:** A section of the American Iris Society (see separate entry). Amateur gardeners and commercial iris businesses interested in reblooming irises. Promotes the culture and improvement of reblooming irises. Encourages membership in national, regional, and local societies. Assembles and broadcasts varietal descriptions. Sponsors slide programs, shows and exhibitions. Maintains Speaker's Bureau; conducts educational programs. **Awards:** Distinguished Service Award. **Type:** recognition. **Computer Services:** database, lists of reblooming iris cultivars by state and USDA zones. **Affiliated With:** American Iris Society. **Publications:** *Checklist of Reblooming Irises*, periodic. Book. Includes registered name of cultivar, hybridizer, year of introduction to commercial market, description of flower, and genetic pedigree. **Price:** $14.00 postage paid. **Circulation:** 900 ● *The Reblooming Iris Recorder*, semiannual. Includes features on culture, varietal comments, advances in breeding, and annual symposium of favorite cultivars. **Price:** $7.00/year; $4.00/back issue; $10.00/3 back issues. **Circulation:** 1,000. **Advertising:** accepted. **Conventions/Meetings:** annual convention - April-May.

22053 ■ Rose Hybridizers Association (RHA)

21 S Wheaton Rd.
Horseheads, NY 14845-1077
Ph: (607)562-8592
E-mail: lpeterso@stny.rr.com
URL: http://www.rosehybridizers.org
Contact: Larry D. Peterson, Treas.
Founded: 1969. **Members:** 200. **Membership Dues:** domestic, $10 (annual) ● international, $12 (annual). **Multinational. Description:** Individuals who hybridize roses as a hobby; professional hybridizers are also members. Provides information to interested individuals and offers free consultation services to members. Maintains trial grounds at headquarters of American Rose Society (see separate entry) in Shreveport, LA. **Libraries: Type:** reference; lending; not open to the public. **Holdings:** 150; archival material, audiovisuals, books. **Subjects:** hybridizing, propagation. **Awards:** Best Seedling. **Frequency:** annual. **Type:** recognition. **Recipient:** for outstanding achievements. **Computer Services:** database, search by topic/author ● online services, website articles and forum. **Publications:** *RHA Newsletter*, quarterly. Pertains to hybridizing of roses. **Price:** included in membership dues. **Circulation:** 200 ● *Rose Hybridizing for Beginners*. Booklet. Covers basics of how to hybridize roses. **Price:** $5.00 ● *Rose Hybridizing: The Next Step*. Booklet. Contains chapters on topics useful to rose hybridizers. **Price:** $12.00. **Conventions/Meetings:** biennial convention.

22054 ■ Seed Savers Exchange (SSE)

3094 N Winn Rd.
Decorah, IA 52101
Ph: (563)382-5990

Fax: (563)382-5872
E-mail: steph@seedsavers.org
URL: http://www.seedsavers.org
Contact: Kent Whealy, Dir.
Founded: 1975. **Members:** 8,000. **Membership Dues:** in U.S., $35 (annual) ● in Canada, $40 (annual) ● outside U.S. and Canada, $50 (annual). **Staff:** 10. **Description:** Vegetable gardeners dedicated to finding, multiplying, and spreading heirloom vegetable and fruit varieties before they are lost. Members trade seeds through the mail, experiment with vegetable varieties and culturing techniques, and report results through the group's publications. Has specific interest in locating vegetable varieties: that have been in families for generations; that families have brought to the U.S. from their homeland; that has been selectively improved over the years; that are no longer available from any seed catalogue; that are unusual, such as genetic mutations; that are extremely disease-resistant, very hardy, of exceptional quality, or having other outstanding characteristics. **Telecommunication Services:** electronic mail, kent@seedsavers.org. **Formerly:** (1979) True Seed Exchange. **Publications:** *Fruit, Berry, and Nut Inventory*, every 3-4 years. Book. Contains inventory of U.S. mail order nurseries, with descriptions. ● *Garden Seed Inventory*. Contains inventory of mail order vegetable seed catalogs in the U.S. and Canada featuring non-hybrid varieties. ● *Harvest Edition*, annual. **Price:** included in membership dues ● *Seed to Seed*. Provides seed saving techniques for vegetable gardeners. ● *Summer Edition*, annual. **Price:** included in membership dues ● *Yearbook*, annual. **Price:** included in membership dues. **Conventions/Meetings:** annual Camp-Out Convention, for members and their guests - in July.

22055 ■ Society for Japanese Irises (SJI)

c/o Dennis Hager, Pres.
PO Box 390
Millington, MD 21651
Ph: (410)928-3147
E-mail: hager@aredee.com
URL: http://www.socji.org
Contact: Dennis Hager, Pres.
Founded: 1951. **Members:** 550. **Membership Dues:** regular, $5 (annual). **Description:** A section of the American Iris Society (see separate entry). Growers and hybridizers of Japanese irises, which are beardless garden irises with large showy flowers developed in Japan. **Libraries:** Type: reference. **Awards:** Payne Award. **Frequency:** annual. **Type:** recognition. ● **Type:** recognition. **Affiliated With:** American Iris Society. **Publications:** *Cumulative Index of Japanese Irises*, annual. **Price:** $5.00 ● *The Japanese Iris* ● *The Review*, semiannual. **Price:** included in membership dues. **Circulation:** 600. **Advertising:** accepted ● Also makes available culture instructions. **Conventions/Meetings:** triennial Garden Tour and Flower Show - tour and show.

22056 ■ Society for Louisiana Irises (SLI)

c/o Richard J. Sloan, Treas.
118 E Walnut St.
Alma, AR 72921-3608
Ph: (479)632-4962
E-mail: rjsloan@mynewroads.com
URL: http://sliris.bizland.com
Contact: Richard J. Sloan, Treas.
Founded: 1941. **Members:** 450. **Membership Dues:** individual, in U.S., $13 (annual) ● family, in U.S., $16 (annual) ● life (individual/family), $200 ● individual, outside U.S., $20 (annual) ● family, outside U.S., $23 (annual). **Description:** Represents amateur growers of Louisiana irises. Promotes, fosters and encourages the planting and cultivation of Louisiana irises. **Awards:** American Iris Society Awards. **Type:** recognition. **Computer Services:** Mailing lists, of members. **Additional Websites:** http://www.louisianas.org. **Formerly:** (1948) Mary Swords Debaillon Louisiana Iris Society. **Publications:** *The Louisiana Iris*, quarterly. Book. Contains check list, cumulative, of registrations and introductions. **Price:** $25.00 plus shipping and handling, in U.S.; $11.50 international, plus shipping and handling ● Newsletter, quarterly. **Advertising:** accepted. Alternate Formats: online.

Conventions/Meetings: annual meeting and tour, includes garden tours, awards banquet, flower show.

22057 ■ Society for Pacific Coast Native Iris (SPCNI)

c/o Terri Hudson, Sec.-Treas.
33450 Little Valley Rd.
Fort Bragg, CA 95437
Ph: (707)964-3907
E-mail: irishud@earthlink.net
URL: http://www.pacificcoastiris.org
Contact: Terri Hudson, Sec.-Treas.
Founded: 1973. **Members:** 450. **Membership Dues:** individual in U.S., $8 (annual) ● individual outside U.S., $12 (annual) ● individual in U.S., $20 (triennial) ● family in U.S., $10 (annual) ● family in U.S., $23 (triennial) ● life, in U.S., $75. **Staff:** 4. **Budget:** $2,000. **National Groups:** 2. **Multinational. Description:** A section of the American Iris Society. Hybridizers and individuals who grow or admire Pacific Coast irises. (Native to the American Pacific Coast, the flower appears in various colors and grows to a height of about 12 inches.) Provides color slides for group shows; distributes seeds. **Libraries:** Type: open to the public. **Holdings:** 46; books, periodicals. **Subjects:** Pacific Coast Iris. **Awards:** Mitchell Award. **Frequency:** annual. **Type:** recognition. **Recipient:** for the best advancement in breeding. **Computer Services:** database, Almanac subject index ● mailing lists. **Boards:** Directors. **Affiliated With:** American Iris Society. **Publications:** *A Guide to Pacific Coast Irises*. Journal. Contains illustrations of the species for identification and provides information on habitat. **Price:** $6.00 each ● *A Revision of the Pacific Coast Irises*. Booklet. Contains the most complete survey of the PCI. **Price:** $8.00/copy ● *Almanac: Society for Pacific Coast Native Iris*, semiannual. Newsletter. Provides information on the culture, origins, hybridization, and display of Pacific Coast irises. Includes research reports. **Price:** included in membership dues; $3.50 each (back issues); $2.00 complete chronological index; $4.00 index by subject or author ● *Hybridization and Specialization in the Pacific Coast Irises*. Booklet. **Price:** $8.00 each; $14.00 both Hybridization and Revision. **Conventions/Meetings:** annual meeting, held in conjunction with AIS.

22058 ■ Society for Siberian Irises (SSI)

c/o Judy Hollingworth, Pres.
124 Sherwood Rd. E
Williamston, MI 48895
Ph: (517)349-8121
E-mail: cyberiris@cablespeed.com
URL: http://www.socsib.org
Contact: Judy Hollingworth, Pres.
Founded: 1960. **Members:** 200. **Multinational. Description:** A section of the American Iris Society (see separate entry). Iris growers; amateur and professional hybridizers; interested individuals. Seeks to improve the quality of the Siberian iris. (The Siberian iris lacks the lower beard-like petals common to most irises.) Seeks to educate the public on Siberian irises. **Publications:** *The Siberian Iris*, semiannual. Articles. Covers genetic research, diseases, insect pests, plant exploration, people hybridizing and cultural practices. **Conventions/Meetings:** annual meeting, held in conjunction with AIS.

22059 ■ Species Iris Group of North America (SIGNA)

c/o Rodney Barton
PO Box 250
Molalla, OR 97038
Ph: (503)829-3102
E-mail: gardens@molalla.net
URL: http://dir.gardenweb.com/directory/sigma
Contact: William Plotner, Pres.
Founded: 1966. **Members:** 700. **Membership Dues:** regular in U.S., $12 (annual) ● regular in U.S., $32 (triennial) ● foreign, $15 (annual) ● foreign, $40 (triennial) ● life, $300. **Multinational. Description:** A section of the American Iris Society (see separate entry). Iris fanciers, libraries, and nurserymen. Promotes the study, conservation, and cultivation of wild species of iris and other members of the iris

family. Conducts round-robin study groups, seed exchange, and speakers' bureau in areas where officers reside. Maintains scientific papers. Maintains slide collection. **Awards:** Founders of SIGNA Medal. **Frequency:** annual. **Type:** medal. **Recipient:** for pure species ● Randolph Perry Medal. **Frequency:** annual. **Type:** medal. **Recipient:** for species crosses. **Computer Services:** Information services, features different irises. **Additional Websites:** http://www.si-gna.org, http://www.badbear.com/signa/signa.pl?Inroducrion. **Affiliated With:** American Iris Society. **Publications:** *An Introductory Guide to Species Iris and SIGNA*, published as needed. Booklet. Features guides for beginner or advanced gardener on working with species iris. **Price:** $5.00 ● *Checklist of Species Iris*, periodic ● *Investigating Iris by Professor Marietta Colasante*, 3/year. Booklet. Contains scientific works on Iris from other languages that are translated into English with comments. **Price:** $9.95 plus postage ● Newsletter, semiannual. **Price:** included in membership dues; $15.00 /year for nonmembers. **Circulation:** 700.

22060 ■ Spuria Iris Society (SIS)

c/o Jim Hedgecock, Pres.
Rte. 1, Box 258
Gower, MO 64454
Ph: (816)424-6436
E-mail: comanche@ccp.com
URL: http://www.spuria.org
Contact: Jim Hedgecock, Pres.
Founded: 1960. **Members:** 250. **Membership Dues:** single, $9 (annual) ● single, $20 (triennial) ● life, $125 ● family, $12 (annual) ● family, $24 (triennial) ● overseas, $15 (annual) ● overseas, $30 (triennial). **Multinational. Description:** A section of the American Iris Society (see separate entry). Amateur and professional hybridizers; interested individuals. Seeks to educate people about Spuria iris, a beardless flower with a tall stem (some grow to six feet in height) found principally in central Asia, but also in the Middle East and Mediterranean regions. Strives to improve the Spuria iris breed. **Awards:** Award of Merit. **Frequency:** annual. **Type:** recognition ● Eric Nies Medal. **Frequency:** annual. **Type:** medal. **Recipient:** for best spuria. **Affiliated With:** American Iris Society. **Publications:** *The Spuria Irises, Introduction and Varietal Listing*, decennial. Book. Lists all spuria irises registered and/or introduced, plus all known species. ● Newsletter, semiannual. **Conventions/Meetings:** annual meeting, held in conjunction with AIS (exhibits).

22061 ■ Tall Bearded Iris Society (TBIS)

PO Box 303
McKinney, TX 75070
Ph: (806)792-1878
E-mail: rhoward3604@sbcglobal.net
URL: http://www.tbisonline.com
Contact: Ramona Howard, Pres.
Membership Dues: household, organization, $10 (annual) ● household, $27 (triennial) ● dual, $15 (annual) ● dual, $41 (triennial) ● life, $300 ● outside U.S., $25 (annual). **Multinational. Description:** Promotes the distribution, cultivation, hybridization, and development of Tall Bearded Irises. Seeks to educate its members and the general public by conducting Iris shows and exhibitions. Maintains a display garden directory. **Publications:** *Tall Talk*. Magazine. **Advertising:** accepted. Alternate Formats: online.

22062 ■ Terrarium Association (TA)

Address Unknown since 2007
Founded: 1974. **Staff:** 2. **Description:** Florists, individuals in the nursery profession, garden club members, schools, and others interested in terraria. Offers instruction on making and maintaining terraria through a series of publications. Maintains how-to photofile and data on terrarium history. **Convention/Meeting:** none. **Publications:** *Bottle Planters* ● *Cacti Succulents for Miniture Desert Landscapes*. Brochure ● *Comprehensive List of Foliage Plants*. Brochure ● *Evolution of the Bottle Garden: A Continuing Saga of Terraria* ● *Guideline for Taking the Guesswork out of Exhibiting and Judging Terrariums in Flower Shows* ● *How to Make a Plant Column* ● *How to Make Par-*

tridgeberry Bowls and Holiday Berry Balls to Give or Hang on the Christmas Tree ● How to Plant a Horizontal Five Gallon Terrarium ● Planting the Big Ones ● Recipe for a Gallon Garden ● Soil Formulas for All Phases of Terrarium Gardening ● The Terrarium Association Answer Sheet to Questions Our Readers Most Frequently Ask ● The Terrarium Association Directory of Plant Sources and Bottle Gardening Supplies ● Pamphlets ● Publishes directional care cards for Brandy snifters and bowls, bottle planters, cactus gardens, and dried arrangements in glass.

Glass

22063 ■ American Carnival Glass Association (ACGA)

c/o Dolores Wagner, Sec.
5951 Fredericksburg Rd.
Wooster, OH 44691-9491
Ph: (330)264-3703
E-mail: wags3191@earthlink.net
URL: http://www.myacga.com
Contact: Dolores Wagner, Sec.
Founded: 1966. **Members:** 500. **Membership Dues:** $25 (annual). **Description:** Collectors of carnival glass, a colorful iridescent glassware, known also as "cinderella glass" and "taffeta glass." Such glassware was produced inexpensively beginning in the 1900's in the U.S. and frequently given away as prizes at carnivals and fairs, hence the name. Encourages study and exchange of carnival glass; determines authenticity of pieces. **Publications:** American Carnival Glass News, quarterly. Newsletter. Contains membership news, auction lists, directory of regional clubs, and club news. **Price:** included in membership dues. **Conventions/Meetings:** annual American Carnival Glass Convention - meeting (exhibits) - always June or July ● annual National Carnival Glass Week - meeting - always first week of October.

22064 ■ American Cut Glass Association (ACGA)

c/o Kathy Emmerson, Exec. Sec.
PO Box 482
Ramona, CA 92065-0482
E-mail: acgakathy@aol.com
URL: http://www.cutglass.org
Contact: Kathy Emmerson, Exec. Sec.
Founded: 1978. **Members:** 2,300. **Membership Dues:** individual, $45 (annual). **Regional Groups:** 19. **National Groups:** 4. **Description:** Collectors of and dealers in American brilliant period cut glass. Seeks to increase knowledge and appreciation of American cut glass as an art form; provides opportunities for personal contact among cut glass enthusiasts. **Publications:** Hobstar, 10/year. Newsletter. **Price:** included in membership dues. **Advertising:** accepted ● Membership Directory, annual ● Also publishes catalog reprints. **Conventions/Meetings:** annual Dealers Show - trade show, with speakers and sale (exhibits) - always July.

22065 ■ Ball Collectors Club (BCC)

c/o Mason Bright, Pres.
497 Fox Dr.
Monroe, MI 48161
Ph: (734)241-0113 (734)269-2783
E-mail: balljars@cheerful.com
Contact: Mason Bright, Pres.
Founded: 1987. **Members:** 130. **Staff:** 1. **Description:** Collectors and admirers of Ball brand fruit jars. Promotes collection and preservation of Ball jars. Serves as a clearinghouse on Ball jars and their collection. **Publications:** Newsletter, periodic. **Conventions/Meetings:** periodic show.

22066 ■ Fenton Art Glass Collectors of America (FAGCA)

PO Box 384
Williamstown, WV 26187-0384
Ph: (304)375-6196

E-mail: fagcainc@wirefire.com
URL: http://users.wirefire.com/fagcainc
Contact: Richard Hunt, Pres.
Founded: 1976. **Members:** 14,000. **Membership Dues:** individual, $20 (annual) ● associate, $5 (annual). **Staff:** 2. **Local Groups:** 20. **Description:** Collectors of Fenton Art glass. (Fenton is the family name of a contemporary glass-making company.) Encourages appreciation of the glass-making industry and the history of Fenton glass. **Libraries: Type:** reference. **Subjects:** glass, especially Fenton Art glass. **Publications:** Butterfly Net, bimonthly. Newsletter. **Price:** included in membership dues. **Advertising:** accepted ● Caught in the Butterfly Net. Book. **Conventions/Meetings:** annual convention - always July/August.

22067 ■ Fostoria Glass Collectors (FGC)

PO Box 1625
Orange, CA 92856
E-mail: fgcglass@fostoriacollectors.org
URL: http://www.fostoriacollectors.org
Contact: Maryann Schneider, Sec.
Founded: 1990. **Members:** 175. **Membership Dues:** individual in U.S., $25 (annual) ● individual in Canada, $32 (annual). **Budget:** $2,000. **Description:** Collectors and admirers of handmade American glassware. Promotes appreciation of handmade American glass products. Serves as a clearinghouse on handmade American glassware and its collection; sponsors research and educational programs; participates in charitable activities; maintains museum. **Libraries: Type:** reference; lending; not open to the public. **Holdings:** 50; archival material. **Subjects:** American handmade glass. **Awards:** Gift. **Frequency:** annual. **Type:** grant. **Recipient:** nonprofit glass museums. **Computer Services:** Mailing lists ● online services. **Publications:** The Glass Works, bimonthly. Newsletter. Contains educational articles. **Price:** included in membership dues. **Advertising:** accepted. Alternate Formats: online. **Conventions/Meetings:** periodic board meeting ● monthly meeting and general assembly, educational program and show and tell.

22068 ■ Fostoria Glass Society of America (FGSA)

PO Box 826
Moundsville, WV 26041
Ph: (304)845-9188
E-mail: decrabb@paonline.com
URL: http://www.fostoriaglass.org
Contact: Donn Crabb, Contact
Founded: 1981. **Members:** 800. **Membership Dues:** voting, $16 (annual). **Local Groups:** 1. **National Groups:** 5. **Description:** Represents Fostoria Glass collectors. Promotes interest in glass collecting. Offers referrals. **Libraries: Type:** open to the public. **Holdings:** archival material, books, periodicals. **Subjects:** glass, glass manufacturing. **Computer Services:** Mailing lists, of members. **Formerly:** (1995) National Glass Clubs Affiliate. **Publications:** Facets of Fostoria, 8/year. Magazine. **Price:** $2.00 for nonmembers, plus postage; included in membership dues. **Circulation:** 750. **Advertising:** accepted. Alternate Formats: online. **Conventions/Meetings:** semiannual Glass Shows - convention and workshop, elegant glass (exhibits).

22069 ■ Glass Art Society (GAS)

3131 Western Ave., Ste.414
Seattle, WA 98121
Ph: (206)382-1305
Fax: (206)382-2630
E-mail: info@glassart.org
URL: http://www.glassart.org
Contact: Pamela Figenshow Koss, Exec. Dir.
Founded: 1971. **Members:** 3,800. **Membership Dues:** individual in U.S., Canada and Mexico, $50 (annual) ● individual outside North America, $65 (annual) ● full-time student in U.S., Canada and Mexico, $25 (annual) ● full-time student outside North America, $35 (annual) ● sponsor, $100 (annual) ● family in U.S., Canada and Mexico, $75 (annual). **Staff:** 5. **Description:** Works to encourage excellence, advance education, and support the worldwide

community of artists who work with glass. **Libraries: Type:** reference. **Holdings:** archival material. **Awards:** Honorary Lifetime Membership Award. **Frequency:** annual. **Type:** recognition ● Lifetime Achievement Award. **Frequency:** annual. **Type:** recognition. **Recipient:** for artists. **Computer Services:** database ● mailing lists. **Publications:** GAS News, bimonthly. Newsletter. **Price:** included in membership dues. **Circulation:** 3,000. **Advertising:** accepted ● Glass Art Society Journal, annual. **Price:** $23.00 for members in U.S., Canada and Mexico; $27.00 for nonmembers in U.S., Canada and Mexico; $28.00 for members in other countries; $32.00 for nonmembers in other countries. **Circulation:** 2,600. **Advertising:** accepted ● Membership Directory and Education Roster, annual ● Resource Guide, annual. **Price:** included in membership dues. **Circulation:** 3,000. **Advertising:** accepted. **Conventions/Meetings:** annual conference (exhibits).

22070 ■ H.C. Fry Glass Society

PO Box 41
Beaver, PA 15009
E-mail: judymc9@comcast.net
URL: http://thenostalgialeague.com/fryglass
Contact: Judy Cleary, Pres.
Membership Dues: local, $12 (annual) ● family, $15 (annual). **Multinational. Description:** Committed to the preservation of information and appreciation of the glass made at the H.C. Fry Glass Company in Rochester, Pennsylvania from 1901 to around 1933. **Committees:** Acquisition. **Publications:** The Shards, quarterly. Newsletter. **Conventions/Meetings:** convention ● monthly meeting - 1st Thursday.

22071 ■ Heart of America Carnival Glass Association (HOACGA)

Address Unknown since 2007
Founded: 1972. **Members:** 1,400. **Membership Dues:** individual/family, $25 (annual). **Staff:** 5. **Budget:** $45,000. **National Groups:** 1. **Description:** Individuals with an interest in carnival glass. Promotes the appreciation of carnival glass through educational programs. **Libraries: Type:** open to the public. **Publications:** Bulletin, monthly ● Membership Directory, periodic. **Conventions/Meetings:** annual symposium (exhibits) - 4th Friday of April; **Avg. Attendance:** 350.

22072 ■ Heisey Collectors of America/National Heisey Glass Museum (HCA)

169 W Church St.
Newark, OH 43055
Ph: (740)345-2932
E-mail: director@heiseymuseum.org
URL: http://www.heiseymuseum.org
Contact: Dick Smith, Pres.
Founded: 1971. **Members:** 3,100. **Membership Dues:** associate, individual, $30 (annual) ● joint, $40 (annual) ● family, $50 (annual) ● patron, $100 (annual) ● sponsor, $250 (annual) ● benefactor, $500 (annual). **Staff:** 5. **Budget:** $350,000. **Regional Groups:** 28. **Local Groups:** 3. **National Groups:** 9. **Multinational. Description:** Collectors and dealers in Heisey glassware, manufactured in Newark, OH from 1896-1957. Promotes the preservation and collection of Heisey glassware; founded the National Heisey Glass Museum in Newark, OH. Holds annual benefit auction. Maintains speakers' bureau. **Libraries: Type:** reference. **Holdings:** 500; books, periodicals. **Subjects:** glass industry. **Committees:** Educational; Museum; Research and Archives. **Publications:** A.H. Heisey and Company: A Brief History ● Encyclopedia of Heisey Glass, 1925-1938 ● Etchings and Carvings, Second Edition ● Heisey by Imperial ● Heisey Candlesticks ● Heisey News, monthly. Newsletter. Includes advertisements, club news, and articles on glass history. **Price:** included in membership dues. ISSN: 0731-8014. **Circulation:** 1,800. **Advertising:** accepted ● Heisey Rose ● Heisey Toothpick Holders ● Heisey's Classic Ridgeleigh ● Heisey's Glassware. Catalog ● Heisey's Lariat and Athena Patterns ● Heisey's Orchid Etching. **Conventions/Meetings:** board meeting and general assembly - always April, June, September ● annual

Heisey Collectors National Convention - convention and assembly (exhibits) - always June.

22073 ■ International Carnival Glass Association (ICGA)
c/o Brian Pitman, Pres.
10750 NW 13th St.
Topeka, KS 66615
Ph: (785)478-9004
E-mail: bpitman@woodsland.com
URL: http://www.internationalcarnivalglass.com
Contact: Brian Pitman, Pres.
Founded: 1967. **Members:** 2,000. **Membership Dues:** household in U.S., $25 (annual) ● household outside U.S., $30 (annual). **Multinational. Description:** Individuals interested in old carnival glass. Promotes the hobby of collecting carnival glass. Members meet annually to display their glass and to buy, sell, and swap items. **Libraries: Type:** reference. **Holdings:** audiovisuals, books. **Publications:** *Carnival Pump*, quarterly. Newsletter. Contains educational articles. **Conventions/Meetings:** annual convention, special display room & displays in members rooms (exhibits) - always July.

22074 ■ National American Glass Club (NAGC)
PO Box 489
Millburn, NJ 07041
E-mail: webmaster@glassclub.org
URL: http://www.glassclub.org
Contact: Larry Steiner, Pres.
Founded: 1933. **Members:** 1,100. **Membership Dues:** single, institution, $25 (annual) ● household, $30 (annual) ● life-double, $500 ● student, $10 (annual) ● sustaining, $35 (annual) ● supporting, $60 (annual) ● donor, $100 (annual) ● life-single, $400. **Regional Groups:** 21. **Description:** Institutions, museums, libraries, historical societies, and individuals. Studies and researches glass, particularly American glass. Conducts educational programs. Maintains 200 volume library of books on antique glass and glassmaking. **Formerly:** (2001) National Early American Glass Club. **Publications:** *Glass Club Bulletin*, 3/year. Covers the history of glass, especially American glassware; articles relate to the manufacture, style, and attributions by collectors. **Price:** included in membership dues. **Circulation:** 1,100. Also Cited As: *NEAGC Bulletin* ● *Glass Shards*, quarterly. Newsletter. Covers association activities and information on glass. Includes calendar of events and chapter news. **Price:** included in membership dues. **Circulation:** 1,100 ● *National Early American Glass Club—Membership Directory*, annual. **Price:** included in membership dues. **Circulation:** 1,100 ● Yearbook. **Conventions/Meetings:** annual seminar.

22075 ■ National Cambridge Collectors (NCC)
PO Box 416
Cambridge, OH 43725-0416
Ph: (740)432-4245
Fax: (740)439-9223
E-mail: david@ourhouseantiques.com
URL: http://www.cambridgeglass.org
Contact: Rick Jones, Pres.
Founded: 1973. **Members:** 1,350. **Membership Dues:** master, $22 (annual) ● associate, $3 (annual). **Staff:** 3. **Regional Groups:** 8. **Description:** Persons appreciative of fine glassware who are interested in the study, preservation, and collection of Cambridge glass (manufactured in Cambridge, OH from 1901-59). Sponsors antique shows, auctions, and special events; conducts educational programs during meetings. **Libraries: Type:** reference. **Publications:** *Cambridge Crystal Ball*, monthly. Newsletter. **Price:** $20.00/year. **Circulation:** 1,000. **Advertising:** accepted ● Also makes available movie. **Conventions/Meetings:** quarterly meeting - always March, June, August, and November, in Cambridge, OH ● seminar.

22076 ■ National Depression Glass Association (NDGA)
PO Box 8264
Wichita, KS 67208-0264

E-mail: president@ndga.net
URL: http://www.ndga.net
Contact: Kent G. Washburn, Pres.
Founded: 1974. **Members:** 920. **Membership Dues:** individual, $20 (annual) ● associate, $5 (annual) ● club, corporate, $30 (annual). **Description:** Individuals interested in promoting depression glass through an exchange of ideas and information. Promotes preservation of glass, glassmaking tools and documents related to glassmaking in the U.S., primarily during the years immediately preceding, during and immediately after the "Great Depression," roughly the time period 1925-1949. **Publications:** *National Depression Glass Association—News and Views*, semimonthly. Newsletter. Contains articles on glass and related topics. Includes information on shows and association activities. **Price:** included in membership dues. **Advertising:** accepted ● Bibliography. Contains list of books about glass. **Conventions/Meetings:** annual Show and Sale - show and convention, with seminars and rare individual collections (exhibits) - always July.

22077 ■ National Duncan Glass Society (NDGS)
525 Jefferson Ave.
Washington, PA 15301
Ph: (724)225-9950
E-mail: museum@linequest.net
URL: http://www.duncan-glass.com
Contact: Tom Bloom, Pres.
Founded: 1975. **Members:** 300. **Membership Dues:** active, $18 (annual) ● additional family member, $3 (annual). **Regional Groups:** 1. **Description:** Aims to study and preserve Duncan and Duncan Miller glass. Maintains a permanent collection and museum in Washington, PA, where the glass was manufactured. Provides speakers; conducts historical research. **Libraries: Type:** reference; lending; open to the public. **Holdings:** archival material, books, clippings, periodicals. **Subjects:** glass and glass-related topics. **Committees:** Memorabilia; Museum; Publicity. **Publications:** *Duncan Catalog with Price Guide*, quarterly. Reprint. Contains reprint of 1943 original. **Price:** $23.00 plus shipping and handling. **Advertising:** accepted ● *Duncan Journal*, quarterly. **Advertising:** accepted. **Conventions/Meetings:** annual Duncan Miller Glass Show and Sale - convention and show (exhibits) - last weekend of July ● monthly meeting, with guest speakers.

22078 ■ National Fenton Glass Society (NFGS)
PO Box 4008
Marietta, OH 45750
Ph: (740)374-3345
Fax: (740)376-9708
E-mail: nfgs@ee.net
URL: http://www.fentonglasssociety.org
Contact: Jim Measell, Contact
Founded: 1990. **Members:** 2,500. **Membership Dues:** individual, premier associate, $20 (annual) ● associate (same household), $2 (annual) ● premier (includes yearly piece of glass), $35 (annual). **Staff:** 1. **Budget:** $35,000. **Regional Groups:** 3. **State Groups:** 4. **Local Groups:** 1. **Description:** Promotes the study and understanding of handmade glass and handmade glass industry. Focuses study on glass made by the Fenton Art Glass Company. Encourages discussion and interaction between individuals interested in Fenton glass. Holds educational seminars, raffles of Fenton glass, and public auctions. Maintains speakers' bureau. Conducts forum to identify and discuss aspects of specific Fenton glass pieces. **Libraries: Type:** reference. **Subjects:** glass. **Awards:** Edtell Award. **Frequency:** annual. **Type:** recognition. **Publications:** *Fenton Flyer*, bimonthly. Newsletter. Contains educational articles and organizational news. **Price:** included in membership dues. **Circulation:** 600. **Advertising:** accepted. **Conventions/Meetings:** annual dinner and banquet, includes an auction of pieces made from the special glass produced for members and a dinner cruise (exhibits) ● annual meeting - last week of July or 1st week of August, in Marietta, OH.

22079 ■ National Imperial Glass Collectors Society (NIGCS)
PO Box 534
Bellaire, OH 43906
E-mail: info@imperialglass.org
URL: http://www.imperialglass.org
Contact: Mr. Mike Wilson, Pres.
Founded: 1977. **Members:** 1,100. **Membership Dues:** individual, $18 (annual) ● associate, $21 (annual). **Local Groups:** 10. **Description:** Individuals and collectors clubs collecting glass produced by Imperial Glass Corporation in Bellaire, OH. Sponsors the National Imperial Glass Museum in Bellaire, Ohio. **Awards: Type:** recognition. **Formerly:** (1977) Imperial Glass Collectors Society. **Publications:** *Imperial Collectors Glasszette*, quarterly. Newsletter. **Advertising:** accepted. **Conventions/Meetings:** annual convention and trade show, with educational seminars (exhibits) - always June.

22080 ■ National Milk Glass Collectors Society (NMGCS)
c/o Barb Pinkston
1306 Stowe St.
Inverness, FL 34450-6853
E-mail: membership@nmgcs.org
URL: http://www.nmgcs.org
Contact: June Sohl, Pres.
Founded: 1988. **Members:** 700. **Membership Dues:** single, $18 (annual) ● associate, $10 (annual) ● family, $28 (annual). **Description:** Collectors of antique milk glass and other interested individuals. Supports and preserves the study and preservation of milk glass. Conducts educational activities. **Libraries: Type:** reference; open to the public. **Publications:** *Opaque News*, quarterly. Newsletter. Includes articles written by members on all aspects of milk glass collecting, including reproductions and how to distinguish new glass from old glass. **Price:** included in membership dues. **Conventions/Meetings:** annual meeting and convention, forum for members to buy, sell, trade, and display milk glass; includes auction, speakers, and presentations (exhibits).

22081 ■ Tiffin Glass Collectors Club
PO Box 554
Tiffin, OH 44883
Ph: (419)448-0200
E-mail: info@tiffinglass.org
URL: http://www.tiffinglass.org
Contact: Ruth Hemminger, Pres.
Founded: 1985. **Members:** 300. **Membership Dues:** individual, $15 (annual). **Description:** Collectors of glasswares produced in Tiffin, OH at Factory R of the U.S. Glass Company. Promotes location, preservation, education, and collection of Tiffin glass. Facilitates exchange of information among members; serves as a clearinghouse on Tiffin glass. Operates Tiffin Glass Museum and Tiffin Glass Shoppe located at 25-27 S. Washington St., Tiffin, Ohio. Conducts tours and retail sales. **Libraries: Type:** not open to the public. **Holdings:** 40; articles, books, business records, clippings, periodicals. **Subjects:** glasswares. **Committees:** Tiffin Glass Museum. **Publications:** *Tiffin Glassmasters*, quarterly. Newsletter. Includes club's news, research articles on glass and glass ID. **Price:** available to members only. **Circulation:** 300. **Advertising:** accepted. **Conventions/Meetings:** semiannual Glass Show, show and sale, educational displays, book sales (exhibits) - always last weekend of June and 1st weekend of November, in Tiffin, OH ● monthly meeting (exhibits) - always second Tuesday in Tiffin, OH.

Gourmets

22082 ■ American Institute of Wine and Food (AIWF)
213-37 39th Ave., Box 216
Bayside, NY 11361
Free: (800)274-2493
Fax: (718)229-2324

E-mail: info@aiwf.org
URL: http://www.aiwf.com
Contact: Tom Potter, Exec. Dir.
Founded: 1981. **Members:** 7,000. **Membership Dues:** student, $25 ● individual, $75 ● dual, $125 ● professional/contributing, $150 ● business/winery/restaurant, $250 ● chapter partner, $500 ● national partner, $2,500. **Staff:** 6. **Local Groups:** 33. **Description:** Represents chefs, restaurateurs, winemakers, journalists, and others interested in the art of wine and fine cuisine. Promotes a broad exchange of information and ideas to benefit all who care about wine and food. Seeks to advance the understanding, appreciation and quality of food and drink. Conducts educational programs. **Computer Services:** Mailing lists, of members. **Programs:** Days of Taste. **Publications:** *American Wine and Food*, bimonthly. Newsletter. **Price:** included in membership dues.● Annual Report, annual. Alternate Formats: online.

22083 ■ Confrerie de la Chaine des Rotisseurs, Bailliage des U.S.A. (CHAINE)
285 Madison Ave.
Madison, NJ 07940-1099
Ph: (973)360-9200
Fax: (973)360-9330
E-mail: chaine@chaineus.org
URL: http://www.chaineus.org
Contact: Clyde Braunstein, Exec. Dir.
Founded: 1950. **Members:** 7,000. **Staff:** 4. **Budget:** $1,300,000. **Regional Groups:** 10. **Local Groups:** 150. **Description:** Encourages the professional and academic pursuit of culinary excellence. Represents laymen, world renowned lecturers, authors, and critics, professionals involved in food preparation, service, and administration in hotels and restaurants, and wine, food, and equipment suppliers. Stresses the interrelation between the amateur and professional. Promotes participation in activities, conventions, and reunions sponsored abroad by similar international organizations. Sponsors Chaine Education Fund, which supports educational and charitable programs on food and hotel education throughout the U.S. (Group's name translates as: Brotherhood of the Chain of Roasters, U.S. Chapter). **Awards:** Bronze Star of Excellence. **Frequency:** annual. **Type:** recognition. **Recipient:** for outstanding service by a Bailli ● Gold Chaine Star of Excellence. **Frequency:** annual. **Type:** recognition. **Recipient:** for outstanding regional or national service ● Gold Mondial Medal. **Frequency:** annual. **Type:** medal. **Recipient:** for outstanding regional or national service ● Mondial Bronze Medal. **Frequency:** annual. **Type:** medal. **Recipient:** for outstanding service by a Bailli ● Mondial Silver Medal. **Frequency:** annual. **Type:** medal. **Recipient:** for outstanding service by a Bailli provincial ● Silver Star of Excellence. **Frequency:** annual. **Type:** recognition. **Recipient:** for outstanding service by a Bailli provincial. **Councils:** National. **Publications:** *Gastronome*, 3/year. Magazine. Records the full range of Chaine activities. **Price:** included in membership dues; $20.00 single copy. **Circulation:** 10,000 ● Newsletters. **Conventions/Meetings:** annual congress ● seminar.

22084 ■ International Barbeque Cookers Association (IBCA)
PO Box 300556
Arlington, TX 76007-0556
Ph: (817)469-1579 (817)457-0599
Fax: (817)860-7755
E-mail: ibcalynn@comcast.net
URL: http://www.ibcabbq.org
Contact: Jeff Shivers, Exec. Dir.
Founded: 1989. **Members:** 500. **Membership Dues:** general, $30 (annual) ● per extra pit, $10 (annual) ● life, $250. **Staff:** 1. **Regional Groups:** 1. **State Groups:** 4. **Description:** Barbeque cooks. Promotes the art of barbeque cooking. Provides rules, guidelines and oversees judging at competition events using any and all meat and/or meats cooked from scratch.

22085 ■ International Chili Society (ICS)
PO Box 1027
San Juan Capistrano, CA 92693

Ph: (949)496-2651
Free: (877)777-4ICS
Fax: (949)496-7091
E-mail: ics@chilicookoff.com
URL: http://www.chilicookoff.com
Contact: Carol Hancock, CEO
Founded: 1970. **Members:** 10,000. **Membership Dues:** regular, in U.S., $42 (annual) ● regular, in Canada and Mexico, $47 (annual) ● international, $62 (annual). **Staff:** 2. **Regional Groups:** 97. **Local Groups:** 350. **Multinational. Description:** Chili enthusiasts who believe that chili cooking is "as American as apple pie". Sponsors chili cook-offs in search of the best chili. Holds 350 competitions with winners proceeding to one of 97 regional or state competitions. Regional and state champions compete at annual cook-off where the winner receives a $25,000 prize. All proceeds go to charity. **Publications:** *All-American Chili Cookbook* ● *ICS Newspaper*, quarterly. Newsletter. **Price:** included in membership dues. **Circulation:** 35,000. **Advertising:** accepted ● *Official Chili Cookbook* ● Magazine, annual. Features program of the World's Championship. **Price:** $2.00. **Conventions/Meetings:** annual World's Championship Chili Cook-Off - competition - always October.

22086 ■ International Connoisseurs of Green and Red Chile (ICGRC)
c/o NMSU Alumni Association
PO Box 30001
MSC 3AS
Las Cruces, NM 88003-8001
Ph: (505)646-3616
Free: (866)678-2586
Fax: (505)646-6123
E-mail: alumni@nmsu.edu
URL: http://alum.nmsu.edu
Contact: Sandra Avalos, Pres.
Founded: 1973. **Members:** 250. **Membership Dues:** aggie level, $35 (annual) ● pete level, $75 (annual) ● crimson, life, $500 ● joint aggie, $50 (annual) ● joint pete, $100 (annual) ● joint crimson, $750. **Staff:** 2. **Local Groups:** 1. **For-Profit. Description:** Enthusiasts of green and red chiles. Conducts research programs. Sponsors competitions.

22087 ■ Kansas City Barbeque Society (KCBS)
11514 Hickman Mills Dr.
Kansas City, MO 64134
Ph: (816)765-5891
Free: (800)963-KCBS
Fax: (816)765-5860
E-mail: kcbs@kcbs.us
URL: http://www.kcbs.us
Contact: Carolyn Wells, Exec. Dir.
Founded: 1986. **Members:** 5,000. **Membership Dues:** individual in U.S., $35 (annual) ● individual outside U.S., $45 (annual) ● family, $50 (annual). **Staff:** 3. **Budget:** $500,000. **Regional Groups:** 6. **Multinational. Description:** Promotes barbeque. Sanctions barbeque competitions and assists state and local civic and charitable organizations in conducting cook-offs. Maintains contact with other barbeque organizations. Sponsors educational programs and speakers' bureau. Compiles statistics. Operates Hall of Flame. **Libraries: Type:** reference; not open to the public. **Holdings:** archival material, audiovisuals, books, clippings, periodicals. **Subjects:** barbeque equipment, manufacturers, and "how to" manuals. **Awards:** Hall of Flame. **Frequency:** annual. **Type:** recognition. **Recipient:** for outstanding achievement in field of BBQ ● Team of the Year. **Frequency:** annual. **Type:** recognition. **Recipient:** for the team earning the most competition points during the calendar year. **Computer Services:** database, members and suppliers. **Publications:** *KC Bullsheet*, monthly. Newspaper. **Price:** included in membership dues. **Circulation:** 5,000. **Advertising:** accepted ● *2006 KCBS Cook's Handbook*, annual. Alternate Formats: online. **Conventions/Meetings:** annual convention and trade show (exhibits).

22088 ■ Terlingua International Chili Championship (TICC)
c/o Alan Dean, Exec. Dir.
112 Leaning Oak Cir.
Johnson City, TX 78636
Ph: (830)868-4313
E-mail: pepperdean@ctesc.net
URL: http://www.chili.org/terlingua.html
Contact: Alan Dean, Exec. Dir.
Founded: 1967. **Staff:** 2. **Multinational. Description:** Individuals (described as "tough-mouthed gourmets" and "chili heads") who meet for the annual Terlingua International Chili Cook-off. Chili cooks from 52 states and territories, Mexico, Canada, and all over the world compete for the title of international chili cooking champion. Aims to improve chili con carne while preserving it according to "old Texas style standards." Conducts charitable programs. **Formerly:** (1988) Chili Appreciation Society International. **Publications:** *Goat Gap Gazette*, monthly. Newsletter. Contains news for chili and barbecue enthusiasts, notices of upcoming cookoffs, and lists of competition winners. **Price:** $20.00/year. **Circulation:** 5,000. **Advertising:** accepted. **Conventions/Meetings:** annual International Convention - convention and competition - always first Saturday in November, Terlingua, TX.

22089 ■ Vinegar Connoisseurs International (VC)
c/o Lawrence Diggs
PO Box 41
Roslyn, SD 57261
Free: (800)342-4519
Fax: (605)486-4536
E-mail: vinegar@vinegarman.com
URL: http://www.vinegarman.com
Contact: Lawrence Diggs, Contact
Founded: 1996. **Members:** 400. **Staff:** 1. **Budget:** $10,000. **Languages:** Chinese, English, German, Japanese, Spanish. **For-Profit. Multinational. Description:** Individuals with an interest in vinegar and its uses. Serves as a clearinghouse for vinegar consumers. Gathers and disseminates information on types of vinegar and their culinary applications. Makes available discounts and special vinegar buying opportunities to members; distributes recipes using vinegar. Conducts research and educational programs; sponsors competitions; maintains speakers' bureau; sponsors competitions. Operates International Vinegar Museum. **Libraries: Type:** reference. **Holdings:** articles, artwork, audio recordings, books, periodicals, video recordings. **Subjects:** vinegar, recipes. **Awards:** Mother of All Vinegar Award. **Frequency:** annual. **Type:** trophy. **Recipient:** for competition winners. **Computer Services:** Information services, education on vinegar. **Publications:** *The Complete Vinegar*. Book. Contains information about vinegar. **Price:** $17.95 paperback. **Conventions/Meetings:** annual festival.

Guitar

22090 ■ European Guitar Teachers Association (EGTA)
c/o Jonathan Leathwood, Journal Ed.
2363 S York St., No. 304
Denver, CO 80210
E-mail: ginettediffley@aol.com
URL: http://www.egtaguitarforum.org/egta.html
Contact: Jonathan Leathwood, Journal Ed.
Multinational. Description: Represents professional guitar players and teachers; promotes further development of guitar education and artistic, the scientific aspects of guitar playing and chamber music, and cultural-political concepts of guitar music.

Hobbies

22091 ■ American Cookie Jar Association (ACJA)
c/o Gary Cottrell, Membership Chm.
304 Clinton St.
Fayetteville, NY 13066

E-mail: dues@cookiejarclub.com
URL: http://www.cookiejarclub.com
Contact: Barb Jensen, Co-Pres.
Membership Dues: regular, $10 ● additional (same household), $5. **Description:** Promotes fun, fellowship, education and the sharing of information among jar collectors. **Computer Services:** database, dealer members ● online services, bulletin board. **Publications:** Newsletter.

22092 ■ Federation of Metal Detector and Archaeological Clubs (FMDAC)
184 Grange Rd.
McClellandtown, PA 15458
Ph: (724)439-1380 (330)364-1608
E-mail: snakemandb@earthlink.net
URL: http://www.fmdac.org
Contact: Duane Biller, Pres.
Founded: 1984. **Membership Dues:** independent, $10 (annual) ● club (per member), $5 (annual). **Description:** Seeks to unite, promote and encourage metal detecting, archaeological and prospecting clubs. Preserves the hobby/sport of metal detecting. Establishes an understanding of the significant relationship between metal detecting and archaeological research. Disseminates technical, educational and social information relating to metal detecting and historical or archaeological discoveries. **Computer Services:** Online services, forum. **Publications:** *Quest.* Newsletter. Alternate Formats: online.

22093 ■ National Polymer Clay Guild (NPCG)
PMB 345
1350 Beverly Rd., 115
McLean, VA 22101
E-mail: info@npcg.org
URL: http://www.npcg.org
Contact: Diane Villano, Pres.
Membership Dues: individual in U.S. and Canada, $30 (annual) ● family in U.S. and Canada, $40 (annual) ● individual/family outside U.S. and Canada, $50 (annual). **Description:** Seeks to educate the public about polymer clay and to study and promote interest in the use of polymer clay as an artistic medium. Promotes polymer clay work to galleries and museums as well as to the public. Develops opportunities for artists to show their work to the public and engage in public-service activities. **Computer Services:** database, listing of local, regional and international guilds ● information services, polymer clay ● online services, chat ● online services, forum. **Telecommunication Services:** electronic mail, npcg@npcg.org ● electronic mail, secretary@npcg.org. **Publications:** *PolyInformer*, quarterly. Newsletter.

Home Exchange

22094 ■ Homelink International
c/o Karl Costabel, Exec. Off.
2937 NW 9th Terr.
Wilton Manors, FL 33311
Ph: (954)566-2687
Free: (800)638-3841
E-mail: homelink@spamcop.net
URL: http://www.homelink-usa.org
Contact: Karl Costabel, Exec. Off.
Founded: 1960. **Members:** 16,000. **Membership Dues:** individual, $80 (annual). **Staff:** 4. **Budget:** $710,000. **Regional Groups:** 26. **Description:** Individuals and families interested in exchanging homes (apartments, cottages, or farms) temporarily for holiday and vacation purposes; members write to each other to make their own exchange or rental arrangements. The club is linked with Homelink International, Cambridge, England; International Home Exchange, Manly, Australia; Sejours, Aix-en-Provence, France; Holiday Service, Memmelsdorf, Germany; LOVW, Groningen, Netherlands; Intercambio de Casas, Madrid, Spain; Taxi-Stop, Ghent, Belgium; Casa Vacanza, Padova, Italy; and West World Holiday Exchange, Vancouver, Canada; these groups issue combined directories of U.S. and European home exchange offerings. **Libraries: Type:**

reference. **Holdings:** 5. **Formerly:** (1997) Vacation Exchange Club; (2003) Man Watchers. **Publications:** *Exchange Book*, quarterly. Directory. Lists 15,000 families in 50 countries seeking home exchange travel and holiday arrangements. **Price:** included in membership dues. **Conventions/Meetings:** annual congress.

22095 ■ Interval International (II)
PO Box 431920
Miami, FL 33143-1920
Ph: (305)668-3414 (305)666-1884
Free: (888)784-3447
Fax: (305)667-5321
E-mail: customerservice@intervalintl.com
URL: http://www.intervalworld.com
Contact: Craig Nash, Chm./CEO
Founded: 1976. **Membership Dues:** individual, $79 (annual) ● interval gold status, $54 (annual). **For-Profit. Multinational. Description:** Facilitates vacation exchange among members owning time-share properties. Individuals are thus able to exchange the time they own at their "home" resorts for the time owned by others at different resorts in the Interval network. **Publications:** *Interval World.* Magazine. Contains articles on destinations, activities, member benefit updates, vacation bargains and new resorts. ● *Resort Directory.* Gives detailed descriptions of member resorts. **Conventions/Meetings:** semiannual symposium.

Horseback Riding

22096 ■ American Association of Riding Schools (AARS)
8375 Coldwater Rd.
Davison, MI 48423-8966
Ph: (810)496-0360
Fax: (810)658-9733
E-mail: info@ucanride.com
URL: http://www.ucanride.com
Description: Offers riding and horse care program in the United States.

22097 ■ American Riding Instructors Association (ARIA)
28801 Trenton Ct.
Bonita Springs, FL 34134-3337
Ph: (239)948-3232
Fax: (239)948-5053
E-mail: aria@riding-instructor.com
URL: http://www.riding-instructor.com
Founded: 1984. **Membership Dues:** general, $35 (annual) ● life, $750 ● general, $75 (triennial). **Description:** Promotes safe and knowledgeable riding instruction. Encourages instructors to attend the American Riding Instructor Certification program. **Publications:** *Riding Instructor*, quarterly. Magazine. Alternate Formats: online.

22098 ■ Centered Riding (CR)
PO Box 157
Perkiomenville, PA 18074
Ph: (610)754-0633
Fax: (610)754-0634
E-mail: president@centeredriding.org
URL: http://www.centeredriding.org
Contact: Deb Moynihan, Pres.
Membership Dues: supporting, $35 (annual) ● supporting (in Canada and Mexico), $42 (annual) ● supporting (international), $45 (annual) ● business in U.S., $85 (annual) ● business (in Canada and Mexico), $92 (annual) ● business (international), $90 (annual). **Multinational. Description:** Serves as a way of expressing the classical principles of riding, using body awareness, centering and imagery. Educates instructors in the use of Centered Riding techniques. **Publications:** *Centered Riding Instructor Directory*, annual. Also Cited As: *CRID* ● *Centered Riding News*, quarterly. Newsletter. **Advertising:** accepted. Also Cited As: *CRN.*

Horses

22099 ■ American Sulphur Horse Association (ASHA)
2180 Mt. Olive Ch. Rd.
Taylorsville, NC 28681
E-mail: utahoss@msn.com
URL: http://www.americanspanishsulphur.org
Contact: Rob Martin, Pres.
Founded: 2003. **Membership Dues:** full, $10 (annual) ● family, farm and ranch, $15 (annual) ● associate, $5 (annual). **Multinational. Description:** Seeks to preserve, promote and perpetuate the Spanish/Iberian American Sulphur horse. **Computer Services:** database, stallions at stud ● information services, breed standard ● information services, sulphur inspection. **Telecommunication Services:** electronic mail, featheroakranch@socal.rr.com. **Departments:** Administration; Marketing; Membership; Publications; Registry.

22100 ■ National Reined Cow Horse Association (NRCHA)
13181 US Hwy. 177
Byars, OK 74831
Ph: (580)759-4949
Fax: (580)759-3999
E-mail: nrcha@nrcha.com
URL: http://www2.nrcha.com
Contact: Dan Roeser, Pres.
Membership Dues: regular, $65 (annual) ● junior, youth, $40 (annual) ● life, $650 ● international, $115 (annual) ● associate, $35 (annual) ● Canadian, $83 (annual). **Description:** Preserves the old methods of training reined cow horses. Promotes active participation of members in working cow horse events. Encourages junior riders in continuing the old ways of the vaqueros. **Committees:** Affiliates; Ethics; Horse Sales; Judges; Limited Aged Events; Non Pro; Stallion Service Silent Auction; World Show.

22101 ■ North American Model Horse Shows Association (NAMHSA)
PO Box 40
Campbell, TX 75422
E-mail: president@namhsa.org
URL: http://www.namhsa.org
Contact: Amy Peck, Pres.
Membership Dues: individual, $20 (annual) ● individual, $50 (triennial) ● show, $30-$70. **Description:** Promotes the model horse hobby to the public to develop interest, support and recognition. Serves as a unifying organization for cooperation among live shows and as a clearinghouse for information on shows and events. **Awards:** NAMHSA Member Show of the Year. **Frequency:** annual. **Type:** recognition. **Recipient:** to outstanding NAMHSA member live shows. **Computer Services:** Mailing lists.

Housewares

22102 ■ Griswold and Cast Iron Cookware Association (G&C¹CA)
c/o Kathy Tatro, Sec.
PO Box 33688
Portland, OR 97292
E-mail: kattatro@aol.com
URL: http://www.gcica.org
Contact: Kathy Tatro, Sec.
Founded: 1992. **Members:** 958. **Membership Dues:** individual, $20 (annual) ● family, $25 (annual). **Description:** Collectors and enthusiasts of Griswold and cast iron cookware. Promotes collection, use, and proper care of cast iron and Griswold cookware. Facilitates communication among members; serves as a clearinghouse on Griswold and cast iron cookware; conducts campaigns to halt the manufacture and distribution of fake and reproduction cast iron cookware; makes available appraisal services. Sponsors research and educational programs; participates in charitable activities. **Libraries: Type:** reference; not open to the public. **Holdings:** archival material, articles, clippings. **Subjects:** Griswold cookware, cast

iron cookware. **Awards:** Outstanding Member of the Year. **Frequency:** annual. **Type:** recognition. **Publications:** *G&CICA Newsletter*, quarterly. **Price:** included in membership dues. Alternate Formats: online ● Membership Directory, annual. **Conventions/Meetings:** annual convention and workshop, with swap meet and education.

Hovercraft

22103 ■ Hovercraft Club of America (HCA)
PO Box 908
Foley, AL 36536-0908
Ph: (251)946-3800
Fax: (251)946-3800
E-mail: hovermail@hoverclubofamerica.org
URL: http://www.hoverclubofamerica.org
Contact: Sherri L. Galka, Office Admin./Sec.
Founded: 1974. **Members:** 750. **Membership Dues:** individual, $30 (annual) ● family/school/group, $40 (annual). **Staff:** 2. **Regional Groups:** 10. **Description:** Amateur and professional owners and builders of Hovercraft; Hovercraft manufacturers, students, engineers, and enthusiasts. Hovercraft operate commercially as ferries, commuter vehicles, search and rescue craft, and as military assault and logistic transportation. Sports models are produced by amateurs and commercial builders in a variety of sizes; most hold one or two passengers. **Awards:** Hovernaut of the Year. **Frequency:** annual. **Type:** recognition. **Recipient:** for outstanding achievement. **Committees:** Communications; Cruising; Events; Racing; Safety. **Formerly:** (2003) Hoverclub of America. **Supersedes:** American Hovercraft Association. **Publications:** *Hoverclub Roster*, semiannual. Book. Contains member information. ISSN: 1098-1713 ● *Hovercraft Information*. Booklet. Lists manufacturers, parts dealers, groups, clubs, and publications. ● *Hovernews*, bimonthly. Newsletter. Covers the latest in sport hovercraft technology, factory and homebuilt. **Price:** included in membership dues. **Circulation:** 800. **Advertising:** accepted ● *Light Hovercraft Design*. Book. Contains formulas, photos, and technical information. ● *Recreational Hovercraft Safety and Competition Rules*. Booklet. Contains safety rules and regulations. **Conventions/Meetings:** annual Rally and Hover-In (exhibits).

Humor

22104 ■ Absurd Special Interest Group (ASIG)
c/o Hank Roll, Exec. Off.
1306 Lloyd St.
Nanty Glo, PA 15943
E-mail: theatrocity@aol.com
Contact: Hank Roll, Exec. Off.
Founded: 1979. **Members:** 222. **Membership Dues:** subscriber, $12 (annual). **Staff:** 2. **Description:** Members of Mensa interested in absurd humor. Maintains museum; operates speakers' bureau. **Libraries:** **Type:** reference. **Awards:** **Type:** recognition. **Affiliated With:** American Mensa. **Also Known As:** The Sig That Taste Forgot. **Publications:** *Atrocity*, monthly. Newsletter. Contains tasteless humor and absurdities. **Price:** $12.00/year; $20.00 26 issues. **Circulation:** 250. **Advertising:** accepted. **Conventions/Meetings:** competition.

22105 ■ Benevolent and Loyal Order of Pessimists (BLOOP)
PO Box 1945
Iowa City, IA 52244
Ph: (319)351-2973 (319)351-1201
Fax: (319)354-5657
E-mail: dleshtz@ia.net
Contact: Jack Duvall, Pres.
Founded: 1975. **Members:** 1,000. **Membership Dues:** individual, $20. **Staff:** 2. **Description:** A tongue-in-cheek organization of pessimists, founded as a counterpart to optimists' clubs. Sponsors charitable events to raise funds for AIDS-related services and domestic violence programs. Maintains

the motto "In front of every silver lining there's a black cloud.". **Awards:** Meritorious Achievement in Pessimism. **Frequency:** annual. **Type:** recognition. **Recipient:** for specific activities embodying the belief that pessimism equals realism ● Pessimist of the Year Award. **Frequency:** annual. **Type:** recognition. **Recipient:** to a member who most personifies the spirit of pessimism. **Publications:** Newsletter. Contains information of charitable events sponsored by the organization. **Price:** included in membership dues. **Conventions/Meetings:** annual meeting - always Saturday closest to April 15 (IRS deadline for filing tax returns), usually in Iowa City, IA.

22106 ■ Burlington Liars Club (BLC)
PO Box 156
Burlington, WI 53105-0156
Ph: (262)763-4640
URL: http://www.burlingtonhistory.org/Liars_Club.htm
Contact: John Soeth, Pres.
Founded: 1929. **Members:** 110,000. **Membership Dues:** life, $1. **Description:** Perpetuates the American heritage of telling humorous tall tales. **Awards:** Best Lie of the Year. **Frequency:** annual. **Type:** recognition. **Recipient:** to world champion liar. **Publications:** *Championship Lies, Fibs and Prevarications*, periodic. Booklet. Contains brief history of the club and all of the "champion lies" since 1929. **Price:** $3.00 ● Books. **Conventions/Meetings:** annual Champion Liars' Contest - competition.

22107 ■ Institute of Totally Useless Skills (ITUS)
c/o Rick Davis
PO Box 181
Temple, NH 03084
Ph: (603)654-5875
Fax: (509)696-1635
E-mail: rick@schoolshows.com
URL: http://www.totallyuselessskills.com
Contact: Rick Davis, Contact
Founded: 1987. **Members:** 654. **Description:** A tongue-in-cheek organization for individuals devoted to the obtainment of useless and nonpractical skills. Advocates the importance of mastering skills such as advanced eye crossing, yodeling, parlor tricks, paper balancing, spoon playing, pen bouncing, and "weird feelings." Encourages members to "learn everything you'll never need to know." Seeks to bring instant talent to the untalented and to "boldly go where no curriculum has gone before." Sponsors workshops. **Libraries:** **Type:** reference. **Awards:** Practitioner of Uselessness Degree. **Type:** recognition.

22108 ■ International Association of People Who Dine Over the Kitchen Sink
PO Box 221413
Sacramento, CA 95822
E-mail: normh@sinkie.com
URL: http://www.sinkie.com
Contact: Norm Hankoff, Founder
Founded: 1991. **Multinational. Description:** Celebrates the "time honored tradition of saving precious minutes by eating while standing over the kitchen sink or in comparable informal fashion." Donates some proceeds to charities that combat world hunger. If it has anything to do with having a quick bite, it has everything to do with being a "sinkie". **Awards:** "Suspected Closet-Sinkies" List. **Frequency:** annual. **Type:** recognition. **Recipient:** to prominent people suspected of being "Closet-Sinkies". **Also Known As:** Sinkies International. **Publications:** *The Official Sinkies Don't Cook Book*. **Price:** $13.95. **Conventions/Meetings:** annual Sinkie Day - competition - always the day after Thanksgiving.

22109 ■ International Association of Professional Bureaucrats (INATAPROBU)
c/o Dr. Jim H. Boren, Pres./Founder
2400 Jolinda Ln.
Whitesboro, TX 76273
Ph: (903)564-9290
Fax: (903)564-9430

E-mail: jim.boren@cox-internet.com
URL: http://www.jimboren.com/inataprobu.shtml
Contact: Dr. Jim H. Boren, Pres./Founder
Founded: 1968. **Members:** 1,750. **Membership Dues:** individual, $20 (annual). **Staff:** 3. **Budget:** $25,000. **Regional Groups:** 5. **National Groups:** 9. **Languages:** English, Portuguese, Spanish. **Multinational. Description:** Individuals employed by governments, universities, and industry united to spoof bureaucracy in the hope that looking at it with goodnatured humor may bring improvement. Motto of association is "When in doubt, mumble." Aims to foster professional interdigitation and to give recognition to practitioners of the bureaucratic arts. Sponsors international awards banquets, and other activities to enhance the bureaucratic way of life. Maintains 29 coordinating committees. Conducts examination for Certified Professional Bureaucrats (CPB). Maintains hall of fame. **Libraries:** **Type:** reference. **Holdings:** 5,500; artwork, books, clippings, monographs, periodicals. **Subjects:** government, politics, humor. **Awards:** Order of the Bird Award. **Frequency:** semiannual. **Type:** recognition. **Recipient:** for outstanding examples of bureaucratic excellence ● Order of the Egg Award. **Type:** recognition. **Recipient:** for outstanding examples of bureaucratic excellence, 2nd level ● Rejection Scroll. **Frequency:** annual. **Type:** recognition. **Recipient:** for those who undermine the bureaucratic way of life. **Divisions:** Corporate; Governmental; Media. **Subgroups:** Ughy-Ughy-Oooh Society of America, Inc. **Formerly:** (1974) National Association of Professional Bureaucrats. **Publications:** *Bureaucratic Strategies*. Book ● *The Bureaucratic Zoo*. Book ● *Fuzzify*. Book ● *Have Your Way With Bureaucrats*. Book ● *How to be a Sincere Phoney*. Handbook. **Price:** $21.95 hardback; $12.95 paperback ● *The Jim Boren BIRDCAGE: A View of the World From the Bottom of the Cage*, monthly. Newsletter. **Price:** $20.00/year ● *Twiggle*. Book ● *The Ughy-Ughy-Oooh Report*, quarterly. **Price:** $20.00/year ● *When in Doubt, Mumble*. Book. **Conventions/Meetings:** annual meeting, with awards ball ● seminar.

22110 ■ International Banana Club (IBC)
16367 Main St.
Hesperia, CA 92345-3547
Ph: (760)244-5488 (626)321-6262
E-mail: bananaman@bananaclub.com
URL: http://www.bananaclub.com
Contact: L. Ken Bannister, Pres.
Founded: 1972. **Members:** 9,000. **Membership Dues:** life, $15. **Multinational. Description:** Banana enthusiasts in 27 countries with an appreciation of humor. Influences people to smile more often in a world that is "going bananas". Promotes sense of humor, positive outlook, and good health. Organizes occasional parties, picnics, games, photographic outings, seminars, and educational programs on bananas. Maintains museum of over 17000 banana artifacts sent by members, open by appointment only. **Libraries:** **Type:** reference. **Awards:** Bananister Award. **Type:** recognition ● Doctorate of Bananistry Medal. **Frequency:** annual. **Type:** recognition ● International Banana Club Member of the Year. **Frequency:** annual. **Type:** recognition. **Recipient:** for contributions to the association and daily effort to lift other people's spirits ● Master of Bananistry Medal. **Frequency:** annual. **Type:** recognition. **Subgroups:** Banana Busters - South Carolina. **Publications:** *Woddis News*, semiannual. Newsletter. Contains club news and health tips. **Price:** $10.00/year. **Advertising:** accepted. Alternate Formats: online ● *Woddis Newsletter*, semiannual ● Brochure. **Conventions/Meetings:** annual international conference (exhibits).

22111 ■ International Order of the Armadillo (IOA)
PO Box 60305
Jacksonville, FL 32236
Ph: (904)384-8594
Fax: (904)387-1806
Contact: Robert L. Graessle, Coor.
Founded: 1982. **Members:** 2,000. **Membership Dues:** life, $10. **For-Profit. Description:** Individuals interested in the history and habits of the armadillo, a

small, burrowing mammal indigenous to the semitropical regions of the Americas. Seeks to inform the public of the cultural and ecological value of these creatures. Maintains a collection of materials pertaining to the armadillo. **Publications:** Booklet. Details armadillo truth, myth, and legend. ● Catalog. Lists armadillo gift items.

22112 ■ Man Will Never Fly Memorial Society Internationale (MWNFMS)

103 Caribbean Ave.
Virginia Beach, VA 23451-4716
E-mail: webmaster@manwillneverfly.com
URL: http://www.manwillneverfly.com
Founded: 1959. **Members:** 6,000. **Membership Dues:** life, $10. **Description:** Persons in the news media or aviation and "assorted believers." Characterizes itself as a tongue-in-cheek, bottle-in-hand group dedicated to proving that birds fly - men drink. Sponsors annual social event on the eve of the celebration of the anniversary of the alleged first airplane flight by the Wright brothers (Dec. 17, 1903); the society reportedly was founded as a spoof on the First Flight Society, which sponsors the Wright brothers observance. At the Man Will Never Fly gathering, an "unknown international celebrity" discourses on the "unlikely notion that the Wright brothers ever got off the ground." The group gives an annual citation to one or more persons who did the most during the previous year to discourage the idea that flight is a logical thing; in 1959 established an Aviation Hall of Infamy Award. **Awards: Frequency:** annual. **Type:** recognition. **Recipient:** for some aviation goof-off. **Publications:** *Program Announcement*, annual. Newsletter. **Conventions/Meetings:** annual dinner - always December 16, Kill Devil Hills, NC.

22113 ■ National Organization Taunting Safety and Fairness Everywhere (NOTSAFE)

PO Box 5743
Montecito, CA 93150
Ph: (805)969-6217
E-mail: dale93150@aol.com
URL: http://www.notsafe.org
Contact: Dale Lowdermilk, Exec. Dir./Founder
Founded: 1982. **Members:** 7,925. **Membership Dues:** political satire, $25 (annual). **Staff:** 4. **Budget:** $41,000. **For-Profit. Description:** Provides platform from which problems of government "stupidity" can be attacked with wit, satire, and overkill. Describes itself as "the world's most sarcastic organization" and uses wooden nickels with slogans such as "Help Abolish Everything" to humorously lampoon bureaucrats. **Libraries: Type:** not open to the public. **Subjects:** political satire. **Awards:** Stir-the-Pot Award. **Frequency:** annual. **Type:** recognition. **Recipient:** to an individual demonstrating undaunted courage in the face of bureaucratic intimidation. **Computer Services:** database, Spamalistic. **Committees:** Coalition to Ban Cruellers; Rename Obscene American Cities. **Publications:** *Quagmire*, annual. Newsletter. Contains news on membership activities. **Price:** included in membership dues. **Circulation:** 1,500. **Conventions/Meetings:** annual Think-In - meeting - always February in Montecito, CA.

22114 ■ Sarcastics Anonymous (SA)

Address Unknown since 2007
Founded: 1984. **Members:** 280. **Staff:** 2. **Budget:** $25,000. **Description:** Individuals who alienate others through the inappropriate use of sarcastic remarks or put-downs; those who live or work with these individuals. Purpose is to promote the positive uses of humor and laughter as opposed to sarcasm, or what the group sees as inappropriately used humor with the aim of getting the laugh, regardless of the results. Provides information on: the uses and abuses of humor in personal and professional lives; how to live or work with sarcastic people; methods for lessening sarcastic tendencies for members wishing to do so; how to develop their sense of humor if sarcastics choose to continue. Operates speakers' bureau. **Awards: Type:** recognition. **Absorbed:** (1991) Laugh Lovers. **Publications:** *Humor Defense*, quarterly. Newsletter. **Advertising:** not accepted ● Also publishes information sheet. **Conventions/**

Meetings: workshop, on business, education, and health with emphasis on stress reduction and communication.

22115 ■ Society for the Preservation and Enhancement of the Recognition of Millard Fillmore, Last of the Whigs (SPERMFLOW)

37 Hillside Rd.
Stratford, NJ 08084
Ph: (856)627-5118
E-mail: parkow@philafound.org
Contact: Phil Arkow, VP
Founded: 1975. **Members:** 400. **Membership Dues:** life, $10. **Description:** Individuals dedicated to the celebration of mediocrity in American culture, as epitomized by Millard Fillmore (1800-74), 13th president of the U.S. The society considers Fillmore to be the "dullest and unluckiest president we ever had," and says his "only accomplishment" was "keeping Texas from annexing the state of New Mexico in a fit of pre-football hysteria." Collects and disseminates information on mediocre public figures and events. **Libraries: Type:** reference. **Subjects:** mediocrity, whimsy. **Awards:** Medal of Mediocrity. **Frequency:** annual. **Type:** recognition. **Recipient:** for the individual who represents the principles Fillmore "tried to stand for, but usually sat on". **Departments:** Redundancy. **Also Known As:** Millard Fillmore Society. **Publications:** *Fillmore Bungle*, annual. Newsletter. Provides a humorous look at the foibles of American culture. **Circulation:** 300. **Conventions/Meetings:** annual Dearthday Party - meeting - usually January 7.

22116 ■ Universal Perkehner Society

Address Unknown since 2007
Founded: 1988. **Description:** Accepts any horse into special registry for the "misfit breed". Requirements include photograph of horse and a list of "outstanding personality peculiarities". Examples of personality traits include the pursuit of obstacles such as low tree limbs, water, and fences; sudden lameness during shows and prior to sale; daring escapes from the stall; gluttonous appetite; runaway tendencies.

Hunting

22117 ■ Bowhunting Preservation Alliance (BPA)

PO Box 258
Comfrey, MN 56019
Ph: (507)877-5300
Free: (866)266-2776
Fax: (507)877-2149
E-mail: jaymcaninch@archerytrade.org
URL: http://www.archerytrade.org/bowhunting_preservation_alliance.html
Contact: Jay McAninch, Pres./CEO
Founded: 2002. **Description:** Promotes the sport of bowhunting. **Publications:** *Chronic Wasting Disease: Should You Hunt Deer or Elk This Fall?*. Pamphlet ● Proceedings. **Price:** $20.00/copy; $45.00 3 copies; $100.00 100 copies. **Conventions/Meetings:** conference.

22118 ■ International Hunting Land Association (IHLA)

476 Dorothy Ave.
Johnstown, PA 15906-1455
Ph: (814)536-1898
Free: (888)814-4453
Fax: (814)536-1898
E-mail: info@hunt4land.org
URL: http://www.hunt4land.org
Contact: John E. MacEwan, Pres./Chm.
Founded: 1999. **Members:** 175. **Membership Dues:** life, $425 ● regular, $35 (annual) ● associate, $25 (annual). **Staff:** 7. **Description:** Represents hunters. Works to preserve quality hunting and recreational land for the public. **Publications:** *Hunting Land*, quarterly. Newsletter. Contains information about the association and its members. Alternate Formats: online. **Conventions/Meetings:** monthly meeting.

22119 ■ North American Bowhunting Coalition (NABC)

PO Box 493
Chatfield, MN 55923
E-mail: twangdrb@earthlink.net
URL: http://www.nabowhuntingcoalition.com
Contact: Dennis Ballard, Natl. Chm.
Founded: 2005. **Multinational. Description:** Works to promote, preserve and defend the ideals of bowhunting. Maintains a democratic process/structure whereby important bowhunting issues will be identified and efficiently pursued. Advocates for the future welfare of bowhunting in the United States and Canada. Functions as a clearinghouse for essential bowhunter information.

Implements

22120 ■ Cast Iron Seat Collectors Association (CISCA)

604 Washington St.
Woodstock, IL 60098-2251
Ph: (815)338-6464
Fax: (815)338-3556
E-mail: bud@castironseatclub.org
URL: http://www.castironseatclub.org
Contact: Charlotte Traxler, Sec.-Treas.
Founded: 1973. **Members:** 650. **Membership Dues:** regular, in U.S. and Canada, $20 (annual) ● regular, outside U.S. and Canada, $25 (annual). **Description:** Represents collectors of cast iron seats and related farm memorabilia made rare due to scrap drives of past wars. **Formerly:** (1980) National Cast Iron Implement Seat Collectors. **Publications:** *Cast Iron Seat Collectors Newsletter*, quarterly. **Price:** included in membership dues ● Brochures ● Newsletter, quarterly. **Conventions/Meetings:** annual Swap and Sell - meeting, displays of cast iron seats (exhibits) - always last weekend of July.

22121 ■ Mid-West Tool Collectors Association (M-WTCA)

PO Box 355
Humboldt, IA 50548-0355
E-mail: admin@mwtca.org
URL: http://www.mwtca.org
Contact: John Wells, Pres.
Founded: 1968. **Members:** 4,000. **Membership Dues:** regular, in U.S., $25 (annual) ● regular, in Canada, $33 (annual) ● other country, $40 (annual). **Multinational. Description:** Dedicated to study, preservation, and understanding of early tools, implements and devices used by ancestors in homes, shops, farms, and seas. **Awards:** M-WTCA Scholarships. **Frequency:** annual. **Type:** scholarship. **Recipient:** for students seeking a four-year degree. **Committees:** Mt. Vernon. **Publications:** *Gristmill*, quarterly, March, June, September, December. Magazine. Contains articles about tools, makers, users, early industries, etc. **Price:** included in membership dues. Alternate Formats: online. **Conventions/Meetings:** semiannual meeting and lecture (exhibits) ● regional meeting (exhibits).

22122 ■ National Reamer Collectors Association (NRCA)

c/o Wayne Adickes
408 E Reuss
Cuero, TX 77954
E-mail: adickes@sbcglobal.net
URL: http://www.reamers.org
Contact: Wayne Adickes, Contact
Founded: 1980. **Members:** 390. **Membership Dues:** regular, in U.S., $25 (annual) ● international, $27 (annual) ● household in U.S., $12 (annual) ● household in Canada, $14 (annual). **Regional Groups:** 3. **Description:** Collectors and dealers interested in reamers (orange juicers and lemon squeezers). Promotes reamer collecting and disseminates information about reamers. **Publications:** *Quarterly Review*. Newsletter. **Conventions/Meetings:** annual meeting, rare reamers, sales (exhibits) - always July/August.

22123 ■ Potomac Antique Tools and Industries Association (PATINA)
c/o Mr. Hugh M. South, Sec.-Treas.
11166 Wood Elves Way
Columbia, MD 21044
Ph: (410)992-1823
E-mail: hmsouth@comcast.net
URL: http://www.patinatools.org
Contact: Mr. Hugh M. South, Sec.-Treas.
Founded: 1978. **Members:** 300. **Membership Dues:** regular, $12 (annual). **Description:** Antique tool collectors, users, and their families; others interested in antique tools and industries. Seeks to advance understanding and appreciation of the tools, trades, agriculture, household economy, and other aspects of American ancestral life through the dissemination of information. Members conduct research; findings are published in newsletter. Provides educational programs, speakers, and demonstrations to interested public education groups. **Libraries: Type:** reference; lending; not open to the public. **Holdings:** 50; books. **Subjects:** antique tools, old trade catalogs. **Awards: Type:** monetary. **Recipient:** for institutions sponsoring tool-related exhibits and activities. **Publications:** *PATINAGRAM Newsletter*, bimonthly ● Membership Directory, annual. **Conventions/Meetings:** bimonthly meeting (exhibits) ● annual National Auction and Dealer Sale - meeting.

22124 ■ World Atlatl Association (WAA)
c/o Richard Lyons, Treas.
5024 King Rd.
Jeffersonville, IN 47130
Ph: (812)246-9987
E-mail: atlatlin@theremc.com
URL: http://www.worldatlatl.org
Contact: Scott Van Arsdale, Pres.
Founded: 1987. **Members:** 485. **Membership Dues:** individual, $15 (annual) ● family, $20 (annual). **Staff:** 12. **State Groups:** 7. **Description:** Individuals, organizations, institutions, and businesses interested in the atlatl spear thrower. (The atlatl is an ancient hunting weapon, used today as a sporting device.) Encourages the use, practice, promotion, manufacture, and perpetuation of the atlatl. Cooperates with anthropologists and archaeologists to discover, record, and preserve material and information related to the presence of the atlatl in specific regions; makes information available to the public for research. Maintains records, rules, and standards of sportsmanship in atlatl competitions. **Libraries: Type:** reference. **Holdings:** 48; periodicals. **Subjects:** spear throwing. **Awards: Frequency:** periodic. **Type:** fellowship ● Grand Champion Primitive and Modern Equipment - U.S. and Europe. **Frequency:** annual. **Type:** recognition ● International Standard Accuracy ATLATL Contest - U.S. and Europe. **Frequency:** annual. **Type:** recognition. **Recipient:** for attaining the highest scores ● President's Award. **Frequency:** annual. **Type:** recognition. **Telecommunication Services:** electronic mail, devoemertz@sbcglobal.net. **Publications:** *A Brief Coverage of ATLATL Styles, Construction and Usage*. Article. **Price:** $2.00 plus 50 cents postage ● *The Atlatl*, quarterly, every January, April, July, and October. Newsletter. Includes atlatl contest calendar and results, archaeological findings, and study results. **Price:** included in membership dues; $1.50/copy for nonmembers (plus postage). **Circulation:** 485 ● *Bamboo ATLATL Darts*. Article. **Price:** $1.00 plus 50 cents postage. **Conventions/Meetings:** annual convention, membership meeting (exhibits).

Knives

22125 ■ American Edge Collectors Association (AECA)
PO Box 2565
Country Club Hills, IL 60478
Ph: (708)868-7784 (708)672-8838
E-mail: louis_jamison@yahoo.com
URL: http://www.aecaknifeclub.com
Contact: Louis Jamison, Pres.
Founded: 1979. **Members:** 250. **Membership Dues:** regular, $20 (annual) ● associate, $10 (annual). De-

scription: Individuals interested in collecting, trading, dealing, buying, and selling old and new cutlery from swords to pocket knives. Aims to: advance knife collecting and trading as a hobby; promote fair and honest dealings with fellow members and collectors; discourage and condemn the practices of knife counterfeiting, misrepresentation, and exploitation of new and inexperienced collectors or traders. Conducts educational programs. **Libraries: Type:** open to the public. **Awards: Frequency:** annual. **Type:** recognition. **Recipient:** for winners at annual knife show in different categories. **Computer Services:** Mailing lists, members, dealers, and knifemakers. **Publications:** *AECA Newsletter*, monthly. **Price:** included in membership dues. **Advertising:** accepted. **Conventions/Meetings:** annual Knife Show, with displays of knives (custom, factory, collectibles) (exhibits) - always 2nd weekend in September ● monthly meeting and show - always 3rd Sunday (except September).

22126 ■ Case Collectors Club (CCC)
PO Box 4000
Bradford, PA 16701
Free: (800)523-6350
Fax: (814)368-1736
E-mail: casecollectorsclub@wrcase.com
URL: http://www.wrcase.com
Contact: Lisa Boser, Admin.
Founded: 1981. **Members:** 18,600. **Membership Dues:** regular, $12 (annual) ● life, $100. **Staff:** 6. **Description:** Knife collectors. Provides members with information about Case knives. Offers special edition knives annually. **Publications:** *The Case Collector*, quarterly. Magazine. Contains in-depth articles about the history of Case and information on Case products (old and new). **Price:** included in membership dues. **Conventions/Meetings:** biennial SWAP Meet - dinner and convention, knife collectors, Zippo lighters, auction (exhibits).

22127 ■ International Fight'n Rooster Cutlery Club (IFRCC)
PO Box 936
Lebanon, TN 37088
Ph: (615)444-8070
Fax: (615)444-0717
Contact: Frank Buster, Pres.
Founded: 1980. **Members:** 2,000. **Description:** Dealers and collectors of pocket knives and other types of cutlery. Promotes the hobby of knife collecting. (Fight'n Rooster knives are produced by the Frank Buster Cutlery Company.) Sponsors shows at which knife collections are displayed. Disseminates information about availability of special Fight'n Rooster knives. Conducts competitions; Compiles statistics; maintains museum. **Awards: Type:** recognition. **Recipient:** for best displays ● **Type:** recognition. **Recipient:** for ladies and juveniles to encourage prospective collectors. **Publications:** *The International Fight'n Rooster Knife Collector* ● Newsletter, monthly. **Conventions/Meetings:** annual show - always June 5.

22128 ■ Knife Collectors Club (KCC)
2900 S 26th St., US 540 Exit 81
Rogers, AR 72758-8571
Ph: (479)631-0130
Free: (800)255-9034
Fax: (479)631-8493
E-mail: ag@agrussell.com
URL: http://www.k-c-c.com
Contact: A.G. Russell, Pres.
Founded: 1970. **Members:** 5,000. **Membership Dues:** regular, in U.S., $10 (annual) ● regular, in Canada and Mexico, $20 (annual) ● other country, $35 (annual). **Staff:** 5. **Budget:** $250,000. **For-Profit. Description:** Encourages knife collecting; offers discounts on new knives to members. **Convention/Meeting:** none. **Computer Services:** database ● mailing lists. **Publications:** *Mailing*, bimonthly. **Price:** available to members only.

22129 ■ National Knife Collectors Association (NKCA)
PO Box 21070
Chattanooga, TN 37424-0070
Ph: (423)875-6009
Fax: (423)875-6039
E-mail: nkca@aol.com
URL: http://www.nationalknife.org
Contact: Lisa Broyles, Mgr.
Founded: 1972. **Members:** 6,500. **Membership Dues:** regular, .$28 (annual) ● associate, $12 (annual) ● youth (under the age of 18), $5 (annual) ● local club, $60 (annual) ● international, $64 (annual) ● corporate, $1,000 (annual). **Staff:** 2. **Local Groups:** 4. **Description:** Represents knife collectors and knife manufacturers united to promote the knife-collecting hobby. Maintains the National Knife Collectors Museum. **Publications:** *Knife World*, monthly. Newspaper. Contains feature articles, letters, and show dates. **Price:** included in membership dues. ISSN: 0164-7547. **Circulation:** 12,000. **Advertising:** accepted. **Conventions/Meetings:** semiannual meeting.

Lamps

22130 ■ Aladdin Knights of the Mystic Light (AKML)
c/o Dr. J.W. Courter, Bright Knight
3935 Kelley Rd.
Kevil, KY 42053
Ph: (270)488-2116
Fax: (270)488-2119
E-mail: brtknight@aol.com
URL: http://www.aladdinknights.org
Contact: Dr. J.W. Courter, Bright Knight
Founded: 1973. **Members:** 1,750. **Membership Dues:** individual, $25 (annual). **Description:** Collectors, dealers, users, and admirers of Aladdin lamps and memorabilia. Seeks to preserve information on kerosene lighting and electric Aladdin lamps; to encourage Aladdin collecting and camaraderie among collectors. **Awards: Type:** recognition. **Publications:** *Mystic Light of the Aladdin Knights*, bimonthly. Newsletter. **Advertising:** accepted. **Conventions/Meetings:** annual Gathering of Aladdin Knights - meeting (exhibits) ● International Antique Lamp Show.

22131 ■ International Guild of Lamp Researchers
Lamplighters Farm
10111 Lincoln Way W
St. Thomas, PA 17252-9513
E-mail: fgraff@comcast.net
URL: http://www.lampguild.org
Contact: Fil Graff, Sec.
Founded: 1997. **Multinational. Description:** Acknowledges and honors the contributions of dedicated lamp researchers to the growing body of knowledge in the field of antique artificial lighting. Encourages collectors to share their knowledge. Furthers the study of liquid or gaseous-fueled lamps and lighting. **Publications:** *Light International Digest*, annual. Magazine. Alternate Formats: online; CD-ROM.

Magic

22132 ■ International Brotherhood of Magicians (IBM)
11155-C S Towne Sq.
St. Louis, MO 63123-7813
Ph: (314)845-9200
Fax: (314)845-9220
E-mail: office@magician.org
URL: http://www.magician.org
Contact: Fred Casto, Intl. Pres.
Founded: 1922. **Members:** 15,000. **Membership Dues:** active, $40 (annual) ● active, without magazine, $20 (annual) ● youth, $35 (annual) ● youth, without magazine, $15 (annual) ● associate, $10 (annual). **Staff:** 7. **Regional Groups:** 1. **State Groups:** 209. **Local Groups:** 357. **Multinational. Descrip-

tion: Professional and semiprofessional magicians, suppliers, assistants, agents, and others interested in magic. Seeks to advance the art of magic in the field of amusement, entertainment, and culture. Promotes proper means of discouraging false or misleading advertising of effects, tricks, literature, merchandise, or actions appertaining to the magical arts; opposes exposures of principles of the art of magic, except in books on magic and magazines devoted to such art for the exclusive use of magicians and devotees of the art; encourages humane treatment and care of live animals whenever employed in magical performances. **Publications:** *The Linking Ring*, monthly. Journal. **Price:** included in membership dues. **Circulation:** 14,000. **Advertising:** accepted. Alternate Formats: CD-ROM. **Conventions/Meetings:** annual convention and lecture (exhibits).

22133 ■ Magic Collectors' Association (MCA)

PO Box 511
Glenwood, IL 60425-0511
Ph: (708)757-4950
Contact: A. Meyer, Sec.
Founded: 1949. **Members:** 500. **Membership Dues:** in U.S., \$25 (annual) ● Canada & Mexico, \$30 (annual) ● other countries, \$30 (annual). **Staff:** 2. **Description:** Persons interested in the historical aspects of theatrical and performance magic, including conjuring and collecting conjuring books, playbills, magazines, lithographs, or props. Members exhibit collected items at national magic conventions. **Awards: Type:** recognition. **Publications:** *Magicol*, quarterly. Magazine. Includes personality sketches, articles on collections, unusual facts about magic and magicians etc. **Price:** \$5.00 sample issue. **Circulation:** 500. **Advertising:** accepted ● *Index to Magical Issues 1-100, Sept 1959-Aug 1991* ● MAGICOL: The Original Series: Reprint & Indices Vol. 1-3, 1951-52. **Conventions/Meetings:** annual Magic Collectors Weekend - convention, original posters, apparatus and stage illusions on display (exhibits).

22134 ■ Magic Youth International (MYI)

11155C S Towne Sq.
St. Louis, MO 63123
E-mail: murdoch82@aol.com
URL: http://www.magicyouth.com
Contact: Dave Weidemer, Contact
Founded: 1955. **Members:** 250. **Membership Dues:** individual, \$35 (annual) ● junior associate, \$25 (annual). **Staff:** 4. **Budget:** \$2,500. **Multinational. Description:** Fraternal organization designed to bring together young magicians from around the world. "Although operated by young people for young people, any magician young at heart is welcome to join". **Convention/Meeting:** none. **Libraries: Type:** reference. **Absorbed:** (1966) International Club of Magic. **Formerly:** (2004) Magical Youths International. **Publications:** *Top Hat*, quarterly. Magazine. Features profiles of up and coming magicians, magic tricks and essays on improving magic abilities. **Price:** included in membership dues.

22135 ■ Society of American Magicians (SAM)

PO Box 510260
St. Louis, MO 63151
Ph: (314)846-5659
Fax: (314)846-5659
E-mail: rmblowers@aol.com
URL: http://www.magicsam.com
Contact: Richard Blowers, Natl. Admin.
Founded: 1902. **Members:** 8,500. **Membership Dues:** regular, \$65 (annual) ● Canadian/Mexican, \$70 (annual) ● international, \$80 (annual). **Staff:** 1. **Budget:** \$220,000. **Local Groups:** 218. **Multinational. Description:** Represents professional and amateur magicians, manufacturers, collectors, and others interested in magic. Promotes interest in magic as a hobby or profession; conducts lectures and educational programs; sponsors hospital shows. Operates Houdini Hospital Benefit Fund. Maintains SAM Magic Hall of Fame and museum. **Programs:** Magic in Special Education; Veteran's Entertainment. **Publications:** *M-U-M Magazine*, monthly ● *MiSE*

Newsletter. **Conventions/Meetings:** competition ● annual conference.

Marbles

22136 ■ Marble Collectors' Society of America (MCSA)

c/o Stanley A. Block, Chm.
PO Box 222
Trumbull, CT 06611
Ph: (203)261-3223
E-mail: blockschip@aol.com
Contact: Stanley A. Block, Chm.
Founded: 1975. **Members:** 2,100. **Membership Dues:** \$12 (annual). **Description:** Collectors, dealers, museums, and historical societies united for charitable, scientific, literary, and educational purposes. Aims to gather and disseminate information and to perform services to further the hobby of marble collecting. Maintains charitable, educational, and research programs; compiles statistics; offers appraisal service. Contributes collections to museums. Is currently organizing a traveling display for loan to museums. **Publications:** *Marble Mania*, quarterly. Newsletter. **Price:** included in membership dues ● Also publishes price guides, and photographic manuals; plans to publish a comprehensive manual; produces slide presentations and videos.

Matchcover

22137 ■ Denver Strikers Matchcover Club (DSMC)

219 Carroll Ave.
Cheyenne, WY 82009
Ph: (307)632-7374
E-mail: kwscowboy@aol.com
Contact: Ken Schneider, Contact
Founded: 1988. **Members:** 120. **Membership Dues:** ordinary, \$7 (annual). **Budget:** \$840. **Description:** Collectors and admirers of matchbooks and matchboxes. Promotes collection, preservation, and restoration of phillumenic materials. Serves as a clearinghouse on matchbooks and matchboxes; conducts educational programs; sponsors competitions. **Awards:** Denver Striker Award. **Frequency:** semiannual. **Type:** recognition. **Recipient:** for most unusual display of matches. **Publications:** *Denver Striker*, bimonthly. Newsletter. **Price:** \$7.00/year. **Circulation:** 120. **Conventions/Meetings:** semiannual convention (exhibits) - always May and August.

22138 ■ Rathkamp Matchcover Society (RMS)

1509 S Dugan Rd.
Urbana, OH 43078-9209
E-mail: trowerms@ctcn.net
URL: http://www.matchcover.org
Contact: Terry Rowe, Membership Sec.
Founded: 1941. **Members:** 1,400. **Membership Dues:** individual, \$20 (annual) ● family, \$24 (annual) ● individual in Canada and Mexico, \$25 (annual) ● elsewhere, \$35 (annual). **Staff:** 6. **Local Groups:** 31. **Multinational. Description:** Collectors of match book covers (phillumenists). Named after Henry Rathkamp, a collector who gave the hobby direction. Maintains Hall of Fame. **Libraries: Type:** reference. **Holdings:** archival material, books, business records, clippings, periodicals. **Subjects:** match club bulletins, match industry history. **Awards:** Hall of Fame Award. **Frequency:** annual. **Type:** recognition. **Recipient:** for individuals with at least 20 years of membership and has contributed to the society's growth ● Outstanding Collector Award. **Frequency:** annual. **Type:** recognition. **Recipient:** for members who have contributed greatly in the promotion of collecting match book covers in the past year. **Publications:** *Voice of the Hobby*, bimonthly. **Circulation:** 800. **Conventions/Meetings:** annual conference (exhibits) - usually third week in August.

Military

22139 ■ American Society of Military Insignia Collectors (ASMIC)

c/o George Duell, Membership Sec.
526 Lafayette Ave.
Palmerton, PA 18071-1621
Ph: (610)826-5067
Fax: (610)826-5067
E-mail: adjutant@asmic.org
URL: http://www.asmic.org
Contact: George Duell, Membership Sec.
Founded: 1937. **Members:** 2,500. **Membership Dues:** regular, in U.S., \$28 (annual) ● regular, in U.S., \$50 (biennial) ● regular, outside U.S., \$40 (annual) ● regular, outside U.S., \$70 (biennial) ● regular, in Canada and Mexico, \$32 (annual) ● regular, in Canada and Mexico, \$58 (biennial). **Staff:** 4. **Budget:** \$75,000. **Regional Groups:** 7. **Local Groups:** 7. **Multinational. Description:** Represents oldest military insignia collectors group in the U.S. Promotes the collection and preservation of U.S. and foreign military insignia. Disseminates information on the symbolism and historical significance of insignia. Assists veterans and individuals in search of insignia. **Libraries: Type:** reference; not open to the public. **Holdings:** 1,000; books, monographs, periodicals. **Subjects:** military insignia, insignia, heraldry, military history. **Awards:** Best of Show. **Frequency:** annual. **Type:** recognition. **Recipient:** for originality, comprehensiveness of display and attractiveness of display. **Computer Services:** Mailing lists, of members. **Committees:** Catalog; Convention; Distinctive Insignia Catalog Advisory; Editorial; Finance; Grievance; Shoulder Sleeve Insignia Catalog Advisory. **Publications:** *Membership List*, annual. Magazine. Contains addresses and collecting interests of members. **Price:** available to members only. **Circulation:** 2,600 ● *The Newsletter*, quarterly. Contains collectors' trading news and advertisements (classified and display). **Price:** available to members only. **Advertising:** accepted ● *Shoulder Sleeve and Distinctive Identification Insignia Catalogs*, periodic ● *The Trading Post*, quarterly. Journal. Contains illustrations of and information pertaining to military insignias and articles. **Price:** included in membership dues; \$6.00/issue for nonmembers. ISSN: 1437-7665. Alternate Formats: online ● Also publishes 30 different shoulder sleeve and distinctive insignia identification catalogs. **Conventions/Meetings:** annual convention and general assembly (exhibits) - always Labor Day Weekend.

22140 ■ Association of American Military Uniform Collectors (AAMUC)

PO Box 1876
Elyria, OH 44036
Ph: (440)365-5321
E-mail: aamucfl@comcast.net
URL: http://www.naples.net/clubs/aamuc
Contact: Gil Sanow II, Ed.
Founded: 1977. **Members:** 300. **Membership Dues:** regular, in U.S., \$20 (annual) ● regular, outside U.S., \$25 (annual). **Staff:** 8. **Budget:** \$4,000. **State Groups:** 2. **Description:** Collectors of American military and naval uniforms (1776-present). Promotes interest in uniform preservation and heritage along with patriotic interest in the U.S. armed forces. Loans uniform displays by members to various groups, including Boy Scouts of America, Girl Scouts of the U.S.A., American Legion, and Veterans of Foreign Wars of the U.S.A. branches, public schools, libraries, and public exhibitions. Reviews the books on U.S. military uniforms. **Convention/Meeting:** none. **Libraries: Type:** reference. **Awards: Type:** recognition. **Divisions:** Education; Exploration of Military Uniform Regulations; Library Services. **Publications:** *Association of American Military Uniform Collectors— Membership List*, annual. Membership Directory. **Price:** available to members only. **Circulation:** 300 ● *Footlocker*, quarterly. Newsletter. Includes book and museum reviews. **Price:** included in membership dues. **Circulation:** 300. **Advertising:** accepted ● *Military Uniform Collectors Handbook*.

22141 ■ Company of Military Historians (CMH)
PO Box 910
Rutland, MA 01543-0910
Ph: (508)845-9229
E-mail: mail@military-historians.org
URL: http://www.military-historians.org
Contact: David M. Sullivan, Admin.
Founded: 1949. **Members:** 2,500. **Membership Dues:** student in U.S., $15 (annual) ● individual, institutional, $45 (annual) ● family in U.S., $55 (annual) ● individual (life), $500 ● student outside U.S., $20 (annual) ● individual, institutional outside U.S., $50 (annual) ● family outside U.S., $60 (annual). **Staff:** 4. **Description:** Represents professional society of military historians, museologists, artists, writers, journalists, military personnel, teachers, researchers, and other individuals interested in the history of American military units, organization, tactics, uniforms, arms, and equipment. Maintains museum. **Formerly:** (1962) Company of Military Collectors and Historians. **Publications:** *Military Collector and Historian*, quarterly. Journal. Contains information on military organization, unit history, military art and artists, and activities of the society. **Price:** included in membership dues ● *Military Music in America*, periodic ● *Military Uniforms in America*, annual.

22142 ■ Military Vehicle Preservation Association (MVPA)
PO Box 520378
Independence, MO 64052
Ph: (816)833-6872
Free: (800)365-5798
Fax: (816)833-5115
E-mail: hq@mvpa.org
URL: http://www.mvpa.org
Contact: Kay Willard, Mgr.
Founded: 1976. **Members:** 10,500. **Membership Dues:** regular, in U.S., $35 (annual) ● regular, in Canada, $40 (annual) ● overseas, $90 (annual) ● junior, $15 (annual) ● life, $1,000-$1,200. **Staff:** 3. **National Groups:** 56. **Multinational. Description:** Represents individuals and groups interested in the preservation, restoration, maintenance, and enjoyment of historic military vehicles. Informs the public of the historical value of collectible military vehicles; serves as a clearinghouse for technical and historical information. **Awards:** Bart Vanderveen Award. **Frequency:** annual. **Type:** recognition. **Recipient:** to an individual who has contributed the most to the historic preservation of military vehicles ● MVPA Expert Driver Award. **Type:** recognition. **Recipient:** for active members ● MVPA Roll of Honor. **Frequency:** annual. **Type:** recognition. **Recipient:** for individuals or organizations ● President's Recruiter of the Year Award. **Frequency:** annual. **Type:** recognition. **Recipient:** for a member who has recruited the largest number of new members. **Formerly:** (1990) Military Vehicle Collectors Club. **Publications:** *Army Motors*, quarterly. Magazine. Features historic and technical military vehicle information. **Price:** included in membership dues. ISSN: 0195-5632. **Circulation:** 10,500 ● *Supply Line*, bimonthly. Magazine. ISSN: 8750-0124. **Advertising:** accepted ● Also publishes results of research by members. **Conventions/Meetings:** annual competition, with vehicle display and swap meet (exhibits) ● annual meeting and show (exhibits).

22143 ■ Orders and Medals Society of America (OMSA)
PO Box 198
San Ramon, CA 94583
E-mail: dpeck9696@aol.com
URL: http://www.omsa.org
Contact: Douglas Peck, Sec.
Founded: 1950. **Members:** 1,700. **Membership Dues:** regular, in U.S., $35 (annual) ● regular, outside U.S., $60 (annual) ● regular, in Canada, $50 (annual) ● regular, in Mexico, $50 (annual). **Staff:** 20. **Budget:** $74,000. **Local Groups:** 5. **Multinational. Description:** Persons, including 300 members outside the U.S., interested in collecting and studying insignias of the orders of knighthood and merit, the decorations of valor and honor, the medals of distinction and service, and allied material and historical data. **Libraries: Type:** lending; not open to the public. **Holdings:** 1,000. **Awards:** Honorary Membership. **Type:** recognition. **Recipient:** for service to organization's objectives. **Computer Services:** Online services, membership information, publications, society information. **Publications:** *The Journal of the Orders and Medals Society*, bimonthly. Contains articles covering orders and medals, notices of events, and new books. **Price:** included in membership dues. ISSN: 0025-6633. **Circulation:** 1,700. **Advertising:** accepted. Also Cited As: *JOMSA*. **Conventions/Meetings:** annual convention, member-prepared displays (exhibits) - always August.

Mobile Homes

22144 ■ Teton Club International (TCI)
c/o Carole Gilfedder
PO Box 866
Sanbornville, NH 03872-0866
E-mail: webmaster@tetoners.org
URL: http://www.tetoners.org
Contact: Carole Gilfedder, Contact
Membership Dues: regular, $25 (annual). **Multinational. Description:** Promotes Teton RV car. Represents enthusiasts and owners of Teton RV. Helps fellow owners enjoy their Teton RVs to the fullest. Promotes camaraderie and communication with other Teton owners. **Publications:** Newsletter, quarterly. **Price:** included in membership dues. **Conventions/Meetings:** annual rally - 2007 Sept. 17-24, Renfro Valley, KY.

Model Trains

22145 ■ Lionel Collectors Club of America (LCCA)
c/o Louis J. Caponi, Pres.
610 Andrews Ave.
Springfield, PA 19064-3816
Ph: (610)543-1540
E-mail: caponilj@comcast.net
URL: http://www.lionelcollectors.org
Contact: Louis J. Caponi, Pres.
Founded: 1970. **Members:** 8,000. **Membership Dues:** regular in U.S., $30 (annual) ● regular outside U.S., $40 (annual). **Multinational. Description:** Collectors, operators, and dealers of Lionel electric trains. Fosters enjoyment of and research about Lionel trains of all eras. Promotes continuing education for persons in the model railroad hobby. Provides for exchange of trains and train parts among members. **Publications:** *Interchange Track*, bimonthly. Newsletter. Contains new product information, and train set layouts. Alternate Formats: online ● *Lion Roars*, 5/year. Magazine. Contains club news, informative articles and photo essays about train layouts. ● *Roster*. Membership Directory. Alternate Formats: online. **Conventions/Meetings:** annual convention (exhibits).

22146 ■ Lionel Railroader Club (LRRC)
50625 Richard W Blvd.
Chesterfield, MI 48051
Ph: (586)949-4100
Free: (800)4LIONEL
Fax: (586)949-5429
E-mail: talktous@lionel.com
URL: http://www.lionel.com
Contact: Joshua Lionel Cowen, Founder
Founded: 1977. **Members:** 20,000. **Membership Dues:** main level, $20 (annual). **Staff:** 4. **Description:** Children and adults who are enthusiasts of Lionel electric trains. Works to provide information on Lionel trains, train layouts, new products, and games and to act as supply resource through the club's newsletter. **Convention/Meeting:** none. **Libraries: Type:** reference. **Holdings:** archival material. **Publications:** *Inside Track from Lionel*, quarterly. Newsletter. **Circulation:** 20,000.

22147 ■ Marklin Digital Special Interest Group
PO Box 510559
New Berlin, WI 53151-0559
Ph: (262)784-8854
Fax: (262)784-1095
E-mail: tom@marklin.com
URL: http://www.marklin.com
Contact: Dr. Tom C. Marklin, Digital Consultant
Founded: 1987. **Members:** 400. **Membership Dues:** regular, $12 (annual). **Description:** Model train collectors and enthusiasts. Promotes the Marklin Digital model train. Provides information on model trains. Conducts educational programs. **Publications:** *Marklin Digital Newsletter*, bimonthly. **Price:** $12.00/year. **Circulation:** 600.

22148 ■ National Model Railroad Association (NMRA)
4121 Cromwell Rd.
Chattanooga, TN 37421
Ph: (423)892-2846
Fax: (423)899-4869
E-mail: dgann@comcast.net
URL: http://www.nmra.org
Contact: Diane Shaffner, Admin. Assoc.
Founded: 1935. **Members:** 25,000. **Membership Dues:** regular, $48 (annual) ● family, $7 (annual) ● student, $24 (annual). **Staff:** 9. **Budget:** $1,000,000. **Regional Groups:** 17. **Local Groups:** 212. **Description:** Amateur model railroad hobbyists, railroad dealers, manufacturers, and others interested in scale model railroads and equipment. Conducts research and educational programs. Sponsors contests. Develops standards for model railroad equipment. Holds V national convention and national train show each July. **Libraries: Type:** reference. **Holdings:** 3,200; books, periodicals, photographs. **Subjects:** model railroading, railroad technical history. **Awards:** HLM. **Type:** recognition. **Recipient:** for individual from honors committee ● MMR. **Type:** recognition. **Recipient:** for completion of seven certificates of 12. **Computer Services:** database, periodical index and library catalog ● mailing lists. **Publications:** *Index to Photographs of the Southern Pacific; Baltimore and Ohio Louisville and Nashville; Atchison, Topeka and Santa Fe*. Catalog ● *Kentlein-Porter Photo Index*. Catalog ● *NMRA Bulletin*, monthly. Magazine. Highlights association activities; provides modeling and historical information. **Price:** $2.75/issue. ISSN: 0027-9722. **Circulation:** 26,000. **Advertising:** accepted. Alternate Formats: online ● *Official NMRA Standards and Recommended Practices* ● *Official Railway Equipment Register 1953 (reprint)*. Book ● Also publishes data sheets and periodical index supplements. **Conventions/Meetings:** annual convention ● annual meeting (exhibits).

22149 ■ Teen Association of Model Railroaders (TAMR)
c/o Mr. Tim Vermande
6100 Ohio Dr., Apt. 1611
Plano, TX 75024
E-mail: info@tamr.org
URL: http://www.tamr.org
Contact: Mr. Tim Vermande, Contact
Founded: 1964. **Members:** 130. **Membership Dues:** regular, $15 (annual) ● associate, $18 (annual) ● sustaining, $20 (annual). **Staff:** 10. **Budget:** $1,000. **Regional Groups:** 5. **Local Groups:** 20. **Description:** Individuals under 21 years of age who are interested in the fields of model railroading and railfanning; adults may join as associate members but cannot hold elected office. Helps teens plan, build, and operate model railroads. Promotes fellowship among teens. Conducts modeling and photography contests at annual convention. **Libraries: Type:** reference. **Holdings:** 100; books, periodicals, video recordings. **Subjects:** railroads, model railroading. **Awards:** Modeling and Photography Awards. **Frequency:** annual. **Type:** recognition. **Recipient:** based on judge's criteria. **Committees:** Archives; Pass Exchange; Shortline. **Formerly:** (1988) Teen Association of Model Railroading. **Publications:** *HOTBOX*, bimonthly. Newsletter. Includes membership activities and information. **Price:** $15.00. ISSN: 1093-622X.

Circulation: 120. **Advertising:** accepted. Alternate Formats: online• ● *Promotional Brochure.* **Price:** free ● *TAMR Directory of Members*, annual.

22150 ■ Toy Train Collectors Society (TTCS)

c/o Louis A. Bohn, Membership Chm.
109 Howedale Dr.
Rochester, NY 14616-1534
Ph: (585)663-4188
E-mail: jpeszko@aol.com
Contact: Louis A. Bohn, Membership Chm.

Founded: 1978. **Members:** 700. **Membership Dues:** regular, $30 (annual) ● renewal, $18 (annual) ● initial, $12. **State Groups:** 1. **Description:** Individuals interested in the promotion and preservation of toy trains. Sponsors 8 swap meets per year in New York State for model railroad collectors. Maintains speakers' bureau for presentations on the subject of toy trains before civic, professional, and service organizations. Offers educational programs. **Libraries: Type:** reference. **Holdings:** archival material. **Awards: Type:** recognition. **Telecommunication Services:** hotline, (716)667-1548. **Publications:** *Century Limited,* annual. Magazine. Contains articles, news, photos and schedule. **Price:** included in membership dues. **Circulation:** 650 ● *Crew List ● High Baller,* bimonthly. Newsletter. **Price:** included in membership dues. **Circulation:** 650. **Advertising:** accepted ● *TTCS Directory,* annual. Membership Directory. **Conventions/Meetings:** annual meet and show - in fall.

22151 ■ Toy Train Operating Society (TTOS)

136 E Santa Clara St., No. 2
Arcadia, CA 91006
Ph: (626)547-7453
Fax: (626)575-7454
E-mail: ttos@ttos.org
URL: http://www.ttos.org
Contact: Gary Keck, Pres.

Founded: 1966. **Members:** 6,500. **Membership Dues:** regular, $27 (annual). **Staff:** 2. **Budget:** $100,000. **Regional Groups:** 30. **Local Groups:** 20. **Description:** Collectors and operators of toy trains united to share expertise and mutual enjoyment. Conducts charitable program and children's services; sponsors competitions; compiles statistics. Maintains speakers' bureau, and museum. Conducts shows, swap meets, and exhibits. **Libraries: Type:** reference. **Holdings:** archival material, books. **Awards: Type:** recognition. **Publications:** *TTOS Bulletin,* semimonthly ● *TTOS Order Board,* semimonthly. Magazine ● Directory, every 2-3 years ● Reprints. **Conventions/Meetings:** annual Toy Train Show (exhibits) - usually August.

22152 ■ Train Collectors Association (TCA)

PO Box 248
Strasburg, PA 17579-0248
Ph: (717)687-8623
Fax: (717)687-0742
E-mail: tca-office@traincollectors.org
URL: http://www.traincollectors.org
Contact: Bob Keller, Pres.

Founded: 1954. **Members:** 32,000. **Membership Dues:** regular, $32 (annual). **Staff:** 15. **Regional Groups:** 20. **Local Groups:** 25. **Multinational. Description:** Collectors of tin-plate toy trains (mass produced models rather than handcrafted trains). Operates public museum; maintains library; conducts research and educational programs; compiles statistics. **Libraries: Type:** open to the public. **Subjects:** tin-plate toy trains. **Additional Websites:** http://www.tcamembers.org. **Publications:** *National Headquarters News,* bimonthly. Newsletter. Features association news and classified ads from members to buy, sell, or trade trains. **Price:** included in membership dues. ISSN: 1078-0718. **Circulation:** 31,000. **Advertising:** accepted ● *Train Collectors Quarterly.* **Price:** included in membership dues; $3.00/copy to nonmembers. ISSN: 0041-0829. **Circulation:** 31,000. **Conventions/Meetings:** annual convention, operating layouts, static displays of rains.

Models

22153 ■ 1/87 Vehicle Club

PO Box 2701
Carlsbad, CA 92018-2701
E-mail: info@1-87vehicles.org
URL: http://www.1-87vehicles.org

Multinational. Description: Promotes the construction, use and manufacture of prototypically accurate vehicle and equipment models in 1/87 scale. Assists in the exhibition, promotion, manufacturing and production research of vehicles of all kinds in 1/87 scale. **Computer Services:** Mailing lists ● online services, manufacturers directory. **Publications:** Newsletter. Alternate Formats: online.

22154 ■ American Model Yachting Association (AMYA)

c/o Michelle Dannenhoffer, Membership Sec.
558 Oxford Ave.
Melbourne, FL 32935-3010
Free: (888)237-9524
E-mail: membership@amya.org
URL: http://www.modelyacht.org
Contact: Michelle Dannenhoffer, Membership Sec.

Founded: 1970. **Members:** 1,600. **Membership Dues:** adult, $25 (annual) ● family, $27 (annual) ● junior, $12 (annual). **Staff:** 3. **Budget:** $52,000. **Regional Groups:** 6. **Local Groups:** 100. **Description:** Promotes the building and racing of radio-controlled and model sailing yachts. Aims to standardize racing classes and establish rules to govern the conduct of races and racers. Schedules competitive events. Provides information exchange. Encourages fellowship among members. **Awards: Frequency:** annual. **Type:** recognition. **Recipient:** for contribution to model yachting. **Special Interest Groups:** Vintage Model Yacht. **Publications:** *Model Yachting,* quarterly. Newsletter. **Price:** included in membership dues. **Circulation:** 1,600. **Advertising:** accepted. **Conventions/Meetings:** annual meeting.

22155 ■ Circus Model Builders, International (CMB)

c/o Ron Hurst, Sec.
4724 W Pendleton Pl.
Peoria, IL 61615-2841
E-mail: ronrhurst@sbcglobal.net
URL: http://www.circusmodelbuilders.com
Contact: Ron Hurst, Sec.

Founded: 1936. **Members:** 1,600. **Membership Dues:** regular, $35 (annual) ● family in U.S. and Canada, $40 (annual) ● student, $23 (annual) ● junior, $22 (annual) ● auxiliary, $2 (annual) ● family outside U.S. and Canada, $50 (annual). **Staff:** 2. **Regional Groups:** 9. **Local Groups:** 63. **Description:** Individuals 16 years of age or older who own or have built miniature models of circus equipment; youth's age eight to 15 who shows a serious interest in the circus and intend to pursue the hobby of circus model building. Focuses on bringing together circus hobbyists through exchanging ideas, plans, and specifications; and assisting each other in problems of circus model construction. Works to perpetuate the circus as an amusement by designing and constructing circus models and publicly displaying them as a reminder that the circus is a great institution. Bestows honorary membership to individuals who have been active in the circus world or have benefited the organization. **Publications:** *Little Circus Wagon,* bimonthly. Magazine. Includes articles, circus pictures, news and modeling plans contributed by members. **Price:** included in membership dues. **Advertising:** accepted ● *Membership Roster,* biennial. Membership Directory. **Price:** available to members only. **Conventions/Meetings:** annual meeting.

22156 ■ Giant Scale Warbirds Association (GSWA)

PO Box 4469
Columbus, GA 31914-0469
E-mail: giantwarbirds@hotmail.com
URL: http://www.giantwarbirds.org
Contact: Chris Joiner, Founder/Sec.-Treas.

Founded: 1996. **Membership Dues:** general, $20 (annual). **Multinational. Description:** Represents the interests of pilots, builders and enthusiasts of giant scale warbirds. Promotes the hobby of radio controlled giant scale warbird model aviation. Encourages sportsmanship and fellowship through participation in non-competitive fly-ins and public demonstrations. Promotes the construction and flying of 1911-1950 era giant scale warbird model aircraft. Informs the public about the history and heritage of military aircraft. **Telecommunication Services:** electronic mail, fokkerdr1@tds.net ● electronic mail, ckiel32561@aol.com. **Formerly:** (2005) Southern Scale Warbirds Association. **Publications:** *Warbirds Journal,* quarterly. **Price:** included in membership dues. Alternate Formats: online.

22157 ■ International Model Power Boat Association (IMPBA)

PO Box 1951
Huntsville, AL 35807-0951
Ph: (256)684-2986
E-mail: jondne@knology.net
URL: http://www.impba.net
Contact: Bill Zuber, Pres.

Founded: 1949. **Members:** 2,700. **Membership Dues:** senior, $50 (annual) ● family, junior, $20 (annual). **Staff:** 1. **Description:** Clubs and individuals interested in the advancement of model power boat racing. Fosters model boat building, coordination of member clubs, and uniform rules and classes of boats. Supports classes for nitro-powered boats of many hull types; gasoline-mix weed trimmer engine boats; battery-powered classes for both racing and precision events (scale electric). Sanctions races. Supports an International Regatta for power boats where top winners are designated US-1, or National Champion for each class offered. **Awards:** Excellence of Performance Trophy. **Frequency:** annual. **Type:** trophy. **Recipient:** for contestant with the highest score ● President's Cup Trophy. **Frequency:** annual. **Type:** trophy. **Recipient:** for best single performance of two boats in heat racing ● William E. LeFeber Award. **Frequency:** annual. **Type:** recognition. **Recipient:** for outstanding sportsmanship and service to the organization. **Computer Services:** database ● electronic publishing ● mailing lists, of members ● online services, members' forums. **Committees:** Technical. **Divisions:** International Scale. **Publications:** *Roostertail.* Newsletter. Includes organization information, changes in rules, district director reports, racing schedule updates, new records, and race results. **Advertising:** accepted. Alternate Formats: online ● *Rule Book.* **Price:** $12.00 hardcopy ● Directory, annual. **Price:** $12.00. **Circulation:** 2,700. **Conventions/Meetings:** annual board meeting ● annual International Gas NATS - meeting ● annual International Nitro NATS - meeting.

22158 ■ International Plastic Modelers Society/United States Branch (IPMS/USA)

PO Box 2475
North Canton, OH 44720
E-mail: mj@ipmsusa.org
URL: http://www.ipmsusa.org
Contact: Mary Jane Kinney, Office Mgr.

Founded: 1963. **Members:** 4,500. **Membership Dues:** junior, $12 (annual) ● adult, $25 (annual) ● in Canada and Mexico, $30 (annual). **Staff:** 1. **Budget:** $70,000. **Regional Groups:** 11. **Local Groups:** 215. **Description:** Builders of models in most media. Acts as vehicle for exchange of information among members. **Awards:** Chapter of the Year. **Frequency:** annual. **Type:** recognition ● **Type:** recognition. **Recipient:** for superior construction and finish of various modeling subjects (including cars, planes, ships, spacecraft, science fiction subjects, and figures). **Publications:** *IPMS Journal,* bimonthly. **Price:** included in membership dues. **Circulation:** 4,500. **Advertising:** accepted. **Conventions/Meetings:** annual convention and workshop (exhibits) - always July.

22159 ■ International R/C Helicopter Association (IRCHA)

5161 E Memorial Dr.
Muncie, IN 47302-9050
Ph: (765)287-1256

Fax: (765)289-4248
E-mail: secretary@ircha.org
URL: http://www.ircha.org
Contact: Ron Kummer, Pres.
Founded: 1989. **Description:** Dedicated to improving the quality of R/C helicopter pilots.

22160 ■ International Scale Soaring Association (ISSA)
c/o Rick Briggs, Treas./Webmaster
3015 Volk Ave.
Long Beach, CA 90808
Ph: (562)421-4864
E-mail: scalebldr@charter.net
URL: http://www.soaringissa.org
Contact: Rick Briggs, Treas./Webmaster
Membership Dues: general, $15 (annual) ● junior, student, $12 (annual) ● associate, $10 (annual) ● general, $40 (triennial) ● general, $60 (quinquennial). **Multinational. Description:** Fosters and supports all phases of scale and sporting radio-controlled soaring activities. Encourages advancement in the knowledge of all phases of scale radio-controlled soaring. Promotes general interest in soaring flight. Facilitates sharing of information on building and flying techniques for scale gliders. **Publications:** The Towline. Newsletter. Alternate Formats: online.

22161 ■ Kit Collectors International (KCI)
PO Box 38
Stanton, CA 90680
Ph: (714)826-5218
E-mail: kitcollectorsshow@yahoo.com
Contact: Edie Keller, Exec. Dir.
Founded: 1980. **Staff:** 3. **For-Profit. Description:** Individuals and companies involved in the collection of scale-model kits, especially out-of-production kits. Seeks to provide leadership, information, and assistance to model kit collectors worldwide. Fosters interest in and knowledge of scale-model kit collecting. Encourages and facilitates trading, buying, and selling of model kits among members. Advises manufacturers on model trends. Conducts audiovisual program for model clubs. Compiles statistics; maintains museum. **Libraries: Type:** reference. **Subjects:** model catalogs. **Telecommunication Services:** phone referral service, helpline to assist major model companies with customer inquiries about out-of-production kits. **Conventions/Meetings:** Kit Collectors Exposition & Sale - meet (exhibits) - 3/year, always in Buena Park, CA.

22162 ■ National Association of Rocketry (NAR)
PO Box 407
Marion, IA 52302
Free: (800)262-4872
Fax: (319)373-8913
E-mail: nar-hq@nar.org
URL: http://www.nar.org
Contact: Mark Bundick, Pres.
Founded: 1957. **Members:** 5,000. **Membership Dues:** junior, leader, $25 (annual) ● senior, $62 (annual). **Staff:** 1. **Budget:** $350,000. **Local Groups:** 120. **Description:** Promotes safety, education and fun in sport rocketry. Provides membership services to sport rocket flyers of all ages and experience levels; assists educators using rocketry as a learning tool, hobbyists striving to have fun and expand their personal rocketry horizons, and provides valuable input to public safety officials who regulate the hobby. **Awards:** Howard Galloway Spacemodeling Award. **Frequency:** annual. **Type:** recognition. **Recipient:** for outstanding service to all sport rocket flyers ● National Model Rocket Champions. **Frequency:** annual. **Type:** trophy. **Recipient:** for excellence in competition rocket flying in three-age groups and clubs. **Computer Services:** Mailing lists, club leaders sign up for news, announcements and discussions about association business and events. **Committees:** Club Activities; Contest and Records; Education; National Events; Public Affairs; Sport Rocket Regulations; Standards and Testing; Technical Services; Training and Education. **Affiliated With:** Craft and Hobby Association; National Aeronautic Association. **Formerly:** (1958) Model Missile Associa-

tion. **Publications:** The Model Rocketeer, bimonthly. Newsletters. Contains the President's message, committee announcements, other association business, club news and launch schedules. **Circulation:** 5,000 ● Sport Rocketry: America's Complete Sport Rocketry Magazine, bimonthly. Journal. Includes calendar of events and upcoming contests. **Price:** included in membership dues. ISSN: 0883-0991. **Circulation:** 6,000. **Advertising:** accepted. **Conventions/Meetings:** annual convention and workshop, weekend long event with hands on educational sessions, speakers, discussion groups and vendor displays - always late March ● semiannual meeting (exhibits) - always August ● annual National Model Rocket Championships - competition, sport launch for any kind of model or high power rocket, vendor displays and sales, evening activities - late July to early August ● annual National Sport Launch - meeting, sport launch with evening activities - usually late May.

22163 ■ National Association of Scale Aeromodelers (NASA)
c/o Bonnie Rediske, Sec.-Treas.
128 Darnley Dr.
Moon Township, PA 15108
E-mail: rediskejb@aol.com
URL: http://www.nasascale.org
Contact: Bonnie Rediske, Sec.-Treas.
Membership Dues: regular, in U.S., $15 (annual) ● regular, in Canada, $20 (annual) ● international, $25 (annual). **Multinational. Description:** Promotes and advances all phases of scale aeromodeling. Supports and assists scale modelers in their pursuit of excellence in the field of aeromodeling. Encourages the formation of scale clubs. Promotes flying scale competition at all levels. Fosters the training of scale judges for competition. **Telecommunication Services:** electronic mail, onawing@mindspring.com. **Publications:** Replica, bimonthly. Newsletter. Contains modeling tips, contest reports, schedule of events and articles about full-scale aircraft. **Advertising:** accepted. Alternate Formats: online..

22164 ■ National Organization for Racing Radio Control Autos (NORRCA)
11114 Sweet River Dr.
Bakersfield, CA 93311-9115
Ph: (661)328-1481
E-mail: donr@norrca.com
URL: http://www.norrca.com
Contact: Don Risner, Pres.
Founded: 1987. **Members:** 17,000. **Description:** Works to promote tracks/clubs and racers. **Conventions/Meetings:** annual On-Road Nationals - competition.

22165 ■ Navy Carrier Society (NCS)
225 W Orchid Ln.
Phoenix, AZ 85021
E-mail: clflyer@mchsi.com
URL: http://clflyer.tripod.com/ncs/ncs.htm
Contact: Bill Calkins, Pres.
Founded: 1977. **Members:** 104. **Membership Dues:** individual, $6 (annual). **Budget:** $300. **Description:** Promotes the advancement of control line model aircraft navy carrier events. Sponsors competitions; compiles statistics. **Awards:** Eugene Ely Award. **Frequency:** annual. **Type:** recognition. **Recipient:** for highest three event total score ● Rookie of the Year. **Frequency:** annual. **Type:** recognition. **Recipient:** for highest placing modeler who has never competed in a national before. **Publications:** Hi-Low-Landings, bimonthly. Newsletter. **Price:** included in membership dues. **Circulation:** 104. **Advertising:** accepted. **Conventions/Meetings:** annual meeting.

22166 ■ North American Model Boat Association (NAMBA)
c/o Ms. Cathie Galbraith, Exec. Sec.
1815 Halley St.
San Diego, CA 92154
Ph: (619)424-6380
Fax: (619)424-8845

E-mail: cathie.galbraith@namba.com
URL: http://www.namba.com
Contact: Ms. Cathie Galbraith, Exec. Sec.
Founded: 1959. **Members:** 1,500. **Membership Dues:** adult, $45 (annual) ● junior, $25 (annual) ● additional adult (same household), $35 (annual). **Staff:** 1. **Regional Groups:** 10. **Description:** Individuals and clubs interested in promoting the hobby of building and operating radio-controlled model boats. Focuses on the progress and expansion of model boating through fellowship and sportsmanship. Sanctions races; maintains hall of fame; compiles statistics. **Awards:** Hall of Fame. **Frequency:** annual. **Type:** recognition. **Recipient:** for members. **Formerly:** (1971) Western Council of Model Boating; (2000) NAMBA International. **Publications:** PROPWASH, quarterly. Newsletter. Includes technical articles and race reports. **Price:** $10.00/year. **Circulation:** 1,500. **Advertising:** accepted ● Also publishes rulebook. **Conventions/Meetings:** annual Nationals - competition - always eight days in July.

22167 ■ R/C Quarter Scale Association of America (QSAA)
PO Box 13980
Las Vegas, NV 89112
E-mail: donmig@msn.com
Contact: Carol Miguez, Sec.
Founded: 1976. **Members:** 486. **Membership Dues:** family in U.S., $20 (annual) ● individual in U.S., $15 (annual) ● individual outside U.S., $20 (annual) ● family outside U.S., $25 (annual). **Budget:** $2,000. **Regional Groups:** 5. **State Groups:** 1. **Local Groups:** 1. **Multinational. Description:** Promotes excellence in hobby of building and flying 1/4-scale model aircraft. **Publications:** The Quarter Scaler, quarterly. Newsletter. **Price:** included in membership dues; $1.00 for nonmembers. Alternate Formats: online. **Conventions/Meetings:** annual Quarter Fly-In - meeting - held in Las Vegas, Nevada.

22168 ■ Scale Ship Modelers Association of North America (SSMA)
c/o Bruce Ray, Natl. Dir.
6780 Gleason
Kalamazoo, MI 49048
E-mail: biray@ssmana.org
URL: http://www.ssmana.org
Contact: Bruce Ray, Natl. Dir.
Founded: 1988. **Membership Dues:** individual, $20-$40 (annual) ● family, $25-$50 (annual) ● junior, $10-$20 (annual) ● club affiliate, $25-$50 (annual) ● business affiliate, $25-$50 (annual). **Description:** Advocates and encourages scale ship model building. Promotes the hobby of radio control and static ship modeling. Encourages all types of model boating in electric, sail and steam power and the building of plastic and wooden static models. Acts as a clearing house for information concerning the modeling industry. Works with the modeling industry to address the needs of the modeling community. **Publications:** SSMA Journal, quarterly. **Price:** included in membership dues.

22169 ■ Scale Warbird Racing Association (SWRA)
PO Box 328
Muncie, IN 47302
E-mail: johnagon@email.msn.com
URL: http://www.swraracing.com
Contact: John Gonzales, Pres.
Membership Dues: general, $20 (annual). **Description:** Represents individuals interested in the thrill, excitement and nostalgia of racing radio controlled model aircraft of piston-driven warbirds and replicas of the Unlimited "Reno" Racers. Promotes the development and improvement of scale warbird racing and Mini-Reno racing events. Develops and updates unified rules. Coordinates racing dates for events. **Telecommunication Services:** electronic mail, drsherrow@hotmail.com ● electronic mail, manginoaz@msn.com ● electronic mail, wclays@hotmail.com. **Committees:** Race; Rules. **Publications:** The Scatter Pylon. Newsletter. **Price:** for members.

22170 ■ Ships-in-Bottles Association of America (SIBAA)

c/o Don Hubbard, Membership Chm.
PO Box 180550
Coronado, CA 92178
Ph: (619)435-3555
E-mail: hubbarddon@aol.com
URL: http://www.shipsinbottles.org
Contact: Don Hubbard, Membership Chm.
Founded: 1978. **Members:** 425. **Membership Dues:** individual, $25 (annual). **Description:** Promotes the art of building ships-in-bottles and exchanges ideas and information among builders throughout the world. **Formerly:** (1982) International Ships-In-Bottles Association. **Publications:** *Bottle Shipwright*, quarterly. Newsletter. Provides information for people who build or collect ships-in-bottles. **Price:** included in membership dues. **Circulation:** 400. **Conventions/Meetings:** periodic conference (exhibits).

22171 ■ Unlimited Scale Racing Association (USRA)

PO Box 819
Brea, CA 92822
E-mail: hanburys@ameritech.net
URL: http://www.usrainfo.org
Contact: Martin Treat, Pres.
Founded: 1994. **Membership Dues:** regular, in U.S., $50 (annual) ● international, $75 (annual). **Multinational. Description:** Official sanctioning and rules body for sport of Giant Scale Air Racing. **Publications:** *Fly R/C.* Magazine ● Newsletter. **Price:** included in membership dues.

22172 ■ US Scale Masters Association (USSMA)

PO Box 160
Aurora, OR 97002
Ph: (503)678-6036
Fax: (503)678-6036
E-mail: jensendes@centurytel.net
URL: http://www.scalemasters.org
Contact: Earl Aune, Chm.
Membership Dues: champion, $75 (annual) ● classic, $35 (annual) ● youth, $25 (annual). **Description:** Promotes the development and growth of scale aircraft modeling, by bringing people together to have fun while focusing on scale realism, competition and sportsmanship for the enjoyment of all. **Computer Services:** Online services, message board. **Publications:** Newsletter, quarterly. **Price:** included in membership dues.

22173 ■ Western Associated Modelers (WAM)

c/o Doug Barton, Pres.
160 Park Ave.
Woodland, CA 95695
Ph: (530)662-6469
E-mail: yoyoflo@aol.com
URL: http://www.wamsite.com
Contact: Doug Barton, Pres.
Founded: 1947. **Members:** 3,200. **Membership Dues:** adult, $15 (annual) ● junior, $10 (annual). **Description:** Individuals and clubs united to promote the building, flying, and racing of control line, free flight, and radio controlled model planes, and the racing of radio-controlled model cars and boats. Sanctions novice, junior, and senior competitions; maintains competition records; sets safety standards. Arranges insurance coverage for members. Sponsors annual Parade of Champions. Conducts educational programs and children's services. **Affiliated With:** Academy of Model Aeronautics; North American Model Boat Association. **Publications:** *Propwash*, monthly. Newsletter. **Price:** $10.00. **Conventions/Meetings:** competition ● periodic meeting ● monthly meeting - every 2nd Friday.

22174 ■ World Miniature Warbird Association (WMWA)

c/o Ed Irons, Sec./Ed.
7100 Cottonwood Dr.
Grant, FL 32949
Ph: (321)724-0584

E-mail: eirons@harris.com
URL: http://www.wmwa.org
Contact: Dean Di Giorgio, Pres.
Membership Dues: general, $15. **Multinational. Description:** Fosters and advances the construction and operation of radio controlled Warbird Aircraft of all sizes. Creates an atmosphere where pleasure, recreation, fellowship and co-mingling can be fostered among individuals enjoying the sport of building and flying miniature radio controlled Warbird Aircraft. **Telecommunication Services:** electronic mail, icemanjr92@aol.com. **Publications:** *Wings of Eagles*, quarterly. Newsletter. **Price:** included in membership dues.

Motorcycle

22175 ■ All-American Indian Motorcycle Club (AAIMC)

c/o Paul Clement, Treas.
4745 N Jerome Rd.
Maumee, OH 43537
Ph: (440)647-3723
E-mail: paulteri@aol.com
URL: http://www.allamericanindianmotorcycleclub.com
Contact: Ernie Hartman Jr., Pres.
Founded: 1965. **Members:** 300. **Membership Dues:** individual, $15 (annual). **Description:** Promotes restoration, preservation, and exhibition of American-made Indian motorcycles manufactured from 1901 to 1953. **Publications:** *All American Indian Motorcycle News*, quarterly. Newsletter. Alternate Formats: online. **Conventions/Meetings:** quarterly meeting.

22176 ■ American Federation of Motorcyclists (AFM)

6167 Jarvis Ave., No. 333
Newark, CA 94560
Ph: (510)796-7005
Fax: (209)577-2111
E-mail: afm@afmracing.org
URL: http://www.afmracing.org
Contact: Kevin Smith, Pres.
Founded: 1954. **Members:** 1,150. **Membership Dues:** individual, $100 (annual). **Budget:** $500,000. **Regional Groups:** 1. **State Groups:** 1. **Description:** Motorcycle enthusiasts. Large amateur motorcycle roadracing club. Conducts races, classes for all types of motorcycles, and schools for new racers. **Awards:** Class Champions. **Frequency:** annual. **Type:** recognition. **Recipient:** for season point standings ● Top Novice. **Frequency:** annual. **Type:** recognition. **Recipient:** for season point standings ● Top Ten Plates. **Frequency:** annual. **Type:** recognition. **Recipient:** for season point standings. **Publications:** *AFM News*, bimonthly. Newsletter. **Price:** free for members. Alternate Formats: online ● *AFM Rulebook*, annual. Contains competition rulebook. **Price:** free for members. Alternate Formats: online. **Conventions/Meetings:** annual banquet, with awards ceremony - at season's end.

22177 ■ American Historic Racing Motorcycle Association (AHRMA)

2375 Midway Rd. SE
Bolivia, NC 28422
Ph: (910)253-8012
Fax: (910)253-8313
E-mail: ccowell@ahrma.org
URL: http://www.ahrma.org
Contact: Cindy Cowell, Exec. Dir.
Founded: 1986. **Members:** 5,600. **Membership Dues:** nonracing, $30 (annual) ● competition, $40 (annual) ● road racing, $10 (annual). **Staff:** 4. **Budget:** $850,000. **Description:** Individuals interested in vintage racing motorcycles. Promotes and sponsors races and related activities. Conducts educational programs; compiles statistics. **Libraries: Type:** reference. **Holdings:** archival material, business records. **Awards:** National Championships. **Type:** recognition ● Sportsman of the Year. **Frequency:** annual. **Type:** recognition. **Recipient:** for outstanding contributions to the vintage movement. **Computer Services:** Mail-

ing lists, inclusion in newsletter. **Committees:** Eligibility. **Affiliated With:** American Motorcyclist Association. **Absorbed:** (1989) California Vintage Race Group. **Publications:** *AHRMA Handbook*, annual. Contains rules for vintage motorcycle competition. **Price:** $5.00 for nonmembers. **Circulation:** 5,600. **Advertising:** accepted. Alternate Formats: online ● *Vintage Views*, monthly. Newsletter. **Price:** $2.00. **Circulation:** 5,600. **Advertising:** accepted ● Yearbook. **Conventions/Meetings:** semiannual conference and board meeting.

22178 ■ American Voyager Association (AVA)

2015 Powers Dr.
Lewiston, ID 83501
Ph: (208)746-3530
E-mail: avainc@amervoyassoc.org
URL: http://www.amervoyassoc.org
Contact: Duane Ash, Chm.
Founded: 1987. **Members:** 8,500. **Membership Dues:** individual in U.S., $30 (annual) ● individual outside U.S., $40 (annual). **Staff:** 8. **Budget:** $30,000. **State Groups:** 18. **Multinational. Description:** Owners and riders of the Kawasaki Voyager motorcycle. Promotes motorcycle safety and the creation of camaraderie and friendship of all members and the general public, be they riders or non-riders. Facilitates exchange of ideas and information, educational programs, and regional and international rallies. **Awards:** Rally Associated Award. **Frequency:** annual. **Type:** recognition. **Recipient:** for attendance at rallies. **Affiliated With:** American Motorcyclist Association. **Publications:** *Helping Hands Roster*, annual. Directory. **Price:** included in membership dues. **Circulation:** 1,500. **Advertising:** accepted ● *International Roster*, annual. Membership Directory. **Price:** included in membership dues ● *Technical Tips*, annual. Booklet. **Price:** $8.00 ● *Voyagers' Voice*, bimonthly. Newsletter. Contains articles of interest to members. **Price:** included in membership dues. **Circulation:** 1,500. **Advertising:** accepted. Alternate Formats: online. **Conventions/Meetings:** annual International Rally, social and technical ride (exhibits).

22179 ■ Antique Motorcycle Club of America (AMCA)

c/o Dick Winger, Membership Chm.
PO Box 310
Sweetser, IN 46987
Ph: (765)384-5421
Free: (800)782-2622
E-mail: amc@comteck.com
URL: http://www.antiquemotorcycle.org
Contact: Pete Gagan, Pres.
Founded: 1954. **Members:** 11,000. **Membership Dues:** regular, in U.S., $30 (annual) ● regular, in Canada and Mexico, $34 (annual) ● overseas, $40 (annual). **Regional Groups:** 43. **Multinational. Description:** Individuals interested in collecting and restoring antique motorcycles. Holds National Road Rides, National Meets, and Motorcycling Judging. **Libraries: Type:** reference. **Holdings:** 200; books. **Awards: Type:** recognition. **Recipient:** for machines judged at national meets. **Telecommunication Services:** electronic mail, jandmmoore@jps.net. **Publications:** *Antique Motorcycle*, quarterly. Magazine. **Advertising:** accepted ● *Membership Roster*, biennial. Membership Directory. **Conventions/Meetings:** competition and banquet (exhibits) - 9/year ● annual meet.

22180 ■ Ariel Motorcycle Club North America

PO Box 77737
Stockton, CA 95267-1037
Ph: (714)894-5761
Fax: (858)578-1504
E-mail: arielthunder@verizon.net
URL: http://www.arielnorthamerica.org
Contact: Thor Faber, Pres.
Founded: 1968. **Members:** 300. **Membership Dues:** individual in U.S., $15 (annual) ● family, $25 (annual) ● life, $200. **Description:** Owners, restorers, and collectors of Ariel motorcycles. Aims for the preservation and use of Ariel motorcycles. Provides technical information and conducts parts-finding program. Includes activities such as family-oriented rides and

parties. **Formerly:** (2003) Ariel Owners' Motorcycle Club. **Publications:** *Cheval de Fer*, monthly. Newsletter ● *Spirit of the Air*, bimonthly. Newsletter. **Conventions/Meetings:** annual meeting - always May or June.

22181 ■ Blue Knights International Law Enforcement Motorcycle Club (BK)
38 Alden St.
Bangor, ME 04401
Ph: (207)947-4600
Free: (877)254-5362
Fax: (207)947-5814
E-mail: internationaloffice@blueknights.org
URL: http://blueknights.org
Contact: Connie Flanagan, Pres.
Founded: 1974. **Members:** 19,000. **Membership Dues:** law enforcement, $25 (annual). **Staff:** 2. **Regional Groups:** 11. **Local Groups:** 385. **Multinational. Description:** Represents deputy sheriffs, game wardens, local police, parole officers, state troopers, and other law enforcement personnel participating in recreational motorcycling. Works to improve the public image of motorcycle groups. Promotes motorcycle safety and social organization for recreational activities for off-duty police personnel. Encourages family recreational motorcycling; stresses the importance of courtesy, economy, and safety. Sponsors recreational programs for handicapped children. **Formerly:** (1983) Blue Knights. **Publications:** *The Blue Knights News*, quarterly. Magazine. Provides means of communication within the Club. **Advertising:** accepted ● *Roster*, periodic. Newsletter ● Pamphlets. **Conventions/Meetings:** annual convention (exhibits) - always third week in July.

22182 ■ BMW Motorcycle Owners of America (BMW MOA)
PO Box 3982
Ballwin, MO 63022
Ph: (636)394-7277
Fax: (636)391-1811
E-mail: comments@bmwmoa.org
URL: http://www.bmwmoa.org
Contact: Ray Zimmerman, Exec. Dir.
Founded: 1971. **Members:** 37,000. **Membership Dues:** individual in U.S. (additional 8 within the same household), $32 (annual) ● individual outside U.S., $47 (annual). **Staff:** 8. **Local Groups:** 190. **For-Profit. Description:** BMW motorcycle owners organized for pleasure, recreation, safety, and dissemination of information concerning BMW motorcycles. **Awards: Type:** recognition. **Publications:** *BMW Owners Anonymous*, annual ● *BMW Owners News*, monthly. Magazine. **Advertising:** accepted. **Conventions/Meetings:** annual rally - always July.

22183 ■ BMW Riders Association International (BMW RA)
PO Box 120430
West Melbourne, FL 32912-0430
Ph: (321)984-7800
Fax: (321)984-7800
E-mail: admin@bmwra.org
URL: http://www.bmwra.org
Contact: Linda Gotcher, Admin.
Founded: 1971. **Members:** 5,000. **Membership Dues:** regular, in U.S. $25 (annual) ● associate, $5 (annual) ● regular, outside U.S., $35 (annual). **Staff:** 1. **Regional Groups:** 17. **State Groups:** 50. **Local Groups:** 200. **Languages:** English, German. **Multinational. Description:** Represents riders and enthusiasts of BMW motorcycles. Sponsors and promotes events for members. Supports responsible efforts to preserve the rights of motorcyclists and to improve the public image of motorcycling. Provides social and service opportunities. Promotes safe riding. **Libraries: Type:** reference. **Holdings:** periodicals. **Subjects:** BMW motorcycles. **Awards:** Bill Harmer Award. **Frequency:** periodic. **Type:** recognition. **Recipient:** for outstanding service to BMW RA ● Walt Klein Award. **Frequency:** annual. **Type:** recognition. **Recipient:** for signing up members. **Computer Services:** database, membership. **Publications:** *On the Level*, 10/year. Magazine. **Price:** included in membership dues. **Circulation:** 5,000. **Advertising:**

accepted. **Conventions/Meetings:** annual International Rally (exhibits).

22184 ■ British Biker Cooperative (BBC)
PO Box 371021
Milwaukee, WI 53237-2121
Ph: (920)471-4097
E-mail: rwheeler1@new.rr.com
URL: http://www.britishbiker.net
Contact: Rudy Wheeler, Pres.
Founded: 1977. **Members:** 150. **Membership Dues:** general, officer, director, $25 (annual). **Staff:** 15. **Description:** Admirers of British motorcycles. Promotes operation and preservation of British motorcycles. Facilitates exchange of information among members; provides assistance to motorcycle restorers; sponsors social activities. Conducts educational programs; sponsors competitions; participates in charitable activities. **Libraries: Type:** not open to the public. **Holdings:** books, periodicals. **Subjects:** British motorcycles. **Awards:** Motorcycle Show Awards. **Frequency:** annual. **Type:** recognition. **Publications:** *British Steel*, annual. Yearbook. **Advertising:** accepted. **Conventions/Meetings:** periodic board meeting ● annual rally.

22185 ■ British International Motorcycle Association (BIMA)
PO Box 158
Plympton, MA 02367-0158
Ph: (508)946-1144 (508)946-1939
Fax: (508)946-1145
E-mail: tiocbima@aol.com
URL: http://members.aol.com/JohnTIOC/tioc.htm
Contact: John Healy, Contact
Founded: 1987. **Members:** 1,200. **Membership Dues:** in U.S., $18 (annual) ● in Canada, $22 (annual) ● outside U.S., $27 (annual) ● life, in U.S., $200 ● life, in Canada, $250 ● life, outside U.S. and Canada, $300. **Staff:** 3. **Description:** Owners and others interested in the use and preservation of British motorcycles. **Formerly:** British International Motorcycle Association. **Publications:** *Vintage Bike*, quarterly. Magazine. **Price:** included in membership dues. **Advertising:** accepted. **Conventions/Meetings:** annual Daytona Beach Week - meeting (exhibits).

22186 ■ Christian Motorcyclists Association (CMA)
PO Box 9
Hatfield, AR 71945
Ph: (870)389-6196
Fax: (870)389-6199
E-mail: cmausamail@cmausa.org
URL: http://www.cmausa.org
Contact: Mr. John Ogden Sr., Chm.
Founded: 1975. **Members:** 50,000. **Staff:** 15. **Budget:** $1,000,000. **Local Groups:** 400. **Description:** Promotes Christian fellowship among motorcyclists through public worship, ministry, and Christian evangelistic rallies. Improves the image of persons engaged in motorcycling sports. Activities include motorcycle games, fellowship services, gospel and other singing events, and worship services. Sponsors evangelistic schools, state rallies, national rallies, and training programs for its members worldwide. **Awards:** Run for the Sun Award. **Frequency:** annual. **Type:** recognition. **Recipient:** for 10 top fundraisers, 10 top chapters. **Publications:** *HeartBeat*, monthly. Newsletter. Contains general information, announcements, and stories. **Price:** free, for members only. **Circulation:** 50,000. **Advertising:** accepted. **Alternate Formats:** diskette ● Also publishes evangelism tracts focused toward motorcyclists and training books for members. **Conventions/Meetings:** annual Changing of the Colors Rally - meeting - always third week of October ● annual rally (exhibits) - usually fourth week of June.

22187 ■ Combat Veterans Motorcycle Association (CVMA)
1019 Highland Dr.
Liberty, MO 64068

E-mail: cvma@rochester.rr.com
URL: http://combatvet.org
Contact: Robert C. Clements, Contact
Founded: 1999. **Membership Dues:** full, $15 (annual) ● military support, $10 (annual) ● life, $150. **Description:** Promotes interest in various forms of motorcycle activity associated with Veterans. Creates and maintains camaraderie among Combat Veterans. Encourages better understanding of motorcycle riders as a constructive sport among members of the public, press, and law enforcement agency. **Telecommunication Services:** electronic mail, webmaster@combatvet.org.

22188 ■ Cushman Club of America (CCOA)
PO Box 661
Union Springs, AL 36089
Ph: (334)738-3874
E-mail: ccoagene@yahoo.com
URL: http://www.cushmanclubofamerica.com
Contact: Tom O'Hara, Treas.
Founded: 1981. **Members:** 5,250. **Membership Dues:** individual, $25 (annual) ● regular, outside U.S., $35 (annual). **Description:** Represents individuals interested in Cushman motor scooters. Promotes the restoration and preservation of Cushman motor scooters, manufactured from 1936-65 by the Cushman Motor Works in Lincoln, NE. (The scooters gained popularity during World War II, when wartime concerns halted U.S. production of cars for private use). **Publications:** *Cushman Club of America Member Magazine*, bimonthly. **Conventions/Meetings:** annual meet (exhibits).

22189 ■ Deutsches Motorrad Register (DMR)
8663 Grover Pl.
Shreveport, LA 71115
Ph: (318)797-0803
Fax: (318)797-0803
E-mail: mtbrushmore@yahoo.com
Contact: Winston Conway Link, Dir.
Founded: 1982. **Members:** 550. **Membership Dues:** regular, $12 (annual). **Staff:** 2. **Budget:** $4,500. **Description:** Works for the preservation, enjoyment, and use of vintage German motorcycles. Provides parts sources and restoration and technical tips. **Libraries: Type:** reference; lending; not open to the public. **Holdings:** 5,000; archival material, books, periodicals. **Subjects:** motorcycles. **Formerly:** (1989) Deutsche Motorrader Register. **Supersedes:** NSU Register. **Publications:** *Membership List*, annual. Membership Directory ● Magazine, quarterly. Contains information on services available, parts sources, restoration advice, and historical articles. **Price:** included in membership dues. **Circulation:** 600. **Advertising:** accepted ● Also publishes parts source listings. **Conventions/Meetings:** annual rally, swap meet vendors (exhibits) - always August in Pennsylvania.

22190 ■ Gold Star Owners Club (GSOC)
Address Unknown since 2006
Founded: 1973. **Members:** 480. **Description:** Owners and admirers of BSA Gold Star series motorcycles. Promotes the preservation, maintenance, and enjoyment of the BSA Gold Star motorcycle, produced in England by Birmingham Small Arms from 1938 to 1963. Facilitates sale and trade of motorcycles, parts, and accessories among members. Maintains biographical archives and small library. Sponsors competitions. **Awards: Type:** recognition. **Publications:** *Twitter*, bimonthly. Newsletter. **Conventions/Meetings:** annual rally.

22191 ■ Gold Wing Road Riders Association (GWRRA)
21423 N 11th Ave.
Phoenix, AZ 85027
Ph: (623)581-2500
Free: (800)843-9460
Fax: (623)581-3844
E-mail: mike@gwrra.org
URL: http://www.gwrra.org
Contact: Mike Wright, Pres.
Founded: 1977. **Members:** 82,000. **Membership Dues:** individual, $45 (annual) ● individual (associ-

ate), $50 (annual) ● family, $55 (annual) ● associate, $60 (annual). **Staff:** 21. **Budget:** $5,000,000. **Regional Groups:** 11. **State Groups:** 57. **Local Groups:** 950. **Description:** Owners of Honda Gold Wing motorcycles; spouses and dependents of owners. Promotes the pleasure and recreational aspects of Gold Wing motorcycle riding. Coordinates common motorcycle efforts and provides for exchange of information. Strives to improve public acceptance of motorcyclists and motorcycling, educate noncyclists to motorcycling problems, promote safe and skillful riding, and assist in local civic improvement, and police, government, and charity activities. Supports similarly motivated organizations, local Honda dealerships, American Honda, and the Motorcycle Safety Foundation (see separate entry). Informs members of trips, tours, and rallies; offers insurance discounts; compiles statistics. Develops plans for increased member benefits, motorcycle skills course, and a store carrying approved accessories and wearables. Maintains speakers' bureau. **Libraries: Type:** reference. **Holdings:** 200. **Subjects:** cycle-related. **Awards:** Motorcycle Association of the Year. **Frequency:** annual. **Type:** recognition. **Recipient:** for motorcycle safety programs offered by organizations. **Computer Services:** database, IBM 36. **Committees:** Advertising; Benefits; Mechanical; Officer Liaison. **Departments:** Education and Public Relations; Operations and Officer Training. **Programs:** Consumer Education; Cycle Riding Skills; Insurance; Product Evaluations; Safe Riding Techniques. **Publications:** *Gold Book*, annual. Directory. **Price:** $40.00. **Circulation:** 40,000. **Advertising:** accepted. Alternate Formats: online; CD-ROM; magnetic tape ● *Wing World Magazine*, monthly. Includes information on new products, listing of officers, calendar of tours and rallies, and regional news. **Price:** included in membership dues. ISSN: 0745-273X. **Advertising:** accepted ● Also publishes leadership manual and officers' guide, for internal use only. **Conventions/Meetings:** annual Wing Ding - meeting and trade show (exhibits).

22192 ■ Harley Hummer Club (HHC)
c/o Brent Dugan
13 Sylvan Rd.
High Bridge, NJ 08829-1716
E-mail: office@harleyhummerclub.org
URL: http://www.harleyhummerclub.org
Contact: Brent Dugan, Contact
Founded: 1980. **Members:** 500. **Staff:** 8. **Description:** Persons who own or are interested in the restoration of American-made two-stroke Harley-Davidson motorcycles produced from 1948 to 1966. Objective is to aid in the preservation and restoration of these motorcycles. **Libraries: Type:** reference. **Holdings:** papers. **Publications:** *HummerNews*, bimonthly. Newsletter. Contains pictures, stories, tech tips, reprints of historical material, and classified advertisements regarding Hummer-Motorcycles. **Price:** included in membership dues. ISSN: 1077-0062. **Circulation:** 500. **Advertising:** accepted ● *Membership Roster*, annual. Membership Directory.

22193 ■ Harley Owners Group (HOG)
PO Box 453
Milwaukee, WI 53201
Ph: (414)343-4056
Free: (800)258-2464
Fax: (414)343-4515
URL: http://www.harley-davidson.com/selector.asp?hog=true
Founded: 1983. **Members:** 900,000. **Membership Dues:** full, $45 (annual) ● associate, $25 (annual). **Staff:** 33. **Local Groups:** 1,157. **Description:** Harley-Davidson motorcycle owners. Provides benefits, services, and programs to members. Conducts social gatherings, including receptions. **Publications:** *Enthusiast*, 3/year. Magazine. Contains the latest Harley-Davidson news and information, feature articles, and stories. **Price:** included in membership dues ● *HOG Membership Manual*. Contains details on the various programs and benefits of H.O.G. membership. **Price:** free for members ● *HOG Tales*, bimonthly. Magazine. Provides rally information, company updates, production information, and

member profiles. **Price:** included in membership dues ● *HOG Touring Handbook*. Contains maps, dealer locations, climate information, and riding laws. **Price:** included in membership dues. **Conventions/Meetings:** annual rally (exhibits).

22194 ■ Honda Sport Touring Association (HSTA)
c/o Phill Allgood
4040 E 82nd St., Ste.C9
PMB 331
Indianapolis, IN 46250-4209
Ph: (317)890-8858
Fax: (317)841-0111
E-mail: psnomads@ameritech.net
Contact: David Brickner, Pres.
Founded: 1982. **Members:** 2,000. **Membership Dues:** regular, $35 (annual) ● sustaining, $60 (annual) ● life, $600. **Budget:** $70,000. **Regional Groups:** 5. **State Groups:** 35. **Description:** Represents owners and enthusiasts of sport touring motorcycles. Seeks to foster fellowship and mutual assistance among members. Locates after-market accessories and provides feedback on mechanical failure and evaluation of these accessories. Provides technical assistance. Offers safety-oriented programs at state and regional events. **Libraries: Type:** not open to the public. **Holdings:** 100; video recordings. **Subjects:** motorcycling. **Computer Services:** database, Access/Microsoft. **Formerly:** (1987) Honda V-4 Sport Touring Association. **Publications:** *BlueBook Membership Guide*, annual. Membership Directory. **Price:** included in membership dues. **Circulation:** 2,000. **Advertising:** accepted ● *STAReview*, monthly. Newsletter. Includes upcoming rally information and surveys. **Price:** included in membership dues. **Circulation:** 2,000. **Advertising:** accepted. **Conventions/Meetings:** annual STAR National Meeting - regional meeting ● annual STAR Rally - meeting (exhibits) - always June, location varies.

22195 ■ Indian Motor-Cycle Club of America (IMCA)
PO Box 1743
Perris, CA 92572-1743
Ph: (909)780-0421
Fax: (909)780-0857
E-mail: imca@starklite.com
Contact: Robert E. Stark, Pres.
Founded: 1972. **Members:** 980. **Membership Dues:** individual, $25 (annual). **Description:** Owners and enthusiasts of Indian motorcycles, built in Springfield, MA from 1901 to 1953. Provides technical assistance and sources for motorcycles and parts; offers members a discount on specially manufactured parts. Participates in motorcycle rallies. **Publications:** *Pow Wow*, semiannual. Membership Directory. Contains articles and upcoming events. **Advertising:** accepted ● *Smoke Signals*, 10/year. Newsletter. Contains articles and upcoming events. **Advertising:** accepted.

22196 ■ International CBX Owners Association (ICOA)
c/o Bill Herting
6201 Hilltop Ct.
Fort Lee, NJ 07024-2218
E-mail: director@cbxclub.com
URL: http://www.cbxclub.com
Contact: Mike Brown Barone, Natl. Dir.
Founded: 1980. **Members:** 1,150. **Membership Dues:** regular, in U.S., $30 (annual) ● regular, in Canada, $34 (annual) ● overseas, $38 (annual). **State Groups:** 49. **Multinational. Description:** Owners of Honda CBX motorcycles. Works to share technical information and education on the maintenance of the Honda CBX motorcycle. Conducts technical sessions and publishes articles on servicing parts and accessories, product evaluation, and exchange/sales advertisements. **Libraries: Type:** reference. **Subjects:** parts, accessories, sales, factory service. **Publications:** *CB XPRESS*, quarterly. Magazine ● *Travel and Tour Assistance Directory*, annual. **Conventions/Meetings:** annual meeting ● meeting ● rally.

22197 ■ International Norton Owners' Association (INOA)
c/o Suzi Greenway, Pres.
Bellacraine Cooper Rd.
Stockbridge, MI 49285
Ph: (517)851-7437
E-mail: suzi@inoanorton.com
URL: http://www.inoanorton.com
Contact: Suzi Greenway, Pres.
Founded: 1974. **Members:** 4,000. **Membership Dues:** regular, in U.S., $25 (annual) ● associate, $10 (annual) ● regular, in Canada, $40 (annual). **Regional Groups:** 21. **Description:** Represents owners and enthusiasts concerned with the future of the Norton motorcycle. Enhances communication among Norton owners and preserve the Norton motorcycle. Encourages factories to make replacement parts and build new Norton motorcycles. Sponsors regional rallies; compiles statistics. **Formerly:** (1985) U.S. Norton Owners' Association. **Publications:** *Norton News*, 5/year. Magazine. Offers technical assistance, parts and service sources, and a forum for member-originated modifications and maintenance procedures. **Advertising:** accepted ● *Parts-Service-Membership Directory*, annual ● *Technical Digest*. **Conventions/Meetings:** annual Great Lakes Norton Rally.

22198 ■ International Star Riders Association (ISRA)
PO Box 532
Linden, VA 22642
E-mail: membership@star-riders.org
URL: http://www.star-riders.org
Contact: Pam Harrison, Sec.
Description: Represents individuals who love Star motorcycles. **Publications:** *The Star Cruiser*, monthly. Newsletter.

22199 ■ LeMans America (LA)
c/o Donald Boyd, Pres.
8075 Tipsico Trail
Holly, MI 48442
E-mail: lemansameric@earthlink.net
URL: http://www.lemansamerica.com
Contact: Donald Boyd, Pres.
Founded: 1975. **Members:** 500. **Membership Dues:** regular, dealer, associate (non-Suzuki) $20 (annual) ● household, $12 (annual). **Staff:** 12. **Budget:** $20,000. **Regional Groups:** 4. **State Groups:** 34. **Local Groups:** 2. **Description:** Owners of Suzuki motorcycles. Seeks to: improve the quality of motorcycling; improve the public image of riders; provide a social outlet for motorcyclists. Compiles statistics. Provides motorcycle safety training. **Libraries: Type:** reference. **Holdings:** 400; archival material. **Subjects:** Suzuki motorcycles. **Awards: Type:** recognition. **Computer Services:** Information services, technical and restoration information, statistics, provided by designated model chairmen ● mailing lists, of members. **Publications:** *Lemans America Newsletter*, monthly. **Price:** included in membership dues. **Circulation:** 1,000. **Advertising:** accepted ● Directory, annual. **Conventions/Meetings:** annual National Rally - meeting (exhibits).

22200 ■ Motorcycle Events Association (MEA)
2993 Tyrone Blvd. N
St. Petersburg, FL 33710
Ph: (727)343-1049
Free: (866)203-4485
Fax: (727)344-0327
E-mail: info@motorcycleevents.com
URL: http://www.motorcycleevents.com
Membership Dues: individual, $25 (annual) ● family, $40 (annual) ● life (individual), $250 ● life (family), $400. **For-Profit. Description:** Motorcycle enthusiasts who attend or plan to attend major events in the United States. Promotes participation in motorcycle events. Serves as a clearinghouse on motorcycle gatherings; makes available travel discounts to members; sanctions motorcycle events and races. **Publications:** *MotocycleEvents.com*, monthly. Newsletter ● *Motorcycle Events Magazine*, quarterly.

22201 ■ Motorcycle Riders Foundation (MRF)
236 Massachusetts Ave. NE, Ste.510
Washington, DC 20002-4980
Ph: (202)546-0983
Fax: (202)546-0986
E-mail: jeff@mrf.org
URL: http://www.mrf.org
Contact: Jeff Hennie, VP of Government Relations
Founded: 1979. **Membership Dues:** individual, $25 (annual) ● sustaining, $100 (annual) ● joint, $40 (annual). **Description:** Works to continue developing an aggressive independent national advocate for the advancement of motorcycling and its associated lifestyle, which is financially stable and exceeds the needs or motorcycling enthusiasts. **Awards:** MRF Young Activist. **Type:** scholarship. **Recipient:** for members 30 years of age or younger. **Computer Services:** Mailing lists, of members. **Programs:** MRF State Representative; Roadside Assistance. **Publications:** *MRF Reports*, bimonthly. Newsletter. Summary of national motorcycle rights.

22202 ■ Rickman Owners Club International (ROCI)
9911 Central Rd., Ste.R
Apple Valley, CA 92308
Ph: (760)247-0027
E-mail: metissprts@aol.com
Contact: George L. Wineland, Managing Dir.
Founded: 1976. **Members:** 360. **Membership Dues:** regular, $15 (annual) ● outside U.S., $25 (annual). **Staff:** 1. **Budget:** $3,500. **Multinational. Description:** Owners of Rickman motorcycles in 8 countries dedicated to fostering and preserving the marque. (First produced in the early 1960s by Rickman (Engineering) Limited of New Milton, England, the motorcycle is characterized by fiberglass components and nickel-plated frames and is known as the Metisse, or cross-breed. In the middle to late 1960s, the Rickman was the most prominent marque in motocross and road racing. Through 1983 the Rickman was still in very limited production as an endurance racing motorcycle.) Focuses on contemporary models formerly made by M.R.D. Metisse of Bristol, England, under license from Rickman, Wasp Engineering in Hants, England, and Mark III, built by Adrian Moss in England. Facilitates social and technical interaction. Serves as liaison between members and factories; acts as clearinghouse for printed materials, parts, and accessories. Compiles statistics. **Convention/Meeting:** none. **Libraries: Type:** reference. **Holdings:** 23; clippings, photographs. **Subjects:** Rickman history, vintage motorcycling. **Affiliated With:** American Motorcycle Heritage Foundation; American Motorcyclist Association. **Publications:** *Metisse News*, quarterly. Newsletter. **Price:** included in membership dues. **Advertising:** accepted.

22203 ■ Riders for Justice (RFJ)
PO Box 1192
Clifton, CO 81520-1192
Ph: (970)434-4644
E-mail: rfjinfo@ridersforjustice.com
URL: http://www.ridersforjustice.com
Contact: Jay Rademacher, Pres.
Founded: 1986. **Membership Dues:** individual, $20 (annual). **Description:** Promotes the rights of motorcycle riders. Disseminates information. Maintains library; compiles statistics. **Publications:** *Riders for Justice Newspaper*, monthly. **Price:** included in membership dues. **Advertising:** accepted. Alternate Formats: online. **Conventions/Meetings:** monthly meeting.

22204 ■ Rudge Enthusiasts Club (REC)
c/o Charles M. McReynolds, Area Rep.
3338 Barhite St.
Pasadena, CA 91107
Ph: (626)798-7557
Fax: (626)798-8450
E-mail: cmmcreynolds@charter.net
URL: http://www.rudge.ndirect.co.uk
Contact: Charles M. McReynolds, Area Rep.
Founded: 1956. **Members:** 750. **Membership Dues:** regular, $40 (annual). **Staff:** 100. **Budget:** $350,000. **Regional Groups:** 4. **National Groups:** 2. **Multina-**

tional. **Description:** Owners and enthusiasts of Rudge motorcycles, built in England from 1910-40. Promotes maintenance and recognition of Rudge motorcycles. Offers technical queries service; sponsors Rudgespares, a spare parts service. Compiles statistics. **Libraries: Type:** reference. **Holdings:** books. **Subjects:** Rudge motorcycles; includes 75 plus factory drawings on CD. **Awards: Type:** recognition. **Publications:** *The Radial*, quarterly. Journal. **Price:** included in membership dues. **Circulation:** 825. **Conventions/Meetings:** annual meeting - always March, in England ● rally - usually in June, in England.

22205 ■ Triumph International Owners Club (TIOC)
PO Box 158
Plympton, MA 02367-0158
Ph: (508)946-1144
Fax: (508)946-1145
E-mail: tiocbima@aol.com
URL: http://members.aol.com/JohnTIOC/tioc.htm
Contact: John Healy, Contact
Founded: 1978. **Members:** 3,400. **Membership Dues:** first class, $18 (annual) ● in Canada, $22 (annual) ● outside U.S. and Canada, $27 (annual) ● life, in U.S., $200 ● life, in Canada, $250 ● life, outside U.S. and Canada, $300. **Staff:** 3. **Description:** Promotes the use and preservation of Triumph motorcycles. **Formerly:** (2002) Triumph International Owners Association. **Publications:** *Vintage Bike*, quarterly. Magazine. **Price:** included in membership dues. **Circulation:** 2,800. **Advertising:** accepted. **Conventions/Meetings:** annual meeting, rally.

22206 ■ United Sidecar Association (USCA)
c/o Al Roach, Sec.
130 S Michigan Ave.
Villa Park, IL 60181
Ph: (630)833-6732
E-mail: secretary@sidecar.com
URL: http://www.sidecar.com
Contact: Al Roach, Sec.
Founded: 1979. **Members:** 1,600. **Membership Dues:** regular, in U.S. and Canada, $25 (annual) ● international, $40 (annual). **Staff:** 6. **Budget:** $50,000. **State Groups:** 15. **Local Groups:** 20. **Description:** Owners, manufacturers, and distributors of motorcycle sidecars. Organizes local and national rallies for sidecar owners and enthusiasts. Offers exhibits to major motorcycle shows. Sponsors training and instructor programs. **Publications:** *Riding With a Sidecar*. **Price:** $10.00 ● *Sidecar Operator Manual*. **Price:** $10.00 ● *Sidecarist*, every 8 weeks. Magazine. Provides technical and safety information and rally dates. **Price:** included in membership dues. **Advertising:** accepted. **Conventions/Meetings:** annual rally - always June or July.

22207 ■ Velocette Owners Club of North America (VOCNA)
c/o Tom Ross
11830 Ridgecrest Dr.
Riverside, CA 92505
Ph: (951)354-6444
E-mail: venomveeline@charter.net
URL: http://www.velocette.org
Contact: Tom Ross, Contact
Founded: 1976. **Members:** 350. **Membership Dues:** individual, $18 (annual). **Description:** Persons who are interested in the Velocette, a British-made motorcycle. Seeks to restore, preserve, and enjoy Velocettes. Sponsors annual concourse including judging of motorcycles and riding events. Maintains library of manuals and parts lists. **Formerly:** (1981) West Coast Velocette Owners Club. **Publications:** *Fishtail West*, bimonthly. Newsletter ● *Machine Register*, periodic. **Conventions/Meetings:** annual rally.

22208 ■ Vespa Club of America (VCOA)
PO Box 54825
Oklahoma City, OK 73154-4825
E-mail: jd@merryweatherphoto.com
URL: http://www.vespaclubusa.org
Contact: J.D. Merryweather, Pres.
Founded: 1993. **Members:** 900. **Membership Dues:** domestic, $25 (annual) ● overseas, $35 (annual).

Staff: 5. **Description:** Represents Vespa scooter enthusiasts in the U.S. Promotes Vespa scooters. **Awards:** Best Original. **Frequency:** annual. **Type:** recognition ● Best Restoration. **Frequency:** annual. **Type:** recognition. **Publications:** *American Scooterist*, quarterly. Magazine. **Price:** $5.00/back issue. **Advertising:** accepted ● Membership Directory, annual. **Price:** included in membership dues. **Conventions/Meetings:** annual Amerivespa - rally.

22209 ■ Vincent Owners Club - Keystone Section (VOC)
97 Freemansville Rd.
Shillington, PA 19607
Ph: (610)777-4714
E-mail: president998@voc.uk.com
Contact: Bryan Phillips, Pres.
Founded: 1963. **Members:** 3,000. **Membership Dues:** international, $25 (annual) ● section, $5 (annual). **State Groups:** 1. **Local Groups:** 1. **National Groups:** 7. **Description:** Vincent motorcycle enthusiasts. Offers information and mechanical advice on Vincent motorcycles. (Vincents were manufactured until 1955; a world speed record was set on a Vincent in 1955, at 185 mph.) Collects or locates Vincents still in existence; conducts rallies. **Awards: Type:** recognition. **Publications:** *MPH*, monthly. Magazine. Contains international club news. **Price:** included in membership dues. **Circulation:** 3,000. **Conventions/Meetings:** annual North American Meeting (exhibits).

22210 ■ Vintage BMW Motorcycle Owners (VBMWMO)
c/o Roland Slabon, Ed.-in-Chief
PO Box 67
Exeter, NH 03833
Ph: (603)772-9799
E-mail: roland.slabon@vintagebmw.org
URL: http://www.vintagebmw.org
Contact: Roland Slabon, Ed.-in-Chief
Founded: 1972. **Members:** 7,000. **Membership Dues:** regular, in U.S., $25 (annual) ● regular, in Canada and Mexico, $30 (annual) ● elsewhere, $35 (annual). **Staff:** 5. **Budget:** $40,000. **Languages:** English, German. **Multinational. Description:** Represents present and former owners of antique (1923-45), vintage (194854), classic (1955-69), or contemporary BMW motorcycles; other individuals. Works to preserve and enjoy BMW motorcycles. Disseminates information on the history of the marque and sidecars. Provides technical reprints, overseas parts sources, and motorcycle classified advertisements. **Computer Services:** Mailing lists, of members. **Affiliated With:** BMW Riders Association International; BMW Vintage Car Club of America. **Also Known As:** The Vintage BMW Club; Vintage BMW. **Publications:** *Vintage BMW Bulletin*, quarterly. Newsletter. Contains illustrations and classified ads. **Price:** included in membership dues. **Advertising:** accepted. **Conventions/Meetings:** annual May Day Madness - rally and meeting, campout and flea market/swap meet - Memorial Day Weekend ● annual rally, international.

22211 ■ Vintage Motor Bike Club (VMBC)
c/o Joyce Lee
537 W Huntington St.
Montpelier, IN 47359
Ph: (417)881-7411
E-mail: robertcan@cantrellbarnes.com
URL: http://www.cantrellbarnes.com/vmbc.html
Contact: Joyce Lee, Contact
Founded: 1972. **Members:** 2,200. **Membership Dues:** regular, in U.S., $25 (annual) ● regular, outside U.S., $30 (annual). **Staff:** 1. **Budget:** $44,000. **Description:** Owners and individuals interested in motorbikes and scooters that are out of production; dedicated to the preservation and restoration of motorized bicycles and scooters. Compiles statistics. Buys, trades, and sells machines and parts through club newsletter and auctions. **Awards: Type:** recognition. **Publications:** *Vintage Motor Bike Club Magazine*, quarterly. **Price:** included in membership dues. **Advertising:** accepted ● Membership Directory, annual ● Magazine, quarterly ● Newsletter,

quarterly. **Conventions/Meetings:** Annual National Meet - competition (exhibits) - usually July ● annual meet.

22212 ■ Virago Owners Club (VOC)
c/o Paul Boyd, Treas.
1386 Reynolds Cir.
Binghamton, NY 13903
Ph: (607)669-4352
E-mail: voctreas@tny.rr.com
URL: http://www.viragoownersclub.org
Contact: Rick Van Gorder, Pres.
Founded: 1982. **Members:** 600. **Membership Dues:** regular, $21 (annual) ● associate, $14 (annual). **Regional Groups:** 4. **State Groups:** 12. **Local Groups:** 20. **Description:** Owners of the Virago model motorcycles introduced in 1981 by Yamaha. Sponsors local events and national contests. Compiles statistics. Maintains library. **Awards: Type:** recognition. **Computer Services:** database, dealer discount program and list ● information services, parts finding ● mailing lists, of members. **Publications:** VOC Newsletter, bimonthly. **Price:** included in membership dues. **Advertising:** accepted. Alternate Formats: CD-ROM; online. **Conventions/Meetings:** annual meeting.

22213 ■ Women in the Wind (WITW)
c/o Becky Brown, Founder/Treas.
PO Box 8392
Toledo, OH 43605
E-mail: becky@womeninthewind.org
URL: http://www.womeninthewind.org
Contact: Becky Brown, Founder/Treas.
Founded: 1979. **Members:** 1,300. **Membership Dues:** associate, $10 (annual) ● chapter, $15 (annual) ● regular, outside U.S., $20 (annual). **Staff:** 3. **Local Groups:** 52. **Description:** Women motorcyclists and enthusiasts united to promote a positive image of women motorcyclists. Educates members on motorcycle safety and maintenance. Conducts charitable programs. **Awards:** Safe Mileage. **Frequency:** annual. **Type:** recognition. **Recipient:** for riding motorcycles safely with highest mileage. **Publications:** Shootin' the Breeze, bimonthly. Newsletter. Contains membership activities news and calendar of events. **Price:** included in membership dues. **Circulation:** 830. **Conventions/Meetings:** annual conference ● semiannual international conference.

22214 ■ Women's Motorcyclist Foundation (WMF)
7 Lent Ave.
Le Roy, NY 14482-1009
Ph: (585)768-6054
Free: (800)442-3550
Fax: (585)502-0418
E-mail: wmfginsue@aol.com
URL: http://www.womensmotorcyclistfoundation.org
Contact: Gin Shear, Exec. Dir.
Founded: 1984. **Members:** 2,000. **Staff:** 4. **Budget:** $60,000. **Description:** Information and service organization for women motorcyclists. Offers networking opportunities; has sponsored and produced the Pony Express Tour '96, '98, Pony Express Roundup 2000, and Pony Express Relay 2003. **Awards:** Jill Ireland Award. **Frequency:** annual. **Type:** recognition. **Recipient:** for volunteers. **Formerly:** Women Riding For Research. **Conventions/Meetings:** biennial Pony Express Relay: National Motorcycle Ride for Breast Cancer Research - festival, relay ride circumnavigating the continental U.S.

22215 ■ Yamaha 650 Society
27 Green Acres Dr.
Rolla, MO 65401-3910
Ph: (573)368-5852
E-mail: dlawson@fidnet.com
URL: http://beaver.vinu.edu/650.htm
Contact: Don Lawson, Interim Dir.
Founded: 1978. **Members:** 650. **Membership Dues:** in U.S., $20 (annual) ● in Canada, $24 (annual) ● outside U.S. and Canada, $26 (annual). **Staff:** 2. **State Groups:** 50. **Description:** Yamaha 650 twin-cylinder and other motorcycle owners interested in traditional motorcycles made in the same style as Triumph motorcycles. Provides information on me-

chanics, maintenance, new products, and safety. Collects articles and archival material on the Yamaha 650. **Computer Services:** Mailing lists. **Publications:** Yam 650 News, bimonthly. Newsletter. **Circulation:** 650. **Advertising:** accepted. **Conventions/Meetings:** rally - 8/year.

Mouse

22216 ■ American Fancy Rat and Mouse Association (AFRMA)
9230 64th St.
Riverside, CA 92509-5924
Ph: (909)238-5231 (951)685-2350
E-mail: afrma@afrma.org
URL: http://www.afrma.org
Contact: Karen Robbins, Founder
Founded: 1983. **Members:** 200. **Membership Dues:** individual/family, $25 (annual) ● regular, in Canada, $30 (annual) ● overseas, $35 (annual). **State Groups:** 1. **Description:** Enthusiasts and owners of fancy rats and mice. Promotes and encourages the breeding and exhibition of fancy rats and mice, educates the public on their positive qualities as companion animals and provides information on their proper care. Defines and sets the standards as to recognized types of fancy rats and mice. Assures that defined and set standards are strictly enforced in judging, awarding prizes, and organizing shows. Conducts and maintains a recording system of champion rats and mice. Holds displays at county fairs, pet expo, etc. **Awards:** Challenge Trophies. **Frequency:** annual. **Type:** recognition. **Recipient:** for winners of different rat and mouse classes at the annual show. **Publications:** AFRMA Standards and Show Regulations. Booklet. Lists recognized standards of show animals and show rules/regulations, helpful show info and proposed standards of rats/mice. **Price:** $5.00 each, for members; $8.00 for nonmembers. **Circulation:** 200 ● American Fancy Rat and Mouse Association—Directory. Provides show results, lists of award-winning rats/mice, veterinarians, addresses of similar clubs, and other relevant information. **Price:** included in membership dues; $5.00/copy for nonmembers. **Circulation:** 200. **Advertising:** accepted ● American Fancy Rat and Mouse Association—Rule Book. Booklet. Lists rules of association. **Price:** included in membership dues; $5.00/copy for nonmembers. **Circulation:** 200 ● American Fancy Rat & Mouse Association - Brochure ● Breeding Rats and Mice. Booklet. Covers breeding rats and mice. **Price:** $10.00 for nonmembers ● Mouse Genetics. Booklet. Contains articles on mouse genetics from the association's newsletter. **Price:** $15.00 for nonmembers; $10.00 for members ● Rat and Mouse Tales, quarterly. Newsletter. Provides information about basic care, rodent genetics, veterinary medicine, and stories of pets; includes calendar of events and breeders directory. **Price:** included in membership dues; $5.00/issue for nonmembers. **Circulation:** 200. **Advertising:** accepted ● Rat Genetics. Booklet. Contains articles on rat genetics from the association's newsletter. **Price:** $15.00 for nonmembers; $10.00 for members. **Conventions/Meetings:** annual competition - always January ● bimonthly Fancy Rat & Mouse Shows - competition (exhibits) - always Southern California ● semiannual Pet Shows - competition - usually February and October.

22217 ■ Fitzgerald's Fancys: Rat and Mouse Information
210 La Verne Ave.
Long Beach, CA 90803
Ph: (562)439-2002
Fax: (562)987-1904
E-mail: mrtwa1@aol.com
Contact: Roxanne Fitzgerald, Contact
Founded: 1984. **Nonmembership. Multinational. Description:** Breeder of fancy pedigreed rats and mice. Disseminates information on international and domestic clubs, husbandry, health, behavior, etc. **Libraries: Type:** not open to the public. **Holdings:** books, periodicals. **Subjects:** show breeding pet rats, mice.

22218 ■ Rat Fan Club
857 Lindo Ln.
Chico, CA 95973
Ph: (530)899-0605
E-mail: ratlady@ratfanclub.org
URL: http://www.ratfanclub.org
Contact: Debbie Ducommun, Founder
Founded: 1992. **Members:** 350. **Membership Dues:** regular, $25 (annual). **Staff:** 1. **For-Profit. Multinational. Description:** Enthusiasts and owners of rats. Promotes the keeping of rats as pets. Disseminates information on rat care. Provides a forum for exchange of information among members. **Libraries: Type:** reference. **Holdings:** 13. **Subjects:** pet rats. **Publications:** The Rat Report, monthly. Newsletter. Contains information on keeping rats as pets. Includes ideas for toys, games, and health care, as well as stories and photographs from members. **Price:** included in membership dues. ISSN: 1069-2045. **Circulation:** 550. **Advertising:** accepted ● Also publishes Rat Health Care booklet. **Conventions/Meetings:** bimonthly regional meeting - held in Northern California.

22219 ■ Rat and Mouse Club of America (RMCA)
6082 Modoc Rd.
Westminster, CA 92683
E-mail: rmgazette@aol.com
URL: http://www.rmca.org
Contact: Mary Ann Isaksen, Dir.
Membership Dues: regular, $10 (annual). **Regional Groups:** 10. **Multinational. Description:** Promotes domestic rats and mice as pets and responsible pet ownership. **Publications:** Rat and Mouse Gazette, bimonthly. Magazine.

22220 ■ Rat, Mouse, and Hamster Fanciers (RMHF)
783 Solana Dr.
Lafayette, CA 94549
URL: http://www.ratmousehamster.com
Contact: Sylvia Butler, Treas.
Founded: 1984. **Members:** 100. **Membership Dues:** individual (domestic), family, $15 (annual) ● individual (foreign), $24 (annual). **Staff:** 10. **Description:** Individuals interested in raising rats, mice, hamsters, and dwarf hamsters as pets. Facilitates information exchange; conducts educational programs and competitive rodent shows. **Awards: Type:** recognition. **Committees:** Standards. **Publications:** Rat, Mouse, and Hamster Fanciers Standards of Perfection. **Price:** $12.00 for nonmembers, includes postage and handling; $8.00 for members, includes postage and handling; $5.00 for members (price at show); $10.00 for nonmembers (price at show) ● Newsletter, bimonthly. Includes notices of activities and shows. **Price:** $15.00/year. **Circulation:** 100. **Advertising:** accepted. **Conventions/Meetings:** semiannual meeting.

Music

22221 ■ American Pianists Association (APA)
4603 Clarendon Rd., Ste.030
Indianapolis, IN 46208
Ph: (317)940-9945
E-mail: apainfo@americanpianists.org
URL: http://www.americanpianists.org
Contact: Helen Small, Pres./CEO
Founded: 1979. **Membership Dues:** friend (one person), $25-$99 ● friend (two persons with same address), $50-$99 ● supporting friend, $100-$499 ● sustaining friend, $500-$999 ● grand friend (minimum), $1,000. **Staff:** 6. **Budget:** $1,800,000. **Description:** Aims to discover, promote and advance the careers of world-class, classical and jazz pianists, who are citizens of the United States between the ages of 18 and 30. **Awards:** Classical Fellowship Award. **Frequency:** biennial. **Type:** fellowship. **Recipient:** to a classical pianist under the age of 30 ● Jazz Fellowship Award. **Frequency:** biennial. **Type:** fellowship. **Recipient:** to a jazz pianist aged 18 to 30. **Formerly:** (1989) Beethoven Foundation. **Publi-**

cations: Newsletter, quarterly. **Circulation:** 6,000. **Advertising:** accepted. **Conventions/Meetings:** biennial American Jazz Piano Competition and Classical Fellowship Awards.

22222 ■ Antique Phonograph Collectors Club (APCC)
502 E 17th St.
Brooklyn, NY 11226
Ph: (718)941-6835
E-mail: allenamet@aol.com
URL: http://www.phonobooks.com
Contact: Allen Koenigsberg, Ed.
Founded: 1973. **Members:** 2,000. **Staff:** 1. **Description:** Collectors, libraries, and historical societies. Provides accurate information and encourages communication among collectors of antique phonographs and records. Questions and answers by mail; reviews books on the hobby. Provides lectures to local collector groups; lists current research projects of members; offers discounts on large orders of collector publications. **Libraries: Type:** reference; by appointment only. **Holdings:** 500; archival material. **Subjects:** 2100 patents, 5000 cylinder records from the time period 1877-1930. **Computer Services:** Information services, trademark and patent research (historical). **Publications:** *Complete Talking Machine Book* ● *Edison Cylinder Records, 1889-1912.* Catalogs ● *Patent History of the Phonograph, 1877-1912.* Book ● *Trademarks of Recorded Sound, 1893-1929.* Monograph ● Also publishes discographies and posters; republishes trade literature, manuals, and patents pertaining to the history of recorded sound, back issues of *Antique Phonograph Monthly.* Research on the Lindbergh kidnapping and the Leo Frank case.

22223 ■ Carousel Organ Association of America (COAA)
c/o Marge Waters, Treas.
7552 Beach Rd.
Wadsworth, OH 44281
E-mail: info@coaa.us
URL: http://www.coaa.us
Contact: Marge Waters, Treas.
Founded: 1998. **Membership Dues:** regular, in U.S., $30 (annual) ● regular, in Canada and Mexico, $35 (annual) ● overseas, $40 (annual). **Multinational.** **Description:** Dedicated to enjoyment, preservation, knowledge sharing of all outdoor mechanical musical instruments, including band organs, fair and street organs, calliopes, and hand-cranked organs of all sizes. **Telecommunication Services:** electronic mail, wawaters2@aol.com. **Publications:** *Carousel Organ,* quarterly. Journal.

22224 ■ Collectors Record Club (CRC)
61 French Market Pl.
New Orleans, LA 70116
Ph: (504)525-5000
Fax: (504)525-1776
E-mail: info@jazzology.com
URL: http://www.jazzology.com
Contact: George H. Buck Jr., Exec. Off.
Founded: 1949. **Members:** 12,000. **Membership Dues:** life, $5. **Staff:** 3. **Languages:** Arabic, English, French, German. **Description:** Persons interested in authentic jazz and big band music. Promotes the circulation of authentic jazz and big band recordings by providing members with the opportunity of purchasing recordings at a discount. Club uses money from recording sales to make more recordings available on the club's Jazzology label. **Libraries: Type:** reference. **Holdings:** 1,000. **Subjects:** jazz, big band, blues, standards. **Computer Services:** Mailing lists ● online services. **Subgroups:** G.H.B. Jazz Foundation. **Publications:** *Jazz Beat,* quarterly. Magazine. Contains feature stories and lists of new releases. **Price:** free. **Circulation:** 15,000 ● *Jazzfest Quarterly.* Catalogs. Contains jazz, big band, and other unusual recordings. ● Newsletter, 3-4/year.

22225 ■ International Association of Jazz Appreciation (IAOJA)
PO Box 48146
Los Angeles, CA 90048
Ph: (323)295-0644

Fax: (323)751-3323
Contact: William J. Coffey MD, Pres.
Founded: 1982. **Members:** 683. **Staff:** 1. **Budget:** $250,000. **Description:** Enthusiasts of jazz music. Works to preserve and perpetuate jazz through educational programs such as the Jazz Goes to School program, in which public school students, grades K-12, witness lectures and demonstrations on the culture and history of jazz music as it relates to the culture and history of America. Offers consultation on education, presentation, and performance. Maintains speakers' bureau. **Libraries: Type:** not open to the public. **Holdings:** 550; articles, books, periodicals. **Computer Services:** Mailing lists. **Committees:** Education. **Publications:** Newsletter, bimonthly. Includes reviews and a listing of events. **Price:** free for members. **Circulation:** 3,000. **Advertising:** accepted. **Conventions/Meetings:** annual International Jazz Conference - meeting (exhibits).

22226 ■ International Association of Jazz Record Collectors (IAJRC)
c/o Shelley Wruk Finke, Corresponding Sec.
10411 Glenmary Farm Dr.
Louisville, KY 40291
Ph: (502)762-1200
E-mail: musicmail97@bellsouth.net
URL: http://www.iajrc.org
Contact: Shelley Wruk Finke, Corresponding Sec.
Founded: 1964. **Members:** 1,500. **Membership Dues:** individual, $35 (annual) ● family, $40 (annual) ● student, $20 (annual). **Multinational.** **Description:** Collectors of jazz records from many countries. Aims are to: create more recognition for great jazz musicians and stimulate increased public acceptance of jazz as a great American art form; promote communication among collectors, dealers, and musicians; issue publications and records; promote formation of local jazz clubs. Reviews record releases and books; provides information exchange for collectors. Makes special CDs available to members. **Libraries: Type:** lending. **Computer Services:** Mailing lists. **Committees:** CD Program; Convention; Journal Publication; Monograph Publications. **Publications:** *Assessing, Insuring, and Disposing of Jazz Record Collections.* Monograph ● *Herman Chittison—A Bio-Discography.* Monograph ● *IAJRC Journal,* quarterly. **Advertising:** accepted ● *IAJRC Membership Directory,* biennial. **Conventions/Meetings:** annual symposium.

22227 ■ Jazz Nation
PO Box 218362
Houston, TX 77218
Ph: (832)439-3560
E-mail: jazznation@yahoo.com
Contact: Albert Khalis Pride, Pres./Founder
Founded: 1997. **Membership Dues:** citizenship, $20 (annual). **Multinational.** **Description:** Dedicated to promoting, preserving and celebrating jazz music. **Publications:** *Jazz Exodus,* quarterly. Newsletter. **Conventions/Meetings:** meeting.

22228 ■ Lyre Association of North America (LANA)
10001 Kinross Ave.
Silver Spring, MD 20901
Ph: (301)270-2055
Fax: (301)270-2055
E-mail: sembrey@erols.com
URL: http://www.lyreamerica.net
Contact: Samantha Embrey, Treas.
Founded: 1969. **Members:** 84. **Membership Dues:** regular, $35 (annual) ● supporting, $50 (annual). **Description:** Individuals who play the lyre or are interested in lyre music. Promotes lyre music education. Offers course in music studies. **Programs:** Youth Lyre. **Formerly:** (2003) Lyre Association of North America-Esther Centers. **Publications:** *Lyre Newsletter,* semiannual. **Price:** included in membership dues. **Conventions/Meetings:** annual Lyre Conference ● annual meeting.

22229 ■ Musical Box Society International (MBSI)
PO Box 10196
Springfield, MO 65808-0196
Ph: (417)886-8839

Fax: (417)886-8839
E-mail: jbeeman.mbsi@att.net
URL: http://www.mbsi.org
Contact: Jacque Beeman, Admin.
Founded: 1949. **Members:** 2,200. **Membership Dues:** regular (in U.S.), $55 (annual) ● regular (in Canada and Mexico), $65 (annual) ● regular (outside North America), $70 (annual). **Budget:** $167,000. **Local Groups:** 11. **Languages:** English, Japanese. **Description:** Collectors and dealers in 20 countries of antique musical boxes and other mechanical and automatic musical instruments, including player pianos, reproducing pianos, orchestrions, band organs, barrel and paper roll organs, clocks and watches with music works, musical automata, birds, and whistling figures. **Libraries: Type:** reference. **Subjects:** mechanical music. **Formerly:** (1952) Musical Box Hobbyists. **Publications:** *MBSI Mechanical Music,* bimonthly. Newsletter. Includes news, articles, activity calendar, and chapter reports. **Price:** included in membership dues. ISSN: 1071-0191. **Advertising:** accepted ● Membership Directory, biennial. **Advertising:** accepted. **Conventions/Meetings:** annual meeting ● regional meeting, for individual chapters - 30-40/year.

22230 ■ North American Folk Music and Folk Dance Alliance
510 S Main St., 1st Fl.
Memphis, TN 38103
Ph: (901)522-1170
Fax: (901)522-1172
E-mail: fa@folk.org
URL: http://www.folkalliance.org
Contact: Leslie Berman, Pres.
Founded: 1989. **Members:** 2,500. **Membership Dues:** individual, $70 (annual) ● sustaining, $100 (annual) ● partner, $95 (annual) ● small organization, $150 (annual) ● medium organization, $230 (annual) ● large organization, $505 (annual) ● life, $1,000 ● affiliate, $50 (annual). **Staff:** 5. **Regional Groups:** 6. **Multinational.** **Description:** Performers, agents, media, record companies, merchandisers, presenters and other organizations in traditional and contemporary folk music, dance, storytelling, festivals, and related performing arts. Promotes traditional, contemporary, and multicultural folk music and dance and related performing arts through education, networking, advocacy, and field and professional development. **Awards:** Lifetime Achievement Award. **Frequency:** annual. **Type:** recognition. **Also Known As:** Folk Alliance. **Publications:** Newsletter, bimonthly. **Advertising:** accepted. **Conventions/Meetings:** annual conference.

22231 ■ Ricky Martin Worldwide Fan Club (RMWFC)
PO Box 5825
Fullerton, CA 92838
E-mail: jenn@rickymartinmusic.com
URL: http://www.rickymartinmusic.com
Contact: Jenn Naranjo, Contact
Founded: 1994. **Multinational.** **Description:** Fan club devoted to singer Ricky Martin.

22232 ■ Southeastern Historical Keyboard Society (SEHKS)
c/o Martha Clinkscale, Treas.
PO Box 670282
Dallas, TX 75367-0282
E-mail: lpalmer@smu.edu
URL: http://www.sehks.org
Contact: Larry Palmer, Pres.
Founded: 1981. **Members:** 250. **Membership Dues:** student in U.S., $25 (annual) ● individual in U.S., $45 (annual) ● institution or organization in U.S., $45 (annual) ● student outside U.S., $30 (annual) ● individual outside U.S., $50 (annual) ● institution or organization outside U.S., $50 (annual). **Multinational.** **Description:** Promotes the study of early keyboard instruments, specifically the harpsichord, clavichord, fortepiano, and organ prior to 1860. Conducts educational programs and holds an annual conference generally in the USA. **Awards:** Alienor Awards. **Frequency:** quadrennial. **Type:** monetary. **Recipient:** to encourage the creation of new works

for the harpsichord ● Mae and Irving Jurow International Harpsichord Competition Award(s). **Frequency:** quadrennial. **Type:** monetary. **Recipient:** for harpsichordists who are under 33 years of age at the time of the competition. **Programs:** Jurow International Harpsichord Competition. **Publications:** *Early Keyboard Journal*, annual. **Price:** included in membership dues. ISSN: 8998-132X. **Advertising:** accepted. **Conventions/Meetings:** annual Conference and Alienor Awards - competition, competition for new works for the harpsichord plus other presentations and performances (exhibits) - 2008 Mar. 7-9, Winston-Salem, NC ● annual Conference and Jurow Competition, with workshops and Jurow performance competition by judges and others (exhibits).

Needlework

22233 ■ American Bunka Embroidery Association (ABEA)
8677 Brittania Dr.
Fort Myers, FL 33912
Ph: (239)561-8802
E-mail: swflbunka@comcast.net
URL: http://americanbunka.com
Contact: Elery Shaw, Pres.

Membership Dues: regular, $18 (annual). **Multinational. Description:** Represents skilled Bunka stitchers and individuals who are interested in Japanese Bunka. Promotes the art of Japanese Bunka embroidery. Provides opportunities for its members to hone their skills in Japanese Bunka embroidery. **Publications:** Newsletter. **Price:** included in membership dues.

22234 ■ Crochet Guild of America (CGOA)
1100-H Brandywine Blvd.
Zanesville, OH 43701-7303
Ph: (740)452-4541
Free: (877)852-9190
Fax: (740)452-2552
E-mail: cgoa@crochet.org
URL: http://www.crochet.org
Contact: Nancy Brown, Pres.

Founded: 1994. **Membership Dues:** individual in U.S., $35 (annual) ● business, $100-$1,000 (annual) ● regular, in Canada and Mexico, $42 (annual) ● international, $50 (annual). **Description:** Aims to preserve and advance the art of crochet. Educates the public about crochet. Provides education and networking opportunities. Sets a national standard for the quality, art and skill of crochet through creative endeavors. **Libraries: Type:** lending. **Holdings:** 4,987; articles, books, video recordings. **Computer Services:** Information services, crochet resources ● online services, message board. **Committees:** Education; Professional Development. **Programs:** Masters. **Special Interest Groups:** Hooks. **Publications:** *Chain Link*, bimonthly. Newsletter. Includes news of crochet-related activities and crochet patterns. Alternate Formats: online.

Numismatic

22235 ■ American-Israel Numismatic Association (AINA)
PO Box 13063
Silver Spring, MD 20911-0063
E-mail: ainamel@aol.com
URL: http://amerisrael.com
Contact: Mr. Mel Wacks, Pres.

Founded: 1967. **Members:** 2,000. **Membership Dues:** regular, in North America, $18 (annual) ● regular, outside North America, $25 (annual) ● life, $300. **Staff:** 10. **Description:** Cultural and educational organization dedicated to the study and collection of past and present Judaic and Israel numismatics. Develops programs; sponsors seminars, meetings, and other activities that provide news, history, technical, social, and related background to the study of numismatics. Publishes bi-monthly Shekel magazine. **Libraries: Type:** lending. **Holdings:** 34; audio-visuals. **Subjects:** Judaic and Israel numismatics.

Publications: *The Shekel*, bimonthly. Journal. Contains Judaic numismatic articles and information, ancient to modern. **Price:** $18.00 for nonmembers in U.S. and Canada; $25.00 for nonmembers outside U.S. and Canada; $300.00 lifetime subscription for nonmembers; included in membership dues for US and Canada. ISSN: 0087-3486. **Circulation:** 2,000. **Conventions/Meetings:** annual meeting, in conjunction with summer meeting of American Numismatic Association.

22236 ■ American Numismatic Association (ANA)
818 N Cascade Ave.
Colorado Springs, CO 80903-3279
Ph: (719)632-2646
Free: (800)367-9723
Fax: (719)634-4085
E-mail: ana@money.org
URL: http://www.money.org
Contact: Christopher Cipoletti, Exec. Dir.

Founded: 1891. **Members:** 32,000. **Membership Dues:** regular, $36 (annual) ● junior (age 23 and under), $20 (annual) ● senior (age 65 and older), $31 (annual) ● club, $36 ● associate, $13 ● life, $500-$1,250. **Staff:** 30. **Budget:** $3,000,000. **Regional Groups:** 13. **Local Groups:** 670. **Description:** Collectors of coins, medals, tokens, and paper money. Promotes the study, research, and publication of articles on coins, coinage, and history of money. Sponsors correspondence courses; conducts research. Maintains museum, archive, authentication service for coins, and hall of fame. Sponsors National Coin Week; operates speakers' bureau. **Libraries: Type:** reference. **Holdings:** 35,000; archival material. **Subjects:** numismatic. **Awards:** Farrun Zerbe Award. **Frequency:** annual. **Type:** recognition ● Medal of Merit. **Frequency:** annual. **Type:** recognition. **Telecommunication Services:** additional toll-free number, membership, (800)514-2646. **Publications:** *The ABC's of Money - A Numismatic Primer* ● *ANA Grading Guide* ● *ANA Numismatic Correspondence Course* ● *Consumer Alert - Investing in Rare Coins* ● *First Strike Supplement: Emerging Collectors*, quarterly. **Circulation:** 35,800. **Advertising:** accepted ● *The Numismatist: For Collectors of Coins, Medals, Tokens and Paper Money*, monthly. Magazine. Includes feature articles, book reviews, calendar of events, consumer news, and obituaries. Also contains advertisers and annual indexes. **Price:** included in membership dues. ISSN: 0029-6090. **Circulation:** 28,000. **Advertising:** accepted. Alternate Formats: microform; online. **Conventions/Meetings:** annual World's Fair of Money - convention (exhibits) - always July/August.

22237 ■ American Numismatic Society (ANS)
96 Fulton St.
New York, NY 10038
Ph: (212)571-4470
Fax: (212)571-4479
E-mail: info@numismatics.org
URL: http://www.numismatics.org
Contact: Ute W. Kagan, Exec. Dir.

Founded: 1858. **Members:** 2,200. **Membership Dues:** student, $35 (annual) ● basic associate, $50 (annual) ● full associate, $75 (annual) ● life, associate/life, fellow, $7,500 ● life associate, $150 (annual) ● corporate associate, $500 (annual). **Staff:** 15. **Budget:** $1,000,000. **Description:** Collectors and others interested in coins, medals, and related materials. Advances numismatic knowledge as it relates to history, art, archaeology, and economics by collecting coins, medals, tokens, decorations, and paper money. Maintains only museum devoted entirely to numismatics. Presents annual Graduate Fellowship in Numismatics. Sponsors Graduate Seminar in Numismatics, a nine-week individual study program for ten students. **Libraries: Type:** open to the public. **Holdings:** 100,000; books, periodicals, photographs. **Subjects:** numismatics, archaeology, art history, economic history. **Awards:** Huntington Award Medal. **Frequency:** annual. **Type:** recognition. **Recipient:** for excellence in numismatic research ● Saltus Medal Award. **Frequency:** annual. **Type:** recognition. **Recipient:** for excellence in the art of the medal. **Com-**

puter Services: database, collections and membership. **Committees:** East Asian Coins; Greek Coins; Huntington Medal Award; Islamic and South Asian Coins; Library; Medals and Decorations; Medieval and Early Modern European Coins; Modern Coinage and Currency; Roman and Byzantine Coins; Saltus Medal Award. **Formerly:** (1907) American Numismatic and Archaeological Society. **Publications:** *American Coins in North American Collections* ● *American Journal of Numismatics*, annual. **Price:** included in membership dues. ISSN: 0145-1413 ● *American Numismatic Society—Numismatic Studies*, periodic. Book. Includes numbered monograph series of scholarly books containing numismatic data. **Price:** $35.00 each. ISSN: 0078-2718 ● *Ancient Coins in North American Collections*, periodic. Book. Includes numbered monograph series containing details on private and public collections of ancient coins of research value. ISSN: 0291-4019 ● *ANS Magazine*, 3/year. Includes news of numismatic and academic events, feature stories, columns, departments. **Price:** included in membership dues ● $15.00 for nonmembers. **Advertising:** accepted ● *Biennial Indexes to Numismatic Literature, 1947-65* ● *Coinage of the Americas Conference* ● *The Colonial Newsletter*, 3/year. Journal. Focuses on the study of coinages during the Confederation period. **Price:** $45.00 /year for members; $55.00 /year for nonmembers. Alternate Formats: CD-ROM. Also Cited As: *CNL* ● *Index to American Journal of Numismatics* ● *Numismatic Literature*, semiannual. Bibliography. Bibliography containing abstracts of articles worldwide on ancient and modern coins and medals. **Price:** $10.00/year. ISSN: 0029-6031. Alternate Formats: online ● *Numismatic Notes and Monographs* ● *Numismatic Studies* ● *Sylloge Nummorum Graecorum: The Collection of the American Numismatic Society*, periodic. Monograph. Series published in parts detailing all Greek coins in the ANS collection. ISSN: 0271-3993 ● Also makes available videos, color slide sets, medals, and cards illustrating items from the collection. **Conventions/Meetings:** annual Coinage of the Americas Conference - meeting ● meeting - always second Saturday in January, April, and October.

22238 ■ American Society of Check Collectors (ASCC)
473 E Elm St.
Sycamore, IL 60178
E-mail: ilrno2@netzero.com
URL: http://www.asccinfo.com
Contact: Lyman Hensley, Sec.

Founded: 1969. **Members:** 350. **Membership Dues:** regular, $13 (annual) ● regular, in Canada, $17 (annual) ● regular, outside U.S., $23 (annual). **Description:** Represents persons interested in collecting, preserving, and conducting historical research in old and new banking paper such as checks, drafts, certificates of deposit, gold dust receipts, stock and bond certificates, and protectographing material and methods. Formal group operating by correspondence among members. **Formerly:** (1987) Check Collectors Roundtable. **Publications:** *The Check Collector*, quarterly. Papers. **Price:** included in membership dues. ISSN: 1066-3061. **Circulation:** 350. **Advertising:** accepted ● *Membership Roster*, periodic. Membership Directory ● *Security Printers*. Booklet. **Conventions/Meetings:** annual conference - always June.

22239 ■ American Tax Token Society (ATTS)
c/o Carl L. Cochrane, Sec.-Treas.
12 Pheasant Dr.
Asheville, NC 28803
E-mail: clcochrane@prodigy.net
URL: http://www.taxtoken.com
Contact: Carl L. Cochrane, Sec.-Treas.

Founded: 1971. **Members:** 150. **Membership Dues:** in U.S., $8 (annual) ● in U.S. and Canada, $9 (annual) ● UK and Europe, $15 (annual) ● life - in U.S., $160 ● life - in U.S. and Canada, $180 ● life (UK and Europe addresses), $300. **Description:** Collectors and researchers in the field of sales tax tokens. Gathers and disseminates information on numismatic, philatelic, and related items concerning the history and collection of sales taxes, including tokens, checks, scrip, punch cards, coupons, and receipts. Promotes collecting of such items; facilitates communication between collectors; encourages and facilitates research and publication of data on sales taxes and sales tax items. **Affiliated With:** American Numismatic Association. **Publications:** *ATTS Newsletter*, quarterly. **Price:** included in membership dues ● *Checklist and Guide to Sales Tax Tokens*. Catalog. **Conventions/Meetings:** annual conference, held in conjunction with the American Numismatic Association (exhibits).

22240 ■ American Wooden Money Guild (AWMG)
Address Unknown since 2007
Founded: 1975. **Members:** 375. **Membership Dues:** $30 (annual). **National Groups:** 1. **Description:** "Lignadenarists," numismatists, and others interested in wooden money either as collectors or dealers. Issues several wooden nickels annually; maintains collection of wooden money. Issues wood in a limited quantity of 500 specimens. **Publications:** *Encyclopedia of Wooden Money* ● *Old Woody Views*, periodic. Newsletter. Covers the hobby of collecting wooden money. ● Also publishes research results; and has produced slide program. **Conventions/Meetings:** annual meeting, auction.

22241 ■ Armenian Numismatic Society (ANS)
8511 Beverly Park Pl.
Pico Rivera, CA 90660-1920
Ph: (562)695-0380
E-mail: armnumsoc@aol.com
Contact: Y.T. Nercessian, Sec.
Founded: 1971. **Members:** 175. **Membership Dues:** in U.S., $35 (annual) ● outside U.S., $45 (annual). **Staff:** 5. **Budget:** $6,000. **Description:** Individuals interested in the study of Armenian coins or other disciplines related to the study of Armenian antiquity. **Libraries: Type:** by appointment only. **Holdings:** 3,500; articles, books, periodicals. **Subjects:** Armenian numismatics. **Awards:** Armenian Numismatic Memorial Award. **Frequency:** annual. **Type:** recognition. **Recipient:** for articles on Armenian Numismatics. **Computer Services:** database, office use only ● mailing lists, office use only. **Committees:** Armenian Museum. **Formerly:** (1971) Armenian Coin Club; (1974) Armenian Numismatics and Artifact Society. **Publications:** *A Hoard of Copper Coins of Tigranes the Great and a Hoard of Artaxiad Coins*. **Price:** $3.00 plus shipping and handling of $1.25 ● *Armenian Books*. Booklets ● *Armenian Ceramic Art* ● *Armenian Coin Hoards*. **Price:** $8.00 plus shipping and handling of $3 ● *Armenian Coins & Their Values*. **Price:** $40.00 plus shipping and handling of $4 ● *Armenian Numismatic Bibliography & Literature*. **Price:** $50.00 plus shipping and handling of $5 ● *Armenian Numismatic Journal* (in Armenian and English), quarterly. Contains numismatic articles. **Price:** $50.00 /year for members. ISSN: 0884-0180. **Circulation:** 200 ● *Armenian Numismatic Studies*. **Price:** $75.00 plus shipping and handling of $7 ● *Armenian Woven Art* ● *Attribution & Dating of Armenian Bilingual Trams*. **Price:** $7.00 plus shipping and handling of $3 ● *Bank Notes of Armenia*. **Price:** $30.00 plus shipping and handling of $5 ● *Coinage of Cilician Armenia* ● *Coinage of the Armenian Kingdoms of Sophene & Commagene*. **Price:** $6.00 plus shipping and handling of $3 ● *Coinage of the Artaxiads of Armenia* ● *Eighteenth Century Armenian Medals Struck in Holland* ● *Essays on Armenian Numismatics in Memory of Father Clement Sibilian on the Centennial of His Death (the Sibilian volume)*. **Price:** $30.00 plus shipping and handling of $5 ● *Selected Numismatic Studies*. **Price:** $35.00 plus shipping and handling of $5 ● *Selected Numismatic Studies II*. **Price:** $57.00 plus shipping and handling of $5 ● *Thirty Centuries of Armenian Metal Art* ● Also issues a Special Publication series (in Armenian and English). **Conventions/Meetings:** quarterly meeting, with presentation of scholarly papers on Armenian numismatics (exhibits) - always in Los Angeles, CA.

22242 ■ Civil War Token Society (CWTS)
c/o Dale Cade, Sec.
26548 Mazur Dr.
Rancho Palos Verdes, CA 90275
Ph: (310)378-4182
E-mail: cwtpal@aol.net
URL: http://www.cwtsociety.com
Contact: Dale Cade, Sec.
Founded: 1966. **Members:** 1,000. **Membership Dues:** individual, $10 (annual) ● junior, $5 (annual). **Staff:** 1. **Description:** Collectors of civil war tokens issued by merchants to serve as emergency coins when federally-issued coins vanished from circulation after the government suspended specie payments from 1862-64. Many tokens served as advertisements for merchants and their businesses; others contained patriotic inscriptions and designs. Works to promote the educational, historic, and scientific study of Civil War tokens. Sponsors member only auctions and exhibits. Offers slide programs and video tapes to members. Offers Quarterly mail bid auctions for members only. **Libraries: Type:** reference. **Holdings:** articles, books. **Subjects:** Civil War tokens and issuers. **Awards:** CWTS Hall of Fame. **Type:** recognition ● Jack Detwiler Memorial Service Awards. **Frequency:** annual. **Type:** recognition. **Recipient:** for service ● Literary Awards. **Frequency:** annual. **Type:** recognition. **Recipient:** for written articles published in the Journal of the Civil War Token Society. **Publications:** *Civil War Token Journal*, quarterly. Provides information for collectors of Civil War tokens. Includes listings of tokens for sale or wanted. **Price:** included in membership dues. **Circulation:** 1,000. **Advertising:** accepted ● Membership Directory. **Price:** available to members only ● Reprints ● Vols. 1 thru 6 of journal (30 years). **Conventions/Meetings:** annual general assembly, held in conjunction with American Numismatic Association summer meeting (exhibits).

22243 ■ Combined Organizations of Numismatic Error Collectors of America (CONECA)
c/o Mike Ellis, Pres.
PO Box 706
Eureka Springs, AR 72632
Ph: (479)253-5055
E-mail: gmmmike@arkansas.net
URL: http://www.conecaonline.org
Contact: Mike Ellis, Pres.
Founded: 1983. **Members:** 700. **Membership Dues:** regular, $25 (annual) ● young numismatist, $7 (annual). **Staff:** 20. **Description:** Represents coin collectors interested in mint errors and varieties on U.S. and foreign coins. Provides authentication, education, research, and evaluation services; maintains museum and hall of fame; conducts research and educational programs. Compiles statistics. **Libraries: Type:** reference. **Subjects:** error coins and allied fields. **Awards:** Dr. King Award. **Frequency:** annual. **Type:** recognition. **Recipient:** to member ● Literary Award. **Frequency:** annual. **Type:** recognition. **Recipient:** for the most outstanding member ● **Type:** scholarship. **Computer Services:** database, U.S. and world minting varieties. **Programs:** Young Numismatist's. **Affiliated With:** American Numismatic Association. **Formerly:** Collectors of Numismatic Errors; Numismatic Error Collectors of America. **Publications:** *CONECA Handbook*. **Price:** $7.50 for members; $10.00 for nonmembers ● *Errorscope*, bimonthly. Journal. **Price:** included in membership dues. **Advertising:** accepted. **Conventions/Meetings:** competition ● annual Errorama Coin Show and Symposium - show and symposium.

22244 ■ Cuban Numismatic Association (CNA)
c/o Robert Freeman, Treas.
523 Meridian St.
Tallahassee, FL 32301-1281
Ph: (727)531-7337
E-mail: fxputrow@aol.com
URL: http://www.cubannumismaticassociation.com
Contact: Francis X. Putrow, Pres.
Founded: 2004. **Members:** 122. **Membership Dues:** regular, $10 (annual) ● junior, $5 (annual). **Multinational. Description:** Represents individuals interested in collecting Cuban coins, currency, medals, tokens, bonds, casino chips and all other related items. Encourages, promotes and dispenses Cuban numismatic knowledge, culture, education and fraternal relations among the numismatic community. **Affiliated With:** American Numismatic Association; American Numismatic Society; Association of Collecting Clubs; Latin American Paper Money Society. **Publications:** *Cuban Numismatic Association Newsletter*, quarterly. Alternate Formats: online.

22245 ■ Dedicated Wooden Money Collectors (DWMC)
c/o Thiltert Mehl
2084 N Brook Cir.
York, PA 17403
Ph: (717)845-4295 (717)854-0223
Fax: (717)854-0223
Contact: Larry White, Treas.
Founded: 1976. **Members:** 150. **Membership Dues:** regular in U.S., $5 (annual) ● life, $100 ● individual in Canada, $7 (annual) ● junior, $3 (annual). **Staff:** 7. **Budget:** $1,500. **Description:** Wooden money collectors united to advance the knowledge of official and unofficial wooden money along educational, historical, and scientific lines; further cooperation among all persons interested in the issue, circulation, classification, collection, exhibition, use, and preservation of all wooden money; exchange ideas through monthly publication and annual convention. **Libraries: Type:** reference; not open to the public. **Holdings:** 20; archival material. **Subjects:** wooden money. **Awards:** Design Award. **Frequency:** annual. **Type:** recognition. **Recipient:** for the best design of wooden money ● Harold Butner Award. **Frequency:** annual. **Type:** recognition. **Recipient:** for outstanding service to the DWMC ● Literary Award. **Frequency:** annual. **Type:** recognition. **Recipient:** for the best article in the newsletter. **Affiliated With:** American Numismatic Association. **Publications:** *Timber Lines*, monthly, except August. Newsletter. **Price:** free for members. **Circulation:** 150. **Advertising:** accepted. **Conventions/Meetings:** annual convention and meeting, held in conjunction with the American Numismatic Association (exhibits) - usually August.

22246 ■ Early American Coppers (EAC)
PO Box 15782
Cincinnati, OH 45215
E-mail: info@eacs.org
URL: http://www.eacs.org
Contact: Dan Holmes, Pres.
Founded: 1967. **Members:** 1,500. **Membership Dues:** 1st class mail, $25 (annual) ● junior (age 17 or under), $5 (annual). **Regional Groups:** 7. **Description:** Represents collectors and dealers of early American copper coinage. Promotes fellowship, sharing of information, and trading among members. Conducts research. **Libraries: Type:** reference; lending; not open to the public. **Holdings:** books, monographs, periodicals. **Subjects:** early American coppers. **Publications:** *Penny-Wise*, bimonthly. Newsletter. **Price:** included in membership dues. **Conventions/Meetings:** annual convention.

22247 ■ The Elongated Collectors (TEC)
c/o Tristan Davis, Sec.
210 N Leoma Ct.
Chandler, AZ 85225
E-mail: minime8484@hotmail.com
URL: http://www.tecnews.org
Contact: Tristan Davis, Sec.
Founded: 1966. **Members:** 560. **Membership Dues:** individual, $12 (annual) ● junior, $6 (annual) ● associate, $6 (annual) ● foreign, $18 (annual). **Staff:** 6. **Description:** Collectors of elongated coins; interested others. (Elongated coins are coins rolled through hand-cranked jeweler mill type machines consisting of reverse-engraved dies cut in steel rollers, which presses the coin into the die, and due to the pressure stretches the coin into an oblong shape in the process.) Promotes the collection and study of elongated coins; researches the history of such coins. Conducts educational programs; maintains speakers' bureau. **Libraries: Type:** reference; lending. **Holdings:** books, periodicals, video recordings. **Subjects:** history of elongated coins and machines. **Awards:** TEC Medal of Merit Award. **Frequency:** annual. **Type:** recognition. **Recipient:** for significant contributions to hobby; nominations accepted from members

● TEC News Articles Award. **Frequency:** annual. **Type:** recognition. **Recipient:** for collectors who submit articles that are published in TEC news. **Computer Services:** Mailing lists, of members. **Publications:** *TEC News*, quarterly. Newsletter. Includes officers' reports, submitted articles, and advertising. **Price:** included in membership dues. **Circulation:** 525. **Advertising:** accepted. **Conventions/Meetings:** annual meeting, held in conjunction with the American Numismatic Association National Convention.

22248 ■ International Bank Note Society (IBNS)

c/o Marcus Turner, Pres.
PO Box 191
Danville, IN 46122
E-mail: maturner@indy.rr.com
URL: http://www.ibns.it
Contact: Marcus Turner, Pres.
Founded: 1961. **Members:** 2,300. **Membership Dues:** junior, $16 (annual) ● regular, $33 (annual) ● family, $41 (annual). **Budget:** $25,000. **Regional Groups:** 6. **State Groups:** 1. **Multinational. Description:** Collectors of paper currency; professional dealers in bank notes; museums, banks, libraries, and similar organizations. Seeks to promote, stimulate, and advance the educational, scientific, and historical study and knowledge of worldwide bank notes and paper currencies. Conducts educational programs. **Libraries: Type:** reference; lending. **Holdings:** books. **Subjects:** paper money. **Awards:** Bank Note of the Year. **Frequency:** annual. **Type:** recognition. **Recipient:** best issued bank note ● Book of the Year. **Frequency:** annual. **Type:** recognition. **Recipient:** to an author who has produced the finest work in the previous year, which addresses paper money ● **Frequency:** annual. **Type:** recognition. **Recipient:** for research in the bank note field. **Committees:** Note Identification; Research. **Publications:** *International Bank Note Society—Journal*, quarterly. Contains articles and pictorial essays on paper currencies; includes book reviews and classified ads. **Price:** included in membership dues. **Circulation:** 2,200. **Advertising:** accepted. Also Cited As: *IBNS Journal* ● Membership Directory, periodic. Lists members' collecting interests. ● Newsletter, quarterly. **Conventions/Meetings:** periodic meeting (exhibits) ● semi-annual meeting, includes auction during all major coin or paper money conventions and expositions.

22249 ■ John Reich Collectors Society (JRCS)

PO Box 135
Harrison, OH 45030-0135
E-mail: djdavis4@provide.net
URL: http://www.jrcs.org
Contact: David J. Davis, Pres.
Founded: 1984. **Members:** 450. **Membership Dues:** regular, $20 (annual) ● life, $500. **Description:** Individuals interested in early U.S. silver and gold coinage. Promotes the study of numismatics, focusing on U.S. silver and gold coins minted prior to 1838; acts as a source of information and education concerning those coins. **Committees:** Nominating. **Publications:** *Early United States Dimes 1796-1837*. Book ● *Federal Half Dimes 1792-1837*. Book ● *John Reich Journal*, 3/year. **Price:** included in membership dues. Alternate Formats: online ● Books. **Conventions/Meetings:** annual meeting, held in conjunction with American Numismatic Association.

22250 ■ Latin American Paper Money Society (LANSA)

3304 Milford Mill Rd.
Baltimore, MD 21244
Ph: (410)655-3109
E-mail: matzlansa@aol.com
Contact: Arthur C. Matz, Pres./Sec.-Treas./Ed.
Founded: 1973. **Members:** 450. **Membership Dues:** regular, $10 (annual). **Budget:** $2,500. **Languages:** English, Spanish. **Description:** Collectors, dealers, libraries, banks, and others interested in the study of paper money of Latin America and the Iberian Peninsula. **Libraries: Type:** reference. **Holdings:** 600. **Subjects:** numismatics, history, finance. **For-**

merly: Latin American Notaphilic Society. **Publications:** *LANSA Bulletin* (in English and Spanish), 3/year. Journal. Contains historical articles and information for collectors; includes book reviews, and membership directory update. **Price:** included in membership dues. ISSN: 0308-8677. **Circulation:** 450. **Advertising:** accepted ● Catalog ● Membership Directory, annual. Lists members' areas of interest. **Price:** included in membership dues. ISSN: 0308-8677. **Circulation:** 450. **Advertising:** accepted.

22251 ■ Liberty Seated Collectors Club (LSCC)

c/o Leonard Augsburger, Sec.-Treas.
PO Box 261
Wellington, OH 44090
E-mail: john.mccloskey@notes.udayton.edu
URL: http://www.numismalink.com/lscc.html
Contact: Leonard Augsburger, Sec.-Treas.
Founded: 1974. **Members:** 610. **Membership Dues:** individual, $15 (annual). **Staff:** 1. **Budget:** $12,000. **Description:** Collectors of 19th century U.S. silver coins. Promotes study of liberty seated 19th century U.S. silver coins. Determines the rarity and authenticity of these coins; provides identification and descriptions. Offers slide program. **Awards:** K.M. Ahwash Literary Award. **Frequency:** annual. **Type:** recognition. **Recipient:** for the best article published in the club journal. **Publications:** *Gobrecht Journal*, 3/year. Covers rarity, authentication, identification, and description of the coins. **Price:** $5.00/issue. **Circulation:** 700 ● *The Gobrecht Journals/Collective Volume Number I, Number II and Number III*. Books. **Conventions/Meetings:** annual conference - always August.

22252 ■ Lithuanian Numismatic Association (LNA)

PO Box 22696
Baltimore, MD 21203
Ph: (410)233-9279
E-mail: lithnumis@hotmail.com
Contact: Aleksandras Radzius, Dir.
Founded: 1978. **Members:** 130. **Membership Dues:** charter, $15 (annual). **Staff:** 2. **Budget:** $1,500. **Languages:** English, Lithuanian. **Description:** Collects and studies coins and paper money used in Lithuania throughout history. Conducts research; translates Lithuanian source materials into English. **Libraries: Type:** not open to the public. **Holdings:** 500; articles, books, periodicals. **Subjects:** Lithuanian numismatics and history. **Publications:** *The Knight*, bimonthly. Bulletin. Contains current and historical topics in Lithuanian numismatics. **Price:** $15.00/year. **Circulation:** 140. **Advertising:** accepted. **Conventions/Meetings:** annual meeting, in conjunction with numismatic conventions and meetings.

22253 ■ Love Token Society (LTS)

c/o Sidney Gale, Sec.-Treas.
PO Box 2351
Mandeville, LA 70470
Ph: (985)626-3867
E-mail: sidgale@charter.net
URL: http://www.geocities.com/lovetokensociety
Contact: Sidney Gale, Sec.-Treas.
Founded: 1971. **Members:** 275. **Membership Dues:** regular, $12 (annual). **Staff:** 1. **Description:** Represents individuals interested in the collecting and study of love tokens, a coin of the realm taken from circulation smoothed and hand-engraved on one side while retaining its original image on the other; the tokens, usually designed on dime-sized silver coins, became popular during the Civil War and were presented to sweethearts as tokens of love. Works to promote interest in numismatics, particularly in the area of engraved coins; to cultivate friendliness among collectors and dealers of such pieces; and to gather and disperse information on love tokens. Plans to construct a permanent collection for exhibition and to assemble colored slides of rare or multiple pieces. Compiles statistics. **Awards:** Silver Certificate for Local Exhibits. **Type:** recognition. **Recipient:** for love token exhibit at any coin show or event. **Publications:** *Love Letter*, bimonthly. Newsletter. **Price:** included in membership dues. **Circulation:** 350 ●

Love Tokens as Engraved Coins. Book ● Makes available slide programs. **Conventions/Meetings:** annual competition, held in conjunction with ANA (exhibits) - August ● annual conference, held in conjunction with the American Numismatic Association (exhibits) ● annual Fun Show - always January, in Orlando, FL.

22254 ■ Medal Collectors of America (MCA)

c/o John W. Adams, Pres.
99 High St., 11th Fl.
Boston, MA 02110
E-mail: jadams@ahh.com
URL: http://www.medalcollectors.org
Contact: John W. Adams, Pres.
Founded: 1998. **Membership Dues:** general, $20 (annual). **Description:** Promotes the collection of valuable medals. Brings together those interested in collecting, research and publication of research concerning art and historical medals. **Telecommunication Services:** electronic mail, btayman@comcast.net ● electronic mail, medalcollector@nc.rr.com.

22255 ■ North American Collectors (NAC)

16000 Ventura Blvd., Ste.1000
Encino, CA 91436
Ph: (818)370-4020
Free: (800)370-4720
Fax: (818)377-3901
E-mail: davidsimon@northamericancollectors.com
URL: http://collectionagencydirect.com
Contact: David Simon, Pres.
Founded: 1970. **Members:** 1,800. **Membership Dues:** organization/regular, $15 (annual). **Description:** Collectors of proof and other specialty coins such as patterns, pieforts, and low mintage pieces. Seeks to better inform and educate members on the availability of coins, mintage, material, and the future prospects of coins. **Affiliated With:** World Proof Numismatic Association. **Publications:** *How To Order Foreign Coins* ● *Master Pricelist* ● *Proof Collectors Corner*, periodic ● *World Coinage*, periodic.

22256 ■ Numismatic Bibliomania Society (NBS)

c/o David M. Sundman, Sec.-Treas.
PO Box 82
Littleton, NH 03561
E-mail: dsundman@littletoncoin.com
URL: http://www.coinbooks.org
Contact: David M. Sundman, Sec.-Treas.
Founded: 1980. **Members:** 300. **Membership Dues:** regular, in U.S., $15 (annual) ● regular, outside U.S., $20 (annual) ● life, in U.S., $300 ● life, outside U.S., $400. **Description:** Represents numismatic book and catalog collectors. Provides forum for exchange of new information and research on numismatic literature. Conducts seminars. **Publications:** *The Asylum*, quarterly. Journal. **Price:** included in membership dues. **Advertising:** accepted. **Conventions/Meetings:** annual meeting, held in conjunction with American Numismatic Association.

22257 ■ Numismatic Literary Guild (NLG)

c/o Ed Reiter, Exec. Dir.
12 Abbington Terr.
Glen Rock, NJ 07452
E-mail: orchmail@aol.com
URL: http://www.numismaticliteraryguild.org
Contact: Ed Reiter, Exec. Dir.
Founded: 1968. **Members:** 360. **Membership Dues:** regular, $15 (annual). **Description:** Represents editors, publishers, numismatic curators, catalogers, professionals who write numismatic articles and books and amateurs with prominent bylines. Seeks to encourage information exchange and good fellowship among numismatic writers. **Awards:** Best Book Award. **Frequency:** annual. **Type:** recognition ● Best Writer Award. **Frequency:** annual. **Type:** recognition ● Clement F. Bailey Memorial Award. **Frequency:** annual. **Type:** recognition ● Clemy and Maurice Gould Memorial Award. **Frequency:** annual. **Type:** recognition ● **Frequency:** annual. **Type:** recognition. **Recipient:** for audio-visuals. **Committees:** Convention and Entertainment; Judging of Writings. **Publica-**

tions: *A 25-Year History 1968-1993*. Booklet. Covers the NLG's first quarter-century. **Price:** $5.00 ● *Numismatic Literary Guild Newsletter*, quarterly. Includes new member and writer information and book reviews. **Price:** included in membership dues. **Circulation:** 400. **Advertising:** accepted. **Conventions/Meetings:** annual symposium, held in conjunction with American Numismatic Association - always late July or August.

22258 ■ Numismatics International (NI)
PO Box 570842
Dallas, TX 75357-0842
Ph: (940)440-2213
Fax: (940)365-2072
E-mail: rossschraeder@texoma.net
URL: http://www.numis.org
Contact: Charles R. Schraeder, Sec.
Founded: 1964. **Members:** 500. **Membership Dues:** regular, $20 (annual) ● senior (above age 70)/junior (below 18), $15 (annual). **Multinational. Description:** Numismatists, coin dealers, students, and numismatic authors in 35 countries. Works to: encourage and promote the science of numismatics; cultivate fraternal relations among collectors and numismatic students; encourage new collectors and foster the interest of youth in numismatics; stimulate and advance affiliations among collectors and kindred organizations; acquire, share, and disseminate numismatic knowledge including cultural and historical information on coins. Sponsors periodic lectures. Maintains coin collection. **Convention/Meeting:** none. **Libraries: Type:** reference; not open to the public. **Holdings:** 2,400; books, periodicals. **Publications:** *NI Bulletin*, periodic. Contains numismatics-related articles. **Price:** included in membership dues; $2.00/copy for nonmembers. ISSN: 0197-3088 ● Bibliographies ● Booklets ● Reprints.

22259 ■ One Cent International
334 W Magnolia St.
Durant, MS 39063
Ph: (662)653-3262
E-mail: davidalancox@netzero.com
Contact: David A. Cox, Dir.
Founded: 1997. **Membership Dues:** individual, $3 (annual). **Staff:** 1. **Multinational. Description:** Donates numismatic materials and publications that promote economic development and world peace to schools and public libraries worldwide. **Funds:** De Novo Numismatics.

22260 ■ Philippine Collectors Society (PCS)
Address Unknown since 2006
Founded: 1982. **Members:** 200. **Staff:** 3. **Description:** Collectors and organizations interested in Philippine coins, tokens, medals, currency and adult age pen-pals. Provides for the exchange of information on Philippine numismatics. Informs members of news items. Conducts mail auctions. Presently inactive; although sources for data and materials provided. **Publications:** *Philippine Collectors Society—Membership Index*, quarterly. Membership Directory. Lists collectors of Philippine coins, medals, currency, tokens, and marriage eligible pen-pals. **Price:** included in membership dues. **Circulation:** 125. **Advertising:** accepted ● *Philippine Collectors Society—Newsletter*, quarterly. **Price:** included in membership dues. **Circulation:** 200. **Advertising:** accepted. **Conventions/Meetings:** annual conference, held in conjunction with American Numismatic Association.

22261 ■ Professional Currency Dealers Association (PCDA)
c/o Mr. James A. Simek, Sec.
PO Box 7157
Westchester, IL 60154
Ph: (630)889-8207
E-mail: nge3@comcast.net
URL: http://www.pcdaonline.com
Contact: Mr. James A. Simek, Sec.
Founded: 1985. **Members:** 75. **Staff:** 1. **Description:** Dealers of rare paper money and other printed media of exchange including stocks, bonds, fiscal documents, and related ephemera. Promotes the study of and interest in collectible paper media of

exchange; maintains standards in commercial aspects of syngraphics. Sponsors research project to identify U.S. national banks whose large size note issues are undiscovered. **Telecommunication Services:** electronic mail, kfoley2@wi.rr.com. **Publications:** Membership Directory, annual ● Pamphlets. **Conventions/Meetings:** annual meeting, held in conjunction with the Society of Paper Money Collectors and the International Bank Note Society (exhibits) - always in St. Louis, MO.

22262 ■ Professional Numismatists Guild (PNG)
c/o Robert Brueggeman, Exec. Dir.
3950 Concordia Ln.
Fallbrook, CA 92028
Ph: (760)728-1300
Fax: (760)728-8507
E-mail: info@pngdealers.com
URL: http://www.pngdealers.com
Contact: Robert Brueggeman, Exec. Dir.
Founded: 1954. **Members:** 250. **Membership Dues:** full, $400 (annual) ● associate, $200 (annual) ● affiliate, $100 (annual). **Staff:** 2. **Description:** Represents coin dealers who have been involved full-time in the profession for at least five years. Establishes, promotes, and defends ethics in the hobby of numismatics. **Awards:** Abe Kosoff Founders Award. **Frequency:** annual. **Type:** recognition. **Recipient:** to a member who has made a significant contribution to numismatics ● Friedberg Award. **Frequency:** annual. **Type:** recognition. **Recipient:** for best writing on numismatic literature ● Lifetime Achievement Award. **Frequency:** annual. **Type:** recognition. **Recipient:** to a numismatist for his/her devotion to the hobby ● Sol Kaplan Award. **Frequency:** annual. **Type:** recognition. **Recipient:** to an individual aiding law enforcement in solving numismatic crimes. **Computer Services:** Information services, dealers' directory. **Affiliated With:** American Numismatic Association; American Numismatic Society. **Formerly:** (1969) Professional Numismatic Guild. **Publications:** *The Pleasure of Coin Collecting*. Booklet ● *Professional Numismatist Guild Membership Directory*, annual ● *What You Should Know Before You Invest in Coins*. Brochure. **Conventions/Meetings:** periodic convention, coin show (exhibits).

22263 ■ Russian Numismatic Society (RNS)
PO Box 3684
Santa Rosa, CA 95402-3684
Ph: (707)527-1007
Fax: (707)527-1204
E-mail: smoulding@earthlink.net
URL: http://www.russiannumismaticsociety.org
Contact: Alex Basok, Contact
Founded: 1978. **Members:** 350. **Membership Dues:** individual, $20 (annual). **Description:** Collectors and students interested in numismatic and related studies of the past millennium of Russian history. Establishes. Aims to help students and collectors over as wide a range of interests as possible and to exchange knowledge and experience. Shares research drawn from international sources. **Publications:** *Journal of the Russian Numismatic Society*, quarterly. **Price:** $4.00 ● *Membership List*, annual. Membership Directory ● Books ● Reprints. **Conventions/Meetings:** annual meeting - always December, in New York City.

22264 ■ Society of Lincoln Cent Collectors (SLCC)
c/o Dr. Sol Taylor, Pres.
13515 Magnolia Blvd.
Sherman Oaks, CA 91423-1417
Ph: (818)789-7805
E-mail: soltaylor2@aol.com
Contact: Dr. Sol Taylor, Pres.
Founded: 1982. **Members:** 300. **Membership Dues:** regular, $15 (annual). **Description:** Collectors, dealers, and investors interested in Lincoln cents. Promotes and participates in the collecting of Lincoln cents, the longest lasting and most widely collected coinage series in the U.S. Seeks to inform and educate the public regarding the Lincoln cent. Represents members' interests in matters affecting coinage legislation. Sponsors mail bid sales. **Publica-**

tions: *Lincoln Cent Quarterly*. Journal ● *Standard Guide to the Lincoln Cent*. **Conventions/Meetings:** meeting (exhibits) - always first Saturday of February, June, and October; Long Beach, CA.

22265 ■ Society of Paper Money Collectors (SPMC)
c/o Frank Clark, Membership Dir.
PO Box 117060
Carrollton, TX 75011
E-mail: frank_clark@spmc.org
URL: http://www.spmc.org
Contact: Frank Clark, Membership Dir.
Founded: 1961. **Members:** 2,000. **Membership Dues:** junior and regular, in U.S., $30 (annual) ● junior and regular, in Canada and Mexico, $35 (annual) ● regular, outside North America, $40 (annual) ● life, in U.S., $600 ● life, in Canada and Mexico, $700 ● life, outside North America, $800. **Staff:** 20. **Regional Groups:** 10. **Multinational. Description:** Represents collectors of paper money including U.S. currency of various types, foreign currency, obsolete paper money, military currency, checks, stocks, bonds, scrip, and fractional currency. Encourages research about paper money; furnishes information to collectors (information requests must be accompanied by SASE). **Libraries: Type:** reference. **Holdings:** 1,000; archival material, books, monographs, periodicals. **Subjects:** currency, financial documents, banking/finance. **Awards:** D.C. Wismer Award. **Frequency:** annual. **Type:** recognition. **Recipient:** for best paper money book ● Dr. Glenn Jackson Memorial Award. **Frequency:** annual. **Type:** recognition. **Recipient:** for an outstanding article about bank note essays, proofs and specimen ● Founders Award. **Frequency:** annual. **Type:** recognition. **Recipient:** for outstanding achievement during the preceding year ● George W. Wait Memorial Prize. **Frequency:** annual. **Type:** monetary. **Recipient:** for paper money research ● Literary Award. **Frequency:** annual. **Type:** recognition. **Recipient:** for best articles appearing in *Paper Money* ● Nathan Gold Memorial Lifetime Achievement Award. **Frequency:** annual. **Type:** recognition. **Recipient:** to a person who has contributed to the advancement of paper money collecting. **Publications:** *Paper Money*, bimonthly. Magazine. Includes articles about paper money, banking and financial history. **Price:** included in membership dues. ISSN: 0031-1162. **Circulation:** 2,000. **Advertising:** accepted. Alternate Formats: diskette. **Conventions/Meetings:** annual convention and meeting, with speaker and awards (exhibits) - held in June ● annual regional meeting - held in fall.

22266 ■ Society of Private and Pioneer Numismatists (SPPN)
98 Main St., Ste.201
Tiburon, CA 94920
Ph: (415)435-2601
Fax: (415)435-1627
E-mail: info@kagins.com
URL: http://www.kagins.com
Contact: Donald Kagin PhD, Ed.
Founded: 1988. **Members:** 150. **Membership Dues:** regular, $30 (annual) ● initiation, $5. **Description:** Represents coin collectors and historians interested in the private and pioneer gold coinage of the western and southeastern United States, small denomination "fractional" gold coinage of California, gold souvenir tokens, and western mining or banking scrip. Sponsors research and educational programs. **Publications:** *Brasher Bulletin*, quarterly. Newsletter. Contains research reports, news of society activities and major coin auctions, and membership surveys. **Price:** $30.00/year. **Circulation:** 200. **Advertising:** accepted. **Conventions/Meetings:** annual convention (exhibits).

22267 ■ Society of Ration Token Collectors (SRTC)
c/o Samuel M. Hevener, Dir.
3583 Everett Rd.
Richfield, OH 44286-9723

E-mail: samhevener@yahoo.com
Contact: Samuel M. Hevener, Dir.
Founded: 1966. **Members:** 200. **Membership Dues:** individual, $8 (annual). **Description:** Collects information regarding items related to rationing, including both paper and tokens. Researches possible sources in an attempt to locate new information and to verify existing information. Serves as a central station for the collection and dissemination of information, and for communication among members; to promote exchange of ideas and information. Establishes and maintains rationing tokens and currency as a facet of numismatics. Conducts research. Auctions ration material from members' collections to members only. Maintains hall of fame, memorial fund, speakers' bureau, and placement service of ration tokens to new members. Compiles statistics. **Libraries: Type:** reference. **Holdings:** 300; archival material. **Subjects:** WWI - WWII Consumer rationing. **Awards:** President's Certificate of Appreciation. **Type:** recognition. **Recipient:** for public displays/public talks. **Committees:** Canada; England; Germany; Holland; New Zealand; United States. **Also Known As:** Ration Stamp and Book Collecting. **Publications:** *The Ration Board: World War II U.S. and Foreign Homefront Ration Information*, quarterly. Newsletter. Contains information related to the wartime rationing of consumer goods during World War I and World War II. Includes statistics. **Price:** included in membership dues. **Circulation:** 200. **Advertising:** accepted ● *U.S. Ration Currency and Tokens 1942-1945*. Catalog. Lists all U.S. WW II paper and token consumer ration items. **Conventions/Meetings:** competition ● annual conference, held in conjunction with American Numismatic Association - always July or August.

22268 ■ Society for U.S. Commemorative Coins
PO Box 2335
Huntington Beach, CA 92647
Ph: (714)963-6138
E-mail: beedon@earthlink.net
URL: http://www.suscconline.org
Contact: Gary Beedon, Sec.
Founded: 1983. **Members:** 300. **Membership Dues:** adult, $20 (annual) ● junior, $10 (annual). **Staff:** 5. **Description:** Promotes interest in and knowledge of U.S. commemorative coins and related materials. Conducts educational programs. **Libraries: Type:** lending; not open to the public. **Holdings:** audiovisuals, books, clippings, periodicals. **Subjects:** U.S. commemorative coins and related materials. **Publications:** *The Commemorative Trail*, 3-4/year. Journal. **Price:** included in membership dues. **Conventions/Meetings:** periodic Numismatic and Philatelic Exposition - specialty show - January, February, March, April, June, August, September and October.

22269 ■ Solano Silver Round Club (SSRC)
c/o Jan D. Henke
PO Box 3518
Fairfield, CA 94533-0518
Ph: (707)427-0482
Contact: Robert Tadder, Sec.
Founded: 1983. **Members:** 35. **Membership Dues:** junior, $5 (annual) ● regular, $10 (annual). **Description:** Individuals with an interest in silver rounds. Promotes the collection and design of silver rounds and related numismatic materials. Facilitates communication and cooperation among members; serves as a clearinghouse on silver rounds and their collection. **Libraries: Type:** not open to the public. **Holdings:** archival material, artwork. **Subjects:** silver rounds. **Publications:** *Silver Notes*, monthly. Newsletter. **Conventions/Meetings:** monthly meeting.

22270 ■ Token and Medal Society (TAMS)
5225 W SR 36, No. 408
Sanford, FL 32771-9230
E-mail: mlighter@bellsouth.net
URL: http://www.tokenandmedal.org
Contact: Mark Lighterman, Treas.
Founded: 1960. **Members:** 1,400. **Membership Dues:** regular, in U.S. and Canada, $25 (annual) ● regular, outside U.S. and Canada, $30 (annual). **Staff:** 2. **Description:** Represents collectors of

tokens and medals. Promotes study and research on rarity and valuation of tokens and medals. **Libraries: Type:** reference. **Holdings:** 200; audiovisuals, books, periodicals. **Subjects:** American and foreign medals, store cards, many kinds of tokens including telephone, parking, patriotic, Civil War tokens. **Awards:** Catalog Award. **Frequency:** annual. **Type:** medal. **Recipient:** for book cataloging tokens or medals ● Literary Award. **Frequency:** annual. **Type:** recognition. **Recipient:** for best article published in journal ● Medal of Merit. **Frequency:** annual. **Type:** medal. **Recipient:** for service to the organization. **Formerly:** (1961) Society of Token, Medal and Obsolete Paper Money Collectors. **Publications:** *TAMS Journal*, bimonthly. Lists tokens and medals. **Price:** included in membership dues. **Circulation:** 1,700. **Advertising:** accepted ● Membership Directory, periodic ● Reprints. Old numismatic literature. ● Survey. **Conventions/Meetings:** annual convention, held in conjunction with American Numismatic Association (exhibits) - usually August.

22271 ■ Women in Numismatics (WIN)
5175 Gloria St.
Wayne, MI 48184
Ph: (734)721-4991 (734)877-0123
Fax: (407)321-5138
E-mail: cgrellman@aol.com
Contact: Rita Jene Sledz, Sec.
Members: 100. **Membership Dues:** regular, $35 (annual) ● junior, $20 (annual) ● associate, $15 (annual). **Description:** Promotes coin collecting. **Publications:** *Winning Ways*, 3/year. Journal. **Price:** included in membership dues. **Advertising:** accepted. **Conventions/Meetings:** meeting - 3/year, January, April, August.

22272 ■ World Internet Numismatic Society (WINS)
PO Box 220904
St. Louis, MO 63122
E-mail: winspresident@winsociety.org
URL: http://www.winsociety.org
Contact: Ralph J. Huntzinger, Pres.
Multinational. Description: Promotes the study and collection of coins, tokens, medals and currency. Provides education, guidance and assistance to online club members. Encourages information exchange and fellowship among members. **Libraries: Type:** reference. **Holdings:** articles. **Subjects:** numismatics. **Publications:** *The Tarnished Truth*. Newsletter. Contains the latest updates of the organization's activities and interesting articles relating to numismatics. Alternate Formats: online.

22273 ■ World Proof Numismatic Association (WPNA)
PO Box 4094
Pittsburgh, PA 15201-0094
Ph: (412)782-4477
Fax: (412)782-0227
E-mail: worldproofna@aol.com
Contact: Edward J. Moschetti, Pres.
Founded: 1964. **Members:** 2,500. **Membership Dues:** regular or organization, $15 (annual) ● junior, $10 (annual). **Multinational. Description:** Individuals dedicated to the study and collection of proof coins and BU coinage in all metals. Informs and educates members about coinage issues; provides informational background on all types of coinage. Attempts to have mints include "fineness" of gold coin on coin itself, rather than issue a separate "fineness" certificate. **Libraries: Type:** not open to the public. **Holdings:** 200; books. **Subjects:** numismatics. **Awards: Frequency:** annual. **Type:** medal. **Recipient:** for contributions toward the peace and welfare of humanity. **Publications:** *How to Order Foreign Coins*. Book ● *Master Pricelist*, annual. Lists 1,000 coins from all over the world, numismatic books and medals. **Price:** included in membership dues ● *Proof Collectors Corner*, bimonthly. **Price:** included in membership dues.

Origami

22274 ■ Origami USA
15 W 77th St.
New York, NY 10024-5192

Ph: (212)769-5635
Fax: (212)769-5668
E-mail: admin@origami-usa.org
URL: http://www.origami-usa.org
Contact: Tony Cheng, Pres.
Founded: 1980. **Members:** 2,000. **Membership Dues:** junior, $20 (annual) ● family, $50 (annual) ● individual outside North America, $45 (annual) ● contributing, $100 (annual) ● sponsor, $125 (annual) ● patron, $250 (annual) ● benefactor, $500 (annual) ● guardian, $1,000 (annual) ● individual in Canada and Mexico, $40 (annual) ● individual in U.S., $30 (annual). **Staff:** 2. **Budget:** $200,000. **Regional Groups:** 60. **Multinational. Description:** Individuals interested in promoting origami. (Origami is an art of paperfolding that originated in ancient China and was introduced and popularized in the U.S. by Lillian Oppenheimer, author of several children's books.) Sponsors workshops, special sessions, and volunteer training programs. Provides origami services to the American Museum of Natural History. Sponsors exhibitions of origami designed by children for schools, libraries, and cultural institutions. Maintains museum, biographical archive, 2000-volume library of origami instruction books in eight languages, and a study collection of 20000 origami models. **Libraries: Type:** lending; reference; not open to the public. **Holdings:** 2,000. **Subjects:** origami. **Computer Services:** database, origami models and books. **Telecommunication Services:** electronic mail, origami-info@origami-usa.org. **Publications:** *The Paper*, quarterly. Magazine. Includes instructional diagrams, information regarding activities of regional groups and members, and technical information about origami. **Price:** included in membership dues. **Circulation:** 3,000 ● Membership Directory, periodic. **Conventions/Meetings:** annual conference (exhibits) - every June in New York, NY.

Ornithology

22275 ■ Hartz Club of America (HCA)
c/o Robert Wild, Treas.
305 Grosvenor Ct.
Bolingbrook, IL 60440
E-mail: r.wild@comcast.net
URL: http://www2.upatsix.com/hartz
Contact: Ella Galik, Pres.
Membership Dues: regular, in U.S., $15 (annual) ● regular, in Canada, $17 (annual). **Description:** Provides a forum for people interested in breeding Hartz canaries. Provides a medium for the exchange of ideas, methods and other information beneficial to members. Promotes bird shows. **Computer Services:** database, list of breeders ● database, show winners ● information services, Hartz Canary Standard ● information services, show classifications ● information services, Topknot breeding chart. **Telecommunication Services:** electronic mail, ellambg@aol.com. **Publications:** Newsletter, quarterly.

Outdoor Recreation

22276 ■ North American Squirrel Association (NASA)
c/o Tony Christnovich, Founder
PO Box 186
Holmen, WI 54636
Ph: (608)781-3100 (608)781-3636
E-mail: nasasquirrel@yahoo.com
URL: http://www.nasasquirrel.org
Contact: Tony Christnovich, Founder
Founded: 2003. **Description:** Assists the physically challenged and elderly to enjoy hunting and fishing opportunities and recreational activities. Supports individuals and other organizations with similar goals and objectives. Contributes to the education of young people interested in the pursuit of outdoor activities related to hunting, fishing, and conservation.

22277 ■ Wilderness Volunteers (WV)
PO Box 22292
Flagstaff, AZ 86002-2292
Ph: (928)556-0038 (503)525-5870

Fax: (928)222-1912
E-mail: info@wildernessvolunteers.org
URL: http://www.wildernessvolunteers.org
Contact: John Sherman, Pres.
Founded: 1997. **Nonmembership. Description:** Organizes and promotes volunteer service to America's wild lands. Works with public land agencies that supply them with tools and supervision for their projects. Offers a selection of trips with a variety of service projects. Teaches and follows Leave No Trace (LNT) outdoor living skills and ethics. **Telecommunication Services:** electronic mail, john@wildernessvolunteers.org. **Publications:** *Wilderness Volunteers Newsletter*, biennial. Alternate Formats: online.

Pacific

22278 ■ Polynesian Voyaging Society (PVS)
Pier 7, 191 Ala Moana Blvd.
Honolulu, HI 96813
Ph: (808)536-8405
Fax: (808)536-1519
E-mail: pvshawaii@hawaiiantel.net
URL: http://pvs.kcc.hawaii.edu
Contact: Patrick Duarte, Exec. Dir.
Founded: 1973. **Membership Dues:** sailor, $50 (annual) ● steerperson, $100 (annual) ● canoe maker, $250 (annual) ● navigator, $500 (annual) ● astronomer, $1,000 (annual) ● voyaging chief, $2,500 (annual). **Staff:** 5. **Description:** Promotes research on how Polynesian seafarers discovered and settled inhabitable islands in the Pacific Ocean before European explorers arrived in the 16th century; has built and launched two replicas of ancient canoes, Hokule'a and Hawai'iloa. **Publications:** Newsletter, quarterly. Features current and past events, voyages, educational programs, and the people who support the mission and vision of PVS.

Paperweights

22279 ■ International Paperweight Society (IPS)
c/o The Glass Gallery
123 Locust St.
Santa Cruz, CA 95060-3907
Ph: (831)427-1177
Free: (800)538-0766
E-mail: lselman@got.net
URL: http://www.paperweight.com
Contact: Wibarine Favre, Pres.
Founded: 1993. **Members:** 1,000. **Membership Dues:** family, $50 (annual). **Description:** Promotes paperweight collecting. Conducts educational programs. Runs a speakers' bureau. **Conventions/Meetings:** annual meeting and festival, weekend event with artists and collectors.

Pets

22280 ■ RagaMuffin Cat Lovers Society (RCLS)
PO Box 1774
Orange Park, FL 32067-1774
E-mail: ragamuffin@ragamuffincatlovers.com
URL: http://www.ragamuffincatlovers.com
Founded: 2003. **Membership Dues:** associate (owner or fancier), $25 (annual) ● breeder, $40 (annual) ● founder, $100 (annual). **Multinational. Description:** Represents owners, breeders and individuals who love the RagaMuffin breed of cats. Organizes cat shows. **Computer Services:** database, breeder list ● information services, pedigrees ● information services, Ragamuffin resources. **Publications:** Newsletter, quarterly.

22281 ■ Rat Assistance and Teaching Society (RATS)
857 Lindo Ln.
Chico, CA 95973
Ph: (530)899-0605

E-mail: rats@petrats.org
URL: http://www.petrats.org
Contact: Debbie Ducommun, Pres.
Founded: 2002. **Description:** Seeks to educate pet care professionals about pet rats.

Philatelic

22282 ■ Alaska Collectors' Club (ACC)
c/o Jim Zuelow, Pres.
5300 N Paseo del Arenal
Tucson, AZ 85750
E-mail: jimzuelow@aol.com
URL: http://www.alaskacollectorsclub.nl
Contact: Jim Zuelow, Pres.
Founded: 1958. **Members:** 150. **Membership Dues:** $15 (annual). **Description:** Philatelists interested in the postal history of Alaska. Conducts mail auction of philatelic items. Sponsors research on Alaskan postal history. **Libraries: Type:** reference. **Holdings:** 100. **Subjects:** Alaskan history. **Publications:** *Alaskan Collectors Club—Membership Roster*, annual. Membership Directory. **Price:** included in membership dues. **Circulation:** 200. **Advertising:** accepted ● *Alaskan Philatelist*, quarterly. **Price:** included in membership dues. **Circulation:** 200. **Advertising:** accepted.

22283 ■ American Air Mail Society (AAMS)
c/o Stephen Reinhard, Treas.
PO Box 110
Mineola, NY 11501
E-mail: treasurer@americanairmailsociety.org
URL: http://www.americanairmailsociety.org
Contact: Stephen Reinhard, Treas.
Founded: 1923. **Members:** 1,600. **Membership Dues:** individual in U.S., $23 (annual) ● individual outside U.S., $28 (annual) ● life, in U.S., $460 ● life, outside U.S., $560. **Regional Groups:** 20. **Description:** Philatelists collecting air mail stamps and covers. Conducts educational and research programs; maintains hall of fame. **Awards:** George W. Angers Award. **Frequency:** semiannual. **Type:** recognition ● Walter J. Conrath Award. **Frequency:** semiannual. **Type:** recognition. **Computer Services:** Information services, message board. **Absorbed:** Aero Philatelists; Aerophilatelic Federation of the Americas; First Day Cover Collectors Club; Concorde Collectors Club. **Formerly:** Aero Philatelic Society of America. **Publications:** *Aerial Mail Service*. Monograph. **Price:** $15.00 ● *The Air Mails of Canada and Newfoundland*. **Price:** $28.00 for members; $35.00 for nonmembers ● *Airpost Journal*, monthly. **Price:** $23.00/year in U.S.; $28.00/year outside U.S.; $3.00/copy (back issues). ISSN: 0739-0939. **Circulation:** 1,600. **Advertising:** accepted ● *American Air Mail Catalogue*. **Price:** $25.00 for members; $35.00 for nonmembers ● *Ellington-Zwisler Rocket Mail Catalog* ● *Glider Mail*. Handbook. **Price:** $20.00 hardbound; $16.00/copy for members ● *The Pioneer Airplane Mails of the United States*. Book. **Price:** $25.00 hardbound; $20.00/copy for members. **Conventions/Meetings:** semiannual competition and meeting (exhibits) ● annual convention ● semiannual meeting (exhibits) ● annual meeting (exhibits) - always fall.

22284 ■ American First Day Cover Society (AFDCS)
PO Box 16277
Tucson, AZ 85732-6277
Ph: (520)321-0880
Fax: (520)321-0879
E-mail: afdcs@aol.com
URL: http://www.afdcs.org
Contact: Douglas Kelsey, Exec. Dir.
Founded: 1955. **Members:** 4,000. **Membership Dues:** regular, in U.S., $25 (annual) ● regular, outside U.S., $31 (annual). **Local Groups:** 50. **For-Profit. Description:** Philatelists who specialize in the study and collection of U.S. and foreign first day covers (envelopes with postage stamps affixed that have been canceled on the first day they were placed on sale). Conducts research and holds cover clinics. Provides expertise service, lecture and color slide

programs. **Libraries: Type:** reference. **Holdings:** archival material. **Awards:** AFDCS Best FDC Exhibit Award. **Frequency:** annual. **Type:** recognition. **Recipient:** for exhibitors. **Departments:** Sales; Translation. **Affiliated With:** American Philatelic Society. **Publications:** *First Days*, 8/year. Journal. Contains feature and research articles, profiles of cachet makers, society and new member information, book reviews, and catalog listings. **Price:** included in membership dues; $25.00 /year for nonmembers. ISSN: 0428-4836. **Circulation:** 5,000. **Advertising:** accepted ● Handbook, periodic. **Conventions/Meetings:** annual Americover - convention (exhibits).

22285 ■ American Helvetia Philatelic Society (AHPS)
c/o Richard Hall, Sec.
PO Box 15053
Asheville, NC 28813-0053
E-mail: secretary@swiss-stamps.org
URL: http://swiss-stamps.org
Contact: Richard Hall, Sec.
Founded: 1975. **Members:** 400. **Membership Dues:** regular in U.S., $24 (annual). **Multinational. Description:** Stamp collectors who specialize in the philately of Switzerland. Maintains extensive collection of Swiss philatelic literature and translation service. Conducts philatelic auctions. **Study Groups:** Literature; Postal History. **Affiliated With:** American Philatelic Society. **Formed by Merger of:** Helvetia Philatelic Society; Swiss American Stamp Society. **Publications:** *Tell*, bimonthly. Journal. Includes mail auction of postage stamps and related items. **Price:** included in membership dues. **Circulation:** 400. **Advertising:** accepted. **Conventions/Meetings:** periodic competition ● meeting - every 18 months.

22286 ■ American Philatelic Congress (APC)
c/o Mr. Ross A. Towle, Sec.-Treas.
400 Clayton St.
San Francisco, CA 94117-1912
E-mail: rosstowle@yahoo.com
URL: http://www.americanphilateliccongress.org/index.html
Contact: Mr. Ross A. Towle, Sec.-Treas.
Founded: 1935. **Members:** 700. **Membership Dues:** active in U.S., $40 (annual) ● active outside U.S., sustaining in U.S., $50 (annual) ● sustaining outside U.S., $60 (annual) ● patron in U.S., $55 (annual) ● patron outside U.S., $65 (annual). **Description:** Promotes philatelic writing and research. **Libraries: Type:** not open to the public. **Awards:** Barr Award. **Frequency:** annual. **Type:** recognition. **Recipient:** for philatelic writing and oratory ● Colby Award. **Frequency:** annual. **Type:** recognition. **Recipient:** for philatelic writing in periodicals ● Drossos Award. **Frequency:** annual. **Type:** recognition. **Recipient:** for philatelic writing ● Helen August Memorial Award. **Type:** recognition. **Recipient:** for the best article on U.S. postal history or best article on first day covers in 20th century ● Klein Award. **Frequency:** annual. **Type:** recognition. **Recipient:** for philatelic writing ● McCoy Award. **Frequency:** annual. **Type:** recognition. **Recipient:** for philatelic writing ● Meritorious Service Award. **Type:** recognition ● Wagner Award. **Frequency:** annual. **Type:** recognition. **Recipient:** for philatelic writing on 19th Century U.S. postal history. **Absorbed:** (1980) American Academy of Philately. **Publications:** *American Philatelic Congress Book*, annual. Contains original research in philately and postal history. **Price:** $43.00/copy. **Circulation:** 750. **Advertising:** accepted ● *Congress Comments*, 3/year. Newsletter. **Conventions/Meetings:** annual Stamp Show - convention.

22287 ■ American Philatelic Research Library (APRL)
100 Match Factory Pl.
Bellefonte, PA 16823
Ph: (814)933-3803
Fax: (814)933-6128
E-mail: gini@stamps.org
URL: http://www.stamps.org/TheLibrary/lib_AbouttheAPRL.htm
Contact: Virginia Horn, Librarian
Founded: 1942. **Members:** 2,500. **Membership Dues:** general, $18 (annual). **Staff:** 6. **Budget:**

$300,000. **Description:** Stamp collectors, students of postal history, advanced philatelists; authors, editors, and publishers of philatelic reference publications. Encourages greater use and study of philatelic literature; provides facilities for purchase, sale, and exchange of reference material; prepares bibliographies on various philatelic topics such as world postal history; conducts philatelic and postal history research; reviews philatelic books, catalogs, and periodicals. **Convention/Meeting:** none. **Libraries: Type:** open to the public. **Holdings:** 21,000. **Subjects:** stamp collecting, postal history. **Boards:** Trustees. **Affiliated With:** American Philatelic Society. **Formerly:** (1955) Philatelic Library Association; (1968) Philatelic Literature Association. **Publications:** Philatelic Literature Review, quarterly. Journal. Provides information on philatelic history and literature; includes book reviews, indexes, bibliographies, and histories of philatelic publications. **Price:** included in membership dues. **ISSN:** 0270-1707. **Circulation:** 2,500.

22288 ■ American Philatelic Society (APS)
c/o Janet Klug, Pres.
100 Match Factory Pl.
Bellefonte, PA 16823
Ph: (814)933-3803
Fax: (814)933-6128
E-mail: tongajan@aol.com
URL: http://www.stamps.org
Contact: Peter C. Mastrangelo, Exec. Dir.
Founded: 1886. **Members:** 48,000. **Membership Dues:** in U.S., $38 (annual) ● in Canada, $41 (annual) ● outside U.S., $48 (annual). **Staff:** 40. **Budget:** $3,500,000. **Local Groups:** 635. **National Groups:** 200. **Description:** Collectors of postage and revenue stamps, first day covers, postal history, and related philatelic items. Helps members buy and sell stamps; operates expertise service; offers stamp insurance program; circulates slide programs. Maintains hall of fame; offers correspondence courses; accredits judges for philatelic competitions. Conducts philatelic seminars. **Libraries: Type:** lending; reference; open to the public. **Holdings:** 60,000; archival material, artwork, audiovisuals, books, clippings, periodicals. **Subjects:** philately, postal history, geography, history. **Computer Services:** Online services, library. **Committees:** Ethics; Fakes and Forgeries; International Relations; Preservation; Stamp Theft; Translation; Youth Activities. **Affiliated With:** American Philatelic Research Library. **Publications:** The American Philatelist, monthly. Magazine. Includes annual index and index of advertisers, book reviews, new U.S. stamp listings, and calendar of events. **Price:** included in membership dues; $30.00 /year for nonmembers in U.S.; $33.00 /year for nonmembers in Canada and Mexico; $36.00 /year for nonmembers, all other countries. **ISSN:** 0003-0473. **Circulation:** 48,000. **Advertising:** accepted ● Handbooks ● Monographs ● Reports. **Conventions/Meetings:** annual Stampshow - convention (exhibits) - always August.

22289 ■ American Philatelic Society Writers Unit (APSWU)
c/o Mr. George B. Griffenhagen
2501 Drexel St.
Vienna, VA 22180-6906
URL: http://www.stamps.org/directories/affiliat.asp
Contact: Mr. George B. Griffenhagen, Contact
Founded: 1967. **Members:** 300. **Membership Dues:** regular in U.S., $15 (annual) ● regular in Canada and Mexico, $17 (annual) ● regular outside U.S., Canada, and Mexico, $20 (annual). **Staff:** 1. **Budget:** $4,000. **Multinational. Description:** Editors, writers, and columnists who specialize in philatelic subjects. Promotes philatelic writing, aids beginning writers, and helps members with research materials on stamps and related philatelic subjects. Maintains philatelic writers hall of fame. **Libraries: Type:** not open to the public. **Subjects:** back issues of the philatelic communicator only. **Awards:** Philatelic Writers Hall of Fame. **Frequency:** annual. **Type:** recognition. **Recipient:** for outstanding contributions to national or international philately. **Affiliated With:** American Philatelic Society. **Publications:** The

Philatelic Communicator, quarterly. Journal. **Price:** included in membership dues. **Circulation:** 300. **Conventions/Meetings:** semiannual meeting, meets twice a year at annual convention of the American Philatelic Society (exhibits) - always August and spring.

22290 ■ American Plate Number Single Society (APNSS)
c/o Rick Burdsall, Sec.
PO Box 1023
Palatine, IL 60078-1023
E-mail: secretary@apnss.org
URL: http://www.apnss.org
Contact: Rick Burdsall, Sec.
Founded: 1973. **Members:** 350. **Membership Dues:** regular in U.S. and Canada, $8 (annual) ● life, $125 (annual) ● other country, $10 (annual). **Staff:** 12. **Multinational. Description:** Represents collectors of stamp plate number singles and persons interested in plate numbers; a plate number is assigned to the printing plate used by the U.S. Bureau of Engraving and Printing or private security printer to produce sheets of postage stamps. Specializes in the collection and study of the single stamps adjoining the selvage of the sheet with the plate number or numbers. **Libraries: Type:** not open to the public. **Holdings:** 26. **Committees:** Research. **Affiliated With:** American Philatelic Society. **Formed by Merger of:** Herbert's Standard Plate Number Single Catalogue. **Publications:** Herbert's Standard Plate Number Single Catalogue, biennial. Contains check list for U.S. plate number singles. **Price:** $30.00 postpaid for nonmembers; $27.00 postpaid for members. Also Cited As: Herbert's ● Plate Numbers, bimonthly. Newsletter. Includes auction listing and information on new plate number activity. **Price:** included in membership dues. **Advertising:** accepted. **Conventions/Meetings:** annual conference (exhibits).

22291 ■ American Revenue Association (ARA)
c/o Eric Jackson, Pres.
PO Box 728
Leesport, PA 19533-0728
Ph: (610)926-6200
E-mail: eric@revenuer.com
URL: http://www.revenuer.org
Contact: Eric Jackson, Pres.
Founded: 1947. **Members:** 1,300. **Membership Dues:** regular, $21 (annual). **Multinational. Description:** Collectors and dealers of U.S. and foreign revenue and tax stamps and stamped paper and other nonpostal "Cinderella" philatelic material. Administers Vanderhoof Memorial Fund to underwrite publication of booklets pertaining to revenues and Cinderellas. **Libraries: Type:** reference; lending. **Holdings:** 150; books, periodicals. **Subjects:** revenue stamps of the world. **Awards:** Carolynn Cunliffe Memorial Award. **Frequency:** annual. **Type:** recognition. **Recipient:** for outstanding exhibits of fiscals and Cinderellas at local stamp shows. **Departments:** Sales. **Publications:** The American Revenuer, bimonthly. Journal. Features illustrated articles on every phase of fiscal and Cinderella philately. **Price:** included in membership dues. **Circulation:** 1,300. **Advertising:** accepted ● Membership Roster, biennial. Membership Directory ● Pamphlets. Covers fiscal and Cinderella philately. ● Books. **Conventions/Meetings:** annual convention (exhibits).

22292 ■ American Society of Polar Philatelists (ASPP)
c/o Alan Warren, Sec.
PO Box 39
Exton, PA 19341-0039
Ph: (610)321-0740
Fax: (610)321-0219
E-mail: alanwar@att.net
URL: http://www.polarphilatelists.org
Contact: Alan Warren, Sec.
Founded: 1956. **Members:** 400. **Membership Dues:** in U.S. and Canada, $22 (annual) ● outside U.S. and Canada, $30 (annual). **Multinational. Description:** Stamp collectors specializing in polar postal history.

Collections include philatelic items (stamps and covers with special cancellations and cachets) and sometimes related material such as autographs, books, photographs, and maps dealing with polar regions. **Awards:** Honorary Life Membership. **Type:** recognition. **Affiliated With:** American Philatelic Society. **Publications:** Ice Cap News, quarterly. Journal. Contains articles and columns about members and polar postal history. **Price:** $3.00 sample copy. **ISSN:** 0019-1051. **Circulation:** 400. **Advertising:** accepted ● Monographs. **Conventions/Meetings:** annual meeting (exhibits).

22293 ■ American Topical Association (ATA)
PO Box 57
Arlington, TX 76004-0057
Ph: (817)274-1181
Fax: (817)274-1184
E-mail: americantopical@msn.com
URL: http://www.americantopicalassn.org
Contact: Ray Cartier, Exec. Dir.
Founded: 1949. **Members:** 3,400. **Membership Dues:** in U.S., $20 (annual) ● outside U.S., $30 (annual) ● life, $1,000. **Staff:** 2. **Budget:** $120,000. **Local Groups:** 35. **National Groups:** 50. **Multinational. Description:** Persons specializing in the collection of stamps by subject matter (topics) rather than by country of issue; includes members in 90 countries. Maintains photographic slide and lecture service, translation service for 27 languages, and information service on 200 topics. Maintains 50 study units including: Bicycle, Europe, Golf, Lighthouse, Masonic, Mathematical, Medical Subjects, Archaeology (Old World), Napoleon, Religion, Ships, Railroads/Trains, and Windmills. **Awards:** ATA Awards 1st, 2nd, 3rd. **Frequency:** annual. **Type:** recognition. **Recipient:** for 100 best topical stamp exhibits at local, state, regional, national, and international stamp shows. **Committees:** Claims and Credit Screening; Distinguished Topical Philatelist; Heirs and Estates Assistance; Historian; Judges Accreditation; Junior Activities; Slide and Lecture. **Affiliated With:** American Philatelic Society; Professional Convention Management Association. **Publications:** Topical Stamp Collectors Handbooks, quarterly. Alternate Formats: CD-ROM ● Topical Time, bimonthly. Journal. Includes society news, feature articles, reviews, and questions/answers. **Price:** $6.00. **ISSN:** 0040-9332. **Circulation:** 5,000. **Advertising:** accepted ● Membership Directory, quadrennial. **Price:** $25.00. **Circulation:** 2,000. **Advertising:** accepted. **Conventions/Meetings:** annual convention (exhibits).

22294 ■ American Topical Association, Americana Unit (AU)
17 Peckham Rd.
Poughkeepsie, NY 12603
Ph: (845)452-2126
E-mail: info@americanaunit.org
URL: http://www.americanaunit.org
Contact: Dennis M. Dengel, Treas.
Founded: 1951. **Members:** 150. **Membership Dues:** individual in U.S., $6 (annual) ● individual in Canada, $10 (annual) ● individual outside U.S. and Canada, $12 (annual). **Staff:** 4. **Budget:** $2,000. **Description:** A study unit of the American Topical Association and the American Philatelic Society. Works to collect stamps commemorating or picturing Americans or Americana; to research and publish philatelic information concerning the Americana topic; to encourage and support topical stamp exhibitions pertaining to Americana; to share this knowledge and experience with fellow collectors. **Awards:** Merit Award. **Frequency:** annual. **Type:** recognition. **Recipient:** for the best Americana exhibit at the annual convention of the American Topical Association. **Affiliated With:** American Philatelic Society. **Publications:** Americana Philatelic News, quarterly. Newsletter. Lists new postage stamp issues, member news, Americana articles. **Price:** included in membership dues. **ISSN:** 1096-1119. **Circulation:** 200 ● Index to Americana Philatelic News, 1970-85. Article. **Conventions/Meetings:** annual National Topical Stamp Show - meeting, held in conjunction with ATA (exhibits).

22295 ■ American Topical Association, Biology Unit (BU)
c/o Christopher Dahle, Sec.
1401 Linmar Dr. NE
Cedar Rapids, IA 52402
Ph: (319)364-4999
E-mail: chris-dahle@uiowa.edu
URL: http://www.biophilately.org
Contact: Christopher Dahle, Sec.
Founded: 1951. **Members:** 210. **Membership Dues:** individual, $20 (annual) ● life, $300. **Description:** A study unit of the American Topical Association. Individuals in the zoological and botanical fields dedicated to the international cooperative study of biological postage stamps and related material. Conducts biological research. **Publications:** *Biophilately*, quarterly. Journal. Includes periodic membership list. **Conventions/Meetings:** annual meeting (exhibits) - usually June.

22296 ■ Armed Forces Stamp Exchange Club (AFSEC)
c/o Larry O. Sundholm, Exec. Sec.
PO Box 8473
Spokane, WA 99203-0473
Ph: (509)747-0662 (509)747-0654
Fax: (509)747-0662
E-mail: afsec2@juno.com
URL: http://webpages.charter.net/afsec9
Contact: Larry O. Sundholm, Exec. Sec.
Founded: 1954. **Members:** 300. **Membership Dues:** regular, $7 (annual). **Staff:** 1. **Local Groups:** 6. **Description:** Active or retired members of the Armed Forces and their families; veterans; widows and widowers of Armed Forces personnel; employees of the federal government. Works to perpetuate stamp collecting and provide an outlet for members to dispose of and acquire duplicates, accumulations, and other philatelic material. Coordinates sales and exchange circuits; sponsors auctions. **Convention/Meeting:** none. **Publications:** *AFSEC Bulletin*, quarterly. Newsletter. Covers membership activities. **Price:** included in membership dues. **Circulation:** 300. **Advertising:** accepted. Alternate Formats: online ● *Armed Forces Stamp Exchange Club—Membership Directory*. **Price:** included in membership dues.

22297 ■ Associated Collectors of El Salvador (ACES)
c/o Pierre Cahen
PO Box 02-5364
Miami, FL 33102
E-mail: sfes-aces@elsavadorphilately.org
URL: http://www.elsavadorphilately.org
Contact: Ramon de Clairmont, Pres.
Founded: 1975. **Members:** 60. **Membership Dues:** general, $36 (annual) ● collector abroad, $24 (annual). **Staff:** 4. **Languages:** English, Spanish. **Multinational. Description:** Stamp collectors interested in El Salvador. Offers translation and expertization services. Offers new issue service and mail bid sales. **Convention/Meeting:** none. **Libraries: Type:** reference. **Affiliated With:** American Philatelic Society. **Publications:** *El Faro*, quarterly. Journal. Lists new issues of Salvadoran stamps. **Price:** included in membership dues. **Circulation:** 100. **Advertising:** accepted.

22298 ■ Astronomy Study Unit (ASU)
c/o George G. Young
PO Box 632
Tewksbury, MA 01876
Ph: (978)851-8283
E-mail: george-young@msn.com
Contact: George G. Young, Sec.-Treas.
Founded: 1972. **Members:** 65. **Membership Dues:** in U.S. and Canada, $8 (annual) ● outside U.S. and Canada, $10 (annual). **Description:** A study unit of the American Topical Association. Stamp collectors interested in astronomy on stamps. Purpose is to collect and study philatelic material portraying the various aspects of astronomy, astrology, and related subjects and to communicate this knowledge to unit members and other interested persons. **Computer Services:** checklists ● member list. **Affiliated With:**

American Topical Association. **Publications:** *Astrofax*, quarterly. Newsletter.

22299 ■ Bicycle Stamps Club (BSC)
c/o Bill Eubanks, U.S. Treas.
21304 2nd Ave. SE
Bothell, WA 98021-7550
E-mail: tonimaur@bigpond.com
URL: http://members.tripod.com/~bicyclestamps
Contact: Bill Eubanks, U.S. Treas.
Founded: 1985. **Members:** 100. **Membership Dues:** individual, $19 (annual) ● individual, $53 (triennial). **Staff:** 7. **Description:** Philatelists interested in collecting stamps depicting bicycles and cycling themes. **Convention/Meeting:** none. **Affiliated With:** American Topical Association. **Publications:** *Bicycle Stamps*, quarterly. Magazine. Includes information regarding newly discovered bicycle-related stamps. ● Also publishes checklist of all known bicycle stamps worldwide.

22300 ■ Brazil Philatelic Association (BPA)
c/o Mr. Kurt Ottenheimer
462 W Walnut St.
Long Beach, NY 11561-3133
E-mail: oak462@optonline.net
URL: http://www.stamps.org/directories/affiliat.asp
Contact: Mr. Kurt Ottenheimer, Contact
Founded: 1968. **Members:** 200. **Membership Dues:** in U.S., $15 (annual) ● outside U.S., $20 (annual). **Multinational. Description:** Philatelists interested in Brazilian stamps and/or Brazilian postal history. Unites to develop and distribute information relating to philatelic topics of Brazil including stamps, postal stationery, essays and proofs, and postal history. **Libraries: Type:** reference. **Holdings:** 300. **Subjects:** Brazil philately. **Affiliated With:** American Philatelic Society. **Publications:** *Brazil Philatelic*. Bibliography ● *Bulls Eyes*, quarterly. Journal. Includes auction information. **Conventions/Meetings:** annual meeting.

22301 ■ Bullseye Cancel Collectors' Club (BCCC)
c/o Stan Vernon, Sec.-Treas.
2749 Pine Knoll Dr., No. 4
Walnut Creek, CA 94595-2044
E-mail: stanleyvernon@sbcglobal.net
URL: http://www.jeffhayward.com/bccc
Contact: Donald J. Landis, Pres.
Founded: 1999. **Membership Dues:** regular, in U.S., Canada, and Mexico, $15 (annual) ● overseas, $20 (annual). **Multinational. Description:** Represents people with an interest in centered cancels on postage stamps in any portion that the location and the date of the obliteration are readable. Provides a forum for people interested in postage stamps. **Publications:** Bulletin, quarterly, January, April, July and October.

22302 ■ CartoPhilatelic Society
c/o Mr. Alf Jordan, Sec.-Treas.
156 W Elm St.
Yarmouth, ME 04096
E-mail: ajordan@maine.rr.com
URL: http://www.mapsonstamps.com
Contact: Mr. Alf Jordan, Sec.-Treas.
Founded: 1955. **Members:** 128. **Membership Dues:** regular, in U.S., $18 (annual) ● regular, outside U.S., $20 (annual). **Description:** Serves as a study unit of the American Topical Association. Collectors of stamps depicting maps or map themes. Disseminates information on all aspects of map-related stamps; facilitates contact among collectors. **Projects:** CP Index; Maps on Stamps Checklist. **Affiliated With:** American Philatelic Society; American Topical Association. **Formerly:** (2005) Carto-Philatelists. **Publications:** *The New CartoPhilatelist*, quarterly. Journal. Includes book reviews and information about new issues of map stamps. **Price:** $15.00 /year for nonmembers in U.S.; free for members. ISSN: 0891-0758. **Circulation:** 140. **Advertising:** accepted.

22303 ■ Casey Jones Railroad Unit - ATA (CJRRU-ATA)
PO Box 18615
Rochester, NY 14618-8615
E-mail: launa@yosemite.net
URL: http://www.uqp.de/cjr
Contact: Launa J. Droescher, Sec.
Founded: 1950. **Members:** 220. **Membership Dues:** junior, in U.S., $3 (annual) ● individual, in U.S., $10 (annual) ● individual, in Canada and Mexico, $12 (annual) ● other foreign, $15 (annual). **Staff:** 1. **Description:** Collectors of railway stamps, cards, and covers united to promote the betterment of railway philately; other areas of interest include trains, locomotives, and other railroad equipment, and Railroad Post Office postmarks. Conducts research programs; compiles statistics. Makes available mailing list. **Libraries: Type:** reference; open to the public. **Holdings:** 268; books. **Subjects:** locomotives, trains, builders. **Awards:** Distinguished Topical Philatelist-ATA. **Frequency:** annual. **Type:** recognition. **Computer Services:** Mailing lists, of members. **Affiliated With:** American Topical Association. **Formerly:** (1950) Casey Jones Railroad Unit. **Publications:** *The Dispatcher*, bimonthly. Bulletin. Lists newly discovered postage stamps and new members; contains question and answer section. **Price:** included in membership dues. **Circulation:** 240. **Advertising:** accepted. Alternate Formats: online.

22304 ■ Cats on Stamps Study Unit (CSSU)
c/o Mary Ann Brown, Sec.-Treas.
3006 Wade Rd.
Durham, NC 27705
E-mail: mabrown@nc.rr.com
Contact: Mary Ann Brown, Sec.-Treas.
Founded: 1985. **Members:** 130. **Membership Dues:** regular in U.S., Canada and Mexico, $8 (annual) ● elsewhere, $10 (annual). **Description:** Study unit of the American Topical Association. Philatelists interested in the depiction of domestic and wild cats on postage stamps. **Convention/Meeting:** none. **Affiliated With:** American Philatelic Society; American Topical Association. **Publications:** *Cat Mews*, quarterly. Newsletter. **Price:** included in membership dues. ISSN: 0891-8635. **Circulation:** 130. **Advertising:** accepted.

22305 ■ Chemistry and Physics on Stamps Study Unit (CPOSSU)
c/o Prof. Foil A. Miller, Ed.-Emeritus
960 Lakemont Dr.
Pittsburgh, PA 15243
E-mail: michael@cpossu.org
URL: http://www.cpossu.org
Contact: Michael A. Morgan, Pres.
Founded: 1979. **Members:** 220. **Membership Dues:** regular, in U.S., $15 (annual) ● regular, outside U.S., $20 (annual) ● regular, in Canada, $17 (annual). **Description:** Serves as a study unit of the American Topical Association. Scientists and individuals interested in the collection of postage stamps pertaining to chemistry and physics. **Libraries: Type:** reference. **Holdings:** archival material, articles, books, periodicals. **Awards:** Outstanding Worldwide Postage Stamp on Chemistry or Physics. **Frequency:** annual. **Type:** recognition. **Recipient:** for stamp or postal stationary issued on a science or technology theme or honoring a chemist or physicist. **Affiliated With:** American Philatelic Society; American Topical Association. **Formerly:** (1985) Chemistry Study Unit; (1991) Chemistry and Physics Study Unit. **Publications:** *Philatelia Chimica et Physica*, quarterly. Journal. **Price:** included in membership dues. ISSN: 1041-2999. **Circulation:** 230 ● Also publishes lists of chemists on stamps; issues souvenir cards and envelopes for chemistry-related events.

22306 ■ China Stamp Society (CSS)
c/o Paul H. Gault, Sec.
PO Box 20711
Columbus, OH 43220
Ph: (614)451-8034

E-mail: pgault@columbus.rr.com
URL: http://www.chinastampsociety.org
Contact: Paul H. Gault, Sec.
Founded: 1936. **Members:** 750. **Membership Dues:** individual, $21 (annual). **Local Groups:** 6. **Description:** Individuals who collect stamps and study postal history of China and related areas such as Hong Kong, Shanghai and treaty ports, Tibet, Formosa, Taiwan, Korea, Mongolia, Macao, and Manchukuo. Creates a spirit of fraternity among members. Encourages research through mutual exchange of information and assistance. Promotes interest in this branch of philately. Conducts mail auctions, translation service. **Libraries: Type:** not open to the public. **Holdings:** 800; articles, books, periodicals. **Subjects:** China and related areas. **Awards:** China Stamp Society Award. **Frequency:** annual. **Type:** recognition. **Recipient:** for outstanding literary contributions and exhibits. **Publications:** *The China Clipper*, bimonthly. Journal. Includes research and study reports and annual index; aggregate index covering 1936-93 available separately. **Price:** included in membership dues. ISSN: 0885-9779. **Advertising:** accepted ● Also publishes specialized supplements to *The China Clipper*. **Conventions/Meetings:** annual meeting - usually October/November.

22307 ■ Christmas Philatelic Club (CPC)
312 Northwood Dr.
Lexington, KY 40505-2104
E-mail: stamplinda@aol.com
URL: http://www.hwcn.org/link/cpc
Contact: Linda L. Lawrence, Sec.-Treas.
Founded: 1969. **Members:** 225. **Membership Dues:** regular, in North America, $15 (annual) ● regular, outside North America, $22 (annual). **Description:** Individuals interested in collecting all types of philatelic material on the theme of Christmas from around the world. Promotes "the association of Christmas topicalists in an entourage of philatelic activities that are conducive to the members' common growth in knowledge and enjoyment of all aspects of Christmas philately". **Awards:** Ken Mackenzie Writer's Award. **Frequency:** annual. **Type:** recognition. **Recipient:** for best article in the journal, Yule Log. **Computer Services:** Mailing lists. **Telecommunication Services:** electronic mail, cpc@ hwcn.org. **Affiliated With:** American Philatelic Society; American Topical Association. **Publications:** *Yule Log*, bimonthly. Bulletin. **Price:** included in membership dues. ISSN: 0843-7394. **Advertising:** accepted. Alternate Formats: online.

22308 ■ Christopher Columbus Philatelic Society (CCPS)
c/o Leslie Seff
3750 Hudson Manor, Terr. E
Falls Church, VA 22042-3912
E-mail: otharris@midamerica.net
URL: http://ccps.maphist.nl
Contact: Overton T. Harris, Pres.
Founded: 1982. **Members:** 100. **Membership Dues:** regular, in U.S., $20 (annual) ● regular, outside U.S., $24 (annual). **Regional Groups:** 5. **Multinational. Description:** Persons interested in the life and voyages of Christopher Columbus and in the discovery of the New World as depicted in philatelic material. Conducts research and mail auctions. Sponsors international and regional groups. **Affiliated With:** American Philatelic Society; American Topical Association. **Publications:** *Checklist of Columbus Related Postage Stamps*, periodic. Catalogs. Includes articles related to Columbus philately; checklist of Columbian stamps. **Price:** $6.00 for nonmembers; $4.00 for members; free for new members ● *Discovery!*, quarterly. Journal. Includes society news, membership lists, and quarterly index. **Price:** included in membership dues; $5.00/copy for nonmembers. **Circulation:** 200. **Conventions/Meetings:** periodic International Seminar of Columbus Philately - international conference, visits to Columbus related sites.

22309 ■ Citizens' Stamp Advisory Committee (CSAC)
c/o United States Postal Service
1735 N Lynn St., Rm. 5013
Arlington, VA 22209-6432
URL: http://www.usps.com/communications/organization/csac.htm
Contact: Ronald A. Robinson, Chm.
Founded: 1957. **Members:** 15. **Description:** Advisory committee appointed by the Postmaster General to examine requests meeting the established criteria for commemorative stamps and select subjects of general interest with the most appropriate and appealing themes for recommendation to the U.S. Postal Service.

22310 ■ Civil Censorship Study Group (CCSG)
c/o Charles J. LaBlonde
15091 Ridgefield Ln.
Colorado Springs, CO 80921
E-mail: clablonde@aol.com
URL: http://www.postalcensorship.com/ccsg
Contact: Charles J. LaBlonde, Contact
Founded: 1972. **Members:** 200. **Membership Dues:** individual, $20 (annual). **Multinational. Description:** A study group affiliated with the American Philatelic Society. Hobbyists and other interested individuals who promote the study of censorship of civilian mails. **Libraries: Type:** reference. **Holdings:** 400; articles, books, periodicals. **Subjects:** censorship of the mails. **Awards:** Best CCSG Exhibit at a Convention. **Frequency:** periodic. **Type:** recognition. **Affiliated With:** American Philatelic Society. **Publications:** *Catalog of British Empire Civil Censorship Devices.* **Price:** $48.00 section 2, for members; $58.00 section 2, for nonmembers; $32.00 section 3, for members; $34.50 section 3, for nonmembers ● *Civil Censorship in the United States During World War II* ● *Free French Censorship in the Levant* ● Bulletin, quarterly. Covers censorship subjects from all time periods. **Price:** included in membership dues; $20.00 /year for nonmembers. **Advertising:** accepted. **Conventions/ Meetings:** biennial convention - 2008 May, Denver, CO - **Avg. Attendance:** 30; 2010 Nov., Chicago, IL - **Avg. Attendance:** 30.

22311 ■ Collectors Club (CC)
22 E 35th St.
New York, NY 10016-3806
Ph: (212)683-0559
Fax: (212)481-1269
E-mail: collectorsclub@nac.net
URL: http://www.collectorsclub.org
Contact: Wade E. Saadi, Pres.
Founded: 1896. **Members:** 1,000. **Membership Dues:** resident, $190 (annual) ● nonresident, $75 (annual) ● overseas, $95 (annual). **Staff:** 2. **Budget:** $585,000. **Local Groups:** 1. **Description:** Stamp collectors united to promote interest and knowledge of philately among members and the public. Encourages the exchange of information with other philatelic organizations and to enlarge and develop the cultural and historical aspects of philately. Sponsors philatelic research and lectures. Maintains library. Holds public and private exhibitions. **Libraries: Type:** reference. **Holdings:** 200,000; archival material, books. **Subjects:** philately, postal history. **Awards:** Alfred F. Lichtenstein Memorial Award. **Frequency:** annual. **Type:** recognition. **Recipient:** for outstanding service to philately. **Computer Services:** database, membership. **Committees:** Library; Study Group. **Publications:** *Collectors Club Philatelist*, bimonthly. Journal. Covers philately and postal history, both U.S. and foreign. Includes book reviews and library acquisitions list. **Price:** $42.00/year. ISSN: 0010-0838. **Circulation:** 1,300. **Advertising:** accepted. Alternate Formats: online ● Handbooks ● Membership Directory, periodic. **Conventions/Meetings:** annual competition, philatelic exhibits (exhibits) ● meeting - 20/ year on the first and third Wednesday of each month (excluding summer) ● seminar ● workshop.

22312 ■ Collectors of Religion on Stamps (COROS)
c/o Verna Shackleton, Sec.
425 N Linwood Ave., No. 110
Appleton, WI 54914-3476
Ph: (920)734-2417 (920)734-6711
E-mail: corosec@sbcglobal.net
URL: http://my.vbe.com/~cmfourl/coros1.htm
Contact: Verna Shackleton, Sec.
Founded: 1943. **Members:** 250. **Membership Dues:** regular, in U.S., $22 (annual) ● regular, outside U.S., $24 (annual). **Staff:** 10. **Description:** Persons interested in the collection and study of postage stamps whose designs have some religious significance. Maintains slide collections. **Awards:** Ribbons of Merit. **Type:** recognition. **Study Groups:** North American Sovereign Military Order of Malta Philatelic Study Circle. **Affiliated With:** American Philatelic Society; American Topical Association. **Publications:** *The COROS Chronicle*, quarterly. Journal. Includes articles on religious topics, listings of new stamp issues, new member information, and checklists. **Price:** included in membership dues. ISSN: 0746-2433. **Circulation:** 390. **Advertising:** accepted ● Directory, biennial ● Handbooks. **Conventions/Meetings:** competition.

22313 ■ Concorde Collectors Club
Address Unknown since 2007
Founded: 1980. **Membership Dues:** U.S., $20 ● foreign, $25. **Description:** Promotes the study of philatelic activities carried out on concorde jets. **Libraries: Type:** reference. **Holdings:** 1,000; audio recordings, books, clippings, monographs, periodicals, video recordings. **Subjects:** concorde flights carrying mail. **Affiliated With:** American Air Mail Society. **Publications:** *Jack Knight Air Log*, quarterly. Newsletter. **Price:** included in membership dues; $5.00 for nonmembers. **Advertising:** accepted. **Conventions/Meetings:** semiannual congress.

22314 ■ Confederate Stamp Alliance (CSA)
c/o Col. Richard Murphy, Sec.
501 Rosebud Ln.
Greer, SC 29650
E-mail: secretary@csalliance.org
URL: http://www.csalliance.org
Contact: Col. Richard Murphy, Sec.
Founded: 1935. **Members:** 630. **Membership Dues:** regular, in U.S., $24 (annual) ● international, $32 (annual) ● junior in U.S., $14 (annual). **Multinational. Description:** Represents the interests of professional and amateur philatelists and historians interested in the Confederate States of America, especially in its postal history and stamp issues. Promotes fraternity, research and education in Confederate philately. **Libraries: Type:** reference. **Holdings:** archival material. **Awards:** August Dietz Award. **Frequency:** annual. **Type:** recognition. **Recipient:** to the author of best book in Confederate philately ● Haydn Myer Award. **Frequency:** annual. **Type:** recognition. **Recipient:** for service to the Alliance. **Committees:** Authentication. **Affiliated With:** American Philatelic Society. **Publications:** *Confederate Philatelist*, quarterly. Articles. Includes articles on Confederate stamps and postal history, as well as general history and information on the American Civil War. **Price:** $1.75 for nonmembers; included in membership dues. **Advertising:** accepted ● *Muster Roll and Handbook*, biennial. Includes membership listings, constitution and by-laws. **Price:** $1.75 for members. **Circulation:** 650.

22315 ■ Cover Collectors Circuit Club (CCCC)
c/o Renate Thompson, Managing Dir.
241 Beachers Brook Ln.
Cary, NC 27511
E-mail: bandart@bellsouth.net
URL: http://www.geocities.com/coverccc
Contact: Renate Thompson, Managing Dir.
Founded: 1947. **Members:** 25,000. **Membership Dues:** life, $10. **Staff:** 1. **Multinational. Description:** Stamp and philatelic cover collectors. Facilitates exchange of information through correspondence and contact among collectors throughout the world. **Convention/Meeting:** none. **Affiliated With:** American Philatelic Society.

22316 ■ Croatian Philatelic Society (CPS)
PO Box 696
Fritch, TX 79036-0696
Ph: (806)857-0129
E-mail: spahich@hotmail.com
URL: http://www.croatianstamps.com
Contact: Eckrem Spahich, Exec. Sec./Founder
Founded: 1972. **Members:** 800. **Membership Dues:** hobby, $24 (annual). **Languages:** Croatian, English, Serbian, Slovene. **Multinational. Description:** Philat-

elists from more than 30 countries, most of whom are interested in stamps, coins, and the postal history of Central Europe and the Balkans, especially Croatia and Bosnia. Aims to promote interest in and knowledge of the postal history of Croatia, Bosnia, Slovenia, the Balkans, and related areas; to foster and encourage the collection, study, organization, display, and dissemination of such material and knowledge in stamp shows, exhibitions, and publications. Maintains 14 study groups; offers a translation service in 15 languages. Compiles statistics. **Libraries: Type:** reference. **Holdings:** archival material, books. **Committees:** Albania; Austria; Bosnia-Herzegovina; Bulgaria; Croatia; Fiume; Hungary; Macedonia; Montenegro; Romania; Serbia; Slovenia; Trieste; Yugoslavia. **Affiliated With:** American Philatelic Society. **Publications:** *Trumpeter* (in Croatian and English), quarterly. Newsletter. Includes book reviews, numismatic section, and study group directory. **Price:** included in membership dues. ISSN: 0148-673X. **Circulation:** 800. **Advertising:** accepted ● Membership Directory, quarterly. **Conventions/Meetings:** periodic competition ● annual meeting.

22317 ■ Disabled Collectors'
Correspondence Club (DCCC)
c/o Glen Chisholm, Sec.
16878 Laramie Ave.
Oak Forest, IL 60452-4428
URL: http://www.members.aol.com/disabledcc/index.
   html
Contact: Glen Chisholm, Sec.
Founded: 1991. **Members:** 90. **Membership Dues:** individual, $5 (annual). **Description:** Encourages fellowship, enjoyment, and exchanges among disabled stamp collectors. Affiliated with APS and ATA. **Also Known As:** DCCC. **Publications:** *Stampabilities,* quarterly. Newsletter. Includes personal profiles on members, articles, jokes, comments and suggestions, and listings of items for sale. **Advertising:** accepted.

22318 ■ Dogs on Stamps Study Unit
(DOSSU)
c/o Morris Raskin, Sec.
202A Newport Rd.
Monroe Township, NJ 08831-3920
Ph: (609)655-7411
E-mail: mraskin@verizon.net
Contact: Morris Raskin, Sec.
Founded: 1979. **Members:** 300. **Membership Dues:** in U.S., $5 (annual) ● outside U.S., $10 (annual). **Description:** A study unit of the American Topical Association. Individuals interested in the collection and study of stamps depicting dogs. Gathers and disseminates information to members. Sponsors National Dog Week. **Publications:** *DOSSU Journal,* quarterly. Includes new and supplemental listings of dogs on stamps. **Price:** included in membership dues. ISSN: 0882-0236. **Circulation:** 300.

22319 ■ Earth's Physical Features Study Unit
(EPFSU)
c/o Fred W. Klein, Sec.-Treas.
515 Magdalena Ave.
Los Altos, CA 94024
E-mail: epfsu@jeffhayward.com
URL: http://epfsu.jeffhayward.com
Contact: Jeffrey Hayward, Pres.
Founded: 1977. **Members:** 82. **Membership Dues:** regular, in U.S., $15 (annual) ● elsewhere, $25 (annual). **Description:** Serves as a study unit of the American Topical Association. Individuals interested in collecting philatelic material related to the physical features of the earth. Members exchange stamp checklists, information, and stamps. **Study Groups:** Caves; Mountains; Volcanoes; Waterfalls. **Affiliated With:** American Topical Association. **Publications:** *Geology Checklist.* **Price:** $16.00 in U.S.; $20.00 overseas ● *Hot Springs Checklist.* **Price:** $6.00 in U.S.; $10.00 overseas ● *Nature's Wonders,* quarterly. Journal. Includes articles by members and checklists. **Price:** available to members only ● *Volcanoes Checklist* ● *Waterfalls Handbook.* **Price:** $26.00 in U.S.; $35.00 overseas.

22320 ■ Eire Philatelic Association (EPA)
c/o David J. Brennan, Sec.
PO Box 704
Bernardsville, NJ 07924-0704
Ph: (908)766-2728
Fax: (908)766-7783
E-mail: brennan704@aol.com
URL: http://www.eirephilatelicassoc.org
Contact: William A. O'Connor, Pres.
Founded: 1950. **Members:** 550. **Membership Dues:** individual and family in U.S., $12 (annual) ● individual and family in Canada, $15 (annual) ● individual and family in other country, $20 (annual). **Regional Groups:** 10. **Description:** Adults interested in philatelic items from Ireland. Holds mail auctions of Irish stamps and other philatelic matter. Holds informal area meetings in conjunction with large stamp exhibits in major U.S. cities. **Libraries: Type:** reference. **Holdings:** 100; articles, books, periodicals. **Subjects:** Irish philately. **Awards:** Clark Award. **Frequency:** annual. **Type:** recognition. **Recipient:** for outstanding services toward Irish philately. **Committees:** Field; Forged and Bogus Material. **Affiliated With:** American Philatelic Society. **Publications:** *The Revealer,* quarterly. Journal. **Price:** included in membership dues. **Circulation:** 650. **Advertising:** accepted. **Conventions/Meetings:** annual meeting, meeting with philatelic educational program (exhibits).

22321 ■ Errors, Freaks and Oddities
Collector's Club (EFOCC)
7643 Sequoia Dr. N
Mobile, AL 36695-2809
Ph: (251)607-9253
Fax: (251)607-9253
Contact: Jim McDevitt, Pres.
Founded: 1978. **Members:** 175. **Membership Dues:** regular, in U.S., $16 (annual) ● regular, outside U.S., $30 (annual) ● life, $210. **Budget:** $2,000. **Description:** Philatelists interested in the production of postage stamps and the variations that occur as a result of mistakes in, or testing of, production equipment; those interested in errors in stamp designs and cancellations. Objectives are: to learn the causes of EFO (errors, freaks, and oddities) material and to disseminate that information; to be aware of current trends in philately and EFO value determination. Holds periodic auctions; encourages publishing of research efforts; works to assemble catalog of EFOs. **Awards:** Manning Award. **Frequency:** annual. **Type:** recognition. **Affiliated With:** American Philatelic Society. **Publications:** *EFO Collector,* quarterly. Journal. Includes articles relating to EFOs. **Price:** included in membership dues; $16.00 /year for nonmembers. ISSN: 1099-7377. **Circulation:** 225. **Advertising:** accepted. **Conventions/Meetings:** annual competition. ● annual convention, philatelic exhibits (exhibits).

22322 ■ Fine Arts Philatelists (FAP)
19 Ramsey Rd.
Great Neck, NY 11023
Ph: (516)466-6073
E-mail: ebs19@optonline.net
Founded: 1955. **Members:** 100. **Membership Dues:** in U.S., $22 (annual) ● outside U.S., $30 (annual). **Staff:** 10. **Budget:** $3,500. **Multinational. Description:** Represents libraries, museums, and individuals interested in an appreciation for and enjoyment of the fine arts through philately. Researches and assembles handbooks, bibliographies, and articles relating to fine and performing arts philatelic materials. Encourages use of the fine arts in postage stamp designs. **Formerly:** Fine Arts Unit of American Topical Association. **Publications:** *Journal of Fine and Performing Arts Philately,* quarterly. **Price:** $22.00/year in U.S.; $30.00/year outside U.S. **Circulation:** 250. **Advertising:** accepted ● *Paintings on Stamps.* Contains supplements I, II, and Addenda. ● Membership Directory, annual. **Conventions/Meetings:** periodic conference.

22323 ■ France and Colonies Philatelic
Society (FCPS)
c/o Edward Grabowski, Sec.
741 Marcellus Dr.
Westfield, NJ 07090-2012

Ph: (908)233-9318
E-mail: fcpsqs@drunkenboat.net
URL: http://www.drunkenboat.net/FrandCol
Contact: Edward Grabowski, Sec.
Founded: 1941. **Members:** 494. **Membership Dues:** in U.S., $20 (annual) ● outside U.S., $25 (annual). **Multinational. Description:** Collectors of the postage stamps of France, Monaco, and all the French colonies, past and present. **Libraries: Type:** not open to the public. **Awards:** Gerard Gilbert Memorial Award. **Frequency:** annual. **Type:** recognition. **Recipient:** for best English publication related to French philately. **Formerly:** France and Colonies Group. **Publications:** *A Key to the Ink-Color Numbers on French Proofs,* quarterly. Journal. **Price:** $5.00. ISSN: 0897-1293 ● *A Key to the Lozenge Obliterators of French Colonies 1860-1892.* **Price:** $5.00 ● *The Bordeaux Issue.* Book. **Price:** $10.00 plus postage for members; $20.00 for nonmembers ● *The Diverse World of Postal Markings of Bagon/Congo/A.E.F..* **Price:** $5.00 ● *The France and Colonies Philatelist,* quarterly. Journal. Contains news, features and announcements. ● *The French "Departements Conquis" 1791-1815, Their Chronology, Civil Post Offices Having Postmarks, and Typical Postmarks.* **Price:** $5.00 ● *The Postal History of the Commune Revolution, Paris 1871.* **Price:** $20.00 for members; $16.00 for nonmembers ● Also publishes indexes, keys, and lists of postmarks, post offices, and stamps.

22324 ■ Gems, Minerals and Jewelry Study
Unit (GMJSU)
c/o George G. Young, Sec.-Treas.
PO Box 632
Tewksbury, MA 01876
Ph: (978)851-8283
E-mail: george-young@msn.com
URL: http://www.geocities.com/gmjsu
Contact: Alan Dean, Pres.
Founded: 1976. **Members:** 120. **Membership Dues:** in U.S. and Canada, $10 (annual) ● outside U.S. and Canada, $15 (annual). **Description:** A study unit of the American Topical Association. Stamp collectors interested in philatelic materials related to gems, minerals, and jewelry. Exchanges information and materials and promotes philatelic correspondence. Conducts auctions and exhibits. **Affiliated With:** American Topical Association. **Publications:** *Philagems International,* quarterly. Newsletter. **Circulation:** 120. **Advertising:** accepted. **Conventions/Meetings:** periodic meeting.

22325 ■ German Colonies Collectors Group
(GCCG)
c/o J.D. Manville, Sec.-Treas.
PO Box 845
Stevens Point, WI 54481-0845
E-mail: jadeco@charter.net
URL: http://www.gps.nu/studygroup/colonies
Contact: J.D. Manville, Sec.-Treas.
Founded: 1968. **Members:** 250. **Membership Dues:** regular, in U.S., Canada, Mexico, $16 (annual) ● regular, outside U.S. and Canada, $29 (annual). **Staff:** 3. **Multinational. Description:** Study unit of the Germany Philatelic Society. Stamp collectors who specialize in the German colonies and post offices abroad. Exchanges ideas, observations, and information on stamps, cancels, and postal history of the colonies and related seapost and World War I occupations. **Awards:** Col. Davis Award. **Frequency:** annual. **Type:** recognition. **Computer Services:** database ● mailing lists. **Affiliated With:** Germany Philatelic Society. **Publications:** *Vorlaufer,* quarterly. Journal. Contains combined original research, expository and feature articles, and selected translations from less accessible journals. **Price:** $3.00 each. **Conventions/Meetings:** annual meeting.

22326 ■ Germany Philatelic Society (GPS)
PO Box 6547
Chesterfield, MO 63006-6547
E-mail: jason@gps.nu
URL: http://www.gps.nu
Contact: Dr. Jason Manchester, Pres.
Founded: 1949. **Members:** 1,450. **Membership Dues:** in U.S., $30 (annual) ● in Canada and Mexico,

$45 (annual) ● international, $65 (annual). **Staff:** 2. **Local Groups:** 30. **Multinational. Description:** Philatelists interested in collecting and studying postal issues and postal history of the old German states, Germany, its former colonies, offices abroad, plebiscites, and occupied and kindred areas. Presents medals at stamp exhibitions. **Libraries: Type:** reference. **Holdings:** 650; articles, audiovisuals, books, clippings, periodicals. **Subjects:** postal history of Germany from medieval times to the present. **Awards:** Herman L. Halle Research Award. **Frequency:** annual. **Type:** trophy. **Recipient:** for best research exhibit ● President's Award. **Frequency:** annual. **Type:** trophy. **Recipient:** for best German-area exhibit. **Study Groups:** Bavaria; Bohemia and Moravia, General Government; Buildings; Colonies; Danzig; Early Empire; Hand-Overprints; Inflation; Notopfer; Plebiscites; Stadtpost; Third Reich. **Publications:** *German-English Philatelic Dictionary.* Handbook. **Price:** $25.00 for nonmembers; $20.00 for members ● *German Postal Specialist,* monthly. Journal. **Price:** included in membership dues. ISSN: 0016-8823. **Advertising:** accepted ● Also publishes maps of Germany since 1849. **Conventions/Meetings:** annual convention (exhibits) - 2008 Feb. 29-Mar. 2, St. Louis, MO.

22327 ■ Graphics Philatelic Association (GPA)
c/o Bruce L. Johnson, Sec.
115 Raintree Dr.
Zionsville, IN 46077-2012
Ph: (317)733-9737
E-mail: indybruce1@yahoo.com
URL: http://www.graphics-stamps.org
Contact: Mark H. Winnegrad, Pres.
Founded: 1975. **Members:** 160. **Membership Dues:** individual, in North America, $13 (annual) ● individual, outside North America, $23 (annual). **Description:** Study unit of the American Topical Association. Represents people who collect stamps depicting facets of the printing industry including printing equipment and plants, famous printers, papermaking machinery and processes, and printers' marks. **Libraries: Type:** reference. **Holdings:** articles. **Affiliated With:** American Philatelic Society. **Publications:** *Philateli-Graphics,* quarterly. Newsletter. Includes articles, new member information, news of stamp issues, and annual membership list. **Price:** included in membership dues; $2.00 each, for back issues. ISSN: 0739-6198 ● *Printing on Stamps.* Paper ● Monographs. **Conventions/Meetings:** annual meeting.

22328 ■ Haiti Philatelic Society (HPS)
c/o Mr. Ubaldo Deltoro, Sec.-Treas.
5709 Marble Archway
Alexandria, VA 22315-4013
Ph: (703)922-9531
E-mail: u007ubi@aol.com
URL: http://www.haitiphilately.org
Contact: Mr. Ubaldo Deltoro, Sec.-Treas.
Founded: 1975. **Members:** 120. **Membership Dues:** individual, $15 (annual). **Languages:** English, French. **Description:** Individuals interested in the philately of Haiti. Sponsors exhibits and auctions; participates in joint research projects. **Convention/Meeting:** none. **Affiliated With:** American Philatelic Society. **Publications:** *Haiti Philately,* quarterly. Journal. For collectors of Haitian stamps. **Price:** included in membership dues. **Advertising:** accepted.

22329 ■ Hellenic Philatelic Society of America (HPSA)
541 Cedar Hill Ave.
Wyckoff, NJ 07481
Ph: (201)447-6262
Fax: (201)612-9228
Contact: Dr. Nicholas Asimakopulos MD, Sec.
Founded: 1942. **Members:** 200. **Membership Dues:** $20 (annual). **Description:** Collectors interested in philatelic knowledge of classic Hermes heads, modern Greek stamps, covers, postal history of Greece, and material of related countries. Acts as a clearinghouse on Hellenic philately. Participates in

stamp exhibitions. **Committees:** Expertization Committee for Stamps and Covers. **Publications:** *HPSA News Bulletin,* quarterly. **Price:** $20.00/year; $20.00/year outside U.S.; $25.00/year airmail outside U.S. **Circulation:** 250. **Advertising:** accepted ● *Membership List,* periodic. **Conventions/Meetings:** annual convention.

22330 ■ Humor Stamp Club (HSC)
Address Unknown since 2007
Founded: 1985. **Membership Dues:** $10 (annual). **For-Profit. Multinational. Description:** Individuals who collect stamps and have a particular interest in stamps that depict humorous themes, comedians, or famous people with wide grins. Disseminates information regarding humorous stamps issued worldwide; compiles statistics. **Publications:** *How to Recognize a Humor Stamp.* Book. **Price:** $8.50 ● Directory, annual. Lists humorous stamps worldwide. **Price:** included in membership dues. **Advertising:** not accepted. **Conventions/Meetings:** annual meeting - always New York City.

22331 ■ India Study Circle for Philately (ISCP)
PO Box 7326
Washington, DC 20044
Ph: (202)564-6876
Fax: (202)565-2441
E-mail: info@indiastudycircle.org
URL: http://www.indiastudycircle.org
Contact: Gerald Sattin, Pres.
Founded: 1950. **Members:** 750. **Membership Dues:** regular, $30 (annual). **Description:** Philatelists with an interest in the stamps and postal history of India. Facilitates communication and exchange of information among members internationally. Sponsors study groups; maintains collection of research articles on Indian philately. **Libraries: Type:** not open to the public. **Holdings:** 75; articles, books. **Subjects:** stamps and postal history of India and related areas. **Awards:** ISC Award. **Frequency:** periodic. **Type:** recognition ● Roake Trophy. **Frequency:** annual. **Type:** trophy. **Recipient:** for the best article. **Affiliated With:** American Philatelic Society. **Publications:** *Handbook of Indian Philately,* periodic. **Price:** $25.00/issue ● *India Post,* quarterly. Journal. Contains original articles submitted by members of the ISC. **Price:** included in membership dues. **Advertising:** accepted. Alternate Formats: online ● *India Post: Newsletter of the Americas,* annual. Contains items of interest to ISCP's North and South American members. **Price:** included in membership dues ● *India Study Circle for Philately—Member's Guide,* quinquennial. Membership Directory. **Price:** included in membership dues. **Conventions/Meetings:** periodic India Study Circle—North America - convention.

22332 ■ Inter-Governmental Philatelic Corporation (IGPC)
460 W 34th St., 10th Fl.
New York, NY 10001
Ph: (212)629-7979
Fax: (212)629-3350
E-mail: postmaster@igpc.net
URL: http://www.igpc.net
Contact: Samuel Malamud, Pres.
Founded: 1957. **Members:** 3. **Staff:** 30. **For-Profit. Description:** Philatelic agency. Distributes postage stamps, bank notes, and coins of 50 nations to stamp dealers throughout the world. Sponsors competitions. Holds commercial exhibitions. **Convention/Meeting:** none.

22333 ■ International Society for Japanese Philately (ISJP)
PO Box 1283
Haddonfield, NJ 08033
E-mail: isjp@comcast.net
URL: http://www.isjp.org
Contact: Dr. Kenneth Kamholz, Sec.
Founded: 1945. **Members:** 1,137. **Membership Dues:** individual, $12 (annual) ● sustaining, $24 (annual) ● contributing, $18 (annual). **Regional Groups:** 3. **Multinational. Description:** Individuals interested in Japanese philately. Promotes interest in the

Japanese philately and related areas and encourages friendly cooperation among philatelists worldwide. **Convention/Meeting:** none. **Libraries: Type:** lending. **Holdings:** 100. **Subjects:** Japanese philately. **Computer Services:** Information services, journal index ● mailing lists. **Committees:** Expertization; Grievance. **Affiliated With:** American Philatelic Society. **Formerly:** (1951) International Japanese Philatelic Specialists Study Club. **Publications:** *Forgeries.* Alternate Formats: CD-ROM ● *Japanese Philately,* bimonthly. Journal. Covers philately and postal history of Japan. Includes annual index and membership list, maps, news of stamp issues, and obituaries. **Price:** included in membership dues; $15.00 /year for nonmembers. ISSN: 0146-0994. **Circulation:** 1,400. **Advertising:** accepted ● Monograph ● Also publishes cumulative indices to *Japanese Philately,* 1945-92.

22334 ■ International Society of Worldwide Stamp Collectors (ISWSC)
9463 Benbrook Blvd., No. 14
Benbrook, TX 76126
E-mail: executivedirector@iswsc.org
URL: http://www.iswsc.org
Contact: Dr. Terry Myers, Exec. Dir.
Founded: 1984. **Members:** 1,000. **Membership Dues:** adult/dealer/stamp club, $15 (annual) ● youth (under age 18), $10 (annual) ● family, $19 (annual). **Regional Groups:** 4. **Description:** Stamp Collectors. Promotes and encourages stamp collecting for all ages and levels of expertise. Offers Sales Circuits, Swap Circuits, Omni Exchange Circuits, individual stamp trading with worldwide members, ISWSC Mail Sales, stamp identification, translation and other services. Makes stamps available to children and youth leaders at no charge. Maintains youth mentoring program. **Awards:** ISWSC Youth Merit Award. **Type:** recognition. **Recipient:** for outstanding youngsters. **Telecommunication Services:** electronic mail, jseidl@mindspring.com. **Affiliated With:** American Philatelic Society. **Absorbed:** (1986) Worldwide Collectors Club. **Publications:** *Beginners Booklets and Albums.* Includes stamp mini-albums for beginners and activity pages for youth stamp club leaders. ● *The Circuit,* bimonthly. Newsletter. Contains articles, features, advertising, worldwide reports on philatelic activities of organization, Kid's Page, and beginners' column. **Price:** included in membership dues. **Advertising:** accepted ● *ISWSC Roster,* annual. Membership Directory. Includes bimonthly updates. **Price:** available to members only. **Conventions/Meetings:** annual meeting, held in conjunction with stamp shows (exhibits).

22335 ■ International Stamp and Coin Collectors Society (ISCS)
c/o Israel I. Bick, Pres.
PO Box 854
Van Nuys, CA 91408
Ph: (818)997-6496
Free: (866)226-0507
Fax: (818)998-4337
E-mail: iibick@sbcglobal.net
URL: http://www.bick.net
Contact: Israel I. Bick, Pres.
Founded: 1970. **Members:** 1,427. **Staff:** 8. **Budget:** $50,000. **Description:** Stamp collectors. Promotes interest in philately and numismatics as a means to achieve mutual understanding of cultures worldwide. Creates limited edition commemorative and first day covers for sale to members and collectors. Conducts educational forums and displays and produces coin and stamp expositions. **Libraries: Type:** reference. **Holdings:** books, periodicals. **Publications:** *Interstamps,* periodic. Newspaper. **Price:** available to members only. **Advertising:** accepted ● *Stamp Collectors World,* quarterly. Newsletter. **Price:** available to members only. **Advertising:** accepted ● *Stamp Expo Collectors Program,* 10/year. Programs to philatelic shows sponsored by the society. **Price:** included in show registration fee. **Circulation:** 5,000. **Advertising:** accepted. **Conventions/Meetings:** Stamp Coin EXPO - meeting (exhibits) - 14/year.

22336 ■ Israel Plate Block Society (IPBS)
Address Unknown since 2007
Founded: 1978. **Members:** 100. **Description:** Promotes the collection of plate blocks of stamps pertaining to Israel. Encourages formation of study groups; compiles and assembles checklists and information concerning plate blocks. **Affiliated With:** Society of Israel Philatelists. **Publications:** *Israel Plate Block Journal*, quarterly. Includes information on Israeli postal history, new plate block issues, and auction lists. **Price:** available to members only. **Advertising:** accepted. **Conventions/Meetings:** annual meeting.

22337 ■ Jack Knight Air Mail Society (JKMS)
PO Box 1239
Elgin, IL 60121-1239
Fax: (847)948-9440
E-mail: sneulander@attbi.com
URL: http://www.americanairmailsociety.org/html/
   aams_chapters.html
Contact: Stephen Neulander, Pres.
Founded: 1943. **Members:** 350. **Membership Dues:** individual in U.S., $28 (annual) ● individual outside U.S., $33 (annual). **Description:** Collectors of airmail stamps, covers, and other aerophilatelic materials. Focuses on researching aviation pioneers and early airmail flights. Named for Jack Knight (1892-1971), an early airmail flyer who helped in the creation of the society. **Libraries: Type:** reference. **Holdings:** 1,000; archival material. **Subjects:** philatelic items, airline guides dating back to 1920. **Affiliated With:** American Air Mail Society. **Publications:** *Jack Knight Air Log*, quarterly. Journal. **Price:** included in membership dues; $5.00/issue for nonmembers. **Advertising:** accepted. **Conventions/Meetings:** annual conference and symposium, held in conjunction with American Air Mail Society (exhibits) - always May, Chicago, IL.

22338 ■ John F. Kennedy First Day Cover Study Unit (JFK FDC SU)
PO Box 535, Madison Sq. Sta.
New York, NY 10159
Ph: (212)799-8148
Contact: Henry B. Scheuer, Exec.Dir.
Founded: 1982. **Members:** 100. **Description:** Philatelists and postal historians. Purpose is to keep records of philatelic commemorations relating to John F. Kennedy (1917-63). Maintains speakers' bureau and hall of fame. **Convention/Meeting:** none. **Libraries: Type:** reference. **Holdings:** 150. **Subjects:** original research involving Kennedy. **Computer Services:** database ● mailing lists, listing of known covers cancelled on May 29, 1964, the first day of issue for the five-cent John F. Kennedy stamp. **Publications:** *JFK FDC Study Unit Newsletter*, quarterly.

22339 ■ John F. Kennedy Philatelic Society (JFKPS)
Address Unknown since 2006
Founded: 1960. **Description:** Collectors of philatelic material and other memorabilia concerning President John F. Kennedy (1917-1963). Maintains library of books on Kennedy's life. Issues a printed certificate to any collector who displays his collection.

22340 ■ Jugoslavia Study Group (JSG)
1514 N 3rd Ave.
Wausau, WI 54401-1903
Ph: (715)675-2833
E-mail: mjlenard@aol.com
Contact: Michael Lenard, Chm.
Founded: 1974. **Members:** 40. **Staff:** 3. **Description:** Individuals interested in Yugoslavian stamps and postal history; correspondents are asked to study stamps of Yugoslavia and to find varieties and give reasons for their creation. Preserves letters on file. Maintains contact with philatelic societies in Yugoslavia and Germany, Switzerland and England. **Libraries: Type:** open to the public. **Holdings:** 80; books, periodicals. **Subjects:** Yugoslavia philately. **Affiliated With:** Croatian Philatelic Society. **Publications:** *The Trumpeter* (in Croatian and English), quarterly. Magazine. Contains in-depth articles on Yugoslavian area philately. **Price:** $20.00. **Circulation:** 300. **Advertising:** accepted ● Makes available slide pro-

grams on Yugoslav philately. **Conventions/Meetings:** biennial conference.

22341 ■ Junior Philatelists of America (JPA)
PO Box 2625
Albany, OR 97321-0643
Ph: (541)967-7043
Fax: (541)967-9515
E-mail: exec.sec@jpastamps.org
Contact: Jennifer Arnold, Exec.Sec.
Founded: 1963. **Members:** 550. **Membership Dues:** junior, $9 (annual) ● family (add $5 for each additional family member), $9 (annual) ● adult, $15 (annual). **Staff:** 9. **Local Groups:** 10. **Description:** Members in 11 countries. Stamp collectors under age 18; adult and/or junior stamp clubs; adult supporting members. Encourages stamp collecting among youth. Offers stamp research and identification service; pen pal service; various contests throughout the year. **Libraries: Type:** not open to the public. **Awards:** JPA Exhibiting Award. **Frequency:** periodic. **Type:** recognition. **Recipient:** to outstanding junior exhibitors at stamp shows. **Committees:** Awards; Pen Pals; Stamp Clusters; Stamp Identification. **Affiliated With:** American Philatelic Society. **Absorbed:** (1976) Junior Writers Unit, American Philatelic Society. **Formerly:** (1976) Junior Philatelic Society of America. **Publications:** *Getting Started in Stamp Collecting*. Pamphlet ● *How to Avoid Common Mistakes As a Beginning Stamp Collector*. Pamphlet ● *The Philatelic Observer*, bimonthly. Newsletter. Contains articles and games for young stamp collectors; includes book reviews, new member information informative articles, new issue information. **Price:** included in membership dues. ISSN: 0273-5598. **Circulation:** 600. **Advertising:** accepted ● *Search 'n' Find Puzzles for Stamp Collectors*. Pamphlet ● Handbooks.

22342 ■ Korea Stamp Society (KSS)
c/o John E. Talmage, Jr., Sec.-Treas.
PO Box 6889
Oak Ridge, TN 37831
E-mail: jtalmage@usit.net
URL: http://www.pennfamily.org/KSS-USA
Contact: John E. Talmage Jr., Sec.-Treas.
Founded: 1951. **Members:** 150. **Membership Dues:** regular, $25 (annual) ● sustaining, $50 (annual) ● contributor, $85 (annual). **Languages:** English, Korean. **Multinational. Description:** Collectors of philatelic items of Korea, back to the early days of the Korean Kingdom, the occupation by the Japanese forces, the Republic of Korea after 1945, and the Democratic People's Republic of Korea since 1945. Conducts research into all aspects of philately related to postal issues of Korea. **Libraries: Type:** reference. **Holdings:** books, video recordings. **Publications:** *Korean Philately*, quarterly. Journal. Includes trading column for members. **Price:** included in membership dues. ISSN: 1087-5107. **Circulation:** 175. **Advertising:** accepted.

22343 ■ Machine Cancel Society (MCS)
c/o Gary M. Carlson, Sec.
3097 Frobisher Ave.
Dublin, OH 43017-1652
E-mail: gcarlson@columbus.rr.com
URL: http://www.machinecancel.org
Contact: Don Pearson, Pres.
Founded: 1961. **Members:** 500. **Membership Dues:** regular, in U.S., $15 (annual) ● regular, in Canada, $22 (annual) ● in Europe, $24 (annual) ● in Japan, $24 (annual). **Staff:** 4. **Regional Groups:** 1. **Description:** Philatelists interested in envelopes bearing machine cancellations, whether by hand driven or high speed electrically driven equipment. Sponsors quarterly mail auction. Conducts research programs; compiles statistics. **Awards: Type:** recognition. **Recipient:** to members who win for their exhibits of flag cancels at regional and national exhibitions. **Affiliated With:** American Philatelic Society. **Formerly:** (1987) Flag Cancel Society. **Publications:** *Machine Cancel Forum*, quarterly. Newsletter. Contains a variety of articles on all phases of machine cancel collecting. **Price:** included in membership dues; $10.00 /year for nonmembers. **Advertising:** accepted. Alternate Formats: online ● *Roster of Mem-

bers, biennial. Membership Directory ● Produces slide program. **Conventions/Meetings:** annual meeting (exhibits).

22344 ■ Mailer's Postmark Permit Club (MPPC)
c/o Charlie Myers
PO Box 3
Portland, TN 37148-0003
E-mail: cfmyers@mindspring.com
URL: http://www.mppclub.org
Contact: Kenneth M. Davis PhD, Pres.
Founded: 1979. **Members:** 275. **Membership Dues:** regular, in U.S., $7 (annual) ● regular, in Canada and Mexico, $9 (annual) ● life (depends on age), $55-$85. **Multinational. Description:** Promotes interest in mailer's postmark permits which allow individuals to postmark their own mail. Members must obtain applications at post offices where mailings will be made. Mail bearing precancelled postmarks must be presented to authorized postal employees for circulation. **Publications:** *Permit Patter*, bimonthly. Newsletter. **Price:** $6.00/year; $1.00/copy. ISSN: 0892-0311 ● Catalogs ● Membership Directory, annual ● Also publishes checklists of mailer's precancel postmarks.

22345 ■ Maritime Postmark Society (MPS)
c/o Tom Hirschinger, Pres.
PO Box 497
Wadsworth, OH 44282
Ph: (330)336-8227
E-mail: fmcgary@yahoo.com
URL: http://www.judnick.com/judnick/maritimepost-
   marksociety.htm
Contact: Tom Hirschinger, Pres.
Founded: 1939. **Members:** 150. **Membership Dues:** regular in U.S. and Canada, $10 (annual) ● outside U.S. and Canada, $15 (annual). **Multinational. Description:** Represents philatelists interested in the collection and publication of postal history relating to all sea post and maritime mails. Sponsors auctions and offers estate disposal service. **Convention/ Meeting:** none. **Absorbed:** (1939) Universal Ship Cancellation Society, Savannah Chapter. **Formerly:** (1945) International Seapost Cover Club. **Publications:** *Seaposter*, bimonthly. Journal. **Price:** $10.00 in U.S. and Canada; $15.00 outside U.S. and Canada. ISSN: 0048-9891.

22346 ■ Mathematical Study Unit (MSU)
c/o Monty J. Strauss, Pres.
Texas Tech Univ.
Dept. of Mathematics
Lubbock, TX 79409
Ph: (806)742-2580
Fax: (815)550-4139
E-mail: m.strauss@ttu.edu
Contact: Monty J. Strauss, Pres.
Founded: 1979. **Members:** 150. **Membership Dues:** regular, in North America, $12 (annual) ● regular, outside North America, $15 (annual). **Description:** Serves as a study unit of the American Topical Association and the American Philatelic Society (see separate entries). Represents persons interested in stamps dealing with mathematics and related subjects. Promotes education on all aspects of mathematical philately. **Convention/Meeting:** none. **Affiliated With:** American Philatelic Society; American Topical Association. **Publications:** *Philamath*, quarterly. Journal. Covers mathematical philately. **Price:** included in membership dues. **Circulation:** 160. **Advertising:** accepted ● Also publishes a checklist of mathematics on postage stamps.

22347 ■ Medical Subjects Unit (MSU)
c/o Frederick C. Skvara, MD
PO Box 6228
Bridgewater, NJ 08807
Ph: (908)725-0928
Fax: (908)725-0928
E-mail: fcskvara@bellatlantic.net
Contact: Frederick C. Skvara MD, Ed.
Founded: 1958. **Members:** 175. **Membership Dues:** in U.S., $15 (annual) ● outside U.S., $18 (annual). **Multinational. Description:** A study unit of the American Topical Association. Individuals interested

in medical philately. Purposes are: to further the study and collection of stamps and ancillary philatelic material which have a connection, either direct or indirect, with the arts and sciences of medicine and allied subjects; to foster interest in medical philately by compiling and disseminating information. Maintains speakers' bureau. **Awards:** Myrtle Watt Awards. **Frequency:** annual. **Type:** recognition. **Recipient:** for best article in scalpel and tongs and for promoting medical philately. **Telecommunication Services:** electronic mail, rchakrav@vt.edu. **Affiliated With:** American Topical Association. **Publications:** *Scalpel and Tongs*, quarterly. Journal. Illustrated articles and checklist on medically related subjects. **Price:** $15.00 in U.S.; $18.00 outside U.S. ISSN: 0048-9255. **Circulation:** 175. **Advertising:** accepted. Also Cited As: *American Journal of Medical Philately* ● *Scalpel & Tongs*. Articles. **Price:** included in membership dues. **Advertising:** accepted ● Journal, quarterly. **Advertising:** accepted. **Conventions/Meetings:** annual congress, held in conjunction with ATA (exhibits).

22348 ■ Meter Stamp Society (MSS)
c/o Douglas Kelsey, Sec.
PO Box 16178
Tucson, AZ 85732-6178
E-mail: douglask21@aol.com
URL: http://www.meterstampsociety.org
Contact: Douglas Kelsey, Sec.
Founded: 1948. **Members:** 250. **Description:** Individuals interested in the study and collection of U.S. and foreign postage meter stamps. Provides exchanges for topical slogans and meter types and continuous updating of U.S. and Canadian towns that use or have used meters. Provides access to specialists in all phases of meter stamp collecting. **Supersedes:** Meter-Slogan Associates. **Publications:** *Membership Roster*, annual. Membership Directory ● Bulletin, quarterly. **Conventions/Meetings:** periodic meeting.

22349 ■ Metropolitan Air Post Society (MAPS)
c/o Fred Dietz, Pres.
14834 Hadcock Dr.
Sterling, NY 13156-4196
E-mail: bugsmashers@frontiernet.net
URL: http://www.metroairpost.com
Contact: Fred Dietz, Pres.
Founded: 1941. **Members:** 100. **Membership Dues:** individual, $10 (annual). **Multinational. Description:** Represents persons interested in collecting airmail stamps and covers. Promotes the interest in air post history, and the development of aviation, airlines and air mail services. **Awards:** Gus Lancaster Trophy. **Frequency:** annual. **Type:** trophy. **Recipient:** for contribution to aerophilately. **Affiliated With:** American Air Mail Society. **Formerly:** (1970) Metropolitan Airmail Cover Club. **Publications:** *MAPS Bulletin*, quarterly. Contains general aerophilately subjects. **Price:** included in membership dues. **Circulation:** 100. **Conventions/Meetings:** quarterly meeting, held in conjunction with Collector's Club in February, picnic in summer, Philatelic Show in spring ● symposium, research.

22350 ■ Mexico Elmhurst Philatelic Society International (MEPSI)
c/o Geoffrey Goodridge, Circuit Book Mgr.
PO Box 1217
New York, NY 10113
E-mail: treasurer@mepsi.org
URL: http://www.mepsi.org
Contact: Geoffrey Goodridge, Circuit Book Mgr.
Founded: 1935. **Members:** 750. **Membership Dues:** regular, $20 (annual). **Regional Groups:** 9. **Languages:** English, Spanish. **Multinational. Description:** Philatelists interested in the stamps and postal history of Mexico and united for the promotion and dissemination of knowledge of this field. Supports individual and collective research. Maintains library and hall of fame; sponsors competitions; compiles statistics. Conducts auctions and circuit sales. **Libraries: Type:** not open to the public. **Subjects:** Mexico, Mexican philately. **Awards:** Irwin Heiman Memorial Award. **Frequency:** biennial. **Type:** recognition. **Re-**

cipient: for advancing in the field of Mexico philately ● MEPSI Hall of Fame. **Frequency:** periodic. **Type:** recognition. **Recipient:** for individuals who have advanced the field of Mexico philately. **Computer Services:** Mailing lists, of members. **Telecommunication Services:** electronic mail, geoffreygoodridge@mac.com ● electronic mail, circuit@mepsi.org. **Committees:** Catalogue; Expertization. **Departments:** Mexicana Advertising. **Divisions:** Auctions; Circuit Book Sales; Library; Publications. **Affiliated With:** American Philatelic Society. **Publications:** *Mexicana*, quarterly. Journal. **Price:** included in membership dues. **Circulation:** 750. **Advertising:** accepted ● Membership Directory, triennial. Lists officers, members, and services. **Advertising:** accepted ● Publishes many outstanding works on Mexican Philately. **Conventions/Meetings:** annual convention (exhibits).

22351 ■ Military Postal History Society (MPHS)
c/o Ed Dubin, Sec.
PO Box 586
Belleville, MI 48112
E-mail: dubine@comcast.net
URL: http://www.militaryphs.org
Contact: Alfred F. Kugel, Pres.
Founded: 1937. **Members:** 600. **Membership Dues:** in U.S., $21 (annual) ● in Canada and Mexico, $24 (annual) ● other, $26 (annual). **Description:** Represents persons interested in collecting and studying military postal history. Operates mail auction whereby members may buy material or dispose of duplicate items. **Awards:** Best Military Postal History Exhibit. **Frequency:** annual. **Type:** recognition. **Study Groups:** World War I; World War II. **Publications:** *Military Postal History Society Bulletin*, quarterly. **Price:** free for members. **Advertising:** accepted. **Conventions/Meetings:** annual meeting (exhibits).

22352 ■ Mobile Post Office Society (MPOS)
c/o Douglas N. Clark, Sec.
PO Box 427
Marstons Mills, MA 02648-0427
Ph: (508)428-9132
E-mail: dnc@math.uga.edu
URL: http://www.eskimo.com/~rkunz/mposhome.html
Contact: Douglas N. Clark, Sec.
Founded: 1950. **Members:** 480. **Membership Dues:** patron, $53 (annual) ● sustaining in U.S., $30 (annual) ● sustaining, outside North America, $45 (annual) ● regular in U.S., $20 (annual) ● regular, outside North America, $35 (annual) ● family, $5 (annual). **Budget:** $4,000. **Description:** Collectors and students of philately interested in covers, cachets, postmarks, history, and data of U.S. and foreign Highway Post Office, Traveling Post Office, and Railway Post Office routes. Conducts historical research; compiles data; sponsors competitions, cover sales, and auctions; presents awards. **Libraries: Type:** reference; not open to the public. **Holdings:** biographical archives, books, monographs, periodicals. **Subjects:** transportation of the mails. **Awards:** Charles L. Towle Award. **Frequency:** annual. **Type:** medal. **Recipient:** for the best exhibit at annual convention. **Affiliated With:** American Philatelic Society. **Formerly:** (1966) National Highway Post Office Society. **Publications:** *Transit Postmark Collector*, bimonthly. Journal. Includes research articles, society news and auction. ISSN: 0041-1175. **Circulation:** 510. **Advertising:** accepted. **Conventions/Meetings:** annual convention, with a national stamp show (exhibits).

22353 ■ Napoleonic Age Philatelists (NAP)
7513 Clayton Dr.
Oklahoma City, OK 73132-5636
Ph: (405)721-0044
E-mail: krb2@earthlink.net
URL: http://www.nap-stamps.org
Contact: Kenneth R. Berry, Sec.-Treas.
Founded: 1983. **Members:** 65. **Membership Dues:** individual, $12 (annual). **Description:** A study unit of the American Topical Association (see separate entry). Stamp collectors and other individuals inter-

ested in the study of events, places, and people associated with Napoleon Bonaparte (1769-1821), Emperor of the French, as portrayed on stamps. Promotes the study of Napoleon by revealing the stories behind the postage stamps issued to commemorate his life and times; members select stamps on such topical interests as: naval battles of the Napoleonic Wars; art and paintings of the era; cities Napoleon visited; the battles of Napoleon. Maintains biographical data on famous persons of the Napoleonic Age. Compiles statistics and checklists for stamps. **Convention/Meeting:** none. **Affiliated With:** American Topical Association. **Publications:** *Campaign*, quarterly. Newsletter ● *Napoleon Topical Checklist*.

22354 ■ National Duck Stamp Collectors Society (NDSCS)
PO Box 43
Harleysville, PA 19438-0043
E-mail: ndscs@hwcn.org
URL: http://www.hwcn.org/link/ndscs
Contact: Anthony J. Monico, Sec.
Founded: 1992. **Membership Dues:** patron life, $500 ● life, $250 ● junior, $10 (annual) ● associate, $30 (annual) ● regular, $20 (annual) ● regular, $35 (biennial). **Description:** Promotes and encourages the collection and study of migratory waterfowl hunting and conservation stamps. Aims to advance interest in duck stamp collecting and promote educational meetings, lectures and exhibits. Encourages research and articles pertaining to duck stamps. **Publications:** *Duck Tracks*, quarterly. Journal. **Price:** included in membership dues. **Advertising:** accepted. Alternate Formats: online.

22355 ■ Nepal and Tibet Philatelic Study Circle (NTPSC)
6 Rainbow Ct.
Warwick, RI 02889-1118
Ph: (401)738-0466
E-mail: editorofpostalhimal@cox.net
URL: http://fuchs-online.com/ntpsc
Contact: Mr. Colin Hepper, Sec.
Founded: 1970. **Members:** 200. **Membership Dues:** regular, $18 (annual) ● life, $375. **Description:** Philatelists and dealers worldwide with an interest in the stamps and postal history of Nepal and Tibet. Encourages members to participate in national and international exhibitions. Conducts mail auctions of Himalayan stamps and other postal memorabilia. Makes available educational slide shows. **Libraries: Type:** reference. **Awards:** Nepal and Tibet Philatelic Study Circle - Best of Show. **Type:** recognition. **Affiliated With:** American Philatelic Society. **Publications:** *Classic Stamps of Nepal*. Book ● *POSTAL HIMAL*, quarterly. Journal. Provides a forum for the development of new information and research projects. **Price:** included in membership dues. **Circulation:** 350. **Advertising:** accepted ● Membership Directory, biennial ● Articles. **Conventions/Meetings:** competition ● periodic meeting (exhibits).

22356 ■ Palestine Study Group (SG)
Address Unknown since 2007
Founded: 1978. **Members:** 25. **Description:** Currently Inactive. Philatelists interested in Palestine. Conducts research on stamps and postal history from Palestine. **Publications:** none. **Affiliated With:** Society of Israel Philatelists. **Conventions/Meetings:** monthly meeting - always North Brunswick, NJ.

22357 ■ Perfins Club
c/o Ken Rehfield, Sec.
PO Box 125
Greenacres, WA 99016-0125
Ph: (509)924-6375
E-mail: krehfield@peoplepc.com
URL: http://www.perfins.org
Contact: Ed Linn, Pres.
Founded: 1943. **Members:** 650. **Multinational. Description:** Philatelists who are interested in the special field of perforated initials and insignia. Objectives are: to study and disseminate information about all aspects of the use of perforated insignia and security endorsements as applied to postal paper; to

facilitate contact among collectors; to encourage and aid collectors in their efforts to study and form collections of these items. Services include: identification; exchange circuit; sales circuit; auctions; slide presentation; catalogs. **Libraries: Type:** reference. **Holdings:** 450; articles, books, clippings, periodicals. **Subjects:** perfins. **Awards:** Hallock Card Award. **Frequency:** annual. **Type:** recognition. **Recipient:** for outstanding contributions to the field. **Committees:** Foreign Catalog; U.S. Catalog. **Publications:** *The Perfins Bulletin*, 10/year. Includes club news, auction information, new member listings, research reports, survey of member collections, library listing, and roster. **Price:** included in membership dues. ISSN: 8750-1627. **Circulation:** 700. **Advertising:** accepted ● *United States Perfin Catalog*, periodic ● Directory, periodic. **Conventions/Meetings:** annual convention (exhibits).

22358 ■ Philatelic Foundation (PF)
70 W 40th St., 15th Fl.
New York, NY 10018
Ph: (212)221-6555
Fax: (212)221-6208
E-mail: philatelicfoundation@verizon.net
URL: http://www.philatelicfoundation.org
Contact: George J. Kramer, Chm.
Founded: 1945. **Members:** 1,200. **Staff:** 6. **Budget:** $500,000. **Description:** Educational institution chartered by New York State Department of Education for philatelic study and research. Offers philatelic slide programs as an educational aid for schools, organized youth groups, and stamp clubs. Renders opinions on stamps and other philatelic material. Prepares exhibitions for stamp shows. **Libraries: Type:** reference. **Holdings:** archival material, books, photographs. **Subjects:** stamps, postal history, documentary records. **Awards:** Neinken Medal. **Frequency:** annual. **Type:** medal. **Recipient:** for service to the philatelic community. **Committees:** Education; Expert. **Publications:** *Analysis and Counterfeit Leaflets*, periodic ● *Color in Philately*. Book ● *Directory of Audio/Visual Programs*, periodic ● *Foundations of Philately*. Book ● *Opinions*, periodic. Books. Includes case histories of stamps submitted for expertising. **Circulation:** 1,500 ● *Philatelic Focus*, annual. Newsletter. Includes information on expertizing stamps and covers, educational programs, publications, and membership news. ISSN: 0196-5034. **Circulation:** 1,500 ● *The Pony Express - A Postal History*. Book. **Price:** $45.00 additional $5 for shipping ● Booklets. Provides information on issues of the Confederate States of America. ● Also publishes seminar textbook series. **Conventions/Meetings:** seminar, on stamps and postal history.

22359 ■ Philatelic Friends Exchange Circuit (PFEC)
PO Box 93006
Austin, TX 78709-3006
E-mail: pfec_771@hetnet.nl
URL: http://home.hetnet.nl/~pfecsite/index.html
Contact: Bob Olds, Mgr.
Founded: 1984. **Members:** 1,295. **Membership Dues:** collector, $300. **Staff:** 1. **Multinational.** **Description:** Stamp collectors. Promotes the international exchange of philatelic material. **Computer Services:** database, membership. **Publications:** *PFEC Newsletter*, 3-4/year. Contains news about members. **Circulation:** 970. **Conventions/Meetings:** annual congress.

22360 ■ Polonus Philatelic Society (PPS)
PO Box 489
Maryville, IL 62062
E-mail: info@polanus.org
URL: http://www.polonus.org
Contact: Chester Mikucki, Founder
Founded: 1939. **Members:** 250. **Membership Dues:** individual, $25 (annual). **Staff:** 7. **Budget:** $15,000. **Description:** Stamp collectors of Polish origin and individuals who collect Polish stamps or who specialize in Poland, Polonica, or postal history of Poland. Promotes and encourages Polish philately; to obtain the issuance of U.S. postage stamps relating to Poland. Has been instrumental in the issuance of the

following stamps: Poland, Overrun Nation; Paderewski, Champion of Liberty; Polish Millennium; Copernicus. Conducts research and sponsors competitions. Maintains speaker's bureau. **Libraries: Type:** reference. **Holdings:** 250; artwork, books, business records, clippings, periodicals. **Subjects:** Polish philately. **Awards:** Grand Award. **Frequency:** annual. **Type:** recognition. **Recipient:** for excellence in Polish philately. **Publications:** *Polonus Philatelic Bulletin*, quarterly. **Price:** $5.00 each, for nonmembers; $2.00 each, for members. **Circulation:** 250. **Advertising:** accepted ● Brochures ● Catalogs ● Monographs ● Also publishes an index of bulletin articles. **Conventions/Meetings:** annual meeting (exhibits).

22361 ■ Post Mark Collectors Club (PMCC)
c/o Robert J. Milligan, Membership Mgr.
7014 Woodland Oaks Dr.
Magnolia, TX 77354-4898
Ph: (281)259-2735
E-mail: bob.milligan@prodigy.net
URL: http://www.postmarks.org
Contact: Robert J. Milligan, Membership Mgr.
Founded: 1946. **Members:** 500. **Membership Dues:** individual, $18 (annual) ● student (under age 18), associate, $9 (annual). **Regional Groups:** 4. **Description:** Collectors of postmarks, postal markings, and related items. Provides opportunity for exchange of postmarks and hobby information. Maintains museum of two million items, including postmark collections, postal guides, catalogs, philatelic publications, and other materials connected with postmarks at Historic Lyme Village, Bellevue, OH. Maintains 15 departments. **Telecommunication Services:** electronic mail, teamo@mindspring.com. **Affiliated With:** American Philatelic Society. **Absorbed:** (1950) Postal Cancellation Society. **Publications:** *PMCC Bulletin*, 11/year. Includes auction notices, member profiles, membership list updates, new members information, obituaries, postmark service offers, and classified ads. **Price:** included in membership dues. ISSN: 1041-4894. **Circulation:** 550. **Advertising:** accepted ● *Post Mark Collectors Club—Membership Roster*, periodic. Membership Directory. Includes collecting preferences. **Circulation:** 550. **Conventions/Meetings:** annual convention (exhibits) - always August.

22362 ■ Postal Commemorative Society (PCS)
c/o MBI Inc.
47 Richards Ave.
Norwalk, CT 06857
Ph: (203)853-2000
E-mail: hr@mbi-inc.com
URL: http://www.mbi-inc.com/stamps.asp
Contact: Peter Maglathlin, Dir.
For-Profit. Description: Offers members official U.S. first day covers. First day covers are envelopes on which are affixed "First Day of Issue" U.S. commemorative postage stamps. They are cancelled by the post office on the first day of sale at a specially designated postal location.

22363 ■ Postal History Society (PHS)
8207 Daren Ct.
Pikesville, MD 21208
Ph: (410)653-0665
E-mail: kalphyl@juno.com
Contact: Kalman V. Illyefalvi, Sec.-Treas.
Founded: 1951. **Members:** 549. **Membership Dues:** regular, in U.S., $30 (annual) ● regular, outside U.S., $40 (annual). **Budget:** $25,000. **State Groups:** 21. **Languages:** English, German, Hungarian, Italian, Spanish. **Description:** Brings together philatelists, who are interested chiefly in the study and collection of pre-adhesive and adhesive material with postal history connotations. **Awards:** Postal History Medal. **Type:** medal. **Recipient:** for the best postal history exhibit at national stamp shows. **Computer Services:** database ● mailing lists. **Publications:** *Postal History Journal*, 3/year. Contains research articles concerning development of the postal systems of countries worldwide. Includes book reviews and new member listing. **Price:** included in membership dues. ISSN: 0032-5341. **Circulation:** 600. **Advertising:** accepted. Alternate Formats: microform. **Conven-**

tions/Meetings: annual meeting, always in conjunction with a national stamp show (exhibits) - usually fall ● seminar.

22364 ■ Precancel Stamp Society (PSS)
c/o James Hirstein, Sec.
PO Box 4072
Missoula, MT 59806-4072
Ph: (406)543-4305
E-mail: mnhynes@yahoo.com
URL: http://www.precancels.com
Contact: Eugene Byers, Pres.
Founded: 1912. **Members:** 1,100. **State Groups:** 17. **Description:** Represents collectors and dealers of U.S. precanceled stamps. **Affiliated With:** American Philatelic Society. **Absorbed:** (1923) International Precancel Club. **Publications:** *The Precancel Forum*, monthly. Newsletter. Covers collection building, measurement, mounting, meetings, and PSS news. Includes calendar of events and PSS Catalog changes. **Price:** included in membership dues; $17.50 /year for nonmembers. ISSN: 0273-5415. **Circulation:** 1,100. **Advertising:** accepted ● *Precancel Stamp Society—Biennial Yearbook*. Arranged alphabetically and geographically. **Price:** included in membership dues. **Circulation:** 1,100. **Advertising:** accepted. **Conventions/Meetings:** annual meeting (exhibits).

22365 ■ Rossica Society of Russian Philately (RSRP)
c/o Dr. Ed Laveroni, Sec.
PO Box 320997
Los Gatos, CA 95032-0116
E-mail: ed.laveroni@rossica.org
URL: http://www.rossica.org
Contact: Gary Combs, Pres.
Founded: 1929. **Members:** 301. **Membership Dues:** individual, $25 (annual). **Regional Groups:** 3. **Local Groups:** 5. **Multinational. Description:** Stamp collectors and postal historians with an interest in philately of the Russian area, Russian States, and the Soviet Union. Promotes interest in Russian philately and clarifies information concerning Russian postal history. Sponsors lectures, slide shows, and exhibits. **Libraries: Type:** reference. **Holdings:** 12,000; articles. **Subjects:** Russian postal history. **Awards: Type:** recognition. **Recipient:** for exhibits at stamp shows. **Committees:** Expertization; Library. **Affiliated With:** American Philatelic Society. **Also Known As:** Rossica; Rossika. **Publications:** *Journal of the Rossica Society of Russian Philately*, semiannual. Examines research in the philately and postal history of the USSR, Imperial Russia, Mongolia, Tannou Touva, and related areas. Includes book reviews. **Price:** included in membership dues; $10.00/issue for nonmembers. ISSN: 0035-8363. **Circulation:** 500. **Advertising:** accepted ● Directory, periodic ● Monographs ● Also publishes reference works. **Conventions/Meetings:** annual meeting, with guest speaker.

22366 ■ Rotary on Stamps Fellowship (ROS)
c/o Gerald FitzSimmons, Sec.-Treas.
105 Calle Ricardo
Victoria, TX 77904
E-mail: support@rotaryonstamps.org
URL: http://www.rotaryonstamps.org
Contact: Kenichi Hamana, Chm.
Founded: 1955. **Members:** 200. **Membership Dues:** individual, $20 (annual) ● life, $200. **Multinational. Description:** Stamp collectors, primarily members of Rotary International (see separate entry), who specialize in philatelic recognition of Rotary and its worldwide activities. Publicizes local Rotary club philately-related projects; distributes canceled stamps to charitable institutions. **Libraries: Type:** reference. **Holdings:** 20. **Subjects:** stamps of rotary. **Awards:** RoS Exhibit Award. **Frequency:** periodic. **Type:** recognition. **Recipient:** to a member who presents stamp exhibition. **Committees:** Member Sales and Services. **Affiliated With:** American Topical Association; Rotary International. **Formerly:** Rotary on Stamps Unit. **Publications:** *Directory of Rotary-on-Stamps*, periodic ● *PolioPlus - A Philatelic History*. Book. Promotes PolioPlus and the polio eradication

campaign of the Rotary Foundation. **Price:** $20.00 ● *The RoS Bulletin,* bimonthly. Newsletter. Includes new stamp issues and checklists of all stamps issued commemorating the Rotary. **Price:** included in membership dues; $20.00 /year for nonmembers. **Circulation:** 350 ● *The RoS Encyclopedia.* Book. **Price:** $250.00 ● Membership Directory, annual ● Catalog. **Price:** $25.00. **Conventions/Meetings:** annual meeting, in conjunction with RI.

22367 ■ Russian Zone Handoverprint Study and Research Group

c/o Gerald J. de Boer
1108 Eureka Ave.
Davis, CA 95616
Ph: (530)756-1638
Contact: Gerard J. de Boer, Dir.
Founded: 1953. **Members:** 120. **Description:** Stamp collectors interested in the 1948 Currency Reform provisional stamps of the Russian zone of occupied Germany. Provides expertizing service; maintains sales and auction departments to help members buy and sell stamps and covers. Compiles statistics. **Also Known As:** HOP Study Group. **Publications:** Bulletin, 4-5/year ● Catalog, annual. **Conventions/Meetings:** semiannual meeting, held in conjunction with Germany Philatelic Society - always spring and fall.

22368 ■ Ryukyu Philatelic Specialist Society (RPSS)

c/o Carmine J. DiVincenzo, Sec.
PO Box 381
Clayton, CA 94517-0381
E-mail: admin@ryukyustamps.org
URL: http://www.ryukyustamps.org
Contact: Ron Browner, Pres.
Founded: 1969. **Members:** 204. **Membership Dues:** individual in North America, $15 (annual) ● individual outside North America, $18 (annual) ● sustaining, $25. **State Groups:** 2. **Multinational. Description:** Collectors and dealers interested in the postal history of the Ryukyu Islands under U.S. administration (1945-72). **Libraries: Type:** reference. **Holdings:** archival material, articles. **Awards:** Shurei-no-Mon. **Type:** recognition. **Affiliated With:** American Philatelic Society. **Publications:** *From the Dragon's Den,* QRT. Journal. Contains stamps and postal stationery. **Price:** free, for members only. **Advertising:** accepted. **Conventions/Meetings:** meeting (exhibits) - always San Francisco, CA, during Westpex, and Washington, DC, during NAPEX ● quinquennial meeting, held in conjunction with NAPEX ● seminar, held at stamp exhibitions.

22369 ■ St. Helena, Ascension, and Tristan da Cunha Philatelic Society (SHATCPS)

c/o John L. Havill, Sec.-Treas.
205 N Murray Blvd., Apt. No. 221
Colorado Springs, CO 80916
E-mail: jhavill@earthlink.net
URL: http://pages.britishlibrary.net/philatelic
Contact: Mr. Ronald F. Burn, Pres.
Founded: 1976. **Members:** 150. **Membership Dues:** regular, in North America, $20 (annual) ● regular, outside North America, $23 (annual) ● overseas, $25 (annual). **Description:** A study unit of the American Philatelic Society. Stamp collectors and dealers specializing in materials relating to St. Helena, Ascension, and Tristan da Cunha Islands, a British crown colony in the South Atlantic Ocean. Seeks to stimulate interest in and make available postal history and information dealing with these islands; aids members in completing their collections. Maintains small library of books and pamphlets; compiles statistics. **Formerly:** (1987) Station Helena and Dependencies Philatelic Society. **Publications:** *South Atlantic Chronicle,* quarterly. Journal. Contains postal history articles, book reviews, photographs and illustrations of island stamps and events. **Price:** included in membership dues; $4.00/copy for nonmembers, in North America; $5.00/copy for nonmembers, outside North America. **Circulation:** 225. **Advertising:** accepted. Alternate Formats: online ● Directory, an-

nual. Contains specialty Monographs. ● Membership Directory, annual ● Monograph. **Price:** free for members.

22370 ■ Samuel Gompers Stamp Club (SGSC)

7720 T Bellington Ct.
Springfield, VA 22151-2705
Ph: (703)451-7008
Fax: (703)451-4042
E-mail: emschmidt@compuserve.com
Contact: Edwin M. Schmidt, Sec.-Treas.
Founded: 1981. **Description:** Named after one of the early leaders of the American labor movement. Strives to further the collection and creation of trade union topics on stamps. Offers expertise in creating special cancels and postal stations. **Publications:** Newsletter, periodic.

22371 ■ Scandinavian Collectors Club (SCC)

c/o Donald Brent, Exec. Sec.
PO Box 13196
El Cajon, CA 92020
E-mail: dbrent47@sprynet.com
URL: http://www.scc-online.org
Contact: Mats Roing, Pres.
Founded: 1935. **Members:** 930. **Membership Dues:** in North America, $20 (annual) ● in Canada and outside North America, $26 (annual) ● life, $400. **Local Groups:** 17. **Description:** Collectors and dealers in the stamps and postal materials of Scandinavian countries. **Libraries: Type:** reference. **Holdings:** 1,650; articles, audiovisuals, books, periodicals. **Subjects:** philately in general and Scandinavian related. **Awards:** Carl E. Pelander Award. **Frequency:** periodic. **Type:** recognition. **Recipient:** for outstanding work in furthering the aims of SCC and Scandinavian philately ● Earl Grant Jacobsen Award. **Frequency:** periodic. **Type:** recognition. **Recipient:** for Scandinavian philatelic research ● Frederick A. Brofos Award. **Frequency:** annual. **Type:** recognition. **Recipient:** for outstanding articles published in the Posthorn ● Medals and Joanna Taylor Memorial Bowl. **Frequency:** annual. **Type:** recognition. **Recipient:** for Scandinavian exhibits ● SCC Thematic/Topical Award. **Frequency:** annual. **Type:** recognition. **Recipient:** for best thematic exhibit by a member of SCC ● SSC National Award. **Frequency:** annual. **Type:** recognition. **Recipient:** for best Scandinavian exhibit. **Computer Services:** Mailing lists. **Divisions:** Library; Scandinavian Stamp Mart. **Affiliated With:** American Philatelic Society. **Publications:** *The Posthorn,* quarterly. Journal. Includes articles on Scandinavian philately, annual index, member news, new members listing, and obituaries. **Price:** included in membership dues. ISSN: 0551-6817. **Circulation:** 1,000. **Advertising:** accepted. Alternate Formats: online ● Publishes monologues on an occasional basis. **Conventions/Meetings:** periodic regional meeting (exhibits) ● annual show and meeting, membership meeting at a National Stamp Exhibition and Show (exhibits) - 2008 Nov. 21-23, Arlington Heights, IL.

22372 ■ Scouts on Stamps Society International (SOSSI)

PO Box 6228
Kennewick, WA 99336
Ph: (509)735-3731
E-mail: lclay3731@charter.net
URL: http://www.sossi.org
Contact: Mr. Lawrence E. Clay, Exec. Sec.
Founded: 1951. **Members:** 800. **Membership Dues:** regular in U.S., Canada, Mexico, $15 (annual) ● regular outside North America, $18 (annual) ● youth (under 18), $15 (biennial). **Multinational. Description:** Individuals interested in collecting stamps related to the Boy and Girl Scout movement. Promotes international goodwill through scout philately. Donates collections of stamps to the Boy Scout Historical Museum and to GSUSA National Headquarters. **Awards:** Honorary Director. **Frequency:** annual. **Type:** recognition. **Recipient:** for outstanding service to SOSSI and to philately ● SOSSI Distinguished Philatelist Award. **Frequency:** periodic. **Type:** recognition. **Recipient:** for technical philatelic excellence and based on philatelic achievement. **For-**

merly: Scouts on Stamps Society; Youth Organization on Stamps. **Publications:** *SOSSI Journal,* bimonthly. Contains information related to Scout stamp collecting and the organization's activities. **Price:** included in membership dues. ISSN: 1066-6028. **Circulation:** 900. **Advertising:** accepted. **Conventions/Meetings:** annual conference (exhibits).

22373 ■ Ships on Stamps Unit (SOSU)

2117 E 6th St.
Moscow, ID 83843-9709
Ph: (208)882-0257
E-mail: hobbies@turbonet.com
URL: http://www.shipsonstamps.org
Contact: Myron P. Molnau, Pres.
Founded: 1954. **Members:** 150. **Membership Dues:** regular (international), $20 (annual) ● Canada and Mexico, $14 (annual) ● regular in U.S., $12 (annual). **Multinational. Description:** A study unit of the American Topical Association. Individuals who collect stamps depicting watercraft. Disseminates information about watercraft on stamps. **Libraries: Type:** reference. **Holdings:** archival material, articles. **Awards: Frequency:** annual. **Type:** recognition. **Recipient:** for best ship stamp exhibit at annual meeting. **Telecommunication Services:** electronic bulletin board, electronic discussion group on yahoo groups. **Affiliated With:** American Philatelic Society; American Topical Association. **Publications:** *Short Biographies of Ships on Stamps: A-D,* irregular. Report. Contains short histories of named ships that appear on stamps. Alternate Formats: CD-ROM ● *Watercraft Philately,* bimonthly. Newsletter. Covers the hobby of collecting stamps with a ship motif as well as the histories of ships depicted on stamps. Includes book reviews. **Price:** included in membership dues. ISSN: 0004-0471. **Circulation:** 250. **Advertising:** accepted. **Conventions/Meetings:** annual meeting, in conjunction with ATA.

22374 ■ Society of Australasian Specialists/Oceania (SASO)

PO Box 24764
San Jose, CA 95154-4764
Ph: (408)978-0193
E-mail: stulev@ix.netcom.com
URL: http://members.aol.com/stampsho/saso.html
Contact: Stuart Leven, Sec.
Founded: 1978. **Members:** 285. **Membership Dues:** regular in U.S. and Canada, $17 (annual) ● regular outside North America, $24 (annual). **Staff:** 5. **Budget:** $8,000. **Multinational. Description:** Collectors who specialize in the stamps, stationery, and postal history of Australia, Australian states, New Zealand, New Zealand dependencies, and other Oceanic islands. Operates sales department. Functions primarily through correspondence, except in larger cities where informal meetings are held. Associated with similar philatelic clubs in New South Wales and in Great Britain. **Libraries: Type:** reference. **Holdings:** 5,000. **Subjects:** Australian and Pacific Island stamps and postal history. **Awards: Frequency:** annual. **Type:** recognition. **Study Groups:** Tonga and Tincan Mail. **Affiliated With:** American Philatelic Society. **Formed by Merger of:** Society of Australasian Specialists; Oceania Philatelic Society. **Publications:** *Society of Australasian Specialists/Oceania—The Informer,* quarterly. Newsletter. Includes address changes, new member information, obituaries, research reports, and SAS/O mail auction. **Price:** included in membership dues. **Circulation:** 450. **Advertising:** accepted ● Monographs. **Conventions/Meetings:** annual conference, stamps and postal history of Australasia (exhibits).

22375 ■ Society for Costa Rica Collectors (SOCORICO)

4832 SW Lake Grove Cir.
Palm City, FL 34990
E-mail: harbar@adelphia.net
URL: http://www.socorico.org
Contact: Mr. Raul Hernandez, Pres.
Founded: 1963. **Members:** 180. **Membership Dues:** regular, in U.S., $12 (annual) ● regular, outside U.S., $15 (annual). **Staff:** 7. **Budget:** $5,000. **Description:** Collectors of the stamps and postal history of Costa

Rica and other Central American countries. Promotes the philately of these countries through publications and sale of members' material to other members. Offers expertization service on Costa Rica philately to members. Maintains library of books and periodicals on Costa Rica philately. **Libraries: Type:** not open to the public. **Holdings:** 170. **Subjects:** Costa Rica philately. **Affiliated With:** American Philatelic Society. **Publications:** *Airmail Postal History of Costa Rica.* Book. Contains a description of earlier airmail service in Costa Rica. **Price:** $30.00 ● *Costa Rica Postal Catalogue, 1997.* Contains list of old postal issues or related. **Price:** $30.00 ● *Costa Rica Postal Catalogue 2004.* Book. **Price:** $15.00 for members ● *Costa Rica Revenue Stamp Catalog, 1998.* Contains a listing of all revenue stamps census. **Price:** $20.00 ● *History of the Revenue Stamps of Costa Rica.* Book. Contains the history of revenue issues of Costa Rica. **Price:** $30.00 ● *Index of Costa Rican Philatelic Literature, 2000,* decennial. Book. Features a cumulative index of Costa Rica philolely publications. **Price:** $15.00 ● *The Oxcart,* quarterly. Journal. Covers philately of Costa Rica. Includes news of auctions. **Price:** included in membership dues. ISSN: 0737-0954. **Advertising:** accepted. **Conventions/Meetings:** annual meeting, in conjunction with major philatelic exhibition (exhibits).

22376 ■ Society for Hungarian Philately (SHP)

1920 Fawn Ln.
Hellertown, PA 18055-2117
E-mail: info@hungarianphilately.org
URL: http://www.hungarianphilately.org
Contact: Dr. H. Alan Hoover, Pres.

Founded: 1969. **Members:** 200. **Membership Dues:** regular, in U.S. and Canada, $18 (annual) ● regular, outside U.S. and Canada, $25 (annual). **Multinational. Description:** Collectors of philatelic material relating to Hungary. Offers translation service; holds quarterly mail auction. **Publications:** *News of Hungarian Philately,* quarterly. Journal. Features philatelic activity related to Hungary. **Price:** included in membership dues. **Circulation:** 200. **Advertising:** accepted ● Monographs. Includes research in specialty areas. **Conventions/Meetings:** annual meeting (exhibits) - 2008 Aug. 14-17, Hartford, CT.

22377 ■ Society of Israel Philatelists (SIP)

c/o Mr. Michael Bass, Pres.
PO Box 507
Northfield, OH 44067
Ph: (330)467-7446
Free: (800)292-0550
Fax: (330)467-7442
E-mail: mbass@hy-ko.com
URL: http://www.israelstamps.com
Contact: Mr. Michael Bass, Pres.

Founded: 1948. **Members:** 1,300. **Membership Dues:** in U.S., $25 (annual) ● junior in U.S., $12 (annual) ● in Canada and Mexico, $29 (annual) ● other, $38 (annual). **Local Groups:** 26. **Multinational. Description:** Collectors interested in the philately of the Holy Land. Conducts research into the postal systems of the area; participates in exhibitions. **Libraries: Type:** lending; not open to the public. **Holdings:** 2,500. **Computer Services:** Online services, links to dealers, trade forum, collector's forum, philatelic links. **Committees:** Advertising; Education Fund; Endowment Fund; Publicity; Youth Education. **Study Groups:** Holocaust; JNF Study Circle. **Affiliated With:** American Philatelic Society. **Absorbed:** (1967) Israel-Palestine Philatelic Society of America. **Publications:** *The Israel Philatelist,* bimonthly ● Monographs. **Conventions/Meetings:** annual Philatelic Expo - meeting (exhibits) ● annual show, held in conjunction with NOJEX show (exhibits).

22378 ■ Society for Thai Philately (STP)

c/o H.R. Blakeney, Exec. Sec.
PO Box 44142
Oklahoma City, OK 73144-1142
E-mail: hrblakeney@thaiphilately.org
URL: http://www.thaiphilately.org
Contact: H.R. Blakeney, Exec. Sec.

Founded: 1977. **Members:** 175. **Membership Dues:** sustaining, $16 (annual) ● regular, $10 (annual). **Re-**

gional **Groups:** 3. **Local Groups:** 2. **Description:** Philatelists interested in all aspects of Thai philately, including postal stationery, revenues, covers, occupation issues, and forgeries. Promotes the study of the stamps and postal history of Thailand. Sponsors competitions. **Affiliated With:** American Philatelic Society. **Publications:** *Thai Philatelic Handbook* ● *Thai Philately.* Journal. **Price:** $12.00 in U.S., includes postage; $17.00 outside U.S., includes postage. ISSN: 0198-7992. **Circulation:** 250. **Advertising:** accepted ● *Thai Stamps 2000.* Brochure. **Price:** $15.00 in U.S., includes postage. **Conventions/Meetings:** periodic conference.

22379 ■ Space Topic Study Unit

c/o Carmine Torrisi, Sec.
PO Box 780241
Maspeth, NY 11378
E-mail: ctorrisi@nyc.rr.com
URL: http://stargate.1usa.com/stamps
Contact: Carmine Torrisi, Sec.

Founded: 1957. **Members:** 650. **Membership Dues:** individual, $15 (annual). **Staff:** 8. **Budget:** $10,000. **Regional Groups:** 6. **State Groups:** 6. **Local Groups:** 5. **Multinational. Description:** A study unit of the American Philatelic Society (see separate entry). Collectors of stamps dealing with space themes. Promotes space philately and disseminates information. Advises members on mounting, collecting, and exhibiting space material. Conducts space stamp auctions. **Libraries: Type:** reference. **Holdings:** 48. **Subjects:** space. **Awards:** Scholl Award. **Frequency:** annual. **Type:** recognition ● Winick Award. **Frequency:** annual. **Type:** recognition. **Committees:** Fakes and Forgeries; Mars. **Affiliated With:** American Philatelic Society; American Topical Association. **Also Known As:** Space Unit. **Formerly:** (2002) Space Topics Study Group. **Publications:** *The Astrophile,* bimonthly. Journal. Features articles on space, on stamps, and checklists. **Price:** free, for members only. **Circulation:** 650. **Advertising:** accepted. Also Cited As: *Astrophilately.* **Conventions/Meetings:** annual National Topical Stamp Show - meet (exhibits) ● Philadelphia National Stamp Exhibition - show (exhibits).

22380 ■ Sports Philatelists International (SPI)

c/o Margaret A. Jones
5310 Lindenwood Ave.
St. Louis, MO 63109-1758
E-mail: president@sportstamps.org
URL: http://www.sportstamps.org
Contact: Mark C. Maestrone, Pres./Ed.

Founded: 1962. **Members:** 425. **Membership Dues:** in U.S. and Canada, $20 (annual) ● overseas, $30 (annual). **Multinational. Description:** Philatelists united to promote the study and collection of postage stamps and collateral materials dealing with sports and recreation. Supports those organizations promoting and sponsoring amateur sports around the globe and fosters international understanding through mutual interest in sports and philately. Sponsors mail auctions; operates circuit book sales program and translation service; cooperates with leading sports organizations; works to find and collect the sports philatelic information needed by the membership. Conducts research and study groups. **Awards: Type:** recognition. **Affiliated With:** American Philatelic Society; American Topical Association. **Publications:** *Handbook of Basketball Philately.* **Price:** $26.50 in U.S.; $30.00 outside U.S. ● *Handbook of Tennis Philately.* **Price:** $18.00 in U.S.; $20.00 outside U.S. ● *Index for Journal of Sports Philatelists,* annual. **Price:** $20.00 in U.S.; $25.00 outside U.S. ● *Journal of Sports Philately,* quarterly. Contains articles on the Olympics and other sporting events. **Price:** $20.00 /year for nonmembers; included in membership dues; $30.00 for nonmembers overseas. **Advertising:** accepted ● *Membership Handbook,* biennial. Membership Directory ● *Postal History and Vignettes of the 1932 Olympic Games.* Handbook. **Price:** $10.00 in U.S.; $12.00 outside U.S. ● *The Simplified Handbook of Adult Competitive Sports Stamps* ● Also publishes checklists and membership lists. **Conventions/Meetings:** periodic competition ● annual Stamp Show.

22381 ■ Stamps on Stamps Collectors Club (SOSCC)

c/o Michael Merritt, Sec.-Treas.
73 Mountainside Rd.
Mendham, NJ 07945
E-mail: mischu@research.att.com
URL: http://www.stampsonstamps.org
Contact: Gaston Barrette, Pres.

Founded: 1954. **Members:** 100. **Membership Dues:** in U.S., $15 (annual) ● outside U.S., $18 (annual). **Multinational. Description:** Stamp collectors participating in the study of a stamp on stamp and/or centenary topics. **Formerly:** (1963) Stamps on Stamps Unit; (2001) Stamps on Stamps - Centenary Unit. **Publications:** *SOS Signal,* quarterly. Bulletin. Contains valuable information, articles of interest and news. **Price:** included in membership dues; $3.00 each, for nonmembers ● Also publishes auction lists.

22382 ■ Stamps for the Wounded (SFTW-LISC)

c/o Don Montlack
8784 Thames River Dr.
Boca Raton, FL 33433-6274
E-mail: pdgdonm@aol.com
URL: http://35dlions.org/stamps.html
Contact: Don Montlack, Contact

Founded: 1942. **Budget:** $12,000. **Nonmembership. Description:** Collects new and used stamps from US and foreign donors, and collections, to be sorted and distributed to patients in 15 Veterans Administration hospitals and centers. Also collects albums, catalogs, and accessories for distribution to hospitalized servicemen and women so that they may enjoy the philatelic avocation as part of recreational therapy. They are also used in organized therapy sessions.

22383 ■ State Revenue Society (SRS)

c/o Kent Gray
PO Box 67842
Albuquerque, NM 87193
E-mail: kent@staterevs.com
URL: http://www.staterevs.com
Contact: Kent Gray, Contact

Founded: 1959. **Members:** 250. **Membership Dues:** regular, in U.S., $15 (annual) ● regular, outside U.S., $21 (annual). **Description:** Collectors of revenue stamps issued by state and local governments. Records, studies, and catalogs such stamps. **Libraries: Type:** reference. **Holdings:** 230. **Subjects:** U.S. and state revenue stamps and tax laws. **Awards:** Best State Revenue Research Article Award. **Frequency:** annual. **Type:** monetary. **Recipient:** for the most extensive and thoroughly researched article on an aspect of state revenue stamps. **Affiliated With:** American Revenue Association. **Publications:** Directory, biennial. **Price:** $15.00/year. **Circulation:** 300. **Advertising:** accepted ● Also publishes state revenue stamp catalogs. **Conventions/Meetings:** annual meeting, with ARA annual meeting.

22384 ■ Tannu Tuva Collectors' Society (TTCS)

c/o Kenneth R. Simon, Pres.
513 6th Ave. S
Lake Worth, FL 33460
E-mail: fpo09501@yahoo.com
URL: http://www.tuva.tk
Contact: Kenneth R. Simon, Pres.

Founded: 1993. **Members:** 200. **Membership Dues:** regular, $7 ● supporting, $15 ● hero of TUA, $20. **Staff:** 1. **Multinational. Description:** Promotes study of stamps, coins, banknotes, medals, zwaki, postcards, and postal history of Tuva. **Libraries: Type:** reference; not open to the public. **Holdings:** 50. **Subjects:** Tuva and related topics. **Affiliated With:** American Philatelic Society. **Publications:** *The Postal History and Stamps of Tuva (1997).* Book. **Price:** $33.00 post-inclusive for members; $48.00 for nonmembers and libraries ● *TbBA.* Journal. Contains articles and short stories of information.

22385 ■ Third Reich Study Group (TRSG)
c/o Myron Fox, Dir.
4 Arbor Cir.
Natick, MA 01760-2953
E-mail: myronfox1@aol.com
URL: http://gps.nu/studygroup/thirdreich
Contact: Myron Fox, Dir.
Founded: 1962. **Members:** 200. **Membership Dues:** in U.S. and Canada, $22 (annual) ● outside U.S. and Canada, $28 (annual) **Staff:** 4. **Languages:** English, German. **Description:** A study group of the Germany Philatelic Society (see separate entry). Persons interested in the postal history of Germany from 1933 to 1945. Offers Fieldpost Identification inquiry service. Awards plaque for the best Third Reich postal history exhibit; sponsors competitions and bimonthly auction. **Awards:** Bob Houston Memorial Award. **Type:** recognition. **Recipient:** for the best III Reich Exhibit in National Exposition. **Affiliated With:** Germany Philatelic Society. **Publications:** *Back Issue Guide Update.* **Price:** $2.50 each ● *Feldpost Cancellation Guide.* Catalog. Contains study of German WWII military postmarks. **Price:** $3.00 each ● *Third Reich Study Group Bulletin*, quarterly. Journal. **Price:** included in membership dues. **Circulation:** 300 ● *TRSG Handbook and Back Issue Guide.* **Price:** $6.00 each ● *Waffen - SS Feldpost Numbers/Order or Battle.* **Price:** $15.00 each ● Also publishes monographs, catalogs, research articles, literature reviews, abstracts of foreign publications, and survey articles. **Conventions/Meetings:** annual conference (exhibits).

22386 ■ Ukrainian Philatelic and Numismatic Society (UPNS)
PO Box 3
Springfield, VA 22150-0003
Fax: (703)569-0223
E-mail: ingert@starpower.net
URL: http://www.upns.org
Contact: Dr. Ingert Kuzych-Berezovsky, Pres.
Founded: 1951. **Members:** 350. **Membership Dues:** individual, $25 (annual). **Staff:** 7. **Regional Groups:** 1. **Local Groups:** 6. **Languages:** English, German, Ukrainian. **Description:** Collectors of Ukrainian stamps, coins, bank notes, medals, and buttons. Offers periodic Trident Course. Maintains speakers' bureau. Sponsors competitions. **Libraries: Type:** reference. **Holdings:** 250; archival material, books, monographs. **Subjects:** philately, numismatics, heraldry, ethnicity. **Awards:** Eugene Kotyk Award. **Frequency:** annual. **Type:** recognition. **Recipient:** for research and writing excellence ● Heorhiy Narbut Prize. **Frequency:** annual. **Type:** recognition. **Recipient:** for stamp design ● Julian Maksymczuk Award. **Frequency:** annual. **Type:** recognition. **Recipient:** for services to Ukrainian collecting. **Computer Services:** Mailing lists, membership directory, special interest. **Committees:** Expertizing. **Affiliated With:** American Philatelic Society. **Formerly:** (1971) Society of Ukrainian Philatelists. **Publications:** *Trident Visnyk*, bimonthly. Newsletter. **Price:** $1.00/copy. ISSN: 0882-1674. **Circulation:** 350. **Advertising:** accepted ● *Ukrainian Philatelist* (in English and Ukrainian), semiannual. Journal. Includes reviews of philatelic publications. **Price:** $8.00/issue. ISSN: 0198-6252. **Circulation:** 350. **Advertising:** accepted ● *UPNS Membership Directory*, every 2-3 years. **Conventions/Meetings:** annual Ukrainpex - conference (exhibits).

22387 ■ United Nations Philatelists, Inc. (UNPI)
PO Box 146
Morrisville, PA 19067-0146
Ph: (215)295-3143
E-mail: info@unstampz.com
URL: http://www.unpi.com
Contact: Anthony Dewey, Pres.
Founded: 1977. **Members:** 300. **Membership Dues:** regular, in U.S., $22 (annual) ● regular, in Canada, $24 (annual) ● regular, outside U.S., $38 (annual). **Regional Groups:** 4. **Description:** Promotes fellowship and communication among collectors of philatelic material relating to the United Nations and its activities. Develops and disseminates information. **Librar-**

ies: Type: reference. **Holdings:** archival material. **Awards: Frequency:** annual. **Type:** recognition. **Committees:** Archivist; Auctions; Exhibits; Publicity; Website. **Affiliated With:** American Philatelic Society; American Topical Association. **Publications:** *Journal of the United Nations Philatelists*, bimonthly. Includes cancels, meters, show imprints, and auction information. **Price:** included in membership dues. **Circulation:** 400. **Advertising:** accepted. Alternate Formats: online ● Monographs. **Conventions/Meetings:** competition ● annual meeting (exhibits).

22388 ■ United Postal Stationery Society (UPSS)
c/o Stuart Leven, Membership Mgr.
1445 Foxworthy Ave., No. 187
San Jose, CA 95118-1119
E-mail: portvenn@ameritech.net
URL: http://www.upss.org
Contact: Lewis E. Bussey, Pres.
Founded: 1945. **Members:** 1,200. **Membership Dues:** in U.S., $18 (annual) ● outside U.S., contributing (18 years old and above), $25 (annual) ● junior (14-17 years old), $6 (annual) ● life, in U.S., $400 ● life, outside U.S., $600. **Description:** Collectors of postal stationery of the U.S. and the world. Provides member benefits including auctions, sales circuits and slide programs on various specialized collections. **Libraries: Type:** reference. **Holdings:** books, clippings. **Awards: Type:** recognition. **Recipient:** for postal stationery exhibition. **Computer Services:** Information services, discussion chatroom. **Telecommunication Services:** electronic mail, lebarch@aol.com. **Affiliated With:** American Philatelic Society. **Formed by Merger of:** (1945) Postal Card Society of America; International Postal Stationery Society. **Publications:** *Actual Size Illustrations Cutting Knife Handbook.* Catalog. **Price:** $36.00 for members; $45.00 for nonmembers ● *Postal Stationery*, bimonthly. Journal. **Price:** included in membership dues; $3.00 for nonmembers. **Advertising:** accepted ● *Postal Stationery of Peru.* Catalog. **Price:** $12.00 for members; $15.00 for nonmembers ● *Thomas Leavitt-His History and Postal Markings 1875-1892.* Catalog. **Price:** $32.00 for members; $40.00 for nonmembers ● *U.S. Postal Card Catalog.* **Price:** $32.00 for members; $40.00 for nonmembers ● *UPSS Catalog of the 19th Century Stamped Envelopes and Wrappers of the U.S..* **Price:** $28.00 for members; $35.00 for nonmembers ● *UPSS Catalog of the 20th Century Stamped Envelopes and Wrappers of the U.S..* **Price:** $40.00 for members; $50.00 for nonmembers. **Conventions/Meetings:** semiannual convention, held with national stamp shows (exhibits) - always spring and fall. 2008 Feb. 6-8, Sarasota, FL.

22389 ■ U.S. Cancellation Club (USCC)
c/o Roger Rhoads, Sec.-Treas.
6160 Brownstone Ct.
Mentor, OH 44060
E-mail: track@alum.wpi.edu
URL: http://www.geocities.com/Athens/2088/usc-chome.htm
Contact: Roger D. Curran, Pres.
Founded: 1938. **Members:** 500. **Description:** Beginning and advanced philatelists interested in collecting postal markings and cancellations. Conducts research on postal history and markings; operates sales department for purchase or sale of stamps and covers. Maintains loan library of about 150 items pertaining to this philatelic specialty. **Libraries: Type:** not open to the public; lending. **Holdings:** books, periodicals. **Departments:** Research; Sales. **Affiliated With:** American Philatelic Society. **Publications:** *News*, quarterly. Newsletter ● *Roster*, annual. Directory. **Conventions/Meetings:** annual meeting.

22390 ■ U.S. Philatelic Classics Society (USPCS)
102 Old Pawling Rd.
Pawling, NY 12564-2121
Ph: (845)855-1616 (914)450-3791
Fax: (845)855-0817

E-mail: charles.dicomo@uspcs.org
URL: http://www.uspcs.org
Contact: Dr. Charles J. DiComo, Sec.
Founded: 1948. **Members:** 1,200. **Membership Dues:** regular, $27 (annual) ● contributing, $35 (annual) ● sustaining, $50 (annual). **Budget:** $30,000. **Regional Groups:** 3. **Description:** Philatelists and postal historians interested in issues of U.S. postage stamps and the postal history of the period 1847-93, and in the preceding stampless period. Disseminates information concerning discoveries and research of members. Sponsors publication of educational literature of interest to philatelists and postal historians. Conducts seminars. Selects individuals to sign the Distinguished Philatelists Scroll. **Awards:** Dr. Carroll Chase Cup Award. **Frequency:** annual. **Type:** recognition. **Recipient:** for authors of articles, books, or other studies concerning US stamps issued to 1894 industries ● Elliott Perry Cup Award. **Frequency:** annual. **Type:** recognition. **Recipient:** for individuals who have provided significant contributions to research concerning US stamps on Postal History to 1894 ● Lester G. Brookman Cup Award. **Frequency:** annual. **Type:** recognition. **Recipient:** for a member who has given outstanding services to the society ● Stanley B. Ashbrook Cup Award. **Frequency:** annual. **Type:** recognition. **Recipient:** for authors of articles or other studies concerning U.S. Postal History from the Colonial period to 1894. **Affiliated With:** American Philatelic Society. **Absorbed:** (1992) U.S. 1869 Pictorial Research Associates. **Formerly:** The Three Cent 1851-57 Unit. **Publications:** *Cancellations and Killers of the Banknote Era, 1870-1894.* Books ● *Chatter*, quarterly. Newsletter ● *Chronicle of U.S. Classic Postal Issues*, quarterly. **Price:** $24.00 for nonmembers. ISSN: 0009-6008. **Circulation:** 1,250. **Advertising:** accepted ● *Letters of Gold.* Book ● *North Atlantic Mail Sailings, 1840-75* ● *The 1851 Issue of United States Stamps: A Sesquicentennial Retrospective.* Book. **Price:** $125.00 ● *1847 Cover Census.* Book. **Conventions/Meetings:** annual convention and meeting.

22391 ■ United States Stamp Society
c/o Larry Ballantyne, Exec. Sec.
PO Box 6634
Katy, TX 77491-6634
E-mail: stampsjoann@prodigy.net
URL: http://www.usstamps.org
Contact: Larry Ballantyne, Exec. Sec.
Founded: 1930. **Members:** 2,000. **Membership Dues:** regular, $25 (annual). **Staff:** 3. **Budget:** $75,000. **Description:** Collectors of United States stamps. Promotes the study of the philatelic output of the Bureau of Engraving and Printing and postage and revenue stamped paper produced by others for use in the United States and U.S. administered areas. Conducts slide shows and panel discussions. **Awards:** Hopkinson Award. **Frequency:** annual. **Type:** recognition. **Recipient:** for best exhibit at national, regional, and local exhibitions ● Southgate Award. **Frequency:** annual. **Type:** recognition. **Recipient:** for best article in monthly magazine. **Also Known As:** Bureau Issues Association. **Publications:** *Durland Standard Plate Number Catalog*, quadrennial. Provides plate number data for all U.S. stamps. **Price:** $22.00/copy. **Circulation:** 2,000 ● *U.S. Specialist*, monthly. Journal. Contains information on the production, printing, use, and history of U.S. stamps. Includes plate number reports. **Price:** included in membership dues. ISSN: 0164-923X. **Circulation:** 2,000. **Advertising:** accepted. Also Cited As: *The Bureau Specialist* ● Also publishes reference books, papers and pamphlets on various aspects of U.S. stamps, including issues and printing technology. **Conventions/Meetings:** annual meeting (exhibits) ● seminar.

22392 ■ Universal Ship Cancellation Society (USCS)
747 Shard Ct.
Fremont, CA 94539-7419
E-mail: shaymur@flash.net
URL: http://www.uscs.org
Contact: Paul Helman, Pres.
Founded: 1932. **Members:** 1,500. **Membership Dues:** individual, $20 (annual) ● life, $400. **Budget:**

$50,000. **Local Groups:** 25. **Multinational. Description:** Collectors of covers (envelopes) bearing postmarks of United States naval ships and shore stations, merchant ships, and foreign naval and merchant ships, together with historical and statistical information regarding them. Presents numerous awards; maintains photographic archive. **Libraries: Type:** reference. **Holdings:** archival material. **Awards:** Stanton Honeyman Memorial Award. **Frequency:** annual. **Type:** monetary. **Recipient:** for best article in the society's monthly magazine. **Committees:** Cancellation Classification; Naval History. **Publications:** *Catalog of Naval Covers Cachet Makers.* Book ● *Catalog of Naval Postmarks.* Book ● *Membership Roster,* annual ● *USCS Log,* monthly. ISSN: 0279-6139. **Advertising:** accepted. **Conventions/Meetings:** annual convention (exhibits).

22393 ■ Western Cover Society (WCS)

c/o John Drew, Sec.
15370 Skyview Terr.
San Jose, CA 95132
Ph: (408)258-6922
E-mail: jandndrew@aol.com
URL: http://www.westerncoversociety.org
Contact: John Drew, Sec.

Founded: 1950. **Members:** 300. **Membership Dues:** regular, $25 (annual). **Staff:** 10. **Description:** Collectors of letters, envelopes (covers), and written historical material of the West. Purposes are to exchange ideas and information; to preserve historical philatelic relics, maps, pictures, and diaries; to collect and exchange books of the West; to cooperate with museums, libraries, and historical societies; to assist students, writers, and educators. **Libraries: Type:** open to the public. **Affiliated With:** American Philatelic Society. **Publications:** *Western Express,* quarterly. Journal. **Price:** included in membership dues. **Circulation:** 350. **Advertising:** accepted. **Conventions/Meetings:** semiannual meeting - always April, San Francisco, CA, and October, Los Angeles, CA.

22394 ■ Young Stamp Collectors of America (YSCA)

100 Match Factory Pl.
Bellefonte, PA 16823
Ph: (814)933-3820
E-mail: ysca@stamps.org
URL: http://www.stamps.org/ysca/intro.htm

Membership Dues: regular, $10 (annual) ● family, $15 (annual) ● supporting, $20 (annual). **Description:** Promotes stamp collecting for young people. Assists members in acquiring and disposing of philatelic materials. Offers services and programs for the benefit of stamp collecting and of all collectors. **Affiliated With:** American Philatelic Society. **Publications:** Newsletter, quarterly. Alternate Formats: online.

22395 ■ Zeppelin Collectors Club (ZCC)

PO Box A3843
Chicago, IL 60690-3843
Fax: (847)468-0840
E-mail: cganzl@uic.edu
Contact: Cheryl Ganz, Contact

Founded: 1968. **Members:** 300. **Membership Dues:** individual, $20 (annual) ● forman, $25 (annual). **Description:** Individuals interested in the history of airships and collectors of airship philatelic material and memorabilia. Serves as a forum for exchange of information concerning exhibits, special events, awards, and published materials. **Libraries: Type:** not open to the public. **Holdings:** 1,000. **Affiliated With:** American Philatelic Society. **Publications:** *The Zeppelin Collector,* quarterly. Journal. Available as a newsletter insert with the *Journal of the Aerophilatelic Federation of the Americas, Jack Knight Air Log.* **Advertising:** accepted. **Conventions/Meetings:** periodic congress ● quadrennial meeting and symposium.

Photography

22396 ■ Photographic Society of America (PSA)

3000 United Founders Blvd., Ste.103
Oklahoma City, OK 73112-3940
Ph: (405)843-1437
Fax: (405)843-1438
E-mail: hq@psa-photo.org
URL: http://www.psa-photo.org
Contact: Richard Frieders FPSA, Pres.

Founded: 1934. **Members:** 5,000. **Membership Dues:** institution/camera club/individual/photographic organization (in U.S., Canada, and Mexico), $45 (annual) ● institution/camera club/individual/photographic organization (in all other countries), $53 (annual) ● youth (in U.S., Canada, and Mexico), $29 (annual) ● youth (in all other countries), $35 (annual) ● joint (in U.S., Canada, and Mexico), $68 (annual) ● joint (in all other countries), $76 (annual) ● senior (72 and older), $40 (annual) ● individual (over 18), $45 (annual) ● joint senior (in U.S., Canada, and Mexico), $62 (annual) ● joint senior (in other countries), $69 (annual). **Staff:** 2. **Description:** Camera clubs; amateur, advanced amateur photographers. Sponsors competitions. Conducts slide and print contests, provides instruction slide sets, slide analysis, print portfolios, and other technical services. **Libraries: Type:** reference. **Awards: Type:** recognition. **Committees:** International Affairs; International Exhibits; Permanent Print Collections; Progress Medal Award; Scholarship; Special Awards; Travel. **Divisions:** Color Slide; Motion Picture; Nature; Photo-Journalism; Photo-Travel; Pictorial Print; Stereo; Techniques. **Formerly:** Associated Camera Clubs of America. **Publications:** *PSA Journal,* monthly. Provides practical information for amateur photographers. **Price:** included in membership dues. ISSN: 0030-8277. **Advertising:** accepted. Alternate Formats: microform; online. **Conventions/Meetings:** annual conference and workshop (exhibits) ● periodic regional meeting.

Pigeons

22397 ■ American Racing Pigeon Union (ARPU)

PO Box 18465
Oklahoma City, OK 73154-0465
Ph: (405)848-5801
Free: (800)755-ARPU
Fax: (405)848-5888
E-mail: augrow@aol.com
URL: http://www.pigeon.org
Contact: Steve Lawler, Pres.

Founded: 1910. **Members:** 8,500. **Membership Dues:** individual, $25 (annual) ● patron, $20 (annual) ● sponsor, $15 (annual) ● family, $35 (annual) ● junior, $10 (annual) ● life, $300. **Staff:** 4. **State Groups:** 34. **Local Groups:** 700. **Description:** Persons interested in racing homing pigeons. Maintains speakers' bureau and hall of fame. **Libraries: Type:** reference. **Holdings:** video recordings. **Awards:** AU All Distance Champion. **Type:** recognition ● AU Long Distance. **Type:** recognition ● Hall of Fame. **Frequency:** annual. **Type:** recognition. **Recipient:** for outstanding accomplishments of homing pigeons ● President's Cup. **Type:** recognition. **Computer Services:** Mailing lists. **Also Known As:** AU. **Publications:** *American Racing Pigeon Union Up-Date,* quarterly. Newsletter. Includes pigeon health updates and racing rules. **Price:** included in membership dues. **Circulation:** 11,500. **Advertising:** accepted ● *Club Band List Directory,* annual. **Advertising:** accepted. **Conventions/Meetings:** annual meeting and convention, with pigeon suppliers (exhibits) - always fall.

22398 ■ International Federation of American Homing Pigeon Fanciers (IFAHPF)

c/o Val Matteucci, Sec.-Treas.
PO Box 374
Hicksville, NY 11802
Ph: (516)794-3612
Fax: (516)794-6654
E-mail: paul@walshloft.com
URL: http://www.ifpigeon.com
Contact: Richard Smith, Pres.

Founded: 1881. **Members:** 4,200. **Membership Dues:** regular, $15 (annual). **Staff:** 1. **Local Groups:** 200. **Multinational. Description:** Members of affiliated clubs of pigeon fanciers. Promotes the breeding, training, racing, and exhibition of pigeons. **Publications:** *Association News Column in American Racing Pigeon News,* monthly. Newsletter. **Conventions/Meetings:** annual convention.

22399 ■ International Modena Club (IMC)

c/o B. Tim Taylor, Sec.-Treas.
10032 Goodrich Rd.
Bloomington, MN 55437-2413
E-mail: srodders@aol.com
URL: http://www.internationalmodenaclub.com
Contact: Jim Vines, Pres.

Founded: 2003. **Membership Dues:** individual in U.S., individual senior outside U.S., affiliated club, $25 (annual) ● spouse, $10 (annual) ● junior, $15 (annual). **Languages:** English, French, German, Norwegian, Spanish. **Multinational. Description:** Represents Modena pigeon hobbyists around the world. Promotes breeding, maintenance, conditioning and exhibition of Modena pigeons. Serves as a Modena resource center for the Modena hobby worldwide. **Awards:** IMC Diploma Award. **Frequency:** periodic. **Type:** recognition. **Recipient:** for distinguished Modena pigeon breeders. **Telecommunication Services:** electronic mail, jvmodena@valuelinx.net. **Affiliated With:** National Pigeon Association. **Publications:** *IMC Quarterly.* Newsletter. **Price:** included in membership dues. Alternate Formats: online ● Brochure. Alternate Formats: online.

Pipe Smoking

22400 ■ International Association of Pipe Smokers Clubs (IAPSC)

c/o Paul T. Spaniola, Chm.
647 S Saginaw St.
Flint, MI 48502
Ph: (810)235-0581
Fax: (810)235-1300
E-mail: chairman@iapsc.net
URL: http://www.iapsc.net
Contact: Dave Edel, Pres.

Founded: 1949. **Membership Dues:** pipe club, $30 (annual) ● associate, $15 (annual) ● sustaining, $35 (annual). **Description:** Pipe smokers clubs in Brazil, Canada, England, Germany, Israel, Japan, Netherlands, New Zealand, and the United States; associate members are pipe and tobacco shops; sustaining members are pipe, tobacco, and accessory manufacturers. Promotes friendship and fellowship among members. Establishes rules for competitive pipe-smoking. Maintains hall of fame and museum. **Awards:** Pipe Smoker of the Year. **Frequency:** annual. **Type:** recognition. **Recipient:** for pipe smoker or collector. **Publications:** *Agricultural and Mechanical Gazette,* 5/year. **Price:** $10.00/year. **Circulation:** 500. **Advertising:** accepted ● *Annual World Pipe Convention Guide,* annual. **Conventions/Meetings:** annual Worlds Pipe-Smoking Contest and Pipe Show - convention, includes pipe-smoking contest (exhibits) - always October.

22401 ■ The Universal Coterie of Pipe Smokers (TUCOPS)

Address Unknown since 2007

Founded: 1964. **Members:** 5,000. **Multinational. Description:** Persons with a genuine interest in pipe smoking. Informal group with no dues, no meetings other than an occasional get-together when desired by any number of members, no charter, and no obligations. Through its publication, provides members with: quotes about pipes and pipe smoking; correspondence on pipe collecting, pipe exchange/"used wood" market, snuff, cigars, and tobacco tins; tips on where to send for free tobacco, catalogs, and other materials; hints on improving the quality of a pipe, book reviews, auction reports. **Libraries: Type:** reference. **Holdings:** 1,000; archival material, articles, artwork. **Subjects:** pipe smoking memorabilia, tobacco, related topics. **Publications:** *Members' Collecting Directory,* periodic. **Advertising:** not accepted

● *The Pipe Smoker's Ephemeris*, periodic. Journal. Includes book and magazine reviews, new members listing, listing of auctions, shows, swaps, articles on pipes and tobacco, original artwork, etc. ISSN: 0032-0161. Circulation: 5,000. **Advertising:** not accepted ● *The Pipe Smoker's Ephemeris, Book I.* A limited edition, hard cover compendium (1965-1979) of The Pipe Smoker's Ephemeris Journal, contains extra illustrations and is fully indexed. ● *The Pipe Smoker's Ephemeris, Book II.* A limited edition, hard cover compendium (1980-1994) of The Pipe Smoker's Ephemeris Journal, contains extra illustrations and is fully indexed. ● Bibliography ● Reprints. Literature dealing with pipes and pipe smoking.

Poker

22402 ■ National Poker Association (NPA)
2885 W 128th Ave., No. 1423
Denver, CO 80234
Ph: (615)300-7367
E-mail: info@mynpa.org
Contact: Wesley Parker, Pres.
Founded: 1990. **Members:** 1,350. **Membership Dues:** individual, $25 (annual). **Staff:** 2. **Description:** Individuals interested in the formal game of poker as played in casinos and cardrooms. Promotes casino poker as a viable business and activity, and works for the legalization of the game in all states. Casino poker is distinguished by established rules of play, security, and dealer neutrality; the house does not play against participants and therefore has no vested interest in the outcome of the game. Works to improve the public image of poker by marketing it as a game of skill. Offers assistance to cardrooms suffering "political and legal harassment." Conducts legislative activities; writes poker regulations for tribal and state control authorities; compiles industry statistics. Settles poker rules disputes. Offers for a fee: complete poker set up, including equipment selection, implementation of all rules and controls, full personnel training, and promotional/marketing package. **Committees:** Political Action. **Publications:** *Poker for All.* Video. **Price:** $22.00 postage paid. **Conventions/Meetings:** competition, poker tournaments.

22403 ■ World Poker Association (WPA)
848 N Rainbow Blvd., Ste.1000
Las Vegas, NV 89107
Ph: (702)952-2460
Free: (866)371-WPA1
Fax: (702)952-2468
E-mail: info@wpapoker.org
URL: http://www.wpapoker.org
Contact: Jesse Jones, Founder
Founded: 2005. **Members:** 918. **Membership Dues:** non-voting, $10 (annual) ● voting, $50 (annual) ● founding, $1,000 (annual). **Multinational. Description:** Addresses ethical and integrity issues about poker. Establishes fair and consistent rules and procedures and increases the opportunities of individual and organizational members worldwide. Acts as the governing body of tournament poker worldwide. Unites all related tournament poker entities. **Publications:** Newsletter, monthly. **Price:** included in membership dues. Alternate Formats: online.

Political Items

22404 ■ American Political Items Collectors (APIC)
PO Box 55
Avon, NY 14414
Ph: (585)226-2236
E-mail: apic@texas.net
URL: http://www.apic.us
Contact: Harvey Goldberg, Sec.
Founded: 1945. **Members:** 3,200. **Membership Dues:** regular, $28 (annual) ● affiliate, $8 (annual) ● regular, in Canada, $55 (annual) ● regular, outside U.S., $90 (annual). **Staff:** 1. **Regional Groups:** 7.

State Groups: 27. **Local Groups:** 32. **National Groups:** 16. **Description:** Individuals and organizations interested in the collection and preservation of political Americana. Conducts auctions by mail of campaign buttons and other political memorabilia. Sponsors research. **Computer Services:** Mailing lists, of members. **Committees:** Educational; Ethics. **Publications:** *APIC Keynoter*, quarterly. Newsletter ● *APIC Roster*, annual. Handbook. Contains Roster of membership. **Price:** free, for members only. **Circulation:** 2,700. Also Cited As: *APIC Handbook*. **Conventions/Meetings:** biennial meeting (exhibits).

Postcards

22405 ■ Deltiologists of America (D of A)
PO Box 8
Norwood, PA 19074
Ph: (610)485-8572
E-mail: postcardclassics@juno.com
URL: http://www.deltiologists-America.com
Contact: James L. Lowe, Dir.
Founded: 1960. **Members:** 350. **Staff:** 2. **Description:** Collectors and dealers of picture postcards, especially the earlier, antique postcards published worldwide from 1890-1920. Supplies members with information about their hobby, including checklists of sets and series and dealer offerings. Conducts auctions on Ebay. **Libraries: Type:** not open to the public. **Holdings:** 600. **Subjects:** postcards, paper Americana. **Absorbed:** Chrome Card Collectors Club. **Formerly:** (1970) Better Postcard Collectors' Club. **Publications:** *Standard Postcard Catalog*, triennial ● Also publishes guides.

22406 ■ International Federation of Postcard Dealers (IFPD)
PO Box 1765
Manassas, VA 20108-1765
E-mail: mdcgbg@cs.com
URL: http://www.playle.com/ifpd
Contact: Mark Clemens, Treas.
Founded: 1979. **Members:** 150. **Membership Dues:** general, $25 (annual). **Staff:** 9. **Budget:** $10,000. **Multinational. Description:** Accredited postcard dealers. Seeks: to create fellowship among dealers; to keep members informed of upcoming postcard shows and sales; to standardize business practices. **Libraries: Type:** reference. **Subjects:** postcard. **Affiliated With:** American Philatelic Society. **Publications:** *Membership Roster*, annual. Membership Directory. **Circulation:** 8,500. **Advertising:** accepted ● Newsletter, quarterly. **Price:** included in membership dues. **Circulation:** 150. **Conventions/Meetings:** annual meeting (exhibits) - always Saturday before Easter in Dulles, VA ● show - 7/year.

22407 ■ Korea Postcard Collectors Group
c/o Deltiologists of America
PO Box 8
Norwood, PA 19074
URL: http://www.deltiologists-america.com
Contact: James Lewis Lowe, Dir.
Description: Promotes the hobby of collecting Pre-1953 Korean postcards. Educates members about the Korean heritage, its culture and tradition before it was divided into North and South. **Affiliated With:** Deltiologists of America. **Also Known As:** Korea PC Group.

22408 ■ Post Card Collectors Club
Address Unknown since 2007
Founded: 1989. **Membership Dues:** U.S., $20 ● foreign, $25. **Description:** Individuals who collect post cards. Promotes the collection and enjoyment of post cards. Concentration is on antique postcards that show planes. **Libraries: Type:** reference. **Holdings:** 1,000; archival material, clippings, periodicals. **Subjects:** post cards relating to and showing aeronautics. **Affiliated With:** American Air Mail Society. **Publications:** *Air Log*, quarterly. **Price:** $5.00. **Advertising:** accepted.

22409 ■ Postcard History Society (PHS)
1795 Kleinfeltersville Rd.
Stevens, PA 17578-9669
Ph: (717)721-9273
E-mail: midcreek@ptd.net
Contact: Jim Ward, Owner/Publisher/Ed.
Founded: 1975. **Members:** 200. **Membership Dues:** individual, $9 (annual). **Staff:** 2. **Description:** Collectors interested in postcards and world history through the study of the postcard. Stresses the importance of observing both sides of the postcard: the picture, the stamp, the postmark, and other postal markings, and the written message. **Libraries: Type:** not open to the public. **Holdings:** 120; books, periodicals. **Subjects:** postcards. **Publications:** *Journal of the Postcard History Society*, quarterly. Contains illustrations with short articles pertaining to postcards. **Price:** included in membership dues. **Circulation:** 200.

Press

22410 ■ American Amateur Press Association (AAPA)
c/o Kenneth Rystrom, Sec.-Treas.
2951 Archer Dr.
Springfield, OH 45503-1209
Ph: (937)390-3499
E-mail: dtribby@stanfordalumni.org
URL: http://members.aol.com/aapa96/index.html
Contact: Kenneth Rystrom, Sec.-Treas.
Founded: 1936. **Members:** 250. **Membership Dues:** individual, $15 (annual). **Staff:** 1. **Budget:** $5,500. **Regional Groups:** 3. **Description:** Amateur writers and printers who publish small, non-profit journals as a hobby. Encourages and promotes the publication of such journals and maintains central mailing bureau for monthly circulation of members' works; strong elements of both old-fashioned letter press printing and desktop publishing. **Awards:** Laureates. **Frequency:** annual. **Type:** recognition. **Recipient:** for best journal, printing, essay, work of fiction, art work, and poem in annual laureate contest. **Publications:** *American Amateur Journalist*, bimonthly. Contains official reports and articles of interest. **Price:** included in membership dues. ISSN: 1046-0470. **Circulation:** 250. **Conventions/Meetings:** annual convention (exhibits) - always summer.

22411 ■ National Amateur Press Association (NAPA)
c/o William E. Boys, Sec.-Treas.
6507 Westland Dr.
Knoxville, TN 37919
E-mail: wboys@compuserve.com
URL: http://www.amateurpress.org
Contact: Arie C. Koelewyn, Pres.
Founded: 1876. **Members:** 170. **Membership Dues:** regular, $20 (annual). **Regional Groups:** 1. **State Groups:** 2. **Multinational. Description:** Persons with an avocational interest in writing and letterpress printing. Members write for, print, and publish small amateur magazines and papers which are distributed through a central mailing bureau to other members without charge. Promotes the idea of craftsmanship in improving printing and writing techniques. Conducts occasional educational programs in printing craftsmanship. Collections of amateur papers are in the Library of Congress, Washington, DC; American Antiquarian Society (see separate entry), Worcester, MA; New York Historical Society and Special Collection Division, New York University Library. Has participated in the People to People Program and is currently engaged in contributing to displays of the U.S. Information Agency in Europe and Asia. **Publications:** *National Amateur*, quarterly. Journal. Contains organizational news and reports. Alternate Formats: online ● Membership Directory, semiannual. **Conventions/Meetings:** annual meeting.

22412 ■ United Amateur Press Association of America (UAPAA)
c/o Deborah Beachboard, Sec.-Treas.
343 SW Pacific Ave.
Chehalis, WA 98532-2925

E-mail: beachboard@localaccess.com
URL: http://uapaa.jarday.com
Contact: Jean Calkins, Pres.
Founded: 1895. **Members:** 48. **Membership Dues:** individual, $15 (annual). **Description:** Serves as a literary society for amateur and professional writers. Provides a channel for writers to have their work published, including noncommercial material. Maintains library; sponsors competitions. **Affiliated With:** American Amateur Press Association; National Amateur Press Association. **Formed by Merger of:** United Amateur Press Association; United Amateur Press Association of America. **Formerly:** (2003) United Amateur Press Association. **Publications:** *Membership List*, annual. Membership Directory ● *United Amateur*, monthly. **Price:** included in membership dues. **Conventions/Meetings:** annual conference.

Prospectors

22413 ■ Gold Prospectors Association of America (GPAA)
PO Box 891509
Temecula, CA 92589
Ph: (951)699-4749
Free: (800)551-9707
E-mail: info@goldprospectors.org
URL: http://www.goldprospectors.org
Contact: John H. McClintock, Pres.
Founded: 1968. **Members:** 84,000. **Membership Dues:** gold life, $950. **Staff:** 11. **Budget:** $100,000. **For-Profit. Description:** Recreational gold prospectors and miners. Seeks to: promote prospecting as an environmentally compatible operation; further knowledge of gold mining; help small miners attain prospecting success; has established Institute for Legislative Action to preserve the Mining Law of 1872, which upholds Americans' rights to utilize public lands for prospecting. Offers educational classes and seminars on geology, assaying and refining, gold metallurgy, and dowsing. Sponsors shows featuring equipment demonstrations, lectures, gold panning, contests, and displays. Coordinates children's services and participates in charitable programs. Operates hall of fame, maintains speakers' bureau, and sponsors competitions. Holds annual seminar. **Awards: Type:** recognition. **Recipient:** for excellence in prospecting, panning, dredging, and mucking. **Publications:** *Gold Prospector*, bimonthly. Magazine. Provides reports, new product information, lists of dealers and new members, and articles of interest. **Price:** $20.00/year in U.S.; $30.00/year outside U.S. ISSN: 0745-6344. **Advertising:** accepted ● *GPAA Mining Claims Guide* ● *Pick and Shovel Gazette*, quarterly ● *U.S. Mining Laws Handbook* ● Bulletin, periodic ● Journal, annual. **Conventions/Meetings:** Gold Show (exhibits) - 10/year.

22414 ■ Treasure Hunting Research and Information Center (TTA)
Address Unknown since 2006
Founded: 1986. **Staff:** 3. **Description:** Seeks to compile and preserve collections of literature related to treasure hunting, prospecting, lost mines, shipwrecks, and pirates. **Convention/Meeting:** none. **Libraries: Type:** reference. **Holdings:** 2,000. **Subjects:** treasure hunting, prospecting, lost mines, shipwrecks, and pirates. **Also Known As:** Treasure Trove Archives. **Publications:** *Directory of Back Issue Treasure Magazine Buyers, Sellers, and Traders* ● *Directory of Treasure Hunting, Prospecting, and Related Organizations* ● *Treasure Hunting Bibliography and Index to Periodical Articles*.

Publishing

22415 ■ EPIC - Electronically Published Internet Connection
c/o Barbara Woodward, Treas.
PO Box 2278
Glen Rose, TX 76043

E-mail: brennalyons3@mindspring.com
URL: http://www.epicauthors.com
Contact: Ms. Brenna Lyons, Pres.
Founded: 1998. **Members:** 560. **Membership Dues:** regular, $30 (annual). **Multinational. Description:** Represents published authors of e-books and print books, e-publishers, cover artists, editors, publicists, and other industry professionals. Aims to educate the public about e-books (how to buy/read them, what the industry offers, what direction its currently taking and laws that affect e-book publishing and reading), increase communication in the industry, and provide a support network for authors and industry professionals. **Libraries: Type:** reference. **Holdings:** 75; articles. **Subjects:** e-book information, model contract and red flags, laws, marketing and promotion information, e-book statistics. **Awards:** EPPIE Award. **Frequency:** annual. **Type:** trophy. **Recipient:** for e-book excellence; the most inclusive and longest-standing of its kind judged in two rounds ● New Voices Award. **Frequency:** annual. **Type:** recognition. **Recipient:** for middle and high school students who serve as excellent tools for English teachers to add to their yearly curriculum. **Computer Services:** Mailing lists, of members. **Telecommunication Services:** electronic mail, treasurer@epicauthors.com. **Conventions/Meetings:** annual EPICon - conference, with business meetings, three class tracks, editor/agent appointments, bookstore, e-Fiesta, and banquet (exhibits).

Puppets

22416 ■ Puppeteers of America (P of A)
26 Howard Ave.
New Haven, CT 06519
Ph: (203)777-4601
Free: (888)568-6235
E-mail: membership@puppeteers.org
URL: http://www.puppeteers.org
Contact: Paul Mesner, Pres.
Founded: 1937. **Members:** 2,100. **Membership Dues:** single adult, senior couple, $50 (annual) ● couple, $60 (annual) ● family, $70 (annual) ● business, company, $80 (annual) ● youth, senior, full time college student, $30 (annual) ● library, $40 (annual). **Staff:** 4. **Budget:** $200,000. **Regional Groups:** 8. **Local Groups:** 34. **Description:** Amateur and professional puppeteers, educators, recreation directors, youth leaders, therapists, children, and others interested in puppetry. Provides information, encourages performances and builds a community of people who love puppet theater. **Libraries: Type:** reference. **Subjects:** all phases of puppetry, history, performance, education. **Awards:** George Latshaw Award for Writing. **Frequency:** semiannual. **Type:** recognition. **Recipient:** for accomplishments in writing and publishing in field of puppetry ● Jim Henson Award for Innovation. **Frequency:** semiannual. **Type:** recognition. **Recipient:** for innovation in puppetry that is technological, dramaturgical or collaborative in nature ● Marjorie Batchelder McPharlin Award. **Frequency:** semiannual. **Type:** recognition. **Recipient:** for outstanding contributions by puppeteers in the field of education ● President's Award. **Frequency:** semiannual. **Type:** recognition. **Recipient:** for a member who has contributed the most to advance the art of puppetry ● Puppeteers of America Award. **Frequency:** semiannual. **Type:** recognition. **Recipient:** for contributions to the art of puppetry for person/group not immediately involved in the field ● Trustees Award. **Frequency:** semiannual. **Type:** recognition. **Recipient:** for outstanding service to the organization. **Computer Services:** database, available to members only ● mailing lists, available to members only. **Publications:** *Playboard*, bimonthly. Newsletter. Contains organization and membership news. **Price:** included in membership dues ● *Puppetry Journal*, quarterly. Dedicated to happenings in art of puppetry. **Price:** free for members. ISSN: 0033-443X. **Circulation:** 2,000. **Advertising:** accepted ● Membership Directory, annual. Helps its readers contact local guilds, puppetry centers, and over 2,000 puppetry enthusiasts. **Price:** included in membership dues.

Advertising: accepted. **Conventions/Meetings:** annual National Day of Puppetry - meeting, held in all areas of country (exhibits) - last Saturday of April ● semiannual National Puppetry Festival - festival and workshop, with performances, store (exhibits) ● semiannual Regional Festival - meeting and festival, with performances, store (exhibits).

22417 ■ UNIMA-U.S.A., American Center of the Union Internationale de la Marionnette (UNIMA-USA)
c/o Vincent Anthony, Gen. Sec.
1404 Spring St. NW
Atlanta, GA 30309-2820
Ph: (404)873-3089
Fax: (404)873-9907
E-mail: unima@mindspring.com
URL: http://www.unima-usa.org
Contact: Gretchen Van Lente, Pres.
Founded: 1966. **Members:** 550. **Membership Dues:** basic, library, $30 (annual) ● company, $50 (annual) ● couple, $40 (annual) ● student, senior, $20 (annual). **Staff:** 3. **Description:** Promotes world friendship through puppetry. Encourages international exchange of students and artists of puppetry. Strives to encourage and reward excellence in the field of puppetry. Plans conferences on international concerns of puppetry. "Bestows Citation for Excellence in the Art of Puppetry", founded by Jim Henson. **Awards:** Citation for Excellence in the Art of Puppetry. **Frequency:** annual. **Type:** recognition. **Recipient:** for excellence in the art of puppet theatre. **Publications:** *Language of the Puppet*. Book. Contains essays by 19 top puppetry performers artists & scholars. **Price:** $14.95/copy ● *Puppetry International*, semiannual. Magazine. Covers articles pertaining to World Puppetry in theater, films, and new media. **Price:** included in membership dues; $6.00 newsstand price; $13.00/year; $3.00/back issue. **Circulation:** 5,000. **Advertising:** accepted. **Conventions/Meetings:** annual meeting, held in conjunction with Puppeteers of America or Henson Festival of Puppet Theatre.

Rabbits

22418 ■ American Beveren Rabbit Club
c/o Kim Calloway, Pres.
6010 S County Rd., 100 W
Frankfort, IN 46041
Ph: (765)659-4906
E-mail: calloway@mintel.net
URL: http://www.beverens.8m.com
Contact: Kim Calloway, Pres.
Members: 30,000. **Membership Dues:** adult, $5 (annual) ● youth, $3 (annual) ● family (two adults per residence), $7 (annual). **Multinational. Description:** Promotes the domestic rabbit and cavy. **Computer Services:** Online services.

22419 ■ American Fuzzy Lop Rabbit Club (AFLRC)
c/o Muriel Keyes, Sec.
14255 SE Stephens
Portland, OR 97233
E-mail: danceswithwools@comcast.net
URL: http://users.connections.net/fuzzylop
Contact: Paula Grady, Pres.
Founded: 1985. **Members:** 550. **Membership Dues:** single, $17 (annual) ● family, $22 (annual). **Multinational. Description:** Aims to improve breeding, maintain standards, and encourage exhibitions of the American Fuzzy Lop Rabbit. **Publications:** *Fuzzy Lop*, quarterly. Newsletter. **Price:** included in membership dues.

Racing

22420 ■ Buick Street Rod Association (BSRA)
c/o Carter G. Hampton, Sr., Pres.
824 Kay Cir.
Chattanooga, TN 37421-4218

E-mail: webmaster@buickrods.org
URL: http://www.buickrods.org
Contact: Carter G. Hampton Sr., Pres.
Founded: 1993. **Members:** 800. **Membership Dues:** regular, in U.S. and Canada, $35 (annual) ● regular, outside U.S. and Canada, $50 (annual). **Multinational. Description:** Promotes 1948 and older Buick street rods and the growth of street rodding for Buick's as a hobby. **Publications:** *Preporter*, quarterly. Newsletter. **Price:** included in membership dues. **Advertising:** accepted.

22421 ■ East Coast Timing Association (ECTA)

c/o Joe Timney, Pres.
1081 Dexter Corner Rd.
Townsend, DE 19734
Ph: (302)378-3013
E-mail: jtimney@ecta-lsr.com
URL: http://www.ecta-lsr.com
Contact: Joe Timney, Pres.
Membership Dues: individual, $50 (annual) ● life, $500. **Description:** Promotes speed trials involving Bonneville style cars and motorcycles, racing head long over a full mile. **Publications:** Newsletter. **Price:** included in membership dues.

22422 ■ Kustoms of America (KOA)

c/o Jim Hibbs
2812 Lebanon Pike
Nashville, TN 37214
Ph: (615)885-1279
Fax: (615)883-5329
E-mail: jimatkoa@aol.com
URL: http://www.kustomsofamerica.com
Contact: Jim Hibbs, Contact
Founded: 1949. **Members:** 4,300. **Membership Dues:** individual, $32 (annual) ● individual, $55 (biennial) ● individual, $78 (triennial). **Description:** Works to bring Kustoms and Rods vehicles back together. **Publications:** *Styleline*, bimonthly. **Price:** included in membership dues.

22423 ■ MG Vintage Racers (MGVR)

55 Belden Rd.
Burlington, CT 06013
E-mail: mark@mgvr.org
URL: http://www.mgvr.org
Contact: Mark Palmer, Pres.
Founded: 1981. **Members:** 250. **Membership Dues:** regular (with newsletter subscription), $25 (semiannual). **Staff:** 6. **Multinational. Description:** Works to maintain camaraderie and open exchange of information among MG vintage racers; promotes MG vintage racing. **Awards:** Spirit Award. **Frequency:** annual. **Type:** recognition. **Computer Services:** database, for internal use only. **Publications:** *MG Vintage Racers' Newsletter*, quarterly. **Price:** included in membership dues. **Circulation:** 275. Alternate Formats: online.

Radio

22424 ■ Antique Wireless Association (AWA)

PO Box 421
Bloomfield, NY 14469
E-mail: awamembership@rochester.rr.com
URL: http://www.antiquewireless.org
Contact: Geoffrey Bourne, Pres.
Founded: 1952. **Members:** 4,000. **Membership Dues:** in U.S., $20 (annual) ● outside U.S., $25 (annual) ● life, in U.S., $400 ● life, outside U.S., $500. **Staff:** 30. **Regional Groups:** 2. **Multinational. Description:** Radio historians and collectors interested in documenting the history and technology of wireless, the work of its pioneers and early broadcasting, and all phases of communication. Members are primarily concerned with wireless or radio transmitting or receiving apparatus used in wireless telegraphy and/or telephony during the early years of radio broadcasting. Provides speakers' bureau. Maintains museum of 25,000 historical items. Develops and presents historical radio and radio film programs. Sponsors several historical radio meets annually. Has

compiled list of members' private museums and collections. **Libraries: Type:** reference. **Holdings:** 1,000; audio recordings, photographs, video recordings. **Subjects:** early radio (wireless), television, telegraphs. **Awards:** Houck Award. **Frequency:** annual. **Type:** recognition. **Recipient:** for outstanding documentation and presentation of historical radio. **Affiliated With:** American Association of Museums. **Absorbed:** Antique Radio Club of America. **Publications:** *AWA Review*, annual. Covers historical radio and television development. **Price:** $6.00/back issue (volumes 6, 7 and 8); $12.00/back issue (volumes 10 and 13); $14.95/back issue (volumes 14, 15 and 16); $19.95/back issue (volume 17). Alternate Formats: CD-ROM ● *Old Timer's Bulletin*, quarterly. Covers radio and television history. **Price:** included in membership dues. **Circulation:** 5,000 ● Journal, quarterly. **Price:** included in membership dues. Alternate Formats: online; CD-ROM. **Conventions/Meetings:** annual conference - always September, in Rochester, NY.

22425 ■ Friends of Old-Time Radio (FOTR)

PO Box 4321
Hamden, CT 06514
Ph: (203)248-2887
Fax: (203)281-1322
E-mail: jayhick@aol.com
Contact: Jay Hickerson, Pres.
Founded: 1976. **Members:** 500. **Description:** Serves as a loosely-formed organization of individuals who trade and collect recordings of radio shows of the past. **Awards: Type:** recognition. **Recipient:** to individuals who were active in radio between 1930 and 1960. **Publications:** *Hello Again*, bimonthly. Newsletter. **Conventions/Meetings:** annual meeting (exhibits) - always October, in Newark, NJ.

22426 ■ National Lum and Abner Society (NLAS)

c/o Tim Hollis, Sec.
81 Sharon Blvd.
Dora, AL 35062
Ph: (205)674-0101
Fax: (205)674-0190
E-mail: hollis1963@aol.com
URL: http://home.inu.net/stemple
Contact: Tim Hollis, Sec.
Founded: 1984. **Members:** 600. **Membership Dues:** individual, $15 (annual). **Description:** Individuals interested in the Lum and Abner radio series and its creators, Chester Lauck, and Norris Goff. **Libraries: Type:** reference. **Holdings:** archival material, audio recordings. **Awards:** Lum and Abner Memorial Award. **Type:** recognition. **Publications:** *Jot 'Em Down Journal*, quarterly. Newsletter. **Conventions/Meetings:** annual convention - always June, in Mena, AR.

22427 ■ North American Radio Archives (NARA)

c/o Don Aston, Sec.-Treas.
PO Box 1392
Lake Elsinore, CA 92531
Free: (888)33-AVPRO
Fax: (909)244-0022
E-mail: avpro@linkline.com
URL: http://www.avpro-otr.com
Contact: Don Aston, Sec.-Treas.
Founded: 1973. **Members:** 500. **Membership Dues:** regular, $20 (annual). **Description:** 6 Individual collectors, families, colleges, and universities. Seeks to serve the public's interest in radio history and to promote services that will create a greater appreciation and understanding of radio history. Gathers and preserves materials that serve to educate the public, such as original radio broadcasts, books, magazines, and other historical publications. **Convention/Meeting:** none. **Libraries: Type:** reference. **Holdings:** 20,000; audio recordings, books, periodicals. **Subjects:** radio shows. **Publications:** *NARA News*, quarterly. Catalog. Provides lending library information. **Price:** available to members only. **Advertising:** accepted.

22428 ■ Old Time Radio Club (OTRC)

56 Christen Ct.
Lancaster, NY 14086
Ph: (716)683-6199
E-mail: collinsjf@yahoo.com
URL: http://www2.pcom.net/robmcd
Contact: Jerry Collins, Pres.
Founded: 1975. **Members:** 80. **Description:** Admirers of "old time" radio. Promotes preservation and appreciation of historic radio programs. Serves as a clearinghouse on historic radio programming; facilitates exchange of information among members. **Libraries: Type:** reference; not open to the public. **Holdings:** audio recordings, books, clippings, video recordings. **Subjects:** radio history. **Publications:** *Illustrated Press*, monthly. Newsletter ● Makes available reel-to-reel, cassette, and video recordings. **Conventions/Meetings:** monthly meeting - first Monday, not held in July.

22429 ■ Radio Club of America (RCA)

PO Box 621074
Littleton, CO 80162
Ph: (303)948-4921
Fax: (303)972-1653
E-mail: exsec@radioclubofamerica.org
URL: http://www.radio-club-of-america.org
Contact: Philip M. Casciano, Pres.
Founded: 1909. **Members:** 1,200. **Membership Dues:** regular, $185 (annual) ● retired, $100 (annual) ● student, $30 (annual). **Staff:** 2. **Budget:** $10,000. **Regional Groups:** 4. **Description:** Represents radio executives, engineers, and amateurs. Operates museum. **Awards:** Alfred H. Grebe Award. **Type:** recognition. **Recipient:** for major contributions to the advancement of military electronic communications systems ● Allen B. DuMont Citation. **Frequency:** annual. **Type:** recognition. **Recipient:** for contributions in the field of electronics to the science of television ● Armstrong Medal. **Frequency:** annual. **Type:** medal. **Recipient:** for outstanding contribution to radio art and science ● Barry Goldwater Amateur Radio Award. **Type:** recognition. **Recipient:** for contributions to the amateur radio service ● Edgar F. Johnson Pioneer Citation. **Frequency:** annual. **Type:** recognition. **Recipient:** for members who have contributed substantially to the success and development of the club ● Fred M. Link Award. **Frequency:** annual. **Type:** recognition. **Recipient:** for contributions to the advancement and development of land-mobile radio and communications ● Henri Busignies Memorial Award. **Frequency:** annual. **Type:** recognition. **Recipient:** for contributions to the advancement of electronics for the benefit of mankind ● Jack Poppele Broadcast Award. **Frequency:** annual. **Type:** recognition. **Recipient:** for important and long-term contributions to the improvement of radio broadcasting ● Jerry B. Minter Award. **Type:** recognition. **Recipient:** for contributions to the electronics art through innovation in instrumentation, avionics, and electronics ● Lee DeForest Award. **Type:** recognition. **Recipient:** for significant contributions to the advancement of radio communications ● President's Award. **Frequency:** annual. **Type:** recognition. **Recipient:** for unselfish dedication and support to the club ● Ralph Batcher Memorial Award. **Frequency:** annual. **Type:** recognition. **Recipient:** for preserving the history of radio and electronic communications ● RCA Centenarian Award. **Frequency:** periodic. **Type:** recognition. **Recipient:** for any member attaining the age of 100 years ● Sarnoff Citation. **Frequency:** annual. **Type:** recognition. **Recipient:** for significant contributions to electronics communications ● **Type:** scholarship. **Recipient:** for electronics students ● Special Services Award. **Type:** recognition. **Recipient:** for contributions to the advancement of the club. **Formerly:** (1911) Junior Wireless Club, Limited. **Publications:** *Aerogram*, quarterly. Newsletter ● *Radio Club of America - Proceedings*, semiannual. Provides information for persons interested in the history of electronics. **Circulation:** 1,200. **Advertising:** accepted ● Membership Directory, biennial ● Yearbook, decennial. **Conventions/Meetings:** annual meeting - always November, in New York City.

22430 ■ Radio Collectors of America (RCA)
15 Walden Dr.
Walpole, MA 02081
Ph: (508)660-0923
Contact: Wayne Boenig, Sec.
Founded: 1969. **Members:** 40. **Membership Dues:** $7 (monthly). **Staff:** 5. **State Groups:** 1. **Description:** Focuses on the enjoyment, collection, and preservation of radio's heritage. Does not collect old radios nor provide radio hardware information. Maintains library of tapes and electrical transcription discs. Has copies of tapes that are distributed to libraries for the blind across the country through the Carleton E. Morse Radio Programs for the Blind and Handicapped. Accepts donations of tapes or electrical transcription discs of old radio shows in mint condition. Maintains collection of 3000 hours of radio tapes, loaned to members on a rotating basis. **Libraries: Type:** reference. **Holdings:** 2,500; audio recordings. **Subjects:** radio shows. **Programs:** Carlton E. Morse Radio Program for the Blind. **Publications:** Newsletter, monthly. **Conventions/Meetings:** monthly meeting - always fourth Thursday in Quincy, MA.

22431 ■ Society to Preserve and Encourage Radio Drama, Variety and Comedy (SPERDVAC)
PO Box 7177
Van Nuys, CA 91409-7177
Ph: (310)219-0053
Free: (877)251-5771
E-mail: sperdvac@aol.com
URL: http://www.sperdvac.org
Founded: 1974. **Members:** 1,600. **Membership Dues:** first year, $25 ● after first year, $15 (annual). **Staff:** 38. **Budget:** $50,000. **Regional Groups:** 1. **State Groups:** 1. **Local Groups:** 1. **Description:** Individuals and organizations active or interested in radio broadcasting. Preserves "old time" radio and promotes quality radio programming at the national and local levels. Works to preserve radio programs and research materials beginning with radio of the 1920s. Honors individuals who participated in early radio or in the encouragement of new and written history of radio. **Libraries: Type:** reference. **Holdings:** 20,000; audio recordings, papers. **Subjects:** radio programs, radio shows. **Awards: Type:** grant. **Recipient:** to noncommercial radio stations that promote "old time" radio ● Radio Pioneer Award. **Type:** recognition. **Publications:** Radio Gram, monthly. Bulletin. **Circulation:** 2,000. **Advertising:** accepted ● Radiogram, monthly. Newsletter. Includes society updates and information on radio personalities. **Price:** included in membership dues. **Circulation:** 2,000. **Advertising:** accepted. Alternate Formats: CD-ROM ● Reprints ● Also publishes radio logs and scripts. **Conventions/Meetings:** annual dinner (exhibits) - always November, Los Angeles, CA ● monthly meeting - always second Saturday, Los Angeles, CA.

22432 ■ Vintage Radio and Phonograph Society (VRPS)
PO Box 165345
Irving, TX 75016
Ph: (972)353-4862 (972)222-3828
E-mail: president@vrps.org
URL: http://www.vrps.org
Contact: James Sargent, Pres.
Founded: 1974. **Members:** 500. **Membership Dues:** regular, in U.S., Canada, Puerto Rico, and Mexico, $17 (annual) ● all other country, $20 (annual). **Description:** Early ham operators, radio instructors, engineers, television support personnel. Promotes the preservation of early radios, phonographs, and telegraphs. Sponsors periodic lectures on restoration projects, auctions, and restoration contest. **Awards: Type:** recognition. **Formerly:** Southwest Vintage Radio and Phonograph Society. **Publications:** The Reproducer, annual. Newsletter. **Price:** included in membership dues. ISSN: 0742-9088. **Circulation:** 500. **Advertising:** accepted. Alternate Formats: online ● Soundwaves, monthly. Newsletter. Covers member activities; contains calendar of events. **Price:** included in membership dues. **Circulation:** 500. Ad-

vertising: accepted. Alternate Formats: online. **Conventions/Meetings:** annual convention, with auctions (exhibits) - 2007 Nov. 16-18, Mesquite, TX ● semiannual meet ● monthly meeting - always third Saturday in Irving, TX ● annual Spring Auction - meeting.

Railroads

22433 ■ Bridge Line Historical Society (BLHS)
PO Box 13324
Albany, NY 12212
E-mail: president@bridge-line.org
URL: http://bridge-line.org
Contact: Dave Roberts, VP
Founded: 1990. **Members:** 750. **Membership Dues:** CP rail employee/Soo/D&H, $23 (annual) ● regular, $25 (annual) ● corporate/sustaining, $55 (annual) ● family, $29 (annual). **Staff:** 15. **Description:** Preserves and documents the history and activities of the Delaware and Hudson Railroad. Sponsors educational programs. **Libraries: Type:** reference. **Holdings:** archival material. **Subjects:** Delaware and Hudson Railroad. **Awards:** Marv Davis Award. **Frequency:** annual. **Type:** recognition. **Recipient:** for outstanding service to organization. **Publications:** Bulletin, monthly. Contains current and historical railroad information. **Price:** included in membership dues; $3.00/issue for nonmembers. **Circulation:** 1,000. **Conventions/Meetings:** annual festival and convention (exhibits) - usually September or October ● annual meeting - usually spring ● meeting - 5/year.

22434 ■ Central Electric Railfans' Association (CERA)
PO Box 503
Chicago, IL 60690
Ph: (312)346-3723
E-mail: cerabook@flash.net
URL: http://www.cera-chicago.org
Contact: Jeff Wien, VP
Founded: 1938. **Members:** 1,600. **Membership Dues:** active, $35 (annual) ● associate, $27 (annual). **Description:** Hobbyists interested in history, equipment, and operation of urban, rapid transit, suburban, interurban, trunk line, and industrial electric railways. Publishes books, holds monthly meetings and conducts occasional inspection trips. **Publications:** Books, annual. Covers electric railway history, which include photos, maps, and rosters of equipment. **Conventions/Meetings:** monthly meeting - always fourth Friday except July and August, in Chicago, IL.

22435 ■ Mid-Continent Railway Historical Society (MCRHS)
PO Box 358
North Freedom, WI 53951
Ph: (608)522-4261
Free: (800)930-1385
Fax: (608)522-4490
E-mail: inquiries@midcontinent.org
URL: http://www.midcontinent.org
Contact: Jeff Bloohm, Pres.
Founded: 1959. **Members:** 700. **Membership Dues:** regular, $35 (annual). **Staff:** 3. **Budget:** $525,000. **State Groups:** 36. **Description:** Preserves railroad equipment from the 1885-1925 era representative of what was used by railroads of the upper Midwest of the U.S; restores rolling stock to as original an appearance as is realistically possible; operates a steam passenger train in the style and manner of a turn-of-the-century shortline railroad; creates, with new and used material, an authentic turn-of-the-century short-line railroad environment to complement the historic steam train operation; displays, artifacts that relate to the history, skills, equipment, and lore of the railroad industry. **Libraries: Type:** reference. **Holdings:** 1,000; artwork, photographs, video recordings. **Subjects:** railroad industry. **Computer Services:** Mailing lists. **Departments:** Building and Grounds; Car; Communications; Curator; Development; Engineering; Gift Shop; Marketing; Mechanical; Membership; Operating. **Formerly:** (1963)

Railway Historical Society of Milwaukee. **Publications:** Mid-Continent Railway Gazette, quarterly. Magazine. Covers Midwestern railroad history, especially in Wisconsin. Contains news and information for members, board minutes, and calendar of events. **Price:** included in membership dues ● Whistle on the Wind, annual. Contains calendar. **Conventions/Meetings:** annual Members' Meeting - in October.

22436 ■ Pine Creek Railroad (PCKRR)
c/o N.J. Museum of Transportation
PO Box 622
Farmingdale, NJ 07727-0622
Ph: (732)938-5524
E-mail: vicrailroad@netzero.net
URL: http://www.njmt.org
Contact: Victor Crisanto, Chm.
Founded: 1952. **Members:** 500. **Membership Dues:** senior operating, $20 (annual) ● family, $35 (annual) ● individual/junior, $15 (annual). **Staff:** 20. **Budget:** $125,000. **Description:** A division of the N.J. Museum of Transportation. Works to increase interest in the preservation of antique railway equipment. Disseminates information; conducts educational programs. Maintains working railroad display of antique equipment. Operates antique steam and diesel locomotives. Sponsors traveling A/V show and tours of facilities. Maintains library, speakers' bureau, and museum. **Libraries: Type:** not open to the public. **Holdings:** 100; books, periodicals. **Subjects:** railway history, technology, operations. **Publications:** Pine Creek RR Order Board and Trainman's Gazette, quarterly. Newsletter. **Price:** included in membership dues. **Circulation:** 500 ● Also publishes brochures and flyers. **Conventions/Meetings:** annual Christmas Express - meeting - always four weekends starting Thanksgiving weekend ● annual Easter Express - meeting - always Palm and Easter weekend ● Haunted Halloween Express, Nighttime Runs - meeting ● bimonthly meeting - always third Saturday of odd months ● annual Railroaders Weekend - meeting - always Saturday and Sunday after Labor Day.

22437 ■ Railroadiana Collectors Association Incorporated (RCAI)
c/o Bob James, Pres.
17675 W 113th St.
Olathe, KS 66061
Ph: (913)541-8568
E-mail: rdmjames@swbell.net
URL: http://www.railroadcollectors.org
Contact: Bob James, Pres.
Founded: 1971. **Members:** 1,000. **Membership Dues:** regular, $30 (annual). **Regional Groups:** 8. **Description:** Individuals interested in railroadiana collecting and railroad history. Serves as a clearinghouse to establish contact between people of similar interests. Is planning to create a museum; offers specialized education programs. **Divisions:** China Group. **Publications:** Railroadiana Express, quarterly. Magazine. Contains information about all kinds of railroad artifacts in United States. ● Directory, biennial.

Recreation

22438 ■ American Lands Access Association (ALAA)
c/o Peggy Blickfeldt, Pres.
304 E 45th St.
Garden City, ID 83714
E-mail: grumpies@quixnet.net
URL: http://www.gamineral.org/alaa.htm
Contact: Peggy Blickfeldt, Pres.
Founded: 1992. **Membership Dues:** general, $25 (annual). **Description:** Promotes amateur fossil and mineral collecting, recreational prospecting and mining and the use of private lands for educational and recreational purposes. Represents the interests of all amateur collectors and hobbyists to the elected officials, the government regulators and the public land managers. **Affiliated With:** American Federation of Mineralogical Societies.

22439 ■ International Miniature Aircraft Association (IMAA)
c/o Jim Giffin, Pres./AMA Liaison
PO Box 494688
Redding, CA 96049
Ph: (916)760-8291
Fax: (530)275-8151
E-mail: 2giffs@msn.com
URL: http://www.fly-imaa.org
Contact: Jim Giffin, Pres./AMA Liaison
Founded: 1980. **Members:** 155,000. **Membership Dues:** regular in U.S., Canada, Mexico, $20 (annual) ● rest of the world, $30 (annual) ● life - below 45 years old, $400 ● life - 45 to 50 years old, $350 ● life - 51 to 55 years old, $300 ● life - 56 to 65 years old, $250 ● life - over 65 years old, $200. **Multinational.** **Description:** Advances the operation of large scale radio controlled model aircraft in a setting where informality and safety operation prevail. Provides a forum for individuals interested in building and flying large scale radio controlled model aircraft. **Awards:** IMAA Distinguished Services Award. **Type:** recognition. **Recipient:** for outstanding contribution to the founding, development and promotion of the organization. **Computer Services:** database, chapters' addresses. **Publications:** High Flight, quarterly. Newsletter.

22440 ■ North American Stone Skipping Association (NASSA)
PO Box 189
Driftwood, TX 78619
E-mail: jmcghee@austin.rr.com
URL: http://www.yeeha.net/nassa/a1.html
Contact: Jerdone Coleman-McGhee, Contact
Founded: 1989. **Membership Dues:** regular-complete, $15 (annual). **Multinational.** **Description:** Promotes stone skipping as a natural non-competitive recreation and as an internationally standardized competitive sport. Organizes and oversees international competitions. **Computer Services:** Information services, stone skipping trivia.

Recreational Vehicles

22441 ■ Alpenlite Travel Club (ATC)
PO Box 1726
Clackamas, OR 97015
Ph: (503)698-4461
Fax: (503)698-5521
E-mail: alpenliteclub@aol.com
URL: http://www.wrv.com/html/alpen_club_about.html
Contact: Jerry Millspaugh, Contact
Founded: 1986. **Membership Dues:** regular, $52 (annual) ● regular, $71 (biennial). **Description:** Represents Western Recreational Vehicle RV owners. Aims to promote fun, friendship and fellowship. Conducts rallies and caravans. **Additional Websites:** http://www.alpenlitetravelclub.com. **Publications:** The Traveling Echo, bimonthly. Newsletter. **Circulation:** 2,000. **Advertising:** accepted. **Conventions/Meetings:** annual Alpenfest - party.

22442 ■ Alpine Coach Association
5808 A Summitview Ave., No. 337
Yakima, WA 98908
Ph: (509)457-0729
E-mail: kwattsaca@aol.com
URL: http://www.alpinecoach.com/html/alpine_assoc_about.html
Contact: Kay Watts, Sec.
Membership Dues: charter, $47 (annual). **Description:** Association for individuals owning Western Recreational Vehicles. **Publications:** Newsletter, quarterly. **Conventions/Meetings:** annual Homecoming - rally.

22443 ■ American Clipper Owners Club (ACOC)
1880 Countrywood Ct.
Walnut Creek, CA 94598
E-mail: webmaster@americanclipper.com
URL: http://www.americanclipper.com/acoc.htm
Contact: Dr. Robert Cornwell, Exec. Off.
Founded: 1982. **Members:** 469. **Membership Dues:** regular, $20 (annual). **Regional Groups:** 6. **Descrip-tion:** Owners of American Clipper motorhomes and others interested in American Clipper. Provides information useful in maintaining, preserving, and enjoying the Clipper motorhome. Locates parts suppliers; has arranged remanufacture of certain parts. **Publications:** The Clipper Journal, bimonthly. Newsletter. **Conventions/Meetings:** rally - 3/year.

22444 ■ Antique Snowmobile Club of America (ASCOA)
c/o Dave Guenther
32832 County Rd. 39
Pequot Lakes, MN 56472-3722
Ph: (218)543-4146
E-mail: ascoa921@tds.net
URL: http://www.ascoa.org
Contact: John McGuirk, Pres.
Founded: 1976. **Members:** 2,100. **Membership Dues:** regular, $20 (annual). **For-Profit.** **Description:** Persons owning antique snowmobiles. Aims to collect, restore, exhibit, and compete with antique snowmobiles. Makes available for races and shows. **Libraries:** **Type:** reference. **Subjects:** manufacturers' specifications on snowmobiles manufactured prior to 1968. **Awards:** Founders Award. **Frequency:** annual. **Type:** recognition ● Jake Woekner Award. **Frequency:** annual. **Type:** recognition. **Publications:** Iron Dog Tracks, bimonthly. Newsletter. **Price:** $15.00/year. **Circulation:** 1,500. **Advertising:** accepted ● Iron Dog Tracks Magazine ● Bulletin, periodic. **Conventions/Meetings:** semiannual meeting and seminar - always mid-summer and winter ● Winter Enduro - competition.

22445 ■ Avion Travelcade Club
43430 E Florida Ave., Ste.F, PMB 297
Hemet, CA 92544
Ph: (951)927-5902
E-mail: jcavion@juno.com
Contact: Carol Davis, Exec.Sec.
Founded: 1960. **Members:** 900. **Membership Dues:** $35 (annual). **Staff:** 1. **State Groups:** 28. **Description:** Avion RV owners. United to find fellowship and take inexpensive tours.

22446 ■ Beaver Ambassador Club (BAC)
c/o Iris Schmidt, Membership Dir.
3590 Round Bottom Rd.
Cincinnati, OH 45244-3026
Free: (800)445-1732
E-mail: iris.bac@mac.com
URL: http://www.beaveramb.org
Contact: Iris Schmidt, Membership Dir.
Membership Dues: general, $40 (annual). **Description:** Beaver RV owners. Promotes fellowship and cooperation among family motor coach owners. Provides rally activities and conducts other functions. **Affiliated With:** Family Motor Coach Association. **Publications:** BeaverTales, quarterly. Newsletter.

22447 ■ Escapees
100 Rainbow Dr.
Livingston, TX 77351
Ph: (936)327-8873
Free: (888)757-2582
Fax: (936)327-4388
E-mail: clubbusiness@escapees.com
URL: http://www.escapees.com
Contact: Cathie Carr, CEO
Founded: 1978. **Members:** 65,000. **Membership Dues:** regular, $60 (annual) ● initial fee, $70. **Staff:** 90. **State Groups:** 50. **For-Profit.** **Description:** Support network for RVers who travel for extensive periods. Offers short and long term parking at private RV parks, mail and message service, and discounts on affiliated services. Operates speakers' bureau, educational seminars, and compiles statistics on RV lifestyles for research. Affiliated with Escapees CARE, Inc. the first adult day care facility to provide special assistance to RVers. **Libraries:** **Type:** reference. **Holdings:** 11; books, periodicals. **Subjects:** how to travel via recreational vehicles. **Awards:** President's Award. **Frequency:** annual. **Type:** recognition. **Recipient:** for an outstanding volunteer. **Committees:** Rallies. **Publications:** Encyclopedia for RVers. Book. **Price:** $13.00 ● Escapees Discount Parks Directory, annual. **Price:** included in membership dues. **Circulation:** 50,000. **Advertising:** accepted ● Escapees: Magazine for RV'ers, bimonthly. Contains articles on maintenance, book reviews, chapter news, tech articles, how-to articles, product evaluations, and research reports. **Price:** included in membership dues. **Advertising:** accepted ● Escapees—Membership Directory, annual. **Circulation:** 10,000 ● Full-Time RVing: Is It for You?. Booklet ● Handbook for Escapees' Members. Lists benefits of membership, maps and directions to 18 parks, general club information. **Price:** included in membership dues. **Circulation:** 70,000. **Advertising:** accepted ● Home Is Where You Park It. Book. Contains information on RV travel and lifestyle. **Price:** $13.00 ● Survival of the Snowbirds. Book. Deals with RV travel and lifestyle. **Price:** $13.00 ● Thoughts for the Road. Book. Features a collection of inspiring stories with a message. **Price:** $13.00 ● Travel While You Work. Book. Contains information for finding part-time work while traveling. **Price:** $11.00. **Conventions/Meetings:** periodic Chapter Rallies - rally, held in various geographical areas of the U.S., Canada, and Mexico; social events, idea sharing, fun ● Escapade - seminar and lecture, on RVing (exhibits) - 3/year; April, July, September.

22448 ■ Family Motor Coach Association (FMCA)
8291 Clough Pike
Cincinnati, OH 45244
Ph: (513)474-3622
Free: (800)543-3622
Fax: (513)474-2332
E-mail: bsd@fmca.com
URL: http://www.fmca.com
Contact: Don Moore, Pres.
Founded: 1963. **Members:** 95,000. **Membership Dues:** full/family, $45 (annual) ● renewal, $35 (annual). **Staff:** 50. **Budget:** $8,000,000. **Regional Groups:** 340. **Description:** Owners of motor homes used for recreation, travel, and camping. Qualifying vehicles must be self-propelled and self-contained, including all the conveniences of a home (cooking, sleeping, and sanitary facilities), and in which the driver's seat is accessible in a walking position from the living quarters. Aids local chapters and members with information on safety, product analysis, special activities, and news of other members. **Publications:** Family Motor Coaching, monthly. Magazine. Contains travel features and technical information on motor coach mechanics. Includes some association news and calendar of events. **Price:** included in membership dues; $30.00 /year for nonmembers. **ISSN:** 0360-3024. **Circulation:** 100,000. **Advertising:** accepted. **Alternate Formats:** online ● Membership Directory, annual. **Conventions/Meetings:** semiannual National Motorhome Convention (exhibits) - always March and August.

22449 ■ Georgie Boy Owners' Club
PO Box 198
Osceola, IN 46561-0198
Ph: (574)258-0571
Free: (800)262-5178
Fax: (574)259-7105
E-mail: clubs@recclub.com
URL: http://www.georgieboyrvclub.com
Founded: 1986. **Members:** 2,500. **Membership Dues:** individual, $25 (annual) ● individual, $45 (biennial) ● individual, $65 (triennial). **Staff:** 1. **Description:** George Boy RV owners. Activities include international rallies and caravans, state and regional rallies, and local outings planned by the local chapters across the country. **Publications:** The World, quarterly. Newsletter. **Circulation:** 5,000. **Advertising:** accepted. **Alternate Formats:** online. **Conventions/Meetings:** rally (exhibits).

22450 ■ Good Sam Recreational Vehicle Club (GSRVC)
PO Box 6888
Englewood, CO 80155-6888
Free: (800)234-3450

E-mail: info@goodsamclub.com
URL: http://www.goodsamclub.com
Founded: 1966. **Members:** 970,000. **Membership Dues:** individual, $19 (annual) ● individual, $32 (biennial) ● individual, $45 (triennial). **State Groups:** 57. **Local Groups:** 2,300. **For-Profit. Description:** Recreational vehicle enthusiasts who act as "Good Samaritans" on the road by aiding members in distress. Offers free benefits to members, including credit card loss protection, trip routing service, and mail forwarding. Provides comprehensive discount programs on camping fees, RV financing and insurance, tour programs, emergency road service and magazine subscriptions for members. Conducts charitable program. **Publications:** *CyberSam,* monthly. Newsletter. Keeps members up-to-date on subjects focusing on Good Sam Club news. **Price:** included in membership dues. Alternate Formats: online ● *Highways,* monthly. Magazine. Contains information on issues of concern to all RVers. **Price:** included in membership dues. **Advertising:** accepted ● *RV Campground and Services Directory,* annual. **Conventions/Meetings:** annual Samboree - rally (exhibits).

22451 ■ Handicapped Travel Club (HTC)
c/o Roland Winters, Jr., Pres.
604 Twilight St.
Placentia, CA 92870
Ph: (714)524-2700
E-mail: president@handicappedtravelclub.com
URL: http://www.handicappedtravelclub.com
Contact: Roland Winters Jr., Pres.
Founded: 1973. **Members:** 250. **Membership Dues:** $8 (annual). **Staff:** 5. **Budget:** $2,500. **Regional Groups:** 3. **State Groups:** 35. **Description:** Disabled individuals and interested able-bodied persons who travel throughout the U.S. Encourages handicapped people to travel; facilitates interaction among disabled individuals; provides for travel and association among campers. **Libraries: Type:** reference. **Holdings:** articles, business records, photographs. **Awards:** Lifetime Membership. **Frequency:** periodic. **Type:** recognition. **Subgroups:** Local Chapter. **Publications:** *Handicapped Travel Club Newsletter.* **Price:** free for members. Alternate Formats: online. **Conventions/Meetings:** annual National Rally - meeting - 2007 Sept. 19-23, San Dimas, CA.

22452 ■ HitchHikers of America International
PO Box 180
Osceola, IN 46561
Ph: (574)258-0571
Fax: (574)259-7105
E-mail: clubs@recclub.com
URL: http://www.hitchhikerrvclub.com
Contact: Marv Niehoff, Founder
Founded: 1993. **Members:** 2,000. **Membership Dues:** individual, $25 (annual) ● individual, $45 (biennial) ● individual, $65 (triennial). **Staff:** 1. **Description:** Represents owners of HitchHiker brand RVs. Works for the enjoyment of all owners. Participates in stationery rallies, caravans and many other outings. **Publications:** *Thumbs Up,* quarterly. Newsletter. **Conventions/Meetings:** rally (exhibits).

22453 ■ Holiday Rambler Recreational Vehicle Club (HRRVC)
PO Box 587
600 E Wabash
Wakarusa, IN 46573
Ph: (574)862-7330
Free: (877)702-5415
Fax: (574)862-7390
E-mail: hrclub@monacohr.com
URL: http://www.hrrvc.org
Contact: Linda Moran, COO
Founded: 1964. **Members:** 22,000. **Membership Dues:** new, $45 (annual) ● new, $110 (triennial). **Staff:** 5. **Budget:** $600,000. **Regional Groups:** 8. **State Groups:** 49. **Local Groups:** 300. **National Groups:** 5. **Description:** Represents owners of recreational vehicles manufactured by Holiday Rambler Corp. Sponsors social and recreational activities such as rallies, caravans, and tour groups. Offers a scholarship program and children's services;

sponsor competitions. Conducts seminars, workshops, and management leadership training. **Awards: Type:** scholarship. **Affiliated With:** RV Manufacturers' Clubs Association. **Publications:** *Holiday Ramblings,* 8/year. Magazine. Contains club information and member profiles. **Circulation:** 16,000. **Advertising:** accepted. Alternate Formats: CD-ROM; online ● Membership Directory, annual. **Conventions/Meetings:** annual rally (exhibits).

22454 ■ Jayco Travel Club
PO Box 192
Osceola, IN 46561-0192
Ph: (574)258-0571
Free: (800)262-5178
Fax: (574)259-7105
URL: http://www.jaycorvclub.com
Founded: 1968. **Members:** 2,125. **Membership Dues:** regular, $25 (annual) ● regular, $45 (biennial) ● regular, $65 (triennial). **Staff:** 5. **Local Groups:** 100. **Description:** Owners of Jayco recreational vehicles. Provides social events for members, such as rallies, caravans, and campouts. **Formerly:** (2006) Jayco Jafari International Travel Club. **Publications:** *Hitch,* quarterly. Newsletter. **Price:** free. **Conventions/Meetings:** annual Family Reunion and Factory Rally.

22455 ■ Loners of America (LOA)
Rte. 2, Box 2495E
Ellsinore, MO 63937-9536
E-mail: loa-mo@semo.net
Founded: 1987. **Members:** 1,450. **Membership Dues:** $40 (annual). **Staff:** 1. **State Groups:** 30. **Description:** Legally single individuals who enjoy camping and traveling. Promotes fellowship for singles pursuing RV (recreational vehicle) lifestyles or enjoying camping. Organizes campouts and annual rallies. **Publications:** *LOA Membership Directory,* semiannual ● *Loners of America News,* monthly. Newsletter. Contains information on campouts and rallies, clubs news, membership activities, and travel tips. **Price:** included in membership dues ● Brochure. **Conventions/Meetings:** annual National Rally and Membership Meeting - meeting and rally, includes five-day campout.

22456 ■ Loners on Wheels (LOW)
PO Box 1060 - WB
Cape Girardeau, MO 63702
Free: (888)569-4478
Fax: (573)651-8601
E-mail: lonersreply@clas.net
URL: http://www.lonersonwheels.com
Contact: Barb Schow, Pres.
Founded: 1969. **Members:** 2,800. **Membership Dues:** regular, $45 (annual). **Staff:** 6. **Budget:** $90,000. **Regional Groups:** 50. **For-Profit. Description:** Single persons, particularly retirees, who own and travel in recreational vehicles, such as trailers, campers, and motor homes. Provides support and companionship for members while respecting their desire to be alone. Provides local camp-outs and rallies, member news, invitations to visit and park, tips on RV maintenance, and other items helpful to campers, travelers, and dancers. Conducts charitable activities. **Publications:** *Supplementary Directory,* monthly ● Newsletter, monthly. Includes meeting dates and places. **Price:** included in membership dues. **Circulation:** 2,800. **Advertising:** accepted ● Membership Directory, annual. **Conventions/Meetings:** annual meeting.

22457 ■ National African-American RV'ers Association (NAARVA)
1426 W 29th St., Ste.201
Indianapolis, IN 46208
Free: (877)221-2238
E-mail: anne.steele@naarva.com
URL: http://www.naarva.com
Contact: Anne B. Shearer Steele PhD, Pres.
Founded: 1993. **Members:** 1,400. **Membership Dues:** individual, family, $50 (annual). **Local Groups:** 50. **Description:** Promotes camping in recreational vehicles as a way of life and as another means for families to have fun. Provides members special

services, rallies and unique camping environment. Enables members to meet and interact with other RV'ers that share common interests. **Publications:** *The NAARVA Voice.* Newsletter. Alternate Formats: online. **Conventions/Meetings:** annual rally.

22458 ■ National Association of Trailer Owners (NATO)
Address Unknown since 2007
Founded: 1956. **Members:** 600. **Membership Dues:** $70 (annual). **Staff:** 4. **For-Profit. Description:** Mail forwarding for owners of travel trailers, campers, and motor homes; boaters, and people on the go. **Computer Services:** mail forwarding. **Publications:** *Scene Magazine,* monthly. Civic, social and cultural events in the Southwest Florida area. **Price:** $3.00. **Advertising:** accepted.

22459 ■ National Recreational Vehicle Owners Club (NRVOC)
Jack's Br. Rd.
PO Box 520
Gonzalez, FL 32560-0520
Ph: (850)937-8354
Free: (800)281-9186
Fax: (850)937-8356
E-mail: nrvockws@spydee.net
Contact: K.W. Stephens, Natl.Dir.
Founded: 1983. **Members:** 30,684. **Membership Dues:** individual/family, $25 (annual) ● commercial, $100 (annual). **Staff:** 8. **Budget:** $440,000. **Regional Groups:** 8. **State Groups:** 2. **Local Groups:** 7. **National Groups:** 5. **Description:** Recreational vehicle owners; manufacturers, distributors, dealers, and RV park/resort, RV rental and storage owners. Provides service and technical information for those involved with the use or manufacture of recreational vehicles. Supports legislation advantageous to owners and users. Reviews and evaluates RV products. Conducts leadership training and volunteer instruction programs. Organizes rallies, caravans, tours, and cruises. Maintains speakers' bureau; offers charitable program; compiles statistics. **Awards:** Member of the Year. **Frequency:** annual. **Type:** recognition. **Recipient:** member selection by peers. **Affiliated With:** International Family Recreation Association; Recreation Vehicle Industry Association. **Formerly:** (2003) National RV Owners Club. **Publications:** *Living the RVing Lifestyle,* 5/year. Includes club news, calendar of events, legislative news, and member profiles. **Price:** included in membership dues; $20.00 /year for nonmembers. **Circulation:** 23,821. **Advertising:** accepted ● *The NRVOC Update,* monthly. Newsletter ● *Recreation Advisor,* 5/year. Published in conjunction with International Family Recreation Association. **Conventions/Meetings:** competition ● annual rally (exhibits) ● workshop, recreational vehicle use.

22460 ■ RV Manufacturers' Clubs Association (RVMCA)
413 Walnut St.
Green Cove Springs, FL 32043-3443
Ph: (904)529-6575
Free: (866)GO-RVMCA
Fax: (904)284-4472
E-mail: send@rvmcamail.com
URL: http://www.rvmcamail.com
Contact: Jeff Vander Vliet, Pres.
Founded: 1974. **Members:** 24. **Membership Dues:** regular, $25 (annual). **Staff:** 40. **Description:** Directors of manufacturer-supported clubs of recreational vehicle owners. Seeks to keep members informed on current trends in RVing and to foster the interchange of ideas concerning safety, finding suitable campgrounds and rally sites, and increasing membership. Exchanges information on how to organize rallies. Conducts campground surveys. **Formerly:** (1980) KDK; (1991) Recreational Vehicle Club Directors Association. **Publications:** Newsletter, quarterly. **Price:** free ● Magazine, monthly. **Conventions/Meetings:** annual conference (exhibits) ● periodic seminar.

22461 ■ RVing Women (RVW)
PO Box 1940
Apache Junction, AZ 85217-1940
Ph: (480)671-6226
Free: (888)557-8464

Fax: (480)671-6230
E-mail: rvingwomen@juno.com
URL: http://www.rvingwomen.org
Contact: Judy Bozman, Office Mgr.
Founded: 1991. **Members:** 4,000. **Membership Dues:** individual, $45 (annual). **Staff:** 2. **Budget:** $275,000. **Regional Groups:** 2. **State Groups:** 9. **Local Groups:** 1. **Description:** Women with an interest in recreational vehicles. Promotes participation by women in recreational vehicle-related activities. Conducts educational programs. **Publications:** Magazine, bimonthly. **Circulation:** 4,000. **Advertising:** accepted. Alternate Formats: diskette; CD-ROM ● Also publishes Annual Directory of members and Discount Providers Directory. **Conventions/Meetings:** annual Make History in York - convention (exhibits) ● rally - 50/year ● periodic trade show.

22462 ■ Supreme Travel Club
PO Box 191
Osceola, IN 46561
Ph: (574)258-0571
Free: (800)262-5178
Fax: (574)259-7105
E-mail: clubs@recclub.com
URL: http://supremetravelrvclub.com
Founded: 1994. **Members:** 1,000. **Membership Dues:** individual, $25 (annual) ● individual, $45 (biennial) ● individual, $65 (triennial). **Staff:** 1. **Description:** Travel Supreme RV owners. Formed to add enjoyment to RV travels. Conducts rallies, caravans, as well as local chapter activities. **Publications:** Travelers Journal, quarterly. Newsletter. **Conventions/Meetings:** rally (exhibits).

22463 ■ Vagabundos Del Mar RV, Boat and Travel Club
190 Main St.
Rio Vista, CA 94571
Ph: (707)374-5511
Free: (800)474-2252
Fax: (707)374-6843
E-mail: info@vagabundos.com
URL: http://www.wbcci.com
Contact: Fred Jones, VP/Gen. Mgr.
Founded: 1971. **Members:** 10,000. **Membership Dues:** regular, $35 (annual). **Staff:** 1. **Multinational. Description:** Works to share, learn and extend RV travels, and boating fun. Organizes many outings, caravans, and many other activities. **Publications:** Chubasco, monthly. Newsletter.

22464 ■ Wally Byam Caravan Club International (WBCCI)
PO Box 612
Jackson Center, OH 45334
Ph: (937)596-5211
Fax: (937)596-5542
E-mail: creed@wbcci.org
URL: http://www.wbcci.org
Contact: Ms. Cindy Reed, Corporate Mgr.
Founded: 1955. **Members:** 14,000. **Membership Dues:** regular, $55 (annual) ● member-at-large, $70 (annual). **Budget:** $600,000. **Regional Groups:** 12. **Local Groups:** 175. **Description:** Owners of classic Airstream travel trailers and motor homes. Aims are to: provide a satisfying and meaningful travel experience; promote international goodwill; encourage development of outdoor recreational vehicle facilities. Maintains code of ethics for trailer traveling; sponsors unit, regional, national, and international rallies. (Named for Wally Byam, original builder and developer of the Airstream trailer and pioneering leader of Airstream caravans). **Committees:** Caravans; Ethics; International Relations; Legislative; Public Relations. **Publications:** Blue Beret, 10/year ● Directory, annual. **Conventions/Meetings:** annual International Rally - always June 27-July 4.

22465 ■ Winnebago-Itasca Travelers (WIT)
PO Box 268
Forest City, IA 50436-0268
Ph: (641)585-6874
Free: (800)643-4892
Fax: (641)585-6703

E-mail: witclubnews@winnebagoind.com
URL: http://www.winnebagoind.com/clubs/wit
Founded: 1970. **Members:** 19,000. **Staff:** 16. **State Groups:** 45. **Local Groups:** 196. **For-Profit. Description:** Owners of recreational vehicles manufactured by Winnebago Industries, Inc. Seeks for the mutual enjoyment of their vehicles, travel opportunities, new friendships, and activities. Conducts caravans; operates store. **Absorbed:** (1982) Winnebago/Itasca Travelers. **Formerly:** (1987) Winnebago International Travelers. **Publications:** Club News, monthly. Magazine. **Circulation:** 18,400. **Advertising:** accepted ● Membership Directory, annual. **Conventions/Meetings:** competition ● annual Grand National Rally (exhibits) - always Forest City, IA.

Reiki

22466 ■ International Center for Reiki Training (ICRT)
21421 Hilltop St., Unit 28
Southfield, MI 48034
Ph: (248)948-8112
Free: (800)332-8112
Fax: (248)948-9534
E-mail: center@reiki.org
URL: http://www.reiki.org
Contact: William Lee Rand, Pres./Founder
Founded: 1988. **Multinational. Description:** Dedicated to the re-establishment of Reiki energies in the modern world. **Computer Services:** database, Reiki classes. **Publications:** The Book on Karuna Reiki. **Price:** $25.25 ● Japanese Reiki Techniques Workshop. Video. **Price:** $30.00 ● Reiki News, quarterly. Magazine. Contains articles on Reiki. **Price:** $17.00/year in U.S.; $20.00/year in Canada; $25.00/year outside U.S. and Canada. **Advertising:** accepted. Alternate Formats: online ● Reiki Quarterly. Newsletter ● Reiki, The Healing Touch - Workshop Manual. **Price:** $18.95 ● Sacred Reiki Sites of Japan. Video. **Price:** $28.75 ● Spirit of Reiki. Book. **Price:** $19.75 ● Spiritual Healing, Scientific Validation of a Healing Revolution. Book. **Price:** $30.95.

Roller Coasters

22467 ■ American Coaster Enthusiasts (ACE)
1100-H Brandywine Blvd.
Zanesville, OH 43701-7303
Ph: (740)450-1560
Fax: (740)452-2552
E-mail: webmaster@aceonline.org
URL: http://www.ACEonline.org
Contact: Carole Sanderson, Pres.
Founded: 1978. **Members:** 8,000. **Membership Dues:** individual, $60 (annual) ● couple, $80 (annual) ● family, $85 (annual) ● corporate, $90 (annual). **Staff:** 2. **Budget:** $500,000. **Regional Groups:** 26. **Description:** Represents roller coaster enthusiasts interested in history, preservation, and present day operation of roller coasters. Purposes are to: promote, organize, and increase the appreciation of the roller coaster; encourage study and exchange of information by serving as a clearinghouse for data and statistics, designer information, and park updates; develop art of coaster model building, photography, and coaster postcard collecting; aid individual park owners and coaster operators in design decisions. Seeks to save vintage wood coasters from demolition. Establishes an amusement park/roller coaster museum that will contain permanent exhibits, photograph galleries, models, coaster cars, and a rehabilitation workshop. Compiles statistics. **Libraries: Type:** by appointment only. **Holdings:** 25,000. **Subjects:** roller coasters, amusement parks. **Committees:** Archives; Census; Events; Historical; Information Services; Legal; Merchandise; Preservation; Public Relations; Publications; Regional Representative; Registration. **Affiliated With:** International Association of Amusement Parks and Attractions. **Publications:** ACE News, bimonthly. Newsletter. **Price:** included in membership dues. **Circulation:** 4,000. **Advertising:** accepted ● Guide to Ride, periodic.

Magazine. Serves as a guide to North American roller coasters. Includes photos and statistics. **Price:** $20.00 ● International Roller Coaster Census, annual. Directory. **Price:** included in membership dues ● Rollercoaster!, quarterly. Magazine. **Price:** included in membership dues. **Circulation:** 4,000. **Advertising:** accepted. **Conventions/Meetings:** annual Coaster Con - convention and conference (exhibits) ● annual conference.

Sand Castles

22468 ■ International Association of Sand Castle Builders (IASCB)
Address Unknown since 2007
Founded: 1988. **Members:** 200. **Staff:** 1. **Description:** Beach enthusiasts and seashore environment advocates promoting interest in the art of sand castle building worldwide. Provides support and assistance to people engaged in or seeking to become engaged in sand castle building; furthers understanding of the impact humans have on beaches. Maintains speakers' bureau. **Libraries: Type:** reference. **Holdings:** archival material, artwork, clippings. **Subjects:** sand sculpture. **Also Known As:** International Brotherhood of Silica Structure Engineers.

22469 ■ World Sand Sculptors Association
Address Unknown since 2007
Founded: 1991. **Staff:** 10. **Description:** Individuals interested in creating mythical creatures, castles, and other sculptures from sand. Holds sand sculpting competitions; sponsors charitable and educational programs. **Libraries: Type:** reference. **Holdings:** artwork, books, business records, clippings, periodicals. **Subjects:** architecture, sculpture.

Shooting

22470 ■ Fifty Caliber Shooters Association (FCSA)
PO Box 111
Monroe, UT 84754-0111
Ph: (435)527-9245
Fax: (435)527-0948
E-mail: membership@fcsa.org
URL: http://www.fcsa.org
Founded: 1985. **Members:** 3,500. **Membership Dues:** regular, affiliated organization, $40 (annual) ● active military personnel, $20 (annual) ● associate, $10 (annual) ● foreign, $50 (annual) ● life - USA (over 65 years old), $500 ● life - USA (under 65 years old); life - foreign (over 65 years old), $700 ● life - foreign (under 65 years old), $900. **Multinational. Description:** Seeks to unite all persons interested in the .50 BMG cartridge. Advances the sporting uses of the .50 BMG cartridge. Provides research and education to the military, the law enforcement agencies and the public about the .50 BMG cartridge. **Computer Services:** Information services, fifty caliber resources ● information services, schedule of matches ● online services, visitors forum. **Affiliated With:** National Rifle Association of America. **Publications:** Magazine, quarterly.

Special Days

22471 ■ African American Holiday Association (AAHA)
PO Box 43255
Washington, DC 20010
Ph: (202)667-2577
E-mail: aaha@aaha-info.org
Contact: Ayo Handy Kendi, Founder/Dir.
Founded: 1989. **Description:** Perpetuates and preserves culture through traditional and non-traditional holidays, celebrations and rituals. **Telecommunication Services:** electronic mail, info@aaha-info.org.

22472 ■ Golden Glow of Christmas Past
c/o Robert W. Dalluge
6401 Winsdale St.
Golden Valley, MN 55427
E-mail: terryweesner@sbcglobal.net
URL: http://www.goldenglow.org
Contact: Robert W. Dalluge, Contact
Founded: 1980. **Members:** 1,138. **Membership Dues:** US, $45 (annual) ● Canadian, $50 (annual) ● foreign, $55 (annual) ● US, $90 (biennial) ● Canadian, $100 (biennial) ● foreign, $110 (biennial) ● US, $125 (triennial) ● Canadian, $140 (triennial) ● foreign, $155 (triennial). **Multinational. Description:** Represents the interests of collectors of antique Christmas ornaments. Provides a forum for individuals interested in pre-1966 Christmas decorations, including ornaments, Santas, lighting, tinsel, snowmen, feather trees, snow babies and post cards. **Publications:** *The Glow*, bimonthly, in February, April, June, August, October, December. Newsletter. **Price:** included in membership dues.

Sports

22473 ■ American Airgun Field Target Association (AAFTA)
c/o Steve Schulz, Sec.-Treas.
7223 Barnett Rd.
Bethesda, MD 20817
E-mail: steve@acqlog.com
URL: http://www.aafta.org
Contact: Cliff Smith, Chm.
Membership Dues: individual, club, $25 (annual). **Description:** Promotes the Field Target shooting clubs in the United States. Establishes rules and guidelines for competitions. Assists affiliated clubs in conducting regional and national competitions. **Computer Services:** database, club listing ● online services, forum. **Telecommunication Services:** electronic mail, csmith57@tampabay.rr.com. **Publications:** Newsletter, periodic. Features local, regional and international events throughout the shooting season. Alternate Formats: online.

Steam Engines

22474 ■ International Stationary Steam Engine Society (ISSES)
c/o Rick Rowlands, Membership Sec.
2261 Hubbard Rd.
Youngstown, OH 44505
Ph: (330)728-2799
URL: http://www.isses.org
Contact: Geoff Hayes, Pres.
Founded: 1991. **Members:** 250. **Membership Dues:** regular, $20 (annual) ● reduced (senior/student), $27 (annual) ● affiliated society, $33 (annual). **Staff:** 13. **National Groups:** 2. **Description:** Represents active and retired steam power engineers, museum and preservation specialists, students, model builders and hobbyists. Aims to study the history, design, and operation of stationary and marine reciprocating steam engines. Recognizes the role of these engines in industrial history; encourages their preservation. **Computer Services:** database, surviving stationary steam engines in the U.S., Canada, and Great Britain. **Formed by Merger of:** Stationary Engine Society; British Stationary Engine Research Group. **Publications:** *I.S.S.E.S Newsletter*. Contains information on urgent visits to engine sites. **Advertising:** accepted. Alternate Formats: online ● *International Stationary Steam Engine Society Bulletin*, quarterly. Includes information on steam engines in United States, Canada, Great Britain, and other countries. **Price:** $30.00/year ● *Stationary Power*, annual. Journal. Includes research articles on steam power. **Price:** $20.00/year.

22475 ■ Northwest Steam Society (NSS)
c/o Wolfgang Schlager, Pres.
3618 Seeley St.
Bellingham, WA 98226-4368
Ph: (360)647-5112

Fax: (360)647-8876
E-mail: nw-steamboats@comcast.net
URL: http://www.northweststeamsociety.org
Contact: Wolfgang Schlager, Pres.
Founded: 1973. **Members:** 280. **Membership Dues:** regular, $20 (annual). **Languages:** English, German. **Description:** Individuals with a hobby or job that involves steam apparatus, including steamboats, cars, railroads, or models; those whose interest in steam engines is historical. Works to increase members' knowledge of steam technology. Sponsors work sessions and instructions by experts; principal competitions are in steamboat activities such as class racing, "Tug-O-War," and handicap races. Holds annual Steam Gathering. **Awards:** Bill Dessert Trophy. **Frequency:** annual. **Type:** trophy. **Recipient:** to a member who has made an exceptional contribution to the organization or the hobby ● George Ives Trophy. **Frequency:** annual. **Type:** trophy. **Recipient:** to a member who has made an exceptional contribution to the organization or the hobby. **Publications:** *Membership Roster*, annual. Membership Directory. **Price:** free for members. **Advertising:** accepted ● *Steam Gage*, quarterly. Newsletter. **Conventions/Meetings:** annual Membership Meeting - meeting and dinner - always February ● annual Steamboat Meeting - always first weekend of August.

22476 ■ Rough and Tumble Engineers' Historical Association (R&T)
PO Box 9
Kinzers, PA 17535-0009
Ph: (717)442-4249
E-mail: info@roughandtumble.org
URL: http://www.roughandtumble.org
Contact: Warren Wolf, Pres.
Founded: 1948. **Members:** 1,500. **Membership Dues:** individual, $20 (annual) ● family, $25 (annual) ● life, $200. **Budget:** $135,000. **Description:** Individuals interested in old gas and steam engines and farm machinery. "Rough and Tumble" engineers operate saw mills, threshers, road rollers, and other machinery. Maintains museum of antique farm and home equipment, much of it still in working condition. **Awards:** Boy Scout Merit. **Frequency:** annual. **Type:** scholarship. **Publications:** *Demonstrating Show Days*, 8/year ● *The Whistle*, quarterly. Newsletter. **Price:** included in membership dues. **Circulation:** 2,000. **Conventions/Meetings:** semiannual Exposition - meeting (exhibits) - always May and October, Kinzers, PA ● annual reunion and competition - always August, Kinzers, PA.

22477 ■ Steamship Historical Society of America (SSHSA)
1029 Waterman Ave.
East Providence, RI 02914
Ph: (401)274-0805
Fax: (401)274-0836
E-mail: sewen@sshsa.org
URL: http://www.sshsa.org
Contact: Robert C. Cleasby, Pres.
Founded: 1935. **Members:** 2,900. **Membership Dues:** individual, $40 (annual). **Staff:** 2. **Budget:** $200,000. **Regional Groups:** 10. **Description:** Represents professional and amateur historians, collectors, and others interested in steam or other power-driven vessels, past and present. Maintains photo bank (100,000 photos). **Libraries:** Type: open to the public. **Holdings:** 5,000; articles, books, periodicals. **Subjects:** marine subjects. **Formerly:** (1940) American Steamship Historical Society. **Publications:** *Steamboat Bill*, quarterly. Journal. Features articles on the history and present day engine powered vessels, includes book reviews. **Price:** included in membership dues; $30.00 /year for libraries. ISSN: 0039-0844. **Circulation:** 5,000. **Advertising:** accepted. Alternate Formats: microform ● Pamphlets. **Conventions/Meetings:** semiannual convention ● semiannual meeting.

Stone

22478 ■ International Meteorite Collectors Association (IMCA)
c/o Ken Newton, Treas.
115 Maple Ave. N
Lehigh Acres, FL 33936-6482

E-mail: ken@imca.cc
URL: http://www.meteoritecollectors.org
Contact: Ken Newton, Treas.
Membership Dues: general, $20 (annual). **Multinational. Description:** Promotes the collection of authentic meteorites. Upholds the standards of meteorite identification and proper labeling practices. **Computer Services:** Information services, meteorite resources ● mailing lists ● online services, forum.

Swine

22479 ■ National Show Pig Association (NSPA)
c/o Jeff Langemeier, Sec.-Treas.
8737 E 2700th Rd.
Sidell, IL 61876
Ph: (217)493-8037 (620)327-2280
Fax: (620)327-4394
E-mail: aschrag@sunglofeeds.com
URL: http://nationalshowpig.org
Contact: Allen Schrag, Pres.
Membership Dues: youth, $20 (annual) ● breeder, associate, $100 (annual) ● boar stud and feed company, corporate, $1,000 (annual). **Description:** Provides leadership and support to youth who are interested in Show Pig competition. Enhances the youth experiences and opportunities in the Show Pig industry. **Telecommunication Services:** electronic mail, hipoint_jeff@ccsdana.net.

Tarot

22480 ■ American Tarot Association (ATA)
2901 Richmond Rd., Ste.130, No. 123
Lexington, KY 40509-1763
Free: (800)372-1524
Fax: (800)331-7787
E-mail: info@ata-tarot.com
URL: http://www.ata-tarot.com
Contact: Rickey Hite, Membership Coor.
Members: 700. **Membership Dues:** M1, regular mail delivery of ATA newsletter, $30 (annual) ● M2, regular mail delivery of ATA newsletter, $50 (biennial) ● M3, regular mail delivery of ATA newsletter, $70 (triennial) ● I1, Internet mail delivery of ATA newsletter, $20 (annual) ● I2, Internet mail delivery of ATA newsletter, $35 (biennial) ● I3, Internet mail delivery of ATA newsletter, $50 (triennial). **Multinational. Description:** Works to bring together qualified students, teachers and masters of the Tarot, who are willing to subscribe to a high ethical standard, and use the Tarot for the benefit of those for whom they read. Recognizes Tarot as a useful tool for personal growth and spiritual development. **Publications:** *A Mystical System for Reading Tarot*. **Price:** $10.00 via Internet; $15.00 via mail; $15.00 audiotape or CD; $30.00 book and tape or CD ● *A Numerological System for Reading Tarot*. **Price:** $10.00 via Internet; $15.00 via mail; $15.00 audio tape or CD-Rom; $30.00 book and tape or CD-Rom ● *Advanced Tarot Correspondence Course Book*. **Price:** $10.00 via email; $15.00 via mail; $40.00 audio course; $50.00 book and audio ● *An Astrological System for Reading Tarot*. **Price:** $10.00 via Internet; $15.00 via mail; $15.00 audio tape or CD; $30.00 book and tape or CD ● *ATA Quarterly*. Newsletter. **Price:** free for members. **Advertising:** accepted. Alternate Formats: online ● *Intermediate Tarot Correspondence Course Book*. **Price:** $10.00 via Internet; $15.00 via mail; $40.00 audio course (CD or tape); $50.00 book and audio ● *Introduction to Tarot Correspondence*. Book. **Price:** $10.00 via Internet; $15.00 via mail; $40.00 audio (CD or tape); $50.00 book and audio. Alternate Formats: online ● *Tarot Reflections*, monthly. Newsletter. **Price:** free. Alternate Formats: online.

Telegraphy

22481 ■ Morse Telegraph Club (MTC)
c/o Roger Reinke, International Sec.-Treas.
5301 Neville Ct.
Alexandria, VA 22310

Ph: (703)971-4095
E-mail: rwreinke@cox.net
URL: http://www.morsetelegraphclub.org
Contact: Roger Reinke, International Sec.-Treas.
Founded: 1942. **Members:** 2,400. **Membership Dues:** individual, $16 (annual). **Local Groups:** 38. **Description:** Persons proficient or interested in the use of Morse or International code. Perpetuates the tradition of the telegraph profession. Educates members on the use of Morse and International codes; preserves names and records of persons who participated in the development of the telegraph. **Publications:** *Dots and Dashes*, quarterly. Newspaper. Features historical articles and information about telegraphy, with emphasis on landline operation. Contains mailbag and new member listings. **Price:** included in membership dues. **Circulation:** 2,700. **Conventions/Meetings:** semiannual meeting - last Saturday of spring and fall.

Telephones

22482 ■ Antique Telephone Collectors Association (ATCA)
PO Box 1252
McPherson, KS 67460
Ph: (620)245-9555
E-mail: office@atcaonline.com
URL: http://www.atcaonline.com
Contact: Cindy Goldsmith, Office Mgr.
Founded: 1971. **Members:** 1,500. **Membership Dues:** regular, in U.S., $35 (annual) ● regular, in Canada and other country, $40 (annual) ● spousal associate, student (under 18), $10 (annual). **Staff:** 2. **Multinational. Description:** Collectors of antique telephones. Seeks to: promote the collecting of old telephones and related items; publicize the historical significance of the telephone; establish and promote common courtesies and guidelines for members to use when buying, selling, and trading old telephones and equipment. Acts as a means for communication among members. Associated with Museum of Independent Telephony. **Libraries: Type:** reference. **Holdings:** 500. **Awards:** Best in Show in Five Different Categories. **Frequency:** semiannual. **Type:** recognition. **Computer Services:** Online services, listserv resource for members. **Publications:** *Antique Telephone Collectors Association Information Guide for Perspective Members.* Brochure. Covers membership. Contains membership application. ● *Antique Telephone Collectors Association Newsletter*, monthly. Includes information on new members, regional shows and exhibits, and educational information; buy, sell and trade information. **Advertising:** accepted ● *ATCA Membership List*, annual. Membership Directory ● Also publishes other literature. **Conventions/Meetings:** semiannual show (exhibits) - spring and fall.

22483 ■ Telephone Collectors International (TCI)
3805 Spurr Cir.
Brea, CA 92823
Ph: (801)849-6520
Fax: (801)849-6520
E-mail: info@telephonecollectors.org
URL: http://www.telephonecollectors.org
Founded: 1986. **Members:** 450. **Membership Dues:** postal in U.S., $36 (annual) ● postal outside U.S., $44 (annual) ● electronic worldwide, $25 (annual) ● postal in Canada and Mexico, $36 (annual). **Description:** Promotes public education regarding the history of telephony; researches telephone history. Encourages exhibition of antique telephones. **Awards:** Best Phone and Best Display of Show. **Frequency:** biennial. **Type:** trophy. **Special Interest Groups:** Switchers' Quarterly. **Publications:** *Singing Wires*, monthly. Newsletter. Includes photos and articles on antique to retro telephones. **Price:** $35.00/year. **Circulation:** 600. **Advertising:** accepted ● *Switcher's Quarterly*. Newsletter. **Conventions/Meetings:** biennial Antique Telephone Show, displays of antique phones (exhibits).

Textiles

22484 ■ Brazilian Dimensional Embroidery International Guild (BDEIG)
c/o Juanita Chase, Membership Chair
3729 191st Pl. SW
Lynnwood, WA 98036
E-mail: jchasern@comcast.net
URL: http://www.brazilian-dimensional-embroidery.org
Contact: Juanita Chase, Membership Chair
Founded: 1991. **Members:** 400. **Membership Dues:** US bulk mail/e-mail, $30 (annual) ● US first class/Canada, $34 (annual) ● overseas airmail, $40 (annual). **Multinational. Description:** Promotes the art of Brazilian embroidery. Helps members, teachers and students achieve high standards of excellence in Brazilian embroidery. Encourages the knowledge and use of Brazilian embroidery. Promotes positive interaction among those who do Brazilian embroidery. **Awards:** Judy Jensen Award. **Frequency:** annual. **Type:** recognition. **Recipient:** to embroiderers for their outstanding contributions to the guild ● **Frequency:** annual. **Type:** scholarship. **Recipient:** for guild members. **Publications:** Newsletter, quarterly. **Price:** included in membership dues. Alternate Formats: online.

Timepieces

22485 ■ International Watch Fob Association (IWFA)
601 Patriot Pl.
Holmen, WI 54636
Ph: (608)385-7237
E-mail: info@watchfob.com
URL: http://www.watchfob.com
Contact: Louise Harting, Sec.-Treas.
Founded: 1965. **Members:** 700. **Membership Dues:** individual, $15 (annual) ● junior, $10 (annual). **Staff:** 6. **Regional Groups:** 4. **Description:** Collectors of strap-type watch fobs. Encourages and promotes the study of fobs; fosters interest of youth in the subject. Acquires and distributes watch fob information; demonstrates the educational and recreational aspects of fob collecting. Programs include annual spring show for collectors to display, trade, buy, and sell fobs. **Awards: Type:** recognition. **Recipient:** for best displays. **Committees:** Judging; Show. **Publications:** *Membership List*, semiannual, January and June. Newsletter. **Price:** included in membership dues. **Advertising:** accepted ● Newsletter, semiannual. **Conventions/Meetings:** annual meeting (exhibits) - usually Cleveland, OH, area.

22486 ■ National Association of Watch and Clock Collectors (NAWCC)
514 Poplar St.
Columbia, PA 17512-2124
Ph: (717)684-8261 (717)684-5544
Fax: (717)684-0878
E-mail: shumphrey@nawcc.org
URL: http://www.nawcc.org
Contact: Mr. J. Steven Humphrey, Exec. Dir.
Founded: 1943. **Members:** 25,000. **Membership Dues:** individual, $65 (annual) ● additional household, $20 (annual). **Staff:** 37. **Budget:** $2,362,791. **Regional Groups:** 175. **Description:** Collectors, historians, craftsmen, dealers, and others interested in timekeeping devices and horology. Seeks to preserve Horological data, to prepare information about the mechanics of timepieces and their repair, and to aid members in buying or selling watches, clocks, and related items. Offers a clock and watch repair program. **Libraries: Type:** reference. **Holdings:** 28,000. **Subjects:** horology. **Awards: Type:** recognition. **Computer Services:** database, horological ● database, membership listing. **Publications:** *Mart of the NAWCC*, bimonthly. Magazine. Serves as an advertising tabloid for members' horological items. **Price:** included in membership dues. **Circulation:** 30,000. **Advertising:** accepted ● *NAWCC Bulletin*, bimonthly. Magazine. Contains

historical, technical, and how-to articles on clocks, watches, and other items related to the study of time. Includes chapter news. **Price:** included in membership dues. ISSN: 0027-8688. **Circulation:** 30,000. **Conventions/Meetings:** annual Crafts Contest - competition, held in conjunction with the Annual National Convention (exhibits) ● annual seminar.

22487 ■ Self Winding Clock Association (SWCA)
c/o Dr. Bengt Honning
1161 E Marcellus St.
Long Beach, CA 90807-1609
Ph: (562)422-5158
Contact: Dr. Bengt E. Honning PhD, Pres./Libn.
Founded: 1979. **Members:** 250. **Membership Dues:** $25 (annual). **Staff:** 4. **Local Groups:** 1. **Languages:** English, German, Khmer, Swedish. **Description:** Individuals and corporations who are members of the National Association of Watch and Clock Collectors and who are interested in the preservation and promotion of historical horological information, particularly the preservation of information about the Self Winding Clock Company, which operated in New York from 1886 to 1971. Maintains speakers' bureau and museum; compiles statistics. 1996 - Physical Science and Math Library donated, catalogued, available to members Jan. 1997. **Libraries: Type:** reference. **Holdings:** 2,300; periodicals. **Subjects:** horology, chemistry, physics. **Awards:** The SWCA Report. **Frequency:** annual. **Type:** recognition. **Recipient:** for best original research paper published in the *Catalyst*. **Computer Services:** database, available to members only ● mailing lists, PNT mailing. **Committees:** European Liaison; Manuscript. **Affiliated With:** National Association of Watch and Clock Collectors. **Formerly:** (1990) SWCA Library. **Publications:** *Catalyst*, quarterly. Journal. Contains research articles on clock mechanisms and electrical horology, historical data, and electric/battery clock manufacturers. **Price:** included in membership dues. **Circulation:** 200 ● *Membership Roster*, annual. **Price:** available to members only ● Also publishes research papers, available to members only. **Conventions/Meetings:** annual conference - always Long Beach, CA ● annual seminar and convention, horological & scientific (related) exhibits (exhibits) - always Long Beach, CA.

Toys

22488 ■ A.C. Gilbert Heritage Society (ACGHS)
9 Bristol Knoll Rd.
Newark, DE 19711
E-mail: president@acgilbertheritagesociety.com
URL: http://www.acgilbertheritagesociety.com
Contact: Klon Smith, VP
Founded: 1991. **Members:** 400. **Membership Dues:** regular, $25 (annual). **Staff:** 12. **Budget:** $6,000. **Regional Groups:** 7. **Description:** Collects and distributes historical facts and information about the life, inventions, and products of the A. C. Gilbert Co. (The A. C. Gilbert Co. produced mainly scientific toys from the early 1900s through the 1960s, including Erector sets.) Restores Gilbert scientific and educational toys; compiles statistics. **Libraries: Type:** reference. **Holdings:** 100; archival material, books, monographs, periodicals. **Subjects:** inventions, products of the A.C. Gilbert Co. **Awards: Frequency:** periodic. **Type:** recognition. **Recipient:** for outstanding service or accomplishments. **Publications:** Newsletter, quarterly. **Price:** included in membership dues; $2.50/back issue. **Circulation:** 440. **Advertising:** accepted. **Conventions/Meetings:** annual meeting, with scientific toys of A.C. Gilbert Co., except A.F. trains (exhibits).

22489 ■ Antique Toy Collectors of America (ATCA)
Crescent Springs
Covington, KY 41017
E-mail: hettinger@fuse.net
Contact: Susan Hettinger, Sec.
Founded: 1965. **Members:** 300. **Description:** Activities include the research, study and documentation

of antique toys and toy manufacturers. Does not respond to research questions from nonmembers, and does not honor requests to assess the value of toys. Also cannot help in selling toys. Applicants for membership must be sponsored by current members. Contact through email only. **Committees:** Education. **Publications:** *Toy Chest*, 3-4/year. **Price:** available to members only ● Pamphlets ● All publications are available to members, libraries, and museums. Nonmembers should email for list of publications for sale.

22490 ■ Etch-A-Sketch Club
c/o The Ohio Art Co.
1 Toy St.
PO Box 111
Bryan, OH 43506-0111
Ph: (419)636-3141
Free: (800)641-6226
E-mail: info@ohioart.com
URL: http://www.etch-a-sketch.com
Founded: 1976. **Members:** 2,700. **Membership Dues:** regular, in U.S., $4 (triennial) ● regular, outside U.S., $5 (triennial). **Description:** Fans and collectors of Etch-A-Sketch drawing toys. **Publications:** *Etch A Sketch Newsletter*, quarterly. **Price:** included in membership dues. **Advertising:** accepted.

22491 ■ Fisher-Price Collector's Club (FPCC)
1442 N Ogden
Mesa, AZ 85205
E-mail: gasper_b@bellsouth.net
URL: http://www.fpclub.org
Contact: Jacquie Hamblin, Contact
Founded: 1993. **Members:** 200. **Membership Dues:** ordinary, $20 (annual) ● international, $25 (annual). **Multinational. Description:** Represents admirers of toys manufactured by the Fisher-Price Company. Promotes collection and restoration of Fisher-Price toys. Serves as a clearinghouse on Fisher-Price toys and their collection; conducts educational programs; participates in charitable activities. **Awards:** Caring and Sharing Award. **Frequency:** periodic. **Type:** recognition. **Publications:** *Gabby Goose*, 3/year. Newsletter. **Advertising:** accepted. **Conventions/Meetings:** annual convention and festival - always August in East Aurora, NY.

22492 ■ GI Joe Collectors' Club
225 Cattle Baron Parc
Fort Worth, TX 76108
Ph: (817)448-9863
Fax: (817)448-9843
E-mail: brian@mastercollector.com
URL: http://www.mastercollector.com
Contact: Brian Savage, Ed.
Founded: 1986. **Members:** 7,800. **Membership Dues:** individual, in U.S., $36 (annual) ● individual, in Canada, $57 (annual) ● individual, outside U.S. and Canada, $82 (annual). **Description:** Collectors of GI Joe memorabilia. Teaches and informs collectors about the GI Joe doll. Sponsors competitions; produces conventions, author of 3 books on GI Joe; maintains hall of fame and museum. **Libraries: Type:** reference. **Holdings:** books. **Awards:** GI Joe Fan. **Type:** recognition. **Recipient:** for fans. **Additional Websites:** http://www.gijoeclub.com. **Publications:** *Master Collector*, monthly. Newsletter. **Price:** included in membership dues ● *The New Official Guide to GI Joe, 1964-1978*. Book. **Price:** $20.00. **Conventions/Meetings:** annual GI Joe Convention (exhibits).

22493 ■ Toy Car Collectors Association (TCCA)
c/o Dana Johnson Enterprises
PO Box 1824
Bend, OR 97709-1824
Ph: (541)318-7176
E-mail: toynutz@earthlink.net
URL: http://www.toynutz.com
Contact: Mr. Dana Johnson, Chm.
Founded: 1993. **Members:** 60. **Membership Dues:** regular, in U.S., $29 (annual) ● regular, in Canada and Mexico, $39 (annual) ● international (other than Canada & Mexico), $49 (annual) ● regular, in U.S., $54 (biennial) ● regular, in Canada and Mexico, $74 (biennial) ● international (other than Canada &

Mexico), $94 (biennial) ● regular, in U.S., $79 (triennial) ● regular, in Canada and Mexico, $109 (triennial) ● international (other than Canada and Mexico), $139 (triennial). **Staff:** 1. **Multinational. Description:** Provides an international resource center for collectors of diecast, white metal, cast iron, tinplate, resin and other automotive toys and ready-built models worldwide. **Libraries: Type:** not open to the public; reference. **Holdings:** 100; archival material, books, periodicals, photographs, software. **Subjects:** diecast toys, pressed steel, tin, white metal, promo models, automotive toys and models. **Computer Services:** database, listings of retail sources, manufacturers, publications, clubs, auction houses, collector checklists and other services ● online services, worldwide resource center for toy car collectors. **Special Interest Groups:** online discussion group. **Formerly:** (1997) North American Diecast Toy Collectors Association; (2001) Diecast Toy Collectors Association. **Publications:** *TCCA Resource Directory*, annual. Booklet. Provides the latest news about new models and old favorites. **Circulation:** 200. **Advertising:** accepted ● *Toy Car Collector*, bimonthly. Magazine. Features articles and photos of old and new automotive toys and models of all kinds. **Price:** included in membership dues. **Circulation:** 60. **Advertising:** accepted, Also Cited As: *TCCM* ● *Toy Car Collector's Guide*, every 2-3 years. Book. **Price:** $20.00 ● Siku Toys of Germany. Tomica-Japan's Best Diecast Toys.

22494 ■ Toy Stitchers International, Inc. (TSII)
c/o Sharon Tedrow, Pres.
66434 E Bay Rd.
North Bend, OR 97459
E-mail: toystitchers@earthlink.net
URL: http://toystitchers.tripod.com
Contact: Sharon Tedrow, Pres.
Founded: 2002. **Membership Dues:** in U.S., $40 (annual) ● outside U.S., $45 (annual). **Multinational. Description:** Promotes interest in and appreciation of collecting toy sewing machines. Unites all toy sewing machine collectors. Promotes collecting toy sewing machines as a unique and valuable hobby. Raises awareness and appreciation of collecting toy sewing machines. Encourages research and provides information about toy sewing machines. **Publications:** *The Toy Stitcher*, quarterly. Newsletter ● Membership Directory, annual.

22495 ■ Toy Stores Steiff Collectors Club (TSSCC)
c/o The Toy Store Collectors Gallery
Westgate Village
3301 W Central Ave.
Toledo, OH 43606
Ph: (419)531-2839
Free: (800)862-8697
Fax: (419)531-2730
E-mail: info@toystorenet.com
URL: http://www.toystorenet.com
Contact: Beth Savino, Ed.
Founded: 1982. **Members:** 2,500. **Membership Dues:** individual, in U.S., $15 (annual) ● individual, outside U.S., $20 (annual). **Staff:** 3. **Budget:** $5,000. **Description:** Collectors and enthusiasts of Steiff toys. Disseminates collector and historical information on Steiff toys. Collects bears, gollys, and figurines. **Publications:** *Collector's Life*, quarterly. Newsletter. **Price:** $15.00 in U.S.; $20.00 outside U.S. **Circulation:** 2,500. **Alternate Formats:** online. **Conventions/Meetings:** annual Festival of Steiff - meeting and convention, includes antique dealers, auction, and sales (exhibits).

22496 ■ Treasures for Little Children (TLC)
c/o Marion Steinbrunner, Treas.
PO Box 118
Chardon, OH 44024
E-mail: webmaster@treasuresforlittlechildren.com
URL: http://www.treasuresforlittlechildren.com
Contact: Marion Steinbrunner, Treas.
Founded: 1992. **Members:** 250. **Membership Dues:** individual, family, $35 (annual). **Description:** Represents collectors interested in children's antique toy dishes, glassware, furniture, and toy kitchens and

related items. Offers information on acquiring, researching, protecting, and displaying these collectibles. **Formerly:** (1999) Toy Dish Collectors. **Publications:** *Tiny Times*, quarterly. Newsletter. Contains informative articles, pictures, for sale and want section, news. **Price:** included in membership dues. **Conventions/Meetings:** annual convention and meeting, with lecturers, auction, sales room (exhibits) - third or fourth weekend of July.

Tractors

22497 ■ Antique Engine, Tractor, and Toy Association (AETTA)
c/o David C. Semmel
5731 Paradise Rd.
Slatington, PA 18080-4028
Ph: (610)767-4768
Contact: David C. Semmel, Contact
Founded: 1986. **Members:** 500. **Membership Dues:** individual, $6 (annual). **Budget:** $10,000. **Description:** Individuals with an interest in antique tractors, engines, and farm toys. Promotes study and collection of antique farm equipment and farm toys. Conducts educational programs. No museum. **Publications:** Newsletter, quarterly. **Price:** included in membership dues. **Circulation:** 500. **Conventions/Meetings:** monthly board meeting - always third Wednesday of each month, except December ● annual Club Show (exhibits) - Bowers, PA ● monthly meeting.

22498 ■ International Harvester Collectors (IHC)
c/o Bill Swope, Pres.
4731 Liberty Hi Rd.
Cygnet, OH 43413-9778
Ph: (419)655-2945
E-mail: wls_ihc_w6@hotmail.com
URL: http://members.aol.com/ihcollectors
Contact: Bill Swope, Pres.
Founded: 1990. **Members:** 5,000. **Membership Dues:** regular in U.S., $15 (annual) ● regular outside U.S., $25 (annual). **State Groups:** 28. **Description:** Owners and admirers of farm machinery produced by International Harvester. Promotes preservation and restoration of International Harvester equipment. Facilitates communication among members; serves as a clearinghouse on International Harvester tractors and other farm equipment. **Awards:** IHCC Scholarship. **Frequency:** annual. **Type:** scholarship. **Recipient:** to members, children or grandchildren of members. **Publications:** *Harvester Highlights*, quarterly. Magazine. Contains club news, history, ads 50 plus pages, and color photos. **Price:** included in membership dues. **Circulation:** 5,000. **Advertising:** accepted ● *Red Power Round-Up*, annual. Book. Features full color photo documentation of nearly all the exhibits attending the Roundups. **Price:** $25.00/copy. **Conventions/Meetings:** annual convention - always winter ● annual Red Power Round-up - convention and show, antique IH machinery, tractors and trucks (exhibits) - always summer.

22499 ■ National Antique Tractor Pullers Association (NATPA)
c/o Jerry Leek, Pres.
1020 W Steels Corners Rd.
Cuyahoga Falls, OH 44223
Ph: (330)929-0940
URL: http://www.natpa.com
Contact: Jerry Leek, Pres.
Founded: 1995. **Membership Dues:** puller, promoter, $40 (annual) ● social, $30 (annual) ● tractor, $10 (annual). **Description:** Promotes antique tractor pulling. Makes rules for competitions and the safety of antique tractor pulling. **Committees:** Safety.

22500 ■ Two-Cylinder Club
PO Box 430
Grundy Center, IA 50638-0430
Ph: (319)824-6060
Free: (888)782-2582
Fax: (319)824-2662

E-mail: twocyl@iowatelecom.net
URL: http://www.two-cylinder.com
Contact: Jack Bible, Dir.
Founded: 1981. **Members:** 24,000. **Membership Dues:** in U.S. and Canada, $32 (annual) ● outside U.S., $49 (annual). **Description:** Individuals interested in tractors manufactured by John Deere prior to 1973, collectors of John Deere memorabilia. Seeks to preserve and restore antique John Deere tractors and accessories. Assists members in obtaining technical information. **Formerly:** Two-Cylinder Worldwide. **Publications:** *Two-Cylinder*, bimonthly. Magazine. **Price:** $25.00/year. ISSN: 0899-2258. **Circulation:** 24,000. **Advertising:** accepted. Alternate Formats: diskette; CD-ROM. **Conventions/Meetings:** annual Tractor Expo - show, restores antique tractors and implements; travels throughout the country (exhibits).

Transportation

22501 ■ American Vecturist Association (AVA)
c/o Richard Mallicote, Sec.
655 Wintergate Ct.
Alpharetta, GA 30022-5584
URL: http://www.vecturist.com
Contact: Richard Mallicote, Sec.
Founded: 1948. **Members:** 800. **Membership Dues:** regular, in U.S., $22 (annual) ● regular, in Canada, $25 (annual) ● regular, outside U.S. and Canada, $33 (annual). **Staff:** 2. **Budget:** $20,000. **Description:** Collectors of transportation fare tokens as used currently or historically on railroads, street cars, buses, ferries, toll roads, and vehicular and foot bridges. (Vecturist stems from a Latin term meaning passage money.) Promotes general knowledge of the history of urban and intercity transit through a study of metal fare tokens issued by various transportation firms; preserves such tokens and catalog them. Conducts educational programs; compiles statistics. **Libraries: Type:** not open to the public. **Holdings:** 500. **Awards:** The Fare Box Literary Award. **Frequency:** annual. **Type:** recognition. **Publications:** *Atwood- Coffee Catalogue of U.S. and Canadian Transportation Tokens*, 5/year. Catalogs. Lists transportation and parking tokens. **Price:** $100.00/3 Volumes. **Circulation:** 2,500 ● *The Fare Box*, monthly. Newsletter ● Membership Directory, annual. **Conventions/Meetings:** annual convention and conference (exhibits) - 2nd weekend in August.

22502 ■ The Monorail Society (TMS)
36193 Carnation Way
Fremont, CA 94536-2641
E-mail: monorailsociety@comcast.net
URL: http://www.monorails.org
Contact: Kim Pedersen, Pres./Founder
Founded: 1989. **Members:** 4,500. **For-Profit. Multinational. Description:** Engineers, monorail operators, mechanics, manufacturers, and individuals interested in the history, present day operation, and future of the monorail. Promotes the single rail transport system as a low cost, safe, efficient transportation alternative. Encourages study and exchange of information; provides a clearinghouse for dissemination of statistics and data. Develops photograph and video documentation; collects monorail postcards and souvenirs. **Libraries: Type:** reference. **Holdings:** biographical archives. **Awards: Type:** recognition. **Recipient:** for outstanding achievement in the advancement of monorail transit.

22503 ■ National Association of Timetable Collectors (NAOTC)
PO Box 217
Bethpage, NY 11714-0217
E-mail: crts@worldnet.att.net
URL: http://www.rrhistorical-2.com/naotc/index.html
Contact: John Krattinger, Contact
Founded: 1962. **Members:** 500. **Membership Dues:** regular, $20 (annual) ● contributing, individual outside U.S. and Canada, $25 (annual) ● junior (under 18), $15 (annual). **Regional Groups:** 9. **Lo-**

cal Groups: 3. **Description:** Collectors of timetables and related artifacts from railroads, airlines, steamships, and bus lines. Is presently working on a project to compile a catalog of North American timetable issues from 1829 to the present. **Awards:** William L. Wagner Memorial Award. **Frequency:** annual. **Type:** recognition. **Publications:** *The First Edition*, bimonthly. Newsletter. Contains current timetable news. ISSN: 1066-2529 ● *Timetable Collector*, quarterly. Magazine. Includes detailed feature articles and compendium information on past and present timetables. ISSN: 1066-2510 ● Directory, annual. **Conventions/Meetings:** annual meeting and show (exhibits) - always August.

Travel

22504 ■ Arab International Association for Tourism and Automobile Clubs (AIATAC)
Address Unknown since 2007
Languages: Arabic, English. **Description:** Tourism and automobile clubs. Promotes travel as a recreational and educational pastime. Provides discounts, travel information, and other support to travellers.

22505 ■ Bounders United
603 Seagaze Dr., Ste.714
Oceanside, CA 92054
Ph: (760)966-1468
E-mail: buprez@msn.com
URL: http://www.bounder.net
Contact: Patrick Towle, Pres.
Members: 2,800. **Description:** Bounder RV owners. Works to promote and facilitate the ownership and use for pleasure, of Bounder motorhomes. Conducts rally activities and other functions. **Publications:** *Bounder Sounder*, monthly. Newsletter.

22506 ■ Carriage Travel Club
PO Box 246
Millersburg, IN 46543
Ph: (574)642-3622
Free: (800)832-3632
Fax: (574)642-4146
E-mail: cotc@carriageinc.com
URL: http://www.carriageinc.com/Travclub.htm
Contact: Lucy Bontrager, Natl. Treas.
Membership Dues: individual, $25 (annual). **Description:** Represents Carriage RV owners. Promotes fellowship, friendship, and fun. Holds seasonal campouts and rallies. **Publications:** *Campin' Nooz*, bimonthly. Newsletter. **Conventions/Meetings:** Grand National Rally ● Texas National Rally.

22507 ■ Country Coach International (CCI)
PO Box 400
Junction City, OR 97448
Free: (800)537-0622
Fax: (541)998-3712
E-mail: club@countrycoach.com
URL: http://www.countrycoach.com
Contact: Jerry O'Connor, Pres.
Founded: 1984. **Members:** 2,400. **Membership Dues:** regular, $50 (annual). **Description:** Country Coach RV owners. Promotes fellowship, friendship and fun. Holds seasonal campouts and rallies. **Publications:** *Country Coach Destinations*. Magazine. **Price:** included in membership dues. **Conventions/Meetings:** annual reunion and seminar - always summer in Eugene, OR.

22508 ■ Extra Miler Club (EMC)
PO Box 31
Annandale, VA 22003-0031
E-mail: geopathman@aol.com
URL: http://www.extramilerclub.org
Contact: Reid Williamson, Sec.
Founded: 1973. **Members:** 315. **Membership Dues:** open, $12 (annual). **Staff:** 1. **Description:** Avid travelers whose goal is to visit every U.S. county and equivalent jurisdiction. Other travel goals include visiting every state capitol building, all national parks, and points of the highest and lowest elevation in each state. Distributes county outline maps. **Awards:** Extra

Miler 3142 Plaque. **Type:** recognition. **Recipient:** for visiting all 3,142 counties ● 50 States Visited Award. **Type:** recognition. **Recipient:** for visiting all 50 states ● 1000 County Award. **Type:** recognition. **Recipient:** for visiting 1000 counties ● 3000 County Award. **Type:** recognition. **Recipient:** for visiting 3000 counties ● 2000 County Award. **Type:** recognition. **Recipient:** for visiting 2000 counties. **Study Groups:** Alaska-Canada. **Formerly:** (1983) Extra Milers. **Publications:** *The Extra Miler*, quarterly. Newsletter. Includes new members listing; boundary changes; members' progress reports. **Price:** included in membership dues. **Circulation:** 310 ● Also distributes county outline maps. **Conventions/Meetings:** annual conference and convention.

22509 ■ Highpointers Club
c/o Mr. R. Craig Noland, Membership Chm.
PO Box 6364
Sevierville, TN 37864-6364
E-mail: membership@highpointers.org
URL: http://highpointers.org
Contact: Mr. R. Craig Noland, Membership Chm.
Founded: 1987. **Members:** 2,500. **Membership Dues:** in U.S., $20 (quarterly) ● outside U.S., $25 (quarterly). **Staff:** 8. **Budget:** $10,000. **Regional Groups:** 4. **Description:** Seeks to climb to the highest point in each of the fifty states. Compiles statistics. **Libraries: Type:** reference. **Holdings:** 50; archival material. **Subjects:** state high points, climbing, hiking. **Awards:** High Point Count Awards. **Frequency:** periodic. **Type:** recognition ● Vin Hoeman Award. **Frequency:** annual. **Type:** recognition. **Recipient:** for outstanding member. **Committees:** HP Landowner Liaison; Membership Chair; Newsletter Staff; Treasurer. **Publications:** *Highpointers Newsletter*, quarterly. Covers members' achievements and club news. **Price:** included in membership dues. **Circulation:** 2,500. **Conventions/Meetings:** annual banquet (exhibits) - usually held the end of July.

22510 ■ International Airline Passengers Association (IAPA)
PO Box 700188
Dallas, TX 75370-0188
Ph: (972)404-9980
Free: (800)821-4272
Fax: (972)233-5348
E-mail: info.dallas@iapa.com
URL: http://www.iapa.com
Founded: 1960. **Members:** 400,000. **Staff:** 35. **Languages:** English, Spanish. **Description:** Persons who are frequent users of airlines. Represents frequent flyers in matters of safety, comfort, convenience, and economy. Conducts semiannual survey regarding travel preferences and opinions in order to present consumers' viewpoints to airlines and government agencies. Provides discounts on hotels and car rentals. Disseminates travel information through magazines and literature. Compiles statistics. **Convention/Meeting:** none. **Divisions:** Group Publications; Travel Services. **Formerly:** (1969) Airways Club; (1982) Airline Passengers Association. **Publications:** *IAPA World - The World*, quarterly. Newsletter ● *International Member Benefits Directory*, annual ● Directory ● Magazine, quarterly.

22511 ■ Oceanic Society Expeditions (OSE)
Ft. Mason, Quarters 35 N
San Francisco, CA 94123-1394
Ph: (415)441-1106
Free: (800)326-7491
Fax: (415)474-3395
E-mail: office@oceanic-society.org
URL: http://www.oceanic-society.org
Contact: Birgit Winning, Pres.
Founded: 1969. **Members:** 500. **Membership Dues:** regular, $30-$50 (annual) ● contribution, $100-$250 (annual). **Staff:** 12. **Budget:** $100,000. **Description:** Offers the public the opportunity to learn about the national world through Biological Research Expeditions, Whale Watching and Nature Expeditions. **Libraries: Type:** not open to the public. **Holdings:** 300; books, periodicals. **Subjects:** wildlife, marine environment, travel. **Publications:** *Oceanic Society Field Guide to the Gray Whale* ● *Oceanic Society Field*

Guide to the Humpback Whale ● *Whale*, semiannual. Journal. **Price:** included in membership dues ● Catalog, annual. Lists environmental travel opportunities, educational cruises, and research expeditions. **Price:** $2.00 each (for 2 or more copies). **Circulation:** 25,000.

22512 ■ Roving Volunteers in Christ's Service (RVICS)
1800 SE 4th St.
Smithville, TX 78957
Ph: (512)237-2446
Free: (800)727-8914
Fax: (512)237-5119
E-mail: rvics@rvics.com
URL: http://www.rvics.com
Contact: Gale Hickman, Pres.
Description: Retired Christian couples living in recreational vehicles, who are serving the Lord through an organized work ministry. Provides maintenance and service, as well as small construction projects for non-profit Christian colleges, schools, camps, conference grounds, and others. **Publications:** *The Traveler*, quarterly. Newsletter. Alternate Formats: online.

22513 ■ Travel Companion Exchange (TCE)
PO Box 833
Amityville, NY 11701
Ph: (631)454-0880
E-mail: tce@travelcompanions.com
URL: http://www.travelcompanions.com
Contact: Jens Jurgen, Ed.
Founded: 1982. **Members:** 2,000. **Membership Dues:** individual, $298 (annual). **Staff:** 2. **For-Profit.** **Description:** Travel companion network for single, widowed, divorced people in the US and Canada. Finds companions for travel and leisure activities. Offers travel information, and free mail exchange. **Libraries: Type:** not open to the public. **Holdings:** 500. **Subjects:** travel. **Formerly:** (1999) Golden Companions. **Publications:** *Travel Companions*, bimonthly. Newsletter. Contains articles on travel destinations, types of travel, and leisure activities such as sports, hobbies, the Arts, and members' personal accounts. **Price:** $48.00/year. ISSN: 1076-5719. **Circulation:** 5,000.

22514 ■ Travelers' Century Club (TCC)
PO Box 7050
Santa Monica, CA 90406-7050
Ph: (310)458-3454
Fax: (310)395-9511
E-mail: tccclub3@gte.net
URL: http://travelerscenturyclub.org
Contact: Klaus Billep, Chm.
Founded: 1954. **Members:** 1,800. **Membership Dues:** $40 (annual). **Staff:** 2. **Multinational. Description:** International organization of persons who have visited a minimum of 100 nations. **Publications:** *The Centurian*, quarterly ● *Roster of Members*, biennial.

22515 ■ World Ocean and Cruise Liner Society (WOCLS)
PO Box 329
Northport, NY 11768
Ph: (631)261-5556
E-mail: membership@wocls.org
URL: http://www.wocls.org
Contact: George C. Devol, Pres.
Founded: 1980. **Members:** 8,000. **Membership Dues:** regular, in U.S., $30 (annual) ● regular, outside U.S., $36 (annual). **Description:** Ocean and cruise liner passengers and enthusiasts. Purpose is to keep members informed of new ships, itineraries, and special rates in ocean and cruise liner travel. Provides information on topics such as trends in the cruise industry, ships of the past and new ships under construction, and the evolution of contemporary cruise lines; also provides consulting services. **Convention/Meeting:** none. **Awards:** Ship of the Year. **Frequency:** annual. **Type:** recognition. **Publications:** *Ocean and Cruise News*, monthly. Newsletter. Updates the cruise ship industry, including reports on cruise discounts, cruise ships, and ratings of the major cruise ship lines. **Price:** included in member-

ship dues; $2.50/issue; $30.00 /year for nonmembers. **Circulation:** 8,000.

Trucks

22516 ■ American Truck Historical Society (ATHS)
PO Box 901611
Kansas City, MO 64190-1611
Ph: (816)891-9900
Fax: (816)891-9903
E-mail: info@ahts.org
URL: http://www.aths.org
Contact: Katie Cramer Eck, Managing Dir.
Founded: 1971. **Members:** 22,090. **Membership Dues:** individual, $37 (annual) ● company, $225 ● life, $1,000 ● family, $47 (annual). **Staff:** 5. **Budget:** $702,600. **Local Groups:** 83. **Description:** Promotes the dynamic history of trucks, the trucking industry, and its pioneers. **Libraries: Type:** reference. **Holdings:** 2,500; archival material, books, clippings, periodicals, photographs, video recordings. **Subjects:** trucks, trucking industry. **Awards:** Founders Award. **Frequency:** periodic. **Type:** recognition ● Golden Achievement Award. **Type:** recognition. **Recipient:** for members who have been involved in trucking for 50 years or more. **Absorbed:** (1972) U.S. Truck Historical Society. **Publications:** *American Truck Historical Society—Roster*, annual. **Price:** $15.00 ● *Antique Truck Registry*, periodic ● *Wheels of Time*, bimonthly. Magazine. Includes articles on the history of truck manufacturers, users, and the effect on daily living; calendar of events; chapter and directory news. **Price:** included in membership dues; $37.00 /year for nonmembers in U.S. and Canada. **Circulation:** 22,750. **Advertising:** accepted. **Conventions/Meetings:** annual convention and show, with antique truck show (exhibits) - usually May.

22517 ■ Antique Truck Club of America (ATCA)
85 S Walnut St.
Boyertown, PA 19512
Ph: (610)367-2567
Fax: (610)367-9712
E-mail: office@antiquetruckclubofamerica.org
URL: http://www.antiquetruckclubofamerica.org
Contact: Jim Widmann, Pres.
Founded: 1971. **Members:** 2,500. **Membership Dues:** active in U.S., $30 (annual) ● active in Canada, $40 (annual) ● active outside U.S. and Canada, corporate in U.S., $45 (annual). **Regional Groups:** 18. **Description:** Represents persons interested in the restoration of antique (over 25 years old) commercial vehicles including large trucks, pickups, sedan deliveries, hearses, fire engines, and tractors. **Libraries: Type:** reference. **Holdings:** archival material. **Subjects:** specifications and repair. **Awards: Type:** recognition. **Computer Services:** database ● mailing lists ● online services. **Publications:** *Double Clutch*, bimonthly. **Price:** free, for members only. **Advertising:** accepted ● *Membership and Truck Roster*, biennial. Membership Directory. **Conventions/Meetings:** annual show and banquet.

22518 ■ Diamond T Register (DTR)
PO Box 1657
St. Cloud, MN 56302-1657
Ph: (320)632-8664
URL: http://clubs.hemmings.com/frameset.cfm?club=diamondt
Contact: William F. Wielinski, Exec. Off.
Founded: 1978. **Members:** 350. **Membership Dues:** regular in U.S., $16 (annual) ● regular in Canada, $21 (annual) ● regular outside U.S. and Canada, $26 (annual). **Multinational. Description:** Diamond T truck owners, restorers, and historians. Preserves Diamond T trucks. Researches and records the history of their manufacturer, the Diamond T Motor Car Company. The Diamond T Company manufactured automobiles from 1905-11 and trucks from 1911-67. The pre-war Diamond T truck is distinguished by styling and comfort emulating that found in passenger cars. **Awards:** Golden Quill (Old Cars Newspaper).

Type: recognition. **Recipient:** for outstanding club publication. **Publications:** *Salmagundi*, semiannual. Newsletter. Contains periodical of company history, restoration sources and techniques. **Price:** included in membership dues. **Circulation:** 400. **Advertising:** accepted.

22519 ■ North American Truck Camper Owners Association (NATCOA)
c/o Bill Mathews, Co-Founder
12214 Carlsbad Ln.
Jacksonville, FL 32223
E-mail: billm@natcoa.com
URL: http://www.natcoa.com
Contact: Bill Mathews, Co-Founder
Founded: 2005. **Membership Dues:** in North America, $24 (annual) ● in Australia, $25 (annual) ● outside North America and Australia, $12 (annual). **Multinational. Description:** Represents the interests of Truck Camper (TC) consumers and enthusiasts. Promotes the Truck Camper as a Recreational Vehicle (RV) lifestyle and connects manufacturers with consumers via forum. Communicates with TC manufacturers who have the same enthusiasm for truck campering. **Telecommunication Services:** electronic mail, paul@natcoa.com. **Conventions/Meetings:** annual show, with rally (exhibits).

22520 ■ White Owners Register (WOR)
1624 Perkins Dr.
Arcadia, CA 91006
Ph: (626)355-7679
Contact: Robert Scoon, Ed.
Founded: 1970. **Members:** 550. **Multinational. Description:** Individuals interested in restoring White and Indiana vehicles, Cletrac tractors, and Rollin, Rubay (RUBAY), and Templar automobiles. **Convention/Meeting:** none. **Publications:** *The Albatross*, periodic. Newsletter. **Price:** free or with donation.

Wine

22521 ■ Napa Valley Wine Library Association (NVWLA)
PO Box 328
St. Helena, CA 94574-0328
Ph: (707)963-5145
E-mail: info@napawinelibrary.org
URL: http://www.napawinelibrary.org
Contact: Kevin Alfaro, Pres.
Founded: 1963. **Members:** 2,400. **Membership Dues:** individual, $50 (annual) ● life, $1,000. **Description:** Represents persons interested in wines, particularly those of the Napa Valley. Collects, preserves, and makes available books, publications, periodicals, and ephemera concerning Napa Valley wine. Conducts wine tasting courses. **Libraries: Type:** open to the public. **Holdings:** 5,000. **Subjects:** wine. **Publications:** *Napa Valley Wine Library Report*, quarterly. Newsletter. Includes calendar of events. ● Also publishes bibliography of holdings and oral histories. **Conventions/Meetings:** annual Wine Tasting - meeting.

22522 ■ Society of Medical Friends of Wine (SMFW)
c/o Susan Guerguy, Exec. Sec.
511 Jones Pl.
Walnut Creek, CA 94597-3141
Ph: (925)933-9691
Fax: (925)933-9691
E-mail: susanquerguy@sbcglobal.net
URL: http://medicalfriendsofwine.org
Contact: Susan Guerguy, Exec. Sec.
Founded: 1939. **Members:** 330. **Membership Dues:** MD's/DDS's, $150 (annual). **Staff:** 1. **Budget:** $50,000. **Regional Groups:** 1. **Description:** Physicians and surgeons interested in the nutritional and therapeutic values of wine. Works to stimulate scientific research on wine, develop an understanding of its beneficial effects, and encourage an "appreciation of the conviviality and good fellowship that are part of the relaxed and deliberate manner of living that follows its proper use.". **Awards:** Wine

Research Award. **Frequency:** biennial. **Type:** recognition. **Recipient:** for wine research. **Committees:** Editorial; Research. **Publications:** *Society of Medical Friends of Wine—Bulletin*, annual. Covers effects of wine on health and society news; includes book reviews. **Price:** included in membership dues. Alternate Formats: online. **Conventions/Meetings:** quarterly dinner ● annual Vintage Tour.

22523 ■ Society of Wine Educators (SWE)
1212 New York Ave. NW, Ste.425
Washington, DC 20005
Ph: (202)408-8777
Fax: (202)408-8677
E-mail: lairey@societyofwineeducators.org
URL: http://wine.gurus.com
Contact: Lisa Airey, Dir. of Wine Education and Certification

Founded: 1977. **Members:** 1,300. **Membership Dues:** national corporate, $2,500 (annual) ● industry, $500 (annual) ● non-profit, $250 (annual) ● professional, $125 (annual) ● associate, $65 (annual) ● student, $40 (annual). **Staff:** 4. **Budget:** $500,000. **Regional Groups:** 4. **Multinational. Description:** Represents individuals who teach or write about wine for the trade or academic communities; those associated with wineries, restaurants, or the wine retail, wholesale, or import industry; consumers with an interest in wine and wine education. Facilitates the flow of information among wine producers, marketers, retailers, and consumers. **Computer Services:** Mailing lists. **Telecommunication Services:** electronic mail, members@societyofwineeducators.org. **Committees:** Awards; Certificate Program; Chapter Development; Public Relations. **Publications:** *Chronicle*, quarterly. Newsletter ● *Membership List*, periodic. Directory ● *Resource Manual*, biennial. **Price:** $45.00. **Conventions/Meetings:** annual conference (exhibits) - always August.

22524 ■ Women for Winesense (WWS)
PO Box 10549
Napa, CA 94581
Free: (800)204-1616
Fax: (707)255-1119
E-mail: gabrielle@winecountryliving.com
URL: http://www.womenforwinesense.org
Contact: Gabrielle Leonhard, Pres.

Founded: 1990. **Membership Dues:** wine aficionado, $40 (annual) ● professional, $80 (annual) ● student (at least 21 years old), $25 (annual) ● corporate, $5,000 (annual). **Local Groups:** 10. **Description:** Promotes the appreciation and responsible enjoyment of wine. Supports the success and professional development of women in wine and associated industries. **Computer Services:** Information services, wine education resources ● online services, forum. **Boards:** National Advisory. **Divisions:** Mobile, Alabama Chapter; Napa Sonoma, California Chapter; New York City, New York Chapter; Portland, Oregon Chapter; Richmond, Virginia Chapter; Rochester, New York Chapter; San Francisco, California Chapter; San Luis Obispo, California Chapter; Santa Barbara, California Chapter; Seattle, Washington Chapter. **Publications:** Articles. Alternate Formats: online.

Wood

22525 ■ International Wood Collectors Society (IWCS)
c/o William Cockrell, Sec.-Treas.
2300 W Rangeline Rd.
Greencastle, IN 46135-7875
Ph: (765)653-6483

E-mail: iwcs@joink.com
URL: http://woodcollectors.org
Contact: William Cockrell, Sec.-Treas.

Founded: 1947. **Members:** 1,400. **Membership Dues:** individual or couple, $35 (annual) ● new, $90 (triennial) ● new, commercial, $125 (quinquennial) ● life, $500 ● student, $15 (annual) ● sustaining, $50 (annual). **Staff:** 2. **Budget:** $70,000. **Regional Groups:** 4. **State Groups:** 6. **Local Groups:** 6. **National Groups:** 3. **Description:** Scientists, botanists, dendrologists, foresters, wood collectors, hobbyists, and craftsmen. Members help each other find exotic and colorful wood from historic trees and buildings and from different species of trees worldwide and share information on books, tools, and methods of turning and finishing. Encourages the exchange of wood specimens and the adoption of standard methods of sample collecting and standard specimen size. Assists in accurate naming and classification of specimens. Cooperates with institutions, universities, and schools in augmenting their specimen collections. **Libraries: Type:** not open to the public. **Holdings:** 56; periodicals. **Subjects:** botany. **Awards:** Endowment Fund Scholarship. **Frequency:** annual. **Type:** grant. **Recipient:** for educational projects. **Computer Services:** database, educational. **Committees:** Endowment Fund; Executive; Membership; Publication. **Formerly:** (1958) Wood Collectors Society. **Publications:** *A Guide for Developing A Wood Collection*. Book. Contains an explanation on how to start, develop and maintain wood collection. **Price:** $6.00 for members; $8.00 for nonmembers ● *A Guide to Useful Woods of the World (2nd Edition, 2001)*. Book. Highlights the 279 woody species and includes illustration of the key botanical feature and color photographs of the wood. **Price:** $39.95 for members, plus shipping; $44.95 for nonmembers, plus shipping; $7.00 in U.S.; $9.00 in Canada ● *Australian Trees and Shrubs - Common, Local and Scientific Names*. Book. Contains compilation of over 4000 entries, of every known name for some 3500 species of trees and woody plants in Australia. **Price:** $13.00 in U.S. and Canada, includes shipping ● *World of Wood*, bimonthly. Magazine. Includes annual membership list, new member listings, schedule of events, articles written by members, IWCS Wood Data Sheet, and book reviews. **Price:** $6.00/issue; $100.00/year for commercial members. **Advertising:** accepted. **Conventions/Meetings:** annual meeting ● annual Woodfest - regional meeting and seminar, with woodcrafts, wood samples, sawmill demonstrations (exhibits) - in February.

22526 ■ Scrollsaw Association of the World (SAW)
768 Rifle Rd.
Sylvania, GA 30467
Ph: (912)829-5708
Fax: (912)829-5708
E-mail: info@saw-online.com
URL: http://www.saw-online.com
Contact: Ms. Pat Lupori, Sec.

Founded: 1998. **Members:** 1,400. **Membership Dues:** business/professional in U.S., $60 (annual) ● business/professional in North America, $70 (annual) ● business/professional outside North America, $80 (annual) ● family in U.S., individual outside North America, $35 (annual) ● family in North America, $40 (annual) ● family outside North America, $45 (annual) ● individual in U.S., $25 (annual) ● individual in North America, $30 (annual). **Multinational. Description:** Represents individuals interested in the art of the scrollsaw. Provides the base of a community with a variety of means of contact: chat room, message board, event information, etc. Sponsors a number of scrollsaw competitions. Provides methods for members to contact each other. **Awards:** Lifetime Membership. **Frequency:** periodic. **Type:** recognition. **Recipient:** to a person who had a great contribution to

the entire scrolling community ● Most Valuable Member. **Frequency:** annual. **Type:** recognition. **Recipient:** for the member who has contributed to the community of scrolling ● Opportunity Grant. **Frequency:** periodic. **Type:** grant. **Recipient:** to a member of a local chapter to defray the cost of a class that will enhance their knowledge of scrolling techniques ● Patrick Spielman Memorial Scholarship. **Frequency:** annual. **Type:** scholarship. **Recipient:** to a member of the association or an immediate family member of an association member. **Computer Services:** Online services, Pattern Generator. **Additional Websites:** http://www.saw-online.org. **Boards:** Advisors. **Publications:** *Resource Directory*, annual. Contains a listing of all SAW members, current by-laws of the association, and a list of resources available to scrollers. **Advertising:** accepted ● *SAW Dust*, quarterly. Newsletter. Contains information about the association and its members and supplies print patterns.

22527 ■ Woodworking Association of North America (WANA)
Address Unknown since 2006

Founded: 1983. **Members:** 8,500. **Membership Dues:** individual, $25 (annual). **Staff:** 2. **For-Profit. Description:** Individuals (8445) and companies (55) engaged in woodworking. Promotes woodworking as a hobby, occupation, and art form. **Computer Services:** database ● mailing lists. **Publications:** *ShopTalk*, quarterly. Newsletter. Includes woodworking show dates, club information, swap n' source and members only webpage information. **Price:** included in membership dues. **Circulation:** 6,000. **Advertising:** not accepted.

World's Fairs

22528 ■ 1904 World's Fair Society
2605 Causeway Dr.
St. Louis, MO 63125
E-mail: admin@1904worldfairsociety.org
URL: http://www.1904worldsfairsociety.org
Contact: Mr. Mike Truax, Pres.

Founded: 1986. **Members:** 500. **Membership Dues:** individual, $18 (annual) ● individual (joining after July 1), $25 (annual). **Description:** Seeks to preserve the memory and memorabilia of the 1904 Louisiana Purchase Exhibition, a world's fair held in St. Louis, MO, to celebrate the 100th anniversary of the Louisiana Purchase. **Libraries: Type:** open to the public. **Awards:** President's Award. **Frequency:** annual. **Type:** recognition. **Publications:** *World's Fair Bulletin*, monthly. **Conventions/Meetings:** annual Closing Day Celebration - banquet - always December 1 (the closing date of the fair) ● monthly meeting.

Writers

22529 ■ Broad Universe
1121 E Vienna Ave.
Milwaukee, WI 53212
E-mail: info@broaduniverse.org
URL: http://www.broaduniverse.org
Contact: Suzy McKee Charnas, Contact

Founded: 2000. **Membership Dues:** level two, $15 (annual) ● level one, $30 (annual). **Description:** Promotes science fiction, fantasy, and horror written by women. **Computer Services:** database, directory of bookstore contacts ● mailing lists, email discussion group. **Publications:** *The Broadsheet*. Newsletter. Alternate Formats: online ● Brochure. Alternate Formats: online ● Catalog. Contains a list of short stories and books submitted by members. Alternate Formats: online.

Acrobatics

22530 ■ U.S. Sports Acrobatics (USA)
201 S Capitol Ave.
Indianapolis, IN 46225
Ph: (317)829-5667
Fax: (317)237-5069
E-mail: claughon@usa-gymnastics.org
URL: http://www.ussportsacrobatics.com
Contact: Carisa Laughon, Dir.
Founded: 1974. **Members:** 1,200. **Membership Dues:** athlete, $50 (annual) ● coach/judge, $60 (annual) ● club, $100 (annual). **Staff:** 2. **Regional Groups:** 12. **Local Groups:** 78. **Description:** Individuals interested in promoting acrobatics in the U.S. Purposes are to encourage competition and high standards of technique and safety in sports acrobatics; to provide a clearinghouse and distribution center for coaching aids, literature, and research materials to clinics. Conducts clinics; compiles statistics. Offers videotapes of competitions. **Awards:** National Team Award. **Frequency:** annual. **Type:** recognition. **Computer Services:** database, membership. **Committees:** Education & Safety; International Relations; Judges; Technical. **Affiliated With:** United States Olympic Committee; USA Gymnastics. **Formerly:** (1999) U.S. Sports Acrobatic Federation. **Publications:** *Acrosport*, bimonthly. Newsletter. **Price:** $12.00. **Advertising:** accepted. Alternate Formats: diskette ● Bibliographies ● Also publishes rule book, glossary, and training materials. **Conventions/Meetings:** annual International Invitational - convention - always March ● annual National Championships - competition ● semiannual Superclinic - board meeting (exhibits).

Aerobics

22531 ■ Aerobic Training International
Calle D F-14 El Dorado
Rio Piedras, PR 00926
Ph: (787)751-6665 (787)763-5434
Fax: (787)767-3037
E-mail: mendiza@yahoo.com
Contact: Maria Theresa Mendizabal, Co-Dir.
Founded: 1981. **Staff:** 8. **Languages:** English, Spanish. **Description:** Training organization for aerobic teachers and fitness professionals. Promotes the benefits of aerobic exercise; works to enhance the professional status of members. Offers continued credits in ACE. **Conventions/Meetings:** annual Caribbean Heat - convention and workshop, activity aerobic classes (exhibits) - summer or autumn.

22532 ■ NETA - National Exercise Trainers Association (NETA)
5955 Golden Valley Rd., Ste.240
Minneapolis, MN 55422-4472
Ph: (763)545-2505
Free: (800)237-6242
Fax: (763)545-2524
E-mail: neta@netafit.org
URL: http://www.netafit.org
Contact: Susie Supper, Education Dir.
Founded: 1977. **Members:** 120,000. **Staff:** 50. **Budget:** $1,500,000. **Description:** Offers certification and training for Personal Trainers, Group Exercise Instructors. Specialty certificates in Pilates, Yoga and many other fitness related disciplines. **Formerly:** NDEITA - National Dance Exercise Instructors Training Association. **Publications:** *NETA Fitness Professional's Manual*. **Price:** $45.00 ● Audiotapes ● Brochures ● Videos. **Conventions/Meetings:** periodic workshop, on aerobics certification.

22533 ■ United States Competitive Aerobics Federation (USCAF)
8033 Sunset Blvd., No. 920
Los Angeles, CA 90046
Ph: (323)850-3777
Fax: (323)850-7795
E-mail: info@sportaerobics-nac.com
URL: http://www.sportaerobics-nac.com
Contact: Dale Duncan, Contact
Founded: 1989. **Members:** 2,000. **Membership Dues:** senior, $25 (annual) ● youth, $15 (annual). **Description:** Governs and organizes sports fitness and aerobic competitions for youth and adults. Seeks to maintain high standards and consistency in the sport. Conducts educational programs. **Publications:** *The Aerobic Competitor*. Newsletter. **Circulation:** 2,000.

Aerospace

22534 ■ Collegiate Soaring Association (CSA)
4671 Kipling St., No. 68
Wheat Ridge, CO 80033
Ph: (303)432-2137
E-mail: jhpc@hotmail.com
URL: http://www.coloradosoaring.org/ssa/coll/home.htm
Contact: John H. Campbell PhD, Pres.
Founded: 1985. **Members:** 30. **Membership Dues:** group, $20 (annual). **Budget:** $2,000. **Description:** Clubs, schools, and others; soaring groups with a school affiliation or significant student composition. Works to promote soaring (gliding) as an accepted college sport; encourage youth involvement in soaring through glider flight training, technology, and education programs accessible to students; sanction intercollegiate soaring competitions; maintain network of student soaring groups; help start new groups; publicize achievements and contributions and raise funds; research college gliding eras of the 1910s, '30s, and '50s; contact non-U.S. networks. Sponsors competitions; compiles statistics. **Libraries: Type:** reference. **Holdings:** periodicals, photographs. **Subjects:** previous college gliding eras. **Awards:** Gogos Scholarship. **Type:** scholarship. **Recipient:** for college students who are active in CSA ● Robert B. Evans Trophy. **Frequency:** annual. **Type:** trophy. **Recipient:** for best aggregate score in intercollegiate championships. **Computer Services:** Mailing lists, of members. **Telecommunication Services:** electronic mail, csa-soaring@lists.colorado.edu. **Affiliated With:** Soaring Society of America. **Publications:** *Becoming a Soaring Pilot*. Brochure. **Price:** free ● *College Soaring*, quarterly. Newsletter. Includes directory. ● *Rules for Intercollegiate Gliding and Soaring Championships*. **Price:** free ● *Tips on Starting a College Soaring Club*. **Price:** free ● Brochure. **Price:** free. **Conventions/Meetings:** annual Contest Meeting - always fall ● annual convention, held in conjunction with Soaring Society of America (exhibits) - always late February.

22535 ■ International Aerobatic Club (IAC)
EAA Aviation Ctr.
PO Box 3086
Oshkosh, WI 54903-3086
Ph: (920)426-4800
Fax: (920)426-6574
E-mail: iac@eaa.org
URL: http://www.iac.org
Contact: Gerry Molidor, Pres.
Founded: 1970. **Members:** 5,000. **Membership Dues:** basic, in U.S. and Canada, $55 (annual) ● basic (international), $73 (annual). **Staff:** 3. **Local Groups:** 40. **Description:** A division of the Experimental Aircraft Association (see separate entry). Members of EAA with an interest in precision and sport aerobatics. Promotes aerobatics as both a competitive and noncompetitive sport. Provides enthusiasts with the opportunity to meet others with the same interest; offers noncompetitive flyers a chance to participate in organized aerobatics events. Maintains Aerobatics Hall of Fame. Sponsors judges' schools; individual chapters conduct fly-ins, practice sessions, and various social events. **Awards:** Frank Price Cup. **Frequency:** annual. **Type:** recognition. **Recipient:** for outstanding individuals in aerobatics ● Harold E. Neumann Award. **Frequency:** annual. **Type:** recognition. **Recipient:** for outstanding contribution as a chief judge during the prior contest year ● Kathie Jaffe Volunteer Award. **Frequency:** annual. **Type:** recognition. **Recipient:** for an outstanding volunteer during the previous year ● **Frequency:** annual. **Type:** recognition. **Recipient:** for winners of competition ● Robert L. Heuer Award for Judging Excellence. **Frequency:** annual. **Type:** recognition. **Recipient:** for an outstanding aerobatic judge each year. **Affiliated With:** Experimental Aircraft Association. **Publications:** *Sport Aerobatics*, monthly. Magazine. **Price:** included in membership dues. **Circulation:** 6,000. **Advertising:** accepted. **Conventions/Meetings:** competition ● seminar ● annual U.S. National Aerobatic Championship - meeting - always in Denison, TX.

22536 ■ National Air-Racing Group (NAG)
c/o Betty Sherman, Treas.
1932 Mahan
Richland, WA 99352-2121
Ph: (509)946-5690
Fax: (509)946-5690

E-mail: betty.sherman@verizon.net
URL: http://warbird.com/joinnag.html
Contact: Betty Sherman, Treas.
Founded: 1974. **Members:** 1,700. **Membership Dues:** regular, $15 (annual) ● additional individual at same address, $3 (annual). **Description:** Individuals involved in or having an interest in closed-course pylon air racing. Aims to promote the sport of air racing and to train officials prior to races at race sites. Compiles statistics on past race results. **Libraries: Type:** reference. **Holdings:** photographs. **Subjects:** past copies of professional Air-racing, race results. **Committees:** Officiating; Public Relations. **Divisions:** AT-6/SNJ Racing; Biplane; International Formula One Racing; Sport Class Racing; Jet Class Racing; Unlimited Racing. **Affiliated With:** International Council of Air Shows. **Absorbed:** United States Air Racing Association. **Publications:** *Professional Air Racing*, monthly. Newsletter. **Circulation:** 1,200. **Conventions/Meetings:** monthly general assembly - always 2nd Saturday.

22537 ■ National Soaring Foundation (NSF)
PO Box 684
Hobbs, NM 88240
Ph: (505)392-6032 (505)390-9584
URL: http://www.aerobaticsweb.org/SOARING/books/foundatn.htm
Contact: Bob Dittert, Pres.
Founded: 1976. **Members:** 17. **Description:** Soaring pilots interested in advancing the art and science of motorless flight and the preservation of a site for national and regional soaring contests. Sponsors national, regional, and local contests. **Awards:** Soaring Badge. **Type:** recognition. **Recipient:** for pilots of motorless aircraft. **Affiliated With:** Soaring Society of America. **Conventions/Meetings:** annual meeting - always June or July.

22538 ■ Soaring Society of America (SSA)
PO Box 2100
Hobbs, NM 88241-2100
Ph: (505)392-1177
Fax: (505)392-8154
E-mail: info@ssa.org
URL: http://www.ssa.org
Contact: Dennis Wright, Exec. Dir.
Founded: 1932. **Members:** 13,000. **Membership Dues:** full, $64 (annual) ● family, youth, $36 (annual). **Staff:** 8. **Regional Groups:** 4. **Local Groups:** 240. **Description:** Persons interested in the activity of soaring and gliding (building and flying of gliders and sailplanes). Promotes soaring in the U.S. Sanctions soaring contests. Maintains hall of fame and speakers' bureau; supports efforts of the National Soaring Museum. Conducts specialized education and research programs; compiles statistics. **Libraries: Type:** reference. **Subjects:** soaring. **Awards: Type:** recognition. **Committees:** Contest; Development; Governmental Liaison; Member Relations; Technical. **Divisions:** Collegiate Soaring Association; National Soaring Foundation; National Soaring Museum; 1-26 Association; Sailplane Homebuilders Association; Self-Launching Sailplane Pilots Association; Vintage Sailplane Association; Women Soaring Pilots Association. **Affiliated With:** National Aeronautic Association. **Absorbed:** National Gliding Association. **Publications:** *Membership Handbook*, biennial ● *Soaring*, monthly. Magazine ● *Soaring Flight Manual* ● *Technical Soaring*, quarterly. **Conventions/Meetings:** annual convention (exhibits).

22539 ■ U.S. Hang Gliding Association (USHGA)
PO Box 1330
Colorado Springs, CO 80901-1330
Ph: (719)632-8300
Free: (800)616-6888
Fax: (719)632-6417
E-mail: ushga@ushga.org
URL: http://www.ushga.org
Contact: Jayne Depanfilis, Exec. Dir.
Founded: 1971. **Members:** 9,500. **Membership Dues:** individual in U.S., $69 (annual) ● individual outside U.S., $90 (annual). **Staff:** 6. **Budget:** $1,000,000. **Regional Groups:** 13. **Local Groups:**

125. **Description:** Individuals interested in the science and art of ultralight flight. Seeks to explore, promote, and educate others concerning all facets of self-launched ultralight flight, with a particular emphasis on safety education and providing communication for enthusiasts. Includes programs such as: accident review board and achievement awards or ratings for pilots. Conducts instructor certification clinic. **Libraries: Type:** reference. **Awards:** Newsletter of the Year. **Frequency:** annual. **Type:** recognition. **Recipient:** for an outstanding club publication (printed or web-based) that has been supportive to the sport and the sponsoring chapter's activities ● Presidential Citation. **Frequency:** annual. **Type:** recognition. **Recipient:** for an individual who has made a unique and outstanding contribution to the science and technique of foot-launched ultralight flight ● USHGA Exceptional Service Award. **Frequency:** annual. **Type:** recognition. **Recipient:** for outstanding service to the association during the year by any member or non-member. **Computer Services:** Mailing lists. **Boards:** Accident Review. **Committees:** Awards; Competition and Record Attempts; Insurance; National Coordinating; Public Relations; Research and Development; Safety and Training; Site Management; World Team. **Affiliated With:** National Aeronautic Association. **Formerly:** (1971) Peninsula Hang Glider Club; (1972) Southern California Hang Glider Association. **Publications:** *Hang Gliding and Paragliding*, monthly. Magazine. Contains technical and educational articles on activities in the sport of hang gliding. Includes index of advertisers and calendar of events. **Price:** included in membership dues; $35.00 /year for nonmembers. ISSN: 0895-433X. **Circulation:** 9,000. **Advertising:** accepted. **Conventions/Meetings:** competition ● semiannual conference and board meeting.

22540 ■ Vintage Sailplane Association (VSA)
1709 Baron Ct.
Daytona Beach, FL 32128
E-mail: kimobear@aol.com
URL: http://www.vintagesailplane.org
Contact: Barry v W. Crommelin, Sec.
Founded: 1974. **Members:** 550. **Membership Dues:** individual, $20 (annual) ● individual, $35 (biennial) ● individual, $85 (quinquennial). **Description:** Owners, flyers, builders, and restorers of vintage (pre-1958) sailplanes; enthusiasts of aviation history; model airplane builders. Preserves history, artifacts, and aircraft relating to sailplanes. Provides specialized education program in powerless flight history; compiles statistics; records locations of older sailplanes. Supports research efforts of National Soaring Museum and Smithsonian Institution National Air and Space Museum. Sponsors competitions and displays. **Convention/Meeting:** none. **Libraries: Type:** reference. **Holdings:** clippings, periodicals, photographs. **Subjects:** U.S. and international publications on sailplane history, vintage sailplanes, gliders. **Awards:** Glider Restoration Award. **Frequency:** annual. **Type:** monetary. **Affiliated With:** Soaring Society of America. **Publications:** *Bungee Cord*, quarterly. Newsletter. Contains information on the acquisition, restoration, and flying of vintage and classic gliders. **Price:** included in membership dues. ISSN: 0194-6889. **Circulation:** 500. **Advertising:** accepted ● *Bungee Cord Bibliography List* ● Membership Directory.

Aikido

22541 ■ Aikido Association of America (AAA)
1016 W Belmont Ave.
Chicago, IL 60657
Ph: (773)525-3141
Fax: (773)525-5916
E-mail: aikidoamer@gmail.com
URL: http://www.aaa-aikido.com
Founded: 1984. **Description:** Aims to lift American Aikido instruction using traditional Japanese and modern methods of teaching Aikido arts and philosophy. Provides national recognition and accreditation of Aikido dojo and their satellites. Furthers the train-

ing of Aikido students through standardized instruction and intensive, focused training. **Computer Services:** Information services, Aikido resources. **Committees:** National Teaching. **Programs:** Professional Instructor Training. **Publications:** *Aikido World*, quarterly. Newsletter. Includes photos, short articles, book and movie reviews, and news related to Aikido. **Price:** included in membership dues.

22542 ■ Aikido Association of North America (AANA)
5836-38 Henry Ave.
Philadelphia, PA 19128
Ph: (215)483-3000
E-mail: doshinkan@yoshinkai.org
URL: http://www.doshinkan-aikido.org
Contact: Yukio Utada, Pres.
Multinational. Description: Seeks to bring Doshinkan Aikido to the widest possible audience. Seeks to ensure that the caliber of teaching is maintained at the highest level. Maintains a professional teaching staff and standardizes teaching practices. Assists in the formation of new clubs and organizes special classes. Serves as a vehicle for communication among teachers and students of Aikido. **Computer Services:** Information services, Aikido resources. **Publications:** *Doshin Digest*. Magazine. Contains information, training articles and announcements of upcoming products and events. **Price:** free. Alternate Formats: online.

22543 ■ International Aikido Association (IAA)
PO Box 4528
Dallas, TX 75208
Ph: (214)943-7530 (817)737-2223
E-mail: sosasiaa@sbcglobal.net
URL: http://internationalaikido.com
Contact: Bill Sosa Sensei, Chief Instructor
Founded: 1995. **Multinational. Description:** Promotes the practice of Aikido. Provides a non-competitive, family-type atmosphere at dojos, observing traditional values of courtesy and respect. **Publications:** *Aiki, Journey to Self-Mastery*. Book. **Price:** $12.95 plus shipping and handling ● *The Essence of Aikido*. Book ● *Secrets of Police Aikido* (in Bulgarian and English). Book.

22544 ■ United States Aikido Federation (USAF)
c/o Susan McKenzie Wolk, Sec.
98 State St.
Northampton, MA 01060
Ph: (413)586-7122
E-mail: usaf@torontoaikikai.com
URL: http://www.usaikifed.com
Contact: Susan McKenzie Wolk, Sec.
Founded: 1976. **Members:** 8,000. **Regional Groups:** 4. **Local Groups:** 200. **Description:** Aikido clubs and dojos (schools). Provides the proper instruction of aikido, a modern Japanese martial art based on earlier techniques and practiced as a mental and physical discipline and method of self-defense. Develops and improves the practice of aikido; establishes grading standards; represents its members in the International Aikido Federation and the Aikikai Foundation in Tokyo, Japan; registers all Dan (blackbelt) grades with the IAF. **Telecommunication Services:** electronic mail, susanmwolk@comcast.net. **Committees:** Teaching; Technical. **Publications:** *Aikido Celebration '94*. Video. **Price:** $33.00 plus shipping and handling ● *Aikido East*, quarterly. Newsletter. **Price:** $20.00/year. **Advertising:** accepted ● *Aikido: The Power and the Basics Vol. 1*. Video. **Price:** $35.00 plus shipping and handling ● *Aikido: The Power and the Basics Vol. 2*. Video. **Price:** $35.00 plus shipping and handling ● *New Aikido Complete (Ultimate Aikido)*. Book. **Price:** $16.95 plus shipping and handling ● *30th Anniversary Summer Camp*. Video. **Price:** $40.00 plus shipping and handling ● Manuals ● Distributes films. **Conventions/Meetings:** annual meeting ● seminar.

Archery

22545 ■ Archery Shooters Association (ASA)
PO Box 399
Kennesaw, GA 30156

Ph: (770)795-0232
Fax: (770)795-0953
E-mail: info@asaarchery.com
URL: http://www.asaarchery.com
Contact: Laval D. Falks, Natl. Dir.
Membership Dues: individual, $30 (annual) ● life, $350. **Regional Groups:** 5. **Description:** Represents the interests of archery shooters. Promotes archery to the public. **Awards:** Shooter of the Year. **Frequency:** annual. **Type:** recognition. **Computer Services:** database, listing of archers ● online services, forums. **Committees:** Competition. **Conventions/Meetings:** tour.

22546 ■ Christian Bowhunters of America (CBA)

2205 State Rte. 571 W
Greenville, OH 45331-9425
Ph: (937)548-0623
Free: (877)912-5724
URL: http://www.christianbowhunters.org
Contact: Dr. Wally Harder, Ministry Coor.
Founded: 1984. **Members:** 2,500. **Membership Dues:** individual, $25 (annual) ● individual, $40 (biennial) ● individual, $50 (triennial) ● family, $30 (annual) ● family, $50 (biennial) ● family, $65 (triennial) ● life, $300 ● affiliate, $20. **Regional Groups:** 80. **Description:** Nondenominational ministry to the bowhunting and archery world. Seeks to "exalt and serve Jesus Christ by leading lost people to Him, and encouraging Christian growth". **Publications:** *The Christian Bowhunter*, bimonthly. Newsletter. Features articles and pictures of interest to Christian bowhunters. **Price:** included in membership dues. **Circulation:** 5,000. **Advertising:** accepted. Alternate Formats: CD-ROM; online ● Brochure. Includes a membership application. Alternate Formats: online. **Conventions/Meetings:** annual competition, for sport and archery shoots and fellowship.

22547 ■ National Archery Association of the United States (NAA)

1 Olympic Plz.
Colorado Springs, CO 80909-5778
Ph: (719)866-4576 (719)866-4577
Fax: (719)632-4733
E-mail: info@usarchery.org
URL: http://www.usarchery.org
Contact: Bradley R. Camp, Exec. Dir.
Founded: 1879. **Members:** 6,000. **Membership Dues:** associate, youth, full-time student, $30 (annual) ● individual, $50 (annual) ● club, regional, state, $90 (annual). **Staff:** 8. **Budget:** $1,100,000. **Regional Groups:** 4. **State Groups:** 50. **Local Groups:** 350. **National Groups:** 2. **Description:** Individuals and clubs interested in target archery. Standardizes tournament rules, procedures, and rounds. Maintains official records of archers. Sponsors archery matches and awards medals and pins. Selects and trains men's and women's archery teams to represent the U.S. in the Olympic Games and Pan American Games. Selects teams for World Championships and other international meets. **Awards:** Shenk Award. **Frequency:** annual. **Type:** recognition. **Recipient:** for performance at national championship events ● Thompson Medal of Honor. **Type:** medal. **Boards:** Governors. **Affiliated With:** United States Olympic Committee. **Publications:** *USA Archery*, bimonthly. Magazine. **Price:** $30.00/year. **Advertising:** accepted. **Conventions/Meetings:** annual National Target Championship - competition and meeting, with national championship tournament (exhibits).

22548 ■ National Bowhunter Education Foundation (NBEF)

PO Box 180757
Fort Smith, AR 72918
Ph: (479)649-9036
Fax: (479)649-3098
E-mail: mbentz@nbef.org
URL: http://www.nbef.org
Contact: Marilyn Bentz, Exec. Dir.
Founded: 1977. **State Groups:** 50. **Description:** Volunteer bowhunters serving as instructors to educate the public and other bowhunters on the safe

and proper use of the bow as a device for hunting legal game. Maintains International Bowhunter Education Program, which teaches bowhunters the fundamentals of safe bowhunting and appreciation and respect for the environment in which they hunt. Conducts training courses. **Publications:** *Instructor Notebook* ● *International Bowhunter Education Student Manual* ● Also publishes numerous training literature, charts, and videos.

22549 ■ The National Crossbowmen of the U.S.A. (TNC)

c/o Patricia Copley, Sec.-Treas.
38 B Ave.
Richwood, WV 26261
Ph: (954)704-0770
E-mail: boxman@wvadventures.net
URL: http://www.crossbowusa.com
Contact: William G. Pimm Jr., Pres.
Founded: 1960. **Members:** 300. **Membership Dues:** individual, $15 (annual) ● family, $18 (annual) ● corporate, $20 (annual). **Staff:** 6. **Description:** Individuals united to perpetuate, foster, and direct the practice of crossbow archery in accordance with official rules and the spirit and traditions of this ancient sport. Conducts activities such as crossbow competitions as well as research and education in sport and hunting crossbow disciplines. **Affiliated With:** National Archery Association of the United States. **Also Known As:** National Crossbowmen of the United States of America, Inc. **Publications:** *Crossbow Chit Chat*, 3/year. Newsletter. Contains informative articles on current events in the sport of crossbow; includes tournament scores and historical information. **Price:** included in membership dues. **Circulation:** 300. **Advertising:** accepted. **Conventions/Meetings:** competition ● annual meeting, in conjunction with National Archery Association of the U.S. championship tournament.

22550 ■ National Field Archery Association (NFAA)

31407 Outer I-10
Redlands, CA 92373
Ph: (909)794-2133
Free: (800)811-2331
Fax: (909)794-8512
E-mail: nfaarchery@aol.com
URL: http://www.NFAArchery.com
Contact: Marihelen Rogers, Exec. Sec.
Founded: 1939. **Members:** 22,000. **Membership Dues:** regular, $65 (annual) ● life, $450 ● professional, $75 (annual) ● bowhunter, $30 (annual). **Staff:** 4. **Budget:** $910,000. **Regional Groups:** 8. **State Groups:** 50. **Local Groups:** 1,200. **Description:** Field archers and bowhunters. Sponsors field archery schools, three national tournaments, and 16 sectional tournaments; works toward conservation of game and its natural habitat. **Awards:** Bowfisher of the Year. **Frequency:** annual. **Type:** recognition. **Recipient:** for the largest fish caught ● Diamond Buck Award. **Frequency:** annual. **Type:** recognition. **Recipient:** for the largest typical or non-typical mule deer, white deer or blacktail deer caught ● Memorial Scholarship. **Frequency:** annual. **Type:** scholarship. **Recipient:** varies by committee. **Committees:** Competitive Systems; Conservation; Handicap; Hunting Activities; Legal; Rounds; Rules; Tournament; Youth. **Publications:** *Archery*, bimonthly. Magazine. **Price:** $25.00/year; $5.00/issue. **Circulation:** 20,000. **Advertising:** accepted ● *Constitution and By-Laws of Field Archery*, annual. **Conventions/Meetings:** annual conference, business meeting.

22551 ■ Pope and Young Club (PYC)

PO Box 548
Chatfield, MN 55923-0548
Ph: (507)867-4144
Fax: (507)867-4144
E-mail: admin@pope-young.org
URL: http://www.pope-young.org
Contact: Stan Rauch, Conservation Committee Chm.
Founded: 1961. **Members:** 6,500. **Membership Dues:** associate, $35 (annual) ● regular, senior, $125 (annual). **Staff:** 4. **Description:** Bowhunters who feel they have set themselves apart from other hunters in

their choice of weapons and who derive more satisfaction from the quest than the quarry. Seeks to enhance the bowhunter image and promotes the principles of fair chase. Believes bowhunting allows the maximum in hunter participation for a given game harvest. Maintains and is responsible for the authenticity of the Bowhunters Big Game Records of North America. Sponsors photo and art competitions; compiles statistics. (Organization is named for Dr. Saxton Pope and Arthur Young, two pioneering bowhunters of the early 1900s.). **Awards: Type:** recognition. **Telecommunication Services:** electronic mail, pyclub@isl.net. **Committees:** Conservation. **Publications:** *Bowhunting Big Game Records of North America* ● *How to Measure and Score Big Game Trophies* ● Newsletters, quarterly. **Conventions/Meetings:** biennial meeting.

22552 ■ Professional Bowhunter's Society (PBS)

PO Box 246
Terrell, NC 28682
Ph: (704)664-2534
Fax: (704)664-7471
E-mail: probowhunters@adelphia.net
URL: http://www.bowsite.com/pbs
Contact: C. Jack Smith, Sec.-Treas.
Founded: 1965. **Members:** 3,500. **Membership Dues:** associate, $30 (annual) ● regular, $55 (annual) ● life, $1,250. **Staff:** 8. **Description:** Bowhunters who meet membership requirements. Seeks to upgrade, promote, and preserve the sport of bowhunting and to provide an honest representation for the bowhunter at all levels. Works to: ensure the taking of game in a humane and sportsmanlike manner; share experiences, knowledge, and shooting skills; elevate standards of the art; provide training in safety, shooting skills, hunting techniques, information, education files, and speakers' bureau. Conducts charitable, educational, and research programs. **Libraries: Type:** reference. **Holdings:** 1,000; books, films, video recordings. **Awards:** PBS Conservation Program. **Type:** grant. **Computer Services:** database. **Committees:** Conservation; Legislative; National Anti-Crossbow. **Publications:** *PBS Annual*, annual ● *Professional Bowhunter Magazine*, quarterly. Alternate Formats: online. **Conventions/Meetings:** biennial convention (exhibits) - always March ● annual meeting.

22553 ■ United Sportsmans Association of North America (USANA)

224 Sandbridge Rd.
Pittsgrove, NJ 08318
Ph: (856)358-4891
E-mail: goldeneagels@snip.net
URL: http://www.usanamtc.com
Contact: Skip Myers, Pres.
Founded: 1968. **Members:** 2,000. **Membership Dues:** regular, active military, out of state, $110 (annual) ● family, $135 (annual) ● spouse, $35 (annual) ● junior (under 20 years of age), resident, $60 (annual) ● active college student, $70 (annual). **Local Groups:** 5. **Description:** Individuals interested in competing in or learning more about tournament crossbow shooting. Promotes and selects all U.S. national crossbow teams for various shooting events, including world championships. Maintains hall of fame; conducts research and educational programs. **Libraries: Type:** reference. **Holdings:** 150; archival material, audiovisuals, books. **Subjects:** competition shooting. **Absorbed:** (1993) U.S. Armbrust Association. **Publications:** *Shot Heard 'Round the World*, quarterly. Magazine. **Price:** free. **Circulation:** 15,000. **Advertising:** accepted ● *Shot Heard "Round" The World*, annual. Directory. **Price:** free. **Circulation:** 10,000. **Advertising:** accepted ● Newsletters. **Conventions/Meetings:** biennial World Championship - competition (exhibits).

Armwrestling

22554 ■ American Armsport Association (AAA)

176 Dean Rd.
Mooresburg, TN 37811

Ph: (423)272-6162
Fax: (423)272-6162
E-mail: armsport@usit.net
URL: http://www.armsport.com
Contact: Frank Bean, Exec. Dir.
Founded: 1967. **Members:** 6,000. **Membership Dues:** individual, $25 (annual). **Staff:** 2. **State Groups:** 52. **Description:** Sponsors local, state, and national seated and standing arm-wrestling competitions. **Awards: Frequency:** annual. **Type:** recognition. **Committees:** State Directors. **Affiliated With:** World Armsport Federation. **Publications:** *Armbender*, quarterly. Magazine. Includes contest results, photographs, and calendar of events. **Price:** included in membership dues; $25.00 /year for nonmembers. **Advertising:** accepted. **Conventions/Meetings:** semiannual general assembly.

22555 ■ World Armsport Federation (WAF)
176 Dean Rd.
Mooresburg, TN 37811
Ph: (423)272-6162
Fax: (423)272-6162
E-mail: armsport@usit.net
URL: http://www.armsport.com/waf.htm
Contact: Frank Bean, Gen. Sec.
Founded: 1967. **Members:** 73. **Membership Dues:** organization, $25 (annual). **National Groups:** 73. **Description:** Represents national arm wrestling organizations worldwide. Promotes the sport of arm sports. **Affiliated With:** American Armsport Association. **Formerly:** World Armwrestling Federation. **Publications:** *ARMBENDER*, triennial. Journal. **Price:** included in membership dues. **Circulation:** 10,000. **Advertising:** accepted. **Conventions/Meetings:** annual meeting and competition.

Athletics

22556 ■ American Association of Cheerleading Coaches and Advisors (AACCA)
6745 Lenox Center Ct., Ste,318
Memphis, TN 38115
Free: (800)533-6583
URL: http://www.aacca.org
Founded: 1988. **Members:** 50,000. **Membership Dues:** general, $10 (annual). **Description:** Promotes a safe and responsible practice of student cheerleading. Provides a forum for cheerleading coaches across the United States. **Computer Services:** Information services, safety guidelines ● mailing lists. **Publications:** *AACCA Cheerleading Safety Manual*. **Price:** $20.00 plus shipping and handling ● Newsletter. Alternate Formats: online.

22557 ■ Assyrian Chaldean Athletics of North America (ACANA)
c/o Ashur Enwiya, Chm.
8018 W Lyons St.
Niles, IL 60714
Ph: (847)583-8525
E-mail: executivecommittee@acana.us
URL: http://www.acana.us
Contact: Ashur Enwiya, Chm.
Founded: 2004. **Membership Dues:** team, $200 (annual) ● individual, $100 (annual). **Multinational. Description:** Works to serve the ChaldoAssyrian athletes and athletic teams in North America. Promotes and enhances the sports of soccer and basketball, and encourages the participation of athletes from all ages regardless of gender. Provides a venue to exchange ideas that are important to athletes and teams in order to improve themselves. **Publications:** *ACANA News*. Newsletter. Alternate Formats: online.

22558 ■ Dwarf Athletic Association of America (DAAA)
418 Willow Way
Lewisville, TX 75077
Ph: (972)317-8299
Fax: (972)966-0184

E-mail: daaa@flash.net
URL: http://www.daaa.org
Contact: Janet Brown, Exec. Dir.
Founded: 1985. **Members:** 1,050. **Staff:** 1. **Regional Groups:** 13. **Description:** Represents dwarf athletes in the US. Develops, promotes, and provides quality amateur level athletic opportunities. Holds clinics, developmental events and formal competitions at local, regional, and national levels. **Committees:** Sport Tech. **Councils:** Athlete Advisory. **Affiliated With:** Billy Barty Foundation; Disabled Sports USA; Little People of America; United States Olympic Committee. **Conventions/Meetings:** annual Little People of America Conference/National Games (exhibits).

22559 ■ Foundation for Safer Athletic Field Environments (SAFE)
c/o Sports Turf Managers Association
805 New Hampshire St., Ste.E
Lawrence, KS 66044-2774
Free: (800)323-3875
Fax: (800)366-0391
E-mail: stmainfo@sportsturfmanager.org
URL: http://www.stma.org/AboutUs/SAFE
Contact: Kim Heck, Exec. Dir.
Founded: 2000. **Nonmembership. Description:** Supports sports field specific scientific research, educational programs, and environmental concerns to promote user safety. **Awards: Frequency:** annual. **Type:** scholarship. **Recipient:** to students in turf programs. **Conventions/Meetings:** seminar.

22560 ■ North American Sports Federation (NASF)
Box K
Drifton, PA 18221
Ph: (570)454-1952
Fax: (570)453-3855
E-mail: nasf@nasf.net
URL: http://www.nasf.net
Contact: Jake Kislan, Exec. Dir.
Founded: 1994. **Multinational. Description:** Serves as a coordinating body for amateur sports for adults and youth in the sports of softball, volleyball, flag and touch football, soccer, basketball and baseball. Encourages proper training of all officials in each sport, safe playing facilities, and increased participation in amateur programs. Facilitates communication and good sportsmanship among members. **Publications:** *North American Sporting News*. Newspaper.

22561 ■ USA Federation of Pankration Athlima (USAFPA)
1935 S Plum Grove Rd., No. 321
Palatine, IL 60067
Ph: (847)540-9854
E-mail: aaateamusa@webtv.net
URL: http://teamusapankration.com
Contact: John Townsley, Pres.
Founded: 1998. **Membership Dues:** athlete, coach, official, $25 ● club, $50 ● state director (minimum of 12 clubs), $600 ● regional organization, $750 ● national and disabled organization, $3,000 ● public sector, $10. **Description:** Represents men, women and children athletes. Provide classes, training and information for this Olympic sport.

22562 ■ Women Involved in Sports Evolution (WISE)
c/o Pierpont Racquet Club
500 Sanjon Rd.
Ventura, CA 93001
Ph: (805)652-1805 (805)652-1987
Fax: (805)641-0090
E-mail: wisestar@dock.net
URL: http://www.womeninsports.org
Contact: Diane Loring, Exec. Dir.
Founded: 1997. **Members:** 60. **Staff:** 20. **Local Groups:** 1. **Description:** Works to support the continued evolution of advancements in women's sports; provides programs to develop athletic excellence for females of all ages; dedicated to ensuring mainstream media coverage of daily athletic achievements of women. **Libraries: Type:** open to the public. **Awards:** Elenor Lloyd Dees Foundation. **Frequency:** annual. **Type:** grant. **Recipient:** for deserving female

athletes with 2.0 grade point average ● Ventura Rotary Club with Julius Gius Memorial Foundation. **Frequency:** annual. **Type:** grant. **Recipient:** for deserving female athletes with 2.0 grade point average. **Affiliated With:** Women's Sports Foundation. **Conventions/Meetings:** weekly Athletic Performance Program - workshop - January-December in Ventura, California.

Automobile

22563 ■ American Auto Racing Writers and Broadcasters Association (AARWBA)
922 N Pass Ave.
Burbank, CA 91505-2703
Ph: (818)842-7005
Fax: (818)842-7020
E-mail: dustybrandel@gmail.com
URL: http://www.aarwba.org
Contact: Norma Brandel, Pres.
Founded: 1955. **Members:** 500. **Membership Dues:** professional, $45 (annual) ● affiliate, $65 (annual) ● associate, $300 (annual). **Description:** Persons who write, broadcast, or photograph auto racing. Seeks to: upgrade coverage of auto racing; promote the stature of racing; secure better facilities for writers. Conducts contests for top race stories, photography, and broadcasts. **Awards:** Angelo Angelopolous Sportsman. **Frequency:** annual. **Type:** recognition. **Recipient:** for sportsmanship at Indianapolis 500 event ● Bloys Britt. **Frequency:** annual. **Type:** recognition ● Come Back Driver of the Year. **Frequency:** annual. **Type:** recognition. **Recipient:** for a driver returning to motorsports following accidents ● David Overpeck Memorial Scholarship. **Frequency:** annual. **Type:** scholarship. **Recipient:** for an incoming freshman journalism student ● Jigger Hard Luck Award. **Frequency:** annual. **Type:** recognition. **Recipient:** for the driver with the worst luck in qualifying for Indy 500 ● Straight Shooters Award. **Frequency:** annual. **Type:** recognition. **Recipient:** to an individual or group who has distinguished itself by its care for others in the racing community. **Committees:** All American Team; Credentials; Hall of Honor; Legends in Racing. **Publications:** *AARWBA Membership Directory*, annual. **Advertising:** accepted ● *All America Team Banquet Souvenir Program*, annual. **Advertising:** accepted ● *ImPRESSions*, monthly. Newsletter. **Conventions/Meetings:** annual meeting - always May, in Indianapolis, IN.

22564 ■ American Funny Car Series
4003 Freeport Rd.
Sterling, IL 61081
Ph: (815)626-2537 (815)625-2201
E-mail: help@americanfunnycars.com
URL: http://americanfunnycars.com
Contact: Dan Crownhart, Contact
Founded: 1966. **Members:** 320. **Staff:** 5. **Budget:** $160,000. **Description:** Drag racing teams; retail distributors of products related to drag racing; owners of drag racing cars; persons with an interest in the sport. Sponsors drag racing events; provides cars to other associations for races. **Formerly:** (1985) Midwest United Drag Racers Association; (2003) United Drag Racers Association. **Publications:** *United Racer*, quarterly. Newspaper. **Advertising:** accepted. **Conventions/Meetings:** annual conference (exhibits) - always February, in Merrillville, IN.

22565 ■ American Hot Rod Association (AHRA)
N 102 Hayford Rd.
Spokane, WA 99224
Ph: (509)244-3663
E-mail: srp@spokaneracewaypark.com
URL: http://www.spokaneracewaypark.com
Contact: Orville Moe, Exec. VP
Founded: 1956. **Members:** 25,000. **Membership Dues:** driver, owner, $30 (annual). **Staff:** 4. **Regional Groups:** 1. **State Groups:** 17. **Local Groups:** 350. **For-Profit. Description:** Professional and amateur drag racers from the U.S. and Canada. Aims to sponsor a series of national drag racing championships.

Conducts track operators meeting for racetrack owners. Sponsors competitions. Maintains hall of fame. **Awards:** Drivers World Champions. **Frequency:** annual. **Type:** recognition. **Recipient:** for winners of the event. **Committees:** National Rules/International. **Formerly:** (1986) American Drag Racing Association. **Publications:** *AHRA-Drag World*, monthly. Newspaper. Contains auto racing information. **Price:** included in membership dues. **Circulation:** 15,000. **Advertising:** accepted ● *Drag News*, monthly. Newsletter. **Price:** included in membership dues. **Circulation:** 3,000. **Advertising:** accepted ● *Grand American Series of Professional Drag Races*, annual ● *Rule Book*, annual. **Price:** $3.00 plus shipping and handling. **Conventions/Meetings:** annual symposium, related with the automotive industry (exhibits).

22566 ■ American Speed Association (ASA)
c/o Racing Speed Associates, LLC dba ASA Racing
457 S Ridgewood Ave., Ste.101
Daytona Beach, FL 32114
Ph: (386)258-2221
Fax: (386)258-2226
E-mail: info@asa-racing.com
Founded: 1968. **Description:** Promotes short track stock car racing.

22567 ■ Automobile Competition Committee for the United States FIA (ACCUS)
PO Box 100588
Denver, CO 80250
Ph: (303)730-8100
Free: (877)71-ACCUS
Fax: (303)730-8108
URL: http://www.accusfia.us
Founded: 1959. **Members:** 28. **Staff:** 4. **Description:** United States representative on the International Sporting Commission of the International Automobile Federation. National racing organizations and individuals who direct the committee; organization members are Sports Car Club of America, United States Auto Club, National Hot Rod Association, National Association for Stock Car Auto Racing, Championship Auto Racing Teams, Indy Racing League and Professional Sports Car Racing, Grand American Road Racing Association (see separate entries). Coordinates activities between the member organizations and the FIA. Works with manufacturers for international recognition of American-built automobiles. Issues international racing driver and entrant licenses. **Committees:** Car Classification; Public Relations; Safety. **Publications:** *Automobile Competition Committee for the U.S.—Roster of Members*, periodic. Membership Directory. **Conventions/Meetings:** annual meeting.

22568 ■ Automobile Racing Club of America (ARCA)
PO Box 5217
Toledo, OH 43611-0217
Ph: (734)847-6726
Fax: (734)847-3137
E-mail: arca@sprintmail.com
URL: http://www.arcaracing.com
Contact: Shalene Williams, Contact
Founded: 1953. **Members:** 600. **Staff:** 15. **Description:** Sanctions and promotes auto racing in the U.S. **Publications:** *Inside Track*. Newsletter.

22569 ■ Championship Association of Mechanics (CAM)
8435 Georgetown Rd., Ste.200
Indianapolis, IN 46224-0694
Ph: (317)802-0001
Fax: (317)802-0003
E-mail: memberships@racecrews.org
URL: http://www.racecrews.org
Contact: Bernie Myers, Pres.
Founded: 1989. **Members:** 800. **Membership Dues:** full, in U.S., $60 (annual) ● full, in Canada, $75 (annual) ● associate, in U.S., $50 (annual) ● associate, in Canada, $70 (annual). **Staff:** 3. **Description:** Professional association of Indy car racing crew members. Promotes the achievements of Indy crew members and encourages increased media coverage. Provides educational opportunities for improving

technical and management skills. Operates benevolent fund to assist charities. Conducts charitable activities including Special Crew Member program with Special Olympics International. Operates speakers' bureau. **Awards:** CAM special Appreciation. **Frequency:** annual. **Type:** recognition. **Recipient:** for individual ● Coast Fabrication/CAM Rookie of the Year. **Frequency:** annual. **Type:** recognition. **Recipient:** for rookie ● Feather trailers/CAM Transport Driver of the Year. **Frequency:** annual. **Type:** monetary. **Recipient:** for driver ● Firestone/CAM Tire Specialist of the Year. **Frequency:** annual. **Type:** recognition. **Recipient:** for individual ● Lincoln Electric/CAM AJ Watson Award for Fabricator of the Year. **Frequency:** annual. **Type:** recognition. **Recipient:** for individual ● Mechanix Wear/CAM Quick Pit. **Frequency:** annual. **Type:** recognition. **Recipient:** for individual. **Publications:** *CAM News*, periodic ● *CAMAGRAM*, 16/year. Newsletter. Contains information of interest to members and media.

22570 ■ Championship Auto Racing Teams (CART)
5350 Lakeview Pkwy., South Dr.
Indianapolis, IN 46268-5129
Ph: (317)715-4100
Fax: (317)715-4110
E-mail: humanresources@champcar.ws
URL: http://www.champcarworldseries.com
Contact: Dick Eidswick, Chm.
Founded: 1978. **Members:** 2,000. **Staff:** 70. **Languages:** Arabic, Cantonese, Czech, Danish, English, Italian, Japanese, Polish, Portuguese, Russian, Swedish. **Multinational. Description:** Race car owners who compete for series championships. Serves as the scheduling and rule-making body for champcar type motor racing events. Seeks to enhance the sport of automobile racing. Organizes and sanctions annual FedEx Championship Series throughout North America, Australia, Brazil, Japan, England, Germany, and Mexico. **Publications:** *Market Research Brochure*, quarterly ● *Media Guide*, annual ● *Rule Book*, annual. Alternate Formats: online ● *Technical Bulletin*, periodic.

22571 ■ International Hot Rod Association (IHRA)
9 1/2 E Main St.
Norwalk, OH 44857
Ph: (419)663-6666 (419)660-4209
Fax: (419)663-4472
E-mail: comments@ihra.com
URL: http://ihra.com
Contact: Aaron Polburn, Pres.
Founded: 1970. **Members:** 25,000. **Membership Dues:** basic in U.S., basic (foreign), $45 (annual) ● basic, in Canada, $95 (annual) ● all other country, $120 (annual). **Description:** Promotes safety and encourages sportsman participation in drag racing. Strives to become a responsive organization for both promoters and competitors through the sanctioning of numerous drag strips throughout the country. Conducts IHRA World Championship Series for professional and sportsman drag racers. Sponsors competitions and compiles statistics. **Awards:** **Frequency:** annual. **Type:** recognition. **Recipient:** for outstanding achievers in drag racing. **Absorbed:** (1984) Professional Drag Racing Association. **Publications:** *Drag Review*, semimonthly. Magazine. **Price:** included in membership dues. ISSN: 1053-6248. **Advertising:** accepted ● *Official IHRA Rule Book*, annual. **Price:** included in membership dues; $10.00 for nonmembers ● *Souvenir Programs*, monthly. **Conventions/Meetings:** annual banquet.

22572 ■ International Motor Contest Association (IMCA)
1800 W D St.
PO Box 921
Vinton, IA 52349
Ph: (319)472-2201
Fax: (319)472-2218
E-mail: raceimca@imca.com
URL: http://www.imca.com
Contact: Kathy Root, Pres.
Founded: 1915. **Members:** 6,000. **Staff:** 14. **Budget:** $1,500,000. **For-Profit. Description:** Auto race driv-

ers, auto race car owners, and mechanics; auto racing sanctioning body to establish rules, regulations, and specifications. Sanctions competitions for late models, sprint cars, modifieds, and stock cars. Offers extensive auto safety programs; maintains hall of fame. **Awards:** **Frequency:** annual. **Type:** recognition. **Publications:** *Inside IMCA*, monthly. Newsletter. Contains association's activities. **Price:** included in membership dues; $19.95 /year for nonmembers. **Circulation:** 9,000. **Advertising:** accepted ● Yearbook. **Price:** $7.00. **Conventions/Meetings:** annual banquet (exhibits) - always November.

22573 ■ International Motor Sports Association (IMSA)
1394 Broadway Ave.
Braselton, GA 30517
Ph: (706)658-2120
Fax: (706)658-2130
E-mail: webmaster@imsaracing.net
URL: http://www.imsaracing.net
Contact: H. Doug Robinson, Exec. Dir.
Founded: 1969. **Members:** 1,900. **Membership Dues:** basic, in U.S., $5 ● basic, in Canada, $8. **For-Profit. Description:** Governing body for American Le Mans series races: with exotic foreign and domestic prototype sports car. **Libraries:** **Type:** reference. **Holdings:** biographical archives. **Subjects:** driver/team info. **Awards:** **Type:** recognition. **Affiliated With:** Automobile Competition Committee for the United States FIA. **Formerly:** (2002) Professional Sports Car Racing.

22574 ■ National American Motors Drivers and Racers Association (NAMDRA)
PO Box 987
Twin Lakes, WI 53181-0987
Ph: (262)843-4326
Fax: (262)396-9552
E-mail: namdra@juno.com
URL: http://www.namdra.org
Contact: Jock Jocewicz, Contact
Founded: 1978. **Members:** 1,676. **Membership Dues:** $30 (annual). **Staff:** 12. **State Groups:** 7. **Description:** AMC automobile owners. Promotes use of AMC and AMC/Jeep vehicles in drag race competitions; sponsors car shows, swap meets, and races. Serves as a clearinghouse and parts exchange for members. Maintains library of owners' parts, shop manuals and manufacturers. **Libraries:** **Type:** not open to the public. **Holdings:** 85. **Awards:** Golden Quill Award. **Frequency:** annual. **Type:** recognition. **Formerly:** (1983) American Motors Drag Racing Association; (1985) National American Motors Drag Racing Association. **Publications:** *Tough Americans*, monthly. Newsletter. Includes coverage of automobile races and shows, AMC parts and service listings, calendar of events, and member profiles. **Price:** included in membership dues. **Circulation:** 1,700. **Advertising:** accepted. **Conventions/Meetings:** annual AMC Nationals - convention, with drag racing, car show, and swap meet for AMC's only (exhibits) - usually summer.

22575 ■ National Association for Stock Car Auto Racing (NASCAR)
1801 W Intl. Speedway Blvd.
PO Box 2875
Daytona Beach, FL 32120
Ph: (386)253-0611
Fax: (386)258-7646
E-mail: nascar@turner.com
URL: http://www.nascar.com
Contact: Mike Helton, Pres.
Founded: 1947. **Members:** 42,000. **Membership Dues:** $40 (annual). **Staff:** 100. **For-Profit. Description:** Sanctions and supervises stock car races. Compiles statistics. **Awards:** **Type:** recognition. **Publications:** *NASCAR News*, semimonthly. Provides stock car racing schedules and results; includes profiles of drivers, officials, and race tracks. **Price:** included in membership dues; $35.00 /year for nonmembers. **Circulation:** 44,000. **Advertising:** accepted. **Conventions/Meetings:** annual banquet - always December, New York City.

22576 ■ National Auto Racing Historical Society (NARHS)

121 Mt. Vernon
Boston, MA 02108
Ph: (617)723-2661
Fax: (617)723-2333
E-mail: jfreeman@racemaker.com
Contact: Joseph S. Freeman, Communications Dir.
Founded: 1979. **Members:** 25. **Membership Dues:** $10 (annual). **Description:** Auto racing historians. Assists advertising, public relations, and other media personnel in using antique autos or automotive historical themes. **Convention/Meeting:** none. **Publications:** none. **Libraries: Type:** reference. **Holdings:** 1,000. **Subjects:** automotive, automobile racing history. **Affiliated With:** Veteran Motor Car Club of America.

22577 ■ National Hot Rod Association (NHRA)

2035 Financial Way
Glendora, CA 91741
Ph: (626)914-4761
Fax: (626)963-5360
E-mail: nhra@nhra.com
URL: http://www.nhra.com
Contact: Tom Compton, Pres.
Founded: 1951. **Members:** 80,000. **Membership Dues:** in U.S., $64 (annual) ● in Canada and Mexico, $100 (annual) ● overseas, $106 (annual). **Staff:** 200. **Regional Groups:** 7. **Description:** Persons interested in automobiles modified and designed for performance and acceleration. Sets competition rules and construction guidelines; promotes regional and national drag races; conducts world championship points series and certifies official records. Conducts design and safety research; provides automotive data. Emphasizes safety, ingenuity, and sportsmanship in races and on the road; encourages civic activities by local groups. Sanctions racing events at 140 tracks in the U.S. and Canada. Maintains photographic file. Produces 23 television shows based on national racing events. **Computer Services:** database, membership list. **Committees:** Show. **Affiliated With:** Automobile Competition Committee for the United States FIA. **Publications:** *National Dragster*, weekly. Newspaper. Covers industry developments and racing results and personalities; includes indexes of advertisers and NHRA classes. Also contains calendar. **Price:** included in membership dues. **Circulation:** 80,000. **Advertising:** accepted ● *NHRA Fan Guide*. Yearbook. Includes award winner profiles and calendar of national drag racing events. **Price:** $5.00/issue. **Advertising:** accepted ● *NHRA Rulebook*, annual. Includes guide to the rules governing designing and racing a car in sanctioned NHRA drag races. **Price:** included in membership dues; $10.00/issue for nonmembers. **Circulation:** 120,000. **Advertising:** accepted ● Also publishes safety and educational pamphlets and individual event programs.

22578 ■ Northern Late Model Racing Association (NLRA)

c/o Harold Schill Jr., Pres.
1817 8th Ave. N
Grand Forks, ND 58203
Ph: (701)356-5320 (701)282-3002
Free: (800)726-8022
E-mail: harolds@mcneilus.com
URL: http://www.nlra.org
Contact: Harold Schill Jr., Pres.
Founded: 1997. **Members:** 55. **Membership Dues:** voting, $75 (annual) ● non-voting, $25 (annual). **Local Groups:** 1. **Description:** Works for the betterment and advancement of late model cars and all racing vehicles. **Awards:** Point Fund. **Frequency:** annual. **Type:** monetary. **Computer Services:** Online services, message and information board. **Conventions/Meetings:** semiannual meeting - March/December.

22579 ■ Sportscar Vintage Racing Association (SVRA)

257 Dekalb Indus. Way
Decatur, GA 30030
Ph: (404)298-3323

Fax: (404)298-3325
E-mail: kim@svra.com
URL: http://www.svra.com
Contact: Kim Belinc, Registrar
Founded: 1978. **Members:** 2,000. **Membership Dues:** general, $85 (annual) ● dual general, $105 (annual) ● competition license/one lap license driver/one lap license non-driver, $150 (annual) ● dual competition license, $225 (annual). **Staff:** 5. **Budget:** $650,000. **For-Profit. Description:** Serves as sanctioning body for vintage sports car races. **Libraries: Type:** reference. **Awards:** Bob Prouty Award. **Frequency:** annual. **Type:** recognition ● BUBBA Award. **Frequency:** annual. **Type:** recognition ● Charlie Gibson Award. **Frequency:** annual. **Type:** recognition ● Driver of the Year. **Frequency:** annual. **Type:** recognition ● Hugh Kleinpeter Award. **Frequency:** annual. **Type:** recognition ● Most Improved Driver. **Frequency:** annual. **Type:** recognition ● Rookie of the Year. **Frequency:** annual. **Type:** recognition. **Programs:** Driver Orientation. **Publications:** *The Line*, monthly. Newsletter. **Price:** included in membership dues. **Circulation:** 2,000. **Advertising:** accepted. **Conventions/Meetings:** monthly competition (exhibits).

22580 ■ United States Auto Club (USAC)

4910 W 16th St.
Speedway, IN 46224
Ph: (317)247-5151
Fax: (317)247-0123
URL: http://www.usacracing.com
Contact: Rollie Helmling, Pres./CEO
Founded: 1955. **Members:** 5,000. **Staff:** 18. **Description:** Officials, manufacturers' representatives, mechanics, drivers, and car owners. Purposes are to: provide qualified leadership and officiating at major automotive competitions; license personnel; sanction competitions; maintain permanent records of accomplishments; schedule events; execute other functions necessary for the proper control of motorsports in the U.S. **Committees:** Benevolent; Certification; Rules; Safety; Safety Research; Technical. **Divisions:** Certification of Special Events; Dirt Track; F 2000; Midget; National Championship; Sprint; TQ Midget. **Publications:** *U.S. Auto Club—Media Guide/Yearbook*, annual. Directory. Contains lists of drivers, statistics, and race track information, index of advertisers, season wrap-up of all racing divisions, and biographies. **Advertising:** accepted ● *USAC News*, biweekly. Newsletter. Includes USAC race divisions, race reports, drivers, sponsors, and statistics. **Price:** included in membership dues. **Advertising:** accepted ● Also issues press releases. **Conventions/Meetings:** annual meeting - always January, in Indianapolis, IN.

Badminton

22581 ■ USA Badminton (USAB)

1 Olympic Plz.
Colorado Springs, CO 80909
Ph: (719)866-4808
Fax: (719)866-4507
E-mail: usab@usabadminton.org
URL: http://www.usabadminton.org
Contact: Dan Cloppas, Exec. Dir.
Founded: 1936. **Members:** 4,000. **Membership Dues:** adult, $30 (annual) ● junior, $20 (annual) ● family, $65 (annual) ● regular, $80 (triennial) ● junior, $50 (triennial) ● family, $145 (triennial) ● regular, $125 (quinquennial) ● junior, $75 (quinquennial) ● family, $230 (quinquennial) ● life, $750. **Staff:** 4. **Budget:** $550,000. **Regional Groups:** 5. **State Groups:** 50. **Local Groups:** 177. **Description:** National Governing body for the Olympic sport of badminton in the U.S. Assists in development of clubs, associations, and grassroots development upholds rules and status of players, and arranges and manages tournaments. **Committees:** Coaching; Court Officials; Disabled Athletes; Finance; Grassroots Development; Grievance; High School Programs; International Competitions; Juniors; Legal; Membership; NCAA; Olympic Player Development;

Ranking; Senior Council. **Affiliated With:** Badminton World Federation. **Formerly:** (1998) United States Badminton Association. **Publications:** *Badminton USA Magazine*, quarterly. Includes articles on badminton tournaments, drug testing, coaching, and regional news. **Price:** included in membership dues; $15.00 /year for nonmembers. **Circulation:** 2,500. **Advertising:** accepted ● Also publishes Senior Nationals, Adults Nationals, Junior Nationals, US Open, BCD Nationals. **Conventions/Meetings:** semiannual board meeting.

Ball Games

22582 ■ American Roque and Croquet Association (ARL)

PO Box 2304
Richmond, IN 47375-2304
Ph: (765)962-7191 (765)939-2544
Fax: (765)935-2638
E-mail: jackr100@insightbb.com
Contact: Jack R. Roegner, Pres.
Founded: 1902. **Membership Dues:** voting, $5 (annual). **Regional Groups:** 6. **Description:** Individuals interested in promoting the game of roque (a combination game of croquet and billiards). Holds local, state, and national tournaments. Maintains speakers' bureau. Sponsors clinics. **Libraries: Type:** reference. **Holdings:** archival material. **Awards:** National Champion. **Frequency:** annual. **Type:** recognition. **Committees:** Awards; Rules; Tournament. **Divisions:** Croquet; 4-Ball; 2-Ball. **Absorbed:** National Roque Association. **Formerly:** Western Roque Association; (1991) American Roque League. **Publications:** *ARL Player and Club Directory*, annual. **Price:** $25.00. **Advertising:** accepted ● *Roque News*, monthly ● *Roque - Official Rules and Regulations*. **Conventions/Meetings:** annual meeting and competition ● workshop.

22583 ■ National Amateur Dodgeball Association (NADA)

c/o Schaumburg Park District
220 E Weathersfield Way
Schaumburg, IL 60193
Ph: (847)985-2144 (847)985-2115
Fax: (847)985-2461
E-mail: dodgeballusa@parkfun.com
URL: http://www.dodgeballusa.com
Membership Dues: individual, $15 ● collegiate club, $40-$150 ● agency, $200-$300. **Multinational. Description:** Serves as a recreational pursuit for non-traditional sports enthusiasts. Promotes and encourages individual involvement in dodgeball. Conducts tournaments and maximizes members' social enjoyment. **Computer Services:** Information services, dodgeball resources ● mailing lists, of members. **Affiliated With:** National Intramural-Recreational Sports Association. **Publications:** *Official NADA Rule Book*. Booklet. **Price:** $3.00 for members; $2.00 for non-members. **Alternate Formats:** online.

22584 ■ National Paddleball Association (NPA)

7642 Kingston Dr.
Portage, MI 49002
Ph: (269)323-0121
Free: (888)871-1501
Fax: (269)279-6275
E-mail: npa@paddleball.org
URL: http://www.paddleball.org
Contact: Lorri Brigham, Contact.
Founded: 1930. **Members:** 400. **Membership Dues:** individual, $25 (annual). **Description:** Persons interested in the sport of paddleball. Distributes rules and recommends equipment for paddleball games. Conducts educational programs and sanctions tournaments. **Awards:** Earl Riskey Award. **Frequency:** annual. **Type:** recognition. **Recipient:** for contributions to the sport. **Publications:** *NPA Newsletter*, quarterly. Contains tournament information and player profiles. **Price:** included in membership dues. **Circulation:** 600. **Advertising:** accepted. **Conventions/Meetings:** annual National Doubles Tourna-

ment - competition ● annual National Singles Tournament - competition.

22585 ■ United States Floorball Association (USFbA)
4301 Fathom Ct.
Raleigh, NC 27606
Ph: (919)233-7274
Fax: (919)233-7249
E-mail: usafloorball@aol.com
URL: http://www.usafloorball.org
Contact: Ollie Rupp, Pres.
Membership Dues: individual, $50 (annual) ● club, $500 (annual). **Description:** Promotes the sport of floorball in the USA. Organizes training camps, competitions and tournaments. **Computer Services:** Information services, floorball resources.

22586 ■ U.S.A Team Handball
One Olympic Plz.
Colorado Springs, CO 80909
Ph: (719)866-4038
Fax: (719)866-4055
E-mail: mike.cavanaugh@usoc.org
URL: http://www.usateamhandball.org
Contact: Michael D. Cavanaugh, Exec. Dir.
Founded: 1959. **Members:** 1,000. **Membership Dues:** youth, $15 (annual) ● junior, $25 (annual) ● adult, $35 (annual) ● bronze, $50 (annual) ● life, $400. **Staff:** 3. **Budget:** $400,000. **Regional Groups:** 4. **State Groups:** 6. **Local Groups:** 50. **Description:** Schools, universities, players, and coaches. Seeks to develop team handball in the United States. Conducts the National and International Team Handball program of the U.S. and serves as the national governing body, directing the U.S. Team Handball Program for the Olympic games. Maintains clinics and training camps; sponsors competitions. **Awards:** Developmental Grant. **Frequency:** annual. **Type:** grant. **Committees:** Coaching and Methods; Development; Men's and Women's National Olympic Teams; Organizing and Competition; Public Relations; Rules and Referees; Sports Medicine. **Affiliated With:** Boys and Girls Clubs of America; International Handball Federation; Special Olympics. **Formerly:** (1999) U.S. Team Handball Federation. **Publications:** *Fast Break.* **Price:** included in membership dues ● *Handball Happenings*, monthly. Newsletter. Includes updates on local club activities, national and international competitions, election results, and other special events. **Price:** included in membership dues. **Circulation:** 120. **Advertising:** accepted ● *Team Handball-USA*, quarterly. Magazine. Includes news of members, media contacts, and new developments in the sport. **Price:** included in membership dues; $3.00/issue for nonmembers. **Circulation:** 2,000. **Advertising:** accepted ● Books. **Conventions/Meetings:** semiannual board meeting ● biennial congress.

Ballooning

22587 ■ Aeronaut Society (AS)
Address Unknown since 2007
Founded: 1975. **Members:** 100. **Staff:** 2. **Regional Groups:** 2. **Languages:** English, French, German, Spanish. **Description:** Balloon owners, aeronauts, and crew. Maintains speakers' bureau. Sponsors specialized education. Conducts balloon flights in different countries. Provides balloons for films/tv commercials, etc. Provides balloon expert witnesses. Provides and writes books on ballooning, including textbooks on earning a pilot certificate and how to fly a balloon. **Libraries: Type:** reference. **Holdings:** archival material, artwork, audiovisuals, books, clippings, periodicals. **Subjects:** hot-air balloons, gas balloons, airships. **Awards:** Pate' Award. **Frequency:** annual. **Type:** trophy. **Recipient:** best post-balloon-flying picnic. **Computer Services:** Mailing lists. **Formerly:** (1975) International Society of Aeronauts. **Publications:** *Minutes*, monthly. **Advertising:** not accepted ● *Roster*, annual. **Conventions/Meetings:** monthly meeting - every third Wednesday.

22588 ■ Balloon Federation of America (BFA)
PO Box 400
Indianola, IA 50125
Ph: (515)961-8809
Fax: (515)961-3537
E-mail: bfaoffice@bfa.net
URL: http://www.bfa.net
Contact: Sharon Ripperger, Office Mgr.
Founded: 1961. **Members:** 3,000. **Membership Dues:** associate, $55 (annual) ● foreign, $100 (annual) ● in Canada and Mexico, $65 (annual) ● life, $1,000 ● family, $20 (annual). **Description:** Active thermal and gas balloonists who own their own balloons or who belong to clubs that own one or more balloons. Supervises and documents official ballooning competitions and record attempts in the U.S. in accordance with the requirements of the International Aeronautical Federation and the National Aeronautic Association of the U.S.A; ensures that all sanctioned contests are governed in accordance with the FAI Sporting Code; promulgates specific rules relating to balloon competition. **Libraries: Type:** reference. **Holdings:** films. **Awards:** Bill Murtoff Award. **Frequency:** annual. **Type:** recognition. **Recipient:** to a member who has contributed to youth programs or education in the sport of ballooning ● Shields-Trauger Award. **Frequency:** annual. **Type:** recognition. **Recipient:** for special contribution to aerostatics. **Computer Services:** Mailing lists. **Committees:** Awards; Ballooning Journal; Competition; Education; Film and Seminar Library; Gas Balloon Events; Government Liaison; Museum; Public Relations; Safety. **Affiliated With:** National Aeronautic Association. **Publications:** *Ballooning*, bimonthly. Journal. **Price:** included in membership dues. **Advertising:** accepted ● *Skylines*, monthly. Newsletter. **Price:** included in membership dues. **Advertising:** accepted. **Conventions/Meetings:** annual U.S. National Hot Air Balloon Championship - meeting.

22589 ■ Highamerica Balloon Club (HBC)
Address Unknown since 2007
Founded: 1968. **Members:** 300. **Description:** All individuals interested in the sport of ballooning (flying large balloons filled with hot air, capable of lifting and transporting a pilot-passenger in a gondola or similar carrier). **Formerly:** (1977) Balloon Platoon of America. **Conventions/Meetings:** weekly Balloon Launch - meeting.

Baseball

22590 ■ American Amateur Baseball Congress (AABC)
100 W Broadway
Farmington, NM 87401
Ph: (505)327-3120
Fax: (505)327-3132
E-mail: aabc@aabc.us
URL: http://www.aabc.us
Contact: Mike Dimond, Pres.
Founded: 1935. **Staff:** 2. **Regional Groups:** 7. **Local Groups:** 1,800. **Description:** State and regional baseball affiliates in the U.S.A., Puerto Rico, and Canada with 14,000 teams in 7 age divisions. Governing body and service bureau. Provides standard rules of play and eligibility, sanctions tournaments, and performs administrative services. Sponsors 7 annual national age group tournaments: Stan Musial World Series (unlimited age); Connie Mack World Series (18 and under); Mickey Mantle World Series (16 and under); Sandy Koufax World Series (14 and under); Pee Wee Reese World Series (12 and under); Willie Mays World Series (ten and under); Roberto Clemente (8 and under). **Libraries: Type:** reference. **Subjects:** baseball. **Divisions:** Connie Mack; Mickey Mantle; Peewee Reese; Roberto Clemente; Sandy Koufax; Stan Musial; Willie Mays. **Formerly:** (1955) American Baseball Congress. **Publications:** *Amateur Baseball News*, 7/year. Newspaper. **Price:** $5.00 for nonmembers. **Circulation:** 15,000. **Advertising:** accepted. **Alternate Formats:** online ● Handbooks. **Conventions/Meetings:** annual conference - always mid-November.

22591 ■ American Baseball Coaches Association (ABCA)
108 S Univ. Ave., Ste.3
Mount Pleasant, MI 48858-2327
Ph: (989)775-3300
Fax: (989)775-3600
E-mail: abca@abca.org
URL: http://www.abca.org
Contact: Dave Keilitz, Exec. Dir.
Founded: 1945. **Members:** 5,350. **Membership Dues:** individual in U.S., $30 (annual) ● individual in Canada, $35 (annual) ● individual outside U.S. and Canada, $40 (annual). **Staff:** 4. **Budget:** $700,000. **Multinational. Description:** Baseball coaches in high schools, colleges, and universities; interested individuals. Maintains hall of fame for amateur baseball coaches in Louisville, KY. Conducts clinics. Provides baseball publication. **Awards:** All-American Teams. **Frequency:** annual. **Type:** recognition ● Coaches of the Year. **Type:** recognition ● Hall of Fame. **Frequency:** annual. **Type:** recognition ● Honor Awards. **Type:** recognition ● Lefty Gomez Award. **Frequency:** annual. **Type:** recognition. **Committees:** All American/Coach of the Year; Clinic; Divisional; Editorial; Exhibitors; Hall of Fame; Lefty Gomez Award; Legislative Issues; Nominating/Awards; Playing Rules-College; Playing Rules-High School; Professional/Amateur Relations; Research; Summer Leagues; Veterans Hall of Fame. **Affiliated With:** National Association of Intercollegiate Athletics; National Collegiate Athletic Association; National Junior College Athletic Association. **Formerly:** (1984) American Association of College Baseball Coaches. **Publications:** *ABCA Directory & Buyer's Guide*, annual. Includes associations' guides. **Price:** included in membership dues. **Advertising:** accepted ● *Coaching Digest*, semiannual. Article ● *Covering All Bases*, 3/year. Newsletter. Covers association activities. **Price:** included in membership dues. **Advertising:** accepted. **Conventions/Meetings:** annual convention, sporting goods and equipment, coaching clinics, honors banquets (exhibits) - always January.

22592 ■ American Baseball Foundation
2660 10th Ave. S, Ste.620
Birmingham, AL 35205
Ph: (205)558-4235
Fax: (205)918-0800
E-mail: abf@americanbaseball.org
URL: http://www.americanbaseball.org
Contact: E. David Osinski, Exec. Dir.
Founded: 1994. **Members:** 200. **Staff:** 7. **Budget:** $125,000. **Languages:** English, Spanish. **Description:** Works to develop programs for community outreach through sports education. Teaches fundamentals of baseball to youth. Helps build confidence in individuals. Orients coaches, parents and families in nurturing children through recreation, competition and learning. **Awards:** Enchiro Yamamoto Award. **Frequency:** annual. **Type:** recognition. **Recipient:** for lifetime achievement in international baseball ● James R. Andrews Health South Comeback Player of the Year Award. **Frequency:** annual. **Type:** recognition. **Publications:** *The Pitch*, quarterly. Newsletter. Contains program updates. ISSN: 1086-0401. **Circulation:** 4,000.

22593 ■ American Legion Baseball (ALB)
700 N Pennsylvania St.
Indianapolis, IN 46204
Fax: (317)630-1369
E-mail: acy@legion.org
URL: http://www.baseball.legion.org
Contact: Joseph Rivich, Contact
Founded: 1925. **Members:** 100,000. **Staff:** 2. **Budget:** $1,000,000. **State Groups:** 50. **Local Groups:** 5,000. **Description:** Teams of teenagers playing supervised summer baseball under leadership provided by volunteer adult managers and coaches. Teams are locally financed by individuals, service clubs, and commercial business firms. Purposes are to: stimulate greater baseball activity in local communities; help preserve and improve recreational facilities; aid in the development and improvement of the physical fitness of America's youth; combat juvenile delinquency through positive methods.

Conducts coaching clinics, administrative conferences, and annual tournaments. Compiles statistics. **Libraries: Type:** reference. **Awards:** Dr. Irvin L. (Click) Cowger RBI Memorial Award. **Frequency:** annual. **Type:** recognition ● George W. Rulon American Legion Player of the Year. **Frequency:** annual. **Type:** recognition. **Recipient:** to a player with integrity, mental attitude, cooperation, citizenship, sportsmanship, scholastic aptitude, and general good conduct ● Jack Williams Memorial Leadership Award. **Frequency:** annual. **Type:** recognition. **Recipient:** for manager and coach of the National Championship Team ● James F. Daniel, Jr. Memorial Sportsmanship Award. **Frequency:** annual. **Type:** recognition. **Recipient:** to a player who best represents the principles of good sportsmanship ● Louisville Slugger Batting Champion Award. **Frequency:** annual. **Type:** recognition. **Recipient:** to a player compiling the highest batting average during national competition ● Rawlings Big Stick Award. **Frequency:** annual. **Type:** recognition. **Recipient:** for a player compiling the highest number of bases in regional and national competition. **Affiliated With:** U.S.A. Baseball. **Publications:** *Baseball Handbook*, annual. Official American Legion baseball rules. **Circulation:** 15,000. **Advertising:** accepted. **Conventions/Meetings:** annual conference - always Indianapolis, IN.

22594 ■ Association of Professional Ball Players of America (APBPA)
1820 W Orangewood Ave., Ste.206
Orange, CA 92868-2052
Ph: (714)935-9993
URL: http://www.apbpa.org
Contact: Dick Beverage, Sec.-Treas.
Founded: 1924. **Members:** 9,800. **Membership Dues:** individual, $12-$75 (annual). **Staff:** 2. **Description:** Represents baseball players, umpires, coaches, trainers, scouts, and managers. **Conventions/Meetings:** annual meeting.

22595 ■ Babe Ruth Baseball/Softball (BRB)
Babe Ruth League, Inc.
1770 Brunswick Pike
PO Box 5000
Trenton, NJ 08638
Ph: (609)695-1434
Free: (800)880-3142
Fax: (609)695-2505
E-mail: info@baberuthleague.org
URL: http://www.baberuthleague.org
Contact: Mr. Steven Tellefsen, Pres./CEO
Founded: 1951. **Members:** 800,000. **Staff:** 15. **State Groups:** 65. **Local Groups:** 5,500. **Description:** Supervises baseball and softball activity for youths five to eighteen years of age. Conducts eight World Series annually. Sponsors workshops. **Formerly:** (1954) Little Bigger League. **Publications:** *Babe Ruth Baseball Line Drives*, monthly. Newsletter. Includes information about membership activities. **Price:** free ● *Babe Ruth League Bullpen*, quarterly. Newspaper. Includes umpire's tips column and articles on fundraising activities, corporate sponsors, clinics, camps, and local leagues. **Price:** free. **Circulation:** 33,000. **Advertising:** accepted ● Manuals. Includes rules and regulations. ● Also publishes media guide. **Conventions/Meetings:** periodic conference ● annual meeting - always in Fort Lauderdale, FL.

22596 ■ Babe Ruth Birthplace/Sports Legends at Camden Yards
216 Emory St.
Baltimore, MD 21230
Ph: (410)727-1539
Free: (888)438-6909
Fax: (410)727-1652
E-mail: info@baberuthmuseum.com
URL: http://www.baberuthmuseum.com
Contact: Michael Louis Gibbons, Exec. Dir.
Founded: 1973. **Members:** 2,000. **Membership Dues:** student, $35 (annual) ● individual, $45 (annual) ● family, $65 (annual). **Staff:** 20. **Budget:** $750,000. **Description:** Represents the interests of individuals and corporations. Maintains the historic legacy of Babe Ruth, Baltimore's Orioles and Colts,

and local and regional sports at the amateur, collegiate and professional levels, by preserving, exhibiting, interpreting and augmenting its collections for a diverse audience. Promotes the sport of baseball through community outreach events and children's educational programs. Operates speakers' bureau. Conducts charitable program; compiles statistics. Maintains hall of fame and collection of memorabilia, photographs, and ephemera on Ruth, the Orioles, and Maryland baseball. Maintains Baltimore Colts archive and John Unitas' football memorabilia collection. **Additional Websites:** http://www.sportslegendsatcamdenyards.com. **Committees:** Collections; Educational; Finance; Human Resources; Marketing. **Affiliated With:** International Sports Heritage Association. **Formerly:** (2000) Babe Ruth Birthplace Foundation; (2005) Babe Ruth Museum/Sports Legends at Camden Yards. **Publications:** *Score!*, quarterly. Newsletter. Includes calendar of events. **Price:** free. **Circulation:** 1,500 ● Brochures.

22597 ■ Cosmic Baseball Association (CBA)
c/o Journal of the Cosmic Baseball Association
907 6th St. SW, Ste.214
Washington, DC 20024
E-mail: editor@cosmicbaseball.com
URL: http://www.cosmicbaseball.com
Contact: Anne Nelson, Ed.
Founded: 1981. **Description:** Represents individuals interested in "fantasy baseball with a philosophical/political/intellectual focus".

22598 ■ George Khoury Association of Baseball Leagues (GKABL)
5400 Meramec Bottom Rd.
St. Louis, MO 63128
Ph: (314)849-8900
URL: http://www.khouryleague.org
Contact: George G. Khoury, Exec. Dir.
Founded: 1936. **Members:** 850,000. **Description:** Boys and girls seven years of age and older who play baseball or softball in 60,000 leagues organized by local fraternal, church, service or community organizations, or by individuals. Believes good citizens can be built on baseball diamonds much better than in back alleys. Official Khoury rules and regulations are slightly different from those of major leagues to allow for size and ability of players and to enable as many teams as possible to enjoy the thrill of being winners. Conducts end of season playoffs; supplies official forms and certificates to local teams.

22599 ■ International League of Professional Baseball Clubs (ILPBC)
55 S High St., Ste.202
Dublin, OH 43017
Ph: (614)791-9300
Fax: (614)791-9009
E-mail: office@ilbaseball.com
Contact: Randy Mobley, Pres.
Founded: 1884. **Members:** 10. **Description:** Baseball clubs in the U.S. **Conventions/Meetings:** annual meeting.

22600 ■ Little League Baseball and Softball (LLB)
PO Box 3485
Williamsport, PA 17701-0485
Ph: (570)326-1921
Fax: (570)326-1074
E-mail: cdowns@littleleague.org
URL: http://www.littleleague.org
Contact: Stephen D. Keener, Pres./CEO
Founded: 1939. **Members:** 2,900,000. **Membership Dues:** player, $1 (annual). **Staff:** 100. **Regional Groups:** 9. **State Groups:** 50. **Local Groups:** 650. **National Groups:** 65. **Multinational. Description:** Children 5 to 18 years of age. Organizes baseball and softball programs in every state, 104 countries, and U.S. territorial possessions. Operates Challenger Division for disabled children. Sponsors international World Series each August. Offers clinics for managers, coaches, umpires, and administrative personnel. Observes Little League Week on the second week of June. Maintains Peter J. McGovern Little League Baseball Museum in Williamsport, PA. **Computer**

Services: database, list of world series players. **Formerly:** (2004) Little League Baseball. **Publications:** Handbooks ● Manuals. **Conventions/Meetings:** triennial International Congress - meeting and seminar, delegates vote on rules changes (exhibits).

22601 ■ Little League Foundation (LLF)
539 US Rte. 15 Hwy.
PO Box 3485
Williamsport, PA 17701-0485
Ph: (570)326-1921
Fax: (570)326-1074
E-mail: sconnolley@littleleague.org
URL: http://www.littleleague.org
Contact: Howard Paster, Pres.
Founded: 1955. **Members:** 19. **Description:** Seeks to stabilize and ensure the future of the Little League Baseball movement by raising funds through annual drive during Little League Baseball week; funds are used to develop needed facilities and expand Little League services to local leagues. **Affiliated With:** Little League Baseball and Softball. **Publications:** Brochure.

22602 ■ Major League Baseball (MLB)
75 9th Ave., 5th Fl.
New York, NY 10011
Ph: (212)931-7800
Free: (866)800-1275
URL: http://mlb.mlb.com/index.jsp
Contact: Allan H. Selig, Commissioner of Baseball
Founded: 1900. **Members:** 14. **Description:** Major league baseball teams in Anaheim, CA; Baltimore, MD; Boston, MA; Chicago, IL; Cleveland, OH; Dallas-Fort Worth, TX; Detroit, MI; Kansas City, MO; Milwaukee, WI; Minneapolis-St. Paul, MN; New York City; Oakland, CA; Seattle, WA; and Toronto, ON, Canada. Compiles statistics. **Libraries: Type:** reference. **Holdings:** biographical archives. **Awards: Type:** recognition. **Recipient:** for various aspects of outstanding play. **Formerly:** (2006) American League of Professional Baseball Clubs. **Publications:** *All Star Guide*, annual ● *American League Red Book*, annual ● *World Series Media Guide*, annual. **Conventions/Meetings:** annual meeting.

22603 ■ Major League Baseball Players Alumni Association (MLBPAA)
1631 Mesa Ave., Ste.B
Colorado Springs, CO 80906-2956
Fax: (719)477-1875
E-mail: postoffice@mlbpaa.com
URL: http://www.baseball-legends.com
Contact: Brooks Robinson, Pres.
Founded: 1982. **Members:** 5,100. **Membership Dues:** fan, $70 (annual) ● all-star, $120 (annual). **Staff:** 9. **Description:** Sponsors golf tournaments and youth baseball clinics. Offers 35-city "Swing with The Legends" charity golf series, charitable programs and children's services. **Computer Services:** database. **Publications:** *Baseball Alumni News*, quarterly. Newsletter. **Circulation:** 6,000. **Advertising:** accepted. **Conventions/Meetings:** board meeting.

22604 ■ National Amateur Baseball Federation (NABF)
c/o Charles M. Blackburn, Jr., Exec. Dir.
PO Box 705
Bowie, MD 20715
Ph: (301)464-5460
Fax: (301)352-0214
E-mail: nabf1914@aol.com
URL: http://www.nabf.com
Contact: Charles M. Blackburn Jr., Exec. Dir.
Founded: 1914. **Members:** 200,000. **Membership Dues:** organization, $150 (annual). **Staff:** 24. **Regional Groups:** 8. **State Groups:** 50. **National Groups:** 256. **Description:** Amateur baseball associations. Promotes noncommercialized baseball in the U.S. Sponsors tournaments in 8 age groups: 12 years and under; 14 years and under; 16 years and under; 17 and under high school division, 18 years and under; college division, 22 years and under; major division; and 10 and under rookie division. Conducts baseball clinics. Sponsors educational and charitable programs. **Libraries: Type:** reference.

Holdings: archival material, books, business records, periodicals. **Awards:** NABF Scholarship Awards. **Frequency:** annual. **Type:** scholarship. **Recipient:** to an active player member of NABF. **Affiliated With:** U.S.A. Baseball. **Formerly:** (1946) National Baseball Federation. **Publications:** *Behind the Seams*, bimonthly ● *NABF Rule Book*, annual. **Circulation:** 125,000. **Advertising:** accepted ● *National Amateur Baseball Federation Tournament News*, annual. Includes tabloid of game results; lists NABF award winners. **Price:** $3.00/copy. **Circulation:** 125,000. **Advertising:** accepted ● *National Baseball Souvenir Programs*, annual. Covers eight age groups. **Conventions/Meetings:** annual convention (exhibits) - always first weekend of November ● meeting, for special events.

22605 ■ National Association of Professional Baseball Leagues (NAPBL)
PO Box A
St. Petersburg, FL 33731
Ph: (727)822-6937
Fax: (727)821-5819
E-mail: admin@minorleaguebaseball.com
URL: http://web.minorleaguebaseball.com/index.jsp
Contact: Mike Moore, Pres./CEO
Founded: 1901. **Members:** 20. **Staff:** 31. **State Groups:** 20. **Local Groups:** 240. **Languages:** English, Spanish. **Multinational. Description:** Represents 20 professional baseball minor leagues composed of 240 baseball teams. Winter leagues in the Caribbean area are associate members. **Libraries: Type:** reference. **Holdings:** archival material, books, business records, clippings, periodicals. **Subjects:** minor league baseball. **Divisions:** Promotion. **Also Known As:** Minor League Baseball. **Publications:** *Baseball News*, 10/year. Newsletter. Contains articles on Minor League baseball. **Price:** $16.00 includes shipping and handling. **Circulation:** 550 ● *Minor League Baseball Information Guide*, annual. Directory. Lists members, schedules, statistics and honors. **Price:** $14.00. **Conventions/Meetings:** annual Baseball Winter Meetings - convention (exhibits).

22606 ■ National Baseball Congress (NBC)
PO Box 1420
Wichita, KS 67201
Ph: (316)267-3372
Fax: (316)267-3382
E-mail: jerry@wichitawranglers.com
URL: http://www.nbcbaseball.com
Contact: Mr. Jerry Taylor CAA, Dir. of Operations
Founded: 1931. **Members:** 4,000. **Staff:** 14. **Budget:** $250,000. **State Groups:** 50. **For-Profit. Description:** Baseball teams competing in leagues and district tournaments for the right to participate in state and regional tournaments in U.S. to qualify for national tournament. Maintains hall of fame; compiles statistics. Offers educational programs. **Awards: Type:** recognition. **Divisions:** Baseball Equipment; Rule Books. **Publications:** *Official Rules of Baseball*, annual. Booklet. Includes current rules as set forth by major league baseball. **Price:** $1.50. **Circulation:** 100,000. **Advertising:** accepted ● *World Series Annual*, annual. Magazine. Contains tournament results. **Price:** $3.00. **Circulation:** 6,000. **Advertising:** accepted. **Conventions/Meetings:** competition ● annual tour (exhibits) - always August, in Wichita, KS.

22607 ■ National Baseball Hall of Fame and Museum
PO Box 590
Cooperstown, NY 13326
Ph: (607)547-7200
Free: (888)425-5633
Fax: (607)547-2044
E-mail: info@baseballhalloffame.org
URL: http://www.baseballhalloffame.org
Contact: Dale Petroskey, Pres.
Founded: 1936. **Members:** 233. **Membership Dues:** junior, $20 (annual) ● individual, $40 (annual) ● family, $70 (annual) ● sustaining, $100 (annual) ● patron, $250 (annual) ● president's circle, $500 (annual) ● benefactor, $1,000 (annual). **Staff:** 75. **Description:** Represents players who have played a minimum of 10 years and have been retired for 23 years or more;

players who were in the Negro Baseball leagues; former baseball managers, executives, and umpires. **Libraries: Type:** open to the public. **Holdings:** 2,600,000; articles, books, periodicals, photographs, video recordings. **Subjects:** baseball. **Awards:** Hall of Fame Champions. **Frequency:** annual. **Type:** recognition. **Recipient:** for individuals whose contributions played a key role in helping the organization. **Publications:** *Around the Horn*, monthly. Newsletter. Contains news on upcoming events and programs. Alternate Formats: online ● *Memories and Dreams*, quarterly. Newsletter. Contains museum news. **Price:** free. **Circulation:** 9,000 ● Yearbook, annual. **Price:** $9.00/copy. **Circulation:** 15,000. **Advertising:** accepted ● Also publishes Scouting Report, free, for participants in junior membership program.

22608 ■ National Junior Baseball League (NJBL)
c/o Jan Rosenblum
2800 Coyle St., Apt. 205
Brooklyn, NY 11235
Ph: (631)582-5191
E-mail: njbl@optonline.net
URL: http://www.nationaljunior.com
Contact: Frank Sullivan, Commissioner
Founded: 1990. **Staff:** 25. **Description:** Supports and promotes the the the development of baseball players through high level competition.

22609 ■ National Pitching Association (NPA)
PO Box 2350
Del Mar, CA 92014
Free: (866)977-4824
E-mail: info@nationalpitching.com
URL: http://www.nationalpitching.net
Contact: Tom House, Founder
Description: Helps pitchers of all ages safely develop to their fullest potential. Focuses on teaching the mechanics of pitching, strength and conditioning requirements, and nutritional necessities, as well as the mental and emotional elements of the sport. Develops the support group that the pitchers require including their parents and coaches. **Publications:** *The Pitch*, bimonthly. Newsletter.

22610 ■ National Semi-Professional Baseball Association (NSPBA)
c/o Tim Turpin, Dir.
8437 Bell Oaks Dr., No. 184
Newburgh, IN 47630
Ph: (812)430-2725
E-mail: timturp15@aol.com
URL: http://eteamz.active.com/NSPBA
Contact: Tim Turpin, Dir.
Founded: 1982. **Members:** 4,000. **Staff:** 1. **State Groups:** 14. **Description:** Baseball teams concerned with the longevity of the game. Works to improve skills and advance baseball careers for individual members. Sponsors North Atlanta Mustangs amateur team. Conducts: the Fastest Kid on the Bases Contest for individuals aged eight to 30; annual Continental Amateur World Series; annual trip to Cooperstown; Men's Senior Leagues, regional tournaments, and World Series in Chattanooga, TN, Cincinnati, OH, and Tempe, AZ; annual Congress World Series; annual Dizzy Dean World Series Classic in Chattanooga, TN; Roy Hobbs World Series for men over age 40, also over 45 and over 50 world series; National Semi Pro Masters Baseball Association for men age 45 and over tournaments. Holds improvement clinics and provides scholarship consultation. Conducts research; disseminates information. Offers placement services. Baseball scholarship consulting for the 21st century. **Libraries: Type:** reference. **Holdings:** 500; archival material, books, clippings. **Awards:** National Semi Pro Hall of Fame Semi Pro Player. **Frequency:** annual. **Type:** scholarship. **Affiliated With:** National Amateur Baseball Federation; U.S.A. Baseball. **Publications:** *Home Plate*, 3/year ● *Mother's Guide to Youth League Baseball*. Audiotape. **Price:** $20.00 ● *Thinking Baseball: The Winning Edge*. Book ● *12 Secrets of Power Hitting*. Book ● Video. Covers baseball techniques. **Conventions/Meetings:** annual International Tournament - competition - always in Atlanta, GA.

22611 ■ Negro Leagues Baseball Museum (NLBM)
1616 E 18th St.
Kansas City, MO 64108-1610
Ph: (816)221-1920
Free: (888)221-NLBM
Fax: (816)221-8424
E-mail: dmotley@nlbm.com
URL: http://www.nlbm.com
Contact: Don B. Motley, Exec. Dir.
Founded: 1990. **Members:** 3,000. **Membership Dues:** individual major leaguer, $25-$49 (annual) ● individual all-star, $50-$99 (annual) ● individual MVP, $100-$499 (annual) ● Hall of Fame individual, $500-$999 (annual) ● Legacy Team individual, $1,000 (annual). **Staff:** 10. **Budget:** $1,000,000. **Description:** Focuses on preserving and illuminating the history of Negro League Baseball and its affect on American society. Promotes an appreciation of the baseball culture that existed "behind the color barrier." Provides assistance to Negro League veterans in need through merchandising of team memorabilia. Maintains Speaker's Bureau; operates museum; conducts educational programs; compiles statistics. **Libraries: Type:** reference. **Holdings:** archival material, audio recordings, books, clippings, periodicals, video recordings. **Subjects:** Negro League, players. **Awards:** Buck O'Neil Scholarship Award. **Frequency:** annual. **Type:** scholarship. **Recipient:** for academic achievement and involvement in sports - high school seniors. **Publications:** *Silhouettes*, quarterly. Newsletter. **Price:** included in membership dues ● *Year End Review*, annual. **Conventions/Meetings:** annual Legacy Awards Banquet, a tribute honoring the spirit of the past with the stars of the present Awarding the best MLB player, the best Negro player trophy (exhibits) ● Night of the Harvest Moon Children's Festival, provides a safe alternative to Halloween for area youth.

22612 ■ Pony Baseball and Softball
PO Box 225
Washington, PA 15301
Ph: (724)225-1060
Fax: (724)225-9852
E-mail: info@pony.org
URL: http://www.pony.org
Contact: Abraham L. Key III, Pres./CEO
Founded: 1951. **Members:** 28,500. **Staff:** 10. **Budget:** $1,300,000. **Description:** Offers organized and supervised summertime recreational baseball and girls softball programs. Leagues include: Shetland League for players 5-6; Pinto Leagues for players 7-8; Mustang Leagues for players 9-10; Bronco Leagues for players 11-12; Pony Leagues for players 13-14; Colt Leagues for players 15-16; Palomino Leagues for players 17-18. Holds annual World Series for Mustang, Bronco, Pony, Colt, and Palomino baseball leagues and conducts national championship tournaments in girls' softball age categories; series rotate to different cities. Maintains hall of fame and museum. **Awards:** Joe E. Brown Award. **Frequency:** annual. **Type:** recognition. **Recipient:** for established volunteer in the organization ● Wall of Fame. **Frequency:** annual. **Type:** recognition. **Recipient:** for volunteer service. **Committees:** Girls' Softball; Rules; Youth Baseball. **Programs:** Coaches Training; Umpire Registration. **Affiliated With:** U.S.A. Baseball. **Formerly:** (1960) Pony League; (1961) Pony and Colt Boys Baseball; (1976) Boys Baseball. **Publications:** *Pony Baseball Blue Book*, annual. Manual. Organizational manual for amateur youth baseball and girls' softball programs. **Price:** included in membership dues; $5.00 /year for nonmembers. **Circulation:** 100,000. **Advertising:** accepted ● *Pony Baseball Rules and Regulations*, annual. **Price:** included in membership dues; $1.00 /year for nonmembers. **Circulation:** 100,000. **Advertising:** accepted. **Conventions/Meetings:** annual board meeting.

22613 ■ Professional Baseball Athletic Trainers Society (PBATS)
c/o Brian Ebel, ATC
Baltimore Orioles
333 W Camden St.
Baltimore, MD 21201

Fax: (410)825-1623
E-mail: info@pbats.com
URL: http://www.pbats.com
Contact: Jamie Reed, Pres.
Founded: 1983. **Members:** 204. **Description:** Represents athletic trainers working for major and minor league baseball teams. Seeks to improve the health care skills of members. Conducts educational programs for minor league athletic trainers. **Libraries: Type:** reference. **Holdings:** books, video recordings. **Subjects:** athletic training. **Awards:** Minor League Trainer of the Year. **Frequency:** annual. **Type:** recognition ● PBATS Athletic Training Staff of the Year. **Frequency:** annual. **Type:** recognition ● PBATS Scholarship. **Frequency:** annual. **Type:** scholarship. **Recipient:** for Minor League trainers and student athletic trainers. **Subgroups:** National Athletic Trainers Association. **Affiliated With:** National Athletic Trainers' Association. **Publications:** *PBATS Newsletter,* semiannual. Contains articles on the prevention, treatment, and rehabilitation of athletic injuries. **Price:** free. **Circulation:** 20,000. **Conventions/Meetings:** annual seminar, for Minor League trainers - always in December.

22614 ■ Society for American Baseball Research (SABR)
812 Huron Rd., No. 719
Cleveland, OH 44115
Ph: (216)575-0500
Free: (800)964-7227
Fax: (216)575-0502
E-mail: info@sabr.org
URL: http://www.sabr.org
Contact: John Zajc, Exec. Dir.
Founded: 1971. **Members:** 6,800. **Membership Dues:** individual in U.S., $50 (annual) ● individual in Canada and Mexico, $60 (annual) ● individual outside North America, $65 (annual). **Staff:** 2. **Budget:** $400,000. **Regional Groups:** 30. **Description:** Anyone with a genuine interest in baseball statistics and history. Works to establish an accurate historical and statistical account of baseball from its origin; coordinate and facilitate the dissemination of baseball research information; foster the study of baseball as a significant American social and athletic institution. Conducts individual research or as part of committee project. **Libraries: Type:** reference. **Subjects:** baseball. **Awards:** The Bob Davids Award. **Frequency:** annual. **Type:** recognition ● Jack Kavanagh Memorial Youth Baseball Research Award. **Frequency:** annual. **Type:** monetary ● The Lee Allen Award. **Frequency:** annual. **Type:** recognition ● The SABR Baseball Research Award. **Frequency:** annual. **Type:** monetary. **Recipient:** for the best paper by individual under 21 years of age ● The SABR Salute. **Frequency:** annual. **Type:** recognition ● The Seymour Medal. **Frequency:** annual. **Type:** medal ● The Sporting News-SABR Baseball Research Award. **Frequency:** annual. **Type:** monetary ● **Type:** trophy ● The USA Today Baseball Weekly Award. **Frequency:** annual. **Type:** monetary. **Computer Services:** Mailing lists. **Committees:** Ball Parks; Baseball in UK/Europe; Baseball Records; Bibliography; Biographical Research; Business of Baseball; Collegiate; Dead Ball ERA; Latin American Baseball; Minor Leagues; Negro Leagues; 19th Century Baseball; Oral History; Pictorial History; Scouts; Statistical Analysis; Umpire and Rules; Women in Baseball. **Publications:** *Baseball Research Journal: Annual Historical and Statistical Review of the Society for American Baseball Research,* annual. Contains baseball analysis and history featuring articles contributed by members. **Price:** included in membership dues. ISSN: 0734-6891. **Circulation:** 7,000 ● *The National Pastime: A Review of Baseball History,* annual. Journal. Covers baseball biography, history, and statistics; illustrated. **Price:** included in membership dues. ISSN: 0734-6905. **Circulation:** 8,000 ● *SABR Bulletin,* quarterly. Newsletter. Includes plans and accomplishments of society committees and regional groups, baseball histories, association news, booklists, and obituaries. **Price:** included in membership dues. **Circulation:** 6,800. **Advertising:** accepted ● Monographs. **Conventions/Meetings:** annual conference and convention, includes player

panels, research presentations, banquet, and business meeting (exhibits) - June or July.

22615 ■ U.S.A. Baseball (USBF)
Durham Bulls Athletic Park
403 Blackwell St.
Durham, NC 27701
Ph: (919)474-8721
Fax: (919)474-8822
E-mail: info@usabaseball.com
URL: http://mlb.mlb.com/usa_baseball/index.jsp
Contact: Paul V. Seiler, Exec. Dir./CEO
Founded: 1978. **Members:** 17. **Staff:** 7. **National Groups:** 17. **Description:** Representatives of collegiate, high school, and amateur baseball sports councils and athletic associations. Serves as the National Governing Body of amateur baseball in the United States and is a member of the United States Olympic Committee. Selects, trains, and supports the U.S.A. Baseball Team and the U.S.A. Baseball Junior Team which participate in international competitions, including the Olympic Games and Junior World Championships. Carries out regulations of the U.S. Olympic Committee; establishes additional rules and regulations concerning procedures and requirements for approval of baseball games with other countries; sponsors teams for international competitions; develops baseball nationally and internationally. **Libraries: Type:** reference. **Awards:** Golden Spikes Award. **Frequency:** annual. **Type:** recognition. **Recipient:** to top amateur player in America. **Committees:** Ambassador; Athlete Affairs; International Affairs; Junior Team Preparation; Legal Affairs; Medical and Safety; Membership Relations; Senior Team Preparation; Sports Medicine; Umpires; Youth Affairs. **Affiliated With:** United States Olympic Committee. **Absorbed:** (1965) National Committee for Amateur Baseball. **Formerly:** (1993) United States Baseball Federation. **Publications:** *Commemorative Yearbook,* annual. **Conventions/Meetings:** annual board meeting.

Basketball

22616 ■ Continental Basketball Association (CBA)
195 Washington Ave.
Albany, NY 12210
Ph: (518)694-0100
Fax: (518)694-0101
E-mail: info@cbahoopsonline.com
URL: http://www.cbahoopsonline.com
Contact: Gary Hunter, Commissioner
Founded: 1946. **Members:** 8. **Staff:** 4. **Description:** Professional basketball league that administers a professional basketball league. Develops players, coaches, and referees for the National Basketball Association (see separate entry) and provides professional basketball entertainment. Sponsors competitions and compiles league statistics. **Libraries: Type:** reference. **Holdings:** video recordings. **Awards: Type:** recognition. **Publications:** *Continental Basketball Association—Official Guide and Register,* annual. Covers team information, CBA history and news. Includes biographies of management personnel, team schedules, statistics, and rules. **Circulation:** 5,000. **Conventions/Meetings:** meeting - 3/year.

22617 ■ Eastern College Basketball Association
Address Unknown since 2006
URL: http://www.ecac.org
Founded: 1939. **Members:** 292. **Description:** Trains and assigns officials for college basketball games in the eastern U.S. Conducts clinics annually for over 700 officials. **Awards:** Distinguished Achievement Award. **Frequency:** periodic. **Type:** recognition. **Recipient:** to an ECAC athletic administrator who has achieved outstanding success in his or her career and has made an unusual contribution in the interest of intercollegiate athletics ● ECAC Jostens Male and Female Administrators of the Year. **Frequency:** annual. **Type:** recognition. **Recipient:** to administrators from ECAC member schools in recognition of outstanding or meritorious service to the ECAC ● George L. Shiebler Award. **Frequency:** annual. **Type:** recognition. **Recipient:** to an ECAC official who has demonstrated dedication to his avocational activities ● Jostens Institution of the Year. **Frequency:** annual. **Type:** recognition. **Recipient:** to the ECAC institution that best exemplifies the highest standards of collegiate academic and athletic performances. **Affiliated With:** Eastern Collegiate Hockey Association. **Formerly:** (1965) Collegiate Basketball Officials Bureau. **Conventions/Meetings:** annual conference.

22618 ■ International Association of Approved Basketball Officials (IAABO)
PO Box 1300
Germantown, MD 20875-1300
Ph: (301)540-5180
Fax: (301)540-5182
E-mail: jloube@iaabo.org
URL: http://www.iaabo.org
Contact: Paul J. Loube, Exec. Dir.
Founded: 1921. **Members:** 14,000. **Staff:** 2. **Regional Groups:** 184. **State Groups:** 5. **Description:** Basketball officials in 13 countries. Aims to recruit and continually educate basketball officials and clinicians. **Committees:** Board Relations; Foundation; Hall of Fame; Rules Examinations; Visualization and Education. **Publications:** *Sportorials,* 7/year. **Price:** $10.00/year. **Conventions/Meetings:** semiannual meeting - held in spring and fall ● annual workshop and conference.

22619 ■ Metropolitan Intercollegiate Basketball Association (MIBA)
60 E 42nd St., Ste.660
New York, NY 10165-0659
Ph: (212)425-6510
Fax: (212)785-0594
E-mail: jpowers@ncaa.org
URL: http://www.nit.org
Contact: John J. Powers, Exec. Dir.
Founded: 1938. **Members:** 5. **Staff:** 4. **Description:** Athletic directors from Fordham University, Manhattan College, New York University, St. Johns University, and Wagner College. Each March, sponsors the National Invitation Tournament, the oldest postseason national basketball tournament in the U.S., in which 40 teams are invited to participate; each November sponsors the preseason NIT in which 16 teams are invited to participate. Sponsors an All-Star Tour with a team consisting of 12 players from the previous year's NIT teams. Compiles statistics; maintains hall of fame. **Publications:** *College Basketball Sport Release* ● *Tournament Programs* ● Brochure, annual ● Handbook, annual.

22620 ■ Naismith Memorial Basketball Hall of Fame (NMBHF)
1000 W Columbus Ave.
Springfield, MA 01105
Ph: (413)781-6500
Free: (877)4-HOOPLA
E-mail: doleva@hoophall.com
URL: http://www.hoophall.com
Contact: John L. Doleva, Pres./CEO
Founded: 1959. **Members:** 1,000. **Membership Dues:** student, $25 ● individual, $35 ● family, $60 ● preferred, $100. **Staff:** 30. **Description:** Persons who have performed outstanding services to the game of basketball are elected to the Hall of Fame; they include players, coaches, referees, and contributors in various fields of service to the game. Conducts educational programs. Maintains museum. Sponsors NBA Game and Hall of Fame Tip-Off Classic. **Libraries: Type:** reference. **Holdings:** 2,000; archival material, artwork, books, clippings, monographs, periodicals. **Subjects:** basketball. **Awards:** Clair Bee Coach of the Year Award. **Frequency:** annual. **Type:** recognition. **Recipient:** for the active Division I basketball coach who has made the most significant positive contributions to sports during the preceding year ● Frances Pomeroy Naismith Award. **Frequency:** annual. **Type:** recognition. **Recipient:** for the nation's outstanding senior male basketball player under 6 feet tall and the nation's outstanding senior women player under 5 feet 6 inches tall ● John Bunn

Award. **Frequency:** annual. **Type:** recognition. **Recipient:** for a person making great contributions to basketball and sports. **Committees:** Hall of Fame; Licensing and Sponsorship; Public Relations/Marketing. **Publications:** *Naismith Memorial Basketball Hall of Fame—Newsletter*, quarterly. **Price:** included in membership dues ● *Naismith Memorial Basketball Hall of Fame—Official Hall of Fame Book*, annual. Provides information on the career of each member of the Hall of Fame. **Price:** $14.00/copy. **Conventions/Meetings:** semiannual board meeting ● annual Enshrinement Weekend - meeting, includes induction ceremonies and golf tournament.

22621 ■ National Association of Basketball Coaches (NABC)
1111 Main St., Ste.1000
Kansas City, MO 64105-2136
Ph: (816)878-6222
Fax: (816)878-6223
E-mail: jim@nabc.com
URL: http://nabc.cstv.com
Contact: James A. Haney, Exec. Dir.
Founded: 1927. **Members:** 5,000. **Membership Dues:** affiliate, activity, $60 (annual) ● active, $250 (annual) ● associate, $375 (annual) ● international activity, $85 (annual). **Staff:** 12. **Description:** Basketball coaches from colleges, universities, junior colleges, and high schools. Associate and affiliate members are former coaches from colleges, universities, junior colleges, and high schools; athletic directors; conference commissioners; officials; and members of athletic goods manufacturers and promoters. Sponsors research and charitable programs; supports hall of fame. Sponsors a program called "Coaches vs. Cancer" that raises funds for cancer research for American Cancer Society. Within the structure of the organization compose of a 21-member board of directors; a member-congress by NCAA Division I, II and III; a student (athlete) congress; and an honors-court that recognizes academic achievement of student athletes. **Awards:** Cliff Wells Appreciation. **Frequency:** annual. **Type:** recognition ● Divisions I, II and III Player of the Year. **Frequency:** annual. **Type:** recognition ● Golden Anniversary. **Frequency:** annual. **Type:** recognition ● Honors Award. **Frequency:** annual. **Type:** recognition ● Junior College Coach of the Year. **Frequency:** annual. **Type:** recognition ● Merit. **Frequency:** annual. **Type:** recognition ● Metropolitan. **Frequency:** annual. **Type:** recognition ● NABC District Coaches of the Year. **Frequency:** annual. **Type:** recognition ● Newton S. Hillyard Memorial. **Frequency:** annual. **Type:** recognition ● Pete Newell Award. **Frequency:** annual. **Type:** recognition ● Ray Marquette. **Frequency:** annual. **Type:** recognition ● Silver Anniversary All-America Team. **Frequency:** annual. **Type:** recognition. **Committees:** Academics; All-America, Division I and II; All-Star Game; Assistant Coaches; Basketball Rules; Convention; Division I Championships; Division III Championships; Future Legislation; Grief Support; Hall of Fame; High School; Honors; International; Junior College; Officiating; Public Relations; Recruiting; Research; Special Events and Marketing. **Affiliated With:** National Collegiate Athletic Association; U.S.A. Basketball. **Formerly:** (1998) National Association of Basketball Coaches of the United States. **Conventions/Meetings:** annual competition and convention, meetings, clinics, awards show, all-star game (exhibits) ● annual convention, with college and high school basketball games - always March/April ● seminar.

22622 ■ National Basketball Association (NBA)
645 5th Ave., 10th Fl.
New York, NY 10022
Ph: (212)826-7000
Free: (800)NBA-0548
Fax: (212)826-0579
E-mail: fanrelations@nba.com
URL: http://www.nba.com
Contact: David J. Stern, Commissioner
Founded: 1949. **Members:** 30. **Description:** Professional franchise basketball teams. Each team plays 82 regular season games per year. Sponsors All-Star Game. Represents the following teams: Atlanta Hawks; Boston Celtics; Charlotte Bobcats; Chicago Bulls; Cleveland Cavaliers; Dallas Mavericks; Denver Nuggets; Detroit Pistons; Golden State Warriors; Houston Rockets; Indiana Pacers; Los Angeles Clippers; Los Angeles Lakers; Memphis Grizzlies; Miami Heat; Milwaukee Bucks; Minnesota Timberwolves; New Orleans/Oklahoma Hornets; New Jersey Nets; New York Knicks; Orlando Magic; Philadelphia 76ers; Phoenix Suns; Portland Trail Blazers; Sacramento Kings; San Antonio Spurs; Seattle Supersonics; Toronto Raptors; Utah Jazz; and Washington Wizards. Maintains hall of fame. **Divisions:** NBA Properties, Inc. **Absorbed:** (1976) American Basketball Association. **Formed by Merger of:** Basketball Association of America; National Basketball League. **Publications:** *Hoop*, monthly. Magazine. **Conventions/Meetings:** annual meeting.

22623 ■ National Basketball Athletic Trainers Association
c/o Rollin Mallernee, Gen. Counsel
400 Colony Sq., Ste.1750
Atlanta, GA 30361
Ph: (404)875-4000
Fax: (404)892-8560
E-mail: rmallernee@mallernee-branch.com
URL: http://nbata.com
Contact: Rollin Mallernee, Gen. Counsel
Founded: 1974. **Members:** 30. **Description:** Represents athletic trainers working for the 30 National Basketball Association teams. Works to develop and implement new methods of health care for professional basketball players. **Awards:** NBA Athletic Trainer of the Year. **Frequency:** annual. **Type:** recognition. **Recipient:** for special contributions to the science of athletic training ● **Frequency:** annual. **Type:** scholarship. **Recipient:** to student athletic trainers based on academic achievement. **Affiliated With:** National Basketball Association. **Formerly:** (2004) National Basketball Trainers Association. **Conventions/Meetings:** annual meeting - always early June, in Chicago ● workshop, on training.

22624 ■ United States of America Deaf Basketball (USADB)
c/o Lad Baird, Treas.
104 W Rose St.
Sioux Falls, SD 57105
E-mail: usadbpres@mac.com
URL: http://www.usadb.org
Contact: Raymond Kilthau, Pres.
Membership Dues: general, $10 (annual). **Description:** Stimulates healthful, physical, moral and cultural education for deaf sports enthusiasts in the United States. Develops participation in local, regional, and national deaf basketball competitions and recreational events. **Telecommunication Services:** electronic mail, usadbtreasurer@sio.midco.net.

22625 ■ United States Basketball Writers Association (USBWA)
1818 Chouteau Ave.
St. Louis, MO 63103
Ph: (314)421-0339
E-mail: mitch@mvc.org
URL: http://www.sportswriters.net/usbwa
Contact: Joseph F. Mitch, Exec. Dir.
Founded: 1956. **Members:** 1,000. **Membership Dues:** individual, $40 (annual). **Description:** Persons who write about collegiate and professional players for newspapers, magazines, and other communications media. Promotes basketball and cooperates with the National Association of Basketball Coaches of the U.S., the Basketball Hall of Fame, and other organizations promoting the game. Serves in an advisory capacity to the National Collegiate Athletic Association. Works to improve press box services and facilities. **Awards:** Katha Quinn Award. **Frequency:** annual. **Type:** scholarship. **Recipient:** to college students pursuing careers in sports journalism or individuals for their contributions to college basketball ● Oscar Robertson. **Frequency:** annual. **Type:** trophy. **Recipient:** for player of the year. **Committees:** Classification; Ethics; Statistical and Press Service. **Publications:** *The Tip-Off*, monthly. Newslet-ter. Alternate Formats: online ● *USBWA Directory*, annual. **Price:** included in membership dues. **Conventions/Meetings:** annual meeting - always spring, at the site of the NCAA Final Four basketball championship.

22626 ■ U.S.A. Basketball
5465 Mark Dabling Blvd.
Colorado Springs, CO 80918-3842
Ph: (719)590-4800
Fax: (719)590-4811
E-mail: fanmail@usabasketball.com
URL: http://www.usabasketball.com
Contact: Jim Tooley, Exec. Dir.
Founded: 1974. **Members:** 14. **Membership Dues:** individual, $35 (annual). **Staff:** 13. **Description:** Recognized by the International Basketball Federation (FIBA) and the U.S. Olympic Committee (USOC) and the national governing body for men's and women's basketball in the United States. Responsible for selection, training, and fielding of USA teams that compete in FIBA sponsored international competitions (Olympics, World Championship, Jr. World Championship, and Goodwill Games), as well as some national competitions. U.S. amateur teams playing overseas, and all foreign teams in the U.S. **Libraries:** Type: reference. **Subjects:** international competitions. **Formerly:** (1990) Amateur Basketball Association of the United States of America. **Publications:** *Media Guides*, biennial, even-numbered years. Contains information on Olympic and World Championship teams. ● *USA Basketball News*, 3/year. Newsletter ● Also publishes other special publications. **Conventions/Meetings:** annual meeting.

22627 ■ Women's Basketball Coaches Association (WBCA)
4646 Lawrenceville Hwy.
Lilburn, GA 30047
Ph: (770)279-8027
Fax: (770)279-8473
E-mail: wbca@wbca.org
URL: http://www.wbca.org
Contact: Beth Bass, CEO
Founded: 1981. **Members:** 4,100. **Membership Dues:** active a/professional, $145 (annual) ● active b, $115 (annual) ● associate/affiliate, $75 (annual) ● institutional/international, $220 (annual) ● player, $50 (annual) ● retired coach, administrator, $60 (annual). **Staff:** 12. **Budget:** $2,000,000. **Description:** Head basketball coaches, assistants, athletic directors, officials, media personnel, organizations lending financial support to the association, and others interested in women's basketball. Fosters amateur sports competitions at both national and international levels. Promotes a reputable image of women's basketball by developing the game. Works to refine rules, regulations, and procedures that will enhance athletic leadership, sportsmanship, and women's participation in basketball. Encourages education and development of members and players; promotes health and welfare of participants in the sport. **Awards:** All-America Award. **Frequency:** annual. **Type:** recognition ● Jostens-Berenson Service Award. **Frequency:** annual. **Type:** recognition. **Recipient:** to an individual who has maintained a professional lifelong commitment to service for and to the game of women's basketball ● WBCA National Coach of the Year Award. **Frequency:** annual. **Type:** recognition. **Recipient:** to collegiate or high school coach ● WBCA Player of the Year Award. **Frequency:** annual. **Type:** recognition. **Recipient:** to the best women's basketball player in NCAA Division II, Division III, NAIA, Junior and Community College, and High School. **Committees:** Awards Selection; Ethics and Eligibility; Financial and Legal. **Publications:** *At The Buzzer*, monthly. Newsletter ● *Backboard Bulletin*, bimonthly ● *Coaching Women's Basketball*, monthly. Journal. **Price:** $20.00/year. **Circulation:** 4,000. **Advertising:** accepted ● *Fast Break Alert*, monthly. **Conventions/Meetings:** annual convention, provides coaches with opportunity to network and learn from each other (exhibits).

Baton Twirling

22628 ■ Global Alliance of National Baton Twirling and Majorette Associations
PO Box 266
Janesville, WI 53547-0266

Ph: (608)757-0939 (608)754-2238
Fax: (608)754-1986
E-mail: baton@americanbaton.com
Contact: Don Sartell, Coor.
Description: Promotes development of baton twirling throughout the world as a beneficial and worthwhile youth movement. Holds international festivals. **Formerly:** (1999) World Federation of Baton Twirling and Majorette Associations.

22629 ■ National Baton Twirling Association International (NBTAI)
PO Box 266
Janesville, WI 53547
Ph: (608)754-2238
Fax: (608)754-1986
E-mail: baton@americanbaton.com
URL: http://www.americanbaton.com
Contact: Don Sartell, Pres.
Founded: 1945. **Description:** Baton twirlers and majorettes. Devoted to the advancement of baton twirling. Conducts summer baton twirling camps; sanctions local contests; holds national championships. Sponsors teaching and judging workshops. **Awards: Type:** recognition. **Formerly:** (1999) National Baton Twirling Association. **Publications:** *Drum Major*, monthly. Magazine ● *Who's Who*, annual. Book.

22630 ■ United States Twirling Association (USTA)
c/o Ms. Karen Cammer, Exec. Dir.
44 Drexel Dr.
Bay Shore, NY 11706
Ph: (631)961-0499
Fax: (208)474-9067
E-mail: executivedirector@ustwirling.com
URL: http://www.ustwirling.com
Contact: Ms. Karen Cammer, Exec. Dir.
Founded: 1958. **Members:** 7,500. **Membership Dues:** first year individual, $10-$15 (annual) ● full, $30-$60 (annual) ● elite, $50-$80 (annual) ● semi-professional, $35-$65 (annual) ● semi-professional elite, $60-$70 (annual) ● professional, $65-$75 (annual) ● professional elite, $85-$95 (annual) ● family, $15-$30 (annual) ● team (group), $55-$75 (annual) ● team, organizational (each athlete), $3-$5 (annual) ● organizational (group), $155-$175 (annual). **Staff:** 3. **Budget:** $400,000. **Regional Groups:** 6. **State Groups:** 20. **Description:** Twirlers, coaches, judges, and others interested in baton twirling. Establishes rules and regulations for contests and competitions and qualifications for selection of judges. Sponsors national, regional, and state twirling contests. Produces timed march record for use at contests. Conducts teacher/coach workshops and clinics. **Awards:** Charlie Close Scholarship. **Frequency:** annual. **Type:** scholarship. **Recipient:** to a member of the USA world team ● National Champion Savings Bond. **Frequency:** annual. **Type:** monetary. **Recipient:** for outstanding national title ● USTC and USTA World Team Member Scholarship. **Frequency:** annual. **Type:** scholarship. **Recipient:** to a member of the USA world team. **Computer Services:** database ● mailing lists ● online services. **Commissions:** Coaches; Essentials; Events; Judges; Marketing; Public Relation. **Programs:** Benefactor Foundation. **Publications:** *Catch It*, quarterly. Magazine. **Advertising:** accepted ● *On rules*. Book ● *U.S. Trial Handbook* ● Brochures ● Manuals. **Conventions/Meetings:** annual convention (exhibits) - held in fall ● annual National Championships - competition - held in summer ● annual U.S. Trials/Pre-trials - competition - held in spring.

Billiards

22631 ■ American CueSports Alliance (ACS)
101 S Military Ave., Ste.P - No. 131
Green Bay, WI 54303
Ph: (920)662-1705
Free: (888)662-1705
Fax: (920)662-1706

E-mail: jlewis@americancuesports.org
URL: http://www.americancuesports.org
Contact: Cecil Messer, Pres./Chair
Membership Dues: league player, $10 (annual) ● single player, $25 (annual) ● referee, $35 (annual). **Description:** Promotes the sport of billiards. Promotes and sanctions amateur and professional tournaments. Increases the awareness of and participation in the sport to all people. Works with the entire billiards community to increase the overall growth of billiards. Promotes good fellowship and better social understanding of billiards. **Telecommunication Services:** electronic mail, bharris@americancuesports.org ● electronic mail, julie.mitchell@midwest-wd.com. **Conventions/Meetings:** annual National 8-Ball Championships - competition.

22632 ■ Billiard Congress of America (BCA)
4345 Beverly St., Ste.D
Colorado Springs, CO 80918
Ph: (719)264-8300
Fax: (719)264-0900
E-mail: steve@bca-pool.com
URL: http://www.bca-pool.com
Contact: Stephen D. Ducoff, Exec. Dir.
Founded: 1948. **Members:** 2,600. **Membership Dues:** voting, $1,000 (annual) ● associate, $500 (annual) ● retail, $200 (annual) ● room operator/affiliate, $150 (annual) ● recreation, $60 (annual). **Staff:** 10. **Description:** Develops rules for pocket billiards. Serves as national clearinghouse for billiard activities. Compiles statistics. **Awards:** Billiard Hall of Fame Award. **Frequency:** annual. **Type:** recognition. **Recipient:** for greatest players and industry achievement. **Divisions:** Manufacturers; Player (Professional and Amateur); Proprietors; Retailers. **Publications:** *BCA Break* and *BCA Open Table*, quarterly. Newsletter. Covers billiard-related events and tournament results. **Price:** included in membership dues. **Circulation:** 3,500 ● *BCA Proprietor's Manual*. Features preparation and operation of a billiard room. ● *How to Play Pool Right*. Booklet. Includes a video. ● *Official Rules and Records Book*, annual ● Also publishes instructional guides, videos, and prints of billiard greats and charts. **Conventions/Meetings:** annual International Billiard and Home Recreation Expo - trade show (exhibits) - 2008 Apr. 24-26, Charlotte, NC; 2009 Apr. 12-14, Las Vegas, NV; 2011 Apr. 9-11, Las Vegas, NV.

22633 ■ United States Billiard Association (USBA)
1000 Kiely Blvd., No. 86
Santa Clara, CA 95051-4831
Ph: (408)615-7479
E-mail: president@usbilliardassn.org
URL: http://www.usbilliardassn.org
Contact: Bob Jewett, Pres.
Founded: 1989. **Members:** 500. **Membership Dues:** individual, $36 (annual). **Staff:** 2. **Budget:** $7,000. **Description:** Promotes the sport of three-cushion billiards in the U.S. Compiles statistics. Provides instruction and promotional services. Conducts regional and national tournaments. Is the US affiliate of the World Billiard Union (UMB). **Awards:** National 3-Cushion Billiard Championship. **Frequency:** annual. **Type:** recognition. **Recipient:** for sports competition. **Affiliated With:** Billiard Congress of America. **Formed by Merger of:** Billiard Federation of the United States of America; American Billiard Association. **Publications:** Bulletin, monthly. **Conventions/Meetings:** annual board meeting ● annual Regional Qualifiers - competition, regional qualifying events ● annual U.S. National 3-Cushion Championships - competition - first week of February.

22634 ■ United States Professional Poolplayers Association (UPA)
PO Box 21671
Phoenix, AZ 85036
Ph: (602)653-9974
Fax: (602)795-7731
E-mail: upa_tour@yahoo.com
URL: http://www.upatour.org
Contact: Robert Lipson, Pres.
Membership Dues: standard, $25 (annual) ● touring professional, $100 (annual). **Description:** Elevates

the standards of the professional poolplayers' vocation. Enhances the economic well-being of the individual member. Stimulates interest and involvement from major media companies, major advertisers and the general public. Promotes the overall vitality of the sport. **Publications:** *Pro Side*, monthly. Newsletter. **Price:** included in membership dues.

22635 ■ United States Snooker Association (USSA)
220B S San Gabriel Blvd.
San Gabriel, CA 91776-1623
E-mail: ussa@snookerusa.com
URL: http://www.snookerusa.com
Contact: Alan Morris, Exec. Dir.
Founded: 1991. **Membership Dues:** general, $25 (annual). **Description:** Promotes and develops the sport of snooker in the United States. Works to create a structure capable of supporting international championships in the United States. Develops American amateur and professional players. **Publications:** Newsletter. **Price:** included in membership dues.

22636 ■ Women's Professional Billiard Association (WPBA)
PO Box 546
Goodlettsville, TN 37070-0908
Ph: (704)344-8664
Fax: (704)344-8660
URL: http://www.wpba.com
Contact: Kim White, Pres.
Founded: 1976. **Description:** Professional women billiard players and other individuals with an interest in women's billiards. Promotes increased participation by women in billiards; seeks to increase interest in professional women's billiards events. Sanctions, schedules, and conducts amateur and professional women's billiards tournaments; maintains world rankings among professional women billiard players; conducts promotional activities. **Publications:** *WPBA Player Handbook* ● Newsletter, monthly.

22637 ■ World Confederation of Billiard Sports (WCBS)
c/o Stephen D. Ducoff
4345 Beverly St., Ste.D
Colorado Springs, CO 80918
Ph: (719)264-8300
Fax: (719)264-0900
E-mail: steve@bca-pool.com
URL: http://www.billiard-wcbs.org
Contact: Stephen D. Ducoff, Contact
Founded: 1992. **Membership Dues:** associate, $1,000 (annual). **Multinational. Description:** Promotes billiards sports internationally, especially to the youth. Seeks to standardize competitive rules, guidelines and format of play for billiards sports worldwide. Promotes and develops billiards sports based on human rights, democratic principles and social values of universal fraternity and solidarity irrespective of nationality, race, religion, gender or politics.

Blind

22638 ■ Blind Sailing International (BSI)
c/o Carroll Center for the Blind
770 Centre St.
Newton, MA 02458
E-mail: blindsailing@blindsailing.org
URL: http://www.blindsailing.org
Contact: Arthur O'Neill, Chm.
Founded: 1994. **Membership Dues:** general, $50 (annual). **Multinational. Description:** Promotes sailing as a recognized sport for the blind and visually impaired. Serves as the governing body for competitive international sailing for people who are blind or visually impaired. Organizes international regattas. **Telecommunication Services:** electronic mail, webmaster@blindsailing.org. **Publications:** Video. Provides a summary of blind sailing and the 1999 Championship Regatta. **Price:** $25.00.

Boating

22639 ■ American Power Boat Association (APBA)
17640 Nine Mile Rd.
Eastpointe, MI 48021
Ph: (586)773-9700
Fax: (586)773-6490
E-mail: apbahq@apba-racing.com
URL: http://www.apba-racing.com
Contact: Ms. Gloria J. Urbin, Exec. Admin.
Founded: 1903. **Members:** 6,500. **Membership Dues:** associate, $25 (annual). **Staff:** 7. **Regional Groups:** 200. **Description:** Governing body for the promotion of power boat racing in the United States and national authority for world records as compiled by the Union of International Motorboating. Sanctions regattas and formulates rules, conducts speed trials, and tabulates high point scoring of drivers participating in sanctioned events. **Divisions:** Drag; Inboard; Inboard Endurance; Modified Outboard; Offshore; Outboard Performance Craft; Professional Racing Outboard; R/C Model; Special Event; Stock Outboard; Unlimited. **Publications:** *American Power Boat Association Reference Book*, annual. Consists of three racing books and a reference book containing racing records, commissions, and membership directory. **Price:** included in membership dues. **Circulation:** 6,500. **Advertising:** accepted ● *Feel the Power*. Brochure ● *Propeller*, monthly. Magazine. Covers power boat racing events, technology, safety, and racing accomplishments. **Price:** included in membership dues. ISSN: 0194-6218. **Circulation:** 6,500. **Advertising:** accepted ● *Quick Guide* ● *Rule Book and Official Directory*, annual. **Conventions/Meetings:** annual meeting (exhibits) ● seminar.

22640 ■ American Sail Training Association (ASTA)
PO Box 1459
Newport, RI 02840
Ph: (401)846-1775
Fax: (401)849-5400
E-mail: asta@sailtraining.org
URL: http://tallships.sailtraining.org
Contact: David V.V. Wood, Exec. Dir.
Founded: 1973. **Members:** 1,000. **Membership Dues:** junior (associate), $25 (annual) ● individual (associate), $50 (annual) ● family (associate), $75 (annual) ● supporting (associate), affiliate (organizational), $250 (annual) ● business partner (organizational), $400 (annual) ● corporate (organizational), patron (associate), $1,000 (annual) ● sail training organization (based on annual budget), $375-$600 (annual). **Staff:** 5. **Budget:** $650,000. **Languages:** English, Spanish. **Description:** Organizations operating sail training programs; corporations and educational institutions supporting sail training; private citizens with an interest in sailing and sail training. Promotes sail training as an educational and character-building experience for youth of all ages. Seeks to bring together the sail training ships of the world in a spirit of friendship and international goodwill. Sponsors Tall Ships events including sail training rallies. Maintains billet bank/placement service; compiles statistics. **Awards:** ASTA Crew Professional Grant. **Frequency:** 3/year. **Type:** grant. **Recipient:** for individual and group member of ASTA ● ASTA Lifetime Achievement Award. **Frequency:** annual. **Type:** recognition ● ASTA Port City of the Year Award. **Frequency:** annual. **Type:** recognition ● ASTA Sail Trainer of the Year. **Frequency:** annual. **Type:** recognition ● ASTA Sail Training Program of the Year. **Frequency:** annual. **Type:** recognition ● ASTA Sailing Vessel Assistance Grant. **Frequency:** annual. **Type:** grant ● ASTA Sea Education Program of the Year. **Frequency:** annual. **Type:** recognition ● ASTA Volunteer of the Year. **Frequency:** annual. **Type:** recognition ● Black Pearl. **Frequency:** annual. **Type:** scholarship ● Henry H. Anderson, Jr. Sail Training Scholarship. **Frequency:** semiannual. **Type:** scholarship. **Recipient:** for individuals and groups ● Perry Bowl. **Frequency:** annual. **Type:** recognition. **Computer Services:** database, sail training programs and schedules. **Committees:** Races and Ral-

lies; Sail Training and Education; Technical. **Publications:** *American Sail Training Association—Syllabus and Logbook*, periodic. Journal. Includes personal record, educational guide to nautical and marine science for trainees. **Circulation:** 2,000 ● *International Safety Forum Proceedings*, annual. Provides papers and presentations compiled from the International Sail Training Safety Forum. **Price:** included in membership dues. **Circulation:** 3,500 ● *Running Free*, quarterly. Newsletter. Provides information on sail training, sea education, and tall ship activities. **Price:** included in membership dues; $11.95/copy for nonmembers. **Circulation:** 5,500. **Advertising:** accepted ● *Sail Tall Ships!*, annual. Directory. Contains lists of each ship's origin, program, area of operation, training program fees, index and details of ships. **Price:** included in membership dues; $14.95/copy for nonmembers. **Circulation:** 15,000. **Advertising:** accepted. **Conventions/Meetings:** biennial International Safety Forum - meeting, in conjunction with ASTA annual conference ● regional meeting - 3-4/year ● annual Sail Training and Tall Ship Conference - usually November.

22641 ■ American Sailing Association (ASA)
5301 Beethoven St., Ste.265
Los Angeles, CA 90066
Ph: (310)822-7171
Fax: (310)822-4741
E-mail: info@american-sailing.com
URL: http://www.american-sailing.com
Contact: Mr. Harry Mumms, Exec. VP
Founded: 1981. **Members:** 42,150. **Membership Dues:** individual, $39 (annual) ● individual, $69 (biennial) ● regular, outside U.S., $59 (annual) ● family, $75 (annual) ● family, $129 (biennial) ● life, individual, $450 ● life, family, $750. **For-Profit. Description:** Sailing instructors, sailing schools, and students. Promotes sailing safety and internationally recognized standards for sail education. Provides accreditation to sailing schools and instructors nationwide. Offers special boat insurance rate to members. Conducts business seminars and instructor training programs for the sailing industry. **Awards:** Instructor of the Year. **Frequency:** annual. **Type:** recognition ● School of the Year. **Frequency:** annual. **Type:** recognition. **Publications:** *Affiliate News*, bimonthly ● *American Sailing*, bimonthly. Journal ● *Coastal Navigation Manual*. Manuals. Includes topics in cruising and navigation. ● *Let's Go Sailing*. Contains beginners' text. ● *Sailing Fundamentals*. Video.

22642 ■ American Sailing Association Foundation (ASA)
c/o American Sailing Association
5301 Beethoven St., Ste.265
Los Angeles, CA 90066-7052
Ph: (310)822-7171
Fax: (310)822-4741
E-mail: info@american-sailing.com
URL: http://www.american-sailing.com
Contact: Harry Munns, Pres.
Founded: 1982. **Members:** 20,000. **Staff:** 6. **Description:** Sailing enthusiasts. Promotes amateur water sports and fosters sailing education and boating safety. Sponsors Council of Disabled Sailors, a project designed to provide opportunities for handicapped sailors to sail within their physical limitations. Organizes regattas; maintains speakers' bureau; operates library on sailing and the handicapped. **Awards:** School of the Year. **Frequency:** annual. **Type:** recognition. **Affiliated With:** American Sailing Association. **Publications:** *American Sailing*, quarterly. Journal. **Advertising:** accepted.

22643 ■ American Shark Association (ASA)
5435 Wells Curtice Rd.
Canandaigua, NY 14424
E-mail: jpattenaude@cox.net
URL: http://www.sharkcatamaranclass.org
Contact: Jean Pattenaude, Pres.
Founded: 1964. **Members:** 130. **Membership Dues:** active, $30 (annual) ● associate, $15 (annual). **State Groups:** 6. **Description:** Owners of Shark Catamaran Class sailboats. Promotes the Shark Catamaran; provides information on the activities of the class.

Sponsors national championship regattas. **Publications:** *The Shark's Tale*, quarterly. Newsletter. **Conventions/Meetings:** annual Regatta - meeting, gathering of boats across the nation to race each other - always third week of August.

22644 ■ American Y-Flyer Yacht Racing Association (AYFYRA)
7349 Scarborough Blvd., East Dr.
Indianapolis, IN 46256-2052
Ph: (317)849-7588
E-mail: yflyer@juno.com
URL: http://www.yflyer.org
Contact: Paul White, Class Sec.
Founded: 1952. **Members:** 449. **Membership Dues:** active, $30 (annual) ● associate, $25 (annual) ● junior, crew, $10 (annual). **Staff:** 1. **Regional Groups:** 3. **Local Groups:** 33. **Description:** Sailors of Y-Flyer Class racing sailboats. Seeks to maintain the one-design status of the Y-Flyer Class sailboat and promote sailboat racing among members. Holds national senior and junior (under 19 years of age) championships. Bestows awards. **Publications:** *Roster*, annual. Directory ● *Y-Flyer*, bimonthly. Newsletter. **Price:** free for members. **Conventions/Meetings:** annual meeting.

22645 ■ Antique Outboard Motor Club (AOMC)
c/o Department IN
PO Box 2526
Walla Walla, WA 99362
E-mail: memberservices@aomci.org
URL: http://www.aomci.org
Contact: Judy Weber, Chair
Founded: 1965. **Members:** 3,000. **Membership Dues:** regular, in U.S., $50 (biennial) ● regular, in Canada, $63 (biennial) ● regular, outside U.S. and Canada, $67 (biennial). **Regional Groups:** 34. **Multinational. Description:** Represents persons interested in the history, preservation, restoration, and operation of antique outboard motors (built prior to 1950). Offers information services to members including free advertising in club publications for spare parts. Local chapters sponsor water meets on a regional level. **Convention/Meeting:** none. **Publications:** *Antique Outboard Motor Club—Newsletter*, 8/year. Contains classified advertisements for antique outboard motor parts wanted or for sale. Also includes new member information and meet notices. **Price:** included in membership dues. **Circulation:** 3,000. **Advertising:** accepted ● *The Antique Outboarder*, quarterly. Magazine. Covers meets, outboard motor repairs and restoration, racing, and other items of interest to antique outboard motor enthusiasts. **Price:** included in membership dues. **Circulation:** 3,000.

22646 ■ Association of Yachting Professionals (AYP)
Address Unknown since 2007
Description: Aims to define and promote the standards of professionalism and excellence and to achieve a recognized professional status for yacht captains, mates, engineers, stewards/stewardesses, chefs and dockhands. **Publications:** *Wavelength*. Newsletter. **Conventions/Meetings:** biweekly meeting - usually first and third Mondays of the month ● seminar.

22647 ■ Boat Owners Association of the United States (BOAT US)
880 S Pickett St.
Alexandria, VA 22304
Ph: (703)823-9550 (703)461-4666
Free: (800)395-2628
Fax: (703)461-2847
E-mail: mail@boatus.com
URL: http://www.boatus.com
Contact: Richard Schwartz, Chm./Founder
Founded: 1966. **Members:** 600,000. **Membership Dues:** in U.S., $25 (annual) ● outside U.S., $30 (annual). **Staff:** 900. **Description:** Owners or prospective owners of recreational boats. Independent, consumer service organization offering representation, benefits, and programs for boat owners. Services

include: legislative and regulatory representation on issues affecting boaters' interests; marine insurance; magazines; trailering club; marina discounts; long-term boat financing; boating regulations and forms service; charter and group travel services; sale and chartering exchange; marine surveyor and admiralty lawyer reference service; assistance with individual boating problems and towing reimbursement; association flag. Maintains Consumer Protection Bureau, which utilizes comprehensive consumer experience files to pursue individual complaints. **Libraries: Type:** reference. **Holdings:** 15,000; books. **Subjects:** boating. **Telecommunication Services:** electronic mail, boatingsafety@boatus.com. **Absorbed:** (1967) American Yachtmen's Association. **Publications:** *Annual Equipment Catalog*, annual ● *BOAT U.S. Magazine*, bimonthly. Covers current boating issues. Includes legislative and regulatory proposals, classified section, and tax, safety, and consumer news for owners. **Price:** included in membership dues. **Circulation:** 520,000. **Advertising:** accepted ● *Boat U.S. Trailering Magazine*, bimonthly ● *Seaworthy*, quarterly. Journal. Covers loss prevention. Contains actual cases taken from marine insurance claims files. **Price:** $10.00.

22648 ■ Bullseye Association
203 Washington St.
Marblehead, MA 01945
Ph: (508)252-3442
Fax: (508)252-8047
E-mail: awburnham@aol.com
URL: http://www.bullseyeclass.org
Contact: David C. Burnham, Sec.
Founded: 1961. **Members:** 225. **Membership Dues:** $20 (annual). **Budget:** $2,000. **Description:** Owners and those interested in Bullseye Class fiberglass sailboats. Promotes the sailing and racing of Bullseye Class sailboats. Encourages use of the fiberglass Bullseye for family and recreational sailing. Facilitates communication among owners; provides specifications and rules to ensure uniformity and safety in racing. Sponsors regattas, during which technical assistance is provided. Compiles statistics. **Committees:** Technical. **Formerly:** (2003) Bullseye Class Association. **Publications:** *Bullseye Newsletter*, quarterly. **Circulation:** 250 ● *Roster of Boats*, periodic.

22649 ■ Catalina 22 National Sailing Association (CTNSA)
c/o Dora McGee, Sec.-Treas.
3790 Post Gate Dr.
Cumming, GA 30040
Ph: (770)887-9728
Fax: (770)887-9728
E-mail: secretary@catalina22.org
URL: http://www.catalina22.org
Contact: Dora McGee, Sec.-Treas.
Founded: 1971. **Members:** 1,700. **Membership Dues:** general, $25 (annual). **Regional Groups:** 10. **Local Groups:** 129. **Description:** Owners of Catalina 22 sailboats. Promotes safe and enjoyable family sailing; conducts activities through regional and local chapters. **Awards:** Annual Sailing for Family and Leadership. **Frequency:** annual. **Type:** recognition. **Recipient:** for family sailing. **Publications:** *Mainsheet*, quarterly. Magazine. **Conventions/Meetings:** annual National Regatta - meeting - in June.

22650 ■ Catboat Association (CBA)
c/o John L. Greene, Membership Sec.
PO Box 246
Cataumet, MA 02534-0246
Ph: (508)947-5093 (508)563-3715
E-mail: john.greene@catboats.org
URL: http://www.catboats.org
Contact: John L. Greene, Membership Sec.
Founded: 1962. **Members:** 1,700. **Membership Dues:** regular, $20 (annual). **Staff:** 34. **Description:** Owners and enthusiasts of catboats, including decked and noncruising catboats. (A catboat is a boat traditionally fitted with a gaff-rigged sail on a single mast set well up in the "eyes" of the boat.) Objectives are to: promote interest in catboats; exchange information; preserve the history of watercraft. **Librar**-

ies: Type: open to the public. **Holdings:** 141; books, periodicals, video recordings. **Subjects:** catboat design. **Awards:** Broad Axe Award. **Frequency:** annual. **Type:** recognition. **Recipient:** for member ● Dolphin Award. **Frequency:** annual. **Type:** recognition. **Recipient:** for member ● John Killam Murphy Award. **Frequency:** annual. **Type:** recognition. **Recipient:** for member. **Publications:** *The Boy, Me and the Cat*, 3/year. Book. A cruising story. **Price:** $29.95 available to members only. **Circulation:** 1,500 ● *The Catboat Book*. Includes membership directory. **Price:** $15.00 ● *The Catbook and How to Sail Her*. Features rig diagrams and sailing instructions. **Price:** $10.00 ● *Nine Lives*. Video. **Price:** $29.95 ● Bulletin, 3/year. **Price:** available to members only. **Circulation:** 1,500 ● Yearbook. Includes membership directory. **Conventions/Meetings:** annual meeting and workshop, for members only (exhibits) - usually February.

22651 ■ Coronado 15 National Association
c/o Sue Fishman, Sec.-Treas.
547 Garden St.
Sacramento, CA 95815
Ph: (916)359-1442
E-mail: sfishman@winfirst.com
URL: http://www.coronado15.org
Contact: Sue Fishman, Sec.-Treas.
Founded: 1968. **Members:** 510. **Regional Groups:** 8. **Description:** Sailing organizations, collegiate sailing clubs, and individuals that sail Coronado 15 Class sailboats. Encourages a spirit of friendly and competitive growth in the sport of dinghy racing, match racing, team racing, and recreational sailing in the Coronado 15 class of sailboats. Certifies boats as conforming to class specifications. Sponsors Coronado 15 Class regattas. Fosters camaraderie among members. **Awards: Type:** recognition. **Affiliated With:** United States Sailing Association. **Formerly:** (1989) Coronado 15 Class Racing Association; (2003) Coronado 15 Association. **Publications:** *Coronado Comments*, quarterly. Includes directory. ● *Mainsheet Magazine*, quarterly. **Conventions/Meetings:** annual meeting.

22652 ■ Council of Sailing Associations (CSA)
c/o United States Sailing Association
PO Box 1260
15 Maritime Dr.
Portsmouth, RI 02871-0907
Ph: (401)683-0800
Fax: (401)683-0840
E-mail: sbetts1@san.rr.com
URL: http://www.ussailing.org/csa
Contact: Stanton W. Betts, Chm.
Founded: 1897. **Members:** 42,000. **Membership Dues:** youth, $20 (annual) ● adult, $50 (annual) ● family, $75 (annual) ● sustaining (adult), $100 (annual) ● sustaining (family), $125 (annual) ● supporting (adult/family), $250 (annual) ● benefactor (adult/family), $500 (annual) ● patron (adult/family), $1,000 (annual). **Staff:** 30. **Description:** A council of the US Sailing (see separate entry). Represents local yacht clubs that conduct regattas, including local day regattas, national championships, and international regattas. Serves as a central forum for the exchange of views. Aims to provide individual US Sailing members with improved services, better racing, and stronger and more efficient race administration. **Formerly:** (1993) Yacht Racing Associations Council. **Conventions/Meetings:** semiannual conference - always March and October.

22653 ■ Cruising Club of America (CCA)
77 Churchills Ln.
Milton, MA 02186-3522
E-mail: secretary@cruisingclub.org
URL: http://www.cruisingclub.org
Contact: Stephen E. Taylor, Sec.
Founded: 1921. **Members:** 1,200. **Description:** Experienced offshore sailors. Aims to use its collective wisdom and experience to influence "adventurous use of the sea" through its efforts to improve seamanship, the design of seaworthy yachts, safe yachting procedures and environmental awareness. **Awards:** Blue Water Medal. **Frequency:** periodic. **Type:**

medal. **Recipient:** for the most meritorious example of seamanship ● Rod Stephens. **Frequency:** annual. **Type:** recognition. **Recipient:** for sailor and rescuer. **Publications:** Papers. **Conventions/Meetings:** biennial Newport to Bermuda Race - competition - 2008 June 20, Newport, RI ● Safety at Sea - seminar.

22654 ■ Day Sailer Association (DSA)
c/o Patricia Skeen, Sec.
1936 Danebo Ave.
Eugene, OR 97402-1135
Ph: (541)689-2190
Fax: (541)461-3146
E-mail: skeenjp@aol.com
URL: http://www.daysailer.org
Contact: Michael Measures, Pres.
Founded: 1960. **Members:** 500. **Membership Dues:** individual, $25 (annual). **Staff:** 1. **Regional Groups:** 12. **Local Groups:** 50. **Description:** Active members own, co-own, or charter Day Sailer Class yachts; associate members are interested in the promotion of the yachts, but do not own or charter one. Promotes acceptance of the Day Sailer Class yacht group sailing activities within and among Day Sailers. Develops one-design racing under a uniform set of rules. Offers educational programs; compiles statistics. Teaches sailing/water safety. **Libraries: Type:** reference. **Holdings:** 200; archival material, books, business records, periodicals. **Subjects:** sailing. **Awards: Frequency:** annual. **Type:** grant. **Recipient:** for sailing achievements and service ● **Frequency:** annual. **Type:** recognition. **Committees:** Class Race; Design; Editor; Measurement; Nominating; Promotion. **Affiliated With:** United States Sailing Association. **Publications:** *Class Yearbook and Handbook*, annual. **Advertising:** accepted ● *The Day Sailer*, quarterly. Newsletter. Covers association activities, cruising, racing, and fleets. Includes geographic area reports, race results, and regatta schedule. **Price:** included in membership dues. **Circulation:** 550. **Advertising:** accepted ● *Day Sailer Association—Class Handbook*. Covers DSA constitution, by-laws, and specifications for Day Sailer Class yachts. **Price:** included in membership dues. **Circulation:** 550 ● Directory, annual. Lists Day Sailer Class yacht owners by fleet and region. Includes news of awards and officers. ● Also publishes an advertising brochure. **Conventions/Meetings:** annual Mid-Winter Regatta - competition - every 3rd weekend of March ● annual North American Championship - competition.

22655 ■ El Toro International Yacht Racing Association (ETIYRA)
1014 Hopper Ave., No. 419
Santa Rosa, CA 95403-1613
Ph: (707)526-6621
Fax: (707)526-3838
E-mail: steve@swiftsail.net
URL: http://www.eltoroyra.org
Contact: Steve Lowry, Sec.
Founded: 1947. **Members:** 1,000. **Membership Dues:** first skipper in household, $25 (annual) ● second skipper in household, $12 (annual) ● youth (under 18 and only skipper in the household), $15 (annual). **Staff:** 1. **Regional Groups:** 8. **Local Groups:** 75. **National Groups:** 8. **Description:** Owners of approved small sailing craft (8 feet long, with a hull weight of 60-65 pounds), used as yacht tenders and/or for racing. Establishes specifications of El Toro Class craft; sells construction plans. Local fleets of 5 or more class yachts sponsor regattas, and offer training to juniors. Name coined by members of the Richmond, CA Yacht Club in the early 1940s, when members selected the MacGregor "Sabot" to serve as a yacht tender and sailing dinghy. The craft was used during members' regular "bull sessions"; hence, the name El Toro (Spanish for "the bull") was chosen for the boat and a shovel adopted for a sail insignia. **Awards:** Junior, Intermediate, and Senior Championship Awards. **Frequency:** annual. **Type:** trophy. **Recipient:** for winners of championship races. **Publications:** *The Shovel*. Newsletter. **Price:** included in membership dues. **Advertising:** accepted. **Conventions/Meetings:** annual meeting and general assembly - always at site of North American Championship.

22656 ■ FJ United States (FJUS)
c/o Rebecca Wyatt, Sec.-Treas.
6572 Margaret Dr.
Westerville, OH 43082
Ph: (614)865-0145
E-mail: beetlefreak@ameritech.net
URL: http://www.ussailing.net/fjus
Contact: Rebecca Wyatt, Sec.-Treas.
Founded: 1960. **Members:** 100. **Regional Groups:** 5. **Local Groups:** 24. **Description:** Represents sailors who own and sail the International FJ (Flying Junior) one-design class sloop. Sponsors national regattas and sailing or racing clinics. Promotes the FJ class to sailing enthusiasts. Maintains collection of articles on sailing. **Publications:** *FJ U.S.—Jottings*, quarterly. Newsletter. Covers sailing activities of the international FJ Class boats in the United States. Includes calendar of events and regatta results. **Price:** included in membership dues. **Advertising:** accepted ● *Membership List*, annual. Membership Directory ● Brochure. **Conventions/Meetings:** annual Championship - competition.

22657 ■ Flying Scot Sailing Association (FSSA)
1 Windsor Cove, Ste.305
Columbia, SC 29223
Ph: (803)252-5646
Free: (800)445-8629
Fax: (803)765-0860
E-mail: info@fssa.com
URL: http://www.fssa.com
Contact: Courtney C. Waldrup, Exec. Sec.
Founded: 1959. **Members:** 2,500. **Membership Dues:** active, $45 (annual) ● family, $60 (annual) ● junior, $22 (annual) ● associate/sustaining/sponsoring, $35 (annual) ● life, $1,000. **Staff:** 10. **Local Groups:** 135. **Description:** Amateur sailors, owners, and crewmen of Flying Scot Sloops. Promotes the sport of sailing through the sponsorship of regattas and competitions. Compiles statistics. **Awards: Type:** recognition. **Recipient:** for winners of races. **Publications:** *Scots 'n Water*, bimonthly ● *Who's Who in FSSA*, semiannual ● Handbook, semiannual. **Conventions/Meetings:** annual North American Championship - meeting.

22658 ■ Force +5 Class Association (F5CA)
c/o David S. Costanzo, Sec.
110 Baldwin Brook Rd.
Canterbury, CT 06331-1805
E-mail: rjcullen@net.net
URL: http://www.force5.us
Contact: Bob Cullen, Pres.
Founded: 1972. **Members:** 200. **Membership Dues:** $20 (annual). **Description:** Provides a medium of exchange of information among sailors throughout the country. Encourages and fosters the enjoyment of the sporting and recreational aspects of sailing. Sponsors regattas; compiles statistics. **Awards:** Class Champion. **Frequency:** annual. **Type:** recognition ● North American Champion. **Frequency:** annual. **Type:** recognition. **Computer Services:** Mailing lists. **Committees:** Class Rules. **Affiliated With:** United States Sailing Association. **Publications:** *Force 5 Newsletter*, periodic. Includes event notices and technical boating info. **Price:** free with membership. **Advertising:** accepted ● *Regatta Schedule*, annual. **Conventions/Meetings:** annual meeting (exhibits).

22659 ■ Geary 18 International Yacht Racing Association (G18 IYRA)
PO Box 4763
Federal Way, WA 98063
Ph: (253)946-2619
E-mail: stephethom@netscape.net
URL: http://www.geary18.org
Contact: Debra Eckrote, Contact
Founded: 1933. **Members:** 150. **Membership Dues:** regular, $25 (annual). **Staff:** 1. **Regional Groups:** 4. **Description:** Aims to bring together persons interested in cruising and racing small watercraft. Provides inexpensive competition between individual owners of watercraft and fleets representing uniform rules and regulations. Creates local fleets, hold regattas,

and conduct social events. Cooperates with other yachting organizations; establishes rules governing the Annual Geary 18 Championship Series and other sanctioned events; local fleets conduct seminars on boat-building, sailing, and racing programs. Maintains library of scrapbooks of publicity and business papers dating back to 1929. **Committees:** Measurement. **Affiliated With:** United States Sailing Association. **Formerly:** (1960) International Flattie Yacht Racing Association. **Publications:** *Telltale*, bimonthly. **Price:** free for members. **Circulation:** 100 ● Handbook, annual. Includes membership roster. ● Also publishes boat-building plans and building instructions. **Conventions/Meetings:** annual International Championship Regatta - competition and meeting.

22660 ■ Hampton One-Design Class Racing Association (HODCRA)
c/o Charles H. McCoy, Jr., Treas.
1721 Cloncurry Rd.
Norfolk, VA 23505
Ph: (757)423-3109 (757)625-7418
Fax: (757)497-6225
E-mail: mccoy514@juno.com
URL: http://www.shorenet.net/hamptonone/intro.htm
Contact: Charles H. McCoy Jr., Treas.
Founded: 1934. **Members:** 120. **Membership Dues:** active, $50 (annual) ● associate, $25 (annual). **Regional Groups:** 9. **Description:** Member association of the Chesapeake Bay Yacht Racing Association. Recreational sailors of Hampton One-Design Class sailboats. (Hampton sailboats are 18 feet long, are best sailed by two people, and are equally well suited for day sailing or racing.) Seeks to preserve and promote use of Hampton sailboats. Organizes regattas for members; conducts social activities. Holds novice and newcomer racing seminars; membership is concentrated in the Chesapeake Bay area. **Awards:** Hampton One Design Class National Championship. **Frequency:** annual. **Type:** recognition. **Publications:** *The Best on the Bay - Fifty Years of Racing*. Book. **Price:** $30.00 ● *Buoy Room*. Newsletter. **Price:** $1.00 ● *Sea Chest*, periodic, published as necessary. Manual. Features boat specifications and class rules. **Price:** $1.00. **Conventions/Meetings:** annual meeting - always August.

22661 ■ Highlander Class International Association (HCIA)
c/o Bryan Hollingsworth, Exec. Sec.-Treas.
410 Holiday Rd.
Lexington, KY 40502
E-mail: 989bauer@netwalk.com
URL: http://www.sailhighlander.org
Contact: Jamey Carey, Pres.
Founded: 1952. **Members:** 347. **Membership Dues:** active (boat owner)/co-owner, $45 (annual) ● binder, $5 (annual) ● associate, $30 (annual) ● junior, $15 (annual). **Staff:** 2. **Local Groups:** 11. **Description:** Owners of Highlander One-Design Class sailboats. Promotes sailing and racing of Highlander boats. Helps young people develop sailing skills. **Libraries: Type:** open to the public. **Awards:** National Champion. **Frequency:** annual. **Type:** recognition. **Computer Services:** database, membership ● mailing lists, of members. **Committees:** Budget; Measurement; National Race; Nomination; Publicity and Promotion. **Publications:** *The Highlander*, quarterly. Newsletter. Features Highlander Class sailing activities, regatta schedules, racing results, boat improvement, fleet activities. **Price:** included in membership dues. **Circulation:** 336. **Advertising:** accepted ● *Highlander Yearbook*. Includes rules and regulations for Highlander Class sailing races, boat specifications, fleet locations, and championship listings. **Price:** included in membership dues. **Circulation:** 336. **Advertising:** accepted. **Conventions/Meetings:** quarterly board meeting ● competition ● annual meeting - always August.

22662 ■ Inland Lake Yachting Association (ILYA)
PO Box 311
Fontana, WI 53125
Ph: (262)275-6921
Fax: (262)275-3772

E-mail: scowslants@aol.com
URL: http://www.ilya.org
Contact: James A. Smith, Exec. Sec.
Founded: 1897. **Members:** 1,700. **Membership Dues:** regular, $70 (annual) ● family, $200 (annual) ● youth, $40 (annual) ● dinghy, $30 (annual) ● associate, $35 (annual). **Staff:** 2. **Budget:** $140,000. **Regional Groups:** 42. **Description:** Sailing enthusiasts. Sponsors regattas; approves class specifications. Provides sailing instruction. Conducts training in junior sailing. **Awards: Type:** recognition. **Publications:** *Scow Showcase*. Brochure ● *Scow Slants*, quarterly. Newsletter. Provides information about sailing and association news. **Price:** included in membership dues. ISSN: 0195-1424. **Circulation:** 1,600. **Advertising:** accepted. Alternate Formats: online. **Conventions/Meetings:** annual Winter Inland - conference (exhibits) - always January, Wisconsin.

22663 ■ Inter-Collegiate Sailing Association of North America (ICSA)
c/o Capt. Eric Wallischeck
U.S.A. Merchant Marine Acad.
300 Steamboat Rd.
Kings Point, NY 11024-1699
E-mail: sailing@usmma.edu
URL: http://www.collegesailing.org
Contact: Mr. Mitchell Brindley, Pres.
Founded: 1928. **Members:** 7. **Regional Groups:** 7. **Local Groups:** 200. **Description:** Serves as a national governing body of the sport of collegiate sailing, and represents nearly 200 colleges and universities that have recognized varsity sailing teams, sailing clubs, or student activity groups interested in sailing. Includes the Middle Atlantic Intercollegiate Sailing Association, Midwest Collegiate Sailing Association, New England Intercollegiate Sailing Association, Northwest Inter-Collegiate Sailing Association, Pacific Coast Collegiate Sailing Conference, South Atlantic Intercollegiate Sailing Association, and South Eastern Intercollegiate Sailing Association. Promotes yacht racing and the sport of sailing, including intercollegiate sailing competitions and intramural and recreational sailing; schedules and sanctions intersectional competitions; supports development of sailors for U.S. Olympic Sailing Teams. Encourages good sportsmanship and safety afloat; gives instruction in sailing, boat safety and racing tactics. Compiles statistics and maintains College Sailing Hall of Fame. **Awards:** Everett B. Morris Trophy. **Frequency:** annual. **Type:** trophy. **Recipient:** to the outstanding college sailor of the year ● James Rousmaniere Student Leadership Award. **Frequency:** annual. **Type:** recognition. **Recipient:** to an undergraduate who has provided outstanding leadership to his or her team or conference ● Leonard M. Fowle Trophy. **Frequency:** annual. **Type:** trophy. **Recipient:** to the team with the best overall performance ● Robert H. Hobbs Sportsmanship Award. **Frequency:** annual. **Type:** recognition. **Recipient:** to the sportsman or sportswoman of the year. **Committees:** All Academic Sailing Team Selection; All American Selection; Appeals; Budget; Communications; Eligibility; Intersectional Schedule; North American Championships; Rules. **Formerly:** (1949) Inter-Collegiate Yacht Racing Association ● (2000) Inter-Collegiate Yacht Racing Association of North America. **Publications:** *Annual Schedule* ● *Procedural Rules for Inter-Collegiate Sailing Competition*, quadrennial, coincides with the quadrennial Olympic cycle. Pamphlet. Describes the rules for organizing and conducting intercollegiate sailing races. **Price:** $5.00 for non-members; free to member institutions and conferences. **Circulation:** 1,000. **Advertising:** accepted. Alternate Formats: CD-ROM; online ● Also publishes pamphlets on racing rules, procedural rules for dinghy competitions, safety, and equipment. **Conventions/Meetings:** annual North American Championship - competition.

22664 ■ Inter-Lake Yachting Association (I-LYA)
c/o Daniel Van Heeckeren, Advisory Committee Chm.
600 Battles Rd.
Gates Mills, OH 44040

Ph: (440)423-3244 (401)849-0220
E-mail: ddawg@chartermi.net
URL: http://www.i-lya.org
Contact: Jim Dupre, Commodore

Founded: 1885. **Members:** 30,000. **Membership Dues:** club, $125 (annual). **Budget:** $150,000,000. **Regional Groups:** 133. **Description:** Yacht and boat clubs in Michigan, Pennsylvania, Indiana, New York, Ohio, and Ontario, Canada. Holds the largest inland regatta in the world; sponsors regional races. Conducts educational programs; compiles statistics. **Libraries: Type:** reference. **Awards: Frequency:** annual. **Type:** recognition. **Recipient:** for competition winners. **Computer Services:** database. **Committees:** Admiralty; Advisory; Code of Regulations; Intersection Racing; Junior Activities; Long Term Planning; Monument; Political Action; Power Boat Measures; Regatta Support; Sail Yacht Measures; Shore Courtesy. **Affiliated With:** National Boating Federation; National Club Association; United States Sailing Association. **Publications:** Yearbook, annual. Includes notice of races, schedule of ladder events, preliminary racing instructions, roster of members, and sailing charters. **Price:** free. **Circulation:** 6,000. **Advertising:** accepted. **Conventions/Meetings:** semiannual conference and general assembly - always the first weekend of April and December.

22665 ■ Interlake Sailing Class Association (ISCA)

c/o Ron Gall, Sec.-Treas.
2022 Glencove Dr.
Toledo, OH 43609-1945
Ph: (419)356-7296
E-mail: ron.gall@yahoo.com
URL: http://www.interlakesailing.org
Contact: Martin Howell, Pres.

Founded: 1935. **Members:** 250. **Membership Dues:** active, $30 (annual) ● associate, $12 (annual). **Description:** Represents owners and enthusiasts of Interlake Class sailboats. Promotes friendly competition, teaches and assists entry-level sailors, enforces standards, facilitates new and used boat sales and service. **Publications:** Intercom, 5/year. Newsletter. Includes sailing articles, regatta information and results. **Price:** included in membership dues. **Circulation:** 400. **Advertising:** accepted ● Interlake Owner's Handbook, annual. Serves as an introduction to the boat and the association. ● Handbook. **Conventions/Meetings:** annual National Championships - competition, races ● seminar, on sailing.

22666 ■ International 210 Association (ITA)

c/o Greg Sullivan, Pres.
59 Water St.
Hingham, MA 02043
Ph: (781)749-4141
Fax: (617)633-2626
E-mail: g.sullivan@att.net
URL: http://www.210class.com
Contact: Greg Sullivan, Pres.

Founded: 1946. **Members:** 498. **Membership Dues:** regular, $50 (annual). **Regional Groups:** 10. **Description:** Owners of International 210 yachts (326); crew members, former owners, and interested persons (172). Promotes racing of International 210 class sailboats. (International 210 class yachts are approximately 30 ft. long and weigh about 2300 lbs.) Sets and enforces rules and standards; maintains uniformity of 210 class construction and sail specifications. Sanctions vegattas for 210 class yachts. **Libraries: Type:** reference. **Holdings:** archival material, photographs. **Awards:** Raymond C. Hunt Trophy. **Frequency:** annual. **Type:** trophy. **Recipient:** to a winner of sailing vegatta. **Computer Services:** database, membership list. **Also Known As:** 210 Class. **Publications:** Newsletter, quarterly. Reports on international events and 210 Class sailboat race results. **Price:** free, for members only. **Circulation:** 500. **Advertising:** accepted ● Yearbook, annual. Includes history of sanctioned regatta winners. **Conventions/Meetings:** competition ● annual Regatta - meeting.

22667 ■ International 505 Yacht Racing Association, American Section

c/o G. Macy Nelson
401 Washington Ave., Ste.803
Towson, MD 21204
Ph: (757)897-2127
E-mail: gmacynelson@gmacynelson.com
URL: http://www.int505.org
Contact: G. Macy Nelson, Contact

Founded: 1954. **Members:** 150. **Membership Dues:** full, $45 ● associate, $25 ● family, $60. **Regional Groups:** 5. **Description:** Owners of International 505 Class sailing dinghies. Promotes and sponsors competitions in high performance sailing. **Awards:** Dennis Surtees Service Award. **Frequency:** annual. **Type:** recognition. **Recipient:** for 505 sailors with outstanding service to the American Section. **Computer Services:** database, membership. **Publications:** Tank Talk, quarterly. Magazine ● Handbook, annual. **Conventions/Meetings:** annual meeting.

22668 ■ International Blue Jay Class Association (IBJCA)

c/o William K. Dunbar, III, Pres.
937 Lagoon Ln.
Mantoloking, NJ 08738
Ph: (732)295-0238
Fax: (732)295-0238
E-mail: jad25@earthlink.net
URL: http://www.sailbluejay.org
Contact: William K. Dunbar III, Pres.

Founded: 1954. **Members:** 600. **Membership Dues:** individual, $25 (annual). **Description:** Owners, charterers, and enthusiasts in states of Blue Jay Class yachts. Promotes Blue Jay Class racing with emphasis on Junior Training. Seeks to stabilize ownership and racing costs of Blue Jay Class yachts and maintain their one-design features. Formulates rules governing construction and racing; offers a nationals and master's regatta each year. **Awards:** Blue Jay National Championship Regatta. **Frequency:** annual. **Type:** recognition ● Master's Regatta 1st Place. **Type:** recognition ● Perpetual Championship Division. **Type:** recognition ● Perpetual President's Cup Division. **Type:** recognition ● Top Female Skipper. **Type:** recognition. **Measurement. Publications:** Blue Jay Banter, 3-4/year. Newsletter. **Price:** included in membership dues. **Advertising:** accepted ● Class Specifications and Year Book, every 2-3 years. **Conventions/Meetings:** annual board meeting - fall/winter ● annual meeting - at Class National Sailing Championship.

22669 ■ International Catalina 27/270 Association (IC27/270A)

c/o Phil Agur, Sec.
2963 Mt. View Ct.
Cameron Park, CA 95682
Ph: (530)677-6229 (410)721-0322
Fax: (410)293-6616
E-mail: ic27a@sbcglobal.net
URL: http://www.catalina27.org
Contact: Mark Elert, Commodore

Founded: 1971. **Members:** 775. **Membership Dues:** outside North America, $22 (annual) ● in Canada and Mexico, $19 (annual) ● in U.S., $15 (annual). **Description:** Owners and sailors of Catalina 27/270 yachts. Promotes the sailing and racing of Catalina 27/270 yachts; encourages the exchange of information among members. Sponsors competitions; compiles statistics. **Libraries: Type:** open to the public. **Holdings:** photographs. **Affiliated With:** United States Sailing Association. **Formerly:** (1984) Catalina 27 National Association; (2002) International Catalina 27 Association. **Publications:** Mainsheet, quarterly. Magazine. **Conventions/Meetings:** annual Regatta - meeting.

22670 ■ International D.N. Ice Yacht Racing Association (IDNIYRA)

c/o Rob Holman
2626 Sandpiper Rd.
Lambertville, MI 48144
Ph: (734)854-3915

E-mail: bobh@dpdesignandprint.com
URL: http://www.idniyra.org
Contact: Rob Holman, Contact

Founded: 1953. **Members:** 2,000. **Membership Dues:** active, $25 (annual). **National Groups:** 13. **Description:** Owners and part owners of DN ice yachts from 13 countries. Promotes ice yacht racing in the one-design class with boats built to official specifications. Sponsors Gold Cup World Championship and North American Championship regattas. Compiles statistics. (The first DN iceboats were built in 1936 in the Detroit News Hobby Shop, Detroit, Michigan; the boat's name is derived from the newspaper's initials). **Libraries: Type:** open to the public. **Subjects:** DN ice boating. **Publications:** Plans and Specifications ● Runner Tracks. Newsletter ● Think Ice: The DN Ice Boating Handbook. **Price:** $9.00 ● Newsletter, 4-6/year. Contains information on upcoming events, race results, and articles on a wide range of subjects. **Price:** included in membership dues. **Circulation:** 900. **Advertising:** accepted ● Yearbook, annual. **Conventions/Meetings:** annual meeting.

22671 ■ International Etchells Class Association

PO Box 676
Jamestown, RI 02835
Ph: (401)862-1783
E-mail: etchells@att.net
URL: http://www.etchells.org
Contact: Bunny Wayt, Exec. Dir.

Founded: 1969. **Members:** 1,700. **Staff:** 1. **Budget:** $80,000. **National Groups:** 12. **Multinational. Description:** Owners and enthusiasts of Etchells Class sailing yachts. Promotes amateur sailing competition and seeks to maintain the one-design characteristics of the Etchells Class yacht. **Computer Services:** Mailing lists. **Committees:** International Governing; One Design and Technical Control. **Affiliated With:** International Sailing Federation. **Also Known As:** International E-22 Class Association. **Publications:** Etchells Class Yearbook, biennial. Provides rules, results, and rosters of Etchells class yacht competitors. **Price:** included in membership dues; $5.00/copy for nonmembers. **Circulation:** 2,000. **Advertising:** accepted ● Etchells News, quarterly. Newsletter. **Price:** included in membership dues; $15.00 /year for nonmembers. **Advertising:** accepted. **Conventions/Meetings:** annual Etchells World Championship & A.G.M. - meeting and competition.

22672 ■ International Flying Dutchman Class Association of the U.S. (IFDCAUS)

c/o John Sayles, Sec.-Treas.
291 Cromwell Ln.
West Chester, PA 19380
Ph: (610)429-9765
E-mail: ifdcaus@comcast.net
URL: http://www.sailfd.org/USA
Contact: John Sayles, Sec.-Treas.

Founded: 1959. **Members:** 150. **Membership Dues:** regular, in U.S., $25 (annual) ● associate, $35 (annual) ● international, $45 (annual). **Regional Groups:** 10. **Multinational. Description:** Owners of Flying Dutchman Class sailboats; other interested individuals. Promotes ownership and racing of the Flying Dutchman. Holds responsibility for the administration of class rules; issues numbers and approves measurement certificates for the boats. Sponsors national and international regattas throughout the U.S. and Canada. Maintains a list of builders of the Flying Dutchman and a list of available used boats. **Publications:** The Flying Dutchman-The Thrill of Sailing. Video ● International Flying Dutchman Bulletin, quarterly ● Trapeze, quarterly. Newsletter. Includes regatta calendar. **Price:** included in membership dues. **Advertising:** accepted ● Brochure. **Conventions/Meetings:** annual National Championship - competition.

22673 ■ International Hobie Class Association (IHCA)

c/o Lori Mohney, VP
2812 E Shore Dr.
Portage, MI 49002

Ph: (269)327-4565
E-mail: hobie01@sbcglobal.net
URL: http://www.hobieclass.com
Contact: Lori Mohney, VP
Members: 10,000. **Staff:** 2. **Description:** Groups of Hobie One-Design Class sailboat owners who sail together in fleets. Promotes sailing and racing of Hobie Cat sailboats. **Formerly:** (1982) Hobie Class Association. **Publications:** *Hobie Hotline*, bimonthly. Magazine. Lists race results and technical and recreational information. **Price:** $11.97/year. **Advertising:** accepted ● Brochures. **Conventions/Meetings:** semiannual meeting.

22674 ■ International J/22 Class Association
12900 Lake Ave., No. 2001
Lakewood, OH 44107
Ph: (440)796-3100
E-mail: j22@adelphia.net
URL: http://www.j22.org
Contact: Christopher E. Howell, Exec. Sec.
Founded: 1983. **Members:** 500. **Membership Dues:** gold, $100 (annual) ● platinum, $500 (annual) ● international, $45 (annual) ● student, $25 (annual). **Staff:** 1. **Multinational. Description:** Owners, co-owners, and helmsmen of J/22 Class sailboats. (A J/22 is a racer/cruiser that is 22 ft. long.) Promotes one-design sailing events with J/22 sailboats. Gathers and disseminates information to members; regional districts hold annual regattas. **Awards: Type:** recognition. **Conventions/Meetings:** annual Midwinter Championship - competition ● annual North American Championship - competition ● annual World Championship - competition.

22675 ■ International Lightning Class Association (ILCA)
c/o Jan Davis, Exec. Sec.
7625 S Yampa St.
Centennial, CO 80016
Ph: (303)325-5886
E-mail: office@lightningclass.org
URL: http://www.lightningclass.org
Contact: Jan Davis, Exec. Sec.
Founded: 1939. **Members:** 3,600. **Membership Dues:** active, $45 (annual) ● associate, $26 (annual) ● crew, $10 (annual). **Staff:** 1. **Regional Groups:** 510. **Multinational. Description:** Owners and crew of Lightning Class sailing yachts. Promotes Lightning Class yacht racing without geographical limitation, under uniform rules, and between boats of identical design. Conducts fleet, district, area, and world championship competitions. **Awards:** Several Perpetual Trophies. **Type:** trophy. **Recipient:** for winning a championship regatta. **Publications:** *Lightning Flashes*, 10/year. Newsletter. Covers regattas, rules, plans, and other information pertaining to sailing Lightning Class boats. **Price:** included in membership dues; $20.00 /year for nonmembers. ISSN: 0746-7052. **Circulation:** 3,100. **Advertising:** accepted ● Yearbook, annual. Provides reports and articles by champions of various regattas, fleet and district reports, alphabetical listings of active owners of Lightning Class. **Price:** included in membership dues; $12.00/copy for nonmembers. **Circulation:** 2,000. **Advertising:** accepted. **Conventions/Meetings:** semiannual meeting.

22676 ■ International Mobjack Association (IMA)
4803 Croft Ct.
Glen Allen, VA 23060
Ph: (804)346-8761 (757)312-0768
E-mail: mobjack@gmail.com
URL: http://mobjack.tripod.com
Contact: Jerry Desvernine, Pres.
Founded: 1959. **Members:** 200. **Membership Dues:** active, isolated, $30 ● associate, $25. **Regional Groups:** 1. **State Groups:** 7. **Local Groups:** 6. **Multinational. Description:** Represents owners of mobjack sailboats. Promotes racing and use of the mobjack class. **Awards:** National Championship. **Frequency:** annual. **Type:** recognition. **Publications:** *Jack Tar*, semiannual. Newsletter. **Advertising:** accepted ● Directory, semiannual. **Conventions/Meet-**

ings: annual National Championship Regatta - meeting - always third weekend of August.

22677 ■ International Naples Sabot Association (INSA)
c/o Aimee Graham, Sec.-Treas.
PO Box 6808
San Diego, CA 92166
Ph: (949)645-1245
Fax: (949)645-1245
E-mail: napplessabot@hotmail.com
URL: http://www.naples-sabot.org
Contact: Aimee Graham, Sec.-Treas.
Founded: 1946. **Members:** 900. **Membership Dues:** regular, $15 (annual) ● supporting, $10 (annual) ● additional family, $8 (annual). **Staff:** 1. **Regional Groups:** 2. **Local Groups:** 9. **Description:** Sailors of Naples Sabot class yachts. (Naples Sabot yachts are small, sideboard-keeled sailing craft whose total weight may not be less than 95 pounds; their small size and great stability make them an ideal boat for use by children and beginning sailors.) Promotes racing of Naples Sabot yachts; establishes uniform rules to govern Naples Sabot regattas worldwide. Conducts annual regattas in various skill and age classes; compiles statistics; membership is concentrated in Southern California, but is international in scope. **Awards:** Jessica Uniack Memorial Sportsmanship Award. **Frequency:** annual. **Type:** recognition. **Recipient:** for sportsmanship on and off the water. **Computer Services:** Mailing lists, regatta notices. **Committees:** Measurement; Race; Rules. **Formerly:** Naples Sabot One—Design Association. **Publications:** *The Leeboard*, semiannual. Newsletter. Includes calendar of regattas, race results, and fleet and association news. **Price:** included in membership dues. **Circulation:** 800. **Advertising:** accepted ● Yearbook, annual. Includes lists of members and trophy winners, association information, and racing rules. **Price:** included in membership dues. **Conventions/Meetings:** annual general assembly.

22678 ■ International Penguin Class Dinghy Association (IPCDA)
c/o Charles Krafft
8300 Waverly Rd.
Owings, MD 20736
E-mail: jenkins@dmv.com
URL: http://home.dmv.com/~jenkins
Contact: John Jenkins, Sec.
Founded: 1940. **Membership Dues:** regular, $25 (annual) ● family, $30 (annual) ● associate, junior (under 19), $15 (annual). **Description:** Individuals who own, sail, or are interested in Penguin Class Dinghy sailboats. Promotes and develops Penguin Class Dinghy racing and seeks to maintain the one-design features of Penguin Class Dinghies. Conducts local training sessions. **Libraries: Type:** reference. **Committees:** International Measurement; International Race. **Publications:** *Penguin Log*, biennial. Directory ● *Penguin Patter*, quarterly. Newsletter. **Conventions/Meetings:** annual Regatta - meeting.

22679 ■ International Prindle Class Racing Association
c/o Performance Catamarans Inc.
1800 E Borchard Ave.
Santa Ana, CA 92705
Ph: (714)835-6416
Fax: (714)541-6643
E-mail: pcat@performancecat.com
URL: http://www.performancecat.com
Contact: Jack Young, Contact
Founded: 1976. **Members:** 2,921. **Membership Dues:** domestic, $15 (annual) ● international, $30 (annual). **Regional Groups:** 9. **Description:** Owners and crew of NACRA class catamarans. Sponsors an active class program for both racers and recreational sailors. **Affiliated With:** United States Sailing Association. **Formerly:** (1998) International NACRA Class Racing Association. **Publications:** *Performance Sailor*, bimonthly. Newsletter. Covers national and international racing results and schedules. Includes articles on care, equipment, safety, and handling of products. **Price:** free, for members only.

Advertising: accepted. **Conventions/Meetings:** annual North American Championship - meeting.

22680 ■ International Star Class Yacht Racing Association (ISCYRA)
1545 Waukegan Rd., Ste.8
Glenview, IL 60025-2185
Ph: (847)729-0630
Fax: (847)729-0718
E-mail: office@starclass.org
URL: http://www.starclass.org
Contact: Diane C. Dorr, Exec. Sec.
Founded: 1911. **Members:** 4,000. **Membership Dues:** active/isolated active, $60 (annual) ● associate/isolated associate, $30 (annual). **Staff:** 2. **Multinational. Description:** Owners and crew members of Star Class racing yachts (sailboats) and individuals interested in Star boat racing. Promotes the continuance of Star as a one-design racing class. Sanctions regattas. Conducts seminars and clinics. **Libraries: Type:** reference. **Committees:** Class Management; International Governing; Judiciary; Marketing; Race; Technical Advisory. **Affiliated With:** International Sailing Federation; United States Sailing Association. **Publications:** *International Star Class Yacht Racing Association—Log*, annual. Directory. Includes Star Class rules, technical updates, and racing specifications. **Price:** included in membership dues. **Circulation:** 4,000. **Advertising:** accepted ● *Starlights*, quarterly. Magazine. **Price:** included in membership dues. **Circulation:** 3,800. **Advertising:** accepted. **Conventions/Meetings:** annual meeting.

22681 ■ International Sunfish Class Association (ISCA)
PO Box 300128
Waterford, MI 48330-0128
Ph: (248)673-2750
Fax: (248)673-2750
E-mail: sunfishoff@aol.com
URL: http://www.sunfishclass.org
Contact: Terry Beadle, Sec.
Founded: 1955. **Members:** 2,000. **Membership Dues:** individual in U.S., $30 (annual) ● family in U.S., $15 (annual) ● junior, $20 (annual) ● individual outside U.S., $35 (annual) ● junior outside U.S., $25 (annual). **Staff:** 2. **Budget:** $50,000. **National Groups:** 15. **Description:** Sponsors regattas worldwide. Compiles statistics; maintains hall of fame. Registers Sunfish racers worldwide. **Libraries: Type:** not open to the public. **Holdings:** periodicals. **Awards:** World Champion Award. **Frequency:** annual. **Recipient:** qualifications by country and one week of races. **Councils:** World and Advisory. **Affiliated With:** International Sailing Federation; United States Sailing Association. **Formerly:** Alcort Sailfish-Sunfish Class; (1976) AMF Alcort Sailfish-Sunfish Class; (1984) AMF Sunfish Racing Class Association; (1986) International Sunfish Class Association. **Publications:** *Sunfish Regatta Schedule*, annual. **Price:** $3.00. **Circulation:** 2,600. **Advertising:** accepted ● *Windward Leg*, 3/year. Magazine. **Price:** $3.00/issue. **Circulation:** 26,000. **Advertising:** accepted. **Conventions/Meetings:** annual World Championship - competition.

22682 ■ International Thunderbird Class Association (ITCA)
PO Box 1033
Mercer Island, WA 98040-1033
E-mail: dale@wallstreetclothiers.com
URL: http://www.thunderbirdsailing.org
Contact: Dale Dunning, Pres.
Founded: 1962. **Members:** 1,250. **Membership Dues:** general, $10 (annual). **Regional Groups:** 18. **Multinational. Description:** Individuals who own or are interested in International Thunderbird Class sailboats. Promotes the maintenance and one-design class racing of International Thunderbird Class sailboats. Sanctions world and regional regattas. Compiles statistics; a member of the U.S. Yacht Racing Union. **Awards:** World Championship Trophy. **Frequency:** semiannual. **Type:** trophy. **Recipient:** for 1st Place Boat in Championship Regatta. **Computer Services:** Information services, boat resources ● mailing lists, of members ● online services, forum.

Telecommunication Services: electronic mail, wendy.loat@utoronto.ca. **Committees:** Technical. **Formerly:** International Thunderbird Association; Thunderbird Class Association. **Publications:** *International Newsletter*, quarterly ● *International Roster*, biennial. **Conventions/Meetings:** annual meeting - always January.

22683 ■ Jet 14 Class Association (J-14/CA)
26 Pontiac Dr.
Wayne, NJ 07470
Ph: (216)261-9922
E-mail: jet14secretary@comcast.net
URL: http://www.sailingsource.com/jet14
Contact: Dick Kennedy, Sec.-Treas.
Founded: 1955. **Members:** 200. **Membership Dues:** associate, $15 (annual) ● junior, $15 (annual) ● active, $35 (annual). **Description:** Owners and enthusiasts of Jet 14 Class sailboats. (The Jet 14 Class is a planing, one-design, two-man racing dinghy.) Sponsors, organizes, and coordinates the scheduling of district and regional regattas, special regattas, club weekend races, and the national senior and junior championship regattas. Awards individual and perpetual trophies. Sets standards for specifications and measurements. Investigates suggestions and conducts tests on possible improvements in design and performance. Compiles statistics. **Affiliated With:** United States Sailing Association. **Publications:** *Jet Blasts*, quarterly. Newsletter. **Price:** included in membership dues. **Circulation:** 200. **Advertising:** accepted ● *Jet 14 Class Yearbook*. **Conventions/Meetings:** annual meeting ● seminar.

22684 ■ Joshua Slocum Society International (JSSI)
c/o Ted Jones, Commodore
15 Codfish Hill Rd. Extension
Bethel, CT 06801
Ph: (203)790-6616
Fax: (203)778-9917
E-mail: ted@joshuaslocumsocietyintl.org
URL: http://www.joshuaslocumsocietyintl.org
Contact: Ted Jones, Commodore
Founded: 1955. **Members:** 250. **Membership Dues:** active, $35 (annual). **Staff:** 3. **Budget:** $7,500. **Description:** Persons interested in long distance passages in small boats united to record, encourage, and support such voyages. Cosponsors single-handed trans-Pacific and other regattas. Supports junior sailing events and remote sailing for the disabled; the society is named after Captain Joshua Slocum who made the first single-handed, small boat circumnavigation of the world in 1895-98. Maintains Port Captains around the world. **Libraries:** Type: reference. **Holdings:** 1,200. **Subjects:** general long distance voyages. **Awards:** Golden Circle. Type: recognition. **Recipient:** for members who have circumnavigated the world ● Northern Light Award. Type: recognition. **Recipient:** for captains and crew of merchant vessels with outstanding service ● Slocum Award. Type: recognition. **Recipient:** for the most notable single-handed journey ● Voss Award. Type: recognition. **Recipient:** for the most notable crewed journey. **Formerly:** (1989) Slocum Society. **Publications:** *Spray Ahoy!*, 3/year. Newsletter. Provides timely updates on ongoing activities and events, as well as stories about member's adventures. **Price:** $3.00 ● *The Spray Journal*, annual. Contains information about the numerous activities of the society and its members. **Price:** $3.00. **Circulation:** 400. **Advertising:** accepted. **Conventions/Meetings:** annual meeting (exhibits) - usually November.

22685 ■ Lido 14 International Class Association
PO Box 1252
Newport Beach, CA 92663
Ph: (714)437-1370
Fax: (714)437-1374
E-mail: shaddowwoman@sbcglobal.net
URL: http://www.lido14.org
Contact: Sharon Young, Exec. Sec.
Founded: 1958. **Members:** 300. **Staff:** 1. **Regional Groups:** 6. **State Groups:** 5. **Local Groups:** 22.

Description: Yachtsmen, post-secondary schools, and naval recreational centers. Promotes Lido 14 Class racing under uniform rules and regulations; seeks to maintain the one-design features of the Lido 14 Class sloop. Cooperates with other yachting organizations and, in return, insists on strict observance and compliance with association rules. Works to keep the cost of acquisition and upkeep within modest limits without sacrificing high standards of performance and seaworthiness. **Affiliated With:** United States Sailing Association. **Publications:** *Bow Wave*, quarterly. Newsletter. **Advertising:** accepted ● *Roster*, annual. Membership Directory ● Handbook, annual. **Conventions/Meetings:** annual meeting.

22686 ■ MC Sailing Association (MCSA)
c/o Ronald G. Stryker, Exec. Sec.
PO Box 250
Lewis Center, OH 43035-0250
Ph: (740)549-4700
E-mail: secretary@mcscow.org
URL: http://www.mcscow.org
Contact: Ronald G. Stryker, Exec. Sec.
Founded: 1973. **Members:** 600. **Membership Dues:** regular, $25 (annual) ● sustaining, $55 (annual). **Staff:** 1. **National Groups:** 84. **Description:** Sailors and enthusiasts of MC Class racing yachts which are planing-hull scows that can be sailed single-handed or by a crew in most wind conditions. Aims are to: promote the sport and sportsmanship of one-design yacht racing in general and MC Scow racing in particular; set standards and rules regarding chartering, yacht specifications, and racing. **Computer Services:** Mailing lists. **Formerly:** (2003) International MC Class Sailboat Racing Association. **Publications:** *International MC Class Sailboat Racing Association—Yearbook*, annual. **Price:** included in membership dues ● *MC Rule Book*, periodic. Contains articles of incorporation, bylaws and scantlings of MCScow. Alternate Formats: online ● *Touch of Class*, quarterly. Newsletter. **Price:** included in membership dues. **Advertising:** accepted. **Conventions/Meetings:** annual Blue Chip Regatta - competition, national championship - always September ● competition, inter-fleet ● annual Mid-Winter Championship Junior and Masters Regattas - competition ● annual National Championship Regatta - competition - always late summer or early fall.

22687 ■ Midget Ocean Racing Club (MORC)
c/o Rene Valliant
711 Warren Dr.
Annapolis, MD 21403
Ph: (410)263-6632
E-mail: ivalliant@aol.com
URL: http://www.morc.org
Contact: Rene Valliant, Contact
Founded: 1954. **Membership Dues:** regular (skipper/helmsman), $20 (annual) ● associate (crew/helmsman), $5 (annual) ● supporting, $25 (annual) ● contributing, $50 (annual) ● sustaining, $100 (annual) ● sponsoring, $250 (annual) ● benefactor, $500 (annual) ● life, $1,000. **Description:** A group of sailors dedicated to the ideal that different types of boats can be fairly raced using a measurement rule - to handicap, and that differences in boat size should be minimal to help ensure fair racing. **Publications:** Handbook. Alternate Formats: online ● Newsletter, periodic. Alternate Formats: online.

22688 ■ National Boating Federation (NBF)
PO Box 4111
Annapolis, MD 21403-6111
Ph: (253)927-1285
Fax: (360)297-3505
E-mail: ssserval@aol.com
URL: http://www.n-b-f.org
Contact: Marlene Barrington, Pres.
Founded: 1966. **Members:** 20. **Membership Dues:** regular, $200 (annual) ● associate, $100 (annual) ● club, $50 (annual) ● family, $35 (annual) ● individual, $25 (annual). **Budget:** $25,000. **Regional Groups:** 22. **State Groups:** 10. **Local Groups:** 72. **National Groups:** 25. **Description:** Boat and yacht clubs and individual recreational boaters in the U.S. Works to improve and strengthen recreational boating through:

information exchange; promoting safety education and seamanship; development and protection of waterways for safe boating; understanding and cooperation among boaters and state and federal authorities. Promotes a unified voice for the boating public with no commercial interests. Cooperates with United States Power Squadron and U.S. Coast Guard Auxiliary to promote instruction in seamanship and small boat handling. **Libraries:** Type: reference. **Holdings:** books, clippings, monographs. **Subjects:** recreational boating issues. **Awards:** United States Power Squadron and U.S. Coast Guard Auxiliary. **Frequency:** annual. **Type:** trophy. **Recipient:** for excellence in recreational boating education. **Publications:** *The Lookout*, bimonthly. Newsletter. Reports on federal and regional legislative issues affecting recreational boating. **Price:** included in membership dues. **Circulation:** 4,500. **Advertising:** accepted. Alternate Formats: online ● *NBF Success Record* ● *Wallop-Breaux Funding for Boating Safety* ● *What is NBF?*. **Conventions/Meetings:** semiannual conference - always spring and fall.

22689 ■ National Butterfly Association (NBA)
c/o Windwards Boatworks
7005 Hubbard Ave.
Middleton, WI 53562
Ph: (608)831-8771
E-mail: jthayashi@aol.com
URL: http://www.butterflyer.org
Contact: John Hayashi, Contact
Founded: 1964. **Members:** 300. **Membership Dues:** individual, $10 ● additional family, $6. **Staff:** 1. **Description:** Owners of Butterfly sailboats; persons interested in Butterfly sailing. Encourages and maintains the suitability of the one-design Butterfly Class sailboat for use as an economical family racing and junior training boat. Sponsors regattas. **Publications:** *The Butterflyer*, bimonthly. Newsletter. **Conventions/Meetings:** seminar, sailing.

22690 ■ National C Scow Sailing Association (NCSSA)
PO Box 473
Pewaukee, WI 53072
E-mail: mrgone1111@yahoo.com
URL: http://www.cscow.org
Contact: Chris Martin, Sec.
Membership Dues: regular, $30 (annual) ● associate, $15 (annual) ● junior (under 21), $10 (annual). **Multinational. Description:** Promotes Class C Scow racing under uniform rules in all regions of the United States and Canada. Represents amateur sailors. Keeps the cost of the C Scow within modest limits without sacrificing high standards of performance. Conducts yacht races and regattas. **Computer Services:** database, e-mail directory ● information services, boat resources ● online services, bulletin board ● online services, discussion forum. **Committees:** ILYA Class C; Promotion and Publicity; Regatta; Rules. **Publications:** *C World*. Magazine. Alternate Formats: online.

22691 ■ National Class E Scow Association (NCESA)
PO Box 3022
Madison, WI 53704-0022
Ph: (608)347-1480
E-mail: lon@e-scow.org
URL: http://e-scow.org
Contact: Lon Schoor, Sec.-Treas.
Founded: 1959. **Members:** 750. **Membership Dues:** associate crew, $15 (annual) ● regular, skipper, $50 (annual). **Staff:** 2. **Regional Groups:** 5. **Local Groups:** 77. **Description:** Boat owners and skippers; boat crews are associate members. Aims are to: encourage and promote amateur yacht racing and maintain the class as a one-design yacht; adapt and enforce rules and regulations for specifications for the control of the design of Class E Scows; keep these vessels within the financial reach of people of moderate means and avoid the rapid obsolescence of yachts through radical changes in the scantling rules and specifications. **Awards:** Championship. **Frequency:** annual. **Type:** trophy. **Recipient:** for winner of National Regatta. **Committees:** Judicial;

Measurement; Publications; Regatta; Rules. **Publications:** *Digital Reaches*, annual. Newsletter. Summarizes regional regattas. **Price:** included in membership dues. **Advertising:** accepted ● *Fleet Directory*. Alternate Formats: online ● *National Class E Scow Association—Reporter*, annual. Magazine. Summarizes major championship regattas. **Price:** included in membership dues. **Advertising:** accepted. Alternate Formats: online ● *National Class E Scow Association—Yearbook/Rulebook*, annual. **Price:** included in membership dues. **Advertising:** accepted ● *Regatta*, annual. Reports. Alternate Formats: online. **Conventions/Meetings:** competition, in conjunction with the Minnetonka Yacht Club ● annual Regatta - meeting (exhibits) - always September.

22692 ■ National Offshore Department (NAD)
c/o United States Sailing Association
PO Box 1260
15 Maritime Dr.
Portsmouth, RI 02871-0907
Ph: (401)683-0800
Fax: (401)683-0840
E-mail: info@ussailing.org
URL: http://www.ussailing.org
Contact: Charlie Leighton, Exec. Dir.

Description: A department of the U.S. Sailing. Organizations dedicated to the interest of offshore racing in cruiser/racers (yachts that contain cruising accommodations and are used for racing) who are members of the U.S. Sailing group or committees of member yacht racing associations. Purposes are to promote the interests of whose who race Cruiser/Racers in offshore waters, provide a forum for exchange of information, and represent the council's interests before the union. **Formerly:** (1992) National Offshore Council. **Conventions/Meetings:** annual meeting.

22693 ■ National One Design Racing Association (NODRA)
c/o Jolly Booth, Sec.-Treas.
1225 E Bronson St.
South Bend, IN 46615
Ph: (330)644-9305
E-mail: nod747@sbcglobal.net
URL: http://www.nodra.com
Contact: Mark Roberts, Commodore

Founded: 1937. **Members:** 110. **Membership Dues:** full, $40 (annual) ● associate, $15 (annual). **Description:** Sailors and former owners of National One-Design racing boats. Encourages and promotes interest in racing activities; controls design and construction specifications; provides contracts for construction and riggings. **Telecommunication Services:** electronic mail, nod747@aol.com. **Affiliated With:** United States Sailing Association. **Publications:** *The NODS*, 3/year, every mid-winter, summer, fall. Newsletter. Alternate Formats: online ● *Regatta Bulletin*, 3/year ● Newsletter ● Yearbook, annual. **Conventions/Meetings:** biennial Summer Open - meeting.

22694 ■ National Starwind/Spindrift Class Association
PO Box 21262
Columbus, OH 43221
E-mail: crew@starwinds.com
URL: http://www.starwinds.com
Contact: Sue Hull, Exec. Off.

Founded: 1984. **Members:** 150. **Description:** Owners of Starwind and Spindrift sailboats. Provides information exchange on the maintenance of Starwind/Spindrift sailboats. Makes available technical information. **Formerly:** (1991) Starwind/Spindrift 19 Association; (2005) Starwind/Spindrift Association. **Publications:** *Rigging Manual for Starwind 19 Boat* ● Also makes available back issues of *Star Winds* (newsletter).

22695 ■ North American Formula 18 Association (NAF18)
7505 Elkmont Ct.
Wilmington, NC 28411
Ph: (757)851-4815

E-mail: admin@naf18.com
URL: http://www.naf18.com
Contact: Tracie Van Houten, Chair

Membership Dues: regular, $20 (annual). **Multinational. Description:** Represents F18 sailors. Promotes the sports of sailing in North America. Sponsors competitions. **Telecommunication Services:** electronic mail, tracievh@cox.net. **Publications:** Newsletter. Alternate Formats: online.

22696 ■ North American Tornado Association
c/o James Young, USA Measurer
401 County Rd. 413
Granby, CO 80446
Ph: (562)431-9930
E-mail: jim@jy1.com
URL: http://www.tornado.org
Contact: Alain Dubuc, Pres.

Founded: 1970. **Members:** 250. **Description:** Sailors actively racing the Olympic Class of catamaran, the Tornado. Coordinates Tornado activities in the U.S. **Formerly:** (2003) U.S. Tornado Association. **Publications:** *Tornado Watch*, quarterly. Newsletter. Contains racing schedule and Tornado Class standings. **Price:** included in membership dues. **Circulation:** 350. **Advertising:** accepted ● Yearbook. **Conventions/Meetings:** annual meeting.

22697 ■ Olson 30 Class Association (OTCA)
3416 36th Ave. W
Seattle, WA 98199
Ph: (530)416-6100
E-mail: wilsontahoe@sbcglobal.net
URL: http://www.olson30.org
Contact: Ray Wilson, Pres.

Founded: 1978. **Members:** 100. **Membership Dues:** active, $30 (annual) ● associate, $15 (annual). **Regional Groups:** 10. **State Groups:** 15. **Description:** Owners of Olson 30 Class racing sailboats. (The Olson 30 Class is an ultralight sloop that is approximately 30 ft. in length.) Promotes Olson 30 Class boat racing. **Computer Services:** database, boat sales ● mailing lists, of members. **Committees:** Local fleets. **Affiliated With:** United States Sailing Association. **Conventions/Meetings:** annual National Championship/Regatta - meeting.

22698 ■ One-Design Class Council (ODCC)
c/o United States Sailing Association
15 Maritime Dr.
PO Box 1260
Portsmouth, RI 02871-0907
Ph: (401)683-0800
Free: (800)US-SAIL1
Fax: (401)683-0840
E-mail: sdieball@quantumsails.com
URL: http://www.ussailing.org/odcc
Contact: Skip Dieball, Chm.

Founded: 1975. **Members:** 150. **Membership Dues:** organization, $100 (annual). **Description:** A council of the United States Sailing Association. Works to promote and support One-Design Class sailing in the U.S. Represents the interests of the One-Design Class associations within US sailing. Provides an exchange of information between one-design class associations. (Composed of owners of yachts which normally race on a closed course without a handicap system.) Sponsors competitions. **Libraries: Type:** reference. **Awards:** U.S. Sailing One-Design Award. **Frequency:** annual. **Type:** recognition. **Recipient:** for outstanding individuals and organizations in one design sailing. **Computer Services:** Mailing lists, of members. **Committees:** Technical/Safety. **Publications:** *American Sailor*, 10/year. Magazine. **Circulation:** 43,000. **Advertising:** accepted ● *Class Management Handbook*. **Price:** $55.00 for nonmembers; $35.00 for members ● *Fleet Captain's Manual*. Alternate Formats: online ● *SNAX*, quarterly. Newsletter. Alternate Formats: online. **Conventions/Meetings:** annual meeting.

22699 ■ Prindle Class Association (PCA)
c/o Performance Catamarans, Inc.
1800 E Borchard Ave.
Santa Ana, CA 92705
Ph: (714)835-6416

Fax: (714)541-6643
E-mail: pcat@performancecat.com
URL: http://www.performancecat.com
Contact: Jack Young, Class Rep.

Founded: 1972. **Members:** 7,000. **Membership Dues:** international, $30 (annual). **Staff:** 1. **Local Groups:** 100. **Description:** Owners of Prindle Catamarans and their families. To promote the use of Prindle Catamarans and to act as a social organization. Sponsors regional series of regattas. **Publications:** *Performance Sailor*, bimonthly. Newsletter. **Price:** free, for members only. **Advertising:** accepted. **Conventions/Meetings:** annual National Championship Regatta - meeting.

22700 ■ Rhodes 19 Class Association (R-19/CA)
c/o Chuck Becker, Treas.
1100 N Lake Shore Dr., Apt. 3B
Chicago, IL 60611
Ph: (312)642-1006
E-mail: cebecker@aol.com
URL: http://www.rhodes19.org
Contact: Wiley Crockett, Pres.

Founded: 1959. **Members:** 150. **Membership Dues:** active, $35 (annual) ● associate, $15 (annual). **Regional Groups:** 4. **Description:** Owners and charters of the Rhodes 19 sailboat. Works to promote and develop Rhodes 19 Class racing under uniform rules and to maintain the one-design feature of the sailboat. Maintains small library. Sponsors competitions; bestows award for best performance by a novice. **Awards:** Cressy Trophy. **Frequency:** annual. **Type:** trophy. **Recipient:** to the national skipper's second placer ● Don Quixote Trophy. **Frequency:** annual. **Type:** trophy. **Recipient:** to the highest finishing national competitor who has never been listed on top five of any previous National Regatta ● Novice Trophy. **Frequency:** annual. **Type:** trophy. **Recipient:** to the highest finishing National Regatta competitor who has never competed in the previous events ● President's Trophy. **Frequency:** annual. **Type:** trophy. **Recipient:** for class members with significant contributions to the association ● Travel Trophy. **Frequency:** annual. **Type:** trophy. **Recipient:** to the National Regatta competitor who has traveled farthest to attend the championship. **Committees:** Rules. **Publications:** *Mainsheet*, quarterly. Contains association news and regatta notices. **Price:** included in membership dues. Alternate Formats: online ● *The Rule Book*. Alternate Formats: online. **Conventions/Meetings:** annual Class Championship Regatta - meet.

22701 ■ Rhodes Bantam Class Association (RBCA)
2133 Ellis Hollow Rd.
Ithaca, NY 14850
Ph: (607)539-7316
Contact: Kathy Burlitch, Exec. Officer

Founded: 1947. **Description:** Owners of Rhodes Bantam sailboats and other interested individuals. Promotes the sailing and racing of Rhodes Bantam sailboats and enthusiasm in the sport of sailing. Presently inactive. **Conventions/Meetings:** annual International Championship Regatta - meeting - usually first week of August.

22702 ■ San Juan 21 Class Association (SJTCA)
c/o Ken Gurganus, Sec.-Treas.
211 Gloria St.
Greenville, NC 27858-8627
Ph: (252)355-6974
E-mail: kgurganus@suddenlink.net
URL: http://www.sanjuan21.net/national
Contact: Ken Gurganus, Sec.-Treas.

Founded: 1971. **Members:** 400. **Membership Dues:** active, $25 (annual) ● associate/sustaining, $15 (annual). **Staff:** 6. **Budget:** $7,000. **Regional Groups:** 40. **Description:** Owners and skippers of San Juan 21 sailing sloops. Promotes San Juan 21 sailing and one-design racing. Sponsors national, regional, and local regattas and cruising activities. **Awards: Type:** recognition. **Affiliated With:** United States Sailing Association. **Publications:** *Class Handbook*, bimonthly. Newsletter. **Advertising:** accepted ● *Jib-sheet*, bimonthly. **Conventions/Meetings:** annual Nationals - meeting - held concurrently on East and West coasts.

22703 ■ Santana 20 Class Association

c/o Zoe Gilstrap, Sec.
1266 Napa Creek Dr.
Eugene, OR 97404
E-mail: zoegilstrap@yahoo.com
URL: http://www.s20.org
Contact: Zoe Gilstrap, Sec.
Founded: 1977. **Members:** 200. **Membership Dues:** regular, $50 (annual) ● associate, $25 (annual). **Staff:** 1. **Local Groups:** 37. **Description:** Owners of Santana 20 Class sailboats and their families. Aims to promote Santana 20 Class racing and other yachting activities. Cooperates with other yachting associations to ensure strict observance and compliance with the rules of the association. Keeps the costs of buying and maintaining a Santana 20 sloop modest without sacrificing standards of performance and seaworthiness. Promotes a one-design class of Santana 20 sailboats in which racing shall be to determine the skill of the skipper and crew under uniform rules and specifications. Conducts seminars and clinics related to sailing the Santana 20 sloop. Holds local, regional, and national regattas. **Publications:** *Santana 20/20 News*, quarterly. Newsletter. Reports on association activities. **Price:** included in membership dues. **Circulation:** 300. **Advertising:** accepted ● Yearbook, annual. **Conventions/Meetings:** annual meeting.

22704 ■ Seven Seas Cruising Association (SSCA)

2501 E Commercial Blvd., Ste.201
Fort Lauderdale, FL 33308
Ph: (954)771-5660
Fax: (954)771-5662
E-mail: office@ssca.org
URL: http://www.ssca.org
Contact: Kathleen Watt, Pres.
Founded: 1952. **Members:** 10,000. **Membership Dues:** regular, in U.S., bulk mail, $40 (annual) ● regular, in U.S., first class, $47 (annual) ● regular, in Canada, Mexico, $48 (annual) ● regular, outside U.S., surface mail, $49 (annual) ● regular, outside U.S., airmail, $64 (annual). **Staff:** 3. **Description:** Individuals who are interested in the cruising lifestyle, who live aboard, own boats and live ashore, or just dream the cruising lifestyle. Fosters communication and camaraderie among members. **Libraries: Type:** not open to the public. **Holdings:** 1,000. **Subjects:** sailing. **Awards:** Circumnavigation. **Frequency:** periodic. **Type:** recognition ● Service. **Frequency:** annual. **Type:** recognition ● 7 Seas. **Frequency:** annual. **Type:** recognition ● Transocean. **Frequency:** periodic. **Type:** recognition. **Telecommunication Services:** electronic mail, membership@ssca.org ● electronic mail, editor@ssca.org ● electronic mail, board@ssca.org. **Publications:** *Commodores' Bulletin*, monthly. Provides information on sailing trips taken by members. Includes information on prices, locations, navigation equipment, docking, and harbors. **Price:** $25.00 on CD. Alternate Formats: online; CD-ROM ● *Equipment Survey*, by order. Contains cruisers' opinions in equipment and gear based on personal experience. **Price:** $10.00 ● Also publishes cookbook, and call sign. **Conventions/Meetings:** weekly Fort Lauderdale Cruiser's - breakfast - every Sunday ● annual Melbourne GAM - meeting, sailing seminars (exhibits) - always November.

22705 ■ Shields National Class Association

PO Box 236
Newport, RI 02840
Ph: (401)842-6911
E-mail: skipmcgoo@aol.com
URL: http://www.shieldsclass.com
Contact: Skip McGuire, Pres.
Founded: 1966. **Members:** 350. **Description:** Boat owners, crew members, and enthusiasts interested in the racing of Shields Class yachts. Promotes Corinthian racing and attempts to maintain the one-design character of Shields Class yachts. Sponsors national

championship regatta. **Awards:** James B. Moore Jr. Memorial Prize. **Frequency:** annual. **Type:** recognition. **Recipient:** to the crew of the winning yacht ● Shields Class National Championship Institutional Trophy. **Frequency:** annual. **Type:** trophy. **Recipient:** for the best performance by an institutional crew ● Shields National Championship Trophy. **Frequency:** annual. **Type:** trophy. **Recipient:** to the winner of the championship ● Take A Bow Trophy. **Frequency:** annual. **Type:** trophy. **Recipient:** for individual selected by special committee. **Also Known As:** Shields Class Sailing Association. **Formerly:** (2001) Shields Class Association. **Publications:** *Class Handbook*, annual ● *The Masthead*, quarterly. Newsletter. Alternate Formats: online.

22706 ■ Snipe Class International Racing Association (SCIRA)

c/o Jerelyn W. Biehl, Exec. Dir.
2812 Canon St.
San Diego, CA 92106-2742
Ph: (619)224-6998
Fax: (619)224-0528
E-mail: scira@snipe.org
URL: http://www.snipe.org
Contact: Jerelyn W. Biehl, Exec. Dir.
Founded: 1931. **Members:** 5,000. **Membership Dues:** crew, junior, $20 (annual) ● co-owner, $30 (annual) ● senior, $40 (annual) ● family, $55 (annual) ● silver, $60 (annual) ● gold, $100 (annual). **Staff:** 1. **Budget:** $75,000. **Multinational. Description:** Persons interested in racing sailboats of the Snipe Class; owners of Snipe Class sailboats belonging to fleets throughout the world. Competes in regional and international championship races. Conducts youth training sessions. Sponsors competitions. **Committees:** International Rules. **Affiliated With:** International Sailing Federation. **Publications:** *Snipe Bulletin*, quarterly. Newsletter. Contains reports and schedules of regattas. **Price:** $20.00 /year for nonmembers outside U.S.; $10.00 /year for nonmembers in U.S.; included in membership dues. **Circulation:** 2,200. **Advertising:** accepted ● *Snipe Class International Racing Association—Rule Book*, quadrennial. **Price:** included in membership dues; $10.00/copy for nonmembers. **Circulation:** 3,500. **Advertising:** accepted. **Conventions/Meetings:** annual meeting.

22707 ■ Sonar Class Association (SCA)

c/o Sarah Sheldon, Sec.
43 Cottage Farm Rd.
Brookline, MA 02446
Ph: (617)738-1021
Fax: (617)731-7903
E-mail: tallott@silgan.com
URL: http://www.sonar.org
Contact: Anthony Allott, Pres.
Founded: 1980. **Members:** 400. **Membership Dues:** active, $50 (annual) ● associate, $25 (annual). **Description:** Owners or part-owners of Sonar sailboats; associate members are individuals interested in Sonars. (Sonars are 23-foot keel, one-design daysailers.) Seeks to: promote one-design class racing among sailboats; keep one-design standards; cooperate with other sailboat organizations; encourage good sportsmanship. Sponsors competitions. **Libraries: Type:** reference. **Holdings:** articles. **Awards:** European Champion. **Frequency:** annual. **Type:** trophy ● Midwinters Champion. **Frequency:** annual. **Type:** trophy ● National Champion. **Frequency:** annual. **Type:** trophy ● New England Champion. **Frequency:** annual. **Type:** trophy ● World Sonar Champion. **Frequency:** biennial. **Type:** trophy. **Committees:** Measurement; Publicity and Publications; Technical. **Publications:** *The Echo*, monthly. Newsletter. **Conventions/Meetings:** annual meeting.

22708 ■ Swan Owners Association of America (SOA)

17 Oyster Point
Warren, RI 02885
E-mail: secretary@swanowners.com
URL: http://www.swanowners.com
Contact: Bill Kardash, Sec.-Treas.
Membership Dues: active/associate, $100 (annual).
Description: Encourages and promotes interest in

the sport of sailing. Provides a platform for Swan sailboats to participate in cruise and rendezvous events as an organized class. Arranges for formal Swan classes in major sailing regattas. **Computer Services:** Online services, discussion forum. **Telecommunication Services:** electronic mail, commodore@swanowners.com ● electronic mail, treasurer@swanowners.com ● electronic mail, swanowners@yachtsoft.com. **Committees:** Cruising; Program; Regatta; Services. **Publications:** Newsletters. Alternate Formats: online.

22709 ■ T-Ten Class Association (TTCA)

c/o Stan Mehaffey, Exec. Sec.
360 E Randolph St., Apt. 803
Chicago, IL 60601
Ph: (312)861-0766
E-mail: smehaffrey@rcn.com
URL: http://www.tten.com
Contact: Stan Mehaffey, Exec. Sec.
Founded: 1980. **Members:** 144. **Membership Dues:** regular, $50 (annual) ● associate, $20 (annual). **Staff:** 1. **Budget:** $20,000. **Regional Groups:** 4. **Description:** Owners of Tartan Ten sailboats. Promotes the sport of sailing. Sponsors Tartan Ten North American Championship and Mid Winter Regatta. Offers tips on sailing techniques. (The Tartan Ten is a speedy, long, and narrow sailboat that handles easily and can be used in overnight offshore racing as well as weekend cruising.) **Awards:** North American Championship. **Frequency:** annual. **Type:** recognition. **Recipient:** to regatta winner. **Committees:** North American Regatta. **Publications:** *Membership Roster*, annual. Membership Directory. **Price:** included in membership dues. **Advertising:** accepted. Alternate Formats: online ● *TenSpeed News*, 3-4/year. Newsletter. **Price:** included in membership dues. **Circulation:** 200. **Advertising:** accepted. Alternate Formats: online ● Articles. Alternate Formats: online ● Also publishes regatta results. **Conventions/Meetings:** annual competition, held regionally and nationally for sailing ● annual meeting.

22710 ■ Tanzer 16 Class Association

PO Box 26003
Raleigh, NC 27611
E-mail: chris@clal.ca
URL: http://www.clal.ca/tanzer16
Contact: Chris Locke, Contact
Founded: 1982. **Members:** 185. **Local Groups:** 10. **Description:** Owners of Tanzer 16 one-design class sailboats. Promotes family day sailing and class racing of the Tanzer 16. **Formed by Merger of:** Canadian Tanzer 16 Association; U.S. Tanzer 16 Class Association. **Publications:** *Tanzer 16 Handbook*, biennial ● *Tanzer 16 Sailor*, bimonthly. **Conventions/Meetings:** competition - 2-3/year ● annual meeting.

22711 ■ Thistle Class Association (TCA)

c/o Patty Lawrence, Sec.-Treas.
6758 Little River Ln.
Loveland, OH 45140
Ph: (513)583-5080
E-mail: secretary@thistleclass.com
URL: http://www.thistleclass.com
Contact: Patty Lawrence, Sec.-Treas.
Founded: 1946. **Members:** 1,950. **Membership Dues:** family, $45 ● active, $35 ● associate/junior, $15. **Staff:** 1. **Regional Groups:** 16. **Local Groups:** 69. **Description:** Owners and sailors of Thistle Class sailboats. Fosters the sailing and racing of Thistles for sport and pleasure. Sponsors local, regional, and national regattas. Sets standards for specifications, measurements, and regattas. **Awards: Type:** recognition. **Publications:** *Bagpipe*, bimonthly. Journal. Contains sailing news of interest to Thistle sailors. **Advertising:** accepted ● *Constitution and By-Laws*, periodic ● *Roster*, biennial ● Brochures. **Conventions/Meetings:** Midwinter Meeting - always January and March ● annual National Championship - competition.

22712 ■ U.S. Albacore Association (USAA)

c/o Kay Marsh, Membership Sec./Ed.
1031 Graham St.
Bethlehem, PA 18015-2520

E-mail: klmarsh@verizon.net
URL: http://www.albacore.org/usa
Contact: Kay Marsh, Membership Sec./Ed.
Founded: 1965. **Members:** 80. **Membership Dues:** boat owner, $30 (annual) ● non-boat owner, crew, $20 (annual). **Local Groups:** 4. **Description:** Owners of the Albacore Class sailboat; other interested persons. Promotes Albacore sailing; represents the class locally and abroad; encourages control of the design with class rules and licensed builders. Sponsors regattas. **Committees:** Race and Regatta; Specifications. **Formerly:** Albacore Association. **Publications:** *Albacourier*, quarterly. Newsletter ● *International Yearbook*, annual. Includes calendar of events, association and chapter news, and membership directory. Contains USAA constitution and by-laws and Albacore Class rules. **Conventions/Meetings:** annual meeting ● seminar, on boat rigging and racing.

22713 ■ United States J/24 Class Association
7793 Burnet Rd., No. 15
Austin, TX 78757
Ph: (512)266-0033
E-mail: j24class@compuserve.com
URL: http://www.j24class.org/usa
Contact: Nancy Zangerle, Pres.
Founded: 1977. **Members:** 3,600. **Membership Dues:** associate, junior, $30 (annual) ● full, $60 (annual) ● contributing, $100 (annual) ● supporting, $150 (annual) ● sustaining, $200 (annual) ● platinum, $300 (annual). **Staff:** 2. **Multinational. Description:** Experienced amateur sailors and owners or part owners of J/24 sailboats; companies and associations. Works to promote, coordinate, and sponsor amateur sailboat racing activities in the U.S. Seeks to: disseminate information and tips of interest to all J/24 owners and sailors; provide racing rules; sponsor local, regional, and international competitions; offer informal coaching and training to owners and sailors. **Formerly:** (2003) J/24 Class Association. **Publications:** *International J/24*, semiannual. Magazine. **Price:** $6.00. **Advertising:** accepted ● *Rule Book*, semiannual ● *Waterlines*, quarterly. Newsletter. **Price:** available to members only. **Advertising:** accepted. **Conventions/Meetings:** annual meeting.

22714 ■ U.S. Mariner Class Association
c/o Tom Bayer, Sec.-Treas.
PO Box 775
Princeton Junction, NJ 08550
Ph: (609)655-7623
Fax: (609)799-8670
E-mail: wclopp@comcast.net
URL: http://www.usmariner.org
Contact: Bill Clopp, Pres.
Founded: 1965. **Members:** 320. **Membership Dues:** regular, $15 (annual). **Description:** Owners and enthusiasts of Mariner One-Design Class sailboats. Promotes Mariner sailboats for racing and family cruising; encourages safe boating. Sponsors local and regional regattas. **Affiliated With:** United States Sailing Association. **Publications:** *The Cruising Story Book*. **Price:** $12.95 ● *Notice to Mariners*, quarterly. Newsletter. **Price:** included in membership dues. **Advertising:** accepted ● *The Racer's Edge*. Booklet. **Price:** $5.95 ● *Roster*, annual. **Conventions/Meetings:** annual National Regatta - competition.

22715 ■ U.S. Mirror Class Association (USMCA)
c/o John M. Borthwick, Sec.
5305 Marian Dr.
Lyndhurst, OH 44124
Ph: (440)461-7231
E-mail: jmbrbb@aol.com
Contact: John M. Borthwick, Sec.
Founded: 1970. **Members:** 100. **Membership Dues:** individual, $10 (annual). **Regional Groups:** 5. **Description:** Owners of Mirror Class sailboats; other interested individuals. Promotes the sport of sailing and sailboat racing; teaches sailing techniques. (Mirror Class sailboats are 11 feet, two-person dinghies; used for racing and recreational sailing.) Offers children's services. **Computer Services:** Mailing lists, membership. **Publications:** *The Looking Glass*,

quarterly. Newsletter. Includes articles, sailing schedules and boats for sale. **Price:** included in membership dues. **Circulation:** 100. **Advertising:** accepted. Alternate Formats: magnetic tape ● *USMCA Directory*, annual. **Conventions/Meetings:** annual meeting ● annual Regatta Championship - competition - 3rd week of July.

22716 ■ United States Optimist Dinghy Association (USODA)
PO Box 1301
Beach Haven, NJ 08008
Ph: (609)492-9000
Fax: (609)492-1612
E-mail: usoda@usoda.org
URL: http://www.usoda.org
Contact: John Storck Jr., VP
Founded: 1947. **Members:** 3,000. **Membership Dues:** skipper, $35 (annual) ● sustaining, $45 (annual) ● sailor, $65 (annual). **Staff:** 1. **Budget:** $200,000. **Description:** Young people under the age of fifteen who are interested in learning to sail and race. Sponsors national and international competitions. Sends 100 sailors to International Regattas around the world. **Publications:** *OPTINEWS*, 5/year. Magazine. Contains stories and articles. **Advertising:** accepted. **Conventions/Meetings:** annual meeting.

22717 ■ United States Power Squadrons (USPS)
1504 Blue Ridge Rd.
PO Box 30423
Raleigh, NC 27607
Ph: (919)821-0281
Free: (888)367-8777
Fax: (888)304-0813
URL: http://www.usps.org
Contact: Leslie Johnson, Natl. Chief Commander
Founded: 1914. **Members:** 65,000. **Staff:** 23. **Local Groups:** 448. **Description:** Pleasure boat owners and others interested in studying navigation and acquiring boating skills. Offers free instruction in safe boating to the public; conducts courses for members in seamanship, advanced piloting, celestial navigation, marine electronics, engine maintenance, sailing, cruise planning, and meteorology. **Libraries: Type:** not open to the public. **Computer Services:** Mailing lists. **Committees:** Law; Planning; Public Relations. **Publications:** *By Land or By Sea, Cuisine of the United States Power Squadrons*. Book. Includes brief history of the Auxiliaries, Squadrons and USPS. **Price:** $25.00 ● *The Ensign*, monthly. Magazine. **Price:** $10.00/year. **Circulation:** 60,000. **Advertising:** accepted ● Newsletters. Alternate Formats: online ● Annual Report, annual. **Conventions/Meetings:** semiannual Governing Board - meeting - always fall and spring ● annual meeting (exhibits) - always January or February.

22718 ■ United States Sailing Association
PO Box 1260
Portsmouth, RI 02871-0907
Ph: (401)683-0800
Free: (800)US-SAIL1
Fax: (401)683-0840
E-mail: info@ussailing.org
URL: http://www.ussailing.org
Contact: Jim Capron, Pres.
Founded: 1897. **Members:** 50,000. **Staff:** 35. **Regional Groups:** 37. **Local Groups:** 1,800. **Description:** Encourages participation and promotes excellence in sailing and racing in the U.S. Offers training and education programs, supports a wide range of sailing organizations and communities, and provides administration and oversight of competitive sailing across the country, including the US Sailing Teams and the U.S. Olympic and Paralympic Sailing Team. **Awards:** Nathanael G. Herreshoff Trophy. **Frequency:** annual. **Type:** trophy. **Recipient:** to an individual who has made an outstanding contribution to the sport of sailing ● Rolex Yachtsman of the Year Award. **Frequency:** annual. **Type:** recognition. **Recipient:** to outstanding on-the-water achievement within the calendar year. **Affiliated With:** International Sailing Federation; United States Olympic Commit-

tee. **Also Known As:** (2004) U.S. Sailing Association. **Formerly:** (1975) North American Yacht Racing Union; (1992) U.S. Yacht Racing Union. **Publications:** *Racing Rules of Sailing*, annual. Annual Reports. Contains international racing rules of sailing with U.S. sailing prescriptions. **Price:** $29.95/copy. **Circulation:** 50,000. **Advertising:** accepted. Also Cited As: *RRS* ● Also publishes rule books, time allowance tables, and other information pertinent to racing. **Conventions/Meetings:** annual conference.

22719 ■ United States Sailing Foundation (USSF)
c/o United States Sailing Association
PO Box 1260
15 Maritime Dr.
Portsmouth, RI 02871-0907
Ph: (401)683-0800
Free: (800)US-SAIL1
Fax: (401)683-0840
E-mail: info@ussailing.org
URL: http://www.ussailing.org
Contact: Katie Kelley, Contact
Founded: 1958. **Description:** Individuals and organizations contributing through to the support of United States teams in international competition. Aims to see that international competition is open to best sailors, not just those able to afford the expense of representing their country; has contributed to the costs of the USA Sailing Team in the Olympic Games since 1959 and has aided U.S. sailing representatives in the Pan-American Games and international one-design competitions. Assists in research projects to improve the sport. **Affiliated With:** United States Sailing Association. **Formerly:** (1987) United States International Sailing Association. **Publications:** Annual Report, annual. **Conventions/Meetings:** annual meeting.

22720 ■ U.S. Soling Association (USSA)
c/o Jude Kujanson, Admin. Sec.
605 Farmhurst Dr., No. 20
Charlotte, NC 28217
Ph: (704)264-0096
E-mail: judekujanson@earthlink.net
URL: http://www.ussoling.com
Contact: Jude Kujanson, Admin. Sec.
Founded: 1965. **Members:** 400. **Staff:** 1. **Description:** Represents owners and sailors of Soling Class yachts. (The Soling Class is a one-design, three-man racing sloop that is approximately 27 ft. in length). Promotes soling racing; sponsors national and regional regattas. **Libraries: Type:** open to the public. **Holdings:** articles, photographs. **Computer Services:** database, membership list. **Publications:** *The Leading Edge*, quarterly. Newsletter. **Conventions/Meetings:** annual meeting.

22721 ■ United States Wayfarer Association (USWA)
c/o Paul McVey, Treas.
42914 Brookstone Dr.
Novi, MI 48377
Ph: (248)283-2259 (248)960-6575
E-mail: pmcvey@uswayfarer.org
URL: http://www.uswayfarer.org
Contact: Paul McVey, Treas.
Founded: 1963. **Members:** 150. **Membership Dues:** regular, $15 (annual) ● regular, $40 (triennial). **Staff:** 5. **Description:** Represents owners and enthusiasts of Wayfarer sailboats. Promotes use of the sailboats. Provides forum for exchange of information and experiences by members; represents Wayfarer sailors before the Wayfarer International Committee. **Awards:** United States National Champion Trophy. **Frequency:** annual. **Type:** trophy. **Recipient:** for the winner of national regatta. **Publications:** *Skimmer*, quarterly. Newsletter. Covers racing, cruising, and rigging; for one-design sailboat owners. Includes member listing and technical articles. **Price:** included in membership dues. **Circulation:** 250. **Advertising:** accepted. **Conventions/Meetings:** semiannual National Regatta - meeting ● annual North American Championship Regatta - meeting.

22722 ■ United States Windsurfing Association (USWA)

c/o Nat Sidall, Exec. Dir.
PO Box 99
Chelsea, MI 48118
Ph: (734)678-5625
Free: (877)386-8708
E-mail: info@uswindsurfing.org
URL: http://www.uswindsurfing.org
Contact: Nat Sidall, Exec. Dir.

Founded: 1980. **Members:** 4,500. **Membership Dues:** individual, $30 (annual) ● club, $50 (annual) ● life, $1,000 ● individual sponsor, $100 ● family, $40 ● junior, $10 ● discounted, $25 ● business, $75. **Staff:** 4. **Local Groups:** 60. **Description:** Promotes windsurfing for both racers and recreational sailors. Works to help maintain safe waterways and water quality for windsurfers. Fosters communication among members. Issues sail numbers for events and sanctions competitions. **Libraries: Type:** reference. **Subjects:** safety, access, sports marketing, windsurfing, event management, racing rules of sailing. **Awards:** Corpus Christi Bay Trophy. **Frequency:** annual. **Type:** trophy ● Massachusetts Bay Trophy. **Frequency:** annual. **Type:** trophy ● USWA Sportsman of the Year Award. **Frequency:** annual. **Type:** recognition ● USWA Windsurfer of the Year. **Frequency:** annual. **Type:** recognition. **Committees:** Communications; Events; Safety and Water Access. **Formerly:** (1987) United States Board Sailing Association. **Publications:** US Windsurfing News, bimonthly. Newsletter. **Price:** included in membership dues. **Circulation:** 4,500. Alternate Formats: online ● USWA Event Guidelines, triennial. **Conventions/Meetings:** semiannual board meeting ● annual National Championships - competition ● annual Sanctioned National Wave Sailing Championship Series - competition.

22723 ■ United States Yngling Association (USYA)

c/o Bruce Chafee, Pres.
79 Marlborough St.
Boston, MA 02116
Ph: (617)424-6107
E-mail: usa-president@yngling.org
URL: http://usa.yngling.org
Contact: Bruce Chafee, Pres.

Founded: 1976. **Members:** 200. **Membership Dues:** owner/skipper, $30 (annual) ● associate/crew, $15 (annual) ● owner/skipper, $40 (annual). **Description:** Owners and other individuals interested in Yngling Class sailboats. Promotes sailing and racing of the 21-foot boats. **Libraries: Type:** reference. **Formerly:** (2005) North American Yngling Association. **Publications:** Y's Up, quarterly. Newsletter. Contains articles about Yngling sailors and sailing. **Circulation:** 100. **Advertising:** accepted. **Conventions/Meetings:** annual meeting.

22724 ■ U.S.A. Finn Association (USAFA)

Address Unknown since 2007
URL: http://usfinnclass.org

Founded: 1959. **Members:** 100. **Membership Dues:** associate, $30 (annual) ● regular, $60 (annual). **Staff:** 7. **Budget:** $10,000. **Regional Groups:** 5. **Languages:** English, Spanish. **Description:** Boat owners and interested persons associated with single-hand sailboat racing in the Olympic games and on world class levels. Objective is winning medals in the Olympics for the United States. Conducts annual clinics in conjunction with the U.S. Olympic Sailing Committee. **Computer Services:** Online services, online e-mail group of 100 subscribers: finnclass@yahoogroups.com. **Affiliated With:** United States Sailing Association. **Publications:** Solo, quarterly. Newsletter. North American racing reports and class information. **Price:** free with membership for class supporters. **Circulation:** 180. **Conventions/Meetings:** annual National Championship - competition and meeting, with elections.

22725 ■ Windmill Class Association (WCA)

1856 Runnymeade Rd.
Winston-Salem, NC 27104-3110

E-mail: achauvenet@triad.rr.com
URL: http://www.windmillclass.org
Contact: Allen Chauvenet, Sec.

Founded: 1960. **Members:** 300. **Membership Dues:** active (owner/racer), $20 (annual) ● family (owner/racer), $25 (annual) ● associate (builder/supporter), $10 (annual) ● affiliate (club-owned boat), $12 (annual). **Description:** Individuals interested in sailing and racing the Windmill Class sailboat. Promotes competitive sailing and recreational cruising of Windmill Class sailboats; works to maintain its one-design feature. **Publications:** Jouster, bimonthly. Newsletter. Covers sailing events, rigging, boat building, and association news. Includes race results and regatta schedule. **Price:** included in membership dues. **Circulation:** 450. **Advertising:** accepted. **Conventions/Meetings:** annual Regatta - meeting.

22726 ■ Yachting Club of America (YCA)

Box 1040
Marco Island, FL 34146
Ph: (239)642-4448
Fax: (239)642-5284
E-mail: ycaol@hotmail.com
URL: http://www.ycaol.com
Contact: David J. Martindell, Pres.

Founded: 1963. **Members:** 300,000. **Membership Dues:** yacht club, $300 (annual). **Staff:** 10. **Description:** Yachtsmen. Seeks to advance yachting, its facilities, and the relationship between yachting organizations through a viable fraternity of yachtsmen. **Libraries: Type:** reference. **Holdings:** 3. **Publications:** American Yacht Club Burgees, annual. Directory. Includes list of 1500 past and present yacht club burgees (flags or pennants) and photos. **Price:** $20.00/copy ● American Yacht Club Directory. Includes list of 1100 U.S. Yacht Clubs. **Price:** $20.00/copy ● Register of American Yacht Clubs, annual. Directory. Includes list of 950 yacht clubs. **Price:** $35.00/copy.

Bocce

22727 ■ International Bocce Association (IBA)

Address Unknown since 2006

Founded: 1977. **Members:** 6,200. **Budget:** $50,000. **Multinational. Description:** Serves as an international governing body for the game of bocce (an Italian variation of lawn bowling). Standardizes rules, regulations, and the physical contraints pertinent to competitive bocce. Authorizes regional, international, handicapped, senior citizen's, and youth tournaments. Provides resources and technical information regarding equipment and facilities. Helps organize leagues, bocce clinics, and competitons. Trains and registers bocce officials. Maintains speakers' bureau; compiles statistics; conducts research programs. **Awards: Type:** recognition. **Computer Services:** database. **Publications:** Annual Tournament Calendar ● Players and Tournament Directory, periodic ● Rules and Regulations for Competitive Bocce, periodic ● Newsletter, quarterly.

22728 ■ United States Bocce Federation (USBF)

16090 Mays Ave.
Monte Sereno, CA 95030-4213
Ph: (480)354-0625
E-mail: heresjohnny@earthlink.net
URL: http://www.bocce.com
Contact: Mr. John Ross, Pres.

Founded: 1976. **Members:** 5,000. **Membership Dues:** new, $5 (annual) ● individual, $15 (annual) ● senior citizen, school, community group, $50 (annual) ● family, $25 (annual) ● commercial, $250 (annual). **Budget:** $30,000. **Regional Groups:** 4. **State Groups:** 32. **Local Groups:** 85. **Description:** Local groups united to promote the sport of bocce. Conducts research and educational programs for schools and for the handicapped. Offers specialized and amateur training. Develops course material for inclusion in secondary and university curricula. Provides a speaker's bureau. Promotes amateur competition and

selects America's representatives for international competition. **Libraries: Type:** reference. **Holdings:** artwork, audiovisuals, books, clippings, periodicals. **Subjects:** history of bocce, court construction, rules. **Awards: Type:** recognition. **Formerly:** (1986) U.S.A. Federation of Bocce. **Publications:** Index Service, 3/year ● National Bocce, 3/year. Magazine. Contains tournament announcements and articles of general history. **Price:** included in membership dues; $3.00 for nonmembers. **Circulation:** 10,000. **Advertising:** accepted ● Sport of Bocce, periodic. Directory. **Conventions/Meetings:** competition ● seminar.

22729 ■ World Bocce League

188 Indus. Dr., Ste.17 A
Elmhurst, IL 60126
Ph: (630)834-8349
Free: (800)OKB-OCCE
Fax: (630)832-2174
E-mail: mrbocce@worldbocce.org
URL: http://www.worldbocce.org
Contact: Philip Ferrari, Pres.

Founded: 1992. **Members:** 1,000. **Membership Dues:** individual, $25 (annual) ● charter club, $150 (annual) ● commercial, $250 (annual) ● senior, $65 (annual) ● patron, $500 (annual) ● bronze, $1,000 (annual) ● silver, $2,500 (annual) ● gold benefactor, $25,000 ● life benefactor, $50,000. **Staff:** 5. **Budget:** $100,000. **Regional Groups:** 25. **Description:** Works to introduce the game of bocce to the public to promote and preserve Italian heritage. Provides information on constructing bocce courts and rules and regulations of the game; offers training techniques; helps clubs to approach cities to build public facilities; offers discounts on services; hosts tournaments. **Awards:** Humanitarian and Sports Person of the Year. **Frequency:** annual. **Type:** recognition. **Formerly:** (2006) World Bocce Association. **Publications:** Amici, quarterly. Magazine ● Bollentino Newspaper, monthly. **Circulation:** 100,000 ● The Joy of Bocce. Book. **Price:** $12.95/copy ● Official Rules and Regulations for Competitive Bocce. Book. **Price:** $7.50/copy ● Primo. Magazine. Provides questions from bocce enthusiasts and tips for playing bocce. **Circulation:** 50,000 ● Articles. Contains articles written on bocce. **Conventions/Meetings:** annual Super Ball Tournaments - competition (exhibits).

Bodybuilding

22730 ■ International Natural Bodybuilding and Fitness Federation (INBF)

PO Box 4
Pocono Lake, PA 18347
E-mail: downs@exercisegroup.com
URL: http://www.inbf.net
Contact: Steve Downs CSCS, VP

Founded: 2000. **Members:** 3,000. **Membership Dues:** regular, $35 (annual). **Multinational. Description:** Represents the interests of bodybuilding athletes. Promotes natural bodybuilding and fitness. Works to develop the sport of weightlifting and bodybuilding and its athletes at the local, regional and national levels. Organizes and sponsors competitions. **Publications:** Natural Bodybuilding & Fitness, quarterly. Magazine. **Price:** included in membership dues. Alternate Formats: online. Also Cited As: NB&F.

22731 ■ North American Natural Bodybuilding Federation (NANBF)

7026 Alden St.
Shawnee, KS 66216
Ph: (913)268-4133
E-mail: nanbf@everestkc.net
URL: http://www.nanbf.org
Contact: Fred Rowlett, Pres.

Founded: 1994. **Description:** Represents bodybuilding athletes. Promotes the sports of natural bodybuilding and fitness. Promotes drug tested body building shows.

Boomerangs

22732 ■ Free Throwers Boomerang Society (FTBS)

c/o The Jungle Gym Adventure Center
320 London Rd., Ste.101
Delaware, OH 43015

Ph: (740)363-8332
Fax: (740)363-8332
E-mail: leadingedgechet@columbus.rr.com
URL: http://www.leadingedgeboomerangs.com
Contact: Chet Snouffer, Founder/Exec. Dir.
Founded: 1980. **Members:** 300. **Membership Dues:** regular, $20 (annual). **Staff:** 1. **Description:** Boomerang enthusiasts. Promotes boomerang throwing and competition as recreational and sporting activity. Holds instructional sessions; sponsors free throwing events and exhibitions. Maintains speakers' bureau. **Computer Services:** database ● mailing lists. **Affiliated With:** U.S. Boomerang Association. **Also Known As:** Free Throwers. **Publications:** *The Leading Edge*, quarterly. Newsletter. Reports on tournament results, boomerang design, construction, and playing tips. Includes calendar of events. **Price:** included in membership dues. **Circulation:** 350. **Advertising:** accepted ● Also publishes construction plans and listings of clubs, wood sources, and manufacturers. **Conventions/Meetings:** annual competition, largest, longest running tournament in the country - first weekend of August ● annual meeting, tournament - always August, Delaware, OH.

22733 ■ U.S. Boomerang Association (USBA)
3351 236th St. SW
Brier, WA 98036-8421
Ph: (425)485-1672
Fax: (425)485-1672
E-mail: golenom@fc.montgomerybell.com
URL: http://www.usba.org
Contact: Matt Golenor, Pres.
Founded: 1981. **Members:** 550. **Membership Dues:** electronic, $15 (annual) ● premium in U.S., $20 (annual) ● international premium, $25 (annual) ● family, $35 (annual). **Staff:** 9. **Description:** Represents clubs and individuals interested in boomerangs. Works to further the knowledge of boomeranging as an art, science, and sport. Conducts clinics and educational programs for all ages. Maintains listings of manufacturers, local organizations, materials, upcoming events, rules, and rating systems; also maintains speakers' bureau. Compiles statistics. **Libraries: Type:** reference. **Holdings:** archival material. **Subjects:** boomerangs. **Awards: Frequency:** annual. **Type:** recognition. **Computer Services:** Mailing lists, of members. **Publications:** *Boomerangs*, quarterly. Newsletter. **Price:** $15.00. **Circulation:** 550. **Advertising:** accepted. Alternate Formats: online. **Conventions/Meetings:** annual meeting, held with USBA national tournament (exhibits) - always August ● seminar and workshop.

Bowling

22734 ■ American Transportation Bowling Association (ATBA)
c/o William L. Noye
1732 Utah Rd.
Altoona, PA 16602
Ph: (814)946-4995
Fax: (814)946-4995
Contact: William Noye, Exec.Sec.-Treas.
Founded: 1949. **Members:** 1,500. **Staff:** 1. **Regional Groups:** 17. **State Groups:** 9. **Local Groups:** 3. **Description:** People primarily from the transportation industry, although membership is open to all interested persons. **Awards: Frequency:** annual. **Type:** recognition. **Publications:** *Official Schedule of Bowling*, annual. **Advertising:** accepted. Alternate Formats: online. **Conventions/Meetings:** annual Bowling Tournament - meeting - always April/May.

22735 ■ Bowlers to Veterans Link (BVL)
11350 Random Hills Rd., Ste.800
Fairfax, VA 22030
Ph: (703)934-6039
Fax: (703)591-3049
E-mail: bvl@bowlforveterans.org
URL: http://www.bowlforveterans.org
Contact: Elaine Hagin, Chair
Budget: $1,000,000. **Description:** Bowlers providing Veterans Administration hospitals and outreach

centers with cash grants, television sets, entertainment, and recreational materials. **Formerly:** (1978) Bowlers' Victory League.

22736 ■ International Gay Bowling Organization (IGBO)
c/o Sharon Stump, Pres.
6490 W 5th Ave.
Lakewood, CO 80226
Ph: (818)505-1109
E-mail: president@igbo.org
URL: http://www.igbo.org
Contact: Sharon Stump, Pres.
Founded: 1980. **Members:** 13,000. **Membership Dues:** league, $200 (annual) ● basic, $50 (annual) ● associate, $25 (annual). **Description:** Gay bowlers. Promotes the sport of bowling. Facilitates communication among members; sponsors leagues and tournaments; conducts educational programs. **Libraries: Type:** reference. **Awards:** Fellowship Award. **Frequency:** annual. **Type:** recognition. **Recipient:** for individuals who excel in living and promoting IGBO's ideals of unity, communication, fellowship on a local, regional and international level ● Tom Hack Service Award. **Frequency:** annual. **Type:** recognition. **Recipient:** for outstanding support to the organization. **Computer Services:** database, tournament averages ● mailing lists, of members ● online services, forum. **Committees:** Archives; Bid Standards; Deaf and Disabled Bowlers Advisory; Federation of Gay Games; Fellowship; Fundraising; Marketing, Sponsorship and Research; Women's Social. **Publications:** Newsletter, 3/year. **Circulation:** 2,000. **Advertising:** accepted. **Conventions/Meetings:** annual competition.

22737 ■ The National Bowling Association (TNBA)
c/o Ms. Annette R. Samuel, Exec. Sec.-Treas.
9944 Reading Rd.
Cincinnati, OH 45241
Ph: (513)769-1985
Fax: (513)769-3596
E-mail: nationaloffice@tnbainc.org
URL: http://www.tnbainc.org
Contact: Ms. Annette R. Samuel, Exec. Sec.-Treas.
Founded: 1939. **Members:** 26,000. **Staff:** 2. **Local Groups:** 110. **Description:** Seeks to foster good sportsmanship, fellowship, and friendship; increase the interests, talents, and skills of adult and youth bowlers; create national awareness and interest in civic and community programs. Participates in and promotes bowling tournaments and other activities. Sponsors fundraising programs for sickle cell anemia and the United Negro College Fund (see separate entry). Bestows bowling awards, annual special bowling and service awards, and annual national and local scholarship awards. Maintains hall of fame; compiles statistics. **Committees:** Charities; Hall of Fame; History; Junior Bowling; Scholarship. **Formerly:** (1944) Negro National Bowling Association. **Publications:** *Bowler*, quarterly. Magazine ● *NBA History Book* ● *Souvenir Yearbook*, annual. Journal. **Advertising:** accepted ● Newsletter, monthly. **Conventions/Meetings:** annual meeting.

22738 ■ National Duckpin Bowling Congress (NDBC)
c/o Sue Burucker, Exec. Dir./Sec.
4991 Fairview Ave.
Linthicum, MD 21090
Ph: (410)636-2695 (410)444-4058
Fax: (410)636-3256
E-mail: nationalduckpin@aol.com
URL: http://ndbc.org
Contact: Sue Burucker, Exec. Dir./Sec.
Founded: 1927. **Members:** 15,000. **Staff:** 3. **Budget:** $200,000. **Regional Groups:** 7. **State Groups:** 4. **Description:** Rulemaking and governing body for duckpin bowling. Establishes lane certification, individual and league registration, and playing rules and guidelines. Sponsors tournaments. Operates hall of fame; compiles statistics. **Libraries: Type:** reference. **Holdings:** archival material. **Subjects:** duckpin bowling. **Awards:** National Trophy. **Frequency:** annual. **Type:** trophy. **Recipient:** for top average in

country; male and female. **Committees:** Lane Inspection; Research and Development. **Publications:** *Format Book*, annual. **Price:** $3.00 ● *Rule Book*, annual. **Price:** $5.00. **Conventions/Meetings:** annual meeting - always early May ● annual National Duckpin Tournament - competition ● workshop.

22739 ■ Professional Bowlers Association of America (PBA)
719 2nd Ave., Ste.701
Seattle, WA 98104-1747
Ph: (206)332-9688
Fax: (206)654-6030
E-mail: info@pba.com
URL: http://www.pba.com
Contact: Chris Peters, Chm.
Founded: 1958. **Members:** 3,600. **Membership Dues:** standard, $107 (annual) ● full, $239 (annual). **Staff:** 19. **Regional Groups:** 7. **For-Profit. Description:** Professional bowlers. Works to promote the status of the qualified bowler to the rank of professional; also promotes bowling as a major sport. Sponsors tournaments; assists the American Bowling Congress in enforcing its rules and regulations; has established code of ethics. Promotes better understanding between professional bowlers and bowling proprietors, bowling manufacturers, and the communications media. Maintains placement service, hall of fame, school, and insurance programs for members. Compiles statistics. **Libraries: Type:** reference. **Awards: Type:** recognition. **Affiliated With:** United States Bowling Congress. **Publications:** *Official Tour Program*, semiannual ● *Press-Radio-TV Guide*, annual ● Newsletter, quarterly. **Conventions/Meetings:** semiannual board meeting.

22740 ■ United States Bowling Congress (USBC)
5301 S 76th St.
Greendale, WI 53129-1128
Ph: (414)421-6400
Free: (800)514-2695
Fax: (414)421-1194
E-mail: bowlinfo@bowl.com
URL: http://www.bowl.com
Contact: Roger Dalkin, CEO
Founded: 1895. **Members:** 8,000,000. **Membership Dues:** local association (maximum), adult, $10 (annual) ● youth, $9 (annual) ● state association (maximum), $1 (annual). **Staff:** 10. **Budget:** $15,000,000. **State Groups:** 50. **Local Groups:** 2,700. **Description:** Aims to be the unified organization of choice focused on the growth of bowling. Ensures the integrity and protects the future of the sport, provides programs and services and enhances the bowling experience. **Libraries: Type:** reference. **Holdings:** artwork, audiovisuals, books, clippings, periodicals. **Subjects:** bowling. **Awards:** US Bowler Writing Competition. **Frequency:** annual. **Type:** recognition. **Recipient:** for articles about bowling. **Computer Services:** database ● mailing lists. **Programs:** Coaching; Collegiate; High School; Sport; Team USA; Youth. **Absorbed:** (1964) United States Seniors Bowling Association. **Formerly:** (2005) American Bowling Congress. **Publications:** *American Bowler*, quarterly. Magazine. **Price:** included in membership dues. **Circulation:** 1,500,000. **Advertising:** accepted. **Conventions/Meetings:** annual convention, elected representatives of bowlers throughout the country (exhibits).

22741 ■ United States Lawn Bowls Association (USLBA)
c/o Lawn Balls USA
10639 Lindamere Dr.
Los Angeles, CA 90077
E-mail: woodyogden@sbcglobal.net
URL: http://www.bowlsamerica.org
Contact: Colin Smith, Pres.
Founded: 1915. **Members:** 5,000. **Membership Dues:** $10 (annual). **Budget:** $30,000. **Regional Groups:** 7. **Local Groups:** 114. **Description:** Ruling body for lawn bowls in the U.S. Sponsors national, divisional, sectional, and club playdowns. Compiles statistics; maintains Hall of Fame and biographical archives. Sponsors competitions. Offers on-site

instruction and printed training materials. Publishes triennial BOWLS USA magazine. Is developing lawn bowl surfaces. **Libraries: Type:** not open to the public. **Holdings:** archival material. **Awards:** Bowler of the Decade. **Frequency:** periodic. **Type:** recognition. **Recipient:** for the most successful tournament bowler of the last 10 years ● Bowler of the Tournament (National Open Tournament). **Frequency:** annual. **Type:** recognition. **Recipient:** for the most accomplished bowler in the National Open Tournament (by formula) ● U.S. Pairs Champions. **Frequency:** annual. **Type:** recognition. **Recipient:** for first and second place finishers in the United States Championships pairs (male and female) ● U.S. Singles Champions. **Frequency:** annual. **Type:** recognition. **Recipient:** for first and second place finishers in the United States Championships singles (male and female). **Formerly:** (2001) American Women's Lawn Bowls Association; (2001) American Lawn Bowls Association. **Publications:** *Bowls USA*, triennial. Magazine. Features stories, club news and divisional, national and international events. **Price:** $6.00 /year for nonmembers in Canada; free for members. **Circulation:** 6,200. **Advertising:** accepted ● *The Construction of the Lawn Bowling Green, by Dr. Edgar Haley.* Manual. Detailed instruction on how to install a lawn bowling green. **Price:** $15.00 ● *Laws of the Sport of Bowls-USLBA.* Book. Serves as the United States Lawn Bowls Association rule book. **Price:** $2.00. **Advertising:** accepted ● *The Maintenance of the Lawn Bowling Green, by Dr. Edgar Haley.* Manual. Detailed instructions on the care and maintenance of a lawn bowling green. **Price:** $25.00 ● *Official Lawn Bowler's Almanac.* Handbook. **Price:** $2.00 ● Manuals. Introductory and training. **Price:** free for members. Alternate Formats: CD-ROM. **Conventions/Meetings:** annual meeting.

22742 ■ Western Women Premier Bowlers (WWPB)

c/o Mrs. Laura Hardeman, Sec.
938 Redbud Rd.
Chula Vista, CA 91910
E-mail: webmaster@wwpb.com
URL: http://www.wwpb.com
Contact: Mrs. Laura Hardeman, Sec.

Founded: 1965. **Members:** 155. **Membership Dues:** regular, $100 (annual). **Staff:** 3. **Description:** Adult women with a bowling average of 175 or higher in 60 or more games. Aims are to: provide an organization in which women bowlers may participate as tournament competitors and as involved members; develop support among women bowlers for national, state, and local competitions; promote an interest in competitive participation among women bowlers; encourage good fellowship and sportsmanship, thereby creating a desirable public image to promote and elevate bowling as a whole. Conducts 12-15 tournaments per year. **Libraries: Type:** reference. **Holdings:** archival material, books. **Subjects:** program. **Awards:** Merle Matthew's Distinguished Service Award. **Type:** recognition ● WWPB Bowler of the Year. **Frequency:** annual. **Type:** recognition ● WWPB Rookie of the Year. **Frequency:** annual. **Type:** recognition. **Committees:** Bowler and Rookie of the Year; Good Cheer; Pennants and Banner. **Formerly:** (1975) Western Women Bowlers; (1990) Worldwide Women Professional Bowlers; (2007) Western Women Professional Bowlers. **Publications:** *Code of Operations*, annual. Book. **Price:** free to hosting centers. **Circulation:** 200. **Advertising:** accepted ● *Program Book*, annual ● *Squad Room*, 12-15/year. Newsletter. Circulated after each tournament. ● *Tournament Guide for Hosting Centers.* **Conventions/Meetings:** annual meeting - usually November or December ● periodic Tournament of Champions - meeting.

22743 ■ Women's All-Star Association (WASA)

c/o Sharon Nasta, Exec. Dir.
16 Ward Ave.
Toms River, NJ 08755
Ph: (732)367-0257
Fax: (732)367-3949

E-mail: mcwba@aol.com
URL: http://www.wasabowling.com
Contact: Sharon Nasta, Exec. Dir.

Founded: 1971. **Members:** 325. **Membership Dues:** inactive, $10 (annual) ● senior, $30 (annual) ● regular, $40 (annual). **Staff:** 6. **Description:** Amateur and professional women bowlers aged 17 and older with established minimum averages of 170 for one season in a sanctioned (WIBC) bowling league. Provides tournaments for members and promote women bowlers and their accomplishments. Maintains hall of fame and seniors group. Compiles statistics and updates and maintains historical records. Provides 17 tournaments in 5 Eastern states annually plus 8 Senior (50) tournaments annually. **Libraries: Type:** reference. **Holdings:** archival material. **Awards:** Bowler of the Year Award. **Frequency:** annual. **Type:** recognition. **Recipient:** for best bowler of the year based on performance points ● High Average Award. **Frequency:** annual. **Type:** recognition. **Recipient:** for highest bowling average per year ● Rookie of the Year Award. **Frequency:** annual. **Type:** recognition. **Recipient:** for best rookie bowler of the year based on points ● Senior Bowler of the Year. **Frequency:** annual. **Type:** recognition. **Recipient:** for best senior bowler of the year based on points ● Sportswomen of the Year Award. **Frequency:** annual. **Type:** recognition. **Recipient:** for sportsmanship. **Committees:** Awards; Dress Code; Hall of Fame; Legislative. **Publications:** Newsletter, monthly. **Price:** available to members only. **Circulation:** 600 ● Also publishes press releases and provides a program (with directory) at every tournament site. News releases following each event are sent to more than 100 newspapers and magazines. **Conventions/Meetings:** annual meeting, election of board members - always December.

Boxing

22744 ■ American Association for the Improvement of Boxing (AAIB)

86 Fletcher Ave.
Mount Vernon, NY 10552-3319
Ph: (914)664-4571
Fax: (914)664-3164
E-mail: aaib@worldnet.att.net
URL: http://www.aaib.org
Contact: Stephen B. Acunto, Chm.

Founded: 1969. **Members:** 400. **Membership Dues:** general, $20 (annual) ● outside U.S., $25. **Staff:** 15. **Description:** Individuals dedicated to the restoration and improvement of the sport of boxing. Disputes allegations that boxing is a dangerous sport and should be abolished. Recommends that dangers can be minimized through careful regulation. Objectives are to: work for the establishment of uniform rules and a national boxing commission; call for careful regulation of the sport; encourage boxing in high school and college curricula; achieve optimum medical treatment and uniform standards in boxing; gather and disseminate information on all areas of boxing. Conducts studies on equipment and rules; prepares legislative proposals. Maintains speakers' bureau. **Libraries: Type:** reference. **Holdings:** 150; archival material, audiovisuals, books, clippings, monographs, periodicals. **Subjects:** boxing. **Awards:** AAIB College Scholarship. **Frequency:** annual. **Type:** scholarship. **Recipient:** for an outstanding high school senior. **Computer Services:** Mailing lists, of members. **Committees:** Ex-Champion; Ex-Coaches; Legal; Legislative; Medical; Officials; Publicity; Representatives; Scholarship; Union. **Publications:** *American Association for the Improvement of Boxing—Bulletin*, 3/year. **Price:** $20.00. **Circulation:** 750. **Advertising:** accepted ● *American Association for the Improvement of Boxing—Position Papers*, periodic ● *Art of Boxing.* Film ● *Boxerama*, annual. Journal. **Price:** $5.00. **Circulation:** 600. **Advertising:** accepted ● *Boxing, More Than a Sport.* Video ● *Champions Boxing Guide.* Book. **Price:** $20.00 plus 1.95 postage ● *Ring Rhetoric*, 3-4/year. Newsletter ● Monographs ● Also publishes boxing posters and films. **Conventions/Meetings:** bimonthly board

meeting ● annual luncheon, includes awards to current and former champion trainer-sports medicine doctor-authors-journalists (exhibits) ● annual meeting (exhibits).

22745 ■ International Boxing Federation (IBF)

516 Main St., 2nd Fl.
East Orange, NJ 07018
Ph: (973)414-0300
Fax: (973)414-0307
E-mail: mmuhammad@ibfboxing.com
URL: http://www.ibf-usba-boxing.com
Contact: Marian Muhammad, Pres.

Founded: 1983. **Members:** 200. **Membership Dues:** regular, $150 (annual). **Staff:** 5. **Description:** Professional boxers, managers, trainers, referees, and judges. Develops uniformity and minimum safety standards for the sport of boxing. Operates charitable program. Conducts periodic training seminars on judging and refereeing; compiles statistics; maintains speakers' bureau. **Awards:** Best Fight of the Year Award. **Frequency:** annual. **Type:** recognition ● Best Fighter of the Year Award. **Frequency:** annual. **Type:** recognition ● Best Fighter of Unlimited Potential Award. **Frequency:** annual. **Type:** recognition ● Best Punch of the Year Award. **Frequency:** annual. **Type:** recognition. **Computer Services:** database, information on professional boxers around the world. **Committees:** Audit and Compensation; Championship; Medical; Rating. **Publications:** *IBF/USBA Ratings*, monthly ● *IBF/USBA Reporter*, quarterly ● Bulletin, bimonthly. **Conventions/Meetings:** annual conference ● periodic seminar, provides training on judging and refereeing.

22746 ■ International Boxing Hall of Fame Museum (IBHOF)

1 Hall of Fame Dr.
Canastota, NY 13032
Ph: (315)697-7095
Fax: (315)697-5356
URL: http://www.ibhof.com
Contact: Edward P. Brophy, Exec. Dir.

Founded: 1982. **Members:** 300. **Staff:** 3. **Budget:** $150,000. **Description:** Recognizes and honors the achievements of outstanding boxers by maintaining a Boxing Hall of Fame in Canastota, NY, which includes a library of boxing records and literature and a collection of boxing memorabilia. Emphasizes the importance of sports to American society and the role of sports in the development of individual character. Works to provide advice and assistance to organizations contemplating boxing programs in physical fitness competition. **Libraries: Type:** reference. **Holdings:** 100. **Subjects:** boxing. **Affiliated With:** International Boxing Federation. **Publications:** *The Main Event Newsletter*, quarterly. **Conventions/Meetings:** annual Hall of Fame Weekend - meeting, with collector's show (exhibits) - always second week of June, in Canastota, NY.

22747 ■ International Chinese Boxing Association (ICBA)

6205 Coit Rd., Ste.336-194
Plano, TX 75024
E-mail: icbachairman@wwicba.com
URL: http://www.wwicba.com
Contact: GM David M. Grago Sr., Chm.

Membership Dues: active, $25 (annual). **Multinational. Description:** Preserves the legacy of Chinese Martial Arts worldwide. Provides a general curriculum for those looking to begin Chinese Martial Arts but do not know where to concentrate their studies. **Programs:** Distance Learning; Self Defense.

22748 ■ International Female Boxers Association (IFBA)

50B Peninsula Center Dr., No. 120
Rolling Hills Estates, CA 90274
Ph: (310)428-1402
Fax: (310)541-9708
E-mail: info@ifba.com
URL: http://www.ifba.homestead.com
Contact: Rick Kulis, Contact

Founded: 1997. **Multinational. Description:** Promotes female boxing throughout the world as a genuine, professional and athletic competition. Works to develop female boxing into a sport that will persuade Olympic Committees that women's boxing is worthy of being included in future world games. **Computer Services:** database, current ratings. **Publications:** Articles. Alternate Formats: online.

22749 ■ International Veteran Boxers Association (IVBA)

Address Unknown since 2007
Founded: 1963. **Members:** 35,000. **Membership Dues:** club, $25 (annual). **Regional Groups:** 47. **State Groups:** 31. **Local Groups:** 15. **National Groups:** 12. **Description:** Former professional and amateur boxers, referees, boxing judges, and other interested individuals united to raise funds for former boxers in need. Maintains museum and hall of fame. Operates charitable program; compiles statistics. **Libraries: Type:** reference. **Holdings:** archival material. **Awards:** Babe Orlando Award. **Frequency:** annual. **Type:** recognition ● Boxing Hall of Fame. **Type:** recognition ● Boxing Referee Award. **Frequency:** annual. **Type:** recognition ● Boxing Trainer of the Year Award. **Frequency:** annual. **Type:** recognition ● Boxing Writer of Year. **Frequency:** annual. **Type:** recognition ● Fighter of the Year Award. **Frequency:** annual. **Type:** recognition ● Freddie Fiducia Award. **Frequency:** annual. **Type:** recognition ● Humanitarian Award. **Frequency:** recognition ● Irv Silverman Award. **Frequency:** annual. **Type:** recognition ● Joe Poodles Award. **Type:** recognition ● Special Award. **Frequency:** annual. **Type:** recognition. **Recipient:** for individuals who have made a special effort to further the cause of safe boxing ● Steve Belloise Award. **Frequency:** annual. **Type:** recognition. **Publications:** *Boxing Digest*, monthly ● *Boxing World*, monthly ● *Constitution and By Laws* ● *Punch Lines*, monthly. Newsletter ● *Reporter*, monthly ● *Ring Magazine*, monthly ● *Scoop's Corner*, monthly. **Conventions/Meetings:** annual conference and symposium (exhibits) ● annual convention.

22750 ■ Knights Boxing Team - International

12086 Flat Shoals Rd.
Covington, GA 30016-4708
Ph: (770)787-3131
E-mail: hmw3@flash.net
Contact: Don Wade, Exec. Dir.
Founded: 1976. **Members:** 961. **Membership Dues:** individual, $200. **Staff:** 15. **Budget:** $350,000. **Regional Groups:** 1. **State Groups:** 1. **Local Groups:** 1. **Languages:** English, German. **Description:** Provides amateur boxing program for youth age 12 and up. Aims to train young boxers in hopes that some will qualify for the U.S. Olympic Boxing Team. Sponsors training programs. Maintains museum, hall of fame, and speakers' bureau; offers children and adult services. **Libraries: Type:** by appointment only. **Holdings:** 16,000; books, video recordings. **Subjects:** non-fiction, history, biographies, reference, sports, novels. **Awards:** Outstanding American Award. **Frequency:** periodic. **Type:** recognition. **Recipient:** for extraordinary achievement for mankind. **Affiliated With:** American Association for the Improvement of Boxing; Fellowship of Christian Athletes; United States Olympic Committee. **Publications:** *Knights Boxing Team, International—Newsletter*, monthly. **Price:** free. **Circulation:** 18,000 ● *Knights Program*, annual. Yearbooks. **Price:** free. **Circulation:** 25,000. **Conventions/Meetings:** competition ● annual conference (exhibits) - always October 18, Atlanta, GA ● lecture ● seminar.

22751 ■ North American Boxing Federation (NABF)

c/o Rex Ross Walker, Pres.
3300 Airport Rd.
Boulder, CO 80301
Ph: (303)442-0258
Fax: (303)442-0380
E-mail: info@nabfnews.com
URL: http://www.NABFNews.com
Contact: Rex Ross Walker, Pres.
Founded: 1967. **Members:** 550. **Membership Dues:** general-associate, $50 (annual) ● promoter, $125 (annual) ● matchmaker, $100 (annual). **State**

Groups: 37. **National Groups:** 3. **Languages:** English, French, Spanish. **Multinational. Description:** Associate members are selected on the basis of interest in boxing. One of seven regional commissions of the World Boxing Council. Sanctions North American title fights in all divisions. Works as the instrument through which various official supervisory and regulatory bodies can maintain protection for boxers; ensures that the sport of boxing remains free of influence from undesirable elements. Holds seminars for trainers, medical personnel, referees, judges, and others connected with boxing. Studies sports medicine with a view toward maximizing its benefits to boxing. **Awards:** Champion of the Year Award. **Frequency:** annual. **Type:** recognition ● Fight of The Year Award. **Frequency:** annual. **Type:** recognition ● Matchmaker of The Year Award. **Frequency:** annual. **Type:** recognition ● Promoter of the Year Award. **Frequency:** annual. **Type:** recognition. **Computer Services:** database, rankings of NABF rated boxers ● information services, of newsletter. **Telecommunication Services:** electronic mail, cowboy@sombrero.com. **Committees:** Championships; Constitution and Bylaws; Grievance and Appeals; Medical Advisory-legal; Ratings. **Affiliated With:** World Boxing Council. **Publications:** *NABF News* (in English and Spanish), monthly. Newsletter. Monthly boxing report including NABF title fights and upcoming title fights as well as boxing news of interest to the membership. **Price:** included in membership dues. **Circulation:** 600. Alternate Formats: online. **Conventions/Meetings:** annual conference and convention, for all members and others interested in the NABF are welcome, noted speakers and ring officials' seminars are scheduled.

22752 ■ USA Boxing

1 Olympic Plz.
Colorado Springs, CO 80909
Ph: (719)866-4506
Fax: (719)632-3426
E-mail: jstavros@usaboxing.org
URL: http://www.usaboxing.org
Contact: John Stavros, Acting Exec. Dir.
Founded: 1887. **Members:** 35,000. **Staff:** 14. **Budget:** $3,100,000. **Local Groups:** 56. **National Groups:** 3. **Description:** Amateur boxers; boxing referees, judges, timers, administrators, officials, and coaches. Aims to promote and develop Olympic-style boxing in the U.S. Compiles statistics. Sponsors clinics. Maintains hall of fame. **Libraries: Type:** reference. **Holdings:** periodicals, photographs. **Awards:** Boxer of the Year. **Frequency:** annual. **Type:** recognition ● Coach of the Year. **Frequency:** annual. **Type:** recognition ● Official of the Year. **Frequency:** annual. **Type:** recognition ● Physician of the Year. **Frequency:** annual. **Type:** recognition. **Computer Services:** database. **Also Known As:** United States of American Amateur Boxing Federation. **Formerly:** (1980) Senior Men's Boxing Committee of the Amateur Athletic Union; (1991) United States of America Amateur Boxing Federation. **Publications:** *Boxing USA*, biennial. Magazine. Promotes amateur boxing, especially the U.S. Olympic boxing team. **Circulation:** 35,000. **Advertising:** accepted ● *USA Boxing—Annual Guide*. Includes definitions, profiles of leading boxers, and history of the sport. ● *USA Boxing—Official Rules*, semiannual. Includes lists of past and present U.S. champions and rules. **Conventions/Meetings:** periodic competition, national and international ● annual convention - always fall ● periodic seminar.

Camping

22753 ■ American Camp Association (ACA)

5000 State Rd. 67 N
Martinsville, IN 46151-7902
Ph: (765)342-8456
Free: (800)428-CAMP
Fax: (765)342-2065
E-mail: psmith@acacamps.org
URL: http://www.acacamps.org
Contact: Peg L. Smith, CEO
Founded: 1910. **Members:** 6,000. **Membership Dues:** owner/director of camp, $400 (annual) ● other

staff in camp, $300 (annual) ● standard visitor/retiree/professional educator - professional, $150 (annual) ● associate, $100 (annual) ● standard visitor/retiree/volunteer - associate, $50 (annual) ● student, $35 (annual). **Staff:** 30. **Budget:** $3,500,000. **Local Groups:** 24. **Description:** Camp owners, directors, program directors, businesses, and students interested in resident and day camp programming for youth and adults. Conducts camp standards. Offers educational programs in areas of administration, staffing, child development, promotion, and programming. **Libraries: Type:** reference. **Holdings:** 5,000. **Subjects:** camping. **Awards:** Distinguished Service Award. **Frequency:** annual. **Type:** recognition. **Recipient:** for outstanding service in the field ● Hedley S. Dimock Award. **Frequency:** annual. **Type:** recognition. **Recipient:** for individuals who have made significant contributions to camping through related fields ● Honor Award. **Frequency:** annual. **Type:** recognition. **Recipient:** to recognize meritorious service ● Special Recognition Award. **Frequency:** annual. **Type:** recognition. **Recipient:** to groups, organizations or individuals for their efforts to promote camp. **Committees:** Education; Ethics; Standards. **Divisions:** Independent Camps; Not-for-Profit Camps; Religiously Affiliated Camps. **Formerly:** (1910) Camp Directors Association of America; (2006) American Camping Association. **Publications:** *Camping Magazine*, bimonthly. Includes association news, book reviews, legislative news, research reports, new product information, and index of advertisers. **Price:** included in membership dues; $24.95 for nonmembers. **Advertising:** accepted ● *Guide to Accredited Camps*, annual. Directory. Lists 2200 camps accredited by the ACA. Includes information on clientele, fees, and location and a cross-reference guide to program activities. **Price:** $19.95/copy. **Circulation:** 15,000. **Advertising:** accepted ● Books. Covers camp administration, staffing, outdoor skills, ecology, games and nature. **Conventions/Meetings:** annual conference (exhibits).

22754 ■ Camping Women (CW)

PO Box 13261
Sacramento, CA 95813
E-mail: shtaylor@dfg.ca.gov
URL: http://www.campingwomen.org
Contact: Jan Cadotte, Pres.
Founded: 1977. **Members:** 200. **Membership Dues:** regular, $25 (annual). **Local Groups:** 6. **Description:** Individuals seeking to enhance women's camping skills; women interested in camping, backpacking, hiking, canoeing, white water rafting, biking, skiing, birdwatching, and other outdoor activities. Aims are to: provide opportunities for women to experience an outdoor program in a supportive atmosphere; help women develop a sense of "at-homeness" in the outdoors; develop women's camping abilities and leadership skills. Provides skills training in campcraft, watercraft, snow camping, and leadership. **Awards:** Camping Women of the Year. **Frequency:** annual. **Type:** recognition. **Recipient:** to a member who has given exceptional service to the organization at both the chapter and national level. **Publications:** *Camping Women Trails*, 10/year. Newsletter. **Price:** included in membership dues; $8.00 /year for nonmembers in U.S.; $10.00 /year for nonmembers outside U.S. **Advertising:** accepted ● Membership Directory, annual. **Conventions/Meetings:** annual Invitational Camp - meeting - always August.

22755 ■ Christian Camping International/U.S.A. (CCCA)

PO Box 62189
Colorado Springs, CO 80962-2189
Ph: (719)260-9400
Fax: (719)260-6398
E-mail: info@ccca-us.org
URL: http://www.ccca-us.org
Contact: Steve Prudhomme, Chm.
Founded: 1963. **Members:** 1,070. **Staff:** 18. **Budget:** $1,000,000. **Regional Groups:** 25. **Description:** Exists to proclaim the power of the Christian camp and conference experience and to interpret its benefits to the Church and the public at large; and to provide leaders at member organizations with ongoing

encouragement, professional training, and timely resources. **Libraries: Type:** open to the public. **Holdings:** periodicals. **Subjects:** camp/conference management, maintenance, food service, marketing. **Computer Services:** database, membership. **Also Known As:** Christian Camp and Conference Association. **Formerly:** (1986) Christian Camping International. **Publications:** *CampSight*, semiannual. Magazine. Offers glimpses of lives changed through the Christian camp and conference experience. **Price:** $3.95 quantity discounts available. **Circulation:** 20,000. **Advertising:** accepted ● *Executive Briefing*, monthly. Newsletter. Includes calendar of events. **Price:** included in membership dues; $34.00 /year for nonmembers. **Circulation:** 1,150 ● *InSite*, bimonthly. Magazine. **Price:** included in membership dues; $26.95 /year for nonmembers. **Circulation:** 8,500. **Advertising:** accepted. Alternate Formats: online ● Also publishes educational material to present new ideas, to assist in training, and to provide news about legislation and tips on improving and expanding facilities. **Conventions/Meetings:** annual conference (exhibits) - November or December.

22756 ■ Family Campers and RVers (FCRV)
4804 Transit Rd., Bldg. 2
Depew, NY 14043
Ph: (716)668-6242
Free: (800)245-9755
Fax: (716)668-6242
E-mail: fcrvnat@buffnet.net
URL: http://www.fcrv.org
Contact: Eldon Sellers, Natl. Pres.
Founded: 1949. **Members:** 7,000. **Membership Dues:** family, $25 (annual) ● family, C$31 (annual). **Staff:** 3. **Regional Groups:** 7. **State Groups:** 40. **Local Groups:** 1,000. **Multinational. Description:** Family campers and hikers; others interested in outdoor activities. Promotes and enhances the experience of "family" style camping/RVing. **Awards:** Conservation Award. **Frequency:** annual. **Type:** recognition ● Membership Building Award. **Frequency:** annual. **Type:** recognition ● **Type:** scholarship. **Recipient:** for children of members ● Wildlife Award. **Frequency:** annual. **Type:** recognition. **Programs:** Conservation; Disaster Awareness Training; Education; Legislation Awareness; Retirees; Scholarship; Self-Propelled Camping; Teens; Travalongs; Trip Information; Wildlife Refuge; Youth. **Affiliated With:** American Recreation Coalition; Recreation Vehicle Industry Association. **Formerly:** National Campers and Hikers Association. **Publications:** *Camping Today*, monthly. Magazine. Includes calendar of events, discount information, and convention report. **Price:** included in membership dues. ISSN: 8750-1465. **Circulation:** 30,000. **Advertising:** accepted. **Conventions/Meetings:** annual Campvention - convention, includes campout (exhibits).

22757 ■ Light Living Library (LLL)
Address Unknown since 2007
Founded: 1980. **Members:** 400. **Description:** Individuals and families who live for long periods in recreational vehicles or tents and manufacturers of portable all-weather shelters. Disseminates information on woodcraft, backpacking, and survival skills; provides instructions on building low-cost dwellings and household devices. **Publications:** *Dwelling Portably*, 3/year. **Price:** $1.00/issue. **Circulation:** 1,300 ● *Light Living Packet*. **Price:** $2.00 ● *Off the Beaten Path: Guide to Unusual Sources*, annual.

22758 ■ North American Family Campers Association (NAFCA)
PO Box 318
Lunenburg, MA 01462
Ph: (508)867-3215
E-mail: nafcadianne@aol.com
URL: http://www.nafca.org
Contact: Diane Crook, Pres.
Founded: 1957. **Members:** 2,000. **Membership Dues:** individual, $23 (annual) ● individual, $38 (biennial). **Budget:** $34,000. **State Groups:** 6. **Local Groups:** 162. **Description:** Families interested in camping; sustaining members are manufacturers and dealers of camping equipment, campgrounds, and

other services related to family campers. Works to improve camping conditions, inform members about camping areas, equipment, and techniques, promote good camping manners, and foster fellowship among family campers. Encourages and guides development of campgrounds; cooperates with conservation and legislative agencies for the good of camping. Conducts conservation and antilitter programs. **Awards:** Leadership Conference Scholarship. **Frequency:** annual. **Type:** scholarship. **Recipient:** for an outstanding member. **Telecommunication Services:** electronic mail, nafcamarty@verizon.net. **Committees:** Conservation; Leadership Training; State Coordinating. **Formerly:** (1957) New England Camping Association; (1967) New England Family Campers Association. **Publications:** *Campfire Chatter*, monthly. Magazine. Includes news articles, recipes, and president's message. **Price:** included in membership dues. ISSN: 0410-4889. **Circulation:** 7,000. **Advertising:** accepted ● Newsletter, monthly. Contains state news. ● Newsletter, monthly. Contains chapter news. **Conventions/Meetings:** annual general assembly - always last week of July ● annual Leadership Conference - conference and seminar ● show and workshop, camping information ● annual Spring Safari - competition, horseshoe games, volleyball, grunt, and bocce ball (exhibits) - always 3rd weekend of May.

22759 ■ Wilderness Inquiry (WI)
808 14th Ave. SE
Minneapolis, MN 55414-1516
Ph: (612)676-9400 (612)676-9409
Free: (800)728-0719
Fax: (612)676-9401
E-mail: info@wildernessinquiry.org
URL: http://www.wildernessinquiry.org
Contact: Greg Lais, Exec. Dir.
Founded: 1978. **Staff:** 60. **Budget:** $1,800,000. **Description:** Seeks to: integrate disabled and nondisabled people together in outdoor adventures; educate campers in "low-impact" camping techniques which preserve the natural environment. Promotes social interaction between individuals with varying levels of physical and cognitive abilities. Offers study tours in conjunction with the Smithsonian Institute; arranges customized trips for rehabilitation hospitals, community recreation programs, schools and universities, group homes, and private groups. Offers Universal Program Training (UP Training) to other organizations wishing to open their programs to persons with disabilities. Offers workshops. **Computer Services:** Online services, Minnesota state park accessibility guide. **Telecommunication Services:** TDD, (612)-379-3858 ● teletype, (612)676-9475. **Publications:** *Accessibility in the National Wilderness Preservation System*. Proceedings. Contains proceedings of conferences. **Price:** $15.00 ● *Share the Adventure*, periodic. Provides descriptions on wilderness trips. **Price:** free ● *Universal Access: Guidelines for Outfitters Operating on Public Lands*. Manual. **Price:** $15.00 ● *Wilderness Access Decision Tool*. Contains resources for federal land managers. **Price:** $15.00.

Camps

22760 ■ Association of Jewish Sponsored Camps (AJSC)
130 E 59th St.
New York, NY 10022
Ph: (212)751-0477
Fax: (212)755-9183
E-mail: info@jewishcamps.org
URL: http://www.jewishcamps.org
Contact: Rahel Goldberg, Exec.Dir.
Founded: 1963. **Members:** 40. **Staff:** 2. **Budget:** $80,000. **Description:** Participating members are Jewish sponsored organizations that provide camping to the Jewish community of greater New York; cooperating agencies are interested Jewish organizations that do not operate camps. Maintains Jewish Camp Information Services to provide information and referral services to parents, agencies, and organizations interested in placing children in Jewish

sponsored camps. **Computer Services:** database, people interested in Jewish camping ● mailing lists, of camps and people interested in camping ● online services, website. **Boards:** Board of Directors. **Affiliated With:** United Jewish Appeal - Federation of Jewish Philanthropies of New York. **Supersedes:** Jewish Vacation Association. **Publications:** Newsletter, quarterly. **Price:** free. **Conventions/Meetings:** board meeting - every 6 weeks ● seminar - 6/year.

22761 ■ National Association of Therapeutic Wilderness Camps (NATWC)
264 Brown Hill Rd.
Markleysburg, PA 15459
Ph: (724)329-1098
E-mail: natwc@qcol.net
URL: http://www.natwc.org
Contact: Rick McClintock, Membership Chm.
Founded: 1994. **Membership Dues:** individual, $60 (annual) ● student, $40 (annual) ● university/college, $100 (annual) ● organization (based on annual operating budget), $150-$750 (annual). **Description:** Promotes standards for all aspects of therapeutic wilderness camping organizations. Raises public awareness on the effectiveness of outdoor therapeutic treatment with troubled youth. Provides resources for technical assistance, shared training, and shared resources pertaining to therapeutic wilderness camping. **Publications:** *Journal of Therapeutic Wilderness Camping*, periodic.

22762 ■ National Camp Association (NCA)
610 5th Ave.
PO Box 5371
New York, NY 10185-5371
Ph: (212)645-0653 (845)354-5504
Free: (800)966-2267
Fax: (845)000-0000
E-mail: info@summercamp.org
URL: http://www.summercamp.org
Contact: Jeffrey Solomon, Exec. Dir.
Founded: 1982. **Multinational. Description:** Serves as a free advisory service representing sleep away summer camps and programs worldwide. Works to help parents find the right camp for their children. Offers staff placement service and access to camp suppliers. **Computer Services:** Online services, Camp Mall for all camp related supplies and services and staff placement service. **Formerly:** (2001) National Camping Association. **Publications:** *NCA Parents Guide "How To Choose a Summer Camp"*, annual. Journal. **Price:** $3.00/copy. Alternate Formats: online. **Conventions/Meetings:** monthly meeting - every first Saturday, except July and holiday weekends.

Canoeing

22763 ■ American Canoe Association (ACA)
7432 Alban Sta. Blvd., Ste.B-232
Springfield, VA 22150
Ph: (703)451-0141
Fax: (703)451-2245
E-mail: aca@americancanoe.org
URL: http://www.acanet.org
Contact: Ms. Pamela Dillon, Exec. Dir.
Founded: 1880. **Members:** 45,000. **Membership Dues:** individual, $40 (annual) ● family, $60 (annual) ● affiliate club, affiliate business/organization, $225 (annual). **Staff:** 20. **Budget:** $3,000,000. **Regional Groups:** 13. **Local Groups:** 250. **Description:** Promotes the sport of canoeing and kayaking and to the preservation of streams and rivers. Sponsors races, cruises, encampments, and training classes. Provides publications information and offers computerized services on canoe clubs, manufacturers, liveries, and outfitters; promotes safety and skill on the water. Conducts instructor certification and methods workshops. **Libraries: Type:** reference. **Holdings:** books, periodicals. **Awards: Type:** recognition. **Computer Services:** Mailing lists. **Committees:** Canoe Poling; Canoe Sailing; Conservation; Instruction; Marathon; Olympic (flatwater) and Slalom Paddling; Outrigger Canoe; Recreational Canoe and Kayak; Safety; Sea Kayaking; Slalom and Wildwater Racing; Whitewater

Open Canoe. **Affiliated With:** National Safe Boating Council. **Publications:** *American Canoeist*, quarterly. Newsletter. Contains editorials, upcoming events, and articles on conservation, recreation, and safety. ISSN: 0739-8344 ● *Canoeing and Kayaking*. Manual ● *Canoeing and Kayaking for Persons with Physical Disabilities*. Manual ● *Paddler Magazine*, bimonthly. Contains information on places to paddle, skill enhancement, gear reviews, industry updates and profiles of leading paddlers. **Price:** $18.00/year. Alternate Formats: online. **Conventions/Meetings:** annual Camp and Meet - meeting - usually August, Gananoque, ON, Canada ● annual conference and meet.

22764 ■ United States Canoe Association (USCA)
c/o Paula Thiel
53 Ross Rd.
Preston, CT 06365
Ph: (727)823-8000
E-mail: canoechamp@aol.com
URL: http://www.uscanoe.com
Contact: John Edwards, Exec. Dir.
Founded: 1968. **Members:** 4,000. **Membership Dues:** governing (age 18 and over), $20 (annual) ● family, $25 (annual) ● junior (age 5-17), $7 (annual) ● race sponsor/club affiliate/business affiliate, $30 (annual) ● foreign, $5-$10 (annual). **Budget:** $100,000. **Regional Groups:** 4. **State Groups:** 60. **Description:** Represents individuals interested in canoeing. Encourages the growth of recreational and competitional paddling; preserves scenic and wild waters; promotes and disseminates safety standards; develops design criteria for cruising canoes, kayaks, and related gear; teaches paddling skills and water safety; and sponsors recreational canoe trips and races. Serves as the marathon sanctioning body in the United States that has jurisdiction over competitions in cruising or pleasure-type canoes and kayaks. Establishes club affiliates to support the association's Five-Star Program: Competition-Cruising-Conservation-Camping-Camaraderie. Offers insurance program to race participants and spectators. **Awards:** Howie LaBrant Award. **Frequency:** annual. **Type:** trophy. **Recipient:** for significant contribution to world of paddlesports ● Mike Fremont Conservation Award. **Frequency:** annual. **Type:** trophy. **Recipient:** for significant contribution to conservation. **Committees:** Camaraderie; Camping; Canoe News; Competition; Conservation; Cruising; Dragon Boats; Education; Insurance; International; Long Range Planning; Public Relations; Safety; Sailing; Sprints; Swan Boats; Technical Inspection; Triathlon; Voyageur Canoes; Whitewater; Youth Activities. **Publications:** *Canoe News*, bimonthly. Magazine. Contains paddlesports information. **Price:** available to members only. **Advertising:** accepted. Alternate Formats: diskette; online ● *Canoe Plans and Manual* ● *Safety Canoeing*. Video ● Membership Directory, annual. **Conventions/Meetings:** annual convention (exhibits) - always second weekend in January ● annual National Championship - competition, includes marathon and sprint races - always second and third weekend in August ● National Marathon Canoe and Kayak Championship and Adult Sprints - competition, national youth canoe/kayak sprints, national canoe/kayak orienteering championship.

22765 ■ USA Canoe/Kayak (USACK)
301 S Tryon St., Ste.1750
Charlotte, NC 28282
Ph: (704)348-4330
Fax: (704)348-4418
E-mail: dmyarborough@usack.org
URL: http://www.usack.org
Contact: David Yarborough, Exec. Dir.
Founded: 1989. **Members:** 1,600. **Membership Dues:** junior, $25 (annual) ● business affiliate, $50 (annual) ● adult, $55 (annual) ● family, $115 (annual) ● life (individual, family), $500 ● club/organization, $150 (annual). **Staff:** 15. **Description:** Seeks to prepare, train and select the best teams to represent the USA in the Olympic sports of Flatwater sprint and Whitewater slalom canoe and kayak racing. Holds competitions; compiles statistics; conducts educa-

tional programs. **Formerly:** (2005) U.S. Canoe and Kayak Team. **Conventions/Meetings:** annual conference.

Chariot Racing

22766 ■ World Championship Cutter and Chariot Racing Association (WCC&CRA)
c/o J. Victor Adams, Sec./Mgr.
2632 S 4300 W
Ogden, UT 84401
Ph: (801)731-8021
Fax: (801)731-8021
E-mail: jva8021@aol.com
Contact: J. Victor Adams, Sec./Mgr.
Founded: 1964. **Members:** 5,000. **Membership Dues:** association, $125 (annual). **Staff:** 14. **Regional Groups:** 22. **Local Groups:** 9. **Description:** Local chariot and cutter racing associations. Each must have 12 teams and run nine association meets to qualify its teams for the national organization; most are in the western U.S. The races feature teams of horses harnessed to two-wheel cutters or chariots driven by one man. Active November through March. Races are run 440 yards with a weight limit of 275 lbs. (includes driver, chariot, and horse). **Awards:** **Frequency:** annual. **Type:** recognition. **Publications:** *Cutter and Chariot World*, annual. Magazine. **Price:** $5.00. **Advertising:** accepted ● *Cutter Annual*, annual ● *WCC and CRA Racing Annual*, annual. **Advertising:** accepted. **Conventions/Meetings:** periodic competition ● annual meeting (exhibits) - always last two weekends of March.

Chiropractic

22767 ■ United States Sports Chiropractic Federation (USSCF)
1035 Robertson St.
Fort Collins, CO 80524
Ph: (970)224-2282
Fax: (970)224-2282
E-mail: info@usscf.com
URL: http://www.usscf.org
Contact: Dr. Monty Wilburn, Treas.
Membership Dues: general, $75 (annual). **Description:** Serves as a governing body for US sports chiropractors and organizations. Promotes and develops the care of athletes and personnel at international sporting events and activities.

Christian

22768 ■ Christian Golfers' Association (CGA)
1285 Clara Louise Kellogg Dr.
Sumter, SC 29153
Free: (800)784-2171
Fax: (803)773-7757
E-mail: christiangolf@ftc-i.net
URL: http://www.christiangolfer.org
Contact: Tom Winstead Sr., Pres.
Founded: 1996. **Membership Dues:** individual, $30 (annual) ● family, $45 (annual) ● student, $24 (annual). **Description:** Utilizes the game of golf as a platform for evangelizing, witnessing and sharing the gospel of Jesus Christ with other golfing friends and acquaintances while promoting fun, fellowship and common interests among Christian golfing enthusiasts. Encourages and enhances fellowship among Christians who love the game of golf. **Publications:** *On the Green*. Newsletter. **Price:** included in membership dues.

Climbing

22769 ■ American Mountain Guides Association (AMGA)
PO Box 1739
Boulder, CO 80306-1739
Ph: (303)271-0984

Fax: (303)271-1377
E-mail: info@amga.com
URL: http://www.amga.com
Contact: Michael Alkaitis, Exec. Dir.
Membership Dues: student associate, $40 (annual) ● associate, $60 (annual) ● individual, $100 (annual) ● life, $2,500. **Description:** Represents the interests of American mountain guides by providing support, education and standards. Provides aid in the development of skills required by professional mountain guides. Offers training courses and guide certification exams in rock, alpine and ski mountaineering. **Telecommunication Services:** electronic mail, mike@amga.com.

22770 ■ Sheclimbs
c/o Lilly Feldman
296 Country Club Rd.
Avon, CT 06001
E-mail: president@sheclimbs.org
URL: http://www.sheclimbs.org
Contact: Carolyn McHale, Pres.
Founded: 1995. **Membership Dues:** regular, $30 (annual) ● individual in Canada, $40 (annual) ● student/senior, $18 (annual). **Multinational. Description:** Promotes a strong female presence in the climbing community. Supports active, self-reliant participation of women and girls in the sport of climbing. Encourages a spirit of volunteerism, mentoring, and environmental responsibility. Organizes events and participates in service-oriented functions. **Publications:** *Rock Goddess Gazette*, quarterly. Newsletter. Contains trip reports, fiction and chapter events. **Price:** included in membership dues ● Newsletter, monthly. Presents articles of interest and notices of chapter events.

22771 ■ USA Climbing
PO Box 3405
Boulder, CO 80307
Free: (888)944-4244
E-mail: info@usaclimbing.org
URL: http://www.usaclimbing.org
Contact: Jim Concannon, Pres.
Founded: 1998. **Membership Dues:** limited, $48 (annual) ● full, $69 (annual) ● supporting, $37 (annual). **Description:** Promotes the interests of climbing both in the United States and abroad. Promotes and encourages climbers of all ages in competitive climbing. Organizes and promotes competitive climbing events in an atmosphere of camaraderie and respect. **Publications:** *E-News Flash*. Newsletter. **Price:** included in membership dues. Alternate Formats: online ● *Urban Climber*. Magazine ● Membership Directory. **Price:** included in membership dues. Alternate Formats: online.

Coaching

22772 ■ Black Coaches Association (BCA)
Pan Amer. Plz.
201 S Capitol Ave., Ste.495
Indianapolis, IN 46225
Ph: (317)829-5600
Free: (877)789-1222
Fax: (317)829-5601
E-mail: fkeith@bcasports.org
URL: http://www.bcasports.org
Contact: Floyd A. Keith, Exec. Dir.
Founded: 1988. **Members:** 1,500. **Membership Dues:** supporter, $30 (annual) ● associate, coach, $60 (annual) ● platinum (institutional, corporate), $1,500 (annual) ● gold (institutional, corporate), $950 (annual) ● silver (institutional, corporate), $500 (annual) ● bronze (institutional, corporate), $250 (annual). **Staff:** 4. **Budget:** $1,000,000. **Description:** Promotes equitable employment of ethnic minorities in all sports professions; the education, development and scholarship of members and ethnic minority student athletes. Promotes the creation of a positive environment in which issues such as stereotyping, lack of significant media coverage, and discrimination can be exposed, discussed, and resolved. Provides member services. Petitions the NCAA legislative bod-

ies to design, enact, and enforce diligent guidelines and policies to improve professional mobility for minorities. **Awards:** Ethnic Minority Scholarship Program. **Frequency:** annual. **Type:** scholarship. **Recipient:** to graduate students in sports management education programs. **Publications:** *BCA Journal*, quarterly. Magazine. Includes activities and awards updates. **Price:** included in membership dues. **Circulation:** 1,000. **Advertising:** accepted. Alternate Formats: CD-ROM; online. **Conventions/Meetings:** annual convention, for sports professionals and companies (exhibits).

22773 ■ Indoor Soccer Coaches Association (ISCA)
9606 Aero Dr.
San Diego, CA 92123
Ph: (858)836-4422
Fax: (858)836-4421
E-mail: coaches@isca.net
Description: Promotes, educates, provides service and generates interest in the game of indoor soccer. **Conventions/Meetings:** Sports clinics - meeting ● symposium.

22774 ■ National Alliance for Youth Sports (NAYS)
2050 Vista Pkwy.
West Palm Beach, FL 33411
Ph: (561)684-1141
Free: (800)729-2057
Fax: (561)684-2546
E-mail: nays@nays.org
URL: http://www.nays.org
Contact: Fred C. Engh, Pres./CEO
Founded: 1981. **Members:** 150,000. **Membership Dues:** coach, $20 (annual). **Staff:** 27. **Budget:** $3,000,000. **State Groups:** 50. **Local Groups:** 2,000. **Description:** Seeks to improve youth league sports programming in order to make sports a positive, fun experience for all youths; has developed National Standards for Youth Sports and operated Say Yes to Better Sports for Kids program. Conducts research and educational programs. **Awards:** Coach of the Year Award. **Frequency:** annual. **Type:** recognition. **Telecommunication Services:** additional toll-free number, (800)688-KIDS. **Formerly:** (1998) National Youth Sports Coaches Association. **Publications:** *Youth Sports Coach*, periodic. **Conventions/Meetings:** annual conference (exhibits).

22775 ■ National Association of Golf Coaches and Educators
Address Unknown since 2007
URL: http://www.nagce.org
Founded: 1998. **Membership Dues:** patron, U.S., $25 (annual) ● patron, non-U.S., $40 (annual) ● program member, U.S., $50 (annual) ● program member, non-U.S., $75 (annual) ● educational/community member, U.S., $75 (annual) ● educational/community member, Non-U.S., $125 (annual) ● corporate member, U.S., $100 (annual) ● corporate member, Non-U.S., $150 (annual) ● junior member, U.S., $18 (annual) ● junior member, Non-U.S., $25 (annual). **Description:** Mission is to promote the growth of golf among young people and help to enhance the effectiveness of coaches in the sport. **Formerly:** (2003) National Association of Golf Coach Educators.

22776 ■ National High School Athletic Coaches Association (NHSACA)
c/o Gelaine Orvik, Exec. Dir.
PO Box 10065
Fargo, ND 58106
Ph: (701)293-2099
Fax: (701)293-8282
E-mail: office@hscoaches.org
URL: http://www.hscoaches.org
Contact: Gelaine Orvik, Exec. Dir.
Founded: 1965. **Members:** 55,000. **Membership Dues:** state, $25 (annual). **Staff:** 5. **Budget:** $800,000. **Regional Groups:** 8. **State Groups:** 41. **National Groups:** 2. **Description:** High school coaches and athletic directors; athletic directors for school systems; executive secretaries of state high

school coaches; state high school coaches associations. Aims to give greater national prestige and professional status to high school coaching and focuses on promoting cooperation among coaches, school administrators, the press, game officials, and the public. Promotes drug and alcohol abuse prevention through National Training Seminars in Drug Prevention in conjunction with the Drug Enforcement Administration, Washington, DC. Conducts Sports medicine/Medical Aspects of Sports seminars in conjunction with national sports and medical groups, and National College Credit Program for coaches and athletic directors. **Awards:** AD of Year. **Frequency:** annual. **Type:** recognition. **Recipient:** for sport and community service ● Coach of Year. **Frequency:** annual. **Type:** recognition. **Recipient:** for sport and community service (18 sports) ● Hall of Fame. **Frequency:** annual. **Type:** recognition. **Recipient:** for sport and community service. **Computer Services:** Mailing lists. **Conventions/Meetings:** annual conference, holds 80 exhibitors or more (exhibits).

22777 ■ NFHS Coaches Association (NFCA)
c/o National Federation of State High Schools
PO Box 690
Indianapolis, IN 46206
Ph: (317)972-6900
Fax: (317)822-5700
E-mail: tflannery@nfhs.org
URL: http://www.nfhs.org
Contact: Timothy E. Flannery CMAA, Staff Liaison
Founded: 1981. **Members:** 16,000. **Membership Dues:** coach, $30 (annual) ● coach and official (combined), $60 (annual). **Staff:** 2. **Budget:** $500,000. **State Groups:** 51. **Description:** High school, middle school and youth athletic coaches. Promotes professional growth and image of interscholastic sports coaches; provides a forum for coaches to make suggestions on rules and procedures in high school sports in the U.S. Cooperates with state high school athletic associations and uses extensive committee structure to ensure grass roots involvement and input from the local, state, and national levels. Maintains hall of fame. **Awards:** National Coach of the Year Award. **Frequency:** annual. **Type:** recognition. **Recipient:** for best coaching record and role model for athletes. **Committees:** Awards and Recognition; Professional Development; Public Information; Sports. **Affiliated With:** National Federation of State High School Associations. **Formerly:** (2002) National Federation Coaches Association. **Publications:** *Coaches' Quarterly*. Magazine. **Price:** included in membership dues; $15.00 for nonmembers. **Circulation:** 180,000. **Advertising:** accepted.

22778 ■ NFHS Spirit Association
c/o National Federation of State High School Associations
PO Box 690
Indianapolis, IN 46206
Ph: (317)972-6900
Fax: (317)822-5700
E-mail: nslone@nfhs.org
URL: http://www.nfhs.org
Contact: Nicole Slone, Admin. Asst.
Description: Supports coaches of middle and high school cheerleading, pom, dance and drill teams. **Boards:** Advisory. **Formerly:** (2003) National Federation Interscholastic Spirit Association.

22779 ■ Positive Coaching Alliance (PCA)
3430 W Bayshore Rd., Ste.104
Palo Alto, CA 94303
Free: (866)725-0024
Fax: (650)739-0270
E-mail: pca@positivecoach.org
URL: http://www.positivecoach.org
Contact: Jim Thompson, Founder/Exec. Dir.
Founded: 1998. **Membership Dues:** individual, $50 (annual) ● family, $150 (annual) ● life, $5,000. **Description:** Transforms the culture of youth sports to give all young athletes the opportunity for a positive, character-building experience. Provides coaches, parents, and leaders with practical tools to help them involve young people in a positive sports environ-

ment. **Awards:** Double-Goal Coach Awards. **Frequency:** annual. **Type:** recognition. **Recipient:** for Double-Goal coaches who strive to win and help their players develop skills ● Grassroots Leadership Award. **Frequency:** annual. **Type:** recognition. **Recipient:** for coaches who strive to win and help their players develop skills ● Honoring the Game Awards. **Frequency:** annual. **Type:** recognition. **Recipient:** for Youth Sports Organizations (YSOs) that strive to win and help their players develop skills ● Ronald L. Jensen Award for Lifetime Achievement. **Frequency:** annual. **Type:** recognition. **Recipient:** for coaches who strive to win and help their players develop skills. **Publications:** *Momentum*. Newsletter. **Price:** included in membership dues.

22780 ■ United States Elite Coaches' Association for Women's Gymnastics (USECA)
c/o Natalie Duke, Sec.-Treas.
10 Quail Point Pl.
Carmichael, CA 95608
Ph: (916)487-3559
Fax: (916)487-3706
E-mail: coacht@gym.net
URL: http://www.gym.net/useca
Contact: Natalie Duke, Sec.-Treas.
Founded: 1976. **Members:** 500. **Description:** Coaches of women's artistic gymnastics; gymnastics judges and officials. Seeks to promote and enhance coaching and training of elite women gymnasts in the United States. Represents members before national gymnastics governing boards; facilitates exchange of information among members; serves as a clearinghouse on gymnastics coaching and training. **Awards:** USECA Athlete Scholarship. **Frequency:** annual. **Type:** scholarship. **Publications:** Newsletter, 8-12/year.

Community Improvement

22781 ■ Christian Sports International (CSI)
PO Box 254
Zelienople, PA 16063
Ph: (724)453-1400
Fax: (724)473-9461
E-mail: info@csikids.org
URL: http://www.csikids.org
Contact: N. Scott Grinder, Pres.
Founded: 1990. **Staff:** 3. **Multinational. Description:** Seeks to strengthen communities through sports and educational programs that impact children and their families with a message of hope, love and positive moral, ethical and spiritual values. **Programs:** Back to School; Community Awareness; POWER Baseball; POWER Basketball; POWER Football; POWER Golf; POWER Outdoors; POWER Soccer.

Cricket

22782 ■ United States of America Cricket Association (USACA)
PO Box 589
Yonkers, NY 10702
Ph: (301)646-0383
Free: (866)872-2206
Fax: (914)969-0192
E-mail: info@usaca.org
URL: http://www.usaca.org
Contact: Mr. Gladstone Dainty, Pres.
Membership Dues: full, $30 (annual) ● associate, $15 (annual). **Description:** Promotes the game of cricket at all levels in the United States of America. Aims to develop national teams that will be competitive and successful in international competitions. **Computer Services:** Information services, cricket resources. **Telecommunication Services:** electronic mail, gadainty@aol.com.

Croquet

22783 ■ Croquet Foundation of America (CFA)
700 Florida Mango Rd.
West Palm Beach, FL 33406-4461
Ph: (561)478-0760
E-mail: usca@msn.com
URL: http://www.croquetamerica.com
Contact: Rich Curtis, Pres.
Founded: 1978. **Staff:** 4. **Budget:** $150,000. **Description:** Promotes the growth and development of croquet and emphasizes the social and recreational rewards of the sport. Sponsors clinics in conjunction with the United States Croquet Association (see separate entry). Operates charitable and research programs. Maintains U.S. Croquet Hall of Fame. Compiles statistics. Plans include the establishment of a museum. **Affiliated With:** United States Croquet Association. **Publications:** *Bob and Ted's Excellent Croquet Video* ● *Bob and Ted's Most Wanted Croquet Strategy Video.* Includes 3 1/2 hours of croquet strategy explained by the best American coaches in the game. ● *Bob and Ted's Staying Alive - Winning Croquet Tactics.* Video ● *Bob and Ted's "You Make The Call" Video* ● *Croquet Court Design, Planning and Maintenance.* Book ● *Croquet: How to Play the Perfect Game.* Book ● Audiotape. **Conventions/Meetings:** International Croquet Ball - meeting ● U.S. Croquet Hall of Fame Awards Dinner.

22784 ■ United States Croquet Association (USCA)
700 Florida Mango Rd.
West Palm Beach, FL 33406-4461
Ph: (561)478-0760 (585)341-3535
E-mail: usca@msn.com
URL: http://www.croquetamerica.com
Contact: Rich Curtis, Pres.
Founded: 1976. **Membership Dues:** individual, $60 (annual) ● couple, $90 (annual) ● type A club, $250 (annual) ● type B club, $175 (annual) ● type C club, $125 (annual). **Budget:** $400,000. **Regional Groups:** 6. **Description:** Persons interested in organizing and promoting the game of croquet as a serious national sport. Sanctions tournaments throughout the U.S; selects the U.S. National Croquet Team. Maintains U.S. Croquet Hall of Fame in conjunction with Croquet Foundation of America (see separate entry). Conducts specialized education. Compiles statistics. **Awards: Type:** recognition. **Affiliated With:** Croquet Foundation of America. **Publications:** *Croquet Annual,* annual. Magazine. **Advertising:** accepted ● *USCA Bulletin,* bimonthly. Includes calendar of events and list of tournament results. **Price:** included in membership dues. **Circulation:** 5,000. **Advertising:** accepted ● *USCA Croquet News,* quarterly. Newsletter. Features coverage of USCA national, regional, and state title events. ● *USCA Crouquet Directory.* Features comprehensive reference of events, results, Grand Prix tallies, awards, and directory of more than 300 USCA affiliated clubs. ● Also publishes rule books. **Conventions/Meetings:** annual National Club Team Championships - competition ● annual National Single and Doubles Championships - competition.

Curling

22785 ■ United States Curling Association (USCA)
1100 Center Point Dr.
PO Box 866
Stevens Point, WI 54481-2849
Ph: (715)344-1199
Free: (888)287-5377
Fax: (715)344-2279
E-mail: info@usacurl.org
URL: http://www.usacurl.org
Contact: David Garber, Special Projects Coor.
Founded: 1958. **Members:** 13,000. **Membership Dues:** regular, $18 (annual). **Staff:** 6. **Budget:** $900,000. **Regional Groups:** 11. **State Groups:** 25. **Local Groups:** 133. **Description:** Federation of regional curling associations and their member clubs. Promotes curling in the U.S. by sponsoring national curling championships. Represents U.S. curlers in international matters relating to the sport; is active in international competitions. Conducts educational programs to train instructors, officials, coaches, and athletes. Maintains museum and hall of fame. **Committees:** Championships; Marketing and Operations. **Programs:** Competitive. **Affiliated With:** United States Olympic Committee; World Curling Federation. **Formerly:** United States Men's Curling Association. **Publications:** *United States Curling News,* bimonthly. Newsletter. Includes competition results and other curling news. **Price:** $20.00/year. **ISSN:** 0199-2473. **Circulation:** 9,200. **Advertising:** accepted ● *USA Curling Directory and Media Guide,* annual. **Price:** $25.00. **Circulation:** 1,500. **Advertising:** accepted. **Conventions/Meetings:** semiannual meeting and board meeting - April/September.

22786 ■ United States Women's Curling Association (USWCA)
c/o Star Pfiffner, Pres.
North Shore Curling Club
1340 Glenview Rd.
Glenview, IL 60025-3199
Ph: (847)729-7105
E-mail: president@uswca.org
URL: http://www.uswca.org
Contact: Star Pfiffner, Pres.
Founded: 1947. **Members:** 3,000. **Budget:** $50,000. **Local Groups:** 68. **Description:** Women amateur curlers. **Libraries: Type:** reference. **Holdings:** archival material, business records. **Subjects:** curling competitions, administration records. **Affiliated With:** United States Curling Association. **Publications:** *Handbook of Rules and Regulations* ● *North American Curling News,* bimonthly. Newsletter. Contains results of national competition, sites and dates of upcoming Bonspiels, and minutes of executive directors' meetings. **Price:** $7.00/year. **Advertising:** accepted ● *Roster of USWCA,* annual. Membership Directory ● *Some Aspects of Curling.* Booklet. **Conventions/Meetings:** semiannual meeting - always February and September ● annual National Women's Bonspiel - competition ● annual Senior Women's Bonspiel - competition.

Cycling

22787 ■ Adventure Cycling Association
PO Box 8308
Missoula, MT 59802
Ph: (406)721-1776
Free: (800)755-2453
Fax: (406)721-8754
E-mail: info@adventurecycling.org
URL: http://www.adv-cycling.org
Contact: Mr. Jim Sayer, Exec. Dir.
Founded: 1973. **Members:** 40,000. **Membership Dues:** student or senior citizen, $30 (annual) ● individual, $35 (annual) ● family, $45 (annual) ● individual life, $1,000 ● patron, $50 (annual) ● supporting, $100 (annual) ● benefactor, $150 (annual). **Staff:** 24. **Budget:** $2,700,000. **Description:** Originally founded to develop the TransAmerica Coast-to-Coast Bicycle Trail (4450 miles) that was inaugurated in 1976 during the 200th birthday celebration of the U.S. Focuses on the research, maintenance, and mapping of over 20,000 miles of bicycle touring and mountain biking routes. Efforts are aimed at promoting bicycle adventure travel and educating the public in bicycle usage and safety. **Libraries: Type:** reference. **Holdings:** 5,000. **Subjects:** bicycling. **Computer Services:** Online services, publication. **Additional Websites:** http://www.adventurecycling.org. **Programs:** Development of Bicycle Trails and Routes; Group Trips; Leadership Training. **Absorbed:** (1986) Bicycle Forum. **Formerly:** (1980) Bikecentennial; (1994) Bikecentennial: The Bicycle Travel Association. **Publications:** *Adventure Cyclist: The Periodical of Bicycle Adventure,* 9/year. Magazine. Contains information on bicycle travel. **Price:** included in membership dues. **Circulation:** 40,000. **Advertising:** accepted. Alternate Formats: online ● *Cyclists' Yellow Pages,* annual. Directory. Includes government agencies, private organizations, and publications useful to bicyclists for planning bike trips. **Price:** included in membership dues. **Circulation:** 40,000. **Advertising:** accepted ● Also publishes tour catalog, sales catalog, maps, guidebooks, and educational materials. **Conventions/Meetings:** annual meeting - always in Missoula, MT.

22788 ■ American Bicycle Association (ABA)
PO Box 718
Chandler, AZ 85244
Ph: (480)961-1903
Fax: (480)961-1842
E-mail: clayton@ababmx.com
URL: http://www.ababmx.com
Contact: Clayton John, Pres.
Founded: 1977. **Members:** 89,000. **Membership Dues:** associate, $16 (annual) ● pro cruiser, $70 (annual) ● gold, $100 (annual) ● first family, $45 (annual) ● second family, $40 (annual) ● third and additional family, cruiser, $35 (annual). **Staff:** 19. **Local Groups:** 180. **For-Profit. Description:** Bicycle Motocross (BMX) racing enthusiasts. Sanctions thousands of local races across the U.S; administers 20 national competitions each year. **Libraries: Type:** open to the public. **Holdings:** 204; articles, books, periodicals. **Subjects:** BMX racing, product evaluations. **Awards: Type:** trophy. **Recipient:** for 1st, 2nd, and 3rd place race winners. **Absorbed:** (1986) U.S. Bicycle Association. **Publications:** *BMXer,* monthly. Magazine. Covers national racing, product evaluation, member point standings, future events, and buyers' guide. **Price:** $2.50/issue. **Circulation:** 49,000. **Advertising:** accepted. **Conventions/Meetings:** annual Grand Nationals - competition (exhibits) - always Thanksgiving weekend in Oklahoma City, OK ● annual Track Operators Convention/Seminar - convention and seminar ● annual World Cup - competition.

22789 ■ Bicycle Parking Project
PO Box 7342
Philadelphia, PA 19101
Ph: (215)222-1253
Fax: (215)222-1253
E-mail: cyclerecycle@hotmail.com
Contact: John Dowlin, Dir.
Founded: 1988. **Members:** 30. **Membership Dues:** charter, $50. **Description:** Encourages organizations and institutions to provide safe, attractive, and efficient parking facilities for bicycles. Fabricates and promotes new bike parking designs, also retrofits of existing, single-purpose street furniture into bike parking facilities. Publishes annual calendar of bicycle photos. **Formerly:** Bicycling Parking Foundation; (2004) Bicycling Parking Project. **Conventions/Meetings:** workshop and seminar.

22790 ■ Bicycle Ride Directors' Association of America (BRDAA)
c/o Sheila Lyons
755 N Leafwood Ave.
Brea, CA 92821
Ph: (562)690-9693
E-mail: bikeride@roadrunner.com
URL: http://www.brdaa.org
Contact: Sheila Lyons, Contact
Founded: 1987. **Members:** 100. **Membership Dues:** individual, $75 (annual). **Description:** Directors of public bicycle rides. Seeks to organize and unify public bike ride directors for the purpose of establishing a calendar of events, negotiating liability insurance rates, sharing marketing and vendoring ideas, and establishing bike ride standards. Compiles statistics; operates speakers' bureau. **Computer Services:** database, listing of bike ride participants ● mailing lists, of members. **Formerly:** (1987) U.S. Ride Directors Association.

22791 ■ International Christian Cycling Club USA (ICCC)
PO Box 441757
Aurora, CO 80044-1757
Ph: (720)870-3707 (303)283-6719

E-mail: christiancycling@aol.com
URL: http://www.christiancycling.com
Contact: Paul Haller, Pres.
Founded: 1986. **Members:** 700. **Membership Dues:** single, in U.S. and Canada, $30 (annual) ● family, in U.S. and Canada, $40 (annual) ● single, outside U.S. and Canada, $36 (annual) ● family, outside U.S. and Canada, $46 (annual). **Staff:** 2. **Budget:** $50,000. **State Groups:** 7. **For-Profit. Description:** Seeks to unite Christian cyclists for a worldwide testimony in lifestyle, training and sportsmanship. Conducts educational programs; holds competitions; competes as the Wheels of Thunder team; runs a camp every August. Affiliated with the U.S. Cycling Federation. Competes in off-road events, hosts clinics and offers free pasta meals for athletes at events. **Also Known As:** Team Ironclad. **Publications:** *Outspokin'*, quarterly. Newsletter. Includes spiritual challenges, cycling tips, and local and international news. **Price:** included in membership dues. **Circulation:** 800. Alternate Formats: online.

22792 ■ International Mountain Bicycling Association (IMBA)

PO Box 7578
Boulder, CO 80306
Ph: (303)545-9011
Free: (888)442-4622
Fax: (303)545-9026
E-mail: info@imba.com
URL: http://www.imba.com
Contact: Mike Van Abel, Exec. Dir.
Founded: 1988. **Members:** 32,000. **Membership Dues:** supporting, $40 (annual) ● basic, $25 (annual) ● big wheel, $55 (annual) ● family, $75 (annual) ● Fat Tire Friend, $100 (annual) ● Trail Builder, $250 (annual) ● Silver Saddle, $500 (annual) ● Single Track Society, $1,000 (annual) ● dealer, $50 (annual) ● elite dealer, $150 (annual) ● affiliated club (with less than 100 members), $30 (annual) ● affiliated club (with more than 100 members), $60 (annual). **Staff:** 15. **Budget:** $1,700,000. **Local Groups:** 475. **Languages:** English, Italian. **Multinational. Description:** Works to keep trails open for mountain bikes by encouraging responsible riding and supporting volunteer trailwork. **Libraries: Type:** open to the public. **Awards:** Mountain Bike Club Grants. **Frequency:** periodic. **Type:** recognition. **Computer Services:** database. **Telecommunication Services:** electronic mail, membership@imba.com. **Publications:** *IMBA Single Track Update*, monthly. Newsletter. Alternate Formats: online ● *IMBA Trail News*, bimonthly. Newsletter. **Price:** included in membership dues. **Circulation:** 34,000 ● *Trail Solutions: IMBA's Guide to Building Sweet Singletrack*. Book. Contains information on basic trailbuilding techniques. **Price:** $30.00 for members; $35.00 for nonmembers. **Conventions/Meetings:** annual meeting.

22793 ■ International Unicycling Federation (IUF)

PO Box 790
Northbend, WA 98045-0790
E-mail: jfoss@unicycling.com
URL: http://www.unicycling.org/iuf
Contact: John Foss, Dir.
Founded: 1982. **Members:** 1,000. **Description:** Works to encourage and promote the sport of unicycling throughout the world; to sponsor international unicycling conventions and competitions; to establish and maintain international unicycling skills standards and rules for international competitive unicycling; to facilitate communication sand cooperation between national unicycling associations; and, to seek the addition of the sport of unicycling to the Olympic Games. **Committees:** Rules. **Affiliated With:** Unicycling Society of America. **Publications:** *International Competition Rulebook*, semiannual. Handbook ● *Unicycling Magazine*, quarterly. **Conventions/Meetings:** semiannual International Unicycling Convention and World Championships - competition.

22794 ■ League of American Bicyclists

1612 K St. NW, Ste.800
Washington, DC 20006-2850
Ph: (202)822-1333

Fax: (202)822-1334
E-mail: bikeleague@bikeleague.org
URL: http://www.bikeleague.org
Contact: Andy D. Clarke, Exec. Dir.
Founded: 1880. **Members:** 300,000. **Membership Dues:** regular, $30 (annual) ● advocate, $50 (annual) ● silver spoke, $100 (annual) ● family, $45 (annual) ● advocate family, $75 (annual) ● life, $1,000. **Staff:** 12. **Budget:** $2,100,100. **Local Groups:** 500. **Description:** Bicyclists and bicycle clubs. Promotes bicycling for fun, fitness, and transportation, and works through advocacy and education for a bicycle-friendly America. Represents members' interests. Seeks to bring better bicycling to all communities. **Libraries: Type:** reference. **Holdings:** archival material, audiovisuals, books, clippings, monographs, periodicals. **Subjects:** bicycling. **Awards:** Dr. Paul Dudley White Award. **Frequency:** annual. **Type:** recognition. **Recipient:** for persons instrumental in promoting bicycling in the U.S. **Committees:** Consumer Affairs; Effective Cycling; Government Relations; Insurance; Legal Affairs; Touring Information. **Formerly:** (1987) League of American Wheelmen/ Bicycle U.S.A.; (1994) League of American Wheelmen. **Publications:** *Bicycling*, quarterly. Magazine. **Advertising:** accepted ● *BikeLeague News*, bimonthly. Newsletter ● Brochures ● Reports ● Surveys. **Conventions/Meetings:** annual National Bike Summit - workshop and seminar, lobbying day ● annual Rally and Membership Consortium.

22795 ■ National Bicycle League (NBL)

3958 Brown Park Dr., Ste.D
Hilliard, OH 43026-1160
Ph: (614)777-1625
Free: (800)886-BMX1
Fax: (614)777-1680
E-mail: btedesco@nbl.org
URL: http://www.nbl.org
Contact: Bob Tedesco, Managing Dir.
Founded: 1974. **Members:** 42,000. **Membership Dues:** regular/basic, $35 (annual). **Staff:** 20. **State Groups:** 38. **Local Groups:** 140. **Description:** BMX racers. (BMX stands for bicycle motocross, a race of unmotorized bicycles on a tight course of 600 to 1,000 ft. over natural terrain that includes steep hills, sharp turns, and jumps.) Aims to establish rules and regulations for BMX races. Sponsors national competitions; distributes number plates to be earned by the top 40 racers. Maintains file on points earned by members in local races; licenses racers according to age class and proficiency. **Awards:** Bob Warnicke Scholarship Fund. **Frequency:** annual. **Type:** recognition. **Recipient:** for academic performance. **Publications:** *BMX Today*, monthly. Magazine. Covers national, international, state, and local races, schedules, and member point standings. **Price:** $10.00/year. **Advertising:** accepted ● Also publishes rule book. **Conventions/Meetings:** annual Competition Congress - always February.

22796 ■ National Bicycle Tour Directors Association (NBTDA)

PO Box 155
Lanesboro, MN 55949
E-mail: exec@nbtda.com
URL: http://www.nbtda.com
Contact: David Harrenstein, Exec. Dir.
Founded: 1980. **Membership Dues:** general (based on number of riders and duration of the event), $75-$200 (annual). **Description:** Represents the interests of ride directors and individuals interested in bicycle racing and tour events. Works to bring together directors, coordinators and organizers of bicycle tours to share ideas and learn ways to improve their events. Promotes responsible cycling. **Publications:** Newsletter, quarterly. **Price:** included in membership dues.

22797 ■ National Center for Bicycling and Walking (NCBW)

8120 Woodmont Ave., Ste.650
Bethesda, MD 20814
Ph: (301)656-4220
Fax: (301)656-4225

E-mail: info@bikewalk.org
URL: http://www.bikewalk.org
Contact: Bill Wilkinson AICP, Exec. Dir.
Founded: 1977. **Staff:** 5. **Budget:** $300,000. **Description:** Promotes bicycling for transportation and recreation; encourages increased quality and number of local bicycling programs; facilitates communication within the bicycle community. Disseminates information and provides technical assistance to community bicycle activists and city officials involved in bicycle programs. Designs and manages national bicycle promotion campaigns. Studies liability issues; develops guidelines for community bicycle programs; sponsors training seminars and programs for safety and planning professionals; conducts workshops on bicycle safety. Plans to offer advocacy and promotion services to government, industry, consumers, and organizations. **Libraries: Type:** reference. **Holdings:** 5,000. **Subjects:** bicycles and bicycling. **Also Known As:** Pro Bike. **Formerly:** (2000) Bicycle Federation of America. **Publications:** *CenterLines*, biweekly. Newsletter. Alternate Formats: online ● *NCBW Forum*, quarterly. Journal ● *Pro Bike Directory*, periodic ● *Pro Bike News*, monthly. Newsletter ● *Pro Bike Proceedings*, biennial. **Conventions/Meetings:** biennial conference (exhibits).

22798 ■ Randonneurs USA (RUSA)

c/o Mark Thomas, Pres.
13543 160th Ave. NE
Redmond, WA 98052
Ph: (206)612-4700
Fax: (425)702-8881
E-mail: president2006@rusa.org
URL: http://www.rusa.org
Contact: Mark Thomas, Pres.
Founded: 1998. **Membership Dues:** individual, $20 (annual) ● foreign/household, $30 (annual). **Description:** Promotes randonneuring in the USA. Provides service to American randonneurs and randonneuses. **Awards:** R-12 Award. **Frequency:** annual. **Type:** recognition. **Recipient:** for riding a 200 K or longer randonneuring event for 12 consecutive months ● Ultra Randonneur Award. **Frequency:** annual. **Type:** recognition. **Recipient:** for RUSA members who have ridden ten Super Randonneur series. **Publications:** *American Randonneur*, quarterly. Newsletter. Keeps members informed on RUSA and RM activities. Alternate Formats: online.

22799 ■ Tandem Club of America (TCA)

c/o Smith Doss
10708 Cambium Ct.
Raleigh, NC 27613-6304
Ph: (919)847-8437
E-mail: membership@tandemclub.org
URL: http://www.tandemclub.org
Contact: Smith Doss, Contact
Founded: 1976. **Members:** 4,000. **Membership Dues:** regular, in U.S., $15 (annual) ● regular, in Canada, $20 (annual) ● regular, outside U.S. and Canada, $25 (annual). **Staff:** 15. **Regional Groups:** 25. **Description:** Tandem bicycling teams. Seeks to form network of tandem bicyclists and to promote information exchange on tandems, exercise, appreciation of the environment and companionship. **Affiliated With:** League of American Bicyclists. **Publications:** *DoubleTalk*, bimonthly. Newsletter. Available on tape for legally blind members. **Price:** $15.00/year in U.S.; $20.00/year in Canada; $25.00/year in all other countries. **Advertising:** accepted ● Membership Directory, annual. **Price:** available to members only.

22800 ■ Ultra Marathon Cycling Association (UMCA)

PO Box 18028
Boulder, CO 80308-1028
E-mail: director@ultracycling.com
URL: http://www.ultracycling.com
Contact: John Hughes, Managing Dir.
Founded: 1980. **Members:** 1,500. **Membership Dues:** regular, $35 (annual). **Staff:** 7. **Multinational. Description:** Represents cyclists. Promotes, recognizes, and sanctions long-distance cycling (events 100 miles and longer). Sanctions Race Across

America and other ultra marathons. Provides information on training, nutrition and equipment for long-distance cyclists. **Awards:** John Marino Competition. **Frequency:** annual. **Type:** recognition ● Mileage Challenge. **Frequency:** annual. **Type:** recognition. **Recipient:** for high totals of race miles. **Publications:** *Ultra Cycling*, bimonthly. Magazine. Contains articles on training, nutrition and equipment; coverage of ultra cycling events. **Price:** included in membership dues. **Circulation:** 3,000. **Advertising:** accepted ● Directory, annual ● Manual, annual. **Conventions/Meetings:** annual meeting.

22801 ■ Unicycling Society of America (USA)
PO Box 21487
Minneapolis, MN 55421-0487
E-mail: constance.cotter@baesystems.com
URL: http://www.unicycling.org/usa
Contact: Constance Cotter, Pres.
Founded: 1973. **Members:** 1,200. **Membership Dues:** regular, in U.S., $15 (annual) ● regular, in Canada and Mexico, $20 (annual) ● international, $25 (annual). **Description:** Individuals or families who enjoy unicycling as a hobby; professional unicyclists. Fosters social and athletic interest in and promotes the sport of unicycling among youth and adults. Establishes voluntary standards of performance. Bestows unicycle proficiency awards at 10 levels. **Affiliated With:** International Unicycling Federation. **Absorbed:** (1973) Unicyclist's Association of America. **Publications:** *On One Wheel*, quarterly. Magazine. Includes biographies of professional unicyclists, historical articles, announcements of events, club and rider profiles, and unicycling information. **Price:** included in membership dues. **Circulation:** 450. **Advertising:** accepted. **Conventions/Meetings:** annual National Unicycle Convention, local and national (exhibits) - July.

22802 ■ United States Cycling Federation (USCF)
c/o USA Cycling
1 Olympic Plz.
Colorado Springs, CO 80909
Ph: (719)866-4581
Fax: (719)866-4628
E-mail: membership@usacycling.org
URL: http://www.usacycling.org
Contact: Steve Johnson, CEO
Founded: 1921. **Members:** 85,000. **Membership Dues:** adult, $45 (annual) ● 18 and younger, $35 (annual). **Staff:** 30. **State Groups:** 1,091. **Description:** National governing body for cycling in the United States. Supervises and controls all elite and amateur bicycle championships, including road, track, mountain bike, BMX, and cyclo-cross; Compiles national bicycle racing records. Conducts development camps, coaching education, mechanics and officials training. **Awards: Type:** recognition. **Absorbed:** Professional Racing Organization of America; National Off-Road Bicycling Association. **Formerly:** (1975) Amateur Bicycle League of America. **Publications:** *Annual Rule Book*, annual ● *Media Guide* ● *National Championship Program*, annual ● *NORBA Newsletter*, periodic ● *Take the Lead*. Brochure ● *USA Cycling Magazine*, bimonthly. **Conventions/Meetings:** annual meeting - usually September.

22803 ■ United States Handcycling Federation (USHF)
PO Box 3538
Evergreen, CO 80437
Ph: (303)459-4159
Fax: (303)674-0533
E-mail: info@ushf.org
URL: http://www.ushf.org
Contact: Ian L. Lawless, Exec. Dir./Co-Founder
Founded: 1998. **Membership Dues:** junior, $5 (annual) ● individual, supporter, $10 (annual) ● family, $25 (annual) ● non-profit organization/club (based on annual budget), $50-$300 (annual) ● dealer/manufacturer, $75 (annual) ● life - recreational, $100. **Description:** Promotes handcycling as a recreational and competitive sport. Creates cycling opportunities for wheelchair users and athletes with lower-mobility

impairments. Provides coaching and development programs, competitions and community outreach. **Publications:** Newsletter. **Price:** included in membership dues. Alternate Formats: online.

22804 ■ The Wheelmen
c/o Paul Brekus, Treas.
4485 Utica St.
Denver, CO 80212-2436
E-mail: membership@thewheelmen.org
URL: http://www.thewheelmen.org
Contact: Paul Brekus, Treas.
Founded: 1967. **Members:** 1,000. **Membership Dues:** regular, $25 (annual) ● sustaining, $35 (annual) ● family, $1 (annual). **State Groups:** 33. **Description:** Persons interested in early cycles and cycling, high wheel, hard-tired, or pre-1914 pneumatic-tired bicycles. Purposes are to keep alive the heritage of American cycling, promote the restoration and riding of early cycles, and encourage cycling as a part of modern living. Members conduct research on early cycling history, and they restore, preserve, and demonstrate antique bicycles. Members participate in numerous parades and fun rides throughout the year. **Libraries: Type:** not open to the public. **Holdings:** 100. **Subjects:** antique bicycles, parts and accessories. **Awards:** Wheelmen Award. **Frequency:** annual. **Type:** recognition. **Recipient:** for completion of Official High Wheel Tours and for Century Rides (100 miles in one day on a high-wheel or other antique bicycle); also, for contributions to cycling history literature. **Computer Services:** Mailing lists, for organization use only. **Committees:** Historian; Librarian; Membership; Restoration Consultant. **Publications:** Magazine, semiannual. Contains information about antique bicycles (review, history, etc.). **Price:** $25.00/year; $4.00 each (1 to 4 copies); $3.50 each (5 to 24 copies); $3.00 each (more than 25 copies). **Circulation:** 1,000 ● Membership Directory, biennial. Contains antique bicycle events, classified ads for antique bicycles and related items, articles on research about antique bicycles. **Price:** available to members only. **Circulation:** 1,000 ● Newsletter, quarterly. Includes a range of current information such as short stories on meets, antique bicycle book reviews, and schedule of events. **Price:** included in membership dues. **Circulation:** 950. **Advertising:** accepted ● Also publishes information bulletins on special subjects to members, bicycle restoration, parade riding, etc. **Conventions/Meetings:** annual meeting, with rides, business and other seminars, swap meets (exhibits).

22805 ■ Women's Mountain Bike and Tea Society (WOMBATS)
PO Box 757
Fairfax, CA 94978
Ph: (415)459-0980
E-mail: jacquie@batnet.com
URL: http://www.wombats.org
Contact: Jacquie Phelan, Contact
Founded: 1987. **Members:** 350. **Membership Dues:** regular, $60 (annual). **Staff:** 2. **Languages:** English, French, German, Italian, Swedish. **Description:** Women with an interest in mountain bicycle riding. Promotes increased participation by women in mountain biking. Serves as a clearinghouse on mountain biking for women. Conducts mountain biking and trail maintenance and awareness courses; sponsors rides; facilitates exchange of information among members. Makes available equipment discounts to members. **Publications:** Newsletter, quarterly.

Dance

22806 ■ National Dance Education Association (NDEO)
c/o Jane Bonbright, Exec. Dir.
4948 St. Elmo Ave., Ste.301
Bethesda, MD 20814-6065
Ph: (301)657-2880 (301)657-2881
Fax: (301)657-2882

E-mail: info@ndeo.org
URL: http://www.ndeo.org
Contact: Jane Bonbright, Exec. Dir.
Founded: 1997. **Members:** 2,200. **Membership Dues:** professional, $95 (annual) ● student, $35 (annual) ● institutional (high school, studio, school district), $150 (annual) ● business, $350 (annual) ● institutional (college, university), $200 (annual). **Staff:** 4. **Budget:** $500,000. **State Groups:** 50. **National Groups:** 150. **Description:** Strives for quality professional development at national, state, and local levels for all educators teaching dance in the arts. Sponsors institutes, national and regional conferences. Provides world-class teaching resources (books, CDs, videos, etc.), research data bases, Journal in Dance Education, and develops dance standards, curriculum, and assessments for use at national and state levels. **Libraries: Type:** reference. **Holdings:** 200; articles, audio recordings, books, periodicals, video recordings. **Subjects:** dance arts education. **Awards:** Distinguished Public Service Award. **Frequency:** annual. **Type:** recognition. **Recipient:** for outstanding public service to the arts at national and/or state levels ● Leadership Award. **Frequency:** annual. **Type:** recognition. **Recipient:** for qualities of leadership; one who leads with excellence and confidence, and develops leadership skills in others ● Lifetime Achievement Award. **Frequency:** annual. **Type:** recognition. **Recipient:** for exemplary leadership, research, scholarship, and philanthropy and/or service to dance education ● Philanthropic Award. **Frequency:** annual. **Type:** recognition. **Recipient:** for a philanthropic supporter of the arts ● Vision Award. **Frequency:** annual. **Type:** recognition. **Recipient:** for excellence in one's ability to create programs and/or projects that have made an important impact on and contribution to dance education. **Computer Services:** database, national, state ● database, Research in Dance Education. **Affiliated With:** American Alliance for Theatre and Education; American Association for the Advancement of Science; American Association of Colleges for Teacher Education; American Association for Health Education; American Association of School Librarians; American College Dance Festival Association; American Council on the Teaching of Foreign Languages; American Dance Guild; American Dance Therapy Association; American Federation of Teachers; American Library Association; Arts Education Partnership; Association for Childhood Education International; Cecchetti Council of America; Congress on Research in Dance; Council of Chief State School Officers; Dance Critics Association; Dance Notation Bureau; Dance/U.S.A.; Educational Theatre Association; International Association for Dance Medicine and Science; Kennedy Center Alliance for Arts Education Network; Laban/Bartenieff Institute of Movement Studies; MENC: The National Association for Music Education; National Art Education Association; National Assembly of State Arts Agencies; National Assessment of Educational Progress; National Association of Schools of Dance; National Association for Sport and Physical Education; National Center for Education Statistics; National Communication Association; National Council of Teachers of English; National Council of Teachers of Mathematics; National Dance Association; National Dance Education Association; National Education Association; National Endowment for the Arts; National Middle School Association; National Science Teachers Association; National Study of School Evaluation; Society of Dance History Scholars; Teachers of English to Speakers of Other Languages; Wolf Trap Foundation for the Performing Arts; World Dance Alliance; Young Audiences. **Publications:** *Journal of Dance Education*, quarterly. **Price:** $25.00 for members; $55.00 for nonmembers; $75.00 for institutions. **Advertising:** accepted. **Conventions/Meetings:** annual Celebrating the Whole Person - conference (exhibits).

22807 ■ National Dance Teacher's Association (NDTA)
c/o Ronnie Gardner, Pres.
2309 E Atlantic Blvd.
Pompano Beach, FL 33062

Ph: (954)782-7760
E-mail: rg_ndta@comcast.net
URL: http://www.nationaldanceteachers.org
Contact: Ronnie Gardner, Pres.
Founded: 1987. **Membership Dues:** full (single), $50 (annual) ● full (couple), $75 (annual) ● non-participating (single), $25 (annual) ● non-participating (couple), $35 (annual) ● studio staff, $20 (annual). **Description:** Seeks to assist professional dance teachers in the field of ballroom, Latin, country Western, swing, theater arts and other partner or social dances. **Formerly:** National Council of Dance Teachers Organizations. **Publications:** Videos. Contains information on NDTA seminars. **Conventions/Meetings:** quarterly seminar, on the art of dance.

22808 ■ Professional Dancers Federation (PDF)
c/o Richard Booth, Pres.
6830 N Broadway "D"
Denver, CO 80221
Ph: (303)412-1213
Fax: (303)412-8231
E-mail: mariahansen@mac.com
URL: http://www.pdfusa.com
Contact: Richard Booth, Pres.
Founded: 1980. **Membership Dues:** individual, $90 (triennial) ● individual, $65 (biennial) ● individual, $40 (annual). **Description:** Represents professionals involved in competitive dancesport.

Darts

22809 ■ American Darters Association (ADA)
1000 Lake St. Louis Blvd., Ste.310
Lake St. Louis, MO 63367-9932
Ph: (636)625-8621
Fax: (636)625-8919
E-mail: gremick@adadarters.com
URL: http://www.adadarters.com
Contact: Glenn Remick, Pres.
Founded: 1991. **Membership Dues:** general, $20 (annual). **Description:** Serves as the sanctioning body for a nationwide, centrally-controlled dart league. Promotes the sport of darts. **Publications:** Newsletter. Contains championship pictures and statistics, news, tips from the pros and tournament action. **Price:** included in membership dues.

22810 ■ American Darts Organization (ADO)
c/o Katie Harris
230 N Crescent Way, Ste.K
Anaheim, CA 92801-6707
Ph: (714)254-0212
Fax: (714)254-0214
E-mail: adodarts1@aol.com
URL: http://www.adodarts.org
Contact: Buddy Bartoletta, Pres.
Founded: 1976. **Members:** 75,000. **Membership Dues:** individual, $30 (annual) ● youth, $10 (annual). **Staff:** 2. **Budget:** $300,000. **Regional Groups:** 27. **Local Groups:** 300. **Description:** Dart players, manufacturers, and suppliers. Aims to promote the sport of darts. Sanctions 250 dart tournaments annually. Compiles statistics. Conducts 4 playoff systems leading to national titles and international competition. **Libraries:** Type: reference. **Holdings:** 76; periodicals. **Subjects:** darts. **Awards:** ADO Memorial Scholarship Fund. **Frequency:** annual. **Type:** scholarship. **Recipient:** for winners of youth playoff series ● **Type:** trophy. **Computer Services:** database ● mailing lists. **Divisions:** Youth. **Publications:** Double Eagle, quarterly. Newsletter. **Price:** included in membership dues; $15.00 for nonmembers in Canada and Mexico; $20.00 for nonmembers overseas. **Circulation:** 75,000. **Advertising:** accepted. **Conventions/Meetings:** semiannual board meeting (exhibits) ● quarterly meeting, tournament.

22811 ■ AMOA National Dart Association
c/o Wendell J. Walls, CAE, Exec. Dir.
5613 W 74th St.
Indianapolis, IN 46278-1753

Ph: (317)387-1299
Free: (800)808-9884
Fax: (317)387-0999
E-mail: director@ndadarts.com
URL: http://www.ndadarts.com
Contact: Wendell J. Walls CAE, Exec. Dir.
Founded: 1986. **Members:** 60,052. **Membership Dues:** coin-operated vending company, $300-$575 (annual) ● associate (supplier), $5,000 (annual) ● manufacturer, $20,000 (annual). **Staff:** 3. **Budget:** $1,500,000. **Regional Groups:** 305. **State Groups:** 38. **Local Groups:** 3,000. **National Groups:** 16. **Multinational. Description:** Sport associations; manufacturers and vendors. Acts as sanctioning body for the sport of electronic darting. Sets standards for and regulates league darting. Sponsors competitions; compiles statistics. Maintains charitable programs. **Computer Services:** database, players and operators. **Committees:** Awards; Classification; Judicial Education; Legislative; Publicity; Rules; Tournament. **Affiliated With:** Amusement and Music Operators Association. **Publications:** Throw Lines, 3/year. Magazine. Includes league and tournament results and highlights. **Price:** $15.00. **Circulation:** 350,000. **Advertising:** accepted. Alternate Formats: online ● Annual Report, annual ● Also publishes league manuals. **Conventions/Meetings:** biennial Dart Summit - workshop ● annual Team Dart International Tournament - competition.

Disabilities

22812 ■ American Competition Opportunities for Riders with Disabilities (ACORD)
c/o Judy Serie Nagy
5303 Felter Rd.
San Jose, CA 95132
Ph: (408)261-8292 (408)263-3143
Fax: (408)261-9438
E-mail: danivar@aol.com
URL: http://members.aol.com/acordcomp
Contact: Judy Serie Nagy, Contact
Description: Organizes safe and quality horse shows for riders with disabilities. Enables disabled riders to experience the fun and satisfaction of competing in a horse show. **Publications:** Equestrian Update. Newsletter. Alternate Formats: online.

Disabled

22813 ■ Achilles Track Club (ATC)
42 W 38th St., Ste.400
New York, NY 10018-6210
Ph: (212)354-0300
Fax: (212)354-3978
E-mail: info@achillestrackclub.org
URL: http://www.achillestrackclub.org
Contact: Dick Traum, Pres.
Founded: 1983. **Members:** 3,400. **Staff:** 4. **Budget:** $400,000. **Local Groups:** 40. **National Groups:** 43. **Description:** Disabled runners; volunteer coaches. (Membership, though drawn primarily from New York City, also includes international members who are coached by mail.) Seeks to encourage people with all types of disabilities to participate in running, and to improve the self-image of the disabled and demonstrate that they are energetic and capable people. Encourages the disabled to be aerobically fit and to run in competitions beside the able-bodied. Stresses that no previous athletic experience is necessary, just a desire to improve fitness with regular training. Conducts children's programs. Maintains speakers' bureau. (Group is named for the mythical Greek hero whose disability was a vulnerable heel on an otherwise invincible body.) **Convention/Meeting:** none. **Awards:** Albert H. Gordon Award. **Frequency:** annual. **Type:** recognition. **Recipient:** for unusual personal commitment to helping others. **Affiliated With:** New York Road Runners Club. **Publications:** The Achilles Heel and Kid's Bits, 3/year. Newsletter. **Circulation:** 3,440. Alternate Formats: online.

22814 ■ Adaptive Sports Association (ASA)
PO Box 1884
Durango, CO 81302
Ph: (970)259-0374 (970)385-2163
Fax: (970)259-2175
E-mail: info@asadurango.com
URL: http://www.asadurango.org
Contact: Ms. Cheri Pettyjohn, Exec. Dir.
Founded: 1983. **Members:** 420. **Staff:** 10. **Budget:** $235,000. **Description:** Provides ski lessons to people with disabilities. Offers summer sports opportunities to individuals with disabilities including river rafting, kayaking, canoeing, hiking, and fishing. **Formerly:** (1995) Durango/Purgatory Adaptive Sports Association. **Publications:** ASA Program Video. Covers ASA's summer program. Alternate Formats: online ● Membership Newsletter, quarterly ● Newsletter, quarterly. **Price:** $30.00. **Circulation:** 1,600. **Advertising:** accepted ● Handbooks. Alternate Formats: online.

22815 ■ American Association of adaptedSPORTS Programs (AAASP)
PO Box 451047
Atlanta, GA 31145
Ph: (404)294-0070
Fax: (404)294-5758
E-mail: sports@adaptedsports.org
URL: http://www.adaptedsports.org
Contact: Jeffrey D. Hoffman, CEO
Founded: 1996. **Description:** Oversees the partnership of leaders in education and community to lay the foundation for a national network of interscholastic adapted athletic programs. Initiates interscholastic sports leagues for students with physical disabilities or visual impairments in Grades 1 to 12. Serves as the governing body and athletic association for sports programs for disabled students. **Publications:** The adaptedSports Report. Newsletter. Contains news from special sports leagues around the country. **Price:** free. Alternate Formats: online.

22816 ■ American Blind Bowling Association (ABBA)
c/o Linda Keeney, Pres.
320 S Gramercy Pl., Apt. 205
Los Angeles, CA 90020
Ph: (213)384-9613
E-mail: lindakeeney@hotmail.com
URL: http://www.americanblindbowlers.com
Contact: Linda Keeney, Pres.
Founded: 1951. **Members:** 2,000. **Regional Groups:** 4. **State Groups:** 125. **Local Groups:** 140. **Description:** Legally blind men and women, 18 years of age and older, competing in organized tenpin bowling. Promotes bowling as a recreational activity for adult blind persons. Sanctions member leagues; sponsors annual mail-o-graphic. Presents awards. **Publications:** The Blind Bowler, 3/year. **Conventions/Meetings:** annual Championship Blind Bowling Tournament - competition.

22817 ■ American Blind Golf Association (ABGA)
7634 Benassi Dr.
Gilroy, CA 95020
Ph: (408)842-3369
E-mail: americanblindgolf@charter.net
URL: http://www.abdga.org
Contact: Roy Holt, Exec. Dir.
Founded: 2001. **Membership Dues:** life (blind golfers), $50 ● life (supporting), $25. **Description:** Educates the general public about golf for the blind and disabled. Promotes the game of golf to young blind and disabled people through clinics, seminars, tournaments and other educational activities. **Formerly:** (2006) American Blind and Disabled Golf Association.

22818 ■ American Blind Skiing Foundation (ABSF)
2228 Grand Pointe Trail
Aurora, IL 60504
Ph: (312)409-1605

E-mail: absf@absf.org

URL: http://www.absf.org

Contact: Steve Crowe, Treas.

Founded: 1972. **Members:** 175. **Membership Dues:** individual, $20 (annual) ● family, $25 (annual). **Description:** Volunteers who teach downhill and cross-country recreational and competitive skiing to the blind and visually handicapped. Holds giant slalom, downhill, and cross-country races; awards trophies. Travels with blind skiers to skiing areas in Colorado, Wisconsin, and Michigan. Sponsors international races in Canada, World Cup for Disabled in Switzerland, and Olympics for Disabled in Austria. **Publications:** Newsletter. Alternate Formats: online. **Conventions/Meetings:** annual Ski Trip and Show.

22819 ■ American Hearing Impaired Hockey Association (AHIHA)

1143 W Lake St.

Chicago, IL 60607

Ph: (312)226-5880

Fax: (312)829-2098

E-mail: info@ahiha.org

URL: http://www.ahiha.org

Contact: Stan Mikita, Pres.

Founded: 1973. **Members:** 80. **Staff:** 62. **Description:** Hearing impaired boys and men, aged 5 to 26, who wish to play ice hockey. Seeks to develop members' skills and self-confidence, both as hockey players and as individuals, through participation in the annual Stan Mikita Hockey School for the Hearing Impaired. **Publications:** *Locker Room Briefs.* Newsletter.

22820 ■ American Polocrosse Association (APA)

PO Box 915

New Hampton, NY 10958

Ph: (845)856-4265 (845)858-2913

Fax: (845)856-4265

E-mail: info@americanpolocrosse.org

URL: http://www.americanpolocrosse.org

Contact: Laura Humphreys, Sec.

Founded: 1984. **Members:** 563. **Membership Dues:** junior, $30 (annual) ● individual, $60 (annual) ● family, $90 (annual) ● handicap (all ages), $35 (annual) ● foreign, $55 (annual). **Staff:** 2. **Local Groups:** 30. **Description:** Promotes the sport of polocrosse. Provides tournament insurance, umpire training and certification, instructional clinics, sanctions tournaments, selection of teams, international exchanges, and international youth exchanges. **Awards:** Rotating Honorary Awards. **Frequency:** annual. **Type:** recognition. **Recipient:** for the riders and horses. **Telecommunication Services:** electronic mail, lhumphreys@americanpolocrosse.org. **Programs:** Domestic Youth; International; International Youth Exchange. **Publications:** *American Polocrosse*, semiannual. Magazine. **Circulation:** 300. **Advertising:** accepted ● *Off the Racquet*, monthly. Newsletter. **Circulation:** 300. **Advertising:** accepted.

22821 ■ American Wheelchair Bowling Association (AWBA)

c/o Dave Roberts, Exec.Sec-Treas.

PO Box 69

Clover, VA 24534-0069

Ph: (434)454-2269

Fax: (434)454-6276

E-mail: bowlawba@aol.com

Contact: Dave Roberts, Exec.Sec.-Treas.

Founded: 1962. **Members:** 600. **Membership Dues:** associate, $15 (annual) ● life, $150. **Regional Groups:** 12. **Description:** Represents male and female athletes with permanent disabilities who are confined to wheelchairs. Organizes and promotes wheelchair bowling and regulate rules. Provides information about wheelchair bowling. Conducts state and national wheelchair bowling tournaments. Maintains hall of fame and museum; compiles statistics. **Awards: Type:** recognition. **Publications:** *The 11th Frame*, bimonthly ● *Wheelchair Bowling.* Book. **Conventions/Meetings:** annual National Tournament - meeting.

22822 ■ America's Athletes with Disabilities (AAD)

8630 Fenton St., Ste.920

Silver Spring, MD 20910

Ph: (301)589-9042

Free: (800)238-7632

Fax: (301)589-9052

E-mail: info@americasathletes.org

URL: http://www.americasathletes.org

Contact: Deborah Bonsack, Exec. Dir.

Founded: 1985. **Description:** Strives to promote and sponsor sports, recreation, fitness and leisure events for children and adults with physical disabilities. Maintains a National Athlete Registry. **Programs:** Disability Awareness; Youth. **Publications:** *Victory Voice.* Newsletter.

22823 ■ Association of Disabled American Golfers (ADAG)

PO Box 280649

Lakewood, CO 80228-0649

Ph: (303)922-5228

Fax: (303)969-0447

E-mail: adag@usga.org

URL: http://www.golfcolorado.com/adag

Contact: Greg Jones, Pres.

Founded: 1992. **Description:** Represents the interests of individuals dedicated to enhancing full participation in the game of golf for persons with disabilities. Promotes the inclusion of golfers with disabilities into the game of golf. Serves as the clearinghouse for information regarding golfers with disabilities and the golf community.

22824 ■ Challenge Aspen at Snowmass

PO Box M

Aspen, CO 81612

Ph: (970)923-0578

Fax: (970)923-7338

E-mail: possibilities@challengeaspen.com

URL: http://www.challengeaspen.com

Contact: Sarah Williams, Program Dir.

Founded: 1995. **Staff:** 8. **Budget:** $1,200,000. **Description:** Assists people with mental or physical disabilities in appreciating outdoor recreation and cultural activities. Provides volunteer guides and/or instructors to help enjoy the outdoors by skiing, skating, hiking, fishing, horseback riding, swimming, and biking. Offers annual summer camps in art, music and dance productions, and downhill biking. **Programs:** Recreation; Volunteer. **Formerly:** (2000) Blind Outdoor Leisure Development; (2000) BOLD/Challenge Aspen. **Publications:** Brochures.

22825 ■ Disabled Sports USA (DS/USA)

451 Hungerford Dr., Ste.100

Rockville, MD 20850

Ph: (301)217-0960

Fax: (301)217-0968

E-mail: information@dsusa.org

URL: http://www.dsusa.org

Contact: Kirk M. Bauer, Exec. Dir.

Founded: 1967. **Members:** 20,000. **Membership Dues:** individual, $25 (annual) ● challenger, $40 (annual) ● medalist, $100 (annual) ● champion, $250 (annual). **Staff:** 9. **Budget:** $1,500,000. **Regional Groups:** 4. **Local Groups:** 86. **Description:** Promotes sports and recreation opportunities for individuals with physical disabilities. Provides direct services to people with mobility and visual impairments. Offers and sanctions recreational winter and summer programs, including learn-to-ski, learn-to-sail, and learn-to-race clinics, competitive alpine and Nordic skiing, archery, basketball, cycling, lawnbowling, shooting, swimming, table tennis, track and field, volleyball, sailing, and weightlifting. Conducts special programs for children, women, and veterans with disabilities. Offers training and certification of adaptive fitness and adaptive ski instructors. Sponsors U.S. Disabled Ski Team, U.S. Amputee Summer Sports Team, and U.S. Disabled Sports Team. Maintains hall of fame. **Awards:** Diana Golden Fund. **Type:** scholarship. **Recipient:** for young athletes with disabilities in skiing ● Jim Winthers Award. **Frequency:** annual. **Type:** recognition. **Recipient:** for excellence in the field of disabled sports. **Telecommunication Ser-**

vices: TDD, (301)217-0963. **Projects:** Wounded Warrior Disabled Sports. **Affiliated With:** Professional Ski Instructors of America; United States Olympic Committee. **Absorbed:** (1991) United States Amputee Athletic Association. **Formerly:** (1972) National Amputee Skiers Association; (1977) National Inconvenienced Sportsmen's Association; (1989) National Handicapped Sports and Recreation Association; (1998) National Handicapped Sports. **Publications:** *Adaptive Ski Teaching Methods*, quarterly. Newsletter. **Circulation:** 20,000. **Advertising:** accepted ● *Aerobics for Amputees*. Video ● *Aerobics for Cerebral Palsy*. Video ● *Aerobics for Paraplegia*. Video ● *Aerobics for Quadriplegia*. Video ● *Challenge*, quarterly. Magazine. **Price:** included in membership dues. Alternate Formats: online ● *Disabled Children in Physical Education: Learning Through Movement*. Handbook. Overviews proper adapted physical education programs for disabled children. **Price:** $14.95 ● *Fitness Programming and Physical Disabilities*. Manual ● *Manual for Adaptive Fitness Instructors* ● *Manual for Adaptive Ski Instructors* ● *Strengthen Flexibility Exercises for All Types of Disabilities*. Video. **Conventions/Meetings:** annual National Amputee Summer Games - meeting (exhibits) ● annual Ski Spectacular for Disabled Skiers - competition (exhibits) - usually December ● annual Summerfest - festival - usually June ● annual U.S. Disabled Ski Championships - competition.

22826 ■ Handicapped Scuba Association (HSA)

1104 El Prado

San Clemente, CA 92672-4637

Ph: (949)498-4540

Fax: (949)498-6128

E-mail: hsa@hsascuba.com

URL: http://www.hsascuba.com

Contact: Jim Gatacre, Pres.

Founded: 1975. **Members:** 4,000. **Membership Dues:** supporting, $25 (annual) ● sponsoring, $75 (annual) ● patron, $300 (annual). **Staff:** 6. **Budget:** $30,000. **Regional Groups:** 30. **State Groups:** 50. **National Groups:** 34. **Languages:** English, French, German, Italian, Japanese. **Multinational. Description:** Individuals with handicaps and interested others. Aims to advance and promote scuba diving among the handicapped. Seeks to enhance the self-image of handicapped divers by emphasizing their abilities rather than their disabilities. Stresses the importance of education and safety procedures in diving; maintains training agency for handicapped divers. Offers training and certification worldwide for scuba diving instructors in teaching the handicapped. Holds monthly diving excursion and lectures, and conducts four diving vacations per year. Offers instructor referrals worldwide. **Computer Services:** database, instructors ● mailing lists. **Telecommunication Services:** electronic bulletin board, General Electric Network for Information Exchange. **Divisions:** Advisory Directors; Volunteers. **Programs:** Dive Buddy. **Publications:** *Dive Buddy Manual* ● *Freedom in Depth*. Film. **Price:** $30.00 ● *Instructor Training Manual* ● *SQUID*. Film. **Price:** $20.00. **Advertising:** accepted ● *To Fly in Freedom*. Film. **Price:** $30.00 ● Also produces a film about the association with the Cousteau Society (see separate entry). **Conventions/Meetings:** annual convention, for members (exhibits).

22827 ■ International Committee of Sports for the Deaf/DEAFLYMPICS (CISS)

528 Trail Ave.

Frederick, MD 21701

Fax: (301)620-2990

E-mail: info@ciss.org

URL: http://www.deaflympics.com

Contact: Ms. Tiffany Granfors, Exec. Dir.

Founded: 1924. **Members:** 94. **Staff:** 2. **Budget:** $250,000. **Regional Groups:** 4. **Multinational. Description:** National athletic organizations for the deaf. Provides an international sports competition for the deaf patterned after the International Olympic Games. Promotes and develops physical education and the practice of sports among the deaf. Encourages friendly relations between countries with programs in silent sports and countries without programs for deaf athletes. Holds Summer World Games and Winter Games alternately at 2-year intervals for competitors with hearing loss of 55 decibels or more; the committee is recognized by the International Olympic Committee. **Awards:** Gold, Silver, and Bronze Medals. **Frequency:** biennial. **Type:** medal. **Recipient:** for the first, second, and third place winners of each event during the Summer World Games and the Winter Games ● Windex Sportsman and Sportswoman of the Year. **Frequency:** annual. **Type:** recognition. **Recipient:** for an exceptional athlete nominated by National Deaf Sports Federations. **Councils:** Regional Representatives. **Special Interest Groups:** Technical Directors. **Affiliated With:** International Olympic Committee. **Also Known As:** (2000) Deaf Olympics. **Conventions/Meetings:** biennial congress, held concurrently with games (exhibits).

22828 ■ International Wheelchair Road Racers Club (IWRRC)

c/o Joseph M. Dowling, Pres.
30 Myano Ln.
PO Box 3
Stamford, CT 06902
Ph: (203)967-2231
Fax: (203)327-7999
E-mail: dowling007@aol.com
Contact: Joseph M. Dowling, Pres.

Founded: 1981. **Members:** 200. **Description:** Disabled persons, able-bodied persons, rehabilitation institutes, and major road race organizations interested in health and physical fitness for the disabled. Promotes wheelchair road racing in the U.S; assists road race organizations in incorporating wheelchair divisions. Provides educational and technical assistance to race directors and road racers; maintains communications network concerning multi-sports for the disabled. Governs the sport of wheelchair road racing. **Affiliated With:** Wheelchair Sports, USA. **Publications:** Newsletter, semimonthly. **Conventions/Meetings:** periodic meeting.

22829 ■ National Ability Center (NAC)

PO Box 682799
Park City, UT 84068
Ph: (435)649-3991
Fax: (435)658-3992
E-mail: info@nac1985.org
Contact: Meeche White, CEO/Co-Founder

Founded: 1985. **Members:** 5,000. **Membership Dues:** individual, $20 (annual) ● family, $30 (annual). **Staff:** 10. **Budget:** $600,000. **State Groups:** 4. **National Groups:** 2. **Description:** People with disabilities and their families. Promotes the development of lifetime skills for persons with disabilities and their families; works to increase the self-esteem of people with disabilities. Sponsors affordable sports and recreational activities, including cycling, skiing, challenge course, horseback riding, and river rafting, for members. **Telecommunication Services:** electronic mail, meechew@nac1985.org. **Publications:** Ability Bulletin, quarterly. **Advertising:** accepted. **Conventions/Meetings:** meeting.

22830 ■ National Alliance for Accessible Golf (NAAG)

12100 Sunset Hills Rd., Ste.130
Reston, VA 20190
Ph: (703)234-4136
Fax: (703)435-4390
E-mail: info@accessgolf.org
URL: http://www.accessgolf.org
Contact: Trey Holland, Pres.

Founded: 2001. **Description:** Increases participation of people with disabilities in the game of golf. Promotes collaboration among the golf community organizations, people with disabilities and organizations providing service or treatment to people with disabilities. Advances models and resources for persons with disabilities to learn the game of golf. Assists the golf community in resolving issues related to expanding golf access for people with disabilities. **Computer Services:** Mailing lists. **Committees:** Education; Golf Course Operator Tool Kit; Players Tool

Kit. **Projects:** Toolkit for Golf Course Owners and Operators. **Subcommittees:** Corporate Giving/Sponsorship; Friends and Annual Giving; Grants and Contracts. **Task Forces:** Single Rider Car.

22831 ■ National Amputee Golf Association (NAGA)

11 Walnut Hill Rd.
Amherst, NH 03031-1713
Ph: (603)672-6444
Free: (800)633-6242
Fax: (603)672-2987
E-mail: info@nagagolf.org
URL: http://www.nagagolf.org
Contact: Bob Wilson, Exec. Dir.

Founded: 1955. **Members:** 2,400. **Membership Dues:** associate, $35 (annual) ● regular, $25 (annual) ● life (based on age), $100-$800. **Staff:** 2. **Budget:** $150,000. **Regional Groups:** 5. **Description:** Individuals who have lost a hand, foot, or a combination thereof at a major joint. Aims to promote the mental and physical rehabilitation of amputees through the sport of golf. Conducts first swing program for therapists. Organizes local, regional, national, and international tournaments. Compiles statistics. **Libraries: Type:** reference. **Awards: Type:** recognition ● **Type:** scholarship. **Recipient:** to college students demonstrating financial need. **Publications:** Amputee Golfer Magazine, annual. **Price:** included in membership dues. **Circulation:** 6,000. **Advertising:** accepted. Alternate Formats: CD-ROM ● NAGA News, annual. Newsletter. **Price:** included in membership dues. Alternate Formats: online. **Conventions/Meetings:** annual meeting ● annual National Amputee Golf Championship and Robinson Cup - competition.

22832 ■ National Beep Baseball Association (NBBA)

5568 Boulder-Crest St.
Columbus, OH 43235
Ph: (614)442-1444
E-mail: secretary@nbba.org
URL: http://www.nbba.org
Contact: Jeana Weigand, Sec.

Founded: 1975. **Members:** 500. **Membership Dues:** individual, $10 (annual) ● team, $25 (annual). **Local Groups:** 20. **Description:** Blind and visually impaired athletes, sighted volunteers, and others interested in participating in beep baseball. (Beep baseball uses an adapted ball and two adapted bases that emit sounds. Once the batter hits the beeping ball, he or she must get to whichever base buzzes before one of the six defensive players fields the ball. The pitchers, catchers and defensive spotters are usually sighted volunteers.) Promotes the development of amateur beep baseball and other recreational and competitive programs for the blind and visually impaired; improves independence, mobility, communication, and social skills of the blind and visually impaired; educates and promotes community awareness and interaction between the sighted and the blind/visually impaired; holds tournaments. Sponsors speakers' bureau; conducts research programs. **Awards:** Dan Tracy Award. **Frequency:** annual. **Type:** recognition. **Recipient:** to the game official (plate umpire, head scorekeeper, base switch operator, field umpire or base umpire) receiving the most votes from teams, over the course of the world series tournament, for his exceptional volunteer assistance/service during games ● George Haws Sportsmanship Award. **Frequency:** annual. **Type:** recognition ● Jim Quinn Award. **Frequency:** annual. **Type:** recognition. **Recipient:** for outstanding contribution to or promotion of the sport Beep Baseball ● NBBA Top 5 Pitchers List. **Frequency:** periodic. **Type:** recognition ● NBBA Top 30 Players List. **Frequency:** periodic. **Type:** recognition. **Computer Services:** Mailing lists, of members. **Committees:** Ball and Equipment; Budget and Finance; By-Laws; Fund Raising; Hall of Fame; Nominating; Projects; Public Relations; Rules; Tournament. **Publications:** Beep Baseball In A Nutshell, annual. Bulletin. Features a brief description explaining the game and rules. **Price:** free. Alternate Formats: online; CD-ROM; diskette ● History of NBBA. Bulletin ● NBBA Newsletter, quarterly. Includes score statistics, tournament information and rule changes. **Price:** included in membership dues. **Circulation:** 500. Alternate Formats: online. **Conventions/Meetings:** semiannual board meeting - 1st weekend of March (spring) and November (fall) ● annual World Series Tournament - general assembly - always end of July or first week of August.

22833 ■ National Center for Therapeutic Riding (NCTR)

Address Unknown since 2007
Founded: 1973. **Staff:** 5. **Budget:** $250,000. **Description:** Nonprofit center that provides specialized horseback riding lessons to students with disabilities and other individuals from the Washington, DC area. Using the horse as a motivator, classes focus on teaching techniques for the physically handicapped, emotionally disturbed, learning disabled, or mentally retarded person. **Formerly:** (1980) Rock Creek Park Horse Centre. **Publications:** NCTR Horsemanship Manual.

22834 ■ National Deaf Women's Bowling Association (NDWBA)

c/o A. Jane Jacobson, Sec.-Treas.
3314 64th St.
Urbandale, IA 50322
E-mail: ndwbast@gmail.com
URL: http://www.ndwba.com
Contact: Judie Cronlund, Pres.

Founded: 1974. **Members:** 160. **Description:** Represents hearing impaired bowlers. Promotes fellowship and fair play among participants. **Publications:** The Deaf Bowler, 3/year. Magazine. Prints bowling news from all over the country - pertains to deaf bowlers. **Price:** $8.00/year. **Circulation:** 500 ● NDWBA Constitution and By Laws. **Conventions/Meetings:** annual meeting and competition, includes singles, doubles, team, queen's, and world championship tournaments and Senior Citizen World Women's Champ - always July.

22835 ■ National Disability Sports Alliance (NDSA)

25 W Independence Way
Kingston, RI 02881
Ph: (401)792-7130
Fax: (401)792-7132
E-mail: info@ndsaonline.org
URL: http://www.ndsaonline.org
Contact: Jerry McCole, Exec. Dir.

Founded: 1986. **Members:** 3,000. **Membership Dues:** regular, $25 (annual) ● circle of friends, $50 (annual) ● bronze medal club, $100 (annual) ● silver medal club, $250 (annual) ● gold medal club, $500 (annual). **Staff:** 4. **Budget:** $500,000. **Regional Groups:** 30. **State Groups:** 15. **Local Groups:** 100. **Description:** Athletes with cerebral palsy, athletic officials including coaches and administrators, health care professionals, and other interested individuals. Seeks to offer competitive athletic opportunities for athletes with cerebral palsy or traumatic brain injury and stroke survivors; provides support and training assistance to athletes with varying degrees of disability. Organizes multi-sport competitions at the local, regional, national, and international levels; maintains 8-level classification system to ensure that competition is based on the functional level of participants rather than their neurological capability. Selects athletes to represent the U.S. in the Paralympic Games and other international competitions. Provides referral service to assist members in obtaining support for local sports programs; develops fund-raising programs. Operates Youth Sports Program, which provides guidelines and assistance to young people with special needs who wish to learn a sport. Conducts educational clinics and seminars. Compiles statistics; maintains speakers' bureau and library. Plans to make available to members liability insurance and reduced rates on special sports equipment. **Computer Services:** database. **Committees:** Athletes; Medical and Education. **Subcommittees:** Youth Sports. **Affiliated With:** Cerebral Palsy International Sports and Recreation Association; United States Olympic Committee. **Formed by Merger of:** (1986) National Association of Sports for Cerebral Palsy;

(1986) United States Association of Cerebral Palsy Sports. **Formerly:** (2002) United States Cerebral Palsy Athletic Association. **Publications:** *NDSA Classification and Rules Manual* ● *Update*, quarterly. Newsletter. **Circulation:** 3,000.

22836 ■ National Wheelchair Basketball Association (NWBA)

6165 Lehman Dr., Ste.101
Colorado Springs, CO 80918
Ph: (719)266-4082
Fax: (719)266-4082
E-mail: toddhatfield@nwba.org
Contact: Todd Hatfield, Program Mgr.
Founded: 1948. **Members:** 185. **Budget:** $65,000.
Description: Wheelchair basketball teams comprised of individuals with severe permanent physical disabilities of the lower extremities. Seeks to provide opportunities on a national basis for the physically disabled to participate in the sport of wheelchair basketball, with its adjunct psychological, social, and emotional benefits, and to maintain a high level of competition through continuing refinement and standardization of playing rules and officiating. Sponsors sectional and regional tournaments leading up to the National Wheelchair Basketball Tournament. Maintains hall of fame; compiles statistics; participates in charitable activities. **Awards: Frequency:** annual. **Type:** trophy. **Recipient:** to winner of national tournament. **Affiliated With:** U.S.A. Basketball. **Publications:** *National Wheelchair Basketball Tournament Program*, annual ● *Rules and Case Book*, annual ● *Standings and Statistics*, 10/year ● *Directory*, annual. Includes conference officers, team representatives names, and addresses. **Circulation:** 400 ● Newsletter, 12/year. **Conventions/Meetings:** annual meet, for sports model wheelchairs (exhibits).

22837 ■ National Wheelchair Poolplayer Association (NWPA)

9651 Halekulani Dr.
Garden Grove, CA 92841-4911
Ph: (714)636-3371
Free: (866)636-3371
Fax: (714)636-3371
E-mail: jdolezal@cox.net
URL: http://www.nwpainc.org
Contact: Jeff Dolezal, Dir./Acting Pres.
Founded: 1994. **Members:** 400. **Membership Dues:** player/associate/non-player in U.S., $10 (annual) ● player/associate/non-player outside U.S., $15 (annual) ● life - player in U.S., $125 ● life - player outside U.S., $130 ● life - associate/non-player in U.S., $60 ● life - associate/non-player outside U.S., $65. **Multinational. Description:** Works to promote wheelchair pool. Provides opportunities for the physically disabled to participate in the cue sports. Works with other groups, organizations and tournament directors to update rules to include wheelchair players. **Telecommunication Services:** electronic mail, deadstrok1@aol.com. **Publications:** Newsletter. Alternate Formats: online.

22838 ■ National Wheelchair Softball Association (NWSA)

c/o Mike Wheaton, Commissioner
6000 W Floyd Ave., No. 110
Denver, CO 80227
Ph: (303)936-5587
E-mail: nwsainfo@yahoo.com
URL: http://www.wheelchairsoftball.com
Contact: Mike Wheaton, Commissioner
Founded: 1976. **Members:** 24. **Description:** Represents teams that are active in wheelchair softball competitions. Acts as governing agency for the promotion, interpretation, standardization, and continued growth of wheelchair softball. Coordinates efforts of member teams and encourages formation of new teams; protects the interests of members and enforces existing rules and regulations established by member teams. Conducts seminars on wheelchair softball and wheelchair sports; sponsors tournaments. Maintains hall of fame and compiles statistics. **Committees:** Classification; Hall of Fame; Rules; Website. **Conventions/Meetings:** annual meeting - always September.

22839 ■ North American Riding for the Handicapped Association (NARHA)

PO Box 33150
Denver, CO 80233
Ph: (303)452-1212
Free: (800)369-7433
Fax: (303)252-4610
E-mail: narha@narha.org
URL: http://www.narha.org
Contact: Sheila K. Dietrich, Exec. Dir.
Founded: 1969. **Members:** 5,900. **Membership Dues:** individual, $45 (annual) ● spirit club, $25 (annual) ● professional, $70 (annual) ● executive professional, $160 (annual) ● allied, $75 (annual) ● life, $1,500. **Staff:** 15. **Regional Groups:** 11. **National Groups:** 700. **Description:** Individuals and riding centers. Provides therapeutic riding for individuals with disabilities with good safety and proper care; offers appropriate training and certification for instructors working with the disabled. Provides educational programs. **Awards:** Adult Independent Rider Award. **Frequency:** annual. **Type:** recognition ● Professional Achievement Award. **Frequency:** annual. **Type:** recognition ● Therapy Horse Award. **Frequency:** annual. **Type:** recognition ● Volunteer Award. **Frequency:** annual. **Type:** recognition. **Sections:** Equine-Facilitated Mental Health Association. **Publications:** *EFMHA News*, 3/year. Newsletter. **Circulation:** 370 ● *NARHA News*, 8/year. **Price:** included in membership dues. **Circulation:** 4,300. **Advertising:** accepted. Alternate Formats: online ● *NARHA Strides*, quarterly. Magazine. **Price:** included in membership dues. **Circulation:** 4,300. **Advertising:** accepted. **Conventions/Meetings:** annual conference and meeting (exhibits) - always November.

22840 ■ One-Arm Dove Hunt Association (OADH)

PO Box 582
Olney, TX 76374
Ph: (940)564-8867
E-mail: 1armjack@brazosnet.com
URL: http://www.onearmdovehunt.com
Contact: Jack R. Northrup, Co-Founder
Founded: 1972. **Members:** 550. **Staff:** 2. **Description:** Hand or arm amputees who enjoy the sport of shotgun shooting; interested nonamputees. Works to help amputees accept their handicap and to provide fellowship and shooting competitions. Activities include dove hunts, One-Arm Tales, One-Arm Talent, pool Tournament, golf tournament, horseshoe tournament, and dove dinner. **Awards: Type:** recognition. **Publications:** Newsletter, annual. **Circulation:** 600. **Conventions/Meetings:** annual competition - always first weekend following Labor Day, Olney, TX.

22841 ■ Physically Challenged Golf Association (PCGA)

10 E View Dr.
Farmington, CT 06032
Ph: (860)676-2035
Fax: (860)676-2041
E-mail: pcga@townusa.com
URL: http://www.townusa.com/pcga
Contact: Brian A. Magna PT, Exec. Dir.
Founded: 1995. **Membership Dues:** active/associate, $15 (annual) ● golf/health professional, $25 (annual) ● facility, $75 (annual) ● corporate sponsor, $500-$5,000 (annual). **Multinational. Description:** Promotes the game of golf for the physically challenged. Conducts workshops, seminars and clinics for physically challenged golfers and healthcare and golf professionals. **Publications:** Newsletter, quarterly ● Membership Directory.

22842 ■ Praying Hands Ranches (PHR)

c/o Shirley A. Hanson, Exec. Dir.
4825 E Daley Cir.
Parker, CO 80138
Ph: (303)841-4043
Fax: (720)851-7679
E-mail: hansonphr@myawai.com
URL: http://www.prayinghandsranches.org
Contact: Shirley A. Hanson, Exec. Dir.
Founded: 1987. **Description:** Represents the interests of individuals committed to meeting the needs of mentally, emotionally and physically challenged children and adults in a therapeutic ranch environment. Strives to achieve rehabilitation using equine, horticultural, small animal therapies and peer tutor programs. **Programs:** Equine; Harness Driving; Hippotherapy; Horticultural Experience; Small Animal Experience; Troubled Youth.

22843 ■ Ski for Light (SFL)

1455 W Lake St.
Minneapolis, MN 55408
Ph: (612)827-3232
E-mail: info@sfl.org
URL: http://www.sfl.org
Contact: Larry Showalter, Pres.
Founded: 1975. **Regional Groups:** 9. **Nonmembership. Description:** Teaches blind, visually-impaired and mobility-impaired adults how to cross-country ski, in an atmosphere that encourages each participant to realize that the only true limitations to what they can accomplish in life are the limitations that they place on themselves. The organization conducts a week-long program once per year in varying locations, where upwards of 125 blind participants, 10 mobility-impaired participants, and 150 volunteer instructor guides join together for a week of learning, sharing and fun. **Libraries: Type:** reference. **Subjects:** skiing. **Awards:** Jan Haug Award. **Frequency:** annual. **Type:** recognition. **Recipient:** for new disabled skier who has shown real enthusiasm and potential for the sport of cross-country skiing ● **Type:** recognition. **Committees:** Regional Events; Ski for Light International Week. **Affiliated With:** Sons of Norway. **Formerly:** (1980) Ski for Light; (1983) HEALTHsports, Inc. **Publications:** *SFL Bulletin*, quarterly. Contains organizational news. **Price:** free. **Circulation:** 1,000 ● *Ski for Light Event Journal*, annual. Contains schedule of the international week and background information about the program. **Conventions/Meetings:** annual International Ski Event - meeting.

22844 ■ Special Olympics

1133 19th St. NW
Washington, DC 20036
Ph: (202)628-3630
Free: (800)700-8585
Fax: (202)824-0200
E-mail: info@specialolympics.org
URL: http://www.specialolympics.org
Contact: Mr. Bruce Pasternack, Pres./CEO
Founded: 1968. **Members:** 2,250,000. **Staff:** 130. **Budget:** $73,000,000. **Regional Groups:** 7. **State Groups:** 52. **Regional Groups:** 150. **Multinational. Description:** Changes lives by promoting understanding, acceptance and inclusion between people with and without intellectual disabilities. Through year-round sports training and athletic competition and other related programming for more than 2.25 million children and adults with intellectual disabilities in more than 150 countries, Special Olympics has created a model community that celebrates people's diverse gifts. Provides people with intellectual disabilities continuing opportunities to realize their potential, develop physical fitness, demonstrate courage and experience joy and friendship. **Awards:** Hero Award. **Frequency:** quarterly. **Type:** recognition. **Recipient:** for athletes who embody the spirit of the Special Olympics. **Councils:** International Advisory. **Programs:** Athlete Leadership; Healthy Athletes. **Publications:** *Special Olympics Annual Report*, annual. Includes a summary of the past year's program service accomplishments. Alternate Formats: online ● *Spirit*, quarterly. Magazine ● Also publishes informational brochures, guides, instructional manual, and list of state programs. **Conventions/Meetings:** quadrennial World Summer Games - competition - 2007 Oct. 10-19, Shanghai, People's Republic of China - **Avg. Attendance:** 7000.

22845 ■ U.S. Association for Blind Athletes (USABA)

33 N Indus. St.
Colorado Springs, CO 80903
Ph: (719)630-0422 (719)630-0610
Fax: (719)630-0616

E-mail: mlucas@usaba.org
URL: http://www.usaba.org
Contact: Mark Lucas, Exec. Dir.
Founded: 1976. **Members:** 3,000. **Membership Dues:** junior (below 21 years old), $25 (annual) ● adult (21 years old and above), $35 (annual) ● volunteer, $15 (annual) ● life, $200. **Staff:** 3. **Budget:** $550,000. **Regional Groups:** 4. **State Groups:** 49. **Description:** Visually impaired athletes; fully sighted physical educators, coaches, and special education teachers; interested volunteers. Aims to develop individual independence through sports opportunities and athletic competition. Promotes sports for the legally blind and visually impaired, organizes regional, national, and international competitions. Works with other international organizations to promote goodwill and independence through friendly competition; sports contested include alpine skiing, goalball, gymnastics, judo, Nordic skiing, powerlifting, speed skating, 5-side football, swimming, tandem cycling, track and field and wrestling. Sponsors coaches' training seminars, panel discussions, and training groups. Offers children's services; compiles statistics. **Awards:** Copland Scholarship. **Type:** grant. **Computer Services:** database. **Committees:** Athletes; Education and Mainstreaming; Junior Programs; Medical; Sports Technical. **Affiliated With:** American Alliance for Health, Physical Education, Recreation and Dance; International Blind Sports Federation; United States Olympic Committee. **Publications:** *Directory of Organization Representatives*, quarterly ● *USABA Agenda*, monthly. Includes information on upcoming events. ● *Vision*, quarterly. Magazine. Includes results of competitions and calendar of events. **Price:** included in membership dues. **Circulation:** 3,000. **Advertising:** accepted ● Also publishes programs and grant proposals.

22846 ■ United States Blind Golf Association (USBGA)
3094 Shamrock St. N
Tallahassee, FL 32309
Ph: (850)893-4511
Fax: (850)893-4511
E-mail: bob.andrews44@comcast.net
URL: http://www.blindgolf.com
Contact: Bob Andrews, Contact
Founded: 1953. **Members:** 145. **Membership Dues:** totally blind, $25 (annual) ● vision impaired, $15 (annual) ● support/coach, $10 (annual). **Staff:** 1. **Description:** Blind and vision impaired golfers who compete for a national championship and U.S. Open, and various other tournaments around the country and internationally. Tournaments raise funds for various blind charities; blind Junior Golf Program. **Publications:** *The Midnight Golfer*, semiannual. Newsletter. Includes information on blind golf; some international coverage. **Price:** free. **Circulation:** 300 ● Also provides learning packets and information on blind golf. **Conventions/Meetings:** annual National Championship - competition.

22847 ■ U.S. Deaf Cycling Association (USDCA)
c/o Bobby Skedsmo, Sec.-Treas.
247 Jack London Ct.
Pittsburg, CA 94565-3661
Ph: (925)473-9824
E-mail: usdeafcycling@mindspring.com
URL: http://www.usdeafcycling.org
Contact: Beverly Buchanan, Pres.
Founded: 1975. **Members:** 29. **Membership Dues:** general, $5 (annual). **Staff:** 5. **Budget:** $350. **Regional Groups:** 2. **Description:** Promotes recreational and competitive cycling among the deaf and hearing impaired in the U.S. Conducts educational programs; sponsors competitions. **Affiliated With:** USA Deaf Sports Federation. **Publications:** *Breakaway*, annual. Newsletter. Features club activities and special features. **Price:** $1.00. **Circulation:** 30. **Advertising:** accepted.

22848 ■ United States Deaf Ski and Snowboard Association (USDSSA)
c/o Edward Ingham, Pres.
709 8th St. NE
Washington, DC 20002

E-mail: president@usdssa.org
URL: http://www.usdssa.org
Contact: Edward Ingham, Pres.
Founded: 1968. **Members:** 350. **Regional Groups:** 8. **Description:** Promotes recreational and competitive skiing among the deaf and hearing impaired in the U.S. Provides deaf skiers with benefits, activities, and opportunities that will increase their enjoyment of the sport. Encourages ski racing among the deaf and sponsors national and regional races for deaf skiers, including the U.S.A. National Deaf Alpine and Nordic Ski Championships. Assists in the selection, organization, and training of the United States Deaf Ski Teams for international competition such as the World Winter Games for the Deaf. Presents awards; maintains hall of fame; offers children's services. **Telecommunication Services:** teletype, (435)752-2702. **Committees:** Alpine Ski Tryout; Cross Country; Nordic; Speed Skating. **Affiliated With:** USA Deaf Sports Federation. **Publications:** Newsletter, 3/year. **Price:** available to members only. **Conventions/Meetings:** biennial Ski Week - competition, includes races (exhibits).

22849 ■ U.S. Flag Football for the Deaf (USFFD)
PO Box 1453
Silver Spring, MD 20915
E-mail: commissioner@usffd.org
URL: http://www.usffd.org
Contact: Alex Calogar, Commissioner
Founded: 1984. **Members:** 500. **Membership Dues:** individual, $30 (annual). **Staff:** 6. **Budget:** $3,000. **Description:** Hearing-impaired individuals. Organizes flag football games to be played every year across the nation. Compiles statistics and maintains hall of fame. **Libraries:** **Type:** reference. **Holdings:** clippings. **Publications:** *National Sports Organization - AAAD*, bimonthly. Newsletter. **Conventions/Meetings:** annual meeting ● annual USSFD National Championships - competition - 2007 Nov. 2-4, Fremont, CA.

22850 ■ Universal Wheelchair Football Association (UWFA)
c/o John Kraimer
Univ. of Cincinnati
Raymond Walters Coll.
9555 Plainfield Rd.
Cincinnati, OH 45236-1096
Ph: (513)792-8625
Fax: (513)792-8624
E-mail: john.kraimer@uc.edu
URL: http://www.nyc.gov/html/sports/html/uwfa.html
Contact: John Kraimer, Contact
Description: Provides opportunities for the physically disabled to participate in football. Presents the rules of Universal Wheelchair Football. **Telecommunication Services:** teletype, (513)745-8300.

22851 ■ USA Deaf Sports Federation (USADSF)
102 N Krohn Pl.
Sioux Falls, SD 57103-1800
Ph: (605)367-5760 (605)367-5761
Fax: (605)367-4979
E-mail: homeoffice@usdeafsports.org
URL: http://www.usdeafsports.org
Contact: Lawrence Fleischer, Pres.
Founded: 1945. **Members:** 4,000. **Membership Dues:** individual, $16 (annual) ● agency, $40 (annual). **Staff:** 1. **Budget:** $200,000. **Regional Groups:** 8. **State Groups:** 50. **Local Groups:** 200. **National Groups:** 20. **Description:** Provides year-round training to athletes and coordinates athletic competition in a variety of sports at the state, regional, national, and international level. **Libraries:** **Type:** reference. **Subjects:** sports for deaf people. **Awards:** Art Kruger Award. **Frequency:** annual. **Type:** recognition. **Recipient:** for leadership and continuous participation, support and contribution in the federation over an extended period of time ● Athlete of the Year Award. **Frequency:** annual. **Type:** recognition ● Executive Board Award. **Frequency:** annual. **Type:** recognition. **Recipient:** to a deserving individual, corporation or organization providing significant contribution towards

the enhancement of the goals of the federation ● President's Award. **Frequency:** annual. **Type:** recognition. **Telecommunication Services:** TDD, (888)-735-5906. **Affiliated With:** United States Olympic Committee. **Formerly:** (1999) American Athletic Association for the Deaf. **Publications:** *Deaf Sports Review*, annual. Magazine. ISSN: 1059-3063. **Circulation:** 1,000. **Advertising:** accepted ● *USADSF Bulletin*, quarterly. ISSN: 1528-6681. **Circulation:** 1,000. **Advertising:** accepted ● Newsletter. Alternate Formats: online. **Conventions/Meetings:** annual general assembly (exhibits).

22852 ■ Wheelchair Motorcycle Association (WMA)
101 Torrey St.
Brockton, MA 02301
Ph: (508)583-8614
Contact: Dr. Eli Factor, Pres.
Founded: 1975. **Members:** 1,000. **Local Groups:** 1. **Description:** Handicapped persons confined to wheelchairs interested in rediscovering the outdoors; institutional and individual supporters. Researches, develops, and tests off-road vehicles for quadriplegics and other severely handicapped persons. Has audiovisual program showing the use of cycles by the handicapped. **Publications:** *Climb for Independence*, quarterly. Newsletter. **Price:** included in membership dues.

22853 ■ Wheelchair Sports, USA (WSUSA)
PO Box 5266
Kendall Park, NJ 08824
Ph: (732)422-4546
Fax: (732)422-4546
E-mail: wsusa@aol.com
URL: http://www.wsusa.org
Contact: Barbara Chambers, Chair
Founded: 1958. **Members:** 2,000. **Membership Dues:** athlete, coach, patron, $35 (annual) ● club, $200 (annual). **Staff:** 1. **Regional Groups:** 14. **Description:** Men and women athletes with significant permanent neuromuscular-skeletal disability (spinal cord disorder, poliomyelitis, or amputation) who compete in various amateur sports events in wheelchairs. Members compete in regional events and in the annual National Wheelchair Games, which include competitions in track and field (including pentathlon), swimming, archery, shooting, fencing, table tennis, weightlifting, basketball, and rugby. Compiles statistics; maintains hall of fame and speakers' bureau; sponsors competition. **Committees:** Development; International Games Preparation; International Relations; Juniors; Sports Medicine and Science. **Formerly:** (1994) National Wheelchair Athletic Association. **Publications:** *Constitution and By-Laws*, biennial. Newsletter. **Price:** $10.00 for 4 issues; $17.00 for 8 issues. **Circulation:** 3,000. **Advertising:** accepted ● *WSUSA Newsletter*, quarterly. **Price:** $10.00/year. **Advertising:** accepted ● Also publishes rule books. **Conventions/Meetings:** annual Delegate Assembly - meeting - always fall.

Disc Sports

22854 ■ Freestyle Players Association (FPA)
864 Grand Ave.
Box 475
San Diego, CA 92109
E-mail: info@freestyledisc.org
URL: http://www.freestyledisc.org
Contact: Liza Hunrichs, Exec. Dir.
Founded: 1978. **Members:** 150. **Membership Dues:** jammer, $10-$20 (annual) ● platinum, $100 (annual) ● competitor, $30-$35 (annual). **Multinational. Description:** Freestyle disc players and manufacturers. Organizes freestyle competitions; creates competition guidelines. **Awards:** Lowry-Coddington Award. **Frequency:** annual. **Type:** trophy. **Recipient:** for freestyle Frisbee enthusiasts ● **Type:** monetary. **Recipient:** for competitors at events ● Most Improved Player. **Frequency:** annual. **Type:** recognition ● Rookie of the Year. **Frequency:** annual. **Type:** recognition. **Publications:** *FPA Forum*, quarterly.

Newsletter. Alternate Formats: online ● *Zen and the Art of Frisbee Freestyle*. Video. **Price:** $15.95. **Conventions/Meetings:** annual meeting ● periodic meeting, held at tournaments.

22855 ■ International Disc Dog Handlers' Association (IDDHA)
1690 Julius Bridge Rd.
Ball Ground, GA 30107
Ph: (770)735-6200
Fax: (770)735-6287
E-mail: iddha@aol.com
URL: http://www.iddha.com
Contact: Greg Tresan, VP/Exec. Dir.
Membership Dues: life, $150 ● associate, $20 (annual). **Description:** Promotes, advertises, and develops the disc dog as a canine athlete. Sets standards for competition, oversees activities. Maintains records of achievement. Cooperates with other organizations with similar purpose. **Conventions/Meetings:** Canine Disc World Championships - competition.

22856 ■ Riders of the Wind, The Field Events Player's Association (ROW/FEPA)
PO Box 43
Wallops Island, VA 23337
Ph: (757)824-1642
Fax: (757)824-1851
E-mail: snapconger@earthlink.net
Contact: Michael D. Conger, Dir.
Founded: 1980. **Members:** 50. **Membership Dues:** open, $5 (annual) ● sponsor, $100 (annual). **Description:** Frisbee players interested in frisbee as an educational, recreational, and sporting activity. Promotes the advancement of physical and mental fitness by playing frisbee. Provides speakers for sports banquets. Sponsors local, regional, national, and international events. Affiliated with the World Flying Disc Federation (WFDF). **Awards:** Pegasus Award. **Frequency:** annual. **Type:** recognition. **Recipient:** to the best U.S. player in field events play. **Computer Services:** database, world records. **Committees:** International. **Publications:** *The Row*, annual. Directory ● *Tradewinds*, 5/year. **Conventions/Meetings:** annual conference ● annual congress (exhibits).

22857 ■ Ultimate Players Association (UPA)
4730 Table Mesa Dr., Ste.J-200
Boulder, CO 80305
Ph: (303)447-3472
Free: (800)872-4384
Fax: (303)447-3483
E-mail: ed@upa.org
URL: http://www.upa.org
Contact: Sandie Hammerly, Exec. Dir.
Founded: 1979. **Members:** 15,600. **Membership Dues:** regular, $40 (annual) ● college, $30 (annual) ● youth (high school or lower), $20 (annual) ● life, $750. **Staff:** 5. **Budget:** $600,000. **Regional Groups:** 6. **State Groups:** 50. **Local Groups:** 500. **Description:** Serves to promote and support the Sport of Ultimate, a team flying disc sport combining the elements of basketball, football, and soccer. Holds championships in multiple divisions and coordinates outreach activities for all levels of play. **Libraries: Type:** reference. **Holdings:** archival material, articles, papers, photographs. **Subjects:** Frisbee, flying disc sports, ultimate. **Awards:** UPA National Championships. **Frequency:** annual. **Type:** recognition. **Recipient:** for sectional, regional, national competition and sportsmanship ● UPA Spirit of the Game Awards. **Frequency:** annual. **Type:** recognition. **Recipient:** for sectional, regional, national competition and sportsmanship. **Telecommunication Services:** electronic bulletin board. **Divisions:** College Open; College Women; High School Girls, Boys; International; Masters; Mixed; Open; Women. **Publications:** *The Official Rules of Ultimate*, annual. Pamphlet. **Circulation:** 15,000. **Advertising:** accepted ● *UPA Championships*. Videos ● *UPA Newsletter*, quarterly. Contains tournament results from U.S. and overseas, club directory, rules discussions, regional reports and membership benefits information. **Price:** included in membership dues. **Circulation:** 15,600. **Advertis-**

ing: accepted. **Conventions/Meetings:** annual Club Sectional, Regional, National Championships - competition - usually September/October ● annual Junior and College Sectional, Regional, National Championships - competition - usually late April-May.

22858 ■ U.S. Disc Sports Association (USDS)
c/o World Flying Disc Federation
8550 Tujunga Valley St.
Sunland, CA 91040
Ph: (818)353-6339
E-mail: verish@kelvin.jpl.nasa.gov
URL: http://www.cs.rochester.edu/u/ferguson/
ultimate/wfdf/wfdf-about.html
Contact: Beth Verish, Dir.
Founded: 1983. **Members:** 4,500. **State Groups:** 180. **Description:** Flying-disc clubs. (Flying-discs are Frisbees and other discs used in games and tournaments.) Promotes flying-disc play in the U.S; sanctions flying-disc events. Encourages communication between state and U.S. local flying-disc clubs and teams; maintains U.S. flying-disc club registry and official U.S. flying-disc records. Obtains discs for members at discount prices. **Publications:** *U.S. Disc Club Directory*, annual. **Conventions/Meetings:** annual congress, held in conjunction with WFDF.

Diving

22859 ■ Association of Dive Program Administrators (ADPA)
c/o Dick Blankfein, Membership Dir.
New York Aquarium Surf Ave.
W 8th St.
Brooklyn, NY 11224
E-mail: rblankfein@wcs.org
URL: http://www.adso.org
Contact: Derek Smith, Pres.
Membership Dues: individual, $50 (annual). **Description:** Provides a professional forum for the exchange of ideas, information, support and solutions within the community of diving program administrators. Develops a network to facilitate regular and convenient communication between diving programs. Assists and encourages diving programs in maximizing their potential for public education, aquatic conservation efforts and preservation of the environment. Supports and assists diving program administrators in meeting the common challenges of maximizing diver safety, effective use of human resources and professional development. **Telecommunication Services:** electronic mail, gwittken@pdza.org ● electronic mail, hbourbon@neaq.org.

22860 ■ Divers Alert Network (DAN)
Peter B. Bennett Ctr.
6 W Colony Pl.
Durham, NC 27705
Ph: (919)684-2948
Free: (800)446-2671
Fax: (919)490-6630
E-mail: dan@diversalertnetwork.org
URL: http://www.diversalertnetwork.org
Contact: Peter B. Bennett, Founder
Founded: 1980. **Members:** 200,000. **Membership Dues:** individual, $29 (annual) ● family, $44 (annual). **Staff:** 70. **Budget:** $15,000,000. **Languages:** English, French, German, Italian, Portuguese, Spanish. **Description:** Promotes recreational scuba diving safety and health. Develops emergency oxygen equipment and training. **Awards:** Dan/Rolex Award. **Frequency:** annual. **Type:** recognition. **Recipient:** for individual who makes significant contribution to scuba diving safety and health. **Computer Services:** Mailing lists, of members. **Telecommunication Services:** hotline, 24-hour diving emergency, (919)-684-8111. **Publications:** *Alert Diver*, bimonthly. Journal. **Circulation:** 140,000. **Advertising:** accepted ● Annual Report, annual. Alternate Formats: online ● Catalog. Alternate Formats: online.

22861 ■ International Association of Nitrox and Technical Divers (IANTD)
1545 NE 104th St.
Miami Shores, FL 33138-2665
Ph: (305)754-1027

Fax: (509)355-1297
E-mail: iantd@iantd.com
URL: http://www.iantd.com
Contact: Tom Mount, Chm.
Multinational. Description: Fosters openness and development of individual diver responsibilities through aggressive skill refinement and experience in the water. Provides a standard of care for instruction in the diving community. Shares procedures, techniques, and operational methods with divers seeking to expand their diving experiences.

22862 ■ United States Apnea Association (USAA)
87-3184 EA Rd.
Captain Cook, HI 96704
E-mail: matt-bel@hawaii.rr.com
URL: http://www.usaa.freedivers.com
Contact: Matthew Briseno, Dir./Pres.
Membership Dues: regular, $25 (annual) ● associate individual/associate business, $100 (annual). **Multinational. Description:** Promotes and develops freediving or breath-hold diving as an amateur sport, both recreationally and competitively within the United States and abroad. Provides information, education and events to further grow the sport of freediving. **Publications:** Annual Report, annual ● Newsletter. **Price:** included in membership dues. Alternate Formats: online.

22863 ■ United States Professional Diving Coaches Association (USPDCA)
PO Box 268
Milford, OH 45150
E-mail: uspdca@cinci.rr.com
URL: http://www.uspdca.org
Contact: Curt Wilson, Pres.
Founded: 1983. **Members:** 261. **Membership Dues:** regular, $40 (annual). **Description:** Conducts educational programs; offers placement services. **Libraries: Type:** reference. **Holdings:** video recordings. **Subjects:** Olympic diving coverage. **Publications:** Newsletter, bimonthly. Includes membership directory. **Price:** included in membership dues. **Circulation:** 280. **Advertising:** accepted ● Articles. **Conventions/Meetings:** meeting - 3/year.

22864 ■ USA Diving
201 S Capitol Ave., Ste.430
Indianapolis, IN 46225
Ph: (317)237-5252
Fax: (317)237-5257
E-mail: linda.paul@usadiving.org
URL: http://www.usadiving.org
Contact: Debbie Hesse, CEO
Founded: 1981. **Members:** 10,000. **Membership Dues:** athlete (junior, master, senior), family, official, $75 (annual) ● individual, $50 (annual) ● coach, $150 (annual) ● limited athlete, $15 (annual) ● novice athlete, $25 (annual). **Staff:** 8. **Local Groups:** 42. **Description:** Athletes, coaches, officials, and interested individuals. Promotes diving as a sport; conducts diving programs at all levels of competitive ability from beginner to Olympic. Conducts research in sports sciences; compiles statistics. Plans include seminars on topics within the sports sciences area. **Telecommunication Services:** electronic mail, usdiving@usadiving.org. **Affiliated With:** U.S. Aquatic Sports. **Publications:** *Inside USA Diving*, quarterly. Magazine. **Price:** $10.00/year in U.S.; $35.00/year outside U.S. ● *U.S. Diving Directory*, annual ● *U.S. Diving Safety Manual*. Manuals ● Brochures ● Also publishes rule book. **Conventions/Meetings:** annual United States Aquatic Sports - convention (exhibits).

22865 ■ World Diving Coaches Association (WDCA)
Address Unknown since 2007
Founded: 1968. **Members:** 120. **Membership Dues:** olympiad (4 years), $100 (annual). **Description:** Springboard and platform diving coaches and officials. Objectives are to: promote understanding and friendship among diving coaches worldwide; study the needs of world diving; revise rules and procedures necessary for advancement of the sport. Conducts educational and research programs for the enrich-

ment of competitive diving; sponsors periodic competitions. Maintains speakers' bureau; compiles statistics. Plans to develop a library. **Libraries: Type:** not open to the public. **Subjects:** diving, beginning to Olympic training on demand. **Awards:** Sammy Lee Award. **Frequency:** quadrennial. **Type:** recognition. **Recipient:** to the person who has done the most for the sport of diving throughout the world during his life time. **Computer Services:** Mailing lists. **Publications:** Newsletter, 3-4 year. **Advertising:** not accepted. **Conventions/Meetings:** biennial conference and symposium ● periodic meeting.

Dog

22866 ■ International Weight Pull Association (IWPA)

c/o Rodney Martin, Membership Chm.
3407 17th Ave.
Evans, CO 80620
Ph: (970)339-9264
E-mail: info@iwpa.net
URL: http://www.iwpa.net
Contact: Robbie Reed, Pres.

Founded: 1984. **Members:** 300. **Membership Dues:** individual, $40 (annual) ● family, $45 (annual). **Multinational. Description:** Promotes the sport of dog pulling and the working heritage of all dogs. Promotes a program to keep dogs in good physical condition with a constructive outlet for canine competition. **Computer Services:** Information services, dog pull resources. **Publications:** Newsletter. **Price:** included in membership dues. Alternate Formats: online.

22867 ■ National Retriever Club

4379 S Howell Ave., Ste.17
Milwaukee, WI 53207-5053
Ph: (414)481-2760
Fax: (414)481-2743
E-mail: retrievernews@mindspring.com
URL: http://www.working-retriever.com/nrc
Contact: Tony Snow, Sec.-Treas.

Description: Club for owners of working retrievers.

22868 ■ North American Dog Agility Council (NADAC)

11522 S Hwy. 3
Cataldo, ID 83810
E-mail: info@nadac.com
URL: http://www.nadac.com
Contact: Christopher Nelson, Contact

Founded: 1993. **Membership Dues:** associate, $15 (annual) ● associate, $35 (triennial) ● associate, $50 (quinquennial). **Multinational. Description:** Promotes dog agility as an athletic and community sport. Encourages the public to become involved in activities with pets. Promotes responsible pet ownership. Conducts agility dog training and competitions. Sanctions agility trials sponsored by affiliated clubs. **Telecommunication Services:** electronic mail, member@nadac.com. **Publications:** *Exhibitor's Handbook.* **Price:** included in membership dues. Alternate Formats: online ● *Trial Chairperson/Trial Secretary's Handbook.* Alternate Formats: online.

22869 ■ United States Dog Agility Association (USDAA)

PO Box 850955
Richardson, TX 75085
Ph: (972)487-2200
Fax: (972)272-4404
E-mail: info@usdaa.com
URL: http://www.usdaa.com
Contact: Kenneth Tatsch, Pres.

Founded: 1986. **Description:** Promotes dog agility as an athletic, spectator and community sport. Offers a junior handler program for school-age children and their pets. Teaches responsible pet ownership. **Awards:** Agility Top Ten. **Frequency:** annual. **Type:** recognition. **Recipient:** for the best competitors of the year. **Boards:** Regulations and Competition. **Committees:** Event Administration; Hall of Fame; Public Relation and Communication.

22870 ■ United States Mondioring Association (USMRA)

c/o Ann Putegnat, Sec.-Treas.
400 Hidden Oak
Bulverde, TX 78163
Ph: (830)438-3327 (209)892-3114
E-mail: annwp3@yahoo.com
URL: http://www.usmondioring.org
Contact: Augusta Farley, Pres.

Membership Dues: general, $50 (annual). **Description:** Promotes, organizes and administers in the USA the international working dog sport known as mondioring. Promotes sportsmanlike conduct, and fair and humane training at all dog sport activities. Provides opportunities for members to achieve training and trialing goals in mondioring. Develops programs and activities to educate the public about mondioring and the working dog sports. **Telecommunication Services:** electronic mail, ducielroug@aol.com. **Publications:** Newsletter. **Price:** included in membership dues.

22871 ■ World Canine Freestyle Organization (WCFO)

PO Box 350122
Brooklyn, NY 11235-2525
Ph: (718)332-8336
Fax: (718)646-2686
E-mail: wcfodogs@aol.com
URL: http://www.worldcaninefreestyle.org
Contact: Patie Ventre, Founder/Pres.

Founded: 1999. **Membership Dues:** individual, family 4H (up to 3 members), $40 (annual) ● WCFO club, $30 (annual) ● junior, $25 (annual) ● 4H junior, $20 (annual) ● family (up to 3 members), $65 (annual) ● WCFO club family, $48 (annual) ● club (based on number of members), $150-$250 (annual). **Multinational. Description:** Promotes the joys and fun of responsible pet ownership through musical canine freestyle, both as a sport and an entertainment medium. Supports the growth of freestyle on a global basis. Supports and funds the seeking of liaisons with other organizations globally to create international titling and non-titling events. **Publications:** Brochure. Alternate Formats: online ● Books ● Videos.

Dog Racing

22872 ■ American Greyhound Track Operators Association (AGTOA)

Palm Beach Kennel Club
1111 N Cong. Ave.
West Palm Beach, FL 33409
Ph: (561)688-5799
Fax: (801)754-2404
E-mail: feedback@agtoa.com
URL: http://www.agtoa.com
Contact: Richard Winning, Pres.

Founded: 1946. **Members:** 38. **Staff:** 2. **Budget:** $350,000. **State Groups:** 19. **Description:** Owners and operators of Greyhound dog racing pari-mutuel tracks. Promotes uniform policies and activities in relation to the furtherance of Greyhound racing as a sport and as a business enterprise. Compiles statistics; supports hall of fame. **Committees:** Racing Education Foundation. **Publications:** *Greyhound Dog Racing in America,* annual ● *Inside Track,* monthly. Newsletter ● *Summary of State Parimutuel Tax Structures,* annual ● *Track Facts,* annual. Membership Directory. **Price:** free. **Advertising:** accepted. **Conventions/Meetings:** annual conference - usually March.

22873 ■ Greyhound Racing Association of America (GRA/America)

110 W 9th St., No. 813
Wilmington, DE 19801
Free: (800)372-3047
Fax: (443)946-0683

E-mail: admin@gra-america.org
URL: http://www.gra-america.org
Contact: Ron Hevener, Co-Founder/Pres./CEO

Founded: 2002. **Membership Dues:** adult, $35 (annual) ● joint, $50 (annual) ● corporate, $150 (annual) ● life (adult), $750. **Description:** Promotes, protects and enhances the sport of greyhound racing and the greyhound industry through education, example and media for the benefit of the members, fans, supporters and the greyhound racing dogs. **Computer Services:** Information services, greyhound racing resources. **Committees:** Greyhound Adoption. **Programs:** Approved Adoption Group.

22874 ■ International Federation of Sleddog Sports (IFSS)

c/o Tim White, Pres.
881 County Rd. 14
Grand Marais, MN 55604
Ph: (218)387-2712
E-mail: twhite@boreal.org
URL: http://www.sleddogsport.com
Contact: Tim White, Pres.

Founded: 1986. **Members:** 26. **Multinational. Description:** National and international groups representing sled dog racers. Aims to promote public interest in sled dog sports and to integrate them into the mainstream of recognized sporting events; to collaborate with organizations having as their objectives the promotion of sled dog sports; to strive for the uniform development of sled dog sports worldwide; to maintain authority and autonomy of its members; to effectuate the World Championships and other world events. Works to receive the International Olympic Committee's recognition of the sport; organized a showcase event prior to the opening of the 1988 Winter Olympics in Calgary, Canada, in which mushers from around the world competed in an international event for the first time. Organizes and sponsors races. **Affiliated With:** International Sled Dog Racing Association. **Conventions/Meetings:** biennial meeting.

22875 ■ International Sled Dog Racing Association (ISDRA)

c/o Dave Steele, Exec. Dir.
22702 Rebel Rd.
Merrifield, MN 56465
Ph: (218)765-4297
Fax: (218)765-3246
E-mail: dsteele@brainerd.net
URL: http://www.isdra.org
Contact: Dave Steele, Exec. Dir.

Founded: 1966. **Members:** 1,000. **Membership Dues:** individual in U.S., $35 (annual) ● individual in Canada, $40 (annual) ● associate in U.S., $25 (annual) ● associate in Canada, $30 (annual) ● family in U.S., $15 (annual) ● family in Canada, $18 (annual) ● organization, $100 (annual). **Staff:** 5. **Budget:** $55,000. **Regional Groups:** 13. **National Groups:** 42. **Description:** Serves the International Sled Dog Racing community, providing rules, standards, sanctioning programs, points systems, software for running sled dog events, standards for animal welfare and many other services. **Libraries: Type:** reference. **Holdings:** archival material. **Awards:** Point Championship Medals. **Frequency:** annual. **Type:** recognition. **Computer Services:** database ● mailing lists. **Committees:** Animal Welfare; Ethics; Junior Sled Dog Racing; Long Distance Racing; Race Rules; Race Sanctioning; Statistics; Weight Pulls. **Publications:** *Dog & Driver,* bimonthly. Magazine. **Price:** included in membership dues. **Advertising:** accepted. **Conventions/Meetings:** annual meeting (exhibits).

22876 ■ Lakes Region Sled Dog Club (LRSDC)

PO Box 382
Laconia, NH 03247
Ph: (603)524-4314
Fax: (603)527-0897

E-mail: lyman@lrsdc.org
URL: http://www.lrsdc.org
Contact: James Lyman, Pres.
Founded: 1957. **Members:** 50. **Membership Dues:** $10 (annual). **Description:** Persons interested in promoting the sport of sled dog racing throughout the U.S. and Canada. **Awards: Frequency:** annual. **Type:** recognition. **Supersedes:** Laconia Sled Dog Club. **Conventions/Meetings:** annual World Championship Sled Dog Derby - competition.

Drag Racing

22877 ■ National Electric Drag Racing Association (NEDRA)
3200 Dutton Ave., No. 220
Santa Rosa, CA 95407
E-mail: info@nedra.com
URL: http://www.nedra.com
Contact: Brian Hall, Pres.
Membership Dues: regular, $35 (annual) ● corporate, $500 (annual) ● instructor, $35 (annual) ● student, $5 (annual) ● life, $200. **Description:** Increases awareness of electric vehicle performance. Encourages advances in electric vehicle technology through competition. Sanctions safe, silent and exciting electric vehicle drag racing events. **Publications:** *NEDRA Rulebook.* Handbook.

Falconry

22878 ■ North American Falconers Association (NAFA)
c/o Lisa Cherry, Corresponding Sec.
37362 Pourroy Rd.
Winchester, CA 92596-9673
E-mail: nafainfo@n-a-f-a.org
URL: http://www.n-a-f-a.org
Contact: Darryl A. Perkins, Pres.
Founded: 1961. **Members:** 2,800. **Membership Dues:** regular, associate, $35 (annual) ● foreign, $50 (annual). **State Groups:** 33. **Description:** Individuals interested in raptors (birds of prey) and falconry. Promotes scientific study of the raptorial species, their care, welfare, and training; encourages conservation of birds of prey and appreciation of their value in nature; urges recognition of falconry as a legal field sport. Creates North American Peregrine Foundation to promote research in captive breeding of the peregrine falcon and to reintroduce it into native breeding grounds. **Committees:** Conservation; Legal; Technical Advisory. **Affiliated With:** National Rifle Association of America; National Wildlife Federation. **Publications:** *Hawk Chalk,* quarterly. Newsletter. **Price:** available to members only ● Journal, annual. Includes directory. **Conventions/Meetings:** annual Field Meet - meeting (exhibits) - always Thanksgiving week ● annual meeting and meet.

Fencing

22879 ■ Association for Historical Fencing (AHF)
PO Box 2013
Secaucus, NJ 07096-2013
E-mail: secretary@ahfi.org
URL: http://www.ahfi.org
Contact: Maestro Ramon Martinez, Pres.
Membership Dues: individual, associate, professional, $35 (annual) ● institutional, $100 (annual) ● life, $500. **Multinational. Description:** Seeks to preserve the teachings of classical and historical fencing. Raises public awareness of classical and historical fencing. Ensures the availability of qualified masters and instructors in the arts of classical and historical fencing. Promotes the growth of fencing schools and academies. Disseminates knowledge and basic factual materials about classical and historical fencing. **Computer Services:** Information services, classical and historical fencing resources ● information services, tournament rules. **Projects:**

Capo Ferro Translation. **Publications:** *Estafilade,* quarterly. Newsletter. Alternate Formats: online.

22880 ■ Intercollegiate Fencing Association (IFA)
c/o Eastern College Athletic Conference
1311 Craigville Beach Rd.
Centerville, MA 02632
Ph: (508)771-5060
Fax: (508)771-9486
E-mail: sbamford@ecac.org
URL: http://www.ecac.org/league/ifa.asp
Contact: Rudy Keeling, Interim Commissioner
Founded: 1897. **Members:** 12. **Description:** Colleges with men's fencing teams. Establishes rules of competition. **Awards: Type:** recognition. **Recipient:** for team and individual contests in epee, saber, and foil fencing. **Affiliated With:** Eastern Collegiate Hockey Association. **Conventions/Meetings:** competition - usually February or March ● annual meeting.

22881 ■ United States Fencing Association (USFA)
1 Olympic Plz.
Colorado Springs, CO 80909-5780
Ph: (719)866-4511
Fax: (719)632-5737
E-mail: info@usfencing.org
URL: http://www.usfencing.org
Contact: Michael Massik, Exec. Dir.
Founded: 1891. **Members:** 17,000. **Membership Dues:** junior, senior, coach, veteran (competitive), $50 (annual) ● junior, senior, coach, veteran (competitive), $130 (triennial) ● parent associate, associate, coach associate (noncompetitive), $40 (annual) ● life, $1,200 ● family, $100 (annual). **Staff:** 10. **Budget:** $1,900,000. **Regional Groups:** 10. **State Groups:** 66. **Description:** Amateur fencers. Conducts local, national, and international fencing competitions and selects Pan American, World University, World Championship, and Olympic teams. Conducts junior training camps, regional coaches seminars, and annual national coaches' college. Sponsors educational activities. **Commissions:** Medical; Officials; Technical. **Committees:** International Selection; Legal; Media Tools; National Training; Tournament; Training and Development. **Programs:** Junior Development. **Affiliated With:** United States Olympic Committee. **Formerly:** (1981) Amateur Fencers League of American. **Publications:** *American Fencing,* quarterly. Magazine. Includes coverage of the sport of fencing. **Price:** included in membership dues; $16.00 /year for nonmembers; $28.00 /year for nonmembers outside U.S. ISSN: 0002-8436. **Circulation:** 10,000. **Advertising:** accepted. Alternate Formats: microform ● *National Newsletter,* quarterly ● Booklets. Contains educational information. ● Also publishes official rules book. **Conventions/Meetings:** annual National Championships - competition - always June/July.

22882 ■ United States Fencing Coaches Association (USFCA)
c/o Don Badowski, Sec.
138 E Racine Pl.
Mundelein, IL 60060
Ph: (847)444-7811
E-mail: donq@totheescrime.org
URL: http://www.usfca.org/usfca
Contact: Arnold Mercado, Chm.
Founded: 1941. **Members:** 350. **Membership Dues:** associate, $35 (annual) ● moniteur, prevost, master, $50 (annual) ● life, $500. **Staff:** 1. **Description:** Professional society of fencing teachers and coaches and others with an avocational interest in fencing. Works to promote fencing and conduct clinics and research programs. Offers examination for accreditation as instructor, Prevost D'Armes and Fencing master. Maintains hall of fame. **Awards:** All-American (1st and 2nd teams) Award. **Frequency:** annual. **Type:** recognition. **Recipient:** for NCAA performance of athlete ● Coach of the Year Award. **Frequency:** annual. **Type:** recognition. **Recipient:** for outstanding coach. **Boards:** Certification and Accreditation. **Committees:** Amendments; Awards; Publicity. **Affiliated With:** National Collegiate Athletic Association. **For-**

merly: (1981) National Fencing Coaches Association of America. **Publications:** *Swordmaster,* quarterly. Newsletter. **Price:** included in membership dues. **Advertising:** accepted. **Conventions/Meetings:** annual meeting and general assembly ● workshop.

Field Hockey

22883 ■ National Field Hockey Coaches Association (NFHCA)
11921 Meadow Ridge Terr.
Glen Allen, VA 23059
Ph: (804)364-8700
Fax: (804)364-5467
E-mail: jjgoodr@attglobal.net
URL: http://eteamz.active.com/nfhca
Contact: Jennifer J. Goodrich, Exec. Dir.
Membership Dues: head coach (division I/II/III), $150-$200 (annual) ● assistant coach (division I/II/III), $75-$100 (annual) ● high school (head coach and assistant coach), $100 (annual) ● junior high school head coach, club coach, official, administrator, friend, sponsor, $50 (annual) ● junior high school assistant coach, $25 (annual) ● life, $300. **Description:** Stimulates the professional development of coaching leadership within the sport of field hockey. Fosters and promotes the growth of the sport of field hockey. Facilitates public and professional understanding and appreciation of the importance and value of the sport of field hockey. **Awards:** Dita/NFHCA High School Coach of the Year. **Frequency:** annual. **Type:** recognition. **Recipient:** to the outstanding high school coach of the year ● National Academic Squad and Team Award. **Frequency:** annual. **Type:** recognition. **Recipient:** to the outstanding academic squad and team ● NFHCA Hall of Fame. **Frequency:** annual. **Type:** recognition. **Recipient:** to individuals who have made outstanding contributions to the sport of field hockey through their coaching career ● NFHCA Junior Hockey Award. **Frequency:** annual. **Type:** recognition. **Recipient:** for significant contribution to the maintenance and development of a junior hockey program. **Computer Services:** Online services, message boards. **Programs:** Open Collegiate Practice Day. **Conventions/Meetings:** annual convention.

22884 ■ U.S. Field Hockey Association (USFHA)
1 Olympic Plz.
Colorado Springs, CO 80909
Ph: (719)866-4567
Fax: (719)632-0979
E-mail: usfha@usfieldhockey.com
URL: http://www.usfieldhockey.com
Contact: Ms. Sheila Walker, Exec. Dir.
Founded: 1921. **Members:** 12,000. **Membership Dues:** youth (under 12 years old), $25 (annual) ● youth (under 19 years old), $40 (annual) ● adult (19 years and older), coach, umpire, $50 (annual) ● corporate/industry, $500 (annual) ● life (over 40 years old), $500. **Staff:** 16. **Budget:** $2,000,000. **Regional Groups:** 13. **Local Groups:** 324. **Description:** Clubs, schools, and colleges where men and women and boys and girls play field hockey; umpires and interested individuals. National governing body for men's and women's field hockey recognized by the United States Olympic Committee (see separate entry). Seeks to: promote interest in the sport of field hockey through exhibition games, coaching clinics, and technical materials; develop a quality youth sport program for children ages 6 to 13; sponsor annual national tournaments for members; enable national teams to compete internationally; certify and train coaches. **Libraries: Type:** reference. **Holdings:** books, video recordings. **Subjects:** field hockey. **Awards:** Female and Male Sportsman of the Year. **Frequency:** annual. **Type:** recognition. **Computer Services:** database. **Committees:** Coaching; Development; Equipment; Events; Rules; Technical Service; Umpiring. **Affiliated With:** United States Olympic Committee. **Absorbed:** United States of America Field Hockey; Field Hockey Association of America. **Formerly:** U.S.A. Field Hockey Association. **Publica-**

tions: *Coaching Manual* ● *Hockey News*, bimonthly. Newsletter. **Price:** included in membership dues. **Circulation:** 12,000. **Advertising:** accepted ● *Quick-Flicks E-Newsletter*, monthly. Contains program updates, announcements, and exclusive features. **Price:** included in membership dues. Alternate Formats: online ● *Umpiring Manual* ● *Whistle Stop*, semiannual. Newsletter. Features rules updates and interpretations, resource listings, and information on umpiring equipment and apparel. **Price:** included in membership dues. **Circulation:** 3,000. **Advertising:** accepted. **Conventions/Meetings:** annual Hockey Festival - festival and competition, for 100 teams (exhibits) - usually Thanksgiving weekend.

Fishing

22885 ■ American Casting Association (ACA)
c/o Dale Lanser, Exec. Sec.
1773 Lance End Ln.
Fenton, MO 63026-2674
Ph: (636)225-9443
Fax: (636)225-7238
E-mail: info@americancastingassoc.org
URL: http://www.americancastingassoc.org
Contact: Dale Lanser, Exec. Sec.
Founded: 1907. **Members:** 1,500. **Membership Dues:** club, $50 (annual) ● individual, $25 (annual). **Staff:** 1. **Budget:** $25,000. **Regional Groups:** 7. **State Groups:** 5. **Local Groups:** 30. **Description:** Federation of amateur tournament fly and bait casters; also includes colleges and universities teaching angling and casting. Promotes casting and angling as a recreational activity. Coordinates, regulates, and establishes rules for sanctioned tournaments; certifies instructors; works to develop improved fishing tackle; provides instruction in workshops and clinics; compiles statistics. Maintains hall of fame. **Awards:** **Type:** recognition. **Committees:** Conservation; Youth Activities. **Publications:** *Casting Instruction.* Manual ● *Creel*, bimonthly. Bulletin. **Price:** $7.00/year. **Circulation:** 400. **Advertising:** accepted ● *Early Times of Casting, 1750-1900* ● *Golden Years of Casting, 1900-1960.* **Conventions/Meetings:** annual National Tournament for Casting - competition (exhibits) - August.

22886 ■ American League of Anglers and Boaters (ALAB)
225 Reinekers Ln., Ste.420
Alexandria, VA 22314
Ph: (703)519-9691
Fax: (703)519-1872
E-mail: arc@funoutdoors.com
Contact: J. Michael Nussman, Chm.
Founded: 1985. **Members:** 35. **Staff:** 1. **Description:** Seeks to protect and maintain the proper use of U.S. aquatic resources. Acts as advocate of the Sport Fishing and Boating Enhancement Act (PL 98-369) and the Aquatic Resources Trust Fund created by the Act. Encourages participation in recreational boating and sportfishing and assists boating safety efforts. **Conventions/Meetings:** triennial meeting (exhibits).

22887 ■ American Sportfishing Association (ASA)
225 Reinekers Ln., Ste.420
Alexandria, VA 22314
Ph: (703)519-9691
Fax: (703)519-1872
E-mail: info@asafishing.org
URL: http://www.asafishing.org
Contact: Mike Nussman, Pres./CEO
Founded: 1962. **Members:** 600. **Staff:** 19. **Budget:** $80,000. **Description:** Works to ensure healthy and sustainable fisheries resources and increase sportfishing participation through education, conservation, promotion and marketing. **Awards:** Fellowship Award. **Frequency:** annual. **Type:** fellowship. **Recipient:** to promising graduate students in fishery science at selected universities throughout North America ● **Type:** recognition. **Recipient:** for best student paper at annual conference of the American

Fisheries Society. **Formerly:** American Sport Fishing Association; (1988) Sport Fishery Research Foundation. **Publications:** *American Sportfishing*, monthly. Newsletter. Includes coverage issues and news in the sportfishing industry. **Price:** $19.95/year. **Circulation:** 10,000. **Conventions/Meetings:** annual convention, sportfishing show - trade and consumer venues (exhibits).

22888 ■ Association of Northwest Steelheaders (ANWS)
PO Box 22065
Milwaukie, OR 97269
Ph: (503)653-4176
Fax: (503)653-8769
E-mail: anws@nwsteelheaders.org
URL: http://www.nwsteelheaders.org
Contact: Norman Ritchie, Exec. Dir.
Founded: 1960. **Members:** 2,000. **Membership Dues:** regular, $30 (annual) ● family, $40 (annual) ● student, youth, senior, $15 (annual). **Staff:** 1. **State Groups:** 1. **Local Groups:** 21. **Description:** Fishermen in Oregon and Washington. Seeks protection of salmon, trout and steelhead as genetic resources; promotes recreational angling. Works to maintain, restore, and improve fish and wildlife habitat and natural and cultural features; conducts studies and assesses the effects of projects such as hydropower plants grazing, gravel excavation and forest practices on these resources. Monitors and testifies at legislative and agency hearings at both state and federal level. **Publications:** *Northwest Steelheader*, quarterly. Newsletter. **Price:** free. **Circulation:** 5,000. **Advertising:** accepted. **Conventions/Meetings:** annual Hall of Fame - banquet, recognition and fundraiser.

22889 ■ Bass Anglers Sportsman Society (BASS)
PO Box 10000
Lake Buena Vista, FL 32830
Ph: (334)409-5329
Free: (877)BAS-SUSA
Fax: (334)409-5329
E-mail: customerservice@bassmaster.com
URL: http://sports.espn.go.com/outdoors/bassmaster/index
Contact: Mr. Don Rucks, Exec. Dir.
Founded: 1968. **Members:** 600,000. **Membership Dues:** individual, $20 (annual). **Staff:** 110. **Regional Groups:** 45. **Local Groups:** 3,000. **For-Profit. Description:** Individuals who enjoy the sport of bass fishing. Promotes interest in fishing, particularly bass fishing; works to help members improve their fishing skills; strives to enhance fishery resources through management, conservation, and other environmental measures. Provides members with services including boat insurance and discount buying privileges. Produces The Bassmasters, a cable television program. In an effort to prevent pollution of fishing waters, it filed more than 200 antipollution suits in 1970. **Also Known As:** B.A.S.S. **Publications:** *BASS Times*, monthly. Newsletter. **Circulation:** 112,500. **Advertising:** accepted ● *Bassmaster*, 10/year. Magazine. Contains practically everything you need to know to catch more bass and have more fun on the water. **Price:** included in membership dues. **Circulation:** 550,000. **Advertising:** accepted ● *Bassmaster Tour.* Magazine ● *Fishing Tackle Retailer*, 11/year ● *Southern Outdoors*, 9/year. **Conventions/Meetings:** annual Bass Masters Classic - competition (exhibits).

22890 ■ Brotherhood of the Jungle Cock (BJC)
c/o Bosley Wright
PO Box 576
Glen Burnie, MD 21061
Ph: (410)761-7727
Fax: (410)553-0575
Contact: Bosley Wright, Exec.VP
Founded: 1940. **Members:** 700. **Membership Dues:** $15 (annual). **Staff:** 26. **State Groups:** 6. **Description:** Anglers dedicated to teaching youth angling technique, good sportsmanship, and the conservation of game fish. **Conventions/Meetings:** annual meeting, with campfire.

22891 ■ Federation of Fly Fishers (FFF)
215 E Lewis St.
Livingston, MT 59047
Ph: (406)222-9369
Fax: (406)222-5823
E-mail: van@fedflyfishers.org
URL: http://www.fedflyfishers.org
Contact: R.P. Gytenbeek, CEO/Pres.
Founded: 1965. **Members:** 12,000. **Membership Dues:** individual (life), $500 ● couple (life), $750 ● individual, $35 (annual) ● family, $45 (annual) ● youth, $15 (annual) ● senior, $25 (annual) ● retail shop or outfitter, $75 (annual) ● sustaining, $200 (annual) ● virtual, $19 (annual). **Staff:** 7. **Budget:** $800,000. **Regional Groups:** 15. **Local Groups:** 300. **Multinational. Description:** Promotes fly fishing as the most enjoyable and sportsmanlike method of fishing and as the method most consistent with the preservation of fishing waters and game fish. Sponsors research in Whitlock-Vibert Boxes (WVB) for planting eggs in waters. (A WVB is a slotted plastic container used to protect developing fish from predators while allowing more mature fish to leave the confines of the receptacle.) Conducts water quality, specialized education, and fly fishing instruction programs. Supports conservation efforts; maintains 13 councils. Operates and maintains museum. **Libraries: Type:** reference. **Holdings:** 1,500. **Subjects:** fly fishing, conservation. **Awards: Frequency:** annual. **Type:** recognition. **Formerly:** (1981) Federation of Fly Fishermen. **Publications:** *An Outdoor Journal.* Journals. **Price:** $18.95 ● *Carp Are Gamefish.* Book. **Price:** $13.95 ● *The Fly Fisher*, quarterly. Magazine ● *Fly Fishing Always.* Book ● *Fly Fishing for Smallmouth Bass.* Book. **Price:** $16.95 ● *Fly Fishing for Trout Volume 4: Imitating and Fishing Natural Fish Foods.* Book. **Price:** $20.00 ● *The Flyfisher*, quarterly. Magazine. Includes federation news and book reviews. **Price:** included in membership dues. **Circulation:** 13,000. **Advertising:** accepted ● *The Junior Fly Fisher*, quarterly. Journal ● Makes available audiovisual programs. **Conventions/Meetings:** annual International Fly Fishing Conclave and Show - conference, includes educational workshops and programs (exhibits) - first week of August ● National Fly Fishing and Boating Week - workshop - first week of June.

22892 ■ Fishing Has No Boundaries (FHNB)
PO Box 175
Hayward, WI 54843
Free: (800)243-3462
E-mail: info@fhnbinc.org
URL: http://fhnbinc.org
Contact: Bobby Cammack, Founder
Founded: 1986. **Membership Dues:** individual, $25 (annual) ● family, $40 (annual) ● life, $500. **Local Groups:** 17. **Description:** Promotes fishing as a recreational activity for individuals with disabilities. Fulfills a need for positive self image, creating an opportunity for self expression and independence for persons with disabilities. **Programs:** Kidz To Kidz.

22893 ■ Future Fisherman Foundation (F3)
c/o American Sportfishing Association
225 Reinekers Ln., Ste.420
Alexandria, VA 22314-2875
Ph: (703)519-9691
Fax: (703)519-1872
E-mail: info@asafishing.org
URL: http://www.asafishing.org
Contact: Mike Nussman, Pres./CEO
Founded: 1985. **Staff:** 3. **Budget:** $1,000,000. **Nonmembership. Description:** Promotes participation and education in fishing and enhances the environment by educating the public via the media, retailers, schools, and other means. Develops aquatic education support material. Supports the National Fishing Tackle Loaner Program. **Additional Websites:** http://www.futurefisherman.org. **Telecommunication Services:** electronic mail, info@futurefisherman.org. **Programs:** Fishing Tackle Loaner; Hooked On Fishing - Not On Drugs; National Fishing and Boating Education Grants Initiative; National 4-H Sportfishing. **Affiliated With:** American Sportfishing Association; Association of Fish and Wildlife Agencies. **Publica-**

tions: *Aquatic Resource Education Curriculum.*
Price: $25.00 ● *Fishing Fun for Kids.* Booklet. **Price:**
$1.25 ● *Instructor's Guide to Hooked on Fishing -
Not On Drugs* ● *Sport Fishing and Aquatic Resource
Handbook.* **Conventions/Meetings:** annual board
meeting.

22894 ■ Great Lakes Sport Fishing Council (GLSFC)

PO Box 297
Elmhurst, IL 60126-0297
Ph: (630)941-1351
Fax: (630)941-1196
E-mail: staff@great-lakes.org
URL: http://www.great-lakes.org
Contact: Dan Thomas, Pres.
Founded: 1972. **Members:** 325,000. **Membership
Dues:** individual in U.S., $15 (annual) ● individual in
Canada, charter captain in U.S., small business in
U.S., $25 (annual) ● charter captain in Canada, small
business in Canada, $35 (annual) ● associate, club,
$75 (annual) ● corporate, $100 (annual). **Descrip-
tion:** Great Lakes regional sport fishermen and their
families. Disseminates information and provides
educational programs on conservation and sport fishing in the Great Lakes. Represents the interests of
members before regional and federal agencies;
award winning web site with over 400 pages offers
weekly news and is open to the public. **Committees:**
Finance; Legal; Legislative; Membership; Safety;
Steelhead. **Publications:** *Great Lakes Basin Report,*
monthly. Newsletter. **Advertising:** accepted. Alternate
Formats: online. **Conventions/Meetings:** periodic
meeting (exhibits).

22895 ■ International Game Fish Association (IGFA)

IGFA Fishing Hall of Fame and Museum
300 Gulf Stream Way
Dania Beach, FL 33004
Ph: (954)927-2628
Fax: (954)924-4299
E-mail: hq@igfa.org
URL: http://www.igfa.org
Contact: Rob Kramer, Pres.
Founded: 1939. **Members:** 30,000. **Membership
Dues:** junior, $20 (annual) ● regular, $40 (annual) ●
family, $55 (annual) ● life, $1,000 ● contributing, $50
(annual) ● corporate, $595-$2,950 (annual). **Staff:**
35. **Languages:** English, French, German, Spanish.
Multinational. Description: Represents freshwater
and saltwater anglers, angling clubs, and others.
Promotes the study of game fishes. Keeps the sport
of game fishing ethical. Encourages this sport both
as recreation and as a potential source of scientific
data and to make this data available to all interested
individuals. Keeps an attested and current chart of
world record catches. Promotes conservation of
fisheries and resources. Compiles and maintains
freshwater, saltwater, and fly rod records. **Libraries:**
Type: open to the public; reference. **Holdings:**
14,000; books, films, periodicals, photographs. **Subjects:** fish, fishing, oceans, aquatic life. **Absorbed:**
International Spin Fishing Association; Salt Water Fly
Rodders of America. **Publications:** *International Angler,* bimonthly. Newsletter. Includes book and film
reviews; reports on new member clubs, new world
records, conservation and legislation. **Price:** included
in membership dues. ISSN: 0257-1520. **Circulation:**
25,000 ● *News Releases,* periodic ● *World Record
Game Fishes,* annual. Contains articles by scientists
and fishing experts, current world records, species
information, and other reference material. **Price:**
included in membership dues; $14.95/copy for
nonmembers. ISSN: 0194-3340. **Circulation:** 33,000.
Conventions/Meetings: annual International Banquet and Auction, includes auction - usually January.

22896 ■ International Underwater Spearfishing Association (IUSA)

31169 Nassau Ct.
Temecula, CA 92591
E-mail: lspearo26@msn.com
URL: http://www.iusarecords.com
Contact: Larry Carter, Pres.
Founded: 1950. **Membership Dues:** regular, $25
(annual). **Multinational. Description:** Promotes ethi-

cal, safe, and sportsman-like spearfishing practices,
to encourage and support a sense of environmental
responsibility among divers. Establishes uniform
regulations for the compilation of world spearfishing
records. Provides basic spearfishing guidelines for
use in other spearfishing activities. **Awards:** Underwater Spearfishing Athlete of the Year. **Frequency:**
annual. **Type:** recognition. **Computer Services:** Information services, spearfishing records, spearfishing
rules. **Committees:** Records; Scientific.

22897 ■ International Women's Fishing Association (IWFA)

PO Box 21066
Fort Lauderdale, FL 33335-1066
E-mail: devca@comcast.net
URL: http://www.iwfa.org
Contact: Ann Dever, Membership Chair
Founded: 1955. **Members:** 200. **Membership Dues:**
in U.S., $75 (annual) ● international, $85 (annual).
Description: Sport fisherwomen. Promotes angling
competition among women anglers; encourages
conservation; fosters fishing tournaments of all kinds.
Establishes a scholarship trust to help graduate
students further their education in the marine sciences. **Awards:** Ann C. Kunkel Newcomer Award.
Frequency: annual. **Type:** recognition. **Recipient:**
for new members who earned most points ● Scholarship Trust Award. **Frequency:** annual. **Type:** scholarship. **Recipient:** for graduate studies in marine science. **Publications:** *Hooks and Lines,* bimonthly.
Newsletter ● Yearbook, annual. **Conventions/Meet-
ings:** annual meeting - always April.

22898 ■ National Professional Anglers' Association (NPAA)

c/o Dave Landahl
628 James St.
Geneva, IL 60134
Ph: (630)845-2766
Fax: (630)578-1918
E-mail: npaa@npaa.net
URL: http://www.npaa.net
Contact: Tommy Skarlis, Pres.
Founded: 1997. **Members:** 800. **Membership Dues:**
pro, $210 (annual) ● registered, $110 (annual) ● associate, $25 (annual). **Staff:** 4. **Description:** Repre-
sents professional anglers that promotes and edu-
cates its members. Provides a valuable platform for
anglers to become involved in the issues regarding
the sport of competitive angling and fishing industry
in general. **Awards:** Lifetime Membership Award. **Frequency:** annual. **Type:** recognition. **Publications:**
NPAA News, bimonthly. Newsletter. **Price:** included
in membership dues. **Circulation:** 3,000. Alternate
Formats: online ● Membership Directory. Alternate
Formats: online. **Conventions/Meetings:** annual
Members Only Conference, supporting members'
displays.

22899 ■ North American Fishing Club (NAFC)

12301 Whitewater Dr.
Minnetonka, MN 55343
E-mail: memberservices@fishingclub.com
URL: http://www.fishingclub.com
Contact: Steve Pennaz, Exec. Dir.
Founded: 1988. **Members:** 425,000. **Membership
Dues:** individual, $1 (monthly). **Staff:** 16. **For-Profit.**
Description: Fishermen. Seeks to improve the fish-
ing skills of members and promotes enjoyment of the
sport. Provides information about fishing guides/
outfitters; conducts field testing. Maintains Trade-a-
Trip Program. **Computer Services:** database. **Publications:** *Fishing Club Journal,* bimonthly. Newsletter.
Price: $18.00/year ● *North American Fisherman,*
bimonthly. Magazine. Serves as personal guide into
the world of freshwater fishing. **Price:** included in
membership dues. **Circulation:** 425,000. **Advertising:** accepted ● Newsletter, weekly. **Advertising:**
accepted. Alternate Formats: online.

22900 ■ Salmon Unlimited (SU)

5936 N Manton Ave.
Chicago, IL 60646
Ph: (773)736-5757

E-mail: salmonunlimited@sbcglobal.net
URL: http://home.comcast.net/~svoboda519
Contact: Lou Champa, Contact
Founded: 1971. **Members:** 1,000. **Membership
Dues:** family, $35 (annual). **Description:** Salmon
and trout sport fishermen. Works preserve, improve,
and enjoy salmon and trout sport fishing on the Great
Lakes, especially Lake Michigan. Has raised funds to
purchase nearly 2,000,000 chinook and Coho salmon,
rainbow trout, and golden trout for stocking in Illinois
waters of Lake Michigan. Sponsors series of sport
fishing tournaments for members. Maintains speakers' bureau. Kids fishing program. Fishing hotline
gives information on fishing conditions in Illinois
waters of Lake Michigan. Tells depths, locations lures,
colors etc. changed twice a week from April 1st to
Sept. 15th. **Awards:** Big Fish and Master Angler.
Frequency: annual. **Type:** recognition. **Recipient:**
for current members of Salmon Unlimited. **Telecommunication Services:** 24-hour hotline, (773)736-
5761, April 1-October 1. **Committees:** Special
Events; Tournament. **Publications:** *Hook'n Line,*
monthly. Newsletter. Reports on club events, conservation efforts, new products, and research projects.
Price: included in membership dues. **Circulation:**
3,000. **Advertising:** accepted ● *Membership Log,*
annual. Membership Directory ● Also publishes news
releases and reference sheets. **Conventions/Meet-
ings:** monthly lecture and seminar, on sport fishing
techniques and boating safety (exhibits) - every 2nd
Tuesday ● show, sport fishing and boat.

22901 ■ Shore Fishing and Casting Club International (SFCCI)

PO Box 8168
Corpus Christi, TX 78468
Ph: (361)939-7643
E-mail: nkrueger@stx.rr.com
URL: http://www.sfcci.org
Contact: Neal Krueger Jr., Pres.
Membership Dues: single, $24 ● family, $36 ●
student, $12 ● retired, $18 ● corporate, $100. **Multi-
national. Description:** Promotes the sports of fishing and competitive long distance casting to the betterment of the environment. Shares knowledge,
techniques, and data. Seeks to become better
stewards of the precious natural resources. **Telecommunication Services:** electronic mail, webmaster@
sfcci.org.

22902 ■ United Fly Tyers (UFT)

PO Box 2478
Woburn, MA 01888
E-mail: info@unitedflytyers.org
URL: http://www.unitedflytyers.org
Contact: Jared Tausig, Pres.
Founded: 1959. **Members:** 750. **Membership Dues:**
general, $40 (annual). **Regional Groups:** 2. **Descrip-
tion:** Serves individuals who develop, practice, and
carry on the craft of fly tying. Offers educational and
charitable programs. **Libraries: Type:** not open to
the public. **Awards:** F.T. Video of the Year. **Frequency:** annual. **Type:** recognition ● Fly Tying Book
of the Year. **Frequency:** annual. **Type:** recognition ●
Fly Tying Competition. **Frequency:** annual. **Type:**
scholarship. **Recipient:** to the junior winner, 16 years
of age and under. **Committees:** Conservation;
Educational. **Affiliated With:** Federation of Fly Fishers; Trout Unlimited. **Publications:** *Roundtable
Newsletter,* monthly. Includes information on the
monthly meetings. **Price:** included in membership
dues. **Circulation:** 1,500. **Advertising:** accepted.
Conventions/Meetings: monthly general assembly -
1st Thursday of September-May in Burlington, MA.

22903 ■ United States Shore Angling Association (USSAA)

7208 Wisteria Way
Carlsbad, CA 92009
Ph: (760)438-7908
E-mail: ussaa@shoreangling.com
URL: http://www.shoreangling.com
Membership Dues: basic individual, $10 (annual) ●
basic individual plus (includes newsletter), family, $15
(annual) ● full, $30 (annual) ● family plus (includes 2
newsletter), $25 (annual) ● family full, $40 (annual).

Description: Provides a social and competitive environment for both saltwater and freshwater shore angling throughout the United States. Establishes Amateur Shore Angling Clubs comprised of anglers from local communities in each state. **Computer Services:** Information services, fishing tips and techniques ● online services, message board. **Divisions:** Freshwater; Saltwater. **Publications:** Newsletter, quarterly.

Footbag

22904 ■ World Footbag Association (WFA)
PO Box 775208
Steamboat Springs, CO 80477
Ph: (970)870-9898
Free: (800)878-8797
Fax: (970)870-2846
E-mail: wfa@worldfootbag.com
URL: http://www.worldfootbag.com
Contact: Bruce Guettich, Pres.
Founded: 1983. **Members:** 66,000. **Staff:** 4. **Budget:** $275,000. **For-Profit. Multinational. Description:** Footbag enthusiasts and players of organized footbag games. (A footbag, sometimes known by the brand name Hacky Sack, is a palm-sized bag weighing a little more than one ounce that players attempt to keep in the air using their feet and knees.) Promotes: interest in footbags and cooperative and competitive footbag games; fitness and skill development through seminars, workshops, clinics, and national training camps. Has expanded educational programs and classes to include popular games and alternative sports such as juggling, balancing activities, and flying disc events. Introduces footbag techniques and programs to schoolchildren throughout the country. Demonstrates footbag use at stores, trade shows, and festivals. Maintains professional tour teams; certifies instructors and tour team personnel. Sponsors and directs eight regional footbag championships annually. Sanctions festivals and tournaments run by members, community groups, and schools. Conducts research programs. Offers discounts to members on footbag products and events. **Libraries: Type:** open to the public. **Holdings:** 15; articles, books, periodicals. **Subjects:** footbag. **Awards:** Mike Marshall Award. **Frequency:** annual. **Type:** recognition. **Recipient:** for top promoter/player of footbag. **Computer Services:** Mailing lists. **Committees:** International Footbag; Professional Players Agency; Regulatory Committee Controlling Guidelines, Rules and Regulations for Worldwide Organized Footbag Play. **Divisions:** Alternative Sports and New Games. **Supersedes:** National Hacky Sack Footbag Players Association. **Publications:** Footbag Basics. Video. Provides information on footbag training. **Price:** $15.00 ● Footbag World. Magazine. Alternate Formats: online ● Booklet ● Also publishes tournament and festival kits, promotional material, and official player manuals, rules, and regulations. **Conventions/Meetings:** annual World Footbag Championships - competition (exhibits).

Football

22905 ■ American Football Coaches Association (AFCA)
100 Legends Ln.
Waco, TX 76706
Ph: (254)754-9900
Fax: (254)754-7373
E-mail: info@afca.com
URL: http://www.afca.com
Contact: Mr. Adam Guess, Dir. of Administration
Founded: 1922. **Members:** 10,000. **Membership Dues:** active, allied, $60 (annual) ● foreign allied, $100 (annual). **Staff:** 15. **Description:** College, university, professional, junior college, and high school football coaches. Conducts educational programs. **Libraries: Type:** reference; by appointment only. **Holdings:** 300; archival material, archival material, books, periodicals, photographs, video recordings. **Subjects:** coaching techniques, coaching

philosophy. **Awards:** All-American Team. **Frequency:** annual. **Type:** recognition. **Recipient:** for superior performance by a player ● Amos Alonzo Stagg Award. **Frequency:** annual. **Type:** recognition. **Recipient:** to the individual, group, or institution whose services have been outstanding in the advancement of the best interests of football ● Coach of the Year. **Frequency:** annual. **Type:** recognition. **Recipient:** for outstanding coaching performance during the season ● McLaughry Award. **Frequency:** annual. **Type:** recognition. **Recipient:** to a distinguished American (or Americans) for the highest distinction in service to others. **Computer Services:** database, membership. **Boards:** Advisory Board to the NCAA Rules Committee; Review. **Committees:** All-America Team Selection; Assistant Coaches; Coach of the Year; Concessions and Displays; Ethics; Football Operations Directors; Hall of Fame; High School; Luncheon; Meeting Room; Minority Issues; Nominating; Professional Development Series; Program; Public Relations; Registration; Rules; Summer Manual. **Publications:** The Extra Point, quarterly. Newsletter. **Price:** included in membership dues. Alternate Formats: online ● Proceedings Manual, annual. **Price:** included in membership dues ● Summer Manual, annual. **Price:** included in membership dues ● Directory, annual. **Price:** included in membership dues. **Conventions/Meetings:** annual Meeting and Coaches Clinic - convention (exhibits).

22906 ■ American Youth Football (AYF)
1000 S Point Dr., TH-9
Miami, FL 33139
Ph: (305)535-6591
Free: (888)438-2816
E-mail: jlaufer@americanyouthfootball.com
URL: http://www.americanyouthfootball.com
Contact: Jessica Laufer, Exec. Dir.
Founded: 1996. **Members:** 350,000. **Staff:** 8. **Description:** Youth football teams and cheerleader squads. Serves boys and girls in the aforementioned areas, along with their adult supervisors. **Publications:** The Huddle. Newsletter. Alternate Formats: online ● Operations Manuals ● The Pigskin, semiannual. Newsletter ● Rulebooks. Booklets.

22907 ■ Australian Football Association of North America (AFANA)
PO Box 27623
Columbus, OH 43227-0623
Ph: (614)571-8986
E-mail: aussiefb@afana.com
URL: http://www.afana.com
Contact: Rob de Santos, Chm.
Founded: 1996. **Membership Dues:** sustaining, $10 (monthly) ● sustaining, $120 (annual) ● participating, $40 (annual) ● standard, $8 (annual). **Multinational. Description:** Furthers the development and exposure of Australian football in North America. Seeks to improve television coverage of the sport. Facilitates communication and cooperation among members. **Telecommunication Services:** electronic mail, rdesantos@afana.com. **Publications:** Footy News. Newsletter. **Advertising:** accepted. Alternate Formats: online ● Media News and TV Schedules. Newsletter. **Advertising:** accepted. Alternate Formats: online.

22908 ■ Football Writers Association of America (FWAA)
c/o Steve Richardson, Exec. Dir.
18652 Vista Del Sol Dr.
Dallas, TX 75287-4021
Ph: (972)713-6198
E-mail: tigerfwaa@aol.com
URL: http://www.sportswriters.net/fwaa
Contact: Steve Richardson, Exec. Dir.
Founded: 1941. **Members:** 850. **Membership Dues:** individual, $40 (annual). **Description:** Represents newspaper and magazine sportswriters covering high school and college football. **Awards:** All-American Team. **Frequency:** annual. **Type:** recognition. **Recipient:** for outstanding football players of college season ● Bronko Nagurski College Football Defensive Player of the Year. **Frequency:** annual. **Type:** recognition. **Recipient:** for outstanding defensive player ● Eddie

Robinson Coach of the Year. **Frequency:** annual. **Type:** recognition. **Recipient:** for outstanding coach of college season ● Grantland Rice National Championship Team. **Frequency:** annual. **Type:** recognition. **Recipient:** for national champion ● Outland Trophy. **Frequency:** annual. **Type:** trophy. **Recipient:** for outstanding college interior lineman. **Publications:** The Fifth Down, periodic. Newsletter. Contains news and notes about college football and FWAA members. **Price:** included in membership dues. **Circulation:** 850. **Advertising:** accepted. Alternate Formats: online ● Football Writers Association of America—Telephone Directory of Members, annual. **Advertising:** accepted. **Conventions/Meetings:** annual meeting, with press conference (exhibits) - always January.

22909 ■ National Football Foundation and College Hall of Fame (NFF)
433 E Las Colinas Blvd., Ste.1130
Irving, TX 75039
Ph: (972)556-1000
Free: (800)486-1865
Fax: (972)556-9032
E-mail: membership@footballfoundation.com
URL: http://www.footballfoundation.com
Contact: Mr. Steven Hatchell, Pres.
Founded: 1947. **Members:** 12,000. **Membership Dues:** varsity, $40 (annual) ● life, $1,000. **Staff:** 31. **Regional Groups:** 5. **Local Groups:** 119. **Description:** Represents coaches, college athletic directors and sports information directors, sportswriters, broadcasters, telecasters, and business leaders with an interest in football. Honors great ex-players and coaches of college football by election to the College Football Hall of Fame and promotes amateur football in schools and colleges. Researches biography and history of the game, its players, and coaches. Presents scholarships to athletes who continue their studies in graduate schools and athletes pursuing medical education. Runs programs designed to use the power of amateur football in developing scholarship, citizenship and athletic achievement in America's young people. Programs include the College Football Hall of Fame, Play It Smart, Center for Youth Development Through Sport, the NFL/NFF Coaching Academy and scholarships of nearly one million dollars for college and high school scholar-athletes. Tabulates and releases the weekly Bowl Championships Series (BCS) standings to the public and the press in cooperation with six major college football conferences. **Libraries: Type:** by appointment only. **Holdings:** 10,000; audio recordings, books, video recordings. **Subjects:** college football. **Awards:** Chapter Leadership Award. **Frequency:** annual. **Type:** recognition. **Recipient:** to individuals for exceptional stewardship of regional chapters ● College Football Hall of Fame Induction and Enshrinement. **Frequency:** annual. **Type:** recognition. **Recipient:** to individuals achieving first team All America status ● Distinguished American Award. **Frequency:** periodic. **Type:** recognition. **Recipient:** for leadership and significant contribution to amateur football ● Gold Medal. **Frequency:** annual. **Type:** medal. **Recipient:** to an individual with unblemished reputation closely associated with college football ● HealthSouth Draddy Award. **Frequency:** annual. **Type:** monetary. **Recipient:** for postgraduate study ● High School Scholar-Athletes of the Year. **Frequency:** annual. **Type:** recognition. **Recipient:** to student athletes ● John L. Toner Award. **Frequency:** annual. **Type:** recognition. **Recipient:** to athletic director ● MacArthur Trophy. **Frequency:** annual. **Type:** trophy. **Recipient:** to outstanding college football team of the season ● National Scholar-Athlete Awards. **Frequency:** annual. **Type:** monetary. **Recipient:** for postgraduate study ● Outstanding Contribution to Amateur Football. **Frequency:** annual. **Type:** recognition ● Outstanding Official Award. **Frequency:** annual. **Type:** recognition. **Formerly:** (1954) National Football Shrine and Hall of Fame. **Publications:** Footballetter, quarterly. Magazine. **Price:** included in membership dues. **Circulation:** 12,000. **Advertising:** accepted ● Member Update, 3/year. Newsletter ● NSAA News, 3/year. Newsletter. **Conventions/Meetings:** annual Awards Dinner - banquet, silent

auction during and before dinner (exhibits) ● annual Enshrinement Ceremony - meeting, for Hall of Fame inductees ● annual Hall of Fame Awards Dinner.

22910 ■ National Football League (NFL)
280 Park Ave.
New York, NY 10017
Ph: (212)655-5665
Free: (877)635-7467
E-mail: customer_service@nflshop.com
URL: http://www.nfl.com
Contact: Roger Goodell, Commissioner
Founded: 1920. **Members:** 32. **Description:** Professional football teams divided into the American Football Conference and the National Football Conference as a result of the merger with the American Football League in 1970. Each conference is made up of an East, West, North, and South division. **Publications:** *Record and Fact Book*, annual ● Newsletter, weekly. Updates about football teams, upcoming games schedules, league rankings and team records. Alternate Formats: online. **Conventions/Meetings:** annual meeting - always March.

22911 ■ National Football League Alumni (NFL Alumni)
3696 N Fed. Hwy., Ste.202
Fort Lauderdale, FL 33308-6262
Ph: (954)630-2100
Free: (800)878-5437
Fax: (954)630-2535
E-mail: contact@nflahq.org
URL: http://www.nflalumni.org
Contact: Frank W. Krauser, Pres./CEO
Founded: 1967. **Membership Dues:** professional, $160 (annual) ● associate, $220 (annual). **Description:** Former professional football players, coaches, and administrators; individuals who wish to work for sports through youth and for youth through sports. Contributes time, talent, and money to children's charities and programs. Holds Player of the Year awards dinner. Sponsors annual Charity Golf Classic Series consisting of tournaments hosted by local chapters culminating in the Super Bowl of Golf championship tournament. Observes Youth of America Week every fall. Operates Pro Legends, Inc., a marketing, licensing, and public relations subsidiary. **Awards:** Career Achievement. **Frequency:** annual. **Type:** recognition ● Old Hero. **Type:** recognition ● Order of the Leather Helmet. **Frequency:** annual. **Type:** recognition ● Player of the Year Award. **Frequency:** annual. **Type:** recognition. **Formerly:** National Football League Alumni, Inc. **Publications:** *Legends Magazine*, periodic. Contains information published in conjunction with association-sponsored events. **Price:** free. **Advertising:** accepted ● *Pro Legends*, bimonthly. Newsletter. Includes news of charitable activities, lists of award recipients, and obituaries. **Price:** included in membership dues. **Conventions/Meetings:** annual meeting.

22912 ■ National Football League Players Association (NFLPA)
2021 L St. NW, Ste.600
Washington, DC 20036
Ph: (202)463-2200
Free: (800)372-2000
Fax: (202)857-0380
E-mail: webmaster@nflplayers.com
URL: http://www.nflpa.org
Contact: Eugene Upshaw Jr., Exec. Dir.
Founded: 1956. **Members:** 3,500. **Staff:** 87. **Description:** Active and retired players; sports agents. Aims to advance individual negotiations for NFL players. Sponsors charitable events. Conducts research on player issues; compiles salary information and statistics. Maintains speakers' bureau; holds educational seminars for agents. **Awards:** **Type:** recognition. **Recipient:** for outstanding players. **Absorbed:** (1970) American Football League Players Association. **Publications:** *Pipeline to the Pros*, periodic. Newsletter. For college players about to enter the NFL. ● *Playbook*, periodic. Newsletter. Contains current news on player issues. ● *Touchback*, periodic. Newsletter. For retired player members. **Conventions/Meetings:** annual meeting (exhibits).

22913 ■ North American Football League (NAFL)
250 Prairie Center Dr., No. 217
Eden Prairie, MN 55344
Ph: (952)829-7999 (952)829-7222
Free: (888)360-7767
Fax: (952)216-0134
E-mail: info@nafl.org
URL: http://www.nafl.org
Contact: Robert F. Licopoli, Pres./Founder
Founded: 1996. **Members:** 5,000. **Multinational. Description:** Promotes and develops the sport of football. Provides a self-sustaining level of football that allows players to develop skills or simply for the love of the game. Advances the skills and talents of NFL players. Educates team owners and organizes a league where each team operates equally. **Telecommunication Services:** electronic mail, rlicopoli@nafl.org. **Publications:** *The Goal Post*, periodic. Newsletter. Highlights the actions of the league and its' members. Alternate Formats: online.

22914 ■ Pop Warner Football (PWF)
586 Middletown Blvd., Ste.C-100
Langhorne, PA 19047
Ph: (215)752-2691
Fax: (215)752-2879
E-mail: football@popwarner.com
URL: http://www.popwarner.com
Contact: Jon C. Butler, Exec. Dir.
Founded: 1929. **Members:** 370,000. **Membership Dues:** team only, $30 (annual) ● team with cheer squad, $47 (annual) ● flag team with or without cheer squad, $10 (annual). **Staff:** 8. **Regional Groups:** 8. **Local Groups:** 142. **Description:** Represents youths ages 5 to 16 organized into approximately 6600 teams playing tackle and flag football under safety-first rules. Enforces strict safety rules, equipment standards, age and weight limitations. Teams based on age/weight groupings are: Mitey-Mite; Junior Peewee; Peewee; Junior Midget; Midget; Junior Bantam; and Bantam. Provides program which is named for Glenn Scobie (Pop) Warner (1871-1954), who coached football at Cornell, Georgia, Iowa, Pittsburgh, Carlisle, Temple, Stanford, and San Jose State universities. Serves as service agency providing publications, insurance programs, scheduling of inter-league postseason games, and research. **Awards:** All-American Scholar Award. **Frequency:** annual. **Type:** scholarship ● Team Scholastic Award. **Type:** scholarship ● Volunteer of the Year Award. **Frequency:** annual. **Type:** recognition. **Computer Services:** Mailing lists, internal use only ● online services, PWLSREG Registration Days. **Formerly:** (1980) Pop Warner Junior League Football. **Publications:** *Rules and Regulations for Pop Warner Football*, triennial. Includes flag football and cheerleading rules. **Conventions/Meetings:** annual dinner, includes awards presentation - late spring, in Walt Disney World, FL or Disneyland, CA ● National Championship - competition - always early December ● Regional Championship - competition - always late November ● periodic regional meeting ● workshop, coaching certification clinic.

22915 ■ Professional Football Athletic Trainers Society (PFATS)
c/o Steve Antonopulos, Pres.
13655 Broncos Pkwy.
Englewood, CO 80112
Ph: (303)649-9000
E-mail: contact@pfats.com
URL: http://www.edblock.com
Contact: Steve Antonopulos, Pres.
Founded: 1982. **Members:** 90. **Description:** Professional athletic trainers working for National Football League teams. Provides the best possible health care for NFL players. Operates speakers' bureau. **Awards:** Athletic Training Staff of the Year. **Frequency:** annual. **Type:** scholarship. **Recipient:** for student trainers. **Additional Websites:** http://www.pfats.com. **Publications:** *Pro Football Athletic Trainer*, semiannual. **Circulation:** 18,000. **Conventions/Meetings:** semiannual Business Meeting - always February and June ● annual workshop.

22916 ■ Professional Football Researchers Association (PFRA)
12870 Rte. 30, No. 39
North Huntingdon, PA 15642
E-mail: bob2296@comcast.net
URL: http://www.footballresearch.com
Contact: Bob Carroll, Exec. Dir.
Founded: 1979. **Members:** 420. **Membership Dues:** regular, $25 (annual). **Staff:** 1. **Description:** Individuals interested in pro football history and related subjects. Seeks to: foster the study of professional football as a significant social and athletic institution; establish an accurate historical account of professional football; disseminate information. **Awards:** Nelson Ross Award. **Frequency:** annual. **Type:** recognition. **Recipient:** for achievement in pro football history ● Ralph Hay Award. **Frequency:** annual. **Type:** recognition. **Recipient:** for achievement in pro football history. **Publications:** *Coffin Corner*, bimonthly. Newsletter. **Advertising:** accepted ● Membership Directory, annual. **Conventions/Meetings:** annual meeting.

22917 ■ Professional Football Writers of America (PFWA)
12030 Cedar Lake Ct.
Maryland Heights, MO 63043
Ph: (314)453-0755
E-mail: hbalzer@aol.com
URL: http://www.pfwa.org
Contact: Howard Balzer, Sec.-Treas.
Founded: 1962. **Members:** 450. **Membership Dues:** regular, $50 (annual). **Description:** Sportswriters and columnists who cover professional football on a regular basis. Works to strengthen working status of writers. Coordinates working relationships with leagues, clubs, and players' associations. Bestows Dick McCann Award for long and distinguished reporting in the field of pro football; Jack Horrigan Award to the league or club official for his or her qualities and professional style in helping the pro football writers do their job; Good Guy Award to a player for his qualities and professional style in helping the pro football writers do their job. **Publications:** Newsletter, 9/year. **Price:** included in membership dues. **Circulation:** 550. **Conventions/Meetings:** annual meeting - always on Friday preceding the Super Bowl.

22918 ■ United States Flag Football League (USFFL)
c/o John D. Carrigan, Commissioner
117 St. Gallen Ct.
New Bern, NC 28562
Ph: (252)633-1014
Contact: John D. Carrigan, Commissioner
State Groups: 11. **Description:** Promotes and develops the sport of flag football for men ages 18 and over on an amateur basis. (Flag football emphasizes non-contact skills of passing, receiving, and running while providing opportunity for physical contact in the form of blocking.). **Awards:** **Type:** recognition. **Formerly:** (1986) United States Flag Football Association. **Publications:** *USFFL Rule Book*. **Conventions/Meetings:** annual competition, held for championship teams from member state associations - always first weekend in December.

22919 ■ U.S. Flag and Touch Football League (USFTL)
7709 Ohio St.
Mentor, OH 44060
Ph: (440)974-8735
Fax: (440)974-8441
E-mail: usftl@usftl.com
URL: http://www.usftl.com
Contact: Michael Cihon, Exec. Dir./Pres.
Founded: 1988. **Members:** 300,000. **Membership Dues:** youth team, $10 (annual) ● adult team, $20 (annual) ● official, $25 (annual) ● associate, $100 (annual) ● life, $500. **Staff:** 8. **Regional Groups:** 4. **State Groups:** 51. **Description:** Players of flag and touch football and officials. (Flag and touch football are modified versions of standard football in which touching or deflagging is substituted for tackling.) Provides rule books, educational materials, and video tapes to members. Provides trained officials at all

levels of play. Offers recreational athletic opportunities to men, women, boys, girls, and industrial and church groups. Conducts instructional and officials clinics. Maintains a hall of fame and museum; compiles statistics. Offers television coverage of US-FTL events. **Libraries: Type:** reference. **Holdings:** archival material. **Awards:** All American Teams Award. **Frequency:** annual. **Type:** recognition. **Recipient:** based on play at National Flag Football Championships. **Computer Services:** Mailing lists. **Programs:** African American; Armed Forces; Church; Co-Rec; Corporate; 5 on 5; 4 on 4; Hispanic; Law Enforcement; Masters; Men; Women; Youth. **Formerly:** (1994) US Flag Football League. **Publications:** *First & Twenty*, quarterly. Newspaper. Contains information on upcoming tournaments, national rankings, sports medicine articles on flag and touch football. **Price:** $10.00/year. **Circulation:** 20,000. **Advertising:** accepted ● *USFTL Rule Book, Constitution and Officials' Manual*, semiannual. **Price:** $7.50. **Advertising:** accepted ● Also "Northcoast Flag & Touch Newsletter," & "Buckeye Flag & Touch Newsletter" and "USTFL Weekly News & Notes.". **Conventions/Meetings:** annual conference and workshop (exhibits) - always April.

Gay/Lesbian

22920 ■ International Gay Figure Skating Union (IGFSU)

PO Box 945
New York, NY 10116
E-mail: info@igfsu.org
URL: http://www.igfsu.org
Membership Dues: general, $25 (annual). **Multinational. Description:** Coordinates, maintains and tracks the Ice Skating Institute (ISI) membership and testing of members. Coordinates with the Federation of Gay Games, the World OutGames and GLISA. **Computer Services:** Information services, ISI rules.

Golf

22921 ■ All-American Collegiate Golf Foundation (AACGF)

232 Madison Ave., Ste.900
New York, NY 10016
Ph: (212)755-1492
Fax: (212)755-3762
Contact: William Denis Fugazy, Pres.
Founded: 1964. **Description:** Promotes collegiate golf by providing donations to youth-oriented charities and student scholarship funds. Presents achievement awards. **Awards: Frequency:** annual. **Type:** scholarship. **Publications:** *All-American Collegiate Golf Foundation Gala*, annual. Journal. **Advertising:** accepted ● *Day with the All-American*, annual. **Conventions/Meetings:** annual meeting and dinner ● annual Pro-Celebrity Tournament - competition.

22922 ■ American Junior Golf Association (AJGA)

1980 Sports Club Dr.
Braselton, GA 30517
Ph: (770)868-4200
Free: (877)373-2542
Fax: (770)868-4211
E-mail: ajga@ajga.org
URL: http://www.ajga.org
Contact: Stephen A. Hamblin, Exec. Dir.
Founded: 1978. **Members:** 5,000. **Membership Dues:** junior in U.S. and Canada, $195 (annual) ● junior international, $220 (annual) ● CBS in U.S. and Canada, $270 (annual). **Staff:** 53. **Multinational. Description:** Works for the overall growth and development of young men and women through competitive junior golf. Provides exposure vehicle for college scholarships. **Libraries: Type:** reference. **Holdings:** books, clippings, periodicals. **Awards:** HP Scholastic All-American Team. **Frequency:** annual. **Type:** recognition ● Jerry Cole Sportsmanship Award. **Frequency:** annual. **Type:** recognition ● Polo Golf Junior All-American Teams. **Frequency:** annual. **Type:**

recognition ● Polo Golf Players of the Year. **Frequency:** annual. **Type:** recognition. **Publications:** *Golfweek*. Magazine. **Price:** included in membership dues ● *Inside the AJGA*, 8/year. Newsletter. **Price:** included in membership dues. **Circulation:** 7,000. Alternate Formats: online ● Brochure ● Pamphlet ● Newsletter, biweekly. **Price:** free ● Also publishes tournament programs. **Conventions/Meetings:** annual meeting - in February.

22923 ■ Eastern Amputee Golf Association (EAGA)

2015 Amherst Dr.
Bethlehem, PA 18015-5606
Ph: (610)867-9295
Free: (888)868-0992
Fax: (610)867-9295
E-mail: info@eaga.org
URL: http://www.eaga.org
Contact: Bob Buck, Exec. Dir.
Founded: 1987. **Members:** 900. **Membership Dues:** amputee, associate, $15 (annual) ● life, $200. **Multinational. Description:** Works to assist in rehabilitation of amputees and provides for their general welfare through the medium of golf. **Libraries: Type:** open to the public. **Subjects:** amputees. **Awards:** EAGA Scholarships. **Frequency:** annual. **Type:** scholarship. **Recipient:** for an amputee student or a child of amputee member. **Affiliated With:** National Amputee Golf Association. **Publications:** *EAGA Golfers Magazine*, annual. **Advertising:** accepted. Alternate Formats: CD-ROM ● *Instructional Golf Videos*. **Price:** free for members. **Conventions/Meetings:** First Swing - seminar, 22 clinics throughout the year, to teach tips and techniques on adaptive golf ● Golf Tournaments - competition ● Learn to Golf Clinics - meeting, for individuals with disabilities.

22924 ■ Executive Women's Golf Association (EWGA)

300 Ave. of the Champions, Ste.140
Palm Beach Gardens, FL 33418-3620
Ph: (561)691-0096
Free: (800)407-1477
Fax: (561)691-0012
E-mail: mail@ewga.com
URL: http://www.ewga.com
Contact: Pam Swensen, Exec. Dir.
Founded: 1991. **Membership Dues:** classic, $90 (annual) ● regular, in Canada, C$130 (annual) ● premier, $150 (annual) ● executive, $250 (annual). **Description:** Represents career-oriented women golfers. Includes activities such as beginner clinics, etiquette seminars, league play, monthly outings, chapter championship, networking functions, member-guest events, charity tournaments, holiday dinners, and other creative events.

22925 ■ Golf Coaches Association of America (GCAA)

1225 W Main St., Ste.110
Norman, OK 73069
Ph: (405)329-4222
Fax: (405)573-7888
E-mail: gcaa@collegiate.golf.com
URL: http://www.collegiategolf.com
Contact: John Fields, Pres.
Founded: 1958. **Members:** 225. **Membership Dues:** president, $5,000 (3/year) ● platinum, $2,000 (annual) ● hall of fame, $375 ● head coach, $150 ● assistant coach, $100 (annual) ● associate coach, $75 (annual). **Description:** Golf coaches of four-year colleges and universities who are members of the National Collegiate Athletic Association (see separate entry). Supervises college golf so that it will be administered in accordance with the definition of amateurism and the principles of amateur sports; has responsibility for collegiate golf tournaments as set forth by the NCAA; promotes intercollegiate and intramural golf participation; encourages adoption of strict eligibility rules. Selects first, second, and third All-American Golf Teams. Conducts research into conditions and types of competitive golf play. **Awards:** Jack Nicklaus. **Frequency:** annual. **Type:** recognition. **Recipient:** for players who excel throughout the course of entire season. **Formerly:** (1969) NCAA

Golf Coaches Association. **Conventions/Meetings:** annual meeting, in conjunction with NCAA Golf Tournament.

22926 ■ Golf Writers Association of America (GWAA)

c/o Melanie Hauser, Sec.-Treas.
10210 Greentree Rd.
Houston, TX 77042-1232
Ph: (713)782-6664
Fax: (713)781-2575
E-mail: golfwritersinc@aol.com
URL: http://www.gwaa.com
Contact: Melanie Hauser, Sec.-Treas.
Founded: 1946. **Members:** 995. **Membership Dues:** $50 (annual). **Staff:** 1. **Description:** Editors and writers covering golf for newspapers, magazines, and news services. **Awards:** Bartlett Award. **Frequency:** annual. **Type:** recognition ● Ben Hogan Award. **Frequency:** annual. **Type:** recognition ● Player of the Year Award. **Frequency:** annual. **Type:** recognition ● Richardson Award. **Type:** recognition. **Publications:** *Golf Writers Association of America—Membership Directory*, annual ● *Golf Writers Association of America—Newsletter*, 10/year. **Price:** included in membership dues. **Conventions/Meetings:** semiannual meeting and competition, held in conjunction with the U.S. Open Golf Tournament - always April, Augusta, GA, and June (various locations).

22927 ■ Group Fore Golf Foundation (GFGF)

1259 El Camino Real, Ste.153
Menlo Park, CA 94025
Ph: (650)327-5207
Free: (800)947-2632
Fax: (650)327-5208
E-mail: pandagolf@aol.com
Contact: Judy Horst, Exec. Dir.
Founded: 1980. **Description:** Promotes the game of golf and encourages young people to participate in golf. Provides college golf scholarships for women and funds junior golf programs in the U.S. Sponsored by the Women's Professional Golf Tour, which produces and promotes golf tournaments for women professional and amateur golfers on a weekly basis.

22928 ■ International Golf Associates (IGA)

4370 La Jolla Village Dr., 4th Fl.
San Diego, CA 92122
Ph: (858)546-4737
Fax: (619)615-2083
URL: http://www.iga-golf.com
Membership Dues: regular, $90 (annual). **Multinational. Description:** Allows easy and affordable access to golf internationally. **Committees:** Franco-Suisse; Handicap; Social; Tournament. **Formerly:** (2001) International Golf Association. **Publications:** *Franco-Suisse News*, monthly. Newsletter.

22929 ■ International Golf Federation (IGF)

PO Box 708
Far Hills, NJ 07931-0708
Ph: (908)234-2300
Fax: (908)234-2178
E-mail: igfinfo@usga.org
URL: http://www.internationalgolffederation.org
Contact: Stephanie Parel, Joint Deputy Sec.
Founded: 1958. **Members:** 114. **Membership Dues:** individual, $100 (annual). **Staff:** 10. **National Groups:** 108. **Multinational. Description:** Strives to encourage the international development of golf, and to foster friendship and sportsmanship among the peoples of the world through the conduct of the biennial Amateur Team Championships for the Eisenhower Trophy and the Espirito Santo Trophy. Promotes golf as an Olympic sport and acts as the Federation for golf in the Olympic games. **Awards:** Eisenhower Trophy. **Frequency:** biennial. **Type:** trophy. **Recipient:** for international men's team competition ● Espirito Santo Trophy. **Frequency:** biennial. **Type:** trophy. **Recipient:** for international women's team competition. **Committees:** Administrative. **Affiliated With:** International Olympic Committee. **Formerly:** (2003) World Amateur Golf Council. **Publications:** *International Golf Federation—Record Book: World Amateur Team Championships*, biennial.

Lists competitors, pictures, winners, scores, and historical records from the World Amateur Team Championships. **Price:** included in membership dues; free, upon request. **Circulation:** 2,000. Alternate Formats: online. **Conventions/Meetings:** biennial meeting.

22930 ■ Ladies Professional Golf Association (LPGA)
100 Intl. Golf Dr.
Daytona Beach, FL 32124-1082
Ph: (386)274-6200
Fax: (386)274-1099
E-mail: feedback@lpga.com
URL: http://www.lpga.com
Contact: Rae F. Evans, Chair
Founded: 1950. **Members:** 1,600. **Staff:** 70. **Description:** Represents and promotes women golfers, teachers and competitors. Compiles statistics on tournaments, money winnings, and scoring. **Awards: Type:** recognition. **Divisions:** Teaching and Club Professionals; Tournament. **Formerly:** (1948) Women's Professional Golf Association. **Publications:** Crush, semiannual. Magazine. **Price:** $7.99 ● Ladies Professional Golf Association—Schedule Directory, annual. Lists tournament date, venue, purse, defending champion, and contact telephone number. **Price:** free for members ● Player Guide, annual. Includes player biographies, tournament histories and information, LPGA records and statistics, information on LPGA awards, and staff. **Price:** free to LPGA media; $20.00/copy for nonmembers, limited quantity available ● Newsletter, weekly. **Conventions/Meetings:** annual conference (exhibits).

22931 ■ Multicultural Golf Association of America (MGAA)
43 Main St.
PO Box 1081
Westhampton Beach, NY 11978
Ph: (631)288-8255
Fax: (631)288-5734
E-mail: mgaagolf@aol.com
URL: http://www.mgaa.com
Contact: Paul G. David, Exec. VP/Co-Founder
Founded: 1991. **Members:** 1,500. **Membership Dues:** individual, $25 (annual) ● family, $45 (annual) ● small company, $150 (annual) ● large company, $500 (annual). **Staff:** 12. **Description:** Seeks to get more minorities (primarily youth) involved in the sport of golf. Conducts junior golf exhibitions and clinics nationwide to expose youth to the attributes of the sport. **Awards:** MGAA Father of the Year. **Frequency:** annual. **Type:** recognition. **Additional Websites:** http://home.earthlink.net/~pgd58. **Formerly:** (2000) Minority Golf Association of America. **Publications:** Path To The Flag, quarterly. Newsletter. **Price:** free for members and sponsors. Alternate Formats: online. **Conventions/Meetings:** annual Celebrity Golf Classic - competition.

22932 ■ National Advertising Golf Association (NAGA)
c/o John Black, Dir.
207 Chestnut Oaks Cir.
Simpsonville, SC 29681
Ph: (864)573-8653
Fax: (864)582-8228
E-mail: jblack@bmgcorporate.com
URL: http://www.naga.net
Contact: John Black, Dir.
Founded: 1967. **Members:** 1,500. **Description:** Comprises of 16 advertising golf associations. **Publications:** none. **Conventions/Meetings:** annual competition, golf tournament ● annual meeting.

22933 ■ National Association of Golf Tournament Directors (NAGTD)
212 S Henry St.
Alexandria, VA 22314
Ph: (703)549-3543
Free: (888)899-2483
Fax: (703)549-9074

E-mail: nagtd2@aol.com
Contact: Amanda Flangas, Exec.Dir.
Founded: 1996. **Members:** 450. **Membership Dues:** tournament director, $175 (annual) ● supplier, $450 (annual). **Staff:** 4. **Budget:** $25,000. **Description:** Works to provide a forum for education and networking opportunities for directors of golf tournaments. Provides certification programs; offers a tournament reservation service and director referral services. **Awards:** APEX Award. **Frequency:** annual. **Type:** recognition. **Publications:** Leader Board, monthly. Newsletter. **Price:** for members. Alternate Formats: online ● Book. Tournament source book listing members by service and product. **Conventions/Meetings:** annual conference and trade show (exhibits).

22934 ■ National Association of Left-Handed Golfers (NALG)
3249 Hazelwood Dr. SW
Atlanta, GA 30311
E-mail: nalg@mindspring.com
URL: http://www.nalg.org
Contact: Joseph Brogdon, Dir.
Founded: 1936. **Members:** 1,600. **Membership Dues:** individual, $25 (annual). **Staff:** 2. **Budget:** $23,500. **Regional Groups:** 12. **State Groups:** 32. **Local Groups:** 10. **Description:** Golfers who play all shots left-handed. Purposes are: to organize the amateur left-handed golfers of the U.S., Canada, and other countries into a recognized and accepted group; to foster closer acquaintances among all left-handed golfers and to work continuously for a spirit of goodwill and fellowship; to conduct a National Left-Handed Amateur Tournament, a National Lefty-Righty Amateur, one or more Lefty-Partner Tournaments, and any other tournaments approved by the board of governors; to recognize Open, Senior, and Women's champions annually. Maintains hall of fame; compiles statistics. Sponsors annual golf tournaments. **Computer Services:** Mailing lists, of members. **Committees:** Tournament. **Divisions:** Open; Senior; Super Seniors; Women. **Publications:** History of Left-Handed Golf ● Southpaw Activities, 5/year. Newsletter. Includes tournament results, calendar of events, membership profiles, and obituaries. **Price:** included in membership dues. **Circulation:** 1,600. **Advertising:** accepted. **Conventions/Meetings:** annual board meeting.

22935 ■ National Pan-American Junior Golf Association (NPAJGA)
c/o National Pan-American Golf Association
PO Box 7211
Corpus Christi, TX 78467-7211
Ph: (903)569-2638
Fax: (630)604-6985
E-mail: rtreyes@tyler.net
URL: http://npaga.callernetwork.com/main.html
Contact: Raymond T. Reyes, Sec.
Founded: 1998. **Members:** 3,000. **Membership Dues:** corporate, $500 (annual). **Staff:** 3. **Regional Groups:** 41. **State Groups:** 36. **National Groups:** 7. **Description:** Individuals and organizations with an interest in youth golf. Promotes increased participation in the game of golf by children and youth. Provides golf instruction for young people; organizes tournaments including national and international junior championships. **Awards:** Scholarship Awards. **Frequency:** periodic. **Type:** scholarship. **Recipient:** for financial and academic need. **Publications:** El Campo. Newsletter. **Circulation:** 2,900. **Conventions/Meetings:** convention ● annual meeting and convention - usually winter.

22936 ■ National Senior Golf Association (NSGA)
3673 Nottingham Way
Hamilton Square, NJ 08690
Ph: (609)631-8145
Free: (800)282-6772
Fax: (609)584-8905
E-mail: mark@nationalseniorgolf.com
URL: http://www.nsgatour.com
Contact: Liza Price, Pres.
Membership Dues: family, $35 (annual). **Description:** Organizes golf tournaments for amateur golf-

ers. Conducts social events that offer creative activities and recreational choices. Promotes physical fitness among adults. **Publications:** FORE! Seniors, bimonthly. Newsletter. Features events and golf travel and information. Alternate Formats: online. **Conventions/Meetings:** annual competition.

22937 ■ PGA TOUR Tournaments Association (PGATTA)
13000 Sawgrass Village Cir., Ste.36
Ponte Vedra Beach, FL 32082
Ph: (904)285-4222
Fax: (904)273-5726
E-mail: suzanne@pgatta.org
URL: http://pgatta.org
Contact: Suzanne Bohle, Exec. Dir.
Founded: 1970. **Members:** 50. **Staff:** 2. **Budget:** $500,000. **Multinational. Description:** Sponsors major professional golf tournaments held on the regular PGA Tour in the United States and Canada each year. Provides forum for exchange of information and ideas. **Awards: Frequency:** annual. **Type:** recognition. **Computer Services:** Mailing lists. **Committees:** Annual Meeting; Communications; Executive; Finance; Marketing; Operations. **Affiliated With:** International Association of Golf Administrators; National Golf Foundation. **Formerly:** (1970) International Golf Sponsors Association; (1997) American Golf Sponsors; (1998) Professional Golf Tournaments Association; (1999) PGA Tour Directors Association. **Conventions/Meetings:** annual conference, over 75 industry suppliers (exhibits) - always November.

22938 ■ Professional Golf Teachers Association of America (PGTAA)
PO Box 912
La Quinta, CA 92247
Ph: (760)777-1925
Fax: (760)777-1925
E-mail: info@pgtaa.com
URL: http://www.pgtaa.com
Contact: Susan Lotz, Contact
Multinational. Description: Encourages and promotes efficiency in and responsibility in relation to the profession. Promotes uniform practice and discipline among practitioners. Encourages the study of the golf game and profession. Seeks to uphold and improve the standards of professional conduct and qualifications of practitioners. **Publications:** Newsletter, quarterly. Alternate Formats: online.

22939 ■ Professional Golfers' Association of America (PGA)
100 Ave. of the Champions
Palm Beach Gardens, FL 33410
Ph: (561)624-8400
Fax: (561)624-8430
E-mail: info@pga.com
URL: http://www.pga.com
Contact: Jim Awtrey, CEO
Founded: 1916. **Members:** 24,000. **Membership Dues:** plus section dues, $100. **Staff:** 120. **Budget:** $120,000,000. **Regional Groups:** 41. **Description:** Recruits and trains men and women to manage a variety of golf businesses, including golf clubs, courses, and tournaments. Sponsors PGA Championship, PGA Seniors' Championship, Ryder Cup Matches, PGA Grand Slam of Golf, Club Professional Championship, PGA Foundation, and Senior Club Professional Championship; PGA Junior Championship; PGA Assistants Championship. Conducts Professional Golf Management; certifies college programs in golf management at 14 universities. Sponsors winter tournament program for club professionals including tournaments held in south Florida. Offers complementary employment services for PGA members and employers, owns and operates PGA Golf Club and PGA Learning Center. **Libraries: Type:** reference. **Holdings:** films, video recordings. **Awards:** Club Professional of the Year Award. **Frequency:** annual. **Type:** recognition ● Junior Golf Leader Award. **Type:** recognition ● Merchandiser of the Year Award. **Frequency:** annual. **Type:** recognition ● Player of the Year Award. **Frequency:** annual. **Type:** recognition ● Teacher of the Year Award. **Frequency:** annual. **Type:** recognition ● Vardon Trophy.

Type: trophy. **Committees:** Awards; Championship; Club Relations; Education; Junior Golf; National Golf Month. **Departments:** Broadcasting; Career Services; Communications and Public Awareness; Credit Union; Education; Golf Expositions; Golf Promotions; Insurance; Marketing; Member Information Service Center; Personnel; PGA Golf Properties; PGA Travel and Special Events; Player Development; Section Affairs; Tournament. **Publications:** *PGA Magazine*, monthly. Includes PGA tournament news, golf instruction, and profiles of professional golfers and industry leaders, book and video reviews, and statistics. **Price:** included in membership dues; $23.95 /year for nonmembers. ISSN: 1044-1204. **Circulation:** 50,000. **Advertising:** accepted. **Conventions/Meetings:** annual Business Meeting ● annual meeting (exhibits) ● biennial Teaching Summit - meeting.

22940 ■ Professional Putters Association (PPA)

5225 28th St.
Lubbock, TX 79407
E-mail: commissioner@proputters.com
URL: http://www.proputters.com
Contact: Joe Aboid, Commissioner
Founded: 1959. **Members:** 1,200. **Membership Dues:** professional, $150 (annual) ● amateur, $25 (annual). **Staff:** 32. **Description:** Persons over age 18 who compete in national putting tournaments sanctioned by the Association; "Putt Putt" golf course franchise owners, managers, and suppliers. Seeks to recognize, develop, and reward the skills and abilities of America's putters. Sponsors competitions; compiles statistics; presents awards national, regional and local titles and cash prizes. Produces Putt-Putt Golf Courses Championship currently airing on ESPN Series, a television sports show of three half-hour segments. **Libraries: Type:** open to the public. **Holdings:** archival material, periodicals, video recordings. **Awards:** PPA Hall of Fame Award. **Frequency:** annual. **Type:** recognition ● Sportsman of the Year. **Frequency:** annual. **Type:** recognition. **Committees:** Pros Players. **Publications:** *Putt Putt World*, biennial. Magazine. Serves as a consumer publication dedicated to the sport of putting. **Circulation:** 180,000. **Advertising:** accepted ● *Rub of the Green*, annual. Newsletter. Contains reviews tournaments, schedules, players, and statistics. **Circulation:** 1,200. **Advertising:** accepted. Alternate Formats: online.

22941 ■ Puerto Rico Golf Association (PRGA)

58 Caribe St.
San Juan, PR 00907-1909
Ph: (787)721-7742
Fax: (787)723-5760
E-mail: egonzalez@prga.org
URL: http://www.prga.org
Contact: Mr. Luis Elvin Gonzalez, Pres.
Founded: 1954. **Membership Dues:** adult, $25 (annual) ● junior, $10 (annual). **Description:** Professional golfers and golfing enthusiasts. Strives to further the game of golf. Sponsors variety of golfing tours and events. **Programs:** Community Service; Scholarship. **Publications:** *FORE*, quarterly. Newsletter.

22942 ■ United States Golf Association (USGA)

PO Box 708
Far Hills, NJ 07931
Ph: (908)234-2300
Fax: (908)234-9687
E-mail: usga@usga.org
URL: http://www.usga.org
Contact: James T. Snow, Natl. Dir.
Founded: 1894. **Members:** 9,750. **Membership Dues:** individual, junior, $15 (annual) ● dual, $25 (annual) ● champion, $50 (annual) ● eagle club (individual, dual), $100-$125 (annual) ● medal club (individual, dual), $250-$300 (annual) ● honor club (individual, dual), $500-$650 (annual). **Staff:** 200. **Description:** Regularly organized golf clubs and golf courses. Serves as governing body for golf in the United States. Turfgrass Visiting Service promotes scientific work in turf management. Provides data on

rules, handicapping, amateur status, tournament procedure, turf maintenance, and golf balls and implements. Administers Golf House Museum, a collection of memorabilia including clubs of champions, the Moon Club, and paintings, insignia, and portraits of USGA champions. Sponsors USGA Research and Educational Fund. Conducts 13 annual national championships and research programs; sponsors teams for international competitions. **Libraries: Type:** reference. **Holdings:** 10,000. **Awards:** Bob Jones Award. **Type:** recognition ● Golf House Book Award. **Type:** recognition ● USGA Green Selection Award. **Type:** recognition. **Departments:** Green Section. **Programs:** Fellowship. **Affiliated With:** USGA Green Section. **Publications:** *Decisions on the Rules of Golf* ● *Golf Journal*, 9/year ● *Green Section Record*, bimonthly ● *Rules of Golf* ● Brochures. Contains information on rules, course maintenance, and safety. ● Handbook. **Conventions/Meetings:** annual meeting.

22943 ■ United States Golf Teachers Federation (USGTF)

1295 SE Port St. Lucie Blvd.
Port St. Lucie, FL 34952
Ph: (772)335-3216
Free: (888)346-3290
Fax: (772)335-3822
E-mail: info@usgtf.com
URL: http://www.usgtf.com
Contact: Geoff Bryant, Pres.
Founded: 1989. **Members:** 8,000. **Membership Dues:** regular, $185 (annual). **Staff:** 10. **Description:** Represents golf teaching professionals. Offers professional training and certification. **Computer Services:** Mailing lists. **Publications:** *Golf Teaching Pro*, quarterly. Magazine. Contains information on the latest teaching methodology, member benefits, tournament information and marketing strategies. **Circulation:** 10,000. **Advertising:** accepted. Alternate Formats: online ● *Golf Teaching Professionals*, monthly. Newsletter. Alternate Formats: online ● Brochure. Includes information on golf teaching certification courses. **Conventions/Meetings:** biennial World Golf Teachers Cup - conference (exhibits).

22944 ■ USGA Green Section

PO Box 708
Far Hills, NJ 07931
Ph: (908)234-2300
Free: (800)223-0041
Fax: (908)781-1736
E-mail: greensectionemail@usga.org
URL: http://www.usga.org/turf
Contact: James T. Snow, Natl. Dir.
Founded: 1920. **Description:** A department of United States Golf Association. Members are golf clubs and golf course superintendents. Aims to improve maintenance and management of golf courses. Maintains speakers' bureau and museum. Holds rules seminars. **Libraries: Type:** reference. **Holdings:** 8,000; books, periodicals. **Awards:** Green Section Award. **Frequency:** annual. **Type:** recognition. **Recipient:** for outstanding contribution to the game of golf ● Piper and Oakley Award. **Frequency:** periodic. **Type:** recognition. **Recipient:** for individuals who have contributed to the programs of the Green Section. **Publications:** *Golf Journal*, 8/year ● *USGA Green Section Record*, bimonthly ● Directory, periodic. **Conventions/Meetings:** annual conference, held in conjunction with Golf Course Superintendents Association of America.

22945 ■ Western Golf Association (WGA)

1 Briar Rd.
Golf, IL 60029
Ph: (847)724-4600
Fax: (847)724-7133
E-mail: evansscholars@wgaesf.com
URL: http://www.westerngolfassociation.com
Contact: Donald D. Johnson, Exec. Dir.
Founded: 1899. **Members:** 500. **Budget:** $5,000,000. **Description:** More than 500 golf and country clubs. Conducts three national golf championships: the Western Open, Western Amateur, and Western Junior. Supports and administers the Evans

Scholars Foundation, which awards four-year college scholarships to caddies on a competitive basis. **Awards:** Evans Scholarship. **Frequency:** annual. **Type:** scholarship. **Recipient:** for high school students. **Publications:** Annual Report, annual ● Brochure, annual. **Conventions/Meetings:** annual meeting - always May, in Golf, IL.

22946 ■ World Senior Golf Federation

c/o Sherry Clark, Exec. Dir.
PO Box 350667
Westminster, CO 80035-0667
Ph: (303)920-4206
Fax: (303)920-8206
E-mail: worldseniorgolf@comcast.net
URL: http://www.worldseniorgolf.com
Contact: Sherry Clark, Exec. Dir.
Multinational. Description: Encourages the international development of golf. Organizes golf tournaments and conducts social events that offer creative activities and recreational choices. Promotes physical fitness among adults. Fosters friendship and sportsmanship among members. **Telecommunication Services:** electronic mail, rjstone2@sbcglobal.net.

Gymnastics

22947 ■ American Group Gymnastics Association (AGGA)

c/o USA Gymnastics
201 S Capitol Ave.
Pan Am Plz., Ste.300
Indianapolis, IN 46225
Ph: (317)237-5050
Fax: (317)237-5069
E-mail: webmaster@usa-gymnastics.org
URL: http://www.usa-gymnastics.org/gg/2002/whatis-agga.html
Contact: Lynn Moskovitz, Pres.
Membership Dues: coach, $20 (annual). **Description:** Represents the interests of individuals dedicated to the advancement of group gymnastics in the U.S. through the education of coaches and participants in the sport. Promotes group gymnastics events. **Computer Services:** Mailing lists. **Telecommunication Services:** electronic mail, dcapelot@tfb.com.

22948 ■ College Gymnastics Association (CGA)

c/o Dr. Richard Aronson, Exec. Dir.
52 Evelyn Rd.
Needham, MA 02494
Ph: (617)444-3893
E-mail: fallen@huskers.unl.edu
URL: http://tigger.uic.edu/~cjgym
Contact: Dr. Richard Aronson, Exec. Dir.
Founded: 1950. **Members:** 125. **Membership Dues:** $150 (annual). **Description:** Compiles statistics; holds competitions; maintains hall of fame. **Awards:** Assistant Coach of the Year Award. **Frequency:** annual. **Type:** recognition. **Recipient:** for the nominated assistant coach who receives the highest number of votes from CGA active members ● Honor Coach Award. **Frequency:** annual. **Type:** recognition. **Recipient:** for a member-coach of twenty-five years or more who has gained the admiration of his coaching associates ● Nissen-Emery Award. **Frequency:** annual. **Type:** recognition. **Recipient:** for outstanding senior collegiate gymnast ● Special Service Award. **Frequency:** annual. **Type:** recognition. **Recipient:** for a member who had a significant contribution to the CGA and also for a retiring president for his outstanding service. **Computer Services:** database, coaches statistics. **Additional Websites:** http://www.collegegymnastics.org. **Formerly:** (2000) Collegiate Gymnastics Association. **Publications:** Directory ● Also issues weekly stat reports. **Conventions/Meetings:** NCAA Championships - competition ● regional meeting ● annual USA Gymnastics - convention and congress.

22949 ■ Eastern Intercollegiate Gymnastic League (EIGL)
c/o Eastern College Athletic Conference
1311 Craigville Beach Rd.
PO Box 3
Centerville, MA 02632
Ph: (508)771-5060
Fax: (508)771-9486
E-mail: sbamford@ecac.org
URL: http://www.ecac.org
Contact: Steve Bamford, Interim Commissioner
Founded: 1926. **Members:** 8. **Description:** Colleges having men's gymnastic teams. Conducts annual competition; establishes rules. **Affiliated With:** Eastern Collegiate Hockey Association. **Conventions/ Meetings:** annual meeting.

22950 ■ National Association of Collegiate Gymnastics Coaches/Women (NACGC/W)
c/o Mike Lorenzen, Pres.
120 Indian Hill Rd.
Boalsburg, PA 16827
Ph: (814)404-4686
E-mail: mlorenzen@woodwardcamp.com
URL: http://www.collegegymnast.com
Contact: Mike Lorenzen, Pres.
Founded: 1982. **Members:** 300. **Budget:** $50,000. **Description:** Women collegiate gymnastics coaches. **Conventions/Meetings:** annual convention - every May.

22951 ■ National Association of Women's Gymnastic's Judges (NAWGJ)
c/o Carole Ide, Pres.
26 Country Club Ct.
Hilton Head, SC 29926
Ph: (843)682-2652
E-mail: ci.nawgj@adelphia.net
URL: http://www.nawgj.org
Contact: Carole Ide, Pres.
Membership Dues: professional, $55 (annual) ● new judge, $45 (annual) ● associate (non-judge, coach, parent), $35 (annual). **Description:** Supports and promotes women's gymnastics in the United States. Provides professional development, education, communication and representation for members. **Publications:** *National NAWGJ News.* Newsletter.

22952 ■ National Gymnastics Judges Association (NGJA)
c/o Butch Zunich, Pres.
2302 Sand Point
Champaign, IL 61822
Ph: (217)359-4866 (217)384-8517
Fax: (217)384-8550
E-mail: zunich@urbana.css.mot.com
URL: http://www.ngja.org
Contact: Butch Zunich, Pres.
Founded: 1969. **Members:** 900. **Membership Dues:** professional, $50 (annual). **Budget:** $40,000. **Regional Groups:** 4. **Local Groups:** 15. **Description:** Represents judges of men's gymnastic competitions. Trains judges and serves the entire U.S. men's gymnastic community with qualified officials for national and international competition. Conducts full certification courses quadrennially and refresher courses annually. Maintains National Judges Hall of Fame; conducts research programs; compiles statistics; updates and interprets men's gymnastics rules. **Awards:** NGJA Hall of Fame. **Frequency:** annual. **Type:** recognition. **Recipient:** for outstanding members ● Regional Judges Award. **Frequency:** annual. **Type:** recognition. **Recipient:** for outstanding judges. **Boards:** Governing; Technical. **Affiliated With:** International Gymnastic Federation; USA Gymnastics. **Publications:** *Men's Rules Interpretations,* semiannual. Book ● *Rules Interpretations,* annual ● Membership Directory, annual. **Price:** included in membership dues. **Advertising:** accepted ● Newsletter, annual. **Price:** included in membership dues. **Advertising:** accepted. **Conventions/Meetings:** semiannual conference and workshop (exhibits).

22953 ■ USA Gymnastics (USA GYM)
Pan Amer. Plz., Ste.300
201 S Capitol Ave.
Indianapolis, IN 46225
Ph: (317)237-5050
Free: (800)345-4719
Fax: (317)237-5069
E-mail: rebound@usa-gymnastics.org
URL: http://www.usa-gymnastics.org
Contact: Steve Penny, Pres.
Founded: 1963. **Members:** 100,000. **Membership Dues:** instructor, athlete, $44-$49 (annual) ● club, $160 (annual) ● industry, $325 (annual). **Staff:** 40. **Budget:** $13,000,000. **National Groups:** 35. **Description:** National associations or organizations concerned with amateur sports, particularly gymnastics. Conducts national program in gymnastics for Junior Olympics and Junior, Senior, and Elite International level gymnasts. Selects teams for World Championships, World Cup, Pan American Games, Olympic Games, and other international events. Sponsors sessions on training and safety, coaching techniques, and officiating at annual convention. Compiles statistics; conducts research programs. **Libraries: Type:** reference. **Holdings:** archival material. **Awards:** Athlete/Coach of Year. **Type:** recognition ● Hall of Fame. **Type:** recognition ● Star Service. **Type:** recognition. **Computer Services:** Online services. **Committees:** Elite; Foreign Relations; Junior Olympic; Sanctioning; Technical. **Programs:** International; Rhythmic. **Affiliated With:** United States Olympic Committee. **Formerly:** (1993) United States Gymnastics Federation. **Publications:** *Guidance for the Instruction of International Judges of Women's Artistic Gymnastics ● Men's Rules for Competition ● National Compulsory Routines ● Technical Journal,* monthly. **Price:** $25.00 in U.S.; $48.00 in Canada; $60.00 outside U.S. and Canada ● Magazine, bimonthly. **Price:** $19.95 in U.S. ● Manual ● Also publishes English translations of technical manuals.** **Conventions/Meetings:** annual National Congress, gymnastics excellence through education (exhibits).

Handball

22954 ■ United States Handball Association (USHA)
2333 N Tucson Blvd.
Tucson, AZ 85716
Ph: (520)795-0434
Free: (800)289-8742
Fax: (520)795-0465
E-mail: handball@ushandball.org
URL: http://ushandball.org
Contact: Vern Roberts, Exec. Dir.
Founded: 1951. **Members:** 9,000. **Membership Dues:** individual, $35 (annual) ● junior, student, $10 (annual). **Staff:** 5. **Budget:** $1,000,000. **Regional Groups:** 9. **State Groups:** 50. **Local Groups:** 50. **Description:** Handball players, fans, and coaches. Establishes rules, sponsors tournaments, and promotes recognition of handball as an intercollegiate activity. Supports games and tournaments for youngsters. Maintains hall of fame. **Libraries: Type:** open to the public. **Awards:** Hall of Fame. **Frequency:** annual. **Type:** recognition. **Computer Services:** Mailing lists. **Committees:** Civic Activities; Intercollegiate Activities; Rules. **Publications:** *Handball,* bimonthly. **Price:** $30.00 /year for nonmembers; included in membership dues. ISSN: 0046-6778. **Circulation:** 9,000. **Advertising:** accepted. **Conventions/Meetings:** annual National Tournament - meeting (exhibits) - always June.

Hockey

22955 ■ American Hockey Coaches Association (AHCA)
c/o Joe Bertagna, Exec. Dir.
7 Concord St.
Gloucester, MA 01930
Ph: (781)245-4177

Fax: (781)245-2492
E-mail: jbertagna@hockeyeastonline.com
URL: http://www.ahcahockey.com
Contact: Joe Bertagna, Exec. Dir.
Founded: 1947. **Members:** 1,200. **Membership Dues:** allied, $75 (annual) ● amateur, high school, $25 (annual) ● division I, $315 (annual) ● division II-III, $185 (annual). **Description:** Represents university, college, and secondary school ice hockey coaches. Conducts coaches' clinics throughout the U.S. **Awards:** Coach of the Year Award. **Frequency:** annual. **Type:** recognition ● D-3 Player of the Year. **Frequency:** annual. **Type:** recognition ● Joe Burke Award. **Frequency:** annual. **Type:** recognition. **Recipient:** for an individual who has shown great support to girls/women's hockey ● JOFA All-American Teams. **Frequency:** annual. **Type:** recognition ● John Kelley Founders Award. **Frequency:** annual. **Type:** recognition. **Recipient:** for people in coaching profession who contributed to the growth and development of ice hockey ● John Mariucci Award. **Frequency:** annual. **Type:** recognition. **Recipient:** for an exemplary secondary school coach ● Terry Flanagan Award. **Frequency:** annual. **Type:** recognition. **Recipient:** to an assistant coach's career body of work. **Divisions:** College; Independents; Professional; University. **Publications:** *American Hockey Coaches Directory,* annual. **Circulation:** 1,500 ● *Stops and Starts,* 8/year. **Conventions/Meetings:** annual convention (exhibits).

22956 ■ American Hockey League (AHL)
1 Monarch Pl., Ste.2400
Springfield, MA 01144-4004
Ph: (413)781-2030
Fax: (413)733-4767
E-mail: info@theahl.com
URL: http://www.theahl.com
Contact: David A. Andrews, Pres./CEO
Founded: 1936. **Members:** 19. **Staff:** 10. **Budget:** $1,000,000. **Description:** Professional ice hockey league with teams in: Albany, NY; Hartford, CT; Rochester, NY; Syracuse, NY; Hershey, PA; Springfield, MA; Worcester, MA; Providence, RI; Portland, ME; Norfolk, VA; Louisville, KY; Quebec City, QC, Canada; Wilkes-Barre, PA; Cincinnati, OH; Hamilton, ON; Lexington, KY; Lowell, MA; Philadelphia, PA; Saint John, NB, Canada; and St. John's, NFLD Canada. Provides sponsorship packages and licenses merchandise. Compiles scoring statistics weekly during season. **Committees:** Expansion; Marketing; Rules. **Publications:** *Official Rule Book,* annual. Contains the details of all of the playing rules utilized by the AHL. **Price:** $6.00. **Advertising:** accepted ● *Schedule,* annual. Directory. Includes starting times and complete team directory. **Price:** $1.00 ● *2000-01 AHL Official Guide and Record Book,* annual. **Price:** $20.00 each. **Advertising:** accepted ● *Weekly Statistics.* **Price:** $50.00. **Conventions/Meetings:** annual meeting - always mid-July.

22957 ■ Central Collegiate Hockey Association (CCHA)
23995 Freeway Park Dr., Ste.101
Farmington Hills, MI 48335
Ph: (248)888-0600
Fax: (248)888-0664
URL: http://ccha.cstv.com
Contact: Tom Anastos, Commissioner
Founded: 1971. **Members:** 12. **Staff:** 4. **Description:** Colleges with National Collegiate Athletic Association Division I hockey programs including Bowling Green State University, Ferris State University, Lake Superior State University, Michigan State University, Miami University, Northern Michigan University, Ohio State University, University of Alaska Fairbanks, University of Michigan, University of Notre Dame, Western Michigan University, and University of Nebraska Omaha. Provides officiating services. Sponsors playoffs. Compiles statistics. **Awards:** Player of the Week. **Frequency:** weekly. **Type:** recognition. **Recipient:** for the best player of the week based upon performance in a weekend series. **Affiliated With:** National Collegiate Athletic Association. **Publications:** *CCHA Insider,* monthly. Magazine. Contains features, news, and statistics on all 12

member schools. ● *Media Guide*, annual. Contains information regarding the twelve teams in the league. **Price:** $14.00. **Advertising:** accepted. Alternate Formats: CD-ROM; online ● *Press Release*, weekly ● Articles. Alternate Formats: online. **Conventions/ Meetings:** competition ● semiannual Executive Council Meeting, review code of regulations; discuss, pass, and amend legislation.

22958 ■ Eastern College Athletic Conference (ECAC)
1311 Craigville Beach Rd.
Centerville, MA 02632
Ph: (508)771-5060
Fax: (508)771-9481
E-mail: sbamford@ecac.org
URL: http://www.ecac.org
Contact: Mr. Stephen R. Bamford, Interim Commissioner
Founded: 1940. **Members:** 220. **Description:** Administers over 100 postseason events in 35 men's and women's sports. Offers the prestigious Asa S. Bushnell post-graduate internship. Maintains a legislative and compliance service to assist members with the application of NCAA regulations. Assigns officials for Divisions I, II and III in 15 sports. Administers and hosts special events such as the ECAC Lambert Football Poll, the Eastern College Football Banquet, and the NCAA Division III New England Regional Baseball Championship among others. **Awards:** Distinguished Achievement Award. **Frequency:** periodic. **Type:** recognition. **Recipient:** to an athletic administrator who has achieved outstanding success in his/her career ● Dr. Donald Grover Memorial Award. **Frequency:** periodic. **Type:** recognition. **Recipient:** to an athletic trainer who has made a significant contribution to intercollegiate athletics ● ECAC Jostens Institution of the Year. **Frequency:** annual. **Type:** recognition. **Recipient:** to an institution that best exemplifies the highest standards of collegiate academic and athletic performances ● ECAC Jostens Male and Female Administrators of the Year. **Frequency:** annual. **Type:** recognition. **Recipient:** for an outstanding service to ECAC ● ECAC Robbins Scholar-Athlete Award. **Frequency:** annual. **Type:** scholarship. **Recipient:** for one male and one female athlete from division I, II and III member institutions ● George L. Shiebler Award. **Frequency:** annual. **Type:** recognition. **Recipient:** to an ECAC official who has demonstrated dedication to his/her avocational activities ● Katherine Ley Award. **Frequency:** annual. **Type:** recognition. **Recipient:** for an Eastern woman athletic administrator. **Affiliated With:** Eastern Collegiate Hockey Association. **Formerly:** Intercollegiate Ice Hockey Association. **Conventions/Meetings:** annual meeting.

22959 ■ Eastern Collegiate Hockey Association (ECHA)
c/o Marshall Stevenson, Commissioner
18206 Bunker Hill Rd.
Parkton, MD 21120-9435
Ph: (410)704-2963 (410)357-9878
Fax: (410)704-4702
E-mail: mstevenson@towson.edu
URL: http://www.echahockey.com
Contact: Marshall Stevenson, Commissioner
Founded: 1938. **Members:** 278. **Description:** Colleges and universities in 14 New England and Middle Atlantic states and the District of Columbia. Supervises tournaments and championship competitions for men and women either on a conference basis or for the affiliated organizations in baseball, basketball, cross country, fencing, field hockey, football, golf, gymnastics, ice hockey, lacrosse, rowing, soccer, softball, swimming, tennis, track, volleyball, and wrestling. Supervises and appoints game officials. Maintains files on individual and team records; collects statistics. **Publications:** *ECAC Directory and Record Book*, annual ● *ECAC Regulations Handbook*, biennial. **Conventions/Meetings:** annual convention ● semiannual meeting.

22960 ■ Hockey North America (HNA)
PO Box 78
Sterling, VA 20167-0078

Ph: (703)430-8100
Free: (800)446-2539
Fax: (703)421-9205
E-mail: hnasupport@aol.com
URL: http://www.hna.com
Contact: Elliott Root, Pres.
Founded: 2000. **Members:** 4,000. **Staff:** 8. **State Groups:** 13. **For-Profit. Description:** Hockey league. Promotes the sport of hockey. **Formerly:** (2000) Dominion Sports Services, Inc. **Publications:** Brochure. Alternate Formats: online.

22961 ■ USA Hockey
1775 Bob Johnson Dr.
Colorado Springs, CO 80906-4090
Ph: (719)576-8724
Free: (800)566-3288
Fax: (719)538-1160
E-mail: usah@usahockey.org
URL: http://www.usahockey.com
Contact: Ron DeGregorio, Pres.
Founded: 1937. **Members:** 589,907. **Staff:** 75. **Regional Groups:** 12. **Description:** Serves as the national governing body for the sport of ice hockey in the United States. Promotes the growth of ice hockey in America by encouraging, developing, advancing all participants and administering the sport. **Computer Services:** database ● mailing lists. **Committees:** Executive; Finance; Member Service/Insurance; Nominating/Credentials; Player Development; Playing Rules; Risk Management; Safety and Protective Equipment. **Councils:** Adult; International; Junior; Legal; Marketing; Youth. **Affiliated With:** International Ice Hockey Federation; United States Olympic Committee. **Formerly:** (1991) Amateur Hockey Association of the U.S. **Publications:** *Official Guide*, annual ● *Official Playing Rules Book*, biennial ● *Referee's Manual*, periodic ● *USA Hockey Magazine*, 10/year. **Price:** $70.00 for nonmembers. **Circulation:** 450,000. **Advertising:** accepted ● Brochures. Contains instructional materials for players, referees, and coaches. **Conventions/Meetings:** annual convention (exhibits) ● quarterly executive committee meeting.

22962 ■ Western Collegiate Hockey Association (WCHA)
2211 S Josephine, Rm. 302
Denver, CO 80210
Ph: (303)871-4223
Fax: (303)871-4770
E-mail: bmcleod@du.edu
URL: http://wcha.cstv.com
Contact: Bruce M. McLeod, Commissioner
Founded: 1952. **Members:** 10. **Staff:** 5. **Description:** College ice hockey league comprising Colorado College, Michigan Technological University, Northern Michigan University, St. Cloud State University, University of Alaska-Anchorage, University of Denver, University of Minnesota, University of Minnesota-Duluth, University of North Dakota, and University of Wisconsin. Works to continue and improve competition in ice hockey in conjunction with colleges and universities. Administers games; supervises and hires game officials for annual league play; compiles and distributes league records and statistics; conducts annual championship tournament; certifies student athletes; develops league schedules. **Awards:** Frequency: annual. **Type:** recognition. **Telecommunication Services:** electronic mail, clabelle@du.edu. **Affiliated With:** National Collegiate Athletic Association. **Publications:** *News Release*, weekly. **Advertising:** accepted ● Yearbook, annual. **Conventions/Meetings:** annual conference - always April.

Home Study

22963 ■ Home School Sports Network (HSPN)
PO Box 69
Linden, VA 22642
Ph: (540)636-3713

E-mail: info@hspn.net
URL: http://www.hspn.net
Contact: Chris Davis, Founder/Exec. Dir.
Membership Dues: getting started, $15 (annual) ● team/organization, $25 (annual) ● showcase me, $160 (annual) ● founder, $500 (annual). **Description:** Dedicated to offering "Christian homeschool sporting events done in a way that would make God proud." Motto is "Sportsmanship the Way GOD Intended". **Publications:** Newsletter. **Price:** free. Alternate Formats: online.

Horse Driving

22964 ■ American Driving Society (ADS)
PO Box 278
Cross Plains, WI 53528
Ph: (608)237-7382
Fax: (608)237-6468
E-mail: info@americandrivingsociety.org
URL: http://www.americandrivingsociety.org
Contact: Susan Koos Acker, Exec. Dir.
Founded: 1974. **Members:** 3,200. **Membership Dues:** individual in Canada, $65 (annual) ● club, commercial, outside U.S., $60 (annual) ● family, $85 (annual) ● junior, $40 (annual) ● life, $1,000 ● sustaining, $160 (annual). **Staff:** 4. **Budget:** $225,000. **Description:** Persons interested in the sport of driving horses and carriages. Promotes horse and pony driving both competitively and for pleasure; create and maintain public interest in driving events; organize or facilitate the organization of driving events; establish a list of qualified judges. Sponsors educational programs, judge's clinics, and a junior judging program; recognizes driving competitions. Maintains speakers' bureau. **Computer Services:** Mailing lists, of members. **Publications:** *The Wheelhorse*, 8/year. Newsletter. Contains calendar of events, late breaking news, articles, and safety tips. ● *The Whip*, quarterly. Magazine. Contains in-depth educational features, reports on local club and regional activities. **Price:** included in membership dues. **Circulation:** 3,200. **Advertising:** accepted ● Handbook, annual. **Conventions/Meetings:** semiannual conference (exhibits).

Horse Racing

22965 ■ American Barrel Racing Association (ABRA)
PO Box 203
Collinsville, TX 76233
Ph: (817)790-4446 (580)395-0024
E-mail: homeoffice@abra4d.com
URL: http://www.abra4d.com
Contact: Christin Brown-Umsted, Pres.
Founded: 2001. **Membership Dues:** individual, $20 (annual) ● duo, $30 (annual) ● family, $40 (annual). **Description:** Promotes the sport of 4D barrel racing and the horse industry in general, by creating an exciting, yet educational, family atmosphere at all ABRA events. Organizes barrel racers across the United States of America for their mutual protection and benefit. Raises the standards of 4D barrel racing events. **Publications:** *ABRA Heartbeat*. Newsletter. Alternate Formats: online.

22966 ■ American Computer Barrel Racing Association (ACBRA)
c/o Mary Hodson, Pres.
PO Box 213
Catheys Valley, CA 95306
Ph: (209)742-4212
E-mail: bhodson@sierratel.com
URL: http://www.acbra.com
Contact: Mary Hodson, Pres.
Founded: 1985. **Membership Dues:** general/full (per horse), $50 (annual) ● associate/arena operator, $30 (annual). **Description:** Promotes the sport of barrel racing. Fulfills the need of a system that would enable people to compete in barrel racing against horses of their own skill level. Improves the image and popularity of barrel racing with the requirement

that all members shall exercise good sportsmanship and professionalism. **Computer Services:** Online services, message board. **Publications:** Newsletter, monthly. **Price:** included in membership dues.

22967 ■ Arabian Jockey Club (AJC)
10805 E Bethany Dr.
Aurora, CO 80014
Ph: (303)696-4523
Fax: (303)696-4599
E-mail: ajc@arabianracing.org
URL: http://www.arabianracing.org
Contact: Edgar M. Brown, Chm.

Founded: 1987. **Membership Dues:** affiliate, $50 (annual) ● individual, $100 (annual). **Staff:** 3. **Regional Groups:** 11. **Description:** Arabian horse owners, breeders, and racing enthusiasts. Works closely with the Arabian Horse Registry of America to promote and manage the Arabian horse racing industry. Oversees industry code of ethics. Lobbies state legislatures on behalf of the Arabian racing industry; gathers and disseminates information and statistics on Arabian racing; conducts educational seminars. **Computer Services:** database, Arabian racing reports ● online services. **Publications:** *Arabian Jockey Club News*, monthly. Newsletter. Includes racing statistics, calendar of association and racing events, and industry related articles. **Price:** included in membership dues ● *The Arabian Jockey Club Stallion Directory* ● *The Original Racehorse*. Video. **Price:** free ● Brochures.

22968 ■ Barrel Futurities of America (BFA)
c/o Ross Wright, Sec.-Treas.
5650 N Broadway
Norman, OK 73069
Ph: (405)364-0274
Fax: (405)364-8279
E-mail: ross@barrelfuturitiesofamerica.com
URL: http://www.barrelfuturitiesofamerica.com
Contact: Ross Wright, Sec.-Treas.

Founded: 1983. **Members:** 1,000. **Membership Dues:** individual, $85 (annual). **Description:** Organizers of and participants in futurities. Promotes barrel racing. (Barrel futurities involve racing individual horses around barrels; the horses must stay within prescribed boundaries and race against the clock.) Seeks to establish rules and guidelines. Sponsors competitions. Provides training upon request. **Awards:** Top 15 in Derby. **Type:** recognition ● Top 20 in Futurity. **Frequency:** annual. **Type:** recognition. **Committees:** Awards. **Publications:** *The Barrel Horse News*, bimonthly. Magazine. **Conventions/ Meetings:** annual meeting (exhibits).

22969 ■ Harness Horse Youth Foundation (HHYF)
16575 Carey Rd.
Westfield, IN 46074
Ph: (317)867-5877
Fax: (317)867-5896
E-mail: ellen@hhyf.org
URL: http://www.hhyf.org
Contact: Ellen Taylor, Exec. Dir.

Founded: 1976. **Staff:** 1. **Description:** Individuals interested in harness horse racing. Aims to foster interest in harness horse racing among young people and to develop and promote their careers in the sport. Sponsors camps, internships, scholarships, and 4-H programs. **Awards:** Rambling Willie Memorial Scholarship. **Frequency:** annual. **Type:** scholarship. **Recipient:** for students who are pursuing or planning to pursue horse related careers. **Formerly:** (1976) Ohio Standard Breeding Association Youth Foundation. **Publications:** *Careers In Harness Racing*. Booklet ● *Directory to Equine Schools and Colleges*, biennial. **Price:** $12.00 ● *Studying the Standardbred*. Book. **Conventions/Meetings:** annual meeting.

22970 ■ Harness Horsemen International (HHI)
64 Rte. 33
Manalapan, NJ 07726
Ph: (609)259-3717

Fax: (732)683-1578
Founded: 1964. **Members:** 15,000. **Staff:** 2. **Regional Groups:** 28. **Description:** Owners, drivers, trainers, and breeders engaged in harness racing. Works to better harness racing standards. Promotes welfare, insurance, and better purses. Seeks to protect members against unfair policies. **Awards:** Jerome L. Hauck Scholarship. **Frequency:** annual. **Type:** scholarship. **Conventions/Meetings:** semiannual conference.

22971 ■ Harness Racing Museum and Hall of Fame
PO Box 590
Goshen, NY 10924
Ph: (845)294-6330
Fax: (845)294-3463
E-mail: hrm@frontiernet.net
URL: http://www.harnessmuseum.com
Contact: Gail C. Cunard, Dir.

Founded: 1951. **Members:** 1,000. **Membership Dues:** friend, $35 (annual) ● associate, $50 (annual) ● family, $100-$999 (annual) ● corporate (minimum), $1,000 (annual) ● fellow, $1,000-$4,999 (annual) ● benefactor (minimum), $5,000 (annual). **Staff:** 15. **Budget:** $250,000. **Description:** Harness track owners, Standardbred farm owners, drivers, persons working in harness racing, and others interested in the sport. Promotes the study of the history of the American Standardbred. Preserves memorabilia of the harness horse sport. Works with harness tracks and organizations in promoting the sport and making the public aware of the historical significance of the American trotter and its influence upon international harness racing. Conducts traveling exhibits. Elects men and horses to the Living Hall of Fame. Maintains speakers' bureau; compiles statistics. Offers children's services. **Libraries: Type:** reference. **Holdings:** 3,000; archival material. **Subjects:** equine, harness racing. **Awards:** Harness Racing Hall of Fame. **Frequency:** annual. **Type:** recognition. **Recipient:** for significant contribution to the sport of harness racing ● Pinnacle Award. **Frequency:** annual. **Type:** recognition. **Recipient:** for members of the press and public relations professionals. **Computer Services:** database. **Formerly:** (1995) Trotting Horse Museum. **Publications:** *Mail Order Catalog*, annual. Features Harness racing gift items; items can also be purchased online. **Price:** free. **Circulation:** 50,000 ● *Museum News*, quarterly. Brochure. Includes book reviews, historical facts, and current events. **Price:** included in membership dues. **Circulation:** 1,100 ● *Souvenir Journal*, annual. Publication of the Hall of Fame Induction. **Price:** free. **Circulation:** 5,000. **Advertising:** accepted. Alternate Formats: online ● Brochure. **Conventions/Meetings:** annual Hall of Fame Induction Ceremonies - meeting - always first weekend of July, in Goshen, NY.

22972 ■ Harness Tracks of America (HTA)
4640 E Sunrise, Ste.200
Tucson, AZ 85718
Ph: (520)529-2525
Fax: (520)529-3235
E-mail: info@harnesstracks.com
URL: http://www.harnesstracks.com
Contact: Stanley F. Bergstein, Exec. VP

Founded: 1954. **Members:** 36. **Staff:** 4. **Description:** Represents major pari-mutuel harness race tracks in North America. Studies and supports research on aspects of harness track management and the standardbred industry. Informs track management of pertinent legal matters; carries out promotional and research programs. Compiles statistics; maintains speakers' bureau and placement service. **Libraries: Type:** reference. **Holdings:** archival material, audiovisuals, books, business records, clippings, periodicals. **Subjects:** racing and gambling industry. **Awards:** Driver of the Year. **Frequency:** annual. **Type:** recognition ● HTA Scholarships. **Frequency:** annual. **Type:** scholarship ● Messenger Award. **Frequency:** annual. **Type:** recognition ● Nova Award. **Frequency:** annual. **Type:** recognition. **Recipient:** selected by Track Racing Secretaries. **Publications:** *HTA Directory*, annual. Contains listings of all HTA tracks and most racing industry organizations. **Price:**

$15.00. **Circulation:** 2,500. **Advertising:** accepted ● *Track Topics*, weekly. Newsletter. Contains promotional material and highlights industry happenings, trends and developments within gaming industry. ● Executive Newsletter, daily with current hot topics, events, legislation effecting industry worldwide. **Conventions/Meetings:** annual Art Auction - competition, for art with harness racing or standardbred themes - last week September or first week of October ● annual board meeting - late February - early March.

22973 ■ International Barrel Racing Association (IBRA)
PO Box 425
Valley City, OH 44280
Ph: (330)483-9608
Fax: (330)483-9708
E-mail: info@ibra.us
URL: http://ibra.us
Membership Dues: associate/non-contestant, $30 (annual) ● single, $45 (annual) ● family, $95 (annual). **Multinational. Description:** Promotes the sport of barrel racing. Encourages larger participation at local approved shows by working with other associations. Builds outstanding awards program that will recognize and award barrel racers. **Computer Services:** Mailing lists ● online services, chat room ● online services, discussion boards.

22974 ■ International Trotting and Pacing Association (ITPA)
60 Gulf Rd.
Gouverneur, NY 13642
Ph: (315)287-2294
Fax: (315)287-5010
E-mail: ldenesha@twcny.rr.com
Contact: Kathy Denesha, Office Mgr.

Founded: 1964. **Members:** 500. **Membership Dues:** full (before January 1), $55 ● full (after January 1), $60. **Staff:** 1. **Multinational. Description:** Represents persons interested in promoting and developing the Trottingbred breed of light harness ponies for pleasure, profit, and show, and to compete in classified and conditioned racing in both the U.S. and Canada. **Formed by Merger of:** (1976) National Trotting and Pacing Association; IOMI. **Publications:** *Trottingbred* (in English and French), bimonthly. Magazine. **Price:** included in membership dues; $23.50 /year for nonmembers. **Advertising:** accepted. **Conventions/Meetings:** annual board meeting.

22975 ■ The Jockey Club (TJC)
821 Corporate Dr.
Lexington, KY 40503
Ph: (859)224-2700 (212)371-5970
Fax: (859)224-2710
E-mail: amarzelli@jockeyclub.com
URL: http://www.jockeyclub.com
Contact: Alan Marzelli, Pres./COO

Founded: 1894. **Members:** 100. **Staff:** 250. **Description:** Acts as the official breed registry for North American Thoroughbreds. Establishes regulations governing Thoroughbred breeding and the importation of foreign Thoroughbreds for racing purposes; family of companies provide a wide range of technology and information services to the Thoroughbred industry; two charitable foundations fund equine research and assist needy individuals in the thoroughbred industry. **Computer Services:** Online services, interactive registration. **Publications:** *The American Stud Book - Principal Rules and Requirements*. Alternate Formats: online ● *Jockey Club Fact Book*, annual. Alternate Formats: online.

22976 ■ Jockeys' Guild (JG)
PO Box 150
Monrovia, CA 91017-0150
Ph: (626)305-5605
Free: (866)465-6257
Fax: (626)305-5615
E-mail: info@jockeysguild.com
URL: http://www.jockeysguild.com
Contact: John Velazquez, Chm.

Founded: 1940. **Members:** 2,000. **Staff:** 14. **Description:** Represents licensed jockeys in good standing with all racing officials and commissions; limited to flat riding jockeys. Offers financial and medical aid to needy members and their families. **Formerly:** (1946) Jockey's Community Fund and Guild. **Publications:** *The Jockeys' News*, quarterly. Newsletter. **Advertising:** accepted. Alternate Formats: online ● *The Jockeys' News Express* (in English and Spanish). Newsletter. Alternate Formats: online. **Conventions/Meetings:** annual meeting - always December.

22977 ■ Kids to the Cup (KTTC)

2905 Circle Crest Ct.
Prospect, KY 40059
Ph: (626)695-3433
URL: http://www.kidstothecup.com
Contact: Trudy McCaffery, Pres.

Founded: 1999. **Description:** Horse racing fans. Offers education, advice, and support for racing fans between the ages of 8 and 16 years of age. Sponsors trips to racing events. Holds contests. Awards scholarships.

22978 ■ National Association of Off-Track Betting (NAOTB)

978 Park Pl., Box 3000
Pomona, NY 10970
Ph: (845)362-0400
Fax: (845)362-0419
E-mail: naotb@betsrus.com
Contact: Donald J. Groth, Treas.

Founded: 1973. **Members:** 7. **Membership Dues:** professional, $2,000 (annual). **Staff:** 1. **Description:** Legal gambling and off-track betting operations. Lobbies for tax issues and other legislation relevant to gambling and off-track betting; functions as a trade association for issues pertinent to off-track betting operations. **Conventions/Meetings:** semiannual conference and workshop.

22979 ■ National Barrel Horse Association (NBHA)

PO Box 1988
Augusta, GA 30903-1988
Ph: (706)722-7223
Fax: (706)823-3700
E-mail: nbha@nbha.com
URL: http://www.nbha.com
Contact: Sherry Fulmer, Exec. Dir.

Founded: 1992. **Members:** 22,000. **Membership Dues:** regular, family, $62 (annual) ● charter, $48 (annual). **Staff:** 9. **Regional Groups:** 6. **State Groups:** 50. **Local Groups:** 350. **National Groups:** 3. **Description:** Individuals interested in barrel horse racing. Promotes increased interest and participation in the sport of barrel racing. Establishes standard competitive rules for barrel racing and organizes leagues and district, state, national, and international competitions; compiles statistics. **Libraries: Type:** reference. **Holdings:** articles, audio recordings, periodicals, video recordings. **Subjects:** barrel racing. **Publications:** *Barrel Horse News*, monthly. Magazine. Includes racing results and show updates.

22980 ■ National Christian Barrel Racers Association (NCBRA)

7100 Houghton Rd.
Bakersfield, CA 93313
Ph: (661)831-9031
E-mail: ncbra@inthelord.net
URL: http://www.geocities.com/ncbra
Contact: Bill Overton, Pres.

Membership Dues: open, $50 (annual) ● junior (17 and under), $30 (annual) ● apprentice (10 and under), $10 (annual). **Description:** Shares the gospel of Jesus Christ through barrel racing and other related activities. Brings the Gospel of Jesus Christ to the lost and encourages fellowship among believers. Aims to establish outreach ministry teams throughout the Nation. **Additional Websites:** http://www.ncbra.com. **Publications:** Newsletter. Alternate Formats: online.

22981 ■ National Museum of Racing and Hall of Fame (NMR)

191 Union Ave.
Saratoga Springs, NY 12866-3566
Ph: (518)584-0400
Free: (800)562-5394
Fax: (518)584-4574
E-mail: nmrmedia@racingmuseum.net
URL: http://www.racingmuseum.org
Contact: Peter H. Hammell, Dir.

Founded: 1950. **Members:** 2,000. **Membership Dues:** individual, $50 (annual) ● family, $75 (annual) ● contributor, $100 (annual) ● donor, $250 (annual) ● associate, $500 (annual) ● patron, $1,000 (annual) ● benefactor, $1,500 (annual) ● gold cup, $2,500 (annual). **Staff:** 18. **Budget:** $2,200,000. **Description:** Preserves the history and promotes the popularity of Thoroughbred horse racing in the U.S. Maintains collection of art, trophies, silks, and books related to Thoroughbred racing. Conducts research and educational programs. **Libraries: Type:** open to the public. **Holdings:** 5,000; books, periodicals, photographs. **Subjects:** thoroughbred racing. **Publications:** Books ● Newsletter, quarterly. Alternate Formats: online. **Conventions/Meetings:** annual Hall of Fame Induction Ceremony - meeting.

22982 ■ National Steeplechase Association (NSA)

400 Fair Hill Dr.
Elkton, MD 21921
Ph: (410)392-0700
Fax: (410)392-0706
E-mail: info@nationalsteeplechase.com
URL: http://www.nationalsteeplechase.com
Contact: Jonathan E. Sheppard, Chm.

Founded: 1895. **Members:** 2,000. **Membership Dues:** regular, $150 (annual) ● patron, $500 ● historian, $1,000. **Description:** Turf governing body of steeplechase racing. Compiles and enforces rules to cover racing at hunt meetings, license trainers, and riders. **Absorbed:** United Hunts Racing Association. **Formerly:** National Steeplechase and Hunt Association. **Publications:** *American Steeplechasing*, annual. Yearbook ● Newsletter, quarterly.

22983 ■ National Thoroughbred Racing Association (TRC)

800 3rd Ave., Ste.901
New York, NY 10022
Ph: (212)230-9500
Fax: (212)752-3093
E-mail: ntra@ntra.com
URL: http://www.ntra.com
Contact: D.G. Van Clief Jr., Commissioner

Founded: 1987. **Staff:** 6. **Description:** Represents the interests of the Jockey Club, Thoroughbred Racing Associations, and Breeder's Cup Ltd. Seeks to expand and increase public awareness of thoroughbred racing and breeding. Promotes media relations programs. Co-produces monthly TV magazine show, "Thoroughbred World", and ready-to-air TRC Video News Features. Serves as central office for Equine Care Watch, a multi-breed communications project devoted to equine use and care issues. Maintains reference library; compiles statistics. **Publications:** *Post to Post*, bimonthly. Newsletter. Covers information for children. ● *TRC Media Update*, 35/year. Newsletter. Includes polls, television and radio schedules, news, and statistics. **Price:** free to media outlets; $75.00/year to nonmedia subscribers. **Circulation:** 600 ● *Wire to Wire: Enjoying a Day at the Races*.

22984 ■ North American Pt-to-Pt Association (NAPPA)

PO Box 102
Butler, MD 21023
Ph: (410)329-3749
Fax: (410)329-3884
E-mail: info@naptp.com
URL: http://naptp.com
Contact: Ms. Regina Welsh, Exec. Dir.

Membership Dues: adult, $35 (annual) ● junior, $25 (annual) ● family, $50 (annual) ● spectator, $100 (annual) ● master, $500 (annual) ● sponsor, $1,000

(annual) ● hurdle, organization, $250 (annual). **Description:** Protects and preserves the integrity, historic values and pageantry of foxhunting and steeplechase racing. Educates novices on all aspects of foxhunting and steeplechasing.

22985 ■ Oregon Horsemen's Benevolent Protective Association (OHBPA)

10350 N Vancouver Way, No. 351
Portland, OR 97217-7530
Ph: (503)285-4941
Fax: (503)285-4942
E-mail: ohbpa@aol.com
URL: http://www.oregonhbpa.com
Contact: Dick Cartney, Exec. Dir.

Founded: 1940. **Members:** 2,600. **Staff:** 4. **Budget:** $150,000. **Regional Groups:** 25. **Description:** Owners and trainers of thoroughbred horses. Promotes the sport of horse racing. Offers advice on proper racing rules and conditions as they affect horsemen and their employees. Seeks to establish understanding relationship with racing associations, commissions, and the public. **Awards:** Claimer of the Year. **Frequency:** annual. **Type:** recognition. **Conventions/Meetings:** semiannual conference.

22986 ■ Standardbred Owners Association (SOA)

733 Yonkers Ave., Ste.102
Yonkers, NY 10704-2659
Ph: (914)968-3599
Fax: (914)968-3943
E-mail: soaofny@optonoline.net
URL: http://www.soaofny.com
Contact: Joseph A. Faraldo, Pres.

Founded: 1954. **Members:** 1,000. **Membership Dues:** active or associate, $25 (annual). **Staff:** 5. **Description:** Represents owners, trainers, and drivers of Standardbred horses. Promotes the welfare of harness racing in New York. Assists all authorities governing harness racing. Recommends to governing authorities changes in rules or regulations that seem to be in the best interests of the sport of harness racing. Cooperates with all associations conducting harness race meetings. Suggests to such associations possible improvements. Consults with associations and all horsemen interested in the sport of harness racing concerning their mutual problems. Compiles statistics. Provides tax guides for U.S. and Canadian horsemen and offers legal assistance to members concerning harness racing. **Awards: Frequency:** annual. **Type:** scholarship. **Recipient:** for qualified high school graduates ● **Frequency:** annual. **Type:** trophy. **Publications:** *SOA News and Views*, quarterly. Newsletter. Alternate Formats: online. **Conventions/Meetings:** annual meeting - November.

22987 ■ Thoroughbred Club of America (TCA)

PO Box 8098
Lexington, KY 40533
Ph: (859)254-4282
Fax: (859)231-6131
E-mail: info@thoroughbredclubofamerica.com
URL: http://www.thoroughbredclubofamerica.com
Contact: Betty S. Flynn, Exec. Dir.

Founded: 1932. **Members:** 1,350. **Staff:** 2. **Description:** Represents thoroughbred horse breeders, owners, and trainers. **Libraries: Type:** reference. **Holdings:** 1,950; books, periodicals. **Subjects:** current issues of many racing and breeding. **Publications:** *Membership Roster*, annual. Membership Directory. **Conventions/Meetings:** annual dinner - always last quarter ● meeting - 9/year.

22988 ■ Thoroughbred Owners and Breeders Association (TOBA)

PO Box 910668
Lexington, KY 40591
Ph: (859)276-2291 (859)276-2299
Fax: (859)276-2462

E-mail: info@toba.org

URL: http://www.toba.org

Contact: Daniel J. Metzger, Pres.

Founded: 1961. **Members:** 3,000. **Membership Dues:** in U.S., $250 (annual) ● in Canada, $324 (annual) ● outside U.S. and Canada, $349 (annual). **Staff:** 6. **Description:** Owners and breeders of Thoroughbred horses whose aim is to promote and protect Thoroughbred racing and the interests of owners and breeders. Acts as national voice for the breeding and racing industry and as an industry advocate before the public, the media, and state legislatures. Maintains educational program. **Telecommunication Services:** electronic mail, toba@toba.org. **Committees:** Executive; Graded Stakes; Health; Owners. **Formed by Merger of:** American Thoroughbred Breeders Association; American Thoroughbred Owners Association. **Publications:** *Awards Journal*, annual. **Price:** free. **Circulation:** 4,000. **Advertising:** accepted ● *Blood-Horse*, weekly. Magazine. **Price:** included in membership dues ● *Graded Stakes Booklet*, annual ● *Stakes Supplement*, annual ● *Stallion Register*, annual ● *The TOBA Times*, quarterly. Newsletter. **Alternate Formats:** online ● Booklets ● Books ● Membership Directory, annual ● Also publishes other supplemental and statistical issues. **Conventions/Meetings:** annual dinner ● annual meeting.

22989 ■ Thoroughbred Racing Associations (TRA)

420 Fair Hill Dr., Ste.1

Elkton, MD 21921-2573

Ph: (410)392-9200

Fax: (410)398-1366

E-mail: cscherf@tra-online.com

URL: http://www.tra-online.com

Contact: Christopher Scherf, Exec. VP

Founded: 1942. **Members:** 51. **Staff:** 5. **Budget:** $1,000,000. **Description:** Thoroughbred racetracks. Promotes Thoroughbred racing. Compiles statistics on member tracks. **Libraries: Type:** not open to the public. **Holdings:** 500. **Subjects:** horseracing. **Computer Services:** Mailing lists, of members ● online services, job bank. **Affiliated With:** Thoroughbred Racing Protective Bureau. **Publications:** *Simulcast Procedures Manual*. **Alternate Formats:** online ● *Thoroughbred Racing Associations—Directory and Record Book*, annual. Contains listings of member tracks and racing records. **Price:** $17.00. **Circulation:** 3,000. **Conventions/Meetings:** annual board meeting - always February/March.

22990 ■ Thoroughbred Racing Protective Bureau (TRPB)

420 Fair Hill Dr., Ste.2

Elkton, MD 21921

Ph: (410)398-2261

Fax: (410)398-1499

E-mail: trpbinfo@trpb.com

URL: http://www.trpb.com

Contact: Franklin J. Fabian, Pres.

Founded: 1945. **Budget:** $2,000,000. **Description:** National investigative bureau financed by the Thoroughbred Racing Associations (see separate entry). Conducts character investigations of racing licenses and of applicants for positions in racing. Investigates reports of malpractice. Maintains fingerprinting and horse tattooing program and requires that member tracks keep fingerprint records of all officers, officials, employees, and racing participants such as trainers, jockeys, exercise boys, and grooms. **Telecommunication Services:** hotline, (866)847-8772. **Conventions/Meetings:** annual meeting - always February.

22991 ■ United States Team Penning Association (USTPA)

PO Box 4170

Fort Worth, TX 76164-0170

Ph: (817)378-8082

Fax: (817)378-8078

E-mail: angie.grizzel@ustpa.com

URL: http://www.ustpa.biz

Contact: Gary Stanfill, Pres.

Membership Dues: individual, $65 (annual) ● family, $150 (annual) ● youth/official/non-rider, $35 (annual) ● life (individual), $500 ● life (family), $750. **Multinational. Description:** Encourages and promotes the sport of team penning. Establishes and maintains a national association of persons and groups engaged in team penning. Establishes and encourages the use of uniform rules of competition at team penning events. **Computer Services:** Online services, executive forum ● online services, feedback forum. **Telecommunication Services:** electronic mail, president@ustpa.com. **Publications:** *Flags UP!*, monthly. Magazine. **Price:** included in membership dues; $2.25 nominal fee per month. **Alternate Formats:** online ● *USTPA Members Handbook*.

22992 ■ United States Trotting Association (USTA)

750 Michigan Ave.

Columbus, OH 43215

Ph: (614)224-2291

Free: (877)800-USTA

Fax: (614)224-4575

E-mail: customerservice@ustrotting.com

URL: http://www.ustrotting.com

Contact: Eric Sharbaugh, Exec. VP

Founded: 1938. **Members:** 30,000. **Membership Dues:** individual, associate (initial), $66 ● individual, associate, corporate (active), $50 (annual). **Staff:** 80. **Budget:** $8,000,000. **Regional Groups:** 14. **Description:** Owners, trainers, and drivers of Standardbred horses, officials in harness racing, track officers, sponsors of fairs, and other track organizations. Works to improve the breed of trotting and pacing horses, establish rules regulating standards and registration of such horses, licensed drivers and officials, and register drivers' colors. Compiles statistics. **Libraries: Type:** open to the public. **Holdings:** 1,000. **Subjects:** standard bred racing, breeding. **Committees:** Driver/Trainer; Finance; Marketing; Officiating; Owners/Breeders; Pari-Mutuel; Public Relations; Registration; Regulatory; Rules; Stakes/Fairs. **Absorbed:** (1994) Harness Racing Communications. **Formed by Merger of:** (1938) National Trotting Association; (1938) United Trotting Association; American Trotting Association. **Publications:** *Hoof Beats*, monthly. Magazine. Contains articles on harness racing and standardbreds. **Price:** $16.50 /year for members in U.S.; $32.50 /year for nonmembers in U.S.; $28.00 /year for members in Canada; $49.00 /year for nonmembers in Canada. **Circulation:** 16,000. **Advertising:** accepted ● *Membership List*, annual ● *Sires and Dams Book*, annual ● *Trotting and Pacing Guide*, annual. **Conventions/Meetings:** annual board meeting - always early March, in Columbus, OH.

Horseback Riding

22993 ■ American Cutting Horse Association (ACHA)

PO Box 2443

Brenham, TX 77834

Ph: (979)836-3370

Fax: (979)251-9971

E-mail: achacutting@aol.com

URL: http://www.achacutting.org

Contact: Billy Crenshaw, Pres.

Description: Promotes cutting horse contests as a sport; encourages breeding, training and exhibiting cutting horse in the contest arena. **Publications:** Newsletter.

22994 ■ American Horse Trials Foundation (AHTF)

221 Grove Cove Rd.

Centreville, MD 21617

Ph: (443)262-9555

Fax: (443)262-9666

E-mail: ahtf@worldnet.att.net

URL: http://www.ahtf3day.org

Contact: Donna L. Field, Exec. Dir.

Founded: 1987. **Description:** Works to enable three-day event riders with limited financial resources to train and compete at the national and international levels.

22995 ■ Back Country Horsemen of America (BCHA)

PO Box 1367

Graham, WA 98338-1367

Ph: (360)832-2461

Free: (888)893-5161

Fax: (360)832-2471

E-mail: info@backcountryhorse.com

URL: http://www.backcountryhorse.com

Contact: Peg Greiwe, Exec. Sec.

Founded: 1973. **Members:** 16,000. **Membership Dues:** individual, $30 (annual). **Staff:** 2. **Budget:** $55,000. **State Groups:** 20. **Local Groups:** 155. **Description:** Individuals who enjoy riding horses in wilderness and Back Country areas. Promotes the common sense use and enjoyment of horses in the wilderness; seeks to ensure availability of Back Country horse trails. Conducts educational programs on horse care and Back Country and wilderness riding; lobbies public agencies to ensure that public lands remain available for horseback riding. **Libraries: Type:** reference. **Holdings:** books, periodicals, video recordings. **Subjects:** Back Country horsemanship, public lands. **Computer Services:** database ● mailing lists. **Publications:** *Back Country Vet Book*, 5/year. Booklet. Contains veterinary information for the horse in the Back Country. **Price:** $5.00 ● *Guidebook*. **Price:** $1.00/copy, plus shipping and handling. **Advertising:** accepted ● Newsletter, quarterly. **Price:** included in membership dues. **Circulation:** 12,000. **Advertising:** accepted. **Conventions/Meetings:** annual board meeting.

22996 ■ CHA - Certified Horsemanship Association

c/o Polly Barger, Program Dir.

4037 Iron Works Pkwy., Ste.180

Lexington, KY 40511

Free: (800)399-0138

Fax: (859)255-0726

E-mail: pbarger@cha-ahse.org

URL: http://www.cha-ahse.org

Contact: Polly Barger, Program Dir.

Founded: 1967. **Members:** 3,500. **Membership Dues:** youth, $15 (annual) ● individual, $45 (annual) ● life, $750. **Staff:** 5. **Budget:** $300,000. **Regional Groups:** 12. **State Groups:** 12. **Description:** Certifies Riding Instructors. Conducts an Instructor Employment program. **Awards:** Partnership in Safety Award. **Frequency:** annual. **Type:** recognition. **Recipient:** for outstanding support of safety or education in the horse industry ● **Type:** recognition. **Committees:** Clinic Review; College Curriculum; Combined Clinics; Educational Resource; Instructors for Riders with Disabilities; Standards/Site Accreditation; Trail Program; Video. **Formerly:** (1992) Camp Horsemanship Association; (1999) CHA-Association for Horsemanship Safety and Education. **Publications:** *CHA Composite Horsemanship Manual*. Contains illustrations; for all level of riders. ● *The Instructor*, quarterly. Journal. Contains safety tips and information on member activities. **Price:** free for members. **Circulation:** 5,000. **Advertising:** accepted ● *National Membership Directory*, annual ● *Riding Instructors Manual*. Comprehensive manual for horseback riding instructors. ● *Standards for Group Riding Programs*. Book. Categories of operational procedures for beginning and/or evaluation of existing riding programs. ● Four level manuals (illustrated) of Horsemanship for riding students. Horsemanship safety posters. **Conventions/Meetings:** annual conference, five days of workshops and seminars for anyone involved in horsemanship (exhibits) - fall.

22997 ■ Gladstone Equestrian Association (GEA)

PO Box 119

Gladstone, NJ 07934

Ph: (908)470-0500

Fax: (908)453-3332
E-mail: gladstoneeq@gladstonedriving.org
URL: http://www.gladstonedriving.org
Contact: Ellen Marie Ettenger, Contact
Founded: 1985. **Members:** 500. **Membership Dues:** patron, $175-$5,000 (annual). **Staff:** 3. **Budget:** $400,000. **Description:** Individuals with an interest in carriage driving and other equestrian events and activities. Seeks to increase interest and participation in carriage driving and related sports. Sponsors competitions. **Awards: Frequency:** periodic. **Type:** grant. **Recipient:** for competitors requiring assistance to travel to sanctioned competitive events. **Publications:** Newsletter, quarterly. **Price:** included in membership dues. **Conventions/Meetings:** annual Gladstone Driving Event - competition.

22998 ■ Horsemanship Safety Association (HSA)

c/o Ted Marthe
5304 Reeve Rd.
Mazomanie, WI 53560
Ph: (608)767-2593
Fax: (608)767-2590
E-mail: hoofbeat@midplains.net
URL: http://www.horsesafety.net
Contact: Donna Maye West, Exec. Dir.
Founded: 1964. **Members:** 650. **Membership Dues:** instructor, $30 (annual) ● individual, $15 (annual) ● stable and camp club, $95 (annual). **Staff:** 3. **Budget:** $35,000. **Description:** Schools of horsemanship; equine programs at colleges and technical schools; riding instructors and students; medical personnel. To educate equestrians and instructors in safe horsemanship practices. Trains instructors in leadership techniques; conducts group and private lessons for children and adults; sponsors seminars and speaking engagements by certified clinicians. Conducts riding instructor clinics for adults. Certifies instructors at 4 levels: assistant riding instructor, horsemanship safety instructor, associate instructor, and clinic instructor. Certified instructors must renew certification every 3 years. Provides on-site consultation. Offers Expert Witness service. Compiles statistics; maintains library of instructor training manuals, speakers' bureau, and placement service. Operates job placement services. **Libraries: Type:** not open to the public. **Holdings:** 205. **Subjects:** safety in horse sports, instructor education. **Awards:** Horseman of the Year. **Frequency:** annual. **Type:** recognition. **Recipient:** for demonstrating teaching and training techniques related to safety. **Committees:** Certified Clinicians. **Affiliated With:** American Camp Association. **Publications:** *Equestrian Lifeguard's Manual*. Also Cited As: *HSA Instructor's Manual* ● *Horse Science Manual* ● *HSA News*, quarterly. Newsletter. **Conventions/Meetings:** annual conference.

22999 ■ Intercollegiate Horse Show Association (IHSA)

Smoke Run Farm
Hollow Rd., Box 741
Stony Brook, NY 11790
Ph: (613)751-4625
Fax: (613)941-1193
E-mail: glihsa@aol.com
URL: http://www.ihsainc.com
Contact: George Lukemire, VP
Founded: 1967. **Members:** 5,000. **Membership Dues:** college, $150 (annual) ● individual (combined), $30 (annual) ● individual (hunter seat and western), $20 (annual) ● alumni (hunter seat and western), $45 (annual) ● alumni (combined), $55 (annual). **Budget:** $75,000. **Regional Groups:** 30. **Description:** Colleges and universities; individuals. Promotes the education of students in horsemanship and sportsmanship. Provides a basis of competition for intercollegiate riders from beginning through advanced levels. Sponsors clinics, seminars, and other horse-oriented activities. **Libraries: Type:** reference. **Holdings:** books. **Awards:** Grand Champion National Trophy. **Frequency:** annual. **Type:** trophy ● Intercollegiate Equestrian Foundation. **Frequency:** annual. **Type:** recognition. **Recipient:** for team and individual performance ● Senior Athletic Academic Achievement. **Frequency:** annual. **Type:** scholarship. **Recipi-**

ent: for any rider who meets the membership requirements and has a 3.5 grade point average or better ● Senior Athletic Academic Special. **Frequency:** annual. **Type:** monetary. **Recipient:** for those who qualify for the first award. **Telecommunication Services:** electronic mail, recihsa@aol.com. **Committees:** International. **Divisions:** Alumni Fences; Alumni Flat; Intermediate; Intermediate Over Fences; Novice; Novice Over Fences; Open; Open Over Fences; Walk-Trot; Walk-Trot-Canter. **Affiliated With:** United States Equestrian Federation. **Publications:** *Regional Directory*, annual ● Newsletter, semiannual. **Conventions/Meetings:** semiannual board meeting ● annual National Champion Horse Show - always first weekend in May.

23000 ■ International Equestrian Drill Team Alliance (IEDTA)

Address Unknown since 2007
Founded: 1999. **Members:** 200. **Staff:** 1. **Budget:** $350,000. **Regional Groups:** 6. **Description:** Promotes the sport and professionalism of drill and flag teams; disseminates information to drill teams worldwide; provides professional instruction in maneuvers, drills, figures, and patterns. Devises standards of competition regulations; cultivates certification of judiciary standards; develops standardization of terms of drill patterns and figures; assists with the creation of team by-law formats; assists members with legal and financial matters. Provides educational programs, statistics, and children's services. Maintains a speakers bureau. **Publications:** Handbook, biennial. **Price:** $25.00 for adults; $15.00 for children ● Newsletter, monthly. **Price:** for members; $15.00 for nonmembers. **Conventions/Meetings:** quarterly meeting.

23001 ■ International Jumper Futurity (IJF)

PO Box 1445
Georgetown, KY 40324
Ph: (502)535-6787
Fax: (502)535-4412
E-mail: yjcoffice@youngjumpers.com
URL: http://www.youngjumpers.com
Contact: Joyce Matin, Exec. Dir.
Founded: 1989. **Staff:** 2. **Description:** Owners, breeders, and trainers of sport horses. Promotes interest and participation in show jumping and other equestrian events; seeks to improve sport horse bloodlines. Serves as a clearinghouse on North American sport horses; recognizes outstanding equestrian riders, trainers, and breeders. **Libraries: Type:** reference. **Holdings:** archival material, articles, business records, clippings. **Subjects:** sport horses.

23002 ■ International Side Saddle Organization (ISSO)

PO Box 57
Vineland, NJ 08362-0057
Ph: (856)696-8949
Fax: (856)696-8949
E-mail: issoaside@aol.com
URL: http://www.sidesaddle.com
Contact: Linda Bowlby, Pres.
Founded: 1974. **Members:** 650. **Membership Dues:** regular, $35 (annual) ● junior/affiliate, $25 (annual) ● family, $75 (annual) ● life, $350. **For-Profit. Description:** Women who ride sidesaddle; other interested individuals. Organizes all-sidesaddle horse shows and clinics. Conducts seminars; helps handicapped riders. Maintains Hall of Fame and Speaker's Bureau. **Libraries: Type:** reference. **Holdings:** books. **Subjects:** old and rare sidesaddle texts. **Awards:** Breed Awards. **Frequency:** annual. **Type:** trophy. **Recipient:** to a high point rider for a variety of horse breeds as sponsored by individuals ● Champion in Various Categories. **Frequency:** annual. **Type:** trophy. **Recipient:** to a high point rider for a variety of categories such as English activities, Western activities and hunter ● Hall of Fame. **Frequency:** annual. **Type:** recognition. **Recipient:** for service to the organization ● National Champion. **Frequency:** annual. **Type:** trophy. **Recipient:** for success in competition of high point rider ● Special Awards. **Frequency:** annual. **Type:** recognition. **Recipient:** for service to the organization in several categories ● State Awards.

Frequency: annual. **Type:** trophy. **Recipient:** to a high point rider for states and countries who qualify by membership count. **Computer Services:** database ● mailing lists ● online services. **Boards:** Congress. **Formed by Merger of:** (2006) International Side-Saddle Organization and World Sidesaddle Federation, Inc. **Publications:** *Aside World*, quarterly. Magazine. Contains sidesaddle related information. **Price:** included in membership dues. **Circulation:** 1,000. **Advertising:** accepted ● *The Habit and the Horse*. Book ● *Modern Side-Saddle Riding*. Book. **Conventions/Meetings:** annual banquet, includes awards presentation - always January.

23003 ■ National Hunter Jumper Association (NHJA)

PO Box 1015
Riverside, CT 06878
Ph: (203)869-1225
E-mail: wgbrosecroft@aol.com
URL: http://www.nhja.org
Contact: Ellie Estes, Sec.-Treas.
Founded: 1989. **Members:** 806. **Membership Dues:** individual, $20 (annual) ● individual, $50 (triennial) ● life, $250. **Description:** Individuals interested in showing hunters and jumpers in competitions. Represents interests of amateur exhibitors and professional horsemen, competition management, sponsors, bill paying non-competitors, professionals in allied fields, and spectators. Establishes standards and regulations to maintain horse show competitions in a professional manner. Conducts research programs and educational programs. **Affiliated With:** United States Equestrian Federation. **Publications:** *Guidelines for Pony Hunter Distances*. **Price:** $2.00 ● Newsletter, bimonthly. **Price:** included in membership dues. **Circulation:** 1,150. **Conventions/Meetings:** annual meeting.

23004 ■ National Hunter/Jumper Council (NHJC)

4047 Ironworks Pkwy.
Lexington, KY 40511-8483
Ph: (859)258-2472
Fax: (859)231-6662
E-mail: info@nhjc.org
Contact: Sue Pinckney, Dir.
Founded: 1996. **Membership Dues:** full, participating, $30 (annual). **Description:** Represents the interests of USA Equestrian members involved in hunter/jumper activities. **Committees:** Ad-Hoc Safety Helmet; Budget and Finance; Education; Grass Roots; Hunter; Hunter Breeding; Hunter Seat Equitation; Judge's; Jumper; Junior Hunter; Nominating; North American Young Riders and Prix de States Junior Jumper Championships; Planning; Pony Hunter; Show Management; Show Standards; Show Stewards. **Publications:** *The Council Connection*, quarterly. Newsletter. **Price:** included in membership dues ● Membership Directory. **Conventions/Meetings:** monthly conference, calls to handle the business and administration of the council ● annual convention and seminar, held in conjunction with the USA Equestrian Annual Meeting - held in early January.

23005 ■ Trail Riders of Today (TROT)

c/o Michelle Beachley, Membership Chair
26309 Howard Chapel Dr.
Damascus, MD 20872
Ph: (301)351-6211
E-mail: priscillahuffman@verizon.net
URL: http://www.trot-md.org
Contact: Priscilla Huffman, Pres.
Founded: 1980. **Members:** 1,000. **Membership Dues:** single/family, $20 (annual) ● contributing, $30 (annual) ● sustaining, $50 (annual). **Local Groups:** 10. **Description:** Dedicated to the preservation of existing equestrian trails. Works with developers to secure equestrian easements, permit preservation, and re-routing rather than closure of trails. Works to keep public recreational land open to horseback riders. Provides 24 hour certified mounted search and rescue teams for Maryland, Virginia, Delaware, and Pennsylvania. **Publications:** *TROT Newsletter*, bimonthly. Alternate Formats: online ● Membership

Directory, annual ● Also publishes trail maps. **Conventions/Meetings:** quarterly meeting.

23006 ■ United States Dressage Federation (USDF)
4051 Iron Works Pkwy.
Lexington, KY 40511
Ph: (859)971-2277
Fax: (859)971-7722
E-mail: shienzsch@usdf.org
URL: http://www.usdf.org
Contact: Stephan Hienzsch, Exec. Dir./Acting Development Dir.
Founded: 1973. **Members:** 32,000. **Membership Dues:** participating, $62 (annual) ● youth participating, $35 (annual) ● participating - life, $1,000 ● business, $250 (annual). **Staff:** 26. **Budget:** $3,000,000. **Regional Groups:** 9. **Local Groups:** 128. **Description:** Members of local dressage organizations and other interested individuals. Promotes and encourages a high standard of accomplishment in dressage throughout the U.S., primarily through educational programs, and to improve understanding of dressage through educational clinics, forums, and seminars. (In dressage, a horse is trained to execute intricate and highly refined steps and maneuvers. Ideally, the signals from rider to horse are not visible to the spectator.) Certifies dressage instructors. **Libraries:** Type: reference. **Holdings:** audiovisuals. **Awards:** Frequency: annual. Type: recognition. **Recipient:** to an outstanding horse and rider. **Computer Services:** Mailing lists. **Committees:** Awards; Freestyle; Junior/Young Rider. **Councils:** Competition Management; Competitors; Judges; Musical Freestyle; Technical Delegates; Trainers/Instructors. **Affiliated With:** American Horse Council; United States Equestrian Federation. **Publications:** USDF Connection, monthly. Magazine. **Advertising:** accepted ● USDF Directory, annual. Magazine ● Videos. **Conventions/Meetings:** annual conference.

23007 ■ United States Equestrian Federation (USEF)
4047 Iron Works Pkwy.
Lexington, KY 40511-8483
Ph: (859)258-2472
Fax: (859)231-6662
E-mail: lrawls@usef.org
URL: http://www.usef.org
Contact: Mr. John R. Long, CEO
Founded: 1917. **Members:** 77,000. **Membership Dues:** junior, $35 (annual) ● basic, senior, $40 (annual) ● platinum, $85 (annual) ● contributing (non-competing), $25 (annual) ● life, $2,500. **Staff:** 90. **Budget:** $8,000,000. **Regional Groups:** 143. **Description:** Individuals and horse shows. Promotes interest in equestrian sports; establishes and enforces rules governing equestrian competitions; maintains records and sanctions dates for competitions. Administers drugs and medication testing program and research. Provides general and specific assistance on equestrian sports in the U.S. as well as referrals. Conducts educational programs for licensed officials throughout the year. Licenses judges and stewards. National Federation of Equestrian Sports for the U.S. National Governing Body for Equestrian Sports (USOC). **Awards:** Horse of the Year Award. **Frequency:** annual. **Type:** recognition ● Media Awards. **Frequency:** annual. **Type:** recognition. **Computer Services:** Mailing lists. **Telecommunication Services:** electronic mail, jlong@usef.org. **Affiliated With:** International Federation for Equestrian Sports; United States Olympic Committee. **Formed by Merger of:** (2003) U.S.A. Equestrian Association; (2003) United States Equestrian Team. **Formerly:** (2002) American Horse Shows Association. **Publications:** Horse Show, monthly. Magazine. Covers horse showing. **Price:** included in membership dues. **Circulation:** 77,000. **Advertising:** accepted ● Rule Book, biennial ● Pamphlets. **Conventions/Meetings:** annual competition (exhibits) - in January ● annual conference and convention (exhibits) - always January.

23008 ■ United States Eventing Association (USEA)
525 Old Waterford Rd. NW
Leesburg, VA 20176

Ph: (703)779-0440
Fax: (703)779-0550
E-mail: info@useventing.com
URL: http://www.useventing.com
Contact: Jo Whitehouse, CEO
Founded: 1959. **Members:** 12,000. **Membership Dues:** full, $75 (annual) ● family, junior, $50 (annual) ● non-competing, $46 (annual) ● subscribing, $25 (annual) ● life, $1,500. **Staff:** 10. **Budget:** $1,000,000. **Regional Groups:** 10. **Description:** Horsemen and others supporting the objectives of the USCTA. Formulates, distributes, and explains standards, rules, and regulations for the proper conduct of combined training instruction and equestrian combined training competitions. (A combined training competition is composed of two or all three of the following equestrian activities: dressage, cross-country, and show jumping; when all three activities are included the competition is called a horse trial or event.) Sponsors clinics. Assists to provide training opportunities for potential Olympic games competitors. Approves competitions; compiles records and statistics. **Libraries:** Type: reference. **Holdings:** audiovisuals, books, clippings, periodicals. **Subjects:** combined training, "eventing". **Awards:** High Score Award. **Frequency:** annual. **Type:** recognition. **Computer Services:** Mailing lists. **Formerly:** (2002) United States Combined Training Association. **Publications:** Eventing USA, bimonthly. Magazine. **Price:** $25.00. Alternate Formats: online ● Rules for Combined Training, biennial. **Price:** included in membership dues. **Advertising:** accepted ● USCTA News, bimonthly. Magazine. **Price:** included in membership dues; $20.00 /year for nonmembers. **ISSN:** 0744-0103. **Advertising:** accepted ● USCTA Omnibus, quarterly. **Price:** included in membership dues; $10.00/copy for nonmembers. **Advertising:** accepted ● Manuals. **Conventions/Meetings:** annual meeting and convention (exhibits) ● seminar.

23009 ■ United States Hunter Jumper Association (USHJA)
PO Box 13400
Lexington, KY 40583
Ph: (859)225-2055 (859)225-6942
Fax: (859)258-9033
E-mail: sdotson@ushja.org
URL: http://www.ushja.org
Contact: Susan S. Dotson, Exec. Dir.
Founded: 2003. **Membership Dues:** senior active, $55 (annual) ● junior active, $45 (annual) ● associate, $25 (annual) ● affiliate, $100 (annual) ● life, $1,000. **Description:** Aims to advance and represent the hunter and jumper disciplines. Fosters an educated community of equestrians that promotes the welfare of the horse and fairness in competition. Strives to provide its members with the resources they need to achieve their goals. **Awards:** Affiliate Awards. **Frequency:** annual. **Type:** recognition. **Recipient:** for exemplary good horsemanship, sportsmanship, and integrity for the sport and exhibitors ● Amateur Sportsmanship Award. **Frequency:** annual. **Type:** recognition. **Recipient:** for amateur-owner and adult amateur exhibitors who have shown excellence and integrity by supporting their fellow competitors ● Hunterdon Equitation Cup. **Frequency:** annual. **Type:** recognition. **Recipient:** to a rider who has won a USEF medal, ASPCA Maclay, USEF Show Jumping Talent Search, or WIHS Classic ● Rider Recognition Program Award. **Frequency:** annual. **Type:** recognition. **Recipient:** for overall and lifetime money earnings of professional hunter and jumper riders ● USHJA Foundation Awards. **Frequency:** annual. **Type:** recognition. **Recipient:** for outstanding accomplishments of grassroots equestrians and promotion of B and C level competitions. **Publications:** In Stride, bimonthly. Magazine. **Price:** included in membership dues.

23010 ■ United States Pony Clubs (USPC)
4041 Iron Works Pkwy.
Lexington, KY 40511-8483
Ph: (859)254-7669
Fax: (859)233-4652

E-mail: uspc@ponyclub.org
URL: http://www.ponyclub.org
Contact: Peggy Entrekin, Exec. Dir.
Founded: 1954. **Members:** 12,500. **Membership Dues:** corporate, $30-$40 (annual) ● alumni life, $375 ● regular life, $1,000. **Staff:** 17. **Budget:** $1,300,000. **Regional Groups:** 42. **Local Groups:** 627. **For-Profit. Description:** Provides education in riding, mounted sports, horse management, and the care of horses and ponies. Grants certificates of proficiency. Promotes responsibility, moral judgment, leadership, and self-confidence in youth. Sponsors local, regional, and national competitions. Cooperates with the British Horse Society - Pony Club. Offers educational programs. Maintains 20 committees. **Libraries:** Type: reference. **Holdings:** books. **Subjects:** instructions, activities, riding, horse management. **Awards:** Founders Award. **Frequency:** annual. **Type:** recognition. **Recipient:** to volunteer. **Publications:** USPC Handbook and Rules for Eventing Competition. Alternate Formats: online ● USPC News, quarterly. Newsletter. Includes book reviews, competition results, and information about activities. **Price:** included in membership dues; $25.00 /year for nonmembers. **Circulation:** 15,000. **Advertising:** accepted. Alternate Formats: online ● Annual Report, annual. **Price:** included in membership dues. **Advertising:** accepted ● Also publishes publications list, and instructional materials on subjects such as riding, care of tack and equipment, care of horses and ponies, conduct of rallies, mounted games, and other events. **Conventions/Meetings:** semiannual Championships - competition - August and January ● annual conference and board meeting (exhibits) ● annual convention ● triennial festival, with educational information and competition.

Horses

23011 ■ North American Thoroughbred Society (NATBS)
460 Park Ave., 16th Fl.
New York, NY 10022
E-mail: info@hellohorse.com
URL: http://www.hellohorse.com
Membership Dues: national, $70 (annual) ● regional, $25 (annual). **Description:** Promotes, supports, and acknowledges the fullbred North American Thoroughbred.

23012 ■ Sport Horse Owners and Breeders Association (SOBA)
PMB 241
6753 Thomasville Rd., Ste.108
Tallahassee, FL 32312
Ph: (850)893-8532
Fax: (850)893-8954
E-mail: soba@sport-horse.org
Description: Promotes sport horse breeding and sport horse events. **Computer Services:** Mailing lists. **Funds:** All Breed Sport Horse Incentive. **Publications:** Dressage Sires 2000. Yearbook. **Price:** free ● Sport Horse Stallion Directory 2000. **Price:** free. Alternate Formats: online.

Horseshoes

23013 ■ National Horseshoe Pitchers Association of America (NHPA)
c/o Dick Hansen, Sec.-Treas.
3085 S 76th St.
Franksville, WI 53126
Ph: (262)835-9108 (707)538-3128
E-mail: nhpa.sec.trea@worldnet.att.net
URL: http://www.horseshoepitching.com
Contact: Dick Hansen, Sec.-Treas.
Founded: 1909. **Members:** 17,000. **Membership Dues:** adult, $12 (annual) ● junior, $5 (annual). **Staff:** 50. **Budget:** $400,000. **Regional Groups:** 53. **State Groups:** 60. **Local Groups:** 2,000. **National Groups:** 3. **Description:** Fosters, develops, and promotes the sport of horseshoe pitching on all levels, both as recreational pastime and competitive

sport; has established a unified code of rules, equipment, and playing procedures. Makes available game-related items including official shoes, trophies, scoresheets, and ringer charts. Maintains speakers' bureau; compiles statistics. **Awards:** Gene and Mary Van Sant Memorial Award. **Frequency:** annual. **Type:** recognition. **Recipient:** to the Regional Director ● NHPA Achievement Awards. **Frequency:** annual. **Type:** recognition. **Recipient:** for outstanding contributions to the game on a local or statewide level ● NHPA Hall of Fame. **Frequency:** annual. **Type:** recognition. **Recipient:** for an outstanding performance on World Tournament Championship play ● Presidential Award. **Frequency:** annual. **Type:** recognition. **Recipient:** for contributions to the game and the NHPA ● **Type:** scholarship ● Stokes Memorial Award. **Frequency:** annual. **Type:** recognition. **Recipient:** for a person who has done the most during the preceding 3-5 years to promote and build the sport. **Computer Services:** Mailing lists ● online services, message board. **Telecommunication Services:** electronic mail, info@horseshoepitching.com. **Committees:** Hall of Fame. **Absorbed:** (1914) Grand League of American Horseshoe Pitchers; (1921) National Association of Horseshoe and Quoit Pitchers. **Publications:** *Horseshoe Pitching Newsline*, bimonthly. Magazine. Includes tournament results and schedules. **Price:** $12.00/year in U.S.; $20.00/year in Canada. **Circulation:** 3,000. **Advertising:** accepted ● Manual. **Conventions/Meetings:** annual convention ● annual meeting ● annual World Tournament - competition.

Hunting

23014 ■ American Coon Hunters Association (ACHA)
c/o WCCHR Registration Office
PO Box 453
Grayson, KY 41143
Ph: (606)474-9740
E-mail: acha@papadocs.com
URL: http://www.acha-wcchr.com
Contact: Sherry Parker, Contact
Founded: 1948. **Members:** 400. **Budget:** $24,500. **Description:** Represents coon hunters and their hounds. Presents awards to top 20 coonhounds. **Publications:** *Tally Sheets and Award List of World Hunt*, annual ● Brochure, annual ● Newsletter, quarterly. Alternate Formats: online. **Conventions/Meetings:** annual World Championship - competition - always October.

23015 ■ American Crossbow Federation (ACF)
PO Box 251
Glenwood, MN 56334
Ph: (320)634-3660
E-mail: bowtwain@charter.com
URL: http://www.hunting.net/nab
Contact: Daniel James Hendricks, Contact
Founded: 1993. **Members:** 1,200. **Membership Dues:** single, $25 (annual) ● couple, $45 (annual) ● family, $65 (annual) ● life, $500. **Staff:** 3. **Description:** Bowhunters dedicated to the preservation of archery. Promotes "all forms of legal hunting with any legal weapons". Sponsors bowhunts; makes available discount hunting products and services to members; conducts social and educational activities. **Libraries: Type:** reference. **Holdings:** articles, audio recordings, periodicals, video recordings. **Subjects:** Bowhunting, video. **Additional Websites:** http://www.horizontalbowhunter.com. **Formerly:** (2006) North American Bowhunter. **Publications:** *Horizontal Bowhunter*, quarterly. Magazine.

23016 ■ Hunter's Shooting Association (HSA)
N8881 Hwy. D
Belleville, WI 53508
Fax: (413)431-9309
E-mail: info@huntershooter.com
URL: http://www.huntershooter.com
Description: Promotes field marksmanship events, particularly for big game hunters.

23017 ■ International Bowhunting Organization (IBO)
PO Box 398
Vermilion, OH 44089
Ph: (440)967-2137
E-mail: ibo@ibo.net
URL: http://www.ibo.net
Contact: Ken Watkins, Pres.
Founded: 1984. **Membership Dues:** individual in U.S., $25 (annual) ● life, $300 ● individual outside U.S., $15 (annual) ● additional family, $5 (annual). **Multinational. Description:** Promotes the sport of bowhunting. Acts as a political coordinator for the protection and advancement of bowhunting. Functions as a clearinghouse for essential bowhunter information. **Awards:** Shooter of the Year. **Frequency:** annual. **Type:** recognition. **Computer Services:** Information services, bowhunting resources ● online services, forums. **Publications:** *Bow Hunting World*. Magazine. **Price:** $17.00 in Canada and Mexico; $22.00 outside North America. **Conventions/Meetings:** trade show ● World Championship - competition.

23018 ■ International Hunter Education Association (IHEA)
2727 W 92nd Ave., Ste.103
Federal Heights, CO 80260
Ph: (303)430-7233
Fax: (303)430-7236
E-mail: info@ihea.com
URL: http://www.ihea.com
Contact: Ms. Susie Kiefer, Communications Dir.
Founded: 1972. **Members:** 2,000. **Membership Dues:** volunteer instructor, individual, $25 (annual) ● instructor association, $100 (annual) ● life, $375. **Staff:** 5. **Multinational. Description:** Hunting education instructors, and other interested individuals. Seeks to provide leadership and establish safety standards for hunters. Encourages hunters to be responsible, knowledgeable, and involved. Provides professionally trained volunteer instructors to teach mandatory hunting education courses internationally. **Sections:** IHEA Foundation. **Affiliated With:** Association of Fish and Wildlife Agencies. **Formerly:** (1988) North American Association of Hunter Safety Coordinators; (2003) Hunter Education Association. **Publications:** *Hunter and Shooting Sports Education Journal*, 3/year. Magazine. **Price:** included in membership dues. **Circulation:** 70,000. **Advertising:** accepted ● *Hunters Handbook*, annual ● *Hunting Accident Report for North America*, semiannual. **Conventions/Meetings:** annual conference (exhibits) - always early summer.

23019 ■ Masters of Foxhounds Association of America (MFHA)
PO Box 363
Millwood, VA 22646
Ph: (540)955-5680
Fax: (540)955-5682
E-mail: office@mfha.com
URL: http://www.mfha.com
Contact: Mason H. Lampton, Pres.
Founded: 1907. **Membership Dues:** individual, $25 (annual) ● hunt, $100 (annual) ● life, $500. **Multinational. Description:** Members are Masters of Foxhounds. Registers and recognizes formally organized fox and drag hunting organizations in the U.S. and Canada. **Formerly:** American Masters of Foxhounds Association. **Publications:** *Covertside*. Newsletter. **Price:** $10.00/copy ● *Foxhound Studbook*, periodic. **Conventions/Meetings:** annual meeting.

23020 ■ National Hunters Association (NHA)
PO Box 820
Knightdale, NC 27545
Ph: (919)365-7157
Fax: (919)366-2142
E-mail: nhadvs@worldnet.att.net
Contact: D.V. Smith, Pres.
Founded: 1976. **For-Profit. Description:** Membership organization that provides hunting information service, hunting tours, African safaris, survival training, education in hunting and gun safety, and other services to members. Promotes hunter safety and

the preservation of the rights of sportsmen. Conducts wilderness survival courses to provide young people of all ages with knowledge of handling themselves in the wild.

23021 ■ North American Hunting Club (NAHC)
12301 Whitewater Dr.
PO Box 3401
Minnetonka, MN 55343
Ph: (952)988-9333
Free: (877)893-7947
Fax: (952)936-9755
E-mail: namghq@namginc.com
URL: http://www.huntingclub.com
Contact: Gregg Gutschow, Exec. Dir.
Founded: 1978. **Members:** 750,000. **Membership Dues:** individual, $18 (annual) ● life, $350. **Staff:** 45. **Regional Groups:** 1. **For-Profit. Description:** Hunters of game animals and birds of North America. Seeks to improve the hunting skills of members and promote the enjoyment of the sport. Provides information about hunting outfitters. Conducts charitable programs; compiles statistics. **Awards:** Big Game Awards Program. **Frequency:** annual. **Type:** recognition ● Big Game Registry. **Frequency:** biennial. **Type:** recognition. **Publications:** *Hunters Information Series*, bimonthly. Book. Contains encyclopedia series of hunting books. **Price:** $19.95. **Circulation:** 100,000 ● *North American Hunter*, bimonthly. Magazine. Contains incredible hunting adventures all across the US. **Price:** included in membership dues ● *Wild Bounty Cookbook*. Features award-winning recipes for every type of game. **Conventions/Meetings:** biennial Jamboree - meeting (exhibits).

23022 ■ Physically Challenged Bowhunters of America (PCBA)
2152 Rte. 981
New Alexandria, PA 15670-2592
Ph: (724)668-7439 (609)737-7340
Fax: (724)668-7439
E-mail: mkvought@comcast.net
URL: http://www.pcba-inc.org
Contact: Karen Vought, Sec.-Treas.
Founded: 1993. **Members:** 540. **Membership Dues:** youth, $5 (annual) ● individual, $15 (annual) ● corporate, $100 (annual). **Staff:** 11. **Description:** Physically challenged bowhunters. Introduces and promotes participation in the sport of bowhunting by people with physical challenges. Conducts bowhunting and archery education programs; works with archery and bowhunting equipment manufacturers to address the special needs of the physically challenged. Works closely with hospitals, rehabs and doctors, as well as bow groups and manufacturers, to aid in the return to archery and bowhunting for the physically challenged. **Libraries: Type:** reference. **Holdings:** video recordings. **Subjects:** adaptive equipment. **Telecommunication Services:** electronic mail, frankzsk@comcast.net. **Publications:** *Good News*, quarterly. Newsletter. Contains stories of members' success, pictures, and information on adaptive equipment; also available on audiotape for visually impaired. **Price:** included in membership dues. **Circulation:** 900. Alternate Formats: online ● *Overcoming the Challenge Adaptive Equipment Guide*. Video. **Price:** $10.00 plus shipping and handling ($5) ● *The PCBA Story*. Video. **Price:** $10.00 plus shipping and handling ($5). **Conventions/Meetings:** Adaptive Equipment Seminars & Hunts ● annual regional meeting (exhibits) - June.

23023 ■ U.S. Sportsmen's Alliance (USSA)
801 Kingsmill Pkwy.
Columbus, OH 43229
Ph: (614)888-4868
Fax: (614)888-0326
E-mail: info@ussportsmen.org
URL: http://www.ussportsmen.org
Contact: Walter P. Pidgeon Jr., Pres./CEO
Founded: 1978. **Membership Dues:** individual, $25 (annual) ● supporting, $50 (annual) ● sustaining, $100 (annual) ● sponsor, $250 (annual) ● patron, $500 (annual). **Staff:** 11. **Description:** Aims to protect and advance America's heritage of hunting,

fishing and trapping by uniting sportsmen to: protect against legal and legislative attacks by the animal rights movement; win public support for outdoor sports; ensure the future of this heritage by involving families in the outdoor experience; and promote the sportsman's stewardship role in the scientific management of America's fish and wildlife. **Computer Services:** Mailing lists, of members. **Telecommunication Services:** electronic mail, bpidgeon@ussportsmen.org. **Formerly:** (2002) Wildlife Legislative Fund of America. **Publications:** *On Target*, weekly. Newsletter. Reports on sportsmen's news headlines. Alternate Formats: online ● *The Sentry*, monthly. Newsletter. Contains information produced to keep sportsmen and sportswomen aware of issues affecting them. ● Also publishes educational materials.

Jousting

23024 ■ National Jousting Association (NJA)
PO Box 14
Mount Solon, VA 22843
Ph: (434)983-2989
E-mail: jousting@nationaljousting.com
URL: http://www.nationaljousting.com
Contact: Mona Banton, Pres.
Members: 14. **Membership Dues:** club, $25 (annual). **Staff:** 3. **Description:** Represents jousting clubs. (In modern jousting, knights spear small rings with jousting lances, in competitions known as ring tournaments.) Works to advance the sport of jousting and promote the Jousting Hall of Fame and museum. Sponsors National Jousting Competition. **Libraries: Type:** open to the public. **Holdings:** articles. **Conventions/Meetings:** semiannual competition ● annual Jousting Tournament - competition ● annual National Jousting Championship - competition.

Judo

23025 ■ American Judo Association (AJA)
PO Box 1568
Santa Barbara, CA 93102
Ph: (805)569-1388
Fax: (805)569-0267
Contact: Dr. C. Hank Drost, Pres.
Founded: 1979. **Members:** 25. **Description:** Individuals interested in the sport of judo. Objective is to teach, promote, and grade the martial art of judo. Plans to sponsor seminars and professional training. **Awards: Type:** recognition. **Conventions/Meetings:** annual conference.

23026 ■ American Judo and Jujitsu Federation (AJJF)
c/o Central Office Administration
216 F St., No. 16
Davis, CA 95616
Ph: (530)899-1617
Free: (800)850-2553
Fax: (800)850-2553
E-mail: co@ajjf.org
URL: http://www.ajjf.org
Contact: Prof. Tom Ball, Pres./CEO
Founded: 1958. **Members:** 2,500. **Membership Dues:** youth (age 15 and below), $30 (annual) ● adult (age 16-64), $60 (annual) ● senior (age 65 above), $15 (annual). **Staff:** 20. **Budget:** $100,000. **Regional Groups:** 9. **State Groups:** 2. **Local Groups:** 1. **Description:** Judo and jujitsu practitioners and schools. Promotes increased participation in the martial arts; seeks to advance martial arts training procedures. Works to improve the expertise of martial arts practitioners through educational programs; sponsors competitions. **Awards:** Okazaki Scholarship Award. **Frequency:** annual. **Type:** scholarship. **Publications:** *Kiai Echo*, quarterly. Newsletter. Features news and events. **Price:** included in membership dues. **Circulation:** 2,500. **Advertising:** accepted. **Conventions/Meetings:** annual convention and dinner, with classes and mat workouts (exhibits).

23027 ■ United States Judo (USJ)
1 Olympic Plz., Ste.505
Colorado Springs, CO 80909
Ph: (719)866-4730
Fax: (719)866-4733
E-mail: drrontripp@aol.com
URL: http://www.usjudo.org
Contact: Dr. Ron Tripp, Pres.
Founded: 1979. **Members:** 6,000. **Membership Dues:** primary (individual), $50 (annual) ● family, $125 (annual) ● life (bronze, silver, gold, platinum), $1,000-$10,000. **Regional Groups:** 51. **Description:** Judo groups and athletes, referees, judges, and interested individuals. Serves as national governing body for amateur judo in the United States. Promotes the sport of judo and trains athletes for competition. Develops eligibility and safety standards; conducts training courses for referees, coaches, and athletes. Sanctions and sponsors national amateur judo competitions. Maintains placement service; compiles statistics. **Committees:** Development; Junior Olympics; Law and Legislation; Standards and Certification. **Affiliated With:** International Judo Federation; International Olympic Committee; United States Olympic Committee. **Publications:** *United States Judo Times*, periodic. Newsletter. **Conventions/Meetings:** annual meeting - always April, prior to US Senior National Judo Championships ● semiannual meeting - prior to the U.S. International Invitational Judo Championships.

23028 ■ United States Judo Association (USJA)
21 N Union Blvd.
Colorado Springs, CO 80909-5784
Ph: (719)633-7750
Free: (877)411-3409
Fax: (719)633-4041
E-mail: usja@usja-judo.org
URL: http://www.usja-judo.org
Contact: Katrina Davis, Exec. Office Mgr.
Founded: 1954. **Members:** 25,000. **Membership Dues:** regular, $40 (annual) ● life, $400 ● family (based on number of members in the family), $166 (annual) ● foreign address, $10 (annual). **Staff:** 4. **Budget:** $620,000. **Description:** Amateur judo athletes and coaches. Promotes the recreational and physical benefits of judo; advocates practice of the sport to develop sportsmanship, good citizenship, and mental well-being. Encourages public interest and participation in Judo. Seeks the advancement of amateur judo competition in the U.S. and worldwide. Maintains National Judo Hall of Fame. Sanctions local, state, and regional tournaments. Offers training and certification program for coaches and referees. **Libraries: Type:** reference; not open to the public. **Awards:** Judo Coaches of the Year. **Frequency:** annual. **Type:** recognition ● Male and Female Judo Athletes of the Year. **Frequency:** annual. **Type:** recognition ● Most Improved Male and Female Judo Athletes of the Year. **Frequency:** annual. **Type:** recognition. **Committees:** Aikido; Awards; Coach Certification; Jui-do; Jujitsu; Kata Certification; Referee; Tournaments. **Formerly:** Strategic Air Command Judo Association; United States Air Force Judo Association; (1969) Armed Forces Judo Association. **Publications:** *American Judo Magazine*, quarterly. **Advertising:** accepted. Alternate Formats: online ● Handbooks. Contains USJA junior and senior rank systems. **Conventions/Meetings:** annual Junior National Tournament - competition and banquet, senior team championship (exhibits).

23029 ■ United States Judo Federation (USJF)
PO Box 338
Ontario, OR 97914
Ph: (541)889-8753
Fax: (541)889-5836
E-mail: ed@usjf.com
URL: http://www.usjf.com
Contact: Robert Fukuda, Exec. Dir.
Founded: 1952. **Members:** 25,000. **Membership Dues:** life (ages 31 and up), $130-$230 ● primary, $50 (annual) ● secondary, $15 (annual). **Staff:** 3. **Regional Groups:** 32. **Local Groups:** 550. **Descrip-tion:** People interested in the sport of judo. Supervises the technical aspects of the sport such as refereeing, judging, testing of ranks, conducting tournaments, and sponsoring tours. Sponsors teacher's institute; conducts regional and national clinics. **Committees:** Board of Examiners; Insurance; Interscholastic Olympic; Junior Development; Legal; Medical; Official's Certification; Promotion Evaluation; Rank Registration; Standards; Teacher Placement; Women's. **Affiliated With:** International Judo Federation. **Formerly:** (1953) AmateurJudo Association; (1961) Judo Black Belt Federation of the U.S.A. **Publications:** *High School and College Training Manual* ● *JUDO-USA*, quarterly ● *Procedure Book*, periodic ● Handbook, every 18-24 months. Includes rule book. ● Also publishes *High School and College Training Manual*. **Conventions/Meetings:** semiannual meeting - always April and October/November.

Juggling

23030 ■ International Jugglers' Association (IJA)
PO Box 7307
Austin, TX 78713-7307
Ph: (415)596-3307
Fax: (302)397-2345
E-mail: memberships@juggle.org
URL: http://www.juggle.org
Contact: Jim Maxwell, Membership Dir.
Founded: 1947. **Members:** 3,000. **Membership Dues:** adult, $30 (annual) ● youth (below 17 years old), $23 (annual) ● life, $1,500. **Description:** Professional and amateur jugglers. Seeks to preserve and further the art of juggling and promote fellowship among those associated with the art. Sponsors educational programs. **Awards: Type:** recognition. **Publications:** *Juggle*, bimonthly. Magazine. Includes book reviews, calendar of events, club and festival listings, and product reviews. **Price:** included in membership dues; $7.00/copy for nonmembers; $119.00 1 set (from 1981 to 2001). **Conventions/Meetings:** annual festival (exhibits) - usually 3rd week of July.

23031 ■ World Juggling Federation (WJF)
8370 W Cheyenne Ave., No. 109-286
Las Vegas, NV 89129
Ph: (702)866-9516
E-mail: info@thewjf.com
URL: http://www.thewjf.com
Contact: Jason Garfield, Founder/Pres.
Membership Dues: bronze level, $10 (annual) ● silver level, $30 (annual) ● gold level, $75 (annual) ● exclusive club, $250 (annual). **Multinational. Description:** Promotes and advances the sport of juggling. Teaches and helps individuals interested in learning how to juggle. Increases the skill level in juggling. Organizes and produces international juggling conventions and competitions. **Telecommunication Services:** electronic mail, jason@thewjf.com. **Publications:** *WJF Update*. Newsletter. Alternate Formats: online ● Videos. Alternate Formats: online.

Karate

23032 ■ American Amateur Karate Federation (AAKF)
1930 Wilshire Blvd., Ste.1007
Los Angeles, CA 90057
Ph: (213)483-8262
Fax: (213)483-4060
E-mail: aakf@aakf.org
URL: http://www.aakf.org
Contact: Mr. Hidetaka Nishiyama, Pres.
Founded: 1961. **Members:** 241. **Staff:** 6. **Budget:** $247,000. **State Groups:** 12. **Description:** Represents karate clubs and schools representing over 20000 individuals. Serves as a national governing body for karate. Seeks to improve the physical and mental health of the public through the practice of karate; promotes public understanding of karate. Establishes competition standards such as rules,

judging, and athlete qualifications. Sets ranking standards in accordance with international standards. Sanctions and conducts national competitions including the All America Karate Championship; recognizes karate practitioners. Plans and executes karate development programs. Sponsors U.S. team development camp, national summer training course, U.S. regional instructor program, championship ranking and judging programs, and examiner qualification program. **Committees:** Eligibility; Medical; Publicity; Research; Technical. **Formerly:** (1978) All America Karate Federation. **Publications:** *Ranking and Examination Guide*, periodic ● *Times Newsletter*, monthly ● Directory, annual. **Conventions/Meetings:** annual meeting - always July, in La Jolla, CA.

23033 ■ American Kenpo Karate International (AKKI)

PO Box 768
Evanston, WY 82931
Ph: (307)789-4124
E-mail: headquarters@akki.com
URL: http://www.akki.com
Contact: Mr. Paul Mills, Pres./Founder
Founded: 1995. **Membership Dues:** student, $25 (annual) ● school, $125 (annual) ● club, $50 (annual). **For-Profit. Multinational. Description:** Seeks to preserve, honor, and elevate the strength of Kenpo Karate. Sponsors competitions. Maintains educational, charitable, and research programs, children's services, and a speakers' bureau. **Libraries: Type:** not open to the public; by appointment only. **Subjects:** kenpo karate education, professional karate schools. **Awards:** KKI Black Belt Certification. **Type:** recognition. **Formerly:** (2001) Kenpo Karate International. **Publications:** *1st Level Club Manual*. **Price:** $28.00 plus shipping and handling ● *1st Level Knife Manual*. **Price:** $35.00 plus shipping and handling ● *Kenpo Karate-Works*. Newsletter ● *Professional Business Guide*. Book ● Articles. Alternate Formats: online ● Booklets ● Also distributes "Secrets of Kenpo Masters" audio/video library.

23034 ■ Feminist Karate Union (FKU)

1426 S Jackson St.
Seattle, WA 98144
Ph: (206)325-3878
E-mail: info@feministkarateunion.org
URL: http://www.feministkarateunion.org
Contact: Sensei Aleeta Van Petten, Chief Instructor
Founded: 1971. **Members:** 150. **Staff:** 10. **Local Groups:** 2. **Description:** Teaches self-protection, self-defense, and karate to women and other victimized groups including children, senior citizens, physically and/or mentally disabled persons, and battered wives. Offers demonstrations, workshops, seminars, and in-service training to community and educational groups and social service agencies. **Formerly:** (1982) Feminist Karate Union; (1985) Feminist Karate Union/Alternatives to Fear. **Publications:** *Acquaintance Rape* ● *Fear Into Anger: A Manual of Self-Defense for Women* ● *FKU Punchline*. Newsletter. Alternate Formats: online ● *Peace of Mind*.

23035 ■ International Traditional Karate Federation (ITKF)

1930 Wilshire Blvd., Ste.1007
Los Angeles, CA 90057
Ph: (213)483-8261 (213)483-8262
Fax: (213)483-4060
E-mail: office@itkf.org
URL: http://www.itkf.org
Contact: Sensei Hidetaka Nishiyama, Chm.
Founded: 1974. **Members:** 64. **Budget:** $298,000. **Description:** National karate federations. Provides international rules, regulations, and competition standards for traditional karate; sanctions international competitions and seminars. **Telecommunication Services:** electronic mail, itkf@itkf.org. **Affiliated With:** American Amateur Karate Federation. **Publications:** *Official Circular*, biweekly. **Conventions/Meetings:** periodic congress.

23036 ■ Japan Karate-Do Organization (JKO)

3545 Midway Dr., Ste.C
San Diego, CA 92110-4922
Ph: (619)223-7405

Fax: (619)223-9422
E-mail: jkoshihan@aol.com
URL: http://www.jko.com
Contact: Minobu Miki, Contact
Founded: 1972. **Multinational. Description:** Promotes karate worldwide. **Computer Services:** Online services, forum. **Affiliated With:** World Karate Federation. **Conventions/Meetings:** International Karate-Do Championship - competition, with Masters' seminar.

23037 ■ Pan-American Union of Karatedo Organizations (PUKO)

1300 Kenmore Blvd.
Akron, OH 44314
Ph: (330)753-3114
Fax: (330)753-6888
E-mail: usakf@raex.com
Contact: George E. Anderson, Pres.
Founded: 1975. **Members:** 37. **Membership Dues:** national, $100 (annual). **Staff:** 4. **Budget:** $2,000. **National Groups:** 37. **Languages:** English, Portuguese, Spanish. **Description:** National karatedo organizations that are recognized by their home government or the International Olympic Committee. Governing body for the sport of karatedo in the Americas. Seeks to improve quality of karatedo performance, officiating, and instruction. Regulates development of karatedo rules, scoring, and methods of instruction. Conducts karatedo instruction programs; licenses and certifies karatedo instructors. Administers international competitions. **Awards: Type:** recognition ● **Type:** scholarship. **Affiliated With:** World Karate Federation. **Publications:** *Program Booklet*, 3-4/year ● Newsletter, 4-5/year ● Also publishes rulebook, coach's manual, and referee's manual. **Conventions/Meetings:** annual congress ● Pan American Championship - competition.

23038 ■ U.S.A. Karate Federation (USAKF)

1300 Kenmore Blvd.
Akron, OH 44314
Ph: (330)753-3114
Fax: (330)753-6888
E-mail: usakf@raex.com
URL: http://www.usakarate.org
Contact: Patrick M. Hickey, Pres.
Founded: 1986. **Members:** 100,000. **Membership Dues:** regular, in U.S., $20 (annual) ● regular, outside U.S., $28 (annual) ● club, in U.S., $100 (annual) ● club, outside U.S., $150 (annual). **Staff:** 5. **Budget:** $2,000. **Description:** Individuals, corporations, sports organizations, and karate clubs. Serves as a national federation for karate in the U.S. Seeks to promote karate as a sport and to advance karate performance and instruction; certifies karate instructors. Organizes competitions, selects U.S. a national karate team. Conducts classes for karate students and masters. Conducts research; compiles statistics; maintains hall of fame and speakers' bureau. **Awards: Type:** recognition. **Affiliated With:** United States Olympic Committee; World Karate Federation. **Publications:** Book. Provides information on rules. ● Manuals. Provides information for referees and coaches. ● Newsletter, quarterly. **Conventions/Meetings:** biennial meeting ● annual meeting.

23039 ■ World Traditional Karate Organization (WTKO)

c/o Mr. John J. Mullin, Exec. Chm.
138 Bradley Ave.
Staten Island, NY 10314
E-mail: wtko@wtko.org
URL: http://www.wtko.org
Contact: Mr. John J. Mullin, Exec. Chm.
Founded: 2001. **Multinational. Description:** Represents groups and individuals dedicated to the pursuit of excellence and advancement of Shotokan karate. Promotes public awareness and understanding of karate. Preserves the values and principals of Shotokan karate. Fosters Shotokan karate through camps, seminars and championships around the world. **Awards:** Athlete of the Year. **Frequency:** annual. **Type:** recognition. **Recipient:** for Shotokan karate athlete ● Instructors of the Month. **Frequency:** monthly. **Type:** recognition. **Recipient:** for instructors

who have demonstrated extraordinary ability in karate ● Man of the Year. **Frequency:** annual. **Type:** recognition. **Recipient:** to an individual for outstanding contribution to karate. **Telecommunication Services:** electronic mail, jmullinwtko@yahoo.com.

Kart Racing

23040 ■ International Kart Federation (IKF)

1609 S Grove Ave., Ste.105
Ontario, CA 91761
Ph: (909)923-4999
Fax: (909)923-6940
E-mail: support@ikfkarting.com
URL: http://www.ikfkarting.com
Contact: Jack Lehmann, Pres.
Founded: 1957. **Members:** 5,000. **Membership Dues:** regular, outside North America, $50 (annual). **Staff:** 6. **Description:** Persons interested in racing karts. Serves as a source of technical data; sets specifications for karts and rules for racing; promotes nationwide interest in kart racing; provides information on track construction; offers kart track insurance program; establishes national competition schedule. Hosts Grand National championships, June through October. **Publications:** *Karter News*, monthly. Magazine. Reports results of individual races and club news; also includes calendar of events and technical and rule book updates. **Price:** included in membership dues. **Circulation:** 5,000. **Advertising:** accepted. **Conventions/Meetings:** semiannual meeting.

Kite Flying

23041 ■ American Kitefliers Association (AKA)

PO Box 1614
Walla Walla, WA 99362
Free: (800)252-2550
E-mail: aka@aka.kite.org
URL: http://www.aka.kite.org
Contact: Mel Hickman, Exec. Dir.
Founded: 1964. **Members:** 4,200. **Membership Dues:** basic, $30 (annual) ● extra, $38 (annual) ● regular, in Canada or Mexico, $38 (annual) ● overseas (via surface mail), $40 (annual) ● overseas (via airmail), $55 (annual) ● sponsor, $100 (annual). **Budget:** $130,000. **Regional Groups:** 62. **Description:** Represents persons interested in kite building, kiting events, and the advancement of kites. Sponsors specialized education and competitions; provides teachers' packets on kites and kite building. **Libraries: Type:** reference. **Holdings:** archival material. **Awards:** Edeiken Trophy. **Frequency:** annual. **Type:** recognition. **Recipient:** for contributions to kiting. **Committees:** Archives and Records; Festivals and Competitions; Safety and Ethics. **Publications:** *Kiting*, quarterly. Newsletter. Includes kite events, local club activities, and more. **Price:** included in membership dues. **Advertising:** accepted ● Membership Directory, periodic ● Books. Contains competition rules. ● Manuals ● Pamphlets.

Lacrosse

23042 ■ International Lacrosse Federation (ILF)

4117 Gilgo E
Gilgo Beach, NY 11702
Ph: (631)620-4433
E-mail: phobbs@shd.com.au
URL: http://www.intlaxfed.org
Contact: Peter Hobbs, Pres.
Founded: 1974. **Members:** 18. **Staff:** 4. **Budget:** $50,000. **Languages:** Chinese, Czech, English, German, Japanese, Korean, Spanish, Swedish. **Multinational. Description:** International governing body of men's lacrosse; supports international development. **Awards:** Turnbull Trophy. **Frequency:** quadrennial. **Type:** trophy. **Recipient:** world champion. **Conven-**

tions/Meetings: annual conference ● quadrennial World Championships - competition.

23043 ■ United States Intercollegiate Lacrosse Association (USILA)
c/o John Spring, Exec. Dir.
3738 W Lake Rd.
Perry, NY 14530
Ph: (585)237-5886
Fax: (585)237-5886
E-mail: usilajspring@aol.com
URL: http://www.usila.org
Contact: John Spring, Exec. Dir.
Founded: 1883. **Members:** 206. **Membership Dues:** active, $200 (annual). **Staff:** 1. **Budget:** $88,000. **Description:** Colleges and universities. Conducts research programs; sponsors competitions. Compiles statistics. **Awards:** Howdy Myers Man of the Year. **Frequency:** annual. **Type:** recognition. **Recipient:** for untiring devotion to the game of lacrosse ● USILA Scholar All-America Program. **Frequency:** annual. **Type:** scholarship. **Recipient:** for outstanding student athletes from member institutions. **Committees:** All American; Championship Awards; Coach of the Year; Lacrosse Rules; Man of the Year; Officiating; Statistical. **Conventions/Meetings:** annual convention, includes coaching clinic (exhibits) - usually December.

23044 ■ United States Lacrosse Association, Women's Division (USLAWD)
113 W Univ. Pkwy.
Baltimore, MD 21210
Ph: (410)235-6882
Fax: (410)366-6735
E-mail: info@lacrosse.org
URL: http://www.lacrosse.org/womens_div/index.
  phtml
Contact: Steve Stenersen, Exec. Dir.
Founded: 1931. **Members:** 6,000. **Membership Dues:** youth player, $20 (annual) ● official, adult, head coach, $50 (annual) ● high school player, assistant/youth coach, $35 (annual) ● cross participant (18 yrs. and below), $45 (annual) ● fan, $40 (annual) ● cross participant adult, $65 (annual). **Budget:** $200,000. **Regional Groups:** 6. **Local Groups:** 60. **Description:** Promotes the sport of lacrosse for women. Establishes rules for competition; trains umpires; conducts clinics. Sponsors annual national tournament and competitive international events. **Awards:** Beth Allen Award. **Frequency:** annual. **Type:** recognition. **Recipient:** for sportsmanship and leadership ● Heather Albert Award. **Frequency:** annual. **Type:** recognition. **Recipient:** for sportsmanship ● Nancy Chance Award. **Frequency:** annual. **Type:** recognition. **Recipient:** for service ● Val Walchak. **Frequency:** annual. **Type:** recognition. **Committees:** Accreditation; Camps; Clinics; Collegiate Coaches; Fundraising; High School and College All-American; Loan Kits; Manual Revision; Memorial Fund; National Tournament; Rules; Safety; Stick Repair; Tours; Umpiring; U.S. Squad; Youth Lacrosse. **Publications:** *U.S. Women's Lacrosse Association—Newsletter*, 5/year. Includes calendar of events. **Price:** included in membership dues. **Advertising:** accepted ● Books ● Directory, annual ● Manuals. Covers coaching and umpiring. ● Videos. **Conventions/Meetings:** annual meeting - always Memorial Day weekend ● seminar.

23045 ■ U.S. Lacrosse and The Lacrosse Museum and National Hall of Fame
113 W Univ. Pkwy.
Baltimore, MD 21210
Ph: (410)235-6882
Fax: (410)366-6735
E-mail: info@uslacrosse.org
URL: http://www.uslacrosse.org
Contact: Nancy Patrick, Asst. to the Exec. Dir.
Founded: 1998. **Members:** 218,000. **Membership Dues:** youth player, $20 (annual) ● high school player, assistant/youth/club/JV coach, $35 (annual) ● adult player, official, $50 (annual) ● head coach, $50 (annual) ● fan, $40 (annual) ● cross participant (age 18 and above), $65 (annual) ● cross participant (youth/high school), $45 (annual). **Staff:** 41. **Budget:** $10,000,000. **Regional Groups:** 53. **Description:**

Serves as the national governing body of men's and women's lacrosse. Runs the Lacrosse Museum and National Hall of Fame. **Awards:** Camp Scholarship Program. **Frequency:** annual. **Type:** scholarship. **Recipient:** for children to attend summer lacrosse camps ● Excellence in Growing the Game. **Frequency:** annual. **Type:** recognition. **Recipient:** for an individual who supports the US Lacrosse mission and vision ● Outstanding Contribution to the Game. **Frequency:** annual. **Type:** recognition. **Recipient:** for individuals who have consistently contributed to the youth game of lacrosse ● Program Administrator of the Year. **Frequency:** annual. **Type:** recognition. **Recipient:** for an outstanding administrator ● **Type:** recognition. **Recipient:** for officials ● Youth Equipment Grant Program. **Frequency:** annual. **Type:** grant. **Recipient:** for a starting lacrosse program. **Computer Services:** Mailing lists. **Committees:** North-South Game; Publicity; Rules; Secondary Schools. **Formerly:** (1993) The Lacrosse Foundation. **Publications:** *Lacrosse Magazine*, monthly. **Price:** included in membership dues; $5.00 for members (additional copy); $6.00 for nonmembers (additional copy). **Advertising:** accepted. Alternate Formats: online ● *The Parent's Guide to the Sport of Lacrosse*. Pamphlet ● *US Lacrosse Women's Division Collegiate Rulebook*. Handbook. **Conventions/Meetings:** annual Intercollegiate Associates Championship - competition ● annual National Lacrosse Hall of Fame Induction Celebration - meeting ● annual National Youth Festival, includes coaching clinic (exhibits) ● annual US Lacrosse National Convention ● annual Women's Division National Tournament - competition.

Lifesaving

23046 ■ International Association of Dive Rescue Specialists (IADRS)
201 N Link Ln.
Fort Collins, CO 80524
Ph: (970)482-1562
Free: (800)423-7791
Fax: (970)482-0893
E-mail: swatson@iadrs.org
URL: http://www.iadrs.org
Contact: Susan Watson, Dir. of Operations
Founded: 1978. **Members:** 1,000. **Membership Dues:** individual in U.S., $25 (annual) ● individual outside U.S., $40 (annual). **Staff:** 1. **Description:** Water rescue professionals worldwide. Seeks to establish safety measures for water rescue professionals and develop training and certification standards in all aspects of water rescue and recovery work. Gathers and disseminates information and advice. Sponsors specialty type conferences. **Awards:** **Type:** scholarship. **Committees:** Standards. **Publications:** *Association News*, bimonthly. Newsletter. Covers new methods and developments in the field; includes calendar of events, lists of training programs, and product news. **Price:** included in membership dues. **Circulation:** 2,500. **Advertising:** accepted. **Conventions/Meetings:** annual international conference.

Luge

23047 ■ United States Luge Association (USLA/USALuge)
57 Church St.
Lake Placid, NY 12946
Ph: (518)523-2071
Fax: (518)523-4106
E-mail: info@usaluge.org
URL: http://www.usaluge.org
Contact: Amy Chapin, Dir. of Administration
Founded: 1981. **Members:** 600. **Membership Dues:** athletic (class C, G & N), $40 (annual) ● athletic (class B, Y, & O), $30 (annual) ● athletic (class A), $25 (annual). **Staff:** 20. **Budget:** $2,625,000. **Regional Groups:** 3. **Local Groups:** 6. **Languages:** English, German. **Description:** Represents luge athletes and interested individuals. Selects qualified

athletes for the U.S. Olympic Luge Team. Promotes and seeks to improve amateur luge in the U.S; helps defer training expenses for amateur American athletes; sanctions international competitions for junior and senior athletes in men's singles, women's singles, and doubles. Conducts research programs for technical advancement of the sport. Maintains speakers' bureau; compiles statistics. **Libraries:** **Type:** reference. **Holdings:** archival material. **Awards:** Athlete of the Year. **Frequency:** annual. **Type:** recognition. **Recipient:** for top finishers in luge events ● Individual Race Awards. **Frequency:** annual. **Type:** recognition. **Recipient:** for men singles and women doubles ● Justin A. Matarese. **Frequency:** annual. **Type:** recognition ● Sam Venezia Volunteer Spirit Award. **Frequency:** annual. **Type:** recognition. **Recipient:** for top finishers in luge events ● Verizon U.S. Junior National Champion. **Frequency:** annual. **Type:** recognition. **Recipient:** for men singles and women doubles ● Verizon U.S. Senior National Champion. **Frequency:** annual. **Type:** recognition. **Recipient:** for men singles and women doubles. **Computer Services:** database ● mailing lists. **Committees:** National Team; Racing. **Affiliated With:** International Luge Federation; United States Olympic Committee. **Publications:** *The Slider*, quarterly. Newsletter. Contains information on the National Luge Team, sports medicine and science, the Olympic trials, national and international races. **Price:** included in membership dues. **Advertising:** accepted. **Conventions/Meetings:** annual congress - usually June ● seminar, on luge technique, coaching, equipment, rules, and athletic and psychological training.

Marine

23048 ■ Historical Diving Society USA (HDSUSA)
PO Box 2837
Santa Maria, CA 93457
Ph: (805)934-1660
Fax: (805)938-0550
E-mail: hds@hds.org
URL: http://hds.org
Contact: Dan Orr, Chm.
Founded: 1992. **Membership Dues:** student (domestic), $35 (annual) ● individual (domestic), $40 (annual) ● Caribbean, $45 (annual) ● family domestic, diving club, institutional, dive store, $50 (annual) ● overseas, $60 (annual) ● corporate, $100 (annual) ● life, $1,000. **Description:** Identifies, preserves, protects and maintains artifacts and archives associated with the history of diving. Provides a forum for individuals and organizations with an interest in the history of underwater exploits. Organizes meetings and rallies to foster a general awareness of the importance of diving as a significant aspect of technological endeavor. **Affiliated With:** Association of Diving Contractors International. **Publications:** *Historical Diver*, quarterly. Magazine. Features articles covering the history of diving. **Price:** included in membership dues.

Martial Arts

23049 ■ All Japan Ju-Jitsu International Federation (AJJIF)
622 W Colorado St.
Glendale, CA 91204
Ph: (323)512-2538
E-mail: ajjif@yahoo.com
URL: http://www.ajjif.org
Contact: Grand Master Alexey Kunin, Pres.
Founded: 2000. **Membership Dues:** life, $100. **Multinational. Description:** Preserves, protects and promotes disappearing traditional and combat Ju-Jitsu in the world. Establishes support, development, friendship, cooperation, growth, education, and promotion of traditional and classical Ju-Jitsu worldwide. Recognizes and registers all the different styles and families of Ju-Jitsu.

23050 ■ American Chen Style Tai Chi Association (ACT)

300 NE 12 Ave., No. 601
Hallandale Beach, FL 33009
E-mail: info@americanchentaichi.com
Contact: Gaofei Yan, Contact

Founded: 1996. **Membership Dues:** regular, $55 (annual). **Description:** Promotes the Original Large Frame Chen Style Tai Chi Chuan martial arts. **Programs:** Internal Body Changing. **Publications:** *Chen Style Tai Chi Straight Sword Form (JIAN)*. Video. Provides a guide to begin training for JIAN. **Price:** $30.00 plus shipping and handling ● *International Tai Chi Meeting 1998 - Push Hands Competition*. Video. Features tournament rules and matches. **Price:** $28.00 for members, plus shipping and handling; $35.00 for nonmembers, plus shipping and handling ● *Master Chen Quanzhong - Original Chen Style Tai Chi Form and Push Hand*. Video. Demonstrates the Lao Jia (Old Large Frame) Forms and Push Hands. **Price:** $36.00 for members, plus shipping and handling; $45.00 for nonmembers, plus shipping and handling ● *Master Chen Quanzhong - Original Chen Style Tai Chi Weapons Form*. Video. Demonstrates the use of two edged sword, broadsword, spear, and Guan Dao. **Price:** $36.00 for members, plus shipping and handling; $45.00 for nonmembers, plus shipping and handling ● Newsletter. Alternate Formats: online.

23051 ■ American Kempo-Karate Association (AKKA)

PO Box 680037
Charlotte, NC 28216-0037
Free: (800)320-2552
E-mail: info@torakendo.com
URL: http://torakendo.com
Contact: Ray D. Ferrell, Pres./Chief Instructor
Description: Supports and governs the Shorinji Toraken Ryu system of martial arts. Teaches a standardized curriculum on specific rules, regulations and disciplines of Shorinji Toraken Ryu. Provides activities to further and reunite Shorinji Toraken Ryu practitioners and instructors.

23052 ■ American Shorin Kempo Karate Association

c/o Terry L. Bryan, Pres.
1587 York St.
Colorado Springs, CO 80918
Ph: (719)598-0398
Fax: (719)268-2733
E-mail: kyoshibryan@juno.com
URL: http://www.americanblackbeltacademy.com
Contact: Terry L. Bryan, Pres.
Founded: 1970. **Members:** 1,700. **Membership Dues:** regular, $25 (annual). **Staff:** 6. **Budget:** $300,000. **Regional Groups:** 6. **State Groups:** 6. **Multinational. Description:** Offers instruction, certification and on-going study in the martial arts and self-defense. Teaches "Streetwise Self-Defense" program in local schools and offers the program to the general public. Prepares students for threatening situations. Pilot programs are starting nationally and internationally. **Libraries: Type:** open to the public. **Holdings:** audiovisuals, books, business records, periodicals. **Subjects:** martial arts.

23053 ■ American Teachers Association of the Martial Arts (ATAMA)

c/o Dr. T.R. Crimi, PhD, Pres.
11990 Sunset Hill Rd.
Penn Valley, CA 95946
Ph: (530)432-5588
Fax: (530)432-0674
E-mail: ryuzado@aol.com
URL: http://www.atama.us
Contact: Dr. T.R. Crimi PhD, Pres.
Founded: 1981. **Membership Dues:** life, $300 ● adult associate, $55 (annual) ● junior associate, $40 (annual). **Description:** Promotes the practice of martial arts. Seeks to improve the level of competency within the martial arts through mutual exchange of knowledge. Aims to help students become better instructors and to help instructors to become better teachers.

23054 ■ American Wu Shu Society (AWS)

PO Box 5898
Long Island City, NY 11105-5898
E-mail: wusociety@yahoo.com
URL: http://www.wusociety.com
Contact: Edward Aguirre, Pres.
Founded: 1996. **Membership Dues:** individual, $30 (annual) ● school, $100 (annual). **Multinational. Description:** Furthers the advancement of modern Wu Shu in the US and worldwide. Provides information about the arts and ethics of Wu Shu. **Computer Services:** database, members list ● information services, Wu Shu/Sanda resources ● online services, forum. **Publications:** Journal. Alternate Formats: online.

23055 ■ American Yangjia Michuan Taijiquan Association (AYMTA)

PO Box 173
Grand Haven, MI 49417
E-mail: president@aymta.org
URL: http://aymta.org
Contact: Charlie Adamec, Pres.
Membership Dues: regular, $35 (annual) ● family, student, $20 (annual). **Description:** Furthers and promotes the growth of Yangjia Michuan Taijiquan (YMT) as a unique art of self-defense. Seeks to educate the public about the purpose and benefits of practicing Yangjia Michuan Taijiquan. Provides opportunities for its members to develop their skills as potential YMT instructors. **Telecommunication Services:** electronic mail, bofd@aymta.org. **Publications:** Newsletter ● Journal, semiannual. Features articles and information about Yangjia Michuan Taijiquan. **Price:** free for members.

23056 ■ Association of Women Martial Arts Instructors (AWMAI)

PO Box 7033
Houston, TX 77248-7033
Ph: (281)630-5120
E-mail: info@awmai.org
URL: http://www.awmai.org/drupal
Contact: Shihan Sherry McGregor, Exec. Coor.
Membership Dues: general, $25 (annual) ● life, $250. **Description:** Enhances the learning experience and professional recognition of women martial arts instructors. Provides teacher training, school and organizational development, ethical standards, and rank recognition and promotion. **Conventions/Meetings:** annual conference, teacher training; panel discussion.

23057 ■ Combat Martial Art Practitioners Association (CMAPA)

c/o John Frank Brado, Dir./Chief Instructor
2277 E Elm St.
Lima, OH 45804
E-mail: info@combatmartialarts.com
URL: http://www.combatmartialarts.com
Contact: John Frank Brado, Dir./Chief Instructor
Membership Dues: life, $100. **Description:** Supports traditional, reality-based, self-defense-oriented martial arts practitioners regardless of rank, style or other affiliations. Provides standardized rank advancement program so that independent solo practitioners and professional martial arts instructors and school owners can continue their personal and professional development through rank advancement.

23058 ■ International Association of Gay and Lesbian Martial Artists (IAGLMA)

PO Box 590601
San Francisco, CA 94159-0601
E-mail: iaglmaorg@aol.com
URL: http://www.iaglma.org
Contact: Teresa Galetti, Co-Pres.
Founded: 1990. **Members:** 150. **Membership Dues:** individual, $15 (annual) ● family/club/organization, $25 (annual). **Languages:** Dutch, English, Spanish. **Description:** Gay and lesbian martial artists. Promotes participation of homosexual individuals in martial arts. Facilitates communication among members; conducts educational programs; sponsors competitions. Assists in the staging of martial arts events at the Gay Games. **Computer Services:** Mailing lists, of members. **Telecommunication Services:** electronic mail, iaglmaboard@iaglma.org. **Publications:** *IAGLMA Newsletter*, quarterly. Alternate Formats: online. **Conventions/Meetings:** periodic board meeting ● annual meeting.

23059 ■ International Martial Arts League (IMAL)

c/o John Pendergrass, Pres.
12820 N Shore Dr.
Fort Wayne, IN 46818
Ph: (219)625-2389
Free: (800)639-1643
Fax: (219)625-3299
E-mail: imal@earthlink.net
URL: http://martialartsleague.bizland.com
Contact: John Pendergrass, Pres.
Multinational. Description: Promotes and develops the practice of martial arts. Offers martial arts competitions from around the world. Helps promote tournaments. Assists young black belt school owners with promotions and seminars.

23060 ■ International Okinawa Kobudo Association (IOKA)

1666 San Diego St.
Fairfield, CA 94533
Ph: (707)428-7266
Fax: (707)428-7266
E-mail: bolz@okinawabudou.org
URL: http://www.okinawa-budou.org/IOKA
Contact: Shihan Mary H. Bolz, VP
Founded: 1990. **Members:** 350. **Membership Dues:** life, $500. **Multinational. Description:** Works to teach traditional Okinawan weaponry with authentic and practical techniques. Maintains high teaching standards. Provides training, assistance, advancement and support to members. Promotes friendship and cooperation among members.

23061 ■ International Shaolin Kenpo Association (ISKA)

69 Washington St.
Daly City, CA 94014
Ph: (650)755-8996
Fax: (650)755-8996
E-mail: infoforiska@aol.com
URL: http://www.shaolinkenpo.com
Contact: Ralph Castro, Founder/Pres.
Founded: 1982. **Members:** 205. **Regional Groups:** 3. **Multinational. Description:** Promotes the practice and teaching of the martial art of Shaolin Kenpo karate. **Libraries: Type:** reference. **Subjects:** karate. **Awards:** Fighter of the Year. **Frequency:** annual. **Type:** recognition ● Lifetime Achievement. **Type:** recognition ● Student of the Year. **Frequency:** annual. **Type:** recognition. **Committees:** Awards; Events. **Publications:** Newsletter. **Price:** included in membership dues. **Advertising:** accepted. **Conventions/Meetings:** annual California Open Karate Championships - competition.

23062 ■ International Sungja-Do Association (ISA)

c/o George I. Petrotta, Dir./Founder
1366 St. Andrews Blvd.
Florence, SC 29505
Ph: (843)669-1444
E-mail: isahdq@sc.rr.com
URL: http://www.sungjado.org
Contact: George I. Petrotta, Dir./Founder
Founded: 2001. **Membership Dues:** color belt, $15 (annual) ● black belt, $18 (annual) ● life, $35. **Multinational. Description:** Seeks to bring together all affiliated martial arts schools and instructors. Stimulates interest in the various martial arts among all students of Taekwondo, Karate, Kung-fu, Hapkido, Aikido, Aiki-JuJitsu, Jiujtsu, Kempo, Kenpo and other arts. Aims to establish the martial arts in physical education programs and curricula. Establishes and maintains relations with affiliated schools and other authentic martial arts organizations.

23063 ■ International Yang Style Tai Chi Chuan Association

4076-148th Ave. NE
Redmond, WA 98052
Ph: (425)869-1185
Fax: (425)869-1185
E-mail: nancy@yangfamilytaichi.com
URL: http://www.yangfamilytaichi.com
Contact: Yang Zhen Duo, Chm.
Founded: 1998. **Membership Dues:** individual, $30 (annual) ● family, $45 (annual) ● senior, $25 (annual). **Multinational. Description:** Promotes Yang Style Tai Chi Chuan worldwide. Develops new Yang Tai Chi Chuan centers. Increases interaction with other martial arts organizations. Evaluates Tai Chi practitioners' levels of skill. **Computer Services:** Information services, Tai Chi Chuan resources ● online services, discussion board. **Departments:** European Affairs; Membership Services; Outreach and Development; Public Relations; Southern American Affairs; Training Standards. **Publications:** *Tai Chi Chuan*, 3/year. Newsletter.

23064 ■ Japan Aikido Association U.S.A. (JAA/USA)

5752 S Kingston Way
Englewood, CO 80111
E-mail: nettles@tomiki.org
URL: http://www.tomiki.org
Contact: Seiji Tanaka, Chm./Dir.
Founded: 1990. **Members:** 250. **Membership Dues:** individual, $20 (annual) ● large club (up to 20 members), $180 (annual) ● life, $5. **Budget:** $20,000. **Regional Groups:** 50. **Description:** Fosters international amateur sports competition. Seeks to introduce and promote the Japanese martial art Aikido by organizing training camps, exhibitions, and tournaments around the world. Promotes international and intercultural exchange, education, and understanding. **Libraries: Type:** reference. **Holdings:** video recordings. **Subjects:** demonstrations, seminars by 8th degree black belts, tournament coverage. **Awards: Type:** recognition. **Publications:** *The Aikido Times*, quarterly. Newsletter. **Price:** included in membership dues; $10.00/year. **Circulation:** 300. **Advertising:** accepted. **Conventions/Meetings:** biennial International Tournaments - competition (exhibits) - odd years ● biennial National Tournaments - competition (exhibits) - even years.

23065 ■ Martial Arts International Federation (MAIF)

1850 Columbia Pike, Ste.No. 613
Arlington, VA 22204
Ph: (703)693-6331 (703)920-1590
Fax: (703)920-1590
E-mail: info@maintlfed.org
URL: http://www.maintlfed.org
Contact: Bruce R. Bethers, Sec. Gen.
Founded: 1998. **Membership Dues:** life (with affiliate organization), $50 ● life (without affiliate organization), $100 ● group, $250 (annual) ● individual (Kyu grade), $25 (annual). **Multinational. Description:** Promotes and develops the practice of martial arts. Fosters technical excellence, fellowship and human character development. Provides an international forum for martial arts where Nationally Recognized Martial Art Organizations (NRMAO) and International Partner Martial Art Organizations (IPMAO) can debate related issues. Provides training, assistance, advancement and support to members. **Affiliated With:** International Judo Federation; U.S.A. Karate Federation; World Karate Federation; World Taekwondo Federation. **Publications:** Articles. Alternate Formats: online.

23066 ■ Martial Arts USA

1619 Fairway Dr. SW
Jacksonville, AL 36265
Fax: (256)782-8033
E-mail: mausalb@yahoo.com
URL: http://www.martialartsusa.com
Contact: Prof. Lawrence A. Beard, Pres.
Membership Dues: school owner, $25 (annual) ● individual, $55 (annual) ● life, $350. **Description:** Represents the interests of martial artists dedicated

to sharing knowledge with others, building moral character and promoting goodwill. Promotes and develops the practice of martial arts in the USA. Provides training, assistance, support, advancement and certification to members. **Publications:** Newsletter. **Price:** included in membership dues. Alternate Formats: online.

23067 ■ National Association of Professional Martial Artists (NAPMA)

5601 116th Ave. N
Clearwater, FL 33760
Ph: (727)540-0500
Free: (800)973-6734
Fax: (727)540-0806
E-mail: info@napma.com
URL: http://www.napma.com
Contact: Rob Colasanti, VP
Founded: 1995. **Membership Dues:** general, $99 (monthly). **Description:** Aims to increase the number of people benefiting from martial arts instruction. Offers business, marketing and management education to martial arts professionals. Promotes safety and professionalism in the martial arts industry. **Libraries: Type:** reference. **Holdings:** audio recordings, video recordings. **Subjects:** self-defense. **Computer Services:** database, lists of NAPMA schools ● information services, martial arts and other self-defense articles ● online services, member forum. **Departments:** Advertising; Membership Services; Production; Website Administration. **Programs:** Coca Cola; Fitness Kickboxing; Kichen Kids After School; School Support Network. **Publications:** *Martial Arts Professional*, monthly. Magazine. Covers martial arts business and instructor information. ● Newsletter. Alternate Formats: online.

23068 ■ National Women's Martial Arts Federation (NWMAF)

100 Bush St., Ste.1500
San Francisco, CA 94104
Ph: (415)982-9200
E-mail: nwmaf@yahoogroups.com
URL: http://www.nwmaf.org
Contact: Ms. Sally Johnson Van Wright, Chair
Founded: 1972. **Members:** 550. **Membership Dues:** regular in U.S., $40 (annual) ● regular outside U.S., $50 (annual) ● fulltime student, senior in U.S., $25 (annual) ● fulltime student, senior outside U.S., $35 (annual) ● life, in U.S., $375 ● life, outside U.S., $475. **Regional Groups:** 13. **Description:** Female martial artists. Promotes excellence in martial arts. Encourages "the widest range of women" to train in the spirit of building individual and collective strength. Sponsors competitions, educational, and charitable programs. **Libraries: Type:** reference. **Holdings:** archival material. **Awards:** Lifetime Achievement Award. **Type:** recognition. **Committees:** Elections; ST Planning. **Funds:** Scholarship. **Publications:** *Disabilities Directory* ● *Women in the Martial Arts*, quarterly. Newsletter. Includes articles and features on female martial artists, and news about upcoming events. **Price:** included in membership dues. **Advertising:** accepted. Alternate Formats: online ● Brochure. Alternate Formats: online ● Membership Directory. **Price:** included in membership dues ● Video. **Price:** $25.00 ● Videos. **Price:** $10.00. **Conventions/Meetings:** regional meeting ● annual Special Training Conference (exhibits) ● workshop.

23069 ■ North America Wu(Hao) Taiji Federation (NAWTF)

1778 N Plano Rd., Ste.No. 108
Richardson, TX 75081
Ph: (972)680-7888
Fax: (972)680-7889
E-mail: jkwong@chinwoo.com
URL: http://www.wuhaotaiji.com
Contact: Master Jimmy K. Wong, Founder
Founded: 1999. **Membership Dues:** executive, $360 (annual) ● school, $100 (annual) ● instructor, $39 (biennial) ● individual, $18 (biennial). **Multinational. Description:** Promotes the art of Wu(Hao) Taiji in North America. Aims to preserve the Wu(Hao) Taiji standardization. Participates in tournaments in local, national and international levels. Facilitates com-

munication and cooperation among members. **Publications:** Newsletter. **Price:** included in membership dues. Alternate Formats: online.

23070 ■ Pan American Taekwondo Union (PATU)

c/o Mr. David Askinas, VP
One Olympic Plz., Ste.104C
Colorado Springs, CO 80909
Ph: (719)866-4632
Fax: (719)866-4642
E-mail: david.askinas@usa-taekwondo.us
URL: http://www.patu.org
Contact: Mr. David Askinas, VP
Founded: 1977. **Members:** 43. **Membership Dues:** regular, $75 (annual). **Budget:** $75,000. **Multinational. Description:** North, South, and Central American countries having taekwondo federations or associations recognized by the World Taekwondo Federation (see separate entry). Promotes the sport of taekwondo. **Libraries: Type:** reference; not open to the public. **Subjects:** national/international activities. **Commissions:** Coaches; Development; Medical; Referees; Technical. **Publications:** *Directory of the PATU*, biennial. **Price:** available to members only. **Advertising:** accepted ● Newsletter, quarterly. **Price:** available to members only. **Advertising:** accepted. **Conventions/Meetings:** biennial congress and general assembly (exhibits) ● biennial PAN American Taekwondo Championships - competition, held in conjunction with group's biennial congress.

23071 ■ United States of America Wushu-Kungfu Federation (USAWKF)

6313 Harford Rd.
Baltimore, MD 21214
Ph: (410)444-6666
Fax: (410)426-5524
E-mail: usawkf@usawkf.org
URL: http://www.usawkf.org
Contact: Anthony Goh, Contact
Founded: 1993. **Membership Dues:** individual, $25 (annual) ● life - individual, $250 ● school, $100 (annual) ● life - school, $500 ● international/associate, $39 (annual) ● life - international/associate, $390 ● international/associate school, $125 (annual) ● life - international/associate school, $595. **Description:** Seeks to improve the quality and increase the popularity of Wushu-Kungfu in the United States. Represents the United States in the International Wushu Federation. Works for the recognition of Wushu as an Olympic sport. **Computer Services:** database, school directory ● mailing lists. **Committees:** Internal Wushu; Traditional Wushu. **Publications:** Newsletter, quarterly. **Price:** included in membership dues.

23072 ■ United States Hapki Hae

4826 Old Natl. Hwy.
College Park, GA 30337
Ph: (404)768-0507
Fax: (404)768-0402
E-mail: ushapkihaeihf@yahoo.com
URL: http://www.unitedstateshapkihae.com
Contact: Master Shelton R. Moreland, Dir./Founder
Multinational. Description: Seeks to establish a worldwide link between the practitioners of Korean based martial arts systems and their roots in Korea. Seeks to build a mutual relationship of respect and encouragement between the practitioners of all traditional martial arts styles. **Computer Services:** Information services, code of ethics ● information services, Hapkido resources.

23073 ■ United States Martial Arts Association (USMA)

8011 Mariposa Ave.
Citrus Heights, CA 95610-1514
Ph: (916)727-1486
Fax: (916)727-7236
E-mail: psp83@earthlink.net
URL: http://www.mararts.org
Contact: Philip S. Porter, Founder
Membership Dues: life, $50 ● registration of current rank, $25 ● promotion, $25-$400. **Multinational. Description:** Unifies American Martial Arts in spirit by

offering services and guidance to all martial artists. Conducts national and international seminar programs to provide expert instruction on martial arts. **Programs:** American Martial Arts Character Achievement; USMA Community Service; USMA Instructor and Examiner Certification; USMA Martial Arts School Management. **Publications:** Articles. Alternate Formats: online.

23074 ■ United States Muay Thai Association (USMTA)
6535 Broadway, Ste.1K
Riverdale, NY 10471
Fax: (718)549-6122
E-mail: usmta@usmta.com
URL: http://www.usmta.com
Contact: Arjarn Clint Heyliger, Pres.
Founded: 1991. **Membership Dues:** affiliate, $15 (annual) ● associate, $52 (annual) ● standard, $20 (annual) ● international affiliate, $45 (annual) ● fighter, $12 (annual) ● official, $50 (annual). **Description:** Promotes the growth and success of American Muay Thai throughout the North American continent and throughout the world. Regulates Muay Thai competitions in North America. **Awards:** Samai Masamarn Award. **Frequency:** annual. **Type:** recognition. **Recipient:** for outstanding performance of the "Ram Musay" by a US fighter in both amateur and professional leagues. **Computer Services:** database, fighters list ● database, international schools ● database, list of instructors ● database, U.S. schools ● online services, forum. **Publications:** *Muay Thai International*. Magazine. Alternate Formats: online. Also Cited As: *MTI*.

23075 ■ U.S. Taekwondo Union (USTU)
1 Olympic Plz., Ste.104C
Colorado Springs, CO 80909
Ph: (719)866-4632
Fax: (719)866-4642
E-mail: david.askinas@usa-taekwondo.us
URL: http://www.usa-taekwondo.us
Contact: David Askinas, CEO
Founded: 1974. **Members:** 30,000. **Membership Dues:** life, $500 ● athlete, coach, referee, $35 (annual) ● support, $20 (annual). **Staff:** 13. **Budget:** $3,000,000. **State Groups:** 50. **Local Groups:** 900. **Description:** A member of the United States Olympic Committee and the national governing body for the sport of Taekwondo. Amateur Taekwondo athletes and instructors. Promotes Taekwondo programs in the U.S. and represents the U.S. in the Olympics and World Championships and other international competitions under sanction of the World Taekwondo Federation. Offers referee and coaching certification programs; conducts seminars. Sponsors competitions; selects national Olympic Taekwondo teams. **Libraries:** Type: not open to the public. **Awards:** **Frequency:** periodic. **Type:** recognition. **Recipient:** for volunteers, in appreciation of dedicated service. **Formerly:** (1981) United States National Amateur Athletic Union Taekwondo Committee; (1985) National AAU Taekwondo Union of the United States of America. **Publications:** *U.S. Taekwondo Journal*, annual. **Price:** $12.00. **Circulation:** 45,000. **Advertising:** accepted ● *US Referee Seminar*. Manual ● *USTU Club Newsletter*, bimonthly ● Also publishes competition rules and regulations. **Conventions/Meetings:** semiannual National Championships - board meeting and executive committee meeting ● seminar ● annual U.S. Jr. Olympic Taekwondo Championship - competition.

23076 ■ Universal Martial Arts Brotherhood (UMAB)
c/o Grandmaster Eugene A. Humesky, PhD
2427 Buckingham Rd.
Ann Arbor, MI 48104
Ph: (734)971-7040
E-mail: assyahu@webtv.net
URL: http://www.utbtaekwondo.us/page3.htm
Contact: Grandmaster Eugene A. Humesky PhD, Founder/CEO/Chm.
Founded: 1994. **Multinational. Description:** Promotes and develops the practice of martial arts. Provides opportunities for students and instructors to

meet, exchange information, train together and expand the community of Taekwondo practitioners. Expands training to all styles of martial arts.

23077 ■ World Head of Family Sokeship Council (WHFSC)
6035 Ft. Caroline Rd., Ste.22
Jacksonville, FL 32277
Fax: (904)744-4625
E-mail: whfsc@bushido.org
URL: http://www.bushido.org/whfsc
Contact: Frank E. Sanchez, Founder/Exec. Dir.
Founded: 1993. **Members:** 160. **Multinational. Description:** Seeks to bring communication between the different systems of Martial Arts through its grandmasters. Proliferates the growth of the martial arts. Serves as a registering agency for inheritors and student grandmasters. Promotes friendship and cooperation among martial arts enthusiasts and leaders. **Awards:** International Martial Arts Achievement Awards. **Frequency:** annual. **Type:** recognition. **Recipient:** for outstanding individuals in the martial arts community. **Publications:** Newsletter, bimonthly. Alternate Formats: online.

23078 ■ World Jeet Kune Do Federation (WJKDF)
PO Box 52820
Tulsa, OK 74152-0820
E-mail: info@leejkd.com
URL: http://www.leejkd.com
Contact: Prof. Carter Hargrave, Pres.
Founded: 1992. **Members:** 6,000. **Membership Dues:** individual, instructor, $30 (annual) ● JKD School Charter, $75 (annual) ● sister association, $500 (annual) ● life, $75. **Multinational. Description:** Seeks to bring together martial artists and instructors and educate the public with facts about Jeet Kune Do (JKD) and teachings from Bruce Lee's schools. Promotes and teaches original techniques of JKD. Provides training, assistance, support, advancement and certification to members. **Publications:** Videos.

23079 ■ World Martial Arts Association (WMAA)
PO Box 1568
Santa Barbara, CA 93102
Ph: (805)569-1389
Fax: (805)569-0267
URL: http://www.wmaa.com
Contact: Dr. C. Hank Drost, Pres.
Founded: 1979. **Members:** 25. **Description:** Persons interested in the martial arts. Purpose is to teach, promote, and grade the technical aspects of martial arts such as judo, karate, tae kwon do, kung fu, jujitsu, and aikido. **Awards:** Type: recognition. **Recipient:** for special martial arts skills. **Conventions/Meetings:** competition ● annual conference ● seminar.

23080 ■ World Modern Arnis Alliance (WMAA)
PO Box 5
West Seneca, NY 14224
Ph: (716)675-0899
Fax: (716)675-4960
E-mail: wmarnis@wmarnis.com
URL: http://www.wmarnis.com
Contact: Timothy J. Hartman, Pres./Technical Dir.
Membership Dues: individual, $25 (annual) ● individual, $100 (quinquennial) ● school, $75 (annual) ● school, $275 (quinquennial). **Multinational. Description:** Aims to further the growth of Arnis in the world. Seeks to establish standards throughout the Arnis community. Designs specific training programs that will advance the progression of Arnis. **Publications:** Manual. **Price:** included in membership dues.

23081 ■ Zen-do Kai Martial Arts (ZDK)
PO Box 186
Johnstown, NY 12095
Ph: (518)762-4723
Fax: (518)762-4723

E-mail: zendokai@superior.net
URL: http://www.superior.net/~zendokai
Contact: Michael J. Campos, Dir.
Founded: 1974. **Members:** 3,000. **Membership Dues:** individual, $15 (annual). **Description:** Martial art clubs. Teaches Shotokan, Shokukai, Uechi-Ryu, Pentjak-Silat, and Tae Kwon Do styles of karate. Sponsors tournaments and antirape and police training seminars. Conducts demonstrations of the martial arts. Organizes martial arts sports production. Conducts instructor training programs. Provides guest instructors and seminars; maintains hall of fame and speakers' bureau; sponsors competitions. Offers children's services and charitable program. **Libraries:** Type: reference. **Holdings:** 200; books, periodicals. **Subjects:** martial arts. **Awards:** Instructor of the Year Award. **Frequency:** annual. **Type:** recognition. **Computer Services:** Mailing lists. **Councils:** Black Belt. **Formerly:** (1986) Zen-do Kai Martial Arts Association. **Publications:** *The Warrior*, quarterly. Newsletter. Contains membership activities. **Price:** included in membership dues; $6.00 /year for nonmembers. **Circulation:** 500. **Conventions/Meetings:** annual Awards Banquet Weekend, testing, seminars, awards - always March ● annual meeting, martial arts training camp - always July, in Hamilton, NY.

Military Sports

23082 ■ United States Airsoft Corps (USAC)
PO Box 8825
Columbia, SC 29202-8825
Ph: (803)622-7932
E-mail: recruiter@usairsoftcorps.com
URL: http://www.usairsoftcorps.com
Contact: Skip Hudson, Pres.
Membership Dues: youth/basic, $20 (annual) ● full, $50 (annual). **Description:** Aims to create and establish a National Airsoft Team that follows a concept modeled on the US Military. Works to provide combat simulation participants with the war gaming experience. Fosters patriotism and seeks to instill values and sportsmanship. Develops friendships and camaraderie among members. **Telecommunication Services:** electronic mail, swhudson@usairsoftcorps.com. **Publications:** Brochure. Alternate Formats: online.

Motorcycle

23083 ■ American Motorcycle Heritage Foundation (AMHF)
13515 Yarmouth Dr.
Pickerington, OH 43147
Ph: (614)856-2222
Fax: (614)856-2221
E-mail: info@motorcyclemuseum.org
URL: http://www.motorcyclemuseum.org
Contact: Mark Mederski, Exec. Dir.
Founded: 1982. **Staff:** 6. **Budget:** $750,000. **Nonmembership. Description:** Affiliated with the American Motorcyclist Association. Maintains Motorcycle Hall of Fame Museum. Sponsors fundraising activities. Compiles statistics. **Libraries:** Type: not open to the public. **Holdings:** 3,000; artwork, audiovisuals, biographical archives, books, films, periodicals. **Subjects:** American motorcycling, history of the sport of motorcycling. **Awards:** Motorcycle Hall of Fame inductions. **Frequency:** annual. **Type:** recognition. **Recipient:** for significant contributions to all aspects of motorcycling ● Type: recognition. **Affiliated With:** American Association of Museums; American Motorcyclist Association.

23084 ■ American Motorcyclist Association (AMA)
13515 Yarmouth Dr.
Pickerington, OH 43147-8214
Ph: (614)856-1900
Free: (800)262-5646
Fax: (614)856-1920

E-mail: ama@ama-cycle.org
URL: http://www.ama-cycle.org
Contact: Dal Smilie, Chm.

Founded: 1924. **Members:** 200,000. **Membership Dues:** full, $39 (annual) ● extra mile, $49 (annual) ● associate, $15 (annual). **Staff:** 80. **Local Groups:** 1,800. **Description:** Represents motorcycle enthusiasts. Acts as a rulemaking body for motorcycle competition. Promotes highway safety. Maintains museum and hall of fame. **Libraries: Type:** reference. **Holdings:** archival material. **Awards:** AMA Hazel Kolb Brighter Image Award. **Type:** recognition. **Affiliated With:** American Motorcycle Heritage Foundation; International Motorcycling Federation. **Formerly:** American Motorcycle Association. **Publications:** *American Motorcycle Association—Action*, bimonthly. Newsletter. Includes legislative updates. **Price:** free. **Circulation:** 3,000 ● *American Motorcyclist Magazine*, monthly. Journal. Includes information on the technical aspects of motorcycles and government regulations on safety. Also contains competition calendar. **Price:** included in membership dues; $10.00 /year for nonmembers. **Circulation:** 200,000. **Advertising:** accepted. **Conventions/Meetings:** annual meeting.

23085 ■ Continental Motosport Club (CMC)
PO Box 3178
Mission Viejo, CA 92690-3178
Ph: (949)367-1141
Fax: (949)367-1608
E-mail: spcmcmx@aol.com
URL: http://www.cmcmotocross.com
Contact: Stuart H. Peters, Pres.

Founded: 1968. **Members:** 15,000. **Membership Dues:** regular/basic, $35 (annual). **Staff:** 23. **Regional Groups:** 10. **Description:** Licensed riders involved or interested in motocross (motorcycle racing). Sponsors and sanctions regional and national events; compiles statistics. **Awards:** Sunstar Sprocket. **Frequency:** semiannual. **Type:** scholarship. **Formerly:** California Motorama Corporation. **Publications:** *CMCSports*, bimonthly. Newspaper. **Price:** free for members. **Circulation:** 15,000. **Advertising:** accepted ● *Motosports Newspaper*, periodic.

23086 ■ International Brotherhood of Motorcycle Campers (IBMC)
PO Box 375
Helper, UT 84526
Ph: (435)650-3290
E-mail: camp@ibmc.org
URL: http://www.ibmc.org
Contact: Ms. Michelle Goldsmith, Dir.

Founded: 1972. **Members:** 850. **Membership Dues:** individual, $12 (annual) ● international, $14 (annual). **Staff:** 2. **Description:** Families and individuals in 4 countries who enjoy motorcycling and camping. Promotes correspondence and hospitality among members. Compiles statistics on members' motorcycle experiences and preferences. Sponsors campouts. **Formerly:** (1981) Brotherhood of Motorcycle Campers. **Publications:** *The Campfire Ring*, bimonthly. Newsletter. **Price:** included in membership dues ● *Membership List*, annual ● Handbook.

23087 ■ Motor Maids
PO Box 157
Erie, MI 48133
Ph: (419)290-3126
E-mail: cyclethatcher@bex.net
URL: http://www.motormaids.org
Contact: Ms. Brenda Thatcher, Pres.

Founded: 1940. **Members:** 950. **Membership Dues:** individual, $20 (annual). **Regional Groups:** 28. **Description:** Unites women motorcycle riders in promoting motorcycle interest. **Awards:** Dot Robinson Road Run. **Frequency:** annual. **Type:** trophy ● High Mileage Award. **Frequency:** annual. **Type:** trophy. **Formerly:** Motormaids of America. **Publications:** *Advisory Newsletter*, quarterly. **Price:** free, for members only. **Conventions/Meetings:** annual convention - always held in July.

23088 ■ Motorcycle Touring Association (MTA)
N7068 County Rd. C
Casco, WI 54205
Ph: (920)837-7325
Free: (877)833-3687
Fax: (281)752-9507
E-mail: bikenut@centurytel.net
URL: http://www.mtariders.com
Contact: Mr. Keith Yedica, Dir.

Founded: 1984. **Members:** 550. **Membership Dues:** regular, $40 (annual) ● associate, $10 (annual) ● emergency road service, $28 (annual). **Staff:** 4. **Budget:** $25,000. **Description:** Touring motorcyclists' owners group. Provides support group for motorcyclist no matter what brand they ride. There are regional, chapter and an international gatherings. **Awards: Type:** recognition. **Computer Services:** Mailing lists. **Formerly:** (1997) Venture Touring Society; (1998) Motorcycle Touring Society. **Publications:** *Motorcycle Roads*, bimonthly. Newsletter. ISSN: 0883-7821. **Circulation:** 550. **Advertising:** accepted ● *MTA Representatives Handbook*. Alternate Formats: online ● *VTS Tour Directory*, annual ● Brochure. Alternate Formats: online. **Conventions/Meetings:** annual rally and meeting (exhibits).

23089 ■ Scoot-Tours Touring Scooter Riders Association (STTSRA)
532 Farm Rd. 1100
Monett, MO 65708-8316
E-mail: scoot-tours@juno.com
URL: http://www.geocities.com/scoottours
Contact: Sally Reinhardt, Pres.

Founded: 1988. **Members:** 800. **Membership Dues:** individual/family, $30 (annual). **Staff:** 2. **Description:** Scooter enthusiasts united to exchange ideas and enjoy the sport of motor scooter riding. (Motor scooters are low 2- or 3-wheeled automotive vehicles with seats positioned so that the rider does not have to straddle the engine.) Facilitates networking among members. **Libraries: Type:** not open to the public. **Holdings:** 24; articles, books, periodicals. **Subjects:** antique and modern scooters. **Awards: Type:** recognition ● **Type:** trophy. **Publications:** *Membership List*, periodic. Membership Directory ● *Scootin'*, quarterly. Newsletter. Includes information on accessories, trailers, sidecars, and rallies; also contains maintenance tips. **Price:** included in membership dues. **Circulation:** 500. **Conventions/Meetings:** competition ● annual Scootercade - rally (exhibits) ● tour.

23090 ■ WERA Motorcycle Roadracing
2555 Marietta Hwy., Ste.104
Canton, GA 30114
Ph: (770)720-5010
Fax: (770)720-5015
E-mail: wera@wera.com
URL: http://www.wera.com
Contact: Sean P. Clarke, Moderator

Founded: 1973. **Members:** 4,000. **Membership Dues:** provisional novice, novice, expert, $100 (annual) ● associate, $30 (annual). **Staff:** 150. **Regional Groups:** 6. **For-Profit. Description:** Amateur and professional motorcycle racers who compete on the same tracks as auto racers rather than on dirt tracks. Promotes and licenses motorcycle road racing as a sport in the U.S., Canada, and Mexico. Compiles statistics. **Awards:** National Championships. **Frequency:** annual. **Type:** trophy. **Recipient:** for 1st place at finals. **Formerly:** (1996) Western Eastern Roadracer's Association, Inc.; (1996) Western Eastern Roadracers Association. **Publications:** *Fastline*, quarterly. Newsletter. Features member information. **Price:** free for members. **Circulation:** 3,500. **Advertising:** accepted. **Conventions/Meetings:** annual Grand National Finals - meeting, includes Grand National Championship (exhibits).

23091 ■ White Plate Flat Trackers Association (WPFTA)
PO Box 897
Sturgis, SD 57785

E-mail: kannenball20j@aol.com
URL: http://www.wpfta.com
Contact: Denny Kannenberg, Exec. Dir.

Founded: 1980. **Members:** 158. **Description:** Professional motorcycle racers who have been awarded an AMA expert rating for having a good safety record, and a sufficient accumulation of points in events sanctioned by the American Motorcyclist Association (see separate entry). Seeks to preserve the memories and document the racing careers of expert motorcycle racers. Has constructed a monument to the racers. **Conventions/Meetings:** annual meeting - always first Friday following the first weekend in August, Sturgis, SD.

23092 ■ Women On Wheels Motorcycle Association
PO Box 83076
Lincoln, NE 68501
Ph: (402)477-1280
Free: (800)322-1969
E-mail: general@womenonwheels.org
URL: http://www.womenonwheels.org
Contact: Teresa Hakey, Pres./Trustee

Founded: 1982. **Members:** 3,500. **Membership Dues:** full, $30 (annual) ● supporting, $15 (annual) ● child, $10 (annual). **Staff:** 1. **Local Groups:** 90. **Description:** Women motorcyclists. Aims to unite women motorcyclists and to gain recognition from the motorcycle industry concerning the needs of female consumers. Promotes camaraderie of women motorcyclists and participation in motorcycle events. Organizes rallies, interchapter social affairs, fashion activities, and fundraising for public service projects. **Formerly:** (2004) Women on Wheels. **Publications:** *Women On Wheels*, bimonthly. Magazine. Contains stories and articles written by and for membership, and reports on new products and industry events. **Price:** included in membership dues. **Circulation:** 3,000. **Advertising:** accepted ● Brochure. **Circulation:** 10,000 ● Membership Directory, annual. **Conventions/Meetings:** monthly Chapter Meeting ● annual International Ride In - rally (exhibits) - always July.

Native American

23093 ■ Native American Recreation and Sport Institute (NARSI)
c/o Judith G. Shepherd, Founder
116 W Osage
Greenfield, IN 46140
Ph: (317)462-4245
Fax: (317)462-4245
E-mail: gramshep@netusa1.net
URL: http://www.charismapros.com/p/narsi.htm
Contact: Judith G. Shepherd, Founder

Founded: 1996. **Nonmembership. Description:** Provides youth recreation and sport directors and coaches training programs in the U.S. **Publications:** *Native American Recreation*. Newsletter. **Conventions/Meetings:** Native American Youth Recreation and Sports Administration - conference, provides training, clinics, sessions ● North American Youth Recreation and Sport Institute - workshop, classes for youth coaches - variety of dates including special requests.

23094 ■ Native American Sports Council (NASC)
1235 Lake Plaza Dr., Ste.221
Colorado Springs, CO 80906
Ph: (719)632-5282
Fax: (719)632-5614
E-mail: information@nascsports.org
URL: http://www.nascsports.org
Contact: Gene Keluche, Pres.

Description: Promotes development of community-based multi-sports and wellness programs to assist Native communities; supports Native athletes to achieve Olympic status. **Programs:** Sports Wellness Leadership.

Netball

23095 ■ Caribbean American Netball Association (CANA)
PO Box 250-057
Lefferts Sta.
Brooklyn, NY 11225
Ph: (718)634-5377
Fax: (718)634-5377
E-mail: matwilkie@hotmail.com
URL: http://www.cananetball.org
Contact: Matthias Wilkie, Pres.
Founded: 1995. **Description:** Promotes the game of netball throughout the United States. Recognizes potential role as a force for change and empowerment to the young people of the community. Organizes netball league competitions in different communities. **Affiliated With:** United States of America Netball Association.

23096 ■ United States of America Netball Association (USANA)
PO Box 1105
New York, NY 10274-1105
Ph: (561)733-4364
Fax: (561)733-4675
E-mail: netballusa@aol.com
URL: http://www.usanetball.com
Contact: Rev. Edina M. Bayne, Pres.
Founded: 1992. **Local Groups:** 13. **Description:** Promotes netball across the USA through education, training and implementation of the sports in schools, colleges and recreational facilities.

Olympic Games

23097 ■ Greek Olympic Society (GOS)
555 N High St.
Columbus, OH 43215
Ph: (614)224-9020
Fax: (614)224-5032
E-mail: generalinfo@greekcathedral.com
URL: http://www.greekcathedral.com/index.
　cfm?page=GreekOlympicSociety
Contact: Ted Leakas, Pres.
Membership Dues: individual, $50 (annual). **Multinational. Description:** Greek Orthodox, Hellenic community. Provides athletic and educational activities, and social interaction. Hosts annual "Lamb Roast" and other social events. Promotes fraternal fellowship. **Conventions/Meetings:** monthly meeting, brief educational programs arranged; "Kafenio" interactions follow meetings - every 2nd Thursday at 6 PM, except during summer.

23098 ■ Guam National Olympic Committee (GNOC)
PO Box 21809
Barrigada, GU 96921
Ph: (671)647-4662
Fax: (671)646-4233
E-mail: gnoc@teleguam.net
URL: http://www.oceaniasport.com/guam/
Contact: Ricardo C. Blas, Pres.
Founded: 1976. **Description:** Supports and promotes the Olympic movement in Guam. **Publications:** Annual Report, annual.

23099 ■ United States Olympic Committee (USOC)
1 Olympic Plz.
Colorado Springs, CO 80909-5780
Ph: (719)632-5551
Fax: (719)578-4654
E-mail: media@usoc.org
URL: http://www.olympic-usa.org
Contact: Peter Ueberroth, Chm.
Founded: 1921. **Members:** 73. **Staff:** 500. **Budget:** $393,000,000. **State Groups:** 50. **Description:** Federation of sports governing bodies constituting the governing body in the representation of the U.S. in the competitions and events of the Olympic and Pan American games. Works to coordinate, organize,

select, finance, equip, transport, house, and feed team members. Operates three Olympic Training Centers. Supports the Olympic Education Center at Northern Michigan University. **Libraries: Type:** reference. **Holdings:** 5,000; archival material, books. **Subjects:** sports, Olympic games. **Awards: Type:** recognition. **Departments:** Public Information/Media Relations. **Affiliated With:** International Olympic Committee. **Formerly:** United States Olympic Association; (1921) American Olympic Association; (1945) United States of America Sports Federation. **Conventions/Meetings:** annual meeting (exhibits) - usually October/November.

23100 ■ Virgin Islands Olympic Committee
PO Box 1578
Frederiksted, VI 00841
Ph: (340)778-2229
Fax: (340)778-0270
E-mail: virginislandsolympic@attglobal.net
URL: http://www.virginislandsolympics.com
Contact: Hans Lawaetz, Pres.
Founded: 1967. **Description:** Commits to the development of athletes; supports development of sports for all programs and high performance sport in the Virgin Islands.

23101 ■ World Olympians Association (WOA)
The Biltmore
1200 Anastasia Ave., Ste.140
Miami, FL 33134
Ph: (305)446-6440
Fax: (305)446-4523
E-mail: miami@woaoffice.org
URL: http://www.woaolympians.com
Contact: Mr. William A. Toomey, VP (USA)
Founded: 1995. **Multinational. Description:** Seeks to leverage the global network of Olympians and create an entity that benefits the Olympians, the Olympic movement and the general public. Supports and represents the interests of Olympians and contributes to the enhancement of their quality of life. Educates Olympians to become good ambassadors of the Olympic Movement. Promotes the establishment of National Olympians Associations. **Awards:** Osaka Award. **Frequency:** annual. **Type:** recognition. **Recipient:** for individuals who have supported and assisted Olympians and the Olympic Movement. **Publications:** The Flame, quarterly. Magazine. **Price:** $20.00 for nonmembers; free for members. Alternate Formats: online ● What an Olympian Should Know. Manual. Alternate Formats: online ● Newsletters. Alternate Formats: online.

Orienteering

23102 ■ National Association of Competitive Mounted Orienteering (NACMO)
503 171st Ave. SE
Tenino, WA 98589-9711
Ph: (360)264-2727
Free: (800)354-7264
E-mail: arabnacmo@thurston.com
URL: http://www.nacmo.org
Contact: Mr. Walter H. Olsen, Exec. Dir.
Founded: 1981. **Members:** 2,801. **Membership Dues:** individual, $20 (annual) ● family, $30 (annual). **Budget:** $25,000. **Regional Groups:** 5. **State Groups:** 29. **Multinational. Description:** Horse enthusiasts with a special interest in wilderness-type riding. Promotes horseback riding and fellowship among members. Fosters regulation of the sport through a uniform rules system. Offers competitive and noncompetitive mounted orienteering activities. (Mounted orienteering combines horseback riding with map reading and direction-finding.) Provides assistance to members wishing to manage a ride, and informs members of ride dates and locations. Responds to discrepancies and complaints reported by members. Emphasizes competition through orientation skills as opposed to the speed of individual horses. Conducts charitable program. Compiles statistics. **Libraries: Type:** reference. **Holdings:** 2; archival material, audiovisuals, clippings. **Awards:**

High Point of the Year Award. **Frequency:** annual. **Type:** recognition. **Recipient:** for most points earned ● Horse Awards. **Frequency:** annual. **Type:** recognition. **Recipient:** for most points earned ● National Awards. **Frequency:** annual. **Type:** recognition. **Recipient:** for top points per state for riders and horses ● National Junior Rider Award (High Point). **Type:** recognition ● National Short Course Individual Award Male. **Type:** recognition ● National Short Course Team Award. **Type:** recognition ● National Single Rider Female Award. **Frequency:** annual. **Type:** recognition. **Recipient:** for most points earned ● National Single Rider Male Award. **Frequency:** annual. **Type:** recognition. **Recipient:** for most points earned ● National Team. **Frequency:** annual. **Type:** recognition. **Recipient:** for top points per state for riders and horses ● Ride Managers. **Frequency:** annual. **Type:** recognition ● Rider Awards. **Type:** recognition ● State Awards. **Frequency:** annual. **Type:** recognition. **Computer Services:** database, for point scores, rider points, horse points, ride manager points, breed awards ● mailing lists, in-house. **Divisions:** Competitive Driving Orienteering; Competitive Mounted Orienteering; Non-Competitive Mounted Orienteering. **Affiliated With:** American Horse Council. **Publications:** General Rules. **Price:** free. **Circulation:** 1,000. Alternate Formats: online ● How to Lay Out Orienteering Rides ● Introduction ● Meadeow Muffin Reports, 5/year. Newsletter. **Price:** free for members. **Circulation:** 1,000 ● NACMO How to Ride the Sport. Video ● Also offers slide sets (with scripts). **Conventions/Meetings:** annual banquet, held by each state for awards presentation (exhibits) ● competition ● annual meeting - usually 2nd week of March.

23103 ■ United States Orienteering Federation (USOF)
c/o Robin Shannonhouse, Exec. Dir.
PO Box 1444
Forest Park, GA 30298-1444
Ph: (404)363-2110
E-mail: usof@comcast.net
URL: http://www.us.orienteering.org
Contact: Robin Shannonhouse, Exec. Dir.
Founded: 1971. **Members:** 7,000. **Membership Dues:** individual, $30 (annual) ● family, $35 (annual) ● student, $15 (annual) ● junior, $5 (annual) ● life (individual), $600 ● life (family), $700. **Budget:** $100,000. **Local Groups:** 65. **Description:** Individuals interested in the sport of orienteering (finding one's way in the outdoors using map and compass). Purposes are: to promote orienteering activities throughout the U.S; to assist in establishing orienteering clubs; to establish and standardize the rules governing orienteering competitions; to hold annual national championships; to provide incentives for performance and commendable achievement in orienteering; to approve all international orienteering events held in the U.S; to select competitors to represent the U.S. in world championships and other international competitions. **Awards:** U.S. Championship Title. **Frequency:** annual. **Type:** recognition. **Recipient:** for fourteen individuals who display commendable achievement and performance in orienteering competitions. **Committees:** Club Development. **Affiliated With:** International Orienteering Federation; United States Olympic Committee. **Publications:** Coaching Orienteering. Manual. **Price:** free for qualified junior team coaches; $14.50 for individuals, plus shipping and handling ● Orienteering North America, 8/year. Magazine. Includes event schedules and results and information on competition, equipment, health, nutrition, and the recreational values of the sport. **Price:** included in membership dues; $30.00 /year for nonmembers outside U.S.; $24.00 /year for nonmembers in U.S.; $27.00 /year for members in Canada. ISSN: 0886-1080. **Circulation:** 2,300. **Advertising:** accepted. Also Cited As: ONA ● Brochure. **Conventions/Meetings:** annual meeting and workshop.

Outdoor Recreation

23104 ■ Women Outdoors (WO)
55 Talbot Ave.
Medford, MA 02155

E-mail: info@women-outdoors.org
URL: http://www.women-outdoors.org
Contact: Debbi Wright, Pres.
Founded: 1980. **Members:** 400. **Membership Dues:** regular, $25-$35 (annual) ● over 65 or under 18 years old, $15 (annual) ● joint (2 women at same address), $45-$55 (annual) ● life, $500 ● organization/corporation, $75 (annual). **Budget:** $15,000. **State Groups:** 6. **Local Groups:** 7. **Description:** An all volunteer organization of women that sponsors regional chapters across the country with the greatest concentration of members in the Northeast. Aims to provide a supportive and nurturing environment where all women can have fun and challenge themselves while respecting the earth in a community of women who love the outdoors. Local groups hold weekly events like hiking, biking, kayaking and camping. Conducts a national gathering, held annually in New Hampshire. **Libraries: Type:** reference. **Holdings:** 800. **Subjects:** women's adventure travel, nature study. **Awards: Type:** scholarship. **Recipient:** for active involvement in Women Outdoors. **Computer Services:** database, membership and regional contacts. **Committees:** Annual Gathering. **Divisions:** Central Massachusetts Region; Connecticut Region; Greater Boston Region; NY Adirondacks Region; NY Finger Lakes Region; Rhode Island Region; South Florida Region; Wyoming Region. **Publications:** *Campground Comments.* Pamphlet. Features reviews of 500 campgrounds in Canada and Northern U.S. **Price:** $2.00 ● *Women Outdoors Condensed Bibliography.* Pamphlet. Contains reviews of 300 recommended books. **Price:** included in membership dues ● *Women's Adventure and Skill Programs.* Pamphlet. Contains annotated listings for 400 outfitters who provide women's outdoor trips. **Price:** $2.00 ● Bibliography, semiannual. Provides critical reviews of 1,000 books on women's adventure travel, wilderness and country living and nature study. **Price:** $6.00 ● Magazine, biennial. **Price:** included in membership dues. **Circulation:** 300. **Advertising:** accepted. Alternate Formats: online. **Conventions/Meetings:** annual Women Outdoors Gathering - conference, skill development workshops (exhibits) - Memorial Day weekend.

Paintball

23105 ■ American Paintball Players Association (APPA)
c/o Chris Raehl, Coor.
1133 Indus. Blvd., No. 6
Chippewa Falls, WI 54729
Ph: (715)720-9131
E-mail: raehl311@yahoo.com
URL: http://www.paintball-players.org
Contact: Chris Raehl, Coor.
Description: Promotes the sport of paintball; advocates for paintball and paintball-equipment legislation. **Computer Services:** database, paintball information.

23106 ■ National Collegiate Paintball Association (NCPA)
c/o Chris Raehl, Pres.
530 E South Ave.
Chippewa Falls, WI 54729
Ph: (612)605-8323
Fax: (612)605-8323
E-mail: ncpa@college-paintball.com
URL: http://www.college-paintball.com
Contact: Chris Raehl, Pres.
Founded: 1986. **Description:** Promotes paintball at the interscholastic level. Facilitates the creation and growth of college and high school paintball activity and national coordination among college and high school clubs and teams. **Telecommunication Services:** electronic mail, raehl311@yahoo.com.

Parachuting

23107 ■ United States BASE Association (BASE)
c/o Jean Boenish
12619 Manor Dr.
Hawthorne, CA 90250-4313

Ph: (310)676-1935
Contact: Jean Boenish, Dir.
Founded: 1981. **Members:** 5,000. **Staff:** 3. **Regional Groups:** 2. **Description:** Persons interested in the concept of individuals jumping with parachutes off fixed objects, an "esoteric aspect of man's age-old dream of self-flight." To qualify for a BASE award, members must dive off a building, an antenna tower, a span, and an earth formation (hence the acronym BASE); all jumps must involve use of a parachute as a lifesaving device which is not inflated prior to the jump. Objective is to share information, technology, experiences, and opinions about BASE jumping. Dedicated to the safety, advancement, and accurate positive public image of BASE jumpers and the sport, not stunt, of BASE jumping worldwide. Does not advocate breaking the law to accomplish BASE jumps. Conducts research on equipment, technique, and sites and coordinates public presentation. Operates museum; accredits BASE jumpers; compiles statistics; maintains speakers' bureau. The USBA is a member of the BASE Federation, the international council of BASE associations. **Libraries: Type:** reference. **Holdings:** archival material. **Subjects:** fixed-object jumping. **Awards:** BASE Number. **Type:** recognition. **Recipient:** for completion of a BASE jump in each of the four fixed-object categories ● Object Number. **Type:** recognition. **Recipient:** for completion of a BASE jump from a specific fixed object. **Publications:** *AIAA '86: BASEic Sport Parachuting.* Monograph ● *The BASE Monitor,* periodic. Newsletter ● *BASEics.* Handbook ● *USBA Curriculum and Coordination Guide.* Manual. **Conventions/Meetings:** annual Plenum - meeting.

23108 ■ United States Parachute Association (USPA)
5401 Southpoint Centre Blvd.
Fredericksburg, VA 22407
Ph: (540)604-9740
Fax: (540)604-9741
E-mail: uspa@uspa.org
URL: http://www.uspa.org
Contact: Glenn Bangs, Pres.
Founded: 1946. **Members:** 34,000. **Membership Dues:** individual outside U.S., $60 (annual) ● individual (renewal) outside U.S., $58 (annual) ● individual in U.S., $51 (annual) ● individual (renewal) in U.S., $49 (annual) ● life, in U.S., $800. **Staff:** 17. **Budget:** $3,000,000. **Description:** Represents persons interested in skydiving. Promotes safety in skydiving. Sanctions sport competitions including annual National Championships, annual National Collegiate Skydiving Championships; selects and trains the U.S. Skydiving Team for world and international competition. Issues licenses and ratings. Conducts Instructor Rating Program to instruct, test, and rate sport skydiving jumpmasters, instructors, and instructor/examiners. Represents skydivers at all levels of government. **Libraries: Type:** open to the public. **Holdings:** 10,000; articles, books, periodicals. **Subjects:** skydiving. **Awards:** Achievement Awards. **Type:** recognition ● Gold Wing. **Type:** recognition. **Recipient:** for national and international skydivers ● Silver Wing. **Type:** recognition. **Computer Services:** Mailing lists ● online services. **Formerly:** (1946) National Parachute Jumpers-Riggers Association; (1957) Parachute Club of America. **Publications:** *Parachutist,* monthly. Magazine. Covers safety concerns of skydiving. **Price:** $4.50/issue. **Circulation:** 35,000. **Advertising:** accepted ● *Skydiver's Information Manual.* **Price:** $23.50 order of 5 copies; $18.50 order of 50 copies; $15.00 order of 100 copies. Alternate Formats: online. **Conventions/Meetings:** semiannual board meeting ● annual general assembly.

Petanque

23109 ■ Federation of Petanque U.S.A. (FPUSA)
c/o Frank Pipal, Sec.
PO Box 180
Kenwood, CA 95452

E-mail: fpusasecretary@comcast.net
URL: http://www.usapetanque.org
Contact: Mr. John Rolland, Pres.
Founded: 1976. **Members:** 600. **Membership Dues:** adult (members of affiliated petanque clubs), $10 (annual). **Local Groups:** 21. **Description:** Works as a federation of local petanque clubs. Petanque is an outdoor bowling game that originated in ancient Greece and Rome. The modern game evolved in the southern area of France known as Provence. Organized World Championships attract participants from more than 60 federations on all continents. Promotes amateur competition in the sport. It encourages the formation of new clubs and provides a clearinghouse of information on the game's activities throughout the U.S. It also sanctions national tournaments and participates in international competition as a member of the International Governing Body - La Federation Internationale de Petanque et Jeu Provencal - FIPJP. **Libraries: Type:** reference. **Subjects:** petanque. **Absorbed:** (1987) Federation of Petanque of U.S.A. **Formerly:** (1987) American Petanque Association U.S.A. **Publications:** *Federation of Petanque USA— Members' Newsletter,* 3/year. Covers tournaments, tips on playing, and organization activities. **Price:** available to members only. **Advertising:** accepted ● Brochures ● Manual. **Conventions/Meetings:** annual board meeting ● annual competition.

Physical Fitness

23110 ■ American Medical Athletic Association (AMAA)
4405 East-West Hwy., Ste.405
Bethesda, MD 20814
Ph: (301)913-9517
Free: (800)776-2732
Fax: (301)913-9520
E-mail: bbaldwin@americanrunning.org
URL: http://www.amaasportsmed.org
Contact: Barbara Baldwin, Contact
Founded: 1969. **Members:** 5,000. **Membership Dues:** regular, $50 (annual) ● international, $70 (annual) ● supporter, $100 (annual) ● patron, $150 (annual) ● Olympian, $250 (annual). **Staff:** 2. **Local Groups:** 20. **Description:** Physicians and medical professionals or allied fields. Encourages and fosters endurance sports among physicians in the U.S. so that they, in turn, will encourage it among their patients. Conducts medical seminars and educational programs; compiles statistics; sponsors marathons. **Awards: Type:** recognition. **Additional Websites:** http://www.americanrunning.org, http://www.arrms.org. **Telecommunication Services:** electronic mail, amaa@americanrunning.org. **Programs:** Beat the Heat Educational Campaign; Hyponatremia Educational Campaign; The Running Shoe Database; Sport Medicine Professional Referral. **Also Known As:** American Medical Joggers Association. **Publications:** *AMAA Journal,* 3/year. Newsletter. **Conventions/Meetings:** quarterly meeting.

23111 ■ American Running Association (ARA)
4405 East-West Hwy., Ste.405
Bethesda, MD 20814
Ph: (301)913-9517
Free: (800)776-ARFA
Fax: (301)913-9520
E-mail: run@americanrunning.org
URL: http://www.americanrunning.org
Contact: David Watt, Exec. Dir.
Founded: 1968. **Members:** 15,000. **Membership Dues:** individual, $35 (annual) ● international, $55 (annual) ● supporter, $100 (annual) ● patron, $150 (annual) ● Olympian, $250 (annual). **Staff:** 2. **Budget:** $500,000. **Description:** Represents individual runners, exercise enthusiasts, and sports medicine professionals. Promotes running and other aerobic activities; fosters the preventive maintenance concept in health preservation. Serves as a repository for data on running and fitness. Reports on research in exercise physiology and in techniques of increasing total human performance and maintaining physical

fitness. Maintains speakers' bureau. Conducts educational programs and charitable activities. **Libraries: Type:** reference. **Holdings:** 21. **Subjects:** preventive medicine through exercise. **Computer Services:** database ● mailing lists ● online services, member forum. **Programs:** The Clinic; Hyponatremia Educational Campaign; One-on-One, Walk and Run; Running Shoe Database. **Formerly:** (1981) National Jogging Association. **Publications:** *Running and Fit-News*, bimonthly. Newsletter. Provides information on training, nutrition, injury prevention, exercise, and sports medicine. **Price:** included in membership dues; $35.00 /year for nonmembers. **Circulation:** 25,000 ● Brochures. **Conventions/Meetings:** meeting, sports medicine continuing education meetings - 3-4/year.

23112 ■ Aquatic Exercise Association (AEA)

201 Tamiami Trail S, Ste.3
Nokomis, FL 34275
Ph: (941)486-8600
Free: (888)232-9283
Fax: (941)486-8820
E-mail: info@aeawave.com
URL: http://www.aeawave.com
Founded: 1987. **Members:** 6,000. **Membership Dues:** professional in U.S., $65 (annual) ● professional outside U.S., $75 (annual) ● business, $400 (annual) ● elite in U.S., $110 (biennial) ● elite outside U.S., $135 (biennial) **Staff:** 10. **Description:** Aquatic fitness instructors and therapists, pool and club owners, recreation departments, and manufacturers of pool products and services. Fosters members' professional development; serves as a resource center for services and products related to the aquatic fitness and therapy industries. Compiles and disseminates information through educational events and networking opportunities; offers certification to aquatic exercise instructors. Conducts educational programs. **Awards:** Global Aquatic Exercise Awards. **Frequency:** annual. **Type:** recognition. **Recipient:** for excellence in aquatic fitness. **Computer Services:** Mailing lists, available for rental. **Committees:** Awards; Legislation; Research; Speaker Application Review; Written Exam. **Also Known As:** (2005) World Aquatic Coalition, Inc. **Publications:** *AKWA Letter*, bimonthly. Newsletter. Includes information on aquatic fitness research and trends; contains calendar of events. **Price:** included in membership dues. **Circulation:** 6,000. **Advertising:** accepted ● *Aquatic Therapy & Fitness Research Journal*, semiannual. Contains therapy and fitness research related issues. **Price:** $17.00 for members. **Circulation:** 1,000 ● Books ● Videos. **Conventions/Meetings:** annual International Aquatic Fitness Conference, for fitness professionals (exhibits) ● workshop.

23113 ■ National Coalition for Promoting Physical Activity (NCPPA)

1100 H St. NW, Ste.510
Washington, DC 20005
Ph: (202)454-7522 (202)454-7521
Fax: (202)454-7598
E-mail: info@ncppa.org
URL: http://www.ncppa.org
Contact: Sheila Franklin, Dir.
Founded: 1996. **Membership Dues:** lead organization (by invitation only), $10,000 (annual) ● national strategic partner/national non-profit organization, $1,000 (annual) ● state based organization, $500 (annual) ● educational institution/school/community based organization, $100 (annual) ● corporate partner/vendor, $5,000 (annual) ● individual, $50 (annual). **Description:** Aims to unite the strengths of public, private and industry efforts into collaborative partnerships that inspire and empower all Americans to lead more physically active lifestyles. Develops new alliances and partnerships to focus and coordinate public education campaigns, policy development, and media education. Seeks to address issues pertaining to physical activity including health/science, education, environments, population specific outreach and activity behavior. **Computer Services:** database ● landmark reports, statistics and other resources ● database, physical activity information and fact sheets ● information services, public affairs

and policy. **Committees:** Media Relations; Public Affairs; State Coalitions. **Publications:** *Active Communication: A Guide to Reaching the Media*. Handbook. Discusses basic media relations techniques. Alternate Formats: online ● *The Activity Advocate*. Newsletter. Alternate Formats: online ● *NCPPA News*, biweekly. Newsletter. Alternate Formats: online ● *State Coalition Handbook: Strategies and Techniques*. Provides an introduction to the basic components of creating a coalition. Alternate Formats: online.

23114 ■ National Gym Association (NGA)

PO Box 970579
Coconut Creek, FL 33097-0579
Ph: (954)344-8410
Fax: (954)344-8412
E-mail: info@nationalgym.com
URL: http://www.nationalgym.com
Contact: Mr. Andrew Bostinto, Founder/Pres.
Description: Represents athletes, trainers and fitness professionals dedicated to helping athletes live a drug-free lifestyle. Promotes the art and science of natural strength training and bodybuilding. Educates the general public about drugs in sports. **Programs:** NGA Personal Fitness Certification Training. **Publications:** Newsletter. Alternate Formats: online.

23115 ■ National Senior Games Association (NSGA)

PO Box 82059
Baton Rouge, LA 70884-2059
Ph: (225)766-6800
Fax: (225)766-9115
E-mail: nsga@nsga.com
URL: http://www.nsga.com
Contact: Phil Godfrey, Pres./CEO
Founded: 1985. **Membership Dues:** individual, $25 (annual). **Staff:** 9. **Budget:** $1,000,000. **Regional Groups:** 5. **State Groups:** 50. **Local Groups:** 200. **Description:** Promotes fitness, healthy lifestyles, and participation in athletic competition for people over 50 years old. **Awards: Type:** recognition. **Formerly:** (1998) U.S. National Senior Sports Organization. **Publications:** *The Game Plan*, semiannual. Newsletter. **Circulation:** 100,000. **Conventions/Meetings:** biennial U.S. National Senior Sports Classic - competition, multi-sport (exhibits).

23116 ■ North American Network of Women Runners (NANWR)

PO Box 2736
Bala Cynwyd, PA 19004
Ph: (610)668-9886
Fax: (215)848-1130
E-mail: philly@crossroadswomen.net
Contact: Phoebe B. Jones, Dir.
Founded: 1979. **Members:** 500. **Staff:** 8. **State Groups:** 10. **Description:** Women runners, fitness participants, racers, health professionals, women in sports, and women concerned about opportunities for health, fitness, and sport. Dedicated to winning the financial resources that will make athletic careers, physical fitness, and good health accessible to women internationally. Holds low-cost women's workouts with child care in various sports through community, school, and business facilities. **Publications:** Newsletter, quarterly. **Conventions/Meetings:** biennial conference.

23117 ■ United States Water Fitness Association (USWFA)

PO Box 243279
Boynton Beach, FL 33424-3279
Ph: (561)732-9908 (561)732-4252
Fax: (561)732-0950
E-mail: info@uswfa.org
URL: http://www.uswfa.com
Contact: John R. Spannuth, Pres./CEO
Founded: 1989. **Members:** 3,000. **Membership Dues:** facility, $100 (annual). **Staff:** 5. **Budget:** $500,000. **Description:** Promotes aquatics, including water fitness, through activities such as water aerobics, water walking, water running, and deep water exercise. Awards certification for water fitness instructors, program coordinators, and aquatic directors.

Helps to identify and establish trends in water fitness and aquatics. Sponsors National Water Fitness Week, National Water Walking Week, and National and World Water Fitness competitions. Encourages research. Promotes aquatics throughout the country by educating aquatic professionals on the organization and administration of aquatic programming. Maintains speakers' bureau; compiles statistics. **Libraries: Type:** reference. **Holdings:** 300; archival material. **Subjects:** aquatics. **Awards:** Who's Who in Aquatic Leadership in the USA. **Frequency:** annual. **Type:** recognition. **Publications:** *National Aquatics Newsletter*, quarterly. Includes water exercises, aquatics, educational articles, human interest stories, lifestyle management and certification information. **Price:** included in membership dues. **Circulation:** 5,000. **Advertising:** accepted. **Conventions/Meetings:** annual International Aquatics Conference (exhibits).

Polo

23118 ■ Collegiate Equestrian Polo Association (CEPA)

c/o Andres Huertas, Treas./Exec. Dir.
20317 Coulson St.
Woodland Hills, CA 91367
Ph: (818)346-7648
E-mail: andres@cepa-polo.org
URL: http://www.cepapolo.org
Contact: Andres Huertas, Treas./Exec. Dir.
Description: Promotes the spirit of safety, competition, sportsmanship, and friendship among polo players. Provides polo ponies, tack, equipment, money, and instructional materials and coaching. Maintains Clearing House Database of polo resources.

23119 ■ United States Bicycle Polo Association (USBPA)

PO Box 19424
Sacramento, CA 95819-0424
Ph: (916)487-1670
Fax: (916)487-1683
E-mail: usbikepolo@aol.com
URL: http://www.bikepolo.com
Contact: Ron Kraut, Exec. Dir.
Founded: 1942. **Members:** 20. **Staff:** 1. **Budget:** $1,000,000. **Regional Groups:** 4. **Local Groups:** 6. **For-Profit. Description:** Individuals 21 years and older interested in bicycle polo. (Bicycle polo, first played 80 years ago in Ireland, differs from traditional horse polo by: the use of half-size mallets, a field only a third as large as a horse polo field, the limitation to three successive hits compared with unlimited number in regulation polo, and the rule that "riding off" is not allowed since a bicycle is being used.) Provides assistance in organizing competitive events and sponsors national and international annual. Conducts educational programs; compiles statistics and conducts charitable program. Encourages the playing of the sport in preparatory schools and universities. **Awards:** MVP. **Frequency:** annual. **Type:** recognition. **Publications:** *Bicycle Polo Techniques*. **Price:** free ● *Fundamental and Official Rule Book* ● Also distributes *World of Sports*. **Conventions/Meetings:** annual meeting - always New York City.

23120 ■ United States Polo Association (USPA)

4037 Ironworks Pkwy., Ste.110
Lexington, KY 40511
Ph: (859)219-1000
Free: (800)232-USPA
Fax: (859)219-0520
E-mail: uspa@uspolo.org
URL: http://www.uspolo.org
Contact: Peter Rizzo, Exec. Dir.
Founded: 1890. **Members:** 3,500. **Membership Dues:** student/learner, $35 (annual) ● associate, $100 (annual) ● player, $200 (annual) ● club, $300 (annual). **Staff:** 8. **Budget:** $1,000,000. **Description:** Federation of polo clubs in the USA. Conducts polo schools. **Libraries: Type:** reference. **Holdings:** films.

Computer Services: Mailing lists, of members. **Committees:** Club Polo; Constitution; Executive; Finance; Handicap; High Goal; Intercollegiate/Interscholastic; International; Junior Polo; Legal Affairs; Long-Range Planning; Nomination; Promotion; Rules; Safety and Tournament; Social; Television; Tournament; Umpire; Veterinary. **Publications:** *Arena Rules.* Video ● *Outdoor Rules.* Video ● *Polo Magazine,* 10/year ● *Sidelines.* Magazine ● Yearbook ● Also publishes rule book. **Conventions/Meetings:** semiannual meeting.

Powerlifting

23121 ■ North American Powerlifting Federation (NAPF)
c/o Robert Keller, Gen. Sec.-Treas.
PO Box 291571
Davie, FL 33329-1571
Ph: (954)384-4472
Fax: (954)301-3344
E-mail: rhk@verizon.net
URL: http://www.usapowerlifting.com/IPF-NorthAmerica
Contact: Dr. Lawrence Maile, Pres.
Founded: 2000. **Description:** Promotes the sport of powerlifting in North America. Develops standardized competitive rules according to the IPF rules. Promotes, sanctions and supervises North American developmental programs and competitions. Helps organize regional powerlifting in North America and the Caribbean nations. **Telecommunication Services:** electronic mail, lawrence_maile@health.state. ak.us ● electronic mail, lmaile@alaska.com. **Conventions/Meetings:** annual North American Regional Powerlifting Championships - competition - 2008 June, Port of Spain, Trinidad and Tobago; 2009 June, Mexico City, DF, Mexico.

23122 ■ U.S. Powerlifting Federation (USPF)
c/o David Jeffrey, Pres.
PO Box 231
Parkersburg, WV 26102
Ph: (304)489-2428
E-mail: uspf@netassoc.net
URL: http://www.uspf.com
Contact: David Jeffrey, Pres.
Founded: 1981. **Members:** 5,000. **Staff:** 2. **Budget:** $100,000. **Regional Groups:** 8. **State Groups:** 50. **Local Groups:** 250. **Description:** Amateur powerlifters, referees, and officials. (Powerlifting is a sport which consists of three lifts performed with a powerlifting barbell: squat, bench press, and deadlift. Three attempts are made of each lift, and the highest scores in each category are added up for best total.) Regulates and promotes the sport through sanctioned meets and a system of training state and international referees. Sponsors clinics, seminars, and a sports medicine program. Approves officials for international meetings and championships involving powerlifting; coordinates the competition of foreign athletes in powerlifting in the U.S. and sanctions Special Olympics powerlifting meets. Maintains hall of fame; compiles statistics. **Awards: Type:** recognition. **Recipient:** for amateur powerlifters. **Committees:** All-American Awards; Classification Awards; Coaching Techniques; Collegiate; Discipline; Hall of Fame; Law and Legislation; Masters; Men's and Women's Records; Men's and Women's Selections; National Referees; Publicity; Registration; Sports Medicine; Television and Special Events; Women's; Youth Development. **Formerly:** Powerlifting Committee of the Amateur Athletic Union; (1983) U.S. Powerlifting Federation of the AAU. **Conventions/Meetings:** annual meeting (exhibits).

23123 ■ USA Powerlifting (USAPL)
c/o Dr. Larry J. Maile, PhD, Pres.
PO Box 668
Columbia City, IN 46725
Ph: (260)248-4889
Fax: (260)248-4879

E-mail: usapl@fwi.com
URL: http://www.usapowerlifting.com
Contact: Dr. Larry J. Maile PhD, Pres.
Membership Dues: adult, $40 (annual) ● high school division, $30 (annual) ● special Olympian, $10 (annual) ● high school seasonal, high school upgrade, $15 (semiannual). **Description:** Promotes drug-free powerlifting in the United States and around the world. Conducts powerlifting competitions and other related activities to establish the sport and encourage young people and adults to be involved in the sport. **Telecommunication Services:** electronic mail, l-maile@usapowerlifting.com. **Publications:** *Powerlines,* bimonthly. Newsletter. Contains news, information and other related issues for USALP members.

Psychology

23124 ■ Athletic Success Institute (ASI)
c/o William J. Winslow, Dir.
1933 Winward Point
Discovery Bay, CA 94514
Ph: (925)516-8686
E-mail: winslow@athleticsuccess.org
URL: http://www.athleticsuccess.org
Contact: William J. Winslow, Dir.
Founded: 1962. **Languages:** English, French, Spanish. **Description:** Originated by sports psychologists to: enhance the performance of athletes in competitive and recreational sports; enable coaches to better understand and coach athletes; provide athletes with self-knowledge for self-improvement and development. Prepares reports on athletic attitudes of athletes based on results of Athletic Motivation Inventory and Athletic Success Profile, written questionnaires prepared specifically for sports to measure 11 traits related to success: aggressiveness, drive, determination, responsibility, leadership, self-confidence, emotional control, mental toughness, coachability, conscientiousness, and trust. Markets programs to high schools, colleges, amateur athletes, professional teams, and recreational athletes. Maintains software licensing program for sports organizations and consultants. Operates speakers' bureau. **Convention/Meeting:** none. **Computer Services:** database, processing athletic success reports. **Additional Websites:** http://www.athleticsuccessinstitute.com. **Formerly:** (1971) Institute for the Study of Athletic Motivation; (1998) Institute for the Study of Athletic Motivation and Institute of Athletic Motivation; (2003) Institute of Athletic Motivation.

23125 ■ North American Society for the Psychology of Sport and Physical Activity (NASPSPA)
c/o Ann L. Smiley-Oyen, Sec.-Treas.
Iowa State Univ.
Dept. of Kinesiology
244 Forker
Ames, IA 50011
Ph: (515)294-8261
E-mail: asmiley@iastate.edu
URL: http://www.naspspa.org
Contact: Ann L. Smiley-Oyen, Sec.-Treas.
Founded: 1966. **Members:** 500. **Membership Dues:** professional, $60 (annual) ● student, $27 (annual). **Description:** Kinesiologists, psychologists and physical educators. Promotes scientific research and relations within the behavioral sciences with an application to sport psychology, motor learning, control, and development through meetings, investigations, and other activities. **Awards:** Distinguished Scholar Award. **Frequency:** annual. **Type:** recognition ● Early Career Distinguished Scholar Award. **Frequency:** annual. **Type:** recognition ● President's Award. **Frequency:** annual. **Type:** recognition. **Conventions/Meetings:** annual conference, presentation of research by members and invited scholars from related disciplines.

Racing

23126 ■ American Bicycle Racing (ABR)
PO Box 487
Tinley Park, IL 60477-0487

Ph: (708)532-7204
Fax: (773)545-0055
E-mail: ambikerace@aol.com
URL: http://www.ambikerace.com
Contact: Bob Lundberg, Dir.
Membership Dues: general, $25 (annual) ● junior, $10 (annual). **Description:** Promotes and supports bicycle racing throughout the United States. Offers race insurance, membership licenses, educational services and quality racing. **Telecommunication Services:** electronic mail, abrlund@aol.com.

23127 ■ American Mule Racing Association (AMRA)
PO Box 660651
Sacramento, CA 95866-0651
Ph: (916)263-1529
E-mail: ksnider@calexpo.com
URL: http://www.muleracing.org
Contact: Don Jacklin, Pres.
Membership Dues: voting, $25 (annual) ● associate, non-voting, $10 (annual). **Description:** Promotes the racing of mules at recognized distances in the sport of mule racing. **Awards:** Claiming Mule. **Type:** recognition ● Emerging Jockey. **Type:** recognition ● Endurance Champion Rider. **Type:** recognition ● Ironman Jockey. **Type:** recognition ● Leading Claim Owner. **Type:** recognition ● Leading Jockey. **Type:** recognition ● Leading Trainer. **Type:** recognition ● Special Recognition, Mule. **Type:** recognition ● Special Recognition, Person. **Type:** recognition ● Speed Index 74-85. **Type:** recognition ● Speed Index 61 and under. **Type:** recognition ● Speed Index 62-74. **Type:** recognition ● World Champion Sprint Mule. **Type:** recognition ● World Champion 3 Year Old. **Type:** recognition. **Sections:** Cal Bred Organization. **Publications:** Newsletter. **Price:** $10.00 for nonmembers; included in membership dues. **Conventions/Meetings:** annual convention, with awards ● annual meeting.

23128 ■ American Swan Boat Association (ASBA)
312 Duff Ave.
Wenonah, NJ 08090
Ph: (856)468-4646
Fax: (856)468-4646
E-mail: chairman@swanboat.org
URL: http://www.swanboat.org
Contact: Glen F. Green, Chm.
Founded: 1989. **Description:** Promotes national and international amateur sports competitions in Swan Boat racing. Creates and fosters friendship, understanding, camaraderie, cooperation and teamwork among the different people who practice and participate in Swan Boat racing. Supports and develops amateur athletes for Swan Boat competitions.

23129 ■ National Championship Racing Association (NCRA)
c/o C. Ray Hall, Pres.
7700 N Broadway
Wichita, KS 67219
Ph: (316)755-1781
Fax: (316)744-1881
E-mail: jrittenoure@cox.net
URL: http://www.ncraracing.org
Contact: John Rittenoure, Contact
Description: Promotes championship automobile racing.

23130 ■ Southern Automobile Racing Association (SARA)
Address Unknown since 2006
Description: Promotes auto racing in the South.

23131 ■ United Speedways of North America (USNA)
4914 W Genesee
Camillus, NY 13031
Ph: (315)487-6086
Description: Sanctioning body providing dirt track owners, racers and fans in the Northeast region an option in dirt track motor sports entertainment. **Publications:** *Official USNA 2000 Rule Book.*

23132 ■ United States Adventure Racing Association (USARA)
12403 Bluestone Cir.
Austin, TX 78758
Ph: (512)873-1205
Fax: (512)873-1205
E-mail: info@usara.com
URL: http://www.usara.com
Contact: Troy Farrar, Contact
Membership Dues: regular, $35 (annual). **Description:** Guides and assists race directors and committees in conducting fun, safe, and fair events. Seeks to ensure the health, welfare, and safety of participants, spectators, officials, and volunteers. Aids in the continued positive growth of the sport of adventure racing. **Publications:** *Trail Runner.* Magazine. **Price:** included in membership dues; $29.95 for nonmembers.

23133 ■ U.S. Lawn Mower Racing Association (USLMRA)
1812 Glenview Rd.
Glenview, IL 60025
Ph: (847)729-7363
Fax: (847)729-4208
E-mail: mowinfo@letsmow.com
URL: http://www.letsmow.com
Contact: Bruce Kaufman, Pres.
Founded: 1992. **Members:** 500. **Membership Dues:** regular, $35 (annual). **Staff:** 4. **Local Groups:** 20. **Description:** Promotes lawn mower racing as a competitive sport. **Publications:** *Cutting Edge,* annual. Magazine. **Price:** free. **Circulation:** 3,000. **Advertising:** accepted. **Conventions/Meetings:** competition.

23134 ■ Young Racers of America (YRA)
1609 Pleasant Run
Keller, TX 76248
Ph: (817)431-8390
Fax: (817)887-0780
E-mail: info@youngracersofamerica.org
URL: http://www.youngracersofamerica.org
Contact: Ms. Gayla Lutyk, Founder/Pres.
Description: Helps children who have a passion to participate in racing and require financial assistance to compete. Provides safety equipment, transportation, accommodation, safety classes and instructions, and entry fees and registration. Conducts program and education on drug and alcohol awareness. **Telecommunication Services:** electronic mail, gayla.lutyk@youngracersofamerica.org.

Racquetball

23135 ■ Guam Racquetball Federation (GRF)
PO Box 315619
Tamuning, GU 96931-3519
Ph: (671)472-1819
E-mail: sgmflores@hotmail.com
URL: http://guam_racquetballfed1.tripod.com
Contact: Nick Captain, Pres.
Founded: 2000. **Membership Dues:** regular, $30 (annual) ● junior, $5 (annual). **Description:** Aims to teach racquetball to youth; works to maintain excellence in sportsmanship in the training of racquetball. **Telecommunication Services:** electronic mail, isc@netpci.com. **Publications:** Newsletter, periodic.

23136 ■ International Bi-Rak-It Association (USBRA)
Address Unknown since 2007
Founded: 1985. **Members:** 500. **Membership Dues:** lifetime, $500. **Staff:** 12. **Regional Groups:** 4. **State Groups:** 9. **National Groups:** 2. **For-Profit. Multinational. Description:** Promotes the sport of Bi-Rak-It. (Bi-Rak-It is similar to racquetball except that the players use two racquets, one held in each hand.). **Libraries: Type:** open to the public. **Holdings:** articles. **Subjects:** muscle imbalance, fitness management, one-sided Americans in athletics. **Awards:** McCormick Waterford Crystal Award. **Frequency:** annual. **Type:** recognition. **Recipient:** for outstanding BiRakI achievement. **Computer Services:** Mailing

lists. **Boards:** Board of Directors. **Formerly:** United States Bi-Rak-It Association. **Publications:** *Fitness Management,* annual. Brochure. Describes the sport of Bi-Rak-It. **Price:** free. **Advertising:** accepted ● *Tribune Media Services* ● *USHA, AARA, and HSRA articles.* **Conventions/Meetings:** annual convention (exhibits).

23137 ■ International Racquetball Federation (IRF)
1631 Mesa Ave.
Colorado Springs, CO 80906
Ph: (719)477-6934
Fax: (719)634-5198
E-mail: lstonge@internationalracquetball.com
URL: http://www.internationalracquetball.com
Contact: Luke St. Onge, Sec. Gen.
Founded: 1979. **Members:** 91. **Membership Dues:** country, $100 (annual). **Staff:** 9. **Budget:** $1,600,000. **Regional Groups:** 5. **State Groups:** 48. **Local Groups:** 130. **Description:** International sports federation representing over 14 million members. Fosters the promotion, development, and improvement of racquetball throughout the world. Seeks to increase interest and participation in the sport. Helps coordinate the efforts and activities of organizations promoting racquetball; raises funds for the improvement of racquetball. Conducts research projects; serves as a clearinghouse for coaching aids, rules, literature, films, and research materials. Works to establish an effective communications network for the latest developments and techniques in the sport. Trains and certifies officials. Maintains hall of fame and museum. Compiles statistics. **Libraries: Type:** reference. **Holdings:** archival material. **Awards: Type:** recognition. **Affiliated With:** International Olympic Committee. **Publications:** *Racquetball,* bimonthly. Magazine. **Price:** $24.00. **ISSN:** 1060-877X. **Circulation:** 45,000. **Advertising:** accepted. Alternate Formats: online. **Conventions/Meetings:** competition ● biennial World Congress - meeting - always August at the site of the World Racquetball Championships.

23138 ■ United States Racquetball Association (USRA)
1685 W Uintah St.
Colorado Springs, CO 80904-2969
Ph: (719)635-5396
Fax: (719)635-0685
E-mail: jhiser@usra.org
URL: http://www.usra.org
Contact: James Hiser, Exec. Dir.
Founded: 1969. **Members:** 15,000. **Membership Dues:** adult, $35 (annual) ● junior, $20 (annual) ● adult, $100 (triennial) ● life, $1,000. **Staff:** 7. **Budget:** $1,833,061. **State Groups:** 50. **Description:** Represents racquetball players and enthusiasts. Promotes racquetball as a sport; organizes racquetball to be a self-governing sport of, by, and for the players; encourages building of facilities for the sport; conducts racquetball events including annual national and international tournaments. Maintains hall of fame, junior player programs, and charitable programs. **Libraries: Type:** reference. **Awards:** Athletes. **Frequency:** annual. **Type:** recognition ● Hall of Fame. **Frequency:** annual. **Type:** recognition ● Joe Sobek Award. **Frequency:** annual. **Type:** recognition ● John Halverson Fair Play Award. **Frequency:** annual. **Type:** recognition ● Junior Athlete of the Year. **Frequency:** annual. **Type:** recognition ● USRA Presidential Award. **Frequency:** annual. **Type:** recognition ● USRA Scholarship Program. **Frequency:** annual. **Type:** scholarship. **Recipient:** for current member. **Computer Services:** database ● electronic publishing, latest articles regarding events, changes, list of current racquetball events ● online services, membership forms, tournament entry forms, sales, apparel, videos, posters, rulebooks and magazines. **Affiliated With:** Sports Charities USA; United States Olympic Committee. **Also Known As:** (2006) USA Racquetball. **Formerly:** (1968) International Paddle Rackets Association; (1969) International Paddle Association; (1980) International Racquetball Association; (1997) American Amateur Racquetball Association; (2001) United States Amateur Racquetball Association. **Pub-**

lications: *Official USRA Rules.* Alternate Formats: online ● *Racquetball Magazine,* bimonthly. **Price:** included in membership dues; $20.00 /year for nonmembers in U.S.; $35.00 /year for nonmembers outside U.S. **Conventions/Meetings:** annual High Performance Camp - workshop, players are trained by professional racquetball coaches and players on ways to improve skills; very vigorous training ● annual National Singles, National Doubles, National Intercollegiates, National High Schools, National Junior Olympics, and U.S. Open Championships - competition.

Recreation

23139 ■ International Association of Skateboard Companies (IASC)
22431 Antonio Pkwy., Ste.B160-412
Rancho Santa Margarita, CA 92688
Ph: (949)455-1112
Fax: (949)455-1712
URL: http://www.skateboardiasc.org
Contact: John Bernards, Exec. Dir.
Founded: 1995. **Members:** 40. **Membership Dues:** premium (based on company's annual revenue), $500-$7,500 (annual) ● lifestyle, $250 (annual) ● corporate associate, $1,500 (annual) ● donor (bank/financial institution, insurance company), $2,000 (annual). **Staff:** 2. **Budget:** $50,000. **Description:** Promotes the business and sport of skateboarding by providing information and educational materials. Sanctions events, exhibitions, and competitions and helps to provide the sport's best athletes for performances and appearances for television and motion pictures. Compiles statistics. Maintains speakers' bureau. Sponsors educational and research programs. **Libraries: Type:** reference. **Holdings:** archival material, books, periodicals. **Subjects:** skateboarding, contemporary and historical skateboarding manufacturing information. **Computer Services:** Mailing lists ● online services. **Committees:** National Governing Body; Professional Skateboarders; Skateparks. **Publications:** *Grapevine,* monthly. Newsletter. **Circulation:** 40. **Advertising:** accepted. **Conventions/Meetings:** board meeting ● regional meeting ● trade show.

Recreational Vehicles

23140 ■ BlueRibbon Coalition (BRC)
4555 Burley Dr., Ste.A
Pocatello, ID 83202-1945
Ph: (208)237-1008 (208)237-0311
Free: (800)BLUE-RIB
Fax: (208)237-9424
E-mail: broffice@sharetrails.org
URL: http://www.sharetrails.org
Contact: Mr. Greg Mumm, Exec. Dir.
Founded: 1987. **Members:** 10,500. **Membership Dues:** individual, $20 (annual) ● organization, club, business, $100 (annual) ● life, $250. **Staff:** 9. **Budget:** $1,000,000. **Description:** Individuals, organizations and businesses involved in off highway recreation such as snowmobiling, motorcycle trail riding, mountain biking, ATVing, hiking, horseback riding, 4x4ing, rock hounding and boating. Seeks to preserve access for off highway recreation; promotes conservation of natural resources; encourages cooperation among members and government land managers. **Formerly:** (2002) Blue Ribbon Coalition. **Publications:** *BlueRibbon Magazine,* monthly. Covers off highway recreation and political issues. **Price:** $20.00/year. **Circulation:** 19,000. **Advertising:** accepted. **Conventions/Meetings:** semiannual board meeting, board meeting in spring, general membership meeting in fall - spring and fall.

River Sports

23141 ■ America Outdoors (AO)
PO Box 10847
Knoxville, TN 37939

Ph: (865)558-3595
Free: (800)524-4814
Fax: (865)558-3598
E-mail: infoacct@americaoutdoors.org
URL: http://www.americaoutdoors.org
Contact: David Brown, Exec. Dir.
Founded: 1975. **Members:** 650. **Staff:** 3. **Budget:** $500,000. **Description:** Represents professional recreation service outfitters. Seeks to preserve and protect America's lands and waters, to enhance public enjoyment of and safe travel on these resources, and to increase the level of professionalism of persons guiding and making trips along the rivers or trails. Offers professional training; provides directory of outfitters who can assist in the planning and participation of outfitted adventure travel. Sponsors National River Cleanup Week, a national volunteer service project. **Libraries: Type:** reference. **Additional Websites:** http://www.adventurevacation.com. **Absorbed:** Western River Guides Association. **Formerly:** (1991) Eastern Professional River Outfitters Association. **Publications:** *Outfitters Directory and Vacation Guide*, annual. **Circulation:** 20,000 ● *Outfitters Resource Guidebook*, annual. **Price:** free, for members only ● Newsletter, quarterly ● Bulletin, 2-3/month. Provides updates on industry-related issues. Alternate Formats: online. **Conventions/Meetings:** annual Confluence - conference (exhibits).

23142 ■ American Whitewater (AWA)
PO Box 1540
Cullowhee, NC 28723
Ph: (828)293-9791
Free: (866)262-8429
Fax: (828)227-7422
E-mail: info@amwhitewater.org
URL: http://www.americanwhitewater.org
Contact: Mark Singleton, Exec. Dir.
Founded: 1954. **Members:** 8,600. **Membership Dues:** basic, $35 (annual) ● family, $45 ● junior/senior, $25 ● ender club/PCP, $100 ● club, $75 ● life, $750 ● platinum paddler, $250. **Staff:** 7. **Budget:** $1,000,000. **Description:** Members and affiliates interested in whitewater recreation and conservation. Promotes whitewater safety, technique, equipment, and river access programs. Conducts the annual Ocoee River Rodeo, held in June in Tennessee, and the Gauley River Festival, held in September in West Virginia. Conducts research; compiles statistics. Offers computerized services. **Libraries: Type:** reference. **Subjects:** rivers, kayaking, canoeing. **Awards: Type:** recognition. **Computer Services:** Mailing lists. **Telecommunication Services:** electronic mail, nick@amwhitewater.org. **Committees:** Safety. **Affiliated With:** American Rivers. **Formerly:** (2002) American Whitewater Affiliation. **Publications:** *AW Beta*, monthly. Newsletter. Features whitewater news. Alternate Formats: online ● *International Safety Code* ● *Nationwide Whitewater Inventory*. **Price:** $15.00 ● *The Rivers of Chile*. **Price:** $5.00 ● Magazine, bimonthly. Includes new equipment information. **Price:** $25.00 /year for members; $29.00 /year for nonmembers. ISSN: 0300-7626. **Circulation:** 10,000. **Advertising:** accepted ● Articles. Alternate Formats: online.

23143 ■ National Organization for Rivers (NORS)
212 W Cheyenne Mountain Blvd.
Colorado Springs, CO 80906-3712
Ph: (719)579-8759
Fax: (719)576-6238
E-mail: nationalrivers@email.msn.com
URL: http://www.nationalrivers.org
Contact: Eric Leaper, Exec. Dir.
Founded: 1978. **Members:** 6,000. **Membership Dues:** regular, $20 (annual) ● life, $130. **Staff:** 3. **Budget:** $100,000. **Description:** Individuals interested in river sports including kayaking, rafting, canoeing and fishing. Provides information on the conservation of Wilderness Rivers, and the public's legal rights to visit rivers and navigate rivers. Works for safety on private and Commercial River trips. Represents the recreational and conservational concerns of members before government agencies; has challenged the various river access restrictions.

Keeps members abreast of developments regarding popular rivers, techniques in river racing, equipment, and off-season river trips outside the U.S. Maintains speakers' bureau. **Libraries: Type:** not open to the public. **Additional Websites:** http://www.nors.org. **Formerly:** (1995) National Organization For River Sports. **Publications:** *Currents*, quarterly. Magazine. Includes river news, technique articles, book reviews, calendar of events, and safety reports. **Price:** included in membership dues. **Circulation:** 7,000. **Advertising:** accepted ● Booklets ● Videos ● Also publishes how to books about river trips. **Conventions/Meetings:** periodic board meeting.

Rodeo

23144 ■ American Junior Rodeo Association (AJRA)
4501 Armstrong St.
San Angelo, TX 76903
Ph: (325)658-8868
Fax: (325)658-8868
E-mail: ajra1@verizon.net
URL: http://mysite.verizon.net/resp1qhq
Contact: Seth Mahaffey, Pres.
Founded: 1952. **Members:** 450. **Membership Dues:** family, $30-$75 (annual) ● associate, $5 (annual). **Description:** Works to promote young rodeo riders. Holds competitions.

23145 ■ International Gay Rodeo Association (IGRA)
PO Box 460504
Aurora, CO 80046-0504
Ph: (303)595-4472
E-mail: admin.assistant@igra.com
URL: http://www.igra.com
Contact: Tommy Channel, Admin. Asst.
Founded: 1985. **Members:** 22. **Staff:** 1. **Languages:** English, French. **Description:** Gay rodeo associations in the United States and Canada. Promotes public interest in rodeo events and seeks to increase participation in rodeo by gay people. Facilitates communication and cooperation among members; sponsors competitions. **Publications:** *Safety Video*. Covers basic safety practices for rodeo contestants. Alternate Formats: online ● *2005 Rodeo Resource Guidebook*. **Price:** $5.00 each. Alternate Formats: online; CD-ROM.

23146 ■ International Professional Rodeo Association (IPRA)
PO Box 83377
Oklahoma City, OK 73148
Ph: (405)235-6540
Fax: (405)235-6577
E-mail: info@iprarodeo.com
URL: http://iprarodeo.com
Contact: Dale Yerigan, Gen. Mgr.
Founded: 1957. **Members:** 4,000. **Membership Dues:** individual, $50 ● family, $75 ● new, $255. **Staff:** 10. **Budget:** $950,000. **Description:** Promotes rodeo as a sport and profession. Writes rules and policies governing professional rodeo. Conducts surveys on the economic impact of rodeos on the local businesses where they take place. Prepares and conducts professional rodeo judges schools. **Awards:** International Professional Rodeo Association World Champion Award. **Frequency:** annual. **Type:** recognition. **Formerly:** (1963) Interstate Rodeo Association; (1983) International Rodeo Association. **Publications:** *Pro Rodeo World*, monthly. Magazine. **Price:** $25.00/year. **Circulation:** 10,000. **Advertising:** accepted. **Conventions/Meetings:** annual International Finals Rodeo - convention (exhibits) - January.

23147 ■ National Finals Rodeo Committee (NFRC)
101 Pro Rodeo Dr.
Colorado Springs, CO 80919
. Ph: (719)593-8840 (719)528-4747

Fax: (719)548-4876
URL: http://www.prorodeo.com
Contact: Troy Ellerman, Commissioner
Founded: 1958. **Members:** 14. **Description:** Governing board for the National Finals Rodeo, comprising eight representatives of the Professional Rodeo Cowboys Association (see separate entry), a stock contractor representative and contract personnel director, commissioner, rodeo committee representative, two contestant directors, and five representatives of the host city. Produces the "world series" of rodeo to determine the champions in bareback and saddle bronc riding, bull-riding, tie down roping, steer wrestling, and team roping in Las Vegas, NV. **Affiliated With:** Professional Rodeo Cowboys Association. **Formerly:** (1978) National Finals Rodeo Commission. **Conventions/Meetings:** annual meeting.

23148 ■ National High School Rodeo Association (NHSRA)
12001 Tejon St., Ste.128
Denver, CO 80234
Ph: (303)452-0820
Free: (800)46-NHSRA
Fax: (303)452-0912
E-mail: info@nhsra.org
URL: http://www.nhsra.org
Contact: Barb Roskopf, Dir.
Founded: 1949. **Members:** 10,000. **Membership Dues:** contestant, $35 (annual) ● alumnus, $25 (annual) ● associate, $50 (annual). **Staff:** 6. **Budget:** $1,900,000. **State Groups:** 39. **Description:** Federation of 39 state and 4 Canadian provincial and Australian organizations. Sponsors and promotes high school rodeo; organization hosts the NHSRA Finals featuring 1500 state and provincial champions competing in a week-long, 13-performance rodeo. Promotes rodeo as a recognized high school sport; works to develop sportsmanship, horsemanship, citizenship, and character in young people. **Awards: Type:** recognition ● **Type:** scholarship. **Recipient:** for champions and nonwinners. **Committees:** Budget and Finance; Contestant Entertainment; Humane Relations; Insurance; Livestock Inspection; National Sites; Planning and Steering; Public Relations; Queen; Rodeo Personnel; Rodeo Safety; Rules; Youth Advisory. **Publications:** *NHSFR Souvenir Program*. **Advertising:** accepted ● *NHSRA TIMES*, monthly. Newspaper. Contains features on members, columns, results, rules, and educational articles. **Price:** $20.00/year in U.S.; $25.00/year in Canada. ISSN: 0744-3390. **Circulation:** 15,000. **Advertising:** accepted ● *This is High School Rodeo*, annual. Brochure ● *This is High School Rodeo*. Video. **Conventions/Meetings:** annual Delegates Meeting (exhibits) - always summer ● annual Mid-Winter Meeting - conference (exhibits) - always mid-winter.

23149 ■ National Intercollegiate Rodeo Association (NIRA)
2316 Eastgate N, Ste.160
Walla Walla, WA 99362
Ph: (509)529-4402 (337)753-2343
E-mail: info@collegerodeo.com
URL: http://www.collegerodeo.com
Contact: John J. Smith, Commissioner
Founded: 1949. **Members:** 3,000. **Membership Dues:** individual, $245 (annual) ● school, $200 (annual). **Staff:** 5. **Regional Groups:** 11. **Description:** College and university rodeo clubs and individuals participating in college rodeo. Organizes the sport of college rodeo on a national basis; member clubs produce regional rodeos. **Publications:** *Collegiate Arena*, 10/year. Newspaper. **Price:** $22.50/year. **Circulation:** 4,000. **Advertising:** accepted ● *National Intercollegiate Rodeo Association Rulebook*. Alternate Formats: online. **Conventions/Meetings:** annual College National Finals - competition ● semiannual competition.

23150 ■ National Little Britches Rodeo Association (NLBRA)
5050 Edison Ave., Ste.105
Colorado Springs, CO 80915
Ph: (719)389-0333
Free: (800)763-3694

Fax: (719)578-1367
E-mail: info@nlbra.com
URL: http://www.nlbra.com
Contact: Lowell Pfleger, Pres.
Founded: 1952. **Membership Dues:** contestant, $75 ● associate, $75-$200. **Description:** Junior rodeo association for youth aged 8-19 years old. **Libraries: Type:** reference. **Holdings:** clippings. **Subjects:** rodeo. **Awards:** NLBRA Scholarship. **Frequency:** annual. **Type:** scholarship. **Recipient:** for contestant. **Formerly:** (1961) Little Britches Rodeo. **Publications:** *Calendar* ● *NLBRA Rodeo News*. Newsletter. Alternate Formats: online ● Also publishes rule book. **Conventions/Meetings:** annual convention (exhibits) - January.

23151 ■ Professional Armed Forces Rodeo Association (PAFRA)
c/o Bruce A. McCormick, Pres.
208 se 4
Tuttle, OK 73089
Ph: (405)381-0322
E-mail: pafra_pres@msn.com
URL: http://www.pafra2000.com
Contact: Bruce A. McCormick, Pres.
Membership Dues: individual, $65 (annual) ● sponsored competitor, $80 (annual) ● family, $95 (annual) ● associate, $40 (annual) ● star, $20 (annual). **Multinational. Description:** Promotes and provides public understanding of the sport of rodeo, with emphasis upon the military cowboy around the world. Strives to ensure honesty and fairness to both the contestants and the producers. Advertises rodeos being sponsored in accordance with association standards. **Publications:** *PAFRA Newsletter*. **Price:** included in membership dues.

23152 ■ Professional Rodeo Cowboys Association (PRCA)
101 Pro Rodeo Dr.
Colorado Springs, CO 80919-2301
Ph: (719)593-8840
Fax: (719)548-4876
URL: http://www.prorodeo.com
Contact: Troy Ellerman, Commissioner
Founded: 1936. **Members:** 11,375. **Staff:** 70. **Description:** Rodeos (700); contestants, stock contractors, and contract performers (8,752) in the sport of professional rodeo. Acts as rule-making and governing body for professional rodeo; grants approval to and provides leadership for rodeos sponsored by local community groups. Produces annual National Finals Rodeo through the National Finals Rodeo Committee (see separate entry). Maintains the Pro Rodeo Hall of Fame in Colorado Springs, CO; compiles statistics. **Computer Services:** database ● mailing lists. **Telecommunication Services:** hotline, radio, (719)548-4888. **Formerly:** (1936) Cowboys Turtle Association; (1945) Rodeo Cowboys Association; (1975) Professional Rodeo Cowboys Association. **Publications:** *Media Guide*, annual. Handbook. Features complete professional rodeo history and statistics. **Price:** $15.00/copy ● *Prorodeo Sports News*, biweekly. Newsletter. Features rodeo schedule, results, and standings. Includes articles of interest to contestants and fans. **Price:** $37.00/year. **Advertising:** accepted ● *Prorodeo Sports News Year-End Edition*. **Conventions/Meetings:** annual convention and trade show, in conjunction with the National Finals Rodeo (exhibits) - always in Las Vegas, NV.

23153 ■ United States Calf Ropers Association (USCRA)
PO Box 690
Giddings, TX 78942
Ph: (979)542-1239
E-mail: info@uscra.com
URL: http://www.uscra.com
Founded: 1996. **Membership Dues:** fan, $50 (annual) ● showdown, $100 (annual) ● roper's plus, $150 (annual). **Description:** Seeks to give calf ropers a fair and competitive chance to compete in the sport of calf roping. Promotes the sport of calf roping in the United States. **Computer Services:** database,

roping schedule ● database, standings ● information services, rule book ● online services, ropers forum.

23154 ■ Women's Professional Rodeo Association (WPRA)
1235 Lake Plaza Dr., Ste.127
Colorado Springs, CO 80906
Ph: (719)576-0900
Fax: (719)576-1386
E-mail: tdavis5@stx.rr.com
URL: http://www.wpra.com
Contact: Jymmy Kay Davis, Pres.
Founded: 1948. **Members:** 2,000. **Membership Dues:** card/permit, $250 (annual) ● gold card competing, $80 (annual). **Staff:** 3. **Description:** Produces and competes in All Professional Girl Rodeos and Barrel Races in rodeos sanctioned by the Professional Rodeo Cowboys Association. Conducts seminars and clinics on fundamentals of horsemanship and rodeo events. Operates National Cowgirl Hall of Fame. **Libraries: Type:** reference. **Holdings:** films, photographs. **Subjects:** rodeos and horsemanship events. **Awards: Frequency:** annual. **Type:** monetary. **Recipient:** for the top 15 barrel racers ● **Frequency:** annual. **Type:** monetary. **Recipient:** for champions in each of six rodeo events. **Committees:** Awards. **Formerly:** (1980) Professional Women's Rodeo Association; (1981) Girls Rodeo Association. **Publications:** *Procom 101*. Articles. Alternate Formats: online ● *Reference Book*, annual ● *Rule Book*, annual ● *Women's Pro Rodeo News*, monthly. Newsletter. **Price:** $24.00/year. **Circulation:** 3,900. **Advertising:** accepted. **Conventions/Meetings:** annual board meeting - always December, in Las Vegas, NV.

Rope Jumping

23155 ■ American Double Dutch League (ADDL)
PO Box 567
Cherry Hill, NJ 08003-0567
Free: (800)982-ADDL
E-mail: addlnyc@msn.com
URL: http://www.usaddl.org
Contact: Janice Melvin, Pres.
Founded: 1975. **Members:** 40,000. **Staff:** 3. **Budget:** $60,000. **Regional Groups:** 6. **Description:** Individuals promoting the sport of Double Dutch rope jumping. (Double Dutch is a style of rope jumping in which two turners swing two ropes in opposite directions allowing them to touch the ground alternately, eggbeater style, while one or more participants jump through the ropes doing tricks.) Benefits of Double Dutch rope jumping include teamwork, cooperation, healthy competition, physical fitness, leadership, and creativity; the sport can be played by youngsters of all ages and requires only two ropes. Sponsors annual citywide, regional, and worldwide competitive events. Offers certification course for official judges and conducts training seminars and national training program. **Telecommunication Services:** electronic mail, janiceaddlusa@aol.com. **Publications:** *Double Dutch*. Book ● *Official Double Dutch Rule Book*, periodic ● *Official Double Dutch Score Book*, periodic. **Conventions/Meetings:** annual conference - always October.

23156 ■ United States Amateur Jump Rope Federation (USAJRF)
PO Box 569
Huntsville, TX 77342-0569
Ph: (936)295-3332
Free: (800)225-8820
Fax: (936)295-3309
E-mail: info@usajrf.org
URL: http://www.usajrf.org
Contact: Marian Fletcher, Exec. Dir.
Founded: 1995. **Members:** 4,000. **Membership Dues:** adult (18 years and older), $30 (annual) ● youth (under 18 years old), $25 (annual) ● international club or team, $500 ● coach, $40 (annual) ● family, $65 (annual). **Staff:** 2. **Budget:** $250,000. **Regional Groups:** 10. **State Groups:** 50. **Local**

Groups: 1,500. **Description:** Individuals and rope skipping teams. Promotes the benefits of rope skipping as a sport that fosters teamwork, cooperation, physical fitness, and creativity. Organizes competitions, exhibitions, and summer camps. **Programs:** Camps; Conventions; Judging Clinics; Tournaments; Workshops. **Formerly:** (1995) International Rope Skipping Organization. **Publications:** *Rope Skipping News*, quarterly. Newsletter. Contains information about the association. **Circulation:** 3,000. **Advertising:** accepted. **Conventions/Meetings:** National Championship - competition.

Rowing

23157 ■ Eastern Association of Rowing Colleges (EARC)
c/o Eastern College Athletic Conference
1311 Craigville Beach Rd.
Centerville, MA 02632
Ph: (508)771-5060
Fax: (508)771-9486
E-mail: gcaldwell@ecac.org
URL: http://www.ecac.org/league/earc.asp
Contact: Gary Caldwell, Contact
Founded: 1945. **Members:** 16. **Description:** Colleges with rowing teams. Conducts regatta in May for eight-oared shells; establishes rules. **Affiliated With:** Eastern Collegiate Hockey Association. **Conventions/Meetings:** annual Sprints Regatta - competition (exhibits).

23158 ■ Intercollegiate Rowing Association (IRA)
c/o ECAC Rowing Office
1311 Craigville Beach Rd.
Centerville, MA 02632-4129
Ph: (508)771-5060
Fax: (508)771-9486
E-mail: gary.caldwell@tufts.edu
URL: http://rowing.ecac.org/index.html
Contact: Gary Caldwell, Dir.
Founded: 1895. **Members:** 5. **Description:** Colleges sponsoring national intercollegiate rowing championships. **Affiliated With:** Eastern Collegiate Hockey Association. **Conventions/Meetings:** annual meeting ● annual Regatta - competition (exhibits) - always early June at Cooper River Camden, NJ.

23159 ■ Middle States Regatta Association (MSRA)
5035 Pulaski Ave.
Philadelphia, PA 19144
Ph: (215)951-9549
Fax: (215)951-9549
E-mail: msr06@regattaentry.com
Contact: Albert Wacklin, Pres.
Founded: 1899. **Members:** 22. **Description:** Rowing clubs in Philadelphia, PA, New York City, New England, and Washington, DC. Works to advance the sport of rowing. Maintains hall of fame; sponsors competitions. **Awards:** Latrobe Cogswell Point Trophy Award. **Frequency:** annual. **Type:** trophy. **Conventions/Meetings:** annual Regatta - meeting - always first Sunday in June, Philadelphia, PA.

23160 ■ National Rowing Foundation (NRF)
c/o W. Hart Perry, Jr., Exec. Dir.
67 Mystic Rd.
North Stonington, CT 06359
Ph: (860)535-0634
Fax: (860)535-0637
E-mail: natrowing@natrowing.org
URL: http://www.natrowing.org
Contact: W. Hart Perry Jr., Exec. Dir.
Founded: 1966. **Members:** 200. **Staff:** 2. **Budget:** $450,000. **Description:** Seeks to: promote the sport of rowing by financially supporting competition in international regattas and sending a national team to world championship regattas; increase public interest in and awareness of rowing as a competitive sport and a healthy form of exercise; assist in establishment of newly founded rowing organizations. Maintains museum and Rowing Hall of Fame. Conducts

charitable program; members must be US team alumni. **Libraries: Type:** reference. **Holdings:** 600; archival material, books, periodicals. **Subjects:** rowing history. **Awards:** Rowing Hall of Fame. **Frequency:** annual. **Type:** recognition. **Recipient:** for excellence in rowing/service to rowing. **Computer Services:** Mailing lists, of members. **Affiliated With:** Mystic Seaport; United States Rowing Association.

23161 ■ Scholastic Rowing Association of America (SRAA)
c/o Matthew Ledwith
PO Box 528
Berlin, NJ 08009
Ph: (215)641-0589
E-mail: contact@sraa.net
URL: http://www.sraa.net
Contact: Matthew Ledwith, Contact
Founded: 1935. **Members:** 500. **Description:** Individuals, public and private schools, and organizations interested in the sport of rowing. Sponsors annual amateur regatta for school boys and girls. **Awards:** Bronze Medal. **Frequency:** annual. **Type:** medal. **Recipient:** for individual rowers ● Gold Medal. **Frequency:** annual. **Type:** medal. **Recipient:** for individual rowers ● Plaque. **Frequency:** annual. **Type:** recognition. **Recipient:** for schools of winning rowers in various classes of competition ● Silver Medal. **Frequency:** annual. **Type:** medal. **Recipient:** for individual rowers. **Affiliated With:** United States Rowing Association. **Formerly:** (1978) Schoolboy Rowing Association of America. **Conventions/Meetings:** annual Regatta - competition.

23162 ■ United States Rowing Association (USRowing)
2 Wall St.
Princeton, NJ 08540
Ph: (609)751-0700
Free: (800)314-4769
Fax: (609)924-1578
E-mail: members@usrowing.org
URL: http://www.usrowing.org
Contact: Glenn Merry, Exec. Dir.
Founded: 1872. **Members:** 14,000. **Membership Dues:** individual (26 years old and younger), $45 (annual) ● individual (27 years old and older), $60 (annual). **Staff:** 21. **Budget:** $3,700,000. **Description:** Universities, colleges, prep schools, high schools, and rowing clubs; individuals who are competing rowers, former rowers, and rowing enthusiasts. Promotes, fosters, and governs amateur rowing in the U.S. Promulgates rules and regulations governing the sport. Stages men's and women's and Master's National Championship Regattas annually; sanctioning body for all U.S. crews who wish to compete abroad and for all foreign oarsmen (except Canadian and Mexican crews) who row in the U.S. Selects all rowing crews to represent the U.S. in the World Championships, Pan American Games, and the Olympics. Conducts coaching development seminars. Provides educational clinics and material to help train individuals who wish to become judge-referees; licenses judge-referees. **Awards:** Athlete of the Year. **Frequency:** annual. **Type:** recognition ● Jack Kelly Award. **Frequency:** annual. **Type:** recognition ● US Rowing Medal. **Frequency:** annual. **Type:** medal. **Committees:** Executive; International; Judge/Referee; Long Range Planning; Masters; Membership; Sports Medicine and Technology. **Affiliated With:** International Federation of Rowing Associations; United States Olympic Committee. **Absorbed:** (1986) National Women's Rowing Association. **Also Known As:** USRowing. **Formerly:** (1982) National Association of Amateur Oarsmen. **Publications:** *American Rowing*, bimonthly. Magazine. **Price:** available to members only. **Advertising:** accepted ● *MasterStrokes*. Newsletter ● *Rowing Directory*, periodic ● Newsletter, monthly. Alternate Formats: online. **Conventions/Meetings:** competition ● annual meeting (exhibits) - always first week of December.

Rugby

23163 ■ United States Quad Rugby Association (USQRA)
5861 White Cypress Dr.
Lake Worth, FL 33467-6230
Ph: (561)964-1712 (941)924-1804
E-mail: edandcindy@comcast.net
URL: http://www.quadrugby.com
Contact: Ed Hooper, Pres.
Founded: 1988. **Membership Dues:** national team, $350 (annual) ● developing team, $150 (annual). **Multinational. Description:** Helps promote and regulate the sport of quad rugby on both national and international levels. Provides a competitive, unique and original team sport for people with severe disabilities. **Computer Services:** Information services, international rules ● information services, rugby resources. **Publications:** Newsletters. Alternate Formats: online.

23164 ■ United States Rugby Football Union (USARFU)
1033 Walnut St., Ste.200
Boulder, CO 80302
Ph: (303)539-0300
Free: (800)280-6302
Fax: (303)539-0311
E-mail: info@usarugby.org
URL: http://www.usarugby.org
Contact: Dan Lyle, Mgr. of Operations
Founded: 1975. **Members:** 30,000. **Membership Dues:** individual, $10-$25 (annual) ● coach, $10-$25 (annual) ● life, silver eagle, $500 ● life, gold eagle, $1,000. **Staff:** 13. **Budget:** $2,200,000. **Regional Groups:** 1,400. **Local Groups:** 53. **National Groups:** 2. **Description:** Federation comprising the Midwest Rugby Football Union, South Rugby Union, Pacific Coast Rugby Union, Western Rugby Union of the United States, Southern California Rugby Union, Northeast Rugby Union, Mid-Atlantic Rugby Union, and representing 60,000 rugby players. Aims to promote the sport of rugby in the U.S; to establish and administer policies; to represent the U.S. in international rugby affairs. Coordinates activities of the unions, particularly in the areas of coaching, refereeing, representative sides and selections, and communications. Conducts clinics for coaches, referees, and players; fields national team. Resources include books and pamphlets on coaching, refereeing, and playing. Maintains historical records; compiles statistics; conducts charitable program. Sponsors National Club, Collegiate Championships, Military and High School Championships. **Awards: Type:** recognition. **Computer Services:** Mailing lists, name and mailing address for all members. **Publications:** *Touchline*, quarterly. Newsletter. **Price:** available to members only. **Conventions/Meetings:** semiannual board meeting.

Sailboarding

23165 ■ International Mistral Class Organization (IMCO)
c/o Laura Lewandowski
125 Eighth Ave.
Indialantic, FL 32903
Ph: (321)953-5858
Fax: (321)953-5858
E-mail: lalewando@cfl.rr.com
URL: http://www.imco.org
Contact: Laura Lewandowski, Contact
Founded: 1982. **Members:** 500. **Staff:** 2. **Regional Groups:** 10. **State Groups:** 28. **Description:** Sailors of Mistral Class sailboards. (Mistral Class is a one-design sailboard that is 12 ft., 2 inches in length and weighs 35 lbs.) Sponsors races and competitions; compiles statistics. **Formerly:** Mistral Class Association. **Publications:** Newsletter, quarterly. **Conventions/Meetings:** periodic meeting.

Scuba Diving

23166 ■ National Association of Black Scuba Divers (NABS)
PO Box 91630
Washington, DC 20090-1630
Free: (800)521-NABS
Fax: (202)526-2907
E-mail: corrsecy@nabsdivers.org
URL: http://www.nabsdivers.org
Contact: Keshea Madison, Corresponding Sec.
Founded: 1991. **Membership Dues:** life (individual), $500 ● life (family), $650 ● full individual, $30 (annual) ● family, $45 (annual) ● student, $15 (annual) ● non-diver individual, $20 (annual) ● financial supporting, $10 (annual). **Description:** Promotes scuba diving, water sports skills, and environmental awareness and conservation. **Awards: Type:** scholarship. **Recipient:** to college students studying marine and environmental sciences. **Committees:** Awards and Recognition; Science and Education; Youth. **Publications:** Newsletter, quarterly. **Conventions/Meetings:** convention ● Scuba Trips - meeting.

Self Defense

23167 ■ American Self-Protection Association (ASPA)
c/o Dr. Evan S. Baltazzi, Founder
825 Green Gate Oval
Sagamore Hills, OH 44067-2311
E-mail: ebaltazzi@aol.com
URL: http://www.americanselfprotection.org
Contact: Dr. Evan S. Baltazzi, Founder
Founded: 1965. **Members:** 609. **Membership Dues:** undergraduate, $20 (annual) ● black belt, $40 (annual). **State Groups:** 6. **National Groups:** 4. **Languages:** English, French, German, Greek, Italian, Russian, Spanish. **Description:** Functions in YMCAs and schools "to develop and disseminate an American type of self-defense and physical fitness" program and to conduct research in the field of combative arts. (Judo, Aikido, Kickboxing, Stickfighting and Tai-Chi.) Gives presentations to groups and on radio and television. **Awards:** Rank Certificates. **Type:** recognition. **Recipient:** for promotion exams and contributions to ASP. **Publications:** *Basic A.S.P.* Book. Alternate Formats: online ● *Kickboxing: A Safe Sport, A Deadly Defense.* Book. **Price:** $18.00 paperback. Alternate Formats: online ● *Self-Protection Complete, The ASP System.* Book. **Price:** $37.00 plus shipping and handling ($3 in U.S.) ● *Stickfighting.* Book. **Price:** $28.00 hard bound. Alternate Formats: online ● *The World of ASP*, quarterly. Newsletter. **Price:** available to members only. **Conventions/Meetings:** annual meeting.

Shooting

23168 ■ Amateur Trapshooting Association (ATA)
601 W Natl. Rd.
Vandalia, OH 45377
Ph: (937)898-4638
Fax: (937)898-5472
E-mail: ccollier@shootata.com
URL: http://www.shootata.com
Contact: Connie Collier, Exec. Sec.
Founded: 1923. **Members:** 100,000. **Membership Dues:** life, $500 ● $18 (annual) ● sub-junior, junior, $9 (annual). **Staff:** 15. **Budget:** $3,500,000. **Description:** Persons who participate or are interested in the sport of trapshooting. Sanctions and determines rules governing shoots held by local, state, provincial, and worldwide trapshooting associations. Maintains permanent records for each shooter participating in 16 yard, handicap, and doubles classifications in registered class competitions in state and provincial meets; historical exhibit, hall of fame, and museum. **Libraries: Type:** reference. **Awards: Type:** monetary ● **Type:** scholarship ● **Type:** trophy. **Committees:** Central Handicap Executive. **Publications:** *Official Trapshooting Rules*, annual ● *Trap and Field Magazine*, monthly ● *Trap and Field Official ATA Averages*, annual. **Conventions/Meetings:** annual Grand American Tournament - meeting (exhibits) - always August in Vandalia, OH.

23169 ■ American Single Shot Rifle Association (ASSRA)
c/o Keith Foster, Membership Admin.
15770 Rd. 1037
Oakwood, OH 45873

Ph: (419)393-2976
E-mail: shuetzenmeister@assra.com
URL: http://www.assra.com
Contact: John Merz, Pres.
Founded: 1948. **Members:** 2,500. **Membership Dues:** individual in U.S., $35 (annual) ● individual outside U.S., $50 (annual). **Budget:** $65,000. **Regional Groups:** 60. **State Groups:** 42. **Multinational. Description:** Individuals who have an interest in the collection, use, preservation, and study of single shot rifles and their accessories. Devoted to the development and organization of activities that involve the classic single shot rifles in the German-American Schuetzen and Creedmoor tradition. Opposes legislative curtailment of the right to possess and use arms "by decent and peaceful persons as shooters, collectors, and sportsmen"; cooperates with law enforcement agencies in the prevention of illegal or abusive use of arms; provides the public with accurate information on the subject of arms and their accessories. Fosters the use of safe range facilities where members and guests may hold shooting contests and engage in practice and experimental shooting; instructs in the proper handling and safe use of arms and marksmanship; encourages and coordinates research into the historical data and lore of single shot rifles. Sponsors competitions. **Libraries: Type:** reference. **Holdings:** 2,450; archival material. **Subjects:** history of shooting, arms collecting, gunsmithing. **Awards:** National Championships. **Frequency:** annual. **Type:** recognition. **Computer Services:** database. **Publications:** *Single Shot Rifle Journal*, 6/year. Magazine. Contains book reviews, match announcements, and results. **Price:** included in membership dues. ISSN: 0734-5801. **Circulation:** 3,700. **Advertising:** accepted. **Conventions/Meetings:** annual general assembly (exhibits) - always Saturday of Memorial Day weekend, Etna Green, IN.

23170 ■ Cast Bullet Association (CBA)
c/o Ronald Klerk De Reus, Membership Dir.
12857 S Rd.
Hoyt, KS 66440-9116
E-mail: 1pres@castbulletassoc.org
URL: http://www.castbulletassoc.org
Contact: Ronald Klerk De Reus, Membership Dir.
Founded: 1975. **Members:** 1,900. **Membership Dues:** regular in U.S. and Canada, foreign, $17 (annual) ● regular in U.S. and Canada, foreign, $30 (biennial). **Budget:** $40,000. **Regional Groups:** 8. **Description:** Individual shooters interested in the techniques required to achieve accuracy with centerfire rifles and pistols firing fixed ammunition with cast lead alloy bullets. Seeks to: improve the design, quality, and accuracy of bullets cast of lead alloy to the extent that they are equal in effectiveness to jacketed bullets on targets and game; stimulate casting, hand loading, and firing experiments aimed at improved uniformity and accuracy and report findings to members; disseminate technical information to increase the level of knowledge and expertise of cast bullet shooters; enhance the economy and effectiveness of shooting cast bullets by encouraging the continual expansion of civilian rifle shooting as a sport. Compiles statistics. **Libraries: Type:** not open to the public. **Awards: Type:** recognition. **Recipient:** to winners of each rifle classification. **Affiliated With:** National Rifle Association of America. **Publications:** *The Fouling Shot*, bimonthly. Newsletter. Contains match results, new member listings, new product reviews, and results. **Price:** included in membership dues. **Circulation:** 1,900. **Advertising:** accepted ● Newsletters ● Pamphlets. **Price:** available to members only ● Also publishes newsletter subject index. **Conventions/Meetings:** annual National Tournament - competition - always September.

23171 ■ International Benchrest Shooters (IBS)
c/o Joan Borden, Recording Sec.
RR1, Box 250 BB
Springville, PA 18844
Ph: (570)965-2366
Fax: (570)965-2328

E-mail: joan@bordenrifles.com
URL: http://www.international-benchrest.com
Contact: Joan Borden, Recording Sec.
Founded: 1970. **Members:** 1,000. **Membership Dues:** regular in U.S., $40 (annual) ● associate, $10 (annual) ● junior, $5 (annual) ● regular in Canada, $65 (annual) ● regular outside U.S. and Canada, $73-$95 (annual). **Staff:** 1. **Description:** Gunsmiths, research engineers, gun writers, and other interested persons. Develops the ultimate in rifle accuracy. Sponsors tournaments with demonstrations of new inventions or idea developments in the field; also sponsors seminars. **Committees:** Awards; Group; Long Distance; Power Puff; Records; Rimfire; Rules; Score. **Publications:** *IBS Rule Book*. Books. **Price:** $3.00. Alternate Formats: online ● *Precision Shooting Magazine*, monthly. Reports on firearm accuracy and shooting, reloading, and gunsmithing techniques. Includes association news and calendar of events. **Price:** included in membership dues; $37.00 /year for nonmembers in U.S.; $62.00 /year for nonmembers in Canada. **Circulation:** 4,000. **Advertising:** accepted. Alternate Formats: online. Also Cited As: *Accuracy Shooting Magazine*. **Conventions/Meetings:** annual meeting (exhibits).

23172 ■ International Defensive Pistol Association (IDPA)
2232 CR 719
Berryville, AR 72616
Ph: (870)545-3886
Fax: (870)545-3894
E-mail: info@idpa.com
URL: http://www.idpa.com
Contact: Bill Wilson, Pres.
Founded: 1996. **Members:** 12,000. **Membership Dues:** individual, $35 (annual) ● individual (foreign), $55 (annual) ● club affiliation, $50 (annual) ● club affiliation (foreign), $210 (annual) ● corporate sponsor, $200-$2,000 (annual). **Multinational. Description:** Promotes the safe and proficient use of guns and equipment for self defense. Creates a playing field for competitors to test individual skills and abilities. Provides shooters with practical and realistic courses that simulate potentially life threatening encounters. **Computer Services:** database, listing of shooters ● information services, gun-related literature. **Divisions:** Custom Defensive Pistol; Enhance Service Pistol; Enhanced Service Revolver; Stock Service; Stock Service Revolver. **Publications:** *Rulebook*. Booklet. Alternate Formats: online. **Conventions/Meetings:** National Championship - competition.

23173 ■ International Handgun Metallic Silhouette Association (IHMSA)
PO Box 901120
Sandy, UT 84090-1120
Ph: (801)733-2423
Fax: (801)733-2424
E-mail: pres@texasairnet.com
URL: http://www.ihmsa.org
Contact: Mike Stimson, Pres.
Founded: 1976. **Members:** 55,000. **Membership Dues:** basic, $30 (annual) ● family, $7 (annual). **Staff:** 2. **Regional Groups:** 8. **State Groups:** 52. **Local Groups:** 300. **National Groups:** 4. **Description:** Handgun enthusiasts who shoot at metallic silhouettes of chickens, pigs, turkeys, and rams at ranges of 50, 100, 150, and 200 meters, respectively. Sanctions tournaments. **Awards:** Outstanding Service. **Frequency:** annual. **Type:** recognition. **Recipient:** for sportsmanship and volunteerism. **Computer Services:** database ● mailing lists. **Committees:** Evaluations; Physically Challenged; Rules; Safety; Technical. **Publications:** *IHMSANews*, monthly. Newspaper. **Price:** $2.00/issue; free, for members only. **Advertising:** accepted ● Brochures. **Conventions/Meetings:** annual International Championship - competition and meeting, handgun tournament (exhibits) - last week of July or 1st week of August.

23174 ■ National Association of Shooting Sports Athletes (NASSA)
2103 Wheaton Dr.
Richardson, TX 75081

E-mail: pcoach@nassa.org
URL: http://www.nassa.org
Contact: E.C. Wong, CEO/Pistol Venue Dir.
Membership Dues: individual, $25 (annual) ● family, $50 (annual) ● life, $240. **Staff:** 10. **Description:** Provides training to athletes to enhance their shooting skills. Reduces shooting sports-related expenses. Monitors competition among individuals, teams and clubs. **Divisions:** Competition. **Publications:** *Compass*, monthly. Newsletter. Includes shooting tips, advice, news and results of matches. **Advertising:** accepted. Alternate Formats: online.

23175 ■ National Bench Rest Shooters Association (NBRSA)
c/o Mrs. Pat Ferrell, Business Mgr.
2835 Guilford Ln.
Oklahoma City, OK 73120-4404
Ph: (405)842-9585
Fax: (405)842-9575
E-mail: patnbrsa@aol.com
URL: http://www.benchrest.com/nbrsa
Contact: Mrs. Pat Ferrell, Business Mgr.
Founded: 1951. **Members:** 2,200. **Membership Dues:** individual in U.S., club, $50 (annual) ● associate (children under 18; spouses of current members), $10 (annual) ● outside U.S. (surface mail), $61 (annual). **Staff:** 16. **Regional Groups:** 10. **Description:** Rifle enthusiasts interested in precision shooting. Conducts registered shoots and certifies records. Compiles statistics; maintains hall of fame. **Convention/Meeting:** none. **Awards: Type:** recognition. **Special Interest Groups:** Hunter (Shoot for Score); 1,000 Yard Benchrest; Regular Shoot-For-Group Benchrest; Rimfire Shoot-For-Group Benchrest. **Publications:** *NBRSA News*, monthly. Magazine. Contains club shooting match reports, match scores, match statistics, and articles. **Price:** included in membership dues. **Advertising:** accepted.

23176 ■ National Muzzle Loading Rifle Association (NMLRA)
PO Box 67
Friendship, IN 47021
Ph: (812)667-5131
Free: (800)745-1493
Fax: (812)667-5136
E-mail: nmlra@nmlra.org
URL: http://www.nmlra.org
Contact: Roberta Benham, Membership Sec.
Founded: 1933. **Members:** 21,000. **Membership Dues:** regular in U.S., $40 (annual) ● regular outside U.S., $50 (annual) ● family in U.S., $53 (annual) ● family outside U.S., $63 (annual) ● associate, $14 (annual) ● junior, $15 (annual) ● Golden Guardian (regular), $140 (annual) ● Golden Guardian (associate), $114 (annual) ● endowment - life, $1,000 ● patron - life, $1,200 ● benefactor - life, $1,500 ● associate -life, $300. **Staff:** 13. **Budget:** $1,800,000. **Regional Groups:** 240. **Description:** Persons interested in black powder shooting. Seeks to preserve the heritage of black powder shooting and to promote safety in the use of arms. Maintains national range located at Friendship, IN. Offers educational program in hunter safety. **Awards: Frequency:** annual. **Type:** scholarship. **Committees:** Award; Camping; Commercial Row; Field Representatives; Grounds; Memorial; Property; Public Relations; Range Officers; Safety; Scoring; Traffic. **Divisions:** Rendezvous; Territorial. **Publications:** *Muzzle Blasts*, monthly. Magazine. Includes calendar of events, legislative news, member profiles, new products, obituaries, research reports, shoot results, and advertisers' index. **Price:** included in membership dues. ISSN: 0027-5360. **Circulation:** 25,000. **Advertising:** accepted ● Also publishes range rules. **Conventions/Meetings:** annual meeting, fall shoot (exhibits).

23177 ■ National Rifle Association of America (NRA)
11250 Waples Mill Rd.
Fairfax, VA 22030
Ph: (703)267-1600
Free: (800)392-8683

E-mail: membership@nrahq.org
URL: http://www.mynra.com
Contact: Wayne LaPierre, Exec. VP
Founded: 1871. **Members:** 2,800,000. **Membership Dues:** regular, $35 (annual) ● life, $750 ● associate, $10 (annual) ● junior, $24 (annual) ● junior (life), $550. **Staff:** 400. **Budget:** $130,000,000. **State Groups:** 54. **Local Groups:** 14,000. **Description:** Target shooters, hunters, gun collectors, gunsmiths, police officers, and others interested in firearms. Promotes rifle, pistol, and shotgun shooting, hunting, gun collecting, home firearm safety, and wildlife conservation. Encourages civilian marksmanship. Educates police firearms instructors. Maintains national and international records of shooting competitions; sponsors teams to compete in world championships. Also maintains comprehensive collection of antique and modern firearms. Administers the NRA Political Victory Fund. Compiles statistics; sponsors research and education programs; maintains speakers' bureau and museum. Lobbies on firearms issues. **Libraries: Type:** reference. **Holdings:** 5,000. **Subjects:** gun control constitution. **Awards:** Defender of Freedom Award. **Type:** recognition. **Additional Websites:** http://www.nrahq.org. **Divisions:** Competition; Education and Training; Field Services; Hunting and Conservation; Institute for Legislative Action; Law Enforcement Assistance; Public Affairs. **Publications:** *American 1st Freedom.* Magazine. **Price:** included in membership dues; $9.95 for nonmembers ● *American Hunter,* monthly. Magazine. Includes listing of awards presented, legislative news, and wildlife profiles. **Price:** included in membership dues; $5.99 for nonmembers. ISSN: 0092-1068. **Circulation:** 1,260,000. **Advertising:** accepted ● *American Rifleman,* monthly. Magazine. Contains reports on equipment, tournaments, Olympics, collector items, and NRA news. Includes book reviews and calendar of events. **Price:** included in membership dues; $9.95 for nonmembers. ISSN: 0003-083X. **Circulation:** 1,390,000. **Advertising:** accepted ● *InSights,* monthly. Magazine. Includes articles on firearm education and safety and hunting tips. **Price:** included in junior membership dues. ISSN: 0747-007X. **Circulation:** 31,000. **Advertising:** accepted ● *Woman's Outlook.* Journal. **Price:** included in membership dues; $9.95 for nonmembers. **Conventions/Meetings:** annual meeting (exhibits).

23178 ■ National Shooting Sports Foundation (NSSF)
Flintlock Ridge Off. Ctr.
11 Mile Hill Rd.
Newtown, CT 06470-2359
Ph: (203)426-1320
Fax: (203)426-1087
E-mail: info@nssf.org
URL: http://www.nssf.org
Contact: Doug Painter, Pres.
Founded: 1961. **Members:** 3,000. **Staff:** 27. **Budget:** $13,105,000. **Description:** Represents manufacturers of firearms and ammunition, accessories, components, gun sights, hunting clothes, and other reputable firms that make a profit from hunting and shooting; includes outdoor and gun magazine publishers. Fosters a better understanding of and more active participation in the shooting sports. Promotes firearms safety; works with state and federal agencies in providing additional hunting opportunities. Cooperates with private enterprise to create outdoor recreational facilities. Distributes literature concerning firearms safety, conservation, and recreational shooting. Finances educational programs. **Libraries: Type:** reference. **Holdings:** books, reports. **Subjects:** hunting, recreation. **Absorbed:** Sportsmen's Service Bureau. **Publications:** Booklets ● Brochures ● Videos. **Conventions/Meetings:** annual National Hunting and Fishing Day - meeting ● annual Shooting, Hunting, and Outdoor Trade Show - meeting.

23179 ■ National Skeet Shooting Association (NSSA)
5931 Roft Rd.
San Antonio, TX 78253
Ph: (210)688-3371
Free: (800)877-5338

Fax: (512)688-3014
E-mail: nssa@nssa-nsca.com
URL: http://www.mynssa.com
Contact: Don Snyder, Exec. Dir.
Founded: 1935. **Members:** 20,000. **Membership Dues:** regular, $30 (annual) ● associate, $25 (annual) ● life, $500. **Staff:** 30. **Budget:** $925,000. **State Groups:** 54. **Local Groups:** 650. **Description:** Amateur skeet shooters. Registers competitive shoots and supervises them through formulation and enforcement of rules. Honors outstanding individuals whose shooting achievements and contributions to the sport of skeet qualify them for a position of honor in the Skeet Shooting Hall of Fame. Offers computerized services; compiles statistics on skeet shooting. **Additional Websites:** http://www.nssa-nsca.com. **Committees:** All American Selection; Chief Referee; Hall of Fame Nominations; Instruction; Junior World Shoot; Rules and Classification; Safety; World Shoot. **Publications:** *Records Annual,* annual ● *Skeet Shooting Review,* monthly. Magazine. **Price:** included in membership dues; $20.00 /year for nonmembers; $35.00/2 years for nonmembers ● *Sporting Clays: The Shotgun Hunters Magazine,* monthly. **Advertising:** accepted. **Conventions/Meetings:** annual meeting, includes United States Open Tournament ● annual World Championships - competition (exhibits) - always first two weeks of October.

23180 ■ National Sporting Clays Association (NSCA)
5931 Roft Rd.
San Antonio, TX 78253
Ph: (210)688-3371
Free: (800)877-5338
Fax: (210)688-3014
E-mail: nssa@nssa-nsca.com
URL: http://www.mynssa.com
Contact: Don Snyder, Exec. Dir.
Founded: 1989. **Members:** 17,000. **Membership Dues:** associate, $30 (annual) ● regular, $40 (annual) ● junior, $20 (annual) ● regular, outside U.S., $46 (annual) ● life (individual), $500 ● life (husband and wife), $750. **State Groups:** 528. **Description:** Promotion of shooting sports. Acts as the governing body of sporting clays and has an Advisory Council composed of range owners, shooters, and industry persons. Sanctions registered tournaments for member clubs, and uses registered scores to create an impartial classification system for competition. Operates national league and sweepstakes. Conducts championship competitions. Offers Instructor Certification Program to members. **Libraries: Type:** reference. **Holdings:** articles, artwork, books, business records, clippings, periodicals. **Awards:** Collegiate Scholarship. **Frequency:** annual. **Type:** scholarship. **Recipient:** for senior high school student ● **Type:** recognition. **Computer Services:** Mailing lists, of members. **Committees:** All American Selection; Instructor. **Councils:** Advisory. **Programs:** E-Shoot Reporting; Scholarship; Scholastic Clay. **Publications:** *Rule Book.* Alternate Formats: online ● *Sporting Clays Magazine,* monthly. Journal. **Price:** included in membership dues. **Circulation:** 20,000. **Advertising:** accepted ● Pamphlets. Alternate Formats: online ● Report. Alternate Formats: online ● Manuals. Alternate Formats: online ● Brochure. Alternate Formats: online. **Conventions/Meetings:** annual National Delegate Meeting - board meeting, held during National Championship Tournament ● National Sporting Clays Championships - competition, tournament ● regional meeting.

23181 ■ North-South Skirmish Association (N-SSA)
PO Box 361
Bloomfield Hills, MI 48303-0361
Ph: (248)258-9007 (248)447-5909
Fax: (248)447-5944
E-mail: spartan1@attglobal.net
URL: http://www.n-ssa.org
Contact: Bruce Miller, Public Information Off.
Founded: 1950. **Members:** 4,000. **Membership Dues:** regular, $45 (annual). **Staff:** 55. **Regional Groups:** 13. **Local Groups:** 210. **Description:** Aims to: commemorate the heroism and sacrifice of all,

North and South, who fought in the American Civil War, 1861-1865; promote education of the membership and the general public in the history of the Civil War; demonstrate and promote the safe and proper shooting of Civil War firearms and artillery for the public in events known as "skirmishes"; promote, encourage, coordinate research, and preserve information on Civil War firearms, artillery, equipment, uniforms and period dress. **Affiliated With:** National Rifle Association of America. **Publications:** *Skirmish Line,* bimonthly. Magazine. **Conventions/Meetings:** quarterly meeting - always January, August, May, and October ● semiannual National Skirmish - meeting - always May and October, Fort Shenandoah, VA ● monthly Regional Skirmishes - competition.

23182 ■ Pacific International Trapshooting Association (PITA)
PO Box 770
Lebanon, OR 97355
Ph: (541)258-8766
E-mail: sue@shootpita.com
URL: http://www.shootpita.com
Contact: Sharon Gillis, Pres.
Founded: 1928. **Members:** 8,500. **Membership Dues:** individual, $18 (annual). **Multinational. Description:** Sponsors state, provincial, and individual registered trapshoots. **Publications:** Yearbook, annual. **Price:** $10.00. **Conventions/Meetings:** annual meeting (exhibits) - usually last week of July.

23183 ■ United States Practical Shooting Association (USPSA)
PO Box 811
Sedro Woolley, WA 98284
Ph: (360)855-2245
Fax: (360)855-0380
E-mail: office@uspsa.org
URL: http://www.uspsa.org
Contact: Dave Thomas, Exec. Dir.
Founded: 1984. **Membership Dues:** individual, $40 (annual) ● associate, $25 (annual) ● foreign, $50 (annual) ● life, $500 ● life (foreign), $600 ● benefactor, $1,000 (annual) ● foreign associate, $35 (annual). **Description:** Promotes the sport of practical shooting in the U.S. **Affiliated With:** National Shooting Sports Foundation. **Publications:** *Front Sight,* bimonthly. Magazine. Provides information about association business, events, new products, training techniques, etc. **Circulation:** 16,000. **Advertising:** accepted ● *Front Sight Annual,* annual. Magazines. Provides information to those seeking to learn more about USPSA and the sport of practical shooting. **Circulation:** 15,000. **Advertising:** accepted. Alternate Formats: online.

23184 ■ United States Revolver Association (USRA)
RR No. 1, Box 548
Scotrun, PA 18355
Ph: (570)839-6363
E-mail: usra@stroudsburg.com
URL: http://www.usra1.org
Contact: Mr. Joseph Miller, Membership Sec./ Historian
Founded: 1900. **Membership Dues:** adult, $20 (annual) ● life, $300 ● international, $35 (annual). **Staff:** 2. **Multinational. Description:** Contributes to the development of revolver and pistol shooting. Preserves records; encourages and conducts pistol matches between members and clubs of the U.S., as well as marksmen of other countries. **Libraries: Type:** reference. **Holdings:** 500. **Subjects:** shooting. **Publications:** *U.S. HandGunner,* quarterly. Magazine. Contains scores and awards of pistol matches and articles of interest to pistol shooting competitions. **Price:** included in membership dues. ISSN: 0746-6625. **Advertising:** accepted. **Conventions/Meetings:** annual meeting - always first week of December, Taunton, MA.

23185 ■ USA Shooting (USAS)
1 Olympic Plz.
Colorado Springs, CO 80909
Ph: (719)866-4670
Fax: (719)635-7989

E-mail: admin.info@usashooting.org
URL: http://www.usashooting.com
Contact: Robert Mitchell, CEO
Founded: 1994. **Members:** 5,000. **Membership Dues:** club, $35 (annual). **Staff:** 14. **Description:** Represents national team members, national development members, and resident athletes. Governing body for Olympic shooting responsible for training and selecting shooting teams to represent the US at World Cups, World Shooting Championships, Pan American Games and Olympic Games. Annually hosts the National Junior Olympic Shooting Championships, camps, clinics for shooting and training conferences for shooting coaches. **Publications:** *USA Shooting News*, bimonthly. Magazine.

23186 ■ World Fast-Draw Association (WFDA)
c/o Cheryl Short, Sec.
749 9th St.
Calhan, CO 80808
E-mail: wfda@fastdraw.org
URL: http://www.fastdraw.org/wfda
Contact: Cheryl Short, Sec.
Founded: 1976. **Members:** 500. **Membership Dues:** regular, $45 (annual) ● family, $20 (annual). **Multinational. Description:** Preserves and promotes Western fast-draw as an organized sport. Sponsors sanctioned contests during the shooting season (January through November). Provides instruction in selecting equipment and safety procedures and techniques to interested individuals. **Libraries: Type:** reference. **Affiliated With:** National Rifle Association of America. **Formed by Merger of:** (1976) Midwestern Fast-Draw Association; (1976) Western Fast-Draw Association. **Publications:** *Top Gun*, bimonthly. Magazine. Includes sidekick informational update. **Price:** included in membership dues. **Circulation:** 500. **Advertising:** accepted. **Conventions/Meetings:** annual board meeting.

Shuffleboard

23187 ■ American International Shuffleboard
7216 Burns St.
Richland Hills, TX 76118
Ph: (817)284-3499
Free: (800)826-7856
Fax: (817)595-1506
E-mail: lynda@jump.net
Contact: Kelly Stites, Pres.
Founded: 1928. **For-Profit. Description:** Federation of local leagues of men and women who play amateur table shuffleboard. Provides tournament instructions and rules to interested organizations and institutions. Donates trophies to tournaments. **Formerly:** (1993) American Shuffleboard Company. **Publications:** *How to Play Shuffleboard*. **Price:** $5.50/copy. **Conventions/Meetings:** meeting (exhibits) - 8/year.

23188 ■ International Shuffleboard Association (ISA)
c/o Joe Messier, Pres.
390 Santa Fe Trail
North Fort Myers, FL 33917
Ph: (239)543-1235
E-mail: jhmessier@earthlink.net
URL: http://www.trigger.net/~sandy/internat.htm
Contact: Joe Messier, Pres.
Founded: 1979. **Members:** 5. **Membership Dues:** international association, $500 (annual). **Budget:** $10,000. **Regional Groups:** 10. **State Groups:** 16. **Description:** National shuffleboard associations. Objectives are: to encourage the formation of national shuffleboard associations; to provide information on the game of shuffleboard; to encourage construction developments in playing equipment and the improvement of the rules of play. Promotes world championship games and shuffleboard tournaments. Sponsors competitions; compiles statistics; maintains hall of fame; conducts educational programs. **Libraries: Type:** reference. **Holdings:** articles, photographs. **Subjects:** championship teams, historical pictures, future sponsorships, shuffleboard. **Awards:** Hall of

Fame Merit Certificate. **Frequency:** annual. **Type:** recognition. **Recipient:** for service to association. **Boards:** International. **Publications:** *Program-Preview* (in English and Japanese), annual. Report. Includes information about member countries with pictures. **Price:** free for members. **Circulation:** 1,250. **Advertising:** accepted ● *Shuffle Board Training Manual* ● Catalogs. Covers ISA rules. **Conventions/Meetings:** annual banquet and meeting (exhibits).

Skating

23189 ■ International Inline Skating Association (IISA)
PO Box 18309
Cleveland Heights, OH 44118-0309
Ph: (216)261-3438 (216)371-2977
Fax: (910)762-9477
E-mail: director@iisa.org
URL: http://www.iisa.org
Contact: Kalinda Mathis, Exec.Dir.
Founded: 1991. **Description:** Represents inline skate product manufacturers working together to promote and develop the sport of inline skating. Develops educational programs, promotes safe skating and protects and expands access to public skate ways across the country. **Conventions/Meetings:** semiannual Planning Conference.

23190 ■ Professional Skaters Association (PSA)
3006 Allegro Park SW
Rochester, MN 55902
Ph: (507)281-5122
Fax: (507)281-5491
E-mail: office@skatepsa.com
URL: http://skatepsa.com
Contact: Jimmie Santee, Exec. Dir.
Founded: 1938. **Members:** 6,000. **Membership Dues:** new (full), $85 (annual) ● former (full), $130 (annual) ● regular, outside U.S., associate (new), $45 (annual) ● associate (former), intern, $50 (annual) ● family (new), $115 (annual) ● family (former), $170 (annual) ● regular, in Canada and Mexico, $25 (annual) ● skate technician, program director, $125 (annual). **Staff:** 8. **Budget:** $3,000,000. **Regional Groups:** 16. **National Groups:** 50. **Description:** Professional ice skaters engaged in the teaching, coaching and performing of ice skating. Strives to form a cohesive body of all professional ice skaters for the benefit of the profession, to protect the interests of members' pupils, to advance all aspects of both ice figure skating and recreational skating, and to promote high ethical and professional standards in the field. Grades teachers on the basis of on-ice proficiency and oral examination. Operates placement service. **Awards:** Edi Awards. **Frequency:** annual. **Type:** recognition. **Committees:** Competition Meetings; International Coaches; Ratings; Seminar and U.S. Professional Championship; Special Olympics; Sports Medicine; Technical; Volunteer. **Formerly:** Professional Skaters Guild of America. **Publications:** *Coaches Manual* ● *Professional Skater*, bimonthly. Magazine. Covers instruction, competition, and other facets of figure skating; includes association news, competition schedules, and employment opportunities. **Price:** included in membership dues; $19.95 /year for nonmembers in U.S.; $29.00 /year for nonmembers in Canada; $45.00 /year for nonmembers in other countries. ISSN: 0273-5571. **Circulation:** 6,500. **Advertising:** accepted ● *Professional Skaters Association—Membership Directory*, annual. **Price:** included in membership dues; $5.00/copy for figure skating clubs; $50.00/copy for businesses. **Circulation:** 4,000. **Advertising:** accepted ● *Professional Skaters Association—Rating Systems Manual*, periodic. Lists requirements for credentialing figure skating coaches in the United States and other countries. ● *Skaters Handbook*. **Price:** $10.00. **Conventions/Meetings:** annual conference (exhibits) - always May ● Pro Series - competition ● seminar ● trade show ● annual U.S. Open Professional Figure Skating Championship - competition ● workshop.

23191 ■ Skating Association for the Blind and Handicapped (SABAH)
2607 Niagara St.
Buffalo, NY 14207
Ph: (716)362-9600
E-mail: sabah@sabahinc.org
URL: http://www.sabahinc.org
Contact: Sheila O'Brien, Exec. Dir.
Founded: 1977. **Members:** 800. **Membership Dues:** skater, $75 (annual). **Staff:** 9. **Budget:** $700,000. **Regional Groups:** 1. **State Groups:** 3. **Local Groups:** 1. **National Groups:** 5. **Description:** Provides individuals who have physical, mental, or emotional challenges the opportunity to reach their fullest potential through the development of ice skating skills and performing in an annual ice-skating show. **Awards:** Jessica Rose Thomas Award. **Frequency:** annual. **Type:** recognition. **Recipient:** for courage, determination, and accomplishment in ice-skating. **Publications:** *SABAH Scenes*, quarterly. Newsletter. Provides an overview of activities and events in all chapters. **Price:** free for members, families, donors. **Circulation:** 10,000. **Conventions/Meetings:** annual Ice Show, highlights skaters' accomplishments.

23192 ■ Society of Roller Skating Teachers of America (SRSTA)
6905 Corporate Dr.
Indianapolis, IN 46278
Ph: (317)347-2626
Fax: (317)347-2636
E-mail: rsa@rollerskating.com
URL: http://www.rollerskating.com
Contact: Pat Jacques, Chair
Founded: 1945. **Members:** 900. **Membership Dues:** individual, $360 (annual). **Staff:** 1. **Description:** Qualified teachers of all branches of artistic roller skating registered through the Roller Skating Association International, the parent body. Conducts seminars, clinics, and certification programs; acts as forum for ideas on training, competition, and coaching. **Awards:** Teacher of the Year Award. **Frequency:** annual. **Type:** recognition. **Recipient:** for roller skating teachers of SRSTA. **Publications:** *RSA Today-Coaches Edition*, bimonthly. Newsletter. Features articles on skating teachers and coaches, and coaching techniques. **Price:** included in membership dues. **Circulation:** 1,000. **Advertising:** accepted ● Directory, annual ● Newsletter, monthly ● Also publishes study guides. **Conventions/Meetings:** annual conference.

23193 ■ United States Amateur Confederation of Roller Skating (USAC/RS)
c/o USA Roller Sports
4730 South St.
Lincoln, NE 68506
Ph: (402)483-7551
Fax: (402)483-1465
E-mail: rhawkins@usarollersports.org
URL: http://www.usarollersports.org
Contact: Richard Hawkins, Exec. Dir.
Founded: 1937. **Members:** 29,000. **Membership Dues:** individual, $35 (annual) ● club, $50 (annual) ● coach, $50 (annual) ● judge/official, $15 (annual). **Staff:** 15. **Budget:** $2,000,000. **Regional Groups:** 9. **State Groups:** 20. **Local Groups:** 1,250. **Description:** Amateur organization sponsoring competitive roller skating that includes inline skates. Aims to advance roller skating as an amateur sport and to promote its acceptance into the Olympic games. Selects teams to compete in world championships; oversees sponsorship arrangements. Maintains convention roller skating programs in 3 disciplines: Artistic Roller Skating; Roller Hockey; Inline Speed Skating. Provides judges and referees. Researches the fitness and health benefits of roller skating. Compiles statistics; maintains hall of fame and museum. **Libraries: Type:** reference. **Awards: Type:** recognition. **Recipient:** for inter-club competitions and championship competitions. **Affiliated With:** United States Olympic Committee. **Formed by Merger of:** (1994) United States Amateur Roller Skating Association; United States Federation of Amateur Roller Skaters. **Formerly:** United States of America

Confederation. **Publications:** *U.S. Roller Skating*, bimonthly. Magazine. **Price:** $12.00. **Circulation:** 7,000. **Advertising:** accepted ● Directory, annual. **Conventions/Meetings:** annual Championship - meeting (exhibits) ● competition ● seminar.

23194 ■ United States Barrel Jumping Association (USBJA)
Address Unknown since 2007
Founded: 1977. **Members:** 39. **Staff:** 2. **Regional Groups:** 5. **State Groups:** 4. **Local Groups:** 4. **National Groups:** 3. **Description:** Competitors (35) and coaches (4) in the sport of barrel jumping while on ice skates or roller skates. (Barrels are lined up in a straight line, side to side, on the ground, and the object is to jump over as many barrels as possible without touching them.) Compiles statistics. Sponsors annual barrel jumping competition. Maintains charitable program and children's services. **Awards: Type:** recognition. **Formerly:** (1984) Michigan Barrel Jumping Association. **Publications:** Newsletter, quarterly. **Conventions/Meetings:** periodic Coaching and Training Seminar ● biennial conference (exhibits).

23195 ■ United States Figure Skating Association (USFSA)
20 1st St.
Colorado Springs, CO 80906
Ph: (719)635-5200
Fax: (719)635-9548
E-mail: info@usfigureskating.org
URL: http://www.usfsa.org
Contact: Mr. David Raith, Exec. Dir.
Founded: 1921. **Members:** 142,000. **Membership Dues:** individual, $85 (annual) ● regular, in U.S., additional family, $40 (annual) ● regular, outside U.S., $60 (annual) ● regular, in Canada, $50 (annual). **Staff:** 35. **Budget:** $7,500,000. **National Groups:** 450. **Description:** Member clubs with over 142,000 registered members. National governing body for the sport of figure skating in the U.S. Establishes rules and appoints officials for competitions, tests, carnivals, and exhibitions; determines the eligibility of figure skaters. Compiles statistics; maintains World Figure Skating Hall of Fame and Museum. **Committees:** Athletes Advisory; Coaches; Collegiate Program; Collegiate Skating Institute; Competitions; Dance; Eligibility; Finance; Hall of Fame and Museum; International; Judges; Long Range Planning; Membership; Memorial Fund; Precision Skating; Program Development; Rules; Sanctions and Eligibility; Selections; Singles and Pairs; Special Olympics; Sponsorship; Sport Medicine; State Games. **Affiliated With:** Ice Skating Institute; International Skating Union; Professional Skaters Association; Special Olympics; United States Olympic Committee. **Publications:** *Media Guide*, annual. Booklets ● *Rulebook*, annual ● *Skating*, monthly. Magazine. Includes competition results, profiles, and articles on sports medicine. **Price:** included in membership dues; $25.00 /year for nonmembers in U.S.; $35.00 /year for nonmembers in Canada; $45.00 /year for nonmembers outside U.S. ISSN: 0037-6132. **Circulation:** 37,000. **Advertising:** accepted ● Books. **Conventions/Meetings:** annual meeting (exhibits).

23196 ■ U.S. Speedskating (USS)
PO Box 18370
Kearns, UT 84118
Ph: (801)417-5360
Fax: (801)417-5361
E-mail: bcrowley@usspeedskating.org
URL: http://www.usspeedskating.org
Contact: Bob Crowley, Exec. Dir.
Founded: 1966. **Members:** 2,000. **Membership Dues:** individual, $55 (annual) ● 1st year competing athlete, supporter, $30 (annual) ● fan, $15 (annual) ● organizational, $300 (annual). **Staff:** 15. **Regional Groups:** 17. **Description:** Individuals interested in international speed skating. Promotes Olympic speed skating in the U.S. and helps U.S. skaters in international competition, including the Olympic games. Conducts summer camps. **Absorbed:** (2002) Amateur SpeedSkating Union of the United States. **Formerly:** (1983) United States International Skating Association; (1998) United States International Speed-

skating Association. **Publications:** *Ice Chips*, 8/year. Newsletter. **Price:** $10.00/year. **Circulation:** 500 ● *Racing Blade*. Magazine. **Conventions/Meetings:** biennial board meeting ● competition, to select national champions, world competitors, and Olympic team members ● seminar.

23197 ■ USA Roller Sports (USARS)
PO Box 6579
Lincoln, NE 68506-0579
Ph: (402)483-7551
Fax: (402)483-1465
E-mail: rhawkins@usarollersports.org
URL: http://www.usarollersports.org
Contact: Richard J. Hawkins, Exec. Dir.
Founded: 1937. **Members:** 30,000. **Membership Dues:** individual, $35 (annual) ● club, $50 (annual). **Staff:** 16. **Budget:** $2,000,000. **Regional Groups:** 9. **State Groups:** 48. **Local Groups:** 1,160. **National Groups:** 3. **Description:** Amateur roller skaters and inline skaters. Serves as governing body for competitive roller skating, figure skating, hockey, and speed skating in the U.S. Develops rules and requirements; trains and certifies judges and officials; represents U.S. skaters at international conferences. Conducts educational seminars for skaters and coaches. Sponsors local, state, regional, and national championship competitions; qualifies and trains skaters. Maintains museum and hall of fame. Member of the U.S. Olympic committee. **Libraries: Type:** reference. **Holdings:** 4,000. **Subjects:** skating rules, history, roller skating sport. **Awards:** Athlete of the Year. **Frequency:** annual. **Type:** recognition ● Hall of Fame. **Frequency:** annual. **Type:** recognition. **Recipient:** for roller skaters ● Life Membership. **Frequency:** annual. **Type:** recognition. **Formerly:** (1997) U.S. Amateur Confederation of Roller Skating; (2000) U.S.A. Roller Skating. **Publications:** *USA Roller Sports - The Magazine*, quarterly. Contains competitive results, calendar of events, rule and regulation updates, and profiles. **Price:** $12.00/year in U.S.; $14.00/year outside U.S. **Circulation:** 25,000. **Advertising:** accepted ● Also publishes technical manuals; makes available roller skating memorabilia. **Conventions/Meetings:** semiannual board meeting (exhibits) ● annual congress (exhibits).

Skiing

23198 ■ Amateur Ski Instructors Association (ASIA)
28 Park Dr.
Woodstock, NY 12498-1726
Ph: (845)679-4609
E-mail: asiadesk@asiaski.com
URL: http://www.asiaski.com
Contact: Bill Hornbeck, Exec. Dir.
Founded: 1980. **Membership Dues:** individual, $25 (annual) ● family - first two, $50 (annual) ● family - additional, $10 (annual). **Description:** Trains and certifies candidates who are interested in teaching alpine, snowboard and cross country skiing at the amateur level. Encourages and facilitates the upgrading of skiing and riding skills of all skiers through positive programs designed to enhance the safety and enjoyment of skiing. Seeks to provide a continuing education program for certified amateur ski and snowboard instructors. **Affiliated With:** Professional Ski Instructors of America. **Publications:** *Short Swings*, quarterly. Newsletter.

23199 ■ American Birkebeiner Ski Foundation (ABSF)
PO Box 911
Hayward, WI 54843
Ph: (715)634-5025
Free: (800)872-2753
Fax: (715)634-5663
E-mail: birkie@birkie.com
URL: http://www.birkie.com
Contact: Janet Jenkins, Office Mgr.
Founded: 1987. **Members:** 407. **Membership Dues:** individual, $25 (annual) ● family, $40 (annual) ● business, $50 (annual). **Staff:** 6. **Budget:** $750,000. **De-**

scription: Individuals with an interest in the American Birkebeiner cross-country skiing race, held annually in Hayward, Wisconsin. Promotes increased participation in recreational and competitive cross-country skiing among people of all ages; serves as a clearinghouse on the Birkebeiner race. **Publications:** *Birch Scroll*, semiannual. Magazine. **Circulation:** 16,000. **Advertising:** accepted. **Conventions/Meetings:** annual meeting, in conjunction with the American Birkebeiner - always February.

23200 ■ American Cross Country Skiers (AXCS)
PO Box 604
Bend, OR 97709
Ph: (541)317-0217
Fax: (541)317-0217
E-mail: axcs@xcskiworld.com
URL: http://www.xcskiworld.com
Contact: Richard Hunt, Exec. Dir.
Founded: 1998. **Members:** 1,150. **Membership Dues:** ordinary, $35 (annual). **Budget:** $25,000. **Local Groups:** 200. **Description:** Individuals aged 30 or more with an interest in cross country skiing. Promotes increased participation in the sport of cross country skiing and racing. Facilitates communication among members; makes available discount products and services to members; sponsors social events and competitions. Issues racing licenses required for participation in national cross country ski races. **Publications:** *AXCS News*, 2-3/year. Newsletter. **Price:** free for members ● *AXCS Weekly Workout Idea Booklet*, annual. **Price:** included in membership dues. **Conventions/Meetings:** annual National Masters Championships - competition, for skiers 25 and over - in winter.

23201 ■ National Brotherhood of Skiers (NBS)
1525 E 53rd St., Ste.418
Chicago, IL 60615
Ph: (773)955-4100
Free: (866)280-4184
Contact: Rose Thomas Pickrum, Pres.
Founded: 1973. **Members:** 12,000. **Membership Dues:** club, $100 (annual). **Budget:** $125,000. **Regional Groups:** 4. **Local Groups:** 82. **Description:** Minority ski clubs. Promotes winter sports among minorities, with emphasis on youth. Seeks to locate and develop talented ski racers through local, regional, and national competitions. Promotes the development of Olympic-quality minority skiers. Offers two-year athletic scholarships for qualified youth to attend Ski Academies. Encourages participation in United States Ski Association competitions. Supports Building Skills and Talents programs and community-based youth motivational improvement programs. **Publications:** *NBS Directory*, annual ● *NBS Ski Club Guide*, biennial, odd-numbered years ● *Skiers Edge*, quarterly. Newsletter. Alternate Formats: online ● Report, biennial. **Conventions/Meetings:** biennial Summit/Black Ski Summit - meeting - always odd-numbered years.

23202 ■ National Ski Patrol System (NSP)
133 S Van Gordon St., Ste.100
Lakewood, CO 80228
Ph: (303)988-1111
Fax: (303)988-3005
E-mail: nsp@nsp.org
URL: http://www.nsp.org
Contact: Mark Dorsey, Exec. Dir.
Founded: 1938. **Members:** 26,500. **Membership Dues:** associate, $60 (annual). **Staff:** 27. **Budget:** $2,000,000. **Regional Groups:** 10. **Description:** Promotes ski safety and handling of injuries at ski areas. Assists municipal and federal agencies in cold weather disasters and in rescue attempts involving air crashes, mountain accidents, and blizzards; all members are trained in winter emergency care, receive special training in cold weather survival and rescue, must pass Ski Patrol proficiency and toboggan handling tests, and are trained in avalanche recognition and rescue. Maintains inventory of winter rescue equipment and patrol supplies. **Awards: Type:** recognition. **Computer Services:** Mailing lists,

of members. **Committees:** Auxiliary; Avalanche; Legal Advisory; Medical Advisory; Nordic Patrols; Ski Mountaineering; Tele-Communications; Training; Winter Emergency Care. **Publications:** *Ski Patrol Magazine*, quarterly. Covers first aid, skiing techniques, avalanche rescues, training, equipment, and physical conditioning. Includes advertisers' index and book reviews. **Price:** included in membership dues; $15.00 /year for nonmembers. ISSN: 0890-6076. **Circulation:** 35,000. **Advertising:** accepted ● *Winter Catalog*. **Conventions/Meetings:** annual meeting.

23203 ■ Pacific Northwest Ski Association (PNSA)
PO Box 1278
Snoqualmie Pass, WA 98068
Ph: (425)434-0014
Fax: (425)434-0015
E-mail: pnsa@pnsa.org
URL: http://www.pnsa.org
Contact: Sue Johnson, Pres.
Founded: 1930. **Members:** 2,300. **Budget:** $25,000. **Description:** Individuals in Northern Idaho, Oregon, and Washington interested in promotion of good skiing and participation in ski competitions. Sponsors competitions. Maintains Pacific Northwest Ski Education Foundation which bestows awards, grants, and scholarships to qualified ski racers. A division of the United States Ski Association. **Committees:** Alpine; Freestyle; Nordic; Snowboard INGT. **Affiliated With:** United States Olympic Committee. **Publications:** *PNSA Messenger*, 3/year. Newsletter. **Conventions/Meetings:** annual meeting.

23204 ■ Professional Ski Instructors of America (PSIA)
133 S Van Gordon St., Ste.101
Lakewood, CO 80228
Ph: (303)987-9390
Free: (800)222-ISKI
Fax: (303)988-3005
E-mail: psia@psia.org
URL: http://www.psia.org
Contact: Raymond J. Allard, Pres.
Founded: 1961. **Members:** 24,000. **Membership Dues:** professional, $30 (annual). **Staff:** 7. **Budget:** $1,200,000. **Description:** Professional-certified Alpine and Nordic ski teachers. Promotes ski instruction by professional teachers. Developed American Teaching Method (ATM), which has received international recognition. Sponsors and publishes results of educational research through the Professional Ski Instructors of America Educational Foundation; develops clinics and management seminars. Establishes a library of books and publications on ski technique, teaching, and ski history. **Libraries: Type:** not open to the public. **Holdings:** 6; periodicals. **Committees:** Alpine and Nordic Ski Teams; Certification; Children's; Education; Nordic; Ski School Directors; Snowboard Team. **Publications:** *Convention Proceedings*, annual ● *Professional Skier*, 3/year. Journal. Contains ski tips, interviews, and instructional material. **Price:** $25.00/year. **Circulation:** 23,000. **Advertising:** accepted ● *PSIA Accessories Catalog* ● *Ski School Management*, 3/year. Newsletter. **Price:** $6.00/year. **Circulation:** 700. **Advertising:** accepted ● Pamphlets. **Conventions/Meetings:** convention - 3/year.

23205 ■ U.S. Biathlon Association (USBA)
49 Pineland Dr., Ste.301A
New Gloucester, ME 04260
Ph: (207)688-6500
Free: (800)242-8456
Fax: (207)688-6505
E-mail: usbiathlon@aol.com
URL: http://www.usbiathlon.org
Contact: Larry Pugh, Chm.
Founded: 1980. **Members:** 1,000. **Membership Dues:** supporter, current/past BOD officer, competitor, family, amateur club, coach/official, $50 (annual) ● junior competitor, $25 (annual) ● life, $1,000 ● corporate, partnership, organization, $1,000 (annual). **Staff:** 7. **Budget:** $800,000. **Regional Groups:** 5. **Local Groups:** 30. **Description:** Sportsmen and interested individuals involved in cross-country skiing

and rifle marksmanship. Serves as the national governing body for biathlon in the U.S. Sponsors competitions, coaches' clinics, and training camps. Selects biathletes to represent the U.S. in international competitions including the Olympic Games. International Governing Body is known as The International Biathlon Union. **Awards:** Athletes of the Year. **Frequency:** annual. **Type:** monetary. **Recipient:** for athletes, based on performance. **Councils:** Sports Medicine. **Affiliated With:** United States Olympic Committee. **Publications:** *Bi-Lines*, bi-monthly. Bulletin. **Circulation:** 1,200. **Advertising:** accepted. **Conventions/Meetings:** annual National Champs, Team Trials, North American Champs - competition - January-March.

23206 ■ U.S. Ski Coaches Association (USSCA)
PO Box 100
Park City, UT 84060
Ph: (435)649-9090
Fax: (435)649-3613
E-mail: info@ussa.org
URL: http://www.usskiteam.com
Contact: Bill Marolt, Pres./CEO
Founded: 1977. **Members:** 3,500. **Membership Dues:** disabled, Alpine, $50-$125 (annual) ● disabled, cross country, $30-$110 (annual) ● freestyle, $30-$100 (annual) ● jumping, Nordic, $30-$100 (annual) ● snowboard, $50-$100 (annual). **Staff:** 3. **Description:** Alpine, Nordic, and Freestyle ski and snowboard coaches and instructors; persons interested in sports medicine. Promotes the highest standards of Alpine, Nordic, and Freestyle ski coaching. Provides educational and technical materials, supplies, and equipment necessary to the function of the ski coach. Offers courses, clinics, films, and placement service. Provides high standards of certification, recertification, accreditation, and coaching ethics; handles problems of common concern to the ski coaching profession. **Publications:** *The American Ski Coach*, 5/year. Journal. **Circulation:** 3,800. **Advertising:** accepted ● Manuals. **Conventions/Meetings:** annual meeting.

23207 ■ United States Ski and Snowboard Association (USSA)
PO Box 100
1500 Kearns Blvd.
Park City, UT 84060
Ph: (435)649-9090
Fax: (435)649-3613
E-mail: info@ussa.org
URL: http://www.ussa.org
Contact: Bill Marolt, Pres./CEO
Founded: 1976. **Members:** 25,000. **Staff:** 4. **Budget:** $350,000. **Description:** Works as the national governing body for Olympic skiing and snowboarding, and the parent organization of the U.S. Ski and Snowboard Teams. Provides leadership and direction for tens of thousands of young skiers and snowboarders who share an Olympic dream. **Computer Services:** database, data on individual club member make-up (for members only). **Divisions:** Competition; Recreation. **Absorbed:** (1980) Eastern Ski Association. **Formerly:** National Ski Association of America; (1976) Midwest Collegiate Ski Association; (1998) National Collegiate Ski Association; (1999) United States Skiing; (2000) United States Ski Association. **Publications:** *Competitions and Rules Manual*, biennial ● *NCSA Carnival Brochure*, annual ● *Ski Racing*, periodic. Brochure ● Newsletter, bimonthly ● Directory, annual. **Conventions/Meetings:** annual meeting.

23208 ■ United States Ski Team Foundation (USSTF)
1500 Kearns Blvd.
PO Box 100
Park City, UT 84060
Ph: (435)649-9090
Free: (800)809-SNOW
Fax: (435)649-3613

E-mail: info@ussa.org
URL: http://www.usskiteam.com
Contact: Bill Marolt, Pres./CEO
Founded: 1960. **Staff:** 4. **Description:** Works to establish and promote educational programs devoted to the development and training of skiers as a means of healthful recreation and physical fitness. Seeks to stimulate U.S. interest in domestic and international skiing competition. Solicits contributions for, and disburses grants to, the United States Ski Team. Provides tuition assistance to current and former athletes pursuing degrees at institutions of higher education. **Publications:** *Donor Newsletter*, semiannual ● *Media Guide*, annual. **Conventions/Meetings:** semiannual Trustee Meeting.

23209 ■ World Masters Cross-Country Ski Association (WMCCSA)
c/o John Downing, Founder
PO Box 604
Bend, OR 97709
Ph: (541)317-0217
Fax: (541)317-0217
E-mail: jd@xcskiworld.com
URL: http://www.world-masters-xc-skiing.ch
Contact: John Downing, Founder
Founded: 1980. **Members:** 700. **Membership Dues:** regular, $35 (annual) ● shared household, $60 (annual). **Staff:** 1. **Budget:** $18,000. **National Groups:** 11. **Description:** National representatives working to promote masters cross-country skiing worldwide. Sponsors annual worldwide masters competitions for men and women 30 years of age or older. Conducts research and educational programs. Compiles statistics. **Libraries: Type:** reference. **Holdings:** archival material. **Additional Websites:** http://www.xcskiworld.com. **Publications:** *Worldmasters Cross Country Ski Association Newsletter*, 5/year. Covers cross-country skiing news for skiers over 30 years old. **Circulation:** 2,000. **Advertising:** accepted. **Conventions/Meetings:** annual meeting.

23210 ■ Worldloppet/American Birkebeiner (WL)
PO Box 911
Hayward, WI 54843
Ph: (715)634-5025
Free: (800)872-2753
E-mail: birkie@birkie.com
URL: http://www.birkie.com
Contact: Ned Zuelsdorff, Exec. Dir.
Founded: 1979. **Members:** 2,500. **Staff:** 4. **Budget:** $750,000. **Regional Groups:** 1. **State Groups:** 1. **Local Groups:** 1. **Multinational. Description:** Cross-country skiers who seek to complete a loppet, a series of 11 long-distance cross-country ski races held throughout Europe and North America. (The races total a distance of 632 kilometers and require 20,000 miles of air travel. There is no time limit for race completion.) Objectives are to: give skiers a chance to compete against similar skiers; provide international class racers with an alternative to standard international competitions, especially after retirement from national team racing. Crowns Worldloppet champion each year. **Formerly:** (1992) Worldloppet. **Publications:** *Worldloppet Brochure* (in English and German), annual. Directory. Lists European cross-country ski race sites. **Advertising:** accepted. **Conventions/Meetings:** annual meeting - always June.

Snow Sports

23211 ■ American Association of Snowboard Instructors (AASI)
133 S Van Gordon St., Ste.102
Lakewood, CO 80228
Ph: (303)987-2700
Free: (800)222-4754
Fax: (303)988-3005
E-mail: aasi@aasi.org
URL: http://www.aasi.org
Contact: Stephen M. Over, Exec. Dir.
Founded: 1997. **Description:** Promotes the sport of snowboarding through instruction. Supports snow

sport area management by providing a reliable source for training and certification. Develops certification standards and education materials for snowboard instructors. **Computer Services:** Online services, forum. **Affiliated With:** Professional Ski Instructors of America. **Publications:** *Accessories Catalog*. **Price:** for members ● *The Pro Rider*. Magazine. **Price:** for members.

23212 ■ American Council of Snowmobile Associations (ACSA)
271 Woodland Pass, Ste.216
East Lansing, MI 48823
Ph: (517)351-4362
Free: (888)594-7669
Fax: (517)351-1363
E-mail: info@snowmobilers.org
URL: http://www.snowmobilers.org
Contact: Christine Jourdain, Exec. Dir.
Founded: 1995. **Membership Dues:** individual, $10 (annual) ● family, $15 (annual) ● club, $25 (annual) ● business contributor/dealer, $100 (annual) ● business partner, $250 (annual). **Staff:** 1. **Budget:** $200,000. **Regional Groups:** 3. **State Groups:** 27. **Local Groups:** 2,200. **Description:** Offers charitable programs and a speakers' bureau. **Libraries: Type:** reference. **Holdings:** audiovisuals, books. **Subjects:** snowmobiling, environment. **Awards: Frequency:** annual. **Type:** scholarship. **Publications:** *27 Trails*, bimonthly. Newsletter. **Circulation:** 5,000. **Conventions/Meetings:** bimonthly regional meeting.

23213 ■ U.S. Bobsled and Skeleton Federation (USBSF)
196 Old Military Rd.
Lake Placid, NY 12946
Ph: (518)523-1842
Free: (800)BOB-SLED
Fax: (518)523-9491
E-mail: info@usbsf.com
URL: http://www.usbsf.com
Contact: Terry Kent, Exec. Dir.
Founded: 1931. **Members:** 600. **Membership Dues:** public sector, individual, $30 (annual) ● supporting, junior athlete (18 and younger), $25 (annual) ● athlete, $50 (annual) ● coach/official, $40 (annual) ● bobsled and skeleton club, affiliated sport organization, armed force, disable sport organization, $100 (annual). **Staff:** 10. **Budget:** $1,000,000. **Description:** Individuals and organizations with an interest in promoting the sports of bobsledding and skeleton (a form of tobogganing that uses the skeleton sled, which has a light frame and steel runners). Assembles amateur bobsled teams to represent the U.S. at the Winter Olympic Games and other international competitions. Conducts youth and developmental programs. **Awards:** Athlete of the Year. **Frequency:** annual. **Type:** recognition ● National Champion. **Frequency:** annual. **Type:** recognition. **Committees:** Competition; Fund Raising; Judiciary; Public Relations; Technical Marketing; Youth Education. **Affiliated With:** United States Olympic Committee. **Formerly:** (1968) National Bobsled Federation. **Publications:** *Bobserver*, annual. Newsletter. Features USBSF news, race highlights, and athlete information. **Price:** free. **Conventions/Meetings:** annual meeting - always in Lake Placid, NY or Park City, Utah.

Snowshoe Racing

23214 ■ United States Snowshoe Association (USSSA)
c/o Candice Bosworth, Exec. Dir.
678 County Rte. 25
Corinth, NY 12822
Ph: (518)654-7648 (518)643-8806
E-mail: usssa2@adelphia.net
URL: http://www.snowshoeracing.com
Contact: Candice Bosworth, Exec. Dir.
Founded: 1977. **Membership Dues:** individual, $15 (annual) ● club, $50 (annual). **Description:** Promotes the sport of snowshoeing for recreation and serves as the national governing body for amateur snowshoe

racing; encourages development of snowshoe technology. Sets standards for snowshoe racing; provides assistance to persons interested in setting up snowshoe chapters, organizing events, and marking trails. Compiles statistics. **Awards: Type:** recognition. **Publications:** *Snowshoe*, quarterly. Newsletter ● *USSSA Master Snowshoe Instructor Rating Handbook*, periodic ● *USSSA Senior Snowshoe Instructor Rating Handbook*, periodic. **Conventions/Meetings:** annual meeting - always third Saturday of October, in Corinth, NY ● annual National Amateur Snowshoe Racing Championship Competition.

Soap Box Derby

23215 ■ International Soap Box Derby (ISBD)
PO Box 7225
Akron, OH 44306
Ph: (330)733-8723
Fax: (330)733-1370
E-mail: soapbox@aasbd.org
URL: http://ndr.org/AASBD1.htm
Contact: Jeff Iula, Gen. Mgr.
Founded: 1933. **Members:** 10,000. **Staff:** 12. **Budget:** $1,000,000. **Regional Groups:** 13. **State Groups:** 43. **Local Groups:** 160. **National Groups:** 5. **Description:** Serves as a youth racing program sponsored by civic clubs, service organizations, business firms, interested groups, and individuals. Franchises Soap Box Derby programs throughout the U.S. and in several foreign countries. Sponsors hall of fame open during derby week. **Libraries: Type:** reference. **Holdings:** 40; photographs. **Subjects:** soap box derby. **Awards: Type:** scholarship. **Recipient:** to top three finishers of All-American Soap Box Derby. **Additional Websites:** http://www.aasbd. com. **Committees:** National Control Board. **Publications:** *Rule Book*, annual. Provides rules to the race. **Price:** $3.00. **Circulation:** 5,000. **Conventions/Meetings:** annual All-American Soap Box Derby - festival, week-long (exhibits) ● annual competition - always Akron, OH.

23216 ■ National Derby Rallies (NDR)
6644 Switzer Ln.
Shawnee, KS 66203
Ph: (913)962-6360
E-mail: info@ndr.org
URL: http://www.ndr.org
Contact: Terry Henry, Membership Coor./Treas.
Founded: 1977. **Members:** 800. **Membership Dues:** family with 1 child, $40 (annual) ● family with 2 children, $50 (annual) ● family with 3 children, $55 (annual). **Budget:** $100,000. **Description:** Families interested in gravity drag racing, a sport designed for young people ages seven through 21 that involves family-built racing vehicles propelled by gravity. Promotes derby sports and sanctions local soap box derby-type rally racing. Compiles statistics; maintains points standings, sanctions Regional and National Championships. **Libraries: Type:** open to the public. **Awards: Type:** recognition. **Recipient:** for achievement, workmanship, and conduct. **Computer Services:** Information services. **Committees:** Championship; Field Representatives; Rules. **Divisions:** Class I; Junior; Senior Lay-Down; Senior Lean-Forward; Stock. **Publications:** *Official NDR Race Director's Manual*. Manuals ● *Official NDR Rule Book*, biennial. **Price:** included in membership dues ● Newsletter, quarterly. **Advertising:** accepted ● Also publishes championship programs and rule books. **Conventions/Meetings:** board meeting - 4-6/year ● annual conference, corporate board meeting at the National Championships.

Soccer

23217 ■ America Scores
520 8th Ave., Ste.801
New York, NY 10018
Ph: (212)868-9510
Fax: (212)868-9533

E-mail: info@americascores.org
URL: http://www.americascores.org
Contact: Paul Caccamo, Pres./CEO
Description: Comprised of volunteers and soccer fans. Provides inner-city public schools educational fortification through soccer with challenge grants, technical assistance, creative writing, and publications.

23218 ■ American Amputee Soccer Association
1022 Creekside Dr.
Wilmington, DE 19804
Ph: (302)683-0997
E-mail: rgh@ampsoccer.org
URL: http://www.ampsoccer.org
Description: Promotes social interactivity, self-esteem and self-confidence among adult, new and youthful amputees, through recreational and competitive amputee soccer programs. Identifies, develops and trains athletes to represent the United States in international amputee soccer competitions and in Paralympic competitions when the sport achieves that status.

23219 ■ American Youth Soccer Organization (AYSO)
12501 S Isis Ave.
Hawthorne, CA 90250
Free: (800)872-2976
Fax: (310)643-5310
E-mail: suitup@ayso.org
URL: http://www.soccer.org
Contact: Peter MacPhail, Pres.
Founded: 1964. **Members:** 600,000. **Staff:** 50. **Budget:** $5,000,000. **Regional Groups:** 930. **Description:** Represents individuals dedicated to the development of children in America through youth soccer. Develops library. **Committees:** Communications; Education; Marketing; Meetings; National Development; Public Affairs; Volunteer Services. **Publications:** *The ABCs of AYSO - Parents' Handbook*, annual. **Advertising:** accepted ● *AYSO Shorts*, monthly. Newsletter ● *IN-PLAY*, quarterly. Newsletter ● *Play It Safe*, monthly. Newsletter ● *Soccer Now*, quarterly. Magazine. **Conventions/Meetings:** quarterly board meeting ● annual Business Conference (exhibits) ● Regional Training Conference.

23220 ■ Cosmopolitan Soccer League (CSL)
115 River Rd., Ste.1029
Edgewater, NJ 07020
Ph: (201)943-3390
Fax: (201)943-3394
E-mail: cslnysoccer@aol.com
URL: http://www.newyorksoccer.com
Contact: Peter Strumpf, Pres.
Founded: 1923. **Members:** 100. **Staff:** 1. **Description:** Soccer clubs comprising about 300 teams with 5,500 active members. Encourages participation and promotion of soccer among junior players. **Divisions:** Youth. **Affiliated With:** US Soccer. **Formerly:** German-American Football Association. **Conventions/Meetings:** annual meeting.

23221 ■ Eastern College Soccer Association (ECSA)
PO Box 3
Centerville, MA 02632
Ph: (508)771-5060
Fax: (508)771-9486
E-mail: pbuttafuoco@ecac.org
URL: http://www.ecac.org
Contact: Phil Buttafuoco, Commissioner
Founded: 1955. **Members:** 134. **Description:** Trains and assigns officials for college soccer games in the Northeast. **Affiliated With:** Eastern Collegiate Hockey Association. **Formerly:** (1966) Eastern Soccer Officials Bureau; (1967) Eastern College Soccer Officials Bureau. **Conventions/Meetings:** annual meeting ● annual workshop, clinic for officials.

23222 ■ International Gay and Lesbian Football Association (IGLFA)
c/o Brendan Patrick, Treas.
723 ML King Jr. Way
Seattle, WA 98122
E-mail: info@iglfa.org
URL: http://www.iglfa.org
Contact: Tomas Gomez, Pres.
Founded: 1990. **Members:** 2,000. **Membership Dues:** individual, $15 (annual) ● sustaining, $100 (annual). **Budget:** $6,000. **Languages:** English, German, Spanish. **Description:** International association of football (soccer) clubs of gay and lesbian football (soccer) players and friends. Seeks to "foster and augment the self-respect of gay men and lesbians throughout the world and engender respect and understanding from the non-gay world through the medium of football." Organizes Football (soccer) tournaments; assists in the formation of Football (soccer) clubs. **Publications:** *Kick! International* (in English, German, and Spanish), quarterly. Newsletter. **Circulation:** 1,000. **Advertising:** accepted. **Conventions/Meetings:** annual competition and board meeting ● annual House of Delegates Meeting - competition.

23223 ■ National Intercollegiate Soccer Officials Association (NISOA)
541 Woodview Dr.
Longwood, FL 32779-2614
Ph: (407)862-3305
Fax: (407)862-8545
E-mail: svale_dorsey@hotmail.com
URL: http://www.nisoa.com
Contact: Larry Dorsey, Chm.
Founded: 1964. **Members:** 5,000. **Membership Dues:** college soccer referee, $70 (annual) ● high school soccer referee, $15 (annual). **Staff:** 230. **Budget:** $200,000. **State Groups:** 50. **Local Groups:** 124. **Description:** Persons who officiate college soccer games; high school soccer referees. Operates referees' summer training camps. Conducts international cultural exchange program. Sponsors regional clinics; maintains speakers' bureau. Produces audiovisual instructional aids. **Libraries: Type:** reference. **Subjects:** soccer officiation. **Awards:** Distinguished Service Award. **Frequency:** annual. **Type:** recognition ● Hall of Fame Award. **Frequency:** annual. **Type:** recognition ● Honor Award. **Frequency:** annual. **Type:** recognition. **Affiliated With:** National Association of Intercollegiate Athletics; National Christian College Athletic Association; National Collegiate Athletic Association; National Junior College Athletic Association; National Soccer Coaches Association of America; US Soccer. **Publications:** *Alternate Official*, annual. Booklet. **Advertising:** accepted ● *Clinicians Handbook* ● *DSC Manual* ● *Linesmen's Brochure*. Details refereeing and linesmen duties. ● *National Assessment Handbook* ● *NISOA Manual* ● *Soccer Newsletter*, periodic ● Also publishes 130 teaching lesson plans. **Conventions/Meetings:** annual meeting (exhibits) - always July.

23224 ■ National Soccer Coaches Association of America (NSCAA)
6700 Squibb Rd., Ste.215
Mission, KS 66202-3252
Ph: (913)362-1747
Free: (800)458-0678
Fax: (913)362-3439
E-mail: info@nscaa.com
URL: http://www.nscaa.com
Contact: James Sheldon, Exec. Dir.
Founded: 1941. **Members:** 17,250. **Membership Dues:** youth, $50 (annual) ● regular, $70 (annual). **Staff:** 11. **Budget:** $3,000,000. **Regional Groups:** 8. **State Groups:** 50. **Description:** Soccer coaches and interested individuals. Sponsors clinics and diploma programs, provides educational information, awards programs, bi-monthly magazine, and insurance. **Awards:** All-America Award. **Frequency:** annual. **Type:** recognition. **Recipient:** for youth, high school and college players ● Bill Jeffrey Award. **Frequency:** annual. **Type:** recognition. **Recipient:** for long-term service to intercollegiate soccer ● Coach of the Year Award. **Frequency:** annual. **Type:** recognition ● Hall

of Fame. **Frequency:** annual. **Type:** recognition. **Recipient:** for excellence in soccer coaching ● Honor Award. **Frequency:** annual. **Type:** recognition. **Recipient:** for service/achievement/contribution within the association ● Robert W. Robinson Award. **Frequency:** annual. **Type:** recognition. **Recipient:** for long-term service to interscholastic soccer ● Scholar All-America. **Frequency:** annual. **Type:** recognition. **Recipient:** for top scholar-athletes in intercollegiate and interscholastic soccer ● Team Academic Award. **Frequency:** annual. **Type:** recognition. **Recipient:** for team academic excellence at the college and high school levels ● Youth Long-Term Service Award. **Frequency:** annual. **Type:** recognition. **Recipient:** for long-term contributions to youth soccer. **Computer Services:** Mailing lists, full and segmented. **Committees:** All-America Selection; Coach of the Year; Coaching Academy; Ethics; Foundation; Governor's Council; National Rankings; Youth. **Affiliated With:** National Collegiate Athletic Association; US Soccer. **Publications:** *Soccer Journal*, 7/year. Contains soccer coaching and news. **Price:** included in membership dues. ISSN: 0560-517X. **Circulation:** 17,000. **Advertising:** accepted ● *The Technical Area*, biweekly. Newsletter. Contains news updates on association business, promotional information for association partners and coaching tips. **Circulation:** 10,000. Alternate Formats: online. **Conventions/Meetings:** annual convention and lecture, for the association and other organizations (exhibits) - Mid-January. 2008 Jan. 16-20, Baltimore, MD - **Avg. Attendance:** 8500; 2009 Jan. 14-18, St. Louis, MO - **Avg. Attendance:** 9000; 2010 Jan. 13-17, Philadelphia, PA - **Avg. Attendance:** 9500; 2011 Jan. 12-16, Baltimore, MD - **Avg. Attendance:** 9500.

23225 ■ North American Chinese Soccer League (NACSL)
1 Cronssan Ct.
Landenberg, PA 19350
Ph: (302)831-0625
E-mail: szhang@udel.edu
URL: http://www.nacsl.com
Contact: Shangyou Scott Zhang, Acting Pres.
Founded: 1996. **Multinational. Description:** Promotes the soccer program among Chinese students and alumni. Improves the level of play of the competitive soccer players. Organizes a national grand tournament and endorses several regional soccer tournaments each year.

23226 ■ Soccer Association for Youth (SAY)
1 N Commerce Park Dr., Ste.306-320
Cincinnati, OH 45215
Ph: (513)769-3800
Free: (800)233-7291
Fax: (513)769-0500
E-mail: sayusa@saysoccer.org
URL: http://www.saysoccer.org
Contact: Sheila A. Shay, Natl. Exec. Dir.
Founded: 1967. **Members:** 120,000. **Staff:** 5. **Budget:** $900,000. **Regional Groups:** 8. **State Groups:** 85. **Local Groups:** 300. **Description:** Children ages 4 through 18 who are interested in soccer. Supported by a network of coaches, administrators, and sponsors. Seeks to assure maximum participation with even competition at various age levels and to offer equal opportunity regardless of ability or sex. Forms leagues and schedules games; sanctions annual state, area, and local tournaments. Prescribes rules and regulations. Operates coaching and referee training clinics. Distributes supplies and support necessary to form and register teams and leagues; provides discounts on merchandise; and promotes corporate and foundation support. Compiles statistics. **Awards: Type:** recognition. **Committees:** Development; Education and Training; Operations; Rules and Referee. **Also Known As:** SAY Soccer U.S.A. **Publications:** *Center Circle Newsletter*, quarterly. Contains information for soccer club leaders and administrators. **Price:** included in membership dues. **Circulation:** 1,500. **Advertising:** accepted ● *Refereeing Youth Soccer*. Manual ● *Rulebook*, annual. **Price:** $1.50 plus shipping and handling ● *Touchline*, semiannual. Newsletter. **Price:** free. **Circulation:**

200,000. **Advertising:** accepted ● Brochures. **Conventions/Meetings:** annual meeting (exhibits).

23227 ■ United States Indoor Soccer Association (USIndoor)
PO Box 6569
Arlington, VA 22206
Fax: (509)357-7096
E-mail: info@usindoor.com
URL: http://www.usindoor.com
Contact: Donald L. Shapero, Pres./Founder
Founded: 1998. **Membership Dues:** regular, $105 (annual) ● corporate, $650 (annual). **Description:** Promotes the sport of indoor soccer. Serves and protects the interests of its members. Offers a wide range of products and services that support the growing infrastructure of the sport. **Publications:** *Facility Newsletter*, periodic. **Price:** included in membership dues. Alternate Formats: online ● *Goal Indoor*, quarterly. Magazine. **Price:** included in membership dues; $15.00 /year for nonmembers. **Advertising:** accepted ● *Referee Newsletter*, periodic. **Price:** included in membership dues. Alternate Formats: online.

23228 ■ United States Youth Soccer Association
9220 World Cup Way
Frisco, TX 75034
Ph: (972)334-9300
Fax: (972)334-9960
E-mail: troby@usyouthsoccer.org
URL: http://www.usyouthsoccer.org
Contact: Jim Cosgrove, Exec. Dir.
Founded: 1974. **Members:** 3,100,000. **Staff:** 18. **Budget:** $9,000,000. **Regional Groups:** 4. **State Groups:** 55. **Description:** The youth division of United States Soccer Federation (see separate entry). Soccer players between the ages of five and 19. Seeks to develop and promote the game of soccer for young people. Conducts annual workshop on coaching, refereeing, administration, and general league improvement. Stages national championship for boys and girls teams ages 15-18. Provides program for the selection and training of players to represent the U.S. on the national Olympic and youth soccer teams. Compiles statistics. **Awards:** Soccer Start. **Type:** grant. **Recipient:** for ongoing program ● TOP Soccer. **Type:** grant. **Recipient:** for ongoing program. **Computer Services:** database, coaches, state association officers, and local associations. **Committees:** Budget; Bylaws and Policies; Coaching; Database Marketing; Mediation and Disputes Resolution; National Championship; National ODP Championships; Olympic Development; Recreation; Referee; Registrars; Risk Management; Soccer Start; TOP Soccer. **Publications:** *U.S. Youth Soccer Association—National Directory*, annual. Lists national officers, committee persons, and state association officers. **Price:** included in membership dues. **Circulation:** 100 ● *USYSA Newspaper*, quarterly. Includes coaching tips and other information of interest to coaches, schools, referees, and administrators; includes calendar of events. **Price:** free, for members only. **Circulation:** 125,000. **Advertising:** accepted ● Pamphlets ● Videos. **Conventions/Meetings:** annual Coaches Convention - convention and workshop (exhibits) ● annual general assembly (exhibits) - late summer.

23229 ■ US Club Soccer (USCS)
716 8th Ave. N
Myrtle Beach, SC 29577
Ph: (843)429-0006
E-mail: admin@usclubsoccer.org
URL: http://www.usclubsoccer.org
Contact: William Sage, Exec. Dir./CEO
Founded: 2000. **Members:** 1,200. **Membership Dues:** competitive player (U12 and above), $14 (annual) ● competitive player (below U12), $10 (annual) ● recreational player/staff, $8 (annual). **Description:** Represents the interests of individuals committed to the development of competitive soccer clubs. Fosters the growth and development of club soccer programs throughout the United States. Improves the level of play of the competitive soccer players. **Telecom-**

munication Services: electronic mail, bsage@us-clubsoccer.org.

23230 ■ US Soccer (USSF)
1801-1811 S Prairie Ave.
Chicago, IL 60616
Ph: (312)808-1300
Fax: (312)808-1301
E-mail: dflynn@ussoccer.org
URL: http://www.ussoccer.com
Contact: Dan Flynn, CEO/Sec. Gen.
Founded: 1913. **Staff:** 44. **Budget:** $29,000,000.
Regional Groups: 8. **State Groups:** 108. **Description:** State soccer associations representing 3 million members. Promotes soccer with clubs, leagues, schools, and associations. Provides standard rules of play, sanctions tournaments, and assigns officials. Maintains hall of fame and museum. Compiles statistics. **Libraries: Type:** reference. **Holdings:** films, video recordings. **Awards:** U.S. Open Cup. **Frequency:** annual. **Type:** recognition. **Committees:** Appeals; Coaching; Competitions; Credentials; International Games; Marketing; National Soccer Hall of Fame; Referees; Rules. **Affiliated With:** American Youth Soccer Organization; Armed Forces Sports; National Federation of State High School Associations; National Soccer Coaches Association of America; Soccer Association for Youth; Soccer Industry Council of America; Special Olympics. **Formerly:** (1974) United States Soccer Football Association. **Publications:** *Federation News*, quarterly. Newsletter ● *FIFA Laws of the Game/Guide for Referees*, annual ● *U.S. Referee*, quarterly. Available to referee members only. ● *USSF Official Administrative Rulebook*, annual. **Conventions/Meetings:** annual meeting (exhibits).

Softball

23231 ■ Amateur Softball Association of America (ASA)
c/o Virgil Ackerson, Commissioner
605 Rivera
Tonkawa, OK 74653
Ph: (580)628-2475
Fax: (580)628-3211
E-mail: okcommissioner@hotmail.com
URL: http://www.softball.org
Contact: Virgil Ackerson, Commissioner
Founded: 1933. **Staff:** 30. **Budget:** $6,000,000. **Regional Groups:** 15. **State Groups:** 50. **Local Groups:** 49. **Description:** National Governing body for amateur softball in the U.S; regulates 56,000 umpires and more than 260,000 teams. Programs include National Softball Hall of Fame, a Junior Olympic youth softball and clinics and coaching schools. Operates museum and research center. Maintains over 40 rules, awards, eligibility, and administrative committees. **Libraries: Type:** reference. **Awards:** All-American. **Frequency:** annual. **Type:** recognition. **Recipient:** for national tournament performance ● Bertha Tickey Award. **Frequency:** annual. **Type:** recognition. **Recipient:** for best pitcher at women's major nationals. **Telecommunication Services:** electronic mail, bplummer@softball.org. **Committees:** Championship Awards; Coed Softball; Eligibility; Finance; Foreign Relations; Legislative; Modified Rules; Playing Rules; Procedural Codes; Publications and Promotions; Tournament Organizing; Umpire. **Affiliated With:** National Association of Intercollegiate Athletics; National Collegiate Athletic Association; National Federation of State High School Associations; National Intramural-Recreational Sports Association; National Junior College Athletic Association; Special Olympics. **Formerly:** USA Softball; US National and Olympic Teams. **Publications:** *Balls and Strikes Softball Magazine*, biennial. **Circulation:** 275,000. **Advertising:** accepted ● *Inside Pitch*, monthly. Newsletter ● *Merchandise Catalog*, annual ● *Official Rulebook*, annual ● *Umpire Clinic Guide* Directory, annual. **Conventions/Meetings:** annual competition and meeting (exhibits) - held in November ● annual meeting (exhibits).

23232 ■ Cinderella Softball Leagues (CSL)
PO Box 1411
Corning, NY 14830
Ph: (607)937-5469
E-mail: croftjb@hotmail.com
URL: http://corningcinderella.com/index.html
Contact: Dana Gridley, Pres.
Founded: 1958. **Members:** 6,000. **Budget:** $25,000. **Local Groups:** 15. **Description:** Female softball players 19 years old and younger. Seeks to promote the game of softball among girls and to develop girls' softball leagues nationally and internationally. Develops and recommends guidelines for individual leagues. Serves as a regulatory and sponsoring body for the annual Cinderella World Series. Bestows Cinderella Queen Award. Operates five league divisions: T-Ball (8 and under); Preparatory (ages 12 and under); Cinderella (ages 16 and under); Princess (age 19 under). Conducts fundraising activities. Compiles record book of world series games. Plans to establish a hall of fame. **Committees:** Enhancement. **Publications:** *Cinderella Softball Official Program*, annual. Yearbook ● *Official Rule Book*, annual ● Newsletter, annual. **Conventions/Meetings:** conference - 2-3/year.

23233 ■ International Senior Softball Association (ISSA)
9401 East St.
Manassas, VA 20110
Ph: (703)368-1188
Fax: (703)368-3411
E-mail: issa@seniorsoftball.org
URL: http://www.seniorsoftball.org
Contact: R.B. Thomas Jr., Exec. Dir.
Multinational. Description: Promotes and encourages physical fitness and public participation in senior athletic activities. Aims to promote world-class competitions for senior softball. Fosters productive working relationships among other senior softball organizations through coordination and development of amateur senior softball activities. **Publications:** Newsletter. Alternate Formats: online.

23234 ■ International Softball Federation (ISF)
1900 S Park Rd.
Plant City, FL 33563-8113
Ph: (813)864-0100
Fax: (813)864-0105
E-mail: isf@internationalsoftball.com
URL: http://www.internationalsoftball.com
Contact: Don Porter, Pres.
Founded: 1952. **Members:** 124. **Staff:** 8. **Budget:** $1,000,000. **Languages:** English, Spanish. **Multinational. Description:** National softball associations. Encourages the development of softball worldwide and fosters Olympic recognition of the sport. Promotes international competition. **Committees:** Technical Standards; World Championships. **Affiliated With:** Association of Summer Olympic International Federations; General Association of International Sports Federations; International Olympic Committee. **Publications:** *Official Guide and Playing Rules* (in English and Spanish), biennial. Book. **Price:** $6.00. **Advertising:** accepted ● *World Softball*, 3/year. Magazine. **Price:** $7.50/issue ● Newsletter, quarterly. **Conventions/Meetings:** biennial ISF Congress - meeting.

23235 ■ National Softball Association (NSA)
PO Box 7
Nicholasville, KY 40340
Ph: (859)887-4114
Fax: (859)887-4874
E-mail: nsahdqtrs@aol.com
URL: http://www.playnsa.com
Contact: Hugh Cantrell, Pres./CEO
Founded: 1982. **Members:** 375,000. **Membership Dues:** team, individual, $20 (annual). **Staff:** 12. **Regional Groups:** 12. **State Groups:** 50. **Local Groups:** 200. **National Groups:** 12. **Description:** Promotes participation in and enjoyment of amateur softball. Maintains hall of fame. **Awards: Type:** recognition. **Publications:** *Between the Lines*, bimonthly. Magazine. **Price:** $2.00/copy. **Circulation:**

25,000. **Advertising:** accepted. **Conventions/Meetings:** annual convention (exhibits) - usually 2nd week of November, in Lexington, KY on even years.

23236 ■ North American Fastpitch Association (NAFA)
PO Box 566
Dayton, OR 97114
Ph: (503)864-4487
Fax: (503)864-3939
E-mail: nafafastpitch@aol.com
URL: http://www.nafafastpitch.com
Contact: Benjie Hedgecock, Exec. Dir.
Founded: 1993. **Membership Dues:** life, $200. **Multinational. Description:** Promotes men's fastpitch softball. **Computer Services:** Mailing lists. **Publications:** Newsletter.

23237 ■ United States Specialty Sports Association (USSSA)
c/o Don DeDonatis, Exec. Dir./CEO
611 Line Dr.
Kissimmee, FL 34744
Ph: (321)697-3641
Free: (800)741-3014
Fax: (321)697-3647
E-mail: usssadd@aol.com
URL: http://www.usssa.com
Contact: Don DeDonatis, Exec. Dir./CEO
Founded: 1968. **Members:** 3,200,000. **Staff:** 10. **State Groups:** 50. **Description:** Promotes and officiates amateur slo-pitch softball, fastpitch softball, basketball, baseball, volleyball, golf, T-ball, flag football, taekwondo, karate, gymnastics, and soccer all at a national level. Divides participants into categories including men's, women's, church, corporate, mixed, youth, masters, Black American, Hispanic, Native American, and armed forces. These categories allow for wide and varied participation. Many of the sports have national championships for varied levels of skill and expertise. **Libraries: Type:** by appointment only; open to the public; reference. **Holdings:** 4,251; archival material, artwork, periodicals, photographs, reports, video recordings. **Subjects:** history of the association. **Awards:** Best Female Player. **Frequency:** annual. **Type:** trophy ● Best Male Player. **Frequency:** annual. **Type:** trophy ● Best Official. **Frequency:** annual. **Type:** trophy ● CEO Award. **Frequency:** annual. **Type:** recognition. **Recipient:** to members who have made a notable contribution to the association ● Executive of the Year. **Frequency:** annual. **Type:** recognition ● USSSA Scholarship. **Frequency:** annual. **Type:** scholarship. **Computer Services:** Online services, player statistics, tournaments, and insurance information. **Divisions:** Hoop It Up; Let It Fly; T-Ball USA; US Soccer. **Formerly:** (1998) United States of America Slo-Pitch Softball Association. **Publications:** *Directors Mailing List*, annual ● *Official Rule Book*, annual ● *Umpires Case Book*, annual ● *USSSA World Series Almanac*, annual. Annual Report. **Conventions/Meetings:** annual convention, includes a congress (exhibits).

Sports

23238 ■ Access Fund (AF)
PO Box 17010
Boulder, CO 80308
Ph: (303)545-6772
Free: (888)863-6237
Fax: (303)545-6774
E-mail: steve@accessfund.org
URL: http://www.accessfund.org
Contact: Steve Matous, Exec. Dir.
Founded: 1990. **Members:** 15,000. **Membership Dues:** individual, retail, corporate, $35 (annual) ● student, $25 (annual). **Staff:** 10. **Budget:** $1,000,000. **Regional Groups:** 75. **Description:** Dedicated to supporting climber's interests while preserving diverse climbing resources. Works with local climbers and land managers to develop climbing management policies; educates climbers of the environmental impacts of climbing; promotes environmental aware-

ness of climbing areas and sound climbing practices on public and private lands; fosters the development of local climbing groups; purchases threatened lands; supports scientific research. **Awards:** Climbing Preservation Grants. **Frequency:** semiannual. **Type:** grant. **Recipient:** board approval. **Boards:** Directors; Regional Coordinators. **Publications:** *Vertical Times*, bimonthly. Newsletter. Contains current news, area reports, and upcoming events. **Price:** included in membership dues. **Circulation:** 11,000. Alternate Formats: online. Also Cited As: *Access Notes* ● *Virtual Times E-news*, monthly. Newsletter. Provides information regarding climbing access issues. Alternate Formats: online. **Conventions/Meetings:** semiannual Climbers Rendezvous - board meeting and trade show, slide show, auction (exhibits).

23239 ■ Amateur Athletic Union (AAU)

PO Box 22409
Lake Buena Vista, FL 32830-1000
Ph: (407)934-7200
Free: (800)AAU-4USA
Fax: (407)934-7242
E-mail: bdodd@aausports.org
URL: http://www.aausports.org
Contact: Bobby Dodd, Pres./CEO

Founded: 1888. **Members:** 500,000. **Membership Dues:** athlete (youth), $12-$14 (annual) ● non-athlete (youth and adult), $14-$16 (annual) ● athlete (adult), $12-$37 (annual). **Staff:** 40. **Budget:** $5,000,000. **State Groups:** 58. **Local Groups:** 58. **Description:** Seeks to establish, develop, and implement a comprehensive youth sports program for athletes ages three to nineteen. Offers activities in 34 sports and conducts local, association (by state divisions), regional, and national championships. Conducts charitable and specialized education programs. **Libraries: Type:** not open to the public. **Holdings:** 50,000. **Subjects:** sports. **Awards:** AAU James E. Sullivan Memorial Award. **Frequency:** annual. **Type:** recognition. **Recipient:** for athletic achievement and community involvement. **Divisions:** Aerobics; Baseball; Basketball; Chinese Martial Arts; Cross Country; Field Hockey; Golf; Gymnastics; In-Line Hockey; Judo; Jujitsu; Karate; Soccer; Swimming; Table Tennis; Tae Kwon Do; Tennis; Track and Field; Trampoline and Tumbling; Volleyball; Weightlifting; Wrestling. **Programs:** AAU Junior Olympic Games; AAU Sports; Complete Athlete; Physical Fitness; Presidential Sports; President's Challenge Youth Fitness Award. **Affiliated With:** United States Olympic Committee. **Formerly:** AAU/U.S.A. Junior Olympics; AAU Youth Sports Program. **Conventions/Meetings:** annual congress and convention, with booths relating to sports (exhibits).

23240 ■ Amateur Baseball Umpires' Association (ABUA)

810 Baltimore Ave., Ste.100
Kansas City, MO 64105
Ph: (816)474-8677
Fax: (816)474-7329
E-mail: ted@umpire.org
URL: http://www.umpire.org

Membership Dues: individual, $40 (annual). **Description:** Seeks to improve the overall quality of umpiring in the youth, high school and college leagues. Provides members with insurance packages. **Computer Services:** Information services, insurance questions ● online services, ABUA survey ● online services, forum.

23241 ■ American Amputee Hockey Association (AAHA)

150 York St.
Stoughton, MA 02072
Ph: (781)297-1393
Fax: (781)341-8715
E-mail: dcrandell@amputeehockey.org
URL: http://www.usahockey.com/aaha
Contact: David Crandell MD, Pres.

Founded: 2000. **Description:** Seeks to develop opportunities for amputees and other disabled athletes to learn and play competitive hockey. Aims to make Standing Amputee Hockey a Winter Paralympic sport. **Programs:** Youth.

23242 ■ American Lumberjack Association (ALA)

c/o Andrea Furber, Treas.
213 Somerville Rd.
Santa Rosa, CA 95409
E-mail: furbergirl@hotmail.com
URL: http://www.americanlumberjacks.com
Contact: Andrea Furber, Treas.

Members: 250. **Description:** Works to further, upgrade, and standardize lumberjack sports. **Publications:** Newsletter. **Conventions/Meetings:** competition ● semiannual meeting.

23243 ■ American Ski-Bike Association (ASA)

PO Box 40
Lake George, CO 80827
E-mail: postman@ski-bike.org
URL: http://www.ski-bike.org
Contact: Rod Ratzlaff, Dir.

Membership Dues: individual, $15 (annual) ● family, $20 (annual). **Description:** Promotes participation in the sport of Ski-Biking. Seeks to open up new riding areas and bring new people into the sport. **Computer Services:** database, ski areas ● information services, ski-biking resources ● online services, discussion group.

23244 ■ American Turners (AT)

1127 E Kentucky St.
PO Box 4216
Louisville, KY 40204
Ph: (502)636-2395
Fax: (502)636-1935
E-mail: natlturner@aol.com
URL: http://www.americanturners.com
Contact: Shirley Luckhardt, Sec.

Founded: 1848. **Members:** 13,500. **Staff:** 1. **State Groups:** 58. **Local Groups:** 14. **Description:** Promotes health and physical education for the family through gymnastics, swimming, games, bowling, and cultural education through classes in music, painting, and handicrafts. Holds annual national tournaments in gymnastics, volleyball, basketball, softball, swimming, bowling, and cultural activities. **Computer Services:** database ● mailing lists. **Committees:** Bowling; Cultural Education; Health and Physical Education; Legal. **Formerly:** American Gymnastic Union; American Turnerbund. **Publications:** *American Turner Topics*, 5/year. Newsletter. **Price:** $2.25/year. ISSN: 0746-3480. **Advertising:** accepted. **Conventions/Meetings:** semiannual convention ● quadrennial festival ● annual National Council Meeting.

23245 ■ American Volkssport Association (AVA)

1001 Pat Booker Rd., Ste.101
Universal City, TX 78148
Ph: (210)659-2112
Free: (800)830-WALK
Fax: (210)659-1212
E-mail: avahq@ava.org
URL: http://www.ava.org
Contact: Ms. Jacklyn Wilson, Exec. Dir.

Founded: 1976. **Members:** 3,500. **Membership Dues:** individual, $25 (annual) ● family, $30 (annual) ● life, $250-$500 ● spouse, $100 (annual). **Staff:** 7. **Budget:** $500,000. **Regional Groups:** 10. **State Groups:** 17. **National Groups:** 375. **Description:** Organizations that wish to sponsor volkssport events or promote the goals of the national/international volkssport program; volkssports are noncompetitive organized sports activities including bicycling, cross-country skiing, swimming, and walking. Promotes public health, recreation, and fellowship through volkssport events. Compiles statistics. Maintains museum and hall of fame. **Libraries: Type:** reference. **Holdings:** books, clippings, periodicals. **Subjects:** walking, recreation programs. **Awards:** IVV Achievement Awards. **Type:** recognition. **Committees:** Audit; Awards Recognition; Bylaws; Internet and Technology; Marketing; Outyears Convention; Publicity; Standards and Evaluation. **Formerly:** (1979) International People's Sports - U.S.A. **Publications:** *The American Wanderer*, bimonthly. Newspa-

per. Includes award news, calendar of events, and list of chartered members. **Price:** $25.00 /year for individuals; $30.00/year for families. **Circulation:** 5,000. **Advertising:** accepted ● *AVA Checkpoint*, monthly. Newsletter. **Circulation:** 700. Alternate Formats: online ● *Event Handbook*. Alternate Formats: online ● *Policy Manual*. Alternate Formats: online ● *Spirit or Walking*. Brochure ● *Starting Point: The Year-Round Walking Event Book*. **Price:** $15.00 ● Report, biennial. Alternate Formats: online ● Articles. Alternate Formats: online. **Conventions/Meetings:** biennial convention (exhibits).

23246 ■ Association of Recognized IOC International Sports Federations (ARISF)

1631 Mesa Ave., Ste.A
Colorado Springs, CO 80906
Ph: (719)636-2695
Fax: (719)636-3300
E-mail: jan.fransoo@ikf.org
URL: http://www.arisf.org
Contact: Dr. Jan C. Fransoo, Pres.

Founded: 1984. **Members:** 29. **Languages:** Dutch, English, French, Italian, Spanish. **Multinational. Description:** International sports organizations recognized by the International Olympic Committee (IOC). Serves as a forum for the discussion of issues of mutual interest to members; sponsors competitions. **Conventions/Meetings:** annual general assembly.

23247 ■ Athletic Equipment Managers Association (AEMA)

c/o Dorothy Cutting, Office Mgr.
460 Hunt Hill Rd.
Freeville, NY 13068
Ph: (607)539-6300
Fax: (607)539-6340
E-mail: dec13@cornell.edu
URL: http://www.aema1.com
Contact: Dorothy Cutting, Office Mgr.

Founded: 1974. **Members:** 883. **Membership Dues:** active/associate, $75 (annual) ● student, $25 (annual). **Staff:** 1. **Regional Groups:** 10. **For-Profit. Description:** Athletic equipment managers and others who handle sports equipment for junior high and high schools, colleges, recreation centers, and professional sports; individuals involved in athletic management and coaching or the handling or purchasing of athletic, physical education, or recreational equipment. Aims to improve the profession of equipment management and promote a better working relationship among those interested in problems of management. Works collectively to facilitate equipment improvement for greater safety among participants in all sports. Conducts workshops and clinics. Maintains job placement service. **Libraries: Type:** not open to the public. **Holdings:** 400; articles, books, periodicals. **Subjects:** equipment management. **Awards:** College Scholarship. **Type:** scholarship. **Recipient:** to full-time college students with one year collegiate athletic equipment management experience ● Glenn Sharp Award. **Frequency:** annual. **Type:** monetary. **Recipient:** for outstanding member contribution. **Computer Services:** Mailing lists, of members. **Committees:** Certification; Ethics; Exhibits. **Publications:** *Certification Manual*. Contains research articles on topics identified by the role delineation. ● *The Scoreboard*, 3/year. Newsletter. Alternate Formats: online ● Journal. Contains articles from each area of the role delineation. ● Videos. **Price:** $15.00 plus shipping and handling. **Conventions/Meetings:** annual convention and meeting (exhibits) - usually June.

23248 ■ Atlantic Coast Conference (ACC)

PO Drawer ACC
Greensboro, NC 27417-6724
Ph: (336)854-8787
URL: http://theacc.collegesports.com
Contact: John D. Swofford, Commissioner

Founded: 1953. **Members:** 12. **Staff:** 25. **Description:** Clemson University; Duke University; Florida State University; Georgia Institute of Technology; North Carolina State University; University of Maryland; University of North Carolina; University of Virginia; Wake Forest University. Develops athletic competition in both men's and women's sports including baseball, basketball, cross-country, field hockey, football, golf, lacrosse, soccer, swimming, tennis, track and field, volleyball, rowing, softball, and wrestling. Sponsors Drug Education Outreach Program. Compiles statistics; conducts research programs. **Libraries: Type:** reference. **Awards:** All-Conference Award. **Type:** recognition ● Player of the Year Award. **Frequency:** annual. **Type:** recognition ● Rookie of the Year Award. **Frequency:** annual. **Type:** recognition. **Committees:** Student-Athlete Advisory. **Affiliated With:** National Collegiate Athletic Association. **Publications:** *Baseball Media Guides*, annual. **Price:** $10.00. **Circulation:** 2,000 ● *Basketball Media Guides*, annual. **Price:** $15.00. **Circulation:** 2,000 ● *Conference By-Laws* ● *Football Media Guides*, annual. **Price:** $15.00. **Circulation:** 2,000 ● *Non-Revenue Record Book* ● *Press Guides*, annual ● *theacc.com*, weekly. Newsletter. **Price:** free. Alternate Formats: online. **Conventions/Meetings:** annual conference.

23249 ■ Big East Conference (BEC)
222 Richmond St., Ste.110
Providence, RI 02903
Ph: (401)272-9108
URL: http://www.bigeast.org
Contact: Michael A. Tranghese, Commissioner
Founded: 1979. **Members:** 14. **Staff:** 20. **Description:** Boston College; Georgetown University; Notre Dame; Providence College; Rutgers; St. John's University; Seton Hall University; Syracuse University; University of Connecticut; University of Miami; University of Pittsburgh; Villanova University; West Virginia, Virginia Tech; represents the athletic interests of members in 19 sports including basketball, soccer, baseball, softball, field hockey, tennis, volleyball, cross-country, golf, track, and swimming. **Libraries: Type:** reference. **Holdings:** archival material. **Awards:** Big East Scholarship. **Frequency:** annual. **Type:** scholarship. **Recipient:** to student athletes. **Affiliated With:** National Collegiate Athletic Association. **Publications:** *Media Guide*, annual. **Price:** $18.00 ● *Record Book*. **Price:** $8.00. **Conventions/Meetings:** annual meeting.

23250 ■ Big Ten Conference (BTC)
1500 W Higgins Rd.
Park Ridge, IL 60068-6300
Ph: (847)696-1010
Fax: (847)696-1150
URL: http://bigten.cstv.com
Contact: James E. Delany, Commissioner
Founded: 1896. **Members:** 11. **Staff:** 25. **Description:** Represents ten state universities and one private university in the midwestern U.S; administered by university presidents and chancellors who are not employed in the university's athletic program. Regulates and controls conduct of intercollegiate athletics on conference-wide basis; promotes amateur athletics. Sponsors competitions and championships in 24 sports. Maintains Big Ten Communications Department. Compiles statistics; conducts research and educational programs. **Libraries: Type:** reference. **Awards: Type:** recognition. **Publications:** *bigten. com*, weekly. Newsletter. **Price:** free. Alternate Formats: online ● *Conference Record Book*. Alternate Formats: online ● *Football Media Guide* ● *Handbook of Rules and Regulations* ● *Men's Basketball Media Guide* ● *Volleyball Media Guide* ● *Women's Basketball Media Guide*.

23251 ■ Big West Conference (BWC)
2 Corporate Park
Irvine, CA 92606
Ph: (949)261-2525
Fax: (949)261-2528
E-mail: info@bigwest.org
URL: http://www.bigwest.org
Contact: Dennis Farrell, Commissioner
Founded: 1969. **Members:** 10. **Staff:** 8. **Description:** UC Riverside University of Idaho, Cal Poly University, California State University-Northridge, California State University-Fullerton, Long Beach State University; University of California-Irvine, University of California-Santa Barbara, University of

the Pacific, Utah State University. Develops athletic competition in men's and women's sports including basketball, cross-country, volleyball, soccer, softball, swimming, golf, tennis, baseball, and track.

23252 ■ Bowling Inc.
5301 S 76th St.
Greendale, WI 53129
Ph: (414)421-0900
Free: (800)514-2695
Fax: (414)421-3013
E-mail: webmaster@bowl.com
URL: http://www.bowl.com
Contact: David Patrick, Pres./CEO
Founded: 1995. **Staff:** 200. **Description:** A joint project of the American Bowling Congress, the Women's International Bowling Congress, and the Bowling Proprietors Association of America. Promotes increased interest in the sport of bowling, seeks to increase the profitability of bowling alleys and related establishments. Develops and delivers results-oriented marketing and management services for the bowling industry; serves as a clearinghouse on bowling and related industries. Operates Strike Ten Entertainment, which provides marketing services to the bowling industries. Through its shared services division, performs day-to-day business operations of funding companies and others in the bowling industry. **Telecommunication Services:** electronic mail, bowlinfo@bowl.com.

23253 ■ Central Intercollegiate Athletic Association (CIAA)
303 Butler Farm Rd., Ste.102
PO Box 7349
Hampton, VA 23666
Ph: (757)865-0071
Fax: (757)865-8436
E-mail: theciaa@aol.com
URL: http://www.theciaa.com
Contact: Leon G. Kerry, Commissioner/CEO
Founded: 1912. **Members:** 12. **Description:** Colleges and universities holding regional accreditation and membership in the National Collegiate Athletic Association (see separate entry). Promotes the physical welfare of students, fosters athletic games, and recommends regulations to promote clean sports and maintain scholarship. **Telecommunication Services:** electronic mail, leonkerry@aol.com. **Affiliated With:** National Collegiate Athletic Association. **Formerly:** (1949) Colored Intercollegiate Athletic Association. **Publications:** *Central Intercollegiate Athletic Association—Bulletin*, annual ● *The Double A*, semiannual. Newsletter. Includes conference information. **Circulation:** 3,500. **Advertising:** accepted. **Conventions/Meetings:** annual conference.

23254 ■ Citizenship Through Sports Alliance (CTSA)
c/o Ted Breidenthal
810 Baltimore, Ste.100
Kansas City, MO 64105
Ph: (816)474-7264
Fax: (816)474-7329
E-mail: tbreidenthal@sportsmanship.org
URL: http://www.sportsmanship.org
Contact: Ted Breidenthal, Contact
Founded: 1997. **Description:** Promotes fair play from youth leagues to professional sport to reinforce the value of sport as a test of character. Raises awareness of the issue of citizenship in sports. Offers research, resources, community forums and specific strategies that help parents and coaches create a healthy sports environment. **Awards:** Citizenship Through Sports Award. **Frequency:** annual. **Type:** recognition. **Recipient:** for outstanding citizenship, sportsmanship, ethical conduct and community service. **Boards:** Corporate Advisory.

23255 ■ College Athletic Business Management Association (CABMA)
c/o Pat Manak, Asst. Sec.
PO Box 16428
Cleveland, OH 44116
Ph: (440)892-4000
Fax: (440)892-4007

E-mail: pmanak@nacda.com
URL: http://nacda.ocsn.com/cabma/nacda-cabma. html
Contact: Pat Manak, Asst. Sec.
Founded: 1951. **Members:** 500. **Membership Dues:** regular, associate, $100 (annual) ● institutional, $300 (annual). **Description:** Represents collegiate directors of athletics and their assistants; fundraisers for, and ticket, facilities, system managers and business managers of, college and university athletic programs. **Awards:** Manager of the Year. **Frequency:** annual. **Type:** recognition. **Recipient:** to members who have excelled in the execution of their duties. **Formerly:** (1988) College Athletic Business Managers Association. **Conventions/Meetings:** annual convention, in conjunction with National Collegiate Athletic Association (exhibits).

23256 ■ College Sports Information Directors of America (CoSIDA)
c/o Jeff Hodges, Sec.
Univ. of North Alabama
PO Box 5038
Florence, AL 35632
Ph: (256)765-4595
Fax: (256)765-4659
E-mail: sportsinformation@una.edu
URL: http://www.cosida.com
Contact: Jeff Hodges, Sec.
Founded: 1957. **Members:** 1,960. **Membership Dues:** student, $25 (annual) ● active, $50 (annual) ● associate, $55 (annual). **Budget:** $100,000. **Description:** Individuals employed in college and university sports information departments, public relations departments, and news bureaus. Aims "to exchange ideas among members of the sports information profession, and to help increase influence among athletic directors". **Awards:** Arch Ward Memorial Award. **Frequency:** annual. **Type:** recognition. **Recipient:** for contributions to the sports information profession ● Bob Kenworthy Community Service Award. **Frequency:** annual. **Type:** recognition. **Recipient:** for civic involvement and accomplishment outside the sports information office ● CoSIDA Hall of Fame. **Frequency:** annual. **Type:** recognition. **Recipient:** for outstanding contribution to college sports information ● Jake Wade Memorial Award. **Frequency:** annual. **Type:** recognition. **Recipient:** for contributions to college athletics by a newspaperman ● Trailblazer Award. **Frequency:** annual. **Type:** recognition. **Recipient:** for mentoring and helping improve the level of ethnic and gender diversity ● Warren Berg Award. **Frequency:** annual. **Type:** recognition. **Recipient:** to a College Division member. **Formerly:** (1957) Sports Section, American College Public Relations Association. **Publications:** *College Sports Information Directors Directory*, annual. **Circulation:** 11,000. **Advertising:** accepted ● *News Digest*, 11/year. **Conventions/Meetings:** annual conference (exhibits) ● annual workshop (exhibits) - 2008 June 28-July 2, Tampa, FL; 2009 June 21-24, San Antonio, TX.

23257 ■ Collegiate Commissioners Association (CCA)
2201 Arrington Blvd. N
Birmingham, AL 35203
Ph: (205)458-3013
Fax: (205)458-3031
URL: http://www.secsports.com
Contact: Greg Sankey, Sec.-Treas.
Founded: 1939. **Budget:** $75,000. **Description:** Commissioners or executive directors and assistants of the 32 major intercollegiate athletic conferences in the U.S. Seeks to encourage and promote intercollegiate athletics and high standards of sportsmanship as desirable aspects of higher education. **Additional Websites:** http://www.national-letter.org. **Formerly:** (1948) National Association of Football Commissioners; (1965) National Association of Collegiate Commissioners. **Publications:** *Basketball Officials' Manual*, annual. **Advertising:** accepted ● *Football Officials' Manual for 5-Man Crew*, annual ● *Football Officials' Manual for 4-Man Crew*, annual ● *Football Officials' Manual for 7-Man Crew*, annual ● *Football Officials' Manual for 6-Man Crew*, annual ● *Football*

Rules Illustrated for Coaches, Players and Fans, annual ● *Manual of Football Officiating*, annual ● Directory, annual ● Also publishes exams and keys. **Conventions/Meetings:** semiannual conference.

23258 ■ Consolidated Athletic Commission (CAC)

Address Unknown since 2007
Founded: 1948. **Members:** 8. **Description:** Persons who take part in organized leagues of miniature sports (miniature football, miniature basketball) played as table-top games. Compiles statistics and studies the phenomenon of psychokinesis, which CAC believes is involved in its league play. Exchanges statistical data for analysis with the Foundation for Research on the Nature of Man (see separate entry). **Convention/Meeting:** none. **Publications:** *Sportrecord*, periodic. Tabulates records and describes CAC-sponsored events. Includes research reports and statistics. **Price:** included in membership dues. **Circulation:** 10. **Advertising:** accepted.

23259 ■ Council of Ivy Group Presidents (CIGP)

228 Alexander St.
Princeton, NJ 08544
Ph: (609)258-6426
Fax: (609)258-1690
E-mail: brett@ivyleaguesports.com
URL: http://www.ivyleaguesports.com
Contact: Mr. Jeffrey H. Orleans, Exec. Dir.
Founded: 1954. **Members:** 8. **Staff:** 9. **Description:** Brown University; Columbia University; Cornell University; Dartmouth College; Harvard University; Princeton University; University of Pennsylvania; Yale University. Sponsors championships in 33 sports. **Affiliated With:** Eastern Collegiate Hockey Association; National Collegiate Athletic Association. **Formerly:** Ivy League. **Publications:** *Ivy League Directory and Record Book*, annual. **Advertising:** accepted. Alternate Formats: online ● *Ivy League Football Guide*, annual. Magazine. Alternate Formats: online ● *Ivy League Honors*, quarterly. Newsletter ● *Ivy League Men's and Women's Basketball Guide*, annual. Magazine. Alternate Formats: online. **Conventions/Meetings:** semiannual conference.

23260 ■ Federation of Gay Games (FGG)

584 Castro St., Ste.343
San Francisco, CA 94114
Ph: (415)695-0222
Fax: (800)887-1373
E-mail: info@gaygames.org
URL: http://www.gaygames.org
Contact: Kathleen Webster, Co-Pres.
Founded: 1981. **National Groups:** 26. **Nonmembership. Multinational. Description:** Gay athletic federations and sponsors of gay athletic competitions. Promotes increased participation in sports by gay and lesbian individuals by sponsoring the quadrennial Gay Games. Seeks to "foster and augment the self-respect of lesbians and gay men throughout the world and to engender respect and understanding from the non-gay world." Gathers and disseminates information on gay and lesbian athletic competitions worldwide. **Awards:** Tom Waddell Award. **Frequency:** quadrennial. **Type:** recognition. **Recipient:** for individuals who have demonstrated a history of outstanding service in the arts, athletics, or volunteerism. **Formerly:** Gay Games. **Conventions/Meetings:** quadrennial Gay Games Sport and Cultural Festival - competition and festival.

23261 ■ Federation of International Polo (FIP)

9663 Santa Monica Blvd.
PMB 848
Beverly Hills, CA 90210
Ph: (310)472-4312
Fax: (310)472-5220
E-mail: fippolo@aol.com
URL: http://www.fippolo.com
Contact: Glen Holden, Pres.
Founded: 1983. **Membership Dues:** national association (0-99 players), $750 (annual) ● national association (100-500 players), $2,250 (annual) ● national association (more than 500 players), $4,500

(annual). **Multinational. Description:** Seeks to enhance the image of polo and return the sport to the arenas of the Olympic games. Organizes international tournaments worldwide for professionals, amateurs and children while actively promoting the sport of polo throughout the world. **Computer Services:** database, press releases ● information services, polo resources. **Committees:** Children's Polo; Commercial Polo; Nominating; Olympic; Rules; Tournament.

23262 ■ Intercollegiate Association of Amateur Athletes of America (IC4A)

c/o Eastern College Athletic Conference
1311 Craigville Beach Rd.
Centerville, MA 02632
Ph: (508)771-5060
Fax: (508)771-9486
E-mail: stevebartold@aol.com
URL: http://www.ecac.org
Contact: Steve Bartold, Contact
Founded: 1875. **Members:** 97. **Budget:** $35,000. **Description:** Colleges with track and field teams. Establishes meet locations, dates, and rules; appoints officials and certifies records. **Awards: Type:** recognition. **Committees:** Athletic Rules; Games; Records. **Conventions/Meetings:** annual competition, cross country, indoor and outdoor championships ● annual conference.

23263 ■ International Dodge Ball Federation (IDBF)

3451A Washington Ave.
Gulfport, MS 39507
Ph: (228)860-9000
Fax: (228)863-9085
E-mail: marketing@dodge-ball.com
URL: http://www.dodge-ball.com
Contact: Rusty Walker, Founder
Founded: 1996. **Multinational. Description:** Promotes the sport of dodge ball by standardizing rules, courts and equipment. Acts as the central agency responsible for the sanctioning of tournament play. Studies equipment to find better and safer ways to play the game. **Computer Services:** database, state contacts ● information services, game rules. **Telecommunication Services:** electronic mail, customerservice@dodge-ball.com.

23264 ■ International Federation of Competitive Eating (IFOCE)

151 W 25th St., 4th Fl.
New York, NY 10001
Ph: (212)627-5766 (212)352-8651
Fax: (212)627-5430
E-mail: info@ifoce.com
URL: http://www.ifoce.com
Contact: George Shea, Contact
Multinational. Description: Supervises and regulates eating contests. Ensures the safety of the competitive eating sport. Establishes liaisons with individual competitive eating venues and sponsors. **Computer Services:** database, eater profiles ● database, ranking ● database, records ● information services, eating and eater resources. **Telecommunication Services:** electronic mail, gshea@shea-communications.com.

23265 ■ International Gravity Sports Association (IGSA)

638 N Crestview Dr.
Glendora, CA 91741
Ph: (951)532-6378
E-mail: rietema.m@gravity-sports.com
URL: http://www.gravity-sports.com
Contact: Marcus Rietema, Pres.
Founded: 1996. **Multinational. Description:** Promotes fair and unbiased leadership for the sport of gravity racing. Fosters strong and fair competition. Seeks to reduce the hazards associated with the sport. **Computer Services:** database, World Cup events. **Publications:** Booklets. Contains rules and regulations for competitions. Alternate Formats: online.

23266 ■ International Log Rolling Association (ILRA)

711 Glenna Dr.
Hudson, WI 54016
Ph: (715)549-5311
E-mail: admin@uslogrolling.org
URL: http://www.uslogrolling.org
Contact: Chris Fischer, Pres.
Description: Promotes and perpetuates the sport of log rolling. **Publications:** Newsletter, periodic. Alternate Formats: online. **Conventions/Meetings:** periodic competition.

23267 ■ International Medalist Association (IMA)

1 E Chase St., Ste.11
Baltimore, MD 21202
Ph: (240)464-7444
Fax: (212)898-1267
E-mail: president@internationalmedalist.org
URL: http://www.internationalmedalist.org
Contact: Mr. Ronald Freeman MA, Pres.
Languages: Dutch, English, French, Italian, Portuguese, Spanish. **Multinational. Description:** Provides athletic training scholarships to America's elementary and middle school youth who desire to participate in a sport. Recognizes the need to support sports organizations on a regional, national and international level. Supports community outreach programs and facilitates training programs in the areas of coach preparation and athlete development. Utilizes the services of Olympians and Olympic coaches.

23268 ■ International Sports Exchange (ISE)

5982 Mia Ct.
Plainfield, IN 46168
Ph: (317)839-9257
Fax: (317)839-0258
E-mail: iseice@aol.com
Contact: Kermit B. Davis, Exec. Dir.
Founded: 1979. **Description:** Participants include university teams. Promotes international goodwill and cultural exchange through sports. Organizes and sponsors international sports competitions and tours between North American and European teams. Competitions are held in any sport. **Conventions/Meetings:** annual meeting - always February, Chicago, IL.

23269 ■ International Sports Heritage Association (ISHA)

PO Box 3093
Ponte Vedra Beach, FL 32004
Ph: (904)955-0126
Fax: (904)683-2189
E-mail: info@sportsheritage.org
URL: http://www.sportsheritage.org
Contact: Ms. Karen Bednarski, Exec. Dir.
Founded: 1971. **Members:** 150. **Membership Dues:** institution, corporation, $175 (annual). **Staff:** 1. **Multinational. Description:** Educates, promotes and supports organizations and individuals engaged in the celebration of sports heritage. **Awards:** Bill Schroeder Award. **Frequency:** annual. **Type:** recognition. **Recipient:** for distinguished service to IASMHF and/or member organizations. **Formerly:** (1972) Association of Executive Directors of Halls of Fame; (1989) Association of Sports Museums and Halls of Fame; (2006) International Association of Sports Museums and Halls of Fame. **Publications:** *International Sports Heritage Association Membership Directory*, annual. **Advertising:** accepted ● *ISHA Newsletter*, quarterly. **Price:** included in membership dues; $25.00 /year for nonmembers. **Circulation:** 350. **Advertising:** accepted ● *Organizing a Sports Museum/Hall of Fame*. Manual. **Price:** free. **Conventions/Meetings:** annual conference, museum services and materials, professional education (exhibits).

23270 ■ Maccabi USA/Sports for Israel

1926 Arch St. 4R
Philadelphia, PA 19103
Ph: (215)561-6900
Fax: (215)561-5470

E-mail: maccabi@maccabiusa.com
URL: http://www.maccabiusa.com
Contact: Jed Margolis, Exec. Dir.

Founded: 1948. **Members:** 25,000. **Staff:** 6. **Description:** Individuals, groups, and foundations interested in encouraging a program of participation by Jewish youth in sports, related activities and international competitions that create a heightened awareness of Israel and strengthen and encourage Jewish pride and identity. Sponsors United States Maccabiah Games Team, Israel Sports Center for the Disabled, and the Wingate Institute for Physical Education in Israel. Develops, promotes, and supports international, national and regional based athletic activities. Strives to provide Jewish athletes worldwide the opportunity to share heritage and customs in competitive athletic settings. Maintains information bureau and speakers' bureau. Operates International Jewish Sports Hall of Fame; participates in international sports competition. **Awards:** Robert Spivak Lifetime Achievement Award. **Frequency:** periodic. **Type:** recognition. **Committees:** Alumni Association; Budget; ByLaws; Collaborations; Conference; Endowments; Fundraising; Golf. **Formerly:** (1962) United States Committee for Sports in Israel; (1995) United States Committee Sports for Israel. **Publications:** *Commemorative Journal*, quadrennial. Provides a recap of Maccabiah games results, sponsors, athletes. **Advertising:** accepted ● *Maccabiah Games Commemorative Journal* ● *Sportscene*, quarterly. Newsletter. Alternate Formats: online. **Conventions/Meetings:** annual conference.

23271 ■ Miniature Golf Association of the U.S. (MGAUS)

1113 Belle Pl.
Fort Worth, TX 76107
Ph: (817)738-5522 (817)738-3344
Fax: (817)738-6622
E-mail: info@mgaus.org
URL: http://www.mgaus.org
Contact: Steven W. Hix, Exec. Dir.

Founded: 1997. **Members:** 200. **Membership Dues:** manufacturer, developer, $300 (annual) ● operator, $250 (annual). **Staff:** 3. **For-Profit. Description:** Businesses and business people with an interest in the miniature golf industry. Promotes continued growth and success of miniature golf in the United States. Seeks to open lines of communication and provide an effective national forum for the miniature golf industry. Offers educational programs and statistical information; maintains speakers' bureau. **Committees:** MGAUS Standards and Guidelines. **Publications:** *Right Track*, 6-8/year. Newsletter. **Circulation:** 2,500. **Conventions/Meetings:** annual board meeting - usually November.

23272 ■ Mounted Games Across America (MGAA)

15710 Union Chapel Rd.
Woodbine, MD 21797
Ph: (301)432-2819
E-mail: mgaainfo@mountedgames.org
URL: http://www.mountedgames.org
Contact: Donna McCready, Pres.

Founded: 2004. **Membership Dues:** individual, $25 (annual) ● family, $40 (annual) ● sponsor, $50 (annual) ● patron, $100 (annual). **Description:** Introduces and develops the sport of equestrian mounted games within the United States equestrian community. Provides opportunities for mounted games amateur athletes to develop competitive skills. **Computer Services:** database, additional games. **Committees:** Communications; Competition; Governance; Membership; Nominating; Program.

23273 ■ National Academy of Sports (NAS)

Address Unknown since 2007

Founded: 1961. **Members:** 150. **Staff:** 3. **Description:** Sports editors of U.S. newspapers having at least a 100,000-copy daily circulation. **Awards:** Academy Award of Sport. **Type:** recognition. **Recipient:** bestowed to outstanding athletes and teams, as selected by the academy's members.

23274 ■ National Association of Athletic Development Directors (NAADD)

PO Box 16428
Cleveland, OH 44116
Ph: (440)892-4000
Fax: (440)892-4007
E-mail: pmanak@nacda.com
URL: http://nacda.cstv.com/naadd/nacda-naadd.html
Contact: Mike Cleary, Assoc. Exec. Dir.

Founded: 1993. **Members:** 475. **Membership Dues:** institutional, $360 (annual) ● individual, $90 (annual) ● individual college/university, $100 (annual) ● individual affiliate (conference/association/bowl), $125 (annual) ● individual commercial, $250 (annual) ● student, $25 (annual). **Description:** Individuals working with development activities for a college or university athletic department, the professional and educational association for collegiate athletic development and fund raising personnel. Offers educational programs. **Publications:** none. **Awards:** Donor of the Year - College Division. **Frequency:** annual. **Type:** recognition. **Recipient:** for significant contribution to college athletics, through philanthropic support ● Donor of the Year - University Division. **Frequency:** annual. **Type:** recognition. **Recipient:** for significant contribution to college athletics, through philanthropic support ● Fund Raiser of the Year - College Division. **Frequency:** annual. **Type:** recognition. **Recipient:** for a member who has demonstrated significant achievement in athletic fund raising ● Fund Raiser of the Year - University Division. **Frequency:** annual. **Type:** recognition. **Recipient:** for a member who has demonstrated significant achievement in athletic fund raising ● NAADD Postgraduate Scholarships. **Frequency:** annual. **Type:** scholarship. **Recipient:** for collection seniors pursuing degrees and careers in sports administration ● Volunteer of the Year - College Division. **Frequency:** annual. **Type:** recognition. **Recipient:** for significant contributions of time and energy toward raising monies for college athletics ● Volunteer of the Year - University Division. **Frequency:** annual. **Type:** recognition. **Recipient:** for significant contributions of time and energy toward raising monies for college athletics. **Computer Services:** database, membership. **Affiliated With:** National Association of Collegiate Directors of Athletics. **Conventions/Meetings:** annual workshop (exhibits).

23275 ■ National Association of Collegiate Directors of Athletics (NACDA)

PO Box 16428
Cleveland, OH 44116
Ph: (440)892-4000
Fax: (440)892-4007
E-mail: mcleary@nacda.com
URL: http://nacda.cstv.com
Contact: Michael J. Cleary, Exec. Dir.

Founded: 1965. **Members:** 6,100. **Membership Dues:** sustaining, $225-$1,750 ● individual, $75-$375. **Staff:** 10. **Description:** Junior colleges and four-year colleges and institutions conducting an intercollegiate athletics program; interested individuals. Functions as a service organization for athletics administrators of intercollegiate programs. Sponsors national insurance program for member institutions. Conducts management institutes. Maintains hall of fame. Operates the Sears Directors' Cup Program. **Awards:** GeneralSports TURF System AD of the Year Award. **Frequency:** annual. **Type:** recognition. **Recipient:** for commitment and administrative excellence ● James J. Corbett Memorial Award. **Frequency:** annual. **Type:** recognition. **Recipient:** for athletic directors who have demonstrated distinguished service to the profession throughout their career ● John McLendon Memorial Minority Postgraduate Scholarship. **Frequency:** annual. **Type:** scholarship. **Recipient:** for students pursuing postgraduate studies ● NACDA/Continental Airlines AD of the Year. **Frequency:** annual. **Type:** recognition. **Recipient:** for athletic directors on a regional and divisional level who have demonstrated distinguished service to the profession for a year. **Computer Services:** database, membership. **Committees:** Continuing Education; Finance-Management; Honors and Awards; Inter-Association Liaison; Site Selection;

Strategic and Long Range Planning. **Programs:** Facilities, Fund Raising and Marketing Workshop; Management/Leadership Institute. **Affiliated With:** National Association of Athletic Development Directors; National Association of Collegiate Marketing Administrators. **Publications:** *Athletics Administration*, bimonthly. Journal. Reports on sports programs, drugs in college sports, marketing and administration, and other topics related to college athletics. **Price:** included in membership dues; $15.00 /year for nonmembers. ISSN: 0044-9873. **Circulation:** 6,200. **Advertising:** accepted ● *National Association of Collegiate Directors of Athletics—Conference Proceedings*, annual. **Price:** $20.00/copy ● *National Directory of College Athletics*, annual. Separate directories for men's and women's programs; includes listing of administrators and coaches with numbers. **Price:** $38.95/copy. **Advertising:** accepted ● Proceedings. Alternate Formats: online. **Conventions/Meetings:** annual convention (exhibits) ● annual Kickoff Classic - meeting, football game ● annual Pigskin Classic - meeting, football game ● seminar.

23276 ■ National Association of Collegiate Marketing Administrators (NACMA)

PO Box 16428
Cleveland, OH 44116
Ph: (440)892-4000
Fax: (440)892-4007
E-mail: bvecchione@nacda.com
URL: http://www.nacma.com
Contact: Bob Vecchione, Exec. Dir.

Founded: 1990. **Members:** 705. **Membership Dues:** individual, active, $90 (annual) ● institutional (up to 5 individuals), $250 (annual) ● student, intern, $25 (annual) ● affiliate, $150 (annual) ● group affiliate (up to 5 individuals), $375 (annual). **Staff:** 3. **Description:** Represents individuals involved in sports marketing, public relations, or the promotional aspects at a college, university, or athletic conference. **Awards:** Best of Awards. **Frequency:** annual. **Type:** recognition ● Corporate Sponsor of the Year. **Frequency:** annual. **Type:** recognition ● Hall of Fame. **Frequency:** annual. **Type:** recognition ● Host Communications Marketer of the Year. **Frequency:** annual. **Type:** recognition ● Lifetime Achievement Award. **Frequency:** periodic. **Type:** recognition ● Outstanding Corporate Achievement. **Frequency:** annual. **Type:** recognition ● Outstanding Individual Achievement. **Frequency:** annual. **Type:** recognition ● Postgraduate Scholarship. **Frequency:** annual. **Type:** scholarship. **Computer Services:** database, membership ● mailing lists, listserv access. **Affiliated With:** National Association of Collegiate Directors of Athletics; National Collegiate Athletic Association. **Publications:** *NACMA Corner*, 5/year. Articles. **Advertising:** accepted. Also Cited As: *Athletics Administration* ● *NACMA Ideas*, quarterly. Newsletter. Contains information on marketing and promotions. **Circulation:** 584 ● Membership Directory, annual. **Conventions/Meetings:** annual convention (exhibits).

23277 ■ National Association of Intercollegiate Athletics (NAIA)

23500 W 105th St.
Olathe, KS 66061
Ph: (913)791-0044
Fax: (913)791-9555
E-mail: kdee@naia.org
URL: http://www.naia.org
Contact: Steve Baker, Pres./CEO

Founded: 1937. **Members:** 307. **Membership Dues:** college/university, $4,400 (annual). **Staff:** 22. **Budget:** $3,000,000. **Regional Groups:** 14. **Local Groups:** 30. **Description:** Fully accredited four-year colleges and universities. Works to develop intercollegiate athletic programs as an integral part of the total educational program of the college rather than as a separate commercial or promotional adjunct. Organizes and administers all areas of intercollegiate athletics at the national level including rules and standards, sectional, regional, conference, and national competition. Aims toward uniformity and equity in policies and practices. Sponsors 23 national championships for men and women to provide national competitive opportunities for colleges and universities with a similar philosophy of athletics; football, basketball, baseball, golf, soccer, cross country, swimming, wrestling, outdoor track and field, indoor track and field, tennis, volleyball, and softball. Maintains hall of fame in all sports in which there are championship events in the meritorious service area. Compiles statistics. **Committees:** Council of Affiliated Conferences and Independents; Council of Athletics Administrators; Council of Faculty Athletics Representatives; Council of Presidents; National Coordinating. **Divisions:** Men's; Women's. **Affiliated With:** American Council on Education; United States Collegiate Sports Council; United States Olympic Committee. **Formerly:** (1952) National Association of Intercollegiate Basketball. **Publications:** *Fall, Winter and Spring Sports Media Guides*, annual ● *NAIA News*, daily. Newsletter. Alternate Formats: online ● *National Association of Intercollegiate Athletics—Membership Directory*, annual. Alternate Formats: CD-ROM ● *National Association of Intercollegiate Athletics - Official Handbook*, annual. Alternate Formats: CD-ROM ● *National Association of Intercollegiate Athletics—Official Records Book*, annual ● Also publishes statistical reports and ratings. **Conventions/Meetings:** annual congress (exhibits) - always March ● workshop, for coaches, athletic directors, sports information directors, registrars, and chief executive officers.

23278 ■ National Association for Recreational Equality (NARE)

c/o Bankshot Sports
785 E Rockville Pike
PMB 504
Rockville, MD 20852
Ph: (301)309-0260
Free: (800)933-0140
Fax: (301)309-0263
E-mail: info@bankshot.com
URL: http://www.bankshot.com
Contact: Dr. Reeve Robert Brenner, Founder/Pres.
Founded: 1997. **Members:** 250. **Staff:** 3. **Budget:** $100,000. **Regional Groups:** 3. **State Groups:** 30. **Description:** Dedicated to the development and promotion of non-aggressive inclusionary sports for all, including persons in wheelchairs. **Libraries:** Type: reference; open to the public. **Holdings:** articles, artwork, audiovisuals, business records, clippings, monographs. **Subjects:** inclusionary sports and recreation. **Awards:** Arial Anaker Award. **Frequency:** annual. **Type:** recognition. **Recipient:** for good sportsmanship. **Additional Websites:** http://www.nareletsplayfair.org.

23279 ■ National Christian College Athletic Association (NCCAA)

302 W Washington St.
Greenville, SC 29601-1919
Ph: (864)250-1199
Fax: (864)250-1141
E-mail: info@thenccaa.org
URL: http://www.thenccaa.org
Contact: Dan Wood, Exec. Dir.
Founded: 1966. **Members:** 112. **Membership Dues:** associate (Division I), $400 ● associate (Division II), $300. **Staff:** 4. **Budget:** $762,000. **Regional Groups:** 9. **National Groups:** 16. **Description:** Christian colleges. Provides national competition for the Christian college movement in baseball, basketball (men's and women's) cross-country (men's and women's), football, golf, soccer (men's and women's), tennis (men's and women's), men's volleyball, women's volleyball, track and field (men's and women's), and softball. Maintains placement service; compiles statistics. **Awards:** All-American. **Frequency:** annual. **Type:** recognition. **Recipient:** to student athletes ● Hall of Fame. **Frequency:** annual. **Type:** recognition. **Recipient:** for outstanding leadership and/or service ● Scholar Athlete. **Frequency:** annual. **Type:** recognition ● Susan R. Hellings Award. **Frequency:** annual. **Type:** recognition. **Recipient:** to an outstanding women's volleyball player. **Telecommunication Services:** electronic mail, dwood@thenccaa.org. **Publications:** *National Christian College Athletic Association News Update*, quarterly. Newsletter. Includes research updates, statistics, and tournament results. **Price:** free. **Circulation:** 4,750.

Advertising: accepted ● *National Christian College Athletic Association—Official Handbook*, semiannual. Membership Directory. Includes rules manual. **Price:** included in membership dues. **Circulation:** 150 ● Membership Directory, annual. Alternate Formats: online. **Conventions/Meetings:** annual convention (exhibits).

23280 ■ National Collegiate Athletic Association (NCAA)

PO Box 6222
700 W Washington St.
Indianapolis, IN 46206-6222
Ph: (317)917-6222
Fax: (317)917-6888
E-mail: pmr@ncaa.org
URL: http://www2.ncaa.org
Contact: Myles Brand, Pres.
Founded: 1906. **Members:** 1,250. **Membership Dues:** division I provisional, $25 (annual) ● division I reclassifying, $15 (annual) ● division II provisional, $14 (annual) ● division II reclassifying, $7 (annual). **Staff:** 350. **Budget:** $225,000,000. **Description:** Universities, colleges, and allied educational athletics associations devoted to the administration of intercollegiate athletics. Operates statistics service for college football and baseball; women's softball; men and women's basketball; publishing service; film production service. Maintains 42 sports committees including: Men's Football; Men's and Women's Fencing; Men's and Women's Golf; Men's and Women's Lacrosse; Men's and Women's Rifle; Men's and Women's Skiing; Men's and Women's Swimming; Men's and Women's Track and Field; Men's and Women's Volleyball; Men's Wrestling; Women's Softball. Also maintains 22 other committees including: Communications; Eligibility; Honors; Infractions; Legislation and Interpretation; Legislative Review; National Youth Sports Program; Postgraduate Scholarship; Professional Sports Liaison; Recruiting; Research; Review and Planning; Special Events; Student Athlete Advisory; Women's Athletics. **Libraries:** Type: reference. **Holdings:** 10,000; books. **Subjects:** intercollegiate athletics. **Awards:** Byers Postgraduate Scholarship. **Type:** scholarship ● Degree Completion. **Type:** recognition ● Ethnic Minority and Women's Enhancement. **Type:** recognition ● Freedom Forum. **Type:** recognition ● Postgraduate Scholarship. **Type:** scholarship. **Committees:** Academic Requirement; Baseball; Basketball Officiating Improvement; Competitive Safeguards and Medical Aspects of Sports; Financial Aid and Amateurism; Ice Hockey; Men's and Women's Basketball Rules; Men's and Women's Gymnastics. **Publications:** *National Collegiate Athletic Association—Annual Report*, quarterly. Reports on NCAA committees, minutes of Council, President's Commission and Executive Committee meetings, and financial report. **Price:** $8.00/copy for members; $16.00/copy for nonmembers ● *National Collegiate Athletic Association—Convention Proceedings*, annual. Includes transcripts of all business sessions at NCAA Conventions, summaries of roundtables and roster of delegates and visitors. **Price:** $8.00/copy for members; $16.00/copy for nonmembers. ISSN: 0070-3803 ● *NCAA Directory*, annual. Contains roster of members arranged alphabetically. **Price:** $4.00/copy for members; $8.00/copy for nonmembers. ISSN: 0162-1467 ● *NCAA Manual*, annual. Contains all current NCAA legislation: constitution, by laws, interpretations, executive regulations, and enforcement procedures. **Price:** $13.00. ISSN: 0077-3186 ● *NCAA News*, 46/year. Newspaper. Covers college athletics. **Price:** $24.00/year ● Reports. Covers sports programs, finances, and television. **Conventions/Meetings:** annual meeting - always January.

23281 ■ National Council of Youth Sports (NCYS)

7185 SE Seagate Ln.
Stuart, FL 34997
Ph: (772)781-1452
Fax: (772)781-7298
E-mail: youthsports@ncys.org
URL: http://www.ncys.org
Contact: Sally S. Cunningham, Exec. Dir.
Founded: 1979. **Members:** 130. **Membership Dues:** executive, associate (add $75/subsequent executive

or associate individual), $100 (annual) ● allied (add $175/subsequent allied individual), $250 (annual) ● affiliate, $50 (annual). **Description:** Multi-sport corporation. Strengthens performance of youth sport administrators through education. Advocates values of youth sports. **Awards:** Hershey's Strive Award. **Frequency:** annual. **Type:** recognition. **Recipient:** for coaches, administrators and volunteers who have demonstrated to young people that sports teach respect, initiative, values and excellence. **Publications:** *Youth Sports Today*, bimonthly. Newsletter. **Circulation:** 1,100. Alternate Formats: online. **Conventions/Meetings:** annual conference (exhibits).

23282 ■ National Fastpitch Coaches Association (NFCA)

100 G T Thames Dr., Ste.D
Starkville, MS 39759
Ph: (662)320-2155
Fax: (662)320-2283
E-mail: nfca@nfca.org
URL: http://nfca.org
Contact: Lacy Lee Baker, Exec. Dir.
Founded: 1983. **Members:** 4,200. **Membership Dues:** head coach NCAA - division I, $150 (annual) ● head coach NCAA - division II and III, $100 (annual) ● head coach, assistant coach - other leagues, $60 (annual) ● former coach, business, club, umpire, non-coaching, $50 (annual) ● international, $75 (annual). **Description:** Facilitates public and professional understanding and appreciation of the importance of the sport of fastpitch softball. Keeps members informed of current coaching techniques and trends. Provides national and international educational training for fastpitch softball coaches. **Awards:** Diamond Sports Catcher of The Year Award. **Frequency:** annual. **Type:** recognition. **Recipient:** for the top catcher in the NCAA divisions ● National Coaching Staff of the Year. **Frequency:** annual. **Type:** recognition. **Recipient:** for national coaching excellence ● NFCA Hall of Fame. **Frequency:** annual. **Type:** recognition. **Recipient:** selected by hall of fame committee ● NFCA Scholar-Athlete. **Frequency:** annual. **Type:** scholarship. **Recipient:** to an athlete who receives a 3.5 or better GPA on a 4.0 scale. **Computer Services:** Information services, college fastpitch resources ● information services, scoreboard ● information services, softball resources. **Committees:** Awards and Hall of Fame; Bylaws and Resolutions; Camp and Clinic; Diversity; Education and Publications; Ethics; Internet; Nominating. **Publications:** *Fastpitch Delivery*. Newspaper.

23283 ■ National Federation of State High School Associations (NFSHSA)

PO Box 690
Indianapolis, IN 46206
Ph: (317)972-6900
Fax: (317)822-5700
E-mail: sloomis@nfhs.org
URL: http://www.nfhs.org
Contact: Bill Reader, Pres.
Founded: 1920. **Members:** 65. **Membership Dues:** state high school athletic, activity association, $2,500 (annual). **Staff:** 44. **Budget:** $7,200,000. **State Groups:** 51. **Description:** Federation of high school athletic/activities associations from the 50 U.S. states, the District of Columbia, Virgin Islands, 11 Canadian provinces, Bermuda, and Guam representing more than 20,400 high schools. Seeks to protect and supervise the interstate athletic, musical, and speech and debate interests of high schools and coordinate the activities of state associations. Initiates National Federation Interscholastic Speech and Debate Association, National Federation Interscholastic Music Association, National Federation Interscholastic Coaches Association; National Federation Interscholastic Officials Association; and National Federation Interscholastic Spirit Association. Maintains national press service, high school sports hall of fame, and official sports film service. Sponsors experimentation and testing program for sports equipment. **Awards:** Citations. **Type:** recognition. **Recipient:** for members ● Distinguished Service. **Type:** recognition. **Recipient:** for members ● High School Sports Hall of Fame. **Type:** recognition. **Recipient:** for members. **Commit-**

tees: Equity; Governed Sports Rules; National Records; Spirit; Sportsmanship/Citizenship. **Affiliated With:** Amateur Softball Association of America; National Interscholastic Athletic Administrators Association; NFHS Coaches Association; NFHS Music Association; NFHS Officials Association; NFHS Speech, Debate and Theatre Association. **Formerly:** (1970) National Federation of State High School Athletic Associations. **Publications:** *Interscholastic Athletic Administration*, quarterly. Journal. Contains articles on high school sports administration, including sports medicine, philosophy, and management. **Price:** included in membership dues; $12.00 /year for nonmembers. **Advertising:** accepted ● *National Federation News: The National Voice of High School Activities*, 9/year. Newsletter. Reports on high school athletics, speech, and music. Includes articles on athletes, coaches, officials, and major rule changes within given sports. **Price:** included in membership dues; $10.00 /year for nonmembers. **Advertising:** accepted ● *National Federation of State High School Associations—Handbook*, annual. Contains history, policy, programs, statistics, committees, sports participation survey, and federation directory. **Price:** $4.00/copy, plus shipping and handling ● *National High School Sports Record Book*, annual. Contains national records in 15 sports for high school boys and girls; includes game, season, and career records. **Price:** $9.95/copy, plus shipping and handling. **Advertising:** accepted ● Publishes governed sport rulebooks, casebook, and manuals. Also NF Coaches Quarterly and NF Officials Quarterly. **Conventions/ Meetings:** annual Athletic Directors - meeting - in December ● annual Leadership Conference, professional meeting for high school athletic administrators (exhibits) - held in spring, usually April ● annual meeting and board meeting.

23284 ■ National Intramural-Recreational Sports Association (NIRSA)

4185 SW Res. Way
Corvallis, OR 97333-1067
Ph: (541)766-8211
Fax: (541)766-8284
E-mail: nirsa@nirsa.org
URL: http://www.nirsa.org
Contact: Dr. Kent J. Blumenthal CRSS, Exec. Dir.
Founded: 1950. **Members:** 4,315. **Membership Dues:** professional, $133 (annual) ● student, $59 (annual) ● associate, $395 (annual) ● life, $1,224. **Staff:** 11. **Budget:** $1,100,000. **Multinational. Description:** Professionals (2525); institutions (650); students (1000). Promotes and encourages the professional growth of individuals involved in recreational sports; seeks to advance collegiate and military recreational sports programs. Manages Sports Officials' Development Program and Media Center, which provide educational materials. Sponsors specialized workshops. Administers professional development and certification programs. Provides career opportunity listings. **Computer Services:** Mailing lists. **Formerly:** (1973) National Intramural Association. **Publications:** *Flag and Touch Football Rules and Official's Manual*, biennial. **Price:** $5.00/copy. **Advertising:** accepted ● *National Intramural-Recreational Sports Association—Journal*, 3/year. **Price:** included in membership dues; $13.34/copy for nonmembers. **Advertising:** accepted ● *NIRSA Know*, 10/year. Newsletter. **Circulation:** 3,000. Alternate Formats: online ● *Recreational Sports Directory*, annual. Lists more than 2000 recreational sports programs and more than 7000 professionals in colleges and universities in the U.S. and Canada. **Price:** $30.00/copy for educators; $80.00/copy for corporations. **Advertising:** accepted ● Also makes available supplemental slide package. **Conventions/Meetings:** annual conference (exhibits) ● conference, holds 40 state and 6 regional conferences.

23285 ■ National Junior College Athletic Association (NJCAA)

1755 Telstar Dr., Ste.103
Colorado Springs, CO 80920
Ph: (719)590-9788
Fax: (719)590-7324

E-mail: wbaker@njcaa.org
URL: http://www.njcaa.org
Contact: Wayne Baker, Exec. Dir.
Founded: 1938. **Members:** 507. **Staff:** 8. **Budget:** $949,500. **Regional Groups:** 24. **Description:** Junior colleges recognized by the American Association of Community and Junior Colleges (see separate entry). Promotes two-year college athletics on intersectional and national levels. Sponsors intercollegiate insurance program; compiles statistics/rankings on baseball, men's and women's basketball, football, volleyball, softball, soccer, ice hockey, tennis, bowling, golf, lacrosse, swimming and diving, track and field, and wrestling. Sponsors national tournaments for all major intercollegiate sports. **Libraries:** Type: reference. **Holdings:** films. **Awards:** Frequency: annual. Type: recognition. **Recipient:** to student athletes/individuals. **Committees:** Academic Standards; All-American; Championship Events; Eligibility; Health Related Concerns; Service and Recognition; Sports; Strategic Planning. **Divisions:** Men's; Women's. **Affiliated With:** Amateur Softball Association of America; Naismith Memorial Basketball Hall of Fame; National Association for Girls and Women in Sport; United States Collegiate Sports Council; United States Olympic Committee; United States Tennis Association; United States Volleyball Association/USA Volleyball; U.S.A. Baseball; U.S.A. Basketball; USA Swimming; Women's Sports Foundation. **Publications:** *Eligibility Rules of the National Junior College Athletic Association*, annual. Pamphlet. Provides NJCAA eligibility rules for the current year. **Price:** included in membership dues. **Circulation:** 600 ● *Juco Review*, monthly, from September through May. Magazine. Covers sporting events, student athletes, and championship teams at NJCAA colleges. Includes advertisers index. **Price:** included in membership dues; $30.00 /year for nonmembers. ISSN: 0047-2956. **Circulation:** 3,500. **Advertising:** accepted ● *National Junior College Athletic Association—Handbook and Casebook*, annual. Contains organization's rules, regulations, and structure. Includes athletic program statistics and calendar of events. **Price:** included in membership dues; $12.00/copy for nonmembers; $10.00 record book. **Circulation:** 2,000. **Advertising:** accepted ● Handbook, annual. Covers eligibility requirements and sports procedures. **Advertising:** accepted. **Conventions/Meetings:** annual assembly.

23286 ■ North American Bungee Association (NABA)

PO Box 121
Fairview, OR 97024
Ph: (503)520-0303
Fax: (503)674-2232
E-mail: consult@bungee.com
URL: http://www.bungee.com
Contact: Casey Dale, Pres.
Founded: 1991. **Members:** 150. **Membership Dues:** active operator, $500 (annual). **Staff:** 3. **Budget:** $100,000. **Regional Groups:** 3. **State Groups:** 12. **Local Groups:** 15. **Description:** Individuals who enjoy the thrill-seeking sport of bungee jumping; commercial establishments. Serves as a means of communication among participants in bungee jumping, in which a series of rubber cords are fastened to the body and to one of four types of platforms (bridges, towers, cranes, or hot air balloons) and a jump is made, followed by several rebounds. Educates members on the skills and safety precautions involved. Plans to offer training and an insurance plan. **Publications:** *Bungee Cords*, periodic. Newsletter. **Price:** $24.00/year. **Circulation:** 150. **Advertising:** accepted. Alternate Formats: online; CD-ROM. **Conventions/Meetings:** annual Bungee Jump Master - meeting - spring training.

23287 ■ North American Ski Joring Association (NASJA)

PO Box 1745
Red Lodge, MT 59068
E-mail: dave@nasja.com
URL: http://www.nasja.com
Contact: Dave Schilz, Exec. Dir.
Founded: 1999. **Description:** Consolidates the existing ski joring races in the country. Provides equal op-

portunities for competitors to become the National Ski Joring Champions.

23288 ■ Over the Hill Gang, International (OTHGI)

1515 N Tejon St.
Colorado Springs, CO 80907
Ph: (719)389-0022
Fax: (719)389-0024
E-mail: info@othgi.com
URL: http://www.othgi.com
Contact: Arthur P. Foley, Managing Dir.
Founded: 1977. **Members:** 6,000. **Membership Dues:** individual, $50 (annual) ● couple, $80 (annual). **Staff:** 12. **Budget:** $2,000,000. **Local Groups:** 13. **For-Profit. Multinational. Description:** Individuals 50 years of age and older who enjoy the camaraderie of skiing and other recreational activities with friends and share a spirit of adventure. Aims to promote active sports, fitness, and the fellowship of individuals 50 years and older. Primarily a ski organization, but has expanded to include other sports such as rafting, tennis, biking, hiking, and golf. Sponsors adventure tours throughout the U.S., Europe, and the southern hemisphere. Has sponsored fundraising projects to support the Colorado Ski Museum. **Publications:** *Annual Benefits Directory*, annual. Lists discounts on lift tickets, lodging, equipment and transportation. **Price:** included in membership dues. **Circulation:** 6,000. **Advertising:** accepted ● *Annual Trip Catalog*, annual ● *The Legend*, quarterly. Newsletter. Includes calendar of events. **Price:** included in membership dues. **Circulation:** 5,000. **Advertising:** accepted. **Conventions/Meetings:** Anniversary Reunion.

23289 ■ Pacific 10 Conference (PAC-10)

800 S Broadway, Ste.400
Walnut Creek, CA 94596
Ph: (925)932-4411
Fax: (925)932-4601
URL: http://www.pac-10.org
Contact: Thomas C. Hansen, Commissioner
Founded: 1915. **Members:** 10. **Staff:** 29. **Description:** Arizona State University; Oregon State University; Stanford University; University of Arizona; University of California, Berkeley; University of California, Los Angeles; University of Oregon; University of Southern California; University of Washington; Washington State University. Develops athletic programs and encourages high standards of sportsmanship. **Awards:** Cooper Tire/Pac-10 Leadership Award. **Frequency:** annual. **Type:** scholarship. **Recipient:** for student athletes ● Pac-10 Sportsmanship Award. **Frequency:** annual. **Type:** recognition. **Recipient:** for student athletes. **Committees:** Student-Athlete Advisory. **Affiliated With:** National Collegiate Athletic Association. **Publications:** *Media Guides*, annual. Alternate Formats: online ● *Pacific-10 Conference Handbook*, annual ● *Record Book*, annual. Books. Published for each sanctioned sport. Alternate Formats: online ● *Staff Directory*. Alternate Formats: online ● Newsletter. Alternate Formats: online. **Conventions/Meetings:** semiannual conference - always winter and summer.

23290 ■ Protection Sports Association (PSA)

3670 Revolea Beach Rd.
Middle River, MD 21220
E-mail: treesrotties@aol.com
URL: http://www.psak9.org
Contact: Theresa Furrow, Sec.
Membership Dues: general, $100 (annual). **Description:** Provides an outlet for civilian competition in canine obedience and controlled protection. Promotes competition through club trials and championship tournaments. Sets new standard for training excellence in the protection sports. **Computer Services:** Online services, discussion board. **Publications:** Newsletter.

23291 ■ Ride and Tie Association

PO Box 2436
Sequim, WA 98382

E-mail: contact@rideandtie.org
URL: http://www.rideandtie.org
Contact: Don Betts, Pres.
Founded: 1998. **Membership Dues:** life, $500 ●
individual, $25 (annual) ● family, $40 (annual) ●
friend of Ride and Tie, $20 (annual) ● supporting,
$100 (annual) ● one day, $15. **Description:** Disseminates information about the sport of ride and tie
to new and potential participants. Seeks to make
improvements in the level of competition, horsemanship and athletic performance. Establishes rules and
standards for ride and tie competitions for the protection of the human and equine contestants. **Computer
Services:** database, race schedule ● information
services, ride and tie resources. **Telecommunication Services:** electronic mail, rideandtiedon@aol.
com ● electronic mail, media@rideandtie.org. **Publications:** Newsletter, bimonthly. Contains race results,
annual point standings and articles.

23292 ■ RollerSoccer International Federation (RSIF)
PO Box 423318
San Francisco, CA 94142-3318
Ph: (415)864-6879
Fax: (415)437-0859
E-mail: rsif2@rollersoccer.com
URL: http://www.rollersoccer.com
Contact: Zack Phillips, Founder/Pres.
Founded: 1996. **Membership Dues:** general, $5
(annual). **Multinational. Description:** Seeks to
formally promote, develop and govern the sport of
RollerSoccer. Provides a forum for people interested
in the sport. **Computer Services:** Information ser-
vices, rollersoccer resources. **Telecommunication
Services:** electronic mail, zack@rollersoccer.com ●
electronic mail, info2@rollersoccer.com.

23293 ■ Southeastern Conference (SEC)
2201 Richard Arrington Blvd. N
Birmingham, AL 35203
Ph: (205)458-3000
Fax: (205)458-3031
URL: http://www.secsports.com
Contact: Mike Slive, Commissioner
Founded: 1932. **Members:** 12. **Staff:** 21. **Descrip-
tion:** Auburn University; Louisiana State University;
Mississippi State University; University of Alabama;
University of Arkansas; University of Florida; Univer-
sity of Georgia; University of Kentucky; University of
Mississippi; University of South Carolina; University
of Tennessee; Vanderbilt University. Regulates
intercollegiate athletics. **Awards: Type:** recognition.
Committees: TV. **Affiliated With:** National Collegiate
Athletic Association. **Publications:** Media Guides,
annual. Presents information on baseball, basketball,
football, golf, swimming, tennis, and track. ● News
Releases, biweekly. Newsletter. **Conventions/Meet-
ings:** competition ● annual conference - always May.

23294 ■ Southern Conference (SoCon)
702 N Pine St.
Spartanburg, SC 29303
Ph: (864)591-5100
E-mail: jiamarino@socon.org
URL: http://www.soconsports.com
Contact: Mr. John Iamarino, Commissioner
Founded: 1921. **Members:** 9. **Staff:** 10. **Budget:**
$1,000,000. **Description:** Colleges and universities.
Promotes intercollegiate athletics. Compiles statistics;
maintains speakers' bureau; provides educational
and charitable programs. **Libraries: Type:** reference.
Holdings: 1,000; archival material, business records,
clippings, periodicals. **Subjects:** intercollegiate athletics. **Awards:** Commissioner's Cup. **Frequency:** annual. **Type:** recognition. **Recipient:** to the SoCon
school fielding the league's best all-around men's
sports program ● D.S. McAlister Award. **Frequency:**
annual. **Type:** recognition. **Recipient:** to the SoCon
school that has showed great sportsmanship in its
athletic program ● Dave Hart Graduate Scholarship.
Frequency: annual. **Type:** scholarship. **Recipient:** to
a male student-athlete interested in pursuing a graduate degree ● David Knight Graduate Scholarship.
Frequency: annual. **Type:** scholarship. **Recipient:** to
a student-athlete interested in pursuing a graduate

degree ● Dorothy Hicks Graduate Scholarship. **Frequency:** annual. **Type:** scholarship. **Recipient:** to a
female student-athlete interested in pursuing a graduate degree ● Germann Cup. **Frequency:** annual.
Type: recognition. **Recipient:** to the SoCon school
fielding the league's best all-around women's sports
program ● Mike Wood Foundation Graduate Scholarship. **Frequency:** annual. **Type:** scholarship. **Recipient:** to a male/female student-athlete interested in
pursuing a graduate degree ● TIAA-CREF Student-
Athlete of the Year. **Frequency:** annual. **Type:**
scholarship. **Recipient:** to a student-athlete interested in pursuing a graduate degree. **Publications:**
Seasonal Sports Brochures, 3/year. Contains media
information on member schools. **Price:** $15.00. **Cir-
culation:** 1,000. **Advertising:** accepted ● Newsletters. Alternate Formats: online. **Conventions/Meet-
ings:** competition ● semiannual conference.

23295 ■ Southwest Athletic Conference (SWAC)
A.G. Gaston Bldg.
1527 5th Ave. N
Birmingham, AL 35204
Ph: (205)251-7573
Fax: (205)297-9820
E-mail: r.vowels@swac.org
URL: http://www.swac.org
Contact: Mr. Robert C. Vowels Jr., Commissioner
Founded: 1914. **Members:** 8. **Membership Dues:**
university, $1,000 (annual). **Staff:** 9. **National
Groups:** 2. **Multinational. Description:** Baylor
University; Rice University; Southern Methodist
University; Texas A&M University; Texas Christian
University; Texas Tech University; University of
Houston; University of Texas at Austin. Acts as a
regulatory body for men's and women's intercollegiate athletics in baseball, basketball, cross-country,
football, golf, tennis, track, women's soccer, and
swimming. **Awards:** Coach of the Year. **Frequency:**
annual. **Type:** recognition ● Player of the Year. **Frequency:** annual. **Type:** recognition. **Affiliated With:**
National Collegiate Athletic Association. **Publications:** Press Releases, 3/week. **Advertising:** accepted ● Record Book, annual, published separately
for each sanctioned sport. **Conventions/Meetings:**
semiannual conference - always winter and spring.

23296 ■ Sports Charities USA (SCUSA)
21 Tamal Vista Blvd., Ste.209
Corte Madera, CA 94925
Free: (800)874-0740
E-mail: sfsmith@maguireinc.com
URL: http://www.sportscharities.org
Description: Pre-screens national charities working
to promote athletic excellence, sports opportunities
and recreational experiences. Helps givers find
specific charities that are doing the work that they
wish to support. **Publications:** Annual Report.

23297 ■ Sports Hall of Oblivion
PO Box 69025
Pleasant Ridge, MI 48069
Ph: (248)543-9412
E-mail: wheresports@hotmail.com
Contact: Chuck Hershberger, Contact
Founded: 1982. **Description:** Works to preserve the
memory of defunct sports teams, including pro, semi-
pro, college, and high school. Maintains speakers'
bureau and museum; compiles statistics; conducts
research programs. **Libraries: Type:** reference.
Holdings: archival material, books, clippings, periodicals. **Subjects:** defunct sports leagues, teams, players, executives. **Publications:** Book. **Price:** $5.00
each.

23298 ■ Sportsplex Operators and Developers Association (SODA)
PO Box 24263
Westgate Sta.
Rochester, NY 14624-0263
Ph: (585)426-2215
Fax: (585)247-3112

E-mail: info@sportsplexoperators.com
URL: http://www.sportsplexoperators.com
Contact: Don Aselin, Exec. Dir.
Founded: 1981. **Members:** 1,140. **Membership
Dues:** professional, associate, $295 (annual) ● affili-
ate, $100 (annual) ● sustained, $995 ● social, $125
(annual). **Regional Groups:** 6. **Description:** Sports
complex operators, park and recreation directors,
and product and service supply companies. Seeks to
improve the financial performance of sports complexes. Organizes tours of the top sports complexes.
Makes available liability insurance. Fosters communication among members through a referral
service. Offers indoor and outdoor facilities. **Libraries: Type:** reference. **Holdings:** 12; video recordings. **Subjects:** facility walking tours. **Awards:**
Sportsplex of the Year. **Frequency:** annual. **Type:**
recognition. **Recipient:** for state-of-the art sports
complex. **Formerly:** (1995) Sportsplex Owners and
Directors of America; (1997) Sportsplex Operators
and Developers of America. **Publications:** SODA-
site, bimonthly. Magazine. Features articles on
increasing revenue, facility profiles, operating a pro
shop, concessions, and risk management. **Price:** $4.
95. **Circulation:** 1,500. **Advertising:** accepted ●
Sportsplex Planning and Operation Manual. **Conven-
tions/Meetings:** annual convention and trade show
(exhibits) - always January ● annual National Amateur Sports Symposium - symposium and trade show,
covers maximizing concession profits and obtaining
corporate sponsors, facility construction and operation (exhibits) - mid-December.

23299 ■ United States Adult Soccer Association (USASA)
9152 Kent Ave., Ste.C-50
Indianapolis, IN 46216
Ph: (317)541-8564
Fax: (317)541-8568
E-mail: bmccormick@usasa.com
URL: http://www.usasa.com
Contact: Brooks McCormick, Chm.
Description: Develops, promotes and administers
the game of soccer among players within the United
States. Develops amateur athletes for national and
international competitions. Promotes soccer and
physical fitness for all ages. **Computer Services:**
database, image gallery ● online services, message
board. **Committees:** Appeals; Budget; Coaching;
Credentials; Grants; Hall of Fame; Publicity; Referee.

23300 ■ United States Broomball Association (USBA)
26676 Berg Dr.
Monroe, OR 97456
Ph: (541)998-8294
E-mail: webmaster@usbabroomball.com
URL: http://usbabroomball.com
Contact: Craig McDaniel, Pres.
Membership Dues: general, $20 (annual). **Descrip-
tion:** Furthers the development of broomball in the
United States. Offers programs to teach skill training,
refereeing and rule development. **Computer Ser-
vices:** Information services, broomball resources.

23301 ■ United States Collegiate Athletic Association (USCAA)
c/o Mr. Bill Casto, Commissioner
4101 Washington Ave., Bldg. 601
Newport News, VA 23607
Ph: (757)688-5944 (757)380-7961
Fax: (757)688-3750
E-mail: info@theuscaa.com
URL: http://www.theuscaa.com
Contact: Mr. Bill Casto, Commissioner
Founded: 1966. **Members:** 46. **Membership Dues:**
full, $1,250 (annual). **Description:** Provides quality
athletic competition on a regional and national level
for smaller institutions of higher learning and their
student-athletes. Attempts to offer the opportunity for
the student-athlete to develop the mind, body, and
spirit through athletic competition as it strive to
promote integrity, leadership, scholarship, and values
of life. Believes in striving to place the pursuit of
education as one of the main priorities of student-
athletes. Aims to provide opportunities for small col-

leges to compete on an equal level of competition with schools of like size and athletic programs. Seeks to conduct national championships, name All-Americans, scholar athletes, and promote USCAA member schools. The association believes that the integrity and credibility of the organization and its members are paramount in accomplishing its mission. **Awards:** USCAA Academic All-American. **Frequency:** annual. **Type:** recognition. **Recipient:** to student athletes of junior or senior standing who hold a 35 GPA or above and showed a significant contribution to their team ● USCAA All-American. **Frequency:** annual. **Type:** recognition. **Recipient:** for the season's top athletes selected in their respective sport ● USCAA National Championship Trophy. **Frequency:** annual. **Type:** trophy. **Recipient:** to the winner of the USCAA national championship for each sport ● USCAA Player of the Week. **Frequency:** weekly. **Type:** recognition. **Recipient:** for the most valuable players. **Formerly:** (1989) National Little College Athletic Association; (2001) National Small College Athletic Association. **Publications:** *Membership Brochure*, annual ● *Statistics*, weekly ● *USCAA Daily Update*, weekly. Newsletter ● Directory, annual. **Conventions/Meetings:** annual convention.

23302 ■ United States Collegiate Sports Council (USCSC)

c/o Dr. Stanley Brassie, Exec. Dir.
305 Walton St.
Monroe, GA 30655
Ph: (707)267-2681
Fax: (707)206-9120
E-mail: stanbrassie@yahoo.com
Contact: Dr. Stanley Brassie, Exec. Dir.
Founded: 1967. **Members:** 5. **Membership Dues:** national college and university organization, $2,000 (annual). **Staff:** 1. **Budget:** $10,000. **National Groups:** 5. **Description:** Promotes international understanding through collegiate athletics; particularly, encourages increased U.S. participation in the International University Sports Federation events including the World University Games and individual sports championships. Organizes, conducts, and sponsors tours/competitions among foreign universities and American colleges and universities in several sports. **Divisions:** International Competition; International Physical Education Sports Symposium. **Conventions/Meetings:** semiannual meeting.

23303 ■ U.S. Cultural Exchange and Sports Society (USCESS)

Address Unknown since 2007
Founded: 1977. **Membership Dues:** $5 (annual). **Staff:** 14. **Budget:** $630,000. **Regional Groups:** 11. **Description:** Works in conjunction with similar organizations in other countries to coordinate residential cultural exchange programs for young people ages nine to 18; organizes sports activities worldwide. Offers programs in soccer, tennis, painting, gymnastics, ballet, music, martial arts, sailing, track, and other sports and disciplines. Maintains organizational contacts in the South Pacific region, Australia, New Zealand, Canada, Mexico, Tahiti, Japan, Sweden, Ireland, China, Korea, England, Germany, Italy and Netherlands. **Convention/Meeting:** none. **Also Known As:** U.S. Cultural Exchange Society. **Publications:** *U.S. Cultural Exchange and Sports Society—Newsletter*, periodic. **Advertising:** not accepted.

23304 ■ United States Futsal Federation (USFF)

PO Box 40077
Berkeley, CA 94704-4077
Ph: (510)836-8733
Fax: (510)527-8110
E-mail: futsal@futsal.org
URL: http://futsal.com
Contact: Alexander J.C. Para, Pres./CEO
Founded: 1983. **Description:** Acts as the national governing body for the sport of Futsal in the United States. Promotes Futsal in the United States. Encourages and supports amateur athletes. Promotes goodwill through physical fitness. **Computer Services:** Information services, futsal resources. **Committees:** Appeals; Budget and Audit; Coaches;

Credentials; International Games; International Players Selection; Marketing; National Championship.

23305 ■ U.S. Monoski Association (USMA)

5286 Apennines Cir.
San Jose, CA 95138
Ph: (408)603-9632
E-mail: info@usmonoski.org
URL: http://www.usmonoski.org
Contact: David Wells, Founder
Membership Dues: individual, $25 (annual). **Description:** Seeks to create broad recognition and understanding of monoskiing among the general public. Aims to expose thousands of potential new participants to the sport of monoskiing each year. Develops educational materials to assist new monoskiers in mastering the sport. **Computer Services:** Information services, monoskiing resources. **Publications:** *The Fine Line*. Newsletter. Alternate Formats: online.

23306 ■ United States Sports Academy (USSA)

1 Acad. Dr.
Daphne, AL 36526-7055
Ph: (251)626-3303
Free: (800)223-2668
Fax: (251)625-1035
E-mail: academy@ussa.edu
URL: http://www.ussa.edu
Contact: Dr. Thomas P. Rosandich, Pres./CEO
Founded: 1972. **Staff:** 50. **Description:** Works as an independent, non-profit, accredited, special mission sports university created to serve the nation and the world with programs in instruction, research and service. The role of the Academy is to prepare men and women for careers in the profession of sports. This organization is accredited by the Commission on Colleges of the Southern Association of Colleges and Schools to award the Bachelor of Sports Science degree (level II), the Master of Sports Science degree (level III), and the Doctor of Sports Management degree (level V). **Libraries:** Type: reference. **Holdings:** 9,000. **Subjects:** sport management, sport medicine, sport coaching, sport fitness management, sport research. **Awards:** United States Sports Academy Awards of Sport. **Frequency:** annual. **Type:** recognition. **Recipient:** to those who have made significant contributions to sport, in categories as diverse as the artist and the athlete in several different arenas of sport. **Computer Services:** database. **Additional Websites:** http://www.thesportjournal.org. **Departments:** Academic Services; Academy Sports Bookstore; American Sports Art Museum Archives; Communications; Computer Questions; Personnel and Job Openings; Student Services. **Publications:** *The Academy*, quarterly. **Price:** free. **Circulation:** 27,000 ● *The Sport Journal*, quarterly. **Price:** free. ISSN: 1543-9518. **Circulation:** 250,000. **Advertising:** accepted. Alternate Formats: online ● *The Sport Supplement*, quarterly. **Price:** free. **Circulation:** 27,000. Alternate Formats: online.

23307 ■ University Athletic Association (UAA)

30 Corporate Woods, Ste.280
Rochester, NY 14623
Ph: (585)784-8442
URL: http://www.uaa.rochester.edu
Contact: Dick Schultz, Exec. Sec.
Founded: 1986. **Members:** 8. **Staff:** 3. **Description:** College athletic conference in Division III of the National Collegiate Athletic Association. Seeks excellence in athletics while maintaining a perspective which holds the student-athlete and the academic mission of the institution as the center of focus. Members are: Brandeis University; Carnegie Mellon University; Case Western Reserve University; Emory University; New York University; University of Chicago; University of Rochester; Washington University. Compiles statistics. **Awards:** Type: recognition. **Committees:** Athletic Administrators; Delegates. **Councils:** Presidents. **Publications:** *Athlete of the Week*, weekly ● Manual, annual ● Brochures ● Also publishes press releases, standings, statistics, and championship results. **Conventions/Meetings:**

semiannual Athletic Administrators Committee Meeting - always in January and June ● annual Delegates Committee Meeting - always in March ● semiannual Presidents Council - meeting - always in April and October.

23308 ■ Western Athletic Conference (WAC)

9250 E Costilla Ave., Ste.300
Englewood, CO 80112
Ph: (303)799-9221
Fax: (303)799-3888
E-mail: wac@wac.org
URL: http://www.wacsports.com
Contact: Karl Benson, Commissioner
Founded: 1962. **Members:** 9. **Description:** Boise State University, Fresno State University of Hawaii, University of Idaho, Louisiana Tech University, University of Nevada, New Mexico State University, San Jose State University, Utah State University. Administers athletic competition in both men's and women's sports including football, basketball, baseball, cross-country, gymnastics, indoor and outdoor track and field, swimming and diving, tennis, golf, volleyball and softball. **Libraries:** Type: reference. **Awards:** Joe Kearney Award. **Frequency:** annual. **Type:** recognition. **Recipient:** to the top male and female athlete ● Stan Bates Award. **Frequency:** annual. **Type:** recognition. **Recipient:** to the top male and female scholar athletes. **Committees:** Western Athletic Conference Student-Athlete Advisory. **Publications:** *Media Guide*, annual. Handbooks. Covers football, basketball, baseball, volleyball, and softball. **Price:** $15.00. Alternate Formats: online ● Audiotapes. Alternate Formats: online ● Also publishes weekly releases of athletic events according to season.

23309 ■ Women's Sports Foundation (WSF)

Eisenhower Park
East Meadow, NY 11554
Ph: (516)542-4700
Free: (800)227-3988
Fax: (516)542-4716
E-mail: info@womenssportsfoundation.org
URL: http://www.womenssportsfoundation.org
Contact: Donna Lopiano PhD, CEO
Founded: 1974. **Members:** 6,000. **Membership Dues:** individual, $30 (annual). **Staff:** 25. **Budget:** $6,000,000. **Description:** Encourages and supports the participation of women in sports activities for their health, enjoyment, and mental development; educates the public about athletic opportunities and the value of sports for women. Develops educational guides, provides travel and training grants, scholarships and internship program, and supports the enforcement of the Title IX Amendments of the 1972 Equal Education Act and the Amateur Sports Act. Sponsors an information and resource clearinghouse on women's sports and fitness. Maintains International Women's Sports Hall of Fame. Compiles statistics on women's sports and fitness. **Libraries:** Type: reference. **Holdings:** 1,500; archival material, books, clippings, periodicals. **Subjects:** sports, women's sports and fitness. **Awards:** Billie Jean King Contribution Award. **Frequency:** annual. **Type:** recognition. **Recipient:** for corporations, organizations, or individuals who have made significant contributions to the development of women's sports ● Coaches Award. **Frequency:** annual. **Type:** recognition. **Recipient:** for female coaches working with youth, school and college athletes ● Flo Hyman Memorial Award. **Frequency:** annual. **Type:** recognition. **Recipient:** for female athletes who have captured Hyman's dignity, spirit and commitment to excellence ● International Women's Sports Hall of Fame. **Frequency:** annual. **Type:** recognition. **Recipient:** for female coaches or athletes who have made history in women's sports ● Sportswoman of the Year. **Frequency:** annual. **Type:** recognition. **Recipient:** for an individual and team sportswoman whose performances over a 12-month time span have been exceptional ● WBCA Graduate Student of the Year. **Frequency:** annual. **Type:** recognition. **Recipient:** for graduate assistants who have made a contribution to a college women's basketball program. **Computer Services:** Online services, responses to

info requests, memberships, publications. **Additional Websites:** http://www.gogirlgo.com. **Programs:** Community Awards and Grants. **Publications:** *Go-Girl News*, quarterly. Newsletter. Contains information for junior athletes. ● *Parents Guide to Girls Sports* ● *Playing Fair* ● *SportsTalk*, quarterly. Newsletter ● *The Women's Sports Experience*, quarterly. Newsletter ● Newsletter, weekly. Alternate Formats: online. **Conventions/Meetings:** symposium.

23310 ■ World Sport Stacking Association (WSSA)
PO Box 260526
Highlands Ranch, CO 80163-0526
Ph: (303)917-4171
Fax: (303)962-5650
E-mail: info@worldsportstackingassociation.org
URL: http://www.worldsportstackingassociation.org
Contact: Roger Washburn, Chm.

Founded: 2001. **Multinational. Description:** Promotes the standardization and advancement of sport stacking worldwide. Provides a uniform framework for sport stacking events. Sanctions sport stacking competitions and records. **Computer Services:** database, results and records ● information services, game rules and regulations.

Sports Facilities

23311 ■ Stadium Managers Association (SMA)
525 SW 5th St., Ste.A
Des Moines, IA 50309-4501
Ph: (515)282-8192
Fax: (515)282-9117
E-mail: sma@assoc-mgmt.com
URL: http://www.stadiummanagers.org
Contact: Kerry Goodson, Exec. Dir.

Founded: 1990. **Members:** 425. **Membership Dues:** stadium manager, $200 (annual) ● corporate, $500 (annual) ● affiliate, $200 (annual) ● student, $50 (annual). **Description:** Dedicated to the education of its members for the improvement of management of commercial sports facilities for the benefit of the general public. **Computer Services:** Mailing lists, of members. **Conventions/Meetings:** annual seminar.

Sports Officials

23312 ■ National Association of Sports Officials (NASO)
2017 Lathrop Ave.
Racine, WI 53405
Ph: (262)632-5448
Fax: (262)632-5460
E-mail: naso@naso.org
URL: http://www.naso.org
Contact: Barry Mano, Pres.

Founded: 1979. **Members:** 18,500. **Membership Dues:** individual, $94 (annual) ● regular, in Canada and Mexico, $121 (annual) ● international, $153 (annual). **Budget:** $1,300,000. **Description:** Active sports officials, umpires, companies, and individuals interested in sports. Develops programs to assist in the education of sports officials; engages in programs to instruct fans, coaches, players, and the media on the role of sports officials. Conducts clinics and camps; sponsors public service ads. **Awards:** Gold Whistle Award. **Frequency:** annual. **Type:** recognition. **Recipient:** for an outstanding contribution to the community. **Publications:** *Making the Call: The Inner Game of Sports Officiating*. Booklet. **Price:** $2.35 for members; $2.95 for nonmembers ● *News*, monthly. Newsletter ● *Referee*, monthly. Magazine. Contains interviews. **Price:** $44.95 /year for individuals. Alternate Formats: online ● Audiotapes ● Books ● Videos ● Reports, periodic. **Price:** $10.00. Alternate Formats: online. **Conventions/Meetings:** annual National Convention of Sports Officials ● semiannual seminar.

23313 ■ National Association of Sports Officials - Organizations Network (NASO-ON)
2017 Lathrop Ave.
Racine, WI 53405
Ph: (262)632-5448
Free: (800)733-6100
Fax: (262)632-5460
E-mail: naso-on@naso-on.org
URL: http://www.naso.org
Contact: Jim Neeb, Staff Coor.

Founded: 1990. **Members:** 397. **Membership Dues:** organization, $99 (annual). **Staff:** 20. **Description:** Associations and administrative bodies that uses the services of sports officials. Seeks to increase administrative capability and efficiency of member groups. Offers access to legal assistance and liability insurance. Fosters networking among members. **Libraries: Type:** reference. **Additional Websites:** http://www.naso-on.org. **Affiliated With:** National Association of Sports Officials. **Formerly:** (2004) Local Officials' Administration Network. **Publications:** *Guide to Local Association Management*. Covers training, assigning, meeting management, public relations, fund raising, recruiting and retention. **Circulation:** 500. Alternate Formats: online ● *NewsNet*, monthly. Newsletter. Discusses association management, public speaking, meeting presentations, and legal issues. **Conventions/Meetings:** annual National Conference of Sports Officials.

23314 ■ NFHS Officials Association
PO Box 690
Indianapolis, IN 46206
Ph: (317)972-6900
Fax: (317)822-5700
URL: http://www.nfhs.org
Contact: Mary Struckhoff, Asst. Dir.

Founded: 1981. **Members:** 130,000. **Membership Dues:** official, coach, $30 ● coach and official, $60 ● state organization, $12 (annual) ● organization, $20 (annual) ● individual/special group, $30 (annual). **Staff:** 5. **Budget:** $2,000,000. **Regional Groups:** 8. **State Groups:** 51. **Description:** High school, youth league, and college sports officials. Aims to promote the professional growth and image of interscholastic sports officials. Provides a forum for officials to make suggestions on rules and procedures in high school sports in the U.S. Cooperates with state associations and utilizes extensive committee structure to ensure grass roots involvement and input from the local, state, and national levels. Maintains hall of fame. **Awards:** National Distinguished Service Awards. **Frequency:** annual. **Type:** recognition. **Recipient:** for contributions to high school sports. **Committees:** Awards; Member Services; Professional Development; Public Information; Sports. **Affiliated With:** National Federation of State High School Associations; NFHS Coaches Association. **Formerly:** (2001) National Federation Interscholastic Officials Association; (2003) National Federation Officials Association. **Publications:** *Officials' Quarterly*. Magazine. **Price:** included in membership dues. **Circulation:** 180,000. **Advertising:** accepted.

23315 ■ Professional Association of Volleyball Officials (PAVO)
PO Box 780
Oxford, KS 67119
Free: (888)791-2074
Fax: (620)455-3800
E-mail: pavo@pavo.org
URL: http://www.pavo.org
Contact: Marcia Alterman, Exec. Dir.

Founded: 1969. **Members:** 1,950. **Membership Dues:** individual, $45 (annual). **Staff:** 2. **Budget:** $125,000. **State Groups:** 96. **Description:** Officials for girls' and women's volleyball. Works to train and assign ratings to officials for girls' and women's volleyball. **Awards:** PAVO Board Chair of the Year. **Frequency:** annual. **Type:** recognition. **Recipient:** for outstanding local leaders ● PAVO Honor Award. **Frequency:** annual. **Type:** recognition. **Recipient:** for an outstanding contribution through officiating. **Computer Services:** Mailing lists, of members. **Telecommunication Services:** electronic mail, executive.director@pavo.org. **Programs:** Line Judge

Certification. **Formerly:** (1999) Affiliated Boards of Officials. **Publications:** *The Official Word*, 5/year. Newsletter. **Circulation:** 1,900. **Advertising:** accepted. Alternate Formats: online ● *PAVO Officials' Guidebook*, annual ● *Rules Interpretation Newsletters*. Alternate Formats: online ● Manuals, annual ● Videos ● Booklets. **Conventions/Meetings:** annual Officials Convention - always winter. 2007 Dec. 13-15, Sacramento, CA; 2008 Dec. 18-20, Omaha, NE.

Squash

23316 ■ United States Squash Racquets Association (USSRA)
23 Cynwyd Rd.
PO Box 1216
Bala Cynwyd, PA 19004
Ph: (610)667-4006
Fax: (610)667-6539
E-mail: office@us-squash.org
URL: http://www.us-squash.org
Contact: Mr. Kevin Klipstein, CEO

Founded: 1920. **Members:** 8,000. **Membership Dues:** individual, group, $40 (annual) ● junior, $25 (annual) ● club, $75 (annual) ● corporate, $1,000 (annual) ● college and high school team, $250 (annual) ● life, $1,000. **Staff:** 6. **Budget:** $7,000,000. **Regional Groups:** 40. **Description:** Member of United States Olympic Committee. Aims to establish and enforce uniformity in the rules of the game, standardize court specifications and schedules, and conduct tournaments. **Committees:** Instructional Pictures; Junior Activities; Sanctioning; Sustaining. **Affiliated With:** United States Olympic Committee. **Publications:** *National Court Survey*, triennial. Directory. Lists squash courts in the United States. **Price:** $1.00/copy for members; $3.00/copy for nonmembers. **Advertising:** accepted ● *Squash Magazine*, 10/year. Features tournament news, rule changes, and training and fitness information. Includes standings and statistics. **Price:** $29.95 /year for nonmembers; included in membership dues. **Advertising:** accepted ● *U.S. Squash Racquets Association—Official Yearbook*. Directory. Lists the participants and results of the National Squash Championships. Also lists national rankings, officers, and member clubs. **Price:** included in membership dues; $6.00/copy for nonmembers. **Circulation:** 11,000. **Advertising:** accepted ● Videos. **Conventions/Meetings:** semiannual conference and competition.

Surfing

23317 ■ Association of Surfing Professionals (ASP)
PO Box 309
Huntington Beach, CA 92648
Ph: (714)536-3500
Fax: (714)536-4482
E-mail: meg@aspworldtour.com
URL: http://www.aspnorthamerica.org
Contact: Meg Bernardo, Exec. Mgr.

Founded: 1983. **Members:** 1,500. **Staff:** 10. **Regional Groups:** 7. **State Groups:** 2. **National Groups:** 5. **Description:** Surf shops, competitors, judges, sponsors, directors, and members of the communications media serving as the governing body of professional surfing worldwide. Sanctions world surfing tour. Compiles statistics. **Awards:** World Title. **Frequency:** annual. **Type:** recognition. **Publications:** *ASP Media Guide*, annual. Magazine. Includes biographies of surfers, previews of tour events, listing of tour records, and surfer ratings from the previous year. **Price:** $5.00. **Advertising:** accepted ● *ASP Newsletter*, monthly. Includes contest results, point ratings, and world tour schedule. **Price:** included in membership dues. **Circulation:** 1,000. **Conventions/Meetings:** annual meeting.

23318 ■ Eastern Surfing Association (ESA)
PO Box 625
Virginia Beach, VA 23451
Ph: (757)233-1790
Free: (866)SURF-ESA

Fax: (757)233-1396
E-mail: info@surfesa.org
URL: http://www.surfesa.org
Contact: Debbie Hodges, Exec. Dir.
Founded: 1967. **Members:** 10,000. **Membership Dues:** competition, $40 (annual) ● family, $50 (annual) ● noncompetition, general, $20 (annual). **Staff:** 31. **Budget:** $350,000. **Regional Groups:** 25. **Description:** Promotes the sport of surfing through amateur competitions; works to protect public beaches. Sponsors ecology education and scholarship aid programs. Qualifies East Coast amateur athletes to U.S. Championships and U.S. National Team Trials. **Awards:** Dr. Colin J. Couture Award for Volunteerism. **Frequency:** annual. **Type:** recognition. **Recipient:** for volunteers who are working for the betterment of East coast surfing. **Special Interest Groups:** Surfers for Environmental Action. **Publications:** Newsletter, quarterly. **Conventions/Meetings:** annual board meeting - always September, in Cape Hatteras, NC ● annual Eastern Surfing Championships - competition - always September, in Cape Hatteras, NC ● Eastern Surfing Championships Regional Qualifiers Northeast Mid-Atlantic Southeast - competition, for 1200 top ranked east coast athletes vie for east coast titles (exhibits) - 3/year.

23319 ■ International Surfing Association (ISA)
5580 La Jolla Blvd., PMB 145
La Jolla, CA 92037
Ph: (858)551-5292
Fax: (858)551-5290
E-mail: surf@isasurf.org
URL: http://www.isasurf.org
Contact: Fernando Aguerre, Pres.
Founded: 1976. **Members:** 50. **Membership Dues:** current and participatory (ranked no. 17), $1,000 (annual) ● current and participatory (ranked no. 1 to 16), $500 (annual) ● non-voting, non-participatory, $50 (annual). **Staff:** 1. **Budget:** $250,000. **National Groups:** 45. **Multinational. Description:** Comprised of surfers. Dedicated to the development of surfing and body boarding worldwide. Provides guidance and advice to member nations throughout the world. Sanctions, organizes and sponsors surfing, body-boarding competitions worldwide. Works to have the sport of surfing included in the Olympic Games. **Libraries: Type:** open to the public. **Subjects:** surfing world, Olympics updates. **Awards:** Kahuna Award. **Frequency:** annual. **Type:** recognition. **Recipient:** for supporter of ISA. **Committees:** Adaptive Surfing; Body Boarding; Medical; Technical; Water Safety; Women Surfing. **Publications:** ISA Guide, annual. Booklet. Includes general information about ISA and listing of all NGBs Medical information. **Price:** free. **Circulation:** 10,000. **Advertising:** accepted ● ISA Newsletter, quarterly. **Conventions/Meetings:** biennial general assembly ● annual meeting, vote for rulebook changes, executive/financial report ● trade show (exhibits) - 5/year.

23320 ■ National Scholastic Surfing Association (NSSA)
PO Box 495
Huntington Beach, CA 92648
Ph: (714)378-0889
Fax: (714)964-5232
E-mail: jaragon@nssa.org
URL: http://www.nssa.org
Contact: Janice Aragon, Exec. Dir.
Founded: 1978. **Members:** 5,000. **Staff:** 3. **Budget:** $95,000. **Regional Groups:** 5. **State Groups:** 6. **Description:** Students from grade six to college and others interested in the sport of surfing. Aims to provide student surfers with the opportunity to participate in national surfing competitions. Promotes high school and college team competitions and sponsors international cultural exchange trips. Maintains a national team training camp for a chosen group of student surfers. Develops a contest judge training program and evaluation system. **Awards: Frequency:** annual. **Type:** scholarship. **Recipient:** for outstanding student surfers. **Publications:** Surflines, quarterly. Newsletter. Includes surfing results, amateur information, and conference report. **Price:** free.

Circulation: 5,000. **Advertising:** accepted. **Conventions/Meetings:** annual Championship - competition.

23321 ■ Surfrider Foundation (SF)
PO Box 6010
San Clemente, CA 92674-6010
Ph: (949)492-8170
Free: (800)743-7873
Fax: (949)492-8142
E-mail: info@surfrider.org
URL: http://www.surfrider.org
Contact: Mr. Jim Moriarty, Exec. Dir./CEO
Founded: 1984. **Members:** 50,000. **Membership Dues:** student, senior, $15 (annual) ● regular, $25 (annual) ● family, $40 (annual) ● friend, retail, $100 (annual) ● supporter, $200 (annual) ● corporate, benefactor, $500 (annual) ● club, $2,000 (annual) ● life, $1,000. **Staff:** 19. **Budget:** $2,400,000. **Local Groups:** 60. **Description:** Individuals interested in coastal conservation and ocean wave recreation, especially surfing. Works to: preserve and enhance beach environments and coastal ecologies; promote water safety and recreational beach activity; protect such resources, when necessary, through local activism, education, conservation and research. Represented by 56 national chapters and affiliates in Australia, France, Brazil, and Japan. Monitors and participates in coastal zone management and planning. **Libraries: Type:** reference. **Holdings:** books, clippings, periodicals. **Subjects:** coastal environment, pollution, statistics. **Awards:** Pratte Scholarship. **Frequency:** annual. **Type:** recognition. **Recipient:** for students in environmental education attending Humboldt State University. **Publications:** Making Waves, bimonthly. Newsletter. **Circulation:** 40,000. Alternate Formats: online ● Bulletin, bimonthly ● Also offers slide presentations. Annual State of the Beach report. **Conventions/Meetings:** quarterly board meeting.

23322 ■ United States Surfing Federation (USSF)
Address Unknown since 2006
Founded: 1980. **Members:** 7. **Membership Dues:** associate, $500 (annual). **Staff:** 5. **Budget:** $270,000. **Regional Groups:** 4. **State Groups:** 41. **Description:** Confederation of regional and national amateur surfing associations representing 12,000 individuals. Conducts national championships and selects team for international competition. Supervises administration of amateur code; conducts charitable program; operates hall of fame. Members provide scholarships. **Awards:** Nancy Katin Scholarship. **Frequency:** annual. **Type:** scholarship. **Committees:** Competition. **Supersedes:** U.S. Surfing Association. **Publications:** Newsletter, quarterly. **Advertising:** accepted. **Conventions/Meetings:** annual board meeting - always summer ● annual US Championships - competition and trade show (exhibits).

Swimming

23323 ■ American Swimming Coaches Association (ASCA)
5101 NW 21st Ave., Ste.200
Fort Lauderdale, FL 33309
Ph: (954)563-4930
Free: (800)356-2722
Fax: (954)563-9813
E-mail: asca@swimmingcoach.org
URL: http://www.swimmingcoach.org
Contact: John A. Leonard, Exec. Dir.
Founded: 1958. **Members:** 5,000. **Membership Dues:** full, associate, $70 (annual) ● life, in U.S., $400 ● life plus, in U.S., $1,000 ● life, outside U.S., $600 ● life plus, outside U.S., $1,500. **Staff:** 12. **Budget:** $1,200,000. **Description:** Swimming coaches united for informational and educational purposes. Operates Swim America, a learn-to-swim program. Maintains placement service; conducts research programs; compiles statistics. **Awards:** Coach of the Year Award. **Frequency:** annual. **Type:** recognition. **Computer Services:** Mailing lists, of members. **Committees:** Ethics; Intern Coaching; Research. **Publications:** American Swimming Maga-

zine, semiannual. Includes interviews on stroke training and sample workout. ● Journal of Swimming Research, annual ● World Clinic Program ● World Clinic Yearbook ● Magazine, monthly. ISSN: 0747-6000. **Circulation:** 4,000. **Advertising:** accepted ● Newsletter, monthly. Contains information on the coaching profession, awards, and compensation. ● Videos. **Conventions/Meetings:** annual World Clinic - meeting (exhibits) - always September.

23324 ■ College Swimming Coaches Association of America (CSCAA)
c/o Phil Whitten, Exec. Dir.
10115 E Bell Rd., Ste.107
Scottsdale, AZ 85260
Ph: (480)628-5488
Fax: (480)699-4852
E-mail: swimphil@aol.com
URL: http://www.cscaa.org
Contact: Phil Whitten, Exec. Dir.
Founded: 1922. **Members:** 900. **Membership Dues:** division I-III, $150 (annual) ● associate, $25 (annual) ● college swimming official of America, $30 (annual). **Staff:** 3. **Budget:** $50,000. **Description:** College and university swimming and diving coaches organized to promote college swimming. Disseminates information; maintains placement service and hall of fame. **Awards:** Charles MacCaffree Award. **Frequency:** annual. **Type:** recognition. **Recipient:** for persons who have made outstanding contributions to swimming ● National Collegiate Trophy. **Frequency:** annual. **Type:** trophy ● Richard Steadman Award. **Type:** recognition. **Recipient:** for persons who have made outstanding contributions to swimming. **Committees:** All-America Swimming Team; Collegiate and Scholastic Award; Education; 15-25-40 Year Awards; Fort Lauderdale Forum; Research; Special Awards. **Publications:** Top Ten Times, 10/year ● Newsletter, 9/year. **Conventions/Meetings:** annual College Swim Coaches Forum - conference (exhibits) - always fall ● annual meeting.

23325 ■ International Academy of Aquatic Art (IAAA)
c/o Nadine Pietrantoni, VP, Membership
803 E Washington Blvd.
Lombard, IL 60148
E-mail: napietran@comcast.net
URL: http://www.aquatic-art.org
Contact: Nadine Pietrantoni, VP, Membership
Founded: 1955. **Members:** 250. **Membership Dues:** individual, $15 (annual) ● life, $300. **Multinational. Description:** Individuals and teams interested and involved in aquatic art. (Aquatic art is an outgrowth of synchronized swimming and water ballet.) Aims to recognize aquatic art as a performing art and to explore its artistic and creative development. Seeks to establish an academic environment conducive to the full development of aquatic art forms; encourages the development of standards to assist in the evaluation of skill execution and creative choreography/performance. Promotes interest and participation in aquatic art. Sanctions and sponsors aquatic art events and exhibitions. Maintains hall of fame. **Libraries: Type:** reference. **Subjects:** aquatic art. **Awards: Type:** recognition. **Recipient:** for individuals exhibiting distinguished service and performance. **Publications:** The Aquatic Artist, quarterly. Newsletter. **Price:** included in membership dues. **Advertising:** accepted ● Books ● Videos ● Also publishes information packets. **Conventions/Meetings:** symposium ● annual workshop, aquatic art techniques and dance expression, choreography, and music interpretation.

23326 ■ International Gay and Lesbian Aquatics (IGLA)
c/o Bernie LaFianza, Treas.
7423 Hollywood Blvd.
Los Angeles, CA 90046-2819
E-mail: treasurer@igla.org
URL: http://www.igla.org
Contact: Bernie LaFianza, Treas.
Founded: 1987. **Membership Dues:** individual, $15 (annual) ● small team (1-5), $30 (annual) ● medium sized team (6-24), $60 (annual) ● large team (25-49), $125 (annual) ● very large team (50 or more),

$250 (annual). **Local Groups:** 70. **Multinational. Description:** Represents swimming, water polo, synchronized swimming and diving teams that are predominantly gay and lesbian. Aims to promote participation in aquatic sports among lesbians and gay men and friends of the community; and to ensure maintenance of the highest international standards for all Gay Games. Provides a networking source for approximately 70 predominantly gay and lesbian teams in 15 countries. Organizes an annual international championship tournament in swimming, diving, water polo and synchronized swimming and is the governing body for aquatics sports at the quadrennial Gay Games. **Affiliated With:** Federation of Gay Games. **Publications:** *WetNotes*, quarterly. Newsletter. Contains current activities of and matters of interest to the organization. **Price:** included in membership dues. Alternate Formats: online.

23327 ■ International Swimming Hall of Fame (ISHOF)

1 Hall of Fame Dr.
Fort Lauderdale, FL 33316
Ph: (954)462-6536
Fax: (954)522-4521
E-mail: ishof@ishof.org
URL: http://www.ishof.org
Contact: Bruce Wigo, Pres./CEO

Founded: 1965. **Members:** 1,800. **Membership Dues:** platinum, $5,000 (annual) ● junior, $15 (annual) ● contributor, $100 (annual) ● bronze, school/club, $250 (annual) ● silver, non-profit/aquatic related organization, $500 (annual) ● gold, corporate, $1,000 (annual) ● individual, $35 (annual). **Staff:** 10. **Budget:** $1,000,000. **Description:** Businesses and individuals in 23 countries interested in supporting the museum. Promotes aquatic education. Honors and supports swimming, diving, water polo, synchronized swimming, water safety, and aquatic art. **Libraries: Type:** reference. **Holdings:** 49,000; biographical archives, books, photographs, video recordings. **Subjects:** aquatic sports. **Awards:** Aquatic Sports Grants. **Frequency:** annual. **Type:** grant. **Recipient:** for extensive, specific accomplishments ● G. Harold Martin Award. **Frequency:** annual. **Type:** recognition. **Recipient:** for long and exceptional leadership ● Gold Medallion Award. **Frequency:** annual. **Type:** recognition. **Recipient:** to former competitive swimmer ● ISHOF Service Award. **Frequency:** annual. **Type:** recognition. **Recipient:** for outstanding commitment and service ● Paragon Awards. **Frequency:** annual. **Type:** recognition. **Recipient:** for outstanding contributions to competitive swimming ● Presidential Honor. **Frequency:** annual. **Type:** recognition. **Recipient:** for an extraordinary athletic achievement. **Publications:** *Aquatic Sports Books* ● *International Swimming Hall of Fame—News*, quarterly. Newsletter. **Price:** included in membership dues. **Circulation:** 2,500. **Advertising:** accepted. **Conventions/Meetings:** semiannual board meeting ● competition.

23328 ■ National Interscholastic Swimming Coaches Association of America (NISCA)

c/o Arvel McElroy
Olathe South High School
Olathe, KS 66062
Ph: (913)780-7160 (785)841-6624
Fax: (913)780-7170
E-mail: president@nisca.net
URL: http://www.nisca.net
Contact: Mark Onstott, Pres.

Founded: 1934. **Members:** 1,500. **Membership Dues:** individual, $50 (annual) ● special team/joint NISCA, ASCA, CSCA and ISHOF, $150 (annual) ● joint NISCA and CSCA, $70 (annual) ● joint NISCA and ASCA, $110 (annual) ● joint NISCA, ASCA and CSCA, $130 (annual). **Budget:** $100,000. **Description:** Persons engaged in coaching swimming, diving, and related aquatic sports at an intermediate or high school level. Objectives are to: educate youth about aquatic sports for the promotion of health, fitness, and recreation; adopt, improve, and advance aquatics programs for intermediate and secondary schools; promote interscholastic swimming nationally and locally. Fosters cooperation among aquatic agencies and services. Maintains hall of fame; compiles

statistics. **Awards:** Collegiate-Scholastic. **Frequency:** annual. **Type:** recognition ● Hall of Fame. **Frequency:** annual. **Type:** recognition ● Outstanding Service. **Frequency:** annual. **Type:** recognition. **Publications:** *High School Academic All-America*, annual ● *High School Diving All-America*, annual ● *High School Swimming All-America*, annual ● *High School Water Polo All-America*, annual ● *Journal*, bimonthly. Contains association news, rankings of swimmers, and power points standings. Includes rules changes, convention revisions, and annual report. **Advertising:** accepted ● Newsletter, 4-5/year. **Circulation:** 1,500. **Advertising:** accepted. **Conventions/Meetings:** annual conference (exhibits) ● National High School Senior Swimming and Diving Championship - competition.

23329 ■ Polar Bear Club - U.S.A. (PBC-USA)

Coney Island
Staten Island, NY 10305
Ph: (718)356-7741
E-mail: lns92@aol.com
URL: http://www.polarbearclub.org
Contact: Dennis Thomas, VP

Founded: 1903. **Members:** 95. **Description:** Winter swimmers; potential winter swimmers. Group meets every Sunday during the winter on Coney Island, at Stillwell Ave. and the Boardwalk, to swim in the Atlantic Ocean. Advocates program including exercises such as jogging, ball playing, and training to acclimate the body to extreme weather. Has sponsored charitable activities. During summer, members are concerned with maintaining clean waters and beaches. **Formerly:** (1981) Coney Island Polar Bear Club; (1986) Polar Bear Club - Winter Swimmers. **Conventions/Meetings:** quarterly meeting.

23330 ■ Synchro Swimming U.S.A.

201 S Capitol, Ste.901
Indianapolis, IN 46225
Ph: (317)237-5700
Fax: (317)237-5705
E-mail: webmaster@usasynchro.org
URL: http://www.usasynchro.org
Contact: Virginia Jasontek, Pres.

Founded: 1980. **Members:** 5,700. **Membership Dues:** regular, master, $59 (annual) ● collegiate, recreational, $44 (annual) ● seasonal, booster, association official, $29 (annual) ● technical, $69 (annual) ● life, $1,250. **Staff:** 10. **Budget:** $1,400,000. **Regional Groups:** 15. **State Groups:** 58. **Local Groups:** 300. **National Groups:** 300. **Description:** Governing body for synchronized swimming in the US. Guides and supports all competitive and recreational levels of the sport. Selects and trains the National Team athletes who represent the US internationally including the Pan American and Olympic Games. Provides leadership and resources for the promotion and growth of the sport and strives for competitive excellence at all levels and to develop broad-based participation. **Committees:** Development; International; Officials; Technical. **Programs:** American Coaching Effectiveness; Coaches Certification. **Affiliated With:** International Amateur Swimming Federation; U.S. Aquatic Sports; United States Olympic Committee. **Formerly:** (2002) United States Synchronized Swimming. **Supersedes:** Synchronized Swimming Division of the Amateur Athletic Union. **Publications:** *Official Rulebook* ● *Synchro Intro.* Book. Acts as a reference for recreational level coaches. **Price:** $20.00 plus $4 shipping/handling ● *USA Synchro*, monthly. Newsletter. Contains the latest synchro happenings. Alternate Formats: online ● Magazine. Promotes education and knowledge of sport. **Price:** $20.00 in U.S.; $30.00 all other countries. **Circulation:** 5,000. **Advertising:** accepted. **Conventions/Meetings:** competition, on synchronized swimming ● annual US Aquatic Sports Convention, legislative body and members meet for rules revisions, coaching education, committee meetings (exhibits) - always fall.

23331 ■ U.S. Aquatic Sports (USAS)

c/o Debra Turner, Marketing Coor.
7565 Oceanline Dr.
Indianapolis, IN 46214-4118

Ph: (317)829-5787
Fax: (317)829-5779
E-mail: usas@usaquatic.com
URL: http://www.usaquatic.org
Contact: Dale Neuburger, Pres.

Founded: 1980. **Budget:** $55,000. **National Groups:** 5. **Description:** Holds international franchise for swimming, diving, synchronized swimming, and water polo through United States Diving, United States Synchronized Swimming, U.S.A. Swimming, and U.S. Water Polo. Each organization acts as a separate governing body for its sport and provides teams for the Olympic and Pan American Games. U.S. member of International Amateur Swimming Federation. Conducts conventions for the four sports. **Conventions/Meetings:** annual convention (exhibits) - 2008 Sept. 22-28, Atlanta, GA.

23332 ■ United States Masters Swimming (USMS)

PO Box 185
Londonderry, NH 03053-0185
Free: (800)550-SWIM
Fax: (603)537-0204
E-mail: info@usms.org
URL: http://www.usms.org
Contact: Tracy Grilli, Admin.

Founded: 1970. **Members:** 40,500. **Membership Dues:** individual, $15 (annual). **Staff:** 5. **Regional Groups:** 53. **Local Groups:** 504. **For-Profit. Description:** Adults aged 19 years and over interested in participating in swimming for fun, fitness, and competition. Sponsors short course in May and long course in August. Conducts research, educational, and charitable programs. Maintains speakers' bureau. Compiles statistics. Maintains 16 committees and 7 special assignments. **Libraries: Type:** reference. **Awards:** David Yorzyk Memorial Award. **Frequency:** annual. **Type:** recognition. **Recipient:** to an outstanding swimmer of 400-yard individual medley at the Short Course National Championships ● Dorothy Donnelly USMS Service Award. **Frequency:** annual. **Type:** recognition. **Recipient:** to the most talented volunteer ● Newsletter of the Year Award. **Frequency:** annual. **Type:** recognition. **Recipient:** to the most outstanding club newsletter ● Raleigh Area Masters National Championship Award. **Frequency:** annual. **Type:** recognition. **Recipient:** to the most outstanding person in USMS national championship meets ● Ransom Arthur Award. **Frequency:** annual. **Type:** recognition. **Recipient:** for outstanding service ● Speedo/USMS Coach of the Year Award. **Frequency:** annual. **Type:** recognition. **Recipient:** to the most outstanding coach ● USMS Fitness Award. **Frequency:** annual. **Type:** recognition. **Recipient:** for an outstanding contribution to fitness activities within USMS. **Formerly:** (1980) Masters Swimming Committee of the AAU. **Publications:** *Building a Successful Masters Club*. Book. Contains information on how to start and build a masters swim program. **Price:** $6.00. Alternate Formats: online ● *Masters Swimming — What's It All About?*. Brochure ● *Streamlines*. Newsletter. Alternate Formats: online ● *USMS Rule Book*, annual. Includes the names of USMS record holders, rules of competition, administrative operating codes, and national and world records. **Price:** $9.00/copy ● *USMS Swimmer*. Magazine. **Advertising:** accepted. **Conventions/Meetings:** annual convention, part of the United States Aquatic Sports convention (exhibits) - 2008 Sept. 13-17, Atlanta, GA.

23333 ■ United States Swim School Association

PO Box 17208
Fountain Hills, AZ 85269
Ph: (480)837-5525
Fax: (480)836-8277
E-mail: info@usswimschools.org
URL: http://www.usswimschools.org
Contact: Sue Mackie, Exec. Dir.

Founded: 1988. **Members:** 300. **Membership Dues:** domestic school, $300 (annual) ● international school, $200 (annual) ● retired owner, $50 (annual) ● life, $3,000 ● Champion's Club, $250 (annual). **Budget:** $250,000. **Description:** Owners, managers, and staff of swimming schools. Promotes professional operation and effective teaching in swimming programs; gathers and disseminates information on trends and techniques in swimming instruction. Conducts research and educational programs; participates in charitable activities; maintains hall of fame; compiles statistics. **Libraries: Type:** not open to the public. **Holdings:** 275. **Subjects:** swim school management, swim teaching. **Awards:** Guiding Light. **Frequency:** annual. **Type:** recognition. **Recipient:** for outstanding contribution to the organization. **Computer Services:** Mailing lists, of members. **Telecommunication Services:** electronic mail, scott@usswimschools.org. **Committees:** Conference; Ethics; Nominating. **Formerly:** (2004) National Swim School Association. **Publications:** *Making Waves*, quarterly. Newsletter. Alternate Formats: online ● *Swimformation*, quarterly. Newsletter. **Circulation:** 350. **Advertising:** accepted. **Conventions/Meetings:** annual conference (exhibits).

23334 ■ USA Swimming (USS)
1 Olympic Plz.
Colorado Springs, CO 80909
Ph: (719)866-4578
Fax: (719)866-4669
E-mail: media@usaswimming.org
URL: http://www.usswim.org
Contact: Chuck Wielgus, Exec. Dir.
Founded: 1980. **Members:** 286,000. **Membership Dues:** individual, $25 (annual). **Staff:** 65. **Budget:** $15,000,000. **Local Groups:** 59. **Description:** Swimmers, former swimmers, coaches, officials, administrators, and athletic associations. National governing body for competitive amateur swimming. Selects teams for various international competitions including the Olympics. Trains officials; conducts swimming programs for persons five years of age and older on the local, state, regional, national, and international levels. Conducts research and compiles statistics. Maintains speakers' bureau and biographical archives. Conducts Coaches College, a week-long intensive study program to increase the effectiveness of new swimming coaches. **Awards: Type:** recognition. **Recipient:** for swimmers and volunteers. **Computer Services:** Mailing lists, of members. **Sections:** Age Group; Olympic International; Senior. **Supersedes:** Competitive Swimming Committee of the Amateur Athletic Union. **Publications:** *Code of Regulations and Technical Rules*, annual ● *National Qualifier*, 3/year. Newsletter ● *Splash!*, bimonthly. Newsletter ● *United States Swimming Directory*, annual. **Conventions/Meetings:** competition ● annual conference (exhibits).

23335 ■ World Aquatic Babies and Children (WABC)
PO Box 10596
St. Petersburg, FL 33733
Ph: (727)804-3399
Fax: (727)230-7489
E-mail: info@wabcswim.com
URL: http://www.wabcswim.com
Contact: Mr. Steve Graves, Pres.
Founded: 1994. **Membership Dues:** individual - teacher or director, $95 (annual) ● program, $195 (annual). **For-Profit. Multinational. Description:** International individuals and programs united to promote aquatic programs for babies and children. Conducts clinics and biennial conference. Conducts research. Publishes newsletter. **Libraries: Type:** reference. **Subjects:** teaching of swimming skills; teaching of personal water safety; teaching principles and strategies of drowning prevention. **Awards: Frequency:** periodic. **Type:** recognition. **Recipient:** to individuals who made outstanding contributions to the development of baby and childrens aquatic programming (learn to swim skills, personal water safety skills, and drowning prevention strategies) ● Virginia Hunt Newman International Award. **Frequency:** annual. **Type:** recognition. **Recipient:** to an individual who shares the philosophy and spirit of Newman. **Formerly:** (2001) United States Swimming Foundation; (2006) World Aquatic Babies Congress. **Publications:** *WABC Online Newsletter*, periodic. Contains information on teaching swimming, personal

water safety, and drowning prevention. **Advertising:** accepted. Alternate Formats: online. **Conventions/Meetings:** biennial conference, educational conference for professional teachers and program directors working with babies and young children (exhibits).

Table Tennis

23336 ■ U.S.A. Table Tennis (USATT)
1 Olympic Plz.
Colorado Springs, CO 80909-5769
Ph: (719)866-4583
Fax: (719)632-6071
E-mail: usatt@usatt.org
URL: http://www.usatt.org
Contact: Doru Gheorghe, Exec. Dir.
Founded: 1933. **Members:** 7,500. **Membership Dues:** junior, collegiate, $20 (annual) ● individual, $40 (annual) ● household, outside U.S., $60 (annual) ● league, $12 (annual) ● life (over 70), $100 ● life (millennium), $650. **Staff:** 6. **Regional Groups:** 7. **Local Groups:** 250. **For-Profit. Description:** Sanctions more than 300 table tennis tournaments yearly; develops and modifies rules; presents instructional exhibitions. Sends U.S. players to biennial world championships, Pan American Games, and many foreign countries. Maintains hall of fame. Conducts educational programs. **Libraries: Type:** reference. **Holdings:** archival material. **Computer Services:** Mailing lists, of members. **Committees:** Clubs; Coaching; Officials; Tournament Sanctioning. **Affiliated With:** United States Olympic Committee. **Formerly:** (1994) United States Table Tennis Association. **Publications:** *Club Handbook* ● *Instructors Guide* ● *Laws of Table Tennis* ● *Tournament Guide* ● *USA Table Tennis Magazine*, bimonthly. **Price:** included in membership dues; $50.00 for nonmembers outside U.S.; $20.00 for nonmembers in U.S. ISSN: 1068-5782. **Circulation:** 7,000. **Advertising:** accepted. Alternate Formats: online ● *USA Table Tennis Update*. Newsletter ● *USATT Handbook*. **Conventions/Meetings:** quarterly board meeting ● annual U.S. Nationals - competition - always December ● annual U.S. Open - competition - always July.

T'ai Chi

23337 ■ Patience T'ai Chi Association (PTCA)
2620 E 18th St.
Brooklyn, NY 11235
Ph: (718)332-3477
E-mail: contact@patiencetaichi.com
URL: http://www.patiencetaichi.com
Contact: William C. Phillips, Pres./Founder
Founded: 1982. **Members:** 20. **Membership Dues:** regular, $15. **Staff:** 2. **Budget:** $5,000. **Description:** Individuals interested in T'ai Chi (T'ai Chi Ch'uan), a slow-motion exercise, meditation, and movement program for health and relaxation that originated in China during the ninth or tenth century. Offers several classes and lectures on the Yang short form of T'ai Chi Ch'uan. Offers instructional videotapes; grants certification upon completion of courses. Maintains speakers' bureau, and placement service; conducts seminars. **Libraries: Type:** reference. **Holdings:** archival material. **Awards: Type:** recognition. **Conventions/Meetings:** periodic meeting ● annual Tai Chi Family Gathering - conference (exhibits) ● T'ai Chi Weekend - workshop - every weekend.

Tennis

23338 ■ American Medical Tennis Association (AMTA)
1803 Cobblestone Dr.
Provo, UT 84604
Free: (800)326-2682
Fax: (801)374-0135
E-mail: amta@mdtennis.org
URL: http://www.mdtennis.org
Contact: Craig Broome, Pres.
Founded: 1967. **Members:** 200. **Membership Dues:** individual, $50 (annual). **Staff:** 1. **Budget:** $50,000.

Description: Physicians. Plans and conducts tennis tournaments exclusively for physicians and their families. Sponsors educational programs. **Publications:** *AMTA Newsletter*, semiannual. **Conventions/Meetings:** annual meeting ● Omni-Specialty Medical Update - competition.

23339 ■ American Platform Tennis Association (APTA)
PO Box 99
Summit, NJ 07901
Ph: (908)522-0009
Free: (888)744-9490
Fax: (908)934-9257
E-mail: aptahq@platformtennis.org
URL: http://www.platformtennis.org
Contact: Marjorie Hodson, Exec. Dir.
Founded: 1931. **Members:** 8,000. **Membership Dues:** individual, $50 (annual) ● family, $75 (annual) ● junior, $15 (annual) ● life (individual), $750 ● life (husband/wife), $1,000. **Staff:** 1. **Regional Groups:** 6. **Description:** Individuals, tennis clubs, commercial centers, and municipalities. Promotes and regulates the game. Provides officials and sanctions tournaments. **Awards:** National Championships. **Type:** trophy. **Recipient:** for winners of national competitions in open and age group divisions. **Committees:** Communications; Players; Regional Associations. **Publications:** *How to Conduct a Tournament Draw* ● *Platform Tennis Magazine*, 5/year. **Circulation:** 7,500. **Advertising:** accepted. Alternate Formats: online ● *Sportsmanship Booklet* ● Also publishes rules book and a tournament schedule. **Conventions/Meetings:** annual meeting - always May in New York City or New Jersey.

23340 ■ American Tennis Association (ATA)
1100 Mercantile Ln., Ste.115A
Largo, MD 20774
Ph: (301)583-4631
E-mail: info@atanational.com
URL: http://www.atanational.com
Contact: Willis Thomas Jr., Pres.
Founded: 1916. **Members:** 5,000. **Membership Dues:** adult, $25 (annual) ● junior, $12 (annual) ● family, $50 (annual) ● life, $200. **Budget:** $100,000. **Regional Groups:** 50. **State Groups:** 8. **Description:** Persons interested in tennis. Promotes and develops tennis regardless of race. Supports training programs to develop Teaching Professionals. Sponsors training programs for young players; conducts 60 state and local tournaments. **Affiliated With:** Professional Tennis Registry. **Publications:** *ATA News*, quarterly. Newsletter. **Advertising:** accepted. Alternate Formats: online ● *Black Tennis Magazine*, quarterly. **Conventions/Meetings:** annual competition and seminar, national tournament (exhibits).

23341 ■ Gay and Lesbian Tennis Alliance (GLTA)
5510 Curdy Rd.
Howell, MI 48855
E-mail: info@glta.net
URL: http://www.glta.net
Contact: Daniel Merrithew, Sec.
Founded: 1991. **Membership Dues:** club, $125 (annual). **Description:** Gay and lesbian tennis players; organizations conducting tennis tournaments and events for gay and lesbian individuals. Promotes increased participation by gay and lesbian people in tennis. Manages and sanctions tennis matches and tournaments worldwide. Represents the sport of tennis within the Federation of Gay Games. **Telecommunication Services:** electronic mail, secretary@glta.net. **Conventions/Meetings:** annual competition.

23342 ■ Intercollegiate Tennis Association (ITA)
c/o David A. Benjamin, Exec. Dir.
174 Tamarack Cir.
Skillman, NJ 08558-2021
Ph: (609)497-6920
Fax: (609)497-9766

E-mail: ita@itatennis.com
URL: http://www.itatennis.com
Contact: David A. Benjamin, Exec. Dir.
Founded: 1956. **Members:** 2,200. **Membership Dues:** coach (1 program), $125-$305 (annual) ● coach (2 programs), $200-$610 (annual) ● assistant coach, $55-$70 (annual) ● additional assistant coach, junior player/junior parent outside U.S., $75 (annual) ● collegiate parent in U.S., alumni in U.S., $60 (annual) ● collegiate parent outside U.S., alumni outside U.S., association, $95 (annual) ● junior player/junior parent in U.S., $40 (annual) ● corporate, $595 (annual) ● associate in U.S., $70 (annual) ● associate outside U.S., $105 (annual) ● federation, $250 (annual). **Staff:** 6. **Budget:** $1,000,000. **Description:** Serves as the governing body of collegiate tennis. Members include tennis coaches in universities, colleges, junior colleges, and other institutions; auxiliary. Sponsors intercollegiate regional tournaments and national tennis championships; compiles intercollegiate standings for teams, singles and doubles; awards granted to coaches and players in recognition of outstanding sportsmanship, athletic and academic achievement; maintains separate men's and women's tennis halls of fame. Operates endorsement programs with tennis industry companies. **Libraries:** Type: reference. **Holdings:** archival material. **Awards:** Frequency: annual. **Type:** recognition. **Recipient:** for persons who display outstanding sportsmanship or athletic or academic performances. **Committees:** Ethics and Infractions; Men's and Women's Operating; National Tournament; Rules and Rankings. **Divisions:** Junior and Community Colleges; Men's and Women's Collegiate Tennis Hall of Fame; NAIA; NCAA I, II, III. **Formerly:** (1956) National Collegiate Tennis Coaches Association; (1958) Intercollegiate Tennis Coaches Association. **Publications:** *ITA Coaches Directory*, annual. Alternate Formats: online ● *ITA Pages in Tennis Week* ● *The ITCA Guide to Coaching Winning Tennis*. **Conventions/Meetings:** annual Coaches Convention - conference and seminar, includes clinics (exhibits).

23343 ■ International Tennis Hall of Fame (ITHOF)
194 Bellevue Ave.
Newport, RI 02840
Ph: (401)849-3990
Free: (800)457-1144
Fax: (401)849-8780
E-mail: newport@tennisfame.com
URL: http://www.tennisfame.com
Contact: Tony Trabert, Pres.
Founded: 1954. **Members:** 7,500. **Description:** Seeks to foster interest in tennis, its history, and its athletic heroes. Supports junior tennis training programs; conducts amateur and professional grass-court competitions; maintains a museum. Produces video programs. Inducts new Hall of Fame members annually, including administrators, coaches, players, and writers. **Libraries:** Type: reference. **Holdings:** 2,000; books, films, photographs, video recordings. **Subjects:** tennis. **Awards:** Bill Talbert Junior Sportsmanship Awards. **Frequency:** annual. **Type:** recognition. **Recipient:** to junior players who exemplify the qualities of sportsmanship ● Davis Cup and Fed Cup Awards of Excellence. **Frequency:** annual. **Type:** recognition. **Recipient:** to persons who represent the ideals and spirit of the Davis and Fed Cup Competitions ● Golden Achievement Award. **Frequency:** annual. **Type:** recognition. **Recipient:** to individuals who have made important contributions to the field of tennis ● Great Tennis Nation. **Frequency:** biennial. **Type:** recognition. **Recipient:** to countries with rich tennis heritage ● Samuel Hardy Award. **Frequency:** annual. **Type:** recognition. **Recipient:** to a volunteer ● Tennis Educational Merit Awards. **Frequency:** annual. **Type:** recognition. **Recipient:** to men and women who have made notable contributions in the field of tennis. **Formerly:** Tennis Educational Foundation; (1975) National Tennis Educational Foundation; (1989) National Tennis Foundation and Hall of Fame. **Publications:** *Hall of Fame News*, quarterly. Newsletter. **Price:** included in membership dues. **Circulation:** 5,000. **Advertising:** accepted ● Annual Report, annual.

23344 ■ Major Wingfield Historical Society
c/o Stanley Malless, Pres.
5401 Greenwillow Rd.
Indianapolis, IN 46226
Ph: (317)547-1336 (317)545-1717
Free: (800)547-1336
Fax: (317)549-9259
E-mail: smalless@permanentmagnetco.net
Contact: Stanley Malless, Pres.
Founded: 1974. **Members:** 55. **Membership Dues:** regular, honorary, $25 (annual). **Description:** Promotes tennis. Compiles research on tennis for the U.S. Tennis Association. Promotes other tennis projects. Honors Major Walter Clopton Wingfield (1833-1912), who invented the sport of lawn tennis. Compiles statistics. Maintains museum and speakers' bureau. Sponsors educational and research programs. **Libraries:** Type: reference. **Holdings:** archival material, books. **Subjects:** tennis history. **Awards:** Type: recognition. **Computer Services:** Mailing lists. **Affiliated With:** United States Tennis Association. **Formerly:** (2001) Major Wingfield Club. **Publications:** *Edwardian Gentleman: Major Clopton Wingfield*. Book. Contains 300 pages. **Conventions/Meetings:** annual meeting (exhibits).

23345 ■ National Public Parks Tennis Association (NPPTA)
c/o USTA Northern
1001 W 98th St., No. 101
Bloomington, MN 55431
Ph: (952)887-5001
Fax: (952)887-5061
E-mail: bach@northern.usta.com
URL: http://www.northern.usta.com
Contact: Marcia Bach, Pres.
Founded: 1923. **Members:** 77. **Membership Dues:** $100 (annual). **Budget:** $60,000. **State Groups:** 21. **Description:** Public tennis clubs, teams, associations, recreation departments, and other interested tennis groups at the public park level. Encourages public recreation departments and agencies in the operation of an efficient Public Parks Tennis Program. **Publications:** Newsletter, annual. **Conventions/Meetings:** annual Tennis Championships - competition.

23346 ■ National Senior Women's Tennis Association (NSWTA)
PO Box 7115
West Palm Beach, FL 33405
Ph: (561)307-8026
E-mail: nswta10@aol.com
URL: http://www.nswta.com
Contact: Carolyn Nichols, Pres.
Founded: 1974. **Members:** 1,200. **Staff:** 20. **Description:** Women over 30 years of age and others interested in senior women's competitive tennis. Promotes senior women's tennis events. Sponsors a national, intersectional, and team competition event. **Committees:** Team Competition. **Affiliated With:** United States Tennis Association. **Publications:** *National Senior Women's Tennis Association Newsletter*, quarterly. **Conventions/Meetings:** annual meeting - always spring, Houston, TX, during National Senior Women's Clay Court Championship Tournament.

23347 ■ Peter Burwash International Special Tennis Programs (PBISTP)
4200 Res. Forest Dr., Ste.250
The Woodlands, TX 77381
Ph: (281)363-4707
Free: (800)255-4707
E-mail: hq@pbitennis.com
URL: http://www.pbitennis.com
Founded: 1984. **Regional Groups:** 6. **Description:** Promotes worldwide interest in the game of tennis to individuals of every age and ability. Seeks to provide fitness, fun and heightened self-esteem to disabled or imprisoned individuals. Fosters communication between handicapped and nonhandicapped individuals. Increases awareness of the achievements and abilities of disabled persons to the able-bodied public. Offers special tennis instruction to blind, deaf, retarded persons, wheelchair athletes and prison

inmates. Conducts educational programs, demonstrations, shows, tournaments and tennis clinics. Provides teaching and coaching professionals to clubs and hotel facilities worldwide. **Conventions/Meetings:** annual meeting.

23348 ■ Professional Tennis Registry (PTR)
PO Box 4739
Hilton Head Island, SC 29938
Ph: (843)785-7244
Free: (800)421-6289
Fax: (843)686-2033
E-mail: ptr@ptrtennis.org
URL: http://www.ptrtennis.org
Contact: Daniel Santorum, CEO/Exec. Dir.
Founded: 1976. **Members:** 8,000. **Membership Dues:** regular, in U.S. and Canada, $125 (annual) ● regular, outside U.S., $115 (annual) ● affiliate, $75 (annual). **Staff:** 10. **Budget:** $1,500,000. **Languages:** English, French, Italian, Spanish. **Description:** Tests, certifies, and registers international tennis teaching professionals; Certification requires successful completion of a written and on-court examinations. Sponsors workshops, tennis clinics, and charitable program. Holds competitions; compiles statistics; maintains placement service. **Libraries:** Type: reference. **Holdings:** books. **Subjects:** tennis teaching and coaching instruction. **Awards:** Type: recognition. **Formerly:** Professional Tennis Registry - U.S.A.; (2003) United States Professional Tennis Registry. **Publications:** *Courtlines*, bimonthly ● *TennisPro*, bimonthly. Magazine ● *USPTR Membership Directory*, annual ● Also publishes instructors manuals. **Conventions/Meetings:** periodic conference and seminar ● annual symposium.

23349 ■ Sony Ericsson WTA Tour
1 Progress Plz., Ste.1500
St. Petersburg, FL 33701
Ph: (727)895-5000
Fax: (727)894-1982
E-mail: webmaster@wtatour.com
URL: http://www.wtatour.com
Contact: Larry Scott, CEO
Founded: 1975. **Members:** 1,000. **Staff:** 40. **Budget:** $26,000,000. **Multinational. Description:** Works to increase and strengthen the global popularity and stature of the women's professional tennis tour, and to further advance the game as the preeminent sport for women worldwide. **Awards:** Diamond Aces. **Frequency:** annual. **Type:** trophy. **Recipient:** for promoting tennis on and off the court ● Doubles Team of the Year. **Frequency:** annual. **Type:** trophy. **Recipient:** for teams ● Most Impressive Newcomer. **Frequency:** annual. **Type:** trophy. **Recipient:** for the most impressive newcomer of the year ● Most Improved Player. **Frequency:** annual. **Type:** trophy. **Recipient:** for the most improved player of the year ● Player of the Year. **Frequency:** annual. **Type:** trophy. **Recipient:** for players. **Affiliated With:** International Tennis Federation. **Formerly:** (1993) Women's International Professional Tennis Council; (1994) Women's Tennis Council; (1999) COREL WTA Tour; (2000) WTA Tout; (2005) Sanex WTA Tour.

23350 ■ United States Dental Tennis Association (USDTA)
c/o Iris Kenworthy, Exec. Dir.
1414 Rhorer Rd.
Bloomington, IN 47401
Free: (800)445-2524
Fax: (812)336-7376
E-mail: usdta@sbcglobal.net
URL: http://www.dentaltennis.org
Contact: Iris Kenworthy, Exec. Dir.
Founded: 1969. **Members:** 500. **Membership Dues:** dentist, dental specialist, $50 (annual). **Staff:** 1. **Budget:** $20,000. **Description:** Licensed Dentists and Dental Specialists. Conducts national dental education courses. Promotes continuing education programs to improve the members' skills in the practice of dentistry. Encourages dentists to play tennis, regardless of their level of skill, for the betterment of their physical and mental well-being. Sponsors seminars and tennis tournaments. **Awards:** Type: recognition. **Recipient:** for tournament winners. **Com-**

mittees: Hospitality; Publicity; Scientific Program; Tennis. **Affiliated With:** Academy of General Dentistry; American Dental Association. **Publications:** *USDTA Today,* semiannual. Newsletter. Alternate Formats: online ● Membership Directory, annual. Lists all officers and current members. **Price:** included in membership dues ● Also publishes programs for meetings, and brochures to advertise each meeting. **Conventions/Meetings:** annual Desert Dental Classic - general assembly and conference - always November, in Palm Springs, CA or Arizona ● triennial international conference ● annual meeting.

23351 ■ United States National Tennis Academy (USNTA)

3523 McKinney Ave., Ste.208
Dallas, TX 75204
Ph: (214)887-5999
Free: (800)452-8519
Fax: (214)887-4826
E-mail: usnta@usnta.com
URL: http://www.usnta.com
Contact: Mr. S.J. Cockerham, Dir.
Founded: 1982. **Members:** 2,124. **Membership Dues:** active, $47 (annual). **Staff:** 3. **Description:** Trains and certifies tennis teaching professionals. Produces and distributes distance learning teacher training course; individuals who successfully complete the course are designated as Certified Tennis Teaching Professionals. Sponsors educational programs. **Formerly:** (1994) National Tennis Academy. **Publications:** *USNTA News Notes,* monthly. Newsletter. Includes listing of USNTA certified professionals. **Price:** included in membership dues. **Circulation:** 2,053.

23352 ■ United States Professional Tennis Association (USPTA)

3535 Briarpark Dr., Ste.1
Houston, TX 77042
Ph: (713)978-7782
Free: (800)USPTA-4U
Fax: (713)978-7780
E-mail: uspta@uspta.org
URL: http://www.uspta.com
Contact: Tim Heckler, CEO
Founded: 1927. **Members:** 14,500. **Staff:** 25. **Budget:** $5,000,000. **Regional Groups:** 17. **Multinational. Description:** Professional tennis instructors, tennis-teaching professionals and college coaches. Seeks to improve tennis instruction in the United States; maintains placement bureau and library. Offers specialized adult education; sponsors competitions; administers an adult tennis league and a nationwide program to introduce children ages 3-10 to tennis. Sponsors annual "Tennis Across America" program each spring. **Computer Services:** database, sports marketing program administration. **Committees:** Academy; Awards; Education; Ethics; Testing and Classification. **Formerly:** Professional Lawn Tennis Association of United States; (1971) United States Professional Lawn Tennis Association. **Publications:** *ADDvantage,* monthly. Magazine. Provides information on sports science, club/pro relations, and research. Includes reports, tips on industry action, and division news. **Price:** included in membership dues. **Advertising:** accepted ● Directory, annual.

23353 ■ United States Tennis Association (USTA)

70 W Red Oak Ln.
White Plains, NY 10604
Ph: (914)696-7000
Free: (800)990-8782
Fax: (914)696-7167
E-mail: sylvan@usta.com
URL: http://www.usta.com
Contact: D. Lee Hamilton, Exec. Dir./Chief Operating Off.
Founded: 1881. **Members:** 665,000. **Membership Dues:** junior, $18 (annual) ● adult, $40 (annual) ● family, $65 (annual). **Staff:** 225. **Budget:** $155,000,000. **Description:** Federation of local tennis clubs, educational institutions, recreation departments, and other groups and individuals interested in the promotion of tennis. Works to develop tennis as a

means of healthful recreation and physical fitness and maintain high standards of fair play and sportsmanship. Sanctions thousands of tennis tournaments for all age groups throughout the U.S. each year. Sponsors Junior Program for boys and girls under 18 years of age; U.S. national tennis team; national championships for various age groups; National Circuit tournament for pro and amateur players; Davis Cup, Fed Cup, Olympics international matches; and adult recreational leagues. Compiles statistics on leading professional and amateur players. **Libraries: Type:** reference. **Subjects:** tennis. **Awards: Type:** recognition. **Recipient:** for tennis players. **Additional Websites:** http://www.usopen.org, http://www.usatennis.com. **Committees:** Adult/Senior Competition; Awards; Community Development; Davis Cup; Fed Cup; Information Technology; International Competition; Minority Participation; Officials; Olympic; Professional Competition; SERV; Special Populations; Sport Science; Tennis Innovation; Tennis Rules; US Open; USA League Tennis; USA NJTL Tennis; USA Schools Tennis; USA Team Tennis; USA Team Tennis 1-2-3; Wheelchair Tennis; Youth Competition and Training. **Affiliated With:** International Tennis Federation. **Formerly:** (1975) United States Lawn Tennis Association. **Publications:** *Official USTA Yearbook* ● *Tennis Championships Magazine,* periodic ● *Tennis USTA,* annual. Annual Report. **Price:** included in membership dues. **Circulation:** 75,000. **Advertising:** accepted. **Conventions/Meetings:** annual meeting - always August or September in New York, NY ● semiannual meeting.

23354 ■ USA Tennis - NJTL

70 W Red Oak Ln.
White Plains, NY 10604-3602
Ph: (914)696-7000
Free: (800)990-8782
E-mail: njtl@usta.com
URL: http://www.usta.com
Contact: Dan. Limbago, Natl. Mgr.
Founded: 1969. **Members:** 200,000. **Local Groups:** 1,000. **Description:** A community-based introductory youth team program designed to provide all youngsters access to tennis. Motivates and maintains youngsters' interest in not only tennis, but in education. Introduces youngsters to basic strokes, uses a simple scoring method and promotes team play. **Awards:** USTA/NJTL Chapter of the Year. **Frequency:** annual. **Type:** recognition. **Affiliated With:** United States Tennis Association. **Formerly:** (1999) USTA/National Junior Tennis League. **Publications:** *USTA/NJTL On-Court Program Guide,* annual ● *USTA/NJTL Program Development Guide,* annual ● *USTA/NJTL-Tennis Beat,* monthly. Newsletter. **Conventions/Meetings:** competition ● annual meeting and workshop.

23355 ■ WTA Tour Players Association (WTA)

1 Progress Plz., Ste.1500
St. Petersburg, FL 33701
Ph: (727)895-5000
Fax: (727)894-1982
E-mail: kwulff@wtatour.com
URL: http://www.wtatour.com
Contact: Larry Scott, CEO
Founded: 1973. **Members:** 450. **Staff:** 32. **Budget:** $2,000,000. **Description:** Professional women tennis players. Purpose is to represent members with regard to professional tournaments. **Formerly:** (1986) Women's Tennis Association; (1991) Women's International Tennis Association; (1994) Women's Tennis Association. **Publications:** *Getting Started,* annual ● *Inside Women's Tennis,* monthly ● *Media Guide,* annual ● *Players Handbook,* annual ● *Tournament Guide,* annual. **Conventions/Meetings:** annual meeting.

Track and Field

23356 ■ DECA, The Decathlon Association

c/o Dr. Frank Zarnowski, Founder/Exec. Dir.
58 2nd Ave.
Emmitsburg, MD 21727-9169

Ph: (301)447-6122 (301)447-6255
E-mail: zarnowsk@msmary.edu
URL: http://www.decathlonusa.org
Contact: Dr. Frank Zarnowski, Founder/Exec. Dir.
Founded: 1974. **Members:** 380. **Staff:** 1. **Description:** Individuals who enjoy and support the decathlon including athletes, former athletes, coaches, meet directors, and fans. (A decathlon is a 10-event amalgam athletic contest consisting of the 100-meter, 400-meter, and 1500-meter runs, 110-meter high hurdles, discus and javelin throws, high jump, long jump, pole vault, and shot put.) Has established the Decathlon Roll of Honor listing Olympic gold medalists. Maintains files containing results of past decathlon competitions and decathlon training information. **Formerly:** (1993) DECA. **Publications:** *DECA Newsletter,* 8/year. **Price:** $3.00. **Circulation:** 380. Alternate Formats: online ● *The Decathlon: A History of Track and Field's Most Challenging Event.* Book ● *The Decathlon Book,* biennial. **Conventions/Meetings:** annual meeting.

23357 ■ Fifty-Plus Lifelong Fitness

658 Bair Island Rd., Ste.200
Redwood City, CA 94063
Ph: (650)361-8282
Fax: (650)361-8885
E-mail: info@50plus.org
URL: http://www.50plus.org
Contact: Jim Warren, Pres.
Founded: 1980. **Members:** 2,000. **Membership Dues:** regular, $50 (annual). **Staff:** 1. **Budget:** $150,000. **Description:** Men and women aged 50 years and older who exercise regularly. Seeks to provide a basis for exchanging information about exercise and its benefits among the growing number of over-50 exercisers, and to provide a statistical base for health surveys and other long-range studies of the effects of regular exercise. Circulates newsletters as a means of exchanging information and stimulating interest in all aspects of 50-plus exercises. Plans include organizing occasional runs, walks, or get-togethers in various regions. **Libraries: Type:** reference. **Holdings:** 100. **Computer Services:** Mailing lists, of members. **Formerly:** (1991) Fifty-Plus Runners Association; (2005) Fifty-Plus Fitness Association. **Publications:** *Fifty-Plus Bulletin,* quarterly. Contains book reviews and research reports. **Price:** included in membership dues. **Circulation:** 3,000. **Advertising:** accepted. Alternate Formats: online; diskette. **Conventions/Meetings:** annual Fitness Weekend - meeting (exhibits).

23358 ■ International Track and Field Coaches Association (ITFCA)

1705 Evanston St.
Kalamazoo, MI 49008
Ph: (269)349-1008
Fax: (269)387-4461
E-mail: cdales@webtv.com
Contact: George Dales, Pres.
Founded: 1959. **Members:** 1,150. **Membership Dues:** active, honorary, $10 (annual). **Staff:** 2. **Languages:** English, French, Greek. **Multinational. Description:** Facilitates the exchange of knowledge and ideas among track and field coaches worldwide. Collects and disseminates information on topics including new techniques and research concerning track and field sports. Sponsors congresses, clinics, and social activities. **Awards:** Honorary Member. **Type:** recognition. **Recipient:** for active members for 30 years. **Also Known As:** Association International des Entraineurs d'Athletisme. **Publications:** *Congress Reports,* biennial. Contains technical and educational information. **Price:** $20.00. **Circulation:** 1,100. **Advertising:** accepted. Also Cited As: *XIV ITFCA Congress Proceedings/Edmonton 2001.* **Conventions/Meetings:** biennial congress (exhibits).

23359 ■ New York Road Runners Club (NYRRC)

9 E 89th St.
New York, NY 10128
Ph: (212)860-4455 (212)423-2249

E-mail: membership@nyrr.org
URL: http://www.nyrrc.org
Contact: Mary Wittenberg, Pres./CEO
Founded: 1958. **Members:** 34,000. **Membership Dues:** basic, $35 (annual) ● family, $55 (annual) ● junior, senior, $20 (annual) ● international, $45 (annual) ● benefactor, $199 (annual) ● basic, $59 (biennial) ● basic, $139 (5/year) ● basic, $59 (biennial) ● life - supporter, $999 ● life - patron, $5,000. **Staff:** 55. **Budget:** $10,000,000. **Description:** Runners united to promote running for fitness and competition. Sponsors 150 races throughout the year, including New York City Marathon and Triathlon. Conducts classes and clinics for beginning, intermediate, and advanced runners. Organizes evening group runs in New York City boroughs; provides first aid at races and medical consultants at clinics. Gives members discounts on running merchandise and racing entry fees; donates running equipment to charitable programs; conducts program for the homeless. **Libraries: Type:** reference. **Holdings:** 750; films, periodicals, video recordings. **Telecommunication Services:** electronic mail, classes@nyrr.org ● electronic mail, results@nyrr.org ● electronic mail, marathonmailer@nyrr.org. **Programs:** Handicapped Running; Rikers Island; Urban Running. **Affiliated With:** Road Runners Club of America; U.S.A. Track and Field. **Publications:** *New York Runner*, bimonthly. Magazine. Running magazine for members of the NYRRC. **Advertising:** accepted ● Also publishes list of scheduled races. **Conventions/Meetings:** annual meeting and banquet, includes awards.

23360 ■ New York Triathlon Club (NYTC)
PO Box 50
Saugerties, NY 12477-0050
Ph: (845)247-0271
URL: http://www.nytc.org
Founded: 1984. **Members:** 3,000. **Membership Dues:** regular, $25 (annual) ● sponsor, $50 (annual) ● benefactor, $100 (annual) ● life, $500. **Description:** Encourages physical fitness through safe participation in triathlons, which are endurance races consisting of three phases (swimming, bicycling, and running). Acts as clearinghouse of information for all triathletes; sponsors races, seminars, and training clinics. Although membership is concentrated in New York and the eastern seaboard areas, activities are open to people around the world. **Computer Services:** Online services, calendar of events. **Formerly:** (2003) Big Apple Triathlon Club. **Publications:** *Tri-ing Times*, bimonthly.

23361 ■ Road Runners Club of America (RRCA)
8965 Guilford Rd., Ste.150
Columbia, MD 21046-2397
Ph: (410)290-3890
Fax: (410)290-3893
E-mail: office@rrca.org
URL: http://www.rrca.org
Contact: Jean Knaack, Exec. Dir.
Founded: 1958. **Members:** 180,000. **Membership Dues:** individual, $25 (annual) ● club (35 or fewer members), $99 (annual). **Staff:** 3. **Budget:** $797,200. **Regional Groups:** 4. **State Groups:** 47. **Local Groups:** 600. **Description:** Active long-distance runners and other persons who are interested in promoting long-distance running on an amateur basis in the U.S. Works to encourage running, especially road running, by sponsoring championships and other races on the road, track, and cross-country; also sponsors time trials, social runs, jogging, lectures, and demonstrations. Originates Run for Your Life, a physical fitness program of "fun runs" for men, women, and children. Certifies road courses; maintains hall of fame, speakers' bureau, and records of competitions. **Libraries: Type:** open to the public. **Holdings:** periodicals. **Subjects:** running, training, anecdotes. **Awards:** Hall of Fame Award. **Frequency:** annual. **Type:** recognition. **Recipient:** for individual who has made significant contributions, either as an athlete or an administrator ● Jerry Little Memorial Journalism Awards. **Frequency:** annual. **Type:** recognition. **Recipient:** for outstanding club newsletter and club writer of the year ● Journalistic Excellence Award. **Frequency:** annual. **Type:** recognition. **Recipient:** to a professional journalist in the sport of running ● National Volunteer Award Certificate Program. **Frequency:** annual. **Type:** recognition. **Recipient:** to all club volunteers ● Outstanding State Representative. **Frequency:** annual. **Type:** recognition. **Recipient:** for superior service of a state representative ● Roadrunners of the Year Award. **Frequency:** annual. **Type:** recognition. **Recipient:** to male and female runners ● Rod Steele Award. **Frequency:** annual. **Type:** recognition. **Recipient:** for outstanding club volunteer ● Scott Hamilton Award. **Frequency:** annual. **Type:** recognition. **Recipient:** for outstanding RRCA club president. **Computer Services:** database, members. **Committees:** Awards; Children's; Coaching; Computer; Legal; National Championships; Personal Fitness; Trends and Issues; Women's Distance. **Formerly:** (1963) National Road Runners Club. **Publications:** *Foot-Notes*, quarterly. Magazine. **Circulation:** 200,000. **Advertising:** accepted ● Manual. **Conventions/Meetings:** annual convention (exhibits).

23362 ■ United States Cross Country Coaches Association (USCCCA)
c/o Walt Drenth, Pres.
Michigan State Univ.
Jenison Fieldhouse
East Lansing, MI 48824
Ph: (517)355-1640
Fax: (517)432-3339
E-mail: admin@usccca.org
URL: http://www.usccca.org
Contact: Geoff Masanet, Treas.
Members: 70. **Membership Dues:** regular, $30 (annual). **Staff:** 1. **Regional Groups:** 9. **Description:** Professional organization of college and university cross country coaches. Selects 25 member All-American University College Cross Country Team each year. **Awards:** Academic All-Americans in Cross-Country. **Frequency:** annual. **Type:** recognition. **Recipient:** for all American top 30 at Nationals or top 30 Americans at Nationals ● All-Americans. **Frequency:** annual. **Type:** recognition. **Recipient:** for those with academic 3.25 GPA, All American in Nationals or top 12 in Region. **Formerly:** National Collegiate Cross Country Coaches Association. **Publications:** *Minutes*, annual. **Conventions/Meetings:** annual NCAA Cross Country Meet - competition ● annual NCAA Outdoor Track and Field Meet - competition.

23363 ■ United States Modern Pentathlon Association (USA Pentathlon)
1 Olympic Plz.
Colorado Springs, CO 80909-5780
Ph: (719)866-4608 (719)632-5551
Fax: (719)866-4850
URL: http://www.usapentathlon.org
Contact: Cecil Bleiker, Contact
Founded: 1958. **Members:** 400. **Membership Dues:** individual, $35 (annual) ● family, $60 (annual) ● life, $1,000. **Staff:** 3. **Budget:** $650,000. **State Groups:** 1. **Local Groups:** 6. **For-Profit. Multinational. Description:** Concerned with development, training, and selection of pentathlon teams to represent the U.S. in Olympic Games, Pan American Games, World Championships, and other international competitions. Conducts trial competitions, national championships, and international competitions; also conducts, in conjunction with the United States Olympic Committee, development clinics for potential Modern pentathletes. Compiles statistics. **Awards:** Norman Cain Memorial Award. **Frequency:** annual. **Type:** recognition. **Recipient:** for members of the All-American Team. **Affiliated With:** United States Olympic Committee. **Formerly:** (1981) United States Modern Pentathlon and Biathlon Association; (2002) USA Pentathlon. **Publications:** Newsletter, quarterly. Provides information on upcoming events related to athletes. **Price:** included in membership dues. **Circulation:** 1,000. **Advertising:** accepted. **Conventions/Meetings:** quarterly board meeting.

23364 ■ U.S.A. Track and Field (USATF)
1 RCA Dome, Ste.140
Indianapolis, IN 46225
Ph: (317)261-0500
Fax: (317)261-0481
E-mail: bill.roe@usatf.org
URL: http://www.usatf.org
Contact: Bill Roe, Pres.
Founded: 1979. **Members:** 90,000. **Membership Dues:** individual (maximum fee), $20 (annual) ● youth, individual (minimum fee), $12 (annual). **Staff:** 38. **Budget:** $15,000,000. **Local Groups:** 57. **Description:** Athletic clubs, high school and college/university athletic groups, athletic officials, statisticians, and fans. Serves as the national governing body for track and field, long distance running, and race walking. Arranges international competition for U.S. athletes, organizes national championship events, and provides clinics and training camps. Operates professional, nationally-televised track and field series - the Visa Championship Series. Keeps official U.S. athletic records and codifies and enforces athletic rules. Conducts high performance and sports science programs to improve athletic performance. Conducts youth fitness, healthy lifestyle and fair play programs under the "Be A Champion" banner. Inducts honorees into the National Track & Field Hall of Fame honoring retired athletes, coaches, and meritorious contributors in the sports of track and field, race walking, and long distance running. **Awards: Frequency:** annual. **Type:** recognition. **Recipient:** for outstanding performance in and contribution and service to track and field, long distance running, and race walking. **Computer Services:** Online services, events calendar, televised event schedule, membership directory. **Telecommunication Services:** information service, travel agent, (800)955-5822 ● 24-hour hotline, confidential anti-doping hotline, (866)809-8104. **Committees:** Associations; Athletes Advisory; Athletics for the Disabled; Budget & Finance; Coaching Education; Communications; Cultural Exchange; International Competition; Law and Legislation; Masters Long Distance Running; Masters Track and Field Works; Member Services; Men's and Women's Race Walking; Men's Development; Men's Long Distance Running; Men's Track and Field; Officials; Overview Project Group; Public Relations Task Group; Race Walking; Records; Road Running Technical; Rules; Site Selection; Sponsor Support Advisory Task Group; Sports Medicine and Sports Science; Standards; Substance Abuse Education and Testing (Doping Control); U.S. Olympic Festival; Women's Development; Women's Long Distance Running; Women's Track and Field; Youth Athletics. **Councils:** Cross Country Running. **Programs:** Be A Champion; Zero Tolerance. **Affiliated With:** International Association of Athletics Federations. **Formerly:** (1993) The Athletics Congress of the U.S.A. **Publications:** *Competition Rules for Athletics*, annual ● *Fast Forward*, quarterly. Magazine. **Price:** free for members. **Circulation:** 90,000. **Advertising:** accepted ● *Track Technique*, quarterly. Magazine ● *USA Track & Field Media Guide and FAST Annual*, annual. Media guide for sport with elite athlete biographies, performance lists, and extension records section. **Advertising:** accepted. **Conventions/Meetings:** annual convention, annual convention and business meeting; governance and rule making; hall of fame and other ceremonies; expo show and social gatherings (exhibits) - 2007 Nov. 28-Dec. 2, Honolulu, HI - **Avg. Attendance:** 1300; 2008 Dec. 3-7, Reno, NV.

23365 ■ USA Triathlon (USAT)
1365 Garden of the Gods Rd., Ste.250
Colorado Springs, CO 80907-3425
Ph: (719)597-9090
Fax: (719)597-2121
E-mail: info@usatriathlon.org
URL: http://www.usatriathlon.org
Contact: Mr. Skip Gilbert, Exec. Dir.
Founded: 1982. **Members:** 47,000. **Membership Dues:** adult individual, $30 (annual). **Staff:** 16. **Budget:** $800,000. **Regional Groups:** 11. **Description:** National governing body for the sport of triathlon in the U.S. and its representative to the U.S. Olympic Committee and to the International Triathlon Union. Coordinates grassroots and elite triathlon events across the country and works to create interest and participation in those programs; the elite level is

responsible for the selection and training of teams to represent the U.S. in international competition, including the world championship and Olympic games. Conducts national camps and clinics and provides coaching education programs; the developmental level fosters grassroots expansion of the sport, which is facilitated by the sanctioning of age-group events and triathlon clubs. Aims to provide leadership and structure for the growth and development of excellence in multi-sport. Works to inspire fitness as a healthy lifestyle, create a culture for excellence in leadership and competition and be a world leader in the sport. **Awards:** Athlete of the Year Awards. **Frequency:** annual. **Type:** recognition ● Race of the Year Awards. **Frequency:** annual. **Type:** recognition. **Computer Services:** Mailing lists. **Committees:** Age Group; Championship; Insurance; Masters; Medical; Officials; Women's. **Formerly:** (1983) U.S. Triathlon Association. **Publications:** *Official Manual*, annual ● *Race Director Manual*, annual ● *Triathlon Competition Guide*, annual ● *Triathlon Times: Official Newsletter of Triathlon Federation/United States of America*, bimonthly. Contains information on rules, regulations, and race listings. Includes calendar and race results, equipment, safety, and Olympic news. **Price:** included in membership dues. **Circulation:** 20,000. **Advertising:** accepted. Also Cited As: *Triathlon Times*. **Conventions/Meetings:** annual Race Management Conference.

Tractor Pulling

23366 ■ American Tractor Pullers Association (ATPA)
15501 WCR 13
Platteville, CO 80651
Free: (800)750-7048
E-mail: info@papullersonline.com
URL: http://www.atpapullersonline.com
Founded: 1991. **Description:** Serves as a sanctioning body of professional truck and tractor pulling in the United States. Promotes the sport of tractor and truck pulling. **Telecommunication Services:** electronic mail, american.pullers@gte.net.

23367 ■ National Tractor Pullers Association (NTPA)
6155-B Huntley Rd.
Columbus, OH 43229
Ph: (614)436-1761
Fax: (614)436-0964
E-mail: gregg@ntpapull.com
URL: http://www.ntpapull.com
Contact: Keith Theobald, Pres.
Founded: 1969. **Members:** 5,600. **Budget:** $1,800,000. **State Groups:** 30. **Description:** Serves as a division of World Pulling International. Represents competitors and associates. Promotes the sport of tractor and truck pulling (a competition in which contestants try to pull a weighted sled with a tractor or truck farther than their opponents before its weight overcomes the power of their machines). Standardizes rules and competition categories for events and handles promotion and advertising. Operates Pulling Foundation, which makes available scholarships. Maintains hall of fame. **Awards: Type:** recognition ● US Tobacco Hard Charger Award. **Frequency:** annual. **Type:** monetary. **Recipient:** to the NTPA competitor that puts forth the supreme effort. **Committees:** Technical. **Publications:** *Pull! Program and Yearbook*. Magazine. Covers all classes of NTPA competition. Includes an overview of the previous year end points champions and stories on safety, sleds, and vehicles. **Price:** $5.00 plus shipping and handling. **Circulation:** 40,000. **Advertising:** accepted ● *Puller Magazine*, monthly. Includes information on NTPA events, technical updates, and national point standings. Also contains manufacturers' and member state directories. **Price:** $34.95/year in U.S.; $42.95/year in Canada, outside U.S. ISSN: 8750-4219. **Circulation:** 7,500. **Advertising:** accepted ● *Pulling Rules: Official Rule Book*, annual. **Price:** included in membership dues; $4.95 /year for nonmembers. **Circulation:** 6,000. **Advertising:** ac-

cepted. **Conventions/Meetings:** competition ● annual convention and banquet (exhibits) - always 1st week of December.

Trails

23368 ■ Adirondack Forty-Sixers (AFS)
c/o Phil Corell, Treas.
PO Box 180
Cadyville, NY 12918-0180
Ph: (518)293-6401
E-mail: corell46@charter.net
URL: http://www.adk46r.org
Contact: Phil Corell, Treas.
Founded: 1948. **Members:** 6,000. **Membership Dues:** $8 (annual). **Staff:** 12. **Description:** Persons who have climbed all 46 major peaks of the Adirondacks, a mountain area in northeast New York State. (Major peaks are those 4000 feet or more in elevation, according to the Colvin Survey in the late 19th century. While many have trails marked by the New York Department of Environmental Conservation, 20 are officially trail less and about half of these are in remote areas requiring well-laid plans to complete the climbs.) Conducts service activities such as trail maintenance, re-seeding of summits, and litter bag project. Sponsors conservation camp and outdoor leadership workshop. **Libraries: Type:** reference. **Holdings:** 3. **Subjects:** Adirondack Mountains. **Awards:** Certificate of Accomplishment. **Frequency:** annual. **Type:** recognition. **Recipient:** for newly qualified 46ers ● Conservation Service Award. **Frequency:** annual. **Type:** recognition. **Recipient:** for individuals who perform 46, 146 and 346 hours of conservation service-related work. **Affiliated With:** American Hiking Society. **Publications:** *Adirondack Forty-sixer Peaks*, semiannual. Magazine. Contains articles about the Adirondacks. **Price:** included in membership dues; $15.00 for 3 years. **Circulation:** 4,500 ● *Climbing the Adirondack 46*. Booklet ● *Of the Summits, Of the Forests*. Book. **Conventions/Meetings:** semiannual meeting - always May and October, Keene Valley, NY ● annual Outdoor Leadership Workshop.

23369 ■ Adirondack Mountain Club (ADK)
814 Goggins Rd.
Lake George, NY 12845
Ph: (518)668-4447
Free: (800)395-8080
Fax: (518)668-3746
E-mail: adkinfo@adk.org
URL: http://www.adk.org
Contact: Neil F. Woodworth, Exec. Dir.
Founded: 1922. **Members:** 35,000. **Membership Dues:** life - individual, $1,300 ● individual, senior family (65 or older), $50 (annual) ● family (including children under 18), $60 (annual) ● senior (65 or older), student, $40 (annual) ● life - family, $1,950. **Staff:** 38. **Budget:** $2,500,000. **Regional Groups:** 26. **Description:** Persons interested in mountains, trails, camping, and forest conservation, especially in the Adirondack Mountain region of New York state. Conducts various recreational, conservation, and educational activities; and publishes thirty-five guidebooks, maps, and other titles. Maintains trails in the Adirondacks, Catskills, and elsewhere; operates two lodges. Annually sponsors winter mountaineering schools and educational workshops. Provides public information services at 2 locations. Operates 2 full-service lodges (1 year round), campgrounds and cabins. **Libraries: Type:** reference. **Holdings:** 600. **Subjects:** Adirondack region, mountaineering. **Computer Services:** Mailing lists, of members. **Committees:** Bylaws; Conservation; Education and Natural History; Finance; Headquarters; Heart Lake; Human Resources; Investment; Johns Brook Lodge; Lodge; Membership and Development; Outings; Publication; Trails. **Programs:** Educational. **Publications:** *Adirondack*, bimonthly. Magazine. Contains conservation articles, member news, opportunities, and personal essays. **Price:** included in membership dues; $20.00 /year for nonmembers in U.S.; $22.50 /year for nonmembers outside U.S. ISSN: 0001-8236.

Circulation: 19,000. **Advertising:** accepted. Alternate Formats: diskette. Also Cited As: *High Spot 1945* ● *Adirondack Alpine Summits*, 10/year. Book ● *Adirondack Wildguide*. Booklets. **Price:** $20.95 cloth; $16.95 paper ● *An Adirondack Passage*. Books. **Price:** $12.00 ● *Climbing in the Adirondacks*. Books. Provides a guide to rock and ice routes in the Adirondack Park. **Price:** $24.95 ● *Kids on the Trail! Hiking with Children in the Adirondacks*, semiannual. Newsletter. **Price:** $12.95 ● *No Place I'd Rather Be*, 10/year. Book ● Also publishes calendars, educational leaflets, maps, and trail and canoe guides. **Conventions/Meetings:** annual meeting, cultural, artistic exhibits in Lake George Headquarters (exhibits).

23370 ■ Adirondack Trail Improvement Society (ATIS)
PO Box 565
Keene Valley, NY 12943
Ph: (518)576-9949
E-mail: tgoodwin@kvvi.net
URL: http://www.atis-web.com
Contact: Sam Fisk, Pres.
Founded: 1897. **Members:** 420. **Membership Dues:** family, $125 (annual) ● benefactor, $1,000 (annual) ● patron, $500 (annual) ● sponsor, $200 (annual) ● individual, $75 (annual). **Staff:** 20. **Budget:** $110,000. **Description:** Maintains more than 100 miles of trails on state and private property in the High Peaks region of the Adirondacks and around St. Huberts, NY; organizes hiking and camping trips and manages educational programs concerned with the preservation and wise use of the Adirondacks. Operates the High Peaks Camp for boys and girls aged 12 to 15. Maintains communications network and fire-fighting equipment. **Committees:** Conservation; Education; Fund Raising; Trails; Youth. **Publications:** Newsletter, semiannual. **Conventions/Meetings:** annual meeting - always July or August.

23371 ■ American Endurance Ride Conference (AERC)
PO Box 6027
Auburn, CA 95604
Ph: (530)823-2260
Free: (866)271-AERC
Fax: (530)823-7805
E-mail: aerc@foothill.net
URL: http://www.aerc.org
Contact: Mike Maul, Pres.
Founded: 1972. **Members:** 6,200. **Membership Dues:** single, $65 (annual) ● family (2 persons), $75 (annual) ● junior, $35 (annual) ● veterinary, outside U.S., in Canada, $20 (annual) ● additional family, $10 (annual). **Staff:** 4. **Budget:** $450,000. **Regional Groups:** 9. **Description:** Horse and trail ride enthusiasts. Coordinates endurance ride activities on a national level. Distributes endurance ride schedules; maintains lists of names and addresses; advises on how to start and run rides; works to keep trails open for riders. Conducts seminar on endurance riding, horse training and feeding, ride management, veterinarian suggestions, and trails program. Maintains hall of fame; sanctions competitions; compiles statistics. **Libraries: Type:** open to the public. **Subjects:** all aspects of endurance. **Awards:** Rider Mileage Award. **Frequency:** annual. **Type:** trophy. **Recipient:** for horse and/or rider. **Computer Services:** Mailing lists, of members. **Committees:** Championship Ride; Equine Research; International Competition; Ride Sanctioning; Trails Advocacy; Veterinary Guidelines. **Publications:** *Endurance News*, monthly. Magazine. Covers education and statistics; includes a calendar of events. **Price:** $4.00/issue; $40.00/year in U.S.; $60.00/year in Canada and Mexico; $80.00/year in other countries. ISSN: 1044-4408. **Circulation:** 4,200. **Advertising:** accepted ● *Endurance Rider's Handbook*. Alternate Formats: online ● *Yearbook of Endurance*, annual. **Conventions/Meetings:** annual seminar ● annual trade show and convention (exhibits).

23372 ■ American Hiking Society (AHS)
1422 Fenwick Ln.
Silver Spring, MD 20910

Ph: (301)565-6704
Free: (800)972-8608
Fax: (301)565-6714
E-mail: info@americanhiking.org
URL: http://www.americanhiking.org
Contact: Gregory A. Miller PhD, Pres.
Founded: 1977. **Members:** 5,000. **Membership Dues:** individual, club, hiker, $30 (annual) ● pathfinder, $50 (annual) ● trail leader, $100 (annual) ● explorer, $250 (annual) ● senior (60 and above), $25 (annual) ● life (individual), $750 ● life (couple), $1,000. **Staff:** 8. **Budget:** $800,000. **State Groups:** 30. **Local Groups:** 130. **Description:** Works to promote hiking and foot trails in America. **Libraries: Type:** reference; open to the public. **Holdings:** 100. **Subjects:** hiking and trails. **Awards:** AHS Award. **Frequency:** annual. **Type:** recognition ● AHS Business Partner Award. **Frequency:** annual. **Type:** recognition. **Recipient:** for companies that have supported trail development and improvement ● AHS Trail Achievement Award. **Frequency:** annual. **Type:** recognition. **Recipient:** for a successful trail protection initiative ● Bill Wilcox Award. **Frequency:** annual. **Type:** recognition. **Recipient:** for young adult (up to 30 years old) whose volunteer work has resulted in the design, construction, or improvement of a new trail ● Butch Henley Award. **Frequency:** annual. **Type:** recognition. **Recipient:** for an outstanding career or achievement of staff of a non-profit hiking organization ● Glenn T. Seaborg National Public Leadership Award. **Frequency:** annual. **Type:** recognition. **Recipient:** for prominent citizens who have been effective national advocates for the development and improvement of hiking trails ● Jim Kern Award. **Frequency:** annual. **Type:** recognition. **Recipient:** for outstanding service and commitment to American Hiking Society ● Public Service National Award. **Frequency:** annual. **Type:** recognition. **Recipient:** for public officials who have demonstrated special interest in trails ● Richard Douthit Public Service Award. **Frequency:** annual. **Type:** recognition. **Recipient:** for an exemplary service by an employee of a trail managing agency. **Absorbed:** (1978) National Ski Touring Association; (1981) International Backpackers Association. **Publications:** *American Hiker*, bimonthly. Magazine. **Price:** included in membership dues. ISSN: 0279-9472. **Circulation:** 10,000. **Advertising:** accepted ● *America's National Trails: Journey's Across Land and Time.* Book. Contains events revealed by the system's historic trails. **Price:** $9.85 for members; $10.95 for nonmembers ● *Get Outside!*, annual. Directory. Lists volunteer and internship opportunities on public lands. **Price:** $12.95. **Conventions/Meetings:** biennial National Hikers Conference - meeting (exhibits).

23373 ■ American Trails (AT)
PO Box 491797
Redding, CA 96049-1797
Ph: (530)547-2060
Fax: (530)547-2035
E-mail: trailhead@americantrails.org
URL: http://www.americantrails.org
Contact: Pam Gluck, Exec. Dir.
Founded: 1988. **Members:** 1,000. **Membership Dues:** associate, $25 (annual) ● affiliate organization, $50 (annual) ● patron, $250 (annual) ● supporter, $100-$249 (annual). **Staff:** 2. **Description:** Works for the advancement and promotion of a national trails and greenways infrastructure that meets the health, recreation and travel needs of all Americans through education, communication and partnerships. Coordinates the National Trails Symposium every two years; sponsors the National Trails Awards program; implements the National Trails Training Partnership; serves as the lead non-profit in the effort to revitalize the National Recreation Trails program; implements the Universal Trail Assessment Process program; produces the American Trails Magazine, for all trail advocates and managers, and fosters cooperation and communication among all trail users in order to accomplish quality trails and greenways within 15 minutes of every American home or workplace. **Awards:** National Trails Award. **Frequency:** biennial. **Type:** recognition. **Recipient:** for contributions of volunteers, professionals and

other leaders. **Formed by Merger of:** American Trails Network; National Trails Council. **Publications:** *Trail Tracks*, quarterly. Newsletter. Includes legislative updates, conference listings, and articles on grassroots organizing for trail development and shared-use trails. **Price:** included in membership dues. ISSN: 1082-8303. **Circulation:** 1,000. **Advertising:** accepted. Alternate Formats: online ● *Universal Trail Assessment Process: A Survey of State Trail Administrators.* Includes information on attitudes toward accessibility and actions. ● Bibliographies. Alternate Formats: online ● Articles. Alternate Formats: online. **Conventions/Meetings:** biennial symposium.

23374 ■ Appalachian Mountain Club (AMC)
5 Joy St.
Boston, MA 02108
Ph: (617)523-0636
Fax: (617)523-0722
E-mail: information@outdoors.org
URL: http://www.outdoors.org
Contact: Andrew J. Falender, Exec. Dir.
Founded: 1876. **Members:** 92,000. **Membership Dues:** individual, $50 (annual) ● junior, senior, $25 (annual) ● family, $75 (annual). **Staff:** 125. **Budget:** $14,000,000. **Regional Groups:** 12. **Description:** Promotes the protection, enjoyment, and wise use of the mountains, rivers, and trails of the Appalachian region; to cultivate public knowledge of the environment and promote enjoyment of the outdoors throughout the northeastern U.S. Maintains 1400 miles of trails, and operates trail shelters, campgrounds, camps, and an eight unit backcountry hut system for the public. Conducts public service programs and manages a wide range of educational programs focusing on outdoor skills and natural history for school children and adults. **Libraries: Type:** open to the public. **Holdings:** 8,000; books, maps, periodicals, photographs. **Subjects:** mountaineering, conservation, White Mountains, outdoor education and recreation. **Committees:** Conservation; Education; Mountain Leadership and Safety; Research; Trails. **Publications:** *AMC Guide to Huts and Lodges.* Catalog ● *AMC Guide to Outdoor Adventures.* Magazine ● *AMC Outdoors*, monthly. Journal. Includes features, conservation news, chapter activities, and information on workshops and excursions. **Price:** included in membership dues. ISSN: 1052-5319. **Circulation:** 72,000. **Advertising:** accepted ● *Appalachia Journal*, semiannual. Contains articles on hiking, climbing, canoeing, kayaking, mountain history, and the environment. Includes poetry, short fiction, and essays. **Price:** $15.00/year. ISSN: 0003-6587. **Circulation:** 13,000. **Advertising:** accepted ● Also publishes books and maps, including the AMC White Mountain Guide. **Conventions/Meetings:** biennial workshop.

23375 ■ Appalachian Trail Conservancy (ATC)
799 Washington St.
Harpers Ferry, WV 25425
Ph: (304)535-6331
Fax: (304)535-2667
E-mail: info@appalachiantrail.org
URL: http://www.appalachiantrail.org
Contact: David N. Startzell, Exec. Dir.
Founded: 1925. **Members:** 33,000. **Membership Dues:** introductory, student, senior, ATC club, $25 (annual) ● maintainer, $40 (annual) ● individual life, $600 ● trailmaster, $75 (annual) ● pathfinder, $125 (annual) ● joint life, $900. **Staff:** 44. **Budget:** $4,707,000. **Local Groups:** 31. **Description:** Federation of trail and hiking clubs and individuals interested in the Appalachian Trail, a 2,173 mile foot trail extending from Maine to Georgia along the crests of Appalachian range. Manages and protects from incompatible land development the trail and approximately 100,000 acres of federally owned land surrounding it. Maintains museum, archive, land trust, and visitor center. **Awards:** Grants for Outreach. **Frequency:** annual. **Type:** grant. **Computer Services:** Mailing lists, of members. **Formerly:** (2005) Appalachian Trail Conference. **Publications:** *A.T. Journeys: The Magazine of the Appalachian Trail Conservancy*, semiannual. Includes stories of volunteers, hikers,

and trail communities. **Price:** included in membership dues ● *Appalachian Trailway News*, 5/year. Magazine. Contains news and features on the Appalachian Trail. **Price:** $15.00/year; free online. ISSN: 0003-6641. **Circulation:** 34,500. Alternate Formats: online. Also Cited As: *ATN* ● *The Register*, monthly. Newsletter. Published for the volunteers who maintain the Appalachian Trail. **Price:** $5.00/year. **Circulation:** 1,600. Alternate Formats: online ● Also publishes books, trail guidebooks, maps, and other descriptive material for trail users. **Conventions/Meetings:** biennial meeting (exhibits).

23376 ■ Continental Divide Trail Society (CDTS)
3704 N Charles St., No. 601
Baltimore, MD 21218
Ph: (410)235-9610
Fax: (410)243-1960
E-mail: mail@cdtsociety.org
URL: http://www.cdtsociety.org
Contact: James R. Wolf, Dir.
Founded: 1978. **Members:** 250. **Membership Dues:** individual, $10 (annual) ● regular, outside U.S., $12 (annual) ● regular, in Canada, $12 (annual). **Description:** Dedicated to the planning, development, and maintenance of the Continental Divide Trail as a "silent trail" (one laid out with appreciation of its natural environment and sensitivity to yearnings for a sense of contact with wilderness). Stresses personal responsibility to be a good steward, with respect for fellow travelers, for proprietors of the land, and for the creatures of the earth. Scouts terrain; identifies possible trail locations; describes existing feasible routes through publications. Collects bibliographic and photographic materials related to the Continental Divide Trail Corridor. Monitors land use actions of governmental agencies; participates in administrative review procedures. Cooperates with local and regional organizations; encourages grass roots efforts on behalf of the trail. Serves as a clearinghouse for suggestions from trail users. **Publications:** *DIVI-DEnds*, semiannual. Newsletter. **Price:** included in membership dues; $7.50 /year for nonmembers. ISSN: 1069-6660 ● *Guide to the Continental Divide Trail.*

23377 ■ Florida Trail Association (FTA)
5415 SW 13th St.
Gainesville, FL 32608
Ph: (352)378-8823
Free: (877)HIKE-FLA
Fax: (352)378-4550
E-mail: fta@floridatrail.org
URL: http://www.florida-trail.org
Contact: Pete Durnell, Pres.
Founded: 1964. **Members:** 5,000. **Membership Dues:** individual, $25 (annual) ● family, $30 (annual) ● commercial, $100 (annual) ● individual life, $500 ● family life, $750. **Budget:** $125,000. **State Groups:** 1. **Local Groups:** 17. **Description:** Conservationists, hikers, and canoeists interested in the preservation and appreciation of Florida wilderness and scenic areas. Maintains and develops the Florida Trail, which will eventually cover 1400 miles between the Everglades and Pensacola, for hiking and backpacking; the trail will be divided into approximately 30 sections, each about 25 to 50 miles long; more than 25 sections are now completed. Holds beginner weekends for members to discuss and try out equipment and to learn skills for backpacking and canoeing. Sponsors hikes and canoe trips. Operates charitable program. **Libraries: Type:** reference. **Holdings:** 1,000; books, clippings, periodicals. **Subjects:** outdoors. **Awards:** Champion of the Trail Award. **Frequency:** periodic. **Type:** recognition. **Recipient:** to elected officials who support the trail ● Cornelia Burge Award. **Frequency:** annual. **Type:** recognition. **Recipient:** for a member who has made extraordinary progress toward meeting the purposes of the FTA on a state-wide basis ● Friend of the Florida Trail Award. **Frequency:** annual. **Type:** recognition. **Recipient:** to land owners and agencies that support and promote the trail. **Publications:** *Footprint*, bimonthly. Newsletter. **Price:** included in membership dues. ISSN: 1064-681. **Circulation:** 3,200 ● *Hiking Guide to the Florida*

Trail ● *Regional Maps and Trail Guide Packet.* Features information for 9 different regions across the state. **Price:** $25.00 ● *Trail Manual of the Florida Trail.* **Conventions/Meetings:** annual conference and meeting, with hikes (exhibits) - in March ● regional meeting - 3/year, always fall ● seminar ● workshop.

23378 ■ Heritage Trails Fund (HTF)
1350 Castle Rock Rd.
Walnut Creek, CA 94598
Ph: (925)937-7661
Fax: (925)943-7431
Contact: George H. Cardinet, Exec.Dir.
Founded: 1981. **Nonmembership. Description:** Educational and communication-oriented fund that assists individuals and groups with fundraising to improve and maintain parks, open spaces, and multipurpose trails, with emphasis on trails for horseback riding. Publicizes areas not frequently utilized by nature and trail enthusiasts such as those in Lassen Volcanic National Park in California. Participates in programs sponsored by U.S. groups with similar interests. Currently is promoting and assisting in the development of the Bay Ridge Line Trail which will include both new and existing trails in ten counties surrounding San Francisco Bay. **Publications:** Newsletter, quarterly. **Conventions/Meetings:** semiannual Spring Ride ● annual 10-Day Ride - always August.

23379 ■ Intercollegiate Outing Club Association (IOCA)
c/o Michelle Moon, Exec. Sec.
2711 Blanchard
Mount Holyoke Coll.
South Hadley, MA 01075
Ph: (518)833-6816
E-mail: info@ioca.org
URL: http://www.ioca.org
Contact: Michelle Moon, Exec. Sec.
Founded: 1932. **Members:** 4,000. **Regional Groups:** 3. **Description:** Promotes the safe enjoyment of the outdoors and wilderness, while encouraging preservation of wilderness areas. Sponsors activities such as camping, hiking, canoeing, climbing, caving and mountaineering. Allows larger clubs with a lot of expertise and equipment to help smaller clubs with fewer resources become more active. Helps new clubs to get started by providing sample constitutions, bylaws, and ideas. Offers a great chance to meet others who share a love of the outdoors and adventure during events. **Libraries: Type:** reference; by appointment only. **Holdings:** archival material. **Computer Services:** Mailing lists ● online services, with member organizations, trips, and other information. **Publications:** *IOCA News,* monthly. Bulletin. Includes calendar of events. **Price:** included in membership dues. **Circulation:** 50. **Advertising:** accepted ● *IOCAN,* quarterly. Bulletin ● Directory, annual ● Handbook, periodic. **Conventions/Meetings:** annual Spring Conference, for outing clubs; with camping, square dancing and other activities.

23380 ■ IOCALUM
c/o Roland Vinyard, Exec. Sec.
597 State Hwy. 162
Sprakers, NY 12166-4008
Ph: (518)673-3212
Fax: (518)673-3219
E-mail: rvinyard@frontiernet.net
URL: http://www.ioca.org/iocalum
Contact: Roland Vinyard, Exec. Sec.
Founded: 1934. **Members:** 115. **Membership Dues:** individual, $6 (annual). **Staff:** 1. **Budget:** $2,000. **Description:** Alumni of undergraduate collegiate outing clubs. (IOCAlum stands for Intercollegiate Outing Club Association Alumni). Keeps a roster of addresses and information on all alumni, announce outings of interest to members, and keeps members informed about conservation issues, trips for both undergraduate and graduate members, and the activities of other members. **Libraries: Type:** open to the public. **Holdings:** periodicals. **Subjects:** club history. **Computer Services:** database, member's list. **Affiliated With:** Intercollegiate Outing Club Associa-

tion; National Speleological Society. **Publications:** *Bummer's List,* annual, published each year in June. Directory. Lists members who open their homes to other members. ● *IOCAlum Directory,* annual, published each year in June. Includes listing of members, address, phone, email, colleges attended, children, and special interest job. ● *IOCAlum News,* quarterly. Newsletter. **Price:** included in membership dues ● Newsletter, 3-4/year. **Conventions/Meetings:** semiannual conference - always April and October.

23381 ■ Lincoln Heritage Trail Foundation (LHTF)
PO Box 1507
Springfield, IL 62705
Ph: (217)528-5572
Fax: (217)528-5572
Contact: Charles Ott, Pres.
Founded: 1963. **Members:** 442. **Staff:** 5. **Description:** Individuals, organizations, municipalities, and travel writers interested in encouraging travel to historic points of interest along the route of the Lincoln Heritage Trail. (The trail covers a three-state, 2200 mile route from Abraham Lincoln's birthplace in Hodgenville, KY through Indiana, where he spent his boyhood years, to Illinois where he grew to greatness.) Encourages the study of Lincoln history. Maintains speakers' bureau and biographical archives. **Awards: Type:** scholarship. **Recipient:** to fund Lincoln research. **Also Known As:** President Lincoln's Farm. **Publications:** *Lincoln Heritage Trail Newsletter,* 5/year ● *Lincoln Heritage Trail Tour Brokers Reference Guide.* **Conventions/Meetings:** annual meeting.

23382 ■ Montana Outfitters and Guides Association (MOGA)
2033 11th Ave., No. 8
Helena, MT 59601
Ph: (406)449-3578
Fax: (406)449-9769
E-mail: macminard@imt.net
URL: http://www.moga-montana.org
Contact: Mr. Mac Minard, Exec. Dir.
Founded: 1975. **Members:** 200. **Membership Dues:** outfitter, $175-$600 (annual) ● guide, associate, $50 (annual) ● business, $350 (annual). **Staff:** 2. **Budget:** $100,000. **State Groups:** 1. **Description:** Represents outfitters and guides who operate outdoor trips in Montana for hunting, fishing, float boating, and sightseeing parties using saddle and pack animals, boats, and motorized equipment; operators of dude ranches, wagon trains, and cattle drives. Supports standards of service to be provided by members set by licensing board; encourages preservation of back country and wise use of resources, fish, and game. Is conducting a study of the economic impact of industry on Montana. Maintains speaker's bureau. **Committees:** Educational Institute; Fish and Game; Fund Raising; Land and Water; Political Action. **Affiliated With:** America Outdoors. **Formed by Merger of:** Montana Outfitters and Dude Ranchers Association; Bitterroot Outfitters; Treasure State Outfitters. **Publications:** *Membership Roster,* annual. Membership Directory ● *Montana Outfitters and Guides Association,* annual. Directory. **Price:** free. **Advertising:** accepted ● *Outfitter Journal,* semiannual ● Newsletter, monthly. Alternate Formats: online. **Conventions/Meetings:** annual convention, with trade show, auction banquet, speaker session, working group (exhibits) - January.

23383 ■ Mountaineers
300 3rd Ave. W
Seattle, WA 98119
Ph: (206)284-6310 (206)284-8484
Free: (800)573-8484
Fax: (206)284-4977
E-mail: clubmail@mountaineers.org
URL: http://www.mountaineers.org
Contact: Bills Deters, Pres.
Founded: 1906. **Members:** 15,000. **Membership Dues:** individual, senior gold, $73 (annual) ● spouse, $53 (annual) ● family, $130 (annual) ● senior, $36 (annual) ● summit club, $1,000 (annual) ● student, $48 (annual) ● contributing, $100 (annual) ● presi-

dent's club, $150 (annual). **Staff:** 21. **Regional Groups:** 5. **Description:** Persons of all ages interested in exploring and studying the mountains, forests, and watercourses of the Northwest, preserving the history and traditions of the region, and encouraging protective legislation and other conservation activities. Membership is concentrated in the Northwestern U.S. Conducts short hiking, skiing, camping, and mountain climbing trips for members; offers courses in safe mountain climbing. Owns four ski lodges and huts, and a rhododendron preserve of 180-acres near Bremerton, WA. Maintains museum and speakers' bureau. Maintains over 50 committees. **Libraries: Type:** reference. **Holdings:** 6,000; archival material, books, periodicals, video recordings. **Subjects:** mountaineering, conservation, other outdoor activities. **Awards: Type:** recognition. **Computer Services:** database ● mailing lists. **Divisions:** Activities; Conservation; Property. **Publications:** *The Mountaineer,* monthly. Magazine. Features articles, photographs, and news. **Advertising:** accepted. Alternate Formats: online ● Books. Covers hiking, climbing, and other outdoor activities. Includes trail guides. **Conventions/Meetings:** annual Banff Film Festival - meeting - November/December, in Seattle, WA.

23384 ■ National Trail Ride Association
PO Box 379
Big Sandy, TN 38221
Ph: (731)593-5139 (256)390-1124
E-mail: nationaltrailride@earthlink.net
URL: http://www.nationaltrailride.com
Members: 10,000. **Description:** Represents the interests of individuals interested in trail rides and horseback riding. Promotes safe and fun trail riding. Supports and organizes trail rides.

23385 ■ New England Trail Rider Association (NETRA)
PO Box 469
Collinsville, CT 06022
Ph: (860)693-9111
Fax: (860)693-9227
E-mail: support@netra.org
URL: http://www.netra.org
Contact: Jim Mitchell, Contact
Founded: 1971. **Members:** 2,500. **Membership Dues:** individual, $35 (annual) ● family, sustaining, $45 (annual) ● junior, $20 (annual) ● supporting, $80 (annual) ● sponsoring, $150 (annual) ● life, $350. **Staff:** 1. **Budget:** $200,000. **Local Groups:** 33. **Description:** Motorcycle trail riders. Plans trails; organizes trail development at the local and regional level in cooperation with other trail user groups; conducts educational programs and legislative monitoring. Sanctions and oversees recreational and competitive trail riding events. **Libraries: Type:** reference. **Holdings:** films, monographs, photographs. **Subjects:** trails, trail riding. **Awards:** Annual Award. **Frequency:** annual. **Type:** recognition. **Recipient:** for top positions of classes based on ability. **Telecommunication Services:** electronic mail, cdrew@ulbrich.com. **Committees:** Competition; Trail; Youth. **Publications:** *NETRA News,* monthly. Newsletter. **Price:** included in membership dues. **Circulation:** 3,000. **Advertising:** accepted ● *NETRA Rule Book.* Alternate Formats: online ● Also publishes brochure on endurance competition. **Conventions/Meetings:** Awards Ceremony - meeting, related to motorcycles (exhibits) - always in January.

23386 ■ New England Trails Conference (NETC)
c/o Marsha Towns
PO Box 550
Charlestown, NH 03603
E-mail: rspoerl@sugar-river.net
URL: http://www.wapack.org/netrails
Contact: Bob Spoerl, Pres.
Founded: 1916. **Local Groups:** 46. **Description:** Coalition of organizations with an interest in hiking, trail clearing and maintenance, and conservation; includes groups from six New England states and adjacent parts of New York state. Conducts conference that serves as an information clearinghouse on

hiking trails in New England. **Libraries: Type:** reference. **Holdings:** books, maps. **Publications:** *Hiking Trails of New England*, quinquennial. Includes a listing of most trail maintaining organizations and an extensive bibliography of guidebooks and maps. **Price:** $1.25 ● *New England Trails*, annual. Report. Includes detailed information about current trail and shelter conditions. **Price:** $3.00 each. **Conventions/Meetings:** annual conference, member clubs, maps, trail information (exhibits).

23387 ■ North American Trail Ride Conference (NATRC)
PO Box 224
Sedalia, CO 80135
Ph: (303)688-1677
Fax: (303)688-3022
E-mail: natrc@natrc.org
URL: http://www.natrc.org
Contact: Lourie Dinatale, Exec. Admin.
Founded: 1961. **Members:** 2,000. **Membership Dues:** family, $60 (annual) ● adult/associate, $50 (annual) ● junior, $35 (annual) ● life (single), $600 ● life (family), $800. **Regional Groups:** 6. **Description:** Individuals, families, businesses, and groups involved in some aspect of competitive trail riding. Purposes are to: stimulate greater interest in the breeding and use of good horses possessed of stamina and hardiness as qualified mounts for trail use; demonstrate the value of type and soundness and the proper selection of horses for distance riding; learn and demonstrate the proper methods of training and conditioning horses for distance; encourage good horsemanship in all trail riding; and demonstrate the best methods of caring for horses during and after long distance rides without the aid of artificial methods or stimulants. Sanctions competitive rides nationwide; conducts seminars for judging, ride managing, and riding. **Awards: Frequency:** annual. **Type:** recognition. **Recipient:** for winners of regional and national trail riding events. **Computer Services:** Mailing lists. **Committees:** Breed Awards; Horse and Rider Mileage; Insurance; Management; National Drug Advisory; Protest; Riders; Sanction; Student Loan and Scholarships. **Publications:** *Hoof Print*, bimonthly. Newspaper. Includes veterinarian and horsemanship articles, regional news, and ride results and schedule. **Price:** included in membership dues; $10.00 /year for nonmembers. **Circulation:** 2,000. **Advertising:** accepted ● *NATRC Rider's Manual*. **Price:** $15.00 plus $3 shipping and handling. **Conventions/Meetings:** annual lecture and seminar ● annual meeting (exhibits).

23388 ■ North Country Trail Association (NCTA)
229 E Main St.
Lowell, MI 49331-1711
Ph: (616)897-5987
Free: (866)HIK-ENCT
Fax: (616)897-6605
E-mail: ireneszabo@northcountrytrail.org
URL: http://northcountrytrail.org
Contact: John Leinen, Pres.
Founded: 1981. **Members:** 2,800. **Membership Dues:** regular, $30 ● student, $10 ● sponsored, $18 ● organization, $45 ● trail leader, $50 ● pathfinder, $100 ● business, $150 ● patron, $250 ● life, $1,000. **Staff:** 8. **Budget:** $400,000. **Regional Groups:** 25. **State Groups:** 7. **Description:** Promotes, constructs and maintains a nonmotorized connected footpath, to be called the North Country National Scenic Trail; preserves and restores the natural environment of the trail. Acts as a clearinghouse for information on the trail. Promotes cooperation and coordination among individuals and groups using the trail and encourages active volunteer participation in its construction, repair, and clean-up. Stresses trail education for safe and enjoyable use. Sponsors hikes. **Libraries: Type:** reference. **Holdings:** archival material, audiovisuals, books, business records, clippings, periodicals. **Subjects:** national trail system and its parts. **Awards:** Communicator of the Year Award. **Frequency:** annual. **Type:** recognition. **Recipient:** to a volunteer for exemplary work in promoting the organization ● Distinguished Service Award.

Type: recognition. **Recipient:** for significant commitment and accomplishment over three or more years ● Leadership Award. **Frequency:** annual. **Type:** recognition. **Recipient:** to a volunteer demonstrating exceptional leadership ● Lifetime Achievement Award. **Frequency:** annual. **Type:** recognition. **Recipient:** for significant commitment and accomplishment over ten or more years ● Outreach Award. **Frequency:** annual. **Type:** recognition. **Recipient:** to a volunteer contributing to ongoing success of organization ● Rising Star Award. **Frequency:** annual. **Type:** recognition. **Recipient:** to a volunteer, ages 8-18 ● Sweep Award. **Frequency:** annual. **Type:** recognition. **Recipient:** to a volunteer, for work and achievement behind the scenes on behalf of the organization ● Trail Builder of the Year. **Frequency:** annual. **Type:** recognition. **Recipient:** to a volunteer for outstanding development of new trail or facility over the past year ● Trail Maintainer of the Year. **Frequency:** annual. **Type:** recognition. **Recipient:** to a volunteer demonstrating exceptional dedication or achievement over the past year ● Trailblazer Award. **Type:** recognition. **Recipient:** for a business or foundation's far sighted vision and support ● Vanguard Award. **Type:** recognition. **Recipient:** for a legislator or public servant. **Affiliated With:** American Hiking Society; Buckeye Trail Association; Finger Lake Trail Conference; Kekekabic Trail Club; Superior Hiking Trail Association. **Publications:** *Guide to the North Country Trail—Chippewa National Forest.* Book. **Price:** $1.25 ● *Michigan Mapsets* ● *NCT Trail Map Sets* ● *Newsletter of the North Country Trail Association - North Star*, quarterly ● *North Star*, quarterly. Magazine ● Annual Report, annual. **Conventions/Meetings:** annual conference - usually in August, travels from state to state.

23389 ■ Pacific Northwest Trail Association (PNTA)
24854 Charles Jones Memorial Cir., Unit 4
North Cascades Gateway Ctr.
Sedro Woolley, WA 98284
Free: (877)854-9417
Fax: (360)854-7665
E-mail: pnt@pnt.org
URL: http://www.pnt.org
Contact: Jon Knechtel, Dir.
Founded: 1977. **Members:** 300. **Membership Dues:** student or retiree, $15 (annual) ● regular, $25 (annual) ● family, $35 (annual) ● retired family, $20 (annual) ● executive, $100-$499 (annual). **Staff:** 1. **Regional Groups:** 1. **Local Groups:** 4. **Description:** Individuals with an interest in the Pacific Northwest Trail, a 1,200 miles long and horse path connecting Glacier National Park with Olympic National Park. Promotes preservation of the trail and its environment. Conducts trail maintenance activities projects. Maintains speakers' bureau. Created a detailed map of the trail and surrounding territory. **Publications:** *Nor'wester*, annual. Newsletter. **Advertising:** accepted. **Alternate Formats:** online. **Conventions/Meetings:** monthly board meeting.

23390 ■ Rails-to-Trails Conservancy (RTC)
1100 17th St. NW, 10th Fl.
Washington, DC 20036
Ph: (202)331-9696
Fax: (202)331-9680
E-mail: railtrails@railtrails.org
URL: http://www.railtrails.org
Contact: Keith Laughlin, Pres.
Founded: 1986. **Members:** 100,000. **Membership Dues:** individual, $18 (annual) ● supporting, $25 (annual) ● patron, $50 (annual) ● benefactor, $100 (annual) ● advocate, $500 (annual) ● Trailblazer Society, $1,000 (annual). **Staff:** 40. **Budget:** $4,500,000. **State Groups:** 6. **Description:** Represents hikers, runners, bicyclists, cross-country skiers, equestrians, state and local park officials, trail enthusiasts, and interested groups or individuals. Promotes the conversion of abandoned railways into trails for public use and wildlife conservation. Seeks to build a transcontinental trail way network that will preserve the nation's railroad corridor system. Works with the Interstate Commerce Commission in Washington, DC for simplified regulations in the abandonment

process. Encourages the formation of local and state coalitions. Provides written m material, legal advice, and strategy tips. Offers training seminars for public officials. **Computer Services:** Online services. **Publications:** *Rail to Trails*, quarterly. Magazine. **Circulation:** 100,000 ● *700 Great Rail-Trails: A National Directory* ● *Trailblazer*, quarterly. Newsletter. Covers issues, trends, management, and legislative topics regarding conversion of railroad lines into hiking trails. **Price:** included in membership dues. **Circulation:** 85,000. **Advertising:** accepted ● Manuals ● Annual Report, annual. **Alternate Formats:** online. **Conventions/Meetings:** conference (exhibits) - every 18 months.

Trainers

23391 ■ American Athletic Trainers Association and Certification Board (AATA)
146 E Duarte Rd.
Arcadia, CA 91006
Ph: (626)445-1978
Fax: (626)574-1999
E-mail: americansportsmedicine@hotmail.com
Contact: Joe Borland, Contact
Founded: 1978. **Members:** 1,300. **Membership Dues:** certification, $50 (annual). **Staff:** 1. **Languages:** English, Latin, Spanish. **For-Profit. Description:** Aims to qualify and certify active athletic trainers; establish minimum competence standards for individuals participating in the prevention and care of athletic injuries; to inform communities nationwide of the importance of having competent leadership in the area of athletic training. Conducts continuing education and charitable programs; maintains placement service. **Libraries: Type:** reference. **Awards:** Trainer of the Year Award. **Frequency:** annual. **Type:** recognition. **Computer Services:** database. **Publications:** *AATA News Letter*, semiannual. Brochure ● *Chapter Presidents Testing*, biennial ● *Special Bulletin*, periodic ● Newsletter, semiannual. **Price:** included in membership dues. **Advertising:** accepted. **Conventions/Meetings:** annual conference and lecture.

23392 ■ National Athletic Trainers' Association (NATA)
2952 Stemmons Fwy.
Dallas, TX 75247-6196
Ph: (214)637-6282
Free: (800)879-6282
Fax: (214)637-2206
E-mail: mjalbohm@aol.com
URL: http://www.nata.org
Contact: Charles Kimmel Jr., Pres.
Founded: 1950. **Members:** 23,500. **Membership Dues:** certified/associate, $45-$135 (annual) ● student, $27-$80 (annual) ● international certified, $58-$180 (annual) ● international noncertified, $58-$170 (annual). **Staff:** 34. **Budget:** $4,000,000. **Regional Groups:** 10. **Description:** Athletic trainers from universities, colleges, and junior colleges; professional football, baseball, basketball, and ice hockey; high schools, preparatory schools, military establishments, sports medicine clinics, and business/industrial health programs. Maintains hall of fame and placement service. Conducts research programs; compiles statistics. **Libraries: Type:** reference. **Holdings:** archival material. **Awards: Type:** recognition ● **Type:** scholarship. **Computer Services:** Mailing lists, of members. **Committees:** Audio Visual Aids; Career Information; Clinic - Corporate/Industrial Trainers; College Student Trainers; Ethics; Ethnic Minority Advisory Council; Governmental Affairs; Grants and Scholarships; International Games; Licensure; Placement; Professional Education; Research; Secondary School Athletic Trainers. **Publications:** *Convention Daily News*. Paper. **Advertising:** accepted. **Alternate Formats:** online ● *Journal of Athletic Training*, quarterly. **Price:** $32.00/year. ISSN: 1062-6050. **Circulation:** 23,000. **Advertising:** accepted ● *NATA News*, monthly. Magazine. **Price:** included in membership dues. **Circulation:** 21,700. **Advertising:** accepted. **Alternate Formats:** online ●

Survey. **Conventions/Meetings:** annual meeting and symposium (exhibits) - always second week in June.

23393 ■ National Council on Strength and Fitness (NCSF)
PO Box 43-0945
South Miami, FL 33243-0945
Ph: (305)668-8705
Free: (800)772-6273
Fax: (305)666-4622
E-mail: info@ncsf.org
URL: http://www.ncsf.org
Membership Dues: student, $45 (annual) ● professional, $55 (annual) ● international, $75 (annual). **Description:** Promotes advanced scholarship to the principles of lifetime health and fitness; represents certified personal trainers. **Programs:** Adidas 3-Stripes Instructor; Health Insurance; Professional Liability Insurance. **Publications:** NCSF E-News, monthly. Newsletter. **Price:** included in membership dues. Alternate Formats: online ● NCSF News, quarterly. Newsletter. **Price:** included in membership dues. **Conventions/Meetings:** seminar ● workshop.

23394 ■ National Federation of Professional Trainers (NFPT)
PO Box 4579
Lafayette, IN 47903-4579
Ph: (765)471-4514
Free: (800)729-6378
Fax: (765)471-7369
E-mail: info@nfpt.com
URL: http://www.nfpt.com
Contact: Ron J. Clark, Pres./Founder
Founded: 1988. **Members:** 6,000. **Membership Dues:** individual certification, $425 ● individual, $175 ● health club staff, $280. **Staff:** 10. **Regional Groups:** 70. **National Groups:** 100. **For-Profit.** **Description:** Offers affordable, convenient, comprehensive, and applicable information to those seeking personal fitness trainer certification. Offers organizational certification credentials for consumer recognition of competence; provides certified affiliates with ongoing education; establishes a network of support, and provides professional products and services to trainers and consumers; and facilitates and encourages the exchange of ideas, knowledge, business experiences, and financial opportunities between all fitness administrators internationally. Offers educational programs. **Libraries: Type:** open to the public. **Subjects:** personal training. **Awards:** Certification. **Type:** recognition. **Additional Websites:** http://www.personaltrainertoday.com. **Publications:** NFPT Personal Trainer Today, monthly. Magazine. **Circulation:** 6,500. **Advertising:** accepted. Alternate Formats: online. **Conventions/Meetings:** quarterly board meeting ● trade show.

23395 ■ National Strength and Conditioning Association (NSCA)
1885 Bob Johnson Dr.
Colorado Springs, CO 80906
Ph: (719)632-6722
Free: (800)815-6826
Fax: (719)632-6367
E-mail: nsca@nsca-lift.org
URL: http://www.nsca-lift.org
Contact: Bob Jursnick, Exec. Dir.
Founded: 1978. **Members:** 30,000. **Membership Dues:** certified professional, $115 (annual) ● certified international, $115-$200 (annual) ● certified student, married partner, $90 (annual) ● corporate, $415 (annual) ● international, $120-$205 (annual) ● professional, $120 (annual). **Staff:** 29. **Budget:** $2,000,000. **State Groups:** 50. **Multinational.** **Description:** Represents professionals in the sports science, athletic, and fitness industries. Promotes the total conditioning of athletes to a level of optimum performance, with the belief that a better conditioned athlete not only performs better but is less prone to injury. Gathers and disseminates information on strength and conditioning techniques and benefits. Conducts national, regional, state, and local clinics and workshops. Operates professional certification program. **Awards:** Student Assistantship. **Frequency:** annual. **Type:** recognition. **Recipient:** to student assistants.

Computer Services: Mailing lists. **Committees:** Special Interest Groups; State Directors. **Departments:** Conference. **Formerly:** (1981) National Strength Coaches Association. **Publications:** Journal of Strength and Conditioning Research, quarterly. Features research to provide an improved scientific basis for conditioning practices. **Price:** included in membership dues. ISSN: 1064-8011. **Circulation:** 25,000. **Advertising:** accepted. Also Cited As: Journal of Applied Sports Science Research ● National Strength and Conditioning Association Bulletin, bimonthly. Newsletter. Includes book reviews, certification information, and symposia proceedings. **Price:** included in membership dues. **Circulation:** 25,000. **Advertising:** accepted. Alternate Formats: online ● Strength and Conditioning, bimonthly. Journal. Contains peer-reviewed articles on athletic strength training and conditioning practices and concepts. **Price:** included in membership dues. ISSN: 1524-602. **Circulation:** 25,000. **Advertising:** accepted. Alternate Formats: CD-ROM; online ● Manuals ● Videos ● Also publishes position papers. **Conventions/Meetings:** annual conference and trade show (exhibits).

Trucks

23396 ■ Monster Truck Racing Association (MTRA)
14843 April Dr.
Loxahatchee, FL 33470
Ph: (561)383-7290
Fax: (561)784-4691
E-mail: corporate@bigfoot4x4.com
URL: http://www.mtra.us
Contact: Bob Chandler, Chm.
Founded: 1987. **Membership Dues:** associate (Jr.), $25 (annual) ● associate, $50 (annual) ● promoter, $500 (annual) ● sponsor, $250-$450 (annual) ● owner/driver, $250 (annual). **Multinational.** **Description:** Maintains the longevity of monster truck racing sport. Provides safety guidelines for competitors and spectators. **Computer Services:** database, lists of truck inspectors ● information services, car display. **Publications:** MTRA Rule Book, annual. Handbook. Alternate Formats: online ● Newsletter.

Tug of War

23397 ■ United States Amateur Tug of War Association (USATOWA)
1855 Hwy. 69
Verona, WI 53593
Free: (800)TUGOWAR
E-mail: shelbytow@msn.com
URL: http://www.usatowa.homestead.com
Contact: Shelby Richardson, Pres.
Founded: 1978. **Members:** 600. **Description:** Team and individual enthusiasts of tug-of-war. Seeks to promote the sport of tug-of-war at all age levels, standardize rules, establish competitions, and train new teams. Encourages the U.S. Olympic Committee to include the sport of tug-of-war as an Olympic game. Organizes national championship annually. **Absorbed:** (1984) North American Tug of War Federation. **Conventions/Meetings:** annual meeting.

Underwater Sports

23398 ■ Association of Commercial Diving Educators (ACDE)
c/o Santa Barbara City College
721 Cliff Dr.
Santa Barbara, CA 93109-2394
Ph: (805)965-0581
Fax: (805)560-6059
E-mail: info@acde.us
URL: http://www.acde.us/contact.htm
Contact: Don Barthelmess, Treas.
Founded: 1977. **Members:** 6. **Membership Dues:** associate, $250 (annual). **Staff:** 10. **Budget:**

$200,000. **National Groups:** 3. **Description:** Private and community colleges and trade schools operating as a non-profit 501C3 organization to train commercial divers for inshore, offshore, and coastal diving. Works toward standardization in classifying diver training programs through establishment of minimum parameters for curriculum, equipment, and other factors related to excellence in diver training. **Awards:** Tom Devine Memorial Scholarship. **Frequency:** semiannual. **Type:** scholarship. **Publications:** ANSI Standards - Minimum Standards for Commercial Diver Training ANSI/ACDE 01-1998. Alternate Formats: online ● Professional Divers' Logbook ● Pamphlets. **Conventions/Meetings:** semiannual meeting ● annual meeting, held in conjunction with the Association of Diving Contractors.

23399 ■ Institute of Diving (IOD)
17314 Panama City Beach Pkwy.
Panama City Beach, FL 32413
Ph: (850)235-4101
Fax: (850)235-4101
E-mail: momits@aol.com
Contact: Douglas Hough, Dir.
Founded: 1977. **Members:** 615. **Membership Dues:** individual, $25 (annual) ● associate corporation and life, $250 ● corporation, $500. **Staff:** 3. **Budget:** $125,000. **Description:** Sports, commercial, and military divers, and other individuals; organizations and corporations interested in diving and diving-related activities. Acts for the advancement of professional, literary, and scientific knowledge related to human-oriented activity in the undersea environment. Maintains Museum of Man in the Sea; operates diving information exchange program. **Libraries: Type:** reference. **Holdings:** 300. **Subjects:** history, technology under the sea. **Publications:** Newsletter, quarterly. **Price:** included in membership dues. **Advertising:** accepted. **Conventions/Meetings:** annual conference (exhibits) - always in Panama City, FL.

23400 ■ National Association for Cave Diving (NACD)
PO Box 14492
Gainesville, FL 32604
Ph: (352)331-7666 (386)497-3494
Free: (888)565-6223
E-mail: manager@safecaving.org
URL: http://www.safecavediving.com
Contact: Debra A. Green, Operations Mgr.
Founded: 1968. **Members:** 1,000. **Membership Dues:** individual, associate, $35 (annual) ● individual (international), instructor, $50 (annual) ● family, $55 (annual) ● family (international), $65 (annual) ● business facility (new), $110 (annual) ● business facility (new-international), $170 (annual) ● business facility (renew), $90 (annual) ● business facility (renewal-international), $155 (annual). **Staff:** 10. **Languages:** English, Spanish. **Description:** Individuals interested in cave diving. Promotes a greater appreciation of the underwater environment. Encourages training and experience for safe cave diving. Establishes guidelines for equipment and techniques for safe cave diving. Supports the conservation of the submerged cave environment. Supports education and dissemination of accepted cave diving practices. Works to achieve understanding among the members of the cave diving community, the scientific community, and the public. Promotes innovative cave diving techniques, practices, and equipment. Conducts seminars and workshops. **Libraries: Type:** lending; reference; open to the public. **Holdings:** archival material, audio recordings, books, periodicals. **Subjects:** cave diving. **Awards:** Bill McFaden Cartography Award. **Frequency:** annual. **Type:** recognition. **Recipient:** for underwater cave mapping ● Paul Meng Instructor Award. **Frequency:** annual. **Type:** recognition. **Recipient:** for the instructor with the most number of students taught per year ● Steve Gerrard Outstanding Service Award. **Frequency:** annual. **Type:** recognition ● Wakulla Award. **Frequency:** annual. **Type:** recognition. **Recipient:** for safe cave divers. **Committees:** Equipment and Technology; Research, Exploration and Survey. **Programs:** Safety; Sustaining Contributor; Training. **Projects:** Spring and Cave Conservation. **Publications:** The

Art of Safe Cave Diving. Book. Covers all aspects of safe cave diving. **Price:** $34.95 for members; $39.95 for nonmembers ● *Basic Cave Diving: Blueprint for Survival.* Book. **Price:** $7.00 for members; $8.00 for nonmembers ● *NACD Cave Diver Workbook.* **Price:** $25.00 for members; $30.00 for nonmembers ● *NACD Safety Brochure.* Alternate Formats: online ● *NACD Standards and Procedures.* Book. **Price:** $75.00 for members; $75.00 for nonmembers ● Journal. Contains issues related to cave diving. **Price:** included in membership dues. **Advertising:** accepted. Alternate Formats: online. **Conventions/Meetings:** annual seminar, cave diving convention (exhibits) - November.

23401 ■ National Association of Underwater Instructors (NAUI)

PO Box 89789
Tampa, FL 33689-0413
Ph: (813)628-6284
Free: (800)553-6284
Fax: (813)628-8253
E-mail: nauihq@nauiww.org
URL: http://www.naui.org
Contact: Jim Bram, Pres.

Founded: 1960. **Members:** 12,000. **Membership Dues:** active (instructor), $145 (annual) ● active (divemaster, skin diving instructor and assistant instructor), $90 (annual) ● sustaining (instructor), $110 (annual) ● emeritus (instructor, divemaster, skin diving instructor and assistant instructor), $75 (annual). **Staff:** 31. **Budget:** $4,000,000. **Multinational. Description:** Certified instructors of basic, advanced, and specialized courses in underwater diving. Offers instructor certification programs and training programs. Conducts seminars, workshops, and symposia. Sells diving education books. Sponsors competitions; maintains speakers' bureau and placement service; conducts charitable programs. **Libraries: Type:** reference. **Holdings:** 500; books. **Subjects:** diving, diving instruction. **Awards:** Hall of Honor. **Frequency:** annual. **Type:** recognition. **Recipient:** for individuals ● Honorary Membership. **Frequency:** annual. **Type:** recognition. **Recipient:** for individuals ● Outstanding Service. **Frequency:** annual. **Type:** recognition. **Recipient:** for an NAUI member ● Outstanding Training Support. **Frequency:** annual. **Type:** recognition. **Recipient:** for individuals. **Committees:** Instructor Ethics; International; Leonard Greenstone Award. **Publications:** *Sources: The Journal of Underwater Education,* quarterly. **Advertising:** accepted. **Conventions/Meetings:** annual conference (exhibits).

23402 ■ Professional Association of Diving Instructors (PADI)

30151 Tomas St.
Rancho Santa Margarita, CA 92688-2125
Ph: (949)858-7234
Free: (800)729-7234
Fax: (949)858-7264
E-mail: webmaster@padi.com
URL: http://www.padi.com
Contact: Ralph Erickson, Pres.

Founded: 1966. **Members:** 100,000. **Membership Dues:** in U.S., $29 (annual) ● outside U.S. and Canada, $51 (annual) ● in Canada, $40 (annual). **Staff:** 400. **Budget:** $30,000,000. **Regional Groups:** 10. **Languages:** Chinese, English, French, German, Spanish. **For-Profit. Multinational. Description:** Educates and certifies underwater scuba instructors. Sanctions instructor training courses nationwide and in 175 foreign countries. Provides training course criteria, training aids, and national requirements for all aspects of diving instruction. Instructor training courses are held at geographically central locations. Sponsors PADI Travel Network and a retail dive store program. Offers courses in diving specialties; conducts educational programs. Offers placement service; compiles statistics. **Publications:** *Member Handbook and Benefits Directory,* annual ● *Sport Diver,* monthly. Magazine. Alternate Formats: online ● *The Undersea Journal,* quarterly. Trade publication to membership. **Circulation:** 100,000. **Advertising:** accepted. Alternate Formats: diskette. Also Cited As: *Film, Negs* ● Also publishes instructor training manu-

als, pamphlets, brochures, educational books, and other materials. **Conventions/Meetings:** annual meeting (exhibits) - held in January.

23403 ■ Recreational Scuba Training Council (RSTC)

PO Box 11083
Jacksonville, FL 32239-1083
Ph: (904)744-5554
E-mail: info@wrstc.com
URL: http://www.wrstc.com
Contact: David Scoggins, Coor.

Founded: 1986. **Members:** 5. **Membership Dues:** individual, $600 (quarterly). **Description:** Recreational scuba diving associations. Develops certification standards for the sport. **Conventions/Meetings:** quarterly meeting.

23404 ■ Underwater Society of America (USOA)

PO Box 628
Daly City, CA 94017
Ph: (650)583-8492
Fax: (650)583-0614
E-mail: croseusoa@aol.com
URL: http://www.underwater-society.org
Contact: Carol Rose, Pres.

Founded: 1959. **Members:** 2,000. **Membership Dues:** club or council, $15 (annual) ● independent, $20 (annual). **Budget:** $15,000. **Regional Groups:** 30. **Description:** Represents those who participate in and support the sports of skin diving, spearfishing, scuba diving, underwater photography, underwater hockey, and fin swimming; the society is interested in the advancement of underwater exploration, engineering, and science. Sponsors national skin diving, scuba diving, underwater photography, hockey, underwater rugby, and fin swimming competitions. Maintains hall of fame and speakers' bureau; sponsors children's poster contest; conducts research programs; compiles statistics. **Awards:** All American Dive Team Awards. **Frequency:** annual. **Type:** recognition ● Athletes of the Year Award. **Type:** recognition ● NOGI Award. **Frequency:** annual. **Type:** recognition. **Recipient:** to four individuals in the underwater community for distinguished service and for leadership in the arts, science, sports, or education. **Committees:** Competitions; Environmental/Conservation; Fin Swimming National Competitions; Free Diving; Legislation; Public Education; Safety; Scuba Diving; Search and Rescue; Underwater Hockey; Underwater Photography; Underwater Rugby. **Divisions:** Scientific; Sport. **Affiliated With:** National Association for Cave Diving; United States Olympic Committee; World Underwater Federation. **Publications:** *How to Form a Diving Club.* Manual. **Price:** $20.00 ● *Outlines: Underwater Sports,* annual. Brochure ● *Visibility,* quarterly. Newsletter. Includes updates on legislation affecting the sport and industry, competitions held throughout the country, calendar of events, and safety tips. **Price:** included in membership dues. **Circulation:** 2,000. **Advertising:** accepted ● Books ● Also publishes rules and regulations governing underwater sports. **Conventions/Meetings:** annual general assembly and board meeting.

Vaulting

23405 ■ American Vaulting Association (AVA)

8205 Santa Monica Blvd., No. 1-288
West Hollywood, CA 90046
Ph: (323)654-0800
Fax: (323)654-4306
E-mail: nationaloffice@americanvaulting.org
URL: http://www.americanvaulting.org
Contact: Craig Coburn, Office Mgr.

Founded: 1966. **Members:** 1,500. **Membership Dues:** club, $50 (annual) ● affiliate, $35 (annual) ● sustaining, vaulter, $40 (annual) ● alumni/event, $25 (annual) ● family, $125 (annual) ● life, sustaining, $750 ● sustaining, benefactor, $300 (annual) ● sustaining, contributing, $100 (annual). **Budget:** $80,000. **Regional Groups:** 7. **Description:** Vault-

ers, vaulting teams, and interested individuals. Aims to further the sport of vaulting in the U.S. Conducts courses for instructors and judges and offers seminars; provides assistance in securing equipment. **Libraries: Type:** reference. **Holdings:** audiovisuals, books. **Subjects:** vaulting, gymnastics on horseback, educational, historical, national fests. **Awards:** AVA Horse of the Year Award. **Frequency:** annual. **Type:** recognition. **Recipient:** for the most outstanding vaulting horse ● AVA Team Award. **Frequency:** annual. **Type:** recognition. **Recipient:** for the highest average score over three competitions ● High Point Award. **Frequency:** annual. **Type:** recognition. **Recipient:** for consistent competitors ● **Frequency:** semiannual. **Type:** monetary. **Recipient:** to members for promotion of vaulting ● **Frequency:** semiannual. **Type:** recognition. **Computer Services:** database. **Committees:** Competitions; Development; Education; Technical. **Affiliated With:** International Federation for Equestrian Sports; United States Equestrian Federation. **Publications:** *AVA Directory,* annual. **Circulation:** 1,500 ● *AVA Vaulting World,* bimonthly. Magazine. Contains competition results and information on upcoming meetings and clinics. **Price:** $25.00/year in U.S.; $35.00/year outside U.S. **Advertising:** accepted ● *Correct Vaulting* ● *Equestrian Vaulting* ● *Rule Book.* **Price:** $5.00 for members; $10.00 for nonmembers ● *Stretch and Strength.* Videos. Contains promotional and educational material. ● Brochures ● Also publishes manuals, promotional and educational videos. **Conventions/Meetings:** annual conference - usually January.

23406 ■ International Vaulting Club (IVC)

c/o Suzanne E. Detol, VP
34142 SW Johnson School Rd.
Cornelius, OR 97113
Ph: (503)357-9651
Fax: (503)359-3857
E-mail: office@vaultingclub.com
URL: http://www.vaultingclub.com
Contact: Suzanne E. Detol, VP

Membership Dues: ordinary, $20 (annual). **Multinational. Description:** Promotes the sport of vaulting all over the world. Provides all types of information both for members and for the general public and organizations interested in vaulting. Advances the improvement and further growth of the vaulting sport. Provides education and assistance in the field of vaulting. **Telecommunication Services:** electronic mail, sdetol@aol.com.

Volleyball

23407 ■ American Volleyball Coaches Association (AVCA)

1227 Lake Plaza Dr., Ste.B
Colorado Springs, CO 80906
Ph: (719)576-7777
Fax: (719)576-7778
E-mail: kdeboer@avca.org
URL: http://www.avca.org
Contact: Kathy DeBoer, Exec. Dir.

Founded: 1981. **Members:** 3,200. **Staff:** 8. **Budget:** $800,000. **Description:** Professional volleyball coaches united to promote the development of the sport of volleyball. Encourages high standards of competition; fosters public awareness, understanding, and support of the sport; provides a forum for the exchange of ideas among members and educational programs. **Awards:** AVCA All-America Teams. **Frequency:** annual. **Type:** recognition ● AVCA National Player of the Year. **Frequency:** annual. **Type:** recognition ● Game Plan/AVCA Team Academic Award. **Frequency:** annual. **Type:** recognition. **Recipient:** for high school and college volleyball teams ● Tachikara/AVCA National Coach of the Year. **Frequency:** annual. **Type:** recognition ● Tachikara/AVCA Victory Club Awards. **Frequency:** annual. **Type:** recognition. **Recipient:** for member head coaches who have won 100 to 900 volleyball matches. **Computer Services:** Mailing lists. **Formerly:** (1986) Collegiate Volleyball Coaches Association. **Publications:** *AVCA At The Net,* biweekly.

Newsletter. Provides association updates. **Price:** included in membership dues. ISSN: 1045-7186. **Circulation:** 3,300. **Advertising:** accepted. Alternate Formats: online ● *AVCA Volleyball Handbook* ● *Coaching Volleyball*, bimonthly. Journal. Features articles on conditioning, sports psychology, biomechanics, and technique. **Price:** $26.00 /year for individuals; $43.00 /year for institutions. ISSN: 0894-4237. **Circulation:** 3,500. **Advertising:** accepted ● *Dynamic Power Tips*, monthly. Features technical information specifically designated for high school and club coaches. **Price:** free for members ● *National Volleyball Statistics Manual.* **Conventions/Meetings:** annual convention (exhibits) - always December.

23408 ■ United States Volleyball Association/USA Volleyball (USAV/USVBA)
715 S Circle Dr.
Colorado Springs, CO 80910-2368
Ph: (719)228-6800
Free: (888)786-5539
Fax: (719)228-6899
E-mail: postmaster@usav.org
URL: http://www.usavolleyball.org
Contact: Mr. Kerry Klostermann, Sec. Gen.
Founded: 1928. **Members:** 175,039. **Staff:** 30. **Budget:** $8,000,000. **Regional Groups:** 40. **National Groups:** 35. **Description:** Works as a national governing body for the sport of volleyball in the US. **Computer Services:** Mailing lists, of members. **Divisions:** Beach; Disabled; Member Relations; Officials; Regional Operations; Youth and Junior Olympic Volleyball. **Affiliated With:** International Volleyball Federation - Switzerland; United States Olympic Committee. **Publications:** *Official U.S. Volleyball Rule Book*, annual. Features U.S. official rules for indoor and beach volleyball. **Price:** $7.00 rule book; $9.00 guidebook. **Circulation:** 150,000. **Advertising:** accepted ● *Official Volleyball Guide*, annual. Directory. Lists USVBA organizational guidelines. ● *Rotations*, biweekly. Newsletter. **Price:** free (sent via email). Alternate Formats: online ● *Volleyball USA*, quarterly. Magazine. Includes competition results. **Price:** $10.00/year. **Circulation:** 140,000. **Advertising:** accepted ● Also publishes USA coaching accreditation program textbooks and coaching manuals. **Conventions/Meetings:** annual meeting and general assembly, gathering of leadership - usually May.

Walking

23409 ■ National Organization of I Walkers (NOMW)
PO Box 191
Hermann, MO 65041
Fax: (573)486-3945
E-mail: nielsenfit@aol.com
URL: http://www.peternielsen.com/walking.htm
Contact: Peter Nielson, Contact
Founded: 1988. **Members:** 2,500. **Membership Dues:** $20 (annual). **Staff:** 6. **Budget:** $1,500. **Local Groups:** 35. **Description:** Individuals engaged in physical fitness programs involving walking through shopping ls. Sponsors walking events and sports and fitness promotional programs. Conducts charitable programs; compiles statistics. **Convention/Meeting:** none. **Awards:** **Type:** recognition. **Recipient:** for distance milestones. **Computer Services:** database.

Water Polo

23410 ■ Collegiate Water Polo Association (CWPA)
320 W 5th St.
Bridgeport, PA 19405
Ph: (610)277-6787
Fax: (610)277-7382
E-mail: office@collegiatewaterpolo.org
URL: http://www.collegiatewaterpolo.org
Contact: Daniel Sharadin, Commissioner
Founded: 1970. **Members:** 225. **Staff:** 5. **Budget:** $290,000. **National Groups:** 2. **For-Profit. Descrip-**

tion: Coordinates competition in the sport of water polo on the collegiate level. **Awards:** All Academic. **Frequency:** annual. **Type:** recognition. **Recipient:** for 3.2 GPA/completes season of competition in at least 3 games ● Player of the Week. **Frequency:** weekly. **Type:** recognition. **Recipient:** for ability. **Telecommunication Services:** electronic mail, commissioner@collegiatewaterpolo.org. **Affiliated With:** National Collegiate Athletic Association. **Formerly:** Middle Atlantic Water Polo Conference; Eastern Water Polo Association. **Publications:** *Media Guide*, semiannual. **Price:** $2.00. **Circulation:** 4,500. **Advertising:** accepted. Also Cited As: *League Program*. **Conventions/Meetings:** annual meeting - always second Friday of December.

23411 ■ United States Water Polo (USWP)
2124 Maine St., Ste.210
Huntington Beach, CA 92648
Ph: (714)500-5445
Fax: (714)960-2431
E-mail: cramsey@usawaterpolo.org
URL: http://www.usawaterpolo.org
Contact: Christopher Ramsey, CEO
Founded: 1978. **Members:** 30,000. **Membership Dues:** athlete, $50 (annual) ● coach/referee, $90 (annual) ● associate, $20 (annual). **Staff:** 10. **Budget:** $2,000,000. **Regional Groups:** 9. **Description:** Athletes, administrators, officials, and coaches. Promotes the sport of water polo in the U.S. Conducts clinics for athletes, coaches, and referees; sponsors competitions; and maintains hall of fame. **Awards:** **Type:** recognition. **Computer Services:** Online services, message board. **Committees:** Age Group; Athlete Representative; Hall of Fame; Junior Olympics; Men's and Women's International; National Development; National Referees; National Senior Men's Team; National Women's Team; Sports Medicine. **Affiliated With:** International Amateur Swimming Federation. **Supersedes:** Water Polo Committee of the Amateur Athletic Union. **Publications:** *U.S. Water Polo—Annual Rulebook.* Directory. Contains rules, listings of national team and Olympic water polo team members, and annual calendar of events. **Price:** $15.00. **Circulation:** 1,500. **Advertising:** accepted ● *Water Polo Scoreboard*, bimonthly. Magazine. Includes calendar of events and profiles of Olympic and national-level players. **Price:** included in membership dues. **Circulation:** 23,000. **Advertising:** accepted. **Conventions/Meetings:** annual conference, trade show vendors (exhibits).

Water Skiing

23412 ■ American Barefoot Club (ABC)
c/o Kerry Ross, Sec.-Treas.
PO Box 1203
Frederick, CO 80530-1203
Ph: (303)833-5450
E-mail: kerry.ross@lmco.com
URL: http://barefoot.org
Contact: Kerry Ross, Sec.-Treas.
Founded: 1977. **Members:** 2,500. **Description:** Enthusiasts of barefoot water skiing. Serves as the sanctioning body for official activities concerning the sport. Establishes rules and regulations for tournaments and similar events. **Awards:** Man of the Year Award. **Type:** recognition. **Recipient:** to an individual contributing most to the sport in a nonathletic capacity. **Affiliated With:** USA Water Ski. **Conventions/Meetings:** Barefoot National Competition ● annual meeting - usually August.

23413 ■ American Water Ski Educational Foundation (AWSEF)
1251 Holy Cow Rd.
Polk City, FL 33868-8200
Ph: (863)324-2472
Fax: (863)324-3996
E-mail: info@waterskihalloffame.com
URL: http://www.waterskihalloffame.com
Contact: Carole Lowe, Exec. Dir.
Founded: 1968. **Members:** 500. **Staff:** 2. **Budget:** $100,000. **Description:** Works to preserve the

heritage of water skiing and provide water skiing instruction to young and beginning skiers. Promotes competitive and recreational water skiing to the public. Maintains Water Ski Museum Hall of Fame and resource center. Offers charitable program; compiles statistics. **Libraries:** **Type:** open to the public. **Holdings:** 2,000; biographical archives, video recordings. **Subjects:** safety, water skiing instructions. **Awards:** Award of Distinction. **Frequency:** annual. **Type:** recognition. **Recipient:** write for information ● AWSEF Scholarship. **Frequency:** annual. **Type:** scholarship. **Recipient:** for advanced and deserving water skiers ● Hall of Fame. **Frequency:** annual. **Type:** recognition. **Recipient:** write for information. **Telecommunication Services:** electronic mail, awsefhalloffame@cs.com. **Committees:** Film Research; Hall of Fame Selection; Museum Planning; Scholarship. **Affiliated With:** USA Water Ski. **Publications:** *Water Ski Museum/Hall of Fame Newsletter*, annual. Contains historical articles and information on teams, scholarships, other related articles competitions. Includes schedules of events. **Price:** included in membership dues. **Circulation:** 1,000. **Conventions/Meetings:** semiannual board meeting ● annual meeting - midwinter.

23414 ■ International Jet Sports Boating Association and American Watercraft Association (IJSBA)
330 Purissima St., Ste.C
Half Moon Bay, CA 94019
Ph: (714)751-8695
Fax: (714)751-8609
E-mail: info@ijsba.com
URL: http://www.ijsba.com
Contact: Mark Denny, Managing Dir.
Founded: 1982. **Members:** 30,000. **Membership Dues:** associate, $295 (annual) ● international racer, $75 (annual). **Staff:** 9. **Regional Groups:** 8. **Languages:** English, French, Italian, Portuguese, Spanish, Swedish. **Description:** Owners, competitors, dealers, performance product manufacturers, and individuals supporting the sport of personal watercraft. Promotes the recreational and competitive use of certain single- and double-rider motorized watercraft; serves as the major sanctioning body for the sport of personal watercraft. Conducts national racing series and international world championship and other events; sponsors riding clinics and watercraft owners' jamboree fun days. Offers technical information and tips on improving riding skills. Compiles statistics. **Awards:** **Type:** recognition. **Formerly:** International Jet Ski Boating Association. **Publications:** *JetSports*, bimonthly. Magazine. **Price:** $2.50. **Circulation:** 50,000. **Advertising:** accepted. Alternate Formats: CD-ROM; diskette ● Also publishes rulebook and event, club, and publicity guides.

23415 ■ National Collegiate Water Ski Association (NCWSA)
c/o USA Water Ski
755 Overlook Dr.
Winter Haven, FL 33884
Ph: (941)324-4341
Fax: (941)325-8259
E-mail: j_surdej@yahoo.com
URL: http://www.ncwsa.com
Contact: Jeff Surdej, Chm.
Founded: 1968. **Members:** 1,800. **Membership Dues:** club, $30 (annual). **Staff:** 2. **Budget:** $2,000. **Regional Groups:** 6. **Local Groups:** 71. **Description:** Sport division of the American Water Ski Association (see separate entry). Universities, colleges, and junior colleges united to organize, promote, and direct collegiate water skiing. Holds national and regional competitions. Compiles statistics. **Awards:** Team. **Frequency:** annual. **Type:** recognition. **Recipient:** for the winners of national championships. **Affiliated With:** USA Water Ski. **Publications:** Newsletter, monthly. **Conventions/Meetings:** annual meeting - usually second weekend in October.

23416 ■ United States Hydrofoil Association (USHA)
320 Starlight Pl.
Lutherville, MD 21093

E-mail: questions@hydrofoil.org
URL: http://www.hydrofoil.org
Contact: Brad Scott, Pres.
Membership Dues: individual, $25-$60 (annual) ● foreign, $30-$65 (annual) ● family, $40-$65 (annual). **Description:** Helps introduce people to the sport of hydrofoiling. Educates the public on ways to have more fun and improve individual skills in hydrofoiling. **Awards:** Female Athlete of the Year. **Frequency:** annual. **Type:** recognition. **Recipient:** for outstanding performance as female athlete ● Male Athlete of the Year. **Frequency:** annual. **Type:** recognition. **Recipient:** for outstanding performance as male athlete. **Computer Services:** database, records and rankings ● information services, rules and scoring.

23417 ■ USA Water Ski (AWSA)

1251 Holy Cow Rd.
Polk City, FL 33868
Ph: (863)324-4341
Free: (800)533-AWSA
Fax: (863)325-8259
E-mail: usawaterski@usawaterski.org
URL: http://www.usawaterski.org
Contact: Andy Jugan, Exec. Dir.
Founded: 1939. **Members:** 37,500. **Membership Dues:** individual, $60 ● active (under 25), $35 ● individual supporting, $25 ● foreign active, $65 ● foreign federation active/foreign supporting, $30 ● family active head of household, $65 ● family active spouse and children, $30 ● family supporting head of household, $40. **Staff:** 20. **Budget:** $2,500,000. **Regional Groups:** 5. **State Groups:** 50. **Local Groups:** 700. **Description:** Promotes competitive and recreational water skiing in the U.S. Authorizes and establishes rules for competition and certifies performance records in water skiing. Conducts water ski skills program and clinics for instructors and tournament officials. Works closely with sister organization, American Water Ski Educational Association, which maintains museum and hall of fame. Compiles statistics. **Libraries: Type:** reference. **Subjects:** history and development of water skiing. **Computer Services:** Mailing lists. **Committees:** Boat Drivers Rating; Competitive Rules; International Activities; Judges' Rating and Classification; Safety; Skiers' Rating and Classification; Technical; Waterways Education. **Divisions:** American Barefoot Club; American Kneeboard Association; American Wakeboard Association; American Water Ski Association; National Collegiate Water Ski Association; National Show Ski Association; National Water Ski Racing Association; Water Skiers with Disabilities Association. **Affiliated With:** American Water Ski Educational Foundation; United States Olympic Committee. **Formerly:** (2001) American Water Ski Association. **Publications:** *The Water Skier*, 9/year. Magazine. Includes advertisers index, AWSA news, new member profiles, new products and services information, and tournament calendar. **Price:** included in membership dues. ISSN: 0049-7002. **Circulation:** 28,000. **Advertising:** accepted. Alternate Formats: microform; CD-ROM; online ● Booklets ● Directory, periodic ● Also publishes water ski safety information. **Conventions/Meetings:** annual competition.

Water Sports

23418 ■ American Watercraft Association (AWA)

PO Box 1993
Ashburn, VA 20147-9998
Free: (800)913-2921
Fax: (703)421-9889
URL: http://www.awahq.org
Membership Dues: individual, $24 (annual) ● individual, $46 (biennial) ● individual, $67 (triennial) ● affiliate, $10 (annual). **Description:** Promotes the positive image of watercraft sports through proactive community and legislative action. **Publications:** *Jet Sports*. Magazine. Provides a forum for news, tips, rankings, expert advice, questions and answers. **Price:** free for members ● *Ride Magazine*. **Price:** included in membership dues.

23419 ■ World Freestyle Watercraft Alliance (WFWA)

1060 Old Rte. 220 S
Duncansville, PA 16635
Ph: (734)652-1481
URL: http://www.wfwaalliance.com
Contact: Tommy Nuttall, Contact
Multinational. Description: Represents the interests of freestyle riders and athletes around the world. Promotes the sports of Freestyle Water-X. Furthers the sport of freestyle with the use of ramps, sliders, gaps, and free ride areas. **Publications:** Book.

Weightlifting

23420 ■ North American Kettlebell Federation (NAKF)

c/o Lorraine Patten, Treas.
PO Box 478
Pleasant Valley, NY 12569
E-mail: lopa43@hotmail.com
URL: http://www.nakf.net
Contact: Lorraine Patten, Treas.
Membership Dues: regular, $40 (annual). **Multinational. Description:** Promotes the Girevoy Sport (GS) in North America. Works to develop the sport and its athletes. Hosts Kettlebell competition. Facilitates communication and sportsmanship among members. **Telecommunication Services:** electronic mail, nakfmeets@gmail.com.

23421 ■ USA Weightlifting (USAW)

1 Olympic Plz.
Colorado Springs, CO 80909
Ph: (719)866-4508
Fax: (719)866-4741
E-mail: usaw@usaweightlifting.org
URL: http://www.msbn.tv/usavision
Contact: Wesley Barnett, Exec. Dir.
Founded: 1979. **Members:** 3,800. **Membership Dues:** senior/medical/volunteer/referee/administrator, $35 (annual) ● school age, $20 (annual) ● junior, $30 (annual) ● master, $40-$70 (annual) ● coach, $35-$85 (annual). **Staff:** 8. **Budget:** $950,000. **Regional Groups:** 12. **State Groups:** 42. **Local Groups:** 145. **Description:** Males and females aged 12 and older (3500); sustaining members are non-athletes (300). Serves as national governing body for weightlifting. Works to develop the sport of weightlifting and its athletes at the local, regional, and national levels. Sponsors national and international meets; selects teams for the Olympics and the Pan-American Games. Maintains hall of fame. **Awards: Type:** recognition. **Recipient:** for national squad or national junior squad members ● **Type:** scholarship. **Recipient:** for national squad or national junior squad members. **Publications:** *USAW Club and College Directory*. Alternate Formats: online ● *USAW Weekly Report*. Alternate Formats: online ● *Weightlifting USA*, quarterly. Newsletter. Covers events, tournaments, and the Olympic trials. Includes coaching and training tips, medical updates, and tournament results. **Price:** $20.00 domestic; $30.00 international. **Circulation:** 3,800. **Advertising:** accepted ● Videos. Available for coaching weightlifters at various levels. ● Manuals. **Conventions/Meetings:** periodic competition ● annual meeting, includes national championships.

23422 ■ World Association of Benchers and Dead Lifters (WABDL)

PO Box 27499
Golden Valley, MN 55427
Ph: (763)545-8654 (503)901-1622
Fax: (763)544-3776
E-mail: wabdl@bendbroadband.com
URL: http://www.wabdl.org
Contact: Gus Rethwisch, Pres./Records Chm.
Membership Dues: teen, $25 (annual) ● regular, $30 (annual). **Multinational. Description:** Provides opportunities for local, regional and world competitions in the single-lift bench press and dead lift. Provides a drug-free, drug-tested lifting environment. Keeps updated state, national and world records.

Computer Services: database, meet results ● database, state and international contacts ● database, state records ● information services, kilo chart.

Wrestling

23423 ■ National Wrestling Coaches Association (NWCA)

PO Box 254
Manheim, PA 17545-0254
Ph: (717)653-8009
Fax: (717)653-8270
E-mail: mmoyer@nwca.cc
URL: http://www.nwcaonline.com
Contact: Mike Moyer, Exec. Dir.
Founded: 1928. **Members:** 1,700. **Membership Dues:** fan, parent, scholastic/retired coach, official, $30 (annual) ● high school institutional, organization, $60 (annual). **Budget:** $300,000. **Description:** Fans, coaches and officials connected with the sport of amateur wrestling. Seeks to preserve and promote interscholastic and amateur intercollegiate wrestling. **Awards:** All-Academic Award. **Frequency:** annual. **Type:** recognition. **Recipient:** for outstanding achievement ● Coach of the Year. **Frequency:** annual. **Type:** recognition. **Recipient:** for an outstanding coach. **Affiliated With:** National Collegiate Athletic Association. **Formerly:** (1962) American Wrestling Coaches and Officials Association; (1969) National Collegiate Athletic Association of Wrestling Coaches and Officials. **Publications:** *NWCA Newsletter*, quarterly. **Price:** included in membership dues. **Circulation:** 1,800. **Advertising:** accepted. **Conventions/Meetings:** annual Asics/Resilite Convention, athletic apparel and related products used in the sport of wrestling (exhibits).

23424 ■ U.S.A. Wrestling (USAW)

6155 Lehman Dr.
Colorado Springs, CO 80918
Ph: (719)598-8181
Fax: (719)598-9440
E-mail: hthompson@usawrestling.org
URL: http://www.themat.com
Contact: Rich Bender, Exec. Dir.
Founded: 1968. **Members:** 159,000. **Membership Dues:** competitor, $20 (annual) ● coach, $43 (annual) ● club, $40 (annual) ● partner, $30 (annual). **Staff:** 29. **Budget:** $7,105,500. **Regional Groups:** 6. **State Groups:** 49. **Local Groups:** 2,400. **Description:** Represents amateur wrestlers, coaches, officials, and representatives of major school organizations. Serves as national governing body and member of U.S. Olympic Committee (see separate entry). Seeks to develop, improve, and promote the sport of wrestling. Conducts: rules interpretation clinics for mat and pairings officials; sports medicine and wrestling technique clinics; coach certification clinics. Selects and trains wrestlers representing the USA in international competition. Offers speakers' bureau. Produces films on training methods, wrestling technique, and rule interpretation. Conducts research in the areas of sports psychology, physiology, behavior, sports medicine, training technique, and strategy. Compiles statistics and promotes activities. **Libraries: Type:** reference. **Holdings:** archival material, books. **Subjects:** history of wrestling. **Awards:** Athlete of the Year. **Frequency:** annual. **Type:** recognition ● Developmental Coach of the Year. **Frequency:** annual. **Type:** recognition ● Espoir Person of the Year. **Frequency:** annual. **Type:** recognition ● Freestyle Coach of the Year. **Frequency:** annual. **Type:** recognition ● Freestyle Wrestler of the Year. **Frequency:** annual. **Type:** recognition ● Greco-Roman Coach of the Year. **Frequency:** annual. **Type:** recognition ● Greco-Roman Wrestler of the Year. **Frequency:** annual. **Type:** recognition ● Kids/Cadet Person of the Year. **Frequency:** annual. **Type:** recognition ● Man of the Year. **Frequency:** annual. **Type:** recognition ● Official of the Year. **Frequency:** annual. **Type:** recognition ● State Chairperson of the Year. **Frequency:** annual. **Type:** recognition ● Women's Wrestler of the Year. **Frequency:** annual. **Type:** recognition. **Computer Services:** database,

membership. **Committees:** Athletes Advisory; Camps and Clinics; Freestyle Coach Selection; Freestyle Sport; Greco-Roman Coach Selection; Greco-Roman Sport; International Exchange; Legislation; Marketing; Merchandising; Officials; Sports Science; State Organizations; Women's Coach Selection; Women's Sport. **Councils:** Coaches. **Divisions:** FILA Junior University; Juniors; Kids/Cadet; State Championship; U.S. Federation of Wrestling Clubs. **Programs:** Big Brother and Future Freestyle; National Coaches Education; Resident-Northern Michigan University; Resident-USOC. **Affiliated With:** Armed Forces Sports; National Association of Intercollegiate Athletics; National Collegiate Athletic Association; National Federation of State High School Associations; National Junior College Athletic Association; National Wrestling Coaches Association. **Formerly:** (1983) United States Wrestling Federation. **Publications:** *The Complete Coach*, quarterly. Newsletter. Provides coaching tips, techniques and instructional articles. **Advertising:** accepted ● *International Wrestling Rules*, biennial ● *State Leaders Newsletter*, monthly. Includes event schedules and results and association news. **Price:** $24.00/year ● *USA Wrestler*, monthly, Oct, Nov, Feb, Mar, Apr, Jun. Newspaper. Reports on national and international wrestling events; includes profiles and instructional articles. **Price:** $18.00 /year for nonmembers; free for members. **Advertising:** accepted ● Booklets. **Conventions/Meetings:** semiannual board meeting ● annual convention, with National Junior Championships - always mid-July, in Fargo, ND.

23425 ■ Wrestlers WithOut Borders
1463 Shotwell St.
San Francisco, CA 94110
E-mail: info@wrestlerswob.com
URL: http://www.wrestlerswob.com
Contact: Erich Richter, Chm.
Membership Dues: club, $10 (annual). **Multinational. Description:** Promotes freestyle and Greco-Roman wrestling. Represents member clubs as a voting delegate to the Federation of Gay Games. **Computer Services:** Mailing lists. **Telecommunication Services:** electronic mail, chairman@wrestlerswob.com. **Publications:** Newsletter. Alternate Formats: online.

Wristwrestling

23426 ■ United States ArmSports
423 E Washington St.
Petaluma, CA 94952
Ph: (707)537-7373
E-mail: ddevoto@armwrestling.com
URL: http://www.armwrestling.com
Contact: Dave Devoto, Dir.
Founded: 1953. **Staff:** 4. **Description:** Conducts wrist wrestling championships in divisions ranging from bantamweight (under 130 pounds) to heavyweight (unlimited). Conducts contests for both men and women. Maintains Hall of Fame. **Formerly:** (2003) World's Wristwrestling Championship. **Conventions/Meetings:** annual National Championship Tournament - competition - always April or May ● annual World's Championship Tournament - competition - always second Saturday of October, Petaluma, CA.

Yoga

23427 ■ B.K.S. Iyengar Yoga National Association of the U.S. (IYNAUS)
c/o Steve Hornbacher, Membership Chm.
3010 Hennepin Ave. S, No. 272
Minneapolis, MN 55408
Free: (800)889-9642
E-mail: info@bksiyengar.com
URL: http://www.iynaus.org
Contact: Marla Apt, Pres.
Founded: 1990. **Members:** 2,300. **Membership Dues:** regional, $50 (annual) ● international, $62 (annual). **Regional Groups:** 11. **Description:** Works to disseminate and promote the "art, science, and philosophy of Yoga according to the teachings of B.K.S. Iyengar and his family". **Computer Services:** database, list of certified teachers. **Telecommunication Services:** electronic bulletin board. **Committees:** Archives; By-Laws; Certification; Ethics; Events; Newsletter; Nominating; Scholarship. **Publications:** *Certification Manual* ● *What is Iyengar Yoga?*. Brochure. Alternate Formats: online.● *Yoga Samachar*, semiannual. Newsletter. Price: included in membership dues. Alternate Formats: online ● Bulletin, quarterly. **Price:** included in membership dues. Alternate Formats: online.

Administrative Services

23428 ■ Office and Professional Employees International Union (OPEIU)
265 W 14th St., 6th Fl.
New York, NY 10011
Ph: (212)675-3210
Free: (800)346-7348
Fax: (212)727-3466
E-mail: opeiu@opeiu.org
URL: http://www.opeiu.org
Contact: Michael Goodwin, Pres.
Founded: 1945. **Members:** 145,000. **Staff:** 250. **Regional Groups:** 8. **Local Groups:** 300. **Languages:** English, Spanish. **Multinational. Description:** AFL-CIO. Provides representation to employees throughout the U.S. and Canada. **Libraries: Type:** not open to the public. **Subjects:** research. **Awards:** Henderson B. Douglas Award. **Frequency:** annual. **Type:** monetary. **Absorbed:** (1995) Leather Workers International Union. **Formerly:** Office Employees International Union. **Publications:** *Office and Professional Employees International Union-White Collar*, quarterly. Newspaper. Covers labor issues in Canada and the United States including contract language, pay equity, labor law, collective bargaining, and political issues. **Price:** $1.00/year. ISSN: 0043-4876. **Circulation:** 140,000 ● *Steward Update*. Newsletter. Alternate Formats: online. **Conventions/Meetings:** triennial convention (exhibits).

23429 ■ SEIU, District 925, AFL-CIO
2900 Eastlake Ave. E, No. 230
Seattle, WA 98102
Ph: (206)322-3010
Free: (866)734-8925
Fax: (206)322-6842
E-mail: kcook@seiu925.org
URL: http://www.seiu925.org
Contact: Kim Cook, Pres.
Founded: 1981. **Members:** 7,500. **Staff:** 20. **Regional Groups:** 4. **Description:** National union of secretaries, stenographers, typists, clerks, and other office, technical, and professional workers in the U.S. Promotes collective bargaining for office workers and sponsors research and educational programs on pay equality, automation, and career advancement. Seeks to organize the nearly 20 million office workers in the U.S; compiles statistics. **Libraries: Type:** reference. **Affiliated With:** Service Employees International Union. **Publications:** *Stewards Manual*. Book. Alternate Formats: online ● Brochures ● Bulletin, periodic ● Reports. **Conventions/Meetings:** annual meeting.

Agriculture

23430 ■ Farm Labor Organizing Committee (FLOC)
1221 Broadway St.
Toledo, OH 43609
Ph: (419)243-3456

Fax: (419)243-5655
E-mail: info@floc.com
URL: http://www.floc.com
Contact: Baldemar Velasquez, Pres.
Founded: 1967. **Members:** 7,500. **Staff:** 13. **Budget:** $250,000. **Description:** Hispanic migrant farm workers whose home base is Texas or Florida, but who work seasonally in the states of Ohio, Michigan, and Indiana. Seeks to organize these workers into a labor union; concentrates efforts in the Hispanic community of northwest Ohio. Engages in advocacy on behalf of Hispanic resident farm workers; organized the nationwide farm worker boycott of Campbell products in protest of the canners' refusal to negotiate with the farm workers; has contracts with Campbell and its subsidiary Vlasic covering approximately 1800 cucumber and tomato harvesters in Ohio and Michigan; recent contract will eliminate independent contractor system (sharecropping) and consider farm workers as employees. **Publications:** *Dignidad*, periodic. Newsletter. **Conventions/Meetings:** triennial meeting.

23431 ■ Farm Labor Research Project (FLRP)
1221 Broadway St.
Toledo, OH 43609
Ph: (419)243-3456
Fax: (419)243-5655
E-mail: info@floc.com
URL: http://www.floc.com
Contact: Baldemar Velasquez, Pres.
Founded: 1981. **Staff:** 12. **Budget:** $750,000. **Languages:** English, Spanish. **Description:** Engages in charitable, educational, and scientific activities as they relate to farm workers, former farm workers, and their families, who have been deprived of educational opportunities, who are exposed to many occupational hazards, or who have incomes lower than the federal poverty level. Carries on activities in the fields of elimination of sharecropping and implementation of employee status for farm workers, grassroots leadership and conflict-resolution development, pesticide education, and health education and services. **Conventions/Meetings:** triennial meeting.

23432 ■ United Farm Workers of America (UFW)
PO Box 62
Keene, CA 93531
Ph: (818)565-5603 (661)823-6105
E-mail: execoffice@ufwmail.com
URL: http://www.ufw.org
Contact: Arturo S. Rodriguez, Pres.
Founded: 1962. **Members:** 50,000. **Staff:** 75. **Budget:** $5,000,000. **State Groups:** 5. **Languages:** English, Spanish. **Description:** AFL-CIO. Agricultural laborers. Chief purpose is to achieve collective bargaining rights for U.S. farm workers. Seeks to give farm laborers dignity and pride in their work by improving working and safety conditions and wages. Educates farm workers in the political and social arenas. Trains workers in skills needed for work in the fields and in the office of the union; espouses nonviolence. Archives of the union are housed at

Wayne State University Labor Archives, Detroit, MI. **Libraries: Type:** not open to the public. **Holdings:** books, periodicals. **Computer Services:** Mailing lists, donors. **Formerly:** National Farm Workers Association; United Farm Workers Organizing Committee. **Conventions/Meetings:** biennial convention, with health fair (exhibits) - during Labor Day.

Aircraft

23433 ■ Independent Pilots Association (IPA)
3607 Fern Valley Rd.
Louisville, KY 40219
E-mail: comment@ipapilot.org
URL: http://www.ipapilot.org
Contact: Bob Miller, Pres.
Members: 2,200. **Description:** Represents UPS crewmembers that operate UPS aircraft. Work to organize workers to stand up for their rights.

Appliances

23434 ■ Stove, Furnace, Energy, and Allied Appliance Workers Division of the International Brotherhood of Boilermakers (SFEAW)
357 Riverside Dr., Ste.230-B
Franklin, TN 37064
Ph: (615)791-3861
Fax: (615)791-3891
E-mail: drussell@boilermakers.org
URL: http://www.boilermakers.org/2-WhoWeAre/ SFEAW.html
Contact: Newton B. Jones, Intl. Pres.
Founded: 1994. **Members:** 7,500. **State Groups:** 2. **Description:** Serves as energy industry union. **Affiliated With:** AFL-CIO. **Formed by Merger of:** Stove, Furnace and Allied Appliance Workers International Union of North America; International Brotherhood of Boilermakers. **Publications:** *The Broilermaker Reporter*, bimonthly. Newspaper. **Price:** $10.00 3-year subscription ● Journal, annual. **Conventions/Meetings:** quadrennial meeting.

Art

23435 ■ International Association for Professional Art Advisors (IAPAA)
c/o Kimberly Maier, Exec. Dir.
433 Third St., Ste.3
Brooklyn, NY 11215
Ph: (718)788-1425
E-mail: info@iapaa.org
URL: http://www.iapaa.org
Contact: Kimberly Maier, Exec. Dir.
Founded: 1984. **Members:** 145. **Membership Dues:** individual, $200 (annual) ● institution, $1,000 (annual). **Staff:** 1. **Description:** Supports and represents corporate art curators and independent art advisors.

Awards: IAPAA Award for Excellence. **Frequency:** annual. **Type:** recognition. **Recipient:** to an academic institution for an outstanding graduate student whom the institution selects ● IAPAA Scholarship Award. **Frequency:** annual. **Type:** scholarship. **Formerly:** (2003) National Association for Corporate Art Management.

Asian-American

23436 ■ Asian Pacific American Labor Alliance (APALA)
815 16th St. NW
Washington, DC 20006
Ph: (202)508-3733
Fax: (202)508-3716
E-mail: apala@apalanet.org
URL: http://www.apalanet.org
Contact: Juliet Huang, Exec. Dir.
Founded: 1992. **Membership Dues:** individual, $20. **Description:** Asian Pacific American union members. Strives to provide a voice for Asian Pacific American workers in the labor movement, in the community, in the media, and in the public policy arena. **Publications:** *Organizing Civil Rights Economic Justice.* Brochure. Alternate Formats: online ● Newsletter. Alternate Formats: online.

Automotive

23437 ■ International Union, United Automobile, Aerospace and Agricultural Implement Workers of America (UAW)
8000 E Jefferson Ave.
Solidarity House
Detroit, MI 48214
Ph: (313)926-5000
Free: (800)243-8829
Fax: (313)823-6016
URL: http://www.uaw.org
Contact: Ron Gettelfinger, Pres.
Founded: 1935. **Members:** 1,300,000. **Regional Groups:** 12. **Description:** Labor union, affiliated with AFL-CIO. Strives to improve the quality of life of working men worldwide through vigilant political involvement and coordination with world labor organizations. **Computer Services:** Mailing lists, of members. **Departments:** Aerospace; DaimlerChrysler; Ford; General Motors. **Also Known As:** United Auto Workers. **Formerly:** (1962) International Union, United Automobile, Aircraft, and Agricultural Implement Workers of America. **Publications:** *Occupational Health and Safety.* Newsletter ● *Research.* Bulletin ● *Skill,* quarterly ● *Solidarity,* bimonthly. Magazine. Covers labor, economic, social, and political affairs affecting union members. Includes book and film reviews. **Price:** $5.00/year. ISSN: 0164-856X. Circulation: 1,417,000 ● *Updated Epidemiology of Workers Exposed to Metalworking Fluids Provides Sufficient Evidence for Carcinogenicity.* Paper. **Price:** $28.65. **Conventions/Meetings:** triennial meeting.

Aviation

23438 ■ Air Line Employees Association, International (ALEA)
Address Unknown since 2006
Founded: 1951. **Members:** 300. **Staff:** 7. **Local Groups:** 2. **Description:** AFL-CIO airline clerical, reservation, and station employees. **Affiliated With:** Air Line Pilots Association, International. **Formerly:** (1960) Air Line Agents Association. **Publications:** *The Air Line Employee,* bimonthly. **Advertising:** not accepted ● *News Bulletin,* monthly. **Conventions/Meetings:** triennial meeting.

23439 ■ Air Line Pilots Association, International (ALPA)
1625 Massachusetts Ave. NW
Washington, DC 20036
Ph: (703)689-2270

E-mail: communications@alpa.org
URL: http://www.alpa.org
Contact: Pete Janhunan, Media/Public Contact
Founded: 1931. **Members:** 62,000. **Staff:** 412. **Local Groups:** 106. **Multinational. Description:** Conducts collective bargaining activities of airline pilots. Promotes all aspects of aviation safety and security. **Committees:** Political Action. **Affiliated With:** AFL-CIO; Air Line Pilots Association, International; Association of Flight Attendants - CWA. **Absorbed:** (1982) Union of Professional Airmen; (1997) Canadian Air Line Pilots Association. **Formerly:** (1999) Air Line Pilots Association. **Publications:** *Air Line Pilot: The Magazine of Professional Flight Crews,* monthly. Reports on advances in air safety and flight technology, industry developments, aviation history, and association news. Includes book reviews. **Price:** $22. 00/year for student; $32.00 /year for individuals in U.S.; $45.00 /year for individuals outside U.S. ISSN: 0002-242X. **Circulation:** 81,000. **Advertising:** accepted ● Newsletter, periodic ● Also publishes memoranda.

23440 ■ Aircraft Mechanics Fraternal Association (AMFA)
PO Box 51955
Indianapolis, IN 46251
Ph: (317)244-4413
Fax: (317)244-4418
E-mail: info@amfa2000.org
URL: http://www.amfa2000.org
Contact: Steve MacFarlane, Pres.
Founded: 1962. **Members:** 600. **Regional Groups:** 3. **Local Groups:** 1. **Description:** Aims to promote and protect the interests of the members and their profession. **Publications:** *The Grapevine,* monthly ● *National Newsletter,* quarterly. **Conventions/Meetings:** quadrennial meeting.

23441 ■ Allied Pilots Association (APA)
14600 Trinity Blvd., Ste.500
O'Connell Bldg.
Fort Worth, TX 76155-2512
Ph: (817)302-2272
Free: (800)323-1470
E-mail: public-comment@alliedpilots.org
URL: http://www.alliedpilots.org
Contact: John Darrah, Pres.
Founded: 1963. **Members:** 11,000. **Staff:** 50. **Regional Groups:** 9. **Description:** Independent group originating from the Air Line Pilots Association. Collective bargaining agent for the pilots of American Airlines. **Committees:** Comprehensive; Structure. **Publications:** *Flightline,* bimonthly. Magazine. **Conventions/Meetings:** semiannual board meeting.

23442 ■ American Independent Cockpit Alliance (AICA)
67 Water St., Ste.208
Laconia, NH 03247-0278
Ph: (603)528-2552
Free: (800)808-2552
Fax: (603)524-1331
E-mail: pbrady@aicapilot.org
URL: http://www.aicapilot.org
Contact: Pete Brady, Pres.
Founded: 1993. **Membership Dues:** captain, $50 (monthly) ● first officer, $30 (monthly). **Description:** Advances the professional and economic well being of American Airlines pilots. Promotes the professional interest and protects the individual and collective rights of members. Works to negotiate and maintain agreements covering rates of pay, rules and working conditions.

23443 ■ Association of Flight Attendants - CWA (AFA-CWA)
501 3rd St. NW
Washington, DC 20001
Ph: (202)434-1300
Fax: (202)434-1319
E-mail: afatalk@afanet.org
URL: http://www.afanet.org
Contact: Patricia A. Friend, Pres.
Founded: 1945. **Members:** 50,000. **Membership Dues:** individual, $39 (monthly). **Staff:** 75. **Budget:**

$19,000,000. **Local Groups:** 71. **National Groups:** 15. **Multinational. Description:** AFL-CIO. Airline flight attendants united for contract representation, arbitration, communications, government affairs, and membership services. **Libraries: Type:** not open to the public. **Subjects:** Flightlog. **Awards:** AFA Scholarship. **Frequency:** annual. **Type:** scholarship. **Committees:** Air Safety and Health; Collective Bargaining; Communications; Employee Assistance Program; International; Member Services; Political Action. **Affiliated With:** AFL-CIO. **Formerly:** (1973) Steward/Stewardess Division, Air Line Pilots Association; (2004) Association of Flight Attendants. **Publications:** *E-News.* Newsletter. Alternate Formats: online ● *Flightlog,* quarterly. Journal. Includes industry reports and officer messages. **Price:** $18.00/year. ISSN: 0164-8689. **Circulation:** 50,000. **Advertising:** accepted. **Conventions/Meetings:** annual board meeting.

23444 ■ Association of Professional Flight Attendants (APFA)
1004 W Euless Blvd.
Euless, TX 76040
Ph: (817)540-0108
Free: (800)395-2732
Fax: (817)540-2077
E-mail: communications@apfa.org
URL: http://www.apfa.org
Contact: Tommie Hutto-Blake, Pres.
Founded: 1977. **Members:** 21,000. **Membership Dues:** individual, $35 (monthly). **Staff:** 17. **Budget:** $10,000,000. **Description:** Flight attendants. Seeks to obtain optimal conditions of employment for members. Represents members in contract negotiations with airlines, and before government agencies regulating transportation. In 1993, organized a successful strike which forced American Airlines to enter binding arbitration with its flight attendants. **Libraries: Type:** by appointment only. **Holdings:** archival material, articles, clippings, periodicals. **Subjects:** labor issues in the air transportation industries. **Formerly:** (1977) Airline Stewards and Stewardesses Association.

23445 ■ International Association of Machinists (IAM)
9000 Machinists Pl.
Upper Marlboro, MD 20772-2687
Ph: (301)967-4500
E-mail: websteward@goiam.org
URL: http://www.goiam.org
Contact: R. Thomas Buffenbarger, Intl. Pres.
Founded: 1976. **Members:** 730,000. **Local Groups:** 7. **Description:** Flight attendants employed by Continental Airlines and Air Micronesia. **Absorbed:** (1991) Union of Flight Attendants.

23446 ■ International Association of Machinists and Aerospace Workers (IAM)
9000 Machinists Pl.
Upper Marlboro, MD 20772-2687
Ph: (301)967-4500
E-mail: websteward@goiam.org
URL: http://www.goiam.org
Contact: R. Thomas Buffenbarger, Pres.
Founded: 1888. **Members:** 730,000. **Multinational. Description:** Represents the interests of members. **Departments:** Aerospace; Automotive; Collective Bargaining; Employment Services; Human Rights; Safety and Health; Woodworkers. **Absorbed:** (1987) International Die Sinkers Conference; (1991) Pattern Makers' League of North America. **Formerly:** (1965) International Association of Machinists. **Publications:** *IAM Journal.* Magazine ● *The Machinist,* monthly. **Conventions/Meetings:** quadrennial meeting.

23447 ■ National Air Traffic Controllers Association (NATCA)
1325 Massachusetts Ave. NW
Washington, DC 20005
Ph: (202)628-5451
Fax: (202)628-5767

E-mail: dchurch@natcadc.org
URL: http://www.natca.org
Contact: Patrick Forrey, Pres.
Founded: 1987. **Members:** 15,000. **Membership Dues:** associate (FAA employee), $100 (periodic) ● associate (non-FAA employee), $50 (periodic) ● corporate, $500 (annual) ● retired, $35 (annual). **Staff:** 40. **Budget:** $20,000,000. **Regional Groups:** 9. **Local Groups:** 400. **Description:** Independent union. Represents U.S. air traffic controllers and other aviation safety-related professionals. Negotiates on members' behalf with the Federal Aviation Administration. Publications, training, seminars, internet, recruiting and safety/technology are its key components. **Awards:** Archie League Medal of Safety. **Frequency:** annual. **Type:** recognition. **Recipient:** for members' outstanding performance in work ● Sentinel Safety Award. **Frequency:** annual. **Type:** recognition. **Recipient:** for a member of the aviation community outside NATCA who has displayed outstanding achievement in the field of aviation safety. **Computer Services:** database, grievance and membership. **Committees:** Constitution; Finance; Legislative; Organizing; Safety and Technology. **Departments:** Media. **Affiliated With:** AFL-CIO. **Publications:** *The Air Traffic Controller*, bimonthly. Newsletter. Provides regular updates on NATCA's events and priorities. **Circulation:** 17,000. Alternate Formats: online ● *Safety in Numbers*. Brochure. Features the opinion and views of the legislators and other personalities on ATC staffing. ● *Understanding ATC Financing*. Report. Provides a fact-based framework for policy discussions on financing. ● *Voices: A Glimpse Into the Careers of Air Traffic Controllers*. Booklet. Features the challenging and rewarding profession of being an air traffic controller. ● Annual Reports, annual. Provides an in-depth look at NATCA's major initiatives, accomplishments, events etc. ● Brochure. Contains information on the organization's profile and the locations of its members. ● Also publishes quarterly issue reports, annual report, special issue publications, NATCA brochures, and legislative booklets. **Conventions/Meetings:** biennial convention (exhibits).

23448 ■ National Association of Air Traffic Specialists (NAATS)
PO Box 2550
Landover Hills, MD 20784-0550
Ph: (301)459-5595
Fax: (301)459-5597
E-mail: naatspres@aol.com
URL: http://www.naats.org
Contact: Alan Baker, Pres.
Founded: 1959. **Members:** 1,600. **Staff:** 5. **Regional Groups:** 9. **Local Groups:** 150. **Description:** Independent air traffic control specialists employed by the Federal Aviation Administration at flight service stations. Maintains hall of fame; compiles statistics. **Awards: Type:** recognition. **Committees:** NAATS Political Action Fund. **Publications:** *NAATS News*, quarterly. Bulletin. Contains governmental information and obituaries. **Price:** available to members only ● *Regional Newsletter*, monthly. **Conventions/Meetings:** annual meeting ● seminar and regional meeting.

23449 ■ Professional Airways Systems Specialists (PASS)
c/o Tom Brantley, Pres.
1150 17th St. NW, Ste.702
Washington, DC 20036-4603
Ph: (202)293-7277
Fax: (202)293-7727
E-mail: president@passnational.org
URL: http://www.passnational.org
Contact: Tom Brantley, Pres.
Founded: 1977. **Members:** 4,500. **Membership Dues:** retired, $75 (annual) ● associate, $120 (annual). **Staff:** 11. **Budget:** $3,200,000. **Description:** Systems specialists and aviation safety inspectors employed by the Federal Aviation Administration whose responsibilities include legal certification, systems management, installation and maintenance of the National Airspace System and oversight of general and commercial aviation industries. Works

to: promote and improve the profession and working conditions of systems specialists and inspectors; preserve and develop safety standards of the air traffic system within the U.S. and its territories. Includes areas of concern such as: passage of labor and safety legislation; promotion of professional status; improvement of benefits and pay; institution of standards of progression from trainee to journeyman levels; standardization of all employer practices. Testifies before Congress. **Libraries: Type:** reference. **Holdings:** archival material, books, periodicals. **Affiliated With:** International Federation of Air Traffic Safety Electronics Association; National Maritime Union of America. **Formed by Merger of:** District 1 of Marine Engineers Beneficial Association/National Maritime Union and Professional Airways Systems Specialists. **Publications:** *PASS Times*, bimonthly. Newsletter. **Price:** free for members. **Circulation:** 4,300. Alternate Formats: online ● *Whenever You Fly, PASS Ensures Your Safety*. Brochure. Alternate Formats: online. **Conventions/Meetings:** biennial convention, membership convention (exhibits).

23450 ■ Professional Pilots Federation (PPF)
c/o Bert Yetman, Pres.
PO Box 622
Scranton, PA 18503
Ph: (817)481-5318
E-mail: 70641.1413@compuserve.com
URL: http://www.ppf.org
Contact: Bert Yetman, Pres.
Founded: 1991. **Membership Dues:** regular, $35 (monthly) ● associate, $25 (monthly) ● active alumni, $5 (monthly) ● regular, $400 (annual) ● associate, $285 (annual) ● active alumni, $50 (annual). **Description:** Seeks to eliminate or amend the Age 60 Rule on pilots. Sponsors mass mailings by members to educate elected officials to the discriminatory aspect of forced pilot retirement. Initiates court actions against the said rule. **Publications:** Newsletter, monthly. Contains updates on legislative action on the Age 60 Rule. **Price:** free. Alternate Formats: online.

Bakery

23451 ■ Bakery, Confectionery, Tobacco Workers and Grain Millers International Union (BCTGM)
10401 Connecticut Ave.
Kensington, MD 20895
Ph: (301)933-8600
Fax: (301)946-8452
E-mail: bctgmwebmaster@bctgm.org
URL: http://www.bctgm.org
Contact: Frank Hurt, Pres.
Founded: 1978. **Members:** 145,000. **Staff:** 14. **Languages:** English, French. **Description:** Represents bakery, confectionery, and tobacco workers in the industry. Believes that all workers should be treated with dignity, justice and respect on the job. **Libraries: Type:** reference. **Awards: Type:** scholarship. **Formed by Merger of:** Tobacco Workers International Union; Bakery and Confectionery Workers' International Union of America. **Formerly:** (2001) Bakery, Confectionery and Tobacco Workers International Union. **Publications:** *B, C and T News*, 9/year. Newsletter. **Price:** free for members. **Conventions/Meetings:** quadrennial Constitutional Convention.

Baseball

23452 ■ Major League Baseball Players Association (MLBPA)
12 E 49th St., 24th Fl.
New York, NY 10017-8207
Ph: (212)826-0808 (212)826-0809
Fax: (212)752-4378
E-mail: feedback@mlbpa.org
URL: http://www.mlb.com/NASApp/mlb/pa/info
Contact: Donald M. Fehr, Exec. Dir.
Founded: 1966. **Members:** 1,000. **Staff:** 30. **Budget:** $4,600,000. **Description:** Works closely with MLB in

ensuring that the playing conditions for all games involving Major League players, whether the games are played in MLB stadiums or elsewhere, including internationally, meet proper safety guidelines. Serves as the group-licensing agent on behalf of the players. **Programs:** Baseball Tomorrow; Rookie Career Development. **Conventions/Meetings:** annual meeting - always winter.

23453 ■ World Umpires Association (WUA)
PO Box 394
Neenah, WI 54957
URL: http://www.worldumpires.com
Contact: John Hirschbeck, Pres.
Founded: 2000. **Description:** Acts as bargaining agent for major league baseball umpires. **Publications:** Newsletter, monthly.

Beverages

23454 ■ Brewery and Soft Drink Workers Conference - U.S.A. and Canada
25 Louisiana Ave. NW
Washington, DC 20001
Ph: (202)624-6921
Fax: (202)624-8137
E-mail: brewery@teamster.org
URL: http://www.teamster.org/divisions/brewery/brewery.asp
Contact: Dave Laughton, Sec.-Treas.
Founded: 1886. **Members:** 75,000. **Description:** Promotes the interests of brewery and soft drink workers in the United States and Canada. **Affiliated With:** International Brotherhood of Teamsters. **Formerly:** (1976) International Union of United Brewery, Flour, Cereal, Soft Drink and Distillery Workers of America (AFL-CIO). **Publications:** *Teamsters Brewery and Soft Drink News*. Newsletter. Alternate Formats: online ● *What's On Tap*. Newsletter. Alternate Formats: online. **Conventions/Meetings:** quadrennial meeting.

Blacksmiths

23455 ■ International Brotherhood of Boilermakers, Iron Ship Builders, Blacksmiths, Forgers and Helpers (IBB)
753 State Ave., Ste.570
Kansas City, KS 66101
Ph: (913)371-2640
Fax: (913)281-8105
E-mail: dcaswell@boilermakers.org
URL: http://www.boilermakers.org
Contact: Newton B. Jones, Intl. Pres.
Founded: 1880. **Members:** 70,000. **Multinational. Description:** AFL-CIO affiliated labor union representing members in the U.S. and Canada. **Awards:** International Brotherhood Scholarship Program. **Frequency:** annual. **Type:** grant. **Recipient:** to a dependent of a member. **Divisions:** Cement and Building Materials; Construction; Industrial Plants and Shops; Metal Polishers; Railroad; Shipbuilding and Marine; Stove, Furnace, Energy and Allied Appliance Workers Division. **Funds:** Mobilization, Optimization, Stabilization and Training. **Programs:** Apprentice. **Absorbed:** (1996) Metal Polishers, Buffers, Platers and Allied Workers International Union. **Publications:** *The Boilermaker Activist*, quarterly. Newsletter. Contains articles directed to local IBB union officials pertaining to government affairs and internal IBB issues. **Circulation:** 1,200 ● *The Boilermaker Reporter*, quarterly. Newsletter. Includes annual index. **Price:** free for members; $10.00 /year for nonmembers. **Circulation:** 75,000. Alternate Formats: online ● *Membership Roster*, triennial ● *NTL News*, quarterly. **Price:** available to members only. **Circulation:** 5,000. **Conventions/Meetings:** quinquennial meeting.

Broadcasting

23456 ■ American Federation of Television and Radio Artists (AFTRA)
260 Madison Ave., 9th Fl.
New York, NY 10016-2401

Ph: (212)532-0800
Fax: (212)532-2242
E-mail: info@aftra.com
URL: http://www.aftra.com
Contact: Kim Roberts Hedgpeth, Exec. Dir.

Founded: 1937. **Members:** 80,000. **Membership Dues:** initiation, $1,300 ● minimum, $63 (annual). **Local Groups:** 38. **Description:** Advocates on legislative and public policy issues that directly affect members' wages and working conditions; this includes lobbying and support for such issues as ownership consolidation in the broadcast industry, Equal Employment Opportunity laws and regulations, copyright and performance rights issues, "noncompete" restrictions, OSHA and local safety regulations, and more. **Awards:** Heller Memorial Foundation Scholarships. **Frequency:** annual. **Type:** scholarship. **Recipient:** for members and their dependents. **Formerly:** (1952) American Federation of Radio Artists. **Publications:** *Broadcast Bulletin.* Newsletter. Alternate Formats: online ● *Music Notes.* Newsletter. Alternate Formats: online ● *Talent Agency.* Newsletter. Alternate Formats: online ● Magazine, periodic. **Price:** $3.00/year. ISSN: 0004-7676. Alternate Formats: online. **Conventions/Meetings:** biennial meeting.

23457 ■ American Radio Association (ARA)
c/o John F. Lindner, Admin.
360 W 31st St., 3rd Fl.
New York, NY 10001-2727
Ph: (212)239-8600
Fax: (212)594-7484
E-mail: araplans@earthlink.net
URL: http://www.araplans.com
Contact: John F. Lindner, Admin.

Founded: 1948. **Members:** 250. **Membership Dues:** regular, $1,000 (quarterly). **Staff:** 7. **Local Groups:** 3. **Description:** Represents people in maritime communications and electronics aboard U.S. Flag registered vessels. **Affiliated With:** International Longshoremen's Association. **Publications:** *ARA Free Press,* weekly. Newsletter. Reports maritime shipping news. **Price:** free. **Circulation:** 800. Alternate Formats: online. **Conventions/Meetings:** quarterly conference.

23458 ■ National Association Broadcast Employees and Technicians - Communications Workers of America (NABET-CWA)
501 3rd St. NW
Washington, DC 20001-2797
Ph: (202)434-1254
Free: (800)882-9174
Fax: (202)434-1426
E-mail: nabet-cwa@cwa-union.org
URL: http://www.nabetcwa.org
Contact: Alfred Rossi, Pres.

Founded: 1934. **Members:** 10,000. **Staff:** 8. **Budget:** $5,000,000. **Regional Groups:** 6. **Local Groups:** 38. **Description:** Strives to aid workers who are employed in the broadcasting, distributing, telecasting, recording, cable, video, sound recording and related industries in North America. **Computer Services:** database, job search ● database, membership ● database, retirees. **Telecommunication Services:** electronic mail, jclark@cwa-union.org. **Councils:** Sector Executive. **Formerly:** (1940) Association of Technical Employees. **Publications:** *NABET News,* bimonthly. Newsletter. ISSN: 0027-5697. **Circulation:** 12,000. Alternate Formats: online. **Conventions/Meetings:** quadrennial conference.

Building Trades

23459 ■ Building and Construction Trades Department - AFL-CIO
815 16th St., Ste.600
Washington, DC 20006
Ph: (202)347-1461

E-mail: kathy@bctd.org
URL: http://www.buildingtrades.org
Contact: Edward C. Sullivan, Pres.

Members: 4,500,000. **Multinational. Description:** Federation of labor unions in the construction industry including asbestos workers, bricklayers, masons, plasterers, carpenters, electrical workers, elevator constructors, operating engineers, granite cutters, hood carriers, common laborers, ironworkers, carpet, tile and stone workers, painters, decorators, paperhangers, plumbers, steamfitters, roofers, boilermakers, lathers, sheet metal workers, and other related trades. Maintains liaison with Center to Protect Workers Rights that provides independent research and support. **Committees:** Political Education Fund. **Publications:** *The Builder.* Newsletter ● Directory, annual. **Conventions/Meetings:** quinquennial meeting.

23460 ■ International Association of Machinists and Aerospace Workers, Woodworkers District Lodge W1 (IAMA)
25 Cornell Ave.
Gladstone, OR 97027
Ph: (503)656-1475
Fax: (503)657-2254
E-mail: office@woodworkersdist1iam.org
URL: http://www.woodworkersdist1iam.org
Contact: Chuck Macrae, Pres.

Founded: 1937. **Members:** 5,200. **Staff:** 17. **Local Groups:** 10. **Description:** AFL-CIO. Serves as a union that represents woodworkers in the logging, sawmill, plywood, particleboard, hardboard, and tree nursery industries. **Formerly:** International Woodworkers of America, U.S. AFL-CIO; (1987) International Woodworkers of America. **Conventions/Meetings:** biennial convention - usually April or May.

23461 ■ International Union of Bricklayers and Allied Craftworkers (BAC)
620 F St. NW
Washington, DC 20004
Ph: (202)783-3788
Free: (888)880-8222
E-mail: askbac@bacweb.org
URL: http://www.bacweb.org
Contact: John J. Flynn, Pres.

Founded: 1865. **Members:** 106,000. **Languages:** English, French, Spanish. **Description:** Works to improve members' quality of life through access to fair wages, good benefits, safe working conditions, and solidarity among members. **Libraries: Type:** reference. **Awards:** Craft Awards. **Frequency:** annual. **Type:** recognition. **Recipient:** for excellence in trowel trades. **Committees:** Bricklayers Political Action. **Projects:** Millennium Morning. **Formerly:** (1975) Bricklayers, Masons and Plasterers International of American; (2001) International Union of Bricklayers and Allied Craftsmen. **Publications:** *Chalkline,* periodic ● Journal (in English and Spanish), bimonthly. Alternate Formats: online. **Conventions/Meetings:** quinquennial meeting.

23462 ■ International Union of Operating Engineers (IUOE)
1125 17th St. NW
Washington, DC 20036
Ph: (202)429-9100
E-mail: hq_info@iuoe.org
URL: http://www.iuoe.org
Contact: Vincent J. Giblin, Gen. Pres.

Founded: 1896. **Members:** 400,000. **Local Groups:** 170. **Languages:** English, Spanish. **Description:** Represents operating engineers, stationary engineers, nurses, and other health industry workers engaged in a wide variety of occupations. **Committees:** Engineers' Political and Education. **Absorbed:** International Union, United Welders. **Publications:** *International Operating Engineer,* bimonthly. Magazine. Alternate Formats: online. **Conventions/Meetings:** quinquennial meeting.

23463 ■ Laborers' International Union of North America (LIUNA)
905 16th St. NW
Washington, DC 20006
Ph: (202)737-8320 (202)942-2262

Fax: (202)737-2754
E-mail: rgreer@liuna.org
URL: http://www.liuna.org
Contact: Terence M. O'Sullivan, Gen. Pres.

Founded: 1903. **Members:** 840,000. **Languages:** English, Spanish. **Multinational. Description:** Represents Laborers' Union in North America. **Departments:** Construction; Education; Legal; Minority Advancement; Organizing; Political and Legislative; Public Affairs; Public Employee. **Affiliated With:** National Postal Mail Handlers Union. **Publications:** *The Laborer,* bimonthly. Magazine. **Circulation:** 800,000. Alternate Formats: online. **Conventions/Meetings:** quinquennial convention (exhibits).

23464 ■ National Alliance for Fair Contracting (NAFC)
1 N Old State Capitol Plz., Ste.525
Springfield, IL 62701
Ph: (217)522-5414
Free: (866)523-NAFC
Fax: (217)522-6588
E-mail: webmaster@faircontracting.org
URL: http://www.faircontracting.org
Contact: Edward M. Smith, Co-Chm.

Membership Dues: organization, $500. **Description:** Establishes a national communications network and repository of information, resources and strategies on public contracting laws, regulations and enforcement. Promotes and monitors standards and legislation concerning public construction. Improves communication and cooperation between labor, management and government in the public construction industry. Educates all parties to the laws required for competing in public construction projects. **Publications:** *NAFC News.* Newsletter. **Price:** included in membership dues ● Manual. Alternate Formats: online.

23465 ■ Operative Plasterers and Cement Masons International Association of U.S. and Canada (OPCMIA)
14405 Laurel Pl., Ste.300
Laurel, MD 20707
Ph: (301)470-4200
Fax: (301)470-2502
E-mail: opcmiaintl@opcmia.org
URL: http://www.opcmia.org
Contact: John J. Dougherty, Gen. Pres.

Founded: 1864. **Members:** 50,000. **Staff:** 15. **Local Groups:** 93. **National Groups:** 106. **Description:** Represents men and women working in the plastering and cement mason trades throughout the United States and Canada. **Committees:** Plasterers' and Cement Masons' Action. **Publications:** *Plasterer and Cement Mason,* quarterly. Contains trade specific information. ISSN: 0032-0136. **Circulation:** 40,000. **Conventions/Meetings:** quinquennial conference.

23466 ■ United Brotherhood of Carpenters and Joiners of America (UBC)
c/o Carpenters Union Warehouse
14110-D Sullyfield Cir.
Chantilly, VA 20151
Ph: (703)378-9000
Fax: (703)378-9777
E-mail: webmaster@carpenters.org
URL: http://www.carpenters.org
Contact: Douglas J. McCarron, Pres.

Founded: 1881. **Members:** 500,000. **Description:** Represents and offers training to North America's carpenters, cabinetmakers, millwrights, piledrivers, lathers, framers, floorlayers, roofers, drywallers, and workers in forest-products and related industries. **Committees:** Carpenters' Legislative Improvement. **Absorbed:** (1979) Wood, Wire and Metal Lathers' International Union; (1988) Tile, Marble, Terrazzo, Finishers, Shopworkers, and Granite Cutters International Union. **Publications:** *Carpenter,* bimonthly. Magazine. Covers UBC and labor news. **Price:** free for members; $10.00 /year for nonmembers. ISSN: 0008-6843. **Circulation:** 630,000. **Advertising:** accepted. **Conventions/Meetings:** quinquennial meeting.

23467 ■ United Union of Roofers, Waterproofers and Allied Workers (UURWAW)
1660 L St. NW, Ste.800
Washington, DC 20036-5646
Ph: (202)463-7663
Fax: (202)463-6906
E-mail: roofers@unionroofers.com
URL: http://www.unionroofers.com
Contact: Kinsey M. Robinson, Intl. Pres.
Founded: 1903. **Members:** 25,000. **Description:** Affiliates with the AFL-CIO/Building and Construction Trades Department. **Programs:** Apprenticeship; Construction Organizing Membership Education Training. **Formerly:** United Slate, Tile and Composition Roofers, Damp and Waterproof Workers Association. **Publications:** *The Journeyman Roofer and Waterproofer*, quarterly. Magazine. **Conventions/Meetings:** quinquennial meeting.

Chemicals

23468 ■ International Brotherhood of DuPont Workers (IBDW)
PO Box 10
Waynesboro, VA 22980
Fax: (540)337-5442
E-mail: jimflickinger@dupontworkers.com
URL: http://www.dupontworkers.com
Contact: Jim Flickinger, Pres.
Founded: 1979. **Members:** 3,500. **Staff:** 4. **Regional Groups:** 8. **State Groups:** 3. **Local Groups:** 3. **Description:** Trade union representing employees of DuPont Chemical Company and Dupont Dow Elastomers. Seeks to organize all DuPont workers. Conducts contract negotiations, liability advocacy, and job safety research on behalf of members. **Publications:** *IBDW News*, quarterly. Newsletter. Provides updates on issues concerning Dupont and Dupont Dow Elastomers, Bemis and INVISTA union members. **Price:** free for members. Alternate Formats: online. **Conventions/Meetings:** semiannual convention, a forum for the locals of the IBDW to gather and share information and plan a path forward to address issues that affect the IBDW membership (exhibits) - spring and fall.

Christian

23469 ■ Christian Labor Association of the U.S.A. (CLA)
PO Box 65
Zeeland, MI 49464
Ph: (616)772-9164
Fax: (616)772-9830
E-mail: christianlabor@yahoo.com
URL: http://www.cla-usa.org
Contact: Douglas Reese, Pres.
Founded: 1931. **Members:** 3,000. **Membership Dues:** individual, $28 (monthly). **Staff:** 10. **Budget:** $300,000. **Local Groups:** 7. **Description:** Independent. Provides a genuine alternative for workers who want a union that will provide professional representation. **Libraries: Type:** not open to the public. **Holdings:** 200; books, periodicals. **Subjects:** labor law, human resources. **Awards:** Don Leep Memorial Scholarship. **Frequency:** annual. **Type:** scholarship. **Recipient:** for first time post high student, child of member. **Boards:** National. **Publications:** *Christian Labor Herald*, semiannual. Newsletter. Includes news, labor news and updates of CLA. **Price:** free. **Circulation:** 3,000. **Advertising:** accepted.

Collective Bargaining

23470 ■ National Center for the Study of Collective Bargaining in Higher Education and the Professions (NCSCBHEP)
425 E 25th St.
Box 615
New York, NY 10010-2590
Ph: (212)481-7550
Fax: (212)481-5059
E-mail: national.center@hunter.cuny.edu
URL: http://www.hunter.cuny.edu/ncscbhep/index.shtml
Contact: Richard Boris, Dir.
Founded: 1972. **Members:** 60. **Membership Dues:** regular, $385 (annual). **Staff:** 3. **Budget:** $50,000. **Description:** Serves as clearinghouse and forum for institutions and individuals engaged in collective bargaining and the related processes of grievance administration and arbitration in colleges and universities and in other areas of professional employment. Conducts research addressing scholars and practitioners in the field. **Libraries: Type:** reference. **Holdings:** 1,500; archival material, books, reports. **Subjects:** college and university collective bargaining agreements. **Formerly:** National Center for the Study of Collective Bargaining in Higher Education. **Publications:** *Annual Conference*, annual. Proceedings. Contains proceedings of papers given at annual conference. **Circulation:** 300 ● *Collective Bargaining in Higher Education and the Professions, Bibliography*, annual. Lists books and research reports under the categories of faculty, professions and professionals, and information guides. Includes list of acronyms. **Price:** $45.00. ISSN: 0738-1913. **Circulation:** 200 ● *Directory of Faculty Contracts and Bargaining Agents in Institutions of Higher Education*, annual. Compilation and statistical analysis of faculty contracts and bargaining agents in higher education. Statistics given for two- and four-year schools. **Price:** $45.00/copy. ISSN: 0276-7805. **Circulation:** 275 ● *National Center for the Study of Collective Bargaining in Higher Education and the Professions—Newsletter*, quarterly. Analyzes current trends, developments, and major decisions of courts and regulatory bodies. **Price:** $35.00/year. ISSN: 0737-9285. **Circulation:** 200. Alternate Formats: online ● *National Center for the Study of Collective Bargaining in Higher Education and the Professions—Proceedings*, annual. Includes compilation of academic papers presented at the annual conference. **Price:** $45.00/copy. ISSN: 0742-3667. **Circulation:** 200 ● Newsletter, quarterly ● Monographs ● Brochure. Alternate Formats: online. **Conventions/Meetings:** annual conference, with higher education collective bargaining and related topics - always April/May, New York City.

Communications

23471 ■ Communications Workers of America (CWA)
501 3rd St. NW
Washington, DC 20001-2797
Ph: (202)434-1100
Fax: (202)434-1279
E-mail: cwaweb@cwa-union.org
URL: http://www.cwa-union.org
Contact: Larry Cohen, Pres.
Founded: 1947. **Members:** 700,000. **Description:** Telecommunications, printing and news media, public service, health care, cable television, general manufacturing, electronics, gas and electric utilities workers. Works to help with the process of collective bargaining, spelling out wages, benefits and working conditions for its members. **Libraries: Type:** reference; open to the public. **Holdings:** 1,400; articles, books, periodicals. **Subjects:** criminal justice and public policy. **Formerly:** (1966) Vera Foundation. **Publications:** *Catalog of Selected Publications of the Louis Schweitzer Library* ● *Federal Sentencing Reporter*, bimonthly. Journal. Includes cases and commentary on sentencing issues under the federal sentencing guidelines. **Price:** $130.00/year. ISSN: 1053-9867. **Circulation:** 2,400. Also Cited As: *Fed. Sent. R* ● *Just 'Cause*, bimonthly. Newsletter.

Concrete

23472 ■ Cement, Lime, Gypsum, and Allied Workers Division (CLGAW)
c/o James Hickenbotham, Intl. VP
3112 Peters Creek Rd., N Roanoke Plz.
Roanoke, VA 24019
Ph: (540)362-7110
Fax: (540)362-7116
E-mail: union2@rbnet.com
URL: http://www.boilermakers.org/2-WhoWeAre/CL-GAW.html
Contact: James Hickenbotham, Intl. VP
Founded: 1939. **Members:** 10,000. **Local Groups:** 150. **Description:** AFL-CIO. A division of the International Brotherhood of Boilermakers, Iron Shipbuilders, Blacksmiths, Forgers and Helpers (see separate entry). **Affiliated With:** International Brotherhood of Boilermakers, Iron Ship Builders, Blacksmiths, Forgers and Helpers. **Publications:** *Boilermakers/Blacksmiths Reporter*, periodic. **Conventions/Meetings:** periodic meeting.

Construction

23473 ■ Center to Protect Workers' Rights (CPWR)
8484 Georgia Ave., Ste.1000
Silver Spring, MD 20910
Ph: (301)578-8500
Fax: (301)578-8572
E-mail: cpwrwebsite@cpwr.com
URL: http://www.cpwr.com
Contact: Erich J. Stafford, Exec. Dir.
Founded: 1979. **Regional Groups:** 30. **Description:** Serves as research, development and training arm of the Building and Construction Trades Department and the construction unions in the AFL-CIO. Works to develop ways to improve safety and health for construction workers and families. **Affiliated With:** AFL-CIO; Building and Construction Trades Department - AFL-CIO. **Publications:** *Asthma in Heavy & Highway Construction Workers Exposed to Silica*. Report ● *Construction Chart Book*. Report ● *Deaths & Injuries Involving Elevators or Escalators*. Report ● *Patterns of Death among Construction Workers, California, 1979-81*. Report ● Videos ● Brochures.

Domestic Service

23474 ■ International Guild of Professional Butlers
134 W 82nd St., Ste.3b
New York, NY 10024
Ph: (646)290-6527
Fax: (917)441-0064
E-mail: butlersguild@butlersguild.com
URL: http://www.butlersguild.com
Contact: Robert Wennekes, Chm.
Membership Dues: executive, $72 (annual). **Multinational. Description:** Promotes excellence in the private service profession. Brings together employers and candidates who seek similar long term quality relationships. Protects the interests and reputation of its members. Offers recruitment and training of private staff such as butlers, household managers, personal assistants and chefs. **Awards:** Butler of the Year. **Frequency:** annual. **Type:** recognition. **Recipient:** to an individual whose expertise and exemplary dedication has enhanced the image of the private service profession. **Publications:** Newsletter, monthly. **Price:** included in membership dues.

Education

23475 ■ American Association of Classified School Employees (AACSE)
555 New Jersey Ave. NW
Washington, DC 20001
Free: (800)879-4597
E-mail: president@aacse.org
URL: http://www.aacse.org
Contact: Gary A. Rychard, Natl. Pres.
Founded: 1958. **Members:** 200,000. **Membership Dues:** general, $0 (annual). **Staff:** 2. **Budget:** $250,000. **State Groups:** 8. **Description:** Persons employed by public school systems in nonteaching positions. Promotes a spirit of cooperation and

understanding among employees and their employers; fosters adequate financial improvements for public school employees through collective bargaining, legislative channels, and other legal procedures; promotes improved retirement benefits for public school employees; represents public school employees in their employment relations with their employers. **Telecommunication Services:** electronic mail, tolshefs@aft.org. **Committees:** Constitution and Handbook; Legislative; Life Membership; Public Relations. **Publications:** *Federal Update*, monthly. Newsletter. Covers affiliate activities. **Conventions/Meetings:** semiannual board meeting.

23476 ■ American Federation of Teachers (AFT)
555 New Jersey Ave. NW
Washington, DC 20001
Ph: (202)879-4400
Free: (800)238-1133
Fax: (202)879-4545
E-mail: online@aft.org
URL: http://www.aft.org
Contact: Nat LaCour, Sec.-Treas.

Founded: 1916. **Members:** 1,300,000. **Membership Dues:** basic associate, $30 (annual) ● working teacher, $60 (annual). **State Groups:** 43. **Local Groups:** 3,000. **Description:** Affiliated with the AFL-CIO. Works with teachers and other educational employees at the state and local level in organizing, collective bargaining, research, educational issues, and public relations. Conducts research in areas such as educational reform, teacher certification, and national assessments and standards. Represents members' concerns through legislative action; offers technical assistance. Serves professionals with concerns similar to those of teachers, including state employees, healthcare workers, and paraprofessionals. **Libraries: Type:** not open to the public. **Telecommunication Services:** hotline, learning activities, (800)242-5465. **Publications:** *American Educator*, quarterly. Magazine. **Price:** free for members; $8.00 /year for nonmembers. **Circulation:** 800,000. **Advertising:** accepted. Alternate Formats: microform ● *American Teacher*, 8/year. Newspaper. Covers union news; includes conference report. **Price:** $12.00 /year for nonmembers; included in membership dues. **Circulation:** 524,700. **Advertising:** accepted. Alternate Formats: microform ● *Healthwire*, bimonthly. Newsletter. Informs AFT members involved in health care. **Price:** available to members only. **Circulation:** 15,000. **Advertising:** accepted ● *On Campus*, 8/year. Newspaper. Includes news on AFT higher education locals. **Price:** included in membership dues; $12.00 /year for nonmembers ● *PSRP Reporter*, quarterly. Newsletter. **Price:** included in membership dues. **Conventions/Meetings:** biennial convention - 2008 July 10-14, Chicago, IL ● biennial Quest Education Conference - meeting, professional issues conference for educators (exhibits).

23477 ■ Federal Education Association (FEA)
1201 16th St. NW, Ste.117
Washington, DC 20036
Ph: (202)822-7850
Fax: (202)822-7867
E-mail: fea@feaonline.org
URL: http://www.feaonline.org
Contact: H.T. Nguyen, Exec. Dir./Gen. Counsel

Founded: 1956. **Members:** 6,700. **Membership Dues:** active full, $341 (annual) ● active part time, associate, $170 (annual) ● retired life, pre-retired, $85. **Staff:** 14. **Local Groups:** 82. **Description:** Labor union and professional association. Acts as bargaining agent for educators working in overseas schools for children of military personnel and DOD civilian employees. **Computer Services:** Mailing lists. **Committees:** Legislation and Regulations; Transfer. **Affiliated With:** National Education Association. **Formerly:** Overseas Teachers Association; (1995) Overseas EDU Association. **Publications:** *FEA President's Report*, semimonthly. Alternate Formats: online ● *OEA Leader*, periodic ● *OEA News*, periodic ● Journal, quarterly. Alternate Formats: online. **Conventions/Meetings:** annual meeting.

23478 ■ National Council on Teacher Retirement (NCTR)
7600 Greenhaven Dr., Ste.302
Sacramento, CA 95831
Ph: (916)394-2075
Fax: (916)392-0295
E-mail: jmosman@nctr.org
URL: http://www.nctr.org
Contact: Jim Mosman, Exec. Dir.

Founded: 1936. **Members:** 228. **Staff:** 3. **Budget:** $750,000. **State Groups:** 50. **Local Groups:** 16. **Description:** State and local teacher retirement systems; executive secretaries, administrative and investment officers, actuaries, trustees of either state or local retirement systems, teachers, and other persons interested in retirement problems. Conducts research in the operation of teacher retirement systems and the status of retired teachers. **Committees:** Investments; Legislative; Retired Teacher Concerns. **Publications:** Newsletter, monthly ● Proceedings, annual. **Conventions/Meetings:** annual conference.

23479 ■ National Education Association (NEA)
1201 16th St. NW
Washington, DC 20036-3290
Ph: (202)833-4000
Fax: (202)822-7974
E-mail: bobchase@nea.org
URL: http://www.nea.org
Contact: Reg Weaver, Pres.

Founded: 1857. **Members:** 2,800,000. **Staff:** 600. **Budget:** $200,600,000. **State Groups:** 53. **Local Groups:** 14,000. **Description:** Professional organization and union of elementary and secondary school teachers, college and university professors, administrators, principals, counselors, and others concerned with education. **Computer Services:** Mailing lists, of members ● online services, discussion boards. **Committees:** Affiliate Relationships; Benefits; Civil Rights; Educational Support Personnel; Fund for Children and Public Education; Higher Education; Human Relations; Instruction and Professional Development; Legislation; Minority Affairs; National Public Relations; Peace and International Relations; Women's Concerns. **Departments:** Affiliate Capacity Building; Business and Finance; Collective Bargaining and Member Advocacy; Communications; Governance and Policy; Government Relations; Human and Civil Rights; Human Resources; Information Technology Services; School System Capacity; State Affiliate Relations; Student Achievement; Teacher Quality. **Divisions:** Research. **Absorbed:** (1966) American Teachers Association; (1981) NEA Higher Education Council; (1982) Student National Education Association. **Formerly:** (1870) National Teachers Association. **Publications:** *Almanac of Higher Education*, annual. Journal. **Price:** included in membership dues. **Circulation:** 85,000 ● *NEA Higher Education Advocate* ● *NEA Today*, 8/year. Newsletter. Covers news and events affecting public education. **Price:** included in membership dues; $50.00 /year for nonmembers. **Circulation:** 2,400,000. **Advertising:** accepted. Alternate Formats: online ● *Thought and Action*. Journal ● Handbook, annual. **Conventions/Meetings:** annual Representative Assembly - meeting (exhibits) - usually July. 2008 July 1-6, Washington, DC; 2009 July 1-6, San Diego, CA; 2010 July 1-6, New Orleans, LA.

23480 ■ North American Association of Educational Negotiators (NAEN)
c/o OSBA
PO Box 1068
Salem, OR 97308
Ph: (503)588-2800
Fax: (503)588-2813
E-mail: naen@osba.org
URL: http://www.naen.org
Contact: Steve Hengen, Pres.-Elect

Founded: 1970. **Members:** 500. **Membership Dues:** individual, $80 (annual) ● institution, $200 (annual). **Staff:** 1. **Budget:** $75,000. **Description:** School board negotiators, negotiations teams, and individuals in supporting roles representing management.

Purposes are: to unite those who negotiate on behalf of school boards into a single, strong body; to improve the knowledge and performance of management negotiators; to advance professional status; to provide a facility for the effective communication and exchange of information among these individuals. Offers consultation; conducts regional training program. **Formerly:** Association of Educational Negotiators; (1991) National Association of Educational Negotiators. **Publications:** *North American Association of Educational Negotiators—Bulletin*, bimonthly. Includes employment opportunities and directory. **Price:** included in membership dues. **Circulation:** 600 ● Membership Directory, annual. Includes bylaws and services. **Price:** included in membership dues. **Circulation:** 600. **Advertising:** accepted. **Conventions/Meetings:** annual conference - always March. 2008 Mar. 9-12, New Orleans, LA.

Electronics

23481 ■ Federation of Westinghouse Independent Salaried Unions (FWISU)
Address Unknown since 2007
Founded: 1939. **Members:** 12,000. **Description:** Independent. Electrical production workers united to create strength through unified action and to serve as a coordinating agency for member locals. Reviews new or revised position descriptions and evaluations, including local labor agreements, prior to their acceptance or execution. Conducts organizational activities in order to extend the benefits of collective bargaining to other groups of Westinghouse employees. Hears grievances at appeal level and conducts arbitration. **Committees:** Appeal Grievance; National Negotiating. **Publications:** *Regulator*, annual ● *White Collar or Noose*. **Conventions/Meetings:** semiannual meeting - always June and December.

23482 ■ International Brotherhood of Electrical Workers (IBEW)
900 Seventh St. NW
Washington, DC 20001
Ph: (202)833-7000
Fax: (202)728-7676
E-mail: journal@ibew.org
URL: http://www.ibew.org
Contact: Edwin D. Hill, Intl. Pres.

Founded: 1891. **Members:** 750,000. **Staff:** 400. **Description:** AFL-CIO. Represents members working in the field of utilities, construction, telecommunications, broadcasting, railroads and government. **Awards:** IBEW Founders' Scholarships. **Frequency:** annual. **Type:** scholarship. **Recipient:** for working members. **Committees:** Political Action. **Departments:** Computer Services; Education/Research; Human Services. **Publications:** *IBEW Jurisdictional Mapping System and Local Union Directory*. Alternate Formats: online ● Journal, monthly. Covers topics and activities pertaining to local and international unions in the United States and Canada. **Price:** $4.00/year. **Circulation:** 900,000. Alternate Formats: online. **Conventions/Meetings:** quadrennial International Convention - meeting ● meeting - every January.

23483 ■ International Union of Electronic, Electrical, Salaried, Machine, and Furniture Workers (IUE)
501 Third St. NW
Washington, DC 20001
Ph: (202)513-6300 (202)434-1156
Fax: (202)513-6357
E-mail: jdclark@cwa-union.org
URL: http://www.iue-cwa.org
Contact: Jim Clark, Pres.

Founded: 1949. **Members:** 140,000. **Staff:** 150. **Local Groups:** 450. **Description:** AFL-CIO affiliate. Negotiates collective bargaining agreements; maintains apprenticeship programs. Conducts grievance proceedings, organizing, coordinated bargaining, lobbying, and issue campaigns. **Awards: Type:** recognition. **Computer Services:** Mailing lists. **Boards:** General Electric Conference; General Motors Conference; Professional; Technical and Salaried Conference.

Committees: Coordinated Bargaining; International Social Action; Political Education; Robotics and New Technology. **Councils:** Optical Workers; Skilled Trades; Women's. **Departments:** Accounting; Collective Bargaining; Communications; Education; Legal; Legislation; Organizing; Research; Social Action. **Divisions:** Furniture Workers. **Formerly:** (1983) International Union of Electrical, Radio and Machine Workers; (1987) International Union of Electronic, Electrical, Technical, Salaried, Machine, and Furniture Workers. **Publications:** *International Union of Electronic, Electrical, Salaried, Machine, and Furniture Workers—Convention Proceedings*, quinquennial ● *IUE News*, bimonthly. Newsletter. **Price:** $10.00/year. **Circulation:** 165,000 ● *Public Policy Page*, monthly. **Conventions/Meetings:** quinquennial convention (exhibits).

23484 ■ United Electrical, Radio and Machine Workers of America (UE)
1 Gateway Ctr., Ste.1400
Pittsburgh, PA 15222-1416
Ph: (412)471-8919
Fax: (412)471-8999
E-mail: ue@ranknfile-ue.org
URL: http://www.ranknfile-ue.org
Contact: John H. Hovis, Pres.
Founded: 1936. **Members:** 40,000. **Description:** Represents workers in the electrical manufacturing and electronics industries including General Electric and Rockwell International. **Libraries: Type:** reference. **Holdings:** 10,000. **Publications:** *Labor's Untold Story*. Book. **Price:** $18.00 for nonmembers; $9.00 for members ● *Them and Us*. Book. **Price:** $14.00 for nonmembers; $6.00 for members ● *UE News*, 8/year, every 3 weeks. Newspaper. Provides information on organizing and collective bargaining, economic and political viewpoints of UE, and occupational health and safety. **Price:** free for members; $5.00 /year for individuals; $10.00 /year for institutions. **Circulation:** 100,000 ● *United Electrical, Radio and Machine Workers of America—Convention Proceedings*, annual. **Price:** $15.00 for nonmembers. **Circulation:** 100 ● *United Electrical, Radio and Machine Workers of America—Officers' Report*, annual. Covers union activity in collective bargaining, economics, legislation, civil rights, foreign policy, and education. **Price:** $5.00. **Circulation:** 2,000 ● *United Electrical, Radio and Machine Workers of America—Policy*, annual. Booklet. Contains resolutions and reports adopted by delegates to UE's annual convention. **Price:** $5.00. **Circulation:** 5,000. **Conventions/Meetings:** annual meeting.

Emergency Medicine

23485 ■ International Association of EMTs and Paramedics (IAEP)
159 Burgin Pkwy.
Quincy, MA 02169
Ph: (617)376-0220 (617)376-7273
E-mail: breardon@nage.org
URL: http://www.iaep.org
Contact: Beth Reardon, Membership Dir.
Multinational. Description: Represents the interests of EMTs, paramedics, and other related emergency response employees. Works to safeguard the jobs and bargaining rights of members. Promotes legislation that protects the workplace rights of members. Provides financial assistance and supports grassroots lobbying efforts. **Awards:** Edward G. Gillooly Journalism Scholarship. **Frequency:** annual. **Type:** scholarship. **Recipient:** for working people in the field of journalism ● IAEP/NAGE Scholarships. **Frequency:** annual. **Type:** scholarship. **Recipient:** for members ● Marc Lawson Criminal Justice Scholarship. **Frequency:** annual. **Type:** scholarship. **Recipient:** for working people in the field of law enforcement. **Publications:** *Siren*, 3/year. Newsletter. Alternate Formats: online.

Engineering

23486 ■ International Federation of Professional and Technical Engineers (IFPTE)
8630 Fenton St., Ste.400
Silver Spring, MD 20910-3803
Ph: (301)565-9016
Fax: (301)565-0018
E-mail: gjunemann@ifpte.org
URL: http://www.ifpte.org
Contact: Gregory J. Junemann, Pres.
Founded: 1918. **Members:** 51,000. **Membership Dues:** associate, $12 (annual). **Staff:** 16. **Description:** Represents engineers, scientists, architects and technicians. **Affiliated With:** AFL-CIO; Canadian Labour Congress. **Formerly:** (1973) American Federation of Technical Engineers. **Publications:** *The Outlook*, bimonthly. **Circulation:** 400. **Conventions/Meetings:** triennial convention.

Environmental Quality

23487 ■ Alliance for Sustainable Jobs and the Environment (ASJE)
PO Box 1361
Eureka, CA 95502
Ph: (707)498-4481
E-mail: bluegreen@asje.org
URL: http://www.asje.org
Contact: Bob Borck, Labor Co-Chm.
Membership Dues: organizational, $50-$1,000 (annual) ● student, low-income, $15 (annual) ● individual, $35-$250 (annual). **Description:** Aims to promote the protection of workers and the environment. Facilitates campaigns and educational programs that benefit workers and the environment. **Awards:** Restoration Organization of the Year. **Frequency:** annual. **Type:** recognition. **Recipient:** for best restoration organization ● Restoration Project of the Year. **Frequency:** annual. **Type:** recognition. **Recipient:** for best restoration project ● Restoration Worker of the Year. **Frequency:** annual. **Type:** recognition. **Recipient:** for outstanding worker. **Publications:** *Green Worker*. Newsletter. Alternate Formats: online ● Magazine ● Annual Report, annual.

Film

23488 ■ Directors Guild of America (DGA)
7920 Sunset Blvd.
Los Angeles, CA 90046
Ph: (310)289-2070
Free: (800)420-4173
Fax: (310)289-2029
E-mail: darrellh@dga.org
URL: http://www.dga.org
Contact: Jay D. Roth, Exec. Dir.
Founded: 1936. **Members:** 12,500. **Description:** Independent. Negotiates agreements for members. **Libraries: Type:** reference. **Holdings:** 2,422; books, periodicals. **Subjects:** instruction, motion pictures, television, scripts, fiction, video, history. **Awards:** DGA Awards. **Frequency:** annual. **Type:** recognition. **Recipient:** for excellence in directing ● DGA Honors. **Frequency:** annual. **Type:** recognition. **Recipient:** for excellence in directing. **Committees:** Affirmative Action; African-American Steering; Asian-American; Director Mentor; Ethnically Diverse Steering; Latino; Minority; Women's Steering. **Absorbed:** Unit Production Managers Guild of Hollywood; (1964) Assistant Directors Local 161; (1965) Screen Directors International Guild. **Formed by Merger of:** Screen Directors Guild of America; Radio and Television Directors Guild. **Publications:** *Directory of Members*, annual. Membership Directory. Contains contact information for members. **Price:** $25.00. **Circulation:** 15,000. **Advertising:** accepted. Alternate Formats: online ● Magazine, monthly. **Price:** $30.00 in U.S.; $60.00 outside U.S. **Advertising:** accepted. Alternate Formats: online. **Conventions/Meetings:** biennial meeting.

23489 ■ New York Council of Motion Picture and Television Unions (COMPTU)
Address Unknown since 2007
Founded: 1971. **Members:** 40,000. **Regional Groups:** 15. **Local Groups:** 15. **Description:** Writers, performers, artists, technicians, craftsmen, musicians, directors, assistant directors, production managers and coordinators, script supervisors, cameramen, and service personnel. Serves as an umbrella organization for unions and guilds. Promotes and attracts production to the New York area and upholds union standards. **Affiliated With:** American Federation of Musicians of the United States and Canada; American Federation of Television and Radio Artists; Directors Guild of America; International Brotherhood of Electrical Workers; Screen Actors Guild; United Scenic Artists; Writers Guild of America, East. **Formerly:** (1982) Conference of Motion Picture and Television Conference Unions. **Conventions/Meetings:** monthly meeting - always New York City.

Fire Fighting

23490 ■ International Association of Fire Fighters (IAFF)
1750 New York Ave. NW
Washington, DC 20006
Ph: (202)737-8484
Fax: (202)737-8418
E-mail: pr@iaff.org
URL: http://www.iaff.org
Contact: Harold A. Schaitberger, Gen. Pres.
Founded: 1918. **Members:** 267,000. **Staff:** 119. **State Groups:** 50. **Local Groups:** 2,900. **Description:** AFL-CIO, Canadian Labour Congress. Represents professional fire fighters and emergency medical personnel in the United States and Canada. **Committees:** Fire-PAC. **Affiliated With:** Muscular Dystrophy Association. **Publications:** *Frontline News Brief*, biweekly. Newsletter. Alternate Formats: online ● *International Fire Fighter*, bimonthly. Magazine. Union tabloid; includes IAFF media awards and death and injury survey. **Price:** free for members. **Circulation:** 267,000 ● *Local Union Officers Directory*, annual. **Price:** available to members only. Alternate Formats: online. **Conventions/Meetings:** biennial convention - always August.

23491 ■ National Conference of Firemen and Oilers (NCFO)
1023 15th St. NW, 10th Fl.
Washington, DC 20005-2630
Ph: (202)962-0981
Fax: (202)872-1222
E-mail: mail@ncfo.org
URL: http://www.ncfo.org
Contact: George J. Francisco Jr., Pres.
Founded: 1898. **Members:** 30,000. **Description:** Serves as union of boiler operators. **Formerly:** (1919) International Brotherhood of Stationary Firemen. **Publications:** *Firemen and Oilers Journal*, bimonthly ● *The Journal*, quarterly. Newsletter. **Price:** free for members. Alternate Formats: online. **Conventions/Meetings:** quinquennial meeting.

Food

23492 ■ Joint Labor Management Committee of the Retail Food Industry (JLMC)
c/o Robert F. Harbrant, Chm.
3720 Farragut Ave., Ste.301
Kensington, MD 20895-2110
Ph: (301)942-5400
Fax: (301)942-5409
E-mail: harbrant@thejlmc.com
URL: http://www.thejlmc.com
Contact: Robert F. Harbrant, Chm.
Founded: 1974. **Members:** 14. **Staff:** 2. **Description:** National and regional food chains and unions. Serves as forum for initiating and maintaining dialogue on labor relations matters. Seeks to strengthen the ability of the retail and wholesale food industry (labor and management) to reach constructive decisions in collective bargaining. Provides mediation assistance in selected labor disputes. Provides for nationwide discussion of industry issues such as government regulation, (OSHA, ADA, FMLA) management and union work practices, and contract administration. Conducts studies on health and welfare funds cost containment. **Committees:** Execu-

tive; Steering. **Publications:** *Joint Labor Management Communication on Health Care Cost Management.* Book. **Conventions/Meetings:** conference - 4-6/year ● annual executive committee meeting, for corporate and union CEO's ● quarterly Steering Committee Meeting, for labor relations vice-presidents and labor union counterparts.

23493 ■ Research Associates of America (RRA)
1420 K St. NW, Ste.300
Washington, DC 20005
Ph: (202)737-7200
Fax: (202)737-7208
E-mail: raa@fast-raa.com
URL: http://www.fast-raa.com
Contact: Jeffrey L. Fiedler, Pres.
Founded: 1976. **Members:** 15. **Description:** International trade unions representing 3,500,000 individuals working in the food and allied service trades; lobbies on behalf of members. Coordinates local affiliated food and beverage trades councils. **Formerly:** (1983) Food and Beverage Trades Department (of AFL-CIO); (2007) Food and Allied Service Trades Department (of AFL-CIO). **Conventions/Meetings:** quadrennial convention.

23494 ■ United Food and Commercial Workers International Union (UFCW)
1775 K St. NW
Washington, DC 20006
Ph: (202)223-3111
Fax: (202)466-1562
E-mail: press@ufcw.org
URL: http://www.ufcw.org
Contact: Joseph T. Hansen, Intl. Pres.
Founded: 1979. **Members:** 1,400,000. **Regional Groups:** 9. **Local Groups:** 600. **Languages:** English, Spanish. **Multinational. Description:** AFL-CIO. Represents working men and women across the United States and Canada. Protects and improves the quality of life of all workers by achieving better wages, better benefits, and safer working conditions. **Libraries: Type:** reference. **Holdings:** 2,500. **Subjects:** labor. **Awards:** UFCW Scholarship Program. **Frequency:** annual. **Type:** scholarship. **Recipient:** for members and their dependents. **Committees:** Active Ballot Club Political Action. **Departments:** Civil Rights and Community Relations; Collective Bargaining; Communications. **Divisions:** Distillery, Wine and Allied Workers; Food Processing, Packing and Manufacturing; Health Care, Insurance, Finance, and Professional Employees. **Affiliated With:** International Union of Food, Agricultural, Hotel, Restaurant, Catering, Tobacco, and Allied Workers' Associations. **Absorbed:** (1980) Barbers, Beauticians and Allied Industries International Association; (1981) United Retail Workers; (1983) Insurance Workers International Union; (1986) Canadian Brewery and Distillery Workers; (1994) United Garment Workers of America; (1995) Distillery, Wine and Allied Workers International Union; (1996) International Chemical Workers Union. **Formed by Merger of:** (1979) Amalgamated Meat Cutters and Bucher Workmen of North America; Retail Clerks International Union. **Publications:** *UFCW Leadership Update,* monthly ● *Working America,* bimonthly. Magazine. Covers union activities, political and legislative matters, and consumer news. **Price:** included in membership dues. Alternate Formats: online. **Conventions/Meetings:** quinquennial meeting.

Food Service

23495 ■ American Union of Pizza Delivery Drivers (AUPDD)
PO Box 15172
Pensacola, FL 32514
Ph: (850)665-3494 (502)413-6850
E-mail: info@aupdd.org
URL: http://www.aupdd.org
Contact: Jim Pohle, Natl. Pres.
Membership Dues: regular, $20 (monthly). **Description:** Represents workers engaged in the pizza,

restaurant and prepared food industry. Aims to secure improved wages, hours, working conditions, and other economic advantages through organization, negotiations and collective bargaining. Provides educational advancement and training for employees, members, and officers. Safeguards, advances, and promotes the principle of free collective bargaining throughout the world. Advances the rights of workers and consumers, and the security and welfare of all the people. **Telecommunication Services:** electronic mail, jim@aupdd.org.

Footwear

23496 ■ Brotherhood of Shoe and Allied Craftsmen (BSAC)
PO Box 390
East Bridgewater, MA 02333
Ph: (508)378-9300
Fax: (508)378-9800
Contact: Gerald Swimm, Pres.
Founded: 1933. **Members:** 680. **Membership Dues:** $5 (weekly). **Staff:** 1. **Budget:** $65,000. **Description:** Independent labor union.

Forest Industries

23497 ■ Association of Western Pulp and Paper Workers (AWPPW)
1430 SW Clay St.
Portland, OR 97208-4566
Ph: (503)228-7486
Free: (877)992-9779
Fax: (503)228-1346
URL: http://www.awppw.org
Contact: John Rhodes, Pres.
Founded: 1964. **Staff:** 3. **Description:** Affiliated with the United Brotherhood of Carpenters and Joiners of America, AFL-CIO; includes members employed in pulp, paper, paper converting, lumber, plywood and sawmill production, in prefabrication and creation of modular construction units, and in diverse industries like the maritime trades, and the manufacturing, plastics and wood products trades.

Furniture

23498 ■ United Furniture Workers Insurance Fund
1910 Air Lane Dr.
Nashville, TN 37210
Ph: (615)889-8860
Fax: (615)391-0865
URL: http://ufwip.com
Contact: Mr. Harry Boot, Chm.
Founded: 1937. **Members:** 50,000. **Staff:** 45. **Description:** AFL-CIO. A division of International Union of Electronic, Electrical, Salaried, Machine, and Furniture Workers. **Formerly:** (1987) United Furniture Workers of America; (1989) Furniture Workers Division, IUE. **Conventions/Meetings:** biennial meeting.

Glass

23499 ■ Glass Molders, Pottery, Plastics, and Allied Workers International Union (GMP)
608 E Baltimore Pike
PO Box 607
Media, PA 19063-0607
Ph: (610)565-5051
Fax: (610)565-0983
E-mail: gmpiu@gmpiu.org
URL: http://www.gmpiu.org
Contact: John P. Ryan, Intl. Pres.
Founded: 1842. **Members:** 65,000. **Description:** AFL-CIO; CLC. Participates fully in the life of the labor movement. **Programs:** Scholarship. **Formed by Merger of:** International Molders' and Allied Workers' Union; International Brotherhood of Pottery and

Allied Workers. **Publications:** *Horizons,* monthly. Alternate Formats: online.

23500 ■ USWA Flint/Glass Workers Conference
1440 S Byrne Rd.
Toledo, OH 43614
Ph: (419)385-6687
Free: (800)742-8213
Fax: (419)385-8839
URL: http://www.uswa.org
Contact: Tim Tuttle, Chm.
Founded: 1878. **Members:** 17,598. **Staff:** 21. **Budget:** $6,000,000. **Local Groups:** 143. **National Groups:** 5. **Description:** AFL-CIO. **Libraries: Type:** not open to the public. **Holdings:** 2,000. **Awards: Frequency:** annual. **Type:** scholarship. **Recipient:** to 5 children of members based on a lottery drawing. **Boards:** National Executive. **Formerly:** American Flint Glass Workers of North America. **Publications:** *American Flint,* monthly. Magazine. Contains local news and articles. **Circulation:** 14,000 ● Annual Report ● Directory, annual. **Conventions/Meetings:** triennial convention.

Government Employees

23501 ■ American Federation of Government Employees (AFGE)
80 F St. NW
Washington, DC 20001
Ph: (202)737-8700 (202)639-6419
Fax: (202)639-6441
E-mail: comments@afge.org
URL: http://www.afge.org
Contact: John Gage, Natl. Pres.
Founded: 1932. **Members:** 217,500. **Local Groups:** 1,100. **Description:** Federal employees including food inspectors, nurses, printers, cartographers, lawyers, police officers, census workers, OSHA inspectors, janitors, truck drivers, secretaries, artists, plumbers, immigration inspectors, scientists, doctors, cowboys, botanists, park rangers, computer programmers, foreign service workers, airplane mechanics, environmentalists, and writers. Seeks to help provide good government services, while ensuring that government workers are treated fairly and with dignity. Offers legal representation, legislative advocacy, technical expertise, and informational services. Also represents D.C. government workers in various types of jobs. **Additional Websites:** http://www.unionblog.org. **Committees:** Political Action. **Affiliated With:** AFL-CIO. **Publications:** *Government Standard,* bimonthly. Newspaper. Features news and legislative and regulatory information. **Price:** included in membership dues. **Circulation:** 210,000. Alternate Formats: online. **Conventions/Meetings:** triennial meeting.

23502 ■ American Federation of State, County and Municipal Employees (AFSCME)
1625 L St. NW
Washington, DC 20036-5687
Ph: (202)429-1000 (202)659-0446
Fax: (202)429-1293
E-mail: webmaster@afscme.org
URL: http://www.afscme.org
Contact: Gerald W. McEntee, Pres.
Founded: 1936. **Members:** 1,400,000. **Description:** Represents a divers group of service and health care workers in the public and private sectors. Organizes for social and economic justice in the workplace and through political action and legislative advocacy. **Libraries: Type:** reference. **Holdings:** 6,000. **Subjects:** public sector employees, labor law, occupational safety and health. **Committees:** Public Employees Organized to Promote Legislative Equality. **Publications:** *Public Employee,* 8/year. Magazine. Covers pay equity for working women, the federal budget, day care, welfare reform, and other topics. Lists books and other resources. **Price:** available to members only. **Circulation:** 1,400,000. Alternate Formats: online. **Conventions/Meetings:** biennial meeting.

23503 ■ American Foreign Service Association (AFSA)
2101 E St. NW
Washington, DC 20037
Ph: (202)338-4045
Free: (800)704-AFSA
Fax: (202)338-6820
E-mail: member@afsa.org
URL: http://www.afsa.org
Contact: J. Anthony Holmes, Pres.
Founded: 1924. **Members:** 11,000. **Membership Dues:** spouse, $50 (annual) ● retired, $54 (annual) ● life, $1,500. **Staff:** 25. **Budget:** $1,300,000. **Description:** Associate membership is open to individuals and international organizations and corporations interested in foreign affairs, international trade, and economic policy. Conducts international conferences and symposia; holds monthly speaker programs. Operates the Foreign Service Club; sponsors member insurance programs. Maintains speakers' bureau. **Awards:** Harriman. **Frequency:** annual. **Type:** recognition. **Recipient:** for junior officer ● Herter. **Frequency:** annual. **Type:** recognition. **Recipient:** for senior Foreign Service personnel ● Rivkin. **Frequency:** annual. **Type:** recognition. **Recipient:** for midcareer officer ● Tax Harris. **Frequency:** annual. **Type:** recognition. **Recipient:** for Foreign Service specialist. **Departments:** Administration; Awards; Executive; Legal; Member Services; Outreach; Professional Issues. **Formerly:** American Consular Association. **Publications:** *Directory of Retired Members*, periodic. Alternate Formats: online ● *Foreign Service Journal*, monthly. Magazine. Covers foreign policy and professional issues; includes book and periodical reviews, obituaries, and association newsletter. **Price:** $2.50/issue; $25.00/year. ISSN: 0015-7279. **Circulation:** 11,000. **Advertising:** accepted. Alternate Formats: microform.

23504 ■ Associates of the American Foreign Service Worldwide (AAFSW)
5555 Columbia Pike, Ste.208
Arlington, VA 22204-3117
Ph: (703)820-5420
Fax: (703)820-5421
E-mail: office@aafsw.org
URL: http://www.aafsw.org
Contact: Judy Felt, Pres.
Founded: 1960. **Members:** 700. **Membership Dues:** associate, $45 (annual) ● individual, $160 (5/year) ● individual, $40 (annual). **Staff:** 2. **Budget:** $192,070. **Description:** Represents the spouses of employees of Foreign Affairs Agencies (and employees as well). Facilitates the exchange of information pertaining to Foreign Service life. Advances and safeguards the interests of its members. Provides emergency assistance to members of the foreign affairs community. Encourages educational and practical training programs. Develops and maintains archives relating to the association and to the history of Foreign Service spouses and family members. Promotes a better quality of life and fosters an esprit de corps in the foreign affairs community through advocacy and activities. Acts as a networking facilitator and a registered lobbyist. Provides volunteer opportunities. **Libraries: Type:** open to the public. **Holdings:** 200; archival material. **Subjects:** foreign service history, oral history archive. **Awards:** AAFSW Scholarship. **Frequency:** annual. **Type:** scholarship. **Recipient:** for children of foreign service families ● Lesley Dorman Award. **Frequency:** annual. **Type:** recognition. **Recipient:** for sustained outstanding service to the association ● Secretary of State Award for Volunteerism Abroad. **Frequency:** annual. **Type:** recognition. **Recipient:** for volunteer services to U.S. government employees and family members abroad. **Computer Services:** database, membership lists ● online services, information, payment and donation options, livelines e-group. **Caucuses:** Forum. **Committees:** BookFair. **Departments:** Senior Living. **Projects:** Oral History. **Special Interest Groups:** French Language. **Subgroups:** Foreign-Born Spouses; Writers. **Task Forces:** Medical Evacuee Support Network. **Formerly:** (2000) Association of American Foreign Service Women. **Publications:** *Global Link*, monthly. Newsletter. **Price:** included in membership dues. **Cir-**

culation: 1,200. Also Cited As: *AAFSW Newsletter* ● *Realities of Foreign Service Life*. Book. Contains collection of essays by AAFSW members covering every imaginable facet of life in the Foreign Service - the good, the bad, the funny. **Price:** $20.95. **Conventions/Meetings:** annual workshop.

23505 ■ Association of Civilian Technicians (ACT)
12620 Lake Ridge Dr.
Woodbridge, VA 22192-2335
Ph: (703)494-4845
Fax: (703)494-0961
E-mail: tbastas@actnat.com
URL: http://www.actnat.com
Contact: Thomas G. Bastas, Pres.
Founded: 1960. **Members:** 14,000. **Staff:** 10. **Budget:** $1,000,000. **State Groups:** 5. **Local Groups:** 102. **Description:** Civilian technicians of the National Guard. Aids in having National Guard technicians recognized as federal employees (their salaries are paid by the federal government, but they had previously been considered state employees). Full retirement credit for past technician service has been gained; is still seeking to have National Guard technicians considered civilian technicians. **Libraries: Type:** reference. **Holdings:** archival material, business records. **Awards:** Charles J. Collins Memorial Award. **Frequency:** annual. **Type:** recognition. **Recipient:** for outstanding performance and service to National Guard Technicians and ACT ● Frank Cimino Award. **Frequency:** annual. **Type:** recognition. **Recipient:** for outstanding achievement in public relations ● Recruiting Recognition Award. **Frequency:** annual. **Type:** recognition. **Recipient:** for outstanding efforts in continuing the membership goals of the association. **Formerly:** National Guard Civilian Employees Association. **Publications:** *The Technician*, monthly. **Price:** included in membership dues. **Conventions/Meetings:** semiannual conference.

23506 ■ Civil Service Employees Association (CSEA)
143 Washington Ave.
Capitol Sta.
Box 7125
Albany, NY 12224-0125
Ph: (518)257-1000
Free: (800)342-4146
Fax: (518)462-3639
E-mail: donohue@cseainc.org
URL: http://www.csealocal1000.org
Contact: Danny Donohue, Pres.
Founded: 1910. **Members:** 220,000. **Staff:** 350. **Regional Groups:** 6. **State Groups:** 300. **Description:** AFL-CIO. Represents state and local government employees from all public employee classifications. Negotiates work contracts; represents members in grievances; provides legal assistance for on-the-job problems; provides advice and assistance on federal, state, and local laws affecting public employees. Conducts research, training and education programs. Compiles statistics. **Affiliated With:** American Federation of State, County and Municipal Employees. **Publications:** *Workforce*, monthly. Journal. **Circulation:** 220,000 ● Newsletter, periodic. **Conventions/Meetings:** annual meeting.

23507 ■ Gays and Lesbians in Foreign Affairs Agencies USA (GLIFAA)
PO Box 18774
Washington, DC 20036-8774
Ph: (202)232-1588
E-mail: glifaa@hotmail.com
URL: http://www.glifaa.org
Contact: Scott Boswell, Pres.
Founded: 1992. **Members:** 400. **Membership Dues:** full, $35 (annual) ● affiliated, $15 (annual). **Description:** Gay and lesbian employees of U.S. government agencies engaged in international affairs. Works to solidify and expand members' rights in areas including domestic partnership benefits for same-sex partners. Identifies and addresses gay and lesbian issues in the workplace. **Libraries: Type:** reference. **Holdings:** archival material. **Subjects:** gays, lesbians in foreign affairs agencies. **Committees:** Partnership;

Public Relations. **Formerly:** (2003) Gays and Lesbians in Foreign Affairs. **Publications:** Newsletter, bimonthly. **Circulation:** 300. Alternate Formats: online. **Conventions/Meetings:** monthly board meeting.

23508 ■ National Association of Government Employees (NAGE)
159 Burgin Pkwy.
Quincy, MA 02169
Ph: (617)376-0220
Fax: (617)376-0285
URL: http://www.nage.org
Contact: David J. Holway, Pres.
Founded: 1961. **Members:** 195,000. **Description:** Union of civilian federal government employees with locals and members in military agencies, Internal Revenue Service, Post Office, Veterans Administration, General Services Administration, Federal Aviation Administration, and other federal agencies, as well as state and local agencies. Activities include direct legal assistance, information service, legislative lobbying and representation, trained leadership in contract negotiations, employment protection, and insurance. Offers seminars; sponsors competitions. **Libraries: Type:** reference. **Holdings:** books. **Subjects:** labor law, title 5, agency regulations. **Awards: Frequency:** annual. **Type:** scholarship. **Recipient:** to members. **Committees:** Political Action. **Departments:** Training. **Affiliated With:** Service Employees International Union. **Supersedes:** Federal Employees Veterans Association. **Publications:** *The Fednews*, 3/year. Newsletter. Alternate Formats: online. **Conventions/Meetings:** quadrennial meeting.

23509 ■ National Employee Union Information Center (NEUIC)
Address Unknown since 2007
Founded: 1995. **Staff:** 1. **Description:** Collects information on complaints filed against public employee unions. Refers complainants to agencies able to adjudicate and rectify union injustices. Conducts educational programs to make public employees aware of their rights in case of union malpractice. Sponsors research; makes available speakers' bureau; compiles statistics, makes available pertinent recent court decisions. **Libraries: Type:** reference. **Holdings:** 1,500; articles, clippings. **Subjects:** labor union malpractice. **Awards:** Public Employee Advocacy Award. **Frequency:** annual. **Type:** recognition. **Formerly:** (1996) National Public Employee Union Information Center. **Conventions/Meetings:** annual conference, with discussion of recent developments.

23510 ■ National Federation of Federal Employees (NFFE)
1016 16th St. NW, Ste.300
Washington, DC 20036
Ph: (202)862-4400 (202)862-4471
Fax: (202)862-4432
E-mail: guest@nffe.org
URL: http://www.nffe.org
Contact: Richard N. Brown, Pres.
Founded: 1917. **Members:** 20,000. **Staff:** 20. **Regional Groups:** 9. **Description:** Independent. Opposes Social Security coverage for civil service workers. Conducts seminars on labor relations. **Telecommunication Services:** electronic mail, rbrown@nffe.org. **Councils:** Corps of Engineers; Forest Service; General Services Administration; National Guard General; Oklahoma Indian Health Service; Public Affairs; Veterans Administration; Wisconsin National Guard. **Publications:** *Federal Employee*, monthly. Newsletter. **Price:** free for members. **Circulation:** 20,000. **Advertising:** accepted ● Also publishes promotional material. **Conventions/Meetings:** biennial Lobby Week Convention - meeting (exhibits).

23511 ■ National Organization of Federal Employees Against Abuse and Retaliation (NOFEAR)
PO Box 94
Brooklyn, NY 11234
Ph: (718)377-0249

E-mail: nofear.org@lycos.com
URL: http://www.angelfire.com/ny5/nofear
Contact: Ronald Judd Moore, Chm./Organizing
Founder
Founded: 2003. **Description:** Works to "protect the human rights of United States Federal Employees from undue abuses by corrupt Federal Agencies.". **Computer Services:** Online services, message board.

23512 ■ National Organization of Legal Services Workers, UAW Local 2320 (NOLSW)
113 Univ. Pl., 5th Fl.
New York, NY 10003
Ph: (212)228-0992
Free: (800)829-2320
E-mail: ewallace@att.net
URL: http://www.geocities.com/~uaw2320
Contact: Ellen Wallace, Pres.
Founded: 1978. **Members:** 3,000. **Staff:** 9. **Description:** AFL-CIO. Legal service workers including secretaries, attorneys, paralegals, and others employed by state or federally funded legal service agencies and public interest organizations. Negotiates with management for fair salaries and good working conditions. Lobbies for federal funding and quality legal representation for the underprivileged in civil matters. **Computer Services:** Mailing lists. **Formerly:** (1977) Legal Services Staff Association; (1993) National Organization of Legal Services Workers. **Publications:** *Legal Services Worker*, bimonthly. Newsletter. **Conventions/Meetings:** annual meeting.

23513 ■ National Treasury Employees Union (NTEU)
1750 H St. NW, Ste.600
Washington, DC 20006
Ph: (202)572-5500
Fax: (202)572-5640
E-mail: nteu-pr@nteu.org
URL: http://www.nteu.org
Contact: Frank D. Ferris, Natl. Exec. VP
Founded: 1938. **Members:** 145,000. **Staff:** 135. **Budget:** $150,000. **Regional Groups:** 16. **Local Groups:** 240. **Description:** Employees of the federal government. Conducts research and educational training programs. Sponsors Federal Employees Education and Assistance Fund. **Libraries:** Type: reference. **Holdings:** 3,500; archival material, books, business records, periodicals. **Subjects:** labor law. **Absorbed:** (1975) National Customs Service Association. **Formerly:** (1957) National Association of Employees of Collectors of Internal Revenue; (1973) National Association of Internal Revenue Employees. **Publications:** *NTEU Capital Report*, monthly ● *NTEU Steward Update*, monthly. **Price:** free for NTEU Stewards. ISSN: 0194-7001 ● Bulletin, monthly. ISSN: 0279-540X. **Conventions/Meetings:** annual Legislative Conference ● biennial meeting - always August.

23514 ■ NLRB Professional Association (NLRBPA)
1099 14th St. NW, Ste.6604
Washington, DC 20570
Ph: (202)273-1928 (202)273-1749
Fax: (202)273-4270
Contact: Ms. Leslie Rossen, Pres.
Founded: 1962. **Members:** 200. **Description:** Independent legal professionals. Conducts collective bargaining for unit employees. **Committees:** A.D.R.; EEO-Diversity; Grievance; Legislative. **Conventions/Meetings:** annual conference.

Graphic Arts

23515 ■ Graphic Arts Employers of America (GAE)
c/o Printing Industries of America/Graphic Arts Technical Foundation
200 Deer Run Rd.
Sewickley, PA 15143
Ph: (412)741-6860
Fax: (412)741-2311

E-mail: jkyger@piagatf.org
URL: http://www.gain.net
Contact: Jim Kyger, Human Relations Dir.
Founded: 1891. **Members:** 700. **Staff:** 2. **Description:** Serves as a division of Printing Industries of America (see separate entry). Represents graphic communications, imaging, and printing companies who have at least some unionization or are interested in keeping informed on industrial relations issues. Assists management in functioning at optimal efficiency in a unionized environment. Compiles statistics and assists companies that deal with the major printing unions in the U.S. and Canada. Compiles statistics. **Computer Services:** database, production rates, contract information, fringe benefits, spreadsheets, wages and statistics. **Affiliated With:** Printing Industries of America. **Formerly:** (1981) Graphic Arts Union Employers of America. **Conventions/Meetings:** periodic seminar, on industrial relations.

23516 ■ Graphic Communications Conference of the International Brotherhood of Teamsters (GCC/IBT)
1900 L St. NW
Washington, DC 20036
Ph: (202)462-1400
Fax: (202)721-0600
E-mail: webmessenger@gciu.org
URL: http://gciu.org/index.shtml
Contact: George Tedeschi, Pres.
Founded: 1983. **Members:** 140,000. **Description:** AFL-CIO; Serves as a Canadian Labour Congress. **Departments:** Contract/Research; Data Processing; Education; Information; Legislative; Membership; Occupational Safety and Health; Organizing. **Formed by Merger of:** (1992) Graphic Arts International Union; (2005) Graphic Communications International Union; (2005) International Brotherhood of Teamsters; International Printing and Graphics Communications Union. **Publications:** *Graphic Communicator*, bimonthly. Newspaper. Covers membership and trade union activities. **Price:** $12.00/year. **Circulation:** 180,000. Alternate Formats: online. **Conventions/Meetings:** quadrennial international conference.

23517 ■ International Allied Printing Trades Association (IAPTA)
501 3rd St. NW, Ste.950
Washington, DC 20001
Ph: (202)434-1248
Fax: (202)434-1245
E-mail: bboarman@cwa-union.org
URL: http://www.alliedlabel.org
Contact: William J. Boarman, Pres.
Founded: 1911. **Members:** 700,000. **Description:** Local councils of the Printing, Publishing, and Media Workers Sector of the CWA and the Graphic Communications International Union representing 300,000 members. Aims to own and control the use of the Allied Printing Trades Union Label on printed material. **Convention/Meeting:** none. **Affiliated With:** Graphic Communications Conference of the International Brotherhood of Teamsters; Printing, Publishing and Media Workers Sector of the CWA.

23518 ■ International Plate Printers, Die Stampers, and Engravers' Union of North America
3957 Smoke Rd.
Doylestown, PA 18901
Ph: (215)340-2843
Fax: (215)340-2843
Contact: James L. Kopernick, Sec.-Treas.
Founded: 1893. **Members:** 200. **Staff:** 2. **Description:** AFL-CIO. **Affiliated With:** AFL-CIO. **Conventions/Meetings:** biennial meeting and convention.

23519 ■ Printing, Publishing and Media Workers Sector of the CWA
501 3rd St. NW
Washington, DC 20001-2797
Ph: (202)434-1235
Fax: (202)434-1245

E-mail: bboarman@cwa-union.org
URL: http://www.cwa-union.org
Contact: William J. Boarman, Pres.
Founded: 1852. **Members:** 25,000. **Description:** Represents women and men in a diverse range of occupations in daily newspapers, commercial printing and mailing operations, graphic design, specialty manufacturing, publishing and distribution as well as the U.S. Government Printing Office. Provides its members and their families with responsive representation and progressive programs. **Absorbed:** International Mailers Union. **Formerly:** (1987) International Typographical Union. **Conventions/Meetings:** annual conference.

Health Care

23520 ■ AFT Healthcare (AFTHC)
555 New Jersey Ave. NW
Washington, DC 20001
Ph: (202)879-4491
Free: (800)238-1133
E-mail: healthcare@aft.org
URL: http://www.aft.org/healthcare
Contact: Mary Lehman MacDonald, Dir.
Founded: 1978. **Members:** 70,000. **Staff:** 5. **Local Groups:** 117. **Description:** A division of the American Federation of Teachers, AFL-CIO. Represents RNs, LPNs, techs, therapists and other professional and technical employees in the healthcare field in hospitals, nursing homes, clinics, labs, blood banks and other facilities in the public and private sector. Works to improve members' professional standards by promoting continuing education, advancing economic status, and working conditions conducive to high-quality patient care. Advocates for legislation affecting safe and high-quality patient care, national health insurance, health personnel training funds and other state and national healthcare issues. Organizes new members into local unions, and maintains legal defense fund to provide assistance to members whose legal or contractual rights have been violated. **Libraries:** Type: not open to the public. **Holdings:** 5,000; books, periodicals. **Subjects:** education, health issues. **Divisions:** Editorial; Legislative; Organizing; Political Action; Public Relations; Research; Travel; Union Leadership Institute. **Affiliated With:** American Federation of Teachers. **Formerly:** (2000) Federation of Nurses and Health Professionals. **Publications:** *Healthwire*, bimonthly. Newsletter. Includes book reviews. **Price:** included in membership dues. **Circulation:** 76,000. Alternate Formats: online. **Conventions/Meetings:** annual Professional Issues Conference, focusing on issues of concern to healthcare professionals (exhibits).

23521 ■ Association for Behavioral Health and Wellness (ABHW)
c/o Pamela Greenberg, MPP, Pres./CEO
1101 Pennsylvania Ave. NW, 6th Fl.
Washington, DC 20004
Ph: (202)756-7726
Fax: (202)756-7308
E-mail: info@abhw.org
URL: http://www.abhw.org
Contact: Pamela Greenberg MPP, Pres./CEO
Founded: 1994. **Members:** 10. **Staff:** 1. **Budget:** $400,000. **Description:** Managed behavioral healthcare organizations. Works to advance the value of managed behavioral healthcare and promotes the inclusion of mental illnesses and addiction disorders in benefit coverage. **Libraries:** Type: not open to the public. **Formerly:** (2006) American Managed Behavioral Healthcare Association. **Publications:** *Catalog of Special Reports*. Alternate Formats: online. **Conventions/Meetings:** semiannual board meeting.

23522 ■ Committee of Interns and Residents (CIR)
520 8th Ave., Ste.1200
New York, NY 10018-4183
Ph: (212)356-8100
Free: (800)247-8877
Fax: (212)356-8111

E-mail: info@cirseiu.org
URL: http://www.cirseiu.org
Contact: Simon Ahtaridis MD, Pres.
Founded: 1957. **Members:** 11,000. **Staff:** 20. **Description:** Medical and dental interns, residents, chief residents, and fellows (collectively referred to as house staff officers) at 60 member hospitals located in California, Florida, New York, New Jersey, and Washington, DC. Represents house staff in matters pertaining to compensation, benefits, hours, working conditions, and other issues affecting their employment, education, training, and the quality of health services and patient care. **Committees:** Foreign Medical Graduate; Patient Care. **Divisions:** Hospitals. **Formerly:** (1974) Committee of Interns and Residents in New York City. **Publications:** *CIR News,* quarterly. Newsletter. **Conventions/Meetings:** annual convention ● monthly House of Delegates Meeting.

23523 ■ Family Health Care Association of America
c/o James Mark Reynolds, Sr., Pres.
PO Box 222
Jamestown, NC 27282
Ph: (336)987-0108
E-mail: mreynolds@northstate.net
Contact: James Mark Reynolds Sr., Pres.
Founded: 1996. **Members:** 4,401. **Membership Dues:** family, $219 (annual) ● provisional, $27 (annual). **Staff:** 6. **Budget:** $35,000. **Regional Groups:** 1. **State Groups:** 1. **Description:** Provides educational, charitable, and research programs. Offers speakers bureau. **Publications:** none. **Awards:** **Type:** fellowship. **Computer Services:** database. **Conventions/Meetings:** annual board meeting (exhibits) - usually in February.

23524 ■ Union of American Physicians and Dentists (UAPD)
1330 Broadway, Ste.730
Oakland, CA 94612
Ph: (510)839-0193 (510)873-8620
Free: (800)622-0909
Fax: (510)763-8756
E-mail: uapd@uapd.com
URL: http://www.uapd.com
Contact: Gary Robinson, Exec. Dir.
Founded: 1972. **Members:** 10,000. **Membership Dues:** union, $700 (annual). **Staff:** 19. **Budget:** $2,500,000. **Regional Groups:** 1. **State Groups:** 1. **Local Groups:** 3. **Description:** Independent national labor organization made up of self-employed medical doctors and dentists as well as those employed by hospitals, teaching institutions, counties, and municipalities. Seeks to: provide optimum medical care for the people; ensure quality facilities for the provision of medical care; enable physicians to give of themselves, unhindered by extraneous forces, for the welfare of their patients; ensure reasonable compensation for physicians commensurate with their training, skill, and the responsibility they bear for the life and health of their fellow human beings. **Libraries:** **Type:** not open to the public. **Holdings:** 500; articles, books, periodicals. **Subjects:** medicine, medical management, managed care, Medicare, union. **Formerly:** Union of American Physicians and Dentists. **Publications:** *UAPD Report,* monthly. Newsletter. **Price:** included in membership dues ● Reports ● Also publishes materials on socioeconomic issues. **Conventions/Meetings:** triennial convention.

Heating and Cooling

23525 ■ International Association of Heat and Frost Insulators and Asbestos Workers
9602 Martin Luther King Jr. Hwy.
Lanham, MD 20706
Ph: (301)731-9101
Fax: (301)731-5058
E-mail: webmaster@insulators.org
URL: http://www.insulators.org
Contact: James A. Grogan, Gen. Pres.
Description: Serves as labor union for heat and frost insulators and asbestos workers. Assists member-

ship in securing employment; defends the rights of members; advances education and cooperation.

Hispanic

23526 ■ Labor Council for Latin American Advancement (LCLAA)
815 16th St. NW, 4th Fl.
Washington, DC 20006
Ph: (202)508-6919
Fax: (202)508-6922
E-mail: headquarters@lclaa.org
URL: http://www.lclaa.org
Contact: Dr. Gabriela D. Lemus, Exec. Dir.
Founded: 1972. **Local Groups:** 86. **Description:** Strives for social dignity, economic and political justice, and a decent standard of living for Hispanic workers. Seeks to unite the Hispanic labor community in America. Works within the labor movement for voter education, registration, and political participation on the national, regional, and local levels. Maintains speakers' bureau; compiles statistics. **Publications:** *La Voz Latina,* quarterly. **Alternate Formats:** online. **Conventions/Meetings:** biennial meeting.

Hospitality Industries

23527 ■ UNITE HERE
275 7th Ave.
New York, NY 10001-6708
Ph: (212)265-7000
Fax: (202)333-0468
E-mail: feedback@hereunion.org
URL: http://www.unitehere.org
Contact: Bruce S. Raynor, Gen. Pres.
Founded: 1891. **Members:** 370,000. **Local Groups:** 198. **Description:** AFL-CIO. Helps improve working conditions, wages, and benefits across the U.S. and Canada. Organizes the unorganized in the industry. Works with employers to resolve issues in the workplace and in the relevant industry. **Formed by Merger of:** (2004) Hotel Employees and Restaurant Employees International Union and Union of Needletrades, Industrial and Textile Employees. **Formerly:** (1981) Hotel and Restaurant Employees and Bartenders International Union. **Publications:** *Catering Industry Employee,* monthly. Journal. Covers labor and union activities. Includes obituaries and Spanish and French translations of selected sections. **Price:** $5.00/year. ISSN: 0008-7815. **Circulation:** 350,000. **Conventions/Meetings:** quinquennial congress.

Industrial Workers

23528 ■ AFL-CIO
815 16th St. NW
Washington, DC 20006
Ph: (202)637-5000
URL: http://www.aflcio.org
Contact: John Sweeney, Pres.
Founded: 1955. **Members:** 13,300,000. **Staff:** 400. **State Groups:** 51. **Local Groups:** 620. **Description:** Federation of national unions, state federations, city central bodies, and directly affiliated local unions. **Libraries:** **Type:** reference. **Awards:** George Meany Human Rights Award. **Frequency:** annual. **Type:** recognition. **Recipient:** for service to worldwide human rights and dignity ● Murray-Green-Meany Award. **Frequency:** annual. **Type:** recognition. **Recipient:** for distinguished service to America. **Committees:** Civil Rights; Community Services; Economic Research; Education; Field Services; Housing; Information; International Affairs; Legal; Legislation; Maritime; Organization; Political Education; Public Relations; Research; Safety and Occupational Health; Social Security. **Departments:** Building and Construction Trades; Food and Allied Service Trades; Industrial Union; Maritime Trades; Metal Trades; Professional Employees; Public Employee; Transportation Trades; Union Label and Service Trades (see separate entries). **Also Known As:** American Fed-

eration of Labor and Congress of Industrial Organizations. **Formed by Merger of:** American Federation of Labor; Congress of Industrial Organizations. **Publications:** *America at Work,* 11/year. Magazine ● *News,* biweekly ● *Work in Progress,* weekly. Newsletter. **Alternate Formats:** online. **Conventions/Meetings:** biennial meeting.

23529 ■ General Service Employees Union Local 73
1165 N Clark St., Ste.500
Chicago, IL 60610
Ph: (312)787-5868
Fax: (312)337-7768
E-mail: jmisnik@seiu73.org
URL: http://www.seiu73.org
Contact: Joanna Misnik, Communications Dir.
Description: Independent. Represents employees in the public service industries.

23530 ■ Industrial Workers of the World (IWW)
PO Box 23085
Cincinnati, OH 45223
Ph: (513)591-1905
E-mail: ghq@iww.org
URL: http://www.iww.org
Contact: Mark Damron, Gen. Sec.-Treas.
Founded: 1905. **Members:** 2,000. **Membership Dues:** minimum, $6 (monthly) ● regular, $12 (monthly) ● maximum, $18 (monthly). **Staff:** 3. **Budget:** $90,000. **Local Groups:** 40. **National Groups:** 3. **Languages:** English, Finnish, German, Italian, Russian, Spanish. **Description:** Individuals of all nationalities, religions, or political affiliations, who work for wages or salary. Works for the abolition of the wage system, improvement of conditions through militant unionism, and ultimately "the elimination of social and economic problems at their root, through the establishment of a cooperative commonwealth to replace exploitation of this planet and its people for power or profit". Conducts periodic lectures. Maintains historical archives at Wayne State University, Detroit, Michigan. **Committees:** General Defense; International Solidarity. **Also Known As:** Wobblies. **Publications:** *Industrial Worker,* monthly. Newspaper. Covers world labor issues, economic developments, and organization news; includes book reviews. **Price:** included in membership dues; $15.00 /year for nonmembers; $20.00 /year for libraries. ISSN: 0019-8870. **Circulation:** 5,000. **Advertising:** accepted. **Alternate Formats:** microform ● *Little Red Songbook.* **Price:** $10.00/copy ● *One Big Union.* Pamphlet ● *Solidarity Forever: IWW Labor History Calendar.* Monographs. **Price:** $10.00/copy. **Conventions/Meetings:** annual general assembly - usually Labor Day weekend.

23531 ■ International Union of Elevator Constructors (IUEC)
7154 Columbia Gateway Dr.
Columbia, MD 21046
Ph: (410)953-6150
Fax: (410)953-6169
E-mail: contact@iuec.org
URL: http://www.iuec.org
Contact: Mr. Dana A. Brigham, Pres.
Founded: 1901. **Members:** 25,000. **Description:** Represents elevator constructor unions in the U.S. and Canada. Supplies companies with referrals to elevator installers. **Publications:** *The Constructor,* monthly. **Conventions/Meetings:** quinquennial meeting.

23532 ■ International Union of Tool, Die and Mold Makers (IUTDM)
71 E Cherry St.
Rahway, NJ 07065
Ph: (732)388-3323
Contact: Glenn Bower, Pres.
Founded: 1972. **Members:** 125. **Staff:** 2. **Budget:** $50,000. **Description:** Skilled tradesmen in the metalworking field such as toolmakers, diemakers, moldmakers, machinists, and apprentices. Aims to provide better wages, benefits, working conditions and other conditions of employment, and to improve

the trade by approved apprenticeship programs. Conducts regional seminars stressing the cooperation of management and labor. **Absorbed:** (1975) Tool, Die and Mold Makers Guild. **Formed by Merger of:** (1995) Local 747 Union, New Jersey. **Conventions/Meetings:** biennial meeting.

23533 ■ Machinists Non-Partisan Political League (MNPL)
9000 Machinists Pl.
Upper Marlboro, MD 20772-2687
Ph: (301)967-4500
E-mail: websteward@goiam.org
URL: http://www.goiam.org/mnpl.cfm
Contact: Tom Trotter, Dir.
Founded: 1947. **Members:** 500,000. **Regional Groups:** 4. **Local Groups:** 40. **Description:** Elects labor's friends to Congress. Compiles statistics. **Awards: Type:** recognition. **Publications:** *Action*, annual. **Conventions/Meetings:** competition ● annual conference.

23534 ■ Millwright Group (MG)
c/o Specialized Carriers and Rigging Association
2750 Prosperity Ave., Ste.620
Fairfax, VA 22031-4312
Ph: (703)698-0291
Fax: (703)698-0297
E-mail: info@scranet.org
URL: http://www.scranet.org
Contact: Beth A. O'Quinn, VP
Founded: 1982. **Members:** 150. **Description:** A special interest group of the Specialized Carriers and Rigging Association (see separate entry). Represents millwrights (persons who install and maintain industrial machines such as turbines, power generators, and large printing presses). Disseminates information; has assisted in negotiating labor agreements. Maintains speakers' bureau; conducts research; compiles statistics. **Awards: Type:** recognition. **Committees:** Apprenticeship and Training; Jurisdictional Disputes; Negotiating; Safety. **Publications:** *Safety, Industrial Relations, and Government Affairs Special Report*, periodic ● *Directory*, annual ● *Newsletter*, biweekly. **Conventions/Meetings:** annual meeting (exhibits).

23535 ■ National Organization of Industrial Trade Unions (NOITU)
148-06 Hillside Ave.
Jamaica, NY 11435
Ph: (718)291-3434
Fax: (718)526-2920
E-mail: questions@noitu.org
URL: http://www.noitu.org
Contact: Daniel Lasky, Natl. Pres.
Founded: 1958. **Members:** 10,000. **Membership Dues:** industrial semi-skill, $75. **Description:** Industrial trade unions representing 10,000 individuals. Advocates better wages, hours, and conditions for members. Operates medical and dental centers in Manhattan and Long Island, NY for members and their families. Membership concentrated in the Northeastern U.S. **Libraries: Type:** reference. **Subjects:** union craft. **Awards:** Louis Lasky Scholarship Fund. **Type:** scholarship. **Publications:** *Unioncraft*, quarterly. Journal. **Conventions/Meetings:** quinquennial convention ● annual meeting (exhibits) - always December.

23536 ■ United Paperworkers International Union (UPIU)
3340 Perimeter Hill Dr.
Nashville, TN 37202
Ph: (615)834-8590
Fax: (615)831-6791
Contact: Boyd Young, Pres.
Members: 250,000. **Multinational. Description:** Paper industry workers. Strives to help its members raise their wages, improve working conditions, and protect their rights.

Labor

23537 ■ Just Transition Alliance (JTA)
2434 Southport Way, Ste.D
National City, CA 91950
Ph: (619)474-4001
Fax: (619)474-4001
E-mail: justtransition@sbcglobal.net
URL: http://www.jtalliance.org
Contact: Jose T. Bravo, Exec. Dir.
Founded: 1997. **Multinational. Description:** Represents a coalition of labor, economic and environmental justice activists, indigenous people and working-class people of color. Seeks just transition of communities and workers from unsafe workplaces and environments to healthy, viable communities with a sustainable economy. Facilitates communication and cooperation among members. **Publications:** *Info and Action Brief*. Newsletter. Alternate Formats: online.

23538 ■ SweatFree Communities
c/o Bjorn Claeson, Dir.
30 Blackstone St.
Bangor, ME 04401
Ph: (207)262-7277
Fax: (207)262-7211
E-mail: info@sweatfree.org
URL: http://www.sweatfree.org
Contact: Bjorn Claeson, Dir.
Founded: 2003. **Languages:** English, Spanish. **Description:** Assists sweatshop workers. Seeks to improve the lives of all working people and form strong, independent unions. Strives to end sweatshop exploitation by inspiring responsible local purchasing and fostering solidarity between U.S. communities and workers worldwide. **Telecommunication Services:** electronic mail, bjorn@sweatfree.org. **Publications:** Newsletter, monthly. Alternate Formats: online.

23539 ■ Wal-Mart Alliance for Reform Now (WARN)
1344 W Cass St., Ste.A
Tampa, FL 33606
Ph: (813)258-4030
Fax: (813)258-4488
URL: http://www.warnwalmart.org
Contact: Rick Smith, Hd.
Description: Provides the voice for citizens to force Wal-Mart to be "accountable to community standards and values." Strives to affect change in the business practices of Wal-Mart and its affiliated businesses. Works on projects that promote responsiveness on the part of Wal-Mart. **Publications:** Newsletter. Alternate Formats: online.

23540 ■ Wal-Mart Workers of America (WWOA)
1775 K St. NW, Ste.320
Washington, DC 20006
Free: (866)587-2299
Fax: (202)721-8017
E-mail: help@walmartworkersofamerica.com
URL: http://www.wakeupwalmart.com/wwa
Contact: Chris Kofinis, Contact
Description: Represents current and former Wal-Mart and Sam's Club workers dedicated to "improving workplace conditions, ensuring justice, and protecting and defending the rights of all Wal-Mart workers." Works to strengthen Wal-Mart workers' ability to improve their lives. **Publications:** Newsletter, quarterly. Alternate Formats: online.

23541 ■ Wal-Mart Workers Association (WWA)
1344 W Cass St., Ste.A
Tampa, FL 33606
Ph: (813)258-4030
Fax: (813)258-4488
URL: http://www.walmartwork.org
Contact: Rick Smith, Exec. Dir.
Founded: 2005. **Description:** Represents current and past Wal-Mart workers united to "improve the working conditions and living standards of Wal-Mart workers." Creates a workers support network encouraging workers, activists, organizations and the com-

munity to engage in a pro-worker movement. Provides assistance to past and present Wal-Mart workers who have been discriminated against or treated unfairly. **Publications:** *Wal-Mart Worker's News*. Newsletter. Alternate Formats: online.

Labor Studies

23542 ■ Association of Labor Relations Agencies (ALRA)
c/o Les Heltzer, VP of Professional Development
Natl. Labor Relations Bd.
1099 14th St. NW, Ste.11600
Washington, DC 20570
Ph: (202)273-1067
Fax: (202)273-4270
E-mail: lester.heltzer@nlrb.gov
URL: http://www.alra.org
Contact: Marilyn Glenn Sayan, Pres.
Founded: 1952. **Members:** 72. **Membership Dues:** regular, $250 (annual). **Description:** Impartial U.S. and Canadian government agencies and private non-profit agencies responsible for administering labor-management relations laws or services. Encourages and promotes high professional standards in the field of labor-management. Provides a forum for the discussion of labor relations problems and their solutions. Promotes improved employer-employee relationships in the public and private sectors, and the peaceful resolution of employer-employee and labor-management disputes. Works to develop the public's interest in labor relations. Maintains speakers' bureau; conducts educational programs. **Libraries: Type:** not open to the public. **Holdings:** archival material. **Awards: Type:** scholarship. **Committees:** Arrangements; Audit; Grant Administration; Mediation Liaison; Policy and Constitution; Professional Development; Publications and Communications; Technology. **Publications:** *ALRA Advisor*, semiannual. Newsletter. **Circulation:** 450 ● *Directory*. Alternate Formats: online. **Conventions/Meetings:** board meeting - 3/year ● annual conference (exhibits) - usually in July.

23543 ■ Association for Union Democracy (AUD)
104 Montgomery St.
Brooklyn, NY 11225
Ph: (718)564-1114
E-mail: info@uniondemocracy.org
URL: http://www.uniondemocracy.com
Contact: Judith Schneider, Pres.
Founded: 1969. **Members:** 4,000. **Membership Dues:** associate, $30 (annual) ● club, $100 (annual) ● institution, international, $40 (annual). **Staff:** 3. **Budget:** $150,000. **Regional Groups:** 1. **Description:** Aims to further the knowledge and understanding of democratic principles and practices in American labor organizations by research, publications, and conferences and to assist in insuring the legal rights of labor organization members whose rights are threatened or infringed upon. Conducts workshops and disseminates literature on the legal rights of union members and union democracy. **Committees:** Legal Review. **Projects:** Union Democracy Worker Education; Women's; Worker's Rights. **Publications:** *AFL-CIO Codes of Ethical Practices*. **Price:** $3.00 ● *Democracy in a One Party State*. Book. **Price:** $3.00 ● *Democratic Rights for Union Members: A Guide to Internal Union Democracy*. Book. **Price:** $12.00 ● *How to Get an Honest Union Election*. Book. **Price:** $8.00 ● *The Legal Rights of Union Stewards*. Book. **Price:** $13.00 ● *Manual for Survival for Women in Nontraditional Employment*. **Price:** $10.00 ● *Union Democracy Review*, bimonthly. Journal. Contains law development in union democracy, trends in the labor movement, insurgent movements, and contested elections in unions. **Price:** $30.00 /year for individuals in U.S.; $40.00 /year for individuals and institutions outside U.S. (plus shipping and handling). **Circulation:** 4,000. Alternate Formats: online. **Conventions/Meetings:** periodic meeting.

23544 ■ Institute of Labor and Industrial Relations (ILIR)
Univ. of Michigan
Victor Vaughan Bldg.
1111 E Catherine St.
Ann Arbor, MI 48109-2054
Ph: (734)763-3116
E-mail: ilir-info@umich.edu
URL: http://www.ilir.umich.edu
Contact: Lawrence S. Root, Dir.
Founded: 1957. **Staff:** 30. **Description:** Develops and provides information to labor, management, and public communities regarding employment and worker behavior. Aids in solving human problems in industrial society. Conducts: research in worker health (employee assistance programs); research in the trucking industry; economic impact analysis; educational extension service program for labor unions; program which provides training for professional and personal development of workers. Forecasts employment and unemployment trends.

23545 ■ Labor and Employment Relations Association (LERA)
Univ. of Illinois
121 LIR Bldg.
504 E Armory Ave.
Champaign, IL 61820
Ph: (217)333-0072 (217)244-5419
Fax: (217)265-5130
E-mail: leraoffice@uiuc.edu
URL: http://www.lera.uiuc.edu
Contact: Paula D. Wells, Exec. Dir.
Founded: 1947. **Members:** 3,000. **Membership Dues:** regular, $95 (annual) ● family, $10 (annual) ● emeritus, $55 (annual) ● full-time student, $25 (annual) ● contributing, $200 (annual). **Staff:** 3. **Local Groups:** 50. **Description:** Businesspersons, union leaders, government officials, lawyers, arbitrators, academics, and others interested in research and exchange of ideas on social, political, economic, legal, and psychological aspects of labor and employment relations. **Libraries: Type:** open to the public. **Holdings:** books, papers, periodicals. **Awards:** Best Dissertation. **Frequency:** annual. **Type:** monetary. **Recipient:** for post-doctoral students in industrial relations field ● Excellence in Education. **Frequency:** annual. **Type:** recognition. **Recipient:** for outstanding educators ● Lifetime Achievement. **Frequency:** annual. **Type:** recognition ● Susan C. Eaton Scholar-Practitioner Award. **Frequency:** annual. **Type:** recognition ● Young Practitioner. **Frequency:** annual. **Type:** recognition. **Recipient:** for outstanding practitioner ● Young Scholar. **Frequency:** annual. **Type:** recognition. **Computer Services:** Mailing lists, electronic member list, one time use. **Subcommittees:** Collective Bargaining; Dispute Resolution; International/Comparative IR; Labor and Employment Law; Labor Markets/Labor Economics; Labor Union/Labor Studies; Work and Employment Relations. **Formerly:** (2004) Industrial Relations Research Association. **Publications:** *Labor & Employment Relations Association - Annual Proceedings*, annual. Price: $30.00. ISSN: 0277-7347. **Circulation:** 3,000. Alternate Formats: online ● *Labor & Employment Relations Association - Annual Research Volume*, annual. Price: $29.95 ● *Labor & Employment Relations Association—Membership Directory*, quadrennial. Price: $32.00 ● *Labor & Employment Relations Association—Series Newsletter*, quarterly. Contains employment listing and news about local chapters, national meetings, and publication opportunities. Price: free for members. ISSN: 0019-0500. **Circulation:** 3,000. **Advertising:** accepted. Also Cited As: *IRRA Newsletter* ● *Perspectives on Work*, semiannual. Magazine. Contains issues and information regarding the association. Alternate Formats: online. **Conventions/Meetings:** annual board meeting and general assembly - always in January ● annual IRRA National Policy Forum - board meeting and luncheon - spring or summer.

23546 ■ Labor Notes (LN)
7435 Michigan Ave.
Detroit, MI 48210
Ph: (313)842-6262

Fax: (313)842-0227
E-mail: labornotes@labornotes.org
URL: http://www.labornotes.org
Contact: Chris Kutalik, Co-Dir.
Founded: 1979. **Staff:** 6. **Description:** Serves as a labor activist network that provides a forum for information about the labor movement from the rank-and-file point of view. Conducts classes that bring together labor activists from different unions. Reports on union activities. **Formerly:** (2000) Labor Education and Research Project. **Publications:** Magazine, monthly. Covers the labor movement at the grass roots level for union activists. Price: $24.00 /year for individuals in U.S.; $35.00 /year for institutions and supporting members in U.S.; $30.00 /year for individuals outside U.S.; $40.00 /year for institutions and supporting members outside U.S. ISSN: 0275-4452. **Circulation:** 11,000. Alternate Formats: online ● Books. Contains contract concessions, quality of work life, team concept programs, free trade, sexual harassment, workplace organizing, and union democracy. ● Also publishes guide to researching employers. **Conventions/Meetings:** biennial conference, cross-union gathering of rank and file members and labor activists ● workshop.

23547 ■ Labor Project for Working Families (LPWF)
2521 Channing Way, No. 5555
Berkeley, CA 94720
Ph: (510)643-7088
Fax: (510)642-6432
E-mail: lpwf@berkeley.edu
URL: http://www.laborproject.org
Contact: Art Pulaski, Pres.
Founded: 1992. **Staff:** 3. **Description:** Works with unions to develop work and family policies related to child care, elder care, family leave, and flexible work schedules. Provides information to unions, employers, researchers, lawyers, and workers throughout the U.S. Conducts training sessions for unions on various work and family topics, including the Family and Medical Leave Act (FMLA) and California's new Paid Family Leave Law. **Libraries: Type:** reference; by appointment only. **Holdings:** archival material, clippings. **Subjects:** work and family, union contracts. **Computer Services:** database, labor/work and family. **Boards:** National Advisory. **Publications:** *Labor Family News*, quarterly. Newsletter. Price: $25.00/year. Alternate Formats: online.

23548 ■ Labor Research Association (LRA)
330 W 42nd St., 13th Fl.
New York, NY 10001
Ph: (212)714-1677
Fax: (212)714-1674
E-mail: info@lra-ny.com
URL: http://www.lraconsulting.com
Contact: Jeannine Rudolph, Contact
Founded: 1927. **Members:** 3,000. **Staff:** 10. **Description:** Conducts research and provides publications on economic and political issues for trade unions. Sponsors periodic seminars on issues concerning the trade union movement; offers consulting services to labor organizations; compiles statistics. **Awards: Frequency:** annual. **Type:** recognition. **Additional Websites:** http://www.laborresearch.org. **Telecommunication Services:** electronic mail, jrudolph@lra-ny.com. **Departments:** Research. **Publications:** *LRA's Economic Notes*, monthly. Newsletter. Provides economic analyses of interest to trade unionists. Provides updated data and statistics on unions and the economy. Price: $30.00 /year for individuals; $50.00 /year for institutions. ISSN: 0895-5220. **Circulation:** 3,500. Also Cited As: *Economic Notes* ● *Studies and Reports*, periodic ● *Trade Union Advisory*, biweekly. Newsletter. Provides information on economic forecasting designed for trade union leaders. Contains info on the latest activity in unions. Price: $225.00/year. ISSN: 1058-0557. **Conventions/Meetings:** annual dinner, with awards presentations - 3rd Thursday of October ● annual Ernest DeMaio Dinner, with fundraising activities.

23549 ■ National Labor-Management Association
Address Unknown since 2007
Founded: 1977. **Members:** 300. **Membership Dues:** $350 (annual) ● $90 (quarterly). **Staff:** 3. **Budget:** $100,000. **Description:** Promotes and supports labor management cooperation in the public and private sectors. Represents worksites and area coalitions that are working on workplace issues on a daily basis. Provides labor-management cooperation assistance to various industries, including government, health care, education, and building and construction services. Conducts educational programs and workshops. **Libraries: Type:** reference. **Holdings:** 30; video recordings. **Subjects:** labor-management cooperation. **Computer Services:** Online services. **Telecommunication Services:** electronic bulletin board. **Formerly:** (1993) National Association of Labor-Management Committees. **Publications:** *Forward Thinking*, quarterly. Newsletter. **Price:** included in membership dues; $40.00 for nonmembers. **Circulation:** 500. **Advertising:** accepted. Alternate Formats: online ● *NALMC*. Brochure. **Conventions/Meetings:** annual conference ● semiannual National Labor-Manangement Conference, in conjunction with the U.S. Department of Labor and Federal Mediation and Conciliation Services (exhibits) - always Washington, DC.

Law Enforcement

23550 ■ International Brotherhood of Police Officers (IBPO)
159 Burgin Pkwy.
Quincy, MA 02169
Ph: (617)376-0220
Free: (866)412-7762
Fax: (617)376-0285
E-mail: jflynn@nage.org
URL: http://www.ibpo.org
Contact: David J. Holway, Pres.
Founded: 1970. **Description:** AFL-CIO. Law enforcement officers and police departments nationwide dedicated to the welfare and security of law enforcement personnel at the city, state, and national level. Maintains legal department; offers insurance program. Supports labor relations branch; conducts seminars. **Awards: Type:** scholarship. **Computer Services:** Online services, learning center. **Affiliated With:** Service Employees International Union. **Publications:** *Blue Shield*, 3/year. Newsletter. Price: free, for members only. Alternate Formats: online ● *Police Chronicle*, quarterly. Newspaper.

23551 ■ International Union of Police Associations (IUPA)
1549 Ringling Blvd., Ste.600
Sarasota, FL 34236
Ph: (941)487-2560
Fax: (941)487-2570
E-mail: iupa@iupa.org
URL: http://www.iupa.org
Contact: Samuel A. Cabral, Pres.
Founded: 1978. **Members:** 50,000. **Staff:** 12. **Local Groups:** 400. **Multinational. Description:** AFL-CIO. Represents police officers organized to secure just compensation for their service and equitable settlement of their grievances, promote the establishment of just and reasonable work conditions, and encourage the formation of local unions, state and provincial associations, and joint councils. Seeks professionalization of the police officer through collective bargaining seminars and research. Encourages formation of political action committees by locals. Compiles statistics. Monitors national police/labor legislation. **Libraries: Type:** reference. **Awards:** Quill and Badge. **Frequency:** annual. **Type:** scholarship. **Publications:** *Police Union News*, bimonthly. **Conventions/Meetings:** biennial conference (exhibits) - always odd-numbered years ● biennial convention (exhibits) - always even-numbered years.

23552 ■ National Association of Special Police and Security Officers (NASPSO)
1101 30th St. NW, Ste.500
Washington, DC 20007

Ph: (202)625-8306
Fax: (202)582-6006
E-mail: naspso@aol.com
Contact: Caleb A. Gray-Burriss, Pres.
Founded: 1993. Members: 850. Membership Dues: security personnel, $18 (annual). Staff: 6. Budget: $1,700. Description: Special police and security officers. Seeks to improve delivery law enforcement and public safety services; promotes professional advancement of members. Serves as a forum for the exchange of information regarding special police and security services; sponsors educational programs.

23553 ■ National Border Patrol Council (NBPC)
PO Box 678
Campo, CA 91906
Ph: (619)478-5145
Free: (888)583-7237
E-mail: nbpc-info@nbpc.net
URL: http://www.nbpc.net
Contact: T.J. Bonner, Pres.
Members: 6,500. Local Groups: 14. Description: Represents employees of the U.S. Border Patrol. Publications: Educator, bimonthly, odd-numbered months. Newsletter. Circulation: 3,000. Conventions/Meetings: biennial convention - odd-numbered years.

Marine

23554 ■ Industrial Union of Marine and Ship Building Workers of America (IUMSWA)
122 Main St., Ste.4A
Topsham, ME 04086
Ph: (207)721-8996
Fax: (207)721-3249
E-mail: tprovost@iam.org
Contact: Tony Provost, Dir./Business Rep.
Founded: 1933. Members: 12,000. Description: AFL-CIO. Publications: none. Conventions/Meetings: biennial meeting.

23555 ■ International Longshore and Warehouse Union (ILWU)
1188 Franklin St., 4th Fl.
San Francisco, CA 94109
Ph: (415)775-0533
Fax: (415)775-1302
E-mail: info@ilwu.org
URL: http://www.ilwu.org
Contact: Robert McElrath, Pres.
Founded: 1937. Members: 64,000. Regional Groups: 58. Multinational. Description: Maintains and improves the wages, hours and working conditions for its members without discrimination. Educates its members in the history of the American labor movement and in present labor problems and tactics. Secures legislation in the interests of labor and opposes anti-labor legislation. Libraries: Type: reference. Holdings: 3,000. Committees: Automated Dispatch; Barge; Budget; Constitution, Division Bylaws and Caucus Rules; Education; Entry Level; Legislative; Pension. Formerly: (1997) International Longshoremen's and Warehousemen's Union. Publications: Dispatcher, monthly. Newspaper. Covers international and national labor union news. Includes Washington report. Price: $10.00/year. ISSN: 0012-3765. Circulation: 40,000. Alternate Formats: online. Conventions/Meetings: triennial international conference and convention.

23556 ■ International Longshoremen's Association (ILA)
17 Battery Pl., Ste.930
New York, NY 10004
Ph: (212)425-1200
Fax: (212)425-2928
E-mail: jmcnamara@ilaunion.org
URL: http://www.ilaunion.org
Contact: Mr. John Bowers, Pres.
Founded: 1893. Members: 50,000. Description: AFL-CIO. Represents longshoremen. Telecommunication Services: electronic mail, jbowers@il-

aunion.org. Affiliated With: International Organization of Masters, Mates and Pilots, ILA, AFL-CIO. Publications: Longshore News, monthly. Newsletter ● Directory, annual ● Newsletter, monthly. Conventions/Meetings: quadrennial meeting.

23557 ■ International Organization of Masters, Mates and Pilots, ILA, AFL-CIO (MM&P)
700 Maritime Blvd., Ste.B
Linthicum Heights, MD 21090-1941
Ph: (410)850-8700
Free: (877)667-5522
Fax: (410)850-0973
E-mail: iommp@bridgedeck.org
URL: http://www.bridgedeck.org
Contact: Glen P. Banks, Sec.-Treas.
Founded: 1887. Members: 6,753. Staff: 50. Budget: $6,000,000. Regional Groups: 5. Description: AFL-CIO. Sponsors Maritime Institute of Technology and Graduate Studies in Maryland. Funds: Masters, Mates, and Pilots Political Contribution. Publications: Master, Mate and Pilot, 6/year. Magazine. Conventions/Meetings: biennial convention.

23558 ■ Maritime Trades Department, AFL-CIO (MTD)
815 16th St. NW
Washington, DC 20006
Ph: (202)628-6300
Fax: (202)637-3989
E-mail: fpecquex@maritimetrades.org
URL: http://www.seafarers.org/about/mtd.xml
Contact: Francis X. Pecquex, Exec. Sec.-Treas.
Founded: 1946. Members: 30. Description: Federation of maritime transportation labor unions representing over eight million workers including seamen, shipbuilders, carpenters, electrical workers, engineers, fire fighters, oilers, ironworkers, longshoremen, telegraphers, and 23 port maritime councils throughout the U.S., Canada, and Puerto Rico. Initiates action on matters of concern to unions and workers in the maritime and allied fields. Publications: This is the MTD, periodic. Directory ● Newsletter, monthly. Price: $5.00/year. ISSN: 0161-9373. Conventions/Meetings: biennial convention.

23559 ■ National Maritime Union of America
Address Unknown since 2006
Founded: 1988. Members: 20,000. Description: AFL-CIO. Absorbed: (1982) Brotherhood of Marine Officers. Formed by Merger of: National Maritime Union of America; National Marine Engineers' Beneficial Association. Formerly: (1998) Marine Engineers' Beneficial Association. Publications: American Marine Engineer, monthly. Conventions/Meetings: biennial meeting.

23560 ■ Pacific Coast Marine Firemen, Oilers, Watertenders and Wipers Association (MFU)
240 2nd St.
San Francisco, CA 94105
Ph: (415)362-4592 (415)362-4593
Fax: (415)348-8864
E-mail: mfow_president@yahoo.com
URL: http://www.mfoww.org
Contact: Anthony Poplawski, Pres./Sec.-Treas.
Founded: 1883. Members: 1,691. Staff: 2. Description: AFL-CIO. Represents unlicensed engine room employees on U.S.-flag merchant marine vessels under contract. Seeks to improve working and living conditions of members, both on board ship and ashore. Publicizes labor problems. Telecommunication Services: electronic mail, mfow@pacbell.net. Affiliated With: Seafarers' International Union of North America. Also Known As: Marine Firemen's Union. Formerly: Marine Firemen, Oilers and Watertenders of the Pacific; (1907) Pacific Coast Marine Firemen's Union. Publications: The Marine Fireman, monthly. Newspaper.

23561 ■ Sailors' Union of the Pacific (SUP)
450 Harrison St.
San Francisco, CA 94105
Ph: (415)777-3400 (415)778-5491
Fax: (415)777-5088
E-mail: supwelfarerep@hotmail.com
URL: http://www.sailors.org
Contact: Gunnar Lundeberg, Pres.
Founded: 1885. Members: 1,500. Membership Dues: practical sailor, $130 (quarterly). Staff: 15. Regional Groups: 3. Description: AFL-CIO. Unlicensed crewmembers including able-bodied and ordinary seamen, carpenters, cooks, stewards, and engine department personnel who man U.S.-flagged ships. Seeks to develop and maintain skill and seamanship. Works for legislation to revitalize the American merchant marine; assists other labor organizations. Disseminates information regarding the maritime shipping industry and related union activities. Sponsors seamanship school and training programs. Affiliated With: Seafarers' International Union of North America. Formed by Merger of: (1891) Coast Seamen's Union; (1891) Steamship Sailors' Union. Publications: West Coast Sailors, monthly. Newsletter. Circulation: 5,500. Conventions/Meetings: monthly meeting - always 2nd Monday.

23562 ■ Seafarers' International Union of North America (SIUNA)
5201 Auth Way
Camp Springs, MD 20746
Ph: (301)899-0675
Fax: (301)899-7355
E-mail: webmaster@seafarers.org
URL: http://www.seafarers.org
Contact: Michael Sacco, Pres.
Founded: 1938. Members: 85,000. Description: AFL-CIO. Maintains Seafarers/Harry Lundberg School of Seamanship. Absorbed: (1983) Marine Cooks and Stewards Union. Conventions/Meetings: triennial meeting.

Metal

23563 ■ Institute of the Ironworking Industry (III)
1750 New York Ave. NW
Washington, DC 20006
Ph: (202)783-3998 (202)783-8998
Fax: (202)393-1507
E-mail: institueiw@aol.com
URL: http://www.glfea.org/html/wh-iiows2.htm
Contact: John Schlecht, Exec. Dir.
Founded: 1977. Members: 120. Staff: 5. Budget: $500,000. Description: Sponsored by local associations of steel fabricators and erectors and the International Association of Bridge, Structural and Ornamental Iron Workers (see separate entry). Aims to assist iron working industry workers and employers in solving problems of mutual concern that cannot be resolved within the collective bargaining process. Works to study ways of eliminating potential problems that reduce the competitiveness and inhibit the economic development of the industry. Promotes cooperation among the labor and management associations and promotes friendly relations with the public and public officials. Represents the industry before the American Welding Society and ASTM (see separate entries), and before major construction associations involved in improving building process technology. Sponsors task force of manufacturers, fabricators, erectors, and suppliers who coordinate presentations to architectural/engineering design teams and building owners. Maintains ongoing research program on the development of alternative energy sources. Compiles statistics. Libraries: Type: not open to the public. Awards: Type: recognition. Affiliated With: International Association of Bridge, Structural, Ornamental and Reinforcing Iron Workers. Publications: Directory, periodic. Price: available to members only. Conventions/Meetings: semiannual meeting - always spring and fall, in Washington, DC.

23564 ■ International Association of Bridge, Structural, Ornamental and Reinforcing Iron Workers (IABSORIW)
1750 New York Ave. NW, Ste.400
Washington, DC 20006
Ph: (202)383-4800
Fax: (202)638-4856
E-mail: iwmagazine@iwintl.org
URL: http://www.ironworkers.org
Contact: Joseph Hunt, Gen. Pres.
Founded: 1896. **Members:** 130,000. **Local Groups:** 240. **Description:** AFL-CIO. Improves the working environment in order to provide a safe workplace for every worker. **Committees:** Iron Workers Political Action. **Publications:** *Ironworker*, monthly. Magazine. **Conventions/Meetings:** annual convention ● quinquennial meeting.

23565 ■ Metal Trades Department, AFL-CIO (MTD)
815 16th St. NW
Washington, DC 20006
Ph: (202)508-3705
Fax: (202)508-3706
E-mail: metaltradesweb@aol.com
URL: http://www.metaltrades.org
Contact: Ron Ault, Pres.
Founded: 1908. **Members:** 21. **Description:** Federation of labor unions in fields of metals manufacturing, fabrication, and processing, representing over five million individuals including electrical workers, machinists, boilermakers, carpenters, iron workers, molders, sheet metal workers, stove mounters, and others. Coordinates negotiating, organizing, and legislative efforts of metalworking and related crafts and trade unions; works to improve benefits and working conditions for metal trades workers. **Publications:** *Metaletter*, quarterly. Newsletter. ISSN: 0047-6870. Alternate Formats: online. **Conventions/Meetings:** biennial meeting - always odd-numbered years ● biennial National Ship Building Conference - meeting - always even-numbered years.

23566 ■ Sheet Metal Workers' International Association (SMWIA)
1750 New York Ave. NW
Washington, DC 20006
Ph: (202)783-5880
E-mail: info@smwia.org
URL: http://www.smwia.org
Contact: Michael J. Sullivan, Gen. Pres.
Founded: 1888. **Members:** 150,000. **Description:** Aims to establish and maintain desirable working conditions and thus provide comfort, happiness and security to which every citizen is entitled in return for his labor. Gives a "fair day's work for a fair day's pay". **Committees:** Political Action. **Publications:** *Sheet Metal Workers' Journal*, bimonthly. Contains documents of work of the international and its locals in the U.S. and Canada. **Price:** $7.50 for members. ISSN: 1528-2805 ● Directory, annual ● Newsletter, monthly. **Conventions/Meetings:** annual conference.

23567 ■ United Steelworkers of America (USWA)
5 Gateway Ctr.
Pittsburgh, PA 15222
Ph: (412)562-2400
E-mail: webmaster@usw.org
URL: http://www.uswa.com
Contact: Leo W. Gerard, Pres.
Founded: 1937. **Members:** 750,000. **Membership Dues:** associate, $120 (annual) ● student, unemployed, $60 (annual). **Staff:** 475. **Local Groups:** 3,000. **Description:** Works to build a better future for families. Promotes fairness, justice and equality both on the job and in the societies. **Libraries: Type:** reference. **Holdings:** video recordings. **Absorbed:** (1944) Aluminum Workers of America; (1967) International Union of Mine, Mill and Smelter Workers; (1971) United Stone and Allied Products Workers of America; (1972) International Union of District 50, Allied and Technical Workers of the United States and Canada; (1985) Upholsterers' International Union of North America. **Formerly:** (1942) Steel Workers Organizing Committee. **Publications:** *Steelabor*, bimonthly.

Magazine. Reports on legislation and regulation affecting the union, union activities at the national and chapter levels, economic developments, pension news. **Price:** free to members and retirees; $5.00 /year for nonmembers. ISSN: 0039-0941. **Circulation:** 925,000 ● *Steelworker Old Time*, quarterly ● *USWALERTS*. Newsletter. Alternate Formats: online. **Conventions/Meetings:** biennial Constitutional Convention - meeting (exhibits).

Mining

23568 ■ United Mine Workers of America (UMWA)
8315 Lee Hwy.
Fairfax, VA 22031
Ph: (703)208-7200
Fax: (703)208-7200
URL: http://www.umwa.org
Contact: Cecil E. Roberts Jr., Pres.
Founded: 1890. **Members:** 240,000. **Description:** Represents coal miners, clean coal technicians, health care workers, truck drivers and school board employees. Fights for safe workplaces, good wages and benefits, and fair representation. **Formerly:** (2003) International Union United Mine Workers of America. **Publications:** *United Mine Workers Journal*, monthly. Alternate Formats: online. **Conventions/Meetings:** quadrennial meeting.

Newspapers

23569 ■ The Newspaper Guild (TNG)
501 3rd St. NW, Ste.250
Washington, DC 20001-2760
Ph: (202)434-7177 (202)434-1262
Free: (800)585-5TNG
Fax: (202)434-1472
E-mail: guild@cwa-union.org
URL: http://www.newsguild.org
Contact: Linda K. Foley, Pres.
Founded: 1933. **Members:** 36,000. **Staff:** 16. **Budget:** $4,000,000. **Regional Groups:** 7. **Local Groups:** 100. **National Groups:** 2. **Languages:** English, French, Spanish. **Description:** AFL-CIO; Canadian Labour Congress, and International Federation of Journalists. Sponsors Newspaper Guild International Pension Fund that provides retirement benefits to persons employed in the news industry. **Libraries: Type:** reference. **Holdings:** 900; books, periodicals. **Subjects:** labor, news industry. **Awards:** David Barr Scholarship Fund. **Frequency:** annual. **Type:** scholarship. **Recipient:** for studies in labor law ● Heywood Broun Award. **Frequency:** annual. **Type:** recognition. **Recipient:** for outstanding journalistic achievement. **Telecommunication Services:** electronic mail, lfoley@cwa-union.org. **Departments:** Collective Bargaining; Human Rights; Organizing; Research and Information. **Formerly:** (1972) American Newspaper Guild. **Publications:** *Constitution*, annual. Contains the Newspaper Guild constitution. **Price:** $5.00. ISSN: 0017-5408 ● *Guild Reporter*, monthly. Newspaper. **Price:** $30.00 outside U.S.; $20.00 in U.S. and Canada. ISSN: 0017-5404. **Circulation:** 37,000 ● *Newspaper Guild—Proceedings*, annual. **Price:** $5.00/copy ● Directory, semiannual. **Conventions/Meetings:** annual Sector Meeting - usually summer for 2 days.

23570 ■ Wire Service Guild (WSG)
c/o Local 31222 The Newspaper Guild/Communications Workers of America
424 W 33rd St., Ste.260
New York, NY 10001
Ph: (212)869-9290
Fax: (212)840-0687
E-mail: union@newsmediaguild.org
URL: http://www.newsmediaguild.org
Description: Newspaper Guild/Communications Workers.

Organizations Staff

23571 ■ International Civil Service Commission (ICSC)
2 United Nations Plz., 10th Fl.
New York, NY 10017
Ph: (212)963-5465
Fax: (212)963-0159
E-mail: icscmail@un.org
URL: http://icsc.un.org
Contact: Mr. John P. Hamilton, Exec. Sec.
Founded: 1974. **Members:** 15. **Staff:** 45. **Budget:** $5,000,000. **Languages:** English, French, Russian, Spanish. **Description:** Recommends and establishes terms and conditions of employment for approximately 50,000 United Nations system staff, which includes the U.N. and its specialized agencies. Focuses on such issues as salaries, allowances, classification standards, and personnel policies. **Affiliated With:** United Nations. **Also Known As:** Commission de la Fonction Publique Internationle. **Publications:** *Common System*, biennial ● Annual Report, annual. ISSN: 0251-9321. Alternate Formats: online. **Conventions/Meetings:** semiannual meeting - usually March and July, New York, NY.

23572 ■ OAS Staff Association (OASSA)
1889 F St. NW, 8th Fl., Ste.347A
Washington, DC 20006
Ph: (202)458-6230 (202)458-6231
Fax: (202)458-3466
E-mail: staffsecr@oas.org
URL: http://staff.oas.org/english/default.asp
Contact: Mrs. Corina Alvarez, Admin.
Founded: 1928. **Members:** 605. **Staff:** 1. **Languages:** English, French, Portuguese, Spanish. **Multinational. Description:** Staff members of the Organization of American States (see separate entry) General Secretariat. Serves as a union to negotiate employment conditions and labor rights with the OAS administration. **Computer Services:** database. **Formerly:** (2005) Staff Association of the Organization of American States. **Publications:** *Staff News* (in English and Spanish), published as needed. Newsletter. Contains information regarding staff issues. **Price:** available to members only. **Circulation:** 500. **Conventions/Meetings:** annual meeting.

23573 ■ United Nations Staff Union (UNSU)
Secretariat Bldg., Rm. S-0525
New York, NY 10017
Ph: (212)963-7075
Fax: (212)963-3367
URL: http://www.unstaff.org
Contact: Mr. Stephen Kisambira, Pres.
Founded: 1946. **Members:** 11,000. **Staff:** 26,000. **Budget:** $2,000,000. **Regional Groups:** 14. **Local Groups:** 60. **Languages:** Arabic, English, French, Spanish. **Description:** Individuals employed by the United Nations. Engages in collective bargaining to represent the interests of UN employees. **Libraries: Type:** reference; not open to the public. **Holdings:** articles, books, periodicals. **Subjects:** global issues. **Formerly:** (1971) United Nations Staff Association. **Publications:** *UN Staff Report*, every 4-6 weeks. Newspaper. Includes schedule of meeting times and places for UN committees. **Price:** free. **Circulation:** 23,000. **Advertising:** accepted. **Conventions/Meetings:** annual general assembly, for safety and security of UN staff in line of duty.

Paints and Finishes

23574 ■ International Union of Painters and Allied Trades (IUPAT)
1750 New York Ave. NW
Washington, DC 20006
Ph: (202)637-0700 (202)637-0760
E-mail: mail@iupat.org
URL: http://www.ibpat.org
Contact: James A. Williams, Gen. Pres.
Members: 140,000. **Description:** Serves as labor union representing painters and the allied trades.

Awards: S. Frank Raftery Scholarship. **Frequency:** annual. **Type:** scholarship. **Recipient:** to sons, daughters, or legally adopted dependents of IUPAT members in good standing. **Telecommunication Services:** electronic mail, askthegeneralpresident@ iupat.org. **Publications:** *Painters and Allied Trades Journal*, quarterly. **Advertising:** accepted. Alternate Formats: online.

Pensions

23575 ■ Association of Public Pension Fund Auditors (APPFA)
PO Box 2407
ESP Sta.
Albany, NY 12220
E-mail: webmaster@appfa.org
URL: http://www.appfa.org
Contact: Marci Sundbeck, Pres.
Founded: 1991. **Members:** 44. **State Groups:** 25. **National Groups:** 2. **Description:** Aims to unify and encourage cooperation among public pension fund auditors, to provide comprehensive professional development opportunities on pension related topics, to promote and maintain high professional standards for internal auditors of public retirement systems, and to encourage and facilitate research, publication, and dissemination of information among the membership. **Conventions/Meetings:** annual Professional Development - conference.

Performing Arts

23576 ■ Actors' Equity Association (AEA)
165 W 46th St.
New York, NY 10036
Ph: (212)869-8530
Fax: (212)719-9815
E-mail: info@actorsequity.org
URL: http://www.actorsequity.org
Contact: Mark Zimmerman, Pres.
Founded: 1913. **Members:** 41,000. **Membership Dues:** initiation fee, $1,100 ● basic, $118 (annual). **Staff:** 120. **Budget:** $10,000,000. **Description:** Represents American actors and stage managers working in the professional theatre industry. Negotiates wages and working conditions, administered contracts, and enforced the provisions of various agreements with theatrical employers. Maintains Actors' Equity Foundation that makes grants and awards to organizations or charities that work in the best interests of theatre. **Awards: Type:** grant. **Recipient:** for organizations or charities that work in the best interests of the theatre ● **Type:** recognition. **Recipient:** for organizations or charities that work in the best interests of the theatre. **Publications:** *Equity News*, 10/year. Features news and information regarding the union. **Price:** included in membership dues; $20.00 /year for nonmembers. **Conventions/ Meetings:** biennial meeting - always in New York.

23577 ■ American Federation of Musicians of the United States and Canada (AFM)
1501 Broadway, Ste.600
New York, NY 10036
Ph: (212)869-1330
Fax: (212)764-6134
E-mail: presoffice@afm.org
URL: http://www.afm.org
Contact: Thomas F. Lee, Pres.
Founded: 1896. **Members:** 110,000. **Local Groups:** 250. **Languages:** English, French. **Description:** Union representing the interests of professional musicians through collective bargaining, benefits, and services. **Committees:** Political Action Committee TEMPO. **Departments:** Touring, Theater and Booking. **Divisions:** Electronic Media Services; Symphonic Services. **Publications:** *International Musician*, monthly. Magazine. **Price:** $39.00 for nonmembers in U.S.; $54.00 for nonmembers outside U.S. **Advertising:** accepted. **Conventions/Meetings:** biennial convention.

23578 ■ American Guild of Musical Artists (AGMA)
1430 Broadway, 14th Fl.
New York, NY 10018
Ph: (212)265-3687
Fax: (212)262-9088
E-mail: agma@musicalartists.org
URL: http://www.musicalartists.org
Contact: Linda Mays, Pres.
Founded: 1936. **Members:** 5,500. **Budget:** $2,000,000. **Regional Groups:** 11. **Description:** AFL-CIO. Represents opera and classical concert singers, classical ballet and modern dance performers, and affiliated stage directors, stage managers and choreographers. **Convention/Meeting:** none. **Publications:** *AGMAzine*, 3/year. Newsletter. **Price:** included in membership dues. **Circulation:** 6,000.

23579 ■ American Guild of Variety Artists (AGVA)
363 7th Ave., 17 Fl.
New York, NY 10001
Ph: (212)675-1003
Fax: (212)633-0097
Contact: Frances Gaar, Exec.Sec.-Treas.
Members: 5,000. **Regional Groups:** 16. **Description:** AFL-CIO. **Conventions/Meetings:** annual meeting.

23580 ■ American Musicians Union (AMU)
c/o Ben Intorre
8 Tobinct
Dumont, NJ 07628
Ph: (201)384-5378
Contact: Ben Intorre, Pres.Treas.
Founded: 1947. **Membership Dues:** individual, $30 (annual) ● initiation fee, $10. **Description:** Independent musicians, vocalists, and band managers. Promotes the welfare of member musicians and the exchange of information. Offers legal guidance and life insurance. Sponsors lectures. **Publications:** *List of Members in Good Standing*, periodic. Membership Directory. **Advertising:** accepted ● *Quarternote*, quarterly. Newsletter. Includes information on music and instruments, obituaries, new member information, and Drummers Corner. **Price:** included in membership dues; $5.00 /year for nonmembers. **Circulation:** 300. **Advertising:** accepted ● *What You Should Know About AMU*. Pamphlet.

23581 ■ Associated Actors and Artistes of America (4A's)
165 W 46th St.
New York, NY 10036
Ph: (212)869-0358
URL: http://www.aflcio.org/aboutus/unions
Contact: Theodore Bikel, Pres.
Founded: 1919. **Staff:** 1. **Nonmembership. Description:** AFL-CIO. Serves as international body consisting of 7 national unions within the performing arts field, each autonomous in its particular jurisdiction. Includes members such as: Actors' Equity Association; American Federation of Television and Radio Artists; American Guild of Musical Artists; American Guild of Variety Artists; Hebrew Actors' Union; Guild of Italian American Actors; and Screen Actors Guild. **Conventions/Meetings:** biennial convention - always second Thursday of June, in New York City.

23582 ■ Association of Theatrical Press Agents and Managers (ATPAM)
1560 Broadway, Ste.700
New York, NY 10036-2501
Ph: (212)719-3666
Fax: (212)302-1585
E-mail: info@atpam.com
URL: http://www.atpam.com
Contact: Gordon G. Forbes, Sec.-Treas.
Founded: 1928. **Members:** 700. **Membership Dues:** individual, $180 (annual). **Staff:** 7. **Description:** Labor union for theatrical managers, press agents, and marketing directors. **Awards:** Milton Weintraub Scholarship. **Frequency:** annual. **Type:** scholarship. **Recipient:** for members and relatives of members.

Telecommunication Services: electronic mail, gforbes@atpam.com. **Affiliated With:** AFL-CIO. **Publications:** *Hi-Lites*, bimonthly. Newsletter. **Circulation:** 700. **Conventions/Meetings:** meeting - 3/year; always April, June, and October, in New York City.

23583 ■ Guild of Italian American Actors (GIAA)
Canal St. Sta.
PO Box 123
New York, NY 10013-0123
Ph: (212)420-6590
E-mail: info@giaa.us
URL: http://www.giaa.us
Contact: Guy Palumbo, Pres.
Founded: 1937. **Members:** 250. **Membership Dues:** individual, $60 (annual) ● individual (initiation fee), $350 ● senior, minor, $40 (annual) ● senior, minor (initiation fee), $250. **Languages:** English, Italian. **Description:** AFL-CIO. **Affiliated With:** Associated Actors and Artistes of America. **Formerly:** (1998) Italian Actors Union. **Conventions/Meetings:** semiannual meeting, for members only.

23584 ■ International Alliance of Theatrical Stage Employees, Moving Picture Technicians, Artists and Allied Crafts of the United States, Its Territories and Canada (IATSE)
1430 Broadway, 20th Fl.
New York, NY 10018
Ph: (212)730-1770
Fax: (212)730-7809
E-mail: organizing@iatse-intl.org
URL: http://www.iatse-intl.org
Contact: Thomas C. Short, International Pres.
Founded: 1893. **Members:** 105,000. **Local Groups:** 500. **Multinational. Description:** AFL-CIO; Canadian Labour Congress. Conducts training programs in crafts. **Libraries: Type:** reference. **Holdings:** archival material, books, business records, clippings. **Awards:** Alfred W. DiTolla/Richard F. Walsh/Harold P. Spivak Foundation Scholarship. **Frequency:** annual. **Type:** scholarship. **Recipient:** for members' children. **Departments:** Organizing; Stagecraft; Tradeshow and Display. **Formerly:** (1997) International Alliance of Theatrical Stage Employees, Motion Picture Technicians, Artists and Allied Crafts of the U.S. and Canada; (2001) International Alliance of Theatrical Stage Employees, Motion Picture Technicians, Artists and Allied Crafts of the U.S., U.S. Territories and Canada. **Publications:** *Official Bulletin* (in English and French), quarterly. **Price:** included in membership dues; $3.00 /year for nonmembers. ISSN: 0020-5885. **Circulation:** 100,000. Alternate Formats: online. **Conventions/Meetings:** quadrennial convention (exhibits).

23585 ■ International Guild of Symphony, Opera and Ballet Musicians (IGSOBM)
c/o Matthew Kocmieroski, Treas.
12724 19th Ave. NE
Seattle, WA 98125
Ph: (206)524-7050
Fax: (206)524-7015
E-mail: mkocmieroski@hotmail.com
URL: http://www.igsobm.org
Contact: Matthew Kocmieroski, Treas.
Founded: 1985. **Members:** 150. **Local Groups:** 4. **Description:** Serves as an Independent labor union. **Also Known As:** The Guild. **Publications:** *The Guild Forum*, quarterly. Newsletter. Alternate Formats: online.

23586 ■ Screen Actors Guild (SAG)
5757 Wilshire Blvd.
Los Angeles, CA 90036-3600
Ph: (323)954-1600
Free: (800)SAG-0767
Fax: (323)549-6603
URL: http://www.sag.org
Contact: Connie Stevens, Sec.-Treas.
Founded: 1933. **Members:** 120,000. **Budget:** $50,000,000. **Local Groups:** 26. **Description:** Represents actors in film, television, industrials, com-

mercials and music videos. Enhances actors working conditions, compensation and benefits. AFL-CIO. Compiles statistics. **Awards:** The John L. Dales Scholarship Fund. **Frequency:** annual. **Type:** scholarship. **Recipient:** for members and their children ● Screen Actors Guild Awards. **Frequency:** annual. **Type:** recognition. **Recipient:** for best TV and film performances by actors. **Telecommunication Services:** TDD, for deaf performers, (323)549-6648. **Committees:** Affirmative Action; Agents Relations; Film Society; Government Review; Legislative; Performers with Disabilities; Senior Performers; Stuntpersons; Wages and Working Conditions; Women; Young Performers. **Affiliated With:** Associated Actors and Artistes of America; International Federation of Actors. **Publications:** *Hollywood Call Sheet*, bimonthly. Newsletter. Supplements *Screen Actor* magazine; covers official business of the guild and topics of general interest. **Price:** $7.00 /year for nonmembers. ISSN: 1091-8760. **Circulation:** 50,000 ● *Screen Actor*, bimonthly. Magazine. Covers union activities and topics of general interest; includes obituaries. **Price:** included in membership dues; $7.00 /year for nonmembers. ISSN: 1094-317X. **Circulation:** 98,000. **Conventions/Meetings:** semiannual meeting.

23587 ■ Society of Stage Directors and Choreographers (SSDC)
1501 Broadway, Ste.1701
New York, NY 10036-5653
Ph: (212)391-1070
Free: (800)541-5204
Fax: (212)302-6195
E-mail: info@ssdc.org
URL: http://www.ssdc.org/index.php
Contact: Barbara Hauptman, Exec. Dir.
Founded: 1959. **Members:** 1,700. **Membership Dues:** full, $150 (annual) ● initiation, $1,000 (annual) ● associate, $50 (annual). **Staff:** 10. **Budget:** $950,000. **Description:** Independent national labor union representing directors and choreographers in the professional theatre. **Computer Services:** database, membership. **Telecommunication Services:** electronic mail, bhauptman@ssdc.org. **Committees:** Broadway; Dinner Theatre; LORT; Off-Broadway; Outdoor Musical; Resident Stock; Stock. **Publications:** *SSDC Directory*, biennial. **Price:** $10.00 ● *SSDC Notes*, bimonthly. Newsletter. Contains updates on work rules and compensation rates, employment opportunities, and obituaries. **Price:** included in membership dues. **Circulation:** 2,500. **Conventions/Meetings:** semiannual meeting ● seminar.

23588 ■ United Scenic Artists (USA)
29 W 38th St.
New York, NY 10018
Ph: (212)581-0300
Fax: (212)977-2011
E-mail: usamail@usa829.org
URL: http://www.usa829.org
Contact: Beverly Miller, Business Rep.
Founded: 1918. **Members:** 3,000. **Staff:** 20. **Regional Groups:** 3. **State Groups:** 4. **Description:** Provides contracts and benefits for professional scenic designers, scenic artists, costume and lighting designers, diorama and display workers, mural artists, and costume painters employed by television, theatre, motion picture studios, and producers of commercials. **Programs:** Apprenticeship. **Affiliated With:** International Alliance of Theatrical Stage Employees, Moving Picture Technicians, Artists and Allied Crafts of the United States, Its Territories and Canada. **Publications:** Newsletter, monthly. Alternate Formats: CD-ROM; diskette ● Directory, annual. **Conventions/Meetings:** monthly meeting.

Petroleum

23589 ■ Atlantic Independent Union (AIU)
520 Cinnaminson Ave.
Palmyra, NJ 08065
Ph: (856)303-0776
Free: (800)346-4731

Fax: (856)346-0803
E-mail: president@aiuunion.com
Contact: John W. Kerr, Pres.
Founded: 1938. **Members:** 500. **Membership Dues:** oil worker, $24 (monthly). **Staff:** 2. **Local Groups:** 3. **Description:** Labor union representing the oil and chemical industries. Lobbies for favorable legislation; conducts contract negotiation. **Publications:** *AIU News*, quarterly. Newspaper. **Advertising:** accepted. **Conventions/Meetings:** monthly board meeting ● annual meeting.

23590 ■ Distribution Contractors Association (DCA)
101 W Renner Rd., Ste.460
Richardson, TX 75082-2024
Ph: (972)680-0261
Fax: (972)680-0461
E-mail: dca@dca-online.org
URL: http://www.dca-online.org
Contact: Dennis J. Kennedy, Exec. VP
Founded: 1961. **Members:** 150. **Membership Dues:** regular, $2,000 (annual) ● associate, $750 (annual). **Staff:** 4. **Budget:** $750,000. **Description:** Gas distribution pipeline contractors; manufacturers and supply companies serving the pipeline construction industries are associate members; officials of gas utility companies are industry members. Represents members in labor negotiations. Promotes understanding between gas distribution pipeline contractors and gas utility companies; sponsors safety activities; conducts statistical and procedural surveys. **Libraries:** Type: not open to the public. **Awards:** A. Everham Safety Award. **Frequency:** annual. **Type:** recognition. **Recipient:** for safety ● DCA - Dale R. Michels Endowed Scholarship. **Frequency:** annual. **Type:** scholarship. **Recipient:** for employer, spouse or children. **Committees:** Government Relations; Labor; Marketing; Membership; Public Relations; Recognition; Safety; Scholarship; Strategic Planning; Technical. **Affiliated With:** World Federation of Pipe Line Contractors Associations. **Publications:** *DCA Directory & DCA Roster of Officers and Members*, annual. **Advertising:** accepted ● *DCA News*, monthly. Newsletter ● *News Update Letter*, monthly. Contains news updates regarding the association. ● Also publishes safety CD-ROM "New Employee Safety Orientation", NESO. **Conventions/Meetings:** annual convention.

23591 ■ International Union of Petroleum and Industrial Workers (IUPIW)
8131 E Rosecrans Ave.
Paramount, CA 90723
Ph: (562)630-6232
Free: (800)624-5842
Fax: (562)408-1073
E-mail: petroleumworkers@aol.com
Contact: George R. Beltz, Pres.
Founded: 1945. **Members:** 4,000. **Membership Dues:** $25 (monthly). **Description:** AFL-CIO. **Formerly:** (1961) Independent Union of Petroleum Workers; (1974) International Union of Petroleum Workers. **Publications:** *Directory of Officers*, annual ● *IUPIW—Views*, quarterly. Newsletter. Provides information on federal legislation and regulations affecting union members. Includes obituaries. **Price:** included in membership dues; $5.00 /year for nonmembers. **Circulation:** 5,000. **Conventions/Meetings:** quinquennial convention.

Plumbing

23592 ■ United Association of Journeymen and Apprentices of the Plumbing, Pipe Fitting, Sprinkler Fitting Industry of the U.S. and Canada
United Assn. Bldg.
901 Massachusetts Ave. NW
Washington, DC 20001-4397
Ph: (202)628-5823
Fax: (202)628-5024

E-mail: mikeb@uanet.org
URL: http://www.ua.org
Contact: William P. Hite, Gen. Pres.
Founded: 1889. **Members:** 325,000. **Description:** AFL-CIO. Represents the plumbing and pipe fitting industry. Protects members from unjust and injurious competition, and secure through unity of action among all workers of the industry throughout the United States and Canada. **Awards:** Type: recognition. **Committees:** United Association Political Education. **Formerly:** (2002) United Association of Journeymen and Apprentices of the Plumbing and Pipe Fitting Industry of the U.S. and Canada. **Publications:** Journal, monthly. **Conventions/Meetings:** quinquennial meeting.

Police

23593 ■ National Alliance of Police, Security and Corrections Organizations (NAPSCO)
25510 Kelly Rd., Ste.100
Roseville, MI 48066-4932
Free: (866)627-7260
URL: http://www.napsco.org
Contact: David L. Hickey, Chief Operating Off.
Description: Seeks to protect and advance security unions in the U.S. and to advance the professionalism and welfare of security officers through legislation, education, and training.

Postal Workers

23594 ■ American Postal Workers Union (APWU)
1300 L St. NW
Washington, DC 20005
Ph: (202)842-4200 (202)842-8500
Fax: (202)842-4297
E-mail: askthepresident@att.net
URL: http://www.apwu.org
Contact: William Burrus, Pres.
Founded: 1971. **Members:** 320,000. **Staff:** 200. **Budget:** $20,000,000. **State Groups:** 50. **Local Groups:** 1,600. **Description:** AFL-CIO. Works to advance the interest of members. Negotiates, interprets and enforces a national agreement with the U.S. Postal Service. **Libraries:** Type: reference. **Holdings:** archival material, audiovisuals, books, clippings, monographs, periodicals. **Subjects:** collective bargaining. **Awards:** Hallbeck. Type: scholarship. **Departments:** Legislative; Research and Education; Retirees. **Divisions:** Clerk; Delivery; Maintenance; Motor Vehicle; Support Services. **Formed by Merger of:** United Federation of Postal Clerks. **Publications:** *American Postal Worker*, monthly. Newspaper. Covers union information, contact negotiations, and postal legislation. **Price:** $3.00/year. ISSN: 0044-7811. **Circulation:** 268,000 ● *American Postal Workers Union, AFL-CIO—News Service*, periodic. Covers union topics and legislative news. **Circulation:** 24,000. **Conventions/Meetings:** biennial meeting.

23595 ■ National Alliance of Postal and Federal Employees (NAPFE)
1628 11th St. NW
Washington, DC 20001
Ph: (202)939-6325
Fax: (202)939-6389
E-mail: headquarters@napfe.org
URL: http://www.napfe.com
Contact: James M. McGee, Pres.
Founded: 1913. **Members:** 70,000. **Membership Dues:** associate, $60 (annual). **Budget:** $2,000,000. **Regional Groups:** 10. **Local Groups:** 143. **Description:** Independent. Works to eliminate employment discrimination. **Awards:** Type: scholarship. **Recipient:** to dependent children of members. **Committees:** National Alliance for Political Action; Scholarship. **Departments:** Insurance; Labor Relations. **Divisions:** Auxiliary; Federal Credit Union; Management; Research and Program Development; Retirees; Youth. **Affiliated With:** World Confederation of Labour. **Formerly:** (1968) National Alliance of Postal

Employees. **Publications:** *Credit Union Newsletters* ● *National Alliance*, monthly. Magazine. Covers the postal and other branches of the federal service. **Price:** $13.00/year; $1.50/copy. ISSN: 0027-8513. **Circulation:** 15,000. **Advertising:** accepted. Alternate Formats: online ● Monographs. **Conventions/Meetings:** biennial Convocation - meeting.

23596 ■ National Association of Letter Carriers of the U.S.A. (NALC)
100 Indiana Ave. NW
Washington, DC 20001-2144
Ph: (202)393-4695
Fax: (202)737-1540
E-mail: nalcinf@nalc.org
URL: http://www.nalc.org
Contact: William H. Young, Pres.
Founded: 1889. **Members:** 300,000. **Regional Groups:** 15. **State Groups:** 50. **Local Groups:** 2,600. **Description:** AFL-CIO. Provides Collective Bargaining representation for city delivery letter carriers employed by the U.S. Postal Service. Maintains information center. **Libraries:** Type: reference. **Holdings:** 5,000. **Subjects:** labor, postal, economic. **Committees:** Letter Carriers' Political Education. **Departments:** Compensation; Legislation and Political Action; Retirement. **Also Known As:** National Association of Letter Carriers. **Publications:** *Carrying the Mail*. Pamphlet ● *NALC Activist*, quarterly. Features practical information for branch leaders. **Circulation:** 12,000 ● *NALC Bulletin*, biweekly. **Circulation:** 13,000. Alternate Formats: online ● *NALC Retiree*, biweekly. Newsletter. **Price:** free for members; $1.20 /year for nonmembers. ISSN: 8750-863X. **Circulation:** 86,000 ● *Postal Record*, monthly. Magazine. Covers membership and union activities. Includes election notices, state and district news, and obituaries. **Price:** included in membership dues; $16.00 /year for nonmembers. ISSN: 0032-5376. **Circulation:** 310,000. **Conventions/Meetings:** biennial convention - 2008 July 21-25, Boston, MA.

23597 ■ National Association of Postal Supervisors (NAPS)
1727 King St., Ste.400
Alexandria, VA 22314-2700
Ph: (703)836-9660
Fax: (703)836-9665
E-mail: napshq@naps.org
URL: http://www.naps.org
Contact: Ted Keating, Pres.
Founded: 1908. **Members:** 36,000. **Membership Dues:** national, $78 (annual). **Staff:** 4. **Budget:** $3,000,000. **Local Groups:** 375. **Description:** Represents first-line supervisors who work both in facilities where postal employees process mail and where they deliver mail. Promotes and cooperates with USPS and other agencies of the federal government in a continuing effort to improve the service. **Committees:** Supervisors Political Action. **Publications:** *The Postal Supervisor*, monthly. Magazine. **Price:** $18.00 for nonmembers; included in membership dues. ISSN: 0032-5384. **Circulation:** 35,000. Alternate Formats: online. **Conventions/Meetings:** biennial convention - 2008 Sept. 8-12, Louisville, KY; 2010 Aug. 9-13, Orlando, FL.

23598 ■ National League of Postmasters of the United States (NLPM)
One Beltway Ctr.
5904 Richmond Hwy., Ste.500
Alexandria, VA 22303-1864
Ph: (703)329-4550
Fax: (703)329-0466
E-mail: information@postmasters.org
URL: http://www.postmasters.org
Contact: Charles Mapa, Pres.
Founded: 1887. **Members:** 27,000. **Staff:** 35. **Budget:** $12,000,000. **Regional Groups:** 10. **State Groups:** 51. **Description:** Independent. Sponsors the Postmasters Benefit Plan, an insurance program operated under the Federal Employees Health Benefit Program (FEHBP). Represents postmasters and other federal employees before Congress. Conducts annual league forum and national convention for league officer training. **Libraries:** Type: refer-

ence. **Holdings:** archival material. **Awards:** Postmaster of the Year. **Frequency:** annual. **Type:** recognition. **Recipient:** for service to league, postal service and community. **Telecommunication Services:** electronic mail, cmapa@postmasters.org. **Committees:** Code of Governing Rules; Effective Service; Legislative; Membership; Resolutions; Site Selection. **Programs:** Adverse Action Counselors; Area Coordinators; Car Insurance; Credit Union; District Coordinators; Eyecare; Improved Managers Process; Legal Services; Life Insurance; Long-Term Health Care; Supplemental Dental. **Publications:** *PBP News Bulletin*, periodic. Newsletter. Covers activities of Health Benefit Plan available to members. **Circulation:** 20,000 ● *Postmasters Advocate*, bimonthly. Magazine. Covers activities of members and the U.S. Postal Service. **Price:** $24.00/year. ISSN: 0032-5511. **Circulation:** 30,000. **Advertising:** accepted ● *Postmasters Advocate Express*, periodic. Newsletter. **Price:** included in subscription to magazine. ISSN: 0199-7157. **Circulation:** 30,000. **Conventions/Meetings:** annual convention (exhibits) ● annual League Forum - meeting (exhibits) - always February.

23599 ■ National Postal Mail Handlers Union (NPMHU)
1101 Connecticut Ave. NW, Ste.500
Washington, DC 20036-4325
Ph: (202)833-9095
Fax: (202)833-0008
E-mail: markgardner@npmhu.org
URL: http://www.npmhu.org
Contact: John F. Hegarty, Pres.
Members: 50,000. **Description:** AFL-CIO. Operates as a division of Laborers' International Union of North America (see separate entry). Aims to negotiate and enforce a National Agreement with the U.S. Postal Service, a contract that establishes wages, cost-of-living adjustments and other pay increases, working conditions, and fringe benefits for all workers within its jurisdiction. **Formerly:** National Association of Post Office and Postal Transportation Service Mail Handlers, Watchmen and Messengers; (1989) National Post Office Mail Handlers, Watchmen, Messengers, and Group Leaders. **Publications:** *The Mail Handler*, quarterly. Magazine. **Price:** included in membership dues. ISSN: 1098-5689. **Circulation:** 52,000. **Advertising:** accepted. Alternate Formats: online ● *Mailhandlers*, monthly. Newspaper. Contains fact sheets for bulletin boards. **Circulation:** 2,000. **Conventions/Meetings:** quadrennial general assembly ● annual Presidents Meeting.

23600 ■ National Rural Letter Carriers' Association (NRLCA)
1630 Duke St., 4th Fl.
Alexandria, VA 22314-3426
Ph: (703)684-5545
URL: http://www.nrlca.org
Contact: Donnie Pitts, Pres.
Founded: 1903. **Members:** 101,000. **Staff:** 20. **Budget:** $10,000,000. **State Groups:** 47. **Description:** Works to improve the methods used by rural letter carriers, to benefit their conditions of labor with the United States Postal Service (USPS), and to promote a fraternal spirit among its members. **Awards:** Membership Awards. **Frequency:** annual. **Type:** recognition. **Recipient:** for membership increase ● PAC Awards. **Frequency:** annual. **Type:** monetary. **Recipient:** for PAC contributions collected. **Computer Services:** database, membership maintenance. **Committees:** Political Action. **Publications:** *National Rural Letter Carrier*, biweekly. Magazine. Covers all issues related to rural letter carriers. **Price:** included in membership dues. **Advertising:** accepted. Also Cited As: *The RFD News* ● Magazine, biweekly. Contains rural letter carrier matters. **Price:** $15.00. ISSN: 0028-0089. **Circulation:** 100,000. **Advertising:** accepted. Alternate Formats: online. **Conventions/Meetings:** annual meeting (exhibits) - always August.

Professions

23601 ■ Department for Professional Employees, AFL-CIO (DPE)
1025 Vermont Ave., Ste.1030
Washington, DC 20005

Ph: (202)638-0320
Fax: (202)628-4379
E-mail: info@dpeaflcio.org
URL: http://www.dpeaflcio.org
Contact: Paul E. Almeida, Pres.
Founded: 1977. **Members:** 25. **Staff:** 8. **Description:** National and international unions representing people in the arts, sciences, and professions. Seeks to stimulate union activity and cooperation among unions representing professional, technical, and allied white collar employees; to encourage such workers to share fully in organized labor's programs; to engage in legislative and public relations activities on behalf of such workers. **Telecommunication Services:** electronic mail, palmeida@aflcio.org. **Supersedes:** Council of AFL-CIO Unions for Professional Employees. **Publications:** *NewsLine*, monthly. Newsletter. Alternate Formats: online ● Report, biennial. Alternate Formats: online. **Conventions/Meetings:** semiannual convention.

Publishing

23602 ■ Independent Association of Publishers' Employees (IAPE)
14 Washington Rd., Ste.521
Princeton Junction, NJ 08550
Ph: (609)799-1520
Fax: (609)716-0626
E-mail: union@iape1096.org
URL: http://www.iape1096.org
Contact: Virgil Hottender, Pres.
Founded: 1937. **Members:** 2,000. **Staff:** 2. **Budget:** $570,000. **Description:** Represents employees of Dow Jones and Company, and Factiva, Inc. Members working in production are covered by individual contracts in the association's organized sites. Provides assistance to Dow Jones employees regarding terms and conditions of employment including collective bargaining and grievances. **Committees:** Bargaining; Grievance; Job Classification; Women's and Minorities' Rights. **Formerly:** (1946) Dow Jones Employees Association. **Publications:** *Media Matters*, periodic. Newsletter. **Conventions/Meetings:** semiannual board meeting - always spring and fall.

Railroads

23603 ■ American Train Dispatchers Department of the BLE (ATDA)
1370 Ontario St., Ste.1040
Cleveland, OH 44113-1736
Ph: (216)241-2770
Fax: (216)241-6286
E-mail: atdamccann@aol.com
URL: http://www.atda.us
Contact: Mr. F.L. McCann, Intl. Pres.
Founded: 1917. **Members:** 2,000. **Membership Dues:** associate, $25 (annual) ● active extra, $285 (annual) ● active, $570 (annual). **Staff:** 10. **Local Groups:** 40. **Description:** AFL-CIO. **Libraries:** Type: reference. **Formerly:** (2001) American Train Dispatchers Association. **Publications:** *The Train Dispatcher*, quarterly. **Conventions/Meetings:** quadrennial general assembly.

23604 ■ Brotherhood of Locomotive Engineers and Trainmen, A Division of the Rail Conference of the International Brotherhood of Teamsters (BLET)
1370 Ontario St., Mezzanine
Cleveland, OH 44113-1701
Ph: (216)241-2630
Fax: (216)241-6516
E-mail: hahs@ble-t.org
URL: http://www.ble.org
Contact: Don M. Hahs, Natl. Pres.
Founded: 1863. **Members:** 59,000. **Staff:** 30. **Description:** Independent. Offers regional educational seminars. Compiles statistics. **Awards:** Type: recognition. **Telecommunication Services:** electronic mail, execstaff@ble.org. **Departments:** Education and Training. **Task Forces:** Safety. **Affiliated With:**

AFL-CIO. **Formerly:** (1864) Brotherhood of the Footboard; (1976) Grand International Brotherhood of Locomotive Engineers; (1993) International Brotherhood of Locomotive Engineers; (2004) Brotherhood of Locomotive Engineers, International. **Publications:** *Locomotive Engineer*, monthly. Newsletter. **Price:** free to members ● *Locomotive Engineers' Journal*, quarterly. Covers rail industry news and trends, book reviews, obituaries, and conference reports. **Price:** free to members and widows; $9.00 /year for nonmembers. ISSN: 0024-5747. **Circulation:** 55,000. **Conventions/Meetings:** quinquennial meeting.

23605 ■ Brotherhood of Maintenance of Way Employees (BMWE)
20300 Civic Center Dr., Ste.320
Southfield, MI 48076-4169
Ph: (248)948-1010
Fax: (248)948-7150
E-mail: fns@bmwe.org
URL: http://www.bmwe.org
Contact: Freddie N. Simpson, Pres.
Founded: 1887. **Members:** 60,000. **Regional Groups:** 45. **Local Groups:** 965. **Description:** AFL-CIO; Canadian Labour Congress. Represents and protects the rights of rail workers who build and maintain the track and structures on railroads throughout the United States of America. **Awards: Frequency:** annual. **Type:** scholarship. **Recipient:** for promising student member. **Publications:** *Railway Journal*, bimonthly. **Price:** $20.00 in U.S. and Canada. ISSN: 1049-8921. **Circulation:** 60,000. **Advertising:** accepted ● Directory, quarterly. **Conventions/Meetings:** quadrennial meeting.

23606 ■ Brotherhood of Railroad Signalmen (BRS)
917 Shenandoah Shores Rd.
Front Royal, VA 22630-6418
Ph: (540)622-6522
Fax: (540)622-6532
E-mail: signalman@brs.org
URL: http://www.brs.org
Contact: W.D. Pickett, Pres.
Founded: 1901. **Members:** 13,000. **Description:** AFL-CIO. **Publications:** *Signalman's Journal*, bimonthly ● Reports. **Conventions/Meetings:** triennial meeting.

23607 ■ Brotherhood Railway Carmen Division/Transportation Communications Union (BRC/TCU)
c/o Transportation Communications Union
3 Res. Pl.
Rockville, MD 20850
Ph: (301)948-4910
Fax: (301)948-1369
URL: http://www.members.aol.com/tcucarmen
Contact: Richard A. Johnson, Pres.
Founded: 1888. **Members:** 80,000. **Local Groups:** 560. **Description:** AFL-CIO. A division of the Transportation Communications International Union. **Affiliated With:** Transportation Communications International Union. **Formerly:** (1968) Brotherhood Railway Carmen of America; (1986) Brotherhood Railway Carmen of the U.S. and Canada; (1986) Carmen Division of the Brotherhood of Railway, Airline and Steamship Clerks, Freight Handlers, Express and Station Employees. **Publications:** *TCU Interchange*, monthly. **Conventions/Meetings:** quadrennial meeting.

23608 ■ Transportation Communications International Union (TCU)
3 Res. Pl.
Rockville, MD 20850
Ph: (301)948-4910
Fax: (301)948-1872
URL: http://www.tcunion.org
Contact: Robert A. Scardelletti, Intl. Pres.
Founded: 1899. **Members:** 135,000. **Local Groups:** 500. **Multinational. Description:** AFL-CIO; Canadian Labour Congress. Maintains research and educational programs. Maintains Responsible Citizens

Political League as political action arm. **Libraries: Type:** reference. **Subjects:** labor law, labor history, transportation, labor economics. **Committees:** Political Education. **Departments:** Industry Relations; International Affairs; Legal; Legislative; Manpower Training; Publications; Supervisors. **Divisions:** Canadian. **Absorbed:** (1968) Railway Patrolmen's International Union; (1969) Transportation-Communication Employees Union; (1972) United Transport Service Employees; (1976) Guild of Taxi Drivers; (1978) Brotherhood of Sleeping Car Porters; (1981) American Railway and Airline Supervisors Association; (1983) Western Railway Supervisors Association; (1986) Brotherhood Railway Carmen. **Formerly:** Brotherhood of Railway and Steamship Clerks, Freight Handlers, Express and Station Employees; (1987) Brotherhood of Railway, Airline and Steamship Clerks, Freight Handlers, Express and Station Employees. **Publications:** *Action Lines*, monthly. Newsletter. Covers association, industry and legislative news. ● *Convention Proceedings*, quadrennial ● *Interchange*, bimonthly. Magazine. **Price:** $5.00/year. ISSN: 0033-8869 ● *Leadership in Action: A Manual for Handling Discipline Cases in the Railroad Industry* ● *The Winning Edge*, quarterly. **Conventions/Meetings:** quadrennial meeting ● seminar.

23609 ■ United Transportation Union (UTU)
14600 Detroit Ave.
Cleveland, OH 44107-4250
Ph: (216)228-9400
E-mail: president@utu.org
URL: http://www.utu.org
Contact: Paul C. Thompson, Pres.
Founded: 1969. **Members:** 150,000. **Description:** Promotes the interests of people who work in the transportation industry. **Absorbed:** (1985) Railroad Yardmasters of America. **Formed by Merger of:** Brotherhood of Locomotive Firemen and Enginemen; Brotherhood of Railroad Trainmen; Order of Railway Conductors and Brakemen; Switchmen's Union of North America. **Publications:** *United Transportation Union News*, monthly. **Conventions/Meetings:** quadrennial meeting.

Retailing

23610 ■ Retail, Wholesale and Department Store Union (RWDSU)
30 E 29th St.
New York, NY 10016
Ph: (212)684-5300
Fax: (212)779-2809
E-mail: rwdsu@aol.com
URL: http://www.rwdsu.info
Contact: Stewart Applebaum, Pres.
Founded: 1937. **Members:** 130,000. **Description:** Represents workers throughout the United States and Canada. Works in a wide variety of occupations that range from food processing to retail to manufacturing to service and health care. **Additional Websites:** http://www.ufcw.org. **Absorbed:** (1974) Cigar Makers' International Union of America. **Publications:** *Record*, bimonthly. **Conventions/Meetings:** quadrennial meeting.

Rubber

23611 ■ United Steel Workers of America, Rubber/Plastics Industry Conference (R/PIC)
c/o Ron Hoover, Exec. VP
5 Gateway Center
Pittsburgh, PA 15222
Ph: (412)562-2400
E-mail: webmaster@usw.org
URL: http://www.usw.org/usw/program/content/3115.php
Contact: Ron Hoover, Exec. VP
Founded: 1935. **Members:** 90,000. **Regional Groups:** 5. **Local Groups:** 390. **Description:** AFL-CIO, Canadian Labour Congress. **Awards: Type:** scholarship. **Departments:** Arbitration Service; Community Service; Education; Fair Practices; Industrial

Hygiene; Pension and Insurance; Political Education; Public Relations; Research; Safety and Workers' Compensation; Skilled Trades. **Publications:** *United Rubber Worker*, bimonthly. Covers union news and activities; includes obituaries. **Price:** included in membership dues; $5.00 /year for nonmembers. ISSN: 0162-3869. **Circulation:** 160,000.

Security

23612 ■ American Federation of Security Officers
4311 Wilshire Blvd., Ste.302
Los Angeles, CA 90028
Ph: (323)461-3441
Fax: (323)462-8340
E-mail: helpdesk@visualnet.com
URL: http://americanfederationofsecurityofficers.visualnet.com
Contact: Daniel Payne, Sec.-Treas.
Founded: 1947. **Members:** 2,000. **Description:** Independent. Represents security officers. **Conventions/Meetings:** monthly meeting.

23613 ■ International Guards Union of America (IGUA)
Rte. 8, Box 32-14
Amarillo, TX 79118-9427
Ph: (806)622-2424
Fax: (806)622-3500
E-mail: igua@amaonline.com
URL: http://www.amaonline.com/igua
Founded: 1947. **Members:** 1,800. **Staff:** 2. **Regional Groups:** 7. **National Groups:** 40. **Description:** Independent. Represents working guards dedicated to helping other guards. **Conventions/Meetings:** triennial convention.

23614 ■ International Union of Security Officers (IUSO)
2201 Broadway St., Ste.101
Oakland, CA 94612
Ph: (510)625-9913
Free: (800)772-3326
Fax: (510)625-0998
E-mail: seiu247@gmail.com
URL: http://www.seiu247.org
Contact: Steven McClenathan, Pres.
Founded: 1945. **Members:** 10,000. **Staff:** 20. **Description:** Independent. Represents guards and security officers. Seeks to improve wages, hours, and working conditions for security officers and guards. Conducts charitable program and shop steward training program. **Formerly:** (1978) International Union of Guards and Watchmen. **Publications:** Newsletter, bimonthly. **Conventions/Meetings:** quadrennial meeting.

23615 ■ International Union, Security, Police and Fire Professionals of America (SPFPA)
25510 Kelly Rd.
Roseville, MI 48066
Ph: (586)772-7250
Free: (800)228-7492
Fax: (586)772-9644
URL: http://www.spfpa.org
Contact: David L. Hickey, Pres.
Founded: 1948. **Members:** 20,000. **Staff:** 10. **Regional Groups:** 5. **Local Groups:** 200. **Multinational. Description:** Provides services to members. **Libraries: Type:** not open to the public. **Subjects:** unions, labor law. **Awards: Frequency:** annual. **Type:** scholarship. **Departments:** Homeland Security; Information Technology; Organizing; Research and Communication. **Formerly:** (2000) International Union United Plant Guard Workers of America. **Publications:** *The Security Link*, quarterly. Newspaper. Covers contract negotiations of plant security forces nationwide; includes lists of retiring members and obituaries. **Price:** free for members. **Conventions/Meetings:** quinquennial international conference.

23616 ■ Plant Protection Association
302 N Huron
Ypsilanti, MI 48197
Ph: (734)487-5522
Fax: (734)487-5588
E-mail: ppanunion@sbcglobal.net
Contact: Larry Daniel, Pres.
Founded: 1948. **Members:** 500. **Staff:** 6. **Regional Groups:** 2. **Description:** Independent. **Formerly:** (1999) Independent Union of Plant Protection Employees. **Publications:** Newsletter, monthly. **Conventions/Meetings:** annual meeting.

Service

23617 ■ Service Employees International Union (SEIU)
1800 Massachusetts Ave. NW
Washington, DC 20036
Ph: (202)898-3200
Free: (800)424-8592
URL: http://www.seiu.org
Contact: Andrew Stern, Pres.
Founded: 1921. **Members:** 1,800,000. **Languages:** English, Spanish. **Description:** Unites to improve the lives of workers and their families and to create a more just and humane society. **Telecommunication Services:** TDD, (202)898-3481. **Departments:** Communications; Education; Human Rights; International Affairs; Organization; Political; Research. **Absorbed:** (1980) International Jewelry Workers Union. **Formerly:** Building Service Employees' International Union. **Publications:** *Union*, bimonthly ● *Update*, quarterly. **Conventions/Meetings:** quadrennial meeting.

23618 ■ Service Workers United (SWU)
275 7th Ave., 10th Fl.
New York, NY 10001
Ph: (212)265-7000
Free: (888)798-6466
URL: http://www.serviceworkersunited.org
Contact: Kurt Edelman, Pres.
Languages: English, Spanish. **Description:** Seeks to improve the lives of all working people in the service industries. Seeks to obtain optimal conditions of employment for members. Facilitates communication and cooperation among members. **Publications:** *Leader's Edge* (in English and Spanish), quarterly. Newsletter. Contains stories by, for and about SWU shop stewards and other leaders. Alternate Formats: online ● *SWU Voice* (in English and Spanish), periodic. Newsletter. Features members of SWU, speaking about their experiences on the job as new union members. Alternate Formats: online.

Sports

23619 ■ Association of Volleyball Professionals (AVP)
6100 Center Dr., 9th Fl.
Los Angeles, CA 90045
Ph: (310)426-8000
Free: (888)483-2652
Fax: (310)426-8010
E-mail: contact@avp.com
URL: http://web.avp.com/index.jsp
Contact: Doug Willbanks, Contact
Founded: 1983. **Members:** 300. **Staff:** 12. **For-Profit. Description:** Professional Beach Volleyball Tour. Organizes, promotes, executes, and manages tournaments throughout the country. Comprised of the top professional players in the world. Generates sponsorship and pays out player prize money. **Awards:** Best Defensive Player. **Frequency:** annual. **Type:** trophy ● Best Offensive Player. **Frequency:** annual. **Type:** trophy ● MVP. **Frequency:** annual. **Type:** trophy ● Rookie of the Year. **Frequency:** annual. **Type:** trophy. **Additional Websites:** http://www.volleyball.org/avp. **Telecommunication Services:**

hotline, (310)645-7000. **Publications:** *Rule Book* ● Newsletter, monthly. **Price:** free. **Advertising:** accepted. **Conventions/Meetings:** bimonthly board meeting.

23620 ■ National Basketball Players Association (NBPA)
2 Penn Plz., Ste.2430
New York, NY 10121-2400
Ph: (212)655-0880
Fax: (212)655-0881
E-mail: info@nbpa.org
URL: http://www.nbpa.com
Contact: G. William Hunter, Exec. Dir.
Founded: 1962. **Members:** 430. **Staff:** 13. **Description:** Independent association of members of the 29 National Basketball Association teams. Works to improve the performance of NBA players and to represent their interests in collective bargaining with the league. Sponsors educational programs and career counseling. **Awards: Frequency:** annual. **Type:** recognition. **Recipient:** for statistical leaders in basketball. **Affiliated With:** National Basketball Association. **Publications:** *Time Out*, monthly. Newsletter. Covers membership activities. **Price:** free for members only. **Circulation:** 1,200. **Conventions/Meetings:** annual meeting.

23621 ■ Professional Lacrosse Players Association (PLPA)
52 Haynes Rd.
Sudbury, MA 01776
Ph: (401)845-6263
Fax: (401)845-6263
E-mail: plpa@plpa.com
URL: http://www.plpa.com
Contact: Peter E. Schmitz, Pres.
Founded: 1993. **Members:** 178. **Staff:** 4. **Budget:** $35,000. **Description:** Professional lacrosse players participating in the National Lacrosse League. Seeks to obtain optimal conditions of employment for members. Represents members in negotiations with team owners and league officials.

Textiles

23622 ■ Council of the United Textile Workers of America (UTWA)
4207 Lebanon Rd., Ste.200
Hermitage, TN 37076
Ph: (615)889-9221
Fax: (615)885-3102
Contact: Dave Johnson, Pres.
Founded: 1901. **Members:** 20,000. **Budget:** $2,000,000. **Regional Groups:** 5. **State Groups:** 126. **Description:** AFL-CIO. **Affiliated With:** International Confederation of Free Trade Unions. **Publications:** *Textile Challenger*, quarterly. Provides labor, industrial, economic, union, and member news. **Conventions/Meetings:** quadrennial convention.

23623 ■ Textile Converters Association (TCA)
2001 Palmer Ave.
Larchmont, NY 10538
Ph: (914)834-5040
Fax: (914)833-1350
Contact: Sidney Orenstein, Exec.Dir.
Founded: 1958. **Members:** 18. **Staff:** 1. **Description:** Textile converters. Negotiates collective bargaining agreements with labor unions.

Toys

23624 ■ International Union of Allied Novelty and Production Workers (IUANPW)
1950 W Erie St.
Chicago, IL 60622
Ph: (312)738-0822
Free: (800)248-6466

Fax: (312)738-3553
Contact: Mark Spano, Pres.
Members: 22,000. **Description:** AFL-CIO. **Formerly:** (1965) International Union of Doll and Toy Workers of the U.S. and Canada; (1978) International Union of Dolls, Toys, Playthings, Novelties and Allied Products of the U.S. and Canada. **Conventions/Meetings:** quadrennial meeting.

Transportation

23625 ■ Amalgamated Transit Union (ATU)
5025 Wisconsin Ave. NW
Washington, DC 20016-4121
Ph: (202)537-1645
Free: (888)240-1196
Fax: (202)244-7824
E-mail: dispatch@atu.org
URL: http://www.atu.org
Contact: Warren S. George, Pres.
Founded: 1892. **Members:** 180,000. **Description:** Represents transit workers in the United States and Canada. **Committees:** Political Contributions. **Formerly:** (1963) Amalgamated Association of Street, Electric Railway and Motor Coach Employees of America. **Publications:** *In Transit*, bimonthly. Magazine. ISSN: 0019-3291. Alternate Formats: online. **Conventions/Meetings:** triennial meeting.

23626 ■ International Brotherhood of Teamsters (IBT)
25 Louisiana Ave. NW
Washington, DC 20001
Ph: (202)624-6800
URL: http://www.teamster.org
Contact: James P. Hoffa, Pres.
Founded: 1903. **Members:** 1,600,000. **Budget:** $1,400,000. **Local Groups:** 596. **Description:** Workers, retirees, and their family members in transportation, construction, factories, offices, hospitals, public agencies, airlines, movies, convention centers, warehouses, and many other kinds of work places. Fights for a better future for working families. **Libraries: Type:** reference. **Holdings:** 30,000. **Divisions:** Airline; Building Material and Construction Trade; Carhaul; Food Processing; Freight; Industrial Trades; Motion Picture and Theatrical Trade; Parcel and Small Package. **Formed by Merger of:** Team Drivers International Union; Teamsters National Union. **Formerly:** (1940) International Brotherhood of Teamsters, Chauffeurs, Stablemen and Helpers of America. **Publications:** *The New Teamster*, 8/year. Magazine. **Conventions/Meetings:** quinquennial convention.

23627 ■ Teamsters for a Democratic Union (TDU)
PO Box 10128
Detroit, MI 48210
Ph: (313)842-2600
Fax: (313)842-0227
E-mail: webmaster@tdu.org
URL: http://www.tdu.org
Contact: Peter Landon, Contact
Founded: 1976. **Members:** 8,000. **Membership Dues:** individual, $40 (annual) ● individual, $95 (triennial) ● spouse and teamster grossing under $25000, retiree, $25 (annual). **Staff:** 10. **Description:** Rank-and-file members of the International Brotherhood of Teamsters (see separate entry) working to reform the structure and practices of the union and its leadership. Concerns include health insurance fraud, corruption, weak representation, contract negotiations, concessions, and pensions. Initiates coordinated challenges to entrenched leadership, educating members on local and national elections, and sponsoring legal actions. **Absorbed:** (1980) Professional Drivers Council. **Publications:** *Convoy Dispatch*, monthly. Newspaper. **Price:** $35.00/year; included in membership dues. ISSN: 0738-8330. **Circulation:** 60,000. Alternate Formats: online ● Hand-

books. **Conventions/Meetings:** annual Rank and File Convention - always fall.

23628 ■ Transport Workers Union of America (TWU)
1700 Broadway, 2nd Fl.
New York, NY 10019
Ph: (212)259-4900
Fax: (212)265-4537
E-mail: mailbox@twu.org
URL: http://www.twu.org
Contact: James C. Little, Pres.
Founded: 1934. **Members:** 100,000. **Local Groups:** 107. **Description:** Transit, railroad, and airline workers who are members of the AFL-CIO. **Awards:** Michael J. Quill Scholarships. **Frequency:** annual. **Type:** scholarship. **Recipient:** for children of members. **Divisions:** Airline; Gas Utility; Ground Transit; Public Employees; Railroad; University Maintenance. **Publications:** *President's Report*, quadrennial ● *TWU Express*, monthly. Newspaper. **Price:** $2.00/year. ISSN: 0039-8659. Alternate Formats: online ● Also publishes calendar. **Conventions/Meetings:** quadrennial meeting.

Unions

23629 ■ Change to Win (CtW)
1900 L St. NW, Ste.900
Washington, DC 20036
Ph: (202)721-0660
Fax: (202)721-0661
E-mail: info@changetowin.org
URL: http://www.changetowin.org
Contact: Greg Tarpinian, Exec. Dir.
Founded: 2005. **Multinational. Description:** Seeks to renew hope, opportunity and prosperity for American workers and their families. Unites with unions and allies in other countries to negotiate with global corporations to raise living standards and win respect for workers' rights everywhere. Strives to build a movement of working people with the power to provide workers a higher wage, universal health care, a secure retirement and dignity on the job. **Affiliated With:** International Brotherhood of Teamsters; Laborers' International Union of North America; Service Employees International Union; UNITE HERE; United Brotherhood of Carpenters and Joiners of America; United Farm Workers of America; United Food and Commercial Workers International Union. **Publications:** *CtW Connect*. Newsletter. Alternate Formats: online.

23630 ■ Coalition of Black Trade Unionists (CBTU)
PO Box 66268
Washington, DC 20036-6268
Ph: (202)429-1203
Fax: (202)429-1102
URL: http://www.cbtu.org
Contact: Michael Williams, Exec. Dir.
Founded: 1972. **Membership Dues:** rank and file, $30 (annual) ● staff, retired international officer, $75 (annual) ● international officer, $150 (annual) ● retired staff, $37 (annual) ● retired rank and file, $15 (annual). **Description:** Represents members of 76 labor unions united to maximize the strength and influence of black and minority workers in organized labor. Offers voter registration and education, improvement of economic development, and employment opportunities for minority and poor workers. Sponsors regional seminars and holds annual national convention. Conducts coalition-building activities with religious and community based organizations. **Awards:** Addie L. Wyatt Award. **Frequency:** annual. **Type:** recognition. **Recipient:** for active woman in CBTU, her union, her community, politics and other organizations ● CBTU Grasshopper Awards. **Frequency:** annual. **Type:** recognition. **Recipient:** for CBTU members in recognition of their public service or political activism ● Nelson Jack Edwards Award. **Frequency:** annual. **Type:** recognition.

Recipient: for CBTU members in leadership positions. **Committees:** Environmental Justice; International Affairs; Retiree; Women's; Youth. **Publications:** Bulletin, quarterly. **Conventions/Meetings:** annual meeting.

23631 ■ Coalition of Labor Union Women (CLUW)
815 16th St. NW, 2nd Fl. S
Washington, DC 20006
Ph: (202)508-6969
Fax: (202)508-6968
E-mail: info@cluw.org
URL: http://www.cluw.org
Contact: Carol Rosenblatt, Exec. Dir.
Founded: 1974. **Members:** 20,000. **Membership Dues:** regular, associate, $50 (annual) ● new, $35 (annual) ● student, retiree, unemployed, $15 (annual) ● sustaining, $150 (annual) ● supporting, $100 (annual) ● contributing, $75 (annual) ● life, $1,000. **Local Groups:** 75. **Description:** Aims to: unify all union women in order to determine common problems within unions and deal effectively with objectives; promote unionism and encourage unions to be more aggressive in their efforts to bring unorganized women under collective bargaining agreements; inform members about what can be done within the labor movement to achieve equal opportunity and correct discriminatory job situations; educate and inspire union brothers to help achieve affirmative action in the workplace. Seeks to encourage members through action programs of the coalition, to become more active participants in the political and legislative processes of their unions, to seek election to public office or selection for governmental appointive office at local, county, state, and national levels, and to increase their participation in union policymaking. Conducts training programs and project on empowerment of union women. Maintains Coalition of Labor Union Women Center for Education and Research. **Awards: Type:** recognition. **Computer Services:** Mailing lists, email alerts via e-Activist Network. **Telecommunication Services:** electronic mail, csrosenblatt@cluw.org. **Committees:** Education; Minority; Organizing the Unorganized; Political Action. **Programs:** Behind the Label; Legislative Action; Wal-Mart Campaign; Women in the Global Economy. **Publications:** *Bargaining for Family Issues* ● *CLUW News*, 5/year. Newsletter. **Price:** $30.00 for working members; $15.00 for retirees; included in membership dues. ISSN: 0199-8919. Alternate Formats: online ● *Is Your Job Making You Sick?*. **Conventions/Meetings:** biennial convention (exhibits).

23632 ■ Coalition of Labor Union Women Center for Education and Research
815 16th St. NW, 2nd Fl. S
Washington, DC 20006
Ph: (202)508-6969
Fax: (202)508-6968
E-mail: getinfo@cluw.org
URL: http://www.cluw.org
Contact: Carol Rosenblatt, Exec. Dir.
Founded: 1979. **Staff:** 2. **Budget:** $250,000. **Description:** Education arm of the Coalition of Labor Union Women (see separate entry). Promotes the full participation of women in their unions. Provides direction and assistance in the development of union policies and programs that reflect the concerns of women in the workplace. Serves as information and referral clearinghouse. Develops and conducts education and training programs for working women; emphasizes leadership training so that women may become more involved and may advance in the union. Conducts research on issues concerning working women, particularly labor union women. Sponsors Reproductive Rights Project. Maintains speakers' bureau; compiles statistics. **Programs:** Cervical Cancer Prevention Works; Contraceptive Equity; HIV/AIDS Awareness. **Conventions/Meetings:** periodic meeting.

23633 ■ Congress of Independent Unions (CIU)
303 Ridge St.
Alton, IL 62002
Ph: (618)462-2447
Fax: (618)462-5579
Contact: R. Richard Davis, Pres.
Founded: 1958. **Members:** 75,000. **Staff:** 9. **Description:** Members of independent labor unions. Objectives are: to organize nonunionized employees into independent labor unions; to represent independent labor unions; to act as a bargaining agent between labor unions and management. Maintains library. **Publications:** *CIU News*, quarterly. Newsletter. **Conventions/Meetings:** annual meeting.

23634 ■ Industrial Workers of the World Starbucks Workers Union (SWU)
347 Maujer St., Apt. C
Brooklyn, NY 11206
Ph: (917)577-1110
E-mail: starbuckssunion@yahoo.com
URL: http://www.starbucksunion.org
Contact: Tomer Malchi, Contact
Membership Dues: regular, $6 (monthly). **Description:** Represents Starbucks workers around the United States. Works to gain improvements at work including a higher wage, appropriate staffing and guaranteed hours. Facilitates communication and cooperation among members. **Telecommunication Services:** electronic mail, iww.com. **Affiliated With:** Industrial Workers of the World. **Publications:** Bulletins. Alternate Formats: online.

23635 ■ International Labor Organization - U.S.
1828 L St., NW, Ste.600
Washington, DC 20036
Ph: (202)653-7652
Fax: (202)653-7687
E-mail: washilo@ilowbo.org
Founded: 1919. **Staff:** 12. **Description:** National branch of the International Labour Organization. Promotes voluntary cooperation among government, employer, and worker organizations to improve labor conditions and raise living standards. Conducts surveys and research on topics including women in the global workforce. **Libraries: Type:** open to the public. **Subjects:** International Labor Organization only- labor, child labor, women, occupational safety, and health. **Also Known As:** (2000) International Labor Office. **Publications:** *World of Work*, bimonthly. Newsletter. Alternate Formats: online.

23636 ■ International Union of Industrial and Independent Workers (IUIIW)
8131 E Rosecrans Ave., Ste.203
Paramount, CA 90723
Ph: (770)480-4540
Fax: (817)428-9765
E-mail: mitchiuiiw@aol.com
URL: http://www.iuiiw.com
Contact: Joe Beltz, Intl. Pres.
Founded: 1997. **Multinational. Description:** Works to protect the interests and promotes the general welfare of industrial and independent workers. Maintains, protects and advances the economic welfare and collective security of its members. Fosters and extends democratic institutions and civil rights and liberties. Seeks to secure and provide for the exchange of information and advice relative to the benefit and welfare of the members. **Publications:** Newsletter. Alternate Formats: online.

23637 ■ Labor Management Maritime Committee, Inc. (LMMCI)
Address Unknown since 2006
Founded: 1950. **Members:** 7. **Staff:** 2. **Description:** Steamship lines and the AFL_CIO Maritime Committee. **Conventions/Meetings:** annual meeting.

23638 ■ National Conservation District Employees Association (NCDEA)
PO Box 791206
Baltimore, MD 21279-1206
Ph: (202)547-6223
E-mail: cindy.moon@il.nacdnet.net
URL: http://www.ncdea.org
Contact: Cindy Moon, Pres.
Founded: 1992. **Membership Dues:** supporter, $35 (annual) ● advocate, $60 (annual) ● partner, $100 (annual). **Description:** Strengthens and promotes the conservation district programs through assistance, information, and representation. Supports the professionalism of conservation district employees. Assists agencies, associations, organizations, municipalities, groups, or individuals who supports the Conservation organization. **Awards:** Don Aron Scholarship. **Frequency:** periodic. **Type:** scholarship. **Recipient:** for Conservation District employees and their family members pursuing continuing studies in natural resource conservation ● National Conservation District Board Member. **Frequency:** annual. **Type:** recognition. **Recipient:** for outstanding efforts behind the nation's conservation district programs ● National Conservation District Professional. **Frequency:** annual. **Type:** recognition. **Recipient:** for outstanding efforts behind the nation's conservation district programs. **Publications:** Reports. Alternate Formats: online.

23639 ■ National Federation of Independent Unions (NFIU)
1166 S 11th St.
Philadelphia, PA 19147
Ph: (215)336-3300
Free: (888)595-NFIU
E-mail: fjcnfiu@aol.com
URL: http://www.nfiu.org
Contact: Francis J. Chiappardi, Gen. Pres.
Founded: 1963. **Members:** 70,000. **Description:** Federation of more than 300 independent labor unions. Seeks to obtain national recognition and equal representation for independent unions in Washington, DC and elsewhere. Conducts legislative conference. **Committees:** Educational; Legislative. **Formed by Merger of:** Confederated Unions of America; National Independent Union Council. **Publications:** News for Independent Unions, quarterly. **Conventions/Meetings:** annual meeting.

23640 ■ Paper, Allied-Industrial, Chemical and Energy Workers International Union (PACE)
3340 Perimeter Hill Dr.
PO Box 1475
Nashville, TN 37202
Ph: (615)834-8590
Fax: (615)834-7741
E-mail: byoung@paceunion.org
Contact: Boyd Young, Pres.
Founded: 1999. **Members:** 275,000. **Staff:** 100. **Regional Groups:** 10. **Description:** Represents paper manufacturers and oil refiners in the US. Strives to organize workers to stand up for their rights, both in the workplace and in the political arena. **Libraries:** **Type:** open to the public. **Holdings:** 10,000. **Subjects:** labor, labor law. **Publications:** Pacesetter, bimonthly. Magazine. **Price:** free for members. **Circulation:** 275,000. **Conventions/Meetings:** quadrennial convention.

23641 ■ Philippine Workers Support Committee
2252 Puna St.
Honolulu, HI 96817
Ph: (808)595-7362
E-mail: witeck@hawaii.edu
Contact: John Witeck, Coor.
Founded: 1983. **Members:** 60. **Membership Dues:** individual, $10 (annual) ● organization, unions, $25 (annual). **Staff:** 1. **Budget:** $2,000. **Local Groups:** 4. **Description:** Union members and labor supporters. Provides information on the Philippine labor

movement. Organizes solidarity work in support of Philippine workers in the Philippines, North America, and elsewhere. Offers educational and research programs and information and sponsors tours. Maintains speakers' bureau and distributes KMU Correspondence. **Libraries:** **Type:** reference. **Holdings:** audiovisuals, periodicals. **Publications:** KMU Correspondence, published bimonthly, by the Kilusang Mayo Uno labor center in the Philippines and distributed by PWSC in the U.S. (subscription: $20/year for individual, $30/year for institutions, libraries, and overseas subscribers). **Conventions/Meetings:** biennial conference and regional meeting.

23642 ■ Union Label and Service Trades Department, AFL-CIO (ULSTD)
815 16th St. NW
Washington, DC 20006
Ph: (202)508-3700
Fax: (202)508-3701
E-mail: ulstd@unionlabel.org
URL: http://www.unionlabel.org
Contact: Charles E. Mercer, Pres.
Founded: 1909. **Members:** 70. **Staff:** 5. **Description:** Works to promote the official emblems (union labels, shop cards, store cards, and service buttons) of 70 affiliated labor unions. Promotes purchase of union labeled goods and the patronage of union services. Supports boycotts sanctioned by the AFL-CIO Executive Council. **Publications:** Label Letter, bimonthly. Newsletter. **Price:** free for members. ISSN: 0161-9365. Alternate Formats: online ● Bulletin, bimonthly. Covers labor issues. **Price:** free for labor editors. **Circulation:** 800. **Conventions/Meetings:** quadrennial meeting ● annual show.

23643 ■ United Hebrew Trades - New York Division of the Jewish Labor Committee (UHT)
25 E 21st St., 2nd Fl.
New York, NY 10010
Ph: (212)477-0767
Fax: (212)477-1918
E-mail: jlcexec@aol.com
Contact: Syd Bykofsky, Pres.
Founded: 1888. **Membership Dues:** affiliated union local or similar body, $360 (annual). **Staff:** 1. **Description:** Association of union locals working as liaison agency linking local Jewish communal organizations and local labor movement. **Affiliated With:** Jewish Labor Committee. **Formerly:** (1997) United Hebrew Trades of the State of New York; (1998) United Hebrew Trades Division of the Labor Committee; (2001) United Hebrew Trades Division of the Jewish Labor Committee. **Publications:** Labor in the News, 3/year. Newsletter. Contains agency news and labor and Jewish news. **Price:** free. **Circulation:** 2,000. **Conventions/Meetings:** meeting - 10/year.

Utilities

23644 ■ Brotherhood of Utility Workers of New England (BUWNE)
1300 Jefferson Blvd.
Warwick, RI 02886
Ph: (401)738-1223
Fax: (401)738-1180
Contact: Lorie Stenovich, Sec.
Founded: 1934. **Members:** 4,600. **Budget:** $50,000. **Description:** Independent. **Publications:** Labor Lines, quarterly. Newsletter. **Conventions/Meetings:** biennial meeting.

23645 ■ Utility Workers Union of America, AFL-CIO (UWUA)
815 16th St. NW
Washington, DC 20006
Ph: (202)974-8200
Free: (888)843-8982
Fax: (202)974-8201

E-mail: rfarley@aflcio.org
URL: http://www.uwua.net
Contact: Donald Wightman, Pres.
Founded: 1945. **Members:** 50,000. **Staff:** 24. **Regional Groups:** 5. **State Groups:** 4. **Local Groups:** 240. **Description:** Affiliated with the AFL-CIO. Works to unite workers in utility and related industries, to promote through collective bargaining higher wages and improvement in terms and conditions of employment for members, and to secure legislation safeguarding the economic security and social welfare of workers in the industry. Sponsors educational conferences for local officers. **Libraries:** **Type:** reference. **Awards:** National Merit UWUA Scholarship. **Frequency:** annual. **Type:** scholarship. **Recipient:** to members' children. **Publications:** Light, quarterly. Magazine. Contains news of the regions, contract negotiations, union nominations and elections; lists obituaries and retirements. ISSN: 0456-0434. **Circulation:** 60,000. **Conventions/Meetings:** quadrennial meeting (exhibits).

Writers

23646 ■ National Writers Union (NWU)
113 Univ. Pl., 6th Fl.
New York, NY 10003
Ph: (212)254-0279
Fax: (212)254-0673
E-mail: nwu@nwu.org
URL: http://www.nwu.org
Contact: Gerard Colby, Pres.
Founded: 1983. **Membership Dues:** writer (with income less than $4500), $120 (annual) ● writer (with income between $4501 and $15000), $195 (annual) ● writer (with income between $15001 and 30000), $265 (annual) ● writer (with income between $30001 and $45000), $315 (annual) ● writer (with income between $45001 and $60000), $340 (annual). **Staff:** 10. **Budget:** $1,279,905. **Local Groups:** 19. **Languages:** English, Spanish. **Description:** Freelance writers; journalists, authors, poets, and technical and public relations writers who are not represented by any existing union. Engages in collective bargaining and provides other services for members such as grievance handling and health insurance. Works to raise rates and improve treatment of freelance writers by magazine and book publishers. Holds conferences on legal, economic, trade, and craft issues affecting writers. **Telecommunication Services:** electronic mail, gcolby@nwu.org. **Supersedes:** Organizing Committee for a National Writers Union. **Publications:** American Writer, quarterly. Magazine. Contains organization news, classified ads, and listing of latest books by NWU members. **Price:** free for members. **Circulation:** 8,000. **Advertising:** accepted. Alternate Formats: online ● Freelance Writers' Guide. Handbook. **Price:** $29.15 plus shipping and handling ● Newsletters. **Conventions/Meetings:** annual Delegates Assembly - conference.

23647 ■ Writers Guild of America, East (WGAE)
555 W 57th St., Ste.1230
New York, NY 10019
Ph: (212)767-7800
Fax: (212)582-1909
E-mail: info@wgaeast.org
URL: http://www.wgaeast.org
Contact: Mona Mangan, Exec. Dir.
Founded: 1954. **Members:** 4,000. **Staff:** 22. **Budget:** $3,500,000. **Description:** Labor union for professional writers in motion pictures, television and radio. Provides script registration service for literary material. **Awards:** Outstanding Achievement in Broadcast News Graphics. **Frequency:** annual. **Type:** recognition ● Outstanding Achievement in Television, Radio and Screenwriting Award. **Frequency:** annual. **Type:** recognition. **Telecommunication Services:** electronic mail, calbers@wgae.org. **Funds:** Theater Development. **Programs:** Legal Services. **Affiliated With:** Writers Guild of America, West. **Publications:**

Agents List, bimonthly ● *Theatrical and Television Minimum Basic Agreement* ● *Writers Guild of America, East—Newsletter*, 11/year. Includes list of new members. **Price:** $22.00/year. **Advertising:** accepted ● *Writers Guild of America Membership Directory*, biennial ● Reports. **Conventions/Meetings:** annual meeting - always September, New York City.

23648 ■ Writers Guild of America, West (WGA)
7000 W Third St.
Los Angeles, CA 90048
Ph: (323)951-4000
Free: (800)548-4532
Fax: (323)782-4800

E-mail: website@wga.org
URL: http://www.wga.org
Contact: John McLean, Exec. Dir.
Founded: 1954. **Members:** 8,500. **Staff:** 110. **Description:** Labor union for writers in the fields of motion pictures, television, cable, radio, and new technologies. Represents members in collective bargaining and other labor matters. Works to obtain adequate domestic and foreign copyright legislation and to promote better copyright relations between U.S. and other countries. Maintains Writers Guild Foundation to promote excellence in writing through seminars and library provisions of scripts and books on the entertainment industry written by guild members. Sponsors research programs; compiles statistics. **Libraries: Type:** open to the public. **Holdings:** articles, books, films, periodicals, video recordings. **Awards:** Writers Guild. **Frequency:** annual. **Type:** recognition. **Recipient:** for writing and career achievements. **Departments:** National Council; WGAW Board. **Affiliated With:** Writers Guild of America, East. **Formed by Merger of:** Radio Writers Guild; T.V. Writers Guild. **Publications:** *Member News*, monthly. Newsletter. **Price:** free. Alternate Formats: online ● *Writers Guild Directory*, annual ● *Written By*, monthly. Magazine. Contains articles of interest to writers, craft, and business. **Price:** $40.00/year; $5.00/issue. **Advertising:** accepted. **Conventions/Meetings:** annual meeting - always September, Los Angeles, CA.

Afghan

23649 ■ Afghan-American Chamber of Commerce (AACC)
8201 Greensboro Dr., Ste.103
McLean, VA 22102
Ph: (703)442-5005
Fax: (703)442-5008
E-mail: info@a-acc.org
URL: http://www.a-acc.org
Contact: Engr. Atiq Panjshiri, Pres.
Founded: 2002. **Description:** Advocates for the establishment of a democratic system and open-market economy in Afghanistan. Seeks to improve and strengthen business relationships among Afghan and American owned businesses. Extends efforts to protect Afghan-based businesses. Initiates humanitarian endeavors within and outside Afghanistan. **Tele-communication Services:** electronic mail, smajroh@a-acc.org. **Publications:** *Afghanistan, A Companion & Guide.* Book. **Price:** $30.00/copy ● *Doing Business in Afghanistan.* Book. **Price:** $10.00/copy.

Alpine

23650 ■ Alpine Tourist Commission (ATC)
c/o Switzerland Tourism
PO Box 5513
608 5th Ave.
New York, NY 10020
Ph: (212)757-5944
Free: (877)794-8037
Fax: (212)262-6116
E-mail: info@alpseurope.com
URL: http://www.alpseurope.com
Contact: Rafael Enzler, Chm.
Founded: 1954. **Members:** 4. **Description:** Promotes tourist travel to the alpine regions of Austria, Germany, Italy and Switzerland. **Publications:** Newsletter, bimonthly. Contains information on the Alps in Austria, Germany, Italy, and Switzerland. **Price:** free. **Circulation:** 6,000. **Advertising:** accepted.

Anguilla

23651 ■ Anguilla Tourist Board
c/o Mrs. Marie Walker
246 Central Ave.
White Plains, NY 10606
Ph: (914)287-2400
Free: (877)4ANGUILLA
Fax: (914)287-2404
E-mail: atbtour@anguillanet.com
URL: http://www.anguilla-vacation.com
Contact: Mrs. Marie Walker, Contact
Description: Provides tourist information to the public, travel agents, and travel trade publications on Montserrat in the Caribbean West Indies. **Telecommunication Services:** electronic mail, mwturnstyle@aol.com. **Formerly:** (1989) Anguilla Tourist Information Office; (2003) Anguilla Tourist Information and Reservation Office. **Publications:** Publishes informational brochures, posters, and fact sheets.

Arab

23652 ■ American Arab Chamber of Commerce
4917 Schaefer Rd., Ste.215
Dearborn, MI 48126
Ph: (313)945-1700
Fax: (313)945-6697
E-mail: chamber@americanarab.com
URL: http://www.americanarab.com
Contact: Nasser Beydoun, Chm.
Founded: 1992. **Regional Groups:** 2. **Description:** Promotes, assists, and strengthens member businesses, domestically and internationally. **Computer Services:** Mailing lists, of members ● online services, business directory. **Committees:** American Arab Professional; Building Finance; Engineering and Technology; Small Business. **Affiliated With:** Detroit Regional Chamber. **Publications:** *American Arab Business Directory* ● *Community Bridges*, monthly. Newsletter. **Price:** free. **Circulation:** 20,000. **Advertising:** accepted. Alternate Formats: online. **Conventions/Meetings:** seminar.

23653 ■ Bilateral US-Arab Chamber of Commerce
PO Box 571870
Houston, TX 77257-1870
E-mail: info@bilateralchamber.org
URL: http://www.bilateralchamber.org
Contact: Aseel Saqer, Contact
Multinational. Description: Encourages strategic links and joint ventures between business, academic, and government entities. Seeks to increase understanding of the processes of trade between the U.S. and the Middle East and the North African region. Provides access to decision makers within business, trade and government to expand members' presence in the global marketplace. Increases understanding of the political, economic and social issues through educational exchanges and cultural awareness. **Telecommunication Services:** electronic mail, coordinator@bilateralchamber.org ● electronic mail, programs@bilateralchamber.org. **Publications:** Newsletter, quarterly. **Price:** included in membership dues.

Argentina

23654 ■ Argentine-American Chamber of Commerce (AACC)
630 5th Ave., 25th Fl.
Rockefeller Ctr.
New York, NY 10111
Ph: (212)698-2238
Fax: (212)698-2239
E-mail: argentinechamber@argentinechamber.org
URL: http://www.argentinechamber.org
Contact: Claudia Schaefer-Farre, Exec. Dir.
Founded: 1919. **Members:** 500. **Membership Dues:** patron, $5,000 (annual) ● sponsor, $1,500 (annual) ● corporate, $750 (annual) ● individual, $375 (annual). **Staff:** 8. **Description:** Promotes business and trade with Argentina. **Libraries: Type:** reference. **Holdings:** 500. **Computer Services:** Mailing lists, of members. **Publications:** *Argentina Econofax*, weekly. Newsletter. Contains analysis and statistical information of events occurring in Argentina. ● *Argentine Newsletter*, weekly ● Membership Directory, annual. Alternate Formats: online. **Conventions/Meetings:** annual meeting - usually March.

Asian-Indian

23655 ■ Asian Indian Chamber of Commerce (AICC)
ITM Corporate Ctr.
6 Kilmer Rd., Ste.J
Edison, NJ 08817
Ph: (732)777-4666
Fax: (732)777-4668
E-mail: webmaster@aicc.net
URL: http://www.aicc.net
Contact: Seema M. Singh Esq., Pres.
Founded: 1983. **Membership Dues:** basic, $100 (annual) ● premium, $200 (annual) ● life, $1,000 ● corporate (1-5 employees), $500 (annual). **Description:** Assists Asian-Indian business interests by providing a forum to facilitate communication among members of the Asian-Indian business community. Promotes the exchange of ideas and information and awareness of the availability of federal and state assistance programs. Refers businesses to sources of management or technical assistance. Sponsors seminars and workshops.

Australia

23656 ■ Australian Trade Commission (AUSTRADE)
150 E 42nd St., 34th Fl.
New York, NY 10017-5612
Ph: (212)351-6560 (212)351-6566
Fax: (212)867-7710
E-mail: info@austrade.gov.au
URL: http://www.austrade.gov.au
Contact: Chris Knepler, Business Development Mgr.
Staff: 15. **Regional Groups:** 4. **Description:** Works in the promotion of Australian products and investments in the U.S. **Divisions:** Consumer; Investments. **Publications:** *Export Update*, monthly. Newsletter. Alternate Formats: online ● *Trademark*, monthly. Newsletter. Alternate Formats: online.

Austria

23657 ■ Austrian Press and Information Service
3524 Intl. Ct. NW
Washington, DC 20008-3022
Ph: (202)895-6775
Fax: (202)895-6772
E-mail: austroinfo@austria.org
URL: http://www.austria.org
Contact: Christoph Meran, Dir.
Description: Aims to publicize and enhance the image of contemporary Austria in the U.S. Works to call attention to Austrian political and economic achievements and the image of Austria as a highly developed and competitive Western nation. Collaborates and maintains liaison with Austrian consulates in the U.S. and Austro-American associations. Provides public relations assistance to visitors from Austria and to Austrian activities at the United Nations; offers assistance to Austrian students studying in the U.S. Broadcasts weekly news program in German. **Computer Services:** Mailing lists, of members. **Affiliated With:** United Nations. **Publications:** *Austrian Information,* monthly. Magazine ● *Economic News from Austria,* quarterly. Newsletter ● Also issues press releases and produces films, documentary videos, and slide shows.

23658 ■ Austrian Tourist Office (ANTO)
PO Box 1142
New York, NY 10108-1142
Ph: (212)994-6880
Fax: (212)730-4568
E-mail: info@oewnyc.com
URL: http://www.austria.info/xxl/_site/us/_area/
416153/home.html
Contact: Erich Neuhold, Dir.
Founded: 1927. **Members:** 11. **Staff:** 246. **Description:** Promotes tourism from North America to Austria through its marketing and public relations department, as well as a travel information center. **Libraries: Type:** reference. **Holdings:** 200. **Telecommunication Services:** electronic mail, travel@austria.info. **Formerly:** (2002) Austrian National Tourist Office.

23659 ■ Austrian Trade Commission (ATC)
120 W 45th St., 9th Fl.
New York, NY 10036
Ph: (212)421-5250
Free: (800)847-2478
Fax: (212)421-5251
E-mail: newyork@austriantrade.org
URL: http://www.austriantrade.org/usa
Contact: Bruno Freytag, Trade Commissioner
Founded: 1950. **Languages:** English, German, Spanish. **Description:** Promotes U.S.-Austrian trade with particular emphasis on Austrian exports to the U.S; identifies Austrian trade sources to meet U.S. commercial demand. Handles inquiries related to trade between the two nations and deals with issues such as customs duties, trade laws, and licensing. Compiles statistics. Sponsors trade exhibits. **Convention/Meeting:** none. **Libraries: Type:** reference.

23660 ■ U.S. Austrian Chamber of Commerce
165 W 46th St.
New York, NY 10036
Ph: (212)819-0117
Fax: (212)819-0345
E-mail: memberservices@usatchamber.com
URL: http://www.usatchamber.com
Contact: Johannes P. Hofer, Pres.
Founded: 1949. **Members:** 200. **Membership Dues:** associate, individual, $75 (annual) ● corporate, $500 (annual) ● small business, $200 (annual) ● flagship, $1,500 (annual). **Staff:** 2. **Languages:** English, German. **Description:** Hosts receptions and luncheons. Sponsors Viennese Opera Ball, panel discussions, and business assistance. **Libraries: Type:** open to the public. **Holdings:** 4; periodicals. **Awards:** Person

of the Year. **Type:** recognition. **Computer Services:** database, membership. **Affiliated With:** Manhattan Chamber of Commerce. **Publications:** Newsletter, quarterly. **Circulation:** 400. **Advertising:** accepted. Alternate Formats: CD-ROM. **Conventions/Meetings:** semiannual luncheon ● annual Viennese Opera Ball - party - always May in New York City.

Barbados

23661 ■ Barbados Tourism Authority (BTA)
800 2nd Ave.
New York, NY 10017
Ph: (212)986-6516
Free: (800)221-9831
Fax: (212)573-9850
E-mail: btany@barbados.org
URL: http://www.barbados.org
Contact: Rob McChlery, Mgr.
Description: Promotes tourism in Barbados. **Additional Websites:** http://www.barbadostourism.org/btaoff.htm. **Telecommunication Services:** additional toll-free number, in New York state, (800)451-0466. **Formerly:** (1994) Barbados Board of Tourism.

Belgium

23662 ■ Belgian American Chamber of Commerce in the United States
c/o FORTIS Bank
153 E 53rd St., 27th Fl.
New York, NY 10022
Ph: (212)340-6271
Fax: (212)340-6270
E-mail: info@belcham.org
URL: http://www.belcham.org
Contact: Mr. Georges Ugeux, Chm.
Founded: 1925. **Members:** 120. **Membership Dues:** individual, $350 (annual) ● business, $850 (annual) ● corporate, $2,000 (annual). **Staff:** 2. **Regional Groups:** 2. **Languages:** English, Flemish, French. **Description:** Promotes business and trade between Belgium and the United States. **Awards:** Belgian - US Friendship Award. **Frequency:** annual. **Type:** recognition. **Computer Services:** database, Belgian exporters and American importers of Belgian products.

23663 ■ Belgian Tourist Office (BTO)
220 E 42nd St., Ste.3402
New York, NY 10017
Ph: (212)758-8130
Fax: (212)355-7675
E-mail: info@visitbelgium.com
URL: http://www.visitbelgium.com
Contact: Frederique Raeymaekers, Dir.
Founded: 1947. **Staff:** 6. **Description:** Promotes travel and tourism to Belgium. Provides information services, brochures, and slides; maintains speakers' bureau. **Computer Services:** Mailing lists. **Formerly:** Belgian National Tourist Office. **Publications:** *Belgium Newsbreaks,* 5/year. Newsletter. Contains tourist information on Belgium for travel editors, travel industry people, and consumers. **Price:** free ● *Visit Belgium.* Newsletter. Alternate Formats: online ● Also publishes maps and brochures. Internet Access.

Bermuda

23664 ■ Bermuda Department of Tourism
675 3rd Ave.
New York, NY 10017
Ph: (212)223-6106
Free: (800)BER-MUDA
Fax: (212)983-5289

E-mail: travel@bermudatourism.com
URL: http://www.bermudatourism.com
Contact: Toby Dillas, Sales Dir.
Founded: 1913. **Staff:** 21. **Description:** Established by an act of Parliament of the Bermuda government for the purpose of developing and fostering the trade of the islands and generating tourism to Bermuda. **Formerly:** (1969) Bermuda Trade Development Board. **Publications:** *Bermuda Shorts,* quarterly. Newsletter. Encourages tourism. Includes calendar of events and Bermuda hotel and restaurant news. ● *Destination Bermuda,* periodic. Newsletter. Targets the group and incentive travel market.

Brazil

23665 ■ Brazil Tourism Office (BTO)
c/o Brazil Information Center
2141 Wisconsin Ave. NW, Ste.E-2
Washington, DC 20007-6203
Free: (800)727-2945
E-mail: visitbrazil@braziltourism.org
URL: http://www.braziltourism.org
Contact: Robert Falkenburg, Gen. Mgr.
Founded: 1987. **Staff:** 4. **Budget:** $120,000. **Description:** Organizations promoting Brazilian tourism. Coordinates business contacts, organizes schedules, distributes promotional materials, supplies data on international statistics, obtains access to mailing lists, and offers assistance with participation in international events and fairs. Coordinates studies and surveys on the marketing of foreign travel. **Formerly:** Brazilian Tourism Authority; (1988) Brazilian Tourism Foundation. **Publications:** *Your Support Around the World,* annual. Directory. **Price:** free ● Brochures.

23666 ■ Brazilian-American Chamber of Commerce (BACC)
509 Madison Ave., Ste.304
New York, NY 10022
Ph: (212)751-4691
Fax: (212)751-7692
E-mail: info@brazilcham.com
URL: http://www.brazilcham.com
Contact: Sueli C. Bonaparte, Exec. Dir.
Founded: 1968. **Members:** 500. **Membership Dues:** corporate, $850 (annual) ● patron, $10,000 (annual) ● sponsor, $5,000 (annual) ● contributing, $1,650 (annual) ● regular, $400 (annual). **Staff:** 850. **Budget:** $7,500,000. **Languages:** English, Portuguese. **For-Profit. Description:** Corporations, partnerships, financial institutions, and individuals either in the U.S. or Brazil interested in fostering two-way trade and investment between the countries. Compiles statistics and provides special mailings, press releases, information, and business contacts. Maintains files on business and trade information. Sponsors breakfast briefings, luncheons, seminars, and gala dinners. **Libraries: Type:** reference. **Holdings:** 1,500. **Subjects:** business, trade information, Brazilian laws, corporate member information, resume bank. **Awards:** Person of the Year Award. **Frequency:** annual. **Type:** recognition. **Recipient:** for a Brazilian and an American who have rendered outstanding services to the cause of furthering Brazilian and American business ties. **Computer Services:** database, available on ad-hoc basis with Executive Director's approval ● mailing lists. **Committees:** Awards; Banking and Capital Markets; Business Affairs; Editorial and Publications; Legal Affairs; Nominating; Person of the Year Organizational; Trade and Business Investment. **Publications:** *Brazilian-American Business Review/Directory,* annual. Serves as a resource tool for doing business in Brazil. **Price:** $80.00 for nonmembers in U.S.; $100.00 for nonmembers outside U.S.; $150.00 CD-ROM in U.S.; $200.00 CD-ROM outside U.S. **Circulation:** 2,500. **Advertising:** accepted. Alternate Formats: CD-ROM ● *News Bulletin,* bimonthly. **Price:** $85.00/year. **Circulation:** 1,200. **Advertising:** accepted ● Directory. **Price:** $100.00. **Circulation:** 5,000. **Advertising:** accepted ● Report. Alternate Formats: online ● Mem-

bership Directory. Alternate Formats: online. **Conventions/Meetings:** monthly luncheon ● semimonthly seminar and breakfast.

23667 ■ Brazilian Government Trade Bureau of the Consulate General of Brazil in New York (BGTB)
1185 Ave. of the Americas, 21st Fl.
New York, NY 10036
Ph: (917)777-7777 (917)777-7799
Fax: (212)827-0225
E-mail: trade@brazilny.org
URL: http://www.brazilny.org
Contact: Fred Arruda, Dir.
Founded: 1936. **Staff:** 9. **Languages:** English, Portuguese. **Nonmembership. Description:** Commercial Office of the Brazil Consulate in New York. Offers online match between Brazilian exporters of goods and services and U.S. importers. **Libraries: Type:** reference. **Computer Services:** Online services, matching program. **Additional Websites:** http://www.braziltradenet.gov.br. **Departments:** Investments; Trade. **Publications:** Publishes information on Brazilian trade shows and investments.

British

23668 ■ British Trade Office at Consulate-General
c/o British Consulate-General, New York
845 3rd Ave., 9th Fl.
New York, NY 10022
Ph: (212)745-0200
Fax: (212)754-3062
E-mail: trade@uktradeinvestcanada.org
URL: http://www.uktradeinvestcanada.org
Contact: Kerry Appleton, Contact
Staff: 49. **Description:** British government office that promotes trade with the U.S; assists British companies selling in the U.S; aids American companies that wish to import goods from or invest in Britain. **Libraries: Type:** reference. **Holdings:** 500; books. **Additional Websites:** http://www.britainusa.com/ny. **Telecommunication Services:** electronic mail, uktiny@fco.gov.uk. **Formerly:** (1990) British Trade Development Office; (2001) British Trade and Investment Office.

23669 ■ VisitBritain
551 5th Ave., 7th Fl., No. 701
New York, NY 10176-0799
Ph: (212)850-0330
Free: (800)462-2748
Fax: (212)986-1188
E-mail: travelinfo@visitbritain.org
URL: http://www.visitbritain.com/vb3-en-us/?url=/usa
Contact: Rob Franklin, Exec. VP
Founded: 1929. **Description:** Statutory body of the British Parliament under the aegis of the Department of Employment. Works to promote and develop tourism, incentive travel, meetings and conventions, specialized study tours, and industrial and trade fairs to the United Kingdom. Compiles statistics. **Computer Services:** Mailing lists, of members. **Formerly:** British Tourist Authority. **Supersedes:** British Travel Association; British Travel and Holiday Association. **Publications:** *Britain*, annual. Magazine. **Price:** free. **Circulation:** 450,000. **Advertising:** accepted ● *Britainews*, quarterly. Magazine. Includes calendar of events. **Price:** free. **Advertising:** accepted.

Bulgarian

23670 ■ Bulgarian-American Chamber of Commerce (BACC)
1427 N Wilcox Ave.
Hollywood, CA 90028-8123
Ph: (323)962-2414

Fax: (323)962-2010
URL: http://www.bulgarianamericanchamber.org
Contact: Dr. Ogden C. Page, Founder/Pres.
Founded: 1993. **Membership Dues:** basic, $50 (annual) ● bronze, $90 (annual) ● silver, $120 (annual) ● gold, $150 (annual) ● platinum, $180 (annual). **Description:** Strives to empower Bulgarian-American entrepreneurs by promoting economic development within the Bulgarian-American business community. Aims to increase awareness of various economic and commercial opportunities with respect to Bulgaria. Serves as a liaison between Bulgarian-owned businesses and other interested parties. **Publications:** *Bulgarian-American Business Directory*. **Price:** included in membership dues. Alternate Formats: online ● *Who's Who in Bulgarian-American Community*. Directory. Alternate Formats: online ● Newsletter. **Price:** included in membership dues. Alternate Formats: online.

Business

23671 ■ Bulgarian-U.S. Business Council
c/o Chamber of Commerce of the U.S.
1615 H St. NW
Washington, DC 20062-2000
Ph: (202)463-5460
Fax: (202)463-3114
E-mail: europe@uschamber.com
URL: http://www.uschamber.org
Contact: Thomas J. Donohue, Pres./CEO
Founded: 1975. **Members:** 50. **Membership Dues:** firm (with annual revenues over $50 million), $5,000 (annual) ● firm (with annual revenues under $50 million), $3,000 (annual). **Multinational. Description:** Executive firms having significant actual or potential trade involvement with Bulgaria, including coverage of policy issues related to Russia, Ukraine, Belarus, Turkey, Iran, the Caucasus and Central Asia. Provides a forum for discussing trade and investment issues and formulation of policy issues to promote and expand economic relations between the U.S. and Bulgaria. **Libraries: Type:** not open to the public. **Holdings:** articles, books, periodicals. **Subjects:** international trade, investment. **Publications:** *Bridging the Atlantic*. Book. Describes how eight small American businesses succeeded in Europe. **Price:** $19.95 plus shipping and handling ($4/book) ● *Europe and Eurasia Business Committee Dispatch*, weekly. Newsletter. Provides current information on regulations, legislation and specific industries for Central/Eastern Europe, New Independent States, Turkey and Iran. **Price:** included in membership dues; $350.00 for nonmembers. **Conventions/Meetings:** periodic conference and convention.

23672 ■ Central America - U.S. Chamber of Commerce (CAUSCC)
3400 Coral Way, Ste.No. 602
Coral Gables, FL 33145
Ph: (305)569-9113
Fax: (305)529-2608
E-mail: meet@causcc.com
URL: http://www.causcc.com
Contact: Mr. Gabriel E. Pascual, VP
Languages: English, Spanish. **Description:** Businesses in Central America and the United States. Promotes "commercial ties between the U.S. and all Central American countries." Facilitates establishment of international contacts between U.S. and Central American companies; serves as a clearinghouse on trade between the U.S. and Central America; represents members' commercial and regulatory interests.

23673 ■ Guam Chamber of Commerce
Ada Plaza Ctr.
173 Aspinall Ave., Ste.101
Hagatna, GU 96910
Ph: (671)472-6311 (671)472-8001
Fax: (671)472-6202

E-mail: gchamber@guamchamber.com.gu
URL: http://www.guamchamber.com.gu
Contact: Eloise R. Baza, Pres.
Founded: 1924. **Description:** Businesses and trade organizations. Promotes increased international trade and tourism. Gathers and disseminates information; conducts promotional activities; represents members' interests. **Publications:** *Mailing Labels*. Membership Directory. **Price:** $25.00 for members; $50.00 for nonmembers ● *The President's Report*, monthly. Newsletter. **Advertising:** accepted. Alternate Formats: online ● Directory. **Price:** $10.00 for nonmembers; $5.00 for members.

23674 ■ National Gay and Lesbian Chamber of Commerce (NGLCC)
Dupont Cir.
2000 P St. NW, Ste.300
Washington, DC 20036
Ph: (202)419-0440
Fax: (202)419-0443
E-mail: info@nglcc.org
URL: http://www.nglcc.org
Contact: Justin G. Nelson, Co-Founder
Founded: 2002. **Membership Dues:** supporting, $35-$75 (annual) ● national, $100 (annual) ● pioneer, $250 (annual) ● brass pioneer, $500 (annual) ● bronze pioneer, $1,000 (annual) ● silver pioneer, $2,500 (annual) ● gold pioneer, $5,000 (annual) ● platinum pioneer, $10,000 (annual). **Description:** Seeks to expand the economic opportunities and advancements of the Lesbian, Gay, Bisexual and Transsexual (LGBT) business community. Facilitates cooperation among state and local LGBT chambers and business groups. Partners with the financial services sector to enhance opportunities for members to start or grow their business. Provides lobbying efforts for LGBT business causes and non-discriminatory affairs. **Publications:** Newsletter, monthly. Alternate Formats: online.

Business and Commerce

23675 ■ American International Chamber of Commerce (AICC)
1000 S Fremont Ave., A1 Bldg., Ste.1220-99
Alhambra, CA 91803
Ph: (213)255-2066
Fax: (213)634-1489
E-mail: usa@aiccus.org
URL: http://www.aiccus.org
Contact: Inge Sawerthal, Pres.
Membership Dues: VIP company, VIP individual, $2,500 (annual) ● company, not-for-profit organization, $500 (annual) ● company (foreign company not represented in U.S.), $1,000 (annual) ● VIP foreign company, $5,000 (annual) ● individual, $180 (annual). **Multinational. Description:** Promotes the development of trade, commerce and investment between the United States and all countries, with special focus on Asia Pacific countries and China. Fosters and maintains ethical standards in conducting business activities. Provides a forum in which international businesses in the United States can identify and discuss common interests regarding their commercial interests in the United States. **Awards:** Business Consultant Award. **Frequency:** annual. **Type:** recognition. **Recipient:** to a noted consultant or business advocate with a track record of contributing to the advancement of business education ● Business Leader Award for Philanthropy. **Frequency:** annual. **Type:** recognition. **Recipient:** to an individual with a history of giving to one or more major business institutions ● Corporate Contribution Award. **Frequency:** annual. **Type:** recognition. **Recipient:** to a high-profile, major corporate leader with a record of contributing to business and services institutions or initiatives ● Corporate Contribution Membership Award. **Frequency:** annual. **Type:** recognition. **Recipient:** to a high-profile, membership major corporate leader with a record of contributing to business and services institutions or initiatives ● Cultural Artist

Award for Outstanding Contribution to the Arts. **Frequency:** annual. **Type:** recognition. **Recipient:** to an international artist ● Lifetime Achievement Award. **Frequency:** annual. **Type:** recognition. **Recipient:** to a recognized and established scientist with a history of exemplary technical research invention accomplishment in his or her field. **Telecommunication Services:** electronic mail, ingesawerthal@aiccus.org. **Publications:** Magazine, monthly. **Price:** included in membership dues ● Reports.

23676 ■ Australian New Zealand - American Chambers of Commerce (ANZACC)
30 N LaSalle St., Ste.3400
Chicago, IL 60602
Ph: (312)641-5311
Fax: (312)641-5520
E-mail: info@anzaccnational.com
URL: http://www.anzaccnational.com
Contact: Jan McGrath, Natl. Pres.
Multinational. Description: Promotes Australian and New Zealand culture and commerce and the social and economic relationships that exist between Australia, New Zealand, and the United States. Maintains close ties with international business communities in Australia, New Zealand, and the United States. Provides a forum for the discussion of vital issues and dissemination of information on Australian New Zealand-American trade and economic relations.

23677 ■ Cameroon-USA Chamber of Commerce (CamUSA)
PO Box 8842
Jacksonville, FL 32239-0842
Ph: (904)553-4095
Free: (866)231-2838
E-mail: headquarters@cam-usa.us
URL: http://www.cam-usa.us
Contact: Ariel Ngnitedem MBA, Pres./CEO
Membership Dues: individual, $100 (annual) ● small business, $300 (annual) ● NGO, NPO, $500 (annual) ● corporate, $700 (annual) ● VIP, $1,000 (annual). **Multinational. Description:** Promotes trade, investments, cultural exchange, and goodwill between the United States of America and Cameroon. Seeks to help in the fight against poverty in Cameroon. Assists Cameroonian companies to get access to the American market. Aims to maintain and extend a business presence between the two countries for their mutual benefit. Provides professional services that will be helpful in developing and creating business opportunities for its members. **Publications:** Membership Directory. **Price:** included in membership dues.

Business, Minority

23678 ■ National Black Chamber of Commerce (NBCC)
1350 Connecticut Ave. NW, Ste.405
Washington, DC 20036
Ph: (202)466-6888
Fax: (202)466-4918
E-mail: info@nationalbcc.org
URL: http://www.nationalbcc.org
Contact: Harry C. Alford, Pres./CEO
Founded: 1993. **Membership Dues:** chapter, $300 (annual) ● NGO, $400 (annual) ● government agency, $600 (annual) ● President's Club, $5,000 (annual) ● Public Policy Council, $25,000 (annual) ● business (based on annual sales), $300-$15,000 (annual). **Local Groups:** 190. **Description:** Works for the issues of economics and entrepreneurship in the African-American community. **Programs:** Advocacy; AFLAC Entrepreneur of the Year Award Nomination; Banking and Finance; Collegiate; Corporate; E-Commerce; Procurement; World Trade. **Publications:** The Small Business Resource Guide. Journal ● Newsletters ● Annual Report, annual. **Conventions/Meetings:** convention.

Business Tourism

23679 ■ American Chamber of Commerce Executives (ACCE)
4875 Eisenhower Ave., Ste.250
Alexandria, VA 22304
Ph: (703)998-0072

Fax: (703)212-9512
E-mail: mfleming@acce.org
URL: http://www.acce.org
Contact: Michael Fleming, Pres./CEO
Founded: 1914. **Members:** 5,088. **Staff:** 35. **Budget:** $3,000,000. **Description:** Professional society of chamber of commerce executives and staff members. **Awards:** Chairman's Professional Leadership Award. **Type:** recognition ● Communications Evaluation Award. **Type:** recognition. **Recipient:** for magazines and other publications. **Telecommunication Services:** electronic bulletin board, jobwatch, a job listing service for members. **Committees:** Certification Panel; Management Standards. **Formed by Merger of:** American Association of Commercial Executives; Central Association of Commercial Secretaries. **Formerly:** (1949) National Association of Commercial Organization Secretaries. **Publications:** The Chamber Executive, bimonthly. Newsletter. **Price:** $99.00 for nonmembers; $18.95 single copy. **Advertising:** accepted. Alternate Formats: online ● Jobwatch, bimonthly ● Management Information Service, bimonthly ● Who's Who in Chamber Management, annual ● Directory, annual. **Price:** free for members ● Newsletter, weekly. Alternate Formats: online. **Conventions/Meetings:** annual conference (exhibits) ● annual convention.

Caribbean

23680 ■ Caribbean Tourism Organization, American Branch (CTO)
80 Broad St., 32nd Fl.
New York, NY 10004
Ph: (212)635-9530
Fax: (212)635-9511
E-mail: ctony@caribtourism.com
URL: http://www.doitcaribbean.com
Contact: Hugh Riley, Marketing Dir.
Founded: 1951. **Members:** 231. **Staff:** 10. **Languages:** English, French, Spanish. **Description:** A marketing arm of the Caribbean Tourism Organization. Seeks to encourage and assist development in the Caribbean through tourism. **Libraries: Type:** reference. **Holdings:** photographs. **Awards: Frequency:** annual. **Type:** recognition. **Recipient:** for leaders in the travel industry and persons who have made significant contributions to the development of tourism in the Caribbean. **Formed by Merger of:** (1988) Caribbean Tourism Research and Development Center; Caribbean Tourism Association. **Formerly:** (1951) Caribbean Tourist Association. **Publications:** Caribbean Tourism Organization—Regional Statistics, annual. **Price:** $150.00 ● Caribbean Vacation Planner, annual. **Price:** free ● CTO Monitor, monthly. Newsletter. Contains review of trends and statistics. Alternate Formats: online. **Conventions/Meetings:** annual Caribbean Tourism Conference, with arts, crafts, local manufactured products (exhibits) - usually in September ● semiannual trade show - always spring and fall.

23681 ■ Grenada Board of Tourism
PO Box 1668
Lake Worth, FL 33460
Ph: (561)588-8176
Free: (800)927-9554
Fax: (561)588-7267
E-mail: cnoel@grenadagrenadines.com
URL: http://www.grenadagrenadines.com
Contact: Christine Noel, Dir.
Description: Promotes tourism for the West Indies Island of Grenada. Acts as government tourist information service. **Formerly:** (2001) Grenada Board of Tourism. **Publications:** The Visitor Magazine (in English, French, and Spanish), semiannual. Provides general information on the destination, including hotels, restaurants and other services offered. **Advertising:** accepted ● Brochure ● Directory.

23682 ■ Saint Kitts Tourism Authority
414 E 75th St., Ste.5
New York, NY 10021
Ph: (212)535-1234
Free: (800)582-6208
Fax: (212)734-6511
E-mail: newyork@stkittstourism.kn
URL: http://www.stkitts-tourism.com
Contact: Robert Kelly, Dir.
Founded: 1983. **Staff:** 2. **Description:** Promotes the Eastern Caribbean islands of St. Kitts and Nevis as travel and tourist destinations. **Formerly:** (2002) Saint Kitts-Nevis Tourist Office.

23683 ■ Saint Lucia Tourist Board (SLTB)
800 2nd Ave., 9th Fl.
New York, NY 10017
Ph: (212)867-2950
Free: (800)456-3984
Fax: (212)867-2795
E-mail: stluciatourism@aol.com
URL: http://www.stlucia.org
Contact: Odile Devaux, Fulfillment/Enquiries Off.
Staff: 7. **Description:** Promotes tourism in St. Lucia, West Indies. Participates in trade shows and cultural events; conducts educational seminars. Sponsors promotional programs. **Publications:** Newsletter. Alternate Formats: online.

Cayman Islands

23684 ■ Cayman Islands Department of Tourism (CIDT)
c/o Missy Farren & Associates
3 Park Ave., 39th Fl.
New York, NY 10016
Ph: (212)889-9009
Fax: (212)889-9125
E-mail: ldrago@mfaltd.com
URL: http://www.caymanislands.ky
Description: Offices of tourism promoting travel to the Cayman Islands.

Chambers of Commerce

23685 ■ ACCE Communications Council
c/o ACCE
4875 Eisenhower Ave., Ste.250
Alexandria, VA 22304
Ph: (703)998-0072
Fax: (703)212-9512
E-mail: mfleming@acce.org
URL: http://www.acce.org
Contact: Michael Fleming, Pres.
Founded: 1947. **Members:** 400. **Membership Dues:** individual, $75 (annual). **Description:** Communication directors, editors, advertising and business managers, other administrative, executive, and creative personnel connected with chamber of commerce publications and public relations. Maintains Communications Advisory Service in which members assist chambers in developing or improving their communications programs and speakers' bureaus. **Awards: Frequency:** annual. **Type:** recognition. **Recipient:** for effective communications programs. **Affiliated With:** American Chamber of Commerce Executives. **Formerly:** (1972) American Association of Commerce Publications. **Publications:** Communications Executive, bimonthly. Article ● Directory, annual ● Handbook. **Conventions/Meetings:** annual conference and workshop - usually May.

23686 ■ American Chamber of Commerce of Cuba in the U.S. (AmCham Cuba)
10454 Parthenon Ct.
Bethesda, MD 20817
Ph: (301)365-1745
Fax: (301)365-1829
E-mail: amchamcuba@aol.com
Contact: Robert Weekley, Pres.
Founded: 1961. **Members:** 200. **Membership Dues:** individual, $100 (annual) ● corporate, $1,500 (annual) ● friend of American Chamber of Commerce Cuba & smaller corporation, $500 (annual). **Staff:** 1. **Budget:** $40,000. **Languages:** English, Spanish. **Description:** Individuals and corporations. Provides education and opportunities for trade and investment in a post-Castro Cuba. Serves as a clearinghouse on

legislation and regulations affecting U.S.-Cuba. Assists corporations in the United States in planning strategies for investing in and trading with Cuba in the event that the embargo is lifted. Conducts research and educational programs. **Libraries: Type:** lending; reference. **Holdings:** 200; books, clippings, monographs, periodicals. **Subjects:** U.S.-Cuba relations, trade, foreign investment in Cuba. **Computer Services:** database, membership ● mailing lists ● online services. **Committees:** Editorial; Finance; Membership. **Formerly:** Am Cham Cuba. **Publications:** *Cuba News*, monthly. Newsletter. Contains news reports and commentary. **Price:** included in membership dues. ISSN: 1073-7715. Alternate Formats: online. **Conventions/Meetings:** semiannual board meeting, for members and guests - usually April and October, in Washington, DC or Miami, FL ● monthly luncheon ● periodic regional meeting.

23687 ■ American Islamic Chamber of Commerce (AICC)
PO Box 93033
Albuquerque, NM 87199-3033
E-mail: islam@americanislam.org
URL: http://americanislam.org
Languages: Arabic, English. **Description:** Individuals and organizations. Seeks to advance the interests of Islamic-owned businesses in the United States. Conducts business education programs; provides technical and management assistance to Islamic-owned businesses.

23688 ■ American Israel Chamber of Commerce - Southeast Region (AICC)
1150 Lake Hearn Dr., Ste.130
Atlanta, GA 30342
Ph: (404)843-9426
Fax: (404)843-1416
E-mail: aiccse@aiccse.org
URL: http://www.aiccse.org
Contact: Tom Glaser, Pres.
Founded: 1992. **Members:** 450. **Membership Dues:** young professional, $100 (annual) ● individual, $200 (annual) ● business (with less than 25 employees), $350 (annual) ● corporate (with more than 25 employees), $850 (annual) ● patron, $1,500 (annual) ● sponsor, $5,000 (annual). **Staff:** 4. **Languages:** English, Hebrew. **Description:** American and Israeli companies. Promotes increased trade between Israel and the United States, with emphasis on increasing Israeli-American trade involving companies in the southeastern U.S. Facilitates networking and contact development involving Israeli and U.S. corporations; makes available trade mentoring and matchmaking services; sponsors educational programs. **Computer Services:** Electronic publishing ● mailing lists, members' contact information ● online services. **Committees:** Ambassadors; Eagle Star Awards Gala; Israeli Wine Tasting; Medical; Nanotechnology; Professional; Security; Software. **Publications:** *Latest Southeast-Israel Business News*, monthly. Newsletter. **Price:** included in membership dues. Alternate Formats: online ● Membership Directory. Alternate Formats: online.

23689 ■ American-Uzbekistan Chamber of Commerce (AUCC)
1717 N St. NW
Washington, DC 20036
Ph: (202)828-4111
Fax: (202)659-7010
E-mail: aucc@verizon.net
URL: http://www.aucconline.com
Contact: Robert S. Pace, Exec. Dir.
Founded: 1993. **Members:** 75. **Membership Dues:** corporate, $3,000 (annual) ● non-profit, $500 (annual) ● professional, $100 (annual) ● small and medium-sized enterprise, $1,250 (annual). **Staff:** 1. **Budget:** $150,000. **Description:** Brings together companies and individual professionals interested in promoting trade and investment between Uzbekistan and the United States. Represents business and industry to promote growth in interest of the U.S. business community in Uzbekistan. **Libraries: Type:** not open to the public. **Holdings:** 100; articles, books, papers. **Subjects:** central Asia, U.S. business

and non-profit issues, economy of Uzbekistan. **Awards:** Statesmanship Award. **Frequency:** annual. **Type:** recognition. **Publications:** *AUCC Board Report*, monthly. Newsletter. **Circulation:** 20. **Conventions/Meetings:** annual conference, attended by member and non-member firms plus high level U.S. and Uzbek government officials ● monthly meeting.

23690 ■ Austrian Trade Commissions in the United States (ATCUSC)
11601 Wilshire Blvd., Ste.2420
Los Angeles, CA 90025
Ph: (310)477-9988
Fax: (310)477-1643
E-mail: losangeles@austriantrade.org
URL: http://www.austriantrade.org/usa/en
Contact: Christian Kuegerl, Commissioner
Languages: English, German. **Description:** Corporations in Austria, Canada and the United States. Promotes increased trade between the U.S., Canada, and Austria. Works to remove legislative barriers to international trade; represents members before international trade organizations and agencies; facilitates establishment of joint ventures and other international business connections involving members. **Formerly:** (2004) Austrian Trade Commissions in the United States and Canada.

23691 ■ Brazil-U.S. Business Council (BUSBC)
1615 H St. NW
Washington, DC 20062
Ph: (202)463-5485
Fax: (202)463-3126
E-mail: host@brazilcouncil.org
URL: http://www.brazilcouncil.org
Contact: Tom Catania, Chm.
Founded: 1976. **Members:** 73. **Membership Dues:** corporate, $5,000 (annual). **Staff:** 5. **Languages:** English, Portuguese. **Description:** Works to provide a high-level private sector forum for the business communities of both countries to engage in substantive dialogue on trade and investment issues and communicate private sector priorities to both governments. **Task Forces:** Communication; E-Commerce; Investment; Services; Trade. **Publications:** *Brazil Bulletin*, weekly. Newsletter. Contains a summary of the developments in business, politics and economics. **Price:** available to members only. Alternate Formats: online ● *Policy Monitor*, monthly. Report. Contains information on the status of the bills or executive decrees that have impact on its member businesses. Alternate Formats: online ● Reports. **Conventions/Meetings:** annual meeting.

23692 ■ BritishAmerican Business Inc. of New York and London (BABI)
52 Vanderbilt Ave., 20th Fl.
New York, NY 10017
Ph: (212)661-4060
Fax: (212)661-4074
E-mail: mallen@babinc.org
URL: http://www.babinc.org
Contact: Richard Fursland, CEO
Founded: 1920. **Members:** 510. **Membership Dues:** Transatlantic Council in London, 3,855 (annual) ● sponsor in London, 1,540 (annual) ● corporate in London, 700 (annual) ● Transatlantic Council in U.S., $3,750 (annual) ● corporate in U.S., $1,400 (annual) ● associate in U.S., $625 (annual). **Staff:** 11. **Multinational. Description:** Works to increase the trade and investment between the U.S. and the U.K. by offering member companies a full range of transatlantic business services, information, and contacts. **Computer Services:** database, business intelligence ● database, financial information of companies in European countries ● database, top 250000 US and Canadian companies ● mailing lists, available to members only ● online services. **Roundtables:** CEO; Growing Business; Human Resources; Marketing and Communications. **Formerly:** (2001) British-American Chamber of Commerce. **Publications:** *American British Business Handbook*, annual. **Advertising:** accepted. Alternate Formats: online ● *British American Business Handbook*, annual. **Advertising:** accepted. Alternate Formats: online ● *BritishAmerican Busi-*

ness Inc. - Membership Directory, annual. Lists member companies, products, and services. **Price:** free, available to members only. **Circulation:** 15,000. **Advertising:** accepted. Alternate Formats: online ● *Investment News*, monthly. Bulletins. Contains data and information on the economy in NYC, London, UK, US, and Europe. Alternate Formats: online ● *Issue Insight*, bimonthly. Bulletins. Contains policy issues impacting transatlantic businesses and action/ initiatives taken by BABI. Alternate Formats: online ● *Network London*, quarterly. Newsletter. Contains updates on members and organization's activities. **Advertising:** accepted. Alternate Formats: online ● *Network New York*, quarterly. Newsletter. Contains updates on members and organization's activities. **Advertising:** accepted. Alternate Formats: online.

23693 ■ Caribbean American Chamber of Commerce and Industry (CACCI)
63 Flushing Ave.
Brooklyn Navy Yard, Bldg. No. 5, Mezzanine A
Brooklyn, NY 11205
Ph: (718)834-4544
Fax: (718)834-9774
E-mail: rahastick@msn.com
URL: http://www.caribbeantradecenter.com
Contact: Roy A. Hastick Sr., Pres./CEO
Founded: 1985. **Members:** 1,500. **Membership Dues:** small/newly started business, nonprofit organization, $150 (annual) ● medium-size business (with annual sales of less than $3 million), $375 (annual). **Multinational. Description:** Promotes economic development among Caribbean American, African American, Hispanic and other minority entrepreneurs. **Computer Services:** Mailing lists. **Publications:** Membership Directory. Alternate Formats: online. **Conventions/Meetings:** roundtable, international forums ● seminar.

23694 ■ Chamber of Commerce of the Apparel Industry (CCAI)
118 River Rd., Ste.18
Harriman, NY 10926-3022
Ph: (845)781-7337
Fax: (845)781-7340
Contact: Howard Birne, Pres.
Members: 1,300. **Description:** Workers' compensation group authorized by the New York State Insurance Fund.

23695 ■ Colombian Government Trade Bureau (CGTB)
1901 L St. NW, Ste.700
Washington, DC 20036
Ph: (202)887-9000
Fax: (202)223-0526
E-mail: coltrade@coltrade.org
URL: http://www.coltrade.org
Contact: Juan Carlos Botero, Dir.
Founded: 1966. **Staff:** 6. **Languages:** English, Spanish. **Description:** Promotes Colombian companies and their exports to the United States. **Publications:** *Exporters' Directory*, annual.

23696 ■ Council for Community and Economic Research (C2ER)
PO Box 100127
Arlington, VA 22210
Ph: (703)522-4980
E-mail: sam@accra.org
URL: http://www.c2er.org
Contact: Sean McNamara, Admin. Dir.
Founded: 1960. **Members:** 500. **Membership Dues:** research, $250 (annual) ● organizational, $500 (annual). **Description:** Research directors of city, regional, and state chambers of commerce and other community development organizations. Seeks to exchange information and technical ideas on industrial, economic, and community research. Promotes issues vital to the development of the research profession. Offers certification program for research/ economic development professionals. **Libraries: Type:** reference. **Holdings:** reports. **Awards:** Certified Community Research. **Type:** recognition. **Affiliated With:** American Chamber of Commerce Executives; International Economic Development Council.

Also Known As: (1993) American Chamber of Commerce Researchers Association. **Formerly:** (2006) ACCRA. **Publications:** *ACCRA Community Profiles*, quarterly. **Price:** $60.00/issue; $120.00/disk; $200.00/year (book and 4 disks) ● *ACCRA Cost of Living Index*, quarterly. **Price:** $58.00/issue ● *Applied Research in Economic Development*. Journal. **Price:** $35.00. Alternate Formats: online ● *Research in Review*, bimonthly. Newsletter. Provides members with the latest information on the trends and issues affecting community and economic development. ● Membership Directory, annual ● Monographs. **Conventions/Meetings:** annual conference (exhibits) - usually June.

23697 ■ Cyprus Embassy Trade Center (CETC)
13 E 40th St.
New York, NY 10016
Ph: (212)213-9100
Fax: (212)213-2918
E-mail: ctcny@cyprustradeny.org
URL: http://www.cyprustradeny.org
Languages: English, Greek, Turkish. **Description:** Export promotion office representing Cypriot businesses and government agencies. Promotes increased trade between the U.S. and Cyprus. Serves as a clearinghouse on trade with Cyprus; facilitates establishment of international contacts between Cypriot and U.S. companies; makes available professional services; conducts promotional activities.

23698 ■ European - American Business Council (EABC)
1325 G St. NW, Ste.500
Washington, DC 20005
Ph: (202)449-7705
Fax: (202)449-7704
URL: http://www.eabc.org
Contact: Michael C. Maibach, Pres./CEO
Founded: 1989. **Members:** 55. **Membership Dues:** patron, $12,000 (annual). **Staff:** 4. **Multinational. Description:** Represents over 50 major European and North American companies with a focus on promoting trans-Atlantic growth, bilateral trade, and investment in order to foster prosperity and stability between the US and Europe. Committed to fortifying EU-US economic integration, growth and competitiveness. **Committees:** Policy. **Formerly:** (1998) European-American Chamber of Commerce in Washington, DC. **Conventions/Meetings:** semiweekly roundtable.

23699 ■ European-American Chamber of Commerce in the United States (EACC-USA)
12 E 49th St., 24th Fl.
New York, NY 10017
Ph: (212)315-2196
Fax: (212)315-2183
E-mail: lorth@gaccny.com
Contact: Manfred Dransfeld, Pres./CEO
Founded: 1990. **Members:** 5,000. **Staff:** 1. **Description:** American and European corporations and member chambers concerned with trade and economic issues that affect all trade across the Atlantic. Works to enhance the awareness of new opportunities available for both American and European businesses and represents corporations engaged in transatlantic trade. Provides information about the European Single Market. Organizes public events. **Committees:** Foreign Investment; Taxation; Trade. **Conventions/Meetings:** periodic seminar.

23700 ■ Hemispheric Congress of Latin Chambers of Commerce
c/o Latin Chamber of Commerce of USA
1417 W Flagler St.
Miami, FL 33135
Ph: (305)642-3870
Fax: (305)642-0653
E-mail: info@camacol.org
URL: http://www.camacol.org
Contact: Dr. Horacio Aguirre, Contact
Founded: 1981. **Members:** 1,000. **Staff:** 4. **Languages:** English, Spanish. **Description:** Represents chambers of commerce. Promotes the integration of all chambers of commerce in North and South America. **Formerly:** (1995) Permanent Secretariat of the Hemispheric Congress of Latin C.O.C. and Indiana.

23701 ■ Icelandic American Chamber of Commerce (IACC)
800 3rd Ave., 36th Fl.
New York, NY 10022-7604
Ph: (212)593-2700
Fax: (212)593-6269
E-mail: info@icelandnaturally.com
URL: http://www.icelandtrade.com
Contact: Mr. Petur Oskarsson, Exec. Dir.
Founded: 1986. **Members:** 80. **Membership Dues:** individual, $60 (annual) ● corporate, $200 (annual). **Staff:** 1. **Description:** Promotes trade between Iceland and the United States. **Programs:** Iceland Naturally. **Publications:** Newsletter, monthly. **Price:** included in membership dues. **Advertising:** accepted. **Conventions/Meetings:** board meeting - 3-4/year ● triennial conference ● luncheon.

23702 ■ Innovation Norway - United States
655 3rd Ave., Rm. 1810
New York, NY 10017-9111
Ph: (212)885-9700
Fax: (212)885-9710
E-mail: newyork@invanor.no
URL: http://www.innovanor.no/templates/inv_DK-start____56479.aspx
Contact: Arne Hjeltnes, Dir. for Tourism Americas
Founded: 1945. **Staff:** 260. **Languages:** English, Norwegian. **Description:** U.S. branch of the Export Council of Norway. Assists Norwegian companies in marketing their goods and services in the U.S. Provides information to Norwegian exporters on U.S. markets, tariffs and statistics, trade constraints, and distribution channels. Establishes contacts with U.S. authorities, marketing and manufacturing firms, local lawyers, accountants, banks, patent offices, advertising and public relations agencies, consultants, and credit and debt collection agencies. Aids in establishing Norwegian subsidiaries in the U.S. **Also Known As:** (2004) Export Council of Norway; (2004) Norwegian Trade Council. **Formerly:** (1991) Trade Commission of Norway; (2004) Norwegian Trade Council - United States. **Publications:** *Norway Exports*. Contains company presentations. Alternate Formats: online. **Conventions/Meetings:** quarterly meeting.

23703 ■ International Chamber of Commerce - USA (ICC)
c/o US Council for International Business
1212 Ave. of the Americas
New York, NY 10036-1689
Ph: (212)354-4480 (212)703-5078
Fax: (212)575-0327
E-mail: membership@uscib.org
URL: http://www.uscib.org
Contact: Peter M. Robinson, Pres./CEO
Founded: 1919. **Membership Dues:** company (based on total and foreign revenues), $7,500 (annual) ● association (based on number of attorneys), $5,000 (annual) ● associate (with annual revenue of less than $1 million to $10 million), $500-$2,000 (annual). **Multinational. Description:** Corporations and business associations. Represents and offers services to international businesses. Seeks to evaluate and express the consensus of those businesses involved in trade and international investment; represents members before the United Nations and government agencies. Works to secure effective and consistent action in the development and improvement of business conditions worldwide. Conducts research and educational programs. **Additional Websites:** http://www.iccwbo.org.

23704 ■ Ireland Chamber of Commerce U.S.A. (ICCUSA)
556 Central Ave.
New Providence, NJ 07974
Ph: (908)286-1300
Fax: (908)286-1200
E-mail: padmak@iccusa.org
URL: http://www.iccusa.org
Contact: Maurice A. Buckley, Pres./CEO
Founded: 1988. **Membership Dues:** founding, $10,000 (annual) ● corporate, $1,000 (annual) ● professional, $500 (annual) ● individual, $250 (annual). **Multinational. Description:** Irish and American companies engaged in international trade. Promotes increased trade between the United States and the Republic of Ireland. Represents members before international trade and regulatory agencies; lobbies for removal of barriers to trade; facilitates establishment of joint ventures involving members; conducts promotional activities.

23705 ■ Latino American Management Association (LAMA)
419 New Jersey Ave. SE
Washington, DC 20003
Ph: (202)546-3803
Fax: (202)546-3807
Contact: Stephen Denlinger, Pres./CEO
Founded: 1972. **Members:** 500. **Membership Dues:** corporate, $500 (annual). **Staff:** 10. **Budget:** $900,000. **Description:** Corporations. Promotes the interests of Hispanic and other minority-owned business firms through marketing and procurement information, education and training activities, publications, public policy advocacy initiatives, and outreach programs. **Awards:** Businessperson of the Year. **Frequency:** annual. **Type:** recognition. **Recipient:** for business executives whose contributions to the Hispanic community are outstanding ● Corporate Advocate Leadership Award. **Frequency:** annual. **Type:** recognition. **Recipient:** for a corporation that has shown exemplary leadership in its commitment to the Hispanic business community ● Entrepreneur of the Year. **Frequency:** annual. **Type:** recognition. **Recipient:** for a business owner who has demonstrated superior entrepreneurial skills ● Government Advocate Leadership Award. **Frequency:** annual. **Type:** recognition. **Recipient:** for an outstanding public sector individual who has increased the government's use of Hispanic business products and services ● Hispanic Leadership Award. **Frequency:** annual. **Type:** recognition. **Recipient:** for an individual who has had a dramatic impact on the Hispanic business community ● Rising Star Leadership Award. **Frequency:** annual. **Type:** recognition. **Recipient:** for a business owner or corporate manager whose skills signal great potential for future distinction. **Computer Services:** database, membership profiles. **Formerly:** (1990) Latin American Manufacturers Association. **Publications:** *Business Owner's Guide to the Business Opportunity Development Reform Act of 1988*. Includes guides to business development and improvement for business owners. ● *Handbook for Self-Marketing Under the SBA Section 8(A) Program* ● *Watch on Washington*, quarterly. Newsletter. **Advertising:** accepted ● *Watch on Washington Update*, biweekly. **Conventions/Meetings:** annual Issues Conference - always May ● annual Legislative Fly-In - conference - always April ● annual Recognition Dinner - always November.

23706 ■ Lithuanian-U.S. Business Council
c/o Chamber of Commerce of the U.S.
1615 H St. NW
Washington, DC 20062
Ph: (202)463-5460
Fax: (202)463-3114
E-mail: europe@uschamber.com
URL: http://www.uschamber.org
Contact: Thomas J. Donohue, Pres./CEO
Founded: 1975. **Members:** 50. **Membership Dues:** firm (with annual revenues over $50 million), $5,000 (annual) ● firm (with annual revenues under $50 million), $3,000 (annual). **Multinational. Description:** Executive firms having significant actual or potential trade involvement with Lithuania, including coverage of policy issues related to Russia, Ukraine, Belarus, Turkey, Iran, the Caucasus and Central Asia. Provides a forum for discussing trade and investment issues and formulation of policy issues to promote and expand economic relations between the U.S. and Lithuania. **Libraries: Type:** not open to the public.

Holdings: articles, books, periodicals. **Subjects:** international trade, investment. **Publications:** *Bridging the Atlantic.* Book. Describes how eight small American businesses succeeded in Europe. **Price:** $19.95 plus shipping and handling ($4/book) ● *Europe and Eurasia Business Committee Dispatch,* weekly. Newsletter. Provides current information on regulations, legislation and specific industries for Central/Eastern Europe, New Independent States, Turkey and Iran. **Price:** included in membership dues; $350.00 for nonmembers. **Conventions/Meetings:** periodic conference and convention.

23707 ■ National United States-Arab Chamber of Commerce (NUSACC)
1023 15th St. NW, Ste.400
Washington, DC 20005
Ph: (202)289-5920
Fax: (202)289-5938
E-mail: nusacc@aol.com
URL: http://www.nusacc.org
Contact: Mr. David Hamod, Pres.
Founded: 1992. **Membership Dues:** individual, association, corporate 2, $500 (annual) ● corporate 1, $1,000 (annual). **Staff:** 6. **Regional Groups:** 4. **Description:** Individuals, companies, corporations, and associations interested in commercial trade relations with the Arab world. Promotes business between the United States and the Arab world; encourages policies that promote better commercial relations. Conducts research and information services on commercial opportunities, export regulations, and conditions that affect the trade and investment climate. Sponsors trade delegations; holds seminars, conferences, and training sessions; acts as a central information center. Maintains relations with U.S. and Arab governments and agencies to develop, monitor, and recommend relevant legislation. **Libraries:** Type: reference. **Holdings:** books, clippings, periodicals. **Subjects:** U.S.-Arab trade. **Computer Services:** database, U.S.-Arab Datanet. **Affiliated With:** World Trade Centers Association. **Publications:** *A Business Guide to the Kingdom of Saudi Arabia.* Book. Includes information on commercial policy and foreign trade, business regulations and procedures, and key contact. **Price:** $15.00 for members; $20.00 for nonmembers ● *Business in the Arab World.* Survey. Contains series of business profiles with regulations, procedures, and contacts for each Arab country. **Price:** $2.00/profile; $1.00/profile (7 or more) ● *Directory of Participants.* Lists over 400 Arab and American business persons who participated in the first U.S.-GCC Business Conference. **Price:** $12.00 ● *Gulf Business Development Handbook.* Directory. Includes public and private trade resources. **Price:** $5.00 for members; $7.50 for nonmembers ● *Interest and Banking in Islamic Law.* Book. **Price:** $5.00 for members; $7.50 for nonmembers ● *The Quarterly.* Newsletter. Contains guest editorials and Chamber activities. ● *U.S.-Arab Trade Line,* monthly. Bulletin. Contains business leads, certification procedures, and announcements. ● *U.S. Companies Active in the GCC.* Directory. **Conventions/Meetings:** periodic conference.

23708 ■ Norwegian American Chamber of Commerce - New York City (NACC)
800 3rd Ave.
New York, NY 10022
Ph: (212)421-1655
Fax: (212)838-0374
E-mail: nacc@ntcny.org
URL: http://www.nacc.no
Contact: Inger Tallaksen, Gen. Mgr.
Founded: 1915. **Members:** 850. **Membership Dues:** regular corporate, $475 (annual). **Regional Groups:** 8. **Description:** Promotes business and trade among members and between Norway and the United States. Provides networking opportunities and source information. **Awards:** NACC Achievement Award. **Frequency:** annual. **Type:** recognition. **Recipient:** for individuals whose personal conduct exemplifies the highest tradition of community service and involvement ● Trade Award. **Frequency:** annual. **Type:** recognition. **Publications:** *Norwegian Trade Bulletin,* quarterly.

23709 ■ Spain-United States Chamber of Commerce
Empire State Bldg.
350 5th Ave., Ste.2600
New York, NY 10118
Ph: (212)967-2170
Fax: (212)564-1415
E-mail: info@spainuscc.org
URL: http://www.spainuscc.org
Contact: Bisila Bokoko, Exec. Dir.
Founded: 1959. **Members:** 170. **Membership Dues:** corporate, $1,500 (annual) ● sustaining, $1,000 (annual) ● regular, $500 (annual) ● young professional, $100 (annual). **Staff:** 3. **Budget:** $400,000. **Languages:** English, Spanish. **Multinational. Description:** Spanish and U.S. business persons dedicated to the expansion of Spanish-American trade and goodwill. **Libraries:** Type: not open to the public. **Holdings:** 1,600. **Subjects:** trade, economies, statistics. **Awards:** Business Leader of the Year Award. **Frequency:** annual. **Type:** recognition. **Recipient:** for business leadership between Spain and the US. **Also Known As:** Camera de Comercio Espana - Estados Unidos. **Publications:** *Business Directories.* Contains chamber's extensive list and US businesses. **Price:** free for members ● *Spain: The Business Link* (in English and Spanish), semiannual. Magazine. Provides trade, economic and cultural information useful for both Spain and the US. **Price:** $8.00/copy for nonmembers; $22.00 /year for nonmembers; free for members. **Circulation:** 5,000. **Advertising:** accepted. Alternate Formats: online ● *Visa and Work Permits for the USA* (in English and Spanish). Handbook. Includes detailed requirements, documentation, length of stay, and other criteria for visa. **Price:** $50.00/copy for nonmembers; free for members. **Conventions/Meetings:** annual Gala Dinner ● quarterly seminar ● quarterly Tapas and Tarjetas - seminar.

23710 ■ Swedish-American Chambers of Commerce, USA (SACC-USA)
1403 King St.
Alexandria, VA 22314
Ph: (703)836-6560
Fax: (703)836-6561
E-mail: gunilla@sacc-usa.org
URL: http://sacc-usa.org
Contact: Gunilla Girardo, Pres.
Founded: 1906. **Members:** 250. **Membership Dues:** individual, $175 (annual) ● corporate (based on annual revenues), $650-$3,400 (annual). **Staff:** 2. **Regional Groups:** 17. **Languages:** English, Swedish. **Description:** Provides bilateral trade and investments between Sweden and the U.S. **Libraries:** Type: reference. **Holdings:** books, periodicals. **Subjects:** Swedish business, culture and society. **Awards:** Lucia Trade Award. **Frequency:** annual. **Type:** recognition. **Recipient:** for world leaders. **Computer Services:** Mailing lists, of members. **Formerly:** (2001) Swedish-American Chamber of Commerce. **Publications:** *Currents* (in English and Swedish), monthly. Newsletter. **Advertising:** accepted. Alternate Formats: online; magnetic tape ● *Swedish Subsidiaries in U.S.,* annual. **Advertising:** accepted ● Brochures (in English and Swedish). **Circulation:** 2,000. **Advertising:** accepted ● Membership Directory, annual. **Conventions/Meetings:** annual conference and luncheon (exhibits) ● seminar.

23711 ■ U.S. - Angola Chamber of Commerce (USACC)
1100 Connecticut Ave. NW, Ste.1000
Washington, DC 20036
Ph: (202)223-0540
Fax: (202)223-0551
E-mail: contactus@us-angola.org
URL: http://www.us-angola.org
Contact: Paul J. Hare, Exec. Dir.
Founded: 1990. **Members:** 75. **Languages:** English, Portuguese. **Multinational. Description:** Promotes increased trade between the U.S. and Angola. Works to remove legislative barriers to international trade. Represents members before international trade organizations and agencies. Facilitates establishment of joint ventures and other international business connections involving members. **Publications:** *The Angola Report.* Newsletter. Alternate Formats: online.

23712 ■ United States - Azerbaijan Chamber of Commerce (USACC)
1212 Potomac St. NW
Washington, DC 20007
Ph: (202)333-8702
Fax: (202)333-8703
E-mail: chamber@usacc.com
URL: http://www.usacc.org
Contact: Mahir Iskender, Exec. Dir./Sec.
Founded: 1995. **Membership Dues:** associate, $450 (annual) ● regular, $2,500 (annual) ● sustaining, $5,000 (annual) ● benefactor, $8,750 (annual). **Languages:** English, Russian. **Multinational. Description:** American and Azerbaijani businesses. Promotes increased trade between Azerbaijan and the United States; seeks to improve understanding between the peoples of the U.S. and Azerbaijan. Serves as a liaison linking members with governmental and international trade organizations and agencies; serves as a clearinghouse on U.S.-Azerbaijani trade; sponsors trade missions and educational programs; conducts cultural events. **Programs:** Internship. **Projects:** Academic; Azerbaijan Trade and Cultural Center; Humanitarian. **Publications:** *Investment Guide,* annual. Report. Provides information to foreign investors interested in entering Azerbaijan's market. **Advertising:** accepted ● Newsletter, weekly. Alternate Formats: online. **Conventions/Meetings:** periodic conference ● periodic seminar.

23713 ■ U.S. Chamber of Commerce
1615 H St. NW
Washington, DC 20062-2000
Ph: (202)659-6000
Free: (800)638-6582
E-mail: custsvc@uschamber.com
URL: http://www.uschamber.com
Contact: Thomas J. Donohue, Pres./CEO
Founded: 1912. **Members:** 219,200. **Membership Dues:** small business (maximum of 50 employees), $365-$1,395 (annual) ● small business (e-membership), $125 (annual) ● chamber (minimum), $300 (annual) ● association (minimum), $500 (annual). **Staff:** 1,200. **Budget:** $70,000,000. **Regional Groups:** 5. **Description:** National federation of business organizations and companies. Membership includes chambers of commerce, trade and professional associations, and companies. Determines and makes known to the government the recommendations of the business community on national issues and problems affecting the economy and the future of the country. Works to advance human progress through an economic, political, and social system based on individual freedom and initiative. Informs, trains, equips, and encourages members to participate in policy-making at federal, state, and local levels and in legislative and political action at the national level. Produces First Business, a daily business-oriented news broadcast; and It's Your Business, a weekly television debate program. Operates the American Business Network (BizNet), through which the group maintains a video production studio to produce and syndicate programs. Conducts continuing education program for business executives, including satellite seminars and Institutes for Organization Management (courses to improve management skills of chamber of commerce and association executives). Maintains speakers' bureau; compiles statistics; conducts research programs. **Libraries:** Type: reference. **Holdings:** 10,000; articles, books, periodicals. **Subjects:** business, economics. **Awards:** Blue Chip Enterprise Initiative. **Frequency:** annual. **Type:** recognition. **Recipient:** for small to medium sized businesses that have shown evidence of overcoming adversity through perseverance, diligence, innovation, and quality management produced success. **Committees:** Accrediting Board; Associations; Chamber of Commerce; Council on Small Business; Economic Policy; Education, Employment and Training; Employee Benefits; Environment and Energy; Food and Biotechnology; International Policy; Labor Relations; Public Affairs; Regulatory Affairs; Taxation; Technology Policy;

Transportation Infrastructure and Logistics. **Councils:** Legal Affairs. **Divisions:** Broadcast; Center for Leadership Development; Communications; Corporate Relations; Domestic Policy; Economic Policy; International Policy; Media Relations; Publishing; Quality Learning Services. **Affiliated With:** Center for International Private Enterprise; National Chamber Foundation; National Chamber Litigation Center. **Formerly:** (2001) Chamber of Commerce of the United States - U.S. Chamber. **Publications:** *Analysis of Workers' Compensation Laws*, annual. Summary of state workers' compensation laws including benefits provided, coverage, and administration of laws. **Price:** $12.00/copy ● *Congressional Directory*, periodic. Lists members of Congress and their committee and subcommittee assignments. **Price:** $3.00/copy ● *Employee Benefits*, annual ● *Grassroots Information Action Network*. Features legislative issues. Also Cited As: *GAIN* ● *Nation's Business*, monthly. Magazine. Covers national issues, with emphasis on small business. Includes news of important pending legislation. **Price:** $25.00/year. ISSN: 0028-047X. **Advertising:** accepted ● Papers ● Reports ● Also publishes studies; distributes films and slide presentations. **Conventions/Meetings:** annual meeting - always in Washington, DC.

23714 ■ United States-Mexico Chamber of Commerce (USMCOC)

1300 Pennsylvania Ave. NW, Ste.G-0003
Washington, DC 20004-3021
Ph: (202)312-1520
Fax: (202)312-1530
E-mail: news-hq@usmcoc.org
URL: http://www.usmcoc.org
Contact: Albert C. Zapanta, Pres./CEO
Founded: 1973. **Members:** 2,000. **Membership Dues:** associate, $100 (annual) ● individual, $300 (annual) ● corporate (based on annual revenues) $500-$2,000 (annual) ● regional, $2,500 (annual) ● bi-national, $7,500 (annual). **Staff:** 15. **Budget:** $2,000,000. **Regional Groups:** 16. **State Groups:** 10. **Languages:** English, Spanish. **Description:** U.S. businessmen and chambers of commerce in Mexico representing 350,000 companies. Works to promote private sector trade and investment between the United States and Mexico. Offers advice on economic, legal, and trade issues; informs members of long-range advantages of alternative plant locations. Works with both governments on the executive, legislative, and federal levels. Monitors legislation and regulations concerning trade issues critical to business development in both countries. Conducts seminars and luncheons. **Libraries:** Type: reference. **Holdings:** 7,500; articles, books, periodicals. **Subjects:** various U.S. and Mexico topics. **Awards:** Good Neighbor Award. **Frequency:** annual. **Type:** recognition. **Recipient:** for contributions to improved US-Mexico relations. **Programs:** Bajio Cleaner Production Implementation; Ventana Ambiental Mexico; Wiring the Border. **Task Forces:** Business and Commercial Services; Financial and Risk Management; Infrastructure; Manufacturing; Sustainable Development. **Publications:** *Chamber News*, quarterly. Newsletter. **Advertising:** accepted ● *United States-Mexico Chamber of Commerce—Regional Newsletters*, periodic ● *United States-Mexico Chamber of Commerce—Special Report*, periodic. Booklets ● Newsletter (in English and Spanish), periodic. **Advertising:** accepted ● Membership Directory, annual ● Also publishes reference materials. **Conventions/Meetings:** semiannual NFTA Update - meeting - Washington, DC in May; Mexico City in October.

23715 ■ U.S. Pan Asian American Chamber of Commerce (USPAACC)

1329 18th St. NW
Washington, DC 20036
Ph: (202)296-5221 (202)378-1130
Free: (800)696-7818
Fax: (202)296-5225
E-mail: info@uspaacc.com
URL: http://www.uspaacc.com
Contact: Susan Au Allen, Natl. Pres./CEO
Founded: 1984. **Members:** 15,000. **Membership Dues:** national supplier, $250 (annual) ● certified

supplier, $300 (annual) ● non-profit organization, government partner, $2,500 (annual) ● regional corporate, $3,500 (annual) ● regional supplier, $75 (annual) ● national corporate, $5,000 (annual) ● national corporate gold, $10,000 (annual) ● national corporate platinum, $15,000 (annual). **Staff:** 6. **Budget:** $1,000,000. **Regional Groups:** 6. **State Groups:** 6. **Local Groups:** 6. **Languages:** Chinese, English, Hindi, Indian Dialects, Japanese, Korean, Thai, Vietnamese. **Description:** Businesspersons and professionals united to promote contract, education and other opportunities for Asian American businesses and their partners in corporate America and government agencies. Promotes programs and activities to help members pursue owning and growing their business; enter mainstream society; and participate in procurement, commerce, trade, investment and employment opportunities in corporate America and government. Conducts educational and networking activities. Maintains scholarship fund. Holds business colloquies. Sponsors speakers' bureau. Conducts research and charitable programs. Bestows achievement awards. **Awards:** Corporate Of The Year Award. **Frequency:** annual. **Type:** recognition. **Recipient:** to member corporations who have done the most in supplier contracting ● Government Of The Year. **Frequency:** annual. **Type:** recognition. **Recipient:** to government agencies who have done the most business with minority suppliers/contractors ● USPAACC Scholarships. **Frequency:** annual. **Type:** monetary. **Recipient:** to high school seniors who have high GPA and have done community services to enhance the community they lived in ● USPAACC/Wells Fargo Asian Business Awards. **Frequency:** annual. **Type:** monetary. **Recipient:** for Asian businesses based on their annual revenue and contributions they have made to the community. **Computer Services:** database, 4,500 Asian American-owned businesses. **Committees:** Congress Watch; Legislative. **Publications:** *E-News*, bimonthly. Reports ● *East-West Report*, quarterly. Newsletter. Reports on domestic and international events that affect Asian American business and professional interests. **Price:** $25.00/year. **Circulation:** 8,000. **Advertising:** accepted. Alternate Formats: online ● *National Directory of Asian American Organizations and Resource Guide*, annual. Directories ● *Top Asian American Series (in different fields)*, annual. Yearbook. **Conventions/Meetings:** annual CelebrAsian Conference - conference and luncheon, includes expo, Guanxi Opportunity Fair, awards dinner, scholarship awards luncheon, seminars and plenary sessions - 3-day event ● annual Excellence Awards and Scholarships Dinner - dinner and general assembly, brings the best of Asian Americans together to recognize achievements and contributions to American life (exhibits) ● annual Presidential Retreat, gathering of all regional presidents together to come up with strategic plans for the following year ● monthly Procurement Connections Events - regional meeting and luncheon.

23716 ■ United States-Qatar Business Council (USQBC)

1341 Connecticut Ave. NW, Ste.4A
Washington, DC 20036
Ph: (202)457-8555
Fax: (202)457-1919
E-mail: eric@usqbc.org
URL: http://www.qatarbusinesscouncil.org
Contact: Ambassador Patrick N. Theros, Pres./Exec. Dir.
Founded: 1996. **Members:** 15. **Membership Dues:** general, $5,000 (annual). **Staff:** 1. **Budget:** $150,000. **Description:** American companies doing or planning to engage in projects in the State of Qatar and Qatar companies with ties to the United States. Works to promote expanded US-Qatar ties, and to enhance the US-Qatar relationship. **Libraries:** Type: not open to the public. **Publications:** *U.S.-Qatar Journal*, monthly. Alternate Formats: online ● Newsletters, bimonthly.

23717 ■ Venezuelan-American Chamber of Commerce

c/o Hilda Guinand
2332 Galiano St.
Coral Gables, FL 33134

Ph: (305)728-7042
Fax: (305)728-7043
E-mail: info@venezuelanchamber.org
URL: http://www.venamcham.org
Contact: Hilda Guinand, Contact
Founded: 1950. **Members:** 3,132. **Languages:** English, Spanish. **Description:** Promotes trade between the U.S. and Venezuela. Conducts 8 seminars per year. **Computer Services:** database ● mailing lists. **Additional Websites:** http://www.venezuelanchamber.org. **Committees:** Consumer Products; Corporate Finance; Data Systems; Economics; Environmental Affairs; Exports; Foreign Investment and Exchange; Labor Relations; Legislative Affairs; Patents, Trademarks, and Copyrights; Tax. **Also Known As:** Camara Venezolano Americana de Comercio e Industria. **Formerly:** (1976) American Chamber of Commerce. **Publications:** *Business Brief*, monthly. Newsletter ● *Business Venezuela*, bi-monthly. Brochure ● *Living in Venezuela*. Brochure ● *Turismo Venezuela*, annual. Magazine. Includes information on tourism, industry, investment possibilities, and development statistics. **Price:** Bs. 10.00. **Circulation:** 7,000. **Advertising:** accepted ● Yearbook, annual. **Conventions/Meetings:** quarterly luncheon.

23718 ■ Webmaster Resource Centers

7100 W Camino Real Blvd., No. 121
Boca Raton, FL 33433
Ph: (561)226-2530
Fax: (561)226-2543
E-mail: pres@adultchamber.com
URL: http://www.adultchamber.com
Contact: Marc Laffer, Pres.
Founded: 1997. **Members:** 100,000. **Staff:** 6. **Languages:** English, Portuguese, Spanish. **Description:** Business on the world-wide-web. Webster Resource Center. **Computer Services:** Online services, adult web hosting. **Formerly:** (2000) Adult Chamber of Commerce. **Publications:** Newsletter, monthly. Alternate Formats: online.

Chile

23719 ■ North American-Chilean Chamber of Commerce (NACC)

30 Vasay St., Ste.506
New York, NY 10007
Ph: (212)233-7776
Fax: (212)233-7779
E-mail: andean@nyct.net
Contact: David Spencer, Exec. Dir./Sec.
Founded: 1977. **Members:** 120. **Membership Dues:** corporate, $250 (annual) ● individual, $100 (annual). **Staff:** 1. **Languages:** English, Spanish. **Description:** Fosters expanded trade and commerce between businesses in Chile, and the U.S. **Conventions/Meetings:** periodic luncheon.

China

23720 ■ Chinese American Association of Commerce (CAAC)

778 Clay St., Ste.C
San Francisco, CA 94108
Ph: (415)362-4306
Fax: (415)362-1478
Contact: Charlie Chang, Pres.
Founded: 1980. **Members:** 350. **Membership Dues:** $100 (annual). **Languages:** Chinese, English. **Description:** Individuals interested in improving trade between U.S. and the People's Republic of China. Promotes commerce, industry, business interests, and the welfare of the Chinese community in the U.S. Co-organizes small commodity exhibitions; researching the import and export trade between U.S. and the People's Republic of China; offers interpretation services for business tours; assists members in channeling trade complaints and problems to proper authorities in China; provides current trade opportunities and information on commodities and raw material requirements desired by the American market.

Holds regular meetings with the Chinese Consulate General; makes available Chinese trade catalogs and export and import statistics. Sponsors cultural exchange program; assists U.S. business people who wish to visit the Canton Fair. Fosters closer relations among Chinese-American communities through joint outreach ventures in New York City, St. Louis, MO, Houston, TX, Boston, MA, and Los Angeles, CA. Organizes social gatherings. **Publications:** Brochure (in Chinese and English), quarterly. **Circulation:** 500 ● Newsletter, periodic. **Conventions/Meetings:** seminar, provides information on economy, problems in Chinese imports, logistics of transporting products and goods, and trade prospects.

23721 ■ Chinese Chamber of Commerce of Hawaii
42 N King St.
Honolulu, HI 96813
Ph: (808)533-3181
Fax: (808)533-6967
E-mail: info@chinesechamber.com
URL: http://www.ccchi.org
Contact: Edward Pei, Pres.
Founded: 1911. **Members:** 400. **Budget:** $60,000. **Description:** Promotes business and trade between China and the United States. **Committees:** Community and Social Welfare; Legislation, State and Municipal Affairs; Narcissus Festival; Reception and Entertainment; Special Events; Trade, Commercial and Industrial Development. **Publications:** Lantern, monthly. Newsletter ● Narcissus Festival Souvenir Program, annual. **Conventions/Meetings:** semiannual meeting.

23722 ■ United States of America-China Chamber of Commerce (USCCC)
55 W Monroe St., Ste.630
Chicago, IL 60603
Ph: (312)368-9911
Fax: (312)368-9922
E-mail: info@usccc.org
URL: http://www.usccc.org
Contact: Siva Yam, Pres.
Founded: 1993. **Membership Dues:** Chairman's Circle, $10,000 (annual) ● corporate sponsor, $2,000 (annual) ● general, $350 (annual). **Multinational. Description:** Seeks to develop increased U.S.-China trade and investment activities. Provides assistance to American and Chinese companies in locating suitable business partners for trade and investments. Offers services to assist U.S. corporations in hosting visiting delegations from and to China, and in organizing other events in connection with U.S.-China business activities. **Publications:** China Alert. Newsletter. Alternate Formats: online.

Christian

23723 ■ Christian Chamber of Commerce (CCC)
PO Box 48207
Minneapolis, MN 55432
Ph: (763)792-3512
E-mail: news@christianchamber.com
URL: http://www.christianchamber.com
Contact: Michael D.C. Ricker, Pres.
Founded: 1983. **Members:** 300. **Membership Dues:** individual, $30 (annual). **Staff:** 2. **Regional Groups:** 1. **State Groups:** 1. **Local Groups:** 3. **Description:** Christians who own and operate their own businesses; other Christian professionals. Seeks to: identify members in the Christian community; encourage fellowship and cooperation among members, ministries, and other organizations. **Publications:** East Houston CCC Yellow Pages, annual. Book ● North Houston CCC Yellow Pages, annual. Book ● West Houston CCC Yellow Pages, annual. Book ● Membership Directory, weekly.

Colombia

23724 ■ Colombian American Association (CAA)
30 Vesey St., Ste.506
New York, NY 10007

Ph: (212)233-7776
Fax: (212)233-7779
E-mail: andean@nyct.net
URL: http://www.colombianamerican.org
Contact: Linda A. Calvet, Sec.
Founded: 1927. **Members:** 105. **Membership Dues:** corporate, $500 (annual) ● supporting, $2,000 (annual) ● overseas corporate, individual, $250 (annual). **Staff:** 3. **Description:** Facilitates commerce and trade between the Republic of Colombia and the U.S. Fosters and advances cultural relations and goodwill between the two nations. Encourages sound investments in Colombia by Americans and in the U.S. by Colombians. Disseminates information in the U.S. concerning Colombia. **Awards:** Paul E. Calvet Award. **Type:** recognition. **Recipient:** for the development of goodwill and friendship between business people of Colombia and USA. **Computer Services:** Mailing lists, of members. **Formerly:** (1975) Colombian-American Chamber of Commerce. **Publications:** Colombian Newsletter, monthly. Provides economic, financial, business, and political news from Colombia. **Price:** free for members; $65.00 /year for nonmembers. Alternate Formats: online. **Conventions/Meetings:** periodic luncheon, includes reception.

23725 ■ Colombian-American Chamber of Commerce of Greater Miami (COL-AMCHAM)
250 Catalonia Ave., Ste.407
Coral Gables, FL 33134
Ph: (305)446-2542
Fax: (305)446-2038
E-mail: info@colombiachamber.com
URL: http://www.colombiachamber.com
Contact: Ricardo Tribin, Pres.
Founded: 1976. **Members:** 400. **Membership Dues:** student, $20 (annual) ● individual, $150 (annual) ● corporate, $300 (annual) ● benefactor, $2,000 (annual). **Staff:** 5. **Description:** International business interests in Colombia. Promotes investment and encourages cooperation among national and international businesspeople. Provides economic and commercial information on Colombia and the U.S. Maintains close contact with the Colombian government. Evaluates investment and commercial opportunities for Colombia; makes referrals. Offers placement service; conducts charitable program. Maintains speakers' bureau. **Libraries: Type:** reference. **Holdings:** 500; books, clippings, periodicals. **Awards: Type:** recognition. **Recipient:** to a company and individual with outstanding commercial activity in the past year to a charity organization. **Computer Services:** Mailing lists. **Committees:** Activities; Foreign Investment; Policy; Promotion of Private Enterprises System. **Divisions:** Commercial Information; Economic. **Affiliated With:** Association of American Chambers of Commerce in Latin America. **Publications:** Business Colombia, quarterly. Magazine ● Cam ColAm Informa (in English and Spanish), weekly. Bulletin. **Advertising:** accepted ● Who's Who of Colombian-American Business, annual. Newspaper. **Conventions/Meetings:** periodic conference and seminar (exhibits).

Croatian

23726 ■ Croatian-American Chamber of Commerce (CACC)
50-52 49th St.
Woodside, NY 11377
Ph: (718)937-4040
Free: (888)937-4040
Fax: (718)392-6262
E-mail: info@croamchamber.org
URL: http://www.croamchamber.org
Contact: Domagoj Kero, Pres.
Founded: 1998. **Membership Dues:** professional, $200 (annual) ● small business, $500 (annual) ● medium and large-sized corporation, $1,000 (annual) ● gold, $2,000 (annual) ● international company, $3,000 (annual). **Languages:** Croatian, English. **Multinational. Description:** Promotes bilateral business relationships between the United States and Croatia. Promotes the interests of its members who consist of

Croatian professionals, small business owners, large business corporations, and international corporations. Provides its members with business information, assistance in establishing business contacts and advisory services. **Publications:** Newsletter (in Croatian and English). Alternate Formats: online.

Cyprus

23727 ■ Cyprus Tourism Organization (CTO)
13 E 40th St.
New York, NY 10016
Ph: (212)683-5280
Fax: (212)683-5282
E-mail: gocyprus@aol.com
URL: http://www.visitcyprus.org.cy
Contact: Neophytos Christodoulou, Dir.
Founded: 1980. **Staff:** 3. **Languages:** English, Greek. **Description:** Promotes tourism to the island Republic of Cyprus. Sponsors promotions and works with U.S. and Canadian travel agents and tour operators to increase tourism to Cyprus. Provides information concerning Cyprus. **Computer Services:** Mailing lists, of members. **Telecommunication Services:** electronic mail, visitcyprus@cto.org.cy. **Publications:** Cyprus Travellers Handbook, Hotel Guide, annual. Brochures ● Events. Pamphlets ● 10000 Years of History and Civilization. Brochures ● Annual Report, annual. Alternate Formats: online ● Also publishes maps and posters.

Denmark

23728 ■ Danish American Chamber of Commerce (DACC)
1 Dag Hammerskjold Plz.
885 2nd Ave., 18th Fl.
New York, NY 10017
Ph: (212)705-4945
Fax: (212)754-1904
E-mail: daccny@daccny.com
URL: http://www.daccny.com
Contact: Nargis McGuinness, Exec. Dir.
Founded: 1974. **Members:** 200. **Membership Dues:** individual/commercial, $100 (annual) ● corporate, $500 (annual) ● sustaining, $1,500 (annual). **Staff:** 1. **Description:** Danish and American business leaders; firms and institutions. Functions as an advisory board to support and promote commercial relations between the United States and Denmark, in both directions; makes itself available for consultation with the Danish diplomatic representatives in the U.S. and to the U.S. Department of Commerce, as well as to trade groups and members in Denmark and the U.S. Attempts to avoid duplication of governmental activities. **Formed by Merger of:** Danish Luncheon Club of New York; Danish American Trade Council. **Publications:** Newsletter, bimonthly. **Circulation:** 300. **Advertising:** accepted. Alternate Formats: online. **Conventions/Meetings:** annual dinner.

Ecuador

23729 ■ Ecuadorian-American Chamber of Commerce of Greater Miami
1390 Brickell Ave., Ste.220
Miami, FL 33131
Ph: (305)539-0010
Fax: (305)539-8001
E-mail: ecuacham@bellsouth.net
URL: http://www.ecuachamber.com
Contact: Juan Jose Malo, Pres.
Founded: 1988. **Members:** 100. **Membership Dues:** individual, $100 (annual) ● corporate, $275 (annual). **Staff:** 1. **Budget:** $100,000. **Languages:** English, Spanish. **Description:** Business firms, government agencies, and individuals in Ecuador and the U.S. united to promote contact between members, their governments, and international businesses. Sponsors seminars. **Libraries: Type:** reference. **Holdings:** 300. **Subjects:** American and Ecuadorian top-

ics. **Awards:** I. Hagen Latino Americana Award. **Frequency:** annual. **Type:** recognition. **Computer Services:** database, commercial and trade. **Committees:** Executive; Sponsorship. **Affiliated With:** Association of American Chambers of Commerce in Latin America; U.S. Chamber of Commerce. **Publications:** *Ecuadorian-American Chamber of Commerce—Annual Directory.* Membership Directory. Lists members' products and services. Includes Ecuadorian statistics and trademarks. **Price:** S 10. 00/year. Circulation: 2,000 ● *Ecuanotas* (in Spanish), quarterly. Newsletter. Includes chamber news. **Price:** free. **Circulation:** 500 ● *Living in Ecuador.* Book. **Circulation:** 2,000. **Conventions/Meetings:** monthly Economics and Financials - meeting.

Estonia

23730 ■ Estonian American Chamber of Commerce and Industry (EACCI)
c/o Krista Altok Tassa, Pres./Founder
157-61 17th Ave.
Whitestone, NY 11357
Ph: (718)747-3805
Fax: (718)767-8825
E-mail: katassa@eacci.org
URL: http://estonianamericanchamberofcommerce. com
Contact: Krista Altok Tassa, Pres./Founder
Founded: 2002. **Membership Dues:** affiliate, individual, $175 (annual) ● basic corporate (based on number of employees), $500-$1,000 (annual) ● corporate sponsorship, $1,500-$5,000 (annual). **Description:** Facilitates and promotes trade and investment between the United States and Estonia. Provides a forum for business networking and information exchange between the American and Estonian business communities. Strives to further the business interests of its members. **Publications:** *EACCI Newsletter,* quarterly. **Price:** included in membership dues. Alternate Formats: online.

Finland

23731 ■ Finnish American Chamber of Commerce (FACC)
866 UN Plz., Ste.250
New York, NY 10017
Ph: (212)821-0225
Fax: (212)750-4418
E-mail: faccnyc@verizon.net
URL: http://www.facc-ny.com
Contact: Ann-Christine Westerlund, Pres.
Founded: 1958. **Members:** 300. **Membership Dues:** student, $30 (annual) ● individual, young associate, $80 (annual) ● small business, $300 (annual) ● corporate, $550 (annual) ● sustaining, $1,600 (annual). **Staff:** 1. **Regional Groups:** 4. **Languages:** English, Finnish. **Description:** Maintains liaison with similar groups abroad; conducts seminars; arranges meetings with speakers. **Publications:** Newsletter, bimonthly. Covers Finnish-American trade, business, and culture. Includes book reviews and obituaries. **Price:** free. ISSN: 0015-2439. **Circulation:** 2,700. **Advertising:** accepted. **Conventions/Meetings:** monthly meeting.

France

23732 ■ French-American Chamber of Commerce (FACC)
122 E 42nd St., Ste.2015
New York, NY 10168
Ph: (212)867-0123
Fax: (212)867-9050
E-mail: info@faccnyc.org
URL: http://www.ccife.org/usa/new_york
Contact: Serge Bellanger, Pres.
Founded: 1896. **Members:** 4,100. **Membership Dues:** corporate, $2,000 (annual) ● councilor, $750 (annual) ● active, $500 (annual) ● associate, $300

(annual) ● young executive, $200 (annual). **Regional Groups:** 18. **Description:** Promotes trade between the U.S. and France and fosters economic, commercial, and financial relations between the two countries. Functions in an advisory and informative capacity and assists in organizing business contacts for its members. Holds roundtable discussions, business card exchanges, and other events. Sponsors educational programs. **Awards:** Person of the Year Award. **Frequency:** annual. **Type:** recognition. **Recipient:** for individual who has made an outstanding contribution to international business. **Computer Services:** Mailing lists, labels. **Committees:** Special Events. **Departments:** Events and Communications; Trade Assistance; Visitor Exchange. **Formerly:** French-American Chamber of Commerce in the United States; (1977) French Chamber of Commerce in the United States. **Publications:** *French-American Chamber of Commerce—Membership Directory,* annual. **Price:** $100.00/issue. **Circulation:** 4,500. **Advertising:** accepted. Alternate Formats: online ● *French-American News,* 5/year. Newsletter. Includes new publications information. **Price:** available to members only. **Advertising:** accepted. Alternate Formats: online. **Conventions/Meetings:** conference ● luncheon ● seminar.

Gay/Lesbian

23733 ■ National Gay/Lesbian Travel Desk
2790 Wrondel Way
PMB No. 444
Reno, NV 89502
E-mail: nglbtraveldesk@aol.com
Contact: Ira Gruber, Contact
Founded: 1995. **Members:** 4,500. **Budget:** $50,000. **Multinational. Description:** Main objective is to provide free travel stories to gay/lesbian senior, single and alternative newspapers from grant money. Operates Friends Tours for gays/lesbians that are single and do not want to travel alone. Looking for people in North America who want to write about their city. The NG/L Travel Desk will help those individuals with lodgings and food/museum admissions. Expects to have chapters on 64 cities for forthcoming publication, The Gay/Lesbian Guide to Great Cities in North America. **Libraries: Type:** not open to the public. **Holdings:** 1,500; books, periodicals. **Subjects:** gay, lesbian, straight travel publications, travel in North America and internationally. **Publications:** *Gay/Lesbian Guide to Great Cities in North America.* **Conventions/Meetings:** biennial meeting, for stringers ● annual meeting.

Germany

23734 ■ German American Chamber of Commerce
75 Broad St., 21st Fl.
New York, NY 10004-2415
Ph: (212)974-8830 (212)974-8849
Fax: (212)974-8867
E-mail: info@gaccny.com
URL: http://www.gaccny.com
Contact: Armin Kruger, VP/Treas.
Founded: 1947. **Members:** 2,100. **Membership Dues:** blue chip, $2,000 (annual) ● corporate, $1,000 (annual) ● regular, $500 (annual). **Staff:** 35. **Languages:** English, French, German. **Description:** Promotes business and trade between the United States and Germany. **Telecommunication Services:** electronic mail, akruger@gaccny.com. **Publications:** *American Subsidiaries of German Firms,* annual. Directory. **Price:** $120.00/copy; $399.00/copy on CD-ROM. **Advertising:** accepted. Alternate Formats: CD-ROM ● *Business in Industrial Location Germany.* Book ● *Distributorship Agreements in the United States.* Book ● *German American Trade,* monthly. Magazine. **Price:** $5.00/copy; $50.00/year ● *Licensing Technology and Trademarks in the United States.* Book ● *U.S.-German Economic Yearbook,* annual. **Price:** $50.00/copy. **Conventions/Meetings:** annual meeting.

23735 ■ German Convention Bureau (GCB)
122 E 42nd St., Ste.2000
New York, NY 10168-0072
Ph: (212)661-4582
Fax: (212)661-6192
E-mail: gcbny@gcb.de
URL: http://www.gcb.de
Contact: Richard Rheindorf, Dir.
Founded: 1973. **Members:** 220. **Staff:** 13. **Description:** Lufthansa German Airlines, German National Tourist Office, the German Federal Railroad, cities, convention centers, hotels, car rental companies, and ground operators. Promotes Germany as a site for conventions, meetings, seminars, and incentive travel. **Publications:** *A Short Guide on How to Plan and Organise Events in Germany.* Manual ● *Incentive and Event Guide to Germany.* Brochure ● *Meetings Made in Germany.* Brochure ● Also publishes incentive kit.

Greece

23736 ■ American Hellenic Institute (AHI)
1220 16th St. NW
Washington, DC 20036
Ph: (202)785-8430
Fax: (202)785-5178
E-mail: nlarigakis@ahiworld.org
URL: http://www.ahiworld.org
Contact: Nicholas Larigakis, Exec. Dir.
Founded: 1974. **Members:** 1,500. **Membership Dues:** regular, $100 (annual) ● contributing, $150 ● supporter, $250 ● sponsor, $500 ● sustaining, $1,000 ● patron, $2,500 ● benefactor, $5,000 ● grand benefactor, $10,000 ● student, $35. **Staff:** 3. **Description:** Seeks to strengthen political, cultural, trade, commerce, and related matters between the U.S. and Greece, Cyprus, and the American Hellenic community. Conducts research on issues such as Turkish threats to the Aegean, Cyprus, the rule of law, and human rights. Sponsors internship program and seminars. **Libraries: Type:** reference. **Computer Services:** Mailing lists, of members. **Committees:** Public Affairs. **Programs:** College Internship. **Special Interest Groups:** AHI Business Network. **Subgroups:** AHI Foundation. **Publications:** *AHI Report,* 3/year. Newsletter. Alternate Formats: online ● *American Hellenic Who's Who.* Manual. Alternate Formats: online ● *Doing Business in Greece.* **Price:** $250.00 ● *General News.* Newsletters. Alternate Formats: online ● *Greece's Pivotal Role in World War II and its Importance to the U.S. Today.* **Price:** $20.00 ● *Handbook on United States Relations with Greece and Cyprus.* Alternate Formats: online ● *Rule of Law and Conditions on Foreign Aid to Turkey.* Proceedings. Alternate Formats: online ● *United States Foreign Policy Regarding Greece, Turkey and Cyprus - The Rule of Law and American Interests.* Alternate Formats: online ● *Annual Report,* annual. Alternate Formats: online. **Conventions/Meetings:** annual Hellenic Heritage and National Public Service Awards Dinner - conference and dinner.

23737 ■ Hellenic-American Chamber of Commerce
960 Ave. of the Americas, Ste.1008
Atlantic Bank Bldg.
New York, NY 10001-2112
Ph: (212)629-6380
Fax: (212)564-9281
E-mail: hellenicchamber-nyc@att.net
URL: http://www.hellenicamerican.cc
Contact: Andre Gregory, Pres.
Founded: 1947. **Members:** 250. **Languages:** English, Greek. **Description:** Promotes commerce and trade; represents members' interests. **Awards:** George Athans Scholarship Fund. **Type:** scholarship. **Publications:** Journal, annual ● Newsletter, quarterly ● Membership Directory. Alternate Formats: online. **Conventions/Meetings:** annual conference - held in February.

Hispanic

23738 ■ United States Hispanic Chamber of Commerce (USHCC)
2175 K St. NW, Ste.100
Washington, DC 20037
Ph: (202)842-1212
Free: (800)874-2286
Fax: (202)842-3221
E-mail: ushcc@ushcc.com
URL: http://www.ushcc.com
Contact: Michael L. Barrera, Pres./CEO
Founded: 1979. **Members:** 70,000. **Membership Dues:** chamber/association (voting), $100 (annual) ● foreign trade association/chamber of commerce, $300 (annual) ● corporate, $10,000 (annual). **Staff:** 20. **Budget:** $5,000,000. **Regional Groups:** 132. **Languages:** English, Spanish. **Description:** Hispanic and other business firms interested in the development of Hispanic business and promotion of business leadership and economic interests in the Hispanic community. Promotes positive image of Hispanics and encourages corporate involvement with Hispanic firms. Conducts business-related workshops, conferences, and management training; reports on business achievements and vendor programs of major corporations; compiles statistics. **Libraries:** Type: reference. **Holdings:** photographs. **Awards:** Chairman's Award. **Type:** recognition ● Corporate Advisor of the Year (Business & Government). **Frequency:** annual. **Type:** recognition. **Recipient:** for corporate advisors ● Large and Small Chamber of the Year Award. **Frequency:** annual. **Type:** recognition. **Recipient:** for large and small chambers ● President's Award. **Type:** recognition. **Computer Services:** Information services, on Hispanic firms. **Councils:** Corporate Advisory; Small Business. **Publications:** *Chamber Weekly.* Newsletter. Provides information about USHCC initiatives, events and new opportunities for members and Hispanic business owners. **Price:** free. Alternate Formats: online ● *Hispanic Trends,* quarterly. Magazine. Covers convention. **Circulation:** 50,000. **Advertising:** accepted ● *Networking,* quarterly. Magazine. Provides information about the USHCC programs and initiatives and resources for Hispanic businesses. **Price:** included in membership dues. **Circulation:** 50,000. **Advertising:** accepted. **Conventions/Meetings:** annual competition and convention (exhibits) ● annual meeting (exhibits) ● periodic meeting, for networking ● annual regional meeting.

Historic Preservation

23739 ■ National Historic Route 66 Federation
PO Box 1848
Dept. WS
Lake Arrowhead, CA 92352-1848
Ph: (909)336-6131
Fax: (909)336-1039
URL: http://www.national66.org
Contact: David Knudson, Exec. Dir.
Founded: 1994. **Members:** 2,100. **Membership Dues:** trial, in U.S., $35 (annual) ● silver founder in U.S., $70 (annual) ● life, in U.S., $500 ● trial, outside U.S., $45 (annual) ● silver founder, outside U.S., $90 (biennial) ● life, outside U.S., $700. **Staff:** 4. **Description:** Committed to directing attention to the importance of US Highway Route 66, to preserve the historic landmarks and revitalize the economies of communities along the 2,400-mile road. **Awards:** Cyrus Avery. **Frequency:** annual. **Type:** recognition. **Recipient:** for the most promising member of the organization ● John Steinbeck. **Frequency:** annual. **Type:** recognition. **Recipient:** for the most productive member. **Programs:** Adopt A Hundred. **Projects:** Corridor Preservation Act; Route 66 Visitor Center/ Museum Plan. **Publications:** *Federation News,* quarterly. Magazine. Contains current news of Route 66, its history, people and points of interest. **Circulation:** 2,100. **Advertising:** accepted. **Conventions/Meetings:** annual festival, staged at various Route 66 cities.

Hong Kong

23740 ■ Hong Kong Trade Development Council (HKTDC)
219 E 46th St.
New York, NY 10017
Ph: (212)838-8688
Free: (800)832-4583
Fax: (212)838-8941
E-mail: elsweet.rufino@tdc.org.hk
URL: http://www.tdctrade.com
Founded: 1966. **Staff:** 15. **Description:** Quasi-governmental body responsible for promoting Hong Kong trade with the rest of the world and creating a favorable image for Hong Kong as a trading partner and international trade center. Sponsors trade missions and participates in major trade shows around the world. Maintains library of trade publications in both Hong Kong and its North American offices. Compiles statistics. **Convention/Meeting:** none. **Departments:** Accounts. **Divisions:** Marketing; Publicity; Research; Trade Enquiry; Trade Promotion; Trade Services. **Publications:** *Hong Kong Apparel,* quarterly. Brochure. Features review of the apparel industry in Hong Kong. ● *Hong Kong Electronics,* semiannual. Journal ● *Hong Kong Enterprise,* monthly. Journal. Describes Hong Kong products. **Circulation:** 70,000 ● *Hong Kong for the Business Visitor.* Brochure ● *Hong Kong Gifts and Premiums,* annual. Brochure.

Hospitality Industries

23741 ■ Caribbean Society of Hotel Association Executives (CSHAE)
c/o Caribbean Hotel Association
1000 Ponce De Leon Ave., 5th Fl.
San Juan, PR 00907
Ph: (787)725-9139
Fax: (787)725-9108
E-mail: imartinez@caribbeanhotels.org
URL: http://www.caribbeanhotelassociation.com
Contact: Ivette Martinez, Dir.
Founded: 1977. **Members:** 35. **Membership Dues:** professional/association executive, $250 (annual). **Staff:** 5. **Multinational. Description:** Represents and promotes professional development of national hotel association executives. Provides opportunities for discussion, study and conference on subjects of interest to Hotel and Tourism associations. Promotes sound policies for marketing and promotion, administration, management procedures and techniques for Hotel and Tourism associations. Cooperates and counsels with the Caribbean Hotel Association in the best interest of the CHA federation.

India

23742 ■ United States Indian American Chamber of Commerce (USIACC)
c/o Ron Mutch, Exec. Dir.
1725 I St. NW, Ste.No. 300
Washington, DC 20006
Ph: (202)349-1111
Fax: (480)607-9500
E-mail: info@usiacc.com
URL: http://www.usiacc.com
Contact: KV Kumar, Natl. Chm./CEO
Founded: 2003. **Membership Dues:** platinum corporate (one-time payment), $100,000 ● gold corporate (one-time payment), $50,000 ● silver corporate (one-time payment), $25,000 ● silver corporate, $2,000 (annual) ● corporate, trade associate, public sector, $1,000 (annual) ● small business, $250 (annual) ● student, $25 (annual). **Multinational. Description:** Promotes international trade between the United States and India. Fosters business development, community growth and economic development. Aims to strengthen Indian American businesses and associations at local, state and national levels. Monitors legislative policies and programs that affect the Indian American business community and advocates on behalf of Indian American businesses. Expands relationships between the Indian American businesses and professionals. **Telecommunication Services:** electronic mail, ronmutch@usiacc.com ● electronic mail, kvkumar@usiacc.com. **Publications:** Brochure. Alternate Formats: online.

Indonesia

23743 ■ American Indonesian Chamber of Commerce (AICC)
317 Madison Ave., Ste.1619
New York, NY 10017
Ph: (212)687-4505
Fax: (212)687-5844
E-mail: wayne@aiccusa.org
URL: http://www.aiccusa.org
Contact: Wayne Forrest, Pres./Sec./Exec. Dir.
Founded: 1949. **Members:** 180. **Membership Dues:** benefactor, $5,000 (annual) ● sponsor, $1,500 (annual) ● regular, $1,000 (annual) ● associate, $500 (annual). **Description:** Holds briefings on new trade policies in Indonesia and offers orientation workshops to company personnel traveling to Indonesia. **Committees:** Government Relations; Investment. **Publications:** *American Business Directory for Indonesia,* periodic. Contains list of American companies doing business in Indonesia and their agents or partners. **Price:** $60.00 for members; $70.00 for nonmembers ● *Executive Diary.* Analyses issued in response to current events. ● *Indonesia's Countertrade Experience* ● *Members Bulletin,* periodic ● *Outlook Indonesia,* quarterly. Newsletter. **Price:** included in membership dues ● *Sourcing Products in Indonesia: A Guide for Importers.* Contains tips and suggestions for successfully buying products from Indonesia, based on interviews with successful importers. **Price:** $25.00 ● Reports ● Also publishes an index of articles to Indonesia appearing in major Asian publications. **Conventions/Meetings:** periodic luncheon, includes Indonesian and American speakers.

International Standards

23744 ■ Albanian-American Trade and Development Association (AATDA)
159 E 4th St.
Dunkirk, NY 14048
Ph: (954)802-3166
Fax: (716)366-1516
E-mail: aatda@engl.com
URL: http://www.albaniabiz.org
Contact: James V. Elias, Chm./CEO
Founded: 1991. **Members:** 77. **Membership Dues:** ordinary, $50 (annual). **Staff:** 2. **Description:** Businesses and individuals engaged in trade involving the U.S. and Albania. Promotes expansion of trade between Albania and the United States. Facilitates establishment of international contacts by members; lobbies for removal of barriers to trade. **Libraries:** Type: not open to the public. **Holdings:** books, business records, periodicals. **Subjects:** international trade.

Investments

23745 ■ Managed Funds Association (MFA)
2025 M St. NW, Ste.800
Washington, DC 20036-3309
Ph: (202)367-1140
Fax: (202)367-2140
E-mail: hq@mfainfo.org
URL: http://www.mfainfo.org
Contact: John G. Gaine, Pres.
Founded: 1991. **Members:** 700. **Membership Dues:** basic, $2,000 (annual) ● capital, $10,000 (annual) ● sustaining, $40,000 (annual) ● special exception (start-up manager, small firm), $500 (annual). **Staff:** 4. **Description:** Alternative investment professionals including hedge fund managers, fund of funds managers, service providers, and others associated

with non-regulated investment funds. **Awards: Frequency:** annual. **Type:** grant. **Recipient:** for universities, colleges, academic institutions and individuals. **Committees:** Managed Funds Association Political Action. **Publications:** *Foundation for Managed Derivatives Research Reports.* **Price:** $2.00 ● *MFA Journal. Hedge Fund Strategies.* Contains articles by hedge fund managers regarding strategies and market sectors. **Price:** $10.00 for members; $12.50 for nonmembers ● *MFA Reporter.* Newsletter. Alternate Formats: online ● Membership Directory. **Conventions/Meetings:** conference.

Ireland

23746 ■ Tourism Ireland
345 Park Ave., 17th Fl.
New York, NY 10154
Ph: (212)418-0800
Fax: (212)371-9052
E-mail: corporate.usa@tourismireland.com
URL: http://www.irelandvacations.com
Contact: Andrew Coppel, Chm.
Description: Promotes travel to the Republic of Ireland. Conducts advertising and public relations activities; offers information services for tourists. Sponsors educational programs, seminars, and travel workshops. **Additional Websites:** http://www.tourismireland.com. **Telecommunication Services:** electronic mail, corporate.admin@tourismireland.com. **Departments:** Human Resources; Marketing and Technology Support; Marketing Communications; Research and Planning. **Divisions:** Corporate and Industry Communications; Corporate Services; Marketing; Markets and Customer Relations. **Formerly:** (2004) Irish Tourist Board. **Publications:** *Contact,* quarterly. Newsletter. Alternate Formats: online ● *Ireland: Island of Ireland Overseas Visitors.* Booklet. Alternate Formats: online ● Annual Report, annual. Alternate Formats: online ● Brochures. Alternate Formats: online.

Israel

23747 ■ America-Israel Chamber of Commerce and Industry (AICCI)
3 New York Plz., 10th Fl.
New York, NY 10004
Ph: (212)232-8440
Fax: (212)365-3366
E-mail: info@aicci.org
URL: http://www.digitaldreamarts.com/aicci
Contact: Ronny Bassan, Exec. VP
Founded: 1953. **Members:** 500. **Membership Dues:** individual, $375 (annual) ● small business, $750 (annual) ● corporate, $2,000 (annual) ● sponsor, $2,500 (annual). **Staff:** 2. **Description:** Promotes the interests of the U.S.-Israel business community; provides educational programs on trade expansion, bilateral investment, marketing and regional development; maintains close ties with the U.S. and Israeli governments and business leaders and actively participates in forums to advance bilateral trade and investment. **Libraries: Type:** reference. **Awards: Type:** recognition. **Formerly:** American-Israel Chamber of Commerce and Industry. **Publications:** *Economic Horizons,* semiannual ● *Israel Quality,* quarterly ● Newsletter. **Conventions/Meetings:** luncheon ● seminar, provides discussions on U.S.-Israel trade and investment.

23748 ■ Committee for the Economic Growth of Israel (CEGI)
PO Box 2053
Milwaukee, WI 53217
Ph: (414)906-6250
Fax: (414)906-7878
E-mail: elmer.winter@na.manpower.com
URL: http://www.cegi.org
Contact: Elmer L. Winter, Chm.
Founded: 1976. **Members:** 150. **Staff:** 5. **Description:** Businessmen and women. Seeks to expand

business relationships between Israel and the U.S. by promoting investment and joint venture opportunities for U.S. and Israeli companies. Promotes the exchange of technology, research and development, and products from Israel. **Publications:** *CEGI Newsletter,* semimonthly. Contains information for Israeli manufacturers. **Price:** free. **Circulation:** 2,200 ● Also publishes brochures.

Italian

23749 ■ Italian-American Chamber of Commerce (IACC)
500 N Michigan Ave., Ste.506
Chicago, IL 60611
Ph: (312)553-9137
Fax: (312)553-9142
E-mail: info@italianchamber.us
URL: http://www.italianchamber.us
Contact: Fulvio Calcinardi, Exec. Dir.
Founded: 1907. **Members:** 200. **Membership Dues:** company, $500 (annual) ● sustaining, $800 (annual) ● general, $250 (annual) ● young professional (under 35), $100 (annual). **Staff:** 4. **Languages:** English, Italian. **Description:** Promotes trade between Italy and the U.S. and aids Italian organizations and companies to promote their products and/or services in the U.S. Organizes trade missions to Italian trade shows and trade delegations of U.S. businesses in Italy to meet with companies and organizations. Represents CASIC-BIC Sardinia to promote foreign investments in the industrial area of Cagliari, Sardinia. **Libraries: Type:** reference. **Holdings:** 300. **Subjects:** Italian companies. **Awards: Frequency:** annual. **Type:** scholarship. **Recipient:** for full time students, residents of six counties in Illinois, of Italian ancestry between the last year of high school and the last year of a 4-year college or university. **Computer Services:** database, companies in Italy. **Committees:** Business Expo; Dinner Dance; Golf Outing; Legal; Public Relations; Scholarship; Trade with Italy. **Publications:** *The Bulletin,* quarterly. **Price:** free for members; $35.00 for nonmembers. **Circulation:** 1,000. **Advertising:** accepted. Alternate Formats: online ● Newsletter. Alternate Formats: online. **Conventions/Meetings:** annual convention ● bimonthly meeting.

Italy

23750 ■ Italy-America Chamber of Commerce (IACC)
730 5th Ave., Ste.600
New York, NY 10019
Ph: (212)459-0044
Fax: (212)459-0090
E-mail: info@italchamber.org
URL: http://www.italchamber.org
Contact: Franco De Angelis, Sec. Gen.
Founded: 1887. **Members:** 1,000. **Membership Dues:** general, $650 (annual) ● sustaining, $2,000 (annual) ● senior sustaining, $2,500 (annual). **Staff:** 10. **National Groups:** 9. **Languages:** English, Italian. **Description:** Brings together businesses ranging from individual entrepreneurs to large corporations. Advances the interests of its members through contacts and interaction with government agencies, trade associations and leading international organizations. **Libraries: Type:** not open to the public. **Holdings:** 3,000. **Subjects:** U.S.-Italian commerce. **Awards:** Business and Culture Award. **Frequency:** annual. **Type:** recognition. **Recipient:** for Italian companies, businessmen and businesswomen ● Golden Award. **Frequency:** annual. **Type:** recognition. **Recipient:** for economic achievements in international relations. **Computer Services:** database, Italian importers/exporters; access through IACC data system. **Boards:** Export Advisory. **Committees:** Apparel; Consumer Products; Financial Services; Food and Beverage; Freight Forwarders

and Custom Wholesale Brokers; High Tech; Industrial Products; Publicity and Public Relations; Transportation; Women; Young Executive. **Publications:** *IACC Inform,* monthly. Magazine. **Price:** included in membership dues. **Circulation:** 5,000. **Advertising:** accepted ● *Trade With Italy,* bimonthly. Magazine. **Price:** included in membership dues. **Advertising:** accepted. Alternate Formats: online ● *United States - Italy Trade Directory,* annual. **Price:** $150.00. **Circulation:** 15,000 ● US - Italy Trade Directory CD-ROM. **Conventions/Meetings:** annual Networking - convention (exhibits).

Jamaica

23751 ■ Jamaica Tourist Board (JTB)
5201 Blue Lagoon Dr., Ste.670
Miami, FL 33126
Ph: (305)665-0557
Free: (800)233-4582
Fax: (305)666-7239
E-mail: info@visitjamaica-usa.com
URL: http://www.visitjamaica.com
Contact: Anthony King, Regional Mgr.
Staff: 199. **Description:** Participates in travel trade expositions. **Publications:** *Jamaica Newsletter,* periodic. **Price:** free for travel agents. **Conventions/Meetings:** periodic meeting.

Japan

23752 ■ Japan Convention Bureau (JCB)
1 Rockefeller Plz., Ste.1250
New York, NY 10020
Ph: (212)757-5640
Fax: (212)307-6754
E-mail: visitjapan@jntonyc.org
URL: http://www.jnto.go.jp
Contact: Mr. Bruce Kanfer, Convention Dir.
Founded: 1965. **Staff:** 6. **Languages:** English, Japanese. **Description:** An agency of the Japanese government created to promote Japan as a convention site. Encourages and assists U.S. businesses, associations, and special interest groups to hold conventions at Japanese centers; collaborates with companies to promote Japanese convention incentive programs. **Convention/Meeting:** none. **Affiliated With:** Japan National Tourist Organization. **Publications:** *Convention Destination Japan,* semiannual. Book ● *Exhibitors and Events in Japan,* semiannual. Brochure ● *Incentive Destination,* annual. Book ● *Japan International Congress Calendar,* semiannual. Report.

23753 ■ Japan External Trade Organization (JETRO)
1221 Ave. of the Americas
McGraw Hill Bldg., 42nd Fl.
New York, NY 10020
Ph: (212)997-0400
Fax: (212)997-0464
E-mail: jetrony@jetro.go.jp
URL: http://www.jetro.org
Contact: Ryohei Yamamoto, Contact
Founded: 1958. **Staff:** 80. **Languages:** English, Japanese. **Description:** Supports foreign companies in export and/or investment to Japan-related business ventures. Disseminates comprehensive information on the Japanese economy and market through surveys, reports, publications, and newsletters. Conducts trade and investment promotion seminars and symposia. Sponsors trade shows and exhibitions. Provides professional business consultation services and handles trade-related inquiries and provides opportunities for international exchange. **Libraries: Type:** open to the public. **Holdings:** articles, books, periodicals. **Subjects:** doing business with Japan. **Publications:** *Directory of Japanese Affiliated Companies,* biennial. **Price:** $360.00. **Advertising:** accepted ● *Japan Trade Directory,* an-

nual ● *JETRO Spotlight USA*, monthly. Newsletter. Brings relevant and timely articles highlighting business opportunities between the United States and Japan.

23754 ■ Japan Light Machinery Information Center of Central New York (JLMIC)
1221 Ave. of the Ams., 42 Fl.
New York, NY 10020-1079
Ph: (212)997-0444
Fax: (212)944-8315
Contact: Satoshi Miyamoto, Exec.Dir.
Description: Represents the interests of Japanese Light Machinery Industries.

23755 ■ Japan National Tourist Organization (JNTO)
1 Rockefeller Plz., Ste.1250
New York, NY 10020
Ph: (212)757-5640
Fax: (212)307-6754
E-mail: visitjapan@jntonyc.org
URL: http://www.jnto.go.jp
Contact: Minoru Nakamura, Pres.
Founded: 1964. **Staff:** 148. **Description:** Instrument of the Japanese government to promote Japan's tourist industry through overseas publicity, information services, and other related activities. Prepares videos and publicity materials; provides technical assistance to the tourist industry of Japan; conducts market surveys and participates in overseas fairs and exhibitions. Maintains tourist information centers in Tokyo and Kyoto, Japan to aid foreign tourists. Operates 14 overseas offices, including five in the U.S. **Additional Websites:** http://www.japantravelinfo.com. **Formerly:** (1964) Japan National Tourist Association.

23756 ■ Japanese Chamber of Commerce and Industry of Hawaii
Address Unknown since 2007
Founded: 1951. **Members:** 275. **Membership Dues:** individual, $160 (annual). **Staff:** 1. **Budget:** $45,000. **Description:** Promotes business and trade between Japan and the United States of America. **Committees:** Economic Development; Education; Golf; Government Affairs; International Festival; Public Relations and Aloha; Publicity and Newsbulletin. **Publications:** *Oshirase*, bimonthly. Newsletter. **Circulation:** 350. **Advertising:** accepted. **Conventions/Meetings:** annual Hawaii's International Festival of the Pacific - meeting - always July, Hilo, HI ● quarterly meeting.

23757 ■ Japanese Chamber of Commerce and Industry of New York (JCCINY)
145 W 57th St.
New York, NY 10019
Ph: (212)246-8001
Fax: (212)246-8002
E-mail: info@jcciny.org
URL: http://www.jcciny.org
Contact: Susumu Kato, Pres.
Founded: 1932. **Members:** 450. **Membership Dues:** regular, $1,450 (annual) ● associate, individual, $850 (annual). **Staff:** 7. **Description:** Japanese and non-Japanese corporations. Fosters improved trade relations between the U.S. and Japan. Conducts seminars and surveys. **Boards:** Directors. **Committees:** Community Affairs; JCC Fund Committee Municipal Relations; Public Relations. **Task Forces:** US Educators. **Formerly:** (1989) Japanese Chamber of Commerce of New York. **Publications:** *Japan's Industries and Trade: Profiles and Interrelationships with the United States* (in English and Japanese). Pamphlet ● *JCCI Weekly Report, What America Needs to Know About Changing Japan*. Highlights news found in various newspapers pertaining to Japan, the U.S., and the international market. ● *Joining In! A Handbook for Better Corporate Citizenship in the U.S.* ● Membership Directory, annual. **Advertising:** accepted ● Reports. **Conventions/Meetings:** annual dinner, to celebrate US-Japan Alliance - usually fall.

23758 ■ U.S.-Japan Business Council (USJBC)
2000 L St. NW, Ste.515
Washington, DC 20036
Ph: (202)728-0068
Fax: (202)728-0073
URL: http://www.usjbc.org
Contact: Karen Katen, Chair
Members: 70. **Staff:** 3. **Description:** Management leaders of American companies engaged in business activities with Japan. Represents U.S. business interests in an effort to maintain a balance in Japan-U.S. economic and overall relations. Seeks to provide a forum to propose solutions to problems within the Japan-U.S. economic relationship, and stimulate and facilitate business relations between the two countries. Advises U.S. government leaders on economic issues and policies. **Conventions/Meetings:** annual conference, held in conjunction with the Japan-U.S. Business Council - always summer, alternating between Japan and the U.S. ● annual meeting - in April.

Japanese

23759 ■ Honolulu Japanese Chamber of Commerce (HJCC)
2454 S Beretania St., Ste.201
Honolulu, HI 96826
Ph: (808)949-5531
Fax: (808)949-3020
E-mail: info@honolulujapanesechamber.org
URL: http://www.honolulujapanesechamber.org
Contact: Wendy A. Abe, Pres.
Founded: 1900. **Members:** 850. **Membership Dues:** active, $350 (annual) ● associate/Jaycee, $110 (annual) ● supporting, $35 (annual). **Staff:** 5. **Description:** Provides the organizational means for support of functions of groups within the Hawaiian community or Japan-related groups in pursuit of cultural, economic, governmental, and social development. **Committees:** Business, Economic Development and Tourism; Culture; Government Affairs; Information and Technology; Marketing; Program and Community Affairs; Small Business Advocacy; Ways and Means. **Publications:** *Honolulu Japanese Chamber of Commerce—Membership Directory*, annual. Lists members by company, trade, and individuals. Includes summaries of chamber functions, projects, events, and facilities. **Price:** free for members; $20.00 for nonmembers. **Circulation:** 1,200. **Advertising:** accepted ● *Shoko Newsletter*, monthly. Contains information on Hawaiian commerce and chamber activities. Includes information on trade opportunities and new members and calendar of events. **Price:** included in membership dues. **Circulation:** 800. **Advertising:** accepted. **Conventions/Meetings:** annual conference.

Jordan

23760 ■ Jordan Information Bureau (JIB)
3504 Intl. Dr. NW
Washington, DC 20008
Ph: (202)265-1606
Free: (877)80-JIBDC
Fax: (202)667-0777
E-mail: jordaninfo@aol.com
URL: http://www.jordanembassyus.org
Contact: Merissa Khurma, Dir.
Founded: 1975. **Staff:** 9. **Languages:** Arabic, English. **Description:** Provides cultural, economic, and travel information on Jordan. **Libraries: Type:** reference. **Holdings:** books, clippings, periodicals. **Subjects:** Jordan. **Computer Services:** Mailing lists, information. **Telecommunication Services:** electronic mail, jordaninfo1@aol.com. **Publications:** *Facts and Figures* (in Arabic and English), annual. Brochure. Contains full illustrated information about

Jordan, its history, culture, art, tourist spots, and economy. **Price:** free.

Korea

23761 ■ The Korea Society (TKS)
950 3rd Ave., 8th Fl.
New York, NY 10022
Ph: (212)759-7525
Fax: (212)759-7530
E-mail: fred.ny@koreasociety.org
URL: http://www.koreasociety.org
Contact: Frederick F. Carriere, VP/Exec. Dir.
Founded: 1962. **Members:** 1,200. **Membership Dues:** student, $15 (annual) ● individual, $25 (annual) ● joint/family/institution, $50 (annual) ● contributor, $100 (annual) ● sustaining, $250 (annual) ● sponsor, $500 (annual) ● patron, $1,000 (annual). **Staff:** 12. **Budget:** $2,000,000. **Languages:** English, Korean. **Description:** Works to foster increased understanding between the people of the United States and Korea. Promotes improved economic, cultural, and educational exchange through seminars, educational programs, and research. **Libraries: Type:** reference. **Holdings:** 600; articles, books, periodicals. **Subjects:** Korea and U.S. - Korea relations. **Awards:** Peter Ohm Scholarship. **Frequency:** annual. **Type:** scholarship. **Programs:** The Arts; Business Korean Language; Contemporary Issues; Corporate Affairs; Intercultural Outreach; Korean Studies; Special Events; VOICES. **Formerly:** (1973) Korea-America Commerce and Industry Association; (1982) U.S.-Korea Economic Council; (1990) U.S.-Korea Society. **Publications:** *Getting to Know Korea: Resource book for K-12 educators.* Alternate Formats: online ● *The Korea Society Quarterly*. Magazine. **Price:** $15.00/year; $25.00/2 years. Alternate Formats: online ● *The U.S. Korea Review*, bimonthly. Newsletter. Features all subjects on U.S. - Korea relations. **Price:** $15.00/year. **Circulation:** 12,000 ● Annual Report, annual. Alternate Formats: online ● Report. Alternate Formats: online.

23762 ■ Korea Trade Promotion Center (KOTRA)
460 Park Ave., Ste.402
New York, NY 10022
Ph: (212)826-0900
Fax: (212)888-4930
E-mail: kotrany@ix.netcom.com
Contact: Woo Jae Ryang, Pres.
Founded: 1962. **Regional Groups:** 10. **Description:** Works as an agency of the Korean government. Provides information about Korean export commodities and exporters, and import commodities and importers. Sponsors visits of foreign businesspersons to the Republic of Korea; arranges introductions of potential traders to Korean manufacturers and sales and buying missions of traders with the Republic of Korea. Compiles statistics; conducts economic and marketing research for distribution to Korean industry, business, and government; participates in U.S. trade shows. Maintains 35,000 volume international trade library. **Libraries: Type:** reference. **Holdings:** 35,000. **Subjects:** international trade. **Departments:** Area Research; Commodity Research; Exhibition; Overseas Marketing; Public Information; Research and Development; Special Transaction; Trade Promotion. **Publications:** *Daily KOTRA Marketing News* (in English and Korean). Newsletter ● *Korea Trade*, 5/year ● *Korea Trade and Investment*, monthly ● Books ● Pamphlets.

Latin America

23763 ■ Association of American Chambers of Commerce in Latin America (AACCLA)
1615 H St. NW
Washington, DC 20062-2000
Ph: (202)463-5485

Fax: (202)463-3126
E-mail: info@aaccla.org
URL: http://www.aaccla.org
Contact: Tom Mouhsian, Assoc. Dir.
Founded: 1967. **Members:** 22. **Staff:** 4. **Description:** Umbrella organization for American chambers of commerce in Latin America. Represents American chambers of commerce before the congressional and executive branches of the United States government. Conducts lobbying and legislation tracking activities. **Awards:** Eagle of the Americas. **Frequency:** annual. **Type:** recognition. **Affiliated With:** U.S. Chamber of Commerce. **Publications:** *Americas Update*, bi-monthly. Newsletter. Alternate Formats: online ● *Latin American Country Profiles*, annual. **Price:** $55.00 ● *Survey of Investment Climate*, annual. **Price:** $30.00 ● Report. Alternate Formats: online ● Membership Directories. Alternate Formats:. online ● Surveys. Alternate Formats: online. **Conventions/Meetings:** annual Corporate Briefing - meeting - always spring, Washington, DC ● semiannual executive committee meeting ● annual meeting - always Washington, DC. 2007 Sept. 17-19, Washington, DC ● annual Mid-Year Meeting - conference - usually mid-November ● regional meeting and seminar - 4-6/year.

23764 ■ Council of the Americas (CoA)
680 Park Ave.
New York, NY 10021
Ph: (212)249-8950
Fax: (212)249-1880
E-mail: inforequest@as-coa.org
URL: http://www.counciloftheamericas.org
Contact: Susan L. Segal, Pres./CEO
Founded: 1965. **Members:** 260. **Membership Dues:** corporate, $10,000 (annual). **Staff:** 20. **Budget:** $2,000,000. **Languages:** English, Portuguese, Spanish. **Description:** Promotes on behalf of its members, policies and practices favoring free trade and investment, market economies and the rule of law in West Hemisphere. Provides a forum for its members to discuss economic, political and social issues relevant to the Hemisphere with public and private sector leaders. Represents the membership in public policy discussions. Assists members in the achievement of their business objectives in the region. **Committees:** Mexico-U.S. Business. **Councils:** U.S. **Working Groups:** Brazil Study; Energy Action; Peru Action; Trade Advisory. **Affiliated With:** Americas Society. **Formerly:** Council for Latin America. **Publications:** Annual Report, annual. Alternate Formats: online ● Annual Reports, annual. Alternate Formats: online ● Papers. Alternate Formats: online ● Articles ● Brochure. Alternate Formats: online ● Reports. Alternate Formats: online. **Conventions/Meetings:** annual Washington Conference, held at the state department, focus on integration and free trade in the Western Hemisphere.

23765 ■ Latin Chamber of Commerce of U.S.A.
1417 W Flagler St., 3rd Fl.
Miami, FL 33135
Ph: (305)642-3870
Fax: (305)642-0653
E-mail: info@camacol.org
URL: http://www.camacol.org
Contact: William Alexander, Pres.
Founded: 1965. **Members:** 1,900. **Membership Dues:** regular, $200 (annual). **Staff:** 25. **Budget:** $900,000. **Languages:** English, Spanish. **Description:** Provides placement services; compiles statistics. Maintains information and referral service. **Libraries: Type:** reference. **Holdings:** 2,000. **Subjects:** projects realized within the chamber. **Computer Services:** Mailing lists, of members. **Committees:** Building Improvements; Christmas Baskets; Finance; Government Affairs; New Members; Public Relations; Special Events. **Also Known As:** Camara de Comercio Latina de los EEUU. **Formerly:** (1990) Latin Chamber of Commerce. **Publications:** *Revista Camacol* (in English and Spanish), monthly. Magazine. Brings all the past and upcoming events of the

chamber, also provides an informative social issues. **Price:** free for members. **Circulation:** 1,700. **Advertising:** accepted ● Membership Directory. **Conventions/Meetings:** annual Hemispheric Congress - conference and convention, sales of imported and exported products (exhibits) - always held at the end of April ● monthly meeting.

Malaysia

23766 ■ Malaysia Tourism Promotion Board (MTPB)
818 W 7th St., Ste.970
Los Angeles, CA 90017-3431
Ph: (213)689-9702
Free: (800)336-6842
Fax: (213)689-1530
E-mail: mtpb.la@tourism.gov.my
URL: http://www.tourismmalaysiausa.com
Contact: Mr. Mohamed Amin Yahya, VP
Founded: 1984. **Staff:** 6. **Description:** Promotes tourism to Malaysia. Conducts educational presentations. **Formerly:** (1992) Malaysia Tourist Information Center. **Publications:** *Malaysia Tourism News*, monthly. Newsletter ● Books ● Brochures ● Videos ● Also publishes maps and posters.

Mexico

23767 ■ Mexico Tourism Board (MTB)
400 Madison Ave., Ste.11C
New York, NY 10017
Ph: (212)308-2110
Free: (800)446-3942
Fax: (212)308-9060
E-mail: contact@visitmexico.com
URL: http://www.visitmexico.com
Contact: Maria Isabel Lopez, Contact
Founded: 2000. **Staff:** 10. **Languages:** English, Spanish. **Description:** Promotes and provides information on Mexico to travel agents, wholesalers, consumers in Northeastern United States. Conducts seminars and trade shows. **Formerly:** (2004) Mexican Government Tourism Office.

Middle East

23768 ■ American Mideast Business Associates (AMBA)
4 Kansas Rd.
Little Egg Harbor Township, NJ 08087-1037
Ph: (609)296-4783
E-mail: osirisbin@peoplepc.com
Contact: I.F. Yusif CAE, Pres.
Founded: 1951. **Members:** 185. **Membership Dues:** corporate, $10,000 (annual). **Description:** U.S. and Middle Eastern oil, transportation, automotive, finance, machinery, and other firms interested in promoting and expanding trade between the United States, the Middle East, and North Africa. Has cosponsored trade missions covering the Near East, Persian Gulf area, and North Africa. Holds frequent forums and briefings. Offers consultation and translation services to nonmembers for fee. **Awards:** U.S. President's "E" and "E-Star" Awards for Excellence. **Type:** recognition. **Committees:** Programs and Activities. **Formerly:** (1960) American Egyptian Society; (1987) American-Arab Association for Commerce and Industry. **Publications:** *Staff Memoranda* ● Directory, periodic. **Conventions/Meetings:** annual meeting - in the spring ● periodic workshop and conference.

Native American

23769 ■ Native American Indian Information and Trade Center
PO Box 27626
Tucson, AZ 85726-7626

Ph: (520)622-4900
Fax: (520)622-3525
E-mail: info@usaindianinfo.org
URL: http://www.usaindianinfo.org
Contact: Fred Synder, Dir./Consultant
Founded: 1983. **Members:** 2,700. **Staff:** 3. **Budget:** $50,000. **Description:** Acts as a clearinghouse of information on American Indians. Collects and disseminates information at major American Indian events, conferences, and gatherings. Sponsors educational programs, pow wows, and Indian art festivals. **Libraries: Type:** reference. **Holdings:** 5,000. **Subjects:** American Indians. **Awards:** Frequency:** annual. **Type:** scholarship. **Computer Services:** Mailing lists, individuals with an interest in Native Americans. **Committees:** Reservation Creations Woman's Circle Charitable Trust. **Affiliated With:** National Native American (Indian) Cooperative; North America Native American (Indian) Information and Trade Center. **Formerly:** (1999) North American Indian Chamber of Commerce of North America. **Publications:** *Indian America*, quarterly. Contains information packet including flyers, brochures, maps, newspapers, pow wow/event schedules, programs, and reports pertaining to American Indians. **Circulation:** 100,000. **Advertising:** accepted ● *Native American Directory*. Serves as a yellow "Red Pages" on Indians of North America. ● *Pow Wows on the Red Road*. Includes listings of pow wows, rodeos, cultural festival, arts and crafts shows and conventions. **Conventions/Meetings:** annual American Indian Expo - conference - last Sunday in January through 2nd Sunday in February ● annual Indian America Competition Pow Wow - New Year's weekend ● semiannual Native American Month Social Pow Wow - meeting - always Thanksgiving weekend ● Thunder in the Desert - meeting - December 31 through 2nd weekend in January.

Netherlands

23770 ■ Netherlands Board of Tourism and Conventions (NBTC)
355 Lexington Ave., 19th Fl.
New York, NY 10017
Ph: (212)370-7360
Fax: (212)370-9507
E-mail: jwassenaar@holland.com
URL: http://www.nlcongress.nl
Contact: Jort Wassenaar, Contact
Founded: 1971. **Staff:** 15. **Description:** Promotes travel from the United States to the Netherlands as destination for meetings, conventions and incentives. **Formerly:** Netherlands Convention Bureau; (2001) Netherlands Board of Tourism; (2003) Netherlands Convention and Visitors Bureau; (2004) Netherlands Board of Tourism. **Publications:** *Resource Directory*, annual. Contains list of Holland's most useful convention and meeting venues. **Price:** free ● Also publishes brochures and travel literature.

23771 ■ Netherlands Chamber of Commerce in the United States (NLCOC)
267 5th Ave., Ste.301
New York, NY 10016
Ph: (212)265-6460
Fax: (212)265-6402
E-mail: newyork@nlcoc.com
URL: http://www.netherlands.org
Contact: Kersen J. De Jong, Sec.
Founded: 1903. **Members:** 300. **Membership Dues:** corporate, $775 (annual) ● sustaining, $1,550 (annual) ● patron, $3,100 (annual) ● benefactor, $6,200 (annual). **Staff:** 3. **Budget:** $360,000. **Description:** Aims to maintain and expand business relations between The Netherlands and the United States. **Awards:** George Washington Vanderbilt Trophy. **Frequency:** periodic. **Type:** trophy. **Recipient:** for most significant contribution towards the expansion of trade and investments between the United States and The Netherlands. **Computer Services:** database ● mailing lists. **Publications:** Newsletter, monthly. **Price:**

free for members. **Circulation:** 300. **Advertising:** accepted ● Annual Report, annual. **Price:** free. **Circulation:** 300. **Conventions/Meetings:** annual luncheon - 2007 Dec. 7, Amsterdam, Netherlands.

Netherlands Antilles

23772 ■ Bonaire Government Tourist Office (BGTO)
c/o Adams Unlimited Public Relations and Marketing
80 Broad St., 32nd Fl., Ste.3202
New York, NY 10004
Ph: (212)956-5911
Free: (800)266-2473
Fax: (212)956-5913
E-mail: usa@tourismbonaire.com
URL: http://www.infobonaire.com
Contact: Marie Rosa, VP
Founded: 1990. **Description:** Disseminates travel information on Bonaire, Netherlands Antilles. **Formerly:** (1990) Bonaire Tourist Information Office.

23773 ■ Curacao Convention Bureau/Tourist Board
Curacao Tourism Corp.
3361 SW Third Ave., Ste.201
Miami, FL 33145
Ph: (305)285-0511
Free: (800)328-7222
Fax: (305)285-0535
E-mail: northamerica@curacao.com
URL: http://www.curacao-tourism.com
Contact: Joel Grossman, Contact
Description: Facilitates conventions and tourism in Curacao. **Additional Websites:** http://www.ctb.an. **Formerly:** (1968) Curacao Information Center; (1973) Curacao and Bonaire Tourist Boards; (1977) Curacao Tourist Board.

New Zealand

23774 ■ New Zealand Tourism Board (NZTB)
501 Santa Monica Blvd., Ste.300
Santa Monica, CA 90401
Ph: (310)395-7480
Free: (866)639-9325
Fax: (310)395-5453
E-mail: register@nztb.govt.nz
URL: http://www.newzealand.com
Contact: Bruce Lahood, Regional Mgr., North America
Founded: 1901. **Staff:** 160. **Description:** Promotes New Zealand as a desirable site for tourism and international conventions and as a favorable destination for incentive travel programs. Answers inquiries about New Zealand and provides research and source materials. Compiles statistics. **Libraries:** **Type:** reference. **Holdings:** audiovisuals, books. **Awards:** **Type:** recognition. **Computer Services:** database, NZHOST, consumers and travel agents. **Additional Websites:** http://www.tourismnewzealand.com. **Councils:** New Zealand Tourism. **Divisions:** Research; Tourism Development. **Formerly:** (1963) Department of Tourism and Health Resorts; (1990) New Zealand Tourist and Publicity Office. **Publications:** *New Zealand Accommodation Guide*, annual ● *New Zealand Arrival Statistics*, monthly ● *New Zealand Official Vacation Planner*, annual ● *New Zealand Ski Guide*, annual ● *Research Documents*, periodic ● Also publishes transport summary schedules, sight-seeing summary, New Zealand maps and other special interest publications on New Zealand. **Conventions/Meetings:** annual Tourism Rendezvous New Zealand - meeting (exhibits) - always May/June, in New Zealand.

Pakistan

23775 ■ Pakistan Chamber of Commerce USA (PCC-USA)
9700 Club Creek Dr., Ste.E
Houston, TX 77036
Ph: (713)771-9628
Fax: (281)530-8282
E-mail: info@pcc-usa.org
URL: http://www.pcc-usa.org
Contact: Dr. Barkat Charania, Pres.
Founded: 1997. **Membership Dues:** business, corporate, $300 (annual) ● individual self-employed, professional, $50 (annual) ● life, $1,500. **Multinational. Description:** Promotes trade and commerce between Pakistan and United States. Seeks to maintain and promote good relations between the two countries through a strong business community presence in the United States. Cooperates and coordinates with other Chambers of Commerce and Organizations in Pakistan and in the US. Provides social interaction, networking and friendly exchange among members and their families social and cultural functions. Encourages the practice of higher business ethics and moral standards among its members and the rest of the Pakistani American business community. **Affiliated With:** U.S. Chamber of Commerce.

Philippines

23776 ■ Philippine-American Chamber of Commerce (PACC)
1130 Connecticut Ave., Ste.310
Washington, DC 20036
Ph: (202)835-0875
Fax: (202)835-1464
E-mail: twusa1pta@aol.com
Contact: Celia P. Donahue, Pres.
Founded: 1920. **Members:** 101. **Membership Dues:** individual, $50 (annual) ● corporate, $100 (annual). **Staff:** 4. **Description:** Promotes trade and investment between the U.S. and the Philippines. Provides information and services on doing business in the Philippines. **Libraries:** **Type:** open to the public. **Holdings:** 100. **Subjects:** U.S./Philippine business. **Committees:** Business Development; Community Outreach; Fundraising; Media and Publications; Science and Technology; Special Projects; Trade Fair. **Publications:** *Living in the Philippines*. Newsletter ● *Network*, quarterly. Newsletter ● *Philamcham News*, biweekly. Newsletter ● *Philippine Business Quarterly*. **Conventions/Meetings:** monthly luncheon.

Poland

23777 ■ Polish-U.S. Business Council
c/o Chamber of Commerce of the United States
1615 H St. NW
Washington, DC 20062-2000
Ph: (202)659-6000
Free: (800)638-6582
E-mail: eurasia@uschamber.com
URL: http://www.uschamber.com
Contact: Thomas J. Donohue, Pres./CEO
Founded: 1974. **Members:** 30. **Membership Dues:** company (with over 50 million annual revenues), $5,000 (annual) ● company (with under 50 million annual revenues), $3,000 (annual). **Description:** U.S. corporations involved in industry, agriculture, or services. Seeks to expand trade between the U.S. and Poland, and to encourage investment in Poland by U.S. firms. **Formerly:** (1998) Polish-U.S. Economic Council. **Publications:** *Bridging the Atlantic. Book.* Offers tips and suggestions for breaking ground into the European business market. **Price:** $23.95 includes shipping ● *The Eurasia Committee Dispatch*, weekly. Report. Contains latest information from United States Chamber of Commerce on regulations, legislation, etc. **Price:** $200.00/year. **Conventions/Meetings:** periodic conference and workshop - alternates between Poland and the U.S.

Portugal

23778 ■ Portuguese National Tourist Office (PNTO)
590 5th Ave., 4th Fl.
New York, NY 10036-4702
Ph: (212)354-4403
Fax: (212)764-6137
E-mail: tourism@portugal.org
URL: http://www.portugal.org
Contact: Mr. Frederico Costa, Dir.
Description: Provides information about tourism, trade, investment, and other general information about Portugal. **Formerly:** (1972) Portugese Information, Tourist and Trade Office; (1975) Portugese Tourist and Information Office. **Publications:** *Portugal Update*, quarterly. Newsletter. For travel editors, travel writers, and the travel industry.

23779 ■ Portuguese Trade Commission (PTC)
590 5th Ave., 3rd Fl.
New York, NY 10036
Ph: (212)354-4610
Fax: (212)575-4737
E-mail: webmaster@portugal.org
URL: http://www.portugal.org
Contact: Eduardo Souto Moura, Hd.
Budget: $3,000,000. **Description:** Promotes exports from Portugal to the U.S. and helps American importers and businesses find sources in Portugal. **Convention/Meeting:** none. **Additional Websites:** http://www.portugalinbusiness.com. **Formerly:** (1984) Portuguese Government Trade Office. **Publications:** *Export Directory of Portugal*, annual ● Also publishes fact sheets, catalogs, and industry brochures.

Romania

23780 ■ Romanian-American Chamber of Commerce (RACC)
2 Wisconsin Cir., Ste.700
Chevy Chase, MD 20815
Ph: (240)235-6060 (212)471-8453
Fax: (240)235-6061
E-mail: racc@racc.ro
URL: http://www.racc.ro
Contact: Jay McCrensky, Managing Dir.
Founded: 1991. **Members:** 200. **Membership Dues:** individual, $150 (annual) ● corporate, $600 (annual) ● Corporate and Infrastructure Council, $2,500 (annual) ● student, $50 (annual) ● small business/nonprofit organization, $300 (annual). **Staff:** 3. **Description:** Individuals and companies in the United States that either trade with, or invest in, Romania. Promotes free and expanded trade between the U.S. and Romania; seeks to insure continued development of the Romanian economy. Represents members' interests before government agencies and business organizations in both the U.S. and Romania. Gathers and disseminates information about the Romanian economy and investment opportunities. Sponsors trade missions; maintains liaison office in Romania. Assists members in dealing with Romanian business people, officials, and economic entities. Makes available discounts to members on Romanian travel and publications. **Programs:** Custom Member Services. **Publications:** *RACC Newsletter*, quarterly ● *The Romanian Digest*, monthly. Newsletters. Reviews legal and economic developments in Romania. **Circulation:** 4,500. Alternate Formats: online. **Conventions/Meetings:** periodic dinner ● periodic luncheon ● monthly meeting.

23781 ■ Romanian-U.S. Business Council
c/o Chamber of Commerce of the United States
1615 H St. NW
Washington, DC 20062-2000
Ph: (202)659-6000 (202)463-5488
Free: (800)638-6582
Fax: (202)463-3173
URL: http://www.uschamber.com
Contact: Jeffrey C. Crowe, Contact
Founded: 1974. **Members:** 15. **Membership Dues:** company (with annual revenue over $50 million), $5,000 (annual) ● company (with annual revenue under $50 million), $3,000 (annual). **Description:** Advocates American business interests with respect

to U.S. Romanian trade and investments. Provides the American and Romanian business communities with a means of discussing bilateral trade and investment issues and the formulation of policy positions that will promote and expand economic relations between the two countries. Facilitates appropriate legislation and policies regarding trade between the U.S. and Romania. Has sponsored seminars on topics such as possibilities for cooperative commercial efforts in other countries and cooperation in energy development. **Formerly:** Romanian-U.S. Economic Council; (1998) Romanian-U.S. Working Group. **Publications:** *Bridging the Atlantic.* Book. Offers tips, suggestions for breaking ground in the European business market. **Price:** $23.95 includes shipping ● *The Eurasia Business Committee Dispatch*, weekly. Report. Provides the latest information from the U.S. Chamber of Commerce on regulations, legislation, etc. **Price:** $350.00/year. Alternate Formats: online. **Conventions/Meetings:** annual meeting - alternates between U.S. and Romania.

Russian

23782 ■ Russian-American Chamber of Commerce in the USA
970 Sidney Marcus Blvd., Ste.1504
Atlanta, GA 30324
Ph: (404)667-9319
Fax: (678)558-0418
E-mail: info@russianamericanchamber.com
URL: http://www.russianamericanchamber.com
Contact: Sergio Millian, Pres.
Membership Dues: student, investor, associate corporate (located outside U.S.), $300 (annual) ● executive, $1,000 (annual) ● board of directors, $5,000 (annual) ● sponsor, $10,000 (annual). **Staff:** 10. **Multinational. Description:** Promotes trade and cooperation between Russian and American businesses. Serves as a catalyst and facilitator for business energy focused on solving international, national, and regional problems and issues. Provides knowledge relating to U.S. trade, investment and commerce in the Russian and former USSR countries marketplace. Seeks to develop the opportunities of international cooperation between Russian-speaking and non-Russian businesses and organizations all over the world. **Telecommunication Services:** electronic mail, sergio@russianamericanchamber.com. **Publications:** *Russian-American Chamber News.* Newsletter. **Advertising:** accepted ● *Va-Bank Monthly Business Magazine* ● Membership Directory, annual. **Advertising:** accepted.

Scandinavia

23783 ■ Scandinavian Tourist Boards (STB)
PO Box 4649
Grand Central Sta.
New York, NY 10163-4649
Ph: (212)885-9700
Fax: (212)885-9710
E-mail: info@goscandinavia.com
URL: http://www.goscandinavia.com
Languages: Danish, English, Finnish, Icelandic, Norwegian, Swedish. **Description:** National tourist offices of Denmark, Finland, Iceland, Norway, and Sweden. **Formerly:** (1988) Scandinavian National Tourist Offices. **Publications:** Brochure, annual. Contains information about travel and tourism. **Price:** free. **Circulation:** 200,000. **Advertising:** accepted. **Conventions/Meetings:** biennial meeting.

Serbia

23784 ■ Serbian-American Chamber of Commerce
448 W Barry Ave.
Chicago, IL 60657
Ph: (773)388-3404

E-mail: info@serbianamericancommerce.com
URL: http://www.serbianamericanchamberofcommerce.com
Contact: Vlado Bjelopetrovic, Chm./Pres.
Membership Dues: individual, $50 (annual) ● small business, $150 (annual) ● corporation, donation, $250 (annual) ● sponsor, $500 (annual). **Multinational. Description:** Promotes and facilitates business relations between Serbia and the United States. Represents and furthers the interests of its members in trade between the two countries. Gathers and disseminates information on trade and industry. Provides platforms for networking in both countries.

South Africa

23785 ■ South African Tourism
500 Fifth Ave., 20th Fl., Ste.2040
New York, NY 10110
Ph: (212)730-2929
Free: (800)593-1318
Fax: (212)764-1980
E-mail: info.us@southafrica.net
URL: http://www.southafrica.net
Contact: Dr. Felicia Mabuza-Suttle, Pres.
Staff: 9. **Description:** Promotes tourism to South Africa. **Awards:** Tourism Ambassador Award. **Frequency:** annual. **Type:** recognition. **Computer Services:** database ● mailing lists. **Formerly:** (1984) South African Tourist Corporation; (1999) South African Tourism Board. **Publications:** *South Africa Accommodation Guide*, annual. Brochure ● *South Africa Calendar*, annual. Brochure ● *South Africa - Destination Brochure*, annual ● *Travel Planner*, annual. Brochure. **Price:** free. **Advertising:** accepted.

Southern Africa

23786 ■ American-Southern Africa Chamber of Trade and Industry (ASACOT)
1080 Park Ave., Ste.4W
New York, NY 10128-1167
Ph: (212)410-6560
Contact: Dr. Robert John, Dir.Gen.
Founded: 1966. **Members:** 38. **Description:** Corporations involved in trade with and within Angola, Botswana, Lesotho, Malawi, Mozambique, South Africa, Swaziland, Zambia, and Zimbabwe. Furthers the development of trade and investment between the U.S. and the countries of southern Africa; gathers and disseminates information; examines questions pertaining to commercial and industrial relations; promotes and facilitates economic relations between the countries concerned.

Spain

23787 ■ Commercial Office of Spain (COS)
405 Lexington Ave., 44th Fl.
New York, NY 10174-0331
Ph: (212)661-4959
Fax: (212)972-2494
E-mail: bony@mcx.es
Contact: Mr. Javier Sansa, Sr. Trade Commissioner
Staff: 35. **Description:** Promotes the products of Spain in the U.S. Acts as information clearinghouse. Promotes US investment in Spain, and presence of corporations from Spain in USA. **Publications:** *Foods from Spain*, quarterly. Newsletter. **Price:** free. **Advertising:** accepted ● *From Spain*, biennial. Newsletter. Contains activities of the commercial office of Spain. **Price:** free ● *Spain Gourmetour*, semiannual. Magazine. Contains information on food, wine, and travel in Spain. **Price:** $5.00. ISSN: 0214-2937. **Advertising:** accepted ● *Wines from Spain*. Newsletter. **Price:** free. **Advertising:** accepted.

Sri Lanka

23788 ■ Ceylon (Sri Lanka) Tourist Department
Embassy of Sri Lanka
2148 Wyoming Ave. NW
Washington, DC 20008
Ph: (202)483-4025 (202)483-4028
Fax: (202)232-7181
E-mail: slembassy@slembassyusa.org
URL: http://www.slembassyusa.org
Contact: Ambassador Ravinatha Aryasinha, Deputy Chief of Mission
Founded: 1968. **Staff:** 24. **Description:** Promotes tourism from the U.S. and Canada to Sri Lanka, formerly known as Ceylon. Provides brochures, films, slides, and other information on Sri Lanka. **Libraries:** Type: reference. Holdings: 300. Subjects: Sri Lanka. **Publications:** *Sri Lanka Tourist Statistics Magazine*, monthly ● *Sri Lanka Travel Bulletin*, quarterly.

Switzerland

23789 ■ Swiss-American Chamber of Commerce
c/o Mrs. Annemarie Gilman, Admin.
New York Chap.
500 5th Ave., Rm. 1800
New York, NY 10110
Ph: (212)246-7789
Fax: (212)246-1366
E-mail: newyork@amcham.ch
URL: http://www.amcham.ch
Contact: Mrs. Annemarie Gilman, Admin.
Founded: 1967. **Members:** 2,500. **Languages:** English, French, German. **Description:** Represents individuals and corporations with interest in business relations between Switzerland and the United States. **Subgroups:** Doing Business in Switzerland; Doing Business in the U.S.A.; Finance and Investments; Taxes. **Formerly:** American Chamber of Commerce in Switzerland. **Publications:** *Doing Business and Living in Switzerland*, annual. Bibliography. Details English language publications. **Advertising:** accepted ● *Swiss-American Business News*, 11/year. Newsletter ● Papers ● Yearbook ● Also publishes English translations of Swiss laws.

23790 ■ Switzerland Convention and Incentive Bureau (SCIB)
c/o Switzerland Tourism
608 5th Ave.
New York, NY 10020
Ph: (212)757-5944
Fax: (212)262-6116
E-mail: scib.usa@switzerland.com
URL: http://myswitzerland.com/mice
Contact: Marco Walti, Mgr.
Founded: 1964. **Members:** 13. **Staff:** 4. **Description:** Offers assistance in the planning and organizing of meetings, incentives, conventions and other events. Represents ten major destinations and resorts for business travel and two Swiss destination management companies, as well as Swiss International Air Lines Ltd., the new national carrier. **Formerly:** Swiss National Tourist Office; (2001) Switzerland Tourism. **Publications:** *Switzerland Now!*, quarterly. Newsletter. **Circulation:** 5,500 ● *Team-Spirit*. Booklet. Contains information about out of the ordinary places to sleep, eat and rest and unusual ways to get around in Switzerland. Alternate Formats: online ● Newsletter, monthly. Alternate Formats: online ● Video. Contains impressions of Switzerland as a varied and multi-functional event destination.

Tourism

23791 ■ National Federation of Tourist Guide Associations-USA (NFTGA-USA)
c/o Bobbie Gattuso, Pres.
121 Commerce St.
Gretna, LA 70056

Ph: (504)367-8162
E-mail: bobbiegatt@yahoo.com
Contact: Bobbie Gattuso, Pres.
Founded: 1998. **Membership Dues:** profit organization, $200 (annual) ● nonprofit organization, $100 (annual) ● friend, $50 (annual). **Description:** Represents and promotes tourist guide associations in the U.S. **Boards:** Historian and Meeting Facilitator; Membership; Public Relations/Publicity; Publications; Tourism Liaison. **Committees:** Administration/Website; Nominating. **Publications:** Guide Postings. Newsletter. Presents articles of national importance to members. **Price:** included in membership dues. Alternate Formats: online. **Conventions/Meetings:** biennial conference.

Travel

23792 ■ Business Travel Coalition (BTC)
214 Grouse Ln.
Radnor, PA 19087-2730
Ph: (610)341-1850
E-mail: mitchell@businesstravelcoalition.com
URL: http://btcweb.biz
Contact: Kevin P. Mitchell, Chm./Founder
Founded: 1996. **Membership Dues:** recurring silver, $49 (annual) ● recurring gold, $99 (annual) ● recurring platinum, $149 (annual) ● recurring titanium, $2,500 (annual) ● recurring double titanium, $5,000 (annual). **Description:** Works to influence public policy and supplier issues of concern to customers of the business travel industry. **Computer Services:** Information services, daily global business travel news briefing. **Publications:** BTC Travelogue. Alternate Formats: online.

23793 ■ International Galapagos Tour Operators Association (IGTOA)
PO Box 1043
Winchester, MA 01890
E-mail: exd@igtoa.org
URL: http://www.igtoa.org
Contact: David Blanton, Exec. Dir.
Founded: 1997. **Members:** 45. **Membership Dues:** full, $550 (annual) ● associate, friend, $200 (annual) ● non-profit, educational, supporting, $50 (annual). **Staff:** 2. **Budget:** $35,000. **Languages:** English, Spanish. **Description:** Individuals and corporations conducting tours to the Galapagos Islands; educational and scientific institutions with an interest in the Islands and their ecosystems. Promotes tourism with the lowest possible environmental impact; seeks to preserve the unique ecosystems and species indigenous to the Galapagos Islands. Raises funds to support environmental protection initiatives; serves as a clearinghouse on low-impact nature tourism; facilitates communication and cooperation among members. **Awards:** Becario. **Frequency:** annual. **Type:** scholarship. **Recipient:** for Ecuadorian student conducting research for the Charles Darwin Research Station on the Galapagos Islands. **Publications:** IGTOAVoz. Newsletter. Alternate Formats: online.

Turkey

23794 ■ Turkish-American Chamber of Commerce and Industry (TACCI)
c/o Tunc Tuncer, Dir.
730 5th Ave., 9th Fl., Ste.905
New York, NY 10019
Ph: (212)659-7720
Fax: (646)304-1666
E-mail: info@turkishuschamber.com
URL: http://www.turkishuschamber.org
Contact: Tunc Tuncer, Dir.
Founded: 2002. **Membership Dues:** general, $650 (annual) ● premium, $2,000 (annual) ● young executive, $150 (annual). **Multinational. Description:** Promotes bilateral trade, awareness, communications, and social and commercial relationships among

companies that have, or are interested in establishing commercial relations between the USA and Turkey. Seeks to advance the interests of its members through contacts and interaction with government agencies, trade associations, and international organizations. Encourages and assists Chambers of Commerce and other businesses operating in the United States to establish affiliates, subsidiaries, or other business ventures in Turkey. **Telecommunication Services:** electronic mail, director@turkishuschamber.org. **Publications:** Newsletter. Alternate Formats: online.

United States

23795 ■ National Council of State Tourism Directors (NCSTD)
c/o Travel Industry Association of America
1100 New York Ave. NW, Ste.450
Washington, DC 20005-3934
Ph: (202)408-8422
Fax: (202)408-1255
URL: http://www.tia.org/express/ntlcouncil_state_tourism_directors.html
Contact: Todd Davidson, Chm.
Founded: 1969. **Members:** 56. **Staff:** 2. **Description:** Individuals who direct the tourism promotion campaigns for each U.S. state, territory, and the District of Columbia. Acts as a forum for the discussion of issues and concerns. Serves as an industry council of the Travel Industry Association of America. **Awards:** Marketing and Promotion Creativity Award. **Frequency:** annual. **Type:** recognition ● Mercury Awards. **Frequency:** annual. **Type:** recognition. **Recipient:** for excellence in marketing, promotion and individual leadership ● State Travel Director of the Year. **Frequency:** annual. **Type:** recognition ● Trotter Special Service Award. **Frequency:** annual. **Type:** recognition. **Recipient:** for enthusiastic supporters. **Committees:** Awards; Education; Executive. **Formerly:** (1998) National Council of State Travel Directors. **Publications:** Stateside, quarterly. Newsletter. **Price:** available to members only. Alternate Formats: online ● 2004 Survey of US State and Territory Tourism Office Travel Information Center, biennial. Reports. Includes profile of state/territory travel information and welcome center programs and operations. **Price:** $75.00 for members; $125.00 for nonmembers ● 2004 Survey of US State and Territory Tourism Office Website Practices, biennial. Reports. Contains measurement on how tourism offices are using current technology in their marketing and promotion efforts. **Price:** $85.00 for members; $145.00 for nonmembers ● 2004-2005 Survey of State Tourism Offices, annual. Reports. Contains information on tourism development budget and operations of all 50 states. **Price:** $300.00 for members; $495.00 for nonmembers. **Conventions/Meetings:** annual Educational Seminar for State Travel Officials - conference and seminar ● annual meeting.

Venezuela

23796 ■ Venezuelan American Association of the United States (VAAUS)
30 Vesey St., Ste.506
New York, NY 10007
Ph: (212)233-7776
Fax: (212)233-7779
E-mail: andean@nyct.net
URL: http://venezuelanamerican.org
Contact: Montserrat Hernandez, Program Dir.
Founded: 1936. **Members:** 145. **Membership Dues:** corporate, $500 (annual) ● supporting, $2,000 (annual) ● individual, $200 (annual) ● full time student, $85 (annual). **Staff:** 3. **Description:** Financial institutions, businesses, organizations, and individuals interested in the expansion and improvement of trade and trade relations between Venezuela and the

United States. Fosters cultural and commercial relations, facilitates investment between the U.S. and Venezuela, and promotes improved understanding between businesspersons of the two nations. Conducts informal meetings with speakers and discussions. **Awards:** Amistad Award. **Frequency:** periodic. **Type:** recognition. **Recipient:** for promotion of friendship and understanding between Venezuela and the US. **Formerly:** (1975) Venezuelan Chamber of Commerce of the United States. **Publications:** Venezuela News Bulletin, monthly. Provides condensed economic, financial, commercial, and political news from Venezuela. **Price:** included in membership dues; $65.00 for nonmembers. **Conventions/Meetings:** periodic luncheon.

Vietnam

23797 ■ US-Vietnam Chamber of Commerce (UVCC)
PO Box 71274
Oakland, CA 94612
Ph: (510)219-0637 (714)265-7969
E-mail: info@usvnchamber.org
URL: http://www.usvnchamber.org
Contact: Mr. Trung Trinh, Exec. Dir.
Membership Dues: corporate sponsor, $500 (annual) ● business, $50 (annual) ● student, $20 (annual). **Description:** Promotes enhanced business relationships between the United States and Vietnam. Provides assistance to small and medium-sized American companies that are interested in developing business opportunities in the U.S. and Vietnam. Creates and maintains a network within its members to share information and experience in conducting business activities in the U.S. and Vietnam. **Affiliated With:** Federation of International Trade Associations. **Publications:** Newsletter, monthly. **Price:** included in membership dues. Alternate Formats: online ● Brochure. Alternate Formats: online.

Women

23798 ■ National Chamber of Commerce for Women (NCCW)
10 Waterside Plz., Ste.6H
New York, NY 10010
Ph: (212)889-3806 (212)889-3808
Fax: (212)889-3807
E-mail: nccw@aol.com
Contact: R. Wright, Exec.Dir.
Founded: 1977. **Staff:** 3. **Budget:** $130,000. **Description:** Seeks to help women reach their pay comparison goals, career path goals, and business plan goals. **Libraries: Type:** not open to the public. **Awards:** Elizabeth Lewin Fund and Millie Award. **Frequency:** annual. **Type:** monetary. **Recipient:** for women business owners. **Computer Services:** database, business information and research bank. **Committees:** Chamber's Speakers' Bureau; Home-Based Business; National Job Bank Census; Working Women and Consumers in Health Care Industries. **Publications:** Enrich!, bimonthly. Newsletter. Analyzes opportunities, trends, and techniques for women who manage small businesses in commercial space or their homes. **Price:** $96.00. **Circulation:** 5,600. **Advertising:** accepted ● Booklets, annual. **Advertising:** accepted. **Conventions/Meetings:** annual conference (exhibits) - always New York City.

23799 ■ U.S. Women's Chamber of Commerce (USWCC)
1201 Pennsylvania Ave. NW, Ste.300
Washington, DC 20004
Free: (888)418-7922
URL: http://www.uswcc.org
Contact: Margot Dorfman, CEO
Founded: 2001. **Membership Dues:** small business (based on number of employees), $195-$750 (annual) ● regional corporate, $1,675-$10,000 (annual).

Description: Represents the financial interests of its members and small business owners. Seeks to empower women as strong and influential leaders in the corporate world. Supports the advancement of economic opportunities for women.

Youth

23800 ■ U.S. Junior Chamber of Commerce (USJCC)

PO Box 7
Tulsa, OK 74102-0007
Ph: (918)584-2481
Free: (800)JAY-CEES
Fax: (918)584-4422

E-mail: directorcommunications@usjaycees.org
URL: http://www.usjaycees.org
Contact: John Shiroma, Exec. VP

Founded: 1920. **Members:** 115,000. **Staff:** 30. **Budget:** $4,200,000. **State Groups:** 50. **Local Groups:** 2,500. **Description:** Civic service organization of young people, aged 21-39, dedicated to providing leadership training for its members through active participation in local community service programs. Annually selects nation's Four Outstanding Young Farmers, and Ten Healthy American Fitness Leaders; administers International BB Gun Match and shooting education program, anti-youth smoking program, national leadership academy, and Social Security reform Town Hall meeting. Maintains Hall of Fame exhibit hall and museum. **Libraries: Type:** reference. **Holdings:** archival material, clippings, photographs. **Subjects:** U.S. Junior Chamber of Commerce.

Awards: Ten Outstanding Young Americans. **Frequency:** annual. **Type:** scholarship. **Recipient:** for nominated individuals by independent judges. **Computer Services:** Mailing lists. **Committees:** Chapter Development; Corporate Marketing; International Issues, Positions and Resolutions; Member Education; State Development. **Affiliated With:** Junior Chamber International. **Formerly:** (1965) United States Junior Chamber of Commerce; (1990) United States Jaycees. **Publications:** *Directory of State and National Officers*, annual. **Price:** $95.00. **Circulation:** 5,000. **Advertising:** accepted ● *The Jaycee Book*, annual ● *Jaycees Magazine*, quarterly. **Price:** included in membership dues; $15.00 /year for nonmembers. ISSN: 0893-0031. **Circulation:** 120,000. **Advertising:** accepted. Alternate Formats: microform. Also Cited As: *Future*. **Conventions/Meetings:** annual meeting, provides training, awards, socials, and famous speakers (exhibits).

Accounting

23801 ■ Beta Alpha Psi
1211 Ave. of the Americas, 19th Fl.
New York, NY 10036-8775
Ph: (212)596-6090 (212)596-6108
Fax: (212)596-6288
E-mail: bap@bap.org
URL: http://www.bap.org
Contact: Hadassah Baum CPA, Exec. Dir.
Founded: 1919. **Members:** 300,000. **Membership Dues:** student, faculty, honorary, $45 (annual). **Staff:** 2. **Regional Groups:** 199. **Description:** Honorary and professional fraternity - men and women, accounting. Conducts Volunteer Income Tax Assistance Program. Offers accounting assistance to nonprofit organizations. **Awards:** Accountemps/AICPA Student Scholarship. **Frequency:** annual. **Type:** scholarship. **Recipient:** to AICPA student affiliate members ● Best Practices. **Frequency:** annual. **Type:** scholarship ● Manuscript Award. **Frequency:** annual. **Type:** scholarship. **Recipient:** for best student graduate and undergraduate paper ● Outstanding Accountant of the Year Award. **Frequency:** annual. **Type:** recognition ● Outstanding Faculty Development Award. **Frequency:** annual. **Type:** recognition. **Affiliated With:** AACSB International - Association to Advance Collegiate Schools of Business. **Publications:** *Advisory Forum.* Brochure. Includes information about membership. ● *Chapter Directory,* annual. Directories. Contains information about individual chapters. ● Newsletter, semiannual ● Article, annual. Includes financial statements. **Conventions/Meetings:** annual conference - always August.

Adult Education

23802 ■ National Adult Education Honor Society (NAEHS)
PO Box 76571
Highland Heights, KY 41076
Ph: (859)685-8559
Fax: (859)685-8565
E-mail: naehs@fuse.net
URL: http://www.naehs.org
Contact: Lloyd Weaver, Dir.
Founded: 1991. **Membership Dues:** life - student, $15 ● life - charter, $50. **Description:** Seeks to provide recognition to adult education students. Improves student employment opportunities and develops student ambassadors for local adult education programs. Creates adult education awareness with school administrators and state legislators. **Awards:** Student of the Month. **Frequency:** monthly. **Type:** recognition. **Recipient:** for outstanding student.

Advertising

23803 ■ American Advertising Federation Education Services (AAF)
1101 Vermont Ave. NW, Ste.500
Washington, DC 20005
Ph: (202)898-0089
Free: (800)999-AAF1
Fax: (202)898-0159
E-mail: aaf@aaf.org
URL: http://www.aaf.org
Contact: Wally Snyder, Pres./CEO
Founded: 1913. **Members:** 57,000. **Membership Dues:** corporate, $250 (annual). **Staff:** 30. **Description:** Operates as the academic division of the American Advertising Federation (see separate entry). Provides and promotes greater understanding of the functions and values of advertising. Seeks, through advertising education, to stimulate professionalism in the field. Encourages application of the skills, creativity, and energy of advertising in solving social problems. **Awards:** Distinguished Advertising Educator Award. **Frequency:** annual. **Type:** recognition. **Recipient:** to an individual who has demonstrated excellence in teaching, scholarly research, writing and student advertisement ● Diversity Achievement Award. **Frequency:** annual. **Type:** trophy. **Recipient:** to several companies who have shown great strides toward promoting multiculturalism in the advertising industry ● Most Promising Minority Student Award. **Frequency:** annual. **Type:** trophy. **Recipient:** to college students who have been recognized as very promising in the field of advertising, marketing and communications. **Computer Services:** Bibliographic search. **Committees:** Academic; Professional Education. **Formerly:** ADS, National Professional Advertising Society; (1973) AAF/ADS; (1991) AAF College Chapter; (2003) AAF Education Services. **Publications:** *AAF Internship Directory,* annual ● *Communicator,* quarterly. Newsletter. **Circulation:** 7,000. **Conventions/Meetings:** semiannual Academic Meeting ● annual National Student Advertising Competition.

Agricultural Education

23804 ■ Alpha Tau Alpha (ATA)
c/o Dr. Tim Buttles, Sec.-Treas.
Univ. of Wisconsin
320 Ag Sci. Bldg.
River Falls, WI 54022-5001
Ph: (715)425-3555
E-mail: timothy.j.buttles@uwrf.edu
URL: http://ataonline.org
Contact: Dr. Tim Buttles, Sec.-Treas.
Founded: 1921. **Members:** 18,609. **Membership Dues:** life (active and honorary), $15. **Budget:** $1,000. **Regional Groups:** 4. **State Groups:** 46. **Description:** Honorary fraternity in agricultural education. **Awards:** Honorary Membership. **Frequency:** annual. **Type:** recognition. **Also Known As:** National Professional Honorary Agricultural Education Fraternity. **Publications:** *The Alphan,* semiannual. Newsletter. **Price:** free. **Conventions/Meetings:** annual National Collegiate Agricultural Educa-

tion Conference and Alpha Tau Conclave - always 4th week of October in Louisville, KY.

Agricultural Engineering

23805 ■ Alpha Epsilon (AE)
c/o Dr. Joseph L. Purswell, Sec.-Treas.
PO Box 5367
Mississippi State, MS 39762
Ph: (662)320-7480
Fax: (662)320-7589
E-mail: jody_purswell@yahoo.com
URL: http://www.alpha-epsilon.org
Contact: Dr. Joseph L. Purswell, Sec.-Treas.
Founded: 1959. **Members:** 5,056. **Description:** Honor society - agricultural and biological engineering. **Awards:** Outstanding Alpha Epsilon Chapter Award. **Frequency:** annual. **Type:** recognition. **Affiliated With:** American Society of Agricultural and Biological Engineers. **Conventions/Meetings:** annual meeting, held in conjunction with Winter International Meeting of the American Society of Agricultural Engineers - always December.

Agriculture

23806 ■ Alpha Gamma Rho (AGR)
10101 N Ambassador Dr.
Kansas City, MO 64153-1395
Ph: (816)891-9200
Fax: (816)891-9401
E-mail: agr@alphagammarho.org
URL: http://www.alphagammarho.org
Contact: Thomas A. Davis, Pres.
Founded: 1904. **Members:** 57,000. **Staff:** 11. **Budget:** $1,300,000. **Local Groups:** 65. **Description:** Professional fraternity - agriculture. Conducts career development programs and individual chapter retreats and sessions. Compiles statistics. **Awards:** Grand President's Award. **Frequency:** annual. **Type:** recognition. **Recipient:** to agricultural students ● Hall of Fame. **Frequency:** biennial. **Type:** grant. **Recipient:** to agricultural students ● **Type:** scholarship. **Recipient:** to agricultural students. **Committees:** Hall of Fame. **Publications:** *Sickle and Sheaf,* quarterly. Magazine. **Price:** free. **Circulation:** 38,000. **Conventions/Meetings:** annual Leadership Seminar ● workshop.

23807 ■ Alpha Zeta
16020 Swingley Ridge Rd., Ste.300
Chesterfield, MO 63017
Ph: (636)449-5090
Free: (800)225-3629
Fax: (636)449-5051
E-mail: info@alphazeta.org
URL: http://www.alphazeta.org
Contact: Steven C. Drake, CEO
Founded: 1897. **Members:** 102,500. **Membership Dues:** alumni, $38 (annual) ● student, $75 (3/year).

Staff: 3. **Budget:** $250,000. **Regional Groups:** 5. **Local Groups:** 72. **National Groups:** 2. **Description:** Represents students and professionals in the fields of agricultural and natural resources. Provides scholarships, internships, career development workshops and leadership conferences. **Awards:** Advisor of the Year Award. **Frequency:** annual. **Type:** recognition. **Recipient:** for the advisor who has shown exemplary dedication to the organization ● Burkett-Cunningham-Dennis Award. **Frequency:** annual. **Type:** scholarship. **Recipient:** for leadership, scholarship and character ● Founders Cup. **Frequency:** annual. **Type:** recognition. **Recipient:** to the most outstanding active Alpha Zeta chapter ● G.W. Roach Award. **Frequency:** annual. **Type:** scholarship. **Recipient:** for leadership, scholarship and character ● McClure Officer of the Year. **Frequency:** annual. **Type:** recognition. **Recipient:** for outstanding chapter officers ● Middaugh Awards. **Frequency:** biennial. **Type:** recognition. **Recipient:** to chapters for excellence in service to campus, college or agriculture; new member development; chapter development and fundraising ● National Alpha Zeta Scholars Award. **Frequency:** annual. **Type:** scholarship. **Recipient:** for leadership, scholarship and character ● Outstanding Alumni Award. **Frequency:** annual. **Type:** recognition. **Computer Services:** Mailing lists, of members. **Affiliated With:** Professional Fraternity Association. **Publications:** *Alpha Zeta, A Seventy Five Year History* ● *AZ Leader*, monthly ● *AZ News*, quarterly. **Conventions/Meetings:** biennial Conclave - conference, national business meeting ● annual National Ag Leadership Conference, for agriculture.

23808 ■ Gamma Sigma Delta (GSD)
c/o Steven A. Henning, Pres.
Agricultural Economics and Agribusiness
101 Ag. Admin. Bldg.
Louisiana State Univ.
Baton Rouge, LA 70803-5604
Ph: (225)578-2718
E-mail: shenning@agctr.lsu.edu
URL: http://www.gammasigmadelta.org
Contact: Steven A. Henning, Pres.
Founded: 1905. **Members:** 100,000. **Membership Dues:** life, $10. **Budget:** $25,000. **Local Groups:** 51. **Multinational. Description:** Honorary fraternity - men and women, agriculture and related sciences. Works for advancement of agriculture in all its phases, the maintenance and improvement of the relations of agriculture and related sciences to other industries, and the recognition of the responsibilities of those engaged in all aspects of agriculture to humankind. **Libraries: Type:** reference. **Holdings:** archival material. **Awards:** International Award for Distinguished Service in Agriculture. **Frequency:** annual. ● **Type:** monetary ● **Type:** recognition ● **Type:** scholarship. **Publications:** *New Notes*, 3/year. Newsletter ● Newsletter, annual. Alternate Formats: online. **Conventions/Meetings:** biennial Conclave - conference and workshop.

Alumni

23809 ■ Mt. Marty College Alumni Association (MMCAA)
1105 W 8th St.
Yankton, SD 57078
Ph: (605)668-1597 (605)668-1232
Free: (800)658-4552
Fax: (605)668-1607
E-mail: ctudor@mtmc.edu
URL: http://www.mtmc.edu
Contact: Christine Tudor, Dir.
Founded: 1936. **Members:** 8,823. **Budget:** $27,429. **Description:** Graduates of Mt. Marty College; former students who completed at least 24 credit hours at the College. Supports the goals of Mt. Marty College; facilitates communication and good fellowship among members. Conducts fundraising and student recruitment campaigns; sponsors social activities. **Awards:** Distinguished Professional Achievement. **Frequency:**

annual. **Type:** recognition ● Distinguished Service to Church. **Frequency:** annual. **Type:** recognition ● Distinguished Service to Mt. Mary. **Frequency:** annual. **Type:** recognition ● Outstanding Young Alumnus. **Frequency:** annual. **Type:** recognition. **Publications:** *UPDATE*, triennial. Magazine.

23810 ■ Wellesley College Alumnae Association (WCAA)
Green Hall, Rm. 246
106 Central St.
Wellesley, MA 02481-8268
Ph: (781)283-2331 (781)283-2335
Fax: (781)283-3638
E-mail: alumnae@wellesley.edu
URL: http://www.wellesley.edu/Alum
Contact: Alison Greer, Exec. Dir.
Founded: 1880. **Members:** 34,000. **Description:** Promotes activities of the Wellesley College alumnae association. **Awards:** Alumnae Achievement Awards. **Frequency:** annual. **Type:** recognition. **Recipient:** for outstanding achievements ● Syrena Stackpole Award. **Frequency:** annual. **Type:** recognition. **Recipient:** to an alumna for outstanding service to Wellesley College. **Programs:** Travel and Regional. **Publications:** *Wellesley Alumnae Magazine* ● Directory. Alternate Formats: online. **Conventions/Meetings:** reunion ● symposium - summer.

Animal Science

23811 ■ National Block and Bridle Club (B&B)
c/o Dr. Cindy Wood, Natl. Pres.
Dept. of Animal and Poultry Sciences
3400 Litton Reaves Hall, 0306
Virginia Tech
Blacksburg, VA 24061
Ph: (540)231-6936
Fax: (540)231-3010
E-mail: piglady@vt.edu
URL: http://www.asas.org/bandb/index.html
Contact: Dr. Cindy Wood, Natl. Pres.
Founded: 1919. **Description:** Professional society - men and women, animal science. **Awards:** **Frequency:** annual. **Type:** recognition. **Recipient:** for the best chapter ● **Frequency:** annual. **Type:** recognition. **Recipient:** for individuals ● **Type:** scholarship. **Recipient:** for individuals ● **Type:** scholarship. **Additional Websites:** http://www.blockandbridle.org. **Affiliated With:** American Society of Animal Science. **Publications:** Annual Report ● Newsletter, quarterly. **Conventions/Meetings:** annual conference.

Anthropology

23812 ■ Lambda Alpha
Ball State Univ.
Dept. of Anthropology
Muncie, IN 47306-0435
Ph: (765)285-1575
E-mail: 01bkswartz@bsu.edu
URL: http://www.lambdaalpha.com
Contact: Dr. B.K. Swartz Jr., Natl. Exec. Sec.
Founded: 1968. **Members:** 13,000. **Membership Dues:** life, $25. **Staff:** 2. **Local Groups:** 109. **Description:** National collegiate honor society - anthropology. Seeks to encourage and stimulate scholarship and research in anthropology. Acknowledges and honors achievement in the study of anthropology among students, faculty, and others involved in the discipline of anthropology. **Awards:** Charles R. Jenkins Distinguished Service Award. **Frequency:** periodic. **Type:** recognition. **Recipient:** for service ● Lambda Alpha National Dean's List Scholarship. **Frequency:** annual. **Type:** scholarship. **Recipient:** for an outstanding junior anthropology major in an affiliated Lambda Alpha Chapter ● National Lambda Alpha Graduate Overseas Research Grant. **Frequency:** annual. **Type:** grant ● National Lambda

Alpha Scholarship Award. **Frequency:** annual. **Type:** scholarship. **Recipient:** for a graduating senior anthropology major in an affiliated Lambda Alpha chapter. **Councils:** National Executive. **Also Known As:** National Collegiate Honors Society for Anthropology. **Publications:** *Lambda Alpha Annual Newsletter*, annual. Includes annual Honor Roll of inductees. Alternate Formats: online ● *Lambda Alpha Journal*, annual. Scholarly; encourages student publications. **Price:** $10.00/year. Also Cited As: *Journal of Man*.

Architecture

23813 ■ Tau Sigma Delta
c/o Elizabeth I. Louden, Pres.
Coll. of Architecture
PO Box 42091
Texas Tech Univ.
Lubbock, TX 79409-2091
Ph: (806)742-3136
Fax: (806)742-2855
E-mail: elizabeth.louden@ttu.edu
URL: http://www.tausigmadelta.org
Contact: Elizabeth I. Louden, Pres.
Founded: 1913. **Members:** 13,000. **Staff:** 1. **National Groups:** 52. **Description:** Honor society - men and women, architecture, landscape architecture, and allied arts. Presents annual Gold Medal for distinction in design, leadership, and education. **Affiliated With:** Association of College Honor Societies. **Publications:** Newsletter, annual. **Conventions/Meetings:** annual conference, held in conjunction with American Institute of Architects or Association of Collegiate Schools of Architecture.

Arts

23814 ■ Kappa Pi International Honorary Art Fraternity
c/o Ron Koehler, Pres.
400 S Bolivar Ave.
Cleveland, MS 38732
Ph: (662)846-6271
E-mail: koehler@tecinfo.com
URL: http://www.KappaPiArt.org
Contact: Ron Koehler, Pres.
Founded: 1911. **Members:** 6,000. **Membership Dues:** active, alumni, faculty, $10 (annual) ● associate, $25 (annual) ● life, $50 (annual). **Staff:** 2. **Budget:** $50,000. **National Groups:** 170. **Multinational. Description:** Honorary and recognition fraternity - men and women, art. Sponsors art scholarship competitions. **Awards: Type:** scholarship. **Recipient:** for members. **Publications:** *Sketch Book*, annual. Magazine. Contains articles of art interest. **Circulation:** 5,000 ● *Sketch Pad*, annual. Bulletin.

23815 ■ Phi Beta
c/o Cora Willett, Treas.
377 Pearl St.
Jackson, OH 45640-1756
E-mail: treasurer@phibeta.com
URL: http://www.phibeta.com
Contact: Elin Torvik, Pres.
Founded: 1912. **Members:** 400. **Membership Dues:** collegiate, $30 (annual) ● collegiate initiation, $40 ● senior alumnus (with age 65 plus), $35 (annual) ● regular alumnus, $60 (annual) ● alumnus initiation, $75 ● life, $10-$30. **Staff:** 5. **Budget:** $15,000. **Local Groups:** 16. **National Groups:** 2. **Description:** Professional fraternity - creative and performing arts. Encourages high professional standards and supports creative and performing arts endeavors. Sponsors competitions for collegiate members and donates annually to the MacDowell Colony. **Awards: Frequency:** annual. **Type:** monetary. **Affiliated With:** National Communication Association; National Federation of Music Clubs; National Music Council; Professional Fraternity Association. **Publications:** *The Baton*, semiannual. Magazine. **Price:** included in

membership dues; $10.00 /year for nonmembers. **Circulation:** 500. **Advertising:** accepted ● *Rosepetals.* Newsletter. **Price:** available to members only. **Conventions/Meetings:** biennial convention (exhibits).

Arts and Sciences

23816 ■ Phi Beta Kappa
1606 New Hampshire Ave. NW
Washington, DC 20009
Ph: (202)265-3808
Fax: (202)986-1601
E-mail: info@pbk.org
URL: http://www.pbk.org
Contact: John Churchill, Sec.
Founded: 1776. **Members:** 500,000. **Membership Dues:** life (initiation only), $25. **Staff:** 25. **Budget:** $3,000,000. **Regional Groups:** 7. **Local Groups:** 315. **National Groups:** 2. **Description:** Scholarly honor society for men and women in the liberal arts and sciences. Recognizes scholarly achievement and academic excellence through national programs such as the Phi Beta Kappa book awards, Romanell Professorship in Philosophy, Visiting Scholar and Lectureship programs, and through programs of university chapters and alumni associations, including secondary school teachers' workshops, scholarships and awards. Supported by the Phi Beta Kappa Foundation. **Libraries: Type:** not open to the public. **Holdings:** 1,000. **Awards:** Mary Isabel Sibley Fellowship. **Frequency:** annual. **Type:** monetary. **Recipient:** for postdoctoral fellowship in Greek and French cultural studies ● Phi Beta Kappa Book Award. **Frequency:** annual. **Type:** monetary. **Recipient:** for outstanding scholarly books in humanities and social sciences ● Romanell-Phi Beta Kappa Professorship in Philosophy. **Frequency:** annual. **Type:** monetary. **Recipient:** for recent scholarship in philosophy ● Sidney Hook Award. **Frequency:** triennial. **Type:** recognition. **Recipient:** for leadership in the cause of liberal learning. **Computer Services:** database, in-house. **Publications:** *A Handbook for New Members*, triennial. Contains introduction to the society. **Circulation:** 15,000 ● *American Scholar*, quarterly. Journal. Contains essays, poetry, and reviews. **Price:** $25.00/year. ISSN: 0003-0937. **Circulation:** 100,000. **Advertising:** accepted ● *Key Reporter*, quarterly. Newsletter. Includes essays and book reviews. **Price:** included in membership dues; $5.00 /year for nonmembers. ISSN: 0023-0804. **Circulation:** 470,000. **Conventions/Meetings:** triennial convention, convention of delegates from all local affiliates.

Athletics

23817 ■ Sigma Delta Psi
The Citadel
DEAS Hall
171 Moultrie St.
Charleston, SC 29409-6430
Ph: (843)953-7778 (843)953-6809
Fax: (843)953-6809
E-mail: delmastrom@citadel.edu
URL: http://www.citadel.edu
Contact: Mark P. Del Mastro, Founder/Dir./Sec.-Treas.
Founded: 1919. **Members:** 4,700. **Description:** Recognition fraternity - athletics. Sponsors competitions; compiles statistics. **Convention/Meeting:** none. **Additional Websites:** http://www.sigmadeltapi.org. **Affiliated With:** American Alliance for Health, Physical Education, Recreation and Dance; National Intramural-Recreational Sports Association. **Publications:** *Newsbulletin*, 5/year.

Biology

23818 ■ Beta Beta Beta
c/o Kathy W. Roush, Sec.-Treas.
Univ. of North Alabama
PO Box 5079
Florence, AL 35632

Ph: (256)765-6220
Fax: (256)765-6221
E-mail: tribeta@una.edu
Contact: Kathy W. Roush, Sec.-Treas.
Founded: 1922. **Members:** 175,000. **Membership Dues:** regular, graduate, chapter/club honorary, alumna/US, $30 (annual) ● associate, $20 (annual) ● corporate, $500 (annual) ● chapter/club, $300 (annual). **Staff:** 2. **Budget:** $100,000. **Regional Groups:** 15. **Description:** Honorary and professional society - men and women, biology. Seeks to improve the understanding and appreciation of biological study and extend the boundaries of human knowledge through scientific research. **Awards:** C.E. McClung Award. **Frequency:** annual. **Type:** recognition. **Recipient:** for best research paper published in BIOS each year ● Frank G. Brooks. **Frequency:** annual. **Type:** recognition. **Recipient:** for research presentations in each district convention and biennial convention ● John C. Johnson. **Frequency:** annual. **Type:** recognition. **Recipient:** for an outstanding poster presentation in each district convention and biennial convention ● Lloyd M. Bertholf. **Frequency:** annual. **Type:** recognition. **Recipient:** for an outstanding chapter ● Research Grants. **Frequency:** annual. **Type:** grant. **Recipient:** to conduct student research; to TriBeta members only ● Yokley Faculty Service Award. **Frequency:** annual. **Type:** recognition. **Recipient:** for years of service as faculty advisor and/or district director ● Yokley Leadership Award. **Frequency:** annual. **Type:** recognition. **Recipient:** to individuals who have given long-term services as national officers ● Yokley Outstanding Faculty Advisor. **Frequency:** annual. **Type:** recognition. **Recipient:** for an outstanding poster presentation in each district convention and biennial convention. **Programs:** Chapter Donor; Individual Donor. **Also Known As:** TriBeta. **Publications:** *BIOS*, quarterly. Journal. Includes calendar of events, society news, & research papers. **Price:** included in membership dues. ISSN: 0005-3155. **Circulation:** 11,500. **Advertising:** accepted. Alternate Formats: microform; online ● Papers. Alternate Formats: online. **Conventions/Meetings:** biennial convention, scientific convention - always held during June ● annual convention, district scientific conventions - always held during spring.

23819 ■ Phi Sigma
c/o Henry R. Owen, PhD, Pres.
Eastern Illinois Univ.
600 Lincoln Ave.
Charleston, IL 61920
Ph: (217)581-3126 (217)581-6238
Fax: (217)581-7141
E-mail: cfhro@eiu.edu
URL: http://www.phisigmasociety.org
Contact: Henry R. Owen PhD, Pres.
Founded: 1915. **Members:** 50,000. **Membership Dues:** life, $50. **Staff:** 3. **Local Groups:** 67. **Description:** Honor society - pure and applied biological sciences. Chapter programs include lecture series, informal workshops, laboratory visits and demonstrations, field trips, exhibits, and other scientific endeavors and social activities. Presents certificates and awards. **Awards:** Phi Sigma Student Travel Grant Program. **Frequency:** annual. **Type:** monetary. **Recipient:** for presentation of research at a professional meeting. **Affiliated With:** American Association for the Advancement of Science; American Institute of Biological Sciences; Association of College Honor Societies. **Publications:** *BioScience*. Journal. **Price:** included in membership dues. **Conventions/Meetings:** biennial meeting, held in conjunction with American Institute of Biological Sciences.

Broadcasting

23820 ■ Iota Beta Sigma (IBS)
367 Windsor Hwy.
New Windsor, NY 12553-7900
Ph: (845)565-0003

Fax: (845)565-7446
E-mail: ibshq@aol.com
Contact: Fritz Kass, Exec. Dir.
Founded: 1963. **Members:** 5,276. **Membership Dues:** chapter, $10 (annual) ● individual or honorary, $10. **Staff:** 2. **Budget:** $93,063. **Local Groups:** 54. **Description:** College and high school students and graduates who are or were involved in student broadcasting. Promotes radio broadcasting through fellowship. **Awards: Type:** recognition. **Affiliated With:** Intercollegiate Broadcasting System. **Publications:** Newsletter, periodic. **Conventions/Meetings:** competition ● annual Conclave - meeting, held in conjunction with the Intercollegiate Broadcasting System.

23821 ■ National Broadcasting Society - Alpha Epsilon Rho (NBS - AERho)
c/o Jim Wilson, Exec. Dir.
PO Box 4206
Chesterfield, MO 63006
Ph: (314)469-1943
Free: (866)272-3746
Fax: (314)469-1948
E-mail: nbsaerho@swbell.net
URL: http://www.nbs-aerho.org
Contact: Jim Wilson, Exec. Dir.
Founded: 1943. **Members:** 45,000. **Membership Dues:** student, professional, $40 (annual). **Staff:** 3. **Regional Groups:** 6. **Local Groups:** 115. **Description:** Provides opportunities for ethical and responsible leadership, assistance in career development, and opportunities to participate in community service activities. Sponsors media education programs. **Awards:** NBS-AERho Convention Grants. **Frequency:** annual. **Type:** grant. **Recipient:** for outstanding student members in electronic media ● Richard Uray Alpha Epsilon Rho Award for Excellence. **Frequency:** annual. **Type:** recognition. **Recipient:** for outstanding professional activity in the electronic media ● Society Awards. **Frequency:** annual. **Type:** recognition. **Recipient:** for outstanding service to the national broadcasting society. **Formerly:** (1981) Alpha Epsilon Rho. **Publications:** *Signals Online*, quarterly. Newsletter. **Price:** included in membership dues. Alternate Formats: online. **Conventions/Meetings:** annual convention.

Business

23822 ■ Alpha Iota Delta (AID)
c/o Ms. Shirley Groves, Admin. Coor.
Georgia State Univ.
J. Mack Robinson Coll. of Bus.
35 Broad St., Ste.1022
Atlanta, GA 30303
Ph: (404)651-4056
Fax: (404)651-2896
E-mail: dscsgg@langate.gsu.edu
URL: http://www.alphaiotadelta.com
Contact: Dr. Gregory W. Ulferts, Exec. Dir.
Founded: 1972. **Members:** 5,000. **Regional Groups:** 44. **Languages:** English, Spanish. **Description:** Serves as honor society for men and women in decision sciences and information systems. **Publications:** none. **Awards:** Instructional Innovation. **Frequency:** annual. **Type:** recognition. **Recipient:** for innovative education. **Telecommunication Services:** electronic mail, ulfertgw@udmercy.edu. **Affiliated With:** Decision Sciences Institute. **Conventions/Meetings:** annual meeting, held in conjunction with Decision Sciences Institute (exhibits) - always fall.

23823 ■ Alpha Iota Sorority
PO Box 223223
Chantilly, VA 20153-3223
Ph: (703)378-8010
Fax: (703)815-2232

E-mail: kolivek@yahoo.com
URL: http://www.alphaiota.org
Contact: Karen O. Kolosvary, Intl. Sec.
Founded: 1925. **Members:** 1,400. **Membership Dues:** general, $35 (annual). **Staff:** 2. **Regional Groups:** 5. **Local Groups:** 46. **Multinational. Description:** Honorary sorority - business. Helps each member to become a better businesswoman through development of self-confidence, leadership and awareness of responsibility to herself and her community. **Awards: Frequency:** biennial. **Type:** scholarship. **Recipient:** for members. **Publications:** *Note-Book*, quarterly. Newsletter. **Price:** included in membership dues. **Circulation:** 1,400. **Conventions/Meetings:** biennial convention ● annual regional meeting.

23824 ■ Alpha Kappa Psi (AKPsi)
7801 E 88th St.
Indianapolis, IN 46256-1233
Ph: (317)872-1553
Fax: (317)872-1567
E-mail: president@akpsi.com
URL: http://www.akpsi.com
Contact: Dan L. Stubblefield, Pres.
Founded: 1904. **Members:** 180,000. **Membership Dues:** individual, $70 (annual). **Staff:** 11. **Budget:** $1,000,000. **Regional Groups:** 13. **Local Groups:** 192. **Description:** Professional fraternity - business administration. Conducts educational and charitable programs. Focuses on leadership development. **Libraries: Type:** reference. **Holdings:** books, periodicals. **Awards: Type:** monetary ● **Type:** recognition ● **Type:** scholarship. **Publications:** *Diary*, 3/year. Magazine. Contains information on Fraternity and Foundation news; includes educational articles focusing on professional development. **Circulation:** 25,000 ● *Galley*, monthly. Newsletter. **Conventions/Meetings:** biennial convention - always August.

23825 ■ Beta Gamma Sigma (BGS)
125 Weldon Pkwy.
Maryland Heights, MO 63043
Ph: (314)432-5650
Free: (800)337-HNRS
Fax: (314)432-7083
E-mail: bgshonors@betagammasigma.org
URL: http://www.betagammasigma.org
Contact: James A. Viehland, Exec. Dir.
Founded: 1913. **Members:** 500,000. **Membership Dues:** life, $50. **Staff:** 12. **Budget:** $1,250,000. **Regional Groups:** 380. **Local Groups:** 16. **Multinational. Description:** International honor society. For students in business and management at business programs accredited by AACSB International. Supports the advancement of business thought and practice to encourage lifelong learning. **Awards:** Business Achievement Award. **Frequency:** annual. **Type:** recognition. **Recipient:** for outstanding business achievement ● Medallion for Entrepreneurship. **Frequency:** annual. **Type:** recognition. **Recipient:** for outstanding entrepreneurs. **Computer Services:** Online services, community for member networking. **Publications:** *Beta Gamma Sigma Directory*, annual. **Circulation:** 5,000 ● *From the Podium*, periodic ● *International Exchange*, quarterly. Magazine. **Circulation:** 360,000. Alternate Formats: online ● *Invited Essay*, periodic. **Conventions/Meetings:** biennial convention.

23826 ■ Beta Gamma Sigma Alumni
c/o Beta Gamma Sigma
125 Weldon Pkwy.
Maryland Heights, MO 63043
Ph: (314)432-5650
Free: (800)337-HNRS
Fax: (314)432-7083
E-mail: bgshonors@betagammasigma.org
URL: http://www.betagammasigma.org
Contact: Vicki C. Klutts, Assoc. Exec. Dir.
Founded: 1932. **Members:** 2,000. **Membership Dues:** regular, $30 (annual). **Staff:** 2. **Description:** Alumni members of the collegiate national honor society Beta Gamma Sigma. Promotes excellence in business education, ethics, and scholastic achievement and recognition. Local New York chapter. **Awards: Frequency:** annual. **Type:** scholarship. **Re-**

cipient: to outstanding business students chosen by Deans. **Additional Websites:** http://www.bgs-nyc.org. **Affiliated With:** Beta Gamma Sigma. **Also Known As:** (2000) BGSA Chapter; (2000) Beta Gamma Sigma Alumni in New York City. **Publications:** *BGSA Keyboard*, 2-4/year. Newsletter. **Conventions/Meetings:** general assembly (exhibits) - 4-5/year in New York City metro area.

23827 ■ Beta Pi Sigma Sorority
8831 S Michigan
Chicago, IL 60619
E-mail: bpssi@betapisigmasorority.org
URL: http://www.betapisigmasorority.org
Contact: Supreme Basileus Ruth A. Loggins, Pres.
Founded: 1945. **Members:** 1,060. **Staff:** 3. **Budget:** $3,000. **Regional Groups:** 4. **State Groups:** 4. **Local Groups:** 21. **Description:** Business and professional sorority. Conducts civic, cultural, charitable, and educational projects. Cooperates with the Close Up Foundation on the Program for Older Americans. Offers tutoring services. Youth programs partnerships with schools, book donation programs (schools and libraries), and youth programs. **Awards: Type:** recognition ● **Frequency:** annual. **Type:** scholarship. **Recipient:** for college students and colleges. **Affiliated With:** Close Up Foundation. **Publications:** *Olive Grove*, quarterly. Newsletter. Includes schedule of events. **Price:** $5.00/year. **Circulation:** 750. **Advertising:** accepted. **Conventions/Meetings:** biennial meeting and convention - always August; meeting held in even-numbered years, convention in odd-numbered years.

23828 ■ Delta Mu Delta Honor Society (DMD)
9217 Broadway Ave.
Brookfield, IL 60513-1251
Ph: (708)485-8494
Free: (866)789-7067
Fax: (708)221-6183
E-mail: dmd@dmd-ntl.org
URL: http://deltamudelta.org
Contact: Rich L. Sosnowski, Sec./Exec. Dir.
Founded: 1913. **Members:** 120,000. **Membership Dues:** life, $50. **Staff:** 2. **Budget:** $300,000. **Regional Groups:** 7. **Local Groups:** 215. **Description:** Serves as honor society for business administration. **Awards:** A.J. Jablonsky Award. **Frequency:** annual. **Type:** recognition. **Recipient:** for Delta Mu Delta chapters ● Delta Mu Delta Scholarships. **Frequency:** annual. **Type:** scholarship. **Recipient:** for business students at schools that have Delta Mu Delta chapters ● Star Chapter Award. **Frequency:** annual. **Type:** recognition. **Recipient:** to all chapters that meet or exceed national standards for chapter operation and administration. **Committees:** Bylaws and Policies; Extension and Development; Honors and Awards; Investment; Long Range Planning; Public Information and Editorial Review; Scholarships; Standards and Definitions; Triennial Meeting. **Affiliated With:** Association of College Honor Societies; Association of Collegiate Business Schools and Programs. **Publications:** *The Contact*, semiannual. Newsletter. **Circulation:** 300 ● *Directory of Officers and Faculty Advisors*, annual ● *Info Card*, annual. **Circulation:** 5,000 ● *Membership Brochure* ● *The Vision*, semiannual. Newsletter. **Price:** included in membership dues. **Circulation:** 60,000. Alternate Formats: online. **Conventions/Meetings:** triennial congress.

23829 ■ Eta Phi Beta
16815 James Couzens Fwy.
Detroit, MI 48235
Ph: (313)862-0600
Fax: (313)862-6245
URL: http://www.etaphibetanatl.org
Contact: Jean Dade-Batchie, Natl. Pres.
Founded: 1942. **Members:** 8,000. **Regional Groups:** 6. **Description:** Professional sorority - business. Conducts national projects concerning retarded citizens and retarded children. Conducts leadership and career programs and seminars; sponsors competitions. Operates speakers' bureau; provides children's services; maintains charitable program. **Awards: Type:** grant ● **Type:** recognition ● **Type:** scholarship. **Committees:** Archives; Merits and Awards; Queen Bee (scholarship); Talent; Teenage

Pregnancy and Parenting; Youth Career. **Affiliated With:** National Association for the Advancement of Colored People; United Negro College Fund; Young Women's Christian Association of the United States of America YWCA of the U.S.A. **Publications:** *Beeline*, semiannual ● Newsletter, quarterly ● Membership Directory, biennial. **Conventions/Meetings:** biennial conference - always odd-numbered years ● biennial meeting (exhibits).

23830 ■ Future Business Leaders of America - Phi Beta Lambda (FBLA-PBL)
1912 Assn. Dr.
Reston, VA 20191-1591
Ph: (703)860-3334
Free: (800)325-2946
Fax: (703)758-0749
E-mail: general@fbla.org
URL: http://www.fbla-pbl.org
Contact: Ms. Jean M. Buckley, Pres./CEO
Founded: 1942. **Members:** 230,000. **Staff:** 14. **State Groups:** 52. **Local Groups:** 8,000. **Description:** Maintains 4 divisions: Future Business Leaders of America for high school students preparing for business and related careers; Phi Beta Lambda for postsecondary and college men and women enrolled in business or teacher education programs; Professional Division for business persons FBLA - parents and teachers; Middle Level for students in junior high schools. Sponsors educational program and National Student Award program based on national competition for members. **Programs:** National Student Award. **Publications:** *Advisers' Hotline*, 3/year. Newsletter. Covers association activities for advisers, officers, and other organization leaders. **Price:** included in membership dues. **Circulation:** 8,500. **Advertising:** accepted ● *The Middle Level Advisor's Hotline*, 3/year. Newsletter. For junior high school advisors providing career and leadership guidance to students. **Circulation:** 8,500. **Advertising:** accepted ● *PBL Business Leader*, 3/year. Journal. For postsecondary students in Phi Beta Lambda. **Circulation:** 13,000. **Advertising:** accepted ● *Professional Edge*, 3/year. Newsletter. For professionals. **Price:** included in membership dues. **Circulation:** 3,500. **Advertising:** accepted ● *Tomorrow's Business Leader*, quarterly. Journal. For high school students preparing for business careers. Includes advertisers' index, book reviews, calendar of events, and chapter news. **Price:** included in membership dues. ISSN: 0279-9685. **Circulation:** 250,000. **Advertising:** accepted. **Conventions/Meetings:** annual National Leadership Conference, leadership, elections, and competitive events in business and leadership skills.

23831 ■ Iota Phi Lambda
1462 W 113th Pl.
Chicago, IL 60643
Ph: (773)445-1315
Free: (800)982-IOTA
E-mail: membership@iota1929.org
URL: http://www.iota1929.org
Contact: Charlotte M. Maull, Natl. Pres.
Founded: 1929. **Members:** 5,000. **Staff:** 1. **Regional Groups:** 5. **Description:** Business and professional civic sorority. Seeks to: develop leadership expertise among business and professional women; promote increased interest in business education among high school and college girls through planned programs and scholarships; encourage the development of personalities for all areas of leadership through provision of educational opportunities; establish and promote civic and social service activities for youth and adults. Conducts children's services and tutoring sessions. Maintains small library. Provides educational, tutorial, senior citizen, and health programs. **Awards:** Alice Pallen Scholarship. **Type:** scholarship ● Lola M. Parker Achievement Award. **Type:** recognition ● Mahala S. Evans Award. **Type:** recognition. **Affiliated With:** Congressional Black Caucus; Leadership Conference on Civil Rights; National Association for the Advancement of Colored People; National Urban League; United Negro College Fund. **Publications:** *Let's Chat*, semiannual ● Journal, annual ● Membership Directory, biennial ● Proceedings, biennial. **Conventions/Meetings:** biennial Leadership Conference - held in non-convention years.

23832 ■ Phi Chi Theta
c/o Saundra Finley, Exec. Dir.
1508 E Beltline Rd., Ste.104
Carrollton, TX 75006

Ph: (972)245-7202
E-mail: executivedirector@phichitheta.org
URL: http://www.phichitheta.org
Contact: Saundra Finley, Exec. Dir.
Founded: 1924. **Members:** 46,500. **Membership Dues:** individual, $60 (annual) ● one-time initiation fee, $40 ● pledge fee, $10. **Staff:** 1. **Budget:** $150,000. **Regional Groups:** 4. **Description:** Co-ed professional fraternity - business and economics. Maintains hall of fame; sponsors educational programs. **Libraries: Type:** reference. **Awards:** Alumni Achievement Award. **Frequency:** biennial. **Type:** recognition ● Anna E. Hall Scholarship. **Frequency:** annual. **Type:** recognition. **Recipient:** for GPA, Phi Chi Theta and community service ● Helen D. Snow Scholarship. **Frequency:** annual. **Type:** scholarship. **Recipient:** for GPA, Phi Chi Theta and community service ● Key Award. **Frequency:** annual. **Type:** recognition. **Recipient:** on basis of scholarship, activities, and leadership ● Outstanding Advisor Award. **Frequency:** biennial. **Type:** recognition. **Recipient:** to an outstanding collegiate advisor. **Committees:** Professional Programs. **Affiliated With:** AACSB International - Association to Advance Collegiate Schools of Business; Professional Fraternity Association. **Absorbed:** (1973) Epsilon Eta Phi. **Formed by Merger of:** (1924) Phi Kappa Epsilon; (1924) Phi Theta Kappa. **Publications:** The Iris, semiannual. Magazine. **Price:** $5.00/year. **Circulation:** 2,500. **Conventions/Meetings:** biennial convention (exhibits).

23833 ■ Phi Gamma Nu
6745 Cheryl Ann Dr.
Seven Hills, OH 44131-3720
Ph: (216)524-0934
E-mail: exedir@ameritech.net
URL: http://www.phigammanu.com
Contact: Lorraine A. Scott, Exec. Dir.
Founded: 1924. **Members:** 28,000. **Description:** Professional fraternity - business administration and economics. **Affiliated With:** AACSB International - Association to Advance Collegiate Schools of Business; College Fraternity Editors Association; Professional Fraternity Association. **Publications:** The Magazine of Phi Gamma Nu, semiannual ● National Headquarters Bulletin, bimonthly ● Phi Gamma Nu's, annual. Newsletter ● Directory, periodic. **Conventions/Meetings:** triennial congress.

23834 ■ Phi Theta Pi
6552 Bradford Dr.
West Des Moines, IA 50266-2308
Ph: (515)440-2045
E-mail: ptpfrat@mchsi.com
URL: http://www.phithetapi.org
Contact: Mr. David Pierce, Sec.-Treas.
Founded: 1926. **Members:** 24,000. **Membership Dues:** one-time initial fee, $25. **Staff:** 5. **Regional Groups:** 4. **Description:** Honorary fraternity of businessmen and women (includes faculty members). **Awards:** Business Person Of The Year. **Frequency:** annual. **Type:** recognition. **Recipient:** to all alumni members of the fraternity who are in good standing with both the local and national offices ● J. Spencer Borders Scholarship. **Frequency:** annual. **Type:** scholarship. **Recipient:** for active members. **Affiliated With:** Alpha Iota Sorority. **Publications:** The Symbol, quarterly. **Price:** included in membership dues. **Advertising:** accepted ● Membership Directory, biennial. Lists members' names, addresses and phone numbers. **Price:** available to members only, included in membership dues. **Conventions/Meetings:** annual convention and conference (exhibits).

Business Education

23835 ■ Alpha Beta Gamma International (ABG)
75 Grasslands Rd.
Valhalla, NY 10595
Ph: (914)606-6877 (914)606-6554
Fax: (914)606-6481

E-mail: ceo@abg.org
URL: http://www.abg.org
Contact: Dr. John D. Christesen, CEO
Founded: 1970. **Members:** 58,000. **Membership Dues:** honor, academic, social, $30 (annual) ● life, $35. **Staff:** 5. **Budget:** $150,000. **Local Groups:** 200. **Languages:** English, French, Spanish. **Description:** Honor Society - Business. Students enrolled at accredited two-year community, technical, and junior colleges in North America; also initiates distinguished International business persons and academics as honorary members. Sponsors training sessions and cultural and college activities. Maintains speakers' bureau. **Awards: Frequency:** annual. **Type:** scholarship. **Committees:** Alumni Development; Annual Meeting; Awards; Chapter Development; Community Relations; Faculty Executive; National Advisory Board; Ritual; Scholarship. **Formerly:** Alpha Beta Gamma. **Publications:** ABG National Constitution ● About Alpha Beta Gamma. Brochure ● Honors Journal, biennial. Newsletter. Contains news about chapters and winning essays by students. **Price:** free. **Circulation:** 50,000. **Advertising:** accepted. Alternate Formats: online. **Conventions/Meetings:** annual National Leadership Meeting - seminar and symposium, leadership training and lectures - always March or April ● seminar and symposium.

23836 ■ Delta Pi Epsilon (DPE)
c/o Dr. Robert B. Mitchell, Exec. Dir.
PO Box 4340
Little Rock, AR 72214
Ph: (501)219-1866
Fax: (501)219-1876
E-mail: dpe@ipa.net
URL: http://www.dpe.org
Contact: Dr. Robert B. Mitchell, Exec. Dir.
Founded: 1936. **Members:** 2,500. **Membership Dues:** regular, $65 (annual). **Staff:** 2. **Budget:** $250,000. **Local Groups:** 70. **For-Profit. Description:** Professional society - men and women, business education. **Awards:** Research Award. **Frequency:** annual. **Type:** recognition. **Recipient:** for the outstanding doctoral dissertation and master's thesis or seminar paper in business education completed during a particular year ● Research Grants. **Frequency:** annual. **Type:** grant. **Recipient:** for DPE member and chapter. **Telecommunication Services:** electronic mail, rbmitchell@ualr.edu. **Committees:** AdHoc Budget; AdHoc Communications; Awards; National Conference; Publications; Research Awards; Research Projects; Strategic Planning. **Publications:** Delta Pi Epsilon Journal, quarterly. **Price:** $48.00/year; $20.00/single issue; $54.00 for foreign countries. ISSN: 0011-8052. **Circulation:** 5,000 ● Journal of Applied Research for Business Instruction, quarterly. **Price:** $15.00/year; $5.00/single issue ● National Conference Book of Readings. **Price:** $10.00 ● Bulletins. Alternate Formats: online ● Reports. **Conventions/Meetings:** annual meeting.

23837 ■ Pi Omega Pi (POP)
c/o Dr. Lana Carnes, Pres.
Coll. of Bus. and Tech.
Eastern Kentucky Univ.
521 Lancaster Ave.
Bus. and Tech. Center 011
Richmond, KY 40475
Ph: (859)622-8005
Fax: (859)622-2359
E-mail: lana.carnes@eku.edu
Contact: Dr. Lana Carnes, Pres.
Founded: 1923. **Members:** 49,019. **Membership Dues:** life, $40. **Description:** Honor society - men and women, business education. **Awards:** Outstanding Member Award. **Type:** monetary. **Recipient:** to a member, awarded each semester. **Affiliated With:** Association of College Honor Societies. **Publications:** Here and There, quarterly. Newsletter. Contains chapter news. ● This Is Your Society, biennial. **Conventions/Meetings:** competition ● biennial meeting and convention.

Chemistry

23838 ■ Alpha Chi Sigma
2141 N Franklin Rd.
Indianapolis, IN 46219-2497
Free: (800)ALCHEMY

E-mail: anderson@marshall.edu
URL: http://alphachisigma.org
Contact: Sherrie E. Settle, Pres.
Founded: 1902. **Members:** 56,000. **Staff:** 2. **Budget:** $225,000. **Description:** Professional fraternity - chemistry. Offers a leadership program. **Libraries: Type:** reference. **Holdings:** 200. **Subjects:** alchemy, chemistry. **Awards:** Alpha Chi Sigma Scholar. **Frequency:** annual. **Type:** scholarship. **Recipient:** for student ● John R. Kuebler Award. **Frequency:** annual. **Type:** recognition. **Recipient:** for outstanding service to the fraternity and accomplishment in chemistry ● Ronald. T. Pflaum Outstanding Chapter Advisor Award. **Frequency:** annual. **Type:** recognition. **Recipient:** to an outstanding chapter advisor. **Committees:** Boy Scout Activity; Professional Activities; Safety; Scholarship; Student Loans. **Sections:** Collegiate; Professional. **Publications:** Alpha Chi Sigma Fraternity Membership Directory. Alternate Formats: online ● Hexagon, quarterly. Magazine. Alternate Formats: online ● Brochure ● Annual Reports, annual. Alternate Formats: online ● Reports, biennial. Alternate Formats: online. **Conventions/Meetings:** biennial Conclave - convention and workshop.

23839 ■ Iota Sigma Pi
c/o Kathryn Louie, Natl. VP
Univ. of Arizona Coll. of Medicine
1609 N Warren BRL B-110
Tucson, AZ 85724
Ph: (520)626-2044
Fax: (520)626-2383
E-mail: klouie@email.arizona.edu
URL: http://www.iotasigmapi.info
Contact: Kathryn Louie, Natl. VP
Founded: 1902. **Members:** 10,100. **Membership Dues:** student, $15 (annual) ● professional, $35 (annual). **Regional Groups:** 40. **Description:** Professional honor society for chemistry. **Awards:** Agnes Fay Morgan Research Award. **Frequency:** annual. **Type:** recognition. **Recipient:** for a woman chemist under age 40 who has made an outstanding research achievement ● Anna Louise Hoffman Award for Outstanding Achievement in Graduate Research. **Frequency:** annual. **Type:** recognition. **Recipient:** for outstanding achievement in chemical research by a woman graduate student ● Centennial Award for Excellence in Undergraduate Teaching. **Frequency:** annual. **Type:** recognition. **Recipient:** for excellence in teaching chemistry, biochemistry, or chemistry-related field by a woman in an undergraduate institution that does not offer a graduate program in that field ● Gladys Anderson Emerson Scholarship. **Frequency:** annual. **Type:** scholarship. **Recipient:** for a junior/senior college chemistry or biochemisty major who is an Iota Sigma Pi member ● National Honorary Member Award. **Frequency:** triennial. **Type:** recognition. **Recipient:** for an outstanding woman chemist for exceptional and significant achievement in chemistry or an allied field of such nature to merit international recognition ● Undergraduate Award for Excellence in Chemistry. **Frequency:** annual. **Type:** recognition. **Recipient:** for an outstanding woman senior undergraduate student majoring in chemistry ● Violet Diller Award for Professional Excellence. **Frequency:** triennial. **Type:** recognition. **Recipient:** for outstanding contribution to chemistry and allied fields by a woman. **Publications:** The Iotan, 3/year. Newsletter. Alternate Formats: online ● Directory, triennial. **Conventions/Meetings:** triennial Business Meeting.

23840 ■ Phi Lambda Upsilon (PLU)
c/o Dr. Manuel P. Soriaga, Pres.
Dept. of Chemistry
Texas A&M Univ.
College Station, TX 77842-3012
Ph: (979)845-1846
E-mail: soriaga@mail.chem.tamu.edu
URL: http://www.cpac.washington.edu/~campbell/plu
Contact: Dr. Manuel P. Soriaga, Pres.
Founded: 1899. **Members:** 55,000. **Membership Dues:** one-time, $30. **Local Groups:** 50. **Description:** Serves as honor society for students in chemistry, biochemistry, and chemical engineering. **Awards:**

National Fresenius Award. **Frequency:** annual. **Type:** recognition. **Recipient:** for chemist, biochemist or chemical engineer under age 35. **Additional Websites:** http://www.philambdaupsilon.org. **Publications:** *The Register*, annual. Magazine. **Price:** $3.00/year. **Conventions/Meetings:** triennial congress.

Childhood Education

23841 ■ Delta Phi Upsilon
PO Box 8275
Houston, TX 77288-8275
Ph: (713)272-OWLS
E-mail: execdir@dphiu.com
URL: http://www.dphiu.org
Contact: Colen M. Skinner, Exec. Dir.
Founded: 1923. **Members:** 400. **Description:** Recognition fraternity - women and men, childhood education. Conducts philanthropic projects. Operates speakers' bureau. **Awards: Type:** scholarship. **Recipient:** for students and alumni. **Committees:** Bulletin; Extension; Legislative; Research; Scholarship. **Councils:** Associations; Chapters; Grand. **Publications:** *Bulletin-Convention*, biennial ● *Bulletin-Founders' Day*, biennial ● Newsletter, semiannual. **Conventions/Meetings:** biennial conference (exhibits).

Chinese

23842 ■ National Chinese Honor Society (NCHS)
c/o Diane Mammone, Chair
PO Box 249
Barre, MA 01005
E-mail: classk12@yahoo.com
URL: http://www.classk12.org/Files/honor.htm
Contact: Diane Mammone, Chair
Founded: 1993. **Membership Dues:** student, $3. **Description:** Acknowledges the academic achievement, leadership character and community service of students studying Chinese as a second language. Advances Chinese language education. Promotes international relations and understanding of cultural differences.

Classical Studies

23843 ■ Eta Sigma Phi, National Classics Honorary Society
Dept. of Classics
Monmouth Coll.
700 E Broadway
Monmouth, IL 61462
Ph: (309)457-2371
Fax: (815)346-2565
E-mail: toms@monm.edu
URL: http://department.monm.edu/classics/esp
Contact: Thomas J. Sienkewicz, Exec. Sec.
Founded: 1914. **Members:** 1,800. **Membership Dues:** active-one time fee, $20 ● associate-one time fee, $10. **Staff:** 1. **Budget:** $15,000. **Local Groups:** 95. **Languages:** English, Greek, Latin. **Description:** Honorary society - men and women, classics (Latin and Greek). Sponsors competitions in translation of Latin and Greek and scholarships for summer study in Greece and in Italy. **Awards:** Bernice L. Fox Teacher Training Award. **Frequency:** annual. **Type:** scholarship. **Recipient:** for members only ● Eta Sigma Phi Summer Scholarships. **Frequency:** annual. **Type:** scholarship. **Additional Websites:** http://www.etasigmaphi.com. **Publications:** *Nuntius*, semiannual. Newsletter. **Price:** $25.00 one-time fee. **Advertising:** accepted. **Conventions/Meetings:** annual convention.

Communications

23844 ■ Zeta Phi Eta
c/o Joe Arnold, Exec. Dir.
1512 24th Ave., No. 36
Kenosha, WI 53140

Ph: (414)881-7381
E-mail: coed@zetaphieta.org
URL: http://www.zetaphieta.org
Contact: Ms. Lise Simring, Advisory Board Chair
Founded: 1893. **Members:** 15,000. **Membership Dues:** alumni, $30 (annual) ● student, $20 (annual). **Local Groups:** 12. **Description:** Conducts professional discussions, community service events, social and theatrical outings, and workshops. Provides national email listserves and assists members' network with each other when exploring career options. **Libraries: Type:** by appointment only. **Holdings:** archival material, articles, biographical archives, business records, photographs, reports. **Awards:** Distinguished Service Award. **Frequency:** annual. **Type:** recognition. **Recipient:** for two members who have served their chapter extensively over the past year ● Zeta Phi Eta Scholarships. **Frequency:** annual. **Type:** scholarship. **Recipient:** for use in undergraduate or graduate studies; for professional development education. **Boards:** Advisory Board to National Council. **Committees:** ByLaws Review. **Councils:** National. **Funds:** Fundraising and Budget Committee. **Programs:** Extensions and Reactivation Committee. **Projects:** National Service. **Study Groups:** Historian. **Subgroups:** Lost Member Campaign and Member-at-Large Outreach. **Working Groups:** Webmaster and Web Editors. **Affiliated With:** American Alliance for Theatre and Education; North American Interfraternal Foundation; Professional Fraternity Association. **Publications:** *Cameo*, semiannual. Magazine. Contains information about the fraternity. **Price:** included in membership dues; $30.00 for nonmembers. **Conventions/Meetings:** biennial convention.

Computer Science

23845 ■ Upsilon Pi Epsilon Association
c/o Orlando S. Madrigal, PhD, Sec.
158 Wetlands Edge Rd.
American Canyon, CA 94503
Ph: (530)518-8488 (707)648-3249
Fax: (707)647-3560
E-mail: upe@acm.org
URL: http://www.acm.org/upe
Contact: Orlando S. Madrigal PhD, Sec.
Founded: 1967. **Members:** 2,500. **Membership Dues:** $35 (annual). **Staff:** 2. **Budget:** $78,000. **Local Groups:** 170. **Description:** Honor society - computing and information disciplines. Students and faculty involved in computing and information discipline programs worldwide. Recognizes academic excellence in computing science at both the undergraduate and graduate levels; provides speakers. Cosponsors National Scholastic Programming Contest and other student activities in conjunction with other computer-related organizations. **Awards:** UPE Scholarship. **Frequency:** annual. **Type:** scholarship. **Recipient:** to active society members. **Publications:** *Semi-Annual Newsletter*, semiannual. Describes chapter activities during the past year. **Price:** free to all chapters. **Circulation:** 3,000. Alternate Formats: online. **Conventions/Meetings:** annual congress, computer art (exhibits) - last week in February.

Cooperative Extension

23846 ■ Epsilon Sigma Phi (ESP)
c/o Linda D. Cook, Exec. Dir.
PO Box 357340
Gainesville, FL 32635-7340
Ph: (352)378-6665
Fax: (352)375-0722
E-mail: espoffice@espnational.org
URL: http://espnational.org
Contact: Linda D. Cook, Exec. Dir.
Founded: 1927. **Members:** 11,000. **Staff:** 2. **Budget:** $128,000. **State Groups:** 50. **Description:** Serves as a honorary fraternity. Fosters standards of excellence in the Extension System and develops the Extension profession and professional. **Awards:** National Distinguished Service Ruby Award. **Frequency:** annual. **Type:** recognition. **Recipient:** for members ●

National Friends of Extension Awards. **Type:** recognition. **Recipient:** for outstanding public service and support of Extension Service programs ● Professional Development Mini Grants. **Frequency:** annual. **Type:** grant. **Recipient:** for projects that enhance professionalism in the cooperative extension system ● Regional Distinguished Service Ruby Award. **Frequency:** annual. **Type:** recognition. **Recipient:** for regional members. **Committees:** Global Relations; Journal of Extension; Marketing; Member Recruitment and Retention; Member Services; Professional Development; Public Issues; Resource Development and Management. **Publications:** *ESP Connection*, quinquennial. Newsletter. Alternate Formats: online ● Monographs ● Annual Report, annual. Alternate Formats: online ● Brochures. **Price:** free. Alternate Formats: online. **Conventions/Meetings:** annual Professional Development Workshops - meeting and seminar, educational.

Dentistry

23847 ■ Alpha Omega International Dental Fraternity
191 Clarksville Rd.
Princeton Junction, NJ 08550
Ph: (609)799-6000
Free: (800)677-8468
Fax: (609)799-7032
E-mail: headquarters@ao.org
URL: http://www.ao.org
Contact: John Wolffe, Intl. Pres.
Founded: 1907. **Members:** 15,000. **Membership Dues:** in U.S., $180 (annual) ● in Canada, $170 (annual) ● outside North America, $150 (annual) ● student, graduate student, $33 (annual). **Staff:** 4. **Budget:** $500,000. **Local Groups:** 125. **Description:** Professional fraternity - dentistry. Encourages fraternalism and monitors discrimination in dental schools. Maintains the Alpha Omega Foundation, which sends funds to dental schools in Israel and the U.S. Holds continuing education seminars. **Awards: Type:** grant. **Recipient:** for post-graduate dental students ● **Frequency:** annual. **Type:** recognition. **Recipient:** for students with superior scholastic standing. **Publications:** *Alpha Omegan*, quarterly. Magazine. **Price:** free for members ● *AO Today*, quarterly. Newsletter. Provides information on dental education in the United States and Israel. **Price:** included in membership dues. **Circulation:** 11,500. **Conventions/Meetings:** annual congress (exhibits) - always December 25-January 1.

23848 ■ Delta Sigma Delta
296 15th Ave.
Nekoosa, WI 54457
Ph: (715)325-6320
Free: (800)335-8744
Fax: (715)325-3057
E-mail: drjprey@earthlink.net
URL: http://www.deltsig.com
Contact: Dr. John H. Prey, Supreme Scribe
Founded: 1882. **Members:** 29,000. **Membership Dues:** life, $100. **Staff:** 2. **Budget:** $360,000. **State Groups:** 35. **Local Groups:** 34. **National Groups:** 11. **Multinational. Description:** Professional fraternity - dentistry. Maintains museum; offers educational programs. **Awards:** Meritorious Award. **Frequency:** annual. **Type:** recognition. **Recipient:** distinguished service decree. **Computer Services:** Mailing lists. **Publications:** *Alumni Directory*, quadrennial. ISSN: 0011-9474. **Circulation:** 28,000 ● *Desmos*, quarterly. Magazine. Includes chapter news, scientific articles, and announcements. **Price:** free for members. ISSN: 0011-9474. **Circulation:** 26,000. **Conventions/Meetings:** annual conference and meeting.

23849 ■ Omicron Kappa Upsilon (OKU)
c/o Ms. Jan John, Corresponding Sec.
Univ. of Nebraska
Coll. of Dentistry
40th and Holdrege St., Rm. 105
Lincoln, NE 68583-0740
Ph: (402)472-1345

Fax: (402)472-5290
E-mail: jkjohn@unmc.edu
URL: http://www.oku.org
Contact: Ms. Jan John, Corresponding Sec.
Founded: 1914. **Members:** 17,500. **Description:**
Serves as an honorary society of men and women in
the field of dentistry. **Awards:** Chapter Award. **Frequency:** annual. **Type:** recognition. **Recipient:** for
chapter that has created exemplary programs in
promoting excellence at the local level ● Charles
Craig Teaching Award. **Frequency:** annual. **Type:**
recognition. **Recipient:** for young dental educator
who has demonstrated new and innovative teaching
techniques ● Stephen Leeper Award. **Frequency:**
annual. **Type:** recognition. **Recipient:** for dental
educator who has demonstrated exemplary standards
in dental pedagogy. **Publications:** Bulletin, annual.
Conventions/Meetings: annual meeting - always
March.

23850 ■ Psi Omega
1040 Savannah Hwy.
Charleston, SC 29407-7804
Ph: (843)556-0573
Fax: (843)556-6311
E-mail: psiomega@bellsouth.net
URL: http://www.psiomegafraternity.org
Contact: Dr. B. Thomas Kays, Co-Exec. Dir.
Founded: 1892. **Members:** 30,000. **Membership
Dues:** new student, $60 (annual). **Staff:** 3. **Regional
Groups:** 25. **State Groups:** 36. **Description:** Professional fraternity - dentistry. **Libraries: Type:** reference. **Holdings:** archival material, artwork, books,
business records, periodicals. **Awards:** Founders
Award. **Frequency:** annual. **Type:** recognition. **Recipient:** for community service and chapter excellence. **Computer Services:** database, of records for
each chapter, each member and each alumnus. **Publications:** Frater, 3/year. Magazine. **Circulation:**
5,000. **Advertising:** accepted. **Conventions/Meet-
ings:** annual general assembly and workshop, held
in conjunction with American Dental Association
(exhibits) - every fall.

23851 ■ Sigma Phi Alpha (SPA)
c/o Bonnie Branson, Pres.
UMKC School of Dentistry
650 E 25th St.
Kansas City, MO 64108
Ph: (816)235-2053
Fax: (816)235-2157
E-mail: presidentelect@sigmaphialpha.org
URL: http://www.sigmaphialpha.org
Contact: Bonnie Branson, Pres.
Founded: 1958. **Members:** 9,000. **Membership
Dues:** chapter, $55 (annual). **Staff:** 1. **Local Groups:**
163. **Description:** Honorary society, dental hygiene.
Awards: Type: scholarship. **Recipient:** for individu-
als in dental hygiene ● Sigma Phi Alpha Award.
Frequency: annual. **Type:** recognition. **Recipient:**
for dental hygiene students in their final semester.
Also Known As: National Dental Hygiene Honor
Society. **Publications:** Newsletter, annual. **Conven-
tions/Meetings:** annual meeting, held in conjunction
with American Association of Dental Schools and/or
the American Dental Hygienists Association (exhibits).

23852 ■ Xi Psi Phi
c/o Dr. Keith W. Dickey, Supreme Sec.-Treas.
160 S Bellwood Dr., Ste.Z
East Alton, IL 62024-2086
Ph: (618)307-5433
Fax: (618)307-5430
E-mail: gobux27@yahoo.com
URL: http://www.xipsiphi.org
Contact: Dr. Keith W. Dickey, Supreme Sec.-Treas.
Founded: 1889. **Members:** 19,000. **Staff:** 2. **Local
Groups:** 22. **Description:** Professional dental
fraternity - dentistry. Maintains Hall of Fame. Conducts educational programs. **Libraries: Type:** reference. **Holdings:** archival material, periodicals.
Awards: Charlie Reagan Scholarship. **Frequency:**
annual. **Type:** scholarship. **Recipient:** for senior
students with satisfactory academic achievement and
in need of financial assistance ● Reynold L. and Vivian Foutz Scholarship. **Frequency:** annual. **Type:**

scholarship. **Recipient:** for junior students with
academic achievement, community leadership, and
in need of financial assistance. **Computer Services:**
Mailing lists, of members. **Publications:** Magazine,
quarterly. **Price:** $8.00. **Advertising:** accepted. **Con-
ventions/Meetings:** annual board meeting.

Dramatics

23853 ■ Alpha Psi Omega (APO)
c/o Dr. Bret Jones, Natl. Business Mgr.
East Central Univ.
1100 E 14th St.
Ada, OK 74820
Ph: (580)310-5756
E-mail: castcontacts@alphapsiomega.org
URL: http://www.alphapsiomega.org
Contact: Dr. Bret Jones, Natl. Business Mgr.
Founded: 1925. **Members:** 36,000. **Staff:** 3. **Local
Groups:** 800. **Description:** Recognition fraternity for
men and women in dramatics at four-year colleges
and universities. **Awards: Type:** recognition. **Publica-
tions:** The Playbill, annual ● Directory, annual ●
Newsletter, annual. **Conventions/Meetings:** quin-
quennial meeting.

23854 ■ Delta Psi Omega
c/o James Fisher, Natl. Business Mgr.
Wabash Coll.
Theater Dept.
Crawfordsville, IN 47933
Ph: (765)361-6394
E-mail: fisherj@wabash.edu
URL: http://www.wabash.edu/orgs/apodpo
Contact: James Fisher, Natl. Business Mgr.
Founded: 1925. **Members:** 20,000. **Membership
Dues:** honorary, $10. **Local Groups:** 251. **Descrip-
tion:** Honorary fraternity - men and women, dramat-
ics (junior college). **Awards: Type:** recognition. **Pub-
lications:** The Playbill, annual. Newsletter. **Conven-
tions/Meetings:** quinquennial meeting.

Economics

23855 ■ Lambda Alpha International (LAI)
c/o Terry Stevenson, Exec. Dir.
214 N Hale St.
Wheaton, IL 60187
Ph: (630)510-4584
Fax: (630)510-4501
E-mail: lai@lai.org
URL: http://www.lai.org
Contact: Terry Stevenson, Exec. Dir.
Founded: 1930. **Members:** 2,000. **Membership
Dues:** individual (by invitation only), $85 (annual) ●
member-at-large, $125. **Staff:** 2. **Budget:** $100. **Na-
tional Groups:** 22. **Languages:** English, French.
Multinational. Description: Serves as honorary
society for land economics. Offers land economics
archival program at Cornell University. **Libraries:
Type:** reference. **Awards:** Author Award. **Frequency:**
biennial. **Type:** recognition. **Recipient:** for authors
whose literary efforts have contributed to a greater
understanding of land economics internationally ●
Journalism Award. **Frequency:** biennial. **Type:**
recognition. **Recipient:** for journalists whose efforts
have contributed to a greater understanding of land
economics. **Formerly:** International Fraternity of
Lambda Alpha. **Publications:** Keynotes International,
quarterly. Newsletter. Alternate Formats: online ●
Model Manual for Chapter Operations For Lambda
Alpha International. Alternate Formats: online ●
Membership Directory, biennial ● Brochure ● Membership Directory. Alternate Formats: online. **Conven-
tions/Meetings:** biennial meeting and symposium.

23856 ■ Omicron Delta Epsilon (ODE)
PO Box 1486
Hattiesburg, MS 39402
Ph: (601)264-3115
Fax: (601)264-3669

E-mail: information@omicrondeltaepsilon.org
URL: http://www.omicrondeltaepsilon.org
Contact: Dr. William D. Gunther, Exec. Sec.-Treas.
Founded: 1963. **Members:** 115,000. **Membership
Dues:** student (life), $30. **Staff:** 1. **Budget:** $120,000.
Multinational. Description: Serves as an academic
honor society of men and women in economics.
Awards: Frank W. Taussig Article Award. **Frequency:**
annual. **Type:** recognition. **Recipient:** for undergraduates or recent graduates in economics who submit-
ted the best article in any year ● Irving Fisher Article
Award. **Frequency:** annual. **Type:** recognition. **Recipient:** for the best article submitted by a graduate
student or recipient of a doctorate in economics ●
John R. Commons Award. **Frequency:** biennial.
Type: recognition. **Recipient:** for an outstanding
economist ● Outstanding Student Award. **Frequency:**
annual. **Type:** recognition. **Recipient:** for students
who assume leadership roles in their chapter.
Formed by Merger of: (1962) Omicron Delta
Gamma; Omicron Chi Epsilon. **Publications:** The
American Economist, semiannual. Journal. **Price:**
$20.00 /year for individuals; $45.00 /year for institutions in U.S.; $55.00 /year for institutions outside
U.S.; $10.00/year for students. ISSN: 0569-4345.
Circulation: 6,000. **Conventions/Meetings:** biennial
convention, in conjunction with the American Economic Association (exhibits).

Editors

**23857 ■ College Fraternity Editors
Association (CFEA)**
c/o Christine Barnicki, Pres.
330 S Campus Ave.
Oxford, OH 45056
Ph: (513)523-1907
Fax: (513)523-7292
E-mail: ctbarnicki@earthlink.net
URL: http://www.cfea.org
Contact: Christine Barnicki, Pres.
Founded: 1883. **Members:** 200. **Membership Dues:**
regular, $50 (annual). **Description:** Represents edi-
tors of magazines published by men's and women's
general, professional, and honorary national fraternities. Sponsors competitions; conducts specialized
education; compiles statistics. **Awards: Type:** recognition. **Affiliated With:** National Panhellenic Conference; North-American Interfraternity Conference.
Publications: CFEA Bibliography, periodic ● The
Editor's Edition, quarterly ● The Fraternity Editor,
quarterly ● Membership Directory, annual. **Conven-
tions/Meetings:** annual conference and seminar
(exhibits).

**23858 ■ National Pan-Hellenic Editors
Conference (NPEC)**
8777 Purdue Rd., Ste.117
Indianapolis, IN 46268
Ph: (317)872-3185
Fax: (317)872-3192
E-mail: npccentral@npcwomen.org
URL: http://www.npcwomen.org
Contact: Carol Armstrong, Admin. Dir.
Founded: 1902. **Members:** 26. **Description:** Repre-
sents editors of National Panhellenic Conference (see
separate entry) magazines. **Formerly:** Sorority Edi-
tors Conference. **Publications:** NPEC News, peri-
odic. Newsletter. **Price:** available to members only.
Conventions/Meetings: biennial conference.

Education

23859 ■ Alpha Delta Kappa
1615 W 92nd St.
Kansas City, MO 64114
Ph: (816)363-5525
Free: (800)247-2311
Fax: (816)363-4010

E-mail: headquarters@alphadeltakappa.org
URL: http://www.alphadeltakappa.org
Contact: Ms. Janice M. Estell, Exec. Admin.
Founded: 1947. **Members:** 45,000. **Membership Dues:** individual, $25 (annual). **Staff:** 10. **Budget:** $1,200,000. **Regional Groups:** 7. **State Groups:** 50. **Local Groups:** 1,600. **National Groups:** 6. **Multinational. Description:** Honorary organization. Promotes educational excellence, altruism and world understanding. **Awards:** Woman of Distinction. **Frequency:** biennial. **Type:** recognition. **Recipient:** for a woman who has made outstanding contributions to the fields of education, humanities, sciences or arts on a national or international level. **Publications:** *The Alpha Delta Kappan*, semiannual. Magazine. **Price:** $3.00 in U.S.; $10.00 outside U.S. **Circulation:** 50,000 ● *The Columns*, bimonthly. Newsletter. **Conventions/Meetings:** biennial convention - always odd-numbered years. 2009 July 8-11, Greensboro, NC ● biennial regional meeting - always even-numbered years.

23860 ■ Alpha Phi Sigma Honorary Scholastic Society
Address Unknown since 2007
Founded: 1930. **Members:** 20,000. **Membership Dues:** life, $25. **Staff:** 3. **National Groups:** 9. **Description:** Scholastic honor society - men and women, open to all disciplines. **Awards:** Honor Key. **Frequency:** periodic. **Type:** recognition. **Recipient:** for outstanding leadership. **Publications:** *The Key*, periodic. Monograph. **Price:** free to members. **Advertising:** not accepted. **Conventions/Meetings:** biennial conference - always March.

23861 ■ Delphi Foundation
2020 Pennsylvania Ave. NW, No. 355
Washington, DC 20006-1811
Ph: (202)558-2295
Free: (800)587-3728
Fax: (202)318-2277
E-mail: delphi@dlp.org
URL: http://www.dlp.org
Contact: Erik B. Stavlund, Pres.
Founded: 1995. **Description:** Supports the educational mission of the Delta Lambda Phi fraternity. Provides scholarship assistance to gay, lesbian, and bisexual youths. **Convention/Meeting:** none. **Funds:** David L. West Scholarship. **Publications:** *Delphi Report*, annual. Annual Report. **Price:** free.

23862 ■ Kappa Delta Epsilon (KDE)
c/o Mrs. Patricia Clark, Natl. Treas.
619 34th Ave. E
Tuscaloosa, AL 35404
E-mail: sealark7@aol.com
URL: http://www.kappadeltaepsilon.org
Contact: Mrs. Patricia Clark, Natl. Treas.
Founded: 1933. **Members:** 47,518. **Membership Dues:** collegiate, $25 (annual) ● alumni chapter, $10 (annual). **Staff:** 1. **Regional Groups:** 4. **Local Groups:** 50. **Description:** Serves as an honorary professional fraternity - education. Conducts educational programs. **Awards:** Boyd-Orr International Award. **Frequency:** biennial. **Type:** recognition ● Outstanding Chapter Award. **Frequency:** biennial. **Type:** recognition ● Scrapbook Award. **Frequency:** biennial. **Type:** recognition ● Writing Award. **Frequency:** biennial. **Type:** recognition. **Recipient:** for the writers of KDE publication, The Current. **Affiliated With:** Professional Fraternity Association. **Formerly:** Kappa Delta Epsilon Sorority. **Publications:** *Ceremonies of Kappa Delta Epsilon*. Contains history of Dappa Delta Epsilon. **Price:** $5.00/copy ● *The Current*, 3/year. Newsletter. Contains membership and chapter activities news. **Price:** included in membership dues ● *Kappa Delta Epsilon Handbook* ● *Steps in Chartering a Collegiate Chapter*. Brochures ● *Steps in Chartering an Alumni Chapter*. Brochures. **Conventions/Meetings:** biennial conference and general assembly - 3 days usually in November ● biennial regional meeting - even numbered years.

23863 ■ Kappa Delta Pi
3707 Woodview Trace
Indianapolis, IN 46268-1158
Ph: (317)871-4900
Free: (800)284-3167
Fax: (317)704-2323
E-mail: wolfe@kdp.org
URL: http://www.kdp.org
Contact: Michael P. Wolfe, Exec. Dir.
Founded: 1911. **Members:** 57,000. **Membership Dues:** individual, $32 (annual). **Staff:** 22. **Budget:** $2,560,000. **Local Groups:** 620. **Description:** Honor society for men and women. Conducts research projects. Gives scholarships. Publishes scholarly journals and books. **Awards:** Achieving Chapter Excellence. **Frequency:** annual. **Type:** recognition ● Book-of-the-Year Award. **Frequency:** annual. **Type:** recognition ● Distinguished Dissertation Award. **Frequency:** annual. **Type:** recognition ● Graduate and Undergraduate Schools. **Frequency:** annual. **Type:** scholarship ● National Student Teacher of the Year. **Frequency:** annual. **Type:** recognition. **Computer Services:** database. **Boards:** Executive Council. **Affiliated With:** Association of College Honor Societies. **Publications:** *Educational Forum*, quarterly. Journal. **Price:** $16.00/year ● *Kadelpian*, quarterly. Newsletter ● *Kappa Delta Pi Record*, quarterly ● *Lifecycle of the Career Teacher*. Monograph ● *New Teacher Advocate*, quarterly ● *New Teacher Products*. Booklets. **Advertising:** accepted ● *Society Handbook*, biennial. **Conventions/Meetings:** biennial Convocation - conference (exhibits).

23864 ■ National Kappa Kappa Iota
1875 E 15th St.
Tulsa, OK 74104-4610
Ph: (918)744-0389
Free: (800)678-0389
Fax: (918)744-0578
E-mail: kappa@galstar.com
URL: http://www.kappakappaiota.org
Contact: Judy Craig, Co-Chair
Founded: 1921. **Members:** 5,500. **Membership Dues:** new, $25 (annual). **Staff:** 2. **State Groups:** 25. **Local Groups:** 500. **Description:** Professional organization - education. Supports foundations for battered adults and children. Conducts educational programs; compiles statistics. **Awards:** **Type:** recognition ● **Type:** scholarship. **Recipient:** for future teachers and teacher members. **Projects:** National Philanthropic. **Formerly:** (1931) Blue Blue Violet; (1993) Kappa Kappa Iota. **Publications:** *The Kappa Profile*, quarterly. Newsletter. **Price:** free for members. **Circulation:** 7,000. **Conventions/Meetings:** annual convention.

23865 ■ National Sorority of Phi Delta Kappa
8233 S King Dr.
Chicago, IL 60619
Ph: (773)783-7379
Fax: (773)783-7354
E-mail: info@sororitynpdk.org
URL: http://www.sororitynpdk.org
Contact: W. Ruth Branham, Office Mgr.
Founded: 1923. **Members:** 5,000. **Regional Groups:** 5. **Local Groups:** 125. **Description:** Represents women who teach or hold administrative positions in education. Five-point program includes educational conferences (Teach-A-Rama), reading and study centers for youth, youth guidance, scholarship awards, and maintenance of a children's library in Liberia. Offers tutorial programs. **Awards:** **Frequency:** annual. **Type:** recognition. **Recipient:** for two members of the National Association for the Advancement of Colored People. **Committees:** Education and Human Rights; History; International Project; Legal Defense Fund; Legislative Affairs; National Urban League; Wire Service and Schomburg Center for Research and Black Culture. **Councils:** National Council of Negro Women. **Programs:** Assault on Illiteracy. **Publications:** *Krinon*, annual ● Bulletin, quarterly ● Directory, annual. **Conventions/Meetings:** biennial meeting (exhibits).

23866 ■ Phi Theta Kappa, International Honor Society
PO Box 13729
Jackson, MS 39236-3729
Ph: (601)984-3504
Free: (800)946-9996
Fax: (601)984-3550
E-mail: member.services@ptk.org
URL: http://www.ptk.org
Contact: Rod A. Risley, Exec. Dir.
Founded: 1918. **Members:** 1,300,000. **Membership Dues:** life, $45. **Staff:** 54. **Budget:** $6,400,000. **Regional Groups:** 29. **Local Groups:** 1,250. **Multinational. Description:** International honor society - men and women, education (two-year colleges). Administers an alumni association. Sponsors Honors Institute and National Leadership Development Program. **Awards:** Hallmark Award. **Frequency:** annual. **Type:** recognition. **Recipient:** for chapters, members, advisors, and regions ● Nota Bene. **Frequency:** annual. **Type:** scholarship. **Recipient:** for members. **Telecommunication Services:** additional toll-free number, (877)785-1918. **Formerly:** Phi Theta Kappa International; (1987) Phi Theta Kappa. **Publications:** *The Golden Key*, quarterly. Newsletter. Contains information for chapter advisors, chapter and regional officers. ● *Golden Key News Briefs*, weekly. Newsletter. Provides information for and recognition of members, advisors, alumni, and friends. Alternate Formats: online ● *Manual for Members*, annual. Honors anthology showcasing student writings on selected topics. ● *Nota Bene*, annual. Directory. Honors anthology showcasing student writings on selected topics ● *The Phi Theta Kappa Leader*. Newsletter. Contains information for certified faculty of the leadership studies program. Alternate Formats: online ● *Phi Theta Kappa Scholarship Directory*, annual. Contains articles relating to leadership, scholarship, fellowship and service, and Hallmark awards relating to two-year colleges. ● *Visionary*, annual. Journal. Contains articles relating to leadership, scholarship, fellowship and service, and Hallmark awards relating to two-year colleges. ● Brochures. **Conventions/Meetings:** periodic conference ● annual International Convention - always April ● periodic regional meeting.

23867 ■ Pi Lambda Theta
4101 E 3rd St.
PO Box 6626
Bloomington, IN 47407-6626
Free: (800)487-3411
Fax: (812)339-3462
E-mail: office@pilambda.org
URL: http://www.pilambda.org
Contact: Rita J. Jones, Intl. Pres.
Founded: 1910. **Members:** 15,000. **Membership Dues:** professional, $35 (annual) ● full-time student, $25 (annual). **Staff:** 5. **Budget:** $906,200. **Description:** Maintains the highest academic admission standards, and also recognizes certification by the National Board for Professional Teaching Standards. Provides a Career Services Network consisting of a searchable job listing, member resume database, and a network of members who have volunteered to assist other members in job searches. **Awards:** Anna Tracey Memorial. **Type:** monetary. **Recipient:** to a producer of a communications medium ● Distinguished P. Lambda Thetan. **Frequency:** biennial. **Type:** recognition. **Recipient:** for outstanding contribution to the organization ● Distinguished Student Scholar. **Frequency:** biennial. **Type:** recognition. **Recipient:** to an education major who displayed leadership ● Ella Victoria Dobbs Award. **Frequency:** biennial. **Type:** recognition. **Recipient:** for a unique published research ● Excellence in Education. **Frequency:** biennial. **Type:** monetary. **Recipient:** for commitment to excellence in education ● Graduate Student Scholar. **Type:** recognition. **Recipient:** to an outstanding graduate student ● Lillian and Henry Barry Award in Human Relations. **Frequency:** biennial. **Type:** monetary. **Recipient:** for outstanding service to people with disabilities ● Scepter and Key. **Frequency:** biennial. **Type:** recognition. **Recipient:** to a member. **Committees:** Membership; Professional Projects; Publications Advisory Board; Re-

search Awards. **Publications:** *Educational Horizons*, quarterly. Journal. **Price:** $18.00/year in U.S.; $25.00/year outside U.S. ● Newsletter, bimonthly. **Conventions/Meetings:** biennial meeting, participant focused workshops in thematic strands - always July/August.

Engineering

23868 ■ Alpha Pi Mu (APM)
c/o Dr. Robert D. Dryden, Exec. Dir.
PO Box 773
Portland, OR 97207-0773
Ph: (503)297-3604
Fax: (503)297-3694
E-mail: jdryden@cecs.pdx.edu
URL: http://www.alphapimu.eas.pdx.edu
Contact: Dr. Robert D. Dryden, Exec. Dir.
Founded: 1949. **Membership Dues:** initiation; student, faculty, honorary, $38. **Staff:** 1. **Regional Groups:** 72. **Description:** Honor society - men and women, industrial engineering. **Awards: Type:** recognition.

23869 ■ Eta Kappa Nu (HKN)
300 W Adams, Ste.1210
Chicago, IL 60606-5114
Free: (800)406-2590
Fax: (800)864-2051
E-mail: info@hkn.org
URL: http://www.hkn.org
Contact: Dr. J. David Irwin, Pres.
Founded: 1904. **Members:** 200,000. **Membership Dues:** life, $40. **Staff:** 4. **Budget:** $175,000. **Local Groups:** 211. **Description:** Honorary fraternity - electrical engineering; honor society - electrical and computer engineering. **Awards:** Alton B. Zerby and Carl T. Koerner Outstanding Electrical and Computer Engineering Student. **Frequency:** annual. **Type:** recognition. **Recipient:** to students with outstanding scholastic excellence and high moral character ● C. Holmes MacDonald Outstanding Teacher Award. **Frequency:** annual. **Type:** recognition. **Recipient:** for the outstanding E.C.E. professor ● Outstanding Chapter Award. **Frequency:** annual. **Type:** recognition. **Recipient:** for excellence in college chapter programming ● Outstanding Young Electrical Engineer Award. **Frequency:** annual. **Type:** recognition. **Recipient:** to young engineers who have demonstrated significant accomplishments early in their career ● Vladimir Karapetoff Outstanding Technical Achievement Award. **Frequency:** annual. **Type:** recognition. **Recipient:** to a practitioner of electrical or computer engineering who has distinguished him/herself through an invention, development or discovery in the field of electrical or computer technology. **Committees:** Award. **Publications:** *The Bridge*, semiannual. Magazine. **Price:** $60.00 lifetime subscription; included in membership dues; $15.00 3-year subscription. **ISSN:** 0006-9809. **Circulation:** 22,000. **Advertising:** accepted. **Conventions/Meetings:** semiannual Directors' Meeting - usually New Jersey in spring and California in fall.

23870 ■ Kappa Eta Kappa (KHK)
718 E Pearson St.
Milwaukee, WI 53202
Ph: (414)273-9843
E-mail: rosem@msoe.edu
URL: http://www.msoe.edu/st_orgs/khk
Contact: Mark Rose, Pres.
Founded: 1923. **Members:** 20. **Membership Dues:** $30 (monthly). **Regional Groups:** 3. **Description:** Social/professional fraternity - electrical engineering. Conducts regular and special request engineering projects for exposition and private use. **Libraries: Type:** reference; not open to the public. **Holdings:** 400; books, periodicals. **Subjects:** engineering related. **Awards: Type:** recognition ● **Type:** scholarship. **Publications:** *Electron*, quarterly ● *List of Active Members*, semiannual. Directory. **Conventions/Meetings:** annual conference (exhibits).

23871 ■ Keramos
c/o Dr. Robert W. Schwartz, Pres.
Dept. of Ceramic Engg.
222 McNutt Hall
Univ. of Missouri-Rolla
Rolla, MO 65409-0330
Ph: (573)341-6025
Fax: (573)341-6934
E-mail: rwschwar@umr.edu
URL: http://www.ceramics.org/membership/sdc_pages/sdcdisplay.asp?ItemID=3
Contact: Dr. Robert W. Schwartz, Pres.
Founded: 1902. **Members:** 8,000. **Membership Dues:** honorary, student, $10 (annual). **Staff:** 1. **Local Groups:** 12. **Description:** Represents professional fraternity - ceramic engineering. Conducts research, educational, and charitable programs. **Libraries: Type:** not open to the public. **Awards:** Greaves-Walker Roll of Honor Award. **Frequency:** annual. **Type:** recognition. **Recipient:** for outstanding achievement in field of ceramics. **Computer Services:** database. **Publications:** *Keragram*, quarterly. Newsletter. Alternate Formats: online. **Conventions/Meetings:** competition, students compete in scholarship and service excellence ● annual conference.

23872 ■ Omega Chi Epsilon
c/o Richard A. Davis, Exec. Sec.
Univ. Minnesota-Duluth
Chem. Engg. Dept.
176 Engg. Bldg.
1303 Ordean Ct.
Duluth, MN 55812-3025
Ph: (218)726-6162
Fax: (218)726-6907
E-mail: rdavis@d.umn.edu
URL: http://www.omegachiepsilon.org
Contact: Richard A. Davis, Exec. Sec.
Founded: 1931. **Members:** 18,000. **Membership Dues:** active and associate; one-time initiation fee, $15. **Staff:** 8. **Local Groups:** 60. **Description:** Honor society - chemical engineering. Undergraduate and graduate students enrolled in chemical engineering curricula who display high academic achievement. Recognizes academic excellence, leadership, and service; encourages original investigation in chemical engineering; promotes student-faculty dialogue. **Awards:** National Omega Chi Epsilon Award. **Frequency:** annual. **Type:** recognition. **Recipient:** for service. **Affiliated With:** Association of College Honor Societies. **Publications:** *OXE Newsletter*, semiannual, always spring and fall ● Also publishes brochure. **Conventions/Meetings:** annual meeting, held in conjunction with the American Institute of Chemical Engineers.

23873 ■ Phi Alpha Epsilon
c/o Prof. Brian A. Rock, PhD, Faculty Advisor
Univ. of Kansas
Architectural Engg. Prog.
CEAE Dept., Learned Hall
1530 W 15th St., Rm. 2150
Lawrence, KS 66045-7609
Ph: (785)864-3603
E-mail: docrock@ku.edu
URL: http://www.ceae.ku.edu
Contact: Prof. Brian A. Rock PhD, Faculty Advisor
Founded: 1981. **Members:** 1,000. **National Groups:** 6. **Description:** Honor society - men and women, architectural engineering. Encourages chapters to become involved in campus life and community service. **Formerly:** (1984) Kappa Sigma Alpha Epsilon. **Publications:** Brochure ● Newsletter, annual ● Also plans to publish directory. **Conventions/Meetings:** annual conference, in conjunction with the Architectural Engineering Institute within the American Society of Civil Engineers.

23874 ■ Phi Kappa Upsilon Fraternity
21000 W 9 Mile Rd.
Southfield, MI 48075
Ph: (248)356-9591

E-mail: contact@phikapp.com
URL: http://www.phikappupsilon.com
Contact: Andrew Peters, Pres.
Founded: 1932. **Members:** 20. **Staff:** 3. **Description:** Social society - men, engineering and architecture. Works to further the individual and collective welfare of members. Sponsors recreational activities including trips and dinners. Participates in charitable activities. Previously national in scope, the society now has only one local chapter, though alumni reside throughout the U.S. **Libraries: Type:** open to the public. **Holdings:** books, periodicals. **Subjects:** engineering, arch, business. **Awards:** Phi Kappa Upsilon Man of the Year. **Frequency:** annual. **Type:** scholarship. **Publications:** *PhiKapp News*, monthly. Newsletter. **Conventions/Meetings:** weekly meeting, for active members of Delta Chapter ● semimonthly meeting, for Alumni members.

23875 ■ Pi Tau Sigma
c/o Dr. Farrokh Mistree, Natl. Sec.-Treas.
Georgia Inst. of Tech.
Woodruff School of Mech. Engg.
Systems Realization Lab
Atlanta, GA 30332-0405
Ph: (404)894-8412
Fax: (404)894-9342
E-mail: tom.burton@coe.ttu.edu
URL: http://www.pitausigma.net
Contact: Dr. Thomas D. Burton, Pres.
Founded: 1915. **Members:** 100,000. **Membership Dues:** honor, $25. **Staff:** 1. **Budget:** $50,000. **Local Groups:** 160. **Multinational. Description:** Honorary fraternity - men and women, mechanical engineering. **Awards:** Charles Russ Richards Memorial Award. **Frequency:** annual. **Type:** monetary ● Pi Tan Sigma Gold Medal Award. **Frequency:** annual. **Type:** monetary. **Publications:** *The Condenser of Pi Tau Sigma*, annual ● *The Story of Pi Tau Sigma*, biennial. **Conventions/Meetings:** annual convention.

23876 ■ Sigma Gamma Tau (SGT)
c/o Aerospace Engineering Department
Wichita State Univ.
Wichita, KS 67260-0044
Ph: (316)978-5935 (316)978-3410
Fax: (316)978-3307
E-mail: roy.myose@wichita.edu
URL: http://www.engr.wichita.edu/ae/sgt/sgthome.html
Contact: Dr. Roy Myose, Natl. VP
Founded: 1953. **Members:** 20,000. **Membership Dues:** regular, $25. **Staff:** 1. **Budget:** $25,000. **Regional Groups:** 8. **Local Groups:** 50. **Description:** National honor society - aerospace engineering. **Awards:** Amon Andes Honor Undergraduate Student Award. **Frequency:** annual. **Type:** recognition. **Recipient:** for young students' accomplishments as they start their professional careers. **Formed by Merger of:** Tau Omega; Gamma Alpha Rho. **Publications:** Journal, periodic. **Conventions/Meetings:** triennial congress.

23877 ■ Tau Alpha Pi (TAP)
1818 N St. NW, Ste.600
Washington, DC 20036
Ph: (202)350-5762
Fax: (202)265-8504
E-mail: w.sallade@asee.org
URL: http://www.taualphapi.org
Contact: Warren Sallade, Exec. Off.
Founded: 1953. **Members:** 45,000. **Membership Dues:** regular, $35 (annual). **Staff:** 1. **Local Groups:** 96. **Description:** National honor society for engineering technology. **Libraries: Type:** not open to the public. **Awards: Frequency:** annual. **Type:** recognition. **Councils:** College/University Chapters. **Publications:** *Journal of Tau Alpha Pi National Honor Society - Engineering Technologies*, annual. **Price:** free.

23878 ■ Tau Beta Pi Association
PO Box 2697
Knoxville, TN 37901-2697
Ph: (865)546-4578
Fax: (865)546-4579

E-mail: tbp@tbp.org
URL: http://www.tbp.org
Contact: James D. Froula, Exec. Dir.
Founded: 1885. **Members:** 476,000. **Membership Dues:** life, $37. **Staff:** 10. **Budget:** $2,000,000. **Regional Groups:** 16. **Local Groups:** 230. **Description:** Honor society - engineering. Provides grants, scholarships, fellowships, and student loans. Honors students for non-engineering activities as Laureates. Presents national outstanding alumnus, advisor, mentoring, and chapter awards. Teaches personal development and leadership skills. Membership is by invitation only. **Awards:** Distinguished Alumnus. **Frequency:** annual. **Type:** recognition. **Recipient:** for alumni who have continued to live up to the ideals of Tau Beta Pi ● Greater Interest in Government. **Frequency:** quarterly. **Type:** grant. **Recipient:** to chapters for civic projects ● Laureate. **Frequency:** annual. **Type:** monetary. **Recipient:** for a student member of Tau Beta Pi with an exceptional talent in the field of engineering ● National Outstanding Advisor. **Frequency:** annual. **Type:** monetary. **Recipient:** for outstanding Tau Beta Pi chapter advisors ● Tau Beta Pi Fellowship. **Frequency:** annual. **Type:** fellowship. **Recipient:** for outstanding graduate students ● Tau Beta Pi -McDonald Mentoring Award. **Frequency:** annual. **Type:** monetary. **Recipient:** to an outstanding mentor in the academe or in the industry ● Tau Beta Pi Scholarships. **Frequency:** annual. **Type:** scholarship. **Recipient:** for outstanding senior student members. **Affiliated With:** American Association of Engineering Societies; American Society for Engineering Education; Association of College Honor Societies. **Absorbed:** (1974) Sigma Tau. **Publications:** *The Bent of Tau Beta Pi*, quarterly. Journal. Features general engineering articles for engineers/executives in all engineering fields. **Price:** $10.00/year; $60.00 lifetime subscription. ISSN: 0005-884X. **Circulation:** 91,000. **Advertising:** accepted. Alternate Formats: CD-ROM; online ● *The Bulletin of Tau Beta Pi*, 3/year. **Conventions/Meetings:** annual National Convention, engineering recruitment (exhibits) - usually October.

23879 ■ Theta Tau
1011 San Jacinto, Ste.205
Austin, TX 78701
Ph: (512)472-1904
Free: (800)264-1904
Fax: (512)472-4820
E-mail: central@thetatau.org
URL: http://www.thetatau.org
Contact: Michael T. Abraham, Exec. Dir.
Founded: 1904. **Members:** 30,000. **Staff:** 3. **Budget:** $250,000. **Regional Groups:** 6. **Local Groups:** 43. **Description:** Professional fraternity - engineering. Maintains hall of fame. **Libraries: Type:** reference. **Holdings:** 125; books. **Awards:** Alumni Hall of Fame. **Frequency:** annual. **Type:** recognition. **Recipient:** for excellent contributions to the fraternity and/or profession ● Outstanding Student Member Award. **Frequency:** annual. **Type:** recognition. **Publications:** *A History of Theta Tau Fraternity* ● *Chapter Officers Manual* ● *Executive Council Bulletin*, bimonthly ● *The Gear of Theta Tau*, semiannual. Magazine. **Price:** free for members. **Circulation:** 17,000. **Advertising:** accepted ● *Pledge and Membership Manual*, periodic ● Membership Directory, quinquennial. **Conventions/Meetings:** annual convention, general chapters displays only (exhibits) - always mid-August ● annual Leadership Academy - conference, general chapters displays only (exhibits) - always mid-August ● annual Rube Goldberg Machine Contest - competition.

English

23880 ■ Sigma Tau Delta, the International English Honor Society
c/o Dr. William C. Johnson, Exec. Dir.
Dept. of English
Northern Illinois Univ.
DeKalb, IL 60115
Ph: (815)753-1612

E-mail: sigmatd@niu.edu
URL: http://www.english.org
Contact: Dr. William C. Johnson, Exec. Dir.
Founded: 1924. **Members:** 165,000. **Staff:** 5. **Budget:** $290,000. **Regional Groups:** 625. **Multinational. Description:** Honor society - men and women, English. Confers distinction upon students of the English language and literature in undergraduate, graduate, and professional studies. **Awards:** Internships. **Frequency:** annual. **Type:** recognition. **Recipient:** for students, faculty and alumni ● Scholarships. **Frequency:** annual. **Type:** scholarship. **Recipient:** to an outstanding student scholar. **Affiliated With:** Association of College Honor Societies. **Formerly:** Association of College Honor Societies; Sigma Tau Delta. **Publications:** *The Rectangle*, annual. Magazine. Contains information about literary non-fiction, fiction, and poetry. **Price:** $4.00 ● *The Sigma Tau Delta Review*, annual. Journal. Features critical essays on literature, rhetoric and composition, and devoted to pedagogical issues. **Price:** $4.00. **Conventions/Meetings:** annual board meeting (exhibits) ● annual conference - always March ● semiannual executive committee meeting ● regional meeting - 5-6/year.

Environmental Education

23881 ■ Green Leaf National Honor Society
c/o Environmental Studies Program
Univ. of Southern California
Sci. Bldg., Rm. 160
Los Angeles, CA 90089-0740
Ph: (213)740-7770
E-mail: environ@rcf.usc.edu
URL: http://www.usc.edu/dept/LAS/enviro/envgreenleaf3.htm
Contact: Prof. Albert A. Herrera, Dir.
Description: Recognizes and acknowledges students throughout the country who are studying natural environment as college undergraduates. Emphasizes studies in the societal aspects of environmental issues. **Publications:** Newsletter, annual.

Foreign Service

23882 ■ Delta Phi Epsilon, Professional Foreign Service Fraternity
3401 Prospect St. NW
Washington, DC 20007
Ph: (202)337-9702
Fax: (202)333-3725
E-mail: tjb007@comcast.net
URL: http://www.deltaphiepsilon.net
Contact: Charles M. McClees, Pres.
Founded: 1920. **Members:** 7,000. **Regional Groups:** 24. **State Groups:** 4. **Description:** Serves as a professional fraternity for foreign service. Offers placement service. **Libraries: Type:** reference. **Holdings:** 1,000. **Subjects:** international affairs. **Awards:** American Peace Prize. **Frequency:** periodic. **Type:** recognition. **Recipient:** for professional men in Foreign Service. **Funds:** Alumni House. **Publications:** *Alumni Directory*, biennial. Alternate Formats: online ● *The Galley*, annual ● *The Sun*, quarterly ● *The Tramp*, annual. Newsletter. Alternate Formats: online. **Conventions/Meetings:** biennial conference.

23883 ■ Delta Phi Epsilon Professional Foreign Service Sorority
c/o Delta Phi Epsilon Professional Foreign Service Fraternity
3401 Prospect St. NW
Washington, DC 20007
E-mail: tjb007@comcast.net
URL: http://www.deltaphiepsilon.net/Sorority.html
Contact: Kah Yee Teh, Pres.
Founded: 1972. **Members:** 300. **Description:** Students and professionals in diplomacy and foreign trade. Assists women in entering and advancing in these careers. **Additional Websites:** http://www.

geocities.com/foreignservicesorority. **Conventions/Meetings:** biennial conference.

Fraternities and Sororities

23884 ■ Alpha Pi Sigma
PO Box 3814
Torrance, CA 90510
E-mail: aps@alphapisigma.org
URL: http://www.alphapisigma.org
Contact: Jessica Mix, Pres.
Founded: 1990. **Description:** Latina-based sorority. Unites and supports Latina women on each campus.

23885 ■ Association of Fraternity Advisors (AFA)
9640 N Augusta Dr., Ste.433
Carmel, IN 46032
Ph: (317)876-1632
Fax: (317)876-3981
E-mail: info@fraternityadvisors.org
URL: http://www.fraternityadvisors.org
Contact: Sue Kraft-Fussell, Exec. Dir.
Founded: 1976. **Members:** 1,100. **Membership Dues:** regular or affiliate, $90 (annual) ● associate, $190 (annual) ● graduate, retired, $55 (annual). **Staff:** 2. **Budget:** $300,000. **Description:** Represents student personnel professionals working with fraternities and sororities; professional and volunteer staff and officers of fraternities and sororities; local chapter advisers; interested persons. Provides a forum in which members can exchange ideas, work toward common goals, and enhances professional development geared toward working with fraternities and sororities. Compiles statistics. **Libraries: Type:** reference. **Holdings:** archival material. **Awards: Type:** recognition. **Publications:** *Advising Fraternities and Sororities*. Manual. **Price:** $40.00 for members; $55.00 for nonmembers ● *AFA Perspectives*, quarterly. Newsletter ● *Ideas for Practice*. Manual. **Price:** $45.00 for nonmembers; $30.00 for members. **Conventions/Meetings:** annual conference and meeting, held in conjunction with National Interfraternity Conference (exhibits).

23886 ■ Center for the Study of the College Fraternity (CSCF)
Indiana Univ.
900 E 7th St., Ste.371
Bloomington, IN 47405
Ph: (812)855-1228
E-mail: cscf@indiana.edu
URL: http://www.indiana.edu/~sao/cscfsite
Contact: Mr. Steve Velkdamp, Exec. Dir.
Founded: 1979. **Staff:** 2. **Description:** National fraternities and sororities; Panhellenic associations and interfraternity councils; higher education institutions; interested individuals. Seeks to further programs and services devoted to the common needs of college fraternities and sororities and higher education. Supports research related to the Greek system and the development of a resource library. Compiles statistics. **Committees:** Research. **Publications:** *Enhancing the Quality of Greek Life* ● *The Influences of Student Involvement by Sorority Membership* ● *Update*, quarterly. Newsletter. **Conventions/Meetings:** annual board meeting.

23887 ■ Central Office Executives Association of National Pan-Hellenic Conference (COEA/NPC)
3905 Vincennes Rd., Ste.105
Indianapolis, IN 46268-3000
Ph: (317)872-3185
Fax: (317)872-3192
Founded: 1943. **Members:** 26. **Description:** Executive directors of each member group of the National Panhellenic Conference. **Formerly:** (1982) National Panhellenic Association of Central Office Executives; (1985) National Panhellenic Conference of Central Office Executives. **Conventions/Meetings:** annual conference - always October or November.

23888 ■ Delta Kappa Phi
9 Mt. Hope St.
Lowell, MA 01854
Ph: (978)455-1978
URL: http://www.delta-kappa-phi.net
Contact: Kenneth Tucceri, Pres.
Founded: 1898. **Members:** 1,532. **Description:** Serves as fraternity primarily for textile education, but promotes education in engineering, the sciences or liberal arts.

23889 ■ Fraternity Executives Association (FEA)
c/o Sydney N. Dunn, Admin.
1750 Royalton Dr.
Carmel, IN 46032
E-mail: fea.inc@gmail.com
URL: http://www.fea-inc.org
Contact: Robert Biggs, Pres.
Founded: 1930. **Members:** 57. **Membership Dues:** individual, $60 (annual). **Budget:** $100,000. **Description:** Represents executive officers of college social fraternities. **Formerly:** (1970) College Fraternity Secretaries Association. **Publications:** News and Notes, monthly. **Conventions/Meetings:** annual meeting (exhibits).

23890 ■ Kappa Psi Kappa Fraternity (KPK)
108 Forrister St.
Columbia, SC 29223
E-mail: kpsik@kpsikinc.org
URL: http://www.kpsikinc.org
Contact: Sean R. Tirrell, Pres.
Founded: 2001. **Description:** Works to enhance quality of life within the community. **Telecommunication Services:** electronic mail, srtirrell@kpsikinc.org.

23891 ■ Lambda Pi Alumni Association
PO Box 1133
Chico, CA 95927
Ph: (530)332-9347 (831)423-3952
E-mail: gcodiga@pacbell.net
URL: http://www.lambdapi.org
Contact: Grant Codiga, Pres.
Founded: 1944. **Description:** Alumni of Lambda Pi Fraternity. Strives to maintain tradition of leadership and respect in the inter-fraternity community. **Conventions/Meetings:** meeting.

23892 ■ Lambda Theta Phi
565 Main Ave., 2nd Fl.
Passaic, NJ 07055
E-mail: info@lambda1975.org
URL: http://www.lambda1975.org
Contact: Byron Bustos, Pres.
Founded: 1975. **Members:** 6. **National Groups:** 43. **Description:** Fraternity brothers. Provide political and social actions and affirmative role models for the Latino population. Promote scholarships, harmony and respect for all cultures and brotherhood. **Telecommunication Services:** electronic mail, byron.bustos@lambda1975.org.

23893 ■ National Pan-Hellenic Council
3951 Snapfinger Pkwy., Ste.218
Decatur, GA 30035
Ph: (404)592-6145
Fax: (404)592-6129
E-mail: info@nphchq.org
URL: http://www.nphchq.org
Contact: Dr. Michael Bowie, Natl. Pres.
Founded: 1930. **Membership Dues:** council, $100-$200 (annual) ● affiliate, $1,000 (annual) ● associate, $2,000 (annual). **Staff:** 3. **Regional Groups:** 5. **Local Groups:** 415. **National Groups:** 9. **Description:** Umbrella organization for 9 historically black Greek-letter organizations: Alpha Kappa Alpha Sorority, Inc., Alpha Phi Alpha Fraternity, Inc., Delta Sigma Theta Sorority, Inc., Zeta Phi Beta Sorority, Inc., Iota Phi Theta Fraternity, Inc., Kappa Alpha Psi Fraternity, Inc., Sigma Gamma Rho Sorority, Inc., Phi Beta Sigma Fraternity, Inc., Omega Psi Phi Fraternity, Inc. **Awards: Type:** scholarship. **Publications:** The Summit, periodic. Newsletter. Alternate Formats: online. **Conventions/Meetings:** biennial convention and regional meeting, with Greek paraphernalia, corpora-

tions, recruiting (exhibits) - usually October/November ● periodic workshop.

23894 ■ National Panhellenic Conference (NPC)
8777 Purdue Rd., Ste.117
Indianapolis, IN 46268-3000
Ph: (317)872-3185
Fax: (317)872-3192
E-mail: npccentral@npcwomen.org
URL: http://www.npcwomen.org
Contact: Ms. Carol Armstrong, Admin. Dir.
Founded: 1902. **Members:** 26. **Staff:** 2. **Local Groups:** 620. **National Groups:** 26. **Description:** Serves as a federation of college women's social sororities. **Computer Services:** database. **Publications:** Greek Today and Here to Stay ● Listing of Member Groups on Campuses, annual. Membership Directory ● News Bulletin ● NPC Directory, biennial ● PH Factor, semiannual. Bulletin. **Conventions/Meetings:** biennial meeting (exhibits).

23895 ■ North American Interfraternal Foundation (NIF)
1750 Royalton Dr.
Carmel, IN 46032-9620
Ph: (317)767-7657
Fax: (317)571-9686
E-mail: sidneyndunn@nif-inc.net
URL: http://www.nif-inc.net
Contact: Sidney A. Dunn, Exec. Dir.
Founded: 1945. **Staff:** 1. **Budget:** $75,000. **Non-membership. Description:** Promotes the welfare of the North American college fraternity system; collects and disseminates information on fraternity life, history, and problems; cooperates with college fraternities, individual chapters, and colleges and universities in encouraging positive aspects of fraternity life, atmosphere, and practices. **Awards:** Jack Anson Fellowship. **Frequency:** annual. **Type:** recognition. **Recipient:** to fraternal members pursuing graduate studies in student personnel ● James H. McLaughlin. **Frequency:** annual. **Type:** scholarship. **Recipient:** for outstanding fraternal leadership to students enrolled in Canadian universities ● Lloyd G. Balfour Fellowships. **Frequency:** annual. **Type:** fellowship. **Recipient:** to graduate fraternal members who have exhibited academic achievement and leadership ● Mary Louise Roller Panhellenic Scholarship. **Frequency:** annual. **Type:** scholarship. **Recipient:** to women who have exhibited outstanding Panhellenic leadership ● NIF Publications. **Frequency:** annual. **Type:** recognition. **Recipient:** for fraternity magazine articles about student life and the fraternity system. **Formerly:** (2002) National Interfraternity Foundation. **Publications:** NIF Notes, quarterly. Newsletter. Alternate Formats: online.

23896 ■ North-American Interfraternity Conference (NIC)
3901 W 86th St., Ste.390
Indianapolis, IN 46268-1791
Ph: (317)872-1112
Fax: (317)872-1134
E-mail: nic@nicindy.org
URL: http://www.nicindy.org
Contact: Marc Katz, Pres.
Founded: 1909. **Members:** 66. **Description:** Serves as federation of men's general college fraternities in the U.S. and Canada. Collects data and statistics. **Awards:** Award of Distinction. **Frequency:** annual. **Type:** recognition. **Recipient:** for overall leadership and excellence ● Gold Medal Award. **Type:** medal. **Recipient:** for service to youth through the college fraternity. **Affiliated With:** College Fraternity Editors Association; Fraternity Executives Association. **Formerly:** (1999) National Interfraternity Conference. **Publications:** Campus Commentary, 8/year ● Interfraternity Directory, annual. **Conventions/Meetings:** annual meeting (exhibits) - always December.

23897 ■ Professional Fraternity Association (PFA)
345 N Charles St., 3rd Fl.
Baltimore, MD 21201
Free: (888)7714-PFA

Fax: (410)347-3119
E-mail: info@profraternity.org
URL: http://www.profraternity.org
Contact: Andrew Sagan, Exec. Dir.
Founded: 1978. **Members:** 37. **Description:** Supports professional fraternities and sororities to preserve high standards on campus and in professional practice. **Awards:** Career Achievement Award. **Frequency:** annual. **Type:** recognition. **Recipient:** to an active member of a constituent fraternity who has achieved national or international renown ● Faculty Award of Excellence. **Frequency:** annual. **Type:** recognition. **Formed by Merger of:** Professional Panhellenic Association; Professional Inter-fraternity Conference. **Publications:** PFA Directory, annual ● PFA Today, quarterly. Newsletter. **Conventions/Meetings:** annual conference and meeting (exhibits).

23898 ■ Zeta Beta Tau Fraternity (ZBT)
3905 Vincennes Rd., Ste.300
Indianapolis, IN 46268
Ph: (317)334-1898
Fax: (317)334-1899
E-mail: zbt@zbtnational.org
URL: http://www.zbtnational.org
Contact: Jonathan I. Yulish, Exec. Dir.
Founded: 1898. **Members:** 110,000. **Description:** Strives to maintain tradition of leadership and respect in the inter-fraternity community. **Publications:** Chapter and Colony, monthly. Bulletin. Alternate Formats: online ● Manuals. Alternate Formats: online. **Conventions/Meetings:** convention.

French

23899 ■ Pi Delta Phi
c/o Dr. Pamela Park, Exec. Dir.
Box 8350
Dept. of Foreign Languages
Idaho State Univ.
Pocatello, ID 83209
Ph: (208)282-3740
Fax: (208)282-3098
E-mail: parkpame@isu.edu
URL: http://www.pideltaphi.org
Contact: Dr. Pamela Park, Exec. Dir.
Founded: 1906. **Members:** 5,000. **Membership Dues:** life, $25. **Staff:** 1. **Budget:** $40,000. **Regional Groups:** 6. **Local Groups:** 329. **Languages:** English, French. **Description:** Serves as honor society for men and women, French language and literature. Seeks to stimulate and encourage appreciation of France and its people. **Libraries: Type:** not open to the public. **Awards:** Joseph Yedlicka Scholarship Awards. **Frequency:** annual. **Type:** scholarship. **Recipient:** for students who have excelled in their study of French at the university level. **Affiliated With:** Association of College Honor Societies. **Also Known As:** National French Honor Society. **Publications:** Brochure ● Handbook ● Newsletter, semiannual. **Price:** included in membership dues. **Conventions/Meetings:** competition ● triennial conference.

Geography

23900 ■ Gamma Theta Upsilon (GTU)
c/o Lawrence Handley, Exec. Sec.
700 Cajundome Blvd.
Lafayette, LA 70506
Ph: (337)266-8691
Fax: (337)266-8513
E-mail: larry_handley@usgs.gov
URL: http://www.gtuhonors.org
Contact: Lawrence Handley, Exec. Sec.
Founded: 1928. **Members:** 49,500. **Membership Dues:** regular, honorary, $25. **Regional Groups:** 8. **Local Groups:** 244. **Description:** Honor society - geography. Cosponsors Visiting Geographical Scientist Program with Association of American Geographers (see separate entry). **Awards:** Buzzard Scholarship. **Frequency:** annual. **Type:** scholarship. **Recipient:** for graduates and undergraduates ● Excellence in Geography Award. **Frequency:** annual.

Type: recognition ● Maxfield Scholarship. **Frequency:** annual. **Type:** scholarship. **Recipient:** to junior or senior undergraduates with career or graduate school aspirations ● President's Scholarship. **Frequency:** annual. **Type:** scholarship. **Recipient:** to junior or senior undergraduates with career or graduate school aspirations ● Richason Scholarship. **Frequency:** annual. **Type:** scholarship. **Recipient:** to junior or senior undergraduates with career or graduate school aspirations. **Programs:** Visiting Geographical Scientist. **Affiliated With:** Association of American Geographers; Association of College Honor Societies. **Publications:** *The Geographical Bulletin*, semiannual. Journal. Contains student research articles and chapter news. **Price:** included in membership dues for first year members; $5.00 /year for members; $10.00 /year for institutions and alumni ● Also publishes handbook. **Conventions/Meetings:** semiannual meeting, with National Council for Geographic Education and Association of American Geographers (exhibits) - usually in April and October.

Geology

23901 ■ Sigma Gamma Epsilon (SGE)
c/o Dr. Charles J. Mankin, Sec.-Treas.
Univ. of Oklahoma
100 E Boyd, Rm. N-131
Norman, OK 73019
Ph: (405)325-3031
Fax: (405)325-7069
E-mail: cjmankin@ou.edu
URL: http://www.earth.uni.edu/SGE
Contact: Dr. Charles J. Mankin, Sec.-Treas.

Founded: 1915. **Members:** 75,000. **Membership Dues:** student, associate, alumni, honorary, $15 (annual) ● life, $175. **Staff:** 1. **Regional Groups:** 4. **Local Groups:** 100. **Description:** Honorary society recognizing scholarship and professionalism in the earth sciences. Seeks: scholastic, scientific, and professional advancement of its members; cooperation between colleges and universities devoted to the advancement of earth science. **Awards:** Austin Sartin Award. **Frequency:** annual. **Type:** recognition. **Recipient:** for excellent papers ● National Council Award. **Frequency:** annual. **Type:** recognition. **Recipient:** for excellent papers ● W.A. Tarr Award. **Frequency:** annual. **Type:** recognition. **Recipient:** for outstanding achievement. **Publications:** *The Compass: The Earth Science Journal of Sigma Gamma Epsilon*, quarterly. Contains lists of chapters and advisors; includes directory. **Price:** $24.00/year. ISSN: 0894-802X. **Circulation:** 1,600. **Conventions/Meetings:** biennial convention.

German

23902 ■ Delta Phi Alpha (DPA)
c/o Dr. John F. Reynolds, Natl. Sec.-Treas.
Natl. German Honor Soc.
Grainger Bldg. 306
Longwood Univ.
201 High St.
Farmville, VA 23901-1839
Ph: (434)395-2712
Fax: (434)395-2141
E-mail: reynoldsjf@longwood.edu
URL: http://www.deltaphialpha.org
Contact: Dr. John F. Reynolds, Natl. Sec.-Treas.

Founded: 1927. **Members:** 32,000. **Membership Dues:** life, $20 ● chapter, $25 (annual). **Staff:** 2. **National Groups:** 125. **Languages:** English, German. **Description:** Honor society for men and women in German studies. **Awards:** Delta Phi Alpha Scholarship Awards. **Frequency:** annual. **Type:** scholarship. **Recipient:** to undergraduate student members wishing to further their German studies with research and study abroad in a German speaking country. **Publications:** Bulletin, biennial ● Newsletter, periodic. **Conventions/Meetings:** annual National Council - meeting.

Health

23903 ■ University of Colorado Health Sciences Center Alumni Association
4200 E 9th Ave., Box A-080
Denver, CO 80262
Ph: (303)315-8832
Free: (877)HSC-ALUM
Fax: (303)315-7729
E-mail: alumni@uchsc.edu
URL: http://www.uchsc.edu/alumni
Contact: Wende Reoch, Dir.

Description: Serves as ambassadors, advocates and advisors for Colorado University. **Programs:** Dentistry; Nursing; Physical Therapy; Schools of Medicine. **Publications:** *CU Medicine Today*, semiannual. Magazine. **Conventions/Meetings:** annual meeting ● reunion.

History

23904 ■ Phi Alpha Theta
Univ. of South Florida
4202 E Fowler Ave., SOC107
Tampa, FL 33620-8100
Ph: (813)974-8212
Free: (800)394-8195
Fax: (813)974-8215
E-mail: phialpha@phialphatheta.org
URL: http://www.phialphatheta.org
Contact: Graydon A. Tunstall Jr., Exec. Dir.

Founded: 1921. **Members:** 281,000. **Membership Dues:** life, $40. **Staff:** 3. **Budget:** $550,000. **Regional Groups:** 40. **Local Groups:** 880. **Description:** Serves as honor society for men and women, history. **Awards:** Book Awards. **Frequency:** annual. **Type:** recognition. **Recipient:** for the best book in history published by a society member ● Nash History Journal Award. **Type:** recognition ● Paper Prize Awards. **Frequency:** annual. **Type:** recognition. **Recipient:** for outstanding papers by members of the society ● Scholarship. **Frequency:** annual. **Type:** grant. **Telecommunication Services:** electronic mail, phialpha@ptd.net. **Affiliated With:** Association of College Honor Societies. **Publications:** *The Historian*, quarterly. Journal. Includes book reviews and research reports. **Price:** $30.00 for members. ISSN: 0018-2370. **Circulation:** 12,500. **Advertising:** accepted ● *The News Letter*, 3/year. Newsletter. **Price:** $12.00/year. **Conventions/Meetings:** biennial convention ● periodic regional meeting.

Home Economics

23905 ■ Kappa Omicron Nu (KON)
4990 Northwind Dr., Ste.140
East Lansing, MI 48823-5031
Ph: (517)351-8335
Fax: (517)351-8336
E-mail: dmitstifer@kon.org
URL: http://www.kon.org
Contact: Dr. Dorothy I. Mitstifer PhD, Exec. Dir.

Founded: 1990. **Members:** 133,000. **Membership Dues:** individual, $50 (annual). **Staff:** 1. **Budget:** $300,000. **Local Groups:** 115. **Description:** Honor society for men and women in human sciences. Conducts educational programs and supports undergraduate and graduate study and professional research. **Awards:** Dorothy I. Mitstifer Conclave Scholarships. **Frequency:** biennial. **Type:** scholarship. **Recipient:** for chapter adviser attendance ● Eileen C. Maddex Fellowship. **Frequency:** annual. **Type:** fellowship. **Recipient:** for member pursuing a master's degree ● Hettie Margaret Anthony Fellowship. **Frequency:** annual. **Type:** fellowship. **Recipient:** for doctoral research ● Marjorie M. Brown Dissertation Fellowship. **Frequency:** annual. **Type:** fellowship. **Recipient:** for critical science research ● National Alumni Chapter Grant. **Frequency:** annual. **Type:** grant. **Recipient:** for research proposal ● National Alumni Fellowship. **Frequency:** biennial. **Type:** fellowship. **Recipient:** for a member pursuing

a master's degree ● New Initiatives Grant. **Frequency:** annual. **Type:** grant. **Recipient:** for cross specialization and integrative research ● Omicron Nu Research Fellowship. **Frequency:** annual. **Type:** fellowship. **Recipient:** for a member pursuing doctoral degree. **Affiliated With:** Association of College Honor Societies. **Formed by Merger of:** (1990) Kappa Omicron Phi; Omicron Nu. **Publications:** *Kappa Omicron Nu Dialogue*, semiannual. Newsletter. **Price:** $10.00 for nonmembers. ISSN: 1520-4855. **Circulation:** 12,000. Alternate Formats: online ● *Kappa Omicron Nu FORUM*, semiannual. Journal. ISSN: 1520-4820 ● *Kappa Omicron Nu Spotlight*. Newsletter. ISSN: 1528-6029. **Conventions/Meetings:** biennial Conclave - meeting, leadership development for students, professionals, and undergraduate research conference.

23906 ■ Phi Upsilon Omicron (Phi U)
PO Box 329
Fairmont, WV 26555-0329
Ph: (304)368-0612
E-mail: info@phiu.org
URL: http://www.phiu.org
Contact: Susan Rickards, Exec. Dir.

Founded: 1910. **Members:** 87,000. **Membership Dues:** collegiate, honorary, $45. **Staff:** 2. **Budget:** $120,880. **Regional Groups:** 40. **State Groups:** 59. **Description:** Honor society of women and men in family and consumer sciences. **Awards:** Alumni Research Grant. **Frequency:** biennial. **Type:** grant. **Recipient:** to a member supporting post graduate research ● Candle Fellowship. **Type:** fellowship. **Recipient:** for members enrolled in a graduate school ● Diamond Anniversary Fellowship. **Type:** fellowship. **Recipient:** for members enrolled in a graduate program ● Florence Fallgatter Distinguished Service Award. **Frequency:** biennial. **Type:** recognition. **Recipient:** to a member who has made outstanding achievements in family and consumer sciences ● Founders Fellowship. **Type:** fellowship. **Recipient:** for advanced graduate study ● Frances Morton Holbrook Alumni Award. **Frequency:** biennial. **Type:** recognition. **Recipient:** to a member who demonstrated excellence in the family and consumer sciences ● Genevieve Forthun Scholarship. **Type:** scholarship. **Recipient:** for members enrolled in baccalaureate degree programs ● Golden Anniversary Scholarship. **Type:** scholarship. **Recipient:** for members enrolled in baccalaureate degree programs ● Janice Cory Bullock Scholarship. **Frequency:** annual. **Type:** scholarship. **Recipient:** for non-traditional students who want to pursue continuing studies ● Jean Dikerscheid Scholarship. **Type:** scholarship. **Recipient:** to a student pursuing a PhD in family and consumer sciences ● Lillian P. Schoephoerster Scholarship. **Type:** scholarship. **Recipient:** to a member pursuing a baccalaureate degree in family and consumer sciences ● Lucile Rust Scholarship. **Type:** scholarship. **Recipient:** to members enrolled in baccalaureate degree on family and consumer sciences ● Marion Bachtel Collegiate Advisor Award. **Frequency:** annual. **Type:** recognition. **Recipient:** to a collegiate chapter advisor who demonstrated excellence ● Mary Weiking Franken Scholarship. **Type:** scholarship. **Recipient:** to member working toward a baccalaureate degree in family and consumer sciences ● Orinne Johnson Writing Award. **Type:** recognition. **Recipient:** to a collegiate member who submits the best creative writing related to the current professional project theme ● Past President Scholarship. **Type:** scholarship. **Recipient:** for members enrolled in baccalaureate programs ● Presidents Research Fellowship. **Type:** fellowship. **Recipient:** for graduate research at the master's, doctoral or post doctoral level in family and consumer sciences or a related area ● Sarah Thorniley Phillips Leadership Award. **Frequency:** annual. **Type:** recognition. **Recipient:** to undergraduate members for outstanding leadership and participation in collegiate and community programs ● Treva C. Kintner Scholarship. **Type:** scholarship. **Recipient:** to non-traditional student who has completed at least half of the academic work toward a baccalaureate degree in family and consumer sciences. **Affiliated With:** Association of College Honor Societies. **Publications:**

Alumni Newsletter, periodic ● *The Candle*, semiannual. Journal. **Conventions/Meetings:** biennial Conclave - meeting (exhibits) ● annual National Council - meeting.

Honor Societies

23907 ■ Alpha Chi (AX)
Harding Univ.
HU Box 12249
900 E Center Ave.
Searcy, AR 72149-0001
Ph: (501)279-4443
Free: (800)477-4225
Fax: (501)279-4589
E-mail: alphachi@harding.edu
URL: http://www.alphachihonor.org
Contact: Dennis M. Organ, Exec. Dir.
Founded: 1922. **Members:** 300,000. **Membership Dues:** life, $30 ● active alumni program, $15 (annual). **Staff:** 4. **Regional Groups:** 7. **Local Groups:** 300. **Description:** Honor society - college students ranking in the upper ten percent of their class, invited into membership by their local Alpha Chi chapter as juniors, seniors, or graduating seniors. **Awards:** Distinguished Alumni. **Frequency:** biennial. **Type:** recognition. **Recipient:** for distinguished alumni ● Gaston/Nolle Scholarship. **Frequency:** annual. **Type:** scholarship. **Recipient:** to a qualified undergraduate junior Alpha Chi member for senior year of undergraduate study ● President's Cup. **Frequency:** biennial. **Type:** recognition. **Recipient:** for an outstanding chapter ● Pryor Alumni Fellowship. **Frequency:** annual. **Type:** scholarship. **Recipient:** to a qualified active alumnus for graduate study ● Sledge/Benedict Fellowship. **Frequency:** annual. **Type:** fellowship. **Recipient:** for a qualified undergraduate senior Alpha Chi member in the first year of graduate study. **Affiliated With:** Association of College Honor Societies. **Formerly:** (1927) Scholarship Societies of Texas; (1934) Scholarship Societies of the South. **Publications:** *Recorder*, 3/year. Journal. Contains research papers; includes *Directory of Chapters and Sponsors*. **Price:** included in membership dues. ISSN: 0893-889X ● Newsletter, 3/year. **Conventions/Meetings:** biennial convention - always odd-numbered years.

23908 ■ Alpha Kappa Mu
c/o Alpha Kappa Mu Honor Society
101 Longwood Ln.
Greenwood, SC 29646
Ph: (864)229-1546
Fax: (864)223-1638
E-mail: information@alphakappamu.org
URL: http://hierographics.org/alphakappamu.htm
Contact: Dr. Ann W. Morris, Exec. Sec.-Treas.
Founded: 1937. **Members:** 19,260. **Description:** Honor society - men and women, scholarship. **Awards:** **Type:** scholarship. **Recipient:** for graduate students. **Publications:** Journal, quarterly ● Newsletter, 3/year. **Conventions/Meetings:** biennial meeting - always March.

23909 ■ Alpha Sigma Nu
PO Box 1881
Milwaukee, WI 53201-1881
Ph: (414)288-7542 (414)288-7545
Fax: (414)288-3259
E-mail: kate.gaertner@marquette.edu
URL: http://www.marquette.edu/dept/ASN
Contact: Kate Gaertner, Exec. Dir.
Founded: 1915. **Members:** 55,190. **Membership Dues:** life, $50. **Staff:** 3. **Budget:** $192,989. **Regional Groups:** 35. **Multinational. Description:** Scholastic honor society which inducts only 4&percent; of the top juniors and seniors at Jesuit institutions of higher education in the United States, Canada, and Korea. **Awards:** National Jesuit Book Awards. **Frequency:** annual. **Type:** recognition. **Recipient:** for outstanding scholarly publishing achievement by faculty and administrators ● **Type:** scholarship. **Computer Services:** Online services, membership directory. **Committees:** Alumni; Bylaws;

Communications; Investment; Nominations; Standards. **Absorbed:** (1973) Gamma Pi Epsilon. **Formerly:** (1930) Alpha Sigma Tau. **Publications:** Newsletter, semiannual. **Conventions/Meetings:** triennial In the Present, For the Future: Men & Women for Others - conference - always fall.

23910 ■ Association of College Honor Societies (ACHS)
4990 Northwind Dr., Ste.140
East Lansing, MI 48823-5031
Ph: (517)351-8335
Fax: (517)351-8336
E-mail: dmitstifer@achsnatl.org
URL: http://www.achsnatl.org
Contact: Dorothy I. Mitstifer, Exec. Dir.
Founded: 1925. **Members:** 67. **Staff:** 1. **Budget:** $35,000. **Description:** Federation of college honor societies. **Publications:** *ACHS Handbook*, triennial. Booklet. Contains overview of each member organization, history, constitution. Alternate Formats: online. **Conventions/Meetings:** annual meeting (exhibits) - always February.

23911 ■ Blue Key Honor Society
c/o Dr. Christopher M. Sieverdes, Exec. Dir.
7501 Whitehill Ln.
Whitehill Farm
Millersburg, OH 44654-9270
Ph: (330)674-2570
E-mail: csvrds@clemson.edu
URL: http://www.bluekey.org
Contact: Dr. Christopher M. Sieverdes, Exec. Dir.
Founded: 1924. **Members:** 140,000. **Staff:** 5. **Description:** Recognizes honorary fraternity, scholarship, and leadership. **Awards:** Chapter Faculty Advisor Award. **Frequency:** biennial. **Type:** recognition ● Outstanding Chapter Award. **Frequency:** annual. **Type:** recognition. **Recipient:** for leadership, scholarship, and service excellence. **Publications:** *Roster*, biennial ● Newsletter, quarterly. **Conventions/Meetings:** biennial meeting.

23912 ■ Cum Laude Society (CLS)
23490 Caraway Lakes Dr.
Bonita Springs, FL 34135
Ph: (239)390-3257
Fax: (239)390-3245
E-mail: cumlaudesociety@mac.org
URL: http://www.cumlaudesociety.org
Contact: Bruce W. Galbraith, Registrar Gen.
Founded: 1906. **Members:** 350. **Membership Dues:** school, $100 (annual). **Staff:** 2. **Regional Groups:** 8. **Description:** Serves as a federation of local chapters at public and independent secondary schools; academic honor society for junior and senior class members "to encourage learning and sound scholarship in secondary schools." Each chapter may elect students who have had an honor record up to the time of election and who stand in the first fifth of the senior class or in the first tenth of the junior class (the remainder of the standing must be made up by the end of the senior year). **Awards:** Cecil A. Ewing Award. **Type:** recognition. **Recipient:** for devoted and dedicated service. **Computer Services:** database, record of all cum laude initiates. **Formerly:** (1916) Alpha Delta Tau Fraternity. **Publications:** *Proceedings and Handbook of Information*. **Conventions/Meetings:** triennial conference ● annual Officers and Regents - board meeting.

23913 ■ Delta Epsilon Sigma (DES)
c/o Dr. J. Patrick Lee, Sec.-Treas.
11300 NE 2nd Ave.
Barry Univ.
Miami Shores, FL 33161
E-mail: deltaepsilonsigma@mail.barry.edu
URL: http://www.deltaepsilonsigma.org
Contact: Dr. J. Patrick Lee, Sec.-Treas.
Founded: 1939. **Members:** 65,000. **Description:** Honorary scholastic fraternity - men and women. **Awards:** Fitzgerald Fellowship. **Frequency:** annual. **Type:** fellowship. **Recipient:** for senior year members ● Fitzgerald Scholarship. **Frequency:** annual. **Type:** scholarship. **Recipient:** for junior year members ● **Type:** recognition. **Publications:** Journal, 3/year.

Includes essays, poetry, and short fiction. **Circulation:** 14,000. **Conventions/Meetings:** annual competition, writing.

23914 ■ Gamma Beta Phi Society
78A Mitchell Rd.
Oak Ridge, TN 37830
Ph: (865)483-6212
Free: (800)628-9920
Fax: (865)483-9801
E-mail: gbphqs@aol.com
URL: http://www.gammabetaphi.org
Contact: Margaret McCauley, Exec. Dir.
Founded: 1964. **Members:** 100,000. **Membership Dues:** life, $50 ● chapter, $2-$15 (annual). **Staff:** 5. **Budget:** $440,000. **Regional Groups:** 2. **State Groups:** 19. **Local Groups:** 145. **Description:** College honor-service society. College and university students who are in the top 10-20&percent; of their class academically, and who are committed to scholarship, service, and good character. Recognizes excellence in education, promotes leadership ability and character, and aims to foster and improve education through service projects. **Awards:** Aaron W. Todd Certificate of Merit Award. **Frequency:** annual. **Type:** recognition. **Recipient:** for individuals with the highest level of service contribution to the society ● State Award. **Frequency:** annual. **Type:** recognition. **Recipient:** to the state council having the highest percentage of chapters who have received the Distinguished Service Award. **Committees:** National Executive. **Publications:** *GAMBET*. Newspaper ● *Gamma Beta Phi Manual*. Alternate Formats: online ● Newsletter, 3/year. **Conventions/Meetings:** annual convention, national.

23915 ■ Golden Key International Honour Society (GKIHS)
621 North Ave. NE, Ste.C-100
Atlanta, GA 30308
Ph: (404)377-2400
Free: (800)377-2401
Fax: (678)420-6757
E-mail: memberservices@goldenkey.org
URL: http://www.goldenkey.org
Contact: Alexander D. Perwich II, CEO
Founded: 1977. **Members:** 1,500,000. **Membership Dues:** life, $60. **Staff:** 30. **Budget:** $9,000,000. **Regional Groups:** 13. **Local Groups:** 350. **National Groups:** 7. **Multinational. Description:** Academic honour society for College/University high achievers. Recognizes and encourages scholastic excellence and achievement at the undergraduate level. Works to build global communities of academic achievers by providing opportunities for individual growth through leadership, career development, networking, and service. Sponsors educational programs, leadership training, and academic scholarships. **Libraries: Type:** reference. **Holdings:** articles, books. **Subjects:** career topics. **Awards:** Business Achievement Awards. **Frequency:** annual. **Type:** monetary. **Recipient:** for members who excel in the study of business ● Golden Key Graduate Scholar Award. **Frequency:** annual. **Type:** scholarship. **Recipient:** for graduate students. **Telecommunication Services:** electronic mail, alumni@goldenkey.org. **Formerly:** (2001) Golden Key National Honor Society. **Publications:** *Concepts*, annual. Magazine. Contains information on upcoming receptions, scholarships, essays on personal development and current events. ● Newsletter, monthly, every 4th Friday of the month. Highlights information about programs of the society. Alternate Formats: online. **Conventions/Meetings:** annual conference - 2008 July 31-Aug. 3, New Orleans, LA.

23916 ■ Intercollegiate Knights (IK)
PO Box 7264
Provo, UT 84602-7264
Ph: (801)489-0458
E-mail: jim76501@vvm.com
URL: http://www.ik-fraternity.org
Contact: Nolan Smith, Exec. Dir.
Founded: 1919. **Members:** 30,000. **Membership Dues:** individual, $13 (annual). **Staff:** 16. **Description:** Honor society - men and women, scholarship,

leadership, and service. Maintains national archives at Brigham Young University. Sponsors charitable programs administered through the Intercollegiate Knights Foundation. **Awards: Frequency:** annual. **Type:** recognition ● **Frequency:** annual. **Type:** scholarship. **Councils:** National Executive. **Affiliated With:** International Guild of Nobles. **Formerly:** (1919) Knights of the Hook. **Publications:** *The Guidebook,* biennial. Handbook. Includes policies and procedures. ● *National Page Manual,* periodic. Introductory handbook for pledges. ● *The Roll,* annual. Directory ● *The Roundtable.* Yearbook ● *The Shield,* quarterly. Newsletter ● Also publishes meeting minutes. **Conventions/Meetings:** annual convention.

23917 ■ Kappa Gamma Pi
10215 Chardon Rd.
Chardon, OH 44024-9700
Ph: (440)286-3764
Fax: (440)286-4379
E-mail: kgpnews@aol.com
URL: http://www.kappagammapi.org
Contact: Pamela W. Waitinas, Natl. Office Coor.
Founded: 1926. **Members:** 47,000. **Membership Dues:** individual, $30 (annual). **Staff:** 4. **Regional Groups:** 20. **Multinational. Description:** Serves as a national catholic college graduate honor society. Members are honor graduates with outstanding leadership skills and a record of church, school and community service. Members are nominated at the time of graduation from an affiliated college or university, with a baccalaureate degree, master's degree or PhD degree. In addition, there are membership categories for college/university administrators and alumni of affiliated institutions. Kappas serve as a network of morally and spiritually motivated people who support and sustain each other in their search for excellence, justice, compassion and wisdom. **Awards:** Cornaro Scholarship for Graduate Studies. **Frequency:** annual. **Type:** scholarship. **Recipient:** for Kappa Gamma Pi members who are pursuing graduate studies at any accredited university. **Formerly:** (2005) Kappa Gamma Pi National Office. **Publications:** *Kappa Gamma Pi News,* 5/year. Newsletter. **Conventions/Meetings:** biennial convention ● annual Kappa Gamma Pi National Board Meeting and Long Range Planning Meeting.

23918 ■ Mortar Board (MB)
1200 Chambers Rd., Ste.201
Columbus, OH 43212
Free: (800)989-6266
Fax: (614)488-4095
E-mail: mortarboard@mortarboard.org
URL: http://www.mortarboard.org
Contact: Jon Cook, Exec. Dir.
Founded: 1918. **Members:** 226,000. **Membership Dues:** sustaining, $25 (annual). **Staff:** 4. **Budget:** $430,000. **Regional Groups:** 213. **State Groups:** 37. **Description:** Serves as a national honor society for recognizing college seniors (students) who have achieved outstanding scholarship, leadership, and service; mortar Board National Foundation awards annual fellowships to members for graduate study. Offers project grants to selected chapters for service projects. **Libraries: Type:** reference. **Holdings:** archival material, books. **Awards:** Mortar Board Fellowships. **Frequency:** annual. **Type:** fellowship. **Recipient:** to members ● Mortar Board National Citation Award. **Frequency:** annual. **Type:** recognition. **Publications:** *Alumni News,* semiannual. Newsletter. **Price:** $5.00/year. Alternate Formats: online ● *Mortar Board Forum,* semiannual. Magazine. Includes news, alumni profiles, career and scholarship information, and leadership services. **Price:** $5.00/year. **Circulation:** 35,000. **Advertising:** accepted ● Annual Report, annual, usually February. **Conventions/Meetings:** annual conference.

23919 ■ National Alpha Lambda Delta
Box 4403
Macon, GA 31208-4403
Ph: (478)744-9595
Free: (800)9ALPHA-1
Fax: (478)744-9924

E-mail: ald@nationalald.edu
URL: http://www.nationalald.org
Contact: Dr. Glenda Earwood, Exec. Dir.
Founded: 1924. **Members:** 700,000. **Membership Dues:** student, life, $20. **Staff:** 5. **Budget:** $500,000. **National Groups:** 230. **Description:** Freshman Honor society. **Awards:** Fellowships & TROW Scholarships. **Frequency:** annual. **Type:** scholarship. **Recipient:** for undergraduates, graduates, or professional study. **Publications:** *The Flame,* annual. Magazine. **Circulation:** 27,000. **Conventions/Meetings:** annual Leadership Workshop - meeting ● annual workshop, for leadership/programming.

23920 ■ National Association of the Knights of Scorpius, Honorary Leadership Society
PO Box 656513
Fresh Meadows, NY 11365-6513
Ph: (718)357-7075
E-mail: drtomstevens@aol.com
Contact: Dr. Thomas Robert Stevens, Pres.
Founded: 1977. **Members:** 475. **Description:** Honorary society - men and women demonstrating exceptional leadership qualities or leadership potential. Aims to develop the leadership qualities of members and help them achieve academic superiority; provide a forum for discussing and implementing plans to address issues relating to student government and the power struggle between students and administration; strive to keep student leaders free from special interests and administration influence and control. Disseminates information on how to become more responsive and effective leaders. **Awards: Frequency:** annual. **Type:** recognition. **Recipient:** for outstanding members; recipient automatically becomes an honorary member. **Publications:** Newsletter, quarterly.

23921 ■ National Honor Society (NHS)
1904 Assn. Dr.
Reston, VA 20191-1537
Ph: (703)860-0200
Fax: (703)476-5432
E-mail: nhs@nhs.us
URL: http://www.nhs.us
Contact: Rocco Marano, Dir.
Founded: 1921. **Members:** 900,000. **Membership Dues:** school (chartering fee), $100 ● chapter, $66 (annual). **Staff:** 12. **State Groups:** 21. **Local Groups:** 15,000. **Description:** Secondary school students in grades 10, 11, and 12, excelling in scholarship, leadership, service, and character. Founded and directed by National Association of Secondary School Principals. **Awards:** National Honor Society Scholarships. **Frequency:** annual. **Type:** scholarship. **Recipient:** for outstanding members. **Publications:** *Leadership for Student Activities,* 9/year. Magazine. **Price:** included in membership dues. **Circulation:** 40,000. **Conventions/Meetings:** annual conference (exhibits) - always November.

23922 ■ National Junior Honor Society (NJHS)
1904 Assn. Dr.
Reston, VA 20191-1537
Ph: (703)860-0200
Fax: (703)476-5432
E-mail: njhs@njhs.us
URL: http://www.njhs.us
Contact: Rocco Marano, Dir.
Founded: 1929. **Members:** 215,000. **Membership Dues:** school, $85 (annual). **Staff:** 15. **State Groups:** 21. **Local Groups:** 4,000. **Description:** Students in middle or junior high school excelling in scholarship, leadership, service, character, and citizenship. Founded and directed by National Association of Secondary School Principals (see separate entry). **Publications:** *Leadership for Student Activities,* 9/year. Magazine. **Circulation:** 56,000. **Advertising:** accepted. **Conventions/Meetings:** annual conference (exhibits) - always November.

23923 ■ National Valedictorian Honor Society
PO Box 3
Redmond, WA 98073
Ph: (425)836-1000

E-mail: nvhs@valedictorian.org
Contact: John T. Murdock II, Exec.Dir.
Founded: 1996. **Description:** Serves as collegiate honor society for valedictorians. Promotes excellence in education and scholastic achievement. Conducts research projects. **Libraries: Type:** reference. **Holdings:** archival material. **Awards:** Scholar Award. **Frequency:** annual. **Type:** recognition. **Recipient:** for valedictorians who have demonstrated continued excellence in academics. **Committees:** Archives; Awards; Publication/Communications; Research. **Affiliated With:** National Valedictorian Society.

23924 ■ Omicron Delta Kappa Society (ODK)
300 N Broadway
Lexington, KY 40508
Ph: (859)455-8870
Free: (877)635-6437
Fax: (859)455-8874
E-mail: odknhdq@odk.org
URL: http://www.odk.org
Contact: John D. Morgan, Exec. Dir.
Founded: 1914. **Members:** 260,000. **Membership Dues:** life, $50. **Staff:** 7. **Budget:** $350,000. **Regional Groups:** 16. **Local Groups:** 298. **Description:** Serves as honor society for college men and women in their junior or senior year or graduate school. Maintains Omicron Delta Kappa Foundation. **Libraries: Type:** reference. **Holdings:** 290; archival material, books. **Subjects:** leadership. **Awards:** Distinguished Service Award. **Frequency:** biennial. **Type:** recognition. **Recipient:** for exceptional service to society ● Eldridge W. Roark, Jr. Meritorious Service Award. **Frequency:** annual. **Type:** recognition. **Recipient:** for service to society ● Laurel Crowned Circle. **Frequency:** annual. **Type:** recognition. **Recipient:** to an American who has exemplified the ideals of the society ● National Leader of the Year. **Frequency:** annual. **Type:** recognition. **Recipient:** for leaders from province ● Robert L. Morlan Award. **Frequency:** annual. **Type:** recognition. **Recipient:** for outstanding faculty secretary ● Robert W. Bishop Faculty Adviser Award. **Frequency:** annual. **Type:** recognition. **Recipient:** to a faculty adviser who rendered outstanding service to the local circle and the society. **Computer Services:** database. **Committees:** Budget and Finance; Circle Standards; Clay Grant Award; Extension; Leader of the Year; Nominations; Policy and Law; Publications; Robert L. Morlan and Robert Bishop Award; Scholarship. **Affiliated With:** Association of College Honor Societies; Community Leadership Association. **Publications:** *THE CIRCLE,* quarterly. Newsletter. **Circulation:** 35,000 ● *Key Notes,* quarterly. Newsletter. Alternate Formats: online ● Manual, biennial. **Conventions/Meetings:** biennial convention.

23925 ■ Order of the Coif
Law Lib., CB No. 3385
Univ. of North Carolina
Chapel Hill, NC 27599-3385
Ph: (919)962-8501 (919)962-1322
Fax: (919)962-1193
E-mail: sjones2@email.unc.edu
URL: http://www.orderofthecoif.org
Contact: Sandy Jones, Admin. Asst.
Founded: 1902. **Members:** 40,000. **Membership Dues:** one-time fee, $25. **Staff:** 2. **National Groups:** 79. **Description:** Honorary scholastic society - men and women, law. **Libraries: Type:** reference. **Awards:** Biennial Book Award. **Frequency:** biennial. **Type:** monetary. **Telecommunication Services:** electronic mail, laura_gasaway@unc.edu. **Formerly:** (1912) Theta Kappa Nu. **Publications:** *1991 - 1995.* Directory. **Price:** $25.00 ● *1996 - 2000.* Directory. **Price:** $25.00 ● *1902 - 1990.* Directory. **Price:** $175.00 ● *2001 - 06.* Directory. **Conventions/Meetings:** annual executive committee meeting, held in conjunction with Association of American Law Schools - always January.

23926 ■ Phi Beta Delta
c/o David Merchant, Dir. of Publications
1527 New Hampshire Ave. NW
Washington, DC 20036
Ph: (202)483-2512

Fax: (202)483-2657
E-mail: captain@phibetadelta.org
URL: http://www.phibetadelta.org
Contact: David Merchant, Dir. of Publications
Founded: 1986. **Members:** 10,000. **Membership Dues:** individual, $15 (annual). **Budget:** $105,000. **Regional Groups:** 117. **Description:** Honor society - international education. Chapters hold educational and social programs related to international education and exchange. **Awards:** National Book Award. **Frequency:** annual. **Type:** recognition. **Recipient:** for outstanding book related to International Aspects of a Discipline or International Education/Exchange ● National Faculty Award. **Frequency:** annual. **Type:** recognition. **Recipient:** for outstanding contributions to International Education ● National Scholarships. **Frequency:** annual. **Type:** scholarship. **Recipient:** for students ● National Staff Award. **Frequency:** annual. **Type:** recognition. **Recipient:** for outstanding contributions and support for campus of Phi Beta Delta. **Committees:** Development; Scholarships and Awards. **Publications:** *The Medallion*, quarterly. Newsletter. Features member and Chapter News. **Price:** included in membership dues. **Circulation:** 5,000 ● *Phi Beta Delta International Review*, annual. Journal. Contains articles on international education issues and topics. **Price:** included in membership dues. ISSN: 1067-5558. **Conventions/Meetings:** annual conference, with presentations, panels, keynote speeches, awards banquet ● periodic meeting.

23927 ■ Phi Kappa Phi
7576 Goodwood Blvd.
Baton Rouge, LA 70806
Ph: (225)388-4917
Free: (800)804-9880
Fax: (225)388-4900
E-mail: info@phikappaphi.org
URL: http://www.phikappaphi.org
Contact: Perry A. Snyder, Exec. Dir.
Founded: 1897. **Members:** 800,000. **Membership Dues:** individual, $35 (annual). **Staff:** 18. **Budget:** $2,000,000. **Regional Groups:** 5. **Local Groups:** 300. **Description:** Inducts annually approximately 30,000 students, faculty, professional staff, and alumni. Has chapters on nearly 300 select college and university campuses in North America and the Philippines. Membership is by invitation only to the top 10 percent of seniors and graduate students and 7.5 percent of juniors. Faculty, professional staff, and alumni who have achieved scholarly distinction also qualify. Aims to recognize and promote academic excellence in all fields of higher education and to engage the community of scholars in service to others. **Awards:** Phi Kappa Phi Awards of Excellence. **Frequency:** annual. **Type:** recognition. **Recipient:** for scholarly and artistic accomplishments ● Phi Kappa Phi Fellowships. **Frequency:** annual. **Type:** fellowship. **Recipient:** to first-year graduate students, must be a member ● Phi Kappa Phi Literacy Grants. **Frequency:** annual. **Type:** grant. **Recipient:** for chapters and individual members to fund ongoing literacy projects or to create new initiatives ● Phi Kappa Phi Scholar and Artist. **Frequency:** triennial. **Type:** recognition. **Recipient:** to individuals who demonstrate the ideals of the society through their activities, achievements, and scholarship ● Phi Kappa Phi Study Abroad Grants. **Frequency:** annual. **Type:** grant. **Recipient:** for undergraduates to help them as they seek knowledge and experience in their academic fields by studying abroad. **Committees:** Communications; Extension; Fellowship; Investment; Journal Advisory. **Publications:** *In Pursuit of Excellence*. Book ● *Making Heroes of Scholars*. Book ● *Phi Kappa Phi Forum*, quarterly. Magazine. **Conventions/Meetings:** triennial convention.

Insurance

23928 ■ Gamma Iota Sigma
17 S High St., Ste.200
Columbus, OH 43215
Ph: (614)221-1900

E-mail: grand@gammaiotasigma.org
URL: http://www.gammaiotasigma.org
Contact: George A. Gummer, Treas.
Founded: 1965. **Members:** 10,800. **Staff:** 1. **Budget:** $80,000. **Local Groups:** 43. **Multinational. Description:** Fraternity of insurance professionals. Works to promote, encourage, and sustain student interest in insurance as a profession. Co-sponsors research activities. **Awards: Frequency:** annual. **Type:** scholarship. **Publications:** *Sextant*, semiannual. Newsletter. **Conventions/Meetings:** annual International Management Conference.

Japanese

23929 ■ Japanese National Honor Society (JNHS)
c/o Karla Vescovi, Dir.
Lockport Township High School
1333 E 7th St.
Lockport, IL 60441
E-mail: ganbare@yahoo.com
URL: http://www.ncjlt.org/JNHS
Contact: Karla Vescovi, Dir.
Description: Promotes interest in Japanese language study. Recognizes and encourages scholastic achievement and excellence in Japanese study. Collaborates with teachers and administrators in developing and maintaining the standard of Japanese language education. **Telecommunication Services:** electronic mail, ncjlt@japaneseteaching.org.

Journalism

23930 ■ Kappa Tau Alpha (KTA)
c/o Dr. Keith P. Sanders, Exec. Dir.
Univ. of Missouri
Scholarship of Journalism
Columbia, MO 65211-1200
Ph: (573)882-7685
Fax: (573)884-1720
E-mail: umcjourkta@missouri.edu
URL: http://www.missouri.edu/~ktahq
Contact: Dr. Keith P. Sanders, Exec. Dir.
Founded: 1910. **Members:** 59,000. **Membership Dues:** life, $20. **Local Groups:** 93. **Description:** Serves as a national honor society for college majors in journalism and mass communication. Seeks to recognize and promote excellence in scholarship. **Awards:** Chapter Adviser Research Grant Award. **Frequency:** annual. **Type:** grant. **Recipient:** for chapter adviser ● Frank Luther Mott Award. **Frequency:** annual. **Type:** recognition. **Recipient:** for best researched book in journalism and mass communication ● Outstanding Service Award. **Frequency:** annual. **Type:** recognition. **Recipient:** to an individual who has made outstanding accomplishments ● Taft Outstanding Adviser Award. **Frequency:** annual. **Type:** recognition. **Recipient:** to the best chapter adviser ● Top Scholar Awards. **Frequency:** annual. **Type:** recognition. **Recipient:** to the highest ranked (GPA) journalism and mass communication student from each chapter. **Publications:** *KTA Newsletter*, semiannual. Alternate Formats: online. **Conventions/Meetings:** annual meeting, held in conjunction with Association for Education in Journalism and Mass Communication.

23931 ■ Quill and Scroll Society (QSS)
Univ. of Iowa
School of Journalism and Mass Commun.
100 Adler Journalism Bldg., Rm. E346
Iowa City, IA 52242
Ph: (319)335-3457
Fax: (319)335-3989
E-mail: quill-scroll@uiowa.edu
URL: http://www.uiowa.edu/~quill-sc
Contact: Richard P. Johns, Exec. Dir.
Founded: 1926. **Members:** 1,000,000. **Staff:** 5. **Description:** Honor Society high school journalism students recommended for membership by their schools. Seeks to reward individual achievements and to encourage individual initiative in high school

journalism, creative writing, and allied fields. Provides information to editors, staffs, and advisers on all phases of publication work. Other activities include news media evaluation service. Through Quill and Scroll Foundation, the society promotes research and conducts surveys. **Awards:** Edward J. Nell. **Frequency:** annual. **Type:** scholarship. **Recipient:** for national winners in either the Yearbook Excellence Contest or the International Writing/Photography Contest ● Lester G. Benz. **Frequency:** annual. **Type:** recognition. **Recipient:** for journalism teachers and publication advisers who have had at least six semester hours of journalism courses. **Publications:** *Quill and Scroll*, bimonthly. Magazine. For newspaper advisors, students, and principals. **Price:** $15.00/year. **Advertising:** accepted ● Also publishes stylebook. **Conventions/Meetings:** National Writing/Photo Contest - competition ● YearBook Excellence Contest - competition.

23932 ■ Sigma Delta Chi Foundation (SDX)
3909 N Meridian St.
Indianapolis, IN 46208
Ph: (317)927-8000
Fax: (317)920-4789
E-mail: sdx@spj.org
URL: http://www.spj.org
Contact: Steve Geimann, Pres.
Founded: 1961. **Budget:** $500,000. **Description:** Aims to provide assistance for the activities of the Society of Professional Journalists (see separate entry). Funds and supervises professional development seminars, Broadcasting-Taishoff seminar, Pulliam/Kilgore Freedom of Information Internships in Washington, DC, Eugene C. Pulliam Editorial Writing Fellowship, and Project Watchdog, a public-service campaign extolling the virtues of a free press. Sponsors speakers, workshops, and competitions. **Awards:** Eugene C. Pulliam Fellowship. **Frequency:** annual. **Type:** fellowship. **Recipient:** to the outstanding editorial writer ● Eugene S. Pulliam First Amendment Award. **Frequency:** annual. **Type:** recognition. **Recipient:** to individuals who have worked to protect the basic rights provided by the First Amendment ● **Frequency:** annual. **Type:** grant. **Recipient:** for SPJ related project and other journalism related project. **Committees:** Governance/Mission. **Funds:** Chapter Scholarship Fund. **Programs:** Educational. **Conventions/Meetings:** annual meeting (exhibits).

Language

23933 ■ Alpha Mu Gamma National (AMG)
855 N Vermont Ave.
CMB 1009
Los Angeles, CA 90029
Ph: (323)644-9752
Fax: (323)644-9752
E-mail: amgnat@lacitycollege.edu
URL: http://www.lacitycollege.edu/academic/honor/amg/nflw.htm
Contact: Dr. Franklin Triplett, Pres.
Founded: 1931. **Membership Dues:** life, $25. **Staff:** 1. **Regional Groups:** 24. **Local Groups:** 326. **Description:** Collegiate honor society - foreign languages. Sponsors annual National Foreign Language Week. Conducts educational programs. **Awards:** Goddard, Indovia and Krakowski Scholarship. **Frequency:** annual. **Type:** scholarship. **Recipient:** for a member of Alpha Mu Gamma who is planning to continue study of foreign languages ● The James Fonseca Scholarship. **Type:** scholarship. **Recipient:** for the study of Esperanto or Spanish ● Laval University. **Frequency:** annual. **Type:** scholarship. **Formerly:** (2000) Alpha Mu Gamma. **Publications:** *AMG Newsletter*, semiannual. Contains reports, directory, and listing of chapter activities and scholarship awards. **Price:** $5.00/year. **Advertising:** accepted ● Handbook ● Also publishes various folders for National Foreign Language Week. **Conventions/Meetings:** biennial convention ● biennial National Convention - competition ● regional meeting.

23934 ■ Phi Sigma Iota
World Language Educ.
CPR 107
Univ. of South Florida
4202 E Fowler Ave.
Tampa, FL 33620-5500
Ph: (813)974-3658 (813)974-2746
Free: (800)673-5599
Fax: (813)974-6944
E-mail: contact@phisigmaiota.org
URL: http://www.phisigmaiota.org
Contact: Dr. Jacob C. Caflisch III, Pres./Exec. Dir.
Founded: 1922. **Members:** 50,000. **Membership Dues:** new, $30 ● life, $130 ● continuing, $20 (annual). **Staff:** 3. **Budget:** $60,000. **Local Groups:** 348. **Description:** Honor society - foreign languages. Sponsors essay contests in foreign languages. **Awards:** Phi Sigma Iota Scholarship. **Frequency:** annual. **Type:** scholarship. **Recipient:** for PSI members only. **Committees:** Scholarship. **Affiliated With:** Association of College Honor Societies; Modern Language Association of America. **Absorbed:** Alpha Zeta Pi. **Publications:** *The Forum* (in English, French, German, and Spanish), semiannual. Magazine. Features chapter news, employment information, conference reports, and literary articles in foreign languages as well as in English. **Price:** included in membership dues; $5.00 /year for nonmembers. ISSN: 0883-5640. **Circulation:** 5,000. **Advertising:** accepted. Alternate Formats: online. **Conventions/Meetings:** biennial conference, for secretariat and regional VPs - spring.

Law

23935 ■ Delta Theta Phi
38640 Butternut Ridge Rd.
Elyria, OH 44035
Ph: (440)458-4381
Free: (800)783-2600
Fax: (440)458-4380
E-mail: dtpoffice@alltel.net
URL: http://www.deltathetaphi.org
Contact: Catherine K. Smith, Exec. Dir.
Founded: 1913. **Members:** 100,000. **Membership Dues:** student, $60. **Staff:** 3. **Regional Groups:** 9. **Local Groups:** 85. **Description:** Professional fraternity - law. **Libraries:** Type: open to the public. **Holdings:** 117; books, periodicals. **Subjects:** law-related topics, fraternity news, and special features. **Awards:** Alden L. Doud Memorial Award. **Frequency:** annual. **Type:** recognition. **Recipient:** to the student senate with the largest percentage increase as determined by the Master of Rolls ● Century Senate Award. **Frequency:** annual. **Type:** recognition. **Recipient:** to each student senate initiating 100 or more new members during the fiscal year ● Horace L. Lohnes Memorial Award. **Frequency:** annual. **Type:** recognition. **Recipient:** to the student senate with the largest percentage increase as determined by the Master of Rolls ● Outstanding Alumni Senate Award. **Frequency:** annual. **Type:** recognition. **Recipient:** for nomination, service, involvement and reporting ● Outstanding Professor. **Frequency:** annual. **Type:** recognition. **Recipient:** for nomination, involvement and promotion ● Outstanding Student Award. **Frequency:** annual. **Type:** recognition. **Recipient:** for nomination, service, involvement and reporting. **Computer Services:** database. **Committees:** Senates. **Absorbed:** (1989) Sigma Nu Phi. **Formed by Merger of:** (1913) Alpha Kappa Phi; (1913) Theta Lambda Phi; Delta Phi Delta. **Publications:** *Adelphia Law Journal*, annual. Contains authoritative law journal. **Price:** $15.00 ● *The Delta Theta Phi Law Fraternity Directory of Alumni Members*, periodic ● *The Paper Book*, quarterly. **Advertising:** accepted ● *The Syllabus*, periodic. **Conventions/Meetings:** biennial convention and workshop, for alumni and student members - 2nd week in August.

23936 ■ Phi Alpha Delta (PAD)
345 N Charles St.
Baltimore, MD 21201
Ph: (410)347-3118
Fax: (410)347-3119
E-mail: info@pad.org
URL: http://www.pad.org
Contact: Frank C. Patek II, Exec. Dir.
Founded: 1902. **Members:** 240,000. **Membership Dues:** law school and pre-law (initiation), $70. **Staff:** 7. **Budget:** $750,000. **Regional Groups:** 90. **Local Groups:** 380. **Languages:** English, Spanish. **Description:** Professional fraternity - law. Aims to form a strong bond uniting students and teachers of the law. **Awards:** Barbara C. Jordan Public Service Award. **Type:** recognition. **Recipient:** for members only ● Tom C. Clark Equal Justice Under Law Award. **Type:** recognition. **Absorbed:** (1972) Phi Delta Delta. **Publications:** *The Reporter*, quarterly. **Advertising:** accepted. **Conventions/Meetings:** biennial convention (exhibits) - always August, even-numbered years.

23937 ■ Tau Epsilon Rho Law Society (TER)
c/o Alan M. Tepper, Natl. Treas./Exec. Dir.
1951 Old Cuthbert Rd., Ste.413
Cherry Hill, NJ 08034
Ph: (856)429-3901
Fax: (856)429-4846
E-mail: tepesq@erols.com
URL: http://www.ter-law.org
Contact: Alan M. Tepper, Natl. Treas./Exec. Dir.
Founded: 1921. **Members:** 7,500. **Membership Dues:** attorney, $85 (annual). **Staff:** 1. **Regional Groups:** 10. **Description:** Professional society - law. Offers continuing legal education seminars. Maintains placement service; sponsors scholarship and essay competitions. **Awards:** TER Schwartzburg Scholarship Foundation Awards. **Frequency:** annual. **Type:** scholarship. **Recipient:** for the highest and most improved grades of law students. **Computer Services:** database, Lawnet ● mailing lists, of members ● online services, legal referral system. **Formerly:** (1984) Tau Epsilon Rho Law Fraternity. **Publications:** *The Summons*, 3-4/year. **Price:** free for members. **Advertising:** accepted ● Membership Directory, biennial. **Advertising:** accepted. **Conventions/Meetings:** annual convention ● annual meeting - always mid-year.

Legal Education

23938 ■ Phi Delta Phi International Legal Fraternity
1426 21st St. NW
Washington, DC 20036
Free: (800)368-5606
Fax: (202)223-6808
E-mail: contact@phideltaphi.org
URL: http://www.phideltaphi.org
Contact: Tim Wheat, Exec. Dir.
Founded: 1869. **Members:** 200,000. **Membership Dues:** initiation, $75 ● life, $475. **Staff:** 3. **Budget:** $550,000. **Regional Groups:** 32. **State Groups:** 182. **Languages:** English, Spanish. **Multinational.** **Description:** Professional fraternity - law. Promotes professional development and legal ethics. Maintains placement service. Maintains Phi Delta Phi Legal Institute (research arm). **Libraries:** Type: reference. **Holdings:** archival material. **Awards:** Balfour Scholarship. **Frequency:** annual. **Type:** scholarship. **Recipient:** to members only ● J. Will Pless International Graduate of the Year Award. **Frequency:** annual. **Type:** recognition. **Recipient:** to members only. **Publications:** *The Headnoter*. Newsletters ● Membership Directory, quadrennial. **Conventions/Meetings:** biennial convention - always August, odd-numbered years.

Liberal Arts

23939 ■ Phi Sigma Pi National Honor Fraternity
2119 Ambassador Cir.
Lancaster, PA 17603-2391
Ph: (717)299-4710
Fax: (717)390-3054
E-mail: pspoffice@phisigmapi.org
URL: http://www.phisigmapi.org
Contact: Suzanne Schaffer, Exec. Dir./Ed.
Founded: 1916. **Members:** 28,000. **Membership Dues:** collegiate active, $45 (semiannual) ● induction (one-time fee), $95. **Staff:** 10. **Budget:** $845,000. **National Groups:** 100. **Description:** Works for the advancement of scholarship, leadership, and fellowship. **Awards:** **Frequency:** annual. **Type:** scholarship ● Todd Tripod Scholarship. **Frequency:** annual. **Type:** scholarship. **Recipient:** for active undergraduate members who have excelled in embodying the ideals of scholarship, leadership and fellowship. **Computer Services:** database ● mailing lists ● online services. **Boards:** National Council. **Affiliated With:** Professional Fraternity Association. **Publications:** *Alumni Newsletter*, monthly. Alternate Formats: online ● *Collegiate Newsletter*, biweekly. Alternate Formats: online ● *Lampadian*, quarterly. Magazine. Alternate Formats: online ● *Looking for the Opportunity of a Lifetime?*. Brochures ● *Purple and Gold*, quarterly. Newsletter. Alternate Formats: online ● *The Scholar's Province*. Alternate Formats: CD-ROM. **Conventions/Meetings:** annual convention - November ● annual Grand Chapter Conference - meeting, four-day leadership conference and business meeting - usually July ● workshop.

Library Science

23940 ■ Beta Phi Mu
Florida State Univ.
School of Info. Stud.
Tallahassee, FL 32306-2100
Ph: (850)644-8123
Fax: (850)644-9763
E-mail: beta_phi_mu@lis.fsu.edu
URL: http://www.beta-phi-mu.org
Contact: Wayne Wiegand, Exec. Dir.
Founded: 1948. **Members:** 23,000. **Membership Dues:** life, $50. **Staff:** 1. **Multinational.** **Description:** Professional honor society - men and women, library and information studies. **Awards:** Distinguished Service to Library Education Award, American Library Association. **Frequency:** annual. **Type:** monetary ● Doctoral Dissertation. **Frequency:** annual. **Type:** scholarship. **Recipient:** for completion of an approved doctoral dissertation in the field of information studies ● Frank B. Sessa Scholarship. **Frequency:** annual. **Type:** scholarship. **Recipient:** for continuing professional education of a Beta Phi Mu member ● Harold Lancour Scholarship for Foreign Study. **Frequency:** annual. **Type:** scholarship. **Recipient:** for librarian or library school student ● Sarah Rebecca Reed Scholarship. **Frequency:** annual. **Type:** scholarship. **Recipient:** for library students at an ALA accredited school ● Woolls Blanche. **Frequency:** annual. **Type:** scholarship. **Publications:** Newsletter, semiannual. **Circulation:** 23,000. Alternate Formats: online ● Newsletter, semiannual. **Conventions/Meetings:** annual meeting, in conjunction with the American Library Association - always June.

Literature

23941 ■ Lambda Iota Tau (LIT)
Dept. of English
Ball State Univ.
2000 W Univ. Ave.
Muncie, IN 47306-0460
Ph: (765)285-8584 (765)285-8370
Fax: (765)285-3765
E-mail: bhozeski@bsu.edu
URL: http://www.bsu.edu/english/undergraduate/lit
Contact: Prof. Bruce W. Hozeski, Exec. Sec.-Treas.
Founded: 1953. **Members:** 30,000. **Membership Dues:** individual, $30 (quinquennial) ● life, $50. **Staff:** 2. **Budget:** $15,000. **Local Groups:** 98. **Languages:** English, French, German, Spanish. **Description:** College/university literature honor society comprised of men and women; literature of all modern languages, undergraduate and graduate. **Awards:** Scholarships and Publication Awards. **Frequency:** annual. **Type:**

scholarship. **Recipient:** for writing and academic excellence. **Affiliated With:** Association of College Honor Societies. **Publications:** *LIT Journal*, annual. Contains best poems, short stories, essays and critical research from chapters. **Price:** free for members. **Circulation:** 1,100. **Advertising:** accepted ● *LIT Newsletter*, semiannual. **Price:** free. **Advertising:** accepted. **Conventions/Meetings:** periodic conference (exhibits).

Management

23942 ■ Sigma Iota Epsilon (SIE)
c/o Dr. G. James Francis, Pres.
Colorado State Univ.
312 Rockwell Hall - Mgt. Dept.
Fort Collins, CO 80523-1275
Ph: (970)491-6265 (970)491-7200
Fax: (970)491-3522
E-mail: jimf@lamar.colostate.edu
URL: http://www.sienational.com
Contact: Dr. G. James Francis, Pres.
Founded: 1928. **Members:** 40,000. **Membership Dues:** life, $35. **Staff:** 1. **Budget:** $60,000. **Regional Groups:** 5. **State Groups:** 73. **Description:** Honorary and professional fraternity - management. Provides competitions, educational and charitable programs, and speakers' bureau on a local level. Student division of the Academy of Management (see separate entry). **Awards:** Chapter of the Year. **Frequency:** annual. **Type:** monetary. **Recipient:** to the chapter of SIE with the most activity in terms of programs, student support services, recruitment and initiation ● Keith Davis Graduate Scholarship Awards. **Frequency:** annual. **Type:** scholarship. **Recipient:** for member graduate students who write an outstanding paper on an appropriate management subject ● National Scholarship. **Frequency:** 8/year. **Type:** scholarship. **Recipient:** to students who have excelled academically as well as demonstrated excellence in community service. **Computer Services:** database, membership. **Boards:** National Executive. **Affiliated With:** Academy of Management; Professional Fraternity Association. **Publications:** *SIE Gift & Apparel Catalog*, annual. Catalog of SIE merchandise options - includes sweatshirts, t-shirts, mugs, hats, jackets, etc. ● Brochures, biennial. **Conventions/Meetings:** annual Executive Session/Reception - convention, at Academy of Management annual conference - always August 12-15.

Marketing

23943 ■ Mu Kappa Tau (MKT)
1200 Grainger Hall
Univ. of Wisconsin-Madison
975 Univ. Ave.
Madison, WI 53706
E-mail: kthughes@wisc.edu
URL: http://mkt.rso.wisc.edu
Contact: Kim Hugues, Pres.
Founded: 1978. **Members:** 250. **Membership Dues:** general, $60 (annual). **Description:** Students who have declared a marketing major and demonstrate superior academic ability; faculty of marketing department at the University of Wisconsin; honorary members of the business community who are outstanding in the marketing field; university alumni who are former society members. Encourages professional and academic excellence among marketing students and fellowship among marketing students, faculty, and practicing marketing professionals. Offers series of informational evenings cosponsored by business firms; meetings focus on employment opportunities in specific areas of marketing such as consumer goods marketing, industrial goods marketing, marketing research, marketing services, and retailing. Offers seminars where speakers present topics on career planning for marketing majors. Participates in Inter-collegiate Marketing competitions. Offers placement service. Conducts annual Careers in Marketing workshop. **Awards: Type:** recognition ● **Type:** scholarship. **Committees:** Community Service; Fundraising; Marketing Consulting; Promotions; Social; Speaker Series; Special Events. **Publications:** *Mu Kappa Tau Review*, annual ● *Resume Book*, biennial ● Newsletter, monthly.

23944 ■ Pi Sigma Epsilon (PSE)
3747 S Howell Ave.
Milwaukee, WI 53207-3870
Ph: (414)328-1952
Free: (800)761-9350
Fax: (414)328-1953
E-mail: pse@pse.org
URL: http://www.pse.org
Contact: Ann Devine, Exec. Dir.
Founded: 1952. **Members:** 60,000. **Membership Dues:** individual, $60 (annual). **Staff:** 5. **Budget:** $400,000. **Local Groups:** 52. **Description:** Professional fraternity - marketing, sales management, and selling. Conducts marketing, sales, and research projects at universities across the United States and works with corporations to provide employment candidates. **Libraries: Type:** open to the public. **Holdings:** 250. **Subjects:** business and personal development. **Awards:** National Awards Program. **Frequency:** annual. **Type:** grant. **Recipient:** for PSE membership and activity ● **Frequency:** annual. **Type:** scholarship. **Recipient:** for PSE membership and activity. **Computer Services:** database, job board ● database, membership. **Councils:** National. **Affiliated With:** Mu Kappa Tau; Sales and Marketing Executives International. **Publications:** *Dotted Lines*, 3/year. Newsletter. **Advertising:** accepted ● *Dotted Onlines Electronic Newsletter*, bimonthly. **Advertising:** accepted. Alternate Formats: online ● *Journal of Personal Selling and Sales Management*, quarterly. **Advertising:** accepted ● *National Conference in Sales Management Proceedings*, annual. Contains information on the National Conference in Sales Management. **Advertising:** accepted ● *PSE Membership Directory*, periodic. **Advertising:** accepted ● *Training and Consulting Directory* ● Manuals ● Also publishes guides. **Conventions/Meetings:** annual National Sales and Marketing Convention (exhibits) - always March/April.

Mathematics

23945 ■ Kappa Mu Epsilon (KME)
c/o Dr. Don Tosh, Pres.
Dept. of Sci. and Tech.
Evangel Univ.
Springfield, MO 65802
Ph: (417)865-2811
E-mail: toshd@evangel.edu
URL: http://kappamuepsilon.org
Contact: Dr. Don Tosh, Pres.
Founded: 1931. **Members:** 58,935. **Membership Dues:** regular, $20. **Regional Groups:** 6. **Local Groups:** 141. **Description:** Serves as honor society for men and women in mathematics. **Awards:** George R. Mach Distinguished Service Award. **Frequency:** biennial. **Type:** recognition. **Recipient:** to an individual who has made major contributions to the society. **Affiliated With:** Association of College Honor Societies; National Hospice and Palliative Care Organization. **Publications:** *The Pentagon*, semiannual. Journal. Includes student papers, problems and chapter news. **Price:** $5.00/year in U.S.; $7.00/year outside U.S.; $10.00 library rate in U.S.; $5.00/copy of back issues. ISSN: 0031-4870. Alternate Formats: microform ● Brochure, biennial. **Conventions/Meetings:** biennial convention ● regional meeting.

23946 ■ Mu Alpha Theta
c/o University of Oklahoma
601 Elm Ave., Rm. 1102
Norman, OK 73019-3103
Ph: (405)325-4489
Fax: (405)325-7184
E-mail: matheta@ou.edu
URL: http://www.mualphatheta.org
Contact: Kay Weiss, Exec. Dir.
Founded: 1957. **Members:** 65,000. **Membership Dues:** student, $5. **Staff:** 3. **Local Groups:** 1,500.

Description: Honorary club - for high school and junior college mathematics students. **Awards:** Andree Award. **Frequency:** annual. **Type:** monetary. **Recipient:** for students interested in becoming mathematics teachers ● Diane Rubin Award. **Frequency:** annual. **Type:** monetary. **Recipient:** for outstanding Mu Alpha Theta chapters ● Huneke Award. **Frequency:** annual. **Type:** monetary. **Recipient:** for sponsors who have made significant contribution to the organization ● Kalin Award. **Frequency:** annual. **Type:** monetary. **Recipient:** for graduating students who excelled in mathematics ● Sister Scholastica Award. **Frequency:** annual. **Type:** monetary ● Summer Study Grants. **Frequency:** annual. **Type:** scholarship. **Affiliated With:** Mathematical Association of America; National Council of Teachers of Mathematics. **Also Known As:** National High School and Junior College Mathematics Club. **Publications:** Newsletter, semiannual. **Conventions/Meetings:** annual meeting - always August.

23947 ■ Pi Mu Epsilon
c/o Leo J. Schneider, Sec.-Treas.
Dept. of Mathematics and Cmpt. Sci.
John Carroll Univ.
University Heights, OH 44118-4581
Ph: (216)397-4481 (216)397-4351
Fax: (216)397-3033
E-mail: leo@jcu.edu
URL: http://www.pme-math.org
Contact: Leo J. Schneider, Sec.-Treas.
Founded: 1914. **Membership Dues:** life, $20. **Staff:** 1. **Local Groups:** 317. **Description:** Honorary society for men and women in the field of mathematics. Sponsors expository mathematical writing competition and annual student paper sessions. **Awards:** AMS Speaker Awards. **Frequency:** annual. **Type:** monetary. **Recipient:** for the best student speakers at the annual August meeting; five to eight awards given ● Richard V. Andree Award. **Frequency:** annual. **Type:** monetary. **Recipient:** for the authors of the three best student papers published in the Pi Mu Epsilon Journal during a given year ● SIAM Award. **Frequency:** annual. **Type:** monetary. **Recipient:** to 2 student speakers at annual meeting for outstanding presentation on applied mathematics ● SIGMAA-EM Award. **Frequency:** annual. **Type:** monetary. **Recipient:** to 2 student speakers at annual meeting for outstanding presentations on environmental mathematics. **Publications:** *PME Journal*, semiannual. Contains mathematics articles, often written by undergraduate students. **Price:** $10.00 /year for members; $15.00 /year for nonmembers. **Advertising:** accepted. **Conventions/Meetings:** annual meeting.

Medical Education

23948 ■ Phi Delta Epsilon Medical Fraternity (PHIDE)
2655 Collins Ave., Ste.912
Miami Beach, FL 33140
Ph: (305)531-1929
Fax: (305)531-7483
E-mail: phide@phide.org
URL: http://www.phide.org
Contact: Karen Katz, CEO
Founded: 1904. **Members:** 25,000. **Membership Dues:** graduate, $110 (annual) ● new student, $100 (annual) ● returning student, $50 (annual). **Local Groups:** 41. **Multinational. Description:** Serves as professional fraternity for medicine. **Awards:** Myer H. Stolar Public Service Award. **Frequency:** annual. **Type:** recognition. **Recipient:** for outstanding chapter ● Service Award. **Frequency:** annual. **Type:** recognition. **Recipient:** for outstanding student member. **Publications:** *Phi Delta Epsilon News and Scientific Journal*, quarterly. **Conventions/Meetings:** annual meeting.

Medicine

23949 ■ Alpha Epsilon Delta (AED)
c/o National Office
James Madison Univ.
MSC 9015
Harrisonburg, VA 22807

Ph: (540)568-2594
Fax: (540)568-2595
E-mail: aed@jmu.edu
URL: http://www.jmu.edu/orgs/nationalaed
Contact: Mr. T.G. Jackson PhD, Pres.
Founded: 1926. **Members:** 88,600. **Budget:** $220,000. **Regional Groups:** 5. **Description:** Honor society of men and women in the field of premedical study. **Awards:** Distinguished Service Award. **Frequency:** periodic. **Type:** recognition. **Recipient:** for outstanding service in the field of medical and premedical education ● **Type:** monetary ● **Frequency:** annual. **Type:** scholarship. **Recipient:** for members. **Affiliated With:** American Association for the Advancement of Science. **Publications:** The Scalpel, semiannual. Newsletter. Alternate Formats: online ● Newsletter, bimonthly. **Conventions/Meetings:** biennial Gateway to Your Future - convention, for members; with speakers.

23950 ■ Alpha Omega Alpha Honor Medical Society
525 Middlefield Rd., Ste.130
Menlo Park, CA 94025
Ph: (650)329-0291
Fax: (650)329-1618
E-mail: eharris@alphaomegaalpha.org
URL: http://www.alphaomegaalpha.org
Contact: Edward D. Harris Jr., Exec. Sec.
Founded: 1902. **Members:** 72,000. **Regional Groups:** 124. **Description:** Honor society for men and women studying medicine at graduate and postgraduate levels. Sponsors "Leaders in American Medicine" videotape series; underwrites visiting professorships. Sponsors student research, student essay, and medical student service project awards. **Awards:** Distinguished Teacher Award. **Frequency:** annual. **Type:** recognition ● **Type:** fellowship. **Recipient:** for student research ● Student Essay Award. **Frequency:** annual. **Type:** recognition ● Volunteer Clinical Faculty Award. **Frequency:** annual. **Type:** recognition. **Recipient:** for a physician who contributes effectively to the education and training of clinical students. **Formerly:** Alpha Omega Alpha. **Publications:** The Pharos, quarterly. Journal. Contains non-technical articles of medical interest. **Circulation:** 72,000. **Conventions/Meetings:** annual board meeting.

23951 ■ Phi Alpha Sigma
313 S 10th St.
Philadelphia, PA 19107
E-mail: robert.olszewski@jefferson.edu
URL: http://www.phialphasigma.org
Contact: Austin Daly, Pres.
Founded: 1886. **Members:** 120. **Membership Dues:** household, $200 (monthly). **Staff:** 200. **Budget:** $40,000. **Regional Groups:** 1. **State Groups:** 1. **Local Groups:** 1. **Description:** Serves as a professional fraternity - medicine. Various Charity events are held throughout the year to benefit charities such as the Smile Train. **Libraries:** Type: reference; not open to the public. **Holdings:** 250; books. **Subjects:** medicine. **Awards:** fellowship. **Recipient:** for patronage of the organization by an alumni. **Publications:** Bubbling Rales, annual. Newsletter. **Price:** free to alumni. **Circulation:** 650. **Conventions/Meetings:** annual Concilium Magnum - meeting - always in Philadelphia, PA.

23952 ■ Phi Chi Medical Fraternity (PCMF)
Jefferson Medical Coll.
1025 Spruce St.
Philadelphia, PA 19107
E-mail: pjd109@jefferson.edu
URL: http://www.umich.edu/~phichi
Contact: Bryan Hess, Contact
Founded: 1889. **Members:** 40,818. **Staff:** 1. **Budget:** $50,000. **Local Groups:** 12. **Description:** Serves as a professional fraternity for medicine. Maintains Phi Chi Welfare Association, which accepts voluntary contributions to a student loan fund and other services. **Awards:** Frequency: annual. **Type:** recognition ● **Frequency:** annual. **Type:** scholarship. **Computer Services:** Mailing lists. **Additional Websites:** http://www.phi-chi.com/Intro.htm. **Formerly:** (1989)

Phi Chi. **Publications:** Constitution and Statutes ● Officers' Manual ● PC Chronicles, semiannual. Magazine. Provides chapter news and information. **Price:** included in membership dues. **Circulation:** 4,300. **Advertising:** accepted ● Phi Chi Directory ● Phi Chi History, 1889-1989 ● Phi Chi Songs. **Conventions/Meetings:** annual Grand Chapter Meeting - conference.

23953 ■ Phi Rho Sigma Medical Society
PO Box 90264
Indianapolis, IN 46290-0264
E-mail: central_office@phirhosigma.org
URL: http://www.phirhosigma.org
Contact: Martin Wice, Pres.
Founded: 1890. **Members:** 31,260. **Staff:** 1. **Regional Groups:** 13. **State Groups:** 12. **Description:** Professional society - medicine. **Publications:** Journal of Phi Rho Sigma, quarterly. **Price:** free, for members only. **Conventions/Meetings:** annual meeting.

Military

23954 ■ Arnold Air Society (AAS)
AFROTC Det. 770 Clemson Univ.
300 Tillman Hall
Box 341352
Clemson, SC 29634
Ph: (864)656-3254
E-mail: commander@arnold-air.org
URL: http://arnold-air.org/category/aas
Contact: Gen. Richard Bundy Ret., Exec. Dir.
Founded: 1947. **Members:** 3,500. **Budget:** $300,000. **Regional Groups:** 11. **Local Groups:** 147. **Description:** Honorary professional fraternity within AFROTC. Organizes community service projects. Sponsors Silver Wings, a nonmilitary campus service organization. **Awards:** Frequency: annual. **Type:** recognition. **Recipient:** for individuals and squadrons. **Affiliated With:** Air Force Association. **Publications:** Arnold Air Letter, semiannual. Report ● Arnold Air Letter. Newsletter ● Report, biennial. **Conventions/Meetings:** annual Conclave - meeting - held Easter weekend.

23955 ■ National Society of Pershing Rifles (NSPR)
PO Box 17976
Baton Rouge, LA 70893
E-mail: nhq@pershingriflessociety.org
URL: http://NHQ.pershingrifles.com
Contact: P/R Major Gen. Chris Scheuermann, Natl. Commander
Founded: 1894. **Members:** 2,500. **Membership Dues:** charter, $75 (annual). **Staff:** 10. **National Groups:** 40. **Description:** Members range from military to civilian, male to female. Seeks to foster a spirit of friendship and cooperation among men and women in the military department and to maintain a highly efficient drill company. **Libraries:** Type: reference. **Subjects:** U.S. Army Gen. John J. Pershing, history of NSPR. **Awards:** Drill Meet. **Frequency:** annual. **Type:** trophy ● National Rifle Match Trophies. **Frequency:** annual. **Type:** trophy ● **Frequency:** annual. **Type:** scholarship. **Recipient:** for members. **Computer Services:** Mailing lists. **Publications:** Pershing Rifleman, bimonthly. Newsletter ● The PIR Bullet, bimonthly. Newsletter ● Roster of Pershing Rifles Units, annual. **Conventions/Meetings:** annual Fall Commanders Call - conference - fall ● annual Pershing Rifles National Convention - conference - always spring.

23956 ■ National Society of Scabbard and Blade (NSSB)
1018 S Lewis St.
Stillwater, OK 74074-4622
Ph: (405)377-2237 (405)377-4279
Fax: (405)377-2237

E-mail: ddollar@scabbardandblade.org
URL: http://www.scabbardandblade.org
Contact: Maj. Gen.(Ret.) Douglas O. Dollar, Exec. Dir.
Founded: 1904. **Members:** 133,000. **Membership Dues:** regular, in U.S., $20 (annual) ● regular, in U.S., $38 (biennial) ● regular, in U.S., $56 (triennial) ● regular, outside U.S., $55 (annual) ● regular, outside U.S., $95 (biennial) ● regular, outside U.S., $145 (triennial) ● life (40 and under), $360 ● life (41-50), $345 ● life (51-60), $300 ● life (61-70), $250 ● life (71-80), $200 ● life (81 and over), $150. **Staff:** 2. **Budget:** $7,000. **Regional Groups:** 121. **Local Groups:** 121. **Description:** Honorary and recognition fraternity - men and women, military; advanced ROTC; junior ROTC, and all-Service. Maintains speakers' bureau. **Awards:** Award for Excellence in Military Science. **Frequency:** annual. **Type:** recognition. **Recipient:** for outstanding support of Reserve Officers Training Course Program. **Computer Services:** database. **Councils:** National Alumni. **Publications:** The Five Star, quarterly. Newsletter. Contains a variety of articles submitted by members from across the country. **Price:** included in membership dues. **Circulation:** 600. **Advertising:** accepted ● Scabbard and Blade Today, semiannual. Newsletter. **Circulation:** 2,000. **Advertising:** accepted. **Conventions/Meetings:** biennial National Convention - conference (exhibits).

23957 ■ Silver Wings (SW)
c/o University of Illinois at Urbana-Champaign
AFROTC Detachment 190
229 Armory Bldg.
505 E Armory Ave.
Champaign, IL 61820
E-mail: president@silver-wings.org
URL: http://www.silver-wings.org
Contact: Ms. Megan Stark, Pres.
Founded: 1952. **Members:** 800. **Budget:** $50,000. **Regional Groups:** 11. **Local Groups:** 50. **Description:** Works as a national, co-ed, professional organization dedicated to creating proactive, knowledgeable, and effective civic leaders through community service and education about national defense. Its mission includes the following interrelated objectives: a. Personal Development b. Professional Development and c. Civic Awareness. **Libraries:** Type: reference. **Awards:** Frequency: annual. **Type:** recognition. **Recipient:** for individuals and chapters. **Affiliated With:** Air Force Association; Arnold Air Society. **Formerly:** (1998) Angel Flight/Silver Wings. **Publications:** On Silver Wings, semiannual. Magazine ● Silver Wings Manual. Alternate Formats: online. **Conventions/Meetings:** annual Conclave - meeting - held Easter weekend.

Music

23958 ■ Delta Omicron (DO)
c/o Julie Hensley, Exec. Sec.
910 Church St.
Jefferson City, TN 37760
Ph: (865)471-6155
Fax: (865)475-9716
E-mail: doexecsec@aol.com
URL: http://www.delta-omicron.org
Contact: Julie Hensley, Exec. Sec.
Founded: 1909. **Members:** 25,000. **Membership Dues:** alumnus, $30 (annual) ● life, $300. **Local Groups:** 56. **National Groups:** 18. **Description:** Serves as professional fraternity for music. **Awards:** Educational Grants. **Frequency:** annual. **Type:** grant. **Recipient:** for deserving students ● Summer Music Scholarships. **Frequency:** annual. **Type:** scholarship. **Recipient:** for members with good standing and who have paid national dues for the current year. **Committees:** Awards and Citations; Bylaws; Composition Competition; Foundation Education Grants; Fraternity Education; Music Editor; National Patron/ National Honorary Members; Patrons/Patroness. **Publications:** Delta Omicron Instructional Book. Includes fraternity forms and instructions. ● Delta Omicron International Music Fraternity Directory, an-

nual ● *The Epoillac*, triennial. Proceedings. Contains summary and minutes of the conference and business reports of officers and committees. ● *Province President's Manual*. Outlines specific duties of the province president. ● *The Wheel*, quarterly. Journal. Contains articles and information related to the fraternity. **Price:** $5.00/year; $1.25/issue. ISSN: 0043-4752 ● *The Whistle*, annual. Newsletter. Alternate Formats: online. **Conventions/Meetings:** triennial meeting and conference.

23959 ■ Kappa Kappa Psi (KKPSI)
PO Box 849
Stillwater, OK 74076-0849
Free: (800)543-6505
Fax: (405)372-2363
E-mail: kkytbs@kkytbs.org
URL: http://www.kkytbs.org
Contact: Dixie Mosier-Greene, Natl. Admin.
Founded: 1919. **Members:** 3,600. **Membership Dues:** active, associate, conditional, $65 (annual) ● alumnus (life), $250 ● honorary, $30 ● alumnus (National Alumni Association), $25 (annual). **Staff:** 6. **Budget:** $750,000. **Regional Groups:** 6. **Local Groups:** 165. **Description:** Serves as an honorary fraternity - band. **Awards:** A. Frank Martin Award. **Frequency:** semiannual. **Type:** recognition. **Recipient:** for band directors and laymen ● Chapter Leadership Award. **Frequency:** biennial. **Type:** recognition. **Recipient:** for excellent chapter that demonstrates the ideals of the fraternity ● Stanley G. Finck Memorial Award. **Frequency:** biennial. **Type:** recognition. **Recipient:** for individual who exemplifies the spirit of joint cooperation ● William Scroggs Founder's Trophy. **Frequency:** biennial. **Type:** trophy. **Recipient:** to the outstanding chapter in the nation. **Additional Websites:** http://www.kkpsi.org. **Affiliated With:** Tau Beta Sigma. **Publications:** *Membership Education Teaching Manual*. Alternate Formats: online ● *News Notes*, monthly. Newsletter. Alternate Formats: online ● *The Podium*, semiannual. Magazine. **Price:** $10.00 ● Reports. Alternate Formats: online ● Directories. Alternate Formats: online. **Conventions/Meetings:** biennial convention.

23960 ■ Mu Beta Psi
801 15th St. S, Apt. 213
Arlington, VA 22202
Ph: (703)415-4665 (814)450-5334
E-mail: secretary@mubetapsi.org
URL: http://mubetapsi.org
Contact: Mr. Nathaniel Kulyk, Natl. Sec.
Founded: 1925. **Members:** 3,300. **Membership Dues:** brother, $20 (annual). **Local Groups:** 6. **Description:** Comprised of men and women of diverse group with many interests — but with one thing in common: "we share a love for music." Provides a unique opportunity for many students with an active interest in music to work together both musically and socially. Membership in the organization is honorary. Brothers are chosen for their love for music and commitment to the advancement of their educational institution and in the surrounding community. The brothers of the organization provide service to musical organizations on their respective campuses. The organization is also an active fraternity. **Libraries: Type:** not open to the public. **Subcommittees:** Alumni Association. **Publications:** *The Clef*, semiannual. Newsletter. **Price:** free. **Advertising:** accepted. **Conventions/Meetings:** annual convention and general assembly, all chapters, officers, board of trustees.

23961 ■ Mu Phi Epsilon International
4705 N Sonora Ave., Ste.114
Fresno, CA 93722-3947
Ph: (559)277-1898
Free: (888)259-1471
Fax: (559)277-2825
E-mail: mpeieo@aol.com
URL: http://home.muphiepsilon.org
Contact: Gloria Debatin, Exec. Sec-Treas.
Founded: 1903. **Members:** 80,000. **Membership Dues:** college, $23 (annual) ● alumnus, $35 (annual). **Staff:** 1. **Local Groups:** 170. **Description:** Serves as a professional music fraternity. Administers

fraternity philanthropies through Mu Phi Epsilon Foundation. **Libraries: Type:** reference. **Awards:** Povince Senior Achievement, Chapter Achievement. **Frequency:** annual. **Type:** recognition ● **Type:** scholarship. **Recipient:** for outstanding member. **Committees:** Artists, Composers, Musicologists, Educators; Bylaws, Centennial Projects, Membership; Music Librarian, Rules, Education, Service, Therapy in Music. **Formerly:** (2003) Mu Phi Epsilon. **Publications:** *Centennial Edition of Mu Epsilon Composers and Authors*. Directory. **Price:** $32.00 plus shipping and handling ● *The Triangle of Mu Phi Epsilon*, quarterly. Journal. **Conventions/Meetings:** triennial convention.

23962 ■ Phi Beta Mu
c/o Richard C. Crain, Exec. Sec.
7 Surrey Run Pl.
The Woodlands, TX 77384-4786
Ph: (936)321-8946
Fax: (936)271-0667
E-mail: info@phibetamu.org
URL: http://www.phibetamu.org
Contact: Richard C. Crain, Exec. Sec.
Founded: 1938. **Members:** 2,600. **State Groups:** 32. **Multinational. Description:** Honorary fraternity for bandmasters from universities, colleges, high schools, and elementary schools. Recognizes outstanding achievement after five years of activity in the field. Maintains hall of fame. **Awards:** Outstanding Bandmaster Award. **Frequency:** annual. **Type:** recognition. **Publications:** *International Newsletter*, periodic ● *National Membership Roster*, annual. **Conventions/Meetings:** annual meeting - always December, Chicago, IL.

23963 ■ Phi Mu Alpha Sinfonia Fraternity and Foundation National Headquarters
10600 Old State Rd.
Evansville, IN 47711
Ph: (812)867-2433
Free: (800)473-2649
Fax: (812)867-0633
E-mail: lyrecrest@sinfonia.org
URL: http://www.sinfonia.org
Contact: Ryan T. Ripperton, Exec. Dir.
Founded: 1898. **Members:** 120,000. **Membership Dues:** regular, $55 (biennial). **Staff:** 4. **Budget:** $600,000. **State Groups:** 34. **Local Groups:** 203. **Description:** Professional fraternity - music. Sponsors collegiate musical activities. Conducts 34 biennial provincial workshops. **Awards: Type:** recognition. **Commissions:** Standards. **Committees:** Awards; Legislative; Music Outreach; Recruitment/ Expansion; Risk Management. **Councils:** Collegiate Province Representatives; Province Governors. **Affiliated With:** College Fraternity Editors Association; Professional Fraternity Association. **Formerly:** (1934) The Sinfonia Fraternity. **Publications:** *The Red and Black*, monthly. Newsletter. Includes pictures, news from chapters, information about current events in the fraternity and inspirational messages. ● *Sinfonian*, semiannual. Magazine. Contains informative and inspiring articles, news of current and upcoming activities, alumni news and messages from the leadership. **Price:** $5.00/year ● Directory, annual ● Also publishes kits, resource packets, manuals, and handbooks. **Conventions/Meetings:** annual Educational and Legislative Conference (exhibits).

23964 ■ Pi Kappa Lambda (PKL)
c/o Mark Lochstampfor, Exec. Dir.
Capital Univ.
Conservatory of Music
1 Coll. and Main
Columbus, OH 43209
Ph: (614)236-7211
Fax: (614)236-6935
E-mail: pikappalambda@capital.edu
URL: http://pikappalambda.capital.edu
Contact: Mark Lochstampfor, Exec. Dir.
Founded: 1918. **Members:** 57,000. **Membership Dues:** life, $50. **Staff:** 1. **Local Groups:** 189. **Description:** Honor society-men and women, music. Sponsors competitions and charitable and educational programs for chapters. Membership is based

on faculty committee consisting of PKL members and requires high GPA as well as vote on high musicianship. **Computer Services:** database, chapter lists. **Affiliated With:** Association of College Honor Societies. **Publications:** Newsletter, semiannual ● Handbook, biennial. **Conventions/Meetings:** annual board meeting ● biennial conference.

23965 ■ Sigma Alpha Iota International Music Fraternity (SAI)
1 Tunnel Rd.
Asheville, NC 28805
Ph: (828)251-0606
Fax: (828)251-0644
E-mail: nh@sai-national.org
URL: http://www.sai-national.org
Contact: Ruth Sieber Johnson, Exec. Dir.
Founded: 1903. **Members:** 105,000. **Membership Dues:** regular, $250. **Staff:** 7. **Regional Groups:** 57. **Local Groups:** 335. **Description:** College students and alumnae (80,250); honorary members and patronesses (7,750) International Music Fraternity. Promotes music creation, performance, and scholarship. **Libraries: Type:** reference. **Subjects:** music. **Awards:** International American Music Award. **Frequency:** triennial. **Type:** monetary. **Recipient:** for anyone from North, Central or South America. **Committees:** People-to-People Music. **Projects:** Hazel E. Ritchey Loan Fund for Members; Music Therapy; Services for Musicians with Special Needs; Strings. **Publications:** *Pan Pipes*, quarterly. Journal. Contains book and current recording reviews, and chapter news. **Price:** $25.00 in U.S.; $35.00 outside U.S. ISSN: 0889-7581. **Circulation:** 26,000. Alternate Formats: magnetic tape ● *Winter Contemporary American Music*, annual. **Price:** $8.00/issue. **Conventions/Meetings:** triennial convention ● triennial Performance Awards - competition.

23966 ■ Tau Beta Sigma (TBS)
PO Box 849
Stillwater, OK 74076-0849
Free: (800)543-6505
Fax: (405)372-2363
E-mail: kkytbs@kkytbs.org
URL: http://www.kkytbs.org
Contact: Alan Bonner, Natl. Exec. Dir.
Founded: 1946. **Members:** 3,000. **Membership Dues:** active, conditional, $65 (annual) ● life, $250 ● honorary, $30. **Staff:** 6. **Budget:** $700,000. **Regional Groups:** 6. **Local Groups:** 130. **Description:** Serves as a honorary sorority - band. **Awards:** Outstanding Service to Music. **Type:** recognition. **Recipient:** for woman of the sorority who has made a significant contribution to bands through outstanding musicianship ● **Frequency:** biennial. **Type:** recognition ● Stanley G. Finck Memorial. **Frequency:** biennial. **Type:** recognition. **Recipient:** for individuals who exemplify the spirit of joint cooperation ● Wava Banes Tuner. **Frequency:** biennial. **Type:** recognition. **Recipient:** for member who has demonstrated outstanding and continued service. **Additional Websites:** http://www.tbsigma.org. **Programs:** Women in Music Series. **Projects:** Sorority Archives. **Affiliated With:** Kappa Kappa Psi. **Publications:** *The Podium*, semiannual. **Price:** $10.00. **Conventions/Meetings:** biennial convention.

Nursing

23967 ■ Alpha Tau Delta (ATD)
c/o Susan Carson, Pres.
11252 Camarillo St.
Toluca Lake, CA 91602
E-mail: scarson@chla.usc.edu
URL: http://www.atdnursing.org
Contact: Aileen Waltner, Board Member
Founded: 1921. **Members:** 6,000. **Membership Dues:** chapter, $25 (annual) ● member-at-large, $30 (annual). **Staff:** 6. **Regional Groups:** 2. **State Groups:** 12. **Description:** Professional fraternity - nursing. Seeks to further educational standards for the nursing profession. Maintains scholarship program for members only. **Libraries: Type:** reference.

Holdings: archival material. **Awards:** Member of the Year. **Frequency:** annual. **Type:** grant. **Recipient:** for student members ● Miriam Fay Furlong Grant. **Frequency:** annual. **Type:** grant. **Recipient:** for member students ● National Advisor of the Year. **Frequency:** annual. **Type:** recognition. **Computer Services:** database, members. **Committees:** Legislative; Rituals. **Affiliated With:** Professional Fraternity Association. **Publications:** *President's Letter*, quarterly ● *The Pulse.A publication of Alpha Tau Delta*, quarterly. Newsletter. Contains reports, member and chapter news, and calendar of events, CEU, interview and nursing news. **Price:** included in membership dues. **Advertising:** accepted. Alternate Formats: online ● Brochure. **Conventions/Meetings:** biennial convention, for military nursing and graduate nursing education (exhibits) ● workshop and seminar.

23968 ■ Chi Eta Phi Sorority

3029 13th St. NW
Washington, DC 20009
Ph: (202)232-3858
Fax: (202)232-3460
E-mail: chietaphi@erols.com
URL: http://www.chietaphi.com
Contact: Dr. Lillian Stokes, Supreme Basileus
Founded: 1932. **Members:** 8,000. **Staff:** 1. **Description:** Professional sorority - registered and student nurses. Aims to encourage continuing education. Stimulates friendship among members. Develops working relationships with other professional groups for the improvement and delivery of health care services. Operates speakers' bureau on health education. **Libraries: Type:** reference. **Holdings:** biographical archives. **Subjects:** African-American nurses. **Awards:** Aliene Carrington Ewell Scholarship. **Frequency:** annual. **Type:** scholarship. **Recipient:** to deserving undergraduate students pursuing a nursing degree ● Mabel Keaton Staupers National Scholarship Award. **Frequency:** annual. **Type:** scholarship. **Recipient:** for current members of the Chi Eta Phi Sorority and the American Nurses Association. **Computer Services:** Mailing lists, of members. **Programs:** Chi Care Call-programs for the Elderly; Chi Teen/Future Nurses Clubs; Child Care Center; Leadership Development. **Projects:** Back to Sleep Campaign; National Eye Health Education; National Hypertension Awareness; Stay Beautiful, Stay Alive!. **Publications:** *Chi Line News*, semiannual. Newsletter. Includes membership activities. **Price:** available to members only. **Circulation:** 4,000. **Advertising:** accepted. Alternate Formats: online ● *The Directory*, biennial ● *History of Chi Eta Phi Sorority, Inc.* ● *JOCEPS*, annual. Journal. **Price:** $30.00 /year for institutions. **Circulation:** 4,000. **Advertising:** accepted ● *Mary Eliza Mahoney, America's First Black Professional Nurse*. **Conventions/Meetings:** biennial conference and meeting (exhibits).

23969 ■ Sigma Theta Tau International (STTI)

550 W North St.
Indianapolis, IN 46202
Ph: (317)634-8171
Free: (800)634-7575
Fax: (317)634-8188
E-mail: stti@stti.iupui.edu
URL: http://www.nursingsociety.org
Contact: Nancy Dickenson-Hazard, CEO
Founded: 1922. **Members:** 120,000. **Membership Dues:** international (based on income), $50-$400 (annual) ● individual (based on income), $12-$60 (annual). **Staff:** 70. **Budget:** $8,000,000. **Local Groups:** 406. **Multinational. Description:** One of the largest and most prestigious nursing organizations in the world. Committed to fostering nursing excellence, scholarship and leadership to improve health care worldwide, its members promote research-based practice by making resources available to all interested people and institutions. Comprised of chapter honor societies that are located on more than 500 colleges and university campuses in all 50 states, Puerto Rico, Canada, South Korea, Taiwan, Australia, Pakistan, Brazil, Netherlands, and Hong Kong. Members are active in 94 countries and territories. **Libraries: Type:** reference. **Holdings:** 1,318; audio recordings, periodicals, video record-

ings. **Subjects:** nursing. **Awards: Frequency:** biennial. **Type:** recognition. **Recipient:** for research, use of media, technology, community service, publications, and other displays of nursing excellence. **Computer Services:** database, online nursing resources. **Telecommunication Services:** electronic mail, memserv@stti.iupui.edu ● phone referral service, (317)687-2271. **Formerly:** (1985) Sigma Theta Tau. **Publications:** *Directory of Nurse Researchers*. **Price:** $60.00 print; $25.00 compact disc. Alternate Formats: online ● *Journal of Nursing Scholarship*, quarterly. Includes manuscripts, books reviews, and opinion pieces. **Price:** $34.00/year; $56.00/2 years. ISSN: 0743-5150. **Advertising:** accepted. Alternate Formats: microform ● *The Online Journal of Knowledge Synthesis for Nursing (Full-Text Electronic Journal)*. **Price:** $90.00 /year for members; $105.00 /year for nonmembers; $75.00 /year for institutions (small); $350.00 /year for institutions (large) ● *Reflections on Nursing Leadership*, quarterly. Magazine. Includes President's message, executive update, inside the society, feature articles, people and announcements. **Price:** $20.00/2 years. ISSN: 0885-8144. **Circulation:** 125,000. **Advertising:** accepted. **Conventions/Meetings:** biennial Learning and Leading Globally - Members and Chapters - convention (exhibits).

Optometry

23970 ■ Beta Sigma Kappa (BSK)

c/o Dr. Marjorie Ross, Exec. Dir.
24 Bay Pointe
Battle Creek, MI 49017
Ph: (269)963-5342
Fax: (269)962-0987
E-mail: ross@betasigmakappa.org
URL: http://www.betasigmakappa.org
Contact: Dr. Marjorie Ross, Exec. Dir.
Founded: 1925. **Members:** 1,800. **Local Groups:** 17. **Description:** Honorary fraternity - ocular science. **Awards: Type:** recognition ● Research Grants. **Type:** grant. **Recipient:** for students in optometric colleges. **Boards:** Regents. **Councils:** Central World. **Publications:** *Ocularum*, semiannual. **Price:** available to members only. **Conventions/Meetings:** annual breakfast, in conjunction with American Optometric Association.

23971 ■ Omega Delta (OD)

Southern Coll. of Optometry
1245 Madison Ave.
Memphis, TN 38104
Ph: (901)722-3200
Free: (800)238-0180
E-mail: rgraves@sco.edu
URL: http://www.sco.edu
Founded: 1917. **Members:** 90. **Description:** Serves as a professional fraternity - optometry. **Publications:** *Omega Delta Fraternity Directory*, periodic. **Conventions/Meetings:** annual meeting.

Osteopathy

23972 ■ National Osteopathic Women Physician's Association (NOWPA)

ATSU-Kirksville Coll. of Osteophatic Medicine
800 W Jefferson
Kirksville, MO 63501
E-mail: atsu.nowpa@gmail.com
URL: http://www.nowpa.org
Contact: Candace Westgate, Pres.
Founded: 1904. **Members:** 200. **Description:** Professional sorority for women in the field of osteopathy. Gives Grant-in-Aid annually. **Awards: Type:** scholarship. **Recipient:** for junior and senior osteopathic medical students. **Committees:** Education. **Formerly:** (1988) Delta Omega. **Publications:** *The Alpha*, annual. **Conventions/Meetings:** annual luncheon, held in conjunction with American Osteopathic Association.

23973 ■ Sigma Sigma Phi

4810 Snowdrop Dr.
Garland, TX 75043
E-mail: brimelow@airmail.net
URL: http://www.sigmasigmaphi.org
Contact: Deborah Ann Brimelow, Sec.-Treas.
Founded: 1921. **Members:** 3,600. **Description:** Honorary fraternity - osteopathy. Objectives are: to further the science of osteopathic medicine and its practice; to improve scholastic standings of its students; to promote a closer relationship between students and college officials and faculties. Provides financial and supportive aid to chapters at osteopathic medical colleges. **Awards: Type:** recognition. **Recipient:** to persons in the osteopathic profession and others who have contributed to the advancement of osteopathic practice and research. **Affiliated With:** American Osteopathic Association. **Conventions/Meetings:** annual meeting.

23974 ■ Theta Psi

c/o KCOM
A. T. Still Univ. of Hea. Sciences
Dept. of Student and Alumni Services
800 W Jefferson St.
Kirksville, MO 63501
Ph: (660)626-2121
Free: (866)626-ATSU
Fax: (660)626-2483
E-mail: webmaster@atsu.edu
URL: http://www.kcom.edu/newcatalog/organizations/thetapsi.htm
Contact: Fred Hauser, Pres.
Founded: 1903. **Members:** 650. **Description:** Professional fraternity - osteopathy. **Publications:** *Signet*, annual. **Conventions/Meetings:** annual meeting.

Pharmacy

23975 ■ Alpha Zeta Omega (AZO)

4422 Porpoise Dr.
Tampa, FL 33617-8316
E-mail: brucestrell@excite.com
URL: http://www.azo.org
Contact: Vince Paul, Dir.
Founded: 1919. **Members:** 11,000. **Budget:** $35,000. **Description:** Professional fraternity - men and women, pharmacy. Sponsors scholarships, grants-in-aid, and visiting lectureships at colleges where a chapter of AZO is maintained. Raises funds for the "City of Hope" in Los Angeles, CA, the Arthritis Foundation (see separate entry), and the Hebrew University of Pharmacy in Israel. **Awards:** AZO Achievement Medal. **Frequency:** annual. **Type:** medal. **Recipient:** for long and meritorious service to the profession of pharmacy ● **Frequency:** annual. **Type:** grant. **Publications:** *The Azoan and The Azomedic* ● Newsletter, monthly.

23976 ■ Kappa Psi

c/o Kappa Psi Central Office
The Central Off.
Coll. of Pharmacy
SWOSU
100 Campus Dr.
Weatherford, OK 73096
Ph: (580)774-7171
Fax: (580)774-7125
E-mail: taffiney.sherril@wosu.edu
URL: http://www.kappa-psi.org
Contact: Scott F. Long, Exec. Dir.
Founded: 1879. **Members:** 55,000. **Membership Dues:** individual, $35 (annual). **Staff:** 2. **Regional Groups:** 62. **State Groups:** 41. **Description:** Professional fraternity - pharmacy. **Telecommunication Services:** electronic mail, executivedirector@kappa-psi.org. **Publications:** *Constitution and By-Laws*. Manual ● *Handbook and Pledge Manual* ● *The History of Kappa Psi* ● *The Mask*, quarterly. **Conventions/Meetings:** biennial Grand Council Convention - convention and workshop.

23977 ■ Lambda Kappa Sigma (LKS)
W179 S6769 Muskego Dr.
Muskego, WI 53150
Free: (800)557-1913
Fax: (262)679-4558
E-mail: lks@lks.org
URL: http://www.lks.org
Contact: Joan E. Rogala CAE, Exec. Dir.
Founded: 1913. **Members:** 18,000. **Membership Dues:** alumni enrolled in a graduate degree program, $50 (annual) ● retired alumni, $70 (annual). **Staff:** 5. **Budget:** $175,000. **Regional Groups:** 8. **Local Groups:** 60. **Description:** Serves as a professional fraternity for pharmacy. **Awards:** Award of Merit. **Frequency:** biennial. **Type:** recognition. **Recipient:** to a member who has achieved professional advancement, community service, organizational work and academic achievement ● Distinguished Service Award. **Frequency:** biennial. **Type:** recognition. **Recipient:** to a member who has contributed outstanding service ● Ethel J. Health Scholarship Key. **Frequency:** annual. **Type:** scholarship ● **Frequency:** annual. **Type:** grant. **Recipient:** to undergraduate and graduate student members ● Ruth Flaherty Service Award. **Frequency:** annual. **Type:** recognition. **Recipient:** to member who exhibits outstanding chapter service and loyalty. **Committees:** Educational Trust Liaison; Professional Projects; Publicity; Women's Health Issues. **Programs:** Responsible Drinking. **Projects:** Hope. **Task Forces:** Alumnae. **Affiliated With:** American Society of Association Executives; College Fraternity Editors Association; Professional Fraternity Association. **Publications:** *Blue and Gold Triangle*, biennial. Newsletter. **Advertising:** accepted ● *Compounding Was More Fun* ● *LinKS*, periodic. Newsletter ● *Prospectus* ● *Women in Pharmacy Leadership Directory*. **Price:** $25.00 ● Membership Directory, every 4-5 years. **Conventions/Meetings:** biennial meeting and conference (exhibits) - held in August of even years.

23978 ■ Phi Delta Chi
PO Box 83250
Conyers, GA 30013
Free: (800)PDC-1883
E-mail: pdc_executive_director@hotmail.com
URL: http://www.phideltachi.org
Contact: Song You, Grand Pres.
Founded: 1883. **Members:** 50,000. **Membership Dues:** alumnus, $50 (annual). **Staff:** 1. **Budget:** $185,000. **Regional Groups:** 5. **Local Groups:** 54. **Description:** Professional fraternity - pharmacy. Compiles statistics. **Awards:** Albert B. Prescott/Glaxo Wellcome Leadership Award. **Frequency:** annual. **Type:** recognition. **Recipient:** for a pharmacist with less than ten years experience who has displayed exemplary leadership qualities. **Computer Services:** Mailing lists, of members. **Publications:** *The Communicator*, quarterly. Magazine. **Circulation:** 4,500. **Advertising:** accepted ● *Who's Who in Phi Delta Chi*, annual. **Conventions/Meetings:** biennial Grand Council - convention, policy meeting ● biennial Leader Development Seminar - always August.

23979 ■ Rho Chi - Alpha Beta Chapter
Duquesne Univ.
Mylan Scholarship of Pharmacy
600 Forbes Ave.
Pittsburgh, PA 15282
Ph: (412)396-6364
E-mail: harrold@duq.edu
URL: http://www.rhochi.org
Contact: Dr. Marc W. Harrold, Faculty Advisor
Founded: 1922. **Members:** 55,000. **Membership Dues:** honor; one time fee, $25. **Regional Groups:** 8. **Description:** Honor society of the top twenty percent in their class of men and women in pharmacy. Presents annual Rho Chi Lecture. **Formerly:** (1922) Aristolochite Society; (2001) Rho Chi. **Publications:** *History, Constitution and Bylaws*, annual ● Membership Directory, annual. Includes annual supplements. ● Annual Report, annual. **Conventions/Meetings:** annual conference, held in conjunction with American Pharmaceutical Association (exhibits).

Philosophy

23980 ■ Phi Sigma Tau
PO Box 1881
Milwaukee, WI 53201-1881
Ph: (414)288-6857
Fax: (414)288-3010
E-mail: lee.rice@marquette.edu
URL: http://www.marquette.edu/phil/phisigmatau.html
Contact: Dr. Lee C. Rice, Exec. Sec.
Founded: 1955. **Members:** 25,203. **Membership Dues:** student, faculty, honorary, $25. **Staff:** 2. **Budget:** $22,000. **Regional Groups:** 171. **Description:** Honor society - men and women, philosophy. **Publications:** *Dialogue*, semiannual. Journal. Contains student essays in all areas of contemporary philosophical research. **Price:** $5.00. **ISSN:** 9912-2246. **Circulation:** 2,000. **Advertising:** accepted ● Newsletter, 3/year. Contains news of local chapter activities.

Physical Education

23981 ■ Delta Psi Kappa
PO Box 90264
Indianapolis, IN 46290
Ph: (317)334-8720
Fax: (317)334-8721
Contact: Harriet Rodenberg, Exec. Dir.
Founded: 1916. **Members:** 20,000. **Regional Groups:** 15. **State Groups:** 2. **Description:** Professional fraternity - health, physical education, recreation, and dance. **Awards:** **Type:** recognition. **Committees:** Research Award. **Absorbed:** Phi Delta Pi. **Conventions/Meetings:** biennial meeting.

23982 ■ Phi Epsilon Kappa
901 W New York St.
Indianapolis, IN 46202
Ph: (317)278-2410
Fax: (317)278-2041
E-mail: jvessel@iupui.edu
URL: http://www.phiepsilonkappa.org
Contact: Jeff Vessely, Exec. Dir.
Founded: 1913. **Members:** 2,000. **Membership Dues:** collegiate, $15 (annual) ● alumnus, $30 (annual). **Staff:** 2. **Budget:** $75,000. **Regional Groups:** 6. **National Groups:** 55. **Description:** Serves as professional fraternity for physical education, health education and related fields. **Awards:** R.R. Schreiber Distinguished Service. **Frequency:** annual. **Type:** recognition. **Publications:** *Black and Gold Bulletin*, semiannual. Newsletter. **Price:** included in membership dues ● *The Physical Educator*, quarterly. Journal. **Price:** $45.00/year. **ISSN:** 0031-8981. **Conventions/Meetings:** triennial assembly.

Physics

23983 ■ Sigma Pi Sigma
1 Physics Ellipse
College Park, MD 20740
Ph: (301)209-3007
Fax: (301)209-0839
E-mail: sps@aip.org
URL: http://www.aip.org/education/sps/sigpisig.htm
Contact: Dr. Gary White, Dir.
Founded: 1921. **Members:** 75,000. **Membership Dues:** life (plus $45 entrance fee), $25. **Staff:** 9. **Budget:** $300,000. **Regional Groups:** 18. **National Groups:** 460. **Description:** Honor society - men and women, physics. Recognizes and encourages the attainment of high scholarship and potential achievement in physics among outstanding students. **Awards:** Marsh W. White Awards. **Frequency:** annual. **Type:** recognition. **Recipient:** to chapters for projects that popularize physics with the public ● SPS Scholarships. **Frequency:** annual. **Type:** scholarship. **Recipient:** to 19 individuals for the final year of study toward a baccalaureate degree in physics ● Undergraduate Research Awards. **Frequency:** annual. **Type:** recognition. **Recipient:** for undergradu-

ates working on research projects. **Telecommunication Services:** electronic mail, gwhite@aip.org. **Affiliated With:** Society of Physics Students. **Publications:** *Radiations*, semiannual. Magazine. Alternate Formats: online ● *SPS Observer*. Newsletter. **Conventions/Meetings:** annual meeting - always September.

Political Science

23984 ■ Pi Sigma Alpha (PSA)
1527 New Hampshire Ave. NW
Washington, DC 20036-1203
Ph: (202)483-2512
Fax: (202)483-2657
E-mail: office@pisigmaalpha.org
URL: http://www.apsanet.org/~psa
Contact: Dr. James I. Lengle, Exec. Dir.
Founded: 1920. **Members:** 186,000. **Membership Dues:** life, individual, $30. **Staff:** 2. **Budget:** $200,000. **Local Groups:** 587. **Description:** Honor society - men and women, political science. **Awards:** Best Chapter Advisor Awards. **Frequency:** annual. **Type:** recognition. **Recipient:** to long-serving chapter advisors ● Best Chapter Awards. **Frequency:** annual. **Type:** monetary. **Recipient:** to chapters engaged in extraordinary levels of activity ● Best Paper Awards, Undergraduate. **Frequency:** annual. **Type:** recognition ● Best Undergraduate Honors Thesis. **Frequency:** annual. **Type:** recognition. **Recipient:** for members only ● Frank L. Burdette Award. **Frequency:** annual. **Type:** monetary. **Recipient:** for the best paper presented at the APSA annual meeting ● Scholarships for Graduate Study. **Frequency:** annual. **Type:** scholarship. **Recipient:** for members only. **Also Known As:** Pi Sigma Alpha, the National Political Science Honor Society. **Publications:** Newsletter, semiannual. **Price:** available to members only. **Conventions/Meetings:** biennial Business Meeting, held in conjunction with the American Political Science Association - in even numbered years.

Professions

23985 ■ Phi Delta Gamma
1201 Red Mile Rd.
PO Box 4599
Lexington, KY 40544-4599
Ph: (859)255-1848
Fax: (859)253-0779
E-mail: phigam@phigam.org
URL: http://www.phigam.org
Contact: William Martin III, Exec. Dir./Ed.
Founded: 1848. **Members:** 95,000. **Membership Dues:** active, $25 (annual) ● associate, $20 (annual). **Staff:** 1. **Budget:** $29,750. **Regional Groups:** 4. **State Groups:** 9. **Description:** Aims to promote friendships, to reaffirm high ethical standards and values, and to foster personal development in the pursuit of excellence. Provides opportunities to each brother to develop responsibility, leadership and social skills to become a fully contributing member of society. **Libraries:** **Type:** reference. **Holdings:** archival material. **Awards:** Academic Achievement Awards. **Type:** scholarship. **Recipient:** to newly initiated members who earn a 3.0 GPA during their pledging semester ● Peale Scholarship Grant. **Type:** scholarship. **Recipient:** for members choosing careers in the ministry. **Computer Services:** database, membership lists. **Committees:** Education Services. **Publications:** Newsletter, semiannual ● Membership Directory, periodic. **Conventions/Meetings:** biennial Ekklesia - convention and reunion.

23986 ■ Phi Delta Kappa
408 N Union St.
PO Box 789
Bloomington, IN 47402-0789
Ph: (812)339-1156
Free: (800)766-1156
Fax: (812)339-0018

E-mail: information@pdkintl.org
URL: http://www.pdkintl.org
Contact: William Bushaw, Exec. Dir.
Founded: 1902. **Members:** 2,518. **Description:** Serves as a professional fraternity of nonacademic (business and professional) men. Aims to promote quality education as essential to the development and maintenance of a democratic way of life by providing innovative programs, relevant research, visionary leadership, and dedicated service. **Publications:** *Edge*, bimonthly. Magazine. **Price:** $17.95 /year for members; $22.95 /year for nonmembers. Alternate Formats: online ● *PDK Connection*. Newsletter. Contains information on chapter activities. **Price:** free ● *Phi Delta Kappan*, monthly. Journal. **Price:** $58.00/year. **Conventions/Meetings:** annual conference.

Psychology

23987 ■ Psi Beta
c/o Jerry Rudmann, PhD, Exec. Dir.
8918 W 21st St. N, Ste.200, No. 179
Wichita, KS 67205
Free: (888)PSI-BETA
Fax: (714)265-7160
E-mail: jerry@psibeta.org
URL: http://www.psibeta.org
Contact: Jerry Rudmann PhD, Exec. Dir.
Founded: 1981. **Members:** 22,500. **Membership Dues:** life, $50. **Staff:** 2. **Budget:** $84,000. **Regional Groups:** 5. **Local Groups:** 160. **Description:** National honor society - recognizes outstanding achievement of community and junior college psychology students through the Federation of Local College Chapters. Participates in psychology conventions. Provides means for contact with professors in students' areas of interest. Conducts educational programs and sponsors national awards. Promotes excellence in scholarship, leadership, research and community service; a member of the Association of College Honor Societies. **Libraries:** Type: reference. **Holdings:** archival material, business records, periodicals. **Subjects:** psychology. **Awards:** Allyn and Bacon Research Paper Award. **Frequency:** annual. **Type:** monetary. **Recipient:** for 3 original empirical research papers written in APA style ● Ann G. Robinson College Life. **Frequency:** annual. **Type:** recognition. **Recipient:** for a unique promotion of the quality of 2-year college life that has advanced psychology and Psi Beta's mission ● Carol Tracy Community Service Award. **Frequency:** annual. **Type:** monetary. **Recipient:** for an outstanding community service project ● Harcourt College Publishers National Chapter Award. **Frequency:** annual. **Type:** monetary. **Recipient:** for an active chapter that has demonstrated outstanding programming ● Virginia Sexton Faculty Advisor Award. **Frequency:** annual. **Type:** recognition. **Recipient:** for an outstanding service as faculty advisor. **Computer Services:** database, membership. **Councils:** National. **Affiliated With:** American Psychological Association; Association of College Honor Societies; Association for Psychological Science. **Publications:** *Psi Beta Chapter Handbook*, annual. **Price:** $16.00/copy. **Circulation:** 200. Alternate Formats: CD-ROM ● Newsletter, semiannual. **Price:** included in membership dues; $5.00 /year for nonmembers. **Circulation:** 2,200. Alternate Formats: online. **Conventions/Meetings:** annual meeting, in conjunction with the American Psychological Association National Convention - annual business meeting, chapter programs, Innovative Teaching methods.

23988 ■ Psi Chi, the National Honor Society in Psychology
PO Box 709
825 Vine St.
Chattanooga, TN 37401-0709
Ph: (423)756-2044
Fax: (423)265-1529
E-mail: psichi@psichi.org
URL: http://www.psichi.org
Contact: Dr. Virginia Andreoli Mathie, Exec. Dir.
Founded: 1929. **Members:** 510,000. **Membership Dues:** active, $35. **Staff:** 6. **Budget:** $1,000,000.

Regional Groups: 7. Local Groups: 1,050. **Description:** Encourages, stimulates, and maintains excellence in scholarship, and advances the science of psychology. Functions as a federation of chapters located at senior colleges and universities in the USA and Canada. **Awards:** Psi Chi Awards and Grants. **Frequency:** annual. **Type:** recognition. **Recipient:** for Psi Chi members. **Computer Services:** database. **Affiliated With:** American Psychological Association; Association of College Honor Societies. **Publications:** *Eye on Psi Chi*, quarterly. Magazine. **Price:** included in membership dues. ISSN: 0033-2569 ● *Psi Chi Journal of Undergraduate Research*, quarterly. **Conventions/Meetings:** annual regional meeting.

Public Affairs

23989 ■ Pi Alpha Alpha (PAA)
c/o NASPAA
1029 Vermont Ave. NW, Ste.1100
Washington, DC 20005
Ph: (202)628-8965
Fax: (202)626-4978
E-mail: naspaa@naspaa.org
URL: http://www.naspaa.org/initiatives/honor.asp
Contact: Prof. Krishna K. Tummala, Pres.
Founded: 1974. **Members:** 28,754. **Membership Dues:** life, $30. **Staff:** 2. **Budget:** $40,000. **Local Groups:** 130. **Description:** Individuals who demonstrate academic achievement in public affairs and administration programs in member schools of the National Association of Schools of Public Affairs and Administration (see separate entry). Encourages and recognizes outstanding scholarship and accomplishment in public affairs and administration; fosters integrity, professionalism, and creative performance in the conduct of governmental and related public service activities. **Awards:** Chapter and Faculty Awards of Excellence. **Frequency:** annual. **Type:** recognition ● PAA Student Manuscript Award. **Frequency:** annual. **Type:** monetary. **Recipient:** to masters and doctoral students. **Affiliated With:** Association of College Honor Societies; National Association of Schools of Public Affairs and Administration. **Publications:** *PAA Handbook for Chapters* ● Journal. Alternate Formats: online. **Conventions/Meetings:** competition ● biennial meeting, held in conjunction with NASPAA Conference - always October.

Public Health

23990 ■ Delta Omega (DO)
c/o Allison Foster, Exec. Sec.
1101 15th St. NW, Ste.910
Washington, DC 20005
Ph: (202)296-1099
E-mail: afoster@asph.org
URL: http://www.deltaomega.org
Contact: Allison Foster, Exec. Sec.
Founded: 1924. **Members:** 4,000. **Membership Dues:** active, $40 (annual). **Regional Groups:** 18. **Local Groups:** 18. **Description:** Honorary society - men and women, public health. Promotes research and scholarly attainment; sponsors lectures. **Awards:** Social Justice in Public Health. **Frequency:** annual. **Type:** recognition. **Committees:** Awards; Chapter Relations; Governance; Publications. **Publications:** Annual Reports, annual ● Reports. **Conventions/Meetings:** periodic competition ● annual meeting, held in conjunction with American Public Health Association.

Religious Studies

23991 ■ Theta Chi Beta
Syracuse Univ.
Dept. of Religion
501 Hall of Languages
Syracuse, NY 13244-1170

Ph: (315)443-3861
Fax: (315)443-3958
E-mail: jpwaghor@syr.edu
Contact: Prof. Joanne Waghorne, Pres.
Founded: 1915. **Members:** 500. **Description:** Honorary society for faculty and students matriculated at Syracuse University who have excelled in religious studies. Recognizes members of the community for their support of religious studies. Provides funds to augment Syracuse University Library's collections in religious studies. Local chapter of National Honor Society for Religious Studies Theta Alpha Kappa. **Conventions/Meetings:** annual meeting - always spring, Syracuse, NY.

Scholarship

23992 ■ Astronaut Scholars Honor Society (ASHS)
c/o Linn LeBlanc, Exec. Dir., Astronaut Scholarship Foundation
6225 Vectorspace Blvd.
Titusville, FL 32780
Ph: (321)269-6101
Fax: (321)264-9176
E-mail: linn@astronautscholarship.org
URL: http://www.astronautscholars.org
Contact: Larry Bradley PhD, Pres.
Description: Provides educational outreach services to young students. Promotes research, inventions and career development in the field of science and technology. Enhances the knowledge and encourages exchange of information among individuals in science and engineering. **Awards:** Astronaut Scholarships. **Frequency:** annual. **Type:** scholarship. **Recipient:** to outstanding undergraduate and graduate level students in science and engineering. **Telecommunication Services:** electronic mail, webmaster@astronautscholarship.org. **Publications:** *Astronaut Scholars*, annual. Newsletter. Includes activities of past and present scholarship winners. Alternate Formats: online.

Science

23993 ■ Beta Kappa Chi (BKX)
c/o Ms. Deadra James Mackie, Exec. Sec.
PO Box 10046
Baton Rouge, LA 70813
Ph: (225)771-4845
E-mail: mzdjames@aol.com
URL: http://www.betakappachi.org
Contact: Ms. Deadra James Mackie, Exec. Sec.
Founded: 1923. **Members:** 11,871. **Membership Dues:** student, $35 (annual) ● faculty, $40 (annual). **Staff:** 1. **Budget:** $21,947. **Regional Groups:** 5. **Local Groups:** 61. **Description:** Serves as honor society for men and women, science and mathematics. **Awards:** Undergraduate Research Paper Awards. **Frequency:** annual. **Type:** recognition. **Recipient:** for quality of research, ability to present and to be understood by the students. **Councils:** Executive. **Publications:** *Beta Kappa*, semiannual. Newsletter. Contains news about chapters, members and national annual meeting. **Price:** included in membership dues; $35.00 for nonmembers. **Advertising:** accepted ● *The Bulletin*, quarterly. **Advertising:** accepted. **Conventions/Meetings:** annual Brookhaven Joint National Meeting, for graduate schools, scientific companies and government agencies (exhibits) - first week of April.

23994 ■ Lambda Delta Lambda (LDL)
Wayne State Coll.
Carhart Sci. Bldg.
1111 Main St.
Wayne, NE 68787
Ph: (402)375-7000
Free: (800)228-9972
Fax: (402)375-7441

E-mail: info@ldlucdavis.org
URL: http://ldlucdavis.org
Contact: David Peitz PhD, Advisor
Founded: 1925. **Members:** 50. **Description:** Honorary society - men and women, physical science. Supports, through local chapters, sciences open houses, scientific efforts including judging science fairs, promotion of society's planetarium, and small museum. Sponsors lectures. **Convention/Meeting:** none. **Awards: Type:** recognition. **Recipient:** for outstanding teachers. **Additional Websites:** http://wildcat.wsc.edu/clubs/ldl. **Telecommunication Services:** electronic mail, dapeitz1@wsc.edu.

23995 ■ Sigma Delta Epsilon, Graduate Women in Science (SDE/GWIS)

c/o Ms. Marie Drottar, Sec.
PO Box 291
Avon, MA 02322
Ph: (617)697-4947
E-mail: marie_drottar@msn.com
URL: http://www.gwis.org
Contact: Ms. Marie Drottar, Sec.
Founded: 1921. **Members:** 1,200. **Membership Dues:** regular, $50 (annual) ● graduate student, postdoc, emeritus, $20 (annual) ● life, $500. **Budget:** $31,000. **Description:** Professional organization of graduate women in science. Fosters research in science and seeks to increase the participation of women in science. Works to: improve science and mathematics education for women; encourage women with science degrees to enter the workforce; support study of the history of women in science; cooperate with organizations with similar goals; make use of the media to publicize the accomplishments of women in science. Conducts fundraising activities. **Awards:** Eloise Gerry Fellowship. **Frequency:** annual. **Type:** fellowship ● **Type:** recognition. **Committees:** Fellowships; Liaison with Women in Science Societies; Program Development. **Affiliated With:** American Association for the Advancement of Science. **Formerly:** (1977) Sigma Delta Epsilon. **Publications:** *Membership List*, biennial. Membership Directory. **Price:** included in membership dues ● Newsletter, 3/year. **Price:** included in membership dues ● Bulletin, 3/year. **Conventions/Meetings:** annual meeting and symposium - always summer ● annual meeting, held in conjunction with AAAS - always winter.

23996 ■ Sigma Xi, The Scientific Research Society

PO Box 13975
Research Triangle Park, NC 27709
Ph: (919)549-4691
Free: (800)243-6534
Fax: (919)549-0090
E-mail: memberinfo@sigmaxi.org
URL: http://www.sigmaxi.org
Contact: Dr. Philip Carter, Exec. Dir.
Founded: 1886. **Members:** 75,000. **Membership Dues:** regular, $67 (annual) ● student, $25 (annual) ● emeritus, $33 (annual) ● life, $1,350. **Staff:** 40. **Budget:** $5,500,000. **Local Groups:** 516. **Description:** Honorary society for men and women in scientific research. Sponsors national lecturers panel and national forums. **Awards:** Grants-in-Aid of Research. **Frequency:** semiannual. **Type:** grant. **Recipient:** to students from all areas of the sciences and engineering. **Computer Services:** Information services, archive of American scientist articles ● online services, various chapter services. **Absorbed:** (1974) Scientific Research Society of America. **Formerly:** (1978) Sigma Xi. **Publications:** *American Scientist*, bimonthly. Magazine. Includes explanations of research. **Price:** $28.00 individual in U.S.; $35.00 individual in Canada; $42.00 individual outside U.S. and Canada. ISSN: 0003-0996. **Circulation:** 90,044. **Advertising:** accepted ● *Conference Reports* ● *Forum Proceedings* ● *Honor in Science*. Books. Includes guide to ethics and values in research. **Price:** $3.00 ● *The Responsible Researcher: Paths and Pitfalls*. Booklet. Includes ethical issues that have arisen since Honor in Science was first published in 1984. **Price:** $3.00 ● *Science in the News*, daily or weekly. Newsletter. Includes summaries and links to

the top science and technology stories appearing in the mainstream media. **Price:** included in membership dues. **Conventions/Meetings:** annual conference, with workshops on leadership, major issues facing the research enterprise and chapter management (exhibits) ● annual meeting - 2007 Nov. 1-4, Orlando, FL.

23997 ■ Sigma Zeta

c/o Dr. Harold Wilkinson
Millikin Univ.
1184 W Main St.
Decatur, IL 62522
Ph: (651)638-6379
E-mail: hallj@lake.ollusa.edu
URL: http://www.sigmazeta.org
Contact: Jim Hall, Exec. Dir.
Founded: 1925. **Members:** 30,000. **Membership Dues:** student, $25 (annual). **Staff:** 2. **Budget:** $10,000. **Local Groups:** 51. **Description:** Honor society of men and women in science and mathematics. Maintains Sigma Zeta Development Fund. **Libraries: Type:** reference. **Holdings:** 55. **Subjects:** chapter information. **Awards:** Founders Cup Award. **Frequency:** annual. **Type:** recognition. **Recipient:** for local and national chapter involvement ● Sigma Zeta Honor Award. **Frequency:** annual. **Type:** recognition. **Computer Services:** Mailing lists, of members. **Publications:** *The Sigma Zetan*, annual. Journal. Contains information about awards, chapter activities, and convention minutes. **Price:** included in membership dues. **Circulation:** 1,000 ● Handbook. **Conventions/Meetings:** annual Millikin University Convention - conference, scientific research symposium.

Service Fraternities

23998 ■ Alpha Phi Alpha Fraternity

2313 St. Paul St.
Baltimore, MD 21218-5234
Ph: (410)554-0040
Fax: (410)554-0054
E-mail: admin@apa1906.net
URL: http://www.apa1906.net
Contact: Darryl R. Matthews Sr., Gen. Pres.
Founded: 1906. **Members:** 150,000. **Membership Dues:** alumni, $730 (annual) ● college freshman, $640 (annual) ● college sophomore, $565 (annual) ● college junior, $490 (annual) ● college senior, $415 (annual). **Staff:** 12. **Budget:** $1,800,000. **Regional Groups:** 5. **State Groups:** 46. **Local Groups:** 750. **National Groups:** 4. **Description:** Service fraternity founded for people of African descent; the organization has been interracial since 1945. **Computer Services:** Mailing lists. **Publications:** *Sphinx*, quarterly. Magazine. **Circulation:** 15,500. **Advertising:** accepted. Alternate Formats: online ● Directory, annual ● Reports. Alternate Formats: online. **Conventions/Meetings:** annual conference (exhibits) - always August ● biennial convention.

23999 ■ Alpha Phi Omega National Service Fraternity

14901 E 42nd St.
Independence, MO 64055-7347
Ph: (816)373-8667
Fax: (816)373-5975
E-mail: executive.director@apo.org
URL: http://www.apo.org
Contact: Robert London, Exec. Dir.
Founded: 1925. **Members:** 350,000. **Membership Dues:** individual, $55 (annual) ● one-time fee, $15. **Staff:** 8. **Budget:** $500,000. **Regional Groups:** 11. **State Groups:** 50. **Local Groups:** 350. **Description:** Fraternity - service. Works to provide service to campus, community, state, and nation. Provides educational program on leadership development for college students. **Awards:** Daily Point of Light. **Type:** recognition ● Point of Light Foundation. **Type:** recognition. **Boards:** Directors. **Publications:** *National Chapter Bulletin*, periodic ● *Torch and Trefoil*, quarterly. Magazine. **Price:** included in membership dues. **Conventions/Meetings:** biennial conference.

24000 ■ National Beta Club

151 Beta Club Way
Spartanburg, SC 29306-3012
Free: (800)845-8281
Fax: (864)542-9300
E-mail: jburnett@betaclub.org
URL: http://betaclub.org
Contact: Joan J. Burnett, Interim Exec. Dir./CEO
Founded: 1934. **Members:** 417,000. **Membership Dues:** student/junior high school, one-time fee, $13. **Staff:** 19. **Budget:** $3,500,000. **Local Groups:** 7,500. **Description:** Academic-Leadership-Service organization for students. Junior Beta Club includes fifth through ninth grade students; Senior Beta Club includes ninth through 12 grades. Activities and meetings focus on leadership, character development and community service. Local administrators of each school supervise the work of the club, the selection of members, and the operation of the chapter in their school. **Awards:** Beta Scholar Award. **Frequency:** annual. **Type:** scholarship. **Recipient:** for members who display academic excellence, leadership, and community service ● Harris Leadership Award. **Frequency:** annual. **Type:** medal. **Recipient:** for members who display outstanding leadership. **Publications:** *Beta Journal*, bimonthly. Features articles and club news. **Price:** included in membership dues. **Circulation:** 350,000 ● *Beta Reporter*, 5/year. Newsletter. **Conventions/Meetings:** annual convention and competition (exhibits) ● annual National Junior Beta Club Convention - competition ● annual State Conventions.

24001 ■ Phi Beta Sigma Fraternity

145 Kennedy St. NW
Washington, DC 20011-5294
Ph: (202)726-5434
Fax: (202)882-1681
E-mail: president@pbs1914.org
URL: http://www.pbs1914.org
Contact: Paul L. Griffin Jr., Pres.
Founded: 1914. **Members:** 120,000. **Staff:** 6. **Regional Groups:** 7. **Local Groups:** 629. **Description:** Service fraternity. Seeks to develop and translate into functional realities the ideals of brotherhood, service, and scholarship. Promotes three national programs: Bigger and Better Business; Education; Social Action. Offers placement service. **Projects:** National Outreach Foundation. **Subgroups:** Sigma Beta Club; Sigmas Waging War Against Cancer. **Publications:** *The Crescent*, semiannual. Magazine ● *The Crescent Extra*, periodic. Newsletter. **Conventions/Meetings:** annual Conclave - conference (exhibits) ● regional meeting - 7/year.

Service Sororities

24002 ■ Alpha Kappa Alpha (AKA)

5656 S Stony Island Ave.
Chicago, IL 60637
Ph: (773)684-1282
Fax: (773)288-8251
E-mail: exec@aka1908.com
URL: http://www.aka1908.com
Contact: Dr. Betty N. James, Exec. Dir.
Founded: 1908. **Members:** 140,000. **Budget:** $5,000,000. **Regional Groups:** 10. **Description:** Service sorority. Provides community services; compiles statistics. **Libraries: Type:** open to the public. **Subjects:** African-American history. **Awards:** Math and Science Camps. **Frequency:** biennial. **Type:** grant. **Recipient:** for students in grades 9-11 ● **Type:** recognition. **Programs:** Leadership Fellows (for undergraduates); Leadership Intern; Math and Science Camps. **Publications:** *Along the Ivy Line*, 2-3/year. Magazine ● *Ivy Leaf Quarterly*. Magazine. Contains feature stories, membership section, and obituaries. **Price:** included in membership dues; $12.00 /year for nonmembers. **Circulation:** 38,000. **Advertising:** accepted ● *The Ivy Vine*, 2-3/year ● Also publishes heritage series reading booklets and sorority history book. **Conventions/Meetings:** biennial conference, vendors, chapter and business recruitment exhibits (exhibits) - always summer.

24003 ■ Beta Sigma Phi
1800 W 91st Pl.
Kansas City, MO 64114
Ph: (816)444-6800
Free: (800)821-3989
Fax: (816)333-6206
E-mail: service@betasigmaphi.org
URL: http://www.betasigmaphi.org
Contact: Laura Ross Wingfield, Pres., Exec. Council
Founded: 1931. **Members:** 250,000. **Membership Dues:** regular, $24 (annual). **Staff:** 46. **Local Groups:** 11,520. **Description:** Acts as a social, service, and cultural society - all women over age 18. Operates charitable program. Works as a friendship organization. **Awards:** Walter W. Ross Memorial Scholarship. **Frequency:** annual. **Type:** scholarship. **Recipient:** to Beta Sigma Phi's and their children. **Computer Services:** Online services, bulletin board ● online services, download files ● online services, fee payment ● online services, gift orders ● online services, software marketing. **Departments:** Certification; Gifts; Service. **Publications:** The Torch, monthly. Magazine. **Conventions/Meetings:** annual convention and seminar - runs from April-October ● annual State and Province Meetings.

24004 ■ Delta Sigma Theta
1707 New Hampshire Ave. NW
Washington, DC 20009
Ph: (202)986-2400
Fax: (202)986-2513
E-mail: dstemail@deltasigmatheta.org
URL: http://www.deltasigmatheta.org
Contact: Ms. Louise Rice, Pres.
Founded: 1913. **Members:** 175,000. **Budget:** $2,000,000. **Regional Groups:** 7. **Description:** Serves as a public service sorority of Black women. Maintains Delta Research and Educational Foundation. **Committees:** Arts and Letters; Constitution and Bylaws; Heritage and Archives; Housing and Properties; Information and Communications; Program Planning; Scholarship and Standards; Social Action. **Publications:** The Delta, semiannual. Journal. **Price:** free. **Advertising:** accepted ● Delta Newsletter, quarterly. **Price:** free. **Advertising:** accepted ● Also publishes fact sheets. **Conventions/Meetings:** annual meeting (exhibits) ● regional meeting - 7/year.

24005 ■ Epsilon Sigma Alpha (ESA)
363 W Drake Rd.
Fort Collins, CO 80526
Ph: (970)223-2824
Fax: (970)223-4456
E-mail: esainfo@esaintl.com
URL: http://www.esaintl.com
Contact: B.J. Clark, Exec. Dir.
Founded: 1929. **Members:** 20,000. **Membership Dues:** traditional, collegiate, alumnus, $69 (annual) ● senior, $65 (annual) ● legacy, $15 (annual) ● men of ESA, Elan, debutante of ESA, $45 ● life, $650 ● senior, life, $550. **Budget:** $700,000. **Description:** Serves as a leadership service sorority. **Awards:** DIANA Award. **Frequency:** annual. **Type:** recognition. **Recipient:** to the most productive woman in each community ● Outstanding Youth Awards. **Frequency:** annual. **Type:** recognition. **Recipient:** for young people. **Councils:** International. **Also Known As:** ESA International. **Publications:** Jonquil, semiannual. Magazine. **Price:** included in membership dues ● Booklets ● Books ● Bulletins ● Handbooks ● Also publishes guides. **Conventions/Meetings:** annual meeting - always July.

24006 ■ Gamma Alpha Omega Sorority
PO Box 427
Tempe, AZ 85280
Ph: (641)985-5700
E-mail: communications@gammaalphaomega.com
URL: http://www.gammaalphaomega.com
Contact: Marcia A. Torres-Ruiz, Natl. Pres.
Founded: 1993. **Description:** Promotes leadership, scholarship and unity within the sisterhood. Aims to support Hispanic/Latino communities. Improves the education of members and the community at large.

24007 ■ Gamma Sigma Sigma
PO Box 248
Rindge, NH 03461
E-mail: president@gammasigmasigma.org
URL: http://www.gammasigmasigma.org
Contact: D'Ann Brosnahan, Natl. Pres.
Founded: 1952. **Members:** 3,500. **Membership Dues:** undergraduate, alumna, $35 (annual). **Staff:** 1. **Budget:** $250,000. **Regional Groups:** 7. **State Groups:** 20. **Local Groups:** 51. **Description:** Service sorority. Works with charitable organizations. **Awards:** Distinguished Service Award. **Frequency:** annual. **Type:** recognition. **Recipient:** for national involvement ● Ferraro Award. **Frequency:** annual. **Type:** recognition ● Linton Award. **Frequency:** annual. **Type:** recognition ● Powell Award. **Frequency:** annual. **Type:** recognition ● Frequency: annual. **Type:** recognition. **Recipient:** for outstanding service projects ● Scout Award. **Frequency:** annual. **Type:** recognition ● Service Merit Award. **Frequency:** annual. **Type:** recognition. **Recipient:** for outstanding chapters ● Volunteers of Distinction. **Frequency:** annual. **Type:** recognition ● Woman of the Year. **Frequency:** annual. **Type:** recognition. **Recipient:** for national involvement ● Zimmerman Award. **Frequency:** annual. **Type:** recognition. **Publications:** Perspectives, 3/year. Alternate Formats: online. **Conventions/Meetings:** biennial convention ● quarterly meeting (exhibits).

24008 ■ Pi Omicron National Sorority
Address Unknown since 2007
Founded: 1928. **Members:** 338. **Staff:** 1. **Regional Groups:** 1. **State Groups:** 2. **Local Groups:** 20. **National Groups:** 1. **Description:** Purposes are to: provide the opportunity for cultural growth through adult education; sponsor philanthropic projects; lend assistance for worthy and charitable causes. Awards annual scholarship. **Awards: Frequency:** annual. **Type:** scholarship. **Divisions:** Cities' Councils; District; State. **Publications:** The Pharos, semiannual. Newsletter. **Circulation:** 400. **Advertising:** not accepted. **Conventions/Meetings:** biennial meeting - always July.

24009 ■ Sigma Alpha
2713 Ubly Rd.
Bad Axe, MI 48413
E-mail: tsusig_2000@hotmail.com
URL: http://www.sigmaalpha.org
Contact: Jamie Foster, Pres.
Founded: 1978. **Members:** 6,000. **Regional Groups:** 14. **Local Groups:** 87. **Description:** Promotes the members in all facets of agriculture and strengthens the bonds of friendship among them. Strives for achievement in scholarship, leadership, and service, and furthers the development of excellence in women pursuing careers in agriculture. **Awards:** The Emerald Chapter Award. **Frequency:** annual. **Type:** recognition. **Recipient:** to chapters who have promptly submitted all forms, dues and required materials to national board by the due dates ● The Founders Cup Award. **Frequency:** annual. **Type:** trophy. **Recipient:** to the chapter with the highest national point system total for the previous school year; second and third place chapters are also recognized ● The Most Improved Scholarship Award. **Frequency:** annual. **Type:** recognition. **Recipient:** to the chapter with the most improved GPA over the previous year (fall term to fall term) ● The Outstanding Advisor Award. **Frequency:** annual. **Type:** recognition. **Recipient:** for dedication and support of an advisor to the Sigma Alpha Sorority at the collegiate level ● The Outstanding Leader Award. **Frequency:** annual. **Type:** monetary. **Recipient:** to an outstanding leader whose chapter nominates her based on extraordinary accomplishments in Sigma Alpha and elsewhere in her college experiences ● The Outstanding Professional Development Program Award. **Frequency:** annual. **Type:** monetary. **Recipient:** to the chapter with the most successful program of professional skill and knowledge development ● The Outstanding Scholarship Award. **Frequency:** annual. **Type:** recognition. **Recipient:** to the chapter with the highest GPA ● The Outstanding Service Award. **Frequency:** annual. **Type:** monetary. **Recipient:** to the

chapter with the most complete and successful overall service program. **Boards:** Sigma Alpha National Alumni. **Affiliated With:** American Agri-Women; Professional Fraternity Association. **Publications:** Emerald Times, 3/year. Newsletters. Alternate Formats: online. **Conventions/Meetings:** annual convention.

24010 ■ Sigma Gamma Rho Sorority
1000 Southill Dr., Ste.200
Cary, NC 27513
Ph: (919)678-9720
Free: (888)SGR-1922
Fax: (919)678-9721
E-mail: executivedirector@sgrho1922.org
URL: http://www.sgrho1922.org
Contact: Dr. Mynora J. Bryant, Intl. Grand Basileus
Founded: 1922. **Members:** 90,000. **Regional Groups:** 5. **Multinational. Description:** Community service sorority. Sponsors: Project Africa, providing African women with agricultural assistance; Project Reassurance, dealing with teen pregnancy; Teen and Town Vocational Guidance Workshops; the Vocational Guidance and Workshop Center, which provides activities for youth. Conducts competitions. Maintains hall of fame. **Committees:** Achievement and Awards; Health and Welfare; Legislative/Social Action; National Youth Projects; Public Relations; Scholarship. **Publications:** Aurora, quarterly. **Price:** included in membership dues. **Advertising:** accepted ● Behind These Doors, A Legacy ● Directory, periodic. **Conventions/Meetings:** biennial meeting (exhibits).

24011 ■ Zeta Phi Beta Sorority
1734 New Hampshire Ave. NW
Washington, DC 20009
Ph: (202)387-3103
Fax: (202)232-4593
E-mail: ihq@zphib1920.org
URL: http://www.zphib1920.org
Contact: Lois H. Sylver, Natl. Exec. Dir.
Founded: 1920. **Members:** 80,000. **Staff:** 8. **Budget:** $3,200,000. **Regional Groups:** 8. **State Groups:** 47. **Local Groups:** 700. **Description:** Service and social sorority. Maintains Zeta Phi Beta Sorority Educational Foundation. Maintains speakers' bureau and charitable program. **Libraries: Type:** not open to the public. **Awards:** Isabel M. Herson Scholarship in Education. **Frequency:** annual. **Type:** scholarship. **Recipient:** to graduate or undergraduate level students enrolled in a degree program in either elementary or secondary education ● Zora Neale Hurston Scholarship. **Frequency:** annual. **Type:** scholarship. **Recipient:** to graduate students pursuing a degree in anthropology or related fields. **Committees:** Economic Empowerment; Education; Health; U.S. Space Camp Youth. **Affiliated With:** March of Dimes Birth Defects Foundation; National Association for the Advancement of Colored People; National Urban League; United Negro College Fund. **Publications:** Archon, semiannual. Journal. Includes listing of employment opportunities. **Price:** included in membership dues ● National Headquarters Newsletter, quarterly ● Book ● Directory, annual. Provides membership activity information. ● Manuals. **Conventions/Meetings:** biennial meeting (exhibits) ● biennial National Boule - competition (exhibits).

Social Fraternities

24012 ■ Acacia
8777 Purdue Rd., Ste.225
Indianapolis, IN 46268
Ph: (317)872-8210
Free: (888)345-1904
Fax: (317)872-8213
E-mail: acacianat@acacia.org
URL: http://www.acacia.org
Contact: Darold W. Larson, Exec. Dir.
Founded: 1904. **Members:** 47,000. **Staff:** 6. **Budget:** $500,000. **Description:** Serves as a social fraternity. Sponsors Shriner's Burns Institute for Children. **Awards:** George F. Patterson Outstanding Alumnus Award. **Frequency:** annual. **Type:** recognition. **Re-**

cipient: for Acacia alumni. **Publications:** *TRIAD*, semiannual. Magazine. **Conventions/Meetings:** biennial Conclave and Leadership Academy - meeting.

24013 ■ Alpha Chi Rho (AXP)
109 Oxford Way
Neptune, NJ 07753
Ph: (732)869-1895 (732)988-0588
Fax: (732)988-5357
E-mail: hq@alphachiro.org
URL: http://www.alphachirho.org
Contact: Mr. Scott A. Carlson CPA, CEO/Natl. Sec.
Founded: 1895. **Members:** 20,000. **Staff:** 4. **Regional Groups:** 91. **Description:** Social fraternity. Maintains AXP Educational Foundation. **Awards:** Scholarships. **Frequency:** annual. **Type:** scholarship. **Recipient:** for members only. **Publications:** *AXP Alumni Directory*, quinquennial. Alternate Formats: CD-ROM ● *The Garnet and White*, quarterly. Magazine. **Conventions/Meetings:** biennial convention ● annual workshop.

24014 ■ Alpha Delta Gamma (ADG)
946 Sanders Dr.
St. Louis, MO 63126
E-mail: president@alphadeltagamma.org
URL: http://www.alphadeltagamma.org
Contact: James Smith, Natl. Pres.
Founded: 1924. **Members:** 8,000. **Membership Dues:** undergraduate, initiation, $300. **Staff:** 8. **Budget:** $5,000. **Local Groups:** 11. **Description:** Social fraternity. Promotes school involvement, scholastic development service programs, spiritual growth, and social interaction. Provides opportunities in leadership and business to develop well-rounded college graduates that will serve society. **Awards:** Alpha Delta Gamma Education Foundation Scholarship Award. **Frequency:** annual. **Type:** scholarship. **Computer Services:** database, membership. **Publications:** *Alphadelity*, semiannual. Newsletter. Contains alumni news. **Price:** free to all alumni. **Circulation:** 6,000 ● *Alumni Phone Directory*, periodic ● *Red Carnation*, monthly, during the school year. Newsletter. **Conventions/Meetings:** semiannual conference, includes leadership and chapter management training - always spring and fall ● annual convention.

24015 ■ Alpha Delta Phi
6126 Lincoln Ave.
Morton Grove, IL 60053
Ph: (847)965-1832
Fax: (847)965-1871
E-mail: office@alphadeltaphi.org
URL: http://www.alphadeltaphi.org
Contact: Mr. Jonathan C. Vick, Pres.
Founded: 1832. **Members:** 50,000. **Staff:** 2. **Budget:** $200,000. **Regional Groups:** 25. **Description:** Social fraternity. Sponsors literary competitions; maintains placement service, biographical archives, and museum. Conducts educational programs. **Awards:** **Type:** scholarship. **Publications:** *Xaipe*. Newsletter ● Directory, decennial. **Conventions/Meetings:** annual convention ● quarterly meeting.

24016 ■ Alpha Delta Pi
1386 Ponce de Leon Ave. NE
Atlanta, GA 30306
Ph: (404)378-3164
Fax: (404)373-0084
E-mail: info@alphadeltapi.com
URL: http://www.alphadeltapi.org
Contact: Linda Welch Ablard, Exec. Dir.
Founded: 1851. **Members:** 182,500. **Description:** Serves as a social sorority. **Awards:** Clasped Hands Fund Grant. **Frequency:** annual. **Type:** grant. **Recipient:** for needy alumnae ● Competitive Academic Scholarship. **Frequency:** annual. **Type:** scholarship. **Recipient:** for members of the Foundation in good academic standing. **Publications:** *Adelphean*, quarterly. Magazine. Alternate Formats: online ● *The Chronicle*. Newsletter. Features updates on the new policies and procedures, and other matters discussed by Grand Council. Alternate Formats: online ● *Delphi*, quarterly. Newsletter. Encompasses programming ideas for alumnae associations and the latest

information on alumnae policies and procedures. Alternate Formats: online ● *Mane Line*. Newsletter. Features updates of particular interest to current and former officers, including new and departing officers, marriages, births and deaths. Alternate Formats: online ● *Oracle*, monthly. Newsletter. Contains announcements and due dates. Alternate Formats: online. **Conventions/Meetings:** biennial convention (exhibits).

24017 ■ Alpha Epsilon Pi
8815 Wesleyan Rd.
Indianapolis, IN 46268-1171
Ph: (317)876-1913
Fax: (317)876-1057
E-mail: office@aepi.org
URL: http://www.aepi.org
Contact: Mr. Andrew S. Borans, Exec. Dir.
Founded: 1913. **Members:** 77,000. **Staff:** 11. **Regional Groups:** 36. **Local Groups:** 123. **Description:** Social fraternity. Maintains Alpha Epsilon Pi Foundation as philanthropic arm that awards scholarships, loans, and grants. **Publications:** *The Eye of the Lion*, monthly. Newsletter ● *The Lion*, quarterly. Magazine. ISSN: 1041-6935. **Circulation:** 25,000. **Advertising:** accepted ● *Playing It Safe*. Newsletter. Contains information on risk management. **Conventions/Meetings:** annual Anniversary Convention - usually August. 2013 Aug. 7-11, New York, NY.

24018 ■ Alpha Iota Omicron (AIO)
1040 Hampton St.
Atlanta, GA 30318
Ph: (850)832-8864
URL: http://www.aiogt.com
Contact: Pinkesh Patel, Contact
Founded: 1998. **Description:** Promotes brotherhood and South Asian culture. Provides networking and community service. Facilitates communication and cooperation among members.

24019 ■ Alpha Kappa Lambda (AKL)
4735 Statesmen Dr., Ste.F
Indianapolis, IN 46250
Ph: (317)585-4911
Fax: (317)585-4907
E-mail: nhq@akl.org
URL: http://www.akl.org
Contact: Jeremy Slivinski, Natl. Sec.
Founded: 1914. **Members:** 22,000. **Description:** Social fraternity. Sponsors The Alpha Kappa Lambda Educational Foundation. Maintains small library; compiles statistics. Is developing speakers' bureau. Encourages chapter visitations. **Awards:** **Type:** recognition. **Formerly:** (1914) Los Amigos. **Publications:** *AKL in Motion*, monthly ● *Alumni Directory*, periodic ● *Inside AKL*, quarterly. Alternate Formats: online ● *The Logos*, quarterly ● *The Truth and the Word* ● Newsletter, periodic. **Conventions/Meetings:** annual meeting - always August.

24020 ■ Alpha Lambda Tau International Social Fraternity
PO Box 400953
Las Vegas, NV 89140
Ph: (702)362-5276
Fax: (702)362-5276
E-mail: info@altfrat.org
URL: http://www.altfrat.org
Contact: Bro. Michael Knight, Natl. Sec.
Membership Dues: per semester, $50. **Multinational. Description:** Provides social, educational, financial, career and leadership development opportunities for gay, transgendered and bisexual male college students. Facilitates communication and fellowship among members. **Telecommunication Services:** electronic mail, alt@altfrat.org. **Publications:** *The Hyperion*. Newsletter. Alternate Formats: online.

24021 ■ Alpha Phi Delta (APD)
PO Box 200
Struthers, OH 44471
Ph: (330)755-1891

E-mail: apdoffice@apd.org
URL: http://www.apd.org
Contact: Evan Sottosanti, Natl. Pres.
Founded: 1914. **Members:** 15,200. **Membership Dues:** individual, one time fee, $160 ● undergraduate, alumnus, $25 (annual). **Staff:** 1. **Budget:** $125,000. **State Groups:** 22. **Local Groups:** 44. **Languages:** English, Italian. **Description:** Serves as a social fraternity for men. **Awards:** Most Improved Chapter. **Frequency:** annual. **Type:** recognition ● Outstanding Alumni. **Frequency:** annual. **Type:** recognition ● Outstanding Alumni Club. **Frequency:** annual. **Type:** recognition ● Outstanding Chapter. **Frequency:** annual. **Type:** recognition ● Outstanding Community Service. **Frequency:** annual. **Type:** recognition ● Outstanding Undergraduate. **Frequency:** annual. **Type:** recognition. **Committees:** Expansion; Legislative; Resolution; Undergraduate Coordinating. **Divisions:** Central Office; National Council. **Absorbed:** Il Circalo Italiano; Sigma Gamma Phi. **Publications:** *Alumni Directory*, quinquennial. **Price:** $29.95. **Circulation:** 1,000 ● *Chapter Letter*, 10/year ● *Dokime*, quinquennial ● *Ecce Signum: Annual Undergraduate Directory and Handbook*, annual. **Price:** $3.00. **Circulation:** 1,500 ● *History of Alpha Phi Delta Fraternity, 1914-1973*. Book ● *Kleos*, quarterly. Reports on educational materials concerning college and fraternity interests. **Price:** free for members. **Circulation:** 9,500 ● Manuals. Includes topics on chapter management, expansion, and rush procedures. **Conventions/Meetings:** annual convention ● annual Leadership School - meeting.

24022 ■ Alpha Psi Lambda National
PO Box A3152
Chicago, IL 60690-3512
E-mail: apsinbod@yahoo.com
URL: http://www.alphapsilambda.net
Contact: Michelle L. Maday, Natl. Pres.
Founded: 1985. **Description:** Hispanic individuals and individuals interested in Latin culture. Promotes leadership and communication skills. Encourages interaction of men and women from diverse cultural backgrounds. Sponsors career workshops and community clean-up programs. Conducts charitable programs and competitions. Participates in Hispanic Awareness Week. **Publications:** none. **Awards:** Chapter of the Year. **Frequency:** annual. **Type:** recognition. **Recipient:** for a promising chapter ● Hermana of the Year. **Frequency:** annual. **Type:** recognition. **Recipient:** for a promising female member ● Hermano of the Year. **Frequency:** annual. **Type:** recognition. **Recipient:** for a promising male member ● National Member of the Year. **Frequency:** annual. **Type:** recognition. **Recipient:** for an outstanding member ● National Scholarship. **Frequency:** annual. **Type:** scholarship. **Recipient:** for outstanding members.

24023 ■ Alpha Sigma Phi
710 Adams St.
Carmel, IN 46032
Ph: (317)843-1911
Fax: (317)843-2966
E-mail: drew@alphasigmaphi.org
URL: http://www.alphasigmaphi.org
Contact: Drew Thawley, Pres./CEO
Founded: 1845. **Members:** 65,000. **Staff:** 10. **Budget:** $1,250,000. **Local Groups:** 68. **Description:** Aims to better the Man, through the creation and perpetuation of brotherhood founded upon the values of character—Silence, Charity, Purity, Honor, Patriotism. Dedicated to be the co-curricular organization of choice for discerning undergraduate men, through the provision of an enriching brotherhood experience and a full range of character and leadership development opportunities that are: Relevant, Replicable, and Recognizable. Manages archives, museums and records. **Libraries: Type:** reference. **Holdings:** 25,000. **Subjects:** fraternal history, chapter history, member information. **Awards:** Alpha Gamma Upsilon Award. **Frequency:** biennial. **Type:** recognition. **Recipient:** to the chapter that has shown the most significant improvement in fulfilling the mission statement of the fraternity ● Frank F. Hargear Award. **Frequency:** annual. **Type:** recognition. **Recipient:** to

the member who exemplifies the mission statement of the fraternity in his daily actions ● Gary A. Anderson Award. **Frequency:** annual. **Type:** recognition. **Recipient:** to the chapter that best exemplifies the mission statement of the fraternity through its New Member Education Program ● Phi Pi Phi Award. **Frequency:** biennial. **Type:** recognition. **Recipient:** to the chapter that has demonstrated the most outstanding dedication to philanthropy or service. **Absorbed:** Alpha Gamma Upsilon; Alpha Kappa Pi; Phi Pi Phi. **Publications:** *Brotherhood Bulletin*, monthly. Newsletter. **Circulation:** 700 ● *The Tomahawk*, quarterly. **Circulation:** 37,500. **Conventions/Meetings:** annual National Leadership Conference - always August.

24024 ■ Alpha Tau Omega (ATO)
One N Pennsylvania St., 12th Fl.
Indianapolis, IN 46204
Ph: (317)684-1865
Fax: (317)684-1862
E-mail: wsmiley@ato.org
URL: http://www.ato.org
Contact: Wynn R. Smiley, CEO
Founded: 1865. **Members:** 185,000. **Staff:** 20. **Budget:** $2,100,000. **Local Groups:** 140. **Description:** Social and leadership development fraternity. **Libraries: Type:** reference. **Holdings:** 650; archival material, books. **Awards:** Gold and Silver Communication Award. **Frequency:** annual. **Type:** recognition ● **Type:** scholarship ● Thomas Arkle Clark Award. **Type:** fellowship. **Recipient:** for the most outstanding senior candidates with undergraduate degrees ● True Merit Award. **Frequency:** annual. **Type:** recognition. **Recipient:** for best chapters. **Additional Websites:** http://www.atoroadshow.org, http://www.joinato.org. **Publications:** *Alpha Tau Omega Alumni Directory*, quinquennial ● *ATO Leader*, biweekly ● *The Palm of Alpha Tau Omega*, semiannual. **Conventions/Meetings:** biennial meeting.

24025 ■ Beta Chi Theta National Fraternity
9663 Santa Monica Blvd., Ste.498
Beverly Hills, CA 90210
Fax: (208)445-4949
E-mail: feedback@betachitheta.com
URL: http://www.betachitheta.com
Contact: Mujteba Naqvi, Pres.
Founded: 1999. **Local Groups:** 11. **Description:** Represents South Asian community. Facilitates social, political, business and personal interactions within the brotherhood. Promotes academic excellence and South Asian awareness. Advances knowledge and appreciation of South Asian culture and heritage.

24026 ■ Beta Sigma Psi National Lutheran Fraternity
2408 Lebanon Ave.
Belleville, IL 62221
Ph: (618)235-0014
Fax: (618)235-0051
E-mail: office@betasigmapsi.org
URL: http://www.betasigmapsi.org
Contact: Mr. Chad Pfister, Pres.
Founded: 1925. **Members:** 7,500. **Membership Dues:** college, $140 (annual) ● alumni group, $150 (annual). **Staff:** 1. **Budget:** $50,000. **Regional Groups:** 1. **Local Groups:** 20. **Description:** Social fraternity. Provides an environment in which the Lutheran college man can grow spiritually, scholastically, and socially. Undertakes programs to develop Christian leaders and to aid the individual in assuming a satisfying and useful role in society. Through its alumni and undergraduate leadership, Beta Sigma Psi endeavors to assist each member develop character, intellectual awareness, responsibility to chapter, college, community, state, nation, and world, spiritual welfare, brotherhood, integrity; promote friendship and advance justice. Sponsors numerous national and regional meetings for collegiate and alumni members. In addition, Beta Sigma Psi offers education programs for its members in areas ranging from leadership to scholarship to spiritual building to recruitment. **Awards:** Alumni Pastoral Scholarship. **Frequency:** annual. **Type:** scholarship. **Recipient:** to

seminary students who are Beta Sigma Psi alumni ● Alumni Volunteer Service Award. **Frequency:** annual. **Type:** recognition. **Recipient:** to alumni who significantly impact a collegiate chapter, alumni chapter, national committee or national board ● At-large Pastoral Scholarship. **Frequency:** annual. **Type:** scholarship. **Recipient:** to first year seminary students ● Baehr Award. **Frequency:** annual. **Type:** recognition. **Recipient:** to the active chapter/colony producing and displaying the best scrapbook ● Edwards Award. **Frequency:** annual. **Type:** recognition. **Recipient:** to the active chapter exhibiting the best overall management ● Erck Award. **Frequency:** annual. **Type:** recognition. **Recipient:** to the outstanding active member of the Beta Sigma Psi ● Founders' Cup. **Frequency:** annual. **Type:** recognition. **Recipient:** to the active chapter/colony deemed to have the best member education program ● Governor Norbert T. Tiemann Award. **Frequency:** annual. **Type:** recognition. **Recipient:** for a lifetime of exceptional accomplishment in professional endeavors ● Hingst Award. **Frequency:** annual. **Type:** recognition. **Recipient:** to the active chapter or colony that exhibits the top scholastic achievement in the National Fraternity ● Lienemann Award. **Frequency:** annual. **Type:** recognition. **Recipient:** for outstanding service to the fraternity ● Luther Award. **Frequency:** annual. **Type:** recognition. **Recipient:** to a person devoting service to the Lutheran Church ● Welge Award. **Frequency:** annual. **Type:** recognition. **Recipient:** to the active chapter/colony deemed to have the best recruitment program. **Computer Services:** Mailing lists. **Committees:** National Awards; Nominating; Vision for the Future. **Councils:** National Council of Beta Sigma Psi. **Affiliated With:** North-American Interfraternity Conference. **Formerly:** Beta Sigma Psi. **Publications:** *The Gold Rose of Beta Sigma Psi*, 3/year. Magazine. **Circulation:** 7,500. **Advertising:** accepted. **Conventions/Meetings:** biennial convention.

24027 ■ Beta Theta Pi
PO Box 6277
5134 Bonham Rd.
Oxford, OH 45056
Ph: (513)523-7591
Free: (800)800-2382
Fax: (513)523-2381
E-mail: beta@betathetapi.org
URL: http://www.betathetapi.org
Contact: Mr. Stephen B. Becker CAE, Admin. Sec./ Chief Admin. Off.
Founded: 1839. **Members:** 113,000. **Membership Dues:** individual, $265. **Staff:** 28. **Budget:** $2,900,000. **National Groups:** 146. **Description:** Social fraternity. Promotes academic excellence, mutual assistance, friendship, loyalty and brotherhood. **Libraries: Type:** open to the public. **Holdings:** 2,100; books, periodicals. **Subjects:** fraternity history. **Awards:** Beta Foundation Merit Scholarships. **Frequency:** annual. **Type:** scholarship. **Recipient:** for undergraduate and graduate student members of the fraternity ● Beta of the Week. **Frequency:** weekly. **Type:** recognition. **Recipient:** for individuals' accomplishments and achievements ● Francis W. Shepardson Award. **Frequency:** annual. **Type:** recognition. **Recipient:** to brothers who embody the spirit and dedication of Brother Shepardson and epitomize the concept of life long service to the fraternity ● Oxford Cup. **Frequency:** semiannual. **Type:** recognition. **Recipient:** for members of Beta Theta Pi who have brought honor to the fraternity through distinguished service and accomplishments in their chosen professional fields ● Sisson Award. **Frequency:** annual. **Type:** recognition. **Computer Services:** Online services, Beta jukebox. **Committees:** Alumni Affairs; Chapters; Constitution and Jurisprudence; Credentials; Miscellaneous Affairs; Permanent Organization; Registration; Risk Management. **Publications:** *Graphics Manual*. Alternate Formats: online ● *Son of the Stars*. Manual. **Price:** $10.00 plus shipping and handling ● *Songs of Beta Theta Pi*. Book. Alternate Formats: online ● *Style Guide*. Manual ● Magazine, quarterly. **Price:** $30.00. **Circulation:** 95,000. **Advertising:** accepted. Alter-

nate Formats: online. **Conventions/Meetings:** annual convention (exhibits) - always August.

24028 ■ Chi Phi
850 Indian Trail Rd. NW
Lilburn, GA 30047
Ph: (404)231-1824
Fax: (404)237-5090
E-mail: azarian@chiphi.org
URL: http://www.chiphi.org
Contact: Michael Azarian, Exec. Dir.
Founded: 1824. **Membership Dues:** undergraduate, $75 (annual). **Regional Groups:** 7. **Description:** Social fraternity. Supports and participates in national fundraising dealing with all facets of the environment. **Awards:** Chi Phi Scholarship. **Frequency:** annual. **Type:** scholarship. **Recipient:** to deserving undergraduate and graduate members ● Sparks Memorial Medal. **Frequency:** annual. **Type:** medal. **Recipient:** to the man having the highest G.P.A in each chapter and colony. **Councils:** Grand. **Programs:** College of Excellence; Scholarship. **Publications:** *The Chi Phi Chakett*, quarterly. Magazine. Contains alumni and undergraduate items of interest. **Price:** free, for members only. Alternate Formats: online. **Conventions/Meetings:** annual College of Excellence - meeting, leadership school ● semiannual convention.

24029 ■ Chi Psi
147 Maple Row Blvd., Ste.200
Hendersonville, TN 37075
Ph: (615)736-2520
Fax: (615)736-2366
E-mail: co@chipsi.org
URL: http://www.chipsi.org
Contact: Samuel C. Bessey, Exec. Dir.
Founded: 1841. **Members:** 28,000. **Staff:** 5. **Regional Groups:** 15. **Local Groups:** 30. **Description:** Social fraternity. Maintains Chi Psi Educational Trust. Conducts leadership institutes and self-development programs. Operates speakers' bureau and museum. Provides placement services. **Libraries: Type:** reference. **Holdings:** 2,000; archival material. **Awards:** Alumni Recognition Award. **Frequency:** annual. **Type:** recognition. **Recipient:** to alumni members of Chi Psi for continued loyalty and service to the Alpha and the fraternity ● Financial Honor Roll. **Frequency:** annual. **Type:** recognition. **Recipient:** to Alphas who have maintained a budget surplus for the year and displayed fiscal responsibility in all areas of management ● Founders Trophy. **Frequency:** annual. **Type:** trophy. **Recipient:** to Alpha who has made the most significant improvement during the school term ● Goodbody Award. **Frequency:** annual. **Type:** recognition. **Recipient:** to Alpha whose scholastic average compares most favorably with the all men's average on campus and makes the best use of Educational Trust's programs ● Hiram L. Kennicott Literary Award. **Frequency:** annual. **Type:** recognition. **Recipient:** to Alphas who have maintained excellent communications with their alumni directly ● Robert C. Pueble, Jr. Alumnus of the Year Award. **Frequency:** annual. **Type:** recognition. **Recipient:** to Chi Psi alumnus for an exemplary service to or performance of a special project for the Chi Psi Educational Trust ● Stanley Birge Award. **Frequency:** annual. **Type:** recognition. **Recipient:** to a graduating brother for an exemplary service to the fraternity ● Thayer Trophy. **Frequency:** annual. **Type:** trophy. **Recipient:** to Alpha who has made the most outstanding performance in the previous school year, in all areas. **Committees:** Educational Trust Trustees. **Funds:** Alpha Building. **Programs:** Alpha Management Retreat; Career Guidance; Leadership Development; Mentorship; Risk Management Retreat; Self Development. **Publications:** *Chi Psi Membership Directory*, quinquennial ● *Chi Psi Update*, monthly. Newsletter. Alternate Formats: online ● *The Purple and Gold*, quarterly. Magazine. Includes calendar of events. **Price:** included in membership dues. **Circulation:** 20,000. **Conventions/Meetings:** regional meeting - 5/year ● annual Spencer Leadership Institute - convention (exhibits) - always August. 2008 Aug., Hoboken, NJ.

24030 ■ Delta Kappa Epsilon (DKE)
PO Box 17310
Richmond, VA 23226

Ph: (804)330-4040
Free: (800)560-3353
Fax: (202)478-0374
E-mail: dekehq@hotmail.com
URL: http://www.dke.org
Contact: David K. Easlick Jr., Exec. Dir.
Founded: 1844. **Members:** 70,000. **Membership Dues:** alumni, $75 (annual). **Staff:** 3. **Description:** Social fraternity. Provides counseling and advice to undergraduate and alumni groups on chapter operation and management. **Awards:** Lion Trophy. **Frequency:** annual. **Type:** trophy. **Recipient:** to outstanding chapter performance ● **Frequency:** annual. **Type:** recognition. **Recipient:** for undergraduate and alumni ● William M. Henderson Award. **Type:** recognition. **Recipient:** for alumni. **Computer Services:** database, alumni listing by chapter and geographical area. **Publications:** *The Deke Quarterly* ● *Delta Kappa Epsilon Alumni Directory*, every 4-5 years ● Also publishes chapter guides and manuals. **Conventions/Meetings:** annual meeting - always June/July.

24031 ■ Delta Lambda Phi National Social Fraternity
2020 Pennsylvania Ave. NW, No. 355
Washington, DC 20006-1811
Ph: (202)558-2295
Free: (800)587-FRAT
Fax: (202)318-2277
E-mail: nationaloffice@dlp.org
URL: http://www.dlp.org
Contact: Russell Martin, Natl. Sec.
Founded: 1986. **Members:** 1,500. **Membership Dues:** active, $250 (annual) ● new, $265. **Staff:** 1. **Budget:** $10,000. **Local Groups:** 22. **Description:** Social fraternity promoting purposeful and dignified social service and recreational activities for progressive men, irrespective of sexual orientation. **Computer Services:** database. **Formerly:** (2001) Delta Lambda Phi. **Publications:** *Chapter Handbook*, annual. **Price:** included in membership dues ● *Delta Lambda Phi*, quarterly. Newsletter. **Price:** free for members. **Circulation:** 1,000. **Conventions/Meetings:** annual Delta Force - general assembly (exhibits) - always July.

24032 ■ Delta Phi
PO Box 81521
Athens, GA 30608-1521
Ph: (706)552-1444
Fax: (706)552-5444
E-mail: natl_hq@deltaphi.org
URL: http://www.deltaphi.org
Contact: Stu Gittelman, Exec. Dir.
Founded: 1827. **Members:** 7,700. **Membership Dues:** undergraduate brother, $20 (annual). **Description:** Social fraternity. **Publications:** *Delta Phi Record*, periodic ● *The Oracle*. Book. **Price:** $12.50. **Conventions/Meetings:** annual meeting.

24033 ■ Delta Psi
PO Box 876
Ithaca, NY 14851-0876
Ph: (607)533-9994
Free: (888)850-9349
Fax: (607)533-9218
E-mail: stanthony@clarityconnect.com
URL: http://www.deltapsi.org
Contact: Liz Kinast, Exec. Sec.
Founded: 1847. **Members:** 6,000. **Regional Groups:** 10. **Description:** Serves as a social and literary fraternity. **Additional Websites:** http://www.stanthonyhall.org. **Publications:** *Blue Book*, decennial ● Newsletter, semiannual. **Conventions/Meetings:** annual meeting.

24034 ■ Delta Sigma Pi
330 S Campus Ave.
Oxford, OH 45056-0230
Ph: (513)523-1907
Fax: (513)523-7292
E-mail: centraloffice@dspnet.org
URL: http://www.dspnet.org
Contact: William Schilling, Exec. Dir.
Founded: 1907. **Members:** 202,000. **Membership Dues:** life, $65. **Staff:** 14. **Local Groups:** 186. **Description:** Professional fraternity - commerce and business administration. Operates Delta Sigma Pi Leadership Foundation. Maintains museum; sponsors competitions; offers computerized services; compiles statistics. Provides educational and career assistance. **Libraries: Type:** reference. **Awards:** Career Achievement Award. **Frequency:** annual. **Type:** recognition. **Recipient:** for sustained contributions of major importance and numerous accomplishments within a career ● Chapter Advisor of the Year. **Frequency:** annual. **Type:** recognition ● Collegian of the Year. **Frequency:** annual. **Type:** recognition. **Recipient:** for an undergraduate member whose achievements and leadership reflect the highest ideals of the fraternity ● District Director of the Year. **Frequency:** annual. **Type:** recognition ● Lifetime Achievement. **Frequency:** annual. **Type:** recognition. **Recipient:** for sustained contributions of importance to the national fraternity. **Computer Services:** database ● online services, marketplace; event registration and donation online; index of Deltasig newsletters and magazines. **Committees:** Alumni Development; Community Service; Nominations; Organizational Development. **Publications:** *The Deltasig*, quarterly. Magazine ● *DSP News*, monthly. Newsletters. Includes updates and reminders of upcoming events and deadlines. **Price:** $1.00. **Alternate Formats:** online. **Conventions/Meetings:** biennial Grand Chapter Congress - convention, meeting of the supreme governing body of Delta Sigma Pi; election of leaders.

24035 ■ Delta Upsilon
PO Box 68942
Indianapolis, IN 46268-0942
Ph: (317)875-8900
Fax: (317)876-1629
E-mail: ihq@deltau.org
URL: http://www.deltau.org
Contact: Dave Maguire, Exec. Dir.
Founded: 1834. **Members:** 110,000. **Staff:** 16. **Budget:** $1,100,000. **Local Groups:** 80. **Multinational. Description:** Men's non-secret social fraternity. Provides educational programming, service opportunities, social activities, and life skills training. Operates biographical archives and museum. Compiles statistics and resources. **Libraries: Type:** open to the public. **Holdings:** 2,800. **Subjects:** members of Delta Upsilon, fraternity issues. **Awards:** Distinguished Alumni Awards. **Frequency:** annual. **Type:** recognition. **Recipient:** for extraordinary contributions to the community and profession ● Sweepstake Awards. **Frequency:** annual. **Type:** recognition. **Recipient:** for the best Delta Upsilon chapter in North America. **Computer Services:** database ● mailing lists ● online services. **Publications:** *Delta Upsilon Quarterly*. Magazine. Includes fraternity news, industry trends, and alumni information. **Circulation:** 65,000. **Advertising:** accepted ● *Manual of Delta Upsilon*, periodic. **Conventions/Meetings:** annual Leadership Institute - conference, with educational program and legislative meeting - always late summer ● annual President's Academy - conference.

24036 ■ Farmhouse
11020 NW Ambassador Dr., Ste.330
Kansas City, MO 64153
Ph: (816)891-9445
Fax: (816)891-0838
E-mail: fhhq@farmhouse.org
URL: http://www.farmhouse.org
Contact: Jim Griffith CAE, Fraternity Exec. Dir.
Founded: 1905. **Members:** 20,000. **Staff:** 5. **Description:** Serves as a social fraternity. **Publications:** *Pearls and Rubies*, quarterly. Magazine. **Conventions/Meetings:** biennial meeting.

24037 ■ Groove Phi Groove, Social Fellowship
PO Box 8337
Silver Spring, MD 20907
E-mail: info@groove-phi-groove.org
URL: http://www.groove-phi-groove.org
Contact: Chris S. Tomlinson, Gen. Counsel
Founded: 1962. **Members:** 15,000. **Regional Groups:** 12. **Local Groups:** 42. **Description:** Aims to promote academic achievement; to develop creative and effective leadership; to integrate the social, religious, business, civic, and cultural phases of life through interaction and mutually beneficial activity without regard to race, creed, or color. Attempts to study and help solve problems confronting society, especially those of the African-American, in order to uplift and enhance community stature and citizenry. Aims to create a climate of goodwill, brotherhood, and friendship among members and nonmembers, and to "keep alive within the college graduate an interest in college life and the progressive movement emanating there from". **Publications:** *Sword and Spear*, periodic. Newsletter. **Alternate Formats:** online.

24038 ■ Kappa Alpha Order
PO Box 1865
Lexington, VA 24450
Ph: (540)463-1865
Fax: (540)463-2140
E-mail: lswiese@ka-order.org
URL: http://www.ka-order.org
Contact: Larry S. Wiese, Exec. Dir.
Founded: 1865. **Members:** 125,000. **Membership Dues:** regular, $240 (annual). **Staff:** 18. **Budget:** $1,300,000. **Regional Groups:** 21. **Local Groups:** 124. **Description:** Social fraternity. Compiles statistics; maintains biographical records archives and museum. Conducts drug and alcohol awareness programs; operates speakers' bureau. Sponsors competitions. Maintains charitable program. **Libraries: Type:** reference. **Holdings:** 200; archival material, articles, biographical archives, books, papers, photographs. **Subjects:** history of Kappa Alpha, Robert E. Lee, books written by individuals who are KA's. **Awards: Type:** recognition. **Recipient:** to a chapter that meets all the requirements ● **Frequency:** annual. **Type:** scholarship. **Computer Services:** database, names of all members and gift giving accounts ● mailing lists. **Publications:** *Alumni Directory*, periodic ● *History of Kappa Alpha Order*. Book ● *Kappa Alpha Journal*, quarterly ● *Varlet*, annual. Manual. Contains the history of the Kappa Alpha Order. **Conventions/Meetings:** biennial convention, national; for all alumnus and undergraduates; election of new executive council (exhibits).

24039 ■ Kappa Alpha Psi Fraternity
2322-24 N Broad St.
Philadelphia, PA 19132
Ph: (215)228-7184
Fax: (215)228-7181
E-mail: executive_director@kappaalphapsi1911.com
URL: http://www.kappaalphapsi1911.com
Contact: Mr. Richard Lee Snow, Exec. Dir./Chief Operating Off.
Founded: 1911. **Members:** 150,000. **Membership Dues:** alumni, $150 (annual) ● undergraduate, $75 (annual). **Staff:** 10. **Regional Groups:** 12. **Local Groups:** 700. **Multinational. Description:** Social fraternity. Sponsors charitable and educational programs and children's services. Maintains speakers' bureau and placement service; compiles statistics. **Libraries: Type:** reference; by appointment only; open to the public. **Holdings:** archival material, articles, books, periodicals, photographs, video recordings. **Awards: Type:** recognition ● **Type:** scholarship. **Publications:** *Confidential Bulletin*, quarterly ● *The Story of Kappa Alpha Psi* ● Journal, quarterly. **Conventions/Meetings:** biennial Grand Chapter Meeting - conference (exhibits).

24040 ■ Kappa Alpha Society
PO Box 876
Ithaca, NY 14851-0876
Free: (877)895-1825
Fax: (607)533-9218
E-mail: kas@alumnirecords.org
URL: http://www.ka.org
Contact: Sean H. Griffin, Admin.
Founded: 1825. **Members:** 5,000. **Staff:** 3. **Regional Groups:** 11. **Description:** Serves as a social fraternity. **Libraries: Type:** not open to the public. **Formerly:** (1997) Kappa Alpha. **Publications:** *Kap Key*, periodic. Newsletter. **Circulation:** 5,000 ● Newslet-

ter, semiannual. **Conventions/Meetings:** annual Concilium - meeting ● annual New York Dinner - meeting.

24041 ■ Kappa Delta Rho
331 S Main St.
Greensburg, PA 15601-3111
Ph: (724)838-7100
Free: (800)536-KDR1
Fax: (724)838-7101
E-mail: info@kdr.com
URL: http://www.kdr.com
Contact: Joseph Rees II, Exec. Dir.
Founded: 1905. **Members:** 23,000. **Membership Dues:** active, $220 (annual). **Staff:** 5. **Budget:** $475,000. **Regional Groups:** 41. **State Groups:** 3. **Description:** Social fraternity. Strives for promotion of Greek life and/or the fraternity. Maintains Kappa Delta Rho Foundation that generates scholarship grants for Kappa Delta Rho undergraduates. Funds leadership training programs. **Awards:** Ordo Honoris. **Frequency:** annual. **Type:** recognition. **Recipient:** for outstanding alumni who have shown exceptional involvement with the fraternity. **Publications:** *Kappa Delta Rho Alumni Directory*, quinquennial. Membership Directory ● *National Office Memorandum*, periodic ● *Quill and Scroll*, biennial ● *Sentry of Kappa Delta Rho*, monthly. Newsletter. **Conventions/Meetings:** annual Williams Leadership Academy - conference - usually in August.

24042 ■ Kappa Sigma
PO Box 5066
Charlottesville, VA 22905-5066
Ph: (434)295-3193
Fax: (434)296-9557
E-mail: mic@hq.kappasigma.org
URL: http://www.kappasigma.org
Contact: Mitchell B. Wilson, Exec. Dir.
Founded: 1869. **Members:** 230,000. **Staff:** 23. **Regional Groups:** 210. **State Groups:** 210. **Local Groups:** 210. **Description:** Serves as a social fraternity. **Libraries: Type:** reference. **Holdings:** 400; books. **Subjects:** fraternity and members. **Awards:** John Tower Award. **Frequency:** annual. **Type:** recognition. **Recipient:** for a member who brings great honor to Kappa Sigma Fraternity ● Man of the Year. **Frequency:** annual. **Type:** recognition. **Recipient:** for individual who has accomplished significant achievement ● Scholarship/Leadership Awards. **Frequency:** annual. **Type:** scholarship. **Recipient:** for academic and campus/community fraternity involvement. **Computer Services:** Mailing lists, of members. **Funds:** Kappa Sigma Endowment. **Subgroups:** Kappa Sigma Memorial Foundation. **Publications:** *Bononia Docet.* Manual. Features historical, operational and instructional information important to members. **Price:** $5.00. Alternate Formats: online ● *Caduceus*, quarterly. Magazine. Covers news and events of interest to members. ISSN: 1071-6491. Alternate Formats: online ● *Chapter Operations Letter - District Grand Masters Update*, bimonthly ● *Kappa Sigma, A History: 1869-1929.* Book. **Price:** $7.00 ● *Kappa Sigma Directory*, quinquennial ● *Star and Crescent*, quarterly. **Conventions/Meetings:** biennial Conclave - meeting.

24043 ■ Lambda Chi Alpha
8741 Founders Rd.
Indianapolis, IN 46268-1389
Ph: (317)803-7329 (317)803-7339
Fax: (317)875-3828
E-mail: mbauer@lambdachi.org
URL: http://www.lambdachi.org
Contact: Mark A. Bauer, Pres./CEO
Founded: 1909. **Members:** 230,000. **Staff:** 38. **Budget:** $6,000,000. **Regional Groups:** 215. **Description:** General Fraternity. Maintains hall of fame and museum. Founder of the North American Food Drive, which raises more than 1 million pounds of food each year for the needy. **Libraries: Type:** not open to the public. **Holdings:** 500; archival material, books, periodicals. **Subjects:** fraternal history. **Awards:** Bruce Hunter McIntosh Standards for Chapter Excellence Award. **Frequency:** annual. **Type:** recognition. **Recipient:** to chapters that effectively utilize the

standard program ● Graduate Fellowship. **Frequency:** annual. **Type:** scholarship. **Recipient:** to graduate students ● Lewis A. Plourd Fraternity Education Award. **Frequency:** annual. **Type:** recognition. **Recipient:** to chapters whose education programs exemplify excellence ● Order of Interfraternity Service. **Frequency:** biennial. **Type:** recognition. **Recipient:** for an extensive service to fraternal organizations. **Computer Services:** Mailing lists, services for chapters, alumni associations. **Committees:** Impact Leadership Steering. **Special Interest Groups:** Educational Foundation; Lambda Chi Alpha Educational Foundation. **Absorbed:** (1939) Theta Kappa Nu. **Publications:** *Alumni Connections.* Newsletter ● *Cross and Crescent*, quarterly. Magazine. **Price:** $3.00. ISSN: 1930-1278. **Circulation:** 120,000. **Advertising:** accepted. Alternate Formats: online ● *Fraternity Manual.* Alternate Formats: online ● *The Traveler.* Newsletter ● *Update.* Newsletter. Alternate Formats: online ● Bulletin, weekly. Contains news on the activities taking place in the fraternity. Alternate Formats: online ● The Crossed Swords, Emphasis on Recruitment, Updates, Dialogs in Financial Planning the Paedagogus. **Conventions/Meetings:** semiannual assembly, determines fraternity codes and statutes (exhibits) ● annual Educational and Leadership Conclave - workshop, leadership development and training ● annual Leadership Seminar, leadership training conference.

24044 ■ Omega Gamma Delta
89 Longview Rd.
Port Washington, NY 11050-3039
Ph: (516)883-0159
E-mail: rstarleton@aol.com
Contact: Robert Tarleton, Pres.
Founded: 1902. **Members:** 25,000. **Membership Dues:** initiation fee, $25 ● alumni, $10 (annual). **Local Groups:** 106. **Description:** High school men's social fraternity and associated alumni organization. Conducts charitable programs. **Libraries: Type:** reference. **Holdings:** archival material. **Subjects:** history of organization. **Awards:** Gar Davidson Award. **Frequency:** annual. **Type:** recognition. **Recipient:** for outside leadership excellence ● Lee Dowling Award. **Frequency:** annual. **Type:** recognition. **Recipient:** for fraternal leadership/service ● Ray Walsh Award. **Frequency:** annual. **Type:** recognition. **Recipient:** for academic excellence ● Vince Lombardi Award. **Frequency:** annual. **Type:** recognition. **Recipient:** for athletics. **Publications:** *Guide to Omega Gamma Delta*, periodic. Manual ● *Sodalitas Magazine*, bimonthly. **Conventions/Meetings:** annual meeting ● monthly meeting.

24045 ■ Omega Psi Phi Fraternity
3951 Snapfinger Pkwy.
Decatur, GA 30035
Ph: (404)284-5533
Fax: (404)284-0333
E-mail: omegagrace@oppf.com
URL: http://www.oppf.org
Contact: Warren G. Lee Jr., Grand Basileus
Founded: 1911. **Members:** 100,000. **Description:** Serves as a social fraternity. **Awards:** Citizen of the Year. **Frequency:** annual. **Type:** recognition. **Recipient:** for citizens who made unusual contributions to humanity ● Founders Award. **Frequency:** annual. **Type:** recognition. **Recipient:** for a fraternity district member who exhibits Omega's highest ideals for cardinal principles ● Omega Man of the Year Award. **Frequency:** annual. **Type:** recognition. **Recipient:** for graduate or undergraduate fraternity member who made significant contribution to the fraternity ● Superior Service Award. **Frequency:** annual. **Type:** recognition. **Recipient:** for a fraternity member who demonstrated outstanding contributions to his chapter. **Publications:** *Omega Bulletin*, quarterly ● *The Oracle*, quarterly. **Conventions/Meetings:** semiannual Conclave - meeting.

24046 ■ Phi Delta Theta International Fraternity
2 S Campus Ave.
Oxford, OH 45056-1801
Ph: (513)523-6345

Fax: (513)523-9200
E-mail: ghq@phideltatheta.org
URL: http://www.phideltatheta.org
Contact: Robert A. Biggs, Exec. VP
Founded: 1848. **Members:** 218,000. **Membership Dues:** individual, $235. **Staff:** 25. **Budget:** $1,750,000. **State Groups:** 75. **Local Groups:** 184. **Description:** General fraternity. Conducts educational programs. Maintains museum. **Libraries: Type:** reference. **Awards:** Lou Gehrig Award. **Frequency:** annual. **Type:** recognition. **Recipient:** for major league baseball player who best exemplifies the spirit and character of Lou Gehrig. **Publications:** *History of Phi Delta Theta* ● *The Scroll*, quarterly. Magazine ● Directory, periodic ● Manual. **Conventions/Meetings:** annual conference ● biennial convention.

24047 ■ Phi Gamma Delta
1201 Red Mile Rd.
PO Box 4599
Lexington, KY 40544-4599
Ph: (859)255-1848
Fax: (859)253-0779
E-mail: phigam@phigam.org
URL: http://www.phigam.org
Contact: Joan Schmidt, Exec. Admin. Asst.
Founded: 1848. **Members:** 145,000. **Staff:** 17. **Budget:** $1,500,000. **Regional Groups:** 129. **Local Groups:** 71. **Description:** Men's college fraternity. Conducts educational and leadership programs. Operates museum and offers computerized services. **Libraries: Type:** reference. **Holdings:** 1,800; books. **Subjects:** members. **Awards: Type:** recognition ● **Type:** scholarship. **Publications:** Magazine, quarterly. **Circulation:** 90,000 ● Membership Directory, decennial. **Conventions/Meetings:** biennial Ekklesia - convention - always August.

24048 ■ Phi Kappa Sigma (PKS)
2 Timber Dr.
Chester Springs, PA 19425
Ph: (610)469-3282
Free: (888)PKS-INTL
Fax: (610)469-3286
E-mail: web@pks.org
URL: http://www.pks.org
Contact: Hamilton Smith, Exec. Dir.
Founded: 1850. **Members:** 40,000. **Membership Dues:** college student and alumnus (one time), $283. **Staff:** 5. **Budget:** $700,000. **Local Groups:** 69. **Multinational. Description:** Social fraternity. Conducts educational and charitable programs. **Libraries: Type:** not open to the public. **Holdings:** 500; books, periodicals. **Subjects:** American college fraternity/organization history. **Awards:** Baltzer Graduate Scholarship. **Frequency:** annual. **Type:** scholarship ● Carroll K. Simons Outstanding Chapter Award. **Frequency:** annual. **Type:** recognition. **Recipient:** for the best chapter based on performance within the Mitchell Chapter standards process ● Dr. Karlem J. Riess Volunteer of the Year Award. **Frequency:** annual. **Type:** recognition. **Recipient:** for an outstanding volunteer ● Phi Kappa Sigma Foundation Scholarship. **Frequency:** annual. **Type:** scholarship. **Recipient:** for members only. **Computer Services:** Mailing lists, of members only, access to chapter's contact lists. **Additional Websites:** http://www.grandchapter.com. **Publications:** *The Maltese Cross*, annual. Magazine. **Price:** included in membership dues. **Circulation:** 40,000. **Advertising:** accepted. **Conventions/Meetings:** biennial convention, general business of the organization and leadership education (exhibits).

24049 ■ Phi Kappa Tau
5221 Morning Sun Rd.
Oxford, OH 45056-8928
Ph: (513)523-4193
Free: (800)PKT-1906
Fax: (513)523-9325
E-mail: clarkgd@auburn.edu
URL: http://www.phikappatau.org
Contact: David Clark, Pres.
Founded: 1906. **Members:** 82,000. **Membership Dues:** associate (one-time fee), $55 ● one-time initiation fee, $165 ● undergraduate, $50 (annual). **Staff:**

17. **Budget:** $980,000. **Regional Groups:** 26. **National Groups:** 97. **Description:** Social fraternity. Conducts educational and scholarship programs. Sponsors competitions. Maintains biographical archives and museum. **Awards:** Dwight I. Douglass President's Award. **Frequency:** annual. **Type:** recognition. **Recipient:** to a chapter president with general administrative excellence ● Thomas L. Stennis II Award. **Frequency:** annual. **Type:** recognition. **Recipient:** for most outstanding domain program. **Additional Websites:** http://www.auburn.edu/student_info/greeks/phi_kappa_tau/index.html. **Formerly:** (1916) Phrenocon. **Publications:** Alumni Directory, periodic. **Circulation:** 45,000 ● The History of The Phi Kappa Tau Fraternity ● The Laurel of Phi Kappa Tau, quarterly. Magazine. **Circulation:** 45,000. **Conventions/Meetings:** biennial convention ● biennial Leadership Academy - conference.

24050 ■ Phi Kappa Theta National (PhiKaps)
9640 N Augusta Dr., Ste.420
Carmel, IN 46032-9602
Ph: (317)872-9934
Fax: (317)879-1889
E-mail: executiveoffices@phikaps.org
URL: http://www.phikaps.org
Contact: Robert Riggs, Exec. Dir.
Founded: 1889. **Members:** 52,000. **Membership Dues:** regular, $155. **Staff:** 7. **Budget:** $650,000. **Regional Groups:** 55. **State Groups:** 57. **Local Groups:** 6. **Description:** Social fraternity. Maintains membership data. Provides leadership development opportunities. Conducts alumni events; sponsors sporting events. **Awards:** Phi Kappa Theta Awards. **Frequency:** annual. **Type:** recognition. **Recipient:** for completion of awards packet. **Affiliated With:** American Society of Association Executives; College Fraternity Editors Association; Fraternity Executives Association; North-American Interfraternity Conference. **Formed by Merger of:** (1959) Phi Kappa; Theta Kappa Phi. **Publications:** Alumni Directory, quinquennial ● The Pillars, quarterly ● Also publishes The Knight. **Conventions/Meetings:** biennial convention (exhibits) ● biennial National Leadership Conference.

24051 ■ Phi Mu Delta
316 Cherry Hill Blvd.
Cherry Hill, NJ 08002
Free: (888)401-2213
E-mail: hq@phimudelta.org
URL: http://www.phimudelta.org
Contact: Mr. Thomas Murphy, Exec. Dir.
Founded: 1918. **Members:** 10,000. **Staff:** 1. **Description:** Social fraternity. Maintains data banks and archives. **Publications:** The Lion Line, quarterly. Newsletter ● The Triangle, biennial. Magazine. **Conventions/Meetings:** biennial Conclave - meeting.

24052 ■ Phi Sigma Kappa (PSK)
2925 E 96th St.
Indianapolis, IN 46240
Ph: (317)573-5420
Fax: (317)573-5430
E-mail: michael@phisigmakappa.org
URL: http://www.phisigmakappa.org
Contact: Michael Carey, Exec. Dir.
Founded: 1873. **Members:** 115,000. **Membership Dues:** initiation fee, $300. **Staff:** 9. **Budget:** $1,200,000. **National Groups:** 85. **Description:** Social fraternity. Grants foundation scholarships. Maintains library; conducts educational programs. **Programs:** Passages New Member; Sustaining Members. **Absorbed:** (1985) Phi Sigma Epsilon. **Publications:** Phi Sig Insider, monthly. Newsletter. Contains policies and programs affecting fraternity. ● The Signet, quarterly. Magazine. Alternate Formats: online. **Conventions/Meetings:** annual convention - always August.

24053 ■ Pi Beta Phi
1154 Town and Country Commons Dr.
Town and Country, MO 63017-8200
Ph: (636)256-0680
Fax: (636)256-8095

E-mail: centraloffice@pibetaphi.org
URL: http://www.pibetaphi.org
Contact: Emily Russell, Grand Pres.
Founded: 1867. **Members:** 223,969. **Local Groups:** 485. **Description:** Social fraternity. Promotes friendship; develops women of intellect and integrity; cultivates leadership potential and enrich lives through community service. **Publications:** Arrow, quarterly. Magazine. Alternate Formats: online. **Conventions/Meetings:** biennial meeting - always June.

24054 ■ Pi Kappa Alpha
8347 W Range Cove
Memphis, TN 38125
Ph: (901)748-1868
Fax: (901)748-3100
E-mail: pka@pikes.org
URL: http://www.pka.com
Contact: Raymond L. Orians, Exec. VP
Founded: 1868. **Members:** 170,000. **Budget:** $1,300,000. **Description:** Social fraternity. Compiles statistics; promotes philanthropic activities. **Libraries: Type:** reference. **Holdings:** 2,000. **Awards:** Robertson Most Outstanding Undergraduate Award. **Type:** scholarship. **Recipient:** to an outstanding graduating senior. **Publications:** Alumni Directory, quinquennial ● Forum, monthly. Newsletter. Alternate Formats: online ● Garnet and Gold Membership Manual ● The History of Pi Kappa Alpha ● Shield and Diamond Magazine, quarterly. **Conventions/Meetings:** biennial congress (exhibits).

24055 ■ Pi Kappa Phi
2102 Cambridge Beltway Dr., Ste.A
Charlotte, NC 28273
Ph: (704)504-0888
Free: (800)929-1905
Fax: (704)504-0880
E-mail: pikapphq@pikapp.org
URL: http://www.pikapp.org
Contact: Mark E. Timmes, CEO
Founded: 1904. **Members:** 89,000. **Membership Dues:** individual, $60 (biennial) ● chartered chapter, $20 (biennial). **Staff:** 20. **Budget:** $1,600,000. **Regional Groups:** 34. **Local Groups:** 129. **Description:** Serves as a social fraternity. **Computer Services:** Mailing lists. **Affiliated With:** North-American Interfraternity Conference. **Publications:** Educational Manual Series ● Star and Lamp, quarterly. Magazine ● Also publishes educational manuals and organizational guides. **Conventions/Meetings:** annual Mid-Year Leadership Conference ● biennial Supreme Chapter - convention.

24056 ■ Pi Lambda Phi Fraternity (PiLam)
304 Fed. Rd., Ste.113
Brookfield, CT 06804-2420
Ph: (203)740-1044
Free: (800)394-7573
Fax: (203)740-1644
E-mail: headquarters@pilambdaphi.org
URL: http://www.pilambdaphi.org
Contact: Mr. Gary Sanders, Exec. Dir.
Founded: 1895. **Members:** 46,000. **Staff:** 4. **Budget:** $530,000. **Local Groups:** 38. **Multinational. Description:** Works as social fraternity. **Awards:** George A. Beck Outstanding Chapter Award. **Frequency:** annual. **Type:** recognition. **Recipient:** to the most outstanding chapter for the academic school year ● Isadore Halprin Memorial Scholarship Award. **Frequency:** annual. **Type:** recognition. **Recipient:** to the chapter that maintains the highest average grade point average for the academic year ● Jules Lennard Human Relations Award. **Frequency:** annual. **Type:** recognition. **Recipient:** to a chapter or individual who demonstrates the most dedication to human relations and tolerance ● Rafer Johnson Upsilon Achievement Award. **Frequency:** annual. **Type:** recognition. **Recipient:** to an undergraduate member who exhibits excellence in scholarship, athletics, community service, and service to the fraternity ● Snap Melnicker Community Service Award. **Frequency:** annual. **Type:** recognition. **Recipient:** to the chapter that demonstrates the most dedication to community service and philanthropy in the academic year. **Affiliated With:** Fraternity Executives Association; North-

American Interfraternity Conference. **Absorbed:** (1972) Beta Sigma Rho. **Publications:** New Member Manual, triennial. Contains the history of the Fraternity; includes requirements of being a member. **Price:** included in membership dues ● Notes From National, quarterly ● The Paragon, monthly. Newsletter. Contains information of interest to undergraduate chapters. Alternate Formats: online ● Pi Lambda Phi Alumni Directory, quinquennial ● The Tripod, annual. **Conventions/Meetings:** annual convention.

24057 ■ Psi Upsilon
3003 E 96th St.
Indianapolis, IN 46240
Ph: (317)571-1833
Fax: (317)844-5170
E-mail: intl_ofc@psiu.org
URL: http://www.psiu.org
Contact: Mark A. Williams, Exec. Dir.
Founded: 1833. **Members:** 26,000. **Staff:** 4. **Budget:** $700,000. **Multinational. Description:** General fraternity. Provides educational programming. Psi Upsilon Foundation makes available scholarships and other assistance to members. **Libraries: Type:** reference. **Holdings:** archival material, periodicals, photographs. **Awards:** Distinguished Alumni Service Award. **Frequency:** annual. **Type:** recognition. **Recipient:** for alumni whose service have brought honor to fraternity ● Garnet and Gold Award of Excellence. **Frequency:** annual. **Type:** recognition. **Recipient:** for a chapter, provisional chapter, or Owl Club that achieved a chapter GPA of 3.0 or greater, in each semester. **Publications:** The Diamond of Psi Upsilon, quarterly. Magazine. ISSN: 1073-4686. **Circulation:** 23,000 ● The Review of Psi Upsilon, quarterly. Newsletter ● Directory, quinquennial. **Conventions/Meetings:** annual convention, includes Leadership Institute - always summer.

24058 ■ Sigma Alpha Epsilon (SAE)
1856 Sheridan Rd.
Evanston, IL 60201-3837
Ph: (847)475-1856
Free: (800)233-1856
Fax: (847)475-2250
E-mail: editor@sae.net
URL: http://www.sae.net
Contact: Dr. Thomas G. Goodale, Exec. Dir.
Founded: 1856. **Members:** 270,000. **Membership Dues:** life, $645. **Staff:** 30. **Budget:** $3,000,000. **Regional Groups:** 29. **Local Groups:** 211. **Multinational. Description:** International social fraternity. Promotes the highest standards of friendship, scholarship, and service to members. **Libraries: Type:** reference. **Holdings:** 5,000. **Subjects:** Greek life. **Awards:** Distinguished Service Award. **Type:** recognition. **Computer Services:** database ● mailing lists. **Additional Websites:** http://www.thetgi.net, http://www.saeforum.net. **Programs:** The True Gentleman Initiative. **Publications:** Chapter Directory. **Price:** free. **Circulation:** 475,000. **Advertising:** accepted. Alternate Formats: online ● The e-Recorder, monthly. Newsletter. **Circulation:** 10,000. Alternate Formats: online ● Phi Alpha, biennial. Booklet ● The Record, quarterly. Magazine. **Circulation:** 350,000 ● Books. **Conventions/Meetings:** biennial Anniversary Convention - congress, with social sessions (exhibits).

24059 ■ Sigma Alpha Mu
9245 N Meridian, Ste.105
Indianapolis, IN 46260
Ph: (317)846-0600
Free: (888)369-9361
Fax: (317)846-9462
E-mail: samhq@sam.org
URL: http://www.sam.org
Contact: Lawrence D. Schaffer, Pres.
Founded: 1909. **Members:** 56,247. **Staff:** 6. **Description:** Social fraternity. Operates charitable program. **Awards:** Hyman I. Jacobson Award. **Frequency:** annual. **Type:** scholarship. **Recipient:** for top senior scholar in the fraternity. **Publications:** Keyhole. Bulletin ● The Octagonian, quarterly. Magazine. ISSN: 0744-6969. **Conventions/Meetings:** annual conference, leadership conference.

24060 ■ Sigma Beta Rho Fraternity
PO Box 107
New York, NY 10020
E-mail: info@sigmabetarho.com
URL: http://www.sigmabetarho.com
Contact: Gaurav Jhalani, Pres.
Founded: 1996. **Description:** Represents South Asian brotherhood. Promotes betterment and preservation of South Asians in United States. Increases awareness of South Asian culture and community at large.

24061 ■ Sigma Chi International Fraternity
PO Box 469
Evanston, IL 60201
Ph: (847)869-3655
Fax: (847)869-4906
E-mail: feedback@sigmachi.org
URL: http://www.sigmachi.org
Contact: Mark Anderson, Exec. Off.
Founded: 1855. **Members:** 203,000. **Membership Dues:** individual, $35 (semiannual). **Staff:** 35. **Budget:** $3,500,000. **Regional Groups:** 44. **Description:** Social fraternity; works for the value-based development of membership. Maintains museum, member records, and training materials. **Libraries: Type:** reference. **Holdings:** 4,000; archival material. **Awards: Frequency:** annual. **Type:** grant ● **Type:** recognition. **Computer Services:** database, member records. **Formerly:** (2001) Sigma Chi International Corporation. **Publications:** *History*, every 25 years ● *The Magazine of Sigma Chi*, quarterly ● *Norman Shield*, biennial. Manual ● *RiskWatch*, quarterly. Newsletter ● *Sig House*, quarterly. Pamphlet ● *Sig Leader*, quarterly. Newsletter ● *Standard Operating Procedures*, biennial. Manual ● Membership Directory, quinquennial. **Conventions/Meetings:** annual Balfour Leadership Training Workshop ● biennial Grand Chapter - conference and convention ● biennial Grand Council - conference.

24062 ■ Sigma Nu Fraternity
9 Lewis St.
PO Box 1869
Lexington, VA 24450
Ph: (540)463-1869
Fax: (540)463-1669
E-mail: headquarters@sigmanu.org
URL: http://www.sigmanu.org
Contact: James A. Owens, Exec. VP
Founded: 1869. **Members:** 200,000. **Staff:** 32. **Budget:** $2,500,000. **Regional Groups:** 210. **National Groups:** 163. **Description:** Social fraternity. Sponsors professional training. Operates hall of fame and museum. **Libraries: Type:** reference. **Holdings:** 8,500; archival material, books, monographs. **Awards: Frequency:** annual. **Type:** recognition ● **Frequency:** annual. **Type:** scholarship. **Computer Services:** Mailing lists, of members. **Programs:** AlcoholEdu. **Publications:** *The Delta*, quarterly ● *Historic Roll Call of the Legion of Honor - Who's Who in Sigma Nu?* ● *Rock*, bimonthly. Newsletter. Alternate Formats: online. **Conventions/Meetings:** biennial Leadership School - meeting ● workshop.

24063 ■ Sigma Phi Epsilon (SIGEP)
310 S Blvd.
PO Box 1901
Richmond, VA 23218
Ph: (804)353-1901
Fax: (804)359-8160
E-mail: comments@sigep.net
URL: http://www.sigep.org
Contact: Mr. Craig Templeton, Exec. Dir.
Founded: 1901. **Members:** 165,000. **Budget:** $1,200,000. **Description:** Social fraternity. Maintains Sigma Phi Epsilon Educational Foundation and National Housing Corporation. **Committees:** National Leadership; Scholarship Awards; Student Loan. **Publications:** *Commemorative Directory*, quinquennial ● Bulletin, monthly ● Journal, semiannual. Alternate Formats: online ● Newsletter, monthly. **Conventions/Meetings:** biennial Grand Chapter Conclave - meeting - always August.

24064 ■ Sigma Phi Society
205 Lloyd St., Ste.204
Carrboro, NC 27510-1883
E-mail: sigmaphi@sigmaphi.org
URL: http://www.sigmaphi.org
Contact: Derek Fredrickson, Gen.Sec.
Founded: 1827. **Members:** 5,580. **Staff:** 1. **Description:** Social fraternity. Maintains Sigma Phi Educational Foundation. **Awards:** Elihu Root Distinguished Sigma Phi Award. **Frequency:** annual. **Type:** recognition. **Recipient:** for distinguished career achievement ● **Type:** scholarship. **Computer Services:** database ● mailing lists. **Publications:** *Sigma Phi Bulletin*, semiannual. **Circulation:** 5,600 ● *Sigma Phi Catalogue* ● *Sigma Phi Flame*, annual ● *Thesaurus of the Sigma Phi*. **Conventions/Meetings:** annual convention.

24065 ■ Sigma Pi Fraternity, International
PO Box 1897
Brentwood, TN 37024
Free: (800)332-1897
Fax: (615)373-8949
E-mail: exec@sigmapi.org
URL: http://www.sigmapi.org
Contact: Mark S. Briscoe, Exec. Dir.
Founded: 1897. **Members:** 75,000. **Membership Dues:** life, $300. **Staff:** 15. **Budget:** $2,000,000. **State Groups:** 6. **National Groups:** 125. **Description:** Serves as a social fraternity. **Formerly:** Sigma Pi. **Publications:** *Alumni Directory*, quadrennial ● *Emerald of Sigma Pi*, quarterly. **Circulation:** 50,000. **Conventions/Meetings:** biennial Convocation - meeting (exhibits) - always August.

24066 ■ Sigma Pi Phi Fraternity
PO Box 1897
Brentwood, TN 37024-1897
Ph: (212)477-5550
Fax: (212)477-1082
URL: http://www.sigma-pi-phi.net
Contact: Dr. Charles C. Teamer, Grand Sire Archon
Founded: 1904. **Members:** 3,000. **Staff:** 2. **Regional Groups:** 5. **Local Groups:** 97. **Description:** Graduate/professional fraternity. Promotes social and intellectual camaraderie; supports designated social programs. Maintains the Boule Foundation. **Publications:** *Boule Journal*, quarterly ● *Roster*, biennial. **Conventions/Meetings:** biennial congress.

24067 ■ Sigma Tau Gamma
Marvin Millsap HQ Bldg.
PO Box 54
Warrensburg, MO 64093-0054
Ph: (660)747-2222
Fax: (660)747-9599
E-mail: wpbernier@sigmataugamma.org
URL: http://www.sigmataugamma.org
Contact: Bill Bernier, Exec. VP
Founded: 1920. **Members:** 60,000. **Staff:** 9. **Budget:** $700,000. **Regional Groups:** 5. **Local Groups:** 70. **Description:** Serves as a social fraternity. **Awards:** Distinguished Achievement. **Frequency:** annual. **Type:** recognition. **Recipient:** for an alumnus of the fraternity that has achieved distinction in his chosen profession ● Ellsworth C. Dent Man of the Year Award. **Frequency:** annual. **Type:** recognition. **Recipient:** for most outstanding undergraduate leaders ● **Type:** scholarship. **Recipient:** for undergraduate studies. **Publications:** *Chain of Honor*. Manual. Serves as a historical reference and pledge education. ● *Saga*, quarterly ● Membership Directory, decennial. **Conventions/Meetings:** biennial meeting.

24068 ■ Tau Epsilon Phi (TEP)
1000 White Horse Rd., Ste.512
Voorhees, NJ 08043
Ph: (856)782-9837
Fax: (856)782-9849
E-mail: tep@pipeline.com
URL: http://www.tephq.org
Contact: George Hasenberg, Consul
Founded: 1910. **Members:** 44,300. **Staff:** 8. **Budget:** $700,000. **Regional Groups:** 13. **State Groups:** 26. **Local Groups:** 131. **Description:** Social and educational fraternity. Operates hall of fame and museum; conducts charitable program. Maintains Tau Epsilon

Phi Foundation to provide scholarships and student aid funds. **Computer Services:** database, membership management. **Divisions:** Properties. **Publications:** *Geographic Membership List*, 4-5/year. Membership Directory ● *The Plume*, quarterly. **Conventions/Meetings:** biennial congress.

24069 ■ Tau Kappa Epsilon (TKE)
8645 Founders Rd.
Indianapolis, IN 46268
Ph: (317)872-6533
Fax: (317)875-8353
E-mail: tkeogc@tke.org
URL: http://www.tke.org
Contact: Kevin M. Mayeux, CEO
Founded: 1899. **Members:** 236,822. **Membership Dues:** individual, $287. **Staff:** 25. **Budget:** $3,500,000. **Description:** Social fraternity. Maintains charitable program; conducts educational programs on leadership and character development. **Publications:** *The Teke*, quarterly. Magazine. Alternate Formats: online. **Conventions/Meetings:** biennial Conclave - convention - usually held in August, odd-numbered years.

24070 ■ Theta Chi Fraternity
3330 Founders Rd.
Indianapolis, IN 46268-1333
Ph: (317)824-1881
Fax: (317)824-1908
E-mail: ihq@thetachi.org
URL: http://www.thetachi.org
Contact: David L. Westol, CEO
Founded: 1856. **Members:** 156,352. **Budget:** $1,100,000. **Regional Groups:** 155. **State Groups:** 27. **Description:** Social fraternity. Maintains museum. Compiles statistics. **Libraries: Type:** reference. **Holdings:** 500; biographical archives, books. **Awards: Type:** recognition ● **Type:** scholarship. **Programs:** Leadership, Education, and Academic Development. **Publications:** *Alumni Directory*, periodic ● *Alumnus*, monthly. Newsletter. Alternate Formats: online ● *Men Since '56*, monthly. Newsletter ● *The Rattle of Theta Chi*, semiannual. Alternate Formats: online. **Conventions/Meetings:** biennial conference.

24071 ■ Theta Delta Chi
214 Lewis Wharf
Boston, MA 02110
Ph: (617)742-8886
Free: (800)999-1847
E-mail: cfo@tdx.org
URL: http://www.tdx.org
Contact: William Alexander McClung, Exec. Dir.
Founded: 1847. **Members:** 37,500. **Staff:** 5. **Budget:** $400,000. **Regional Groups:** 5. **Local Groups:** 29. **Multinational. Description:** Social fraternity. Conducts charitable and educational programs. Sponsors Theta Delta Chi Educational Foundation and Theta Delta Chi Founder's Corporation. **Libraries: Type:** reference. **Holdings:** 1,000; books, periodicals. **Subjects:** fraternity history and happenings, works by members. **Awards:** Alumni of the Year. **Frequency:** annual. **Type:** recognition. **Recipient:** for members ● **Frequency:** annual. **Type:** scholarship. **Recipient:** for members. **Computer Services:** database ● online services. **Boards:** Educational Foundation; Founders' Corporation; Grand Lodge. **Publications:** *CFO Update*, monthly. Newsletter. **Price:** free for members. **Circulation:** 37,500. Alternate Formats: online ● *Shield*, quarterly. Journal ● *Theta Delta Chi Directory*, every 4-5 years ● *Theta Delta Chi Handbook*. Contains information about new members. **Conventions/Meetings:** annual convention, includes new elections and new information - always first weekend in August.

24072 ■ Theta Xi
PO Box 411134
St. Louis, MO 63141-3134
Ph: (314)993-6294
Free: (800)783-6294
Fax: (314)993-8760

E-mail: txhq@thetaxi.org
URL: http://www.thetaxi.org
Contact: James E. Vredenburgh, Exec. Dir.
Founded: 1864. **Members:** 64,000. **Membership Dues:** life, $230 ● student, $90 (annual). **Staff:** 5. **Budget:** $540,000. **Regional Groups:** 8. **Local Groups:** 55. **Description:** College social fraternity. Sponsors charitable and educational programs. **Libraries: Type:** reference. **Holdings:** audiovisuals, clippings. **Awards:** Most Improved Chapter. **Frequency:** annual. **Type:** trophy ● Outstanding Chapter. **Frequency:** annual. **Type:** recognition. **Subgroups:** Theta Xi Foundation. **Absorbed:** Kappa Sigma Kappa. **Publications:** *The Quest for Theta Xi Fraternity*, semiannual. **Price:** $10.00/copy. Alternate Formats: online ● *Theta Xi Alumni Directory*, triennial ● *The UNICORN*, semiannual. Magazine. **Price:** free for life members and contributors. **Circulation:** 24,155. Alternate Formats: online ● Also publishes operations programming guides. **Conventions/Meetings:** biennial Anniversary Convention - convention and workshop ● Regional Leadership and Educational Conferences.

24073 ■ Zeta Beta Tau (ZBT)
3905 Vincennes Rd., Ste.300
Indianapolis, IN 46268-3057
Ph: (317)334-1898
Fax: (317)334-1899
E-mail: zbt@zbtnational.org
URL: http://www.zbt.org
Contact: Jonathan I. Yulish, Exec. Dir.
Founded: 1898. **Members:** 100,000. **Membership Dues:** initial, $310. **Staff:** 8. **Budget:** $900,000. **Description:** Serves as a social fraternity. **Absorbed:** Phi Sigma Delta. **Publications:** *Chapter and Colony.* Bulletin. Alternate Formats: online ● *The Deltan, AZBT Review*, semiannual. Magazine. Alternate Formats: online ● *Good and Welfare*, monthly. Newsletter. Alternate Formats: online ● Manuals. Alternate Formats: online ● Brochures. Alternate Formats: online. **Conventions/Meetings:** annual convention, leadership school - always July.

24074 ■ Zeta Psi Fraternity of North America
15 S Henry St.
Pearl River, NY 10965
Ph: (845)735-1847
Free: (800)477-1847
Fax: (845)735-1989
E-mail: exec.director@zetapsi.org
URL: http://www.zetapsi.org
Contact: Andy O'Brien, Exec. Dir.
Founded: 1847. **Members:** 24,000. **Budget:** $400,000. **Description:** Social fraternity. Sponsors Leadership Training Institute, providing professional training and seminars. Maintains Zeta Psi Educational Foundation and Zeta Psi Foundation of Canada. **Formerly:** (1988) Zeta Psi. **Publications:** *The Circle of Zeta Psi*, semiannual. Magazine. Contains chapter news. **Price:** included in membership dues. **Circulation:** 24,000. **Advertising:** accepted ● *Zeta Update*, 9/year ● Membership Directory, quinquennial. **Conventions/Meetings:** annual meeting - always August.

Social Sciences

24075 ■ Pi Gamma Mu (PGM)
1001 Millington St., Ste.B
Winfield, KS 67156
Ph: (620)221-3128 (620)221-3276
Fax: (620)221-7124
E-mail: pgm@sckans.edu
URL: http://www.pigammamu.org
Contact: Sue Watters, Exec. Dir.
Founded: 1924. **Members:** 228,000. **Membership Dues:** international, $40 (annual). **Staff:** 3. **Budget:** $184,000. **Regional Groups:** 4. **Multinational. Description:** Honor society - social science. Encourages the study of the social sciences among graduate and undergraduate students and faculty members in colleges and universities throughout the world. **Awards:** Guest Lectureship. **Frequency:** annual. **Type:** grant. **Recipient:** for social science topics ●

Frequency: annual. **Type:** scholarship. **Recipient:** for winner of graduate studies in social sciences competition. **Affiliated With:** American Association for the Advancement of Science; Association of College Honor Societies. **Formerly:** (1980) National Social Science Honor Society. **Publications:** *International Social Science Review*, semiannual. Journal. Contains articles and book reviews on social science topics by students and faculty. **Price:** included in membership dues; $10.00 /year for nonmembers. ISSN: 0278-2308. **Circulation:** 4,500. **Advertising:** accepted ● *Pi Gamma Mu Newsletter*, bimonthly. Contains chapter news. **Price:** included in membership dues; $10.00 /year for nonmembers. ISSN: 8750-4855. **Conventions/Meetings:** triennial convention.

Social Sororities

24076 ■ Alpha Chi Omega
5939 Castle Creek Pkwy., North Dr.
Indianapolis, IN 46250
Ph: (317)579-5050
Fax: (317)579-5051
E-mail: info@alphachiomega.org
URL: http://www.alphachiomega.org
Contact: Vicky Harrison, Archivist/Ritual Coor.
Founded: 1885. **Members:** 171,890. **Membership Dues:** new, $199 ● sisterhood packet, $21 ● national per capita, $140 (annual) ● per semester charge, $70 ● per quarter charge, $46 ● certificate, $7 ● badge, $31 ● communication/technology, $5. **Staff:** 30. **Regional Groups:** 132. **Description:** Social sorority. Sponsors Alpha Chi Omega Foundation. **Awards:** Award of Achievement. **Frequency:** biennial. **Type:** recognition ● Love and Loyalty Grants. **Frequency:** annual. **Type:** grant. **Recipient:** for leadership developments ● Opportunity Grants. **Frequency:** annual. **Type:** grant. **Recipient:** to organizations that support victims of domestic violence. **Publications:** *Lyre*, quarterly ● Brochure. Alternate Formats: online. **Conventions/Meetings:** biennial meeting - always June.

24077 ■ Alpha Epsilon Phi
11 Lake Ave. Extension, Ste.1A
Danbury, CT 06811
Ph: (203)748-0029
Fax: (203)748-0039
E-mail: execdir@aephi.org
URL: http://www.aephi.org
Contact: Faith Frank, Pres.
Founded: 1909. **Members:** 50,000. **Description:** Social sorority. **Publications:** *Columns of Alpha Epsilon Phi*, quarterly. **Conventions/Meetings:** biennial meeting.

24078 ■ Alpha Gamma Delta
3905 Vincennes Rd., Ste.105
Indianapolis, IN 46268
Ph: (317)879-9328
Fax: (317)415-0335
E-mail: jcretin@alphagammadelta.org
URL: http://www.alphagammadelta.org
Contact: Julie Waitman Cretin, Exec. Dir.
Founded: 1904. **Members:** 102,000. **Local Groups:** 168. **Description:** Social sorority. Promotes academic excellence, leadership development, high ideals and sisterhood. **Conventions/Meetings:** biennial meeting.

24079 ■ Alpha Omicron Pi
5390 Virginia Way
Brentwood, TN 37027
Ph: (615)370-0920
Fax: (615)371-9736
E-mail: aoiihq@alphaomicronpi.org
URL: http://www.alphaomicronpi.org
Contact: Kimberly Altenus, Exec. Dir.
Founded: 1897. **Members:** 100,000. **Staff:** 30. **Regional Groups:** 10. **State Groups:** 165. **Local Groups:** 112. **Description:** Social sorority. Conducts charitable, research, and educational programs. **Libraries: Type:** reference. **Computer Services:** data-

base, accounting and membership. **Publications:** *The Piper*, monthly. **Price:** free for members. **Circulation:** 100,000. **Advertising:** accepted ● *To Dragma*, quarterly. **Price:** included in initiation fee. **Circulation:** 100,000. **Advertising:** accepted ● Directory, annual. **Conventions/Meetings:** biennial meeting (exhibits).

24080 ■ Alpha Phi International Fraternity
1930 Sherman Ave.
Evanston, IL 60201
Ph: (847)475-0663 (847)475-4786
Fax: (847)475-6820
E-mail: fraternity@alphaphi.org
URL: http://www.alphaphi.org
Contact: Susan Zabriskie, Exec. Dir.
Founded: 1872. **Members:** 95,000. **Membership Dues:** individual, $50 (annual). **Staff:** 15. **Budget:** $2,300,000. **Regional Groups:** 8. **State Groups:** 175. **Local Groups:** 140. **Multinational. Description:** Social sorority. Promotes growth in character; unity of feeling, sisterly affection, and social communion among members. Seeks the highest ideal of womanhood. **Awards:** Professor of Year. **Frequency:** annual. **Type:** grant. **Publications:** *Alpha Phi Quarterly*. Magazine. **Advertising:** accepted. **Conventions/Meetings:** biennial convention - always June.

24081 ■ Alpha Sigma Alpha
9550 Zionsville Rd., Ste.160
Indianapolis, IN 46268
Ph: (317)871-2920
Fax: (317)871-2924
E-mail: asa@alphasigmaalpha.org
URL: http://www.alphasigmaalpha.org
Contact: Nancy Coleman, Exec. Dir.
Founded: 1901. **Members:** 60,000. **Staff:** 12. **National Groups:** 150. **Description:** Serves as a general sorority. **Publications:** *Phoenix*, quarterly. Magazine. **Conventions/Meetings:** biennial convention.

24082 ■ Alpha Sigma Tau (AST)
1929 Canyon Rd.
Birmingham, AL 35216
Ph: (205)978-2179
Fax: (205)978-2182
E-mail: headquarters@alphasigmatau.org
URL: http://www.alphasigmatau.org
Contact: Patricia Klausing Simmons, Pres.
Founded: 1899. **Members:** 37,099. **Staff:** 4. **Regional Groups:** 101. **Description:** Social sorority. **Awards:** Alumnae Top Tau Award. **Frequency:** annual. **Type:** recognition. **Recipient:** for outstanding service and commitment to the chapter and the sorority ● Collegiate Top Tau Award. **Frequency:** annual. **Type:** recognition. **Recipient:** for academic achievement, participation in campus activities, and service to the sorority ● Elizabeth Wilson Award. **Frequency:** annual. **Type:** recognition. **Recipient:** for chapter excellence ● Pearls of Alpha Sigma Tau Award. **Frequency:** annual. **Type:** recognition. **Recipient:** for members who have given special contributions within their communities and/or professions ● **Frequency:** annual. **Type:** scholarship. **Recipient:** for members only. **Publications:** *The Anchor*, semiannual. Magazine ● *Crest*, semiannual. Newsletter. **Conventions/Meetings:** biennial convention.

24083 ■ Alpha Xi Delta Women's Fraternity
8702 Founders Rd.
Indianapolis, IN 46268
Ph: (317)872-3500
Fax: (317)872-2947
E-mail: fhq@alphaxidelta.org
URL: http://www.alphaxidelta.org
Contact: Sara L. Nash, Exec. Dir.
Founded: 1893. **Members:** 120,000. **Membership Dues:** individual, $115. **Staff:** 21. **Budget:** $2,000,000. **Local Groups:** 278. **Description:** Social sorority. **Publications:** *The Quill of Alpha Xi Delta*, 3/year. Magazine. **Circulation:** 67,000. **Advertising:** accepted. Alternate Formats: online. **Conventions/Meetings:** biennial convention (exhibits).

24084 ■ Chi Omega
3395 Players Club Pkwy.
Memphis, TN 38125
Ph: (901)748-8600
Fax: (901)748-8686
E-mail: chiomega@chiomega.com
URL: http://www.chiomega.com
Contact: Anne Emmerth, Exec. Dir.
Founded: 1895. **Members:** 300,000. **Local Groups:** 175. **Description:** Social sorority. **Publications:** *Eleusis*, quarterly. **Conventions/Meetings:** biennial meeting.

24085 ■ Delta Delta Delta
2331 Brookhollow Plaza Dr.
PO Box 5987
Arlington, TX 76005-5987
Ph: (817)633-8001
Fax: (817)652-0212
E-mail: info@trideltaeo.org
URL: http://www.tridelta.org
Contact: Laura C. Simic CFRE, Pres.
Founded: 1888. **Members:** 179,000. **Staff:** 20. **Description:** Social sorority. **Awards:** Graduate Scholarships. **Frequency:** annual. **Type:** scholarship. **Recipient:** for graduate members ● Undergraduate Scholarships. **Frequency:** annual. **Type:** scholarship. **Recipient:** to sophomore and junior members. **Computer Services:** Online services, inCircle (social networking tool). **Programs:** Annual Giving; Philanthropy; Scholarship; Social Development. **Publications:** *The Trident*, quarterly. Magazine. Alternate Formats: online. **Conventions/Meetings:** biennial convention - always even-numbered years.

24086 ■ Delta Gamma
PO Box 21397
Columbus, OH 43221-0397
Ph: (614)481-8169
Fax: (614)481-0133
E-mail: webmaster@deltagamma.org
URL: http://www.deltagamma.org
Contact: Mary Sterling Barlow, Exec. Dir.
Founded: 1873. **Members:** 19,000. **Membership Dues:** college student, $40 (annual) ● alumnae, $17 (annual). **Staff:** 49. **Budget:** $3,200,000. **Regional Groups:** 144. **Multinational. Description:** Social sorority. Serves as channel for philanthropic activities. Sponsors regional and national seminars for alumnae and collegiate officers. **Libraries: Type:** reference. **Holdings:** archival material. **Awards:** Patricia Peterson Danielson Award. **Frequency:** annual. **Type:** recognition. **Recipient:** for outstanding contributions of a chapter ● **Frequency:** annual. **Type:** scholarship. **Computer Services:** database, membership records ● information services, chapter profiles. **Publications:** *Anchora*, quarterly. Magazine. Contains alumni and collegiate news. **Price:** included in membership dues. **Circulation:** 120,000. Alternate Formats: online ● *History of Delta Gamma Series*, every 10 years ● *Shield*, triennial ● Manuals. **Conventions/Meetings:** biennial convention - always June ● biennial seminar, for officer training - always June in Columbus, OH.

24087 ■ Delta Phi Epsilon (DPHIE)
16A Worthington Dr.
Maryland Heights, MO 63043
Ph: (314)275-2626
Fax: (314)275-2655
E-mail: info@dphie.org
URL: http://www.dphie.org/home.shtml
Contact: Donna Bruening, Pres.
Founded: 1917. **Members:** 40,000. **Staff:** 10. **Budget:** $750,000. **Local Groups:** 78. **Description:** Social sorority. Maintains career network. Provides research funds for cystic fibrosis and anorexia nervosa and related eating disorders. Provides educational programs to undergraduate women. Raises funds for several charitable organizations. Provides leadership training at the undergraduate and alumnae level. Organizes alumnae groups throughout country, supports local chapters, and participates in charitable activities. **Libraries: Type:** reference. **Holdings:** archival material, audiovisuals, business records, clippings, periodicals. **Awards:** Scholarship Grants for

Undergraduate or Graduate Study. **Frequency:** annual. **Type:** scholarship. **Recipient:** for members, through Delta Phi Epsilon Educational Foundation. **Publications:** *Triad Magazine*, semiannual. **Conventions/Meetings:** biennial convention.

24088 ■ Delta Xi Phi Multicultural Sorority (DXP)
PO Box 5218
Chicago, IL 60680-5218
E-mail: deltaxiphi@yahoo.com
URL: http://www.geocities.com/~deltaxiphi/index.html
Contact: Diane Abundabar, Pres.
Founded: 1994. **Description:** Promotes community service, sisterhood and friendship among members. Advances women through higher education programs. Increases multicultural awareness on campuses and in the community. **Telecommunication Services:** electronic mail, president@deltaxiphi.org.

24089 ■ Delta Zeta (DZ)
202 E Church St.
Oxford, OH 45056
Ph: (513)523-7597
Fax: (513)523-1921
E-mail: dzs@dzshq.com
URL: http://www.deltazeta.org
Contact: Cynthia Winslow Menges, Exec. Dir.
Founded: 1902. **Members:** 138,000. **Description:** Serves as social sorority. **Awards:** Betsy B. and Garold A. Leach Scholarship for Museum Studies. **Frequency:** annual. **Type:** scholarship. **Recipient:** for member pursuing a course of study that could lead to a career in museum work ● Gertrude Houk Fariss Scholarship. **Frequency:** annual. **Type:** scholarship. **Recipient:** to active members pursuing a graduate degree in fields of journalism or education ● Woman of the Year. **Frequency:** annual. **Type:** recognition. **Recipient:** to a member who has achieved national recognition in her chosen career. **Committees:** Academics; Awards; Constitution, Code of Regulations and Bylaws; Field Activities; History; Judiciary; Music; Program Development. **Absorbed:** (1941) Beta Phi Alpha; (1946) Phi Omega Pi; (1956) Delta Sigma Epsilon; (1962) Theta Upsilon. **Publications:** *The LAMP of Delta Zeta*, quarterly. Magazine. ISSN: 0887-2554. Alternate Formats: online. **Conventions/Meetings:** biennial meeting.

24090 ■ Gamma Phi Beta
12737 E Euclid Dr.
Centennial, CO 80111
Ph: (303)799-1874
Fax: (303)799-1876
E-mail: info@gammaphibeta.org
URL: http://www.gammaphibeta.org
Contact: Patricia Crowley, Exec. Dir.
Founded: 1874. **Members:** 130,000. **Staff:** 17. **Multinational. Description:** Social sorority. Operates networking service for members who are traveling or moving. Promotes scholarship, leadership and community service. **Awards: Frequency:** annual. **Type:** fellowship. **Recipient:** for Gamma Phi Beta graduate students ● **Type:** grant. **Recipient:** to women students in financial need ● **Frequency:** annual. **Type:** scholarship. **Recipient:** for Gamma Phi Beta undergraduates. **Publications:** *Alumnae Directory*, quinquennial ● *THE CRESCENT*, quarterly. Magazine. **Price:** included in membership dues. **Circulation:** 90,000. Alternate Formats: online. **Conventions/Meetings:** biennial convention.

24091 ■ Kappa Alpha Theta
8740 Founders Rd.
Indianapolis, IN 46268
Ph: (317)876-1870
Fax: (317)876-1925
E-mail: info@kappaalphatheta.org
URL: http://www.kappaalphatheta.org
Contact: Jennifer Pendleton, Exec. Dir.
Founded: 1870. **Members:** 170,000. **Staff:** 30. **Local Groups:** 124. **Description:** Social sorority. Conducts educational programs. **Libraries: Type:** reference. **Awards:** Fraternity Grant. **Frequency:** annual. **Type:** grant. **Recipient:** for members ● **Type:**

recognition. **Funds:** Student Loan. **Programs:** Educational Leadership Consultant. **Publications:** Magazine, quarterly ● Membership Directory. Alternate Formats: online. **Conventions/Meetings:** biennial conference ● annual meeting.

24092 ■ Kappa Delta (KD)
3205 Players Ln.
Memphis, TN 38125-8897
Ph: (901)748-1897
Free: (800)536-1897
Fax: (901)748-0949
E-mail: kappadelta@kappadelta.org
Contact: Bonnie Purvis Warren, Natl. Pres.
Founded: 1897. **Members:** 186,000. **Staff:** 18. **Regional Groups:** 477. **Local Groups:** 123. **Description:** Serves as a social sorority. **Awards:** Corre Anding Stegall Collegiate Leadership Award. **Frequency:** annual. **Type:** recognition. **Recipient:** to the top echelon of Kappa Delta student leaders ● Order of the Emerald Honors. **Frequency:** biennial. **Type:** recognition. **Recipient:** to members who have given exceptional service to the sorority ● Order of the Pearl. **Frequency:** biennial. **Type:** recognition. **Recipient:** to members who have made outstanding contributions to their communities in nonsorority capacity. **Publications:** *Alumnae Advisor*, monthly. Newsletter. Alternate Formats: online ● *The Angelos*, quarterly. Magazine. **Circulation:** 90,000. **Advertising:** accepted ● *KD Dialogue*, bimonthly. Newsletter. Alternate Formats: online ● *KD Edge*. Newsletter ● Brochure. Alternate Formats: online. **Conventions/Meetings:** biennial convention (exhibits).

24093 ■ Kappa Kappa Gamma
PO Box 38
Columbus, OH 43216-0038
Ph: (614)228-6515
Free: (866)KKG-1870
Fax: (614)228-7809
E-mail: kkghq@kappa.org
URL: http://kappakappagamma.org
Contact: Ms. Lauren Paitson, Exec. Dir.
Founded: 1870. **Members:** 200,000. **Staff:** 30. **Budget:** $2,010,000. **Regional Groups:** 131. **Local Groups:** 350. **Description:** Social sorority. Maintains Heritage Museum with exhibit pertaining to the history of women and sorority memorabilia. Sponsors charitable activities. **Libraries: Type:** reference. **Holdings:** archival material. **Subjects:** history of organization. **Awards:** Alumnae Achievement Awards. **Type:** recognition ● Kappa Kappa Gamma Foundation Scholarship. **Frequency:** annual. **Type:** scholarship. **Recipient:** to qualified Kappa members. **Councils:** Associate; Fraternity. **Funds:** Rose McGill. **Programs:** Kappa Trainer. **Publications:** *Alumnae Newsletter*, monthly. Alternate Formats: online ● *The Key*, quarterly. Magazine. Alternate Formats: online ● Manuals ● Proceedings, biennial ● Membership Directory. Alternate Formats: online. **Conventions/Meetings:** biennial conference - 2008 June 25-29, Phoenix, AZ.

24094 ■ Phi Beta Chi
PO Box 65426
West Des Moines, IA 50265
E-mail: phibxhq@aol.com
URL: http://www.phibetachi.org
Contact: Amy Johnson, Exec. Dir.
Founded: 1978. **Members:** 2,400. **Staff:** 1. **Budget:** $30,000. **Regional Groups:** 10. **Description:** College women who will be "caring, responsible, contributing chapter members." Celebrates the Lutheran heritage. Sponsors annual Founders Day. Conducts community service programs that reflect the Lutheran heritage. **Awards:** Academic Scholarship. **Frequency:** annual. **Type:** scholarship. **Publications:** *The Ellipse*, semiannual. Magazine. **Conventions/Meetings:** annual convention ● quarterly National Executive Council Meetings - board meeting.

24095 ■ Phi Epsilon Phi
c/o Bernice O'Leary, Exec. Sec.
PO Box 4096
Burlingame, CA 94011-4096
Ph: (650)347-1765

Fax: (650)347-1765
URL: http://www.communitysororities.org/pep.html
Contact: Bernice O'Leary, Exec. Sec.
Founded: 1937. **Members:** 300. **Membership Dues:** individual, $65 (annual). **Staff:** 1. **Regional Groups:** 15. **State Groups:** 17. **Description:** Social and educational sorority. Conducts charitable program. **Awards:** Best Chapter Attendance at Convention. **Frequency:** annual. **Type:** recognition ● Best Educationals. **Frequency:** annual. **Type:** recognition ● Best Minutes. **Frequency:** annual. **Type:** recognition ● Best Treasurer Reports. **Frequency:** annual. **Type:** recognition. **Committees:** Philanthropy Project. **Publications:** *Circumference Newsletter*, quarterly. **Conventions/Meetings:** quarterly board meeting, business of sorority ● annual convention ● workshop.

24096 ■ Phi Mu Fraternity
400 Westpark Dr.
Peachtree City, GA 30269
Ph: (770)632-2090
Fax: (770)632-2135
E-mail: cbyford@phimu.org
URL: http://phimu.org
Contact: Ms. Cara Dawn Byford, Dir. of Member Services
Founded: 1852. **Members:** 100,000. **Staff:** 15. **Description:** Social sorority sponsors charitable and educational activities; offers placement service. Conducts competitions. **Awards:** **Type:** recognition. **Committees:** The Campaign for Phi Mu. **Publications:** *Aglaia*, quarterly. Magazine. **Circulation:** 100,000 ● Also publishes a directory of rush participants and in-house newsletters. **Conventions/Meetings:** biennial convention.

24097 ■ Phi Sigma Sigma
8178 Lark Brown Rd., Ste.202
Elkridge, MD 21075-6424
Ph: (410)799-1224
Fax: (410)799-9186
E-mail: phisighq@phisigmasigma.org
URL: http://www.phisigmasigma.org
Contact: Sandy Grossman, Grand Archon
Founded: 1913. **Members:** 54,992. **Staff:** 9. **National Groups:** 110. **Description:** Social sorority. Aims to inspire the personal development of each sister and perpetuate the advancement of womanhood. **Awards:** **Type:** recognition. **Publications:** *Sphinx*, quarterly. Magazine. **Circulation:** 22,000. Alternate Formats: online. **Conventions/Meetings:** annual meeting - always August.

24098 ■ Sigma Delta Tau (SDT)
714 Adams St.
Carmel, IN 46032
Ph: (317)846-7747 (317)575-5578
Fax: (317)575-5562
E-mail: nationaloffice@sigmadeltatau.com
URL: http://www.sigmadeltatau.com
Contact: Ann Stringer Braly, Exec. Dir.
Founded: 1917. **Members:** 35,000. **Membership Dues:** active, $65 (annual). **Description:** Social sorority. Presents awards and scholarships. Offers career networking for alumnae, placement services, and educational loans. Maintains charitable program. Supports the National Committee for the Prevention of Child Abuse. **Publications:** *SDT 75th Anniversary Alumnae Directory* ● *The Torch*, semiannual. Magazine.● Bulletin, monthly. **Conventions/Meetings:** Regional Leadership Conference ● workshop.

24099 ■ Sigma Kappa
8733 Founders Rd.
Indianapolis, IN 46268
Ph: (317)872-3275
Fax: (317)872-0716
E-mail: info@sigmakappa.org
URL: http://www.sigmakappa.org
Contact: Barbara Collins Wilmer, Pres.
Founded: 1874. **Members:** 138,900. **Staff:** 14. **Description:** Social sorority. **Absorbed:** Pi Kappa Sigma. **Publications:** *Sigma Kappa Savvy*, monthly. Newsletter. Alternate Formats: online ● *Sigma Kappa Triangle*, quarterly. Magazine. Alternate Formats: online ● *Virtual Violet*, monthly. Magazine. Alternate

Formats: online ● Annual Report, annual. Alternate Formats: online. **Conventions/Meetings:** biennial convention (exhibits).

24100 ■ Sigma Kappa Foundation
8733 Founders Rd.
Indianapolis, IN 46268
Ph: (317)872-3275
Fax: (317)872-0716
E-mail: alewis@sigmakappa.org
URL: http://www.sigmakappafoundation.org
Contact: Allison K. Lewis, Exec. Dir.
Founded: 1989. **Staff:** 3. **Description:** Educational foundation of Sigma Kappa (see separate entry). Financially supports leadership and educational programs. Conducts research, educational, and charitable programs. **Awards:** Alzheimer's Disease Research Grant. **Frequency:** annual. **Type:** grant. **Recipient:** to fund Alzheimer's disease research ● Graduate Scholarships. **Frequency:** 11/year. **Type:** scholarship. **Recipient:** to members attending graduate school ● House Directors School Grant. **Frequency:** semiannual. **Type:** grant. **Recipient:** to Sigma Kappa national housing corporation for the education of volunteers on how to provide a safe and healthy living environment for collegiate members ● Leadership Education Grant to Sigma Kappa Sorority. **Frequency:** annual. **Type:** grant. **Recipient:** for educational and leadership programs ● Undergraduate Scholarships. **Frequency:** annual. **Type:** scholarship. **Recipient:** to members. **Committees:** Alumnae Heart Fund; Building; Bylaws, Policy and Procedure; Development; Educational Area Review; Investment; Philanthropy; Scholarship; Sister to Sister Disaster Recovery Fund. **Publications:** *Foundation Gram*, periodic. Newsletter ● *Giving Benefits*. Brochure. Alternate Formats: online ● *Informational*. Brochure. Alternate Formats: online ● *New Member*. Brochure. Alternate Formats: online ● Annual Report, annual. **Conventions/Meetings:** periodic board meeting.

24101 ■ Sigma Sigma Sigma (SSS)
225 N Muhlenberg St.
Woodstock, VA 22664-1424
Ph: (540)459-4212
Fax: (540)459-2361
E-mail: trisigma@trisigma.org
URL: http://www.sigmasigmasigma.org
Contact: Ms. Marcia Cutter, Exec. Dir.
Founded: 1898. **Members:** 89,000. **Staff:** 11. **State Groups:** 106. **Local Groups:** 98. **Description:** Social National Panhellenic Society for college women and alumnae. Conducts philanthropic play therapy project for children at University of North Carolina Hospital (Chapel Hill, NC) and Children's Medical Center (Dallas, TX). Maintains Sigma Sigma Sigma Foundation. Sponsors leadership schools. **Awards:** **Type:** recognition. **Recipient:** for individuals and chapters. **Computer Services:** database, membership, career, and historical ● mailing lists. **Departments:** Alumnae; Collegiate; Membership Development; Panhellenic; Publications; Treasury. **Affiliated With:** National Panhellenic Conference. **Publications:** *The Triangle of Sigma, Sigma, Sigma*, 3/year. Magazine. **Price:** free, for members only. **Circulation:** 46,000. **Conventions/Meetings:** triennial convention, only for official jewelry (exhibits).

24102 ■ Theta Phi Alpha
27025 Knickerbocker Rd.
Bay Village, OH 44140-2300
Ph: (440)899-9282
Free: (877)THETA-PH
Fax: (440)899-9293
E-mail: info@thetaphialpha.org
URL: http://www.thetaphialpha.org
Contact: Susan Check, Natl. Staff Exec.
Founded: 1912. **Members:** 10,000. **National Groups:** 40. **Description:** Social sorority. Sponsors annual Founders Day; conducts fundraising projects for charitable organizations. **Committees:** Float Building; Garment; Greek Week; Historian; Memoirs; Publicity; Social Spirit. **Publications:** *The Compass of Theta Phi Alpha*, quarterly. Magazine. **Conventions/Meetings:** biennial convention.

24103 ■ Zeta Tau Alpha (ZTA)
3450 Founders Rd.
Indianapolis, IN 46268
Ph: (317)872-0540
Fax: (317)876-3948
E-mail: zetataualpha@zetataualpha.org
URL: http://www.zetataualpha.org
Contact: Deb Ensor, Exec. Dir.
Founded: 1898. **Members:** 190,000. **Description:** Serves as a social sorority. **Publications:** *Themis*, quarterly. Magazine. **Price:** $2.00/year. Alternate Formats: online. **Conventions/Meetings:** biennial meeting.

Sociology

24104 ■ Alpha Kappa Delta (AKD)
c/o Marc Matre, Sec.-Treas.
Box U-1147
Mobile, AL 36688
Ph: (251)461-1700 (251)460-6348
Fax: (251)460-7925
E-mail: mmatre@jaguar1.usouthal.edu
URL: http://www.alpha-kappa-delta.org
Contact: Marc Matre, Sec.-Treas.
Founded: 1920. **Members:** 60,000. **Membership Dues:** life, $40 ● undergraduate/graduate student, $20 (annual) ● non-student, $40 (annual). **Budget:** $50,000. **Description:** Honorary society - men and women, sociology. Promotes scholarships in Sociology. **Publications:** *Sociological Inquiry*, quarterly. Journal. Contains research reports. **Price:** included in membership dues; $21.00 /year for nonmembers. ISSN: 0038-0245. **Circulation:** 2,000 ● Handbook ● Newsletter, quarterly. **Conventions/Meetings:** competition, for undergraduate papers ● symposium, research.

24105 ■ Honors Program Student Association of the American Sociological Association (HPSA)
c/o University of Wisconsin-Parkside
PO Box 2000
Kenosha, WI 53141-2000
Ph: (202)383-9005
E-mail: honors@asanet.org
URL: http://www.asanet.org/page.
ww?section=Students&name=Students3-column
Contact: Dr. Dennis M. Rome, Contact
Founded: 1972. **Members:** 150. **Description:** Individuals who have completed the Honors Program of the American Sociological Association. Facilitates communication among members; assists sociology students. **Affiliated With:** American Sociological Association. **Publications:** *Honors Student Handbook*, annual ● *The Network*, quarterly. Newsletter. **Conventions/Meetings:** semiannual meeting (exhibits) ● workshop.

Sororities

24106 ■ Delta Sigma Chi Sorority
114-75 226th St.
Cambria Heights, NY 11411
Free: (866)439-6489
E-mail: info@dsc1996.org
URL: http://dsc1996.org
Contact: Mercedes Feliciano, Co-Founder/Exec. Dir.
Founded: 1996. **Description:** Promotes community service, academic excellence and empowerment among women of different cultural backgrounds. Stimulates friendship among members. **Telecommunication Services:** electronic mail, national@dsc1996.org ● electronic mail, director@dsc1996.org.

24107 ■ Delta Tau Lambda Sorority (DTL)
PO Box 7714
Ann Arbor, MI 48107
E-mail: dtl-info@deltataulambda.org
URL: http://www.deltataulambda.org
Contact: Darilis Garcia-McMillan, Pres.
Founded: 1994. **Description:** Aims to build and strengthen the Latina's position in the community.

Promotes academic excellence and community service. Fosters education, research and support of breast cancer, diabetes, HIV/AIDS and mental health related concerns. **Awards:** Lydia Cruz and Sandra Maria Ramos Scholarship. **Frequency:** annual. **Type:** scholarship. **Recipient:** to a graduating high school Latina senior attending 2 or 4 years higher learning institution. **Telecommunication Services:** electronic mail, webmaster@deltataulambda.org.

24108 ■ Gamma Gamma Chi Sorority
PO Box 15283
Alexandria, VA 22309
Ph: (703)780-7611
Fax: (703)780-7620
E-mail: info@gammagammachi.org
URL: http://gammagammachi.org
Contact: Dr. Althia F. Collins, Pres./Exec. Dir.
Founded: 2005. **Description:** Promotes sisterhood, scholarship, leadership and community service. Aims to increase the involvement of members in their respective communities. Provides assistance and support to Muslim women. **Publications:** Newsletter. Alternate Formats: online.

24109 ■ Kappa Phi Gamma Sorority
3439 Woodbrook Ln.
Sugar Land, TX 77478
E-mail: kpgregents@yahoo.com
URL: http://www.kappaphigamma.org
Contact: Jasmine Bharj, Regent
Founded: 1998. **Description:** Promotes scholastic and ethical standards among South Asian women. Encourages unity, friendship and allegiance among collegiate women of different backgrounds. Improves and disseminates knowledge about South Asian race and culture. **Awards:** Emerald Endowment. **Frequency:** annual. **Type:** scholarship. **Recipient:** to an incoming freshman who has demonstrated excellence in scholarship, leadership and service.

24110 ■ Lambda Psi Delta Sorority (LPsiD)
PO Box 260128
Hartford, CT 06126
E-mail: nationals@lamdapsidelta.org
URL: http://www.lambdapsidelta.org
Contact: Elizabeth Castro, Pres.
Founded: 1997. **Description:** Promotes sisterhood and community outreach. Empowers women through leadership, intellectual development and cultural awareness. Encourages women to participate in educational, cultural, political and public service activities. **Publications:** Tiger's Tale, quarterly. Newsletter. Alternate Formats: online.

Spanish

24111 ■ Sigma Delta Pi
The Citadel
171 Moultrie St.
Charleston, SC 29409-0002
E-mail: delmastrom@citadel.edu
URL: http://www.sigmadeltapi.org
Contact: Mark P. Del Mastro, Founder/Dir.
Founded: 1919. **Membership Dues:** life (active, honorary, graduate/alumnus), $25. **Regional Groups:** 500. **Languages:** English, Spanish. **Description:** Honorary society - men and women, Spanish language and literature. **Awards:** Capitulos de Honor y Merito. **Frequency:** annual. **Type:** recognition. **Recipient:** for chapters with outstanding activities ● Premio Minaya Alvar-Fanez. **Frequency:** annual. **Type:** monetary. **Recipient:** for the most productive chapter adviser. **Publications:** Entre Nosotros (in English and Spanish), annual. **Price:** free for chapters. ISSN: 1092-6526. **Circulation:** 520 ● Reports, annual.

Speech

24112 ■ Delta Sigma Rho - Tau Kappa Alpha (DSR-TKA)
c/o Dr. Frank M. Thompson, Sec.
Univ. of Alabama
Dept. of Commun. Stud.
PO Box 870172
Tuscaloosa, AL 35487-0172

Ph: (205)348-6010 (205)348-8077
Fax: (205)348-8080
E-mail: fthompso@ccom.ua.edu
URL: http://www.ua.edu
Contact: Dr. Frank M. Thompson, Sec.
Founded: 1963. **Members:** 24,000. **Local Groups:** 180. **Description:** Honorary society - men and women, forensics. Sponsors national debate and individual event competitions. **Awards:** Speaker of the Year Award. **Type:** recognition. **Additional Websites:** http://www.mnsu.edu/spcomm/dsr-tka/dsr-tka.htm. **Affiliated With:** Association of College Honor Societies. **Formed by Merger of:** Delta Sigma Rho; Tau Kappa Alpha. **Publications:** Speaker and Gavel, quarterly. **Conventions/Meetings:** annual conference.

Technology

24113 ■ Epsilon Pi Tau (EPT)
Bowling Green State Univ.
Tech. Bldg.
Bowling Green, OH 43403-0296
Ph: (419)372-2425
Fax: (419)372-9502
E-mail: ept@bgsu.edu
URL: http://www.epsilonpitau.org
Contact: Dr. Jerry Olson, Interim Exec. Dir.
Founded: 1929. **Members:** 18,000. **Membership Dues:** regular, $25 (annual). **Staff:** 1. **Budget:** $120,000. **Regional Groups:** 5. **National Groups:** 119. **Multinational. Description:** Members are science and technology professionals, executives in business, industry, education and government, leaders of professional organizations in technology, students in associate, bachelor's and higher degree science and technology professional preparation and advancement programs, practicing engineers, technologists, technicians, supervisors, managers, private entrepreneurs, inventors, scientists, social scientists, public and vocational school teachers and administrators, college and university faculty, researchers and administrators. Objectives are to promote and recognize the achievement of academic excellence, the values and contributions of professionals in technology, to provide a medium for the professional development and recognition of individuals for leadership and achievement in the technology professions, to enhance the status of practitioners in technology professions, to foster and encourage the acceptance of the ideals of technical competence, social proficiency, and research, and to advance understanding, appreciation and awareness of technology as both an enduring and influential human endeavor and an integral element of culture. **Awards:** W. E. Warner. **Frequency:** annual. **Type:** monetary. **Affiliated With:** International Association for Science, Technology and Society; International Technology Education Association; National Association of Industrial Technology; World Council of Associations for Technology Education. **Publications:** The Epsilon Pi Tau Preceptor, semiannual. Magazine. Contains items on leadership, technology, development, relevant Web sites, events and news of the organization, its chapters and members. **Price:** included in membership dues. ISSN: 1540-9910. **Circulation:** 15,000. **Advertising:** accepted. Alternate Formats: online ● Journal of Technology Studies, annual, updated continuously on the website. Combines all articles produced on the website. **Price:** $20.00 in U.S.; $30.00 outside U.S. ISSN: 1071-6084. Alternate Formats: online. Also Cited As: Journal of Epsilon Pi Tau. **Conventions/Meetings:** annual meeting.

Theatre

24114 ■ Theta Alpha Phi
PO Box 14773
Columbus, OH 43214
Ph: (614)447-8045
E-mail: pat_y2kus@yahoo.com
URL: http://www.bgsu.edu/studentlife/organizations/
  theta-alpha-phi
Contact: Amanda Sterling, Sec.
Founded: 1919. **Members:** 49,028. **Membership Dues:** student, $35 (annual). **Staff:** 6. **Local Groups:**

30. **Description:** Recognition fraternity for men and women involved in college theatre. **Convention/Meeting:** none. **Publications:** The Cue, annual. Includes directory.

Transportation

24115 ■ Delta Nu Alpha Transportation Fraternity (DNA)
1451 Elm Hill Pike, Ste.255
Nashville, TN 37210
Ph: (615)360-6863
Fax: (615)360-1891
E-mail: carolh24@msn.com
URL: http://deltanualpha.org
Contact: Carol Hackett, Contact
Founded: 1940. **Members:** 500. **Membership Dues:** silver, $75 (annual) ● student, $35 (annual) ● gold, $125 (annual). **Staff:** 4. **Regional Groups:** 6. **State Groups:** 48. **Local Groups:** 22. **Description:** Serves as professional fraternity - transportation with the focus of transportation, logistics, and supply chain education. **Awards:** Maxwell Powell Award. **Frequency:** annual. **Type:** recognition. **Recipient:** for individual who has contributed to the betterment of the organization on an on-going basis throughout the years ● Student Scholarships. **Frequency:** annual. **Type:** scholarship. **Recipient:** for outstanding professional or student in transportation ● Transportation Person of the Year. **Frequency:** annual. **Type:** recognition. **Recipient:** for outstanding person in the field of transportation, supply chain, and logistics given during annual transportation conference. **Publications:** The Alphian Connection, monthly. Newsletter. Contains organization and industry's specific information. Alternate Formats: online ● Journal of Transportation Management, periodic. **Conventions/Meetings:** annual Transportation Education Conference - conference and seminar (exhibits) - always fall.

Veterinary Medicine

24116 ■ Phi Zeta
c/o Dr. James E. Smallwood, Sec.-Treas.
APR Dept.
Coll. of Veterinary Medicine
North Carolina State Univ.
Raleigh, NC 27606
Ph: (919)513-6223
Fax: (919)513-6465
E-mail: ed_smallwood@ncsu.edu
URL: http://www.cvm.missouri.edu/Phizeta
Contact: Dr. James E. Smallwood, Sec.-Treas.
Founded: 1925. **Local Groups:** 27. **Description:** Honor society for veterinary medicine. **Conventions/Meetings:** annual conference and meeting.

Vocational Education

24117 ■ Iota Lambda Sigma (ILS)
c/o Anna Skinner, Exec. Sec.-Treas.
607 Pkwy. W
Oregon, OH 43616
Ph: (419)693-6860
Fax: (419)693-6859
E-mail: ilsgrandchapter@aol.com
URL: http://www.iotalambdasigma.com
Contact: Anna Skinner, Exec. Sec.-Treas.
Founded: 1927. **Members:** 2,500. **Membership Dues:** regular and at large, $10 (annual) ● life, $562. **Description:** Serves as a professional and honorary fraternity - trade and industrial education, business education, distributive education, home economics, health occupations, technical education, and technology. **Awards:** Outstanding Chapter of the Year. **Frequency:** annual. **Type:** recognition ● Outstanding Teacher Award. **Frequency:** annual. **Type:** recognition ● Presidential Plaque. **Frequency:** annual. **Type:** recognition. **Recipient:** to grand chapter presidents at the end of their successful terms ● Raymond L.

Christensen Distinguished Service Award. **Frequency:** annual. **Type:** recognition. **Recipient:** for members with at least 10 continuous years and have a record of commitment to excellence and service ● **Type:** scholarship. **Recipient:** for graduate studies. **Publications:** *Communicator*, quarterly. **Advertising:** accepted ● Directory, periodic ● Handbooks ● Annual Report, annual. **Conventions/Meetings:** annual National Advisory Committee and Grand Chapter - meeting, held in conjunction with American Vocational Association - always December.

24118 ■ National Technical Honor Society (NTHS)
PO Box 1336
Flat Rock, NC 28731
Ph: (828)698-8011 (828)698-8239
Free: (800)801-7090
Fax: (828)698-8564

E-mail: requests@nths.org
URL: http://www.nths.org
Contact: C. Allen Powell, Exec. Dir./Co-Founder
Founded: 1984. **Members:** 50,000. **Membership Dues:** individual, $20 (annual) ● honorary, $30 (annual). **Staff:** 7. **Budget:** $650,000. **State Groups:** 8. **Local Groups:** 1,400. **Description:** Honor students engaged in occupational and vocational-technical programs at secondary, postsecondary, public, or private schools in the U.S. Promotes vocational-technical education, career development, skilled workmanship, and individual qualities such as leadership and honesty. Works to strengthen the link between vocational-technical institutions and business and industry. Encourages and assists students with their career goals; recognizes student achievement; supplies letters of recommendation. Conducts educational programs and placement service. **Awards:** Jon H. Poteat Scholarships. **Frequency:**

annual. **Type:** scholarship. **Recipient:** to student members who consistently exemplify the seven character attributes of the NTHS ● NTHS/DECA Scholarships. **Frequency:** annual. **Type:** scholarship. **Recipient:** to high school students who are members of both DECA and NTHS ● NTHS/FBLA-PBL Scholarships. **Frequency:** annual. **Type:** scholarship. **Recipient:** to students who have outstanding achievement ● NTHS/HOSA Scholarships. **Frequency:** annual. **Type:** scholarship. **Recipient:** for active HOSA members who are also current NTHS members in good standing ● NTHS/SkillsUSA Scholarships. **Frequency:** annual. **Type:** scholarship. **Recipient:** to students who are active dues-paying members of both SkillsUSA and NTHS. **Formerly:** (2003) National Vocational-Technical Honor Society. **Publications:** *The Artisan.* Newsletter. **Price:** free. Alternate Formats: online. **Conventions/Meetings:** annual National Leadership Conference (exhibits).

Actors

24119 ■ Aldo Ray Fan Club (ARFC)
Address Unknown since 2007
Founded: 1986. **Members:** 160. **Description:** Fans of film actor Aldo Ray (1926-1991). Disseminates information about Ray's career (must include stamped, self-addressed envelope for response). Compiles statistics. **Libraries: Type:** reference. **Holdings:** archival material. **Publications:** Newsletter, semiannual ● Also publishes special announcements.

24120 ■ American Friends of Henry Irving
Penthouse North
29 Washington Sq. W
New York, NY 10011
Ph: (212)533-5018
E-mail: jeannekey@aol.com
Contact: Jenny O'Casey, Exec.Dir.
Founded: 1985. **Members:** 76. **Staff:** 2. **Budget:** $25,000. **Description:** Honors the memory of actor Sir Henry Irving and his associates. **Libraries: Type:** not open to the public. **Holdings:** 123. **Subjects:** Irving, Lyceum theatre, peer actors. **Also Known As:** (1995) Henry Irving Aficionados. **Publications:** *Quarterly Vampire Empire*. Newsletter.

24121 ■ Andrea McArdle Fan Club (AMFC)
2352 B South St.
Elgin, IL 60123
Ph: (847)695-3163
E-mail: rwhite6305@aol.com
URL: http://andreamcardle.homestead.com
Contact: Christopher White, Pres.
Founded: 1979. **Members:** 100. **Description:** Individuals interested in the career of Andrea McArdle (1963-), actress and singer best known for her role in the Broadway musical Annie. Organizes periodic fundraisers for charitable organizations. **Convention/Meeting:** none. **Publications:** *Andrea*, quarterly. Newsletter. **Price:** included in membership dues. **Circulation:** 100. **Advertising:** accepted.

24122 ■ Ann-Margret's Official Fan Club
5664 Cahuenga Blvd., Ste.336
North Hollywood, CA 91601
E-mail: ann-margret@fansource.com
URL: http://www.fansource.com/a-m.htm
Contact: Kathy Bartels, Dir.
Membership Dues: individual, $15 (annual). **Multinational. Description:** Serves as a Fan club devoted to Ann-Margret; members receive a welcome letter from Ann-Margret, biography, filmography, discography, information about Ann-Margret's autobiography, two 8x10 black and white photos.

24123 ■ Barbara Bain International (BBI)
c/o Ms. Terry S. Bowers, Pres.
603 N Clark St.
River Falls, WI 54022-1404

E-mail: frozendestiny75@hotmail.com
URL: http://www.barbarabain.net
Contact: Ms. Terry S. Bowers, Pres.
Founded: 1979. **Members:** 60. **Multinational. Description:** Individuals interested in the acting career of Barbara Bain, 3-time Emmy winner for her role in the popular television series Mission: Impossible and star of Space: 1999. Informs members of the current activities of Bain. **Formerly:** (1993) Landau-Bain Fan Association. **Publications:** Newsletter, bimonthly. **Price:** included in membership dues ● Also publishes Fanzines based on Ms. Bain's Space: 1999 and Mission Impossible characters currently available. SASE or 2 IRC's for information.

24124 ■ Barbara Eden's Official Fan Club
PO Box 5556
Sherman Oaks, CA 91403
E-mail: barbaraclub@fansource.com
URL: http://www.fansource.com
Contact: Marie Levesque, Contact
Founded: 1977. **Members:** 300. **Membership Dues:** subscription, $15 (annual). **Description:** Individuals interested in the activities of actress Barbara Eden. Informs members of upcoming appearances. Compiles statistics of Eden's T.V. and film credits from 1956 to present. **Convention/Meeting:** none. **Formerly:** (1992) Barbara Eden International Fan Club. **Publications:** *Barbara Eden Official Fan Club—Newsletter*, periodic. Includes television and movie credit updates and photos. **Price:** included in membership dues.

24125 ■ Barry Bostwick Fan Club (BBFC)
Address Unknown since 2006
Founded: 1981. **Members:** 300. **Membership Dues:** individual, $5 (annual). **Description:** Fans of actor Barry Bostwick (1945-), whose career includes Broadway, movies, and television mini-series. Serves as a forum for the exchange of information, photos, and other Bostwick memorabilia. Disseminates information about Bostwick's current activities and schedule of appearances. **Libraries: Type:** reference. **Holdings:** biographical archives. **Publications:** *Barry Bostwick Fan Club Newsletter*, 2-4/year. **Price:** included in membership dues. **Advertising:** not accepted.

24126 ■ Betty White Fan Club (BWFC)
c/o Kay Daly
3552 Fed. Ave.
Los Angeles, CA 90066
E-mail: bettywhiteonline@ruemcclanahan.com
URL: http://www.geocities.com/goldengirlskatie/
betspets.html
Contact: Kay Daly, Contact
Founded: 1971. **Members:** 120. **Membership Dues:** regular, in U.S., $15 (annual) ● regular, outside U.S., $20 (annual). **Description:** Fans of actress Betty White (1922-), who won two Emmy awards for her portrayal of Sue Ann Nivens on the Mary Tyler Moore Show (1973-77) and who won an additional Emmy for her portrayal of Rose on the NBC television series The Golden Girls. Disseminates information on

White's activities. Supports animal welfare charities. Maintains biographical archive. **Convention/Meeting:** none. **Telecommunication Services:** electronic mail, kdaly10288@aol.com. **Also Known As:** Bets' Pets. **Publications:** *Bets' Petletter*, quarterly. Bulletin. **Advertising:** accepted ● *Bets' Pets Roundup*, semiannual. Journal.

24127 ■ Beyond the Rainbow
PO Box 31672
St. Louis, MO 63131
Ph: (314)799-1724
Fax: (314)909-6617
E-mail: elaine@beyondtherainbow2oz.com
URL: http://www.beyondtherainbow2oz.com
Contact: Elaine Willingham, Founder
Founded: 1985. **Members:** 2,000. **Staff:** 4. **For-Profit. Description:** Admirers and friends of actress/singer Judy Garland (1922-69), best known for her role as Dorothy in the film The Wizard of Oz. Offers sale of Oz collectibles. Disseminates information on special events regarding Judy Garland, L. Frank Baum and the Wizard of Oz. **Awards:** ILL Humanities Council 1999. **Type:** grant. **Recipient:** for Dorothy Gage Project. **Publications:** *All Things Oz*. Book. Contains 352 pages of stunning illustrations and profoundly wise text. **Price:** $19.99 ● *Cooking In Oz*. Covers 100 years of Oz history, plus recipes. **Conventions/Meetings:** periodic OzRendezvous - convention (exhibits).

24128 ■ Bruce Boxleitner's Official Fan Club
PO Box 5513
Sherman Oaks, CA 91403
E-mail: bruce@fansource.com
URL: http://www.fansource.com/boxleitner.htm
Contact: Bruce Boxleitner, Contact
Founded: 1991. **Members:** 200. **Membership Dues:** subscription, $15 (annual). **Staff:** 1. **Description:** Admirers of actor Bruce Boxleitner, whose career includes the hit television series "Scarecrow and Mrs. King" and "Babylon J." Keeps members informed of Boxleitner's career projects and club activities. **Publications:** Newsletter, periodic. Updates Bruce's Career. **Price:** included in membership dues.

24129 ■ Conrad Veidt Society (CVS)
c/o Barbara Peterson
407 Kingston Ct.
Yorktown, VA 23693
E-mail: nocturne_cvs@yahoo.com
URL: http://www.geocities.com/Hollywood/Studio/
7624/Official.html
Contact: Barbara Peterson, Contact
Founded: 1990. **Members:** 150. **Membership Dues:** general, $30 (annual) ● contributing, $60 (annual) ● life, $100. **Staff:** 2. **Description:** Admirers of Conrad Veidt (1893-1943), the veteran actor whose career linked silent German impressionism with Hollywood of the 1940s. He refused to star in Nazi propaganda films, left Hitler's Germany, and aided the Allied cause through his war-time films. Veidt is ironically remembered best by many for his portrayals of Nazis in American films, including Casablanca, in which he

starred as Major Strasser. Promotes the public appreciation and preservation of Veidt and his films; supported retrospectives and film festivals in London, Berlin, and the United States in 1993, the centennial of Veidt's birth. **Libraries: Type:** open to the public. **Holdings:** clippings, papers, photographs. **Subjects:** collections of Conrad Veidt's personal memorabilia donated to Pacific Film Archive, University of California at Berkeley. **Additional Websites:** http://www. geocities.com/Hollywood/Studio/7624/alltext/Choices. html. **Publications:** *Conrad Veidt Society Newsletter*, periodic. Reports current events of interests. **Price:** included in membership dues. **Circulation:** 150. **Advertising:** accepted. Alternate Formats: online ● *Nocturne.* Journal. **Price:** $4.00 for nonmembers; included in membership dues. Alternate Formats: online.

24130 ■ Danny Cooksey Fan Club (DCFC)
Address Unknown since 2007
Founded: 1981. **Members:** 1,300. **Membership Dues:** $10. **Description:** Fans of singer and actor Danny Cooksey (1975-), who has appeared on numerous television shows including the comedy series "Diff'rent Strokes" and "Salute Your Shorts," and is lead singer of the heavy metal band Lucy's Milk. Works to promote Cooksey and his career. Disseminates information about Cooksey's activities. Operates children's services. **Awards: Type:** recognition. **Affiliated With:** International Fan Club Organization. **Publications:** Newsletter, 3-4/year ● Also publishes updates on Cooksey's appearances. **Conventions/Meetings:** annual Christmas Party ● competition.

24131 ■ David Birney International Fan Club (DBIFC)
c/o Bret Adams, Ltd.
Artists Agency
488 W 44th St.
New York, NY 10036
Ph: (212)265-5630
Fax: (212)265-2212
E-mail: badamsltd@aol.com
URL: http://davidbirney.com
Contact: Ruth K. Becht, Pres.
Founded: 1978. **Members:** 100. **Staff:** 12. **Multinational. Description:** Fans of actor David Birney (1939-), best known for his role as Salieri in the stage production of Amadeus and his appearance in the television show Bridget Loves Bernie, which ran from 1972 to 1973. Works to keep members advised of Birney's public appearances; helps members obtain tickets to such events. Supports Birney's volunteer work; holds contests. Tours with various plays. Most recently "The Diaries of Adam and Eve". Equus, Moon for the Mis Begotten. **Libraries: Type:** reference. **Holdings:** archival material. **Publications:** *The Birney Bulletin*, semiannual. Updates on Birney's personal life and career and Birney's responses to members' questions. ● *The Christmas Tree.* Audiotape. **Price:** $15.00 plus shipping and handling.

24132 ■ Dinah Shore Memorial Fan Club
c/o Kay Daly, Pres.
3552 Fed. Ave.
Los Angeles, CA 90066
E-mail: kdaly10288@aol.com
URL: http://www.dinahshorefanclub.com/dsclub.htm
Contact: Kay Daly, Pres.
Founded: 1952. **Membership Dues:** regular, in U.S., $12 (annual) ● regular, outside U.S., $16 (annual). **Description:** Fan club honoring singer, entertainer Dinah Shore. **Publications:** *Dinah's Digest*, annual. Journal. **Price:** included in membership dues ● *The Shoreline*, quarterly. Newsletter. **Price:** included in membership dues. **Advertising:** accepted ● Booklet. **Price:** included in membership dues.

24133 ■ Fans of Leonard Nimoy and DeForest Kelley
383 Yallow Pine Dr.
Bailey, CO 80421-1871
Ph: (303)816-0083

E-mail: lguyer@aol.com
URL: http://members.tripod.com/~Nimoy_Kelley/ index.html
Contact: Laura Guyer, Exec. Off.
Founded: 1989. **Members:** 450. **Staff:** 1. **Description:** Follows the careers of actor, director, and producer Leonard Nimoy (1931-) and actor DeForest Kelley (1920-1999), best known for their roles in the Star Trek television and motion picture series. Compiles and disseminates information related to the current activities and personal appearances of Nimoy and information related to the career of Kelley. **Convention/Meeting:** none. **Libraries: Type:** reference. **Holdings:** 100; archival material, audiovisuals, books, clippings, periodicals. **Computer Services:** database ● mailing lists. **Publications:** Newsletter, monthly. **Circulation:** 100. **Advertising:** accepted.

24134 ■ Far Beyond the Stars
c/o Gayle Stever, Club Coor.
PO Box 11261
Scottsdale, AZ 85271-1261
E-mail: gsstever@aol.com
URL: http://www.sidcity.net
Contact: Gayle Stever, Club Coor.
Founded: 1995. **Members:** 250. **Membership Dues:** regular in North America, $25 (annual) ● regular outside North America, $35 (annual). **Staff:** 5. **Description:** Represents admirers of actor and director Alexander Siddig, Armin Shimerman and Nana Visitor. Promotes Siddig's, Shimerman's and Visitor's careers. Conducts fundraising activities benefiting Siddig's, Shimerman's and Visitor's favorite charities; facilitates communication among members. **Additional Websites:** http://www.nanavision.com. **Formerly:** (1999) Doctor's Exchange. **Publications:** Newsletter, bimonthly. **Price:** included in membership dues.

24135 ■ Friends of Debbie Reynolds Fan Club (FDRFC)
5713 Rosario Blvd.
North Highlands, CA 95660
Ph: (916)331-0247
E-mail: mail@debbiereynoldsonline.com
URL: http://www.debbiereynoldsonline.com
Contact: Debbie Reynold, Contact
Founded: 1979. **Members:** 150. **Description:** Fans and admirers of film actress and entertainer Debbie Reynolds (1932). Makes available to members photographs of Reynolds and information on her career and public appearances. **Libraries: Type:** open to the public. **Holdings:** articles.

24136 ■ Friends of Hopalong Cassidy Fan Club
6310 Friendship Dr.
New Concord, OH 43762-9708
E-mail: lbates1205@cs.com
URL: http://www.hopalong.com/f_friends.asp
Contact: Laura Bates, Founder
Founded: 1991. **Members:** 545. **Membership Dues:** individual, $20 (annual). **Staff:** 2. **Multinational. Description:** Fans of William Boyd, who played Western hero Hopalong Cassidy in movies (1930s and 1940s) and television (1949-51). Seeks to perpetuate the memory of William Boyd and his work as Hopalong Cassidy. Group has participated in erecting a monument at Boyd's former school, naming a sidewalk after him, and purchasing his boyhood home for preservation. Sponsors festival in Cambridge, Ohio, 1st weekend in May. **Publications:** *Hoppy Talk*, quarterly. Newsletter. **Price:** included in membership dues. **Circulation:** 600. **Advertising:** accepted. **Conventions/Meetings:** annual Hopalong Cassidy Festival, includes collector's show and sale (exhibits) - always Cambridge, OH.

24137 ■ Friends of Lainie Kazan (Folks)
Address Unknown since 2007
Founded: 1990. **Members:** 2,000. **Membership Dues:** individual, $2 (annual). **Staff:** 1. **Description:** Admirers of actress Lainie Kazan. Promotes interest in Kazan's life and career. Gathers and disseminates information on Kazan's work; keeps members abreast of Kazan's current activities and appearance itiner-

ary. **Computer Services:** database ● mailing lists. **Publications:** *Folks*, periodic. Newsletter. **Price:** included in membership dues. **Advertising:** not accepted.

24138 ■ Gale Storm Appreciation Society
c/o Richard A. Bullis, Pres.
6119 3rd Ave. S
St. Petersburg, FL 33707
Ph: (727)381-1056
E-mail: rbullis@tampabay.rr.com
URL: http://galelore.tripod.com/GaleStormFanClub. html
Contact: Richard A. Bullis, Pres.
Membership Dues: regular, $18 (annual). **Description:** Fan club honoring actress, singer, and entertainer Gale Storm. **Additional Websites:** http://www. galestormappreciationsociety.us. **Publications:** Newsletter, quarterly. **Price:** included in membership dues. Alternate Formats: online.

24139 ■ Gary's Web International (GWI)
PO Box 2202
Rancho Cucamonga, CA 91729
Ph: (714)296-4835
E-mail: sinisefans@sinisefans.org
URL: http://www.sinisefans.org/gwi
Contact: L. Loschin, Chair
Founded: 1996. **Members:** 400. **Budget:** $300. **Description:** Admirers of actor Gary Sinise. Promotes appreciation of theatre and film; seeks to advance Sinise's career. Facilitates communication and good fellowship among members. **Computer Services:** Mailing lists, free discussion and announcement lists. **Publications:** Newsletter, quarterly. **Price:** free.

24140 ■ International Sybil Jason Fan Club
c/o Gary L. Heckman, Pres.
745 S 31st St.
Lincoln, NE 68510
Ph: (402)477-7875
E-mail: mikescaife@btinternet.com
URL: http://www.mikescaife.btinternet.co.uk/sybil.htm
Contact: Gary L. Heckman, Pres.
Founded: 1984. **Members:** 95. **Membership Dues:** regular, in U.S., $12 (annual) ● regular, outside U.S., $17 (annual). **Staff:** 2. **Description:** Admirers of Sybil Jason, first child star of Warner Brothers Pictures from 1935-40. Co-stared with Shirley Temple, Al Jolson, Dick Powell, Humphrey Bogart, Jane Wyman, and others. **Libraries: Type:** open to the public. **Holdings:** 19; articles, papers, photographs. **Subjects:** early Hollywood. **Also Known As:** Official Sybil Jason Fan Club. **Publications:** *Sybil Jason Fan Club Newsletter*, quarterly. Includes autograph, 8x10 signed photograph of Jason, letters from, and articles about Sybil Jason. **Price:** included in membership dues. **Advertising:** accepted. **Conventions/Meetings:** quinquennial party and convention, held at Warner Brothers Studio (exhibits).

24141 ■ Jane Powell Fan Club (JPFC)
847 S Carpenter Ave.
Oak Park, IL 60304
Ph: (708)386-2587
E-mail: tonymakara@yahoo.co.uk
URL: http://thegirlmostlovely.freehomepage.com
Contact: Ron Parker, Pres.
Founded: 1969. **Members:** 5,000. **Description:** Fans of singer/actress Jane Powell (1929-), whose film credits include Seven Brides for Seven Brothers and The Girl Most Likely. Enables members to assist one another in finding Powell memorabilia.

24142 ■ Jeanette MacDonald International Fan Club (JMIFC)
c/o Clara B. Rhoades, Co-Pres.
1617 SW Indian Trail
Topeka, KS 66604-1951
Ph: (785)271-7468
E-mail: talemaker1@aol.com
URL: http://www.jeanettemacdonaldfanclub.com/ jmifc__membership_mail_form.htm
Contact: Clara B. Rhoades, Co-Pres.
Founded: 1937. **Members:** 1,990. **Membership Dues:** individual, $14 (annual) ● family, $15 (annual).

Staff: 2. **Description:** Seeks to perpetuate the memory of Jeanette MacDonald (1907-1965), a singer and actress who performed on Broadway, in movies, opera, TV, and radio from 1929 to 1963. After leaving films, she appeared in stage operettas and recitals/concerts until 1959, and on television in 1963. Sponsors a therapy fund to provide aid to crippled children and club members in need. Conducts charitable programs and research on the work of MacDonald and her husband, actor and composer Gene Raymond. Provides information and materials on Jeanette MacDonald's and Raymond's lives and activities, including photographs, tapes, records, and books. Compiles statistics; operates museum. **Libraries: Type:** reference. **Holdings:** 802; archival material, clippings, films. **Subjects:** Jeanette MacDonald, Gene Raymond. **Committees:** Archives; Information; Library; Research. **Departments:** Blind; Goodwill; Translators. **Publications:** *Golden Comet Magazine*, semiannual. **Price:** included in membership dues ● *La Petite Comet*, semiannual ● *Lookin' in and Cookin' in with the MacRaymonds*. Book ● *Private Thoughts on Marriage/Life/Career of the Raymonds* ● *Recipes* ● Bulletin, periodic. **Price:** included in membership dues. **Conventions/Meetings:** annual Clan Clave - meeting, with film showings (exhibits) - always end of June, Los Angeles, CA.

24143 ■ Jon-Erik Hexum Fan Club (JEHFC)
c/o Alan J. Carell, Sec.
3003 NE Knott St.
Portland, OR 97212-3536
URL: http://www.geocities.com/Hollywood/Hills/1744/
 Jon_Erik_Hexum.html
Contact: Alan J. Carell, Sec.
Founded: 1986. **Members:** 525. **Staff:** 2. **Description:** Individuals interested in the life and career of actor Jon-Erik Hexum (1957-84), whose most notable roles were in the NBC television series *Voyagers*, (1982 to 1983) and *Cover Up* (1984); and in the films *Making of a Male Model* (1983) and *The Bear* (1984). Seeks to preserve Hexum's memory and to commemorate his life. Facilitates communication among members; acts as a clearinghouse for Hexum memorabilia. Maintains photo and print archives. Supports THS Scholarship Fund for the performing arts. **Libraries: Type:** reference. **Holdings:** archival material, clippings. **Awards:** Jon-Erik Hexum Performing Arts Award. **Frequency:** annual. **Type:** scholarship. **Recipient:** for Tenefly High School students. **Publications:** *Good Guy - A Biography*. Book. Features the biography of Jon-Erik Hexum's life and career, illustrated. ● *He's Not Coming Back*. Booklet. Features the analysis of Hexum's shooting, its news coverage, and aftermath. **Price:** $4.00/copy ● *Hex-Nut*, periodic. Newsletter ● *Meetings and Recollections*. Booklet ● *Photo Catalogue*. **Price:** $16.00/copy ● *Trying Out His Parts*. Booklet. Describes Hexum's college years (1976-1980). **Price:** $3.00/copy ● Also publishes roster of *Hexum's T.V,* movie credits, pictorial biography, and a bibliography of news and feature coverage of Hexum's career.

24144 ■ June Wilkinson Fan Club (JWFC)
c/o Scott Hughes, Pres.
7901 Iroquois Ct.
Woodridge, IL 60517-3332
Ph: (630)985-4714
E-mail: jwilkinson@ameritech.net
URL: http://members.tripod.com/junewilkinson0
Contact: Scott Hughes, Pres.
Founded: 1997. **Membership Dues:** every two newsletter issues, in U.S., $15 ● every two newsletter issues, outside U.S., $18. **Description:** Admirers of stage actress and film star June Wilkinson. Promotes appreciation of Wilkinson's work. Serves as a clearinghouse on Wilkinson's career; facilitates exchange of information among members. **Computer Services:** Mailing lists. **Publications:** *The June Wilkinson Newsletter*. **Price:** included in membership dues.

24145 ■ Laura Hendler Fan Club (LHFC)
c/o Ronald Rubinovitz
PO Box 112
Lawrence, NY 11559-0091
Contact: Ronald Rubinovitz, Pres.
Founded: 1985. **Membership Dues:** $10 (annual). **Description:** Fans of television actress Laura Hendler.

24146 ■ Leslie Charleson Fan Club (LCFC)
c/o General Hospital - ABC, Inc.
4151 Prospect Ave.
Los Angeles, CA 90027
E-mail: lcfc@lesliecharleson.net
URL: http://www.lesliecharleson.net
Contact: Leslie Charleson, Honorary Pres.
Founded: 1989. **Membership Dues:** regular, in U.S., $20 (annual) ● regular, outside U.S., $25 (annual). **Description:** Fans of actress Leslie Charleson, who appears as Monica Quartermaine in the television daytime drama General Hospital. Promotes Charleson's career; keeps members informed of Charleson's public and media appearances; encourages members to exchange letters. (Distinct from club of the same name in West Hollywood, CA, which disbanded in 1988.).

24147 ■ Linda Gray's Official Fan Club
PO Box 5064
Sherman Oaks, CA 91403
E-mail: linda@fansource.com
URL: http://www.fansource.com/gray.htm
Contact: Kathy Bartels, Dir.
Founded: 1991. **Members:** 200. **Membership Dues:** subscriber, $15 (annual). **Staff:** 1. **Regional Groups:** 1. **Description:** Fans of actress Linda Gray, who played Sue Ellen Ewing on the television show Dallas. Promotes Gray's career and provides members with information on her personal and professional activities. **Convention/Meeting:** none. **Additional Websites:** http://www.lindagray.com. **Publications:** *Linda Gray's Official Fan Club Newsletter*, periodic. Updates members on Linda's activities. **Price:** included in membership dues.

24148 ■ Lindsay Wagner's Official Fan Club
PO Box 5002
Sherman Oaks, CA 91403
E-mail: lindsayclub@fansource.com
URL: http://www.fansource.com
Founded: 1978. **Members:** 700. **Membership Dues:** regular, $19 (annual). **Staff:** 1. **Description:** Admirers of actress Lindsay Wagner, whose career has includes both television and movie most notably The Paper Chase (1973) and ABC-TV's Bionic Woman (1976-78). Keeps members informed regarding Wagner's current projects and the club's activities. **Convention/Meeting:** none. **Publications:** Newsletter, periodic.

24149 ■ Louise Brooks Society (LBS)
1518 Church St.
San Francisco, CA 94131-2018
E-mail: lbs@pandorasbox.com
URL: http://www.pandorasbox.com
Founded: 1994. **Members:** 1,400. **Multinational.** **Description:** Aims to celebrate and honor Louise Brooks (1906-1985) by stimulating interest in her life and films. Maintains comprehensive website devoted to any silent film star. **Libraries: Type:** not open to the public; reference. **Holdings:** 250; archival material, articles, biographical archives, books, clippings, periodicals. **Subjects:** Louise Brooks, silent film, film history, photoplay editions, Hollywood, Jazz Age, popular culture of the 1920's, Ziegfeld Follies, Weimar Berlin, Lulu - character and myth, G.W. Pabst, Frank Wedekind, Denishawn, Ruth St. Denis, dance history, literary tributes, musical tributes, cinematic tributes. **Computer Services:** Bibliographic search ● online services. **Telecommunication Services:** electronic mail, newsoflulu-subscribe@yahoogroups.com. **Publications:** *News of Lulu*. Newsletter. **Price:** included in membership dues. **Alternate Formats:** online.

24150 ■ Malcolm Wain Fan Club (MWFC)
PO Box 9235
Whittier, CA 90608
Ph: (562)698-2878
Contact: Mike Haberecht, Contact
Founded: 1999. **Members:** 30. **Membership Dues:** charter, $10 (annual). **Description:** Admirers of actor Malcolm Wain, stage, screen and television actor (Alberto on George Lopez Show). Promotes appreciation of Wain's work. Gathers and disseminates

information on Wain's career and appearance schedule; facilitates communication among members.

24151 ■ Mamie Van Doren Fan Club (MVDFC)
c/o Bob Bethia, Pres.
1067 Lake View Terr.
Azusa, CA 91702
E-mail: p422b@aol.com
URL: http://www.mamievandoren.com/fanclub.html
Contact: Bob Bethia, Pres.
Founded: 1986. **Members:** 200. **Membership Dues:** regular, in U.S., $15 ● regular, outside U.S., $25. **Staff:** 3. **Description:** Fans of actress Mamie Van Doren (1931-), who appeared in B movies in the 1950s and 1960s, including Running Wild, Born Reckless, and Sex Kittens Go to College. Informs members of Van Doren's public appearances. Holds annual charitable auction. **Convention/Meeting:** none. **Publications:** *mmmMamie!*. Magazine ● Journal, annual ● Journal, annual. **Price:** included in membership dues; $25.00 /year for nonmembers outside U.S. **Advertising:** accepted.

24152 ■ Mark Slade Fan Club (MSFC)
38 Joppa Rd.
Worcester, MA 01603
E-mail: msfc@juno.com
Contact: Kathy Lewis, Pres.
Founded: 1980. **Members:** 100. **Membership Dues:** in U.S. and Canada, $18 (annual) ● outside U.S. and Canada, $26 (annual). **Staff:** 1. **Description:** Fans of actor and writer Mark Slade, best known for his roles in the television series High Chaparral and The Wackiest Ship in the Army, as well as the movie Benji. Mostly inactive, but still answers fan mail and letters, and have all issues of the newsletter available, plus memorabilia. Some members correspond and vacation together worldwide. **Convention/Meeting:** none. **Libraries: Type:** reference. **Holdings:** 68; archival material, books, clippings, periodicals, photographs, video recordings. **Subjects:** Mark Slade's TV shows and movies. **Telecommunication Services:** electronic mail, hcdg@yahoogroups.com. **Publications:** *The Mark Slade Fan Club Newsletter*, 3-4/year. **Circulation:** 100.

24153 ■ Mary Jo Cattlett Fan Club (MCFC)
PO Box 112
Lawrence, NY 11559-0091
Ph: (516)791-1573 (917)593-3713
Contact: Ronald Rubinovitz, Pres.
Founded: 1987. **Members:** 100. **Membership Dues:** $10 (annual). **Description:** Fans of Mary Jo Cattlett, comedienne/actress who starred in Different Strokes and performs at night clubs. Keeps members informed about Cattlett's career developments.

24154 ■ Michael Crawford International Fan Association (MCIFA)
2272 Colorado Blvd., PMB No. 1367
Los Angeles, CA 90041
E-mail: email@mcifa.com
URL: http://www.mcifa.com
Contact: Bobbee Cline, Exec. Dir.
Founded: 1990. **Membership Dues:** full, $36 (annual) ● full, $65 (biennial) ● full, $93 (triennial) ● associate, $12 (annual). **Multinational.** **Description:** Supports the charitable causes in which Michael Crawford is an advocate. Fosters fellowship among members. Supports Michael Crawford's career. Keeps members informed of Michael Crawford's professional activities through access to a 24-hour telephone hotline.

24155 ■ Michele Lee Fan Club/Michele Lee Online (MLFC)
c/o Peter Roth, Pres.
4000 Warner Blvd.
Burbank, CA 91522
URL: http://www.micheleleeonline.com
Contact: Peter Roth, Pres.
Founded: 1985. **Members:** 100. **Membership Dues:** in the United States, $15 (annual). **Staff:** 15. **Languages:** English, French. **Description:** Fans of Michele Lee (1942-), singer and actress most known for her role of Karen in the television series Knots

Landing. Informs members of Lee's activities. **Convention/Meeting:** none. **Computer Services:** Mailing lists. **Formerly:** (2000) Michele Lee Fan Club. **Publications:** *M3*, 5/year. Newsletter. **Price:** included in membership dues. **Circulation:** 100. **Advertising:** accepted.

24156 ■ Nick Mancuso Fan Network
c/o Arrista Pottle, Pres.
116 Sharon Ave.
Sebring, FL 33872
E-mail: nmfn@hotmail.com
URL: http://www.actordatabase.com/nickmancuso
Contact: Arrista Pottle, Pres.
Founded: 1994. **Members:** 57. **Membership Dues:** individual in U.S., $12 (annual) ● individual outside U.S., $15 (annual). **Staff:** 1. **Multinational. Description:** Seeks to share information about actor Nick Mancuso. Operates as "Official" fan club. **Libraries: Type:** reference; not open to the public. **Holdings:** articles, clippings, photographs, video recordings. **Subjects:** Nick Mancuso, Stingray, Matrix. **Publications:** Newsletter, 1-3/year. Contains project updates, memorabilia, articles from members and photo addresses listed. **Price:** included in membership dues; $1.00/back issue (plus $2.00 postage per order). **Advertising:** accepted.

24157 ■ Official International Michael York Fan Club (OIMYFC)
c/o Alexandria Banevicius
3424 Knox Pl., Apt. 3G
Bronx, NY 10467
E-mail: ken@michaelyork.net
URL: http://michaelyork.net
Contact: Alexandria Banevicius, Contact
Founded: 1973. **Members:** 8,098. **Membership Dues:** individual, $8 (annual). **Staff:** 4. **Description:** Fans and admirers of British actor Michael York (1942-), who has appeared in many stage, television, and film productions. Promotes York's career and keeps members informed of his activities. **Convention/Meeting:** none. **Libraries: Type:** open to the public. **Holdings:** 1; periodicals. **Subjects:** Michael York's career. **Publications:** *Yorker*, periodic. Journal ● Bulletin, 3/year. **Price:** included in membership dues ● Newsletter, 3/year.

24158 ■ Official Michael Biehn Fan Club (OMBFC)
c/o Ed Limato
8942 Wilshire Blvd.
Beverly Hills, CA 90211
E-mail: info@michaelbiehnfanclub.com
URL: http://www.michaelbiehnfanclub.com
Contact: Ed Limato, Contact
Founded: 1997. **Members:** 400. **Description:** Admirers of actor Michael Biehn. Promotes appreciation of Biehn's life and work. Gathers and disseminates information on Biehn's career and upcoming activities; facilitates communication among members. **Libraries: Type:** reference. **Holdings:** articles, clippings. **Subjects:** Michael Biehn.

24159 ■ Peter Breck Fan Club (PBFC)
Box 70
Mecklenburg, NY 14863-0070
URL: http://tv.groups.yahoo.com/group/peterbreckfanclub
Contact: Marilyn Bieler, Pres.
Founded: 1985. **Members:** 185. **Membership Dues:** individual, $10. **Description:** Fans of actor Peter Breck (1929-). (Breck's credits include starring roles in the television western series Big Valley, Black Saddle, and Maverick.) Aims to unite Peter Breck fans worldwide. Provides referrals to sources of videotapes and films of episodes of Breck's television series, as well as stills, pressbooks, and posters from his movies. Holds fan gatherings at western film festivals. **Convention/Meeting:** none. The club is officially authorized by Mr. Breck.

24160 ■ Peter Sellers Appreciation Society (PSAS)
c/o Jason Simos, US Rep.
221 E 50th St., Apt. No. 7E
New York, NY 10022
E-mail: info@petersellersappreciationsociety.com
URL: http://www.petersellersappreciationsociety.com
Contact: Jason Simos, US Rep.
Membership Dues: Europe, EUR 26 (annual) ● rest of the world, EUR 35 (annual). **Multinational. Description:** Represents fans of British comedian, actor, and performer Richard Henry "Peter" Sellers. Strives to promote, protect, remember and revere Peter Sellers' name and his works. Provides education and information on the life and works of Peter Sellers. **Telecommunication Services:** electronic mail, j.simos@petersellersappreciationsociety.com. **Publications:** *PSAS Magazine*, quarterly. **Price:** included in membership dues.

24161 ■ Rita Hayworth Fan Club
c/o Caren Roberts-Frenzel
3943 York Ave. S
Minneapolis, MN 55410
E-mail: pwfrenzel@aol.com
URL: http://claudia79.tripod.com/fanclub.html
Contact: Caren Roberts-Frenzel, Contact
Description: Works to honor actress Rita Hayworth. **Computer Services:** Online services, message board. **Publications:** Newsletter, bimonthly. Contains rare photos and information about Rita Hayworth. **Price:** $20.00/year in U.S.; $25.00/year outside U.S. **Advertising:** accepted.

24162 ■ Robert Redford Fan Club (RRFC)
517 William St.
Dunmore, PA 18510
Ph: (570)343-5702
URL: http://www.reelclassics.com/Actors/Redford/redford.htm
Contact: Trudy J. Hoffman, Pres.
Founded: 1962. **Members:** 450. **Membership Dues:** in U.S., $7 (annual) ● outside U.S., $10 (annual). **Description:** Fans of motion picture actor and director Robert Redford (1937-). Seeks to promote Redford's acting career. Makes available to members photographs and biographical information. **Publications:** *The Red Book*, annual. Journal ● *RRFC Newsletter*, annual.

24163 ■ Sharon Gless Fan Club (U.S.) (SGFC)
c/o Gail M. Reese, Pres.
PO Box 91915
Los Angeles, CA 90009
E-mail: sgfcus@aol.com
URL: http://www.sharonglessfans.net.ms
Contact: Gail M. Reese, Pres.
Founded: 1984. **Members:** 1,500. **Description:** Fans and admirers of actress Sharon Gless (1943-); the CBS network television series "Cagney and Lacey" (1982-88); "The Trials of Rosie O'Neill" (1990-92); "Cagney and Lacey" made-for-TV-movies: "The Return" (1994); "Together Again" (1995); "The View Through the Glass Ceiling" (1995); "True Convictions"(1996); and theatrical productions "Watch on the Rhine" (1989); "Misery" (1993); "Chapter Two" (1996). Disseminates information on Gless's career and activities. Supports the Sharon Gless Scholarship Fund at the University of Southern California in Los Angeles, CA. **Convention/Meeting:** none. **Libraries: Type:** not open to the public. **Holdings:** articles, clippings. **Subjects:** Sharon Gless, Tyne Daly, Cagney and Lacey, The Trials of Rosie O'Neill, made-for-TV-movies, theatrical plays. **Computer Services:** Mailing lists, for members only. **Formerly:** (1988) Sharon Gless as Cagney Fan Club. **Publications:** *Gless Times*, quarterly. Newsletter. Covers Gless's professional activities. Features raffles and memorabilia auctions. **Price:** included in membership dues.

24164 ■ Shatner and Friends International
PO Box 1345
Studio City, CA 91604
E-mail: sfi@williamshatner.com
URL: http://www.williamshatner.com
Contact: William Shatner, Contact
Membership Dues: regular, in U.S., $24 (annual) ● regular, in Canada, $26 (annual) ● foreign, $32 (annual). **Description:** Fans and admirers of actor William Shatner (1931-), best known for his portrayal of Capt. James T. Kirk in the original Star Trek television series and the five subsequent Star Trek feature films. Raises funds for charities supported by Shatner. Promotes friendship among members. **Formerly:** (2002) William Shatner Connection. **Publications:** Newsletter, quarterly.

24165 ■ Skidrow Joe Fan Club (SJFC)
PO Box 211
East Prairie, MO 63845
Ph: (573)649-2211
Fax: (573)649-2211
Contact: Tommy Loomas, Pres.
Founded: 1980. **Members:** 300. **Description:** Fans of actor and comedian Joe Silver (1922-), star of television, movies, and theatre. Career highlights include the television series Mr. Imagination and the Red Buttons Show, the films Diary of a Bachelor, Deathtrap, and You Light Up My Life, and the Broadway shows Heads or Tails, Lenny, and The World of Sholom Aleichem. Promotes Silver's career. **Convention/Meeting:** none. **Publications:** Newsletter, quarterly ● Also publishes comic book and promotional materials.

24166 ■ Stefanie Powers' Official Fan Club
PO Box 5087
Sherman Oaks, CA 91403
E-mail: stefanie@fansource.com
URL: http://www.fansource.com/powers.htm
Contact: Stefanie Powers, Contact
Founded: 1990. **Staff:** 1. **Description:** Admirers of actress Stefanie Powers, whose career includes both television and movies; most notable television hit series "Hart to Hart." Keeps members informed regarding Ms. Power's current project and club activities and work of the William Holden Wildlife Foundation. **Convention/Meeting:** none. **Publications:** Newsletter, periodic. **Price:** included in membership dues.

24167 ■ Tom Mix International Fan Club (TMIFC)
c/o John Samorajczyk
19205 Seneca Ridge Ct.
Gaithersburg, MD 20886
Ph: (301)869-1755
Contact: John Samorajczyk, Pres.
Founded: 1986. **Members:** 250. **Membership Dues:** bw membership kit, $10 ● color kit, $15. **Staff:** 4. **Local Groups:** 3. **Description:** Fans of western serial actor Tom Mix and other western heroes from Fawcett comics (Rocky Lane, Gene Autry, Hopalong Cassidy, and Monte Hale); individuals interested in western nostalgia. Promotes the memory of Tom Mix and the straight shooter tradition. Conducts educational seminars and children's programs. **Libraries: Type:** not open to the public. **Computer Services:** database. **Publications:** *Nostalgia Review*, periodic. Contains Fawcett comic reprints. ● *Tom Mix Archives*. Reprint ● *Tom Mix Nostalgia Newsletter*, 3/year. **Price:** $10.00; $5.00/issue for nonmembers. **Advertising:** accepted.

24168 ■ We Love Lucy/International Lucille Ball Fan Club
PO Box 56234
Sherman Oaks, CA 91413-1234
Fax: (818)981-0757
E-mail: info@lucyfan.com
URL: http://www.lucyfan.com
Contact: Thomas J. Watson, Contact
Founded: 1977. **Members:** 1,500. **Membership Dues:** individual, $28 (annual). **Description:** Individuals organized to pay tribute to the comedic talents of Lucille Ball (1911-89) and to her I Love Lucy television series and other productions of Desilu Studios. Organizes social gatherings. Holds annual auction; proceeds are donated to a children's charity. **Libraries: Type:** reference. **Holdings:** archival material, photographs. **Subjects:** Lucille Ball's career. **Publications:** *Lucy Fan Magazine*, quarterly. **Advertising:** accepted. **Conventions/Meetings:** annual Loving Lucy - convention (exhibits).

24169 ■ Zuzu News
c/o Zuzu Appearances
PO Box 145
Carnation, WA 98014
E-mail: zuzu@zuzu.net
URL: http://www.zuzu.net
Founded: 1994. **Members:** 3,000. **Description:**
Fans of the child actress Karolyn Grimes, who
portrayed Zuzu Bailey in "It's A Wonderful Life",
among other roles. Keeps members informed of
Karolyn Grimes many public appearances. **Formerly:**
(1999) Zuzu Society. **Publications:** Newsletter,
semiannual. Alternate Formats: online.

Animals

24170 ■ Princess Kitty Fan Club (PKFC)
PO Box 430784
Miami, FL 33243-0784
Ph: (305)665-1639
Fax: (305)661-0528
E-mail: karen90@attglobal.net
Contact: Karen Payne, Pres.
Founded: 1987. **Members:** 85. **Languages:** English,
French, Spanish. **Description:** Individuals and
organizations who admire domestic cat Princess Kitty,
a former stray turned professional model and actor
billed as the "The Smartest Cat in the World."
Promotes appreciation of the unique achievements of
Princess Kitty through videos, television programming, newsletters, and books. Disseminates information on Princess Kitty's life and career, and on cat
training, pet care and pet loss. Provides cat training/
behavior modification demonstrations. Encourages
adoption and rehabilitation of strays. Operates speakers' bureau. Publishes newsletters and books. **Librar-**
ies: Type: reference. **Holdings:** 200; archival material. **Subjects:** cats, cat training. **Awards: Type:**
recognition. **Affiliated With:** International Platform
Association. **Publications:** The Adventures of Gray-
dog. Book. Contains fictional tale of a puppy's first
year. ● Incredible Cat Tricks Starring Princess Kitty.
Video. **Price:** $19.95 plus shipping and handling ●
Pawprints: Princess Kitty Fan Club Newsletter,
semiannual. Provides tips on cat care and training
and information about club activities. Includes book
and film reviews. **Price:** included in membership
dues. **Circulation:** 85 ● Princess Kitty's Cat Training
Tips. Booklet ● Princess Kitty's Pawprints (For Pet
Lovers Only!). Book. Provides information on pet
care, cat training, and games for children and adults.

Beatles

24171 ■ Beatles Connection (BC)
Address Unknown since 2007
Founded: 1980. **Members:** 1,901. **Membership**
Dues: individual, $20 (annual). **Description:** Fans of
the British rock 'n' roll group, the Beatles (1958-70).
Makes charitable contributions. **Libraries: Type:**
reference; open to the public. **Subjects:** Beatles.
Awards: Type: recognition. **Publications:** Beatles
Connection, bimonthly. Newsletter. **Advertising:** ac-
cepted. **Conventions/Meetings:** periodic competi-
tion ● annual meeting.

24172 ■ Beatles Fan Club: Good Day
Sunshine (BFCGDS)
315 Derby Ave.
Orange, CT 06477
Ph: (203)891-8131 (203)795-4737
Fax: (203)891-8433
E-mail: liverpooltour@aol.com
Contact: Charles F. Rosenay, Pres.
Founded: 1978. **Members:** 36,000. **Membership**
Dues: $15 (annual). **Description:** Fans of the Beat-
les (1958-70). Purpose is to disseminate information
about the Beatles and their music to fans. Produces
Beatles conventions in several cities; charters group
tours to "Beatlesland" (London and Liverpool, En-
gland); books Beatles sound-alike bands worldwide.
Maintains speakers' bureau. **Publications:** Beatles
Magazine, bimonthly. Includes book and record

reviews, collectors columns, and convention reports.
Price: included in membership dues. ISSN: 1041-
4118. **Circulation:** 5,200. **Advertising:** accepted.
Conventions/Meetings: periodic Beatles Expo -
convention (exhibits).

24173 ■ Beatles Fans Unite
c/o Maureen A. Lowry, Pres.
PO Box 50123
Cicero, IL 60804-0123
E-mail: getback@beatlesfansunite.com
URL: http://www.beatlesfansunite.com
Contact: Maureen A. Lowry, Pres.
Founded: 1992. **Members:** 100. **Membership Dues:**
regular, in U.S., $14 (annual) ● regular, in Canada,
$16 (annual) ● regular, outside U.S. and Canada,
$25 (annual). **Staff:** 2. **Regional Groups:** 1. **State**
Groups: 1. **Local Groups:** 1. **Description:** Individu-
als with an interest in the Beatles. Encourages social-
izing among members; no library is maintained; does
not bestow awards. **Publications:** Newsletter,
bimonthly. Contains information, artwork, poetry, and
reviews. **Circulation:** 100. **Advertising:** accepted.
Conventions/Meetings: quadrennial meeting.

24174 ■ Working Class Hero Beatles Club
(WCH)
Address Unknown since 2007
Founded: 1968. **Members:** 500. **Membership Dues:**
in U.S., $20 (annual) ● outside U.S., $30 (annual).
Staff: 20. **Description:** Fans and enthusiasts of the
British rock group the Beatles, which comprised
Ringo Starr (1940-), John Lennon (1940-1980), Paul
McCartney (1942-), and George Harrison (1943-
2001). Compiles statistics. **Formerly:** Beatles Live
Peace in Pepperland; Beatles Peace Followers. **Pub-**
lications: "Working Class Hero Beatles Club", 3/year.
Newsletter. Includes book and record reviews, Beatles news, and members contributions. **Price:** included
in membership dues; $10.00/year for nonmembers in
the U.S. **Circulation:** 500. **Advertising:** accepted.

Broadcasters

24175 ■ Leo Lassen Legacy Project
Address Unknown since 2007
Founded: 2000. **Members:** 232. **Staff:** 3. **Budget:**
$75,000. **State Groups:** 43. **Local Groups:** 4. **Na-**
tional Groups: 10. **Description:** Dedicated to
promoting sports announcer Leo Lassens' contributions to the world of baseball.

Cartoons

24176 ■ Bushmiller Society
PO Box 2250
Amherst, MA 01004-2250
Ph: (413)259-1627
Fax: (413)259-1812
E-mail: service@deniskitchen.com
URL: http://www.deniskitchen.com
Contact: Steven Krupp, Pres.
Founded: 1981. **Members:** 240. **Membership Dues:**
regular, $35 (annual). **Staff:** 1. **For-Profit. Descrip-**
tion: Admirers of Ernie Bushmiller, American cartoon-
ist (1905-1982), who created 'Nancy & Sluggo';
promotes legacy through publications and exhibits.
Libraries: Type: reference; not open to the public.
Holdings: archival material, artwork, audiovisuals,
books, clippings, periodicals. **Subjects:** Bushmiller's
career and creations. **Conventions/Meetings:** annual meeting.

24177 ■ National Fantasy Fan Club for
Disneyana Enthusiasts (NFFC)
PO Box 19212
Irvine, CA 92623-9212
Ph: (714)731-4705
E-mail: info@nffc.org
URL: http://www.nffc.org
Contact: Ms. Kendra Trahan, Pres.
Founded: 1984. **Members:** 5,000. **Membership**
Dues: individual, family in U.S., $29 (annual). **Bud-**

get: $135,000. **Regional Groups:** 32. **Description:**
Fans and collectors of anything to do with Walt Disney products. Promotes enjoyment of any past,
present, or future Disney cartoon characters, films,
amusement parks, and merchandise. **Libraries:**
Type: reference. **Holdings:** video recordings. **Sub-**
jects: recordings from the conventions available to
members and the Walt Disney archives. **Publica-**
tions: Fantasy Line Express, monthly. Newsletter.
Includes photos, news and information on the world
of Disney and various club happenings. **Price:**
included in membership dues. **Advertising:** accepted. **Conventions/Meetings:** semiannual convention (exhibits).

24178 ■ Official Betty Boop Fan Club
(OBBFC)
10550 Western Ave., No. 133
Stanton, CA 90680-6909
Ph: (714)816-0717
E-mail: bboopfans@aol.com
URL: http://www.bettyboopfanclub.org/index.html
Founded: 1986. **Members:** 2,000. **Staff:** 1. **Multina-**
tional. Description: Collectors of Betty Boop memo-
rabilia; businesses that sell Betty Boop collectibles.
(The Betty Boop character debuted in 1930.) Informs
members of Betty Boop events and news stories, as
well as availability of merchandise. **Libraries: Type:**
reference. **Holdings:** 39. **Subjects:** Betty Boop.

24179 ■ Official Gumby Fan Club (OGFC)
c/o Toon's Station, Inc.
5 Hanley Ct.
Tabernacle, NJ 08088
Ph: (609)268-6680
Free: (877)988-6900
Fax: (609)268-0730
E-mail: info@patchcollectibles.com
URL: http://www.officialgumbyfanclub.com
Founded: 2000. **Members:** 10,000. **Multinational.**
Description: Fans of the animated character Gumby
who was created in 1956 by Art Clokey and currently
appears in a syndicated cartoon series. Makes available discounts on Gumby-related items; keeps
members informed of the character's public and
media appearances. Updates on Gumby news, collectibles and items. **Additional Websites:** http://
gumbyfanclub.com. **Publications:** Gumby Gram,
periodic. Newsletter.

24180 ■ Pogo Fan Club and Walt Kelly
Society (PFCWKS)
c/o Spring Hollow Books
6908 Wentworth
Richfield, MN 55423
E-mail: info@pogo-fan-club.org
URL: http://www.pogo-fan-club.org
Contact: Steve Thompson, Contact
Founded: 1984. **Members:** 1,200. **Membership**
Dues: general, $5 (annual) ● subscriber, $25 (annual). **Staff:** 3. **Budget:** $20,000. **Description:** Rep-
resents fans of the comic strip Pogo and its creator,
cartoonist Walt Kelly, who are dedicated to the
research and remembrance of his life and career.
Provides referral and appraisal services. **Libraries:**
Type: reference. **Holdings:** 3,000; artwork, audio
recordings, books, clippings, periodicals, video
recordings. **Subjects:** Walt Kelly, Pogo comic strip,
cartoon history. **Publications:** The Fort Mudge Most,
bimonthly. Newsletter. Contains analysis and discussion of Walt Kelly's life and career as well as reprints
of scarce material. **Price:** $25.00/year. **Circulation:**
450. **Advertising:** accepted. **Conventions/Meet-**
ings: annual Pogofest Classic Comics Forum -
conference (exhibits) - always third weekend of
October in Waycross, GA.

Comedy

24181 ■ Abbott and Costello International
Fan Club (ACFC)
c/o Bill Honor
PO Box 5566
Fort Wayne, IN 46895-5566

E-mail: acqtrly@aol.com
URL: http://members.aol.com/ACQtrly/index.html
Contact: Bill Honor, Contact
Founded: 1986. **Members:** 56,756. **Membership Dues:** individual, international, $22 (annual) ● individual, in U.S., $17 (annual) ● individual, in Canada, $19 (annual). **Staff:** 8. **Budget:** $45,000. **Regional Groups:** 17. **State Groups:** 50. **Local Groups:** 71. **Languages:** English, French, Polish. **Description:** Fans and admirers of the comedy team of Bud Abbott (1896-1974) and Lou Costello (1906-59), which attained peak popularity on both the stage and screen, as well as on radio, from 1941 to 1951. Seeks to keep alive the spirit of good-natured buffoonery which characterized their works. Conducts research and charitable programs; makes available children's services. Maintains hall of fame and library; operates speakers' bureau. Supplies funds for cancer research in children case studies on the international level. **Awards:** Bud and Lou Award/Scholarship Fund. **Frequency:** annual. **Type:** scholarship. **Formerly:** (1992) Abbott and Costello Fan Club. **Publications:** *I'm A Bad Boy.* Newsletter. **Advertising:** accepted. Alternate Formats: CD-ROM. **Conventions/Meetings:** annual Fan Fair - meeting (exhibits).

24182 ■ **Abbott and Costello Official Fan Club**
c/o Bill Honor
PO Box 5566
Fort Wayne, IN 46895-5566
E-mail: acqtrly@aol.com
URL: http://members.aol.com/acqtrly
Contact: Bill Honor, Contact
Founded: 1986. **Members:** 3,200. **Membership Dues:** in U.S., $17 (annual) ● in Canada, $19 (annual) ● international, $22. **Regional Groups:** 6. **Description:** Seeks to perpetuate the memory of burlesque, film and TV comedians Bud Abbott (1897-1974) and Lou Costello (1906-59); is sanctioned by the families of Abbott and Costello. **Libraries: Type:** reference; not open to the public. **Holdings:** 2,456; archival material, articles, audio recordings, clippings, photographs, video recordings. **Computer Services:** Online services, latest news, membership information, TV listings, video releases. **Publications:** *Abbott and Costello Quarterly.* Magazine. Contains rare interviews with family and friends. Features a collector's page and bulletin board services. **Price:** included in membership dues. **Circulation:** 4,200. **Advertising:** accepted ● Also provides a membership kit containing membership card, photo, and other materials.

24183 ■ **Damfinos: The International Buster Keaton Society**
PO Box 1632
Layton, UT 84041
E-mail: moviegirl1926@yahoo.com
URL: http://www.busterkeaton.com
Contact: Patricia Eliot Tobias, Pres.
Founded: 1992. **Members:** 500. **Membership Dues:** in Canada, $40 (annual) ● outside U.S., $50 (annual) ● in U.S., $35 (annual). **Staff:** 2. **Budget:** $15,000. **Multinational. Description:** Lawyers, doctors, archaeologists, film scholars and show business professionals. Promotes film preservation and original research about the American history in the 20th century, primarily as it affected film and vaudeville. **Libraries: Type:** reference; by appointment only; not open to the public. **Holdings:** articles, artwork, biographical archives, books, clippings, papers. **Subjects:** Buster Keaton, film history, history of humor, health benefits of laughter. **Awards:** The Buster Award. **Frequency:** periodic. **Type:** recognition. **Recipient:** to a person or persons who best represent the qualities Buster Keaton displayed in his films or in his life. **Telecommunication Services:** electronic mail, patriciatobias@aol.com. **Publications:** *The Keaton Chronicle*, quarterly. Newsletter. Covers everything from current news pertaining to Buster Keaton to original research about his life and films. **Price:** $5.00/back issue, for members. **Circulation:** 500. **Advertising:** accepted. **Conventions/Meetings:** annual convention (exhibits) - early October, Muskegon, MI.

24184 ■ **International Jack Benny Fan Club (IJBFC)**
PO Box 11288
Piedmont, CA 94611
E-mail: president@jackbenny.org
URL: http://www.jackbenny.org
Contact: Laura Leff, Contact
Founded: 1980. **Members:** 2,300. **Membership Dues:** regular mail subscription, $12 (annual) ● e-mail subscription, $6 (annual). **Staff:** 1. **Budget:** $8,000. **Regional Groups:** 3. **Multinational. Description:** Fans of the comedian Jack Benny. Seeks to further the comedy of Jack Benny and his associates. Provides access to his works. **Libraries: Type:** not open to the public. **Holdings:** 1,000; archival material, books, clippings, periodicals, video recordings. **Subjects:** shows, appearances, tributes, interviews. **Awards:** Jack Bloom Pasadena Chapter. **Frequency:** annual. **Type:** recognition. **Recipient:** to active member for four or more years. **Publications:** *Jack Benny Times*, 3/year. Newsletter. **Price:** included in membership dues. ISSN: 1087-6154. **Circulation:** 400. **Advertising:** accepted. Alternate Formats: online.

24185 ■ **National Phyllis Diller Fan Club (NPDFC)**
Address Unknown since 2007
Founded: 1982. **Members:** 888. **Membership Dues:** $10 (annual). **Staff:** 3. **Budget:** $40,500. **Regional Groups:** 10. **State Groups:** 13. **Local Groups:** 1. **National Groups:** 1. **Description:** Admirers of actress and comedienne Phyllis Diller. Promotes appreciation of Diller's work. Serves as a clearinghouse on Diller's career; organizes trips to Diller performances. **Libraries: Type:** reference. **Holdings:** archival material, audio recordings, books, periodicals, video recordings. **Subjects:** Phyllis Diller's life and career. **Computer Services:** Mailing lists, show dates for Ms. Diller sent out bi-monthly ● online services. **Also Known As:** (2000) Diller Fan Club. **Publications:** *PhyllDiller Alert*, quarterly. Newsletter. Diller related publication. **Price:** free with membership. **Circulation:** 2,500. **Advertising:** accepted. **Conventions/Meetings:** annual meeting and convention.

24186 ■ **Three Stooges Fan Club (TSFC)**
PO Box 747
Gwynedd Valley, PA 19437
Ph: (267)468-0810
Fax: (215)368-3595
E-mail: garystooge@aol.com
Contact: Gary Lassin, Pres.
Founded: 1974. **Members:** 2,300. **Membership Dues:** regular, $9 (annual). **Description:** Fans of the Three Stooges, a popular slapstick comedy team of film and television, starring brothers Moe Howard (1897-1975), Curly Howard (1903-52), and Shemp Howard (1895-1955), and Larry Fine (1902-75) and, later, Joe Besser (1907-88). Works to keep the comedy of the Three Stooges alive. Seeks to keep members informed of the availability of memorabilia for sale or exchange. Conducts research on Three Stooges' careers, films, and collectibles. **Publications:** *The 3 Stooges Journal*, quarterly. Contains film reviews, interviews, information on collectible items, and rare photographs. **Price:** included in membership dues. **Circulation:** 2,300. **Advertising:** accepted. **Conventions/Meetings:** periodic convention (exhibits).

24187 ■ **W.C. Fields Fan Club (WCFFC)**
c/o Ted Wioncek, Pres.
Dept. EOA
PO Box 506
Stratford, NJ 08084-0506
E-mail: wcfieldsfanclub@comcast.net
URL: http://www.webtrec.com/wcfields
Contact: Ted Wioncek, Pres.
Founded: 1992. **Members:** 600. **Membership Dues:** individual in U.S., $15 (annual) ● individual in Canada, $18 (annual) ● other country, $26 (annual). **Staff:** 2. **Description:** Works to keep the spirit of the actor/comedian W.C. Fields alive. **Libraries: Type:** reference; not open to the public; by appointment only. **Holdings:** articles, artwork, audiovisuals, books, clippings, periodicals. **Subjects:** W.C. Fields (January 29, 1880-December 25, 1946). **Publications:** *Lompoc Picayune-Intelligencer*, quarterly. Newsletter. **Advertising:** accepted. **Conventions/Meetings:** annual Doodah Parade and Famous Comedian's Fan Club Show - convention, with memorabilia from many famous comedian fan clubs (exhibits) - first Saturday after income tax deadline, Ocean City, New Jersey.

Country Music

24188 ■ **Shon Branham Fan Club (SBFC)**
c/o Vondol Bailey, Pres.
206 Doel Bean
Kirbyville, TX 75956
Ph: (409)423-3319
E-mail: vbailey@kirbyvillecisd.org
URL: http://www.ifco.org/shon_branham/shon_branham.htm
Contact: Vondol Bailey, Pres.
Founded: 1994. **Members:** 110. **Membership Dues:** individual, $10 (annual). **Description:** Admirers of country music artist Shon Branham. Seeks to advance Branham's career; promotes communication and good fellowship among members. Serves as a clearinghouse on Branham and his career; sponsors social activities. **Publications:** Newsletter, quarterly. Contains schedule of activities. **Price:** free for members. **Conventions/Meetings:** annual dinner - always first Saturday in November.

Crosby, Bing

24189 ■ **International Crosby Circle (ICC)**
5608 N 34th St.
Arlington, VA 22207
Ph: (703)241-5608
E-mail: wig@club-crosby.org
URL: http://www.crosby-circle.org.uk
Contact: Wig Wiggins, Contact
Founded: 1966. **Membership Dues:** $20 (annual). **Multinational. Description:** Fan club honoring late singer, actor, entertainer Bing Crosby. **Computer Services:** Information services, Bing Crosby Information File for members. **Publications:** *Bing*, 3/year, spring, summer, and winter. Journal. Includes text and photographs. ● *Bing Calendar*.

Elvis Presley

24190 ■ **Asian Worldwide Elvis Fan Club**
PO Box 19132
Houston, TX 77224-9132
E-mail: nwn4@wt.net
URL: http://www.elvisworldwide.com
Contact: Will McDaniel, Pres.
Founded: 1977. **Members:** 250. **Staff:** 4. **State Groups:** 3. **Description:** Fans of rock 'n' roll singer Elvis Presley (1935-77). Seeks to perpetuate the memory and music of the singer. **Formerly:** (1991) Elvis Worldwide Memorial Fan Club; (2004) Elvis Worldwide Fan Club. **Publications:** *Elvis Worldwide Fan Club*, quarterly. Newsletter. Contains information about Elvis and club members. **Price:** included in membership dues. **Circulation:** 500. **Advertising:** accepted. Alternate Formats: online. **Conventions/Meetings:** semiannual meeting - always January 8 and August 16 in Memphis, TN.

24191 ■ **Elvis' Angels Fan Club**
10152 La Hwy. 1
Mooringsport, LA 71060-8948
Ph: (318)687-8743
E-mail: elvisluv7@aol.com
URL: http://www.elvisangels.com
Contact: Dianne P. Mitchell, Pres.
Founded: 1997. **Members:** 100. **Membership Dues:** in U.S., $12 (annual) ● outside U.S., $12 (annual). **Description:** Serves as a fan club for Elvis Presley. **Awards:** Make-A-Wish Foundation of Louisiana. **Fre-**

quency: annual. **Type:** monetary. **Telecommunication Services:** electronic mail, info@elvisangels.com. **Publications:** Newsletter, quarterly. **Conventions/Meetings:** monthly meeting - 3rd Saturday, except August and December.

24192 ■ Elvis Fever Fan Club (EFFC)
Address Unknown since 2007
Founded: 1957. **Membership Dues:** in U.S., $15 (annual) ● outside U.S., U.S. funds, $20 (annual). **Staff:** 6. **Multinational. Description:** Admirers of the life and career of Elvis Presley. Promotes appreciation of Elvis' music and theatrical performances. Works to support the memory of Elvis "in a positive and dignified manner." Supports charitable organizations; sponsors social activities. **Libraries: Type:** open to the public. **Publications:** *Elvis Fever Folio*, quarterly. Magazine. **Price:** included in membership dues. **Advertising:** not accepted.

24193 ■ Elvis Forever TCB Fan Club (EFTCBFC)
Address Unknown since 2007
Founded: 1977. **Members:** 3,702. **Membership Dues:** individual U.S., $20 (annual) ● individual in Canada, $25 (annual) ● individual outside U.S. and Canada, $32 (annual). **Description:** Fosters the remembrance of the life and works of vocalist and entertainer Elvis Presley (1935-77). Maintains charitable program. Compiles statistics. (TCB in the group's title refers to "Taking Care of Business," Presley's motto.). **Libraries: Type:** reference. **Holdings:** biographical archives. **Awards: Type:** recognition. **Publications:** *Elvis Forever TCB Newsletter*, semiannual ● Plans to publish directory. **Conventions/Meetings:** annual meeting.

24194 ■ Elvis Presley Memorial Society (EMS)
315 Cypress Glen Dr.
Mount Juliet, TN 37122
Ph: (615)758-0913 (615)416-5218
Fax: (615)453-4473
E-mail: sfetcho@comcast.net
Contact: Sue Fetcho, Pres.
Founded: 1978. **Members:** 100. **Description:** National association of fans and admirers of rock 'n' roll musician and singer Elvis Presley (1935-77). Carry out "the generosity that was Elvis." Conducts fundraising activities, movie nights, and picnics. The society has contributed to charities such as Sudden Infant Death Syndrome of Central New York, Ronald McDonald House in Syracuse, NY, and the Elvis Presley Memorial Trauma Center in Memphis, TN. **Publications:** none.

24195 ■ Elvis Teddy Bears (ETB)
Address Unknown since 2007
Founded: 1976. **Members:** 89. **Membership Dues:** $6 (annual). **Description:** Fans of singer and entertainer Elvis Presley (1935-77). **Publications:** *The Proud Mary*, quarterly. Newsletter. **Price:** included in membership dues. **Advertising:** accepted.

24196 ■ Elvis - The Legend Continues Fan Club (ELCFC)
c/o David Lewis, Pres.
4221 Crestview Dr.
Chattanooga, TN 37415
Ph: (615)867-6722
E-mail: davidtcb1@aol.com
URL: http://www.elvis2001.net/elvis_2001_fan_club_index.htm
Contact: David Lewis, Pres.
Founded: 1997. **Members:** 60. **Membership Dues:** regular, $15 (annual) ● international, $25 (annual). **Staff:** 1. **Regional Groups:** 1. **Description:** Admirers of Elvis Presley. Seeks to preserve the memory and image of Elvis Presley. Facilitates communication and good fellowship among members; assists charitable organizations. **Publications:** *Elvis The Legend Continues Fan Club Newsletter*, 3/year. Includes the latest news in the Elvis world. **Price:** included in membership dues. **Advertising:** accepted. Alternate Formats: online. **Conventions/**

Meetings: semiannual meeting - January and August, Memphis, TN.

24197 ■ ElvisNet Elvis Presley Fan Club (ElvisNet EPFC)
c/o The Presley Connection
PO Box 680444
Prattville, AL 36068
E-mail: presleyconnect@aol.com
URL: http://www.elvisnet.com
Contact: Terri Hancock, Contact
Founded: 1994. **Members:** 450. **Description:** Fans of Elvis Presley. Seeks to provide a means for Elvis fans around the world to exchange information via the internet. **Telecommunication Services:** electronic mail, tcbterri@aol.com. **Publications:** *ElvisBiz*, monthly. Newsletter.

24198 ■ Presley-ites Fan Club International (PFC)
c/o Kathy Ferguson, Pres.
6010 18th St.
Zephyrhills, FL 33540-2702
Ph: (813)788-9133
Fax: (813)782-5112
URL: http://www.greenearth.com/netpage/presleyites
Contact: Kathy Ferguson, Pres.
Founded: 1972. **Members:** 35. **Staff:** 1. **Description:** Individuals who admire the music and career of Rock and Roll singer/guitarist Elvis Presley (1935-77). Seeks to establish January 8 (Presley's birthday) as a national day of recognition. Raises money to help fund the Elvis Presley Memorial Trauma Center in Memphis, TN, and other charitable causes; disseminates information regarding the activities of its members; advertises the availability of Elvis Presley records and memorabilia for sale. **Libraries: Type:** open to the public. **Subjects:** music.

24199 ■ TCB for Elvis Fan Club (TCBEFC)
Address Unknown since 2007
Founded: 1977. **Members:** 100. **Membership Dues:** individual, $12 (annual). **Description:** Individuals interested in perpetuating the memory and music of rock 'n' roll singer and entertainer Elvis Presley (1935-77). Supports charities in Presley's name; sponsors annual Christmas party for needy children. (TCB refers to Presley's motto "Taking Care of Business.").

24200 ■ We Remember Elvis Fan Club (WREFC)
1215 Tennessee Ave.
Pittsburgh, PA 15216
Ph: (412)561-7522
Contact: Priscilla A. Parker, Pres.
Founded: 1982. **Members:** 900. **Membership Dues:** in U.S., $12 (annual) ● in Canada, $14 (annual) ● outside U.S. and Canada, $28 (annual). **Description:** Fans of rock 'n' roll singer and entertainer Elvis Presley (1935-77). Seeks to perpetuate Presley's memory; conducts charitable activities in Presley's name. Sponsors picnics and other social activities to commemorate Presley's birthday. Supports campaign to have Presley awarded the Presidential Medal of Freedom. Also supports the movement for a permanent Day of Recognition for Elvis Aaron Presley, to be held on January 8th. **Formerly:** (1982) Elvis' Little Buddies. **Publications:** *We Remember Elvis Fan Club Newsletter*, 5/year. **Price:** $12.00/year in U.S.; $14.00 Canada; $28.00/year overseas. **Circulation:** 900. **Conventions/Meetings:** annual Spring Festival - convention, dealer set-ups, guest speaker, charity auction, dinner & dance (exhibits).

Entertainers

24201 ■ Dean Martin Fan Center (DMFC)
PO Box 660212
Arcadia, CA 91066-0212
E-mail: webdir@deanmartinfancenter.com
URL: http://www.deanmartinfancenter.com
Contact: Neil T. Daniels, Pres.
Members: 12,000. **Membership Dues:** regular, in U.S., $30 (annual) ● in Australia, Japan, China, $45

(annual) ● other country, $35 (annual). **Staff:** 8. **Multinational. Description:** Fans of Dean Martin. Official organization that gathers and provides information on Dean Martin and his work in television, radio, motion pictures, recordings and stage work. Serves as a place for friends, family, co-workers and fans to come together. **Publications:** *Dean Martin Fan Center Magazine*, 3-4/year. Newsletter.

24202 ■ Elvira Fan Club (EFC)
PO Box 38246
Hollywood, CA 90038
E-mail: scott@elvira.com
URL: http://www.elvira.com
Founded: 1982. **Members:** 5,000. **Membership Dues:** individual in U.S., $18 (annual). **Staff:** 3. **Multinational. Description:** Fans of Elvira, Mistress of the Dark, entertainer and hostess of a horror film television series, star of feature films. **Publications:** *Bad Dog Andy*, periodic. Book. Features illustrated story of a more-than-mischievous Dalmatian. **Price:** $8.00/copy; $28.00/copy for hardback ● Newsletter, annual.

24203 ■ Joni James International Fan Club
PO Box 7207
Westchester, IL 60154-7207
E-mail: joni-fanclub@jonijames.com
URL: http://jonijames.com/fans/fans.html
Contact: Wayne Michael Brasler, Pres./Ed.
Founded: 1987. **Members:** 20,000. **Description:** Admirers of Joni James. Disseminates information on James' current activities and career. **Publications:** *Joni*, quarterly. Newsletter. Includes news about James' current activities, career, answers to fans' questions, and photographs.

Fan Clubs

24204 ■ Crazy4Clay Gang (C4CG)
PO Box 853
Independence, KY 41051
Ph: (859)356-0837
Fax: (859)356-0837
E-mail: crazy4clay@aol.com
Contact: Lori Steuart, Pres.
Membership Dues: regular, in U.S., $20 (annual) ● regular, outside U.S., $25 (annual). **Multinational. Description:** Official fan club for country music artist Clay Walker. **Publications:** *e-Newsletter*. **Price:** included in membership dues. Alternate Formats: online ● Newsletter, quarterly. **Price:** included in membership dues.

24205 ■ Kevin Sorbo's Official Fan Club
PO Box 1418
Aliquippa, PA 15001
E-mail: webmaster@kevinsorbo.net
URL: http://www.kevinsorbo.net
Description: Serves as a fan club devoted to Kevin Sorbo. Provides initial membership kit package, including welcome letter, biography, written interview, button and bumper sticker, color membership card, and autographed color 8x10 photo for members. **Publications:** Newsletter. Contains current information of Kevin's activities.

Fiction

24206 ■ Friends of Freddy (FOF)
PO Box 912
Greenbelt, MD 20768-0912
Ph: (301)345-2774
E-mail: kevin.parker@wap.org
URL: http://www.freddythepig.org
Contact: Kevin Parker, Corresponding Sec.
Founded: 1984. **Members:** 400. **Membership Dues:** regular, in U.S., $25 (biennial) ● regular, in Canada, $30 (biennial) ● regular, outside U.S. and Canada, $37 (biennial) ● regular, in U.S., $45 (quadrennial) ● regular, in Canada, $55 (quadrennial) ● regular, outside U.S. and Canada, $69 (quadrennial) ● charter (all back issues in addition to current member-

ship), $45 (periodic). **Multinational. Description:** Fans of the 26-volume children's book series, *Freddy the Pig*, created by Walter R. Brooks (1886-1958). The series was first published in 1927 and centered on the adventures of Freddy and his barnyard companions, who can speak and are human in nature. Works to: perpetuate the memory of Freddy and other writings by Brooks; initiate the reprinting and reissue of the Freddy series; increase the popularity of the series. Encourages members to participate in school and library book donation programs. Acts as a research network on Brooks and his works. Offers social activities. Operates Walter R. Brooks Memorial Fund. Provides children's services; maintains biographical archives. Sponsors contests; compiles statistics. **Additional Websites:** http://www. friendsoffreddy.org. **Committees:** Book Promotion - Canada; Book Promotion - United States of America; Brooks Memorial Tribute; Library. **Publications:** *Bean Home Newsletter*, quarterly. Explores the literary aspect of the series; contains biographical information on Brooks; monitors the sales of reissued books. ISSN: 0882-4428. **Circulation:** 400. **Advertising:** accepted. **Conventions/Meetings:** biennial convention, for all Friends of Freddy members and anyone else interested in the books (exhibits) - always October in even years, Upstate New York.

24207 ■ International Frankenstein Society (IFS)
29 Washington Sq. W, Penthouse N
New York, NY 10011
E-mail: robertqclark@yahoo.com
Contact: Dr. Jeanne Keyes Youngson, Pres./Founder
Founded: 1980. **Members:** 2,220. **Staff:** 2. **Budget:** $30,000. **For-Profit. Description:** Division of the Vampire Empire with members from 15 countries. Works to bring together enthusiasts of Frankenstein, the main character and title of the novel by Mary Shelley. Promotes exchange of information; sponsors "ethical, social, moral, and educational activities mixed with good fun.". **Libraries: Type:** reference. **Holdings:** 145; archival material. **Subjects:** Frankenstein, Shelley, Golem, Vampires, Bram Stoker. **Publications:** *Frankenstein Gold Book* ● *The Vampire Empire*, quarterly. Newsletter. Contains Frankenstein news. **Conventions/Meetings:** annual Open House - meeting, held at Christmas (exhibits).

24208 ■ Mystery Readers International (MRI)
PO Box 8116
Berkeley, CA 94707-8116
Ph: (510)845-3600
E-mail: janet@mysteryreaders.org
URL: http://www.mysteryreaders.org
Contact: Janet A. Rudolph, Dir./Ed.
Founded: 1975. **Members:** 2,000. **Membership Dues:** individual, $28 (annual) ● individual outside North America, $40 (annual). **Staff:** 5. **Description:** Readers, editors, publishers, fans, critics, and writers of mystery novels. Seeks to enrich the lives of mystery readers. Provides opportunities for members to meet with mystery people, including writers of mystery novels and policemen. **Libraries: Type:** not open to the public. **Holdings:** 10,000. **Subjects:** mystery. **Awards:** Macavity Awards. **Frequency:** annual. **Type:** recognition. **Recipient:** for best novel, best first novel, best short story, and best critical/ biographical novel. **Publications:** *Mystery Readers Journal*, quarterly. ISSN: 1043-3473. **Circulation:** 2,000. Alternate Formats: online. **Conventions/Meetings:** annual Left Coast Crime - meeting, held in conjunction with other mystery conventions ● monthly regional meeting.

24209 ■ The Vampire Empire
29 Washington Sq. W, Penthouse N
New York, NY 10011-9180
E-mail: vampirempire145@hotmail.com
URL: http://www.benecke.com/vampire.html
Contact: Dr. Jeanne Keyes Youngson, Founder/Pres.
Founded: 1965. **Members:** 1,500. **Membership Dues:** regular outside U.S., $35 (annual) ● regular in U.S., $30 (annual). **Staff:** 6. **Budget:** $25,000. **For-Profit. Description:** Individuals interested in the literary and fictional aspects of Bram Stoker's book

Dracula, as well as characters and personalities in the horror, magic, and fantasy genres. Maintains the Dracula Museum. Distributes first-edition books in good condition for collection purposes. Provides booksearch service. Sponsors charitable programs; compiles statistics. **Libraries: Type:** reference. **Holdings:** 2,430; archival material, books, photographs. **Subjects:** horror genre, biography. **Divisions:** Booksearch Service; Clipping Service; The Dracula Museum; Dracula Press; The Halloween Connection; International Frankenstein Society; News-Journal; Picture Collection; Research; Research Library; Special Interest; Undead Treasure Trove; Vampire Bookshop; Vampire Information Referral Service; Werewolves. **Affiliated With:** Bram Stoker Memorial Association; Bram Stoker Society - Ireland. **Formerly:** (2001) Count Dracula Fan Club. **Publications:** *The Bizarre World of Vampires*. Book. Non-fiction. **Price:** included in membership dues ● *Count Dracula and the Unicorn*. Book. **Price:** $5.00/copy ● *Do Vampires Exist?*. Monograph. **Price:** $3.99/copy ● *Dracula Made Easy* ● *The Dracula News Journal*. Newsletter ● *How to Become a Vampire in Six Easy Lessons*. Book. **Price:** $3.99/copy ● *Letterzine* ● *Private Files of a Vampirologist: Case Histories and Letters*. Book. **Price:** included in membership dues; $20.00/copy for nonmembers ● *Undead Undulations*. Newsletter ● *The Vampire Empire Handbook*, biennial. **Price:** included in membership dues ● *Vampire Empire Quarterly*. Includes nonfiction vampire news. **Price:** included in membership dues; $4.00/copy for nonmembers. **Circulation:** 3,000. **Advertising:** accepted ● *Vampires of Folklore* ● Monographs ● Newsletter, quarterly. Includes Super Sweepstakes, members' participation projects, book & movie reviews, lists of recommended books, out of print books for sale, mailings. ● Also publishes limited edition vampire stories. **Conventions/Meetings:** annual Christmas Open House - party, weeklong open house in December to view the Vampire-Santa Tree ● Poetry Competitions.

Film

24210 ■ International Network of Somewhere in Time Enthusiasts (INSITE)
c/o Jo Addie, Pres.
8110 S Verdev Dr.
Oak Creek, WI 53154
Ph: (708)579-3749
E-mail: jo@somewhereintimejunk.tv
URL: http://www.somewhereintime.tv
Contact: Jo Addie, Pres.
Founded: 1990. **Members:** 900. **Membership Dues:** bronze in U.S., $24 (annual) ● silver, $50 (annual) ● gold, $75 (annual) ● platinum, $100 (annual) ● bronze outside U.S., $30 (annual). **Description:** Individuals interested in the movie Somewhere in Time. **Publications:** Newsletter, quarterly. **Price:** included in membership dues. **Circulation:** 1,000. **Advertising:** accepted. **Conventions/Meetings:** annual Somewhere in Time Weekend - convention, featuring memorabilia, vintage items, and posters (exhibits) - always Mackinac Island, MI.

24211 ■ The Official Austin Powers Collector's Club
Address Unknown since 2007

Membership Dues: includes $5 coupon for first purchase, $25. **Description:** For fans of the Austin Powers movies.

24212 ■ Old Time Western Film Club (OTWFC)
Address Unknown since 2007

Founded: 1970. **Members:** 500. **Regional Groups:** 3. **State Groups:** 3. **Local Groups:** 1. **Description:** Fans of old time western films. Seeks to perpetuate the memory of old western film stars of the silent and sound eras. Offers specialized education program. Maintains museum and hall of fame. **Libraries: Type:** reference. **Holdings:** archival material, books, films, photographs. **Publications:** Newsletter, bimonthly.

Conventions/Meetings: meeting (exhibits) - always fourth Saturday of January, March, May, August, and October.

24213 ■ Sons of the Desert (SOD)
c/o Laurel and Hardy Museum
PO Box 99
Harlem, GA 30814
Ph: (706)556-3448
URL: http://www.sotd.org
Contact: Lori Jones-McCaffery, Contact
Founded: 1964. **Members:** 8,000. **Local Groups:** 5. **National Groups:** 125. **Multinational. Description:** Works to study the persons and films of Stan Laurel and Oliver Hardy. Encourages the preservation and showing of Laurel (1890-1965) and Hardy (1892-1957) films. Local groups are called Tents and derive their names from Laurel and Hardy films such as Way Out West of Los Angeles, CA and The Bacon Grabbers of Chicago, IL. **Publications:** *Intra-Tent Journal*, quarterly. Contains national and convention news, tent news, occasional features. **Price:** $17.00 for individuals. **Circulation:** 2,000. Also Cited As: *ITJ*. **Conventions/Meetings:** biennial convention (exhibits) - summer.

Gone With the Wind

24214 ■ Gone With the Wind Society (GWWS)
c/o Herb Bridges
PO Box 192
Sharpsburg, GA 30277
Ph: (770)253-4934 (770)253-4446
E-mail: herb-gwtw@mindspring.com
Contact: Herb Bridges, Contact
Founded: 1985. **Members:** 500. **Description:** Fans of the book and movie Gone With the Wind. Conducts educational, research and charitable programs; maintains museum and speakers' bureau. **Libraries: Type:** reference; by appointment only. **Holdings:** books, clippings. **Publications:** *The Scarlet Letter*, quarterly. Newsletter. **Circulation:** 500. **Advertising:** accepted. **Conventions/Meetings:** periodic convention and lecture, with book signings (exhibits).

Humor

24215 ■ Marx Brotherhood
335 Fieldstone Dr.
New Hope, PA 18938-1012
E-mail: majordomo@lists.panix.com
URL: http://www.marx-brothers.org
Contact: Paul G. Wesolowski, Dir.
Founded: 1978. **Members:** 400. **Membership Dues:** fraternal/social, $10 (annual). **Staff:** 1. **Budget:** $5,000. **Description:** Persons interested in the Marx Brothers. Seeks to educate the public about the lives and careers of Groucho (1890-1977), Chico (1887-1961), and Harpo (1888-1964) Marx, three brothers whose zany, anarchistic comedy style was featured in Hollywood films of the 1930s and 1940s. The act originally included brothers Gummo (1892-1977) and Zeppo (1901-79). Assists authors, actors, producers, and other artists interested in accurately depicting the Marx Brothers. Provides members with research services. Maintains museum. **Libraries: Type:** not open to the public. **Holdings:** 150; articles, books, photographs. **Formerly:** (1994) Marx Brothers Study Unit. **Publications:** *Freedonia Gazette: The Magazine Devoted to the Marx Brothers*, semiannual. Journal. Devoted to the lives and careers of the Marx brothers and their effect on popular culture. Includes biographical information. **Price:** included in membership dues; $10.00 /year for nonmembers. ISSN: 0748-5247. **Circulation:** 400. **Advertising:** accepted. **Conventions/Meetings:** annual Open House - general assembly, contains Marxabilia (exhibits) - always New Hope, PA.

Iglesias, Julio

24216 ■ American Friends of Julio Iglesias Fan Club (AFOJIFC)
PO Box 1425
La Mirada, CA 90637-1425

E-mail: afojifc_star@hotmail.com
URL: http://www.juliomusic.com/fans.htm
Contact: Millie Lucker, Co-Pres.
Founded: 1984. **Members:** 500. **Membership Dues:** individual, $17 (annual) ● foreign, $25 (annual). **Staff:** 2. **Local Groups:** 1. **Multinational. Description:** Admirers of singer Julio Iglesias. Seeks to advance Iglesias' career. Informs members of Iglesias' activities and upcoming appearance schedule.

24217 ■ Julio - America Fan Club
c/o Barbara Rush
400 Dutch Neck Rd., No. H-8
East Windsor, NJ 08512
E-mail: julio-america@mindspring.com
URL: http://www.juliomusic.com/fans.htm
Contact: Pat Riesner, Co-Pres.
Description: Serves as a fan club for Julio Iglesias.

24218 ■ Official Julio Iglesias International Fan Club
PO Box 611930
Miami, FL 33261
Ph: (305)940-8449
Fax: (305)940-8003
E-mail: jifanclub@fm-comm.com
URL: http://www.juliomusic.com
Contact: Elizabeth Hernandez, Dir.
Multinational. Description: Fan club for Julio Iglesias.

Music

24219 ■ Aerosmith's Official Fan Club (AOFC)
Aero Force One
4 Brussels St.
Worcester, MA 01610
Ph: (508)791-3807
E-mail: customerservice@aeroforceone.com
URL: http://www.aeroforceone.com
Membership Dues: gold level, $29 (annual) ● platinum level, $59 (annual). **Description:** Admirers of the rock band Aerosmith. Promotes appreciation of Aerosmith's music. Serves as a clearinghouse on Aerosmith's history and current itinerary; facilitates communication and camaraderie among members; sponsors social activities. **Computer Services:** Mailing lists, of members ● online services, message board. **Publications:** Newsletter. Alternate Formats: online.

24220 ■ Air Supply Fan Club (ASFC)
c/o Julie Wolfe
PO Box 3367
Beverly Hills, CA 90212-0367
Ph: (310)535-6949
E-mail: luv@airsupplymusic.com
URL: http://www.airsupplymusic.com
Contact: Julie Wolfe, Contact
Membership Dues: life, $20 ● life (international), $25. **Description:** Fans of Air Supply, an Australian pop band whose members include Russell Hitchcock (1949-) and Graham Russell (1950-), and which scored numerous hits including Lost in Love, The One That You Love, and Making Love Out of Nothing at All.

24221 ■ Alabama Fan Club (AFC)
PO Box 680529
Fort Payne, AL 35968-1606
Ph: (256)845-1646
Free: (800)557-8223
Fax: (256)845-5650
E-mail: guestbook@thealabamaband.com
URL: http://www.thealabamaband.com
Founded: 1971. **Members:** 300,000. **Membership Dues:** regular, $20 (annual). **Description:** Fans of the southern-rock band Alabama. Promotes Alabama's music; provides concert and ticket information; makes available Alabama memorabilia. Maintains Museum. **Publications:** Newsletter, 3/year. **Conventions/Meetings:** annual meeting.

24222 ■ Alan Jackson Fan Club
PO Box 121945
Nashville, TN 37212-1945
Ph: (615)321-5221
Fax: (615)321-2112
E-mail: ajfc@alanjackson.com
URL: http://www.alanjackson.com/rose_fans.php
Membership Dues: platinum in U.S., $15 (annual) ● platinum in Canada, $20 (annual) ● platinum international, $25 (annual) ● platinum in U.S., $30 (biennial) ● platinum in Canada, $40 (biennial) ● platinum international, $50 (biennial). **Multinational. Description:** Fan club dedicated to Alan Jackson. Membership includes platinum membership card, 8x10 photo, and fact sheets. **Publications:** Real World News. Newsletter. **Price:** included in membership dues. Alternate Formats: online.

24223 ■ Always Patsy Cline World Wide Fan Organization (APC)
PO Box 2236
Winchester, VA 22604
Ph: (540)535-1148
Fax: (540)535-1148
E-mail: alwayspc@visuallink.com
URL: http://www.patsycline.info/apc.html
Contact: Bill Cox, Contact
Founded: 1993. **Members:** 925. **Membership Dues:** single, $13 (annual) ● couple, $21 (annual) ● foreign, single, $16 (annual) ● foreign, couple, $26 (annual). **Staff:** 15. **Description:** Fans of country singer Patsy Cline (1932-1963). Seeks to perpetuate the memory of Cline. Maintains biographical archives, hall of fame, and information on Cline's recordings. **Affiliated With:** International Fan Club Organization. **Publications:** Newsletter, quarterly. **Conventions/Meetings:** annual Patsy Cline Weekend - meeting - always in Labor Day weekend.

24224 ■ Amy Beth Fan Club (ABFC)
c/o T. Parravano, Pres./CEO
Peridot Records
PO Box 8846
Cranston, RI 02920
Ph: (401)785-2677
E-mail: amybeth_e@yahoo.com
URL: http://www.peridotrecords.com/home.html
Contact: T. Parravano, Pres./CEO
Founded: 1996. **Members:** 50. **Membership Dues:** ordinary, $10 (annual). **Staff:** 2. **Description:** Admirers of country musician Amy Beth. Promotes interest in music, with particular emphasis on country music. Gathers and disseminates information on Amy Beth's life and career; sponsors song contests and other social activities. **Libraries: Type:** reference. **Holdings:** archival material, articles, clippings. **Subjects:** discography, musical recordings. **Publications:** Amy Beth Newsletter, biennial. Contains facts and information about Amy Beth. **Price:** free. **Advertising:** accepted. **Conventions/Meetings:** Music Conventions.

24225 ■ Annie Sims International Fan Club
PO Box 816
Bastrop, TX 78602-0816
E-mail: anniefan@austin.rr.com
URL: http://www.anniesims.com
Contact: Jan Foster, Pres.
Members: 1,000. **Membership Dues:** regular, $15 (annual). **Multinational. Description:** Represents the interests of the fans of American country singer Annie Sims. Promotes appreciation of Sims' music. Provides information on upcoming concert tours and other activities of the country singer. Facilitates communication and cooperation among members. **Publications:** Newsletter, quarterly. **Price:** included in membership dues.

24226 ■ Art Greenhaw Official International Fan Club
c/o Marilyn McKay, Pres.
105 Broad St.
Mesquite, TX 75149
Ph: (972)285-5441
Fax: (972)285-5442

E-mail: art@artgreenhaw.com
URL: http://www.artgreenhaw.com
Contact: Marilyn McKay, Pres.
Membership Dues: in U.S., $10 (annual) ● outside U.S., $15 (annual). **Multinational. Description:** Represents fans of Art Greenhaw, lead singer of the country band, The Light Crust Doughboys. Fosters acknowledgement and appreciation for the works done by Art Greenhaw. Keeps members informed of upcoming concert tours and other activities concerning Art Greenhaw and his band, The Light Crust Doughboys. **Publications:** Newsletter, quarterly. **Price:** included in membership dues. Alternate Formats: online.

24227 ■ Asleep At The Wheel Fan Club
PO Box 463
Austin, TX 78767
Ph: (512)444-9885
Fax: (512)444-4699
E-mail: aatw@gte.net
URL: http://www.asleepatthewheel.com/set_fans.html
Contact: Ray Benson, Dir.
Membership Dues: regular, in U.S., $12 (annual) ● regular, outside U.S., $15 (annual). **Description:** Serves as a fan club dedicated to Asleep At The Wheel. Includes autographed band photo, biography, and card that entitles 10 percent merchandise discount for members. **Publications:** As The Wheel Turns, quarterly. Newsletter. Contains up-to-date information on upcoming tours and concerts, insider information on band members, available merchandise, and latest albums. Alternate Formats: online.

24228 ■ Beach Boys Fan Club (BBFC)
631 N Stephanie St., No. 546
Henderson, NV 89014
E-mail: ktsa@beachboysfanclub.com
URL: http://www.beachboysfanclub.com
Contact: Brian Wilson, Contact
Founded: 1973. **Members:** 1,500. **Description:** Represents fans of the pop group The Beach Boys. **Also Known As:** Beach Boys Freaks United. **Publications:** Beach Boys Fan Club News Sheet, 5/year. Newsletter.

24229 ■ Beautiful Music Friends (BMF)
Address Unknown since 2006
Founded: 1983. **Members:** 150. **Membership Dues:** $5 (annual). **Staff:** 4. **Description:** Admirers and supporters of the musical career of Barry Manilow (1946). Organizes fundraising events and programs for children. **Libraries: Type:** open to the public. **Publications:** Beautiful Music Friends, 3/year. Newsletter. Covers Manilow's life and career. **Advertising:** not accepted. **Conventions/Meetings:** annual conference (exhibits).

24230 ■ Bessie Smith Society (BSS)
c/o Dan T. Lewis
Franklin and Marshall Coll.
PO Box 3003
Lancaster, PA 17604-3003
Ph: (717)291-4044 (717)291-3900
Fax: (717)291-4143
Contact: Dan Lewis, Advisor
Members: 50. **Staff:** 1. **Budget:** $7,600. **Local Groups:** 1. **Description:** Admirers of blues singer Bessie Smith, who attained her greatest success in the 1920s and 30s.

24231 ■ Bill Deal and the Rhondels Fan Club (BDRFC)
c/o Robert J. McKenzie, Pres.
114 Prince George Dr.
Hampton, VA 23669-3604
Ph: (757)838-2059
E-mail: thejudge@pcdocs.net
Contact: Robert J. McKenzie, Pres.
Membership Dues: individual, $20 (annual). **Description:** Admirers of the popular music group Bill Deal and the Rhondels, whose hits included "May I" and "I've Been Hurt," both of which were released in 1969. Promotes interest in the band's music and career. Serves as a clearinghouse on Bill Deal and the Rhondells recordings and other memorabilia;

keeps members informed regarding the band's appearance schedule and the availability of collectible items pertaining to Bill Deal and the Rhondells. **Libraries: Type:** reference. **Holdings:** archival material, articles, books, clippings, periodicals. **Subjects:** Bill Deal and the Rhondells music and memorabilia.

24232 ■ Billy "Crash" Craddock Fan Club (BCCFC)
c/o Judy Plummer, Pres.
4101 Pickfair Rd.
Springfield, IL 62703
E-mail: jplumm1@netzero.net
URL: http://www.ifco.org/Billy_Crash_Craddock/billy_crash_craddock.htm
Contact: Judy Plummer, Pres.
Membership Dues: individual in U.S. and Canada, $12 (annual) ● individual outside U.S. and Canada, $14 (annual). **Description:** Represents fans of country music singer Billy "Crash" Craddock, best known for his song "Rub It In". **Publications:** Newsletter, monthly. Covers membership activities. **Price:** included in membership dues.

24233 ■ Billy Ray Cyrus Spirit
PO Box 1206
Franklin, TN 37065
Ph: (931)486-3326
Fax: (931)486-3356
E-mail: brcspirit@bellsouth.net
URL: http://www.billyraycyrus.com
Contact: Tish Cyrus, Dir.
Membership Dues: regular, $20 (annual). **Multinational. Description:** Fan club dedicated to Billy Ray Cyrus. Membership includes 8x10 photo, biography, and merchandise order form. **Publications:** Newsletter, quarterly. Contains tour dates, photos and information about Billy Ray's career.

24234 ■ Bing's Friends and Collectors Society (BFCS)
c/o Hobie Wilson, Pres./Ed.
236 Andrieux St.
Sonoma, CA 95476-6909
Ph: (707)996-0257
Fax: (707)996-0257
E-mail: bingsfriends81@sbcglobal.net
URL: http://www.geocities.com/one_sonoma_rose/BingsHomePage.html?1121136749218
Contact: Hobie Wilson, Pres./Ed.
Founded: 1981. **Members:** 126. **Membership Dues:** domestic, $12 (annual) ● foreign, $16 (annual). **Staff:** 2. **Description:** Record and film collectors who amass memorabilia pertaining to Bing Crosby (1903-77). Seeks to keep the memory of Crosby alive. **Publications:** Bing's Friends and Collectors' Society Newsletter, bimonthly. Contains articles related to Crosby and his career and members classified ads. **Price:** included in membership dues. **Advertising:** accepted. **Conventions/Meetings:** annual banquet (exhibits) - always October.

24235 ■ Bob Homan Fan Club (BHFC)
PO Box 653
Yakima, WA 98907-0653
Ph: (509)453-1228
E-mail: musicbob@yvn.com
Contact: Mrs. Dorothy Sawyer, Pres.
Founded: 1950. **Members:** 125. **Membership Dues:** regular, $5 (annual). **Description:** Fans of country singer Bob Homan (1930 to present). Promotes Homan and his band, Four Your Pleasure and the Bob Homan-Al Maletta Duo. **Publications:** Bob Homan Fan Club—Newsletter, annual, every summer. Includes membership news, new members information, and recipes. **Price:** included in membership dues ● Homan Hi-Lites, semiannual, each spring and fall. Journal. Provides information on country music; includes obituaries and recipes. **Price:** included in membership dues. **Conventions/Meetings:** quinquennial Potluck and Get-Together - meeting.

24236 ■ Bonnie Lou Bishop International Fan Club (BLBIFC)
Address Unknown since 2007
Founded: 1981. **Members:** 200. **Description:** Fans of country music singer Bonnie Lou Bishop. Purpose is to promote Bishop's music and career. Holds parties, dances, and picnics for members. **Affiliated With:** International Fan Club Organization. **Formerly:** (1987) Bonnie Lou Bishop Fan Club. **Publications:** Bulletin, semiannual ● Newsletter, semiannual. **Conventions/Meetings:** periodic Fan Fair - meeting.

24237 ■ Brooks and Dunn Fan Club
PO Box 120669
Nashville, TN 37212-0669
Ph: (615)248-6772
E-mail: fanclub@brooks-dunn.com
URL: http://www.brooks-dunn.com
Contact: Terry Miller, Contact
Membership Dues: regular, $15 (annual). **Multinational. Description:** Fan club dedicated to Brooks & Dunn. Membership includes autographed color photo, card, biography, merchandise ordering information, and tour schedules. **Publications:** Newsletter, quarterly. **Price:** included in membership dues.

24238 ■ Buddy Holly Memorial Society (BHMS)
Address Unknown since 2006
Founded: 1976. **Members:** 5,500. **Description:** Fans of Buddy Holly (1936-59) and his band, the Crickets. Purpose is to conduct research about and disseminate information on Holly and his band to fans. Maintains museum. Compiles statistics. **Libraries: Type:** reference. **Holdings:** archival material, audio recordings, photographs, video recordings. **Publications:** Rockin' 50's: The True Rock 'n' Roll Era, bimonthly. Magazine. For collectors and fans. Contains book reviews and information on new products; lists television shows and record charts of the era. **Price:** $30.00 US plus Canada; $42.00 Europe. ISSN: 0738-7717. **Circulation:** 1,700. **Advertising:** accepted. **Conventions/Meetings:** annual meeting - always September 1-7, Lubbock, TX.

24239 ■ Carla Riggs-Hall International Fan Club
202 Master St.
Elizabethtown, KY 42701
E-mail: ruffles11@hotmail.com
URL: http://www.angelfire.com/ky/studioc
Founded: 1980. **Members:** 250. **Membership Dues:** fan, $20 (annual). **Staff:** 3. **State Groups:** 9. **Description:** Promotes the music career of Carla Riggs-Hall. Sponsors benefit performances. **Publications:** Newsletter, semiannual. **Price:** included in membership dues. **Circulation:** 250. **Advertising:** accepted. **Conventions/Meetings:** annual Fan Club Party, in conjunction with Fan Fair Week (exhibits) - always June.

24240 ■ Cecilia Lee International Fan Club (CLIFC)
Address Unknown since 2007
URL: http://www.geocities.com/cecilialeesings/
Founded: 1984. **Members:** 700. **Membership Dues:** $5 (annual). **Staff:** 5. **State Groups:** 7. **Description:** Production companies; fans. To promote the career of Cecilia Lee (1966-), a country/pop/gospel singer who plays eight instruments including the banjo, flute, saxophone, fiddle, guitar, bass, mandolin and piano. **Computer Services:** Mailing lists, labels. **Committees:** State Representatives. **Affiliated With:** International Fan Club Organization. **Formerly:** (1985) Cecilia Lee Fan Club. **Publications:** Cecilia Lee Fan Club Newsletter, quarterly ● Bulletin, periodic ● Directory, periodic ● Also publishes appearance schedule. **Conventions/Meetings:** semiannual meeting (exhibits).

24241 ■ Charley Pride Fan Club (CPFC)
PO Box 670507
Dallas, TX 75367
E-mail: johndaines@charleypride.com
URL: http://www.charleypride.com
Contact: John Daines, Contact
Founded: 1983. **Members:** 550. **Membership Dues:** regular, in U.S., $10 (annual) ● regular, outside U.S.,

$13 (annual). **Description:** Fans of country music singer Charley Pride (1939-). Aims to promote Pride's music and career by attending concerts, buying records, and soliciting airplay of his music from radio stations. **Publications:** GID Newsletter, quarterly. **Conventions/Meetings:** annual breakfast.

24242 ■ Chet Atkins Appreciation Society (CAAS)
c/o Mark Pritcher, Pres.
3716 Timberlake Rd.
Knoxville, TN 37920
Ph: (865)577-2828
Fax: (865)687-2065
E-mail: feedback@misterguitar.com
URL: http://www.misterguitar.com/caas
Contact: Mark Pritcher, Pres.
Founded: 1983. **Members:** 850. **Membership Dues:** individual, $10 (annual). **Description:** Guitarists and fans of country music guitarist Chet Atkins (1924-2001). Unites fans of Atkins and promotes the Atkins fingerstyle technique of guitar playing. (The Atkins fingerstyle technique is similar to that used in classical guitar, but adapted to popular music, and consists of playing the melody of a song with three fingers while playing the rhythm with the thumb.) Disseminates information about Atkins' music to fans. **Computer Services:** Mailing lists, of members. **Publications:** Mister Guitar, quarterly. Newsletter. **Conventions/Meetings:** annual meeting (exhibits) - always July or August, in Nashville, TN.

24243 ■ Chicago Fan Club (CFC)
PO Box 195
Landing, NJ 07850
E-mail: ctaronni16@aol.com
URL: http://www.ctaofficialfanclub.com
Contact: Bob Dillon, Pres.
Membership Dues: regular, in U.S., $24 (annual) ● regular, in Canada, $25 (annual) ● regular, outside U.S. and Canada, $33 (annual). **Description:** Represents fans of the pop music group Chicago, whose members have included Robert Lamm (1944-), Peter Cetera (1944-), Terry Kath (1946-1978), Lee Loughnane (1946-), Walter Parazaider (1945-), James Pankow (1947-), Daniel Seraphine (1948-), Laudir De Oliveira (1948-), and Donnie Dacus. Recordings include Saturday in the Park, Just You and Me, and Color My World.

24244 ■ Chicago True Advocates (CTA)
PO Box 195
Landing, NJ 07850
Ph: (516)933-7153
E-mail: ctaronni16@aol.com
URL: http://www.ctaofficialfanclub.com
Contact: Bob Dillon, Pres.
Members: 3,000. **Membership Dues:** regular in U.S., $24 (annual) ● regular in Canada, $25 (annual) ● other, $33 (annual). **Staff:** 10. **Description:** Admirers of the musical group Chicago. Promotes appreciation of Chicago's music. Gathers and disseminates information on Chicago and its concert schedule; provides ticket purchasing services to members. **Computer Services:** Mailing lists. **Publications:** Scrapbook, quarterly. Newsletter. **Price:** included in membership dues. **Alternate Formats:** CD-ROM. **Conventions/Meetings:** annual convention, membership meeting with meet and greet with the band.

24245 ■ Chris LeDoux International Fan Club (CLIFC)
PO Box 41052
San Jose, CA 95160
Ph: (408)997-8340
E-mail: info@chrisledoux.com
URL: http://www.chrisledoux.com
Contact: Warner H. Heyer, Pres.
Founded: 1978. **Members:** 1,500. **Membership Dues:** in U.S., $14 (annual) ● outside U.S., $17 (annual). **Description:** Represents country music fans and other individuals interested in the musical activities and career of "cowboy-country" musician Chris LeDoux (1948-). Offers recordings and memorabilia. **Affiliated With:** International Fan Club Organization.

Publications: *Gold Buckle Dreams-The Rodeo Life of Chris LeDoux* ● Newsletter, quarterly ● Yearbook, annual.

24246 ∎ Chuck Negron Fan Club
PO Box 1562
Concord, NH 03302-1562
E-mail: fanclub@negron.com
URL: http://www.negron.com
Contact: Joan Zeledon, Pres.
Founded: 1995. **Members:** 280. **Membership Dues:** regular, in U.S., $20 (annual) ● regular, outside U.S., $24 (annual) ● international, $29 (annual). **Description:** Promotes the career and music of Chuck Negron, former lead singer of Three Dog Night. Provides a weekly chat on America Online and a library on CompuServe. **Convention/Meeting:** none. **Publications:** *Negron News*, quarterly. Newsletter. Contains articles and photos. **Price:** included in membership dues. Alternate Formats: online.

24247 ∎ Circle Club - The Official Fan Club of the Grand Ole Opry (GOOFC)
2804 Opryland Dr.
Nashville, TN 37214
Ph: (615)871-6779 (615)871-5043
Free: (800)SEE-OPRY
Fax: (615)871-6166
URL: http://www.opry.com
Founded: 1987. **Members:** 2,500. **Membership Dues:** regular, $10 (annual). **Staff:** 2. **Description:** Individuals interested in the Grand Ole Opry, the country music radio show first broadcast from Nashville, TN in 1925. Promotes interest in the Opry and country music. **Libraries: Type:** reference; open to the public. **Formerly:** (2001) Grand Ole Opry Fan Club. **Publications:** *Circle Club*, quarterly. Newsletter. **Price:** included in membership dues. **Circulation:** 2,500. **Conventions/Meetings:** annual meeting, brunch for members with Opry stars meet and greet - always June.

24248 ∎ Cliff Richard Fan Club of America (CRFCUSA)
3 Kelley Rd.
Acton, MA 01720-3614
E-mail: scrfanusa@yahoo.com
URL: http://www.cliffrichard.info
Contact: Ms. Heidi J. Schmelzer, Co-Dir.
Founded: 1979. **Members:** 130. **Membership Dues:** regular, $22 (annual). **Local Groups:** 4. **Description:** Fans of British pop-rock singer and recording artist Sir Cliff Richard (1940-). Informs members of Richard's activities and appearances; makes available sources for obtaining Richard's recordings, concert tickets, books, and merchandise; timely reports on record releases. **Additional Websites:** http://home.att.net/~crfcusa. **Formerly:** (1989) Cliff Richard Movement - USA. **Publications:** *The Cliff Connection*, quarterly. Newsletter. Covers Cliff Richard's concerts, performances, and current activities, with input from members. **Price:** included in membership dues. **Advertising:** accepted ● *Dynamite International*, bimonthly. Newsletter. Covers Richard's concerts, performances, and current activities. **Price:** included in membership dues ● Also disseminates biography and discographies.

24249 ∎ Connie Francis International Fan Club (CFFC)
c/o Pat Niglio
100 Caton Ave., Ste.5J
Brooklyn, NY 11218
E-mail: webmaster@conniefrancis.com
URL: http://www.conniefrancis.com/fanclub.html
Contact: Mike Church, Contact
Founded: 1985. **Members:** 300. **Membership Dues:** domestic, Canadian, $21 (annual) ● foreign, $30 (annual). **Description:** Friends and fans of singer Connie Francis (1938-) whose hits include Where the Boys Are, Who's Sorry Now, and Lipstick on Your Collar. Keeps members informed of Francis' career. **Publications:** Bulletin, periodic ● Newsletter, quarterly. **Price:** $15.00/year in U.S.; $17.00/year outside U.S.

24250 ∎ Connie Stevens Fan Club (CSFC)
c/o Betty A. Moran, Pres.
2500 Gaither St. SE
Hillcrest Heights
Temple Hills, MD 20748-3030
Ph: (301)894-9342
URL: http://www.geocities.com/Connie_Stevens_Fan_Club/Welcome.html
Contact: Betty A. Moran, Pres.
Founded: 1975. **Members:** 150. **Staff:** 6. **Description:** Fans of singer and actress Connie Stevens (1938-). Works to promote Stevens' career and keep members informed of her activities. **Publications:** *Stevens Star Journal*, annual ● Newsletter, 3/year.

24251 ∎ Cowsills Fan Club (CFC)
PO Box 83
Lexington, MS 39095
E-mail: cowsillfan@gmail.com
URL: http://www.cowsill.com
Founded: 1990. **Members:** 300. **Multinational. Description:** Promotes the career of the family musical group the Cowsills. Formed in the mid-1960's, the Cowsills produced such hits as The Rain, the Park, and Other Things and the theme from the rock musical Hair. All seven Cowsill siblings are still involved in performing, recording, songwriting, and producing.

24252 ∎ David Allan Coe Fan Club (DACFC)
783 Rippling Creek
Nixa, MO 65714
E-mail: wizard@dilligaf.com
URL: http://www.officialdavidallancoe.com
Contact: Bill Quisenberry, Contact
Founded: 1990. **Members:** 1,500. **Membership Dues:** individual, in U.S., $15 (annual) ● individual, outside U.S., $18 (annual). **Staff:** 2. **Description:** Fans of country-western singer and guitarist David Allan Coe (1939-). Keeps members informed of Coe's career and activities, album releases, and public appearances. **Convention/Meeting:** none. **Publications:** *David Allan Coe Newsletter*, quarterly. **Price:** included in membership dues.

24253 ∎ David Ball International Fan Club
c/o Susan Collier, Public Relations Off.
6204 Jocelyn Hollow Rd.
Nashville, TN 37205
Ph: (615)356-0375
Fax: (615)714-7974
URL: http://www.davidball.com
Contact: Susan Collier, Public Relations Off.
Membership Dues: regular, in U.S., $15 (annual) ● regular, outside U.S., $18 (annual). **Multinational. Description:** Fan club dedicated to David Ball. Membership includes biography, membership card and button, bumper sticker, autographed 8x10 photo, welcome letter, tour schedules, and merchandise offerings. **Publications:** Newsletter, quarterly. **Price:** included in membership dues.

24254 ∎ Davy Devotees - The Official Fan Club for Davy Jones (DDOFCDJ)
c/o Abby Alterio, Pres./Ed.
10930 Stratford Way
Fishers, IN 46038
E-mail: davydevotees@sbcglobal.net
URL: http://www.geocities.com/davydevotee/dd2.html
Contact: Abby Alterio, Pres./Ed.
Founded: 1996. **Members:** 1,500. **Staff:** 1. **Description:** Admirers of singer and musician Davy Jones, a member of the 1960s popular group, The Monkees. Promotes appreciation of Jones' music and many other ventures. Facilitates exchange of information among members; serves as a clearinghouse on Jones' career and current itinerary. **Awards:** Crave the Dave Award. **Type:** recognition. **Recipient:** for web pages. **Computer Services:** Mailing lists, of members. **Publications:** Newsletter, periodic. Includes tour dates, concert reviews, and pictures. **Price:** free. Alternate Formats: online.

24255 ∎ Debbie Harry Collector's Society (DHCS)
124 S Locust Point Rd.
Mechanicsburg, PA 17055-9709
E-mail: blk@debbieharry.net
URL: http://debbieharry.net
Contact: Barry L. Kramer, Contact
Founded: 1987. **Members:** 205. **Description:** Fans and collectors of memorabilia relating to rock singer Debbie Harry (1945-) and her former group Blondie. Seeks to produce and preserve an accurate historical record of the careers of Harry, Blondie, and all their associates by compiling lists of records and live appearances and through the collection of video recordings, interview transcripts, promotional materials, and magazine articles. Assists members in expanding their collections and staying informed about current projects. **Computer Services:** Mailing lists ● online services, data files available on website. **Additional Websites:** http://blondie.net. **Publications:** *Deborah Harry Archive Report*, periodic. Alternate Formats: online ● *Fan Mail*, periodic. Newsletter. Contains information about Harry's current projects, interview transcripts, accounts of concert experiences, and technical information. **Price:** $3.00 plus postage. **Circulation:** 150.

24256 ∎ Del Shannon Appreciation Society (DSAS)
PO Box 44201
Tacoma, WA 98444-0201
E-mail: briancyoung@comcast.net
URL: http://www.delshannon.com
Contact: Brian C. Young, Contact
Founded: 1981. **Members:** 1,000. **Membership Dues:** regular, $50 (annual). **Description:** Individuals who enjoy the music of singer/songwriter Del Shannon (1939-90), whose recordings include Runaway, Hats Off to Larry, and Little Town Flirt. Serves as a forum for the exchange of information and musical recordings among members. **Publications:** *And The Music Plays On*, quarterly. Magazine. Contains information on the music and career of Del Shannon. **Price:** $30.00/year. **Circulation:** 1,000. **Conventions/Meetings:** annual Del Shannon Days - festival, summerfest with live music (exhibits).

24257 ∎ Diamond Rio Fan Club (DRFC)
PO Box 2195
Hendersonville, TN 37077-2195
Fax: (615)824-6101
E-mail: fancluboffice@diamondrio.com
URL: http://www.diamondrio.com
Contact: Scarlet Morgan, Pres.
Founded: 1991. **Members:** 5,000. **Membership Dues:** regular, in U.S., $20 (annual) ● international, $25 (annual). **Description:** Fans of the band Diamond Rio. **Publications:** *Rockin Rio News*, quarterly. Newsletter. Alternate Formats: online.

24258 ∎ Dinah Shore Fan Club (DSFC)
c/o Kay Daly, Pres.
3552 Fed. Ave.
Los Angeles, CA 90066
E-mail: kdaly10288@aol.com
URL: http://www.dinahshorefanclub.com
Contact: Kay Daly, Pres.
Founded: 1952. **Members:** 100. **Membership Dues:** regular, in U.S., $12 (annual) ● regular, outside U.S., $16 (annual). **Description:** Admirers of singer/actress Dinah Shore (1917-1994), who attained her peak musical popularity in the mid-1940s and achieved national prominence once again as the host of the television programs The Dinah Shore Show and Dinah's Place in the early 1970s. Acts as a center of information on Shore's career; aids members in locating Shore's recordings and memorabilia; supports various charitable organizations. **Also Known As:** Dinah Shore Memorial Fan Club. **Publications:** *Dinah's Digest*, annual. Journal ● *The Shore Line*, quarterly. Bulletin.

24259 ∎ Dolly Parton's Fan Club
708 Dollywood Ln.
Pigeon Forge, TN 37863
URL: http://www.oprynorth.com/dolly_parton's%20fan%20club.htm
Description: Serves fans club devoted to singer and actress Dolly Parton.

24260 ■ Dollywood Foundation (DWF)
1020 Dollywood Ln.
Pigeon Forge, TN 37863
Ph: (865)428-9607
Fax: (865)428-9612
E-mail: ccrouse@dollyfoundation.com
URL: http://www.dollywoodfoundation.com
Contact: Christy Crouse, Regional Dir.
Founded: 1988. **Staff:** 3. **Description:** Fans and supporters of country singer and actress Dolly Parton, who appeared in the films Best Little Whorehouse in Texas, 9-to-5, Steel Magnolias, and Straight Talk. Seeks to support children, the underprivileged, and public education in the local community and the East Tennessee/Smoky Mountain area. Conducts educational programs. Promotes education and educational programs for children in Sevier County. Has current program, which is the "Imagination Library." Provides a monthly book to Sevier County children (from birth to age 5) from Ms. Parton and the foundation program, which is designed to promote reading and parental involvement in the early years of a child's life. **Libraries: Type:** reference. **Holdings:** 60. **Awards: Type:** recognition ● **Type:** scholarship. **Formerly:** (1987) Dolly Parton Fan Club; (1989) Dollywood Ambassadors; (1992) Dollywood Ambassadors and Dollywood Foundation.

24261 ■ Donna Fargo International Fan Club (DFIFC)
c/o Linda Cottingham, Coor.
PO Box 210877
Nashville, TN 37221-0877
Ph: (615)662-9484
Fax: (615)662-9484
E-mail: llc927@comcast.net
URL: http://www.donnafargo.com/index2.html
Contact: Linda Cottingham, Coor.
Founded: 1986. **Members:** 1,000. **Membership Dues:** regular, in U.S., $15 (annual) ● regular, in Canada, $18 (annual) ● regular, outside U.S. and Canada, $30 (annual). **Staff:** 4. **Description:** Fans of entertainer Donna Fargo, best known for the songs Happiest Girl in the Whole U.S.A. and Funny Face. **Affiliated With:** International Fan Club Organization. **Formerly:** Donna Fargo Fan Club. **Publications:** The Fargo Express, quarterly. Newsletter. Features career activities of Donna Fargo. Includes Fargo's performance itinerary, swap column, pen pal listing, and current news. **Price:** included in membership dues; $14.00 for nonmembers in Canada; $17.00 for nonmembers international. **Circulation:** 1,300. **Conventions/Meetings:** annual Fan Fair and Fan Club Meeting (exhibits).

24262 ■ Donny Osmond International Network (DOIN)
51 W Center St., No. 424
Orem, UT 84057
E-mail: questions@donny.com
URL: http://www.donny.com
Contact: Tina Salmon, Contact
Founded: 1985. **Members:** 2,500. **Membership Dues:** regular, $13 (annual). **Description:** Fans and admirers of singer Donny Osmond (1957-). Keeps members informed of Osmond's career and activities. **Computer Services:** Mailing lists. **Formerly:** (1989) Donny Osmond Fan Club. **Publications:** Donny Osmond Official Fan Club Newsletter, quarterly. **Price:** included in membership dues. **Conventions/Meetings:** annual Get Together - reunion.

24263 ■ Doors Collectors Club
c/o TDM Inc.
PO Box 1441
Orem, UT 84059-1441
Ph: (801)224-7390
Free: (800)891-1736
Fax: (801)224-5723
E-mail: dcm@doors.com
URL: http://www.doors.com
Contact: Kerry Humpherys, Founder
Founded: 1988. **Members:** 9,000. **Membership Dues:** individual, $15 (annual). **Staff:** 3. **Budget:** $90,000. **For-Profit. Description:** Fans of the rock music group The Doors. Explores the music through

articles, interviews and reviews; Morrison vs. Miami petition. Live show audio trades; free e-mail newsletter; and an online memorabilia list of hard to find Doors collectibles. **Libraries: Type:** reference; not open to the public. **Holdings:** archival material, articles, artwork, audiovisuals, clippings, periodicals. **Subjects:** The Doors. **Computer Services:** Mailing lists, of members. **Publications:** The Doors Collectors Magazine, annual. Explores the music and magic of the Doors. **Price:** $15.00 in U.S. **Circulation:** 5,000. **Advertising:** accepted ● Strange Days, bimonthly. Newsletter. Alternate Formats: online. **Conventions/Meetings:** annual convention.

24264 ■ Eddy Raven Fan Club
PO Box 2476
Hendersonville, TN 37077
Ph: (615)230-7414
E-mail: info@eddyraven.com
URL: http://www.eddyraven.com/fanclub.php
Membership Dues: regular, in U.S. and Canada, $20 (annual) ● overseas, $25 (annual). **Multinational. Description:** Fan club dedicated to Eddy Raven. Membership includes membership card, 8x10 photo, and biography club badge. **Publications:** Newsletter. Alternate Formats: online.

24265 ■ Engelbert's "Goils" (EG)
c/o Dot Gillberg, Co-Pres.
22249 Berry Dr.
Cleveland, OH 44116
Ph: (440)331-5601
E-mail: ddgil@sbcglobal.net
URL: http://www.engelbert.com/fanclubs.html
Contact: Dot Gillberg, Co-Pres.
Founded: 1971. **Members:** 200. **Membership Dues:** individual, family in U.S., $25 (annual) ● individual, family outside U.S., $30 (annual). **Staff:** 2. **Description:** Admirers of the music and career of singer Engelbert Humperdinck (1936-). Promotes the music of Humperdinck; disseminates information regarding his concert schedule and recent activities; supports various charitable programs. Primarily active in the Cleveland, OH, area, although membership is international. **Formerly:** (1980) Humperdinck "Goils". **Publications:** Goil Talk, bimonthly. Newsletter. **Price:** $25.00/year in U.S.; $30.00/year outside U.S.

24266 ■ Engelbert's Golden Eagles (EGE)
Address Unknown since 2007
Founded: 1984. **Members:** 68. **Membership Dues:** $23 (annual). **Staff:** 3. **Regional Groups:** 175. **State Groups:** 3. **Local Groups:** 1. **National Groups:** 120. **Description:** Fans of singer Engelbert Humperdinck (1936-) united to promote Humperdinck and foster sales of his recordings. Reports on Humperdinck's itinerary, record releases, television appearances, and information published in the media. Activities include road trips to attend Humperdinck's concerts and decorate his dressing room. Donates funds to medical associations. Maintains hall of fame; conducts charitable activities, educational programs, and children's services. **Libraries: Type:** reference. **Holdings:** 30; articles. **Subjects:** dates of concert written articles and up-to-date concepts of T.V. shows. **Awards:** Engelbert's Golden Eagles. **Frequency:** monthly. **Type:** recognition. **Publications:** Becoming a Movie Star, quarterly. Video. **Price:** included in membership dues. ISSN: 2300-. **Advertising:** accepted ● Engelbert News, quarterly. Newsletter. Includes research reports on charities, pictures, program books, and information on other clubs' activities. **Price:** $23.00/year. **Advertising:** accepted ● Engelbert's Golden Eagles Flash News, periodic. Bulletin. **Advertising:** accepted ● Fan Club Directory, annual ● Point Blank ● Also publishes Humperdinck biography and discography. **Conventions/Meetings:** annual meeting, meetings to spread different news on Engelbert, parties to celebrate Humperdinck's birthday and showbiz anniversary date - usually Las Vegas.

24267 ■ Engel's Angels in Humperdinck Heaven Fan Club (EAHHFC)
3024 4th Ave.
Baltimore, MD 21234-3208

E-mail: jean3024@yahoo.com
URL: http://groups.yahoo.com/group/engelsangels
Contact: Jean Marshalek, Pres.
Founded: 1971. **Members:** 90. **Budget:** $1,000. **Local Groups:** 1. **Multinational. Description:** Fans of Engelbert Humperdinck (1936-), nightclub entertainer whose hit songs include Release Me and After the Loving. Supports and promotes Humperdinck's career through online newsletter. **Libraries: Type:** not open to the public. **Additional Websites:** http://www.engelbert.com/fanclubs.html. **Committees:** Telephone; Video. **Publications:** The Guardian Engel, periodic. Newsletter. **Price:** free. **Circulation:** 100. Alternate Formats: online.

24268 ■ Ethel Delaney International Fan Club (EDIFC)
301 Firestone Dr.
Las Vegas, NV 89145
E-mail: russdelaney@juno.com
URL: http://etheldelaney.bizland.com
Contact: Sandra S. Delaney, Pres.
Founded: 1965. **Members:** 500. **Description:** Fans of the music of Ethel Delaney and Company. Promotes the history and career of Delaney and country music, especially yodeling. Reports country music news; acts as booking agency. Participates in annual Grand Ole Opry birthday celebration and awards show; is represented at Country Music Association annual meeting. **Publications:** Yodel-Gram, quarterly. Newsletter. **Conventions/Meetings:** annual Fan Fair - meeting (exhibits) - always June in Nashville, TN ● annual Grand Ole Opry Birthday Celebration - meeting - always October ● annual Reunion of Professional Entertainers - meeting - always June ● annual Western Music Association - meeting (exhibits) - always November in Las Vegas, Nevada.

24269 ■ Face the Music Fan Club (FTMFC)
c/o Katrina Walker, Pres.
PO Box 6061-572
Sherman Oaks, CA 91413
E-mail: ftmprez@yahoo.com
URL: http://www.facethemusicfanclub.com
Contact: Katrina Walker, Pres.
Founded: 1994. **Members:** 720. **Staff:** 5. **Description:** Individuals interested in the solo careers of the members of the band, New Kids on the Block. Seeks to advance the careers of former NKOTB band members. Facilitates communication and good fellowship among members; keeps members informed of the appearance schedules of former NKOTB members. **Publications:** Face the Music Magazine (in Dutch, English, Finnish, French, and Spanish), quarterly. Newsletter. Includes news, photos, interviews and more. Alternate Formats: online.

24270 ■ Florence Ballard Fan Club (FBFC)
PO Box 360502
Los Angeles, CA 90036
E-mail: info@florenceballardfanclub.com
URL: http://www.florenceballardfanclub.com
Contact: Alan White, Pres.
Founded: 1985. **Members:** 300. **Membership Dues:** in U.S. and Canada, $15 (annual) ● outside U.S., $20 (annual). **Multinational. Description:** Music fans and collectors. Purpose is to serve as a living memorial to Florence Ballard (1943-76). (Ballard was a member of the original pop/soul trio the Supremes, which also included Diana Ross (1944-) and Mary Wilson (1944-), and who recorded a string of hits in the 1960s and early '70s. Ballard was replaced by Cindy Birdsong (1939-) in 1967 and then pursued a solo recording career.) Seeks to: keep Ballard's memory alive in a positive light; honor Ballard's musical contributions and achievements; conduct research and disseminate information concerning Ballard's life and career; collect memorabilia related to Ballard and the original Supremes. **Libraries: Type:** open to the public. **Holdings:** 200. **Subjects:** Florence Ballard, The Supremes, Motown, Diana Ross, Mary Wilson. **Awards:** Florence Ballard Award. **Type:** scholarship. **Recipient:** for a performing arts major. **Publications:** Florence Ballard, quarterly. Newsletter. Contains photographs, clippings, essays, and

book and music reviews pertaining to Ballard and members of the original Supremes. **Price:** $5.00/issue. **Circulation:** 500. **Advertising:** accepted ● *Florence Ballard Souvenir Program*, annual. Booklet. Contains club and biographical information. **Price:** $5.00/issue. **Circulation:** 500. **Advertising:** accepted. **Conventions/Meetings:** biennial Florence Ballard Exhibition - show.

24271 ■ FR-ENGE International
c/o Marion E. Scowcroft, Pres.
124 Bradford Rd.
Pittsford, NY 14534
E-mail: frengeint@hotmail.com
Contact: Marion E. Scowcroft, Pres.
Founded: 1975. **Members:** 62. **Membership Dues:** regular, in U.S., $15 (annual) ● regular, outside U.S., $20 (annual). **Description:** Individuals who admire the music and career of singer Engelbert Humperdinck (1936-). Provides members with information on Humperdinck's upcoming concert schedule; promotes attendance at his live performances; organizes transportation for members who live in areas not visited by his tours. Supports charitable causes. **Convention/Meeting:** none. **Libraries:** Type: reference. Holdings: archival material, audio recordings. **Subjects:** Engelbert Humperdinck. **Formerly:** (1992) FR-ENGE. **Publications:** *ENGE N PRESS INTERNATIONAL*, 4-6/year. Newsletter. Includes record and concert reviews. **Price:** $15.00/year in U.S.; $20.00/year outside U.S. **Circulation:** 62. **Advertising:** accepted ● Newsletter, bimonthly. **Price:** $15.00/year in U.S.; $20.00/year outside U.S. **Advertising:** accepted.

24272 ■ Frankie Laine Society of America (FLSOA)
c/o Vicki Lockridge, Pres.
N Torrance Sta.
PO Box 7996
Torrance, CA 90504
URL: http://www.frankielaine.com/fl_fans.shtml
Contact: Vicki Lockridge, Pres.
Founded: 1949. **Members:** 200. **Membership Dues:** in U.S., $12 (annual) ● outside U.S., $15 (annual). **Description:** Admirers of singer Frankie Laine (1913-), best known for his hit That's My Desire. (Laine was most popular in the late '40s and the '50s, but still tours today.) Promotes Laine and keeps members apprised of his appearances. **Convention/Meeting:** none. **Publications:** Newsletter, 3-5/year.

24273 ■ Friends of the Cassidys (FOTC)
c/o Cheryl Corwin, Pres.
1647 Crystal Downs St.
Banning, CA 92220
Ph: (562)493-0718 (562)505-8717
Fax: (562)493-9718
E-mail: fotcprez@socal.rr.com
URL: http://www.geocities.com/Hollywood/2001/fotc.html
Contact: Cheryl Corwin, Pres.
Founded: 1977. **Members:** 125. **Membership Dues:** in U.S., $13 (annual) ● in Canada, $16 (annual) ● overseas, $20 (annual). **Staff:** 13. **Description:** Fans of pop singer Shaun Cassidy (1959-), David Cassidy (1950-), Patrick Cassidy (1962-), Ryan Cassidy (1966-), Marty Ingels (1936-), and Shirley Jones (1934-). Provides tour information and career information on each member of the family. Conducts annual collection for Leukemia Society. **Convention/Meeting:** none. **Committees:** Fan Club. **Formerly:** (1993) Friends of Shaun Cassidy Fan Club. **Publications:** *The Cassidy Focus*, monthly. Newsletter. Features updates on family members; membership participation requested. **Price:** $1.25 ● *Friends' Focus*, monthly. Includes members' comments and reviews. **Price:** included in membership dues. Also Cited As: *Friends of Shaun Cassidy Fan Club—Newsletter: Shaun's Love Letter*.

24274 ■ Friends of Dennis Wilson (FODW)
c/o Christine Duffy
1381 Maria Way
San Jose, CA 95117
Ph: (408)379-4998
Contact: Christine M. Duffy, Pres.
Founded: 1983. **Members:** 200. **Membership Dues:** individual, $7 (annual) ● $12 (biennial). **Staff:** 4. **Budget:** $500. **Regional Groups:** 2. **Description:** Fans and admirers interested in the life and career of singer and musician Dennis Wilson (1944-83), who was a member of the pop band the Beach Boys; fans of the singing group Jan and Dean "Brian's Business" 1946-1998, "Carl's Corner" new columns. Seeks to: perpetuate the music of Wilson; promote and encourage concerts and recordings of the Beach Boys. Conducts research on Wilson's life and attempts to uncover unreleased Beach Boys recordings. Provides children's services; conducts charitable "World Vision" programs. **Convention/Meeting:** none. **Libraries:** Type: open to the public. Holdings: 75; articles, articles, periodicals. **Subjects:** reviews, poems, birthdays. **Awards:** National Association (Fan Club). Frequency: annual. Type: recognition ● R&R Hall of Fame (Fan Club). Type: recognition ● Who's Who (Fan Club). Frequency: annual. Type: recognition. **Publications:** *Dennymania*, quarterly. Magazine. Includes music reviews, feature articles, poems, trivia, trade ads, news, and pen pal section. **Price:** $5.00 included in membership dues. **Circulation:** 125. **Advertising:** accepted.

24275 ■ Friends of Guy Clark (FGC)
PO Box 1
Yorkville, CA 95494-0001
Ph: (707)894-5446
E-mail: jezmues@yahoo.com
Contact: Jo Ann Aronson, Contact
Founded: 1985. **Members:** 2,000. **Staff:** 1. **Description:** Fans of country music songwriter and performer Guy Clark (1941-), who wrote and recorded the songs L.A. Freeway and Desperados Waiting for a Train. Encourages communication among fans; informs members of Clark's appearances. **Computer Services:** Mailing lists. **Publications:** *Friends of Guy Clark Newsletter*, semiannual. **Price:** free. **Circulation:** 2,000. **Advertising:** accepted. **Conventions/Meetings:** periodic meeting, for social purposes.

24276 ■ Friends of Julio International (FOJI)
28 Farmington Ave.
Longmeadow, MA 01106-1433
Fax: (413)567-9530
E-mail: foji@attbi.com
URL: http://www.FOJIfanclubforJULIO.homestead.com/FOJIfanclub.html
Founded: 1986. **Members:** 95. **Membership Dues:** regular, in U.S., $20 (annual) ● regular, in Canada, $22 (annual) ● in Europe, $25 (annual) ● in Asia, $30 (annual). **Description:** Fans of singer and performer Julio Iglesias (1943-). Seeks to keep members informed of Iglesias' appearances, concert reports, other news on Iglesias. Encourages participation in other organizations. Contributes to the American Paralysis Association and the United Nations Children's Fund. **Libraries:** Type: reference. Holdings: books, clippings. **Subjects:** relating to the life and career of Julio Iglesias. **Affiliated With:** U.S. Fund for UNICEF. **Formerly:** (1987) Friends of Julio. **Publications:** *Friends of Julio International Newsletter*, quarterly. Contains tour dates, concert reports, and Julio's current activities. **Price:** included in membership dues. **Circulation:** 100. **Advertising:** accepted ● Also sends updates via postcards and flyers to members. **Conventions/Meetings:** periodic meeting (exhibits).

24277 ■ Friends of Paul Overstreet
PO Box 320
Pegram, TN 37143
Ph: (615)952-3999
Free: (800)931-PAUL
Fax: (615)952-3151
URL: http://www.pauloverstreet.com
Multinational. Description: Serves as a fan club dedicated to Paul Overstreet.

24278 ■ Gary Morris Fan Club (GMFC)
c/o Gary Morris Productions
PO Box 187
Chromo, CO 81128
Ph: (970)264-6791
Fax: (270)447-2488
E-mail: diane@garymorris.com
URL: http://garymorris.com
Contact: Betty Urbanek, Pres.
Founded: 1981. **Members:** 450. **Membership Dues:** regular, in U.S., $15 (annual) ● regular, outside U.S., $20 (annual). **Staff:** 1. **Description:** Represents fans of country singer Gary Morris (1948-), whose best known recordings include Wind Beneath My Wings, I'll Never Stop Loving You, and Baby Bye Bye. Morris has also starred in the Broadway production of Les Miserables and appeared in an off-Broadway production of La Boheme and the television series The Colbys. **Telecommunication Services:** electronic mail, garymorris@garymorris.com. **Publications:** *Gary Morris Song Book* ● Newsletter, bimonthly. **Price:** included in membership dues.

24279 ■ Gene Pitney International Fan Club (GPIFC)
6201 - 39th Ave.
Kenosha, WI 53142
E-mail: pitneyfan@aol.com
URL: http://www.Gene-Pitney.com
Contact: David P. McGrath, Exec. Off.
Founded: 1961. **Members:** 1,000. **Membership Dues:** regular, in U.S., $25 (annual) ● in United Kingdom, 25 (annual) ● regular, in Canada, $40 (annual). **Description:** Fans of pop singer Gene Pitney (1941-), famous for the song Only Love Can Break a Heart. Works to promote Pitney's record releases and tours. **Computer Services:** Online services. **Formerly:** (1987) Gene Pitney Fan Club. **Publications:** Newsletter, semiannual. **Circulation:** 1,000. **Advertising:** accepted. **Conventions/Meetings:** annual meeting - always in United Kingdom.

24280 ■ Gene Summers International Fan Club (GSIFC)
222 Tulane St.
Garland, TX 75043-2239
E-mail: genesummers@altavista.com
URL: http://www.rockabillyhall.com/GeneSummers.html
Contact: Steve Len, Pres.
Founded: 1957. **Members:** 1,500. **Staff:** 3. **Languages:** English, French, German. **Description:** Fans of rockabilly artist Gene Summers and of 1950s rockabilly and rock 'n' roll. Promotes Summers and his music; keeps members informed of Summers' activities and recordings. Maintains speakers' bureau, biographical archives, and photographical archives of Summers and other 1950s rock artists. Summers was enshrined in the Rockabilly Hall of Fame in 1997. **Libraries:** Type: reference. Holdings: archival material. **Subjects:** rockabilly music, 1950's rock and roll, 1950's rhythm and blues music. **Publications:** *Geneagers Club Bulletin*, semiannual. **Conventions/Meetings:** semiannual meeting.

24281 ■ Genesis Information (GI)
c/o Brad Lentz
PO Box 12311
Overland Park, KS 66282
Fax: (913)345-2940
Contact: Brad Lentz, Exec. Officer
Description: Fans of the rock music group Genesis. **Telecommunication Services:** hotline, (913)345-2002.

24282 ■ George Strait Fan Club (GSFC)
PO Box 2119
Hendersonville, TN 37077
Ph: (615)824-7176
Fax: (615)826-7052
E-mail: customerservice@georgestraitfans.com
URL: http://www.georgestraitfans.com
Contact: Anita O'Brian, Pres.
Founded: 1983. **Members:** 20,000. **Membership Dues:** by email, $15 (annual) ● by mail, foreign by email, $20 (annual) ● foreign by mail, $25 (annual). **Staff:** 5. **Description:** Represents fans of country-western musician and vocalist George Strait (1952-), who was named male vocalist of the year in 1985, 1986, 1989, 1990, 1996 and 1997 by both the

Academy of Country Music and the Country Music Association (see separate entries); and who received the Entertainer of the Year Award numerous times. **Publications:** *Strait Talk*, monthly. Newsletter. Includes calendar of events, concert reviews, photographs, and correspondence. **Price:** $15.00/year. **Conventions/Meetings:** annual conference.

24283 ■ **Glenn Miller Birthplace Society (GMBS)**
107 E Main St.
PO Box 61
Clarinda, IA 51632
Ph: (712)542-2461
Fax: (712)542-2461
E-mail: gmbs@heartland.net
URL: http://www.glennmiller.org
Contact: Marvin Negley, Pres.
Founded: 1976. **Members:** 1,500. **Membership Dues:** regular in U.S., $25 (annual) ● regular outside U.S., $30 (annual). **Staff:** 1. **Description:** Persons interested in the music of bandleader Glenn Miller (1904-44), or the big band music of the 1930s-40s. Encourages commemorative activities to honor Miller, who was assumed killed when his plane was reported missing during WWII while enroute from England to Paris, France to perform for the Allied troops. Maintains archives. Offers a scholarship program for high school seniors and first year college students interested in music. **Awards:** Glenn Miller Scholarship. **Frequency:** annual. **Type:** scholarship. **Recipient:** for promising young talent in any field of applied music ● **Type:** scholarship. **Recipient:** for high school graduates or college freshmen. **Computer Services:** Mailing lists. **Publications:** *Glenn Miller Calendar*, annual. **Price:** $10.00 for members, plus shipping and handling; $12.00 for nonmembers, plus shipping and handling ● *Miller Notes*. Newsletter. Provides information on former band members, books, recordings, scholarship activities, and society festival schedules and activities. **Circulation:** 1,600. **Advertising:** accepted. **Conventions/Meetings:** annual Glenn Miller Festival - festival and conference, with concerts, history presentations, dances (exhibits) - always 2nd weekend in June, Clarinda, IA.

24284 ■ **Gram Parsons Foundation (GPF)**
c/o Gram's Place
3109 N Ola Ave.
Tampa, FL 33603
Ph: (813)221-0596
Fax: (813)221-0596
E-mail: gramspl@aol.com
URL: http://www.grams-inn-tampa.com/history.htm
Contact: Mark Holland, Founder/Dir.
Founded: 1980. **Staff:** 1. **Regional Groups:** 9. **State Groups:** 4. **Description:** Fans of country/rock singer/ songwriter Gram Parsons (1946-73), who was a member of the Byrds and the Flying Burrito Brothers before performing as a solo act. Seeks to preserve and promote Parsons' music. Maintains hall of fame and museum. Offers placement service; compiles statistics; educational programs. Operates Gram's Place, a bed and breakfast guesthouse and artist retreat. **Libraries: Type:** reference; lending; open to the public. **Holdings:** archival material, artwork, audiovisuals, books, clippings, periodicals. **Subjects:** Gram Parsons, music. **Computer Services:** Mailing lists. **Additional Websites:** http://www.gramparsons.com. **Formerly:** (1993) Gram Parsons Memorial Foundation. **Conventions/Meetings:** periodic meeting.

24285 ■ **Hank Williams International Fan Club**
c/o Mary H. Wallace, Public Relations Chair
PO Box 280
Georgiana, AL 36033
Ph: (334)376-9821 (334)376-0038
E-mail: hanksr@greenlynk.com
Contact: Mary H. Wallace, Public Relations Chair
Founded: 1992. **Members:** 1,000. **Membership Dues:** in U.S., $12 (annual) ● outside U.S., $18 (annual). **Staff:** 3. **Description:** Admirers of country singer Hank Williams. Promotes study of and interest in Williams's life and career. Serves as a clearing-

house on Williams and associated memorabilia; keeps members abreast of the activities of Hank Williams. Facilitates communication among members. **Computer Services:** Mailing lists. **Formerly:** (2002) Hank Williams, Sr. International Fan Club. **Publications:** *Hank Williams International Society and Fan Club Newsletter*, 3/year. Contains articles and facts regarding Hank Williams. **Price:** included in membership dues. **Circulation:** 1,000. **Advertising:** accepted. **Conventions/Meetings:** annual Celebration - party, country music festival - always first weekend of June ● annual Salute - meeting - always first weekend in June ● annual show - always mid-June.

24286 ■ **Hank Williams Jr. Fan Club (HWJFC)**
PO Box 1849
Madison, TN 37115
Ph: (615)865-8671
URL: http://www.hankjr.com
Founded: 1964. **Membership Dues:** regular, in U.S., $20 (annual) ● regular, outside U.S., $25 (annual). **Description:** Represents the fans of country singer Hank Williams, Jr. **Publications:** *Bocephus News*, annual. Newsletter. Includes pictures and news of Williams' career. **Price:** included in membership dues. **Circulation:** 46,000. Also Cited As: *Fan Club Newsletter*.

24287 ■ **Harry Connick, Jr. Fan Club (HCJFC)**
323 Broadway
Cambridge, MA 02139
Ph: (617)868-5858 (424)288-2000
Fax: (617)354-2396
E-mail: info@harryconnickjr.com
URL: http://www.harryconnickjr.com
Founded: 1990. **Membership Dues:** general, $15 (annual). **Multinational. Description:** Represents individuals interested in the work of actor, singer, composer, producer, and instrumentalist Harry Connick, Jr.

24288 ■ **Hearts in Harmony - World Family of John Denver (HIH-WFJD)**
c/o Dottie Honer, Exec. Officer
5214 Stump Rd.
Pipersville, PA 18947-1014
Ph: (215)766-7363
E-mail: kurthhoner@msn.com
URL: http://www.john-denver.org
Contact: Dottie Honer, Exec. Officer
Founded: 1992. **Members:** 840. **Membership Dues:** in U.S., $25 (annual) ● in Canada, $29 (annual) ● outside U.S. and Canada, $33 (annual). **Staff:** 2. **Regional Groups:** 1. **Languages:** Dutch, English, French, German, Italian, Norwegian, Portuguese, Russian, Spanish. **Description:** Fans of singer and songwriter John Denver (1943-1997). Disseminates information about Denver. Sponsors charitable programs and children's services. **Libraries: Type:** open to the public. **Holdings:** 2. **Subjects:** discography, biography. **Formed by Merger of:** (1992) John Denver Heart to Heart Fan Club; Partners in Harmony, World Family of John Denver. **Publications:** Newsletter, quarterly. **Price:** $24.00/year, in U.S.; $28.00/year, in Canada; $32.00/year, overseas. **Circulation:** 840. **Advertising:** accepted ● Also publishes discography, calendars, biography, memorabilia lists, and photos; makes available records. **Conventions/Meetings:** annual John Denver International Fan Convention, photos, back issues, merchandise and memorabilia (exhibits).

24289 ■ **Helen Forrest Fan Club (HFFC)**
Address Unknown since 2007
Founded: 1976. **Members:** 370. **Description:** Fans of jazz singer Helen Forrest. Promotes Forrest's career and disseminates information about her recordings. **Convention/Meeting:** none. **Libraries: Type:** not open to the public. **Holdings:** audio recordings. **Subjects:** Helen Forrest. **Publications:** Newsletter, annual.

24290 ■ **Hillbilly Hits Fan Club**
c/o Mr. Tracy Pitcox
1701 S Bridge St.
Brady, TX 76825

Ph: (325)597-1895
Fax: (325)597-0515
E-mail: tracy@hillbillyhits.com
URL: http://www.hillbillyhits.com
Contact: Mr. Tracy Pitcox, Contact
Founded: 1989. **Members:** 700. **Membership Dues:** individual, $7 (annual) ● couple, $10 (annual). **Staff:** 11. **Description:** Division of the Heart of Texas Country Music Association. Dedicated to promoting traditional country music and its artists, including Kitty Wells, Jack Greene, Johnny Bush, Justin Tubb, Leona Williams, Johnny Duncan, Tony Douglas, and Johnny Wright. Sponsors a weekly radio show that promotes country music. Sponsors charitable and research programs. Maintains museum and hall of fame. **Libraries: Type:** open to the public. **Holdings:** archival material, articles, books, clippings, periodicals. **Subjects:** country music. **Awards:** B.R. Turner Humanitarian Award. **Frequency:** annual. **Type:** recognition. **Computer Services:** Mailing lists, of members. **Publications:** *Hillbilly Hits Fan Club Newsletter*, monthly ● *Hillbilly Hits Newsletter*, monthly. Brochure. Promotes upcoming events; recounts past activities. **Price:** included in membership dues. **Circulation:** 500. **Advertising:** accepted. **Conventions/Meetings:** annual convention and board meeting, gathering of members and guests with emphasis on traditional country music (exhibits) - every third Saturday of March ● annual party.

24291 ■ **International Al Jolson Society (IAJS)**
c/o Tom Nestor, Treas.
1709 Billingshurst Ct.
Orlando, FL 32825
E-mail: jolsonvp@optonline.net
URL: http://www.jolson.org
Contact: Mr. Jan Hernstat, Pres.
Founded: 1950. **Members:** 1,100. **Membership Dues:** individual, $20 (annual). **Staff:** 20. **Budget:** $12,000. **Regional Groups:** 5. **Description:** Admirers of Al Jolson (1886-1950), American Broadway entertainer and actor. Perpetuates the memory and entertainment of "the World's Greatest Entertainer." Promotes annual Jolson Day (May 26). Coordinates charity projects. Maintains audio and video tape department, including material from rare records, radio broadcasts, historic film footage and unused sound track recordings. Society is distinct from another group of the same name. **Libraries: Type:** open to the public. **Holdings:** 90; periodicals. **Subjects:** Al Jolson. **Awards:** Irvin Warwick Memorial Award. **Type:** recognition. **Recipient:** for exceptional service to society. **Computer Services:** Mailing lists. **Telecommunication Services:** electronic mail, jolsonfan@aol.com. **Affiliated With:** Association for Recorded Sound Collections. **Publications:** *Jolson Journal*, semiannual. Contains articles, stories, pictures, and news of other fans, their activities, and Jolson memorabilia for sale. **Price:** included in membership dues. **Circulation:** 1,150. **Advertising:** accepted ● *Jolson Journalette*, quarterly. Newsletter. Lists materials for sale and events of the IAJS. **Price:** included in membership dues. **Circulation:** 1,100 ● *Special Bulletin*, periodic. **Conventions/Meetings:** annual Al Jolson Festival, with Jolson memorabilia (exhibits) - always May.

24292 ■ **International Fan Club Organization (IFCO)**
PO Box 40328
Nashville, TN 37204-0328
Ph: (615)371-9596
Fax: (615)371-9597
E-mail: 4info@ifco.org
URL: http://www.ifco.org
Contact: Kay Johnson, Pres.
Founded: 1967. **Members:** 400. **Membership Dues:** regular, in U.S., $33 (annual) ● regular, outside U.S., $45 (annual) ● individual, $25 (annual). **Staff:** 3. **Budget:** $110,000. **For-Profit. Description:** Represents presidents of fan clubs and radio air personalities around the world. Seeks to advance country music and aids in the establishment of country music fan clubs. Promotes the history of country music while developing new sounds and artists. Sponsors semian-

nual fan artist tour and country music showcase. Maintains speakers' bureau; conducts research; compiles statistics. **Awards:** Tex Ritter Award. **Frequency:** annual. **Type:** recognition. **Recipient:** to a country music personality or business leader. **Computer Services:** Mailing lists, labels. **Telecommunication Services:** information service, (900)454-9100. **Publications:** *Club House*, quarterly. Bulletin. Provides news updates. **Price:** $25.00/year in U.S. and Canada; $30.00/year outside U.S. and Canada. **Circulation:** 1,500 ● Journal, quarterly ● Also publishes periodic news bulletins. **Conventions/Meetings:** annual show (exhibits).

24293 ■ International Sinatra Society (ISS)
Address Unknown since 2007
Founded: 1974. **Members:** 3,000. **Membership Dues:** $25 (quarterly). **Regional Groups:** 4. **Description:** Promotes and discusses the career of singer and recording artist Frank Sinatra (1915-98). Monitors and reports on the activities of Sinatra's career. **Libraries: Type:** open to the public. **Holdings:** 129. **Publications:** *International Sinatra Society—Newsletter*, bimonthly. Includes calendar of events, record reviews, and reprints of concert reviews from various newspapers and periodicals. **Price:** included in membership dues. **Advertising:** not accepted ● *Sinatra Journal*, annual. **Conventions/Meetings:** periodic convention.

24294 ■ International Traditional Country Music Fan Club (ITCMFC)
PO Box 161
Watauga, TN 37694
Ph: (423)542-5543
E-mail: itcmfc@preferred.com
URL: http://www.itcmfc.com
Contact: Beecher O'Quinn Jr., Pres.
Founded: 1996. **Membership Dues:** regular in U.S., $10 (annual) ● regular outside U.S., $12 (annual). **Multinational. Description:** Aims to preserve and promote traditional country, bluegrass, and gospel music. Strives to keep the traditional country music alive and well. Promotes the music performed by country music legends and emerging artists. **Telecommunication Services:** electronic mail, itcmfc@charter.net. **Publications:** Newsletter, 3/year. **Price:** included in membership dues.

24295 ■ International Willie Nelson Fan Club
PO Box 7104
Lancaster, PA 17604-7104
E-mail: klausdog@hotmail.com
URL: http://www.geocities.com/SouthBeach/Shores/5498/wnindex.html
Contact: Christine DaMore, Pres.
Membership Dues: standard in U.S., $20 (annual) ● standard outside U.S., $23 (annual) ● renewal in U.S., $15 (annual) ● renewal outside U.S., $18 (annual). **Multinational. Description:** Fans of country music singer and songwriter Willie Nelson (1933-), popular for such songs as On the Road Again and Georgia on My Mind. Nelson has also appeared in films including The Electric Horseman and Honeysuckle Rose. Makes available Nelson memorabilia. **Publications:** *Willie's World*, quarterly. Newsletter. Includes itinerary. **Price:** included in membership dues.

24296 ■ Jana Jae Fan Club (JJFC)
PO Box 35726
Tulsa, OK 74153
Ph: (918)786-8896
Free: (800)526-2523
URL: http://www.janajae.com
Contact: Evelyn Deal, Pres.
Founded: 1977. **Members:** 200. **Membership Dues:** individual, $10 (annual). **Staff:** 6. **Description:** Fans and admirers of Jana Jae, violinist, singer and fiddle player of symphonic and country-western music. Provides members with information on Jae's events and activities. Offers educational programs and a speaker's bureau. **Publications:** Newsletter, quarterly.

24297 ■ Jeff Carson International Fan Club
PO Box 1332
Franklin, TN 37065
Ph: (615)321-5080
E-mail: lcavanaugh@curb.com
URL: http://www.jeffcarson.net
Contact: Liz Cavanaugh, Contact
Founded: 1994. **Members:** 800. **Membership Dues:** ordinary, $10 (annual). **Staff:** 2. **Description:** Admirers of the life and career of recording artist Jeff Carson. Promotes appreciation of Carson's music. Keeps members abreast of Carson's activities and performance itinerary. **Computer Services:** Mailing lists, of members. **Publications:** Newsletter, periodic.

24298 ■ Jerry Jeff Walker Fan Club (JJWFC)
c/o Tried and True Music
PO Box 39
Austin, TX 78767
Ph: (512)477-0036
Fax: (512)477-0095
E-mail: walter@jerryjeff.com
URL: http://www.jerryjeff.com
Contact: Laura Lewis, Contact
Founded: 1986. **Members:** 40,000. **Staff:** 3. **Description:** Fans of songwriter and performer Jerry Jeff Walker (1942-), best known for composing and recording Mr. Bojangles (1968). Promotes the work and music of Walker; informs members of upcoming activities and events. Sells Walker's albums and souvenirs. **Also Known As:** The Tried and True Warriors. **Publications:** *Jerry Jeff Walker Newsletter*, 3/year. **Price:** free. **Circulation:** 40,000. Alternate Formats: online. **Conventions/Meetings:** annual Jerry Jeff Walker Birthday Weekend - meeting, includes concerts and events for fans of Jerry Jeff Walker - always March in Austin, TX.

24299 ■ Jimi Hendrix Information Management Institute (JIMI)
3369 Morgan St.
West Lafayette, IN 47906
Ph: (765)464-3175 (765)283-7685
Fax: (765)463-1487
E-mail: kvoss1@verizon.net
Contact: Kenneth L. Voss, Curator
Founded: 1984. **Members:** 1,400. **Membership Dues:** individual, $15 (annual) ● international, $20 (annual). **Staff:** 1. **Budget:** $90,000. **For-Profit. Description:** Fans of rock music guitarist Jimi Hendrix (1942-70), winner of five gold albums (symbolizing sales of $1 million) and considered one of the most influential guitarists in rock history. Disseminates information on Hendrix; serves as a clearinghouse for collectors and fans. Provides articles and memorabilia to members. Operates museum and speakers' bureau. Conducts research programs. **Libraries: Type:** reference. **Holdings:** 65; archival material, articles, audio recordings, books, photographs, video recordings. **Subjects:** Jimi Hendrix. **Computer Services:** database, lists of albums, affiliates, films, fans, and foundations. **Also Known As:** (2000) VooDoo Child. **Publications:** *Voodoo Child*, quarterly. Newsletter. Provides reviews and listings of items for sale. **Price:** included in membership dues. **Circulation:** 1,400. **Advertising:** accepted. **Conventions/Meetings:** annual convention (exhibits) - always November 27 (Hendrix's Birthday).

24300 ■ Jimmy Kish "The Flying Cowboy" Fan Club (JKFCFC)
PO Box 140316
Nashville, TN 37214
Ph: (615)889-6675
E-mail: kishranch@comcast.net
Contact: Ruth Kish, Pres.
Founded: 1981. **Members:** 2,500. **Description:** Represents fans of Jimmy Kish "The Flying Cowboy" (1925-), Western country disc jockey, entertainer, singer, guitarist, song writer, square dance caller, and airplane pilot since 1953. Promotes Kish and his music; maintains Pegasus Records in Nashville, TN.

24301 ■ Joe Diffie Fan Club (JDFC)
PO Box 479
Velma, OK 73491-0479
Ph: (580)444-2315
E-mail: diffie@texhoma.net
URL: http://www.joediffie.com
Contact: Flora Diffie, Pres.
Founded: 1990. **Members:** 5,000. **Membership Dues:** regular, in U.S. and Canada, $15 (annual) ● other country, $20 (annual). **Staff:** 2. **Description:** Fans of the country singer Joe Diffie. Seeks to keep fans informed on the singer's activities. **Awards: Frequency:** annual. **Type:** scholarship. **Recipient:** for two high school students who go to Joe Diffie's Alma Mater. **Publications:** *The Diffie Defender*, quarterly. Newsletter. **Conventions/Meetings:** annual party (exhibits).

24302 ■ John Berry's Fan Club
c/o Sandie Rogers
47 Autumn View Dr.
Windham, ME 04062
Ph: (207)892-2067
Free: (877)438-5646
Fax: (207)892-2067
E-mail: johnberryfanclub@verizon.net
URL: http://www.johnberry.net
Contact: Mr. Terry Oliver, Mgr.
Membership Dues: regular, in U.S., $15 (annual) ● regular, outside U.S., $20 (annual). **Multinational. Description:** Fan club dedicated to John Berry. **Computer Services:** Mailing lists. **Additional Websites:** http://www.johnberry.com. **Publications:** Newsletter, 3/year. **Price:** included in membership dues.

24303 ■ John Gary International Fan Club
7 Briarwood Cir.
Richardson, TX 75080
Fax: (214)231-5761
E-mail: jasongary@attbi.com
URL: http://www.johngary.com
Contact: Jason Gary, Contact
Founded: 1963. **Members:** 600. **Membership Dues:** regular, $25 (annual). **Staff:** 4. **State Groups:** 45. **National Groups:** 3. **Multinational. Description:** Individuals interested in the life and career of singer John Gary, performer of romantic tunes and traditional Irish folk ballads and finalist in the U.S. Olympic archery trials. Seeks to promote Gary's career. **Libraries: Type:** open to the public. **Holdings:** 1; articles, books. **Subjects:** ecology, philosophy, song lyrics, poetry. **Telecommunication Services:** electronic mail, leegary@webtv.net. **Boards:** Community Concerts; MESA; Richardson Symphony. **Affiliated With:** American Cancer Society. **Formerly:** (1998) John Gray International Fan Club; (2004) John Gary Memorial Fan Club. **Publications:** *Gallery Gazette*, quarterly. Newsletter. Contains news of remastered albums on LDs, photos, and members' activities. **Price:** included in membership dues.

24304 ■ John Mellencamp Official International Fan Club
PO Box 6777
Bloomington, IN 47407-6777
E-mail: feedback@mellencamp.com
Contact: Joyce Logan, Pres.
Membership Dues: in U.S. and Canada, $25 (annual) ● outside North America, $30 (annual). **Description:** Fans of the singer John Mellencamp. **Publications:** *Minutes to Memories*. Newsletter. **Price:** included in membership dues.

24305 ■ Johnny Len Fan Club (JLFC)
PO Box 1714
Manitowoc, WI 54221-1714
Ph: (920)682-4414
Contact: Karen R. Brouchoud, Pres./Sec.
Founded: 1969. **Members:** 60. **Membership Dues:** individual, $9 (annual). **Description:** Fans of country music vocalist and rhythm guitarist Johnny Len (1943-). Purpose is to promote the music and career of Len. **Publications:** Journal, quinquennial ● Newsletter, monthly. **Conventions/Meetings:** annual meeting - always first Sunday in August, Manitowoc, WI.

24306 ■ Johnny Mathis East Coast Fan Club (JMECFC)
Address Unknown since 2007
Founded: 1957. **Membership Dues:** $20 (annual). **Staff:** 3. **Description:** Admirers of singer Johnny Mathis. Promotes appreciation of Mathis and his music. Serves as a clearinghouse on Mathis' career and performance and appearance schedules; facilitates communication among members. **Libraries: Type:** by appointment only. **Holdings:** clippings. **Subjects:** Johnny Mathis, music. **Publications:** *Johnny Mathis Year End Booklet*, annual. Contains reviews, photos and activities of previous year. **Price:** for members only. **Advertising:** not accepted ● Newsletter, quarterly. **Conventions/Meetings:** biennial convention.

24307 ■ Kate Smith Commemorative Society
PO Box 3575
Cranston, RI 02910
Ph: (401)461-7457 (207)793-2547
E-mail: ssann@juno.com
URL: http://www.katesmith.org
Contact: Mr. Louis Sann, Contact
Founded: 1967. **Members:** 250. **Membership Dues:** individual, $15 (annual). **Staff:** 4. **Budget:** $3,000. **Multinational. Description:** Fans of American singer Kate Smith (1907-86), famous for her rendition of God Bless America, which became her trademark. Promotes interest in the musical career of Kate Smith. **Libraries: Type:** reference. **Holdings:** archival material, photographs. **Subjects:** letters sheet music, advertising material, records, broadcasts. **Awards: Type:** recognition. **Formerly:** (1977) Friends of Kate Smith; (1989) Kate Smith/God Bless America Foundation. **Publications:** *The Times of Kate Smith*, semiannual. Journal. **Price:** $15.00. **Circulation:** 250 ● *The Times of Kate Smith Newsletter*, semiannual. Contains membership activities and listings of Smith's music. **Circulation:** 250. **Conventions/Meetings:** annual Kate Smith Festival, features Kate Smith memorabilia (exhibits) - always spring.

24308 ■ Kathy Mattea Fan Club
PO Box 1776
Orem, UT 84059-1776
Ph: (801)229-7048 (801)785-7019
Fax: (801)229-7130
E-mail: matteahead@aol.com
URL: http://www.mattea.com/MatteaFanClubHome.html
Contact: Sue Phelps, Pres.
Membership Dues: in U.S. and Canada, Mexico, $15 (annual) ● foreign, $20 (annual). **Multinational. Description:** Fan club dedicated to Kathy Mattea. Membership includes autographed 8x10 black and white photo, fact sheet, itinerary, official fan club pin, biography, merchandise order form, two backstage passes per calendar year. **Computer Services:** Mailing lists, Kathy's-Clowns on Yahoo Groups. **Publications:** *Street Talk*, 3/year. Newsletter. **Price:** included in membership dues. **Conventions/Meetings:** annual festival, for members.

24309 ■ Kenny Chesney Fan Club (KCOFC)
PO Box 1911
Charlottesville, VA 22903
E-mail: kennychesneyfanclub@musictoday.com
URL: http://www.kennychesney.com
Founded: 2003. **Membership Dues:** regular, $25 (annual). **Multinational. Description:** Fan club dedicated to Kenny Chesney. Membership includes card, 8x10 photo, tour schedules, fact sheet, welcome letter, merchandise offerings. **Additional Websites:** http://www.kennychesneyfanclub.com. **Publications:** Newsletter. **Price:** included in membership dues.

24310 ■ Kingston Korner (KK)
705 S Washington St.
Naperville, IL 60540-3535
Ph: (630)305-0770
Free: (800)232-7328
Fax: (630)305-0782

E-mail: amy@rediscovermusic.com
URL: http://www.rediscovermusic.com
Contact: Allan Shaw, Pres.
Founded: 1978. **Members:** 1,200. **For-Profit. Description:** Fans of popular folk music, particularly that of the Kingston Trio, a group whose original members included Donald D. Guard (1934-1991), Nicholas W. Reynolds (1933-), and Robert C. Shane (1934-). The Kingston Trio, best known for their recording of the folk song Tom Dooley, later broadened their repertoire from traditional American and English folk songs to include contemporary protest songs. Seeks to promote popular folk music. Keeps members informed of concert itineraries and recordings of the Kingston Trio and other folk groups. **Libraries: Type:** reference. **Holdings:** 2; archival material, books. **Subjects:** popular folk music. **Telecommunication Services:** electronic mail, allan@folkera.com. **Publications:** *I Come For To Sing*. Book. **Price:** $25.00 ● *Kingston Trio on Record*, annual. Book. **Price:** $17.95 ● *Rediscover Music Catalogue*, annual.

24311 ■ KISS Rocks Fan Club (KRFC)
c/o Jon Rubin, Pres./Founder
2 Tudor City Pl.
New York, NY 10017
E-mail: jon@kissrocks.net
URL: http://www.kissrocks.net
Contact: Jon Rubin, Pres./Founder
Founded: 1984. **Members:** 50. **For-Profit. Multinational. Description:** Fans of the rock music group KISS, whose original members included Ace Frehley (1951-), Paul Stanley (1952-), Gene Simmons (1949-), and Peter Criss (1947-). Disseminates information about the music and activities of KISS via sale and trade of band memorabilia and merchandise. Sponsors merchandise locating service and fan merchandise website on the Internet, specializing in rare and original KISS memorabilia. **Computer Services:** Mailing lists. **Publications:** *KISS Rocks Merchandise Catalog*. Features rare KISS memorabilia and merchandise for sale and trade, available on the Internet. **Price:** free. Also Cited As: *KISS Rocks*.

24312 ■ Kitty Wells-Johnny Wright-Bobby Wright International Fan Club (WWWFC)
PO Box 1189
Madison, TN 37116
Ph: (615)865-1900 (615)865-6543
Fax: (615)865-1900
E-mail: kitty@kittywells.com
URL: http://www.kittywells.com
Contact: Doris J. Trott, Pres.
Founded: 1981. **Members:** 3,500. **Membership Dues:** in U.S., $10 (annual) ● outside U.S., $15 (annual). **Description:** Fans of country music vocalist and guitarist Kitty Wells (1919-), vocalist and guitarist Johnny Wright (1914-), and their son, vocalist and musician Bobby Wright (1942-). Purpose is to promote the careers of these performers and to disseminate information about their music and activities to members. Operates the KW-JW Family Country Junction museum in Madison, TN. **Libraries: Type:** reference. **Holdings:** archival material. **Formerly:** (1985) Kitty Wells Appreciation Society. **Supersedes:** Kitty Wells/Johnny Wright Fan Club. **Publications:** *The Honky Tonk Angels*. Book. **Price:** $12.95. ISSN: 0963-2684 ● *WWWFC Newsletter*, quarterly. Provides career and touring information. **Price:** included in membership dues. **Conventions/Meetings:** annual meeting, held in conjunction with International Country Music Fan Fair - always June, Nashville, TN.

24313 ■ Lennon Sisters Fan Club (LSFC)
Address Unknown since 2006
Founded: 1979. **Members:** 340. **Membership Dues:** individual, $15 (annual). **Description:** Fans of the vocal group the Lennon Sisters, which includes Dianne (1939-), Peggy (1941-), Kathy (1943-), Janet (1946-) Lennon, and Mimi Lennon (1955-). Promotes and supports the Lennons' musical careers. **Publications:** *Lennonews*, 2-3/year. Newsletter. **Advertising:** not accepted. **Conventions/Meetings:** periodic meeting.

24314 ■ Lesley Gore Fan Club (LGFC)
PO Box 1548
Ocean Pines, MD 21811
Ph: (410)208-6369
Fax: (410)208-6967
URL: http://www.patswayne.com/lesley/lesfan.htm
Contact: Jack Natoli, Pres.
Founded: 1965. **Members:** 500. **Membership Dues:** in U.S., $9 (annual) ● Canadian citizen, $15 (annual) ● outside U.S. and Canada, $15 (annual). **Description:** Admirers of entertainer Lesley Gore (1946-), best known for the song It's My Party. **Convention/Meeting:** none. **Libraries: Type:** reference. **Holdings:** archival material. **Subjects:** Lesley Gore. **Publications:** *Along the Way With Lesley Gore*, quarterly. Newsletter ● Also publishes membership packet including biographical information and record list.

24315 ■ Linda Davis Fan Club
c/o Linda Davis Inc.
PO Box 767
Hermitage, TN 37076
E-mail: info@lindadavis.com
URL: http://www.lindadavis.com
Description: Serves as fan club devoted to country music singer Linda Davis.

24316 ■ Lorrie Morgan International Fan Club
PO Box 121739
Nashville, TN 37212
Ph: (615)332-8947
E-mail: fanclub@lorrie.com
URL: http://www.lorrie.com
Contact: Kelly Sanson, Pres.
Membership Dues: regular, in U.S., $15 (annual) ● regular, outside U.S., $20 (annual). **Multinational. Description:** Fan club devoted to Lorrie Morgan. Distributes to members an 8x10 autographed picture, membership card entitling member to 3 backstage visits per year, current touring schedule, current biography, birthday and Christmas cards from Lorrie. **Publications:** *The Lorrie Story*, quarterly. Newsletter.

24317 ■ Lou Christie International Fan Club (LCIFC)
c/o Harry Young, Pres.
PO Box 260172
St. Louis, MO 63126
E-mail: sentaur@hotmail.com
URL: http://members.aol.com/DennisKQV/christie.htm
Contact: Harry Young, Pres.
Founded: 1977. **Members:** 632. **Membership Dues:** $11 (annual). **Staff:** 5. **Description:** Fans of rock 'n' roll vocalist and composer Lou Christie (1943-), who wrote and performed the 1966 pop hit Lightning Strikes. Studies Christie's career. Plans to establish a museum and hall of fame. **Libraries: Type:** reference. **Holdings:** archival material. **Additional Websites:** http://www.geocities.com/SunsetStrip/Palladium/9229/lounews.htm. **Publications:** *Lightning Strikes: The Lou Christie Newsletter*, semiannual. Contains reprints of press items from 1962 to the present, and original articles. Includes discographical updates and performance and record reviews. **Price:** included in membership dues. ISSN: 1068-8404. **Circulation:** 620. **Advertising:** accepted ● Also publishes offprints and special interest publications. **Conventions/Meetings:** annual meeting (exhibits) - always February 19.

24318 ■ Lucio Fan Club (LFC)
PO Box 148492
Nashville, TN 37214
E-mail: brebiz@yahoo.com
URL: http://luciofanpage.50megs.com/luciofanpage-main.index.html
Contact: Sue Fetcho, Pres.
Founded: 1988. **Members:** 100. **Membership Dues:** individual, $10 (annual). **Description:** Admirers of performing artist Lucio. Promotes interest in Lucio's career and activities. Serves as a clearinghouse on Lucio. **Publications:** *The Official Lucio Fan Club*, 3/year. Newsletter. **Advertising:** accepted. **Conventions/Meetings:** annual Fan Club Party - always June.

24319 ■ Mariah Carey Official International Fan Club
c/o The Fan Emporium
PO Box 679
Branford, CT 06405
E-mail: fnemporium@aol.com
Membership Dues: in U.S. and Canada, $22 (annual) ● outside North America, $28 (annual). **Multinational. Description:** Fans of the singer Mariah Carey. **Convention/Meeting:** none. **Publications:** Newsletter. **Price:** included in membership dues.

24320 ■ Martina McBride Fan Club (MMFC)
PO Box 291627
Nashville, TN 37229-1627
Fax: (615)754-5584
E-mail: fanrelations@martina-mcbride.com
URL: http://www.martina-mcbride.com
Contact: Tracy Weaver, Dir. Fan Relations
Founded: 1992. **Members:** 4,500. **Membership Dues:** regular, in U.S., $15 (annual) ● regular, outside U.S., $20 (annual). **Staff:** 2. **Description:** Admirers of the life and work of country singer Martina McBride. Promotes appreciation of McBride's career. Serves as a clearinghouse on McBride's itinerary; facilitates communication among members. **Computer Services:** Mailing lists. **Telecommunication Services:** electronic bulletin board. **Publications:** Solid Ground, 3/year. Newsletter. **Price:** included in membership dues. **Circulation:** 4,500. Alternate Formats: online. **Conventions/Meetings:** annual meeting, fan fair booth exhibit and photo-op (exhibits) - always June in Nashville, TN.

24321 ■ Marty Stuart Fan Club
c/o Jim Hill
PO Box 129
Hendersonville, TN 37075-0129
E-mail: martystuartfc@msn.com
URL: http://www.martystuart.net
Contact: Marty Stuart, Contact
Founded: 1988. **Members:** 3,000. **Membership Dues:** regular, $15 (annual). **Staff:** 1. **Description:** Fans of country music singer Marty Stuart. **Publications:** Marty Party News, quarterly. Newsletter. **Price:** included in membership dues.

24322 ■ Mel Tillis Fan Club
c/o Mel Tellis Enterprise
PO Box 305
Silver Springs, FL 34489
E-mail: fanclub@meltillis.com
URL: http://www.meltillis.com/fanclub/default.htm
Founded: 1969. **Members:** 280. **Membership Dues:** regular, $10 (annual). **For-Profit. Multinational. Description:** Admirers of country music performer Mel Tillis (1932-), whose hit songs include Coca-Cola Cowboy and Ruby, Don't Take Your Love to Town. Promotes Tillis' career; makes available souvenirs and memorabilia. **Convention/Meeting:** none. **Publications:** Newsletter, 8-10/year. Includes Mel Tillis news, concert itinerary, and Mel Tillis stories. **Price:** included in membership dues.

24323 ■ Michael Bolton Platinum Club (MBPC)
c/o Fan Asylum
PO Box 7149
San Francisco, CA 94120
E-mail: info@michaelboltonclub.com
URL: http://www.michaelboltonclub.com
Founded: 1983. **Members:** 22,000. **Membership Dues:** individual, $40 (annual) ● individual (renewal), $30 (annual). **Staff:** 6. **Description:** Fans of the singer-songwriter Michael Bolton. **Convention/Meeting:** none. **Libraries: Type:** reference. **Holdings:** clippings. **Subjects:** reviews. **Computer Services:** Mailing lists, of members. **Publications:** Bolton Beat, monthly. Newsletter. **Price:** included in membership dues ● Bolton, Behind the Scenes, quarterly. Magazine. **Price:** included in membership dues. **Circulation:** 20,000. **Advertising:** accepted. Alternate Formats: online; CD-ROM.

24324 ■ Mills Brothers Society (MBS)
Address Unknown since 2006
Founded: 1995. **Members:** 377. **Membership Dues:** in U.S., $18 (annual) ● in Canada and Mexico, $19 (annual) ● outside North America, $20 (annual). **Staff:** 1. **Budget:** $9,100. **Regional Groups:** 3. **Description:** Admirers of the Mills Brothers vocal group and their backup musicians. Promotes appreciation of the Mills Brothers' music. Serves as a clearinghouse on the Mills Brothers and American popular music during their career; provides annual record auction, membership directory; offers for sale limited inventory of Mills-related merchandise. **Libraries: Type:** reference; by appointment only; not open to the public. **Holdings:** archival material, articles, audio recordings, clippings, periodicals, video recordings. **Subjects:** The Mills Brothers and related music and musicians. **Awards:** Patrick J. Marra, Sr. Award. **Frequency:** annual. **Type:** recognition. **Recipient:** Society member most dedicated to preservation and promotion of the music of The Mills Brothers. **Also Known As:** Society for the Preservation and Promotion of The Mills Brothers' Musical History. **Publications:** Remembering The Mills Brothers, quarterly. Newsletter. Bio/discographical info about TMB and members. **Price:** included in membership dues. ISSN: 1082-4707. **Circulation:** 550. **Advertising:** not accepted. **Conventions/Meetings:** annual convention, memorabilia displays, recordings, pictures, sheet music.

24325 ■ National Pat Boone Fan Club (NPBFC)
c/o Ms. Chris Bujnovsky, Pres.
1025 Park Rd.
Leesport, PA 19533
E-mail: chrisb926@juno.com
Contact: Ms. Chris Bujnovsky, Pres.
Founded: 1956. **Members:** 130. **Membership Dues:** in U.S., $10 (annual) ● outside U.S., $12 (annual). **Staff:** 4. **Description:** Fans of actor and singer Charles Eugene "Pat" Boone (1934-). Promotes Boone's career; disseminates information about the activities and recordings of Boone. Sponsors charity drives and makes contributions in Boone's name. Offers pen pal columns to bring members together. **Convention/Meeting:** none. **Formerly:** National Association of Pat Boone Fan Clubs; (1956) National Association of Pat Boone Fan Clubs. **Publications:** Then and Now, 3/year. Newsletter. Includes itinerary, record releases, and "Bits and Pieces" about the members and Pat. Also includes pen pal list and book and record list. **Price:** included in membership dues. **Circulation:** 130.

24326 ■ Norma Zimmer National Fan Club (NZNFC)
Address Unknown since 2007
Founded: 1961. **Membership Dues:** $6 (annual). **Description:** Fans and admirers of singer and author Norma Zimmer, who is best known as the "Champagne Lady" on the nationally syndicated Lawrence Welk Show. Keeps fans informed of Zimmer's television and public appearances and other activities. **Publications:** Bulletin, quarterly.

24327 ■ North American Toyah Fan Club (NATFC)
Address Unknown since 2007
Founded: 1982. **Members:** 100. **Membership Dues:** full, $15. **Description:** Fans of British singer/actress Toyah Willcox (1958-). Keeps members informed about her career. Offers mail order service for Willcox records, tapes, videos, posters, and shirts. Compiles statistics. **Convention/Meeting:** none. **Libraries: Type:** reference. **Holdings:** biographical archives. **Subjects:** Toyah Willcox. **Formerly:** (1986) Intergalactic Ranch House. **Publications:** American Newsletter, quarterly. **Price:** $8.00/year. **Advertising:** not accepted ● Toyah's Shadow, quarterly. Newsletter. **Price:** $7.50/year.

24328 ■ Oak Ridge Boys International Fan Club (ORBIFC)
88 New Shackle Island Rd.
Hendersonville, TN 37075
Ph: (615)824-4924 (615)824-4970

Fax: (615)822-7078
E-mail: omt@oakridgeboys.com
URL: http://www.oakridgeboys.com/Pages/places_main.html
Contact: Jim Halsey, Contact
Founded: 1978. **Members:** 10,000. **Membership Dues:** individual, $15 (annual). **Staff:** 1. **Description:** Individuals interested in the lives and careers of Joe Bonsall (1948-), Duane Allen (1943-), Richard Sterban (1943-), and William Lee Golden (1937-), who make up the country music group The Oak Ridge Boys. **Publications:** Fan Club Newsletter. **Circulation:** 10,000. **Advertising:** accepted. **Conventions/Meetings:** annual party, includes open house - always June.

24329 ■ Official Lane Brody and Eleni Global Fan Club
c/o Eddie Bayers, Gen. Mgr.
PO Box 24775
Nashville, TN 37202
Fax: (615)834-8354
E-mail: lane@lanebrody.com
URL: http://www.lanebrody.com
Contact: Eddie Bayers, Gen. Mgr.
Founded: 1985. **Members:** 10,000. **Staff:** 2. **Multinational. Description:** Fans of country music singer and songwriter Lane Brody, best known for the songs Over You and The Yellow Rose and the jazz artist Eleni, who is Lane Brody recording under her given name. Works to promote and disseminate information about Brody's and Eleni's public appearances. **Divisions:** Walden's Puddle Wildlife Rehabilitation Center. **Affiliated With:** The American Chestnut Foundation; American Humane Association; American Society for the Prevention of Cruelty to Animals; Animal Place; Animal Protection Institute of America; Defenders of Wildlife; Doris Day Animal League; Equality Now; Farm Sanctuary; Friends of Animals; Fund for Animals; Greenpeace U.S.A.; In Defense of Animals; International Fund for Animal Welfare; Last Chance for Animals; National Anti-Vivisection Society; National Audubon Society; National Wildlife Federation; Nature Conservancy; Ocean Conservancy; People for the Ethical Treatment of Animals; Pet Savers Foundation; Physicians Committee for Responsible Medicine; United Poultry Concerns; World Society for the Protection of Animals. **Formerly:** (1999) Official Lane Brody Global Fan Club. **Publications:** Lane Brody Global Fan Club Newsletter. Includes frequent e-mailings of updates. **Conventions/Meetings:** annual Fan Fair Getogether - meeting - always June.

24330 ■ Official Mary Wilson Message Board and Fan Club (MWFC)
2305 W Ruthrauff Rd., No. L-14
Tucson, AZ 85705-1985
URL: http://www.marywilson.com/fan_club_reg.html
Founded: 2001. **Members:** 265. **Membership Dues:** general, $20 (annual). **Description:** Represents admirers of Mary Wilson. Gathers and disseminates information on Mary Wilson's life and career. **Formerly:** Supremes International Fan Club; (2003) Mary Wilson Fan Club. **Publications:** Newsletter, quarterly.

24331 ■ Original Four Aces and Al Alberts Archive
c/o Walt Gollender
PO Box 1655
Orange, NJ 07051
Ph: (973)868-1995
E-mail: waltgollender@yahoo.com
URL: http://www.waltgollender.biz
Contact: Walt Gollender, Contact
Founded: 1952. **Staff:** 1. **For-Profit. Description:** Fans of the original vocal group The Four Aces, and Al Alberts. Maintains a hall of fame and museum. Offers a speakers' bureau; available to show 1950's TV clips of group's major Network appearances. Sells some 460 rare glossy photos. **Libraries: Type:** reference; open to the public; by appointment only. **Holdings:** archival material, articles, audiovisuals, periodicals. **Subjects:** radios shows, TV spots, live concerts and interviews with The Four Aces and Al Alberts.

24332 ■ Pam Tillis Fan Club
PO Box 128575
Nashville, TN 37212
E-mail: ptfannet@mindspring.com
URL: http://www.pamtillis.com
Membership Dues: regular, in U.S. and Canada, $15 ● regular, outside U.S., $20. **Multinational. Description:** Fan club devoted to country music singer Pam Tillis. **Publications:** Newsletters ● Articles.

24333 ■ Pat Compton Fan Club (PCFC)
c/o Pat Compton, Pres.
PO Box 463
Dickson, TN 37056
Ph: (615)441-1509 (615)441-4938
Free: (800)445-9882
Contact: Pat Compton, Pres.
Founded: 1990. **Members:** 200. **Membership Dues:** in U.S., $12 (annual) ● regular, outside U.S., $15 (annual). **Staff:** 1. **Description:** Admirers of country singer Pat Compton. Promotes Compton's art and career. Serves as a clearinghouse on Compton's performance itinerary. **Libraries: Type:** not open to the public. **Affiliated With:** International Fan Club Organization. **Publications:** Pat Compton Fan Club Newsletter, quarterly. **Price:** included in membership dues.

24334 ■ Pat Shea International Fan Club (PSIFC)
PO Box 991
Orchard Park, NY 14127
Free: (888)862-7107
E-mail: carolmac@patshea.com
URL: http://www.patshea.com
Contact: Carol MacDonald, Pres.
Founded: 1989. **Members:** 500. **Membership Dues:** regular, in U.S., $10 (annual) ● regular, outside U.S., $12 (annual). **Staff:** 3. **Budget:** $2,500. **Regional Groups:** 1. **Description:** Admirers of country musician Pat Shea. Promotes appreciation of Shea's creative talent and musical expression. Keeps members informed regarding Shea's achievements and concert schedule. **Libraries: Type:** reference; by appointment only. **Holdings:** 5; archival material, articles, business records, clippings. **Subjects:** Pat Shea. **Publications:** Pat Shea News, quarterly. Newsletter. **Price:** included in membership dues. **Circulation:** 500. **Conventions/Meetings:** annual Anniversary Party - regional meeting, with Pat Shea memorabilia (exhibits).

24335 ■ Patti Page Appreciation Society (PPAS)
c/o Rene Paquette, Pres.
4565 S Atlantic Ave., Ste.5103
Ponce Inlet, FL 32127
Ph: (386)756-6682
E-mail: renep@cfl.rr.com
URL: http://www.misspattipage.com
Contact: Rene Paquette, Pres.
Founded: 1985. **Members:** 200. **Membership Dues:** regular, $15 (annual). **Staff:** 1. **Description:** Fans and admirers of singer-entertainer Patti Page (1927-) in the U.S., United Kingdom, Canada, Australia, and the Netherlands. Keeps members informed of Page's career. Provides biographical information, an itinerary of concerts, a discography, and record chart listings. Maintains biographical archives; compiles statistics. Bestows Fan of the Year Award. **Libraries: Type:** open to the public. **Holdings:** 8. **Awards:** Fan of the Year. **Frequency:** annual. **Type:** recognition. **Publications:** The Rage, semiannual. Newsletter. Includes update on Page's career, information on album availability and membership activities, and trivia questions. **Price:** $5.00 past issues.

24336 ■ Perry Como Circle (PCC)
Address Unknown since 2007
Founded: 1956. **Members:** 150. **Membership Dues:** full, $10 (annual). **Staff:** 2. **Budget:** $1,500. **For-Profit. Description:** Fans of singer Perry Como. Seeks to share Perry Como by trading material relating to the singer such as records, photos, article, tapes and videos. Conducts yearly charity drive. **Convention/Meeting:** none. **Libraries: Type:** open to

the public. **Publications:** The Como Courier, semiannual. Newsletter. **Advertising:** accepted ● Also publishes a record list.

24337 ■ Phantom Blue Phan Club (PBPC)
PMB No. 1674
8306 Wilshire Blvd.
Beverly Hills, CA 90211
E-mail: mark@phantomblue.com
Contact: Mark Dawson, CEO
Founded: 1994. **Members:** 10,381. **Staff:** 14. **Description:** Admirers of the all-female rock group Phantom Blue. Promotes interest in, and appreciation of, the music of Phantom Blue. Facilitates communication among members; serves as a clearinghouse on Phantom Blue and its itinerary. **Libraries: Type:** reference. **Subjects:** Phantom Blue.

24338 ■ Phil Collins Information (PCFC)
Address Unknown since 2006
Founded: 1981. **Members:** 50,000. **Description:** Fans of singer Phil Collins (1951-), who is also a member of the rock music group Genesis. **Telecommunication Services:** electronic bulletin board, (913)345-2002. **Formerly:** (1991) Phil Collins Fan Club. **Publications:** Phil Collins Information, periodic. **Advertising:** accepted.

24339 ■ Purple Flower Gang (PFG)
c/o Cindy Bryant, Pres./Ed.
1803 Lucas St.
Muscatine, IA 52761
E-mail: pfg@machlink.com
URL: http://purpleflowergang.tripod.com
Contact: Cindy Bryant, Pres./Ed.
Founded: 1987. **Members:** 150. **Membership Dues:** in U.S. and Canada, $10 (annual) ● outside U.S. and Canada, $15 (annual). **Description:** Fans of the Monkees, a 1960s pop-rock group comprising Davy Jones (1945-), Micky Dolenz (1945-), Peter Tork (1942-), and Michael Nesmith (1942-). Promotes the careers of the group's members. **Publications:** Monkee Shines, quarterly. Newsletter. Contains reviews, features, news updates, and pen pal and editorial columns. **Advertising:** accepted.

24340 ■ Ray Price International Fan Club
c/o Sandra Orwig, Pres.
4205 Catalina Ln.
Harrisburg, PA 17109
E-mail: rpfc40@aol.com
URL: http://www.raypricefanclub.net
Contact: Sandra Orwig, Pres.
Founded: 1961. **Members:** 2,000. **Membership Dues:** regular, in U.S., $10 ● regular, outside U.S., $12. **Staff:** 1. **Description:** Individuals who admire the music of country-western singer/songwriter and guitarist Ray Price (1926-). **Formerly:** International Ray Price Fan Club; (2004) Fans and Friends of Ray Price. **Publications:** The Little Feather, quarterly. Newsletter. **Conventions/Meetings:** annual meeting, held in conjunction with International Country Music Fan Fair - always June, in Nashville, TN.

24341 ■ Razzy Bailey Fan Club (RBFC)
PO Box 727
Goodlettsville, TN 37070-0727
Ph: (615)884-0901
Fax: (615)851-7126
E-mail: razzy@razzybailey.com
Founded: 1972. **Description:** Represents fans of country singer Razzy Bailey. Promotes and supports Bailey's career.

24342 ■ REG - The International Roger Waters Fan Club
128 Onyx Dr.
Watsonville, CA 95076
E-mail: regpinky@rogerwaters.org
URL: http://www.rogerwaters.org
Contact: Michael Simone, Pres.
Founded: 1991. **Membership Dues:** regular, in U.S., $22 (annual) ● regular, outside U.S., $28 (annual). **Multinational. Description:** Represents fans of British rock musician and songwriter Roger Waters.

Promotes recognition, awareness, acknowledgement and appreciation for Roger Waters. Keeps members informed of the upcoming concert tours and other related activities concerning Roger Waters. **Publications:** REG Magazine, 3-4/year. **Price:** included in membership dues; $5.00/back issue for nonmembers, plus shipping and handling.

24343 ■ Rick Springfield Support Club: Human Touch
c/o Gail Plaskiewicz, Pres.
214 Johnson St.
Torrington, CT 06790
Ph: (860)482-4831
E-mail: wait4nite@aol.com
Contact: Gail Plaskiewicz, Pres.
Founded: 1984. **Members:** 11. **Membership Dues:** regular, in U.S., $15 (annual) ● regular, outside U.S., $18 (annual). **Description:** Seeks to raise awareness and disperse information about Rick Springfield. Encourages friendship between members. Sponsors charitable programs. **Convention/Meeting:** none. **Computer Services:** Online services. **Publications:** Newsletter, monthly. **Price:** included in membership dues.

24344 ■ Rick's Loyal Supporters (RLS)
c/o Vivian Acinelli, Ed.
4530 E Four Ridge Rd.
Imperial, MO 63052
E-mail: viv4rls@aol.com
URL: http://www.rickspringfield.net
Contact: Vivian Acinelli, Ed.
Founded: 1989. **Members:** 2,000. **Membership Dues:** regular, in U.S., $20 (quarterly) ● regular, in Canada and Mexico, $24 (annual) ● regular, outside U.S. and Canada, Mexico (if airmail, fee is $25 annually), $34 (annual). **Staff:** 3. **Description:** Fans of the singer, songwriter, musician, and actor Rick Springfield. Promotes Rick Springfield. Sponsors charity programs. **Additional Websites:** http://www.rick-springfield.com. **Publications:** Newsletter, quarterly. Features stories, poems, puzzles, raffles, photos, classified ads and fan participation. **Advertising:** accepted.

24345 ■ Ricky Skaggs International Fan Club (RSIFC)
c/o Skaggs Family Records
PO Box 2478
Hendersonville, TN 37077
Ph: (615)264-8877
Fax: (615)264-8899
E-mail: info@skaggsfamilyrecords.com
URL: http://www.skaggsfamilyrecords.com
Contact: Rachel Warren, Admin.
Founded: 1989. **Members:** 500. **Membership Dues:** regular, in U.S., $10 (annual) ● regular, outside U.S., $13 (annual). **Staff:** 1. **Description:** Admirers of the musical career of country-western singer/songwriter Ricky Skaggs (1954). Provides information regarding Skaggs' recent activities and plans. **Publications:** Newsplash, quarterly. Newsletter. Includes updates and information. **Price:** free for members ● Ricky Skaggs Newsletter, quarterly.

24346 ■ Rockapella Center
c/o PKA Management, Inc.
236 Huntington Ave., 5th Fl.
Boston, MA 02115
Ph: (617)861-4129
Fax: (617)236-0499
E-mail: rockapella@pkamanagement.com
URL: http://www.rockapella.com
Contact: Keith Garde, Contact
Founded: 1996. **Membership Dues:** regular, in U.S., $20 (annual) ● regular, in Canada and in North America, $25 (annual). **Description:** Fans of the pop group Rockapella. **Computer Services:** Mailing lists, of members. **Formerly:** Rockapella Fan Club.

24347 ■ Ronny and the Daytonas Fan Club (RDFC)
c/o Robert J. McKenzie, Pres.
114 Prince George Dr.
Hampton, VA 23669-3604

Ph: (757)838-2059
E-mail: thejudge@pcdocs.net
URL: http://thejudgeschambers.net
Contact: Robert J. McKenzie, Pres.
Founded: 1982. **Members:** 200. **Membership Dues:** individual, $20 (annual). **Staff:** 2. **Budget:** $4,000. **Description:** Admirers of the popular music group Ronny and the Daytonas, which produced hit songs in the mid-1960s including "Little GTO" and "Sandy". Promotes interest in the lives and careers of the band's members. Gathers and disseminates information on Ronny and the Daytonas recordings and memorabilia; informs members of the band's appearance schedule. **Libraries: Type:** reference. **Holdings:** archival material, articles, artwork, books, clippings, periodicals. **Subjects:** Ronny and the Daytonas.

24348 ■ Roy Rogers - Dale Evans Collectors Association (RRDECA)
PO Box 1166
Portsmouth, OH 45662
Ph: (740)353-0900
URL: http://www.sciotocountyohio.com/royrogers.htm
Contact: Nancy Horsley, Exec. Sec.
Founded: 1982. **Members:** 1,250. **Membership Dues:** individual, $20 (annual). **Staff:** 5. **Budget:** $23,000. **Regional Groups:** 1. **Description:** Individuals interested in artifacts and memorabilia relating to Roy Rogers (1911-1998) and Dale Evans (1912-2001), husband and wife team of country-western singers who also appeared on NBC's Roy Rogers Show (1951-57). Serves as a clearinghouse of information on Rogers' memorabilia. Conducts charitable programs and children's services; maintains museum. **Libraries: Type:** open to the public. **Subjects:** Roy Rogers/Dale Evans and family, other western stars. **Awards:** Golden Horseshoe Award. **Frequency:** annual. **Type:** recognition. **Recipient:** for special stars attending the festival ● Roy Rogers Scholarship. **Frequency:** 3/year. **Type:** scholarship. **Recipient:** for attendees of Shawnee State University and members of 4-H for at least one year. **Publications:** *Roy Rogers/Dale Evans Newsletter*, periodic. Contains news of Rogers and Evans, items for sale or trade, pen pals, and festival events. **Price:** included in membership dues; $5.00/issue. **Circulation:** 1,500. **Advertising:** accepted. **Conventions/Meetings:** annual Roy Rogers Festival - competition, with Roy Rogers/Dale Evans and other Western stars' memorabilia (exhibits) - always first weekend of June in Portsmouth, OH.

24349 ■ Sammy Kershaw Fan Club
817 18th Ave. S
Nashville, TN 37203
Fax: (615)320-9557
E-mail: sk@intlwebdesign.com
URL: http://www.sammykershaw.com/fanclub.html
Membership Dues: regular, in U.S., $15 (annual) ● regular, outside U.S., $20 (annual). **Multinational. Description:** Serves as a fan club dedicated to Sammy Kershaw. Members receive colored photo and biography. **Computer Services:** Mailing lists, for members. **Publications:** Newsletter. **Price:** included in membership dues.

24350 ■ Sawyer Brown International Fan Club (SBIFC)
5200 Old Harding Rd.
Franklin, TN 37064-9406
Ph: (615)799-2229
Fax: (615)799-9312
E-mail: elaine@shockink.com
URL: http://www.sawyerbrown.com/fanclub.html
Contact: Jackie Combs, Pres.
Founded: 1985. **Members:** 10,000. **Membership Dues:** regular, $25 (annual). **Staff:** 4. **Regional Groups:** 1. **State Groups:** 1. **Local Groups:** 1. **Description:** Represents fans of the country music band Sawyer Brown, whose members include Mark Miller, Duncan Cameron, Jr., Gregg Hubbard, Joe Smyth, and Jim Scholten. Disseminates information on itineraries and merchandise. **Awards:** CMA Horizon Award. **Frequency:** annual. **Type:** recognition. **Recipient:** for ACM 1997 Vocal ● TNN/MCN

Vocal Band of the Year. **Frequency:** annual. **Type:** recognition. **Recipient:** for MCN-TNN 1993-97. **Formerly:** Sawyer Brown Fan Club. **Publications:** *Gypsies on Parade*, periodic. Newsletter.

24351 ■ SMV Fan Club (SMVFC)
Address Unknown since 2007
Founded: 1995. **Members:** 22. **Membership Dues:** individual (& 8 37 cent stamps), $10 (annual). **Budget:** $32. **Description:** Admirers of the music of 1960s girl groups the Supremes, Marvelettes, and Martha and the Vandellas. Promotes appreciation of Motown girl groups and their music. Gathers and disseminates information on Motown girl groups; sponsors social activities; organized letter-writing campaign advocating induction of the Marvelettes into the Rock and Roll Hall of Fame. **Also Known As:** Supremes, Marvellettes, and Martha and the Vandellas Fan Club. **Publications:** Newsletter, quarterly. Last issue will be published December 2005, after 10 years running.

24352 ■ Sparks International Official Fan Club (SIOFC)
PO Box 25038
Los Angeles, CA 90025
E-mail: store@allsparks.com
URL: http://www.allsparks.com
Contact: Mary Martin, Sec.
Founded: 1973. **Members:** 10,080. **Membership Dues:** regular, $15 (annual). **Staff:** 2. **Regional Groups:** 1. **Description:** Fans in 18 countries of the U.S. rock duo Sparks, comprised of brothers Ron and Russell Mael. Keeps members informed of Sparks' activities. **Convention/Meeting:** none. **Libraries: Type:** reference. **Holdings:** 20; archival material. **Publications:** *Sparks Newsletter*, bimonthly.

24353 ■ Surfun: The Official Jan and Dean Fan Club
328 Sumner Ave.
Sumner, WA 98390
E-mail: surfun1@aol.com
URL: http://www.jananddean.com
Contact: Lori Brown, Contact
Founded: 1986. **Members:** 200. **Membership Dues:** overseas, $20 (annual) ● in Canada and Mexico, $17 (annual) ● in U.S., $15 (annual). **Staff:** 1. **Multinational. Description:** Keeps fans informed of current tour information, recordings, and news. **Convention/Meeting:** none. **Additional Websites:** http://www.jananddean-janberry.com/surfun.html. **Publications:** Newsletter, quarterly. **Price:** included in membership dues. **Circulation:** 200. **Advertising:** accepted.

24354 ■ Suzy Bogguss Fan Club
c/o Suzy Bogguss Concerts
Suzy Fan Mail
PMB 186
8161 Hwy. 100
Nashville, TN 37220
E-mail: suzy@bogguss.com
URL: http://www.bogguss.com
Contact: Janene DiRico-Cable, Pres.
Membership Dues: regular, in U.S., $12 (annual) ● regular, outside U.S., $16 (annual). **Multinational. Description:** Fan club devoted to Suzy Bogguss. Members receive an 8x10 glossy photo, tour itinerary, and membership card. **Publications:** Newsletter, quarterly. **Conventions/Meetings:** breakfast.

24355 ■ Tammy Wynette International Fan Club (TWIFC)
PO Box 3225
Brentwood, TN 37024
E-mail: info@tammywynette.com
Founded: 1967. **Members:** 1,500. **Membership Dues:** individual in U.S., $12 (annual) ● in Canada, $15 (annual) ● inside United Kingdom, 1,050 (annual) ● outside U.S. and Canada, $15 (annual). **Multinational. Description:** Fans of country music singer Tammy Wynette (1942-1998). Provides information about Wynette. **Publications:** *1st Lady News*, quarterly. Newsletter. Includes appearance schedule.

Conventions/Meetings: annual meeting - always Nashville, TN.

24356 ■ Tanya Tucker Fan Club (TTFC)
PO Box 158
Arrington, TN 37014
Ph: (615)395-0117
Fax: (615)395-0117
E-mail: info@tanyatucker.com
URL: http://www.tanyatucker.com
Contact: Tanya Tucker, Contact
Founded: 1979. **Members:** 3,000. **Membership Dues:** in U.S., $20 (annual) ● in Canada, $25 (annual) ● outside U.S. and Canada, $30 (annual). **Staff:** 1. **For-Profit. Multinational. Description:** Fans of country singer Tanya Tucker (1958-), whose hits include Strong Enough to Bend, Highway Robbery, and Delta Dawn at the age of 13. **Libraries: Type:** open to the public. **Holdings:** photographs. **Computer Services:** Online services, mail order. **Publications:** *Tanya Tucker "TNT Explosion" Newsletter*, semiannual. **Circulation:** 3,000. **Advertising:** accepted.

24357 ■ Terri Clark Fan Club
c/o Spalding Entertainment
PO Box 128136
Nashville, TN 37212
E-mail: fanclub@terriclark.com
URL: http://www.terriclark.com
Membership Dues: regular, $24 (annual). **Multinational. Description:** Fan club dedicated to Terri Clark. Membership includes 8x10 photo, card, and biography. **Computer Services:** Mailing lists. **Publications:** Newsletter, quarterly. Includes tour itinerary and tour merchandise offers. ● Journal.

24358 ■ Tex Ritter Fan Club (TRFC)
c/o Sharon L. Richards-Sweeting, Pres.
828 Wandering Creek Dr.
Bothell, WA 98021
Ph: (425)482-0127
E-mail: sharons55@juno.com
URL: http://www.surfnetinc.com/chuck/ritter2b.htm
Contact: Sharon L. Richards-Sweeting, Pres.
Founded: 1968. **Members:** 75. **Membership Dues:** individual in U.S., $10 (annual) ● individual outside U.S., $15 (annual). **Staff:** 1. **Multinational. Description:** Fans of country and western singer Tex Ritter (1905-74). Furthers recognition of Ritter's humanitarian, musical, and acting contributions. Compiles statistics; supports museum. **Libraries: Type:** reference. **Holdings:** archival material, photographs. **Subjects:** life and achievements of Tex Ritter. **Publications:** *The Gringo*, 3/year. Newsletter. **Price:** included in membership dues. **Circulation:** 75. **Advertising:** accepted. **Conventions/Meetings:** annual Tex Ritter Roundup - general assembly and festival (exhibits) - usually third weekend in August.

24359 ■ T.G. Sheppard International Fan Club (TGSIFC)
5123 Secor Rd., No. 6
Toledo, OH 43623-2326
E-mail: miss.lou@prodigy.net
URL: http://www.tgsheppard.com
Contact: Lou Girardot, Pres.
Founded: 1977. **Members:** 1,900. **Membership Dues:** in U.S., $10 ● in Canada, $12 ● outside U.S. and Canada, $15. **Staff:** 1. **Description:** Fans of country music performer T.G. Sheppard (1944-), whose songs include Last Cheater's Waltz and Finally. Promotes Sheppard's career; makes available photographs, souvenirs, and memorabilia. **Awards:** New Artist Award. **Type:** recognition. **Publications:** *Friends of T.G. Sheppard Newsletter*, quarterly. Includes welcome letter, concert itinerary, 8x10 photo, magnets, and membership card. ● *T.G. Sheppard Newsletter*, periodic. **Conventions/Meetings:** annual Get Together - dinner and show, held in conjunction with concerts.

24360 ■ **Toby Keith International Fan Club (TKIFC)**
c/o MusicCityNet
214 Overlook Ct., Ste.120
Brentwood, TN 37027
E-mail: mail@tobykeith.com
URL: http://tobykeith.musiccitynetworks.com
Membership Dues: regular, $25 (annual). **Multinational. Description:** Fan club dedicated to Toby Keith. Membership includes membership card, autographed 8x10 color photo, official button, biography, discography, discounts on merchandise. **Computer Services:** Mailing lists. **Publications:** *Toby Times.* Newsletter. **Conventions/Meetings:** annual party, reservations required.

24361 ■ **Tom Jones "Tom Terrific" Fan Club (TJTTFC)**
c/o Margaret Mariotti, Pres.
411 Coram Ave.
Shelton, CT 06484-3134
Ph: (203)924-1553
Fax: (203)924-1553
E-mail: tjttfc@aol.com
URL: http://www.tjfanclub.com
Contact: Margaret Mariotti, Pres.
Founded: 1978. **Members:** 500. **Membership Dues:** individual, $10 (annual) ● senior, $8 (annual). **Staff:** 2. **Multinational. Description:** Represents fans of entertainer Tom Jones (1940-), whose hits include It's Not Unusual and She's a Lady. Supports charitable programs. **Convention/Meeting:** none. **Publications:** Newsletter, quarterly. **Advertising:** accepted ● Bulletin, periodic.

24362 ■ **Tracy Byrd Online Fan Club (TBOFC)**
PO Box 120795
Nashville, TN 37212
Ph: (615)297-7002
E-mail: fanclubhs1@aol.com
URL: http://tracybyrd.musiccitynetworks.com
Membership Dues: regular, $20 (annual). **Multinational. Description:** Fan club dedicated to Tracy Byrd. Membership includes autographed 8x10 color photo, biography, fact sheet, bumper sticker, button, card, merchandise offerings, 2 Meet & Greets. **Publications:** Newsletter, 3/year.

24363 ■ **Trisha Yearwood Fan Club**
PO Box 120895
Nashville, TN 37212
E-mail: yearwdhead@aol.com
URL: http://members.aol.com/YearwdHead/index.html
Membership Dues: general, $20 (annual). **Multinational. Description:** Fan club dedicated to country music singer Trisha Yearwood. **Additional Websites:** http://trishayearwood.com/fans/index.html.

24364 ■ **Vince Gill Fan Club (VGFC)**
PO Box 700
Grover, MO 63040
E-mail: members@vincegill.com
URL: http://www.vincegill.com
Membership Dues: regular, $24 (annual). **Multinational. Description:** Fan club dedicated to Vince Gill. Membership includes 8x10 photo, fact sheet, membership card, and free gift. **Computer Services:** Mailing lists, of members. **Publications:** Newsletter, quarterly. Contains itineraries and merchandise offerings. **Price:** included in membership dues.

24365 ■ **Wade Hayes Fan Network**
PO Box 128546
Nashville, TN 37212
E-mail: wade_hayes@sonynashville.com
URL: http://www.sonynashville.com/WadeHayes/fanclub/fanclub.htm
Description: Serves as a fan club dedicated to Wade Hayes.

24366 ■ **Wolfpack Fan Club (WFC)**
PO Box 292797
Nashville, TN 37229-2797
Ph: (615)780-3579 (615)367-0458
Free: (888)345-WOLF
Fax: (615)367-1320
E-mail: wolftalk@comcast.net
URL: http://www.steppenwolf.com
Contact: Charlie Wolf, Pres.
Founded: 1992. **Members:** 3,500. **Membership Dues:** life in U.S. (plus $4.05 shipping and handling fee), $25 ● life outside U.S. (plus $9.75 shipping and handling fee), $25. **Staff:** 2. **National Groups:** 3. **Description:** Admirers of the rock-and-roll band, Steppenwolf. Promotes appreciation of Steppenwolf's music; facilitates communication among members. Serves as a clearinghouse on Steppenwolf and its members; keeps members abreast of Steppenwolf's current activities; sponsors social events. **Telecommunication Services:** electronic mail, wolfpackfanclub@yahoo.com.

24367 ■ **Wynonna International Fan Club**
PO Box 128229
Nashville, TN 37212
Ph: (615)234-2889
E-mail: wystaff@wynonna.com
URL: http://home.flash.net/~wynonna
Founded: 1985. **Members:** 5,000. **Membership Dues:** regular, $20. **For-Profit. Description:** Fans of country music singer Wynonna Judd, Naomi Judd, and Ashley Judd. **Libraries: Type:** open to the public. **Holdings:** 90. **Subjects:** newsletters. **Publications:** *Wy's World,* quarterly. Newsletter. **Price:** included in membership dues. **Circulation:** 5,000. **Conventions/Meetings:** annual Fan Club Party - meeting.

24368 ■ **ZZ Top International Fan Club, Inc. (ZZTIFCI)**
PO Box 19744
Houston, TX 77224-9744
Ph: (713)461-9851
Fax: (713)461-9854
URL: http://www.lowpft.com/zztifc.html
Founded: 1983. **Description:** Admirers of the rock group ZZ Top. Makes available ZZ Top rock merchandise. **Publications:** *Top Newzz.* Newsletter. Includes interviews and photographs. **Price:** available to members only ● Catalog.

Sinatra, Frank

24369 ■ **Sinatra Society of America (SSA)**
PO Box 2705
Toluca Lake, CA 91610
E-mail: fssociety@aol.com
Contact: Charles Pignone III, Pres.
Founded: 1976. **Members:** 4,000. **Membership Dues:** individual, $25 (annual). **Description:** Individuals who admire singer/actor Frank Sinatra (1915-1998), whose musical career spanned 50 years and countless styles, and whose acting career featured several major motion pictures, including Guys and Dolls. Seeks to enhance members' enjoyment of Sinatra's artistry. **Libraries: Type:** reference. **Holdings:** audio recordings, video recordings. **Publications:** *Sinatra Society of America Newsletter,* bimonthly. **Conventions/Meetings:** periodic meeting (exhibits).

Sports

24370 ■ **Atlanta Flames Fan Club (AFFC)**
c/o Betsy Watkins, VP
3297 Wiltshire Dr.
Avondale Estates, GA 30002-1640
E-mail: jpw45@bellsouth.net
URL: http://www.geocities.com/affc00/affc.htm
Contact: Joe P. Watkins, Pres.
Founded: 1972. **Members:** 25. **Membership Dues:** out-of-state, $8 (annual) ● junior, $5 (annual) ● regular, $10 (annual) ● family, $16 (annual). **Descrip-**tion: Hockey fans. Promotes the game of hockey, especially in the Southeastern U.S. (The Atlanta Flames hockey club competed in the National Hockey League from the 1972-73 season through the 1979-80 season; the franchise then moved to Calgary, AB, Canada, and left the southeastern region of the U.S. without representation in the NHL.) Works to raise funds for childhood cancer research. **Awards:** Howard Cochran Award. **Frequency:** annual. **Type:** recognition ● The Lonely Seal. **Frequency:** annual. **Type:** recognition. **Committees:** Charity; Hospitality; Trips. **Affiliated With:** National Hockey League Booster Clubs Association. **Publications:** *Fireline,* quarterly. Newsletter. Alternate Formats: online. **Conventions/Meetings:** annual convention.

24371 ■ **Blackhawk Standbys, Inc. (BSI)**
c/o Nika Alex, Financial Sec.
11555 Settlers Pond Way, Unit 2B
Orland Park, IL 60467
Ph: (708)479-7967
E-mail: hummelfriend@msn.com
URL: http://www.blackhawkstandbys.homestead.com
Contact: Gladys Wheeler, Pres.
Founded: 1944. **Members:** 135. **Membership Dues:** active, $20 (annual) ● inactive, $15 (annual). **Staff:** 11. **Budget:** $15,000. **Regional Groups:** 1. **State Groups:** 1. **Local Groups:** 1. **Description:** Fans who promote and support the Chicago Blackhawks hockey team. Sponsors charitable and educational programs; maintains children's services. Member of the National Hockey League Booster Clubs Association. **Awards:** Most Valuable Player Award. **Frequency:** annual. **Type:** recognition. **Recipient:** for most valuable contribution to team overall ● Player of the Year Award. **Frequency:** annual. **Type:** recognition. **Telecommunication Services:** electronic mail, standbyn3@hotmail.com. **Affiliated With:** National Hockey League Booster Clubs Association. **Also Known As:** Chicago Blackhawk Standbys. **Formerly:** Chicago Standbys Fan Club. **Publications:** *Wigwam,* monthly. Newsletter. Includes upcoming events. **Price:** included in membership dues. **Circulation:** 100. **Advertising:** accepted. Alternate Formats: online. **Conventions/Meetings:** annual National Hockey League Booster Club Convention - conference - always second weekend of August.

24372 ■ **Blueliners**
PO Box 805
St. Louis, MO 63188
E-mail: blueliners@aol.com
URL: http://www.blueliners.org
Contact: Jim DeCourcy, Pres.
Founded: 1967. **Members:** 250. **Description:** Fans who promote and support the St. Louis Blues hockey team. Operates charitable program. Member of the National Hockey League Booster Clubs Association. **Awards:** Amateur Hockey Awards. **Frequency:** annual. **Type:** recognition. **Affiliated With:** National Hockey League Booster Clubs Association. **Formerly:** (2002) Saint Louis Blueliners. **Publications:** *Bluenotes,* monthly. Newsletter. **Circulation:** 300. **Conventions/Meetings:** monthly meeting - every first Wednesday, 7:00 PM at Affton Ice Rink, Affton, MO, USA.

24373 ■ **Bobby Labonte Fan Club (BLFC)**
PO Box 358
Trinity, NC 27370
Free: (877)426-2295
E-mail: fanclub@bobbylabonte.com
URL: http://www.bobbylabonte.com
Contact: Trisha Reilly, Mgr.
Members: 2,500. **Membership Dues:** individual, $26 (annual) ● family, $31 (annual). **Description:** Admirers of NASCAR driver Bobby Labonte. Promotes interest in auto racing. Serves as a clearinghouse on Labonte's career and activities; produces Labonte memorabilia. **Publications:** Newsletter, quarterly. **Circulation:** 30,000.

24374 ■ **Buffalo Sabres Booster Club (BSBC)**
PO Box 1065
Cheektowaga, NY 14225

E-mail: bufsabbc@aol.com
URL: http://hometown.aol.com/bufsabbc/boosterclub.htm
Founded: 1970. **Members:** 150. **Membership Dues:** youth, $10 (annual) ● individual, $20 (annual) ● family, $30 (annual). **Description:** Fans who promote and support the Buffalo Sabres hockey team. Conducts charitable activities; member of the National Hockey League Booster Clubs Association. **Awards: Frequency:** annual. **Type:** recognition. **Publications:** *Sabre Points*, monthly. Newsletter. **Price:** free for members. **Advertising:** accepted. **Conventions/Meetings:** annual meeting, held in conjunction with the NHLBCAS (exhibits) - always second weekend of August.

24375 ■ Cleveland Hockey Booster Club (CHBC)

c/o Dorothy Michalko, First VP
13118 Tyler Ave.
Cleveland, OH 44111
E-mail: clevelandhockeybc@yahoo.com
URL: http://www.angelfire.com/oh5/chbc/index.html
Contact: Mary Dejak, Pres.
Founded: 1948. **Members:** 155. **Membership Dues:** single, $15 (annual) ● family, $25 (annual). **Staff:** 13. **Description:** Individuals who promote and support the sport of hockey. Sponsors youth hockey in the area. Member of the National Hockey League Booster Clubs Association. **Libraries: Type:** reference. **Holdings:** clippings. **Subjects:** hockey in Cleveland since 1950. **Awards:** Jock Callander Scholarship. **Frequency:** annual. **Type:** scholarship. **Recipient:** to area youth. **Telecommunication Services:** electronic mail, dmdejak@aol.com. **Formerly:** (1980) Cleveland Barons Booster Club. **Publications:** *Puck Eater*, monthly. Newsletter. Includes the association's activities. **Price:** free for members. **Conventions/Meetings:** monthly meeting - every 1st Tuesday.

24376 ■ Club E: The Dale Earnhardt Fan Club

Address Unknown since 2007
Founded: 1986. **Members:** 45,000. **Membership Dues:** individual, $20 (annual). **Budget:** $50,000. **Description:** Fans of the late race car driver Dale Earnhardt. Holds contests; offers discounts at Action owned trailers; produces collectable diecast pieces and other fan club-related products. **Computer Services:** database ● mailing lists. **Publications:** *The Intimidator*, quarterly. Newsletter. **Circulation:** 100,000. **Advertising:** not accepted.

24377 ■ Dale Jarrett Fan Club (DJFC)

1915 Fairgrove Church Rd. SE
Newton, NC 28658
Ph: (828)464-8818
Free: (888)325-3527
Fax: (828)465-5088
E-mail: djfanclub@dalejarrett.com
URL: http://www.dalejarrett.com/fanclub.asp
Contact: Blair Phillips, Mgr.
Members: 8,000. **Membership Dues:** standard, $30 (annual) ● standard (Canadian), $40 (annual). **Description:** Admirers of NASCAR driver Dale Jarrett. Promotes interest in auto racing. Serves as a clearinghouse on Jarrett's career and activities; produces Jarrett memorabilia. **Publications:** Newsletter, quarterly. **Circulation:** 10,000. **Conventions/Meetings:** semiannual convention.

24378 ■ Devils Fan Club (DFC)

PO Box 504
East Rutherford, NJ 07073-0504
Ph: (201)768-9680
Fax: (973)402-5627
E-mail: president@devilsfanclub.org
URL: http://www.devilsfanclub.org
Contact: Trudy Stetter, Pres.
Founded: 1982. **Members:** 1,500. **Membership Dues:** adult, $20 (annual) ● junior, $15 (annual) ● family, $50 (annual). **Staff:** 13. **Description:** Member of the National Hockey League Booster Clubs, Inc. Promotes and supports the New Jersey Devils hockey team and the sport of ice hockey. Conducts charitable programs. **Awards:** Most Valuable Player

Award. **Frequency:** annual. **Type:** recognition. **Recipient:** to new Jersey Devils' player of the year ● Rookie of the Year. **Frequency:** annual. **Type:** recognition. **Recipient:** for the most valuable rookie of the year ● Stedman Cup. **Frequency:** annual. **Type:** recognition. **Recipient:** for the MVP of Garden State Games ice hockey tournament. **Computer Services:** database ● mailing lists. **Committees:** Amateur Hockey; Charities; Game Night Table; Hospitality; Nominating; Special Events; Trips. **Affiliated With:** National Hockey League Booster Clubs Association. **Formerly:** Devils Fan Club; (1993) New Jersey Devils Fan Club. **Publications:** *Burning Issues*, 10/year. Newsletter. **Price:** included in membership dues. **Circulation:** 2,100. **Advertising:** accepted. **Conventions/Meetings:** annual Dinner with the Devils, with NHL Devils players for members only ● annual Garden State Games - tour, open to young men and women from ages seven through high school ● meeting - 10/year.

24379 ■ Elton Sawyer Fan Club (ESFC)

Address Unknown since 2007
Founded: 1994. **Members:** 150. **Membership Dues:** individual, $15 (annual) ● family (up to 4), $18 (annual). **Staff:** 2. **Description:** Admirers of NASCAR automobile racers Elton Sawyer and Patty Moise. Promotes interest in the NASCAR circuit; encourages the success of Sawyer and Moise. Facilitates communication among members; gathers and disseminates information on Sawyer and Moise and their careers. Makes available autographed souvenirs. **Formerly:** (2001) Elton Sawyer - Patty Moise Fan Club: **Publications:** *Fan Club News*, 3/year. Newsletter. **Price:** included in membership. **Advertising:** not accepted.

24380 ■ Hartford Whalers Booster Club (HWBC)

PO Box 273
Hartford, CT 06141
Ph: (860)225-0265
E-mail: alan_m_victor@sbcglobal.net
URL: http://www.whalerwatch.com
Contact: Alan M. Victor, Pres.
Members: 50. **Membership Dues:** basic, $10 (annual). **Description:** Educational, charitable, social organization promoting sport of ice hockey in Connecticut. Sponsors FANniversary party, charity fundraiser and scholarship event. **Affiliated With:** National Hockey League Booster Clubs Association. **Publications:** *Whaler Watch*, monthly. Newsletter. Lists upcoming activities and events. Alternate Formats: online. **Conventions/Meetings:** quarterly meeting ● annual NHL Booster Club Convention - meeting, held in conjunction with NHLBCA - always second week of August.

24381 ■ Los Angeles Kings Booster Club (LAKBC)

Staples Center
1111 S Figueroa St., Ste.3100
Los Angeles, CA 90015
Ph: (310)712-5435
E-mail: info@lakingsboosters.org
URL: http://www.lakings.com
Contact: Janet Raines, Pres.
Founded: 1985. **Members:** 900. **Description:** Fans who promote and support the Los Angeles Kings hockey team. Sponsors charitable programs. Member of the National Hockey League Booster Clubs Association. **Publications:** *The Booster Shot*, monthly. Newsletter. Features activities of members. **Price:** included in membership dues.

24382 ■ National Hockey League Booster Clubs Association (NHLBCA)

PO Box 805
St. Louis, MO 63188
Ph: (314)895-9466
E-mail: blueliners@aol.com
URL: http://www.blueliners.org/about.html
Contact: Jim DeCourcy, Pres.
Founded: 1968. **Members:** 26. **Membership Dues:** $15 (annual). **Description:** Booster clubs for teams in the National Hockey League. Fosters goodwill

among NHL teams and their respective booster clubs. **Publications:** none. **Libraries: Type:** reference. **Holdings:** archival material. **Awards: Type:** recognition. **Conventions/Meetings:** competition ● monthly meeting - every first Wednesday.

24383 ■ New York Islanders Booster Club (NYIBC)

PO Box 502
Hicksville, NY 11802-0502
Ph: (631)547-6942
E-mail: webmaster@nyiboosterclub.org
URL: http://www.nyiboosterclub.org
Contact: Maryann Filangieri, Treas.
Founded: 1972. **Members:** 420. **Membership Dues:** adult, $20 (annual) ● teen, $15 (annual) ● child (below 12 years old), $10 (annual). **Staff:** 21. **Description:** Fans who promote and support the New York Islanders hockey team. Member of the National Hockey League Booster Clubs Association. Sponsors charitable programs. **Libraries: Type:** reference. **Awards:** Most Popular Player. **Frequency:** annual. **Type:** recognition ● Most Valuable Player. **Type:** recognition. **Telecommunication Services:** electronic mail, isles25@aol.com. **Affiliated With:** National Hockey League Booster Clubs Association. **Publications:** *Center Ice*, monthly. Newsletter. **Price:** included in membership dues. **Circulation:** 450. **Advertising:** accepted. **Conventions/Meetings:** annual dinner, includes dance ● monthly meeting - October through April in Westbury, NY.

24384 ■ New York Rangers Fan Club (NYRFC)

GPO Box 8713
New York, NY 10116-8713
E-mail: president@nyrfanclub.com
URL: http://www.nyrfanclub.com
Contact: Kerry Tricarico, Pres.
Founded: 1950. **Members:** 650. **Membership Dues:** individual, $25 (annual) ● family, $55 (annual). **Budget:** $14,500. **Description:** Fans who promote and support the New York Rangers hockey team. Conducts charitable and social activities. Member of the National Hockey League Booster Clubs Association. **Committees:** Advertising. **Affiliated With:** National Hockey League Booster Clubs Association. **Formerly:** Rangers Fan Club. **Publications:** *The Rangers Review*, monthly. Newsletter. **Price:** included in membership dues. **Circulation:** 700. **Advertising:** accepted. Alternate Formats: online. **Conventions/Meetings:** annual banquet, dinner, dance, and awards ceremony with New York Rangers hockey team ● monthly meeting.

24385 ■ Philadelphia Flyers Fan Club (PFFC)

3601 S Broad St.
Philadelphia, PA 19148
E-mail: flyers212a@verizon.net
URL: http://www.flyersfanclub.org
Contact: Joe Fisher, Pres.
Description: Fans who promote and support the Philadelphia Flyers hockey team. Conducts charitable activities. Member of the National Hockey League Booster Clubs Association. **Telecommunication Services:** electronic mail, webmaster@flyersfanclub.org. **Publications:** *The Puck*, periodic. Newsletter. **Conventions/Meetings:** annual meeting, in conjunction with the NHLBCA - always second week of August.

24386 ■ Pittsburgh Penguins Booster Club (PPBC)

PO Box 903
Pittsburgh, PA 15230
E-mail: pens_bc@mailcity.com
URL: http://members.tripod.com/~pens_bc
Contact: Melinda Harty, Pres.
Founded: 1948. **Members:** 205. **Membership Dues:** full, $20 (annual) ● out of town, $10 (annual). **Description:** Fans who promote and support the Pittsburgh Penguins hockey team. Sponsors charitable program. Member of the National Hockey League Booster Clubs Association. **Awards:** Bob Johnson Scholarship. **Frequency:** annual. **Type:** scholarship. **Recipient:** for a high school senior

involved in hockey with a high grade point average. **Formerly:** Pittsburgh Hornets Booster Club. **Publications:** *The Waddler*, monthly. Newsletter. Includes upcoming events. **Price:** free for members. **Conventions/Meetings:** annual AHL Booster Clubs - convention - always weekend after Labor Day in September ● monthly meeting ● annual NHL Booster Clubs - convention - always 2nd weekend in August.

24387 ■ Red Wing For'em Club (RWFC)
PO Box 230
Eastpointe, MI 48021
E-mail: sportscards9@comcast.net
URL: http://www.redwingforemclub.org
Contact: Lorraine Curmi, Pres.
Founded: 1949. **Members:** 300. **Membership Dues:** active, $25 (annual) ● associate, $15 (annual). **Description:** Hosts annual picnic, bowling parties, and other events. Plans many road trips to see Red Wings play in other arenas across North America. Sells raffle tickets each year with the grand prize of a pair of season tickets for the regular season; all the monies raised from this effort go to charities. **Publications:** *Fanfare*, monthly. Newsletter. Contains articles about events, press releases, stats, and news of other booster club activities. **Price:** included in membership dues. **Conventions/Meetings:** annual NHL Booster Clubs Convention - meeting.

24388 ■ Washington Capitals Fan Club (WCFC)
PO Box 4671
Capitol Heights, MD 20791-4671
E-mail: paulcschneider@hotmail.com
URL: http://www.capsfanclub.org
Contact: Paul Schneider, Sec.
Founded: 1974. **Description:** Represents fans who promote and support the Washington Capitals hockey team; member of the National Hockey League Booster Clubs Association (see separate entry).

Star Trek

24389 ■ Klingon Strike Force
Address Unknown since 2007
Founded: 1978. **Members:** 150. **Membership Dues:** to join, $5 (annual) ● for newsletter (hard copy), $12 (annual). **Staff:** 4. **Budget:** $300. **Description:** Fans of the television series Star Trek and Star Trek: The Next Generation and Deep Space Nine and Star Trek Voyager. Members engage in role playing with other groups and role-playing dealing with Klingon covert and overt activities. Conducts projects to expand and expound on Klingon culture, mythology, and language. **Libraries: Type:** reference. **Holdings:** archival material, artwork, audiovisuals, books, periodicals. **Subjects:** Star Trek materials. **Awards:** Commendation and Promotion. **Frequency:** quarterly. **Type:** recognition. **Recipient:** level of participation. **Computer Services:** Mailing lists, informational. **Publications:** *Battle Lines*, bimonthly. Newsletter. Club newsletter, updates & some fiction & art. **Price:** $12.00/year. **Circulation:** 100. **Advertising:** accepted. Alternate Formats: online ● *KSF Covert Operations Manual*. Available at conventions only. ● Booklets available to members composed of their contributions of art & writing on aspects of Klingon Society, flora, fauna, etc.

24390 ■ Star Trek: The Official Fan Club
253 Granby St.
Norfolk, VA 23510-1813
Free: (866)375-TREK
E-mail: editor@startrek.com
URL: http://www.startrek.com/startrek/view/community/fanclub.html
Founded: 1980. **Members:** 150,000. **Membership Dues:** regular in U.S., $20 (annual). **Staff:** 59. **For-Profit. Description:** Fans of the syndicated science fiction television series Star Trek, which aired from 1966-69 and the current series, Star Trek: The Next Generation as well as Star Trek: Deep Space Nine and Star Trek: Voyager. Keeps members informed about the program, cast members, and movie spin-

offs. Compiles statistics. Offers exclusive merchandise and forwards fan mail to Star Trek personalities. **Libraries: Type:** reference. **Holdings:** archival material. **Formerly:** (1985) Star Trek III: the Official Fan Club. **Publications:** *Quark's Bazaar*, bimonthly. Catalog. Bound in Star Trek Communicator. ● *Star Trek Communicator*, bimonthly. Magazine. Contains book reviews, interviews with cast members, and movie updates. **Price:** included in membership dues; $19.95 /year for nonmembers. ISSN: 1080-3793. **Circulation:** 250,000. **Advertising:** accepted. Alternate Formats: online.

24391 ■ STARFLEET
PO Box 94288
Lubbock, TX 79493-4288
E-mail: webmaster@sfi.org
URL: http://www.sfi.org
Contact: Greg Trotter, Chief of Staff
Founded: 1974. **Members:** 7,000. **Membership Dues:** individual in U.S., $15 (annual) ● family of 2, $22 (annual) ● family of 3 or more, individual outside U.S., $25 (annual) ● family outside U.S., $30 (annual). **Regional Groups:** 16. **Local Groups:** 225. **Description:** Individuals interested in science-fiction motion pictures and television programs, particularly the science fiction television and movie series Star Trek. Conducts community service activities and charitable and educational activities. **Libraries: Type:** reference; lending. **Holdings:** archival material, audiovisuals, biographical archives. **Awards: Frequency:** annual. **Type:** scholarship ● Starfleet Scholarship Program. **Frequency:** annual. **Type:** recognition. **Computer Services:** Mailing lists. **Publications:** *STARFLEET Communique*, bimonthly. Magazine. Includes book and movie reviews and information on local club activities. **Price:** included in membership dues. **Advertising:** accepted. **Conventions/Meetings:** annual international conference (exhibits).

24392 ■ Starfleet Command (SFC)
PO Box 33565
Indianapolis, IN 46203-0565
E-mail: sfc@sfcommand.com
URL: http://www.starfleet-command.com
Contact: Mark A. Bischoff, Pres.
Founded: 1974. **Members:** 2,500. **Membership Dues:** individual, $15 (annual) ● household of 2, $24 (annual) ● household of 3 or more, $30 (annual) ● life (individual), $150 ● life (household of 2), $175 ● life (household of 3 or more), $200. **Staff:** 25. **Regional Groups:** 12. **State Groups:** 1. **Local Groups:** 100. **Multinational. Description:** Fans of science fiction television series Star Trek, which aired from 1966-69, and the current television series Star Trek: The Next Generation and Deep Space Nine; individuals interested in science fiction in general; space enthusiasts. Promotes the peaceful exploration and use of space; supports the establishment of a permanent working space station or moon base. Seeks to raise public awareness of the importance of space exploration, and encourages youth participation in Space Camp activities. Encourages the support of environmental, conservation, and resource management programs. Serves as a forum for exchange of ideas and information. Conducts charitable activities and supports environmental organizations. Offers pen pal service, including overseas contacts. **Libraries: Type:** reference. **Holdings:** archival material. **Subjects:** Trek and space related material. **Awards:** Chapter of the Year. **Frequency:** annual. **Type:** recognition ● Member of the Year. **Frequency:** annual. **Type:** recognition. **Computer Services:** database ● mailing lists. **Committees:** Space Activities. **Publications:** *Starfleet Communications*, quarterly. Newsletter. Reports on organization news and activities, science and space related issues, and updates about Star Trek. **Price:** included in membership dues. **Circulation:** 2,000. **Advertising:** accepted ● Brochure. Alternate Formats: online. **Conventions/Meetings:** annual meeting (exhibits).

24393 ■ Trekville U.S.A./International (TUSA)
c/o Jay S. Hastings, Pres.
1021 S 9th Ave.
Scranton, PA 18504

Ph: (570)343-7806
E-mail: fltadmankh@aol.com
URL: http://www.geocities.com/trekvilleisa
Contact: Jay S. Hastings, Pres.
Founded: 1985. **Members:** 230. **Staff:** 15. **Regional Groups:** 1. **State Groups:** 15. **Local Groups:** 6. **National Groups:** 6. **Description:** Fans of the original Star Trek science fiction television series, which aired from 1966-69, Star Trek: The Animateds, the theatrical Star Trek movies, and the current television series, Star Trek: The Next Generation, Star Trek: Deep Space Nine, and Star Trek: Voyagerm, Star Trek Enterprise, Star Trek novels. Aims to keep fans abreast of events dealing with Star Trek and its actors. **Libraries: Type:** reference. **Boards:** Admiralty. **Councils:** Department Chief. **Formerly:** Trekville U.S.A.

24394 ■ United Federation of Planets, International (UFPI)
PO Box 3157
Chula Vista, CA 91909-3157
E-mail: ccom@ufpi.org
URL: http://www.ufpi.org
Contact: Mr. David Nottage, Commander-in-Chief
Founded: 1995. **Members:** 154. **Membership Dues:** first time - individual/family primary, $17 ● regular - individual/family primary, $15 (annual) ● subspace - individual/family primary, $6 (annual) ● additional family, $1 (annual) ● foreign, $10 (annual). **Regional Groups:** 1. **State Groups:** 6. **Local Groups:** 11. **Multinational. Description:** Fans of science fiction in general, but built on the core beliefs of Star Trek; originally started as a Star Trek fan club celebrating Star Trek fandom, but has expanded its vision and purpose to celebrate all of science fiction fandom, in all of its diverse forms (gaming, fiction, costuming, etc.) Promotes ideals presented and upheld by Star Trek, including respect for all life forms, a concept referred to by the group as IDIC (or "infinite diversity through infinite combinations"). Maintains community services including reading programs, aid to the homeless, children's charities, and other types of charities. **Awards:** Deltan Distinguished Service Ribbon. **Frequency:** annual. **Type:** recognition. **Recipient:** for outstanding service and performance of duties at the fleet level ● International Cadet of the Year. **Frequency:** annual. **Type:** recognition. **Recipient:** to a UFPI cadet (member under the age of 18) for sustained level of activity within UFPI ● International Member of the Year. **Frequency:** annual. **Type:** recognition. **Recipient:** to a member of UFPI for sustained dedication in working for UFPI ● International Ribbon of Honor. **Frequency:** annual. **Type:** recognition. **Recipient:** for truly exceptional individuals ● James T. Kirk Award for Original Thinking. **Frequency:** annual. **Type:** recognition. **Recipient:** for one or numerous ideas that have proven to be of great benefit to the UFPI ● Joint Service Commendation. **Frequency:** annual. **Type:** recognition. **Recipient:** for numerous and outstanding joint service activities with other fandom organizations ● Nebula Commendation. **Frequency:** annual. **Type:** recognition. **Recipient:** for commendable actions ● Order of the Phoenix. **Frequency:** annual. **Type:** recognition. **Recipient:** for the highest level of performance of duties within the UFPI ● Partner Commendation. **Frequency:** annual. **Type:** recognition. **Recipient:** to the significant individuals who deserve recognition for their support of their partner's hobby in fandom ● Praentares Ribbon of Commendation. **Frequency:** annual. **Type:** recognition. **Recipient:** for superior performance and service. **Telecommunication Services:** electronic bulletin board, electronic list. **Special Interest Groups:** Astronomy; Charity and Fundraising; Collecting Memorabilia; Fan Fiction. **Publications:** *The Universal Translator*, bimonthly. Newsletter. Updates members about recent Sci-Fi news and items of interest. Contains news on members, chapters, and UFPI leadership activities. **Price:** free for members. **Circulation:** 154. Alternate Formats: online. **Conventions/Meetings:** annual general assembly and meeting, discussion of past and upcoming business and presentation of awards (exhibits).

Star Wars

24395 ■ Jedi Knights of Orange County
12291 Meade St.
Garden Grove, CA 92841
Ph: (760)244-9593 (714)539-7272
E-mail: darklighter@intlaccess.com
URL: http://home.earthlink.net/~jkoc
Contact: Carol Ann Alves, Membership Chair
Founded: 1977. **Members:** 50. **Membership Dues:** associate, $4 (annual). **Description:** Star Wars/science fiction fans. Works to meet people who share an interest in the movie, Star Wars and other types of science fiction. Conducts monthly business meetings. **Libraries: Type:** not open to the public. **Holdings:** archival material, artwork, papers, periodicals, photographs. **Telecommunication Services:** electronic mail, jkoc@earthlink.net. **Committees:** Games; Programs; Publicity and PR; Social. **Formerly:** (2006) Jedi Knights/Science Fiction. **Publications:** L-Saber, monthly. Newsletter. Publishes minutes from previous meeting, articles on events, member artwork or articles event announcements with maps and convention information. Alternate Formats: online. **Conventions/Meetings:** monthly meeting - always third Sunday in Garden Grove, CA.

Stoker, Bram

24396 ■ Vampire Pen Pal Network
PO Box 290328
Brooklyn, NY 11229-0328
E-mail: vizeprez@benecke.com
URL: http://benecke.com/vampire.html
Contact: Eric Held, Exec. Off.
Founded: 1975. **Members:** 110. **Staff:** 4. **Budget:** $1,500. **Description:** Represents individuals interested in Dracula/vampires and Bram Stoker. **Telecommunication Services:** electronic mail, vampire-empire145@hotmail.com. **Publications:** A Joint Venture of the Vampire Empire and the Vampire Information Exchange.

Television

24397 ■ Air, Sea, and Space Club (ASSC)
19205 Seneca Ridge Ct.
Gaithersburg, MD 20886
Ph: (301)869-1755
Contact: John Samorajczyk Jr., Exec. Officer
Founded: 1987. **Members:** 250. **Membership Dues:** bw membership kit, $10 ● color kit, $15. **Staff:** 4. **Description:** Fans of fictional characters from radio and television programs such as Buck Rogers and Captain Silver. Also includes Jimmie Allen (air), Lance O'Casey (sea), Rocketman, Rocketeer, Space Ace (space), Capt. Marvel, Spy Smasher, and other Fawcett comic heroes. **Publications:** America's Greatest Comix, periodic ● Fawcett Adventures ● Nostalgia Review Vols. I-III, annual. **Price:** included in membership dues. **Circulation:** 250. **Advertising:** accepted.

24398 ■ American Bandstand Fan Club
c/o David Frees, Pres.
PO Box 131
Adamstown, PA 19501
Ph: (717)738-2513
E-mail: popfrosty@webtv.net
URL: http://fiftiesweb.com/bandstnd.htm
Contact: David Frees, Pres.
Founded: 1960. **Members:** 1,006. **Membership Dues:** in U.S., life, $15 ● outside U.S., life, $25. **Description:** Fans of American Bandstand, a television series that showcased teenage music, dances, and styles. The show enjoyed an audience of up to 20 million viewers. **Awards:** Goldmine Service Award. **Type:** recognition. **Additional Websites:** http://www.fiftiesweb.com/davey-frees.htm. **Formerly:** (1989) American Bandstand Memory Club; (1997) 1950s American Bandstand Fan Club. **Publications:** AB Regulars Directory. Booklet ● American Bandstand Regulars Reunion. Video ● Bandstand

Boogie, semiannual. Contains information on American Bandstand performers of the 1950s and 60s and their current activities. Includes photographs. **Price:** $2.00/copy. **Circulation:** 1,000. **Advertising:** accepted ● Dave's Collectibles Collectors Catalog.

24399 ■ The Andy Griffith Show Rerun Watchers Club (TAGSRWC)
9 Music Sq. S
PMB 146
Nashville, TN 37203
E-mail: anewsome@aol.com
URL: http://www.mayberry.com/tagsrwc
Contact: Jim Clark, Founder
Founded: 1979. **Members:** 20,000. **Local Groups:** 1,200. **Description:** Individuals devoted to watching and promoting the airing of reruns of the The Andy Griffith Show. (The show, which originally ran from 1960 to 1968, is aired daily in about 100 television markets nationwide.) Encourages members to write to television stations that air reruns of the show and express their appreciation. Facilitates communication among members on matters relating to the show. Sponsors occasional polls and lectures. Maintains collection of items relating to The Andy Griffith Show. **Awards:** Mayberry Friendship Award. **Frequency:** annual. **Type:** recognition. **Computer Services:** Mailing lists. **Publications:** The Button, 3/year. Newsletter. Provides chapter news, merchandise news, and event news. **Price:** $10.00/2 years. **Circulation:** 5,000 ● eBullet, bimonthly. Newsletter. Contains information about what's going on in and around Mayberry. **Price:** free. Alternate Formats: online. **Conventions/Meetings:** periodic meeting.

24400 ■ Dark Shadows Official Fan Club (DSOFC)
PO Box 92
Maplewood, NJ 07040
E-mail: pansyfaye@darkshadowsfestival.com
URL: http://www.darkshadowsfestival.com
Contact: Ann Wilson, Exec. Dir.
Founded: 1982. **Members:** 30,000. **Multinational. Description:** Clubs in three countries that publish newsletters and magazines dedicated to the preservation of the memory of the 1960s television show Dark Shadows and the 1990s revival series. Seeks to keep members informed regarding the lives of cast members. Donates convention proceeds to various charities; Maintains archives of memorabilia issued in relation to the show and the subsequent MGM movies House of Dark Shadows and Night of Dark Shadows. Compiles statistics. **Libraries: Type:** reference. **Holdings:** archival material. **Also Known As:** Dark Shadows Fan Information Service. **Formerly:** (1992) World Federation of Dark Shadows Clubs. **Publications:** Shadowgram, periodic. Newsletter. Provides current events information and Dark Shadows news. **Price:** $12.00/4 issues ● World of Dark Shadows, periodic. Magazine. Includes commentaries, reviews, photos and classified ads for collectors. **Price:** $12.00/issue ● Also publishes episode summaries and other materials. **Conventions/Meetings:** semiannual Dark Shadows Festival (exhibits) ● annual meeting.

24401 ■ Flight Patrol Fan Club (FPFC)
19205 Seneca Ridge Ct.
Gaithersburg, MD 20886
Ph: (301)869-1755
Contact: John Samorajczyk, Pres.
Founded: 1986. **Members:** 200. **Membership Dues:** bw membership kit, $10 ● color kit, $15. **Staff:** 4. **Local Groups:** 3. **For-Profit. Description:** Captain Midnight fans and "air-minded nostalgia buffs." Works to perpetuate the memory of Captain Midnight and the Secret Squadron tradition. Seeks to educate young people about Captain Midnight. Sponsors speakers' bureau; provides children's services. Offers seminars on the use of nostalgia in therapy and education. **Libraries: Type:** reference. **Holdings:** 1,000. **Computer Services:** database. **Publications:** Captain Midnight Comic, periodic ● Flight Patrol Newsletter, 3/year. **Price:** included in membership dues; $10.00/3 issues $5.00/issue for nonmembers. **Advertising:** accepted ● Reprints.

24402 ■ F.U.G.I.T.I.V.E.S.
Address Unknown since 2007
Founded: 1991. **Members:** 50. **Membership Dues:** individual in U.S., $20 (annual) ● individual in Canada, $25 (annual) ● outside U.S. and Canada, $30 (annual). **Staff:** 2. **Local Groups:** 1. **Multinational. Description:** Friends United for Great Intelligent Television and an Inspiring Video Entertainment Series (F.U.G.I.T.I.V.E.S.)—fans of the television series the Fugitive. Seeks to continue the run of Dr. Richard Kimble by promoting the moral and ethical values of the character through charitable programs and community activities. This is a special interest group as opposed to a typical fan club. **Libraries: Type:** reference; not open to the public; by appointment only. **Holdings:** articles, artwork, audiovisuals, books, clippings, periodicals. **Subjects:** The Fugitive (TV series and movie), actor David Janssen. **Awards:** "Kimble" - Fugitive of the Year. **Frequency:** annual. **Type:** recognition. **Recipient:** for promoting the philosophy of the Fugitive. **Publications:** Stafford Chronicle, quarterly. Newsletter. Covers news pertaining to the TV series and film. Includes member profiles and an information exchange and support system between members. **Price:** $20.00/yr. in U.S.; $25.00/yr. in Canada; $30.00/yr. outside U.S. **Circulation:** 50. **Advertising:** accepted. **Conventions/Meetings:** annual convention, features FUGITIVE/David Janssen related artwork, photos, and memorabilia (exhibits) - last weekend in July ● quarterly meeting, with dinner and newsletter printing and collating - January, April, July, and October 15th (approximately). Austin, TX.

24403 ■ Galaxy Patrol Fan Club (GPFC)
Address Unknown since 2007
Founded: 1986. **Members:** 160. **Membership Dues:** $8 (annual). **Staff:** 2. **Description:** Fans of children's television shows from 1948 to the present, especially science fiction shows such as Space Patrol, Tom Corbett Space Cadet, and Captain Midnight. Facilitates communication among members. Gathers and disseminates information; collects and preserves historic children's T.V. programs. Conducts research. Maintains biographical archives and library; compiles statistics. **Convention/Meeting:** none. **Libraries: Type:** open to the public. **Holdings:** archival material. **Subjects:** past issues of all newsletters over 15 years. **Publications:** Galaxy Patrol Newsletter, quarterly. Contains 8-12 pages with reviews of books and video tapes. **Price:** $8.00/year. **Circulation:** 160. **Advertising:** accepted ● Galaxy Patrol Space-O-Gram, quarterly. Newsletter.

24404 ■ Gilligan's Island Fan Club (GIFC)
12429 Dormouse Rd.
San Diego, CA 92129
E-mail: willyg@gilligansisle.com
URL: http://www.gilligansisle.com
Contact: Willy Gilligan, Pres.
Founded: 1987. **Members:** 180. **Membership Dues:** regular, $15 (annual). **Staff:** 5. **State Groups:** 3. **Description:** Represents fans of the television situation comedy Gilligan's Island, which was aired on the CBS television network from 1964 to 1967. Aims to study the origination and production of the series. Recognizes individuals involved directly and indirectly in the production of the show; has presented plaques to honor cast members and the creator of the series. Serves as a referral service for the Gilligan's Island Fan Club - The Original. Makes available photographs and membership cards. **Convention/Meeting:** none. **Libraries: Type:** open to the public. **Holdings:** 10; articles, books.

24405 ■ Guiding Light Fan Club (GLFC)
c/o Mindi Schulman, Pres.
PO Box 455
Lynbrook, NY 11563-0455
E-mail: oglfc@aol.com
URL: http://www.officialglfanclub.com
Contact: Mindi Schulman, Pres.
Founded: 1980. **Members:** 850. **Membership Dues:** regular, in U.S., $28 (annual) ● regular, in Canada, $35 (annual) ● regular, outside U.S. and Canada, $40 (annual). **Staff:** 6. **Description:** Fans and view-

ers of the CBS television network's daytime drama Guiding Light, which first aired on radio on Jan. 25, 1937. Seeks to establish and maintain viewers loyalty to and interest in the show and its cast members. Makes available bumper stickers and photographs of cast members. Compiles statistics. **Libraries: Type:** reference. **Holdings:** archival material. **Computer Services:** database, membership. **Telecommunication Services:** electronic bulletin board, Prodigy, GL fan club. **Publications:** Springfield Journal, quarterly. **Price:** included in membership dues. **Conventions/ Meetings:** annual meeting, with Charity fundraiser.

24406 ■ Lost in Space Fannish Alliance (LISFAN)
c/o Flint Mitchell
PO Box 510442
St. Louis, MO 63151-0442
Ph: (314)416-4071
E-mail: lisfanpress@hotmail.com
URL: http://www.webspawner.com/users/lostinspace-fan
Contact: Flint Mitchell, Contact
Founded: 1981. **Members:** 1,200. **Description:** Individuals interested in the television show Lost In Space which ran from 1965 to 1968 and starred Jonathan Harris (1914-), June Lockhart (1925-), and Guy Williams (1925-89). Offers LIS information and memorabilia. Offers pen-pal service. **Publications:** Lost In Space Times/Catalog, quarterly ● You Can Build the Lost in Space Robot, published about once every 3-4 years. Book. Contains photos and instructions on how to build a Lost in Space robot. **Price:** $19.95. **Circulation:** 4,000 ● Magazine, monthly. **Price:** $66.00/year; $3.00/copy. **Advertising:** accepted. **Conventions/Meetings:** semiannual meeting (exhibits).

24407 ■ Magic of Bewitched Fan Club (MBFC)
c/o Gina Hill-Meyers, Pres.
PO Box 26734
Fresno, CA 93729
Ph: (559)433-1727
E-mail: gmeyers@fresnomail.com
Contact: Gina Hill-Meyers, Pres.
Founded: 1992. **Members:** 100. **Membership Dues:** $25 (semiannual). **Description:** Fans of the television series Bewitched. Works to promote interest in the show and cast. Facilitates exchange of information; offers episode guides, photos, and videotapes. **Libraries: Type:** reference. **Holdings:** video recordings. **Publications:** The Magic of Bewitched. Book. Written by society President, available at amazon. com or Barnes and Noble books. ● Newsletter, quarterly. **Price:** $30.00/year.

24408 ■ Magnum Memorabilia
c/o David Romas, Dir.
438 Leroy St.
Ferndale, MI 48220
E-mail: ac2942@wayne.edu
Contact: David Romas, Dir.
Founded: 1989. **Members:** 2,000. **Staff:** 1. **Multinational. Description:** Serves as research/production foundation and full-service fan information clearinghouse devoted to the analysis, collection, and creation of the popular media text Magnum, PI. Compiles statistics. Offers educational and research programs. **Libraries: Type:** reference; open to the public. **Holdings:** 2,000; archival material, audiovisuals, books, business records, clippings, periodicals. **Subjects:** Magnum, PI. **Conventions/Meetings:** annual Series Premiere Anniversary Celebration - meeting - in December.

24409 ■ Man from U.N.C.L.E. Fan Club
c/o Sue Cole, Pres.
PO Box 1733
Oshkosh, WI 54903
E-mail: cgs@prodigy.net
URL: http://www.manfromuncle.org/clubs.htm
Contact: Sue Cole, Pres.
Founded: 1998. **Members:** 715. **Membership Dues:** basic in U.S., $25 (annual) ● basic in Canada, $35 (annual) ● basic outside U.S. and Canada, $50 (an-

nual). **Staff:** 1. **Regional Groups:** 5. **Description:** Fan club for the Man from U.N.C.L.E. Provides UNCLE ID card, membership certificate, communicator pen, and triangular badge. Continues to revive interest in the 1960's cult TV series Man & Girl from U.N.C.L.E. Petitions Mr. Felton and others involved in the series to create new movie and or new series based upon original characters. **Libraries: Type:** open to the public. **Holdings:** archival material, books, periodicals. **Awards: Frequency:** monthly. **Type:** monetary. **Recipient:** for needy individuals. **Also Known As:** U.N.C.L.E. Headquarters Inc. **Publications:** UNCLE, quarterly. Newsletter. Offers free classified ads for members. ● Catalog. Offers merchandise.

24410 ■ New Jetsons Fan Club (NJFC)
PO Box 02222
Detroit, MI 48202
E-mail: yul_tolbert@hotmail.com
URL: http://timeliketoons.tripod.com/new_jetsons_fan.htm
Contact: Yul Tolbert, Pres./Founder
Founded: 1997. **Members:** 2. **Staff:** 1. **Budget:** $100. **Description:** Admirers of the animated television series The New Jetsons, a remake of the original 1960s series, which aired in the mid-1980s. Facilitates communication among fans of The New Jetsons. Serves as a clearinghouse on The New Jetsons and related series. **Publications:** Newsletter, periodic. Includes episode discussions, fan fiction, and news on Jetsons fanform. **Price:** free.

24411 ■ Official Gilligan's Island Fan Club (OGIFC)
12429 Dormouse Rd.
San Diego, CA 92129
E-mail: thurshowell@aol.com
URL: http://www.gilligansisle.com
Contact: Louie Knaiger, Pres.
Founded: 1972. **Members:** 3,000. **Staff:** 10. **Regional Groups:** 12. **State Groups:** 50. **Local Groups:** 2. **National Groups:** 14. **Description:** Fans of the television series Gilligan's Island, which aired during 1964-1967. Promotes interest in the show and the cast. Offers sales of Gilligan's Island memorabilia. **Convention/Meeting:** none. **Libraries: Type:** reference. **Holdings:** 27; archival material, books, photographs, video recordings. **Subjects:** Gilligan's Island series, animation, reunions, promo materials. **Awards:** Globe International Gold Award. **Frequency:** biennial. **Type:** recognition. **Recipient:** for website graphics, artwork and information. **Working Groups:** Gilligan Islanders. **Formed by Merger of:** (1994) Gilligan's Island Fan Club; Original Gilligan's Island Fan Club. **Formerly:** Gilligan's Island Fan Club (The Original). **Publications:** Gilligan's Island. Book. **Price:** $75.00 ● Gilligan's Island Newsletters, monthly. Includes letters from members, classified ads. **Price:** free. **Circulation:** 32,000. **Advertising:** accepted ● Inside Gilligan's Island. Book. Includes updated information about the Gilligan's Island Musical and the movie. **Price:** $13.95.

24412 ■ Official Red Dwarf Fan Club (ORDFC)
c/o Jupiter Mining Company
PO Box 3152
Waquoit, MA 02536
E-mail: reddwarf@jupitermining.com
URL: http://www.reddwarffanclub.com
Contact: Jennifer Gould, Membership Coor.
Founded: 1991. **Members:** 3,000. **Membership Dues:** individual in U.S. and Canada, $25 (annual). **Staff:** 10. **Description:** Admirers of the British science fiction comedy series Red Dwarf. Promotes interest in Red Dwarf and its cast and writers. Serves as a clearinghouse on Red Dwarf; sponsors social activities. **Telecommunication Services:** electronic mail, jenny@reddwarffanclub.com. **Publications:** Better Than Life, quarterly. Newsletter. Contains information on Red Dwarf. **Circulation:** 3,000. **Conventions/Meetings:** annual Dimension Jump - convention - always in United Kingdom.

24413 ■ Once Upon A Time (The Prisoner Fan Club) (OUAT)
515 Ravenel Cir.
Seneca, SC 29678
E-mail: lawrence@carol.net
URL: http://www.virtualportmeirion.com/ouat/ouat/ouatflyer.htm
Contact: David Lawrence, Exec. Off.
Founded: 1979. **Description:** Fans of the British television series The Prisoner which aired from 1967 to 1968. The allegorical drama, which starred Patrick McGoohan, depicted one man's struggle for freedom of thought while captive in an authoritarian society. Seeks to provide members with information concerning the television series. Promotes continued airing of the series in syndication. **Convention/Meeting:** none. **Libraries: Type:** reference.

24414 ■ Rin Tin Tin Fan Club
c/o Ms. Daphne Hereford, VP/Founder
PO Box 27
Crockett, TX 75835
Ph: (936)545-0471
E-mail: info@rintintin.com
URL: http://www.rintintin.com
Contact: Ms. Daphne Hereford, VP/Founder
Founded: 1970. **Members:** 100. **Membership Dues:** regular, in U.S., $25 (annual) ● regular, outside U.S., $40 (annual). **For-Profit. Description:** Promotes the breeding, raising, and training of German Shepherds. Runs the Rin Tin Tin Museum, with more than 8,000 pieces of German Shepherd or Rin Tin Tin memorabilia. **Libraries: Type:** open to the public; by appointment only. **Holdings:** archival material, books, clippings, periodicals. **Subjects:** German Shepherd memorabilia. **Awards:** Dog of the Year. **Frequency:** annual. **Type:** recognition. **Publications:** Rinty's News, quarterly. Newsletter. **Price:** included in membership dues; $25.00 for nonmembers in U.S.; $40.00 for nonmembers outside U.S. **Circulation:** 100. **Advertising:** accepted ● Brochure.

24415 ■ S.H.A.D.O. - USECC
c/o Commander Helen Weber
514 Delaware Ave.
Lansdale, PA 19446-3417
URL: http://www.ufoseries.com/shado-usecc.html
Contact: Commander Helen Weber, Contact
Founded: 1979. **Members:** 100. **Membership Dues:** regular in U.S., $28 (annual) ● regular outside U.S., $38 (annual). **Staff:** 3. **Description:** Admirers of the television program UFO. Promotes increased recognition of UFO; facilitates communication among members. Serves as a clearinghouse on UFO and its writers, producers, and cast; conducts social activities. **Publications:** COMMUNIQUE, quarterly. Newsletter. Contains non-fiction articles, latest news, cast updates. **Price:** $28.00 in U.S.; $38.00 outside U.S. **Circulation:** 100.

24416 ■ Six of One Club: The Prisoner Appreciation Society
871 Clover Dr.
North Wales, PA 19454-2749
Ph: (215)699-2527
E-mail: sixofone@netreach.net
URL: http://www.ThePrisonerAppreciationSociety.com
Contact: Bruce A. Clark, Coor.
Founded: 1977. **Members:** 3,000. **Multinational. Description:** Represents devotees of the British television series The Prisoner, which ran from 1967 to 1968 and starred Patrick McGoohan; the drama allegorized an individual's struggle for identity and freedom of thought in an authoritarian society overrun by bureaucracy. Studies and analyzes the 17 episodes of the series. Offers 3 volumes of soundtrack music on compact disc. **Publications:** In the Village, quarterly. Magazine. Contains episode analysis, interviews, and production details. **Price:** included in membership dues. **Circulation:** 3,000 ● The Making of the Prisoner ● The Prisoner Episode Guide ● The Prisoner of Portmeirion ● Prisoner Portmeirion Production ● Village World ● Videos. Contains series of interviews with those involved with The Prisoner TV series. **Conventions/Meetings:** an-

nual conference - always late August or early September, in Portmeirion, Wales.

24417 ■ U.N.C.L.E. HQ

c/o Darlene Kepner, Sec.
856 Buttercup Dr.
Lakeland, FL 33801-6297
URL: http://www.unclehq.com
Contact: Darlene Kepner, Sec.

Founded: 1976. **Members:** 500. **Membership Dues:** $11 (annual). **Staff:** 2. **Description:** Fans of The Man from U.N.C.L.E., a popular television series of the 1960s that followed the seriocomic adventures of secret agents Napoleon Solo and Illya Kuryakin, and The Girl from U.N.C.L.E., its short-lived spinoff. Lobbies for the airing of U.N.C.L.E. reruns and the creation of new episodes. Holds fan gatherings at conventions with themes relating to spy shows. Donates materials to the Felton Files at the University of Iowa, in Iowa City. Maintains pen pal service and charitable programs. **Publications:** *Annual Yearbook*, annual ● *HQ Newsletter*, quarterly. Offers tips on obtaining memorabilia; lists current activities of the show's cast. **Conventions/Meetings:** bimonthly SPY-CON - meeting (exhibits).

24418 ■ United Network Command

c/o Stan Warpechowski, Pres.
231 Niagara St.
Buffalo, NY 14201-2336
E-mail: openchanneld@volcanomail.com
URL: http://www.geocities.com/napsolo81
Contact: Stan Warpechowski, Pres.

Founded: 1994. **Members:** 300. **Membership Dues:** individual, $15 (annual). **Staff:** 1. **Multinational. Description:** Caters to the most diehard of fans of the Sixties action-adventure series "The Man from U.N.

C.L.E." (1964-68) and "The Girl from U.N.C.L.E." (1966-67). Covers varied details on the programs with episode synopses, magazine articles, actor profiles, guest star information, and more. Considered a special interest group more than a fan club; does not believe a new movie would do justice to the classic series which was popular but eventually superceded in quality by series like I Spy and The Wild Wild West; does not gather petitions. **Libraries: Type:** not open to the public. **Holdings:** articles, books. **Subjects:** the TV series, stars, producers, directors, guest stars, input by Glenn Magee. **Publications:** Magazine, periodic. Merchandise offered if and when available, but must qualify as authentic tie-ins. **Price:** included in membership dues. **Circulation:** 300. **Advertising:** accepted.

24419 ■ The World of Dark Shadows (TWODS)

PO Box 17666
Temple City, CA 91780
E-mail: kathleener@aol.com
URL: http://zurc2.com/TWODS/index.html
Contact: Kathleen Resch, Ed.

Founded: 1975. **Members:** 1,000. **Description:** Fans of the supernatural ABC television serial, Dark Shadows, that aired from 1966-71. Promotes syndication of the program and promotes the careers of the actors involved with the show. Conducts festivals; compiles statistics. **Libraries: Type:** reference. **Holdings:** biographical archives. **Publications:** *Dark Shadows Concordances*, periodic. Journal. Covers the storyline from the television series. ● Journal, semiannual. **Conventions/Meetings:** annual Dark Shadows Festival - symposium (exhibits).

24420 ■ Young and the Restless Fan Club (YRFC)

c/o CBS Television
7800 Beverly Blvd., Ste.3305
Los Angeles, CA 90036
URL: http://www.soapcentral.com/yr/fanclubs.php
Founded: 1985. **Members:** 1,200. **Membership Dues:** regular in U.S., $18 (annual) ● regular in Canada, $19 (annual) ● regular outside U.S. and Canada, $27 (annual). **Languages:** English, French. **Description:** Fans of the daytime television drama The Young and the Restless, which first aired in 1973. Works to promote the show and its stars. Reports on cast on- and offscreen activities. **Publications:** *The Young and The Restless Fan Club Journal*, 3/year. Shows actor's interviews and behind the scenes information. **Circulation:** 1,200 ● Also distributes cast photos, cast list, and fan merchandise. **Conventions/Meetings:** biennial meeting, silent auctions, photo taking, autograph session, questions and answers with actors (exhibits) - always summer in Los Angeles, CA.

Writers

24421 ■ Fans of Oz (FOO)

c/o Vampire Empire
29 Washington Sq. W, PHN, Ste.C
New York, NY 10011-9180
E-mail: robertqclark@yahoo.com
Contact: Jane Oz, Exec. Off.

Founded: 1990. **Members:** 75. **Staff:** 2. **Budget:** $1,000. **Multinational. Description:** Promotes collecting of Oz books and memorabilia. **Libraries: Type:** not open to the public. **Holdings:** archival material, articles, books. **Subjects:** Oz. **Publications:** *VE Quarterly*. Includes occasional articles about Baum, the movie, and personalities affiliated with Oz.